ENCARTA®
WORLD ENGLISH DICTIONARY

ENCARTA®
WORLD ENGLISH
DICTIONARY

St. Martin's Press New York

A BLOOMSBURY REFERENCE BOOK
Created from the Bloomsbury Database of World English

First published in the United States of America in 1999 by
St. Martin's Press
175 Fifth Avenue
New York, NY 10010

Library of Congress Cataloging-in-Publication Data

Soukhanov, Anne H., 1943-
Encarta world English dictionary.
p. cm.
The symbol for registered trademark follows "Encarta" in title.
ISBN 0-312-22222-X
1. English language-Dictionaries. I. Title.
PE1628.S5824 1999
423 - - dc21 99-15350
CIP

Typeset by Selwood Systems, Midsomer Norton, Bath, United Kingdom
Printed in the United States of America

Contents

WORLD ENGLISH AND LANGUAGE CONSULTANTS

Robert Allen
Editor and lexicographer

David Blair
Senior Lecturer, Department of Linguistics, Macquarie University (Australia)

Robert B. Costello
Editor and lexicographer

Professor Nikolas Coupland
Centre for Applied English Language Studies, University of Wales (English in Wales)

Tony Deverson
Senior Lecturer, Department of English, University of Canterbury, New Zealand (New Zealand)

Dr. Scott Delancey
Department of Linguistics, University of Oregon (Native American English)

Professor Margery Fee
Department of English, University of Vancouver; author, *Oxford Guide to Canadian Usage* (Canada)

Professor Joshua Fishman
City University of New York (Yiddish)

Jonathon Green
Author of a history of lexicography *Chasing the Sun: Dictionary-makers and the Dictionaries They Made*, and Britain's leading slang lexicographer, author of the *Cassell Dictionary of Slang* (A Brief History of Dictionaries and Dictionary Makers)

Dr. Eva Hertel
English Language and Linguistics, TU Chemnitz (East Africa)

Betty Kirkpatrick
Editor and lexicographer, editor *Roget's Thesaurus*

Jacqueline Lam
Senior Lecturer, Hong Kong University of Science and Technology (Hong Kong)

Naomi C. Losch
Assistant Professor in Hawaiian, Department of Hawaiian and Indo-Pacific Languages, University of Hawaii at Manoa (Hawaiian English)

Dr. Catherine Macafee
University of Aberdeen (Scottish, Northern Irish)

Rajend Mesthrie
Senior Lecturer, Department of Linguistics, University of Capetown (South Africa)

Mark Newbrook, Ph.D.
Senior Lecturer, Department of Linguistics, Monash University (Malaysia and Singapore)

Dr. Mark Sebba
Department of Linguistics, Lancaster University (U.K. Black English)

Professor Geneva Smitherman
University Distinguished Professor; Director, African American Language and Literacy Program; Director, "My Brother's Keeper" Program, Department of English, Michigan State University (African American English)

Kamal Keskar Sridhar
Associate Professor, Department of Linguistics, State University of New York, Stony Brook (South Asia)

Dr. Loreto Todd
Senior Lecturer, English Department, University of Leeds (Irish)

Professor Don Winford
Department of Linguistics, Ohio State University (Caribbean)

SUBJECT CONSULTANTS

Professor Clark Adams
Department of Wildlife and Fisheries Sciences, Texas A & M University (Hunting)

Michael Allaby
Writer and science consultant (Life Sciences)

Professor Christopher Arnison
Royal Agricultural College (Agriculture)

Dr. Tallis Barker
(Music)

Dr. Alan Barnard
University of Edinburgh (Anthropology)

Professor Joseph Bel Bruno
Dartmouth College, Hanover, New Hampshire (Chemistry)

Professor David Bjorklund
Department of Psychology, Florida Atlantic University (Psychology)

Professor Donald Black,
College of Food and Natural Resources, University of Massachusetts (Agriculture)

Dr. Sheila Blair
Editor for Islam and Central Asia, *The Dictionary of Art* (Arabic Words and Places)

Dr. Clive Bloom
Middlesex University (Media)

Allan Brooks
Editor and writer; member, US Government technical committees (Engineering)

Charles Butcher
Specialist writer and editor (Chemical Engineering)

Edward Butcher
Editor (Currencies)

Colin Callander
Editor, *Golf Monthly* (Golf)

Col. John A. Calabro
Professor of English, US Military Academy, West Point (Military)

Professor Paul A. Carling
University of Lancaster (Geography)

Dr. Christopher Chippendale
Museum of Archaeology and Anthropology, University of Cambridge (Archaeology)

Timothy Collings
Motor racing correspondent, Reuters and *Daily Telegraph* (Motor Sports)

Robert B. Costello
Editor and lexicographer (Computing/Foreign Words and Phrases)

Professor Helen Cowie
Roehampton Institute, London (Psychology)

Michael Crane
Director, British Isles Backgammon Association (Backgammon)

Dr. Andrew Dalby
Honorary Librarian, Institute of Linguists, author, *Bloomsbury Dictionary of Languages* (Languages)

Robert Day
Chairman, Suffolk Advanced Motorcyclists Group (DIY, Motorcycles)

Col. Michael Dewar
Formerly Institute of Strategic Studies (Military)

Professor Robert Ditton
Department of Wildlife and Fisheries Sciences, Texas A & M University (Ecology)

Professor Bethany K. Dumas
Department of Linguistics, Language and Law, University of Tennessee (Law)

Dr. Roy Evans
Formerly Faculty of Education, Roehampton Institute, London (Education)

Alan Ewert, Ph.D
University of Northern British Columbia (Mountaineering/Climbing)

Nancy Flynn
Cornell University (Botany)

Professor Bruce Ganem
Department of Chemistry, Cornell University (Chemistry)

Professor James Gramman
Department of Recreation, Park, and Tourism Sciences, Texas A & M University (Leisure)

Fayal Greene
Gardening writer and editor (Gardening)

Professor Lynne Goldstein
Professor and Chair, Department of Anthropology, Michigan State University; editor, *American Antiquity* (Anthropology and Archaeology)

Dr. Jeremy Gray
Open University (Mathematics)

Steven Griffiths
UK civil servant (Transport/Environment)

Professor Trevor Griffiths
Programme Director, School of Arts and Humanities, University of North London (Theater)

Andrew Howard
Middlesex University (Politics)

Alastair Hudson
Queen Mary and Westfield College, University of London (Law)

Philip Johanssson
Naturalist and writer (Zoology)

Bridget Jones
Cookery editor and writer, member of the Guild of Food Writers (Food)

Professor Darlene Juschka
University of Toronto (World Religions)

David Kemp
VP and Euro Director, London, ABN-AMRO Bank N.V. (Currencies)

Alison Kervin
Editor, *Rugby World* (Rugby)

Professor Ira Konigsberg
University of Michigan, Ann Arbor; author, *Complete Film Dictionary* (Cinema)

Dr. John Laurence
Boyce Thomson Institute, Cornell University (Botany)

Professor Bryan Lawson
School of Architecture, University of Sheffield (Architecture)

Professor Andrew Leclair
Newman Laboratory, Cornell University (Physics)

Becky Lee, Ph.D.
Centre for Religion, University of Toronto (Christianity and the Bible)

Professor Franklin M. Loew
President, Becker College, Worcester, MA; formerly Dean of Veterinary Medicine, Tufts and Cornell Universities (Veterinary Science)

Alastair McIver
Editor, *Tennis World* (Tennis)

Jeffrey McQuain
Writer and researcher, *New York Times*; word columnist and researcher; author, *Power Language* and *Never Enough Words* (Politics)

Carolyn Marcus
Gardening writer and editor (Gardening)

Anthony Middleton
Formerly editor, RAF in-house publications service; formerly, Technical Publications Editor, GEC-Marconi (Engineering)

Mark Miller
Editor (Literature)

Martyn Moore
Editor, *Practical Photography* (Photography)

Philip D. Morehead
Chicago Lyric Opera (Music)

Professor David Morton
School of Biomedical Science and Ethics, University of Birmingham (Veterinary Science)

Professor Bruce Murphy
Faculty of Veterinary Medicine, University of Montreal (Biology)

Adrian Napper
formerly Dept of Architecture, Edinburgh College of Art (Building and Construction)

Susan North
Department of Textiles and Dress, Victoria and Albert Museum (Fashion)

Kathleen O'Grady
Trinity College, University of Cambridge (Religion and Mythology)

Professor Alex Orenstein
City University of New York (Philosophy)

Professor Anthony Pellegrini
Department of Educational Psychology, University of Minnesota (Education)

Michael Quinion
Lexicographer and editor (New Words)

John Ross
Writer and editor (Computing)

Dr. Edward Ruddell
Department of Parks, Recreation, and Tourism, University of Utah (Martial Arts)

Richard Soffe
Seale-Hayne Faculty of Agriculture, Food and Land Use, University of Plymouth (Agriculture)

Professor Tony Spybey
Department of Sociology, Staffordshire University (Sociology)

Professor Peter N. Stearns
Dean, College of Humanities and Social Sciences, Carnegie Mellon University; author, *Encyclopedia of World History* (History)

Professor James M. Steele
School of Architecture, University of Southern California; author, *Architecture Today* (Architecture and Building)

Professor Robert Strong
Department of Economics, University of Maine (Finance)

Peter Timmer
University College London (Computing)

Dr. Amos Turk
Professor Emeritus, Department of Chemistry, City College of New York (Chemical Engineering)

Dr. Heather Valencia
University of Stirling (Judaism)

Michael J. Walsh
Librarian, Heythrop College, University of London (the Bible)

Rosemary Wilkinson
Freelance writer and editor (Crafts and Design)

Gillian Williams
Editor, *Ski and Board* magazine (Skiing)

John Williams
Sir Norman Chester Centre for Football Research, University of Leicester (Soccer)

Ellen Wohl
Associate Professor, Colorado State University (Geography)

Professor Philip C. Wright
University of New Brunswick (Business and Management)

Dr. Robert Youngson
Author *Royal Society of Medicine Encyclopedia of Family Health,* formerly consultant advisor on ophthalmology to British Army (Medicine and Pharmacology)

EDITORIAL CONTRIBUTORS

LEXICOGRAPHERS

Sandra Anderson
Debra Bailey
David Barnett
Peter Blanchard
Jane Bradbury
Callum Brines
Pat Bulhosen
Dewayne Crawford
Steve Curtis
David A. Daniel
Dana Darby Johnson
George Davidson
Jessica Feinstein
Rosalind Fergusson
Scott Forbes
Lora Goldman
Jennifer Goss Duby
Alice Grandison
David Hallworth
Orin Hargraves
Ruth Hein
Archie Hobson
Lucy Hollingworth
Katy Isaacs
Stanley A. Kurzban
Barbara Kelly
Imogen Kerr
Rachel P. King
Virginia Klein
Paul Lagassé
Duncan Marshall
Patricia Marshall
Michael Mayor
Héloïse McGuinness
Martin Mellor
Sara Montgomery
Justyn Moulds
Michael Munro
Lynne Murphy
Claire Needler
Susan R. Norton
Dr. Julia Penelope
Luisa Plaja
Julia B. Plier
Elaine Pollard
Deborah M. Posner
Jenny Roberts
Mairi Robinson
Jane Rogoyska
Howard Sargeant
Anne Seaton
Tom Shields
Martin Stark
Penny Stock
Fraser Sutherland
Katharine Turok
Dr. Donald Watt
Holly Webber
Pamela White

SCIENCE AND TECHNICAL EDITORS

Rich Cutler
Pam England
Robert Hine
Ruth Koenigsberg
Alan D. Levy
Ann Marie Menting
Dr. Ruth Salomon
James E. Shea
Martin Tolley

PRONUNCIATIONS

Dr. Phillip Backley
Valerie Boulanger
C. Rodolfo Celis
Kimberley Farrar
Sharon Goldstein
Phil Harrison
Esther Hurrell
Bettina Isensee
Dinah Jackson
Nicholas Jones
Dr. John M. Kirk
Rafal S. Konopka
Rima McKinzey
Scott Montgomery
Susan Rennie
Dr. Mary Rigby
Susan Sharpe
Misty Shock

ETYMOLOGIES

Anna Berge
Titus Bicknell
Pietro Bortone
Anne Corlett
Dr. Julia Cresswell
Dr. Jim Girsch
Kerstin Hoge
Andrew Horton
Martha Mayou
Fred McDonald
Dr. Robert Mory
Cerywss O'Hare
Joseph Patwell
Edward Pettit
Sean Pollack
Anne Seaton
Susan Shephard
Dr. Susan Sigalas
Dr. Roger Woodard
David M. Weeks, Ph.D
Jason Zerdin

ADDITIONAL CONTRIBUTORS

LANGUAGE ANALYSIS

Ruth Blackmore
Richard Breheny
Roland Chambers
Rosalind Combley
Alison Crann
Kay Cullen
Gill Francis
Elizabeth Manning
Diane Nicholls
Christina Rammell
Alison Renshaw
Laura Wedgeworth
Emily Young

PROOFREADERS

Stuart Fortey
Bruce Frost
Katherine Carson
Debra Goring
Isabel Griffiths
Margaret Hill
Ruth Hillmore
Margaret Jull Costa
Irene Lakhani
Laura Lawrie
Jill Leatherbarrow
Julie Marsh
Margaret Mullen
Paula Parish
Kathy Seed
John Wheelwright

EDITORIAL, KEYBOARDING AND ADMINISTRATIVE ASSISTANCE

Charlotte Adams
Sara Al-Bader
Neil Atherton
Lanfranca Attanasio
Simon Beattie
Alistair Bruce
Joan Carpenter
Barry Day
(Database Assistant)
Anna Degotardi
Sarah Faherty
Emma Harrison
Fiona Henderson
Angela Jackson
Andy Lacey
Una McGovern
Soraya Moeng
Fearghus Ó Conchúir
Elizabeth Partington
Melanie Poyo
James Randall
Lucy Reiter
Ian Ronayne
Ian Rowley
Walter Hepburne Scott
Laura Stoddart
Melanie Tate
Rachael Tuley
Kamala Wickramasinghe
Harriet Wynne Finch

Corpus material
Nigel Clifford

GEOGRAPHICAL AND BIOGRAPHICAL ENTRIES

Consultants
John Bowman, Editor-in-Chief, *Cambridge Dictionary of American Biography*

Maggy Hendry, Editor, *Macmillan Encyclopedia of Women* (revised edition)

Professor Howard Nenner, Department of History, Smith College, Consultant and associate editor, *New Dictionary of National Biography*

Sarah Waldram

Managing Editor
Stephen Adamson

Compilers and editors
Trevor Anderson
Richard Beatty
Ian Crofton
Duncan Brewer
Susan Johnson
Keith Lye
Richard O'Neill
Rebecca Palmer
Eileen Ramchandran
Theodore Rowland-Entwistle
Eleanor Stanley
Lucilla Watson

ILLUSTRATIONS

Coordinator
Gill Paul

Picture Researcher
Elaine Willis

Illustrators
Wendy Bramwell
Chris Lyon
Annabel Milne
Sylvie Rabbe
Beatriz Waller
David Wood

Tables
Jeffrey Petts
Ruth Bateson

Annotations
Andrew Clarke

Maps
Digital Wisdom Publishing Ltd

Illustrations Assistants
Dawn Boulton
Elizabeth Geary

DESIGN

Jacket and Text Design
William Webb

Frontmatter Design
Simon Mercer, Mercer Design

Foreword

Anne H. Soukhanov
U.S. General Editor

WHEN RALPH WALDO EMERSON said that "the English language is the sea which receives tributaries from every region under heaven," he could not have predicted that, by the start of the twenty-first century, 1.5 billion people worldwide would speak English in varying degrees of proficiency. Nor could he have predicted the existence of the Internet and e-mail, which, in a very short recent period, have brought English speakers around the globe into a greater, yet closer union, through instant verbal contact. This sea-change in communications technology has effected a sea-change in our language, the ways we must now use it—and with whom we use it.

The *Encarta World English Dictionary* has been written by over 320 scholars in 20 nations, working simultaneously for almost three years. We edited the Dictionary using proprietary computer compilation software and a 50-million word corpus showing English in all its varieties worldwide in typical printed contexts. We consulted with one another from the West Coast to Canada to the Orkney Islands to Australia to New Zealand to the Blue Ridge Mountains of Virginia, using e-mail. The result of this unique, first-time partnership among global scholars is, for North Americans, a comprehensive record of English—but one with a world view.

Of course, the Dictionary records in detail all the things sought by people on a daily basis—spellings, pronunciations, meanings, contextual examples (made up and quoted) of the words in action, word histories, matters of good and bad usage, matters of dialect, and synonymy. In so doing the ***Encarta World English Dictionary*** is a clear mirror onto the culture of our people as a whole and individually in their diversity. And since words and changing meanings evolve as a result of the hopes, dreams, and actions of the people using the language, this Dictionary is truly a linguistic artifact for the people, of the people, by the people of the United States of America and indeed Canada.

Yet the ***Encarta World English Dictionary*** is also a window upon other cultures: it includes thousands of English words used by English speakers the world over—English words, all right, but not U.S. words. These are words that we and our children do and will encounter with increasing frequency as we correspond with others in far-flung lands via e-mail. Make no mistake: we are in the age of *World English*—the complex of varieties of the English language spoken in our neighbor Canada, the Caribbean, Australia, New Zealand, the Pacific Rim, Africa, Southeast Asia, Southwest Asia, the United Kingdom, and yes, the United States.

If, for example, you receive an e-mail from a Canadian citizen in which a *bagman* working for a political party is mentioned, would you understand that *fundraiser* is meant? Should someone from Southern Asia volunteer his or her *biodata*, would you know that the person means *curriculum vitae*? The *Encarta World English Dictionary* includes these and many more such World English terms as main entries or components of its World English essays covering all the major Englishes spoken today. Thus the ***Encarta World English Dictionary*** brings you closer to your counterparts in other lands by giving you the tools required for better understanding. As Steven Pinker has said in *The Language Instinct,* "You and I belong to a species with a remarkable ability: we can shape events in each other's brains with exquisite precision" just "by making noises with our mouths."

In terms of fast-changing U.S. English, the Dictionary brings you up to date on thousands of new words and new meanings of preexisting words. Examples are *drag and drop, street virus, Auschwitz Lie, Dayton Accords, dead cat bounce, mitigation specialist, New Man, full monty*, and *Generation Y*, not to mention new senses of *Easter egg* and *dot*.

Today's dictionary users are typically in a hurry, not wishing to pore over line after line of small type to find the meaning sought. Thus, the ***Encarta World English Dictionary*** contains unique "quick definitions" in small-capital letters, which give you the gist of a word's meaning, especially in multisense entries, so that you can skim the definitions, find what you want quickly, and then read the full definition that follows at your discretion. In another attempt to make this Dictionary easy to use, we have insisted that all science, medical, and technological definitions be written in language that the average educated reader can understand. This policy of accessibility parallels other current trends, such as plain-language movements in the fields of law, medicine, and pharmacy. The definition at the entry *gene* makes the point. By the same token, we realized that most people are mystified by complex pronunciation symbols; hence, our pronunciation system avoids confusing diacritics. This simplified pronunciation system makes the Dictionary ideal for broadcast media people as well as for general users.

Etymologies, or word histories, give, when possible, the century-date of a word's first English occurrence, together with its basic developmental history. When applicable, English words are traced thousands of years back to Indo-European, our ancestral language; at *hail* (the ice pellets), for example, you will learn that the term is ultimately from an Indo-European word that also produced a Greek word meaning "pebble." Word origin essays further link one word to others, giving you a deeper dimension to their genealogies. For instance, if you turn to *energy*, you will find that the words *irk, liturgy, organ, orgy, surgeon,* and *work* all share with it the same Indo-European base. And when a particular word has a very interesting or disputed history, the Dictionary goes into details; see the mystery at *flamingo*.

The Dictionary contains regional English notes at many terms still restricted in their currency to certain geographic areas of North America. The words *hilahila* meaning "bashful, shy, or ashamed"(Hawaii), *farmer's match* (Midwest), *flitter* meaning "fritter" (Appalachian Highlands), and the sense of *Easter lily* meaning "trillium" (Washington State) are but a few examples.

The ***Encarta World English Dictionary*** devotes particular attention to matters of good usage, its Usage notes having been written by publishing professionals conversant with the real-time, real-life problems encountered by writers wishing to use the language with felicity, precision, and accuracy. The Usage notes at *arguably, data, finalize,* and *one* make the point. Strong notes and warning labels involving racial, ethnic, gender, and other sensitivity traps are included at certain stigmatized terms.

Language is an artifact of our culture, domestic and international, and so the ***Encarta World English Dictionary***, unlike any other, ties matters of culture—music, dance, drama, literature, films, painting, sculpture, even comics and cartoons—to headwords with which the titles, characters, or expressions associated with these artistic works are obviously linked. Thus, at the entry *enigma* you will find a Cultural Note that reveals a surprising historical tie-in between the title of a famous classical music piece and a World War II encryption machine. At *pilgrim* you will see that *slough of despond, vanity fair,* and *muckrak(er)* all derive from John Bunyan's *Pilgrim's Progress*.

From the quoted illustrations at entries such as *edge city* to the biographies of personages such as *Jacqueline du Pré, Janet Reno*, and *John Glenn* to the geographic entries for places like *Kosovo, Bosnia-Herzegovina*, and *Hong Kong,* the ***Encarta World English Dictionary*** brings a now globalized language back to its people—the people who created it, and who continue, as I write this, to shape it. May it serve you and your children well in the coming years, and may it bring about better international understanding as World English becomes *the* lingua franca of the twenty-first century.

Anne H. Soukhanov
U.S. General Editor
Bedford, Virginia
April 1999

Introduction to the First Edition

Dr. Kathy Rooney

THE ENGLISH LANGUAGE has changed. One in five of the world's population speaks English. Approximately 375 million people speak English as their first language. Over 375 million people speak English as their second language. English is the main international language of business, pop music, sports, advertising, academic conferences, travel, airports, air-traffic control, diplomacy, science, and technology. It is estimated that English is the language of over 80 percent of the information stored in the world's computers and 85 percent of Internet home pages, and that English is the first language of 68 percent of Web users.

The *Encarta World English Dictionary* is the first dictionary to be able to reflect this new world status of the English language, bringing together not only the two main spelling forms of the language (American English and British English), but also all the other main varieties of our language—from Canada, Australia, New Zealand, Africa, Asia, the Caribbean, and the Pacific Rim.

The Database from which the *Encarta World English Dictionary* is derived is the first dictionary database to have been written in both of the main spelling forms of English at the same time. This gives the Dictionary a truly world perspective. The great dictionaries of the past have all been firmly rooted in their specific cultural heritage—Oxford on the one hand, and, in the United States, the multitude of Websters on the other. In writing the *Encarta World English Dictionary* we have gone beyond such national boundaries and created a dictionary that accurately reflects the worldwide presence of the English language today. The Dictionary has been compiled by a team of over 320 dictionary editors (lexicographers), word-history experts (etymologists), pronunciation specialists (phoneticians), and over 120 special subject and World English consultants. Our team has been drawn from around the world and has included, for example, a Canadian poet, the manager of a meditation center in rural Maryland, and a telecommuting mother of twins from the Orkney Islands, off the northernmost coast of Scotland.

The *Encarta World English Dictionary* is first and foremost a dictionary of the modern English language. The audience for this dictionary is diverse, worldwide, encompassing a wide range of ages and backgrounds. It is also a multimedia audience, for the Dictionary is the first written with both print and electronic publications in view, and the first to be published simultaneously around the world and in both print and electronic formats. For this reason we have made the language of the definitions as natural as possible, and we have tried to avoid dictionary jargon where feasible. We have tried to create clear, informative, and readable definitions that our readers will understand without difficulty. Our goal has been to write our definitions in natural English, to use a level of vocabulary more accessible than the entry term, and to differentiate a word from its near-synonyms while making the user aware of any nuances that generally attach to a sense. Our definitions identify and focus clearly on the characteristics that distinguish and differentiate a word from related terms and include features that are picked up in similes and metaphorical usage.

Where other dictionaries might be described as literary, based on historical principles, or scientific, the *Encarta World English Dictionary* should be described as modern. Its focus is on the language needs of general dictionary users today. These needs encompass both the newest scientific and slang terms and literary or historical language that users of the Dictionary may encounter in their reading. Our guiding principle has been to define the language that our readers are likely to encounter in their everyday lives.

There are in the region of one million words in the English language today, and this total continues to grow, especially in areas such as technology, science, popular culture, and business. The *Encarta World English Dictionary* gives a picture of the language today, and, as our Corpus grows, we will continue to monitor and expand the Dictionary to reflect new coinages and senses. The *Encarta World English Dictionary* has over 100,000 headwords (the words you look up), including

10,000 biographical and geographical entries, and over 3.5 million words of text.

Dictionary editors require hard data to make sure that the definitions they write are based on good linguistic evidence. For earlier dictionary writers such evidence has been garnered and stored on cards or slips of paper. In recent years the advent of the computer has meant that such cumbersome and time-consuming methods have been replaced by computerized corpora. A corpus is like a huge filing cabinet, filled with millions of words of real language (taken from fiction, nonfiction, and journalism, for example). Software developed specifically for this project has enabled our editors to call up examples of the use of any term at the touch of a computer key. The Corpus of World English was created specifically for the *Encarta World English Dictionary* and contains over 50 million words of English from around the world. The *Encarta World English Dictionary* is the first dictionary compiled for speakers of U.S. English for which its editors have been able to use a corpus.

Computers have been vital not only in helping us find the evidence for our definitions but also in enabling us to communicate effectively with our far-flung team. This dictionary is the first to have made maximum use of the Internet not only as a source of language evidence but also as a fundamental means of communication among members of the compilation team. Every evening from our offices we e-mailed our team batches of work. These were then returned to us by e-mail.

People use dictionaries to find out what words mean, and often these words are scientific or technical. However, many dictionaries define such terms in ways that can seem just as technical as the term itself. In writing the *Encarta World English Dictionary* we have tried to bring the same criteria of clarity and transparency to our scientific and technical definitions that have characterized our approach to other definitions. We have applied these criteria across all our specialized entries. In doing so, we combined the skills of our technical definers with contributions from our many subject advisers who checked the accuracy of our definitions and patiently answered thousands of queries. Thus, the *Encarta World English Dictionary* tries to paint a word picture that the reader can understand by keeping use of specialist terminology to a minimum.

Our research has indicated that today's dictionary users want to find the information they are seeking quickly. In response to that need we have developed the "quick definition" feature that is unique to this Dictionary. Quick definitions appear in small capital letters at all entries with more than one sense. They give a brief gloss of the headword for the user who does not want, or need, the full picture. They provide a thumbnail sketch rather than an analysis of the meaning. The quick definitions are also important in helping readers to navigate through the many senses of a long entry.

When deciding on the order of sense categories, our general principle has been "most frequent first, least frequent last" as judged by current usage and evidence from our Corpus of World English. This is to make certain that the most common senses occur early in the entry, to make the text of the Dictionary easy to use. We have, however, in some instances overridden this principle where more frequent senses clearly develop out of a less frequent (probably more technical) sense. Senses within the same part of speech are grouped together in an entry. Informal and slang senses usually come before dated or archaic senses but after stylistically neutral senses.

In sense division, we have tried to strike a balance midway between broad and narrow categorization of senses. The primary consideration has always been ease of use by the reader. We have applied a similar priority when deciding which words and senses should be expanded by example phrases and sentences. We have tried to include these wherever they will help the reader grasp the meaning more easily.

The pronunciation system has been especially developed for the *Encarta World English Dictionary* to provide a system that speakers of English will find easy to decode. Rather than using the International Phonetic Alphabet (IPA), an excellent system for learners of our language, we felt that we should provide a more up-to-date system that our users, mainly speakers of the English language, would find easier to understand. Syllabication dots are included at all entries to help users to break words in the correct place.

Language is a powerful tool, one that can hurt and offend. In writing the ***Encarta World English Dictionary*** we have been at pains to write definitions that convey the meaning of the word in an appropriately clear but sensitive way. Since the Dictionary is a snapshot of the language today, we include some terms that a few users may find offensive or even highly offensive. It has been our policy throughout to indicate clearly when such terms are likely to cause offense. A number of lexical entries labeled *offensive* or *taboo* must be defined as entries in any adult dictionary that attempts to cover the whole range of the language. However, in writing the Dictionary, we have tried to avoid sexist, ethnic, ethnocentric, ethnophobic, ageist, racist, or physiologically stereotypical language in the definitions, examples, and other elements of the text.

Since the English language has a fascinating history, we have paid particular attention to tracing the histories of words (**etymologies**). Our etymologies are written in clear language, avoiding symbols and abbreviations wherever possible. They show not only the origins of the word but also its relationship to other words and the reasons why the word has its particular origin. We have also included hundreds of extended word-history essays. In addition to extended paragraphs on word histories, we have included similar brief essays on usage, synonyms, World English, regional English, and cultural notes. The essays form a stepping stone from the Dictionary text into the wider world of cultural reference.

Writing the ***Encarta World English Dictionary*** has been a huge challenge. Over 320 people have worked on the project. I would like to thank all of them most sincerely for their commitment and dedication at all stages. I would also like to thank our international publishing partners who have shared with us the excitement of writing this completely new Dictionary of the world's language—English.

Kathy Rooney
April 1999

How to use the *Encarta World English Dictionary*

Faye Carney

INTRODUCTION

A dictionary is a complex amalgam of different elements that relate to what users want from a dictionary—spelling, pronunciation, meaning, examples of use, advice on grammar or usage, and the explanation of the origins of a word. This section outlines briefly the different elements in the text, so that you can find what you want in the *Encarta World English Dictionary* quickly and easily.

THE PAGE

Guide Words

Each page has two **guide words** that show, on the left, the first **boldface** dictionary entry on that page, and, on the right, the last, so that you can quickly find the word you are looking for.

Pronunciation Key

Each double-page spread shows the **pronunciation key** along the foot of the page for ease of reference. (For full details on the **Pronunciation System**, see p. xxi.)

Text Layout

The text is designed in three columns for maximum coverage and legibility. Important elements of the text appear in **boldface** type. Quick definitions appear in SMALL CAPITALS. Full definitions appear in roman type and examples and quotations in *italic type*.

Illustrations

Illustrations appear as close as possible to the entries to which they refer. Over 4,000 items are illustrated in this Dictionary in more than 3,500 single and composite images and tables.

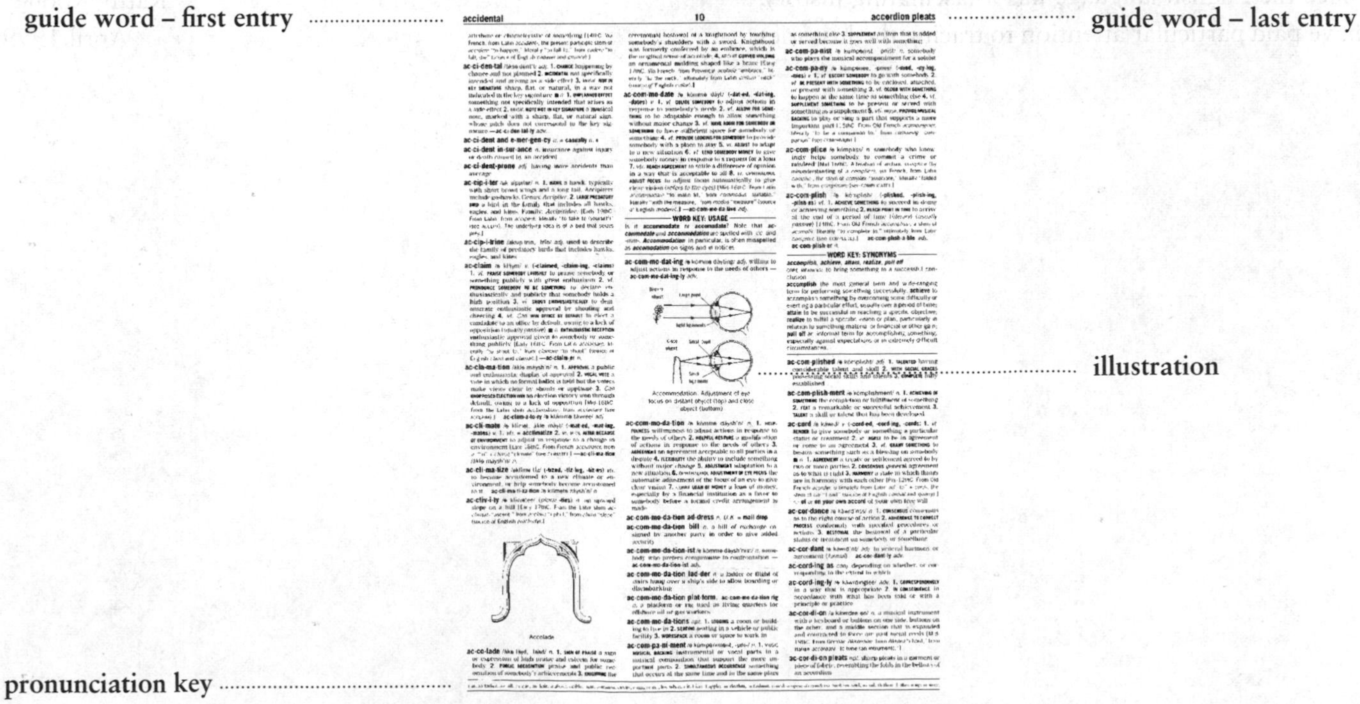

THE TEXT

The text of a dictionary combines many different elements, which are explained briefly here.

Headwords

The *Encarta World English Dictionary* contains over 100,000 headwords (the words you look up), including approximately 10,000 entries about people and places—the biographical and geographical entries.

Syllabication

Syllable breaks are indicated by centered dots in the headword to show where it is advisable to break words at the end of a line of writing.

Alphabetical order

Headwords are listed in strict letter order, ignoring punctuation and other characters:

box bed *n.*
box·board *n.*
box calf *n.*
box cam·er·a *n.*
box can·yon *n.*
box·car *n.*
box coat *n.*
box el·der *n.*

Biographical and geographical entries are listed alphabetically. Wherever one name appears in more than one entry, the entries appear in alphabetical order following the comma with a pronunciation of the first occurrence of the name:

Ad·ams, Abigail
Ad·ams, Ansel
Ad·ams, Gerry
Ad·ams, Henry
Ad·ams, John
Ad·ams, John Quincy
Ad·ams, Samuel

Phrasal verbs are listed with their root verb. See pp xviii.

Words with the same spelling

Words with the same spelling (**homographs**) but with different pronunciations or origins (**etymologies**) are listed with superscript numbers to differentiate them. The order of these numbers broadly reflects usage and frequency.

bow[1] /bō/ *n.* 1. **LOOPED KNOT** a knot in which the loops remain visible, e.g., in tied shoelaces or in ribbons used for decorating gifts or hair. ◊ **bow tie** 2. SPORTS, ARMS **WEAPON FOR FIRING ARROWS** a weapon used to fire arrows, consisting of a curved, flexible piece of wood and a taut string fastened to the two ends 3. MUSIC **ROD FOR PLAYING STRINGED INSTRUMENTS** a rod with horsehair tightly stretched between the two ends, used for playing stringed instruments 4. **CURVED SHAPE OR PART** a rounded or semicircular shape, e.g., a part of a building or a loop in a river 5. **FRAME OF GLASSES** the frame for a pair of glasses, or the part of the frame that curls around the ear 6. ARCHERY, HIST = **bowman**[1] (*literary*) 7. = **rainbow** ■ **bows** *npl.* ARCHERY, HIST **ARCHERS** bowmen or archers considered as a group (*literary*) ■ *v.* (**bowed, bow·ing, bows**) 1. *vti.* **BEND SOMETHING INTO BOW SHAPE** to bend, or bend something, into a rounded or bow shape 2. *vti.* MUSIC **DRAW BOW ACROSS STRINGED INSTRUMENT** to draw a bow across the strings of a stringed instrument 3. *vt.* MUSIC **INDICATE BOWING FOR MUSIC** to mark a piece of music to indicate which notes are to be played with the bow moving in one direction across the strings and which are to be played with it moving in the opposite direction [Old English *boga*. Ultimately from a prehistoric Germanic word meaning "to bend," which is also the ancestor of English *bow*[2], *bight*, and *bagel*.]

bow[2] /bow/ *v.* (**bowed, bow·ing, bows**) 1. *vti.* **BEND HEAD OR BODY FORWARD** to bend the head forward, or to bend forward from the waist, as a signal of respect, greeting, consent, submission, or acknowledgment ○ *bowing her head in shame* 2. *vti.* **BEND SOMETHING OR DROOP** to bend something over so that it droops, or to be bent in this way ○ *branches bowed down with fruit.* 3. *vi.* **YIELD TO SOMETHING OR SOMEBODY** to accept something and yield to it, often unwillingly ○ *bowed to the demands of pressure groups* ■ *n.* **BENDING FORWARD OF UPPER BODY** a bending forward of the upper part of the body to show respect, acknowledgment, subservience, courtesy, or greeting [Old English *būgan* (source also of English *buxom*). Ultimately from an Indo-European word meaning "to bend," which is also the ancestor of English *bow*[1].] ◇ **bow and scrape** to be excessively polite or attentive in an attempt to ingratiate yourself with somebody

bow[3] /bow/ *n.* 1. SHIPPING **FRONT PART OF VESSEL** the front section of a boat or other vessel 2. ROWING **PERSON IN BOW** the rower or oar closest to the front of a boat [Early 17thC. From Low German *boog* or Middle Dutch *boeg*.]

Pronunciation

Our pronunciation system has been developed specifically for the ***Encarta World English Dictionary***. It relies on familiar combinations of letters of the alphabet, so that you can use it without constant reference to a table of explanations and symbols. The system is explained in full on pp. xxi-xxii.

Variant spellings

The Dictionary takes note wherever a word has more than one possible spelling **variant**. Such entries appear in **boldface type** following their headword.

fa·la·fel /fə laáf'l/, **fe·la·fel** *n.* a deep-fried ball of ground chickpeas seasoned with onions and spices, often eaten in pita bread with lettuce and yogurt or tahini sauce. It was originally a Middle Eastern dish. [Mid-20thC. Via Egyptian Arabic *falāfil* from Arabic *fulful* "pepper."]

fe·la·fel *n.* = **falafel**

Inflections

Inflections are forms of words that are different from the headword. These include the different tenses of verbs, the comparative and superlative forms of adjectives, and irregular plurals of nouns. These forms are shown after the pronunciation where the inflection applies to the whole headword or at a specific sense or group of senses as appropriate.

gam·bol /gámb'l/ *vi.* (**-boled** *or* **-bolled, -bol·ing** *or* **-bol·ling, -bols**) **LEAP PLAYFULLY** to leap or skip about playfully ■ *n.* **PLAYFUL LEAPING** an instance of leaping about playfully [Mid-16thC. Alteration of GAMBADE.]

gas /gass/ *n.* (*plural* **gas·es** *or* **gas·ses**) 1. CHEM **SUBSTANCE SUCH AS AIR** a substance such as air that is neither a solid nor a liquid at ordinary temperatures and that has the ability to expand indefinitely 2. UTIL, GEOL **FOSSIL FUEL** a combustible gaseous substance such as natural gas or propane, used as a fuel 3. AUTOMOT **GASOLINE** gasoline for internal-combustion engines 4. AUTOMOT **CAR ACCELERATOR** the pedal used for accelerating a motor vehicle (*informal*) ○ *step on the* *gas* **5.** MIL, CRIMINOL **GAS FOR POISONING OR ASPHYXIATING** a gaseous mixture used as a poison, irritant, or asphyxiating agent **6.** PHARM **ANESTHETIC** a gaseous substance used as an anesthetic **7.** PHYSIOL **FLATULENCE** gaseous product of digestion (*informal*) **8.** MINING **METHANE AND AIR** the highly explosive product of methane combined with air **9. SOMEBODY OR SOMETHING ENTERTAINING** somebody or something such as an experience that is very thrilling or entertaining (*slang*) **10. NONSENSE** meaningless empty talk (*slang*) ■ *v.* (**gassed, gas·sing, gas·es** *or* **gas·ses**) **1.** *vt.* **TO HARM SOMEBODY WITH GAS** to attack, injure, or kill a person or animal with a poisonous, irritating, or asphyxiating gas **2.** *vi.* **RELEASE GAS** to give off gas or a gas **3.** *vi.* **TALK IDLY** to talk too much, especially about unimportant matters (*informal*) [Mid-17thC. From Dutch, coined by the Flemish chemist J. B. van Helmont (1577–1644), based on Greek *khaos* "empty space" (source of English *chaos*).] —**gas·sing** *n.*

ga·teau /ga tő, gaa-/ (*plural* **-teaux** *or* **-teaus**), **gâ·teau** (*plural* **-teaux** /-tő/) *n.* **1. RICH CAKE** a rich cake, usually consisting of several layers held together with a cream filling **2. BAKED FOOD** food baked and served in a form resembling a cake [Mid-19thC. From French, "cake."]

Important irregular inflections also appear as headwords in their own right:

fo·ra *npl.* plural of **forum**

laid past tense, past participle of **lay**[1]

Parts of Speech

Parts of speech labels, in *italic type*, indicate the linguistic function of the headword. They are:

abbr.	abbreviation
adj.	adjective
adv.	adverb
aux. v.	auxiliary verb
conj.	conjunction
contr.	contraction
def. art.	definite article
indef. art.	indefinite article
interj.	interjection
modal v.	modal verb
n.	noun
npl.	plural noun
prefix	prefix
prep.	preposition
pron.	pronoun
symbol	symbol
suffix	suffix
tdmk.	trademark
v.	verb
vi.	intransitive verb
vr.	reflexive verb
vt.	transitive verb
vti.	transitive and intransitive verb

Abbreviations and Acronyms

Abbreviations and acronyms are grouped together according to their punctuation and their status as either an abbreviation or symbol. Our Corpus has shown that punctuation within abbreviations varies considerably. This Dictionary gives the most common form; important variants are also shown. Senses are ordered alphabetically.

q[1] /kyoo/ (*plural* **q's**), **Q** (*plural* **Q's** *or* **Qs**) *n.* **1. 17TH LETTER OF ENGLISH ALPHABET** the 17th letter of the modern English alphabet **2. SPEECH SOUND CORRESPONDING TO LETTER "Q"** the speech sound that corresponds to the letter "Q" **3. LETTER "Q" WRITTEN** a written representation of the letter "Q"

q[2] *symbol.* PHYS **1.** electric charge **2.** heat *n.* 1.

Q *abbr.* **1.** CHESS queen **2.** MONEY quetzal

q. *abbr.* **1.** quart **2.** quarter **3.** quarterly **4.** quarto **5.** question **6.** query **7.** quire **8.** MEASURE quintal

Q. *abbr.* **1.** quartermaster **2.** quarto **3.** Quebec **4.** queen

When an abbreviation is more frequently used than its full form, we give the definition at the abbreviation:

DNA *n.* a nucleic acid molecule in the form of a twisted double strand (**double helix**) that is the major component of chromosomes and carries genetic information. DNA, which is found in all living organisms except some viruses, is self-replicating and is responsible for passing along hereditary characteristics from one generation to the next. Full form **deoxyribonucleic acid**

Senses

Many words have more than one sense. The different senses are indicated by sense numbers that appear in **boldface** type. Senses are ordered according to usage and frequency; they are grouped according to part of speech (all noun senses together, all verb senses together, and so on).

The symbol [■] introduces a new part of speech within an entry.

ra·di·ant /ráydee ənt/ *adj.* **1. SHOWING HAPPINESS** expressing joy, energy, or good health in a pleasing way **2. SHINING** lit with a bright or glowing light **3.** PHYS **EMITTED AS WAVES** used to describe light, heat, or other energy emitted in the form of waves or rays ○ *radiant heat* **4.** PHYS **EMITTING RADIANT ENERGY** emitting light, heat, or other energy in the form of waves or rays ■ *n.* **1. HEATING ELEMENT** an element in a heater that gives out radiant heat **2.** ASTRON **METEOR SHOWER'S POINT OF ORIGIN** a point in space from which a meteor shower appears to originate [15thC. From Latin *radiant-*, the present participle stem of *radiare* "to RADIATE."] —**ra·di·ant·ly** *adv.*

Undefined Terms (Runons)

At the end of many entries there are additional **boldface** entries that have no definitions. These are called undefined runons, and they consist of the headword plus a standard derivative suffix such as *–ly* or *–ness*, or the headword shown in another part of speech. They do not require definitions because they correlate almost exactly in meaning and usage with the main entry. Where appropriate, runons have been given pronunciations, for example, where their stress pattern is different from that of the headword.

fluff·y /flúffee/ (**-i·er, -i·est**) *adj.* **1. SOFT AND LIGHT** consisting of something soft and light to the touch such as wool or feathers **2. DOWNY OR FEATHERY** covered in something soft and light to the touch such as down or feathers **3.** COOK **SOFT AND LIGHT IN TEXTURE** soft and light in texture because air has been beaten or whisked in —**fluff·i·ly** *adv.* —**fluff·i·ness** *n.*

Where we have had sufficient evidence from our Corpus that a potential runon in fact has a different pattern of linguistic behavior, that term has been defined fully.

Subject Labels

Many senses define terms belonging to specific subject areas. **Subject area labels** indicate the subject area to which a sense belongs. The subject labels signpost the different senses in an entry and help you find your way through it.

mark·ing /maárking/ *n.* **1.** ZOOL **MARK OR MARKS** a mark or pattern of marks that occurs naturally, e.g., on an animal's coat (*often used in the plural*) **2.** AIR **AIRCRAFT**

IDENTIFYING MARK an identifying mark, usually a colored symbol, on an aircraft (*often used in the plural*) **3.** EDUC **ASSESSMENT AND GRADING OF WRITTEN WORK** a teacher's correction and assessment of students' written work

Quick Definitions

The **quick definitions**, like subject labels, are designed to guide you through longer entries. They appear in SMALL CAPITALS and act as a brief summary of the full definition so that you can easily find your way to the appropriate sense.

ease /eez/ *n.* **1.** LACK OF DIFFICULTY lack of difficulty in doing or achieving something ○ *defeated the challenger with ease* **2.** LACK OF AWKWARDNESS lack of awkwardness, stiffness, or self-consciousness in social situations ○ *He felt totally at ease with her.* **3.** COMFORT AND AFFLUENCE a comfortable and leisured state free from problems and restrictions, especially those caused by poverty ○ *a life of ease* **4.** RELAXATION a state of comfort and relaxation **5.** RELIEF FROM WORRY OR PAIN freedom or relief from worry or pain

Definitions

The definitions in the *Encarta World English Dictionary* explain the meaning of the sense clearly and comprehensibly and differentiate it from related terms and words meaning almost the same thing.

o·a·sis /ō áyssiss/ (*plural* **-ses** /-seez/) *n.* **1.** GEOG FERTILE LAND IN DESERT fertile ground in a desert where the level of underground water rises to or near ground level, where plants grow and travelers can replenish water supplies **2.** PLACE OR TIME OF RELIEF a place or period that gives relief from a troubling or chaotic situation [Early 17thC. Via late Latin from Greek. Probably ultimately of Egyptian origin.]

Specialist Terminology

The Dictionary includes as headwords the main specialized language you are likely to encounter in general publications and consumer magazines, as well as the principal terminology likely to be encountered by college students.

lig·a·ture /líggəchər, liggə choor/ *n.* **1.** SOMETHING USED FOR TYING something that is used for binding things or tying things up **2.** TYING PROCESS the process of binding something or tying something up **3.** BOND a unifying link or bond (*formal*) **4.** SURG SURGICAL THREAD FOR TYING OFF A DUCT a piece of surgical thread used to tie off a duct or blood vessel in order to cut off the supply of body fluid normally running through it **5.** PRINTING, LING CHARACTER CONSISTING OF JOINED LETTERS a character or piece of type, e.g., æ, that consists of two or more letters joined together **6.** MUSIC = **tie** *n.* 8 **7.** MUSIC SYMBOL IN MEDIEVAL MUSIC a symbol indicating a group of notes to be sung to one syllable in the notation of medieval music **8.** MUSIC REED-HOLDER ON WOODWIND INSTRUMENT on a woodwind instrument, a band, usually made of metal, that holds the reed to the mouthpiece [14thC. Via Old French from, ultimately, Latin *ligare* "to bind" (see LIGAMENT).]

Dated and Archaic Language

The Dictionary includes usages that are no longer current but that you may encounter in works of literature, such as prominent obsolete, archaic, or dated terms.

jo·rum /jáwrəm/, **jo·ram** *n.* a large drinking bowl or its contents (*archaic*) [Mid-18thC. Origin uncertain: perhaps named for *Joram*, who took silver, gold, and brass vessels to King David (II Samuel 8:10).]

Examples

The *Encarta World English Dictionary* has thousands of illustrative examples that clarify the definitions and place them in context. These are drawn from our Corpus of World English.

The symbol [○] introduces examples.

nar·row /nérrō/ *adj.* **1.** SMALL IN WIDTH having a small width, especially in comparison to height or length ○ *a narrow gap* **2.** LIMITED IN SIZE limited or restricted in size or scope ○ *a narrow range of options* **3.** NARROW-MINDED limited and usually inflexible in outlook ○ *a narrow view of events* **4.** JUST ENOUGH FOR SUCCESS barely sufficient for success ○ *a narrow victory* ○ *a narrow escape*

Citations

The Dictionary also includes many quotations taken from written sources (**citations**) such as fiction, nonfiction, and journalism. These citations are drawn from our Corpus of World English.

en·tan·gle·ment /in táng g'lmənt, en-/ *n.* **1.** COMPLICATED PERSONAL SITUATION a complicated situation involving two or more people **2.** CONFUSION confusion or a confused situation ○ *"He sat with his mouth full of toast and his eyes sparkling with mischief, watching my intellectual entanglement."* (Arthur Conan Doyle, *The Valley of Fear*; 1915) **3.** TANGLED THING a mass of tangled objects

Word Origins

The principal aim of the word origins (**etymologies**) in the Dictionary is to present the etymology of the entries with as much accuracy as present-day knowledge will permit, in a way that is accessible and interesting to the general reader. Etymologies have as far as possible been written in plain English, with few abbreviations or technical terms. Where possible, etymologies include the date when the headword was first recorded, an account of the word's origin, and other relevant information likely to be of interest to readers. Many words have a story that is not obvious from the standard bare bones etymology. Where possible, we tell it.

nail *n.*
[Old English *nægl*. Ultimately from an Indo-European word denoting a fingernail or toenail that is also the ancestor of English *onyx* and *ungulate*. The meaning "fastener" evolved in prehistoric Germanic.]

In writing the etymologies, we have put particular stress on three themes. Firstly, the etymological connections between English words, both the obvious and the more remote, such as that between *nail* and *onyx* above.

nau·ti·cal *adj.*
[Mid-16thC. Via Latin from Greek *nautikos*, from *nautēs* "sailor," from *naus* "ship" (source of English *astronaut*, *nausea*, and *noise*).]

Secondly, where possible we explain any ultimate metaphor that underlies the meaning of a modern English word:

na·ive *adj.*
[Mid-17thC. From French *naïve*, feminine of *naïf*, from Latin *nativus* "born" (source of English *native*). The underlying idea is of the innocence or gullibility of the newborn.]

Thirdly, we explain why a word is used with a particular meaning. This may be because of a development of meaning in English or in a source language, from an association with a person or place, or from some visual image or stereotype. We call these "Why?" etymologies, since telling an interesting story is a key feature of the word histories in the Dictionary.

nam·by-pam·by /nàmbee pámbee/ *adj.* (*informal*) **1.** WEAK feeble, childish, and weak **2.** SILLY silly, sentimental, or overly sensitive ■ *n.* (*plural* **nam·by-pam·bies**) NAMBY-PAMBY PERSON somebody who is considered weak or silly (*informal*) [Mid-16thC. Originally a mocking nickname for the English poet Ambrose Philips (1674–1749), who wrote feebly sentimental pastorals; based on *Amb(rose).*]

chor·tle /cháwrt'l/ *n.* GLEEFUL LAUGH a noisy gleeful laugh ■ *vi.* (**-tled, -tling, -tles**) GIVE A CHORTLE to laugh in a noisy gleeful way [Late 19thC. Blend of CHUCKLE and SNORT, originated by Lewis CARROLL in *Through the Looking-Glass* (1872).] —**chor·tler** *n.*

gra·ham flour *n.* unbolted whole-wheat flour [Named for Dr. Sylvester *Graham* (1794–1851), a North American dietary reformer.]

We have also included additional interesting information about the word's origin or transmission into English, for example:

nain·sook /náyn sòòk/ *n.* a lightweight cotton fabric used for babywear and lingerie, originally from India [Late 18thC. From Hindi *nainsukh*, literally "pleasure to the eye."]

Function Words

Function words are grammatical words that include the common prepositions, adverbs, conjunctions, and pronouns (*up, down, at, so, what, when, many, such, a, the,* and so on); the modal verbs and auxiliaries; and verbs such as *be, come, do, get, give,* and *have*.

Speakers of a language rarely look up common terms such as these. They tend to look up rare or archaic senses; technical and specialist senses, such as the nautical use of *after*; dialectal terms, or senses from other varieties of English, such as Irish *I'm after going to town;* senses that present a style or usage problem, such as *a* or *an* used before "h"; least frequently of all, users might want to verify grammar points, for example, whether *after* is an adverb or a preposition.

An introductory summary of the word's "core," or central, meaning appears at the start of the entry. Remaining senses appear in the usual way, except that parts of speech may be combined at one sense. Senses are ordered by frequency.

no² /nō/ CORE MEANING: an adjective used to indicate that there is not any or not one person or thing ○ *There is nothing in walking distance: no post office, no bank.* ○ *I had no choice in the matter.* ○ *They pay no attention to me.*
adj. **1.** NOT AT ALL used to indicate that somebody or something does not have any of the characteristic or identity mentioned ○ *She's no fool.* **2.** NOT not exceeding a particular amount or quality (*used with comparative adjectives and adverbs*) ○ *The issue was no less important to us than you.* [12thC. Shortening of NONE.]

Foreign Words and Phrases

Based on information in our Corpus of World English, foreign words and phrases are included in the A-Z list as entries if they have established English pronunciations and are used without being explained in contemporary literature, journalism, general writing, or general conversation.

jeu d'e·sprit /zhòò de spreé/ (*plural* **jeux d'e·sprit** /zhòò de spreé/) *n.* a witticism, especially one that appears in a work of literature (*literary*) [Early 18thC. From French, literally "game of spirit or wit."]

Cross-References

The *Encarta World English Dictionary* contains two main types of cross-references.

Direct cross-references

A direct cross-reference takes the place of a definition, and indicates that the information you need is given at another entry in the alphabetical sequence of headwords that has the same meaning.

car·ney, carnie *n.* = **carny¹**
em·i·nen·cy /émmenensee/ *n., adj.* = **eminence** *n.* 1

The sign (=) refers from a variant to its main form. *Plural of, past tense of,* and so on refer from an inflected form to its root word. *Abbr of, symbol for,* and *full form of* refer from an abbreviation or acronym or symbol to its full form, or vice versa.

Indirect cross-references

The symbol [◊] indicates an indirect cross-reference to another entry where you will find additional relevant information:

car·ni·vore /kaárne vàwr/ *n.* **1.** FLESH-EATING ANIMAL an animal that eats other animals. ◊ **herbivore, omnivore**

Idioms and Phrases

Phrases and idioms are important lexical groups that are typically underrepresented in dictionaries. The *Encarta World English Dictionary* gives particular attention to such items.

car·pet /kaárpet/ *n.* **1.** FLOOR COVERING thick fabric for covering a floor **2.** PIECE OF FLOOR COVERING a piece of thick, heavy fabric covering the floor of a room or area **3.** LAYER OR COVERING a layer or covering (*literary*) ○ *a carpet of snow* ■ *vt.* (**-pet·ed, -pet·ing, -pets**) **1.** COVER FLOOR WITH CARPET to cover a floor, or the floor of a room, with a carpet ○ *We could carpet every room in the house with the money she spent on that rug.* **2.** COVER to cover something in a layer (*literary*) ○ *The valley was carpeted with flowers.* [14thC. Via Old French *carpite* or medieval Latin *carpita* from, ultimately, Latin *carpere* "to pluck." The underlying idea is of a cloth made from plucked or unraveled fabric.] ◇ **roll out the red carpet** to give a special welcome to a distinguished visitor ◇ **sweep something under the carpet** to conceal or ignore something that needs attention

Idioms and phrases are preceded by the symbol [◇].

Phrasal Verbs

The Dictionary gives phrasal verbs fuller treatment than they have traditionally received in dictionaries for native speakers. Phrasal verbs are verb-plus-particle combinations in which the total meanings are not literally the sum of the parts. They appear after the root form of the verb (**carry away** comes after **carry**, and so on).

carry away *vt.* to make somebody become less controlled, reasonable, or attentive by arousing his or her emotion or interest (*usually passive*) ○ *I was completely carried away by the beauty of it.*
carry back *vt.* to transfer something such as a tax credit so that it is calculated against the previous year's income
carry forward *vt.* **1.** TRANSFER ITEM IN ACCOUNT OR CALCULATION to transfer an item to the next section or column in accounts or in a calculation **2.** TRANSFER SOMETHING TO NEXT YEAR to transfer something, such as a tax credit or liability, so that it is calculated against the next year's income
carry off *vt.* **1.** REMOVE SOMEBODY OR SOMETHING to take something or somebody away with determination or purpose, or by force ○ *carried him off, kicking and screaming, to his crib* **2.** WIN to win a prize (*informal*) ○ *She carried off the award for best newcomer.* **3.** DO SOMETHING SUCCESSFULLY OR WELL to succeed in doing something well or producing a good effect ○ *He was nervous about chairing the meeting, but carried it*

off in style. ○ *It's a very sophisticated outfit, but she can't quite carry it off.*

Illustrations

The *Encarta World English Dictionary* illustrates over 4,000 items. The main function of the illustrations is to help the reader by adding to and complementing the text, providing additional context for the definition, and placing the definition in its context.

Style Level and Register

The Dictionary uses *italic* labels to indicate style, register, and currency:

Currency

archaic	not used since before World War II
dated	used at some stage between 1945 and 1990 but no longer part of the current idiom

Register

literary	used in literature and poetry and for special effect, but not used in everyday contexts
formal	used in formal situations and formal writing, but inappropriate in everyday contexts
technical	marks specialist terms that have an everyday equivalent
informal	used in relaxed conversation or writing but avoided in more formal contexts; often has an innocuous or euphemistic feel
humorous	pompous or formal or dated terms typically used for humorous effect
disapproving	marks a derogatory attitude on the part of the speaker
slang	highly informal, completely inappropriate in formal contexts, and often with a crude edge
babytalk	used by adults when talking to young children and babies
nonstandard	not considered part of correct or educated usage, though current in spoken usage

Offensiveness

insult	a pejorative term that would be likely to insult or upset somebody if it is said directly to the person
offensive	likely to be offensive to many people, for example, because it is racist or sexual
taboo	for classic taboo words referring to sex and bodily functions

Some lexical entries commonly regarded as offensive or taboo require inclusion in a dictionary of this size and scope. However, the editors have attempted to ensure that these and other offensive or potentially offensive lexical items and areas of reference are not used in the defining language and other elements of the text.

Words not universally regarded as offensive but likely to give offense in varying degrees are qualified accordingly: *often considered offensive*, *sometimes considered offensive*, and *offensive in some contexts*.

Offensive terms have been defined by a gloss rather than a substitutable definition.

World English and Regional Varieties of English

In the *Encarta World English Dictionary* we have attempted to give a world view of the English language. We have included information on the two main spelling forms of English—American and British—as well as reflecting words and patterns of usage from a world perspective:

> **caisse pop·u·laire** /kèss poppyoō láir/ (*plural* **caisses pop·u·laires** /kèss poppyoō láir/) *n. Quebec* in Quebec and other French-speaking parts of Canada, a financial institution resembling a credit union [From French]

> **hi·la·hi·la** *adj. Hawaii* bashful, shy, or ashamed [From Hawaiian]

Usage Notes

The Usage Notes serve one of three main purposes. They spell out useful syntactic information beyond the basic part of speech, for example, *takes a singular verb*; they give information on the typical users of a word or phrase, for example, *used mainly by children*; and they give information on the speaker's attitude or tone of voice, for example, *often used ironically*.

> **non·pro·lif·er·a·tion** /nònprə liffə ráysh'n/ *n.* the practice of limiting the production or spread of something, especially nuclear weapons (*often used before a noun*) ○ *nonproliferation agreements*

Trademarks, Servicemarks, Trade Names, and Proprietary Terms

The Dictionary includes words on the basis of their usage in the English language today. Words that are known to have current trademark or proprietary registrations have been given the part of speech *tdmk*.

Word Keys

The *Word Keys* are a feature of the *Encarta World English Dictionary* that has allowed the editors to provide more information on an aspect of a word than is possible within the scope of the standard dictionary entry.

Word History Essays

Over 400 word history essays give additional information of etymological or language-historical interest that is not directly relevant to the etymology of a particular headword, for example, at ***fluent***:

> **WORD KEY: ORIGIN**
> The Latin word *fluere*, from which ***fluent*** is derived, is also the source of English *affluent, effluent, flu, fluctuate, fluid, fluorides, flush, fluvial, flux, influence, mellifluous*, and *superfluous*.

World English and Regional Essays

The World English coverage in the Dictionary is underpinned by a number of essays on specific varieties of English, both regional and from around the world:

flit·ter[2] /flíttər/ *n.* any one of various types of fritter or small cake (*regional*) [alteration of FRITTER]

WORD KEY: REGIONAL NOTE

In the Appalachian Highlands, ***flitter*** identifies a pancake or flapjack; especially in the Piedmont South, it signals a fritter cake, often containing fruit or meat, fried in deep fat; in the Highlands, it also designates a fritter of fried corn meal.

Car·ib·be·an Eng·lish *n.* the variety of English spoken in the Caribbean islands

WORD KEY: WORLD ENGLISH

The English language as used in the Caribbean region, also called *West Indian English*. The islands and coasts of the Caribbean, since their discovery by Columbus in 1492, have, since that time, been claimed, disputed, settled, and governed by the Spanish, Portuguese, French, British, Dutch, Danish, and Americans with obvious, long-term, varied effects on the languages spoken there. In the second half of the 20th century, most of the territories are independent, but colonization has created a complex inheritance. In such mainland areas as Belize and Guyana, indigenous languages survive, but not on the islands, and in all territories there is a complex continuum between the standard forms of English (American and British), Dutch, French, and Spanish on the one side and their creole varieties on the other. In general terms, the creoles mix European lexical items with varying degrees of African structural features. In most Anglo-Caribbean territories, although school-based standard English is the official language it is a minority form and, in states like Belize and Guyana, English mixes with a range of other languages. Apart from Barbados and Guyana, ***Caribbean English*** is usually non-rhotic (i.e., r is not pronounced in such words as art, door, worker).

Usage Essays

The Usage Essays complement the Usage Notes by providing more extended attention to particularly thorny usage problems:

WORD KEY: USAGE

home or **house**? Many consider ***home*** an affectation when used anywhere that ***house*** would be appropriate (*Home for Sale*). ***Home*** is nonetheless useful to express the idea of dwelling places of various sorts, including apartments and condominiums, hogans and huts, and other dwellings that are not accurately described as houses. ***House***, in many contexts, suggests a single-family dwelling. For example, if *The tornado destroyed 17 homes* is meant to convey that 17 residential structures were demolished, the word should have been ***houses***. *Most homes in town lost electricity*, however, no doubt refers to households of all descriptions, so here ***homes*** is the better choice.

Synonym Essays

The Synonym Essays help distinguish between words that are close in meaning:

WORD KEY: SYNONYMS

necessary, ***essential***, ***vital***, ***indispensable***, ***requisite***, ***needed***

CORE MEANING: used to describe something that is required

necessary used to describe something that must be done or provided, or to indicate that somebody's presence is required; **essential** used to emphasize that something is necessary, for example, because a process could not take place without it; **vital** a very emphatic word used to stress that something is urgently necessary; **indispensable** literally suggesting somebody who or something that cannot be done without, but also often used simply to indicate that something is desirable or useful; **requisite** a formal word used especially to suggest that something has been made necessary by a particular circumstance; **needed** used to describe something that is required or desired but implying less urgency than the other words in the group.

Cultural Notes

Cultural Notes are a unique feature in the Dictionary. They form a bridge from a particular sense of a word to its wider cultural context. They typically refer to titles of books, movies, plays, and musical pieces, especially those that have passed into the language.

WORD KEY: CULTURAL NOTE

The Last of the Mohicans, a novel by writer James Fenimore Cooper (1826). The most popular of Cooper's evocative accounts of frontier life, it is set in mid-18th-century North America during the wars between Britain and France. It describes the attempts of frontiersman Hawkeye and his Mohican companions, Chingachook and Uncas, the last of their people, to protect a British family from the French and their Huron allies.

WORD KEY: CULTURAL NOTE

Home Alone, a movie by Chris Columbus (1990). A comedy set in Chicago at Christmas time, it portrays the adventures of a young boy, Kevin (Macauley Culkin), who is inadvertently left at home by his family when they go on vacation in Europe. Delighting in his newfound independence, the boy manages not only to take care of himself but also to outwit a pair of hapless burglars. In U.S. popular culture, *Home Alone* soon came to mean not only children left alone by negligent traveling parents but also the parents themselves, as this headline indicates: "'Home Alone' Parents Indicted by States on 64 Criminal Counts" *Washington Post* (February 10, 1993).

Pronunciation Guide

Pronunciations in the *Encarta World English Dictionary* are given in a pronunciation system specially developed for the Dictionary. It relies on familiar combinations of letters of the alphabet so that it can be interpreted without constant reference to a table of explanations. The only symbol taken from outside the ordinary alphabet is the *schwa* /ə/, which stands for the sound represented by **a** in **approve** and **megabyte**. In the Dictionary the pronunciations follow the headword or sense number and appear between forward slashes / /.

Pronunciation Key

a	at
aa	father
aw	all
ay	day
air	hair
b, bb	but, ribbon
ch	chin
d, dd	do, ladder
ə	about, edible, item, common, circus
e	egg
ee	eel, happy, medium
f, ff	fond, differ
g, gg	go, giggle
h	hot
hw	when
i	it
ī	ice
j, jj	juice, pigeon
k	key, thick
l, ll	let, silly
m, mm	mother, hammer
n, nn	not, funny
ng	song
o	odd
ō	open
o͝o	good
oo	school
ow	owl
oy	oil
p, pp	pen, happy
r, rr	road, carry, hard
s, ss	say, lesson
sh	sheep
th	thin
<u>th</u>	this
t, tt	tell, butter
u	up
ur	urge
v, vv	very, savvy
w	wet
y	yes
z, zz	zoo, blizzard
<u>zh</u>	vision

´ over a vowel indicates the syllable with the strongest (primary) stress.

` over a vowel indicates the syllable with medium (secondary) stress.

’ before /l/, /m/, or /n/ shows that the consonant is syllabic (takes the function of a vowel).

I. Consonants.

The following are used to describe the sound they usually stand for in ordinary spelling:
/b d f g h j k l m n p r s t v w y z/.

befriend	/bi frénd/
hug	/hug/
strap	/strap/
milk	/milk/
jazz	/jaz/
yes	/yess/

The following two-consonant combinations (**consonantal digraphs**) also denote the sound they stand for in ordinary spelling: /ch ng th/.

church	/church/
thing	/thing/
shop	/shop/

For the sound in **"the"** (**voiced dental fricative**) we have used <u>th</u>:

mother	/mú<u>th</u>ər/
that	/<u>th</u>at/

For the central sound in "vision" (**voiced palatoalveolar fricative**) we use <u>zh</u>:

vision	/ví<u>zh</u>’n/
pleasure	/plé<u>zh</u>ər/

Doubling

This Dictionary uses double consonants to show many sounds in the middle of words because English spelling normally doubles letters in these positions. Consonants are doubled when they are preceded by the stressed vowels /á, é, í, ó, ú, o͝o/ or /à, è, ì, ò, ù, o͝o/ and followed by either a vowel or a syllabic consonant, or by /l, r, y, or w/:

rubber	/rúbbər/
petrol	/péttrəl/
travel	/trávv’l/
inward	/ínnwərd/
deputy	/déppyətee/
supposition	/sùppə zísh’n/
teakettle	/tée kett’l/

In order to show clearly that /s/ is required, not /z/, we double the /s/ additionally at the end of a syllable and with voiced consonants:

face	/fayss/
miscue	/miss kyo͞o/
mincer	/mínssər/

But not with voiceless consonants:

wasp	/wosp/
first	/furst/
tax	/taks/

The consonant /k/ is not doubled:

flicker	/flíkər/
tackle	/ták’l/

There is no doubling of the two-consonant combinations /ch, sh, th, ng, <u>th</u>, <u>zh</u>/:

touching	/túching/
passion	/pásh’n/
rhythm	/rí<u>th</u>’m/
measure	/mé<u>zh</u>ər/
hanger	/hángər/

II. Vowels

The traditional short vowels /a, e, i, o, u/ denote the sounds they usually stand for in ordinary spelling:

cat	/kat/
head	/hed/
myth	/mith/
swan	/swon/
double	/dúbb’l/

For the short vowel as in "put", we use /o͝o/:

good	/go͝od/
could	/ko͝od/
full	/fo͝ol/

For the weak vowel as in the first syllable of "along and the second syllable of "butter" we use the symbol /ə/ (schwa):

along	/ə lóng/
butter	/búttər/
flattering	/fláttəring/

For the vowel in "goose" and "soup" we use /oo/:

food	/food/
move	/moov/
rude	/rood/

When this is preceded by a y-sound (**palatal semivowel**) we use /yoo/:

music	/myo͞ozik/
acute	/ə kyo͞ot/
sinuous	/sínnyoo əss/

In words such as "sure" and "pure" we have used /oor/ and /yoor/ respectively:

poor	/poor, pawr/
cure	/kyoor/
during	/do͝oring, dyo͝oring/

For the diphthongs in "gray", "flee", and "boy", th respellings /ay/, /ee/, and /oy/ are used:

great	/grayt/
niece	/neess/
voice	/voyss/

For the diphthongs in "high", "low", and "cow" w use /ī/, /ō/, and /ow/ respectively:

write	/rīt/
goat	/gōt/
micro	/mīkrō/
loud	/lowd/
frown	/frown/

For the vowel of "nurse", we use /ur/:

turn	/turn/
stern	/sturn/
first	/furst/

For the stressed vowel of "father" we use /aa/:

father	/fáathər/
bravado	/brə vaádō/

For the vowel of "start" in words where there is an "r" in the spelling, we use /aar/:

farm	/faarm/
starry	/stáaree/

We have used /aw/ for the vowel of "thought":

thought	/thawt/
tall	/tawl/
cross	/krawss/
frothy	/fráwthee/

For the vowel of "north" in words where there is an "r" in the spelling, we have used /awr/:

short	/shawrt/
war	/wawr/
sport	/spawrt/
sore	/sawr/
story	/stáwree/

For the vowels in "near" and "square" we have used /eer/ and /air/ respectively:

beer	/beer/
beard	/beerd/
weary	/wéeree/
declare	/di kláir/
scarce	/skairss/
vary	/váiree/

For the vowels in "fire" and "sour", we have used /īr/ and /owr/:

inspire	/in spī́r/
virus	/vī́rəss/
shower	/shówr/
dowry	/dówree/

Consonants that take the place of a vowel in a syllable (syllabic consonants) are preceded by /'/:

apple	/ápp'l/
garden	/gaárd'n/
station	/stáysh'n/
dental	/dént'l/
rhythm	/ríth'm/

In the vowel at the end of words such as "happy", we have used /ee/. The same applies to vowels such as the central one in "various":

happy	/háppee/
coffee	/káwfee/
various	/váiree əss/
radiate	/ráydee àyt/

III. Stress

Single syllable words (monosyllables) have no stress marks. In words with more than one syllable (polysyllables) we have indicated the primary stress with an acute accent:

another	/ə núthər/
collide	/kə lī́d/
cosmetic	/koz métik/

There are two types of secondary stress. We have used a grave accent to show those that occur after the main stress (posttonic stresses) as well as those that occur before the main stress (pretonic stresses).

agriculture	/ággri kùlcher/
seventeen	/sèvv'n téen/
academic	/àkə démmik/

IV. When are pronunciations given?

The Encarta World English Dictionary shows pronunciations at headwords except where the headword is made up of separate or hyphenated words that are given pronunciations elsewhere in the Dictionary. Thus we include pronunciations for all entries that are different headwords with the same spelling (homographs) such as bank or bow. Capitalized forms of headwords are not given a pronunciation unless they are geographic or biographical entries. In geographic and biographical entries where the names are repeated, the first occurrence only is given a pronunciation. Important variants in pronunciation are covered in the Dictionary, as are changes in pronunciation or stress in undefined entries (runons) and pronunciations of plural or other forms where the pronunciation or stress changes from that of the headword.

V. Spacing.

As it is easier to work out the pronunciation of a word if longer respellings are broken up into easily processed pieces, we have inserted spaces within the respelling of a word in the following cases:

(i) before a stressed syllable or other syllable containing a strong vowel (which means, for this purpose, any vowel other than /ə i ō oo yoo ŏŏ/):

allow	/ə lów/
detect	/di tékt/
unknown	/ùn nṓn/
celebrate	/séllə bràyt/
cucumber	/kyŏŏ kùmbər/

(ii) between the elements of a compound in which each element retains its usual pronunciation:

bedtime	/béd tīm/
getaway	/gét ə wày/

(iii) between any two successive vowel or diphthong symbols:

conveyance	/kən váy ənss/
chaos	/káy oss/

(iv) between /ur/ and a vowel or diphthong symbol:

furry	/fúr ee/

(v) between /ng/ and a following /g/:

anger	/áng gər/

VI. Foreign pronunciations

In occasional cases — particularly proper names — we have used the following to indicate non English sounds:

/hl/	as in Welsh Llangollen
/kh/	as in Scottish loch, German Bach, Spanish Gijón
/N/	to show nasalization of the preceding vowel as in the French pronunciation of un bon vin blanc /öN boN vaN blaaN/
/ö/	as in French boeuf, German schön
/ü/	as in French rue, German gemütlich

Abbreviations and Symbols

b.	born
C	century (in etymologies)
cgs	centimeter-gram-second
cl	centiliter(s)
d.	died
cm	centimeter(s)
cu.	cubic
e.g.	for example
fl	flourished
fl.	fluid
ft.	foot/feet
gal.	gallon(s)
in.	inch(es)
kg	kilogram(s)
km	kilometer(s)
kmph	kilometers per hour
l	liter(s)
lb.	pound(s)
m	meter(s)
mi.	mile(s)
ml	milliliter(s)
mm	millimeter(s)
mph	miles per hour
oz	ounce(s)
sq.	square
pt.	pint(s)
yd.	yard(s)

■ precedes new part of speech

○ precedes illustrative example

◇ precedes idiomatic phrase

= precedes direct cross-reference

⇨ precedes cross-reference to related entry

History of the English Language – a brief overview

Main contributors:
Professor Christian J. Kay
Professor of English Language
University of Glasgow

Professor Lee Pederson
Charles Howard Candler
Professor of English Language
Emory University

Additional contribution:
Anne H. Soukhanov

THE FIRST PEOPLE to speak the language we now know as English began to arrive in the British Isles around 450 A.D. They came from various parts of what are now Germany, Holland, and Denmark, speaking Germanic dialects that were to form the basis of English dialects in Britain. These people are collectively called the Anglo-Saxons, and their language is known as Anglo-Saxon or Old English. This language, first spoken by a few thousand people, is thus the ancestor of all the varieties of English spoken by millions around the world today.

Written records of Old English survive from the seventh century A.D. At first sight their language may seem like a foreign language to speakers of Modern English. However, if you look at the following Old English sentence, and at its literal translation into Modern English below, you should see some of the connections between the two as well as the kinds of changes that have occurred.

Þæt hus feoll and hys hryre wæs mycel.

The house fell and its destruction was great.

Some of the words in this sentence have changed only slightly in spelling and pronunciation, like *hus* "house" and *feoll* "fall;" one word *and* has not changed at all. The Old English alphabet had letters that have disappeared from Modern English, such as [þ], called "thorn" and pronounced /th/, and [ð], called "ash" and pronounced /a/. The Old English word *þæt* is thus the same as Modern English "that," although its use was somewhat different. Other words, such as *hryre*, have disappeared altogether or survive only in some varieties, mainly in Scots; *mycel*, for example, survives as the Scottish *mickle*, meaning "a little."

This short example shows you two things. The first is that many of our most basic words come from Old English: words for things in the world around us, such as *earth*, *sun*, *moon*, and *stars*; words for relationships, such as *mother* and *father*; words for many physical and mental activities, such as *run, love* and *think*. The second point is that English has changed considerably since Anglo-Saxon times, especially in its grammar and in the enormous growth of its vocabulary.

Languages change for two main reasons. The first of these is contact with other languages or varieties. The second, and often related, reason is changes in the social and cultural context in which speakers operate. The worldwide presence of the English language today bears testament not only to its shared heritage but also to the energetic independence of the many varieties that make up today's phenomenon of World English. Thus, twentieth-century speakers of English may speak any one of a number of varieties—for example, American, Canadian, British, or Australian. These varieties have a long tradition of mutual interconnections and influence that we will trace briefly here.

Even before they came to England, the Germanic peoples had made contact with the Romans, borrowing such words as *cheese* and *copper*. In England they encountered the Celtic peoples, whose language is still spoken in parts of Ireland, Wales, and Scotland. Many Celtic place names and geographic terms survive, as in *Dunedin*, the Celtic name for the Anglo-Saxon Edinburgh. More important from the point of view of the general development of English were the waves of invasions by Scandinavian Vikings that started in the late eighth century. Some came simply to plunder, but others settled down. Unlike the Celts, their language was quite similar to that of the Anglo-Saxons, making communication between the two groups possible. They added many everyday words to English, such as *sky*, *egg*, and *law*, the verb *to take*, and the pronoun *they*. Grammatical changes, such as the *-s* ending in such forms as *she walks*, spread into English from Scandinavian areas.

By far the most important contact, however, was the Norman Conquest of 1066, when the Norman-French Duke William defeated the Anglo-Saxon King Harold at the Battle of Hastings and became King William I of England. French became the language of government, although the bulk of the population continued to speak English. As the Norman nobles took over the lands of their Anglo-Saxon predecessors, communication between French and English speakers became increasingly necessary, and, as in any bilingual situation, the languages influenced each other. By the end of this period, generally known as Middle English, English was much more recognizably the language we know today. Thus in the late fourteenth century, the poet Geoffrey Chaucer wrote of one of his characters:

He was a verray parfit gentil knyght.

He was a very perfect gentle knight.

The words *he*, *was*, *a*, and *knyght* are Old English in origin, but *verray*, *parfit*, and *gentil* were borrowed into English from French and from there can be traced back to Latin. *Knyght* has changed in meaning since Old English, where it meant a boy or servant, while the use of *gentle* to mean noble or courteous differs somewhat from its modern meaning. Such changes in the meanings of words are typical of the way languages develop. These Middle English borrowings from French show the beginnings of one of the most characteristic features of modern English—its large and varied vocabulary. French words come from many vocabulary areas, such as government, law, religion, the arts, and courtly life.

A magnifying glass shows a detail of 'The Wyf of Bathe' in a first edition of Chaucer's Canterbury Tales. Printed in 1477.

Sometimes words from both sources survive side by side, as with *kingly* (Old English) and *royal* (French). Sometimes their meanings are differentiated, as in *calf* (Old English) and *veal* (French), originally the animal, but developing to mean only the meat.

Because French and Latin were the official languages during the early Middle English period, English was slow to develop a standard form in speech or writing. There was considerable diversity in the way people spoke, and when English began to be written again, the scribes tended to write the words as they were pronounced. The spelling and grammar in their manuscripts can often help us reconstruct how people spoke in different regions.

From the point of view of Modern English, continuing changes in grammar are also significant. In Old English grammatical relationships between words were expressed mainly by changing their endings, as in many of the world's languages. This system began to break down through contact with Scandinavian speakers, whose language had the same system but different endings, and the process was accelerated by the contact with French. At the end of this process English began to move toward its present system of expressing such relationships largely through word order and the use of prepositions. It also lost its system of grammatical gender and began to develop the complex system of verb forms that we know today.

By the end of the Middle English period, generally put at around 1500, a more uniform written language was emerging, a development greatly assisted by the rapid spread of printed books at this time. The printers were less tolerant of spelling variation than the medieval scribes had been, and a standardized system began to emerge. Unfortunately for modern users of English, this system predated various changes in the pronunciation of vowels, especially a series known as the Great Vowel Shift. This situation led to apparently illogical spelling variations such as *make/maid*, *flood/food*, or *great/dream*; in the first pair, the vowels used to be pronounced differently, whereas in the others they were once the same.

Early Modern English saw major grammatical patterns being established. Shakespeare and his contemporaries in the late sixteenth century could use either older forms such as "Why go you?" or "He speaks not," or newer ones such as "Why do you go?" and "He does not speak." They could choose between the older "Thou goest, he goeth" or the more modern "You go, he goes." They could express wishes through the old subjunctive form, "Long live the Queen," or the newer "May the Queen live long." In all these cases the older forms were in decline and died out as modern English progressed. At the same time, the verbal group developed, producing forms unavailable to Shakespeare, such as "When are you going?" or "He would have been surprised."

Vocabulary has also continued to grow throughout Modern English. Partly as a result of the renaissance of learning in Europe, the Early Modern period saw an upsurge in Latin borrowings in order to develop terminologies for new approaches to subjects such as science, philosophy, and medicine. Formal prose styles developed, often favoring Latinate words above native ones: *fraternal* might be considered more elegant than the native *brotherly*, or *illuminate* preferred to *light up*. English thus acquired a multilayered vocabulary, able to express a concept at different stylistic levels. This process of borrowing, changing, or inventing words to accommodate new intellectual developments continues to this day, as can be seen from the vocabulary of industrialization in the nineteenth century or of computers or space travel in the twentieth into the twenty-first.

During the Early Modern period English-speaking traders and adventurers were also setting out to explore the world, reaching the Americas, Africa, India, the Far East, and later Australia and New Zealand. Exotic objects were collected or described, and words such as *chocolate*, *wigwam*, *banana*, *gorilla*, *tea*, and *outback* were added to the language. Like their ancestors before them, some of the invaders settled down, thus laying the foundations of English as a world language and contributing to its continual development.

The same factors of contact and context underlie the process of linguistic change that formed American speech and writing. Through four centuries of cultural evolution, American English developed its distinctive pattern, reflecting the unique social experience of a people. As Horace Gregory explained in his preface to William Carlos Williams's *In the American Grain*, "Our nationality which answers to the name of American is neither at the center of a huge continent nor is it floating loosely around its East, West, and Tropical coastlines and harbors. It is a language." The Colonial American period of the seventeenth century marked the settlements of the Atlantic Seaboard communities, the focal areas of major regional dialects: Northern (Boston 1630), Midland (Philadelphia 1701), Greater New York (New York City 1644),

Title page of the original Bodleian copy of the First Folio edition of Shakespeare (1623).

and Southern (Newport News 1621; Charleston 1670). All of these varieties began with the same energetic, fluid, and unsettled code called Early Modern English, but each American dialect selected somewhat differently among the alternatives provided in the source language. From these early options came such distinctive forms as Northern in *broom, roof*, and *root*, and Midland *poke* ("sack"). With these English forms emerged the loanwords from Native American such as *moose*, *hickory*, *squash*, and *terrapin*; from Dutch *coleslaw*, *cruller*, *sleigh*, and *snoop*; and from French *bateau*, *portage*, *prairie*, and *rapids*.

The Frontier period of the eighteenth century extended American speech westward to include the Old Frontier delimited by Pittsburgh in the northwest and Knoxville in the southwest. This period framed the greatest variety of cultural interaction and the most remarkable demographic movement in American history, including the settlement of the Interior South through the Shenandoah Valley and, later, of Kentucky and the Ohio Valley through the Cumberland Gap. This process carried Midland (East Pennsylvania) speech across the Appalachian Highlands to the Piedmont and then south and westward. During this period, the German and Scotch-Irish influences combined with earlier French and Native American loans, especially along the Frontier. Familiar forms from this period reflect sources in German: *clook* "brood hen," *flitch* "fritter," *pannhas* "scrapple," and *smearcase* "cottage cheese"; and Scotch-Irish: *brickle* "brittle," *donsie* "sick, peaked," *redd up* "clean up (the house)," and *scoot over* "make room for."

The nineteenth century began with the Louisiana Purchase and ended with the Spanish-American War. Between those events the divisiveness of Sectionalism emerged across the country, but, nowhere more ominously than in those conflicts that led to the Civil War. But the isolation of the South had a profound impact on its dialects. Immediately after the Civil War technology developed equipment that made agriculture possible in the arid sections of the West and Southwest. The period also witnessed the rise of regional literature, from Harriet Beecher Stowe in the Northeast, George Washington Harris in the South Midlands of Tennessee, Joel Chandler Harris in the South, and Mark Twain in the West, a literary progression that began with local colorists and concluded with *The Adventures of Huckleberry Finn*. Interaction with Mexico began with the acquisition of Texas and much of the Southwest. Although Spanish loans appeared in the previous eras, the largest number occurred in the nineteenth and twentieth centuries. Among the earlier forms are Louisiana French *bayou*, *levee*, and *picayune*; and Spanish *buckaroo* (from *vaquero*), *lariat* (from *la reata*), *pronto*, and *stampede*.

The language of twentieth-century America combines the resources of its past with the factors of contact and context in an urban setting. Here, linguistic change reflects the reorganization of inner cities, from Boston to Los Angeles, involving the emergence of the rural Southern-based Black English and Latino dialects from several sources including Puerto Rico, Cuba, and Mexico. The process also involves a sharp contrast between rural and urban varieties, resulting in a national suburban speech community. This means that the language and culture of suburban New York, Chicago, and San Francisco have more in common with one another in speech and society than they have with any immediate rural communities. These developments explain the emergence of social dialects based on social class and caste. Although most of the old regional dialects endure, most have fewer speakers today as megalopolitan areas have emerged from Massachusetts to Washington, D.C. or Gary, Indiana, through Chicago to Milwaukee, Wisconsin. Contrary to the assumption that it obliterates differences of language and culture, modern American urbanization expands and unifies communities by bringing together formerly discrete communities and suburbs. Such new social contexts make linguistic change inevitable.

The same patterns of a heritage gained from a country's first settlers, borrowings from local languages and peoples, and continuing development and change in response to geographic, cultural, social, and other factors characterize the continuing changes to the English language in its many manifestations today. Australian and New Zealand Englishes have been enriched by words from Aboriginal and Maori traditions; the English of South Asia bears testament to the many local languages and varied cultural heritage of that vast subcontinent. South Africa's Anglo-Dutch heritage yields a multiplicity of words from that dual background as well as from local languages. In the many territories of the Pacific Rim the same process has given rise to a continuing enrichment of English with new words and senses.

In the early years of a new millennium English can reasonably be regarded as the first worldwide *lingua franca* since Latin. This Dictionary has been written to reflect this phenomenon. It will fall to our dictionary editors to monitor the continuing development of the English language in its manifold forms around the world.

A Brief History of Dictionaries and Dictionary Makers

Jonathon Green

THE FIRST DICTIONARY, a very distant ancestor of today's CD-ROMs and spellcheckers, was a list of words committed to a clay tablet around 2000 B.C. The conquest of Sumeria (roughly in the region of today's Iraq) by the neighboring territory Akkad required, as such things do, that the conquerors absorb the language of the conquered. In this case the Akkadians were particularly anxious to take on board the sophistication of the Sumerian legal system. So the tablets were filled with glossaries of legal, and soon other, words offering the Sumerian term followed by the Akkadian term.

Such early compilations, however, remained isolated. It was only in the fourth century B.C. that the Greeks took up dictionary making. They feared that the language of Homer was becoming "dead," even to scholars, and began to compile glossaries of his more obscure vocabulary. This same process was repeated later by the Romans, who also were seeking to preserve the language of their "dead" authorities and authors.

From then through the scholars of Byzantium, of the Middle Ages, and of the Renaissance, the flow of dictionaries was maintained, mainly as bilingual glossaries that translated words from one language into another. One of the most ambitious was the *Calepine*, first created by the monk Ambrosio Calepino in 1502. Edition followed edition, and at its peak its massive folio pages encompassed words in no less than 11 discrete languages for every single entry.

Precursors to today's English dictionaries first appeared in the eighth century. Four glossaries (the *Corpus*, the *Leiden*, the *Epinal*, and the *Erfurt* (named for the libraries that now hold them) are each dedicated to translating the vocabulary of a single text and were written to give scholars access to what were seen as the harder words of specific, usually ecclesiastical texts by translating the original Latin into Anglo-Saxon English.

ALPHABETICAL ORDER

Early glossaries were usually based only on "A-order." This meant that all the words starting with the same letter were listed together, but with no attempt to refine the order further. It would take several centuries before full alphabetization was finally in place.

Over subsequent centuries the production of such text-specific lists began to be amalgamated, offering scholars translations of more than one work in the same list. Such lists, it should be noted, were rudimentary. All these dictionaries—some 20 major works between 1440 and 1600—were bilingual, the usual mix being Latin-English, although some involved European languages. One of these, John Florio's *A World of Words* (1598), introduced so many new English words in his translations that it provided a huge step in English dictionary making in itself.

WORDS FOR WORD BOOKS

Among the titles given to word books have been an *abecedarium* (an alphabetical order), an *alveary* (beehive), a *catholicon* (cure-all), an *ortus* (garden), a *medulla* (marrow or pith), a *glossary*, a *manipulus* (handful), a *sylva* (wood), a *promptuarium*, a *vocabulary*, and a *vulgar* (common thing).

By 1700 *dictionary*, from the medieval Latin *dictionarius*, a repertory of words, had won out, and ever since it has been the predominant term.

In 1604 the first dictionary that defined rather than translated words appeared. Robert Cawdrey's *Table Alphabeticall, Contayning and Teaching the True Writing and Understanding of Hard Usuall English Words* was the first true English-English dictionary. It contained barely 3,000 entries, and its goal was to explain the meanings of difficult words.

Cawdrey had many successors who formed major way stations in the development of lexicography in English. Among the "hard words" lexicographers were John Bullokar (in 1616), Henry Cockeram (1623), Thomas Blount (1656), Edward Philips (1658), and Elisha Coles, whose dictionary, appearing in 1676, would be the first mainstream English work to include slang (the dedicated collection of which had begun in Copland's *Hye Way to the Spittel House* in 1531). These were in response to the emergence in the seventeenth century of a middle class and a surge in literacy.

If the seventeenth century had reflected the expansion of literacy beyond the universities and churches, then the eighteenth reflected that of England itself beyond its own territorial borders. The century that saw the expansion and consolidation of the British colonies demanded new efforts to establish English as a major language, specifically as a rival to French. The creation in 1635 of the *Académie Française* and the publication in 1694 of its authoritative *Dictionnaire* promoted much comment across the Channel. Such literary figures as John Dryden, Robert Hooke, Daniel Defoe, and Jonathan Swift variously called for some form of English Academy and, if established, suggested that its primary task would be to produce a purified version of truly standard English.

Samuel Johnson

These ruminations led in 1746 to the commissioning by a group of booksellers (who, as was the custom, were also publishers) of one Samuel Johnson, then best-known as an essayist and parliamentary writer for the *Gentleman's Magazine*, to prepare a *Dictionary of the English Language*. That dictionary, which appeared in 1755, represents a great turning point in English-language dictionary making.

Lexicography is an ever developing craft, for the language does not reform and reappear mint-new in time for every successive lexicon. Johnson used his predecessors, especially Nathaniel Bailey, whose own major work, the *Universal Etymological English Dictionary*, published in 1730, provided massive assistance in compiling the basic word lists. Nor did Johnson invent any of the processes seen to such advantage in his work, namely etymology, illustrative citations, and basic guides to pronunciation. All of these had been attempted before, but Johnson brought them together and did so more skillfully than had ever been done before.

Johnson did not, however, fix the language, as he and his publishers had once felt was feasible. Instead, recognizing reality, he would declare that such fantasies were "the dreams of a poet doomed at last to wake a lexicographer" and that thus to pursue perfection was reminiscent of ancient tribes who would "chace the sun, which, when they had reached the hill where he seemed to rest, was still beheld at the same distance from them." Language changes and lexicographers, now as much as then, must reflect such changes in their work. Johnson's decision to accept such a reality has influenced the growth of English ever since.

In a nice twist of coincidence, the very first U.S. dictionary, *The School Dictionary* (1798), was written by one Samuel Johnson, a teacher. And others would follow, among them titles from this Johnson and his coeditor the Reverend John Elliott (1800), from another preacher Caleb Alexander (1800), from Richard Coxe (1813) and, in 1807, from Sarah Rowson, a British actor who had quit London and gained a new reputation as a best-selling U.S. novelist.

The first major U.S. dictionary, Noah Webster's *American Dictionary of the English Language,* appeared in 1828. Webster was a New England schoolteacher whose *Blue Back Speller* (1788) sold an astounding 82 million copies within a century of its publication. He was a great pioneer of U.S. English, as opposed to British English. For him the establishment of a national language, based upon but independent of its source, was as politically important as the American Revolution itself. In *Dissertations on the English Language* (1789), Webster wrote: "Several circumstances render a future separation of the American tongue from the English necessary and unavoidable." The spelling of such terms as *theater* for "theatre" and *color* for "colour" is Webster's legacy.

The *Oxford English Dictionary* (*OED*) is arguably still the world's greatest dictionary on historical principles (offering the usage history and development of a word as well as definition and etymology). Conceived in 1857, it would override a false start (in 1865) to begin once more in 1878 with the appointment of James Murray, a self-educated schoolteacher and philologist, as its editor. The first 352-page section, offering words from A to Ant, appeared in 1884 and the dictionary was eventually completed in 1928 after Murray's death.

With the exception of Webster, lexicography has never really been a solo craft. Even Johnson had his assistants, the eight "harmless drudges" who did the basic work of compilation, while the *OED* lists dozens of individuals, from Murray's coeditors through to the ranks of subeditors and readers, all enlisted on the great work. Today's dictionaries, the products of publishers (whether academic or popular), are rarely associated with a single individual. Modern lexicography is in every sense a corporate endeavor—the hundreds of individuals enlisted for this project are typical. Such a finely tuned exercise may have sacrificed a degree of idiosyncrasy (after all, is not the decision by one individual to compile a dictionary, "chasing the panting syllable" as one poet had it, somewhat eccentric in itself?), but has gained an infinity of expertise. It may be less romantic, but today's user wants accuracy and information first. And not only have dictionaries become available on computer, whether on a CD-ROM or online via the Internet, but computers are central to every stage of the production. The great dictionaries of the past depended on armies of amateur readers, scanning texts for examples of usage. Today's compilers have the great corpora, literally "bodies" of real language, available for consultation. Such a corpus was compiled for this Dictionary, ensuring that every nuance of a word's existence can be laid down, and backed up with illustrative quotations. Not only that, but the keyboarding of a great dictionary into a permanent, if evolving, database, renders the great consumers of the lexicographer's time—inserting new and updating old entries and inserting and verifying cross-references—infinitely simpler than the most sophisticated of preelectronic systems could ever manage.

Noah Webster

Perhaps the most important aspect of lexicographic change, and never more so than as illustrated here, is the change in the word list itself. All these earlier dictionaries tried to be language-specific; not so today. World English is the name of the modern game. This Dictionary, as users will find, has responded to that new situation in ways hitherto untried. Aimed at a worldwide audience, incorporating multinational expertise in its compilation and in the entries that have been produced, it is proof in itself of the extent to which English has long since burst through its territorial confines.

The lexicographer is not and never has been in Johnson's ironic, now hackneyed phrase, a "harmless drudge." Lexicographers hold a strange position, employed in an unglamorous task, yet occupying a position of power and influence by virtue of defining what the words in our language mean. That those words, once confined to a small elite of scholars, are now the property of many differing millions and available in myriad variations is both a challenge and a reward to the dictionary maker.

World English

Tom McArthur

AT THE TURNING POINT of a new century and millennium, English is the most used—and studied—language in the history of the human race. At the beginning of the twentieth century, it was already one of the foremost languages of the world, because it was the main language of both the British Empire and the United States of America. At that time it had significant competition from other widespread European languages such as French, German, Russian, and Spanish and, beyond Europe, from Mandarin Chinese, Arabic, and Swahili that all still belong, with English, in the prestigious club of world languages. However, since World War II, although all the other world languages have continued to be widely used, English has been alone in becoming—ever more notably with each passing decade—the sole universal language, the world's *lingua franca*.

Noting its growing role, scholars and other observers have for some time been giving distinctive labels to this runaway language. Increasingly, since occasional use in the 1930s, it has come most commonly to be known as "World English"—whence the name of this dictionary. Since around 1980, this term has also been put into the plural, as "World Englishes," so as to highlight proliferating varieties that are often called simply "the Englishes," and, in Asia and Africa, "the New Englishes." Since at least the 1970s, the language complex has also been called "International English," and, in the 1990s, the term "Global English" has proved fashionable, to accompany and blend in with the current economic buzzword *globalization*.

Describing and cataloging any language is difficult, but in the past the relatively limited scope and roles of the world's languages have allowed us to suppose that the grammars, dictionaries, and other works associated with them are comprehensive. But the scale and variety of present-day English do not permit any such comfortable illusion. Even the population statistics of World English are uncertain, ranging hazily from over three hundred million people who are assumed to be native speakers to over a billion users of English of all kinds, from the most informed and fluent to the most casual and halting. The unnumbered varieties and uses of this language (whether thought, spoken, written, typed, printed, broadcast, taped, telephoned, faxed, e-mailed, or disseminated on the World Wide Web) are so complex that no individual, group, or system can catch them all. Even the most extensive and flexible computer corpus currently imaginable cannot encompass all the registers and usages of the standard language, let alone all the rest.

Even so, however, and paradoxically, there is a manifest need to say something as comprehensive as possible about World English, including its immense wealth of words, past, present, and potential. Although the task is fraught with difficulty, publishers of dictionaries must inevitably respond to the challenge, part of which is to acknowledge the nature and impact of the phenomenon being described, and this has been the primary goal of the ***Encarta World English Dictionary***.

The *study* of English is an international industry. Tens of thousands of scholars and teachers engage in it throughout the world, instructing a student population of hundreds of millions while producing innumerable books, periodicals, dissertations, articles, reports, conference proceedings, class notes, textbooks, newsletters, and Internet materials. Their total output is more than any of them can digest; indeed, few will see—or even be informed about—every proceeding or document that touches on their special interests *within* the language and its literatures. But again, simply to say this and turn away is not enough. If anything, we now need more and better guidance and discrimination from the makers of dictionaries than ever in the past. The millennial challenge is to make even fuller, clearer, and more appropriate dictionaries of English, both benefiting from the technological revolution that has accompanied and helped drive the enlargement of English, and acknowledging that English is larger than any of the communities in which it is used. Members of those communities need to be fully aware of the nature of the

ENGLISH AROUND THE WORLD

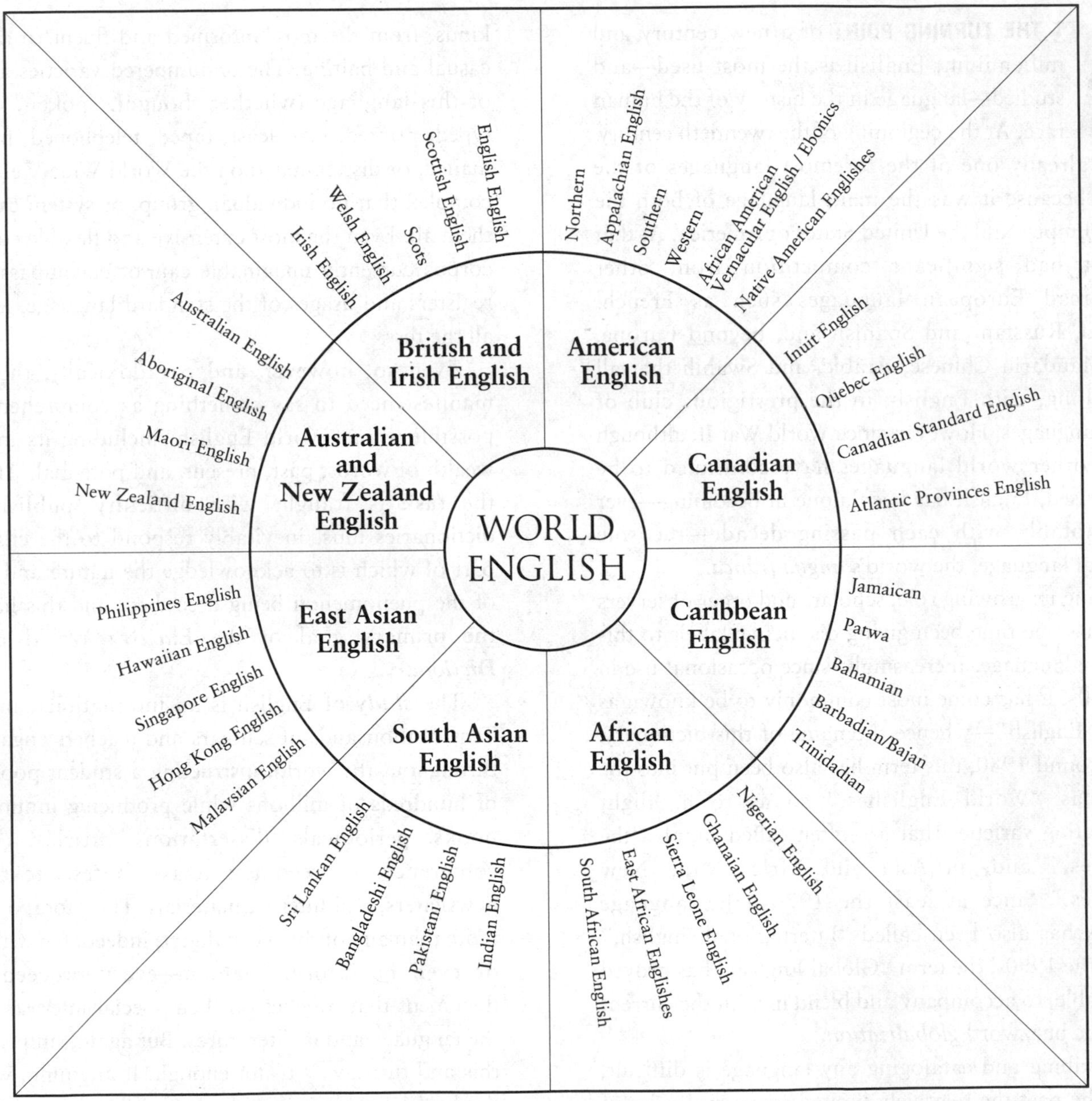

There are many varieties of World English; some of the main ones are included in this diagram.

international linguistic resource at their disposal.

One outcome of this unique and often unnerving state of affairs is that no one can even think today about who "owns" the language or its many varieties. The English language has become a global resource. As such, it does not owe its existence—or its future—to any nation, group, or individual. Inasmuch as a language belongs to any individual or community, English is the possession of every individual and community that wishes to use it, wherever they are in the world. It is in effect as democratic and universal an institution as humankind has ever possessed.

Aa

a[1] /ay/ (*plural* **as** *or* **a's**), **A** (*plural* **As** *or* **A's**) *n.* **1. FIRST LETTER IN ENGLISH ALPHABET** the first letter and first vowel of the alphabet in modern English, and in other languages that also use the Latin alphabet **2. SOUND OF "A"** any speech sound represented by the letter "a" **3. "A"-SHAPED OBJECT** something shaped like the capital letter "A" **4. LETTER "A" WRITTEN** a written representation of the letter "a" **5.** CHESS **FIRST VERTICAL ROW OF CHESSBOARD** used to refer to the first vertical row of squares from the left on a chessboard ◇ **from A to B** from one place to another ◇ **from A to Z 1.** extremely thoroughly **2.** all the way from the beginning to the end

a[2] *(stressed)* /ay/; *(unstressed)* /ə/ CORE MEANING: the indefinite article, used before a singular countable noun to refer to one person or thing not previously known or specified, in contrast with "the," referring to somebody or something known to the listener ○ *I need a new car.*
indef art. **1. INDICATES A TYPE** used before a noun to indicate that somebody or something has some of the same qualities as the person or thing mentioned ○ *a doormat* **2. ONE** used instead of "one" with words of measurement ○ *a teaspoonful of salt* **3. PER** in each or in every ○ *twice a day* **4. INDICATES SOMEBODY NOT KNOWN PERSONALLY** used to indicate somebody not personally known, but known of ○ *There's a Mr. O'Flynn here to see you.* **5. ANY** used in negative structures to emphasize a complete absence of something ○ *He doesn't have a hope!* [Old English, shortening of *ān* (see ONE)]

WORD KEY: USAGE

a or **an**? *A* is the form of the indefinite article used before words that are pronounced with an initial consonant sound (even if the spelling does not begin with a consonant): *a banana*; *a hunk*; *a ewe*. *An* is used before words that begin with a vowel sound (even if an unpronounced consonant comes first): *an elephant*; *an heir*. The same rule regarding sound rather than spelling applies to abbreviations: *a CD* but *an LP*. The practice of using ***an*** before words beginning with *h* and an unstressed syllable (for example *an hotel*, *an historic occasion*) is falling out of use, and it is much more usual now to hear *a hotel* and *a historic occasion*, with the *h* sounded in each word.

---

a[3] *symbol.* PHYS acceleration

a[4] *abbr.* **1.** MEASURE acre **2.** about **3.** MEASURE are

A[1] /ay/ (*plural* **As** *or* **A's**) *n.* **1.** MUSIC **6TH NOTE IN C MAJOR** the sixth note of a scale in C major. The A above middle C is often used to tune instruments and is standardized at a frequency of 440 hertz. **2.** MUSIC **SOMETHING THAT PRODUCES AN A** a string, key, or pipe tuned to produce the note A **3.** MUSIC **SCALE BEGINNING ON A** a scale or key that starts on the note A **4.** MUSIC **WRITTEN SYMBOL OF A** a graphic representation of the tone of A **5. TOP GRADE** the highest standing or grade ○ *straight As for the semester.* ➪ **alpha 6.** MED **HUMAN BLOOD TYPE** a human blood type of the ABO system, containing the A antigen. A person with this type of blood can donate to people of the same group or of the AB group, and can receive blood from people with this type or with type O.

A[2] (*plural* **As** *or* **A's**) *symbol.* **1.** COMPUT 10 (*used in hexadecimal notation*) **2.** PHYS mass number **3.** MEASURE ampere **4.** activity

A[3] /ay/ (*plural* **As** *or* **A's**) *abbr.* **1.** academy **2.** adult **3.** answer

A., Å *symbol.* angstrom

a- *prefix.* in a particular place, condition, or manner ○ *abed* ○ *adrift* ○ *aloud* [Old English, from *an*, an alternative for *on* "ON"]

A1, A-1, A-one *adj.* **1. TOP-NOTCH** in excellent or first-rate condition (*informal*) **2. FULLY SEAWORTHY** used to describe a ship as being well equipped and in excellent condition [Mid-19thC. Originally from Lloyd's Register, an annual British shipping list; *A* indicated a hull in first-class condition, *1* that the ship was well provisioned and equipped.]

aa /áa àa/ *n.* solidified lava with a rough jagged surface and sharp angular features [Mid-19thC. From Hawaiian *a-'a.*]

AA *abbr.* **1.** MIL air-to-air **2.** EDUC achievement age

A.A. *abbr.* **1.** antiaircraft **2.** Associate of Arts

AAA *abbr.* American Automobile Association

A.A.A. *abbr.* American Arbitration Association

AAAL *abbr.* American Academy of Arts and Letters

AAAS *abbr.* American Association for the Advancement of Science

a.a.e. *abbr.* according to age and experience

AAF *abbr.* Army Air Forces

aah /aa/ *interj.* **EXPRESSING EMOTION** used to express surprise, pleasure, satisfaction, or sympathy (*informal*) ■ *vi.* (**aahed, aah·ing, aahs**) **SAY "AAH"** to say "aah" (*informal*) ➧ **ooh** ■ *n.* **UTTERANCE OF "AAH"** an exclamation of "aah" expressing surprise, pleasure, satisfaction, or sympathy (*informal*) [Lengthened form of AH]

AAM *abbr.* air-to-air missile

A & M *abbr.* Agricultural and Mechanical

A & R *abbr.* artists and repertoire

Aardvark

aard·vark /áard vaark/ *n.* a burrowing mammal with a long snout, powerful claws, long tongue, and heavy tail. It eats termites and is native to southern Africa. Latin name: *Orycteropus afer.* [Late 18thC. From Afrikaans, literally "earth pig."]

aard·wolf /áard wòolf/ (*plural* **-wolves** /-vz/) *n.* a striped nocturnal mammal related to the hyena that lives in southern Africa and feeds mainly on termites. Latin name: *Proteles cristatus.* [Mid-19thC. From Afrikaans, literally "earth wolf."]

Aar·on /áirən/ *n.* in the Bible, the first Jewish high priest and elder brother of Moses. With Moses, he led the Israelites out of Egypt but died before reaching the Promised Land.

Aar·on /áirən/, **Hank** (*b.* 1934) U.S. baseball player. He broke many batting records during a 23-year career, including Babe Ruth's career total of home runs, with the Milwaukee Braves, Atlanta Braves, and Milwaukee Brewers. Full name **Henry Louis Aaron**

Aar·on's beard *n.* = **rose of Sharon** [Named for AARON, who had a long beard (see Psalms 133:2), because of the flower's prominent hairy stamens]

Aar·on's rod *n.* an plant found in Asia, Europe, and North America that has tall smooth stems and yellow flowers [Named for the rod bearing the name of AARON, which was said to have flowered (see Numbers 17:8)]

AARP *abbr.* American Association of Retired Persons

A.A.S. *abbr.* **1.** American Academy of Sciences **2.** Associate in Applied Sciences

AAU *abbr.* Amateur Athletic Union

AAUP *abbr.* American Association of University Professors

AAVE *abbr.* African American Vernacular English

Ab /aab/ *n.* = **Av** [Late 18thC. From Hebrew *'āḇ.*]

AB[1] *abbr.* Alberta

AB[2] *n.* a human blood type of the ABO group, containing the A and B antigens. A person with this type of blood can donate to somebody of the same group and receive blood from somebody with this type or with type O, A, or B.

a.b. *abbr.* BASEBALL at bat

A.B. *abbr.* Bachelor of Arts

ab- *prefix.* away from, off ○ *aboral* [From Latin. Ultimately from an Indo-European base meaning "off, away," which is also the ancestor of English *off*, *ebb*, and *post-*.]

a·ba /ə bàa, a-/ *n.* **1. SYRIAN CLOTH** a cloth made in Syria using hair from goats or camels **2. MIDDLE EASTERN GARMENT** a loose sleeveless outer garment worn by boys and men in the Middle East [Early 19thC. From Arabic *'abā.*]

ABA *abbr.* **1.** American Basketball Association **2. ABA, A.B.A.** American Bar Association **3.** American Booksellers Association

ab·a·ca /àbbə káa, àbəkə/ *n.* **1. PLANT YIELDING FIBER** a large plant from whose leaves Manila hemp is produced. It is related to the banana. Latin name: *Musa textilis.* **2.** = **Manila hemp** [Mid-18thC. Via Spanish from Tagalog *abaká.*]

ab·a·ci plural of **abacus**

a·back /ə bák/ *adv.* **1. WITH WIND PRESSING AGAINST SAILS** with the wind blowing against the forward part of a sail or sails, so that a vessel cannot move ahead **2. BACKWARD** backward or toward the back (*archaic*) [Old English *on bæc* "toward the back, backward"] ◇ **taken aback** surprised and unsure how to react

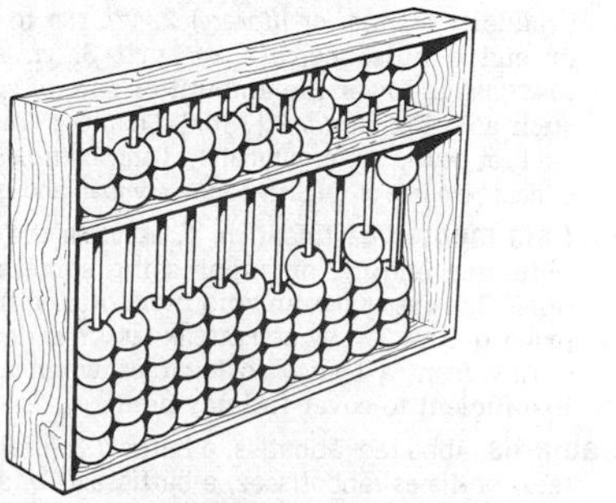

Abacus

ab·a·cus /ábbəkəs/ (*plural* **-cus·es** *or* **-ci** /-sī, -kī/) *n.* **1.** MATH **COUNTING DEVICE** a mechanical device for making calculations consisting of a frame mounted with rods along which beads or balls are moved **2.** ARCHIT

FLAT TOP OF COLUMN a flat slab at the top of a column [14thC. Via Latin from Greek *abakos* "board strewn with dust on which to draw or write" (later "slab, table"), of uncertain origin: probably ultimately from Hebrew *'ābāq* "dust."]

A·ba·dan /aàbə daán, àbbə dán/, **Ā·bā·dān** city in Iran. It is a major petroleum-refining and shipping center. Population: 40,000 (1996).

a·baft /ə báft/ *adv.* **AT THE REAR** toward the rear of a ship or boat ■ *prep.* **BEHIND** to the rear of an area on a ship or boat [14thC. From Old English *an* (see ON) + *be* (see BY) + *æftan* "behind."]

A·ba·kan /aàbə kaan/ city and administrative center of the autonomous republic of Khakassa in northeastern Russia. Population: 158,200 (1992 est.).

ab·a·lo·ne /àbbə lṓnee/ *n.* an edible sea mollusk that breathes through holes in its ear-shaped shell. The pearly interior of the shell is used for making jewelry. Genus: *Haliotis.* [Mid-19thC. Via American Spanish *abulón* from Shoshonean *aulun.*]

ab·am·pere /ab ám peer/ *n.* the centimeter-gram-second unit of electromagnetic current equal to ten amperes

a·ban·don /ə bándən/ *v.* (**-doned, -don·ing, -dons**) **1.** *vt.* **LEAVE SOMEBODY BEHIND** to leave somebody or something behind for others to look after, especially somebody or something meant to be a personal responsibility ○ *pets abandoned by their owners* **2.** *vt.* **LEAVE A PLACE BECAUSE OF DANGER** to leave a place or vehicle, especially for reasons of safety and without intending to return soon ○ *Drivers caught in the snowstorm had to abandon their vehicles.* **3.** *vt.* **RENOUNCE SOMETHING** to renounce or reject something previously done or used ○ *The practice was abandoned long ago.* **4.** *vt.* **GIVE UP CONTROL OF SOMETHING** to surrender control of something completely to somebody else ○ *As troops closed in the town was abandoned to its fate.* **5.** *vt.* **HALT SOMETHING IN PROGRESS** to stop doing something before it is completed, usually because of difficulty or danger **6.** *vt.* INSUR **GIVE UP TO INSURER** to surrender part of an insured property to the insurer in order to make a claim for total loss **7.** *vr.* **GIVE IN TO EMOTION** to give yourself over to a powerful emotion ○ *He abandoned himself to his grief.* ■ *n.* **LACK OF RESTRAINT** complete lack of inhibition or self-restraint [14thC. From Old French *abandoner,* from *a bandon,* literally "under control," from, ultimately, Latin *bannum* "proclamation." The underlying idea is of giving up control.] —**a·ban·don·ment** *n.*

a·ban·doned /ə bándənd/ *adj.* **1. EMPTY** left empty because of not being used or lived in anymore **2. ALONE** left alone without being cared for or supported **3. UNRESTRAINED** without restraint or self-control

a·base /ə báyss/ (**a·based, a·bas·ing, a·bas·es**) *vt.* to make somebody feel belittled or degraded (*literary*) [14thC. From Old French *abaissier,* from *baissier* "to lower," ultimately from Latin *bassus* "short of stature."] —**a·base·ment** *n.* ◇ **abase yourself** to behave in a way that lowers your sense of dignity or self-esteem (*literary*)

a·bash /ə básh/ (**a·bashed, a·bash·ing, a·bash·es**) *vt.* to make somebody feel ashamed, embarrassed, or uncomfortable [14thC. From the Anglo-Norman stem *abaïss-,* from, ultimately, Old French *baïr* "to astound."] —**a·bash·ed·ly** /ə báshədlee/ *adv.* —**a·bash·ment** *n.*

a·bate /ə báyt/ (**a·bat·ed, a·bat·ing, a·bates**) *v.* **1.** *vti.* **BECOME LESS** to lessen or make something lessen gradually (*formal or literary*) **2.** *vti.* **END** to suppress or end a nuisance, act, or writ **3.** *vt.* FIN **REDUCE SOMETHING** to lower the amount or rate of something such as a tax (*formal*) [13thC. From Old French *abatre* "to beat down," from, ultimately, Latin *batt(u)ere* "to fight or beat" (source of English *battle, combat,* and *debate*).]

a·bate·ment /ə báytmənt/ *n.* **1. REDUCING** the action of reducing, ending, or suppressing something, e.g., noise **2.** FIN **DEDUCTION** an amount deducted from a full price or tax **3.** LAW **DECREASE IN LEGACY** a decrease in outlay from a legacy to legatees when assets are insufficient to cover full payment

ab·a·tis /ábbə tee, ábbətiss, ə báttiss/ (*plural* **-tis** /ábbə teez/ *or* **-tis·es** /ábbətissəz, ə báttissəz/) *n.* a rampart made of felled trees placed so that their bent or sharpened branches face out toward the enemy [Mid-18thC. From French, from Old French *abatre* "to beat down, fell" (see ABATE).]

ab·at·toir /ábbə twaar, -twaár/ *n.* a place where animals are slaughtered for their meat and by-products [Early 19thC. From French, formed from *abattre* "to fell," from Old French *abatre* (see ABATE). The underlying sense is "place where things are knocked down."]

ab·ax·i·al /a báksee əl/ *adj.* used to describe the underside of a leaf or other surface that faces away from the stem. ◊ **adaxial**

Abba /ábbə/ *n.* **1. GOD** a name used to address God in the New Testament **2. BISHOP OR PATRIARCH** a title given to bishops and patriarchs in the Syrian Orthodox and Coptic Churches [14thC. Via ecclesiastical Latin and New Testament Greek from Aramaic *'abbā* "father."]

ab·ba·cy /ábbəssee/ (*plural* **-cies**) *n.* the rank, jurisdiction, or term of office of an abbot or abbess [15thC. From ecclesiastical Latin *abbacia,* from the stem *abbat-* (see ABBOT).]

Claudio Abbado

Ab·ba·do /ə baádō/, **Claudio** (*b.* 1933) Italian conductor. He began his career with the La Scala Opera, Milan, Italy, but since 1989 has been artistic director of the Berlin Philharmonic Orchestra, Germany.

Ab·bas /ábbəss/ (566?–653) Arabian merchant. He was instrumental in spreading the tenets of Islam. The prophet Muhammad was his nephew.

Ab·bas I, Shah of Persia (1571–1629). A member of the Safavid dynasty, he ruled from 1588 until his death. Known as **Abbas the Great**

Ab·ba·sid /ə básid, ábbə sid/ *n.* a member of a dynasty that ruled an Islamic empire from Baghdad from 750 to 1258. Descended from Muhammad's uncle, Abbas, they wielded little political power, but were great patrons of Islamic art and culture. —**Ab·ba·sid** *adj.*

ab·ba·tial /abáysh'l/ *adj.* relating to an abbey, abbot, or abbess [Late 17thC. From French, or from medieval Latin *abatialis,* both from the ecclesiastical Latin stem *abbat-* (see ABBOT).]

ab·bé /á bay/ *n.* an abbot or member of a religious order in a French-speaking area [Mid-16thC. Via French from the ecclesiastical Latin stem *abbat-* (see ABBOT).]

ab·bess /ábbəss/ *n.* the nun in charge of a convent [13thC. From Old French *abbesse,* ultimately from the ecclesiastical Latin stem *abbat-* (see ABBOT).]

Ab·be·ville /ábbə vìl, -veel/ city in southwestern Louisiana, southwest of Baton Rouge. Population: 11,460 (1996).

Ab·be·vil·le·an /ab víllee ən, àbbə-/ *adj.* relating to or typical of early Lower Paleolithic culture in Europe [Mid-20thC. From French *Abbevillien,* named for the town of *Abbeville* in northern France, where artifacts from this period were discovered.]

ab·bey /ábbee/ (*plural* **-beys**) *n.* **1. MONASTERY OR CONVENT** a building or buildings occupied by monks under an abbot or nuns under an abbess, especially the church building **2. CHURCH** a church that is or was used by a community of monks or nuns [13thC. From Old French *ab(b)eïe,* from, ultimately, the ecclesiastical Latin stem *abbat-* (see ABBOT).]

Ab·bey /ábbee/, **Edwin Austin** (1852–1911) U.S. painter and illustrator who produced panels for the Boston Public Library (1890–1902) and murals at Pennsylvania State Capitol (1911).

ab·bot /ábbət/ *n.* the monk in charge of a monastery [Pre-12thC. Via ecclesiastical Latin *abbat-,* stem of *abbas,* from, ultimately, Aramaic *'abbā* "father."] —**ab·bot·ship** *n.*

Ab·bott /ábbət/, **Berenice** (1898–1991) U.S. photographer who was known especially for her portrait photography.

Ab·bott, George Francis (1887–1995) U.S. playwright, producer, and director. He was a major figure in the Broadway theater, whose productions included *Call Me Madam* (1950), *The Pajama Game* (1954), and *Damn Yankees* (1955).

Ab·bott, Sir John (1821–93) Canadian politician. He was prime minister of Canada (1891–92) and the mayor of Montreal (1887–89). Full name **Sir John Joseph Caldwell Abbott**

abbr., ab·brev. *abbr.* abbreviation

ab·bre·vi·ate /ə breevee ayt/ (**-at·ed, -at·ing, -ates**) *vt.* **1. SHORTEN WORD** to shorten a word by leaving out some of its letters or sounds **2. SHORTEN TEXT** to shorten a piece of text by cutting sections or paraphrasing it [15thC. From Latin *abbreviat-,* the past participle stem of *abbreviare* "to shorten" (source of English *abridge*), from, ultimately, *brevis* "short" (source of English *brief*).] —**ab·bre·vi·a·tor** *n.*

ab·bre·vi·a·tion /ə breevee áysh'n/ *n.* **1. REDUCED FORM** a shortened form of a word or phrase **2. REDUCTION** the shortening of a word or phrase to be used to represent the full form

WORD KEY: USAGE

Types of abbreviation There are four main kinds of abbreviation: shortenings, contractions, initialisms, and acronyms. **1** Shortenings of words usually consist of the first few letters of the full form and are sometimes spelled with a final period when they are still regarded as abbreviations, for example, *cent.* = century, *foll.* = following (in page references). In many cases they form words in their own right, and in these cases the period is omitted, for example, *gym* = gymnasium, *hippo* = hippopotamus, *limo* = limousine. Such shortenings are often but not always informal in nature. Some become the standard forms, and the full forms are then regarded as formal or technical, for example, *bus* = omnibus, *taxi* = taxicab, *deli* = delicatessen, *zoo* = zoological garden. Sometimes shortenings are altered to facilitate their pronunciation or spelling: *bike* = *bicycle* **2** Contractions are abbreviated forms in which letters from the middle of the full form have been omitted, for example, *Dr.* = doctor, *St.* = saint. Such forms are invariably followed by a period. Another kind of contraction is the type *can't* = cannot, *didn't* = did not, *you've* = you have, with an apostrophe marking the omission of letters. **3** Initialisms are made up of the initial letters of words and are pronounced as separate letters: *CIA* (or *C.I.A.*), *NYC, pm* (or *p.m.*), *US* (or *U.S.*). Practice varies with regard to periods, with current usage increasingly in favor of omitting them, especially when the initialism consists entirely of capital letters. **4** Acronyms are initialisms that have become words in their own right, and are pronounced as words rather than as a series of letters, for example, *AIDS, laser, scuba, UNESCO.* In many cases the acronym becomes the standard term and the full form is only used in explanatory contexts.

ABC[1] *n. U.K.* = **ABCs** ◇ **as easy as ABC** extremely easy

ABC[2] *abbr.* **1.** American Broadcasting Company **2.** atomic, biological, and chemical **3.** Advanced Booking Charter

ABC[3] (*plural* **ABCs**) *n.* an offensive term for a Chinese person born in the United States (*offensive*) [Acronym for American-born Chinese]

ab·cou·lomb /ab kóo lom, -koolōm/ *n.* the centimeter-gram-second unit of electrical charge equal to ten coulombs

ABCs *npl.* **1. ALPHABET** the alphabet, especially when this also refers to the most basic aspects of reading and writing **2. ESSENTIALS** the most basic facts or essential elements of a particular subject

ABD *n.* a doctoral candidate who has completed all requirements for a degree except the submission of a completed thesis. Full form **all but dissertation**

Abd al-Ha·mid /àd daal hámmid/ = **Abdul Hamid II**

Abd Al·lah /aab daálə/ (1846–99) Sudanese nationalist resistance leader who led the uprising against the Egyptian administration of the Sudan and was defeated by Lord Horatio Kitchener.

Abd-ar-Rah·man Khan /aàbdər rə maán kaán/, **emir of Afghanistan** (1844?–1901). During his rule (1880–1901) he helped to establish the Durand Line (1893), which fixed the Afghani-Indian border.

ab·di·cate /ábdi kayt/ (**-cat·ed, -cat·ing, -cates**) *v.* **1.** *vti.* **RESIGN POSITION** to give up a high office formally or officially, especially the throne **2.** *vt.* **NEGLECT A DUTY** to fail to fulfill a duty or responsibility ○ *The company* *seems to have abdicated all responsibility in this matter.* [Mid-16thC. From Latin *abdicat-*, the past participle stem of *abdicare* "to renounce," from *dicare* "to proclaim" (source of English *dedicate, indicate,* and *predicate*).] —**ab·di·ca·tion** /àbdi káysh'n/ *n.* —**ab·di·ca·tor** /ábdi kaytər/ *n.*

ab·do·men /ábbdəmən/ *n.* **1.** **BODY SECTION CONTAINING STOMACH** the part of the body of a vertebrate that contains the stomach, intestines, and other organs. In mammals it is situated between the pelvis and the thorax. **2.** **BELLY** the surface of the body of a vertebrate around the stomach **3.** **REAR PART OF INSECT** the elongated portion of the body of an arthropod, located behind the thorax. It is usually segmented. [Mid-16thC. From Latin, of unknown origin.]

ab·dom·i·nal /ab dómmin'l/ *adj.* **OF ABDOMEN** relating to, located in, or occurring in the abdomen ■ **ab·dom·i·nals** *npl.* **ABDOMINAL MUSCLES** the muscles that form the wall of the abdomen (*informal*) [Mid-18thC. From modern Latin *abdominalis*, from Latin *abdomen*.] —**ab·dom·i·nal·ly** *adv.*

ab·du·cens nerve /àbb dóoss'nz-, àbb dyóoss'nz-/ *n.* a nerve conveying impulses from the brain to the muscle that moves the eye laterally in its socket, one of a pair of cranial nerves [*Abducens* from modern Latin, literally "leading out," from the present participle of *abducere* (see ABDUCT)]

ab·duct /ab dúkt/ (**-duct·ed, -duct·ing, -ducts**) *vt.* **1.** **SNATCH SOMEBODY AWAY** to take somebody away by force or deception **2.** **PULL SOMETHING AWAY** to pull something, e.g., a muscle, away from the midpoint or midline of the body or of a limb. ◊ **adduct** [Early 17thC. From Latin *abduct-*, the past participle stem of *abducere* "to lead out," from *ducere* "to lead" (source of English *duct, conduct,* and *educate*).] —**ab·duc·tion** *n.*

Ab·dul Ha·mid II /àb dóol hámmid/ (1842–1918) Ottoman sultan. He suspended the constitution (1877) and fought Western influences. He was deposed by the Young Turks' revolt (1909).

Ab·dul-Jab·bar /əb dóol jə báar/, **Kareem** (*b.* 1947) U.S. basketball player. He retired in 1989 as the NBA's all-time leading scorer. Born **Ferdinand Lewis Alcindor, Jr.**

Ab·dul·lah /əb dúllə/, **King of Jordan** (*b.* 1962). He was commander of the Jordanian army's Special Forces and succeeded his father Hussein in 1999. Full name **Abdullah bin Hussein**

Ab·dul·lah ibn Hus·sein, King of Jordan (1882–1951). He was emir of Transjordan (1921–46) and the first king of the modern state of Jordan (1946–51).

Ab·dul Rah·man /ab dóol ráamən/, **Tunku** (1903–90) Malayan politician. He was the first prime minister of the Federation of Malaya (1957–63) and of Malaysia (1963–70).

a·beam /ə béem/ *adv.* to or at the side of a ship, boat, or aircraft, especially at right angles to its length

a·be·ce·dar·i·an /ày bee see dáiree ən/ *n.* somebody who is learning the basics of literacy or a subject [Early 17thC. From medieval Latin *abecedarium* "book containing the alphabet," from, ultimately, the names of the first four letters of the alphabet.]

a·bed /ə béd/ *adv.* in or confined to bed (*archaic*)

A·bed·ne·go /ə bédnə gō/ *n.* in the Bible, one of Daniel's companions thrown into Nebuchadnezzar's furnace (Daniel 3:12–20)

A·bel /áyb'l/ *n.* in the Bible, a shepherd and the second son of Adam and Eve, who was killed by his brother Cain (Genesis 4)

Ab·e·lard /ábbə laard, aabə laar/ (1079–1142) French philosopher and theologian. He was an influential teacher and writer on theology, ethics, and dialectics. His love affair with his pupil Héloïse scandalized her family, who ordered his castration. Both took religious orders. Their later correspondence became a literary classic.

a·bele /ə béel/ *n.* = **white poplar** [13thC. Directly or via Dutch *abeel* from Old French *a(u)bel*, from, ultimately, Latin *albus* "white" (source of English *albino, albumen,* and *album*).]

a·be·li·a /ə béelee ə/ *n.* a shrub originally from eastern Asia but now widespread that has white, pink, or purple tubular flowers. Genus: *Abelia.* [Mid-19thC. From modern Latin, named for the English botanist Clarke *Abel* (1780–1826).]

A·be·lian group /ə béelyən-/ *n.* an algebraic group in which the result of the operation is independent of the sequence of the operands, e.g., ab = ba or a+b = b+a [Mid-19thC. Named for the Norwegian mathematician Niels *Abel* (1802–29), whose research contributed to the concept.]

a·bel·mosk /áyb'l mosk/ *n.* a tropical Asian plant of the mallow family with yellow-and-red flowers. Latin name: *Abelmoschus moschatus.* [Late 18thC. Via modern Latin *abelmoschus*, from Arabic *abu'l misk*, literally "father of musk."]

Ab·e·na·ki /àabə naakee, àbbə nákee/ (*plural* **-ki** *or* **-kis**), **Ab·na·ki** /àab naakee, àb nákee/ (*plural* **-ki** *or* **-kis**) *n.* a member of a Native American people who originally lived throughout New England and southeastern Canada, but who now live only in parts of Maine and southern Quebec [Early 18thC. Via French *Abénaqui* from Montagnais *ouabanăkionek* "people of the eastern country."] —**Ab·e·na·ki** *adj.*

A·be·o·ku·ta /àybi ō kóotə/ city and port in southwestern Nigeria. It is the capital of Ogun state. Population: 367,900 (1990 est.).

Ab·er·deen /ábbər deen, àbbər déen/ **1.** city and port in western Washington, situated where the Chehalis River flows into Grays Harbor. Population: 16,598 (1996). **2.** city in northeastern South Dakota in the James River valley. Population: 25,088 (1996). **3.** city northeast of Baltimore, Maryland, near Aberdeen Proving Ground, a military testing base. Population: 13,090 (1996). **4.** city, port, and industrial center in northeastern Scotland, located at the mouth of the Dee and Don rivers. It is known as the Granite City as many of its buildings are constructed of granite. Population: 217,260 (1996).

Ab·er·deen An·gus (*plural* **Ab·er·deen An·gus**) *n.* = **Angus** [Mid-19thC. Named for *Aberdeenshire* and *Angus*, counties in Scotland where the breed originated.]

Ab·er·nath·y /ábbər nàthee/, **Ralph David** (1926–90) U.S. civil rights leader who succeeded Martin Luther King, Jr. as leader of the Southern Christian Leadership Conference (SCLC) (1968–77).

ab·er·rant /ə bérənt/ *adj.* deviating from what is normal or desirable [Mid-16thC. From Latin *aberrant-*, the present participle stem of *aberrare* (see ABERRATION).] —**ab·er·rance** *n.* —**ab·er·rant·ly** *adv.*

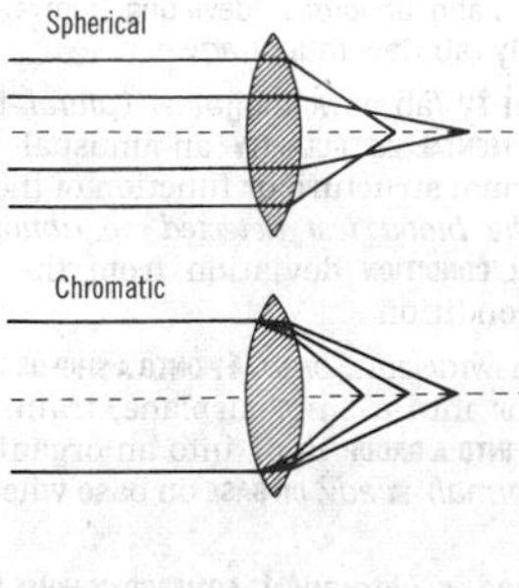

Aberration: Lenses with defects causing distorted image (top) and image with colored edges (bottom)

ab·er·ra·tion /àbbə ráysh'n/ *n.* **1.** **DEVIATION** a departure from what is normal or desirable ○ *in a moment of aberration* **2.** **LAPSE** a temporary departure from somebody's normal mental state **3.** OPTICS **OPTICAL DEFECT** a defect in a lens or mirror, causing a distorted image or one with colored edges **4.** ASTRON **APPARENT DISPLACEMENT IN STAR'S POSITION** a small periodic change in the apparent position of a star or other astronomical object, caused by the motion of the Earth around the Sun [Late 16thC. From the Latin stem *aberration-*, from *aberrare* "to go astray," from *errare* "to wander, err" (source of English *error* and *erratic*).] —**ab·er·ra·tion·al** *adj.*

a·bet /ə bét/ (**a·bet·ted, a·bet·ting, a·bets**) *vt.* to assist somebody to do something, especially something illegal [14thC. From Old French *abeter* "to urge, stimulate," from *beter* "to hound or drive on." Originally "to urge"; "to assist" came from the legal phrase "to aid and abet."] —**a·bet·tor** *n.*

a·bey·ance /ə báy ənss/ *n.* **1.** **SUSPENSION** temporary inactivity or nonoperation ○ *a law that has fallen into abeyance* **2.** **OWNERLESSNESS** a condition in which legal ownership of an estate has not been established [Late 16thC. From Old French *abeance* "expectation, desire," from *abaer* "to desire," from *baer* "to gape" (source of English *bay*), from medieval Latin *batare*.] —**a·bey·ant** *adj.*

ab·far·ad /ab férr ad, -əd/ *n.* the centimeter-gram-second unit of electrical capacitance equal to 10^9 farads

ab·hen·ry /ab hénree/ (*plural* **-ries**) *n.* the centimeter-gram-second unit of electrical conductance equal to 10^{-9} of a henry

ab·hor /ab háwr/ (**-horred, -hor·ring, -hors**) *vt.* to dislike or reject something very strongly (*formal*) [15thC. From Latin *abhorrere* "to shrink back in horror," from *horrere* "to shudder," literally "to bristle" (source of English *horrid* and *horror*).] —**ab·hor·rer** *n.*

ab·hor·rence /ab háwrəns/ *n.* **1.** **AVERSION** a feeling of loathing for or intense disapproval of something **2.** **OBJECT OF REPUGNANCE** somebody or something that is loathed or detested ○ *The idea became an abhorrence to her.*

WORD KEY: SYNONYMS

See Synonyms at ***dislike***.

ab·hor·rent /ab háwrənt/ *adj.* **1.** **REPUGNANT** arousing strong feelings of repugnance or disapproval (*formal*) ○ *a practice abhorrent to nearly everyone* **2.** **INCOMPATIBLE** incompatible or conflicting with something (*literary*)

A·bib /aavéev/ *n.* the first month of the ancient Hebrew calendar, corresponding to Nisan in the modern Jewish calendar [Mid-16thC. From Hebrew *'ābīb* "ear of corn."]

a·bide /ə bíd/ (**a·bode** /ə bód/ *or* **a·bid·ed, a·bode** *or* **a·bid·ed, a·bid·ing, a·bides**) *v.* **1.** *vt.* **TOLERATE SOMETHING** to find somebody or something acceptable or bearable ○ *couldn't abide his superior attitude* **2.** *vt.* **AWAIT SOMETHING** to wait for somebody or something (*archaic*) **3.** *vi.* **DWELL** to live or reside in a place (*archaic*) **4.** *vt.* **WITHSTAND SOMETHING** to endure or withstand something (*archaic*) [Old English *ābīdan* "to wait for or expect," from *bīdan* "to wait" (see BIDE)] —**a·bid·ance** *n.* —**a·bid·er** *n.*

a·bid·ing /ə bíding/ *adj.* permanent or long-lasting ○ *my abiding memory of her* —**a·bid·ing·ly** *adv.*

Ab·i·djan /àbbi jaan/ city and cultural and commercial capital of the Côte d'Ivoire. Population: 2,700,000 (1990 est.).

ab·i·et·ic ac·id /àbbee èttik-/ *n.* a yellowish powder extracted from rosin and used in making varnishes, lacquers, and soaps. Formula: $C_{20}H_{30}O_2$. [*Abietic* from the Latin stem *abiet-* "fir," from which rosin is obtained]

Ab·i·gail /ábbi gayl/ *n.* in the Bible, a woman who averted a hostile attack by David and his followers by taking provisions to them. She later married David. (1 Samuel 25)

Ab·i·lene /ábbə leen/ **1.** city in central Texas that is a center for agricultural products and the oil industry. Population: 108,476 (1996). **2.** city in east-central Kansas on the bank of the Great Smoky Hill River. Population: 6,520 (1996).

a·bil·i·ty /ə bíllətee/ (*plural* **-ties**) *n.* **1.** **BEING ABLE** the capacity to do something or perform successfully ○ *It has the ability to perform well on really rough terrain.* **2.** **TALENT** a particular talent or acquired skill ○ *a student with great musical abilities* **3.** **EXCEPTIONAL SKILL OR INTELLIGENCE** a high degree of general skill or competence ○ *We need people of your ability.* [14thC. Via Old French *ablete* from Latin *habilitas* "suitability, aptness," from *habilis* (see ABLE). The underlying sense is of suitable or sufficient power to do something.]

WORD KEY: SYNONYMS

ability, skill, competence, aptitude, talent, capacity, capability

CORE MEANING: the necessary skill, knowledge, or experience to do something

ability the most general term, covering both natural and acquired skills or knowledge; **skill** proficiency gained through training or experience; **competence** the ability to do something reasonably but not outstandingly well; **aptitude** a natural inclination toward a subject or area of activity; **talent** an unusual natural ability to do something extremely easily or well; **capacity** ability that may not actually have been tested; **capability** the potential ability of a person or machine to do something complex or demanding.

ab in·i·ti·o /àbi níshi ō/ *adv.* **1.** **FROM THE BEGINNING** from the beginning (*formal*) **2.** EDUC **FROM SCRATCH** without any previous knowledge of a subject ○ *study Spanish ab initio* [Early 17thC. From Latin.]

a·bi·o·gen·e·sis /àybī ō jénnəssiss/ *n.* the hypothesis that life can come into being from nonliving materials [Late 19thC. From Greek *abios* "without life," from *bios* "life" + GENESIS.] —**a·bi·o·ge·net·ic** /àybī ō jə néttik/ *adj.* —**a·bi·o·ge·net·i·cal** *adj.* —**a·bi·o·ge·nist** /-jénnist/ *n.*

a·bi·o·sis /àybī óssəss/ *n.* the state of not containing or supporting life

a·bi·ot·ic /àybī óttik/ *adj.* **1.** ECOL **PHYSICAL NOT BIOLOGICAL** used to describe the physical and chemical aspects of an organism's environment **2.** BIOL **FREE OF LIVING THINGS** not containing or supporting life —**a·bi·ot·ic·al·ly** *adv.*

ab·ject /áb jekt, ab jékt/ *adj.* **1. MISERABLE** allowing no hope of improvement or relief **2. HUMBLE** extremely or excessively humble, e.g., in making an apology or request **3. DESPICABLE** utterly despicable or contemptible [15thC. From Latin *abjectus*, past participle of *abjicere* "to throw away, reject," from *jacere* "to throw" (source of English *eject*, *ejaculate*, and *trajectory*). The underlying sense is "rejected."] —**ab·jec·tion** /ab jéksh'n/ *n.* —**ab·ject·ly** /áb jektlee/ *adv.* —**ab·ject·ness** /-nəss, ab jéktnəss/ *n.*

ab·jure /ab jo͝or/ (**-jured, -jur·ing, -jures**) *vt.* **1. FORMALLY RENOUNCE SOMETHING** to give up a previously held belief, especially when this is done formally or solemnly **2. DENY YOURSELF SOMETHING** to abstain from, reject, or avoid something (*literary*) [15thC. From Latin *abjurare*, "to deny on oath," from *jurare* "to swear."] —**ab·ju·ra·tion** /àbjə ráysh'n/ *n.* —**ab·jur·er** /ab jo͝orər/ *n.*

Ab·khaz /ab kaáz/ *n.* LANG a language spoken in the country Georgia, belonging to the Abkhaz-Adyghean group of languages. Abkhaz is spoken by between 80,000 and 100,000 people. [Mid-19thC. From *Abkhaz*, a territory in the Caucasus.] —**Ab·khaz** *adj.*

Ab·kha·zi·a /ab káyzhə, -zhee ə/ autonomous republic in the country Georgia, bordered to the north by Russia and to the southwest by the Black Sea. Area: 3,320 sq. mi./8,600 sq. km. Population: 537,500 (1990 est.).

abl. *abbr.* GRAM ablative

ab·late /ə bláyt/ (**-lat·ed, -lat·ing, -lates**) *vt.* **1.** MED **REMOVE TISSUE** to remove diseased or unwanted tissue from the body by surgical or other means **2.** GEOL **MELT SNOW AND ICE** to remove or reduce snow and ice from a glacier by melting and evaporation [15thC. From Latin *ablat-*, the past participle stem of *auferre* (see ABLATIVE).]

ab·la·tion /ə bláysh'n/ *n.* **1.** MED **REMOVAL OF TISSUE** the removal of diseased or unwanted tissue from the body by surgical or other means **2.** SPACE TECH **MELTING OF SPACECRAFT'S OUTER SURFACE** the melting or erosion of the protective outer surface of a spacecraft during reentry through the earth's atmosphere **3.** GEOL **MELTING OF SNOW AND ICE** the removal of snow and ice by melting and sublimation from a glacier or iceberg

ab·la·tive /ábblətiv/ *adj.* **GRAMMATICAL CASE** used to describe a case, used for nouns, pronouns, and adjectives in some inflected languages, that indicates the source, agent, or instrument of action of the verb ■ *n.* **ABLATIVE CASE OR WORD** the ablative case, or a word or form in this case [15thC. Directly or via French *ablatif* from Latin *ablativus*, from ablatus, past participle of auferre "to carry away." The case originally expressed "direction from."]

ab·la·tor /ə bláytər/ *n.* a heat shield on a spacecraft

ab·laut /áb lowt/ *n.* in Indo-European languages, a regular change of vowels in a related series of words or forms, e.g., "sing," "sang," "sung" [Mid-19thC. From German, from *ab* "off" + *Laut* "sound."]

a·blaze /ə bláyz/ *adj.* **1. ON FIRE** burning strongly **2. BRIGHTLY LIT** very brightly lit **3. SHOWING STRONG EMOTION** displaying great emotion or excitement, especially in the face

a·ble /áyb'l/ (**a·bler, a·blest**) *adj.* **1. IN A POSITION TO DO SOMETHING** physically or mentally equipped to do something, especially because of circumstances and timing ○ *Were you able to reach her before she left?* **2. CAPABLE OR TALENTED** having the necessary resources or talent to do something ○ *a very able administrator* [14thC. Via Old French *(h)able* from Latin *habilis* "easy to hold or handle," from *habere* "to have, to hold."]

WORD KEY: SYNONYMS

See Synonyms at ***intelligent***.

-able *suffix.* **1.** capable of or fit for ○ *readable* **2.** tending to ○ *changeable* [From Latin *-abilis*] —**-ability** *suffix.*

a·ble-bod·ied /-bóddid/ *adj.* healthy and physically strong

a·ble-bod·ied sea·man (*plural* **a·ble-bod·ied sea·men**) *n.* a member of a ship's crew, especially the crew of a merchant ship, who possesses basic skills and qualifications

a·bled /áyb'ld/ *adj.* having unrestricted physical or mental functions. ◊ **differently abled**

a·ble·ism /áyb'liz'm/ *n.* discrimination in favor of those who are not considered to be physically or mentally challenged —**a·ble·ist** *adj.*, *n.*

a·ble sea·man (*plural* **a·ble sea·men**) *n.* a member of a ship's crew who possesses basic skills and qualifications

a·bloom /ə blo͞om/ *adj.* blooming or flowering

ab·lu·tion /ə blo͞osh'n/ *n.* **RITUAL WASHING** the ritual cleansing of a priest's hands or body, or of sacred vessels, during a religious ceremony ■ **ab·lu·tions** *npl.* **WASHING YOURSELF** the act of washing the hands or the whole of the body (*formal or humorous*) [14thC. Directly or via French from the Latin stem *ablution-*, from *abluere* "to wash away, wash clean," from *luere* "to wash" (source of English *dilute*).] —**ab·lu·tion·ar·y** *adj.*

a·bly /áyblee/ *adv.* in a skillful or competent way

ABM *n., abbr.* antiballistic missile

Ab·na·ki *n., adj.* = **Abenaki**

ab·ne·gate /ábnə gàyt/ (**-gat·ed, -gat·ing, -gates**) *vt.* to give up or renounce something (*formal*) [Early 17thC. From Latin *abnegat-*, the past participle stem of *abnegare* "to refuse, reject," from *negare* "to deny" (source of English *deny, negative*, and *renegade*).] —**ab·ne·ga·tion** /àbnə gáysh'n/ *n.* —**ab·ne·ga·tor** /ábnə gàytər/ *n.*

ab·nor·mal /ab náwrm'l, əb-/ *adj.* unusual or unexpected, especially in a way that causes alarm or anxiety ○ *Doctors operated on the lung and found nothing abnormal.* [Mid-19thC. Alteration of ANORMAL, modeled on Latin *abnormis* "deviating from a rule."] —**ab·nor·mal·ly** /ab náwrm'lee/ *adv.*

ab·nor·mal·i·ty /àb nawr mállətee/ (*plural* **-ties**) *n.* **1. PHYSICAL OR MENTAL IRREGULARITY** an unusual variation from a normal structure or function of the mind or body ○ *The blood test detected no abnormalities.* **2. ABNORMAL CONDITION** deviation from the usual or expected condition

a·board /ə báwrd/ *adv., prep.* **1. ONTO A SHIP OR VEHICLE** on, onto, in, or into a ship, airplane, train, or other vehicle **2. INTO A GROUP** in or into an organization or group (*informal*) ■ *adv.* **ON BASE** on base when playing baseball

a·bode[1] /ə bṓd/ *n.* (*literary*) **1. SOMEBODY'S HOME** the house or other place where a particular person lives **2. STAY** a period of living somewhere [13thC. Formed from ABIDE; the underlying meaning is of staying, hence "a place where somebody stays."] ◇ **of no fixed abode** *U.K.* having no permanent place in which to live (*formal*)

WORD KEY: SYNONYMS

See Synonyms at ***residence***.

a·bode[2] past participle, past tense of **abide**

ab·ohm /a bṓm/ *n.* the centimeter-gram-second unit of electrical resistance equal to 10^{-9} of an ohm

a·boi·teau /ábwo tṓ/ (*plural* **aboiteaux** /ábwo tṓ/) *n. Can* a sluice gate in a dike that prevents sea water from flowing in but allows flood water to flow out

a·bol·ish /ə bóllish/ (**-ished, -ish·ing, -ish·es**) *vt.* to put an end to something, e.g., a law ○ *"Critics of advertising usually forget that if it were eliminated or abolished, other methods would necessarily be substituted for it."* (Daniel Starch, *Principles of Advertising*; 1923) [15thC. Via French *aboliss-*, the stem of *abolir*, from Latin *abolere* "to destroy."] —**a·bol·ish·a·ble** *adj.* —**a·bol·ish·er** *n.* —**a·bol·ish·ment** *n.*

ab·o·li·tion /àbbə lísh'n/ *n.* **1. ACT OF OUTLAWING SOMETHING** the act of officially ending a law, regulation, or practice **2. ab·o·li·tion, Abo·li·tion ENDING OF SLAVERY** the official ending of the practice of slavery [Early 16thC. Directly or via French from the Latin stem *abolition-*, from abolere "to destroy" (see ABOLISH).] —**ab·o·li·tion·ar·y** *adj.*

ab·o·li·tion·ist *n.* **1. ab·o·li·tion·ist, Abo·li·tion·ist OPPONENT OF SLAVERY** somebody who campaigned against slavery during the 18th and 19th centuries **2. SOMEBODY WHO SEEKS TO BAN SOMETHING** somebody who supports the abolition of a practice —**ab·o·li·tion·ism** *n.*

ab·o·ma·sum /àbbə máyss'm/ (*plural* **-sa** /-sə/) *n.* the fourth and final chamber of the multi-stomach digestive system of cattle and other ruminants, where enzymatic or true digestion takes place [Late 17thC. From the idea of being separate from the omasum.]

A-bomb *n.* an atomic bomb [Mid-20thC. Contraction.]

a·bom·i·na·ble /ə bómminəb'l, -bómnəb'l/ *adj.* **1. LOATHSOME** extremely repugnant or offensive **2. UNPLEASANT** of a very poor quality, or very unpleasant to experience [14thC. Via Old French from Latin *abominabilis*, from *abominari* "to shun something as being a bad omen," from *omen* "omen."] —**a·bom·i·na·bly** *adv.*

WORD KEY: ORIGIN

From the 14th to the 17th centuries ***abominable*** was often spelled *abhominable* because of a widely held belief that it was derived from Latin *ab hominem*, literally "away from humankind," hence "unnatural, beastly." Shakespeare puns on this sense when Hamlet speaks of incompetent actors who "imitate humanity abominably."

A·bom·i·na·ble Snow·man *n.* = **yeti**

a·bom·i·nate /ə bómmi nayt/ (**-nat·ed, -nat·ing, -nates**) *vt.* to dislike and disapprove of somebody or something intensely (*formal*) [Mid-17thC. From Latin *abominat-*, the past participle stem of *abominari* (see ABOMINABLE).] —**a·bom·i·na·tor** *n.*

a·bom·i·na·tion /ə bòmmi náysh'n/ *n.* **1. SOMETHING HORRIBLE** an object of intense disapproval or dislike **2. SOMETHING SHAMEFUL** something that is immoral, disgusting, or shameful **3. INTENSE DISLIKE** a feeling of intense dislike or disapproval towards somebody or something (*literary*)

ab·o·rig·i·nal /àbbə ríjj'nəl/ *adj.* **INDIGENOUS** existing from the earliest known times ○ *the aboriginal rainforest* ■ *n.* **ORIGINAL INHABITANT** a member of a people that has lived in an area from the earliest known times [Mid-17thC. Formed from *aborigines* (see ABORIGINE).] —**ab·o·rig·i·nal·i·ty** /àbbə rijjə nállə tee/ *n.* —**ab·o·rig·i·nal·ly** /-ríjj'nlee/ *adv.*

WORD KEY: SYNONYMS

See Synonyms at ***native***.

Ab·o·rig·i·nal *n.* **1. EARLY CANADIAN** a member of any of the peoples that inhabited Canada before the arrival of European settlers **2. EARLY AUSTRALIAN** a member of any of the indigenous peoples that inhabited Australia before the arrival of European settlers ■ *adj.* **OF ABORIGINALS** relating to the earliest inhabitants of Canada or Australia

ab·o·rig·i·ne /àbbə ríjjənee/ *n.* a person, animal, or plant that has lived in an area from the earliest known times [16thC. Back-formation from Latin *aborigines*, the pre-Roman inhabitants of Latium, from *ab origine* "from the beginning."]

Ab·o·rig·i·ne *n.* an Aboriginal inhabitant of Australia

a·born·ing /əbáwrning/ *adv.* while being born, created, or realized

a·bort /ə báwrt/ (**a·bort·ed, a·bort·ing, a·borts**) *v.* **1.** *vti.* **REMOVE FETUS** to remove an embryo or fetus from the womb in order to end a pregnancy **2.** *vi.* **HAVE MISCARRIAGE** to give birth to an embryo or fetus before its independent survival is possible. Survival is usually possible at 24 weeks for human fetuses, but may occur earlier. (*technical*) **3.** *vti.* **END PREMATURELY** to bring something to an end or come to an end at an early stage **4.** *vti.* **ABANDON MISSION** to end a space flight or similar mission before it is completed **5.** *vti.* COMPUT **QUIT COMPUTER PROGRAM** to abandon a computer program, command, or operation before it has finished [Mid-16thC. From Latin *abort-*, the past participle stem of *aboriri* "to miscarry," from *oriri* "to come into being" (source of English *origin*).]

a·bor·ti·fa·cient /ə bàwrtə fáysh'nt/ *adj.* used to describe a drug or device that causes abortion —**a·bor·ti·fa·cient** *n.*

a·bor·tion /ə báwrsh'n/ *n.* **1. OPERATION TO END PREGNANCY** an operation or other intervention to end a pregnancy by removing an embryo or fetus from the womb **2.** = **miscarriage** (*technical*) **3. CANCELLATION** the ending of a flight or mission before it is completed

4. OFFENSIVE TERM something so badly done or made that it is a complete failure (*offensive*)

a·bor·tion·ist /ə báwrsh'nist/ *n.* an offensive and disapproving term for somebody who performs abortions, especially suggesting the illegality of the procedure

a·bor·tive /ə báwrtiv/ *adj.* **1.** UNSUCCESSFUL failing to reach completion **2.** BIOL DISRUPTED IN DEVELOPMENT used to describe an organ that has had its development terminated —**a·bor·tive·ly** *adv.*

ABO sys·tem *n.* a system that classifies human blood by dividing it into the four groups A, B, AB, and O. Classification is based on the presence or absence of two chemical groups (**antigens**), A and B, on the red blood cells.

a·bound /ə bównd/ (**a·bound·ed, a·bound·ing, a·bounds**) *vi.* **1.** BE PLENTIFUL to be present in large numbers or quantities **2.** BE WELL SUPPLIED to contain something in large numbers or amounts [14thC. Via Old French *abunder* from Latin *abundare* "to overflow," from *undare* "to surge," from *unda* "wave" (source of English *inundate, redundant,* and *surround*).] —**a·bound·ing** *adj.* —**a·bound·ing·ly** *adv.*

a·bout /ə bówt/ CORE MEANING: a grammatical word that refers to different sides or aspects of something from some point of orientation ○ (prep) *a book about a dog* ○ (adv) *There's a lot of laziness about.*
1. *prep.* IN CONNECTION WITH in connection with or relating to ○ *think about problems* **2.** *prep.* APPROXIMATELY close to in number, time, or degree ○ *inviting about 15 people* **3.** *prep.* DOING OR ATTENDING TO with or in an activity ○ *go about your business* **4.** *prep.* CLOSE BY placed, located, or happening close by or around ○ *frantic activity going on all about us* **5.** *prep.* AROUND around or on a place or person ○ *a red scarf about her neck* **6.** *adv., prep.* IN VARIOUS PLACES positioned here and there ○ *scattered about the house* **7.** *adv., prep.* IN DIFFERENT DIRECTIONS from place to place in different directions or in no particular direction ○ *children running about everywhere* **8.** *adv.* IN CIRCULATION available or in circulation ○ *there was never much money about* **9.** *adv.* INTO A REVERSED POSITION in or to the opposite direction ○ *the wrong way about* **10.** *adv.* ALL AROUND on every side of or all the way around ○ *"He proceeded to the banks of the Hudson, and looked about among the vessels."* (Jules Verne, *Around the World in 80 Days*; 1873) **11.** *adv.* USED AS INTENSIFIER used to emphasize a statement, usually when expressing impatience or anger (*informal*) ○ *Well, it's about time you showed up!* **12.** *adv.* NAUT TO OPPOSITE TACK on or to the opposite tack [Old English *onbūtan* "on or around the outside of," from *on* (see ON) + *būtan* (see BUT)] ◇ **be what something** *or* **somebody is (all) about** to be what something or somebody involves or has as a purpose (*informal*) ◇ **be about to** be on the point of doing something ○ *The game was about to start.* ◇ **not about to** used to emphasize that somebody is certainly not going to do something (*informal*) ○ *I'm not about to apologize!*

a·bout-face *vi.* (**a·bout-faced, a·bout-fac·ing, a·bout-fac·es**) TURN AROUND to turn to face in the opposite direction (*usually used as a command*) ■ *n.* **1.** REVERSAL a sudden and complete reversal of a previous opinion or policy **2.** TURN a turn to face in the opposite direction

a·bout-ship (**a·bout-shipped, a·bout-ship·ping, a·bout-ships**) *vi.* to turn to a new tack in sailing

a·bout-turn *vi.* (**a·bout-turned, a·bout-turn·ing, a·bout-turns**), *n.* U.K. = **about-face**

a·bove /ə búv/ CORE MEANING: a grammatical word indicating a position directly overhead, on top of, or higher than something ○ (prep) *The bird flew up above the trees.* ○ (adv) *gazing at the sky above*
1. *prep., adv.* MORE THAN greater than an amount or level ○ *100 pounds above the ideal body weight* **2.** *prep., adv.* SUPERIOR TO higher in status or power ○ *A general is above a colonel.* **3.** *prep.* TOO GOOD FOR too good or important to be affected by or involved in something ○ *They felt they were above small town gossip.* **4.** *prep.* BEYOND not subject to something negative such as criticism or reproach ○ *"He wanted her to know that here too his conduct should be above suspicion."* (George Eliot, *Middlemarch*; 1872) **5.** *prep.* IN POSITION OF HIGHER RESPECT in a position that is valued more or considered more important than other people or things ○ *We put your needs above everything else.* **6.** *prep.* TOO DIFFICULT outside or beyond somebody's understanding ○ *The lecture was completely above me.* **7.** *prep.* LOUDER THAN OTHER NOISE louder than or over another sound ○ *She couldn't hear him above the roar of the band.* **8.** *prep.* NORTH OF lying north of a place ○ *a small town just above Seattle* **9.** *prep.* UPSTREAM FROM lying upstream from a place **10.** *adv., adj.* IN A PREVIOUS PLACE IN WRITING in a previous place, or further toward the top of the page in a piece of writing (*often used in hyphenated compounds*) ○ *using the information from the table above* **11.** *adv.* RELIG IN HEAVEN to or in heaven (*literary*) ○ *pray to God above* [Old English, from *an* (see ON) + *bufan* "above," ultimately from an Indo-European root that is also the ancestor of English *up, open, eaves,* and *opal*] ◇ **above all** used to indicate the most important thing or the main point of a statement

a·bove·board /ə búv bawrd/ *adj.* OPEN TO SCRUTINY honest, legal, and without deception ■ *adv.* **a·bove·board, a·bove board** OPENLY honestly, legally, and without deception [Late 16thC. Originally a gambling term indicating that the player's hands were above the *board* or gaming table and that nothing was being concealed.]

a·bove-the-ti·tle *adj.* shown in movie credits before the title is seen, and therefore in a starring role ○ *an above-the-title mention*

ab o·vo /àb ṓ vō/ *adv.* from the very beginning (*literary*) [Late 16thC. From Latin, literally "from the egg."]

abp., Abp. *abbr.* archbishop

ab·ra·ca·dab·ra /àbbrəkə dábbrə/ *interj.* MAGIC WORD a word spoken by magicians and conjurors supposedly to ensure the success of a trick ■ *n.* **1.** MAGIC SPELL a magical charm or spell **2.** GIBBERISH deliberately nonsensical language [Mid-16thC. Via Latin from, ultimately, Greek, possibly from abraxas, a series of letters with the value 365 (the days of the year) in numerological theory. Originally a cabbalistic word and formerly usedas a talisman or charm against fever.]

a·brade /ə bráyd/ (**a·brad·ed, a·brad·ing, a·brades**) *vti.* to wear something away or be worn away by friction [Late 17thC. From Latin *abradere*, from *radere* "to scrape" (source of English *erase, raze,* and *razor*).]

A·bra·ham /áybrə hàm/, **A·bram** /áybrəm/ *n.* the first patriarch in the Bible who was asked by God to sacrifice his son, Isaac, and was rewarded for being prepared to do so. He is seen by Jewish people as the father of the Hebrews through his son Isaac, and by Muslims as the father of Arab peoples through his son Ishmael.

A·bra·ham, Plains of plateau in the city of Quebec over the St. Lawrence River. It was the scene of a battle between British and French forces in 1759.

A·bra·hams /áy brə hàms/, **Harold** (1899–1978) British athlete. His victory in the 100 meters at the 1924 Paris Olympic Games was featured in the motion picture *Chariots of Fire* (1981).

a·bran·chi·ate /ay brángkee ət/, **a·bran·chi·al** /-əl/ *adj.* without gills

ab·ra·sion /ə bráyzh'n/ *n.* **1.** WEARING AWAY the process of wearing away by friction **2.** MED SCRAPED AREA OF SKIN an area on the skin, or some other surface of the body, that has been damaged by scraping or rubbing ○ *dental abrasion* **3.** GEOG WEARING AWAY OF ROCK the erosion of bedrock by continuous friction caused by rock fragments in water, wind, or ice [Mid-17thC. From the Latin stem *abrasion-*, from *abradere* (see ABRADE).]

ab·ra·sive /ə bráyssiv, -ziv/ *adj.* **1.** USING FRICTION using friction and roughness of texture to smooth or clean a surface ○ *an abrasive cleaner* **2.** HARSH IN MANNER aggressively direct and insensitive ■ *n.* SMOOTHING SUBSTANCE a substance used to smooth or polish a surface by grinding or scraping. Typical abrasives include sandpaper, pumice, and emery. [Mid-19thC. From Latin *abras-*, the past participle stem of *abradere* (see ABRADE).]

ab·re·act /àbbree ákt/ (**-act·ed, -act·ing, -acts**) *vt.* to release unconscious tension by talking about or reliving the events that caused it —**ab·re·ac·tion** *n.*

a·breast /ə brést/ *adv.* IN LINE side by side and facing the front ■ *adj.* WELL INFORMED up to date with something

ab·ri /ábbree/ *n.* a place of refuge or shelter, e.g., a dugout [Early 19thC. Via French from Latin *apricum* "open place."]

a·bridge /ə bríj/ (**a·bridged, a·bridg·ing, a·bridg·es**) *vt.* **1.** SHORTEN SOMETHING to shorten a text, e.g., by cutting or summarizing it ○ *abridged for television* **2.** CUT SOMETHING SHORT to reduce something in scope or extent ○ *They abridged the meeting as best they could.* **3.** RESTRICT SOMETHING to deprive somebody of rights or privileges (*archaic*) [14thC. Via Old French *abreg(i)er* from Latin *abbreviare* "to shorten" (source of English *abbreviate*), from, ultimately, *brevis* "short" (source of English *brief*).] —**a·bridg·a·ble** *adj.* —**a·bridged** *adj.* —**a·bridg·er** *n.*

a·bridg·ment /ə bríjmənt/, **a·bridge·ment** *n.* **1.** SHORTENED VERSION a shortened version of a novel, play, or other work **2.** ABRIDGING the process of abridging a work **3.** CURTAILMENT a curtailment or reduction of something

a·broach /ə brṓch/ *adj.* opened or tapped so that liquid can be drawn off

a·broad /ə bráwd/ *adv.* **1.** AWAY FROM YOUR OWN COUNTRY in or to a foreign country or countries **2.** IN CIRCULATION in public or into general circulation **3.** EVERYWHERE over a wide area **4.** OFF TARGET wide of the mark (*literary*) ■ *n.* OTHER COUNTRIES foreign countries (*informal*) [Coined from A- + BROAD. The original sense was "widely, over a wide area," hence "away from home, in a foreign country."]

ab·ro·gate /ábbrə gàyt/ (**-gat·ed, -gat·ing, -gates**) *vt.* to repeal or abolish something formally and publicly (*formal*) [Early 16thC. From Latin *abrogat-*, the past participle stem of *abrogare*, "to repeal a law," from *rogare* "to ask, to propose a law" (source of English *arrogant, interrogate,* and *prerogative*).] —**ab·ro·ga·tion** /àbbrə gáysh'n/ *n.*

WORD KEY: SYNONYMS

See Synonyms at ***nullify***.

a·brupt /ə brúpt/ *adj.* **1.** SUDDEN sudden and unexpected **2.** BRUSQUE brief and making no effort to be friendly **3.** DISCONNECTED not passing smoothly from topic to topic **4.** STEEP with a sudden steep slope **5.** GEOL PROJECTING used to describe a rock layer that is steeply inclined and stands out from surrounding rocks [Late 16thC. From Latin *abruptus* "broken off, steep," past participle of *abrumpere* "to break off," from *rumpere* "to break" (source of English *disrupt, interrupt,* and *rupture*).] —**a·brupt·ly** *adv.* —**a·brupt·ness** *n.*

a·brup·tion /ə brúpsh'n/ *n.* the sudden breaking off of a part from a larger mass (*formal*) [Early 17thC. From the Latin stem *abruption-*, from *abrumpere* (see ABRUPT).]

A·bruz·zi /aa brŏŏtsee, ə-/ agricultural region of central southern Italy consisting of the provinces of L'Aguila, Chieti, Pescara, and Teramo. Area: 4,168 sq. mi./10,794 sq. km. Population: 1,249,388 (1991).

abs /abz/ *npl.* the abdominal muscles, or exercises done to firm them (*informal*) [Late 20thC. Shortening.]

ABS[1] *n.* a type of strong plastic (**copolymer**) used for making molded casings and car parts. Full form **acrylonitrile-butachene-styrene**

ABS[2] *abbr.* anti-lock braking system

Ab·sa·lom /ábsə lom/ *n.* in the Bible, the third son of David, King of Israel. He rebelled against his father and was killed by Joab (2 Samuel 13–18).

ab·scess /áb sess/ *n.* PUS-FILLED CAVITY a pus-filled cavity resulting from inflammation and usually caused by bacterial infection ■ *vi.* (**-scessed, -scess·ing, -scess·es**) FORM AN ABSCESS to form an abscess or be the site where one develops [Mid-16thC. From Latin *abscessus*, from *abscedere* "to go away (referring to bodily humors going away in the pus)," from *cedere* "to go" (source of English *cede* and *ancestor*).] —**ab·scessed** *adj.*

ab·scis·ic ac·id /ab sìssik-/ *n.* a plant hormone that promotes dormancy in buds and seeds, retardation of growth, and shedding of leaves, flowers, and fruits. Formula: $C_{15}H_{20}O_4$.

ab·scis·sa /ab síssə/ (*plural* **-sas** *or* **-sae** /-síssee/) *n.* the horizontal coordinate or x-coordinate of a point in a two-dimensional system of Cartesian coordinates. It is the distance from the vertical axis or y-axis measured along a line parallel to the horizontal axis or x-axis. ◊ **ordinate** [Late 17thC. From modern Latin *abscissa linea*, literally "line cut off."]

ab·scis·sion /ab sízh'n/ *n.* **1.** DETACHMENT OF PARTS FROM PLANTS the natural process by which leaves or other parts are shed from a plant **2.** CUTTING OFF the act of suddenly cutting something off [Early 17thC. From the Latin stem *abscission-*, from *abscindere* "to cut off," from *scindere* "to cut up or divide" (source of English *rescind*).]

ab·scond /ab skónd, əb-/ (**-scond·ed, -scond·ing, -sconds**) *vi.* **1.** RUN AWAY to run away secretly, especially in order to avoid arrest or prosecution **2.** ESCAPE to escape from a place of detention [Mid-16thC. From Latin *abscondere* "to hide or put away," from *condere* "to stow." Originally "to hide"; the underlying meaning is of making oneself scarce.] —**ab·scond·er** *n.*

ab·seil /áb sayl/ *vi.* **(-seiled, -seil·ing, -seils)** *U.K.* = **rappel** ■ *n. U.K.* = **rappel** [Mid-20thC. From German *abseilen*, from *ab* "down" + *Seil* "rope."] —**ab·seil·er** *n.*

ab·sence /ábs'ns/ *n.* **1. NOT BEING PRESENT** the fact of somebody's not being in a particular place **2. TIME AWAY** a period during which somebody is away **3. NONEXISTENCE** the lack or nonexistence of a particular quality or feature ○ *in the absence of any fresh information* [14thC. Via French from Latin *absentia*, from *abesse* (see ABSENT[1]).]

ab·sent[1] /ábs'nt/ *adj.* **1. NOT PRESENT** not attending a place or event, especially when expected to ○ *absent from school* **2. INATTENTIVE** not paying attention ■ *prep.* **WITHOUT** in the absence of ○ *Absent a definite refusal, I decided to proceed.* [14thC. From Latin *absent-*, the present participle stem of *abesse*, literally "to be away," from *esse* "to be."]

ab·sent[2] /ab sént/ **(-sent·ed, -sent·ing, -sents)** *vr.* to stay away from or leave something such as an event or occasion ○ *She absented herself from the gathering and went outside.* [14thC. Directly or via French *absenter* from Latin *absentare* "to keep or be away," from *absent-* (see ABSENT[1]).]

ab·sen·tee /àbs'n tée/ *n.* somebody who is not present or not attending an event

ab·sen·tee bal·lot *n.* a ballot sent by somebody who is unable to attend to vote in person at the voting place

ab·sen·tee·ism /àbs'n tée iz'm/ *n.* persistent absence from work or some other place without good reason

ab·sen·tee land·lord *n.* a landlord who lives away from the accommodations rented out, especially one who neglects the needs of tenants

ab·sen·tee vot·er *n.* somebody who votes by mail because of being unable to cast a ballot at the voting place

ab·sent·ly /ábs'ntlee/ *adv.* in an inattentive or absent-minded way

ab·sent-mind·ed *adj.* tending to be preoccupied or forgetful —**ab·sent-mind·ed·ly** *adv.* —**ab·sent-mind·ed·ness** *n.*

ab·sent with·out leave *adj.* absent from military duties without permission, but not assumed to have deserted

ab·sinthe /ábssinth/, **ab·sinth** *n.* **1. TYPE OF DRINK** a highly alcoholic liqueur tasting of aniseed and made from wormwood and herbs. Absinthe is now banned in most Western countries because of its toxicity. **2.** = **wormwood** [Early 17thC. Via French from, ultimately, Greek *apsinthion* "wormwood"; not of Indo-European origin.]

ab·so·lute /ábssə lòot, àbssə lóot/ *adj.* **1. OUT-AND-OUT** used to emphasize the strength of the speaker's feeling on the subject ○ *an absolute fool* **2. UNBOUNDED** to the very greatest degree possible ○ *absolute confidence in her ability to win* **3. DESPOTIC** having total power and authority ○ *to rule as an absolute monarch* **4. INDEPENDENT AND UNMODIFIABLE** not dependent on or qualified by anything else ○ *absolute truth* **5. TOTAL AND UNEQUIVOCAL** completely unequivocal and not capable of being viewed as partial or relative ○ *No absolute correlation has been established.* **6.** GRAM **GRAMMATICALLY INDEPENDENT** not syntactically dependent on the main clause of a sentence, e.g., "It being sunny" in the sentence "It being sunny, they went to the pool" **7.** GRAM **WITHOUT DIRECT OBJECT** used without an explicit direct object. The usage of "satisfy" is absolute in the sentence "We aim to satisfy." **8.** GRAM **USED AS NOUN** used without an explicit noun. "The rich and the poor" are absolute adjectival usages. **9.** PHYS **MEASURED RELATIVE TO VACUUM** involving or relating to measurements made relative to the vacuum state **10.** PHYS **ACCORDING TO STANDARDIZED MEASURES** relating to or using fundamental units of length, time, mass, and charge **11.** PHYS **MEASURED RELATIVE TO ABSOLUTE ZERO** measured on or relating to a scale that has as its lowest temperature absolute zero, the point at which all molecular motion ceases **12.** LAW **FULL AND UNCONDITIONAL** complete and in no way conditional on any future evidence or behavior **13.** LAW **OWNED OUTRIGHT** having unconditional ownership of a title or property, unrestricted by trusts or entails (*often used after a noun*) **14.** MATH **ALWAYS TRUE ALGEBRAICALLY** true for all values of a variable in an algebraic expression **15.** MATH **CONSTANT IN VALUE** not changing in value in varying mathematical expressions **16.** MATH **WITHOUT VARIABLES** not containing an algebraic variable ■ *n.* **1. UNQUESTIONABLE RULE** a principle or value that is held to be always true or valid **2. ab·so·lute, Ab·so·lute** PHILOS **ULTIMATE REALITY** in some schools of philosophy, the one ultimate reality that does not depend on anything, and is not relative to anything else [14thC. From Latin *absolutus* "freed," the past participle of *absolvere* "to set free" (see ABSOLVE). The underlying idea is of setting something free from defect and making it complete.]

ab·so·lute ceil·ing *n.* the maximum height above sea level at which an aircraft can maintain horizontal flight

ab·so·lute·ly /ábssə lòotlee, àbssə lóot-/ *adv.* **1. TOTALLY** used to give strong emphasis to what is being said **2. THAT'S RIGHT** used in speech or dialogue as an emphatic way of agreeing with the other speaker **3. NOT IN RELATIVE WAY** in a way that is independent of circumstances and never variable or modified **4.** LAW **UNCONDITIONALLY** with no conditions or restrictions, especially constitutional or legal ones **5.** GRAM **WITH NO GRAMMATICAL OBJECT** used syntactically with an implied direct object or noun head

WORD KEY: USAGE

Some people dislike the use of ***absolutely*** to mean "very" or "completely" (*That is absolutely disgraceful.*) and regard it as an affectation. Even more controversial is its use to mean simply "yes" or "I agree with you." It has some relevance of meaning in uses such as "Do you like it?" "Yes, absolutely," but has less to justify it when used with answers that are factual rather than judgmental: *"Have you been to Paris?" "Yes, absolutely."*

ab·so·lute ma·jor·i·ty (*plural* **ab·so·lute ma·jor·i·ties**) *n.* the winning total of votes that amounts to more than half of the votes available

ab·so·lute mu·sic *n.* music whose meaning is derived solely from the music itself and which does not evoke another source, e.g., a visual scene. ◊ **program music**

ab·so·lute pitch *n.* **1. GOOD MUSICAL EAR** the ability to identify the pitch of a single note without reference to any other sound **2. PITCH MEASURED BY VIBRATION** the exact pitch a tone is expected to have, measured by its rate of vibrations per second

ab·so·lute tem·per·a·ture *n.* temperature derived from the laws of thermodynamics rather than being primarily derived from properties of substances

ab·so·lute val·ue *n.* **1. NUMBER IGNORING PLUS OR MINUS SIGN** the magnitude of a number, irrespective of whether it is positive or negative. It is symbolized by placing the number within vertical bars, thus $|7| = |-7| = 7$. **2.** = **modulus**

ab·so·lute ze·ro *n.* the temperature at which hypothetically all molecular motion ceases, equal to 0 degrees K and equivalent to -273.16°C or -459.69°F

ab·so·lu·tion /àbssə lóosh'n/ *n.* **1. FORGIVENESS** forgiveness for somebody's sins, especially in a Christian church **2. PRAYER OF FORGIVENESS** a spoken blessing used in a Christian church to grant absolution to somebody [13thC. Via French from the Latin stem *absolution-* "acquittal, perfection," from *absolvere* (see ABSOLVE).]

ab·so·lut·ism /ábssə lòotizzəm/ *n.* **1.** POL **POLITICAL SYSTEM** a political system in which the power of a ruler is unchecked and absolute **2. SOMETHING ABSOLUTE** a standard, principle, or theory that is absolute **3.** PHILOS **THEORY OF OBJECTIVE VALUES** a philosophical theory in which values such as truth or morality are absolute and not conditional upon human perception **4.** CHR **PREDESTINATION** a strict form of the doctrine of predestination —**ab·so·lut·ist** *n., adj.*

ab·solve /əb zólv, -sólv/ **(-solved, -solv·ing, -solves)** *vt.* **1. PRONOUNCE SOMEBODY BLAMELESS** to state publicly or officially that somebody is not guilty and not to be held responsible **2. RELIEVE SOMEBODY OF OBLIGATION** to release somebody from an obligation or requirement **3. FORGIVE SOMEBODY** to forgive somebody's sins, especially in a Christian church service or sacrament [15thC. From Latin *absolvere* "to set free," literally "to loosen away," from *solvere* "to loosen" (source of English *dissolve* and *soluble*).] —**ab·solv·a·ble** *adj.* —**ab·solv·er** *n.*

WORD KEY: SYNONYMS

See Synonyms at ***excuse***.

ab·sorb /əb sáwrb, -záwrb/ **(-sorbed, -sorb·ing, -sorbs)** *vt.* **1. TAKE SOMETHING UP** to soak up a liquid or take in nutrients or chemicals gradually **2. NOT TRANSMIT SOMETHING** to take up light, noise, or energy and not transmit it at all **3. ENGROSS SOMEBODY** to hold somebody's attention or occupy somebody's time completely **4. INCORPORATE SOMETHING INTO WHOLE** to incorporate something into a larger entity in such a way that it loses much of its own identity **5. TAKE SOMETHING IN MENTALLY** to see, read, or hear something and realize its implications mentally **6. ADAPT** to adapt to changing situations without being adversely affected **7. REQUIRE SOMETHING IN QUANTITY** to require something in considerable quantities, usually without significant results ○ *absorbing a huge amount of money* **8. NOT PASS SOMETHING ON** to accept increased costs without passing them on to customers [15thC. Via French *absorber* from Latin *absorbere* "to swallow," from *sorbere* "to suck in."] —**ab·sorb·a·ble** *adj.* —**ab·sorb·er** *n.*

ab·sorb·ance /əb sáwrbəns, -záwrb-/ *n.* the capacity of a substance to absorb radiation

ab·sorbed /əb sáwrbd, -záwrbd/ *adj.* so interested in something that all of the attention is focused on it —**ab·sorb·ed·ly** *adv.*

ab·sorb·ent /əb sáwrbənt, -záwrb-/ *adj.* **1. ABLE TO ABSORB LIQUID** capable of soaking up liquid **2. NONREFLECTIVE** capable of absorbing light, noise, or energy instead of reflecting it (*often used in combination*) [Early 18thC. From Latin *absorbent-*, the present participle stem of absorbere "to swallow" (see ABSORB).] —**ab·sorb·en·cy** *n.* —**ab·sorb·ent** *n.*

ab·sorb·ent cot·ton *n.* cotton that has had the natural wax removed, making it absorbent and suitable for medical and cosmetic use, e.g., as dressings or swabs

ab·sorb·ing /əb sáwrbing, -záwrb-/ *adj.* occupying the attention completely —**ab·sorb·ing·ly** *adv.*

ab·sorp·tance /əb sáwrptənss, -záwrp-/ *n.* a measure of the ability of an object or substance to absorb radiant energy, equal to the ratio of the absorbed energy to the total energy reaching the object or substance. Symbol α [Mid-20thC. Formed from Latin *absorptus*, the past participle of *absorbere* "to swallow" (see ABSORB).]

ab·sorp·tion /əb sáwrpsh'n, -záwrp-/ *n.* **1. PREOCCUPATION** a state in which the whole attention is occupied **2. SOAKING UP** the uptake of liquid into the fibers of a substance **3. NONREFLECTION** the ability of a substance to absorb light, noise, or energy, or the fact that it does so **4. INCORPORATION** the incorporation of something into a larger group or entity **5.** PHYSIOL **ASSIMILATION BY THE BODY** the passage of material through the lining of the intestine into the blood or through a cell membrane into a cell **6.** PHYS **REDUCTION IN RADIATED ENERGY** the reduction in the intensity of radiated energy within a medium caused by converting some or all of the energy into another form **7.** IMMUNOL **REMOVAL OF ANTIBODIES** the elimination of antibodies or antigens by the use of a chemical reagent [Late 16thC. From the Latin stem *absorption-*, from *absorptus*, the past participle of *absorbere* "to swallow" (see ABSORB).] —**ab·sorp·tive** *adj.*

ab·sorp·tion spec·trum *n.* the pattern of dark bands that is seen when electromagnetic radiation passes through an absorbing medium and is observed with a spectroscope. It is the result of unequal absorption of the radiation as it passes through the medium.

ab·squat·u·late /ab skwóchə làyt/ **(-lat·ed, -lat·ing, -lates)** *vi.* (*regional archaic humorous*) **1. ABSCOND** to leave, especially in a hurry or under suspicious circumstances **2. DIE** to die **3. ARGUE** to argue [Mid-19thC. A humorous formation modeled on English words of Latin origin, as if from Latin *ab* "away" + English SQUAT + *-ulate* (as in CONGRATULATE), literally meaning the reverse of SQUAT, that is, "to depart in a hurry."]

ab·stain /əb stáyn/ **(-stained, -stain·ing, -stains)** *vi.* **1. REFRAIN FROM SOMETHING** to choose deliberately not to do something **2. NOT VOTE** not vote for or against a proposal when a vote is held [14thC. Via Old French *abstenir* from Latin *abstinere*, literally "to hold yourself away," from *tenere* "to hold" (source of English *tenant* and *continue*).] —**ab·stain·er** *n.*

ab·ste·mi·ous /əb stéemee əss/ *adj.* not indulging in or involving excessive eating or drinking [Early 17thC. From Latin *abstemius*, from *abs-* "away from" + *temetum* "intoxicating liquor," of unknown origin.] —**ab·ste·mi·ous·ly** *adv.* —**ab·ste·mi·ous·ness** *n.*

ab·sten·tion /əb sténsh'n/ *n.* **1. NOT DOING SOMETHING** the deliberate choice not to do something **2. NOT VOTING** a vote or voting neither for nor against a proposal [Early 16thC. From the late Latin stem *abstention-*, from Latin *abstentus,* the past participle of *abstinere* (see ABSTAIN).]

ab·sti·nence /ábstənənss/ *n.* restraint from indulging a desire for something, e.g., alcohol or sexual relations [14thC. Via Old French from Latin *abstinentia,* from *abstinent-,* the present participle stem of *abstinere* (see ABSTAIN).] —**ab·sti·nent** *adj.* —**ab·sti·nent·ly** *adv.*

ab·stract *adj.* /áb strakt, ab strákt/ **1. NOT CONCRETE** not relating to concrete objects but expressing something that can only be appreciated intellectually **2. THEORETICAL** based on general principles or theories rather than on specific instances ○ *abstract arguments* **3.** ARTS **NONREPRESENTATIONAL** not aiming to depict an object but composed with the focus on internal structure and form **4.** MUSIC **CONCEPTUAL** used to describe music that is intended to have no programmatic or emotional content **5. WITH IRREGULAR PATTERN** decorated with irregular areas of color that do not represent anything concrete **6. IMPERSONAL** emotionally detached or distanced from something ■ *n.* /áb strakt, ab strákt/ **1. PRINTED SUMMARY** a summary of a longer text, especially of an academic article **2. INTELLECTUAL CONCEPT** a concept or term that does not refer to a concrete object but that denotes a quality, an emotion, or an idea **3.** ARTS **ABSTRACT ARTWORK** a work of art, especially a painting, in an abstract style ■ *vt.* /ab strákt/ (**-stract·ed, -stract·ing, -stracts**) **1. CONCEPTUALIZE SOMETHING** to develop a line of thought from a concrete reality to a general principle or an intellectual idea **2. SUMMARIZE SOMETHING** to make a summary of the main points of an argument or some information **3. EXTRACT SOMETHING** to remove something from a place, usually with some difficulty **4. STEAL SOMETHING** to steal something by taking it unobtrusively (*used euphemistically*) **5.** ENVIRON **PUMP WATER** to remove water from a river or other source for industrial use [14thC. From Latin *abstractus,* the past participle of *abstrahere* "to drag away," from *trahere* "to drag" (source of English *tractor, trail,* and *treat*).] —**ab·stract·er** /ab stráktər/ *n.* —**ab·stract·ly** /áb straktlee, ab stráktlee/ *adv.* —**ab·stract·ness** /áb straktnəss, ab stráktnəss/ *n.*

ab·stract·ed /ab stráktəd/ *adj.* **1. PREOCCUPIED** in deep thought and not concentrating on surroundings **2. TAKEN OUT OF SOMETHING** extracted or separated from something —**ab·stract·ed·ly** *adv.* —**ab·stract·ed·ness** *n.*

ab·stract ex·pres·sion·ism *n.* a school of painting, originating in New York in the 1940s, that combined abstract forms with spontaneity of artistic expression

ab·strac·tion /ab stráksh'n/ *n.* **1. GENERALIZED CONCEPT** a generalized idea or theory developed from specific concrete examples of events **2. GENERALIZING PROCESS** the forming of general ideas or concepts from specific concrete examples **3. PREOCCUPATION** a state in which somebody is deep in thought and not concentrating on his or her surroundings **4.** PHILOS **CONCEPTUALIZATION** the philosophical process by which people develop concepts either from experience or from other concepts **5.** ARTS **ABSTRACT ART** an abstract painting or sculpture **6. EXTRACTION** the removal or theft of something, usually with some difficulty **7.** ENVIRON **PUMPING WATER FROM RIVER** the pumping of water from a river or other source for industrial use

ab·strac·tion·ism /ab stráksh'n ìzzəm/ *n.* the principles and practice of abstract art —**ab·strac·tion·ist** *n.*

ab·stract mu·sic *n.* = **absolute music**

ab·stract noun *n.* a noun signifying a concept, quality, or other abstract idea

ab·stract of ti·tle *n.* a summary of the details about the ownership of a piece of land, including all conveyances and any burdens or charges on it

ab·struse /ab stróoss/ *adj.* obscure and not easily understood [Late 16thC. Directly or via French from Latin *abstrusus,* the past participle of *abstrudere,* literally "to thrust away," from *trudere* "to thrust" (source of English *intrude*).] —**ab·struse·ly** *adv.* —**ab·struse·ness** *n.*

WORD KEY: SYNONYMS

See Synonyms at ***obscure.***

ab·surd /əb súrd, -zúrd/ *adj.* **1. LUDICROUS** ridiculous because of being irrational, incongruous, or illogical ○ *an absurd notion* **2. MEANINGLESS** lacking any meaning that would give purpose to life ■ *n.* **ab·surd, Ab·surd MEANINGLESSNESS** the condition of living in a meaningless universe where life has no purpose, especially as a concept in certain 20th-century philosophical movements. ◊ **Theater of the Absurd** [Mid-16thC. Via French from Latin *absurdus* "inharmonious," literally "away from the (right) sound," from assumed *surdos* "sound."] —**ab·surd·ly** *adv.* —**ab·surd·ness** *n.*

ab·surd·ism /əb súrdizzəm, -zúrd-/, **Ab·surd·ism** *n.* the idea that the universe is without meaning or rational order and that human beings, in attempting to find a sense of order, must come into conflict with the universe —**ab·surd·ist** *n., adj.*

ab·surd·i·ty /əb súrdətee/ (*plural* **-ties**) *n.* **1. LUDICROUSNESS** ridiculousness or silliness **2. SOMETHING LUDICROUS** something that is that is irrational, incongruous, or illogical

ABT *abbr.* American Ballet Theater

A·bu Ba·kr /áaboo báakər/ (573–634) Arabian religious leader who was the first caliph of Islam. He was responsible for uniting Arabia and spreading Islam.

A·bu Dha·bi /áa boo dáabee/ capital of the United Arab Emirates, on the southern shore of the Persian Gulf. Population: 363,432 (1989).

a·build·ing /ə bílding/ *adj.* in the process of being built

A·bu·ja /áa bóo jáa/ official capital of Nigeria since December 1991. It is located in the Federal Capital Territory in central Nigeria. Population: 305,900 (1992).

A·bu·kir, Bay of /ábоо kéeə, áaboo kéeə/, **A·bou·kir, A·bū Qīr** a bay in the Nile Delta that was the site of Nelson's defeat of the French fleet in 1798

a·bun·dance /ə búndənss/ *n.* **1. LARGE AMOUNT** a more than plentiful quantity of something **2. AFFLUENCE** a lifestyle with more than adequate material provisions **3. FULLNESS** a fullness of spirit that overflows **4.** CHEM, GEOL **RATE OF INCIDENCE** the extent to which an element is present in the earth or in rocks of a particular type **5.** PHYS **PROPORTION OF ISOTOPE ATOMS** the proportion of one isotope of an element, expressed by number of atoms, to the total quantity of the element [14thC. Via Old French from Latin *abundantia,* from *abundant-* (see ABUNDANT).]

a·bun·dant /ə búndənt/ *adj.* **1. PLENTIFUL** present in great quantities **2. WELL-SUPPLIED** providing a more than plentiful supply of something **3. FOUND IN QUANTITY** existing in large quantities [14thC. From Latin *abundant-,* the present participle stem of *abundare* "to overflow" (see ABOUND).] —**a·bun·dant·ly** *adv.*

a·buse *n.* /ə byóoss/ **1. MALTREATMENT** the physical, sexual, or psychological maltreatment of a person or animal **2. IMPROPER USE** the illegal, improper, or harmful use of something, or an illegal, improper, or harmful practice **3. INSULTS** insulting or offensive language **4. DRUG USE** the harmful or illegal nonmedicinal use of drugs or alcohol ■ *v.* /ə byóoz/ (**a·bused, a·bus·ing, a·bus·es**) **1.** *vt.* **MISUSE SOMETHING** to use something in an improper, illegal, or damaging way **2.** *vt.* **MALTREAT SOMEBODY** to maltreat a person or animal physically, sexually, or psychologically **3.** *vt.* **INSULT SOMEBODY** to speak insultingly or offensively to somebody **4.** *vr.* **MASTURBATE** to masturbate (*disapproving*) [15thC. Via French *abus* from Latin *abusus,* the past participle of *abuti* "to use up, misuse," from *uti* "to use."]

WORD KEY: USAGE

abuse or **misuse**? Both as a verb and as a noun, ***abuse*** is more morally loaded than **misuse**; **alcohol misuse** is a factual statement about alcohol wrongly used, whereas **alcohol abuse** implies a judgment about the user. This difference has been greatly emphasized by the use of ***abuse*** (both noun and verb) with reference to violence or sexual acts committed on children; the alternative word **misuse** would be meaningless here.

WORD KEY: SYNONYMS

See Synonyms at ***misuse.***

a·bus·er /ə byóozər/ *n.* **1. SOMEBODY WHO MALTREATS ANOTHER** somebody who physically, sexually, or psychologically maltreats a person or an animal **2. DRUG USER** somebody who uses drugs or alcohol in a way that may be addictive, harmful, or illegal

A·bu Sim·bel /áa boo símbəl, àa boo sím bél/ *n.* the site of two carved rock temples in southern Egypt, built in the reign of Ramses II in the 13th century B.C. They were moved to higher ground in the 1960s to avoid possible damage from the construction of the Aswan High Dam.

Great Temple of Ramses II

a·bu·sive /ə byóossiv/ *adj.* **1. INSULTING** calculated to insult or offend somebody ○ *abusive language* **2. HARMFUL** involving physical or psychological damage ○ *an abusive relationship* **3. IMPROPERLY USED** involving illegal, improper, or harmful activities ○ *using abusive methods to secure power* —**a·bu·sive·ly** *adv.* —**abu·sive·ness** *n.*

a·but /ə bút/ (**a·but·ted, a·but·ting, a·buts**) *vti.* to touch or be adjacent to something along one side [15thC. Partly from Anglo-Latin *abuttare,* from *butta* "ridge or strip of land"; partly from Old French *aboter* "to aim at," from *boter* "to strike," from Germanic.]

a·bu·ti·lon /ə byóot'l òn/ *n.* = **flowering maple** [Late 16thC. Via modern Latin from Arabic *ubutilun.*]

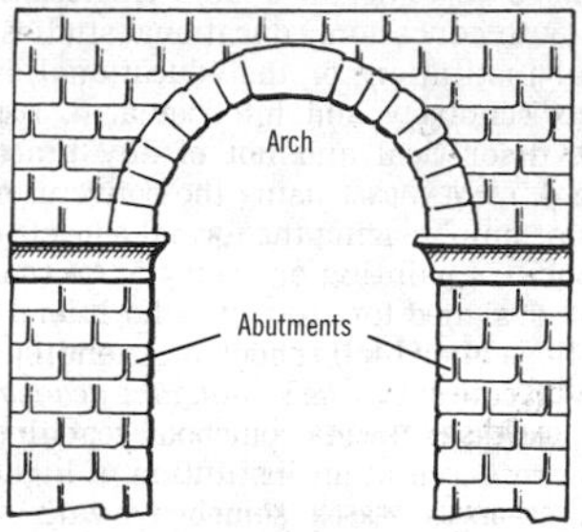

Abutment

a·but·ment /ə bútmənt/ *n.* **1. ADJACENCY** the immediate adjacency of two objects or pieces of land **2. MEETING POINT** the point at which two things abut **3. MAKING THINGS ABUT** the positioning of two things so that they abut **4. SUPPORT STRUCTURE** a structure that supports the end of a bridge or dam, or that bears the thrust of an arch or vault

a·but·tals /ə bútt'lz/ *npl.* the boundaries of a piece of land in relation to an adjoining piece of land

a·buzz /ə búz/ *adj.* filled with buzzing or a sound like it, often as a result of lively conversation or activity

ab·watt /áb wòt/ *n.* the centimeter-gram-second unit of electrical power, equal to 10^{-7} of a watt

a·bysm /ə bízzəm/ *n.* a chasm, void, or other abyss (*archaic*) [14thC. Via Old French *abisme* from medieval Latin *abysmus,* an alteration of late Latin *abyssus* (see ABYSS).]

a·bys·mal /ə bízm'l/ *adj.* **1. HORRIBLE** appallingly bad or extremely severe **2. VERY DEEP** similar to the great depth of an abyss **3. DEEP-SEA** extremely deep or found at extreme depths (*archaic*) —**a·bys·mal·ly** *adv.*

a·byss /ə bíss/ *n.* **1. CHASM** a chasm or gorge so deep or vast that its extent is not visible **2. ENDLESS SPACE** something that is immeasurably deep or infinite **3. TERRIBLE SITUATION** a situation of apparently unending awfulness **4. HELL** hell thought of as a bottomless pit [14thC. Via late Latin *abyssus* from Greek *abussos,* literally "bottomless," from *bussos* "bottom." Ultimately from an Indo-European word that is also the ancestor of English *bathos.*]

a·bys·sal /ə bíss'l/ *adj.* found in the very deepest areas of the oceans or on the deep ocean floor

Ab·ys·sin·i·a /ábbə sínniə/ *n.* former name for **Ethiopia** —**Ab·ys·sin·i·an** *adj., n.*

Ab·ys·sin·i·an cat *n.* a domestic cat belonging to a breed with dark brown or black markings on its short-haired brown coat

ab·ys·so·pe·la·gic /ə bìssōpə lájjik/ *adj.* relating to or living in the water just above the deep ocean floor [Ultimately from Greek *abussos* "abyss" (see ABYSS) + *pelagikos* "of the sea" (see PELAGIC)]

Ac[1] *symbol.* actinium

Ac[2] *abbr.* BIBLE Acts of the Apostles

AC *abbr.* **1. AC, a.c.** ELEC ENG alternating current. ◊ **DC 2.** BEVERAGES appellation contrôlée **3.** air conditioning

ac. *abbr.* acre

A.C. *abbr.* ante Christum

ac- *prefix.* = **ad-** (*used before c, k, and q*)

-ac *suffix.* person affected with a condition ○ *amnesiac* [Via modern Latin *-acus* from Greek *-akos*]

A/C *abbr.* **1. A/C, a/c** ACCT account **2. A/C, a/c** ACCT account current **3.** air conditioning

a·ca·cia /ə káyshə/ (*plural* **-cias** *or* **-cia**) *n.* **1. FLOWERING TREE** a tropical or subtropical shrub or tree that has small fluffy yellow globular flowers, narrow leaves, and dark fruit pods. Genus: *Acacia.* **2. TREE LIKE TRUE ACACIA** any tree or shrub like acacia proper, e.g., the locust **3.** = **gum arabic** [14thC. Via Latin from Greek *akakia*, of uncertain origin: perhaps from Egyptian.]

ac·a·deme /ákə deem/ *n.* (*formal*) **1.** = **academia 2. ACADEMIC INSTITUTION** a place of learning, especially a college or university [Late 16thC. Partly from Latin *academia*, and partly from its Greek source *Akademeia* (see ACADEMY).]

ac·a·de·mi·a /àkə deemee ə/ *n.* scholars and students of the academic world and their activities [Mid-20thC. From Latin (see ACADEMY).]

ac·a·dem·ic /àkə démmik/ *adj.* **1. EDUCATIONAL** connected with education, educational studies, an educational institution, or the educational system **2. SCHOLARLY** scholarly and intellectual **3. IRRELEVANT IN PRACTICE** theoretical and not of any practical relevance **4. CONVENTIONAL** using the conventional techniques or emphasizing the formal aspects of an art form such as painting or poetry **5. FOR COLLEGE-BOUND STUDENTS** designed for students who intend to study at a college after high school, or attending a school with such courses ○ *She's taking the academic track.* ■ *n.* **1. UNIVERSITY TEACHER** somebody teaching or conducting research at an institution of higher learning **2. SCHOLARLY PERSON** somebody with scholarly background or attitudes —**ac·a·dem·i·cal** *adj.* —**ac·a·dem·i·cal·ly** *adv.*

ac·a·de·mi·cian /àkədə mísh'n, ə kàddə-/ *n.* a member of an academy or society concerned with the arts or sciences

ac·a·dem·i·cism /àkə démməsìzzəm/ *n.* artistry that relies on conventional techniques or emphasizes the formal aspects of an art form such as painting or poetry

ac·a·dem·ic year *n.* the annual cycle of teaching and study at an educational institution. It usually starts more than half way through the calendar year and is divided into semesters or quarters.

a·cad·e·mism /ə káddəmizzəm/ *n.* = **academicism**

a·cad·e·my /ə káddəmee/ (*plural* **-mies**) *n.* **1. SOCIETY** a formal society whose purpose is to promote a particular aspect of knowledge or culture **2. SPECIALIZED SCHOOL** an educational institution devoted to a particular subject **3. PRIVATE HIGH SCHOOL** a secondary or high school, usually a private one (*usually used in school names*) **4. ACADEMIC WORLD** the academic community, especially scholars at colleges and universities [Mid-16thC. Via Latin *academia* from Greek *Akademeia*, the school of philosophy founded by Plato, named for the park on the outskirts of Athens where he taught.]

A·cad·e·my *n.* the school Plato founded to teach his philosophy

A·cad·e·my Award *n.* an award given annually by the Academy of Motion Picture Arts and Sciences for work in filmmaking or acting. The statuette awarded is called an Oscar.

A·ca·di·a /ə káydee ə/ *n.* a former French colony in North America that comprised present-day New Brunswick, Nova Scotia, Prince Edward Island, and parts of Quebec and New England

A·ca·di·an /ə káydee ən/ *n.* **1. SOMEBODY FROM ACADIA** one of the French settlers who colonized Acadia after 1604, most of whom were deported elsewhere in North America, especially to Louisiana, by the British authorities between 1755 and 1762 **2. FRENCH CANADIAN LIVING IN MARITIMES** a French-speaking inhabitant of the Canadian provinces of New Brunswick, Nova Scotia, or Prince Edward Island **3.** = **Acadian French** [Early 18thC] —**A·ca·di·an** *adj.*

A·ca·di·a Na·tion·al Park park in northeastern Maine, partially on Mount Desert Island. It was established in 1919 as Lafayette National Park, but the name was changed in 1929. Area: 41,819 acres/16,924 hectares.

A·ca·di·an French, **A·ca·di·an** *n. Can* the form of French spoken in the Canadian provinces of New Brunswick, Nova Scotia, and Prince Edward Island —**A·ca·di·an French** *adj.*

a·cal·cu·lia /àykal kyoolee ə/ *n.* an inability, or the loss of the ability, to carry out basic arithmetic calculations [Early 20thC. Coined from A- "not" + Latin *calculare* "to calculate" (see CALCULATE) + -IA.]

a·can·thi plural of **acanthus**

acantho- *prefix.* thorn ○ *acanthopterygian* [From Greek *akanthos* "thorn plant" (see ACANTHUS)]

a·can·tho·ceph·a·lan /ə kànthə séffələn/ *n.* = **spiny-headed worm** [Mid-19thC. Coined from ACANTHO- + Greek *kephalē* "head" (see CEPHALO-).] —**a·can·tho·ceph·a·lan** *adj.*

ac·an·thop·ter·yg·i·an /àkən thoptə ríjjee ən/ *n.* a fish with spiny-rayed fins and toothed scales. Mackerel, perch, and bass are acanthopterygians. Superorder: Acanthopterygii. [Mid-19thC. Ultimately from Greek *akantha* "thorn" + *pterugion* "fin," literally "small wing," from *pterux* "wing."] —**ac·an·thop·ter·yg·i·an** *adj.*

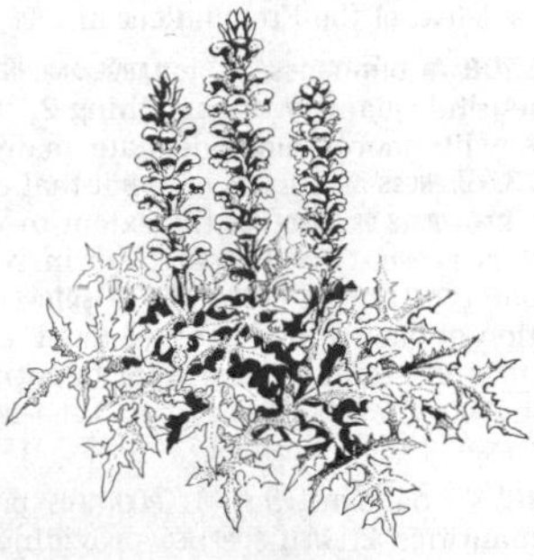

Acanthus

a·can·thus /ə kánthəss/ (*plural* **-thus·es** *or* **-thi** /-thī/ *or* **-thus**) *n.* **1.** PLANTS **PLANT WITH SPINY LEAVES** a Mediterranean shrub or perennial plant with spiny leaves and white or purple flowers. Bear's breech is a variety of acanthus. Genus: *Acanthus.* **2.** ARCHIT **LEAF DESIGN** a design characteristic of the capital of a Corinthian column, representing acanthus leaves [Mid-16thC. Via Latin, from Greek *akanthos*, from Greek *akantha* "thorn."]

a cap·pel·la /aa kəpéllə, à kəpéllə/ *adv.*, *adj.* without accompaniment from musical instruments [Late 19thC. From Italian *a cappella*, literally "by the choir," that is, "in the style of church music."]

Ac·a·pul·co /àkə pōōlkō, aàkə pōol-/ seaport and resort on the Pacific coast in southern Mexico. Population: 592,187 (1990).

ac·a·ri plural of **acarus**

ac·a·ri·a·sis /àkə rī́ əssəss/ *n.* infestation of the skin with mites

ac·a·rid /ákərid/ *n.* a mite or tick. Order: Acarina.

ac·a·roid res·in /ákəroyd-/, **ac·a·roid gum** /ákəroyd-/ *n.* a red resin exuded by certain grass trees, used in making varnishes and coating paper

ac·a·rol·o·gy /àkə róllәjee/ *n.* the branch of zoology devoted to the study of the mites and ticks —**ac·a·rol·o·gist** *n.*

ac·a·ro·pho·bi·a /àkərə fṓbee ə/ *n.* abnormal fear of mites or ticks

ac·a·rus /ákə rəss/ (*plural* **-ri** /-rī/) *n.* a mite or tick (*technical*) [Mid-17thC. Via modern Latin, from Greek *akari* "mite," literally "too short to cut, tiny," ultimately from the stem *kar-* "to cut."]

a·cat·a·lec·tic /ay kàtt'l éktik/ *adj.* **METRICALLY COMPLETE** having the full number of syllables in the final foot of a line of verse ■ *n.* **METRICALLY COMPLETE VERSE** a line of verse that has the full number of syllables in the final foot [Late 16thC. Via late Latin *acatalecticus* from Greek *akatalektos* "complete," from *katalektos* "incomplete."]

a·cau·dal /ay káwd'l/, **a·cau·date** /-dayt/ *adj.* without a tail (*technical*)

a·cau·les·cent /àykaw léss'nt, àkaw-/ *adj.* with no stem or with a stem that is very short

a·cau·line /ay káw lin, -līn/ *adj.* with no stem (*technical*)

acc. *abbr.* **1.** GRAM accusative **2.** ACCT account

ac·cede /ak seed/ (**-ced·ed, -ced·ing, -cedes**) *vi.* **1. ASSENT** to give consent or agreement to something **2. COME TO POWER** to attain an important and powerful position **3. SIGN TREATY** to become a party to an international agreement or treaty [15thC. From Latin *accedere*, literally "to come to," from *cedere* "to come" (source of English *cease* and *ancestor*).] —**ac·ced·ence** *n.* —**ac·ced·er** *n.*

ac·cel. *abbr.* accelerando

ac·cel·er·an·do /ak sèllə rándō, aa chèllə raándō/ *adv.*, *adj.* with gradually increasing speed (*used as a musical direction*) [Early 19thC. From Italian, "accelerating."]

ac·cel·er·ant /ak séllərənt/ *n.* **1. COMBUSTIBLE SUBSTANCE** a substance that is used to intensify a fire **2.** = **accelerator** *n.* **3**

ac·cel·er·ate /ək séllə ràyt/ (**-at·ed, -at·ing, -ates**) *vti.* **1. GO FASTER** to move increasingly quickly, or cause something to move faster **2. PROGRESS FASTER** to happen or develop faster, or cause something to happen or develop faster **3.** PHYS **INCREASE VELOCITY** to cause an increase in the velocity of something, or experience an increase in velocity [Early 16thC. From Latin *acceleratus*, the past participle of *accelerare* "to quicken," from *celer* "quick" (source of English *celerity*).] —**ac·cel·er·at·ed** *adj.* —**ac·cel·er·a·tive** /ak séllə ràytiv/ *adj.*

ac·cel·er·a·tion /ak sèllə ráysh'n/ *n.* **1. INCREASE IN VELOCITY** the rate at which something increases in velocity **2. INCREASE IN RATE OF PROGRESS** an increase in the rate at which something happens or develops **3. ACT OF ACCELERATING** something's accelerating, or the causing of something to accelerate **4.** PHYS **INCREASE IN VELOCITY** the rate of increase in the velocity of something. Symbol *a*

ac·cel·er·a·tion clause *n.* a clause in the terms of a loan or mortgage stipulating that payments must be made earlier in particular circumstances

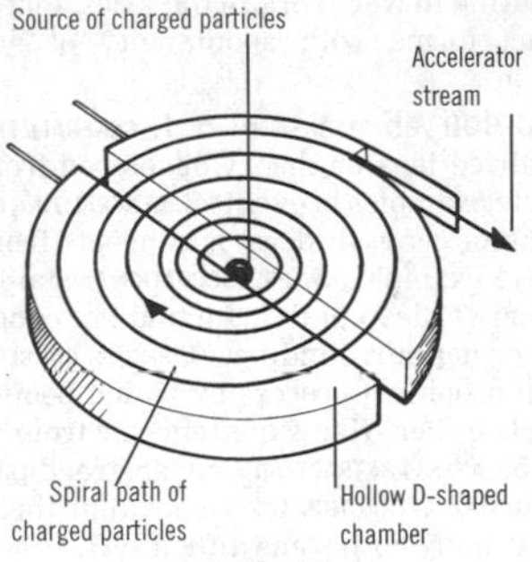

Accelerator

ac·cel·er·a·tor /ək séllə ràytər/ *n.* **1. SPEED-INCREASING CONTROL** a pedal or other control mechanism used to cause a vehicle to increase speed **2.** NUCLEAR PHYS **DEVICE FOR GIVING PARTICLES HIGH VELOCITIES** a machine used to increase the velocity, and hence the kinetic energy, of subatomic particles or nuclei, usually in preparation for collision with a target **3. CHEMICAL THAT SPEEDS UP REACTION** a substance that increases the rate of a chemical reaction

ac·cel·er·a·tor card, **ac·cel·er·a·tor board** *n.* a circuit board that adds a faster central processing unit or a special coprocessor to a computer

ac·cel·er·om·e·ter /ək sèllə rómmətər/ *n.* an instrument or device for measuring acceleration

ac·cent *n.* /ák sent/ **1. MANNER OF PRONUNCIATION** a way of pronouncing words that indicates the place of origin or social background of the speaker ○ *a Southern accent* **2. INTONATION** a way of using intonation or inflection to convey the speaker's mood or character ○ *He answered with an accent of bitterness.* **3. STRESS ON SYLLABLE** a greater emphasis in pronouncing a syllable within a word or a word within a phrase **4. MARK ABOVE LETTER** a symbol used in print or writing to indicate stress or the pronunciation of a vowel **5. MAIN EMPHASIS** an aspect of a situation, issue, or state of affairs that is emphasized ○ *the accent is on safety* **6. CONTRASTING DETAIL** a contrasting decorative feature used to add interest ○ *a blue room with green accents in the furnishings* **7. STYLE** a distinctive style that is characteristic of a particular person, region, or artistic school **8.** MUSIC **STRESS ON NOTES** stress placed on particular notes in a piece of music, or the symbol printed above the notes to indicate this stress **9.** MATH **MATHEMATICAL SYMBOL** a superscript symbol, ' or ", used to indicate a unit of measure such as feet and inches respectively or minutes and seconds of an arc respectively ■ *vt.* /ák sent, ak sént/ **(-cent·ed, -cent·ing, -cents) 1. EMPHASIZE SOMETHING** to stress something, e.g., by pronouncing a word or syllable more prominently **2. MARK SOMETHING WITH AN ACCENT** to mark a letter, word, or something else with a written or printed accent [Early 16thC. Via French, from Latin *accentus*, from *ad* "to" + *cantus* "singing" (source of English *cantor, chant*, and *incentive*), a literal translation of Greek *prosōidia* "accompanied song."]

ac·cent light·ing *n.* lighting that highlights an area or feature of a room, e.g., a painting or an alcove

ac·cen·tor /ak séntər/ *n.* a Eurasian and African songbird distinguished from a house sparrow by its thin finely pointed bill. Hedge sparrows are one type of accentor. Family: Prunellidae.

ac·cen·tu·al /ak sénchoo əl/ *adj.* **1. OF ACCENT** involving or associated with accent or stress **2.** POETRY **BASED ON STRESS** employing a structure based on the number of stresses in a poetic line instead of on the number of syllables. ◊ **syllabic** —**ac·cen·tu·al·ly** *adv.*

ac·cen·tu·ate /ak sénchoo àyt/ **(-at·ed, -at·ing, -ates)** *vt.* **1. DRAW ATTENTION TO SOMETHING** to make a feature of something more noticeable **2. STRESS SOMETHING** to emphasize a syllable, word, or phrase when saying it [Mid-18thC. From medieval Latin *accentuatus*, the past participle of *accentuare* "to emphasize," from Latin *accentus* (see ACCENT).] —**ac·cen·tu·a·tion** /ak sènchoo áysh'n/ *n.*

ac·cept /ak sépt/ **(-cept·ed, -cept·ing, -cepts)** *v.* **1.** *vt.* **TAKE SOMETHING OFFERED** to take something that is offered, e.g., a gift or payment **2.** *vti.* **SAY YES TO INVITATION** to reply in the affirmative to an invitation **3.** *vti.* **TAKE ON DUTY** to agree to take on a duty, responsibility, or position **4.** *vt.* **BELIEVE SOMETHING** to acknowledge that something is true **5.** *vt.* **ENDURE SITUATION** to tolerate something without protesting or attempting to change it **6.** *vt.* **COME TO TERMS WITH SOMETHING** to acknowledge a fact or truth and come to terms with it **7.** *vt.* **TAKE BLAME FOR SOMETHING** to admit the blame or responsibility for something **8.** *vt.* LAW, COMM **AGREE TO TERMS** to indicate formal agreement to the terms and conditions in a contract **9.** *vt.* **ALLOW SOMEBODY TO JOIN** to allow somebody to join an organization or attend an institution **10.** *vt.* **PROCESS SOMETHING** to be able to process something or be operated by something ○ *old machines that won't accept the new cards* **11.** *vt.* **BE WELCOMING TO SOMEBODY** to treat somebody as a member of a group or social circle **12.** *vt.* **RECEIVE SOMETHING FOR REVIEW** to receive something such as a report for official action or review **13.** *vt.* **AGREE TO MARRY SOMEBODY** to reply in the affirmative to a marriage proposal (*dated*) [14thC. Via French *accepter* from Latin *acceptare*, from *accipere*, literally "to take to (yourself)," from *capere* "to take" (source of English *catch* and *occupy*).]

ac·cept·a·ble /ak séptəb'l/ *adj.* **1. ADEQUATE** considered to be satisfactory **2. APPROVED OF** likely to gain somebody's approval **3. WELCOME** likely to please the person who receives it —**ac·cept·a·bil·i·ty** /ək sèptə bíllətee/ *n.* —**ac·cept·a·ble·ness** /-b'lnəss/ *n.* —**ac·cept·a·bly** /ək séptəblee/ *adv.*

ac·cept·a·ble dai·ly in·take *n.* the highest daily intake level of a chemical that, if continued over the whole life of a person, appears to pose no health risk

ac·cep·tance /ak séptənss/ *n.* **1. SAYING YES** a written or verbal indication that somebody agrees to an invitation **2. TAKING OF A GIFT** the willing receipt of a gift or payment **3. WILLINGNESS TO BELIEVE** willingness to believe that something is true **4. COMING TO TERMS WITH SOMETHING** the realization of a fact or truth resulting in somebody's coming to terms with it **5. TOLERATION** the tolerating of something without protesting **6. SOCIAL TOLERANCE** willingness to treat somebody as a member of a group or social circle **7. POSITIVE RESPONSE TO APPLICATION** an offer to allow somebody to join an organization or attend an institution **8.** LAW, COMM **AGREEMENT TO TERMS** formal agreement, in writing or verbally, showing that somebody assents to the terms and conditions in a contract **9.** COMM **AGREEMENT TO PAY** a formal agreement by a debtor to pay a draft or bill of exchange when it becomes payable

ac·cep·tant /ak séptənt/ *adj.* receiving something willingly (*formal*)

ac·cep·ta·tion /àksep táysh'n/ *n.* **1. GENERAL ACCEPTANCE** a generally favorable reception of something **2. ACCEPTED MEANING** the sense in which a word or phrase is generally understood

ac·cept·ed /ak séptəd/ *adj.* widely used and recognized

ac·cept·er *n.* **1. SOMEBODY ACCEPTING** somebody or something that accepts something **2.** = **acceptor** *n.* 1, **acceptor** *n.* 2

ac·cept·ing house (*plural* **ac·cept·ing hous·es**) *n.* a financial institution that guarantees bills of exchange

ac·cep·tor /ak séptər/ *n.* **1. ac·cep·tor, ac·cep·ter** COMM **SOMEBODY ACCEPTING DEBT** somebody who accepts liability for a bill of exchange **2. ac·cep·tor, ac·cep·ter** ELECTRON ENG **IMPURITY IMPROVING CONDUCTIVITY** an impurity added to a semiconductor to increase its conductivity. The metallic element gallium is often used in this way. **3.** CHEM **ATOM ACCEPTING ELECTRONS** an atom or group of atoms that accepts electrons to form a coordinate bond during the formation of a chemical compound. ◊ **donor**

ac·cess /áksess/ *n.* **1. ENTRY OR APPROACH** the possibility or means of entering or approaching a place **2. OPPORTUNITY FOR USE** the opportunity or right to experience or make use of something **3. RIGHT TO MEET SOMEBODY** the right or opportunity to meet somebody **4. OUTBURST** a sudden strongly felt burst of emotion (*literary*) ○ *"With a sudden access of tenderness he flung his arm about me."* (Rider Haggard, *She*; 1887) **5.** COMPUT **RIGHT TO USE COMPUTER** the right or ability to log on to a computer system or use a computer program ○ *software that allows network access* ■ *vt.* **(-cessed, -cess·ing, -cess·es) 1. ENTER PLACE** to find a way or means of entering or approaching a place **2. GET INFORMATION** to have the opportunity or right to experience or make use of something **3.** COMPUT **CALL UP** to retrieve data or a computer file ○ *the program can be accessed using the correct password* [14thC. Directly or via Old French *acces* from Latin *accessus*, the past participle of *accedere* "to come near" (see ACCEDE).]

WORD KEY: USAGE

access or **accession**? The essential difference is that ***access*** refers to a right whereas ***accession*** refers to a process (and is normally used in the special ways mentioned). If you have ***access*** to a library you are allowed to use it, consult the books, and perhaps borrow them. An ***accession*** to a library is a new book that has been bought for people with ***access*** to the library to use. ***Accession*** to the throne is the process by which an heir to the throne becomes king or queen. Somebody who wants to meet the new mayor would have to seek ***access*** to him or her after his or her ***accession*** to office. You might have an ***access*** of strong feeling such as joy or anger, but you would have an ***accession*** of strength.

WORD KEY: USAGE

What things can you **access**? There is normally no problem with using ***access*** as a verb in computing contexts (although even this is objected to by some people), but there is more resistance to using it in general contexts such as accessing bank accounts or items of information.

ac·ces·sa·ry *n.* = **accessory**

WORD KEY: USAGE

See Usage note at ***accessory***.

ac·cess bro·ker *n.* somebody with connections to high officials in a political administration who uses those connections for lobbying

ac·cess code *n.* a sequence of letters or numbers that have to be keyed in to allow somebody access to something such as a building or a telephone network

ac·ces·si·ble /ək séssəb'l/ *adj.* **1. EASILY REACHED** easy to enter or reach physically **2. EASILY UNDERSTOOD** able to be appreciated or understood without specialist knowledge **3. EASILY AVAILABLE** able to be obtained, used, or experienced without difficulty **4. APPROACHABLE** not aloof and not difficult to talk to or meet with **5. SUSCEPTIBLE** susceptible to or likely to be influenced by something **6.** LOGIC **OBSERVABLE FROM ANOTHER WORLD** able to be referred to from another possible world, so that the truth value of statements about it can be given —**ac·ces·si·bil·i·ty** /ək sèssə bíllətee/ *n.* —**ac·ces·si·bly** /-blee/ *adv.*

ac·ces·sion /ak sésh'n/ *n.* **1. TAKING UP POSITION** the assumption of an important position, usually a position of power **2.** INTERNAT LAW **ACCEPTANCE OF TREATY** the formal acceptance by a state of an international treaty or convention **3. ASSENT** agreement or consent, usually when given unwillingly **4. SUDDEN MOOD** a sudden and unexpected display of a particular mood or emotion (*literary*) **5. ADDITION TO COLLECTION** an item added to a collection **6.** LAW **INCREASE TO PROPERTY** addition to property by natural growth or by improvement **7.** LAW **RIGHT TO INCREASE IN PROPERTY** the right of an owner to add to a property by natural growth or improvement ■ *vt.* **(-sioned, -sion·ing, -sions) CATALOG ADDITIONS TO COLLECTION** to make a formal record of an addition to a collection —**ac·ces·sion·al** *adj.*

WORD KEY: USAGE

See Usage note at ***access.***

ac·ces·sor·ize /ak séssə rīz/ **(-ized, -iz·ing, -iz·es)** *v.* **1.** *vti.* **DECORATE AN OUTFIT** to wear or use items such as gloves, hats, and handbags to complete an outfit of clothing **2.** *vt.* **PROVIDE WITH ACCESSORIES** to fit accessories to something

ac·ces·so·ry /ak séssəree/, **ac·ces·sa·ry** *n.* (*plural* **-ries**) **1. OPTIONAL PART** an optional part that may be fitted to something to perform an additional function or enhance performance **2. FASHION ARTICLE** an item of clothing that is worn or used for a fashionable effect with an outfit ○ *"designers who create neckties as fashion accessories"* (*International Herald Tribune*; June 1997) **3.** LAW **CRIMINAL HELPER** somebody who aids somebody else to commit a crime or avoid arrest but who does not participate in the crime itself ■ *adj.* **1. ADDITIONAL** supplementary or subsidiary to the main thing **2.** LAW **ASSISTING IN CRIME** aiding a criminal act although not participating in the crime itself —**ac·ces·so·ri·al** /àkse sáwree əl/ *adj.* —**ac·ces·so·ri·ly** /ak séssərəlee/ *adv.* —**ac·ces·so·ri·ness** /-rinəss/ *n.*

WORD KEY: USAGE

accessory or **accessary**? ***Accessory*** is now the normal spelling in the two main meanings of the word, "an extra attachment" and "somebody who is involved in a crime in addition to the person who commits the crime." ***Accessary*** is an older spelling, and you will still find it used, especially in legal contexts.

ac·ces·so·ry af·ter the fact (*plural* **ac·ces·so·ries af·ter the fact**) *n.* somebody who aids and abets somebody who has committed a crime

ac·ces·so·ry a·part·ment *n.* a self-contained apartment within a family home, usually rented to a relative

ac·ces·so·ry be·fore the fact (*plural* **ac·ces·so·ries be·fore the fact**) *n.* somebody who incites or aids somebody to commit a crime but who is not present during the crime

ac·ces·so·ry nerve *n.* the eleventh cranial nerve, associated with the pharynx and muscles in the throat, larynx, palate, neck, and back

ac·cess time *n.* the time taken by a computer to locate and retrieve data

ac·ciac·ca·tu·ra /aa chaàkə toórə/ (*plural* **-ras** *or* **-re** /-ray/) *n.* MUSIC a brief grace note sounded at the same time as or just before a principal note [Early 19thC. From Italian, "crushing sound."]

ac·ci·dence /áksidənss/ *n.* the area of traditional grammar dealing with the inflections of words [15thC. From late Latin *accidentia* (plural) "things that happen" (taken as singular), from Latin *accident-* (see ACCIDENT).]

ac·ci·dent /áksidənt, áksi dent/ *n.* **1. CHANCE** the way things happen without any planning, apparent cause, or deliberate intent **2. CRASH** a collision or similar incident involving a moving vehicle, often resulting in injury or death **3. MISHAP** an unplanned and unfortunate event that results in damage, injury, or upset of some kind **4. CHANCE HAPPENING** an event that happens completely by chance, with no planning or deliberate intent **5. FAILURE TO REACH TOILET** an incident when somebody, particularly a small child, is incontinent (*used euphemistically*) **6. UNPLANNED PREGNANCY** a child conceived in an unplanned way **7.** PHILOSOPHY **NONESSENTIAL ATTRIBUTE** a nonessential attribute or characteristic of something [14thC. Via French, from Latin *accident-*, the present participle stem of *accidere* "to happen," literally "to fall to," from *cadere* "to fall, die" (source of English *cadaver* and *chance*).]

ac·ci·den·tal /àksə dént'l/ *adj.* **1. CHANCE** happening by chance and not planned **2. INCIDENTAL** not specifically intended and arising as a side effect **3.** MUSIC **NOT IN KEY SIGNATURE** sharp, flat, or natural, in a way not indicated in the key signature ■ *n.* **1. UNPLANNED EFFECT** something not specifically intended that arises as a side effect **2.** MUSIC **NOTE NOT IN KEY SIGNATURE** a musical note, marked with a sharp, flat, or natural sign, whose pitch does not correspond to the key signature —**ac·ci·den·tal·ly** *adv.*

ac·ci·dent and e·mer·gen·cy *n.* = **casualty** *n.* 4

ac·ci·dent in·sur·ance *n.* insurance against injury or death caused by an accident

ac·ci·dent-prone *adj.* having more accidents than average

ac·cip·i·ter /ak síppitər/ *n.* **1. HAWK** a hawk, typically with short broad wings and a long tail. Accipiters include goshawks. Genus: *Accipiter*. **2. LARGE PREDATORY BIRD** a bird in the family that includes all hawks, eagles, and kites. Family: *Accipitidae*. [Early 19thC. From Latin, from *accipere*, literally "to take to (yourself)" (see ACCEPT). The underlying idea is of a bird that seizes prey.]

ac·cip·i·trine /aksípitrin, -trīn/ *adj.* used to describe the family of predatory birds that includes hawks, eagles, and kites

ac·claim /ə kláym/ *v.* (**-claimed, -claim·ing, -claims**) **1.** *vt.* **PRAISE SOMEBODY LAVISHLY** to praise somebody or something publicly with great enthusiasm **2.** *vt.* **PRONOUNCE SOMEBODY TO BE SOMETHING** to declare enthusiastically and publicly that somebody holds a high position **3.** *vi.* **SHOUT ENTHUSIASTICALLY** to demonstrate enthusiastic approval by shouting and cheering **4.** *vt. Can* **WIN OFFICE BY DEFAULT** to elect a candidate to an office by default, owing to a lack of opposition (*usually passive*) ■ *n.* **ENTHUSIASTIC RECEPTION** enthusiastic approval given to somebody or something publicly [Early 16thC. From Latin *acclamare*, literally "to shout to," from *clamare* "to shout" (source of English *claim* and *clamor*).] —**ac·claim·er** *n.*

ac·cla·ma·tion /àklə máysh'n/ *n.* **1. APPROVAL** a public and enthusiastic display of approval **2. VOCAL VOTE** a vote in which no formal ballot is held but the voters make views clear by shouts or applause **3.** *Can* **UNOPPOSED ELECTION WIN** an election victory won through default, owing to a lack of opposition [Mid-16thC. From the Latin stem *acclamation-*, from *acclamare* (see ACCLAIM).] —**ac·clam·a·to·ry** /ə klámmə tàwree/ *adj.*

ac·cli·mate /ə klīmət, áklə màyt/ (**-mat·ed, -mat·ing, -mates**) *v.* **1.** *vti.* = **acclimatize 2.** *vi.* BIOL **ALTER BECAUSE OF ENVIRONMENT** to adjust in response to a change in environment [Late 18thC. From French *acclimater*, from *a-* "to" + *climat* "climate" (see CLIMATE).] —**ac·cli·ma·tion** /àklə máysh'n/ *n.*

ac·cli·ma·tize /əklīmə tīz/ (**-tized, -tiz·ing, -tiz·es**) *vti.* to become accustomed to a new climate or environment, or help somebody become accustomed to it —**ac·cli·ma·ti·za·tion** /ə klīmətə záysh'n/ *n.*

ac·cliv·i·ty /ə klívvətee/ (*plural* **-ties**) *n.* an upward slope on a hill [Early 17thC. From the Latin stem *acclivitat-* "ascent," from *acclivis* "uphill," from *clivus* "slope" (source of English *proclivity*).]

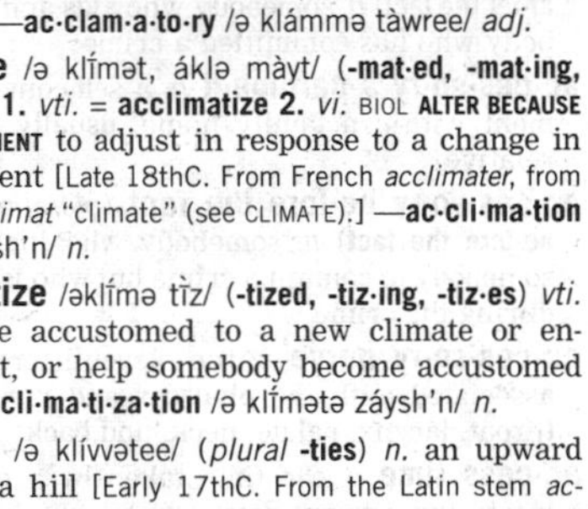

Accolade

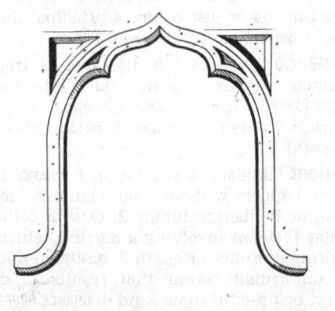

ac·co·lade /ákə làyd, -làad/ *n.* **1. SIGN OF PRAISE** a sign or expression of high praise and esteem for somebody **2. PUBLIC RECOGNITION** praise and public recognition of somebody's achievements **3. KNIGHTING** the ceremonial bestowal of a knighthood by touching somebody's shoulders with a sword. Knighthood was formerly conferred by an embrace, which is the original sense of accolade. **4.** ARCHIT **CURVED MOLDING** an ornamental molding shaped like a brace [Early 17thC. Via French, from Provençal *acolada* "embrace," literally "to the neck," ultimately from Latin *collum* "neck" (source of English *collar*).]

ac·com·mo·date /ə kómmə dàyt/ (**-dat·ed, -dat·ing, -dates**) *v.* **1.** *vt.* **OBLIGE SOMEBODY** to adjust actions in response to somebody's needs **2.** *vt.* **ALLOW FOR SOMETHING** to be adaptable enough to allow something without major change **3.** *vt.* **HAVE ROOM FOR SOMEBODY OR SOMETHING** to have sufficient space for somebody or something **4.** *vt.* **PROVIDE LODGING FOR SOMEBODY** to provide somebody with a place to stay **5.** *vi.* **ADJUST** to adapt to a new situation **6.** *vt.* **LEND SOMEBODY MONEY** to give somebody money in response to a request for a loan **7.** *vti.* **REACH AGREEMENT** to settle a difference of opinion in a way that is acceptable to all **8.** *vi.* OPHTHALMOL **ADJUST FOCUS** to adjust focus automatically to give clear vision (*refers to the eyes*) [Mid-16thC. From Latin *accommodare* "to make fit," from *commodus* "suitable," literally "with the measure," from *modus* "measure" (source of English *modern*).] —**ac·com·mo·da·tive** *adj.*

WORD KEY: USAGE

Is it **accommodate** or **accomodate**? Note that ***accommodate*** and ***accommodation*** are spelled with *-cc-* and *-mm-*. ***Accommodation***, in particular, is often misspelled as ***accomodation*** on signs and in notices.

ac·com·mo·dat·ing /ə kómmə dàyting/ *adj.* willing to adjust actions in response to the needs of others —**ac·com·mo·dat·ing·ly** *adv.*

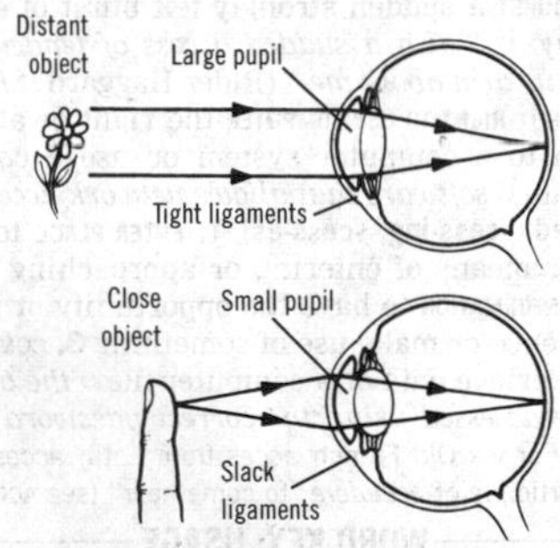

Accommodation: Adjustment of eye focus on distant object (top) and close object (bottom)

ac·com·mo·da·tion /ə kòmmə dáysh'n/ *n.* **1. HELPFULNESS** willingness to adjust actions in response to the needs of others **2. HELPFUL GESTURE** a modification of actions in response to the needs of others **3. AGREEMENT** an agreement acceptable to all parties in a dispute **4. FLEXIBILITY** the ability to include something without major change **5. ADJUSTMENT** adaptation to a new situation **6.** OPHTHALMOL **ADJUSTMENT OF EYE FOCUS** the automatic adjustment of the focus of an eye to give clear vision **7.** COMM **LOAN OF MONEY** a loan of money, especially by a financial institution as a favor to somebody before a formal credit arrangement is made

ac·com·mo·da·tion ad·dress *n. U.K.* = **mail drop**

ac·com·mo·da·tion bill *n.* a bill of exchange cosigned by another party in order to give added security

ac·com·mo·da·tion·ist /ə kòmmə dáysh'nist/ *n.* somebody who prefers compromise to confrontation —**ac·com·mo·da·tion·ist** *adj.*

ac·com·mo·da·tion lad·der *n.* a ladder or flight of stairs hung over a ship's side to allow boarding or disembarking

ac·com·mo·da·tion plat·form, **ac·com·mo·da·tion rig** *n.* a platform or rig used as living quarters for offshore oil or gas workers

ac·com·mo·da·tions *npl.* **1. LODGING** a room or building to live in **2. SEATING** seating in a vehicle or public facility **3. WORKSPACE** a room or space to work in

ac·com·pa·ni·ment /ə kúmpənimənt, -pni-/ *n.* **1.** MUSIC **MUSICAL BACKING** instrumental or vocal parts in a musical composition that support the more important parts **2. SIMULTANEOUS OCCURRENCE** something that occurs at the same time and in the same place as something else **3. SUPPLEMENT** an item that is added or served because it goes well with something

ac·com·pa·nist /ə kúmpənist, -pnist/ *n.* somebody who plays the musical accompaniment for a soloist

ac·com·pa·ny /ə kúmpənee, -pnee/ (**-nied, -ny·ing, -nies**) *v.* **1.** *vt.* **ESCORT SOMEBODY** to go with somebody **2.** *vt.* **BE PRESENT WITH SOMETHING** to be enclosed, attached, or present with something **3.** *vt.* **OCCUR WITH SOMETHING** to happen at the same time as something else **4.** *vt.* **SUPPLEMENT SOMETHING** to be present or served with something as a supplement **5.** *vti.* MUSIC **PROVIDE MUSICAL BACKING** to play or sing a part that supports a more important part [15thC. From Old French *acompaignier*, literally "to be a companion to," from *compaing* "companion" (see COMPANION).]

ac·com·plice /ə kómpliss/ *n.* somebody who knowingly helps somebody to commit a crime or misdeed [Mid-16thC. Alteration of archaic *complice* (by misunderstanding of *a complice*), via French, from Latin *complic-*, the stem of *complex* "associate," literally "folded with," from *complicare* (see COMPLICATE).]

ac·com·plish /ə kómplish/ (**-plished, -plish·ing, -plish·es**) *vt.* **1. ACHIEVE SOMETHING** to succeed in doing or achieving something **2. REACH POINT IN TIME** to arrive at the end of a period of time (*literary*) (*usually passive*) [14thC. From Old French *accompliss-*, a stem of *acomplir*, literally "to complete to," ultimately from Latin *complere* (see COMPLETE).] —**ac·com·plish·a·ble** *adj.* —**ac·com·plish·er** *n.*

WORD KEY: SYNONYMS

accomplish, achieve, attain, realize, pull off

CORE MEANING: to bring something to a successful conclusion

accomplish the most general term and wide-ranging term for performing something successfully; **achieve** to accomplish something by overcoming some difficulty or exerting a particular effort, usually over a period of time; **attain** to be successful in reaching a specific objective; **realize** to fulfill a specific vision or plan, particularly in relation to something material or financial or other gain; **pull off** an informal term for accomplishing something, especially against expectations or in extremely difficult circumstances.

ac·com·plished /ə kómplisht/ *adj.* **1. TALENTED** having considerable talent and skill **2. WITH SOCIAL GRACES** possessing social skills and talents **3. COMPLETE** fully established

ac·com·plish·ment /ə kómplishmənt/ *n.* **1. ACHIEVING OF SOMETHING** the completion or fulfillment of something **2. FEAT** a remarkable or successful achievement **3. TALENT** a skill or talent that has been developed

ac·cord /ə káwrd/ *v.* (**-cord·ed, -cord·ing, -cords**) **1.** *vt.* **RENDER** to give somebody or something a particular status or treatment **2.** *vi.* **AGREE** to be in agreement or come to an agreement **3.** *vt.* **GRANT SOMETHING** to bestow something such as a blessing on somebody ■ *n.* **1. AGREEMENT** a treaty or settlement agreed to by two or more parties **2. CONSENSUS** general agreement as to what is right **3. HARMONY** a state in which things are in harmony with each other [Pre-12thC. From Old French *acorder*, ultimately from Latin *ad* "to" + *cord-*, the stem of *cor* "heart" (source of English *cordial* and *quarry*).] ◇ **of** *or* **on your own accord** of your own free will

ac·cor·dance /ə káwrd'nss/ *n.* **1. CONSENSUS** consensus as to the right course of action **2. ADHERENCE TO CORRECT PROCESS** conformity with specified procedures or actions **3. BESTOWAL** the bestowal of a particular status or treatment on somebody or something

ac·cor·dant /ə káwrd'nt/ *adj.* in general harmony or agreement (*formal*) —**ac·cor·dant·ly** *adv.*

ac·cord·ing as *conj.* depending on whether, or corresponding to the extent to which

ac·cord·ing·ly /ə káwrdinglee/ *adv.* **1. CORRESPONDINGLY** in a way that is appropriate **2. IN CONSEQUENCE** in accordance with what has been said or with a principle or practice

ac·cor·di·on /ə káwrdee ən/ *n.* a musical instrument with a keyboard or buttons on one side, buttons on the other, and a middle section that is expanded and contracted to force air past metal reeds [Mid-19thC. From German *Akkordion*, from *Akkord* "chord," from Italian *accordare* "to tune (an intrument)."]

ac·cor·di·on pleats *npl.* sharp pleats in a garment or piece of fabric, resembling the folds in the bellows of an accordion

ac·cost /ə kóst/ (**-cost·ed, -cost·ing, -costs**) *vt.* to approach and stop somebody in order to speak, especially in an aggressive, insistent, or suggestive way [Late 16thC. Via French from, ultimately, Latin *accostare* "to adjoin," from *costa* "rib, side" (source of English *coast*). The underlying sense is "to be alongside."]

ac·couche·ment /àà koosh màaN, ə kóoshmənt/ *n.* the period of confinement for childbirth (*archaic*) [Late 18thC. From French, formed from *accoucher* (see ACCOUCHEUR).]

ac·coucheur /àkoo shúr/ *n.* a male midwife or obstetrician (*archaic*) [Mid-18thC. From French, formed from *accoucher*, from *coucher* "to lay down" (source of English *couch*).]

ac·count /ə kównt/ *n.* **1.** REPORT a written or verbal report of something **2.** EXPLANATION an explanation of something that has happened, especially one given to somebody in authority **3.** BANKING BANK ARRANGEMENT an arrangement in which a customer keeps money in a bank or other financial institution and is offered certain services in exchange **4.** BANKING MONEY IN BANK the money that a customer keeps in a bank **5.** FIN FINANCIAL ARRANGEMENT an arrangement with a store, company, stockbroker, or other business, which provides certain financial services, e.g., credit **6.** BUSINESS CUSTOMER a customer who has a regular business relationship with a company **7.** BUSINESS BUSINESS ON SOMEBODY'S BEHALF an area of business handled by a company on behalf of another, e.g., advertising, design, or publicity ■ **ac·counts** *npl.* ACCT LIST OF FINANCIAL INFORMATION a detailed list of everything that a company or individual earns or spends, kept primarily for tax purposes ■ *vt.* (**-count·ed, -count·ing, -counts**) CONSIDER to consider something, somebody, or yourself to have a specified quality (*dated*) [14thC. From Old French *aconte* "a counting up," from *aconter*, from, ultimately, Latin *computare* "to sum up" (source of English *computer*).] ◇ **by all accounts** according to what most people say ◇ **call somebody to account** to demand that somebody explain what he or she has done ◇ **of no account** of no importance ◇ **on account** on credit ◇ **on account of** because of ◇ **on no account** for no reason, whatever the circumstances ◇ **on somebody's account** out of concern for somebody's well-being ◇ **take account of something, take something into account** to consider something when making a decision

account for *vi.* **1.** EXPLAIN to provide an explanation for something ○ *And how do you account for the hole in the wall?* **2.** BE RESPONSIBLE FOR to be responsible for something or be an important factor in something ○ *Export sales account for at least half of our total business.* **3.** KILL OR DESTROY to be responsible for killing, destroying, or neutralizing somebody or something

ac·count·a·ble /ə kówntəb'l/ *adj.* **1.** RESPONSIBLE responsible to somebody else or to others, or responsible for something **2.** ABLE TO BE EXPLAINED capable of being explained (*formal*) —**ac·count·a·bil·i·ty** /ə kòwntə bíllətee/ *n.* —**ac·count·a·ble·ness** /-b'lnəs/ *n.* —**ac·count·a·bly** /-blee/ *adv.*

ac·count·an·cy /ə kówntənsee/ *n.* the work or profession of an accountant

ac·count·ant /ə kówntənt/ *n.* somebody who is responsible for maintaining and checking the business records of an individual or organization and preparing forms and reports for tax or other financial purposes

ac·count ex·ec·u·tive *n.* somebody employed by a company, especially in advertising or public relations, to handle all of the business of an individual client

ac·count·ing /ə kównting/ *n.* the activity, practice, or profession of maintaining and checking the business records of an individual or organization and preparing forms and reports for tax or other financial purposes

ac·counts pay·a·ble *npl.* a record that shows how much a company owes suppliers for the purchase of supplies or services on credit

ac·counts re·ceiv·a·ble *npl.* a record that shows how much is owed to a company by customers who have purchased supplies or services on credit

ac·cou·ter /ə kóotər/ (**-tered, -ter·ing, -ters**), **ac·cou·tre** (**-tred, -tring, -tres**) *vt.* to equip and clothe somebody, especially for military purposes [Mid-16thC. Via French *accoutrer* "to equip with something, especially clothes," from, ultimately, assumed Latin *consutura* "sewn together," from *sutura* "sewn" (source of English *suture*).]

ac·cou·ter·ment /ə kóotərmənt/, **ac·cou·tre·ment** /ə kóotrə mənt/ *n.* **1.** ACCESSORY an accessory or piece of equipment associated with a particular object, task, or role **2.** PIECE OF MILITARY EQUIPMENT a piece of military equipment carried by soldiers in addition to their standard uniform and weapons

ac·cra /ə kráa, ákrə/ *n.* in Caribbean countries, a fritter made of stripped salted fish mixed with flour batter and then deep-fried [Late 19thC. From Yoruba *àkàrà* "bean cake."]

Ac·cra /ə kráa, ákrə/ capital of Ghana. It is located on the Gulf of Guinea in southeastern Ghana. Population: 953,500 (1990).

ac·cred·it /ə kréddət/ (**-it·ed, -it·ing, -its**) *vt.* **1.** GIVE AUTHORITY to give somebody the authority to perform a function (*usually passive*) **2.** GIVE OFFICIAL RECOGNITION TO SOMEBODY officially to recognize a person or organization as having met a standard or criterion (*usually passive*) **3.** APPOINT AS ENVOY to appoint somebody as an envoy or ambassador representing his or her government or country [Early 17thC. From French *accréditer* "to believe (firmly)," from *crédit* (see CREDIT).] —**ac·cred·i·ta·tion** /ə krèdde táysh'n/ *n.*

ac·crete /ə kréet/ (**-cret·ed, -cret·ing, -cretes**) *vti.* to become bigger, or make something become bigger, especially by adding to what is there or by two or more things growing together [Late 18thC. From Latin *accret-*, the past participle stem of *accrescere* from *crescere* "to grow."]

ac·cre·tion /ə kréesh'n/ *n.* **1.** INCREASE an increase in size or amount as a result of something accumulating or being added gradually, or something accumulated in this way **2.** LAW ADDITION something added to something else, e.g., a fund or account, from an external source **3.** ASTRON ATTRACTION OF MATTER BY GRAVITY a process in which matter revolving around an astronomical object is gradually pulled in and added to the body's mass **4.** GEOL INCREASE IN LANDMASS a process by which a body of rock or a landmass increases in size as a result of material accumulating on or around it **5.** GEOL INCREASE IN SIZE OF CONTINENTS a process by which the size of a continent increases as a result of the moving together and deforming of tectonic plates —**ac·cre·tion·ar·y** *adj.*

ac·cre·tion disk *n.* a band of matter revolving around and being pulled into an astronomical object that has an intense gravitational field, e.g., a star or black hole

ac·cru·al /ə króo əl/ *n.* something that has accrued

ac·cru·al meth·od *n.* a method of accounting that counts income or expenses at the time they are earned or incurred, irrespective of when money is received or paid out. ◊ **cash method**

ac·crue /ə króo/ (**-crued, -cru·ing, -crues**) *v.* **1.** *vi.* COME INTO SOMEBODY'S POSSESSION to come into somebody's possession, often over a period of time **2.** *vi.* INCREASE to increase in amount or value **3.** *vt.* GATHER TOGETHER to gather together an amount, especially over a period of time **4.** *vi.* LAW BECOME ENFORCEABLE to become legally enforceable (*refers to claims or rights*) [15thC. Via Anglo-Norman from, ultimately, Latin *accrescent-* (see ACCRETE).] —**ac·crue·ment** *n.*

acct. *abbr.* account

ac·cul·tur·ate /ə kúlchə ràyt/ (**-at·ed, -at·ing, -ates**) *v.* **1.** *vi.* TAKE ON OTHER CULTURE to absorb and assimilate the culture of another group of people or another individual **2.** *vt.* CHANGE CULTURE OF SOMEBODY to change somebody's cultural behavior and thinking through contact with another culture [Mid-20thC. Back-formation from ACCULTURATION.] —**ac·cul·tur·a·tive** /ə kúlchə ràytiv/ *adj.*

ac·cul·tur·a·tion /ə kùlchə ráysh'n/ *n.* **1.** CULTURAL CHANGE a change in the cultural behavior and thinking of an individual or group through contact with another culture **2.** ABSORPTION OF CULTURE the process by which somebody absorbs the culture of a society from birth onward [Late 19thC. Coined from AC- + CULTURE + -ATION.] —**ac·cul·tur·a·tion·al** *adj.*

ac·cu·mu·late /ə kyóomyə làyt/ (**-lat·ed, -lat·ing, -lates**) *v.* **1.** *vti.* COLLECT to gather something together or collect something, or gather together or collect, over a period of time **2.** *vi.* INCREASE to gather, grow, or increase over a period of time [15thC. From Latin *accumulat-*, the past participle stem of *accumulare* "to heap up in addition," from *cumulus* "heap."] —**ac·cu·mu·la·ble** /ə kyóomyələb'l/ *adj.*

WORD KEY: SYNONYMS

See Synonyms at ***collect***.

ac·cu·mu·la·tion /ə kyòomyə láysh'n/ *n.* **1.** PROCESS OF GATHERING the process of gathering together and increasing in amount over a period of time **2.** COLLECTION OF THINGS a number of things that have collected or been collected over a period of time **3.** FIN GROWTH THROUGH INTEREST the growth of a sum by the addition of earned interest

ac·cu·mu·la·tive /ə kyóomyələtiv, -myə làytiv/ *adj.* **1.** TENDING TO ACCUMULATE tending to gather or collect things **2.** GROWING BY ADDITIONS growing by gradual additions —**ac·cu·mu·la·tive·ly** *adv.* —**ac·cu·mu·la·tive·ness** *n.*

ac·cu·mu·la·tor /ə kyóomyə làytər/ *n.* **1.** COMPUT MEMORY FOR SHORT-TERM STORAGE a section of memory in a computer or calculator in which the results of a calculation are temporarily held **2.** *U.K.* = **storage battery**

ac·cu·ra·cy /ákyərəssee/ *n.* **1.** CORRECTNESS the correctness or truthfulness of something **2.** ABILITY TO AVOID ERRORS the ability to be precise and avoid errors

ac·cu·rate /ákyərət/ *adj.* **1.** CORRECT giving a correct or truthful representation of something ○ *Their account of the incident was not entirely accurate.* **2.** FREE FROM ERRORS precise or free from errors ○ *an accurate typist* **3.** PROVIDING INFORMATION TO ACCEPTED STANDARD providing correct information in accordance with an accepted standard [Late 16thC. Via Latin *accuratus* "done with care," from, ultimately, *cura* "care" (source of English *curious*, *procure*, and *secure*).] —**ac·cu·rate·ly** *adv.* —**ac·cu·rate·ness** *n.*

ac·curs·ed /ə kúrst, -səd/, **ac·curst** /ə kúrst/ *adj.* (*archaic or literary*) **1.** DOOMED enduring the effects of a curse **2.** HORRIBLE horrible or hateful [12thC. Formed from *a-* "on" (from Old English *ar-*) + CURSE.] —**ac·curs·ed·ly** /ə kúrsədlee/ *adv.* —**ac·curs·ed·ness** *n.*

accus. *abbr.* accusative

ac·cu·sa·tion /àkyə záysh'n/ *n.* **1.** ALLEGATION a claim that somebody has done something illegal, wrong, or undesirable **2.** ACT OF ACCUSING the accusing of somebody, or the state of having been accused of something

ac·cu·sa·tive /ə kyóozətiv/ *n.* **1.** GRAMMATICAL CASE a grammatical case that identifies the direct object of a verb or certain other grammatical parts in some inflected languages and that affects nouns, pronouns, and adjectives **2.** WORD OR PHRASE IN ACCUSATIVE a word or phrase in the accusative ■ *adj.* IN ACCUSATIVE in or relating to the accusative [15thC. From Latin *accusativus*, from *accusare* (see ACCUSE). The grammatical meaning comes from a mistranslation of Greek *ptōsis aitiatikē* "case denoting causation," as "case denoting the accused."] —**ac·cu·sa·tive·ly** *adv.*

ac·cu·sa·to·ri·al /ə kyòozə táwree əl/, **ac·cu·sa·to·ry** /-tàwree/ *adj.* **1.** CLAIMING WRONGDOING containing or suggesting a claim that somebody has done something wrong (*formal*) **2.** LAW RELYING ON PROOF PROVIDED BY PROSECUTOR used to describe a legal system in which the prosecution is required to provide proof beyond reasonable doubt against an accused person, with the evidence being assessed by an impartial judge and jury. ◊ **inquisitorial** —**ac·cu·sa·to·ri·al·ly** *adv.*

ac·cuse /ə kyóoz/ (**-cused, -cus·ing, -cus·es**) *v.* **1.** *vti.* CONFRONT AND BLAME to confront somebody with a charge of having done something illegal, wrong, or undesirable **2.** *vt.* LAW CHARGE to charge somebody formally with having committed a crime (*often passive*) [14thC. Via French, from Latin *accusare* "to call somebody to account," from *ad causa* "to the (legal) case." The underlying idea is to take somebody to court.] —**ac·cus·er** *n.*

ac·cused /ə kyóozd/ *n.* the person or people being charged in a criminal case

ac·cus·ing /ə kyóozing/ *adj.* containing or suggesting a claim that somebody has done something wrong —**ac·cus·ing·ly** *adv.*

ac·cus·tom /ə kústəm/ (**-tomed, -tom·ing, -toms**) *vt.* to make yourself or somebody else become used to something through frequent or prolonged contact or use [15thC. From Anglo-Norman *acustomer*, from *custome* "habit" (see CUSTOM).]

ac·cus·tomed /ə kŭstəmd/ *adj.* 1. **USED TO SOMETHING** used to or familiar with something 2. **HABITUAL** habitual or usual

AC/DC *adj.* 1. ELEC **POWERED BY BATTERY OR ELECTRICAL OUTLET** able to be powered by battery or by connection to an electrical outlet. Full form **alternating current/direct current** 2. **BISEXUAL** bisexual (*slang offensive*)

ace /ayss/ *n.* 1. CARDS **PLAYING CARD** a playing card that has a single mark on it, or the single mark itself 2. **SINGLE-SPOTTED SIDE** a single-spotted side of a die or domino, or the single spot itself 3. TENNIS **WINNING SERVE** a serve that an opponent cannot reach 4. GOLF **HOLE IN ONE** the hitting of a golf ball into a hole in one stroke, or a hole at which only one stroke was taken 5. AIR FORCE **FIGHTER PILOT** a top fighter pilot, especially one who has shot down a number of enemy aircraft 6. **SOMEBODY WITH AN EXCEPTIONAL SKILL** somebody who is outstandingly good at a particular activity, e.g., a sport (*informal*) 7. **BEST FRIEND** somebody who is a best friend (*slang*) ■ *vt.* (**aced, ac·ing, ac·es**) 1. TENNIS **BEAT WITH SERVE** to beat an opponent by serving an ace 2. GOLF **PLAY HOLE IN SINGLE STROKE** to play a hole with only one stroke 3. **DEFEAT SOUNDLY** to defeat an opponent convincingly (*slang*) 4. **SCORE HIGH GRADE** to score an A in a course or examination (*slang*) ○ *aced all her finals* ■ *adj.* **EXCELLENT** excellent (*informal*) [14thC. Via French *as* from Latin, "unit, unity." Originally the lowest score, one, in dice; its connotations of "excellence" come from the powerful status of the ace in cards.] ◇ **be coming up aces** to be flourishing or successful (*informal*) ○ *She's hot, coming up aces with every movie she makes.* ◇ **ace in the hole** an advantage that is reserved for use until it is most needed (*informal*) ◇ **hold all the aces** to have all the advantages (*informal*) ◇ **within an ace of** very close to

Ace *tdmk.* a trademark for a type of elastic bandage

ACE[1] /ays/ *n.* an enzyme causing high blood pressure. Its action can be controlled by drugs as a treatment for heart disease. [Late-20thC. Acronym of angiotensin-converting enzyme.]

ACE[2] *abbr.* American Council on Education

-acean *suffix.* = **-aceous**

ACE in·hib·i·tor *n.* a drug that counters the effects of an enzyme that causes high blood pressure

a·cen·tric /ay séntrik/ *adj.* 1. **LACKING CENTER** without a center 2. **WITHOUT CENTROMERE** used to describe a chromosome that lacks the structure at which the two arms of a chromosome join (**centromere**). ◊ **acrocentric, metacentric, telocentric**

-aceous, -acean *suffix.* resembling or related to ○ *herbaceous* [Formed from modern Latin *-aceus*, from Latin]

a·ceph·a·lous /ay séffələs/ *adj.* used to describe an animal that has no head [Mid-18thC. Via medieval Latin, from Greek *akephalos* "without a head," from *kephalē* "head" (see CEPHAL-).]

a·ce·qui·a /aa sáykee ə/ *n.* *Southwest U.S.* an irrigation canal or ditch [Mid-19thC. Via Spanish from Arabic *sāqīah* "irrigation stream."]

ac·er /áysər/ *n.* a Eurasian and North American tree or shrub grown as an ornamental for its foliage. Genus: *Acer.*

a·cerb *adj.* = **acerbic** [Early 17thC. From Latin *acerbus* (see ACERBIC).]

ac·er·bate /ássər bàyt/ (**-bat·ed, -bat·ing, -bates**) *vt.* (*formal*) 1. **ANNOY SOMEBODY** to annoy or irritate somebody 2. **MAKE SOMETHING BITTER** to make something taste bitter [Mid-18thC. From Latin *acerbat-*, the past participle stem of *acerbare* "to make harsh," from *acerbus* (see ACERBIC).]

a·cer·bic /ə sérbik/, **a·cerb** /ə sérb/ *adj.* bitter or sharp in tone, taste, or manner [Mid-19thC. Formed from Latin *acerbus* "harsh," from, ultimately, an Indo-European word that is also the ancestor of English *acid, acne,* and *oxygen.*] —**a·cer·bi·cal·ly** *adv.*

a·cer·bi·ty /ə sérbətee/ *n.* bitterness or sharpness in tone, taste, or manner [Late 16thC. Directly or via French *acerbité* from Latin *acerbitas*, from *acerbus* (see ACERBIC).]

acet- *prefix.* = **aceto-** (*used before vowels*)

ac·e·tab·u·lum /àssə tábbyələm/ (*plural* **-lums** *or* **-la** /-lə/) *n.* 1. ANAT **CAVITY ON HIPBONE** the curved cavity on the side of the hipbone where the end of the thighbone fits 2. ZOOL **ROUND SUCKER** a round cup-shaped sucker found on flatworms, leeches, and mollusks such as the octopus [14thC. From Latin, literally "a vinegar cup" but also used to mean "a cup-shaped cavity," formed from *acetum* "vinegar" (see ACETIC).] —**ac·e·tab·u·lar** *adj.*

ac·e·tal /ássət'l, ássə tàl/ *n.* 1. **COLORLESS CHEMICAL SOLVENT** a colorless volatile liquid used in perfumes and as a solvent. Formula: $C_6H_{14}O_2$. 2. **ORGANIC COMPOUND** an organic compound similar to acetal that contains a particular chemical group. Formula: $-CH(OR_1)OR_2$.

ac·et·al·de·hyde /àssə táldə hīd/ *n.* a colorless volatile liquid with a distinctive smell, used in the manufacture of other chemicals, especially acetic acid, acetic anhydride, and butanol. Formula: C_2H_4O.

a·cet·a·mide /ə séttə mīd, àssət á-/ *n.* a white crystalline solid that absorbs water readily and is used in the manufacture of other chemicals. Formula: CH_3CONH_2.

a·cet·a·min·o·phen /ə seétə mínnəfən, àssətə-/ *n.* a crystalline compound used to relieve pain and reduce fever. Formula: $C_8H_9NO_2$.

ac·et·an·i·lide /àssə tánn'l īd/ *n.* a white crystalline compound used to relieve pain and reduce fever, and in manufacturing other chemicals, dyes, and rubber. Formula: C_8H_9NO. [Mid-19thC. Coined from ACETYL + ANILINE + -IDE.]

ac·e·tate /ássə tàyt/ *n.* 1. **DERIVATIVE OF ACETIC ACID** a salt or ester of acetic acid 2. = **cellulose acetate** 3. **PRODUCT CONTAINING ACETATE** a product made of or containing acetate

a·ce·tic /ə seétik/ *adj.* containing, producing, or made from vinegar or acetic acid [Late 18thC. From French *acétique*, from Latin *acetum* "vinegar." Ultimately from the same Indo-European ancestor as English *acute, acrid,* and *acid.*]

a·ce·tic ac·id *n.* a colorless acid with a pungent odor that is the main component of vinegar and is used in manufacturing drugs, dyes, plastics, fibers, and other products. Formula: CH_3COOH. ◊ **glacial acetic acid**

a·ce·tic an·hy·dride *n.* a colorless liquid with a pungent odor, used in the manufacture of aspirin and plastics

a·ce·ti·fy /ə seétə fee, -séttə-/ (**-fied, -fy·ing, -fies**) *vti.* to turn into, or cause something to turn into, acetic acid or vinegar —**a·ce·ti·fi·ca·tion** /ə seétəfə káysh'n, -séttə-/ *n.* —**a·ce·ti·fi·er** /ə seétə fīr, ə séttə fīr/ *n.*

aceto-, acet- *prefix.* acetic acid ○ *acetify* [From Latin *acetum* "vinegar" (see ACETUM)]

ac·e·tone /ássətōn/ *n.* a colorless flammable liquid with a pleasant smell, widely used as a solvent for paints and nail polish, and in manufacturing chemicals. Formula: C_3H_6O.

ac·e·tone bod·y *n.* = **ketone body**

a·ce·tous /ə seétəs, ássə-/ *adj.* like, containing, or producing acetic acid or vinegar [14thC. From late Latin *acetosus*, from Latin *acetum* "vinegar" (see ACETIC).]

a·ce·tyl /ə seét'l, ássə-/ *n.* relating to or containing the chemical group derived from acetic acid. Formula: CH_3CO-. —**ac·e·tyl·ic** /àssə tíllik/ *adj.*

a·cet·y·late /ə sétt'l àyt/ (**-lat·ed, -lat·ing, -lates**) *vt.* to introduce the acetyl group into a compound —**a·cet·y·la·tion** /ə sètt'l áysh'n/ *n.*

a·ce·tyl·cho·line /ə seèt'l kṓ leen, àssət'l-/ *n.* a white crystalline compound released from the ends of nerve fibers and involved in the transmission of nerve impulses. Formula: $C_7H_{17}NO_3$.

a·ce·tyl·cho·lin·es·ter·ase /ə seèt'l kōlən éstərayz/ *n.* an enzyme, present in blood and some nerve endings, that aids the breakdown of acetylcholine and suppresses its stimulatory effect on nerves

a·ce·tyl co·en·zyme A, a·ce·tyl CoA *n.* a coenzyme derived from fatty acids, carbohydrates, and amino acids during metabolism

a·cet·y·lene /ə sétt'lən, -l een/ *n.* a colorless gaseous flammable hydrocarbon used in welding and in manufacturing chemicals. Formula: C_2H_2. —**a·cet·y·len·ic** *adj.*

a·cet·y·lide /ə sétt'l īd/ *n.* any chemical compound derived from acetylene and containing a metal atom. Many of these compounds are very explosive.

a·ce·tyl·sal·i·cyl·ic ac·id /ə seèt'l sálli síllik-, àssət'l sálli sìllik-/ *n.* the drug aspirin (*technical*)

ac·ey-deuc·y /àysi dóossee/ *n.* a version of backgammon in which a dice throw of one or two wins an additional turn [Formed from ACE and DEUCE]

A·chae·a /ə keé ə/, **A·cha·ia** /ə kī ə, ə káy ə/ *n.* 1. **MODERN GREEK ADMINISTRATIVE AREA** an administrative area in modern Greece 2. **ANCIENT GREEK PROVINCE** in ancient Greece, a province in the northern Peloponnesus

A·chae·an /ə keé ən, ə kī-, ə káy-/, **A·cha·ian** *n.* 1. **MEMBER OF ANCIENT HELLENIC PEOPLE** a member of an ancient Hellenic people thought to have founded the Mycenean civilization on the Peloponnesus 2. **SOMEBODY FROM ACHAEA** somebody who lives in or was born in the modern Greek an administrative area of Achaea —**A·chae·an** *adj.*

ach·a·la·sia /àkə láyzhə, -láyzhee ə/ *n.* a failure of certain smooth muscle bands, e.g., in the gullet, to relax [Early 20thC. Coined from A- + Greek *khalasis* "relaxation," from *khalan* "to loosen."]

ache /ayk/ *n.* **CONSTANT PAIN** a feeling of constant dull pain ■ *vi.* (**ached, ach·ing, aches**) 1. **FEEL PAIN** to feel or be the site of a dull constant pain 2. **YEARN** to yearn for the presence of somebody or something 3. **WANT BADLY** to want something very much (*informal*) ○ *aching to tell her the news* [Old English *æce* (noun), *acan* (verb), of uncertain origin: perhaps ultimately from an Indo-European word meaning "fault." The *ch* spelling arose from a mistaken association with Greek *akhos* "pain."]

WORD KEY: SYNONYMS

See Synonyms at ***pain***.

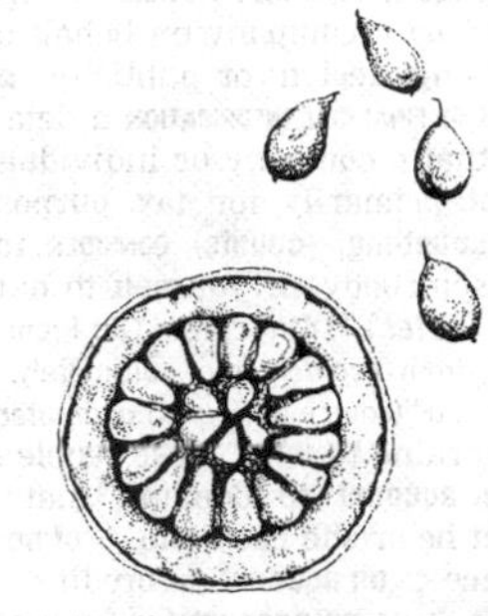

Achene: Cross section of the fruit of the dog rose

a·chene /ə keén/, **a·kene** *n.* a dry single-seeded fruit that does not open to release its seed. Dandelions and sunflowers have achenes. [Mid-19thC. From modern Latin *achaenium*, literally "not gaping," from Greek *khainein* "to gape."]

Ach·er·on /ákə rōn/ *n.* in Greek mythology, one of the rivers that ran through Hades. ◊ **Styx, Lethe**

Ach·e·son /áchəss'n/, **Dean** (1893–1971) U.S. lawyer and statesman who was prominent in the development of the Truman Doctrine, the Marshall Plan, and NATO.

A·cheu·li·an /ə shoólee ən/ *n.* a period of the Paleolithic era during which people made symmetrical stone hand axes [Early 20thC. Named for the French village of Saint-Acheul near Amiens in Picardy, where a large number of distinctive tools were found in the 19thC.] —**A·cheu·li·an** *adj.*

a·chieve /ə cheév/ (**a·chieved, a·chiev·ing, a·chieves**) *vt.* to succeed in doing or gaining something, usually with effort [14thC. From French *achever* "to bring to an end, bring to a head," from *a chief*, literally "to a head" (see CHIEF).] —**a·chiev·a·ble** *adj.*

WORD KEY: SYNONYMS

See Synonyms at ***accomplish***.

a·chieved /ə cheévd/ *adj.* showing great skill or accomplishment

a·chieved sta·tus *n.* social importance within a culture that an individual gains through personal effort rather than by inheriting it

a·chieve·ment /ə cheévmənt/ *n.* 1. **SUCCESS** something that somebody has succeeded in doing, usually with effort 2. **FINISHING WELL** the act or process of finishing something successfully 3. HERALDRY **FULL COAT OF ARMS** a full coat of arms that includes standing figures such as lions or unicorns (**supporters**), the family symbol (**crest**), and the family motto 4. SOCIOL **EARNED SOCIAL STATUS** social status gained through personal merit rather than as a result of the circumstances into which somebody is born

a·chieve·ment age *n.* the age at which a child should be able to perform a particular task successfully

a·chiev·er /ə chēevər/ *n.* **1.** **SUCCESSFUL PERSON** somebody who is successful and motivated to go on being successful **2.** **SOMEBODY WHO DOES SOMETHING SUCCESSFULLY** somebody who succeeds in doing or gaining a particular thing

A·chil·les /ə kílleez/ *n.* in Greek mythology, the principal hero of the Trojan War, made invulnerable by being dipped in the river Styx as a baby by his mother, except for the heel she held him by. He killed the Trojan hero Hector before being fatally wounded in the heel with an arrow fired by Paris.

A·chil·les heel *n.* a weakness that seems small but makes somebody fatally vulnerable

A·chil·les jerk *n.* a reflex action of the foot, which jerks downward when the lower leg muscles contract

A·chil·les ten·don *n.* the tendon that connects the heelbone to the calf muscles

a·chir·al /ày kī́rəl/ *adj.* used to describe a molecule that does not have either left-handed or right-handed configuration **(chirality)**

a·chlor·hy·dri·a /áy klawr hī́dree ə/ *n.* an absence of or reduction in hydrochloric acid in the gastric juice —**a·chlor·hy·dric** *adj.*

a·chon·drite /ày kón drìt/ *n.* a stony meteorite that does not contain rounded grains **(chondrules)** —**a·chon·drit·ic** /ày kon dríttik/ *adj.*

a·chon·dro·pla·sia /ày kóndrə pláyzhə, -zhee ə/ *n.* a genetic disorder in which cartilage fails to develop into bone at the early stages of development, resulting in dwarfism [Late 19thC. Coined from Greek *akhondros* "without cartilage" + -PLASIA.] —**a·chon·dro·plas·tic** /ày kóndrə plástik/ *adj.*

ach·ro·mat /ákrə màt/ *n.* **1.** PHYS = **achromatic lens** **2.** OPHTHALMOL = **monochromat** [Early 20thC. Back-formation from ACHROMATIC.]

ach·ro·mat·ic /àkrə máttik/ *adj.* **1.** **WITHOUT COLOR** without color and therefore white, gray, or black in appearance **2.** PHYS **WITHOUT SPECTRUM COLORS** able to reflect or refract light without spectral color separation **3.** BIOL **NOT EASILY STAINED** used to describe cells not easily stained with standard dyes **4.** MUSIC **WITHOUT SHARPS OR FLATS** using a scale with no sharps or flats —**ach·ro·mat·i·cal·ly** *adv.* —**ach·ro·ma·tic·i·ty** /àkrəmə tíssətee/ *n.* —**a·chro·ma·tism** /-tìzm/ *n.*

ach·ro·mat·ic col·or *n.* a color with no hue or chromatic component

ach·ro·mat·ic lens *n.* a composite lens in which two or more lenses with different properties are combined to prevent distortion **(chromatic aberration)**

ach·y /áykee/ (**-i·er, -i·est**) *adj.* feeling or being the site of a constant dull pain —**ach·i·ness** *n.*

a·cic·u·la /ə síkyələ/ (*plural* **-lae** /-lee, -lī/) *n.* a needle-shaped part, e.g., a spine, bristle, or crystal (*technical*) [Mid-19thC. From late Latin, literally "little needle."] —**a·cic·u·late** *adj.* —**a·cic·u·lat·ed** /ə síkyə làytəd/ *adj.*

ac·id /ássid/ *n.* **1.** CHEM **SOUR-TASTING SUBSTANCE** a compound, usually water-soluble, that releases hydrogen ions when in solution. An acid reacts with a base to form a salt, has a pH less than 7, and turns blue litmus red. Acids are corrosive and have a sour taste. ◊ **alkali** **2.** DRUGS = **LSD** (*slang*) **3.** **SHARPNESS** a sharp, bitter, or sarcastic quality in speech or writing ■ *adj.* **1.** **RELATING TO AN ACID** with the properties of or containing an acid **2.** **SHARP** sharp, bitter, or sarcastic **3.** METEOROL **POLLUTED** used to describe rain or snow that contains dilute acid resulting from pollution **4.** GEOL **HIGH IN SILICA** used to describe igneous rocks that have a high silica content [Late 17thC. Directly or via French, from Latin *acidus*, from *acere* "to be sour."] —**ac·id·ly** *adv.*

WORD KEY: ORIGIN

The Indo-European word from which ***acid*** comes is also the ancestor of English *acacia, acme, acne, acrid, acrobat, acute, alacrity, eager, edge, oxygen,* and *vinegar.*

ac·id dep·o·si·tion *n.* a deposit of water vapor formed in the atmosphere, e.g., dew, rain, snow, hail or fog, that is high in acid content because of atmospheric pollution

ac·id·head /ássid hèd/ *n.* somebody who takes the illegal drug LSD regularly (*slang*)

a·cid·ic /ə síddik/ *adj.* **1.** **SOUR-TASTING** sour or bitter in taste **2.** CHEM **FORMING ACID IN WATER** forming an acid in water

a·cid·i·fi·ca·tion /ə sìddəfə káysh'n/ *n.* the process of becoming acid, e.g., when soil or water is polluted by acid rain [Late 18thC]

a·cid·i·fy /ə síddə fī/ (**-fied, -fy·ing, -fies**) *vti.* to turn something acid, or become acid —**a·cid·i·fi·a·ble** *adj.* —**a·cid·i·fi·er** *n.*

ac·i·dim·e·ter /àssə dímmətər/ *n.* an instrument for measuring the amount of acid in a solution —**a·cid·i·met·ric** /ə sìddə méttrik/ *adj.* —**ac·i·dim·e·try** /àssə dímmətree/ *n.*

a·cid·i·ty /ə síddətee/ (*plural* **-ties**) *n.* **1.** **EXTENT TO WHICH SOMETHING IS ACID** the concentration of an acid in a substance, often measured in terms of pH **2.** = **hyperacidity**

ac·id jazz *n.* a mixture of funk, jazz, and soul music that first appeared in the 1980s

a·cid·o·phil /ə síddə fìl, a síddə-, ə síddə-/, **a·cid·o·phile** *n.* **1.** **ACID-LOVING ORGANISM** a microorganism or plant that flourishes in an acid environment **2.** BIOL **CELL TAKING UP ACIDIC DYE** a cell that stains readily with acidic dyes

ac·i·do·phil·ic /àssidō fíllik, ə sìddə-/ *adj.* **1.** BIOL **EASILY STAINED BY ACID DYE** used to describe cells that are easily stained by an acid dye **2.** MICROBIOL, BOT **FLOURISHING IN ACID ENVIRONMENT** used to describe microorganisms or plants that flourish in an acid environment

ac·i·doph·i·lus milk /àssi dóffələss-/ *n.* milk fermented using bacterial cultures, used to treat digestive disorders

ac·id pro·te·ase *n.* a protein-digesting enzyme that has maximum activity in the acid environment of the stomach

Barnaby's

Acid rain: Detail of tree in Norway damaged by acid rain

ac·id rain *n.* rain that contains dilute acid derived from burning fossil fuels and that is potentially harmful to the environment

ac·id rock *n.* a type of electric rock music popular in the late 1960s, with instrumental effects and lyrics suggesting or promoting psychedelic experiences

ac·id test *n.* a decisive test that establishes the worth or credibility of something [From the use of nitric acid to test gold]

WORD KEY: USAGE

An ***acid test*** is one that is definitive or conclusive. The phrase, popularized by President Woodrow Wilson, has been sometimes criticized as being trite and overused; nevertheless, it continues to be widely used, especially by journalists and politicians: *The treatment accorded Russia by her sister nations in the months to come will be the acid test of their good will.*

a·cid·u·late /ə síjjə làyt/ (**-lat·ed, -lat·ing, -lates**) *vti.* to make something slightly acid, or become slightly acid —**a·cid·u·la·tion** /ə sìjjə láysh'n/ *n.*

a·cid·u·lous /ə síjjələss/ *adj.* **1.** **SOUR-TASTING** slightly sour in taste (*formal*) **2.** **CUTTING** cutting and sharp in speech or tone [Mid-18thC. Formed from Latin *acidulus*, from *acidus* (see ACID).]

ac·id-washed *adj.* treated with chlorine acid to make the fabric look worn and washed-out and feel softer

ac·i·er·ate /ássee ə ràyt/ (**-at·ed, -at·ing, -ates**) *vt.* to make iron into steel by combining it with carbon and other elements [Mid-19thC. From French *aciérer*, from *acier* "steel."] —**ac·i·er·a·tion** /àssee ə ráysh'n/ *n.*

ac·i·nus /ássənəss/ (*plural* **-ni** /-nī/) *n.* **1.** **SMALL GLANDULAR SAC** a rounded sac, containing secretory cells, found at the ends of the ducts in an exocrine gland **2.** ANAT = **alveolus** **3.** **PART OF BLACKBERRY** one of the small globes **(drupelets)** that make up an aggregate fruit such as a blackberry or raspberry [Mid-18thC. From Latin, "berry growing in a cluster, kernel."] —**ac·i·nar** *adj.* —**ac·i·nous** *adj.*

ack. *abbr.* acknowledge

ack-ack /ák àk, àk ák/ *n.* (*informal*) **1.** **ANTIAIRCRAFT GUN** an antiaircraft gun **2.** **ANTIAIRCRAFT FIRE** antiaircraft fire [In military jargon ANTIAIRCRAFT was abbreviated to "AA," which became "ack-ack" from the use of "ack" for the letter "a" when spelling out messages]

ack·ee *n.* = **akee**

ac·knowl·edge /ək nóllij/ (**-edged, -edg·ing, -edg·es**) *v.* **1.** *vti.* **ADMIT SOMETHING** to admit or accept that something exists, is true, or is real **2.** *vti.* **SHOW AWARENESS OF SOMETHING** to respond to something such as a greeting or message to show it has been noticed or received **3.** *vti.* **SHOW APPRECIATION OF SOMETHING** to show appreciation or express thanks for something such as a letter or gift **4.** *vt.* **RECOGNIZE SOMETHING LEGALLY** to recognize or admit the existence, rights, or authority of somebody or something, especially in a legal context **5.** *vt.* **THANK SOMEBODY OFFICIALLY** to give official or public recognition of the help somebody has given or the work somebody has done [15thC. Probably formed from KNOWLEDGE on the model of obsolete English *aknow* "to recognize, acknowledge" (formed from KNOW).] —**ac·knowl·edg·a·ble** *adj.* —**ac·knowl·edg·er** *n.*

ac·knowl·edged /ək nóllijd/ *adj.* known or widely accepted as having a particular status

ac·knowl·edg·ment /ək nóllijmənt/, **ac·knowl·edge·ment** *n.* **1.** **ACT OF ACKNOWLEDGING** the act of acknowledging something, or the condition of being acknowledged **2.** **SIGN OF RECOGNITION** a sign showing that somebody has seen or heard somebody else's greeting or presence **3.** **INDICATION OF RECEIPT** a letter or other message sent to say that something has been received **4.** **THANKS** an expression of thanks or appreciation for something **5.** **OFFICIAL RECOGNITION** official or public recognition of the help somebody has given or the work somebody has done ■ **ac·knowl·edg·ments** *npl.* **AUTHOR'S THANKS** a section at the beginning or end of a book or other piece of writing where an author thanks those who have helped

a·clin·ic line /ay klínnik-/ *n.* = **magnetic equator** [*Aclinic* formed from Greek *aklinēs* "not leaning," from *klinein* "to lean"]

ACLU *abbr.* American Civil Liberties Union

ac·me /ákmee/ *n.* the highest point of perfection or achievement [Late 16thC. From Greek *akmē*, literally "highest point." Ultimately from the same Indo-European ancestor that produced English *acid, edge,* and *oxygen.*]

ac·ne /áknee/ *n.* a disease of the skin giving rise to blackheads and pimples on the face, neck, and shoulders. It often affects adolescents. [Mid-19thC. From Latin, a misreading of Greek *akmē* (see ACME).] —**ac·ned** *adj.*

a·coe·lo·mate /ə séelə màyt/ *n.* an organism such as a flatworm or jellyfish with no cavity **(coelom)** between its digestive tract and outer wall

ac·o·lyte /ákə lìt/ *n.* **1.** RELIG **ASSISTANT TO CLERIC** somebody, especially a young person, who assists a member of the clergy in the performance of rites **2.** **ASSISTANT** a follower or assistant ○ *the acolytes of this powerful leader* [14thC. Directly or via Old French, from ecclesiastical Latin *acolytus*, from Greek *akolouthos* "follower," from *a-* "together" + *keleuthos* "path" (source of English *anacoluthon*).]

A·con·ca·gua /àkən kaágwə, aàkən-/ highest mountain in the Andes and in the western hemisphere, located in western Argentina near the Chilean border. Height: 22,834 ft./6,960 m.

ac·o·nite /ákə nìt/ *n.* **1.** **PLANT WITH HOODED FLOWERS** a plant with poisonous roots that grows in northern temperate regions and has purplish blue or white hooded flowers. Monkshood and wolfsbane are types of aconite. Genus: *Aconitum.* **2.** = **winter aconite** **3.** **EXTRACT OF PLANT ROOT** an extract of the dried poisonous root of some aconite plants, used in the past as a drug [Mid-16thC. Directly or via French, from Latin *aconitum*, from Greek *akoniton*, of unknown origin.]

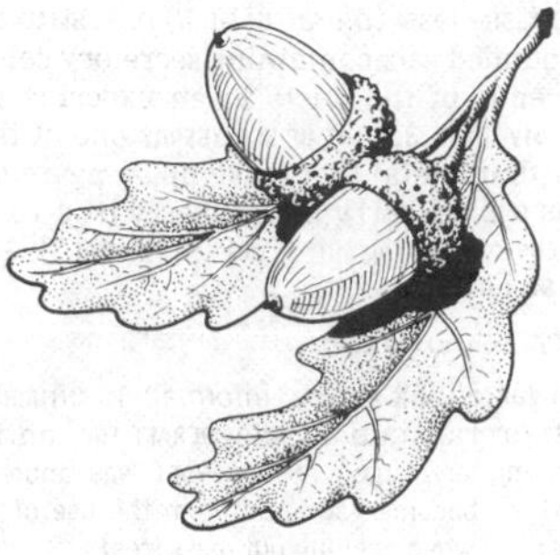

Acorn

a·corn /áy kàwrn/ *n.* the hard fruit of an oak tree, consisting of a smooth single-seeded nut that is set in a cup-shaped base and ripens from green to brown [Old English *æcern,* possibly formed from *æcer* "open land" (source of English *acre*). The word was later interpreted as "oak-corn," as if meaning "fruit of the oak."]

a·corn bar·na·cle *n.* a marine organism that attaches itself to rocks and catches food using tendrils that protrude from a hole in the top of its conical shell. Latin name: *Balanus balanoides.*

Acorn squash

a·corn squash (*plural* **a·corn squash·es** *or* **a·corn squash**) *n.* an acorn-shaped winter squash with a ridged dark-green rind and yellow or orange flesh

a·corn worm *n.* a small burrowing sea animal that looks like a worm and has an acorn-shaped snout that it uses to dig for food on the ocean floor. Phylum: Chordata.

a·cou·chi /ə kooshee/ (*plural* **-chis** *or* **-chies**), **a·cou·chy** (*plural* **-chies**) *n.* an agile South American rodent similar to an agouti. Genus: *Myoprocta.* [Late 18thC. Via French, from Tupi.]

a·cous·tic /ə kóostik/, **a·cous·ti·cal** /-stik'l/ *adj.* **1.** RELATING TO SOUND relating to, involving, or typical of sound, hearing, or the study of sound **2.** DESIGNED FOR USE WITH SOUND designed to control sound, absorb it, or carry it better **3.** MUSIC NOT AMPLIFIED used to describe music or a musical instrument that is not amplified electronically ■ *n.* **1.** MUSICAL INSTRUMENT WITHOUT AMPLIFICATION a musical instrument that is not electronically amplified, usually a guitar (*informal*) **2.** = **acoustics** [Early 18thC. From Greek *akoustikos,* from *akouein* "to hear," from the same Indo-European ancestor as English *hear* and *caution.*] —**a·cous·ti·cal·ly** *adv.*

ac·ous·ti·cian /àkoo stísh'n/ *n.* a specialist in the study of sound

a·cous·tic nerve *n.* = **auditory nerve**

a·cous·tic rock *n.* rock music intended to be played mainly on unamplified instruments

a·cous·tics /ə kóostiks/ *n.* STUDY OF SOUND the scientific study of sound (*takes a singular verb*) ■ *npl.* SOUND-CARRYING ABILITY the characteristic way in which sound carries or can be heard within a particular enclosed space, e.g., an auditorium

a·cous·tic tile *n.* a ceiling or wall tile designed to stop or diminish the transmission of sound

a·cous·to·e·lec·tric /ə kóostō i léktrik/ *adj.* = **electroacoustic** —**a·cous·to·e·lec·tric·al·ly** *adv.*

ACP *n.* a group of over forty nonaligned developing countries with aid-related and economic links. Full form **African, Caribbean and Pacific (countries)**

ac·quaint /ə kwáynt/ (**-quaint·ed, -quaint·ing, -quaints**) *vt.* **1.** MAKE AWARE to make somebody, or yourself, aware of or familiar with something **2.** INTRODUCE SOMEBODY to introduce somebody or make somebody known to somebody else (*dated or formal*) [13thC. Via French *acointier* "to make known" from Latin *accognoscere* "to know perfectly," from *cognoscere* "to know" (source of English *cognition* and *quaint*).]

ac·quain·tance /ə kwáyntəns/ *n.* **1.** SOMEBODY KNOWN somebody who is known slightly rather than intimately **2.** KNOWLEDGE knowledge, usually slight, of somebody or something —**ac·quain·tance·ship** *n.* ◇ **make somebody's acquaintance** to meet somebody for the first time

ac·quaint·ed /ə kwáyntəd/ *adj.* **1.** FAMILIAR having some, often not very much, knowledge of something **2.** KNOWN known to somebody or to each other from a previous introduction

ac·qui·esce /àkwee éss/ (**-esced, -esc·ing, -esc·es**) *vi.* to agree to or comply with something passively rather than expressing approval or support [Early 17thC. From Latin *acquiescere* "to remain resting," hence "to agree tacitly," from *quiescere* "to rest" (source of English *coy* and *quiet*).] —**ac·qui·es·cence** *n.* —**ac·qui·es·cent** *adj.* —**ac·qui·es·cent·ly** *adv.*

WORD KEY: SYNONYMS

See Synonyms at ***agree.***

ac·quire /ə kwír/ (**-quired, -quir·ing, -quires**) *vt.* **1.** GET SOMETHING to get or obtain possession of something **2.** DEVELOP SOMETHING to learn or develop something ○ *a habit I acquired in the Army* **3.** AEROSP LOCATE BY RADAR to locate an object such as an aircraft by the use of radar or another detector [15thC. Via Old French *acquerre* from Latin *acquirere* "to get something extra," from *quaerere* "to try to get or obtain" (see QUERY).] —**ac·quir·a·ble** *adj.* —**ac·quired** *adj.* —**ac·quir·er** *n.*

WORD KEY: SYNONYMS

See Synonyms at ***get.***

ac·quired char·ac·ter, ac·quired char·ac·ter·is·tic *n.* a characteristic that an organism develops in response to its environment and that cannot be passed on to the next generation

ac·quired im·mune de·fi·cien·cy syn·drome, ac·quired im·mu·no·de·fi·cien·cy syn·drome *n.* full form of **AIDS**

ac·quired taste *n.* a liking that develops for something that seems unpleasant at first

ac·quire·ment /ə kwírmənt/ *n.* **1.** ACT OF ACQUIRING SOMETHING the act or process of acquiring something **2.** LEARNED SKILL something learned or attained, especially a skill

ac·qui·si·tion /àkwi zísh'n/ *n.* **1.** ACQUIRING act of acquiring something **2.** NEW POSSESSION something that has recently been bought or obtained **3.** SKILL DEVELOPMENT developing a new skill, practice, or way of doing things ○ *language acquisition* **4.** AEROSP LOCATING BY RADAR the location of an object such as an aircraft by the use of radar or some other detector ■ **ac·qui·si·tions** *npl.* **1.** FIN COMPANY DEPARTMENT the department in a company responsible for taking over other businesses ○ *I work in acquisitions and mergers.* **2.** ADDITIONS DEPARTMENT the department of a library or museum responsible for obtaining and taking care of new items [14thC. From the Latin stem *acquisition-,* from *acquisit-,* the past participle stem of *acquirere* (see ACQUIRE).]

ac·quis·i·tive /ə kwízzətiv/ *adj.* **1.** EAGER TO POSSESS THINGS eager to acquire things, especially possessions **2.** QUICK TO LEARN curious, eager, and quick to learn ○ *an acquisitive mind* [Mid-17thC. Formed from the Latin stem *acquisit-* (see ACQUIRE), on the model of French *acquisitif.*] —**ac·quis·i·tive·ly** *adv.* —**ac·quis·i·tive·ness** *n.*

ac·quit /ə kwít/ (**-quit·ted, -quit·ting, -quits**) *v.* **1.** *vt.* LAW DECLARE INNOCENT to declare officially that somebody is not guilty of a charge or accusation **2.** *vr.* BEHAVE to conduct yourself in a particular way (*formal*) ○ *The band acquitted itself well at the performance.* **3.** *vt.* FREE FROM OBLIGATION to free somebody from a duty or obligation (*formal*) **4.** *vt.* REPAY to repay something such as a debt (*old*) [13thC. Via Old French *a(c)quiter* from assumed Latin *acquitare,* literally "to bring to rest," hence "to set free," from *quies* "quiet" (source of English *quiet* and *aquiesce*).] —**ac·quit·ter** *n.*

WORD KEY: SYNONYMS

See Synonyms at ***excuse.***

ac·quit·tal /ə kwítt'l/ *n.* a judgment given by a judge or jury that somebody is not guilty of a charge or accusation

ac·quit·tance /ə kwítt'ns/ *n.* release from a debt or obligation, or a written receipt or other record of this (*formal*)

a·cre /áykər/ *n.* UNIT OF AREA a unit of area used in some countries, including the United States and the United Kingdom, equal to 4,840 sq. yd./4,046.86 sq. m ■ **a·cres** *npl.* **1.** LAND land, especially a large amount of land **2.** LARGE AMOUNT a large amount or area of something (*informal*) [Old English *æcer.* Ultimately probably "area over which plowing oxen can be driven in a day," from an Indo-European ancestor (source also of English *acorn* and *agriculture*) meaning "to drive."]

WORD KEY: CULTURAL NOTE

A Thousand Acres, a novel by Jane Smiley (1991). A retelling of *King Lear* set in the Midwest, it exposes the tragedies of alcoholism and emotional and environmental abuse behind the rural idyll of a family farm. The novel won the Pulitzer Prize in literature and a National Book Critics' Circle Award, and was made into a movie in 1997.

a·cre·age /áykərij, áykrij/ *n.* land, or an area of land, measured in acres

a·cre-foot (*plural* **a·cre-feet**) *n.* the volume of water that would cover an area of one acre to a depth of one foot, equivalent to 43,560 cu. ft./1,233.5 cu. m

a·cre-inch *n.* one-twelfth of an acre-foot, or the volume of water that would cover an area of one acre to a depth of one inch, equivalent to 3,630 cu. ft./102.8 cu. m

ac·rid /ákrəd/ *adj.* **1.** UNPLEASANTLY PUNGENT unpleasantly strong and bitter in smell or taste **2.** BITTER sharp or bitter in tone or character [Early 18thC. Formed from the Latin stem *acri-* "sharp, pungent," modeled on ACID (which has the same Indo-European ancestor).] —**a·crid·i·ty** /ə kríddətee/ *n.* —**ac·rid·ly** /ákrədlee/ *adv.* —**ac·rid·ness** *n.*

ac·ri·dine /ákrə deen, -din/ *n.* a colorless crystalline solid used in manufacturing dyes and pharmaceuticals. Formula: $C_{13}H_9N$. [Late 19thC. From German *Acridin,* from the Latin stem *acri-* (see ACRID).]

ac·ri·fla·vine /àkrə fláy veen, -fláyvin/ *n.* an orange-brown crystalline solid used in solution as an antiseptic. Formula: $C_{14}H_{14}N_3Cl$.

ac·ri·mo·ni·ous /àkrə mónee əs/ *adj.* full of or displaying anger and resentment —**ac·ri·mo·ni·ous·ly** *adv.* —**ac·ri·mo·ni·ous·ness** *n.*

ac·ri·mo·ny /ákrə mōnee/ *n.* bitterness and resentment, especially in speech, attitude, or tone [Mid-16thC. Directly or via French, from Latin *acrimonia,* from the stem *acri-* (see ACRID).]

acro- *prefix.* top, tip, height ○ *acrocentric* ○ *acrophobia* [From Greek *akros* "extreme, topmost." Ultimately from an Indo-European base meaning "sharp, pointed," which is also the ancestor of English *edge, acute, acid,* and *acme.*]

ac·ro·bat /ákrə bàt/ *n.* **1.** GYMNAST ENTERTAINER a performer of gymnastic feats as entertainment **2.** FACILE CHANGER OF OWN OPINIONS somebody whose opinions or positions change readily to suit the circumstances [Early 19thC. Via French from, ultimately, Greek *akrobatos* "walking on tiptoe," from *akros* (see ACRO-) + *bainein* "to walk" (source of English *base* and *basis*).] —**ac·ro·bat·ic** /àkrə báttik/ *adj.* —**ac·ro·bat·i·cal·ly** *adv.*

ac·ro·bat·ics /àkrə báttiks/ *n.* (*takes a singular or plural verb*) **1.** GYMNASTICS the skill or performance routines of an acrobat **2.** ACTIVITY REQUIRING AGILITY an activity that requires great skill or agility **3.** VIRTUOSO PERFORMANCE performance of something that is marked by virtuosic skill ○ *verbal acrobatics in her closing argument*

ac·ro·cen·tric /àkrō séntrik/ *adj.* used to describe a chromosome that has arms of unequal length because the structure at which the two arms join (**centromere**) is located toward one end. ◊ **acentric**

ac·ro·ceph·a·ly /àkrō séffəlee/ *n.* = **oxycephaly** —**ac·ro·ce·phal·ic** /àkrō sə fállik/ *adj.* —**ac·ro·ceph·a·lous** /-séffələss/ *adj.*

ac·ro·dont /ákrə dònt/ *adj.* used to describe the teeth of some reptiles that have no roots and are joined to the jawbone, or reptiles with teeth of this type

ac·ro·lect /ákrə lèkt/ *n.* the language variety among a group of related varieties that is closest to the standard form of the language

a·cro·le·in /ə królee in/ *n.* a colorless poisonous

pungent aldehyde used in manufacturing chemicals and pharmaceuticals. Formula: CH_2:CHCHO.

ac·ro·lith /ákrə lìth/ *n.* a statue, especially in ancient Greece, with only the hands, feet, and head made in stone, the body being wooden

ac·ro·meg·a·ly /àkrō méggəlee/ *n.* a disease of adults that is caused by overproduction of growth hormones, resulting in abnormal enlargement of the bones of the hands, feet, jaw, nose, and ribs —**ac·ro·me·gal·ic** /àkrō mə gállik/ *adj.*

a·cro·mi·on /ə krṓmee òn, -ən/ (*plural* **-a** /-ə/) *n.* a bony projection from the outer end of the spine of the shoulder blade, to which the collarbone is attached [Late 16thC. From Greek *akrōmion*, from *akros* (see ACRO-) + *ōmos* "shoulder."]

ac·ro·nym /ákrənim/ *n.* a word formed from the initials or other parts of several words, e.g., "NATO," from the initial letters of "North Atlantic Treaty Organization" [Mid-20thC. Literally "tip-name."] —**ac·ro·nym·ic** /àkrə nímmik/ *adj.* —**a·cron·y·mous** /ə krónnəməss/ *adj.*

WORD KEY: USAGE

See Usage note at ***abbreviation.***

a·crop·e·tal /ə króppət'l/ *adj.* used to describe leaves or flowers that grow in order from the base of a plant or stem toward the apex. ◊ **basipetal** —**a·crop·e·tal·ly** *adv.*

ac·ro·pho·bi·a /àkrə fṓbee ə/ *n.* an abnormal fear of being in high places —**ac·ro·pho·bic** *adj.*

a·crop·o·lis /ə króppəliss/ *n.* the fortified citadel of a city in ancient Greece [Early 17thC. From Greek *akropolis*.]

A·crop·o·lis /ə króppəliss/ *n.* the ancient citadel of Athens in Greece that was the religious focus of the city. It contains the remains of several classical temples, including the Parthenon.

ac·ro·some /ákrə sṑm/ *n.* a structure at the end of a sperm cell that releases enzymes to digest the cell membrane of an egg, enabling the sperm to penetrate the egg

a·cross /ə kráws, -króss/ CORE MEANING: a grammatical word indicating that somebody or something is on the opposite side of something or moves or reaches from one side to the other ○ (prep) *I live across the street from you.* ○ (adv) *a bridge wide enough to walk across*

1. *prep.* IN SPITE OF BOUNDARIES in such a way that boundaries or borders are transcended ○ *united across cultures* 2. *adj., adv.* SO AS TO CROSS SOMETHING in such a way as to intersect or form a cross with something ○ *placed one board across the other* 3. *prep.* THROUGHOUT all over something or somewhere ○ *all across the state* 4. *adv.* MEASURED IN WIDTH as measured from one side of something to the other ○ *about an inch across* 5. *adv.* HORIZONTALLY ON CROSSWORD in a horizontal position in a crossword puzzle ○ *couldn't find the solution to 3 across.* ◊ **down** [13thC. Via Old French *à croix* or *en croix* "transversely," literally "at cross" or "in cross," from Latin *crux* (see CROSS).]

a·cross-the-board *adj., adv.* COMPREHENSIVE affecting everyone or everything equally or proportionally ■ *adj.* WINNING IF PLACING IN A RACE wagering an equal amount to win if a horse or other competitor finishes first, second, or third

a·cros·tic /ə króstik/ *n.* a number of lines of writing, especially a poem or word puzzle, in which particular letters, e.g., the first, in each line spell a word or phrase [Late 16thC. Via French *acrostiche* from Greek *akrostikhis*, from *akros* "outermost" + *stikhos* "line of verse" (formed from *steikhein* "to go").] —**a·cros·ti·cal·ly** *adv.*

ac·ry·late res·in /ákrə làyt-/ *n.* a resin derived from acrylic acid or other related acids and used in paints, sizing, adhesives, and plastics [*Acrylate* formed from ACRYLIC]

a·cryl·ic /ə kríllik, a-/ *n.* 1. SYNTHETIC FIBER a synthetic textile fiber produced from acrylonitrile 2. SOMETHING MADE WITH ACRYLIC ACID something containing or made from acrylic acid 3. PAINT a paint containing acrylate resin, used especially in painting pictures ■ *adj.* RELATING TO ACRYLIC ACID relating to, derived from, or containing acrylic acid

a·cryl·ic ac·id *n.* a colorless corrosive acid used in the manufacture of acrylate resins. Formula: $C_3H_4O_2$.

a·cryl·ic re·sin *n.* = **acrylate resin**

ac·ry·lo·ni·trile /ákrəlō nī́t rīl, -nī́trəl, -nī́ treel/ *n.* a colorless toxic liquid used in making acrylic fibers and resins, rubber, and thermoplastics. Formula: C_3H_3N. [Late 19thC. Coined from ACRYLIC + NITRILE.]

act /akt/ *n.* 1. SOMETHING DONE something that somebody does 2. DOING SOMETHING the action of carrying something out 3. PART OF PLAY one of the main sections of a play or other dramatic performance 4. ONE OF SEVERAL PERFORMANCES a short performance, especially one that is part of a varied program or show ○ *The next act is a barbershop quartet.* 5. PERFORMER the performer or performers who take part in an act 6. PERSONAL BEHAVIOR somebody's actions or behavior considered as entertainment or used as an assessment of that person's worth (*informal*) ○ *a class act* 7. PRETENSE behavior that is intended to impress or deceive other people 8. POL STATEMENT OF INSTRUCTION REGARDING LAW a record or statement of the decision made by a law-making or judicial body such as Congress 9. FORMAL RECORD a formal written record of the proceedings of a society, committee, or elected group 10. PHILOS SOMETHING DONE INTENTIONALLY something brought about by human will ■ *v.* (**act·ed, act·ing, acts**) 1. *vi.* DO SOMETHING to do something to change a situation, e.g., to solve a problem or prevent one arising 2. *vti.* BEHAVE IN CERTAIN WAY to adopt a particular way of behaving ○ *You've been acting funny all morning.* ○ *Stop acting the fool.* ○ *"I even liked him when he was "difficult" and official, because I thought I knew why he acted like that."* (Paul Scott, *The Jewel in the Crown*; 1966) 3. *vi.* PRETEND to behave in a way intended to impress or deceive other people 4. *vi.* FUNCTION AS SOMETHING to serve a particular purpose or perform a particular function ○ *The ozone layer acts as a barrier against harmful radiation.* 5. *vi.* REPLACE SOMEBODY to be a substitute for somebody or something else ○ *Since the director cannot attend, his deputy will act for him.* 6. *vi.* HAVE AN EFFECT to create, produce, or bring about an effect or result ○ *Once the medicine acts, you'll feel better.* 7. *vti.* PLAY A ROLE to play the part of a character in a dramatic performance ○ *a chance to act Othello* 8. *vi.* BE ACTOR to pursue a career in films or drama 9. *vti.* PERFORM SOMETHING OR BE PERFORMED to stage a dramatic performance, or be capable of being staged ○ *The company will act a different play tomorrow night.* [14thC. Directly or via French *acte* from Latin *actus* and *actum* "public transaction," both from the past participle stem of *agere* "to do" (source of English *agent* and *prodigal*).] —**act·a·ble** *adj.* ◇ **a hard** *or* **tough act to follow** somebody or something that sets a standard difficult to reach by others who come later ◇ **catch somebody in the act** to see or meet somebody just as he or she is doing something, especially something wrong ◇ **clean up your act** to improve your behavior ◇ **get in on the act** to join in something in order to share in its success or profit (*informal*) ◇ **get your act together** to do something to become more organized (*informal*)

WORD KEY: USAGE

act or **action**? Both ***act*** and ***action*** mean "something done," but ***action*** tends to emphasize the process of doing whereas ***act*** denotes the deed itself: *Terrorist action has increased. It was an act of terrorism.* ***Acts*** are more often associated with people, whereas ***actions*** can refer to machines (especially to denote the way a machine works).

act on, act up·on *vi.* 1. DO AS SUGGESTED to be guided by somebody's advice or suggestion 2. HAVE AN EFFECT to have an effect on something

act out *vt.* 1. PERFORM SOMETHING to perform something or portray it in action 2. PSYCHIAT MISBEHAVE TO EXPRESS FEELING to express a negative feeling or impulse by behaving in a socially unacceptable way

act up *vi.* to cause trouble or pain

Act·ae·on /ak tée ən/ *n.* in Greek mythology, a hunter who was turned into a stag after inadvertently catching sight of the goddess Artemis bathing

ACTH *n.* a hormone produced by the pituitary gland that stimulates the adrenal cortex to produce steroid hormones. Full form **adrenocorticotropic hormone**

ac·tin /áktin/ *n.* a protein that is essential for cell movement and the maintenance of cell shape. It is a constituent of the structure of cells and muscle tissue and combines with myosin during muscle contraction. [Mid-20thC. Formed from Latin *actus* (see ACT).]

actin- *prefix.* = **actino-** (*used before vowels*)

ac·ti·nal /áktənəl/ *adj.* 1. RELATING TO MARINE ANIMAL'S MOUTH AREA used to describe the side of a marine animal such as a jellyfish or sea anemone from which the arms or tentacles radiate, or on which the mouth area is situated 2. WITH TENTACLES with rays or tentacles

act·ing /ákting/ *n.* PERFORMING IN PLAYS the art, profession, or performance of an actor ■ *adj.* 1. TEMPORARY carrying out certain duties or doing somebody else's job temporarily ○ *the acting manager* 2. WITH DIRECTIONS FOR STAGING including directions in a play's text to be used in staging a performance ○ *a copy of the acting edition of the play*

ac·tin·i·an /ak tínee ən/ *n.* a sea anemone (*technical*) [Late 19thC. Formed from modern Latin *Actinia*, genus name, from Greek *aktin-* "ray," from its radial form.]

ac·tin·ic /ak tínik/ *adj.* relating to radiation such as ultraviolet radiation that produces a chemical effect —**ac·tin·i·cal·ly** *adv.*

ac·tin·ide /áktə nīd/ *n.* chemical element in the series of radioactive elements beginning with actinium and ending with lawrencium [Mid-20thC. Formed from ACTINIUM, on the model of LANTHANIDE.]

ac·tin·ism /áktənizəm/ *n.* the property of radiation that makes it possible to effect photochemical changes

ac·tin·i·um /ak tínee əm/ *n.* a radioactive silvery white metallic chemical element found in pitchblende, and used as a source of alpha rays. Symbol **Ac** [Early 20thC. Formed from the Greek stem *aktin-* "ray."]

actino-, **actin-** *prefix.* 1. radial ○ *actinomorphic* 2. radiation [From Greek *aktin-*, the stem of *aktis* "ray of light"]

ac·tin·o·lite /ak tínə līt/ *n.* a green or grayish green mineral consisting of calcium magnesium iron silicate. It is a member of the amphibole group.

ac·ti·no·mere /ak tínə meer/ *n.* ZOOL = **antimere**

ac·ti·nom·e·ter /àktə nómmətər/ *n.* a device for measuring the intensity of radiation, especially that from the Sun —**ac·ti·no·met·ric** /àktənō méttrik/ *adj.* —**ac·ti·nom·e·try** /àktə nómmətree/ *n.*

ac·ti·no·mor·phic /àktənō máwrfik/, **ac·ti·no·mor·phous** /-máwrfəs/ *adj.* spreading out symmetrically around a central point and so making identical halves when divided along any vertical axis. Tulips and starfish are actinomorphic. —**ac·ti·no·mor·phy** /áktənō mawrfee/ *n.*

ac·ti·no·my·cete /àktənō mī́ seet, -mī seét/ *n.* a rod-shaped or filamentous bacterium belonging to a large group that includes some that cause diseases and some that are the sources of antibiotics. Order: Actinomycetales. [Early 20thC. Back-formation from modern Latin *actinomycetes*, coined from ACTINO- + Greek *mukēs* "fungus."] —**ac·ti·no·my·ce·tous** *adj.*

ac·ti·no·my·cin /àktənō mī́sin/ *n.* an antibiotic used mainly to treat childhood cancers

ac·ti·no·u·ra·ni·um /àktənōyoo ráynee əm/ *n.* the only naturally occurring radioactive isotope of uranium that is naturally fissile. It is used in nuclear reactors and weapons.

ac·tion /ákshən/ *n.* 1. DOING SOMETHING TOWARD GOAL the process of doing something in order to achieve a purpose 2. SOMETHING DONE something that somebody or something does 3. MOVEMENT the way somebody or something moves or works, or the movement itself ○ *the action of a piston* 4. VERVE energetic activity ○ *a woman of action* 5. LAW LEGAL PROCEEDINGS legal proceedings in a court to obtain compensation for something or to enforce a right ○ *decided not to take action* 6. EVENTS the important events in any form of narrative composition such as a novel or film 7. FUNCTION OR INFLUENCE the way in which something functions, or the effect it produces ○ *the action of water on stone* 8. MIL FIGHTING DURING WAR a small battle, or the fighting that takes place during a war ○ *wounded in action* ○ *a campaign of brief actions* 9. EXCITING OR PROFITABLE ACTIVITY involvement in something that brings excitement, profit, or pleasure (*informal*) ○ *a piece of the action* 10. OPERATING MECHANISM the operating parts of a mechanism or instrument, e.g., a watch or piano 11. MUSIC SPACE UNDER STRINGS the space between the fingerboard and strings of a string instrument such as a violin or a guitar 12. PHYS FORCE the force applied to a body 13. PHYS PROPERTY OF SYSTEM USED IN DYNAMICS twice the average kinetic energy of a system in a given time multiplied by the time 14. PHILOSOPHY **VOLUNTARY BEHAVIOR** voluntary or intended behavior, as opposed to forced behavior ■ *interj.* CINEMA **START PERFORMING** a command from a film director telling actors to begin acting as filming has begun

WORD KEY: USAGE

Can **action** be used as a verb? The use of ***action*** as a verb, as in *Criticism was leveled at the way the operation was actioned*, has crept into ordinary usage from business jargon. It is disliked by many people because they maintain, with good reason, that simpler words such as **do**, **achieve**, and **complete** are just as effective and a good deal less pretentious. The use is particularly unwelcome in cases such as **to action dismissal**, as in *Dismissal will be actioned if any employee violates this rule*, when a simple verb is available (*Any employee who violates this rule will be dismissed.*). It is always better to use the more straightforward word when this conveys the meaning just as well.

ac·tion·a·ble /áksh'nəb'l/ *adj.* giving a basis for somebody to take legal action

ac·tion chess *n.* = **speed chess**

ac·tion·er /ákshənər/ *n.* a movie that features a great deal of usually extreme action (*informal*) ○ *a made-for-TV actioner with a little-known cast*

ac·tion group *n.* a group of people formed to achieve some purpose, e.g., to support or oppose a proposal

ac·tion paint·ing *n.* a technique used by artists of the Abstract Expressionism movement in which paintings are created by splashing, dripping, spattering, or smearing paint

ac·tion po·ten·tial *n.* a temporary change in electrical potential that occurs between the inside and the outside of a nerve or muscle fiber when a nerve impulse is transmitted

ac·tion re·play *n. U.K.* = **Instant replay**

ac·tion sta·tions *npl. U.K.* MIL = **battle stations** ■ *interj. U.K.* MIL = **battle stations**

ac·ti·vate /áktə vàyt/ (**-vat·ed, -vat·ing, -vates**) *v.* 1. *vt.* **MAKE SOMETHING ACTIVE** to make something active, or set something in motion 2. *vi.* **BECOME ACTIVE** to become active or begin to operate 3. *vt.* PHYS **MAKE SOMETHING RADIOACTIVE** to make something radioactive 4. *vt.* CHEM **MAKE SOMETHING REACTIVE** to increase the rate of a chemical reaction, e.g., by applying heat 5. *vt.* CHEM **INCREASE POWER OF ADSORPTION** to treat a substance such as charcoal so as to increase its capacity for adsorption 6. *vt.* INDUST **PURIFY WITH AIR** to purify sewage by aerating it 7. *vt.* **MOBILIZE MILITARY** to set up or mobilize a military unit ○ *activate the National Guard* —**ac·ti·va·tion** /áktə váysh'n/ *n.* —**ac·ti·va·tor** /-vaytər/ *n.*

ac·ti·vat·ed car·bon, **ac·ti·vat·ed char·coal** *n.* a highly adsorbent powdered or granular form of carbon, used to purify liquids and gases through adsorption, to extract chemicals, to recover solvents, and as an antidote to some poisons

ac·ti·vat·ed sludge *n.* aerated sewage containing microorganisms added to untreated sewage to purify it by accelerating its bacterial decomposition

ac·ti·va·tion en·er·gy *n.* the energy needed to make molecules of a substance take part in a chemical reaction

ac·tive /áktiv/ *adj.* 1. **MOVING ABOUT** moving about, working, or doing something as opposed to resting or sleeping 2. **BUSY** full of or involved in busy activity ○ *an active life* 3. **DOING SOMETHING** carrying out some action or process, or able to do so ○ *an active ingredient* 4. **SHOWING ENERGY AND INVOLVEMENT** marked by involvement, energy, or action ○ *played an active part* 5. **NEEDING AND USING ENERGY** requiring a lot of energy and movement ○ *active pastimes* 6. GEOL **NOT EXTINCT** used to describe a volcano that is not extinct and still erupts occasionally 7. GRAM **RELATING TO ROLE OF VERB'S SUBJECT** used to describe a verb whose subject is the person or thing performing the action described by the verb. ◊ **passive** 8. ASTRON **SHOWING VARIABLE SURFACE FEATURES** used to describe the Sun when it is displaying large numbers of dark patches (**sunspots**) and bright patches (**faculae**) and high variability in radio-wave emissions 9. COMM **USED TO PRODUCE PROFIT** producing or being used to produce profits or dividends 10. FIN **TRADING IN LARGE VOLUME** being bought and sold in large quantities 11. FIN **INVOLVING FREQUENT TRADING** used to describe a form of portfolio management in which the manager adds value to the portfolio by frequent trades 12. ELECTRON ENG **WITH POWER SOURCE** used to describe electronic networks and components that contain a power source and are capable of operating ■ *n.* GRAM **VERB VOICE** the active voice of a verb —**ac·tive·ness** *n.*

WORD KEY: SYNONYMS

See Synonyms at ***busy***.

ac·tive du·ty, **ac·tive ser·vice** *n.* full-time service in the armed forces with full pay and benefits

ac·tive im·mu·ni·ty *n.* immunity generated by the production of antibodies within a body when it is exposed to antigens

ac·tive-ma·trix dis·play *n.* a flat liquid-crystal display with high color resolution that is particularly suited to use in laptop and notebook computers

ac·tive ser·vice *n.* = **active duty**

ac·tive site *n.* the part of an enzyme or antibody molecule that reacts with the substance the enzyme acts on (**substrate**) or the substance that gives rise to the antibody (**antigen**)

ac·tive trans·port *n.* a process in which energy is used to move a chemical substance across a cellular membrane from a region of low concentration to a region of high concentration

ac·tive vo·cab·u·lar·y (*plural* **ac·tive vo·cab·u·lar·ies**) *n.* the range of words that somebody normally uses in speech or writing, as opposed to words he or she understands when used by others

ac·tiv·ism /áktə vìzzəm/ *n.* vigorous and sometimes aggressive action in pursuing a political or social end —**act·i·vist** *n., adj.* —**ac·tiv·is·tic** *adj.*

ac·tiv·i·ty /ak tívvətee, -itee/ (*plural* **-ties**) *n.* 1. **SOMETHING SOMEBODY DOES** something that somebody takes part in or does (*often used in the plural*) 2. **PHYSICAL EXERCISE** energetic physical movement or exercise 3. **STATE OF DOING SOMETHING** work, movement, or whatever somebody or something is doing ○ *Activity in the newsroom has reached fever pitch.* 4. CHEM **MEASURE OF POTENTIAL FOR CHEMICAL REACTION** a measure of the ability of a chemical substance to undergo a chemical reaction 5. **NATURAL PROCESS** a process or function that takes place naturally in a living organism ○ *activities such as eating or sleeping* 6. EDUC **LEARNING EXPERIENCE** an educational exercise designed to provide direct experience of something ○ *an activity to accompany the geography lesson* 7. NUCLEAR PHYS **RADIOACTIVITY** radioactivity (*technical*) Symbol *A*

act of con·tri·tion *n.* a short prayer of penitence

act of faith *n.* an action motivated by belief in something for which there is no concrete evidence

act of God *n.* a sudden uncontrollable event produced by natural forces, e.g., an earthquake or a tornado

ac·to·my·o·sin /áktə mī́ əsən/ *n.* a protein complex of actin and myosin that is found in muscle cells and that is partly responsible for muscular contraction

ac·tor /áktər/ *n.* 1. **PERFORMER IN PLAYS** somebody who acts in plays, movies, or television 2. **SOMEBODY WHO PRETENDS** somebody who pretends to be somebody else or to feel something so as to impress or deceive

ac·tress /áktrəs, -tris, -tres/ *n.* 1. **PERFORMER IN PLAYS** a woman or girl who acts in plays, movies, or television 2. **WOMAN WHO PRETENDS** a woman or girl who behaves in a way intended to deceive or impress others

Acts of the A·pos·tles *n.* the fifth book of the New Testament, in which the resurrection of Jesus Christ and the early history of the Christian church are described (*takes a singular verb*) See table at **Bible**

ac·tu·al /ákchoo əl/ *adj.* 1. **REAL** real and existing as fact ○ *Is that her actual title?* 2. **USED FOR EMPHASIS** used for emphasis, e.g., to stress that somebody or something being referred to is genuinely the person or thing involved ○ *This is the actual place where Lincoln stood.* 3. **EXISTING NOW** existing or occurring at the moment ○ *actual as opposed to projected income*

WORD KEY: USAGE

Actual should normally be used when it contrasts with some other condition such as "ideal" or "imagined" rather than as a mere intensifier often without any real meaning: *He wanted to know what actual damage had been done.* In this sentence ***actual*** could be removed without any significant change to the sense. But in the sentence *The actual total was much higher*, ***actual*** is legitimately used to mark a contrast with projected or estimated totals.

ac·tu·al·i·ty /ákchoo állətee/ (*plural* **-ties**) *n.* 1. **WHAT IN FACT IS** something that is real, as opposed to what is expected, intended, or feared ○ *Let's deal with actualities.* 2. **EVERYTHING THAT REALLY EXISTS OR HAPPENS** everything that does or could exist or happen in real life

ac·tu·al·ize /ákchoo-/ (**-ized, -iz·ing, -iz·es**) *vt.* 1. **MAKE REAL** to make something real or actual, or make something come about ○ *expectations actualized by deeds* 2. **PORTRAY** to portray or represent something realistically —**ac·tu·al·i·za·tion** /àkchoo ə lə záysh'n/ *n.*

ac·tu·al·ly /ákchoo əlee/ *adv.* used to emphasize that something really is so or really exists, e.g., when it may be hard to believe or contrasts with what has already been said ○ *He's actually over 35, although he looks much younger.*

WORD KEY: USAGE

Actually, like ***actual***, is used most effectively when it contrasts with what is theoretical or only apparent: *It sounds difficult but it's actually quite straightforward.* It is regarded as poor style to use it as a kind of sentence filler with no real meaning, although this is more acceptable in informal conversation, in which such fillers help to maintain the flow and balance of the sentence and to avoid bluntness: *Actually, I prefer her to her cousin.*

ac·tu·ar·i·al /àkchoo áiree əl, àkshoo-, àkchoo-/ *adj.* 1. **RELATING TO CALCULATION OF RISK** relating to the statistical calculation of risk or life expectancy for insurance purposes 2. **RELATING TO ACTUARIES** relating to actuaries and their work

ac·tu·ar·i·al sci·ence *n.* the branch of statistics that deals with the calculation of risk, life expectancy, and insurance premiums

ac·tu·ar·y /ákchoo eree, ákshoo-/ (*plural* **-ies**) *n.* a statistician who calculates insurance premiums, risks, dividends, and annuity rates

ac·tu·ate /ákchoo àyt/ (**-at·ed, -at·ing, -ates**) *vt.* 1. **MAKE ACT** to make somebody act or behave in a certain way (*often used in the passive*) ○ *actuated by self-interest* 2. **MAKE WORK** to make a device move or start working (*formal*) [Late 16thC. From medieval Latin *actuatus*, the past participle of *actuare* "to cause something to be done," from Latin *actus* (see ACT).] —**ac·tu·a·tion** /àkchoo áysh'n/ *n.* —**ac·tu·a·tor** /-àyter/ *n.*

ACT-UP /ákt up/ *n.* an AIDS activist organization in the United States and Britain. Full form **Aids Coalition To Unleash Power**

a·cu·i·ty /ə kyoo͝ atee/ *n.* keenness of hearing, sight, or intellect [Mid-16thC. Directly or via French *acuité* from medieval Latin *acuitas*, from Latin *acuere* (see ACUTE).]

a·cu·le·ate /ə kyoo͝lee ət/ *adj.* 1. **STINGING** used to describe an insect that has a sting 2. **PRICKLY** used to describe a plant or plant part that has prickles [Mid-17thC. From Latin *aculeatus*, from *aculeus*, "a small needle," from *acus* (see ACUTE).]

a·cu·men /ə kyoo͝mən, ákyə-/ *n.* quick insight, or the ability to make quick accurate judgments of people or situations ○ *political acumen* [Late 16thC. From Latin, "point, sharpness," formed from *acuere* "to sharpen."]

a·cu·mi·nate *adj.* /ə kyoo͝mənət, -nayt/ used to describe leaves that taper to a sharp point [Late 16thC. From late Latin *acuminatus*, the past participle of *acuminare* "to sharpen to a point," from Latin *acumen* (see ACUMEN).]

ac·u·pres·sure /ákyoo preshər/ *n.* a form of alternative therapy similar to acupuncture that uses manual pressure rather than needles [Mid-19thC. "Acu-" from ACUPUNCTURE.]

ac·u·punc·ture /ákyoo pungkchər/ *n.* a method, originally from China, of treating disorders by inserting needles into the skin at points where the flow of energy is thought to be blocked (**meridians**) [Late 17thC. "Acu-" from Latin *acus* "needle."] —**ac·u·punc·tur·ist** *n.*

a·cute /ə kyoot/ *adj.* 1. **VERY GREAT OR BAD** extremely serious, severe, or painful ○ *an acute financial crisis* 2. **PERCEPTIVE** keenly perceptive and intelligent ○ *an acute grasp of foreign affairs* 3. **SENSITIVE** very powerful and sensitive to detail ○ *acute eyesight* 4. GEOM **LESS THAN 90 DEGREES** used to describe an angle that is less than 90 degrees 5. GEOM **WITH ANGLES LESS THAN 90 DEGREES** used to describe a triangle that has three

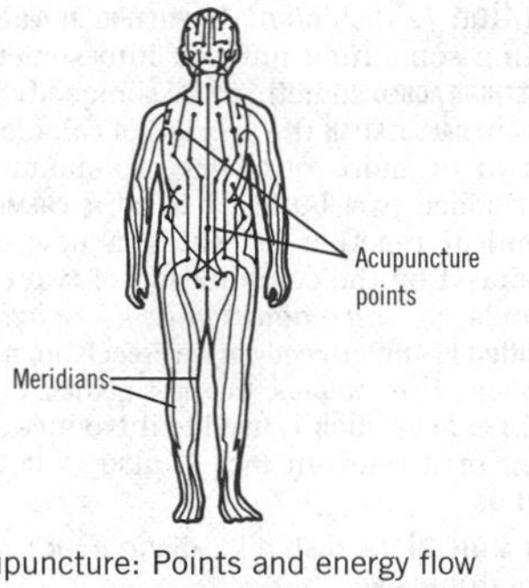

Acupuncture: Points and energy flow paths (meridians) in the human body

internal angles of less than 90 degrees **6.** MED **SEVERE AND OF SHORT DURATION** used to describe a disease that is brief, severe, and quickly comes to a crisis **7.** BOT **POINTED** used to describe leaves that end in a short narrow point ■ *n.* **a·cute, a·cute ac·cent** LANG **MARK ABOVE LETTER** in some languages, a mark placed above a letter, as in *á* and *ó*, to show it is sounded in a particular way. In Spanish, the acute indicates a stressed syllable, as in *cupón*, in French a particular pronunciation of *e*, as in *blé*, and in classical Greek a vowel sounded at a higher pitch. [14thC. From Latin *acutus* (source of English *ague*), the past participle of *acuere* "to sharpen," from *acus* "needle" (source of English *acuity* and *cute*.] —**a·cute·ly** *adv.* —**a·cute·ness** *n.*

a·cute dose *n.* a fatal amount of radiation received over a short period

a·cy·clic /ay sī́klik, -síklik/ *adj.* **1.** CHEM **WITH ATOMS FORMING CHAIN STRUCTURE** having a molecular structure in which the atoms are arranged in a string whose ends do not meet (**open chain**) rather than being arranged in a ring **2.** BOT **WITH PARTS IN SPIRAL ARRANGEMENT** used to describe flowers that have their parts arranged in a spiral rather than a whorl

a·cy·clo·vir /ay sī́klə veer/ *n.* an antiviral drug used to treat genital herpes and cold sores. It works by interfering with viral reproduction, thereby reducing infection.

ac·yl /áy s'l/ *adj.* relating to or containing the chemical group derived from a carboxylic acid, e.g. the acetyl group

a·cyl·a·tion /ày sə láysh'n/ *n.* the introduction of an acyl group into a chemical compound

ad[1] /ad/ *n.* an advertisement [Mid-19thC. Shortening.]

ad[2] *abbr.* TENNIS advantage

AD *abbr.* Alzheimer's disease

a.d. *abbr.* BANKING after date

A.D. *adv.* used to indicate a date that is a specified number of years after the birth of Jesus Christ. Full form **anno Domini.** ◊ **CE, BC, BCE**

WORD KEY: USAGE

Before or after the date? Because of its meaning, **A.D.** is traditionally put before the numeral to which it relates, so that it makes grammatical sense if understood in its expanded form: A.D. *1453*. In practice, **A.D.** is often put after the numeral, being then understood as a word in its own right, and it is normally acceptable to put it after the identification of a century, as in *the fifth century* A.D.

ad-, ac-, af-, ag-, at-, ap- *prefix.* **1.** to, toward ○ *adsorb* ○ *advance* **2.** near ○ *adrenal* [From Latin *ad* "toward, near." Ultimately from an Indo-European word that is also the ancestor of English *at*.]

-ad *suffix.* to, toward ○ *cephalad* [From Latin *ad* (see AD-)]

A·da /áydə/ *n.* a high-level general-purpose programming language used for military and other complex programming applications. Ada programs are highly readable and therefore easy to maintain. [Late 20thC. Named for the English mathematician Augusta *Ada* Byron, Countess of Lovelace (1815–52).]

ADA *abbr.* **1.** Americans with Disabilities Act **2.** American Dental Association

ad·age /áddij/ *n.* a traditional saying that expresses something taken as a general truth ○ *"Oysters are said to be best in months containing the letter R, according to an old adage."* (Barbara Sturm, *Living Page*; 1997) [Mid-16thC. Via French, from Latin *adagium*, from *ad* "to" + a variant of *aio* "I say."]

a·da·gio /ə daájee ō, -zhee ō, -j ō/ *adv.* **SLOWLY** slowly, but faster than lento (*used as a musical direction*) ■ *n.* (*plural* **adagios**) **MUSICAL PIECE** a movement or piece of music played or marked adagio [Late 17thC. From Italian, literally "at ease."] —**a·da·gio** *adj.*

Ad·am /áddəm/ *n.* in the Bible, the first man, created by God ◇ **not know somebody from Adam** to have never met or seen somebody before

Ad·am /áddəm/, **Adolphe Charles** (1803–56) French composer who wrote sixty operas and the ballet *Giselle* (1841).

Ad·am, Robert (1728–92) British architect and interior designer who built grand neoclassical country and town houses, including Kenwood House (1768) and Osterley Park (1778).

ad·a·mant /áddəmənt, -mant/ *adj.* **SET IN OPINION** very determined and not influenced by appeals to reconsider ○ *"They did their best to persuade her, but Mother was adamant."* (Gerald Durrell, *Birds, Beasts and Relatives*; 1969) ■ *n.* **LEGENDARY STONE** a extremely hard legendary stone, sometimes identified as diamond or lodestone (*archaic*) [Pre-12thC. Via Old French *adamaunt* and the Latin stem *adamant-* "adamant, steel, diamond," from Greek *adamas*, literally "unbreakable," from *daman* "to break down."] —**ad·a·mant·ly** *adv.*

ad·a·man·tine /àddə mánt een, -īn, -'n/ *adj.* (*literary*) **1. UNYIELDING** extremely hard or unyielding **2. HARD AND BRILLIANT** like a diamond in hardness and brilliance

Abigail Adams

Ad·ams /áddəmz/, **Abigail** (1744–1818) U.S. feminist. She married John Adams, second president of the United States. Her letters to him were published by her grandson.

Ad·ams, Ansel (1902–84) U.S. photographer, noted for his dramatic photographs of the American landscape.

Ad·ams, Gerry (*b.* 1948) Northern Irish politician and president of Sinn Fein, the political wing of the Irish Republican Army. He was elected to the British Parliament (1983–92, 1997) but declined to take his seat. He is seen as having played an important part in the negotiations to end violence in Northen Ireland.

Ad·ams, Henry (1838–1918) U.S. historian. His works include *History of the United States during the Administrations of Jefferson and Madison* (1889–91). His autobiography *The Education of Henry Adams* was published privately (1904) and later for a general readership (1918) and won a posthumous Pulitzer Prize (1919).

Ad·ams, John (1735–1826) U.S. statesman and second president of the United States. He served from 1797 until 1801 and was one of the committee that drafted the Declaration of Independence (1776).

John Adams

John Quincy Adams

Ad·ams, John Quincy (1767–1848) U.S. statesman and sixth president of the United States. He served from 1825 until 1829. As secretary of state to President James Monroe (1817–25), he formulated the Monroe Doctrine opposing foreign intervention in the American continents.

Ad·ams, Samuel (1722–1803) American revolutionary leader. He was a signatory to the Declaration of Independence (1776), and governor of Massachusetts (1794–97).

Ad·am's ap·ple *n.* the hard lump at the front of the throat formed by the thyroid cartilage of the larynx [From the belief that it results from the forbidden apple being stuck in Adam's throat]

Ad·am's nee·dle *n.* a North American yucca cultivated for its spiny pointed leaves and spikes of white flowers. Latin name: *Yucca filamentosa.* [From the spines on its leaves, in allusion to Adam and Eve sewing fig leaves together to cover themselves (Genesis 3:7)]

A·da·na /ádənə, ə dáná/ city in southern Turkey and capital of the province of the same name. Population: 1,047,300 (1994 est.).

a·dapt /ə dápt/ (**a·dapt·ed, a·dapt·ing, a·dapts**) *v.* **1.** *vti.* **CHANGE SOMETHING TO MEET REQUIREMENTS** to change, or change something, to suit different conditions or a different purpose ○ *adapted the novel for radio* **2.** *vti.* **ADJUST TO SOMETHING** to make or become used to a new environment or different conditions **3.** *vt.* **REWRITE BOOK OR PLAY** to rewrite a book or a play so that it can be made into a film or a television program [15thC. Via French *adapter* and Latin *adaptare*, literally "to fit to," from, ultimately, *aptus*, "attached" (source of English *apt*).]

a·dapt·a·ble /ə dáptəb'l/ *adj.* **1. CHANGING EASILY** able to adjust easily to changes and new conditions **2. ADJUSTABLE** capable of being modified to suit different purposes or conditions ○ *adaptable for different voltages* —**a·dapt·a·bil·i·ty** /ə dàptə bíllətee/ *n.* —**a·dapt·a·ble·ness** /ə dáptəb'lnəs/ *n.*

ad·ap·ta·tion /à dap táysh'n, àddəp-/, **ad·ap·tion** /ə dápshən/ *n.* **1. ADAPTING** the process or state of changing to fit new circumstances or conditions, or the resulting change **2. SOMETHING ADAPTED TO FIT NEED** something that has been modified for a purpose ○ *a film adaptation of a novel* **3.** BIOL **CHANGE TO SUIT ENVIRONMENT** the development of physical and behavioral characteristics that allow organisms to survive and reproduce in their habitats **4.** PHYSIOL **DIMINISHING SENSORY RESPONSE** the diminishing response of a sense organ to a sustained stimulus —**ad·ap·ta·tion·al** *adj.* —**ad·ap·ta·tion·al·ly** *adv.*

a·dapt·er /ə dáptər/, **a·dapt·or** *n.* **1. ELECTRIC CONNECTOR** a device used to connect an electrical appliance to a power source with a different voltage or a different plug shape, or several appliances to one outlet **2. DEVICE FOR CONNECTING UNLIKE PARTS** a device for connecting two nonmatching parts **3. SOMEBODY OR SOMETHING THAT ADAPTS** somebody who or something that changes something or is able to adjust to suit different conditions

a·dap·tion *n.* = **adaptation**

a·dap·tive /ə dáptiv/ *adj.* able to be adjusted for use in different conditions —**a·dap·tive·ly** *adv.*

a·dap·tive ra·di·a·tion *n.* the developmental diversification of a group of organisms from an original ancestral form or group into several different forms that adapt to different environments

a·dap·tive re·use *n.* a use of a building that is different from its original or previous use, often involving conversion work

a·dap·tor *n.* = **adapter**

A·dar /ə dáar/ *n.* in the Jewish calendar, the sixth month of the civil year and the twelfth month of the religious year. It is 29 or 30 days long. In leap years it is renamed Adar Rishon. [14thC. From Hebrew *ădār*.]

A·dar Rish·on /-ríshon/ *n.* in the Jewish calendar, the name given to the month of Adar during a leap year, when an additional month **(Adar Sheni)** follows it

A·dar She·ni /-sháynee/ *n.* a thirteenth month added to the Jewish calendar after Adar in leap years. It is 29 days long. [*Sheni* from Hebrew *šēnī*, "second"]

a·dax·i·al /ad áksee əl/ *adj.* used to describe the upper side of a leaf or other surface that faces toward the stem. ◊ **abaxial**

ADC *abbr.* **1.** Aid to Dependent Children **2. ADC, a.d.c.** Air Defense Command **3.** analog-to-digital converter

Ad·cock /ád kòk/, **Fleur** (*b.* 1934) New Zealand poet, author of *The Inner Harbour* (1979). Full name **Kareen Fleur Adcock**

add /ad/ (**add·ed, add·ing, adds**) *v.* **1.** *vt.* UNITE OR COMBINE THINGS to put something into or join something onto something else ○ *I'll add your name to the list.* **2.** *vti.* MATH FIGURE TOTAL to calculate the total of two or more numbers or amounts **3.** *vt.* PUT IN INGREDIENT to mix in an ingredient that is part of a recipe ○ *Add six eggs to the flour.* **4.** *vt.* INTRODUCE SOMETHING to give something a particular quality or more of a particular quality ○ *The flowers add a touch of cheerfulness.* **5.** *vi.* INTENSIFY SOMETHING to increase the effect of something ○ *This adds to our problems.* **6.** *vt.* SUPPLEMENT SPEECH OR WRITING to say or write something else after you have written or said something ○ *"Don't forget your umbrella," she added.* [14thC. From Latin *addere*, from *dare* "to give" (source of English *data, edit*, and *vendor*).] —**add·a·ble** *adj.*

add up *v.* **1.** *vti.* MAKE TOTAL to calculate the total of two or more numbers or amounts, or reach a total **2.** *vi.* MAKE SENSE to make a sensible or believable story or explanation ○ *His story just doesn't add up.* **3.** *vi.* FORM LARGE AMOUNT to make a large total or amount ○ *If everyone gives a little, it soon adds up.*

add up to *vi.* to amount to or result in a particular sum or thing

ADD *abbr.* attention deficit disorder

add. *abbr.* **1.** addendum **2.** MATH addition **3.** address

Ad·dams /áddəmz/, **Charles** (1912–88) U.S. cartoonist, noted for his humorous and macabre drawings in *The New Yorker* magazine.

Ad·dams, Jane (1860–1935) U.S. reformer and feminist. A Nobel peace laureate (1931), she founded Hull House, Chicago, (1889) ultimately the largest settlement house.

Addax

ad·dax /ádd aks/ (*plural* **-dax·es** *or* **-dax**) *n.* an antelope that has long spiraling horns and lives in desert regions of North Africa. Latin name: *Addax nasomaculatus.* [Late 17thC. From Latin, from an African word.]

ad·dend /ádd end, ə dénd/ *n.* a number that is to be added [Late 17thC. Shortening of ADDENDUM.]

ad·den·dum /ə déndəm/ (*plural* **-da** /-də/) *n.* **1.** SOMETHING ADDED something that is or has been added **2.** SUPPLEMENT a supplement to a book or magazine [Late 17thC. From Latin, formed from *addere* (see ADD).]

Adder

add·er[1] /áddər/ *n.* somebody or something that adds, especially an electronic device that adds numbers

ad·der[2] /áddər/ *n.* a small venomous snake, common in Europe, that is dark gray with a black zigzag pattern on its back. Latin name: *Vipera berus.* [Old English *nǣd(d)re* "snake." The initial *n* was lost when "a nadder" was misanalyzed as "an adder." Ultimately from an Indo-European word that also produced German *Natter* "adder."]

Adder's tongue

ad·der's tongue *n.* **1.** FERN WITH POINTED FROND a fern found in the northern hemisphere that has a spore-bearing stalk at the base of a pointed frond. Genus: *Ophioglossum.* **2.** PLANTS = **dogtooth violet** [From the resemblance of the stalk to a snake's tongue]

ad·dict /áddikt/ *n.* **1.** SOMEBODY CRAVING A DRUG somebody who is physiologically or mentally dependent on a drug or other substance liable to have a damaging physiological or psychological effect **2.** ENTHUSIAST somebody who is devoted to something ○ *soap opera addicts* [Mid-16thC. From Latin *addictus*, the past participle of *addicere* "to award, devote," from *dicere* "to say" (source of English *dictionary, dictate*, and *verdict*).]

ad·dict·ed /ə díktəd/ *adj.* **1.** DEPENDENT physiologically or mentally dependent on tobacco, alcohol, or other substance **2.** VERY ENTHUSIASTIC very interested in something and devoting a lot of time to it ○ *addicted to football*

ad·dic·tion /ə díksh'n/ *n.* **1.** DRUG DEPENDENCE a state of physiological or psychological dependence on a substance, especially an illegal drug or one liable to have a damaging effect **2.** DEVOTION great interest in something to which a lot of time is devoted

ad·dic·tion·ol·o·gy /ə dikshən óllǝjee/ *n.* the study and treatment of addictions —**ad·dic·tion·ol·o·gist** *n.*

ad·dic·tive /ə díktiv/ *adj.* making somebody an addict, or able or likely to do so —**ad·dic·tive·ly** *adv.*

ad·dic·tive per·son·a·li·ty (*plural* **ad·dic·tive per·son·a·li·ties**) *n.* a personality predisposed toward becoming addicted to something

add-in *n.* = **add-on**

Ad·dis Ab·a·ba /adiss ábbəbə/ capital of Ethiopia. Population: 1,912,500 (1990).

Ad·di·son /áddis'n/ village in northeastern Illinois, west of Chicago. Population: 33,580 (1996).

Ad·di·son, Thomas (1793–1860) British physician who correctly ascribed the symptoms of Addison's disease to adrenal malfunction.

Ad·di·son's dis·ease *n.* a wasting disease characterized by bronzing of the skin, low blood pressure, and weakness. It is caused by underactivity of the adrenal glands. [Mid-19thC. Named for Thomas ADDISON.]

ad·di·tion /ə dísh'n/ *n.* **1.** PUTTING IN OR ON the act of adding something onto or into something else **2.** SOMETHING ADDED something or somebody that is added **3.** MATH CALCULATION the process of calculating the sum of two or more numbers or amounts **4.** ANNEX a part added to a building **5.** CHEM CHEMICAL REACTION a chemical reaction in which a new compound is produced by the combination of two or more compounds ○ *an addition-type reaction.* ◊ **substitution** [14thC. Directly or via French, from the Latin stem *addition-*, from *additus*, the past participle of *addere* (see ADD).] ◇ **in addition 1.** used to introduce an additional point or a relevant fact **2.** also ◇ **in addition to** as well as

ad·di·tion·al /ə dísh'n'l, -díshn'l/ *adj.* added on to something else

ad·di·tion·al·ly /ə dísh'nəlee, -díshnəlee/ *adv.* **1.** FURTHER further to what has just been said ○ *Additionally, each machine is checked hourly.* **2.** EVEN MORE to an even greater extent (*literary*) ○ *"The atmosphere of the place was heavy and moldy, being rendered additionally oppressive by the closing of the door which led into the church."* (Wilkie Collins, *The Woman in White*; 1860) **3.** ALSO as well as

ad·di·tive /áddətiv/ *n.* SOMETHING ADDED something added to something else to alter or improve it in some way, e.g., to change the color or texture of food ■ *adj.* INVOLVING ADDING SOMETHING involving or produced by addition or by the addition of something (*formal*) [Late 17thC. From late Latin *additivus*, from *additus* (see ADDITION).]

ad·di·tive i·den·ti·ty (*plural* **ad·di·tive i·den·ti·ties**) *n.* a quantity that, when added to another, leaves it unchanged. For ordinary numbers this is zero.

ad·di·tive in·verse *n.* a number or quantity that gives zero when added to another. For example, the additive inverse of 3 is –3.

ad·di·tive print·ing *n.* a process in printing in which colors are produced by adding proportionate amounts of three primary colors

ad·dle /ádd'l/ (**-dled, -dling, -dles**) *vti.* **1.** BEFUDDLE to confuse or muddle somebody, or become confused or muddled **2.** ROT to make something rotten or spoiled [Old English *adela* "filth, liquid manure." Ultimately from a prehistoric Germanic word that is also the ancestor of Dutch *aal* "liquid manure."]

ad·dle·pat·ed /ádd'l paytid/, **ad·dle·brain·ed** /-braynd/, **ad·dle·head·ed** /-hedid/ *adj.* with a mind that is muddled and confused (*dated informal*)

add-on, add-in *n.* a piece of equipment that can be added to another, e.g., a computer system, to expand its capabilities

ad·dress *n.* /ə dréss, á drèss/ **1.** PHYSICAL LOCATION the number, street name, and other information that describes where a building is or where somebody lives **2.** WRITTEN FORM OF ADDRESS the address of a person or organization when written on a letter or an item of mail **3.** FORMAL TALK a formal speech or report **4.** COMPUT NUMBER FOR LOCATION a number that specifies a location in a computer's memory ■ **ad·dress·es** *npl.* COURTSHIP attention paid to somebody that is intended as courtship (*archaic*) ■ *v.* /ə dréss/ (**-dressed, -dress·ing, -dress·es**) **1.** *vt.* WRITE DIRECTIONS ON to write or print on an item of mail details of where it is to be delivered **2.** *vt.* SPEAK OR MAKE SPEECH TO to say something to somebody, or make a speech to an audience **3.** *vr.* BEGIN JOB to set about doing some task ○ *"Through this program of action we address ourselves to putting our own national house in order"* (Franklin D. Roosevelt, *First Inaugural Address*; 1933) **4.** *vt.* DEAL WITH to face up to and deal with a problem or issue ○ *failure to address the main issue* **5.** *vt.* SPORTS, DANCE FACE to move to face or stand facing a target in a sport or a partner in a dance ○ *address the target* **6.** *vt.* GOLF AIM GOLF CLUB to take up the correct stance before hitting a golf shot ○ *address the ball* [14thC. Via Old French *adresser* and assumed Vulgar Latin *addrictiare*, literally "to direct to," from, ultimately, Latin *directus* (see DIRECT).] ◇ **of no fixed address** having no permanent place in which to live

ad·dress·a·ble /ə dréssəb'l/ *adj.* **1.** RESOLVABLE capable of being dealt with or resolved (*formal*) **2.** TELECOM ALL-CHANNEL used to describe a cable television system that allows the user to decode any broadcast channel —**ad·dress·a·bil·i·ty** /ə drèssəbílləteе/ *n.*

ad·dress·ee /àd res ée, ə drèss-/ *n.* a person or organization to whom an item of mail is to be delivered

ad·duce /ə do͞os, ə dyo͞os/ (**-duced, -duc·ing, -duc·es**) *vt.* to offer something as evidence, reason, or proof (*formal*) [15thC. From Latin *adducere* "to bring forward," from *ducere* "to lead" (source of English *abduct, duke,* and *seduce*).] —**ad·duce·a·ble** *adj.*

ad·duct /ə dúkt, a-/ *vt.* (**-duct·ed, -duct·ing, -ducts**) PULL TOWARD AXIS to pull a leg or arm toward the central line of the body or a toe or finger toward the axis of a leg or arm. ◊ **abduct** ■ *n.* CHEMICAL COMPOUND a chemical compound formed by the combination of two or more different compounds or elements in an addition-type reaction [Mid-19thC. Back-formation from ADDUCTION, which came directly or via French from the Latin stem *adduction-*, from *adductus*, the past participle of *adducere* (see ADDUCE).] —**ad·duc·tion** *n.* —**ad·duc·tive** *adj.*

ad·duc·tor /ə dúktər/ *n.* a muscle that pulls a leg or arm toward the central line of the body or a toe or finger toward the axis of a leg or arm [Early 17thC. From modern Latin, formed from Latin *adductus*, the past participle of *adducere* (see ADDUCE).]

-ade *suffix.* **1.** a sweetened drink ○ *orangeade* **2.** an action ○ *cannonade* [Via Old French from, ultimately, Latin *-ata*, feminine of *-atus* (see -ATE)]

Ad·e·laide /ádd'l àyd/ city in southeastern Australia, situated on the Gulf of St. Vincent. It was founded in 1836. Population: 978,100 (1996).

A·den /áad'n, áyd'n/ **1.** former British colony and protectorate that became part of South Yemen in 1967 and is now part of Yemen. Area: 75 sq. mi./195 sq. km. **2.** port and second largest city of Yemen, situated on a peninsula that juts into the Gulf of Aden. Population: 562,000 (1995).

aden- /áad'n, áyd'n/ *prefix.* = **adeno-** (*used before vowels*)

Ad·en·au·er /ádd'n òw ər/, **Konrad** (1876–1967) German statesman and the first chancellor of the Federal Republic of Germany (1949–63). He led West Germany into NATO in 1955.

ad·e·nec·to·my /àdd' néktəmee/ (*plural* **-mies**) *n.* the surgical removal of a gland

ad·e·nine /ádd' neen, -nin/ *n.* a component of nucleic acids, energy-carrying molecules such as ATP, and certain coenzymes that carries hereditary information in DNA and RNA. Chemically, it is a purine base. Formula: $C_5H_5N_5$. Symbol **A**

ad·e·ni·tis /àdd' nítəs/ *n.* inflammation of a gland or a lymph node

adeno-, aden- *prefix.* gland ○ *adenovirus* [From Greek *adēn*. Ultimately related to Latin *inguen* "groin" (source of English *inguinal*).]

ad·e·no·car·ci·no·ma /àddinō kaàrs'n ṓmə/ (*plural* **-mas** *or* **-ma·ta** /-ṓmətə/) *n.* **1.** MALIGNANT TUMOR IN GLAND a malignant tumor in glandular tissue. Breast cancers are often adenocarcinomas. **2.** TUMOR RESEMBLING GLAND a malignant tumor with cells arranged in patterns similar to those of a gland —**ad·e·no·car·ci·nom·a·tous** *adj.*

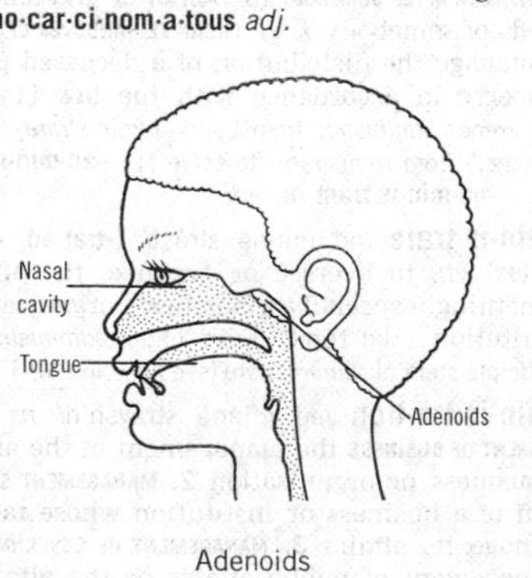

Adenoids

ad·e·noid /ádd'n òyd/ *adj.* **1.** RELATING TO GLANDS relating to or similar to a gland **2.** CONCERNING LYMPHOID TISSUE relating to lymphoid tissue **3.** = **adenoidal** *adj.* 1 ■ **ad·e·noids** *npl.* THROAT TISSUE a mass of tissue at the back of the throat. If they become enlarged, breathing can be restricted through the nose.

ad·e·noi·dal /àdd'n óyd'l/ *adj.* **1.** AFFECTED BY ENLARGED ADENOIDS displaying symptoms caused by enlarged adenoids, e.g., a nasal voice or breathing difficulties **2.** RELATING TO ADENOIDS used to describe the adenoids

ad·e·noi·dec·tom·y /àdd'noy déktəmee/ (*plural* **-ies**) *n.* surgical removal of adenoids

ad·e·no·ma /àdd'n ṓmə/ (*plural* **-mas** *or* **-ma·ta** /-mətə/) *n.* **1.** BENIGN TUMOR IN GLAND a benign tumor in glandular tissue **2.** TUMOR-LIKE GLAND a benign tumor with cells arranged in patterns similar to those found in a gland —**ad·e·nom·a·toid** *adj.*

ad·e·nop·ath·y /àdd'n óppəthee/ (*plural* **-no·path·ies**) *n.* a diseased condition, e.g., inflammation or enlargement, in a gland or lymph node

a·den·o·sine /ə dénnə seen, -s'n/ *n.* a compound of adenine and a ribose that is a component of nucleic acids and energy-carrying molecules such as ATP. Formula: $C_{10}H_{13}N_5O_4$. [Early 20thC. A blend of ADENINE and RIBOSE.]

a·den·o·sine di·phos·phate full form of **ADP**

a·den·o·sine mon·o·phos·phate full form of **AMP**

a·den·o·sine tri·phos·pha·tase *n.* an enzyme occurring in living organisms that aids the breakdown of ATP into ADP with the release of energy that is used by cells

a·den·o·sine tr·iphos·phate full form of **ATP**

ad·en·o·sis /àdd' nṓs əs/ *n.* **1.** ENLARGED OR ABNORMAL GLANDS the enlargement of a gland, or the abnormal formation of glandular tissue **2.** GLAND DISEASE any disease characterized by adenosis

ad·e·no·vi·rus /àddinō vírəs/ *n.* a virus that causes respiratory infections in humans [From its occurrence in adenoid tissue when first discovered]

a·den·yl·ate cy·clase /ə dénnələt-/, **a·den·yl cy·clase** /àddənīl-/ *n.* an enzyme involved in the formation of cyclic AMP from ATP

a·dept *adj.* /ə dépt/ SKILLFUL highly proficient or expert ■ *n.* /ádd ept/ SKILLED PERSON somebody who is highly proficient or expert at something [Mid-17thC. From Latin *adeptus*, the past participle of *adipisci* "to acquire," from *apisci* "to pursue." The underlying idea is of having acquired a skill.] —**a·dept·ly** /ə déptlee/ *adv.* —**a·dept·ness** *n.*

ad·e·quate /áddəkwət/ *adj.* **1.** ENOUGH sufficient in quality or quantity to meet a need **2.** JUST BARELY ENOUGH just barely sufficient in quality or quantity to meet a need or qualify for something [Late 16thC. From Latin *adaequatus*, the past participle of *adaequare* "to make equal, to match," from *aequus* "even" (source of English *equal*).] —**ad·e·qua·cy** *n.* —**ad·e·quate·ly** *adv.* —**ad·e·quate·ness** *n.*

WORD KEY: SYNONYMS

See Synonyms at ***sufficient*** and ***enough***.

A·der /aa dáir/, **Clément** (1841–1926) French engineer who constructed a steam-powered aircraft and made the first heavier-than-air powered flight (1890).

à deux /aa dö/ *adv., adj.* involving only two people and therefore private [Late 19thC. From French.]

ADH *abbr.* antidiuretic hormone. ◗ **vasopressin**

ADHD *abbr.* attention deficit hyperactivity disorder

ad·here /əd heér, ad-/ (**-hered, -her·ing, -heres**) *vi.* **1.** OBEY to follow a rule or instructions exactly, or keep to an agreement **2.** SUPPORT to hold firmly to a belief, idea, or opinion **3.** STICK FIRMLY to stick firmly to a surface or an object [15thC. Directly or via French *adhérer* from Latin *adhaerere*, from *haerere* "to stick" (source of English *cohere* and *hesitate*).] —**ad·her·ence** *n.*

ad·her·ent /əd heérənt, ad-, əd hérrənt/ *n.* SUPPORTER somebody who supports a particular cause or leader ■ *adj.* STICKY able to stick firmly to a surface or an object (*formal*)

ad·he·sion /əd heézh'n, ad-/ *n.* **1.** STICKING POWER the ability to stick firmly to something **2.** NON-SLIPPINESS the ability to make firm contact with a surface without slipping **3.** SUPPORT loyal support for a cause or a leader **4.** PHYS INTERMOLECULAR ATTRACTION the intermolecular attraction between substances that are unlike and in surface contact, causing them to cling together **5.** JOINING OF BODY PARTS the joining of normally unconnected body parts by bands of fibrous tissue [15thC. Directly or via French, from the Latin stem *adhaesion-*, from *adhaes-*, the past participle stem of *adhaerere* (see ADHERE).]

WORD KEY: USAGE

See Usage note at ***adherence***.

ad·he·sive /əd heésiv, ad-, əd heéziv, ad-/ *n.* GLUE a substance used to stick things together ■ *adj.* STICKY able to stick to something or to stick things together [Late 17thC. Formed from the Latin stem *adhaes-* (see ADHESION).] —**ad·he·sive·ly** *adv.* —**ad·he·sive·ness** *n.*

ad hoc /ad hók, -hṓk/ *adj.* done or set up solely in response to a particular situation or problem and without considering wider issues ○ *ad hoc measures* [Mid-17thC. From Latin, "to this."] —**ad hoc** *adv.*

ad hoc com·mit·tee *n.* **1.** TEMPORARY COMMITTEE a temporary committee formed for a particular need **2.** POL CONGRESSIONAL COMMITTEE a congressional committee that is not permanent, but is formed by members of various other committees to address a specific issue or problem

ad hoc·ism /ad hókizəm, -hṓkizəm/, **ad hock·er·y** /ad hókəree, -hṓkəree/ *n.* making decisions or implementing measures according to the nature and needs of each specific case individually rather than on the basis of a set, planned policy (*disapproving*)

ad hom·i·nem /ad hómmə nem, -hómmənəm/ *adj.* appealing to people's emotions and prejudices rather than their ability to think (*formal*) [Late 16thC. From Latin, "to the person."] —**ad hom·i·nem** *adv.*

ADI *abbr.* acceptable daily intake

ad·i·a·bat·ic /àddee ə báttik, àydee-, ày dī-/ *adj.* used to describe a thermodynamic process that happens without loss or gain of heat [Late 19thC. Formed from Greek *adiabatos* "impassable," from *diabainein*, "to go through" (source of English *diabetes*).] —**ad·i·a·bat·i·cal·ly** *adv.*

a·dieu /ə dyo͞o, ə do͞o/ *interj., n.* (*plural* **a·dieux** /ə dyo͞oz, ə do͞oz/ *or* **a·dieus** /ə dyo͞oz, ə do͞oz/) used to say goodbye ○ *"... the more gentle adieus of her sisters were uttered without being heard"* (Jane Austen, *Pride And Prejudice*; 1813) [14thC. From French, literally "(I commend you) to God."]

A·di Granth /aàdi grúnt/ *n.* the principal Sikh scripture, which contains the teachings of the first five gurus and also poems and hymns [From Sanskrit *ādigrantha* literally "first book," from *grantha* "tying, work of literature"]

ad in·fi·ni·tum /ad ìnfə nítəm/ *adv.* endlessly, or for so long as to seem endless [Early 17thC. From Latin, "to infinity."]

ad in·ter·im /àd íntərim/ *adv.* TEMPORARILY for the meantime ■ *adj.* TEMPORARY done or created for the meantime only [From Latin, literally "to the meanwhile"]

ad·i·os /àddee áws, aàdee-/ *interj.* used to say goodbye (*informal*) [Mid-19thC. From Spanish, literally "to God" (see ADIEU).]

ad·ip·ic ac·id /ə dìppik-/ *n.* a white crystalline solid used in making nylon and in the production of other chemicals. Formula: $C_6H_{10}O_4$. [Mid-19thC. *Adipic* formed from the Latin stem *adip-* "fat" (see ADIPO-), because the acid was originally made by oxidizing fats.]

adipo- *prefix.* fat, fatty ○ *adipocyte* [From Latin *adip-*, the stem of *adeps* "fat," of unknown origin]

ad·i·po·cere /áddi pō seèr/ *n.* a brownish, waxy substance, consisting primarily of fatty acids, that is produced by postmortem chemical changes to body fat over time or as a result of prolonged immersion in water [Early 19thC. From French, from the Latin stem *adip-* (see ADIPO-) + French *cire* "wax."]

ad·i·po·cyte /áddipə sìt/ *n.* a cell that synthesizes and stores fat [Mid-20thC. Coined from modern Latin *adiposus* "of fat" (from the Latin stem *adip-* "animal fat") + -CYTE.]

ad·i·pose /áddə pṑss/ *adj.* FATTY containing fat ■ *n.* FAT fat found in tissue just below the skin and surrounding major organs, acting as an energy reserve and providing insulation and protection [Mid-18thC. From modern Latin *adiposus* "fatty."] —**ad·i·pose·ness** *n.* —**ad·i·pos·i·ty** /àddə póssətee/ *n.*

ad·i·pose tis·sue *n.* connective tissue in animal bodies that contains fat

a·dip·sin /ə dípsin/ *n.* a protein that is believed to control appetite, and so is used to treat obesity [Late 20thC. Coined from *adipsia* "abstaining from liquids."]

Ad·i·ron·dack chair /àddə ráwn dak-/ *n.* a wooden armchair usually used outdoors, having wide slats and a slanted seat and back [Late 20thC. Named for the ADIRONDACK MOUNTAINS; from the use of such chairs in that area.]

Ad·i·ron·dack Moun·tains /àddə ráwn dak-/, **Ad·i·ron·dacks** mountain chain in northeastern New York State, known for spectacular scenery and recreational activities. The highest peak is Mount Marcy 5,344 ft./1,629 m.

ad·it /áddət/ *n.* a nearly horizontal shaft used for giving access to a mine or for drainage [Early 17thC. From Latin *aditus* "approach, entrance," from the past participle of *adire* "to go toward," from *ire* "to go."]

adj. *abbr.* **1.** GRAM adjective **2.** MATH adjoint **3.** adjunct **4.** BANKING, INSUR adjustment **5. adj., Adj.** MIL adjutant

ad·ja·cen·cy /ə jáyss'nsee/ (*plural* **-cies**) *n.* **1.** SOMETHING ADJACENT something that is near or adjoining **2.** BEING ADJACENT the state of being near or adjoining

ad·ja·cent /ə jáyss'nt/ *adj.* **1.** NEIGHBORING near or close, especially adjoining **2.** MATH SHARING EDGES used to describe either a pair of vertices in a graph that have common edges, or a pair of edges in a graph that have a common vertex [15thC. From Latin *adjacent-*, the present participle stem of *adjacere* "to lie near," from *jacere* "to lie."]

WORD KEY: USAGE

adjacent or **adjoining**? Two houses are said to be ***adjoining*** when they are next to each other with a common wall. ***Adjoining*** tables are next to each other end to end, forming one surface (they are, to use a more technical word, **contiguous**). ***Adjacent*** houses, on the other hand, can have a space between them or even be on opposite sides of the road, as long as there is nothing significant between them (for example, another house) and they are close enough for you to pass easily from one to the other. ***Adjacent*** tables are next to each other but not necessarily touching. Note also that ***adjoining***, being a form of a verb, can govern an object (*the house adjoining ours*), whereas ***adjacent*** needs the addition of *to* (*the house adjacent to ours*).

ad·ja·cent an·gle *n.* either of the two angles that are formed by the intersection of two straight lines and lie on the same side of one line

ad·jec·ti·val /àjjək tív'l/ *adj.* relating to or functioning as an adjective —**ad·jec·ti·val·ly** *adv.*

ad·jec·tive /ájjəktiv/ *n.* WORD QUALIFYING NOUN a word that qualifies or describes a noun or pronoun ■ *adj.* **1.** ACTING AS ADJECTIVE relating to, forming, or functioning as an adjective **2.** LAW PRACTICED IN COURT relating to court practice and procedure rather than the principles of law [14thC. Via French *adjectif* from Latin *adjectivus*, from, ultimately, *adjicere*, literally "to throw to," from *jacere* "to throw."] —**ad·jec·tive·ly** *adv.*

ad·join /ə jóyn/ (**-joined, -join·ing, -joins**) *v.* **1.** *vti.* BORDER to be next to or share a common border with something, especially an area of land ○ *The two properties adjoin.* **2.** *vt.* CONNECT to attach or add on something (*archaic*) [14thC. Via Old French *ajoin-*, the stem of *ajoindre*, from Latin *adjungere* "to join to," from *jungere* "to join."]

ad·join·ing /ə jóyning/ *adj.* situated next to or touching something or each other

WORD KEY: USAGE

See Usage note at ***adjacent.***

ad·joint /ájjoynt/ *n.* a matrix formed from a given square matrix, each element being derived from its cofactors, the determinants of the given matrix obtained by removing the row and column containing the element [Late 16thC. From French, the past participle of *adjoindre* (see ADJOIN).]

ad·journ /ə júrn/ (**-journed, -journ·ing, -journs**) *v.* **1.** *vti.* POSTPONE PROCEEDINGS to suspend the business of a court, legislature, or committee temporarily or indefinitely, or become suspended temporarily or indefinitely ○ *The court adjourned at one o'clock.* **2.** *vti.* POSTPONE to postpone a meeting to another time, or become postponed **3.** *vt.* DEFER to defer a matter or an action to another time **4.** *vi.* MOVE AS GROUP to move together from one place to another **5.** *vi.* STOP WORKING to stop working (*informal*) [14thC. From Old French *ajourner*, from the phrase *à jorn (nomé)* "to an (appointed) day."]

ad·journ·ment /ə júrnmənt/ *n.* a temporary or indefinite cessation of the business of a court, legislature, or committee

Adjt., **adjt.** *abbr.* adjutant

ad·judge /ə júj/ (**-judged, -judg·ing, -judg·es**) *vt.* **1.** MAKE DECLARATION ABOUT to judge somebody or something in a particular way ○ *She was adjudged to be an accomplished musician.* **2.** LAW DETERMINE JUDICIALLY to decide something in a judicial proceeding **3.** LAW DECREE LEGALLY to pronounce something by law [14thC. Via Old French *ajuger* from Latin *adjudicare* (see ADJUDICATE).]

ad·ju·di·cate /ə jóodi kàyt/ (**-cat·ed, -cat·ing, -cates**) *vti.* **1.** LAW DECIDE LEGALLY to reach a judicial decision on something **2.** DECIDE ABOUT to make an official decision about a problem or dispute [Early 18thC. From Latin *adjudicat-*, the past participle stem of *adjudicare* "to award in arbitration," from the stem *judic-* "judge."] —**ad·ju·di·ca·tive** /ə jóodi kàytiv, ə jóodikətiv/ *adj.* —**ad·ju·di·ca·tor** /-kàytər/ *n.*

ad·ju·di·ca·tion /ə jòodi káysh'n/ *n.* a judicial decision, sentence, or decree

ad·junct /ájjungkt/ *n.* **1.** SOMETHING EXTRA ADDED ON something inessential added to something else **2.** ASSISTANT somebody who assists and is subordinate to somebody else **3.** GRAM INESSENTIAL PART OF SENTENCE a part of a sentence that is not the subject or predicate ■ *adj.* ATTACHED TEMPORARILY TO A STAFF assigned temporarily or as an auxiliary member to the staff of an institution ○ *an adjunct professor of art history* [Early 16thC. From Latin *adjunctus*, the past participle of *adjungere* (see ADJOIN).] —**ad·junc·tion** /ə júngksh'n/ *n.* —**ad·junc·tive** *adj.*

ad·ju·ra·tion /àjjə ráysh'n/ *n.* **1.** FORMAL OATH a solemn oath **2.** SUPPLICATION an earnest appeal —**ad·jur·a·to·ry** /ə jóorə tàwree/ *adj.*

ad·jure /ə jóor/ (**-jured, -jur·ing, -jures**) *vt.* **1.** COMMAND SOLEMNLY to order somebody to do something, especially under oath **2.** MAKE APPEAL to make an earnest appeal to somebody [14thC. From Latin *adjurare* "to swear by oath," from *jurare* "to swear" (see JURY).] —**ad·jur·er** *n.*

ad·just /ə júst/ (**-just·ed, -just·ing, -justs**) *v.* **1.** *vt.* CHANGE SLIGHTLY to make slight changes in something to make it fit or function better **2.** *vti.* ADAPT TO NEW CIRCUMSTANCES to adapt to a new environment or condition **3.** *vt.* DECIDE AMOUNT OF MONEY OWED to decide what sums are payable in the settlement of an insurance claim [Early 17thC. Via obsolete French *adjuster* from assumed Vulgar Latin *adjuxtare* "to put close to," from Latin *juxta* "close" (source of English *juxtapose*).] —**ad·just·a·ble** *adj.* —**ad·just·a·bly** *adv.*

ad·just·a·ble rate mort·gage *n.* a mortgage on which interest is payable at a rate that varies according to a predetermined formula. The interest is typically tied to another interest rate such as the prime rate.

ad·just·er /ə jústər/, **ad·jus·tor** *n.* somebody who assesses the validity of an insurance claim on behalf of an insurance company and authorizes appropriate payment, repairs, or other action

ad·just·ment /ə jústmənt/ *n.* **1.** ACT OF BEING ADJUSTED the act of being or becoming adjusted **2.** SLIGHT CHANGE a slight change intended to make something fit or function better **3.** DEVICE FOR ADJUSTING SOMETHING a device for adjusting something

ad·ju·tant /ájjətənt/ *n.* an officer who acts as an administrative assistant to a commanding officer [Early 17thC. From Latin *adjutant-*, the present participle stem of *adjutare*, literally "to keep on helping" (source also of English *aid*), from *adjuvare* (see ADJUVANT).]

ad·ju·tant gen·er·al (*plural* **ad·ju·tants gen·er·al**) *n.* **1.** SENIOR MILITARY ADMINISTRATIVE OFFICER an army general reponsible for administration and personnel **2.** ADMINISTRATIVE OFFICER OF A MILITARY UNIT the adjutant of a military unit commanded by a general staff

ad·ju·tant stork *n.* a carrion-eating stork of Southeast Asia with a pink neck and soft white feathers on its underside. Latin name: *Leptoptilos dubius* and *Leptoptilos javanicus.* [From the similarity of its walk to that of a military staff officer]

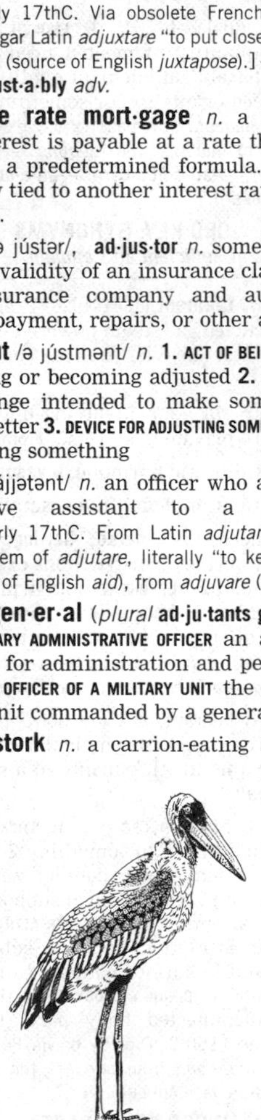

Adjutant stork

ad·ju·vant /ájjəvənt/ *n.* **1.** MED DRUG-ENHANCING AGENT a drug or agent added to another drug or agent to enhance its medical effectiveness **2.** MED ANTIGEN-ENHANCING DRUG a substance injected along with an antigen to enhance the immune response stimulated by the antigen **3.** HELPING AGENT something that helps or assists ■ *adj.* SUPPLEMENTARY helping by supplementing [Late 16thC. Directly or via French, from Latin *adjuvant-*, the present participle stem of *adjuvare* "to give help to," from *juvare* "to help."]

Ad·ler /ádlər/, **Alfred** (1870–1937) Austrian psychiatrist who stressed the importance of the inferiority complex. His books include *The Neurotic Constitution* (1912).

Ad·ler, Stella (1902–92) U.S. actress who taught Method acting at her school, the Stella Adler Conservatory of Acting.

ad lib /àd líb/ *adj.* = **ad libitum** ■ *adv.* **1.** = **ad libitum 2.** OFF THE CUFF without any advance preparation [Early 19thC. Shortening of AD LIBITUM.]

ad-lib /àd líb/ *vti.* (**ad-libbed, ad-lib·bing, ad-libs**) IMPROVISE SPEECH OR PERFORMANCE to make up a speech or a musical or dramatic performance on the spot without a fixed text or score ■ *adj.* UNPLANNED improvised or made up on the spot ■ *n.* IMPROVISED REMARK IN PERFORMANCE something said by an actor or other performer that is not in the script [Early 20th C. From AD LIB.] —**ad-lib·ber** *n.*

ad li·bi·tum /àd líbbətəm/ *adj., adv.* to be performed at the discretion of the performer, or in a speed or style of the performer's choice [Early 17thC. From Latin, literally "at your pleasure."]

ad lit·em /àd lítəm/ *adj.* LAW appointed by a court to represent a minor [Mid-18thC. From Latin, literally "for the purpose of a lawsuit."]

Adm. *abbr.* **1.** Admiral **2.** Admiralty

ad·man /ád màn/ (*plural* **-men** /-mèn/) *n.* somebody who works in the advertising business (*informal*)

ad·meas·ure /ad mézhər/ (**-ured, -ur·ing, -ures**) *vt.* to divide something up to be shared out [14thC. Via Old French *amesurer* from medieval Latin *admensurare* "to apply a measure to."]

ad·min·is·ter /əd mínnəstər/ (**-tered, -ter·ing, -ters**) *v.* **1.** *vti.* BE IN CHARGE OF to manage the affairs of a business, organization, or institution **2.** *vt.* DISPENSE to preside over the dispensation of something ○ *He administered justice in the fairest possible manner.* **3.** *vt.* GIVE AS MEDICATION to give somebody a measured amount of a medication, often also physically introducing it into the body **4.** *vt.* PERFORM AS RITUAL to carry out a set ritual or religious ceremony on behalf of an individual or group **5.** *vi.* SUPERVISE OATH-TAKING to oversee the taking of an oath by somebody **6.** *vi.* LOOK AFTER SOMEBODY to look after and tend to the needs of somebody **7.** *vt.* ORGANIZE HANDOVER OF PROPERTY to manage the distribution of a deceased person's property in accordance with the law [14thC. Via Old French *aministrer* from Latin *administrare* "to serve, manage," from *ministrare* "to serve."] —**ad·min·is·tra·ble** *adj.* —**ad·min·is·trant** *n., adj.*

ad·min·is·trate /əd mínnə stràyt/ (**-trat·ed, -trat·ing, -trates**) *vti.* to oversee or organize the affairs of something, especially a business, organization, or institution [Mid-16thC. From Latin *administrat-*, past participle stem of *administrare* (see ADMINISTER).]

ad·min·is·tra·tion /əd mìnnə stráysh'n/ *n.* **1.** MANAGEMENT OF BUSINESS the management of the affairs of a business or organization **2.** MANAGEMENT STAFF the staff of a business or institution whose task is to manage its affairs **3.** MANAGEMENT OF GOVERNMENT the management of public affairs or the affairs of a government **4.** STAFF OF GOVERNMENT a government's staff whose task is to manage its affairs **5.** TERM OF OFFICE the duration of a particular office, usually a political one **6.** GOVERNMENT a government, especially its executive branch **7.** U.S. GOVERNMENT AGENCY a United States government agency or board **8.** LEGAL DISPOSAL OF ESTATE the disposal or management of a deceased person's estate or an estate held in trust **9.** ADMINISTERING SOMETHING TO SOMEBODY the act of administering something such as an oath, medicine, or sacrament

ad·min·is·tra·tive /əd mínnə strὰytiv/ *adj.* relating to the administration of a business or organization —**ad·min·is·tra·tive·ly** *adv.*

ad·min·is·tra·tive law *n.* the area of law dealing with the affairs of agencies of the executive branch of a government, and with the judicial review of public bodies generally

ad·min·is·tra·tor /əd mínnə strὰytər/ *n.* **1. MANAGER IN ORGANIZATION** somebody whose job is to administer the affairs of a business or organization **2. MANAGER OF ESTATE** somebody appointed by a court to manage the estate of a deceased person, especially when there is no competent executor

ad·mi·ra·ble /ádmərəb'l/ *adj.* deserving to be admired [15thC. From Latin *admirabilis*, from *admirari* (see ADMIRE).] —**ad·mi·ra·ble·ness** *n.* —**ad·mi·ra·bly** *adv.*

Admiral butterfly

ad·mi·ral /ádmərəl/ *n.* **1. NAVAL COMMANDER** the officer in command of a navy or fleet **2. SENIOR NAVAL OFFICER** a naval rank above vice admiral and below Admiral of the Fleet **3. NAVAL OFFICER** a high-ranking naval officer entitled to fly a personal flag **4. ADMIRAL'S FLAGSHIP** an admiral's flagship (*archaic*) **5.** ZOOL **BRIGHTLY COLORED BUTTERFLY** a brightly colored butterfly of temperate regions. Family: Nymphalidae. ◊ **red admiral, white admiral** [13thC. Via French *amiral* from, ultimately, Arabic *amir-al*, literally "commander of" in such phrases as *amir-al-bahr* "commander of the sea."] —**ad·mi·ral·ship** *n.*

Ad·mi·ral of the Fleet *n.* an officer holding the highest rank in the U.S. Navy or the Royal Navy

ad·mi·ral·ty /ádmərəltee/ (*plural* **-mir·al·ties**) *n.* the office or jurisdiction of an admiral

Ad·mi·ral·ty Is·lands /ádmərltee-/ island group in the Bismarck Archipelago, north of New Guinea in the western Pacific Ocean. Manus is the group's largest island. Area: 829 sq. mi./2,072 sq. km.

ad·mi·ra·tion /àdmə ráysh'n/ *n.* **1. HIGH REGARD** a feeling of pleasure and approval, and, often, wonder **2. OBJECT OF HIGH REGARD** something or somebody regarded with a feeling of pleasure, approval, and, often, wonder

WORD KEY: SYNONYMS

See Synonyms at ***regard***.

ad·mire /əd mír/ (**-mired, -mir·ing, -mires**) *vt.* **1. BE PLEASED BY** to regard somebody or something with a feeling of pleasure, approval, and, often, wonder **2. RESPECT** to have a high opinion of somebody or something, e.g., a quality or attribute [Late 16thC. Directly or via French *admirer* from Latin *admirari* "to wonder at," from *mirari* "to wonder" (source of English *miracle*).] —**ad·mir·er** *n.*

ad·mir·ing /əd míring/ *adj.* full of admiration for somebody or something —**ad·mir·ing·ly** *adv.*

ad·mis·si·ble /əd míssəb'l/ *adj.* **1. ALLOWABLE** allowed to be done **2. ALLOWED TO COME IN** able or deserving to enter **3. ALLOWED TO BE GIVEN IN COURT** accepted as evidence in court [Early 17thC. Directly or via French, from medieval Latin *admissibilis*, from the Latin stem *admiss-* (see ADMISSION).] —**ad·mis·si·bil·i·ty** /əd mìssə bíllətee/ *n.* —**ad·mis·si·ble·ness** /-bəlnəs/ *n.* —**ad·mis·si·bly** *adv.*

ad·mis·sion /əd mísh'n/ *n.* **1. ENTRY** the right, ability, or permission to enter **2. FEE FOR ENTRY** a fee paid for entrance to a place or event **3. CONFESSION** a confession to having committed a crime or having made a mistake **4. DECLARATION** an acknowledgment that something is true [15thC. From the Latin stem *admission-*, from *admiss-*, the past participle stem of *admittere* (see ADMIT).] —**ad·mis·sive** *adj.*

WORD KEY: USAGE

admission or **admittance**? Both words mean "permission or right to enter." ***Admission*** is the usual word, whereas ***admittance*** is largely restricted to formal or official contexts, for example, signs and notices: *Admission is by ticket only. No admittance.* ***Admission*** is the only word of the two that can by itself mean "the price charged for entrance" and that can be used before another noun in this meaning: *admission money; admission ticket.*

ad·mit /əd mít/ (**-mit·ted, -mit·ting, -mits**) *v.* **1.** *vti.* **ACKNOWLEDGE TRUTH** to acknowledge that something is true ○ *You must admit it is a tempting offer.* **2.** *vt.* **ALLOW TO ENTER** to allow somebody or something entrance or access ○ *"Admits one"* **3.** *vti.* **CONFESS** to confess to having committed a crime or having made a mistake **4.** *vti.* **OFFER POSSIBILITY** to permit the possibility of something ○ *Their conduct admits of only one explanation.* [14thC. From Latin *admittere*, literally "to let go into," from *mittere* "to let go." The sense "to confess" probably evolved from "letting a confession enter your speech."]

ad·mit·tance /əd mítt'ns/ *n.* **1. PERMISSION TO GO IN** the permission or right to enter a place **2. ENTRANCE TO PLACE** physical entry to a place **3.** PHYS **MEASURE OF FLOW OF CURRENT** the reciprocal of impedance, a measure of the ability of an electrical current to flow

WORD KEY: USAGE

See Usage note at ***admission.***

ad·mit·ted·ly /əd míttədlee/ *adv.* as must be acknowledged

ad·mix /əd míks, ad míks/ (**-mixed, -mix·ing, -mix·es**) *vt.* to mix something into something else [Early 16thC. Origin uncertain: probably a back-formation from ADMIXTURE.]

ad·mix·ture /əd míkschər, ad-/ *n.* **1. PRODUCT OF MIXING** something produced by mixing something into something else **2. INGREDIENT** something added to something else by mixing **3. PROCESS OF MIXING INGREDIENTS** the mixing of something into something else [Early 17thC. Formed from MIXTURE.]

ad·mon·ish /əd mónnish/ (**-ished, -ish·ing, -ish·es**) *vt.* **1. REBUKE** to rebuke somebody mildly but earnestly **2. ADVISE** to advise somebody to do or, more often, not to do something [14thC. Anglicization of Old French *amonester* from assumed Vulgar Latin *admonere*, from Latin *monere* "to warn" (source of English *monitor*).] —**ad·mon·ish·er** *n.*

ad·mo·ni·tion /àdmə nísh'n/ *n.* **1. REBUKE** a mild but earnest rebuke **2. ADVICE** advice for or against doing something

ad·mon·i·to·ry /əd mónnə tàwree/ *adj.* **1. REBUKING** mildly reproving **2. ADVISORY** advising somebody to do or not to do something

ad nau·se·am /ad náwzee əm/ *adv.* to an extreme or annoying extent [Mid-17thC. From Latin, literally "to sickness."]

ad·nex·a /ad néksə/ *npl.* adjoining structural parts of the body [Late 19thC. From Latin, from, ultimately, *adnectere* "to tie together," from *nectere* "to tie."] —**ad·nex·al** *adj.*

ad·nom·i·nal /əd nómmən'l/ *n.* a word that modifies a noun [Mid-19thC. Formed from Latin *adnomen*, alteration of *agnomen* "agnomen."]

a·do /ə dóo/ *n.* excited activity or bother [14thC. Contraction of northern English dialect *at do*, a form of "to do," from Old Norse *at* "to" + DO.] ◇ **without further ado** without wasting any time

WORD KEY: CULTURAL NOTE

Much Ado About Nothing, a play by William Shakespeare (1598?). A comedy set in the court of the Duke of Messina in Sicily, it tells of the love of a soldier, Claudio, for the Duke's daughter, Hero, and the eventually unsuccessful attempts of Claudio's enemy, Don John, to prevent their marriage.

a·do·be /ə dóbee/ *n.* **1. EARTHEN BRICK** brick made from earth and straw and dried by the sun **2. BUILDING MADE OF ADOBE** a structure made with adobe bricks **3. EARTH THAT FORMS ADOBE** earth used to make adobe bricks [Mid-18thC. Via Spanish, from Arabic *at-tūb* "the bricks."]

a·do·be flat *n.* a gently sloping plain of clay soil deposited by desert floods

a·do·bo /aa dó bō, ə-/ (*plural* **-bos**) *n.* a Philippine dish of marinated meat or fish seasoned with vinegar, garlic, soy sauce, and spices [Mid-20thC. From Spanish.]

ad·o·les·cence /àddə léss'ns/ *n.* **1. TIME PRECEDING ADULTHOOD** the period from puberty to adulthood in human beings **2. INTERMEDIATE STAGE OF DEVELOPMENT** the stage in the development of something such as a civilization before its reaching maturity

ad·o·les·cent /àddə léss'nt/ *n.* **SOMEBODY IN PERIOD PRECEDING ADULTHOOD** somebody who has reached puberty but is not yet an adult ■ *adj.* **1. EXPERIENCING ADOLESCENCE** going through the period of adolescence ○ *adolescent males* **2. HAPPENING DURING ADOLESCENCE** typically occurring during the period of adolescence **3. IMMATURE** typical of somebody who is immature [15thC. Via French, from Latin *adolescent-*, the present participle stem of *adolescere* "to be nourished, grow up" (source also of English *adult*), from *alere* "to nourish."]

WORD KEY: SYNONYMS

See Synonyms at ***young***.

Ad·o·nai /aádō ní/ *n.* a name used in Judaism to speak the unspeakable name of YHWH, God [14thC. From Hebrew *'ădōnay*.]

A·don·is /ə dónniss, -dṓ-/ *n.* **1. YOUNG MAN IN GREEK MYTHOLOGY** in Greek mythology, a handsome youth loved by Aphrodite and Persephone. He was killed while hunting boar, but was allowed by Zeus to divide his time between Aphrodite on earth and Persephone in the underworld. **2. A·don·is, a·do·nis HANDSOME YOUTH** an extremely handsome young man [Late 16thC. From Greek *Adōnis*, from, ultimately, Phoenician *ædōnī* "my lord."]

a·dopt /ə dópt/ (**a·dopt·ed, a·dopt·ing, a·dopts**) *vt.* **1. LEGALLY RAISE ANOTHER'S CHILD AS YOUR OWN** to raise a child of other biological parents as if it were your own, in accordance with formal legal procedures **2. CHOOSE AND DECIDE TO USE** to take up something such as a plan, idea, cause, or practice and use or follow it **3. TAKE OVER** to take over something such as an idea that originated elsewhere and use it as your own **4. ASSUME WAY OF ACTING** to assume a particular attitude or way of behaving **5. START USING** to take on and use a new name or title **6. VOTE IN FAVOR OF** to vote to accept something such as a committee's decision or a congressional bill **7. CHOOSE REQUIREMENT** to officially select something as a requirement [15thC. Directly or via French *adopter* from Latin *adoptare* "to choose for oneself," from *optare* "to choose" (see OPT).] —**a·dopt·a·ble** *adj.* —**a·dopt·er** *n.*

WORD KEY: USAGE

adopted or **adoptive**? Parents who adopt a child have an ***adopted*** child, and the child has ***adoptive*** parents. It is easy to confuse these two words but it is important to remember the distinction.

a·dopt·ed /ə dóptəd/ *adj.* used to describe a child who has been adopted

a·dop·tee /ə dòp tée/ *n.* a child who has been adopted

a·dop·tion /ə dópsh'n/ *n.* **1. LEGAL PROCEDURE FOR ADOPTING A CHILD** a formal legal process to adopt a child **2. INSTANCE OF ADOPTING SOMEBODY OR SOMETHING** an instance of adopting somebody or something such as an idea, name, or attitude

a·dop·tive /ə dóptiv/ *adj.* used to describe a parent who adopts a child or somebody related to another by adoption

WORD KEY: USAGE

See Usage note at ***adopt.***

a·dor·a·ble /ə dáwrəb'l/ *adj.* charming, lovable, and usually very attractive —**a·dor·a·bil·i·ty** /ə dàwrə bíllətee/ *n.* —**a·dor·a·ble·ness** /-bəlnəss/ *n.* —**a·dor·a·bly** /-əblee/ *adv.*

ad·o·ra·tion /àddə ráysh'n/ *n.* **1. LOVE** great love and esteem **2. WORSHIP** religious worship of God, a god, or a spirit

a·dore /ə dáwr/ (**a·dored, a·dor·ing, a·dores**) *vt.* **1. LOVE DEEPLY** to love somebody intensely **2. WORSHIP** to worship God, a god, or a spirit **3. LIKE VERY MUCH** to like something or somebody very much (*informal*) [14thC. Via Old French, from late Latin *adorare*, literally "to pray to," from Latin *orare* "to pray" (see ORATE).] —**a·dor·er** *n.*

a·dor·ing /ə dáwring/ *adj.* showing love or admiration for somebody —**a·dor·ing·ly** *adv.*

a·dorn /ə dáwrn/ (**a·dorned, a·dorn·ing, a·dorns**) *vt.* **1. EMBELLISH** to add decoration or ornamentation to something **2. ENHANCE** to add to the beauty or glory of something or somebody [14thC. Via Old French, from Latin *adornare* "to embellish with ornaments," from *ornare* "to embellish" (see ORNATE).] —**a·dorn·er** *n.*

a·dorn·ment /ə dáwrnmənt/ *n.* **1. DECORATING** the act of adorning something **2. SOMETHING DECORATIVE** a decorative item or material added to something to make it more attractive

ADP[1] *n.* a chemical compound (**nucleotide**) in living organisms that is formed when another nucleotide (**ATP**) breaks down to release energy that is used by cells. Full form **adenosine diphosphate**

ADP[2] *abbr.* automatic data processing

ADR *abbr.* STOCK EXCH American depositary receipt

ad rem /ad rém/ *adv.* to the point or purpose [Late 16thC. From Latin, literally "to the matter or business."] —**ad rem** *adj.*

adren- *prefix.* = **adreno-** (*used before vowels*)

ad·re·nal /ə dreén'l/ *adj.* **1. ON THE KIDNEYS** relating to or on the kidneys **2. RELATING TO ADRENAL GLANDS** used to describe parts or effects of the adrenal glands ■ *n.* = **adrenal gland** [Late 19thC. Coined from AD- + RENAL.] —**ad·re·nal·ly** *adv.*

ad·re·nal·ec·to·my /ə dreén'l éktəmee/ (*plural* **-mies**) *n.* the surgical removal of one or both of the adrenal glands

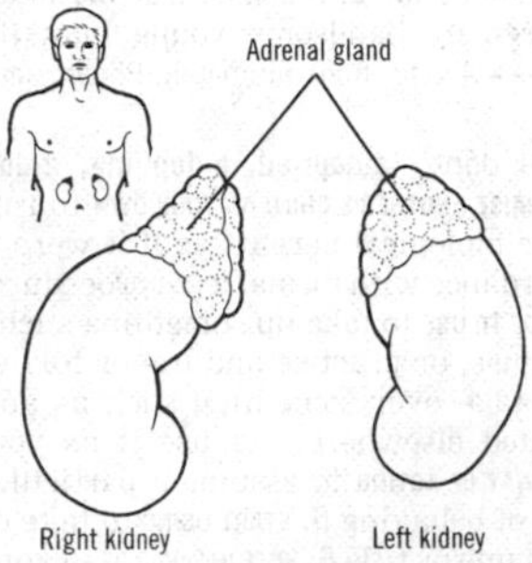

Adrenal glands

ad·re·nal gland *n.* an endocrine gland located above each kidney. The inner part (**medulla**) of each gland secretes epinephrine and the outer part (**cortex**) secretes steroids.

Ad·ren·a·lin *tdmk.* a trademark for epinephrine

a·dren·a·line /ə drénn'lən/ *n.* a hormone secreted in the adrenal gland that raises blood pressure, produces a rapid heartbeat, and acts as a neurotransmitter when the body is subjected to stress or danger (*often used informally*) ○ *get the adrenaline pumping* [Early 20thC. Coined from ADRENAL + -INE.]

ad·re·nal·ize /ə drénn'l ìz/ (**-ized, -iz·ing, -iz·es**) *vt.* to get somebody stirred up and ready for action

ad·re·ner·gic /àddrə núrjik/ *adj.* producing or activated by epinephrine or a similar substance —**adren·er·gi·cal·ly** *adv.*

adreno-, **adren-** *prefix.* pertaining to adrenaline or the adrenal glands ○ *adrenochrome* [Coined from AD- + RENAL, because the adrenal glands are next to the kidneys]

a·dre·no·cor·ti·cal /ə dreénō káwrtək'l/ *adj.* involving, located in, or produced by the cortex of the adrenal glands

ad·re·no·cor·ti·co·ster·oid /ə dreénō káwrtikō steér òyd, -sté ròoyd/ *n.* **1. HORMONE PRODUCED BY ADRENAL GLANDS** a steroid hormone obtained from the cortex of the adrenal glands **2. SYNTHETIC STEROID DRUG** a drug with similar physiological effects to the natural steroid produced by the cortex of the adrenal glands

ad·re·no·cor·ti·co·troph·ic = **adrenocorticotropic**

ad·re·no·cor·ti·co·trop·ic /ə dreénō káwrtikō tróppik/, **ad·re·no·cor·ti·co·troph·ic** /-tróffik/ *adj.* used to describe hormones or drugs that stimulate the cortex of the adrenal glands to produce corticosteroids

ad·re·no·cor·ti·co·trop·ic hor·mone *n.* full form of **ACTH**

ad·re·no·cor·ti·co·trop·in /ə dreénō káwrtikō trópin/, **ad·re·no·cor·ti·co·troph·in** /-trófin/ *n.* = **ACTH**

ad·re·no·leu·ko·dys·tro·phy /ə dreénō lookə dístrəfee/ *n.* a hereditary disorder of the nervous system in boys that affects the adrenal glands

ad·re·no·lyt·ic /ə dreén'l íttik/ *adj.* **STOPPING EPINEPHRINE EFFECTS** blocking the action of the adrenergic nerves or inhibiting the response to epinephrine ■ *n.* **INHIBITORY DRUG** an adrenolytic drug or agent

A·dri·an /áydree ən/ city in southeastern Michigan, southwest of Detroit. Population: 22,262 (1996).

A·dri·at·ic Sea /àydree áttik-/ arm of the Mediterranean Sea, east of Italy. Area: about60,000 sq.mi./155,000 sq.km.

a·drift /ə dríft/ *adj., adv.* **1. FLOATING WITHOUT DIRECTION** floating freely without being steered in a particular direction **2. WITHOUT PURPOSE** living life without a goal

a·droit /ə dróyt/ *adj.* displaying physical or mental skill [Mid-17thC. From French *à droit* "by right, properly." The meaning "skillful" evolved from the idea of "doing something properly or well."] —**a·droit·ly** *adv.* —**a·droit·ness** *n.*

ad·sci·ti·tious /àdsə tíshəss/ *adj.* added to something rather than being inherent or essential (*formal*) [Early 17thC. Formed from Latin *adscit-*, the past participle stem of *adsciscere* "to admit, adopt."]

ADSL *abbr.* asymmetrical digital subscriber line

ad·sorb /əd sáwrb, -záwrb/ (**-sorbed, -sorb·ing, -sorbs**) *vti.* to undergo or cause something to undergo adsorption [Late 19thC. Back-formation from ADSORPTION.] —**ad·sorb·able** *adj.*

ad·sor·bate /əd sáwrbət, -záwrbət, -sáwr bàyt/ *n.* a substance that is adsorbed

ad·sor·bent /əd sáwrbənt, -záwr-/ *adj.* **CAPABLE OF ADSORBING** able to adsorb ■ *n.* **ADSORBING SUBSTANCE** a substance capable of adsorbing

ad·sorp·tion /əd sáwrpsh'n, -záwrp-/ *n.* the process by which a layer of atoms or molecules of a substance, usually a gas, is formed on the surface of a solid or liquid [Late 19thC. Blend of AD- and ABSORPTION.] —**ad·sorp·tive** *adj.*

ad·u·lar·i·a /àjjə lérree ə/ *n.* a white or transparent variety of the mineral orthoclase, used as a gemstone. Formula: $KAlSi_3O_8$. [Late 18thC. Formed from French *adulaire*, from *Adula*, the name of mountains in the Swiss Alps where the mineral was first found.]

ad·u·late /ájjə làyt/ (**-lat·ed, -lat·ing, -lates**) *vt.* to admire or flatter somebody excessively [Mid-18thC. Back-formation from ADULATION.] —**ad·u·la·tor** *n.*

ad·u·la·tion /àjjə láysh'n/ *n.* excessive flattery or admiration [14thC. Directly or via French, from the Latin stem *adulation-*, from *adulari* "to flatter."]

ad·u·la·to·ry /ájjələ tàwree/ *adj.* excessively admiring and flattering

a·dult /ə dúlt, á-/ *adj.* **1. COMPLETELY GROWN** fully developed and mature **2. FOR SOMEBODY MATURE** involving, typical of, or meant for mature people **3. UNSUITABLE FOR CHILDREN** considered unsuitable for young people because of pornography, violence, or sexually explicit language ■ *n.* **1. FULLY GROWN LIFE FORM** a fully mature person, animal, plant, or other form of life **2. SOMEBODY LEGALLY AN ADULT** somebody who has reached the age of legal majority, generally 18 years of age in the United States [Mid-16thC. From Latin *adultus*, the past participle of *adolescere* (see ADOLESCENT).] —**a·dult·ness** *n.*

a·dult child (*plural* **a·dult chil·dren**) *n.* somebody who is an adult in age but, because of a psychiatric disorder, thinks and behaves more like a child

a·dult ed·u·ca·tion *n.* = **continuing education**

a·dul·ter·ant /ə dúltərənt/ *n.* something that makes something else less pure —**a·dul·ter·ant** *adj.*

a·dul·ter·ate /ə dúltə ràyt/ *vt.* (**-at·ed, -at·ing, -ates**) **MAKE IMPURE** to make something less pure by adding inferior or unsuitable elements or substances to it ■ *adj.* **1. IMPURE** made less pure **2.** = **adulterous** (*literary*) [Mid-16thC. From Latin *adulterat-*, the past participle stem of *adulterare* "to change, corrupt, commit adultery," from *alterare* "to alter" (see ALTER).] —**a·dul·ter·a·tion** /ə dùltə ráysh'n/ *n.* —**a·dul·ter·a·tive** /-ràytiv, -rətiv/ *adj.*

a·dul·ter·er /ə dúltərər/ *n.* somebody who commits adultery [Early 16thC. Formed from earlier *adulter* "to commit adultery," from Latin *adulterare* (see ADULTERATE).]

a·dul·ter·ess /ə dúltərəs/ *n.* a woman who commits adultery [Early 17thC. Via Old French *a(v)outresse* from *a(v)outrer* "to commit adultery," from Latin *adulterare* (see ADULTERATE).]

a·dul·ter·ine /ə dúltə rìn, -reén, -rin/ *adj.* **1. IMPURE** characterized by adulteration **2. BORN IN ADULTERY** born from an adulterous relationship **3. ILLEGAL** not within the law

a·dul·ter·ous /ə dúltərəss/ *adj.* relating to or involved in adultery [Early 17thC. Formed from earlier *adulter* "adulterer" from Latin *adulterare* (see ADULTERATE).] —**a·dul·ter·ous·ly** *adv.*

a·dul·ter·y /ə dúltəree/ *n.* voluntary sexual relations between a married person and somebody other than his or her spouse [15thC. Directly and via Old French *avout(e)rie* from Latin *adulterare* (see ADULTERATE).]

a·dult·hood /ə dúlt hòod, á-/ *n.* the age or state of legal majority

a·dult-on·set di·a·be·tes *n.* a form of diabetes mellitus that develops slowly in some adults as the body becomes unable to use insulin effectively

ad·um·brate /áddəm bràyt, ə dúm-/ (**-brat·ed, -brat·ing, -brates**) *vt.* **1. SKETCHILY INDICATE** to give an incomplete or faint outline or indication of something **2. FORESHADOW** to give a vague indication or warning of something to come **3. CONCEAL** to overshadow and obscure something [Late 16thC. From Latin *adumbrat-*, the past participle stem of *adumbrare* "to overshadow," from *umbra* "shade."] —**ad·um·bra·tion** /àddəm bráysh'n/ *n.* —**ad·um·bra·tive** /-tiv, ə dúmbrətiv/ *adj.* —**ad·um·bra·tive·ly** /ad úmbrətivlee/ *adv.*

adv. *abbr.* **1.** adverb **2.** adverbial **3.** advertisement **4.** advisory

ad val. *abbr.* ad valorem

ad va·lo·rem /àd və láwrəm/ *adj., adv.* in proportion to the value of something [Late 17thC. From Latin.]

ad·vance /əd vánss/ *v.* (**-vanced, -vanc·ing, -vanc·es**) **1.** *vti.* **MOVE AHEAD** to move forward in position **2.** *vt.* **SUGGEST** to put something forward as a proposal **3.** *vt.* **GIVE BEFOREHAND** to supply something or part of something, especially money, before it is due **4.** *vt.* **LEND MONEY OR GOODS** to supply money or goods on credit **5.** *vti.* **RISE IN STATUS** to rise in rank or position **6.** *vt.* **BRING FORWARD IN TIME** to make something happen earlier than originally expected **7.** *vti.* **PROGRESS** to further the progress or improvement of something, e.g., a cause, or undergo such progress or improvement **8.** *vti.* **RISE IN AMOUNT** to increase in price, rate, or amount ■ *n.* **1. DEVELOPMENT** a progress or improvement **2. PAYMENT AHEAD OF TIME** a sum of money paid before it is due **3. MOVEMENT AHEAD** a forward movement in position **4. FRIENDLY APPROACH** an approach made to somebody in an attempt to form a relationship or come to an agreement (*often used in the plural*) **5. PROVIDING SOMETHING BEFORE BEING PAID** the act of supplying money or goods before payment is received **6. SOMETHING RECEIVED BEFORE BEING PAID FOR** a quantity of money or goods supplied before payment is made or repayments begin **7. LOAN** a loan of money **8. PRICE RISE** an increase in price or rate ■ *adj.* **1. AHEAD OF TIME** made, given, or sent ahead of time **2. GOING IN FRONT** going ahead of the main group [13thC. Via Old French *avancer* from assumed Vulgar Latin *abantiare*, from *abante* "(from) before," from Latin *ante* "before."] —**ad·vanc·er** *n.* ◇ **in advance** before a particular event takes place

ad·vanced /əd vánst/ *adj.* **1. MORE HIGHLY DEVELOPED** at a higher stage of development or progress than other similar people or things **2. FAR ALONG** at a point late in the progress or development of something **3. FUTURISTIC** considered to be radical or ahead of its time

ad·vanced de·gree *n.* a university degree higher than a bachelor's

ad·vanced stand·ing *n.* the status of a college student who has been granted credit for courses taken or demonstrated knowledge acquired elsewhere

ad·vance guard *n.* a body of troops sent ahead of a main force to prepare an area for operations

ad·vance man (*plural* **ad·vance men**) *n.* somebody employed by a politician or other public figure to travel ahead on trips to organize timetables, publicity, security, and other arrangements

ad·vance·ment /əd vánsmənt/ *n.* **1. PROMOTION** a promotion in rank or position **2. ADVANCING** an act or instance of moving ahead **3. DEVELOPMENT** an improvement or progress in something **4.** LAW **USE OF LEGACY BEFORE DUE** the use of money from a legacy by or on behalf of its beneficiary before the person is strictly entitled to it

ad·vance par·ty (*plural* **ad·vance par·ties**) *n.* **1. MILITARY FORCE SENT ON AHEAD** a group of soldiers or units sent ahead of a larger force to prepare an area for operations **2. SMALL GROUP SENT AHEAD** a small group sent on ahead of any main party, e.g., on an expedition

ad·vance poll *n.* in Canada, an early vote held for voters who will be absent from their regular polling place on election day

ad·van·tage /əd vántij/ *n.* **1. SUPERIOR POSITION** a superior or favorable position in relation to somebody or something **2. FACTOR FAVORING SOMEBODY** a circumstance or factor that places somebody in a favorable position in relation to others ○ *These children have the advantage of a stable home.* **3. PROFIT** a benefit or gain ○ *Their mistakes in the race worked to our advantage.* **4.** TENNIS **POINT AFTER DEUCE** in tennis, the point scored after deuce ■ *vt.* (**-taged, -tag·ing, -tag·es**) **BENEFIT SOMEBODY** to put somebody in a superior or favorable position in relation to other people [14thC. Alteration of Old French *avantage*, from *avant* "before," from assumed Vulgar Latin *abante* (see ADVANCE).] ◇ **take advantage of somebody** to use somebody in a selfish way in order to achieve a personal benefit, usually by exploiting a weakness ◇ **take advantage of something** to make use of something that is available for personal benefit ◇ **to advantage** in a way that emphasizes the positive aspects of somebody or something

ad·van·ta·geous /àdvən táyjəss/ *adj.* **1. GIVING AN ADVANTAGE** giving an advantage **2. USEFUL** of use or benefit —**ad·van·ta·geous·ly** *adv.* —**ad·van·ta·geous·ness** *n.*

ad·vect /əd vékt/ (**-vect·ed, -vect·ing, -vects**) *vt.* to transfer something by advection [Mid-20thC. Back-formation from ADVECTION.]

ad·vec·tion /əd véksh'n/ *n.* the horizontal transfer of a property such as heat, caused by air movement [Early 20thC. From the Latin stem *advection-*, from *advehere* "to carry to," from *vehere* "to carry" (see VEHICLE).]

ad·vent *n.* the arrival of something important or awaited

Ad·vent *n.* **1. FOUR WEEKS BEFORE CHRISTMAS** the four-week period leading up to Christmas, beginning on the fourth Sunday before Christmas Day **2. COMING OF JESUS CHRIST** in Christian theology, the coming of Jesus Christ [Pre-12thC. From Latin *adventus* "arrival," from, ultimately, *advenire*, literally "to come to," from *venire* "to come" (see VENUE).]

Ad·vent·ist /ád ventist, ad véntist/ *n.* a member of any of several Christian denominations, e.g., the Seventh-Day Adventists, who believe that the Second Coming of Jesus Christ is imminent —**Ad·vent·ism** *n.*

ad·ven·ti·tia /àdvən tíshə/ *n.* the outer covering of an organ or body part, especially that of a blood vessel [Late 19thC. From Latin, from the neuter plural of medieval Latin *adventitius* (see ADVENTITIOUS).]

ad·ven·ti·tious /àdvən tíshəss/ *adj.* **1. FROM OUTSIDE** added from an outside and often unexpected source rather than intrinsic **2.** BIOL **UNUSUALLY POSITIONED** developing in an unusual position, as does, e.g., a root growing downward from a branch [Early 17thC. From medieval Latin *adventitius* "coming from outside," alteration of Latin *adventicius*, from *adventus* (see ADVENT).] —**ad·ven·ti·tious·ly** *adv.* —**ad·ven·ti·tious·ness** *n.*

ad·ven·tive /əd véntiv/ *adj.* **NOT INDIGENOUS** used to describe a plant or animal found in an environment where it is not native and is not fully established ■ *n.* **NON-INDIGENOUS PLANT OR ANIMAL** an adventive plant or animal —**ad·ven·tive·ly** *adv.*

Ad·vent Sun·day *n.* the fourth Sunday before Christmas, marking the start of Advent. It is regarded as the beginning of the Christian ecclesiastical year.

ad·ven·ture /əd vénchər/ *n.* **1. EXCITING EXPERIENCE** an exciting or extraordinary event or series of events **2. BOLD UNDERTAKING** an undertaking involving uncertainty and risk **3. INVOLVEMENT IN BOLD UNDERTAKINGS** the participation or willingness to participate in things that involve uncertainty and risk ○ *Where's your sense of adventure?* **4. FINANCIAL SPECULATION** a risky or speculative financial undertaking ■ *v.* (**-tured, -tur·ing, -tures**) **1.** *vt.* **RISK** to risk something **2.** *vt.* **RISK SAYING** to risk saying something that other people may disagree with or find offensive **3.** *vi.* **RISK DANGER** to dare to go somewhere new or engage in something dangerous [13thC. Via French *aventure* from Latin *adventurus* "about to arrive," the future participle of *advenire* (see ADVENT). The sense "exciting event" evolved from "what arrives by chance" via "hazardous undertaking."]

WORD KEY: CULTURAL NOTE

The Adventures of Huckleberry Finn, a novel by Mark Twain (1884). Conceived as a sequel to *Tom Sawyer*, it focuses on subsequent events in the life of Tom's friend Huckleberry Finn. With its realistic portrayal of frontier life, it is generally seen as a more adult book than its predecessor.

ad·ven·tur·er /əd vénchərər/ *n.* **1. SOMEBODY IN SEARCH OF ADVENTURE** somebody who takes part in exciting or risky activities **2. SOMEBODY PURSUING MONEY OR POSITION** somebody who uses unscrupulous means in order to gain wealth or social position **3. SPECULATOR** somebody who seeks wealth through financial speculation

ad·ven·ture·some /əd vénchərsəm/ *adj.* willing or eager to participate in risky or exciting activities —**ad·ven·ture·some·ly** *adv.* —**ad·ven·ture·some·ness** *n.*

ad·ven·tur·ess /əd vénchərəss/ *n.* a woman who uses unscrupulous means in order to gain wealth or social position (*dated*)

ad·ven·tur·ism /əd vénchə rìzzəm/ *n.* reckless intervention by one government in the affairs of another —**ad·ven·tur·ist** *n.*

ad·ven·tur·ous /əd vénchərəss/ *adj.* **1. DARING** willing or eager to participate in risky or exciting activities **2. RISKY** involving risk —**ad·ven·tur·ous·ly** *adv.* —**ad·ven·tur·ous·ness** *n.*

ad·verb /ád vùrb/ *n.* a word that modifies a verb, an adjective, another adverb, or a sentence, e.g., "happily," "very," or "frankly" [15thC. Directly or via French, from Latin *adverbium*, which was modeled on Greek *epirrhēma* "added word."]

ad·ver·bi·al /ad vúrbee əl/ *adj.* **RELATING TO ADVERB** relating to or functioning as an adverb ■ *n.* **ADVERB** an adverb, or a phrase or clause that functions as an adverb —**ad·ver·bi·al·ly** *adv.*

ad ver·bum /ad vúrbəm/ *adv.* word for word [From Latin, "in accordance with the word"]

ad·ver·sar·i·al /àdvər sáiree əl/ *adj.* **1. RELATING TO ADVERSARIES** relating to conflict or adversaries **2.** *U.K.* = **adversary**

WORD KEY: USAGE

adversarial or **adversative** Not until the twentieth century did ***adversarial*** begin to come into use; formerly, ***adversative*** was the only possible choice. Now, however, ***adversarial*** has almost wholly superseded ***adversative***, except in reference to grammar and such adversative conjunctions as *but* and *yet*, and in connection with the stringent methods employed by certain military schools: *"This 'adversative education,' as they call it, is designed to break the cadet of flabby, undisciplined habits acquired early in life and to remake him into a soldier."*

ad·ver·sar·y /ádvər sèrree/ *n.* (*plural* **-ies**) **OPPONENT** somebody who opposes somebody else in a conflict, contest, or debate ■ *adj.* **CONTESTING** involving conflicting parties or interests, in relation to a legal proceeding [14thC. Via Old French, from Latin *adversarius* "enemy," from *adversus* (see ADVERSE).]

WORD KEY: SYNONYMS

See Synonyms at ***opponent***.

ad·ver·sa·tive /əd vúrsətiv/ *n.* a word, phrase, or clause that expresses opposition or contrast, e.g., "but" or "although" [Mid-16thC. Directly or via French, from late Latin *adversativus* "opposed," from Latin *adversus* (see ADVERSE).] —**ad·ver·sa·tive** *adj.* —**ad·ver·sa·tive·ly** *adv.*

ad·verse /ad vúrs, ád vùrs/ *adj.* **1. ANTAGONISTIC** acting with or characterized by opposition or antagonism **2. HARMFUL** creating unfavorable or undesirable results **3. CONTRARY** creating momentum in a direction opposite from that desired **4.** BOT **FACING THE STEM** used to describe a leaf or flower that faces the main stem [14thC. Via Old French, from Latin *adversus* "turned against, hostile," from the past participle of *advertere* (see ADVERT[1]).] —**ad·verse·ly** /ad vúrslee/ *adv.* —**ad·verse·ness** *n.*

WORD KEY: USAGE

adverse or **averse**? Both words mean "opposed" in different ways. ***Adverse*** is normally used before an abstract noun such as *circumstances* or *conditions* when these are unfavorable or likely to cause difficulties. ***Averse*** describes people who are disinclined to do something or have a strong dislike that is specified by the word that follows *to*: *He was averse to flattery.* ***Averse*** is never used attributively (i.e. before a noun), as ***adverse*** normally is.

ad·verse pos·ses·sion *n.* the possession or occupation of land or property without the owner's permission as a method of acquiring legal ownership

ad·ver·si·ty /ad vúrsətee/ (*plural* **-ties**) *n.* **1. MISFORTUNE** hardship and suffering **2. ADVERSE HAPPENING** an extremely unfavorable experience or event

ad·vert[1] /ad vúrt/ (**-vert·ed, -vert·ing, -verts**) *vi.* to call attention or make reference to something [15thC. Via Old French *advertir* "to notice," from Latin *advertere* "to turn toward," from *vertere* "to turn."]

ad·vert[2] /ád vùrt/ *n.* *U.K.* an advertisement (*informal*) [Mid-19thC. Shortening.]

ad·ver·tence /ad vúrt'ns/ *n.* the act of paying attention to or being mindful of something

ad·ver·tise /ádvər tìz/ (**-tised, -tis·ing, -tis·es**) *v.* **1.** *vti.* **PRAISE COMMERCIAL PRODUCT** to publicize the qualities of a product, service, business, or event in order to encourage people to buy or use it **2.** *vti.* **PUBLICLY ANNOUNCE AVAILABILITY OR NEED** to publicize something such as a job opening or item for sale in a newspaper or on the radio, television, or Internet ○ *advertise for a new roommate* **3.** *vt.* **TELL OTHERS ABOUT** to make something known to others [15thC. From Old French *advertiss-*, the stem of *advertir* (see ADVERT[1]). The meaning "to publicize" evolved from "to notice" via "to warn" and "to give notice of."] —**ad·ver·tis·er** *n.*

ad·ver·tise·ment /àdvər tízmənt, -tìz-, əd vúrtəs-/ *n.* **1. PUBLIC ANNOUNCEMENT** a public announcement in a newspaper or on the radio, television, or Internet advertising something such as a product for sale or an event **2. ACT OF ADVERTISING** the act of advertising something

ad·ver·tis·ing /ádvər tìzing/ *n.* **1. PUBLIC PROMOTION OF SOMETHING** the promotion through public announcements in newspapers or on the radio, television, or Internet of something such as a product, service, event, or vacancy in order to attract or increase interest in it **2. BUSINESS OF PRODUCING ADVERTISEMENTS** the business of producing advertisements **3. ADVERTISEMENTS** advertisements considered collectively

ad·vice /əd víss/ *n.* **1. RECOMMENDATION ABOUT ACTION** somebody's opinion about what another person should do ○ *I followed her advice and changed jobs.* **2. OFFICIAL INFORMATION** formal or official information about something, usually received from a distance (*often used in the plural*) [13thC. Via French *avis* "opinion" from, ultimately, Latin *ad (meum) visum* "in (my) view or opinion"; *visum* is the past participle of *videre* "to see."]

ad·vis·a·ble /əd vízəb'l/ *adj.* being a sensible or desirable thing to do —**ad·vis·a·bil·i·ty** /əd vìzə bíllətee/ *n.* —**ad·vis·a·ble·ness** /-b'lnəss/ *n.* —**ad·vis·a·bly** /-əblee/ *adv.*

ad·vise /əd víz/ (**-vised, -vis·ing, -vis·es**) *v.* **1.** *vti.* **OFFER ADVICE** to offer advice to somebody ○ *We were advised to leave.* **2.** *vt.* **RECOMMEND** to suggest or recommend something **3.** *vt.* **INFORM** to make somebody aware of something **4.** *vi.* **SEEK ADVICE** to seek advice or information [14thC. Via Old French *aviser*, from *avis* "opinion." Ultimately from Latin *ad (meum) visum* (see ADVICE).]

WORD KEY: USAGE

advise = "inform" The use of the verb ***advise*** to mean "inform" is widely regarded as commercialese and is best avoided in general usage: *Please advise us of [better: let us know] your new address. I will advise them [better: inform them] of the new time of the meeting.*

WORD KEY: SYNONYMS

See Synonyms at ***recommend***.

ad·vis·ed·ly /əd vízədlee/ *adv.* after careful consideration

ad·vi·see /əd vì zée/ *n.* somebody who receives advice

ad·vis·er /əd vízər/, **ad·vi·sor** *n.* **1. GIVER OF ADVICE** somebody who gives advice **2. SOMEBODY ADVISING STUDENTS** somebody who advises students on academic matters such as course choices [Early 17thC. Formed from ADVISE.]

ad·vi·so·ry /əd vízəree/ *adj.* **1. GIVING ADVICE** providing or of the nature of advice **2. HAVING THE FUNCTION OF GIVING ADVICE** having the function of giving advice, usually with the implication that the advice given need not be followed ■ *n.* (*plural* **-ries**) **1. INFORMATIONAL BULLETIN** a report that gives facts or data and sometimes advice about a subject, e.g., about economic conditions **2. WARNING OF SOMETHING TO COME** an advance notice of something, e.g., a warning of impending severe weather ○ *traffic advisory*

ad·vo·caat /àdvō kaát/ *n.* an alcoholic beverage similar to eggnog, containing eggs, sugar, and brandy [Mid-20thC. From Dutch "advocate," because it was supposed to help clear the throat.]

ad·vo·ca·cy /ádvəkəssee/ (*plural* **-cies**) *n.* active verbal support for a cause or position [14thC. Via Old French *advocacie* from, ultimately, Latin *advocatus* (see ADVOCATE).]

ad·vo·cate *vt.* /ádvə kàyt/ (**-cat·ed, -cat·ing, -cates**) **SUPPORT** to support or speak in favor of something ○ *a tireless advocate of social reform* ■ *n.* /ádvəkət, -kàyt/ **1. SOMEBODY GIVING SUPPORT** somebody who supports or speaks in favor of something **2. HELPER** somebody who acts or intercedes on behalf of another **3.** LAW **LEGAL REPRESENTATIVE** somebody, e.g., a lawyer, who pleads another's case in a legal forum [14thC. Via Old French *avocat* "advocate" from, ultimately, *advocare* "to call to," from Latin *vocare* "to call" (source of English *vocation* and *revoke*).] —**ad·vo·ca·tor** *n.* —**ad·voc·a·to·ry** /ad vókə tàwree, ádvə kàytəree/ *adj.*

WORD KEY: SYNONYMS

See Synonyms at ***recommend***.

advt. *abbr.* advertisement

A·dy·ghe /aádi gay, -gáy/, **A·dy·gei** *n.* a language spoken in the northwestern region of the republic of Georgia, belonging to the Abkhaz-Adyghean group of languages. Adyghe is spoken by about 100,000 people. —**A·dy·ghe** *adj.*

ad·y·tum /áddətəm/ (*plural* **-ta** /-tə/) *n.* the most sacred part in an ancient temple, restricted to priests [Early 17thC. Via Latin, from Greek *adutos*, literally "not to be entered," from *duein* "to enter."]

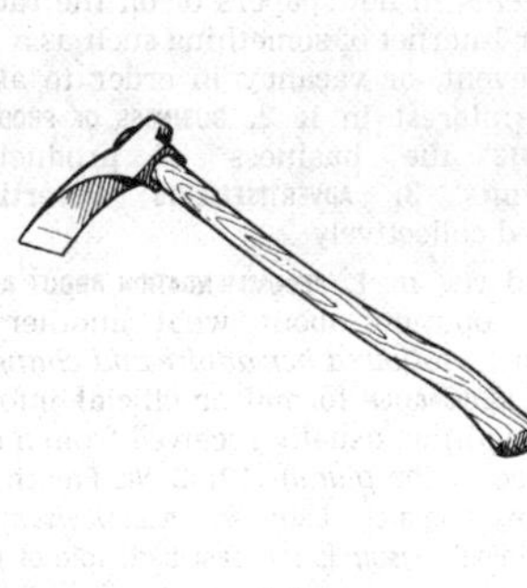

Adz

adz /adz/, **adze** *n.* a tool similar to an ax, with an arched blade set at right angles to the handle, used for trimming and shaping wood [Old English *adesa* or *eadesa*, of unknown origin]

ad·zu·ki bean /ad zóoki/, **a·du·ki bean** /a dóokee-/, **a·zu·ki bean** /a zóokee-/ *n.* **1. ASIAN BEAN PLANT** a bean belonging to a species grown especially in China and Japan. Latin name: *Vigna angularis*. **2. SWEET BEAN** a small slightly sweet red-brown bean, the seed of the adzuki plant, used in sweet dishes in Asian cooking and in western vegetarian cooking [*Adzuki* from Japanese *azuki* "red bean"]

AEC *abbr.* Atomic Energy Commission

ae·cid·i·o·spore *n.* = **aeciospore**

ae·cid·i·um *n.* = **aecium**

ae·ci·o·spore /éesee ə spàwr, -shee-/, **ae·cid·i·o·spore** /-síddee ə-/ *n.* a spore produced in the reproductive organ **(aecium)** of a rust fungus and containing two genetically distinct rust nuclei [Early 20thC. Coined from AECIUM + SPORE.]

ae·ci·um /éeshee əm, éesee əm/ (*plural* **-a** /-ə, -ə/), **ae·cid·i·um** /ee síddiəm/ (*plural* **-a** /-ə/) *n.* a cup-shaped reproductive organ **(fruiting body)** produced by some rust fungi in the tissue of their host plant, in which spores **(aeciospores)** are formed [Early 20thC. Via modern Latin, from Greek *aikia* "injury"; from the harm caused by the fungi.]

a·e·des /ay éedeez/ (*plural* **-des**) *n.* a tropical and subtropical mosquito that can transmit serious diseases, e.g., yellow fever and dengue. Latin name: *Aedes aegypti*. [Early 20thC. From modern Latin, genus name, from Greek *aēdēs* "unpleasant," because it carries diseases.]

ae·dile /ée dìl/ *n.* a magistrate in ancient Rome responsible for public works and buildings, games, markets, and the grain and water supplies [Mid-16thC. From Latin *aedilis*, from *aedes* "building" (source of English *edifice*).]

Ae·ge·an Sea /i jée ən-/ arm of the Mediterranean Sea containing numerous islands divided into three main groups, the Cyclades, Dodecanese, and Sporades. Area: about 69,000 sq. mi./179,000 sq. km.

ae·gis /éejiss/, **e·gis** *n.* in Greek mythology, the shield of Zeus or Athena [Early 17thC. Via Latin, from Greek *aigis* "goatskin shield of Zeus."] ◇ **under the aegis of somebody** *or* **something** with the support or protection of somebody or something (*formal*)

Ae·ne·as /i née əss/ *n.* in Greek and Roman mythology, a Trojan hero who escaped after the fall of Troy and spent seven years traveling before settling near the site of Rome in Italy. His travels are the subject of Virgil's *Aeneid*.

Ae·o·li·a = **Aeolis**

ae·o·li·an *adj.* = **eolian**

Ae·o·li·an /ee ṓlee ən, -ṓlyən/, **E·o·li·an** *n.* **1. MEMBER OF HELLENIC PEOPLE** a member of an ancient Hellenic people who lived in Aeolis and Lesbos about 1100 B.C. **2.** LANG = **Aeolic** ■ *adj.* **1. OF AEOLIS** relating to or typical of Aeolis, or its people or culture **2. OF AEOLUS** relating to Aeolus

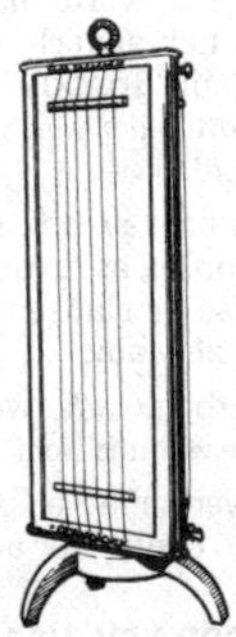

Aeolian harp: 18th-century French three-sided aeolian harp

ae·o·li·an harp, **Ae·o·li·an harp** *n.* a box-shaped musical instrument, a type of zither, with strings tuned in unison to produce their fundamental tones and harmonics when the wind blows over them [*Aeolian* formed from AEOLUS, from Greek *aiolos* "fast-moving"]

Aeolic /ee ṓlik/, **Eolic** *n.* a dialect of Ancient Greek that was spoken mainly in Aeolis, Thessaly, and Boeotia

Ae·o·lis /ée ə liss/, **Ae·o·li·a** /ee ṓlee ə/ ancient region on the northwestern coast of Asia Minor, settled by the Aeolian Greeks about 1100 B.C.

Ae·o·lus /ée ə ləss/ *n.* in Greek mythology, the god of wind

ae·on *n.* = **eon**

aer- *prefix.* = **aero-** (*used before vowels*)

aer·ate /ái ràyt/ (**-at·ed, -at·ing, -ates**) *vt.* **1. EXPOSE TO AIR** to allow circulating air to reach or penetrate something **2. PUT GAS INTO A LIQUID** to charge a liquid with a gas, especially with carbon dioxide when making bubbly and gaseous drinks **3.** = **oxygenate** [Late 18thC. Formed from Latin *aer* "air," from Greek *aēr* (see AERO-).] —**aer·a·tion** /air ráysh'n/ *n.* —**aer·a·tor** /ái ràytər/ *n.*

aer·en·chy·ma /ai réngkəmə/ *n.* the spongy tissue in some aquatic plants that keeps them afloat and helps in the exchange of gases [Late 19thC. Coined from Greek *aēr* "air" + *egkhuma* "infusion."]

aeri- *prefix.* = **aero-**

aer·i·al /áiree əl/ *adj.* **1. RELATING TO AIR** consisting of, typical of, or relating to the air **2. IN AIR** living, happening, or moving in the air ○ *a plant with aerial roots* **3. LIGHT IN WEIGHT** like the air in being light and insubstantial **4. IMAGINARY** existing only in the imagination **5. INVOLVING AIRCRAFT** done by or involving aircraft ○ *an aerial bombardment* ■ *n.* **1.** = **antenna** **2.** HOCKEY **HIGH BALL IN FIELD HOCKEY** in field hockey, a ball passed by being raised off the ground ■ **aerials** *npl.* **MID-AIR SKI-JUMP ACROBATICS** acrobatic movements that a ski-jumper performs while in the air (*informal*) [Early 17thC. Formed from Latin *aerius*, from Greek *aerios*, from *aēr* "air."]

aer·i·al·ist /áiree əlist/ *n.* an acrobat who performs on a tightrope or trapeze

aer·i·al lad·der *n.* a mechanically extending ladder used to reach high places, especially one on a fire engine

aer·i·al per·spec·tive *n.* the use in painting of gradations in color and definition to suggest distance

aer·ie /áiree, ée-/, **eyr·ie, aer·y** (*plural* **-ies**), **eyr·y** (*plural* **-ies**) *n.* **1. BIRD OF PREY'S NEST** the nest of an eagle or other bird of prey, usually built in a high, inaccessible place **2. SECURE BUILDING** a building, especially a stronghold, in a high inaccessible place [15thC. Via medieval Latin *aeria* from Old French *airie*, from, ultimately, Latin *area* "level ground" (source of English *area*).]

aer·i·form /áirə fàwrm/ *adj.* **1. GASEOUS** existing as air or gas **2. INSUBSTANTIAL** having no substance or material form

ae·ro /áirō/ *adj.* used in aircraft or aeronautics

aero-, **aeri-**, **aer-** *prefix.* **1.** Air, atmosphere, gas ○ *aerodynamic* **2.** aviation ○ *aerospace* [From Greek *aēr* "air"]

aer·o·bal·lis·tics /àirō bə lístiks/ *n.* the branch of ballistics that deals with projectiles fired or dropped from aircraft (*takes a singular verb*) —**aer·o·bal·lis·tic** *adj.*

aer·o·bat·ics /àirō báttiks/ *n.* the flying of an aircraft in daring maneuvers, often as an entertainment (*takes a singular or plural verb*) [Early 20thC. Coined from AERO-, modeled on ACROBATICS.] —**aer·o·batic** *adj.*

aer·obe /ái rōb/ *n.* a microorganism that requires oxygen for metabolism [Late 19thC. Coined from AERO- + Greek *bios* "life."]

aer·o·bic[1] /ai rṓbik, ə-/ *adj.* **1. NEEDING OXYGEN** living or taking place only in the presence of oxygen **2. GIVING OXYGEN** having or providing oxygen [Late 19thC. Formed from French *aérobie*, coined by Louis Pasteur from Greek *aēr* "air" + *bios* "life."] —**aerobically** *adv.*

aer·o·bic[2] /ai rṓbik, ə-/ *adj.* **1. SPEEDING UP RESPIRATION** increasing respiration and heart rates ○ *aerobic exercise* **2. OF AEROBICS** used in or relating to aerobics [Mid-20thC. From AEROBICS.]

aer·o·bic res·pi·ra·tion *n.* the breakdown of foodstuffs to create energy in a process that requires the presence of oxygen. ◊ **anaerobic respiration**

aer·o·bics /ai rṓbiks, ə-/ *n.* (*takes a singular or plural verb*) **1. FITNESS EXERCISES** an active exercise program done to music, often in a class **2. ACTIVITIES THAT SPEED UP RESPIRATION** exercises, e.g., walking, jogging, bicycling, and swimming, that increase respiration and heart rates [Mid-20thC. Coined by Dr. Kenneth H. Cooper from AEROBIC on the model of *gymnastics*.]

aer·o·bi·ol·o·gy /àirō bī óllәjee/ *n.* the study of airborne biological materials and organisms, e.g., airborne allergens and disease-causing microorganisms —**aer·o·bi·o·log·i·cal** /àirō bī ə lójjik'l/ *adj.* —**aer·o·bi·o·log·i·cal·ly** *adv.*

aer·o·bi·o·sis /àirō bī óssiss/ *n.* life in the presence of oxygen [Early 20thC. Via modern Latin from, ultimately, Greek (see AEROBIC).]

aer·o·drome /érrədrōm/ *n.* U.K. = **airdrome**

aer·o·dy·nam·ic /àirō dī námmik/ *adj.* **1. DESIGNED TO REDUCE AIR RESISTANCE** designed to reduce air resistance, especially to increase fuel efficiency or maximum speed **2. OF AERODYNAMICS** involving or typical of aerodynamics —**aero·dy·nam·i·cal·ly** *adv.*

aer·o·dy·nam·ics /àirō dī námmiks/ *n.* **STUDY OF OBJECTS MOVING THROUGH AIR** the study of moving gases, especially the study of the forces experienced by objects moving through air (*takes a singular verb*) ■ *npl.* **AERODYNAMIC PROPERTIES** the aerodynamic properties of an object (*takes a plural verb*) —**aer·o·dy·nam·i·cist** /àirō dī námmisist/ *n.*

aer·o·dyne /áirō dīn/ *n.* an aircraft that is heavier than air and depends on motion to lift off the ground [Early 20thC. Back-formation from AERODYNAMIC.]

aer·o·em·bo·lism /àirō émbə lizzəm/ *n.* = **air embolism**

aer·o·foil /érrəfoyl/ *n.* U.K. = **airfoil**

aer·o·gram /áirō gràm/, **aer·o·gramme** *n.* a letter designed for airmail consisting of a single sheet of lightweight paper that, once written on, can be folded and sealed to form an envelope [Late 19thC. Modeled on TELEGRAM.]

aer·og·ra·phy /ai róggrəfee/ *n.* the study of atmospheric conditions

aer·o·lite /áirō līt/ *n.* a meteorite with a high silicate content [Early 19thC. Coined from AERO- + -LITE.] —**aer·o·lit·ic** /áirō líttik/ *adj.*

aer·ol·o·gy /ai róllәjee/ *n.* the study of the lower layers of the Earth's atmosphere —**aer·o·log·ic** /áirə lójjik/ *adj.* —**aer·o·log·i·cal** *adj.* —**aer·ol·o·gist** /ai róllәjist/ *n.*

aer·o·mag·net·ic /áirō mag néttik/ *adj.* relating to the study or measurement of the earth's magnetic field from aircraft —**aer·o·mag·net·i·cal·ly** *adv.* —**aer·o·mag·net·ics** *n.*

aer·o·me·chan·ics /áirō mə kánniks/ *n.* the study of gases in motion and in equilibrium, including the study of the mechanical effects of gases upon objects (*takes a singular verb*) —**aer·o·me·chan·i·cal** *adj.* —**aer·o·me·chan·i·cal·ly** *adv.*

aer·o·med·i·cine /áirō médissin/ *n.* = **aviation medicine** —**aer·o·med·i·cal** *adj.*

aer·o·me·te·or·o·graph /áirō meetee áwrə gràf/ *n.* an instrument on board an aircraft that records temperature, atmospheric pressure, and humidity

aer·om·e·ter /ai rómmətər/ *n.* an instrument for measuring the mass or density of air or another gas [Late 18thC. From French *aéromètre*.]

aer·o·naut /áirə nàwt/ *n.* somebody who flies an aircraft that is lighter than air, e.g., a balloon or blimp [Late 18thC. From French *aéronaute*, from *aéro-* (from Greek *aēr* "air") + Greek *nautēs* "sailor" (source of English *nautical* and *astronaut*).]

aer·o·nau·ti·cal /áirə náwtik'l/, **aer·o·nau·tic** /áirə náwtik/ *adj.* relating to aircraft or their flight [Early 19thC. From French *aéronautique* (see AERONAUT).] —**aer·o·nau·ti·cal·ly** *adv.*

aer·o·nau·tics /áirə náwtiks/ *n.* the science that deals with aircraft and their flight (*takes a singular verb*)

aer·o·neu·ro·sis /áirō nŏŏ rőssiss/ *n.* anxiety and fatigue in airline pilots brought on by prolonged periods of flying

aer·o·pause /áirə pàwz/ *n.* the part of the Earth's upper atmosphere above which air is too thin for aircraft to fly

aer·o·pha·gy /ai róffəjee/, **aer·o·pha·gia** /áirə fáyjə/ *n.* the abnormal spasmodic swallowing of air, a common cause of flatulence and belching [Late 19thC. Modeled on French *aérophagie*.]

aer·o·pho·bi·a /áirə fṓbee ə/ *n.* an abnormal fear of drafts of air —**aer·o·pho·bic** /áirə fṓbik/ *adj.*

aer·o·phyte /áirə fīt/ *n.* = **epiphyte**

aer·o·plane /érrəplayn/ *n.* U.K. = **airplane**

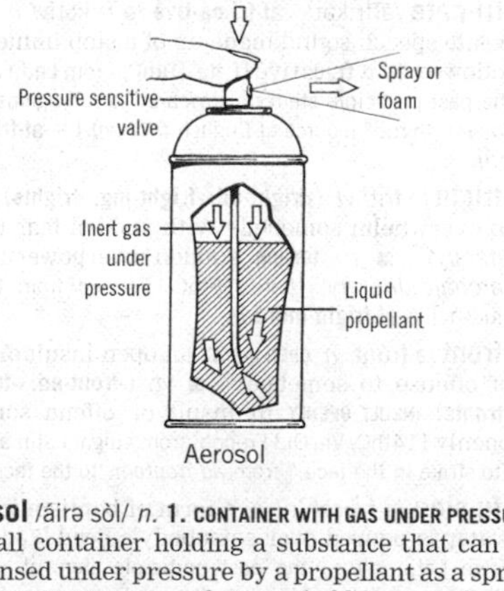

Aerosol

aer·o·sol /áirə sòl/ *n.* **1.** CONTAINER WITH GAS UNDER PRESSURE a small container holding a substance that can be dispensed under pressure by a propellant as a spray **2.** SUBSTANCE SPRAYED a substance held in a small container from which it can be dispensed under pressure by a propellant as a spray **3.** SUSPENSION OF PARTICLES IN GAS a suspension of solid or liquid particles in a gaseous medium

aer·o·space /áirō spàyss/ *n.* ATMOSPHERE AND OUTER SPACE the Earth's atmosphere and outer space ■ *adj.* OF AIRCRAFT AND SPACECRAFT relating to the design, manufacture, and flight of vehicles or missiles that fly in and beyond the Earth's atmosphere

aer·o·space med·i·cine *n.* the branch of medicine concerned with disorders associated with flight both inside and outside the Earth's atmosphere

aer·o·stat /áirō stàt/ *n.* a gas-filled aircraft such as a dirigible or balloon [Late 18thC. From French *aérostat*, from *aéro-* "AERO-" + Greek *statos* "standing" (source of English *static*).] —**aer·o·stat·ic** /áirō státtik/ *adj.*

aer·o·stat·ics /áirō státtiks/ *n.* **1.** PHYS STUDY OF GASES IN EQUILIBRIUM the study of gases in equilibrium and objects in equilibrium in gases **2.** AEROSP STUDY OF DIRIGIBLES AND BALLOONS the science of aircraft that are lighter than air, e.g., dirigibles and balloons

aer·o·ther·mo·dy·nam·ics /áirō thúrmō dī námmiks/ *n.* the study of the heat exchange between gases and solid objects, especially between air and aircraft flying at high velocity (*takes a singular verb*) —**aer·o·ther·mo·dy·nam·ic** *adj.*

aer·y[1] /áiree/ (**-i·er, -i·est**) *adj.* insubstantial and unworldly [Late 16thC. From Latin *aerius*, ultimately derived from Greek *aēr* "air" (source of English *air*).]

aer·y[2] *n.* = **aerie**

Aes·cu·la·pi·an /èskyə láypee ən/ *adj.* relating to medicine and the healing arts [Early 17thC. Formed from Latin *Aesculapius*, the Roman god of medicine.]

aes·cu·la·pi·an snake *n.* a long slender brown nonvenomous snake found in forests in Europe and western Asia. Latin name: *Elaphe longissima.* [From the common depiction of Aesculapius (see AESCULAPIAN) in antiquity with such a snake]

Ae·sop /ée̍ssəp, ée sòp/ (*fl.* 6th century B.C.) Greek writer and reputedly a former slave. His fables were popularized by the Roman poet Phaedrus (1st century A.D.).

aes·the·sia /es théezee ə/, **es·the·sia** *n.* the ability to feel or experience through the senses [Early 18thC. Via modern Latin from Greek *aisthēsis* "perceiving," from *aisthesthai* "to perceive" (see AESTHETIC).]

aes·thete /és thèet/, **es·thete** *n.* somebody who has or affects a highly developed appreciation of beauty, especially in the arts [Late 19thC. Back-formation from AESTHETIC, modeled on ATHLETE.]

aes·thet·ic /es théttik/, **es·thet·ic** *adj.* **1.** PHILOSOPHY RELATING TO AESTHETICS relating to the philosophical principles of aesthetics **2.** ARTS APPRECIATING BEAUTY sensitive to or appreciative of art or beauty **3.** ATTRACTIVE pleasing in appearance ■ *n.* SET OF PRINCIPLES a set of principles [Early 19thC. From Greek *aisthētikos* "perceptual," from *aisthesthai* "to perceive" (source of English *anesthetic*, literally "without feeling"). The sense "relating to perception of beauty" evolved from "perception."] —**aes·thet·i·cal·ly** *adv.*

aes·the·ti·cian /èsthə tísh'n/, **es·the·ti·cian** *n.* **1.** SOMEBODY WHO STUDIES BEAUTY a student or devotee of the principles of art or beauty **2.** PERSON GIVING BEAUTY TREATMENTS a person who gives beauty treatments to people

aes·thet·i·cism /es thétti sìzzəm/, **es·thet·i·cism** *n.* **1.** DERIVATION OF MORAL PRINCIPLES FROM BEAUTY the philosophical doctrine that all moral principles are derived from beauty **2.** BELIEF IN IMPORTANCE OF AESTHETICS the belief that the principles of aesthetics are of the highest importance in the arts **3.** LOVE OF BEAUTY appreciation of and devotion to beauty

aes·thet·i·cize /es thétti sìz/ (**-cized, -ciz·ing, -ciz·es**), **es·thet·i·cize** (**-cized, -ciz·ing, -ciz·es**) *vt.* to show something in its best or most artistic light

aes·thet·ics /es théttiks/, **es·thet·ics** *n.* **1.** STUDY OF BEAUTY the branch of philosophy dealing with the study of aesthetic values such as the beautiful and the sublime (*takes a singular verb*) **2.** STUDY OF ART the study of the rules and principles of art (*takes a singular verb*) **3.** IDEA OF BEAUTY a particular idea of what is beautiful or artistic (*takes a singular or plural verb*) **4.** HOW SOMETHING LOOKS how something looks, especially when considered in terms of how pleasing it is (*takes a singular or plural verb*) [Early 19thC. Via modern Latin *aesthetica*, from Greek *aisthētikos* (see AESTHETIC), perhaps modeled on ATHLETICS.]

aes·thet·ic sur·ge·ry, **es·thet·ic sur·ge·ry** *n.* = **cosmetic surgery**

aes·ti·val *adj.* = **estival**

aes·ti·vate *vi.* = **estivate**

aes·ti·va·tion *n.* = **estivation**

AET, **A.E.T.** *abbr.* aminoethylisothioronium

ae·ti·ol·o·gy *n.* = **etiology**

AEW *abbr.* airborne early warning (aircraft)

AF *abbr.* **1.** air force **2.** Anglo-French **3.** autofocus

Af. *abbr.* **1.** Africa **2.** African

a.f. *abbr.* audio frequency

af- *prefix.* = **ad-** (*used before f*)

a·far /ə fáar/ *adv.* FAR AWAY at, to, or from a great distance (*literary*) ■ *n.* PLACE FAR AWAY a great distance away [14thC. From A + FAR.]

AFB *abbr.* Air Force Base

AFC *abbr.* **1.** automatic flight control **2.** automatic frequency control

AFDC *abbr.* Aid to Families with Dependent Children

a·feard /ə féerd/, **a·feared** *adj.* afraid (*regional dated*) [Old English, the past participle of *afǣren* "to frighten," from *fǣren* "to fear"]

a·feb·rile /ay fébb rīl, -féeb-/ *adj.* having no fever, or marked by absence of fever

af·fa·ble /áffəb'l/ *adj.* good-natured, friendly and easy to talk to [15thC. Via French, from Latin *affabilis* "easy to speak to," from *(af)fari* "to speak (to)" (source of English *fable*, *fame*, and *fabulous*).] —**af·fa·bil·i·ty** /àffə bíllətee/ *n.* —**af·fa·bly** /-blee/ *adv.*

af·fair /ə fáir/ *n.* **1.** BUSINESS MATTER a matter that has been attended to or that needs attention, especially business ○ *a family affair* **2.** OCCURRENCE an event or occurrence that has been referred to or is known about ○ *that odd affair at work last week* **3.** SOCIAL EVENT a social event **4.** SOMETHING OF A PARTICULAR KIND an object or item of a particular kind ○ *The house is a ramshackle affair.* **5.** SEXUAL RELATIONSHIP a sexual relationship between two people not married to each other **6.** SCANDALOUS INCIDENT an incident that attracts public attention or notoriety ■ **af·fairs** *npl.* BUSINESS TO ATTEND TO professional, public, or personal business [12thC. Via French, literally "to do," from, ultimately, Latin *facere* (source of English *fact* and *fashion*).]

af·faire de coeur /ə fàir də kúr/ (*plural* **af·faires de coeur** /ə fàir də kúr/) *n.* a love affair or romantic attachment [Early 19thC. From French, literally "affair of the heart."]

af·fect[1] /ə fékt/ (**-fect·ed, -fect·ing, -fects**) *vt.* **1.** INFLUENCE to act upon or have an effect on somebody or something **2.** MOVE EMOTIONALLY to move somebody emotionally **3.** CAUSE DISEASE to infect or damage somebody or something with disease [14thC. From Latin *affect-*, the past participle stem of *afficere* "to act on," from *facere* "to do" (source of English *fact* and *fetish*).]

WORD KEY: USAGE

affect or **effect**? The first thing to notice is that ***affect*** is only a verb, whereas ***effect*** is a noun and verb. What causes confusion is that they are both pronounced the same way and have meanings that are closely related. If one thing ***affects*** another, it has an ***effect*** on it. Notice also that you can ***affect*** (cause a change in) people as well as things, but you can only ***effect*** (bring about) things. *The election effected major changes in the government.*

af·fect[2] /ə fékt/ (**-fect·ed, -fect·ing, -fects**) *vt.* **1.** PRETEND TO BE to give the appearance or pretense of something **2.** ADOPT SOMETHING to adopt a use, style, or manner as your own **3.** ACT LIKE SOMEBODY to imitate somebody else's style or character **4.** COME TO BE OR HAVE to assume a particular form or state ○ *affect a liquid state* [15thC. Directly or via French *affecter* from Latin *affectare* "to strive for," from *affect-*, the past participle stem of *afficere* (see AFFECT[1]).] —**af·fect·er** *n.*

af·fect[3] /á fèkt/ *n.* an emotion or mood associated with an idea or action, or the external expression of such a feeling ○ *blunted affect* [Late 19thC. Via German *Affekt*.]

af·fec·ta·tion /à fek táysh'n/ *n.* **1.** BEHAVIOR INTENDED TO IMPRESS feigned or unnatural behavior that is often meant to impress others **2.** ACT INTENDED TO IMPRESS an appearance or manner assumed or put on as a show or pretense, often to impress others [Mid-16thC. Directly or via French, from the Latin stem *affection-* "influence," from *affectare* (see AFFECT[2]).]

af·fect·ed /ə féktəd/ *adj.* **1.** INFLUENCED BY SOMETHING acted upon or influenced by something or somebody **2.** MOVED EMOTIONALLY emotionally moved by something **3.** INFECTED OR DAMAGED infected or damaged by disease **4.** TRYING TO IMPRESS behaving in an unnatural way intended to impress others **5.** INTENDED TO IMPRESS done or assumed with the intention of impressing others —**af·fect·ed·ly** *adv.* —**af·fect·ed·ness** *n.*

af·fect·ing /ə fékting/ *adj.* able to stir the emotions —**af·fect·ing·ly** *adv.*

af·fec·tion /ə fékshən/ *n.* FONDNESS fond or tender feeling toward somebody or something ■ **af·fect·ions** *npl.* FEELINGS feelings of fondness or tenderness, sometimes as opposed to reason [12thC. Via Old French *affectation* "emotion," from the Latin stem *affection-* "inclination," from, ultimately, *afficere* (see AFFECT[1]).] —**af·fec·tion·al** *adj.* —**af·fec·tion·al·ly** *adv.*

WORD KEY: SYNONYMS

See Synonyms at ***love***.

af·fec·tion·ate /ə fékshənət/ *adj.* having or showing affection [15thC. Directly or via French, from Latin *affectionatus* "devoted," from the stem *affection-* (see AFFECTION).] —**af·fec·tion·ate·ly** *adv.* —**af·fec·tion·ate·ness** *n.*

af·fec·tive /ə féktiv/ *adj.* **1.** PSYCHOL OF EMOTIONAL EXPRESSION relating to an external expression of emotion associated with an idea or action **2.** = **affecting** [15thC. Via French *affectif* from late Latin *affectivus*, from Latin *affect-*, the past participle stem of *afficere* (see AFFECT[1]).] —**af·fec·tive·ly** *adv.* —**af·fec·tiv·i·ty** /à fek tívvətee/ *n.*

af·fec·tive dis·or·der *n.* a prolonged emotional disturbance, e.g., depression

af·fect·less /ə féktləss/ *adj.* feeling or showing no emotion —**af·fect·less·ness** *n.*

Affenpinscher

af·fen·pin·scher /áffən pìnchər/ *n.* a European breed of small dogs with wiry hair and a tufted muzzle [Early 20thC. From German, literally "ape terrier."]

af·fer·ent /áffərənt/ *adj.* used to describe nerves that carry impulses from the outer body toward the brain or spinal cord, or blood vessels that carry blood to an organ [Mid-19thC. From Latin, the present participle stem of *afferre* "to bring toward."] —**af·fer·ently** *adv.*

af·fet·tu·o·so /ə fèchoo ṓssō/ *adv., adj.* played or sung musically with feeling (*used as a musical direction*) [Early 18thC. From Italian, ultimately from Latin *affect-*, the past participle stem of *afficere* "to act on" (see AFFECT[1]).]

af·fi·ance /ə fī́ ənss/ (**-anced, -anc·ing, -anc·es**) *vt.* to promise yourself or somebody else in marriage to somebody (*formal*) (*often passive*) [14thC. Via Old French *afiancer* from *afiance* "trust," from, ultimately, medieval Latin *affidare* "to trust" (source of English *affidavit*).]

af·fi·da·vit /àffi dáyvit/ *n.* a written declaration made on oath before somebody authorized to administer oaths, usually setting out the statement of a witness for court proceedings [Late 16thC. From medieval Latin, literally "he or she has sworn," a form of *affidare* "to trust, affirm," from, ultimately, *fidus* "faithful" (source of English *fidelity*).]

af·fil·i·ate *v.* /ə fíllee àyt/ (**-at·ed, -at·ing, -ates**) **1.** *vti.* COMBINE ORGANIZATIONS to come, or bring a person or group, into a close relationship with another, usually larger, group **2.** *vt.* DETERMINE SOMETHING'S ORIGIN to determine the origin of something ■ *n.* /ə fíllee ət, -àyt/ ASSOCIATE a group that is closely connected with a larger group, or an individual who combines with others to form a group [Mid-18thC. From Latin *affiliare* "to adopt as a son," from *filius* "son" (source of English *filial*).] —**af·fil·i·at·ed** *adj.* —**af·fil·i·a·tion** /ə fíllee áysh'n/ *n.*

af·fine /ə fī́n, a-/ *n.* **1.** MATH TYPE OF GEOMETRIC TRANSFORMATION a geometric transformation that maps points and parallel lines to points and parallel lines **2.** ANTHROP RELATIVE a relative by marriage [Early 20thC. From Latin *affinis* (see AFFINITY).] —**af·fi·nal** /ə fī́n'l/ *adj.*

af·fined /ə fī́nd/ *adj.* joined by close relationship (*formal*)

af·fin·i·ty /ə fínnitee/ (*plural* **-ties**) *n.* **1.** FEELING OF IDENTIFICATION a natural liking for or inclination toward somebody or something, or a feeling of identification with somebody or something **2.** SOMEBODY ATTRACTIVE somebody to whom somebody else is attracted **3.** CONNECTION a similarity or likeness that connects persons or things **4.** ANTHROP KINSHIP BY MARRIAGE a relationship by marriage rather than blood **5.** BIOL, LANG SIMILARITY IN STRUCTURE a similarity in structure between groups that may suggest a common origin **6.** CHEM LIKELIHOOD OF CHEMICAL REACTION a measure of the likelihood of a chemical reaction taking place between two substances **7.** IMMUNOL ANTIGEN-ANTIBODY ATTRACTION the attraction between an antigen and an antibody [14thC. Via Old French *afinité* "close relationship" from, ultimately, Latin *affinis*, literally "bordering on something," from *finis* "border" (source of English *finish* and *confine*).]

af·firm /ə fúrm/ (**-firmed, -firm·ing, -firms**) *v.* **1.** *vti.* DECLARE POSITIVELY to declare positively that something is true ○ *They affirmed their continued support for the initiative* **2.** *vt.* CONFIRM to confirm something as binding or valid **3.** *vi.* LAW MAKE A FORMAL STATEMENT to make a statement formally but not under oath [13thC. Via Old French, from Latin *affirmare* "to strengthen," from *firmus* "firm" (source of English *firm* and *farm*).] —**af·firm·a·ble** *adj.* —**af·firm·a·bly** *adv.* —**af·fir·mant** *n.* —**af·firm·er** *n.*

af·fir·ma·tion /àffər máysh'n/ *n.* **1.** ASSERTION OF TRUTH an assertion of truth **2.** SOMETHING SAID TO BE TRUE something asserted as being true **3.** LAW FORMAL LEGAL DECLARATION a formal declaration acceptable in a court, usually made by somebody who has a conscientious objection to taking an oath **4.** POSITIVE STATEMENT OF ACHIEVEMENT a positive statement asserting that a goal the speaker or thinker wishes to achieve is already happening ○ *Start the day by repeating 20 times the affirmation "I am a nonsmoker."* [15thC. Directly or via French, from the Latin stem *affirmation-*, from *affirmare* (see AFFIRM).]

af·fir·ma·tive /ə fúrmətiv/ *adj.* **1.** TRUE confirming or asserting that something is true **2.** INDICATING AGREEMENT indicating agreement or giving assent **3.** LOGIC RELATING TO A TYPE OF PROPOSITION relating to or being a categorical proposition in which the predicate's extension is contained partially or wholly within the subject, e.g., "All humans are mammals" ■ *n.* **1.** POSITIVE ASSERTION a positive assertion **2.** WORD CONVEYING AGREEMENT a word or statement conveying agreement or approval **3.** SIDE FOR A PROPOSITION the side in a debate that supports a proposition ■ *interj.* MIL YES a signal codeword expressing agreement or compliance —**af·fir·ma·tive·ly** *adv.*

af·fir·ma·tive ac·tion *n.* a policy or program aimed at countering discrimination against minorities and women, especially in employment and education

af·fix *vt.* /ə fíks/ (**-fixed, -fix·ing, -fix·es**) **1.** FASTEN TO SOMETHING ELSE to fasten something to something else **2.** ADD ON TO SOMETHING to add something at the end of something, e.g., a signature to a document **3.** ATTRIBUTE TO SOMEBODY to ascribe something, e.g., responsibility or blame, to somebody ■ *n.* /áffiks/ **1.** LING PART ADDED TO A WORD a form added to the beginning, middle, or end of another word that creates a derivative word or inflection **2.** SOMETHING ATTACHED something attached or added [Mid-16thC. Directly or via French *affixer* from medieval Latin *affixare*, literally "to keep on fastening to," from Latin *affigere* "to fasten to," from *figere* "to fasten" (source of English *fix*).] —**af·fix·a·ble** *adj.* —**af·fix·er** *n.*

af·fla·tus /ə fláytəss/ *n.* creative inspiration, usually thought of as divine (*literary*) [Mid-17thC. From Latin, literally "act of blowing on," from, ultimately, *flare* "to blow" (source of English *flatulent*). The underlying sense is of divine breath infusing a mortal being.]

af·flict /ə flíkt/ (**-flict·ed, -flict·ing, -flicts**) *vt.* to cause severe mental or physical distress to somebody [14thC. From Latin *afflict-*, the past participle stem of *affligere*, literally "to strike down," hence "to cause to suffer," from *fligere* "to strike" (source of English *profligate*).] —**af·flict·er** *n.* —**af·flic·tive** *adj.* —**af·flic·tive·ly** *adv.*

WORD KEY: USAGE

afflict or **inflict**? The chief difference is in the grammatical construction: you ***inflict*** something unpleasant on somebody, whereas you ***afflict*** somebody (or, more usually, somebody is ***afflicted***) with or by something unpleasant. *The government will inflict a new hardship on students when it abolishes the student loans. The population was afflicted with a series of food shortages.*

af·flic·tion /ə flíkshən/ *n.* **1.** DISTRESS a condition of great physical or mental distress **2.** CAUSE OF DISTRESS something that causes great physical or mental distress [14thC. Via Old French from the Latin stem *affliction-*, from *affligere* (see AFFLICT).]

af·flu·ence /áffloo ənss/, **af·flu·en·cy** /-ənsee/ *n.* an abundance of material wealth [14thC. Via French, from Latin *affluentia*, from *affluent-*, the present participle stem of *affluere* (see AFFLUENT).]

af·flu·ent /áffloo ənt/ *adj.* WEALTHY having an abundance of material wealth ■ *n.* **1.** WEALTHY PEOPLE people who are financially well off ○ *restaurants and clubs frequented by the affluent* **2.** GEOG STREAM FLOWING INTO ANOTHER a stream or river that flows into another [15thC. Via Old French, from, ultimately, Latin *affluere* "to flow toward," from *fluere* "to flow" (source of English *fluid*).] —**af·flu·ent·ly** *adv.*

WORD KEY: CULTURAL NOTE

The Affluent Society, a book by U.S. economist John Kenneth Galbraith (published 1958). One of Galbraith's most widely read works, it attacks what he views as the American obsession with production and material goods and urges greater government expenditure on the country's infrastructure and public services.

af·flux /á flùks/ *n.* an inward flow or flow toward a point, especially of blood in the body [Early 17thC. From medieval Latin *affluxus*, from *affluere* (see AFFLUENT).]

af·ford /ə fáwrd/ (**-ford·ed, -ford·ing, -fords**) *vt.* **1.** BE ABLE TO BUY to be able to meet the cost of something without unacceptable difficulty **2.** BE ABLE TO DO to be able to do or provide something without unacceptable or disadvantageous consequences **3.** BE ABLE TO SPARE to be able to spare something without unacceptable or disadvantageous consequences **4.** PROVIDE to supply or provide something (*formal*) [Old English *geforþian* "to accomplish," from *forþian* "to further." The sense "to be able to buy" evolved from the idea of "having enough money to accomplish something."]

af·ford·a·ble /ə fáwrdəb'l/ *adj.* able to be paid for, done, or spared without unacceptable difficulty or disadvantageous consequences —**af·ford·a·bil·i·ty** /ə fàwrdə bíllətee/ *n.* —**af·ford·a·bly** /-blee/ *adv.*

af·for·est /ə fáwrəst/ (**-est·ed, -est·ing, -ests**) *vt.* to convert land not previously forested into forest by planting trees [Early 16thC. From medieval Latin *afforestare*, from *foresta* (partial source of English *forest*).] —**af·for·es·ta·tion** /ə fàwrə stáysh'n/ *n.*

af·fray /ə fráy/ *n.* a fight or violent disturbance in a public place [14thC. Via Anglo-Norman *afrayer* "to disturb" from assumed Vulgar Latin *exfridare*, literally "to take out of peace." Ultimately of prehistoric Germanic origin.]

af·fri·cate /áffrikət/, **af·fri·ca·tive** /ə fríkətiv/ *n.* a composite speech sound made up of a stop immediately followed by a fricative [Late 19thC. From Latin *affricat-*, the past participle stem of *affricare* "to rub against," from *fricare* "to rub" (source of English *friction*).] —**af·fri·ca·tive** *adj.*

af·fright /ə frī́t/ *vt.* (**-fright·ed, -fright·ing, -frights**) FRIGHTEN to overwhelm somebody with sudden fear (*archaic literary*) ■ *n.* TERROR sudden overpowering fear (*archaic literary*) [Late 16thC. Formed from the verb FRIGHT.] —**af·fright·ment** *n.*

af·front /ə frúnt/ *n.* OPEN INSULT an open insult or giving of offense to somebody ■ *vt.* (**-front·ed, -front·ing, -fronts**) INSULT OPENLY to insult or offend somebody openly [14thC. Via Old French, from Vulgar Latin *affrontare* "to strike in the face," from *ad frontem* "to the face."]

af·fu·sion /ə fyóozh'n/ *n.* a form of baptism in which water is poured over somebody's head [Early 17thC. From Latin *affus-*, the past participle stem of *affundere* "to pour on," from *fundere* "to pour" (source of English *foundry*).]

af·ghan /áf gàn/ *n.* **1.** BLANKET a knitted or crocheted blanket or shawl, often with geometric designs **2.** CARPET a large carpet woven in a geometric design [Early 18thC. From Pashto *afghānī* "of Afghanistan."]

Af·ghan *n.* **1.** PEOPLES SOMEBODY FROM AFGHANISTAN somebody who was born or raised in Afghanistan, or who is a citizen of Afghanistan **2.** LANG = **Pashto** **3.** ZOOL = **Afghan hound** ■ *adj.* OF AFGHANISTAN relating to or typical of the Republic of Afghanistan, or its people or culture

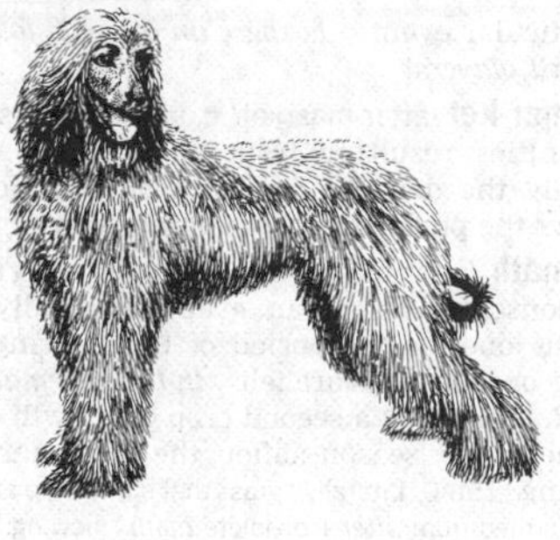

Afghan hound

Af·ghan hound, **Af·ghan** (*unmarked inflection* **-ghans**) *n.* a tall dog with a long silky coat, belonging to a breed originally developed in Afghanistan as hunting dogs and sheepdogs

af·ghan·i /af gánnee, -gáanee/ (*plural* **-is**) *n.* **1.** see table at **currency 2.** COIN WORTH AN AFGHANI a coin worth one afghani [Early 20thC. From Pashto *afghānī.*]

Afghanistan

Af·ghan·i·stan /af gánni stàn/ former monarchy in southwestern Asia, which became a republic in 1973. Language: Pashto, Dari (Persian). Currency: Afghani. Capital: Kabul. Population: 23,738,085 (1997). Area: 251,825 sq. mi./652,225 sq. km.

Af·ghan·i·sti·za·tion /af gànnì stə záysh'n, -ganí-/ *n.* the process of becoming, or coming to be seen as, a remote and marginal place [Late 20thC. Formed from AFGHANISTAN, from the political and social disintegration there after the breakup of the Soviet Union.]

a·fi·cio·na·da /ə fìshə naádə, ə fìshiə-/ *n.* a woman who is enthusiastic and knowledgeable about something

a·fi·cio·na·do /ə fìshə naádō, ə fìshee ə-/ (*plural* **-dos**) *n.* **1.** ENTHUSIAST somebody who is enthusiastic and knowledgeable about something **2.** BULLFIGHTING ENTHUSIAST a devotee of bullfighting [Mid-19thC. Via Spanish, literally "somebody who likes something," from, ultimately, the Latin stem *affection-* (see AFFECTION).]

a·field /ə feéld/ *adv., adj.* **1.** AWAY distant from home or customary surroundings **2.** OFF THE POINT off the point or subject

a·fi·ko·men /àafi kṓmən/ *n.* in Judaism, the unleavened bread that completes the festive meal (**Seder**) on the first night of Passover [Late 19thC. Via Hebrew *aphīqōmān* from Greek, "festival."]

a·fire /ə fír/ *adj., adv.* **1.** ABLAZE on fire or blazing **2.** PASSIONATE passionately interested in something

AFL *abbr.* **1.** American Federation of Labor **2.** American Football League

a·flame /ə fláym/ *adj.* **1.** ABLAZE in flames or blazing **2.** IMPASSIONED highly aroused or impassioned

af·la·tox·in /àfflə tóksin/ *n.* a toxic compound produced by a mold fungus in agricultural crops, especially peanuts, and in animal feeds that have not been carefully stored. It can cause hepatitis and liver cancer. [Mid-20thC. Coined from modern Latin *Aspergillus flavus* + TOXIN.]

AFL-CIO *abbr.* American Federation of Labor and Congress of Industrial Organizations

a·float /ə flṓt/ *adj., adv.* **1.** FLOATING ON WATER floating on water **2.** ON BOARD SHIP on board a ship or at sea **3.** FLOODED covered with water **4.** DRFITING PURPOSELESSLY without purpose or guidance **5.** IN CIRCULATION circulating among the public **6.** FINANCIALLY SOLVENT free of debt or financial problems

a·flut·ter /ə flúttər/ *adj., adv.* **1.** EXCITED in a state of agitation or excitement **2.** FLAPPING flapping or waving, e.g., as a flag does in the breeze

a·foot /ə fóot/ *adj., adv.* **1.** HAPPENING in the process of happening **2.** ON FOOT on foot or by walking [13thC. Partly modeled on Old Norse *á fótum* "on foot."]

a·fore /ə fáwr/ *adv., prep., conj.* before (*regional*) [Old English *onforan*, from *foran* "in front, before" (source also of English *before*)]

a·fore·men·tioned /ə fáwr mènshənd/ *adj.* MENTIONED EARLIER previously mentioned (*formal*) ■ *n.* THE PREVIOUSLY MENTIONED the previously mentioned person or people (*formal*)

a·fore·said /ə fáwr sèd/ *adj.* previously named (*formal*)

a·fore·thought /ə fáwr thàwt/ *adj.* thought about or planned beforehand

a for·ti·o·ri /aa fàwrtee áwree, ay fàwrtee ō rī/ *adv.* for an even stronger reason [Early 17thC. From Latin, literally "from the stronger (reason)," from *fortis* "strong."]

a·foul /ə fówl/ *adj., adv.* **1.** INTO CONFLICT in or into trouble or conflict with somebody or something **2.** ENTANGLED entangled or in collision with something

Afr. *abbr.* Africa ■ *abbr.* African

a·fraid /ə fráyd/ *adj.* **1.** FRIGHTENED frightened or apprehensive about something **2.** RELUCTANT feeling hesitation or disinclination toward something **3.** REGRETFUL regretful that something is or is not the case [14thC. Originally the past participle of AFFRAY, modeled on Anglo-Norman *affrayé.*]

WORD KEY: CULTURAL NOTE

Who's Afraid of Virginia Woolf?, a play by American dramatist Edward Albee (1962). Albee's first full-length play examines the sour relationship between a middle-aged, underachieving academic and his embittered wife. A dinner party with a younger, not dissimilar, couple forces them to confront the reality of their past and present.

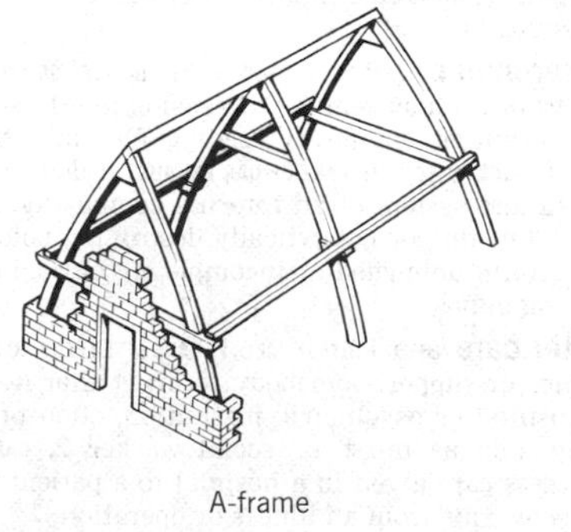

A-frame

A-frame *adj.* SHAPED LIKE A built in the shape of a capital letter A ■ *n.* A-SHAPED BUILDING a building shaped like a capital letter A, with a triangular front and back and a roof that slopes to the ground forming the sides of the building

af·reet /á freét, ə freét/, **af·rit** *n.* an evil spirit or powerful monster in Arabian mythology [Late 18thC. From Arabic *afrīt.*]

a·fresh /ə frésh/ *adv.* once again, especially from the beginning

Af·ri·ca /áffrikə/ the second largest continent, lying south of Europe with the Atlantic Ocean to the west and the Indian Ocean to the east. Population: 728,000,000 (1995). Area: 11,699,000 sq. mi./30,330,000 sq. km.

Af·ri·can /áffrikən/ *adj.* OF AFRICA relating to or typical of any of the countries of the African continent, or their peoples or cultures ■ *n.* **1.** SOMEBODY FROM AFRICA somebody who was born or who lives in Africa **2.** SOMEBODY OF AFRICAN DESCENT somebody descended from any of the peoples of Africa [Pre-12thC. From Latin *Africanus*, from, ultimately, *Afri* "the ancient inhabitants of North Africa."]

Af·ri·can A·mer·i·can *n.* an American of African descent —**African American** *adj.*

WORD KEY: USAGE

African American, **Afro-American**, or **Black**? ***African American*** has vigorously overtaken ***Afro-American*** as a term descriptive of Black Americans. Similarly, *Chinese American* is now more common than *Sino-American*, and *Italian American* than *Italo-American*. Unlike the others of these compounds, of course, ***African American***, along with *Asian American*, refers to a continent, not a country. This lack of parallelism perhaps explains why ***African American*** and *Asian American* seldom appear in discussions of international relations, whereas both forms of the compounds that pair another country with the United States often do (*Franco-American dialogue* and *French-American friendship*). Other limitations on the use of ***African American*** have to do with the stress it lays on African heritage. Although Blacks with Caribbean or Hispanic backgrounds may be able to trace their ancestry to Africa, they do not necessarily regard themselves as ***African Americans,*** any more than the descendants of Spanish immigrants to Argentina consider themselves Spanish. ***Black*** is broader in application, referring as well to non-Americans. *People of color* is broader still, referring to non-whites of whatever origin and nationality. *Colored people* is redolent of other times or other places and is not recommended.

Af·ri·can A·mer·i·can Ver·nac·u·lar Eng·lish *n.* the variety of English spoken by many African Americans

WORD KEY: WORLD ENGLISH

African American Vernacular English, or **AAVE**, is the term used by scholars for the widespread and varied African American usages also called *Ebonics*, *Afro-American English*, *American Black English*, *Black English*, *Black English Vernacular*, and *Black Vernacular English*. Originating in the pidgin of the slave trade and Plantation Creole in the U.S. Southern states, African American Vernacular English considerably influenced U.S. Southern English and, in the late 19th and the 20th centuries, spread by migration through much of the nation. It therefore has both rural and urban components. It has also come to be associated with the language of blues, jazz, and rap music.

As with African English, African American Vernacular English is "non-rhotic" or *r*-dropping: *r* is not pronounced in words such as *art*, *door*, and *worker*. Its other characteristics – some going back to similar features of African languages – are these: (1) the use of *d* and *t* instead of *th*, as in *dem* for *them* and *tree* for *three*; 2. *l*-dropping, as in *hep* for *help*, *sef* for *self*, and *too* for *tool*; (3) consonant reduction at the ends of some words (including tense endings), as in *wha* for *what*, *jus* for *just*, and *pas* for *past*; (4) use of *-n* for *-ing*, as in *runnin* for *running*; (5) multiple negatives, as in *no way nobody can do it*; (6) verb aspects marked for intermittent, momentary, or continuous action rather than tense per se, the tense time being apparent from the contexts, as in *he be laughin* for *he is always laughing* and *he run* for *he runs*; and (7) dropping of the verb *to be* in some constructions, as in *she sick* and *he gone* for *she is sick* and *he has gone*.

African American Vernacular English expressions have contributed to the rich texture of American English, these terms being typical: *yam* (sweet potato), *goober* (peanut), *okra*, *gumbo* (the soup and the river mud), *tote* (carry), *juke*, *mumbo jumbo*, *hey/hip*, and *boogie woogie.* All these are rooted in African languages. In its more urban settings, African American Vernacular English's contributions are also many, these few examples making the point: *dis* (to disrespect), *igg* (to ignore), *chill out* (to stop behaving stupidly), *'tude* (attitude), *the Man* (the police), *hang-up* (a problem), *rap* (to talk), *make it* (succeed), *kicks* (pleasure), and the sense of *bad* meaning variously "good," "extraordinary," and "beautiful." See also ***African English.***

Af·ri·can buf·fa·lo (*plural* **Af·ri·can buf·fa·los** *or* **Af·ri·can buf·fa·loes** *or* **Af·ri·can buf·fa·lo**) *n.* a reddish-brown to black wild buffalo found in Africa. There are two species, the Cape buffalo and the smaller forest, or dwarf, buffalo. Latin name: *Synceros caffer* and *Synceros nanus.*

Af·ri·can Ca·na·di·an *n.* a Canadian of African descent —**Af·ri·can Ca·na·di·an** *adj.*

Af·ri·can dai·sy (*plural* **Af·ri·can dai·sies**) *n.* a plant with colorful flowers resembling large daisies. The name is used for several different plants originating in Africa.

Af·ri·can·der *n.* = **Afrikander**

Af·ri·can Eng·lish *n.* the variety of English spoken in Africa

Af·ri·can green·heart (*plural* **Af·ri·can green·hearts** *or* **Af·ri·can green·heart**) *n.* a leguminous tree of African tropical forests that is the source of commercially important timber. Latin name: *Cylicodiscus gabunensis.*

Af·ri·can·ism /áfrikənizzəm/ *n.* a cultural characteristic typical of Africa or Africans, especially a linguistic feature, usually when found in a non-African language

Af·ri·can·ist /áfrikənist/ *n.* somebody who specializes in African affairs, cultures, or languages

Af·ri·can·ized bee *n.* an aggressive honeybee that was accidentally hybridized in Brazil from African and European strains and has spread north into Mexico and southern Texas

Af·ri·can lil·y (*plural* **Af·ri·can lil·ies**) *n.* a southern African plant of the lily family that has rounded heads of funnel-shaped blue, or sometimes white, flowers. Latin name: *Agapanthus africanus.*

Af·ri·can ma·hog·a·ny (*plural* **Af·ri·can ma·hog·a·nies**) *n.* **1.** AFRICAN TREE LIKE MAHOGANY an African tree that produces wood similar in appearance to that of tropical American mahogany. Genera: *Khaya* and *Entandrophragma.* **2.** WOOD LIKE MAHOGANY the hard wood of the African mahogany tree. It is used for making the same types of products as true mahogany, e.g., furniture.

Af·ri·can mil·let *n.* = **pearl millet**

Af·ri·can Na·tion·al Con·gress *n.* full form of **ANC**

African violet

Af·ri·can vi·o·let *n.* a tropical African plant grown as a houseplant for its violet, white, or pink flowers and fleshy leaves. Genus: *Saintpaulia.*

Af·ri·kaans /àffri kaáns, -kaánz/ *n.* SOUTH AFRICAN LANGUAGE one of the 11 official languages of South Africa, also spoken in Namibia. It is descended from the Dutch spoken by 17th-century settlers. Afrikaans is spoken by about 10 million people. ■ *adj.* OF AFRIKANERS relating to or typical of the Afrikaner people, or their culture or language [Early 20thC. From Dutch "African."]

Af·ri·kan·der /àffri kándər/, **Af·ri·can·der** *n.* **1.** AGRIC BREED OF S AFRICAN BEEF CATTLE a long-horned humpbacked animal with a reddish color, belonging to a South African breed of beef cattle **2.** AGRIC BREED OF S AFRICAN SHEEP a sheep belonging to an indigenous South African breed **3.** PEOPLES AFRIKANER an Afrikaner (*archaic*) [Variant of AFRIKANER]

Af·ri·ka·ner /àffri kaánər/ *n.* AFRIKAANS-SPEAKING SOUTH AFRICAN a South African whose first language is Afrikaans, usually descended from 17th century settlers (**Boers**) ■ *adj.* OF AFRIKAANS-SPEAKING SOUTH AFRICANS relating to or typical of the Afrikaans-speaking population of South Africa [Early 19thC. From Afrikaans, formed from *Afrikaan* "African person" on the model of *Hollander* "Dutch person."]

af·rit *n.* = **afreet**

Af·ro /áffrō/ *n.* (*plural* **-ros**) HAIRSTYLE WITH TIGHT CURLS a hairstyle with rounded thick curls ■ *adj.* OF AFRICA of African origin or style [Mid-20thC. From AFRO-AMERICAN or AFRO-.]

Afro- *prefix.* Africa, African ○ *Afro-Cuban* [From Latin *Afr-*, the stem of Afer "an African"]

Af·ro-A·mer·i·can *n., adj.* = **African American**

WORD KEY: USAGE

See Usage note at ***African American.***

Af·ro-A·sian *adj.* relating to the continents of Africa and Asia or their peoples or shared cultural phenomena

Af·ro-A·si·at·ic *n.* a family of more than 200 languages spoken across North Africa and the Middle East, consisting of the Semitic, Berber, Cushitic, Chadic, and Egyptian subfamilies. About 250 million people speak an Afro-Asiatic language. — **Afro-Asiatic** *adj.*

Af·ro-Car·ib·be·an *n.* somebody of African descent who lives or used to live in the Caribbean, or whose family used to live there

Af·ro-Cu·ban *adj.* relating to Cuban culture as influenced by Africa, especially a style of jazz based on Cuban interpretations of African rhythms

aft /aft/ *adv., adj.* toward or at the rear of a ship, submarine, or aircraft [Early 17thC. Shortening of ABAFT.]

AFT *abbr.* American Federation of Teachers

aft. *abbr.* afternoon

af·ter /áftər/ *prep.* **1.** LATER THAN later in time than **2.** BEHIND behind in order or place **3.** IN PURSUIT OF in pursuit of or looking for **4.** REGARDING about or regarding **5.** FOLLOWING FROM subsequent to and considering **6.** LIKE in imitation or in the manner of somebody or something **7.** AGREEING WITH in agreement with or in conformity to **8.** PAST THE HOUR OF past the hour of ■ *adv.* **1.** LATER later in time or place **2.** NAUT, AIR FURTHER BACK further toward the rear of a ship, submarine, or aircraft ■ *conj.* FOLLOWING A TIME WHEN following a time when, and sometimes as a result ■ *adj.* **1.** SUBSEQUENT later in time **2.** NAUT, AIR REAR nearer to the rear of a ship, submarine, or aircraft [Old English *æfter.* Assumed to be a comparative form, literally "further away," from an Indo-European base meaning "away, off" (ancestor also of English *off*).] ◇ **after all 1.** used to emphasize something that should be taken into consideration in spite of what has happened or been said **2.** used to show that in the end something happened, was done, or was recognized in spite of expectations to the contrary or efforts to prevent it

af·ter·beat /áftər beet/ *n.* = **backbeat**

af·ter·birth /áftər bùrth/ *n.* the placenta and fetal membranes expelled from the womb after a birth [Late 16thC. Perhaps modeled on German *Aftergeburt.*]

af·ter·burn·er /áftər bùrnər/ *n.* **1.** DEVICE FOR INCREASING JET'S THRUST a system for increasing the thrust of an aircraft jet engine by feeding fuel into the hot exhaust gases **2.** PART OF CAR EXHAUST a device in the exhaust system of an internal combustion engine for burning or catalytically destroying potentially harmful unburned or incompletely burned carbon compounds

af·ter·care /áftər kàir/ *n.* MED **1.** CARE AFTER LEAVING HOSPITAL care or support somebody receives after leaving a hospital or psychiatric institution, often provided by a home nurse or social worker **2.** CARE AFTER ILLNESS care given in a hospital to a patient who is recovering from an illness or operation

af·ter·clap /áftər klàp/ *n.* a belated, unexpected, and usually adverse consequence of something thought to be over and done with

af·ter·damp /áftər dàmp/ *n.* gaseous fumes remaining in a mine after an explosion of firedamp

af·ter·deck /áftər dèk/ *n.* the part of the main open deck of a ship that extends from the bridge or midships to the stern

af·ter·ef·fect /áftər i fèkt/ *n.* **1.** DELAYED RESULT an effect, usually unpleasant, that follows its cause after an interval of time ○ *The stock markets are still showing the aftereffects of last month's rise in interest rates.* **2.** PHYSIOL SECONDARY REACTION a secondary response that follows the primary response to a physiological stimulus **3.** PSYCHOL DELAYED REACTION a delayed reaction to a psychological stimulus

af·ter·glow /áftər glō/ *n.* **1.** LIGHT GLOW radiated light that remains visible after a source of light or energy has been removed, e.g., the glow sometimes seen in the sky after sunset **2.** GOOD FEELING a feeling of pleasure or a favorable impression that remains after a positive experience ○ *In the afterglow of the victory, we forgot our leading scorer had been injured.*

af·ter·im·age /áftər ìmmij/ *n.* a visual image that remains briefly after light stimulation has ended

af·ter·life /áftər līf/ *n.* **1.** RELIG LIFE AFTER DEATH a form of existence believed to continue after death **2.** LATER STAGE OF LIFE the period of somebody's life that follows a particular event ○ *Is there an afterlife for retired football players?*

af·ter·mar·ket /áftər maàrkət/ *n.* subsequent sales opportunities resulting from an original sale, especially the demand for parts and services that follows the purchase of something such as a car

af·ter·math /áftər màth/ *n.* **1.** PERIOD FOLLOWING BAD EVENT the consequences of an event, especially a disastrous one, or the period of time during which these consequences are felt ○ *in the aftermath of the war* **2.** SECOND CROP a second crop or growth of grass in the same season, after the first harvest or mowing [15thC. Literally "grass that springs up after mowing," formed from *after* + obsolete *math* "mowing."]

WORD KEY: REGIONAL NOTE

To refer to a second cutting of growth after the first growth of hay has been cut, ***aftermath*** is used principally in the New England and Delaware regions. It is also recorded in the South of the United States, beside *second cutting,* ***lattermath,*** and the dominant Gulf States term *volunteer* and *volunteer crop. Aftermath* is less common in the Midwest and Upper Midwest, where *second crop* prevails. Another New England term, *aftergrass,* has little currency beyond the northeastern states.

af·ter·most /áftər mōst/, **aft·most** /áft mōst/ *adj.* nearest to the stern of a ship

af·ter·noon /áftər noón/ *n.* **1.** TIME DAYTIME BETWEEN MIDDAY AND EVENING the period of the day between noon and evening **2.** LATTER PART a latter part of something, especially of somebody's life (*literary*) ■ *interj.* GREETING a greeting used to say "good afternoon" (*informal*)

af·ter·noons /áftər noónz/ *adv.* during the afternoon, or every afternoon (*informal*)

af·ter·pains /áftər pàynz/ *npl.* pains experienced by some women just after giving birth, similar to labor pains and caused by contractions of the uterus

af·ter·piece /áftər peess/ *n.* a short entertainment, usually comic, performed after a play

af·ter·sen·sa·tion /áftər sen sàysh'n/ *n.* any sense impression, e.g., an aftertaste or afterimage, that remains after the immediate stimulus has been removed

af·ter·shave /áftər shàyv/ *n.* a liquid applied after shaving, to soothe and scent the skin of the face

af·ter·shock /áftər shòk/ *n.* **1.** SMALL EARTHQUAKE a small earthquake, usually one of several, that follows a larger one after a period of time **2.** DELAYED REACTION a delayed psychological or physical reaction to a serious event or trauma

af·ter·taste /áftər tàyst/ *n.* **1.** PERSISTING TASTE a taste left in the mouth by food or drink after swallowing **2.** UNPLEASANT FEELING a feeling or sensation, especially an unpleasant one, left behind after an experience

af·ter-tax *adj.* remaining after paying or deducting money for taxes

af·ter·thought /áftər thawt/ *n.* something not thought of, said, or done originally, but added afterward

af·ter·ward /áftərwərd/, **af·ter·wards** /-wərdz/ *adv.* at a later time or after an event that has been mentioned previously ○ *Let's have breakfast now and go skiing afterward.*

af·ter·word /áftər wùrd/ *n.* a short concluding section added at the end of a literary work, which may be either an epilogue or a commentary of some kind

aft·most *adj.* = **aftermost**

AFTRA /áftrə/ *abbr.* American Federation of Television and Radio Artists

Ag *symbol.* silver [Shortening of Latin *argentum* "silver"]

A.G., AG *abbr.* **1.** Adjutant General **2.** Attorney General

ag- *prefix.* = **ad-** (*used before g*)

a·ga /aágə, ággə/, **a·gha** *n.* used as a title for a military commander or important official in Islamic countries, especially during the Ottoman Empire ○ *the Aga Khan* [Mid-16thC. From Turkish *aghā*, literally "chief, master, lord."]

a·gain /ə gén/ *adv.* **1.** ANOTHER TIME at another time or on another occasion, repeating what has happened or been done before ○ *I hope to come here again some day.* **2.** AS BEFORE to the place, person, or state where somebody or something was earlier ○ *Will I ever be able to walk again?* **3.** IN ADDITION in addition to a previously mentioned quantity ○ *You'll need all that and half as much again.* **4. DIFFERENTLY** on the other hand ○ *You may be right, but again you may be wrong.* **5. MOREOVER** similarly and in addition (*formal*) ○ *Again, that is something that the court must take into account.* **6. IN RESPONSE** in return or response (*archaic*) [Old English *ongēan*, literally "in a direct line with, facing" or "back to a starting point," from a prehistoric Germanic compound formed from the ancestor of German *gegen* "against, towards"] ◇ **again and again** repeatedly

a·gainst /ə génst/ CORE MEANING: a preposition indicating opposition to or conflict with somebody or something, either physically or intellectually ○ (prep) *a battle against cancer*
prep. **1. IN COMPETITION WITH** with somebody or something as an opponent in a competitive situation, especially in sports ○ *Iowa against UCLA in the Rose Bowl* **2. IN CONTACT WITH BY LEANING** in a position such that part or all of something touches another object or surface, by leaning or resting on the side of it rather than resting on top of it ○ *I leaned against a tree.* **3. INTO SUDDEN CONTACT OR COLLISION WITH** so as to briefly touch or suddenly collide with a usually stationary object while in movement ○ *banged his head against the beam* **4. IN THE OPPOSITE DIRECTION OF** in the opposite direction to the movement, angle, or position of something or somebody ○ *to swim against the current* **5. SEEN IN CONTRAST WITH** seen in contrast with something, e.g., a color that is behind or surrounding something ○ *The dark green pines are lovely against the blue sky.* **6. IN RELATION TO EVENTS** in relation to, or contrasted with, a set of events or circumstances ○ *Government actions makes sense against the background of rising tensions.* **7. AS PROTECTION FROM** in order to prevent or avoid something, or to be protected from something ○ *vaccinate against disease* **8. IN PAYMENT OF** in partial or total payment of, or as a charge on ○ *I'd like to put this money against the amount I owe you.* **9. AS A DISADVANTAGE TO** to the disadvantage of somebody or something ○ *Will you hold it against me if I don't come to your party?* **10. COMPARED WITH** in comparison with something ○ *weighed the cost of hiring someone against that of promoting existing staff* **11. CONTRARY TO** contrary to or not approved or allowed by something or somebody ○ *It's against the law.* **12. IN PREPARATION FOR** in preparation for something, usually an expected unpleasant event (*dated*) ○ *to save against hard times* **13. OPPOSITE** opposite to or facing something (*archaic*) [14thC. Formed from earlier *agenes* (from Old English *ongēan*, the ancestor of AGAIN + the adverbial suffix *-es*) + *-t*, modeled on such words as *amidst*.]

A·ga Khan III /àagə kaán/ (1877–1957) religious leader, born in Karachi, Pakistan. He was imam of the Isma'ili Muslim religious group and president of the League of Nations Assembly (1937).

A·ga Khan IV (*b.* 1936) Swiss-born Muslim leader. He became imam of the Ismaili religious group in 1957. Born **Karim al Hussaini Shah**

a·ga·ma /ə gáymə, ággə-/ *n.* **1. SMALL LIZARD** a small long-tailed, often colorful lizard native to tropical Africa and Asia. Genus: *Agama.* **2.** = **agamid** [Late 18thC. Via modern Latin and Spanish from, probably, Carib *mami* "lizard."]

Ag·a·mem·non /àggə mém nòn, -nən/ *n.* the commander of the Greek army in the Trojan War. When Agamemnon returned from the war, he was murdered by his wife Clytemnestra and her lover Aegisthus. His death was later avenged by his son Orestes.

a·gam·ic /ay gámmik/, **ag·a·mous** /-gámməs/ *adj.* used to describe an organism that multiplies asexually [Mid-19thC. Formed from Greek *agamos* "unmarried," from *gamos* "marriage."] —**a·gam·i·cal·ly** *adv.*

a·ga·mid /ággəmid/ *n.* a small long-tailed insect-eating lizard found in tropical regions of Africa and Asia. Family: Agamidae. [Late 19thC. From modern Latin *Agamidae*, family name, ultimately from *agama* (see AGAMA).]

a·gam·o·gen·e·sis /ay gàmmə jénnəssiss, àggəmō-/ *n.* asexual reproduction, e.g., by cell division or budding [Mid-19thC. Coined from Greek *agamos* "unmarried" + -GENESIS.]

a·gam·o·sper·my /ay gámmə spùrmee, ággəmō-/ *n.* the asexual formation of seeds without fertilization [Mid-20thC. Coined from Greek *agamos* "not married" + SPERM + Y².]

ag·a·mous *adj.* = **agamic**

ag·a·pan·thus /àggə pánthəss/ (*plural* **-thus** *or* **-thus·es**) *n.* = **African lily** [Late 18thC. From modern Latin, formed from Greek *agapē* "love" + *anthos* "flower" (source of English *anthology*).]

a·gape¹ /ə gáyp/ *adv., adj.* (*literary*) **1. WIDE OPEN** opened quite widely ○ *The door to the room was agape.* **2. OPEN-MOUTHED** with the mouth wide open, usually in surprise or wonder

a·ga·pe² /aa gaápee/ *n.* **1. NONSEXUAL LOVE** love that is wholly selfless and spiritual **2.** CHR **CHRISTIAN LOVE** selfless love felt by Christians for their fellow human beings **3.** CHR **CHRISTIAN COMMUNAL MEAL** a communal meal held by a Christian community, especially in early Christian times, in commemoration of the Last Supper [Mid-17thC. From Greek *agapē* "brotherly love."]

a·gar /áagər, áy-/, **a·gar-a·gar** *n.* **1.** FOOD **GELLING AGENT FROM SEAWEED** an extract of seaweed in powder form used as a gelling agent in vegetarian cooking and commercially as a thickener **2.** BIOL **GEL FOR GROWING MICROORGANISMS** a gel culture medium based on a seaweed extract, widely used for growing microorganisms in laboratories [Late 19thC. From Malay *agar-agar* "jelly."]

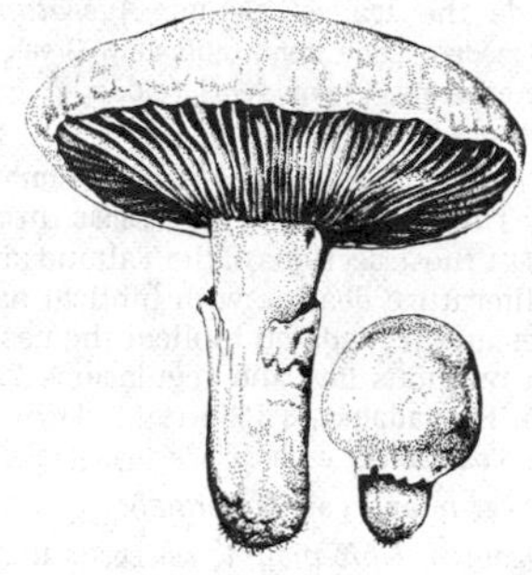

Agaric

ag·a·ric /ággərik, ə gérrik/ *n.* a fungus with a large cap resembling an umbrella with numerous radiating gills on the underside. Some types are edible and some are poisonous. Family: Agaricaceae. [15thC. Directly or via French, from Latin *agaricum*, from Greek *agarikon* "tree fungus," of uncertain origin: perhaps named for *Agaria* in Sarmatia, an ancient region of eastern Europe.]

ag·a·rose /ággə rōss, -rōz/ *n.* a complex carbohydrate (**polysaccharide**) obtained from agar and used in chromatography and electrophoresis as a medium in which a substance being analyzed can be separated into its component molecules

Ag·as·si /ággəssee/, **Andre** (*b.* 1970) U.S. tennis player. He won Wimbledon in 1992 and gold in the Atlanta Olympics in 1996.

Ag·as·siz, Louis (1807–73) Swiss-born U.S. naturalist and glaciologist who became Professor of Natural History at Harvard (1848), and developed theories on the occurrence of Ice Ages. Full name **Jean Louis Rodolphe Agassiz**

ag·ate /ággət/ *n.* **1. TYPE OF CHALCEDONY** a hard fine-grained form of chalcedony with variously colored bands, markings, and areas of clouding, often used as a gemstone **2. TOY MARBLE** a playing marble made of agate or of glass that looks like agate [Late 16thC. Via French, from, ultimately, Greek *akhatēs*, perhaps named for *Achates*, a river in Sicily.]

ag·ate·ware /ággətwair/ *n.* **1. TYPE OF POTTERY** decorative pottery made using a cross section of layers of clay of contrasting colors **2. TYPE OF METALWARE** a variety of metalware, such as pots and pans, with an enamel surface decorated to resemble agate

a·ga·ve /ə gaávee, -gáy-/ (*plural* **-ves** *or* **-ve**) *n.* a plant native to hot dry areas of North and South America that has spiny-edged leaves and a single tall stalk with clusters of flowers. Some species are grown as ornamentals, and others are grown for their fiber (**sisal**) and sap, which is used in making tequila and other alcoholic drinks. Genus: *Agave.* [Late 18thC. Via Latin, from Greek *Agauē*, the mother of Pentheus in Greek mythology, whose name meant literally "illustrious" or "brilliant."]

A·ga·wam /ággə waám/ city in southwestern Massachusetts, situated on the west bank of the Connecticut River. Population: 27,323 (1990).

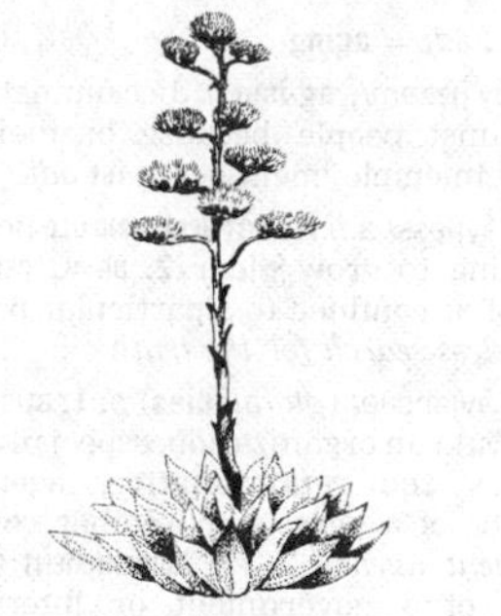

Agave

agcy. *abbr.* agency

age /ayj/ *n.* **1. HOW OLD SOMEBODY OR SOMETHING IS** the length of time that somebody or something has existed, usually expressed in years **2. STAGE OF LIFE** one of the stages or phases in the lifetime of somebody or something ○ *She lived to a ripe old age.* **3. LEGAL ADULTHOOD** the age at which somebody is legally considered to be an adult **4. BEING OLD** the state of being advanced in years ○ *the wisdom of age* **5. age, Age HISTORICAL ERA** a period in history, especially a long period or one associated with and named for a distinctive characteristic, achievement, or influential person ○ *the space age* **6. age, Age** GEOL **GEOLOGIC ERA** a relatively short division of recent geologic time, shorter than an epoch ○ *the Ice Age* **7.** EDUC **LEVEL OF DEVELOPMENT** a level of development equivalent to that of an average person of the stated age ○ *a reading age of 7* **8. GENERATION** a generation of people (*literary*) ○ *the greatest writer of her age* ■ **ag·es** *npl.* **1. LONG TIME** a very long time (*informal*) **2. HISTORY** human history ○ *People have warred with one another throughout the ages.* ■ *v.* (**aged, ag·ing** *or* **age·ing, ag·es**) **1.** *vti.* **GROW OR CAUSE TO GROW OLD** to become old, develop the characteristics of being old, or cause somebody or something to become or seem old ○ *Too much sun ages the skin.* **2.** *vti.* FOOD **IMPROVE SOMETHING OVER TIME** to cause a food or wine to mature, develop a desired flavor, or become more tender, or to become improved in this way over time ○ *The wine is aged in oak barrels.* **3.** *vt.* ELECTRON ENG **STABILIZE SOMETHING THROUGH USE** to stabilize an electronic device by using it [13thC. Via Old French *aage* from the Latin stem *aetat-* "period of life," ultimately from an Indo-European base that also produced English *eon.*] ◇ **come of age** to reach the age when somebody is legally considered an adult ◇ **of a certain age** no longer young (*humorous*)

-age *suffix.* **1.** action or result of an action ○ *breakage* ○ *coinage* **2.** collection of things ○ *signage* **3.** housing ○ *orphanage* **4.** condition, office ○ *brigandage* ○ *peerage* **5.** charge ○ *dockage* [Via French from assumed Vulgar Latin *-aticum*, formed from Latin *-aticus*, suffix forming adjectives]

ag·ed /áyjəd, áyjd/ *adj.* **1. OLD** very advanced in years **2. OF PARTICULAR AGE** of the stated age ○ *a person aged 50* **3. IMPROVED WITH TIME** stored for a period of time in order to mature and produce the best flavor ○ *well-aged wine* **4. ERODED** showing evidence of advanced erosion ■ *npl.* **OLD PEOPLE** people of advanced years, especially those whose physical or mental health has diminished [15thC. Probably modeled on French *âgé* "aged."] —**ag·ed·ly** /ayjədlee/ *adv.* —**ag·ed·ness** /-nəss/ *n.*

age dis·crim·i·na·tion *n.* discrimination against people because of their age, particularly in employment

A·gee /áyjee/, **James** (1909–55) U.S. poet, novelist, screenwriter, and film critic. He co-wrote *Let Us Now Praise Famous Men* with Walker Evans (1941) and wrote the screenplay for *The African Queen* (1951).

age-grade *n.* ANTHROP a group of people in a society who are the same sex and approximately the same age. Age-grades and the relationships between them are an important part of the organization of certain cultures.

age group *n.* a group of people whose ages are approximately the same or fall within a stated range

age·ing *n., adj.* = **aging**

age·ism /áy jìzzəm/, **ag·ism** *n.* discrimination or prejudice against people because of their age, particularly in employment —**age·ist** *adj.*

age·less /áyjləss/ *adj.* 1. NOT BECOMING OLD never growing or seeming to grow older 2. OF ALL GENERATIONS not typical of or confined to a particular period of time ○ *the ageless search for the truth*

a·gen·cy /áyjənsee/ (*plural* **-cies**) *n.* 1. BUSINESS COMPANY ACTING AS AGENT an organization, especially a company, acting as the representative, agent, or subcontractor of a person or another company ○ *an employment agency* 2. POL GOVERNMENT ORGANIZATION a division of a government or international organization that carries out administrative duties ○ *a United Nations agency* 3. OFFICE OF AGENCY the building or offices where an agency is located 4. ACTION OR OPERATION the action, medium, or means by which something is accomplished 5. LAW LEGAL RELATIONSHIP a legal relationship involving a person (**the principal**) and another who acts for the person (**the agent**), or the area of the law concerned with such relationships ○ *The case hinges on a question of agency.* [Mid-17thC. From medieval Latin *agentia*, from the Latin stem *agent-* (see AGENT).]

a·gen·cy shop *n.* a workplace in which a union represents both union and nonunion workers and requires payments from nonunion workers

a·gen·da /ə jéndə/ *n.* 1. LIST OF THINGS TO DO a formal list of things to be done in a particular order, especially a list of things to be discussed at a meeting 2. MATTERS NEEDING ATTENTION the various matters that somebody needs to deal with at a given time ○ *What's your agenda for today?* 3. SOMEBODY'S PARTICULAR MOTIVE an underlying personal viewpoint or bias ○ *Of course she's in favor, but then she has her own agenda.* ■ plural of **agendum** [Early 17thC. From Latin, the plural of *agendum* "thing to be done," from *agere* "to do" (see AGENT).] ◇ **set the agenda** to be the major influence or force affecting something ○ *It is the environmental lobby that is setting the agenda in this round of negotiations.*

WORD KEY: USAGE

Is **agenda** singular or plural? Although ***agenda*** is strictly speaking a plural noun meaning "items to be dealt with," the singular form ***agendum*** is not used, and ***agenda*** is used in the singular as if it were "a list of things to be done," with a plural form ***agendas***: *The agenda for tomorrow's meeting has been changed. This item has appeared on a number of previous agendas.*

A·gen·da 21 *n.* the global environmental program and statement of principles agreed to at the Earth Summit in Rio de Janeiro in 1992

a·gen·dum /ə jéndəm/ (*plural* **-dums** *or* **-da** /-ə/) *n.* an item on an agenda (*formal*) [Early 17thC. From Latin (see AGENDA).]

a·gen·e·sis /ay jénnəsiss/ *n.* the incomplete development or total absence of a body part ○ *ovarian agenesis*

a·gent /áyjənt/ *n.* 1. BUSINESS SOMEBODY REPRESENTING ANOTHER somebody representing somebody else in business, usually under contract, especially in buying and selling property or insurance, or in arranging work in entertainment or publishing 2. GOVERNMENT EMPLOYEE somebody who is employed by a government or other organization as an investigator, guard, or representative ○ *a federal agent* 3. CAUSATIVE SUBSTANCE something, e.g., a chemical substance, organism, or natural force, that causes an effect ○ *a cleansing agent* 4. MEANS EFFECTING RESULT the means by which an effect or result is produced ○ *As CEO you will be expected to be the main agent of change.* 5. SPY somebody who works undercover as a spy or agent provocateur (*informal*) 6. COMPUT COMPUTER PROGRAM a program that works automatically on routine tasks specified by a user, e.g., sorting e-mail or monitoring the Internet [15thC. From Latin *agent-*, the present participle stem of *agere* "to drive, lead, act, do."] —**a·gen·tial** /ay jénshəl/ *adj.*

WORD KEY: ORIGIN

The Latin word *agere* from which ***agent*** is derived is also the source of English *act, active, actual, agile, agitate, ambiguous, cachet, cogent, essay, exact, examine,* and *squat.*

A·gent Or·ange *n.* a herbicide, now understood to be extremely toxic, that was sprayed from the air by the U.S. military during the Vietnam War to defoliate the jungle and expose enemy forces [From the color-coded orange stripe on the drums in which the toxin was stored]

a·gent pro·vo·ca·teur /a zhaaN praw váwkə tür/ (*plural* **a·gents pro·vo·ca·teurs** /a zhaaN praw váwkə tür/) *n.* somebody employed to gain the trust of suspects and then tempt them to do something illegal so that they can be arrested and punished [From French, literally "provocative agent"]

a·gent·ry /áyjəntree/ *n.* an agent's office or work

Age of A·quar·i·us *n.* an astrological era in which increased spirituality and harmony is said to characterize people's lives

age of con·sent *n.* the age at which somebody is legally old enough to consent to marriage or sexual intercourse

Age of Rea·son *n.* the period from the mid- to late 18th century during which there was an emphasis on rationalism in philosophy, religion, and society

age-old *adj.* dating from a very long time ago and still in existence

ag·er·a·tum /àjjə ráytəm/ (*plural* **-tum** *or* **-tums**) *n.* a low-growing plant grown in gardens for its thick clusters of blue, white, or purplish flowers that almost hide the leaves. Genus: *Ageratum.* [Mid-16thC. Via modern Latin from, ultimately, Greek *agēratos* "ageless, everlasting," from *gēras* "old age" (source of English *geriatric*).]

Ag·ga·dah /aà gaa daà, ə gaàdə/ (*plural* **-doth** /aà gaa dáwt, ə gaà dòt/) *n.* JUDAISM 1. RABBINIC LITERATURE ON BIBLICAL STORIES those sections of the Talmud and other rabbinic literature dealing with biblical narrative and stories and legends on biblical themes, rather than with religious law and regulations 2. = **Haggadah** *n.* 1, **Haggadah** *n.* 3 [Mid-19thC. From Rabbinic Hebrew *haggādāh* "tale," especially "edifying tale."]

ag·gie[1] /ággee/ *n.* an agate (*informal*)

ag·gie[2] /ággee/ *n.* (*informal*) 1. AGRICULTURAL STUDENT a student at an agricultural school, college, or university 2. AGRICULTURAL SCHOOL an agricultural school, college, or university

ag·gior·na·men·to /ə jàwrnə méntō/ *n.* the process of modernizing Roman Catholic Church ritual and policy [Mid-20thC. From Italian, from *aggiornare* "to bring up to date," ultimately from Latin *diurnum* "day."]

ag·glom·er·ate *vti.* /ə glómmə ràyt/ (**-at·ed, -at·ing, -ates**) 1. FORM A MASS to collect together into a mass 2. GEOL COLLECT IN ROUND MASS to gather or accumulate something in a roughly ball-shaped mass ■ *n.* /ə glómmərət/ 1. JUMBLED COLLECTION a jumbled mass or collection of something (*formal*) 2. GEOL VOLCANIC ROCK rock produced by a volcanic eruption, consisting of fragments of different rock types, sizes, and shapes set in fine-grained solidified volcanic ash ■ *adj.* /ə glómmərət/ IN ROUND MASS gathered into or forming a rounded mass [Mid-17thC. From Latin *agglomerat-*, past participle stem of *agglomerare* "to heap up," literally "to wind or add onto a ball," ultimately from the stem *glomer-* "ball" (source of English *conglomerate*).] —**ag·glom·er·a·tive** /ə glómmə ràytiv, ə glómmərətiv/ *adj.* —**ag·glom·er·a·tor** *n.*

ag·glom·er·a·tion /ə glòmmə ráysh'n/ *n.* 1. JUMBLED MASS a jumbled or confused mass of separate elements 2. GATHERING THINGS TO FORM MASS the process of gathering things together to form a mass

ag·glu·ti·nate *vti.* /ə glóot'n àyt/ (**-nat·ed, -nat·ing, -nates**) 1. ADHERE OR CAUSE SOMETHING TO ADHERE to be joined or glued together, or cause things to stick to each other 2. BIOL, IMMUNOL CLUMP OR CAUSE CELLS TO CLUMP to cause cells such as red blood cells or bacteria to form clumps, or stick together in clumps 3. LING FORM COMPOUND WORD to combine simple words together without changing their form to make a new word, or be combined in a new word in this way ■ *n.* /ə glóot'nət/ BIOL = **agglutination** *n.* 4 [Mid-16thC. From Latin *agglutinat-*, the past participle stem of *agglutinare* "to fasten with glue," ultimately from *gluten* "glue" (see GLUTEN).] —**ag·glu·tin·a·bil·i·ty** /ə glóot'nə bíllətee/ *n.* —**ag·glu·tin·a·ble** /-ə b'l/ *adj.* —**ag·glu·ti·nant** /-ənt/ *n., adj.*

ag·glu·ti·na·tion /ə glóot'n áysh'n/ *n.* 1. ADHESION the gluing together or uniting of separate elements or objects 2. CLUMPED MASS a group, clump, or mass formed by the gluing together or uniting of separate elements or objects 3. BIOL, IMMUNOL CLUMPING OF CELLS the formation of clumps of cells, e.g., red blood cells or microorganisms, in the presence of particular antibodies ○ *platelet agglutination* 4. BIOL CELL CLUMP clumps of cells, e.g., red blood cells or microorganisms, formed in the presence of particular antibodies 5. LING COMPOUND WORD FORMATION the process of forming compound words, derivatives, or inflections by combining simple words or word components without alteration

ag·glu·ti·na·tive /ə glóot'n àytiv, ə glóot'nətiv/ *adj.* 1. ABLE TO AGGLUTINATE able or likely to agglutinate 2. LING FORMING WORDS BY AGGLUTINATION forming words by combining simple words or word components without alteration ○ *an agglutinative language*

ag·glu·ti·nin /ə glóot'nin/ *n.* a substance that causes cells to clump together, e.g., an antibody or lectin

ag·glu·tin·o·gen /ágloo tínnəjən, ə glóot'nəjən/ *n.* an antigen responsible for the formation of a specific agglutinin

ag·grade /ə gráyd/ (**-grad·ed, -grad·ing, -grades**) *vt.* to build up a land surface or streambed through the natural deposition of material. ◊ **degrade** [Early 20thC. Back-formation from *aggradation*, from AG- + DEGRADATION.] —**ag·gra·da·tion** /àggrə dáysh'n/ *n.* —**ag·gra·da·tion·al** *adj.*

ag·gran·dize /ə grán dīz, ággrən-/ (**-dized, -diz·ing, -diz·es**) *vt.* 1. ENLARGE OR EXTEND SOMETHING to increase the size or scope of something 2. IMPROVE STATUS OF SOMETHING to increase or improve the power, wealth, influence, or status of somebody or something, especially by deliberate plan 3. EXAGGERATE GREATNESS OF SOMEBODY to make somebody or something seem bigger or better than is actually the case, especially through exaggerated praise (*formal disapproving*) ○ *aggrandizing the value of her accomplishments* [Mid-17thC. From French *agrandiss-*, the stem of *agrandir*, from *grandir* "to increase," ultimately from Latin *grandis* "great" (see GRAND).] —**ag·gran·dize·ment** /ə grándizmənt, -dīzmənt/ *n.* —**ag·gran·diz·er** *n.*

ag·gra·vate /ággrə vayt/ (**-vat·ed, -vat·ing, -vates**) *vt.* 1. ANNOY SOMEBODY to irritate or anger somebody, especially with a continuing or trivial annoyance (*informal*) 2. MAKE SOMETHING WORSE to make something that is already bad or serious worse or more severe [Mid-16thC. Probably via Old French, from Latin *aggravat-*, the past participle stem of *aggravare* "to make heavier," ultimately from *gravis* "heavy" (see GRAVE).] —**ag·gra·vat·ing** *adj.* —**ag·gra·vat·ing·ly** *adv.* —**ag·gra·va·tor** *n.*

WORD KEY: USAGE

Can **aggravate** mean "annoy?" The use of ***aggravate*** to mean "annoy" or "irritate" is still disliked by many people, despite a history of usage dating back to the 17th century: *We were aggravated by the continuous loud noise from the street. Their bad behavior is very aggravating.* Except in informal conversation it is usually better to use an alternative word such as **annoy, exasperate**, or **irritate**.

ag·gra·vat·ed /ággrə vaytid/ *adj.* having features that make it a worse criminal offense ○ *aggravated assault*

ag·gra·va·tion /àggrə váysh'n/ *n.* 1. IRRITATION a feeling of exasperation or irritation, especially when caused by a continuing problem 2. SOURCE OF IRRITATION somebody or something that causes continuing exasperation, irritation, or trouble 3. WORSENING the worsening of an already bad situation, or something that or somebody who makes a bad situation worse ○ *Exercising before you have fully recovered may lead to an aggravation of your condition.* 4. *U.K.* TROUBLE annoyance or bother, often aggressive in nature (*informal*) ○ *I get a lot of aggravation from dissatisfied customers.*

ag·gre·gate *adj.* /ággrəgət, -gàyt/ 1. FORMING A TOTAL collected together from different sources and considered as a whole (*formal*) 2. GEOL RESEMBLING ROCK used to describe a mixture of minerals or rock fragments that resembles rock ○ *an aggregate structure* ■ *n.* /ággrəgət, -gàyt/ 1. SUM TOTAL a total or whole made up of different parts from often disparate sources (*formal*) ○ *The political party was an aggregate of many diverse groups.* 2. CONSTR INGREDIENTS OF CONCRETE broken stone, gravel, and sand used in road construction and, when mixed with cement and water, for making concrete 3. GEOL MINERAL MIXTURE RESEMBLING ROCK a mixture of minerals or rock fragments that resembles rock ■ *v.* /ággrə gàyt/ (**-gat·ed, -gat·ing, -gates**) 1. *vti.* UNITE to come together, or bring different things together, into a total, mass, or whole ○ *Aggregate the different totals to get the overall cost.* **2.** *vt.* MATH **ADD UP TO A NUMBER** to amount or add up to a particular number ○ *The company's earnings aggregate $175,000.* [15thC. From Latin *aggregat-*, past participle stem of *aggregare* "to add to," literally "to bring into the flock," ultimately from the stem *greg-* "flock" (source also of English *gregarious*).] —**ag·gre·gate·ly** /ággrəgətlee/ *adv.* —**ag·gre·ga·tive** /ággrə gàytiv/ *adj.* —**ag·gre·ga·tor** /-gàytər/ *n.* ◇ **in the aggregate** considered or taken together as a whole

ag·gre·ga·tion /àggrə gáysh'n/ *n.* a total or collection of different things added together, or the process of adding them together

ag·gress /ə gréss/ (**-gressed, -gress·ing, -gress·es**) *vi.* to attack first, or begin a fight, argument, or war (*formal*) [Late 16thC. Via obsolete French *aggresser* from Latin *aggress-*, the past participle stem of *aggredi* "to approach, attack," literally "to walk to," from *gradi* "to walk."]

ag·gres·sion /ə grésh'n/ *n.* **1. ATTACK** hostile action, especially a physical or military attack, directed against another person or country, often without provocation **2. HOSTILE ATTITUDE OR BEHAVIOR** threatening behavior or actions [Early 17thC. Directly or via French, from the Latin stem *aggression-*, from *aggress-* (see AGGRESS).]

ag·gres·sive /ə gréssiv/ *adj.* **1. LIKELY TO HARM** showing a readiness or having a tendency to attack or do harm to others **2. ATTACKING** attacking or taking action without provocation or without waiting for an enemy to make the first move **3. ASSERTIVE** characterized by or exhibiting determination, energy, and initiative ○ *an aggressive investment policy* **4.** MED **SPREADING QUICKLY** used to describe a disease process or pathological growth, e.g., a tumor, that is fast-growing or spreading to other parts of the body —**ag·gres·sive·ly** *adv.* —**ag·gres·sive·ness** *n.*

WORD KEY: USAGE

One *g* or two? Note that the correct spelling of ***aggressive*** and ***aggression*** is with *-gg-* and *-ss-*.

ag·gres·sor /ə gréssər/ *n.* a person or country that attacks or starts a war, fight, or argument, often without being provoked [Mid-17thC. From late Latin, formed from *aggress-* (see AGGRESS).]

ag·grieve /ə greév/ (**-grieved, -griev·ing, -grieves**) *vt.* **1. CAUSE DISTRESS TO SOMEBODY** to cause somebody pain, trouble, or distress (*formal*) **2.** LAW **INFLICT INJURY ON SOMEBODY** to inflict an actionable injury on somebody [13thC. Via Old French *agrever* "to make heavier," from Latin *aggravare* (see AGGRAVATE). The modern spelling is modeled on *grieve*.]

ag·grieved /ə greévd/ *adj.* **1. UPSET** distressed or angry because of being treated badly or unfairly **2.** LAW **WRONGED** suffering from injustice, especially a denial of legal rights ○ *Compensation was awarded to the aggrieved party.* —**ag·griev·ed·ly** /ə greévədlee/ *adv.* —**ag·griev·ed·ness** /-nəss/ *n.*

ag·gro /ággrō/ *n. U.K.* (*slang*) **1. THREATENING BEHAVIOR** threatening behavior, especially troublemaking or fighting ○ *we don't want any aggro* **2. DIFFICULTY** trouble or difficulty ○ *He's having a lot of aggro with that car.* [Mid-20thC. Shortening of AGGRAVATION or AGGRESSION.]

a·gha *n.* = **aga**

A·gha Mo·ham·mad Khan /áágə mə hámməd kaán/, **Shah** (1742–97) Iranian ruler who was self-proclaimed Shah (1796–97). He founded the Qajar dynasty, which reigned from 1762 until 1925.

a·ghast /ə gást/ *adj.* overcome with shock and dismay [13thC. From the past participle of obsolete *agast* "to frighten," ultimately from Old English *gǣst* "spirit, ghost" (source also of English *ghastly* and *ghost*).]

AGI *abbr.* adjusted gross income

ag·ile /áj'l/ *adj.* **1. NIMBLE** able to move quickly and with suppleness, skill, and control **2. MENTALLY QUICK** able to think quickly and intelligently [Late 16thC. Via French, from Latin *agilis* "that can be moved easily, nimble, quick," from *agere* "to move, do" (see AGENT).] —**ag·ile·ly** *adv.* —**ag·ile·ness** *n.*

a·gil·i·ty /ə jíllətee/ *n.* **1. PHYSICAL NIMBLENESS** a combination of physical speed, suppleness, and skill **2. MENTAL ALERTNESS** a combination of mental quickness, alertness, and intelligence [15thC. Via French, from the Latin stem *agilitat-*, from *agilis* (see AGILE).]

a·gin /ə gín/ *prep.* against (*regional*)

ag·ing /áyjing/, **age·ing** *n.* **1. GROWING OLD** the process of growing old, especially of acquiring the physical and mental characteristics of old age **2. MATURING PROCESS** the natural or chemically assisted process of bringing foods to maturity or of making materials like wood appear older ■ *adj.* **BECOMING OLD** growing old or elderly ○ *caring for an aging parent*

ag·ism *n.* = **ageism**

ag·i·ta /ájjitə/ *n.* acid indigestion

ag·i·tate /ájji tàyt/ (**-tat·ed, -tat·ing, -tates**) *v.* **1.** *vt.* **MAKE SOMEBODY ANXIOUS** to make somebody feel anxious, nervous, or disturbed **2.** *vi.* **AROUSE PUBLIC INTEREST** to attempt to arouse public feeling, interest, or support for or against something such as a cause **3.** *vt.* **MOVE SOMETHING VIOLENTLY** to cause something to move vigorously or violently, e.g., by shaking or blowing it ○ *Agitate the mixture until the sediment is thoroughly dispersed.* [Late 16thC. From Latin *agitat-*, the past participle stem of *agitare* "to move to and fro," from *agere* "to drive, move."] —**ag·i·ta·tive** /ájji tàytiv/ *adj.*

ag·i·tat·ed /ájji taytid/ *adj.* anxious, nervous, or upset and unable to relax —**ag·i·tat·ed·ly** *adv.*

ag·i·ta·tion /àjji táysh'n/ *n.* **1. ANXIETY** nervous anxiety **2. PUBLIC CAMPAIGNING** actions intended to arouse public feeling, interest, or support for or against something such as a cause **3. SHAKING** vigorous or violent shaking, stirring, or other disturbance of something, especially a liquid ○ *Observe the mixture after agitation.* —**ag·i·ta·tion·al** *adj.*

ag·i·ta·to /àjji taátō/ *adj., adv.* in a restless, tense, or excited manner (*used as a musical direction*) [Early 19thC. Via Italian, from, ultimately, Latin *agitat-* (see AGITATE).]

ag·i·ta·tor /ájji tàytər/ *n.* **1. SUPPORTER OF CAUSE** somebody who attempts to arouse feeling or interest for or against something, especially a political cause **2. APPARATUS CAUSING MOVEMENT** a machine or machine part that causes vigorous movement in a liquid or other substance

ag·it·prop /ájjit pròp/ *n.* **1. PROPAGANDA** political propaganda, especially pro-Communist, and especially when disseminated through literature, drama, music, or art **2. PROPAGANDIST ART** artistic work or works serving as a vehicle for political propaganda [Early 20thC. From Russian, from *agitatsiya* "agitation" + *propaganda* "propaganda."]

A·gla·ia /ə gláy ə, ə glí ə/ *n.* in Greek mythology, one of the three Graces who lived on Mount Olympus and tended the goddess Aphrodite. Aglaia was the daughter of Zeus and Euronyme.

a·gleam /ə gleém/ *adj.* glowing, gleaming, or emitting a soft light (*literary*) ○ *She was laughing, her eyes agleam.*

ag·let /ágglət/ *n.* **1. END OF SHOELACE** a plain or ornamental metal or plastic sheath covering the end of a shoelace or ribbon **2. METAL DECORATION FOR CLOTHING** a metallic ornament such as a stud, cord, or pin worn on clothing [15thC. From French *aiguillette* (see AIGUILLETTE).]

a·gley /ə gláy, ə glí/ *adv., adj. Scotland, N England* awry or askew ○ *"The best laid schemes o' mice and men/ Gang aft agley"* (Robert Burns, *To a mouse*; 1785) [Late 18thC. Formed from A- + *gley* "to squint" (of unknown origin).]

a·glim·mer /ə glímmər/ *adj.* glimmering with light (*literary*)

a·glit·ter /ə glíttər/ *adj.* glittering or sparkling with light (*literary*)

ag·loo *n.* = **aglu**

a·glow /ə glṓ/ *adj.* radiating light, warmth, excitement, or happy emotion

ag·lu /ágloo/ (*plural* **-lus**), **ag·loo** (*plural* **-loos**) *n. Can* a breathing hole that a seal has made in sea ice [Late 19thC. From Inuktitut.]

a·gly·cone /ə glí kòn/, **a·gly·con** /-kòn/ *n.* a nonsugar compound that is produced from the reaction of a glycoside with water. Alcohols and phenols are aglycones. [Early 20thC. From German *Aglykon*, from Greek *glukus* "sweet" (see GLUCOSE).]

ag·nail /ág nàyl/ *n.* **1.** = **hangnail 2. SWELLING NEAR NAIL** a painful swelling near the nail of a toe or finger [Old English *angnægl*, formed from *ang-* "narrow, painful" + *nægl* "nail"]

ag·nate /ág nayt/ *n.* **RELATIVE WITH SAME MALE ANCESTOR** a relative who is descended from a common male ancestor, especially through the male line (*formal*) ■ *adj.* (*formal*) **1.** = **patrilineal 2. RELATED** related or akin in any way [15thC. From Latin *agnatus*, literally "born in addition," from Old Latin *gnatus*, the past participle of *gnasci* "to be born" (source of English *innate* and *nativity*).] —**ag·nat·ic** /ag náttik/ *adj.* —**ag·nat·i·cal·ly** *adv.* —**ag·na·tion** /ag náysh'n/ *n.*

Ag·new /ágnoo/, **Spiro T.** (1918–96) U.S. politician. He was Richard Nixon's vice-president (1969–73) and was forced to resign after admitting to tax evasion.

Ag·ni /úgnee/ *n.* the Hindu god of fire [From Sanskrit, "fire, the fire-god"]

ag·no·lot·ti /ànnyə lóttee, àgnə-/ *npl.* small pieces of semicircular pasta stuffed with meat, cheese, or other filling and sealed at the edges [Late 20thC. From Italian dialect, an alteration of Italian *anellotto*, literally "little ring."]

ag·no·men /ag nṓmən/ (*plural* **-nom·i·na** /-mənə/ *or* **-no·mens**) *n.* a fourth name that was occasionally bestowed on somebody as an honor in ancient Rome [Mid-17thC. From Latin, literally "additional name," from *(g)nomen* "name."]

Ag·non /aág nàwn/, **Shmuel Yosef** (1888–1970) Austrian-born Israeli author whose novels include *The Bridal Canopy* (1919) and *The Day Before Yesterday* (1945).

ag·no·sia /ag nṓzhə/ *n.* the total or partial loss of the ability to recognize familiar people or objects, usually caused by brain damage [Early 20thC. From Greek *agnōsia*, literally "lack of knowledge," from *gnōsis* "knowledge."]

ag·nos·tic /ag nóstik/ *n.* **1. SOMEBODY DENYING GOD'S EXISTENCE IS PROVABLE** somebody who believes that it is impossible to know whether or not God exists **2. SOMEBODY DENYING SOMETHING IS KNOWABLE** somebody who doubts that a particular question has a single correct answer or that a complete understanding of something can be attained ○ *I'm an agnostic concerning the validity of modern educational methods.* [Mid-19thC. Coined (reputedly by the English biologist and religious skeptic T. H. Huxley (1825–95) in 1869, although an earlier use of the word has been recorded) from A- + GNOSTIC.] —**ag·nos·tic** *adj.* —**ag·nos·ti·cal·ly** *adv.*

ag·nos·ti·cism /ag nóstə sìzzəm/ *n.* the belief that it is impossible to know whether or not God exists

Ag·nus Dei /aag nŏŏss dáy ee, aágnəss dáy ee, àg nŏŏss dáy ee, àgnəss dáy ee/ *n.* **1. LAMB WITH CROSS** a lamb, usually depicted with a halo and holding a cross and banner, used as a symbol of Jesus Christ **2. CHRISTIAN PRAYER** a Christian prayer that begins in Latin with the words "Agnus Dei," or "Lamb of God," part of the liturgy of the Mass **3.** MUSIC **MUSIC FOR AGNUS DEI PRAYER** a musical setting of the Christian prayer beginning "Agnus Dei" [15thC. From Latin, literally "Lamb of God."]

a·go /ə gṓ/ *adv., adj.* before the present time ○ *He only left about five minutes ago.* [14thC. From the past participle of Old English *āgān* "to go away, pass by," from *gān* "to go."]

WORD KEY: USAGE

ago and **since** If ***ago*** is used it should be followed by **that** and not **since** in a following clause: *It was several weeks ago that I saw them.* If ***ago*** is left out, then **since** is used: *It is several weeks since I saw them.* Note also that in sentences of this type, ***ago*** is preceded by a verb in the past tense (*was*) and **since** by a verb in the present tense.

a·gog /ə gόg/ *adj.* intensely interested, excited, or eager ○ *agog at the new twist to the scandal* [15thC. Probably based on Old French *en gogues* "enjoying yourself," literally "in enjoyment"; the origin of *gogues* is unknown.]

-agog *suffix.* = **-agogue**

à go·go /ə gṓ gō/ *adj.* (*dated informal*) **1. GALORE** as much as anybody could want ○ *caviar à gogo* **2.** in a whirl of activity ○ *The club was completely à gogo by nine in the evening.* [Mid-20thC. From French, "joyfully," from *en gogues* "enjoying oneself" (see AGOG) by repeating the *go-*.]

-agogue, **-agog** *suffix.* substance promoting the flow of something ○ *galactagogue* [Via French from, ultimately, Greek *agōgos* "a drawing off," from *agein* "to lead"]

a·gon /á gòn, áa gòn/ (*plural* **a·gons** *or* **a·gon·es** /à gōniz/) *n.* **1.** CONFLICT a conflict, especially one between the main characters in a drama or other work of literature (*formal*) **2.** GREEK FESTIVAL in ancient Greece, a festival featuring sports, musical, or theatrical competitions, e.g., the Olympic, Pythian, Nemean, and Isthmian games [Early 17thC. From Greek *agōn* "contest," from *agein* "to lead, conduct, celebrate."]

ag·o·nal /ággən'l/ *adj.* involving intense pain, especially the pain or throes of death

a·gon·es plural of **agon**

ag·o·nist /ággənist/ *n.* **1.** ANAT MUSCLE ACTING AGAINST ANOTHER a muscle whose action is balanced by that of another associated muscle. ◊ **antagonist 2.** BIOCHEM DRUG MIMICKING BODILY CHEMICAL a drug, hormone, or other substance that triggers a response in a particular body tissue or group of cells by binding to specific receptor molecules on or inside the cells. ◊ **antagonist 3.** COMPETITOR somebody involved in a struggle, contest, or competition with somebody else (*formal*) [Early 17thC. From Greek *agōnistēs* "contestant, actor," from *agōn* (see AGON).]

ag·o·nistes /àggə nísteez/ *adj.* used after a name to indicate that somebody is engaged in a fundamental struggle, especially a moral one (*literary*) [Late 17thC. From Greek *agōnistēs* (see AGONIST).]

ag·o·nis·tic /àggə nístik/, **ag·o·nis·ti·cal** /àggə nístik'l/ *adj.* **1.** TRYING FOR EFFECT striving to achieve an effect but appearing contrived or exaggerated (*literary*) **2.** ARGUMENTATIVE tending to argue and eager to win an argument (*literary*) **3.** OF GREEK CONTESTS relating to the ancient Greek sports, musical, or theatrical contests **4.** ZOOL AGGRESSIVE characteristic of aggressive interaction between individuals, usually of the same species [Mid-17thC. Via late Latin, from Greek *agōnistikos*, from *agōnistēs* (see AGONIST).] —**ag·o·nis·ti·cal·ly** *adv.*

ag·o·nize /ággə nīz/ (**-nized, -niz·ing, -niz·es**) *v.* **1.** *vi.* SPEND TIME WORRYING to think about something intensely and anxiously, usually in great detail and for a long time, before making a decision ○ *to agonize over the answer to every question* **2.** *vti.* SUFFER OR CAUSE SOMEBODY PAIN to suffer, or cause somebody to suffer, extreme pain or mental anguish **3.** *vi.* STRUGGLE to make a desperate or strenuous effort (*literary*) [Late 16thC. Directly or via French, from late Latin *agonizare*, modeled on Greek *agōnizesthai* "to take part in a contest," from *agōn* (see AGON).]

ag·o·nized /ággə nīzd/ *adj.* expressing or characterized by severe pain or anxiety ○ *an agonized scream* ○ *an agonized search for the missing person*

ag·o·niz·ing /ággə nīzing/ *adj.* **1.** VERY PAINFUL extremely painful **2.** CAUSING DIFFICULTY OR UNPLEASANTNESS causing much difficulty or unpleasantness ○ *an agonizing decision* —**ag·o·niz·ing·ly** *adv.*

ag·o·ny /ággənee/ (*plural* **-nies**) *n.* **1.** GREAT PAIN OR ANGUISH intense physical pain or mental anguish **2.** INTENSE EMOTION a consuming emotion ○ *in an agony of indecision* **3.** STRUGGLE an intense struggle or contest (*formal*) **4.** SUFFERING PRECEDING DEATH a period of struggle or suffering immediately preceding death (*archaic*) ○ *last agony* [14thC. Directly or via French, from Latin *agonia*, from Greek *agōnia* "(mental) struggle, anguish," from *agōn* "contest" (see AGON).] ◇ **prolong the agony** to make a period of misfortune or anxiety last longer than necessary

ag·o·ny col·umn *n.* a newspaper column of personal advertisements, usually inquiring about missing relatives or friends (*archaic*)

ag·o·ra[1] /ággərə, ə gáwrə/ (*plural* **a·go·ras** *or* **a·go·rae** /-ree/) *n.* an open space in a town where people gather, especially a marketplace in ancient Greece [Late 16thC. From Greek, "marketplace, place of assembly," from *ageirein* "to assemble."]

a·go·ra[2] /àagə ráa/ (*plural* **-rot** /-rṓt/) *n.* **1.** see table at **currency 2.** COIN WORTH AN AGORA a coin worth one agora [Mid-20thC. From Hebrew *agōrāh* "small coin."]

ag·o·rae plural of **agora**[1]

ag·o·ra·pho·bi·a /àggərə fṓbee ə/ *n.* a condition characterized by an irrational fear of public or open spaces [Late 19thC. Coined from Greek *agora* "open place" (see AGORA[1]) + -PHOBIA.] —**ag·o·ra·pho·bic** *adj., n.*

a·go·rot plural of **agora**[2]

a·gou·ti /ə gṓotee/ (*plural* **-tis** *or* **-ties**) *n.* **1.** TROPICAL RODENT a tropical rodent native to Central and South America that is similar in size to a rabbit and has short ears and clawed feet. Genus: *Dasyprocta.* **2.** STRIPED FUR an irregularly striped pattern in the individual hairs of the fur of an agouti [Early 17thC. Via French or Spanish, from Tupi-Guarani *akutí.*]

agr. *abbr.* agriculture

Ag·ra /áagrə/, **Āg·ra** city in Uttar Pradesh state, northern India. It is famous as the site of the Taj Mahal. Population: 955,674 (1991).

a·gran·u·lo·cy·to·sis /ay grànyəlō sī tṓsiss/ *n.* a serious and sometimes fatal acute illness characterized by a decrease in granular white blood cells, and lesions of the throat, gastrointestinal tract, and skin. The condition often occurs as a toxic effect of certain drugs. [Early 20thC. Coined from A- + GRANULOCYTE + -OSIS.]

ag·ra·pha /ággrəfə/ *npl.* sayings of Jesus Christ not recorded in the Bible but found in other early Christian writings [Late 19thC. From the plural of Greek *agraphon* "unwritten."]

a·graph·i·a /ə gráffee ə, ay-/ *n.* loss of the ability to write, resulting from neurological damage such as a brain lesion [Mid-19thC. Coined from A- + Greek *graphia* "writing."] —**a·graph·ic** *adj.*

a·grar·i·an /ə gráiree ən/ *adj.* **1.** OF RURAL LIFE dominated by or relating to farming or rural life **2.** OF LAND relating to land, especially its ownership and cultivation **3.** PRO-FARMER promoting the interests of farmers, especially by seeking a fairer or more equitable basis of land ownership ○ *an agrarian political party* ■ *n.* LAND REFORMER somebody, often a member of an agrarian political movement, who believes in the fair distribution of land, especially the redistribution of large amounts of land owned by the rich [Early 17thC. Formed from Latin *agrarius*, from the stem *agr-* "field" (see AGRICULTURE).]

a·grar·i·an·ism /ə gráiree ənizzəm/ *n.* a political movement or philosophy that promotes the interests of the farmer, especially the redistribution of land owned by the rich or government

a·gree /ə grée/ (**a·greed, a·gree·ing, a·grees**) *v.* **1.** *vi.* BE IN ACCORD to have the same opinion about something as somebody or each other ○ *Scientists don't agree about what causes these reactions.* **2.** *vi.* CONSENT to consent to or approve something ○ *They agreed to a postponement.* **3.** *vi.* ADMIT AS TRUE to admit that something is true ○ *I had to agree that the room looked better with a coat of paint.* **4.** *vti.* DECIDE to come to an understanding or reach a settlement regarding something ○ *Do you think we can agree on a plan?* **5.** *vi.* BE CONSISTENT to be consistent in content, meaning, or characteristics with something ○ *The witnesses' stories agree in most details with the accused's.* **6.** *vi.* BE SUITABLE to suit or be good for somebody ○ *The climate doesn't agree with me.* **7.** *vi.* LING MATCH GRAMMATICALLY to have the same grammatical number, case, person, or gender, especially in the same sentence [14thC. Via French *agréer* "to please" from, ultimately, Latin *ad* "to" + *gratus* "pleasing."]

WORD KEY: SYNONYMS

agree, consent, concur, acquiesce, assent

CORE MEANING: to accept an idea, plan, or proposed action that has been put forward

agree the most general and wide-ranging term; **consent** a slightly more formal term for **agree**, also often used to mean to give formal permission to, and sometimes indicating willingness rather than enthusiasm; **concur** a formal term suggesting that somebody has reached agreement independently, often regarding a statement or opinion; **acquiesce** a somewhat formal term that suggests a lack of enthusiasm and commitment, or an initial reluctance and reservation that may have been overcome by some form of external persuasion; **assent** the most formal term, indicating full support, often a statement or opinion.

a·gree·a·ble /ə grée əb'l/ *adj.* **1.** PLEASING pleasing to the senses or to somebody's taste ○ *The climate here is very agreeable.* **2.** FRIENDLY pleasant, friendly, and ready to please others ○ *an agreeable companion* **3.** WILLING TO COMPLY willing to consent to or consider something ○ *If the committee is agreeable, you can start work straight away.* **4.** SATISFACTORY good enough or suitable for somebody (*formal*) ○ *Let us make an arrangement agreeable to both sides.* [14thC. From French, formed from *agréer* (see AGREE).] —**a·gree·a·bil·i·ty** /ə grèe ə bíllətee/ *n.* —**a·gree·a·bly** /-b'lee/ *adv.*

a·greed /ə gréed/ *adj.* **1.** DETERMINED BY CONSENSUS previously decided and assented to by two or more people ○ *the agreed procedure* **2.** SHARING OPINION sharing the same view as somebody else or others ○ *Are we all agreed on the proposal?* ■ *interj.* YES used to confirm agreement with somebody else

a·gree·ment /ə gréemənt/ *n.* **1.** FORMAL CONTRACT a contract or arrangement, either written or verbal and sometimes enforceable by law **2.** ACT OR STATE OF AGREEING the reaching or sharing of the same opinion that somebody or others hold ○ *Do we have your agreement on this issue?* **3.** CONSENSUS OF OPINION a situation in which everyone accepts the same terms or has the same opinion ○ *everyone is in agreement* **4.** CONSENT consent, or an answer of yes ○ *my parents' agreement to the marriage* **5.** GRAM GRAMMATICAL CORRESPONDENCE correspondence of the number, case, gender, or person of one word with that of another word, especially in the same sentence

agri *prefix.* = **agro-**

ag·ri·busi·ness /ággri bìznəss/ *n.* the operations and businesses that are associated with large-scale farming

agri·chem·i·cal *n.* = **agrochemical**

ag·ri·cul·tur·al /àggri kúlchərəl/ *adj.* **1.** OF AGRICULTURE involving or relating to agriculture ○ *agricultural equipment* ○ *agricultural college* **2.** FARMING-CENTERED with farming as the dominant way of life ○ *one of the earliest agricultural communities* —**ag·ri·cul·tur·al·ly** *adv.*

ag·ri·cul·ture /ággri kùlchər/ *n.* the occupation, business, or science of cultivating the land, producing crops, and raising livestock [15thC. Directly or via French, from Latin *agricultura*, from *agri* "of the land" (from the stem *agr-* "field, land") + *cultura* "cultivation."] —**agri·cul·tur·ist** /àggri kúlchərist/ *n.*

ag·ri·mo·ny /ággrə mōnee/ (*plural* **-ny** *or* **-nies**) *n.* **1.** PLANT WITH SPINY FRUITS a perennial plant that has compound leaves, spikes of small yellow flowers, and spiny fruits. Genus: *Agrimonia.* **2.** = **hemp agrimony** [Pre-12thC. Via Old French, from Latin *agrimonia*, a misreading of *argemonia*, from Greek *argemōnē* "poppy."]

agro-, **agri-** *prefix.* **1.** soil ○ *agrology* **2.** agriculture ○ *agroindustrial* [From Latin *agri* (a form of *ager*) and Greek *agros* "field." Ultimately from an Indo-European word meaning "field," which is also the ancestor of English *acre*.]

ag·ro·bi·ol·o·gy /àggrō bī óllәjee/ *n.* the branch of biology concerned with agricultural production, especially crop growth —**ag·ro·bi·o·log·i·cal** /àggrō bī ə lójjik'l/ *adj.* —**ag·ro·bi·o·log·i·cal·ly** *adv.* —**ag·ro·bi·ol·o·gist** /-óllәjist/ *n.*

ag·ro·chem·i·cal /àggrō kémmik'l/, **ag·ri·chem·i·cal** /àggri-/ *n.* **1.** CHEMICAL FOR FARMING a chemical used in farming, e.g., a fertilizer or pesticide **2.** CHEMICAL FROM PLANT a chemical that is extracted or derived from an agricultural product

ag·ro·for·est·ry /àggrō fáwrəstree/ *n.* **1.** AGRIC FORESTRY COMBINED WITH FARMING the method or practice of integrating the raising of trees into farming to provide fuel, fruits, forage, shelter for animals or crops, and other benefits **2.** FORESTRY FORESTRY FOR TIMBER ONLY forestry conducted purely to produce timber, without any regard for sporting or recreational pursuits

ag·ro·in·dus·tri·al /àgrō in dústree əl/ *adj.* **1.** FOR AGRICULTURE AND INDUSTRY relating to the production or provision of materials needed by both agriculture and industry, e.g., water **2.** OF INDUSTRIAL AGRICULTURE used in, produced by, or involved in the industrial processing of agricultural products

ag·ro·nom·ic /àggrə nómmik/, **ag·ro·nom·i·cal** /àggrə nómmik'l/ *adj.* **1.** OF STUDY OF SOILS AND PLANTS relating to the scientific study of soil management, land cultivation, and crop production **2.** IMPORTANT FOR CROP QUALITY used to describe plant characteristics that are important during growth and development of a crop, e.g., height and stem strength

ag·ro·nom·ics /àggrə nómmiks/ *n.* the branch of economics that is concerned with the use and productivity of land (*takes a singular verb*) [Mid-19thC. Coined from AGRO- + ECONOMICS.]

a·gron·o·my /ə grónnəmee/ *n.* the science of soil management, land cultivation, and crop production [Early 19thC. Via French *agronomie* from, ultimately, Greek *agronomos* "overseer of land," from *agros* "land" + *-nomos* "dispensing, administering."] —**a·gron·o·mist** *n.*

a·ground /ə grównd/ *adj., adv.* onto or on ground, especially a shore, a reef, rocks, or the bottom of shallow water

agt. *abbr.* 1. agent 2. agreement

a·guar·di·en·te /àa gwaardee éntee, àa gwaard yén tày/ *n.* rough brandy distilled in Spain, Portugal, or Latin America, sometimes flavored with anise [Early 19thC. From Spanish, from *agua* "water" + *ardiente* "fiery."]

A·guas·ca·lien·tes /àagwəss kaalee én tàyss/ state in central Mexico on the Anahuac plateau. The resort city of Aguascalientes is its capital. Population: 862,335 (1995). Area: 2,158 sq. mi./5,589 sq. km.

a·gue /áy gyoō/ *n.* 1. FEVER a feverish condition involving alternating hot, cold, and sweating stages, especially as a symptom of malaria 2. ATTACK OF FEVER a fever or shivering fit (*archaic*) [14thC. Via French, from medieval Latin *acuta*, short for *febris acuta*, literally "sharp fever."] —**a·gu·ish** /áy gyoō ish/ *adj.* —**a·gu·ish·ly** *adv.* —**a·gu·ish·ness** *n.*

A·gui·nal·do /àa gi naáldō/, **Emilio** (1869–1964) Filipino politician who led the fight for independence from Spain (1896–98) and fought against U.S. occupation (1899–1901).

ah /aa/, **ahh** *interj.* 1. EXPRESSING EMOTION used to express emotions ranging from blissful contentment to acute discomfort to disgust, depending on the speaker's tone of voice ○ *Ah, Mom, do I have to?* ◊ **aah** 2. EXPRESSING RECOGNITION used to express surprise or recognition and understanding ○ *Ah, I see.* ■ *vi.* SAY "AH" to say "ah." ◆ **ooh** ■ *n.* UTTERANCE OF "AH" an exclamation of "ah" expressing any of various emotions

a.h., **A.h.** *abbr.* ampere-hour

A.H., **AH** *adv.* used in the Muslim calendar to indicate the number of years from the Hegira (A.D. 622). Full form **anno Hegirae**

a·ha /aa haá/ *interj.* used when discovering something, especially to express triumphant satisfaction or excitement ○ *Aha, I caught you in the act!* [14thC. Formed from AH + HA.]

AHA *abbr.* alpha-hydroxy acid

a·head /ə héd/ *adv., adj.* 1. IN FRONT in front of somebody or something ○ *They are in the white car just ahead.* 2. FORWARD onward or in a forward direction ○ *Keep walking straight ahead and it'll be on your left.* 3. TO THE FUTURE in or into the future ○ *We expect more news in the weeks ahead.* 4. EARLIER before or in advance of something or somebody ○ *You need to learn to plan ahead!* 5. IN BETTER SHAPE in or into a more advanced or desirable state ○ *Our company is definitely ahead compared to competition.* 6. IN FIRST PLACE in a winning position in a contest or competition ○ *They were ahead by 6 points.* ◇ **ahead of** 1. in front of 2. at an earlier time than 3. in a more advanced or advantageous position than ◇ **get ahead** to succeed, do well, or advance financially (*informal*)

a·hem /ə hém/ *interj.* used in writing to indicate the sound of a quiet cough made to attract attention, express disapproval or doubt, or gain time [Mid-18thC. An imitation of the sound.]

ahh *interj.* = **ah**

a·him·sa /ə hím saá/ *n.* the Hindu, Buddhist, and Jainist philosophy of revering all life and refraining from harm to any living thing [Late 19thC. From Sanskrit, from *a-* "without" + *himsā* "injury."]

a·his·tor·i·cal /ày hi stáwrik'l/, **a·his·tor·ic** /ày hi stáwrik/ *adj.* not concerned with or not taking into account history or historical development, especially when examining a phenomenon that changes over time

AHL *abbr.* American Hockey League

a·hold /ə hṓld/ *n.* a firm grasp on something, usually with the hand (*informal*) ◇ **get ahold of** 1. get somebody or something or reach somebody by phone or similar means (*informal*) 2. to regain emotional control after a shock or state of distress, fear, anxiety, or excitement (*informal*)

-aholic *suffix.* addicted to ○ *workaholic* [From ALCOHOLIC]

a·hoy /ə hóy/ *interj.* 1. EXPRESSING GREETING used by sailors to greet another ship or person or to attract attention ○ *Ahoy there!* 2. REGISTERING A SIGHTING used by sailors to announce that something, usually another ship or land, is in sight [Mid-18thC. Probably a blend of AHA and HOY.]

Ah·ri·man /aárimən/ *n.* the spirit of evil in Zoroastrianism, and opponent of Ormadz [Via Persian, from, ultimately, Avestan *angrō mainiiuš* "evil spirit"]

A·hu·ra Maz·da /ə hoōrə mázdə/ *n.* = **Ormazd** [From Avestan *ahurō mazdā*, literally "wise lord"]

AI *abbr.* 1. artificial insemination 2. artificial intelligence

AIB *abbr.* American Institute of Banking

aid /ayd/ *vti.* (**aid·ed, aid·ing, aids**) GIVE HELP TO SOMEBODY to provide somebody or something with help or with what is needed to achieve something ○ *Better sewage systems aid in the fight against cholera.* ■ *n.* 1. MONEY OR SUPPLIES financial or material assistance, e.g., that provided by a government or international organization, especially in times of crisis 2. ASSISTANCE anything done or provided that assists somebody or something ○ *I wouldn't have made it without the aid of my friends.* 3. SOMEBODY OR SOMETHING HELPFUL somebody or something, e.g., a device, resource, or material, that helps or assists with something ○ *visual aids such as maps* ○ *This book is an aid to surfing the Internet.* 4. ASSISTANT an assistant or aide 5. MIL MILITARY AIDE an officer's aide-de-camp 6. HIST PAYMENT TO LORD a monetary payment by a vassal to an English feudal lord 7. HIST SUBSIDY FOR ENGLISH KING a special subsidy formerly granted to the English king by parliament. Aids for extraordinary expenses were granted from the time of the Norman Conquest into the 18th century. [15thC. Via French, from Latin *adjutare* "to help" (see ADJUTANT).] ◇ **aid and abet** to assist somebody in commission of a crime

AID *abbr.* 1. Agency for International Development 2. acute infectious disease 3. artificial insemination by donor (*dated*)

aide /ayd/ *n.* 1. ASSISTANT an assistant to somebody in public office or to somebody providing a professional service ○ *a congressional aide* 2. = **aide-de-camp** [Late 18thC. Shortening of AIDE-DE-CAMP.]

WORD KEY: SYNONYMS

See Synonyms at ***assistant***.

aide-de-camp /àyd də kámp/ (*plural* **aides-de-camp** /àydz də kámp/), **aide** /ayd/ *n.* a military officer acting as a confidential assistant to a general or senior officer [Late 17thC. From French, literally "camp assistant."]

aide-mé·moire /àyd mem waár/ (*plural* **aide-mé·moire** /àyd mem waár/ *or* **aide-mé·moires** *or* **aides-mé·moire**) *n.* (*formal*) 1. BRIEF SUMMARY a brief written summary or outline of the items on an agenda for a meeting or on which agreement was reached in a meeting 2. MEMORY AID something, e.g., a mnemonic device, book, or document, that is an aid to remembering something else [Mid-19thC. From French, literally "help-memory."]

AIDS /aydz/ *n.* a disease of the immune system caused by infection with the retrovirus HIV, which destroys certain white blood cells and is transmitted through blood or bodily secretions such as semen. Patients lose the ability to fight infections, often resulting in death from secondary causes such as pneumonia or Kaposi's sarcoma. [Late 20thC. Acronym formed from *Acquired Immune Deficiency Syndrome*.]

AIDS-re·lat·ed com·plex *n.* the set of symptoms associated with infection by HIV, including weight loss and fever

aid sta·tion *n.* a military medical installation for troops in the field

ai·grette /ay grét, áy gret/, **ai·gret** *n.* 1. PLUME OF FEATHERS a tuft of long upright plumes, especially the tail feathers of an egret, worn on the head or on a hat for decoration 2. JEWELRY RESEMBLING PLUME OF FEATHERS a piece of jewelry that resembles a plume of feathers, usually worn on the head or on a hat [Mid-17thC. From French, literally "egret, heron" (see EGRET).]

ai·guille /ay gweél/ *n.* a mountain peak or large rock that is tall and sharply pointed [Early 19thC. From French, literally "needle."]

ai·guil·lette /àygwi lét/ *n.* a decorative cord worn on the shoulder of some military uniforms [Mid-16thC. From French, literally "little needle," from *aiguille* "needle." The word originally denoted a metallic pin worn as an ornament.]

AIH *abbr.* artificial insemination by husband

Ai·ken /áykən/ city in west fcentral South Carolina. It was the site of a Civil War battle in 1865. Population: 22,834 (1996).

Aiguille: Teton Mountains, Jackson Hole, Wyoming

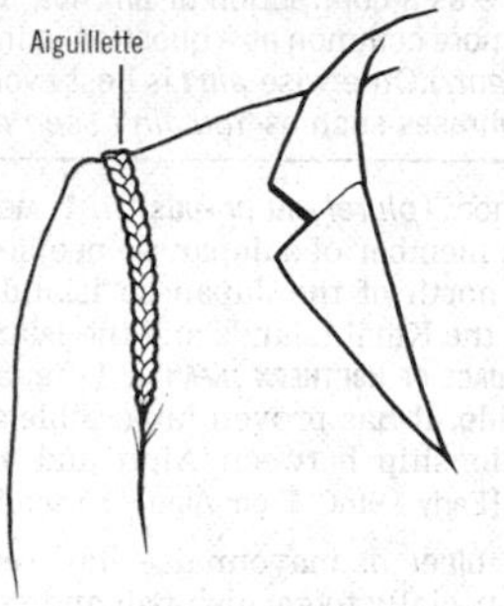

Aiguillette

Ai·ken, Conrad Potter (1889–1973) U.S. writer, poet, and critic. He won the Pulitzer Prize (1930) for *Selected Poems* (1929).

ai·ki·do /ī ki dō, ī kee-/ *n.* a martial art originating in Japan that is similar to judo but incorporates blows made with the hands and feet [Mid-20thC. From Japanese, literally "way of coordinated breathing."]

ail /ayl/ (**ailed, ail·ing, ails**) *vt.* to cause something to be wrong with somebody or something, or cause somebody to feel ill ○ *This soup is good for whatever ails you.* [Old English *eglian.* Ultimately from an Indo-European word meaning "to be afraid or distressed," which is also the ancestor of English *awe*.]

ai·lan·thus /ay lánthəs/ *n.* an Asian tree or shrub with long feathery leaves, winged fruit, and dense flower clusters. Tree-of-heaven is a type of ailanthus. Genus: *Ailanthus.* [Early 19thC. Via modern Latin, genus name, from Amboinese *ai lanto*, literally "tree of heaven," influenced by plant names ending in *-anthus*.]

ai·le·ron /áylə ròn/ *n.* a hinged flap on the trailing edge of an aircraft wing, used to control banking or rolling movements [Early 20thC. From French, literally "small wing," from *aile* "wing," from Latin *ala*.]

Ai·ley /áylee/, **Alvin** (1931–89) U.S. dancer and choreographer. He founded the Alvin Ailey Dance Theater (1958).

ail·ing /áyling/ *adj.* 1. IN POOR CONDITION performing below an expected standard ○ *The nation's ailing steel industry.* 2. ILL suffering from or weakened by an illness (*dated*)

ail·ment /áylmənt/ *n.* a mild illness or injury, especially a persistent one

WORD KEY: SYNONYMS

See Synonyms at ***illness***.

ai·lu·ro·phile /ī loōrə fīl, ay-/ *n.* somebody who loves cats [Mid-20thC. Coined from Greek *ailuros* "cat" + -PHILE.]

ai·lu·ro·phobe /ī loōrə fōb, ay-/ *n.* somebody who hates or has an abnormal fear of cats [Early 20thC. Coined from Greek *ailuros* "cat" + -PHOBE.] —**ai·lu·ro·pho·bi·a** *n.*

aim /aym/ *v.* (**aimed, aim·ing, aims**) 1. *vi.* PLAN TO DO SOMETHING to intend or plan to do something 2. *vt.* DIRECT A MESSAGE to target words, a message, an action, or a product at a particular person or group 3. *vti.* POINT AN OBJECT to point a weapon or object or direct a blow at somebody or something ■ *n.* 1. INTENTION a plan to do or achieve something 2. ACT OF AIMING an act or manner of aiming ○ *Take aim and fire.* 3. SKILL IN AIMING skill at hitting a target ○ *Her aim was perfect.* 4. DEGREE OF ACCURACY the level of accuracy of a weapon ○ *This pistol's aim is off.* 5. TARGET something at which a weapon or other object is aimed (*archaic*) [14thC. From Old French *esmer* "to estimate" and *aesmer* "to aim at," both ultimately from Latin *aestimare* (see ESTIMATE).]

AIM *abbr.* American Indian Movement

aim·less /áymləss/ *adj.* without purpose or direction —**aim·less·ly** *adv.* —**aim·less·ness** *n.*

a·i·na /aa eenə/ *n. Hawaii* land or country [20thC. From Hawaiian *'āina.*]

ain't /aynt/ *contr.* a contraction of "am not," "is not," "are not," "have not," or "has not" (*nonstandard*)

WORD KEY: USAGE

When can you say **ain't**? ***Ain't*** is one of the most informal verb contractions in English, and it is widely disliked because it is associated with uneducated speech of a kind that many people disfavor. It is slightly more acceptable as a contraction of *am not*, and in the form **ain't I?** is more common as a question in informal English (*Ain't I right?*).Otherwise ***ain't*** is best avoided, except in allusive phrases such as *You ain't seen nothing yet.*

Ai·nu /ī nōō/ (*plural* **-nu** *or* **-nus**) *n.* **1.** MEMBER OF JAPANESE PEOPLE a member of a Japanese people who now live in the north of the Japanese island of Hokkaido, and on the Kuril Islands and the island of Sakhalin **2.** LANGUAGE OF NORTHERN JAPAN a language spoken in Hokkaido. It has proven impossible as yet to show a relationship between Ainu and any other language. [Early 19thC. From Ainu, "person."] —**Ai·nu** *adj.*

ai·o·li /ī ōlee/ *n.* mayonnaise flavored with garlic, used especially to garnish fish and vegetables [Early 20thC. Via French, from Provençal, formed from *ai* "garlic" and *oli* "oil."]

air /air/ *n.* **1.** GASES FORMING ATMOSPHERE the mixture of gases, mainly nitrogen and oxygen, that forms the Earth's atmosphere **2.** ATMOSPHERE IN OPEN SPACE the atmosphere of an open space as opposed to that of an enclosed space ○ *in the open air* **3.** ATMOSPHERE WE BREATHE the particular atmosphere in a place or enclosed space ○ *fresh air* **4.** SKY the sky or the empty space above the earth ○ *it flew through the air and landed at our feet* **5.** TRAVEL IN AIRCRAFT travel in or transportation by aircraft (*often used before a noun*) ○ *sending the package by air* ○ *an air terminal* **6.** AURA an aura or particular quality ○ *an air of sadness about him* **7.** SOMEBODY'S DISTINCTIVE QUALITY a distinctive quality in somebody's appearance or manner ○ *her air of superiority* **8.** MUSIC MELODY a melody or tune, especially a light or cheerful one **9.** = **air conditioning 10.** LIGHT WIND a very light wind ■ **airs** *npl.* AFFECTATION affected manners or conduct meant to impress others ○ *He's always putting on airs.* ■ *adj.* OF ZODIAC SIGNS relating to the Aquarius, Gemini, or Libra signs of the zodiac ■ *v.* (**aired, air·ing, airs**) **1.** *vti.* BROADCAST OR BE BROADCAST to be broadcast or broadcast something on radio or television ○ *aired in the spring* **2.** *vt.* MAKE KNOWN to express something such as an opinion or complaint ○ *air your views* **3.** *vti.* EXPOSE TO AIR to be exposed to the air, or expose something to the air in order to dry it, remove dampness from it, cool it, or ventilate it [13thC. Partly via Old French and Latin, from Greek *aēr* "atmosphere" (see AERO-), and partly via French, "nature, place of origin," from Latin *ager* "field" and *area* "open space."] ◇ **clear the air** to remove the tension, uncertainty, or misunderstanding from a situation ◇ **give air to something** to express something verbally ◇ **in the air** happening or about to happen ○ *The rumor is that a merger is in the air.* ◇ **off (the) air** not being broadcast on radio or television, e.g., because a person or program has stopped or finished broadcasting ◇ **on (the) air** being broadcast on radio or television ◇ **take the air** to go for a walk (*formal*) ◇ **up in the air** undecided or uncertain ◇ **vanish into thin air** to disappear completely ◇ **walk on air** to be extremely happy

air bag *n.* **1.** SAFETY DEVICE a safety device in an automobile consisting of a bag that automatically inflates on impact to protect the occupant of the seat **2.** INFLATABLE RESCUE BAG a strong inflatable bag used to bring sunken items to the surface or by rescue workers to lift heavy machinery or debris under which somebody is trapped

air ball *n.* a shot in basketball that misses not only the net but the rim and backboard (*informal*)

air base *n.* a place from which military aircraft operate

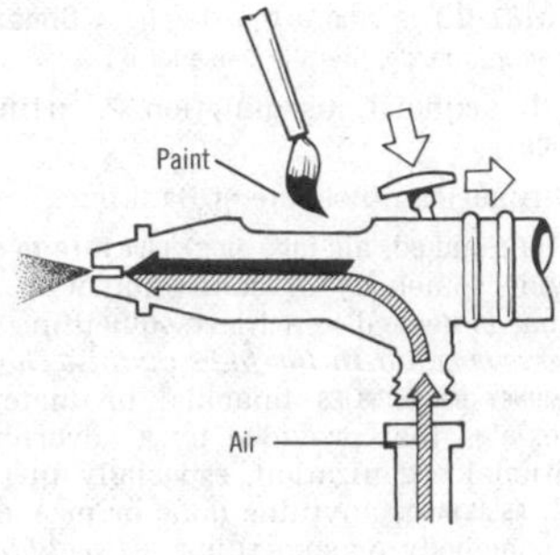

Airbrush

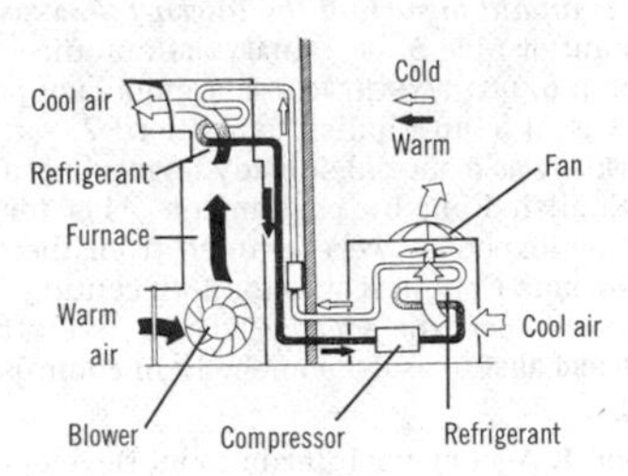

Air conditioning

air blad·der *n.* **1.** FISH'S BUOYANCY ORGAN an air-filled sac above the alimentary canal in most fishes that regulates buoyancy and, in some, aids in respiration **2.** AIR-FILLED SAC IN SEAWEED an air-filled sac that aids buoyancy in certain types of seaweed

air·boat /áir bōt/ *n.* = **swamp boat** [So called because it is driven with a propellor and steered with a rudder like an airplane's]

air·borne /áir bàwrn/ *adj.* **1.** CARRIED BY AIR carried along by movements of air **2.** BY AIRCRAFT carried out or transported by aircraft **3.** IN FLIGHT in flight or in the air

air brake *n.* **1.** AIR-OPERATED BRAKE a brake operated by compressed air, especially in a heavy motor vehicle **2.** AIRCRAFT BRAKE a flap or small parachute on an aircraft operated to increase drag and thus slow the aircraft

air·brush /áir brùsh/ *n.* PAINT SPRAYING DEVICE a device for spraying paint using compressed air ■ *vt.* (**-brushed, -brush·ing, -brush·es**) PAINT WITH AIRBRUSH to paint something or alter or improve a picture using an airbrush ○ *The blemish had been airbrushed out.*

air·burst /áir bùrst/ *n.* an explosion of a bomb, shell, or missile in the air

air cham·ber *n.* **1.** SPACE ENCLOSING AIR an enclosed space with air in it **2.** CHAMBER IN HYDRAULIC SYSTEM a chamber in a hydraulic system in which air expands and compresses to control the flow of a fluid

air-con·di·tion (**air-con·di·tioned, air-con·di·tion·ing, air-con·di·tions**) *vt.* to cool and control the humidity and purity of the air circulating in a building with an air conditioner —**air con·di·tioned** *adj.*

air con·di·tion·er *n.* a device for cooling and controlling the humidity and purity of the air circulating in a building

air con·di·tion·ing *n.* a system for cooling and controlling the humidity and purity of the air circulating in a building

air-cool (**air-cooled, air-cool·ing, air-cools**) *vt.* to cool something, especially an engine, by a flow of air rather than a water system —**air-cooled** *adj.*

Air Corps *n.* the airborne division of the United States Army that later became a separate service as the United States Air Force

air cor·ri·dor *n.* a specified route that aircraft should take through airspace in which flying is restricted

air cov·er *n.* the provision of an airborne defense for ground forces against an enemy air attack, or the aircraft providing the defense

air·craft /áir kràft/ (*plural* **-craft**) *n.* any vehicle capable of flight

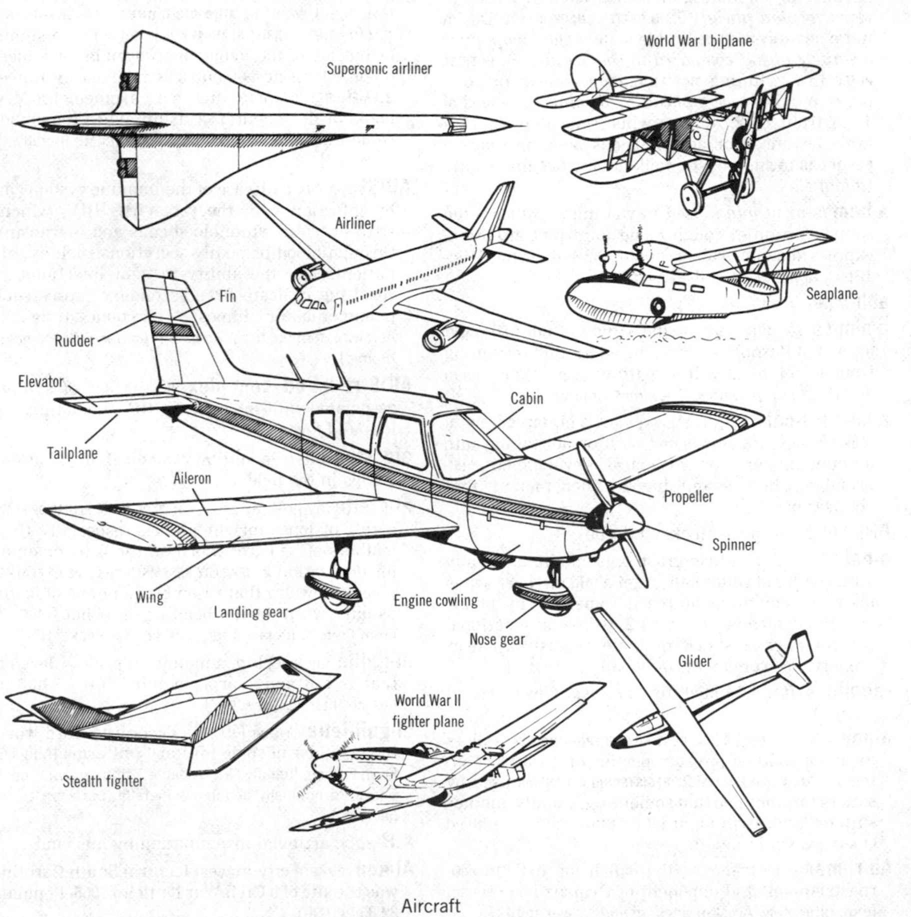

Aircraft

air·craft car·ri·er *n.* a warship with a long flat deck designed to allow aircraft to take off and land on it

air·crew /áir kro͞o/ *n.* the pilot, navigator, and other crew members of an aircraft

air cur·tain *n.* a stream of air directed across a doorway, especially to prevent drafts

air cush·ion *n.* **1.** AIR BENEATH HOVERCRAFT the pocket of air that is forced down to support a hovercraft **2.** AIR SUSPENSION a type of suspension that uses enclosed air to absorb shocks —**air-cush·ioned** *adj.*

air cush·ion ve·hi·cle *n.* = **hovercraft**

air dam *n.* a device for reducing the air resistance of a vehicle, especially a strip of metal or plastic fitted across the width of a car below the front bumper

air·date /áir dàyt/ *n.* the date on which a radio or television program is scheduled to be broadcast

air di·vi·sion *n.* a unit of the United States Air Force of a size between a wing and an air force

air door *n.* a strong current of air directed upward in an entrance to take the place of a door

air·drome /áir drōm/ *n.* a small airfield with limited facilities [Early 20thC. Coined from AIR + DROME.]

air·drop /áir dròp/ *n.* PARACHUTE LANDING a landing of troops or supplies by parachute from an aircraft ■ *vt.* (**-dropped, -drop·ping, -drops**) LAND BY PARACHUTE to land troops or supplies by parachute from an aircraft

air-dry *v.* (**air-dried, air-dry·ing, air-dries**) DRY BY AIR to dry something by exposing it to air ■ *adj.* TOTALLY DRY dry to the point where continued exposure to air will remove no further moisture

Airedale

Aire·dale /áir dàyl/, **Aire·dale ter·ri·er** *n.* a large terrier belonging to a breed with rough tan-colored hair and a black patch on the back [Late 19thC. Named for the district of *Airedale* in West Yorkshire, England.]

air em·bo·lism *n.* the presence of air in a blood vessel resulting from injury, from moving too rapidly from high to lower atmospheric pressure, or from using a heart-lung machine during cardiopulmonary bypass

air·fare /áir fàir/ *n.* the price of a trip in an aircraft

air·field /áir fèeld/ *n.* **1.** AREA FOR AIRCRAFT an area where aircraft can take off and land **2.** AIRPORT an airport or air base

air·flow /áir flō/ *n.* a flow of air, especially around a moving vehicle

air·foil /áir fòyl/ *n.* a part of an aircraft's or other vehicle's surface, e.g., an aileron, wing, or propeller, that acts on the air to provide lift or control

air force *n.* **1.** AIRCRAFT BRANCH OF ARMED SERVICES a military organization that uses aircraft in war, especially a branch of a nation's armed forces **2.** U.S. AIR FORCE BODY a unit of the United States Air Force of a size between a division and a high-level command, e.g., the United States European Command

Air Force One *n.* the official airplane of the President of the United States

air·frame /áir fràym/ *n.* the whole body of an aircraft, apart from its engines [Mid-20thC. Coined from AIRCRAFT + FRAME.]

air·freight /áir fràyt/ *n.* **1.** TRANSPORTATION OF GOODS BY AIR the transportation of freight by air **2.** CHARGE FOR AIRFREIGHT the charge made for transporting freight by air ■ *vt.* (**-freight·ed, -freight·ing, -freights**) TRANSPORT GOODS BY AIR to transport goods by air

air gas *n.* = **producer gas**

air·glow /áir glō/ *n.* a faint light observed in the night sky from low latitudes, caused by photochemical reactions generated by solar radiation in the upper atmosphere

air gui·tar *n.* an imaginary guitar held by somebody pretending to play a real instrument, especially when miming to rock music (*informal*)

air gun *n.* a pistol or rifle that fires a projectile by releasing compressed air

air·head[1] /áir hèd/ *n.* an unintelligent and superficial person (*slang insult*)

air·head[2] /áir hèd/ *n.* an area in enemy territory captured and held by airborne forces and used when flying troops and supplies in or out of the territory [Mid-20thC. Formed from AIR, on the model of BEACHHEAD.]

air hole *n.* **1.** VENTILATION HOLE a hole to allow the passage of air **2.** HOLE IN ICE an unfrozen area in the surface of a frozen body of water, especially one where aquatic mammals surface to breathe **3.** = **air pocket** *n.* 1

air·i·ly /áirilee/ *adv.* **1.** LIGHT-HEARTEDLY in a carefree or light-hearted way as if something was unimportant **2.** LIGHTLY in a delicate or light way

air·i·ness /áirinəss/ *n.* **1.** CASUALNESS carefree or light-hearted casualness **2.** SPACIOUSNESS the quality of being spacious or having plenty of fresh air

air·ing /áiring/ *n.* **1.** DRYING exposure to air or heat, especially for drying, removal of dampness, or ventilation **2.** MAKING SOMETHING KNOWN the exposure to public attention of somebody's opinions or ideas **3.** RADIO OR TELEVISION BROADCAST a radio or television broadcast

air·ish /áirish/ *adj.* used to describe weather that is chilly or cool (*regional*)

air jack·et *n.* **1.** INSULATION an air-filled casing around a machine to insulate it against heat loss or gain **2.** = **life jacket**

air-kiss (**air-kissed, air-kiss·ing, air-kiss·es**) *vt.* greet somebody by making a kissing gesture near to, but not actually making contact with, his or her cheek (*informal*) ○ *The guests were welcomed in a flurry of air-kissing and delighted squeals.* —**air-kiss** *n.*

air lane *n.* a regular route used in air travel

air lay·er·ing *n.* a plant propagation method in which a growing branch is cut or stripped of bark and the area wrapped in moist compost to encourage root formation

air·less /áirləss/ *adj.* **1.** WITH STALE AIR with stale rather than fresh air **2.** WITHOUT AIR completely lacking any air **3.** STILL without wind or movement of air

air·lift /áir lìft/ *n.* AIR TRANSPORT the transport of people or things by air, especially when alternative means cannot be used ■ *vt.* (**-lift·ed, -lift·ing, -lifts**) TRANSPORT BY AIR to transport people or things by air, especially when alternative means cannot be used

air·line /áir līn/ *n.* **1.** SYSTEM OF FLYING a system of commercial scheduled flights transporting people and goods, or a company that operates such a system **2.** SOURCE OF AIR a tube through which air is passed under pressure

air·lin·er /áir līnər/ *n.* a large commercial passenger-carrying aircraft

air·lock /áir lòk/ *n.* **1.** AIRTIGHT CHAMBER an airtight chamber between two areas of differing air pressure in which air pressure can be altered to match that of either area **2.** OBSTRUCTION IN FLOW OF LIQUID an obstruction to the flow of a liquid in a pipe, caused by a bubble of air

air·mail /áir màyl/ *n.* **1.** SENDING OF MAIL BY AIR the system of transporting letters and packages in aircraft **2.** MAIL SENT BY AIR mail transported in aircraft ■ *adj.* SENT BY AIR sent by airmail ■ *vt.* (**-mailed, -mail·ing, -mails**) SEND BY AIR to send something, e.g., a letter or package, by airmail

air·man /áirmən/ (*plural* **-men** /áirmən/) *n.* **1.** MEMBER OF U.S. AIR FORCE an enlisted person in the United States Air Force, who holds a rank above airman basic and below airman first class, or the rank itself **2.** PILOT a pilot, especially of a military aircraft

air·man ba·sic (*plural* **air·men ba·sic**) *n.* an enlisted person who holds the lowest rank in the United States Air Force, or the name of the rank itself

air·man first class (*plural* **air·men first class**) *n.* an enlisted person in the United States Air Force who holds a rank above airman and below sergeant, or the name of the rank itself

air mass *n.* a large body of air with temperature, pressure, and moisture uniform throughout its mass but changed by the environment through which it passes

Air Medal *n.* a decoration for meritorious conduct in the air awarded by the United States Army, Navy, or Air Force

air mile *n.* = **nautical mile**

air·mo·bile /áir mōb'l, -beel, -bīl/ *adj.* able to be transported into a combat zone by air, especially by helicopter

air·pack /áir pàk/ *n.* a device consisting of a portable supply of oxygen connected to a face mask that allows somebody to enter an area where the air is unsafe to breathe

air·park /áir paark/ *n.* a small airport, usually close to a business or industrial center

air pi·ra·cy *n.* the hijacking of an aircraft in flight

air pis·tol *n.* a pistol that fires a projectile by releasing compressed air or another gas

air·plane /áir plàyn/ *n.* a vehicle with wings and a jet engine or propellers, that is heavier than air, and is able to fly [Late 19thC. From French *aéroplane*, from *aéro-* "AERO-" + *-plane*, of uncertain origin: possibly from *plan* "flat" or *planer* "to soar," or from Greek *planos* "wandering."]

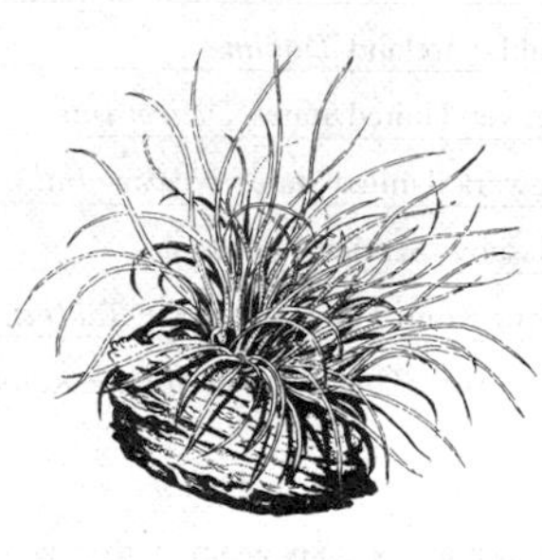

Air plant

air plant *n.* a plant that obtains nutrients and moisture from the air and rain, especially one grown as a houseplant for the novelty value of its requiring no soil or compost. ◊ **epiphyte**

air·play /áir plày/ *n.* the playing on radio of a piece of recorded music

air pock·et *n.* **1.** DOWNWARD AIR CURRENT a small area of lower air density or a downward air current that makes an aircraft abruptly lose height **2.** AIR BUBBLE IN FLUID an air bubble that impedes the flow of liquid or gas, e.g., in a pipe

air po·lice *n.* the military police of an air force

air pop·per *n.* a container for cooking popcorn that uses heated air

air·port /áir pàwrt/ *n.* an area where civil aircraft may take off and land, especially one equipped with surfaced runways and facilities for handling passengers and cargo

air·pow·er /áir pòwr/ *n.* military capability in terms of combat power delivered from the air

air pres·sure *n.* = **atmospheric pressure**

air pump *n.* a device for compressing air or forcing it into or out of something

air qua·li·ty in·dex (*plural* **air quality in·dex·es** *or* **air qua·li·ty in·dic·es**) *n.* a numerical scale that indicates how polluted the air is

air rage *n.* disruptive or aggressive behavior by passengers aboard an aircraft that is liable to endanger the aircraft's safety

air raid *n.* an attack by aircraft on something on the ground, especially a non-military target

air ri·fle *n.* a rifle that fires a projectile by releasing compressed air or another gas

air rights *npl.* rights to build in or otherwise use space above an existing structure

air sac *n.* **1.** = **alveolus** *n.* 1 **2.** AIR-FILLED CAVITY IN BIRD an air-filled cavity in a bird, formed as an extension of the respiratory system and growing into the bones, that aids respiration and decreases bone

CODES OF SELECTED INTERNATIONAL AIRPORTS

Code	City	Country	Airport
AKL	Auckland	New Zealand	*Auckland Intl.*
AMS	Amsterdam	Netherlands	*Schipol*
ATL	Atlanta	United States	*William B. Hartsfield Intl.*
BFS	Belfast	Northern Ireland	*Belfast Intl.*
BHX	Birmingham	England	*Birmingham*
BNE	Brisbane	Australia	*Brisbane Intl.*
CBR	Canberra	Australia	*Canberra*
CCU	Calcutta	India	*Dum Dum Intl.*
CDG	Paris	France	*Charles De Gaulle*
CGX	Chicago	United States	*O'Hare*
CHC	Christchurch	New Zealand	*Christchurch Intl.*
CMB	Colombo	Sri Lanka	*Katunayake*
CPT	Cape Town	South Africa	*Cape Town*
DAC	Dhaka	Bangladesh	*Zia Intl.*
DEL	Delhi	India	*Indira Ghandi Intl.*
DFW	Dallas/Fort Worth	United States	*Dallas/FortWorth Intl.*
DUB	Dublin	Ireland	*Dublin*
DVX	Denver	United States	*Denver Intl.*
EWR	Newark	United States	*Newark Intl*
GLA	Glasgow	Scotland	*Glasgow*
HKG	Hong Kong	Hong Kong	*Kai-Tal Intl.*
JFK	New York	United States	*John F. Kennedy*
NB	Johannesburg	South Africa	*Johannesburg*
KHI	Karachi	Pakistan	*Quaid-E-Azam Intl*
KIN	Kingston	Jamaica	*Norman Manley*
KTP	Kingston	Jamaica	*Tinson*
LAX	Los Angeles	United States	*Los Angeles Intl.*
LGA	New York	United States	*La Guardia*
LGW	London	England	*Gatwick*
LHR	London	England	*Heathrow*
MAN	Manchester	England	*Manchester*
MEL	Melbourne	Australia	*Melbourne*
MIA	Miami	United States	*Miami*
PER	Perth	Australia	*Perth*
SEA	Seattle	United States	*Seattle-Tacoma Intl.*
SIN	Singapore	Singapore	*Singapore*
SYD	Sydney	Australia	*Kingsford Smith*
WAS	Washington	United States	*Dulles*
WLG	Wellington	New Zealand	*Wellington Intl.*
YMX	Montreal	Canada	*Mirabel Intl.*
YOW	Ottawa	Canada	*MacDonald-Cartier Intl.*
YUL	Montreal	Canada	*Dorval Intl.*
YVR	Vancouver	Canada	*Vancouver Intl.*
YYZ	Toronto	Canada	*Lester B. Pearson Intl.*

Airport

mass **3.** RESPIRATION AID IN INSECT a thin-walled bulge (**diverticulum**) that aids respiration, located in the tubes that transport air through the bodies of some insects

air·screw /áir skroō/ *n. U.K.* a propeller on an aircraft

air-sea res·cue *n.* a rescue at sea in which aircraft are used

Airship

air·ship /áir shìp/ *n.* an aircraft that is lighter than air, powered, and navigable

air·show /áir shṑ/ *n.* a public exhibition at an airfield of aircraft in flight and on the ground

air show·er *n.* **1.** BLAST OF AIR a process during which people who work in a clean environment stand in jets of air to remove dust or particles from their clothes **2.** DEVICE FOR GIVING AIR SHOWERS a device for giving air showers

air·sick·ness /áir sìknəss/ *n.* motion sickness caused by air travel —**air·sick** *adj.*

air·side /áir sīd/ *n.* the area of an airport where the aircraft take off and land, load, or unload

air sock *n.* = **windsock**

air·space /áir spàyss/ *n.* **1.** SPACE ABOVE TERRITORY the part of the atmosphere directly over an area of land or water, especially a part over which a state claims jurisdiction **2.** FLYING SPACE the space in the air that a flying aircraft occupies or needs to maneuver

air speed *n.* the speed of an aircraft in relation to the air through which it moves

air splint *n.* a type of splint consisting of an inflatable cylinder that surrounds the injured limb

air spray *n.* = **aerosol** *n.* 1, **aerosol** *n.* 2

air spring *n.* = **air cushion** *n.* 1

air sta·tion *n.* a small airfield with facilities for maintenance of aircraft

air·stream /áir strēem/ *n.* **1.** WIND a wind, especially one blowing at a high altitude **2.** = **airflow**

air strike *n.* an attack by aircraft on something on the ground, especially an enemy position or formation [Late 20thC] —**airstrike** *vt.*

air·strip /áir strìp/ *n.* a place for aircraft to take off and land that has no facilities and is often temporary

air stripping *n.* a technique for removing pollutants from water by breaking the water into minute particles

air tax·i *n.* a small commercial aircraft used for brief flights between places that do not have regularly scheduled flights

air ter·mi·nal *n.* an airport building with facilities for passengers, where disembarking passengers are received and outward-bound passengers leave to board an aircraft

air ter·ror·ism *n.* the use of actions such as skyjacking, aircraft bombing, and other terrorist acts in an attempt to achieve a political objective or get international publicity

air·tight /áir tīt/ *adj.* **1.** IMPERMEABLE BY AIR not allowing air in or out **2.** FLAWLESS without flaws or vulnerable points

air·time /áir tīm/ *n.* **1.** TIME ON AIR the amount of time given to a program or subject in radio or television broadcasting **2.** TIME OF BROADCAST the time at which an item is scheduled to be broadcast

air-to-air *adj.* moving or passing from one aircraft to another while in flight

air-to-sur·face *adj.* moving or passing from a flying aircraft to a point on the ground

air traf·fic *n.* the movement of aircraft in a particular area

air-traf·fic con·trol *n.* the system or organization responsible for directing the movement of aircraft over a particular area, operated by ground staff in radio contact with pilots —**air traf·fic con·trol·ler** *n.*

air ves·i·cle *n.* an air-filled cavity between cells that assists buoyancy in certain aquatic plants, e.g., seaweed

air walk *n.* a high-level passageway connecting two buildings, usually made from a transparent material

air·waves /áir wàyvz/ *npl.* radio waves as used in broadcasting

air·way /áir wày/ *n.* **1.** BREATHING PASSAGE a passage for air from the nose or mouth to the lungs **2.** TUBE TO KEEP AIRWAY OPEN a device for keeping an unconscious person's airway open, incorporating a tube inserted into the throat **3.** VENTILATION PASSAGE a passage for ventilation in a mine or tunnel **4.** AIR ROUTE an air route, especially one used by regular commercial flights (*often used in the plural*)

air·wor·thy /áir wùrthee/ *adj.* in good enough condition to be safe to fly [Early 19thC. Modeled on SEAWORTHY.] —**air·wor·thi·ness** *n.*

air·y /áiree/ (**-i·er, -i·est**) *adj.* **1.** ROOMY having plenty of space **2.** VENTILATED having plenty of fresh air **3.** CAREFREE carefree or lighthearted and unconcerned **4.** ETHEREAL ethereal or illusory **5.** OF AIR connected with, like, or taking place in the air **6.** GRACEFUL light and graceful in movement **7.** HIGH IN THE AIR at a great height in the sky

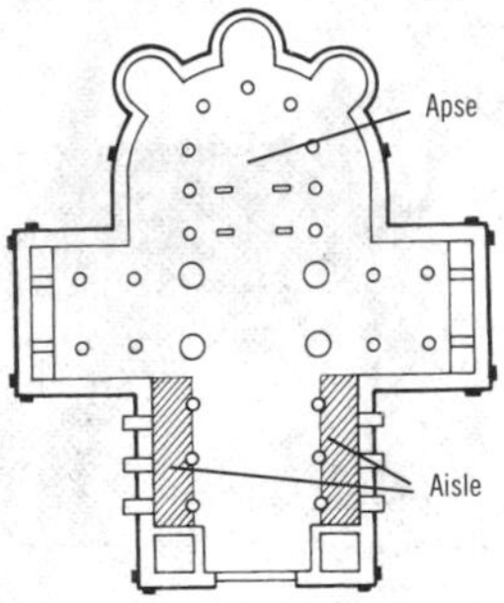

Aisle

aisle /īl/ *n.* **1.** PASSAGEWAY BETWEEN SEATS a passageway between areas of seating, especially in a church, theater, or passenger vehicle **2.** PASSAGEWAY BETWEEN GOODS a passageway between stacks or displays of goods, especially in a supermarket or warehouse **3.** DIVISION IN CHURCH an area of a church separated from the nave or central area by pillars, especially one forming a passage between seats [14thC. Alteration of Old French *ele* "wing," from Latin *ala*, under the influence of ISLE and, later, French *aile* "wing."] ◇ **rolling in the aisles** laughing very heartily

aitch /aych/ *n.* the letter "h," or its sound [Mid-16thC. From French *hache*, via late Latin *ach* from Latin *ah*, an alteration of *ha*.]

a·jar /ə jaár/ *adj., adv.* neither shut nor wide open ○ *left the door ajar* [Late 17thC. Formed from an obsolete word meaning "turn," from Old English *cierr*. The underlying meaning is "turning on its hinges."]

A·jax /áy jàks/ *n.* in Greek mythology, a powerful warrior who fought in the Trojan War as leader of the Salaminian forces

AK *abbr.* Alaska

a.k.a., **aka** *abbr.* also known as

A·kan /aá kaán/ (*plural* **A·kan** *or* **A·kans**) *n.* **1.** PEOPLES MEMBER OF AFRICAN PEOPLE a member of a people who live in southern Ghana, the southeastern Ivory Coast, and parts of Togo **2.** LANGUAGE OF WESTERN AFRICA a language spoken in Ghana and Ivory Coast, belonging to the Kwa group of Niger-Congo languages. Akan is spoken by about eight million people. [Late 17thC. From Twi *akaŋ*.] —**A·kan** *adj.*

a·kar·y·ote /ay kérri ṓt/ *n.* a cell that has no nucleus —**a·kar·y·ot·ic** /ay kèrree óttik/ *adj.*

AKC *abbr.* American Kennel Club

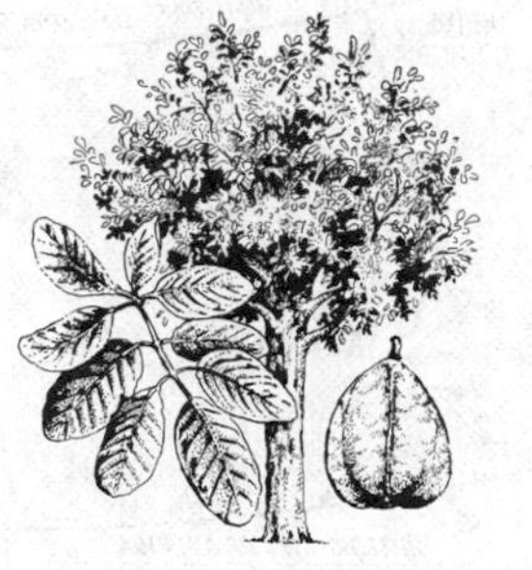

Akee

ak·ee /ákee, ə kée/ (*plural* **-ees** *or* **-ee**), **ac·kee** (*plural* **-k·ees** *or* **-kee**) *n.* **1. AFRICAN TREE** an evergreen tree of the soapberry family that is native to tropical western Africa and cultivated in the Caribbean and Florida for its fruit. Latin name: *Blighia sapida.* **2. FRUIT** the red pear-shaped fruit of the akee tree, edible when ripe but poisonous at other times and with poisonous seeds [Late 18thC. Origin uncertain: possibly from Kru.]

a·kene *n.* = **achene**

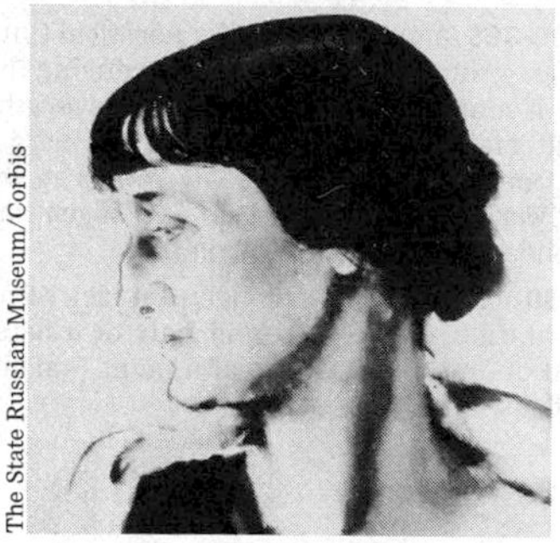

The State Russian Museum/Corbis

Anna Akhmatova: Detail of portrait (1928) by Nikolai Tyrsa

Akh·ma·to·va /ak maátəvə, àkmə tṓvə/, **Anna** (1889–1966) Russian poet. She was a leading figure in an early 20th-century movement that advocated precision and brevity in poetic language. Pseudonym **Anna Andreyevna] Gorenko**

A·ki·ba ben Jo·seph /aa kée baa bən jṓzəf, -jóssəf/ (A.D.50?–135?) Palestinian Jewish rabbi. He lived near Jaffa and was executed by the Romans about 135.

Ak·i·hi·to /aáki hée tō/, **Emperor of Japan** (*b.* 1933). He succeeded his father, Hirohito, in 1989.

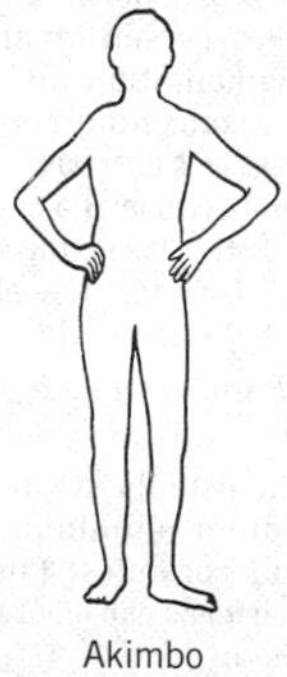

Akimbo

a·kim·bo /ə kímbō/ *adj., adv.* **1. WITH HANDS ON HIPS** with the hands on the hips and the elbows turned outward **2. ARCHED** bent or arched [14thC. Origin uncertain.]

a·kin /ə kín/ *adj.* **1. SIMILAR** similar or closely related to something **2. RELATED** related by blood **3. WITH COMMON ORIGIN** used to describe languages that share a common origin or ancient forms

a·ki·ne·sia /ày kə néezhə, ày kī-/ *n.* the loss or reduction of the normal power of movement [Mid-19thC. From Greek "lack of movement," from, ultimately, *kinein* "to move" (see KINETIC).] —**a·ki·net·ic** /ày ki néttik/ *adj.*

A·ki·ra Yo·shi·mu·ra /a kéerə yṓshi mŏorə/ (*b.* 1927) Japanese writer whose prize-winning novels and nonfiction works include *Journey to the Stars* (1966) and *Von Siebold's Daughter* (1978).

A·ki·ta[1] /ə kéetə/ capital city of Akita Prefecture on the Sea of Japan, northwestern Honshu Island, Japan. Population: 302,362 (1990).

A·ki·ta[2] /ə kéetə/ *n.* a large powerful dog with a broad head, deep muzzle, and curled tail, belonging to a Japanese breed

Ak·kad /á kàd, aá kaád/ ancient region situated in central northern Mesopotamia that corresponds approximately to biblical Babylonia. It was most influential during the third millennium B.C.

Ak·ka·di·an /ə káydiən/ *n.* **1.** PEOPLES **SOMEBODY FROM AKKAD** somebody who was born or lived in the ancient city or region of Akkad **2.** LANG **EXTINCT MIDDLE EASTERN LANGUAGE** the extinct Semitic language of Mesopotamia. It was written in cuneiform. [Mid-19thC. Formed from *Akkad,* a city in ancient Babylonia.] — **Ak·ka·di·an** *adj.*

ak·ra·sia /ə kráyzhə/ *n.* weakness of will, especially a failure to act according to a sense of moral obligation [From Greek, variant of *akrateia,* literally "powerlessness," from *kratos* "strength" (see -CRACY)] —**ak·rat·ic** /ə kráttik/ *adj.*

Ak·ron /ákrən/ city in northeastern Ohio noted for its rubber products. Population: 221,886 (1994).

A·ku·ta·ga·wa Ry·u·no·su·ke /aá koōta gaáwə rŏonə sŏokee/, **A·ku·ta·ga·wa Ry·ū·no·su·ke** (1892–1927) Japanese author, noted for his macabre stories set in Japan's feudal era, e.g., *Rashomon* (1917).

ak·va·vit *n.* = **aquavit**

Al *symbol.* aluminum

AL *abbr.* **1.** Alabama **2.** American League **3.** Albania (*international vehicle registration*)

al. *abbr.* **1.** alcohol **2.** alcoholic

-al[1] *suffix.* relating to or characterized by ○ *delusional* [Via French from Latin *-alis*]

-al[2] *suffix.* action, process ○ *disposal* [Via Old French *-aille* from Latin *-alia,* neuter plural of *-alis*]

-al[3] *suffix.* aldehyde ○ *chloral* [From ALDEHYDE]

à la /aá laa, állə/, **a la** *prep.* in the style of somebody or something [Late 16thC. From French, shortening of *à la mode de* "in the fashion of."]

Ala. *abbr.* Alabama

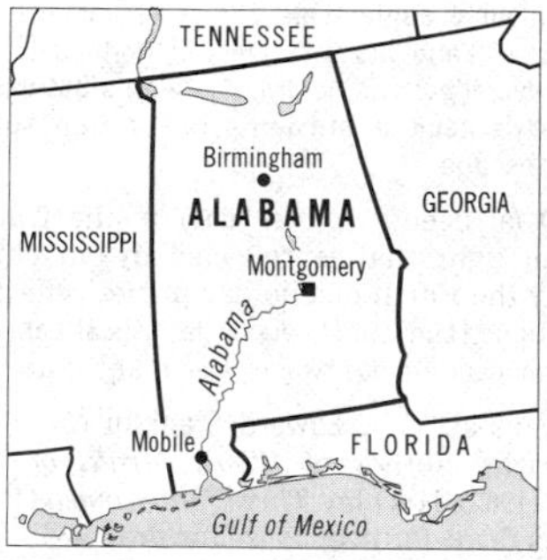

Alabama

Al·a·bam·a /állə bámmə/ **1.** state of the southeastern United States, bounded by Georgia, the Gulf of Mexico, Mississippi, and Tennessee. Capital: Montgomery. Population: 4,319,154 (1997). Area: 52,237 sq. mi./135,293 sq. km. **2.** river flowing from central Alabama southwest to the Tombigbee River north of Mobile. Length: 315 mi./507 km. —**Al·a·ba·man** *adj., n.* —**Al·a·bam·i·an** /állə bámmee ən/ *adj., n.*

al·a·bas·ter /állə bástər/ *n.* **1. TYPE OF GYPSUM** a type of gypsum, usually white or translucent, used for sculpture and decorative work **2. TYPE OF CALCITE** a hard semitranslucent type of calcite, which sometimes has bands ■ *adj.* **OF ALABASTER** made of alabaster, or white and translucent like alabaster [14thC. Via Old French, from, ultimately, Greek *alabastros.*]

à la carte /aá laa kaárt, allə kaárt/, **a la carte** *adj., adv.* with each dish on a menu priced separately [Early 19thC. From French, literally "by the menu."]

a·lack /ə lák/ *interj.* used to express regret (*archaic or literary*) [15thC. Formed from LACK, on the model of ALAS.]

a·lac·ri·ty /ə lákrətee/ *n.* promptness or eager and speedy readiness [Early 16thC. From Latin *alacritas,* formed from *alacer* "lively."] —**a·lac·ri·tous** *adj.*

al-Adha /àl aádə/ *n.* = **Eid-ul-Adha**

à la grecque /aá laa grék/, **a la grecque** *adj.* cooked in a sauce made with olive oil, lemon, usually wine, and herbs and served cold [From French, "in the Greek style"]

à la king /aá laa kíng/, **a la king** *adj.* cooked in a cream sauce with peppers and mushrooms

a·la·me·da /àllə méedə, -máy-/ *n. Southwest U.S.* a public promenade shaded by trees [Late 18thC. From Spanish, formed from *álamo* "poplar tree."]

A·la·me·da /àllə méedə/ city and port in western California, situated on an island south of Oakland. Population: 76,042 (1996).

al·a·mo /álləmō/ *n. Southwest U.S.* a poplar tree, especially a cottonwood [Mid-19thC. From Spanish.]

Al·a·mo /álləmō/ chapel built at the San Antonio mission in Texas in 1744. It was besieged by Mexican forces in 1836 and all 182 Texan defenders were killed.

a·la·mode /aálə mṓd, àllə-/ *n.* a light silk used especially for shawls [Mid-17thC. From French *à la mode,* literally "in the style."]

à la mode /aá laa mṓd/, **a la mode** *adj.* **1. WITH ICE CREAM** served with ice cream **2. FASHIONABLE** in the latest fashion (*dated*) [Late 16thC. From French, literally "in the style."]

Al·a·mo·gor·do /àlləmə gáwrdō/ city in southern New Mexico, northeast of the site of the first atomic bomb explosion, on July 16 1945. Population: 29,036 (1996).

al·a·nine /állə néen/ *n.* a crystalline water-soluble amino acid that is a constituent of various proteins and can also be produced by humans and animals. Formula: $C_3H_7NO_2$. [Mid-19thC. From German *Alanin,* from *Aldehyd* "aldehyde."]

a·la·nu·i /ə lə nŏoee/ (*plural* **-is**) *n. Hawaii* a street [20thC. From Hawaiian *alanui.*]

a·lar /áylər/, **a·la·ry** /-ree/ *adj.* used to describe a part of an animal or plant that is shaped like a wing or is associated with such a part [Mid-19thC. From Latin *alaris,* from *ala* "wing."]

a·larm /ə laárm/ *n.* **1. WARNING DEVICE** a device for giving a warning of danger **2. SECURITY DEVICE** a security device fitted to property, especially a house or car, to make a warning sound if a break-in or theft is attempted **3. SOUND OF SECURITY OR WARNING DEVICE** the sound made by a security or warning device **4.** = **alarm clock 5. FEAR** fear caused by perception of imminent danger **6. CALL TO ARMS** a summons to prepare to fight (*archaic*) **7.** FENCING **CHALLENGE MADE BY STAMPING** a warning or challenge to a fencer made by stamping the leading foot ■ *vt.* (**a·larmed, a·larm·ing, a·larms**) **1. FRIGHTEN** to make somebody frightened or apprehensive **2. WARN** to give somebody warning of danger **3. FIT WITH WARNING DEVICE** to fit a building or vehicle with a security warning device [Early 16thC. Via French, from Italian *all' arme* "to arms!".] —**a·larmed** *adj.*

a·larm clock, **a·larm** *n.* a clock that can be set to sound an alarm at a desired time, especially to wake somebody

a·larm·ing /ə laárming/ *adj.* frightening or disturbing —**a·larm·ing·ly** *adv.*

a·larm·ist /ə laármist/ *n.* **1. SOMEBODY SPREADING FEAR** somebody who spreads unnecessary fear or warnings of danger **2. SOMEBODY EASILY SCARED** somebody who becomes afraid easily ■ *adj.* **SPREADING FEAR** liable to make people feel unnecessarily fearful or worried —**a·larm·ism** *n.*

a·larm re·ac·tion *n.* the initial response of a person or animal to stress, including an increased heart rate and hormonal activity

a·la·rum /ə laárəm, ə láirəm/ *n.* an alarm (*archaic*) [Variant of ALARM]

a·las /ə láss/ *interj.* **EXPRESSING SORROW** used to express sorrow or pity ■ *adv.* **UNFORTUNATELY** unfortunately or regrettably [13thC. Via French *hélas* from, ultimately, Latin *lassus* "weary" (see LASSITUDE).]

Alas. *abbr.* Alaska

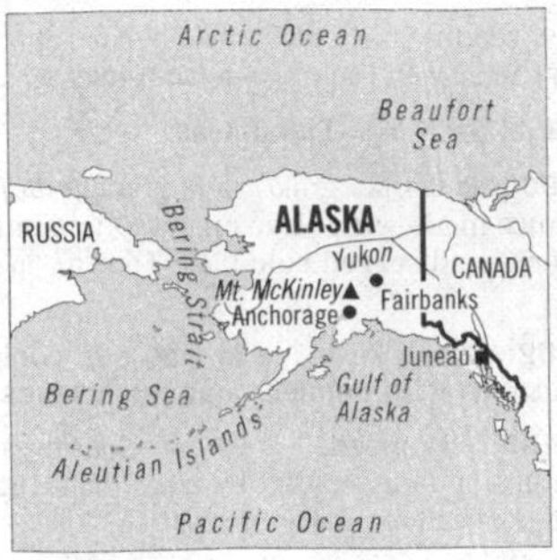

Alaska

A·las·ka /ə láskə/ U.S. state of northwestern North America, bordered by Canada and the Pacific and Arctic oceans. Capital: Juneau. Population: 609,311 (1997). Area: 615,230 sq. mi./1,593,438 sq. km. —**A·las·kan** *adj., n.*

A·las·ka High·way *n.* a road built in 1942 from Dawson Creek, British Columbia, to Fairbanks, Alaska. Former name **Alcan Highway**

A·las·kan king crab *n.* = **king crab** *n.* 1

A·las·kan mal·a·mute *n.* = **malamute**

A·las·kan North Slope region of northern Alaska, extending from the Arctic Ocean south to the Brooks Range

A·las·ka Range mountain range in southern Alaska, extending in a 400 mi./640 km semicircle north of Anchorage. It includes the highest peak in North America, Mount McKinley 20,320 ft./6,194 m.

A·las·ka Stan·dard Time *n.* the local standard time in the ninth zone west of the Greenwich meridian, calculated at 135° west and used throughout Alaska apart from the western Aleutian Islands

a·las·tor /ə lástər/ *n.* an avenging deity, frequently evoked in Greek tragedy [Late 16thC. From Greek, literally "somebody who is not forgotten," from *lath-*, the stem of *lanthanesthai* "to forget" (see LANTHANUM).]

a·late /áy làyt/, **a·lat·ed** /-təd/ *adj.* used to describe insects with wings or seeds with parts resembling wings [Mid-17thC. From Latin *alatus*, from *ala* "wing."]

alb /alb/ *n.* a long white robe with long sleeves worn by priests [Pre-12thC. Via ecclesiastical Latin *(vestis) alba* "white (garment)" from Latin *albus* "white."]

Alb. *abbr.* Albania ■ *abbr.* Albanian

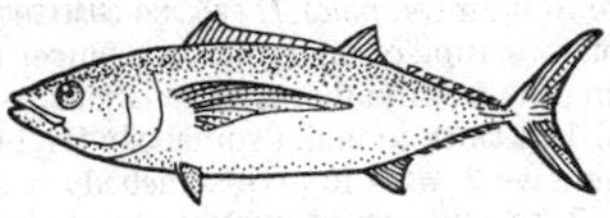
Albacore

al·ba·core /álbə kàwr/ (*plural* **-core** *or* **-cores**) *n.* a large tuna with a long pectoral fin, found in the warm waters of the Atlantic and Pacific and used as a food fish. Latin name: *Thunnus alalunga.* [Late 16thC. From Portuguese *albacor*, of uncertain origin: possibly from Arabic *al-bakrah* "young camel" or *al-bakūra* "premature."]

Al·ba·ni·a /al báyniə/ republic in southeastern Europe, bordering the Adriatic Sea. A former Communist country, it became a parliamentary democracy in 1991. Language: Albanian. Currency: lek. Capital: Tirana. Population: 3,260,000 (1995). Area: 11,100 sq. mi./28,748 sq. km.

Al·ba·ni·an /al báynee ən/ *n.* **1.** LANG **LANGUAGE OF ALBANIA** the official language of Albania, also spoken in parts of Serbia, Croatia, Macedonia, Italy, and Greece. A distinct branch of the Indo-European languages, Albanian is spoken by about four million people. **2.** PEOPLES **SOMEBODY FROM ALBANIA** somebody who was born or raised in Albania, or who is a citizen of Albania

Albania

■ *adj.* **OF ALBANIA** relating to or typical of Albania, or its culture or people

Al·ba·ny /áwlbənee/ **1.** capital of New York, situated on the western bank of the Hudson River. Population: 103,564 (1996). **2.** city in west central Oregon, on the east bank of the Willamette River, south of Salem. Population: 37,919 (1996). **3.** city in southwestern Georgia, situated on the Flint River. Population: 78,591 (1996). **4.** river in Ontario, Canada, flowing northeast into James Bay. Length: 610 mi./982 km.

Albatross

al·ba·tross /álbə tròss/ (*plural* **-tross·es** *or* **-tross**) *n.* **1.** **LARGE SEABIRD** a large long-winged seabird that inhabits cool southern oceans and spends most of its life in flight. Family: Diomedeidae. **2.** **OPPRESSIVE BURDEN** an oppressive burden or hindrance **3.** *U.K.* GOLF = **double eagle** [Late 17thC. Alteration (under the influence of Latin *albus* "white") of Portuguese *alcatraz*, from Arabic *al-ġaṭṭās* "the diver."] ◇ **an albatross around somebody's neck** a burden from which somebody cannot escape

al·be·do /al beédō/ (*plural* **-dos**) *n.* the fraction of incident light that is reflected by an object, especially the Earth or another planet reflecting the Sun's light [Mid-19thC. Via ecclesiastical Latin, "whiteness," from Latin *albus* "white" (see ALB).]

Al·bee /áwlbee, ál-/, **Edward Franklin** (*b.* 1928) U.S. playwright, author of *Who's Afraid of Virginia Woolf?* (1962). His play *Three Tall Women* (1991) won him his third Pulitzer Prize for drama.

al·be·it /awl beé it/ *conj.* used to add information that is different to what you have already said ○ *a difficult, albeit rewarding job* [14thC. Formed from ALL + BE + IT, meaning literally "all though it may be."]

Al·be·marle Sound /álbə maàrl/ inlet of the Atlantic Ocean, in northeastern North Carolina. Kitty Hawk, where the Wright brothers first flew, is on the barrier island that separates the shallow sound from the ocean.

Al·be·rich /álbərich/ *n.* in medieval German legend, king of the dwarves and guardian of the treasures of the Nibelung

Al·bers /álbərz, áwl-/, **Josef** (1888–1976) German painter and designer. He taught at the Bauhaus school of design. After 1933 he worked in the United States.

Al·bert /álbərt/, **Prince, Prince Consort** (1819–61) German-born prince consort to Queen Victoria. A supporter of technological innovation and patron of the arts, he organized the Great Exhibition (1851). The proceeds enabled the building of several museums and the Royal Albert Hall (1871).

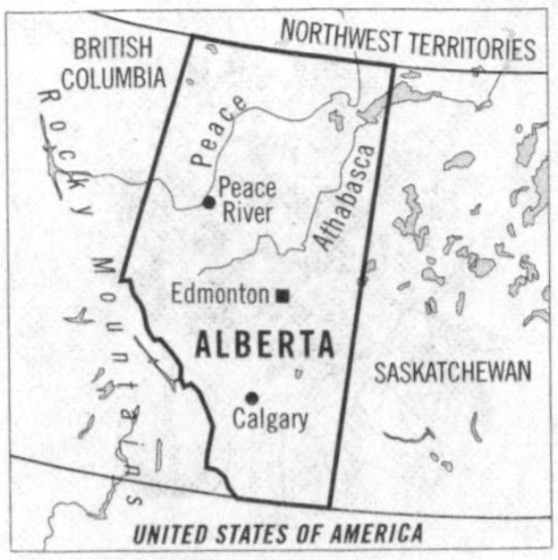

Alberta

Al·ber·ta /al búrtə/ Canada's westernmost Prairie Province and a leading producer of oil and natural gas. Capital: Edmonton. Population: 2,696,826 (1996). Area: 255,287 sq. mi./661,190 sq. km.

al·ber·tite /álbər tìt/ *n.* a solid black variety of bitumen found in oil-bearing rock strata [Mid-19thC. Named for *Albert* County, New Brunswick, in Canada, where it was originally found.]

al·bes·cent /al béss'nt/ *adj.* becoming white or whitish [Early 18thC. Via the Latin stem *albescent-* from, ultimately, *albus* (see ALB).]

Al·bi·gen·ses /àlbi jén seèz/ *npl.* a heretical Christian religious group in southern France during the 12th and 13th centuries. They believed that everything in the material world is evil. [Early 17thC. From medieval Latin, formed from *Albiga*, the city of Albi in southern France, where the group originated.] —**Al·bi·gen·sian** /àlbi jénshən/ *adj.* —**Al·bi·gen·sian·ism** *n.*

al·bi·nism /álbi nìzzəm/ *n.* congenital lack of normal pigmentation in the skin and hair of a person or animal or in the coloration of a plant —**al·bi·nis·tic** /àlbi nístik/ *adj.*

Albino: Dwarf Russian hamsters with albino shown right

al·bi·no /al bínō/ (*plural* **-nos**) *n.* **1.** **PERSON OR ANIMAL LACKING PIGMENTATION** a person or animal whose skin and hair lack pigmentation and whose irises are pink because of a congenital condition **(albinism)** **2.** **PLANT LACKING NORMAL COLORATION** a plant that lacks normal coloration because of a congenital condition **(albinism)** [Early 18thC. Via Portuguese, from, ultimately, Latin *albus* "white" (see ALB).] —**al·bin·ic** /al bínnik/ *adj.* —**al·bin·o·tic** /àlbi nóttik/ *adj.*

Al·bi·on /álbee ən/ ancient name for England or the island of Britain

al·bite /ál bìt/ *n.* a usually white form of feldspar consisting of sodium aluminum silicate, used in making glass and ceramics. Formula: $NaAlSi_3O_8$. [Early 19thC. Formed from Latin *albus* "white" (see ALB).] —**al·bit·ic** /al bíttik/ *adj.*

ALBM *abbr.* air-launched ballistic missile

Al·bright /áwl brìt/, **Ivan Le Lorraine** (1897–1983) U.S. painter. He is best known for his macabre painting of the title character for the movie *The Picture of Dorian Gray* (1945).

Al·bright, Madeleine (*b.* 1937) U.S. stateswoman. She became the highest-ranking woman in American politics in 1997, when she became secretary of state.

al·bum /álbəm/ *n.* **1.** **BLANK BOOK** a book or binder with blank pages or pockets in which valuable or fragile items like postage stamps, photographs, mementos, or autographs are kept **2.** **MUSIC RECORDING** a music recording, sometimes including more than one disk or cassette, issued as an individual item **3.** **RECORD**

Madeleine Albright

HOLDER a cardboard holder for phonograph records, similar to a book in shape **4.** *U.K.* **COLLECTION** a collection in book form of short literary or musical pieces or pictures (*dated*) [Early 17thC. From Latin, "blank tablet," from *albus* "white."]

WORD KEY: ORIGIN

The Latin word *albus* from which ***album*** is derived is also the source of English *alb, albino, albumen, auburn,* and *daub.*

al·bum·blatt /álbəm blàt/ (*plural* **-blatts** or **-blät·ter** /-blèttər/) *n.* a short light instrumental piece popular in the 19th century, usually bound together in a set with other similar pieces [From German, literally "page from an album"]

al·bu·men /al byóomən/ *n.* **1. WHITE OF EGG** the clear water-soluble protein that surrounds the yolk of an egg and provides nutrition for the embryo (*technical*) **2. EGG-WHITE PROTEIN** the protein component of egg white, which includes albumin [Late 16thC. From Latin, formed from *albus* "white" (see ALB).]

al·bu·min /al byóomin/ *n.* a water-soluble protein coagulated by heat. Albumins are found in many animal and plant tissues, especially egg white, blood plasma, and milk.

al·bu·mi·noid /al byóomə nòyd/ *adj.* **LIKE ALBUMIN** resembling or having the characteristics of albumin ■ *n.* = **scleroprotein** —**al·bu·mi·noi·dal** *adj.*

al·bu·mi·nous /al byóomənəss/ *adj.* connected with, like, or containing albumin

al·bu·mi·nu·ri·a /àl byoomə nóoree ə/ *n.* the presence of albumin in urine, usually an indication of kidney disease

Al·bu·quer·que /álbə kùrkee/ city and tourist resort on the Rio Grande and the largest city in New Mexico. Population: 419,681 (1996).

alc. *abbr.* **1.** alcohol **2.** alcoholic

Al·ca·ic /al káy ik/ *adj.* **CONTAINING FOUR FOUR-FOOT LINES** in poetry, written in the metrical form of a stanza of four lines, each containing four feet ■ *n.* **POETRY TYPE** a poem or lines written in the Alcaic form (*often used in the plural*) [Mid-17thC. Via late Latin from, ultimately, Greek *Alkaios,* the lyric poet credited with inventing the form.]

al·cai·de /al kídee/, **al·cay·de** *n.* **1. FORTRESS COMMANDER** a commander of a fortress in a Spanish-speaking area **2. PRISON GOVERNOR** a governor of a prison in a Spanish-speaking area [Early 16thC. Via Spanish, from Arabic *al-kā'id* "the commander."]

al·cal·de /al kaáldee/ *n.* the mayor or chief magistrate of a town in a Spanish-speaking area [Mid-16thC. Via Spanish, from Arabic *al-kādī* "the judge."]

Al·can High·way /ál kàn/ *n.* former name for **Alaska Highway** [From *Alcan,* a contraction of *Alaska-Canada*]

Al·ca·traz /álkə tràz/ island in San Francisco Bay, California, site of a federal prison from 1933 to 1963. It has been part of Golden Gate National Recreation Area since 1972.

al·cay·de *n.* = **alcaide**

al·caz·ar /al kázzər, álkə zaár, aálkə zaár/ *n.* fortress or palace in Spain, especially one built by the Moors [Early 17thC. Via Spanish, from Arabic *al-kaṣr* "the castle," ultimately from Latin *castrum* "camp" (source also of English *castle*).]

Al·ces·tis /al séstiss/ *n.* in Greek mythology, daughter of Pelias and wife of Admetus, King of Phaerae. She died to save her husband's life but was later rescued from Hades by Hercules.

al·che·mist /álkəmist/ *n.* somebody who practices alchemy —**al·che·mis·tic** /àlkə místik/ *adj.*

al·che·mize /álkə mìz/ (**-mized, -miz·ing, -miz·es**) *vt.* to transform something into gold or into a much purer or brighter form by alchemy

al·che·my /álkəmee/ *n.* **1. PREDECESSOR OF CHEMISTRY** an earlier and unscientific form of chemistry, seeking to transform base metals into gold and to discover a life-prolonging elixir, a universal cure for disease, and a universal solvent (**alkahest**) **2. TRANSFORMING OR ENCHANTING POWER** a power supposedly like alchemy, especially of enchantment or transformation [14thC. Via Old French *alquemie* and medieval Latin *alchimia* from Arabic *al-kīmiyā* "the chemistry," ultimately from Greek *khēmeia.*] —**al·chem·ic** /al kémmik/ *adj.* —**al·chem·i·cal** *adj.*

ALCM *abbr.* air-launched cruise missile

Alc·me·ne /alk ménnee/ *n.* in Greek mythology, wife of Amphitryon. While her husband was away at war, Zeus visited Alcmene disguised as Amphitryon. She later gave birth to two sons, Hercules and Iphicles.

Al·cock /áwl kòk, aál-/, **Sir John William** (1892–1919) British aviator. With Arthur Brown, he made the first transatlantic flight, from Newfoundland to Ireland, which took 16 hours 27 minutes.

al·co·hol /álkə hàwl/ *n.* **1. LIQUID FOR DRINKS AND SOLVENTS** a colorless liquid, produced by the fermentation of sugar or starch, that is the intoxicating agent in fermented drinks and is used as a solvent. Formula: C_2H_5OH. **2. DRINKS WITH ALCOHOL** intoxicating drinks containing alcohol **3. ORGANIC COMPOUND** any organic compound containing one or more hydroxyl groups bound to carbon atoms [Mid-16thC. Via medieval Latin, "fine powder, distilled essence of a substance," from Arabic *al-kuḥl* "the antimony powder" (source of English *kohl*).]

al·co·hol·ic /àlkə háwlik/ *adj.* **1. CONTAINING ALCOHOL** connected with or containing alcohol **2. CAUSED BY ALCOHOL** caused by alcohol consumption ○ *alcoholic dehydration* **3. ADDICTED TO ALCOHOL** addicted to drinking beverages containing alcohol ■ *n.* **ALCOHOL ADDICT** somebody who is addicted to drinking alcohol

al·co·hol·ic·i·ty /àlkə haw líssətee/ *n.* the amount of alcohol contained in something

al·co·hol·ism /álkə haw lìzzəm/ *n.* **1. ADDICTION TO ALCOHOL** dependence on alcohol to an extent that adversely affects behavior and social or work function and produces withdrawal symptoms when intake is stopped or reduced **2. ALCOHOL POISONING** a physical disorder caused by the toxic effects of excessive alcohol consumption

Al·co·ran /álkə rán/ *n.* = **Koran** —**Al·co·ran·ic** *adj.*

Al·cott /áwlkət, ál-/, **Amos Bronson** (1799–1888) U.S. transcendentalist and writer who founded the Concord Summer School of Philosophy and Literature in 1879.

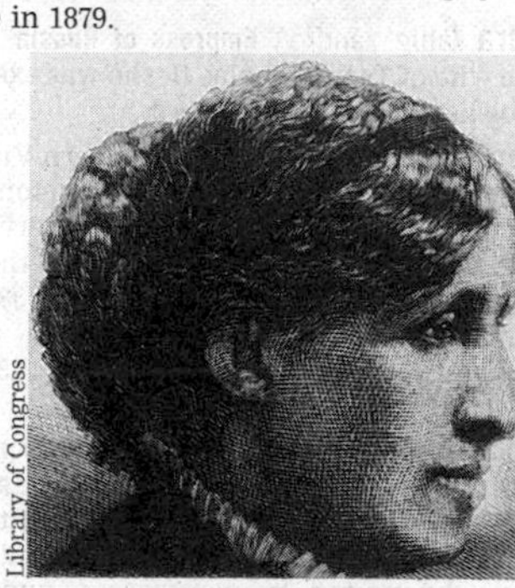

Louisa May Alcott

Al·cott, Louisa May (1832–88) U.S. novelist. Her novels include her most famous book, *Little Women* (1868), and its sequels.

al·cove /ál kòv/ *n.* **1. INTERNAL RECESS** a recess in the wall of a room **2. EXTERNAL RECESS** a recess in an exterior wall, usually with a roof or some covering structure **3. SECLUDED PLACE** a shady or secluded place in a garden [Late 16thC. Via French *alcôve* and Spanish *alcoba* from Arabic *al-kubba* "the vault, the arch."]

Ald. *abbr.* alderman

Al·deb·a·ran /al débbərən/ *n.* the brightest star in the constellation Taurus and one of the brightest stars in the sky

al·de·hyde /áldə hìd/ *n.* a highly reactive organic compound produced by the oxidation of an alcohol and having a CHO group, especially acetaldehyde [Mid-19thC. Contraction of modern Latin *alcohol dehydrogenatum* "dehydrogenated alcohol."] —**al·de·hy·dic** /àldə híddik/ *adj.*

al den·te /àl dén tay, àl déntee/ *adj.* cooked just long enough to be firm rather than soft [From Italian, literally "to the tooth"]

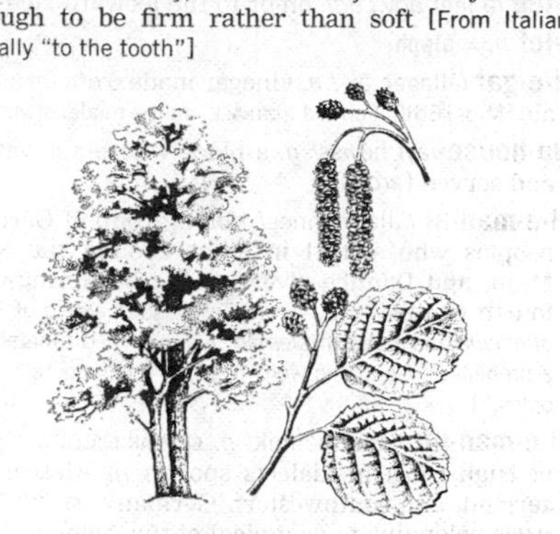

Alder

al·der /áwldər/ *n.* **1. DECIDUOUS TREE** a deciduous tree or shrub with male catkins and cone-shaped fruits, common in wet places in northern temperate areas. Genus: *Alnus.* **2. WOOD OF THE ALDER** the wood of the alder tree, valuable for use in underwater structures as it resists rot when wet . It is also used for carving and furniture making. [Old English *alor.* Ultimately from an Indo-European base meaning "reddish-brown," which is also the ancestor of English *elm* and *elk.*]

al·der·man /áwldərmən/ (*plural* **-men** /-mən/) *n.* **1. MEMBER OF TOWN LEGISLATING BODY** a member of the legislating body of a town or city in the United States or Canada **2. ENGLISH SENIOR COUNCIL MEMBER** a senior member of an English or Welsh local council before the local government reorganization of 1974 **3.** = **ealdorman** [Old English *ealdorman,* from *ealdor* "an elder" + MAN] —**al·der·man·ic** /àwldər mánnik/ *adj.* —**al·der·man·cy** *n.*

Al·der·ney /áwldərnee/ *n.* a cow belonging to a breed of small dairy cattle originally from the Channel Islands

Al·dis lamp /áwldiss-/ *n.* a signaling device in the form of a portable lamp used to flash messages in Morse code [Early 20thC. Named for the British inventor A. C. W. *Aldis,* who designed it.]

Aldm. *abbr.* alderman

al·do·hex·ose /àldō hék sōss/ *n.* a six-carbon sugar, e.g., glucose or mannose, that contains a CHO group [Early 20thC. Contraction of ALDEHYDE + HEXOSE.]

al·dol /ál dàwl/ *n.* **1. LIQUID USED IN SOLVENTS AND PERFUMES** a colorless or pale yellow oily liquid used chiefly in making chemicals to accelerate the vulcanization of rubber, as a solvent, and in making perfumes. Formula: $C_4H_8O_2$. **2. ORGANIC COMPOUND** a colorless liquid formed by the condensation of acetaldehyde and used in organic synthesis and in denaturing alcohol

al·dol·ase /áldə làyss/ *n.* an enzyme that aids the breakdown of fructose [Mid-20thC. From German, coined from *Aldol* "aldol" + *-ase* "-ase."]

al·dose /ál dōss/ *n.* a sugar (**monosaccharide**) that contains a CHO group

al·dos·ter·one /al dóstə rōn/ *n.* a steroid hormone, secreted by the adrenal cortex, that controls the balance of salt and water in the body

al·dos·ter·on·ism /al dóstərə nìzzəm/ *n.* a condition caused by abnormally high secretion of aldosterone by the adrenal cortex, characterized by weakness, high blood pressure, and excessive fluid intake and urinary output

Al·drin /áwldrin/, **Buzz** (*b.* 1930) U.S. astronaut. He was the second man to walk on the Moon (1969). Full name **Edwin Eugene Aldrin, Jr.**

ale /ayl/ *n.* an alcoholic drink made from rapidly fermented malt to which hops have been added [Old English *ealu.* From a prehistoric Germanic word possibly meaning "intoxicating drink."]

a·le·a·to·ry /áylee ə tàwree/ *adj.* **1. DEPENDING ON CHANCE** depending on chance or contingency **2. a·le·a·to·ry, a·le·a·to·ric HAVING RANDOM NOTES** having the sequence of given notes or passages in a piece of music chosen at random by the performer or left to chance [Late 17thC. Via Latin *aleatorius* from, ultimately, *alea* "dice," of unknown origin.]

A·lec·to /ə léktō/ *n.* in Greek mythology, one of the three Furies. The others were Megaera and Tisiphone.

a·lee /ə lée/ *adv., adj.* on or to the leeward side

a·lef *n.* = **aleph**

al·e·gar /álləgər, áy-/ *n.* vinegar made from fermented ale [Mid-16thC. Formed from ALE, on the model of VINEGAR.]

ale·house /áyl hòwss/ *n.* a place where ale was sold and served (*archaic*)

Al·e·man·ni /àllə mánnee/ *npl.* a group of Germanic peoples who settled in areas around the Rhine, Main, and Danube rivers at the beginning of the fourth century A.D. [From Latin (source also of French *allemand* and Spanish *alemán* "German"). Ultimately from a prehistoric Germanic word possibly meaning "all the peoples."]

Al·e·man·nic /àllə mánnik/ *n.* **GERMAN DIALECTS** a group of High German dialects spoken in Alsace, Switzerland, and southwestern Germany ■ *adj.* **OF ALEMANNI** belonging to or typical of the Alemanni

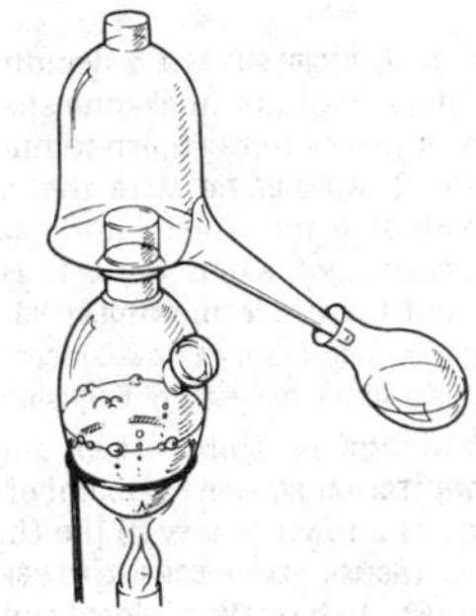

Alembic

a·lem·bic /ə lémbik/ *n.* an apparatus formerly used in distillation [14thC. Via Old French and medieval Latin *alembicus* from Arabic *al-'anbīḳ* "the still," from Greek *ambix* "cup."]

a·leph /áa lèf, áaləf/, **a·lef** *n.* the first letter of the Hebrew alphabet, written as an apostrophe and pronounced as a glottal stop. See table at **alphabet** [14thC. Via Hebrew *'ālep* from, ultimately, Canaanite *'alp* "ox," which started with this sound.]

A·lep·po /ə léppō/ city in northwestern Syria, northeast of Homs, an important center on an ancient trade route to the East. Population: 1,542,000 (1994). Formerly **Beroea**

a·lert /ə lúrt/ *adj.* **1. WATCHFUL** watchful and ready to deal with whatever happens **2. MENTALLY LIVELY** clear-headed and responsive ■ *n.* **1. WARNING OF DANGER** an alarm or warning of danger **2. TIME OF DANGER** a period of time during which an alert remains in force ■ *v.* (**a·lert·ed, a·lert·ing, a·lerts**) **WARN** to make somebody aware of possible dangers or difficulties ○ *Police have alerted the public to the danger.* [Late 16thC. Via French *alerte* from Italian *all'erta,* literally "on the lookout."] —**a·lert·ly** *adv.* —**a·lert·ness** *n.* ◇ **on red alert** prepared for any trouble or danger that may occur ◇ **on the alert** watchful and ready to deal with whatever happens

Al·es·san·dri Pal·ma /allə sàndri pálmə, -saàndri paálmə/, **Arturo** (1868–1950) Chilean statesman who served as the president of Chile three times, in 1920–24, 1925, and 1932–38.

a·leth·ic /ə léthik, -léeth-/ *adj.* relating to the philosophical concepts of truth and possibility and especially to the branch of logic that formalizes them [Late 20thC. Formed from Greek *alētheia* "truth," from *alēthēs* "true," literally "not hidden."]

al·eu·rone /állyə rōn/, **al·eu·ron** *n.* a protein occurring as granules in various plants, especially in seeds [Mid-19thC. Alteration of Greek *aleuron* "wheat flour."] —**al·eu·ron·ic** /àllyə rónnik/ *adj.*

A·leut /ə lóot, àllee óot/ (*plural* **A·leut** *or* **A·leuts**) *n.* **1. PEOPLES MEMBER OF AN ALASKAN PEOPLE** a member of a Native American people who live in the Aleutian Islands and southwestern coastal Alaska **2. LANG ESKIMO-ALEUT LANGUAGE** a Native American language spoken in the Aleutian Islands and coastal parts of Alaska, belonging to the Eskimo-Aleut group. Only a few hundred people now speak Aleut. [Late 18thC. From Russian.] —**A·leut** *adj.*

A·leu·tian /ə lóosh'n/ *adj.* relating to or typical of the Aleutian Islands, or their people or culture

A·leu·tian Is·lands chain of islands stretching westward for about 1,100 mi./1,800 km from the tip of the Alaska Peninsula and separating the Pacific Ocean from the Bering Sea to the north

A·leu·tian Range mountain range on the east coast of the Alaska Peninsula that includes the Katmai National Park and Preserve

A·leu·tian Trench ocean trench at the western end of the Aleutian Islands. Depth: 26,574 ft./8,100 m.

A lev·el *n.* **1. SCHOOL EXAMINATION** the advanced level of any subject studied to gain a General Certificate of Education qualification in England, Wales, and Northern Ireland **2. EXAMINATION PASSING GRADE** a passing grade in an examination in a subject studied at A level [Shortening of *Advanced level*]

a·lev·in /állәvin/ *n.* a young salmon or trout with the yolk sac still attached [Mid-19thC. Via French, from assumed Vulgar Latin *allevamen,* literally "something that is raised," from Latin *levare* (see LEVER).]

ale·wife /áyl wīf/ (*plural* **-wives** /-wīvz/) *n.* **1. MIGRATING HERRING** a herring that migrates up rivers to spawn. It appears off the Atlantic coast of North America in early summer and can be eaten as food. Latin name: *Alosa pseudoharengus.* **2. WOMAN ALE-SELLER** a woman who sold ale, especially one who kept an alehouse (*archaic*) [14thC. From ALE + WIFE "woman." The application to the fish is perhaps an illusion to its large belly.]

a·lex·an·der /àllig zándər/ *n.* a cocktail made from crème de cacao, sweet cream, and gin or brandy [Early 20thC. From the name *Alexander.*]

A·lex·an·der II /àllig zándər/, **Tsar of Russia** (1818–81). He enacted many reforms and sold the Russian lands in North America (now Alaska) to the United States in 1867.

A·lex·an·der III, Pope (1105?–81). He was pope from 1159 to 1181, during which time he imposed penance on Henry II of England for the murder of St. Thomas à Becket. Born **Rolando Bandinelli**

A·lex·an·der (the Great), King of Macedonia (356–323 B.C.). He conquered most of the ancient world from Asia Minor to Egypt and India.

A·lex·an·der, Grover Cleveland (1887–1950) U.S. baseball player who pitched for various teams (1911–29) and was voted into the Baseball Hall of Fame in 1938.

A·lex·an·der tech·nique *n.* a method of improving the posture that involves developing awareness of it [Mid-20thC. Named for the Australian physiotherapist Frederick *Alexander* (1869–1955), who developed the technique.]

A·lex·an·dra /àllig zándrə/, **Empress of Russia** (1872–1918). The wife of Tsar Nicholas II, she was executed by the Bolsheviks at Ekaterinberg.

A·lex·an·dria /àllig zándriə/ **1.** city in eastern Virginia on the Potomac River, south of Washington, D.C. Population: 117,586 (1996). **2.** city and Mediterranean seaport in northern Egypt, on the delta of the Nile River. Founded by Alexander the Great in 332 B.C., it was a major cultural center of the ancient world, renowned for its library. Population: 3,380,000 (1992).

Al·ex·an·dri·an /àllig zándriən/ *adj.* **1. OF ALEXANDER THE GREAT** of or relating to Alexander the Great **2. RELATING TO IDEAS IN EARLY ALEXANDRIA** relating to the literary, philosophical, and scientific theories and ideas in Alexandria during the 3rd century B.C. and later, when Alexandria was home to a famous library **3. SCHOLARLY BUT UNORIGINAL** scholarly and pedantic rather than creative or imaginative and original

al·ex·an·drine /àllig zándrin, -zán drèen/ *n.* **1. ENGLISH VERSE FORM** in English poetry, a line of verse that has six iambic feet and usually a caesura after the third foot **2. FRENCH VERSE FORM** in French poetry, a line of verse that has twelve syllables and usually a caesura after the sixth syllable ■ *adj.* **LIKE OR IN ALEXANDRINES** typical of or written in alexandrines [Late 16thC. From French, named for the romance *Alexandre* about Alexander the Great, which was written in this meter.]

al·ex·an·drite /àllig zán drīt/ *n.* a green chrysoberyl used as a gemstone [Mid-19thC. From German *Alexandrit,* named for *Alexander* II (1818–81), Tsar of Russia, because it was discovered on the day of his majority.]

a·lex·i·a /ə léksee ə/ *n.* a loss of the ability to read, caused by a disorder of the central nervous system [Late 19thC. Coined from A- + Greek *lexis* "speech" + -IA, under the influence of Latin *legere* "to read."]

a·lex·in /ə léksin/ *n.* in biochemistry, a complement (*dated*) [Late 19thC. Via German, from Greek *alexein* "to ward off."]

Al·fa *n., adj.* = **Alpha** [Variant of ALPHA]

al·fal·fa /al fálfə/ *n.* a European and Asian plant in the pea family, widely grown as a hay and forage crop. Latin name: *Medicago sativa.* [Mid-19thC. Via Spanish, from Arabic *al-faṣfaṣa,* literally "the best kind of fodder."]

Al Fa·tah /àl fáttə/ *n.* = **Fatah** [Late 20thC. From Arabic *al* "the" + an acronym formed from *Ḥ(arakat) T(aḥrīr) F(ilastīn)* "Movement for the Liberation of Palestine" (resembling *fataḥ* "conquer").]

al·fil·a·ri·a /al fillə rée ə/, **al·fil·e·ri·a** *n.* a European plant of the geranium family that has pink or purple flowers. It is regarded as a weed in Europe but is grown for forage in the western United States. Latin name: *Erodium cicutarium.* [Mid-19thC. Alteration of American Spanish *alfilerillo,* literally "little pin," from Spanish *alfiler* "pin," from Arabic *al-ḵilāl* "thorn."]

al-Fit·r /al fíttər/ *n.* = **Eid-ul-Fitr**

al·for·ja /al fáwr haà/ *n.* *Southwest U.S.* a saddlebag [Early 17thC. Via Spanish from Arabic *al-ḵurj* "saddlebag."]

Al·fred (the Great) /álfrəd/, **King of Wessex** (849–901). He reigned from 871, reconquering Danish territories in England. He also translated several Latin works into English.

al·fre·do /al fréddō/ *adj.* served with a rich sauce made from cream, butter, and Parmesan cheese [Late 20thC. Origin unknown.]

al·fres·co /al fréskō/ *adv.* **OUTDOORS** outdoors or in the open air ■ *adj.* **LOCATED OUTDOORS** taking place or located outdoors [Mid-18thC. From Italian, literally "in the fresh (air)."]

alg. *abbr.* algebra

Alg. *abbr.* Algeria ■ *abbr.* Algerian

al·ga /álgə/ (*plural* **-gae** /-jèe/ *or* **-gas**) *n.* a mainly aquatic photosynthetic organism that differs from plants in not having true leaves, roots, or stems and includes the seaweeds. Algae were once considered to be plants but are no longer classified as such. [Mid-16thC. From Latin, "seaweed," of uncertain origin.] —**al·gal** /álgəl/ *adj.*

al·gal bloom *n.* an excessive growth of algae on or near the surface of water, occurring naturally or as a result of an oversupply of nutrients from organic pollution

al·gar·ro·ba /àlgə rṓbə/, **al·ga·ro·ba** *n.* **1.** = **carob 2.** = **honey mesquite 3. FRUIT** the edible fruit of the carob or the mesquite [Late 16thC. Via Spanish from Arabic *al-ḵarrūba* "the carob."]

al·ge·bra /áljəbrə/ *n.* **1. MATHEMATICS USING LETTERS AS SYMBOLS** a branch of mathematics in which symbols, usually letters of the alphabet, are used to represent unknown numbers and in doing so generalize arithmetic **2. STUDY OF MATHEMATICAL STRUCTURES** the study of structures in mathematics such as groups, rings, fields, and categories [Mid-16thC. Via Italian and medieval Latin from Arabic *al-jabr,* literally "the reuniting," in the title of the treatise "The science of reunion and equation," by the mathematician al-Khwarizmi.] —**al·ge·bra·ist** /àlji bráy ist/ *n.*

al·ge·bra·ic /àljə bráyik/ *adj.* **1. RELATING TO ALGEBRA** involving or relating to algebra **2. USING ONLY FINITE NUMBERS OR OPERATIONS** relating to or using only finite numbers, expressions, and operations —**al·ge·bra·i·cal·ly** *adv.*

Al·ger /áljər/, **Horatio** (1832–99) U.S. writer and clergyman. He was author of many novels, including *Ragged Dick* (1867) and *Tattered Tom* (1871).

Al·ge·ri·a /al jéeriə/ country in northwestern Africa. It became independent from France in 1962. Language: Arabic. Currency: Algerian dinar. Capital: Algiers. Population: 29,830,371 (1997). Area: 919,595 sq. mi./2,381,741 sq. km. —**Al·ge·ri·an** *adj., n.*

-algia *suffix.* pain ○ *neuralgia* [Formed from Greek *algos* "pain," of uncertain origin]

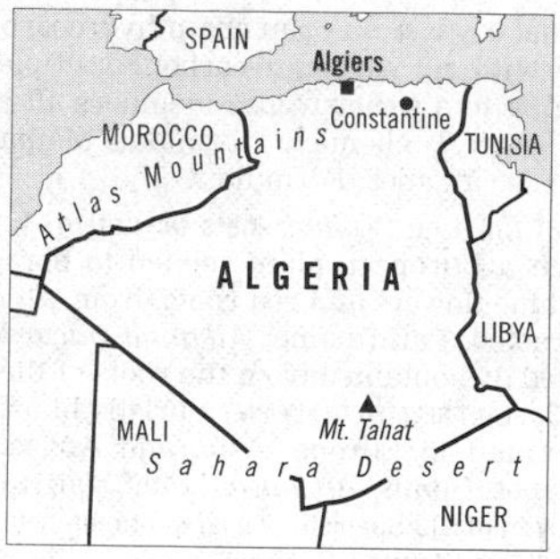

Algeria

al·gi·cide /álji sīd/ *n.* a substance that kills algae or prevents them from growing —**al·gi·ci·dal** /álji sīd'l/ *adj.*

al·gid /áljid/ *adj.* used to describe an episode during a severe fever when the patient's body temperature suddenly drops to an abnormally low level [Early 17thC. From Latin *algidus*, from *algere* "to be cold."] —**al·gid·i·ty** /al jíddətee/ *n.*

Al·giers /al jeérz/ capital, chief port, and largest city of Algeria. Population: 2,168,000 (1995).

al·gin /áljin/ *n.* a viscous liquid, especially alginic acid or an alginate, obtained from seaweed and used as a thickener or emulsifier in the manufacture of plastics or in food [Late 19thC. Formed from ALGA + -IN, suffix denoting organic compounds (compare INSULIN).]

al·gi·nate /áljə nàyt, áljənət/ *n.* a salt or ester of alginic acid. Alginates are often used as thickeners or emulsifiers in plastics or food.

al·gin·ic ac·id /al jìnnik-/ *n.* an insoluble powdery acid obtained from brown seaweed and used in making food, pharmaceuticals, cosmetics, and textiles. Formula: $(C_6H_8O_6)_n$.

algo- *prefix.* pain ○ *algophobia* [From Greek *algos* "pain," of uncertain origin]

al·goid /ál gòyd/ *adj.* resembling or relating to algae

AL·GOL /ál gòl/, **Al·gol** *n.* a high-level computer programming language that employs algebraic symbols and is designed for use in solving mathematical and scientific problems [Mid-20thC. Contraction of algorithm-oriented language.]

al·go·lag·ni·a /àlgō lágnee ə/ *n.* the attainment of sexual pleasure through inflicting or experiencing pain (*technical*) [Early 20thC. Formed from Greek *algos* "pain" and *lagneia* "lust."] —**al·go·lag·nic** /-lág nik/ *adj.* —**al·go·lag·nist** *n.*

al·gol·o·gy /al góllәjee/ *n.* the branch of botany concerned with the scientific study of algae —**al·go·log·i·cal** /àlgə lójjik'l/ *adj.* —**al·gol·o·gist** /-gólləjist/ *n.*

Al·gon·ki·an *n.* = **Algonquian**

Al·gon·kin *n.* = **Algonquin**

Al·gon·qui·an /al góngkee ən, -kwee-/ (*plural* **-an** *or* **-ans**), **Al·gon·ki·an** /-kee-/ (*plural* **-an** *or* **-ans**) *n.* **1.** LANG **GROUP OF N AMERICAN LANGUAGES** a group of over thirty related North American languages that are, or used to be, spoken in central and eastern Canada, and parts of the central and eastern United States. Algonquian includes the languages of the Arapaho, Blackfoot, Cheyenne, Delaware, Fox, Ojibwa, Sauk, and Shawnee peoples. **2.** PEOPLES **MEMBER OF ALGONQUIAN-SPEAKING PEOPLE** a member of an Algonquian-speaking Native American people [Late 19thC. Formed from ALGONQUIN.] —**Al·gon·qui·an** *adj.*

Al·gon·quin[1] /al góngkin, -kwin/ (*plural* **-quin** *or* **-quins**), **Al·gon·kin** /-kin/ (*plural* **-kin** *or* **-kins**) *n.* **1.** PEOPLES **MEMBER OF ABORIGINAL PEOPLE OF E CANADA** a member of a group of Aboriginal peoples living along the Ottawa and St. Lawrence rivers in eastern Canada. Historically, the Algonquin were allies of the French against the Iroquois. **2.** LANG **ALGONQUIAN LANGUAGE** a North American language spoken in Quebec and Ontario. About 3,000 people speak Algonquian dialects, which are closely related to Ojibwa. [Early 17thC. From Canadian French, of Algonquian origin.] —**Al·gon·quin** *adj.*

Al·gon·quin[2] /al góngkin, -kwin/ village in northeastern Illinois. Population: 18,019 (1996).

al·go·pho·bi·a /àlgə fóbee ə/ *n.* an abnormally intense fear of pain

al·go·rism /álgə rìzzəm/ *n.* an algorithm (*dated*) [13thC. Via Old French, and medieval Latin from Arabic *al-Kwārazmī*, name of the mathematician Abū Ja'far Muhammad ibn Mūsā, (780?–850?), who introduced it to the West.]

al·go·rithm /álgə rìthəm/ *n.* **1. PROBLEM-SOLVING PROCEDURE** a logical step-by-step procedure for solving a mathematical problem in a finite number of steps, often involving repetition of the same basic operation **2. PROBLEM-SOLVING COMPUTER PROGRAM** a logical sequence of steps for solving a problem, often written out as a flow chart, that can be translated into a computer program [Late 17thC. Variant of ALGORISM, under the influence of Greek *arithmos* "number."] —**al·go·rith·mic** /àlgə ríthmik/ *adj.*

Al·ham·bra[1] /al hámbrə/ citadel and palace in Granada, Spain, built for Moorish kings in the 12th and 13th centuries

Al·ham·bra[2] /al hámbrə/ city in southwestern California, northeast of Los Angeles. Population: 83,644 (1996).

Muhammad Ali

A·li /aa leé/, **Muhammad** (*b.* 1942) U.S. boxer, three times world heavyweight champion (1964–71, 1974–78, 1978–80). Former name **Cassius Clay**

A·li·a /aálee ə/, **Ramiz** (*b.* 1925) Albanian politician who was president of Albania (1985–92).

a·li·as /áylee əss, áyləss/ *adv.* **ALSO KNOWN AS** otherwise or also known as ■ *n.* **1. NAME TAKEN** an assumed name **2.** COMPUT **FILE OR DIRECTORY NAME** a name assigned to file or directory, e.g., to make it more convenient to locate or manipulate [15thC. From Latin, "otherwise."]

al·i·bi /állə bī/ *n.* (*plural* **-bis**) **1. ACCUSED'S CLAIM OF HAVING BEEN ELSEWHERE** a form of defense against an accusation in which the accused person claims to have been somewhere other than at the scene of the crime when the crime was committed **2. SOMEBODY USED TO ESTABLISH ALIBI** somebody or something used to prove that somebody else was elsewhere at the time that a crime was committed **3. EXCUSE** an explanation offered to justify something (*informal*) ■ *vt.* (**-bied, -bi·ing, -bis**) **PROVIDE ALIBI FOR SOMEBODY** to provide an alibi or excuse for somebody [Late 17thC. From Latin, "elsewhere."]

WORD KEY: USAGE

alibi = "excuse" ***Alibi*** should only be used informally in the weakened meaning "excuse or pretext," because it has a precise legal meaning that is in danger of being compromised. In any case it often sounds silly and affected when **excuse** is the more natural word to use: *He used his illness as an excuse (not as an alibi) for leaving work early.*

A·lice /álliss/ city in southeastern Texas, west of Corpus Christi. Population: 20,599 (1996).

Al·ice-in-Won·der·land /állis in wúndərland/ *adj.* absurd, fantastic, or completely at odds with reality [Early 20thC. From the well-known fantasy by Lewis Carroll (1832–98), *Alice's Adventures in Wonderland* (1865).]

al·i·cy·clic /àlli sīklik, -sík-/ *adj.* used to describe organic compounds that have carbon atoms joined in a string (**open chain**) as well as in rings. ◊ **aliphatic** [Late 19thC. Blend of ALIPHATIC and CYCLIC.]

a·li·en /áylyən, -lee ən/ *n.* **1. EXTRATERRESTRIAL BEING** a being from another planet or another part of the universe, especially in works of science fiction **2. FOREIGN RESIDENT OF COUNTRY** somebody who is a citizen of a country other than the one in which he or she lives or happens to be **3. OUTSIDER** somebody who does not belong to, is not accepted in, or does not feel part of a particular group or society ■ *adj.* **1. STRANGE** outside somebody's normal or previous experience and seeming strange and sometimes threatening **2. INCONSISTENT WITH SOMETHING** not in keeping or totally incompatible with the nature of something or somebody ○ *The idea was alien to her nature.* **3.** LAW **FOREIGN** not a citizen of, or not belonging to, the country in question **4. EXTRATERRESTRIAL** from another world or part of the universe, or involving or relating to extraterrestrial beings ■ *vt.* (**-ened, -en·ing, -ens**) LAW = **alienate** *v.* 4 [14thC. Via Old French or directly from Latin *alienus*, from *alius* "other" (see ALIAS).]

al·ien·a·ble /áylyənəb'l, áylee ən-/ *adj.* capable of being transferred by a legal process to another owner —**al·ien·a·bil·i·ty** /àylyənə bíllətee, àylee ənə-/ *n.*

al·ien·ate /áylyə nàyt, áylee ə-/ (**-at·ed, -at·ing, -ates**) *vt.* **1. MAKE SOMEBODY UNFRIENDLY** to cause somebody to change his or her previously friendly or supportive attitude and become unfriendly, unsympathetic, or hostile ○ *His selfishness alienated all of his friends.* **2. MAKE SOMEBODY FEEL DISAFFECTED** to make somebody feel that he or she does not belong to or share in something, or is isolated from it (*often passive*) ○ *People like that often feel alienated from society.* **3. TURN SOMETHING AWAY** to cause something, especially somebody's affections, to be directed at somebody or something else **4.** LAW **TRANSFER OWNERSHIP TO SOMEBODY** to transfer the ownership of a property or right to somebody [15thC. From Latin *alienat-*, the past participle stem of *alienare* "to make somebody else's, alienate" (see ALIEN).] —**al·ien·a·tor** *n.*

al·ien·a·tion /àylyə náysh'n, àylee ə-/ *n.* **1. ESTRANGEMENT** the process of causing somebody to become unfriendly, unsympathetic, or hostile, or somebody's estrangement from or unfriendly attitude toward somebody else **2. WITHDRAWN STATE** a feeling of being isolated or withdrawn, or of not belonging to or sharing in something ○ *prey to feelings of alienation* **3.** PSYCHOL **FEELING OF UNREALITY** a psychological condition in which somebody comes to feel divorced from the objective world or parts of his or her own personality or feel that he or she is unreal **4.** LAW **TRANSFER OF PROPERTY** the transfer of property or a right to somebody

al·ien·ee /àylyə neé, àylee ə-/ *n.* somebody to whom property or a right is transferred by a legal process

al·ien·ist /áylyənist, áylee ə-/ *n.* **1. PSYCHIATRIST IN LEGAL SYSTEM** an expert witness, usually a psychiatrist, who is accepted by a court of law as qualified to assess the psychological state of people appearing in court **2. PSYCHIATRIST** a psychiatrist (*archaic*) [Mid-19thC. Via French, from, ultimately, Latin *alienare* "to estrange, make irrational" (see ALIENATE).]

al·ien·or /áylyə nàwr, -lee ə-/ *n.* somebody who transfers property or a right to somebody else by a legal process

a·li·form /áylə fàwrm, állə-/ *adj.* shaped like a wing (*technical*) [Early 18thC. Coined from Latin *ala* "wing" (see ALA) + -FORM.]

A·li·ghie·ri ♦ **Dante**

a·light[1] /ə līt/ (**a·light·ed** *or* **a·lit** /ə lít/, **a·light·ed** *or* **a·lit, a·light·ing, a·lights**) *vi.* **1. GET OUT OF VEHICLE** to step down from a vehicle onto the ground or a platform, or dismount from a horse or bicycle ○ *The VIPs alighted from their train.* **2. LAND** to land or settle after a flight ○ *A crow alighted on a branch.* **3. FIND BY CHANCE** to happen to find, spot, or come to rest on something ○ *to alight on a suitable candidate* [Old English *alīhtan*, from *a-* "away, up, out," and *līhtan* "to make lighter, lighten" (see LIGHT[1])]

a·light[2] /ə līt/ *adj.* **1. FULL OF ENERGY** filled with or radiating energy, excitement, interest, or pleasure ○ *His face was alight with joy.* **2. LIT UP** lit up or full of light ○ *The sky was alight with fireworks.* **3. ON FIRE** on fire or burning ○ *Try to keep the fire alight.* [Old English *aliht* "illuminated," past participle of *alihtan*, "to light up" (see LIGHT[1])]

a·lign /ə līn/ (**a·ligned, a·lign·ing, a·ligns**), **a·line** (**a·lined, a·lin·ing, a·lines**) *v.* **1.** *vt.* **BRING SOMETHING INTO LINE** to place something in a line, or in an orderly spatial relationship, e.g., parallel, with something else **2.** *vti.* **BRING INTO CORRECT POSITION** to bring something, e.g., different parts of a machine or structure, into the correct position with respect to each other or something else, or come into this position **3.** *vti.* **DECLARE SUPPORT FOR SOMEBODY OR SOMETHING** to declare your support, or the support of somebody or something you represent, for a particular person, group, argument, or point of view ○ *The country aligned itself with NATO.* **4.** *vi.* FORM LINE to become arranged in a line [15thC. Via Old French *alignier* from, ultimately, Latin *linea* "line."] —**a·lign·er** *n.*

a·lign·ment /ə línmənt/, **a·line·ment** *n.* **1.** LINEAR OR ORDERLY ARRANGEMENT the arrangement of something in a straight line or in an orderly position relative to something else **2.** POSITIONING OF SOMETHING FOR PROPER PERFORMANCE the correct position or positioning of different components relative to one another, so that they perform properly ○ *the wheels are out of alignment* **3.** SUPPORT OR ALLIANCE support for, or a political alliance with, a particular person, group, or point of view ○ *shifting alignments within the legislature* **4.** GROUND PLAN a ground plan, especially one showing the course of a road or railroad track

a·like /ə lík/ *adj.* SIMILAR similar in appearance or character ○ *They're so alike, it's difficult to tell them apart.* ■ *adv.* THE SAME in a similar or the same way ○ *The disaster affects young and old alike.* [Old English *gelíc* "alike, similar." Ultimately from a prehistoric Germanic word meaning "body, form."] —**a·like·ness** *n.*

al·i·ment *n.* /álləmənt/ SOMETHING THAT SUSTAINS something that feeds, sustains, or supports something else (*formal*) ■ *vt.* /állə mént/ (**-ment·ed, -ment·ing, -ments**) SUPPORT to provide sustenance or support to somebody or something (*formal*) [15thC. Via French, from Latin *alimentum*, from *alere* "to nourish."] —**al·i·men·tal** *adj.* —**al·i·men·tal·ly** *adv.*

al·i·men·ta·ry /állə méntəree/ *adj.* (*formal*) **1.** OF FOOD OR NUTRITION relating to food or nutrition **2.** PROVIDING SUSTENANCE OR SUPPORT providing nourishment, sustenance, support, or maintenance

al·i·men·ta·ry ca·nal *n.* the tubular passage between the mouth and the anus, including the organs through which food passes for digestion and elimination as waste

al·i·men·ta·tion /álləmən táysh'n/ *n.* (*formal*) **1.** NOURISHMENT the providing of food or nourishment **2.** SUPPORT the providing of maintenance or support —**al·i·men·ta·tive** /állə méntətiv/ *adj.*

al·i·mo·ny /állə mōnee/ *n.* **1.** FINANCIAL SUPPORT TO EX-SPOUSE money paid regularly by one marriage partner to the other as ordered by a court after a legal separation or divorce, or during proceedings for divorce or separation **2.** MAINTENANCE something that provides somebody with a living [Early 17thC. From Latin *alimonia* "subsistence" (see ALIMENT).]

a·line *vti.* = **align**

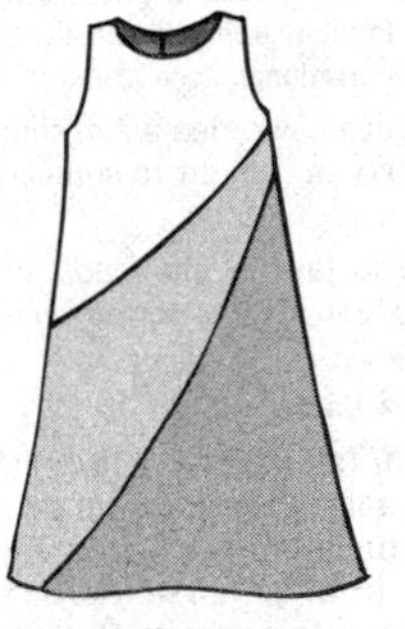

A-line

A-line *adj.* resembling the outline of the letter A, especially in a garment by flaring out from the top to the bottom ○ *an A-line dress*

a·line·ment *n.* = **alignment**

al·i·phat·ic /állə fáttik/ *adj.* used to describe organic compounds that have carbon atoms linked in a string (**open chain**). ◊ **alicyclic** [Late 19thC. Formed from the Greek stem *aleiphat-* "fat," because the term was originally applied to fatty acids (see LIPID).]

al·i·quant /állə kwònt, -kwənt/ *adj.* used to describe a number or quantity that can not divide another number or quantity without leaving a remainder. ◊ **aliquot** [Late 17thC. From Latin *aliquantum* "somewhat."]

al·i·quot /állə kwòt, -kwət/ *adj.* DIVIDING INTO SOMETHING EXACTLY used to describe a number or quantity that will divide another number or quantity without leaving a remainder. ◊ **aliquant** ■ *n.* ALIQUOT PART an aliquot part, including fractional parts, e.g., $\frac{1}{2}$, $\frac{1}{4}$, or $\frac{1}{8}$ [Late 16thC. Via French, from Latin, "a certain number."]

A list *n.* the people most sought after or most in demand for any activity, e.g., as guests at social functions or for recruitment to a team or organization (*hyphenated when used before a noun*)

a·lit past tense and past participle of **alight**

a·lit·er·ate /àylíttərət/ *n.* somebody who, though usually able to read, is completely uninterested in reading and literature —**a·lit·er·acy** /àylíttərəssee/ *n.* —**a·lit·er·ate** /-rət/ *adj.*

a·live /ə lív/ *adj.* **1.** LIVING living, especially still living, and not dead **2.** OF ALL PEOPLE LIVING of all people currently living (*usually used with a superlative*) ○ *the luckiest person alive* **3.** STILL IN EXISTENCE still existing, continuing, or functioning ○ *The movement remained alive by going underground.* **4.** SWARMING WITH SOMETHING full of or swarming with people or animals ○ *The floor of the tent was alive with ants.* **5.** FULL OF LIFE full of energy and vigor, and with a zest for and interest in life **6.** ANIMATED active or animated, especially full of busy activity or a sense of excitement ○ *The place doesn't come alive till after midnight.* **7.** STILL INTERESTING still interesting, relevant, or vividly imaginable for people in the present day **8.** AWARE OF SOMETHING sensitive to or aware of things ○ *alive to the danger involved in the operation* [Old English *on life*, literally "in life" (compare AFIRE)] —**a·live·ness** *n.* ◇ **alive and kicking** still active, healthy, or functioning vigorously

WORD KEY: SYNONYMS

See Synonyms at *living*.

a·li·yah /aa lee yaa, aali yaa/ (*plural* **-yahs** /aali yóss/ *or* **-yot** /aali yót/ *or* **-yoth** /aali yót/) *n.* travel to Israel by a Jew in order to take up residence [Mid-20thC. From Hebrew, literally "ascent."]

a·liz·a·rin /ə lízzərin/ *n.* an orange-red or brownish yellow crystalline compound, now made from coal tar but originally extracted from madder root, used as a dye and in making other dyes. Formula: $C_{14}H_8O_4$. [Mid-19thC. From French *alizarine*, probably ultimately from Arabic *alizari* "madder."]

al-Kadr *n.* = **Lailat-ul-Qadr**

al·ka·les·cent /álkə léss'nt/ *adj.* slightly alkaline or becoming alkaline —**al·ka·les·cence** *n.*

al·ka·li /álkə lī/ (*plural* **-lis** *or* **-li**) *n.* **1.** ACID-NEUTRALIZING CHEMICAL SUBSTANCE a chemical substance that is soluble in water, neutralizes acids, and forms salts with them. An alkali has a pH above 7 and turns red litmus paper blue. **2.** SOLUBLE SALT HARMFUL TO CROPS a soluble mineral salt found in arid soils and some natural waters that is detrimental to agriculture **3.** SODA ASH the soluble part of ashes of marine plants [14thC. Via medieval Latin, from Arabic *al-kalī* "ashes of saltwort," from which it was first obtained.]

al·ka·li met·al *n.* a metallic element belonging to the group comprising lithium, sodium, potassium, rubidium, cesium, and francium. Alkali metals are soft, white, and highly reactive, and their hydroxides are alkalis. Alkali metals also make up group 1 of the periodic table.

al·ka·lim·e·ter /álkə límmətər/ *n.* an instrument used for measuring the concentration of alkalis in a solution —**al·ka·lim·e·try** *n.* —**al·ka·li·met·ric** /álkəli métrik/ *adj.* —**al·ka·li·met·ri·cal·ly** *adv.*

al·ka·line /álkəlin, -līn/ *adj.* having the properties of an alkali, or containing an alkali or alkalis

al·ka·line-earth met·al, **al·ka·line earth** *n.* a metallic element belonging to the group comprising beryllium, magnesium, calcium, strontium, barium, and radium that makes up group 2 of the periodic table

al·ka·lin·i·ty /álkə línnətee/ *n.* the concentration of alkali in a solution, measured in terms of pH

al·ka·lize /álkə līz/ (**-lized, -liz·ing, -liz·es**) *vti.* to make something alkaline, or become alkaline

al·ka·loid /álkə lòyd/ *n.* a nitrogen-containing alkaline compound found in plants and used in medicines, drugs, or as a poison. Strychnine, nicotine, and quinine are alkaloids. [Early 19thC. Formed from ALKALI, because their chemical properties are similar to it.] —**al·ka·loid·al** /álkə lóyd'l/ *adj.*

al·ka·lo·sis /álkə lóssiss/ *n.* an abnormally high level of alkalinity in the blood, other body fluids, or body tissues, causing a high blood pH —**al·ka·lot·ic** /álkə lóttik/ *adj.*

al·kane /ál kàyn/ *n.* an open-chain hydrocarbon compound with no carbon-to-carbon multiple bonds, belonging to a series whose members all have the same general chemical formula. Methane and ethane are alkanes. Formula: C_nH_{2n+2}.

al·ka·net /álkə nèt/ (*plural* **-nets** *or* **-net**) *n.* **1.** EUROPEAN DYE PLANT a European plant related to borage, with small blue flowers and red roots, from which a dye is extracted. Latin name: *Alkanna tinctoria.* **2.** RED DYE a red dye obtained from the roots of the alkanet plant **3.** PLANT RELATED TO ALKANET a bristly blue-flowered plant found in Europe, Asia, and Africa, related to alkanet. Genus: *Anchusa.* [14thC. Origin uncertain: probably from Old Spanish *alcaneta*, ultimately from Arabic *al-ḥinnā'* (see HENNA).]

al·kene /ál keen/ *n.* an open-chain hydrocarbon compound containing one carbon-to-carbon double bond, belonging to a series whose members all have the same general chemical formula. Ethylene is an alkene. Formula: C_nH_{2n}.

al·ky /álkee/ (*plural* **-kies**), **al·kie** *n.* an offensive term for somebody who is an (**alcoholic**) or who drinks to excess (*slang offensive*) [Mid-20thC. Shortening.]

al·kyd /ál kid/, **al·kyd res·in** *n.* a sticky resin that is prepared from phthalic acid and glycerol and becomes liquid or plastic when heated, used in paints and lacquer [Early 20thC. Coined from ALKYL + ACID.]

al·kyl /ál kəl/ *adj.* used to describe a hydrocarbon group derived from an alkane, e.g. the ethyl group [Late 19thC. From German, formed from *Alkohol* "alcohol" + -YL.]

al·kyl·a·tion /álkə láysh'n/ *n.* the addition of one or more alkyl groups to a chemical compound through replacement of a hydrogen atom

al·kyne /ál kīn/ *n.* an open-chain hydrocarbon compound containing one carbon-to-carbon triple bond, belonging to a series whose members all have the same general chemical formula. Formula: C_nH_{2n-2}.

all /awl/ CORE MEANING: a grammatical word used to indicate that the whole of a particular thing, amount, group, or area is involved or affected ○ (adj) *all men and all women* ○ (pron) *All of the computers are down.* ○ (pron) *All that glitters is not gold.*

1. *adj.* THE WHOLE OF used to indicate that the whole of a particular amount, area, quantity, or thing is involved or affected ○ *All Europe was cold this winter.* **2.** *adj.* EVERY every one of ○ *all men over 30* **3.** *adj.* ANY any whatever (*used after a negative word such as "refuse" or "deny"*) ○ *Deny all connection with the plot.* **4.** *adj.* MOST the greatest possible ○ *with all speed* **5.** *adj.* CHARACTERIZED BY dominated in mood or character by something (*informal*) ○ *He was all smiles.* **6.** *adj.* USED UP finished or used up, especially of food or drink (*regional*) **7.** *adv.* VERY very, completely, or totally (*informal*) ○ *I got all confused.* **8.** *pron.* EVERY ONE OR THE WHOLE the whole number or amount (*takes a plural verb*) ○ *All of us are going to the game.* **9.** *pron.* EVERYTHING OR EVERYONE the whole quantity or group ○ *All that glitters is not gold.* **10.** *n.* SOMEBODY'S BEST EFFORT the greatest amount of somebody's ability or effort ○ *He gave his all in the performance.* [Old English *eall*. From a prehistoric Germanic word meaning "all," which is also the ancestor of English *also*.] ◇ **all along** from the beginning, or for the whole time that something else was taking place ◇ **(all) in all** when everything has been taken into account ◇ **all of** only, or no more than (*informal*) ◇ **all square** in a situation where all debts and obligations to each other have been cleared and nobody owes anybody anything ◇ **all that 1.** very, particularly, or to that extent (*informal*) (*usually used in negative statements or questions*) ○ *I'm not all that worried about it.* **2.** extraordinarily good or admirable (*slang*) ○ *She is definitely all that!* ◇ **all the same 1.** nevertheless **2.** used to indicate that it is unimportant to the speaker which of two or more things is done or chosen ◇ **all there** fully alert, aware of what is going on, and able to handle it (*informal*) ◇ **all very well** used to indicate that there is some kind of objection or drawback, despite the fact that somebody else is apparently satisfied with the situation ○ *That's all very well, but it's still my responsibility.* ◇ **be all over somebody** to be extremely or excessively friendly or effusive toward somebody (*informal*) ◇ **be all over something** to have something, especially a project or a problem, completely under control (*informal*)

WORD KEY: USAGE

all or **all of**? There is a choice between ***all*** and ***all of*** when the following noun is qualified by *the, this, that, these, those*, or a possessive adjective such as *my* and *your*: *All my life I've wanted to be a singer. I've been a singer all of my life. All these things worried them. All of these things worried them.* Generally ***all*** is preferred, but the balance and flow of a particular sentence also plays a part.

WORD KEY: REGIONAL NOTE

On its own meaning "all gone, used up," ***all*** is a German loanword that occurs primarily in the territory of the Pennsylvanian Dutch (southeastern Pennsylvania) and neighboring states. It is used especially of quantifiable amounts of food and drink: "the meat is all; potatoes are yet," indicates that the meat is all gone, but the potatoes remain.

al·la breve /àllə brév, ààlə bré vày/ *n.* = **cut time** ■ *adv.* **AT DOUBLE SPEED** at twice the normal speed (*used as a musical direction*) [From Italian, literally "according to the breve"] —**al·la breve** *adj.*

Al·lah /állə, ààlə/ *n.* in Islam, the name of God [Late 16thC. From Arabic *'allāh*.]

al·la·man·da /àllə mándə/ (*plural* **-das** *or* **-da**) *n.* an evergreen shrub of tropical America, cultivated for its attractive trumpet-shaped yellow or purple flowers. Genus: *Allamanda*. [Late 18thC. Named for the Swiss scientist J. N. S. *Allamand*.]

all-A·mer·i·can *adj.* **1. TYPICALLY OF THE UNITED STATES** typical of the United States, its people, or their way of life, or representing them at their best **2. SPORTS BEST IN THE UNITED STATES** selected and honored as the best amateur player or athlete in the United States in a particular position or event ○ *an all-American linebacker* **3. MADE OF U.S. COMPONENTS** made up entirely of people from the United States, or of materials or components from the United States **4. OF ALL THE AMERICAS** including all the countries of North and South America or representatives from them ○ *an all-American agreement* ■ *n.* **1. BEST U.S. ATHLETE** a player or athlete chosen as being the best in a position or event in the United States **2. TEAM OF BEST U.S. PLAYERS** a team made up of U.S. players or athletes selected for their excellence in a particular position or event

Al·lan /állən/, **Sir Hugh** (1810–82) Scottish-born Canadian businessman and shipping mogul. He was head of the company that built Canada's cross-continental railroad.

al·lan·to·is /ə lántō iss/ (*plural* **-i·des** /állən t-y diz/) *n.* a membranous sac that grows from the lower gut in mammal, bird, and reptile embryos. In mammals, it combines with the chorion to form the umbilical cord and placenta. [Mid-17thC. Via modern Latin from, ultimately, Greek *allantoeidēs* "sausage-like," because of its shape.] —**al·lan·to·ic** /àllən tṓ ik/ *adj.*

al·lar·gan·do /àa laar gáan dō/ *adv.* at a gradually slower tempo, with a broadening, stately sound (*used as a musical direction*) [Late 19thC. From Italian, literally "broadening."] —**al·lar·gan·do** *adj.*

all-a·round *adj.* **1. WITH MANY ABILITIES** able to do many things well, or useful in a number of different ways, not specialized ○ *the best all-around player for both offense and defense* **2. ALL-INCLUSIVE** broad or comprehensive in scope ○ *for all-around news coverage* **3. IN ALL DIRECTIONS** in all directions

al·lay /ə láy/ (**-layed, -lay·ing, -lays**) *vt.* **1. CALM AN EMOTION OR WORRY** to calm a strong emotion, e.g., anger, or diminish and set at rest somebody's fears or suspicions **2. RELIEVE PAIN** to relieve or reduce the severity of pain or a painful emotion [Old English *ālecgan* "to lay aside" (see LAY). The meaning was influenced by Old French *aleger* "to lighten" and *aleier* "to moderate."] —**al·lay·er** *n.* —**al·lay·ment** *n.*

all-can·di·dates meet·ing *n. Can* a public meeting during which all candidates for an elected office explain their policies and answer questions from the audience

all-choice *adj.* used to describe a school system that allows people to choose a particular school to attend

all clear *n.* **1. SIGNAL THAT DANGER IS OVER** a signal that a period of danger is over, especially one sounded on a siren after an air raid **2. SIGNAL TO PROCEED** a signal or notification that something may proceed ○ *We've got the all clear to start building.*

al·le·ga·tion /àllə gáysh'n/ *n.* **1. UNPROVED ASSERTION** an assertion, especially relating to wrongdoing or misconduct on somebody's part, that has yet to be proved or supported by evidence **2. ALLEGING** the alleging of something, especially wrongdoing **3. DECLARATION** an assertion made as a plea or excuse

al·lege /ə léj/ (**-leged, -leg·ing, -leg·es**) *v.* **1.** *vti.* **ASSERT WITHOUT PROOF** to state or assert something, especially to accuse somebody of wrongdoing, without offering proof of it or with a view to proving it later ○ *The prosecutor alleged that Simmons knew about the planned robbery.* **2.** *vti.* **AFFIRM** to state something positively ○ *allege that a watch has been stolen* **3.** *vti.* **GIVE SOMETHING AS REASON** to put something forward as a reason or excuse for your actions or conduct (*formal*) ○ *He declined the invitation, alleging a prior appointment.* **4.** *vt.* **REFER TO SOMETHING** to cite or quote something or somebody as an authority (*archaic*) [14thC. Via Anglo-Norman "to declare before a legal tribunal," from, ultimately, assumed Vulgar Latin *exlitigare* "to clear of charges" (see LITIGATE).] —**al·lege·a·ble** *adj.* —**al·leg·er** *n.*

al·leged /ə léjd/ *adj.* claimed but not yet proven to have taken place, have been committed, or be as described —**al·leg·ed·ly** /ə léjjədlee/ *adv.*

WORD KEY: USAGE

alleged and **accused** ***Alleged*** is often used to describe a crime or wrongdoing and denotes uncertainty about whether it happened at all or whether a particular person is responsible for it: *The alleged fraud took place over a number of months.* It is also used to describe somebody who is associated with a crime, not necessarily as the culprit: *The claims of the alleged victims were vigorously denied in court by the defendant.* In this use ***alleged*** differs from ***accused***, which is normally used with a neutral word: *The accused was taken into custody by the police.*

Al·le·ghe·ny /àllə gáynee/ river in Pennsylvania and New York, flowing north from its headwaters in Pennsylvania into New York before turning south again to join the Monongahela River at Pittsburgh to create the Ohio River. Length: 325 mi./523 km.

Al·le·ghe·ny Moun·tains, **Al·le·ghe·nies** western mountain range of the Appalachian Mountains, in Pennsylvania, Maryland, West Virginia, and Virginia. The range is the divide between those rivers emptying into the Gulf of Mexico and those flowing into the Atlantic Ocean.

Al·le·ghe·ny Pla·teau high plateau region of the eastern United States, stretching from New York's Mohawk Valley southward through Pennsylvania, Maryland, West Virginia, and Virginia to the Cumberland Plateau

Al·le·ghe·ny spurge *n.* a low-growing creeping evergreen plant belonging to the box family and found in the southern United States. It is grown for its mottled foliage or for ground cover. Latin name: *Pachysandra procumbens*.

al·le·giance /ə léejənss/ *n.* **1. LOYALTY TO RULER OR STATE** a subject's or citizen's loyalty to a ruler or state, or the duty of obedience and loyalty owed by a subject or citizen **2. DEVOTED SUPPORT** loyalty to or support for a particular person, cause, or group ○ *The game was a treat for all fans, whatever their allegiance.* **3. FEUDAL OBLIGATION** the feudal obligation of vassals to their liege lord [14thC. Via Anglo-Norman, from Old French *ligeance*, from *lige* "liege" (see LIEGE).] —**al·le·giant** *adj.*

al·le·gor·i·cal /àllə gáwrik'l/, **al·le·gor·ic** *adj.* **1. USING ALLEGORY** expressing something through allegory, or intended to be understood as an allegory **2. TYPICAL OF ALLEGORY** used in or relating to allegory —**al·le·gor·i·cal·ly** *adv.*

al·le·go·rize /àllə gaw rīz, álləgə-/ (**-rized, -riz·ing, -riz·es**) *v.* **1.** *vti.* **EXPRESS SOMETHING AS ALLEGORY** to express something in the form of an allegory **2.** *vt.* **INTERPRET SOMETHING AS ALLEGORY** to interpret or treat something as an allegory —**al·le·go·ri·za·tion** /àllə gáw rə záysh'n, àlləgərə-/ *n.* —**al·le·go·riz·er** /àllə gaw rīzər, állәgə rīzər/ *n.*

al·le·go·ry /állə gàwree/ (*plural* **-ries**) *n.* **1. SYMBOLIC WORK** a work in which the characters and events are to be understood as representing other things and symbolically expressing a deeper, often spiritual, moral, or political meaning **2. SYMBOLIC EXPRESSION OF MEANING IN STORY** the symbolic expression of a deeper meaning through a story or scene acted out by human, animal, or mythical characters ○ *the poet's use of allegory* **3. GENRE** allegories considered as a literary or artistic genre **4. SYMBOLIC REPRESENTATION** a symbolic representation of something [14thC. Via Latin from, ultimately, Greek *allegorein*, literally "to say otherwise," from *allos* "other" and *agoreuein* "to speak in public."] —**al·le·go·rist** *n.*

al·le·gret·to /àllə gréttō/ *adv.* **FAIRLY QUICKLY** at a fairly quick tempo (*used as a musical direction*) ■ *n.* (*plural* **-tos**) **PIECE OF MUSIC PLAYED ALLEGRETTO** a piece of music, or a section of a piece, played allegretto [Mid-18thC. From Italian, literally "less than allegro."] —**al·le·gret·to** *adj.*

al·le·gro /ə léggrō/ *adv.* **QUICKLY** at a quick and lively tempo (*used as a musical direction*) ■ *n.* (*plural* **-gros**) **PIECE OF MUSIC PALYED ALLEGRO** a piece of music, or a section of a piece, played allegro [Late 17thC. From Italian, literally "lively."] —**al·le·gro** *adj.*

al·lele /ə léel/ *n.* one of two or more alternative forms of a gene, occupying the same position (**locus**) on paired chromosomes and controlling the same inherited characteristic [Mid-20thC. From German *Allel*, shortening of *Allelomorph* "allelomorph."] —**al·le·lic** *adj.* —**al·le·lism** *n.*

allelo- *prefix.* one another ○ *allelopathy* [From Greek *allēlon*, which was formed from *allos* "other" (see ALLO-)]

al·le·lo·chem·i·cal /ə léelə kémmik'l/ *n.* a chemical produced by one plant that is toxic to another

al·le·lo·morph /ə léelə màwrf, -léllə-/ *n.* = **allele** [Early 20thC. Coined from the Greek stem *allēl-* "one another" + -O- + -MORPH.] —**al·le·lo·mor·phic** /ə lèelə máwrfik, -lèllə-/ *adj.* —**al·le·lo·mor·phism** /-fizzəm/ *n.*

al·le·lop·a·thy /àllə lóppəthee/ *n.* the release into the environment by one plant of a substance that inhibits the germination or growth of other potential competitor plants of the same or another species [Mid-20thC. Coined from the Greek stem *allēl-* "one another" + -O- + -PATHY.] —**al·lelo·path·ic** /ə lèelə páthik, -lèllə-/ *adj.*

al·le·lo·tox·in /ə lèelə tóksin/ *n.* = **allelochemical** [Late 20thC]

al·le·lu·ia *interj., n.* = **hallelujah**

al·le·mande /állə mànd, -mánd/ *n.* **1. DANCE MOVEMENT** a movement used in country dancing or square dancing that involves partners changing positions, often by interlinking arms **2. MUSICAL MOVEMENT FORMING PART OF SUITE** a stately piece of music in moderate tempo and four-four time, often used as the opening movement of a baroque or classical suite **3. DANCE POPULAR IN 18THC** a stately dance of German origin popular in France in the 18th century [Late 17thC. From French, "German."]

all-em·brac·ing *adj.* including all or everything without discrimination

Al·len /állən/ city in northeastern Texas. It is a suburb of Dallas. Population: 31,177 (1996).

Al·len, Ethan (1738–89) U.S. soldier who led the Green Mountain Boys to victory at Fort Ticonderoga (1775) during the American Revolution.

Al·len, Fred (1894–1956) U.S. comedian and comic writer who was known for his satirical radio show *Allen's Alley* (1932–49). Real name **John Florence Sullivan Allen**

Al·len, Woody (*b.* 1935) U.S. movie director, actor, screenwriter, playwright, and humorous essayist. His movies include the Academy Award-winning *Annie Hall* (1977). Full name **Allen Stewart Konigsberg**

A·llen·de Gos·sens /aa yèn day gáw sens/, **Salvador** (1908–73) Chilean politician. He was a founder of the Chilean socialist party and was president (1970–73).

Al·len key *n. U.K.* = **Allen wrench** [See ALLEN SCREW]

Al·len screw *n.* a screw with a hexagonal recess in its head that allows it to be turned using an Allen wrench [Mid-20thC. Named for the *Allen* Manufacturing Company of Hartford, Connecticut.]

Al·len·town /állən tòwn/ city in eastcentral Pennsylvania. It is home to Muhlenberg College. Population: 102,211 (1996).

Al·len wrench *n.* a tool in the form of an L-shaped rod, hexagonal in cross section, made in different sizes to turn corresponding sizes of Allen screws [See ALLEN SCREW]

al·ler·gen /állərjən/ *n.* any substance that causes an allergic reaction —**al·ler·gen·ic** /àllər jénnik/ *adj.*

al·ler·gic /ə lúrjik/ *adj.* **1.** HAVING ALLERGY having an allergy to a substance ○ *allergic to cat hair* **2.** CAUSED BY ALLERGY typical of or caused by an allergy ○ *an allergic reaction* **3.** HAVING A DISLIKE having a strong dislike for or aversion to something or somebody (*informal*) ○ *allergic to loud music*

al·ler·gist /állərjist/ *n.* a physician who specializes in allergies and their treatment

al·ler·gy /állərjee/ (*plural* **-gies**) *n.* **1.** HYPERSENSITIVITY TO A SUBSTANCE unusual sensitivity to a normally harmless substance that, when breathed in, ingested, or brought into contact with the skin, provokes a strong reaction from the person's body. The body is sensitized by the immune system's response to the first exposure to the substance, and the reaction takes place only upon subsequent exposures. **2.** AVERSION a strong dislike for or aversion to something (*informal*) ○ *an allergy to housework* [Early 20thC. From German *Allergie*, from Greek *allos* "other" (see ALLO-), on the model of *Energie* "energy."]

al·le·thrin /állə thrìn/ *n.* a clear or amber-colored viscous liquid used as an insecticide. Formula: $C_{19}H_{26}O_3$. [Mid-20thC. Blend of ALLYL and PYRETHRIN.]

al·le·vi·ate /ə léevee àyt/ (**-at·ed, -at·ing, -ates**) *vt.* to make something, e.g., pain or hardship, more bearable or less severe [Early 16thC. From late Latin *alleviat-*, the past participle stem of *alleviare*, literally "to lighten," from Latin *levis* "light" (see LEVITY).] —**al·le·vi·a·tion** /ə lèevee áysh'n/ *n.* —**al·le·vi·a·tive** /-àytiv/ *adj.* —**al·le·vi·a·tor** *n.* —**al·le·vi·a·to·ry** /-ə tàwree/ *adj.*

al·ley[1] /állee/ (*plural* **-leys**) *n.* **1.** NARROW PASSAGE a narrow passageway or lane, especially one running between or behind buildings **2.** = **bowling alley 3.** SMALL STREET a short or narrow street, often in a poor neighborhood **4.** BASEBALL OUTFIELD ZONE IN BASEBALL in baseball, the zones between the normal position of the center fielder and those of the right and left fielders **5.** TENNIS PART OF TENNIS COURT either of the two spaces, one on each side of a court, between the singles and doubles sidelines **6.** PATH IN GARDEN OR PARK a path or walk in a garden or park, especially one between trees or shrubs [14thC. From Old French *alee* "a walk," ultimately from Latin *ambulare* (see AMBULATE).] ◇ **up** *or* **down somebody's alley** completely suited to somebody's interest, expertise, or line of work

al·ley[2] /állee/ *n.* a large playing marble [Early 18thC. Variant of *ally*, a shortening of ALABASTER, from which they were originally made.]

al·ley ball *n.* the game of basketball as played informally in urban neighborhoods (*slang*)

al·ley cat *n.* **1.** HOMELESS CAT a homeless or stray cat, usually in poor condition or half wild, that lives on the streets **2.** DISREPUTABLE PERSON somebody thought to resemble an alley cat, especially in having loose morals or being disreputable or fierce-tempered

al·ley-oop /állee óop/ *interj.* ENCOURAGEMENT ON GETTING UP used as a word of encouragement when somebody is leaping, getting up, or being helped up, or something is being lifted (*dated*) ■ *n.* (*plural* **al·ley-oops**) **1.** TYPE OF MOVE IN BASKETBALL a play in basketball in which a player jumps up to receive a pass over the basket and immediately puts the ball into the net from above **2.** TYPE OF PASS IN BASKETBALL a pass in basketball aimed to allow a player to jump up to receive it over the basket [Early 20thC. Coined from French *allez* "come on!" + *houp* "upsadaisy!".]

al·ley·way /álli wày/ *n.* an alley or narrow passageway

all-fired *adv.* in an excessive or inordinate way (*informal*) ○ *Don't act so all-fired high and mighty.* [Early 19thC. Alteration of "hell-fired."]

All Fools' Day *n.* = **April Fools' Day**

all fours *n.* CARDS = **seven-up** ◇ **on all fours** crawling along or crouched down on the hands and knees ◇ **on all fours with** consistent or comparable with something (*informal*)

all get-out ◇ **as** *or* **like all get-out** as much, as fast, or as intensely or violently as is possible (*informal*)

all hail *interj.* a greeting, welcome, or shout of acclamation, usually addressed to a person of high rank or distinction (*archaic*)

All·hal·lows /awl hállōz/ (*plural* **-lows**), **All·hal·low·mas** /-hállōməss/ *n.* All Saints' Day (*archaic*) (*takes a singular verb*) [Old English *ealra hálgena*, literally "of all saints," from *hálga* "saint," from *hálig* "holy" (see HOLY)]

All·hal·lows' Eve *n.* Halloween (*archaic*)

all·heal /áwl heèl/ (*plural* **-heals** *or* **-heal**) *n.* a plant traditionally believed to have healing powers, e.g., valerian or selfheal

al·li·ance /ə lī́ ənss/ *n.* **1.** ASSOCIATION OF GROUPS WITH COMMON AIM an association of two or more groups, individuals, or nations who agree to cooperate with one another to achieve a common goal **2.** FORMING OF ALLIANCE the establishment of or participation in an alliance with somebody **3.** MEMBERS OF ALLIANCE the nations, individuals, or groups that make up an alliance ○ *the enemy alliance* **4.** CLOSE RELATIONSHIP a close relationship, based on the possession of similar aims or characteristics, between two or more people or things, especially a love affair [13thC. From Old French *aliance*, from *alier* "to ally" (see ALLY).]

Al·li·ance /ə lī́ ənss/ city in northeastern Ohio on the Mahoning River, southeast of Cleveland. Population: 22,846 (1996).

al·lied /ə lī́d, állīd/ *adj.* **1.** JOINED WITH OTHERS IN ALLIANCE joined in an alliance with other nations, groups, or individuals by agreement or treaty **2.** ASSOCIATED having a close relationship or connection with each other ○ *allied banks* **3.** OF SIMILAR TYPE of a similar or related type ○ *sociology and allied studies*

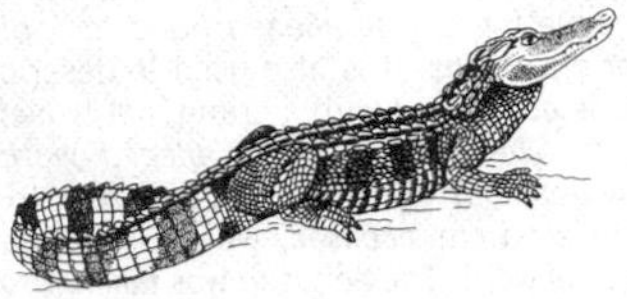

Alligator

al·li·ga·tor /álli gàytər/ *n.* **1.** (*plural* **-tors** *or* **-tor**) ZOOL LARGE REPTILE a large reptile that lives near water, has thick scaly skin, powerful jaws, a long tail, and a shorter and broader snout than a crocodile. There are two species of alligators, one found in the southern United States, the other found in China. Genus: *Alligator*. **2.** INDUST LEATHER FROM ALLIGATOR SKIN leather made from alligator skin **3.** TOOL OR MACHINE WITH MOVABLE JAW a tool or machine with a strong, movable, often toothed jaw for gripping or crushing ■ *vi.* (**-tored, -tor·ing, -tors**) CRACK to develop cracks or blisters ○ *Paint alligators in hot sun.* [Mid-16thC. Alteration of Spanish *el lagarto*, literally "the lizard," from Latin *lacertus* (source of English *lizard*).]

al·li·ga·tor clip *n.* a narrow clasp with a spring and serrated jaws for making temporary electrical connections [From the fact that it resembles an alligator's jaws]

al·li·ga·tor pear *n.* = **avocado** [Mid-18thC. Alteration of American Spanish *aguacate* "avocado," possibly because of the rough dark skin of some varieties.]

al·li·ga·tor snap·ping tur·tle, **al·li·ga·tor snap·per** *n.* a large freshwater snapping turtle of the Gulf States of the United States. It is the largest North American freshwater turtle. Latin name: *Macroclemys temmincki*.

all-im·por·tant *adj.* extremely or vitally important or necessary

all-in·clu·sive *adj.* including or encompassing everything that is expected or appropriate

al·lit·er·ate /ə líttə ràyt/ (**-at·ed, -at·ing, -ates**) *v.* **1.** *vi.* BEGIN WITH SAME SOUND to begin words that are consecutive or close to each other with the same or a similar sound, or to contain alliteration **2.** *vti.* USE ALLITERATION to use alliteration in speaking or writing, or arrange words or construct sentences so as to achieve the effect of alliteration [Late 18thC. Back-formation from ALLITERATION.] —**al·lit·er·a·tive** /ə líttərətiv/ *adj.* —**al·lit·er·a·tive·ly** *adv.*

al·lit·er·a·tion /ə lìttə ráysh'n/ *n.* a poetic or literary effect achieved by using several words that begin with the same or a similar consonants, as in "Whither wilt thou wander, wayfarer?" ◊ **assonance** [Early 17thC. Via medieval Latin from, ultimately, Latin *littera* "letter" (see LETTER).]

all-night *adj.* lasting, open, or available throughout the night, or throughout a particular night ○ *all-night negotiations*

all-night·er *n.* a study or work session, entertainment, or other event that lasts throughout an entire night (*informal*)

allo- *prefix.* other, different, alternate ○ *allosteric* ○ *allophone* [From Greek *allos* "other" (source of English *allegory* and *parallel*). Ultimately from an Indo-European word meaning "other of more than two," which is also the ancestor of *else* and *alias*.]

al·lo·cate /állə kayt/ (**-cat·ed, -cat·ing, -cates**) *vt.* to give something to a particular person, or set something aside for a particular purpose, when dividing something between different people or projects ○ *Each team member has been allocated a specific task.* [Mid-17thC. From medieval Latin *allocat-*, the past participle stem of *allocare*, literally "to put in place" (see LOCUS).] —**al·lo·ca·ble** /álləkəb'l/ *adj.* —**al·lo·cat·a·ble** /állə káytəb'l/ *adj.* —**al·lo·ca·tor** *n.*

al·lo·ca·tion /állə káysh'n/ *n.* **1.** ACT OF ALLOCATING the assignment or earmarking of something ○ *allocation of duties* **2.** SOMETHING ALLOCATED a thing, amount, or share of something allocated to somebody or something ○ *The department has already used its entire allocation.*

al·loch·thon·ous /ə lókthənəss/ *adj.* ◊ **autochthonous 1.** GEOL NOT IN ORIGINAL POSITION used to describe features of the landscape or elements of its geological structure that have been moved to their current position by tectonic forces **2.** BIOL INTRODUCED used to describe flora, fauna, or inhabitants that have moved to the region in which they are found from elsewhere [Early 20thC. Formed from Greek *allochthon*, from ALLO- + *khthōn* "soil" + -OUS.]

al·lo·cu·tion /állə kyóosh'n/ *n.* a formal speech or address, especially one that contains an authoritative statement on a subject or an exhortation to somebody (*formal*) [Early 17thC. From the Latin stem *allocution-*, from *alloqui*, literally "to speak to," from *loqui* "to speak" (see LOQUACIOUS).]

al·log·a·my /ə láwgəmee, a-/ *n.* the process of cross-fertilization in flowering plants —**al·log·a·mous** *adj.*

al·lo·ge·ne·ic /álləjə née ik/, **al·lo·gen·ic** /állə jénnik/ *adj.* used to describe tissues that are genetically different and therefore incompatible when transplanted [Mid-20thC. Coined from ALLO- + Greek *genea* "race" (see GENEALOGY).] —**al·lo·ge·ne·ic·al·ly** *adv.*

al·lo·graft /állə gràft/ *n.* a graft of tissue from one member of a species to a genetically different member of the same species. ◊ **homograft**

al·lo·graph /állə gràf/ *n.* **1.** SOMETHING WRITTEN ON SOMEBODY'S BEHALF something, especially a signature, written by one person on another's behalf **2.** GRAM REPRESENTATION OF PHONEME a letter or combination of letters that is one of a set that can be used to represent the same speech sound (**phoneme**), as, e.g., "s," "ss," and "c" in English

al·lom·er·ism /ə lómmə rìzzəm/ *n.* a similarity in the structure of the crystals of substances that are chemically different —**al·lom·er·ous** *adj.*

al·lom·e·try /ə lómmətree/ *n.* measurement of the rate of growth of a part or parts of an organism relative to the growth of the whole organism. This rate determines the organism's final shape. —**al·lo·met·ric** /állə méttrik/ *adj.*

al·lo·mone /állə mṓn/ *n.* a chemical substance produced by a plant in response to attack by other organisms [Late 20thC. Coined from ALLO- + PLANT HORMONE.]

al·lo·morph /állə màwrf/ *n.* **1.** GRAM REPRESENTATION OF MORPHEME a letter or combination of letters that is part of a set used to represent the same basic grammatical element (**morpheme**) of a language, as, e.g., "-ed" and "-t" both form the English past tense **2.** VARIANT FORM OF CHEMICAL COMPOUND any of the differing crystalline forms of the same chemical compound or element, especially of a mineral [Mid-20thC. Coined from ALLO- + MORPHEME.] —**al·lo·mor·phic** /állə máwrfik/ *adj.* —**al·lo·mor·phism** /-fizzəm/ *n.*

al·lo·nym /állə nìm/ *n.* the name of another person, especially that of a significant historical figure, assumed by somebody, especially a writer (*formal*) [Mid-19thC. From French *allonyme*, from Greek *allos* "other" and *onoma* "name."] —**al·lon·y·mous** /ə lónnəməss/ *adj.* —**al·lon·y·mous·ly** *adv.*

al·lop·a·thy /ə lόwpəthee, a-/ *n.* the treatment of a disease by using remedies whose effects differ from those produced by that disease. This is the principle of mainstream medical practice, as opposed to that of homeopathy. —**al·lo·path** /állәpath/ *n.* —**al·lo·path·ic** /àllə páthik/ *adj.* —**al·lo·path·i·cal·ly** *adv.*

al·lo·pat·ric /àllə páttrik/ *adj.* used to describe species or populations that do not interbreed because they are geographically isolated from one another [Mid-20thC. Coined from ALLO- + Greek *patra* "homeland," from *patēr* "father" (see PATRI-).] —**al·lo·pat·ri·cal·ly** *adv.* —**al·lop·a·try** /ə lóppətree/ *n.*

al·lo·phane /állə fàyn/ *n.* an amorphous mineral, hydrated aluminum silicate, that occurs in a variety of colors [Early 19thC. From Greek *allophanēs*, literally "appearing otherwise" (because it changes color when heated), from *allos* "other" and *phainesthai* "to appear" (see PHENOMENON).]

al·lo·phone /állə fōn/ *n.* **1.** SIMILAR SPEECH SOUND one of the slightly differing forms that the same single speech sound (**phoneme**) can take **2.** QUEBEC IMMIGRANT an immigrant in Quebec who speaks neither English nor French as a first language [Mid-20thC. Coined from ALLO- + PHONEME.] —**al·lo·phon·ic** /àllə fónnik/ *adj.* —**al·lo·phon·i·cal·ly** *adv.*

al·lo·pu·ri·nol /àllō pyóorə nòl/ *n.* a drug that reduces the level of the enzyme that produces uric acid in the blood, used in treating gout [Mid-20thC. Coined from ALLO- + PURINE.]

all-or-none *adj.* functioning or taking effect either completely or not at all

all-or-noth·ing *adj.* **1.** INVOLVING COMPLETE SUCCESS OR FAILURE bound to result either in complete success or total failure, with no possibility of anything in between **2.** UNCOMPROMISING totally and uncompromisingly dedicated to the achievement of something, or unwilling to accept anything less than all ○ *an all-or-nothing approach to negotiating*

al·lo·saur·us /àllə sáwrəss/ *n.* a very large carnivorous theropod dinosaur of the late upper Jurassic period, fossil remains of which have been found in North America. Genus: *Allosaurus.* [Late 19thC. From modern Latin *Allosaurus*, genus name, from Greek *allos* "other"+ *saurus* "lizard."]

al·lo·ster·ic /àllə stérrik/ *adj.* used to describe changes in the activity of proteins, especially enzymes, resulting from their combining with other substances at sites other than those where they are usually biochemically active —**al·lo·ster·i·cal·ly** *adv.* —**al·los·ter·y** /ə lóstəree/ *n.*

al·lot /ə lót/ (**-lot·ted, -lot·ting, -lots**) *vt.* **1.** GIVE AS SHARE to give something to a somebody as his or her share of what is available or what has to be done ○ *I was allotted the task of sweeping up.* **2.** EARMARK to earmark or reserve something for a particular purpose ○ *alloting ten shelves for books* [15thC. From Old French *aloter*, from *lot* "portion," of Germanic origin.] —**al·lot·ter** *n.*

al·lot·ment /ə lótmənt/ *n.* **1.** SOMETHING ALLOTTED a thing, amount, or share allotted to somebody or something **2.** ALLOTTING OF SOMETHING the assignment or earmarking of something ○ *the allotment of shares*

al·lo·trans·plant /àllō tráns plànt/ *vt.* (**-plant·ed, -plant·ing, -plants**) TRANSPLANT BETWEEN GENETICALLY DIFFERENT INDIVIDUALS to transplant an organ or body tissue from one member of a species to a genetically different member of the same species ■ *n.* SOMETHING TRANSPLANTED an organ or piece of body tissue transplanted from one member of a species to a genetically different member of the same species

al·lo·trope /állə trōp/ *n.* one of several different forms in which a chemical element occurs, each of which differs in its physical properties but not in the kind of atoms in its composition. Diamonds and coal are allotropes of carbon. [Late 19thC. Formed from ALLO- + -TROPE.] —**al·lo·trop·ic** /àllə trόpik/ *adj.* —**al·lo·trop·i·cal·ly** *adv.*

al·lot·ro·pism *n.* = **allotropy**

al·lot·ro·pous /ə lóttrəpəss/ *adj.* used to describe flowers in which the nectar is accessible to all species of insect

al·lot·ro·py /ə lóttrəpee/, **al·lot·ro·pism** /ə lóttrə pìzzəm/ *n.* the existence in more than one form (**allotrope**) of the same chemical element, each form differing in physical properties but having the same chemical properties

all'ot·ta·va /àllə taávə/ *adv.* to be played an octave higher or lower than written (*used as a musical direction*) [Early 19thC. From Italian, literally "on the octave."] —**all'ot·ta·va** *adj.*

al·lot·tee /ə lò tée, àllə tée/ *n.* somebody to whom something is allotted

all out *adv.* with maximum effort, at full power, or at top speed

all-out *adj.* involving the maximum possible effort or every available resource ○ *an all-out attempt to break the record*

all o·ver *adv.* (*informal*) **1.** EVERYWHERE everywhere **2.** STRESSING PARTICULAR ACTIONS OF SOMEBODY used to stress that a particular description or action is utterly typical of the person or type of person stated ○ *That's Jackie all over: late again!*

all-o·ver *adj.* covering the whole surface area of something ○ *an all-over tan*

al·low /ə lów/ (**-lowed, -low·ing, -lows**) *v.* **1.** *vt.* LET SOMEBODY DO SOMETHING to give permission for something to happen or somebody to do something, or take no action or make no rule to prevent it ○ *I can't allow you to throw this chance away.* **2.** *vt.* LET SOMEBODY ENTER OR BE PRESENT to let somebody or something enter or be present in a place ○ *Children are not allowed after nine o'clock.* **3.** *vt.* LET SOMEBODY HAVE SOMETHING to let somebody or yourself have something, often a benefit or pleasure of some kind ○ *Allow yourself a few minutes to catch your breath.* **4.** *vt.* CREDIT SOMEBODY MONEY FOR SOMETHING to give or credit somebody with an amount of money as a discount or in exchange for something ○ *How much will you allow on our old machine?* **5.** *vt.* ALLOCATE SOMETHING to set aside or make available something such as a period of time or amount of material for a particular purpose ○ *Allow extra for shrinkage.* **6.** *vi.* MAKE PROVISION FOR SOMETHING to take something into consideration or make provision for it when making a plan or decision ○ *The schedule doesn't allow for any delays.* **7.** *vt.* ADMIT to admit something or accept it to be true or valid (*formal*) ○ *You must allow that it was rather harsh.* **8.** *vi.* PRESENT AS POSSIBLE to present something as possible or reasonable (*formal*) ○ *The events allow of only one interpretation.* **9.** *vi. Southern U.S.* SAY OR THINK to state or suppose ○ *He allowed it was time to go.* [14thC. Via Old French *allouer* from Latin *allaudare* "to praise" and medieval Latin *allocare* "to assign" (see ALLOCATE).] —**al·low·a·ble** *adj.* —**al·low·a·bly** *adv.* —**al·lowed** *adj.*

al·low·ance /ə lówənss/ *n.* **1.** MONEY GIVEN TO CHILDREN a small sum of money paid regularly by parents to a child so that the child can make his or her own purchases **2.** BUDGETED AMOUNT an amount of something, especially money, given out at regular intervals or for a specific purpose ○ *a mileage allowance as well as expenses* **3.** MECH ENG AMOUNT OF VARIATION ALLOWED a small amount of variation permitted in the dimensions of closely fitting machine parts **4.** DISCOUNT money deducted from the selling price of something by the seller as a discount or in exchange for something **5.** SPORTS HANDICAP a handicap or advantage in certain sports, especially horse-racing **6.** TOLERATION the allowing of something to happen, or the toleration of it ■ *vt.* (**-anced, -anc·ing, -anc·es**) **1.** GIVE SOMEBODY ALLOWANCE to restrict somebody to a fixed regular amount of something **2.** HAND SOMETHING OUT to supply something, especially an amount of money, in limited amounts (*archaic*) ◇ **make allowance** *or* **allowances (for somebody** *or* **something) 1.** to take a charitable view of somebody or something and take mitigating circumstances into account **2.** to take something into consideration when making a plan, decision, or judgment

al·low·ed·ly /ə lówədlee/ *adv.* admittedly or by general agreement ○ *Allowedly, the salary is modest.*

al·loy *n.* /á lòy/ **1.** METALL MIXTURE OF METALS a substance that is a mixture of two or more metals, or of a metal with a nonmetallic material **2.** DEBASING ADDITION something that detracts from the value or quality of the thing it is added to or mixed with ○ *The movie is weakened by the alloy of sentimentality.* **3.** BLEND any mixture, amalgam, or compound of different materials ■ *vt.* /ə lóy, á lòy/ (**-loyed, -loy·ing, -loys**) **1.** METALL MIX METALS to mix one metal with another, or mix a metal with a nonmetallic material **2.** DEBASE SOMETHING to detract from the quality, purity, or value of something by being added to it or by adding an inferior material to it ○ *principles alloyed with cynicism* **3.** COMBINE SOMETHING to mix or combine different things [Mid-17thC. Via Old French dialect *allai* (noun) and *allayer* (verb) from, ultimately, Latin *alligare* "to bind to" (see LIGATURE).]

WORD KEY: SYNONYMS

See Synonyms at ***mixture***.

all-points bul·le·tin *n.* a message broadcast to all police in a particular area, usually containing urgent information or a warning

all-pur·pose *adj.* suitable for a wide variety of uses

all right *adj.* **1.** SATISFACTORY generally good, satisfactory, or pleasing (*hyphenated when used before a noun*) ○ *Everything's going to be all right.* **2.** JUST ADEQUATE just about acceptable or adequate, but not very good ○ *The new job's all right, I guess.* **3.** UNINJURED not injured or unwell **4.** IN GOOD CONDITION in good condition or order, and not defective or damaged ■ *interj.* YES used to express agreement or approval ○ *"Will you come along?""All right."* ■ *adv.* **1.** SATISFACTORILY in a generally good, satisfactory, or pleasing way ○ *My old drill still works all right.* **2.** CERTAINLY without any doubt ○ *He's his father's son all right.*

WORD KEY: USAGE

Is it **all right** to use **alright**? It depends on your point of view. Some people think this one-word spelling is justified by the analogy of **already** and **altogether**, and that it is sometimes useful to be able to distinguish between ***all right*** and ***alright*** (just like **altogether** and **all together**): *The answers were alright (= satisfactory). The answers were all right (= all correct).* Though alright is generally considered nonstandard it is often used in informal writing.

all round *adv.* **1.** IN EVERY RESPECT in every respect or taking everything into consideration ○ *I think, all round, it was a pretty successful effort, don't you?* **2.** INVOLVING EVERYONE for, from, or involving everyone

all-round *adj.* U.K. = **all-around**

All Saints' Day, All Saints *n.* November 1, the day in the Christian calendar set aside to celebrate the lives of saints

All Souls' Day, All Souls *n.* November 2, the day in the Roman Catholic Church calendar set aside for prayer for the souls of those who have died and are believed to be in purgatory

Allspice

all·spice /áwl spìss/ *n.* **1.** (*plural* **-spices** *or* **-spice**) TREES TROPICAL TREE WITH AROMATIC BERRIES an evergreen tree from tropical America that is related to myrtle and has clusters of white flowers and aromatic berries. Latin name: *Pimenta dioica.* **2.** COOK SPICE the ground dried berries of the allspice tree, used as a spice [From the fact that it is thought to combine the flavors of cinnamon, cloves, and nutmeg]

all-star *adj.* MADE UP OF STAR PERFORMERS made up mainly or completely of very famous and talented performers or players ■ *n.* MEMBER OF ALL-STAR TEAM a member of an all-star team

All·ston /áwlstən/, **Washington** (1779–1843) U.S. artist and writer, author of the Gothic novel *Monaldi* (1841).

all-suite *adj.* used to describe a hotel room that has a sitting room and kitchenette as well as the standard features of hotel accommodation

all-ter·rain bike *n.* a bicycle or motorcycle designed for use in open country as well as on roads

all-ter·rain ve·hi·cle *n.* a motor vehicle designed for use on rough, sandy, or marshy ground, as well as on roads. It usually has only one seat.

all-time *adj.* having never yet been bettered, or the best, greatest, or most popular ever ○ *an all-time record for this distance*

all told *adv.* when everything or everyone is counted, included, or taken into account ○ *A dozen people made it, all told.* [TOLD in the early sense "counted"]

al·lude /ə lo͞od/ (**-lud·ed, -lud·ing, -ludes**) *vi.* to mention something or somebody, usually briefly, without giving a precise name or explicit identification but usually making clear by other means who or what is being referred to ○ *I presume you are alluding to the alleged financial discrepancy.* [Mid-16thC. From Latin *alludere*, literally "to play to," formed from *ludere* "to play" (see LUDICROUS).]

WORD KEY: USAGE

She alluded to her husband by name. This is a self-contradiction, because ***allude*** means "to refer indirectly." When the reference is direct, the word to use is **refer**. So if she mentioned "the man at home looking after the children," she was ***alluding*** to her husband, whereas if she mentioned "George" or "my husband" directly, she was **referring** to him.

al·lure /ə lo͝or/ *n.* **HIGHLY ATTRACTIVE QUALITY** an attractive or tempting quality possessed by somebody or something, often a glamorous and sometimes rather dangerous one ○ *They couldn't resist the allure of the big city.* ■ *vti.* (**-lured, -lur·ing, -lures**) **ATTRACT POWERFULLY** to exert a very powerful and often dangerous attraction on somebody [15thC. From Anglo-Norman *alurer*, Old French *aloirrier, aleurier*, literally "to bring to the bait," from *leure* "bait" (see LURE). Originally a term of falconry.] —**al·lure·ment** *n.*

al·lur·ing /ə lo͝oring/ *adj.* extremely attractive, tempting, or glamorous, and able to arouse strong desire in people —**al·lur·ing·ly** *adv.*

al·lu·sion /ə lo͞ozh'n/ *n.* **1. INDIRECT REFERENCE** a reference that is made indirectly, subtly suggested, or implied ○ *a poem typical of its period in its use of classical allusions* **2. ACT OF ALLUDING** the act of making an indirect reference to somebody or something [Early 17thC. Directly or via French, from the late Latin stem *allusion-*, from Latin *allus-*, the past participle stem of *alludere* (see ALLUDE).]

WORD KEY: USAGE

allusion, delusion, or **illusion**? ***Allusion*** and ***illusion*** are the closest in sound but the furthest apart in meaning: an ***allusion*** is a process of alluding, that is, an indirect reference to a person, thing, or event (*The story contained an allusion to his childhood in Africa*), whereas an ***illusion*** is a false or misleading impression or perception, either by the senses or by the mind: *The shimmering effect on a hot road is an optical illusion. By shutting himself in his room for hours he kept up an illusion of studying hard.* ***Illusion*** and ***delusion*** are similar in meaning, but ***delusion*** denotes something somebody falsely believes, often harmfully, rather than a wrong impression that somebody receives: *Visitors often suffer under the delusion that the weather is always hot here.*

al·lu·sive /ə lo͞osiv, -ziv/ *adj.* **1. MAKING AN ALLUSION** that makes or contains an indirect reference to something or somebody **2. CHARACTERIZED BY ALLUSIONS** characterized by the use of indirect references or subtle suggestion —**al·lu·sive·ly** *adv.* —**al·lu·sive·ness** *n.*

al·lu·vi·a plural of **alluvium**

al·lu·vi·al /ə lo͞ovee əl/ *adj.* used to describe the environment, action, and sedimentary deposits of rivers or streams

al·lu·vi·on /ə lo͞ovee ən/ *n.* **1. MOVEMENT OF SEA AGAINST SHORE** the flow or wash of the sea or other body of water against a shore **2. FORMATION OF LAND** the expansion of a land area through the buildup of alluvial deposits or the receding of a body of water [Mid-16thC. Via French, from the Latin stem *alluvion-*, from *alluvius* (see ALLUVIUM).]

al·lu·vi·um /ə lo͞ovee əm/ (*plural* **-ums** *or* **-a** /-ə/) *n.* sediment deposited by running water, especially the type of soil formed in river valleys and deltas from material washed down by the river [Mid-17thC. From Latin, a form of *alluvius* "washed against," from, ultimately, *lavere* "to wash" (see LAVATORY).]

all-weath·er *adj.* usable in or able to stand up to all types of weather

al·ly /ə lī́, á lī/ *v.* (**-lied, -ly·ing, -lies**) **1.** *vti.* **JOIN IN MUTUALLY SUPPORTIVE ASSOCIATION** to join, or enlist somebody, in an association with one or more other states, organizations, or individuals for mutual help and support or the achievement of a common purpose **2.** *vt.* **AFFILIATE SOMETHING** to connect something with something else through similarity or common features (*usually passive*) ○ *These plants are allied to lilies.* **3.** *vti.* **CONNECT THROUGH MARRIAGE** to connect individuals or families, or to form a connection with another individual or family, through marriage or a similar tie ■ *n.* (*plural* **-lies**) **1. MEMBER OF ALLIANCE** a person, group, or state that is joined in an association with another or others for mutual help and support or the achievement of a common purpose **2.** BIOL **RELATED ORGANISM** an organism that is closely related to another [14thC. Via Old French *al(e)ier* from Latin *alligare*, literally "to bind to," from *ligare* "to bind" (see LIGATE).]

al·lyl /állәl/ *adj.* used to describe a chemical compound containing a chemical group consisting of three carbon and five hydrogen atoms. Formula: C_3H_5N. [Mid-19thC. Coined from Latin *allium* "garlic" (because it was first obtained from garlic) + -YL.]

al·lyl al·co·hol *n.* a colorless, strong-smelling liquid that is used in the preparation of chemical products such as resins and plasticizers

Al·ma·gest /álmə jest/ *n.* **1. ASTRONOMY TEXT** a text on astronomy written by Ptolemy in the second century A.D. setting out his view of the universe with the Earth at its center surrounded by spheres **2. Al·ma·gest, al·ma·gest MEDIEVAL TREATISE ON ASTRONOMY** an important medieval treatise on a subject, especially on astronomy, astrology, or alchemy [14thC. Via Old French from, ultimately, Arabic *al-mijistī*, literally "the greatest," from Greek *megistē* "greatest," superlative of *megas* "great" (see MEGA-).]

al·ma ma·ter /aálmə maátər, àl-/, **Al·ma Ma·ter** *n.* **1. PLACE WHERE SOMEBODY WAS EDUCATED** the school, college, or university that somebody formerly attended **2. COLLEGE SONG** a song used as the anthem of a school, college, or university [From Latin, literally "bounteous mother," a title given by the Romans to several goddesses associated with abundance]

al·ma·nac /áwlmə nak, álmə-/ *n.* **1. CALENDAR** an annual publication that includes a calendar for the year as well as astronomical information and details of anniversaries and events **2. BOOK OF DATA** an annually published book of information relating to a particular subject or activity ○ *a sports almanac* **3. PRACTICAL GUIDEBOOK** a book, often but not always published annually, containing practical information on a particular subject ○ *a home winemaker's almanac* [14thC. From medieval Latin *almanac(h)*, of uncertain origin: perhaps from assumed Spanish Arabic *al-manākh*, literally "the almanac."]

al·man·dine /álməndeen/, **al·man·dite** /-dīt/ *n.* a deep red garnet consisting of iron aluminum silicate, used as a gemstone. Formula: $Fe_3Al_2Si_3O_{12}$. [15thC. Via French, alteration of *alabandine*, from Latin *alabandina (gemma)* "(gem) of Alabanda," from *Alabanda*, city in Asia Minor where the gem was originally cut and polished.]

Al·ma·ty /al maátee/ city and former capital of Kazakhstan, in the southeastern part of the country, east of Bishkek in Kyrgyzstan. Population: 1,180,000 (1993). Former name **Alma-Ata**

al·might·y /awl mítee/ *adj.* **1. ALL-POWERFUL** having supreme unquestionable power over everything ○ *the almighty dollar* **2. EXTREME** extreme or excessive of its kind (*informal*) ○ *an almighty falling-out* ■ *adv.* **EXTREMELY** to an extreme or excessive degree (*informal*) ○ *almighty rude* [Old English *ælmeahtig*, from *æl* "completely" (see ALL) + *meahtig* "mighty" (see MIGHTY)] —**al·might·i·ness** *n.*

Al·might·y /awl mítee/ *n.* God ○ *pray to the Almighty*

al·mond /aámənd, aál-, ám-, ál-/ *n.* **1. NUT** an edible, oval-shaped, brown-skinned nut that is widely used in cooking, particularly to flavor desserts, cakes, and cookies **2. SMALL TREE PRODUCING ALMONDS** a small tree native to west Asia but widely cultivated, with pink flowers and green fruits containing a hard pit, the kernel of which is edible. Latin name: *Prunus dulcis.* **3. YELLOWISH GRAY** a yellowish gray color, like that of an almond kernel **4. ALMOND-SHAPED OBJECT** something oval and pointed in shape like an almond ■ *adj.* **1. ALMOND-SHAPED** oval and pointed in shape like an almond **2. OF YELLOWISH GRAY** yellowish gray in color, like an almond kernel [14thC. Via Old French *alemande, a(l)mande* from, ultimately, Greek *amugdalē*, of unknown origin.]

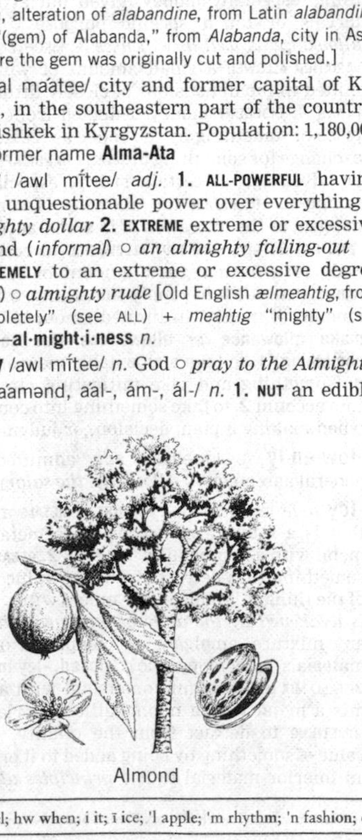

Almond

al·mo·ner /álmənər, aám-/ *n.* **1.** *U.K.* **HOSPITAL SOCIAL WORKER** in the past, somebody affiliated with a hospital as a social worker for its patients **2. GIVER OF MONEY AS CHARITY** in former times, somebody who distributed alms to the needy, especially on behalf of a church, monastery, or wealthy family [15thC. Alteration of obsolete *aumener*, which came via Old French *aumoner* from assumed late Latin *almosinarius*, from ecclesiastical Latin *eleemosynarius* "connected with alms," from *eleemosyna* (see ALMS).]

al·most /áwlmōst, awl mṓst/ *adv.* not exactly, not yet, or not in fact, but very close to being or happening as described ○ *I almost wrecked the car.*

alms /aamz, aálmz/ *npl.* in former times, money or other assistance given to the poor as charity [Pre-12thC. Via assumed Vulgar Latin *alimosina* from ecclesiastical Latin *eleemosyna*, from Greek *eleēmosynē* "compassionateness," from, ultimately, *eleos* "compassion, mercy."]

alms·house /aámz hows, aálmz-/ (*plural* **-hous·es**) *n.* = **poorhouse**

al·ni·co /álni kō/ (*plural* **-coes**) *n.* an alloy of iron, aluminum, and nickel together with one or more of cobalt, copper, and titanium, used for making strong permanent magnets [Mid-20thC. Coined from ALUMINUM + NICKEL + COBALT.]

al·o·ca·sia /àlə káyzhə/ *n.* a plant of the arum family, native to tropical Asia but grown elsewhere as a houseplant for its large heart-shaped or arrow-shaped leaves. Genus: *Alocasia.* [Mid-19thC. Alteration of earlier *colocasia*, a related plant, from, ultimately, Greek *kolokasia* "Egyptian water lily."]

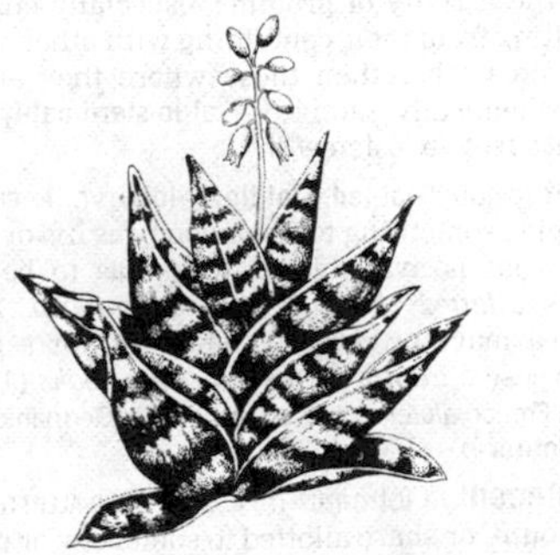

Aloe

al·oe /állō/ *n.* a plant native to southern Africa that has fleshy toothed leaves and red or yellow flowers. Genus: *Aloe.* [14thC. Via Latin, from Greek *aloē*, probably of Asian origin. As ALOES pre-12thC.]

al·oes /állōz/ *n.* (*takes a singular verb*) **1. LAXATIVE MADE FROM ALOE** a bitter-tasting laxative drug made from the leaves of some species of aloe **2. aloes, aloes wood** the fragrant wood of an Asian tree from which a resin is obtained that is used in making perfumes. Latin name: *Aquilaria agallocha.*

al·oe ver·a /-veérə/ *n.* **1. MEDITERRANEAN PLANT** a Mediterranean species of aloe. Latin name: *Aloe barbadensis.* **2. SOOTHING PLANT EXTRACT** an extract from the leaves of the aloe vera plant, used in drugs and cosmetics for its emollient and soothing qualities [From modern Latin, literally "true aloe"]

a·loft /ə lóft/ *adv.* **1. HIGH UP** upward, high up, or in a higher position **2. IN OR INTO SHIP'S RIGGING** in or into the rigging of a sailing ship [13thC. From Old Norse *á lopt(i)*, literally "in the air," from *lopt* "air, sky" (see LOFT).]

a·log·i·cal /ay lójjik'l/ *adj.* that cannot be dealt with by, or has nothing to do with, logic [Late 17thC. Formed from A- "not" + LOGICAL.] —**a·log·i·cal·ly** *adv.* —**a·log·i·cal·ness** *n.*

a·lo·ha /ə lṓ aa, -haa, aa-/ *interj. Hawaii* used as a greeting or farewell [Early 19thC. From Hawaiian, literally "love, affection."]

a·lo·ha shirt *n.* = **Hawaiian shirt**

A·lo·ha State *n.* the state of Hawaii (*informal*)

al·o·in /állō in/ *n.* a bitter-tasting yellow crystalline derivative of aloe used in making laxative drugs [Mid-19thC. Coined from ALOE + -INE.]

a·lone /ə lṓn/ CORE MEANING: a grammatical word meaning without any other person or thing nearby ○ (adj) *I like to be alone sometimes.* ○ (adv) *wandering alone in the wilderness*

1. *adv.* **WITHOUT HELP FROM OTHERS** without help or support from anybody or anything else ○ *I can't do this job alone.* 2. *adj.* **UNIQUE IN SOME RESPECT** used to describe the only one of a group to do, achieve, or think something ○ *Am I alone in thinking this?* 3. *adj.* **DONE WITHOUT OTHERS** carried out by somebody or assigned to somebody without the assistance or company of others 4. *adv., adj.* **WITHOUT COMPANY** without any other person or thing nearby or in attendance, for company, or to give assistance ○ *She left with the others but returned alone.* [13thC. From the phrase *all one* "completely by oneself."] —**a·lone·ness** *n.*

a·long /ə láwng/ CORE MEANING: a preposition indicating that something is situated or moves over all or part of the length of something ○ *came racing along the path*

1. *prep.* **PARALLEL WITH** following a course or line parallel with or beside ○ *freighters sailing along the coastline* 2. *prep.* **SIMILAR TO** in accordance with or similar to ○ *new questions along the same lines* 3. *adv.* **WITH SOMEBODY** with you, with somebody, or with the rest of the group when going somewhere ○ *I asked if I could come along.* ○ *Next time you come, bring your guitar along.* 4. *adv.* **FORWARD** forward, onward, or in a particular direction ○ *Move along there!* 5. *adv.* **AT OR TO A PLACE** arriving at or coming or going to a particular place ○ *There'll be a bus along in a minute.* [14thC. From Old English *andlang*, literally "against the long," from *lang* "long."] ◇ **along with** together with, or as well as

a·long·shore /ə láwng shàwr, -shawr/ *adv.* **BESIDE A SHORE** near to, beside, or along a shore ○ *The water was too shallow to bring the ship alongshore.* ■ *adj.* **BEING NEAR SHORE** located on or near a shore or moving along a shore

a·long·side /ə láwng sīd, ə láwng sī́d/ *prep.* **a·long·side, a·long·side of BY THE SIDE OF** close up against, near, or parallel to the side of ○ *pulled the boat alongside the pier* ■ *adv.* **BY THE SIDE** in or into a position along or by the side of something

A·lon·so /ə láwn zō/, **Alicia** (*b.* 1921) Cuban ballerina and choreographer who was instrumental in establishing the National Ballet of Cuba. She was also a dance teacher.

a·loof /ə lo͞of/ *adj.* 1. **REMOTE IN MANNER** uninvolved or unwilling to become involved with other people or events, often out of a sense of lofty superiority to them 2. **PHYSICALLY REMOTE** physically distant or apart from somebody or something ○ *an aloof pine tree at the summit of the mountain* [Mid-16thC. Origin uncertain: probably from earlier *a luff* "in a windward direction," hence "away from the shore," modeled on Dutch *te loef*, the underlying idea being "steering clear of something."] —**a·loof·ly** *adv.* —**a·loof·ness** *n.*

al·o·pe·cia /àllə pe͞esh ə, -pe͞eshee ə/ *n.* loss or the absence of hair, especially from the human head [14thC. Via Latin, from Greek *alōpekia*, literally "fox mange" (thought by the Greeks to resemble human baldness), from the stem *alōpek-* "fox."] —**al·o·pe·cic** /àllə pe͞eshik/ *adj.*

a·loud /ə lówd/ *adv.* 1. **AUDIBLY** using an audible speaking voice ○ *reading aloud* 2. **LOUDLY** in a loud voice ○ *cried aloud for mercy*

alp /álp/ *n.* a high mountain. ◊ **Alps** [15thC. Via French *Alpes* "Alps" from Latin, from Greek *Alpeis*.]

al·pac·a /al pákə/ *n.* 1. (*plural* **-as** *or* **-a**) **S AMERICAN MAMMAL** a domesticated, long-haired South American mammal of the camel family, related to the llama and similar in appearance. Latin name: *Lama pacos.* 2. **WOOL FROM ALPACA** wool or cloth made from the long shaggy hair of the alpaca 3. **GLOSSY CLOTH** a thin glossy fabric made from cotton, wool, or rayon to simulate cloth made from the wool of the alpaca [Late 18thC.

Alpaca

Via Spanish, from Aymara *alpako*, from *pako* "reddish brown," from the color of its hair.]

al·pen·glow /álpən glō/ *n.* a reddish glow on snow-covered mountain peaks at sunset or sunrise, caused by reflected weak sunlight. ◊ **afterglow** [Late 19thC. Partial translation of German *Alpenglühen*, literally "glowing of the Alps."]

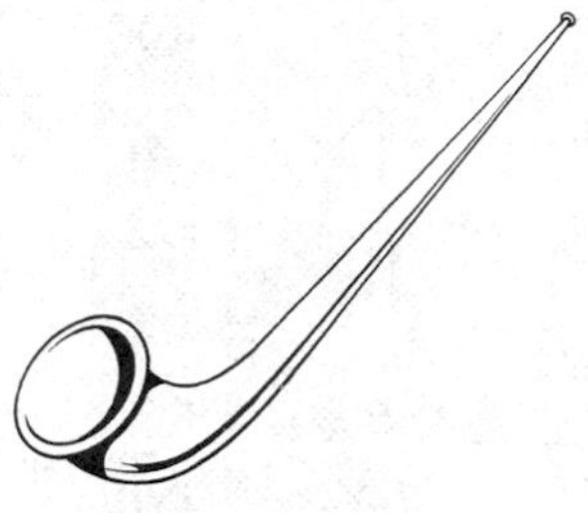

Alpenhorn

al·pen·horn /álpən hàwrn/, **alp·horn** /álp-/ *n.* a traditional wooden wind instrument with a very long tube curving up at the end, originally blown by herders in the Swiss Alps to call cattle [Late 19thC. From German, literally "horn of the Alps."]

al·pen·stock /álpən stòk/ *n.* a long staff with an iron spike at one end, used by mountain climbers until largely superseded by the ice ax [Early 19thC. From German, literally "staff of the Alps."]

al·pes·trine /al péstrin/ *adj.* used to describe a plant that grows at high altitudes [Late 19thC. Formed from Latin *alpestris* "alpine," from *Alpes* (see ALP).]

al·pha /álfə/, **al·fa** *n.* 1. **1ST LETTER OF GREEK ALPHABET** the first letter of the Greek alphabet (Α, α), represented in the English alphabet as "a." See table at **alphabet** 2. RADIO **CODE WORD FOR LETTER "A"** a code word for the letter "A," used in international radio communications 3. **al·pha, Al·pha** ASTRON **BRIGHTEST STAR** the brightest or main star in a constellation (*followed by the Latin genitive*) ○ *Alpha Centauri* ■ *adj.* 1. **MOST IMPORTANT** first or most important ○ *the alpha male in a group of chimpanzees* 2. **ALPHABETICAL** relating to or being in alphabetical order ○ *in alpha order* 3. CHEM **RELATING TO THE NEAREST ATOM** used to describe the atom nearest to a designated atom or group of atoms in an organic molecule 4. CHEM **RELATING TO THE MAJOR FORM OF ELEMENT** used to describe the major form of a chemical element with more than one physical form (**allotrope**) [13thC. Via Latin, from Greek, from Hebrew or Phoenician *āleph* "ox, leader," name of the first letter of the Phoenician and Hebrew alphabets, originally shaped to resemble an ox's head.]

al·pha and o·me·ga *n.* 1. **BEGINNING AND END** the beginning and end of something 2. **MOST IMPORTANT PART** the most important aspect of something [From their being the first and last letters of the Greek alphabet]

al·pha·bet /álfə bet/ *n.* 1. **LETTERS USED TO REPRESENT LANGUAGE** a set of letters, usually listed in a fixed order, used in writing a language and representing its basic speech sounds ○ *the Cyrillic alphabet* 2. **SYMBOLS FOR COMMUNICATING** a set of symbols representng units used in communication, especially speech sounds or words ○ *the alphabet in Braille* 3. **BASIC PRINCIPLES** the basic principles of something (*formal*) 4. *Malaysia, Singapore* **LETTER OF ALPHABET** an individual letter of an alphabet [Early 16thC. Via late Latin *alphabetum* from Greek *alphabētos*, from Greek *alpha* and *bēta*, the first and second letters of the alphabet, taken as a name for the whole alphabet).]

al·pha·bet·i·cal /àlfə béttik'l/, **al·pha·bet·ic** /àlfə béttik/ *adj.* 1. **IN ORDER OF ALPHABET LETTERS** arranged or listed in the customary order of the letters of the alphabet 2. **RELATING TO AN ALPHABET** based on, typical of, or relating to an alphabet —**al·pha·bet·i·cal·ly** *adv.*

al·pha·bet·ize /álfəbət īz/ (**-ized, -iz·ing, -iz·es**) *vt.* 1. **PUT IN ALPHABETICAL ORDER** to arrange words or items in alphabetical order 2. **PROVIDE WITH ALPHABET** to provide a language with, or express something in the form of, an alphabet —**al·pha·bet·i·za·tion** /àlfə bet ə záysh'n/ *n.* —**al·pha·bet·iz·er** /álfəbət-zər/ *n.*

al·pha·bet soup *n.* a confusing mass of letters, especially a list of obscure abbreviations

al·pha-block·er *n.* a drug used to treat high blood pressure and some other conditions, such as an enlarged prostate. The nervous stimulation that constricts blood vessels, and hence increases blood pressure, is blocked by such drugs.

al·pha de·cay *n.* a radioactive decay process in which an alpha particle is emitted from a nucleus

al·pha-fe·to·pro·tein *n.* a protein in the liver of a human fetus, the presence of which in abnormally high or low quantities in the amniotic fluid may indicate spina bifida or Down syndrome

al·pha-hy·drox·y ac·id *n.* an organic acid in which a hydroxyl acid is bonded to a carbon atom. Compounds of this type are frequently used as ingredients in skin care products.

al·pha·nu·mer·ic /àlfənoo mérrik/, **al·pha·nu·mer·i·cal** /àlfənoo mérrik'l/, **al·pha·mer·ic** /-fə mérrik/ *adj.* consisting of both letters and numbers or using both as symbols ○ *an alphanumeric code* [Mid-20thC. Blend of ALPHABET and NUMERIC.] —**al·pha·nu·mer·i·cal·ly** *adv.*

al·pha par·ti·cle *n.* a particle consisting of two neutrons and two protons that is identical to the helium nucleus and is emitted during certain radioactive transformations

al·pha ray *n.* a stream of alpha particles

al·pha-re·cep·tor *n.* a protein molecule in the membrane of a cell that specifically binds epinephrine, norepinephrine, or related substances and triggers a response, e.g., a nerve impulse, in the cell

al·pha rhythm *n.* the pattern of electrical activity in the brain of somebody awake but relaxed or drowsy, registering on an electroencephalograph at a reading between 8 and 13 hertz

al·pha test *n.* a first test on a new or upgraded piece of software or hardware, carried out by the manufacturer under laboratory conditions [From the idea of being "first in a series," hence "preliminary"] —**alpha-test** *vt.*

alp·horn *n.* = **alpenhorn**

al·pine /ál pīn/ *adj.* 1. **TYPICAL OF HIGH MOUNTAINS** relating to, typical of, or found in high mountains ○ *an alpine climate* 2. BOT **SITUATED OR GROWING ABOVE TIMBERLINE** used to describe the zone of vegetation on high mountains between the timberline and snow line and any plant that grows in or originates from that zone 3. **USED IN MOUNTAINEERING** used in or involving mountain climbing ■ *n.* **MOUNTAIN PLANT** a plant that originates from or can grow in the alpine zone on mountains, above the timberline [From Latin *alpinus*, from *Alpes* (see ALP)]

Al·pine *adj.* 1. GEOG **OF THE ALPS** relating to the Alps and those who live in them 2. **Al·pine, al·pine** SKIING **RELATING TO DOWNHILL SKIING** used to describe competitive skiing on steep downhill courses, especially downhill and slalom events

al·pine-style *adj.* used to describe a type of mountaineering in which the climbers carry all the necessary equipment with them on a single ascent to a mountain summit —**al·pine-style** *adv.*

al·pin·ist /álpənist/ *n.* a mountain climber, especially one who climbs in the Alps or mountains of similar height [Late 19thC. From French *alpiniste*, from Latin *alpinus* (see ALPINE).] —**al·pin·ism** *n.*

Alps /álps/ mountain range in southern Europe, extending about 500 mi./800 km from southeastern France to Austria. The highest peak is Mont Blanc. Height: 15,771 ft./4,807 m.

al-Quds /al ko͞odz/ *n.* the Islamic name for Jerusalem, the third most important of the sacred sites of Islam

MAJOR ALPHABETS OF THE WORLD

Phoenician
20 letters, no cases

Letter	Transliteration	Name
𐤀	[']	'aleph
𐤁	[b]	bēth
𐤂	[g]	gaml, gimel
𐤃	[d]	dag, dāleth
𐤄	[ḥ]	hē
𐤅	[w]	wāw
𐤆	[z]	zayin
𐤇	[ḥ]	ḥēth
𐤉	[y]	yōdh
𐤊	[k]	kaph
𐤋	[l]	lāmedh
𐤌	[m]	mēm
𐤍	[n]	nahš, nūn
𐤎	[s]	samekh
𐤏	[']	'ayin
𐤐	[p]	pē
𐤒	[q]	qōph
𐤓	[r]	rōsh, rēsh
𐤔	[th,š]	thann, shin
𐤕	[t]	tāw

Early Greek
21 letters, no cases

Letter	Transliteration	Name
Α	[a]	alpha
Β	[b]	beta
Γ	[g]	gamma
Δ	[d]	delta
Ε	[ĕ]	e (psilon)
Ϝ	[w]	wau, digamma
Ι	[z]	zēta
Η	[h,ē]	ēta
Ϛ	[i,y]	iōta
Κ	[k]	kappa
Λ	[l]	lambda
Μ	[m]	mu
Ν	[n]	nu
Ξ	[ks]	xi
Ο	[ŏ]	o (micron)
Π	[p]	pi
Ϙ	[q]	koppa
Ρ	[r]	rhō
Σ	[s]	sigma
Τ	[t]	tau
Υ	[ū,w]	u (psilon)

Hebrew
23 letters, no cases

Letter	Transliteration	Name
א	[']	'aleph/alef
ב	[b,bh]	bēth
ג	[g,gh]	gimel
ד	[d,dh]	dāleth
ה	[h]	hē
ו	[w]	wāw/vāv
ז	[z]	zayin
ח	[ḥ]	ḥeth
ט	[ṭ]	ṭeth
י	[y]	yod/yodh
כך	[k,kh]	kāph
ל	[l]	lāmedh
מם	[m]	mēm
נן	[n]	nūn
ס	[s]	samekh
ע	[']	'ayin
פף	[p,ph]	pē
צץ	[ṣ]	sadhe/sade
ק	[q]	qōph
ר	[r]	rēsh
שׂ	[ś]	sin
שׁ	[šh]	shin
ת	[t,th]	tāv/tāw

Classical Roman
23 letters, capitals only

A
B
C
D
E
F
G
H
I
K
L
M
N
O
P
Q
R
S
T
V
X
Y
Z

Modern Greek
24 letters[1]

Letter	Transliteration	Name
Αα	[a]	alpha
Ββ	[b]	beta
Γγ	[g,n]	gamma
Δδ	[d]	delta
Εε	[e]	epsilon
Ζζ	[z]	zēta
Ηη	[ē]	ēta
Θθ	[th]	thēta
Ιι	[i]	iota
Κκ	[k]	kappa
Λλ	[l]	lambda
Μμ	[m]	mu
Νν	[n]	nu
Ξξ	[x]	xi
Οο	[o]	omicron
Ππ	[p]	pi
Ρρ	[r,rh]	rhō
Σσς	[s]	sigma[4]
Ττ	[t]	tau
Υυ	[y,u]	upsilon
Φφ	[ph]	phi
Χχ	[kh]	chi/khi
Ψψ	[ps]	psi
Ωω	[ō]	ōmega

Cyrillic
31 letters[2]

Letter	Transliteration
Аа	[a]
Бб	[b]
Вв	[v]
Гг	[g]
Дд	[d]
ЕеЁё	[e,ё][5]
Жж	[zh]
Зз	[z]
ИиЙй	[i][6]
Кк	[k]
Лл	[l]
Мм	[m]
Нн	[n]
Оо	[o]
Пп	[p]
Рр	[r]
Сс	[s]
Тт	[t]
Уу	[u]
Фф	[f]
Хх	[kh]
Цц	[ts]
Чч	[ch]
Шш	[sh]
Щщ	[shch]
Ъъ	["]
Ыы	[y]
Ьь	[']
Ээ	[e]
Юю	[yu]
Яя	[ya]

Modern Arabic
28 letters[3]

Letter	Transliteration	Name
ا ـا	[']	'alif
ب ـب ـبـ بـ	[b]	bā
ت ـت ـتـ تـ	[t]	tā
ث ـث ـثـ ثـ	[th]	thā
ج ـج ـجـ جـ	[j]	jīm
ح ـح ـحـ حـ	[ḥ]	ḥā
خ ـخ ـخـ خـ	[kh]	khā
د ـد	[d]	dāl
ذ ـذ	[dh]	dhāl
ر ـر	[r]	rā
ز ـز	[z]	zāy
س ـس ـسـ سـ	[s]	sīn
ش ـش ـشـ شـ	[sh]	shīn
ص ـص ـصـ صـ	[ṣ]	ṣād
ض ـض ـضـ ضـ	[ḍ]	ḍād
ط ـط ـطـ طـ	[ṭ]	ṭā
ظ ـظ ـظـ ظـ	[ẓ]	ẓā
ع ـع ـعـ عـ	[']	'ayn
غ ـغ ـغـ غـ	[ġ]	ghayn
ف ـف ـفـ فـ	[f]	fā
ق ـق ـقـ قـ	[q]	qāf
ك ـك ـكـ كـ	[k]	kāf
ل ـل ـلـ لـ	[l]	lām
م ـم ـمـ مـ	[m]	mīm
ن ـن ـنـ نـ	[n]	nūn
ه ـه ـهـ هـ	[h]	hā
و ـو	[w]	wāw
ى ـى ـيـ يـ	[y]	yā

Notes

1 In the modern Greek alphabet, each letter has an upper-case and lower-case form.
2 In the Cyrillic alphabet, each letter has an upper-case and lower-case form.
3 In the modern Arabic alphabet, each letter has between two and four forms each.
4 The Classical and modern Greek letter *sigma* has two lower-case forms.
5 The Cyrillic letter *e* has two forms, each with upper case and lower case.
6 The Cyrillic letter *i* has two forms, each with upper case and lower case.

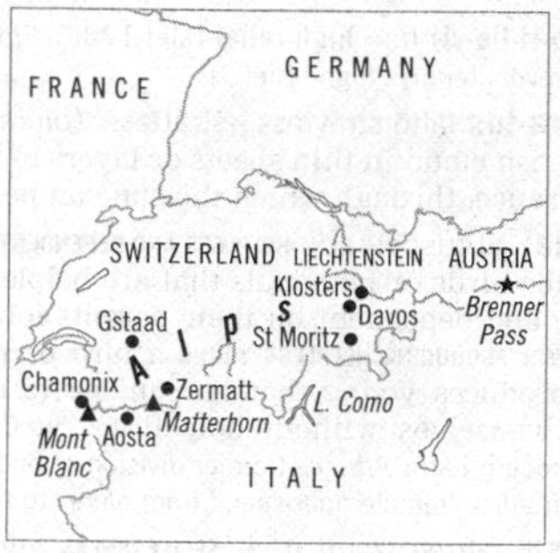

Alps

al·read·y /awl réddee, áwl redee/ CORE MEANING: an adverb indicating that something has happened before now, happened in the past before a particular time, or will have happened by or before a particular time in the future ○ *I already know what you're going to say.* ○ *She had already left when I arrived.*
adv. **1.** UNEXPECTEDLY EARLY by or at an earlier time than expected ○ *Have you finished already?* **2.** USED TO GIVE EMPHASIS used after a command, exclamation, or other statement to give it emphasis or express exasperation (*informal*) ○ *Enough already!* [14thC. From the phrase *all ready* "completely ready"; the meaning evolved via "ready for something" to "beforehand."]

al·right /awl rīt, áwl rīt/ *adv.* SATISFACTORY generally good, satisfactory, or pleasing (*informal*) ■ *adj.* PLEASANT generally good, satisfactory, or pleasant (*informal*)

WORD KEY: USAGE
See Usage note at ***allright.***

ALS *abbr.* amyotrophic lateral sclerosis

A.L.S. *abbr.* autograph letter, signed

Al·sace /al sáss/ region and former province of France, situated west of the River Rhine. Capital: Strasbourg. Population: 1,642,000 (1990). Area: 3,197 sq. mi./8,280 sq. km.

Al·sace-Lor·raine /-lə ráyn/ area of France on the German border, now divided into two administrative regions, Alsace and Lorraine. The area was disputed by France and Germany between 1871 and 1945. Population: 3,930,100 (1990). Area: 12,288 sq. mi./31,827 sq. km.

Al·sa·tian /al sáysh'n/ *n.* **1.** SOMEBODY FROM ALSACE somebody who was born or who lives in Alsace **2.** *U.K.* ZOOL = **German shepherd** ■ *adj.* FROM ALSACE from Alsace, or typical of Alsace or its people [Late 19thC. Formed from medieval Latin *Alsatia* "Alsace."]

al se·gno /aal sáyn yō/ *adv.* MUSIC used in a musical score to indicate that the performer should continue playing from a point marked elsewhere in the score by a sign [Late 18thC. From Italian, literally "to the sign."]

al·sike clo·ver /àl sak-, -sīk-/ *n.* a European perennial clover with white or pink flowers, widely grown for forage. Latin name: *Trifolium hybridum.* [Mid-19thC. Named for *Alsike*, a town near Uppsala in Sweden, where it was first found.]

al·so /áwlsō/ *adv.* **1.** IN ADDITION used to indicate that something is true or is the case in addition ○ *got his picture in the paper and also won a prize.* ◊ **too, as well 2.** LIKEWISE OR SIMILARLY like or in the same way as somebody or something else ○ *Her nephew was also called John.* ○ *When they withdraw their forces, we will also withdraw ours.* **3.** MOREOVER and in addition to that (*used to modify a whole sentence or clause*) ○ *Also, you must complete the task in one hour.* [Old English *ealswā, allswā.* The main modern sense, "in addition," evolved from "just so, in exactly this way" via "similarly."]

al·so-ran *n.* **1.** LOSING RUNNER a horse or other entrant in a race that does not finish in any of the winning places **2.** LOSING COMPETITOR a losing entrant in any contest **3.** SOMEBODY UNIMPORTANT somebody of little or no consequence or significance [Because newspaper racing results formerly listed horses that finished fourth or lower under the heading "Also Ran"]

al·stroe·me·ri·a /àlstrə méeree ə/ (*plural* **-as** *or* **-a**) *n.* a tuberous South American plant of the amaryllis family, cultivated for its brightly and variously colored flowers that last for a long time when cut. Genus: *Alstroemeria.* [Late 18thC. From modern Latin, genus name, named for Klas von *Alstroemer* (1736–96), Swedish naturalist.]

Alt *abbr.* Alt key

alt. *abbr.* **1.** alteration **2.** alternate **3.** altitude **4.** alto

alt- *prefix.* = **alto-** (*used before vowels*)

Al·ta. *abbr.* Alberta

Al·ta·de·na /àltə déenə/ urban community in southwestern California in the San Gabriel Mountains. Population: 42,658 (1990).

Al·ta·ic /al táy ik/ *n.* a family of languages that consists of Turkic, Mongolic, and Tungusic. It is sometimes thought that Altaic languages form part of a wider Ural-Altaic family. [Mid-19thC. Named for the ALTAI MOUNTAINS.] —**Altaic** *adj.*

Al·tai Moun·tains /àl tī-/ mountains in central Asia, on the Kazakhstan-Mongolia border, south of Russia and north of China

Al·ta·mon·te Springs /àltə mŏnt-/ city in east-central Florida, near Orlando. Population: 38,379 (1996).

Altar: Roman Catholic Church altar

al·tar /áwltər/ *n.* **1.** RAISED CEREMONIAL RELIGIOUS STRUCTURE a raised structure, typically a flat-topped rock or a table of wood or stone, or raised area where sacrifices are offered or other religious ceremonies performed **2.** COMMUNION TABLE the table or other raised structure in a Christian church on which the bread and wine of the Eucharist are prepared [Pre-12thC. From Latin *altare*, from *altaria* "burnt offerings," from, probably, *adolere* "to burn up."] ◇ **lead somebody to the altar** to marry somebody (*dated informal*)

al·tar call *n.* an appeal by an evangelist for worshipers to come forward and make a profession of faith

al·tar cloth *n.* a cloth covering for the top of a church altar, or sometimes for its top, front, and sides

al·tar·piece /áwltər pees/ *n.* a work of art placed above and behind an altar

al·tar rail *n.* a rail in front of a church altar separating the chancel from the rest of the church

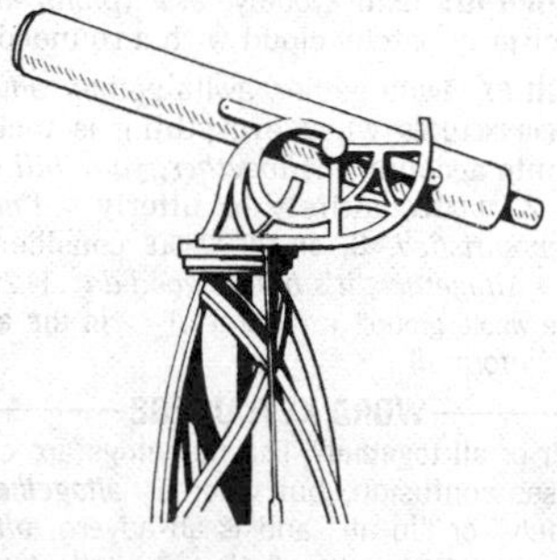
Altazimuth

alt·az·i·muth /al tázməth, -tázzə-/ *n.* **1.** TELESCOPE an instrument, incorporating a telescope that can move vertically and horizontally, used to measure the altitude and azimuth of a celestial body **2.** SURVEYING INSTRUMENT an instrument similar to a theodolite used in surveying to measure horizontal and vertical angles [Mid-19thC. Blend of ALTITUDE and AZIMUTH.]

al·ter /áwltər/ (**-tered, -ter·ing, -ters**) *v.* **1.** *vt.* ADJUST GARMENT FOR BETTER FIT to make adjustments to a piece of clothing so that it fits better ○ *The pants are fine but the jacket will have to be altered.* **2.** *vti.* CHANGE to make changes to something or somebody, or be changed or become different ○ *We'll have to alter our plans.* **3.** *vt. U.S., Aus* CASTRATE to castrate or spay an animal (*informal*) [14thC. Via French, from late Latin *alterare*, from Latin *alter* "other," source also of English *alternate, altercation,* and *altruism.*] —**al·ter·a·bil·i·ty** /àwltərə bíllətee/ *n.* —**al·ter·a·ble** /áwltərəb'l/ *adj.*

WORD KEY: SYNONYMS
See Synonyms at ***change.***

al·ter·a·tion /àwltə ráysh'n/ *n.* **1.** CHANGE a change, modification, or adjustment made to something, especially a garment **2.** DIFFERENCE difference in something resulting from change ○ *I don't see any alteration in the patient's condition.* **3.** PROCESS OF CHANGING the process of changing something or of being changed ○ *undergoing alteration*

al·ter·cate /áwltər kàyt/ (**-cat·ed, -cat·ing, -cates**) *vi.* to engage in a heated argument or confrontation [Mid-16thC. From Latin *altercat-*, the past participle stem of *altercari* "to dispute", from *alter* (see ALTER). The underlying idea is of taking turns speaking with another.]

al·ter·ca·tion /àwltər káysh'n/ *n.* a heated argument, quarrel, or confrontation

al·ter e·go /àwltər éegō/ (*plural* **al·ter e·gos**) *n.* **1.** ALTERNATIVE PERSONALITY a second side to an individual's personality, different from the one that most people know **2.** VERY CLOSE FRIEND a very close and trusted friend [From Latin, literally "other self," used by Cicero, a translation of Greek *allos egō, heteros egō*]

al·ter·nate *v.* /áwltər nàyt/ (**-nat·ed, -nat·ing, -nates**) **1.** *vi.* FOLLOW IN INTERCHANGING PATTERN to follow each other and take each other's place in a regular pattern of events ○ *as night alternates with day* **2.** *vi.* FLUCTUATE to shift back and forth, especially regularly or constantly, between one state and another ○ *Her mood alternates between elation and despair.* **3.** *vt.* ARRANGE THINGS IN INTERCHANGING PATTERN to arrange things, or cause things to happen, in a regular pattern in which one thing always follows the other ○ *a design alternating black tiles with white* **4.** *vi.* BE AN UNDERSTUDY to act as an understudy for another performer ■ *adj.* /áwltərnət/ **1.** ARRANGED IN ALTERNATING PATTERN arranged or happening in a regular pattern in which the one thing alternates with the other ○ *alternate spells of sun and showers* **2.** EVERY OTHER every other or second of a series ○ *They babysit for each other on alternate weekends.* **3.** SERVING AS A BACKUP different from and serving, or able to serve, as a substitute for something else ○ *The band decided to go with the song's alternate title.* **4.** BOT NOT ALIGNED used to describe flowers, buds, or leaves that are arranged singly and at different levels on either side of the stem of a plant, as opposed to being in pairs or groups ■ *n.* /áwltərnət/ **1.** SOMEBODY WHO FILLS IN somebody who acts as a substitute for somebody else ○ *An alternate for the first-string quarterback played the entire first half.* **2.** = **alternative** *n.* 1 [Early 16thC. From Latin *alternat-*, the past participle stem of *alternare* "to do things one after another," from *alternus* "one after another," from *alter* (see ALTER).] —**al·ter·nate·ness** /áwltərnətnəss/ *n.*

al·ter·nate an·gle *n.* one of a pair of angles on opposite sides and at opposite ends of a line that cuts two other lines

al·ter·nate·ly /áwltərnətlee/ *adv.* **1.** INTERCHANGING by following one immediately after the other in a regular repeated pattern or sequence ○ *Driving downtown was restricted to cars with odd and even license plate numbers alternately by day of the month.* **2.** = **alternatively**

al·ter·nat·ing cur·rent *n.* an electric current that regularly reverses direction

al·ter·na·tion /àwltər náysh'n/ *n.* **1.** PROCESS OF ALTERNATING a process of change in which one thing follows, or is made to follow, another in a regular repeated pattern **2.** LOGIC PROPOSITION a proposition of the form "p or q," that is, either sentence "p" is true or sentence "q" is true

al·ter·na·tion of gen·er·a·tions *n.* the existence in the life cycle of an organism of two or more alternating forms or reproductive modes, e.g., sexual and asexual cycles

al·ter·na·tive /awl túrnətiv/ *n.* **1.** OTHER POSSIBILITY something different from, and able to serve as a substitute for, something else ○ *You could take the bus as an alternative to driving.* **2.** POSSIBILITY OF CHOOSING the possibility of choosing between two different things or courses of action ○ *We gave you the alternative; you decided to stay.* **3.** OPTION either one of two, or one of several, things or courses of action to choose between ○ *I can't decide which of the two alternatives is worse.* ■ *adj.* **1.** = **alternate** *adj.* 3 **2. MUTUALLY EXCLUSIVE** of which only one can be true, or only one can be used or chosen, or take place at any one time ○ *There are two alternative theories as to why this phenomenon occurs.* **3. UNCONVENTIONALLY NONTRADITIONAL** outside the establishment or mainstream, and often presented as being less institutionalized or conventional, or more natural or economical with resources ○ *alternative methods of painting* **4.** LOGIC = **disjunctive**

al·ter·na·tive com·e·dy *n.* any form of comedy characterized by subject matter and a style of presentation deliberately made different from mainstream comedy —**al·ter·na·tive co·me·di·an** *n.*

al·ter·na·tive en·er·gy *n.* any form of energy obtained from the sun, wind, waves, or another natural renewable source, in contrast to energy generated from fossil fuels

al·ter·na·tive life·style *n.* a way of living adopted by people who reject the prevailing lifestyle e.g., because they consider it to be too materialistic or too dependent upon technology

al·ter·na·tive·ly /awl túrnətivlee/ *adv.* or instead of that ○ *Alternatively, you could drive there.*

al·ter·na·tive med·i·cine *n.* the treatment of illness using remedies not considered part of mainstream medicine, e.g., homeopathy or naturopathy

al·ter·na·tive press *n.* newspapers and periodicals that reflect nontraditional viewpoints and lifestyles

al·ter·na·tive school *n.* an educational establishment with a curriculum and methods that are nontraditional

al·ter·na·tor /áwltər nàytər/ *n.* a device that generates alternating current, especially in a car

al·tho /awl thṓ/ *conj.* although (*informal*)

Althorn

alt·horn /ált hawrn/ *n.* an alto brass wind instrument of either the saxhorn or the flügelhorn family, used mainly in brass or military bands [Mid-19thC. From German, literally "alto horn," from *Alt* "alto" + *Horn* "horn."]

al·though /awl thṓ/ *conj.* granting or in spite of the fact that ○ *Although the children were sleepy, they kept watching the movie.* [14thC. From ALL in the sense "even" + THOUGH.]

WORD KEY: USAGE

although or **though**? In many uses ***although*** and ***though*** are interchangeable. ***Although*** is more usual when introducing a clause at the beginning of a sentence, but apart from this ***though*** is a generally more versatile word capable of occupying different positions in a sentence and having more grammatical flexibility. It is the only choice in the phrases **as though** and **even though**, and in the following types of use: *I don't like them, though. It is true though that they have been kind to us. The chair, though damaged, could still be used. We enjoyed the day out, cold though it was.*

alti- *prefix.* = **alto-**

al·tim·e·ter /al tímmətər, áltə meetər/ *n.* an instrument that shows height above sea level, especially one mounted in an aircraft and incorporating an aneroid barometer that senses differences in pressure caused by changes in altitude —**al·ti·met·ric** /áltə méttrik/ *adj.* —**al·tim·e·try** /al tímmətree/ *n.*

al·ti·pla·no /àlti plaá nō/ (*plural* **-nos**) *n.* a high plateau, especially in Mexico or the Andes of South America [Early 20thC. From American Spanish, literally "high plain."]

al·ti·tude /áltətood/ *n.* **1. HEIGHT ABOVE SEA LEVEL** the height of something above a particular specified level, especially above sea level or the Earth's surface **2. HIGH PLACE** a place or region situated high above sea level (*often used in the plural*) **3.** GEOM **DISTANCE** in a geometrical figure, the perpendicular distance from the vertex to the base **4.** ASTRON **ANGLE CELESTIAL BODY IS ABOVE HORIZON** the angle of a celestial body above an observer's horizon, measured from the horizon along the circle passing through the object and the point above the observer **5. HIGH RANK OR POSITION** a high rank or high position in a society or group [14thC. From Latin *altitudo*, from *altus* "high" (source of English *haughty*). Ultimately from an Indo-European word meaning "to grow," the underlying idea being "growing tall."] —**al·ti·tu·di·nal** /àltə tóodən'l/ *adj.*

al·ti·tude sick·ness *n.* a condition caused by low levels of oxygen in the air at high altitudes, resulting in nausea and breathlessness

Alt key *n.* a key on a computer keyboard that can be pressed together with another key to change the function of the latter

AKG London

Robert Altman

Alt·man /áwltmən/, **Robert** (*b.* 1925) U.S. movie director and screenwriter who is known for the movies *M*A*S*H* (1970) and *The Player* (1992).

al·to /áltō/ (*plural* **-tos**) *n.* **1.** = **contralto** *n.* 1 **2. HIGHEST MALE VOICE** the highest singing voice for an adult male, achieved by using falsetto **3. ALTO SINGER** somebody who sings with an alto or contralto voice **4. INSTRUMENT BETWEEN SOPRANO AND TENOR** in a family of instruments, the instrument whose size and pitch fall between the soprano and tenor instruments [Late 16thC. Via Italian, literally "high," from Latin *altus* (see ALTITUDE).]

alto-, alti-, alt- *prefix.* high, altitude ○ *altocumulus, altimeter* [From Latin *altus* "high, deep" (source also of English *altitude*). Ultimately from an Indo-European base meaning "to grow," which is also the ancestor of *old*.]

al·to clef *n.* the C clef indicating that middle C is on the third line of the staff

al·to·cu·mu·lus /áltō kyóomyələss/ (*plural* **-li** /-lī/) *n.* white or gray patchy cloud with a rounded outline

al·to·geth·er /àwltə géthər, áwltə gèthər/ *adv.* **1. WITH EVERYTHING INCLUDED** when everything is included or taken into account ○ *Altogether, your bill comes to $75.99.* **2. TOTALLY** entirely or utterly ○ *I'm not altogether satisfied.* **3. ON THE WHOLE** considered as a whole ○ *Altogether, it's been a good day.* [12thC. From ALL "the whole group" + TOGETHER.] ◇ **in the altogether** naked (*informal*)

WORD KEY: USAGE

altogether or **all together**? The meanings are close and this causes confusion, but whereas ***altogether*** means "completely" or "in all" and is an adverb, ***all together*** means "everyone together," that is, "all at the same place or time" and functions as an adjectival phrase. Usually the word *all* can be removed without affecting the grammar or the sense: *They arrived all together at nine. The plates are all together on a separate shelf.*

al·to·ist /áltō ist/ *n.* a musician who plays an alto saxophone

Al·ton /áwlt'n/ city on the eastern banks of the Mississippi River, in southwestern Illinois. Population: 31,562 (1996).

Al·too·na /al tóonə/ city in south central Pennsylvania, in the heart of the state's coalmining region. Population: 50,101 (1996).

al·to-re·lie·vo /áltō ri leé vō/ (*plural* **al·to-re·lie·vos** *or* **al·to-re·lie·vi** /-vee/), **al·to-ri·lie·vo** (*plural* **al·to-ri·lie·vos** *or* **al·to-ri·lie·vi**) *n.* = **high relief** [Mid-17thC. From Italian *alto-rilievo*, literally "high-relief."]

al·to·stra·tus /áltō stráytəss, -stráttəss/ (*plural* **-ti** /-tī/) *n.* grayish cloud in thin sheets or layers of uniform appearance, through which the sun can be seen

al·tri·cial /al tríshəl/ *adj.* **HELPLESS AND DEPENDENT** used to describe birds or mammals that are helpless when young and dependent on their parents for food ■ *n.* **ANIMAL PRODUCING HELPLESS YOUNG** a bird or mammal that produces young that are unable to move or feed themselves without help [Late 19thC. Formed from modern Latin *Altrices* (former division of birds), plural of Latin *altrix* "female nourisher," from *alere* "to nourish."]

al·tru·ism /áltroo ìzəm/ *n.* **1. SELFLESSNESS** an attitude or way of behaving marked by unselfish concern for the welfare of others **2. BELIEF IN ACTING FOR OTHERS' GOOD** the belief that acting for the benefit of others is right and good [Mid-19thC. Via French *altruisme* from Italian *altrui* "that which belongs to other people," from, ultimately, Latin *alter* "other."] —**al·tru·ist** /áltroo ist/ *n.* —**al·tru·is·tic** /àltroo ístik/ *adj.* —**al·tru·is·ti·cal·ly** *adv.*

ALU *abbr.* arithmetic logic unit

al·u·la /állyələ/ (*plural* **-lae** /-lee/) *n.* a bastard wing (*technical*) [Late 18thC. From modern Latin, literally "little wing," formed from Latin *ala* "wing."] —**al·u·lar** *adj.*

al·um[1] /álləm/ *n.* **1. COLORLESS SOLID** a colorless crystalline solid that turns white in air. It is used as an astringent, in water purification, to dress leather, and to make pigments and dyes. Formula: $KAl(SO_4)_2.12H_2O$. **2. COMPOUND STRUCTURALLY SIMILAR TO ALUM** an inorganic chemical compound with a structure similar to that of alum [14thC. Via Old French, from Latin *alumen* (see ALUMINUM).]

al·um[2] /ə lúm/ *n.* a graduate of a school, college, or university (*informal*) [Mid-20thC. Shortening.]

a·lu·mi·na /ə lóomənə/ *n.* white or colorless aluminum oxide, found naturally as corundum and in bauxite. It is used as a catalyst and an abrasive, and in the manufacture of artificial sapphires and rubies. Formula: Al_2O_3. [Late 18thC. Coined from the Latin stem *alumin-* (see ALUMINUM), on the model of words such as SODA and MAGNESIA.]

a·lu·mi·nate /ə lóomənət/ *n.* any salt of aluminum and a metallic oxide

a·lu·mi·nif·er·ous /ə lòomə níffərəss/ *adj.* that contains or is a source of alumina or aluminum

al·u·min·i·um /àlə mínnee əm/ *n.* U.K. = **aluminum**

a·lu·mi·nize /ə lóomə nīz/ (**-nized, -niz·ing, -niz·es**) *vt.* to treat or coat something with aluminum

a·lu·min·o·ther·my /ə lòomənō thúrmee/ *n.* a process for extracting a metal from its oxide that involves burning the oxide together with aluminum powder

a·lu·mi·nous /ə lóomənəss/ *adj.* **1. RESEMBLING ALUMINUM** resembling aluminum or alum **2.** = **aluminiferous** [15thC. Formed from Latin *aluminosus*, from the stem *alumin-* (see ALUMINUM).]

a·lu·mi·num /ə lóomənəm/ *n.* a light metallic element that is silvery white, ductile, malleable, and resistant to corrosion. The commonest metal found in the Earth's crust, aluminum occurs naturally only in compounds such as bauxite. Symbol **Al** [Early 19thC. From Latin *alumin-*, the stem of *alumen* "alum." Coined by the British chemist Sir Humphrey Davy, who discovered the metal.]

a·lu·mi·num foil *n.* aluminum in the form of a very thin sheet, used especially for wrapping food that is to be baked or roasted in an oven

a·lu·mi·num hy·drox·ide *n.* a white solid used as an antacid, catalyst, and drying agent, and in making glass and ceramics. Formula: $Al(OH)_3$ or $Al_2O_3.3H_2O$.

a·lu·mi·num ox·ide *n.* = **alumina**

a·lu·mi·num sid·ing *n.* aluminum used as a protective surface on the outer walls of frame buildings

a·lu·mi·num sul·fate *n.* a white crystalline solid used in making paper and textiles and in water purification. Formula: $Al_2(SO_4)_3$.

a·lum·na /ə lúmnə/ (*plural* **-nae** /-nī, -nee/) *n.* a female graduate or former student of a school, college, or university [Late 19thC. From Latin, feminine form of ALUMNUS.]

a·lum·nus /ə lúmnəs/ (*plural* **-ni** /-nī, -nee/) *n.* a male graduate or former student of a school, college, or university [Mid-17thC. From Latin, literally "pupil, foster-child," formed from *alere* "to nourish" (source of English *adolescent, adult,* and *alimony*).]

al·um·root /álləm root/ *n.* a North American plant of the saxifrage family with small bell-shaped flowers, dark green round or heart-shaped leaves, and astringent roots. Genus: *Heuchera.* [From the astringency of the roots]

al·u·nite /állyə nīt/ *n.* a white, gray, or reddish mineral composed of hydrated potassium aluminum sulfate, formed by alteration of volcanic rocks and used in the production of fertilizers [Mid-19thC. From French, formed from *alun* "alum" from, ultimately, Latin *alumen* (see ALUMINUM).]

Al·va·ra·do, Pedro de (1486–1541) Spanish explorer who served with Hernán Cortés in the conquest of Mexico (1519) and was governor of Guatemala (1530).

al·ve·o·lar /al veé ələr, -veélər, -vee ṓlər/ *adj.* **1.** ANAT **RELATING TO AIR SAC IN LUNG** relating to the air sacs in the lungs (**alveoli**) **2.** ANAT **RELATING TO THE JAWBONE** relating to the part of the upper or lower jaw that contains the roots of the teeth **3.** PHON **WITH TONGUE NEAR UPPER TEETH RIDGE** used to describe a consonant that is sounded with the tongue touching or close to the ridge behind the teeth of the upper jaw ■ *n.* PHON **ALVEOLAR CONSONANT** an alveolar consonant, e.g., "t," "d," or "s" in English —**al·ve·o·lar·ly** *adv.*

al·ve·o·lus /al veé ələss/ (*plural* **-li** /-lī/) *n.* **1.** **AIR SAC IN LUNG** a tiny thin-walled air sac found in large numbers in each lung, through which oxygen enters and carbon dioxide leaves the blood **2.** **TOOTH SOCKET** a socket in the jaw bone in which a tooth is rooted [Late 17thC. From Latin, literally "little cavity," formed from *alveus* "cavity," from *alvus* "belly."]

Al·vin /álvin/ city in eastern Texas, south of Houston. Population: 20,579 (1996).

al·ways /áwl wayz, -wiz/ *adv.* **1.** **EVERY TIME OR CONTINUOUSLY** used to indicate that something happens or is done at all times, either continuously, repetitively, or on every occasion ○ *She's almost always late.* **2.** **THROUGH ALL PAST OR FUTURE TIME** throughout all past time or all future time, or for as long as anyone can remember and as long as anyone can foresee ○ *I will always love you.* **3.** **IF NECESSARY** if necessary, or if there is no other or no better option ○ *I could always stay an extra day if you need help.* [14thC. From Old English *ealne weg*, literally "all the way," originally "covering the complete distance," later "perpetually."] ◇ **for always** for all time

Al·yce clo·ver /álləs-/ *n.* a low-growing spreading tropical plant grown as a pasture and hay crop in the southern United States. Latin name: *Alysicarpus vaginalis.* [Mid-20thC. Origin uncertain: "Alyce" probably by folk etymology (by association with the forename *Alice*) from modern Latin *Alysicarpus*, genus name, from Greek *halusis* "chain" + *karpos* "fruit."]

a·lys·sum /ə líssəm/ *n.* **1.** = **sweet alyssum 2.** = **basket-of-gold** [Mid-16thC. Via modern Latin, genus name, from, ultimately, Greek *alysson* "madwort" (a plant believed to cure rabies), formed from *alyssos*, literally "without madness," from *lyssa* "rabies."]

Alz·heim·er's dis·ease /áalts hīmərz-/, **Alzheimer's** *n.* a degenerative disorder that affects the brain and causes senile dementia [Early 20thC. Named for Alois *Alzheimer* (1864–1915), German neurologist, who described it in 1907.]

am[1], **AM** *abbr.* amplitude modulation

am[2] (*stressed*) /am/; (*unstressed*) /əm/ *v.* 1st person present singular of **be** [Old English *eom.* Ultimately from an Indo-European verb meaning "to be" (source also of French *être*).]

Am *abbr.* **1.** BIBLE Amos **2.** americium

Am. *abbr.* American

a.m., **A.M.** *adj., adv.* in the period between midnight and noon. Full form **ante meridiem**

A.M. *abbr.* **1.** anno mundi **2.** Artium Magister

AMA *abbr.* American Medical Association

A·ma·do /ə maádō, ə maá dṑ/, **Jorge** (*b.* 1912) Brazilian novelist and politician. His works include *Dona Flor and Her Two Husbands* (1969).

a·mah /aámə, -maa, aamaá/ *n.* a children's nurse, woman domestic servant, or office cleaner and attendant in an Asian country [Mid-19thC. Via Portuguese *ama* "nurse" from medieval Latin *amma* "mother" (probably originally a nursery word).]

a·mal·gam /ə málgəm/ *n.* **1.** **MIXTURE** a blend of two or more elements or characteristics **2.** DENT **FILLING MATERIAL FOR TEETH** a substance used as filling for tooth cavities, consisting of a paste of powdered mercury, silver, and tin that quickly hardens [15thC. Directly or via French, from medieval Latin *amalgama*, of uncertain origin: probably ultimately from Greek *malagma* "emollient," from, ultimately, *malakos* "soft." Originally in English, "soft alloy."]

WORD KEY: SYNONYMS

See Synonyms at ***mixture***.

a·mal·ga·mate /ə málgə màyt/ (**-mat·ed, -mat·ing, -mates**) *vti.* **1.** **COMBINE** to combine two or more organizations or things into one unified whole, or join together to form one unified whole **2.** METALL **ALLOY WITH MERCURY** to alloy a metal with mercury, or be alloyed with mercury —**a·mal·ga·ma·tive** *adj.* —**a·mal·ga·ma·tor** *n.*

a·mal·ga·ma·tion /ə màlgə máysh'n/ *n.* **1.** COMM **BUSINESS MERGER** a combination of two or more business concerns so as to form one **2.** **RESULT OF COMBINING THINGS** something that is a combination of different things or results from their amalgamation **3.** **COMBINING THINGS** the process of amalgamating things into a unified whole **4.** METALL **METAL EXTRACTION FROM ORE** a method of extracting a precious metal from an ore by using mercury to form an amalgam with the metal

a·man·dine /aámən deén, -deén, ámmən-/ *adj.* filled, cooked, or served with almonds [Mid-19thC. From French, formed from *amande* "almond."]

a·man·ta·dine /ə mántə deen/ *n.* a drug used to combat viral infection, particularly certain types of influenza, and also to treat Parkinson's disease. It helps reduce the tremor of Parkinson's disease by promoting the release of dopamine in the brain. [Mid-20thC. Blend of AMINE and ADAMANTANE.]

a·man·u·en·sis /ə mànnyoo énsiss/ (*plural* **-ses** /-seez/) *n.* **1.** **SCRIBE** somebody employed by an individual to write from his or her dictation or to copy manuscripts **2.** **WRITER'S ASSISTANT** a writer's assistant with research and secretarial duties [Early 17thC. From Latin, formed from *a manu*, literally, "by hand" (in the phrase *servus a manu* "slave, servant with secretarial duties").]

am·a·ranth /ámmə rànth/ (*plural* **-ranths** *or* **-ranth**) *n.* **1.** **FLOWERING PLANT WITH DROOPING FLOWERHEADS** a plant with long drooping heads of small green, red, or purple flowers. Some types are grown as a grain crop or as a leafy vegetable. Genus: *Amaranthus.* **2.** **LEGENDARY FLOWER** a flower, that, according to legend, never fades **3.** **FOOD DYE** a synthetic red food dye [Mid-16thC. Via either French *amarante* or modern Latin *amaranthus* from Latin *amarantus*, from Greek *amarantos*, literally "not corruptible, not fading."]

am·a·ran·thine /ámmə rán thən, -thīn/ *adj.* **1.** **UNDYING** undying or unfading, like the legendary amaranth (*literary*) **2.** **DARK REDDISH PURPLE** of a dark reddish purple color

am·a·ret·to /ámmə réttō/ (*plural* **-tos**) *n.* an Italian almond-flavored liqueur [Mid-20thC. From Italian, literally "little bitter (one)," formed from *amaro* "bitter," from Latin *amarus* (source of English *maraschino* and *morello*).]

Am·a·ril·lo /àmmə ríllō/ city in northwestern Texas, near the center of the Texas Panhandle. Population: 169,588 (1996).

Amaryllis

am·a·ryl·lis /ámmə rílləss/ (*plural* **-lis·es** *or* **-lis**) *n.* **1.** **SOUTHERN AFRICAN PLANT** a southern African plant grown from a bulb for its large red, pink, or white trumpet-shaped flowers that appear facing in opposite directions at the head of a single stalk. Latin name: *Amaryllis belladonna.* **2.** **TROPICAL AMERICAN PLANT** a tropical American plant related to the southern African amaryllis. Genus: *Hippeastrum.* [Late 18thC. Via modern Latin from, ultimately, Greek *Amarullis*, name of a shepherdess in pastorals such as those of Theocritus, Virgil, and Ovid.]

a·mass /ə máss/ (**a·massed, a·mass·ing, a·mass·es**) *vti.* to gather things together or collect them over time until they form a large pile, collection, or fund, or accumulate or be collected in this way ○ *amassed a fortune in the 1950s* [15thC. From French *amasser*, from *masser* "to gather into a mass," from, ultimately, Latin *massa* (see MASS "body of matter").] —**a·mass·a·ble** *adj.* —**a·mass·er** *n.* —**a·mass·ment** *n.*

WORD KEY: SYNONYMS

See Synonyms at ***collect***.

am·a·teur /ámmətùr, -tər, -chŏor/ *n.* **1.** **SOMEBODY DOING SOMETHING FOR PLEASURE** somebody who does or takes part in something for pleasure rather than for pay ○ *a talented amateur golfer* **2.** **UNSKILLED PERSON** somebody who has only limited skill in, or knowledge of, an activity ○ *Whoever fixed your car must have been an amateur.* **3.** **SOMEBODY WHO LOVES SOMETHING** somebody who loves or is greatly interested in something (*literary*) ○ *She is an amateur of classical sculpture.* ■ *adj.* **1.** **BY AMATEURS** for, by, or consisting of amateurs **2.** **NOT DONE WITH SKILL** unskillful or unprofessional, or done in an unskillful or unprofessional way [Late 18thC. Via French, from Latin *amator* "lover" from *amare* "to love" (source of English *enamor*).]

am·a·teur·ish /ámmə túrish, -chŏor-/ *adj.* lacking the skill of a professional, or unskillfully or unprofessionally done —**am·a·teur·ish·ly** *adv.* —**am·a·teur·ish·ness** *n.*

am·a·teur·ism /ámmətərizəm, -choor-/ *n.* amateur status, participation by amateurs, or the principle that something should reserved for amateurs ○ *one of the last bastions of true amateurism in sports*

am·a·tol /ámmə tòl/ *n.* an explosive made from ammonium nitrate and TNT and used in bombs [Early 20thC. Coined from AMMONIUM + TOLUENE.]

am·a·to·ry /ámmə tàwree/, **am·a·to·ri·al** /-ree əl/ *adj.* relating to, involving, expressing, or typical of physical love ○ *amatory adventures* [Late 16thC. From Latin *amatorius*, from *amator* (see AMATEUR).]

am·au·ro·sis /à maw róssəss/ *n.* partial or complete blindness, especially when there is no obvious damage to the eye [Mid-17thC. From Greek *amaurōsis*, from *amauroun* "to darken," from *amauros* "dark."] —**am·au·rot·ic** /à maw ráwtik/ *adj.*

a·mau·tik /ə mówtik/, **a·mau·ti** /-tee/ *n.* *Can* among the Inuit, a woman's jacket that has a fur-lined hood for carrying an infant or small child [From Inuktitut]

a·maze /ə máyz/ *vt.* (**a·mazed, a·maz·ing, a·maz·es**) **1.** **FILL SOMEBODY WITH WONDER** to fill somebody with wonder, astonishment, or extreme surprise ○ *We were amazed at the news.* **2.** **BEWILDER SOMEBODY** to bewilder or stupefy somebody (*archaic*) ■ *n.* **AMAZEMENT** a state of astonishment or bewilderment (*archaic*) [Old English *āmasian* "to stupefy, stun" (source of English *maze*), of uncertain origin: perhaps from Old Norse] —**a·mazed** *adj.* —**a·maz·ed·ly** /ə máyzədlee/ *adv.* —**a·maz·ed·ness** /-nəss/ *n.*

a·maze·ment /ə máyzmənt/ *n.* **1.** **ASTONISHMENT** a strong feeling of wonder or surprise at the extraordinariness of something **2.** **BEWILDERMENT** bewilderment or confusion (*archaic*)

a·maz·ing /ə máyzing/ *adj.* **1.** **CAUSING AMAZEMENT** so extraordinary or wonderful as to be barely believable or cause extreme surprise ○ *an amazing escape* **2.** **OUTSTANDING** outstandingly good, skillful, or admirable (*informal*) ○ *an amazing concert* —**a·maz·ing·ly** *adv.*

am·a·zon /ámmə zòn/ *n.* a parrot of tropical America that typically has green plumage. Genus: *Amazona.* [Late 19thC. Named for the AMAZON.]

Am·a·zon[1] /ámmə zòn, -əzən/ *n.* **1.** **MYTHOLOGICAL WARRIOR** in Greek mythology, a member of a group of women warriors who lived in Scythia or elsewhere at the northern limits of the world. They fought in the Trojan war on the side of Troy. **2.** **Am·a·zon, a·ma·zon** **STRONG WOMAN** a tall, physically strong, or strong-willed woman —**Am·a·zo·ni·an** /ámmə zṓneean/ *adj.*

Am·a·zon[2] /ámmə zòn, -əzən/ the world's second longest river. It flows east from northern Peru, traversing northern South America and emptying into the Atlantic Ocean in Brazil. Length: about 4,000 mi./6,400 km. —**Am·a·zo·ni·an** *adj.*

Amazon

Am·a·zon·as /ámə zṓnəss/ state in northwestern Brazil. It has many cattle ranches and produces rubber and jute. Population: 2,390,102 (1996). Area: 609,039 sq. mi./1,577,820 sq. km.

Am·a·zon dol·phin *n.* a freshwater dolphin with a long snout found in the upper reaches of the Amazon and Orinoco rivers. Latin name: *Inia geoffrensis.*

am·a·zon·ite /ámmə zo nīt/ *n.* a green or bluish green mineral, a form of microcline used as a gemstone [Named for the AMAZON[2], where similar green stones were formerly found]

Amb. *abbr.* ambassador

am·bas·sa·dor /am bássədər, -dàwr/ *n.* **1. DIPLOMATIC REPRESENTATIVE** a diplomatic official of the highest rank sent by one country as its long-term representative to another **2. OFFICIAL REPRESENTATIVE** somebody who serves as an official representative of something, e.g., a movement ○ *visiting this country as an ambassador for a fund dedicated to saving endangered species* **3. UNOFFICIAL REPRESENTATIVE** somebody or something regarded as an unofficial representative or a symbol of something ○ *The swallow is an ambassador of spring.* [14thC. Via French *ambassadeur* from Italian *ambasciator,* from, ultimately, Latin *ambactus* "vassal," from a Gaulish word meaning "servant" (source of English *embassy*).] —**am·bas·sa·do·ri·al** /am bàssə dáwree əl/ *adj.* —**am·bas·sa·dor·ship** /am bássədər shìp/ *n.*

WORD KEY: CULTURAL NOTE

The Ambassadors, a novel by Henry James (1903). Sometimes regarded as James' masterpiece, it tells the story of Lambert Strether, a middle-aged editor sent by his wealthy New England patron and fiancée to Paris to persuade her expatriate son Chad to return home.

am·bas·sa·dor at large (*plural* **am·bas·sa·dors at large**) *n.* an ambassador not assigned to one particular foreign country

am·beer /ám beer/ *n. Southern U.S.* saliva in the mouth containing the juice of chewed tobacco [Mid-19thC. Origin uncertain: perhaps a blend of AMBER and BEER, from its color and foaminess.]

WORD KEY: REGIONAL NOTE

The term ***ambeer*** is limited to the tobacco-producing regions of the southeastern United States. But its main meaning, given here, is commonplace throughout the rural South.

am·ber /ámbər/ *n.* **1. YELLOW FOSSIL RESIN** a hard translucent fossil resin varying in color from yellow to light brown, used for making jewelry and ornaments **2. BROWNY YELLOW COLOR** a yellow to brown color **3. SIGNAL FOR CAUTION** in a system of traffic signals, the yellow-colored light that advises caution. A car at an amber must halt if it safely can, but a train may proceed with caution. ■ *adj.* **YELLOWISH-BROWN** of a yellowish-brown color [14thC. Via French *ambre* from Arabic *anbar* "ambergris," the original sense in English, from a perceived similarity between the two.]

am·ber·gris /ámbər gris, -grees/ *n.* a gray waxy substance, consisting mainly of cholesterol, secreted from the intestines of the sperm whale. It is found floating in tropical waters or on beaches and is used in perfume-making. [15thC. From French *ambre gris,* literally "gray amber."]

am·ber·jack /ámbər jak/ (*plural* **-jacks** *or* **-jack**) *n.* a large sea fish found in warm Atlantic waters that has golden markings. Genus: *Seriola.*

am·ber·oid /ámbə royd/, **am·broid** /ámbroyd/ *n.* a synthetic form of amber made by heating and compressing valueless small pieces of amber with other resins

ambi- *prefix.* both ○ *ambiversion* [From Latin *ambi* "around, on both sides." Ultimately from an Indo-European base that is also the ancestor of English *by, umlaut,* and *amphi-.*]

am·bi·ance /ámbee əns/, **am·bi·ence** *n.* the typical atmosphere or mood of a place ○ *a restaurant with a welcoming ambiance* [Mid-20thC. From French *ambiance.*]

am·bi·dex·ter·i·ty /àmbi dek stérrətee/ *n.* **1. ABILITY TO USE EITHER HAND** the ability to use either hand with equal skill **2. SKILLFULNESS** general skillfulness, especially with the hands **3. DECEIT** dishonesty, deceit, or double-dealing (*literary*)

am·bi·dex·trous /àmbi dékstrəss/ *adj.* **1. USING EITHER HAND** able to use either the right or the left hand with equal skill **2. SKILLFUL IN MANY WAYS** very skillful and versatile [Mid-17thC. Formed from late Latin *ambidexter,* literally "right-handed on both sides," formed from Latin *dexter* "right-handed" (see DEXTROUS), from the traditional association of the right hand with skill.] —**am·bi·dex·trous·ly** /àmbi dékstrəsslee/ *adv.*

am·bi·ence *n.* = **ambiance**

am·bi·ent /ámbiənt/ *adj.* **IN SURROUNDING AREA** in the immediately surrounding area ○ *ambient temperature* ■ *n.* **ambient, ambient music BACKGROUND MUSIC** a type of music that is usually instrumental and repetitive and often contains soothing electronic sounds. It is used to create an atmosphere of calm or relaxation. [Late 16thC. Directly or via French, from Latin *ambire,* literally "to go around" (see AMBITION).]

am·bi·gu·i·ty /àmbi gyóōətee/ (*plural* **-ties**) *n.* **1. DOUBT ABOUT MEANING** a situation in which something can be understood in more than one way and it is not clear which meaning is intended **2. STATEMENT WITH MORE THAN ONE MEANING** an expression or statement that has more than one meaning

am·big·u·ous /am bíggyooəss/ *adj.* **1. HAVING MORE THAN ONE MEANING** having more than one possible meaning or interpretation ○ *an ambiguous response* **2. CAUSING UNCERTAINTY** causing uncertainty or confusion ○ *an ambiguous result* [Early 16thC. Formed from Latin *ambiguus* "undecided," from *ambigere* "to wander around," from *agere* "to lead" (source of English *agent*).] —**am·big·u·ous·ly** *adv.* —**am·big·u·ous·ness** *n.*

WORD KEY: USAGE

ambiguous or **ambivalent**? Both words describe uncertainty in understanding what something or somebody means. The principal difference is that ***ambivalent*** is used of people and their attitudes, whereas ***ambiguous*** refers to something said or written. If people are ***ambivalent*** about disarmament, they are unsure about the advantages and disadvantages and cannot easily decide between the various arguments, whereas if a political leader makes an ***ambiguous*** statement about disarmament, then the statement has more than one possible meaning.

am·bi·sex·u·al /àmbi sékshooəl/ *adj.* **1. OF BOTH SEXES** used to describe secondary sexual characteristics that are common to both sexes **2. ATTRACTED TO BOTH SEXES** sexually responsive or attracted to both sexes **3.** = **unisex** —**am·bi·sex·u·al·i·ty** /àmbi sekshoo àllətee/ *n.*

am·bi·son·ics /àmbi sáaniks/ *n.* a recording and reproduction system that uses separate channels and speakers to create the effect of being surrounded by sound (*takes a singular verb*) —**am·bi·son·ic** *adj.*

am·bit /ámbit/ *n.* the scope, extent, or limits of something ○ *within the ambit of the court's jurisdiction* [Late 16thC. From Latin *ambitus* "circuit," from *ambire* (see AMBITION).]

am·bi·tion /am bísh'n/ *n.* **1. DESIRE FOR SUCCESS** a strong feeling of wanting to be successful in life and achieve great things **2. AIM OR GOAL** an aim or objective that somebody is trying to achieve [14thC. Via French, from Latin *ambitio,* from *ambire* "to canvass for votes, go around," from *ire* "to go" (source of English *exit*).]

am·bi·tious /am bíshəss/ *adj.* **1. HAVING STRONG DESIRE FOR SUCCESS** having a strong desire to be successful in life **2. NEEDING GREAT EFFORT TO SUCCEED** sounding impressive but difficult to achieve because very high standards have been set or a great deal of work is required ○ *an ambitious plan to increase market share* **3. STRONGLY DESIROUS** with a strong desire to have or do something ○ *ambitious to be the youngest person ever to win the championship* —**am·bi·tious·ly** *adv.* —**am·bi·tious·ness** *n.*

am·biv·a·lence /am bívvələns/ *n.* **1. CONFLICT OF IDEAS OR ATTITUDES** the presence of two opposing ideas, attitudes, or emotions at the same time **2. UNCERTAINTY** a feeling of uncertainty about something due to a mental conflict [Early 20thC. From German *Ambivalenz,* which was modeled on *Äquivalenz* (see EQUIVALENCE).]

am·biv·a·lent /am bívvələnt/ *adj.* having mixed, uncertain, or conflicting feelings about something

WORD KEY: USAGE

See Usage note at ***ambiguous.***

am·bi·ver·sion /àmbi vúrzhən/ *n.* a personality pattern that has characteristics of both introversion and extroversion —**am·bi·vert** /ámbivurt/ *n.*

am·ble /ámb'l/ *vi.* (**-bled, -bling, -bles**) **WALK SLOWLY** to walk slowly in a relaxed way ○ *"I took off shoes and socks and ambled along carrying them, enjoying the evening sun."* (Dick Francis, *The Danger;* 1983) ■ *n.* **SLOW WALK** a slow and relaxed walk or style of walking [14thC. Via French *ambler* from Latin *ambulare* "to walk."] —**am·bler** *n.*

am·blyg·o·nite /am blíggə nīt/ *n.* a white or grayish green mineral consisting of lithium aluminum fluorophosphate. It is an important source of lithium. [Early 19thC. Formed from *amblygon* "obtuse-angled triangle," from, ultimately, Greek *amblugōnios* "obtuse-angled." From the shape of its crystals.]

am·bly·o·pi·a /àmbli ṓpiə/ *n.* an impairment of the vision in one eye that is not caused by structural damage or physical defect [Early 18thC. Via modern Latin, from Greek *ambluōpia,* literally "dim-sightedness."] —**am·bly·o·pic** *adj.*

am·bo /ámb-/ (*plural* **-bos** *or* **-bo·nes** /am bṓneez/) *n.* a stand or pulpit in early Christian churches from which the lessons or other parts of the service were read [Mid-17thC. Via medieval Latin from, ultimately, Greek *ambōn* "raised edge (of a dish)."]

am·bo·nes plural of **ambo**

am·brette /am brét/ (*plural* **-brette** *or* **-brettes**) *n.* = **abelmosk** [Mid-19thC. From French, literally "a little ambergris," from *ambre* (see AMBER). From its musk-scented seeds.]

am·broid *n.* BOT = **amberoid**

Am·brose /ámbrōz/, **St.** (340?–397) Roman priest and theologian. As bishop of Milan from 374 he combatted Arianism and introduced much Greek theology to the West.

am·bro·sia /am brṓzhə/ *n.* **1. FOOD OF THE GODS** in classical mythology, the food of the gods, which was supposed to make those who ate it immortal **2. SOMETHING DELICIOUS** a substance that tastes or smells delicious (*literary*) **3. FRUIT AND COCONUT DISH** a dessert or salad made from oranges, bananas, and coconut [Mid-16thC. Via Latin, from Greek, from *ambrotos* "immortal," from an archaic form of *brotos* "mortal."]

am·bro·sial /am brṓzhəl/, **am·bro·sian** /-zhən/ *adj.* (*literary*) **1. DELICIOUS-TASTING** delightful to taste or smell **2. ASSOCIATED WITH GODS** associated with the gods —**am·bro·sial·ly** *adv.*

am·bry /ámbree/ (*plural* **-bries**), **aum·bry** /áwmbree/ (*plural* **-bries**) *n.* **1. RECESS IN CHURCH** a small recess near the altar in a church, where sacred vessels are kept **2.** *U.K.* **SMALL CUPBOARD** a small cupboard or pantry (*archaic*) [14thC. Via French *armarie* from Latin *armarium* (see ARMOIRE).]

ambs·ace /áymz àyss/, **ames·ace** *n.* (*archaic*) **1. DOUBLE ACE** the lowest throw at dice, with the single spot uppermost on both dice **2. BAD LUCK** bad luck or worthlessness [13thC. Via Old French *ambes as,* literally "both ace," from Latin *ambas as.*]

am·bu·lac·rum /àmbyə láykrəm/ (*plural* **-ra** /-rə/) *n.* any one of the five radial areas on the underside of a starfish, sea urchin, or similar animal, along which the blood vessels and nerves run and through which the feet extend [Early 19thC. From Latin, "avenue," formed from *ambulare* (see AMBULATE).] —**am·bu·lac·ral** *adj.*

am·bu·lance /ámbyələns/ *n.* a vehicle designed and equipped for carrying people to and from a hospital [Mid-19thC. From French, from *hôpital ambulant* "field hospital," literally "walking hospital," from, ultimately, Latin *ambulare* (see AMBULATE).]

am·bu·lance chas·er *n.* (*slang disapproving*) **1. LAWYER BENEFITING FROM ACCIDENTS** a lawyer who, in order to earn large fees, seeks out accident victims and encourages them to claim heavy damages **2. OVERLY AGGRESSIVE LAWYER** a lawyer considered to be overly aggressive and perhaps unethical [Origin uncertain: probably from the late-19thC practice of disreputable lawyers in New York City of commissioning ambulance drivers and police officers to inform them of accidents] —**am·bu·lance chas·ing** *n.*

am·bu·lant /ámbyələnt/ *adj.* **1. TRAVELING** moving around from place to place **2.** MED = **ambulatory** [Early 17thC. Via French from, ultimately, Latin *ambulare* (see AMBULATE).]

am·bu·late /ámbyə làyt/ (**-lat·ed, -lat·ing, -lates**) *vi.* to walk or move from one place to another (*formal*) [Early 17thC. From Latin *ambulat-*, the past participle stem of *ambulare* "to walk" (source of English *alley*, *amble*, and *pram*).] —**am·bu·la·tion** *n.*

am·bu·la·to·ry /ámbyələ tàwree/ *adj.* **1.** MED **MOBILE** used to describe a patient who is able to walk and does not have to be kept in bed **2. WALKING OR MOVING** walking or moving around, or done while walking or moving (*formal*) ○ *ambulatory activities* **3. RELATING TO WALKING** relating to or equipped for walking (*formal*) **4.** LAW **REVOCABLE** able to be revoked ○ *an ambulatory will* ■ *n.* (*plural* **-ries**) ARCHIT **WALKWAY IN CHURCH OR CLOISTER** an aisle at the end of a choir or chancel in a church, or a covered walkway of a cloister —**am·bu·la·to·ri·ly** /àmbyələ táwrəlee/ *adv.*

am·bus·cade /ámbə skàayd/ *n.* **AMBUSH SET** fan ambush set for somebody (*literary*) ■ *vt.* (**-cad·ed, -cad·ing, -cades**) **AMBUSH SOMEBODY** to ambush somebody (*literary*) [Late 16thC. Via French *embuscade* and Italian *imboscata* from, ultimately, assumed Vulgar Latin *imboscare* (see AMBUSH).] —**am·bus·cad·er** *n.*

am·bush /ámbŏŏsh/ *n.* **1. SURPRISE ATTACK** an unexpected attack from a concealed position **2. CONCEALMENT BEFORE ATTACK** a concealment before a surprise attack ○ *They lay in ambush and waited for their victims.* **3. SOMEBODY WAITING IN AMBUSH** one or more people concealed in order to make a surprise attack **4. PLACE OF CONCEALMENT BEFORE ATTACK** a hiding place used in an ambush ■ *v.* (**-bushed, -bush·ing, -bush·es**) **1.** *vt.* **ATTACK** to attack somebody or something suddenly from a concealed position **2.** *vi.* **HIDE BEFORE ATTACK** to wait in a hiding place to attack somebody or take something by surprise [14thC. Via Old French *embusche* from, ultimately, assumed Vulgar Latin *imboscare*, literally "to hide in a bush," from assumed *boscus* "bush" (related to English *bush*).] —**am·bush·er** *n.*

a·me·ba *n.* = **amoeba**

am·e·bi·a·sis /amə bíəssiss/, **am·oe·bi·a·sis** *n.* an infection or disease affecting the bowel, caused by an amoeba *Entamoeba histolytica*

ame·bic dys·en·ter·y, a·moe·bic dys·en·ter·y *n.* an inflammation of the colon causing diarrhea of varying degrees of severity that results from infection by an amoeba *Entamoeba histolytica*

a·me·bo·cyte *n.* = **amoebocyte**

a·me·boid *adj.* = **amoeboid**

a·me·lio·rate /ə méeliə ràyt/ (**-rat·ed, -rat·ing, -rates**) *vti.* to improve something or make it better (*formal*) [Mid-18thC. Alteration of MELIORATE (on the model of French *améliorer*).] —**a·me·lio·ra·ble** /ə méelee ərəb'l/ *adj.* —**a·me·lio·rant** *n.* —**a·me·lio·ra·tive** *adj.* —**a·me·lio·ra·tor** *n.*

a·me·lio·ra·tion /əmeeliə ráyshən/ *n.* **1. PROCESS OF IMPROVEMENT** the act of improving something, or the process of getting better **2. IMPROVEMENT MADE** an improvement in something or somebody

a·men /ay mén, aa-/ *interj.* **1. SO BE IT** said or sung at the end of a prayer or hymn to affirm its content **2. EXPRESSING STRONG AGREEMENT** used to express strong agreement ○ *amen to that* ■ *n.* **AFFIRMATION IN A PRAYER** an indication, at the end of a prayer or hymn, that the person praying or singing affirms its content [Pre-12thC. Via late Latin and Greek, from Hebrew *'āmēn* "truly," from *'āman* "to confirm."]

a·me·na·ble /ə méenəb'l/ *adj.* **1. WILLING TO COOPERATE** responsive to suggestion and likely to cooperate **2. ACCOUNTABLE** required to account for your behavior to an authority **3. LIABLE TO BE JUDGED** likely or available to be tested or judged [Late 16thC. From Anglo-Norman, from Old French *amener*, literally "to bring to," from, ultimately, Latin *minari* "to threaten," from *minae* "threats."] —**a·me·na·bil·i·ty** /ə meenə bíllətee/ *n.* —**a·me·na·ble·ness** /ə méenəb'lnəss/ *n.* —**a·me·na·bly** *adv.*

a·men cor·ner *n.* **1. SEATS FOR MOST DEVOUT** the part of some Protestant churches where the most fervent worshipers sit **2. ENTHUSIASTIC SUPPORTERS** a group of supporters or followers who tend to agree with everything their leader says (*informal*) ○ *As usual, enthusiastic support for the bill came from the sponsoring senator's amen corner.* [From the practice of responding to the preacher's prayers by saying "amen"]

WORD KEY: USAGE

The term ***amen corner*** has traditionally been used in certain Protestant churches to describe the area set aside for members of the congregation who tend to make verbal responses, including the response *Amen*. By extension the term has come to mean, outside the world of religious worship, any area where strong support and high feeling are expressed on behalf of a speaker or performer.

a·mend /ə ménd/ (**a·mend·ed, a·mend·ing, a·mends**) *v.* **1.** *vt.* **IMPROVE OR CORRECT SOMETHING** to make changes to something, especially a piece of text, in order to improve or correct it **2.** *vt.* **REVISE LEGISLATION** to revise or alter formally a motion, bill, or constitution **3.** *vi.* **BEHAVE BETTER** to improve your behavior [13thC. Via French *amender* from, ultimately, Latin *emendare* "to correct," from *menda* "error" (source of English *emend* and *mendicant*).]

WORD KEY: USAGE

amend or **emend**? The normal word to use in general contexts is ***amend***. ***Emend*** is normally restricted to the correction of errors in a printed or written text. *The ambiguous wording at the beginning of the document needs amending (= changing to something clearer). By emending two words (= suggesting alternatives to them because they may have been copied wrongly) it is possible to make the sentence intelligible.*

a·men·da·to·ry /ə méndə tàwree/ *adj.* intended or serving to correct or improve something

a·mend·ment /ə méndmənt/ *n.* **1. ALTERATION TO SOMETHING** a change, correction, or improvement to something **2. CHANGE TO LEGAL INSTRUMENT** an addition or alteration to a motion, bill, or constitution **3. PROCESS OF CHANGING OR IMPROVING SOMETHING** the process of changing, correcting, or improving something ○ *The bill was passed without amendment.*

a·mends /ə méndz/ *n.* something done or given as compensation for a wrong (*takes a singular or plural verb*) ○ *a desire to make amends after the misunderstanding* ○ *No amends were forthcoming even after we had proven that they were in the wrong.* [14thC. From Old French *amendes*, the plural of *amende* "reparation," from *amender* (see AMEND).]

a·men·i·ties /ə ménəteez, -méen-/ *npl.* **1. SOCIAL PLEASANTRIES** any gestures and words of courtesy or pleasantness ○ *The secretary of state and the foreign minister engaged in the usual diplomatic amenities before signing the treaty.* **2. ATTRACTIVE EXTRAS** the features that, when taken together, make a place such as a hotel or resort attractive to guests or customers ○ *among the usual amenities such as phones in every room of the hotel* **3. TOILET** a toilet, as in a hotel (*used euphemistically*)

a·men·i·ty /ə ménətee, -méen-/ (*plural* **-ties**) *n.* **1. PUBLIC FACILITY** a useful or attractive feature or service, e.g., leisure facilities (*often used in the plural*) **2. PLEASANTNESS** an experience of pleasantness or attractiveness ○ *thoroughly enjoyed the amenity of the clean mountain air in the summer* [14thC. Directly or via French *aménité* from Latin *amoenitas*, from *amoenus* "pleasant."]

a·men·or·rhe·a /ay mènə réėə/, **a·men·or·rhoe·a** *n.* the abnormal absence or suppression of menstruation —**a·men·or·rhe·ic** *adj.*

a·men·sa·lism /ay ménsə lìzzəm/ *n.* an interaction between populations of two species that harms one but not the other [Origin uncertain: probably coined from COMMENSALISM]

a·ment /ámmənt, áy-/ *n.* BOT a catkin (*technical*) [Mid-18thC. From Latin *amentum* "strap."]

Amer. *abbr.* American

Am·er·a·sian /amə ráyzhən/ *n.* **SOMEBODY OF AMERICAN AND ASIAN DESCENT** somebody of mixed American and Asian parentage ■ *adj.* **OF MIXED PARENTAGE** having mixed American and Asian parentage [Mid-20thC. A blend of AMERICAN and ASIAN.]

a·merce /ə múrs/ (**a·merced, a·merc·ing, a·merc·es**) *vt.* (*archaic*) **1. PUNISH WITH FINE** to punish somebody with a fine **2. PUNISH ARBITRARILY** to punish somebody in an arbitrary way [14thC. From Anglo-Norman *amercier* "to place at one's mercy (as to the amount of a fine)," from Old French *a merci*, literally "at (one's) mercy."] —**a·merce·a·ble** *adj.* —**a·merce·ment** *n.*

A·mer·i·ca /ə mérrikə/ **1.** = **United States 2. N, S, AND CENTRAL AMERICA** a landmass comprising North America, South America, and Central America **3. N. AMERICA** North America (*informal*) [Early 16thC. From *Americus*, Latinized form of the first name of *Amerigo* Vespucci (1454–1512), Italian navigator.]

WORD KEY: USAGE

Sensitivity trap. The use of ***America*** to mean North America is liable to cause offense to Canadians, and should be avoided.

A·mer·i·can[1] /ə mérrikən/ *n.* **SOMEBODY FROM UNITED STATES** somebody who was born in or is a citizen of the United States ■ *adj.* **1. OF THE UNITED STATES** relating to or typical of the United States, its people, its culture, or the form of English spoken there **2. OF THE AMERICAN CONTINENT** relating to or typical of North, South and Central America [Mid-16thC. From modern Latin *Americanus*, from AMERICA.] —**A·mer·i·can·ness** *n.*

A·mer·i·can[2] /ə mérrikən/ river in north central California flowing southward to join the Sacramento River at Sacramento. Gold discovered along the river in 1848 spurred the California Gold Rush. Length: 30 mi./48 km.

A·mer·i·ca·na /ə mèri kaánə/ *n.* **1. COLLECTIBLE ITEMS FROM UNITED STATES** things from or about the United States, especially items that are valued by collectors (*takes a singular or plural verb*) **2. CULTURE OF UNITED STATES** the culture of the United States (*takes a singular verb*)

A·mer·i·can cha·me·leon *n.* = **anole**

A·mer·i·can cheese *n.* a smooth processed cheese with a mild taste similar to cheddar

A·mer·i·can chest·nut *n.* a North American deciduous tree with rough bark that produces catkins and spiny-covered nuts. Almost annihilated by a blight, it is now found chiefly as shoots from old stumps. Latin name: *Castanea dentata.*

A·mer·i·can dream, A·mer·i·can Dream *n.* the idea that everyone in the United States has the chance to achieve success and prosperity regardless of their background

A·mer·i·can ea·gle *n.* = **bald eagle**

A·mer·i·can elm *n.* a North American elm tree with large spreading branches and winged fruits, often grown for shade or ornament. Once characteristic of U.S. streets and lawns, it has largely disappeared because of Dutch elm disease. Latin name: *Ulmus americana.*

A·mer·i·can Eng·lish *n.* the form of English that is spoken in the United States

WORD KEY: WORLD ENGLISH

With a population of over 260 million, the United States is the largest and most influential English-speaking country in the world, and English has been in use within its present borders for over 400 years. American English can be described in terms of three groups: (1) The dialect divisions Northern, Coastal Southern, Midland, and Western; (2) Distinctive urban varieties, as in New York and New Orleans; (3) Vernacular forms such as African American English and Jewish English. Because many (especially immigrant) Americans have at least one language other than English, they may casually mix English with those languages, as in the remark *Sometimes I start a sentence in English y termino en español* ("... and end in Spanish"). Spanish is the most prominent other language, and the hybrid variety *Spanglish* has distinctive forms in New York, Florida, Texas, California, and Puerto Rico. Although English is the administrative language of the nation, is culturally dominant, and is the statutory official language in many states, it is not statutory at the federal level – a situation that has engendered no small controversy.

The history of American English falls into three broad periods: (1) *Colonial* 1607–1776, dominated by British English norms; (2) *National* 1776–1898, exhibiting a vigorous and growing independence that included dictionaries and style guides; and (3) *International* 1898-, marked by a steadily increasing worldwide influence and prestige. American English tends to be nasal and, apart from three areas (eastern New England,

New York City, and the Southern states), it is "rhotic" (*r* is pronounced in words such as art, door, and worker) and "retroflex" (*r* pronounced with the tip of the tongue curled back and raised). The spelling, punctuation, grammar, vocabulary, and idiom of standard American English have been established since the late 19th century; it differs in many ways from British English and other varieties, with the exception of Philippine English, which follows the U.S. model, and Canadian English, which has features of both American English and British English). See ***African American Vernacular English, Canadian English, Hawaiian English, Philippine English.***
Although standard American and British English are similar, there are significant differences in pronunciation, grammar, and vocabulary. With pronunciation, the two Englishes differ chiefly in vowel quality, stress and voice timbre. For example, Americans pronounce the *a* in words such as *ask, grass,* and *path* in a flat short manner, as in *gasoline,* whereas British English speakers use a broad *a,* as in *father,* when saying these words. American English speakers rather clearly articulate certain unaccented syllables, such as *-ary* in *secretary,* whereas British English speakers clip them to yield pronunciations such as *secret'ry.* American English often places stress on the first syllables of certain words, such as *laboratory* and *excess,* whereas British English moves the stress to medial or terminal positions, as in their pronunciations /lə bórrətri/ and /ek séss/. The reverse is also true with words such as *garage,* in which the U.S. stress is on the last syllable, whereas the U.K. stress is on the first syllable. As for spelling, Americans use, for example, *aluminum, center, encyclopedia, color, fulfill,* and *tire* whereas British speakers use *aluminium, centre, encyclopaedia, colour, fulfil,* and *tyre.* In terms of vocabulary, the two Englishes can and do diverge markedly: American English uses *molasses, snow pea, truck stop,* and *zucchini,* while British English uses *treacle, mangetout, transport cafe,* and *courgette* for the same things. By preference or established convention, American English tends to prefer *store, defog, visor,* and *rooster,* while British English prefers *shop, demist, peak* and *cock.* American and British English are also set apart by sets of words sharing elements in common, yet being distinctively different words for the same things. American English speakers say *talk show, fish stick, substitute teacher,* and *moving van,* while speakers of British English say *chat show, fish finger, supply teacher,* and *removal van.* The two Englishes also have sets of words covering the same subject matter, yet not having the same specific meanings. A prime example is the food term *biscuit,* which, in British English, is the equivalent of U.S. *cookie,* while *biscuit* in American English is a small, round, light pastry. Finally, there are words mutually exclusive to each English, based upon historical, socia,l and cultural differences: for example, *inside the Beltway* referring to people, opinions, and issues close to the nation's capital, is U.S. English only, whereas *Questions in the Commons* or *Question Time,* the period when members of the British Parliament may question government ministers, is British English only. Finally, the idiomatic expressions used in both varieties of English can and do differ: *a tempest in a teapot* is American English; *a storm in a teacup* is British English.

A·mer·i·can Falls part of Niagara Falls on the Niagara River on the U.S. side of the boundary with Canada. About two-thirds of the water volume for Niagara Falls passes over American Falls. Height: 182 ft./55 m.

A·mer·i·can foot·ball *n.* = **football**

A·mer·i·can Fork city in northern Utah, beside Utah Lake, southeast of Salt Lake City and northwest of Provo. Population: 19,451 (1996).

A·mer·i·can fox·hound *n.* a small dog bred in the United States, with drooping ears and a smooth black, tan, and white coat. It is smaller than the English foxhound.

A·mer·i·can fries, A·mer·i·can fried po·ta·toes *npl.* boiled potatoes, sliced and pan-fried

A·mer·i·can gothic, A·mer·i·can Goth·ic *adj.* depicting or representing hard work, frugality, and conservative social attitudes associated with rural and small-town United States [Named for a 1930 painting by the Iowan painter Grant Wood (1892–1942), which depicts a dour farm couple and their surroundings]

A·mer·i·can In·di·an *n.* a Native American (*dated*)—**A·mer·i·can In·di·an** *adj.*

A·mer·i·can·ism /ə mérrikənizzəm/ *n.* **1. U.S. EXPRESSION OR FEATURE** a word, phrase, or custom that originated

Corbis-Bettmann

American Gothic (1930) by Grant Wood

in, or is regarded as characteristic of, the United States **2. LOYALTY TO UNITED STATES** strong affection or support for the United States

A·mer·i·can·ist /ə mérrikənist/ *n.* **1. AUTHORITY ON UNITED STATES** an expert on the life, history, language, or culture of the United States **2. SPECIALIST IN NATIVE AMERICAN LANGUAGES** somebody who is a student of or specialist in the languages and cultures of Native Americans

A·mer·i·can·ize /ə mérrikə nīz/ (**-ized, -iz·ing, -iz·es**) *vti.* to give something the form, style, or qualities associated with or used in the United States, or to take on such qualities —**A·mer·i·can·i·za·tion** /ə mèrikə nī záyshən/ *n.*

A·mer·i·can kes·trel *n.* = **sparrow hawk** *n.* 2

A·mer·i·can Le·gion *n.* an organization of veterans of the U.S. armed services, founded in 1919

A·mer·i·can pit bull ter·ri·er *n.* = **pit bull terrier**

A·mer·i·can plan *n.* a pricing system used in hotels and resorts in which there is a fixed per-day charge for room and meals

A·mer·i·can Re·vised Ver·sion *n.* = **American Standard Version**

A·mer·i·can Rev·o·lu·tion *n.* the war in which the American colonies won independence from Great Britain (1775–83)

A·mer·i·can sad·dle horse *n.* a high-stepping saddle horse, originally bred in Kentucky and trained to walk, trot, canter, gallop, and pace

A·me·ri·can Sa·mo·a U.S. territory, consisting of a group of South Pacific islands, in the Samoan island chain. Pago Pago is the seat of government. Population: 59,566 (1996). Area: 77 sq. mi./200 sq. km.

A·mer·i·can short·hair *n.* a domestic cat belonging to a breed with a broad head and short thick coat

A·mer·i·can Sign Lan·guage *n.* a system of communication used by people with impaired hearing that uses signs made with the hands

A·mer·i·can Staf·ford·shire ter·ri·er *n.* = **pit bull terrier**

A·mer·i·can Stan·dard Code for In·for·ma·tion In·ter·change *n.* COMPUT full form of **ASCII**

A·mer·i·can Stan·dard Ver·sion *n.* a United States revision of the King James Bible, published in 1901

A·mer·i·can War of In·de·pend·ence *n.* = **American Revolution**

A·mer·i·can wa·ter span·iel *n.* a dog with a tightly curled brown coat belonging to a breed used for hunting. The dog is an excellent swimmer and uses its tail as a rudder.

A·mer·i·cas /ə mérrikəz/ = **America** 2

am·er·i·ci·um /àmə rísshiəm/ *n.* a white radioactive metallic chemical element used as a source of alpha particles to make other artificial radioactive elements. Symbol **Am** [Mid-20thC. Named for *America,* where it was first produced.]

A·me·ri·cus /ə mérrikəss/ city southeast of Columbus, in southwestern Georgia. It is an agricultural trading center. Population: 16,606 (1996).

A·mer·ind /ámə rìnd/ *n.* a proposed grouping of languages, defined by some linguists as all those that were spoken in the Americas before the arrival of Europeans, except the Eskimo-Aleut and Na-Dené families

Am·er·in·di·an /àmə ríndiən/ *n., adj.* a Native American (*dated*) [Late 19thC. A blend of AMERICAN and INDIAN.] —**Am·er·in·dic** /àmə ríndik/ *adj.*

Ames /aymz/ city in central Iowa, home to Iowa State University of Science and Technology. Population: 47,698 (1996).

ames·ace *n.* = **ambsace**

Am·es·lan /ámmə slàn/ *n.* = **American Sign Language** [Late 20thC. Acronym.]

Ames test /áymz-/ *n.* a test used to determine the cancer-causing potential of a chemical or other agent by measuring its effect on bacteria [Late 20thC. Named for the U.S. biochemist Bruce N. *Ames* (born 1928), who developed it.]

am·e·thop·ter·in /àmmi thóptərin/ *n.* = **methotrexate**

am·e·thyst /ámməthəst/ *n.* **1.** MINERALS **VIOLET QUARTZ GEMSTONE** a translucent violet variety of quartz used as a gemstone **2.** MINERALS **PURPLE GEMSTONE** a purple variety of corundum used as a gemstone **3.** COLORS **BLUISH-PURPLE** a bluish-purple color ■ *adj.* **1.** MINERALS **OF AMETHYST** made of or containing amethyst **2.** COLORS **OF BLUISH-PURPLE COLOR** of a bluish-purple color [13thC. Via Old French and Latin, from Greek *amethustos,* literally "not intoxicating," from, ultimately, *methu* "wine" (source of English *methyl*). From the belief that it prevented drunkenness.] —**am·e·thys·tine** /àmə thíst īn/ *adj.*

am·e·tro·pi·a /àmi trṓpiə/ *n.* a condition such as myopia or astigmatism in which a refractive error prevents the eye from focusing light on the retina [Mid-19thC. Coined from Greek *ametros* "irregular," literally "without measure" (formed from *metron* "measure") + -OPIA.] —**am·e·trop·ic** /àmi tráapik/ *adj.*

Amex /ámmeks/, **AMEX** *abbr.* American Stock Exchange

Am·har·ic /am hárrik/ *n.* the official language of Ethiopia, belonging to the Semitic branch of Afro-Asiatic languages. Amharic is written in Ethiopic script. It has nearly 15 million native speakers, with as many more speaking it as a second language. [Early 19thC. Formed from *Amhara,* the name of a province in northwestern Ethiopia.] —**Am·har·ic** *adj.*

Am·herst /ám ərst/ **1.** city north of Springfield, in southwestern Massachusetts. It is home to Amherst College and the University of Massachusetts. Population: 35,468 (1996). **2.** city west of Cleveland, near Lake Erie, in northern Ohio. Population: 11,311 (1996).

Am·herst /ám hùrst/, **Jeffrey, Baron** (1717–97) British colonial North American administrator. He was governor-general of the British-held American territories (1760–63).

a·mi·a·ble /áymiəb'l/ *adj.* **1. FRIENDLY AND PLEASANT** friendly and pleasant to be with **2. WITH FRIENDLY FEELINGS** characterized by friendly feelings [14thC. Via French, from late Latin, *amicabilis* "AMICABLE," influenced in meaning by French *aimable* "lovable" (from Latin *amabilis,* from *amare* "to love").] —**a·mi·a·bil·i·ty** /àymiə bíllətee/ *n.* —**a·mi·a·ble·ness** /áymiəb'lnəss/ *n.* —**a·mi·a·bly** *adv.*

am·i·an·thus /àmee ánthəss/ *n.* a type of asbestos with thin silky fibers [Early 17thC. Via Latin, from Greek *amiantos,* literally "undefiled," from *miainein* "to defile."]

am·i·ca·ble /ámmikəb'l/ *adj.* characterized by or done in friendliness, without anger or bad feelings ○ *an amicable divorce* [15thC. From late Latin *amicabilis,* from Latin *amicus* "friend" (source also of English *enemy*), from *amare* "to love."] —**am·i·ca·bil·i·ty** /àmikə bíllətee/ *n.* —**am·i·ca·ble·ness** /ámmikəb'lnəss/ *n.* —**am·i·ca·bly** *adv.*

am·ice /ámmiss/ *n.* a length of white fabric worn by a Christian priest around the neck and shoulders [13thC. Origin uncertain: probably via Old French *amit* from Latin *amictus* "cloak," from *amicire* "to cover," from *iacere* "to throw."]

am·i·cus cu·ri·ae /ə meékəss kyṓoree ée/ (*plural* **am·i·ci cu·ri·ae** /-kī-/), **a·mi·cus** (*plural* **-ci**) *n.* somebody who is not a party to a legal case but whose counsel provides information to the court on the legal issues involved [Early 17thC. From modern Latin, literally "friend of the court."]

a·mid /ə míd/, **a·midst** /ə mídst/ *prep.* **1. WITHIN OR AMONG** surrounded by things or people ○ *a small lake amid the hills* **2. WHILE SOMETHING IS HAPPENING** used to indicate the circumstances or events around or accompanying something ○ *I sat down amid roars of laughter.* [12thC. Formed from an earlier form of MIDDLE.]

am·ide /á mìd, ámmid/ *n.* **1. INORGANIC DERIVATIVE OF AMMONIA** any inorganic compound derived from ammonia and containing the NH_2 ion **2. ORGANIC DERIVATIVE OF AMMONIA** any organic compound derived from ammonia, formed by the replacement of one or more hydrogen atoms with acyl groups [Mid-19thC. Formed from AMMONIA.] —**a·mid·ic** /ə míddik/ *adj.*

am·i·dol /ámmi daal/ *n.* a colorless, water-soluble, crystalline compound used as a photographic developer. Formula: $C_6H_8N_2O·2HCL$. [Late 19thC. From German, a trademark.]

a·mid·ships /ə mídships/, **a·mid·ship** *adv., adj.* near or in the middle of a boat or ship

a·midst *prep.* = **amid**

a·mi·go /ə meégō/ (*plural* **-gos**) *n.* a friend (*used especially in Spanish-speaking regions*) [Mid-19thC. Via Spanish, from Latin *amicus* "friend."]

Idi Amin

A·min /aa meén/, **Idi** (*b.* 1925) Ugandan politician. Under his presidency (1971–79), approximately 70,000 Asians were expelled from Uganda, and up to 300,000 Ugandans were killed.

a·mine /ə meén, á meen/ *n.* any organic derivative of ammonia formed by the replacement of hydrogen with one or more alkyl groups [Mid-19thC. Formed from AMMONIA.]

-amine *suffix.* amine ○ *tryptamine* [From AMINE]

a·mi·no /ə meénō/ *adj.* used to describe a chemical compound containing the NH_2 group of atoms

amino- *prefix.* containing a NH_2 group combined with a nonacid radical ○ *aminophenol* [Formed from AMINE]

a·mi·no ac·id *n.* an organic acid containing one or more amino groups, especially any of a group that make up proteins and are important to living cells. Some can be synthesized by the body (**nonessential amino acids**) and others must be obtained through the diet (**essential amino acids**).

a·mi·no·ben·zo·ic ac·id /ə meénō ben zṓ ik ássid/ *n.* any of three crystalline solids derived from benzoic acid, especially para-aminobenzoic acid, which is used in sunscreen lotions. Formula: $C_7H_7NO_2$.

a·mi·no·pep·ti·dase /ə meénō péptə dayss/ *n.* an enzyme bound to the lining of the small intestine, where it breaks down dietary peptides into amino acids

a·mi·no·phe·nol /ə meénō feénaal/ *n.* any of three white soluble organic compounds used in dyes and photographic developers. Formula: C_6H_7NO.

a·mir *n.* = **emir**

A·mish /áamish/ *npl.* MEMBERS OF U.S. PROTESTANT GROUP members of a Protestant group who migrated from Europe to the United States and Canada in the 18th century. The Amish seek to maintain a traditional rural way of life. ■ *adj.* OF THE AMISH relating to or typical of the Amish people or their culture [Late 19thC. Origin uncertain: probably from German *amisch.* Named for Jacob *Ammann* or *Amen,* a 17thC Swiss Mennonite preacher.]

a·miss /ə míss/ *adv.* INCORRECTLY incorrectly or inappropriately ○ *Things began to go amiss after she left.* ■ *adj.* WRONG incorrect, inappropriate, or not as it should be ○ *We knew immediately from the disorder in the house that something was amiss.* [13thC. From Old Norse *á mis,* literally "so as to miss."] ◇ **take something amiss** to be upset or offended by something, even though no offense was intended

a·mi·to·sis /áymī tṓssiss/ *n.* cell division by simple division of the nucleus and cytoplasm, without the appearance of chromosomes [Late 19thC. Formed from MITOSIS.] —**a·mi·tot·ic** /-táwtik/ *adj.*

am·i·trip·tyl·ine /àmi tríptə leen/ *n.* an antidepressant drug with sedative effects, also used to treat chronic pain

am·i·ty /ámmətee/ *n.* friendliness and peaceful relations (*formal*) [15thC. Via French *amitié* from medieval Latin *amicitas,* from Latin *amicus* "friend" (see AMICABLE).]

Am·man /aa maán/ capital of the Hashemite Kingdom of Jordan, in the northwestern part of the country, northeast of the Dead Sea. Population: 1,000,000 (1994).

am·me·ter /ámm eètər/ *n.* an instrument used for measuring electric current in amperes [Late 19thC. Coined from AMPERE + -METER.]

am·mine /ámm een/ *n.* a chemical compound containing one or more ammonia molecules attached to a salt or similar compound through coordinate bonds [Late 19thC. Formed from AMMONIA.]

am·mo /ámmō/ *n.* ammunition (*informal*) [Early 20thC. Shortening.]

am·mo·coete /ámmə seèt/, **am·mo·cete** *n.* the filter-feeding larva of the lamprey [Mid-19thC. From modern Latin *Ammocoetes,* genus name originally given to the larva, from Greek *ammos* "sand" + *koitē* "bed."]

am·mo·nate /ámmənàyt/ *n.* = **ammine**

am·mo·nia /ə mṓnyə/ *n.* 1. PUNGENT GAS a colorless gas with a pungent odor that is highly soluble in water. It is used in refrigeration and in the manufacture of fertilizers, explosives, plastics, and other chemicals. Formula: NH_3. 2. AMMONIA SOLUTION a solution of ammonia in water, used as a household cleaner and in the manufacture of a wide range of products including fertilizers and textiles [Late 18thC. From modern Latin, from Latin *sal ammoniacus,* literally "salt of Ammon," from, ultimately, Greek *Ammōn* "Ammon," an Egyptian god near whose temple ammonia and ammoniac were said to be obtained.]

am·mo·ni·ac /ə mṓnee àk/ *n.* a strong-smelling brownish yellow gum resin obtained from an Asian plant of the carrot family, used in medicine and as a porcelain cement. = **ammoniacal** [14thC. Via French from, ultimately, Latin *ammoniacus* (see AMMONIA).]

am·mo·ni·a·cal /ámmə nī́ ək'l/, **am·mo·ni·ac** /əmṓnee ak/ *adj.* containing or resembling ammonia

am·mo·ni·ate /ə mṓnee àyt/ (**-at·ed, -at·ing, -ates**) *vt.* to treat or combine something with ammonia or an ammonia compound —**am·mo·ni·a·tion** /ə m-nee áyshən/ *n.*

am·mo·nia wa·ter *n.* = **ammonia** *n.* 2

am·mon·i·fi·ca·tion /ə maánəfə káyshən/ *n.* 1. TREATING OR MIXING WITH AMMONIA the treatment with ammonia or the combination of something with ammonia 2. FORMATION OF AMMONIA the formation of ammonia or ammonia compounds through the bacterial decomposition of organic compounds

am·mon·i·fy /ə maánə f-/ (**-fied, -fy·ing, -fies**) *vti.* to treat something with ammonia or to undergo ammonification —**am·mon·i·fi·er** *n.*

am·mo·nite[1] /ámmə nìt/ *n.* 1. EXTINCT SEA ANIMAL an extinct marine mollusk with a flat partitioned spiral shell 2. FOSSILIZED AMMONITE SHELL the fossilized shell of an ammonite [Mid-18thC. From modern Latin *ammonites,* from medieval Latin *cornu Ammonis,* literally "horn of Ammon." From its resemblance to ram's horns, which characterize representations of the Egyptian god Ammon.] —**am·mo·nit·ic** /àmə níttik/ *adj.*

am·mo·nite[2] /ámmənìt/ *n.* 1. FERTILIZER a mixture of dried animal wastes, used as a fertilizer 2. EXPLOSIVE an explosive consisting of ammonium nitrate and TNT [Mid-20thC. Coined from AMMONIUM + NITRATE.]

Am·mon·ite /ámmə nìt/ *n.* a member of an ancient Semitic people in the Bible who lived between the Syrian desert and the Jordan River from the 13th to the 6th centuries B.C. They were constant enemies of the Israelites. [Mid-16thC. From late Latin, from Hebrew *'Ammōn* "Ammon (son of Lot)."]

am·mo·ni·um /ə mṓneeəm/ *n.* relating to or containing the NH_4+ ion derived from ammonia [Early 19thC. Formed from AMMONIA.]

am·mo·ni·um bi·car·bon·ate *n.* a white crystalline solid that is used in baking powder. Formula: NH_4HCO_3.

am·mo·ni·um car·bon·ate *n.* a white crystalline solid that is used in smelling salts, baking powder, and dyeing. Formula: $(NH_4)_2CO_3$.

am·mo·ni·um chlo·ride *n.* a white crystalline solid that is used as a soldering flux, in dry batteries, and in medicine as an expectorant. Formula: NH_4Cl.

am·mo·ni·um hy·drox·ide *n.* a solution of ammonia in water

am·mo·ni·um ni·trate *n.* a colorless crystalline solid that is used as a fertilizer and in herbicides, insecticides, and explosives. Formula: NH_4NO_3.

am·mo·ni·um sul·fate *n.* a colorless crystalline solid that is used in fertilizers and to purify water. Formula: $(NH_4)_2SO_4$.

am·mo·noid /ámmə nòyd/ *n.* = **ammonite**[1] *n.* 1 [Mid-19thC. From modern Latin *Ammonoidea,* order name, which was formed from *ammonites* "ammonite."]

Am·mons /ámmənz/, **Archie Randolph** (*b.* 1926) U.S. poet, an important exponent of the tradition of transcendentalism in U.S. poetry.

am·mu·ni·tion /àmyə nísh'n/ *n.* 1. BULLETS AND MISSILES bullets, shells, missiles, and other projectiles used as weapons 2. EXPLOSIVE MATERIAL bombs, grenades, and other explosive devices or substances used as weapons 3. SUPPORTING FACTS facts and information that can be used to support a point of view in an argument [Late 16thC. From French, an alteration (due to mistaking "la munition" for "l'amunition") of *munition* (see MUNITION).]

am·ne·sia /am neézhə/ *n.* loss of memory as a result of shock, injury, psychological disturbance, or medical disorder [Late 18thC. From Greek *amnēsia,* an alteration of *amnēstia* "forgetfulness," from *amnēstos,* literally "not remembered," from *mnasthai* "to remember."] —**am·ne·si·ac** /am neézee àk/ *n., adj.* —**am·nes·tic** /-néstik/ *adj.*

am·nes·ty /ámnəstee/ *n.* (*plural* **-ties**) 1. PARDON a general pardon, especially for those who have committed political crimes 2. PROSECUTION-FREE PERIOD a period during which crimes can be admitted or illegal weapons handed in without prosecution ■ *vt.* (**-tied, -ty·ing, -ties**) PARDON SOMEBODY to grant amnesty to somebody [Late 16thC. Via French from, ultimately, Greek *amnēstia* (see AMNESIA). The underlying idea is of forgetting a wrongdoing.]

am·ni·a plural of **amnion**

am·ni·o /amneeō/ (*plural* **-os**) *n.* an amniocentesis (*informal*) [Late 20thC. Shortening.]

am·ni·o·cen·te·sis /àmneeō ssen teéssiss/ (*plural* **-ses**) *n.* a test performed to determine the health, sex, or genetic constitution of a fetus by taking a sample of amniotic fluid through a needle inserted into the womb of the mother [Mid-20thC. Coined from AMNION + Greek *kentēsis* "pricking" (from *kentein* "to prick").]

am·ni·og·ra·phy /àmnee aágrəfee/ *n.* an X-ray of the womb, taken after a substance that will be shown up by the X-rays has been injected into the bloodstream [Mid-20thC. Coined from AMNION + -GRAPHY.]

am·ni·on /ámnee aan/ (*plural* **-ons** *or* **-a** /-ə/) *n.* 1. INNER MEMBRANE SURROUNDING EMBRYO the inner of the two membranes enclosing the embryo of a bird, reptile, or mammal and its surrounding fluid. ◊ **chorion** 2. EMBRYO SAC the fluid-filled sac within which the embryo of a bird, reptile, or mammal develops [Mid-17thC. From Greek, "caul," literally "a small lamb," from *amnos* "lamb."] —**am·ni·ot·ic** /àmnee aátik/ *adj.*

am·ni·ote /ámneeōt/ *n.* any vertebrate that develops from an embryo within an amnion, e.g., a bird, reptile, or mammal [Early 20thC. From modern Latin *Amniota,* from AMNION.]

am·ni·ot·ic flu·id /àmnee ottik-/ *n.* the fluid that surrounds a fetus while it is developing. It is the fluid that flows out in the "breaking of the water" before a baby is born.

am·ni·ot·ic sac *n.* = **amnion** *n.* 2

am·o·bar·bi·tal /àmō baárbi tal/ *n.* a colorless crystalline barbiturate used as a sedative and hypnotic [Mid-20thC. Coined from AMYL + BARBITAL.]

a·moe·ba /ə meébə/ (*plural* **-bas** *or* **-bae** /ə meébee/), **a·me·ba** (*plural* **-bas** *or* **-bae** /-bee/) *n.* a single-celled organism found in water and in damp soil on land, and as a parasite of other organisms. Lacking a fixed form and supporting structures, an amoeba consists of a protoplasmic mass in a thin membrane, and forms temporary projections (**pseudopodia**) in order to move. Genus: *Amoeba.* [Mid-19thC. Via modern Latin, genus name, from Greek *amoibē* "change," from *ameibein* "to change." From its changing shape.] —**a·moe·bic** *adj.*

am·oe·bi·a·sis *n.* = **amebiasis**

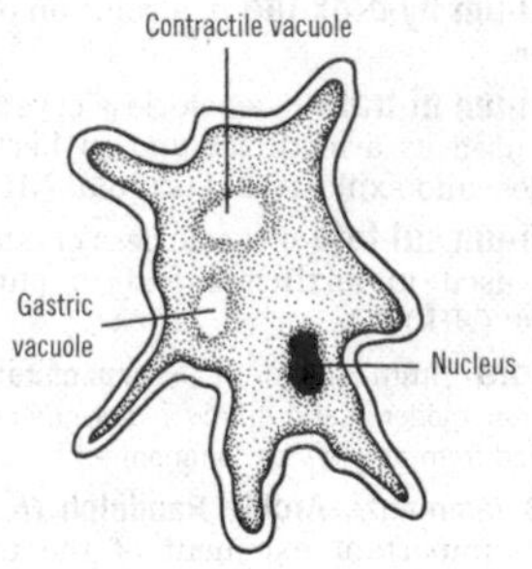

Amoeba

a·moe·bic dys·en·ter·y *n.* = **amebic dysentery**

a·moe·bo·cyte /ə mēebə ss-t/, **a·me·bo·cyte** *n.* a cell that moves like an amoeba, e.g., a blood cell that can engulf particles

a·moe·boid /ə mēe bòyd/, **a·me·boid** *adj.* resembling an amoeba, especially in the manner of moving

a·mok /ə múk, ə mók/, **a·muck** /ə múk/ *adj.* **OUT OF CONTROL** frenzied and out of control ■ *adv.* **1. OUT OF CONTROL** in a very frenzied way ○ *rioters running amok* **2. CONFUSEDLY** in or into a confused or disorganised state [Early 16thC. Directly or via Portuguese *am(o)uco* "homicidally violent Malay" from Malay *amuk* "fighting frenziedly."]

a·mo·le /ə mṓ lay/ *n.* **1. PLANT PART USED AS SOAP** the root or other part of certain North American plants, used as a substitute for soap **2.** (*plural* **-les** *or* **-le**) **PLANT YIELDING SOAP SUBSTITUTE** a plant of which the roots or other parts can be used as a substitute for soap. Agave and yucca are amoles. [Mid-19thC. Via Mexican Spanish from Nahuatl *ahmōlli* "soap."]

a·mong /ə múng/, **a·mongst** /-múngst/ CORE MEANING: a preposition indicating that something or somebody is surrounded by people, things, ideas, or circumstances ○ *You're among friends here.*
prep. **1. OF A GROUP** of the stated group or class ○ *Her carvings are among the world's finest.* **2. IN A GROUP** in or by the particular group stated ○ *a widely-held notion among physicists* **3. BETWEEN GROUP MEMBERS** by, between, or to each person or thing in a group ○ *divided among six of us* **4. IN ADDITION TO** in addition to other things or people ○ *The photos showed, among other things, a birthday party.* [Old English *on (ge)mong*, from *on* "in" + *(ge)mong* "crowd." Ultimately from an Indo-European word that is also the ancestor of English *mingle* and *mongrel*.]

a·mon·til·la·do /ə màantə làadō/ (*plural* **-dos**) *n.* a pale medium-dry sherry from Spain [Early 19thC. From Spanish. Named for the Spanish town *Montilla*, where sherry of this type is made.]

a·mor·al /ay máwrəl/ *adj.* **1. OUTSIDE SCOPE OF MORALITY** not concerned with or amenable to moral judgments **2. WITHOUT MORAL STANDARDS** not caring about good behavior or morals —**a·mor·al·ism** *n.* —**a·mor·al·i·ty** /ày mə rállətee/ *n.* —**a·mor·al·ly** /ay mórəlee/ *adv.*

WORD KEY: USAGE

See Usage note at ***immoral.***

am·o·ret·to /àmə réttō/ (*plural* **-ti** /-réttee/) *n.* an artistic representation of a small naked boy or winged cherub as a symbol of love [Early 17thC. From Italian, literally "a small cupid," from *amore* "love," from Latin *amor* (see AMOROUS).]

am·o·rist /ámmərist/ *n.* somebody who writes about love or who is in love (*literary*) [Late 16thC. Formed from French *amour* "love" or Latin *amor* (see AMOROUS).]

Am·o·rite /ámmə r-t/ *n.* **MEMBER OF SEMITIC PEOPLE IN BIBLE** a member of an ancient Semitic people in the Bible who lived in Mesopotamia, Syria, and Palestine between approximately 2,600 and 1,200 B.C. ■ *adj.* **OF THE AMORITE PEOPLE** relating to or typical of the Amorite people or their culture [Mid-16thC. Formed from Hebrew *&csq;ĕmōrī*, from, ultimately, Akkadian *Amurru(m)*, literally "West," the name of the land inhabited by the Amorites.]

am·o·rous /ámmərəss/ *adj.* showing or feeling romantic love or sexual attraction [14thC. Via Old French, from medieval Latin *amorosus*, from Latin *amor* "love" (source of English *amateur*).] —**am·or·ous·ly** *adv.* —**am·or·ous·ness** *n.*

a·mor·phism /ə máwr fìzzəm/ *n.* **1. LACK OF SHAPE OR FORM** the lack of shape, form, structure, or classifying features **2.** CHEM, GEOL **LACK OF CRYSTALLINE STRUCTURE** the absence of crystalline structure, e.g., in mineral or chemical compounds or rocks

a·mor·phous /ə máwrfəss/ *adj.* **1. WITHOUT SHAPE** without any clear shape, form, or structure **2. NOT CLASSIFIABLE** not obviously belonging to any particular category or type **3.** CHEM, GEOL **WITHOUT CRYSTALLINE STRUCTURE** without a crystalline structure [Mid-18thC. Via modern Latin, from Greek *amorphos*, literally "without shape," from *morphē* "shape."] —**a·mor·phous·ly** *adv.* —**a·mor·phous·ness** *n.*

am·or·ti·za·tion /àmərtə záysh'n/ *n.* the reduction of a debt by making payments in installments or regular transfers, or the money used for this. ◊ **amortize** *v.* 2

am·or·tize /ámmər t-z/ (**-tized, -tiz·ing, -tiz·es**) *vt.* **1. REDUCE DEBT BY INSTALLMENTS** to reduce a debt by making payments against the principal balance in installments or regular transfers **2. WRITE OFF COST OF ASSET** to write off the cost of an asset over a period of time in a statement of accounts **3. TRANSFER PROPERTY** to transfer land or other assets to an ecclesiastical body (*archaic*) [14thC. Via the French stem *amortiss-* "to alienate in mortmain" from assumed Vulgar Latin *admortire* "to deaden," from the Latin stem *mort-* "death."] —**am·or·tiz·a·ble** *adj.*

A·mos /áymass/ **HEBREW PROPHET** a Hebrew prophet in the Bible who lived in the 8th century B.C. and delivered judgments against Judah, Samaria, and Israel ■ *n.* **BOOK IN BIBLE** a book of the Bible that contains the prophecies of Amos. See table at **Bible**

a·mount /ə mównt/ (**a·mount·ed, a·mount·ing, a·mounts**) *n.* a quantity or degree of something, considered as a unit or total [14thC. From Old French *amonter* "to rise," from *amont* "upward," from Latin *ad montem*, literally "to the mountain."]

WORD KEY: USAGE

amount or **number**? ***Amount*** is normally used with singular forms of words or meanings that have no plural, that is, so-called uncountable or mass nouns such as *coal, happiness,* and *warfare,* whereas ***number*** is used with plural nouns such as *books, questions,* and *ships. a large amount of coal. any amount of happiness. a large number of books. a good number of cheeses (= types of cheese). an excessive number of questions.* In everyday speech, ***amount*** is sometimes used when ***number*** is strictly called for: *a large amount of books.* This should be avoided in formal speaking and writing.

amount to *vi.* **1. ADD UP TO** to come to a particular total when added up **2. BE EQUIVALENT TO** to be equivalent to something ○ *Their statement amounts to nothing more than a slick evasion.*

a·mour /ə mŏŏr/ *n.* a love affair, especially one that is clandestine (*dated*) [14thC. Via French, from Latin *amor* "love."]

a·mour-pro·pre /àmŏŏr prŏprə/ *n.* self-respect or estimation of your true worth (*formal*) [Late 18thC. From French, literally "self-love."]

A·moy /ə móy/ *n.* the dialect of Chinese spoken on the island of Xiamen and in neighboring areas in southeastern China [Mid-19thC. Named for *Amoy* (XIAMEN).]

amp /amp/ *n.* **1. AMPERE** an ampere **2. AMPLIFIER** an amplifier (*informal*) [Late 19thC. Shortening.]

AMP *n.* a chemical compound (**nucleotide**) occurring in living organisms that is formed from another nucleotide, ATP, and affects the function of genes and enzymes. Full form **adenosine monophosphate.** ◊ **cyclic AMP**

am·per·age /ámpərij/ *n.* the number of amperes measured in an electric current

am·pere /ámpir/ *n.* the basic unit of electric current in the SI system, equal to a current that produces a force of $2x10^{-7}$ newtons per meter between two parallel conductors in a vacuum. Symbol **A** [Late 19thC. Named for the French physicist André-Marie *Ampère* (1775–1836), who first distinguished between electrical current and voltage.]

am·pere-hour *n.* a measure of quantity of electricity equal to the amount of electricity that passes in one hour through a conductor with a current of one ampere

am·per·sand /ámpər sànd/ *n.* the symbol "&," meaning "and" [Mid-19thC. From *and per se and*, literally "(the character) "&" by itself (means) and." The character "&" itself is a conventionalized printed version of an abbreviation used for Latin *et* "and."]

am·phet·a·mine /am féttə meen/ *n.* a white crystalline compound, or any of its derivatives, formerly used as a stimulant of the central nervous system to treat conditions such as depression, and as an appetite suppressant. Excessive use of amphetamines can cause dangerous side effects and dependency. [Mid-20thC. Contraction of *alpha-methylphenethylamine*.]

amphi- *prefix.* both ○ *amphibious* [Via Latin from, ultimately, Greek *amphi* "on both sides." Ultimately from an Indo-European base that is also the ancestor of English *by, umlaut,* and *ambi-*.]

am·phi·ar·thro·sis /àm fee aar thróssiss/ (*plural* **-ses** /-sseez/) *n.* a joint that permits only a small amount of movement, such as a joint between vertebrae

am·phib·i·an /am fíbbeeən/ *n.* **1. LAND ANIMAL THAT BREEDS IN WATER** a cold-blooded vertebrate that spends some time on land but must breed and develop into an adult in water. Frogs, salamanders, and toads are amphibians. Class: Amphibia. **2. AIRCRAFT OR VEHICLE** an aircraft or vehicle designed to operate on land or water [Mid-19thC. Formed from modern Latin *Amphibia*, class name, from Greek *amphibion* "amphibious being," from *amphibios* (see AMPHIBIOUS).] —**am·phib·i·an** *adj.*

am·phib·i·ous /am fíbbeeəss/ *adj.* **1. LIVING ON LAND AND IN WATER** used to describe an animal that lives in water during early development and on land as an adult **2. ON LAND AND IN WATER** taking place or operating both on land and in water ○ *made an amphibious assault on the island* ○ *amphibious vehicles* **3. OF MIXED TYPE** with two different qualities or features resulting in a mixed type [Mid-17thC. From Greek *amphibios*, literally "living on both (land and water)," from *bios* "life" (source of English *biology*).] —**am·phib·i·ous·ly** *adv.* —**am·phib·i·ous·ness** *n.*

am·phi·bole /ámfə bōl/ *n.* a hydrous silicate mineral containing aluminum, calcium, iron, magnesium, and sodium, singly or in combination. Hornblende, tremolite, and asbestos are amphiboles. [Early 19thC. From French, ultimately from Greek *amphibolos* "ambiguous," literally "throwing in both directions," from *ballein* "to throw"; because the mineral is able to appear in a variety of forms.] —**am·phi·bol·ic** /àmfə bóllik/ *adj.*

am·phib·o·lite /am fíbbə līt/ *n.* a metamorphic rock consisting mainly of amphibole with some plagioclase

am·phib·ol·o·gy /àmfə bólləjee/ (*plural* **-gies**), **am·phib·o·ly** /am fíbbəlee/ (*plural* **-lies**) *n.* a phrase or sentence that can be interpreted in two ways, usually because of the grammatical construction rather than the meanings of the words themselves. The phrase "the boy on the chair with a broken leg" is an amphibology. [Late 16thC. From late Latin *amphibologia* "ambiguity," coined from Latin *amphibolia* + Greek *-logia* "speech."] —**am·phib·o·log·i·cal** /àm fibbə lójjik'l/ *adj.* —**am·phib·o·log·i·cal·ly** *adv.* —**am·phib·o·lous** /am fíbbələss/ *adj.*

am·phi·brach /ámfə bràk/ *n.* a metrical foot of three syllables with the stress on the second syllable, or of one long syllable between two short syllables. The word "contentment" and the phrase "a mushroom" are amphibrachs. [Late 16thC. Via Latin *amphibrachys* from Greek *amphibrakhus* "short on both sides," from *brakhus* "short."] —**am·phi·brach·ic** /àmfə brákik/ *adj.*

am·phic·ty·on /am fíktee ən, -òn/ *n.* a representative of an ancient Greek state or community at the council of a religious alliance (**amphictyony**) [Late 16thC. From Greek *amphiktuones*, originally *amphiktiones* "nearby dwellers," from *ktizein* "to settle, found."]

am·phic·ty·o·ny /am fíktee ənee/ (*plural* **-nies**) *n.* a group of neighboring states or communities in ancient Greece that shared responsibility for shrines and temples. The amphictyony maintaining the shrine of Apollo at Delphi is a famous example. —**am·phic·ty·on·ic** /am fiktee ónnik/ *adj.*

am·phi·go·ry /ámfə gàwree, am fíggəree/ (*plural* **-ries**), **am·phi·gou·ri** /àmfə goo rée/ (*plural* **-ris**) *n.* a nonsensical piece of writing, usually in verse [Early 19thC. From French *amphigouri*, probably coined from Greek *amphi-* "all around" and, perhaps, French *allégorie* "allegory."]

am·phim·a·cer /am fímməssər, ámfə màyssər/ *n.* a metrical foot of three syllables with the stress on the first and third syllables, or of one short syllable between two long syllables. The phrase "happy days" is an amphimacer. [Late 16thC. Via Latin, from Greek *amphimakros* "long on both sides," from *makros* "long."]

am·phi·mix·is /àmfə míksiss/ *n.* sexual reproduction involving the fusion of reproductive cells (**gametes**) from two organisms [Late 19thC. From modern Latin, coined from Greek *amphi-* "on both sides" + *mixis* "mingling," from *mignunai* "to mix."] —**am·phi·mic·tic** *adj.*

am·phi·ox·us /àmfee óksəss/ (*plural* **-i** /-ók sī/ *or* **-us·es**) *n.* = **lancelet** [Mid-19thC. From modern Latin, literally "sharp at both sides," from Greek *amphi-* "at both sides" + *oxus* "sharp" (source of English *oxygen*).]

am·phi·pod /ámfə pòd/ *n.* a small freshwater or marine crustacean with a thin body and without a carapace. Beach fleas are amphipods. Order: Amphipoda. [Mid-19thC. Formed from modern Latin *Amphipoda,* order name, from Greek *amphi-* "both" + *pous* "foot," because there are two types of feet in this order.] —**am·phi·po·dous** /am fíppədəss/ *adj.*

am·phip·ro·style /àmfə prṓ st-l/ *n.* a classical temple or other building with a set of columns at each end but not at the sides [Early 18thC. Via French and Latin, from Greek *amphiprostulos* "with pillars at both ends," from *prostulos* "having pillars" (see PROSTYLE).]

am·phis·bae·na /àmfiss beénə/ (*plural* **-nae** /-nee/ *or* **-nas**) *n.* **1. LIZARD WITHOUT LEGS** a legless lizard usually found in tropical America with a rounded tail resembling a second head. Family: Amphisbaenidae. **2. MYTHOLOGICAL SERPENT** in classical mythology, a poisonous snake that has a head at each end of its body, allowing it to move in either direction [14thC. Via Latin, from Greek *amphisbaina,* literally "going both ways," from *amphis* "both ways" + *bainein* "to go."] —**am·phis·bae·nic** *adj.*

am·phi·sty·lar /àmfə stílər/ *adj.* used to describe a building, especially a classical temple, that has a set of columns on both ends or sides [19thC. Formed from AMPHI- + Greek *stulos* "column."]

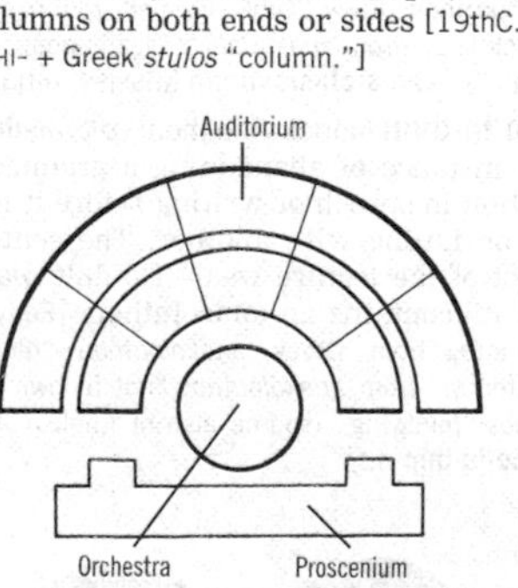

Amphitheater

am·phi·the·a·ter /àmfə theé ətər/ *n.* **1.** ARCHIT **CIRCULAR BUILDING** a round or oval building without a roof that has a central open space surrounded by tiers of seats, especially one used by the ancient Romans for public entertainments **2.** SPORT **PLACE FOR SPORTS** a large enclosure where sporting activities or public entertainments take place **3.** GEOL **ROUND HOLLOW IN LAND** a circular area of level ground surrounded by hills or rising ground, usually a natural feature of the landscape **4. SEATING FOR SPECTATORS** a gallery of seats arranged in semicircular tiers for the audience in a theater or lecture room **5. LECTURE ROOM** a lecture hall or operating room where seating is arranged in semicircular tiers [Mid-14thC. Via Latin, from Greek *amphitheatron* , literally "theater on both sides" (because the typical classical Greek theater had seating on one side only), from *theatron* "theater" (see THEATER).] —**am·phi·the·at·ric** /àmfə thee áttrik/ *adj.* —**am·phi·the·at·ri·cal·ly** *adv.*

am·phi·the·a·tre *n.* U.K. = **amphitheater**

am·pho·ra /ámfərə/ (*plural* **-rae** /-ree/ *or* **-ras**) *n.* a jar, usually made of clay, with a narrow neck and two handles, used by ancient Greeks and Romans for holding oil or wine [15thC. Via Latin from, ultimately, Greek *amphiphoreus,* from *amphi-* "on both sides" + *phoreus* "bearer," from *pherein* "to bear"; from its two handles.] —**am·pho·ral** *adj.*

am·pho·ter·ic /àmfə térrik/ *adj.* able to react chemically as either an acid or a base [Mid-19thC. Formed from Greek *amphoteroi* "both of two," the comparative form of *amphō* "both."]

Amphora

amp hr *abbr.* ampere-hour

am·pi·cil·lin /àmpə síllin/ *n.* a semisynthetic form of penicillin, used especially in the treatment of respiratory infections [Mid-20thC. Blend of AMINO- and PENICILLIN.]

am·ple /ámpəl/ (**-pler, -plest**) *adj.* **1. MORE THAN ENOUGH** as much or as many as required, usually with some left over **2. LARGE** large, especially in physical size (*often used euphemistically*) [15thC. Via French, from Latin *amplus* "large, plentiful."] —**am·ple·ness** *n.*

WORD KEY: SYNONYMS

See Synonyms at ***sufficient*** and ***enough.***

am·plex·us /am pléksəss/ *n.* the mating posture of a pair of frogs or toads, in which the male clasps the female from behind during egg release and fertilization [Mid-20thC. From Latin, "an embracing," from the past participle of *amplecti* "to embrace."]

am·pli·con /ámpli kòn/ *n.* a nucleic acid fragment that is the product of the artificial large-scale reproduction of genetic material

am·pli·dyne /ámplə dīn/ *n.* a specialized direct-current generator in which small changes in power input produce large changes in output. It is used especially in servo systems. [Mid-20thC. Blend of AMPLIFIER + Greek *dynamis* "power" (see DYNAMIC).]

am·pli·fi·ca·tion /àmpləfi káysh'n/ *n.* **1. ENLARGEMENT OF SOMETHING** the act or process of making something larger, greater, or stronger **2. PROCESS OF MAKING LOUDER** the act or process of making something louder **3. ADDITION OF DETAIL** the act or process of making a spoken or written account fuller or clearer **4. DETAIL ADDED** a detail, explanation, or illustration added to a spoken or written account to make it fuller or clearer **5.** ELECTRON ENG **INCREASE IN SIGNAL MAGNITUDE** the increase in the magnitude of a signal produced by an amplifier **6.** GENETICS **GENE REPRODUCTION** the artificial large-scale reproduction of genes or DNA sequences

am·pli·fi·er /ámplə fīr/ *n.* **1. SOUND-INCREASING APPARATUS** a device that makes sounds louder, especially one used to increase the sound level of musical instruments **2. SIGNAL ENHANCER** an electronic device that increases the magnitude of a signal, voltage, or current

am·pli·fy /ámplə fī/ (**-fied, -fy·ing, -fies**) *v.* **1.** *vti.* **INCREASE** to become larger, greater, or stronger, or make something such as an emotion or sensation become larger, greater, or stronger **2.** *vti.* **MAKE LOUDER** to become louder, or make a sound become louder, by electronic or other means **3.** *vti.* **ADD DETAIL** to make a spoken or written account fuller, clearer, or more detailed **4.** *vt.* **EXAGGERATE** to make something seem greater or larger than it is **5.** *vti.* ELECTRON ENG **INCREASE SIGNAL** to increase the magnitude of a signal using an amplifier, or undergo such an increase [15thC. Via French *amplifier* from Latin *amplificare* "to enlarge," from *amplus* "large" (source of English *ample*) + *fic-*, a form of the stem of *facere* "to make."] —**am·pli·fi·a·ble** /ámplə fī əb'l/ *adj.*

WORD KEY: SYNONYMS

See Synonyms at ***increase.***

am·pli·tude /ámplə tood/ *n.* **1. LARGENESS** a largeness in size, volume, or extent **2. BREADTH** a breadth of range **3. ABUNDANCE** an amount that is more than required **4.** PHYS **DISTANCE FROM MEAN POINT** the furthest distance that a vibrating or oscillating system such as a pendulum travels from a mean or zero point **5.** ELECTRON ENG **SIGNAL'S MAXIMUM VALUE** the maximum value of an alternating signal **6.** MATH **ANGLE OF VECTOR REPRESENTING COMPLEX NUMBER** the angle between a vector representing a complex number and the positive real axis [Mid-16thC. Via French, from Latin *amplitudo* "size, greatness, grandeur," from *amplus* (see AMPLE).]

am·pli·tude mod·u·la·tion *n.* the modulation of the amplitude of a radio wave in such a way as to encode the wave with audio or visual information

am·ply /ámplee/ *adv.* to a more than adequate degree

am·poule /ám pyo͞ol/, **am·pule, am·pul** *n.* a small sealed glass container that holds a measured amount of a medicinal substance to be injected [Early 20thC. Via French, from Latin *ampulla* (see AMPULLA); the spelling may be a revival of an earlier form of the word, borrowed from Old French in the 13thC.]

am·pul·la /am po͝ollə, -púl-/ (*plural* **-lae** /am po͝o lèe, -púlee/) *n.* **1. VESSEL FOR HOLY LIQUID** a small container for a consecrated substance, especially oil, water, or the wine used at the Christian Eucharist **2. ANCIENT ROMAN BOTTLE** a round two-handled bottle used by the ancient Romans to hold wine, oil, or perfume [Late 14thC. From Latin, literally "little amphora," from *ampora,* a variant of *amphora* (see AMPHORA).]

am·pu·tate /ámpyə tàyt/ (**-tat·ed, -tat·ing, -tates**) *vti.* to cut off a limb or other appendage of the body, especially in a surgical operation [Mid-16thC. From Latin *amputat-*, the past participle stem of *amputare* "to cut around," from *ambi-* "around" + *putare* "to cut."] —**am·pu·ta·tion** /àmpyə táysh'n/ *n.* —**am·pu·ta·tor** /ámpyə taytər/ *n.*

am·pu·tee /àmpyə tée/ *n.* somebody who has had a limb or part of a limb cut off

am·ri·ta /am reétə/, **am·ree·ta** *n.* **1. DRINK BESTOWING IMMORTALITY** in Hindu mythology, a substance prepared by the gods that makes those who drink it immortal **2. IMMORTALITY** immortality gained by drinking amrita [Late 18thC. From Sanskrit *amṛta,* literally "without death," from *mṛta* "death."]

Am·rit·sar /əm rítsər/ city in Punjab state in northwestern India. It is a holy city for Sikhs. Population: 709,456 (1991).

Am·ster·dam /ámstər dàm/ **1.** capital and commercial center in the Netherlands, situated where the River Amstel flows into the Ijsselmeer. Population: 724,096 (1994). **2.** city in east central New York , on the Mohawk River. Population: 19,843 (1996).

amt. *abbr.* amount

am·trac /ám tràk/, **am·track** *n.* a flat-bottomed motor vehicle that can move on land or water, used to transport troops from ship to shore in preparation for an attack [Mid-20thC. Blend of AMPHIBIOUS and TRACTOR.]

amu *abbr.* atomic mass unit

a·muck *adj., adv.* = **amok**

A·mu Dar·ya /àa moo daárya/ river in central and western Asia flowing from the Pamir plateau toward the Aral Sea. Length: 1,580 mi./2,540 km.

am·u·let /ámmyələt/ *n.* **1. LUCKY JEWELRY** a piece of jewelry worn to provide protection against evil, injury, disease, or bad luck **2. LUCKY OBJECT** an ordinary object that is supposed to provide protection against bad luck or negative forces [Late 16thC. From Latin *amuletum.*]

A·mun /aamən/ *n.* a supreme god of ancient Egypt. Amun was originally a local god of Thebes, but was elevated during the eighteenth dynasty.

A·mund·sen /ámməndsən/, **Roald** (1872–1928) Norwegian explorer. He was the first person to reach the South Pole (1911).

A·mund·sen Gulf body of water in Canada between Banks and Victoria Islands and the Northwest Territories coast. Length: 250 mi./403 km.

A·mur /aa mo͝or/ river in east central Asia that forms the boundary between Manchuria and Siberia before flowing north into the Tatar Strait. Length: 1,786 mi./2,874 km.

a·muse /ə myo͞oz/ (**a·mused, a·mus·ing, a·mus·es**) *v.* **1.** *vti.* **MAKE SOMEBODY LAUGH** to make somebody smile or laugh or think that something is funny **2.** *vt.* **KEEP SOMEBODY HAPPILY OCCUPIED** to keep somebody occupied or entertained by providing entertainment or an interesting task **3.** *vt.* **DECEIVE SOMEBODY BY DISTRACTION** to distract somebody's attention, usually in order to trick or deceive (*archaic*) [15thC. From French *amuser* "to cause to stare stupidly," from *muser* "to stare stupidly" (see MUSE). The modern senses evolved from "to deceive" via "to divert somebody's attention."] —**a·mused** *adj.*

WORD KEY: ORIGIN

The history of the word ***amuse*** is very similar to that of *distract* and *divert*: all three have moved from the notion of "leading the mind astray" in a negative sense to the notion of "entertainment." In the case of ***amuse*** the earlier connotations have been entirely lost.

a·muse·ment /ə myo͞ozmənt/ *n.* **1. FEELING SOMETHING IS FUNNY** the feeling that something is funny or entertaining **2. RECREATIONAL ACTIVITY** an enjoyable activity such as a game, a hobby, or a form of entertainment **3. RIDE OR GAME** a ride, game, or other attraction found in an amusement park or a video arcade **4. KEEPING HAPPILY OCCUPIED** the act of keeping somebody or a group of people occupied or entertained

a·muse·ment park *n.* an outdoor area with a variety of mechanical rides, games, and other attractions that people pay to use

a·muse·ment tax *n.* a tax, often levied locally, on various forms or places of amusement

a·mus·ing /ə myo͞ozing/ *adj.* causing somebody to smile or laugh or be amused, often in a subdued way —**a·mus·ing·ly** *adv.* —**a·mus·ing·ness** *n.*

Am·vets /ám vèts/, **AM·VETS** *n.* a private organization of U.S. veterans of World War II and the Korean and Vietnam wars

a·myg·da·la /ə mígdələ/ (*plural* **-lae** /-lee/) *n.* an almond-shaped mass of gray matter, one in each hemisphere of the brain, associated with feelings of fear and aggression and important for visual learning and memory [Pre-12thC. Via Latin, from Greek *amugdalē* "almond," the original sense in English.]

a·myg·da·lin /ə mígdəlin/, **a·myg·da·line** /-lin, -līn/ *n.* a white crystalline bitter-tasting sugar derivative **(glycoside)** found in the seeds of many plants of the rose family such as apricots, almonds, and peaches [Mid-19thC. Coined from Latin *amygdala* "almond" (see AMYGDALA) + -IN.]

am·yl /ámm'l/ *adj.* relating to or containing any of eight possible forms of a chemical group with the same basic formula. Formula: C_5H_{11}–. [Mid-19thC. Coined from Latin *amylum*, from Greek *amulon* "finely ground meal," from, ultimately, *mulē* "mill" + -YL.]

amyl- *prefix.* = **amylo-** (*used before vowels*)

am·y·la·ceous /ámmə láyshəss/ *adj.* having or resembling starch (*technical*)

am·yl ac·e·tate *n.* a colorless volatile liquid that smells like pears. It is used as a flavoring and as a solvent for paints and lacquers. Formula: $CH_3CO_2C_5H_{11}$.

am·yl al·co·hol *n.* a colorless alcohol, or a mixture of any of the eight related amyl alcohols, used in the synthesis of other chemicals and drugs and as a solvent. Formula: $C_5H_{12}O$.

am·y·lase /ámmə làyss, -làyz/ *n.* an enzyme, found in plants, animal saliva, and pancreatic juice, that aids the conversion of starch and glycogen to simple sugars such as glucose

am·yl ni·trite *n.* a pale yellow fragrant liquid used mainly as an inhalant to dilate blood vessels in the treatment of angina pectoris. Formula: $C_5H_{11}NO_2$.

amylo-, **amyl-** *prefix.* starch ○ *amylosin* [From Latin *amylum* "starch" (see AMYLUM)]

am·y·loid /ámmə lòyd/ *n.* **1. WAXY PROTEIN** a waxy translucent substance composed of complex protein fibers and polysaccharides that is formed in body tissues in some degenerative diseases, e.g., Alzheimer's disease **2. STARCHY SUBSTANCE** a substance that resembles starch in composition or function ■ *adj.* **STARCHY** resembling a starch (*technical*)

am·y·loid·o·sis /àmmə loy dṓssiss/ *n.* a condition marked by the accumulation of a protein-based substance **(amyloid)** in the body's organs and tissues

am·y·lo·pec·tin /àmmə lō péktin/ *n.* an insoluble component of starch that is a carbohydrate polymer with a highly branched structure, high molecular weight, and an inability to gel readily in aqueous solution. ◊ **amylose**

am·y·lop·sin /àmmə lópsin/ *n.* an enzyme **(amylase)** found in pancreatic juice that aids the conversion of starch to maltose [Late 19thC. Coined from AMYLO- + TRYPSIN.]

am·y·lose /ámmə lòss, -lòz/ *n.* a soluble component of starch that is an unbranched carbohydrate polymer formed of glucose units, with a tendency to form gels in aqueous solution. ◊ **amylopectin**

a·my·o·to·ni·a /ày mī ə tṓnee ə/ *n.* an abnormal lack of muscle tension

a·my·o·tro·phic lat·er·al scle·ro·sis /ə mīə trṓfik-/ *n.* a fatal degenerative disease of the nervous system marked by progressive muscle weakness and atrophy. It is a form of motor neuron disease.

a·my·o·tro·phy /ày mī óttrəfee/ *n.* a degeneration of the muscles caused by nerve disease [Late 19thC. Coined from A- + MYO- + -TROPHY.]

an[1] /ən/ *adj.* used instead of "a," the indefinite article, in front of words with an initial vowel sound [Old English, a stressless form of the numeral *ān* "one" (source also of English *a*)]

WORD KEY: USAGE

See Usage note at ***a***.

an[2] /an, ən/, **an'** *conj.* if (*archaic*) [12thC. Reduced form of AND in the sense "if."]

AN *abbr.* airman, Navy

an. *abbr.* **1.** anno **2.** ante

an- *prefix.* = **a-** *prefix.* (*used before vowels*)

-an[1] *suffix.* **1.** of or relating to ○ *Minoan* ○ *agrarian* **2.** A person of or resembling a certain kind ○ *librarian* [Via Old French from Latin *-anus*, a suffix forming nouns and adjectives]

-an[2] *suffix.* an unsaturated carbon compound ○ *benzofuran* [Alteration of -ANE]

an·a[1] /ánnə, áanə/ (*plural* **-a** *or* **-as**) *n.* **1. COLLECTION OF ITEMS** a collection of things connected with a famous person, place, or period, especially spoken or written information, anecdotes, or sayings **2. COLLECTIBLE ITEM** an item in an ana

an·a[2] /ánnə/ *adv.* of each of the ingredients specified in a medical prescription in equal amounts [From the Greek prefix *ana-* "up, back, again," from the preposition and adverb *ana* "up"]

ANA *abbr.* American Newspaper Association

ana- *prefix.* **1.** up, upward ○ *anamorphic* **2.** back, backward, away ○ *anaphase* **3.** again ○ *anaplastic* [From Greek *ana.* Ultimately from an Indo-European word meaning "on," which is also the ancestor of English *on.*]

-ana *suffix.* a collection of objects or information about a topic, person, or place ○ *Shakespeareana* [Via modern Latin from Latin, neuter plural of *-anus* "pertaining to"]

an·a·bap·tism /ánnə báp tìzzəm/ *n.* the advocacy of adult baptism on the grounds that only as adults can people responsibly accept and declare their faith [See ANABAPTISM]

An·a·bap·tism *n.* the doctrines or beliefs of the Anabaptists [Mid-16thC. Via ecclesiastical Latin *anabaptismus* from Greek *anabaptismos* "second baptism," from *baptismos* "baptism."]

An·a·bap·tist /ànnə báptəst/ *n.* a member of a 16th-century Protestant movement promoting the doctrine of adult baptism on the grounds that only adults can accept and declare their faith on their own behalf [Mid-16thC. From ecclesiastical Latin *anabaptista*, which was formed from Greek *ana-* "again, afresh" + *baptistēs* "baptizer" (see BAPTIZE).] —**An·a·bap·tist** *adj.*

a·nab·a·sis /ə nábbəsiss/ (*plural* **-ses** /-seez/) *n.* the advance of an army, especially a large-scale march or expedition moving inland from the coast. The term derives from an account by Xenophon of the unsuccessful advance of a troop of Greek mercenaries led by Cyrus the Younger across Asia Minor in 401–400 B.C. [Early 18thC. From Greek, "going up, ascent," from *anabainein* "to go up," from *bainein* "to go."]

an·a·bat·ic /ànnə báttik/ *adj.* used to describe winds that move or blow upward during the daytime as warm air rises up mountain slopes. ◊ **katabatic** [Mid-20thC. From Greek *anabatikos* "relating to mounting," from *anabainein* "to go up, mount," from *bainein* "to go."]

an·a·bol·ic /ànnə bóllik/ *adj.* used to describe a metabolic process in which energy is used to construct complex molecules from simpler ones [Late 19thC. Blend of ANA- and METABOLIC.]

an·a·bol·ic ster·oid *n.* **1. SYNTHETIC HORMONE** a synthetic steroid hormone that increases muscle mass and strength. It is sometimes used by weightlifters and other athletes. **2. HORMONE** a naturally occurring hormone that promotes tissue growth

a·nab·o·lism /ə nábbə lìzzəm/ *n.* a metabolic process in which energy is used to construct complex molecules from simpler ones in the synthesis of needed compounds and tissues [Late 19thC. Blend of ANA- and METABOLISM.]

a·nab·o·lite /ə nábbə lìt/ *n.* a product or substance resulting from the metabolic process of anabolism

a·na·branch /ánnə bràngk/ *n.* a stream that separates from a river and follows its own course before re-entering the same river further downstream [Mid-19thC. Blend of *anastomosing* (from ANASTOMOSE) and BRANCH.]

a·nach·ro·nism /ə nákrə nìzzəm/ *n.* **1. CHRONOLOGICAL MISTAKE** something from a different period of time, e.g., a modern idea or invention wrongly placed in a historical setting in fiction or drama **2. SOMETHING OUT OF TIME** a person, thing, idea, or custom that seems to belong to a different time in history **3. MAKING OF CHRONOLOGICAL MISTAKE** the representation of somebody or something out of chronological order or in the wrong historical setting [Mid-17thC. Via French *anachronisme* from, ultimately, late Greek *anakhronizesthai*, literally "to be timed backward," from *khronos* "time."] —**a·nach·ro·nous** /ə nákrənəss/ *adj.* —**a·nach·ro·nous·ly** *adv.*

a·nach·ro·nis·tic /ə nàkrə nístik/ *adj.* **1. CHRONOLOGICALLY WRONG** belonging to a time other than the one being represented, especially in fiction or drama **2. NOT APPROPRIATE TO THE TIMES** out-of-date or inappropriate at the time in question —**a·nach·ro·nis·ti·cal·ly** *adv.*

an·a·clit·ic /ànnə klíttik/ *adj.* characterized by strong emotional dependence on a mother or other nurturing person, especially to the extent of exhibiting or causing serious developmental and psychological disturbances [Early 20thC. Formed from Greek *anaklitos* "for reclining," from *anaklinein* "to lean upon," from *klinein* "to lean."] —**an·a·cli·sis** /ànnə klīssiss, ə nákləssiss/ *n.*

an·a·co·lu·thon /ànnəkə lo͞o thòn/ (*plural* **-tha** /-lo͞othə/) *n.* an instance of abandoning a grammatical construction in speech or writing before it is complete and continuing with another. The sentence "The subject of the lecture was – I didn't really understand it" contains an anacoluthon. [Early 18thC. Via late Latin, from Greek *anakolouthon* "illogicality, inconsistency," from *anakolouthos* "not following," from *akolouthos* "following" (source also of English *acolyte*).] —**an·a·co·lu·thic** *adj.*

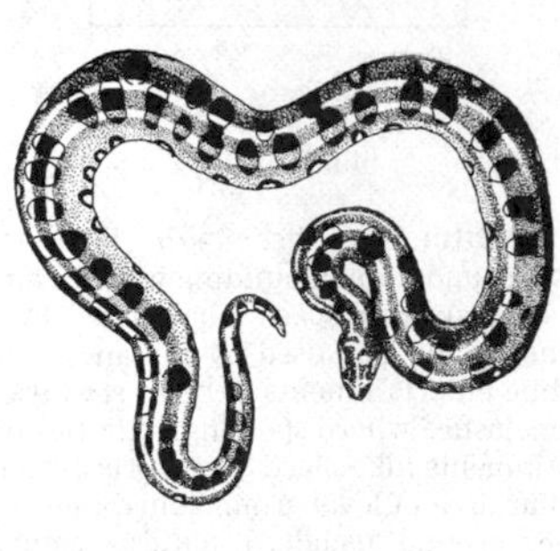

Anaconda

an·a·con·da /ànnə kóndə/ *n.* a South American nonvenomous snake, the largest in the boa family, that lives in or near water and in trees. It can grow to a length of more than 30 ft./9 m. Latin name: *Eunectes murinus.* [Mid-18thC. Origin uncertain: perhaps from Sinhalese, an alteration of *henakandayā*, literally "lightning snake."]

An·a·con·da /ànnə kóndə/ city northwest of Butte, in southwestern Montana; home to the world's largest ore-smelting plant until 1980. Population: 10,093 (1996).

A·nac·re·on /ə nákreeən/ (570?–478 B.C.) Greek lyric poet. He is well known for celebrating love and wine in his verse.

A·nac·re·on·tic /ə nàkree óntik/, **a·nac·re·on·tic** *adj.* **WITH ANACREON'S STYLE OR THEMES** written in the style or treating the subjects of the Greek poet Anacreon ■ *n.* **TYPE OF POEM** an Anacreontic poem [Early 17thC. Via Latin *Anacreonticus* from Greek *Anakreont-*, the stem of *Anakreōn* (see ANACREON).]

an·a·cru·sis /ànnə kro͞osiss/ (*plural* **-ses** /-seez/) *n.* **1.** POETRY **UNSTRESSED SYLLABLES** one or more unstressed syllables at the beginning of a line of verse that are not considered part of the metrical pattern of the line **2.** MUSIC **UNACCENTED NOTES** one or more unaccented notes immediately before the first downbeat of a bar [Mid-19thC. Via modern Latin, from, ultimately, Greek *anakrouein* "to strike up (a tune)," from *krouein* "to strike."] —**a·na·crus·tic** /ànnə kro͞ostik/ *adj.*

an·a·da·ma bread /ànnə dámmə-/ *n.* a type of yeast-raised cornbread that was originally made in New England [Origin unknown]

an·a·dem /ánnə dèm/ *n.* a garland or wreath worn on the head (*archaic or literary*) [Early 17thC. Via Latin, from Greek *anadēma* "headband," from *anadeein* "to bind up," from *deein* "to bind" (source of English *diadem*).]

an·a·di·plo·sis /ànnə də plṓsiss/ (*plural* **-ses** /-eez/) *n.* the rhetorical repetition of the last word or words of one phrase or sentence at the beginning of the next. The sentence "He was tormented by fears – fears that were soon to be realized" uses anadiplosis. [Late 16thC. Via Latin, from, ultimately, Greek *anadiploein*, literally "to double back," from *diploein* "to double."]

a·nad·ro·mous /ə náddrəməss/ *adj.* used to describe fish such as salmon and shad that return from the sea to the rivers where they were born in order to breed. ◊ **catadromous** [Mid-18thC. Formed from Greek *anadromos* "running up (a river from the sea)," from *dromos* "a running."]

a·nae·mi·a *n.* = **anemia**

a·nae·mic *adj.* = **anemic**

an·aer·obe /ánnə rṑb/ *n.* a microorganism that does not require oxygen for metabolism [Late 19thC. Back-formation from French *anaérobie* "living without air," coined by Louis Pasteur, from Greek *an-* "not" + French *aéro-* "air" + Greek *bios* "life."]

an·aer·o·bic /ànnə rṓbik/ *adj.* **1. NOT NEEDING OXYGEN** living or taking place in the absence of oxygen, especially not requiring oxygen for metabolism **2. LACKING OXYGEN** having or providing no oxygen — **an·aer·o·bic·al·ly** *adv.*

an·aer·o·bic proc·ess *n.* a chemical or biological process such as decay or decomposition that does not require oxygen. Such processes are often used to dispose of wastes while generating useful gases.

an·aer·o·bic res·pi·ra·tion *n.* the production of energy from foodstuffs without the presence of oxygen. Anaerobic respiration occurs in some yeasts and bacteria, and in muscle tissue during strenuous exercise when oxygen is insufficient. ◊ **aerobic respiration**

an·aer·o·bi·o·sis /ànnerō bī óssiss/ *n.* life in the absence of free or atmospheric oxygen [Late 19thC. Coined from ANAEROBIC + -BIOSIS.] —**an·aer·o·bi·ot·ic** /ànnerō bī óttik/ *adj.*

an·aes·the·sia *n.* = **anesthesia**

an·aes·thet·ic *n.* = **anesthetic**

an·aes·thet·ics *n. U.K.* = **anesthesiology**

an·a·glyph /ánnə glìf/ *n.* **1. CARVED DECORATION** a decoration carved in low relief, so that the shape of the design projects only slightly from the background **2. THREE-DIMENSIONAL PICTURE** a three-dimensional visual effect created by dyeing each of two images a different color, usually red and green, and then viewing them through complementary-colored filters, one over each eye [Late 16thC. From Greek *anagluphē* "low-relief sculpture," literally "upward carving," from *gluphein* "to carve."] —**an·a·glyph·ic** /ànnə glíffik/ *adj.* — **an·a·glyp·tic** /-glíptik/ *adj.*

a·nag·nor·i·sis /ànag náwrəssìss/ (*plural* **-ses** /-seez/) *n.* in literature, especially Greek tragedy, the principal character's discovery or acknowledgment of some fact that leads to the resolution of the plot [Late 18thC. Via Latin, from Greek, "recognition," formed from *anagnōrizein*, literally "to know thoroughly," from *gnōrizein* "to get knowledge of."]

an·a·go·ge /ánnə gṑjee/, **an·a·go·gy** /-gōjee/ (*plural* **-gies**) *n.* **1. SPIRITUAL INTERPRETATION** a spiritual or mystical interpretation of a word or passage, especially in a sacred text, in contrast to a literal or moral interpretation **2. ALLEGORICAL INTERPRETATION IN BIBLE** an allegorical interpretation of a passage in the Bible as an allusion to or foreshadowing of people or events in the New Testament [18thC. Via Latin, from Greek *anagōgē* "reference," from *anagein*, literally "to take back," from *agein* "to take" (source of English *pedagogue*).] —**an·a·gog·ic** /ànnə gójjik/ *adj.* —**an·a·gog·i·cal** *adj.* —**an·a·gog·i·cal·ly** *adv.*

an·a·gram /ánnə gràm/ *n.* **1. WORD REARRANGED TO FORM ANOTHER** a word or phrase that contains all the letters of another word or phrase in a different order. "Astronomers" is an anagram of "no more stars." **2. WORD GAME** a word game that involves the forming of anagrams (*takes a singular verb*) [Late 16thC. Directly or via French *anagramme* from modern Latin *anagramma*, probably from Greek *anagrammatismos* "transposition of letters," from *anagrammatizein* (see ANAGRAMMATIZE).] —**an·a·gram·mat·ic** /ànnəgrə máttik/ *adj.* —**an·a·gram·mat·i·cal·ly** *adv.*

an·a·gram·ma·tize /ànnə grámmə tīz/ (**-tized, -tiz·ing, -tiz·es**) *vt.* to rearrange the letters of a word or phrase to form a different word or phrase [Late 16thC. Origin uncertain: perhaps directly from Greek *anagrammatizein* "to rearrange the letters of a word," from *gramma* "letter."]

An·a·heim /ánnə hīm/ city in southwestern California. It is home to Disneyland. Population: 288,945 (1996).

a·nal /áyn'l/ *adj.* **1.** ANAT, ZOOL **RELATING TO ANUS** relating to or situated near the anus **2.** PSYCHOANAL **RELATING TO CHILDHOOD INTEREST IN DEFECATION** in Freudian theory, relating to a stage of childhood psychosexual development during which the focus is on the anal region and functions **3. OBSESSIVELY SELF-CONTROLLED** in Freudian theory, relating to adult personality traits, e.g., obsessive neatness, stubbornness, and frugality, that are considered to have originated during or be characteristic of the anal stage of development [Mid-18thC. From modern Latin *analis*, from *anus* "ANUS."] —**a·nal·ly** *adv.*

a·nal. *abbr.* **1.** analogous **2.** analogy **3.** analysis **4.** analytic

a·nal·cime /ə nál seem/, **a·nal·cite** /ə nálsīt/ *n.* a white or light-colored mineral, a form of zeolite composed of hydrated silicate of sodium and aluminum and found in crystal form in igneous rock [Early 19thC. Via French, coined from Greek *analkimos*, literally "not strong" (in reference to the mineral's weak electric current), from *alkimos* "strong," from *alkē* "strength."] — **a·nal·cim·ic** /ánn'l símmik/ *adj.*

an·a·lects /ánnə lèkts/, **an·a·lec·ta** /ànnə léktə/ *npl.* passages selected from one or more literary or philosophical works, especially when published as a collection [Early 17thC. Via Latin, from Greek *analekta* "collected, or selected, things," from, ultimately, *analegein*, literally "to gather up," from *legein* "to gather."] — **an·a·lec·tic** *adj.*

an·a·lem·ma /ànnə lémmə/ (*plural* **-mas** *or* **-ma·ta** /-mətə/) *n.* a scale, found on some sundials and globes, that is shaped like a figure eight and marked to indicate the declination of the sun and to allow the calculation of apparent solar time [Mid-17thC. Via Latin, "sundial, pedestal of a sundial," from Greek *analēmma* "pedestal, support," from *analambanein* "to take up, support," from *lambanein* "to take."]

an·a·lep·tic /ànnə léptik/ *adj.* **STIMULANT** restorative or invigorating, especially after an illness ■ *n.* **STIMULANT DRUG** a drug that has a stimulating effect on the central nervous system [Mid-17thC. Via Latin, from Greek *analēptikos* "restorative," from *analambanein* (see ANALEMMA).]

an·al·ge·si·a /ànn'l jeézee ə, -jeézhə/ *n.* MED **1. UNAWARENESS OF PAIN** the lack of sensibility to pain while somebody is conscious **2. PAIN CONTROL** treatment to control pain [Early 18thC. Via modern Latin, from Greek *analgēsia* "lack of feeling, insensibility," from, ultimately, *algeein* "to feel pain," from *algos* "pain."] —**an·al·get·ic** /ànn'l jéttik/ *adj.*

an·al·ge·sic /ànn'l jeézik, -jeéssik/ *adj.* **PAIN-RELIEVING** used to describe a type of medication that alleviates pain without loss of consciousness ■ *n.* **PAIN-RELIEVING MEDICATION** a type of medication that alleviates pain without loss of consciousness

a·nal in·ter·course *n.* = **sodomy**

an·a·log /ánnə lawg/, **an·a·logue** *n.* **SIMILAR CHEMICAL** a chemical with a similar structure to another but differing slightly in composition ■ *adj.* **USING PHYSICAL REPRESENTATION** relating to a system or device that represents data variation by a measurable physical quantity. ◊ **digital** *adj.* 4 [Mid-20thC. Variant of ANALOGUE.]

an·a·log clock, **an·a·logue clock** *n.* a clock that shows the time by means of hands on a dial

an·a·log com·put·er, **an·a·logue com·put·er** *n.* a computer that uses a variable physical quantity such as voltage to represent data

an·a·log·i·cal /ànnə lójjik'l/ *adj.* relating to or working by means of analogy [Late 16thC. Formed directly or via French *analogique* from Latin *analogicus*, from Greek *analogikos* (see ANALOGOUS).] —**an·a·log·i·cal·ly** *adv.*

a·nal·o·gist /ə nálləjist/ *n.* somebody who uses analogy as a form of reasoning, to provide an explanation, or to support an argument

a·nal·o·gize /ə nállə jīz/ (**-gized, -giz·ing, -giz·es**) *v.* **1.** *vt.* **DRAW COMPARISONS** to compare two things that are similar in some respects, especially in order to explain something or to support an argument **2.** *vi.* **USE ANALOGY** to make use of an analogy

a·nal·o·gous /ə nálləgəss/ *adj.* **1. SIMILAR** similar in some respects, allowing an analogy to be drawn **2.** BIOL **EQUIVALENT BUT INDEPENDENTLY EVOLVED** used to describe body parts and organs that have equivalent functions but that evolved independently of one another in different plants or animals. The wings of birds, bats, and insects, e.g., are analogous. [Mid-17thC. Via French *analogue* or Latin *analogus* from Greek *analogos*, from *analogon* "in due ratio," from *ana* "according to" + *logos* "ratio."] —**a·nal·o·gous·ly** *adv.* —**a·nal·o·gous·ness** *n.*

WORD KEY: USAGE

Some things are more **analogous** than others. ***Analogous***, correctly used, should include a notion of **analogy**, that is, of directly corresponding features: *The Commission has set up guidelines for broadcasters that are analogous to those for journalists.* It is better to avoid it when the comparison is only general and when more straightforward words such as **similar**, **equivalent**, **comparable**, or **corresponding** would serve as well: *The new system is analogous to that used in the electronics industry.*

an·a·log re·cord·ing, **an·a·logue re·cord·ing** *n.* the recording of sound onto vinyl or tape by converting the audio waveform into analogous variations in shape or magnetization

an·a·logue /ánn'l òg/ *n.* **1. CORRESPONDING THING** a thing, idea, or institution that is similar to or has the same function as another ○ *"They had no exact analogue for our word 'home,' any more than they had for our Roman-based 'family.'"* (Charlotte Perkins Gilman, *Herland*; 1915) **2.** BIOL **EQUIVALENT BUT INDEPENDENTLY EVOLVED ORGAN** a body part or organ that has an equivalent function to one in a different plant or animal but that evolved independently. The wings of birds, bats, and insects, e.g., are analogues. **3.** CHEM = **analog** *n.* **4.** FOOD **FOOD SUBSTITUTE** a food or dish made to resemble another by the substitution of inferior ingredients ■ *adj.* = **analog** [Early 19thC. Via French, from Greek *analogon* (see ANALOGOUS).]

an·a·log watch, **an·a·logue watch** *n.* a watch that shows the time by means of hands on a dial

a·nal·o·gy /ə nálləjee/ (*plural* **-gies**) *n.* **1. COMPARISON** a comparison between two things that are similar in some respects, often used to help explain something or make it easier to understand **2. SIMILARITY** a similarity in some respects **3.** BIOL **EQUIVALENCE BETWEEN INDEPENDENTLY EVOLVED PARTS** equivalence in biological function between body parts or organs that have evolved independently in different plants and animals **4.** LOGIC **FORM OF REASONING** a form of logical inference, reasoning that if two things are taken to be alike in a particular way, they are alike in certain other ways **5.** LING **STANDARDIZATION OF LINGUISTIC FORMS** the development or production of linguistic forms and patterns that resemble those already predominating in a language [15thC. Via French *analogie* or Latin *analogia* from Greek *analogia* "proportion," from *analogos* (see ANALOGOUS).]

an·al·pha·bet·ic /a nàlfə béttik/ *adj.* (*formal*) **1. NOT ALPHABETICAL** not in alphabetical order **2. ILLITERATE** not knowing how to read or write ■ *n.* **ILLITERATE PERSON** somebody who does not know how to read or write (*formal*) [Late 19thC. Formed from Greek *analphabētos* "not knowing the alphabet," from *alphabētos* "alphabet."]

a·nal-re·ten·tive *adj.* = **anal** *adj.* 3 —**a·nal re·ten·tion** *n.* —**a·nal-re·ten·tive** *n.* —**a·nal-re·ten·tive·ness** *n.*

a·nal sex *n.* = **sodomy**

a·nal·y·sand /ə nállə sànd, -zànd/ *n.* somebody who is undergoing psychoanalysis [Mid-20thC. Formed from ANALYZE, on the model of *operand*.]

a·nal·y·sis /ə nálləssiss/ (*plural* **-ses** /-seez/) *n.* **1. SEPARATION INTO COMPONENTS** the separation of something into its constituents in order to find out what it contains, to examine individual parts, or to study the structure of the whole **2. LIST OF PARTS** a statement giving details of all the constituent elements of something and how they relate to each other **3. CLOSE EXAMINATION** the examination of something in detail in order to understand it better or draw conclusions from it **4. ASSESSMENT** an assessment, description, or explanation of something, usually based on careful consideration or investigation **5.** MATH **BRANCH OF MATHEMATICS** the branch of mathematics dealing with differential calculus, functions, and limits **6.** LING **WAY OF EXPRESSING GRAMMATICAL RELATIONSHIPS** the use of function words or word order, rather than inflectional forms, to express grammatical relationships in a language **7.** = **psychoanalysis** [Late 16thC. Via medieval Latin, from Greek *analusis* "a breaking up into elements," from *analuein* "to unloose, dissolve into elements," from *luein* "to loosen."]

a·nal·y·sis of var·i·ance *n.* the analysis of the difference in outcomes of an experiment to determine the factors contributing to the variations

an·a·lyst /ánn'list/ *n.* **1. EXPERT WHO EXAMINES SOMETHING** somebody with specialist knowledge or skill who studies or examines something by separating it into its constituent elements and gives an assessment, description, or explanation of it **2.** = **psychoanalyst** [Mid-17thC. From French *analyste*, from *analyse* "analysis" (see ANALYZE).]

an·a·lyt·ic /ànnə líttik/, **an·a·lyt·i·cal** /-líttik'l/ *adj.* **1. OF ANALYSIS** connected with or involving analysis **2. USING ANALYSIS** able or inclined to separate things into their constituent elements in order to study or examine them, draw conclusions, or solve problems **3.** LOGIC **TRUE BY MEANING ALONE** true by definition or by virtue of the meaning of the words used **4.** MATH **DIFFERENTIABLE AT ALL POINTS IN DOMAIN** used to describe a function of a complex variable that is differentiable at all points in its domain **5.** LING **USING FUNCTION WORDS** expressing grammatical relationships by means of function words or word order rather than inflections [Late 16thC. Via late Latin, from Greek *analutikos*, from *analuein* (see ANALYSIS).] —**an·a·lyt·i·cal·ly** *adv.*

an·a·lyt·i·cal bal·ance *n.* an accurate scales used in laboratories for weighing minute objects or quantities

an·a·lyt·i·cal re·a·gent *n.* a substance processed to be virtually free of impurities

an·a·lyt·ic ge·om·e·try *n.* a branch of mathematics dealing with geometric properties using algebraic operations and notation to locate points within a coordinate system

an·a·lyt·ic phi·los·o·phy *n.* a 20th-century philosophy primarily concerned with resolving philosophical problems through the analysis and clarification of language

an·a·lyt·ic psy·chol·o·gy *n.* a system of psychoanalysis based on the psychological theories of Carl Jung

an·a·lyt·ics /ànnə líttiks/ *n.* the branch of logic involved with the analysis of propositions (*takes a singular or plural verb*)

an·a·lyze /ánn'l īz/ (**-lyzed** *or* **-lyzed, -lyz·ing** *or* **-lyz·ing, -lyz·es**) *vt.* **1. BREAK DOWN INTO COMPONENTS** to find out what something is made up of by identifying its constituent parts **2. EXAMINE STRUCTURE** to study or examine the structure of something or how its constituent parts are put together **3. STUDY CLOSELY** to examine something in great detail in order to understand it better or discover more about it **4.** GRAM **EXPRESS BY USING FUNCTION WORDS** to express grammatical relationships by using function words or word order rather than inflectional endings **5.** = **psychoanalyze** [Early 17thC. Origin uncertain: possibly a back-formation from ANALYSIS, or from French *analyse* "analysis" used as a verb; in either case reinforced by French *analyser* "to analyze."] —**an·a·lyz·a·ble** *adj.* —**an·a·ly·za·tion** /ànn'lə záysh'n/ *n.* —**an·a·lyz·er** /ánn'l īzər/ *n.*

an·am·ne·sis /ànnəm néessiss, à nam-/ (*plural* **-ses** /-seez/) *n.* **1.** PSYCHOL **RECOLLECTION** a recollection of past events (*technical*) **2. CASE HISTORY** the medical or psychiatric history of a patient, especially in the patient's own words [Late 16thC. From Greek, "remembrance," from *anamimnēskein*, literally "to call back to mind," from *mimnēskein* "to call to mind."]

an·am·nes·tic /ànam néstik/ *adj.* showing a secondary immunological response to an antigen at some time after initial immunization [Early 18thC. From Greek *anamnēstikos*, ultimately from *anamimnēskein* (see ANAMNESIS).] —**an·am·nes·ti·cal·ly** *adv.*

an·a·mor·phic /ànnə máwrfik/ *adj.* relating to or producing image distortion caused by unequal magnification along different perpendicular axes

an·a·mor·pho·sis /ànnə mawr fóssiss, ànnə máwrfəssiss/ (*plural* **-ses** /-seez/) *n.* **1. DISTORTED IMAGE** a distorted image or drawing of a distorted image that appears normal when viewed with or reflected from a special device **2. IMAGING PROCESS** the process of making distorted images by means of special mirrors or other devices [Mid-18thC. From Greek, "transformation," from *anamorphoein*, literally "to change shape again," from *morphoein* "to change shape," from *morphē* "shape."]

an·a·pest /ánnə pèst/, **an·a·paest** *n.* a metrical foot of three syllables with the stress on the third syllable, or of two short syllables followed by a long syllable. The word "unconcerned" and the phrase "up the hill" are anapests. [Late 16thC. Via Latin, from Greek *anapaistos* "struck backward" (from its being a reversed dactyl), the past participle of *anapaiein*, from *paiein* "to strike."] —**an·a·pes·tic** /ànnə péstik/ *adj.*

an·a·phase /ánnə fàyz/ *n.* a late stage of cell division during which chromosomes move to the poles of the spindle. ◊ **prophase, metaphase, telophase** [Late 19thC. Coined from Greek *ana-* "up, back" + PHASE.]

a·naph·o·ra /ə náffərə/ *n.* **1. REPETITION FOR EFFECT** the use of the same word or phrase at the beginning of several successive clauses, sentences, lines, or verses, usually for emphasis or rhetorical effect. "She didn't speak. She didn't stand. She didn't even look up when we came in" is an example of anaphora. (*formal*) **2.** GRAM **REFERRING BACK** reference to a word or phrase used earlier, especially to avoid repeating the word or phrase by replacing it with something else such as a pronoun. In the sentence "I told Paul to close the door and he did so," the clause "he did so" makes use of anaphora. **3.** CHR **PART OF EUCHARIST** the offering of the bread and wine at the Eucharist [Late 16thC. Via Latin, from Greek, "reference, repetition," from *anapherein*, literally "to carry back," from *pherein* "to carry."] —**a·naph·o·ric** /ànnə fáwrik/ *adj.* —**a·naph·or·i·cal·ly** *adv.*

a·naph·o·re·sis /ànnəfə réessiss/ *n.* the movement toward the anode of suspended particles in solution

an·aph·ro·dis·i·a /ə nàffrə dízzee ə, -dízhə/ *n.* absence or reduction of sexual desire [20thC. From Greek, "inability to inspire love," from *aphrodisios* "relating to love" (see APHRODISIAC).]

an·aph·ro·dis·i·ac /ə nàffrə dízzee àk/ *adj.* **REDUCING SEXUAL DESIRE** tending to reduce sexual desire ■ *n.* **DRUG REDUCING SEXUAL DESIRE** a drug, herb, or other substance that reduces sexual desire [Early 19thC. Formed from Greek *aphrodisiakos* "inspiring love, sexual" (see APHRODISIAC).]

an·a·phy·lac·tic /ànnəfə láktik/ *adj.* relating to or caused or characterized by extreme sensitivity to a substance (**anaphylaxis**) —**an·a·phy·lac·ti·cal·ly** *adv.*

an·a·phy·lac·tic shock *n.* a sudden severe and potentially fatal allergic reaction in somebody sensitive to a particular substance, marked by a drop in blood pressure, difficulty in breathing, itching, and swelling

an·a·phy·lax·is /ànnəfə láksiss/ *n.* **1. EXTREME SENSITIVITY** extreme sensitivity to a particular substance such as a specific protein or drug **2.** = **anaphylactic shock** [Early 20thC. From modern Latin, coined from Greek *ana-* "again" (because a substance is reintroduced) + *-phylaxis* "guarding, watching."] —**an·a·phy·lac·toid** /ànnəfə lák tòyd/ *adj.*

an·a·pla·sia /ànnə pláyzhə/ *n.* the reversion of cells, usually within a tumor, to a simpler or less differentiated form

an·a·plas·tic /ànnə plástik/ *adj.* relating to or characterized by the loss of distinctive cell features (**anaplasia**)

an·a·ptyx·is /ànnəp tíksiss, ànnap-/ *n.* the insertion of a weak vowel sound between two consonants in order to make a word or phrase easier to pronounce [Late 19thC. Via modern Latin, from Greek *anaptuxis* "an unfolding," from *anaptussein* "to unfold," from *ptussein* "to fold."]

an·arch /á naàrk/ *n.* somebody who supports or instigates anarchy (*archaic*) [Mid-17thC. Back formation from ANARCHY.]

an·ar·chic /a naàrkik, ə-/, **an·ar·chi·cal** /-kik'l/ *adj.* **1. LAWLESS** showing no respect for established laws, rules, institutions, or authority **2. CHAOTIC** characterized by a lack of organization or control **3. ENCOURAGING ANARCHY** likely to cause the overthrow of a formal system of government or a breakdown of law and order —**an·ar·chi·cal·ly** *adv.*

an·ar·chism /ánnər kìzzəm/ *n.* **1. DOCTRINE REJECTING GOVERNMENT** an ideology that rejects the need for a system of government in society and proposes its abolition **2. ACTIONS OF ANARCHISTS** behavior intended to overthrow or weaken a society's formal system of government **3. RESISTANCE TO CONTROL** resistance to all forms of authority or control

an·ar·chist /ánnərkist/ *n.* **1. SUPPORTER OF ANARCHISM** somebody who rejects the need for a system of government in society and proposes its abolition **2. LAWLESS PERSON** somebody who tries to overthrow a society's formal system of government or behaves in a generally lawless manner and encourages others to do the same (*disapproving*) —**an·ar·chis·tic** /ànnər kístik/ *adj.*

an·ar·chy /ánnərkee/ *n.* **1. LACK OF GOVERNMENT** the absence of any formal system of government in a society **2. CHAOTIC SITUATION** a situation in which there is a total lack of organization or control [Mid-16thC. Via medieval Latin *anarchia*, from Greek *anarkhia*, from *anarkhos* "without a ruler," from *arkhos* "ruler."]

an·ar·thri·a /a naàrthree ə/ *n.* the loss of the ability to articulate words [Late 19thC. Via modern Latin, from Greek, formed from *anarthros* "inarticulate, disjointed," from *arthron* "joint."] —**an·ar·thric** *adj.*

an·ar·throus /a naàrthrəss/ *adj.* used or occurring without a definite or indefinite article [Early 19thC. Formed from Greek *anarthros*, literally "not articulated," from *arthron* "article, joint."]

an·a·sar·ca /ànnə saàrkə/ *n.* the accumulation of watery fluid in connective tissue and cavities, resulting in swelling (**edema**) [14thC. Via medieval Latin, from the Greek adjective *anasarx*, applied by Galen, a Greek physician, to dropsy, representing the phrase *ana sarka* "throughout the flesh."] —**an·a·sar·cous** *adj.*

A·na·sa·zi /aànə saàzee, ànnə-/ (*plural* **-zis** *or* **-zi**) *n.* a member of an ancient Native American people [Mid-20thC. From Navajo *anaasází*, literally "enemy ancestors."]

A·na·sa·zi cul·ture *n.* a highly developed ancient culture of the southwestern United States. It was centered in the broad plateau where present-day Arizona, New Mexico, Colorado, and Utah meet.

A·na·sta·sia /ànnə stáyzhə/, **Grand Duchess** (1901–18). The daughter of Tsar Nicholas II, she died when the Bolsheviks executed the Romanovs (July 1918), but many women claimed to be her thereafter. Born **Anastasia Nikolaevna Romanovna**

an·as·tig·mat /a nàstíg màt, ànnə stíg màt/ *n.* a lens or combination of lenses free from astigmatism [Late 19thC. From German, a back-formation from *anastigmatisch* "anastigmatic," from, ultimately, medieval Latin *stigmaticus* (see STIGMATIC).]

an·as·tig·mat·ic /ànnə stig mátik, a nàstig mátik/ *adj.* used to describe a lens that is corrected for or free from astigmatism

a·nas·to·mose /ə nástə mōz, -mòss/ (**-mosed, -mos·ing, -mo·ses**) *vt.* to join blood vessels or other tubular parts in a surgical operation (**anastomosis**) [Late 17thC. Origin uncertain: probably a back-formation from ANASTOMOSIS, perhaps on the model of ANKYLOSE and METAMORPHOSE.]

a·nas·to·mo·sis /ə nàstə mṓssiss/ (*plural* **-ses** /-seez/) *n.* **1. NATURAL JOINT** the connection or place of connection of two or more parts of a natural branching system, e.g., of blood vessels, leaf veins, stems of woody plants, or rivers **2.** MED **SURGICAL UNION OF TUBULAR PARTS** the surgical union of two hollow organs, e.g., blood vessels or parts of the intestine, to ensure continuity of the passageway **3. NETWORK OF FUNGAL FILAMENTS** a fusion between fungal filaments (**hyphae**) to form a network [Early 17thC. Via modern Latin, from Greek, "outlet, opening, interconnection of openings," from *anastomoein* "to supply with a mouth or opening," from *stoma* "mouth" (source also of English *stomach*).] —**a·nas·to·mot·ic** /ə nàstə móttik/ *adj.*

a·nas·tro·phe /ə nástrəfee/ *n.* an alteration of the normal order of words or phrases in a grammatical construction, usually for rhetorical effect. Coleridge's "The helmsman steered; the ship moved on; yet never a breeze up blew" ends with an anastrophe. [Mid-16thC. From Greek, "a turning back, inversion," formed from *stroph-*, the stem of *strephein* "to turn."]

anat. *abbr.* **1.** anatomical **2.** anatomy

an·a·tase /ánnə tàyss, -tàyz/ *n.* a blue or yellowish brown mineral consisting of titanium dioxide, which occurs in igneous rock [Early 19thC. Via French, from Greek *anatasis* "extension" (from the elongated crystals), from, ultimately, *teinein* "to stretch."]

a·nath·e·ma /ə náthəmə/ *n.* **1.** OBJECT OF LOATHING somebody or something that is greatly disliked or detested and is therefore shunned **2.** RELIG ECCLESIASTICAL CURSE a curse from a religious authority that denounces something or excommunicates somebody **3.** GENERAL CURSE any forceful curse or denunciation **4.** RELIG SOMEBODY OR SOMETHING FORMALLY DENOUNCED somebody or something cursed, denounced, or excommunicated by a religious authority [Early 16thC. Via ecclesiastical Latin, from Greek, "something devoted to evil," earlier "something devoted," variant of *anathēma* "votive offering," from *anatithenai* "to set up."]

a·nath·e·ma·tize /ə náthəmə tìz/ (**-tized, -tiz·ing, -tiz·es**) *vti.* to formally curse, denounce, or excommunicate somebody or something [Mid-16thC. Via ecclesiastical Latin *anathematizare* "to ban, curse" from Greek *anathematizein* "to dedicate to evil," from *anathemat-*, the stem of *anathema* (see ANATHEMA.)] —**a·nath·e·ma·ti·za·tion** /ə nàthəmətə záysh'n/ *n.*

An·a·to·li·a /ànnə tṓlee ə/ *n.* the Asian part of Turkey, forming the westernmost peninsula of Asia

An·a·to·li·an /ànnə tṓlee ən/ *n.* **1.** PEOPLES SOMEBODY FROM ANATOLIA somebody who was born or who lives in Anatolia **2.** LANG EXTINCT MIDDLE EASTERN LANGUAGE GROUP a group of extinct languages spoken more than 3,000 years ago in central and western Turkey. They form a branch of the Indo-European language family. —**An·a·to·li·an** *adj.*

An·a·to·li·an Pla·teau /anə tṓlee ən-/ mountainous region extending from Kurdistan to Turkey

an·a·tom·i·cal /ànnə tómmik'l/, **an·a·tom·ic** /-tómmik/ *adj.* relating to or showing the physical structure of animals or plants —**an·a·tom·i·cal·ly** *adv.*

an·a·tom·i·cal·ly cor·rect *adj.* having an accurate representation of the genitals and other bodily details

a·nat·o·mist /ə náttəmist/ *n.* a student of or expert on the physical structure of animals or plants, especially the structure of the human body

a·nat·o·mize /ə náttə mìz/ (**-mized, -miz·ing, -miz·es**) *vt.* **1.** = **dissect** *v.* 1 **2.** ANALYZE IN DETAIL to analyze or examine something in great detail, thus revealing features that are not obvious —**a·nat·o·mi·za·tion** /ə nàttəmə záysh'n/ *n.*

a·nat·o·my /ə náttəmee/ (*plural* **-mies**) *n.* **1.** PHYSICAL STRUCTURE OF ORGANISM the physical structure, especially the internal structure, of an animal, plant, or other organism, or of any of its parts **2.** STUDY OF STRUCTURE OF BODY the branch of science that studies the physical structure of animals, plants, and other organisms **3.** BODY the human body (*informal*) **4.** BOOK ABOUT ANATOMY a book or other written work about the physical structure of animals, plants, or other organisms **5.** ANALYSIS a detailed analysis of something [14thC. Via French *anatomie* and late Latin *anatomia* from Greek *anatomē* "cutting up" from, ultimately, *temnein* "to cut" (source of English *atom*).]

WORD KEY: ORIGIN

From the 16th century to the early 19th century ***anatomy*** was used to mean "skeleton," and in this sense it was often misanalyzed as *an atomy*, as if the initial *an-* were the indefinite article: "My bones... will be taken up smooth, and white, and bare as an atomy," Tobias Smollett (1755).

An·ax·ag·o·ras /à nak sággərəss/ (500?–428 B.C.) Greek philosopher. He stated that matter was infinitely divisible and was the first person to explain solar eclipses.

A·nax·i·man·der /ə nàksə mándər/ (611?–547? B.C.) Greek philosopher. He put forward an evolutionary theory of the origins of life, claiming that human beings evolved from more primitive species.

A·nax·i·me·nes /à nak símmə neez/ (570?–500? B.C.) Greek philosopher. He believed that the universe consisted of air or vapor in various stages of condensation, and that the movement of air changed the structure of physical objects.

ANC *n.* a South African political party founded in 1912 that fought against apartheid. It formed South Africa's first multiracial, democratically elected government in 1994. Full form **African National Congress**

an·ces·tor /án sèstər, ánsèstər/ *n.* **1.** DISTANT RELATION SOMEBODY IS DESCENDED FROM somebody from whom somebody else is directly descended, especially somebody more distant than a grandparent **2.** FORERUNNER a predecessor of somebody, e.g., in the development of a certain art form **3.** BIOL EARLIER SPECIES an animal or plant from which a species has evolved **4.** EARLIER MODEL a device that was an earlier form of a modern invention or was used as a basis for developing it [14thC. Via Old French *ancestre* from Latin *antecessor*, literally "somebody who goes before," from *cess-*, the past participle stem of *cedere* (see CEDE).]

an·ces·tral /an séstrəl/ *adj.* belonging to former generations of somebody's family, or inherited from them [15thC. From Old French *ancestrel*, from *ancestre* (see ANCESTOR).] —**an·ces·tral·ly** *adv.*

an·ces·tress /án sess tress, ánssəss-/ *n.* a woman from whom somebody is directly descended, especially somebody more distant than a grandmother (*dated*)

an·ces·try /án sèstree, ánsès-/ *n.* somebody's ancestors regarded as a line linking the modern generation to its past [14thC. Alteration of Old French *ancesserie*, from *ancessour*, from Latin *antecessor* (see ANCESTOR).]

An·chi·ses /an kí̄ seez/ *n.* in Greek and Roman mythology, a Trojan prince and the father of Aeneas by the goddess Aphrodite. In later life, Anchises was saved during the Greek sack of Troy when Aeneas carried him from the burning city on his back.

Anchor

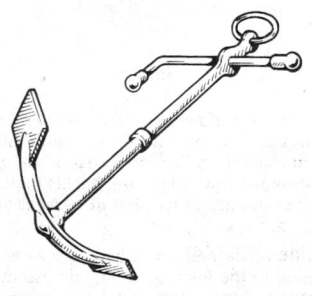

an·chor /ángkər/ *n.* **1.** NAUT DEVICE TO HOLD SHIP IN PLACE a heavy, traditionally double-hooked, device for keeping a ship or floating object in place **2.** DEVICE KEEPING OBJECT IN PLACE any device that keeps an object in place **3.** SOMETHING DEPENDABLE somebody who or something that provides a sense of stability ○ *She was my anchor during the crisis.* **4.** BROADCAST PRESENTER OF NEWS PROGRAM a presenter on a news program, providing links between the studio and reporters on location. ◊ **anchorman, anchorwoman 5.** SPORTS SOMEBODY POSITIONED LAST the team member who is responsible for the last leg in a relay race or farthest to the rear in a tug of war **6.** MOUNTAINEERING SOMETHING CLIMBER IS TIED TO a rock feature, piton, or other feature to which a climber is tied ■ *adj.* ATTACHING used for securing or connecting something ■ *vt.* (**-chored, -chor·ing, -chors**) **1.** HOLD SOMETHING IN PLACE to hold something securely in place **2.** BROADCAST BE NEWS PROGRAM'S PRESENTER to be the presenter on a news program [Pre-12thC. Via Latin *ancora* from Greek *agkura*. Ultimately from an Indo-European base meaning "to bend, hook," which is also the ancestor of English *angle* and *ankle*.] ◇ **at anchor** held on the water by an anchor

an·chor·age /ángkərij/ *n.* **1.** PLACE TO HOLD BOATS SECURE a place in or near a harbor where boats moored **2.** CHARGE FOR ANCHORING BOAT a charge for anchoring a boat in a harbor **3.** SOMETHING HOLDING OBJECT IN PLACE any device used to hold an object in place **4.** ANCHORING the securing of a ship with an anchor **5.** SECURITY a source of stability, or a stable condition

An·chor·age /ángkərij/ city and port in southern Alaska, at the eastern end of Cook Inlet. Population: 253,649 (1994).

an·cho·rite /ángkər rìt/ *n.* somebody who lives a life of prayer, either alone or as part of a religious community [15thC. Via medieval Latin *anc(h)orita* from, ultimately, ecclesiastical Greek *anakhōrētēs*, from Greek *anakhōrein*, literally "to withdraw," from *ana-* "away" + *khōrein* "to move."]

an·chor·man /ángkər màn/ (*plural* **-men** /-mèn/) *n.* **1.** BROADCAST MALE NEWS ANCHOR a man who is an anchor for a news program **2.** SPORTS MALE ANCHOR ON SPORTS TEAM a man who is the anchor in a relay race or for a tug-of-war team

an·chor·per·son /ángkər pùrs'n/ (*plural* **-per·sons** *or* **-peo·ple**) *n.* = **anchor** *n.* 4

an·chor store *n.* a large retail store, such as a department store, that is a major store in a shopping center and is intended to attract shoppers who will patronize the smaller stores

an·chor·wom·an /ángkər wòomən/ (*plural* **-en** /-wìmmən/) *n.* **1.** BROADCAST WOMAN WHO PRESENTS NEWSCAST a woman who is an anchor for a news program **2.** SPORTS WOMAN WHO ANCHORS SPORTS TEAM a woman who is the anchor in a relay race or for a tug-of-war team

an·cho·vy /án chòvee, an chṓvee/ (*plural* **-vies** *or* **-vy**) *n.* a small silvery edible sea fish that travels in large schools. It is widely used in Mediterranean cooking and is often sold salted and canned in oil. Family: Engraulidae. [Late 16thC. From Spanish *anchova*, of uncertain origin.]

an·cien ré·gime /aaN syaaN ray zheem/ (*plural* **an·ciens ré·gimes** /aaN syaaN ray zheem/) *n.* **1.** PRE-REVOLUTIONARY FRENCH SOCIETY the political and social system of France before the revolution of 1789 **2.** FORMER SYSTEM any former system or administration, or outmoded way of doing things [Late 18thC. From French, literally "old regime."]

an·cient /áynshənt/ *adj.* **1.** OF DISTANT PAST belonging to the distant past, especially to the time before the collapse of the Western Roman Empire in A.D. 476 **2.** OLD very old ■ *n.* **1.** SOMEBODY FROM PAST CIVILIZATION somebody who belonged to a civilization in the distant past **2.** SOMEBODY OLD a very mature or venerable person ■ **an·cients** *npl.* **1.** PEOPLE OF ANCIENT WESTERN CIVILIZATIONS the people who lived in one of the ancient civilizations, especially Greece and Rome **2.** ANCIENT GREEK AND ROMAN AUTHORS the authors of ancient Greece and Rome, whose writings form the basis of the classics as a subject of study [14thC. Via French *ancien* from assumed Vulgar Latin *anteanus*, from Latin *ante* "before."] —**an·cient·ness** *n.*

An·cient Greek *n.* the forms of the Greek language spoken from about 1500 B.C. to about A.D. 500

an·cient his·to·ry *n.* **1.** STUDY OF OLD CULTURES the study of the civilizations that flourished in the distant past, especially those of Greece and Rome **2.** THINGS THAT HAPPENED IN PAST things that happened a long time ago (*informal*)

An·cient Mar·i·ner *n.* somebody who talks at length about subjects, often obsessively (*informal humorous*) [From the title of the poem by Samuel Taylor Coleridge]

An·cient of Days *n.* a name for God, used in the Authorized Version of the Bible (Daniel 7: 9) [Translation of Latin *antiquus dierum*]

an·cil·lar·y /ánssə lèree/ *adj.* **1.** SUBORDINATE in a position of lesser importance **2.** PROVIDING SUPPORT providing support for somebody or something, e.g., nontechnical assistance to people who work in an industry or profession ■ *n.* (*plural* **-ies**) **1.** SUBORDINATE PART a subordinate part or element, e.g., a branch of an organization **2.** NONTECHNICAL SUPPORT EMPLOYEE a worker who provides nontechnical assistance or support to the core workers in an industry or profession [Mid-17thC. Formed from Latin *ancilla* "handmaid," feminine of *anculus* "manservant."]

an·cy·lo·sto·mi·a·sis /ángkə lōstə mí əssiss, ánsə-/, **an·ky·lo·sto·mi·a·sis** *n.* a tropical disease caused by infestation of the small intestine by hookworms, with symptoms of anemia and tiredness [Late 19thC. Formed from modern Latin *Ancyclostoma*, genus of hookworms, from Greek *agkulos* "hooked" + *stoma* "mouth."]

and (*stressed*) /and/; (*unstressed*) /ənd, ən/ CORE MEANING: a conjunction used to indicate an additional thing, situation, or fact. "And" in this case links words and phrases of the same grammatical value. ○ *a sister and two brothers* ○ *We need to clean*

the house and pack our suitcases. ○ *switching back and forth between different systems*
conj. **1.** THEN used to link two verbs or statements about events to indicate that the second follows the first ○ *Just add water and stir.* **2.** AS A RESULT used to introduce a situation or event that is a consequence of something just mentioned ○ *Their work was excellent and won several awards.* **3.** USED TO STRESS REPETITION OR CONTINUITY used to link identical words or phrases in order to emphasize repetition or continuity ○ *It gets better and better.* **4.** PLUS used to link two numbers or quantities to indicate that they are to be added together ○ *One and one are two.* **5.** BUT used to introduce a contrasting statement ○ *Make sure you eat enough fruit and avoid refined sugar.* **6.** MOREOVER used to introduce a statement that continues or adds weight to a statement just made ○ *Kim needed clothes, and I hadn't been paid in weeks.* **7.** USED TO CONNECT IDEAS used to connect clauses or sentences, especially in spoken conversation ○ *I like Pierre, the head waiter, but the work's hard. And they pick on me sometimes.* **8.** INDICATES AN INFINITIVE VERB used instead of "to" before an infinitive verb, usually with verbs such as "try," "go," and "come" (*informal*) ○ *I usually try and visit her once a week.* **9.** IF used to introduce a conditional clause (*archaic*) ○ *and it please you* [Old English *and, ond* (related to Dutch *en* and German *und*)] ◇ **and how** an interjection meaning "absolutely" or "certainly," usually following or answering a statement (*informal*)

WORD KEY: USAGE

and at the beginning of a sentence The notion that ***and*** should not be used at the beginning of a sentence is a mistaken notion arising from too literal an understanding of the "joining" function of conjunctions: the same objection is also raised with regard to **but**. If it is overdone the effect is of poor style, but this is not a matter of grammatical correctness, and the position of ***and*** at the beginning of a sentence can often be an effective way of drawing attention to what follows: *"You can't get away with this," he threatened. And we knew he meant it.*

AND /and/ *n.* a word used in computer technology to link two or more items that must occur together [Mid-20thC. From AND.]

And. *abbr.* Andorra

An·da·lu·sia /àndə lóozhə, -shee ə/ autonomous region of southern Spain bordered by the Mediterranean Sea and the Atlantic Ocean. It contains the historic cities of Seville, Granada, and Cadiz and many examples of Moorish architecture. Population: 6,940,522 (1991). Area: 33,694 sq. mi./87,268 sq. km. Spanish **Andalucía** —**An·da·lu·si·an** *adj., n.*

an·da·lu·site /àndə lóo s-t/ *n.* a hard mineral of various colors consisting of aluminum silicate. Some forms are used as gemstones. [Early 19thC. Named for ANDALUSIA, where the mineral was first found.]

An·da·man Is·lands /ándəmən-/ northern part of the Indian union territory of the Andaman and Nicobar Islands, situated between the Bay of Bengal and the Andaman Sea. The Andaman Islands consist of five large islands and about 200 islets. Population: 240,089 (1991). Area: 2,500 sq. mi./6,475 sq. km.

an·dan·te /an dántee, aan dáan tay, -tee/ *adj., adv.* SLOWLY at a moderate musical tempo but slower than moderato (*used as a musical direction*) ■ *n.* MUSIC PLAYED ANDANTE a title given to certain musical pieces or movements that are to be played andante [Early 18thC. From Italian, "walking," the present participle of *andare* "to go, walk."]

an·dan·ti·no /àan daan tée nō/ *adj., adv.* FAIRLY SLOWLY at a moderate musical tempo slightly faster than andante (*used as a musical direction*) ■ *n.* (*plural* **-nos**) MUSIC PLAYED ANDANTINO a title given to certain musical pieces or movements that are to be played andantino [Early 19thC. From Italian, literally "little andante."]

An·der·sen /ándərsən/, **Hans Christian** (1805–75) Danish writer. His fairy tales include "The Snow Queen" (1844) and "The Ugly Duckling" (1843).

An·der·son 1. city in east central Indiana. It is the site of Native American burial mounds. Population: 59,131 (1996). **2.** city located on the Piedmont in northwestern South Carolina. Population: 26,429 (1996).

Marian Anderson

An·der·son, Marian (1897–1993) U.S. contralto. She was the first Black singer to appear at the Metropolitan Opera in New York City (1955).

An·der·son, Maxwell (1888–1959) U.S. playwright and screenwriter. He wrote the verse plays *Elizabeth the Queen* (1930) and *Mary of Scotland* (1933).

An·der·son, Philip W. (*b.* 1923) U.S. physicist. He shared the Nobel Prize in physics in 1977.

An·der·son, Sherwood (1876–1941) U.S. writer. His most famous work is the short-story collection *Winesburg, Ohio* (1919).

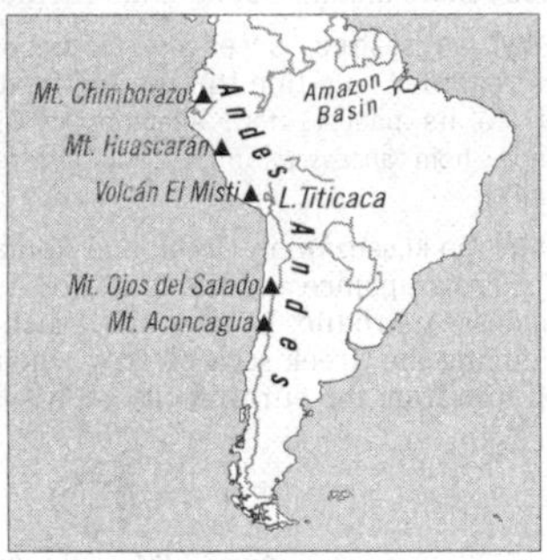

Andes

An·des /ándeez/ huge South American mountain system that extends north to south along the western coast from Panama to Tierra del Fuego. It consists of several ranges and has its highest point at Aconcagua 22,835 ft./6,960 m. —**An·de·an** /ándee ən/ *adj., n.*

an·de·sine /ándə zeen/ *n.* a hard colorless mineral belonging to the feldspar group, an essential component of andesite [Because it is found in the ANDES]

an·de·site /ándə zīt/ *n.* a fine-grained grayish volcanic rock characterized by feldspar minerals [Because it is found in the ANDES] —**an·de·sit·ic** /àndə zíttik/ *adj.*

And·hra Pra·desh /àandrə prə désh/ Indian state, situated in the southeast of the country facing the Bay of Bengal. Capital: Hyderabad. Population: 71,800,000 (1994). Area: 106,195 sq. mi./275,045 sq. km.

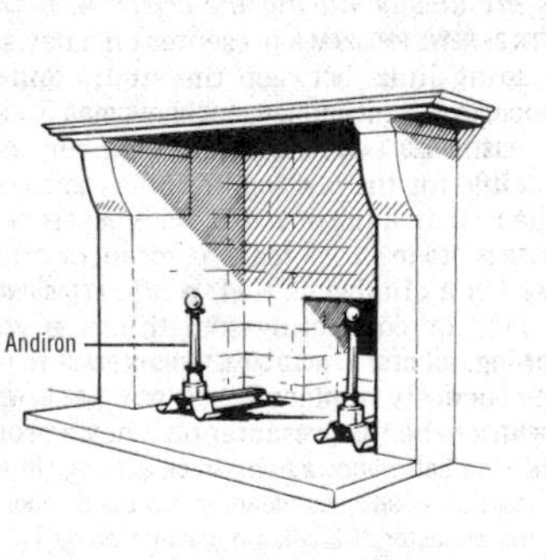

Andiron

and·i·ron /ánd ìərn/ *n.* either of a pair of metal stands used to hold logs in a fireplace [14thC. Alteration (influenced by IRON) of Old French *andier*, ultimately of Celtic origin.]

and/or /ən dáwr/ *conj.* a short way of saying that either or both of two options may be valid ○ *Bring mosquito netting and/or bug repellent.*

WORD KEY: USAGE

When to use **and/or**? ***And/or*** is a useful device to express three possibilities in a concise form: *A and/or B* gives the three possibilities A only, B only, or both A and B. On the other hand, it is not a particularly elegant expression and is usually more appropriate to legal and business usage. An alternative that is often preferable in general contexts is the type *A or B or both.*

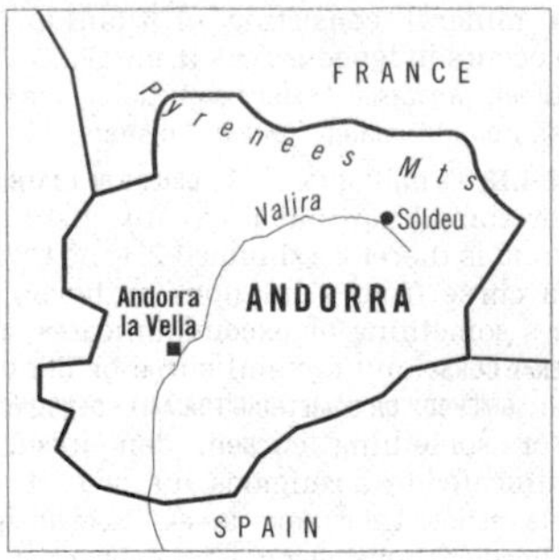

Andorra

An·dor·ra /an dáwrə/ co-principality in the Pyrenees Mountains between France and Spain. Language: Catalan. Currency: French franc. Currency: Spanish peseta. Capital: Andorra la Vella. Population: 64,000 (1997). Area: 181 sq. mi./468 sq. km. —**An·dor·ran** *adj., n.*

An·dor·ra la Vel·la /-lə vélla/ capital of the principality of Andorra. Population: 20,437 (1990).

An·do·ver /án dōvər, ándəvər/ town in northeastern Massachusetts, north of Boston. It is home to Phillips Academy, one of the oldest preparatory schools in the country. Population: 30,891 (1996).

andr- *prefix.* = **andro-** (*used before vowels*)

an·dra·dite /an dráa dīt/ *n.* a type of garnet consisting of calcium iron silicate of various colors. It is used as a gemstone. [Mid-19thC. Named for the Brazilian geologist and independence leader José Bonifácio de *Andrada* e Silva (1763?–1838).]

An·dre /áan drày/, **Carl** (*b.* 1935) U.S. sculptor. He is known for abstract minimalist sculptures made of mass-produced objects such as bricks and metal plates.

An·dré, John (1750–80) British soldier and spy. He conspired to turn over West Point to the British (1780), but was captured and hanged.

An·dre·a·nof Is·lands /àndree ánəf-, -nòf-/ group of islands forming part of the Aleutian Islands

An·drews /án drooz/, **Edwin Howard** (1890–1954) U.S. engineer. He invented electronic circuitry, which became the basis of radio and television transmission.

An·drews, Julie (*b.* 1935) British-born U.S. actor and singer. She made her Broadway debut in the musical *My Fair Lady* (1956) and starred in the popular films *Mary Poppins* (1964) and *The Sound of Music* (1965). Real name **Julia Elizabeth Wells**

andro-, **andr-** *prefix.* male, masculine ○ *androgen* [From Greek, formed from *andr-*, the stem of *anēr* "man"]

An·dro·cles /ándrə kleez/ *n.* a legendary Roman slave who was forced to fight a lion, which spared his life after recognizing Androcles as the man who had once removed a thorn from its paw

an·droe·ci·um /an dréeshee əm, -shəm/ (*plural* **-a** /-shee ə, -shə/) *n.* the set of stamens in a single flower [Mid-19thC. From modern Latin, from Greek *andro-* "man, male" + *oikion* "house." The underlying sense is "housing for the male part of the flower."] —**an·droe·cial** /an dréesh'l/ *adj.*

an·dro·gen /ándrəjən/ *n.* a natural or artificial steroid that acts as a male sex hormone. Androgens are responsible for the development of male sex organs and secondary sexual characteristics. Testosterone and androsterone are androgens. —**an·dro·gen·ic** /àndrə jénnik/ *adj.*

an·drog·e·nize /an drójjə nīz/ (**-nized, -niz·ing, -niz·es**) *vt.* to cause a female to acquire some male sexual characteristics —**an·drog·e·ni·za·tion** /an dròjjənə záysh'n/ *n.*

an·dro·gyne /ándrə jìn/ *n.* **1.** ANDROGYNOUS PERSON somebody who gives the impression of having both a male and a female sexual identity **2.** BOT = **hermaphrodite** [Mid-16thC. Via French and Latin from Greek *androgunos*, from *andro-* "man" + *gunē* "woman."]

an·drog·y·nous /an drójjənəss/ *adj.* **1.** BLENDING MASCULINE AND FEMININE neither male nor female in appearance but having masculine and feminine traits that give an impression of ambiguous sexual identity **2.** BOT WITH BOTH MALE AND FEMALE FLOWERS used to describe a plant species in which both male and female flowers occur in the same flower head **3.** = **hermaphrodite** [Early 17thC. Formed from Latin *androgynus* "hermaphrodite" (see ANDROGYNE).] —**an·drog·y·nous·ly** *adv.* —**an·drog·y·ny** *n.*

an·droid /án dròyd/ *n.* in science fiction, a robot that looks and behaves like a human being [Early 18thC. From modern Latin *androides*, from Greek *andro-*, the stem of *anēr* "man."]

An·drom·a·che /an drómməkee/ *n.* in Greek mythology, a princess of Troy and the wife of Hector. She led the Trojan women throughout the Trojan War, and was celebrated in myth and literature for her dignity and faith after the deaths of her husband and son in the war.

an·drom·e·da /an drómmədə/ (*plural* **-da** *or* **-das**) *n.* an evergreen shrub of the heath family with drooping flower clusters. Genera: *Andromeda* and *Pieris*. [Mid-18thC. From modern Latin, genus name.]

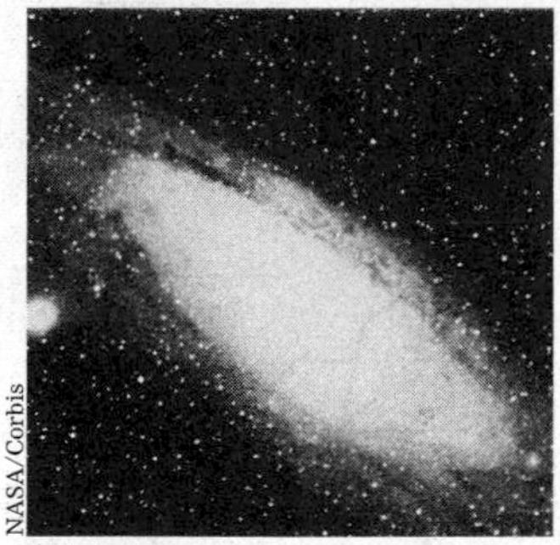

Andromeda Galaxy: Photographed from the Palomar Observatory, California Institute of Technology

An·drom·e·da /an dráwmədə/ *n.* **1.** MYTHOL WIFE OF PERSEUS in Greek mythology, the daughter of Cassiopeia, who was saved from a sea monster by her future husband, Perseus **2.** ASTRON CONSTELLATION IN NORTHERN HEMISPHERE a constellation in the northern hemisphere between the constellations of Cassiopeia and Pegasus. It contains a spiral galaxy, the **(Andromeda Galaxy)**, that can be seen with the naked eye.

An·dro·pov /an dró pòv/, **Yuri** (1914–84) Soviet statesman. He was general secretary of the Communist Party of the Soviet Union from 1982. Full name **Yuri Vladimirovich Andropov**

An·dros /ándrəss/, **Sir Edmund** (1637–1714) British colonial administrator. He governed the British North American colonies of New England (1686–89), Virginia (1692–98), and Maryland (1693–94).

an·dros·ter·one /an dróstə rōn/ *n.* a steroid that is a weak male sex hormone, produced by the metabolism of other hormones such as testosterone, and normally present in both male and female urine. Formula: $C_{19}H_{30}O_2$. [Mid-20thC. Coined from ANDRO- + STEROL + -ONE.]

-andry *suffix.* **1.** The condition of having a particular number of males or husbands ○ *polyandry* **2.** The condition of having a particular number of stamens ○ *monandry* [From Greek *-andria*, from *andr-*, the stem of *anēr* "man"] —**-androus** *suffix.*

-ane *suffix.* a saturated hydrocarbon ○ *methane* [Coined on the model of *-ene*, *-ine*, and *-one*, suffixes used in the names of other hydrocarbon derivatives]

a·near /ə néer/ *prep.* NEAR near to (*archaic or literary*) ○ *"I wouldn't ever go anear that house again"* (Mark Twain, *The Adventures of Huckleberry Finn*; 1884) ■ *adv.* NEARBY nearby (*archaic or literary*)

an·ec·dot·al /ànnək dṓt'l/, **an·ec·dot·ic** /-tik/ *adj.* **1.** BASED ON ANECDOTES OR HEARSAY consisting of or based on secondhand accounts rather than firsthand knowledge or experience or scientific investigation **2.** OF ANECDOTES relating to anecdotes or in the form of anecdotes —**an·ec·do·tal·ly** *adv.*

an·ec·dote /ánnək dòt/ *n.* a short personal account of an incident or event [Early 18thC. Directly or via French from modern Latin *anecdota*, from Greek *anekdota*, literally "things unpublished," from *an-* "not" + *ekdidonai*, "to publish" (literally "to give out").]

an·ec·dot·ic *adj.* = **anecdotal**

an·e·cho·ic /ànnə kṓ ik/ *adj.* producing or characterized by few or no echoes

a·ne·mi·a /ə néemee ə/, **a·nae·mi·a** *n.* **1.** MED BLOOD DEFICIENCY a blood condition in which there are too few red blood cells or the red blood cells are deficient in hemoglobin, resulting in poor health **2.** WEAKNESS lack of vitality or courage [Early 19thC. Via modern Latin, from Greek *anaimia*, literally "being without blood," from *haima* "blood."]

a·ne·mic /ə néemik/, **a·nae·mic** *adj.* **1.** MED HAVING ANEMIA having some form of anemia **2.** SICK-LOOKING pale and not looking well **3.** WEAK lacking vitality, strength, or courage

anemo- *prefix.* wind ○ *anemography* [From Greek *anemos* "wind." Ultimately from an Indo-European base meaning "to breathe," which is also the ancestor of English *animal* and *unanimous*.]

an·e·mog·ra·phy /ànnə móggrəfee/ *n.* the process of measuring wind speed

an·e·mom·e·ter /ànnə mómmətər/ *n.* an instrument that measures the force and direction of the wind

an·e·mom·e·try /ànnə mómmətree/ *n.* the process of measuring the force and direction of the wind —**an·e·mo·met·ri·cal** /ànnəmə méttrək'l/ *adj.*

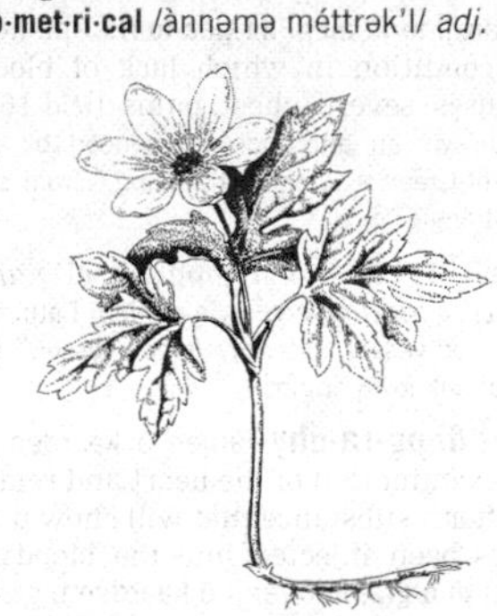

Anemone

a·nem·o·ne /ə némmənee/ (*plural* **-nes** *or* **-ne**) *n.* **1.** BOT FLOWERING PLANT a perennial flowering plant of the buttercup family. Many anemone species grow wild and popular varieties are deep red, purple, and pink with black centers. Genus: *Anemone.* **2.** ZOOL ♦ **sea anemone** [Mid-16thC. Via Latin from Greek *anemōnē*, of uncertain origin.]

a·nem·o·ne fish *n.* a small colorful damselfish with stinging cells, found on tropical coral reefs in close association with sea anemones. Genus: *Amphiprion.*

an·e·moph·i·lous /ànnə móffələss/ *adj.* used to describe a plant species that is pollinated by the wind —**an·e·moph·i·ly** *n.*

an·en·ceph·a·ly /àn en séffəlee/ *n.* the absence of all or a part of the brain and part of the skull at birth —**an·en·ce·phal·ic** /àn ensə fállik/ *adj.*

an·er·gy /á nurjee, ánnə-/ *n.* decreased immunity or lack of immunity to an antigen [Late 19thC. From modern Latin *anergia*, from Greek *an-* "without" + *ergon* "work."] —**an·er·gic** /a núrjik/ *adj.*

an·er·oid /ánnə ròyd/ *adj.* not containing or using liquid [Mid-19thC. From French *anéroïde*, from Greek *a-* "without" + *nēron* "water, liquid."]

an·er·oid ba·rom·e·ter *n.* an instrument for indicating atmospheric pressure on a circular dial. You tap an aneroid barometer to ensure an up-to-date reading.

an·es·the·sia /ànnəss théezhə/, **an·aes·the·sia** *n.* **1.** MED MEDICALLY INDUCED INSENSITIVITY TO PAIN induced loss of sensitivity to pain in all or a part of the body for medical reasons. Methods include drugs, acupuncture, and hypnosis. The procedure may render the patient unconscious **(general anesthesia)** or merely numb a body part **(local anesthesia)**. **2.** MED LOSS OF SENSATION the loss of sensation caused by damage to a nerve **3.** APATHY a state of apathy or mindlessness [Early 18thC. Via modern Latin, from Greek *anaisthēsia*, literally "lack of sensation," from *aisthēsis* "feeling, sensation" (see AESTHETIC).]

an·es·the·si·ol·o·gist /ànnəss theezee óllәjəst/, **an·aes·the·si·ol·o·gist** *n.* a doctor qualified to administer anesthetics to patients. ◊ **anesthetist**

an·es·the·si·ol·o·gy /ànnəss theezee óllәjee/, **an·aes·the·si·ol·o·gy** *n.* the branch of medicine that deals with the study and use of anesthetic substances

an·es·thet·ic /ànnəss théttik/, **an·aes·thet·ic** *n.* SUBSTANCE THAT DULLS PAIN a substance that reduces sensitivity to pain and may cause unconsciousness, especially a drug used in medicine ■ *adj.* PAIN-REDUCING relating to or producing loss of sensation and unconsciousness [Mid-19thC. Formed from Greek *anaisthētos*, literally "without feeling," from *aisthētos* "capable of feeling" (see AESTHETIC).] —**an·es·thet·ic·al·ly** *adv.*

a·nes·the·tist /ə nésthətəst/, **a·naes·the·tist** *n. U.K.* = **anesthesiologist**

a·nes·the·tize /ə nésthətìz/ (**-tized, -tiz·ing, -tiz·es**), **a·naes·the·tize** (**-tiz·ed, -tiz·ing, -tiz·es**) *vt.* to administer an anesthetic to somebody —**an·es·the·ti·za·tion** /ə nèsthətə záysh'n/ *n.*

an·es·trous /an éstrəss/ *adj.* **1.** NOT ACTIVE SEXUALLY used to describe a female mammal that is sexually inactive between breeding periods **2.** WITHOUT SEXUAL ACTIVITY used to describe the period of sexual inactivity between breeding periods in certain female mammals

an·es·trus /an éstrəss/ *n.* the period of sexual inactivity between the breeding periods of certain female mammals

an·eu·ploid /ánnyə plòyd/ *adj.* used to describe a cell or organism with fewer or more chromosomes than usual —**an·eu·ploid** *n.* —**an·eu·ploid·y** *n.*

an·eu·rysm /ánnyə rìzzəm/, **an·eu·rism** *n.* a fluid-filled sac formed when the wall of an artery abnormally dilates [From Greek *aneurusma* "dilation, swelling," from *aneurunein* "to widen out," from *ana-* "through" + *eurus* "wide"] —**an·eu·rys·mal** /ánnyə rízm'l/ *adj.*

a·new /ə nóo, -nyóo/ *adv.* **1.** AGAIN again or once more **2.** IN NEW WAY in a new way or form that is unlike the previous one [14thC. From *a-* (an eroded form of *of*) + NEW; probably modeled on Old French *de neuf, de nouveau*.]

an·frac·tu·os·i·ty /àn frakchoo óssətee/ (*plural* **-ties**) *n.* (*literary*) **1.** TWIST a twist or turn, e.g., in a road or in the plot of a novel **2.** TWISTINESS the twisting, turning nature of something

an·frac·tu·ous /an frákchoo əss/ *adj.* with much twisting and turning (*literary*) [Late 16thC. From late Latin *anfractuosus*, from Latin *anfractus* "bending," from *ambi-* "around" + *fract-*, the past participle stem of *frangere* "to break" (see FRANGIBLE).]

Ang. *abbr.* Angola

an·gel /áynjəl/ *n.* **1.** RELIG HEAVENLY BEING a divine being who acts as a messenger of God. According to a medieval hierarchy, the nine classes of heavenly being are, in ascending order, angels, archangels, principalities, powers, virtues, dominations, thrones, cherubim, and seraphim. **2.** PICTURE OF HEAVENLY BEING a picture of an angel as a human figure with wings **3.** KIND PERSON somebody who is kind or beautiful **4.** GUARDIAN AND GUIDE a spirit that protects and offers guidance **5.** CHR MEMBER OF LOWEST ANGELIC ORDER a member of the lowest order of angels in the medieval Christian celestial hierarchy, ranked below archangels **6.** MONEY OLD ENGLISH COIN a gold coin that was a unit of currency in England from 1465 to the early 17th century [13thC. Via Old French from, ultimately, Greek *aggelos* "messenger."]

WORD KEY: SYNONYMS

See Synonyms at ***backer***.

an·gel dust *n.* DRUGS the illegal hallucinogenic drug phencyclidine (*slang*) [From its white color]

An·gel Falls the world's highest waterfall, located in southeastern Venezuela in the Guiana Highlands. Height: 3,212 ft./979 m.

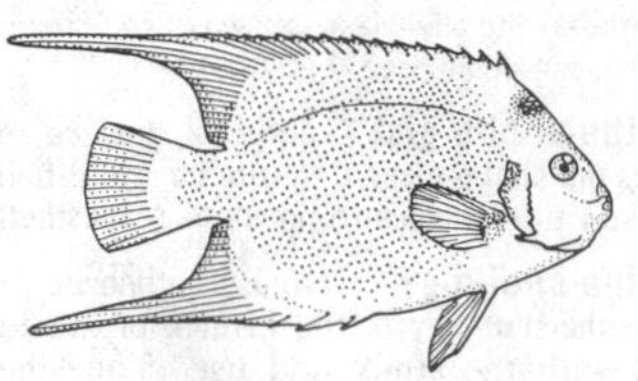

Angelfish

an·gel·fish /áynjəl fish/ (*plural* **-fish** *or* **-fish·es**) *n.* **1.** **TROPICAL FRESHWATER FISH WITH STRIPED BODY** a freshwater fish found in the tropical waters of South America. It has a broad striped body and large fins, and is often kept in aquariums. Latin name: *Pterophyllum scalare.* **2.** **TROPICAL MARINE FISH** a brightly colored tropical marine fish that has a broad flat body. Family: Chaetodontidae and Pomocanthidae. **3.** = **angel shark** [Mainly from the fish's long winglike fins]

an·gel food cake, **an·gel cake** *n.* a whitish light-textured cake with a delicate flavor, made with egg whites but without yolks

an·gel·ic /an jéllik/, **an·gel·i·cal** /-jéllik'l/ *adj.* **1.** **KINDLY** very kind or beautiful **2.** **OF ANGELS** relating to angels —**an·gel·i·cal·ly** *adv.* —**an·gel·i·cal·ness** *n.*

an·gel·i·ca /an jéllikə/ (*plural* **-cas** *or* **-ca**) *n.* **1.** PLANTS **TALL HOLLOW-STEMMED FLOWERING PLANT** a tall hollow-stemmed flowering plant of the carrot family. Angelicas have white or greenish flowers and are found mainly in Europe and Asia. Genus: *Angelica.* **2.** COOK **CANDIED STEMS OF ANGELICA PLANT** the bright green, candied stems of the angelica plant, used to decorate cakes and cookies [Early 16thC. From medieval Latin, short for *herba angelica*, literally "angelic plant"; perhaps from its traditional use as a remedy for poison and contagion.]

an·gel·i·cal *adj.* = **angelic**

An·gel·i·co /an jélli kō/, **Fra** (1400?–55) Italian religious painter. He became a Dominican monk. He is noted for his frescoes in Florence, including the *Annunciation* and the *Coronation of the Virgin.* Born **Guido di Pietro**

An·gel of Death *n.* = **Azrael**

an·gel of mer·cy *n.* somebody who brings welcome assistance

Maya Angelou

An·ge·lou /ánjə lōō/, **Maya** (*b.* 1928) U.S. writer. Her novels and poetry are notable for their depiction of assertive African American women.

an·gel shark *n.* a small shark with a flat body, broad head, and enlarged pectoral fins, giving it the appearance of a ray. Genus: *Squatina.* [From its winglike pectoral fins]

An·ge·lus /ánjələss/, **an·ge·lus** *n.* **1.** **ROMAN CATHOLIC PRAYERS** in the Roman Catholic Church, a set of prayers to commemorate the Annunciation and the Incarnation **2.** **BELL ANNOUNCING ANGELUS** a bell rung to announce the time for the Angelus [Mid-17thC. From Latin *Angelus domini* "the angel of the Lord," the first words of the prayer.]

an·ger /áng gər/ *n.* **GREAT ANNOYANCE** a feeling of extreme annoyance ■ *vti.* (**-gered, -ger·ing, -gers**) **BECOME OR MAKE GREATLY ANNOYED** to become or make somebody extremely annoyed [13thC. From Old Norse *angr* "trouble, sorrow." Ultimately from an Indo-European base meaning "tight, painful," which is also the ancestor of English *anxious, anguish, hangnail,* and *angina.*]

WORD KEY: SYNONYMS

anger, annoyance, resentment, indignation, fury, rage, ire, wrath

CORE MEANING: a feeling of strong displeasure in response to an assumed injury

anger the most general term; **annoyance** a feeling of irritation, milder or more fleeting than anger; **resentment** subdued anger caused by a sense of unfair treatment, and a powerlessness to remedy this; **indignation** anger based on a condemnation of something considered wrong or unfair; **fury** an intense form of anger that suggests lack of control and potential to do violence; **rage** violent anger, more intense than fury; **ire** a literary term for *anger*; **wrath** a literary or formal term for strong anger, often with overtones of a desire for revenge.

WORD KEY: CULTURAL NOTE

Look Back in Anger, a play by English dramatist John Osborne (1956). Seen at the time of its first performances as a landmark play that reflected the disaffection of many young people, this domestic drama focuses on Jimmy Porter, a working-class graduate who feels stifled by the middle-class family into which he has married and trapped by traditional social conventions.

An·ge·vin /ánjəvin/ *adj.* **1.** **OF ANJOU** relating to the Anjou region in France **2.** **OF ANJOU AND PLANTAGENET DYNASTIES** relating to the House of Anjou, especially the branch that includes the Plantagenet kings of England [Mid-17thC. Via French from medieval Latin *Andegavinus*, from *Andegavia* "Anjou."]

an·gi·na /an jīnə/, **an·gi·na pec·to·ris** /-péktəriss/ *n.* a medical condition in which lack of blood to the heart causes severe chest pains [Mid-16thC. From Latin, "quinsy," an alteration (influenced by *angere* "to squeeze") of Greek *agkhonē* "strangling," from *agkhein* "to squeeze, strangle."]

angio- *prefix.* **1.** blood or lymph vessel ○ *angiogram* **2.** pericarp ○ *angiosperm* [Via modern Latin from Greek *aggeion* "blood vessel," literally "small vessel," from *aggos* "vessel," of unknown origin]

an·gi·o·car·di·og·ra·phy /ànjee ō kaardee óggrəfee/ *n.* X-ray examination of the heart and related blood vessels after a substance that will show up when X-rayed has been injected into the bloodstream —**an·gi·o·car·di·o·graph·ic** /ànji ō kaardee ə gráffik/ *adj.*

an·gi·o·gen·e·sis /ànjee ō jénnəssəss/ *n.* the formation of new blood vessels, e.g., in an embryo or as a result of a tumor

an·gi·o·gram /ánjee ə gram/ *n.* an X-ray photograph of a blood vessel

an·gi·og·raph·y /ànjee óggrəfee/ *n.* X-ray examination of blood vessels after a substance that will show up when X-rayed has been injected into the bloodstream —**an·gi·o·graph·ic** /ànjee ə gráffik/ *adj.*

an·gi·ol·o·gy /ànjee óllәjee/ *n.* the branch of medicine that deals with blood vessels and the lymphatic system

Angkor

an·gi·o·ma /ànjee ṓmə/ (*plural* **-mas** *or* **-ma·ta** /-mətə/) *n.* a benign tumor made up of blood or lymph vessels —**an·gi·o·ma·tous** *adj.*

an·gi·op·a·thy /ànjee óppəthee/ (*plural* **-thies**) *n.* a disease of the blood vessels or lymph vessels

an·gi·o·plas·ty /ánjee ə plàstee/ (*plural* **-ties**) *n.* a surgical operation to clear a narrowed or blocked artery

an·gi·o·sar·co·ma /ànjee ō saar kṓmə/ *n.* a malignant tumor consisting of vascular cells, often in the liver

an·gi·o·scope /ánjee ə skōp/ *n.* a long fine surgical viewing instrument threaded into a patient's blood vessels, to allow surgeons to observe and perform operations without large incisions [Late 20thC] —**an·gi·os·co·py** /ànjee os kəpee/ *n.*

an·gi·o·sperm /ánjee ə spùrm/ *n.* a plant in which the sex organs are within flowers and the seeds are in a fruit. ◊ **gymnosperm** [Early 19thC. Coined from ANGIO- + Greek *sperma* "seed."]

an·gi·o·ten·sin /ànjee ō ténsən/ *n.* a hormone that causes blood pressure to rise, formed in the blood by a series of processes that can be influenced by drugs [Mid-20thC. Coined from ANGIO- + HYPERTENSION + -IN.]

Ang·kor /áng kàwr/, **Âng·kôr** ancient capital city of early Khmer civilization, now deserted but noted for its temples and monuments, built 850–900. It is in present-day northwestern Cambodia. Area: 5 sq. mi./13 sq. km.

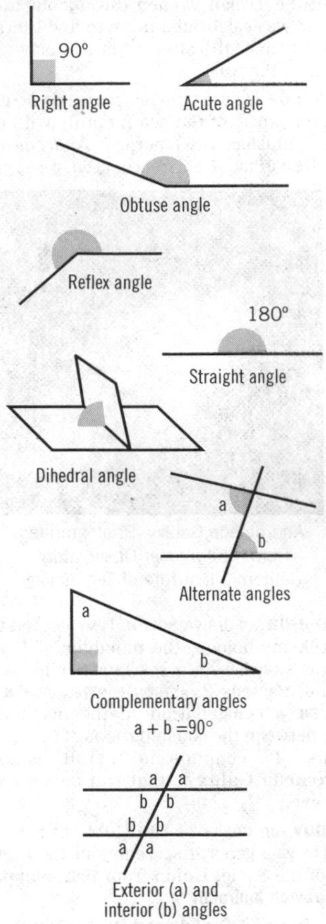

Angle

an·gle[1] /áng g'l/ *n.* **1.** **SPACE BETWEEN DIVERGING LINES** the space between two diverging lines or planes, or a measure of the space **2.** **FIGURE FORMED BY DIVERGING LINES** a figure formed by two lines diverging from a common point or two planes diverging from a common line **3.** = **solid angle** **4.** **PART THAT STICKS OUT** a projecting part of something **5.** **POSITION FOR VIEWING SOMETHING** a position from which somebody can look at something ○ *a sculpture seen from three angles* **6.** **WAY OF CONSIDERING SOMETHING** a way of looking at a situation ○ *Consider the matter from this angle.* ■ *v.* (**-gled, -gling, -gles**) **1.** *vi.* **CHANGE DIRECTION SHARPLY** to turn in a sharply different direction **2.** *vti.* **DIRECT OR PLACE OBLIQUELY** to direct or place something obliquely, or move or be placed obliquely **3.** *vt.* **PRESENT SOMETHING WITH BIAS** to present something with a particular audience in mind or in order to express a particular point of view [14thC. Directly or via French from Latin *angulus* "corner." Ultimately from an Indo-European base meaning "to bend, hook," which is also the ancestor of *angle*[2], *ankle,* and *anchor.*]

an·gle[2] /áng g'l/ (**-gled, -gling, -gles**) *vi.* **1.** **FISH WITH ROD** to fish with a hook, line, and rod **2.** **ATTEMPT TO GET SOMETHING** to attempt to obtain a compliment or an advantage (*informal*) [Old English *angul* "fishhook." Ultimately from an Indo-European base meaning "to bend, hook," which is also the ancestor of English *angle*[1], *ankle*, and *anchor*.]

An·gle /áng g'l/ *n.* a member of a Germanic people who invaded and settled throughout eastern and northern England in the 5th and 6th centuries A.D. [Pre-12thC. From Latin *Angli*, literally "people from *Angul*" in North Germany (source also of *English*), of Germanic origin; ultimately related to *angle*[1].]

an·gle bar *n.* = **angle iron**

an·gle brack·et *n.* one of a pair of marks, < or >, used to enclose text

an·gle i·ron *n.* an iron or steel bar that is L-shaped in cross section

an·gle of at·tack *n.* the acute angle between the direction of airflow and the line linking the leading and trailing edges of an aircraft wing

an·gle of bank *n.* the angle between the lateral and horizontal axes of an aircraft in flight

an·gle of dip *n.* PHYS = **dip**

an·gle of in·ci·dence *n.* the angle between an incoming ray of light and the line perpendicular to the surface at the point of arrival

an·gle of re·flec·tion *n.* the angle between a reflected ray of light and the line perpendicular to the surface at the point of reflection

an·gle of re·frac·tion *n.* the angle between a refracted ray of light and the line perpendicular to the surface at the point of refraction

an·gle of re·pose *n.* the maximum slope or angle at which unconsolidated material such as sand can be made into a mound before it begins to slide

an·gle of yaw *n.* the acute angle between the direction in which an aircraft is flying and its own longitudinal axis

an·gle plate *n.* an L-shaped metal plate used to support a framework

an·gler /áng glər/ *n.* **1.** SOMEBODY WHO GOES FISHING somebody who fishes with a hook, line, and rod **2.** ZOOL = **anglerfish**

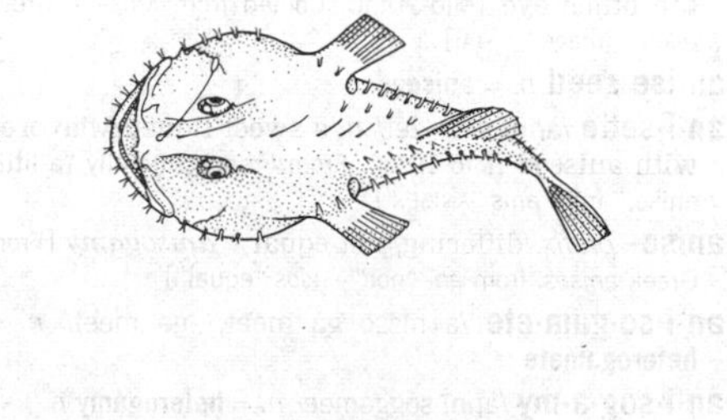

Anglerfish

an·gler·fish /áng glər fish/ (*plural* **-fish** *or* **-fish·es**) *n.* a marine fish that uses a long dorsal fin extending over its mouth to attract prey. Order: Lophiiformes.

An·gle·sey /áng g'lsee/ island off the coast of northwestern Wales in the county of Gwynedd. Population: 67,200 (1995). Area: 276 sq. mi./620 sq. km.

an·gle·site /áng g'l sìt/ *n.* a colorless, white, or lightly tinted mineral consisting of lead sulfate

An·gli·an /áng glee ən/ *adj.* OF ANGLES relating to the Angles ■ *n.* LANG GROUP OF OLD ENGLISH DIALECTS a group of dialects of Old English that includes Mercian and Northumbrian. ◊ **Kentish, West Saxon** [Early 18thC. Formed from Latin *Angli* "the Angles" (see ANGLE).]

An·gli·can /áng glәkən/ *adj.* OF ANGLICAN CHURCH relating to the Anglican Church ■ *n.* MEMBER OF ANGLICAN CHURCH somebody who belongs to an Anglican denomination [Early 17thC. Via medieval Latin *Anglicanus* "English" from, ultimately, Latin *Angli* "Angles" (see ANGLE); from its originally denoting the Church of England.]

An·gli·can Church, An·gli·can Com·mun·ion *n.* a group of Christian churches including the Churches of England and Ireland, as well as the Protestant Episcopal Church

An·gli·can·ism /áng glәkə nìzzəm/ *n.* the doctrines of the Church of England and other Anglican churches

An·gli·cism /áng glə sìzzəm/, **an·gli·cism** *n.* **1.** BRITISH ENGLISH WORD a term that is peculiar to British English as opposed to other varieties of English **2.** ENGLISH WORD IN FOREIGN LANGUAGE an English word or phrase used in a foreign language [Mid-17thC. Formed from medieval Latin *Anglicus* "English" (see ANGLICAN).]

An·gli·cize /áng gli sìz/, **an·gli·cize** (**-cized, -ciz·ing, -ciz·es**) *vti.* to become or make somebody or something more English [Early 18thC. Formed from medieval Latin *Anglicus* "English" (see ANGLICAN).] —**An·gli·ci·za·tion** /àng glissi záysh'n/ *n.*

An·glin /áng glin/, **Margaret** (1876–1958) Canadian actor. She was a stage performer in Canada, Australia, and the United States.

an·gling /áng gling/ *n.* the sport of catching fish with a hook, line, and rod

An·glo /áng glō/ (*plural* **-glos**), **an·glo** (*plural* **-glos**) *n.* (*informal*) **1.** NON-HISPANIC WHITE PERSON an English-speaking white person in the United States who is not of Hispanic origin **2.** *Can* NON-FRENCH-SPEAKING CANADIAN an English-speaking person in Canada, especially in Quebec [Early 19thC. From ANGLO-.]

Anglo- *prefix.* England, the English ○ *Anglophile* [From Latin *Angli* "Angles" (see ANGLE)]

An·glo-A·mer·i·can *n.* a citizen of the United States or Canada whose ancestors were originally from Britain and whose language and culture derive from Britain

An·glo-French *adj.* relating to the links that exist between France and Great Britain

An·glo-In·di·an *adj.* FROM INDIAN LANGUAGE introduced into English from an Indian language ■ *n.* **1.** SOMEBODY WITH BRITISH AND INDIAN ANCESTRY somebody of mixed English or British and Indian descent **2.** BRITISH PERSON RESIDENT IN INDIA an English or British person who has lived a long time in India, especially during the time when India was a British colony

An·glo-I·rish *npl.* people of English descent who were born or live in Ireland —**An·glo-I·rish** *adj.*

An·glo-Nor·man *adj.* HIST ENGLISH AND NORMAN connected with the 11th-century Norman conquerors of England ■ *n.* **1.** HIST NORMAN IN ENGLAND a Norman inhabitant of England after 1066 **2.** LANG FRENCH SPOKEN IN MEDIEVAL ENGLAND the form of Norman French spoken in medieval England

An·glo·phile /áng glə fìl/ *n.* somebody who greatly admires England or the English —**An·glo·phil·i·a** /àng glə fíllee ə/ *n.* —**An·glo·phil·ic** /-fíllik/ *adj.*

An·glo·phobe /áng glə fōb/ *n.* somebody who hates England or the English —**An·glo·pho·bi·a** /àng glə fōbee ə/ *n.* —**An·glo·pho·bic** /-fōbik/ *adj.*

An·glo·phone /áng glə fōn/, **an·glo·phone** *n.* SPEAKER OF ENGLISH somebody who speaks English, especially as a first language ■ *adj.* WHERE ENGLISH IS MOTHER TONGUE where English is spoken by most people as their first language

An·glo-Sax·on *n.* **1.** PEOPLES MEMBER OF GERMANIC PEOPLE a member of one of the West Germanic peoples who settled in Britain from the fifth century A.D. and were dominant until 1066. They included the Angles, Saxons, and Jutes. **2.** LANG = **Old English 3.** WHITE ENGLISH NATIVE SPEAKER somebody who is white, speaks English as a first language, and has connections with an English-speaking country ■ *adj.* **1.** LANG FROM OLD ENGLISH used to describe a word in Modern English that comes from Old English **2.** OF ENGLISH SPEAKERS relating to white English speakers [Early 17thC. From modern Latin *Anglo-Saxones* "Anglo-Saxons," a translation of Old English *Angulseaxe* "English Saxon" (as opposed to one living on the continent of Europe).]

ang mo /áng mó/ (*plural* **ang mos**) *n. Malaysia, Singapore* an inhabitant of the West, especially western Europe or North America (*informal*) [From Hokkien, literally "red hair"]

An·go·la /ang gṓlə/ republic in west central Africa that gained its independence from Portugal in 1975. Language: Portuguese. Currency: kwanza. Capital: Luanda. Population: 10,548,000 (1997). Area: 481,530 sq. mi./1,246,700 sq. km. —**An·go·lan** *adj., n.*

an·go·ra /ang gáwrə/ *n.* **1.** SILKY-HAIRED ANIMAL a rabbit, goat, or cat belonging to a breed with long silky fur **2.** WOOL FROM ANGORA HAIR wool made from the hair of an angora goat or rabbit (*often used before a noun*) ◊ **mohair** [Early 19thC. From ANGORA.]

an·gos·tu·ra /àng gə stŏŏrə/, **an·gos·tu·ra bark** *n.* the bitter aromatic bark of either of two South American citrus trees, used as a flavoring in bitters and

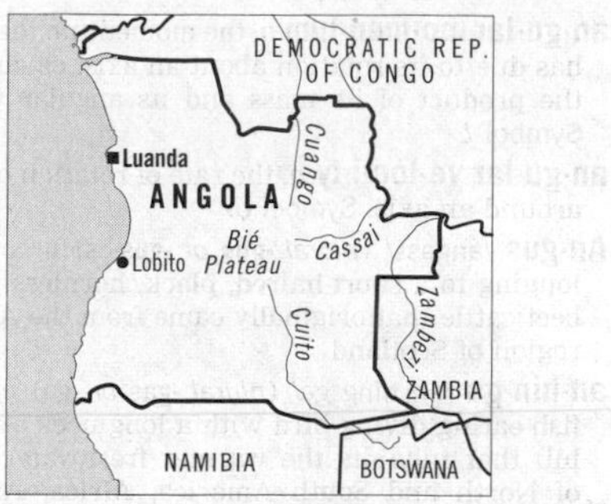

Angola

formerly used medicinally to relieve fever [Named for the city of *Angostura* (Ciudad Bolívar) in Venezuela]

an·gri·ly /áng grəlee/ *adv.* **1.** WITH ANGER in a way that conveys extreme annoyance or displeasure **2.** STORMILY in a stormy threatening way

an·gry /áng gree/ (**-gri·er, -gri·est**) *adj.* **1.** FEELING VERY ANNOYED feeling extremely annoyed, often about an insult or a wrong **2.** EXPRESSING ANNOYANCE expressing extreme annoyance ○ *"Low growls and angry snarls assailed our ears on every side..."* (Edgar Rice Burroughs, *The Gods of Mars*; 1913) **3.** STORMY stormy-looking **4.** INFLAMED inflamed and painful-looking [14thC. Formed from ANGER.]

an·gry young man *n.* **1. an·gry young man, An·gry Young Man** LITERAT, THEATER REBELLIOUS WRITER a member of a group of British male writers in the 1950s who were hostile to authority. The setting for their works is typically working-class, and the central character typically a male loner. (*often used in the plural*) **2.** REBELLIOUS YOUNG MAN a young man who is hostile to authority

angst /angkst, angst, aangkst, aangst/ *n.* **1.** PHILOSOPHY EXISTENTIALIST DREAD in existentialist philosophy, a feeling of dread arising from an awareness of free choice **2.** ANXIETY any feeling of dread or anxiety [Early 20thC. From German. Ultimately from an Indo-European base meaning "tight, painful," which is also the ancestor of English *anguish* and *anger*.]

WORD KEY: SYNONYMS

See Synonyms at ***worry***.

ang·strom /ángstrəm/, **ang·strom u·nit** *n.* a unit of length equal to one ten-billionth of a meter (10^{-10} m), used to measure the wavelengths of electromagnetic radiations. Symbol ° [Late 19thC. Named for the Swedish physicist and astronomer Anders Jonas *Ångström*, (1814–84).]

An·guil·la /ang gwíllə/ one of the Leeward Islands, in the West Indies. It is east of Puerto Rico. Area: 35 sq. mi./91 sq. km.

an·guish /áng gwish/ *n.* EXTREME ANXIETY extreme anxiety or emotional torment ■ *vti.* (**-guished, -guish·ing, -guish·es**) FEEL OR CAUSE SOMEBODY ANGUISH to feel or cause somebody to feel anguish [12thC. Via Old French *anguis* from, ultimately, Latin *angustus* "narrow, tight." Ultimately from an Indo-European base meaning "tight, painful," which is also the ancestor of English *anxious*, *anger*, *hangnail*, and *angina*.]

an·guished /áng gwisht/ *adj.* **1.** WITH ANGUISH feeling or showing extreme anxiety or torment **2.** CAUSING ANGUISH producing extreme anxiety or other torment

an·gu·lar /áng gyələr/ *adj.* **1.** THIN thin and bony **2.** AWKWARD AND UNGAINLY stiff, awkward, and ungainly **3.** SHARPLY DEFINED used to describe an object with a lot of angles **4.** MATH MEASURED BY ANGLES measured by an angle or rate of change of an angle [14thC. From Latin *angularis*, from *angulus* (see ANGLE[1]).]

an·gu·lar ac·cel·er·a·tion *n.* the rate at which the rotation of a rotating body changes. Symbol α

an·gu·lar dis·place·ment *n.* the angle through which something has been rotated about an axis, usually measured in radians

an·gu·lar fre·quen·cy *n.* the frequency of a repeating rotation expressed in radians per second, or the frequency of an oscillation multiplied by 2π. Symbol ω

an·gu·lar·i·ty /àng gyə lérrətee/ (*plural* **-ties**) *n.* **1.** THIN BONY QUALITY the thin and bony appearance of somebody's body **2.** SHARP ANGLE a sharp corner or angle (*often used in the plural*)

an·gu·lar mo·men·tum *n.* the momentum that a body has due to its rotation about an axis, calculated as the product of its mass and its angular velocity. Symbol *L*

an·gu·lar ve·loc·i·ty *n.* the rate of rotation of a body around an axis. Symbol *ω*

An·gus /ángəss/ (*plural* **-gus** *or* **-gus·es**) *n.* a cow belonging to a short-haired, black, hornless breed of beef cattle that originally came from the Aberdeen region of Scotland

an·hin·ga /an híng gə/ (*plural* **-gas** *or* **-ga**) *n.* BIRDS a fish-eating diving bird with a long neck and sharp bill that inhabits the warmer freshwater regions of North and South America, Africa, Asia, and Australia. Family: Anhingidae. [Mid-18thC. Via Portuguese from Tupi *áyinga*.]

An·hui /aán hweé/, **An·hwei** province in east central China surrounded by the provinces of Jiangsu, Zhejiang, Jiangxi, Hubei, and Henan. Capital: Hefei. Population: 59,550,000 (1994). Area: 54,015 sq. mi./139,899 sq. km.

an·hy·dride /an hī́ drīd, -drid/ *n.* a chemical compound formed when water molecules are removed from another compound [Mid-19thC. Formed from ANHYDROUS.]

an·hy·drite /an hī́ drīt/ *n.* a colorless or lightly tinted mineral consisting of anhydrous calcium sulfate, used in cement and fertilizers. Formula: $CaSO_4$. [Early 19thC. Formed from ANHYDROUS.]

an·hy·drous /an hī́ drəss/ *adj.* used to describe compounds that contain no water, or crystals that lack chemically bound water (**water of crystallization**) [Early 19thC. From Greek *anudros*, literally "waterless," from *hudōr* "water" (see HYDRO-).]

a·ni /aa neé/ (*plural* **a·nis** *or* **a·ni**) *n.* a black long-tailed bird of the cuckoo family that has a heavy arched bill and lives in tropical America. Anis lay eggs in a communal nest. Genus: *Crotophaga*. [Early 19thC. Via Spanish *aní* or Portuguese *ani* from Tupi *anū*.]

An·i·ak·chak Na·tion·al Mon·u·ment and Pre·serve /ànnee ák chàk-/ national park in southwestern Alaska. One of its outstanding natural features is the Aniakchak Crater, a volcanic crater 2,000 ft./610 m deep.

an·ic·ca /ə níkə/ *n.* in Buddhism, the cycle of birth, life, and death [Via Pali from Sanskrit *anitya-* "not eternal," from *nitya-* "constant, perpetual"]

an·il /ánnil/ (*plural* **-ils** *or* **-il**) *n.* a West Indian shrub with small reddish yellow flowers that is the source of indigo dye. Latin name: *Indigofera suffruticosa*. [Late 16thC. Via French, Portuguese, Arabic, and Persian from, ultimately, Sanskrit *nīla-* "dark blue."]

an·ile /á nīl, áy-/ *adj.* typical of or resembling a woman of advanced years [Mid-17thC. From Latin *anilis*, from *anus* "venerable woman."]

an·i·line /ánn'lən/ *n.* a colorless poisonous oily liquid that is used in the manufacture of dyes, resins, pharmaceuticals, and explosives. Formula: $C_6H_5NH_2$. [Mid-19thC. Formed from *anil* the indigo plant, because it was first obtained by distilling indigo with alkali.]

an·i·line dye *n.* a synthetic dye derived from aniline

a·ni·lin·gus /àyni líng gəss/ *n.* the practice of stimulating the anus with the tongue or mouth [Mid-20thC. From modern Latin, formed from Latin *anus* "anus," on the model of CUNNILINGUS.]

an·i·ma /ánnəmə/ *n.* **1. INNER SELF** in Jungian psychology, the true inner self as opposed to the outer persona **2. MALE'S FEMININE SIDE** in Jungian psychology, the feminine aspect of the male personality [Early 20thC. From Latin, "breath, soul, spirit" (source also of English *animate* and *unanimous*).]

an·i·mad·ver·sion /ànnə mad vúrzh'n/ *n.* a critical comment or comments, especially those reproaching somebody

an·i·mad·vert /ànnə mad vúrt, -məd-/ (**-vert·ed, -vert·ing, -verts**) *vi.* to comment critically or unfavorably [Mid-17thC. From Latin *animadvertere*, literally "to turn the mind toward," from *animus* "mind" + *advertere* "to turn toward" (see ADVERT[1]).]

an·i·mal /ánnəm'l/ *n.* **1. LIVING ORGANISM WITH INDEPENDENT MOVEMENT** a living organism that is distinguished from plants by independent movement and responsive sense organs **2. MAMMAL** a land mammal other than a human being **3. BRUTISH PERSON** somebody who is vulgar or brutish **4. INSTINCT-DRIVEN INNER SELF** the instinctive inner self as opposed to the one subject to self-restraint **5. PERSON OR THING** any particular person or thing (*informal*) ■ *adj.* **1. FROM ANIMALS** derived from animals **2. INSTINCTIVE** belonging to the realm of instincts and urges [14thC. From Latin *animale*, from *animalis* "living, breathing," from *anima* "breath, life, soul" (see ANIMA).]

an·i·mal crack·er *n.* a small cookie in the shape of an animal

an·i·mal hus·band·ry *n.* the branch of agriculture concerned with breeding and rearing farm animals

an·i·mal·ism /ánnəm'l ìzzəm/ *n.* **1. PREOCCUPATION WITH PHYSICAL SIDE OF LIFE** preoccupation with physical rather than spiritual needs **2. THEORY OF HUMANS' NONSPIRITUAL NATURE** the theory that human beings are driven by physical appetites rather than spiritual needs **3. TYPICAL ANIMAL BEHAVIOR** behavior that is typical of animals —**an·i·mal·is·tic** /ànnəmə lístik/ *adj.*

an·i·mal·ist /ánnəm'l ìst/ *n.* **1. SOMEBODY PREOCCUPIED WITH PHYSICAL NEEDS** somebody who is preoccupied with physical rather than spiritual needs **2. SOMEBODY DENYING HUMANS' SPIRITUAL NATURE** somebody who holds that human beings are driven by physical appetites rather than spiritual needs **3. ANIMAL RIGHTS SUPPORTER** somebody who believes in animal rights and is prepared to take part in militant action to protect them (*informal*)

an·i·mal·i·ty /ànnə málləteé/ *n.* **1. ANIMAL CHARACTERISTICS** the characteristics of animals, as opposed to plants **2.** = **animalism** *n.* 1

an·i·mal·ize /ánnəmə līz/ (**-ized, -iz·ing, -iz·es**) *vt.* to bring out somebody's brutal or instinctive nature —**an·i·mal·i·za·tion** /ànnəmə lə záysh'n/ *n.*

an·i·mal lib·er·a·tion *n.* the movement to free animals from human exploitation (*often used before a noun*)

an·i·mal mag·net·ism *n.* somebody's strong physical attractiveness (*informal humorous*)

an·i·mal pro·tein *n.* animal tissue processed for commercial or industrial use

an·i·mal starch *n.* = **glycogen**

an·i·mal wel·far·ist *n.* somebody who believes in the rights of animals

an·i·mate *vt.* /ánnə màyt/ (**-mat·ed, -mat·ing, -mates**) **1. MAKE LIVELY** to make somebody or something lively **2. INSPIRE SOMEBODY** to rouse or inspire somebody to take action or to have strong feelings **3. PRESENT SOMETHING USING ANIMATION TECHNIQUES** to present or record something in the form of a sequence of moving still images **4. MAKE SOMEBODY ACTIVE** to arouse somebody or something into activity **5. CAUSE TO LIVE** to bring somebody or something to life ■ *adj.* /ánnə mət/ **1. PHYSICALLY ALIVE** in a physically live state, as opposed to being dead or inert **2. FULL OF LIVELINESS** full of liveliness or energy [14thC. From Latin *animat-*, the past participle stem of *animare* "to give life to," from *anima* (see ANIMA).]

WORD KEY: SYNONYMS

See Synonyms at ***living***.

an·i·mat·ed /ánnə màytəd/ *adj.* **1. LIVELY OR BUSY** full of liveliness or activity **2. FILMED AS MOVING SEQUENCE OF STILLS** in the form of a sequence of moving still images —**an·i·mat·ed·ly** *adv.*

an·i·ma·tion /ànnə máysh'n/ *n.* **1. LIVELINESS** liveliness in the way somebody speaks or behaves **2. PRODUCTION OF ANIMATED FILMS** the making of movies by filming a sequence of slightly varying drawings or models so that they appear to move and change when the sequence is shown **3. ANIMATED MOVIE OR PICTURES** a movie or pictures consisting of a series of drawn, painted, or modeled scenes

a·ni·ma·to /aànə maátō/ *adj., adv.* to be played in a lively animated manner (*used as a musical direction*) [Early 18thC. Via Italian from, ultimately, Latin *animare* (see ANIMATE).]

a·ni·ma·tor /ánnə màytər/ *n.* **1. MAKER OF ANIMATED MOVIES** somebody who makes animated movies, or who provides a technical or artistic skill needed to produce animations **2. SOMEBODY OR SOMETHING ADDING LIVELINESS** somebody or something that makes things lively, exciting, or interesting

an·i·ma·tron·ics /ànnəmə trónniks/ *n.* the use of computer technology and a form of radio control to animate puppets or other models, e.g., for a movie (*takes a singular verb*) [Late 20thC. A blend of ANIMATE and ELECTRONICS.] —**an·i·ma·tron·ic** *adj.*

an·i·mé /ánni mày/ *n.* any of various resins from tropical American trees, used in varnishes and scents [Late 16thC. Via French from Tupi *wana'ni*.]

an·i·mism /ánnə mìzzəm/ *n.* **1. BELIEF THAT NATURE HAS A SOUL** the belief that things in nature, e.g., trees, mountains, and the sky, have souls or consciousness **2. BELIEF IN ORGANIZING FORCE IN UNIVERSE** the belief that a supernatural force animates and organizes the universe **3. BELIEF IN EXISTENCE OF SEPARATE SPIRIT** the belief that people have spirits that do or can exist separately from their bodies [Mid-19thC. Formed from Latin *anima* "soul."] —**an·i·mist** *adj., n.* —**an·i·mis·tic** /ànni místik/ *adj.*

an·i·mos·i·ty /ànnə móssəteé/ (*plural* **-ties**) *n.* a feeling or spirit of hostility and resentment [15thC. Directly or via French *animosité* from late Latin *animositas* "spiritedness," from *animosus* "spirited," from *animus* (see ANIMUS).]

WORD KEY: SYNONYMS

See Synonyms at ***dislike***.

an·i·mus /ánnəməss/ *n.* **1. HOSTILITY** a feeling or display of animosity **2. DISPOSITION** an attitude or feeling that motivates somebody's actions **3. FEMALE PERSONALITY'S MALE SIDE** in Jungian psychology, the masculine aspect of the female personality [Early 19thC. From Latin, "mind, spirit."]

an·i·on /á nī ən/ *n.* a negatively charged ion, especially one that is attracted to an anode, either during electrolysis or within a vacuum tube [Mid-19thC. A blend of ANODE and ION.] —**an·i·on·ic** /ànnī ónnik/ *adj.* —**an·i·on·i·cal·ly** *adv.*

an·ise /ánniss/ *n.* **1. PLANT WITH LICORICE-FLAVORED SEEDS** an aromatic Mediterranean plant with licorice-flavored seeds (**aniseed**), used in medicines and for flavoring food and drinks. Latin name: *Pimpinella anisum*. **2.** = **aniseed** [13thC. Via French *anis* and Latin *anisum* from Greek *anison*.]

an·i·seed /ánni seéd/ *n.* the licorice-flavored seeds of anise, used whole or in ground spice mixtures as a flavoring in foods, especially candy and cakes, and in drinks, e.g., pastis and ouzo

an·i·sei·ko·ni·a /a nìsī kṓnee ə/ *n.* a defect in the lens of one eye that results in its seeing an image that differs in size and shape from the image seen by the other eye [Mid-20thC. Coined from ANIS- + Greek *eikōn* "image" + -IA.]

an·ise seed *n.* = **aniseed**

an·i·sette /ánni sét, -zét/ *n.* a sweet liqueur flavored with aniseed [Mid-19thC. From French, literally "a little anise," from *anis* "ANISE."]

aniso- *prefix.* differing, not equal ○ *anisogamy* [From Greek *anisos*, from *an-* "not" + *isos* "equal"]

an·i·so·gam·ete /a nìssō gá meét, -gə meét/ *n.* = **heterogamete**

an·i·sog·a·my /ànnī sóggəmee/ *n.* = **heterogamy** *n.* 1 —**an·i·so·gam·ic** /ànnīsə gámmik/ *adj.* —**an·i·sog·a·mous** /-sóggəməss/ *adj.*

an·i·sole /ánni sōl/ *n.* a colorless liquid with a pleasant smell that is used as a solvent and a flavoring. Formula: $C_6H_5OCH_3$. [Mid-19thC. Coined from ANISE + -OLE.]

an·i·so·mer·ic /a nìssə mérrik/ *adj.* used to describe a chemical compound that does not form structurally different molecules (**isomers**)

an·i·so·met·ric /a nìssə méttrik/ *adj.* **1. ASYMMETRIC** not isometric or symmetrical ○ *an anisometric particle* **2.** CRYSTALS **SHAPED IRREGULARLY** used to describe a crystal that does not have three perpendicular axes of equal length and is therefore not regular

an·i·so·me·tro·pi·a /a nìssə mə trṓpee ə/ *n.* lack of balance between each eye's ability to refract light [Late 19thC. Coined from ANISO- + Greek *metron* "measure" + -OPIA.] —**an·i·so·me·trop·ic** /a nìssə mə tróppik/ *adj.*

an·i·so·trop·ic /a nìssə tróppik/ *adj.* used to describe something with physical properties that are different in different directions, e.g., crystals that are not symmetrical or regular, especially ones measuring differently along each of two or more axes —**an·i·so·trop·i·cal·ly** /a nìssə tróppikəlee/ *adv.* —**an·i·sot·ro·pism** /-sóttrə pìzzəm/ *n.* —**an·i·sot·ro·py** /-pee/ *n.*

An·jou[1] /ánzhoo, -joo/, **An·jou pear** *n.* a variety of pear with green skin and firm flesh [Named for ANJOU, where it was originally grown]

An·jou[2] /ánzhoo, -joo/ former province in western France in the lower Loire valley. Once ruled by the English kings, it was claimed for France in 1481.

An·ka·ra /ángkərə/ capital of Turkey, in the north central part of the country, on the Ankara River, northwest of Adana and southeast of Bursa. Population: 2,782,200 (1994). Former name **Angora**

an·ker·ite /ángkə rīt/ *n.* a white, gray, brown, or reddish mineral that resembles dolomite and contains calcium, magnesium, iron, and sometimes manganese [Mid-19thC. From German *Ankerit.* Named for its discoverer, the Austrian mineralogist M. J. *Anker* (1772–1843).]

ankh /angk/ *n.* a symbol consisting of a cross with a loop for the top extension and a short crossbar, used in ancient Egypt to signify life [Late 19thC. From Egyptian, literally "life."]

an·kle /ángk'l/ *n.* **1. JOINT BETWEEN FOOT AND LEG** the joint that connects the bones of the leg with the highest bone in the foot **2. SLIM PART OF LEG ABOVE ANKLE** the slender part of the leg immediately above the ankle [14thC. From assumed Old Norse *ankula,* which replaced Old English *anclēow* (both related to English *anchor* and *angle*).]

an·kle·bone /ángk'l bōn/ *n.* = **talus**[1] *n.*

an·kle boot *n.* a boot that extends up to the ankle but not much beyond

an·klet /ángklət/ *n.* **1. ANKLE BRACELET** a piece of jewelry or some other ornament worn around the ankle **2. SHORT SOCK COMING JUST ABOVE ANKLE** a sock that extends up to the ankle but not much beyond

an·ky·lo·saur /ángkələ sàwr/ *n.* a plant-eating dinosaur with short legs, a heavy thickset body, and bony dorsal plates. It lived during the Cretaceous period. [Late 20thC. From modern Latin *Ankylosaurus,* genus name, from Greek *agkulōsis* (see ANKYLOSIS) + *sauros* "lizard."]

an·ky·lose /ángkə lṑss, -lṑz/ (**-losed, -los·ing, -los·es**) *vti.* to fuse together and become stiff, or cause bones to fuse together and a joint to become stiff as a result of injury or disease. This is sometimes done surgically to relieve pain and allow injuries to heal. [Late 18thC. Back-formation from ANKYLOSIS.]

an·ky·los·ing spon·dy·li·tis /àngkə lōssing-, -lōz-/ *n.* a disease of the spine that causes the vertebrae to form a solid inflexible column

an·ky·lo·sis /àngkə lṓssiss/ (*plural* **-los·es** /-sēez/) *n.* **1. FUSION OF BONES** the fusion of the bones of a joint, often in an abnormal position as a result of disease or injury, or intentionally through surgery **2. STIFFNESS OF JOINT BONES** stiffness or immobility in a joint caused by bones fusing together as a result of disease or injury or arising from surgery to join one bone or part to another [Early 18thC. Via modern Latin from Greek *agkulōsis* "stiffening of the joints," from *agkuloun* "to bend," from *agkulos* "bent."] —**an·ky·lot·ic** /àngkə lóttik/ *adj.*

an·ky·lo·sto·mi·a·sis *n.* = **ancylostomiasis**

an·lage /áan laagə/ (*plural* **-la·gen** /-laagən/ *or* **-la·ges**) *n.* **1.** EMBRYOL **PART IN EMBRYONIC STAGE** a part or organ in its earliest stage of development **2. BASIS FOR SOMETHING** something, often a principle, on which something else is based or founded (*literary*) [Late 19thC. From German, literally "layout."]

Ann, Cape /an-/ cape on a peninsula of northeastern Massachusetts, jutting 9 mi./14 km into the Atlantic Ocean at the northern edge of Massachusetts Bay

ann. *abbr.* **1.** annals **2.** annual **3.** annuity

an·na /áanə, ánnə/ *n.* a copper coin formerly used in the Indian subcontinent, worth one-sixteenth of a rupee [Early 17thC. From Hindi *ānā.*]

an·nal /ánn'l/ *n.* a single entry in a record of historical events, or a record of the events of a single year in history (*dated*) [Early 17thC. Back-formation from ANNALS.]

an·nal·ist /ánn'list/ *n.* somebody who compiles annals

an·nals /ánn'lz/ *npl.* **1. ANNUAL RECORDS** a record of events arranged chronologically by year **2. RECORDED HISTORY** history in general, as it is recorded in books and other documents ○ *Her achievements have secured her place in the annals of our nation.* **3. LEARNED JOURNAL** a periodical that records events and reports in a specific field of research [Mid-16thC. Directly or via French from Latin *annales,* from *annalis* (see ANNUAL).]

An·nam /ə nám, á nàm/ region in Vietnam, forming a narrow strip along the South China Sea. It became a protectorate of France in 1883 and was autonomous after World War II, until Vietnam was partitioned in 1954. —**An·na·mese** /ànnə mēez, -mēess/ *adj., n.*

An·nan /a naán, ánnən/, **Kofi** (*b.* 1938) Ghanaian statesman. He was elected secretary general of the United Nations in 1997.

An·nan·dale /ánnən dàyl/ city in New York State, situated on the Hudson River

An·nap·o·lis /ə náppəliss/ capital of Maryland, situated near Chesapeake Bay. Population: 33,234 (1996). ■ *n.* NAVY **U.S. NAVAL ACADEMY** the U.S. Naval Academy, which is located in Annapolis. ◊ **West Point**

An·na·pur·na /ànnə pŏŏrnə, -púr-/ mountain in the Himalayan range in north central Nepal, one of the world's highest peaks. Height: 26,504 ft./8,078 m.

Ann Ar·bor /àn áarbər/ city in southeastern Michigan, home to the main campus of the University of Michigan. Population: 108,758 (1996).

an·nat·to /ə náttō/ (*plural* **-tos**) *n.* **1.** INDUST **DYE FROM SEEDCASE PULP** a yellowish red dye made from the pulp enclosing the seeds of a small tropical tree, used to color fabric and food products **2.** TREES **SMALL FLOWERING TREE** a small tropical American tree with pink or red flowers and seeds encased in a pulpy substance used to make annatto dye. Latin name: *Bixa orellana.* [Early 17thC. From Carib.]

an·neal /ə nēel/ *v.* **1.** *vti.* METALL, CRAFT **MAKE SOMETHING STRONGER THROUGH HEATING** to subject an alloy, metal, or glass to a process of heating and slow cooling to make it tougher and less brittle **2.** *vti.* CELL BIOL **SEPARATE STRANDS OF NUCLEIC ACID** to subject nucleic acid to a process of heating and cooling in order to separate strands **3.** *vt.* **MAKE SOMETHING MORE RESOLUTE** to make something, especially an opinion, a feeling, or an intention, stronger, firmer, or more resolute (*literary*) [Old English *onǣlan,* from *ǣlan* "to burn." Originally in the meaning "to set on fire."]

an·ne·lid /ánnəlid/ *n.* an invertebrate organism with a flat body that is divided into segments. Earthworms and leeches are annelids. Phylum: Anelida. [Mid-19thC. From modern Latin *Annelida,* phylum name, from French *annelés* "ringed," from, ultimately, Latin *an(n)ulus* (see ANNULUS).]

an·nex *vt.* /ə néks, a-, á nèks/ (**-nexed, -nex·ing, -nex·es**) **1. ADD SOMETHING TO SOMETHING** to attach something subsidiary to a larger thing (*usually passive*) ○ *The new pool will be annexed to the gymnasium.* **2. TAKE OVER TERRITORY** to take over territory and incorporate it into another political entity, e.g., a country or state **3. ATTACH A QUALITY TO SOMETHING** to add something as a consequence, quality, or condition (*usually passive*) ○ *Annexed to his feeling of guilt was a sense of having let everybody down.* **4. STEAL** to take something without permission (*informal*) ○ *He returned to find that his assistant had annexed his chair.* ■ *n.* /á nèks/ **1.** BUILDING **AUXILIARY BUILDING** a building added on to another building or serving as an auxiliary building to a larger one **2. ATTACHED DOCUMENT** an appendix, epilogue, or other additional material attached to a larger document [14thC. Via French *annexer* from Latin *annectere* "to tie together," from *nectere* "to tie" (source of English *connect* and *nexus*).]

an·nex·a·tion /à nek sáysh'n/ *n.* **1. ADDITION OF SOMETHING** the addition of something to a larger whole **2. TAKING POSSESSION OF TERRITORY** the incorporation of a territory into another country, state, or other political entity **3. SOMETHING ADDED** something that has been added to a larger whole, especially a territory that has been incorporated into another country or state —**an·nex·a·tion·al** *adj.* —**an·nex·a·tion·ism** *n.* —**an·nex·a·tion·ist** *n.*

an·nexe /á nèks/ *n. U.K.* = **annex**

An·nie Oak·ley /ànnee ṓklee/ (*plural* **An·nie Oak·leys**) *n.* a free ticket for something [Early 20thC. Named for Annie OAKLEY. From the resemblance of a punched ticket to a playing card riddled with bullets.]

an·ni·hi·late /ə nī́ ə làyt/ (**-lat·ed, -lat·ing, -lates**) *v.* **1.** *vt.* **DESTROY SOMETHING** to destroy something completely, especially so that it ceases to exist **2.** *vt.* **DEFEAT SOMEBODY** to defeat somebody easily and convincingly (*informal*) **3.** *vt.* **MAKE SOMETHING INVALID** to declare something to be void or ineffective (*archaic*) **4.** *vi.* NUCLEAR PHYS **BE DESTROYED IN PARTICLE COLLISION** to be mutually destroyed when a particle collides with a corresponding antiparticle [Early 16thC. From late Latin *annihilat-,* the past participle stem of *annihilare* "to reduce to nothing," from Latin *nihil* "nothing" (source of English *nil*).] —**an·ni·hi·la·ble** /ə nī́ ələ b'l/ *adj.* —**an·ni·hi·la·tive** /ə nī́ ə làytiv, -lətiv/ *adj.* —**an·ni·hi·la·tor** *n.*

an·ni·hi·la·tion /ə nī́ ə láysh'n/ *n.* **1. DESTRUCTION** the complete destruction of something **2. DEFEAT OF OPPONENT** the complete and convincing defeat of an opponent (*informal*) **3.** NUCLEAR PHYS **DESTRUCTIVE COLLISION OF PARTICLE AND ANTIPARTICLE** the process in which a particle combines with its antiparticle, destroying both and releasing their energy in the form of radiation or other particles ○ *annihilation radiation*

An·nis·ton /ánnistən/ city in northeastern Alabama, south of Gadsden. Population: 25,774 (1996).

an·ni·ver·sa·ry /ànnə vúrsəree/ (*plural* **-ries**) *n.* **1. ANNUAL OBSERVATION OF PAST EVENT** a date that is observed on an annual basis because it is the same date as an important event in a past year, often the date of somebody's wedding **2. ANNUAL RITUAL** a celebration or other commemorative ritual marking the date of an important event, often a wedding [13thC. Directly or via French *anniversaire* from medieval Latin *anniversarium,* from Latin *anniversarius* "returning yearly," from *annus* "year" + *versus,* the past participle of *vertere* "to turn."]

an·no Dom·i·ni /ànnō dómmi nə, ànnō dómminee/ *adv.* full form of **A.D.** [Mid-16thC. From Latin, literally "in the year of the Lord."]

anno He·gi·rae /ánnō hə jī́ree, ànnō héjjəree/ *adv.* full form of **A.H.** [Late 19thC. From Latin, literally "in the year of the Hegira."]

an·no·na /ə nṓnə/ (*plural* **-nas** *or* **-na**) *n.* any one of several tropical American and African trees from which fruits such as the cherimoya, custard apple, soursop, and sugar apple are obtained. Genus: *Annona.* [Via modern Latin and American Spanish from Arawak]

an·no·tate /ánnə tàyt/ (**-tat·ed, -tat·ing, -tates**) *vt.* to add critical or explanatory notes to a text (*often passive*) [Mid-18thC. Via Latin *annotat-,* the past participle stem of *annotare* "to note down," from, ultimately, *nota* "mark" (source of English *note*).] —**an·no·ta·tive** *adj.* —**an·no·ta·tor** *n.*

an·no·ta·tion /ànnə táysh'n/ *n.* **1. ADDITION OF NOTES** the adding of explanatory or critical notes to a text **2. EXPLANATORY NOTE** an explanatory or critical comment that has been added to a text

an·nounce /ə nówns/ (**-nounced, -nounc·ing, -nounc·es**) *v.* **1.** *vt.* **TELL SOMETHING PUBLICLY** to declare or report something publicly **2.** *vt.* **SAY SOMETHING** to say something in a formal, forceful, or aggressive way **3.** *vt.* **DECLARE ARRIVAL OF SOMEBODY OR SOMETHING** to tell others formally that somebody or something has arrived **4.** *vt.* **SIGNIFY OR FORETELL SOMETHING** to be a sign that something has arrived or is imminent **5.** *vt.* **SERVE AS PRESENTER OF SOMETHING** to act as a presenter of something, e.g., a television or radio show **6.** *vti.* **DECLARE CANDIDACY** to declare an intention to run for a public office **7.** *vi.* BROADCAST **BE AN ANNOUNCER** to act as an announcer on television or radio [15thC. Via French *annoncer* and Latin *annuntiare* from, ultimately, *nuntius* "messenger" (source of English *nuncio, pronounce,* and *renounce*).]

an·nounce·ment /ə nównsmənt/ *n.* **1. PUBLIC DECLARATION** a public statement giving people information or news, or the making of the statement **2. WRITTEN NOTICE** a formal written notice, often a card or newspaper item, giving the news of a birth, wedding, or other event

an·nounc·er /ə nównsər/ *n.* **1. SOMEBODY MAKING ANNOUNCEMENTS** somebody who makes public announcements, e.g., on a public address system at an airport or railroad station **2.** BROADCAST **TV OR RADIO COMMENTATOR** somebody who provides informative comment on something, usually a television or radio commentator who gives news bulletins, running commentary on sports, or program information

an·noy /ə nóy/ (**-noyed, -noy·ing, -noys**) *v.* **1.** *vt.* **IRRITATE SOMEBODY** to make somebody feel impatient or angry **2.** *vt.* **HARASS SOMEBODY** to harass or bother somebody repeatedly **3.** *vi.* **BE IRRITATING** to be a source of irritation ○ *Barking dogs are bound to annoy.* [13thC. Via Old French *anoier* from late Latin *inodiare* "to make loathsome," from Latin *in odio* "in hatred."]

WORD KEY: SYNONYMS

annoy, irritate, exasperate, vex, irk

CORE MEANING: to cause a mild degree of anger in somebody

annoy to cause anything from slight impatience to anger in somebody; **irritate** to annoy somebody repeatedly or continuously, often over a period of time; **exasperate** to arouse strong impatience in somebody by seeming to disregard his or her wishes; **vex** a more dated term than *annoy* suggesting distinct confusion or even mild distress; **irk** a more formal term suggesting that the annoyance is tiresome.

an·noy·ance /ə nóy əns/ *n.* **1.** FEELING OF IRRITATION feelings of mild anger and impatience **2.** NUISANCE something that causes somebody to be mildly angry or impatient ○ *Living in this neighborhood is not without its annoyances.*

WORD KEY: SYNONYMS

See Synonyms at ***anger.***

an·noy·ing /ə nóy ing/ *adj.* causing mild anger or impatience —**an·noy·ing·ly** *adv.*

an·nu·al /ányyoo əl/ *adj.* **1.** ONCE A YEAR happening once a year **2.** FOR PERIOD OF ONE YEAR based on or accumulating over one year **3.** BOT DYING AFTER ONE SEASON used to describe a plant that flowers, produces seed, and dies in one growing season ■ *n.* **1.** BOT PLANT THAT DIES AFTER ONE SEASON a plant that flowers, produces seed, and dies in one growing season **2.** = **yearbook** **3.** PUBL YEARLY BOOK OR MAGAZINE a book or magazine published once a year, especially one for children [14thC. Directly or via French *annuel* from late Latin *annualis*, a blend of Latin *annuus* and *annalis* "yearly," from *annus* "year."]

an·nu·al·ize /ányyoo ə lìz/ (**-ized, -iz·ing, -izes**) *vt.* **1.** MAKE FIGURES APPLY TO A YEAR to calculate or adjust figures so that they reflect a period of a year **2.** DO SOMETHING YEARLY to put something on, or change something to, a once-a-year schedule ○ *Let's annualize the newsletter.*

an·nu·al·ly /ányyoo əlee/ *adv.* every year or once a year

an·nu·al meet·ing *n.* a yearly meeting of the stockholders of a corporation or members of a foundation, when officers and directors may be elected and other votes taken. At an annual meeting the officers usually report on matters such as the financial health of the organization.

an·nu·al re·port *n.* a document that outlines and analyzes the activities, especially the financial dealings, of a company or other organization over the past year

Annual ring: Cross section through pine log

an·nu·al ring *n.* a sheath of cells forming concentric rings in the cross-section of a woody stem or trunk, the result of the yearly growth spurt that begins in the spring. The age of a tree can be determined by counting its annual rings.

an·nu·i·tant /ə nóo itənt/ *n.* somebody who is entitled to receive an annuity

an·nu·i·ty /ə nóo itee/ (*plural* **-ties**) *n.* **1.** MONEY PAID AT REGULAR INTERVALS an amount of money paid to somebody yearly or at some other regular interval **2.** INVESTMENT PAYING ANNUAL SUM a type of investment that pays the investor a set amount of money each year for a number of years, often the investor's lifetime **3.** CONTRACT FOR ANNUAL PAYMENT the right to receive or the obligation to pay an annuity [15thC. Via French *annuité* from medieval Latin *annuitas*, from Latin *annuus* (see ANNUAL).]

an·nul /ə núl/ (**-nulled, -nul·ling, -nuls**) *vt.* **1.** LAW MAKE SOMETHING INVALID to render a legal document or agreement invalid **2.** RELIG DECLARE MARRIAGE INVALID to declare that a marriage was never a true marriage in the eyes of the church, e.g., because one of the parties was not completely committed to it **3.** DESTROY SOMETHING to wipe out or destroy the effect or existence of something ○ *not able to annul my fears* [14thC. Via Old French *anuller* from late Latin *annullare* "to make into nothing," from Latin *nullus* "nothing" (source of English *null*).]

WORD KEY: SYNONYMS

See Synonyms at ***nullify.***

an·nu·lar /ányyələr/ *adj.* shaped like or forming a ring [Late 16thC. Directly or via French *annulaire* from Latin *an(n)ularis*, from *an(n)ulus* (see ANNULUS).]

an·nu·lar e·clipse *n.* a solar eclipse in which all but the outermost rim of the sun is blocked by the moon, leaving a ring of sunlight visible around the moon

an·nu·lar lig·a·ment *n.* a ring-shaped ligament that surrounds an ankle joint or a wrist joint and holds other ligaments in place

an·nu·late /ányələt, -layt/, **an·nu·lat·ed** *adj.* with ring-shaped parts, or consisting of rings [Early 19thC. From Latin *an(n)ulatus*, from *an(n)ulus* (see ANNULUS).]

an·nu·la·tion /ànnyə láysh'n/ *n.* **1.** FORMATION OF RINGS the formation of rings or ring-shaped parts **2.** RING-SHAPED PART any part that is shaped like a ring

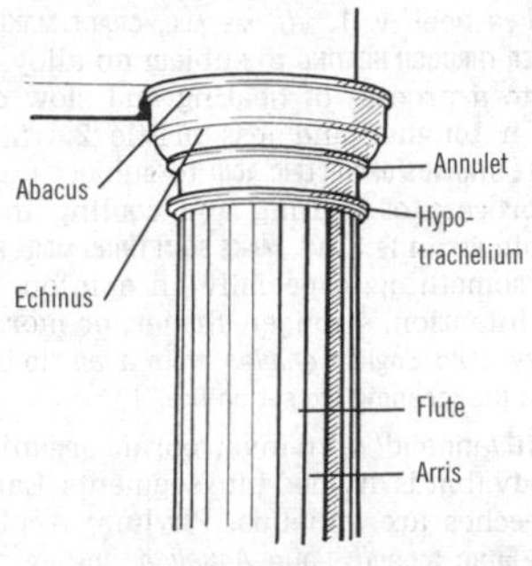

Annulet

an·nu·let /ányələt/ *n.* ARCHIT a ring-shaped molding around a column [Late 16thC. Formed from Latin *an(n)ulus* (see ANNULUS).]

an·nu·li plural of **annulus**

an·nul·ment /ə núlmənt/ *n.* **1.** LAW VOIDING OF SOMETHING the process or result of making a legal document or agreement void or invalid **2.** RELIG RULING THAT MARRIAGE IS INVALID a ruling that a marriage was never a true marriage in the eyes of the church

an·nu·lus /ányələss/ (*plural* **-li** /-lì/ *or* **-lus·es**) *n.* **1.** BIOL RING-SHAPED PART any ring-shaped part or arrangement of parts in a plant or animal, e.g., a growth ring on fish scales **2.** MATH AREA BETWEEN CONCENTRIC CIRCLES the area bounded by two concentric circles [Mid-16thC. From Latin *an(n)ulus*, literally "a small ring," from *anus* "ring."]

an·nun·ci·ate /ə núnsee àyt/ (**-at·ed, -at·ing, -ates**) *vt.* to announce or proclaim something (*archaic*) [14thC. From Latin *annuntiat-*, the past participle stem of *annuntiare* (see ANNOUNCE).]

an·nun·ci·a·tion /ə nùnsee áysh'n/ *n.* the announcing of something, or an announcement (*archaic*)

Annunciation (1513?) by Lucas Cranach the Elder

An·nun·ci·a·tion *n.* **1.** GABRIEL'S VISIT TO MARY in the Bible, the archangel Gabriel's visit to the Virgin Mary to announce that she had been chosen to be the mother of Jesus Christ (Luke 1:26–38) **2.** CHRISTIAN FESTIVAL March 25, celebrated in the Christian calendar as the feast of the Annunciation

an·nun·ci·a·tor /ə núnsee àytər/ *n.* **1.** ANNOUNCER somebody who makes announcements (*archaic*) **2.** ELEC ENG ELECTRONIC SIGNALING DEVICE an electronic signaling device, e.g., a switchboard device that indicates the source of incoming telephone calls

an·nus hor·ri·bi·lis /ánnəss hə ríbbəliss/ (*plural* **an·ni hor·ri·bi·les** /à nī hə ríbbə leez/) *n. U.K.* a year of great unhappiness or misfortune (*formal*) [Late 20thC. From Latin, "horrible year."]

an·nus mi·ra·bi·lis /ánnəss mi rábbəliss/ (*plural* **an·ni mi·ra·bi·les** /à nī mi rábbə leez/) *n.* a year that is remarkable for its great events (*formal*) [Mid-17thC. From Latin, "wonderful year."]

an·ode /á nōd/ *n.* **1.** NEGATIVE TERMINAL the negative terminal of a battery **2.** POSITIVE ELECTRODE the positive electrode in an electrolytic cell [Mid-19thC. Formed from Greek *anodos*, literally "way up," from *hodos* "way."]

an·o·dize /ánnə dìz/ (**-dized, -diz·ing, -diz·es**) *vt.* to coat a metal, e.g., aluminum, with a protective or decorative oxide by making the metal the anode of an electrolytic cell —**an·o·di·za·tion** /ànnədi záysh'n/ *n.*

an·o·don·tia /ànnə dónshə, -shee ə/ *n.* the abnormal absence of some or all teeth because the teeth have never developed [Late 19thC. Coined from AN- + -ODONTIA.]

an·o·dyne /ánnə dìn/ *n.* **1.** PHARM PAINKILLER a medication such as aspirin or codeine that relieves pain or distress **2.** COMFORTING THING something that soothes, comforts, or relaxes (*literary*) ■ *adj.* **1.** PHARM PAIN-KILLING bringing relief from pain or discomfort **2.** SOOTHING serving to soothe, relax, or comfort (*literary*) ○ *the anodyne effects of a weekend in the mountains after a hard workweek* **3.** BLAND harmless, inoffensive, or uncontroversial to the point of being dull (*literary*) ○ *a rather anodyne speech, given the nature of the crisis* [Mid-16thC. Via Latin from Greek *anōdunos* "without pain," from *odunē* "pain."]

an·oes·trous *n.* ZOOL U.K. = **anestrous**

an·oes·trus *n.* ZOOL U.K. = **anestrus**

a·noint /ə nóynt/ (**a·noint·ed, a·noint·ing, a·noints**) *vt.* **1.** BLESS SOMEBODY WITH OIL to rub oil or ointment on a part of somebody's body, usually the head or feet, as part of a religious ceremony, e.g., in a Christian baptism **2.** ORDAIN SOMEBODY to install somebody officially or ceremonially in a position or office [14thC. Via Old French *enoint*, the past participle of *enoindre*, from Latin *inungere*, from *ungere* "to smear" (source of English *ointment* and *unctuous*).] —**a·noint·ment** *n.*

a·noint·ing of the sick *n.* in the Roman Catholic Church, the sacrament of anointing people who are very sick, praying for their recovery, and offering confession and absolution of sins

a·no·le /ə nṓlee/ *n.* any one of several tree-climbing, chiefly tropical lizards that can change color. Genus: *Anolis.* [Early 18thC. Via modern Latin *Anolis*, genus name, from, ultimately, Carib *anoli.*]

a·nom·a·lis·tic month /ə nommə listik-/ *n.* the average time taken by the Moon to orbit the Earth once, starting from the point in its orbit at which it is nearest the Earth, measured as 27.554 days

a·nom·a·lis·tic year *n.* the time taken by the Earth to orbit the Sun once, starting from the point in its orbit at which the Earth is nearest the Sun, measured as 365.26 days

a·nom·a·lous /ə nómmələss/ *adj.* **1.** ABNORMAL deviating from the norm or from what people expect ○ *We're getting anomalous readings on the heart monitor.* **2.** UNUSUAL strange and difficult to identify or classify ○ *"Individuals would occasionally give rise to new species having anomalous habits."* (Charles Darwin, *On the Origin of Species*; 1859) [Mid-17thC. Formed from late Latin *anomalus*, from Greek *anōmalos* "uneven," from *homalos* "even."]

a·nom·a·ly /ə nómməlee/ (*plural* **-lies**) *n.* **1.** IRREGULARITY something that deviates from the norm or from expectations ○ *looking for anomalies in the patient's blood tests* **2.** PECULIARITY something strange and difficult to identify or classify ○ *The space probe has encountered an anomaly.* **3.** ASTRON ANGLE IN PLANET'S ORBIT the angle between a planet's position, the Sun, and the point in the planet's orbit when it is closest to the Sun

an·o·mic /ə nómmik, ə nṓmik/ *adj.* **1.** SOCIOL **UNSTABLE BECAUSE OF MORAL BREAKDOWN** unstable because moral and social codes have been eroded or abandoned ○ *an anomic society* **2.** PSYCHOL **AFFECTED BY ALIENATION** feeling alienated from society and disoriented by the perceived absence of a social or moral framework ■ *n.* PSYCHOL **SOMEBODY AFFECTED BY ALIENATION** somebody who feels a sense of alienation and disorientation as a result of the perceived absence of a social and moral framework

an·o·mie /ánnəmee/, **an·o·my** *n.* **1.** SOCIOL **SOCIAL INSTABILITY** instability in society caused by the erosion or abandonment of moral and social codes **2.** PSYCHOL **SOCIAL ALIENATION** a feeling of disorientation and alienation from society caused by the perceived absence of a supporting social or moral framework [Late 16thC. Via French from Greek *anomia* "lawlessness," from *anomos* "lawless," from *nomos* "law."]

a·non /ə nón/ *adv.* (*archaic or literary*) **1. ANOTHER TIME** at an unspecified future time ○ *I'll see you anon.* **2. SOON** in a short while ○ *more of these grotesque escapades anon* [Old English *on ān*, literally "in one"]

a·non. *abbr.* anonymous

an·o·nym /ánnə nìm/ *n.* **1. UNNAMED AUTHOR** an author whose name is not known or not given **2. PSEUDONYM** a name used by somebody to hide his or her identity [Early 19thC. From French *anonyme* "ANONYMOUS."]

an·o·nym·i·ty /ánnə nímmətee/ (*plural* **-ties**) *n.* **1. FREEDOM FROM IDENTIFICATION** the state of not being known or identified by name, e.g., as the author or donor of something **2. LACK OF DISTINCTIVENESS** a lack of distinctive features that makes things seem bland or interchangeable ○ *detested the anonymity of the downtown hotels* **3. UNNAMED PERSON** somebody who is unnamed or unacknowledged as the doer of something **4. STATE OF BEING UNNOTICED** the state of blending into a crowd and going unnoticed ○ *I always preferred the anonymity of the big city.*

a·non·y·mous /ə nónnəməss/ *adj.* **1. UNNAMED** whose name is not known or not given **2. WITH NAME WITHHELD** with the performer's, maker's, or creator's identity withheld **3. INDISTINCTIVE** lacking individuality or distinctiveness ○ *a quirkiness unsuited to an anonymous shopping mall* **4. PREVENTING IDENTIFICATION** obscuring somebody's identity, or allowing somebody to go unnoticed ○ *a thief who lost his pursuers in an anonymous crowd* [Early 17thC. Formed from late Latin *anonymus*, from Greek *anōnumos* "unnamed," from *onuma* "name."] —**a·non·y·mous·ness** *n.*

a·non·y·mous FTP *n.* a method of connecting to a computer on the Internet that allows files to be accessed and downloaded without needing a password

a·non·y·mous·ly /ə nónnəməsslee/ *adv.* without being named or acknowledged

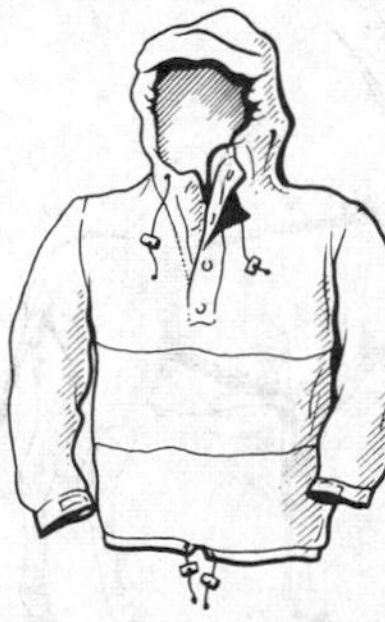

Anorak

an·o·rak /ánnə rak/ *n.* a warm thick waterproof hip-length jacket with a hood [Early 20thC. From (Greenlandic) Inuit *annoraaq*.]

an·o·rec·tic /ánnə réktik/ *adj.* **RELATING TO PATHOLOGICAL APPETITE LOSS** relating to, affected by, or causing pathological loss of appetite ■ *n.* **APPETITE-SUPPRESSING MEDICATION** a type of medication that suppresses the appetite, used in treating any disorder marked by overeating [Late 19thC. Formed from Greek *anorektos* "without appetite," from *orexein* "to desire."]

an·o·rex·i·a /ánnə réksee ə/ *n.* **1.** = **anorexia nervosa 2. CONTINUAL APPETITE LOSS** persistent loss of appetite [Late 16thC. Via modern Latin from Greek, "lack of appetite," from *orexis* "appetite," from *orexein* (see ANORECTIC).]

an·o·rex·i·a nerv·o·sa /-nər vṓssə/ *n.* an eating disorder, marked by an extreme fear of becoming overweight and leading to excessive dieting to the point of serious ill-health and sometimes death [From modern Latin, literally "nervous anorexia"]

an·o·rex·ic /ànnə réksik/ *adj.* **1. OF ANOREXIA NERVOSA** relating to or affected by anorexia nervosa **2. VERY THIN** extremely thin, especially unhealthily or unattractively so (*informal*) ■ *n.* **SOMEBODY WITH ANOREXIA** somebody who is affected by loss of appetite or by anorexia nervosa

an·or·thite /a náwr thìt/ *n.* a rare white, gray, or reddish gray variety of the mineral feldspar, occurring mainly in igneous rocks and used in making glass and in ceramics. Formula: $CaAl_2Si_2O_8$. [Mid-19thC. Coined from AN- + ORTH- + -ITE. From its oblique crystals.] —**an·or·thi·tic** /à nawr thíttik/ *adj.*

an·or·tho·site /a náwrthə sìt/ *n.* a coarse-grained igneous rock comprising at least 90% feldspar [Mid-19thC. Formed from French *anorthose* "type of feldspar," from Greek *anorthos*, literally "not straight." From its oblique crystals.] —**an·or·tho·si·tic** /a nàwrthə síttik/ *adj.*

an·os·mi·a /a nózmee ə/ *n.* absence or loss of the sense of smell [Early 19thC. Coined from AN- + Greek *osmē* "smell" + -IA.] —**an·os·mic** *adj.*

an·oth·er /ə nú*th*ər/ *adj., pron.* **1. ONE MORE** an additional ○ *need another person to help* ○ *May I have another?* **2. ONE THAT IS DIFFERENT** somebody who or something that is completely separate or different from the one mentioned ○ *We need another accountant because ours is moving.* ○ *This one is too dark; I would prefer another.* **3. SOME OTHER** some other one, or any other one

an·ov·u·lant /a nóvvyələnt/ *n.* **DRUG PREVENTING OVULATION** a drug that prevents a woman from ovulating, e.g., a birth-control pill ■ *adj.* **PREVENTING OVULATION** used to describe a drug that prevents ovulation [Mid-20thC. Coined from AN- + OVULATE + -ANT.] —**an·o·vu·la·to·ry** /a nóvvyələ tàwree, -nṓv-/ *adj., n.*

an·o·vu·la·tion /anòvvyə láysh'n, -ṑv yə-/ *n.* the state of not ovulating because of a medical condition, suppression by drugs, or menopause

an·ox·e·mi·a /à nok séemee ə/ *n.* a deficiency of oxygen in the blood flowing through the arteries [Late 19thC. Coined from AN- + OX- + -EMIA.] —**an·ox·e·mic** *adj.*

an·ox·i·a /a nóksee ə/ *n.* = **hypoxia** [Mid-20thC. Coined from AN- + OX- + -IA.] —**an·ox·ic** *adj.*

ans. *abbr.* answer

an·sate /án sàyt/ *adj.* with a handle or a part shaped like a handle [Late 19thC. From Latin *ansatus*, from *ansa* "handle."]

an·sate cross *n.* = **ankh**

ANSI /ánsee/ *abbr.* American National Standards Institute

An·so·ni·a /an sṓnee ə, -sṓnyə/ city in southern Connecticut, on the Naugatuck River. Population: 17,865 (1996).

an·swer /ánsər/ *n.* **1. RESPONSE TO QUESTION** the information requested by a question **2. WAY OF SOLVING SOMETHING** the solution to a problem ○ *trying to find an answer to our ecological problems* **3. RESPONSE TO ACTION** a response to something that somebody says or does ○ *She had no answer to her opponent's lethal backhand.* **4. CORRESPONDING THING** something designed to match or correspond to something else ○ *The Space Needle is Seattle's answer to the Eiffel Tower.* **5.** LAW **PLEA IN COURT** a defendant's plea in response to a charge, lawsuit, or summons ■ *v.* (**-swered, -swer·ing, -swers**) **1.** *vti.* **REPLY TO SOMETHING** to reply to something written or spoken **2.** *vti.* **RESPOND TO CALL** to respond to a summons, e.g., a ringing telephone, a doorbell, or somebody calling your name **3.** *vti.* **DO SOMETHING IN REACTION** to do something as a reaction to an attack, criticism, or bad situation **4.** *vti.* **CORRESPOND TO SOMETHING** to match something or correspond to it ○ *We haven't found anyone who answers to that description.* **5.** *vt.* **MEET A NEED** to fulfill a need or wish **6.** *vi.* **SERVE A PURPOSE** to be adequate in meeting a requirement or serving a purpose ○ *an upturned box that answers for a seat* **7.** *vt.* LAW **RESPOND TO CHARGE IN COURT** to offer a plea in response to a charge, lawsuit, or summons ○ *The defendant will now answer the charges.* [Old English *andswaru*. Ultimately from a prehistoric Germanic word meaning "to swear against." The underlying idea is of making a sworn statement rebutting a charge.] ◇ **know** *or* **have all the answers** to be admirably knowledgeable about a subject, or be irritatingly eager to demonstrate or claim superior knowledge

WORD KEY: SYNONYMS

answer, reply, rejoinder, retort, riposte

CORE MEANING: something said, written, or done in acknowledgment of a question, remark, or other stimulus

answer the most general term, used as an acknowledgment of, or reaction to, questions, letters, actions, and situations; **reply** a more restricted term than *answer*, used especially with reported speech; **rejoinder** a slightly more formal term than *reply*, used to indicate a consdered reaction to a proposal, or a critcism or challenge a reply to a reply; **retort** a sharp reply, often to some form of criticism or accusation; **riposte** the most formal or literary term, used to indicate a quick or witty answer.

answer back *vti.* to reply to somebody boldly or with impudence when silence is expected

answer for *vi.* **1. EXPLAIN MISTAKE OR FAULT** to give an excuse or explanation for a wrong that has been committed ○ *You'll have to answer for this broken window.* **2. RECEIVE PUNISHMENT FOR SOMETHING** to be punished for a wrongdoing ○ *They'll answer for their carelessness when the case comes to trial.* **3. GUARANTEE SOMEBODY'S RELIABILITY** to give an assurance about somebody's good character ○ *She can be trusted, but I can't answer for the rest of the team.*

answer to *vi.* to be obliged to give somebody reasons for your behavior, or be obliged to accept criticism or punishment from somebody

an·swer·a·ble /ánsərəb'l/ *adj.* **1. SOLVABLE** having a possible solution or a correct response **2. ACCOUNTABLE** responsible for something, or obliged to explain your actions to somebody ○ *You're answerable to your boss for any losses you incur.* **3. ABLE TO BE DENIED** able to be argued against or disproved ○ *Is the charge answerable?* —**an·swer·a·bil·i·ty** /ànsərə bíllətee/ *n.* —**an·swer·a·bly** /ánsərəblee/ *adv.*

an·swer·back /ánsər bàk/ *n.* a response in a two-way radio transmission

an·swer·ing ma·chine *n.* a recording device that is connected to a telephone and can be activated to play a message to callers and record messages from them

an·swer·ing ser·vice *n.* a business that receives telephone calls on behalf of other individuals and organizations and takes messages for them

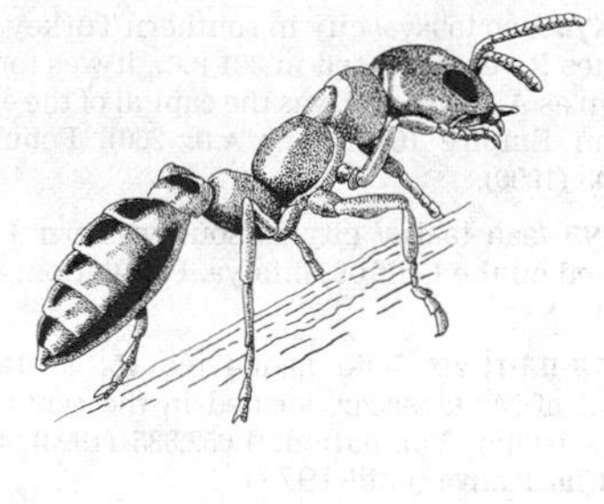

Ant (life size ×50)

ant /ant/ *n.* an insect that lives in complex well-organized colonies and is noted for its ability to carry objects heavier than itself. Male ants have wings, as do fertile females (**queens**) after mating. Family: Formicidae. [Old English *æmette*. Ultimately from a prehistoric Germanic word meaning "to cut off," which also produced German *Ameise* "ant."] ◇ **have ants in your pants** to be excited or impatient about something (*informal*)

ant. *abbr.* **1.** antiquarian **2.** antiquity **3.** antonym

Ant. *abbr.* Antarctica

ant- *prefix.* = **anti-** (*used before vowels*)

-ant *suffix.* **1.** performing a particular action ○ *dessiccant* **2.** being in a particular state ○ *hesitant* [From Latin *-ant-*, the stem of *-ans*, a present participle ending] —**-ance** *suffix.* —**-ancy** *suffix.*

an·ta /ántə/ (*plural* **-tas** *or* **-tae** /-tee/) *n.* a thicker end of the side wall of a Greek temple that forms one side of a porch [Mid-18thC. Back-formation from Latin *antae* "square pilasters."]

Anta

ant·ac·id /ant ássid/ *adj.* NEUTRALIZING ACIDITY preventing, counteracting, or neutralizing acidity, especially in the stomach ■ *n.* ANTI-ACIDITY DRUG a drug that reduces or neutralizes stomach acid

an·tae plural of **anta**

an·tag·o·nism /an tággə nìzzəm/ *n.* **1.** HOSTILITY hostility or hatred causing opposition and ill will **2.** OPPOSITION opposition between forces or principles ○ *the antagonism between good and evil* **3.** PHYSIOL NEUTRALIZING INTERACTION the interaction between two or more chemical substances in the body that diminishes the effect each of them has individually **4.** PHYSIOL MUSCLE OPPOSITION the opposing force that usually exists between pairs of muscles

an·tag·o·nist /an tággənist/ *n.* **1.** OPPONENT somebody or something opposing or in a conflict with another ○ *several antagonists locked in a power struggle* **2.** ARTS CHARACTER IN CONFLICT WITH HERO a major character in a book, play, or movie whose values or behavior are in conflict with those of the protagonist or hero **3.** PHARM NEUTRALIZING AGENT a substance, often a drug, that nullifies the effect another substance has on the body **4.** PHYSIOL OPPOSING MUSCLE a muscle that acts with and limits the action of another muscle

WORD KEY: SYNONYMS

See Synonyms at ***opponent.***

an·tag·o·nis·tic /an tàggə nístik/ *adj.* showing or expressing hostility —**an·tag·o·nis·ti·cal·ly** *adv.*

an·tag·o·nize /an tággə nìz/ (**-nized, -niz·ing, -niz·es**) *vt.* to cause a person or animal to be hostile [Mid-17thC. From Greek *antagōnizesthai*, literally "to struggle against," from *agōnizesthai* "to struggle," from *agōn* "contest" (source of English *agony*).]

An·ta·kya /aan taákyə/ city in southern Turkey on the Orontes River. Founded in 301 B.C., it was formerly known as Antioch and was the capital of the eastern Roman Empire (64 B.C. – A.D. 260). Population: 124,443 (1990).

An·tal·ya /aan taálya/ city in southwestern Turkey, situated on the Gulf of Antalya. Population: 378,208 (1990).

An·ta·na·na·ri·vo /àntə nannə reé vō, aàntə naa-/ capital of Madagascar, located in the central part of the island. Population: 1,052,835 (1993). Former name **Tananarive** (until 1977)

Ant·arc·tic /an taárktik, -aártik/ *n.* the region lying south of the Arctic Circle. ◊ **Arctic** —**Ant·arc·tic** *adj.*

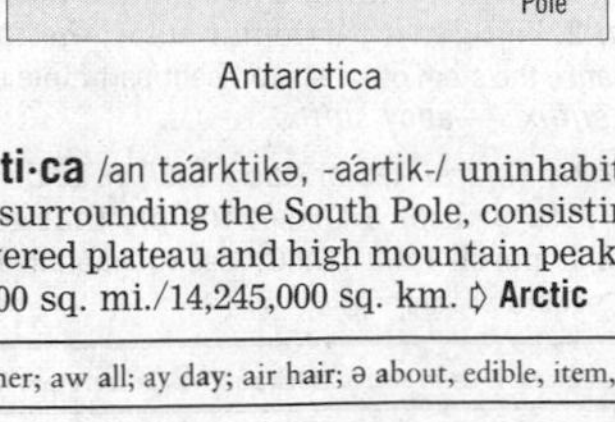

Antarctica

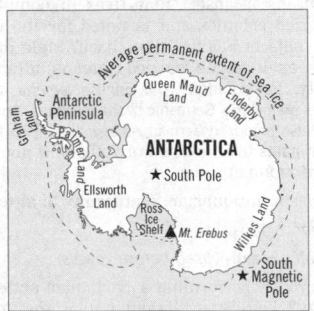

Ant·arc·ti·ca /an taárktikə, -aártik-/ uninhabited continent surrounding the South Pole, consisting of an ice-covered plateau and high mountain peaks. Area: 5,500,000 sq. mi./14,245,000 sq. km. ◊ **Arctic**

Ant·arc·tic Cir·cle parallel of latitude at 66° 30" S, encircling Antarctica and its surrounding seas, marking the northern limit of the area in which the sun does not set during the summer solstice and does not rise during the winter solstice

Ant·arc·tic Cur·rent ocean current circling Antarctica. Moving eastward, it circulates water from one ocean to another.

Ant·arc·tic O·cean the waters that surround the South Pole and Antarctica, consisting of the waters of the southern Atlantic, Indian, and Pacific oceans. Depths exceed 20,000 ft./6,000 m.

ant bear *n.* = **aardvark**

ant cow *n.* an aphid that excretes a substance similar to honey (**honeydew**) that is eaten by certain ants

an·te /ántee/ *n.* **1.** STAKE an amount a card player puts into the gambling pot before cards are dealt **2.** CONTRIBUTION PAID IN ADVANCE any sum of money that is paid in advance as a contribution (*informal*) ■ *vti.* (**-ted, -te·ing, -tes**) CONTRIBUTE TO GAMBLING POT to put forward betting stakes before cards are dealt [Early 19thC. From Latin, literally "before."] ◇ **up the ante 1.** to increase the amount of money required to do or get something (*informal*) **2.** to demand more, or try to get more from a situation (*informal*)

ante up *vti.* to pay money that is due to be paid (*informal*) ○ *We know you've got the cash, so ante up now!*

ante- *prefix.* before, in front ○ *antechamber* [From Latin *ante* (source also of English *ancient*). Ultimately from an Indo-European base meaning "front," which is also the ancestor of *end, until,* and *anti-*.]

Anteater

ant·eat·er /ánt eètər/ *n.* **1.** TROPICAL MAMMAL THAT FEEDS ON ANTS a long-snouted mammal of Central and South America that has no teeth but has long claws and a sticky tongue for catching prey, usually ants and termites. Family: Myrmecophagidae. **2.** = **pangolin 3.** = **echidna 4.** = **aardvark**

an·te·bel·lum /ànti béllәm/ *adj.* **1.** BEFORE ANY WAR preceding any war, or characteristic of the time preceding any war **2.** BEFORE CIVIL WAR belonging or relating to the time before the Civil War [Mid-19thC. From Latin *ante bellum* "before the war."]

an·te·cede /ànti seéd/ (**-ced·ed, -ced·ing, -cedes**) *vt.* to precede something in time or order ○ *Economic depressions often antecede wars.* [Early 17thC. From Latin *antecedere*, literally "to go before," from *cedere* (see CEDE).]

an·te·ce·dence /ànti seéd'ns/ *n.* an earlier position in time, order, or importance

an·te·ce·dent /ànti seéd'nt/ *n.* **1.** THING COMING BEFORE something that happened or existed before something else ○ *The book deals with the historical antecedents of the revolution.* **2.** GRAM WORD THAT SUBSEQUENT WORD REFERS TO a word or phrase that a subsequent word refers back to. "Mary" is the antecedent of "her" in the sentence "I'll give this to Mary if I see her." **3.** LOGIC CLAUSE EXPRESSING CONDITION the first part of a conditional proposition, which states the condition and is the p component in a proposition phrased "if p then q" ■ **an·te·ce·dents** *npl.* **1.** ANCESTORS somebody's ancestors **2.** SOMEBODY'S HISTORY the events or circumstances in somebody's past ○ *He's done pretty well for himself, considering what we know of his antecedents.* ■ *adj.* OCCURRING EARLIER IN TIME happening or existing before something else (*formal*) ○ *A high fever is usually an antecedent condition to other effects of the disease.* [14thC. Directly or via French from Latin *antecedent-*, the present participle stem of *antecedere* (see ANTECEDE).] —**an·te·ce·dent·ly** *adv.*

an·te·cham·ber /ánti chàymbər/ *n.* a small room leading into a larger main room and often used as a waiting area [Mid-17thC. From French *antichambre*, a translation of Italian *anticamera*, literally "room in front."]

an·te·choir /ánti kwìr/ *n.* an area at the entrance to the choir in a church, reserved for clergy and choir members

an·te·date /ánti dàyt/ *vt.* (**-dat·ed, -dat·ing, -dates**) **1.** OCCUR EARLIER THAN SOMETHING to exist or happen at an earlier date than something else ○ *These tapestries antedate the development of synthetic dyes.* **2.** PUT EARLIER DATE ON SOMETHING to assign something a date that is earlier than its true or original date ○ *This vase was mistakenly antedated to the Ming dynasty.* ■ *n.* EARLIER DATE a date assigned to something that is earlier than its true or original date

an·te·di·lu·vi·an /ànti də loóvee ən/ *adj.* **1.** FROM TIME BEFORE FLOOD in or from the time before the biblical Flood **2.** OUTDATED extremely old-fashioned or out-of-date (*informal*) ○ *an antediluvian notion of women's rights* [Mid-17thC. Formed from Latin *diluvium* "flood" (source of English *deluge*).]

WORD KEY: SYNONYMS

See Synonyms at ***old-fashioned.***

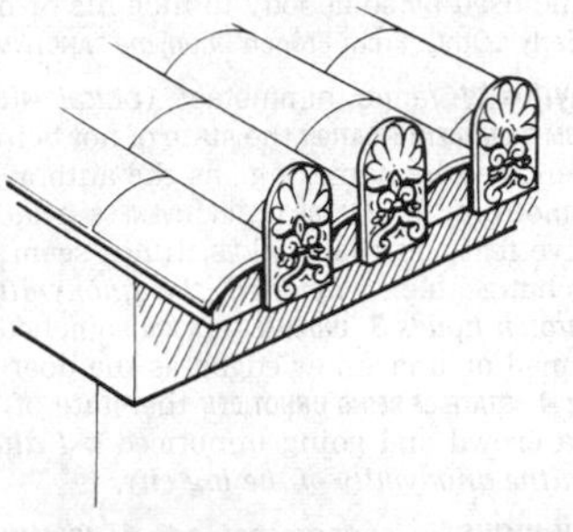

Antefix

an·te·fix /ánti fiks/ (*plural* **-fix·es** *or* **-fix·a** /-fiksə/ *or* **-fix·ae** /-seè/) *n.* an ornamental edging on the eaves of ancient buildings with tiled roofs that hides the joints of the roof tiles [Mid-19thC. From Latin *antefixum*, from *antefigere* "to fasten before," from *figere* "to fasten."] —**an·te·fix·al** /ànti fíks'l/ *adj.*

an·te·lope /ántə lōp/ (*plural* **-lopes** *or* **-lope**) *n.* **1.** HORNED MAMMAL a ruminant mammal with smooth brown or gray hair, two-toed hooves, and unbranched horns, native to Africa and southwestern Asia. Antelopes include the impala, springbok, and gazelles. Family: Bovidae. **2.** = **pronghorn** [15thC. Via Old French *antelop* "mythical creature with sawlike horns said to live on the banks of the Euphrates" from, ultimately, medieval Greek *antholops*.]

Antelope

an·te·me·rid·i·an /ànti mə ríddee ən/ *adj.* relating to or taking place in the morning

an·te me·rid·i·em /-mə ríddee əm/ *adj., adv.* full form of **a.m.** [Mid-16thC. From Latin, "before noon."]

an·te·mor·tem /ànti máwrtəm/ *adj.* existing or happening before death (*formal*) [Late 19thC. From Latin *ante mortem* "before death."] —**an·te mor·tem** *adv.*

an·te·na·tal /ànti náyt'l/ *adj.* = **prenatal** —**an·te·na·tal·ly** *adv.*

an·ten·na /an ténnə/ (*plural* **-nae** /-nee/ *or* **-nas**) *n.* **1.** ZOOL THIN SENSOR ON ORGANISM'S HEAD a thin movable sensory organ found in pairs on the heads of some organisms, including insects and crustaceans **2.**

INQUIRING SENSE somebody's inquisitive or inquiring sense (*informal*) (*often used in the plural*) **3.** BROADCAST DEVICE FOR SENDING AND RECEIVING RADIO WAVES a metallic piece of equipment of variable shape, used in the sending and receiving of television or radio signals [Mid-17thC. From Latin, literally "pole supporting a sail."] —**an·ten·nal** *adj.*

an·te·pen·di·um /ànti péndee əm/ (*plural* **-ums** *or* **-a** /-ə/) *n.* a decorative cloth that hangs on the front of an altar or lectern [Late 16thC. From medieval Latin, from Latin *pendere* "to hang."]

an·te·pe·nult /ànti peé nult, ánti pi núlt/ *n.* the third from last syllable in a word ○ *The antepenult is stressed in the word "superfluous."*

an·te·pe·nul·ti·mate /ànti pi núltəmət/ *adj.* THIRD FROM LAST third from last in a series ○ *the antepenultimate word in the paragraph* ■ *n.* = **antepenult**

an·te·ri·or /an teéree ər/ *adj.* **1.** IN FRONT at or near the front of something (*formal*) ○ *an anterior view of the building* **2.** EARLIER existing or happening before something else (*formal*) **3.** ANAT NEAR FRONT OF BODY situated at or near the front of the body or of a body part **4.** BOT AWAY FROM STEM used to describe a leaf or flower part that is situated furthest away or facing away from the stem of a plant [Mid-16thC. Directly or via French from Latin, "earlier," from *ante* "before."] —**an·te·ri·or·i·ty** /an teéree áwrətee/ *n.* —**an·te·ri·or·ly** /an teéree ərlee/ *adv.*

an·te·room /ánti ròom, -ròom/ *n.* a subsidiary room that opens into a larger main room, often used as a waiting area

an·te·type /ánti tìp/ *n.* an earlier form of something ○ *"Antiochus Epiphanes, the biblical antetype of the Antichrist"* (Rollan McCleary, *The Dead Sea Scrolls in Astrology*; 1997)

an·te·ver·sion /ànti vúrzh'n/ *n.* the abnormal tilting forward of an organ, especially the uterus, without bending

ant·he·li·on /ant heélyən, an theé-/ (*plural* **-a** /-yə/ *or* **-ons**) *n.* a luminous spot appearing occasionally in the sky opposite the Sun [Late 17thC. From Greek, literally "opposite the sun," from *hēlios* "sun."]

ant·he·lix /ant heéliks, an theé-/ (*plural* **-lix·es** /-liksiz/ *or* **-li·ces** /-lə seéz/), **an·ti·he·lix** (*plural* **-lix·es** *or* **-li·ces**) *n.* a ridge of cartilage located behind the folded edge (**helix**) of the outer ear and running more or less parallel to it

ant·helm·inth·ic /ànt hel mínthik/ *adj.* CONTROLLING PARASITIC WORMS able to reduce or eliminate parasitic worm populations ■ *n.* SUBSTANCE FOR CONTROLLING PARASITIC WORMS a natural or pharmaceutical substance that reduces or eliminates parasitic worm populations

ant·hel·min·tic /ànt hel míntik, àn thel-/, **ant·hel·min·thic** /ànt hel mínthik/ *adj.* DESTRUCTIVE TO PARASITIC WORMS used to describe a drug that destroys parasitic worms or flushes out intestinal parasitic worms ■ *n.* SUBSTANCE KILLING PARASITIC WORMS a substance that kills parasitic worms or allows the natural discharge of intestinal parasitic worms [Late 17thC. Formed from the Greek stem *helmint-* "worm."]

an·them /ánthəm/ *n.* **1.** SONG OF ALLEGIANCE a song praising and declaring loyalty to something, e.g., country, cause or organization ○ *a rock anthem* **2.** CHR SHORT HYMN FOR CHOIR a short hymn with words from the Bible, sung by a choir as part of a church service **3.** CHR RELIGIOUS SONG WITH PARTS a religious song with parts for different singers or groups, especially a church hymn with parts sung by different members of the congregation, e.g., a responsorial psalm [Pre-12thC. Via late Latin *antiphona* "antiphon" from Greek *antiphōnos* "responsive," from *phonē* "sound" (source of English *phonetic* and *telephone*).]

an·the·mi·on /an theémee ən/ (*plural* **-a** /-ə/) *n.* a motif of radiating leaves resembling those of the honeysuckle or palm, found in classical Greek art and design [Mid-19thC. Via Greek, literally "a small flower," from, ultimately, *anthos* "flower."]

an·ther /ánthər/ *n.* a male flower part, the top part of a stamen, that bears the pollen in pollen sacs. ◊ **filament** [Early 18thC. Via Latin, literally "medicine made from (the pollen-bearing part of) flowers," from Greek *anthēra* "flowery," from *anthos* "flower."]

an·ther·id·i·um /ànthə ríddee əm/ (*plural* **-a** /-ə/) *n.* the male reproductive organ in algae, ferns, fungi, and mosses

Anthemion

an·the·sis /an theéssiss/ *n.* **1.** BLOOMING OF FLOWER the opening of a flower bud **2.** FLOWERING PERIOD the period of time between the opening of a flower and the formation of the fruit [Mid-19thC. Via modern Latin from Greek *anthēsis* "bloom," from *anthein* "to flower," from *anthos* "flower."]

ant·hill /ánt hìl/ *n.* a mound of earth formed by ants during the construction of their nest

antho- *prefix.* flower ○ *anthozoan* [From Greek *anthos*]

an·tho·cy·a·nin /ánthō sí ənin/ *n.* a water-soluble pigment that produces blue, violet, and red colors in flowers, fruits, leaves, and other plant parts [Mid-19thC. Coined from ANTHO- + CYANINE.]

an·tho·di·um /an thố dee əm/ (*plural* **-a** /-ə/) *n.* BOT = **capitulum** [Mid-19thC. From modern Latin, from Greek *anthōdēs* "flowerlike," from *anthos* "flower."]

an·thol·o·gize /an thóllə jìz/ (**-gized, -giz·ing, -giz·es**) *v.* **1.** *vt.* PUT WRITINGS INTO COLLECTION to gather works from different writers or other artists, e.g., songwriters or painters, into a collection, or include somebody's work in a collection **2.** *vi.* COMPILE ANTHOLOGY to compile or publish an anthology

an·thol·o·gy /an thóllə jee/ (*plural* **-gies**) *n.* **1.** COLLECTION OF DIFFERENT WRITERS' WORKS a book that consists of essays, stories, or poems by different writers **2.** PRINTED COLLECTION OF ANY ARTISTIC WORK a printed collection of works from different artists, e.g., a collection of songs or prints of paintings **3.** ANY COLLECTION anything that brings together various things or ideas ○ *The quilt is an anthology of tributes to those who have died of AIDS.* [Mid-17thC. Via medieval Latin from medieval Greek *anthologiā*, literally "collection of flowers," from Greek *anthos* "flower."] —**an·thol·o·gist** *n.*

Susan B. Anthony

An·tho·ny /ánthənee/, **Susan B.** (1820–1906) U.S. social reformer. She helped to found the National American Woman Suffrage Association (1869). Full name **Susan Brownell Anthony**

an·tho·phi·lous /an thóffələss/ *adj.* used to describe an insect that feeds on or lives among flowers

an·tho·zo·an /ánthə zố ən/ *n.* a marine invertebrate animal with a roundish hollow body. Corals and sea anemones are anthozoans. Class: Anthozoa. [Late 19thC. Formed from modern Latin *Anthozoa*, class name, from ANTHO- + Greek *zōia* "animals."] —**an·tho·zo·ic** *adj.*

an·thra·cene /ánthrə seén/ *n.* an aromatic crystalline solid with a faint blue glow, obtained by distilling coal tar and used to make dyes and chemicals, e.g., alizarin. Formula: $C_{14}H_{10}$. [Mid-19thC. Formed from Greek *anthrax* "coal."]

an·thra·ces plural of **anthrax**

an·thra·cite /ánthrə sìt/ *n.* a hard shiny black type of coal that is clean-burning, high in carbon content, and low in volatile matter [Early 19thC. Via Latin from Greek *anthrakitēs*, from *anthrax* "coal."] —**an·thra·cit·ic** /ànthrə síttik/ *adj.*

an·thrac·nose /an thrák nòss/ *n.* a fungal disease of beans and vines that produces dark sunken spots on fruit, stems, and leaves [Late 19thC. From French, from Greek *anthrax* "coal" + *nosos* "disease."]

an·thra·co·sis /ànthrə kṓssiss/ *n.* MED pneumoconiosis caused by long-term inhalation of coal dust [Mid-19thC. Formed from Greek *anthrax* "coal."]

an·thra·quin·one /ànthrə kwí nōn, -kweé nōn/ *n.* a yellow crystalline chemical that is used in the manufacture of dyes. Formula: $C_{14}H_8O_2$. [Late 19thC. A blend of ANTHRACENE and QUINONE.]

an·thrax /án thràks/ (*plural* **-thra·ces** /-thrə seéz/) *n.* **1.** FATAL DISEASE a highly infectious fatal bacterial disease of mammals, especially cattle and sheep, that causes skin ulcers and is transmittable to humans by inhalation and through feces and infected meat **2.** SKIN SORE CAUSED BY ANTHRAX an open sore on the skin that results from infection with anthrax [14thC. From Greek, "coal." Originally in the meaning "carbuncle" (from its resemblance to a burning coal).]

an·throp. *abbr.* **1.** anthropological **2.** anthropology

anthropo- *prefix.* human being ○ *anthropocentric* [From Greek *anthrōpos* (source of English *misanthrope* and *philanthropy*)]

an·thro·po·cen·tric /ànthrəpə séntrik/ *adj.* **1.** TREATING HUMANS AS PREEMINENT regarding humans as the universe's most important entity **2.** FROM POINT OF VIEW OF HUMANKIND seeing things in human terms, especially judging things according to human perceptions, values, and experiences ○ *anthropocentric responses to the condition of animals* —**an·thro·po·cen·tri·cal·ly** *adv.* —**an·thro·po·cen·trism** *n.*

an·thro·po·gen·e·sis /ànthrəpə jénnəsiss/, **an·thro·po·gen·y** /ànthrə pójjənee/ *n.* the scientific study of the origin of humankind and how it has developed

an·thro·po·gen·ic /ànthrəpə jénnik/, **an·thro·po·ge·ne·tic** /ànthrəpəjə néttik/ *adj.* **1.** CAUSED BY HUMANS relating to or resulting from the influence humans have on the natural world **2.** RELATING TO ORIGIN OF HUMANKIND relating to the origin and development of human beings

an·thro·po·gen·y *n.* = **anthropogenesis**

an·thro·poid /ánthrə pòyd/ *adj.* **1.** ZOOL RELATING TO APES used to describe monkeys and apes **2.** LIKE HUMANS physically resembling human beings or human parts **3.** RESEMBLING AN APE rough-mannered, clumsy, ugly, or unintelligent, as apes are sometimes characterized (*informal*) ■ *n.* **1.** PRIMATE an animal belonging to the group that includes monkeys, gibbons, great apes, and humans. Suborder: Anthropoidea. **2.** = **anthropoid ape**

an·thro·poid·al /ànthrə póyd'l/ *adj.* = **anthropoid** *adj.* 1

an·thro·poid ape *n.* a tailless animal with long arms and a highly developed brain that belongs to the family that includes the gorillas, chimpanzees, orangutans, and gibbons

an·thro·po·log·i·cal /ànthrəpə lójjik'l/ *adj.* relating to the study of humankind, especially the study of cultures —**an·thro·po·log·i·cal·ly** *adv.*

an·thro·po·log·i·cal lin·guis·tics *n.* a branch of linguistic research that investigates the relationship between language and culture (*takes a singular verb*)

an·thro·pol·o·gy /ànthrə póllәjee/ *n.* **1.** ANTHROP STUDY OF HUMANKIND the study of humankind in all its aspects, especially human culture or human development. It differs from sociology in taking a more historical and comparative approach. **2.** CHR CHRISTIAN DOCTRINE CONCERNED WITH HUMANKIND the parts of Christian doctrine that are concerned with the nature, origin, and destiny of humankind —**an·thro·pol·o·gist** *n.*

an·thro·pom·e·try /ànthrə pómmətree/ *n.* the study of human body measurements. The uses of anthropometry include the creation of ergonomic furniture designs and the examination and comparison of populations. —**an·thro·po·met·ric** /ànthrəpə méttrik/ *adj.* —**an·thro·po·met·ri·cal** *adj.* —**an·thro·po·met·ri·cal·ly** *adv.* —**an·thro·pom·e·trist** /ànthrə pómmitrist/ *n.*

an·thro·po·mor·phism /ànthrəpə máwr fizzəm/ *n.* the attribution of a human form, human characteristics, or human behavior to nonhuman things such as gods in mythology and animals in children's stories —**an·thro·po·mor·phic** *adj.* —**an·thro·po·mor·phi·cal·ly** *adv.*

an·thro·po·mor·phize /ànthrəpə máwr fīz/ (**-phized, -phiz·ing, -phiz·es**) *vt.* to give a nonhuman thing a human form or human characteristics ○ *Mythology and children's stories anthropomorphize animals and inanimate objects.* —**an·thro·po·mor·phi·za·tion** /ànthrəpə mawrfə záysh'n/ *n.*

an·thro·po·mor·phous /ànthrəpə máwrfəss/ *adj.* **1.** HUMAN IN SHAPE with the shape of the human body or a human body part **2.** ATTRIBUTING HUMAN QUALITIES TO NONHUMAN THINGS relating to the attribution of human characteristics to nonhuman things, e.g., gods or animals

an·thro·pop·a·thism /ànthrə póppə thìzzəm/, **an·thro·pop·a·thy** /-thee/ *n.* the attribution of human emotions to a nonhuman thing, e.g., a god or an object of worship [Mid-19thC. Coined from ANTHROPO- + -PATHY + -ISM.]

an·thro·poph·a·gus /ànthrə pófføgəss/ (*plural* **-gi** /-jī/) *n.* somebody who eats the flesh of other human beings (*technical*) [Mid-16thC. Via Latin from Greek *anthrōpophagos*, literally "man-eating," from *anthrōpos* (see ANTHROPO-).] —**an·thro·po·phag·ic** /ànthrəpə fájjik/ *adj.* —**an·thro·poph·a·gous** /ànthrə pófføgəss/ *adj.* —**an·thro·poph·a·gy** /-jee/ *n.*

an·thur·i·um /an thóoree əm/ *n.* a tropical evergreen American plant cultivated for its glossy heart-shaped red or white flowers enclosing a spike of yellow florets. Genus: *Anthurium*. [Mid-19thC. From modern Latin, genus name, from Greek *anthos* "flower" (see ANTHO-) + *oura* "tail."]

an·ti /ántī, -tee/ *adj.* OPPOSED TO SOMETHING expressing or holding an opposing view, particularly regarding a political issue or moral principle (*informal*) ○ *She's very anti smoking.* ■ *n.* (*plural* **-tis**) SOMEBODY WHO DISAGREES somebody who holds or expresses an opposing view, particularly regarding a political issue or principle (*informal*) ○ *Are you a pro or an anti?* [Late 18thC. From ANTI-.]

anti-, **ant-** *prefix.* against, opposite ○ *anticonvulsive* [Via Latin from, ultimately, Greek *anti* "opposite, against"]

an·ti·a·bor·tion /àntī ə báwrsh'n, àntee-/ *adj.* opposed to the practice of abortion or to its legalization —**an·ti·a·bor·tion·ist** *n.*

an·ti·ad·re·ner·gic /àntī áddrə núrjik, àntee-/ *adj.* COUNTERACTING EPINEPHRINE blocking or counteracting the physiological effects of epinephrine ■ *n.* ANTI-ADRENERGIC DRUG a drug that counteracts the effects of epinephrine

an·ti·air·craft /àntī áir kràft, àntee-/ *adj.* designed and used to destroy enemy aircraft

an·ti·a·li·as·ing /àntī áylee əssing, àntee-/ *n.* smoothing the jagged edges of diagonal lines in computer-generated images by varying the color or shades of gray at the edges

an·ti·an·xi·e·ty /àntī ang zī ətee, àntee-/ *adj.* preventing or relieving anxiety

an·ti·a·part·heid /àntī ə paárt hīt, àntee ə paár tàyt, -paárt hàyt/ *adj.* expressing or working in opposition to apartheid, particularly as it was legally enforced in South Africa between 1948 and 1991

an·ti·ar·rhyth·mic /àntī ə ríthmik, àntee-/ *adj.* COUNTERACTING IRREGULAR HEART BEAT preventing or correcting irregularities in the heart's action ■ *n.* ANTI-ARRHYTHMIC DRUG a drug that prevents or corrects irregularities in the heart's action

an·ti·art *n.* EARLY 20TH-CENTURY ART MOVEMENT the rebellion against easel painting and conventional art launched by the Dada movement during World War I. The term is meant to indicate the movement's rejection of conventional artistic practices and bourgeois tastes. ■ *adj.* OPPOSED TO CONVENTIONAL ART rejecting established artistic conventions

an·ti·at·om /àntī àttəm, àntee-/ *n.* an atom made up of antiparticles

an·ti·bac·ter·i·al /àntī bak téeree əl, àntee-/ *adj.* ACTING AGAINST GROWTH OF BACTERIA preventing, killing, or reducing the growth of bacteria ■ *n.* AGENT ACTING AGAINST BACTERIA an agent that prevents, kills, or reduces the growth of bacteria

an·ti·bal·lis·tic mis·sile /àntī bə lístik-, àntee-/ *n.* a missile used to prevent a ballistic missile from reaching its target by destroying it in flight

An·tibes /oN téeb/ port and resort southwest of Nice in the Alpes-Maritimes Department in the Provence-Alpes-Côte d'Azur Region of France. Population: 63,000 (1990).

an·ti·bi·o·sis /àntī bī óssiss, àntee-/ *n.* a relationship between organisms that is harmful to one of them, e.g., the production by one microorganism of chemicals that harm another [Late 19thC. Coined from ANTI-, on the model of *symbiosis*.]

an·ti·bi·ot·ic /àntī bī óttik, àntee-/ *n.* AGENT THAT DESTROYS BACTERIA a substance that is able to kill or inactivate bacteria in the body. Antibiotics are derived from microorganisms, especially fungi, or are synthetically produced. They have no effect against viruses. ■ *adj.* WORKING AS AN ANTIBIOTIC able to kill bacteria or render them inactive [Mid-19thC. Coined from ANTI- + BIOTIC.] —**an·ti·bi·ot·i·cal·ly** *adv.*

an·ti·bod·y /ánti boddee/ (*plural* **-ies**) *n.* a protein produced by B cells in the body in response to the presence of an antigen, e.g., a bacterium or virus. Antibodies are a primary form of immune response in resistance to disease and act by attaching themselves to a foreign antigen and weakening or destroying it. [Early 20thC. Translation of German *Antikörper*, a contraction of *anti-toxischer Körper* "antitoxic body" or a similar phrase.]

an·ti·busi·ness /àntī bíznəss, àntee-/ *adj.* working against or opposing the interests or development of business, especially large corporations

an·ti·bus·ing /àntī bússing, àntee-/ *adj.* opposed to the policy or practice of transporting children by bus (**busing**) to schools outside their district in order to achieve an ethnic balance in individual schools

an·tic /ántik/ *n.* CLOWN an actor or performer playing a crazily comic role (*archaic*) ■ **an·tics** *npl.* SILLY PRANKS amusing, frivolous, or eccentric behavior ■ *adj.* STRANGE ludicrously or amusingly strange and eccentric (*archaic*) [Early 16thC. Via Italian *antico* "old, old-fashioned" from Latin *anticus, antiquus*.] —**an·ti·cal·ly** *adv.*

an·ti·can·cer /àntī kánsər, àntee-/ *adj.* preventing or arresting the development of cancer

an·ti·cat·a·lyst /àntī kátt'list, àntee-/ *n.* **1.** ENG, CHEM = **inhibitor 2.** SUBSTANCE TO PREVENT ACTION OF CATALYST a substance that inhibits or prevents the action of a catalyst

an·ti·cath·ode /àntī ká thōd, àntee-/ *n.* the anode in a vacuum tube, e.g., an X-ray tube, toward which electrons flow

an·ti·choice *adj.* against the principle or practice of legally sanctioned abortion

an·ti·cho·lin·er·gic /àntī kōlə núrjik, àntee-/ *adj.* BLOCKING NERVE IMPULSES blocking impulses from the part of the nervous system that controls heartbeat, blood pressure, and other responses to stress, by neutralizing the effects of acetylcholine ■ *n.* SUBSTANCE THAT BLOCKS NERVE IMPULSES an agent with an anticholinergic effect

an·ti·cho·lin·es·ter·ase /àntī kōlə néstə ràyss, àntee-, -ràyz, àntee-/ *n.* a substance that blocks the activity of the enzyme cholinesterase, increasing the concentration of acetylcholine in the body

An·ti·christ /àntī krīst, ántee-/ *n.* **1.** ANTAGONIST OF JESUS CHRIST an antagonist of Jesus Christ, expected by the early Christians to spread evil throughout the world, but then to be overcome by the second coming of Christ **2. An·ti·christ, an·ti·christ** ANY OPPONENT OF JESUS CHRIST any person or power opposed to Jesus Christ [Pre-12thC. Via ecclesiastical Latin from Greek *antikhristos*.]

an·tic·i·pant /an tíssipənt/ *adj.* **1.** ACTING IN ADVANCE working or taking action in advance **2.** FEELING ANTICIPATION expecting or looking forward to something [Early 16thC. From Latin *anticipant-*, the present participle stem of *anticipare* (see ANTICIPATE).]

an·tic·i·pate /an tíssi pàyt/ (**-pat·ed, -pat·ing, -pates**) *vt.* **1.** ACT BEFOREHAND TO ADDRESS SOMETHING IMMINENT to imagine or consider something before it happens and make any necessary preparations or changes **2.** EXPECT SOMETHING to think or be fairly sure that a certain thing will happen or come **3.** LOOK FORWARD TO SOMETHING to feel excited, hopeful, or eager about something that is going to happen **4.** PREVENT SOMETHING to imagine or consider something that might happen and take action to prevent it **5.** START SOMETHING AHEAD OF TIME to say or do something before it becomes fashionable or comes into widespread use (*formal*) **6.** USE SOMETHING NOT YET RECEIVED to make use of something before it has actually been received (*formal*) [Mid-16thC. From Latin *anticipare*, literally "to catch beforehand," from *capere*.] —**an·tic·i·pat·a·ble** *adj.* —**an·tic·i·pa·tor** *n.*

WORD KEY: USAGE

Anticipating trouble If you ***anticipate*** trouble, it often just means that you are expecting or foreseeing trouble, whereas its proper meaning is that you are taking steps to prevent trouble, that is, "forestalling" rather than "expecting" it.

an·tic·i·pa·tion /an tìssi páysh'n/ *n.* **1.** EXPECTANT WAITING the feeling of looking forward, usually excitedly or eagerly, to something that is going to happen **2.** FIN PREMATURE USE OF FUNDS the seizure or use of funds before they are legally available, especially from a trust fund **3.** MUSIC NOTE PLAYED BEFORE CHORD a note related to a chord that is played just before the chord itself

an·tic·i·pa·tive /an tíssi pàytiv, an tíssipətiv/ *adj.* expecting or looking forward to something —**an·tic·i·pa·tive·ly** *adv.*

an·tic·i·pa·to·ry /an tíssipə tàwree/ *adj.* experienced or done in the expectation of a future event

an·ti·cler·i·cal /àntī klérrik'l, àntee-/ *adj.* opposed to the involvement by the church or clergy in politics and public affairs —**an·ti·cler·i·cal·ism** *n.*

an·ti·cli·max /ántī klī màks, ántee-/ *n.* **1.** DISAPPOINTING END AFTER BIG BUILDUP an ordinary or unsatisfying event that follows an increasingly exciting, dramatic, or unusual series of events or a period of increasing anticipation and excitement **2.** LITERAT SUDDEN LOWERING OF TONE an unexpected change in tone or subject matter from the high-minded, serious, or compelling to the trivial, comic, or dull —**an·ti·cli·mac·tic** /àntī klī máktik, àntee-/ *adj.* —**an·ti·cli·mac·ti·cal·ly** *adv.*

an·ti·cli·nal /àntī klīn'l, ántee-/ *adj.* **1.** OF ARCHING ROCK LAYERS relating to, or in the form of, layers of sedimentary rock pushed up into an arch shape (**anticline**) by movements in the earth's crust **2.** BOT PERPENDICULAR TO PLANT SURFACE used to describe a plant cell layer that is perpendicular to the surface of a plant part [Early 19thC. Coined from ANTI- + Greek *klinein* "to lean," on the model of *incline*.]

an·ti·cline /ánti klīn/ *n.* an arch-shaped formation of layers of sedimentary rock folded upward by movements in the earth's crust [Mid-19thC. Back-formation from ANTICLINAL.]

an·ti·clock·wise /àntī klók wīz, àntee-/ *adj., adv.* *U.K.* = **counterclockwise**

an·ti·co·ag·u·lant /àntī kō ággyələnt, àntee/ *adj.* STOPPING BLOOD CLOTTING preventing the normal clotting process of blood ■ *n.* SUBSTANCE THAT STOPS BLOOD CLOTTING a natural or synthetic agent that prevents blood clots from forming

an·ti·co·don /àntī kō dòn, àntee-/ *n.* a unit of genetic code, comprising a set of three nucleotides in transfer RNA involved in the formation of a specific protein

an·ti·co·in·ci·dence /àntī kō ínsid'ns, àntee-/ *adj.* used to describe an electronic circuit that produces an output pulse if one, but not both, of its input terminals receives a pulse within a specified time frame

an·ti·com·pet·i·tive /àntī kəm péttitiv, àntee-/ *adj.* likely or certain to discourage competition

an·ti·con·vul·sant /àntī kən vúlsənt, àntee-/ *adj.* CONTROLLING CONVULSIONS preventing or reducing the incidence of seizures, e.g., in epilepsy ■ *n.* DRUG FOR CONTROLLING CONVULSIONS a drug for preventing or reducing the incidence of seizures, e.g., in epilepsy —**an·ti·con·vul·sive** *n., adj.*

An·ti·cos·ti Is·land /ánti kósti-/ island in the Gulf of St. Lawrence, Quebec, Canada. Its abundant forests shelter diverse wildlife. Area: 3,066 sq. mi./7,941 sq. km.

an·ti·crime /àntī krīm, ántee-/ *adj.* designed to prevent or reduce the incidence of crime in a particular area or among particularly vulnerable groups of people

an·ti·cy·clone /àntī sī klōn, ántee-/ *n.* a large system of atmospheric high pressure marked by circulating winds moving clockwise from the center in the northern hemisphere and counterclockwise in the southern hemisphere, bringing generally settled weather —**an·ti·cy·clon·ic** /àntī sī klónnik, àntee-/ *adj.*

an·ti·dem·o·crat·ic /àntī démmə kráttik, àntee-/ *adj.* opposed to or working in a way that undermines democratic procedures or policies, especially the political institution of representative government

an·ti·de·pres·sant /àntī di préss'nt, àntee-/ *n.* DRUG TO CONTROL DEPRESSION a drug used to prevent or reduce depression ■ *adj.* CONTROLLING DEPRESSION acting to prevent or reduce depression —**an·ti·de·pres·sive** *adj.*

an·ti·di·ar·rhe·al /àntī dī ə rée əl, àntee-/, **an·ti·di·ar·rhoe·al** *adj.* CONTROLLING DIARRHEA preventing or reducing diarrhea ■ *n.* DRUG FOR CONTROLLING DIARRHEA a drug for preventing or reducing diarrhea

an·ti·di·u·ret·ic /àntī dī ə réttik, àntee-/ *adj.* CONTROLLING URINE OUTPUT preventing the excessive output of urine ■ *n.* DRUG FOR CONTROLLING URINE OUTPUT a drug for preventing or reducing the excessive output of urine

an·ti·dote /ánti dōt/ *n.* **1.** SUBSTANCE THAT COUNTERACTS POISON a substance that counteracts the effect of a poison or toxin **2.** WELCOME RELIEF OR REMEDY something that will take away or reduce the bad effects of something experienced earlier [15thC. Via Latin from Greek *antidoton,* from *antididonai,* literally "to give against," from *didonai* "to give" (see DOSE).] —**an·ti·dot·al** /ánti dōt'l/ *adj.* —**an·ti·dot·al·ly** *adv.*

an·ti·dump·ing /àntī dúmping, àntee-/ *adj.* opposed to or restricting the importation of cheaply produced goods that undercut domestic producers' prices

an·ti·e·lec·tron /àntī i lék tròn, àntee-/ *n.* = **positron**

an·ti·e·met·ic /àntī i méttik, àntee-/ *adj.* PREVENTING VOMITING acting to prevent vomiting ■ *n.* DRUG PREVENTING VOMITING a drug that prevents vomiting

an·ti·fed·er·al·ist /àntī féddərəlist, àntee-/ *n.* **1.** **an·ti·fed·er·al·ist, An·ti·fed·er·al·ist** HIST HISTORICAL OPPONENT OF U.S. CONSTITUTION somebody who did not agree that the U.S. Constitution should be formally approved and recognized at the time it was drawn up **2.** SOMEBODY OPPOSED TO FEDERALISM somebody who disagrees with a political system or philosophy that calls for division of power between a central government and regional governments ■ *adj.* AGAINST FEDERALISM hostile to the idea or practice of federalism —**an·ti·fed·er·al·ism** *n.*

an·ti·fer·ro·mag·net·ic /àntī férrō mag néttik, àntee-/ *adj.* used to describe substances that behave like paramagnetic substances with respect to their permeability but behave like ferromagnetic substances when their temperature is changed —**an·ti·fer·ro·mag·net** /àntī férrō mágnət, àntee-/ *n.* —**an·ti·fer·ro·mag·net·ism** *n.*

an·ti·fer·til·i·ty /àntī fər tíllətee, àntee-/ acting to reduce or destroy the ability to reproduce

an·ti·foul·ing paint /àntī fówling-, àntee-/ *n.* a very poisonous type of paint used to prevent barnacles and other organisms from growing on the bottoms of boats or ships

an·ti·freeze /ánti frēez/ *n.* a liquid that lowers the freezing point of another liquid. An antifreeze such as ethylene glycol is added to or substituted for the water in a vehicle's engine to stop it from freezing in winter.

an·ti·fun·gal /àntī fúng'l, àntee-/ *adj.* preventing or reducing the growth of fungi, or killing fungi

an·ti·gen /ántijən/ *n.* a substance, usually a protein, on the surface of a cell or bacterium that stimulates the production of an antibody [Early 20thC. Via German from French *antigène,* from *anti-* "anti-" + Greek *-genēs* (see -GEN).] —**an·ti·gen·ic** /ànti jénnik/ *adj.* —**an·ti·gen·i·cal·ly** *adv.* —**an·ti·ge·nic·i·ty** /ànti jə níssətee/ *n.*

an·ti·gog·lin /ànti gógglin/ *adv.* (*regional*) **1.** ASKEW askew **2.** CATER-CORNERED diagonally [Late 19thC. Of uncertain origin; possibly from ANTI- + *goggle* in a British dialect sense "to tremble, shake."]

WORD KEY: REGIONAL NOTE

Both senses of *antigoglin* are common in the southern, South Midland, and western United States. These regions share several synonyms, none of which is easily distinguished in meaning from the others: *angly, antigoglin, blasy, catawampus, crossways,* and *diagonally.*

An·tig·o·ne /an tíggənee/ *n.* in Greek mythology, the daughter of Oedipus and Jocasta. She killed herself after being condemned to death by Creon, king of Thebes, for cremating her brother's body.

An·tig·o·nus I /an tíggənəss/ (382–301 B.C.) Greek general. He secured a large part of Asia Minor after the breakup of Alexander the Great's empire in 323 B.C.

an·ti·grav·i·ty /àntī grávvətee, àntee-/ *n.* HYPOTHETICAL FORCE CANCELING GRAVITATIONAL FORCE a hypothetical force that would cancel the force of gravity ■ *adj.* OPPOSING GRAVITATIONAL FORCE counteracting the effects of gravity or of high acceleration

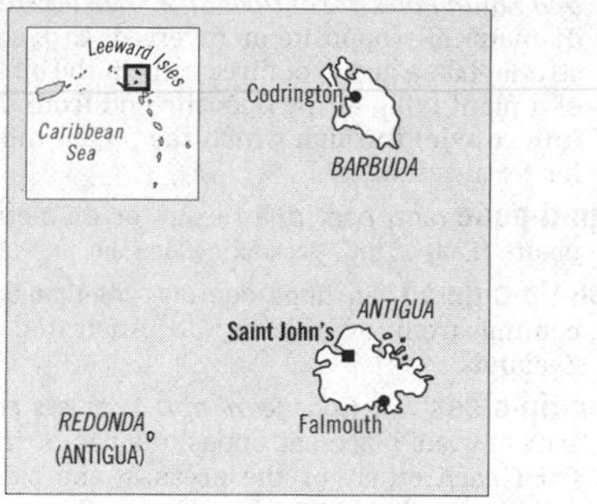

Antigua and Barbuda

An·ti·gua and Bar·bu·da /an téegə ənd baar bóodə/ island nation in the Leeward Isles, east of Puerto Rico and north of Venezuela in the Caribbean Sea. Language: English. Currency: East Caribbean dollar. Capital: Saint John's. Population: 63,739 (1997). Area: 170 sq. mi./440 sq. km. —**Antiguan** *adj., n.*

an·ti·he·lix *n.* = **anthelix**

an·ti·he·ro /ánti hèerō/ (*plural* **-roes**) *n.* somebody who is the central character in a story but who is not brave, noble, or morally good as heroes traditionally are —**an·ti·her·o·ic** /ànti hi rṓ ik/ *adj.* —**an·ti·her·o·ism** /ànti hérrō ìzzəm/ *n.*

an·ti·his·ta·mine /ànti hístəmin, -mèen, àntī-min, -mèen/ *n.* a drug that blocks cell receptors for histamine, either to prevent allergic effects such as sneezing and itching or to reduce the rate of certain secretions in the stomach —**an·ti·his·ta·min·ic** /ànti hístə mínnik, àntī-/ *adj.*

an·ti·hy·per·ten·sive /àntī hīpər ténsiv, àntee-/ *adj.* CONTROLLING HIGH BLOOD PRESSURE preventing or reducing abnormally high blood pressure ■ *n.* DRUG THAT CONTROLS HYPERTENSION an agent or means used to prevent or reduce abnormally high blood pressure

an·ti-in·flam·ma·to·ry (*plural* **an·ti-in·flam·ma·to·ries**) *n.* a drug that acts to reduce inflammation. Aspirin and corticosteroids are anti-inflammatories. —**an·ti-in·flam·ma·to·ry** *adj.*

an·ti·knock /ànti nók/ *n.* a substance used to reduce or stop faulty fuel combustion in vehicle engines, a problem identified with a knocking sound

An·ti-Leb·a·non Moun·tains mountain range running from north to south in Lebanon, parallel to the Mediterranean coast

an·ti·lep·ton /àntī lép tòn, àntee-/ *n.* the antiparticle of a lepton

an·ti·lock brake /àntī lók-/ *n.* an electronically controlled brake or braking system designed so that the vehicle's wheels do not lock if the driver brakes very suddenly

an·ti·log·a·rithm /àntī lóggə rìthəm, àntee-/, **an·ti·log** /ánti lòg, àntī-/ *n.* a number for which the logarithm is a given number, so for $\text{logarithm}_a b = c$, then $\text{antilogarithm}_a c = b$

an·ti·ma·cas·sar /ànti mə kássər/ *n.* a washable piece of fabric, usually embroidered, placed over the back of an armchair to keep it clean where heads rub against it (*dated*) [Mid-19thC. Coined from ANTI- + *Macassar,* a brand of hair oil.]

an·ti·mag·net·ic /àntī mag néttik, àntee-/ *adj.* used to describe a material that does not become permanently magnetized in a magnetic field

an·ti·ma·lar·i·al /àntī mə láiree əl, àntee-/ *adj.* CONTROLLING MALARIA preventing or curing malaria ■ *n.* DRUG FOR CONTROLLING MALARIA a drug that prevents or cures malaria

an·ti·masque /ánti màsk/, **an·ti·mask** *n.* an interlude in or prelude to a 17th-century masque that contrasts with the main performance and often involves grotesque costumes and dancing

an·ti·mat·ter /ánti màttər, ántee-/ *n.* a hypothetical form of matter composed of subatomic particles (**antiparticles**) that correspond to and can annihilate other elementary particles

an·ti·mere /ánti mèer/ *n.* a part of a radially symmetrical animal that is the opposite of a corresponding part of the animal —**an·ti·mer·ic** /ànti mérrik/ *adj.*

an·ti·me·tab·o·lite /àntī mə tábbə līt, àntee-/ *n.* a substance that disrupts cell growth by taking the place of a normal nutrient metabolite with similar properties. Some antimetabolites are effective in treating certain cancers.

an·ti·mis·sile mis·sile /àntī míss'l-, àntee-/ *n.* a missile used to prevent another missile from reaching its target by destroying it in flight

an·ti·mi·tot·ic /àntī mī tóttik, àntee-/ *adj.* preventing or reducing the rate of cell division (**mitosis**) —**an·ti·mi·tot·ic** *n.*

an·ti·mo·ni·al /àntə mṓnee əl/ *adj.* CONTAINING ANTIMONY used to describe drugs that contain antimony ■ *n.* SUBSTANCE CONTAINING ANTIMONY a drug or other substance containing antimony

an·ti·mo·ny /ántə mṑnee/ *n.* a toxic crystalline chemical element that occurs in metallic and nonmetallic forms. The metallic form is silver-white, brittle, and lustrous, and is used in alloys and electronics. [15thC. From medieval Latin *antimonium,* of uncertain origin.]

an·ti·ne·o·plas·tic /àntī nee ō plástik, àntee-/ *adj.* preventing or inhibiting the growth of cancers —**an·ti·ne·o·plas·tic** *n.*

an·ti·neu·tri·no /àntī noo trée nō, àntee-/ (*plural* **-nos**) *n.* the antiparticle of a neutrino. When a neutrino and an antineutrino are brought together mutual annihilation occurs.

an·ti·neu·tron /àntī nóo tròn, àntee-/ *n.* the antiparticle of a neutron. When a neutron and an antineutron are brought together mutual annihilation occurs.

ant·ing /ánting/ *n.* a behavioral practice in which birds pick up ants in their beaks and rub them on their feathers to spread fluids repellent to parasites

an·ti·node /ánti nṑd/ *n.* a point of maximum amplitude of a wave characteristic in a system in which the wave form is stationary in time

an·ti·no·mi·an /ànti nṓmee ən/ *n.* CHRISTIAN BELIEVING SALVATION DEPENDS ON FAITH somebody who maintains that Christians are not bound by established laws, especially moral laws, but should rely on faith and divine grace for salvation ■ *adj.* **1.** OPPOSING FIXED MORAL LAWS disagreeing with the philosophy that the same fixed rules of morality and other laws should apply to everybody **2.** HOLDING ANTINOMIAN BELIEFS holding or relating to the view that Christians are not bound by established laws, especially moral laws, but should rely on faith and divine grace for salvation [Mid-17thC. Formed from medieval Latin *Antinomi* "Antinomians," from Latin *antinomia* (see ANTINOMY).]

an·ti·no·mi·an·ism /ànti nṓmee ə nìzzəm/ *n.* **1.** CHRISTIAN MORAL DOCTRINE the Christians philosophy that they are not bound by established laws, especially moral laws, but should rely on faith and divine grace for salvation **2.** FLEXIBLE CONCEPT OF MORALITY the belief that it is impossible to apply a universal moral code because it will have a different meaning for different people

an·tin·o·my /an tínnəmee/ (*plural* **-mies**) *n.* **1.** PHILOS PARADOXICAL RESULT two apparently correct and reasonable statements or facts that do not agree and therefore produce a contradictory and illogical conclusion **2.** LAW LEGAL DISCREPANCY a contradiction between two laws, principles, or authorities [Late 16thC. Via Latin from Greek *antinomia,* literally "against law," from *nomos* "law, rule."] —**an·ti·nom·ic** /ànti nómmik/ *adj.*

an·ti·nov·el /àntī nòvv'l, àntee-/ *n.* a work of fiction that lacks the elements traditionally used in a novel, especially one with no coherent plot and characters, or in which the writer's perspective is deliberately inconsistent —**an·ti·nov·el·ist** *n.*

an·ti·nu·cle·ar /àntī nóoklee ər, àntee-/ *adj.* **1.** AGAINST USE OF NUCLEAR POWER opposed to nuclear weapons or power **2.** IMMUNOL DESTROYING CELLS reactive with or destructive to cell nuclei

an·ti·nu·cle·on /ántī nóoklee òn, àntee-/ *n.* an antiproton or antineutron. When a nucleon and an antinucleon are brought together mutual annihilation occurs.

an·ti·nuke /àntī nóok, àntee-/ *adj.* antinuclear (*informal*) ○ *an antinuke demonstration*

An·ti·och /ántee òk/ city in northwestern California, on the San Joaquin River. Population: 76,293 (1996).

an·ti·on·co·gene *n.* a recessive gene that is thought to suppress cancers by limiting cell multiplication

an·ti·ox·i·dant /àntī óksid'nt, àntee-/ *n.* any substance that inhibits the destructive effects of oxidation, e.g., in the body or in foodstuffs and plastics

an·ti·par·al·lel /àntī pérrə lèl, àntee-/ *adj.* parallel but opposite in linear or rotational direction

an·ti·par·ti·cle /ántī paártik'l, ántee-/ *n.* an elementary particle with the same mass as its corresponding particle but having opposite values for other properties such as charge. When an antiparticle and its particle interact mutual annihilation occurs.

an·ti·pas·to /ànti paástō, -pás-/ (*plural* **-ti** /-tee/) *n.* any of various different foods served at the beginning of an Italian meal or as a snack, especially cooked meats and sliced sausage, marinated fish, or vegetables [Early 17thC. From Italian, literally "before food."]

an·tip·a·thet·ic /àntipə théttik, an tìppə-/ *adj.* **1. FEELING DISLIKE FOR SOMETHING OR SOMEBODY** feeling or expressing anger, hostility, strong opposition, or disgust, especially toward a particular person or thing **2. REPULSIVE** stirring up or causing strongly negative feelings such as anger, hostility, or disgust [Early 17thC. From ANTIPATHY, modeled on PATHETIC.] —**an·tip·a·thet·i·cal·ly** *adv.*

an·tip·a·thy /an típpəthee/ (*plural* **-thies**) *n.* **1. STRONGLY NEGATIVE FEELING** anger, hostility, fixed opposition, or disgust directed toward a particular person or thing **2. OBJECT OF LOATHING** a source of somebody's anger, hostility, fixed opposition, or disgust [Late 16thC. Via French *antipathie* from, ultimately, Greek *antipathēs*, literally "feeling the opposite," from *pathos* "feeling" (see PATHOS).]

WORD KEY: SYNONYMS

See Synonyms at ***dislike***.

an·ti·pe·ri·od·ic /àntī peeree óddik, àntee-/ *adj.* preventing the periodic recurrence of symptoms or of a disease such as malaria —**an·ti·pe·ri·od·ic** *n.*

an·ti·pe·ri·stal·sis /àntī perri stáwlsiss, àntee-/ (*plural* **-ses** /-seez/) *n.* contractions of the intestine in the reverse direction to what is usual, tending to cause vomiting —**an·ti·pe·ri·stal·tic** *adj.*

an·ti·per·son·nel /àntī pùrsə nél, àntee-/ *adj.* intended to injure and kill enemy personnel rather than to blow up buildings, structures, arsenals, or missiles

an·ti·per·spi·rant /àntī púrspərənt, àntee-/ *n.* **SUBSTANCE TO CONTROL SWEATING** an astringent preparation applied especially under the arms to help prevent perspiration. Antiperspirants are produced in many forms, including aerosols, roll-ons, and sticks. ■ *adj.* **CONTROLLING SWEATING** used to reduce or prevent perspiration

an·ti·phon /ántə fòn/ *n.* **1. MUSIC SUNG IN ALTERNATING PARTS** a hymn or psalm performed by two groups of singers chanting alternate sections **2. SECTION OF FORMAL CHURCH SERVICE** a short piece of biblical or devotional text that is chanted or sung before or after a psalm verse in a Roman Catholic or Anglican church service **3. RESPONSE** a response or reply (*literary*) [15thC. Via ecclesiastical Latin *antiphona* (source of English *anthem*) from Greek *antiphōnos*, literally "sounding in response," from *phōnē* (see -PHONE).]

an·tiph·o·nal /an tíffən'l/ *adj.* **1. PERFORMED IN ALTERNATING SECTIONS** sung, played, or recited by two or more groups performing alternate sections **2. WITH RESPONSES** with alternating phases or responses, as in an antiphon ■ *n.* = **antiphonary** —**an·tiph·o·nal·ly** *adv.*

an·tiph·o·nar·y /an tíffə nèrree/ (*plural* **-ies**) *n.* a book, often large and richly decorated, containing antiphons or anthems to be sung or chanted responsively

an·tiph·o·ny /an tíffənee/ (*plural* **-nies**) *n.* **1.** = **antiphon** *n.* 1 **2. MUSIC PERFORMED IN ALTERNATING SECTIONS** responsive chanting, recitation, or singing, e.g., of liturgical antiphons **3. RESPONSE IN MUSIC** a musical response or answering phrase [Formed from ANTIPHON]

an·tiph·ra·sis /an tíffrəssiss/ *n.* the use of a word or phrase to mean the opposite of its usual or literal sense, e.g., saying on a rainy day, "What a great day for a picnic!" [Mid-16thC. Via late Latin from, ultimately, Greek *antiphrazein*, literally "to express oppositely," from *phrazein* "to declare" (see PHRASE).]

an·tip·o·dal /an típpəd'l/ *adj.* **1. ON SPHERE'S OPPOSITE SIDE** used to describe a point at the opposite end of the diameter of a sphere to another point ○ *The North and South Poles are antipodal.* **2. DIAMETRICALLY OPPOSITE** diametrically opposite or reversed ■ *n.* BOT **EMBRYO CELLS IN PLANT** a group of three cells in the embryo sac of a plant lying at the opposite end from the canal (**micropyle**) through which the pollen tube enters for fertilization

an·ti·pode /ánti pòd/ *n.* an exact or diametrical opposite [Early 17thC. Back-formation from ANTIPODES.]

an·tip·o·de·an /an tìppə dée ən/, **An·tip·o·de·an** *adj.* coming from or relating to Australia or New Zealand

an·tip·o·des /an típpədeez/ *npl.* **1. PLACES AT OPPOSITE SIDES OF WORLD** places at opposite sides of the world from each other, or the areas at the side of the world opposite from a given place **2. OPPOSITES** two points, places, or things that are diametrically opposite each other [14thC. Via French or late Latin from Greek *antipodes*, literally "those who have their feet opposite," from *pod-*, the stem of *pous* "foot."]

An·tip·o·des /-/ *n.* Australia and New Zealand, from the perspective of the United Kingdom or Europe (*informal*)

an·ti·pol·lu·tion /àntī pə lóosh'n, àntee-/ *adj.* designed to stop or reduce pollution of the environment

an·ti·pope /ánti pòp/ *n.* somebody who claims or is declared to be pope, even though a pope chosen by the orthodox canonical system already holds office [15thC. Via French *antipape* from medieval Latin *antipapa*, from *papa* "pope," on the model of *antichristus* "antichrist."]

an·ti·pro·ton /àntī prò tòn, àntee-/ *n.* the antiparticle of a proton. When a proton and an antiproton are brought together mutual annihilation occurs.

an·ti·pru·rit·ic /àntī proo ríttik/; /àntee-/ *adj.* **CONTROLLING ITCHING** preventing or reducing itching ■ *n.* **AGENT FOR CONTROLLING ITCHING** a drug or other agent that prevents or reduces itching

an·ti·psy·chi·a·try /àntī sī kí ətree, ànti sì-/ *n.* a way of treating people with psychiatric disorders that is derived from psychoanalysis and is opposed to the conventional medical mode, which uses medication

an·ti·psy·chot·ic /àntī sī kóttik, àntee-/ *adj.* **REDUCING PSYCHOSIS** counteracting or alleviating the symptoms of a psychiatric disorder such as schizophrenia ■ *n.* **DRUG THAT REDUCES PSYCHOSIS** a drug that counteracts or alleviates the symptoms of a psychiatric disorder such as schizophrenia

an·ti·py·ret·ic /àntī pī réttik, àntee-/ *adj.* **REDUCING FEVER** acting to reduce fever ■ *n.* **DRUG THAT REDUCES FEVER** a drug or other agent that reduces fever —**an·ti·py·re·sis** /àntī pī réessis, ànti-/ *n.*

an·tiq. *abbr.* **1.** antiquarian **2.** antiquity

an·ti·quar·i·an /ànti kwáiree ən/ *adj.* **IN THE ANTIQUES BUSINESS** dealing with or relating to antiques or antiquities, especially rare and old books ■ *n.* = **antiquary** —**an·ti·quar·i·an·ism** *n.*

an·ti·quark /ántī kwàwrk, ántee-/ *n.* the antiparticle of a quark. When a quark and an antiquark are brought together mutual annihilation occurs.

an·ti·quar·y /ánti kwèrree/ (*plural* **-ies**) *n.* a collector, scholar, or seller of antiques or antiquities [Mid-16thC. From Latin *antiquarius*, from *antiquus* (see ANTIQUE).]

an·ti·quate /ánti kwàyt/ (**-quat·ed, -quat·ing, -quates**) *vt.* **1. MAKE SOMETHING OLD-FASHIONED** to cause something to become out of date or old by replacing it with something newer **2.** = **antique** [Late 16thC. Via ecclesiastical Latin *antiquare* "to make old" from, ultimately, Latin *antiquus* (see ANTIQUE).]

an·ti·quat·ed /ánti kwàytəd/ *adj.* quaint, extremely out of date, or badly in need of updating or replacing —**an·ti·quat·ed·ness** *n.*

WORD KEY: SYNONYMS

See Synonyms at ***old-fashioned***.

an·tique /an téek/ *n.* (*plural* **-tiques**) **1. OLD ITEM** a collectible decorative or household object, often a piece of furniture, which is valued because of its age **2. CLASSICAL ART** the style, traditions, and qualities of ancient times, usually specifically the art and sculpture of ancient Greece and Rome ■ *adj.* **1. MADE LONG AGO** old and often valuable, of interest to collectors, and characteristic of a particular period and style of manufacture **2. FROM CLASSICAL TIMES** derived from a period of ancient history, especially ancient Greece or Rome, or stylistically typical of such a period (*formal*) **3. ANCIENT** very old or old-fashioned (*informal*) ■ *vt.* (**-tiqued, -tiqu·ing**) **MAKE SOMETHING APPEAR OLD** to treat something, especially a new object, so that it looks antique or worn with time [15thC. Via French from Latin *antiquus* "old" (source of English *antic*).] —**an·tique·ly** *adv.* —**an·tique·ness** *n.*

an·tiq·ui·ty /an tíkwətee/ (*plural* **-ties**) *n.* **1. ANCIENT HISTORY** ancient history, especially the period of time during which the ancient Greek or Roman civilizations flourished **2. OLDNESS** the state of being very old or ancient ○ *a sculpture of great antiquity* **3. OLD OBJECT** an object, especially something collectible, decorative, valuable, or interesting, that dates from a previous era **4. PEOPLE OF ANCIENT TIME** the people of ancient civilizations, especially those of ancient Greece or Rome

an·ti·ra·cism /àntī ráy sìzzəm, àntee-/ *n.* policies, views, or actions that oppose racial prejudice and discrimination and promote racial equality —**an·ti·ra·cist** *adj.*, *n.*

an·ti·re·jec·tion /àntī rə jékshən, àntee-/ *adj.* designed to prevent the immune system from rejecting a newly grafted organ or tissue

an·ti·roll bar *n.* a cross-mounted metal bar incorporated in the suspension system of a motor vehicle, designed to prevent the vehicle from swinging dangerously or overturning

an·ti·sat·el·lite /àntī sátt'l ìt, àntee-/ *adj.* designed to destroy or incapacitate satellites

an·ti-Se·mit·ic *adj.* hating or discriminating against Jewish people

an·ti-Sem·i·tism *n.* policies, views, or actions that harm or discriminate against Jewish people —**an·ti-Sem·ite** /àntī sé mìt, ànti-/ *n.* —**an·ti-Se·mit·ic** /àntī sə míttik, ànti-/ *adj.*

an·ti·sense /àntī séns, àntee-/ *adj.* relating to or having a strand of DNA complementary to other genetic material and used in genetic engineering to regulate the expression of a trait

an·ti·sep·sis /ànti sépsiss/ *n.* **1. ELIMINATION OF MICROORGANISMS** eliminating or reducing the spread of microorganisms causing disease or decay, especially with chemicals **2. ABSENCE OF MICROORGANISMS** the condition of being free from microorganisms

an·ti·sep·tic /ànti séptik/ *adj.* **1. CONTROLLING INFECTION** reducing or preventing infection, especially by the elimination or reduction of the growth of microorganisms **2. DULL** unexciting and unimaginative ■ *n.* **AGENT FOR CONTROLLING INFECTION** an agent that prevents or reduces infection, especially by eliminating or reducing the growth of microorganisms —**an·ti·sep·ti·cal·ly** *adv.*

an·ti·se·rum /ànti seerəm/ (*plural* **-rums** *or* **-ra** /-sìrrə/) *n.* an animal or human blood serum containing one or more specific ready-made antibodies and used to provide immunity against a disease or to counteract venom

an·ti·sex·ist /àntī séksist, àntee-/ *adj.* opposed to discrimination on the basis of sex, particularly discrimination against women —**an·ti·sex·ism** *n.*

an·ti·slav·er·y /àntī sláyvəree, àntee-/ *adj.* in favor of abolishing the slave trade or preventing people from keeping slaves

an·ti·smog /àntī smóg, àntee-/ *adj.* designed to stop or reduce smog

an·ti·smok·ing /àntī smṓking, àntee-/ *adj.* established or designed to stop people from smoking, especially in public places

an·ti·so·cial /àntī sṓsh'l, àntee-/ *adj.* **1. NOT CARING ABOUT OTHERS** annoying, inconsiderate, or indifferent to the comfort or needs of neighbors, or to society as a whole **2. NOT SOCIABLE** preferring not to spend time with other people —**an·ti·so·cial·i·ty** /àntī sṓshee állətee, àntee-/ *n.* —**an·ti·so·cial·ly** /àntī sṓsh'lee, àntee-/ *adv.*

an·ti·spas·mod·ic /àntī spaz móddik, àntee-/ *adj.* **CONTROLLING SPASMS** preventing or reducing the number and frequency of spasms ■ *n.* **DRUG FOR CONTROLLING SPASMS** a drug or other agent or means that prevents or relieves muscle spasms

an·ti·stat·ic /àntī státtik, àntee-/, **an·ti·stat** /ánti stàt/ *adj.* preventing or controlling the effects of static electricity

An·tis·the·nes /an tísthə neez/ (444?–365? B.C.) Greek philosopher. He believed that happiness depends on moral virtue and founded the Cynic school of philosophy.

an·tis·tro·phe /an tístrəfee/ *n.* **1. MOVEMENT IN ANCIENT GREEK DRAMA** the second of two movements made by the chorus in a classical Greek drama, or the section of an ode sung during this movement. The chorus moves back in the opposite direction after the first movement (**strophe**). **2. SECOND METRICAL FORM IN POEM** the second type of metrical form in a poem that alternates two contrasting metrical forms [Mid-16thC. Via late Latin from Greek *antistrophē*, from *anti-strephein*, literally "to turn back," from *strophē* (see STROPHE).] —**an·ti·stroph·ic** /ánti stróffik/ *adj.* —**an·ti·stroph·i·cal·ly** *adv.*

an·ti·sub·ma·rine /àntī súbmə reen, àntee-/ *adj.* designed to destroy or incapacitate submarines

an·ti·sway bar *n.* = **anti-roll bar**

an·ti·tank /àntī tángk, àntee-/ *adj.* designed to destroy or incapacitate military tanks

an·tith·e·sis /an títhəssiss/ (*plural* **-ses** /-seez/) *n.* **1. DIRECT OPPOSITE** the complete or exact opposite of something **2. FIGURE OF SPEECH** a use of words or phrases that contrast with each other to create a balanced effect **3.** PHILOS **CONTRASTING PROPOSITION** a proposition that is the opposite of another already proposed [Early 16thC. Via late Latin from, ultimately, Greek *antitithenai*, literally "to set against," from *tithenai* "to set" (see THESIS).]

an·ti·thet·i·cal /ànti théttik'l/, **an·ti·thet·ic** /ànti théttik/ *adj.* **1. DIAMETRICALLY OPPOSED** expressing or constituting the complete or exact opposite (*formal*) ○ *policies that are antithetical to the prevailing mood of the country* **2.** PHILOSOPHY **CONTRASTING WITH EARLIER PROPOSITION** amounting or relating to a proposition that is the opposite of another already proposed [Late 16thC. Formed from Greek *antithetikos*, from *antitithenai* (see ANTITHESIS).] —**an·ti·thet·i·cal·ly** *adv.*

an·ti·tox·ic /ànti tóksik/ *adj.* acting to counteract toxins

an·ti·tox·in /ànti tóksin/ *n.* **1. ANTIBODY OPPOSING TOXIN** an antibody produced in response to a particular toxin **2.** = **antiserum**

an·ti·trade /ánti tràyd/ *n.* a wind in the planetary wind system that is above the trade winds and blows in the opposite direction from them

an·ti·tra·gus /an títtrəgəss, ànti tráygəss/ (*plural* **-gi** /an títtrə jī, -gī, ànti tráy jī, -gī/) *n.* a bump of cartilage just below the opening of the external ear

an·ti·trust /àntī trúst, àntee-/ *adj.* intended to oppose trusts and cartels, e.g., from using monopolistic business practices to make unfair profits

an·ti·tus·sive /àntī tússiv, àntee-/ *adj.* **CONTROLLING COUGHING** preventing or alleviating coughing ■ *n.* **MEDICINE FOR CONTROLLING COUGHING** a drug that prevents or alleviates coughing

an·ti·type /ánti tīp/ *n.* **1. LATER OF ASSOCIATED BIBLICAL PAIR** somebody or something seen as being foreshadowed by or having striking similarities to an earlier person or thing (**type**) in the Bible **2. OPPOSITE TYPE** an opposite or contrasting type [Early 17thC. Via late Latin from Greek *antitupos*, literally "corresponding as an impression (to the die in which it was cast)," from *tupos* (see TYPE).] —**an·ti·typ·i·cal** /ànti típpik'l/ *adj.*

an·ti·u·to·pi·a *n.* a place, society, or state that is the opposite of perfect in every way (*literary*) —**an·ti·u·to·pi·an** *adj.*

an·ti·ven·in /àntī vénnin, àntee-/, **an·ti·ven·om** /àntī vénnəm, àntee-/ *n.* **1. ANTIBODY TO VENOM** an antitoxin to the venom of a particular animal or insect **2. SERUM COUNTERACTING VENOM** an antiserum containing antibodies to venom [Early 20thC. Coined from ANTI- + VENOM + -IN.]

an·ti·vi·ral /àntī vīrəl, àntee-/ *adj.* **FOR USE AGAINST VIRUSES** capable of eliminating or inactivating viruses ■ *n.* **AGENT USED AGAINST VIRUSES** a drug or other agent used to eliminate or inactivate a virus

an·ti·vi·rus /àntī vīrəss, àntee-/ *adj.* **1.** MED = **antiviral** *n.* **2.** COMPUT **FOR REMOVING COMPUTER VIRUSES** used to describe a utility program that identifies and removes viruses in a computer's memory or on disks before damage occurs to the computer system

an·ti·vi·ta·min /àntī vītəmin, àntee-/ *n.* a substance that inhibits the effects of a vitamin

an·ti·war /àntī wáwr, àntee-/ *adj.* wanting to prevent a war or bring a war to an end

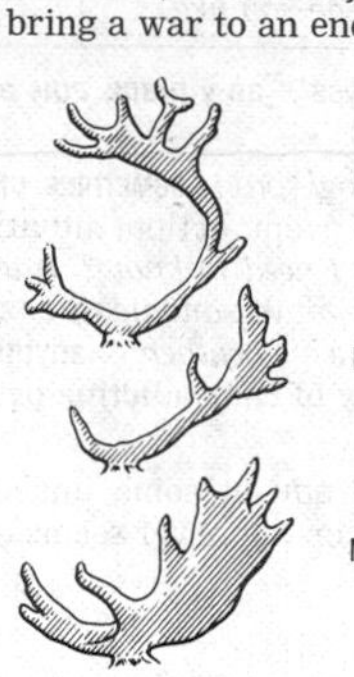

Antler

ant·ler /ántlər/ *n.* a solid bony branched horn found in pairs on the head of animals, especially males, of the deer family, including caribou and elk. Antlers are shed each year. [14thC. From an Anglo-Norman variant of Old French *antoillier*, of uncertain origin: possibly from assumed Vulgar Latin *anteocularе*, literally "in front of the eye" from Latin *oculus* (see OCULAR).] —**ant·lered** *adj.*

ant li·on *n.* a nocturnal insect that resembles the damselfly when adult. The larvae lie buried under sand at the bottom of a cone-shaped pit and trap insects such as ants. Family: Myrmeleontidae. [Translation of Greek *murmēko-leōn*; from its usual prey and its fierce-looking jaws]

An·to·fa·gas·ta /àan tō fə gáastə/ city in northern Chile on the fringes of the Atacama Desert. It is an important center for mining copper and nitrates. Population: 225,316 (1992).

An·to·nel·lo da Mes·si·na /àntə néllō daa mə seé naa/ (1430?–79) Italian painter who was influenced by Flemish realism.

An·to·ni·nus Pi·us /àntə nīnəss pī əss/ (86–161) Roman emperor. He succeeded Hadrian and conducted a peaceful and prosperous reign (138–161). Full name **Titus Aurelius Fulvius Boionius Arrius Antoninus**

an·to·no·ma·sia /àntənə máyzhə/ *n.* **1. USING TITLE INSTEAD OF NAME** the use of a title or formal description such as "Your Highness" or "His Excellency" in place of somebody's proper name **2. USING PROPER NAME FOR GENERAL IDEA** the use of a proper name as a common noun to refer to somebody or something with associated characteristics, e.g., in calling a handsome young man "an adonis" [Mid-16thC. Via Latin from, ultimately, Greek *antonomazein* "to name instead," from *anti-* "against, instead" + *onoma* "name" (see ONOMASTIC).]

An·to·ny /ántənee/, **Mark** (83?–30 B.C.) Roman politician and genera.l He fought in Rome's last civil war allied with Cleopatra and was defeated by Octavian.

an·to·nym /ántə nìm/ *n.* a word that means the opposite of another word. For example, "hot" is the antonym of "cold." [Mid-19thC. From French *antonyme*, from Greek *anti-* "against, opposite" + *onuma* "name."] —**an·to·nym·ic** /àntə nímmik/ *adj.* —**an·ton·y·mous** /an tónnəməss/ *adj.* —**an·ton·y·my** /-mee/ *n.*

an·tra /ántrə/ plural of **antrum**

an·tre /ántər/ *n.* a cavern or cave (*literary*) [Early 17thC. Via French from Latin *antrum* (see ANTRUM).]

an·trum /ántrəm/ (*plural* **-tra** /ántrə/) *n.* a cavity within a bone, especially a sinus cavity [Early 19thC. Via Latin, "cave," from Greek *antron*.]

ant·sy /ántsee/ (**-si·er, -si·est**) *adj.* (*informal*) **1. NERVOUS** tensely nervous or apprehensive **2. FIDGETY** moving or squirming around in a restless, bored, or impatient way [Mid-20thC. Origin uncertain: probably from the expression *to have ants in your pants*.]

Ant·werp /ántwərp/ leading port of Belgium, situated on the Schelde river estuary 55 mi./88 km from the sea. Population: 455,852 (1996).

a·ñu /aá noo, -nyoo, á noo, -nyoo/, **an·yu** /aá nyoo, á-/ *n.* **1.** S AMERICAN **PLANT** a twining plant of the nasturtium family, found in the Andes, with edible tubers and large yellow flowers with red spurs. Latin name: *Tropaeolum tuberosum*. **2. EDIBLE TUBERS OF AÑU** the edible tubers of the añu plant, eaten in Peru, Bolivia, and Chile [Via American Spanish *añú* from Quechua *áñu*]

A·nu·bis /ə nóobiss/ *n.* in Egyptian mythology, a god represented with the head of a jackal, who leads the dead to judgment

a·nu·ran /ə nóorən/ *n.* an amphibian such as a frog or toad that does not have a tail as an adult and has long powerful hind legs. Order: Anura. [Late 19thC. Formed from modern Latin *Anura*, order name, from Greek *an-* "without" + *oura* "tail."]

an·u·re·sis /ànnyə reéssiss/ *n.* inability to pass urine (*archaic*) [Late 19thC. Coined from AN- + Greek *ourēsis* "urination," from *ourein* "to urinate" (see URETER).] —**an·u·ret·ic** /ànnyə réttik/ *adj.*

a·nu·ri·a /a nyóoree ə, ə-, a nóoree ə, ə-/ *n.* inability of the kidneys to form urine, leading to a buildup of toxic waste in the blood —**a·nu·ric** *adj.*

a·nu·rous /ə nóorəss/ *adj.* without a tail

a·nus /áynəss/ *n.* ANAT, ZOOL the opening at the lower end of the alimentary canal through which feces are released [15thC. From Latin, literally "ring."]

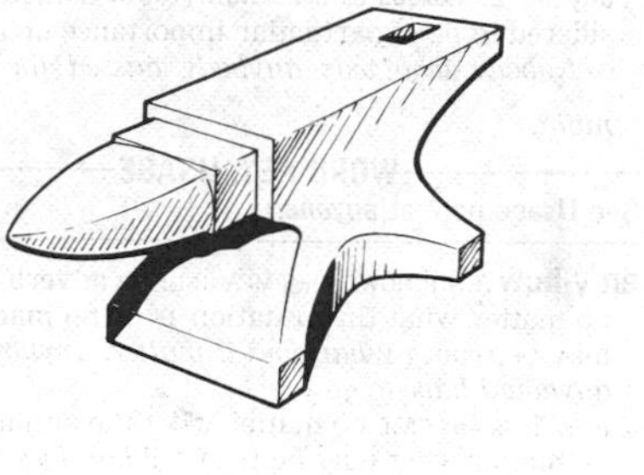

Anvil

an·vil /ánvil/ *n.* **1. METALWORKER'S HAMMERING BLOCK** a sturdy piece of iron onto which heated metal is placed to be beaten into the required shape, especially by a blacksmith **2.** ANAT = **incus** [Old English *anfilte, anfealt*. Ultimately from an Indo-European word meaning "to beat," which is also the ancestor of English *pelt* and *felt*.]

an·vil tech·nique *n.* a prehistoric method of making chipped stone tools that involves striking a stone repeatedly against a static boulder used as an anvil

anx·i·e·ty /ang zī ətee/ (*plural* **-ties**) *n.* **1. FEELING OF WORRY** nervousness or agitation, often about something that is going to happen **2. SOMETHING THAT WORRIES SOMEBODY** a subject or concern that causes worry **3. STRONG WISH TO DO SOMETHING** the strong wish to do a particular thing, especially if the wish is unnecessarily or unhealthily strong **4.** PSYCHIAT **EXTREME APPREHENSION** a state of abnormal and intense apprehension or fear of real or imagined danger, manifested physiologically as increased heart rate, sweating, trembling, weakness, and stomach or intestinal discomfort [Early 16thC. Via French *anxiété* from, ultimately, Latin *anxius* (see ANXIOUS).]

WORD KEY: SYNONYMS

See Synonyms at ***worry***.

anx·i·e·ty dis·or·der *n.* a psychiatric disorder causing feelings of persistent anxiety, e.g., panic disorder or post-traumatic stress disorder

anx·i·e·ty neu·ro·sis (*plural* **anx·i·e·ty neu·ro·ses**) *n.* a persistent panic disorder characterized by emotional distress, constant worry, a strong tendency to avoid specific situations, and overaction of the sympathetic nervous system

anx·i·o·lyt·ic /àngzee ə líttik/ *adj.* **RELIEVING ANXIETY** with the effect of relieving anxiety ■ *n.* **DRUG FOR RELIEVING ANXIETY** a drug that relieves anxiety [Mid-20thC. Coined from ANXIETY + -LYTIC.]

anx·ious /ángkshəss, ángshəss/ *adj.* **1. FEELING NERVOUS** worried or afraid, especially about something that is going to happen or might happen **2. EAGER** wanting very much, or in a desperate or nervous way, to do or receive something **3. PRODUCING ANXIETY** producing feelings of fear, uncertainty, or nervousness [Early

17thC. From Latin *anxius*, from *anx-*, the past participle stem of *angere* "to torment," literally "to strangle."] — **anx·ious·ly** *adv.* —**anx·ious·ness** *n.*

an·y /énnee/ CORE MEANING: a grammatical word used to indicate one, some, or several, when the quality, type, or number is not important ○ (adj) *Do you have any German beer?* ○ (pron) *for any who wish to enter*
1. *adj., pron.* **EVEN ONE OR A LITTLE** even one or even the least amount (*used in negative statements*) ○ *I don't want any dessert.* ○ *I didn't see any.* ○ *This isn't any of your business.* **2.** *adj., pron.* **EVERY** every person or thing stated, no matter who or what ○ *Any financial advisor would agree.* **3.** *adj.* **WITHOUT LIMIT** an unlimited or indefinite amount or number of ○ *any number of foods including soups, stews, and salads* **4.** *adv.* **AT ALL** to even the smallest extent or degree ○ *Is it getting any louder?* ○ *I still don't like him any.* [Old English *ǣnig*. Ultimately from an Indo-European word meaning "one of a kind," which is also the ancestor of English *unique* and *inch*.]

WORD KEY: USAGE

Singular or plural? ***Any*** used as a pronoun is followed by a singular or plural verb depending on the sense: *Any of these suggestions is acceptable. Are any of the children coming?* (*Is any of the children coming?* implies that one is expected, with uncertainty as to which).

an·y·bod·y /énni bòddee, énni bùddee/ *pron.* **1.** = **anyone 2. FAMOUS OR IMPORTANT PERSON** somebody considered to be of particular importance or influence ○ *Nobody who was anybody missed the opening night.*

WORD KEY: USAGE

See Usage note at ***anyone.***

an·y·how /énni hòw/ CORE MEANING: an adverb meaning no matter what the situation is or no matter what may be true ○ *What does it matter, anyhow?* ○ *and anyhow I have to go*
adv. **1. IN ANY CASE** no matter what the situation is or no matter what may be true ○ *What does it matter, anyhow?* **2. IN A CARELESS WAY** in a haphazard, careless, or untidy way ○ *ideas produced anyhow* **3. IN ANY MANNER** in any manner or by any means whatever ○ *Just do it anyhow.* **4. NEVERTHELESS** in spite of something ○ *I asked him to wait, but he left anyhow.*

an·y·more /ènni máwr/, **an·y more, an·y long·er** *adv.* **1. STILL** at present and continuing from a point in the past (*used in negative statements or questions*) ○ *They sure don't make them like this anymore!* **2. FROM NOW ON** from the present and ongoing (*used in negative statements or questions*) ○ *I'm not tolerating this anymore.* **3. NOWADAYS** these days (*regional nonstandard informal*) (*used in positive sentences*) ○ *We always use a taxi anymore.*

WORD KEY: USAGE

anymore or ***any more***? The adverbs ***any more*** (written as two words) and ***anymore*** (written as one word) are equally standard in American English and some other varieties (for example, South African English) Both forms are used after a negative or a question: *She doesn't live here anymore. Do you eat out any more?* In dialectal usage ***anymore*** is often used positively, usually in the sense of "currently": *All that kids do anymore is watch TV.*

WORD KEY: REGIONAL NOTE

Used in the positive sense, "nowadays," as in *asparagus is expensive anymore*, ***anymore*** recurs over much of the United States. It is strongest in the South Midland states of Kentucky and Indiana, but is also fairly common in the Upper and Lower Midwest, from Minnesota to Oklahoma, and in the Blue Ridge region of Virginia.

an·y·one /énni wùn/ CORE MEANING: an indefinite pronoun used to mean one or more people, when exactly which person or which people is not known or not important ○ *Can I get anyone more coffee?* ○ *Did anyone show up?* ○ *There isn't anyone home.*
pron. **1. EVERY PERSON** any or every particular person who could be named or thought of ○ *more qualified than anyone in the business* **2. EVEN ONE PERSON** used to emphasize the unlikelihood of finding even one person to match the stated description or criteria ○ *Why would anyone want to hurt me?* **3. UNIMPORTANT PERSON** an unimportant and unknown person ○ *It's not just anyone, it's your sister!*

WORD KEY: USAGE

anyone or **any one**? ***Anyone*** is somewhat more common than ***anybody*** (which has the same meaning), and is used only of a person: *Has anyone seen my pen?* The words ***any*** and ***one*** are written separately when they are meant to retain their distinct meanings, and in this case ***any one*** can be used of a person or thing: *Any one of them could have started the fire. The tables are all free, so you can sit at any one you like.*

an·y·place /énni plàyss/, **an·y place** *adv.* at, in, or to any place (*informal*)

an·y·thing /énni thìng/ *pron.* **SOMETHING UNSPECIFIED OR UNKNOWN** any object, event, action, situation, or fact ○ *Is there anything I need to know?* ■ *adv.* **AT ALL** in any way (*used in negative statements or questions*) ○ *He isn't anything like his brother.* ◇ **anything but** used as an emphatic way of contradicting or negating a statement

an·y·time /énni tìm/ *adv.* at some undecided time, whenever you like, or whenever seems appropriate (*informal*)

an·yu *n.* = **añu**

an·y·way /énni wày/ CORE MEANING: an adverb meaning no matter what the situation is ○ *Anyway, we have to pay whether it was accidental or not.* ○ *Recycling, according to some anyway, is like a new religion.*
adv. **1. IN ANY CASE** no matter what **2. REGARDLESS OF SOMETHING** in spite of the situation already stated ○ *I knew it would be a sad movie but I went anyway.* **3. IN A CARELESS WAY** in a careless, haphazard, or lazy way ○ *According to my mother, packing is a skilled operation, not throwing your clothes into a case just anyway.* **4. an·y·way, an·y way BY ANY MEANS** in any manner or way (*informal*) ○ *We have to teach our children moral values anyway we can.*

an·y·ways /énni wàyz/ *adv.* anyway (*regional*)

an·y·wear /énni wair/ *n.* clothing that can be worn for both casual and more formal occasions (*informal*)

an·y·where /énni hwàir/ CORE MEANING: an indefinite pronoun and adverb referring to one or many places unknown or unspecified ○ (pron-indef) *Is there anywhere you prefer?* ○ (pron-indef) *Anywhere we live now will seem warm.* ○ (adv) *She can sleep anywhere.*
1. *pron.* **SOME UNIDENTIFIED PLACE** one or many places unknown or unspecified **2.** *adv.* **TO ANY PLACE** to one or many places unknown or unspecified ○ *I'll follow you anywhere!* **3.** *adv.* **AT OR IN ANY PLACE** at or in any place there is, or any place with the stated description ○ *We couldn't find her anywhere.* ○ *will live anywhere with a beach* ◇ **anywhere from... to** used to state an approximate measurement of something by stating the smallest and largest possible measurements ○ *weighing anywhere from six to ten pounds*

any·wheres /énni hwàirz/ *adv.* a regional alternative for anywhere (*regional nonstandard*)

an·y·wise /énni wìz/ *adv.* in any way or in any case (*regional*) (*usually used in negative statements*) ○ *With or without them, I wouldn't go anywise.*

An·zac /án zàk/ *n.* **1.** *ANZ* **WORLD WAR I SOLDIER** a soldier who served in the Australian and New Zealand Army Corps in World War I **2.** *Aus* **AUSTRALIAN SOLDIER** an Australian soldier

An·zi·o /ánzi ō/ port and resort on the western coast of Italy 37 mi./60 km south of Rome. Heavy fighting occurred there during World War II when Allied forces secured a beachhead in January 1944. Population: 32,383 (1991).

a/o, A/O, a.o. *abbr.* account of

ao dai /òw dī, aw-/ *n.* a long tunic worn over pants by Vietnamese women. It has a high neck and is slit at both sides below the waist. [Mid-20thC. From Vietnamese *ào dài* "long blouse."]

A-OK /ày ō káy/, **A-o·kay** *adj.* in excellent condition or working order (*informal*) [Mid-20thC. From *all (systems) OK*.]

AOR *abbr.* adult-oriented rock

a·o·rist /áyərist/ *n.* a verb tense used to express a past action in an unqualified way, without specifying whether that action was repeated, continuing, or completed or how long it lasted, found especially in classical Greek [Late 16thC. From Greek *aoristos* "indefinite," from *a-* "not" + *horistos* "delimited," from *horizein* "to delimit" (see HORIZON).] —**a·o·ris·tic** /ày ə rístik/ *adj.* —**a·o·ris·ti·cal·ly** *adv.*

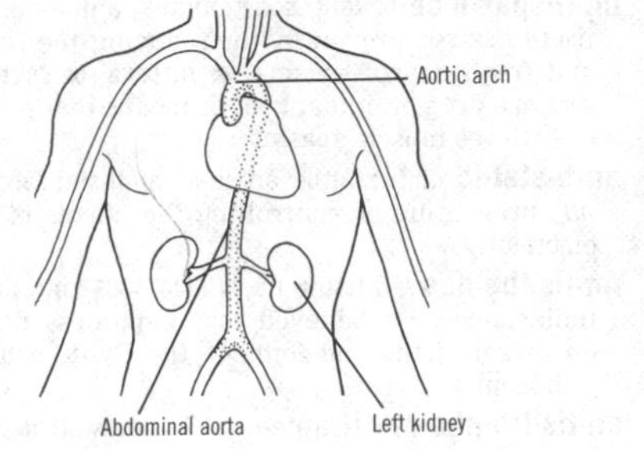

Aorta

a·or·ta /ay áwrtə/ (*plural* **-tas** *or* **-tae** /-tee/) *n.* the main artery in mammals that carries blood from the left ventricle of the heart to all the branch arteries in the body except those in the lungs [Mid-16thC. Via modern Latin from Greek *aortē*, from *aeirein* "to raise"; perhaps from the notion that the heart was held up by the aorta.] —**a·or·tal** *adj.* —**a·or·tic** *adj.*

a·or·tic arch *n.* **1. CURVED SECTION OF MAIN ARTERY** the section of the largest artery (**aorta**) in the body that forms the curve between the ascending and descending parts. As it leaves the heart, the aorta goes upward and then bends back on itself to form the arch. **2. SET OF PAIRED ARTERIES** a set of paired curved arteries, one of several in the vertebrate embryo that begin in the aorta, rise through the pharynx, and join with the dorsal arterial system

a·or·tic valve *n.* the valve in the largest artery (**aorta**) in the body at the point where it leaves the heart. It allows the blood to flow out but not back into the heart.

a·or·tog·ra·phy /ày awr tóggrəfee/ *n.* the X-ray examination of the largest artery (**aorta**) in the body after a substance that will be shown up by the X-rays has been injected into the bloodstream — **a·or·to·graph·ic** /ày awrtə gráffik/ *adj.*

a·ou·dad /ów dàd, aa ŏŏ-/ *n.* a wild North African sheep that has long curved horns and a long fringe of hair on the neck and forelegs. Latin name: *Ammotragus lervia.* [Early 19thC. Via French from Berber *udād*.]

AP *abbr.* **1.** advanced placement **2.** Air Police **3.** American plan **4.** MIL antipersonnel **5.** PUBL Associated Press

ap. *abbr.* apothecary

a.p. *abbr.* **1.** FIN additional premium **2.** PHARM before a meal (*used in prescriptions*) **3.** PUBL author's proof

ap-[1] *prefix.* = **ad-** (*used before p*)

ap-[2] *prefix.* = **apo-** (*used before vowels and h*)

a·pace /ə páyss/ *adv.* **1. QUICKLY** at a good or fast pace **2. ABREAST** at a sufficient rate to keep up with or be alongside somebody or something [14thC. From Old French *a pas*, literally "on step."]

A·pach·e /ə páchee/ (*plural* **-e** *or* **-es**) *n.* **1.** PEOPLES **MEMBER OF NOMADIC NATIVE AMERICAN PEOPLE** a member of one of six nomadic Native American peoples who used to live in the southwestern United States and northern Mexico. A number of Apache peoples live in Arizona, Oklahoma, and New Mexico. **2.** LANG **ATHABASKAN LANGUAGE** a Native American language spoken in parts of New Mexico, Oklahoma, and Arizona, belonging to the Athabaskan group. Apache is spoken by about 50,000 people. [Mid-18thC. From American Spanish, of uncertain origin: perhaps ultimately from Zuñi *Ápachu*, literally "enemy."] —**A·pach·e** *adj.*

A·pach·e·an /ə páchee ən/ *adj.* **1.** PEOPLES **OF APACHE PEOPLE** relating to or typical of the Apache people or their culture **2.** LANG **OF APACHE AND RELATED LANGUAGES** relating to a subgroup of Athabaskan languages that includes Apache and Navajo

Ap·a·lach·i·co·la /àppə làchi kṓlə/ river in western Florida, formed at the Georgia border by the confluence of the Chattahoochee and Flint rivers. It flows southward into the Gulf of Mexico at Apalachicola Bay. Length: 90mi./145 km.

Ap·a·lach·i·co·la Na·tion·al For·est national forest in the panhandle of western Florida that includes Bradwell Bay Wilderness. Area: 564,000 acres/228,250 ha.

ap·a·nage *n.* = **appanage**

ap·a·re·jo /àppə ráy hō, -ō/ (*plural* **-jos**) *n.* *Southwest U.S.* a padded leather saddle used for carrying goods on a horse or mule [Mid-19thC. Via American Spanish, literally "equipment," from, ultimately, Latin *apparare* "to prepare" (see APPARATUS).]

a·part /ə paárt/ CORE MEANING: a grammatical word meaning separated in space or time ○ (adv) *scheduled appointments a month apart* ○ (adv) *living apart* ○ (adj) *hard to be apart* ○ (adj) *sitting with legs apart*

1. *adv.* NOT TOGETHER separated in space or time ○ *She placed the chairs some distance apart.* **2.** *adv.* INTO PIECES into separate parts or sections ○ *take the machine apart* **3.** *adv.* MOVING AWAY AFTER BEING TOGETHER away from somebody or something after previously being together ○ *We've drifted apart over the years.* **4.** *adv.* REMOVED FROM CONSIDERATION set aside or excluded from consideration, or taken as an exception ○ *The orange flowered tie apart, it was a pretty cool outfit.* **5.** *adv.* INTO DIFFICULTY into a poor or difficult condition **6.** *adv.* OF A SEPARATE KIND different and consequently separate from others ○ *a world apart* **7.** *adj.* SEPARATED away from each other in position or location ○ *with legs apart* ○ *think of her all the time we're apart* [14thC. From Old French *a part,* literally "to the side."] ◇ **apart from 1.** with the exception of somebody or something **2.** in addition to something, or besides something

a·part·heid /ə paárt hīt, -hàyt/ *n.* a political system in South Africa from 1948 to the early 1990s that separated the different peoples living there and gave particular privileges to those of European origin [Mid-20thC. From Afrikaans, literally "separateness," from Dutch *apart* "separate," from French.]

a·par·ti·cle *n.* = **alpha particle**

a·part·ment /ə paártmənt/ *n.* **1.** HOME IN LARGER BUILDING a self-contained residence, situated with other similar units in a larger building **2. a·part·ment, a·part·ment build·ing, a·part·ment house** BUILDING OF RESIDENTIAL APARTMENTS a building, often large or high-rise, made up of a number of separate apartments **3.** ROOM a single room in a residential building (*formal*) ■ **a·part·ments** *npl.* *U.K.* SPECIAL ROOMS IN BIG BUILDING a suite of adjoining rooms used for a particular purpose, e.g., as an office, entertainment suite, or place to live (*formal*) [Mid-17thC. Via French *appartement* from, ultimately, Italian *a parte* "apart," literally "to the side"; the underlying sense is "separate place."]

ap·a·tet·ic /àppə téttik/ *adj.* used to describe protective camouflage coloring [Late 19thC. Via Greek *apatētikos* "deceptive" from, ultimately, *apatē* "deceit," of unknown origin.]

ap·a·thet·ic /àppə théttik/ *adj.* not taking any interest in anything, or not bothering to do anything [Mid-18thC. Formed from APATHY, on the model of *pathetic.*] — **ap·a·thet·i·cal·ly** *adv.*

WORD KEY: SYNONYMS

See Synonyms at ***impassive***.

ap·a·thy /áppəthee/ *n.* **1.** LACK OF ENTHUSIASM OR ENERGY lack of interest in anything, or the absence of any wish to do anything **2.** EMOTIONAL EMPTINESS inability to feel normal or passionate human feelings or to respond emotionally [Early 17thC. Via French *apathie* from, ultimately, Greek *apathēs,* literally "without feeling," from *pathos* "feeling" (see PATHOS).]

ap·a·tite /áppə tīt/ *n.* a glassy calcium-phosphate mineral, belonging to a group that ranges from colorless to purple, green, or brown in color, used in making fertilizers and as a source of phosphorus [Early 19thC. Formed from Greek *apatē* "deceit"; from its diversity of form and color.]

APB *abbr.* all-points bulletin

ape /ayp/ *n.* **1.** TAILLESS PRIMATE any tailless primate such as a chimpanzee, gorilla, or orangutan. Family: Pongidae. **2.** PRIMATE any primate (*informal*) **3.** = **monkey 4.** IMITATOR an imitator or mimic of somebody or something **5.** CLUMSY PERSON a clumsy or unintelligent person (*informal*) ■ *vt.* (**aped, ap·ing, apes**) IMITATE SOMEBODY OR SOMETHING to copy somebody or something in an absurd or mindless way [Old English *apa*] ◇ **go ape** to lose self-control, because of either anger or excitement (*slang*)

WORD KEY: SYNONYMS

See Synonyms at ***imitate***.

a·peak /ə peék/ *adj., adv.* NAUT in a vertical position or direction [Late 16thC. From French *à pic,* literally "at the peak."]

APEC /áy pek/ *abbr.* Asia-Pacific Economic Co-operation

ape-man /áyp màn/ (*plural* **ape-men** /-mén/) *n.* **1.** EXTINCT PRIMATE a nontechnical name for any of various extinct primates believed to be ancestors of modern humans. ◊ **hominid 2.** ROUGH, COARSE, UNSOPHISTICATED MAN a rough or coarse man, or one with primitive or unsophisticated instincts (*informal disapproving*)

Ap·en·nines /áppə nīnz/ mountain range that forms the backbone of peninsular Italy. It extends about 800 mi./1,290 km from the area north of Genoa to the toe of Italy. The highest peak is Monte Corno 9,554 ft./2,912 m.

a·per·çu /àapər soó, -syoó/ *n.* (*formal*) **1.** INSIGHT a revealing glimpse or insight **2.** SUMMARY a concise outline or summary [Early 19thC. From French, literally "something perceived."]

a·pe·ri·ent /ə peéree ənt/ *adj.* WITH A LAXATIVE EFFECT mildly stimulating the opening and emptying of the bowels ■ *n.* LAXATIVE SUBSTANCE a mild laxative [Early 17thC. From Latin *aperient-,* the present participle stem of *aperire* (see APERTURE).]

a·pe·ri·od·ic /áy peeree áwdik/ *adj.* **1.** IRREGULAR happening at irregular intervals ○ *aperiodic floods* **2.** PHYS NOT EXHIBITING RESONANCE used to describe a mechanical or electrical system that does not exhibit resonance when a periodic disturbance is applied — **a·pe·ri·od·i·cal·ly** *adv.* —**a·pe·ri·o·dic·i·ty** /áy peeriə díssitee/ *n.*

a·pé·ri·tif /aà perə teéf, aa pèrrə teéf, ə pèrrə teéf/ *n.* an alcoholic beverage to be drunk before a meal [Late 19thC. Via French from, ultimately, Latin *apertus,* the past participle of *aperire* (see APERTURE).]

ap·er·ture /áppər choor/ *n.* **1.** NARROW OPENING a small narrow opening **2.** OPENING THROUGH LENS OR MIRROR a fixed or adjustable opening in a device, e.g., a camera or microscope, that lets light pass through a lens or mirror **3.** DIAMETER OF APERTURE the diameter of an aperture, e.g., in a camera [Mid-17thC. Formed from Latin *apert-,* the past participle stem of *aperire* "to open" (source of English *overt*).] —**ap·er·tur·al** *adj.*

WORD KEY: SYNONYMS

See Synonyms at ***opening***.

ap·er·ture card *n.* a card for mounting microfilmed pages

ap·er·ture pri·or·i·ty *n.* the system in a semi-automatic camera in which the user sets the lens aperture and the camera then selects the appropriate shutter speed automatically

ap·er·ture stop *n.* = **f-stop**

ape·shit *adj.* unreasonably angry or excited (*slang taboo*)

a·pex /áy peks/ (*plural* **a·pex·es** *or* **a·pi·ces** /áppə seez, áy-/) *n.* **1.** HIGHEST POINT the highest point of something **2.** HIGHEST POINT OF SOMEBODY'S CAREER the most successful part of something, especially somebody's career or life **3.** TIP OF SOMETHING the tip or top of something, especially something that is pointed, e.g., a triangle [Early 17thC. From Latin.]

Apex /áy pèks/, **APEX** *n.* a system whereby air tickets are available at a reduced price when bought a certain period of time in advance [Abbreviation of "advance-purchase excursion"]

Ap·gar score /áp gaar-/ *n.* a score that is given after assessing the condition of a newborn baby in the five areas of heart rate, breathing, skin color, muscle tone, and reflex response. Each area has a maximum of two points. [Named for the U.S. physician Virginia *Apgar* (1909–74), who developed it]

a·phaer·e·sis /ə férrəssəss/, **a·pher·e·sis** *n.* the loss of a syllable from the beginning of a word, e.g., in "coon" for "raccoon" [Mid-16thC. Via late Latin from Greek *aphairesis,* from *aphairein* "to take away," from *hairein* "to take" (source of English *heresy*).] —**aph·ae·ret·ic** /àffə réttik/ *adj.*

a·pha·gi·a /ə fáyjee ə, -jə/ *n.* the inability or refusal to swallow

a·pha·ki·a /ə fáykee ə/ *n.* a medical condition in which the internal crystalline lens of the eye is absent [Mid-19thC. Formed from Greek *phakos* "lentil," because of its shape.]

aph·a·nite /áffə nīt/ *n.* an igneous rock with mineral components that are too fine to be seen by the naked eye [Early 19thC. Formed from Greek *aphanēs* "unseen," from *phan-,* the stem of *phainesthai* "to appear" (see PHENOMENON).] —**aph·a·nit·ic** /àffə níttik/ *adj.*

a·pha·sia /ə fázhee ə, -zhə/ *n.* the partial or total loss of the normal ability to produce and understand speech as a result of brain damage caused by injury or disease [Mid-19thC. From Greek, from *aphatos* "speechless," from *phanai* "to speak."] —**a·pha·sic** /ə fáyzik/ *adj.*

a·phe·lan·dra /àffə lándrə/ *n.* an evergreen shrub, native to tropical America, that has shiny leaves and brightly colored flowers. It is often grown as a house plant. Genus: *Aphelandra.*

a·phe·li·on /ə feélyən/ (*plural* **-a** /-ə/) *n.* the point in the orbit of a planet, comet, or other celestial body that is farthest from the Sun [Mid-17thC. From modern Latin *aphelium,* from Greek *apo-* "away" + *hēlios* "sun" (see HELIO-).] —**a·phe·lian** *adj.*

a·pher·e·sis /ə férrəssəss/ *n.* **1.** MED RETRANSFUSION OF TREATED BLOOD the retransfusion of a donor's or patient's own blood from which certain constituents have been removed **2.** LING = **aphaeresis**

aph·e·sis /áffəssəss/ *n.* the loss of an unstressed vowel at the beginning of a word, e.g., in "round" for "around" [Late 19thC. From Greek, literally "letting go," from *aphienai,* literally "to send away," from *hienai* "to send" (see CATHETER).] —**a·phet·ic** /ə féttik/ *adj.* — **a·phet·i·cal·ly** *adv.*

a·phid /áy fid/ *n.* an insect that has specially adapted mouthparts for piercing and sucking the sap from plants. Many aphids transfer viruses from plant to plant as they feed. Family: Aphididae. [Late 19thC. From modern Latin *aphid-,* the stem of *Aphis,* genus name.] —**a·phid·i·an** /ə fíddee ən/ *adj.* —**a·phid·i·ous** *adj.*

a·phid li·on *n.* a larva of a green lacewing, or of other insects belonging to the same family, that feeds on aphids and other insects

a·pho·ni·a /ày fṓnee ə, ə-/ *n.* the loss of the voice as a result of injury or disease of the larynx or mouth or of various psychological conditions [Late 17thC. Formed from Greek *aphōnos,* literally "having no voice," from *phōnē* "voice" (see -PHONE).] —**a·phon·ic** /ày fáwnik/ *adj.*

aph·o·rism /áffərìz'm/ *n.* a succinct statement expressing an opinion or a general truth ○ *Jerome Kern's famous aphorism "Irving Berlin has no place in American music – he is American music"* [Early 16thC. Via French from, ultimately, Greek *aphorizein* "to define," from *horizein* "to delimit" (see HORIZON).] — **aph·o·rist** *n.* —**aph·o·ris·tic** /àffə rístik/ *adj.* —**aph·o·ris·ti·cal·ly** *adv.*

aph·o·rize /áffə rīz/ (**-rized, -riz·ing, -riz·es**) *vi.* to speak or write using aphorisms

a·pho·tic /ày fṓtik/ *adj.* used to describe those parts of the ocean that are not reached by sunlight, or plants that grow there without photosynthesizing

aph·ro·dis·i·ac /àffrə dízzee àk, -deéz-/ *n.* SOMETHING AROUSING PHYSICAL DESIRE something that arouses or intensifies physical desire ■ *adj.* ABLE TO INCREASE PHYSICAL DESIRE able to arouse or intensify physical desire [Early 18thC. From Greek *aphrodisiakos* "arousing sexual desire," from *aphrodisia* "sexual pleasures," from *Aphroditē* (see APHRODITE).] —**aph·ro·di·si·a·cal** /àffrədi zī́ ək'l/ *adj.*

Aph·ro·di·te /àffrə dī́tee/ *n.* in Greek mythology, the goddess of love and beauty. She was the daughter of Zeus. Roman equivalent **Venus**

A·pi·a /ə peéə, aápee ə/ capital of Western Samoa, on northern Upolu Island in the South Pacific Ocean, northeast of Nuku'alofa in Tonga. Population: 34,126 (1991).

a·pi·an /áypee ən/ *adj.* relating to or resembling bees [Early 19thC. From Latin *apianus,* from *apis* "bee," of unknown origin.]

a·pi·ar·i·an /àypee érree ən/ *adj.* related to bees or beekeeping

a·pi·a·rist /áypee ərəst/ *n.* somebody who keeps bees, often for commercial purposes

a·pi·ar·y /áypee èree/ (*plural* **-ies**) *n.* a place where beehives are kept and bees are raised for their honey [Mid-17thC. From Latin *apiarium* "beehive," from *apis* "bee," of unknown origin.]

ap·i·cal /áppək'l, áy-/ *adj.* **1. FORMING TOP** used to describe the top of something **2.** PHON **USING TOP OF TONGUE** used to classify a consonant that is pronounced with the tip of the tongue, e.g., "t" or "d" [Early 19thC. Formed from Latin *apic-*, the stem of *apex* "apex."] —**ap·i·cal·ly** *adv.*

ap·i·cal dom·i·nance *n.* the inhibition exerted on the growth of lateral buds by the terminal bud of a growing plant shoot

ap·i·cal mer·i·stem *n.* the zone of actively dividing tissue at the tip of a shoot or root that produces new tissue, mainly to increase length

a·pi·ces plural of **apex**

a·pic·u·late /ə píkyələt/ *adj.* used to describe a leaf that has a short broad tip [Early 19thC. Formed from modern Latin *apiculus*, literally "little apex," from *apex* "apex."]

a·pi·cul·ture /áypə kùlchər/ *n.* the keeping of bees, especially for commercial purposes [Mid-19thC. Coined from Latin *apis* "bee" + CULTURE.] —**a·pi·cul·tur·al** *adj.* —**a·pi·cul·tur·ist** *n.*

a·piece /ə peéss/ *adv.* to or for each one ○ *gold watches, from $150 to $550 apiece* [Mid-16thC. Formed from A + PIECE.]

ap·ish /áypish/ *adj.* **1. BOORISH** silly, ridiculous, or boorish **2. IMITATIVE** imitating somebody else or somebody's style —**ap·ish·ly** *adv.* —**ap·ish·ness** *n.*

a·pla·cen·tal /àyplə sént'l/ *adj.* used to describe mammals such as marsupials that do not develop a placenta

ap·la·nat·ic /àpplə náttik/ *adj.* used to describe a lens that does not have, or is corrected for, spherical aberration and so produces a clear undistorted image [Late 18thC. Formed from Greek *planasthai* "to wander" (source of English *planet*).]

a·pla·sia /ə pláyzh ə, -zhee ə/ *n.* the absence or defective development of an organ, part of an organ, or tissue

a·plas·tic /ay plástik/ *adj.* unable to develop new cells or tissue

a·plas·tic a·ne·mia *n.* severe anemia in which the capacity of bone marrow cells to generate red blood cells is diminished

a·plen·ty /ə pléntee/ *adj.* in large or excessive amounts ○ *There are apples aplenty for all of you.*

ap·lite /á plīt/ *n.* a light-colored, fine-grained igneous rock [Late 19thC. Via German *Aplit* from, ultimately, Greek *haplous* "single," because of its chemical composition (see HAPLOID).] —**ap·lit·ic** /a plíttik/ *adj.*

a·plomb /ə pláwm, ə plúm/ *n.* confidence, skill, and poise, especially in difficult or challenging circumstances [Early 19thC. From French *à plomb* "perpendicular," literally "according to the plumb line."]

ap·ne·a /áppnee ə/, **ap·noe·a** *n.* a temporary suspension or absence of breathing [Early 18thC. Via modern Latin from Greek *apnoia*, literally "not breathing," from *pnein* "to breathe."]

ap·neu·sis /ap nóossəss/ *n.* an abnormal form of breathing caused by brain damage, in which each full inhalation is held for a prolonged period —**ap·neus·tic** *adj.*

ap·noe·a *n.* = **apnea**

APO *abbr.* Army Post Office

apo-, **ap-** *prefix.* away from, detached ○ *apolune* ○ *apocarp* [From Greek *apo* "off, away." Ultimately from an Indo-European base that is also the ancestor of English *of*, *off*, *after*, and *aft*.]

Apoc. *abbr.* **1.** Apocalypse **2.** Apocrypha

a·poc·a·lypse /ə pa̋akə lips/ *n.* **1. TOTAL DESTRUCTION** the total destruction or devastation of something, or an instance of this **2. REVELATION OF FUTURE** a revelation made concerning the future [13thC. Via late Latin from Greek *apokalupsis* "revelation," from *apokaluptein* "to uncover," from *kaluptein* "to cover."]

WORD KEY: CULTURAL NOTE

Apocalypse Now, a movie by Francis Ford Coppola (1979). This surreal, hallucinatory account of the Vietnam War is based loosely on Joseph Conrad's *Heart of Darkness*. It follows an American captain on his mission to assassinate a rebel officer, played by Marlon Brando, conducting his own independent war in the heart of the jungle.

A·poc·a·lypse *n.* = **Revelation**

a·poc·a·lyp·tic /ə pa̋akə líptik/ *adj.* **1. PREDICTING DISASTER** warning about or predicting a disastrous future or outcome ○ *an apocalyptic scenario of global warming* **2.** BIBLE **RELATING TO THE APOCALYPSE** relating to the events in the Book of Revelation in the Bible **3. INVOLVING DESTRUCTION** involving widespread destruction and devastation —**a·poc·a·lyp·ti·cal·ly** *adv.*

a·poc·a·lyp·ti·cism /ə pa̋akə líptəsìz'm/ *n.* the belief that the end of the world is coming, with the resulting triumph of good over evil, as prophesied in the biblical Book of Revelation

a·poc·a·lyp·tist /ə pókə líptist/ *n.* a believer in the prophecies in the biblical Book of Revelation or in the eventual triumph of good over evil [Mid-19thC. Formed from Greek *apokaluptein* (see APOCALYPSE).]

ap·o·car·pous /àppə ka̋arpəss/ *adj.* used to describe a flower that has separate carpels [Mid-19thC. Coined from APO- + Greek *karpos* "fruit."] —**ap·o·car·py** /áppə kaarpee/ *n.*

ap·o·chro·mat /àppə krṓmət/ *n.* a lens that is corrected for chromatic aberration by incorporating different types of glass

ap·o·chro·mat·ic /àppəkrō máttik/ *adj.* used to describe a lens that has been corrected for chromatic aberration —**a·po·chro·ma·tism** /àppə krṓmə tìzzəm/ *n.*

a·poc·o·pe /ə páwkəpee/ *n.* the loss or omission of one or more syllables from the end of a word, e.g., the shortening of "kind of" to "kinda" [Mid-16thC. Via late Latin from Greek *apokopē*, literally "cutting off," from *koptein* "to cut" (see COMMA).] —**a·poc·o·pate** *vt.*

ap·o·crine /áppəkrin, áppə krīn, áppə kreen/ *adj.* used to describe glands that secrete part of their secreting cells with the secretory products [Early 20thC. Coined from APO- + Greek *krinein* "to separate" (see CRITIC).]

A·poc·ry·pha /ə páwkrəfə/ *n.* **1. BIBLICAL WRITINGS OF DISPUTED AUTHENTICITY** books of the Bible that are included in the Vulgate and Septuagint versions of the Christian Bible, but not in the Protestant Bible or the Hebrew canon (*may be singular or plural*) See table at **Bible 2. EARLY CHRISTIAN WRITINGS** a group of Christian writings dating from the early centuries A.D. that are not included in the New Testament [14thC. Via ecclesiastical Latin from, ultimately, Greek *apokruphos*, literally "hidden away," from *kruptein* "to hide" (see CRYPT).]

a·poc·ry·phal /ə páwkrəf'l/ *adj.* **1. NOT TRUE** probably not true, but widely believed to be true **2. OF THE APOCRYPHA** relating to the Apocrypha —**a·poc·ry·phal·ly** *adv.*

ap·o·dal /áppəd'l/, **ap·o·dous** /áppədəss/ *adj.* without limbs, feet, or pelvic fins. Eels and snakes are apodal organisms. [Mid-18thC. Formed from the Greek stem *apod-* "footless," from *pous* "foot" (see PODIUM).]

ap·o·dic·tic /àppə díktik/, **ap·o·deic·tic** /-dík-/ *adj.* demonstrably or indisputably true [Mid-17thC. Via Latin from, ultimately, Greek *apodeiknunai* "to demonstrate," from *deiknunai* "to show" (see DEICTIC).] —**ap·o·dic·ti·cal·ly** *adv.*

a·pod·o·sis /ə páwdəssəss/ (*plural* **-ses** /-seez/) *n.* the main clause explaining the consequence in a conditional statement, e.g., "we can watch the film" in "If you come early, we can watch the film." In logic the apodosis is the "q" component of propositions of the form "if p then q." [Early 17thC. Via late Latin from, ultimately, Greek *apodidonai*, literally "to give back" (see DOSE).]

ap·o·dous *adj.* = **apodal**

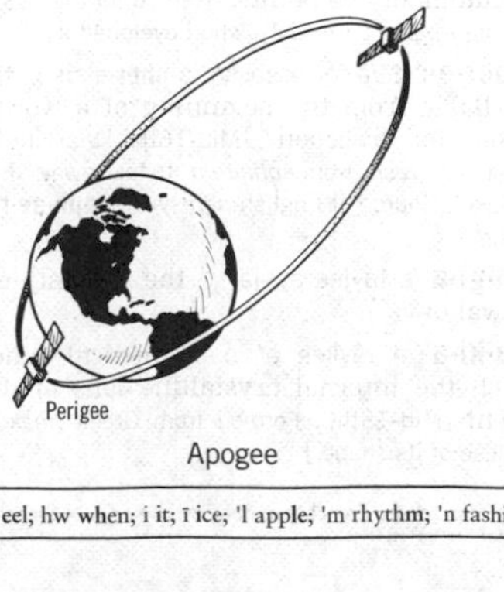

Apogee

ap·o·en·zyme /àppō én zìm/ *n.* the protein component of an enzyme that determines the enzyme's specific function but has no physiological effect until it becomes attached to another compound (**coenzyme**)

a·pog·a·my /ə páwgəmee/ *n.* the development of an embryo without prior fertilization. Apogamy occurs in some ferns, algae, and fungi. —**ap·o·gam·ic** /àppə gámmik/ *adj.*

ap·o·gee /áppə jee/ *n.* **1. CULMINATION** the best or greatest point **2.** ASTRON **POINT IN ORBIT FARTHEST FROM EARTH** the point when the Moon, or a satellite or other object orbiting around the Earth, is farthest from the center of the Earth [Late 16thC. Via French from, ultimately, Greek *apogaios* "away from the earth," from *gaia* "earth" (source of English *geo-*).] —**ap·o·ge·an** /àppə jée ən, áppə jee ən/ *adj.*

a·po·lit·i·cal /àypə líttək'l/ *adj.* having no interest in politics, or not concerned with politics —**a·po·lit·i·cal·ly** *adv.*

A·pol·lo /ə páwlō/ *n.* **1. GREEK GOD OF PROPHECY** in Greek mythology, the god of prophecy, sunlight, music, and healing, also worshiped by the Romans **2. A·pol·lo** (*plural* **-los**), **a·pol·lo** (*plural* **-los**) **HANDSOME MAN** a very handsome young man (*literary*) [Via Latin from Greek *Apollōn*]

Ap·ol·lo·ni·an /àppə lṓnee ən/ *adj.* **1. RELATING TO APOLLO** relating to Apollo or the worship of Apollo **2. ORDERLY** calm, ordered, and balanced [Early 17thC. Formed from Latin *Apollonius*, from *Apollo* "Apollo."]

a·pol·o·get·ic /ə pàwlə jéttik/ *adj.* **1. EXPRESSING APOLOGY** expressing apology or contrition for something **2. DEFENSIVE** defending something in speech or writing [Mid-17thC. Via French and Latin from, ultimately, Greek *apologeisthai* "to speak in your own defense," from *apologia* "defense" (see APOLOGY).] —**a·pol·o·get·i·cal·ly** *adv.*

a·pol·o·get·ics /ə pàwlə jéttiks/ *n.* a branch of theology that is concerned with proving the truth of Christianity (*takes a singular verb*)

ap·o·lo·gi·a /àppə lṓjee ə, ə pōlə jée ə/ *n.* a formal, usually written, defense or justification of a belief, theory, or policy (*formal*) [Late 18thC. From Latin (see APOLOGY).]

a·pol·o·gist /ə póllәjəst/ *n.* somebody who argues to defend or justify a particular doctrine or ideology

a·pol·o·gize /ə páwlə jīz/ (**-gized, -giz·ing, -giz·es**) *vi.* **1. EXPRESS REMORSE FOR SOMETHING** to say you are sorry for something that has upset or inconvenienced somebody else **2. ACKNOWLEDGE THAT SOMETHING IS NOT IDEAL** to acknowledge that something is not as it should be, especially when you feel embarrassed or guilty about it **3. DEFEND FORMALLY** to defend something formally in writing or speech [Late 16thC. From Greek *apologizesthai*, from *apologia* (see APOLOGY).] —**a·pol·o·giz·er** *n.*

ap·o·logue /áppə làwg/ *n.* a fable that is intended to teach a moral lesson, especially one that has animals as characters [Mid-16thC. Via French or late Latin from Greek *apologos* "story," from *logos* "speech" (see LOGOS).]

a·pol·o·gy /ə póllәjee/ (*plural* **-gies**) *n.* **1. STATEMENT EXPRESSING REMORSE** a written or spoken statement expressing remorse for something **2. INFERIOR EXAMPLE** an inferior or poor example of something (*humorous*) ○ *I can't work in this apology for an office!* **3. FORMAL JUSTIFICATION** a formal defense or justification of something [Mid-16thC. Via French *apologie* and Latin *apologia* from Greek "speech in defense," literally "speaking off," from *logos* "speech" (see LOGOS).]

a·po·lune /áppə lo͞on/ *n.* the point in the orbit of a spacecraft circling the Moon when it is farthest from the Moon's center [Mid-20thC. Coined from APO- + Latin *luna* "moon" (see LUNAR), on the model of English *apogee*.]

ap·o·mic·tic /àppə míktik/ *adj.* used to describe an organism that reproduces asexually —**ap·o·mict** /áppə mìkt/ *n.* —**ap·o·mic·tic·al·ly** /àppə míktək'lee/ *adv.*

ap·o·mix·is /àppə míksiss/ *n.* asexual reproduction in organisms that are also able to reproduce sexually, in which embryos are formed without fertilization or the creation of specialized reproductive cells [Early 20thC. Formed from Greek *mixis* "mingling" (see AMPHIMIXIS).]

ap·o·neu·ro·sis /àppō nə rṓssəss/ (*plural* **-ses** /-seez/) *n.* a broad sheet of fibrous tissue or expanded tendon that joins muscles together or connects muscle to bone [Late 17thC. Via modern Latin from, ultimately, Greek *aponeurousthai* "to become like a tendon," from *neuron* "sinew" (see NEURON).] —**ap·o·neu·rot·ic** /àppō nə ráwtik/ *adj.*

a·poph·a·sis /ə páwfəssəss/ *n.* the rhetorical device of alluding to something by denying that it will be mentioned, e.g., in "I will not bring up the question of age now that you are forty" [Mid-17thC. Via late Latin from Greek *apophasis* "to deny," literally "to speak off," from *phanai* "to speak" (see -PHASIA).]

ap·o·phthegm *n.* = **apothegm**

a·poph·y·ge /ə páwfəjee/ *n.* the outward curve at the top of an architectural column where it joins the capital, or at the bottom where it joins the base [Mid-16thC. From Greek *apophugē*, literally "fleeing away," from *pheugein* "to flee." The underlying idea is of the column escaping into its base.]

a·poph·yl·lite /àppə fíllīt, ə páwfə līt/ *n.* a crystalline mineral that is white, pale pink, or pale green and is composed of hydrated potassium, calcium silicate, and fluorine [Early 19thC. Coined from APO- + Greek *phullon* "leaf" (see PHYLLO-), because it peels when heated.]

a·poph·y·sis /ə póffəssiss/ (*plural* **-ses** /-seez/) *n.* **1.** BIOL **NATURAL SWELLING ON ANIMAL OR PLANT** a natural swelling or outgrowth on an animal or plant, e.g., a bony protuberance on a vertebra **2.** GEOL **OFFSHOOT FROM ROCK** a small offshoot or network of veins from a large igneous mass of rock such as granite [Late 16thC. Via modern Latin from, ultimately, Greek *apophuein*, literally "to grow out," from *phuein* "to grow" (see PHYSICS).] — **a·poph·y·sate** *adj.* —**a·poph·y·si·al** /ə pòffə sée əl/ *adj.*

ap·o·plec·tic /àppə pléktik/ *adj.* **1. FURIOUS** overcome with anger **2.** MED **EXHIBITING SYMPTOMS OF STROKE** having the symptoms of a stroke (*archaic*) [Early 17thC. Via French or late Latin from Greek *apoplēktikos*, from *apoplēxia* (see APOPLEXY).] —**ap·o·plec·ti·cal·ly** *adv.*

ap·o·plex·y /áppə plèksee/ *n.* **1. ANGRY FIT** a fit of anger **2.** MED **STROKE CAUSED BY BRAIN HEMORRHAGE** a cerebral stroke, usually caused by a hemorrhage in the brain (*archaic*) [14thC. Via French and Latin from Greek *apoplēxia*, from *apoplēssein*, literally "to strike completely," from *plēssein* "to strike" (see PLECTRUM).]

a·po·ri·a /ə páwree ə/ *n.* a confusion in establishing the truth of a proposition [Mid-16thC. Via late Latin from, ultimately, Greek *aporos*, literally "without passage," from *poros* "passage" (see PORE[1]).] —**a·po·ret·ic** /àppə réttik/ *adj.*

a·port /ə páwrt/ *adv., adj.* on or toward the port or left-hand side of a ship as you face forward

ap·o·se·mat·ic /àppə se máttik/ *adj.* used to describe natural colors and bright markings on an animal that warn predators that it is poisonous ○ *aposematic coloration*

ap·o·si·o·pe·sis /àppə sī ə péessiss/ (*plural* **-ses** /-seez/) *n.* a sudden break in speaking, giving the impression that the speaker does not want to or cannot continue, e.g., in the sentence "On Tuesday morning I came in just as I always do, and I saw— I can't go on" [Late 16thC. Via Latin from, ultimately, Greek *aposiopan* "to stop speaking," from *siopē* "silence."] —**ap·o·si·o·pet·ic** /àppə sī ə péttik/ *adj.*

ap·o·spor·y /àppə spàwree, ə páwsparee/ *n.* the process of asexual reproduction without the occurrence of cell division (**meiosis**) or spore formation, in certain ferns and mosses [Late 19thC. Coined from APO- + SPORE + -Y.]

a·pos·ta·sy /ə páwstəsee/ *n.* the renunciation of a religious or political belief or allegiance [14thC. Via French from, ultimately, Greek *apostasis*, literally "standing away," from *histanai* "to stand" (source of English *prostrate* and *system*).]

a·pos·tate /ə páw stàyt, -stət/ *n.* somebody who has renounced a religious or political belief or allegiance [14thC. Via French and Latin from Greek *apostatēs*, literally "somebody caused to stand away," from *stat-*, related to *histanai* "to cause to stand."]

a·pos·ta·tize /ə páwstə tīz/ (**-tized, -tiz·ing, -tiz·es**) *vi.* to renounce a religious faith, a political party, a set of principles, or a moral allegiance (*formal*)

a pos·te·ri·o·ri /àa paws teeree áw ree, ày—rī/ *adj., adv.* deriving knowledge from experience, or reasoning from observed facts or events back to their causes [From Latin, literally "from what comes later"]

a·pos·til /ə páwstəl/ *n.* an annotation, comment, or note in a margin (*archaic*) [Early 16thC. From Old French *apostille* "marginal note," a variant of *postille* (see POSTIL).]

a·pos·tle /ə páwss'l/ *n.* **1. STRONG BELIEVER IN SOMETHING** somebody who believes strongly in an idea or cause and tries to persuade others to share it ○ *an apostle of free trade* **2. PROMINENT CHRISTIAN MISSIONARY** a prominent Christian missionary, especially one who is responsible for first converting a nation **3. OFFICIAL IN MORMON CHURCH** a member of the 12-person administrative council of the Church of Jesus Christ of Latter-Day Saints [Pre-12thC. Via ecclesiastical Latin from Greek *apostolos*, literally "somebody sent out," from *stellein* "to send" (source of English *epistle*).] — **a·pos·tle·ship** *n.*

A·pos·tle *n.* one of the 12 followers of Jesus Christ chosen by him to preach the news about Christianity

A·pos·tles' Creed *n.* a statement of Christian belief ascribed to the Apostles and dating from around A.D. 500. It is frequently used in services in Eastern Orthodox, Episcopalian, and Lutheran churches.

a·pos·to·late /ə pósta làyt, ə póstələt/ *n.* **1. WORK OF AN APOSTLE** the duties or mission of an apostle **2. GROUP OF PEOPLE PROPAGATING RELIGION** a group involved in converting new followers to a religion or doctrine [Mid-17thC. From ecclesiastical Latin *apostolatus*, from *apostolus* "apostle" (see APOSTLE).]

ap·os·tol·ic /àppə stóllik/ *adj.* **1. RELATING TO POPE** relating to, given by, or on behalf of the pope **2. RELATING TO APOSTLES** connected with the Apostles or their teachings, or contemporary with them [Mid-16thC. Via French and ecclesiastical Latin from, ultimately, Greek *apostolos* "apostle" (see APOSTLE).] —**ap·os·tol·i·cal** *adj.* —**ap·os·tol·i·cal·ly** *adv.*

ap·os·tol·ic del·e·gate *n.* a representative of the pope who is sent to a country that has no formal diplomatic relations with the Vatican

Ap·os·tol·ic Fa·ther *n.* a Christian church leader of the first or second century A.D. who was contemporary with or lived shortly after the Apostles

Ap·os·tol·ic See *n.* the area of jurisdiction (**see**) of the pope

ap·os·tol·ic suc·ces·sion *n.* the doctrine of some Christian denominations that the ordination of bishops follows in an unbroken line of succession from the Apostles, providing the basis of their spiritual authority

a·pos·tro·phe[1] /ə páwstrəfee/ *n.* the punctuation mark (') used to show where letters are omitted from a word, to mark the possessive, and sometimes to form the plural of numbers, letters, and symbols [Mid-16thC. Via French from, ultimately, Greek *apostrophos*, literally "turned away," formed from *apostrephein* "to turn away," from *strephein* "to turn" (see STROPHE).]

a·pos·tro·phe[2] /ə páwstrəfee/ *n.* a speech, especially in the form of a digression, addressing an absent or imaginary person or a personification of an abstract or inanimate entity [Mid-16thC. Via Latin from, ultimately, Greek *apostrephein* (see APOSTROPHE[1]).] — **ap·os·troph·ic** /àppə stróffik/ *adj.*

a·pos·tro·phize /ə páwstrə fīz/ (**-phized, -phiz·ing, -phiz·es**) *vti.* to address an absent or imaginary person or a personified abstraction

a·poth·e·car·ies' meas·ure *n.* a system of liquid volume measure formerly used in pharmacy and based on the minim, fluid dram, fluid ounce, and pint

a·poth·e·car·ies' weight *n.* a system of weights formerly used in pharmacy and based on a troy ounce equal to 480 grains and a pound equal to 12 ounces

a·poth·e·car·y /ə páwthə kèrree/ (*plural* **-ies**) *n.* (*archaic*) **1. PHARMACIST** a pharmacist **2. PHARMACY** a pharmacy [14thC. Via Old French from, ultimately, Greek *apothēkē* "storehouse" (source of English *boutique*), formed from *apotithenai* "to put away," from *tithenai* "to put."]

ap·o·the·ci·um /àppə théeshee əm, -ssee əm/ (*plural* **-a** /-ə, -ə/) *n.* a disk-shaped or cup-shaped spore-bearing structure found in certain fungi, including the fungal component of most lichens [Early 19thC. Via modern Latin from Greek *apothēkē* (see APOTHECARY).] — **ap·o·the·cial** /àppə théesh'l/ *adj.*

ap·o·thegm /áppə thèm/, **ap·o·phthegm** *n.* a terse saying that embodies an important truth, e.g., "Haste makes waste" [Mid-16thC. From Greek *apophthegma*, formed from *apophtheggesthai* "to speak plainly," from *phtheggesthai* "to speak."] —**ap·o·theg·mat·ic** /àppə theg máttik/ *adj.* —**ap·o·theg·mat·i·cal·ly** *adv.*

a·poth·e·o·sis /ə pàwthee óssəss/ (*plural* **-ses** /-sseez/) *n.* **1. HIGHEST LEVEL OF GLORY OR POWER** the highest point of glory, power, or importance **2. BEST EXAMPLE OF SOMETHING** the best or most glorious example of something ○ *the apotheosis of romantic music* **3. TRANSFORMATION INTO GOD** the transformation of a human being into a god [Late 16thC. Via late Latin from, ultimately, Greek *apotheoun*, literally "to make into a god completely," from *theos* "god" (see THEO-).]

ap·o·the·o·size /ə póthee ə sīz, àppə thée ə sīz/ (**-sized, -siz·ing, -siz·es**) *vt.* **1. MAKE SOMEBODY INTO A GOD** to elevate somebody to the status of a god **2. GLORIFY** to glorify or exalt somebody or something

ap·o·tro·pa·ic /àppətrə páy ik/ *adj.* intended to ward off evil or bad luck [Late 19thC. Formed from Greek *apotropaios*, from *apotrepein*, literally "to turn away" from *trepein* "to turn" (see -TROPOUS).] —**ap·o·tro·pa·i·cal·ly** *adv.* —**ap·o·tro·pa·ism** *n.*

app /ap/ *n.* COMPUT = **application** *n.* **6** (*informal*)

app. *abbr.* **1.** apparatus **2.** PUBL appendix **3.** appointed **4.** apprentice

ap·pal *vt.* U.K. = **appall**

Ap·pa·la·chi·a /àppə láychee ə, -láchə/ *n.* the region in the United States that includes the southern Appalachian Mountains, extending roughly from southwestern Pennsylvania through West Virginia and parts of Kentucky and Tennessee to northwestern Georgia

Ap·pa·la·chi·an /àppə láychee ən, -láchən/ *adj.* **1. RELATING TO APPALACHIAN MOUNTAINS** in, from, or relating to the Appalachian Mountains **2. OF APPALACHIA** relating to or typical of Appalachia, or its people or culture ■ *n.* **SOMEBODY FROM APPALACHIA** somebody who lives in or was born or raised in Appalachia [Late 17thC. Formed from *Apalachee*, the name of a Native American people of the southeastern United States.]

Ap·pa·la·chi·an Moun·tains, **Ap·pal·a·chi·ans** North American mountain system, stretching from southeastern Canada to central Alabama. Major ranges include the White, Green, Catskill, Allegheny, Blue Ridge, Great Smoky, and Cumberland mountains. The highest point is Mount Mitchell 6,684 ft./2,037 m.

Ap·pa·la·chi·an tea *n.* = **withe rod**

Ap·pa·la·chi·an Trail *n.* a hiking path in the eastern United States, extending about 2,050 mi./3,298 km from Mount Katahdin in central Maine to Springer Mountain in northern Georgia. It is one of the longest continuous mountain trails in the world.

ap·pall /ə páwl/ (**-palled, -pall·ing, -palls**) *vt.* to make somebody feel shock, horror, or disgust [Mid-16thC. From Old French *apallir* "to grow pale or faint," from *pale* "PALE."]

ap·palled /ə páwld/ *adj.* feeling or appearing to be shocked by something dreadful or awful ○ *an appalled look*

ap·pall·ing /ə páwling/ *adj.* **1. DREADFUL AND SHOCKING** causing shock or horror **2. VERY BAD** very bad, or much worse than expected —**ap·pall·ing·ly** *adv.*

Ap·pa·loo·sa /àppə lóosə/, **ap·pa·loo·sa** *n.* a saddle horse with white hair and dark patches, first bred in northwestern North America. It was much used in the past by Native Americans. [Mid-19thC. Origin uncertain; perhaps an alteration of *Palouse*, a river in the northwestern United States.]

ap·pa·nage /áppənij/, **ap·a·nage** *n.* **1. SOURCE OF REVENUE GIVEN BY SOVEREIGN** a source of revenue e.g., land given by a sovereign for the maintenance of a member of the royal family, especially a younger son **2. NATURAL OR EXPECTED ACCOMPANIMENT TO SOMETHING** a thing that naturally or usually accompanies something else [Early 17thC. Via French from, ultimately, medieval Latin *appanare*, literally "(to give) bread to," from *panis* "bread" (see PANTRY).]

ap·pa·rat /àppə ráat, àap-/ *n.* the administrative organization or staff of the Communist Party in the former Soviet Union and other Communist states [Mid-20thC. Via Russian from German, "apparatus."]

ap·pa·ra·tchik /àppə ráachik, àap-/ *n.* **1. UNQUESTIONINGLY LOYAL SUBORDINATE** a subordinate who is unquestioningly loyal to a powerful political leader or organization **2. COMMUNIST FUNCTIONARY** a member of the administrative organization or staff (**apparat**) of the Communist Party in the former Soviet Union and other Communist states [Mid-20thC. From Russian.]

ap·pa·ra·tus /àppə ráttəss, -ráy-/ (*plural* **-tus·es** *or* **-tus**) *n.* **1.** EQUIPMENT a piece of machinery, a tool, or a device used for a particular purpose **2.** SYSTEM ALLOWING SOMETHING TO FUNCTION the system or structure in which a process occurs or an organization functions ○ *a complex bureaucratic apparatus* **3.** ANAT SYSTEM OF ORGANS a group or system of organs that work together to perform a particular function [Early 17thC. From Latin, literally "something prepared," the past participle of *apparare* "to prepare," from *parare* (see PARE).]

WORD KEY: SYNONYMS

See Synonyms at ***implement***.

ap·pa·ra·tus crit·i·cus /àppə ratəss kríttəkəss, -ráytəss-/ *n.* = **critical apparatus** [Mid-19thC. From modern Latin, literally "critical apparatus."]

ap·par·el /ə pérrəl/ *n.* **1.** CLOTHING clothing or garments, especially outer or decorative clothing ○ *Olympics-related sports apparel* **2.** NAUT SHIP'S EQUIPMENT a ship's gear and equipment ■ *vt.* (**-eled, -el·ing, -els**) CLOTHE to dress somebody, especially in formal clothes (*archaic*) [13thC. Via Old French *apareil* "preparation" from, ultimately, Latin *apparare* (see APPARATUS). The sense "clothing" evolved via "equipment for performing a particular function."]

ap·par·ent /ə pérrənt/ *adj.* **1.** CLEAR TO SOMEBODY clearly seen or understood **2.** SEEMING appearing to show particular qualities, feelings, or attributes that may not be genuine ○ *her apparent indifference* **3.** PHYS DIRECTLY OBSERVED BUT NEGLECTING MODIFYING FACTORS directly observed or measured but not taking into account factors or effects that should be allowed for, e.g., distortion caused by the measuring instruments themselves [14thC. Via Old French *aparant*, the present participle of *aparoir* (see APPEAR).] —**ap·par·ent·ness** *n.*

WORD KEY: SYNONYMS

See Synonyms at ***evident***.

ap·par·ent ho·ri·zon *n.* = **horizon** *n.* 1

ap·par·ent·ly /ə pérrəntlee/ *adv.* according to what seems to be the case but may not actually be so

ap·par·ent mag·ni·tude *n.* = **magnitude**

ap·par·ent wind /-wind/ *n.* a combination of the actual wind and the wind created by a ship's motion

ap·pa·ri·tion /àppə rísh'n/ *n.* **1.** APPEARANCE OF SOMETHING GHOSTLY an appearance of a ghost or something ghostly **2.** APPEARANCE OF SOMETHING UNLIKELY an appearance of something or somebody unexpected or strange (*humorous*) [15thC. Via French from, ultimately, Latin *apparere* (see APPEAR).] —**ap·pa·ri·tion·al** *adj.*

ap·pas·sion·a·to /ə pàssyə náa tō/ *adj., adv.* to be performed in an impassioned way (*used as a musical direction*) [From Italian, literally "impassioned"]

ap·peal /ə péel/ *n.* **1.** EARNEST OR URGENT REQUEST an earnest or urgent request to somebody for something ○ *an emotional appeal for forgiveness* **2.** CAMPAIGN TO RAISE MONEY a request or campaign to raise money or resources ○ *The hospital has launched an appeal for funds.* **3.** ATTRACTION the quality that makes somebody or something attractive ○ *The movie's appeal lies in its humor and charm.* **4.** FORMAL REQUEST a formal request to a higher authority requesting a change in or confirmation of a decision ○ *An appeal to the boss might solve the matter.* **5.** LAW HEARING OF CASE BEFORE SUPERIOR COURT the hearing of part or the whole of a previously tried case by a superior court, a request for a hearing, or the right to have such a hearing ■ *v.* (**-pealed, -peal·ing, -peals**) **1.** *vi.* REQUEST MONEY to ask for or campaign to raise money or resources ○ *The charity is appealing for books and toys.* **2.** *vi.* EARNESTLY REQUEST SOMETHING to make an earnest and urgent request for something ○ *We are appealing to the public to let us know if they see anything suspicious.* **3.** *vi.* MAKE A FORMAL REQUEST TO SUPERIOR to make a formal request to a higher authority requesting a change in or confirmation of a decision ○ *You will have to appeal to a senior officer.* **4.** *vi.* ATTRACT OR FASCINATE SOMEBODY to be interesting or attractive ○ *Starting up my own business really appeals to me.* **5.** *vti.* LAW APPLY TO SUPERIOR COURT FOR HEARING to apply to a superior court for a hearing of the whole or part of a case previously tried in a lower court **6.** *vi.* SPORTS CHALLENGE UMPIRE'S DECISION to challenge the decision of an umpire or referee [14thC. Via Old French *apeler* from, ultimately, Latin *appellare* "to address, entreat," related to *pellere* "to push."] —**ap·peal·er** *n.* ◇ **on appeal** at the stage of a court case that involves reconsideration of the decision made at the original trial

WORD KEY: ORIGIN

Latin *pellere*, from which ***appeal*** is derived, is also the source of English *compel, dispel, expel, impel, propel, pulse, repeal,* and *repel.*

ap·peal·a·ble /ə péeləb'l/ *adj.* LAW having the right to be heard before a higher court with the possibility of a changed judgment

ap·peal·ing /ə péeling/ *adj.* **1.** ATTRACTIVE attractive and pleasing or interesting **2.** REQUESTING HELP OR SYMPATHY appearing to request help or sympathy ○ *a timid, appealing glance* —**ap·peal·ing·ly** *adv.*

ap·pear /ə péer/ (**-peared, -pear·ing, -pears**) *v.* **1.** *vi.* COME INTO VIEW to come into view, or become visible ○ *The main menu will appear whenever you turn on the computer.* **2.** *vi.* BEGIN TO EXIST to come into existence ○ *When did this rash appear?* **3.** *vi.* BECOME AVAILABLE FOR SALE to become available, especially as a product for sale ○ *Cheaper and better printers have appeared on the market.* **4.** *vti.* SEEM LIKELY to seem likely or true ○ *The police appear to be looking for three men.* **5.** *vi.* BE SEEN IN PUBLIC to come before the public, especially to perform a duty or to act ○ *His dream was to appear on Broadway.* **6.** *vi.* LAW BE IN LAW COURT OFFICIALLY to be present in a court of law as a defendant, plaintiff, witness, or legal adviser ○ *due to appear in court next week* **7.** *vi.* FORMALLY PRESENT YOURSELF TO SOMEBODY to formally present yourself to somebody after receiving an official request ○ *He was ordered to appear in the police chief's office.* [13thC. Via Old French *aparoir* from Latin *apparere*, literally "to show, become visible to," from *parere* "to show."]

ap·pear·ance /ə péerənss/ *n.* **1.** COMING INTO EXISTENCE the act of emerging, arriving, or coming into existence ○ *the appearance of the first daffodils* **2.** WAY SOMEBODY OR SOMETHING LOOKS the way somebody or something looks or seems to other people ○ *an attractive appearance* **3.** OUTWARD ASPECT an outward aspect of somebody or something that creates a particular impression (*often used in the plural*) ○ *The place gives the appearance of prosperity.* ○ *I know the dog looks friendly, but don't be fooled by appearances.* **4.** PERFORMANCE OR EXHIBITION IN PUBLIC a performance or exhibition before a public audience ○ *It was the band's first U.S. appearance.* **5.** ATTENDANCE IN COURT attendance in court as a defendant, plaintiff, witness, or legal adviser ○ *The prospect of an appearance in court was daunting.* ◇ **keep up appearances** to maintain an appearance of well-being despite difficulties ◇ **put in an appearance at something** to attend something, often only for a short time or to fulfill an obligation

ap·pease /ə péez/ (**-peased, -peas·ing, -peas·es**) *vt.* **1.** PACIFY to pacify somebody, especially by acceding to demands **2.** SATISFY NEED to satisfy or relieve something, especially a physical appetite [14thC. From Old French *apaisier*, from *pais* "peace" (see PEACE).] —**ap·peas·a·ble** *adj.* —**ap·peas·a·bly** *adv.* —**ap·peas·er** *n.*

ap·pease·ment /ə péezmənt/ *n.* **1.** PACIFICATION OF POTENTIALLY HOSTILE NATION the political strategy of pacifying a potentially hostile nation in the hope of avoiding war, often by granting concessions **2.** GRANT OF CONCESSIONS an attempt to stop complaints or reduce difficulties by making concessions

ap·pel /ə pél/ *n.* **1.** FENCER'S WARNING STAMP OF FOOT a stamp of the foot that signals a fencer's intention to start attacking **2.** BLOW WITH FENCING BLADE in fencing, a sharp blow with the blade made to procure an opening [From French, literally "call"]

ap·pel·lant /ə péllənt/ *n.* LAW the person or group of people in a legal action who appeal a judicial decision in a higher court or a different jurisdiction [Late 16thC. From Old French *apelant*, the present participle of *apeler* (see APPEAL).]

ap·pel·late /ə péllət/ *adj.* LAW having the jurisdiction to hear appeals and review the decisions of lower courts [Mid-18thC. From Latin *appellatus*, the past participle of *appellare* (see APPEAL).]

ap·pel·late court *n.* LAW a court with the power to review and reverse the decisions of lower courts

ap·pel·late ju·ris·dic·tion *n.* LAW the power vested in an appellate court authorizing it to review the decisions of lower courts

ap·pel·la·tion /àppə láysh'n/ *n.* the name or title by which something or somebody is known (*formal*) [15thC. Via French, "naming," from, ultimately, Latin *appellare* (see APPEAL).]

ap·pel·la·tion con·trô·lée /aa pèllaáa syawN kawNtrō láy/ (*plural* **ap·pel·la·tions con·trô·lées** /aa pèllaáa syawN kawNtrō láy/) *n.* a certification for French wine that guarantees its origin and verifies that it meets production regulations [From French, literally "controlled name"]

ap·pel·la·tive /ə péllətiv/ *n.* **1.** = **appellation** (*formal*) **2.** GRAM = **common noun** ■ *adj.* **1.** RELATING TO NAME connected with a name or title **2.** USED AS COMMON NOUN used as a common noun to describe a class of things —**ap·pel·la·tive·ly** *adv.*

ap·pend /ə pénd/ (**-pend·ed, -pend·ing, -pends**) *vt.* **1.** ADD EXTRA INFORMATION to add extra information to something, especially to attach extra information to a document **2.** ADD AUTHORIZED SIGNATURE TO AGREEMENT to add an authorized signature to a bill or an official agreement as one of the final parts of the ratification or agreement process (*formal*) ○ *All principals to the sale must append their signatures.* **3.** ATTACH SOMETHING to attach something or fasten it to something else [Mid-17thC. From Latin *appendere*, literally "to hang upon" (source of English *penthouse*), from *pendere* "to hang" (see PENDANT).]

ap·pend·age /ə péndij/ *n.* **1.** SECONDARY ATTACHMENT something fastened to something else as a small or secondary attachment ○ *feeling like an appendage of your family* **2.** ZOOL PROJECTING BODY PART a body part or organ e.g., a tail, wing, or fin that projects from the main part of the body

ap·pen·dant /ə péndənt/ *n.* **1.** ATTACHMENT something that is attached or added to something larger or more important **2.** LAW SOMETHING ADDED TO LEGAL DOCUMENT a secondary document that is attached to the main body of a legal document, e.g., a codicil altering the terms of a will ■ *adj.* ATTACHED attached or added to something larger or more important [Early 16thC. Via Old French *apendant* from, ultimately, Latin *appendere* (see APPEND).]

ap·pen·dec·to·my /àppən déktəmee/ (*plural* **-mies**) *n.* a surgical operation to remove the appendix [Late 19thC. Coined from the Latin stem of *appendix* "APPENDIX" + -ECTOMY.]

ap·pen·di·ces plural of **appendix**

ap·pen·di·ci·tis /ə pèndə sítiss/ *n.* an inflammation of the appendix, causing severe pain

ap·pen·di·cle /ə péndək'l/ *n.* a small appendage (*archaic*) [Early 17thC. From Latin *appendicula*, literally "small appendix," from *appendix* "APPENDIX."]

ap·pen·dic·u·lar /àppən díkyələr/ *adj.* **1.** ASSOCIATED WITH LIMBS used to describe body parts that are associated with the limbs ○ *appendicular muscles* **2.** OF APPENDIX used to describe the appendix [Mid-17thC. Formed from Latin *appendicula*.]

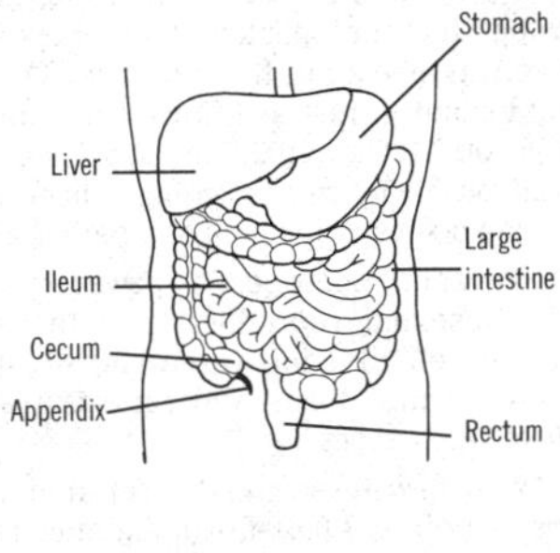

Appendix

ap·pen·dix /ə péndiks/ (*plural* **-dix·es** *or* **-di·ces** /-di seez/) *n.* **1.** ANAT SMALL OUTGROWTH FROM LARGE INTESTINE a blind-ended tube leading from the first part of the large intestine (**cecum**), near its junction with the small intestine. In humans it is small, occurs in the lower right-hand part of the abdomen, and contains cells of the immune system. **2.** ADDITIONAL INFORMATION ACCOMPANYING MAIN TEXT a collection of separate material at the end of a book or document **3.** PROJECTING PART a part that projects from something larger [Mid-16thC. From Latin, from *appendere* (see APPEND).]

ap·per·ceive /àppər séev/ (**-ceived, -ceiv·ing, -ceives**) *vt.* to comprehend or assimilate something, e.g., a new idea, in terms of previous experiences or perceptions [Late 19thC. Back-formation from APPERCEPTION.]

ap·per·cep·tion /àppər sépsh'n/ *n.* the comprehension or assimilation of something, e.g., a new idea, in terms of previous experiences or perceptions [Mid-18thC. From the modern Latin stem *apperception-*, literally "toward perception," from Latin *perceptio* "perception" (see PERCEPTION).] —**ap·per·cep·tive** *adj.*

ap·per·tain /àppər táyn/ (**-tained, -tain·ing, -tains**) *vi.* to belong or relate to something (*formal*) ○ *another issue that appertains to the policy under discussion* [14thC. Via Old French *apartenir* from, ultimately, late Latin *appertinere*, literally "to belong completely to," from *pertinere* "to belong to" (see PERTAIN).]

ap·pe·stat /áppə stàt/ *n.* the region of the brain that controls appetite and eating [Coined from APPETITE + -STAT]

ap·pe·tence /áppət'ns/, **ap·pe·ten·cy** /-tənsee/ (*plural* **-cies**) *n.* a desire or longing for something [Early 17thC. Via French from Latin *appetentia*, from *appetent-*, the present participle stem of *appetere* (see APPETITE).]

ap·pe·tite /áppə tìt/ *n.* **1. DESIRE FOR FOOD** a natural desire for food **2. STRONG DESIRE** a strong desire or craving for something [14thC. Via French from Latin *appetitus* "desire," from *appetere*, literally "to seek after," from *petere* "to seek" (see PETITION).] —**ap·pe·ti·tive** /áppə tìtiv, ə péttətiv/ *adj.*

ap·pe·tiz·er /áppə tìzər/ *n.* **1. FOOD SERVED BEFORE MAIN COURSE** a small dish of food served at the beginning of a meal to stimulate the appetite **2. STIMULATING SAMPLE** a sample of something that is meant to stimulate an interest [Mid-19thC. Formed from earlier *appetize* "to give an appetite," a back-formation from APPETIZING.]

ap·pe·tiz·ing /áppə tìzing/ *adj.* appealing to or stimulating the appetite [Mid-17thC. Anglicization of French *appétissant*, from *appétit* (see APPETITE).] —**ap·pe·tiz·ing·ly** *adv.*

ap·plaud /ə pláwd/ (**-plaud·ed, -plaud·ing, -plauds**) *v.* **1.** *vti.* **CLAP HANDS** to clap hands as a sign of welcome, appreciation, or approval **2.** *vt.* **EXPRESS APPROVAL** to praise somebody or something ○ *applauded the students' achievement* [15thC. Directly and via French from Latin *applaudere*, literally "to clap at," from *plaudere* "to clap" (source of English *plaudit* and *explode*).] —**ap·plaud·a·ble** *adj.* —**ap·plaud·er** *n.* —**ap·plaud·ing** *adj.* —**ap·plaud·ing·ly** *adv.*

ap·plause /ə pláwz/ *n.* the clapping of hands to express welcome, enjoyment, appreciation, or approval [Late 16thC. From Latin *applausus*, from *applaus-*, the past participle stem of *applaudere* (see APPLAUD).]

Apple

ap·ple /ápp'l/ *n.* **1. FIRM ROUND FRUIT WITH CENTRAL CORE** a firm round fruit with a central core, red or green skin, and white flesh **2. FRUIT TREE** a deciduous Eurasian tree that has white or pink flowers and produces apples. Latin name: *Malus pumila.* [Old English *æppel*] ◇ **the apple of somebody's eye** somebody or something very much loved and favored by another person

Ap·ple·baum /ápp'l bàwm/, **Louis** (*b.* 1918) Canadian composer and conductor. He was a prolific composer for film, theater, television, and radio.

ap·ple but·ter *n.* a smooth spread made of stewed apples flavored with spices

ap·ple·cart /ápp'l kaàrt/ *n.* in former times, a street vendor's cart from which apples were sold ◇ **upset the applecart** to spoil a plan or arrangement

ap·ple green *n.* a bright green color with a light tinge of yellow —**ap·ple-green** *adj.*

ap·ple·jack /ápp'l jàk/ *n.* **1. BRANDY** a brandy distilled from cider **2. BEVERAGE** an alcoholic beverage made from the liquid remaining after cider has been frozen

ap·ple mag·got *n.* the larva of a fruit fly that bores into and feeds on the fruit of apple trees. Latin name: *Rhagoletis pomonella.*

ap·ple of Pe·ru *n.* an ornamental annual plant that has pale violet-blue, bell-shaped flowers. Latin name: *Nicandra physalodes.*

ap·ple pan·dow·dy *n. New England* a type of apple pie or deep-dish apple cobbler sweetened with molasses

ap·ple pie *n.* a dessert made by cooking sliced apples in a pastry case ◇ **Mom and apple pie** the virtues, e.g., neighborliness and civic pride, that Americans believe have traditionally characterized U.S. culture

ap·ple-pie *adj.* characteristic of or embodying the virtues that Americans believe to be typical of U.S. culture, e.g., neighborliness, civic pride, and honesty (*informal*) ○ *apple-pie honesty* ◇ **in apple-pie order** neat and tidy

ap·ple-pol·ish (**ap·ple-pol·ished, ap·ple-pol·ish·ing, ap·ple-pol·ish·es**) *vti.* to try to win favor by flattering somebody (*slang*) —**ap·ple pol·ish·er** *n.*

ap·plesauce /ápp'l sàwss/ *n.* **1. CONDIMENT MADE FROM APPLES** a sauce of sweetened stewed apples, often served with pork **2. NONSENSE** silly nonsense (*informal*)

ap·plet /ápplət/ *n.* **1. LIMITED COMPUTER PROGRAM** a simple computer program that performs a single task and is run from within a larger application **2. COMPUTER PROGRAM TRANSFERRABLE OVER INTERNET** a small piece of computer code, often embedded within a Web page, that can be transferred over the Internet and executed by the recipient's computer

Ap·ple·ton /ápp'ltən/ city in east central Wisconsin, on the Fox River. Population: 65,862 (1996).

Ap·ple·ton lay·er *n.* = **F region** [Named for the British physicist Edward V. *Appleton* (1892–1965), who discovered it.]

Ap·ple Val·ley city in southeastern Minnesota, south of St. Paul. Population: 42,949 (1996).

ap·pli·ance /ə plí əns/ *n.* **1. DOMESTIC ELECTRICAL MACHINE** an electrical device or machine such as a vacuum cleaner that is used for a particular purpose in the home **2. DEVICE FOR STRAIGHTENING TEETH** a device made of metal bands or wires that is connected to the teeth and tightened in order to make them straighter **3. PUTTING SOMETHING INTO EFFECT** the act of putting something into effect

WORD KEY: SYNONYMS

See Synonyms at ***implement.***

ap·pli·ca·ble /áplikəb'l/; /ə plíkəb'l/ *adj.* affecting, connected with, or relevant to a particular person, group of people, or situation [Mid-16thC. Via French from, ultimately, Latin *applicare* "to apply" (see APPLY).] —**ap·pli·ca·bil·i·ty** /àpplikə bíllətee/ *n.* —**ap·pli·ca·bly** /ápplәkəblee/ *adv.*

ap·pli·cant /ápplәkənt/ *n.* somebody who formally applies for something, e.g., a job, a grant of money, or admission to a university [Early 19thC. From Latin *applicant-*, the present participle stem of *applicare* (see APPLY).]

WORD KEY: SYNONYMS

See Synonyms at ***candidate.***

ap·pli·ca·tion /àpplə káysh'n/ *n.* **1. FORMAL REQUEST FOR SOMETHING** a formal and usually written request for something, e.g., a job, a grant of money, or admission to a university **2. USE OF SOMETHING** the use something is put to or the process of putting it to use **3. RELEVANCE** the relevance or value that something has, especially when it is applied to a certain field or area ○ *the industrial applications of biochemical research* **4. SPREADING LIQUID ON SURFACE** the act of spreading a liquid such as paint or medicine on a surface **5. HARD WORK** concentration and hard work **6.** COMPUT **COMPUTER SOFTWARE** a computer program or piece of software designed to perform a specific task [15thC. Via French from, ultimately, Latin *applicare* (see APPLY).]

ap·pli·ca·tive /ápli kàytiv, ə plíkətiv/ *adj.* capable of being applied [Mid-17thC. Formed from Latin *applicat-*, the past participle stem of *applicare* (see APPLY).] —**ap·pli·ca·tive·ly** *adv.*

ap·pli·ca·tor /ápplə kàytər/ *n.* a device used to apply a liquid or powder to a surface [Mid-17thC. Formed from Latin *applicat-*, the past participle stem of *applicare* "to apply" (see APPLY).]

ap·pli·ca·to·ry /ápplikə tàwree, ə plíkə tàwree/ *adj.* easily or suitably applied [Mid-17thC. Formed from Latin *applicat-*, the past participle stem of *applicare* (see APPLY).]

ap·plied /ə plíd/ *adj.* able to be put to practical use, especially as a branch of a subject that has both practical and theoretical aspects

ap·plied an·thro·pol·o·gy *n.* the branch of anthropology concerned with the solution of practical problems such as drought relief or economic development

ap·plied lin·guis·tics *n.* the branch of linguistics that applies the results of research to practical areas of language such as translation, language disorders, or teaching second languages (*takes a singular verb*)

ap·plied psy·chol·o·gy *n.* the branch of psychology in which theory is applied to real-life situations, e.g., in the workplace or in medical settings

ap·pli·qué /àppli káy/ *n.* **FABRIC PIECES SEWN ON FABRIC** shaped pieces of fabric sewn on a foundation fabric to form a design or pattern ■ *vt.* (**-quéd, -qué·ing, -qués**) **SEW FABRIC PIECES ON FABRIC** to form a design or pattern by sewing shaped pieces of fabric on a foundation fabric [Mid-18thC. From French, literally "applied."]

ap·ply /ə plí/ (**-plied, -ply·ing, -plies**) *v.* **1.** *vi.* **MAKE A FORMAL REQUEST FOR SOMETHING** to make a formal, usually written, request for something ○ *How do I apply for a tax refund?* **2.** *vt.* **USE SOMETHING** to make use of something to achieve a result ○ *He applied his first-aid skills to help the accident victims.* **3.** *vi.* **BE RELEVANT** to be relevant to somebody or something ○ *The requirement applies only if you are over 65.* **4.** *vt.* **SPREAD SOMETHING** to spread a liquid or other material over a surface ○ *Apply a thin layer of cream to the face and neck.* **5.** *vt.* **WORK HARD** to work hard or spend a significant amount of time on something ○ *I could have done better if I'd applied myself a little more.* [14thC. Via Old French *aplier* from Latin *applicare* "to fold toward," from *plicare* "to fold" (see PLY).] —**ap·pli·er** *n.*

ap·pog·gia·tu·ra /ə pòjjə tóorə/ (*plural* **-ras** *or* **-re** /-ray/) *n.* in music, an ornamental dissonant note resolving, usually downward by a step, into a principal note [Mid-18thC. From Italian, literally "something supported by another."]

ap·point /ə póynt/ (**-point·ed, -point·ing, -points**) *vt.* **1. SELECT SOMEBODY FOR POSITION OR JOB** to select a person or a group of people for an official position or to do a particular job ○ *She's been appointed director.* **2. AGREE UPON A TIME OR PLACE** to fix or agree upon a particular time or place for something to happen (*formal*) **3.** LAW **GIVE CERTAIN POWERS TO TRUSTEE** to authorize a trustee to transfer trust property to particular beneficiaries [14thC. From Old French *apointier* "to arrange, settle," from *a point*, literally "to a point."]

ap·point·ed /ə póyntəd/ *adj.* decorated, furnished, or equipped (*usually used in combination*) ○ *a well-appointed apartment*

ap·point·ee /ə pòyn tée/ *n.* **1. SOMEBODY SELECTED FOR JOB** somebody who is selected for an office or position or to perform a particular job **2.** LAW **TRUSTEE RESPONSIBLE FOR TRUST PROPERTY** a trustee with the power to transfer trust property to particular beneficiaries

ap·point·ive /ə póyntiv/ *adj.* **1. FILLED BY APPOINTMENT** being or relating to a position to which somebody is appointed **2.** LAW **RELATING TO TRUST PROPERTY** relating to trust property that is managed by a trustee with the power to transfer it to beneficiaries

ap·point·ment /ə póyntmənt/ *n.* **1. ARRANGEMENT TO MEET SOMEBODY** an arrangement to have a meeting or to be somewhere at a particular time **2. CHOICE OF SOMEBODY FOR JOB** the selection of somebody for a position, office, or job **3. POSITION OR JOB** a position, office, or job to which somebody is appointed **4. SOMEBODY APPOINTED TO JOB** somebody who has been appointed to a position, office, or job **5.** LAW **SELECTION OF TRUSTEE** the selection of a trustee to whom power is given to transfer trust property to beneficiaries ■ **appointments** *npl.* **FURNITURE AND FITTINGS** the furniture, accessories, and equipment belonging to a particular place

ap·point·ment book *n.* a book, usually with pages labeled according to the days of a calendar year, used to keep notes of appointments

appointment TV *n.* television programs that viewers watch regularly and are loyal to

ap·poin·tor /ə póyntər/ *n.* LAW somebody responsible for selecting a trustee to supervise and transfer trust property

Ap·po·mat·tox /àppə máttəks/ **1.** city in central Virginia. The courthouse there was the site of the 1865 Confederate surrender to the Union Army. Population: 1,838 (1996). **2.** river in southeastern Virginia that flows eastward into the James River at Hopewell. Length: 135 mi./217 km.

ap·port /ə páwrt/ *n.* **1.** PRODUCTION OF OBJECTS AT SÉANCE the production of objects at a spiritualist's séance, supposedly by paranormal means **2.** OBJECT PRODUCED AT SÉANCE an object produced at a spiritualist's séance, supposedly by paranormal means [15thC. From French *aport*, literally "bringing to," from *aporter* "to carry to," from *porter* "to carry" (see PORT).]

ap·por·tion /ə páwrsh'n/ (**-tioned, -tion·ing, -tions**) *vt.* to divide and allocate something among different people or groups [Late 16thC. Via French from, ultimately, Latin *portio* "portion" (see PORTION).]

ap·por·tion·ment /ə páwrsh'nmənt/ *n.* **1.** ALLOCATION the division and allocation of something among people or groups **2.** DISTRIBUTION OF LEGISLATIVE SEATS the distribution of seats in the U.S. House of Representatives or a state legislature, based proportionally on the population of states or electoral districts **3.** ALLOCATION OF TAXES the distribution of direct federal taxes to the states in proportion to their population

ap·pose /ə pṓz/ (**-posed, -pos·ing, -pos·es**) *vt.* to be placed near something, or place or move something next to something else [Late 16thC. Formed from Latin *apponere*, on the model of English *compose* and *expose*.]

ap·po·site /áppəzit/ *adj.* especially well suited to the circumstances [Early 17thC. From Latin *appositus*, the past participle of *apponere* "to add to, put near," from *ponere* "to put" (see POSITION).] —**ap·po·site·ly** *adv.* —**ap·po·site·ness** *n.*

ap·po·si·tion /àppə zísh'n/ *n.* **1.** JUXTAPOSITION the relative position of two things that are next to each other **2.** GRAM RELATIONSHIP BETWEEN NOUN PHRASES the relationship between two usually consecutive nouns or noun phrases that refer to the same person or thing and have the same relationship to other sentence elements. In the sentence "My son, an actor, lives with me," the phrase "My son, an actor" is an example of apposition. **3.** BIOL CELL GROWTH IN LAYERS cell growth in which layers of material are deposited on already existing ones —**ap·po·si·tion·al** *adj.* —**ap·po·si·tion·al·ly** *adv.*

ap·pos·i·tive /ə pózzətiv/ *adj.* used to describe words or phrases that refer to the same person or thing and have the same relationship to other sentence elements —**ap·pos·i·tive** *n.* —**ap·pos·i·tive·ly** *adv.*

ap·prais·al /ə práyz'l/ *n.* **1.** EVALUATION a judgment or opinion of something or somebody, especially one that assesses how effective or useful something or somebody is **2.** VALUATION an estimate of the value of something

ap·praise /ə práyz/ (**-praised, -prais·ing, -prais·es**) *vt.* **1.** VALUATE SOMETHING to give an estimate of how much money something is worth **2.** ASSESS MERITS OR QUALITY to give an opinion of somebody's merits or something's quality [15thC. Alteration of APPRIZE, on the model of PRAISE.] —**ap·prais·a·ble** *adj.* —**ap·praise·ment** *n.*

WORD KEY: USAGE

appraise or **apprise**? ***Appraise***, meaning "to assess, evaluate," is used with reference to people or (more usually) the things they do or achieve. *She appraised their work at the end of each week.* ***Apprise***, meaning "inform," is a more formal word and is used with reference to people. *He apprised them of the decisions.*

ap·prais·er /ə práyzər/ *n.* somebody whose job is to make appraisals of valuables, e.g., antiques, jewels, and silver

ap·pre·cia·ble /ə préeshəbəl/ *adj.* large or important enough to be noticed ○ *There is no appreciable difference between them.* —**ap·pre·cia·bly** *adv.*

ap·pre·ci·ate /ə préeshee ayt/ (**-at·ed, -at·ing, -ates**) *v.* **1.** *vt.* FEEL GRATITUDE to feel grateful for something ○ *I'd appreciate it if you didn't repeat this to anyone.* **2.** *vt.* VALUE SOMEBODY OR SOMETHING HIGHLY to recognize and like the qualities in somebody or something **3.** *vt.* UNDERSTAND SOMETHING to understand fully the meaning or importance of a particular situation **4.** *vi.* GAIN IN VALUE to increase in value, especially over time [Mid-17thC. From late Latin *appretiare* "to value, estimate, rate, appraise," from *pretium* "money spent, worth, value" (source of English *price*).]

WORD KEY: USAGE

Proper contexts. Language critics' opinions on **appreciate** vary widely. Some critics, explaining that the word's etymology has to do with accurate valuation, say proper use requires it to be used only in neutral contexts (*I appreciate your position*). Others, pointing out that *appreciation* is admiration or gratitude, say it should be used only in favorable contexts (*I appreciate your honesty*). Still others argue that the verb's object should always be a noun (*I appreciate your annoyance*), not a clause (*I appreciate how angry you are*). Certainly it is worth remembering the verb's continuing ties to the ideas of valuation and gratitude, and worth remembering, too, that no one objects to *recognize* or *realize* or *understand* in negative contexts or before clauses.

ap·pre·ci·a·tion /ə prèeshee áysh'n/ *n.* **1.** GRATEFULNESS a feeling or expression of gratitude ○ *a token of my appreciation* **2.** POSITIVE OPINION a favorable opinion of something **3.** VALUING SOMETHING HIGHLY recognition and liking of something's qualities **4.** FULL UNDERSTANDING a full understanding of the meaning and importance of something **5.** GROWTH IN VALUE an increase in value, especially over time

ap·pre·cia·tive /ə préeshətiv/ *adj.* expressing or feeling gratitude or approval —**ap·pre·cia·tive·ly** *adv.* —**ap·pre·cia·tive·ness** *n.*

ap·pre·hend /àppri hénd/ (**-hend·ed, -hend·ing, -hends**) *vt.* **1.** ARREST SOMEBODY to put somebody suspected of wrongdoing into legal custody **2.** UNDERSTAND SOMETHING to grasp the importance, significance, or meaning of something **3.** BECOME AWARE OF SOMETHING to become aware of something by use of the senses (*formal*) **4.** BE FEARFUL OF SOMETHING to await an impending disaster or other calamity with fear or dread (*formal*) [14thC. Directly or via Old French from Latin *apprehendere* "to take hold of," from *prehendere* "to seize" (see PREHENSILE).]

ap·pre·hen·si·ble /àppri hénsəb'l/ *adj.* capable of being understood

ap·pre·hen·sion /àppri hénshən/ *n.* **1.** DREAD a feeling of anxiety or fear that something bad or unpleasant will happen **2.** ARREST the taking of a criminal suspect into custody (*formal*) **3.** IDEA an idea formed by observation or experience **4.** ABILITY TO UNDERSTAND the power or ability to grasp the importance, significance, or meaning of something (*formal*) [14thC. Directly or via Old French from the late Latin stem *apprehension-*, from *apprehens-*, the past participle stem of Latin *apprehendere* (see APPREHEND).]

ap·pre·hen·sive /àppri hénsiv/ *adj.* **1.** FEARFUL worried that something bad will happen **2.** AWARE aware or cognizant of something nonphysical, e.g., implications or results (*formal*) —**ap·pre·hen·sive·ly** *adv.* —**ap·pre·hen·sive·ness** *n.*

ap·pren·tice /ə préntiss/ *n.* **1.** TRAINEE somebody who works under a skilled professional in order to learn an art, craft, or trade and become qualified in it **2.** INEXPERIENCED PERSON a novice or amateur ■ *vt.* (**-ticed, -tic·ing, -tic·es**) MAKE SOMEBODY APPRENTICE to give somebody work as an apprentice to a skilled professional ○ *He was apprenticed to a master electrician for five years.* [14thC. From Old French *aprentis*, from *aprendre* "to learn," from Latin *apprehendere* (see APPREHEND).]

WORD KEY: SYNONYMS

See Synonyms at ***beginner***.

ap·pren·tice·ship /ə préntis shìp/ *n.* **1.** TIME SPENT AS APPRENTICE the period of time that an apprentice spends training **2.** STATUS OF APPRENTICE an apprentice's status or conditions of employment

ap·pressed /ə prést/ *adj.* used to describe a part of a plant that is pressed closely against another part without being joined to it ○ *appressed leaves* [Late 18thC. Formed from Latin *appressus*, the past participle of *apprimere* "to press to," from *premere* "to press" (see PRESS).]

ap·prise /ə príz/ (**-prised, -pris·ing, -pris·es**) *vt.* to inform or give notice to somebody about something (*formal*) [Late 17thC. From French *appris*, the past participle of *apprendre* "to make learn, teach" (see APPRENTICE).]

WORD KEY: USAGE

See Usage note at ***appraise.***

ap·prize /ə príz/ (**-prized, -priz·ing, -prizes**) *vt.* to value something very highly, e.g., because of its monetary worth (*formal*) [15thC. Via Old French *aprisier* from Latin *appretiare* (see APPRECIATE).]

ap·proach /ə prṓch/ *v.* (**-proached, -proach·ing, -proach·es**) **1.** *vti.* MOVE CLOSER to move closer to somebody or something ○ *He motioned to us to approach.* **2.** *vt.* ASK SOMEBODY to speak to somebody with a view to asking for something **3.** *vt.* TREAT SOMETHING IN PARTICULAR WAY to deal with something in a particular way ○ *How did she approach the problem?* **4.** *vt.* BORDER ON SOMETHING to be almost at a particular level or state **5.** *vti.* COME CLOSER IN TIME to come nearer in time to something ○ *As spring approaches I notice people smiling more.* **6.** *vi.* GOLF HIT BALL FROM FAIRWAY TO GREEN to make a golf shot from the fairway toward a green **7.** *vi.* TENNIS COME TO NET come in toward the net in tennis ■ *n.* **1.** COMING a coming nearer in space or time **2.** METHOD a way of doing or solving something **3.** MAKING OF CONTACT an informal request, offer, suggestion, or proposal made to somebody (*often used in the plural*) **4.** SIMILAR THING one thing that is very similar in its nature or qualities to another **5.** ACCESS a way of reaching or gaining access to a building or place **6.** AIRCRAFT'S COURSE TO LANDING SITE the path that an aircraft follows as it prepares to land **7.** GOLF SHOT FROM FAIRWAY TO GREEN a golf shot made from the fairway toward the green **8.** TENNIS MOVEMENT TOWARD NET movement of a tennis player toward the net **9.** BOWLING PLAYER'S PREPARATION TO RELEASE BOWLING BALL the steps somebody takes before releasing the ball in bowling, or the part of the bowling alley used for doing this [14thC. Via Old French *aproch(i)er* from late Latin *appropiare* "to go nearer to," from *propius* "nearer" (see PROPINQUITY).]

ap·proach·a·ble /ə prṓchəb'l/ *adj.* **1.** INVITINGLY FRIENDLY friendly and easy to talk to **2.** EASILY ACCESSIBLE able to be reached with ease, especially in terms of transportation **3.** USER-FRIENDLY easy for nonspecialists to understand —**ap·proach·a·bil·i·ty** /ə prṑchə bíllətee/ *n.* —**ap·proach·a·ble·ness** /ə prṓchəb'lnəss/ *n.*

ap·proach·ing /ə prṓching/ *adj.* coming near in space or time

ap·proach shot *n.* **1.** TENNIS SHOT HIT DEEP INTO OPPONENT'S COURT a tennis shot hit deep into the opponent's court, designed to give the player time to approach the net for the next shot **2.** GOLF = **approach** *n.* 7

ap·pro·ba·tion /àpprə báyshən/ *n.* **1.** EXPRESSION OF APPROVAL approval, consent, or appreciation **2.** OFFICIAL SANCTION the official approving, authorizing, or sanctioning of something —**ap·pro·ba·tive** /àpprə bàytiv, ə prṓbətiv/ *adj.* —**ap·pro·ba·to·ry** /àpprə báytəree/ *adj.*

ap·pro·pri·a·ble /ə prṓpriəb'l/ *adj.* able or likely to be appropriated

ap·pro·pri·ate *adj.* /ə prṓpree ət/ FITTING suitable for the occasion or circumstances ■ *vt.* /ə prṓpree àyt/ (**-at·ed, -at·ing, -ates**) **1.** TAKE SOMETHING FOR OWN USE to take or use something forcefully or without permission **2.** USE MONEY FOR PARTICULAR PURPOSE to set aside an amount of money for a particular use [15thC. From late Latin *appropriatus*, the past participle of Latin *appropriare* "to make your own," from *propius* "own" (source of English *proper*).] —**ap·pro·pri·ate·ly** *adv.* —**ap·pro·pri·ate·ness** *n.* —**ap·pro·pri·a·tive** /ə prṓpree àytiv/ *adj.* —**ap·pro·pri·a·tor** /-àytər/ *n.*

ap·pro·pri·a·tion /əprṑpree áysh'n/ *n.* **1.** TAKING SOMETHING FOR OWN USE the taking or using of something forcefully or without permission **2.** MONEY FOR PARTICULAR PURPOSE a sum of money that has been set aside from a budget, especially a government budget, for a particular purpose (*often used in the plural*)

ap·prov·al /ə pro͞ov'l/ *n.* **1.** GOOD OPINION a favorable opinion or feeling about something **2.** OFFICIAL SANCTION formal or official agreement or permission ◇ **on approval** with the opportunity to try something before deciding whether you really want to buy it

ap·prove /ə pro͞ov/ (**-proved, -prov·ing, -proves**) *v.* **1.** *vi.* LIKE SOMEBODY OR SOMETHING to have a favorable opinion of somebody or something **2.** *vt.* GIVE SOMETHING OFFICIAL AGREEMENT OR ACCEPTANCE to agree officially to something, or accept that something has reached a required standard **3.** *vt.* **PROVE SOMETHING** to prove something by trial or testing (*archaic*) [14thC. Via Old French from Latin *approbare* "to assent to as good," from *probus* "good" (source of English *probity*).] —**ap·prov·a·ble** *adj.*

ap·proved /ə pro͞ovd/ *adj.* **1. GENERALLY ACCEPTED** accepted by most people as appropriate or correct **2. OFFICIALLY SANCTIONED** officially accepted or permitted

ap·prox. *abbr.* **1.** approximately **2.** approximate

ap·prox·i·mal /ə próksim'l/ *adj.* used to describe, or relating to, teeth that are side by side or set close together

ap·prox·i·mate *adj.* /ə próksəmət/ **1. NEARLY EXACT** not quite exact, but only slightly more or less in number or quantity **2. SIMILAR** similar in nature, appearance, or characteristics to something else ■ *v.* /ə próksə màyt/ (**-mat·ed, -mat·ing, -mates**) **1.** *vti.* **BE SIMILAR TO SOMETHING** to be or become similar to something in nature, size, or extent **2.** *vt.* **ESTIMATE SOMETHING** to make or provide an estimate, usually a rough estimate, of something **3.** *vti.* **COME OR BRING CLOSE** to come or bring something close to something else [15thC. From late Latin *approximatus*, the past participle of *approximare* "to draw near to," from Latin *proximus* "near" (source of English *proximity*).] —**ap·prox·i·mate·ness** *n.*

ap·prox·i·mate·ly /ə próksəmətlee/ *adv.* not exactly, but nearly or roughly

ap·prox·i·ma·tion /ə pròksə máysh'n/ *n.* **1. ROUGH CALCULATION** a figure that is not exact, but is only slightly higher or lower than a given amount **2. SIMILAR THING** something that is very similar to something else **3. ESTIMATION** the guessing or estimating of an amount or number ○ *figures arrived at by approximation*

appt. *abbr.* appointment

ap·pulse /ə púlss/ *n.* a near approach of two celestial bodies that does not result in a partial concealment or an eclipse [Early 17thC. From Latin *appulsus*, the past participle of *appellere* "to drive to, force toward," from *pellere* "to drive."]

ap·pur·te·nance /ə púrt'nənss/ *n.* **1. ACCESSORY** an accompanying part or feature of something (*formal*) (*often used in the plural*) ○ *an athletic club with all the usual appurtenances* **2.** LAW **MINOR RIGHT** a legal right or privilege attached to a property and inherited with it ■ **ap·pur·te·nan·ces** *npl.* **EQUIPMENT** the equipment needed for a particular activity (*formal*) [14thC. Via Anglo-French from, ultimately, late Latin *appertinere* (see APPERTAIN).] —**ap·pur·te·nant** *adj.*

APR *abbr.* annual percentage rate

Apr., Apr *abbr.* April

a·prax·i·a /ay práksee ə/ *n.* loss of the ability to perform complex movements, often as a result of brain damage, e.g., following a stroke [Late 19thC. Via German from Greek, "inaction."] —**a·prax·ic** /ay práksik/ *adj.*

a·près-ski /aà pray skée/ *n.* **SOCIALIZING AFTER SKIING** social activities taking place after skiing ■ *adj.* **AFTER SKIING** taking place during or appropriate to the period of time after skiing [Mid-20thC. From French, literally "after skiing."]

Apricot

a·pri·cot /áppri kòt, áy-/ *n.* **1. FRUIT** a small round fruit with a soft furry yellowish orange skin and a single pit **2. FRUIT TREE** a tree widely cultivated in temperate climates for its small yellowish orange fruits. Latin name: *Prunus armeniaca.* **3. YELLOWISH-ORANGE COLOR** a pale yellowish-orange color, like that of an apricot ■ *adj.* **YELLOWISH ORANGE** of a pale yellowish-orange color, like an apricot [Mid-16thC. Via obsolete Catalan *abrecoc* from Arabic *al-barqūq*, literally "the apricot."]

WORD KEY: ORIGIN

The *apricot* got its name because the Romans regarded it as a type of early-ripening peach. They therefore applied to it the epithet *praecocus* (a variant of *praecox*, from which English gets *precocious*). This passed via Byzantine Greek *berikokkia* into Arabic where, with the definite article *al*, it became *al-birqūq* or *al-barqūq*. Catalan adopted this as *abrecoc*, which is how English acquired the word (the earliest recorded English spelling is *abrecock*). The final *-t* came soon after, from French.

A·pril /áyprəl/ *n.* in the Gregorian calendar, the fourth month of the year, made up of 30 days [14thC. From Latin *Aprilis*, from Etruscan *apru*, from Greek *Aphrō*, a shortening of *Aphroditē* (see APHRODITE).]

A·pril fool *n.* **1. TARGET OF JOKE** somebody who is the victim of a practical joke on April Fools' Day **2. JOKE PLAYED ON SOMEBODY** a practical joke played on somebody on April Fools' Day ■ *interj.* **ANNOUNCING THAT JOKE HAS BEEN PLAYED** used to tell somebody that he or she has been the victim of an April Fools' Day joke

A·pril Fools' Day *n.* April 1, traditionally a day on which people play practical jokes on other people

a pri·o·ri /aà pree áwree, ày prī áwrī/ *adj.* **1. BASED ON SOMETHING KNOWN** working from something that is already known or self-evident to arrive at a conclusion **2. ASSUMED** known or assumed without reference to experience **3. MADE BEFOREHAND** conceived or formulated before investigation or experience [Mid-17thC. From Latin, literally "from the previous (one, cause, hypothesis)."] —**a pri·o·ri** *adv.* —**a·pri·or·i·ty** /aà pree áwrətee/ *n.*

a·pron /áyprən/ *n.* **1. PROTECTIVE GARMENT TIED OVER CLOTHES** a garment worn over the front of clothes to keep them clean during working, especially cooking. An apron is usually tied around the waist and often has a bib to cover the chest. **2.** TECH **PROTECTIVE PART** a shield or plate attached to a machine that protects the user from flying debris **3. PROJECTING EDGE** the projecting edge of a platform, e.g., a theater stage, dock, or loading bay **4.** AIR **PAVED AREA AT AIRPORT** the paved area immediately in front of airport buildings, on which aircraft are loaded and unloaded **5.** GOLF **BORDER AROUND GREEN** the outer edge of a green on a golf course **6.** BOXING **AREA OUTSIDE BOXING RING ROPES** the part of the floor of a boxing ring that is outside the ropes **7.** GEOG **LOW-ANGLED SURFACE** a gently sloping surface of sand, gravel, or bare rock, usually in front of a mountain range **8.** INDUST **CONVEYOR BELT MADE OF SLATS** a conveyor belt made of slats loosely attached to each other in a way that allows the belt to go around curves **9.** TRANSP = **skirt** *n.* 7 [14thC. From Old French *naperon*, literally "small cloth," from *nape* "tablecloth," from Latin *mappa* "napkin" (source of English *napkin*). The original phrase "a napron" was later construed as "an apron."]

a·pron stage *n.* a stage that juts out into the auditorium

ap·ro·pos /àpprə pṓ/ *adj.* **JUST RIGHT** appropriate in a particular situation (*formal*) ■ *prep.* **IN REGARD TO** on the subject of (*formal*) ○ *We've had further correspondence from them apropos our application for funds.* ■ *adv.* **INCIDENTALLY** by the way (*formal*) ○ *Apropos, do you think we should delay the announcement?* [Mid-17thC. From French *à propos*, literally "to the purpose," a translation of Latin *ad propositum*.]

a·pro·tic /ay prṓtik/ *adj.* used to describe a solvent that is unable to donate protons [Mid-20thC. Coined from A- + PROTON + -IC.]

apse /aps/ *n.* **1.** ARCHIT **ROUNDED PROJECTION ON BUILDING** a semicircular projecting part of a building, especially the east end of a church that contains the altar **2.** ASTRON = **apsis** [Early 19thC. From Latin *apsis* (see APSIS).] —**ap·si·dal** /ápsid'l/ *adj.*

ap·sis /ápsiss/ (*plural* **-si·des** /-deez/) *n.* **1.** ASTRON **NEAREST OR FARTHEST POINT IN ORBIT** either of the two points in an orbit that are nearest to and farthest from the center of gravitational attraction **2.** ARCHIT = **apse** [Late 16thC. Via Latin from Greek *(h)apsis* "rim of a wheel, wheel, arch, vault," perhaps from *haptein* "to fasten."] —**ap·si·dal** *adj.*

apt /apt/ *adj.* **1. VERY APPROPRIATE** especially suited to the circumstances **2. LIKELY** often doing something and likely to do it again **3. QUICK TO LEARN** enthusiastic and quick to learn new things [14thC. Directly or via Old French from Latin *aptus*, past participle of *apere* "to fit, fasten, join."] —**apt·ly** *adv.* —**apt·ness** *n.*

WORD KEY: USAGE

See Usage note at ***likely.***

WORD KEY: ORIGIN

The Latin word *apere* from which ***apt*** is derived is also the source of English *adapt, adept, attitude, copulate, couple,* and *inept.*

apt. *abbr.* apartment

ap·ter·al /áptərəl/ *adj.* **1. WITHOUT COLUMNS** used to describe a classical temple that has no columns along its sides **2. WITHOUT AISLES** used to describe a church that has no aisles [Mid-19thC. Formed from Greek *apteros* "wingless," from *pteron* "wing, feather" (source of English *pterodactyl*).]

ap·ter·ous /áptərəss/ *adj.* used to describe an insect that has no wings [Late 18thC. Formed from Greek *apteros* (see APTERAL).]

ap·ter·yx /áptəriks/ *n.* = **kiwi** [Early 19thC. From modern Latin, coined from Greek *a-* "without" + *pterux* "wing."]

ap·ti·tude /ápti to͞od/ *n.* **1. POTENTIAL TO ACQUIRE SKILL** a natural talent or ability for something, especially one that is not yet fully developed **2. QUICKNESS IN LEARNING** quickness and ease in learning

WORD KEY: SYNONYMS

See Synonyms at ***ability*** and ***talent.***

ap·ti·tude test *n.* a test to determine how readily somebody is likely to be able to develop certain skills, especially in order to do a particular kind of work

APWU *abbr.* American Postal Workers Union

ap·y·rase /áppə ràyss, -ràyz/ *n.* an enzyme that aids the breakdown of ATP, yielding phosphate and energy [Mid-20thC. Contraction of ADENYLPYROPHOSPHATASE, its chemical name.]

ap·y·rex·i·a /ày prī réksee ə, àppə-/ *n.* absence of fever, or a period during which a patient experiences no fever [Mid-17thC. Via modern Latin from Greek *apurexia*.] —**ap·y·ret·ic** /àyprī réttik, àppə-/ *adj.* —**ap·y·rex·i·al** *adj.*

AQ *abbr.* EDUC achievement quotient

aq. *abbr.* **1.** aqua **2.** GEOL aqueous

A·qa·ba, Gulf of /aákəbə/ northeastern arm of the Red Sea, bordered by Egypt's Sinai Peninsula on the east, Israel on the north, and Saudi Arabia on the west. It is of great strategic importance in the Middle East, as it provides Israel with its only access to the Red Sea. Length: 100 mi./160 km.

Aq·mo·la /aak móllə, -máwlə/ former name for **Astana**

aqua /aákwə, ák-/ *n.* (*plural* **aq·uae** /aákwee, ák-, aák wī, ák-/ *or* **aq·uas**) **1. WATER** water, especially when used as a solvent (*technical*) **2.** = **aquamarine** ■ *adj.* = **aquamarine** [14thC. From Latin. Ultimately from an Indo-European base that is also the source of the "i" in *island.*]

aqua- *prefix.* water ○ *aquanaut* [From Latin *aqua* (see AQUA)]

aq·ua·crop /ákwə krop/ *n.* a crop produced by deliberate cultivation of organisms that live in the sea or fresh water, e.g., fish produced by fish-farming [Late 20thC. Coined from AQUACULTURE + CROP.]

aq·ua·cul·ture /aákwə kùlchər, ákwə-/, **aq·ui·cul·ture** /aákwi-, ákwi-/ *n.* **1. FARMING FISH AND AQUATIC PLANTS** the farming of marine and freshwater plants and animals for human consumption **2.** = **hydroponics** [Mid-19thC. Modeled on AGRICULTURE.] —**aq·ua·cul·tur·al** /aákwə kúlchərəl, àkwə-/ *adj.* —**aq·ua·cul·tur·ist** *n.*

aq·ua·dy·na·mic /àkwə dī námmik/ *adj.* having a smooth or streamlined surface in order to reduce drag when passing through water [Late 20thC. Modeled on AERODYNAMIC.]

aq·uae plural of **aqua**

aq·ua for·tis /-fáwrtiss/ *n.* nitric acid (*archaic*) [15thC. From Latin, literally "strong water."]

Aq·ua-Lung *tdmk.* a trademark for an underwater breathing apparatus used by divers

aq·ua·ma·rine /aákwə mə réen, àk-/ *n.* **1. GREENISH-BLUE GEMSTONE** a greenish-blue variety of the mineral beryl, used as a gemstone **2. GREENISH BLUE** a greenish-blue color ■ *adj.* **GREENISH-BLUE** of a greenish-blue color [Late 16thC. From Latin *aqua marina* "sea water" (the color of the stone).]

aq·ua·naut /aákwə nàwt, ák-/ *n.* somebody with training and equipment to spend long periods working or swimming underwater [Late 19thC. Coined from AQUA- + Greek *nautēs* "sailor," on the model of ARGONAUT.]

aq·ua·pho·bi·a /áakwə fṓbee ə, àk-/ *n.* an abnormal fear of water

aq·ua·plane /áakwə plàyn, ák-/ *n.* **WATER-SKIING BOARD** a water-skiing board on which somebody stands while being towed by a motorboat ■ *vi.* **(-planed, -plan·ing, -planes) 1. RIDE ON AN AQUAPLANE** to ride on an aquaplane **2.** *U.K.* = **hydroplane**

aq·ua re·gi·a /àkwə reéjee ə, àkwə reéjə/ *n.* a fuming, highly corrosive mixture of nitric and hydrochloric acid that is used to dissolve metals, including gold [Early 17thC. From Latin, literally "royal water," so called because it can dissolve gold and other "noble" metals.]

aq·ua·relle /áakwə rél, àk-/ *n.* **1. WATERCOLOR PAINTING TECHNIQUE** a painting technique that uses transparent washes of watercolor **2. PAINTED PICTURE** a painting produced using the aquarelle technique [Mid-19thC. Via French from obsolete Italian *acquarella* "watercolor," from *acqua* "water."] —**aq·ua·rel·list** *n.*

a·quar·i·a plural of **aquarium**

A·quar·i·an /ə kwáiree ən/ *n.* = **Aquarius** *n.* 3 —**A·quar·i·an** *adj.*

a·quar·ist /ə kwáirist/ *n.* somebody who takes care of an aquarium as a hobby or a profession

a·quar·i·um /ə kwáiree əm/ (*plural* **-ums** *or* **-a** /-ə/) *n.* **1. CONTAINER FOR FISH** a water-filled transparent container, often box-shaped, in which fish and other aquatic animals and plants are kept **2. AQUATIC ZOO** a building in which fish and other aquatic animals are kept and shown to the public [Mid-19thC. Formed from Latin *aquarius* (see AQUARIUS) on the model of VIVARIUM.]

A·quar·i·us /ə kwáiree əss/ *n.* **1.** ASTRON **CONSTELLATION IN SOUTHERN HEMISPHERE** a constellation in the sky of the southern hemisphere between Pisces and Capricornus **2.** ZODIAC **11TH SIGN OF ZODIAC** the 11th sign of the zodiac, represented by a man pouring water, and lasting from approximately January 20 to February 18. Aquarius is classified as an air sign and its ruling planets are Saturn and Uranus. **3.** ZODIAC **SOMEBODY BORN UNDER AQUARIUS** somebody whose birthday falls between January 20 and February 18 [14thC. From Latin, "water carrier," a noun use of *aquarius* "of water," from *aqua* (see AQUA).] —**A·quar·i·us** *adj.*

aq·ua·ro·bics /àkwə rṓbiks/ *n.* aerobic exercises done to music in a swimming pool (*takes a singular or plural verb*) [Late 20thC. Blend of AQUA- and AEROBICS.]

a·quat·ic /ə kwáatik/ *adj.* **1. OF WATER** connected with, consisting of, or dependent upon water **2. LIVING IN WATER** living or growing in water **3. DONE IN WATER** played or performed in or on water ■ *n.* **WATER PLANT OR ANIMAL** a plant or animal that lives or grows in water —**a·quat·i·cal·ly** *adv.*

a·quat·ics /ə kwáatiks/ *n.* sports played in or on water (*takes a singular or plural verb*)

aq·ua·tint /áakwə tìnt, ák-/ *n.* **1. ETCHING METHOD** a method of etching a copper plate in which the prints produced from it show areas similar to watercolors. This effect is produced by varying the etching times used for different areas of the plate. **2. ETCHED PICTURE** an etching produced by the aquatint process [Late 18thC. Via French *aquatinte* from Italian *acquatinta*, literally "tinted water."] —**aq·ua·tint·er** *n.* —**aq·ua·tint·ist** *n.*

a·qua·vit /áakwə veèt, ákwə-/ *n.* a potato- or grain-based liquor flavored with caraway seeds, produced in Scandinavia [Late 19thC. Via Danish, Norwegian, Swedish *aquavit* from Latin *aqua vitae* (see AQUA VITAE).]

aq·ua vi·tae /ákwə vítee/ *n.* a strong liquor, especially brandy [14thC. From Latin, literally "water of life."]

aq·ue·duct /áakwə dùkt, ák-/ *n.* **1. CHANNEL FOR WATER** a pipe or channel for moving water to a lower level, often across a great distance **2. STRUCTURE CARRYING CANAL** a structure in the form of a bridge that carries a canal across a valley or river **3.** ANAT **CHANNEL CARRYING FLUID IN BODY** a channel in an organ or body part through which fluid passes [Mid-16thC. Via medieval Latin *aqueductus*, from Latin *aquae ductus* "water conveyance."]

a·que·ous /áykwee əss, ákwee-/ *adj.* **1. WATERY** containing, dissolved in, or consisting mostly of water **2.** GEOL **FORMED FROM MATERIAL CARRIED BY WATER** used to describe rocks or deposits that are formed from material carried by water [Mid-17thC. From medieval Latin *aqueus*, from Latin *aqua* (see AQUA).]

Aqueduct: Ancient Roman aqueduct in Tarragona, Spain

a·que·ous hu·mor *n.* the transparent fluid that circulates in the eye chamber between the back of the cornea and the front of the iris and pupil. It also permeates the vitreous humor behind the lens.

aqui- *prefix.* water ○ *aquifer* [From Latin *aqua* (see AQUA)]

aq·ui·cul·ture *n.* = **aquaculture**

aq·ui·fer /ákwifər/ *n.* a layer of permeable rock, sand, or gravel through which groundwater flows, containing enough water to supply wells and springs

aq·ui·line /ákwi l-n/ *adj.* **1. THIN AND CURVED** thin, curved, and pointed like an eagle's beak **2. OF EAGLES** resembling or connected with eagles [Mid-17thC. From Latin *aquilinus*, from *aquila* "eagle."] —**aq·ui·lin·i·ty** /àkwi línnitee/ *n.*

A·qui·no /ə keé nō/, **Corazon** (*b.* 1933) Filipino government leader. She was president of the Philippines (1986–92) after the uprising against Ferdinand Marcos.

Aq·ui·taine /ákwi tàyn/ region of France, situated in the southwest. It includes the departments of Dordogne, Gironde, Landes, Lot-et-Garonne, and Pyrénées-Atlantiques. It corresponds roughly to the same as the Roman administrative region of Aquitania. Capital: Bordeaux. Population: 2,795,800 (1990). Area: 15,949 sq. mi./41,308 sq. km.

a·quiv·er /ə kwívvər/ *adj.* quivering, especially from excitement or agitation

Ar *symbol.* argon

AR *abbr.* Arkansas

ar. *abbr.* **1.** arrival **2.** arrive

Ar. *abbr.* Arabia ■ *abbr.* **1.** Arabian **2.** Arabic

-ar *suffix.* of, relating to, or resembling ○ *nebular* [Via Old French *-ar* from Latin *-aris*, an alternative for *-alis*]

Ar·ab /árrəb/ *n.* **MEMBER OF SEMITIC PEOPLE** a member of a Semitic Arabic-speaking people who live throughout North Africa and the Middle East ■ *adj.* = **Arabian** [14thC. Via Old French and Latin from the Greek stem *Arab-* from Arabic *arab*.]

WORD KEY: USAGE

Arab, Arabic, Arabian ***Arab*** denotes a person, and is also used attributively (i.e. before a noun) as a kind of adjective (*the Arab people, Arab fears*). ***Arabian*** is an adjective referring to Arabia in geographical terms (*the Arabian peninsula , an Arabian camel*); and ***Arabic*** is a noun and adjective meaning the language (*She speaks Arabic and knows Arabic literature*). ***Arabic*** is written with a capital initial letter in ***Arabic numerals*** (1, 2, 3, etc.), and with a small initial letter in the term **gum arabic**, a substance obtained from African acacia trees.

Ar·ab. *abbr.* Arabia ■ *abbr.* **1.** Arabian **2.** Arabic

ar·a·besque /àrrə bésk/ *n.* **1.** DANCE **BALLET POSTURE** a ballet position in which the dancer stands on one leg with the other extended back and both arms stretched out, usually one forward and the other backward **2.** ARTS **ORNATE DESIGN** an intricate and often symmetrical design, or style of design, incorporating curves, geometric patterns, leaves, flowers, and animal shapes **3.** MUSIC **MUSIC WITH ORNATE MELODY** a piece of classical music characterized by decorative melody. The term is often applied to 19th-century compositions for solo piano. [Early 17thC. Via French from Italian *arabesco* "in the Arabian style."]

A·ra·bi·a /ə ráybiə/ peninsula of southwestern Asia, bordering the Persian Gulf, the Arabian Sea, and the Red Sea. Area: 1,160,000 sq. mi./3,000,000 sq. km.

A·ra·bi·an /ə ráybee ən/ *adj.* **OF ARABIA** relating to or typical of Arabia, or its peoples or cultures ■ *n.* **1. SOMEBODY FROM ARABIA** somebody who was born or raised in one of the countries of the Arabian Peninsula **2.** = **Arabian horse**

WORD KEY: USAGE

See Usage note at ***Arab***.

A·ra·bi·an cam·el *n.* = **dromedary**

A·ra·bi·an horse *n.* a horse belonging to a breed native to Arabia and known for its intelligence, graceful build, and speed

A·ra·bi·an Pen·in·su·la = **Arabia**

A·ra·bi·an Sea part of the Indian Ocean, extending from the Arabian Peninsula to the Indian subcontinent

Ar·a·bic /árrəbik/ *n.* **SEMITIC LANGUAGE OF MIDDLE EAST** a Semitic language that is the official language of several countries of North Africa and the Middle East. It is spoken by about 150 million people, with around a further 175 million using it as a second language. ■ *adj.* **1. OF ARABIA** relating to or typical of Arabia, or its people or culture **2. OF ARABIC** relating or belonging to the Arabic language

WORD KEY: USAGE

See Usage note at ***Arab***.

a·rab·i·ca /ə rábbikə/ *n.* **1.** PLANTS **COFFEE SPECIES** a widely grown species of coffee bush producing high-quality coffee. Latin name: *Coffea arabica*. **2. KIND OF STRONG FLAVORED COFFEE** coffee made with arabica coffee beans [Early 20thC. From modern Latin, species name, "Arabic."]

Ar·a·bic nu·mer·al *n.* any of the symbols 0, 1, 2, 3, 4, 5, 6, 7, 8, and 9 that are used to represent numbers

a·rab·i·nose /ə rábbi n-ss, árrəbi n-ss/ *n.* a sugar (**aldose**) derived from various plant gums and used in culturing. Formula: $C_5H_{10}O_5$. [Late 19thC. Coined from GUM ARABIC + -IN + -OSE.]

Ar·ab·ist /árrəbist/ *n.* **1. EXPERT ON ARABS** a student of or expert on the Arabs, their language, or their culture **2. SUPPORTER OF ARABS** somebody who favors Arab causes or political positions

ar·a·ble /árrəb'l/ *adj.* **SUITABLE FOR GROWING CROPS** capable of being cultivated for growing crops ■ *n.* *U.K.* **LAND SUITABLE FOR CULTIVATION** land that is fit for planting crops [15thC. Via Old French from Latin *arabilis*, from *arare* "to plough."] —**ar·a·bil·i·ty** /àrrə bíllətee/ *n.*

Ar·ab League *n.* a political and economic association of Arab states, formed in 1945

ar·a·chi·don·ic ac·id /àrrəki dónnik-/ *n.* an unsaturated fatty acid found in most animal fats and considered essential in human nutrition. Formula: $C_{20}H_{32}O_2$. [Early 20thC. "Arachidonic" coined from the modern Latin stem *arachid-* "peanut" (from Greek *arakhos* "type of leguminous plant") + -ONE + -IC.]

a·rach·nid /ə ráknid/ *n.* a member of a large class of animals that includes spiders, scorpions, and mites. Arachnids have four pairs of legs and a body with two segments. Class: Arachnida. [Mid-19thC. From modern Latin *Arachnida*, class name, from Greek *arakhnē* "spider."] —**a·rach·ni·dan** *adj.*

a·rach·noid /ə rák nòyd/ *n.* **1.** ANAT **MEMBRANE IN SPINAL CORD** the middle of the three membranes that envelop the brain and spinal cord **2.** ZOOL = **arachnid** ■ *adj.* ZOOL **LIKE AN ARACHNID** resembling or related to an arachnid [Mid-18thC. Via modern Latin from Greek *arakhnoeidēs* "cobweblike," from *arakhnē* (see ARACHNID).]

a·rach·nol·o·gy /ə ràk nóllәjee/ *n.* the branch of zoology concerned with the study of spiders and other arachnids [Mid-19thC. Coined from Greek *arakhnē* "spider" + -LOGY.] —**a·rach·nol·o·gist** *n.*

a·rach·no·pho·bi·a /ə ràknə fṓbee ə/ *n.* an abnormally strong fear of spiders [Early 20thC. Coined from Greek *arakhnē* "spider" + -PHOBIA.] —**a·rach·no·phobe** *n.* —**a·rach·no·pho·bic** *adj.*

Ar·a·fat /érrə fàt/, **Yasir** (*b.* 1929) Palestinian leader. He became chairman of the Palestine Liberation Organization (1968) and shared the 1994 Nobel Peace Prize with Itzhak Rabin.

A·ra·fu·ra Sea /èrrə foórə-/ area of the Pacific Ocean between the northern coast of Australia, New Guinea, and eastern Indonesia

a·rag·o·nite /ə rággə n-t/ *n.* a colorless, blue to violet, or yellow mineral consisting of calcium carbonate. Formula: $CaCO_3$. [Late 18thC. Named for *Aragon*, the region in northeastern Spain where it was first found.]

Barnaby's
Yasir Arafat

A·ra·ka·wa Shu·sa·ku /aarə ka̋awə shoo sa̋akoo/ (*b.* 1936) Japanese artist whose Western-style paintings influenced early conceptual art. He moved to the United States in 1961.

a·ra·li·a /ə ráylee ə/ (*plural* **-as** *or* **-a**) *n.* a plant widely grown as a houseplant for its ornamental leaves. Genera: *Aralia* and *Polyscias.* [Mid-18thC. From modern Latin, genus name.]

Ar·al Sea /àrrəl-/ inland sea straddling the Kazakhstan-Uzbekistan border in western Asia, east of the Caspian Sea. Area: 25,660 sq. mi./66,458 sq. km. Depth: maximum 223 ft./68 m.

Ar·a·ma·ic /àrrə máy ik/ *n.* a major language of the ancient Near East, dating from about 300 B.C. and still spoken in parts of Syria, Iraq, Iran, and other countries. It belongs to the Semitic group of languages and is spoken by between 50,000 and 100,000 people. [Mid-19thC. Formed from Greek *Aramaios* "of Aram" (the Biblical name for ancient Syria).] —**Ar·a·ma·ic** *adj.*

Ar·an Is·lands /àrrən-/ group of three islands, Inishmoor, Inishmaan, and Inisheer, situated at the mouth of Galway Bay in western Ireland. Population: 803 (1981). Area: 18 sq. mi./47 sq. km.

A·rap·a·ho /ə ráppə h-/ (*plural* **-ho** *or* **-hos**), **A·rap·a·hoe** (*plural* **-hoe** *or* **-hoes**) *n.* **1.** PEOPLES **MEMBER OF NATIVE AMERICAN PEOPLE** a member of a North American people who originally lived by hunting buffalo on the Great Plains, and who now live mainly in Colorado, Wyoming, and Montana **2.** LANG **ALGONQUIAN LANGUAGE** a North American language of the Algonquian family of languages. Arapaho is spoken by about 1,500 people. [Early 19thC. From Crow *alappahó*, literally "many tattoo marks."] —**A·rap·a·ho** *adj.*

Ar·a·rat, Mount /árrə ràt/ mountain in eastern Turkey, which rises in two peaks, Great Ararat 16,854 ft./5,137 m and Little Ararat 12,840 ft./3,914 m. According to the Bible, it is the landing place of Noah's Ark.

Ar·au·ca·ni·an /àrraw káynee ən/ *n.* **1.** PEOPLES **MEMBER OF NATIVE AMERICAN PEOPLE** a member of a South American people who live in central Chile and areas of western Argentina **2.** LANG **SOUTH AMERICAN LANGUAGE** a South American language spoken in parts of Chile and western Argentina. Araucanian is spoken by about 300,000 people. [Early 19thC. Formed from Spanish *Araucanía*, a region of Chile.] —**Ar·au·ca·ni·an** *adj.*

ar·au·car·i·a /à raw káiriə/ (*plural* **-as** *or* **-a**) *n.* a coniferous tree that is native to the southern hemisphere but widely grown elsewhere. Norfolk Island pine and monkey puzzle are types of araucaria. Genus: *Araucaria.* [Mid-19thC. From modern Latin, genus name, coined from *Arauco*, a province in central Chile.]

Ar·a·wak /árrə wàwk/ (*plural* **-wak** *or* **-waks**) *n.* **1.** PEOPLES **MEMBER OF SOUTH AMERICAN PEOPLE** a member of a South American people who live mainly on the coast of Guyana, but also in parts of Surinam and French Guiana **2.** LANG **ARAWAKAN LANGUAGE** a South American language of the Arawakan family, spoken in Guyana and neighboring countries [Mid-18thC. From Carib *aruac.*]

Ar·a·wa·kan /àrrə wáwkən/ (*plural* **-kan** *or* **-kans**) *n.* **1.** PEOPLES **MEMBER OF NATIVE AMERICAN PEOPLE** a member of a Native American people who live throughout South America and the West Indies **2.** LANG **SOUTH AMERICAN LANGUAGE FAMILY** a family of languages that includes Guajiro, spoken by widely scattered communities in Central and South America. About 300,000 people speak an Arawakan language. —**Ar·a·wa·kan** *adj.*

arb /aarb/ *n.* = **arbitrageur** (*slang*) [Late 20thC. Shortening.]

ar·ba·lest /a̋arbələst/, **ar·ba·list** *n.* a large medieval crossbow used to propel stones, arrows, and other missiles, often by mechanical means [Pre-12thC. Via Old French *arbaleste* from late Latin *arcuballista*, from *arcus* "bow" + *ballista* (see BALLISTA).] —**ar·ba·lest·er** *n.*

Ar·benz Guz·man /a̋arbənz go͝ozmən/, **Jacobo** (1913–71) Guatemalan politician. He was president of Guatemala from 1950 until 1954, when he was ousted during a coup.

ar·bi·ter /a̋arbətər/ *n.* **1.** **SOMEBODY MAKING JUDGMENT** somebody who has the power and authority to settle a dispute or decide an issue **2.** **INFLUENTIAL PERSON OR THING** somebody or something with great influence over what people say, think, or do [14thC. Directly or via Old French *arbitre* from Latin *arbiter* "judge, umpire."]

ar·bi·tra·ble /a̋arbitrəb'l/ *adj.* able to be settled, or likely to be best settled, by arbitration

ar·bi·trage /a̋arbə traazh/ *n.* **SIMULTANEOUS BUYING AND SELLING** the simultaneous buying and selling of the same negotiables or commodities in different markets in order to make an immediate riskless profit ■ *vi.* (**-traged, -trag·ing, -trages**) **ENGAGE IN ARBITRAGE** to participate in arbitrage [Mid-19thC. From French, formed from *arbitrer* "to judge," from Latin *arbitrari* (see ARBITRATE).]

ar·bi·tra·geur /a̋arbi traa zhúr/ *n.* somebody who engages in arbitrage [Mid-19thC. From French.]

ar·bi·tral /a̋arbətrəl/ *adj.* relating to arbiters or arbitration, or arising from the intervention of an arbitrator

ar·bi·trar·y /a̋arbə trèrree/ *adj.* **1.** **BASED ON PERSONAL WHIM** based solely on personal wishes, feelings, or perceptions, rather than on objective facts, reasons, or principles **2.** **RANDOMLY CHOSEN** chosen or determined at random **3.** LAW **NOT ACCORDING TO RULE** based on the decision of a particular judge or court rather than accordance with any rule or law **4.** **AUTHORITARIAN** with unlimited power **5.** MATH **ASSIGNED NO SPECIFIC VALUE** used to describe a constant that is not assigned a specific value [15thC. From Latin *arbitrarius* "uncertain, depending on the judgment of an arbiter" (a term in Roman law), from *arbiter* "judge" (source of English *arbiter*).] —**ar·bi·trar·i·ly** /a̋arbə trérrəlee/ *adv.* —**ar·bi·trar·i·ness** /-inəss/ *n.*

ar·bi·trate /a̋arbi tràyt/ (**-trat·ed, -trat·ing, -trates**) *v.* **1.** *vti.* **SETTLE DISPUTE BETWEEN OTHERS** to act as a judge in a dispute between others **2.** *vt.* **ASK SOMEBODY TO SETTLE DISPUTE** to submit a dispute to be decided by a third party [Late 16thC. From Latin *arbitrat-*, the past participle stem of *arbitrari* "to judge, decide," from *arbiter* "judge" (source of English *arbiter*).]

ar·bi·tra·tion /a̋arbi tráysh'n/ *n.* the process of resolving disputes between people or groups by referring them to a third party, either agreed on by them or provided by law, who makes a judgment —**ar·bi·tra·tion·al** *adj.*

ar·bi·tra·tor /a̋arbi tràytər/ *n.* somebody designated to hear both sides of a dispute and make a judgment

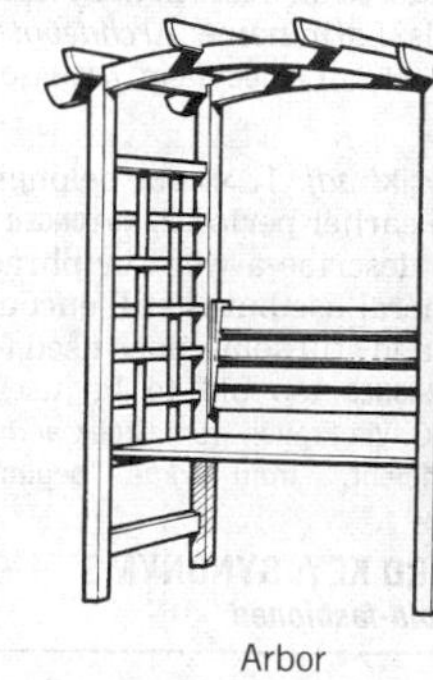
Arbor

ar·bor[1] /a̋arbər/ *n.* **1.** **SHADY PLACE** a shaded place formed by the leaves and branches of trees and plants that interweave naturally or are trained to grow around a trellis **2.** GARDENING a trellis or other structure used to support plants that form an arbor [14thC. Via Old French *(h)erb(i)er* from Latin *herbarium* (see HERBARIUM).]

ar·bor[2] /a̋arbər/ *n.* **1.** **AXLE ON MACHINE OR POWER TOOL** a shaft, axle, or spindle on a machine or a power tool, e.g., a lathe **2.** **SUPPORTING PIECE** a machine part that holds an object being worked on, or the tools being used to work on the object **3.** INDUST **REINFORCING PART OF MOLD** a part that reinforces the core of a mold used to cast metal [Mid-17thC. Via Old French *arbre* from Latin *arbor* "tree, mast, lever, shaft."]

Ar·bor Day *n.* in the United States, a day set aside for the planting and appreciation of trees. It is typically the last Friday in April, but the date varies from state to state.

ar·bo·re·al /aar báwree əl, -bőr-/ *adj.* **1.** **LIVING IN TREES** used to describe a species that lives in trees **2.** **OF TREES** relating to, resembling, or consisting of trees —**ar·bo·re·al·ly** *adv.*

ar·bo·re·ous /aar báwree əss, -bőr-/ *adj.* covered with trees

ar·bo·res·cent /a̋arbə réss'nt/ *adj.* resembling a tree, especially in developing branches or similar parts [Mid-17thC. From Latin *arborescent-*, the present participle stem of *arborescere* "to grow into a tree," from *arbor* "tree."] —**ar·bo·res·cence** *n.*

ar·bo·re·tum /a̋arbə réetəm/ (*plural* **-tums** *or* **-ta** /-tə/) *n.* an area planted with many types of trees for study, display, and preservation [Mid-19thC. From Latin, "place grown with trees, plantation of trees," from *arbor* "tree."]

ar·bo·ri·cul·ture /a̋arbəri kùlchər, aar báwri-/ *n.* the cultivation of trees and shrubs for study, or ornamentation, or profit [Mid-19thC. Blend of ARBOR and AGRICULTURE.] —**ar·bo·ri·cul·tur·al** *adj.* —**ar·bo·ri·cul·tur·ist** *n.*

ar·bor·i·o /aar báwri ō/ (*plural* **-os**), **ar·bor·i·o rice** *n.* a short-grained rice, used to make risotto and other Italian dishes [Late 20thC. From Italian.]

ar·bor·ist /a̋arbərist/ *n.* an expert in the cultivation and care of trees

ar·bo·rize /a̋arbə r-z/ (**-rized, -riz·ing, -riz·es**) *vi.* to develop many branching parts or formations —**ar·bo·ri·za·tion** /a̋arbə ri záyshən/ *n.*

ar·bor·vi·tae /a̋arbər vítee, -véetī/ (*plural* **-taes**), **ar·bor vi·tae** (*plural* **ar·bor vi·taes**) *n.* a coniferous tree of the cypress family with flat closely fitted leaves resembling scales. It is native to Asia and North America and is widely grown as an ornamental. Genus: *Thuja.* [Mid-17thC. From Latin, literally "tree of life."]

ar·bour *n.* U.K. = **arbor**[1]

ar·bo·vi·rus /a̋arbə v-rəss/ *n.* a virus transmitted by bloodsucking arthropods, e.g., ticks and fleas. The viruses that cause encephalitis, yellow fever, and dengue are arboviruses. [Mid-20thC. Contraction of ARTHROPOD-BORNE VIRUS.] —**ar·bo·vi·ral** /a̋arbə vírəl/ *adj.*

Ar·bus /a̋arbəss/, **Diane** (1923–71) U.S. photographer, known for her unconventional and occasionally morbid portraits of unusual characters.

ar·bu·tus /aar byo͞otəss/ (*plural* **-tus·es** *or* **-tus**) *n.* **1.** = **trailing arbutus** **2.** **EUROPEAN SHRUB** a southern European shrub or tree cultivated for its white or pink flowers and reddish fruits. Genus: *Arbutus.* [Mid-16thC. From Latin, "wild strawberry," from the shape of the leaves.]

arc /aark/ *n.* **1.** **CURVE** a curved or semicircular line, direction of movement, or arrangement of items **2.** GEOM **SECTION OF CIRCLE** a section of a circle, ellipse, or other curved figure **3.** ASTRON **VISIBLE PART OF CELESTIAL BODY'S PATH** a section of the path that a planet or other celestial body appears to follow, especially that between rising above the horizon and disappearing below it **4.** ELEC ENG **ELECTRIC DISCHARGE** a luminous discharge caused by an electric current flowing across a gap in an electrical circuit **5.** GEOL = **island arc** ■ *vi.* (**arced, arc·ing, arcs**) **1.** **FORM OR MOVE IN ARC** to form a curve or move along a curved path **2.** ELEC ENG **SPARK ACROSS GAP** to produce a luminous discharge across a gap in an electrical circuit [14thC. Via Old French from Latin *arcus* "bow, curve" (source of English *arch*).]

ARC *abbr.* AIDS-related complex

ar·cade /aar káyd/ *n.* **1.** **AVENUE OF STORES** a covered passage with stores on both sides **2.** **ENCLOSED AREA WITH GAME MACHINES** an enclosed area where people can play on coin-operated game machines such as pinball machines, video games, or slot machines **3.** **PASSAGEWAY WITH ARCHES** a passageway or building with a series of arches and supporting columns **4.** **SERIES OF ARCHES** a series of arches and the columns supporting them [Mid-18thC. Via French from Italian *arcata*, from, ultimately, Latin *arcus* "bow, curve, arch" (source of English *arch*).]

Ar·ca·di·a[1] /aar káydee ə/ *n.* **1. RURAL PARADISE IN CLASSICAL LITERATURE** the imagined rural paradise used as the setting for much Greek and Roman poetry and some Renaissance literature **2. Ar·ca·di·a, ar·ca·di·a IMAGINED PLACE OF RURAL BLISS** a place in which people are imagined or believed to enjoy a perfect life of rustic simplicity [Late 19thC. Via Latin from Greek *Arkadia*, a mountainous district in Peloponnesus.] —**Ar·ca·di·an** *adj.*

Ar·ca·di·a[2] /aar káydee ə/ **1.** mountainous region in the central Peloponnesus in Greece **2.** city in southwestern California, a suburb of Los Angeles. Population: 50,483 (1996). —**Ar·ca·di·an** *adj., n.*

ar·ca·na /aar káynə/ *n.* **TAROT DIVISION** either of two divisions of a pack of tarot cards ■ *npl.* plural of **arcanum**

ar·cane /aar káyn/ *adj.* **1. MYSTERIOUSLY OBSCURE** requiring secret knowledge to be understood **2. HARD TO FATHOM** difficult or impossible to understand [Early 16thC. From Latin *arcanus* (see ARCANUM).] —**ar·cane·ly** *adv.* —**ar·cane·ness** *n.*

WORD KEY: SYNONYMS

See Synonyms at ***obscure***.

ar·ca·num /aar káynəm/ (*plural* **-na** /-nə/) *n.* (*usually used in the plural*) **1. SECRET KNOWN TO FEW** a secret known only to the members of a small select group **2. SECRET OF NATURE** a secret of nature, of the kind that was sought by alchemists [Late 16thC. From Latin, a noun use of the neuter form of *arcanus* "closed, secret," from *arca* "box" (source of English *ark*).]

AKG London

Arc de Triomphe, Paris, France

Arc de Tri·omphe /àark də trée ōNf/ *n.* a triumphal arch at the end of the Avenue des Champs Elysées in Paris, France, completed in 1835. It was commissioned by Napoleon to commemorate military victories, and is now used as a war memorial.

arc fur·nace *n.* a furnace in which an electric arc supplies the heat

arch[1] /aarch/ *n.* **1. CURVED STRUCTURE** a curved structure that forms the upper edge of an open space, e.g., a window, a doorway, or the space between a bridge's supports **2. PASSAGE UNDER ARCH** an entrance or passageway under an arch **3. ARCH SHAPE** the shape of an arch, resembling an inverted U, or an object with such a shape ○ *the arch of his eyebrows* **4. ANAT CURVED BODY PART** a body part with the shape of an arch, especially the bony structure in the foot **5. GEOG CURVED ROCK FORMATION** a naturally occurring arch-shaped span of rock found in arid, especially desert, regions ■ *v.* (**arched, arch·ing, arch·es**) **1.** *vt.* **FORM SOMETHING INTO CURVED SHAPE** to form something into the shape of an arch ○ *Arch your back and let your arms take your weight.* **2.** *vi.* **MOVE IN CURVING LINE** to follow a trajectory in the shape of an arch **3.** *vt.* **CROSS** to extend across something **4.** *vt.* **BUILD SOMETHING IN ARCH SHAPE** to build something in the shape of an arch or with arch-shaped supports [13thC. Via Old French *arche* from, ultimately, Latin *arcus* "bow, curve, arch" (source also of English *arc*).]

arch[2] /aarch/ *adj.* **1. KNOWINGLY PLAYFUL OR MISCHIEVOUS** expressing playfulness, mischief, or shared humor in a knowing way **2. MOST EXTREME** greatest, especially most hostile [Mid-16thC. From ARCH-. The sense "mischievous" developed from its use in such phrases as "arch knave" and "arch wag."] —**arch·ly** *adv.* —**arch·ness** *n.*

arch. *abbr.* **1.** architecture **2.** architect **3.** archaic **4.** archaism **5.** archipelago **6.** archery **7.** archbishop

arch- *prefix.* **1.** chief, most important ○ *archrival* **2.** extreme ○ *archconservative* [Via Old English *ærce-* and Old French *arche* from, ultimately, Greek *arkhi-* "first, chief" (see ARCHI-)]

-arch *suffix.* leader, ruler ○ *matriarch* [Via Old French and late Latin from, ultimately, Greek *arkhos*, from *arkhein* "to rule")] —**-archic** *suffix.* —**-archy** *suffix.*

Ar·chae·an *n., adj.* = **Archean**

ar·chae·bac·te·ri·a /àarki bak téeri ə/ *npl.* members of one of two distinct lines of the most primitive living single-celled organisms —**ar·chae·bac·te·ri·al** *adj.*

archaeo-, **archae-**, **archeo-** *prefix.* ancient ○ *archaeoastronomy* [Via modern Latin from Greek *arkhaios*]

ar·chae·o·as·tron·o·my /àarkee ō ə strónnəmee/, **ar·che·o·as·tron·o·my** *n.* the study of the astronomical beliefs, practices, and discoveries of prehistoric and ancient cultures —**ar·chae·o·as·tron·o·mer** *n.* —**ar·chae·o·as·tro·nom·i·cal** /àarkee ō astrə nómmik'l/ *adj.*

ar·chae·o·bot·a·ny /àarkee ō bótt'nee/, **ar·che·o·bot·a·ny** *n.* the scientific study of excavated plant remains from ancient times —**ar·chae·o·bot·a·nist** *n.*

ar·chae·o·log·i·cal /àarkee ə lójjik'l/, **ar·che·o·log·i·cal, ar·chae·o·log·ic** /-lójjik/, **ar·che·o·log·ic** *adj.* relating to archaeology, or carried out for the purposes of archaeology —**ar·chae·o·log·i·cally** *adv.*

ar·chae·o·lo·gy /àarkee óllәjee/, **ar·che·o·lo·gy** *n.* the scientific study of ancient cultures through the examination of their material remains, e.g., buildings, graves, tools, and other artifacts usually dug up from the ground —**ar·chae·ol·o·gist** *n.*

ar·chae·o·mag·net·ism /àarkee ō mágnətizzəm/, **ar·che·o·mag·net·ism** *n.* a method of dating excavated artifacts by measuring the degree of their magnetization

ar·chae·om·e·try /àarkee ómmətree/, **ar·che·om·e·try** *n.* the systematic dating of archaeological objects —**ar·chae·o·met·ri·cal** /àarkee ə méttrik'l/ *adj.* —**ar·chae·o·met·ri·cal·ly** *adv.* —**ar·chae·om·e·trist** /-ómmətrist/ *n.*

Archaeopteryx

ar·chae·op·ter·yx /àarkee óptəriks/ *n.* an extinct bird of the Jurassic period that had the feathers of modern birds but the jaw and sharp teeth of reptiles. It has been considered an evolutionary link between reptiles and birds. Latin name: *Archaeopteryx lithographica.* [Mid-19thC. Coined from ARCHAEO- + Greek *pterux* "wing."]

ar·cha·ic /aar káy ik/ *adj.* **1. ANCIENT** belonging or relating to a much earlier period **2. NO LONGER IN ORDINARY LANGUAGE** used to describe a word or phrase that is no longer in general use but is still encountered in older literature and still sometimes used for special effect **3. OLD-FASHIONED** too old to be useful or efficient [Mid-19thC. Via French from Greek *arkhaikos*, from *arkhaios* "old, ancient," from *arkhē* "beginning."] —**ar·cha·i·cal·ly** *adv.*

WORD KEY: SYNONYMS

See Synonyms at ***old-fashioned***.

ar·cha·ic smile *n.* a facial expression typical of ancient Greek sculpture, in which the edges of the mouth are upturned but the rest of the face is fairly blank

ar·cha·ism /àarkee ìzzəm/ *n.* **1. OLD FORM** a word, expression, practice, or method from an earlier time that is no longer used **2. USE OF OLD THINGS** the use of expressions, techniques, and fashions from an earlier period [Mid-17thC. Via modern Latin from Greek *arkhaismos*, from *arkhaizein* "to copy the ancients, give an archaic air to," from *arkhaios* (see ARCHAIC).] —**ar·cha·ist** *n.* —**ar·cha·is·tic** /àarkee ístik/ *adj.*

ar·cha·ize /àarkee-z/ (**-ized, -iz·ing, -iz·es**) *vt.* to cause something to seem much older than it is by using old forms or styles —**ar·cha·iz·er** *n.*

arch·an·gel /àark àynjəl/ *n.* **1. PRINCIPAL ANGEL** a chief or principal angel **2. RANK ABOVE ANGEL IN MEDIEVAL CLASSIFICATION** a member of the second-lowest rank in the medieval order of celestial beings, ranking above angels and below principalities **3.** = **angelica** [Pre-12thC. Via Anglo-Norman from, ultimately, ecclesiastical Greek *arkhaggelos*, from Greek *arkhi-* "chief" (see ARCH-) + *aggelos* (see ANGEL).] —**arch·an·gel·ic** /àark an jéllik/ *adj.*

arch·bish·op /aarch bíshəp/ *n.* a bishop of the highest rank, who heads an archdiocese or an ecclesiastical province

arch·bish·op·ric /aarch bíshəprik/ *n.* **1. AREA ARCHBISHOP IS RESPONSIBLE FOR** the area of an archbishop's jurisdiction **2. ARCHBISHOP'S STATUS** the status or term of office of an archbishop [Pre-12thC. From ARCHBISHOP + Old English *rice* "realm."]

archbp. *abbr.* archbishop

arch·con·ser·va·tive /àarch kən súrvətiv/ *n.* somebody who has extremely conservative political views

archd. *abbr.* **1.** archdeacon **2.** archduke

arch·dea·con /aarch déekən/ *n.* a member of the clergy who ranks just below a bishop and assists the bishop with ceremonial and administrative duties —**arch·dea·con·ate** *n.* —**arch·dea·con·ship** /-ship/ *n.*

arch·dea·con·ry /aarch déekənree/ (*plural* **-ries**) *n.* the status or term of office of an archdeacon

arch·di·o·cese /aarch dīəssəss/ *n.* the area for which an archbishop has ecclesiastical responsibility —**arch·di·oc·e·san** /àarch dī óssəssən/ *adj.*

arch·du·cal /aarch dóok'l/ *adj.* relating or belonging to archdukes, archduchesses, or archduchies

arch·duch·ess /àarch dúchəss/ *n.* **1. ARCHDUKE'S WIFE** an archduke's wife or widow **2. AUSTRIAN PRINCESS** a princess of the former Austrian imperial family

arch·duch·y /aarch dúchee/ (*plural* **-ies**) *n.* the land ruled by an archduke or archduchess

arch·duke /aarch dóok/ *n.* a senior duke in some countries. The title was used especially in Austria and granted to the eldest son of the emperor. [Early 16thC. Via Old French *archeduc* from late Latin *archidux*, from *archi-* "chief, first" + *dux* "leader" (source of English *duke*).]

Ar·che·an /aar kée ən/, **Ar·chae·an** *adj.* **1. OF OLDEST ROCK** used to describe the oldest known kinds of rock. They are mostly igneous. **2. OF EARLIEST GEOLOGICAL PERIOD** used to describe the earliest geological period of time, dating from about four billion years ago ■ *n.* **ARCHEAN ERA** the Archean era [Late 19thC. Coined from Greek *arkhaios* "old, ancient" + -AN.]

arched /àarcht/ *adj.* **1. CURVED** with a curved top in the shape of an arch **2. WITH AN ARCH ATTACHED** having or including an arch, e.g., as a support

ar·che·go·ni·a plural of **archegonium**

ar·che·go·ni·ate /àarki gónee ət/ *adj.* **WITH ARCHEGONIA** bearing archegonia ■ *n.* **PLANT WITH ARCHEGONIA** a plant that bears archegonia

ar·che·go·ni·um /àarki gónee əm/ (*plural* **-a** /-ə/) *n.* the female reproductive organ of mosses, ferns, liverworts, and most gymnosperms. It contains a single egg cell. [Mid-19thC. Via modern Latin from Greek *arkhegonos*, from *arkhe-* "chief, first" + *gonos* "people" (source of English *gonad*).] —**ar·che·go·ni·al** *adj.*

arch·en·e·my /àarch énnəmee/ (*plural* **-mies**) *n.* **1. WORST ENEMY** somebody's main or worst enemy **2. arch·en·e·my, Arch·en·e·my SATAN** the Devil

ar·chen·ter·on /aar kéntə ròn, -tərən/ *n.* a digestive cavity in animal embryos that develops into the gut [Late 19thC. Coined from Greek *arkhē* "beginning"+ *enteron* "intestine."] —**ar·chen·ter·ic** *adj.*

archeo- *prefix.* = **archaeo-**

ar·che·o·log·i·cal *adj.* = **archaeological**

ar·che·ol·o·gy *n.* = **archaeology**

arch·er /àarchər/ *n.* somebody who has been trained to use a bow and arrow [13thC. Via Anglo-Norman from Old French *archier*, from, ultimately, Latin *arcus* "bow, curve" (source of English *arch*, *arcade*, and *arc*).]

Arch·er *n.* ZODIAC = **Sagittarius**

arch·er·fish /àarchər fish/ (*plural* **-fish** *or* **-fish·es**) *n.* a freshwater fish of Australia and Southeast Asia that hunts insects by spitting water at them. Family: Toxotidae.

arch·er·y /áarchəree/ *n.* **1. SHOOTING WITH BOW AND ARROW** the activity of shooting with a bow and arrow **2. TROOP OF ARCHERS** a troop of soldiers armed with bows and arrows **3. ARCHERS' WEAPONS** the bows and arrows used by archers

Ar·ches Na·tion·al Park /áarchəz-/ park in south eastern Utah, noted for its natural stone arches, created by erosion. Established as a national monument in 1929, it became a national park in 1971. Area: 73,379 acres/29,695 hectares.

ar·che·spo·ri·um /áarki spáwree əm/ (*plural* **-a** /-ə/) *n.* the tissue that gives rise to spore-producing cells in a sporangium in fungi [Late 19thC. Coined from *arche-*, an alteration of ARCHI- + SPORE + -IUM.]

ar·che·typ·al /áarki tīp'l/ *adj.* **1. TYPICAL** typical of its kind, or providing a perfect example or model of something ○ *the archetypal bachelor* **2. RELATING TO ARCHETYPES** relating to archetypes —**ar·che·typ·al·ly** *adv.*

ar·che·type /áarki tīp/ *n.* **1. TYPICAL SPECIMEN** a typical, ideal, or classic example of something ○ *It was described as an archetype of the interior design of the period.* **2. ORIGINAL MODEL** something that served as the model or pattern for other things of the same type ○ *The film was one of the archetypes of the American Western.* **3.** PSYCHOL **IMAGE FROM COLLECTIVE UNCONSCIOUS** in Jungian psychology, an inherited memory represented in the mind by a universal symbol and observed in dreams and myths **4.** ARTS **RECURRING SYMBOL** an image or symbol that is used repeatedly in art or literature [Mid-16thC. Via Latin *archetypum* from Greek *arkhetupon* "first molded as a model," from *arkhe-* "first, chief" + *tupon* "mold, model."] —**ar·che·typ·ic** /áarki típik/ *adj.* —**ar·che·typ·i·cal** *adj.* —**ar·che·typ·i·cal·ly** /áarki típik'lee, áarkə-/ *adv.*

arch·fiend /áarch féend/ *n.* **1. EXTREMELY WICKED CREATURE** an extremely wicked person or creature **2. arch·fiend, Arch·fiend** SATAN the Devil

archi- *prefix.* **1.** chief, most important ○ *archimage* **2.** primitive, primary ○ *archenteron* [Via French *archi-* from, ultimately, Greek *arkhi-*, from *arkhein* "to be first, rule"]

ar·chi·di·ac·o·nal /áarki dī ákən'l/ *adj.* relating to the work or position of an archdeacon [15thC. Formed from Latin *archidiaconus* (see ARCHDEACON).]

ar·chi·di·ac·o·nate /áarki dī ák'nət, -ákə nayt/ *n.* an archdeacon's position, area of jurisdiction, or term of office [Mid-18thC. Ultimately from Latin *archidiaconus* (see ARCHDEACON).]

Ar·chie /áarchee/ *n.* a database that Internet users can access in order to search for files and programs that they can download using File Transfer Protocol [Late 20thC. Coined from ARCHIVE + -IE, on the model of the male name *Archie.*]

ar·chi·e·pis·co·pal /áarkee ə pískəp'l/ *adj.* relating to archbishops or archdioceses [Early 17thC. Formed from ecclesiastical Latin *archiepiscopus* "archbishop," from ecclesiastical Greek *arkhiepiskopos.*] —**ar·chi·e·pis·co·pal·i·ty** /áarkee ə pískə pálləteе/ *n.* —**ar·chi·e·pis·co·pal·ly** /-pískəpəlee/ *adv.* —**ar·chi·e·pis·co·pate** /-pət/ *n.*

arch·im·age /áarch ímij/ *n.* a powerful magician [Late 16thC. From Greek *arkhimagos* "chief of the magi," from *arkhe-* "first, chief" + *magos* "sorcerer" (see MAGI).]

ar·chi·man·drite /áarkə mán drīt/ *n.* in the Eastern Orthodox Church, a senior priest who heads a monastery or group of monasteries [Mid-17thC. Directly or via French from ecclesiastical Latin *archimandrita*, from ecclesiastical Greek *arkhimandritēs*, from *arkhi-* "first, chief" + *mandra* "enclosure, monastery."]

Ar·chi·me·de·an screw /áarkə mee déeən-/ *n.* an ancient method of raising water using either a large screw inside a sloping tube or a spiral tube curling around a sloping axis. Water is carried upward when the screw or tube is turned. [Named for ARCHIMEDES, who invented it]

Ar·chi·me·des /áarkə meé deez/ (287–212 B.C.) Greek mathematician. He wrote on geometry, arithmetic, and mechanics.

Ar·chi·me·des' prin·ci·ple *n.* the principle stating that an object immersed in a liquid experiences an upward thrust equal to the weight of liquid it displaces. Light objects float because they displace more than their own weight in water, whereas heavy objects sink because they displace less.

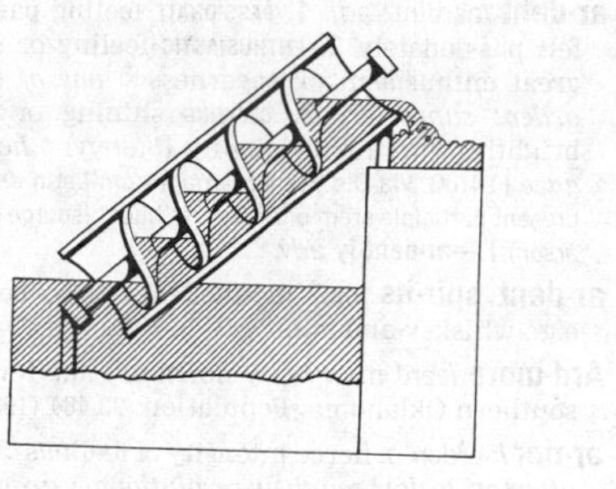

Archimedean screw

Ar·chi·me·des' screw *n.* = **Archimedean screw**

ar·chine /aar shéen/ *n.* a unit of length equal to about 28 in./71 cm, used formerly in Russia and Turkey [Mid-18thC. From Russian.]

ar·chi·pel·a·go /áarkə péllə gō/ (*plural* **-gos** *or* **-goes**) *n.* **1. ISLANDS** a group or chain of islands (*often used in place names*) **2. SEA WITH ISLANDS** an area of sea with many islands [Early 16thC. From Italian *arcipelago*, from Greek *arkhi-* "chief, main" + *pelagos* "sea." First applied to the Aegean Sea.] —**ar·chi·pe·lag·ic** /áarkəpə lájjik/ *adj.*

ar·chit. *abbr.* architecture

ar·chi·tect /áarkə tèkt/ *n.* **1.** ARCHIT **BUILDING DESIGNER** somebody whose job is to design buildings and advise on their construction **2. CREATOR** the person who created or invented something ○ *the architect of her own fortune* [Mid-16thC. Directly or via French and Italian from Latin *architectus*, from Greek *arkhitektōn* "chief builder," from *tektōn* "builder" (source of English *tectonics*).]

ar·chi·tec·ton·ic /áarkə tek táwnik/ *adj.* **1.** ARCHIT **OF ARCHITECTURE OR ARCHITECTURAL QUALITIES** relating to architecture or the qualities, e.g., design and structure, that architecture requires **2.** PHILOS **OF CLASSIFICATION OF KNOWLEDGE** relating to the classification of knowledge used in metaphysics [Mid-17thC. Via Latin from Greek *arkhitektonikos*, from *arkhitektōn* (see ARCHITECT).] —**ar·chi·tec·ton·i·cal·ly** *adv.*

ar·chi·tec·ton·ics /áarkə tek táwniks/ *n.* (*takes a singular verb*) **1.** ARCHIT **SCIENCE OF ARCHITECTURE** the science of architecture **2. STRUCTURAL DESIGN OF COMPLEX THING** the way in which the parts of a complex object or system fit together ○ *the architectonics of a good novel* **3.** PHILOS **CLASSIFICATION OF KNOWLEDGE** in metaphysics, the classification of knowledge

ar·chi·tec·tur·al /áarkə tékchərəl/ *adj.* **1.** ARCHIT **RELATING TO BUILDING DESIGN** relating to the style of buildings or the job of designing them ○ *the architectural merits of the building* **2.** COMPUT **OF COMPUTER SYSTEM DESIGN** relating to the architecture of a computer

ar·chi·tec·tur·al·ly /áarkə tékchərəlee/ *adv.* with regard to architecture as a science or an art, or in a way that involves architecture or its principles ○ *Architecturally, the city is unique.*

ar·chi·tec·ture /áarkə tékchər/ *n.* **1. BUILDING DESIGN** the art and science of designing and constructing buildings **2. BUILDING STYLE** a particular style or fashion of building, especially one that is typical of a period of history or of a particular place **3.** COMPUT **STRUCTURE OF COMPUTER SYSTEM** the design, structure, and behavior of a computer system, microprocessor, or system program, including the characteristics of individual components and how they interact ○ *network architecture*

ar·chi·trave /áarkə tràyv/ *n.* **1. SLAB ON COLUMNS** in classical architecture, the lowest section of an entablature, which comes into contact with the top of the columns **2. DOOR OR WINDOW FRAME** a decorative strip of wood or plaster forming a frame around a door or window [Mid-16thC. Via French from Italian, "main beam," from *trave* "beam," from the Latin stem *trab-*.]

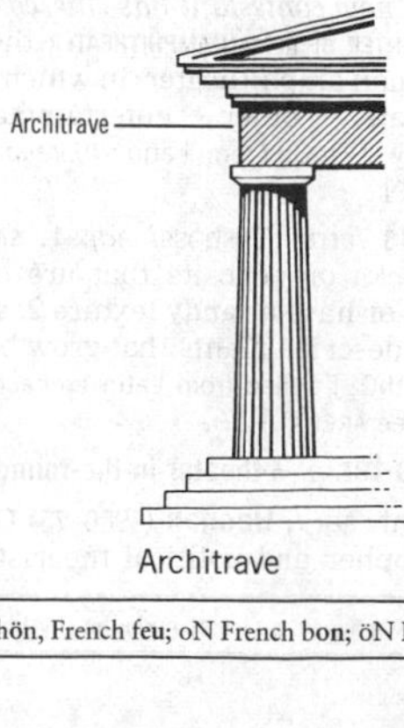

Architrave

ar·chi·val /aar kīv'l/ *adj.* kept in an archive, or relating to the storage of records in an archive

ar·chive /áar kīv/ *n.* **1. COLLECTION OF DOCUMENTS** a collection of documents such as letters, official papers, photographs, or recorded material, kept for their historical interest (*often used in the plural*) ○ *archive material* ○ *We'll have to check the archives.* **2. PLACE WHERE ARCHIVES ARE HELD** the building or room that houses archives ○ *Duke University houses the Duke Papyrus Archive.* ○ *the Harvard Economics Symposium Archive* **3.** COMPUT **BACKUP COMPUTER FILE** a copy of computer files kept, often in compressed form, on tape or disk for long-term storage **4.** COMPUT **COMPUTER FILE OF COMPRESSED FILES** a computer file that contains other files in compressed form **5.** COMPUT **DIRECTORY ACCESSED USING FILE TRANSFER PROTOCOL** a directory of files that Internet users can access using anonymous File Transfer Protocol ○ *The report was filed in an archive for distribution on the Internet.* ■ *vt.* (**-chives, -chived, -chived, -chiv·ing**) **1. PUT DOCUMENT IN ARCHIVE** to store a document in an archive **2.** COMPUT **STORE DATA OUTSIDE HARD DISK** to transfer data from a computer's hard disk to a tape or disk for long-term storage **3.** COMPUT **COMBINE AND COMPRESS COMPUTER FILES** to store copies of multiple computer files in compressed form in a single file [Early 17thC. Via French from Latin *archiva*, from Greek *arkheia* "things kept at the public office," plural of *arkheion* "ruler's house, public office," from *arkhē* "beginning, government."]

ar·chi·vist /áarkəvist, áar kīvist/ *n.* somebody employed to collect, catalog, and take care of the items in an archive

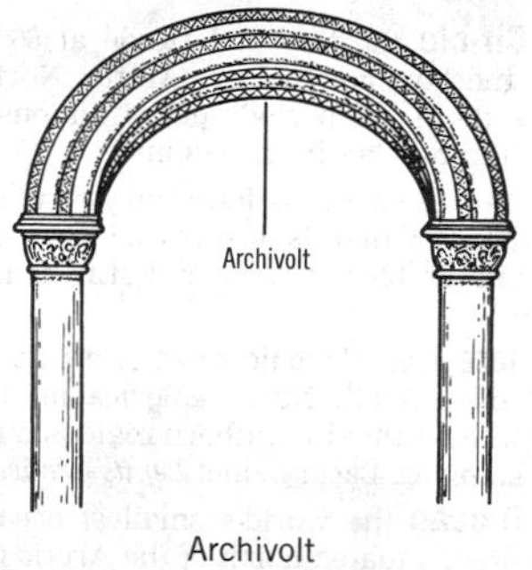

Archivolt

ar·chi·volt /áarkə v-lt/ *n.* **1. MOLDING AROUND ARCH** a decorative molding or band on the face of an arch **2. UNDERSIDE OF ARCH** the underside of an arch [Mid-17thC. Directly or via French *archivolte* from Italian *archivolto*, from, ultimately, Latin *arcus* "arch" + *volta* "vault."]

ar·chon /áar kawn/ *n.* one of the nine chief magistrates in ancient Athens [Late 16thC. From Greek *arkhōn*, from *arkhein* "to rule."] —**ar·chon·ship** *n.*

arch·priest /áarch préest/ *n.* **1. BISHOP'S SENIOR ASSISTANT** a title formerly given to the most senior Roman Catholic priest belonging to a cathedral chapter, who acted as the bishop's principal assistant **2. SPECIAL ROMAN CATHOLIC TITLE** in the Roman Catholic Church, a title given to a priest who has a specific important duty or function **3. HIGH-RANKING EASTERN ORTHODOX PRIEST** in the Eastern Orthodox Church, a priest with the highest rank that a married priest can have [14thC. Via Old French *archeprestre* from late Latin *archipresbyter* "chief priest." The modern spelling is based on ARCH- and PRIEST.]

arch·ri·val /áarch rīv'l/ *n.* somebody's main or most dangerous rival

archt. *abbr.* architect

arch·way /áarch wày/ *n.* an entrance or passage under one or more arches, or an arch that forms an entrance

Ar·chy·tas /aar kītəss/ (*fl.* early 4thC B.C.) Greek mathematician. He calculated the mathematical relationships of musical notes and scales.

Ar·cim·bol·do /áarchim báwldō/, **Giuseppe** (1530?–93) Italian painter and designer. He produced pictures of fantastic heads composed of items such as vegetables and animals.

arc lamp, **arc light** *n.* an intensely bright electric lamp with numerous uses, e.g., in floodlights

ar·co /áarkō/ *adv.* played using the bow of a stringed instrument, usually after a passage played by plucking the strings (**pizzicato**) (*used as a musical direction*) [Mid-18thC. From Italian, "bow."] —**ar·co** *adj.*

arc·tic /áarktik, áartik/ *adj.* VERY COLD extremely cold (*informal*) ■ *n.* OVERSHOE a high waterproof overshoe with a warm lining [14thC. Via Old French *artique* from, ultimately, Greek *arktikos*, from *arktos* "bear," also "the constellation Ursa Major (the Great Bear)," which points to the northern Pole Star.]

Arc·tic /áarktik/ *n.* the region that lies around the North Pole, including the Arctic Ocean and its islands and parts of North America, Asia, and Europe. The area is extremely cold, and its border is generally considered to be the Arctic Circle. ◊ **Antarctic** —**Arc·tic** *adj.*

arc·tic char *n.* a fish of the salmon family, similar to a trout, that is found in the lakes and streams of the northern hemisphere. Latin name: *Salvelinus alpinus.*

Arctic Circle

Arc·tic Cir·cle the line of latitude at 66°30'N that marks the boundary of the Arctic. North of this latitude there are periods of continuous night in the winter and day in the summer.

arc·tic fox *n.* a small fox found in Arctic regions. It has thick fur that is brownish-gray in summer and white or blue in winter. Latin name: *Alopex lagopus.*

arc·tic hare (*plural* **arc·tic hares** *or* **arc·tic hare**) *n.* a large hare of Arctic North America and Greenland with white fur that in southern regions turns brown in the summer. Latin name: *Lepus arcticus.*

Arc·tic O·cean the world's smallest ocean, mostly ice-covered, situated north of the Arctic Circle and surrounding the North Pole. Area: 5,427,000 sq.mi./14,055,930 sq. km. Depth: 17,880 ft./5,500 m.

arc·tic tern (*plural* **arc·tic terns** *or* **arc·tic tern**) *n.* a black-headed seabird that breeds in Arctic regions and migrates to southern Africa, South America, and the Antarctic. Latin name: *Sterna paradisaea.*

arc·ti·id /áarktee id/ (*plural* **-ids** *or* **-id**) *n.* a small to medium-sized moth. There are 8,000 species of arctiid, including the tiger moth. Family: Arctiidae. [From modern Latin *arctiidae*, genus name, from Greek *arktos* "bear"]

arc·to·phile /áarktō fīl/ *n.* somebody who collects or likes teddy bears [Late 20thC. Coined from Greek *arktos* "bear" + -PHILE.]

Arc·tu·rus /aark tŏŏrəss/ *n.* the brightest star in the constellation Boötes and the fourth brightest star in the sky

ar·cu·ate /áarkyə ət, -àyt/ *adj.* in the shape of an arc or a bow [15thC. From Latin *arcuatus*, from *arcus* "bow, arch" (source of English *arch*).] —**ar·cu·ate·ly** *adv.*

arc weld·ing *n.* the joining of metal components by fusing them with heat from an electric arc struck between two electrodes

ARD *abbr.* acute respiratory disease

-ard, **-art** *suffix.* somebody who characteristically has a given quality ○ *dullard* [From Old French; of Germanic origin]

Ar·dennes /aar dén/ forested and thinly populated plateau in southeastern Belgium, extending into Luxembourg and northeastern France. The Battle of the Bulge took place in the Ardennes in 1944. The highest peak is Botrange, near Belgium's border with Germany 2,277 ft./694 m.

ar·dent /áard'nt/ *adj.* **1.** PASSIONATE feeling passion, or felt passionately **2.** ENTHUSIASTIC feeling or showing great enthusiasm or eagerness ○ *one of his most ardent supporters* **3.** GLOWING shining or glowing brightly, with a fiery quality (*literary*) ○ *her ardent gaze* [14thC. Via Old French *ardant* from Latin *ardent-*, the present participle stem of *ardere* "to burn" (source of English *arson*).] —**ar·dent·ly** *adv.*

ar·dent spir·its *npl.* distilled alcoholic beverages, e.g., whiskey and rum

Ard·more /áard màwr/ city north of Lake Murray, in southern Oklahoma. Population: 23,484 (1996).

ar·dor /áardər/ *n.* fierce intensity of feelings ○ *repeated attempts to dampen their revolutionary ardor* [14thC. Via Old French from Latin *ardor*, from *ardere* "to burn" (see ARDENT).]

ar·dour *n.* U.K. = **ardor**

ar·du·ous /áarjoo əss/ *adj.* **1.** DIFFICULT AND TIRING requiring hard work or continuous strenuous effort **2.** STEEP OR DEMANDING very difficult to traverse, endure, or overcome [Mid-16thC. From Latin *arduus* "steep, difficult," the sense "difficult" developing from the fact that anything steep is difficult and tiring to climb.] —**ar·du·ous·ly** *adv.* —**ar·du·ous·ness** *n.*

WORD KEY: SYNONYMS

See Synonyms at ***hard.***

are[1] /aar/ the plural and second person singular present tense of the verb "be" [Old English *earon*. Of prehistoric Germanic origin.]

are[2] /aar/ *n.* a metric unit of area, equal to 100 sq. m. There are one hundred ares in a hectare. [Late 18thC. Via French from Latin *area* (see AREA).]

ar·e·a /áiree ə/ *n.* **1.** MEASUREMENT OF SURFACE the extent of part of a surface enclosed within a boundary, or the extent of the surface of all or part of a solid. The area of a square or rectangle can be calculated by multiplying together the lengths of two adjacent sides. **2.** PART OF SURFACE a distinct part of the surface of something, especially a piece of land ○ *The storms resulted in flooding over a large area.* **3.** SPACE OR PART FOR SPECIFIC FUNCTION a space, part, or surface of something, especially when intended for a specific use ○ *an area of the brain used for memory* **4.** REGION OR DISTRICT a region or district, either a distinct political or administrative division or a place that has particular qualities or features **5.** SUBJECT a particular subject, field of knowledge, or sphere of activity ○ *in the area of genetic research* **6.** SOCCER = **penalty area** [Mid-16thC. From Latin, "flat piece of unoccupied land," of unknown origin.]

ar·e·a bomb·ing *n.* = **carpet bombing**

ar·e·a code *n.* digits indicating a particular area of a country that are dialed before the local number in calls from outside that area. In the United States and Canada, area codes have three digits. ○ *For long distance calls, dial "1" plus the area code and number.*

ar·e·a·way /áiree ə wày/ *n.* an area of lowered ground outside a basement, created to allow more light into basement windows or direct access to the basement from outside

a·re·ca /ə réekə, árri-/ *n.* a tall Southeast Asian palm tree with white flowers. Genus: *Areca.* [Late 16thC. Via Portuguese from Malayalam *aṭekka.*]

a·reg plural of **erg**[2]

a·re·na /ə rée nə/ *n.* **1.** STADIUM an indoor or outdoor area, surrounded by seating for spectators, where shows or sports events take place **2.** SCENE OF ACTIVITY a place or situation where there is conflict or intense activity ○ *A new contestant has entered the political arena.* **3.** CENTER OF ROMAN AMPHITHEATER the open area inside a Roman amphitheater, in which gladiatorial contests and other entertainments were staged [Early 17thC. From Latin *(h)arena* "sand, sand-strewn place."]

ar·e·na·ceous /àrrə náyshəss/ *adj.* **1.** SANDY used to describe rocks or deposits that are composed of sand grains or have a sandy texture **2.** SUITED TO SANDY SOIL used to describe plants that grow best in sandy soil [Mid-17thC. Formed from Latin *arenaceus* "of sand," from *arena* (see ARENA).]

a·re·na the·a·ter *n.* = **theater-in-the-round**

A·rendt /árrənt, áar-/, **Hannah** (1906–75) German-born U.S. philosopher and political theorist. Her major works include *Origins of Totalitarianism* (1951) and *Eichmann in Jerusalem* (1963).

ar·e·nic·o·lous /àrrə níkələss/ *adj.* living, burrowing, or thriving in sand [Mid-18thC. Coined from Latin *arena* "sand" + *-cola* "inhabiting" + -OUS.]

aren't /áarnt/ *contr.* (*informal*) **1.** ARE NOT short form of "are not" ○ *They aren't coming.* **2.** AM NOT short form of "am not," which can only be used in questions ○ *I'm allowed to go too, aren't I?*

WORD KEY: USAGE

Use of **aren't.** English is deficient in not having a convenient contracted form of *am I not?* (The logically expected form **amn't I** is used in some parts of Scotland and Ireland but has never been part of standard English.) There is no contraction for the type *I am not* that corresponds to **I don't** and **I haven't** (as distinct from **I'm not**, which places greater emphasis on the *not*), and this is why the nonstandard form **ain't** tends to be used for want of anything better, although it is extremely informal. (See the Usage Note at ***ain't.***).

a·re·o·la /ə rée ələ/ (*plural* **-lae** /-lee/ *or* **-las**) *n.* **1.** ANAT DARK AREA AROUND NIPPLE the small circular dark area around the nipple in humans **2.** MED CIRCULAR AREA a small circular area, e.g., an inflamed ring around a spot [Mid-17thC. From Latin, literally "little area."] —**a·re·o·lar** *adj.* —**a·re·o·late** /ə rée ələt/ *adj.* —**a·re·o·la·tion** /-láysh'n/ *n.*

ar·e·ole /árree ōl/ *n.* **1.** BIOL SMALL CLEARLY DEFINED SPACE a small clearly defined space, e.g., that between veins on a leaf **2.** BOT PIT ON SURFACE OF CACTUS a depression on the surface of a cactus that the spines, hairs, or flowers grow from [Mid-19thC. Via French from Latin *areola* (see AREOLA).]

A·re·qui·pa /èrrə kéepə, àa-/ city in southern Peru in the Andes. It is an important commercial center. Population: 620,471 (1993).

A·res /áireez/ *n.* in Greek mythology, the god of war and the son of Zeus and Hera. Roman equivalent **Mars**

a·rête /ə ráyt, a-, ə rét, a-/ *n.* a narrow ridge of bare rock situated between two or more deep smooth-sided semicircular areas (**cirques**), found in a mountainous area that has been glaciated [Early 19thC. Via French from Latin *arista* "ear of corn, fish bone, spine," from its shape.]

ar·e·thu·sa /àrree thŏŏzə, èrr-/ *n.* = **swamp pink** [Named for the mythical Greek nymph *Arethusa*, who changed into a spring when pursued by the river god Alpheus]

ar·gal *n.* = **argol**

ar·ga·li /áargəlee/ (*plural* **-li**) *n.* a large wild sheep found in the dry mountainous areas of central and northern Asia. Latin name: *Ovis ammon.* [Late 18thC. From Mongolian.]

ar·gent /áarjənt/ *n.* **1.** SILVER the metal or the color silver (*archaic or literary*) **2.** HERALDRY COLOR ON COAT OF ARMS the color white or silver on a coat of arms [14thC. Via French from Latin *argentum* "silver." Ultimately from an Indo-European word meaning "shining, white," which is also the ancestor of English *argil* and *argue.*] —**ar·gent** *adj.*

ar·gen·tic /aar jéntik/ *adj.* containing silver with a valence of 2

ar·gen·tif·er·ous /àarjən tífərəss/ *adj.* used to describe rocks or deposits containing silver

Argentina

Ar·gen·ti·na /àarjən téenə/ republic that occupies most of the southern tip of South America. It was settled by the Spanish in the 16th century and became independent in 1816. Language: Spanish. Currency: austral. Capital: Buenos Aires. Population: 35,797,981 (1997). Area: 1,073,518 sq. mi./2,780,400 sq. km. Official name **Argentine Republic**

Ar·gen·ti·na /àar hen téenə/, **La** (1888–1936) Argentine dancer. She reintroduced Spanish dancing as a popular art form in the 20th century. Real name **Antonia Merce**

ar·gen·tine /áarjən tīn, -teen/ *adj.* **SILVERY** silvery in color (*archaic or literary*) ■ *n.* **SILVER** the metal silver, or any material that looks like silver

Ar·gen·tine /áarjən t-n, -teen/ *n.* **1.** = **Argentina 2.** = **Argentinean** *adj.* ■ *adj.* = **Argentinean** *n.*

Ar·gen·tin·e·an /àarjən tí nee ən/ *n.* **SOMEBODY FROM ARGENTINA** somebody who was born in or is a citizen of Argentina ■ *adj.* **OF ARGENTINA** relating to or typical of Argentina, or its people or culture

ar·gen·tite /áarjən tīt/ *n.* a gray to black mineral consisting of silver sulfide crystallized in cubic form. Formula: Ag_2S. [Mid-19thC. Coined from Latin *argentum* "silver" + -ITE.]

ar·gil /áarjəl/ *n.* clay, especially potter's clay [14thC. Via Old French *argille* from Greek *argillos* "clay." Ultimately from an Indo-European word meaning "shining, white."]

ar·gil·la·ceous /àarjə láyshəss/ *adj.* used to describe sedimentary rock that is made up of fine silt or clay particles

ar·gil·lite /áarjə līt/ *n.* rock that is made up of clay or silt particles, especially a hardened mudstone

ar·gi·nase /áarjə nàyss, -nàaz/ *n.* an enzyme in the liver that aids the breakdown of the amino acid arginine, producing urea for excretion

ar·gi·nine /áarjə neen/ *n.* an amino acid, obtained by animals from their diet, that is one of the constituents of protein. It is derived from guanidine in plant and animal tissue. Formula: $C_6H_{14}N_4O_2$. [Late 19thC. From German, perhaps formed from Greek *arginoeis* "bright-shining, white."]

Ar·give /áar gīv, -jīv/ *adj.* **1. GREEK** relating to or typical of ancient Greece, especially the city of Argos **2. OF ARGOS** relating to the city of Argos ■ *n.* **1. ANCIENT GREEK** somebody from ancient Greece (*literary*) **2. OF CITIZEN OF ARGOS** somebody from the city of Argos [Mid-16thC. From Latin *Argivus* "of Argos."]

Ar·go /áargō/ *n.* a large constellation in the southern hemisphere, now usually regarded as consisting of the smaller constellations of Puppis, Vela, Carina, and Pyxis

ar·gol /áar gàwl, áarg'l/, **ar·gal** /áarg'l/ *n.* a deposit of potassium hydrogen tartrate, formed in wine casks and sometimes used to manufacture cream of tartar [14thC. From Anglo-Norman *argoile*, of unknown origin.]

ar·gon /áar gàwn/ *n.* a chemical element in the form of an inert gas that makes up about one percent of the Earth's atmosphere. Argon is used in electric lights and as a gas shield in welding. Symbol **Ar** [Late 19thC. From Greek, from *argos* "inactive, idle," from *a-* "without" + *ergon* "work" (source of English *ergonomics* and *allergy*).]

ar·go·naut /áargə nàwt/ *n.* ZOOL = **paper nautilus** [Mid-19thC. From modern Latin *Argonauta*, its genus name. From the fact that it drifts through the oceans (like Jason's ARGONAUTS).]

Ar·go·naut *n.* **1. GREEK HERO** one of the heroes in Greek mythology who sailed with Jason to find the Golden Fleece **2. Ar·go·naut, ar·go·naut ADVENTURER** an adventurer, especially somebody who took part in the Californian gold rush of 1849 [Late 16thC. Via Latin *argonauta* from Greek *argonautēs* "sailor in the ship Argo."]

ar·go·sy /áargəsee/ (*plural* **-sies**) *n.* **1. LADEN MERCHANT SHIP** a large richly laden merchant ship, or a fleet of richly laden ships (*literary*) **2. RICH STORE** a rich plentiful store or supply of something (*archaic or literary*) [Late 16thC. Probably from Italian *Ragusea* "(ship from) Ragusa" (now Dubrovnik in Croatia), which was an important port at the time.]

ar·got /áargət, -gō/ *n.* jargon used by a particular group [Mid-19thC. From French, originally meaning the jargon of criminals, of unknown origin.] —**ar·got·ic** /aar góttik/ *adj.*

ar·gu·a·ble /áargyoo əb'l/ *adj.* **1. PLAUSIBLE OR POSSIBLE** able to be supported or proved with evidence or arguments ○ *an arguable case for global warming* **2. OPEN TO DISPUTE** not obviously true or accurate, and therefore likely to be questioned or argued about ○ *It's arguable whether he really is the world's best guitarist.*

ar·gu·a·bly /áargyoo əblee/ *adv.* used to mean that a statement is open to dispute but could be defended in an argument ○ *This is arguably the best restaurant in town.*

WORD KEY: USAGE

arguably, debatably, disputably ***Arguably***, which is the most common of the three words, tends to emphasize the affirmative position and suggests that the speaker is asserting that which is arguable: *arguably the most influential legislator in the county. Debatably* is the most nearly neutral of the three: *It was a debatably rude thing to do Disputably*, the least common word, tends to emphasize the potential for disagreement: *The cause was disputably his work habits, although some say it was his temper that got him into trouble.*

ar·gue /áargyoo/ (**-gued, -gu·ing, -gues**) *v.* **1.** *vi.* **EXPRESS DISAGREEMENT** to express disagreement with somebody, especially continuously or angrily **2.** *vti.* **GIVE REASONS FOR SOMETHING** to give reasons for an opinion in order to support it ○ *You could argue that this calls for greater freedom, not less.* **3.** *vti.* **DISCUSS SOMETHING** to discuss something in all its aspects **4.** *vt.* **PERSUADE SOMEBODY** to persuade somebody to do something by giving reasons ○ *argued her out of leaving* **5.** *vti.* **PROVIDE EVIDENCE FOR SOMETHING** to be evidence or a sign of something [14thC. Via French *arguer* from Latin *argutari* "to assert repeatedly," from *arguere* "to make clear, assert."] —**ar·gu·er** *n.*

WORD KEY: SYNONYMS

See Synonyms at ***disagree.***

ar·gu·fy /áargyə fī/ (**-fied, -fy·ing, -fies**) *vi. Southern U.S.* to argue about something that is unimportant (*informal*)

ar·gu·ment /áargyəmənt/ *n.* **1. QUARREL** a disagreement in which different views are expressed, often angrily **2. REASON** a reason put forward in support of a point of view ○ *the arguments for and against the planned development* **3. STATED POINT OF VIEW** the main point of view expressed in a book, report, or speech **4. DISCUSSION** debate or discussion about whether something is correct **5.** LING **NOUN ELEMENT IN CLAUSE** any of the noun elements in a clause that relate directly to the verb, such as the subject or object **6.** PHILOS **LOGICAL STATEMENTS WITH CONCLUSION** a unit of reasoning moving from premises that provide evidence to a conclusion **7.** MATH **VARIABLE ELEMENT** an independent variable whose value determines the value of a mathematical expression **8.** COMPUT **FEATURE CONTROLLING COMPUTER PROGRAM** a value that modifies how a command or function operates in a computer program

ar·gu·men·ta plural of **argumentum**

ar·gu·men·ta·tion /àargyəmən táysh'n, -men-/ *n.* **1. DEBATE** a process of debating or discussing something **2. LOGICAL REASONING** reasoning that proceeds methodically from a statement to a conclusion

ar·gu·men·ta·tive /àargyə méntətiv/ *adj.* **1. INCLINED TO DISAGREE** tending to disagree and argue **2. CHARACTERIZED BY DISAGREEMENT** characterized by disagreement or argument —**ar·gu·men·ta·tive·ly** *adv.* —**ar·gu·men·ta·tive·ness** *n.*

ar·gu·men·tum /àargyə méntəm/ (*plural* **-ta** /-tə/) *n.* a series of statements or a demonstration that leads to a logical conclusion (*formal*) [Mid-17thC. From Latin, "argument, rationale," from *arguere* (see ARGUE).]

ar·gu·men·tum ad hom·i·nem /-ad hómmi nem, -hómmənəm/ *n.* criticism of an opponent's character or motives, rather than of the person's argument, opinion, or beliefs (*formal*) [From Latin, literally "argument to the person"]

Ar·gus /áargəss/ *n.* **1. HUNDRED-EYED GIANT** in Greek mythology, a giant with a hundred eyes. He was sent by the jealous Hera to watch over her husband's mistress, Io, but was later lulled to sleep and killed by Hermes. **2. WATCHFUL PERSON** somebody who is very alert and watchful (*literary*)

Ar·gus-eyed *adj.* extremely alert and seeing everything (*literary*)

ar·gyle /áar gīl, aar gī́l/, **ar·gyll** *adj.* **WITH DIAMOND PATTERN** knitted with a pattern of colored diamonds ■ *n.* **SOCK OR SWEATER WITH DIAMOND PATTERN** a sock or sweater made in an argyle design [Mid-20thC. From its being based on the tartan of the branch of the Campbell clan who lived in Argyll in Scotland.]

Argyle

ar·hat /áarhət/ *n.* a Buddhist who has reached the highest state of peace and enlightenment. ◊ **arahat** [Late 19thC. Via Pali from Sanskrit, "deserving, meritorious."] —**ar·hat·ship** *n.*

a·ri·a /áaree ə/ *n.* a melody sung solo or as a duet in an opera, oratorio, or cantata [Early 18thC. Via Italian from Latin *aer* "air" (see AIR).]

Ar·i·ad·ne /àrree ádnee/ *n.* in Greek mythology, the daughter of King Minos of Crete. She gave Theseus the ball of thread which he used to find his way out of the labyrinth after killing the Minotaur.

Ar·i·an[1] /áiree ən/ *n.* = **Aries** *n.* 2 —**Ar·i·an** *adj.*

Ar·i·an[2] /áiree ən/ *n.* a follower of the ancient Greek Christian theologian Arius, who argued that Jesus Christ was the highest created being, but was not divine. This doctrine was pronounced heretical in the 4th century A.D. —**Ar·i·an·ism** *n.*

A·ri·as /aáree aàss/, **Arnulfo** (1901–88) Panamanian political leader. As president of Panama (1940–41, 1949–51, and 1968), he was noted for his authoritarian policies.

A·ri·as San·chez /-saán chez/, **Oscar** (*b.* 1941) Costa Rican statesman. He was president of Costa Rica (1986–90) and won the Nobel Peace Prize (1987).

a·ri·bo·fla·vi·no·sis /ay rībə flayvə nṓsəss/ *n.* a condition caused by a dietary deficiency of vitamin B_2 (**riboflavin**). The symptoms are mouth lesions and excessive oiliness of the skin and hair. [Mid-20thC. Coined from A- + RIBOFLAVIN + -OSIS.]

ar·id /árrid, érr-/ *adj.* **1. WITH LOW RAINFALL** used to describe a region in which annual rainfall is less than 10 in./25 cm **2. DULL** completely lacking in interest or excitement [Mid-17thC. Directly or via French from Latin *aridus*, from *arere* "to be dry."] —**a·rid·i·ty** /ə rídətee/ *n.* —**ar·id·ness** /árridniss, érr-/ *n.*

WORD KEY: SYNONYMS

See Synonyms at ***dry.***

ar·id zone *n.* either of two zones of latitude that are between 15° and 30° north and south of the equator, consisting mostly of desert or semidesert

Ar·i·el /áiree əl/ *n.* ASTRON the third largest satellite of Uranus and the second nearest to the planet

Ar·ies /ái reez, -ree eez/ *n.* **1.** ZODIAC **FIRST SIGN OF THE ZODIAC** the first sign of the zodiac, represented by a ram and lasting from approximately March 21 to April 19. Aries is classified as a fire sign and its ruling planet is Mars. **2.** ZODIAC **SOMEBODY BORN UNDER ARIES** somebody whose birthday falls between March 21 and April 19 **3.** ASTRON **CONSTELLATION** a zodiacal constellation of the northern hemisphere lying between Pisces and Taurus [Pre-12thC. From Latin *aries* "ram."] —**Ar·ies** *adj.*

a·ri·et·ta /àaree éttə, àrree-, èrree-/ *n.* a short simple aria in an opera, oratorio, or cantata [Early 18thC. From Italian, literally "little aria."]

a·right /ə rī́t/ *adv.* well, or in the correct or proper way (*archaic*)

A·rik·a·ra /ə ríkərə/ (*plural* **-ras** *or* **-ra**) *n.* a member of a Native American people who used to live in the Missouri River valley, but who now live in western North Dakota

ar·il /árrəl, érr-/ *n.* a fleshy, often brightly colored seed covering in some plants. It draws attention to the seed and aids dispersal by birds. [Mid-18thC. Via modern Latin *arillus* from medieval Latin *arilli* "dried grape pips," of unknown origin.] —**ar·iled** *adj.* —**ar·il·late** /árrə layt, érr-/ *adj.*

a·ri·o·so /aàree ōsō, -ṓssō/ *adj., adv.* **SONGLIKE** with intense lyricism or feeling ■ *n.* (*plural* **-sos**) **SHORT LYRICAL PIECE** a short lyrical aria or instrumental work [Early 18thC. From Italian, literally "like an aria."]

a·rise /ə rī́z/ (**a·rose** /ə rṓz/, **a·ris·en** /ə rìzən/, **a·ris·ing, a·ris·es**) *vi.* **1. OCCUR** to happen or come into existence, or be noticed or heard ○ *When did the problem arise?* **2. BE CAUSED BY SOMETHING** to happen or exist as a result of something **3. BECOME ACTIVE OR VOCAL** to rise from a quiet, inactive, or subjugated state to become active, vocal, or rebellious (*literary*) **4. GO UP** to move upward to a higher place or level (*archaic or literary*) **5. STAND UP** to stand up from a sitting, lying, or kneeling position (*archaic or literary*) **6. GET OUT OF BED** to get out of bed (*archaic or literary*) [Old English *arisan* "to rise up," from the same prehistoric Germanic ancestor as English *rise*]

a·ris·ta /ə rístə/ (*plural* **-tae** /-tay, -tee/) *n.* **1.** BOT = **awn** (*technical*) **2.** INSECTS **BRISTLE** a bristly part of the antennae of some flies [Late 17thC. From Latin, "ear of grain," of unknown origin.]

Ar·is·tar·chus of Sa·mos /èrri staárkəss-/ (310?–250? B.C.) Greek astronomer. He proposed that the Earth rotates on its axis and orbits the Sun.

Ar·is·tide /aàri steéd/, **Jean-Bertrand** (*b.* 1953) Haitian political leader. He was elected president of the independent republic of Haiti (1991–96) in Haiti's first free elections since 1804.

Ar·is·ti·des the Just /àrri stī́ deez-/ (530–468 B.C.) Greek soldier-statesman. He commanded the Athenian land forces at Salamis against the Persians.

Ar·is·tip·pus /àrri stíppəss/ (435?–360? B.C.) Greek philosopher. A student of Socrates, he founded the Cyrenaic school of hedonism, believing that pleasure is the highest good.

ar·is·toc·ra·cy /àrris tókrəsee, èrr-/ (*plural* **-cies**) *n.* **1. PEOPLE OF HIGHEST CLASS** people of noble families or the highest social class **2. SUPERIOR GROUP** a group acknowledged to be superior to all others of the same kind **3. GOVERNMENT BY ELITE** government of a country by a small group of people, especially a hereditary nobility **4. STATE GOVERNED BY ARISTOCRACY** a state governed by an aristocracy [15thC. Via French *aristocratie* from Greek *aristokratia* "rule by the best," from *aristos* "best" + *kratos* "power, rule" (see -CRACY). The connotations of social class developed in the mid-17thC.]

a·ris·to·crat /ərístə kràt/ *n.* **1. MEMBER OF ELITE SOCIAL CLASS** a member of the highest social class in a country **2. SUPPORTER OF ARISTOCRATIC RULE** a member of a governing aristocracy, or somebody who supports government by aristocracy **3. SUPERIOR PERSON** a person, thing, or group believed to be superior to all others of the same kind

aris·to·crat·ic /ə rìstə kráttik/ *adj.* **1. TYPICAL OF ESTABLISHED WEALTH OR NOBILITY** typical of people belonging to noble or wealthy families, e.g., in having a grand lifestyle or elegant manners **2. OF CLASS OF NOBLES** belonging or relating to the highest social class, especially the nobility —**a·ris·to·crat·i·cal·ly** *adv.*

Ar·is·toph·a·nes /àrri stóffə neèz/ (448?–385 B.C.) Greek dramatist. He satirized social and intellectual pretensions in plays such as *The Birds* (414 B.C.) and *The Clouds* (423 B.C.).

Ar·is·to·te·li·an /àrristə teélee ən, èrr-/ *adj.* **RELATING TO ARISTOTLE** expressing or based on the ideas of the Greek philosopher Aristotle ■ *n.* **FOLLOWER OF ARISTOTLE** a follower of Aristotle's philosophy

Ar·is·to·te·li·an log·ic *n.* the system of logic developed by Aristotle, based on the kind of reasoning (**syllogism**) that reaches a conclusion from two independent statements with a common factor

Ar·is·tot·le /àrri stótt'l/ (384–322 B.C.) Greek philosopher and scientist. He was among the most influential of philosophers in Western history.

a·rith·me·tic *n.* /ə ríthmə tìk/ **1. BASIC MATH** the branch of mathematics that deals with addition, subtraction, multiplication, and division **2. CALCULATION USING BASIC MATHEMATICS** one or more calculations using basic mathematics **3. USE OF NUMBERS** the use of numbers in calculation, or educational exercises involving this **4. ABILITY TO DO ARITHMETIC** somebody's ability to add, subtract, multiply, and divide (*informal*) ■ *adj.* /àrrith méttik/ **ar·ith·met·ic RELATING TO ARITHMETIC** using, involving, or based on arithmetic [13thC. Via Old French *arismetique* from, ultimately, Greek *arithmētikē (tekhnē)* "counting (art)," from *arithmein* "to reckon," from *arithmos* "number."] —**ar·ith·met·i·cal** /àrrith méttik'l, èrr-/ *adj.* —**ar·ith·met·i·cal·ly** *adv.* —**a·rith·me·ti·cian** /ə rìthmə tísh'n/ *n.*

ar·ith·met·ic log·ic u·nit *n.* the circuit in a computer's central processing unit that makes decisions based on the results of calculations

ar·ith·met·ic mean *n.* the average of a set of numbers, calculated by adding them together and then dividing their sum by the number of terms

ar·ith·met·ic pro·gres·sion *n.* a sequence of numbers in which a constant figure (**common difference**) is added to each term to give the next. For example, 3, 8, 13, 18 is an arithmetic progression in which the common difference is 5.

-arium *suffix.* a place or device connected with something ○ *herbarium* [From Latin, neuter of *-arius*]

Ariz. *abbr.* Arizona

Arizona

Ar·i·zo·na /àrri zṓnə/ state in the southwestern United States, bounded by New Mexico, Mexico, California, Nevada, and Utah. Capital: Phoenix. Population: 4,554,966 (1997). Area: 114,000 sq. mi./295,274 sq. km. —**Ar·i·zo·nan** *adj., n.* —**Ar·i·zo·ni·an** *adj., n.*

Ar·ju·na /áar jə nə/ *n.* major character in the *Mahabharata.* Serving as his charioteer, Krishna explains Hindu doctrine to him.

ark /aark/ *n.* **1. NOAH'S SHIP** the ship that, according to biblical accounts, Noah was instructed to build by God to save his family and the animals from the Flood **2. SANCTUARY** a place providing refuge **3. ark, Ark** = **Ark of the Covenant 4. ark, Ark CABINET CONTAINING TORAH SCROLLS** a cupboard in a synagogue in which the scrolls of the Torah are kept [Old English *ærc,* via prehistoric Germanic from Latin *arca* "chest, box"] ◇ **out of the ark** extremely old or old-fashioned (*informal*)

WORD KEY: CULTURAL NOTE

Schindler's Ark, a novel by Thomas Keneally (1982). It tells the true story of a German industrialist, Oskar Schindler, who helped thousands of Jews avoid the Nazi death camps by employing them in his factories. It was made into a movie called *Schindler's List* by Steven Spielberg in 1993.

Ark. *abbr.* Arkansas

Ar·ka·del·phi·a /aàrkə délfee ə/ city in southwestern Arkansas, on the Ouachita River. Population: 10,472 (1996).

Ar·kan·san /aar kánz'n/ *c.* somebody who lives in or was born or raised in Arkansas —**Ar·kan·san** *adj.*

Arkansas

Ar·kan·sas /aárkən sàw/ **1.** southern U.S. state, bordered by Missouri, the Mississippi River, Louisiana, Texas, and Oklahoma. Capital: Little Rock. Population: 2,522,819 (1996). Area: 53,182 sq. mi./137,741 sq. km. **2.** major river of the central United States, rising in central Colorado and flowing south and eastward to join the Mississippi River in southeastern Arkansas. The main cities along its course are Tulsa, Oklahoma, and Little Rock, Arkansas. Length: 1,460 mi./2,350 km.

Ar·kan·sas Post Na·tion·al Me·mo·ri·al national park in east central Arkansas. It is located on the site of the first permanent settlement established in 1686 by the French in the lower Mississippi River valley. Area: 389 acres/157 hectares.

Ar·kan·saw·yer /aárkən sàwyər/ *n.* = **Arkansan** (*regional*) [Early 20thC. Formed from ARKANSAS + *-yer* in SAWYER.]

WORD KEY: REGIONAL NOTE

Arkansawyer is, apparently, preferred by natives of Arkansas to the more familiar ***Arkansan.***

Ark of the Cov·e·nant, Ark of the Tes·ti·mo·ny *n.* the chest in which, according to biblical accounts, Moses placed the two stone tablets containing the Ten Commandments. The Hebrews treasured it as the most sacred sign of God's presence among them.

ark·ose /aárkōss, -ōz/ *n.* a coarse-grained sedimentary rock rich in feldspar and quartz [Mid-19thC. From French, probably coined from Greek *arkhaios* "ancient" (source of English *archaic*).]

Ar·len /aárlən/, **Harold** (1905–86) U.S. composer. He wrote the scores for many movies and Broadway musicals.

Arles /aarl/ city in the Bouches-du-Rhône Department in the Provence-Alpes-Côte-d'Azur Region in France, situated northwest of Marseilles. It was a major Roman city, and after the 10th century was the capital of a kingdom of the same name. Population: 52,593 (1990).

Ar·ling·ton /aárlingtən/ **1.** city in northeastern Virginia, near Washington, D.C., site of Arlington National Cemetery and the Pentagon. Population: 175,334 (1996). **2.** city situated between Fort Worth and Dallas in northeastern Texas. Population: 294,816 (1996).

Ar·ling·ton Heights city in northeastern Illinois, a northern suburb of Chicago. Population: 76,740 (1996).

arm[1] /aarm/ *n.* **1. UPPER LIMB** a limb attached to the shoulder of the human body **2. PART OF GARMENT** the part of a piece of clothing that covers the arm **3. PART OF CHAIR** a side piece of a seat designed to support the arms **4. ANIMAL'S LIMB** a part of an animal's body that is similar to the human arm, or a flexible limb in an invertebrate such as an octopus **5. LONG PROJECTING PART OF SOMETHING** a part of something that is similar to a human arm in function or appearance ○ *an arm of the sea* **6. DIVISION OF LARGER GROUP** a branch of an organization, especially a section of the armed forces [Old English *arm, earm.* Ultimately from an Indo-European word meaning "fit, join."] ◇ **an arm and a leg** a lot of money (*informal*) ○ *It would cost an arm and a leg to repair.* ◇ **arm in arm** holding each other affectionately by linking arms ◇ **at arm's length** in a position or situation that avoids involvement or familiarity ◇ **put the arm on somebody 1.** to try to force somebody to do something (*informal*) **2.** to borrow money from somebody (*informal*) ◇ **twist somebody's arm** to try to persuade somebody to do something against his or her will ◇ **with open arms** in a friendly and welcoming way ◇ **would give your right arm for something** would be willing to do or give almost anything to get something that you want (*informal*)

arm[2] /aarm/ *v.* (**armed, arm·ing, arms**) **1.** *vti.* **EQUIP WITH WEAPONS** to equip somebody or a country with weapons **2.** *vt.* **ACTIVATE** to prepare a weapon so that it is ready to use **3.** *vt.* **PROVIDE WITH TOOLS** to provide somebody with the information or equipment needed to do something ○ *armed myself with statistics before the meeting* ■ *n.* **WEAPON** a weapon, especially one used in warfare (*often used in the plural*) ■ **arms** *npl.* **1. WARFARE** fighting and military activity **2.** = **coat of arms** [12thC. Via Old French *armer* from Latin *armare,* from *arma* (plural) "weapons."] ◇ **be up in arms** to protest or complain angrily ◇ **lay down your arms** to stop fighting ◇ **take up arms** to enter, or prepare to enter, a battle

ARM *abbr.* adjustable rate mortgage

ar·ma·da /aar maádə/ *n.* a large fleet of ships [Mid-16thC. Via Spanish from, ultimately, medieval Latin *armata* (see ARMY).]

Armadillo

ar·ma·dil·lo /aàrmə díló/ (*plural* **-los** *or* **-lo**) *n.* a burrowing mammal with a hard-plated body, found in temperate and tropical regions of the Americas. Armadillos are related to anteaters and sloths. Family: Dasypodidae. [Late 16thC. From Spanish, literally "little armed man," from, ultimately, Latin *armare* "to arm" (see ARM[2]).]

Ar·ma·ged·don /aàrmə gédd'n/ *n.* **1.** BIBLICAL BATTLE BETWEEN GOOD AND EVIL in the Bible, the battle between the forces of good and evil that is predicted to mark the end of the world and precede the Day of Judgment. (Revelation 16:16). **2.** ALL-DESTROYING WAR any final and decisive war or conflict, e.g., a worldwide nuclear war [Early 19thC. Via late Latin from, ultimately, Hebrew *har megiddōn* "hill of Megiddo."]

Ar·magh /aar maá/ historic county of Northern Ireland, in the province of Ulster. Area: 258 sq. mi./667 sq. km.

ar·ma·ment /aármәmәnt/ *n.* **1.** MILITARY WEAPONS the guns and other weapons on a military aircraft, vehicle, or ship (*often used in the plural*) **2.** PROCESS OF ARMING the provision of weapons and equipment in preparation for war **3.** FORCE EQUIPPED FOR WAR a military force equipped for war (*archaic*) [Late 17thC. From Latin *armamentum*, from *armare* (see ARM[2]).]

ar·ma·men·tar·i·um /aàrmə men térree əm/ (*plural* **-ums** *or* **-a** /-ə/) *n.* the complete range of equipment, medications, and techniques that a medical practitioner has at his or her disposal [Late 19thC. From Latin, "arsenal, armory," formed from *armare* (see ARM[2]).]

Ar·ma·ni /aar maánee/, **Giorgio** (*b.* 1934) Italian fashion designer. He founded the Giorgio Armani fashion design company in 1975.

ar·ma·ture /aármәchәr, -tòor, -chòor/ *n.* **1.** ELEC ENG MOVING PART IN ELECTROMAGNETIC DEVICE the moving part in an electromagnetic device, wound with coils that carry a current. In a generator, an electric current is induced in the coils when they revolve through a magnetic field. **2.** KEEPER FOR MAGNET a bar of soft iron or steel placed across the poles of a magnet to maintain its strength **3.** BIOL PROTECTIVE PART a protective outer covering or structure, e.g., quills on a porcupine or spines on a plant **4.** SCULPTURE FRAMEWORK FOR A SCULPTURE a framework that supports a sculpture while it is being modeled [15thC. Via French from Latin *armatura* (source also of English *armor*), from *armat-*, the past participle stem of *armare* (see ARM[2]). The original meaning was "armor."]

arm·band /aárm bànd/ *n.* a band of fabric worn around the upper arm

arm candy *n.* a good-looking woman with whom a man does not have a relationship who accompanies him to a social event by prior arrangement, often for a fee (*slang humorous*)

arm·chair /aárm chàir/ *n.* CHAIR WITH ARMRESTS a chair with arms, especially a comfortable upholstered chair ■ *adj.* WITH NO FIRST-HAND EXPERIENCE with no direct experience, only theoretical knowledge ○ *an armchair tourist*

armed /aármd/ *adj.* **1.** EQUIPPED WITH WEAPONS equipped with one or more weapons ○ *armed robbers* **2.** USING WEAPONS involving the use of weapons ○ *armed conflict* **3.** WITH EXPLODING MECHANISM ACTIVE prepared and ready for use as a weapon, especially with a fuse or detonator activated **4.** PROVIDED WITH NECESSARY THINGS equipped with the information or tools needed to achieve something ○ *armed with the latest statistics*

armed forc·es *npl.* the combined bodies of troops of a country who fight on land, at sea, or in the air

Armenia

Ar·me·ni·a /aar meénee ə/ country in southwestern Asia between the Black and the Caspian seas, surrounded by Azerbaijan, Azerbaijan-Nakcivan enclave, Iran, Turkey, and Georgia. Language: Armenian. Currency: dram. Capital: Yerevan. Population: 3,433,629 (1997). Area: 11,506 sq. mi./29,800 sq. km.

Ar·me·ni·an /aar meénee ən/ *n.* **1.** PEOPLES SOMEBODY FROM ARMENIA somebody who was born or raised in Armenia, or who is a citizen of Armenia **2.** LANG LANGUAGE OF ARMENIA the national language of Armenia, also spoken in Turkey and in many other parts of the world. It forms a distinct branch of Indo-European and is spoken by about six million people. —**Ar·me·ni·an** *adj.*

arm·ful /aármfòol/ *n.* the amount of something that can be carried with one or both arms

arm·hole /aárm hōl/ *n.* either of the holes at the top of a garment for the wearer's arms to go through

ar·mi·ger /aármijər/ *n.* **1.** HERALDRY SOMEBODY WITH COAT OF ARMS somebody entitled to have a coat of arms (*archaic*) **2.** MIL MEDIEVAL SQUIRE a squire who carried a medieval knight's armor [Mid-16thC. From Latin, "bearing weapons," formed from *arma* "weapons" (see ARM[2]).]

Armillary sphere

ar·mil·lar·y sphere /aàrmə lérree-, aar mìlləree-/ *n.* a spherical model of the universe, first used by early Greek astronomers, in which the relative positions of the Earth and other celestial bodies are represented by intersecting metal rings ["Armillary" from modern Latin *armillaris*, from Latin *armilla* "arm bracelet," literally "little shoulder," from *armus* "shoulder"]

Ar·min·i·an /aar mínnee ən/ *adj.* OPPOSING CALVINISM relating to or following the Protestant theologian Arminius or his doctrines, which rejected the Calvinist view of absolute predestination ■ *n.* FOLLOWER OF ARMINIANISM a follower of Arminius or his doctrines [Early 17thC. Formed from *Arminius*, Latinized surname of Jakob Hermandszoon (1560–1609).] —**Ar·min·i·an·ism** *n.*

ar·mi·stice /aármistiss/ *n.* a truce in a war to discuss terms for peace [Early 18thC. Directly or via French from modern Latin *armistitium*, literally "stoppage of weapons," coined from Latin *arma* "weapons."]

Ar·mi·stice Day *n.* the former annual celebration of the armistice that ended World War I on November 11, 1918. In 1954 it was incorporated into the observance of Veterans Day.

arm·let /aármlət/ *n.* **1.** BAND WORN ON ARM a band worn on the upper arm **2.** GEOG NARROW STRIP OF WATER a short narrow arm of a lake or the sea

arm·load /aárm lōd/ *n.* an amount of something that can be carried with one or both arms

arm·lock /aárm lòk/ *n.* a tight immobilizing grip around one or both of somebody's upper arms, e.g., in wrestling or judo

ar·moire /aarmwaár/ *n.* a tall cupboard or wardrobe, often ornately decorated. Originally, an armoire was used for storing weapons. [Late 16thC. Via French from, ultimately, Latin *armarium* "chest," from *arma* (plural) "weapons, tools."]

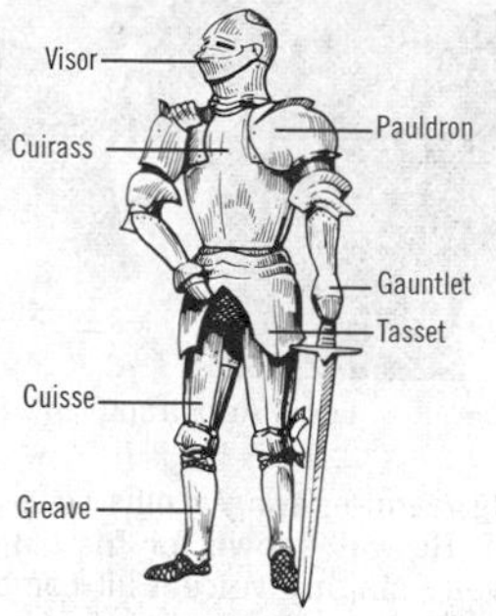

Armor

ar·mor /aármər/ *n.* **1.** MIL PROTECTION FOR SOLDIERS protective clothing of metal or leather worn in battle by soldiers in former times **2.** MIL PROTECTION FOR MILITARY VEHICLES the protective layer of metal covering military vehicles, ships, and aircraft **3.** BIOL COVERING ON PLANTS OR ANIMALS a protective layer covering an animal or plant **4.** PROTECTION anything that gives protection or acts as a safeguard **5.** GEOG GRAVEL ON RIVER BED a surface layer of gravel in a river bed preventing erosion of the material below **6.** HERALDRY COATS OF ARMS coats of arms or the symbols and designs used on them [13thC. From French *armure* from Latin *armatura* (see ARMATURE).]

ar·mored /aármərd/ *adj.* **1.** WITH PROTECTIVE METAL COVERING with a protective metal covering to protect from bullets or missiles **2.** WITH ARMORED VEHICLES using armored vehicles **3.** WITH PROTECTIVE COVERING with a natural protective covering, e.g., a shell

ar·mored car *n.* **1.** CIVILIAN VEHICLE PROTECTED BY ARMOR any vehicle, e.g., a security van, with an extra layer of thick metal to protect the occupants from bullets or other weapons **2.** LIGHT MILITARY VEHICLE a lightweight military vehicle that is lightly armored and used mainly for reconnaissance

ar·mor·er /aármərər/ *n.* **1.** MAKER OF WEAPONS AND ARMOR somebody who makes and repairs armor and weapons **2.** SOLDIER MAINTAINING SMALL ARMS a soldier who repairs and maintains small arms

ar·mo·ri·al /aar máwree əl/ *adj.* relating to coats of arms or decorated with a coat of arms ○ *armorial bearings* [Late 16thC. Formed from obsolete *armory* "heraldry," from Old French *armoi(e)rie*, from *armoier* "to blazon," from *armes* (plural) "weapons" (see ARM[2]).]

ar·mor plate *n.* strong metal sheets used for protecting military vehicles, aircraft, and ships —**ar·mor-plat·ed** *adj.*

ar·mor·y /aárməree/ (*plural* **-ies**) *n.* **1.** STORE FOR WEAPONS a building in which weapons are stored **2.** COLLECTION OF WEAPONS a store or collection of weapons **3.** BUILDING FOR MILITARY TRAINING a building used for drilling and training militia **4.** RESOURCES OF ANY KIND a range of equipment and skills available to somebody, used especially in dealing with opponents **5.** ARMS FACTORY a factory where arms are manufactured [14thC. From Old French *armoi(e)rie* "weaponry" (see ARMORIAL).]

ar·mour *n.* U.K. = **armor**

Ar·mour /aármər/, **Philip Danforth** (1832–1901) U.S. business executive. He revolutionized the meat-packing business and founded Armour & Company in 1870.

ar·mour·y /aárməree/ (*plural* **-ies**) *n.* **1.** U.K. = **armory** **2. ar·mour·y, ar·mour·ies** *Can* = **armory** *n.* 3

arm·pit /aárm pìt/ *n.* **1.** HOLLOW UNDER ARM the hollow area under the arm where it joins the body **2.** WORST PLACE a place that is the worst of its kind (*slang*)

arm·rest /aárm rèst/ *n.* a projecting part, e.g., on a chair, designed to support the arm of somebody sitting down

arm's-length *adj.* without close contact or an intimate relationship ○ *the companies' arm's-length trading arrangement*

arms race *n.* the competition between countries for superiority in the number and power of weapons held

Louis Armstrong

Arm·strong /áarm strawng/, **Louis** (1900–71) U.S. jazz musician. He was known for his trumpet playing and gravelly singing voice. Full name **Daniel Louis Armstrong**. Known as **Satchmo**

Barnaby's
Neil Armstrong

Arm·strong, Neil (*b.* 1930) U.S. astronaut. He was the first person to set foot on the Moon (1969).

arm-twist·ing *n.* heavy-handed or unfair pressure on somebody to do something

arm wres·tling *n.* a contest of strength between two people in which they sit opposite each other with one elbow each on a table, clasp hands, and try to force the opponent's hand onto the table

ar·my /áarmee/ (*plural* **-mies**) *n.* **1.** BRANCH OF ARMED FORCES the branch of a country's armed forces trained to fight on land **2.** LARGE ARMED GROUP any trained or armed fighting force **3.** LARGE ORGANIZED GROUP a large group that has been organized to do a particular thing ○ *an army of volunteers* **4.** LARGE NUMBER OF THINGS a very large number of things [14thC. Via French *armée* from medieval Latin *armata* (source of English *armada*), from the past participle of Latin *armare* "to arm" (see ARM[2]).]

ar·my ant *n.* any nomadic tropical ant that forages in large groups

ar·my brat *n.* a person who is born into, or grows up in, the family of a member of the army ○ *As an army brat, she's lived all over the world.*

ar·my post *n.* a piece of land owned and occupied by the army, used for housing and training personnel

ar·my·worm /áarmi wùrm/ *n.* the larva of any insect that travels in large migratory groups destroying vegetation and crops

Arn·hem /áarn hèm, áarnəm/ city in the eastern Netherlands. It was the scene of a major battle in World War II, when Allied airborne troops fought unsuccessfully to secure Rhine bridges in September 1944. Population: 133,670 (1994).

Arn·hem Land region in northern Australia, situated between the Roper and South Alligator rivers in the Northern Territory, and the site of one of Australia's largest Aboriginal reserves

ar·ni·ca /áarnikə/ (*plural* **-cas** *or* **-ca**) *n.* **1.** PLANT WITH YELLOW FLOWERS a perennial plant found in northern Europe, usually with yellow flowers like daisies. Genus: *Arnica*. **2.** TREATMENT FOR BRUISES a liquid preparation made from the dried flower heads of arnica, used in alternative medicine for treating bruises and sprains [Mid-18thC. From modern Latin, of unknown origin.]

Ar·no /áarnō/ chief river of the Tuscany region in central Italy. It rises in the Tuscan Apennines and flows through of Florence and Pisa. Length: about 150 mi./240 km.

Ar·nold /áarnəld/, **Benedict** (1741–1801) U.S. officer and traitor. His plan to surrender West Point to the British (1780) during the American Revolution made his name synonymous with treachery.

Ar·nold, Matthew (1822–88) British poet and critic. He was professor of poetry at Oxford (1857), and in addition to poetry wrote critical and religious works.

Ar·nold, Thomas (1795–1842) British educator. He was the father of Matthew Arnold, and the influential reforming headmaster of Rugby school (1828–42).

ar·oid /árr òyd, érr-/ *adj.* belonging to the arum family of perennial plants [Late 19thC. Coined from ARUM + -OID.]

a·ro·ma /ə rṓmə/ *n.* **1.** SMELL a smell, especially a pleasant smell **2.** QUALITY a subtle impression or quality [12thC. Via Latin from Greek, "spice."]

WORD KEY: SYNONYMS

See Synonyms at *smell*.

a·ro·ma·ther·a·py /ə rṓmə thérrəpee/ *n.* the use of oils extracted from plants to alleviate physical and psychological disorders, usually through massage or inhalation [Mid-20thC. From French *aromathérapie*.] —**a·ro·ma·ther·a·pist** *n.*

ar·o·mat·ic /àrrō máttik, èrrō-/ *adj.* **1.** WITH PLEASANT SMELL with a distinctive and pleasant smell **2.** CHEM OF CLASS OF CHEMICAL COMPOUNDS used to describe a class of organic chemical compounds that contain one or more rings of carbon atoms and undergo chemical reactions that are characteristic of benzene. About half of all organic compounds are aromatic. ◊ **aliphatic** ■ *n.* FRAGRANT SUBSTANCE OR PLANT an aromatic substance or plant [14thC. Via French *aromatique* from, ultimately, Greek *arōma* "spice."] —**ar·o·mat·i·cal·ly** *adv.*

a·ro·ma·tize /ə rṓmə tīz/ (**-tized, -tiz·ing, -tiz·es**) *vt.* **1.** MAKE FRAGRANT to make something fragrant, or release the fragrance of something **2.** CHEM CONVERT TO AROMATIC COMPOUND to convert a nonaromatic (**aliphatic**) compound to an aromatic compound —**a·ro·ma·ti·za·tion** /ə rṓmə tī záysh'n/ *n.*

A·roos·took /ə ro͝ostək, -ro͞os-/ river in northern Maine that flows northeastward into New Brunswick, Canada, and empties into the St. John River. It is a source of hydroelectric power. Length: 140 mi./225 km.

a·rose past tense of **arise**

a·round /ə równd/ CORE MEANING: a grammatical word used to indicate that something surrounds a place or object or is situated on or moves around all sides of it ○ (prep) *She came in and looked at the mess all around her.* ○ (prep) *A crumbling wall still stood around the old town.* ○ (adv) *From this spot you could see the countryside for miles around.*

1. *prep.* TO THE OTHER SIDE OF moving or looking to the other side of ○ *around the corner* **2.** *adv.* IN OPPOSITE DIRECTION in the opposite direction ○ *turned around and walked away* **3.** *adv.* PRESENT present or existing ○ *since computers have been around* **4.** *adv., prep.* FROM PLACE TO PLACE from place to place, in every or most parts ○ *rushing around* **5.** *adv., prep.* IN THE VICINITY in the vicinity, especially with no particular purpose or intent ○ *hanging around* **6.** *adv., prep.* HERE AND THERE in various unspecified parts of a place or area ○ *traveled around the country* **7.** *adv., prep.* APPROXIMATELY approximately ○ *around $600 a month* [13thC. Formed from A- "on" + ROUND, probably on the model of Old French *a la reond* "in the round, roundabout."] ◇ **have been around** to have had enough experience of life and the ways of the world not to be easily deceived (*informal*)

a·round-the-clock *adj.* happening constantly with no breaks, for 24 hours a day

a·rous·al /ə rówz'l/ *n.* **1.** AROUSING OF EMOTION OR ACTIVITY the arousing of a feeling, response, or desire ○ *the arousal of feelings of jealousy* **2.** SEXUAL DESIRE feelings of sexual desire **3.** WAKING UP waking up from sleep, unconsciousness, or a similar state

a·rouse /ə rówz/ (**a·roused, a·rous·ing, a·rous·es**) *v.* **1.** *vt.* STIMULATE to evoke a feeling, response, or desire **2.** *vt.* STIMULATE SEXUAL DESIRE IN SOMEBODY to cause feelings of sexual desire in somebody **3.** *vt.* ANGER to make somebody angry **4.** *vti.* WAKE UP to wake up, or wake somebody up from sleep or unconsciousness (*formal*) [Late 16thC. Formed from ROUSE.]

AKG London
Jean Arp

Arp /aarp/, **Jean** (1887–1966) French sculptor. A cofounder of the Dada movement (1916), he produced organic abstract sculpture based on natural forms. Also known as **Hans Arp**

ar·peg·gi·o /aar péjjee ō, -péjjō/ (*plural* **-os**) *n.* a sounding of the notes of a chord one after the other in rapid succession, rather than simultaneously [Early 18thC. From Italian, formed from *arpeggiare* "to play on the harp," from *arpa* "harp."]

ar·que·bus *n.* = **harquebus**

arr. *abbr.* **1.** MUSIC arranged **2.** arrives **3.** arrived **4.** arrival

ar·raign /ə ráyn/ (**-raigned, -raign·ing, -raigns**) *vt.* **1.** LAW CHARGE SOMEBODY IN COURT to bring somebody to court to answer a criminal charge (*usually passive*) **2.** ACCUSE SOMEBODY to call somebody to account for a fault or mistake [14thC. Via Anglo-Norman *arainer* from assumed Vulgar Latin *adrationare* "to call to account," literally "to reason to," from Latin *ratio* "reason," (source of English *reason*). The "g" was probably introduced to give an appearance of Latin origin.] —**ar·raign·er** *n.*

ar·raign·ment /ə ráynmənt/ *n.* LAW the legal process involved in bringing somebody before a court of law to answer a criminal charge

Ar·ran /érrən/ island in the Firth of Clyde in western Scotland. It is noted for its mountain scenery. Area: 169 sq.mi./433 sq.km.

ar·range /ə ránj/ (**-ranged, -rang·ing, -rang·es**) *v.* **1.** *vt.* PREPARE FOR SOMETHING to do what is necessary to make something happen in the future ○ *arrange a meeting* **2.** *vt.* PUT SOMEBODY OR SOMETHING IN ORDER to put people or things in a position or order ○ *The flowers had been beautifully arranged.* **3.** *vt.* MAKE AGREEMENT FOR SOMETHING TO HAPPEN to make an agreement so that something can happen or somebody can have something ○ *She's arranged for the plumbers to start next week.* **4.** *vti.* MUSIC ADAPT MUSIC to adapt a piece of music for playing or singing in a different manner (*often passive*) [Mid-18thC. From Old French *arangier*, literally "to put in a line to," from *rangier* "to put in a line" (see RANGE).] —**ar·range·a·ble** *adj.* —**ar·rang·er** *n.*

ar·ranged /ə ráynjd/ *adj.* brought about by agreement or planning ○ *an arranged marriage*

ar·range·ment /ə ráynjmənt/ *n.* **1.** PREPARATION something that has to be done so that something else can happen in the future, or the making of such preparations (*often used in the plural*) **2.** AGREEMENT an agreement made with somebody to do something, or the making of such an agreement **3.** PLEASING DISPLAY a group of things organized in a way that is meant to be attractive, or the arranging of such a group **4.** ORGANIZATION the way in which something is organized **5.** MUSIC MUSICAL ADAPTATION a version of a piece of music adapted for playing or singing in a different manner, or the scoring of such a version

ar·rant /érrənt/ *adj.* used to emphasize that somebody or something is an extreme example of something disapproved of ○ *That comment was arrant nonsense.* [Mid-16thC. Alteration of ERRANT "wandering"; from its frequent application to roving vagabonds.] —**ar·rant·ly** *adv.*

ar·ras /árrəs/ *n.* a tapestry used as a wall hanging or hanging screen [15thC. From Anglo-Norman *draps d'Arras* "cloth of Arras," named for *Arras*, a town in the Pas-de-Calais, northern France, which was famous for the manufacture of woolens and tapestry.]

ar·ray /ə ráy/ *n.* **1.** COLLECTION a large number or wide range of people or things ○ *a dazzling array of talent*

2. STRIKING ARRANGEMENT a group of things arranged in an impressive or structured way ○ *an array of Greek sculptures* **3. FINE CLOTHES** fine, expensive, or impressive clothes (*literary*) **4.** TELECOM **GROUP OF ANTENNAS** a group of antennas arranged to increase their effectiveness **5.** MATH **SET OF NUMBERS ARRANGED IN ORDER** a set of numbers or symbols, e.g., experimental data, usually arranged in a particular order **6.** LAW **JURORS** a panel of jurors, or the group of people from whom a jury is selected **7.** COMPUT **DATA STRUCTURE** an arrangement of items of computerized data in tabular form for easy reference. A computer program references an item by naming the array and the item's position in it. ■ *vt.* **(-rayed, -ray·ing, -rays) 1. ARRANGE SOMETHING** to arrange something for display or in readiness for use (*formal*) (*usually passive*) **2. DEPLOY TROOPS** to arrange troops for battle (*literary*) (*usually passive*) **3. DRESS SOMEBODY** to dress somebody in particular clothes (*literary*) (*often passive*) [14thC. Via Anglo-Norman from Old French *arei*, from *areer* "to array," from assumed Vulgar Latin *arredare* "to arrange," from Latin *ad* "to" + a prehistoric Germanic word meaning "to prepare."]

ar·rear·age /ə reérij/ *n.* **1. REMAINING DEBT** the debt that remains after part of an overdue debt has been paid **2. BEING IN ARREARS** the state of being overdue in the payment of a debt

ar·rears /ə reérz/ *npl.* unpaid debts, especially debts accumulating as a result of the debtor's failure to make regular payments [15thC. From the obsolete adverb *arrear* "to the rear, overdue," which came via Old French from medieval Latin *adretro*, from Latin *ad* "to" + *retro* "backward, behind" (source of English *retro*).] ◇ **in** or **into arrears** behind in making regular payments of money owed

ar·rest /ə rést/ *vt.* **(-rest·ed, -rest·ing, -rests) 1. TAKE SOMEBODY INTO CUSTODY** to seize and take somebody into legal custody **2. STOP OR SLOW SOMETHING** to stop or slow a process (*formal*) ○ *a mechanism that arrests the motion of the flywheel* **3. TAKE HOLD OF SOMETHING** to capture suddenly and hold something, especially somebody's attention (*formal*) **4. SEIZE SOMETHING LEGALLY** to seize something by legal authority (*formal*) ■ *n.* **1. TAKING OF SOMEBODY INTO CUSTODY** the seizing and taking of somebody into legal custody ○ *a case of wrongful arrest* **2. CUSTODY** the state of being held in legal custody ○ *You're under arrest!* **3. SUDDEN STOP** a sudden stopping of the movement or operation of something **4. LEGAL SEIZURE** the legal seizure or detention of something (*formal*) [14thC. Via Old French from assumed Vulgar Latin *arrestare* "to cause to stop," literally "to stop to," from Latin *restare* "to stop, stay behind" (see REST "remainder").] —**ar·rest·ment** *n.*

ar·rest·ee /ə rès teé/ *n.* somebody who is under arrest

ar·rest·er /ə réstər/, **ar·res·tor** /ə réstər, -awr/ *n.* **1.** NAVY **DEVICE TO STOP LANDING AIRCRAFT** one of a set of cables on an aircraft carrier used to slow and stop landing aircraft **2.** LAW **ARRESTING OFFICER** somebody who takes a suspect into legal custody **3. SOMETHING THAT ARRESTS** somebody or something that arrests, e.g., by causing something to stop or somebody to pause

ar·rest·ing /ə résting/ *adj.* looking so attractive or unusual that people's attention is immediately caught —**ar·rest·ing·ly** *adv.*

ar·rest·ing ca·ble *n.* one of a set of cables strung across the deck of an aircraft carrier to catch the tailhook of a landing aircraft and bring it to a halt (*usually used in the plural*)

ar·rest of judg·ment *n.* the withholding of judgment in a legal action if there appears to be a good reason to question its appropriateness, e.g., because of a lack of jurisdiction

ar·res·tor *n.* = **arrester**

ar·rhyth·mi·a /ə ríthmee ə, ay-/ *n.* an irregularity in the normal rhythm or force of the heartbeat [Late 19thC. From Greek, formed from *arruthmos*, literally "without measure," from *rhuthmos* "measure" (see RHYTHM).]

ar·rhyth·mic /ə ríthmik, ay-/ *adj.* **1. IRREGULAR** used to describe a heartbeat that has an irregular rhythm **2. LACKING RHYTHM** without a regular or recognizable rhythm —**ar·rhyth·mi·cal·ly** *adv.*

ar·ri·ère-pen·sée /àrree air poN sáy/ *n.* (*formal*) **1. RESERVATION** a mental reservation **2. INTENTION** an unspoken intention [Early 19thC. From French, literally "behind-thought," from the concealing of the thought.]

ar·ris /érrəs/ (*plural* **-ris** or **-ris·es**) *n.* a sharp edge or ridge made by the meeting of two surfaces on an architectural column or molding [Late 17thC. Via early modern French *areste* "sharp edge" from Latin *arista* (see ARĘTE).]

ar·ri·val /ə rív'l/ *n.* **1. ARRIVING** the reaching of a place after coming from another place ○ *Her arrival caused a buzz of comment.* **2. NEWCOMER** somebody or something recently arriving at a place or joining a group ○ *a late arrival* **3. PASSENGER VEHICLE ARRIVING SOMEWHERE** an aircraft, train, or bus arriving at an airport or station **4. TIME OF ARRIVING** the time when somebody or something reaches a place after coming from another place ○ *date of arrival* **5. BEGINNING** the moment when something begins or becomes important ○ *The arrival of television changed the world.* **6. BIRTH** the birth of a baby **7. REACHING OF SOMETHING** the achieving or reaching of something after much work or effort ○ *Their arrival at a decision seems unlikely.*

ar·rive /ə rív/ **(-rived, -riv·ing, -rives)** *vi.* **1. GET TO PLACE** to reach a place after coming from another place **2. BE DELIVERED** to be delivered or brought to somebody or something ○ *She's waiting for the mail to arrive.* **3. BECOME AVAILABLE OR COMMON** to become available or common **4. BEGIN** to begin or happen after a period of time or waiting **5. BE BORN** to be born **6. WORK OUT SOLUTION** to reach a decision after thinking about or discussing a problem ○ *How did you arrive at the idea of using strings?* **7. SUCCEED** to become successful or famous (*informal*) ○ *You haven't arrived until you've eaten in this restaurant.* [12thC. Via Old French from assumed Vulgar Latin *arripare*, literally "to come to shore," from Latin *ripa* "shore" (source of English *river*).] —**ar·riv·er** *n.*

ar·ri·ve·der·ci /àrrive dáirchee, ə reève-/ *interj.* goodbye for now [Late 20thC. From Italian *a rivederci*, literally "until we see each other again," from *rivedere* "to see again."]

ar·ri·viste /àri veést, -víst/ *n.* somebody who has recently become influential or socially prominent, especially somebody suspected of self-serving or unscrupulous motives (*disapproving*) [Early 20thC. From French, literally "somebody who arrives."]

ar·ro·gance /érrəgəns/ *n.* a strong feeling of proud self-importance that is expressed by treating other people with contempt or disregard

ar·ro·gant /érrəgənt/ *adj.* feeling or showing proud self-importance and contempt or disregard for others [14thC. Via French from Latin *arrogant-*, the present participle stem of *arrogare* "to claim for yourself," literally "to ask to," from *rogare* "to ask" (see ROGATION).] —**ar·ro·gant·ly** *adv.*

WORD KEY: SYNONYMS

See Synonyms at ***proud***.

ar·ro·gate /érrə gàyt/ **(-gat·ed, -gat·ing, -gates)** *vt.* (*formal*) **1. CLAIM SOMETHING WITHOUT RIGHT** to take or claim something for yourself without the right to do so ○ *arrogating the powers of the General* **2. ASSIGN SOMETHING TO ANOTHER** to assign or attribute something to another in a way that is not warranted [Mid-16thC. From Latin *arrogat-*, the past participle stem of *arrogare* (see ARROGANT).] —**ar·ro·ga·tion** /èrrə gáysh'n/ *n.* —**ar·ro·ga·tor** /-gàytər/ *n.*

ar·ron·disse·ment /ə róndissmənt, -mòN/ (*plural* **-ments** /ə róndissmənt, -mòN/) *n.* **1. SUBDIVISION OF FRENCH ADMINISTRATIVE DISTRICT** an administrative area in France that is a major subdivision of an administrative district **2. AREA OF FRENCH CITY** an administrative area in some large cities in France, including Paris [Early 19thC. From French, formed from *arrondiss-*, a stem of *arrondir* "to make round."]

ar·row /érrō/ *n.* **1. MISSILE SHOT FROM BOW** a long thin missile pointed at one end and usually with feathers at the other, fired from a bow **2. DIRECTION SIGN** a direction sign consisting of a horizontal stroke finishing in the middle of a V shape [Old English *arwe*. From the Old Norse stem *örv-*. Ultimately from an Indo-European word that also produced English *arc* and *archer*. The original meaning may have been "bow," and by extension "thing belonging to the bow."] —**ar·row·y** *adj.*

ar·row ar·um (*plural* **ar·row ar·um** or **ar·row ar·ums**) *n.* a perennial plant with arrow-shaped leaves that grows in eastern North America. Latin name: *Peltandra virginica*.

ar·row·head /érrō hed/ *n.* **1. POINT OF ARROW** a sharp pointed tip attached to an arrow **2. AQUATIC PLANT** an aquatic plant with arrow-shaped leaves and clusters of white flowers, native to Asia and North America. Genus: *Sagittaria*.

ar·row-poi·son frog *n.* a brightly colored South American frog whose skin glands produce poison. The frogs are used by local peoples as a source of poison for their arrow tips. Family: Dendrobatidae.

ar·row·root /érrō root/ (*plural* **-root** or **-roots**) *n.* **1.** PLANTS **WEST INDIAN PLANT** a West Indian plant with white flowers and rhizomes that yield an edible starch. Latin name: *Maranta arundinacea*. **2.** FOOD **EDIBLE RHIZOME** the edible rhizome of the arrowroot plant **3. STARCH** starch from the rhizomes of the arrowroot plant, used as a thickener for clear sauces and in cookies [Late 17thC. By folk etymology from Arawak *aru-aru*, literally "meal of meals," from the use of the tubers to absorb poison from arrow wounds.]

ar·row·wood (*plural* **ar·row-woods** or **ar·row-wood**) *n.* a shrub with tough, straight stems that were previously used by Native Americans to make arrows. Genus: *Viburnum*.

ar·row worm *n.* a marine invertebrate animal that has an arrow-shaped body and spines on its head for catching prey. Phylum: Chaetognatha. [From the shape of the head with its curved bristles on either side, suggesting an arrow]

ar·roy·o /ə róy ō/ (*plural* **-os**) *n.* *Southwest U.S.* **1. DRY GULCH** a steep-sided dry gulch in a desert area, that is wet only after heavy rain **2.** a small stream of running water [Mid-19thC. Via Spanish from, ultimately, Latin *arrugia* "mineshaft," of unknown origin.]

arse /aars/ *n.* *U.K.* = **ass**[2] (*taboo offensive*) [Old English *ærs*, *ears*. Ultimately from an Indo-European word meaning "buttocks" that is also the ancestor of *anuran* and *squirrel*.]

arse-lick·er *n.* *U.K.* = **ass kisser** (*taboo offensive*)

ar·se·nal /áarsən'l, -nəl/ *n.* **1. ARMAMENTS** a stockpile of weapons and military equipment **2. WEAPONS STOREHOUSE** a building where weapons and military equipment are stored **3. RESOURCES** a supply of methods or resources ○ *arsenal of teaching strategies* [Early 16thC. Directly or via French from Italian *arzanale*, from Venetian Italian *arzanà*, from, ultimately, Arabic *dār-(aṣ-)ṣinā'a* "workshop, factory," literally "house of the manufacture."]

WORD KEY: ORIGIN

Arsenal is derived from an Arabic word *dār-(aṣ-)ṣinā'a*, meaning "workshop" or "factory." When the original Arabic word was borrowed into Venetian Italian, the initial *d* was lost, possibly because it was misinterpreted as the Italian preposition *de* "of." The word came to mean "dock possessing naval stores," and the dockyard in Venice, which in the 15th century was the leading naval power in the Mediterranean, is known to this day as the *Arzenale*. The Romance languages retain this meaning in words from the same ancestor that still show the Arabic *d*, in Italian *darsena* "dock," for example; in English too, "dockyard" was the original sense, giving way in the late 16th century to "military storehouse."

ar·se·nate /áarsənət, áarsnət, -ə nayt/ *n.* any salt of arsenic acid [Early 19thC. Coined from ARSENIC + -ATE.]

ar·se·nic /áarsnik, áarsənik/ *n.* **1. POISONOUS ELEMENT** a steel-gray poisonous solid chemical element that is a brittle crystalline metalloid used in alloys. Symbol **As 2.** = **arsenic trioxide** ■ *adj.* **CONTAINING ARSENIC** relating to or containing arsenic with a valence of 5 [14thC. Via French from, ultimately, Greek *arsenikon* "yellow orpiment," from Arabic *az-zarnīk*, literally "the orpiment," from, ultimately, Persian *zar* "gold."]

WORD KEY: ORIGIN

The term ***arsenic*** was originally applied to the lemon-yellow mineral arsenic trisulphide, hence it's origin in *zar*, the Persian word for gold. The Arabic derivative of this word was misinterpreted by foreign listeners as including the definite article *al*, and in Greek the supposed beneficial effects on virility led the term to be associated by folk etymology with the similar-sounding words *arsenikos*, "masculine," and *arsēn*, "manly." In English the word still referred to the mineral at first (for which *orpiment* was the other current name), and it is not until the early 17th century that it becomes used for white arsenic or arsenic trioxide. The element arsenic itself was isolated and so named at the start of the 19th century.

ar·sen·ic ac·id /aar sénnik ássid/ *n.* a white crystalline solid that contains arsenic. It is poisonous and is used to make arsenates and insecticides. Formula: H_3AsO_4.

ar·sen·i·cal /aar sénnik'l/ *adj.* **RELATING TO ARSENIC** relating to or containing arsenic ■ *n.* **SUBSTANCE CONTAINING ARSENIC** a substance, e.g., a drug or insecticide, that contains arsenic

ar·sen·ic tri·ox·ide /áarsnik trī ók sīd, aar sénnik trī ók sīd/ *n.* a white solid that contains arsenic. It is poisonous and is used as an insecticide, rat poison, and weed killer, and in making glass and pigments. Formula: AS_2O_3.

ar·se·nide /áarsə n-d/ *n.* a chemical compound of arsenic and a metal [Mid-19thC. Coined from ARSENIC + -IDE.]

ar·se·ni·ous /aar séenee əs/ *adj.* relating to or containing arsenic with a valence of 3 [Early 19thC. Coined from ARSENIC + -IOUS.]

ar·se·no·py·rite /áarsənō pīr īt, aar sénō-/ *n.* a gray-to-white mineral with metallic luster consisting of a sulfide of iron and arsenic. Formula: FeAsS. [Mid-19thC. Coined from ARSENIC + PYRITE.]

ar·ses plural of **arsis**

ar·sine /aar séen, áar seen/ *n.* a colorless poisonous gas with an odor like garlic, used to make organic compounds and transistors and as a chemical weapon. Formula: AsH_3. [Late 19thC. Coined from ARSENIC + -INE.]

ar·sis /áarsiss/ (*plural* **-ses** /-seez/) *n.* ◊ **thesis** *n.* 7 **1. SHORT SYLLABLE** in classical Greek and Roman verse, the short syllable or syllables in a metrical foot **2. ACCENTED SYLLABLE** in modern accentual verse, the accented syllable in a metrical foot [14thC. Via late Latin, "raising of the voice to greater force, accented part of the metrical foot," from Greek *arsis* "raising (of the foot in beating time)."]

ar·son /áars'n/ *n.* the burning of a building or other property for a criminal or malicious reason [Late 17thC. Via legal Anglo-Norman *arsoun* from, ultimately, Latin *arsus*, the past participle of *ardere* "to burn" (source of English *ardent* and *ardor*). Ultimately from an Indo-European word meaning "to burn," which is also the ancestor of English *ash* and *arid*.]

ar·son·ist /áars'nist/ *n.* somebody who sets fire to a building or other property for a criminal or malicious reason

art[1] /aart/ *n.* **1. CREATION OF BEAUTIFUL THINGS** the creation of beautiful or thought-provoking works, e.g., in painting, music, or writing **2. BEAUTIFUL OBJECTS** beautiful or thought-provoking works produced through creative activity **3. BRANCH OF ART** a branch or category of art, especially one of the visual arts **4. ARTISTIC SKILL** the skill and technique involved in producing visual representations **5. STUDY OF ART** the study of a branch of the visual arts **6. CREATION BY HUMANS** creation by human endeavor rather than by nature **7. TECHNIQUES OR CRAFT** the techniques used by somebody in a particular field, or the use of those techniques ○ *the art of the typographer* **8. ABILITY** the skill or ability to do something well **9. CUNNING** the ability to achieve things by deceitful or cunning methods (*literary*) ■ **arts** *npl.* **1. FORMS OF CREATIVE BEAUTY** the activities enjoyed for the beauty they create or the way they present ideas, e.g., painting, music, and literature **2. NONSCIENTIFIC SUBJECTS** nonscientific and nontechnical subjects at school or college [13thC. Via French from the Latin stem *art-* "skill" (source of English *artisan* and *artificial*). Ultimately from an Indo-European word meaning "to fit together."] ◇ **have something down to a fine art** to be able to do something very skillfully

WORD KEY: ORIGIN

The Latin stem *art-* is also the source of the English words *artificial*, *artisan*, and *inert*.

art[2] /aart/ 2nd person present singular of **be** (*archaic or literary*)

art. *abbr.* **1.** article **2.** artificial **3.** artillery **4.** artist

-art *suffix.* = **-ard**

ar·tal plural of **rotl**

art dec·o /-dékō/, **Art Dec·o** *n.* a style of architecture, interior design, and jewelry most popular in the 1930s that used geometrical designs and bold colors and outlines [Mid-20thC. From French, shortening of *Arts Décoratifs*, literally "decorative arts," from *Exposition Internationale des Arts Décoratifs et Industriels Modernes* "International Exposition of Modern Decorative and Industrial Arts," held in Paris in 1925.]

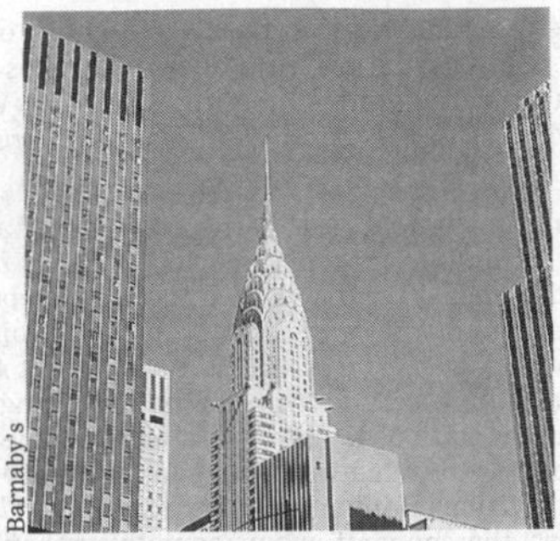

Art deco: Chrysler Building, New York City (1930), designed by William van Alen

art di·rec·tor *n.* the person in charge of the sets and costumes when something is being filmed or photographed

ar·te·fact *n.* = **artifact**

ar·tel /aar tél/ *n.* a workers' or producers' cooperative in imperial Russia or the Soviet Union [Late 19thC. From Russian *artel*, of uncertain origin.]

Ar·te·mis /áartəmiss/ *n.* in Greek mythology, the goddess of hunting and the moon, and of childbirth. She was the daughter of Zeus and the sister of Apollo. Roman equivalent **Diana**

ar·te·mis·i·a /áartə mízhee ə/ (*plural* **-as** *or* **-a**) *n.* an aromatic plant found in the northern hemisphere that has grayish-green leaves and many small flower heads. Genus: *Artemisia*. [14thC. Via Latin from Greek, "wormwood," literally "plant sacred to *Artemis*," goddess of childbirth and fertility. Perhaps from the medicinal use of the herb for diseases of the womb.]

ar·te·ri·al /aar téeree əl/ *adj.* **1. OF ARTERIES** relating to, affecting, or used in arteries **2. OXYGENATED** used to describe the bright red blood in the arteries that has absorbed oxygen **3. MAIN** constituting a main route in a road, rail, or river system —**ar·te·ri·al·ly** *adv.*

ar·te·ri·al·ize /aar téeree ə l-z/ (**-ized, -iz·ing, -iz·es**) *vt.* to convert venous blood into arterial blood by replenishing its oxygen —**ar·te·ri·al·i·za·tion** /aar téeree ə lə záysh'n/ *n.*

arterio- *prefix.* artery, arterial ○ *arteriovenous* [From Greek *artēria* (see ARTERY)]

ar·te·ri·o·gram /aar téeree ə gram/ *n.* an X-ray of the arteries made after a substance that shows up on an X-ray has been injected into the bloodstream

ar·te·ri·og·ra·phy /aar téeree óggrəfee/ *n.* examination of the arteries by X-raying them after injecting into the bloodstream a substance that shows up on an X-ray —**ar·te·ri·o·graph·ic** /aar téeree ə gráffik/ *adj.*

ar·te·ri·ole /aar téeri l/ *n.* a blood vessel that branches off from an artery [Mid-19thC. From French *artériole*, literally "little artery," from *artère* "artery," from Latin *arteria* (see ARTERY).] —**ar·te·ri·o·lar** /aar téeree ṓlər/ *adj.*

ar·te·ri·o·scle·ro·sis /aar téeree ō sklə rṓssiss/ *n.* the arterial disease atherosclerosis (*dated*) —**ar·te·ri·o·scle·rot·ic** /-sklə róttik/ *adj.*

ar·te·ri·o·ve·nous /aar téeree ō véenəss/ *adj.* involving both a vein and an artery

ar·te·ri·tis /áartə rítəs/ *n.* inflammation of the walls of an artery

ar·ter·y /áartəree/ (*plural* **-ies**) *n.* **1. TYPE OF BLOOD VESSEL** a blood vessel that is part of the system carrying blood under pressure from the heart to the rest of the body **2. MAIN ROUTE** a main route in a road, rail, or river system [14thC. Via Latin from Greek *artēria* "windpipe," of uncertain origin. The Greeks called arteries "windpipes" because they regarded them as air ducts branching from the trachea; since arteries do not contain blood after death, it was supposed that their function was conveying air.]

ar·te·sian well /aar téezh'n-/ *n.* a well drilled through impermeable rocks into strata where water is under enough pressure to force it to the surface without pumping [Mid-19thC. "Artesian" from French *artésien*, literally "of Artois" (*Arteis* in Old French), a region in northeastern France where such wells were first drilled in the 18thC.]

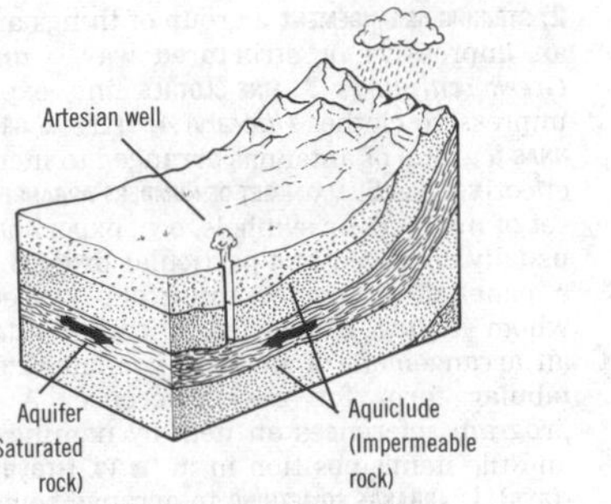

Artesian well

art film *n.* a serious, independently made film that is not aimed at a mass audience

art form *n.* **1. ARTISTIC MEDIUM** a creative activity or type of artistic expression that is intended to be beautiful or thought-provoking **2. SOMETHING DONE ARTISTICALLY** something that is done in such a sophisticated or skillful way that it can be seen as artistic ○ *He's turned the answering of questions without actually saying anything into an art form.*

art·ful /áartf'l/ *adj.* **1. CUNNING** using subtle and clever means to achieve things **2. PERFORMED WITH CLEVERNESS** performed with cleverness and subtlety **3. SKILLFUL** done skillfully or with taste —**art·ful·ly** /áartfəlee/ *adv.* —**art·ful·ness** /-f'lnəss/ *n.*

art gal·ler·y (*plural* **art gal·ler·ies**) *n.* **1. MUSEUM OF ART** a building where works of art are displayed **2. PLACE SELLING ART** an establishment that displays and sells works of art

art house (*plural* **art hous·es**) *n.* a theater where art films are shown

arthr- *prefix.* = **arthro-** (*used before vowels*)

ar·thral·gia /aar thráljə, -jee ə/ *n.* pain in a joint —**ar·thral·gic** *adj.*

ar·threc·to·my /aar thréktəmee/ (*plural* **-mies**) *n.* the surgical removal of a joint

ar·thrit·ic /aar thríttik/ *adj.* **WITH ARTHRITIS** affected by arthritis ■ *n.* **SOMEBODY WITH ARTHRITIS** somebody who has arthritis —**ar·thrit·i·cal·ly** *adv.*

ar·thri·tis /aar thrítəss/ *n.* a medical condition affecting a joint or joints, causing pain, swelling, and stiffness [Mid-16thC. Via Latin from Greek *arthritis* "joint disease," from *arthron* "joint." Ultimately from an Indo-European word meaning "to fit together," which is also the ancestor of English *read* and *logarithm*.]

arthro-, arthr- *prefix.* joint ○ *arthroscopic* [From Greek *arthron*. Ultimately from an Indo-European base meaning "to fit together," which is also the ancestor of English *arm*, *article*, and *art*.]

ar·thro·gram /áarthrə gràm/ *n.* an X-ray of the inside of a damaged joint made after a substance that shows up on an X-ray has been injected into the joint

ar·throg·ra·phy /aar thróggrəfee/ *n.* examination of the inside of a damaged joint by X-raying it after injecting a substance that shows up on an X-ray

ar·throp·a·thy /aar thróppəthee/ *n.* an abnormality or disease of a joint

ar·thro·plas·ty /áarthrə plàstee/ (*plural* **-ties**) *n.* surgical repair of a joint or replacement of a joint or part of one by metal or plastic parts. The most common operations are hip and knee replacements.

ar·thro·pod /áarthrə pòd/ *n.* an invertebrate animal that has jointed limbs, a segmented body, and an exoskeleton made of chitin. Insects, arachnids, centipedes, and crustaceans are arthropods. Phylum: Arthropoda. [Late 19thC. From modern Latin *Arthropoda*, phylum name, from Greek *arthron* "joint" (see ARTHRITIS) + the stem *pod-* "foot" (see -POD).] —**ar·thro·pod** *adj.* —**ar·throp·o·dal** /aar thrápəd'l/ *adj.* —**ar·throp·o·dous** /-thrápədəs/ *adj.*

ar·thros·co·py /aar thróskəpee/ (*plural* **-pies**) *n.* inspection of the inside of a joint of the body using an endoscope —**ar·thro·scope** /áarthrəsk-p/ *n.* —**ar·thro·scop·ic** /áarthrə skóppik/ *adj.* —**ar·thro·scop·ic·al·ly** /-skóppikəlee/ *adv.*

ar·thro·sis /aar thrṓsiss/ (*plural* **-ses** /-seez/) *n.* **1.** JOINT BETWEEN BONES a joint between two bones (*technical*) **2.** JOINT DISEASE a degenerative disease of a joint [Mid-17thC. Via Latin from Greek *arthrōsis*, from *arthroun* "to articulate," from *arthron* "joint" (see ARTHRITIS). The sense "joint disease" is modeled on other disease names ending in -OSIS.]

ar·throt·o·my /aar thróttəmee/ (*plural* **-mies**) *n.* a surgical operation that involves cutting into a joint of the body

Ar·thur /áarthər/, **Chester A.** (1829–86) U.S. statesman and 21st president of the United States. A Republican president (1881–85), he enacted sweeping civil service reforms (1883) that lost him the support of his party. Full name **Chester Alan Arthur**

Ar·thur I *n.* in medieval legend, a king of the Britons whose court was based at Camelot. He was the leader of the Knights of the Round Table. —**Ar·thu·ri·an** /aar thóoree ən/ *adj.*

Artichoke

ar·ti·choke /áartəch-k/ (*plural* **-chokes** *or* **-choke**) *n.* **1.** PLANT WITH EDIBLE FLOWER BUDS a plant native to Europe and Asia that has flowers that resemble thistles. Latin name: *Cynara scolymus.* **2.** FLOWER BUD EATEN AS VEGETABLE the flower bud of an artichoke plant, parts of which can be eaten after cooking **3.** = **Jerusalem artichoke** [Mid-16thC. From Northern Italian *articiocco*, *arciciocco*, from Italian *arcicioffo*, from Spanish *alcarchofa*, from Arabic *al-karšūf(a)*, literally "the artichoke."]

ar·ti·cle /áartik'l/ *n.* **1.** NEWSPAPER OR REFERENCE PIECE a piece of nonfiction writing in a newspaper, magazine, or reference book ○ *an article on ecology* **2.** ITEM an object or item, especially one that is part of a group ○ *articles of clothing* **3.** LAW LEGAL PARAGRAPH a section of a legal document that deals with a particular point **4.** GRAM WORD BEFORE NOUN a word used with a noun that specifies whether the noun is definite or indefinite. In English the indefinite articles are "a" and "an," and the definite article is "the." ■ *vt.* (**-cled, -cling, -cles**) LAW BIND SOMEBODY BY CONTRACT to bind somebody by the articles of a contract, especially somebody training in the legal profession [12thC. Via French from Latin *articulus* "joint, section," literally "little joint," from *artus* "joint, limb." The sense "section of a text" came from the idea of a joint as a section of a limb. The meaning "item" is a 19th-century development.]

Ar·ti·cle 15 *n.* a punishment under part of the U.S. Uniform Code of Military Justice that allows commanders to punish certain offenses without bringing the offender to trial

ar·ti·cle of faith *n.* **1.** BASIC RELIGIOUS BELIEF any one of the items that must be believed as part of a creed or statement of faith **2.** DEEPLY HELD BELIEF something that somebody believes completely

ar·tic·u·la·ble /aar tíkyələb'l/ *adj.* able to be expressed clearly in words

ar·tic·u·lar /aar tíkyələr/ *adj.* relating to or involving a joint of the body [15thC. From Latin *articularis*, from *articulus* "joint" (see ARTICLE).] —**ar·tic·u·lar·ly** *adv.*

ar·tic·u·late *adj.* /aar tíkyə lət/ **1.** ELOQUENT able to express thoughts, ideas, and feelings coherently **2.** COHERENT spoken or expressed clearly **3.** ABLE TO SPEAK possessing the power of speech **4.** ANAT JOINTED with joints or jointed segments, as in the bodies of higher vertebrates and arthropods (*technical*) ■ *v.* /aar tíkyə làyt/ (**-lat·ed, -lat·ing, -lates**) **1.** *vi.* SPEAK INTELLIGIBLY to utter intelligible speech **2.** *vt.* COMMUNICATE SOMETHING to express thoughts, ideas, or feelings coherently ○ *unable to articulate his grief* **3.** *vti.* SPEAK DISTINCTLY to pronounce something or speak clearly **4.** *vti.* JOIN TO ALLOW MOVEMENT to form the kind of joint that allows movement [Mid-16thC. From Latin *articulatus*, the past participle of *articulare* "to divide into joints, speak distinctly," from *articulus* "joint" (see ARTICLE).] —**ar·tic·u·la·cy** *n.* —**ar·tic·u·late·ly** *adv.* —**ar·tic·u·late·ness** *n.*

ar·tic·u·lat·ed /aar tíkyə làytəd/ *adj.* made up of two or more sections connected by a joint that can pivot ○ *an articulated bus*

ar·tic·u·lat·ed lor·ry (*plural* **ar·tic·u·lat·ed lor·ries**) *n. U.K., NZ* a truck made up of two parts, tractor and trailer, connected by a joint that can pivot

ar·tic·u·la·tion /aar tìkyə láysh'n/ *n.* **1.** SPEECH the pronouncing of words, or the manner in which they are pronounced **2.** COMMUNICATION the coherent expression of thoughts, ideas, or feelings **3.** JOINTING the connection of the different parts of something by joints, or the way the parts fit together **4.** ANAT ANIMAL'S JOINT a joint in an animal (*technical*) **5.** BOT PLANT NODE a node of a plant, or the space on a stem between two nodes (*technical*) —**ar·tic·u·la·tive** /aar tíkyələtiv/ *adj.* —**ar·tic·u·la·to·ry** /-tíkyələ tawree/ *adj.*

ar·tic·u·la·tor /aar tíkyə laytər/ *n.* **1.** COMMUNICATOR somebody who speaks or expresses things clearly **2.** PHON VOCAL ORGANS a part of the vocal organs that helps form speech sounds

ar·tic·u·la·to·ry pho·net·ics *n.* the branch of phonetics that deals with how speech sounds are made

ar·ti·fact /áarti fakt/, **ar·te·fact** *n.* **1.** OBJECT MADE BY HUMAN an object made by a human being, e.g., a tool or ornament, especially one that has archeological or cultural interest **2.** METHOD-DEPENDENT RESULT something that appears to exist because of the way a thing, data, or the like is examined, e.g., an abnormal behavior that is produced by a behavioral test **3.** FOREIGN SUBSTANCE something in a biological specimen that is not present naturally but has been introduced or produced during a procedure [Early 19thC. From Latin *arte*, a form of *ars* "skill" (see ART) + *factum* "thing made" (see FACT).]

ar·ti·fice /áartəfəss/ *n.* (*formal*) **1.** CLEVER TRICK a clever trick or stratagem **2.** CLEVERNESS the use of clever stratagems or tricks **3.** INSINCERE BEHAVIOR the deceiving of people in a clever or subtle way [Early 17thC. Via French from, ultimately, Latin *artificium* "craft, art, cunning," from the stem *artific-* "artisan, contriver," from the stem *art-* "skill" (see ART) + *facere* "to make" (see FACT).]

ar·tif·i·cer /aar tíffəsər/ *n.* (*dated*) **1.** SKILLED WORKER somebody whose work requires manual skill **2.** INVENTOR somebody who invents or devises things [14thC. Via Anglo-Norman (with influence from medieval Latin *artificiarius*) from, probably, Old French *artificien*, from, ultimately, Latin *artificium* "craft, cunning."]

ar·ti·fi·cial /àartə físh'l/ *adj.* **1.** MADE BY HUMANS made by human beings rather than occurring naturally **2.** SYNTHETIC made in imitation of something natural **3.** INSINCERE without sincerity or spontaneity (*disapproving*) ○ *an artificial smile* **4.** NOT SPONTANEOUS produced as a result of human action rather than arising spontaneously ○ *an artificial barrier to social advancement* [14thC. Directly or via Old French from Latin *artificialis*, from *artificium* "craft, cunning" (see ARTIFICE).] —**ar·ti·fi·ci·al·i·ty** /àartəfishee álletee/ *n.* —**ar·ti·fi·cial·ly** /àartə físhəlee/ *adv.*

ar·ti·fi·cial climb·ing *n.* climbing on indoor or other human-made environments such as special walls designed and built for this

ar·ti·fi·cial ho·ri·zon *n.* an instrument that displays, usually pictorially, the amount of pitch or bank of an aircraft relative to the horizon

ar·ti·fi·cial in·sem·i·na·tion *n.* a method of inducing pregnancy in a female mammal by injecting sperm into the womb. The technique is used in agriculture to improve the breeding of livestock.

ar·ti·fi·cial in·tel·li·gence *n.* **1.** DEVELOPMENT OF INTELLIGENT MACHINES a branch of computer science devoted to the development of computer programs that will allow machines to perform functions normally requiring human intelligence **2.** COMPUTER INTELLIGENCE the ability of computers to perform functions that normally require human intelligence

ar·ti·fi·cial·ize /àartə físhə l-z/ (**-ized, -iz·ing, -izes**) *vt.* to give something an artificial appearance or quality —**ar·ti·fi·cial·i·za·tion** /àartəfishələ záysh'n/ *n.*

ar·ti·fi·cial lan·guage *n.* a language that has been invented for international communication or for use with computers. The best known artificial language is Esperanto.

ar·ti·fi·cial res·pi·ra·tion *n.* any method of forcing air into the lungs of somebody who has stopped breathing, especially the method that involves blowing air into the mouth. Another formerly used method involved pushing down rhythmically on the chest.

ar·ti·fi·cial se·lec·tion *n.* selection by humans of animals and plants with desirable characteristics for use in breeding over several generations. ◊ **natural selection**

ar·ti·fi·cial sweet·en·er *n.* a synthetic sugar substitute used as an ingredient in low-calorie drinks or food or added to drinks such as coffee or tea by dieters or people with diabetes

ar·til·ler·y /aar tílləree/ *n.* **1.** POWERFUL GUNS large-caliber guns, e.g., cannons, howitzers, missile launchers, and mortars **2.** SOLDIERS USING POWERFUL GUNS soldiers who specialize in operating large, powerful firearms, regarded as a group or unit **3.** CATAPULTS catapults and other large mechanical weapons once used by armies (*archaic*) [14thC. From French *artillerie*, from *artiller* "to equip, arm," from (with influence by folk etymology from *art* "skill") *atillier* "to equip, arm," of uncertain origin.]

ar·til·ler·y·man /aar tíllərimən/ (*plural* **-men** /-mən/) *n.* a soldier in an artillery unit

ar·til·ler·y plant *n.* a tropical American plant with fleshy leaves and stamens that discharge their pollen by exploding. Latin name: *Pilea microphylla.*

ar·ti·o·dac·tyl /àartee ō dákt'l/ *n.* any herbivorous, hooved mammal with an even number of toes on each foot. Cows, sheep, and deer are artiodactyls. Order: Artiodactyla. [Mid-19thC. From modern Latin *Artiodactyla*, order name, literally "even-toed ones," which was coined from Greek *artios* "even, fitting" + *daktylos* "finger, toe."] —**ar·ti·o·dac·ty·lous** *adj.*

ar·ti·san /áartəzən/ *n.* somebody who is skilled at a craft [Mid-16thC. Via French from Italian *artigiano*, from, ultimately, Latin *artit-*, the past participle stem of *artire* "to instruct in the arts," from the stem *art-* "work of art, skill" (see ART).] —**ar·ti·san·ship** *n.*

art·ist /áartist/ *n.* **1.** CREATOR OF ART somebody who creates art, especially paintings, drawings, or sculptures **2.** SKILLED PERSON somebody who does something with great skill and creativity ○ *an artist with a basketball* **3.** PERFORMER a member of the performing arts ○ *a well-known recording artist* **4.** CUNNING PERSON somebody who is very good at doing something, especially something involving cunning or deceit (*slang*) ○ *a ripoff artist* [Late 16thC. Via French *artiste* from Italian *artista*, from *arte* "art" (see ART).]

ar·tiste /aar téest/ *n.* **1.** PERFORMER a professional entertainer, especially a singer or dancer **2.** ARTISTIC PRETENDER somebody who would like to be regarded as artistic (*ironic*) [Early 19thC. From French, "artist" (see ARTIST).]

ar·tis·tic /aar tístik/ *adj.* **1.** GOOD AT ART good at a form of creative expression **2.** OF ART involving or typical of art or artists ○ *the artistic tradition of a nation* **3.** TASTEFUL showing taste, skill, and imagination ○ *artistic flower arrangements* **4.** APPRECIATIVE OF ART able to appreciate the beauty and worth of art ○ *lacking an artistic eye* —**ar·tis·ti·cal·ly** *adv.*

ar·tis·tic di·rec·tor *n.* somebody responsible for the artistic content of an enterprise in one of the performing arts

art·ist·ry /áartəstree/ *n.* **1.** ARTISTIC ABILITY the creative ability and skill of an artist, or the expression of this **2.** GREAT SKILL great ability and skill in doing something

art·less /áartləss/ *adj.* **1.** WITHOUT DECEPTION without guile or deception **2.** TOTALLY NATURAL completely natural and unforced **3.** INELEGANT lacking skill, knowledge, or elegance —**art·less·ly** *adv.* —**art·less·ness** *n.*

WORD KEY: SYNONYMS

See Synonyms at ***naive.***

art mu·sic *n.* music composed in the classical tradition rather than in a folk or pop style

art nou·veau /àart noo vṓ, àar-/, **Art Nou·veau** *n.* a style of art, architecture, and decoration popular in the 1890s that used stylized natural forms and flowing lines [Early 20thC. From French, literally "new art."]

art run·ner *n.* an art dealer who acts as a broker by bringing prospective buyers and sellers together

arts and crafts *n.* the hand production of decoratively designed everyday objects, especially as a skilled craft or as part of a educational or rehabilitation program (*takes a singular or plural verb*)

Arts and Crafts *n.* a movement in the late 19th and early 20th centuries in Britain and the United States that stressed the value of artisanship

arts med·i·cine *n.* a medical specialty that deals with the disorders and injuries sustained by performers, e.g., musicians

art song *n.* a lyric song composed in the classical tradition

art·sy /aártsee/ (**-si·er, -si·est**), **art·y** /-tee/ (**-i·er, -i·est**) *adj.* pretentiously or self-consciously artistic (*informal disapproving*)

art·sy-craft·sy /-kráftsee/ *adj.* decorated in a excessively artistic or cute way, especially seeking to produce an impression of rural craft (*informal*) [Early 20thC. Formed from the phrase ARTS AND CRAFTS.]

art·sy-fart·sy /-faártsee/ *adj.* pretentiously artistic in a elitist or self-indulgent way (*slang disapproving*)

art·wear /aárt wair/ *n.* jewelry or clothing designed and made by an artist

art·work /aárt wurk/ *n.* **1.** WORK OF ART a work or works of art **2.** ILLUSTRATION FOR PRINTING the illustrations that are to be printed in a publication

art·y *adj.* = **artsy** (*informal disapproving*)

art·y. *abbr.* artillery

A·ru·ba /ə ro͝obə/ island off the Venezuelan coast, formerly a Dutch dependency and since 1986 a self-governing part of the Netherlands. Language: Dutch, Papamiento. Capital: Orangestad. Population: 67,794 (1996). Area: 75 sq. mi./193 sq. km.

a·ru·gu·la /ə ro͝ogyələ/ (*plural* **-las** *or* **-la**) *n.* a Mediterranean herb of the mustard family, with pungently flavored leaves that are often eaten in salads. Latin name: *Eruca vesicaria*. [Mid-20thC. Origin uncertain: probably from dialectal Italian.]

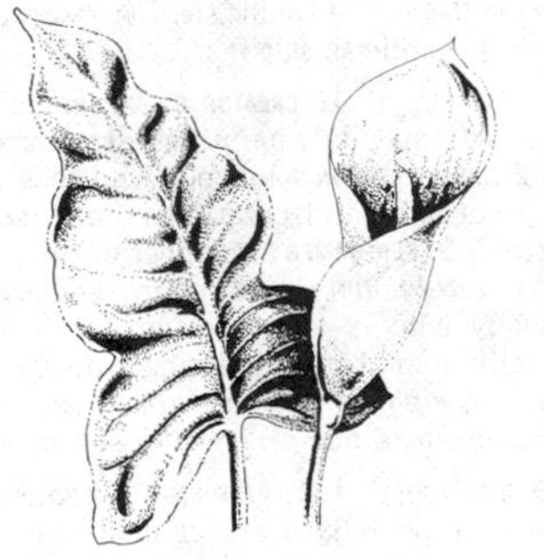

Arum

ar·um /áirəm/ (*plural* **-ums** *or* **-um**) *n.* a European perennial plant that grows from tubers and has arrow-shaped leaves. Genus: *Arum*. [14thC. Via Latin from Greek *aron*, of unknown origin.]

ar·um lil·y (*plural* **ar·um lil·ies** *or* **ar·um lil·y**) *n.* = **calla lily**

A·run·ach·al Pra·desh /aàrə naák'l prə désh/, **A·ru·nā·chal Pra·desh** union state of India. Situated in northeastern India, it has borders with Tibet and Myanmar. Capital: Itanagar. Population: 965,000 (1994). Area: 32,333 sq. mi./83,743 sq. km.

a·rus·pex *n.* = **haruspex**

ARV *abbr.* BIBLE American Revised Version

-ary *suffix.* of or relating to ○ *functionary* [Via Old French *-arie* from Latin *-arius*]

Ar·y·an /áiree ən/ *n.* **1.** LANG INDO-EUROPEAN LANGUAGE the hypothetical parent language of the Indo-European languages (*dated*) **2.** LANG INDO-EUROPEAN ANCESTOR somebody who spoke the hypothetical parent language of the Indo-European languages (*dated*) **3.** ETHNOL INDO-EUROPEAN DESCENDANT somebody belonging to a people thought to be descended from the Indo-Europeans, especially a speaker of an Iranian or Indic language (*dated*) **4.** POL NAZI IDEAL in Nazi ideology, a Caucasian person of non-Semitic descent regarded as racially superior ■ *adj.* **1.** LANG OF INDO-EUROPEAN belonging to or typical of any of the Indo-European languages or their hypothetical parent language (*dated*) **2.** POL REFERRING TO NAZI IDEAL in Nazi ideology, belonging to or characteristic of the supposed Aryan race [Mid-19thC. Formed from Sanskrit *ārya* "noble, of good family," originally a national name denoting the worshipers of the gods of the Brahmans. Ultimately from an Indo-European word meaning "lord, ruler," which is also the ancestor of English *else*.]

ar·yl /érrəl/ *adj.* used to describe a chemical group derived from benzene or another aromatic hydrocarbon

ar·y·te·noid /èrrə teé nòyd, ə rítt'n òyd/ *adj.* **ar·y·te·noid, ar·y·te·noid·al 1.** RELATING TO LARYNX CARTILAGE used to describe either of the two small cartilages of the larynx to which the vocal cords are attached **2.** RELATING TO LARYNX MUSCLE used to describe any of the small muscles of the larynx ■ *n.* ARYTENOID CARTILAGE OR MUSCLE an arytenoid cartilage or muscle [Early 18thC. Via modern Latin from Greek *arutainoeidēs*, literally "ladle-shaped," from *arutaina* "ladle, funnel," from *aruein* "to draw water."]

as /áz/ CORE MEANING: a grammatical word indicating simultaneity, causality, comparison, or the identity or function of somebody or something ○ (conj) *Once again, as I started my interview, the telephone rang.* ○ (conj) *I'll drop the book in, as I'll be passing your house anyway.* ○ (conj coord) *Here, take this pencil as it's sharper than yours.* ○ (prep) *Data is stored on the disk as magnetic patterns, much as music is stored on an audio tape or cassette.*

1. *conj.* AT THE TIME THAT used to indicate that something happens at the same time as something else ○ *A woman stands near the water's edge as two large golden retrievers frolic in the river.* **2.** *conj.* WHAT that which ○ *Do as you like!* **3.** *conj.* BECAUSE seeing that ○ *I'm not sure where we are in mathematics, as I've been absent for the last week.* **4.** *conj.* USED FOR COMPARISON used to compare things, people, or situations ○ (conj-coord) *Marvin's eyes are as big as saucers.* ○ (conj-subord) *The little Honda races toward its destination as fast as its little engine will take it.* **5.** *conj.* EMPHASIZES AMOUNTS used to indicate that an amount is small or large **6.** *conj.* INTRODUCES CLAUSE used to introduce a short clause referring to a previous or subsequent statement ○ *As you know, I have been in this job for a long time.* **7.** *conj.* IN THE WAY THAT used to indicate the way that something happens or exists ○ *Did everything go as planned?* **8.** *conj.* IN THE SAME WAY THAT used to indicate that something happens or exists in the same way as something else ○ *Her attitude to life was very practical, as her mother's had been.* **9.** *conj.* DESPITE in spite of ○ *Hard-working as she is, she can't compete with the others* **10.** *prep.* TIME WHEN used to indicate a stage in somebody's life ○ *As a teenager I was quite overweight.* [12thC. From Old English *ealswā* "exactly so" (see ALSO).] ◇ **as against** used to indicate comparison or contrast between two facts or amounts ◇ **as ever** used to indicate that a situation is the same as usual ◇ **as far as** to the extent to which a situation holds or is relevant ◇ **as for, as to** used to introduce a topic related to what has been mentioned before ◇ **as from, as of** on and after a given date or time (*formal*) ◇ **as if, as though 1.** in a way that suggests something ○ *He looked as though he'd been crying.* **2.** used to indicate that the speaker is saying something ridiculous ○ *As if I'd say a thing like that!* ◇ **as is** in the present condition, with whatever faults there may be ◇ **as it were** used to indicate qualification, uncertainty, or lack of definiteness in a statement (*formal*) ◇ **as such 1.** used to indicate that a word or phrase does not apply exactly to a situation (*often used with a negative*) ○ *I have no qualifications as such, but I feel I could do the job.* **2.** used to indicate that something is being considered separately ○ *After the earthquake, the village as such virtually ceased to exist.* ◇ **as regards** on the topic of ◇ **as to** with reference to ◇ **as yet** used to indicate that a situation has lasted up to the present time ○ *She has never once mentioned the terrible accusation nor has she, as yet, said that she is sorry for all the pain it inflicted.* ◇ **as you were** a military command to return to the same position as before ◇ **as how** used to mean "that" in the phrases "seeing as how" and "allowed as how" (*informal*) ○ *Seeing as how they were almost finished, I waited.* ○ *She allowed as how I had helped her more than anybody.* ◇ **as long as 1.** provided that ○ *You can go, as long as you're home by midnight.* **2.** because or seeing that ○ *As long as we're here we may as well look around.* ◇ **as much again** twice as much ◇ **as per** in accordance with

WORD KEY: USAGE

As meaning "in the capacity of" In this use, the preposition ***as*** is used to show the capacity in which somebody or something exists or acts: *She has a job as a copywriter. As a doctor I understand these problems.* Care has to be taken to avoid false links with the ***as*** clause, when these result in ambiguity or apparent absurdity: *As a journalist, you know I do not like being asked such questions.* (Which is the journalist?) There is less of a problem with the type *As students their rent was reduced*, since despite the logical connection no one is going to be fooled into thinking that the students and the rent are the same; but the style is poor and the sentence would be better rephrased as (for example) *Since they were students, their rent was reduced.*

As *symbol.* arsenic

AS *abbr.* **1.** BANKING after sight **2.** American Samoa **3. AS, A.S.** Anglo-Saxon **4.** antisubmarine **5.** Associate in Science

As. *abbr.* **1.** Asia **2.** Asian

ASA[1] *adj.* used to indicate the speed of photographic film

ASA[2] *abbr.* American Standards Association

As·ad·ha /aásh adə/ *n.* INDIAN RELIG in the Hindu calendar, the fourth month of the year, made up of 29 or 30 days and falling in approximately June to July. It is followed in certain leap years by an extra month (**Dvitiya Asadha**).

as·a·fet·i·da /àssə féttədə, -feét-/, **as·a·foet·i·da** *n.* a bitter, brownish, acrid-smelling resin extracted from the roots of certain Asian plants, used in Indian cooking [14thC. From medieval Latin, from *asa* (from Persian *āzā* "mastic," of unknown origin) + *foetida* "fetid," (see FETID).]

a·sa·na /aásənə/ *n.* a posture used in yoga [Mid-20thC. From Sanskrit *āsana* "manner of sitting," from *āste* "he sits."]

ASAP, asap *abbr.* as soon as possible

ASAT, Asat *abbr.* MIL anti-satellite

as·bes·tos /as béstəss, az-/ *n.* a fibrous silicate mineral widely used for its chemical inertness and heat-resistant properties until discovered to be a cause of certain cancers [Early 17thC. From Greek *asbestos* "unslaked lime," literally "inextinguishable," from *sbestos* "extinguished," from *sbennunai* "to extinguish."] —**as·bes·tine** *adj.*

as·bes·to·sis /às bes tṓssiss, àz-/ *n.* inflammation of the lungs caused by prolonged inhalation of asbestos fibers [Early 20thC. Coined from ASBESTOS + -OSIS.]

As·bur·y /ázbəree/, **Francis** (1745–1816) British-born U.S. Methodist missionary who became leader of the U.S. Methodist Episcopal Church (1785).

As·bur·y Park city and resort in eastern New Jersey. Population: 16,799 (1990).

ASCAP *abbr.* American Society of Composers, Authors, and Publishers

a·scared /ə skáird/ *adj.* *Southern U.S.* frightened (*nonstandard*)

as·ca·ri·a·sis /àskə rī́ əssiss/ *n.* infestation of the intestines by common roundworms or related nematode worms (**ascarids**) [Late 19thC. Coined from ASCARID + -IASIS.]

as·ca·rid /áskərid/ *n.* a parasitic nematode worm such as the common roundworms. Family: Ascaridae. [Late 17thC. Back-formation from *ascarides*, the plural of modern Latin *ascaris*, from Greek *askaris* "intestinal worm," from *askarizein* "to jump," an alteration of *skarizein* "to jump, throb." From the worms' squirming.]

ASCE *abbr.* American Society of Civil Engineers

as·cend /ə sénd/ (**-cend·ed, -cend·ing, -cends**) *v.* **1.** *vi.* MOVE UPWARD to go upward, usually vertically or into the air **2.** *vti.* CLIMB to climb up something, e.g., a hill or stairway ○ *The climber let down a rope so the others could ascend.* **3.** *vi.* LEAD UPWARD to rise or lead to a higher level **4.** *vt.* TAKE UP POSITION to succeed to an important position, especially as a monarch (*formal*) **5.** *vti.* RISE THROUGH IN CAREER to rise through the ranks to a higher status ○ *She ascended the ranks all the way to general.* [14thC. From Latin *ascendere*, literally "to climb to," from *scandere* "to climb" (see SCAN).] —**as·cend·a·ble** *adj.*

as·cen·dance /ə séndəns/, **as·cen·dence** *n.* **1. COMING INTO POWER** succeeding or rising to a powerful position **2.** = **ascendancy**

as·cen·dan·cy /ə séndənsee/, **as·cen·den·cy** *n.* a position of power or domination over others

as·cen·dant /ə séndənt/, **as·cen·dent** *adj.* **1. MOVING UPWARD** moving upward (*literary*) **2. DOMINANT** having a position of power or domination over others (*formal*) **3.** BOT = **ascending** *adj.* 2 ■ *n.* ASTROL **POINT ON ECLIPTIC** in astrology, the point on the ecliptic or the sign of the zodiac that is rising in the east at a particular time —**as·cend·ence** *n.* —**as·cend·en·cy** *n.*

as·cend·er /ə séndər/ *n.* **1. SOMEBODY OR SOMETHING THAT ASCENDS** somebody or something that ascends something **2.** PRINTING **LETTER PART EXTENDING UPWARD** the part of a lowercase letter, e.g., h, d, or b, that projects above the body of the letter **3.** PRINTING **LETTER WITH ASCENDER** a letter with an ascender —**as·cend·ent** *n., adj.*

as·cend·ing /ə sénding/ *adj.* **1. MOVING UP** moving upward, especially on a scale **2. as·cend·ing, as·cen·dant** BOT **GROWING UPWARD** used to describe a plant part that grows upward

as·cen·sion /ə sénsh'n/ *n.* an act of ascending something (*formal*) [14thC. Via French from the Latin stem *ascension-*, from *ascens-*, the present participle stem of *ascendere* (see ASCEND).] —**as·cen·sion·al** *adj.*

As·cen·sion *n.* according to Christianity, the rising of Jesus Christ from earth to heaven after the Resurrection

As·cen·sion Day *n.* the Thursday, forty days after Easter, when Christians celebrate the rising of Jesus Christ from earth to heaven after the Resurrection

As·cen·sion Is·land island in the South Atlantic Ocean to the northwest of Saint Helena, by which it is administered as a British dependency. Population: 1,007 (1988). Area: 34 sq. mi./88 sq. km.

as·cent /ə sént/ *n.* **1. CLIMB** an act of climbing a mountain or hill ○ *the ascent of Everest* **2. UPWARD MOVEMENT** an upward vertical movement **3. UPWARD SLOPE** an upward slope **4. WAY UP MOUNTAIN** a climbers' route up a mountain or hill **5. RISE TO IMPORTANCE** the process by which somebody becomes more important, successful, or powerful [Late 16thC. Formed from ASCEND, on the model of DESCEND, DESCENT.]

as·cer·tain /àssər táyn/ (**-tained, -tain·ing, -tains**) *vti.* to find out something with certainty (*formal*) [Late 16thC. From Old French *acertain-*, a stem of *acertener*, from *certain* CERTAIN.] —**as·cer·tain·a·ble** *adj.* —**as·cer·tain·a·bly** *adv.* —**as·cer·tain·ment** *n.*

as·cet·ic /ə séttik/ *n.* **SOMEBODY WHO LEADS AUSTERE LIFE** somebody who chooses an austere life of self-denial ■ *adj.* **1. AUSTERE** choosing or reflecting austerity and self-denial **2. RELATING TO ASCETICISM** relating to asceticism as a way of life [Mid-17thC. Directly or via medieval Latin from Greek *askētikos*, from *askētēs* "monk, hermit," from *askein* "to exercise."] —**as·cet·i·cal·ly** *adv.*

as·cet·i·cism /ə sétta sizzəm/ *n.* austerity and self-denial, especially as a principled way of life

Asch /ash/ **f, Sholem** *or* **Shalom** (1880–1957) Russian-born U.S. writer. He wrote in Hebrew and later primarily in Yiddish. Many of his works, such as *Salvation* (1934), were translated into English.

as·ci plural of **ascus**

as·cid·i·a plural of **ascidium**

as·cid·i·an /ə síddee ən/ (*plural* **-ans** *or* **-an**) *n.* a marine invertebrate animal that has a body with openings through which water passes. Sea squirts are ascidians. Class: Ascidiacea. [Mid-19thC. Formed from modern Latin *Ascidia*, genus name, from Greek *askidion*, literally "little wineskin," from *askos* "wineskin, leather bag," of unknown origin.]

as·cid·i·um /ə síddee əm/ (*plural* **-a** /-ə/) *n.* a part of a plant or fungus shaped like a pitcher [Mid-18thC. Via modern Latin from Greek *askidion* (see ASCIDIAN).]

ASCII /áskee/ *n.* a standard that identifies the letters of the alphabet, numbers, and various symbols by code numbers for exchanging data between different computer systems. Full form **American Standard Code for Information Interchange**

ASCII art *n.* illustrations using only ASCII characters, often used to decorate or enliven e-mail

ASCII file *n.* a computer file that contains text or data consisting only of ASCII characters. ◊ **binary file**

as·ci·tes /ə sí teez/ *n.* an abnormal accumulation of fluid (**serous fluid**) in the peritoneal cavity, causing abdominal swelling [14thC. Via late Latin from Greek *askitēs* "dropsy," from *askos* "wineskin, leather bag," of unknown origin.] —**as·cit·ic** /ə síttik/ *adj.*

asco- *prefix.* ascus ○ *ascocarp* [Via modern Latin from Greek *askos* "wineskin, leather bag," of unknown origin]

as·co·carp /áskə kaarp/ *n.* a fleshy structure in certain fungi (**ascomycetes**) containing sexually produced spores (**ascospores**) in a membranous spore case (**ascus**)

as·co·go·ni·um /àskə gōnee əm/ (*plural* **-a** /-ə/) *n.* a female reproductive part in certain fungi (**ascomycetes**)

a·sco·ma /ə skṓmə/ (*plural* **-ma·ta** /-mətə/) *n.* = **ascocarp**

as·co·my·cete /áskō mī seet, -mī-/ *n.* a fungus that produces spores sexually inside a membranous, often cylindrical, spore case (**ascus**). Yeasts and truffles are ascomycetes. Class: Ascomycetes. —**as·co·my·ce·tous** /às kō mī séetəss/ *adj.*

a·scor·bate /ay skáwrbət/ *n.* any salt of ascorbic acid

a·scor·bic ac·id /ə skàwrbik-/ *n.* = **vitamin C** [Mid-20thC. *Ascorbic*, literally "not scorbutic," coined from A- + SCORBUTIC.]

as·co·spore /áskə spawr/ *n.* a fungal spore produced sexually in a membranous spore case (**ascus**) —**as·co·spor·ic** /àskə spáwrik, -spṓrik/ *adj.* —**as·co·spo·rous** /àskə spáwrəss, ass kóspərəss/ *adj.*

as·cot /áskət, ás kot/ *n.* a broad cravat with square ends, often held in place with an ornamental stud

as·cribe /ə skríb/ (**-cribed, -crib·ing, -cribes**) *vt.* (*formal*) **1. GIVE SOMETHING AS CAUSE** to believe or say that something was caused by something else that is named ○ *ascribed the defeat to a series of miscalculations* **2. GIVE SOMEBODY AS AUTHOR** to believe or say that something was originally written or said by somebody who is named ○ *a poem no longer ascribed to Shakespeare* **3. GIVE SOMETHING AS CHARACTERISTIC** to believe that something that is named belongs to or is typical of a person or group ○ *to ascribe contentment to the unambitious* [15thC. From Latin *ascribere* "to add to in writing," literally "to write to," from *scribere* "to write."] —**as·crib·a·ble** *adj.*

as·cribed sta·tus *n.* the status that an individual possesses by reason of age, sex, ethnic background, family background, or another factor outside the control of the individual

as·crip·tion /ə skrípsh'n/ *n.* **1. ATTRIBUTION** the attributing of a relationship between something and somebody or something else (*formal*) **2. STATEMENT OF ATTRIBUTION** a statement that assigns or attributes something to somebody or something else (*formal*) **3.** SOCIOL **SOCIAL STATUS BY BIRTH** the social status derived from the circumstances into which somebody is born [Late 16thC. From the Latin stem *ascription-*, from *ascript-*, the past participle stem of *ascribere* (see ASCRIBE).]

ASCU *abbr.* Association of State Colleges and Universities

as·cus /áskəss/ (*plural* **-ci** /-sī, -s kee/) *n.* a membranous spore case formed by certain fungi (**ascomycetes**) that contains eight sexually produced spores (**ascospores**) [Mid-19thC. Via modern Latin from Greek *askos* "wineskin, leather bag," of unknown origin.]

ASDE *abbr.* Airport Surface Detection Equipment

ASE *abbr.* American Stock Exchange

-ase *suffix.* enzyme ○ *polymerase* [From DIASTASE]

ASEAN /ássee an/ *abbr.* Association of Southeast Asian Nations

a·seis·mic /ay sízmik/ *adj.* **1. NOT HAVING EARTHQUAKES** not subject to earthquakes **2. ABLE TO WITHSTAND EARTHQUAKES** built to withstand earthquakes

a·seis·mic creep *n.* movement of tectonic plates below the Earth's crust that is not caused by earthquakes or other seismic disturbance

a·sep·sis /ay sépsiss/ *n.* **1. GERM-FREE CONDITION** a condition in which no living disease-causing microorganisms are present **2. ELIMINATION OF GERMS** the process or methods of bringing about a condition in which no disease-causing microorganisms are present

a·sep·tic /ay séptik/ *adj.* **1. WITHOUT DISEASE-CAUSING MICROORGANISMS** free of disease-causing microorganisms **2. PREVENTING INFECTION** designed to prevent infection from pathogenic microorganisms —**a·sep·ti·cal·ly** *adv.* —**a·sep·ti·cism** *n.*

a·sex·u·al /ay sékshoo əl, -sh'l/ *adj.* **1.** BIOL **WITHOUT SEX-LINKED FEATURES** lacking any apparent sex or sex organs **2.** BIOL **WITHOUT SEXUAL FUSION** used to describe reproduction in which there is no fusion of male and female sex cells (**gametes**), e.g., vegetative reproduction or budding **3. SEXUALLY INACTIVE** without sexual desire or activity —**a·sex·u·al·i·ty** /ay sèkshoo állətee/ *n.* —**a·sex·u·al·ly** /ay sékshoo əlee, -shəlee/ *adv.*

asg. *abbr.* **1.** assigned **2.** assignment

As·gard /áz gaard, ás-/ *n.* in Norse mythology, the home of the gods and of heroes killed in battle

asgd. *abbr.* assigned

as·gmt. *abbr.* assignment

ash[1] /ash/ *n.* **1. REMAINS OF FIRE** the powdery substance that is left when something has been burned (*often used in the plural*) **2.** GEOL **VOLCANIC DUST** fine-grained lava that erupts from a volcano in a gas cloud before settling on the ground, or that flows out ■ **ash·es** *npl.* **BURNED REMAINS OF BODY** the remains of somebody's body after it has been cremated ■ *adj.* **SILVERY GRAY** of a silvery gray color [Old English *æsce*. Ultimately from an Indo-European word meaning "to burn, be dry," which is also the ancestor of English *arid*, *ardent*, and *azalea*.] ◇ **rise (like a phoenix) from the ashes** to come into existence or popularity again, seemingly from a state of ruin or destruction

Ash

ash[2] /ash/ (*plural* **ash·es** *or* **ash**) *n.* **1. DECIDUOUS TREE** a deciduous tree that has compound leaves with paired leaflets, winged fruits, and clusters of small flowers. It is found widely in temperate regions. Genus: *Fraxinus*. **2. HARD WOOD OF ASH** the hard durable wood of the ash tree, used to make furniture and tool handles **3.** LING **SYMBOL FOR VOWEL SOUND** the character "æ" representing the vowel sound of the modern English word "pad," used in Old English and the International Phonetic Alphabet [Old English *æsc* (related to German *Esche* and Old Norse *askr*)]

a·shamed /ə sháymd/ *adj.* **1. FULL OF SHAME** feeling full of shame **2. EMBARRASSED** embarrassed or regretful ○ *I'm ashamed to say I didn't acknowledge their invitation.* [Old English *āscamod*, from *sceamu* "shame" (source of English *shame*)]

A·shan·ti /ə shántee, -shaán-/ (*plural* **-ti** *or* **-tis**), **A·shan·te** (*plural* **-te** *or* **-tes**) *n.* **1. AREA IN GHANA** a former kingdom and present-day administrative area in central Ghana **2.** PEOPLES **MEMBER OF GHANAIAN PEOPLE** a member of a Ghanaian people who live mainly in Ashanti **3.** LANG **AFRICAN LANGUAGE** a language spoken in central Ghana, now often regarded as a form of Akan [Early 18thC. From Twi *Asante*.] —**A·shan·ti** *adj.*

ash blond, ash blonde *adj.* **LIGHT BLOND** light or whiteish blond in color ■ *n.* **FAIR-HAIRED PERSON** somebody with ash blond hair

ash·cake /ásh kàyk/ *n.* a small cornmeal patty that is cooked over an open fire or in hot ashes (*regional*)

ash·can /ásh kàn/ *n.* **1.** = **trash can 2.** MIL **DEPTH CHARGE** a depth charge (*slang*)

Ash·can school *n.* an early 20th century school of U.S. painters whose works focused on the everyday life of cities and city dwellers, depicted realistically

Ash·croft, Dame Peggy (1907–91) British actress who played leading theatrical roles from the 1930s to the 1950s. Her films include *A Passage to India* (1984). Real name **Peggy Edith Margaret Emily Ashcroft**

Ash·down /ásh dòwn/, **Paddy** (*b.* 1941) British politician. A former Royal Marine, he became an MP

Dame Peggy Ashcroft

(1983) and leader of the Liberal Democrat Party (1988–99).

Ashe /ash/, **Arthur** (1943–93) U.S. tennis player who was the first African American men's tennis champion. Full name **Arthur Robert Ashe, Jr.**

ash·en[1] /ásh'n/ *adj.* **1. VERY PALE** extremely pale in appearance **2. LIKE ASHES** resembling or consisting of ashes

ash·en[2] /ásh'n/ *adj.* relating to the ash tree, or made from its wood (*literary*)

Ashe·ville /ásh vìl/ city in western North Carolina, near the foothills of the Great Smoky Mountains. Population: 64,067 (1996).

Ash·ke·naz·i /aáshkə naázee, àshkə-/ (*plural* **-im** /-naázim/) *n.* a member of a Jewish community originating in Germany and northern Europe, as distinguished from a Jewish person of Spanish or Portuguese origin (**Sephardi**) [Mid-19thC. From modern Hebrew, formed from medieval Hebrew *Ashkenaz* "Germany," from Hebrew *Ashkĕnāz*, name of a grandson of Noah.] —**Ash·ke·naz·i** *adj.* —**Ash·ke·naz·ic** *adj.*

Ash·kha·bad /aáshkə baád/ capital of Turkmenistan, located in the southern part of the country near the Turkmenistan-Iran border and the Kara Kum desert. Population: 517,200 (1993).

Ash·land /áshlənd/ **1.** city in northeastern Kentucky, on the Ohio River. Population: 22,918 (1996). **2.** city in north central Ohio. Population: 21,502 (1996).

ash·lar /áshlər/, **ash·ler** *n.* **1. STONE SLAB USED FOR FACING** a thin slab of squared stone, used for facing walls or building **2. MASONRY USING THIN SLABS OF STONE** masonry using thin slabs of squared stone as facing material [14thC. Via Old French *aisselier* "plank" from, ultimately, medieval Latin *axicellus*, from Latin *axis* "plank, axletree" (source of English *axis* and *axle*).]

ash·lar·ing /áshləring/ *n.* the construction of a building using ashlars

Ash·or·a /ə shṓrə/ *n.* an Islamic festival celebrated on the tenth day of Muharran

a·shore /ə sháwr/ *adv.* to the land from the water, or on land as opposed to a ship or boat ○ *All but the captain went ashore.*

ash·ram /aáshrəm/ *n.* **1. HINDU RETREAT** a retreat for the practice of yoga or other Hindu disciplines **2. SPIRITUAL COMMUNITY** a commune or communal house whose members share spiritual goals and practices [Early 20thC. From Sanskrit *āśramaḥ* "hermitage."]

Ash·ta·bu·la /àshtə byóolə/ city in extreme northeastern Ohio, beside Lake Erie. Population: 21,315 (1996).

Ash·ton-War·ner /áshtən wáwrnər/, **Sylvia** (1908–84) New Zealand novelist and teacher, author of *Spinster* (1958).

Ash·to·reth /áshtə rèth/ *n.* MYTHOL ➧ **Ishtar**

ash·tray /ásh trày/ *n.* an open receptacle for the ash from a cigarette, cigar, or pipe and for cigarette butts

Ash·ville /ásh vìl/ city in western North Carolina, near the foothills of the Great Smoky Mountains. Population: 64,067 (1996).

Ash Wednes·day *n.* a Christian religious holiday that marks the first day of Lent, the period preceding Easter [So called because of the Roman Catholic custom of marking the heads of penitents with ashes on this day]

ash·y /áshee/ (**-i·er, -i·est**) *adj.* **1. EXTREMELY PALE** extremely pale or grayish in appearance (*literary*) **2. LIKE ASH** resembling or covered in ash

A·sia /áyzhə/ the world's largest continent, bordered by the Ural and Caucasus mountains and the Arctic, Pacific, and Indian oceans. Area: 17,350,000 sq. mi./44,936,000 sq. km.

A·sia·dol·lar /áyzhə dòllər, áyshə-/ *n.* a United States dollar used in Asian banks and currency markets

A·sia Mi·nor peninsula in the extreme west of Asia, roughly corresponding to Asian Turkey

A·sian /áyzh'n, -sh'n/ *adj.* **OF ASIA** relating to or typical of any of the countries of Asia, or their peoples or cultures ■ *n.* **SOMEBODY FROM ASIA** somebody who was born in or is a citizen of any of the countries that form the continent of Asia [Via Latin from Greek *Asianos*, from *Asia* "Asia"]

A·sian A·mer·i·can *n.* somebody who was born in Asia and is a citizen of the United States, or whose ancestors came from any of the countries that form the continent of Asia —**A·sian A·mer·i·can** *adj.*

WORD KEY: USAGE

See Usage note at ***African American.***

A·sian cock·roach *n.* a pale brown cockroach of medium size commonly found around dwellings in warm and temperate climates. Latin name: *Blattella asahinai.*

A·sian flu *n.* influenza that occurs in sporadic worldwide epidemics, caused by a virus strain thought to have originated in China in the mid-1950s and related strains

A·sian·ize /áyzh'n īz, -sh'n-/ (**-ized, -iz·ing, -iz·es**) *vt.* **1. MAKE ASIAN** to make somebody or something Asian, e.g., in cultural characteristics **2. MAKE ASIAN-OWNED** to bring something under Asian ownership or control —**A·sian·i·za·tion** /àyzh'nə záysh'n, -sh'nə-/ *n.*

A·sian pear *n.* = **sand pear**

A·sia-Pa·ci·fic *n.* a commercial region encompassing the countries of Asia and the Pacific Rim

A·si·at·ic /àyzhee áttik, àyzee-/ *adj.* used to describe things Asian, e.g., flora, fauna, or climate conditions ○ *Asiatic plants and animals* ○ *parts of the Asiatic steppes* [Early 17thC. Via Latin from Greek *Asiatikos*, from *Asia* "Asia."]

A·si·at·ic buf·fa·lo (*plural* **A·si·at·ic buf·fa·lo** *or* **A·si·at·ic buf·fa·loes** *or* **A·si·at·ic buf·fa·los**) *n.* an ox of Southeast Asia, with large upturned horns, now widely domesticated and rare in the wild. Latin name: *Bubalus bubalis.*

A·si·at·ic chol·er·a *n.* = **cholera**

A·si·at·ic cock·roach *n.* = **Asian cockroach**

a·side /ə sī́d/ *adv.* **1. AWAY OR TO ONE SIDE** away from somebody or something, or to one side ○ *Stand aside and let the people through.* **2. OUT OF THE WAY** out of the way, or away from the area of main concern ○ *brush aside all criticism* **3. IGNORED** ignored for the sake of argument ○ *Budget constraints aside, is the deadline feasible?* **4. FOR FUTURE USE** for special or future use ○ *put aside some money each week* ■ *n.* **1.** THEATER **ACTOR'S COMMENT** a remark made by an actor, usually to the audience, that the other characters on stage supposedly cannot hear **2. CONFIDENTIAL COMMENT IN UNDERTONE** a spoken remark not directed to all listeners and usually made in a quiet voice **3. DIGRESSION** a digression from a main point

a·side from *prep.* **1. IN ADDITION TO** in addition to or besides somebody or something ○ *Aside from his medical practice he is also a lawyer.* **2. OTHER THAN** except for or not considering the stated thing ○ *Aside from the cold weather, I love it here.*

As·i·mov /ázzi mòf, -màwf/, **Isaac** (1920–92) Russian-born U.S. scientist and writer, author of around 500 books for young people, including textbooks and science fiction.

as·i·nine /áss'n īn/ *adj.* **1. RIDICULOUS** utterly ridiculous or lacking sense **2. LIKE AN ASS** relating to or resembling an ass [15thC. From Latin *asininus*, from *asinus* "ass."] —**as·i·nine·ly** *adv.* —**as·i·nin·i·ty** /àss'n ínnətee/ *n.*

ask /ask/ (**asked, ask·ing, asks**) *v.* **1.** *vti.* **QUESTION SOMEBODY** to put a question to somebody ○ *Ask them how long it will take.* **2.** *vti.* **MAKE REQUEST** to make a request for something ○ *They asked me for my opinion.* **3.** *vt.* **INVITE SOMEBODY** to invite somebody to a social event ○ *Only close friends were asked to dine.* **4.** *vt.* **REQUIRE** to require somebody to give or contribute something ○ *The job asks a lot more of me than I expected.* **5.** *vt.* **NAME AS PRICE** to name an amount as an acceptable price ○ *They're asking $100,000 for the house.* [Old English *āscian.* Ultimately from an Indo-European word meaning "to wish."] ◇ **for the asking** available at no cost ○ *apples for the asking*

ask after *vi.* to inquire about somebody's welfare ○ *She asks after the children whenever we meet.*

ask for *v.* **1.** *vti.* **REQUEST SOMETHING** to request that something be provided ○ *I asked for a cup of coffee.* **2.** *vi.* **REQUEST SOMEBODY'S APPEARANCE** to request somebody's appearance ○ *A visitor is asking for you.* **3.** *vi.* **REQUEST TELEPHONE CONVERSATION WITH SOMEBODY** to request that somebody be called to the telephone ○ *The caller is asking for the manager.* **4.** *vi.* **INVITE SOMETHING UNPLEASANT** to behave in a way that deserves something unpleasant ○ *You're asking for a lot of problems if you do that.*

ask in *vt.* to invite somebody to enter or participate in something

ask out *vt.* to invite somebody to go on a date

a·skance /ə skáns/ *adv.* **1. SUSPICIOUSLY** with doubt or suspicion ○ *"They surveyed each other askance, feeling that they were rivals, and mentally calculating each other's chances."* (Horatio Alger, Jr., *Ragged Dick*; 1868) **2. OBLIQUELY** sideways, or out of the side of the eye (*archaic*) [15thC. Origin unknown.]

as·ka·ri /áskəree, ə skaáree/, **as·kar** /áskər/ *n.* a soldier or police officer in various Arab or Muslim countries of eastern Africa [Late 19thC. From Arabic *askarī* "soldier."]

a·skew /ə skyóo/ *adj., adv.* at an angle ○ *with his hat askew*

ask·ing price *n.* the price set by a seller before any negotiation

ASL *abbr.* American Sign Language

a·slant /ə slánt/ *adv.* sloping or at an angle ○ *books all aslant on the shelves*

a·sleep /ə sléep/ *adj.* **1. NOT AWAKE** in or into a state of sleep **2. NOT ALERT** not alert enough to function or operate properly ○ *asleep on the job* **3. NUMB** numb for lack of proper blood circulation

a·slope /ə slṓp/ *adj., adv.* at a sloping angle

ASM *abbr.* air-to-surface missile

As·ma·ra /aaz maárə/ capital and largest city of Eritrea. It is also the name of one of the ten provinces within Eritrea. Population: 367,300 (1991).

a·so·cial /ay sṓsh'l/ *adj.* **1. UNWILLING TO MIX SOCIALLY** disinclined or averse to human social interaction **2. NOT INTERACTING SOCIALLY** lacking a need or capacity for social interaction **3. UNSUITED TO SOCIETY** not acceptable in normal society, or showing a lack of consideration for others

asp[1] /asp/ *n.* **1. SNAKE THAT KILLED CLEOPATRA** a small poisonous snake that caused the death of Cleopatra. It is thought to have been a member of the cobra family found in Africa, Asia, and Europe. Latin name: *Naja haje.* **2. SOUTHERN EUROPEAN VIPER** a snake of the viper family, resembling a small adder, found in southern Europe **3.** = **horned viper** [Directly or via Old French *aspe* from Latin *aspis*, from Greek, of unknown origin]

asp[2] /asp/ *n.* an aspen tree (*archaic*) [Old English *æspe* (see ASPEN)]

as·par·a·gin·ase /ə spárrəjə nayss, -nayz/ *n.* an enzyme that aids the breakdown of the amino acid asparagine, producing aspartic acid and ammonia

as·par·a·gine /ə spérrə jeen/ *n.* an amino acid found in many plant seeds that can also be produced by humans and animals. Formula: $C_4H_8N_2O_3$. [Early 19thC. Formed from ASPARAGUS, from which it was first obtained.]

as·par·a·gus /ə spérrəgəss/ (*plural* **-gus**) *n.* **1. PLANT**

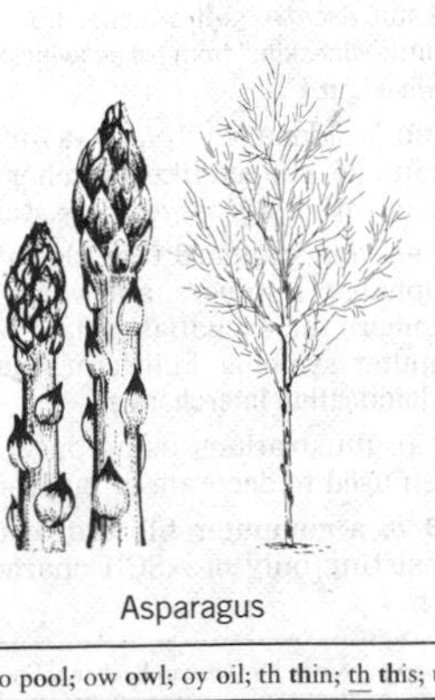
Asparagus

CULTIVATED FOR EDIBLE SHOOTS a perennial plant that is widely cultivated for its edible young shoots. Latin name: *Asparagus officinalis.* **2.** SUCCULENT VEGETABLE the spear-shaped young shoots of the asparagus plant, cooked and served as a vegetable [Pre-12thC. Via Latin from Greek *asparagos*, of unknown origin.]

as·par·a·gus fern *n.* a South African plant with feathery leaves, small white flowers, and purplish black berries that is grown as a houseplant. Its foliage is used in bouquets. Latin name: *Asparagus setaceus.*

as·par·tame /áspər tàym, ə spaár-/ *n.* a synthetic sweetener, many times sweeter to the taste than sugar, that is a protein produced from aspartic acid [Late 20thC. Coined from ASPARTIC ACID + *-ame*, of uncertain origin.]

a·spar·tate /ə spaár tàyt, áspər-/ *n.* a salt or ester of aspartic acid

as·par·tic ac·id /ə spaártik-/ *n.* an amino acid occurring in many plant proteins that can also be produced by humans and animals. Formula: $C_4H_7NO_4$. [Mid-19thC. From French *aspartique*, from *asparagus* "asparagus," from Latin (see ASPARAGUS).]

A.S.P.C.A. *abbr.* American Society for the Prevention of Cruelty to Animals

as·pect /á spèkt/ *n.* **1.** ONE SIDE OR PART a facet, phase, or part of a whole ○ *consider the various aspects of the problem* **2.** APPEARANCE the appearance of something to the mind or eye ○ *The stone has a greenish aspect in this light.* **3.** VIEWPOINT a particular view or point of view ○ *seeing life from a new aspect* ○ *the aspect of the mountain from the river* **4.** EXPOSURE exposure to a particular direction, weather, or other influence ○ *This plant requires a sunny aspect.* **5.** ASTRON ANGLE BETWEEN TWO CELESTIAL BODIES the apparent angular separation of two celestial bodies, especially as observed from the Earth **6.** ASTROL POSITIONS OF PLANETS IN ASTROLOGY in astrology, the relative positions of the stars and planets, believed to influence human affairs **7.** GRAM GRAMMATICAL CATEGORY a grammatical category of verbs that considers qualities of action independent of tense. In English, the progressive and perfect aspects are recognized. **8.** LOOK a look or gaze (*archaic*) [14thC. From Latin *aspectus*, the past participle of *aspicere*, literally "to look at," from *specere* (see SPECTACLE).]

as·pect ra·tio *n.* **1.** SCREEN IMAGE WIDTH-HEIGHT RATIO in television and the movies, the ratio of the width of the picture on the screen to its height. This ratio was 4:3 until the 1950s, when it increased in the movies to 1.85:1 in the United States and 5:3 in Europe. **2.** AEROSP RATIO OF WING LENGTH TO BREADTH the ratio of the length of an aircraft's wing to the mean distance between the front and back edge of the wing. Aircraft operating at low speeds, such as gliders, need a high aspect ratio and have long narrow wings while for supersonic flight a low aspect ratio is created by swinging the wings back.

as·pec·tu·al /a spékchoo əl/ *adj.* relating to the aspects of a verb

as·pen /áspən/ (*plural* **-pens** *or* **-pen**) *n.* a tree of the poplar family, common in the northern United States and Europe, with leaves that rustle and flutter in the breeze [14thC. Formed from Old English *æspe*. The word was originally an adjective meaning "made of aspen wood."]

As·pen /áspən/ city in the Rocky Mountains, at an elevation of about 7,900 ft./2,410 m in west central Colorado. It is a popular ski resort. Population: 5,245 (1996).

as·per /áspər/ *n.* a minor unit of currency in Turkey, 120 of which are worth a piastre [Via French *aspre* from, ultimately, Greek *aspros* "newly minted," from Latin *asper* "rough" (source of English *asperity*)]

as·per·ges /a spúrjiz/ *n.* a religious ceremony of the Roman Catholic Church in which holy water is sprinkled over the altar, clergy, and congregation before High Mass [Late 16thC. From Latin, literally "thou shalt sprinkle," the first word of the rite.]

as·per·gill *n.* = **aspergillum** [Mid-19thC. Anglicization of Latin *aspergillum* (see ASPERGILLUM).]

as·per·gil·lo·sis /àspərji lṓssiss/ *n.* a disease affecting mucous membranes, lungs, and sometimes bones that is caused by infection with the fungus *Aspergillus*

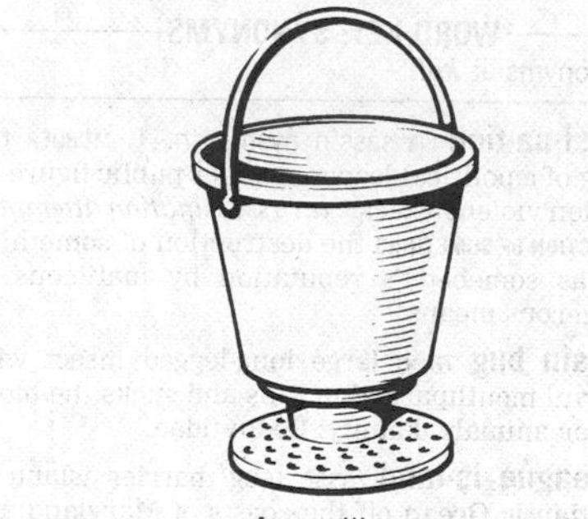

Aspergillum

as·per·gil·lum /àspər jílləm/ (*plural* **-la** /-lə/ *or* **-lums**), **as·per·gill** /àspər jíl/ (*plural* **-gil·la** *or* **-gills**) *n.* a brush or perforated container for sprinkling holy water [Mid-17thC. From modern Latin, literally "little sprinkler," formed from Latin *aspergere* "to sprinkle."]

as·per·i·ty /a spérrətee/ (*plural* **-ties**) *n.* **1.** HARSHNESS OR SEVERITY harshness or severity of manner or tone (*formal*) **2.** ROUGHNESS the roughness of a surface (*literary*) **3.** HARDSHIP something that is hard to bear because of its harshness or severity **4.** PHYS AREA WHERE TWO LOAD-BEARING SURFACES TOUCH a region of contact between two load-bearing flat surfaces [13thC. Via French *asperité* from, ultimately, Latin *asper* "rough," of unknown origin.]

a·sper·mi·a /ay spúrmee ə/ *n.* a medical condition in which no spermatozoa are present in the seminal fluid [Mid-19thC. Coined from A- + Greek *sperma* "seed" + -IA.] —**a·sper·mic** *adj.*

as·perse /ə spúrs/ (**-persed, -pers·ing, -pers·es**) *vt.* to malign somebody by spreading harmful information or making false accusations (*formal*) [15thC. From Latin *aspers-*, the past participle stem of *aspergere*, literally "to spatter on," from *spargere* (see SPARGE). The underlying meaning is "to sling mud."] —**as·pers·er** *n.* —**as·per·sive** *adj.* —**as·per·sive·ly** *adv.*

as·per·sion /ə spúrzh'n, -sh'n/ *n.* **1.** SLANDEROUS REMARK a statement that attacks somebody's character or reputation (*often used in the plural*) **2.** MAKING OF SLANDEROUS REMARKS the making of defamatory remarks

as·per·so·ri·um /àspər sáwree əm/ (*plural* **-ria** /-ree ə/) *n.* RELIG = **aspergillum** [Mid-19thC. From medieval Latin, formed from Latin *aspers-*, the past participle stem of *aspergere* (see ASPERSE).]

as·phalt /ás fàwlt/ *n.* **1.** SEMISOLID BITUMINOUS SUBSTANCE a brownish black solid or semisolid substance used in paving, waterproofing, and fungicides. It occurs naturally in some oil-bearing rocks and can be obtained as a byproduct of petroleum distillation. **2.** MATERIAL USED FOR SURFACING ROADS paving material composed mainly of asphalt and gravel or crushed rock that hardens on cooling and is used for making roads and sidewalks ■ *vt.* (**-phalt·ed, -phalt·ing, -phalts**) COVER SOMETHING WITH ASPHALT to surface a roadway, sidewalk, or other area with asphalt [14thC. Via late Latin from Greek *asphaltos*, of uncertain origin.] —**as·phal·tic** /as fáwltik/ *adj.*

as·phal·tite /as fáwl tìt, às-/ *n.* solid asphalt containing little inorganic material and occurring naturally in veins and beds below the surface of the ground

as·phalt jun·gle *n.* a big city or urban area with much paving and little natural landscape

a·spher·ic /ay sféerik, ày sfér-/, **a·spher·i·cal** *adj.* not perfectly spherical

as·pho·del /ásfə dèl/ (*plural* **-dels** *or* **-del**) *n.* **1.** FLOWERING PLANT a perennial plant of the lily family, native to southern Europe, that has long clusters of white, pink, or yellow flowers. Genera: *Asphodelus* and *Asphodeline.* **2.** PLANT RESEMBLING TRUE ASPHODEL a plant similar to asphodel proper, e.g., bog asphodel **3.** MYTHOL FLOWER OF HADES in Greek mythology, the flower of Hades that was sacred to Persephone [Middle English. Via Latin *asphodilus* (source of English *daffodil*) from Greek *asphodelos*, of unknown origin.]

as·phyx·i·a /as fíksee ə, əs-/ *n.* suffocation as a result of physical blockage of the airway or inhalation of toxic gases, causing a lack of oxygen and unconsciousness [Early 18thC. Via modern Latin from Greek *asphuxia*, literally "lack of pulse," from *sphuxis* "heartbeat," from *sphuzein* "to throb."]

as·phyx·i·ant /as fíksee ənt, əs-/ *adj.* SUFFOCATING causing oxygen deficiency and suffocation ■ *n.* CAUSE OF SUFFOCATION an agent that causes asphyxia, e.g., a toxic gas

as·phyx·i·ate /as fíksee àyt, əs-/ (**-at·ed, -at·ing, -ates**) *vti.* to deprive a person or animal of oxygen, or be deprived of oxygen, usually leading to unconsciousness or death —**as·phyx·i·a·tion** /as fíksee áysh'n, əs-/ *n.* —**as·phyx·i·a·tor** /as fíksee àytər, əs-/ *n.*

as·pic /áspik/ *n.* a cold jelly often used as a mold for fish, meat, eggs, or vegetables [Late 18thC. From French, literally "asp," an alteration of Old French *aspe* (see ASP[1]). Possibly so called because the colors in the jelly were thought to resemble the snake's.]

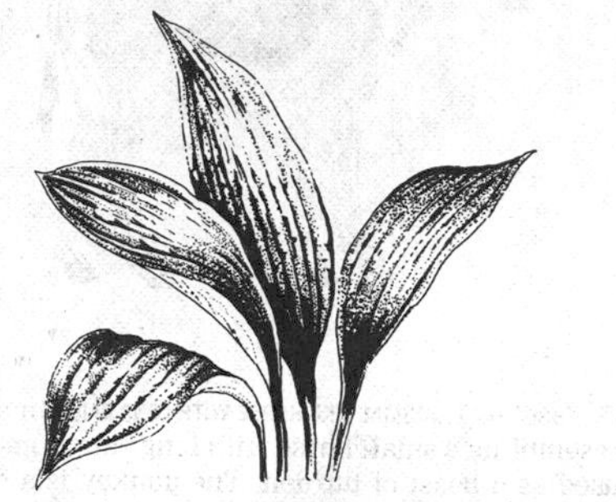

Aspidistra

as·pi·dis·tra /àspi dístrə/ *n.* an Asian plant of the lily family that has large glossy leaves and small brownish flowers and is commonly grown as a houseplant. Genus: *Aspidistra.* [Early 19thC. Via modern Latin, genus name, from Greek *aspid-*, the stem of *aspis* "shield," because of the shape of the plant's leaves.]

as·pi·rant /áspərənt, ə spírənt/ *n.* ASPIRING PERSON somebody who seeks or hopes to attain something ○ *an aspirant to the presidency* ■ *adj.* ASPIRING seeking or hoping to attain something

WORD KEY: SYNONYMS

See Synonyms at ***candidate.***

as·pi·rate *vt.* /áspə ràyt/ (**-rat·ed, -rat·ing, -rates**) **1.** PRONOUNCE WHILE BREATHING OUT to pronounce a sound or word while breathing out, e.g., the letter h at the beginning of such words as "house" and "hat" in standard English **2.** REMOVE LIQUID to remove liquid or gas by suction, especially from a body cavity ○ *using a syringe to aspirate the fluid from the cyst* **3.** INHALE SOMETHING to inhale something, especially a liquid, into the lungs ■ *n.* /áspərət/ **1.** BREATHY LETTER a sound pronounced while breathing out, e.g., the sound of the letter h at the beginning of many English words **2.** MATTER REMOVED matter removed by aspirating ■ *adj.* BREATHY SOUNDING pronounced while breathing out [Late 17thC. From Latin *aspirat-*, the past participle stem of *aspirare*, literally "to breathe toward," from *spirare* (see SPIRIT).]

as·pi·ra·tion /àspə ráysh'n/ *n.* **1.** AMBITION a desire or ambition to achieve something **2.** BREATHY PRONUNCIATION pronunciation accompanied by breathing out **3.** SUCTION the withdrawal by suction of fluids or gases from the body or a body cavity **4.** INHALATION drawing matter into the lungs along with the breath —**as·pir·a·to·ry** /ə spírə tàwree/ *adj.*

as·pi·ra·tion·al /àspi ráyshən'l, -shnəl/ *adj.* showing a desire or ambition to achieve something, especially self-improvement or material success ○ *the aspirational working class*

as·pi·ra·tor /áspə ràytər/ *n.* an apparatus for drawing out fluids or gases by suction

as·pire /ə spír/ (**-pired, -pir·ing, -pires**) *vi.* **1.** HAVE PARTICULAR AMBITION to seek to attain a particular goal ○ *aspire to the priesthood* **2.** FLY HIGH to soar to a great height (*literary*) [14thC. From Latin *aspirare* "to breathe toward." The underlying metaphor is of projecting or breathing your desires toward something.] —**as·pir·er** *n.* —**as·pir·ing** *adj.*

as·pi·rin /áspirin, -prin/ (*plural* **-rins** *or* **-rin**) *n.* **1.** PAIN RELIEVER a drug derived from salicylic acid that is used to relieve pain and inflammation, to lower fever, and to reduce the risk of blood clotting within an artery. Formula: $C_9H_8O_4$. **2.** TABLET CONTAINING ASPIRIN a tablet containing aspirin [Late 19thC. From German, formed from a contraction of *acetylierte Spirsäure* "acetylated spiraeic acid" (the former name of salicylic acid).]

asp vi·per *n.* = **asp**[1] *n.* 2

a·squint /ə skwínt/ *adv.* from the corner of the eye, as if suspiciously

As·quith /áskwith/, **Herbert Henry** (1852–1928) British statesman and Liberal prime minister (1908–16). His government introduced old-age pensions and national insurance.

ASR *abbr.* airport surveillance radar

Ass

ass[1] /ass/ *n.* **1.** ANIMAL LIKE HORSE WITH LONG EARS an animal resembling a small horse with long ears, sometimes used as a beast of burden. The donkey is a domesticated descendant of the wild ass. Genus: *Equus.* **2.** OFFENSIVE TERM an offensive term for an unintelligent, thoughtless, or ridiculous person (*slang insult*) [Old English *assa,* via an unknown Celtic source from Latin *asinus* (source of English *asinine* and *easel*)]

ass[2] /ass/ *n.* (*taboo offensive*) **1.** BUTTOCKS a person's buttocks or anus **2.** OFFENSIVE TERM an offensive term for sexual intercourse [Euphemistic respelling of ARSE] ◇ **cover your ass** to behave in a way that ensures you will not be blamed for something later (*taboo offensive*) ◇ **haul ass** to move or start to move quickly (*taboo offensive*) ◇ **have your ass in a sling** *or* **bind** to be in trouble (*taboo offensive*) ◇ **kick (some) ass** to behave aggressively or violently in order to get what you want (*taboo offensive*) ◇ **kiss ass** to be very polite or obsequious to somebody in authority (*taboo offensive*) ◇ **not know your ass from your elbow** to be very ignorant (*taboo offensive*)

As·sad /aa saád/, **Hafez al-** (*b.* 1928) Syrian government leader. He seized power in 1970 and was elected president of Syria in 1971.

as·sa·gai *n.* = **assegai**

as·sail /ə sáyl/ (**-sailed, -sail·ing, -sails**) *vt.* **1.** ATTACK SOMEBODY to attack somebody vigorously with words or actions ○ *assailed by an angry mob* **2.** TROUBLE OR BESET SOMEBODY to overwhelm the mind or senses of somebody ○ *"Low growls and angry snarls assailed our ears on every side."* (Edgar Rice Burroughs, *The Gods of Mars*; 1913) [13thC. Via Old French *asaill-,* the stem of *asalir,* from assumed Vulgar Latin *assalire,* literally "to leap at," from Latin *salire* "to leap."] —**as·sail·a·ble** *adj.* —**as·sail·er** *n.* —**as·sail·ment** *n.*

as·sail·ant /ə sáylənt/ *n.* somebody who violently attacks somebody else, usually causing physical injury

As·sam /a sám/ union state of India, situated in the northeastern part of the country. Capital: Dispur. Population: 24,200,000 (1994). Area: 30,285 sq. mi./78,438 sq. km.

As·sam·ese /àssə meéz, -meéss/ (*plural* **-ese**) *n.* **1.** PEOPLES SOMEBODY FROM ASSAM somebody who was born in or lives in the state of Assam in northeastern India **2.** LANG INDIC LANGUAGE a language spoken in the state of Assam in northeastern India and in Bangladesh. It belongs to the Indic group of Indo-European languages and is written in Bengali script. Assamese is spoken by about 11 million people. —**As·sam·ese** *adj.*

as·sas·sin /ə sáss'n/ *n.* a killer, especially of a political leader or other public figure [Mid-16thC. Via French from, ultimately, Arabic *ḥašīšīn,* literally "hashish users," denoting a group of 11th-century Ismaili Muslims who murdered Christian leaders.]

as·sas·si·nate /ə sáss'n àyt/ (**-nat·ed, -nat·ing, -nates**) *vt.* **1.** MURDER SOMEBODY to kill somebody, especially a political leader or other public figure, by a sudden violent attack **2.** RUIN SOMETHING to harm or destroy something such as somebody's reputation maliciously or treacherously —**as·sas·si·na·tor** *n.*

WORD KEY: SYNONYMS

See Synonyms at ***kill.***

as·sas·si·na·tion /ə sàss'n áysh'n/ *n.* **1.** MURDER the killing of a political leader or other public figure by a sudden violent attack ○ *an assassination attempt* **2.** DESTRUCTION OF SOMETHING the destruction of something such as somebody's reputation by malicious or treacherous means

as·sas·sin bug *n.* a large long-legged insect with powerful mouthparts that kills and sucks the blood of other animals. Family: Reduviidae.

As·sa·teague Is·land /ássə teeg/ barrier island in the Atlantic Ocean off the coasts of Maryland and Virginia, which share ownership. It is noted for its wild ponies, traditionally rounded up each July. Area: 39,733 acres/16,079 hectares.

as·sault /ə sáwlt/ *n.* **1.** PHYSICAL OR VERBAL ATTACK a violent physical or verbal attack **2.** LAW ATTACK OR FEAR OF BODILY HARM an unlawful threat of bodily violence or harm to somebody else, or an attempt to do such violence or harm **3.** LAW RAPE the offense of raping somebody **4.** ATTEMPT TO DESTROY SOMETHING a campaign or series of actions that aims to challenge or destroy something ○ *The proposals are under assault by various special interest groups.* ■ *vt.* (**-sault·ed, -sault·ing, -saults**) **1.** LAW ATTACK SOMEBODY to attack somebody physically or verbally in a violent way **2.** MIL MAKE MILITARY ATTACK ON PLACE to attack a place with a military force [Via Old French *assaut* from assumed Vulgar Latin *assaltus,* the past participle of *assalire* (see ASSAIL)] —**as·sault·er** *n.*

as·sault and bat·ter·y *n.* the crime of attacking somebody, carried out by violent means, e.g., by hitting or knocking to the ground

as·sault course *n. U.K.* = **obstacle course**

as·saul·tive /ə sáwltiv/ *adj.* extremely aggressive or disposed to attack

as·say /á sày, a sáy/ *n.* **1.** ANALYSIS OF SOMETHING an examination and analysis of something **2.** CHEM CHEMICAL ANALYSIS chemical testing carried out to determine the composition of a substance or the concentration of various components in a substance **3.** SAMPLE OF MATERIAL a sample of material for analysis **4.** ATTEMPT AT SOMETHING an attempt to do something (*archaic*) ■ *vt.* (**-sayed, -say·ing, -says**) **1.** EXAMINE SOMETHING to examine or test something with a view to evaluating it **2.** CHEM ANALYZE to analyze a substance such as a metal or ore in order to discover its components **3.** ATTEMPT TO DO SOMETHING to attempt to do something (*literary*) [The noun is from Old French *assai* "test"; the verb from Old French *assaier* "to test," variant of *essaier* (see ESSAY)] —**as·say·a·ble** /ə sáyəb'l/ *adj.* —**as·say·er** *n.*

ass-back·wards *adj., adv.* in a way that is the reverse of what is usual, normal, or correct (*taboo offensive*)

as·se·gai /ássə gī/, **as·sa·gai** *n.* a slender hardwood spear with an iron tip, used especially by the Zulu peoples of southern Africa [Early 17thC. Via obsolete French *azagaie* from, ultimately, Berber *zaġāya* "spear."]

as·sem·blage /ə sémblij/ *n.* **1.** GATHERING TOGETHER a gathering of things or people at one point ○ *a law to forbid the assemblage of unruly mobs* **2.** COLLECTION a collection of people or things ○ *an assemblage of ideas* **3.** SCULPTURE ARTISTIC ARRANGEMENT OF MISCELLANEOUS ITEMS a work of art made from a collection of different objects

as·sem·blag·ist /ə sémblijist/ *n.* a sculptor who creates assemblages

as·sem·ble /ə sémb'l/ (**-bled, -bling, -bles**) *v.* **1.** *vt.* PUT COMPONENTS TOGETHER to fit the parts of something together to make a finished whole ○ *assembled a model* **2.** *vti.* COLLECT TOGETHER to bring people or things together or gather together in one place ○ *A crowd began to assemble.* [Via French *assembler,* from assumed Vulgar Latin *assimulare,* literally "to put together," from Latin *simul* "together"] —**as·sem·bled** *adj.*

WORD KEY: SYNONYMS

See Synonyms at ***build*** and ***collect.***

as·sem·bler /ə sémblər/ *n.* **1.** INDUST FITTER OF PARTS a person, machine, or company that puts together the parts of a machine or piece of equipment when it is being built **2.** COMPUT COMPUTER PROGRAM a computer program that converts assembly language into machine language **3.** COMPUT = **assembly language**

as·sem·bly /ə sémblee/ (*plural* **-blies**) *n.* **1.** FITTING COMPONENTS TOGETHER the putting together of parts to make a finished product **2.** GATHERING the coming together of people for a common purpose ○ *freedom of assembly* **3.** EDUC SCHOOL MEETING a regular formal gathering of all the students in a school for a special program **4.** **as·sem·bly, As·sem·bly** LEGISLATIVE MEETING a group of people meeting as a deliberative or lawmaking body **5.** COMPONENTS a set of components before they are put together to make a finished product **6.** MILITARY GATHERING the gathering together of a military unit prior to an event or operation **7.** MILITARY SIGNAL a signal for soldiers or other personnel to gather **8.** COMPUT TRANSLATION OF COMPUTER LANGUAGE the translation of assembly language into machine language [14thC. From French *assemblée,* the feminine past participle of *assembler* (see ASSEMBLE).]

WORD KEY: SYNONYMS

See Synonyms at ***meeting.***

as·sem·bly lan·guage *n.* a low-level computer language that consists of mnemonic codes and symbolic addresses corresponding to machine-language instructions

as·sem·bly line *n.* a series of work stations at which individual steps in the assembly of a product are carried out by workers or machines as the product is moved along

as·sem·bly·man /ə sémbliman/ (*plural* **-men** /-mən/) *n.* a member of a legislative assembly

As·sem·bly of God *n.* an Evangelical Christian Church founded in the United States in 1914

as·sem·bly·wom·an /ə sémbli wŏŏmmən/ (*plural* **-en** /-wìmmin/) *n.* a woman member of a legislative assembly

as·sent /ə sént/ *vi.* (**-sent·ed, -sent·ing, -sents**) AGREE TO SOMETHING to agree to something or express agreement ○ *She will never assent to their marriage.* ■ *n.* EXPRESSION OF AGREEMENT an expression of agreement or acceptance [13thC. Via Old French *assenter* from, ultimately, Latin *assentire,* literally "to feel toward."] —**as·sent·er** *n.* —**as·sent·ing·ly** *adv.*

WORD KEY: SYNONYMS

See Synonyms at ***agree.***

as·sen·ta·tion /àss'n táysh'n, à sen-/ *n.* agreement, especially in an insincere manner (*literary*)

as·sent·ed /ə séntəd/, **as·sent·ing** *adj.* used to describe securities that are bought or held with the understanding that proposed changes may affect their status or number

as·sen·ti·ent /ə sénshee ənt/ *adj.* AGREEING agreeing or accepting (*formal*) ■ *n.* SOMEBODY WHO AGREES a person or party that agrees (*formal*) [Mid-19thC. From Latin *assentient-,* the present participle stem of *assentire* (see ASSENT).]

as·sent·ing *adj.* FIN = **assented**

as·sert /ə súrt/ (**-sert·ed, -sert·ing, -serts**) *v.* **1.** *vt.* CLAIM to state something as being true ○ *She asserted that she had never seen the man before.* **2.** *vt.* INSIST ON RIGHTS to insist on or exercise your rights ○ *He asserted his Fifth Amendment rights and refused to testify.* **3.** *vr.* BEHAVE FORCEFULLY to exercise and emphatically reveal your power, influence, and prerogatives ○ *New management quickly began to assert itself two days after the takeover.* **4.** *vr.* BECOME KNOWN OR EFFECTIVE to start to have an effect or become noticeable ○ *Their relationship went well until the age difference began to assert itself.* [Early 17thC. From Latin *assert-,* the past participle stem of *asserere,* literally "to join to," from *serere* (see SERIES).] —**as·sert·a·ble** *adj.* —**as·ser·ter** *n.*

as·ser·tion /ə súrsh'n/ *n.* **1.** EMPHATIC STATEMENT a strong statement that something is true **2.** ACT OF STATING SOMETHING EMPHATICALLY stating emphatically that something is true ○ *denied them the assertion of their rights*

as·ser·tive /ə súrtiv/ *adj.* **1.** ACTING CONFIDENTLY confident in stating your position or claim ○ *Modern education encourages the assertive student.* **2.** STRONG AND PRONOUNCED forcefully strong and noticeable ○ *an assertive flavor* —**as·ser·tive·ly** *adv.*

as·ser·tive·ness /ə súrtivnəss/ *n.* willingness to be forceful if a situation requires it

as·ser·tive·ness train·ing *n.* teaching people how to overcome shyness and assert themselves

as·sess /ə séss/ (**-sessed, -sess·ing, -sess·es**) *vt.* **1. JUDGE** to examine something in order to judge or evaluate it ○ *not enough information to assess whether the event occurred* **2. DETERMINE AMOUNT** to calculate a value based on various factors ○ *Insurance adjustors are assessing the damage.* **3.** FIN **CALCULATE VALUE FOR TAX** to calculate the value of something in order to establish how much tax must be paid ○ *property assessed at $300,000* **4.** LAW **CHARGE AS AMOUNT** to present a demand for payment, e.g., of a fine or penalty ○ *We were assessed $750 in court costs.* [Via Old French *assesser* from Latin *assess-*, the past participle stem of *assidere*, literally "to sit beside," from *sedere* "to sit" (see SEDENTARY)] —**as·sess·a·ble** *adj.*

as·sessed val·ue *n.* the value of a property that serves as the basis for tax calculation

as·sess·ment /ə séssmənt/ *n.* **1. EVALUATION** a judgment about something based on an understanding of the situation ○ *a fair assessment of the project* **2. PROPERTY VALUATION** a calculation of the value of something in order to know how much tax must be paid **3. AMOUNT CALCULATED** an amount assessed, e.g., on property **4. EDUCATIONAL EVALUATION** a method of evaluating student performance and attainment

as·ses·sor /ə séssər/ *n.* **1. SOMEBODY WHO CALCULATES** somebody who calculates amounts to be paid or assessed for tax or insurance purposes **2.** LAW **JUDGE'S ASSISTANT** a judge's or magistrate's assistant in some jurisdictions, typically somebody with specialized expertise in a given subject

as·set /á sèt/ *n.* **1. SOMEBODY OR SOMETHING USEFUL** somebody or something that is useful and contributes to the success of something **2. VALUABLE THING** a property to which a value can be assigned ■ **as·sets** *npl.* **1. OWNED ITEMS** the property that is owned by a particular person or organization **2.** LAW **SEIZABLE PROPERTY** the property of a person that can be taken by law for the settlement of debts or that forms part of a dead person's estate **3.** FIN **BALANCE SHEET ITEMS** the items on a balance sheet that constitute the total value of an organization [Mid-16thC. Via Anglo-Norman *assetz* "sufficient goods" (to settle an estate) from, ultimately, Latin *ad satis*, literally "to sufficiency."]

as·set-strip·ping *n.* the practice of buying a company cheaply and making a profit by selling all its assets individually —**as·set-strip·per** *n.*

as·sev·er·ate /ə sévvə ràyt/ (**-at·ed, -at·ing, -ates**) *vt.* to state something earnestly or solemnly (*formal*) [Mid-16thC. From Latin *asseverat-*, the past participle stem of *asseverare*, from *severus* (see SEVERE).] —**as·sev·er·a·tion** /ə sèvvə ráysh'n/ *n.*

ass·hole /áss hōl/ *n.* **1. STUPID PERSON** a contemptible person (*taboo insult*) **2. ANUS** the anus (*taboo offensive*)

as·sib·i·late /ə síbbi làyt/ (**-lat·ed, -lat·ing, -lates**) *v.* **1.** *vt.* **UTTER SOMETHING WITH HISS** to utter something with a hissing sound like that of the letter s or z **2.** *vi.* **CHANGE INTO HISSING SOUND** to be transformed into a hissing sound (**sibilant**) [Mid-19thC. From Latin *assibilat-*, the past participle stem of *assibilare*, literally "to hiss at," from *sibilare* (see SIBILANT).] —**as·sib·i·la·tion** /ə sìbbi láysh'n/ *n.*

as·si·du·i·ty /àssi dóo ətee/ *n.* **GREAT CARE** great care and attention in doing something ■ **as·si·du·i·ties** *npl.* **ATTENTIVE BEHAVIOR** constant attentiveness shown toward somebody

as·sid·u·ous /ə síjjoo əss/ *adj.* undeviating in effort and care [Mid-16thC. Formed from Latin *assiduus*, from *assidere* (see ASSESS), in a late sense "to apply oneself."] —**as·sid·u·ous·ly** *adv.* —**as·sid·u·ous·ness** *n.*

WORD KEY: SYNONYMS

See Synonyms at ***careful***.

as·sign /ə sín/ *vt.* (**-signed, -sign·ing, -signs**) **1. GIVE SOMEBODY TASK OR DUTY** to give somebody a particular job to do ○ *assign homework* **2. SEND SOMEBODY TO DO SOMETHING** to send somebody to work in a particular place or with a particular group of people ○ *I assigned him to the maintenance department.* **3.** MIL **ORDER A SOLDIER** to put a soldier or military unit under a particular command **4.** LAW **TRANSFER PROPERTY** to transfer property or rights to another by an official act **5. SET SOMETHING ASIDE FOR SOMETHING** to designate something for a particular use ○ *The new radio station has been assigned a frequency by the authorities.* **6.** COMPUT **PLACE A VALUE** to designate a value for a computer memory location corresponding to a named variable ■ *n.* LAW = **assignee** *n.* 1 [14thC. Via French *assigner* from Latin *assignare*, from *signare* "to mark out, designate," from *signum* (see SIGN).] —**as·sign·a·bil·i·ty** /ə sìnə bíllətee/ *n.* —**as·sign·a·ble** /ə sínəb'l/ *adj.* —**as·sign·a·bly** /-blee/ *adv.* —**as·sign·er** *n.*

as·sig·na·tion /àssig náysh'n/ *n.* **1. LOVERS' MEETING** an appointment to meet with a lover, especially secretly **2. ASSIGNING SOMEBODY OR SOMETHING** the act of giving somebody a particular job or designating something for a particular use **3.** LAW = **assignment** *n.* 4 [Via French from the Latin stem *assignation-*, from *assignare* (see ASSIGN)]

as·signed coun·sel *n.* a lawyer who has been appointed by the court to represent a defendant

as·signed risk *n.* a risk assigned to one of a pool of insurers by state law, the risk being otherwise unacceptable

as·sign·ee /ə sī née, à sī-/ *n.* **1. SOMEBODY RECEIVING RIGHT OVER PROPERTY** somebody to whom a right over property is given or transferred **2. PROXY** a person appointed to act for another

as·sign·ment /ə sínmənt/ *n.* **1. TASK** a specific task assigned or undertaken ○ *All team members have received their assignments.* **2. APPOINTMENT** a position, duty, or job for which somebody is chosen ○ *an assignment in Japan* **3.** LAW **LEGAL TRANSFER DOCUMENT** a document, e.g., a deed, that effects a legal transfer of rights **4.** LAW **LEGAL TRANSFER** the transfer of a right in or over property to another

as·sign·ment work·er *n.* a part-time, freelance, or temporary employee

as·sign·or /ə sínər, ə sí nàwr/ *n.* somebody who transfers rights in or over property to another

as·sim·i·la·ble /ə símmiləb'l/ *adj.* capable of being integrated or assimilated —**as·sim·i·la·bil·i·ty** /ə sìmmilə bíllətee/ *n.* —**as·sim·i·la·bly** /-blee/ *adv.*

as·sim·i·late /ə símmi làyt/ (**-lat·ed, -lat·ing, -lates**) *v.* **1.** *vti.* SOC SCI **INTEGRATE** to integrate somebody into a larger group, so that differences are minimized or eliminated, or become integrated in this way **2.** *vt.* PHYSIOL **ABSORB NUTRIENTS** to incorporate digested food materials into the cells and tissues of the body ○ *assimilate protein* **3.** *vti.* PHON **SOUND LIKE ADJACENT SOUND** to make a speech sound similar to an adjacent sound or to become similar to an adjacent sound [15thC. From Latin *assimilat-*, the past participle stem of *assimilare*, literally "to make the same," from *similis* "like."] —**as·sim·i·la·tor** *n.*

as·sim·i·la·tion /ə sìmmi láysh'n/ *n.* **1. ACT OF BECOMING PART OF SOMETHING** the process of becoming part of or more like something greater **2.** SOC SCI **INTEGRATION INTO GROUP** the process in which one group takes on the cultural and other traits of a larger group **3. LEARNING PROCESS** the integration of new knowledge or information with what is already known **4.** PHYSIOL **NUTRIENT CONVERSION** incorporation of nutrients into the cells and tissues of plants and animals involving digestion, photosynthesis, and root absorption **5.** PHON **SPEECH SOUND CHANGE** the changing of a speech sound under the influence of an adjacent sound

as·sim·i·la·tion·ism /ə sìmmi láysh'n ìzzəm/ *n.* a policy of assimilating differing ethnic or cultural groups —**as·sim·i·la·tion·ist** *n.*, *adj.*

as·sim·i·la·to·ry /ə símmilə tàwree/, **as·sim·i·la·tive** /ə símmi làytiv, -lətiv/ *adj.* connected with or capable of assimilation

As·sin·i·boin /ə sínnə boyn/ (*plural* **-boin** *or* **-boins**), **As·sin·i·boine** (*plural* **-boine** *or* **-boines**) *n.* **1.** PEOPLES **MEMBER OF NATIVE AMERICAN PEOPLE** a member of an Aboriginal people of North America who originally occupied lands in northern parts of the Great Plains, and whose members now live mainly in Saskatchewan, Alberta, and Montana **2. NORTH AMERICAN LANGUAGE** a language spoken in parts of southern and western Canada and Montana by the Assiniboin people. It belongs to the Siouan language family. [Late 17thC. Via Canadian French from Ojibwa *assini:-pwa:n*, literally "stone Sioux."] —**As·sin·i·boin** *adj.*

As·sin·i·boine /ə sínni bòyn/ river flowing from southeastern Saskatchewan, Canada, southwestward into Manitoba and the Red River at Winnipeg. Length: 665 mi./1,070 km.

As·si·si /ə sée sée, -zée/ town in central Italy, famous as the birthplace of St. Francis in 1182. The Basilica of St. Francis suffered considerable earthquake damage in 1997. Population: 24,700 (1990).

As·si·si em·broi·der·y *n.* a type of embroidery in which designs are outlined, some design areas are left open, and the background is filled in with cross-stitch

as·sist /ə síst/ *v.* (**-sist·ed, -sist·ing, -sists**) **1.** *vti.* **HELP SOMEBODY** to help somebody to do or accomplish something ○ *a program to assist new parents* **2.** *vi.* **ATTEND SOMETHING** to attend something or be present (*archaic*) ■ *n.* **1.** SPORTS **TEAM PLAYER HELP** an act by a player in a sport that enables a teammate to score or achieve a successful defensive play **2. ACT OF HELPING** an act or series of actions helping another [15thC. Via French *assister* from Latin *assistere*, literally "to stand beside," from *sistere* "to stand," from *stare* (see STATION).] —**as·sist·er** *n.*

as·sis·tance /ə sístənss/ *n.* help given or made available to another ○ *technical assistance*

as·sis·tant /ə sístənt/ *n.* **HELPER** somebody, especially a subordinate, who helps somebody else to do something ■ *adj.* **1. HELPING** subordinate to or helping another ○ *an assistant teacher* **2. HELPFUL** serving to help or be useful

WORD KEY: SYNONYMS

assistant, helper, deputy, aide, right-hand man or woman

CORE MEANING: somebody who helps another person in carrying out a task

assistant somebody who works to somebody else's instructions, often in a paid capacity; **helper** a more informal term than "assistant," usually implying unpaid voluntary help; **deputy** an officially designated chief assistant authorized to act on a superior's behalf; **aide** an assistant in a military context, now extended to cover an executive assistant in political or commercial contexts; **right-hand man** *or* **woman** a trusted deputy who a superior relies on particularly for support and advice.

as·sis·tant pro·fes·sor *n.* a member of a college or university faculty ranking typically above an instructor and below an associate professor

as·sis·tant·ship /ə sístənt shìp/ *n.* an academic position that provides financial support in exchange for services, typically for a graduate student

as·sist·ed con·cep·tion *n.* = **assisted reproduction**

as·sist·ed liv·ing *n.* **1. RESIDENTIAL CARE FOR SENIORS** the provision of independent residential care for individual seniors needing some help with their daily living and medications, provided in a homelike environment **2. RESIDENTIAL-CARE SETTING FOR SENIORS** a freestanding facility, or a part of a nursing home, where residents live to varying degrees of independence

as·sist·ed re·pro·duc·tion *n.* the use of a technique, e.g., in vitro fertilization, to aid human reproduction in cases where this is problematic

as·sist·ed su·i·cide *n.* the suicide of a patient, usually somebody who is terminally ill, that is aided by a caregiver or especially a physician, by the express wish and consent of the patient

as·size /ə síz/ *n.* **INQUEST** a judicial inquest, or the verdict of the jurors involved ■ **as·sizes** *npl.* **PERIODIC COURTS** periodic judicial proceedings that were held formerly in the counties of England and Wales and presided over by itinerant judges. They were replaced by the Crown Courts in 1971. [Middle English. Via Old French *assise*, the past participle of *asseoir* "to settle," from Latin *assidere* (see ASSESS).]

ass kis·ser *n.* somebody who flatters or slavishly carries out the orders of a superior in order to gain favor (*taboo offensive*)

assn., **assoc.** *abbr.* association

as·so·ci·a·ble /ə sṓshee əb'l, -shəb'l/ *adj.* capable of being linked or associated —**as·so·ci·a·bil·i·ty** /ə sṓshee ə bíllətee, -shə bíllətee/ *n.*

as·so·ci·ate *v.* /ə sṓshee àyt, ə sṓssee-/ (**-at·ed, -at·ing, -ates**) **1.** *vt.* **CONNECT THINGS IN MIND** to connect one thing with another in the mind **2.** *vi.* **SPEND TIME WITH SOMEBODY** to spend time together with somebody ○ *Before the race she associated only with other skiers.* **3.** *vr.* **JOIN AS PARTNER** to join other people in a professional or social relationship ○ *Two artists were associated with the design firm.* **4.** *vi.* **FORM AN ASSOCIATION** to form an association ■ *n.* /ə sṓshee ət, -àyt, ə sṓssee-/ **1. PARTNER** a partner in business or other undertaking ○ *my associates in the firm* **2. CONNECTED PERSON** somebody who is seen with or known to spend time with another ○ *I couldn't identify any of his associates.* **3. MEMBER** a member of a club, e.g., or of a law firm, especially a newly licensed attorney, who does not have full status, rights, or privileges **4.** HOLDER OF DEGREE a holder of an associate degree ■ *adj.* /ə sṓshee ət, -àyt, ə sṓssee-/ **1.** ALLIED joined with others in purpose on an equal or nearly equal basis **2.** SECONDARY with subordinate status or less than full membership in an organization ○ *an associate member* [14thC. From Latin *associat-*, the past participle stem of *associare*, from *socius* "ally, companion" (see SOCIAL).] —**as·so·ci·ate·ship** /ə sṓshee ət shìp, ə sṓssee-/ *n.* —**as·so·ci·a·tor** /ə sṓshee àytər, ə sṓssee-/ *n.*

as·so·ci·ate de·gree *n.* a degree earned on completion of a two-year program of study at a community college, junior college, technical school, or other institution of higher education

as·so·ci·ate jus·tice *n.* **1.** JUDGE a judge of a court, other than the presiding judge or chief justice **2.** STATE COURT JUDGE a judge on any of several high state courts

as·so·ci·ate pro·fes·sor *n.* a member of a college or university faculty ranking typically above an assistant professor and below a professor

as·so·ci·a·tion /ə sṓssee áysh'n, ə sṓshee-/ *n.* **1.** GROUP a group of people or organizations joined together for a purpose ○ *form an association to represent dairy farmers* **2.** CONNECTION a linking or joining of people or things ○ *She hasn't profited from her association with him.* **3.** COMING TOGETHER coming together and social interaction between people ○ *freedom of association* **4.** PSYCHOL PSYCHOLOGICAL CONNECTION a connection of ideas, memories, or feelings with each other, or with events. ◊ **free association 5.** LINKED IDEA a thought, idea, or feeling that is linked with an event **6.** CHEM GROUPING OF MOLECULES the formation of groups of loosely bound molecules **7.** ECOL GROUPING OF ORGANISMS a major ecological community dominated by one or more species, e.g., oak and hickory in a deciduous forest —**as·so·ci·a·tion·al** *adj.*

as·so·ci·a·tion·ism /ə sṓssee áysh'n ìzzəm, ə sṓshee-/ *n.* a psychological theory that explains complex thought and feelings in terms of associations with simpler elements —**as·so·ci·a·tion·ist** *n.* —**as·so·ci·a·tion·is·tic** *adj.*

as·so·ci·a·tive /ə sṓshee àytiv, ə sṓssee-, -ətiv/ *adj.* **1.** OF PSYCHOLOGICAL CONNECTIONS connected with the association of ideas, or of ideas with events and experiences **2.** MATH, LOGIC GIVING SAME RESULT IN ANY ORDER giving the same result irrespective of the order taken, thus since a + (b + c) = (a + b) + c, addition is associative. Multiplication is also associative but subtraction and division are not. —**as·so·ci·a·tive·ly** *adv.*

as·so·ci·a·tive learn·ing *n.* a learning process in which separate ideas and beliefs are linked in order to increase learning effectiveness

as·so·ci·a·tive mem·o·ry *n.* computer memory organization in which stored information is accessed by its content rather than by memory address

as·soil /ə sóyl/ (**-soiled, -soil·ing, -soils**) *vt.* (*archaic*) **1.** ABSOLVE SOMEBODY to absolve somebody **2.** ATONE to atone for something [13thC. Via Anglo-Norman *assoilier* from, ultimately, Latin *absolvere* (see ABSOLVE).]

as·so·nance /áss'nəns/ *n.* the similarity of two or more vowel sounds or the repetition of two or more consonant sounds, especially in words that are close together in a poem [Early 18thC. Via French from Latin *assonare*, literally "to respond to," from *sonare* "to sound."] —**as·so·nant** *adj.*

as·sort /ə sáwrt/ (**-sort·ed, -sort·ing, -sorts**) *v.* **1.** *vt.* SORT to sort things by type or category **2.** *vi.* FIT INTO GROUP to fit into a particular group [15thC. From Old French *assorter*, from *sorte* "a sort" (see SORT).] —**as·sort·er** *n.*

as·sort·ed /ə sáwrtəd/ *adj.* **1.** VARIOUS consisting of various kinds ○ *arrived with assorted excuses* **2.** ARRANGED arranged in groups

as·sort·ment /ə sáwrtmənt/ *n.* a collection of various kinds ○ *an assortment of drawings*

A.S.S.R., ASSR *abbr.* Autonomous Soviet Socialist Republic

asst. *abbr.* assistant

as·std. *abbr.* **1.** assisted **2.** assorted

as·suage /ə swáyj/ (**-suaged, -suag·ing, -suag·es**) *vt.* to provide relief from something distressing or painful ○ *Constant reassurance could not assuage their fears.* [13thC. Via Old French *assuagier* from assumed Vulgar Latin *assuaviare*, literally "to sweeten," from Latin *suavis* "sweet" (see SUAVE).] —**as·suage·ment** *n.* —**as·suag·er** *n.* —**as·sua·sive** /ə swáysiv, -ziv/ *adj.*

as·sum·a·ble /ə sóomәb'l/ *adj.* **1.** FIN TRANSFERABLE used to describe a financial obligation that can be taken over by somebody else **2.** ABLE TO BE ASSUMED that can be supposed or taken for granted —**as·sum·a·bly** *adv.*

as·sume /ə sóom/ (**-sumed, -sum·ing, -sumes**) *vt.* **1.** SUPPOSE to think that something is true even though you have no evidence for it ○ *Don't assume that all has been revealed.* **2.** TAKE RESPONSIBILITY FOR SOMETHING to start being responsible for something ○ *She assumed all of her brother's debts when he died.* **3.** ADOPT SOMETHING to adopt or take on something ○ *spirits that assume the form of animals* **4.** TAKE ON ROLE to take on a particular role or function ○ *assumed the office of mayor* **5.** PRETEND SOMETHING to put on a pretense of something, usually in order to hide your true feelings ○ *He assumed an air of indifference.* [From Latin *assumere*, literally "to take up," from *sumere* (see SUMPTUOUS)] —**as·sum·er** *n.*

WORD KEY: SYNONYMS

See Synonyms at ***deduce***.

as·sumed /ə sóomd/ *adj.* **1.** EXPECTED taken for granted ○ *an assumed increase in expenditure* **2.** ARTIFICIAL not genuine or true ○ *Better to express your feelings than sit there with an assumed smile.* —**as·sum·ed·ly** /ə sóomədlee/ *adv.*

as·sumed name *n.* a false name, especially one used by somebody doing something illegal

as·sum·ing /ə sóoming/ *adj.* EXPECTING TOO MUCH expecting too much of other people ■ *conj.* ON THE ASSUMPTION THAT if it is assumed that —**as·sum·ing·ly** *adv.*

as·sump·sit /ə súmpsit/ *n.* **1.** CONTRACT OFF THE RECORD an oral or written agreement, contract, or promise that exists without being on the record or under seal **2.** LEGAL ACTION an attempt to recover damages from a breached assumpsit [Late 16thC. From Latin, literally "he has undertaken."]

as·sump·tion /ə súmpshən/ *n.* **1.** SOMETHING TAKEN FOR GRANTED something that is believed to be true without proof ○ *Make no assumptions before looking at the evidence.* ○ *"Cruelty will be slyly advocated by the assumption that its only opposite is sentimentality."* (C. S. Lewis, *Reflections on the Psalms*; 1961) **2.** TAKING SOMETHING FOR GRANTED believing something to be true without proof **3.** ADOPTING SOMETHING taking something upon yourself ○ *With the assumption of power comes responsibility.* **4.** TAKING RESPONSIBILITY FOR SOMETHING taking over responsibility for something **5.** INCLINATION TO HIGH EXPECTATIONS the tendency to expect too much **6.** LOGIC UNPROVED STARTING POINT something taken as a starting point of a logical proof rather than given as a premise [From the Latin stem *assumption-*, from *assumpt-*, the past participle stem of *assumere* (see ASSUME)]

Assumption (1649–50) by Nicolas Poussin

As·sump·tion, As·sump·tion of the Vir·gin Mar·y *n.* **1.** MARY'S JOURNEY TO HEAVEN the ascent of the Virgin Mary to heaven at her death, as believed by some Christians **2.** CHRISTIAN FEAST a Christian feast that celebrates the Assumption, commemorated on August 15

as·sump·tive /ə súmptiv/ *adj.* predicated on an assumption or a set of assumptions

as·sur·ance /ə shóorəns/ *n.* **1.** PLEDGE OR PROMISE a declaration that inspires or is intended to inspire confidence ○ *They gave us every assurance it would arrive on time.* **2.** CONFIDENCE confidence in your ability or status ○ *He steered the ungainly machine with smooth assurance.* **3.** CERTAINTY freedom from uncertainty ○ *took heart in the assurance that the problem was solved* **4.** MAKING SOMETHING CERTAIN making something certain or overcoming doubt **5.** *U.K.* INSUR INSURANCE AGAINST CERTAINTY insurance against something that is certain to happen, e.g., death, rather than something that might happen, e.g., loss of or damage to property ○ *life assurance*

as·sure /ə shóor/ (**-sured, -sur·ing, -sures**) *vt.* **1.** MAKE SOMEBODY CONFIDENT to overcome somebody's doubt or disbelief about something ○ *I can assure you that every word is true.* **2.** CONVINCE SOMEBODY to convince somebody of something ○ *assured us of her sincerity* **3.** MAKE SOMETHING CERTAIN to make something certain ○ *Proper planning assures that the job will be done right.* **4.** *U.K.* INSUR INSURE AGAINST CERTAINTY to insure somebody against something that is certain to happen, e.g., death, rather than something that might happen, e.g., loss of or damage to property [14thC. Via French *assurer* from assumed Vulgar Latin *assecurare*, literally "to make secure," from Latin *securus* (see SECURE).] —**as·sur·a·ble** *adj.* —**as·sur·er** *n.*

WORD KEY: USAGE

assure, ensure or **insure**? You use ***assure*** when you are referring to somebody being made sure about something, and ***ensure*** when you are referring to something that you want to be sure of. *I assure you it doesn't hurt. She wanted to ensure that it wouldn't hurt.* ***Insure*** is used chiefly in connection with insurance (i.e. financial protection), but it is also a variant spelling of ***ensure***.

as·sured /ə shóord/ *adj.* **1.** GUARANTEED certain to happen ○ *an assured victory* **2.** SELF-CONFIDENT confident about your abilities or other qualities ○ *the most assured conductor the orchestra had ever seen* —**as·sur·ed·ly** /ə shóorədlee/ *adv.* —**as·sur·ed·ness** /ə shóorədnəss/ *n.*

as·sy. *abbr.* assembly

As·syr·i·a /ə séeree ə/ ancient Mesopotamian kingdom with a large empire extending southward and eastward, at its height from the ninth to the seventh centuries B.C.

As·syr·i·an /ə sírree ən/ *n.* **1.** LANG AKKADIAN DIALECT the Akkadian language, particularly in the form that is recorded in cuneiform tablets from Assyria **2.** PEOPLES SOMEBODY FROM ASSYRIA somebody who lived in Assyria —**As·syr·i·an** *adj.*

AST *abbr.* Atlantic Standard Time

a·sta·ble /ay stáyb'l/ *adj.* **1.** UNSTABLE lacking stability **2.** ELEC OSCILLATING BETWEEN STATES oscillating between two unstable states

Fred Astaire

A·staire /ə stáir/, **Fred** (1899–1987) U.S. dancer and actor who was known for his performances in Broadway musicals and movies. He famously partnered Ginger Rogers. Real name **Fred Austerlitz**

As·ta·na /ə staánə/ capital of Kazakhstan. It is situated in the northern part of the country, on the Ishim River. Population: 281,000 (1990). Former name **Aqmola** (until 1998)

As·tar·te /əstaártee/ *n.* MYTHOL ◆ **Ishtar**

a·sta·sia /ə stáyzhə/ *n.* inability to stand caused by a lack of muscle coordination [Late 19thC. From Greek, "unsteadiness," from *astatos*, literally "not standing," from *statos* "standing."]

a·stat·ic /ay státtik/ *adj.* unsteady because of poor muscle coordination [Early 19thC. Formed from Greek *astatos* "unstable," from *statos* "standing."] —**a·stat·i·cal·ly** *adv.* —**a·stat·i·cism** /ay státtissiz'm/ *n.*

a·stat·ic gal·va·nom·e·ter *n.* an instrument for measuring electric current (**galvanometer**) that is not significantly affected by the Earth's magnetic field

as·ta·tine /ástə teen/ *n.* a highly unstable radioactive element, the heaviest in the halogen series, found naturally in trace amounts. It is produced artificially and used in medicine as a radioactive tracer. Symbol **At** [Mid-20thC. Formed from Greek *astatos* (see ASTATIC).]

as·ter /ástər/ *n.* **1.** PLANTS **GARDEN PLANT WITH DAISYLIKE FLOWERS** an annual plant of the daisy family, grown for its white, pink, or violet flowers **2.** CELL BIOL **STAR-SHAPED STRUCTURE IN CELL** a star-shaped structure seen during cell division **(mitosis)** [Early 18thC. Via Latin from Greek *astēr* "star" (source of English *asterisk* and *disaster*). Ultimately from an Indo-European word that is also the ancestor of English *star*.]

-aster *suffix.* one that is inferior ○ *criticaster* [From Latin]

as·te·ri·at·ed /a steéree aytəd/ *adj.* used to describe a crystal that reflects light in a star shape [Early 19thC. Formed from Greek *asterios* "starry."]

as·ter·isk /ástərisk/ *n.* **1.** PRINTING **STAR-SHAPED SYMBOL (*)** a star-shaped symbol (*) used in printing **2.** LING **ASTERISK AS LINGUISTIC SYMBOL** an asterisk used to mark a sound, form, or structure that is believed to have existed but is unrecorded, or that is wrong or ungrammatical ■ *vt.* **(-isked, -isk·ing, -isks) MARK SOMETHING WITH ASTERISK** to mark a printed or written item with an asterisk [14thC. Via late Latin from Greek *asteriskos*, literally "little star," from *astēr* "star" (see ASTER).]

as·ter·ism /ástərizzəm/ *n.* **1.** PRINTING **PRINTER'S MARK OF THREE ASTERISKS** a triangle formed of three asterisks to call the reader's attention to a following passage **2.** ASTRON **STAR CLUSTER** a cluster of stars that is smaller than a constellation **3.** CRYSTALS **STAR-SHAPED REFLECTION IN CRYSTALS** an optical effect appearing as a star in the light reflected from certain crystals [Late 16thC. From Greek *asterismos* "constellation," from *astēr* "star" (see ASTER).]

a·stern /ə stúrn/ *adv.* **1. IN OR TO THE STERN** in, on, to, or toward the stern of a ship or boat ○ *The deckhand walked astern.* **2. WITH STERN FOREMOST** into a position with the stern pointing in the direction of motion ○ *Bring the captain's gig astern.* ■ *adj.* **BEHIND BOAT** positioned behind a boat ○ *The astern line has been cut.*

as·ter·oid /ástə royd/ *n.* **1.** ASTRON **ROCKY OBJECT ORBITING SUN** an irregularly shaped rock that orbits the Sun, mostly in a band **(asteroid belt)** between the orbits of Mars and Jupiter. Asteroids range in size from the largest, Ceres, with a diameter of 580 mi./930 km down to dust particles. **2.** ZOOL **STARFISH** a starfish (*technical*) [Early 19thC. From Greek *asteroeidēs* "star-like," from *astēr* "star" (see ASTER).] —**as·ter·oid·al** /àstə róyd'l/ *adj.*

as·the·ni·a /as theéniə/ *n.* a condition marked by loss of strength in the body [Late 18thC. Via modern Latin from, ultimately, Greek *asthenēs* (see ASTHENIC).]

as·then·ic /as thénnik/ *adj.* **1. PHYSICALLY WEAK** showing abnormal physical weakness **2. OF SLENDER BUILD** having a slender and lightly muscled build [Late 18thC. From Greek *asthenikos*, from *asthenēs*, literally "without strength," from *sthenos* "strength," of unknown origin.]

as·then·o·sphere /as thénnə sfeer/ *n.* a weak zone in the upper part of the Earth's mantle where rock can be deformed in response to stress, resulting in movement of the overlying crust [Early 20thC. Coined from Greek *asthenēs* (see ASTHENIC) + -SPHERE.]

asth·ma /ázmə/ *n.* a chronic disease of the respiratory system, sometimes caused by allergies, with symptoms including coughing, sudden difficulty in breathing, and a tight feeling in the chest [14thC. Via medieval Latin from Greek, from *azein* "to breathe hard."]

asth·mat·ic /az máttik/ *adj.* **1. WITH ASTHMA** affected with or prone to attacks of asthma **2. OF ASTHMA** relating to the respiratory difficulties associated with asthma ■ *n.* **SOMEBODY WITH ASTHMA** somebody who is affected with or prone to attacks of asthma [Early 16thC. Via Latin *asthmaticus* from Greek *asthmatikos*, which was formed from, ultimately, *azein* (see ASTHMA).] —**asth·mat·i·cal·ly** *adv.*

a·stig·ma·tism /ə stígmətizzəm/ *n.* **1. VISUAL DEFECT** a visual defect caused by the unequal curving of one or more of the refractive surfaces of the eye, usually the cornea. It prevents light rays lying in certain planes from coming to a focus on the retina, thus producing blurred vision. **2. OPTICAL LENS DEFECT** a defect in a lens or mirror that prevents light rays

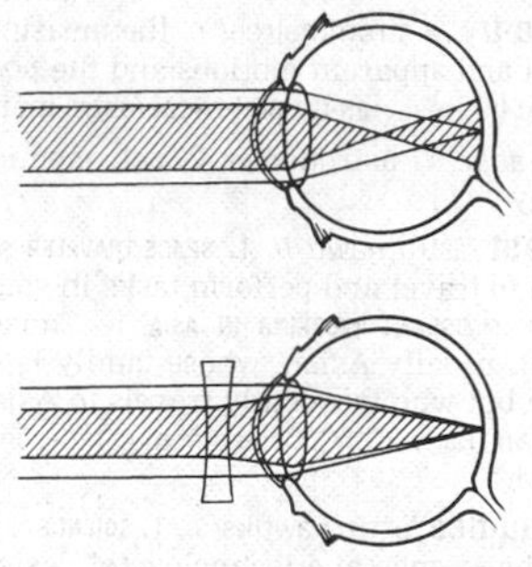

Astigmatism: Visual defect in the eye causing blurred vision (top) and corrected with concave lens (bottom)

from meeting at a single point, producing an imperfect image [Mid-19thC. Formed from the Greek stem *stigmat-* "point."] —**as·tig·mat·ic** /àstig máttik/ *adj.* —**as·tig·mat·i·cal·ly** /-tiklee/ *adv.*

a·stil·be /ə stílbee/ (*plural* **-bes** *or* **-be**) *n.* a perennial plant with attractive plume-shaped flowers. It was originally found in eastern Asia but now is widely cultivated in shady damp gardens. Genus: *Astilbe*. [Mid-19thC. From modern Latin, genus name, literally "not glittering," from Greek *a-* "not" + *stilbos* "glittering."]

a·stir /ə stúr/ *adj.* **1. UP AND ABOUT** awake and moving around, especially out of bed ○ *The children were astir early as usual.* **2. MOVING** moving around ○ *leaves astir in the breeze*

As·ti spu·man·te /àasti spoo maántee/ *n.* sparkling white wine from Asti in northwestern Italy

as-told-to *adj.* used to describe an autobiography written by a professional author using conversations with the person whose life is documented (*informal*) ○ *another as-told-to book* [From the phrase sometimes used in the subtitles of such books]

a·ston·ied /ə stónnid/ *adj.* in a confused or shocked condition (*archaic or literary*) [14thC. Past participle of earlier *astone* (see ASTOUND).]

a·ston·ish /ə stónnish/ (**-ished, -ish·ing, -ish·es**) *vt.* to amaze somebody to a great degree [Early 16thC. Formed from a variant of earlier *astone* (see ASTOUND).] —**a·ston·ish·ing** *adj.* —**a·ston·ish·ing·ly** *adv.*

a·ston·ish·ment /ə stónnishmənt/ *n.* great amazement, often eliciting shock ○ *He was on time, to my astonishment.*

As·tor, John Jacob (1763–1848) German-born U.S. fur trader, property millionaire, and founder of the Astor family and fortune. He endowed the Astor Library, now part of the New York Public Library.

As·tor, Nancy, Viscountess (1879–1964) American-born British politician. She was the first woman member of Parliament (elected 1919).

As·to·ri·a /ə stáwriə/ city and port in northwestern Oregon. The Lewis and Clark Expedition ended here in 1806. Population: 9,844 (1996).

a·stound /ə stównd/ (**a·stound·ed, a·stound·ing, a·stounds**) *vt.* to overwhelm and stun somebody with sudden surprise ○ *astounded by the viciousness of the attacks* [14thC. Alteration of earlier *astoned*, past participle of *astone* "to stun," via Old French *estoner* (source of English *stun*) from assumed Vulgar Latin *extonare*, literally "to thunder out."] —**a·stound·ing** *adj.* —**a·stound·ing·ly** *adv.*

astr- *prefix.* = **astro-** (*used before vowels*)

a·strad·dle /ə strádd'l/ *prep., adv.* with one leg or part on either side of something

as·tra·gal /ástrəg'l/ *n.* **1. TYPE OF DECORATIVE MOLDING** a narrow convex molding, often taking the form of beads **2. MOLDING ON DOUBLE DOORS** a small, convex, usually semicircular molding attached to one or both meeting stiles of a pair of double doors to prevent drafts or the passage of light, noise, or smoke [Mid-17thC. Via French from Greek *astragalos* (see ASTRAGALUS).]

as·trag·a·lus /ə strággələss/ (*plural* **-li** /-lee/) *n.* ANAT = **talus** [Mid-16thC. Via Latin from Greek *astragalos*. Ultimately from an Indo-European word meaning "bone," which is also the ancestor of English *osteo-*, *oyster*, and *ostracize*.]

as·tra·khan /àastrə kaan, -kan/ *n.* fur fabric originally made from the expensive curly black or gray fleece of lambs from Astrakhan, southern Russia, now usually made from acrylic fibers. It is used for hats and trimming coats.

as·tral /ástrəl/ *adj.* **1. RELATING TO STARS** relating to, characteristic of, or consisting of stars **2. ABOVE MATERIAL WORLD** in theosophical belief, belonging to the ethereal region that is believed to exist throughout and at a higher level than the material world, in which personal auras are said to be perceived **3. EXALTED** likened to stars, e.g., in height or distance from ordinary places or people ○ *the astral position of king or president* [Early 17thC. Via late Latin *astralis* from, ultimately, Greek *astron* "star," from *astēr* (see ASTER).] —**as·tral·ly** *adv.*

as·tral bod·y (*plural* **as·tral bod·ies**) *n.* in theosophical belief, a second body, not directly perceivable by the human senses, believed to coexist with and survive the death of the physical body

as·tral plane *n.* in theosophical belief, a level of existence where the spirit goes between death and entry into the spirit world

as·tral pro·jec·tion *n.* in theosophical belief, the ability to send the astral body outside of the physical body, while both remain connected

a·stray /ə stráy/ *adv.* **1. OFF RIGHT PATH** away from the right path ○ *went astray and ended up lost* **2. INTO ERROR OR SIN** in or into an evil or undesirable course of life ○ *a young man who was led astray* [13thC. From Old French *estraie*, past participle of *estraier* "to stray" (see STRAY).]

a·stride /ə strī́d/ *prep.* **1. WITH LEGS AROUND** on top of and with a leg on each side of something ○ *astride a horse* **2. EXTENDING ACROSS** extending across in terms of influence or power ○ *a military colossus astride the world* ■ *adv.* **WITH LEGS APART** with legs spread wide apart ○ *He stood menacingly at the exit, arms folded and legs astride.*

as·trin·gent /ə strínjənt/ *n.* **PORE-CLOSING SUBSTANCE** a substance used on the skin to draw tissue together ■ *adj.* **SHARP AND ACIDIC IN TONE** speaking or writing in a manner that is critical and hurtful in tone and content [Mid-16thC. From Latin *astringent-*, the present participle stem of *astringere*, literally "to bind to," from *stringere* "to bind."] —**as·trin·gen·cy** *n.* —**as·trin·gent·ly** *adv.*

astro-, **astr-** *prefix.* **1.** star, the stars, outer space ○ *astrobiology* **2.** aster of a cell ○ *astrosphere* [From Greek, from *astron* "star," from *astēr* (see ASTER)]

as·tro·bleme /ástrə bleem/ *n.* a depression, usually circular, on the surface of the Earth that is caused by the impact of a meteorite [Mid-20thC. Coined from ASTRO- + Greek *blēma* "wound from a missile."]

as·tro·chem·is·try /àstrō kémmistree/ *n.* the application of the principles of chemistry to celestial bodies and interstellar space —**as·tro·chem·ist** *n.*

as·tro·com·pass /ástrō kùmpəss/ *n.* a nonmagnetic navigational instrument used to determine the position of true north relative to a celestial body

as·tro·cyte /ástrə sīt/ *n.* a star-shaped cell in the central nervous system's supportive tissue **(glia)**

as·tro·cy·to·ma /àstrō sī tṓmə/ (*plural* **-mas** *or* **-ma·ta** /-mətə/) *n.* a commonly occurring malignant brain tumor made up of star-shaped cells **(astrocytes)**

as·tro·dome /ástrə dōm/ *n.* a transparent dome on an aircraft or spacecraft through which celestial observations are made in order to navigate

as·tro·dy·nam·ics /àstrō dī námmiks/ *n.* the study of the effects of gravitational and other forces on the motion of natural and artificial bodies in outer space (*takes a singular verb*) —**as·tro·dy·nam·ic** *adj.*

as·tro·ge·ol·o·gy /àstrō jee óllәjee/ *n.* the study of the origin, history, and structure of cosmic bodies other than the Earth —**as·tro·ge·ol·o·gist** *n.*

as·trol. *abbr.* **1.** astrologer **2.** astrological **3.** astrology

as·tro·labe /ástrə layb/ *n.* an early instrument used to observe the position and determine the altitude of the Sun or other celestial body. The astrolabe was used for navigation from the Middle Ages until the 18th century when it was replaced by the sextant. [14thC. Via Old French and medieval Latin from Greek *astrolabon*, literally "to take a star."]

as·trol·o·gy /ə stróllәjee/ *n.* the study of the positions of the Moon, Sun, and other planets in the belief that their motions affect human beings [14thC. Via

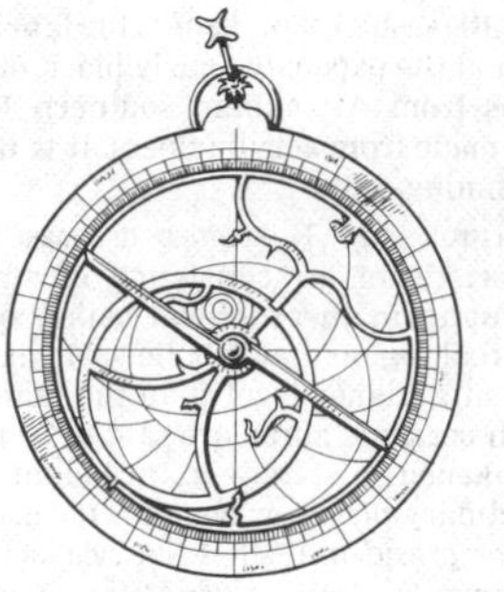

Astrolabe

Aries
21 March-
20 April
Taurus
21 April-
21 May
Gemini
22 May-
21 June
Cancer
22 June-
22 July
Leo
23 July-
23 August
Virgo
24 August-
23 September
Libra
24 September-
23 October
Scorpio
24 October-
22 November
Sagittarius
23 November-
21 December
Capricorn
22 December-
20 January
Aquarius
21 January-
18 February
Pisces
19 February-
20 March
子
Rat
1936-1948-1960
1972-1984
丑
Ox
1937-1949-1961
1973-1985
寅
Tiger
1938-1950-1962
1974-1986
卯
Rabbit
1936-1951-1963
1975-1987
辰
Dragon
1940-1952-1964
1976-1988
巳
Snake
1941-1953-1965
1977-1989
午
Horse
1942-1954-1966
1978-1990
未
Sheep
1943-1955-1967
1979-1991
申
Monkey
1944-1956-1968
1980-1994
酉
Rooster
1945-1957-1969
1981-1993
戌
Dog
1946-1958-1970
1982-1994
亥
Wild Boar
1947-1959-1971
1983-1995

Astrological signs

French from, ultimately, Greek *astrologia*, literally "account of the stars," which was coined from *astro-* "ASTRO-" + *-logia* (see -LOGY). Used scientifically for "observation of the stars."] —**as·trol·o·ger** /ə strólləjər/ *n.* —**as·tro·log·i·cal** /àstrə lójjik'l/ *adj.* —**as·tro·log·i·cal·ly** /-lójjiklee/ *adv.* —**as·trol·o·gist** /ə strólləjist/ *n.*

as·trom·e·try /ə strómmətree/ *n.* the measurement of the real and apparent motions and the positions of celestial bodies —**as·tro·met·ri·cal** /àstrə méttrik'l/ *adj.*

as·tron. *abbr.* **1.** astronomer **2.** astronomical **3.** astronomy

as·tro·naut /ástrə nawt/ *n.* **1.** SPACE TRAVELER somebody trained to travel and perform tasks in space **2.** *Can* CANADIAN IMMIGRANT WORKING IN ASIA a Canadian immigrant, usually Asian, whose family is settled in Canada but who frequently travels to Asia to work (*informal*) [Early 20thC. Coined from ASTRO-, on the model of *aeronaut*.]

as·tro·nau·tics /àstrə náwtiks/ *n.* **1.** SCIENCE OF SPACECRAFT DESIGN the science and technology of designing and building spacecraft (*takes a singular verb*) **2.** SPACECRAFT OPERATION the skills and activities associated with the operation of a spacecraft (*takes a plural verb*) [Early 20thC. Coined from ASTRO-, on the model of *aeronautics*.] —**as·tro·nau·tic** *adj.* —**as·tro·nau·ti·cal·ly** *adv.*

as·tro·nav·i·ga·tion /àstrō navvi gáysh'n/ *n.* **1.** NAVIGATION IN SPACE the navigation of a spacecraft among celestial bodies, especially stars **2.** = **celestial navigation** —**as·tro·nav·i·gate** /àstrō návvi gayt/ *vti.* —**as·tro·nav·i·ga·tor** /-gaytər/ *n.*

as·tron·o·mer /ə strónnəmər/ *n.* somebody who specializes in studying celestial bodies

as·tro·nom·i·cal /àstrə nómmik'l/ *adj.* **1.** IMMEASURABLY GREAT immeasurably numerous, high, or great (*informal*) ○ *reached astronomical proportions* **2.** RELATING TO ASTRONOMY relating to the science of astronomy —**as·tro·nom·i·cal·ly** *adv.*

as·tro·nom·i·cal clock *n.* a clock that shows astronomical information such as the phases of the Moon

as·tro·nom·i·cal tel·e·scope *n.* a telescope used to view celestial objects

as·tro·nom·i·cal twi·light *n.* the period of time during which the Sun is at 18° below the horizon

as·tro·nom·i·cal u·nit *n.* a unit of astronomical distances especially within the solar system, equal to the mean distance between the Earth and the Sun, about 93 million mi./150 million km

as·tro·nom·i·cal year *n.* = **solar year**

as·tron·o·my /ə strónnəmee/ *n.* the scientific study of the universe, especially of the motions, positions, sizes, composition, and behavior of celestial objects. These objects are studied and interpreted from the radiation they emit and from data gathered by interplanetary probes. [13thC. Via Old French and Latin from Greek *astronomia*, literally "star-arranging," from *astro-* "ASTRO-" + *-nomia* (see -NOMY).]

as·tro·pho·tog·ra·phy /àstrōfə tóggrəfee/ *n.* the art of photographing celestial objects and events for astronomical studies

as·tro·phys·ics /àstrō fízziks/ *n.* the study of the physical properties, origin, and development of celestial objects and events (*takes a singular verb*) —**as·tro·phys·i·cal** *adj.* —**as·tro·phys·i·cally** *adv.* —**as·tro·phys·i·cist** *n.*

As·tro·Turf *tdmk.* a trademark for synthetic turf resembling grass

As·tu·ri·as /a stóoree əss, ə-/, **Miguel Angel** (1899–1974) Guatemalan writer, author of antiimperialist novels rooted in Native American tradition. He won the 1967 Nobel Prize.

as·tute /ə stóot/ *adj.* shrewd and discerning, especially where personal benefit is to be derived ○ *an astute investor* [Early 17thC. From Latin *astutus*, from *astus* "cleverness, skill."] —**as·tute·ly** *adv.* —**as·tute·ness** *n.*

a·sty·lar /ay stílər/ *adj.* used to describe a classical building that has no columns [Mid-19thC. Formed from Greek *astulos* "without pillars," from *stulos* "pillar."]

A·sun·cion /aa sóon syáwn/ capital of Paraguay and of the Asuncion and Central departments and the largest city in Paraguay, located on the Paraguay River. Population: 502,426 (1992).

a·sun·der /ə súndər/ *adv.* into separate parts, pieces, or places (*formal*) [Old English *onsundran*, literally "into parts," from *on* "into" + *sundran* "parts," from a prehistoric Germanic base that is also the ancestor of English *sundry*]

a·su·ra /ússoorə/ *n.* in Hindu myth, a member of a class of nonhuman beings who are enemies of heavenly beings [From Sanskrit, "demon," originally "mighty Lord"]

ASV *abbr.* BIBLE American Standard Version

As·vi·na /ásh vin/ *n.* in the Hindu calendar, the seventh month of the year, falling in approximately the same time as September to October

As·wān /a swaán, á swaan/ city on the Nile River in southern Egypt. The Aswan High Dam, south of the city, holds back Lake Nasser. Population: 220,000 (1992 est.).

a·swarm /ə swáwrm/ *adj.* full of moving living beings (*literary*)

a·swirl /ə swúrl/ *adj.* moving with a swirling or twirling motion (*literary*)

a·swoon /ə swóon/ *adj.* experiencing a swoon or faint (*literary*)

a·syl·lab·ic /àyssi lábbik/ *adj.* used to describe a speech sound that does not constitute a syllable

a·sy·lum /ə sīləm/ *n.* **1.** SHELTER AND PROTECTION protection or safety from danger or imminent harm provided by a sheltered place ○ *They sought asylum in a neutral country.* **2.** PROTECTION FROM EXTRADITION protection and immunity from extradition **3.** MENTAL HEALTH FACILITY an institution for people with psychiatric disorders (*dated offensive*) **4.** HIST PLACE OF SANCTUARY a place that once offered shelter to criminals and debtors, especially a church [15thC. Via Latin from Greek *asulon* "refuge," from *asulos*, literally "without right of seizure," from *sulon* "right of seizure."]

a·sym·met·ri·cal /ày si méttrik'l/, **a·sym·met·ric** /-méttrik/ *adj.* **1.** NOT SYMMETRICAL not arranged in a symmetrical way ○ *an asymmetrical flower arrangement* **2.** CHEM WITH PARTICULAR SPATIAL ARRANGEMENT OF ATOMS used to describe a carbon atom with four different atoms or radicals attached. This results in molecules with the same structure but a different spatial arrangement of their atoms (**stereoisomerism**). **3.** ELEC ENG WITH VARYING CONDUCTIVITY used to describe a substance or a device that exhibits varying or different conductivities for currents flowing through it in different directions **4.** AEROSP WITH UNEQUAL THRUST FROM ENGINES unbalanced because of unequal thrust from two or more sources, e.g., when one engine of a pair is not functioning properly **5.** LOGIC, MATH NOT INTERCHANGEABLE used to describe a relation between two things where the first has a relation to the second, but the second cannot have the same relation to the first —**a·sym·met·ri·cal·ly** *adv.*

a·sym·me·try /a símmətree/ *n.* **1.** BEING ASYMMETRICAL the condition of being asymmetrical in arrangement ○ *some asymmetry in the design* **2.** LOGIC, MATH UNRECIPROCAL RELATION BETWEEN TWO THINGS a relation between two things where the first has a relation to the second, but the second cannot have the same relation to the first. Asymmetry is illustrated in the statement "A is the father of B," since B cannot be the father of A.

a·symp·to·mat·ic /ay sìmtə máttik/ *adj.* not showing or producing indications of a disease or other medical condition ○ *Although the blood tests were positive, she remained asymptomatic for some time.* —**a·symp·to·mat·i·cal·ly** *adv.*

as·ymp·tote /ássimp tōt, ássim-/ *n.* a line that draws increasingly nearer to a curve without ever meeting it [Mid-17thC. Via modern Latin from Greek *asumptōtos*, literally "not adapted to fall together," from *sun-* "together" + *ptōtos* "adapted to fall" , literally "to fall together" (see SYMPTOM).] —**as·ymp·tot·ic** /àssimp tóttik, àssim-/ *adj.* —**as·ymp·tot·i·cal·ly** /-iklee, -klee/ *adv.*

a·syn·ap·sis /àyssi nápsiss/ *n.* the failure of chromosomes that are alike (**homologous**) to pair during cell division (**meiosis**)

a·syn·de·ton /ə síndi ton/ (*plural* **-ta** /-tə/) *n.* the leaving out of conjunctions in sentence constructions in which they would usually be used. ◊ **parataxis** [Mid-16thC. Via late Latin from, ultimately, Greek *asundetos*, literally "not bound together," from *sundein* "to bind together" (source of English *syndetic*).] —**as·yn·det·ic** /àssin déttik/ *adj.* —**as·yn·det·i·cal·ly** /àssin dètt-/ *adv.*

a·syn·er·gy /ay sínnərjee/, **a·sy·ner·gia** /ày si núrjə/ *n.* a failure of coordination between different muscle groups so that delicate, skilled, or rapid movements become impossible [Mid-19thC. Formed from Greek *sunergia* (see SYNERGY).] —**a·syn·er·gic** /ay sínnərjik/ *adj.*

a·sys·to·le /ay sístəlee/ *n.* the absence of any heartbeat —**a·sys·tol·ic** /ày si stóllik/ *adj.*

at[1] *(stressed)* /at/; *(unstressed)* /ət/ CORE MEANING: a preposition used to indicate general position or location. In order to be more precise about exact physical location, other prepositions such as "on," "over," "under," and "by" are used instead. ○ *a conference at the school* ○ *Someone's at the door.* ○ *I work at home.*

prep. **1. ATTENDING** attending regularly ○ *not at school yet* **2. FROM AN INTERVAL OF** used to describe the position of something by indicating its distance or angle ○ *She followed them at a distance.* **3. INDICATES WHEN SOMETHING HAPPENS** used to indicate the time or age when something happens ○ *Lunch is at noon.* **4. DURING AN EVENT** while present during an event ○ *had a good time at the carnival* **5. INDICATES RATE OR FREQUENCY** used to indicate the rate, frequency, level, or price of something ○ *driving at 65 miles per hour* **6. TOWARD** to or in the direction of somebody or something ○ *He glanced over at her.* **7. AS A REACTION TO** used to indicate what somebody is reacting to ○ *amazed at what had happened* **8. IN THE STATED ACTIVITY** used to indicate an activity or subject that a judgment about somebody relates to ○ *an expert at windsurfing* **9. IN A CONDITION OR STATE** indicating the state or condition that somebody or something is in ○ *at risk of infection* **10. DOING** engaged or occupied in ○ *hard at work* **11. IN THE MANNER OF** used to indicate how something is done ○ *set off at a run* **12. INDICATES REPEATED ACTIONS** used to indicate the object of a repeated action ○ *She just picks at her food.* **13. ACCORDING TO SOMEBODY'S WISHES** in response to or based on somebody's wish or decision ○ *Spend this money at your discretion.* [Old English *æt.* Ultimately from an Indo-European word that is also the ancestor of Latin *ad* "to, toward" (source of English *aid*).] ◇ **where it's** *or* **something is at** where all the action and excitement is happening (*informal*) ◇ **at all** in any way, to any extent, or under any conditions ○ *don't like it at all*

at[2] /at/ (*plural* **at**) *n.* **1.** see table at **currency 2. COIN WORTH AN AT** a coin worth one at [Mid-20thC. From Thai.]

At *symbol.* astatine

AT *abbr.* **1.** antitank **2.** automatic transmission **3. AT, A.T.** Atlantic Time

at. *abbr.* **1.** airtight **2.** atomic **3.** PHYS, MEASURE atmosphere

at- *prefix.* = **ad-** (*used before t-*)

At·a·brine *tdmk.* a trademark for the antimalarial drug quinacrine

A·ta·ca·ma De·sert /aatə kaámə-/ barren, arid, sparsely populated plateau in northern Chile known for its once enormously abundant nitrate and copper resources. Area: 140,000 sq. mi./363,000 sq. km.

at·a·ghan *n.* = **yataghan**

A·ta·hual·pa /aàtə waálpə/ (1500?–33) Inca king. The last ruler of the Inca Empire (1525–32), he was executed for having his co-ruling brother Huascar assassinated.

at·a·man /áttə màn/ *n.* a Cossack chieftain [Mid-19thC. Via Russian from Turkic, literally "great father."]

at·a·mas·co lil·y /áttə más kō-/ (*plural* **at·a·mas·co lil·ies**) *n.* a plant found in the southeastern United States that grows from a bulb and has one large flower, usually white or pinkish, on a tall stalk. Latin name: *Zephyranthes atamasco.* [Mid-18thC. *Atamasco* from Virginia Algonquian *attamusco.*]

atar *n.* = **attar**

at·a·rac·tic /áttə ráktik/, **at·a·rax·ic** /-ráksik/ *adj.* **TRANQUILIZING** used to describe a drug or other agent that produces calm and peace of mind ■ *n.* **TRANQUILIZER** a tranquilizer (*technical*) [Mid-20thC. Formed from Greek *ataraktos,* literally "not disturbed," from *tarassein* "to disturb."]

at·a·rax·i·a /áttə ráksee ə/ *n.* freedom from worry or any other preoccupation [Mid-19thC. From Greek, from *ataraktos* (see ATARACTIC).]

at·a·rax·ic *adj., n.* = **ataractic**

A·ta·türk /áttə tùrk/**, Mustafa Kemal** (1881–1938) Turkish statesman. He was the founder and the first president of the republic of Turkey (1923–38).

at·a·vism /áttəviz'm/ *n.* **1. REAPPEARANCE OF GENETIC FEATURE** the recurrence of a genetically controlled feature in an organism after it has been absent for several generations, usually because of an accidental recombination of genes **2. SOMEBODY WITH ATAVISM** an individual showing atavism [Mid-19thC. Via French from Latin *atavus,* literally "beyond a grandfather," from *avus* "grandfather."]

AKG London

Mustafa Kemal Ataturk

at·a·vis·tic /àttə vístik/ *adj.* **1. RELATING TO GENETIC REAPPEARANCE** relating to or displaying the recurrence of a genetic feature that has been absent for several generations **2. PRIMITIVE** relating to or displaying the kind of behavior that seems to be a product of primitive impulses long since suppressed by society's rules —**at·a·vis·ti·cal·ly** *adv.*

a·tax·i·a /ə táksee ə/, **a·tax·y** /ə táksee/ *n.* loss of the ability to coordinate the movements of muscles [Late 19thC. Via modern Latin from Greek, literally "without order," from *taxis* "order" (see TAXIS).] —**a·tax·ic** *adj.*

ATB *abbr.* all terrain bike

At·chi·son /áchiss'n/ city on the Missouri River northeast of Topeka, in northeastern Kansas. Population: 10,000 (1996).

ate past tense of **eat**

-ate *suffix.* **1.** having, characterized by ○ *lobate* **2.** office, rank ○ *archdeaconate* **3.** to act on in a particular way ○ *fluoridate* **4.** a chemical compound derived from a particular element or compound ○ *borate* [From Latin *-atus,* past participle ending of verbs in "-are"]

A-team *n.* **1. U.S. SPECIAL FORCES UNIT** a unit of 12 soldiers in the United States Special Forces **2. BEST PEOPLE** a group of people who are the very best of their type [From A "first one in a series," modeled on "A-detachment"]

at·e·lec·ta·sis /àtt'l éktəssiss/ *n.* **1. COLLAPSE OF A LUNG** a partial or total collapse of a lung **2. NONEXPANSION OF LUNGS AT BIRTH** a condition in which the lungs fail to expand completely at birth [Mid-19thC. Coined from Greek *atelēs* "incomplete" + *ektasis* "extension."]

at·el·ier /àtt'l yáy, ə tèl-/ *n.* a studio or workshop where an artist works [Late 17thC. Via French, literally "carpenter's workshop," from, ultimately, late Latin *astella* "board."]

a·te·moy·a /aàtə móyə, àttə-/ *n.* **1. TROPICAL FRUIT** a cone-shaped or heart-shaped green fruit that has edible sweet white flesh **2. TROPICAL FRUIT TREE** the tree on which the atemoya fruit grows, found in the Philippines. The tree is a cross between cherimoya and sweetsop. [Early 20thC. Blend of Philippine English *ate* "sweetsop" and CHERIMOYA.]

a tem·po /aa témpō/ *adv., adj.* in or back into a previous musical tempo (*used as a musical direction*) [From Italian, literally "in time"]

a·tem·po·ral /ay témpərəl, -témprəl/ *adj.* independent of or unaffected by time

a·ten·ol·ol /ə ténnə làwl/ *n.* a medication that is used to treat high blood pressure and angina

ATF *abbr.* **1.** (Bureau of) Alcohol, Tobacco, and Firearms **2.** automatic transmission fluid

Ath·a·bas·ca /athə báskə/ river flowing northeast from the Rocky Mountains in Alberta, Canada, into Lake Athabasca. Length: 765 mi./1,231 km.

Ath·a·bas·ca, Lake fourth largest lake in Canada, bridging the border of Alberta and Saskatchewan. Area: 3,064 sq. mi./7,936 sq. km.

Ath·a·bas·kan /àthə báskən/, **Ath·a·pas·kan** /àthə páskən/ *n.* **1.** LANG **GROUP OF NORTH AMERICAN LANGUAGES** a group of languages spoken in northwestern Canada and parts of Alaska, Oregon, and California. It includes Apache and Navajo and is a branch of the Na-Dene family. About 180,000 people speak an Athabaskan language. **2.** PEOPLES **SPEAKER OF AN ATHABASKAN LANGUAGE** a member of one of the Athabaskan-speaking peoples [Mid-19thC. Named for Lake ATHABASCA.] —**Ath·a·bas·kan** *adj.*

Ath·a·na·sian Creed /àthə náyzh'n-, -náysh'n-/ *n.* a 5th-century Christian statement of belief of unknown authorship, formerly attributed to St. Athanasius, Greek patriarch of Alexandria.

Ath·a·pas·kan *n., adj.* = **Athabaskan**

a·the·ism /áythiizzəm/ *n.* disbelief in the existence of a God or gods [Late 16thC. Via French from, ultimately, Greek *atheos* "godless," from *theos* (see THEO-).]

a·the·ist /áythiist/ *n.* somebody who does not believe in a God or gods

a·the·is·tic /àythee ístik/, **a·the·is·ti·cal** /-ik'l/ *adj.* relating to or characteristic of atheists or atheism —**a·the·is·ti·cal·ly** *adj.*

ath·e·ling /áthəling/ *n.* an Anglo-Saxon nobleman or prince, usually the heir to a throne [Old English *æþeling.* Ultimately from a prehistoric Germanic word meaning "noble," which is also the ancestor of English *edelweiss.*]

a·the·mat·ic /ày thi máttik/ *adj.* used to describe music that is not based on themes or tunes

A·the·na /ə théenə/, **A·the·ne** /ə théenee/ *n.* in Greek mythology, the goddess of wisdom and warfare, and the patron goddess of Athens. She was born from Zeus's head. Roman equivalent **Minerva**

ath·e·nae·um /àthə née əm/, **ath·e·ne·um** *n.* **1. INSTITUTION ADVOCATING LEARNING** an institution that encourages learning, e.g., an academy of science **2. READING ROOM OR LIBRARY** any institution where reading materials are made available to the public, e.g., a library [Mid-18thC. Via Latin from Greek *Athēnaion,* the temple of Athena in Athens, which was used for teaching.]

A·the·na·go·ras I /ə théenə gáwrəss/ (1886–1972) Turkish religious leader. He was patriarch of the Orthodox Church (1948–72).

ath·e·ne·um *n.* = **athenaeum**

Ath·e·ni·an /ə théenee ən/ *n.* **SOMEBODY FROM ATHENS** somebody from the ancient or modern city of Athens in Greece ■ *adj.* **OF ATHENS** relating to or typical of the ancient or modern city of Athens in Greece, or its people or culture

Ath·ens /áthənz/ **1.** capital and largest city of Greece, situated in the southeastern part of the country. Population: 3,096,775 (1991). **2.** city in northeastern Georgia, on the Oconee River. It is a commercial and agricultural center and home to the country's oldest chartered state university. Population: 45,734 (1990). **3.** city in southeastern Ohio, on the south bank of the Hocking River, southeast of Columbus. Population: 21,094 (1996).

a·the·o·ret·i·cal /àythee ə réttik'l/ *adj.* without a theoretical basis

a·ther·man·cy /a thúrmənssee/ *n.* the inability of a substance to transmit infrared radiation or radiant heat [Mid-19thC. Formed from Greek *athermantos,* literally "not heated," from *thermainein* "to heat."]

ath·er·o·gen·e·sis /àtharō jénnəssiss/ *n.* the origination and formation of fatty deposits (**atheromas**) in arteries [Mid-20thC. Coined from ATHEROMA + -GENESIS.] —**ath·er·o·gen·ic** *adj.* —**ath·er·o·gen·i·ci·ty** /àthərōjə níssətee/ *n.*

ath·er·o·ma /àthə rṓmə/ (*plural* **-mas** *or* **-ma·ta** /-mətə/) *n.* an accumulation in the inner lining of an artery of a plaque of cholesterol and other constituents (**atheromatous plaque**) [Late 16thC. Via Latin from, ultimately, Greek *athērē* "porridge," from its texture.] —**ath·er·o·ma·to·sis** /àthə rōmə tṓssiss/ *n.* —**ath·er·om·a·tous** /àthə rómmətəss, -rṓmətəss/ *adj.*

ath·er·o·scle·ro·sis /àthərōsklə rṓssiss/ *n.* a common arterial disease in which raised areas of degeneration and cholesterol deposits (**plaques**) form on the inner surfaces of the arteries. These tend to obstruct blood flow when the blood clots on the roughened plaques. [Early 20thC. Coined from ATHEROMA + SCLEROSIS.] —**ath·er·o·scle·rot·ic** /àthərōsklə róttik/ *adj.* —**ath·er·o·scle·rot·i·cal·ly** /-iklee/ *adv.*

ath·et·o·sis /àthə tṓssiss/ *n.* a condition characterized by involuntary slow movements of the fingers, toes, hands, and feet and usually caused by a brain lesion [Late 19thC. Formed from Greek *athetos,* literally "without a place," from *tithenai* "to place" (see THESIS).]

a·thirst /ə thúrst/ *adj.* **1. EAGER** eager or longing for something (*literary*) **2. THIRSTY** thirsty (*archaic*) [Old English *ofþyrst,* formed from the past participle of *ofþyrstan* "to thirst greatly," from *þurst* (see THIRST)]

ath·lete /áth leet/ *n.* somebody who has the necessary abilities to participate in physical exercise, especially in competitive situations such as games, races, and matches [15thC. Via Latin from Greek *athlētēs*, from *athlein* "to contend for a prize." Originally used in English for "wrestler."]

ath·lete's foot *n.* a contagious fungal infection affecting the feet [From the fact that it flourishes in the heat and dampness of athletes' shoes]

ath·let·ic /ath léttik/ *adj.* 1. OF ATHLETES OR ATHLETICS relating to athletes, athletics, or other sports activities ○ *athletic uniforms* 2. MUSCULAR AND STRONG possessing a large skeletal structure and having strong muscles ○ *an athletic build* [Early 17thC. Via French and Latin from Greek *athlētikos*, from *athlētēs* (see ATHLETE).] —**ath·let·i·cal·ly** *adv.* —**ath·let·i·cism** *n.*

ath·let·ics /ath léttiks/ *n.* 1. SPORTS ACTIVITIES activities such as sports and exercises that require physical skill and strength (*takes a singular or plural verb*) 2. METHODS OF ATHLETIC TRAINING the methods, systems, or principles of training and practice for activities involving athletics (*takes a plural verb*) 3. *U.K.* = **track and field** (*takes a singular or plural verb*)

ath·let·ic shoe *n.* a shoe designed to be worn during athletic activities or exercising

ath·let·ic sup·port·er *n.* = **jockstrap**

ath·o·dyd /áthədid/ *n.* a simple tubular jet engine [Mid-20thC. Contraction of *aero-thermodynamic duct.*]

at-home, **at home** *n.* an informal social gathering in somebody's own home

a·thwart /ə thwáwrt/ *prep.* 1. ACROSS so as to be across or positioned crosswise over something 2. OPPOSING so as to oppose or obstruct something

a·thwart·ships /ə thwáwrt ships/ *adv.* from one side of a ship to the other

a·tilt /ə tílt/ *adv., adj.* in or into a slanting position ○ *Her hat was atilt on her head.*

a·tin·gle /ə tíng'l/ *adj.* feeling a tingling sensation, often associated with excitement (*literary*) ○ *atingle with anticipation*

-ation *suffix.* an action or process, or the result of it ○ *alienation* [Via French from the Latin stem *-ation-*, a suffix forming nouns from verbs in *-are*]

-ative *suffix.* ◊ **-ate**

At·kin·son /átkinsən/, **Brooks** (1894–1984) U.S. theater critic. He was the drama critic for the *New York Times* from 1925 to 1960.

At·lan·ta /at lántə, ət-/ capital of Georgia, and its largest city. It was an important Civil War battle site. Population: 401,907 (1996).

at·lan·tes /ət lán teez, at lán teez/ plural of **atlas** *n.* 3

At·lan·tic /ət lántik/ *adj.* OF THE ATLANTIC OCEAN relating to or situated in or near the Atlantic Ocean ■ *n.* 1. = **Atlantic Ocean** 2. WEST AFRICAN LANGUAGE GROUP a group of languages of West Africa, considered by many linguists to be related to one another and to belong to the Niger-Congo language family [15thC. Via Latin from Greek *Atlantikos*, from *Atlas* (see ATLAS).]

At·lan·tic Cit·y city in southeastern New Jersey, on the Atlantic Ocean, noted for its beaches and gambling casinos. Population: 38,361 (1996).

At·lan·tic In·tra·coas·tal Wa·ter·way system of protected inland waterways along the Atlantic Ocean coast, stretching from Cape Cod, Massachusetts, to southern Florida. It is mostly used by pleasure boats.

At·lan·ti·cism /ət lántissiz'm/ *n.* a doctrine assuming that both western Europe and the United States can benefit politically and economically from cooperation, especially in military matters

At·lan·tic O·cean, **At·lan·tic** the world's second largest ocean, which separates Europe and Africa from North and South America. Area: about 31,800,000 sq. mi./82,362,000 sq. km.

At·lan·tic Prov·in·ces Canadian provinces of New Brunswick, Nova Scotia, Prince Edward Island, and Newfoundland

At·lan·tic Rim *n.* those regions that have shores on the Atlantic Ocean, especially the north Atlantic

At·lan·tic salm·on (*plural* **At·lan·tic salm·on** *or* **At·lan·tic salm·ons**) *n.* a species of salmon that lives in northern Atlantic waters, swims up rivers in North America and Europe to spawn, and is valued as food. Latin name: *Salmo salar.*

At·lan·tic Stan·dard Time, **At·lan·tic Time** *n.* the standard time in the fourth time zone west of Greenwich, England, and reckoned at 60° West. It is used, e.g., in Puerto Rico and the Canadian Maritime Provinces.

At·lan·tic yam *n.* the wild yam, whose tuberous roots are cooked and eaten as a vegetable like potatoes. Genus: *Dioscorea.* (*regional*)

WORD KEY: REGIONAL NOTE

Atlantic yam in the sense of wild yam is recorded only in Kansas.

At·lan·tis /at lántiss, ət-/ *n.* in ancient mythology, an idyllic island that sank in an earthquake

at·las /átləss/ *n.* 1. MAP BOOK a book containing maps and vital statistics relating to geographic regions 2. ANAT TOP BONE IN THE NECK the vertebra that is at the top of the spinal column and supports the skull 3. (*plural* **-lan·tes**) ARCHIT FIGURE OF MAN USED AS SUPPORT a figure of a man, either standing or kneeling, used as a support for the upper part of a classical building [Late 16thC. From Greek.]

At·las /áttləss/ *n.* in Greek mythology, a Titan who was forced by Zeus to support the heavens on his shoulders as a punishment

At·las ce·dar *n.* an evergreen tree from northern Africa, widely grown as an ornamental for its green to silvery-blue foliage. Latin name: *Cedrus atlantica.* [Named for the ATLAS MOUNTAINS where it grows]

at·las moth *n.* a large moth of tropical Asia and Australia, with a wingspan of 10 in./25 cm or more and strongly hooked and boldly patterned wings. Latin name: *Attacus atlas.*

At·las Moun·tains system of mountain ranges that extends through Morocco, Algeria, and Tunisia. The highest peak is Jebel Toubkal in Morocco. Height: 13,665 ft./4,165 m.

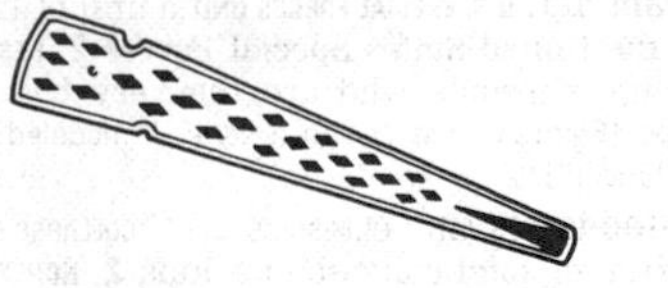

Atlatl

at·la·tl /át latt'l, aat laat'l/ *n.* a spear-throwing device, usually a stick equipped with a thong or socket, used to steady the butt of the spear during the throwing motion [Late 19thC. From Nahuatl *ahtlatl.*]

ATM *n.* an electronic machine, usually situated outside a bank, that enables customers to withdraw paper money or carry out other banking procedures on insertion of an encoded plastic card. Full form **automated teller machine**

WORD KEY: USAGE

Risk of redundancy: Relatively new and conceivably puzzling acronyms, such as *ATM, GPS,* and *PIN,* tempt the user to orient the listener or reader with an additional word such as *machine, system,* or *number.* A moment's thought will reveal that the resulting expression is redundant: *ATM machine* is equivalent to *automated teller machine machine.* Whenever it seems likely the acronym alone will not be understood, it may be accompanied by the full form (*automated teller machine, or ATM*) or the full form may be used alone instead.

atm. *abbr.* 1. atmosphere 2. atmospheric

at·man /áatmən/ *n.* in Hinduism, the essence of an individual [Late 18thC. From Sanskrit *ātman* "breath, spirit" (source of English *mahatma*).]

At·man /áatmən/ *n.* in Hinduism, Brahman regarded as the Universal Soul

atmo- *prefix.* gas, vapor ○ *atmolysis* [From Greek *atmos* "breath, vapor." Ultimately from an Indo-European word meaning "to blow," which is also the ancestor of English *fan.*]

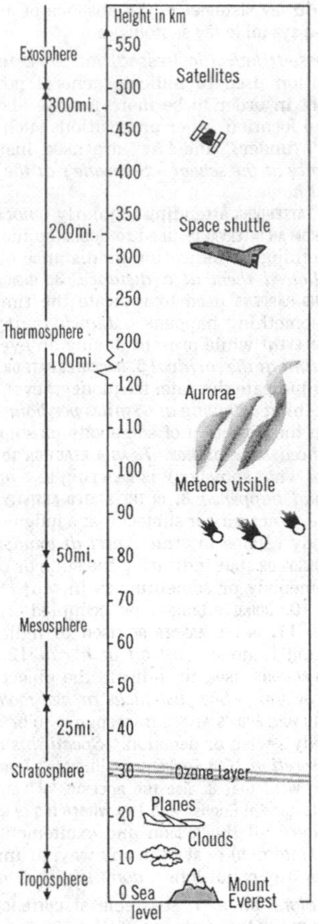

Atmosphere: Divisions of the Earth's atmosphere

at·mos·phere /átmə sfeer/ *n.* 1. GAS AROUND CELESTIAL BODY the mixture of gases that surrounds a celestial body such as the Earth 2. AIR OR CLIMATE the air or climate in a given place 3. MOOD OR TONE a prevailing emotional tone or attitude, especially one associated with a specific place or time ○ *"The atmosphere of the place was heavy and moldy, being rendered additionally oppressive by the closing of the door which led into the church."* (Wilkie Collins, *The Woman in White*; 1860) 4. MOOD OR TONE OF ARTWORK the prevailing tone or mood of a work of art 5. INTERESTING MOOD OF PLACE an interesting or exciting mood existing in a particular place ○ *a jazz club with lots of atmosphere* 6. PHYS UNIT OF PRESSURE a unit of pressure defined as the pressure that will support a 760 mm column of mercury at 0°C at sea level, equal to 1.01325 x 10^5 newtons per square meter [Mid-17thC. From modern Latin *atmosphaera*, literally "sphere of vapor," from Greek *atmos* (see ATMO-) + Latin *sphaera* (see SPHERE).]

at·mos·pher·ic /àtməs férrik, àtməs féerrik/, **at·mos·pher·i·cal** /àtməs férrik'l, àtməs féerrik'l/ *adj.* 1. RELATING TO ATMOSPHERE relating to the atmosphere of a celestial body or of a particular place ○ *atmospheric pollution* 2. ELICITING TONE OR AESTHETIC QUALITY evoking or producing an emotional tone or aesthetic quality ○ *a mural with a misty atmospheric effect* —**at·mos·pher·i·cal·ly** *adv.*

at·mos·pher·ic pres·sure *n.* the downward pressure exerted by the weight of the overlying atmosphere. It has a mean value of one atmosphere at sea level but decreases as elevation increases.

at·mos·pher·ics /àtməs férriks, àtməs féerriks/ *n.* STUDY OF ATMOSPHERIC INTERFERENCE the study of electromagnetic radiation emanating from natural sources in the atmosphere (*takes a singular verb*) ■ *npl.* (*takes a plural verb*) 1. ATMOSPHERIC INTERFERENCE WITH ELECTRONIC SIGNALS static on a radio or flickering white spots (**snow**) on a television screen caused by electromagnetic radiation from natural sources in the atmosphere 2. PREVAILING MOOD the mood or atmosphere suffusing a situation, group, or place

at. no. *abbr.* atomic number

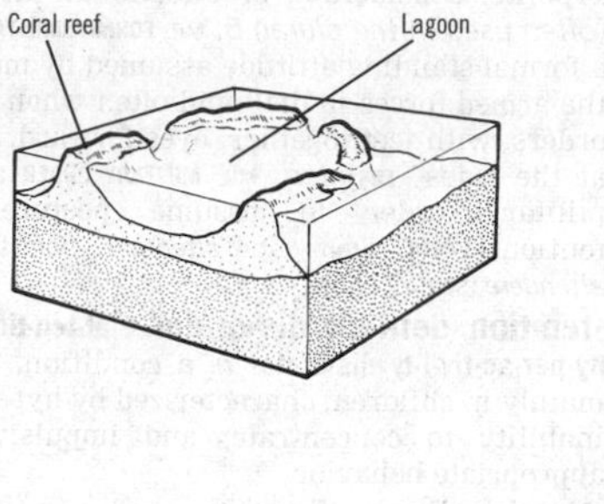

Atoll

a·toll /á tol/ *n.* a ring-shaped coral reef and small island, enclosing a lagoon and surrounded by open sea (*often used in placenames*) ○ *Bikini Atoll* [Early 17thC. From Maldivian *atolu.*]

at·om /áttəm/ *n.* **1. SMALLEST PART OF ELEMENT** the smallest portion into which an element can be divided and still retain its properties, made up of a dense, positively charged nucleus surrounded by a system of electrons. Atoms usually do not divide in chemical reactions except for some removal, transfer, or the exchange of specific electrons. **2. VERY SMALL AMOUNT** a very small part or amount ○ *not an atom of truth* **3. PARTICLE OF MATTER IN GREEK PHILOSOPHY** the basic particle of matter, indestructible and indivisible, first proposed by ancient Greek philosophers as the fundamental component of the universe [16thC. Via Latin *atomus* from Greek *atomos*, literally "unable to be cut," from *temnein* "to cut" (source of English *tome, anatomy,* and *epitome*).]

at·om bomb *n.* = **atomic bomb**

a·tom·ic /ə tómmik/ *adj.* **1. BASED ON NUCLEAR ENERGY** based on or using nuclear energy **2. RELATING TO ATOM** relating to an atom or atoms ○ *atomic theory* **3. TINY** extremely small **4.** LOGIC **UNANALYZABLE** used to describe a proposition, sentence, or formula that cannot be analyzed into a coherent structure —**a·tom·i·cal·ly** *adv.*

A·tom·ic Age *n.* the present era, starting with 1945 and the first use of atomic weaponry, considered in terms of the discovery, uses, and social implications of nuclear energy

a·tom·ic bomb *n.* an explosive device whose destructive power is due to the uncontrollable release of energy from the fission of heavy nuclei, usually uranium-235 or plutonium-239, by neutrons sustaining a rapid chain reaction

a·tom·ic clock *n.* an extremely accurate timekeeping device regulated by the natural regular oscillations of an atom or molecule. An atomic clock powered by a hydrogen atom (**maser**) is accurate to 1 part in 2 quadrillion.

a·tom·ic cock·tail *n.* a radioactive substance in liquid form, used to diagnose or treat cancer (*informal*)

a·tom·ic en·er·gy *n.* = **nuclear energy**

a·tom·ic heat *n.* a value obtained by multiplying the specific heat of an element by its atomic weight

at·o·mic·i·ty /áttə míssitee/ *n.* **1. ATOMIC COMPOSITION** the number of atoms in a molecule of a chemical element **2. ATOMIC NATURE** the state of being composed of atoms **3.** = **valence** *n.* 1

a·tom·ic mass *n.* = **relative atomic mass**

a·tom·ic mass u·nit *n.* a unit of mass defined as one twelfth of the mass of a carbon-12 atom, equal to 1.66×10^{-27} kg. It is useful for expressing the masses of atoms and molecules.

a·tom·ic num·ber *n.* the number of protons in the nucleus of an atom of an element. The atomic number of all the isotopes of an element is the same and determines that element's position in the periodic table. ○ *The atomic number of carbon is 6.* Symbol **Z**

a·tom·ic re·ac·tor *n.* = **nuclear reactor** (*dated*)

a·tom·ic the·o·ry *n.* any theory proposing that matter is composed of atoms

a·tom·ic vet·er·an *n.* a former member of a military group who was exposed to radioactivity during the use or testing of nuclear weapons in or after World War II

a·tom·ic weight *n.* relative atomic mass (*dated*)

at·om·ism /áttəmiz'm/ *n.* the theory that all matter in the universe is made up of small, individual, finite, and indivisible particles —**at·om·ist** *n.*

at·om·ize /áttə mīz/ (**-ized, -iz·ing, -iz·es**) *v.* **1.** *vt.* **SEPARATE SOMETHING INTO ATOMS** to reduce something to atoms or separate something into free atoms **2.** *vt.* **DESTROY SOMETHING** to destroy something with atomic weapons **3.** *vti.* **MAKE INTO SPRAY** to convert a liquid into fine particles or to spray particles converted in this way —**at·om·i·za·tion** /áttəmi záysh'n/ *n.*

at·om·iz·er /áttə mīzər/ *n.* a device that converts a liquid into a fine spray

at·om smash·er *n.* a device that speeds up subatomic particles (*informal*) [From the fact that it creates collisions between atomic nuclei in order to break them down into subatomic particles]

a·to·nal /ay tṓn'l/ *adj.* used to describe music in which the notes are not related by any mode or key —**a·to·nal·ly** *adv.*

a·to·nal·ism /ay tṓn'lizzəm/ *n.* the process of composing music in an atonal style or using atonality —**a·to·nal·ist** *n., adj.*

a·to·nal·i·ty /ày tō nállətee/ *n.* in music, the fact of consisting of notes that are not related by any mode or key

a·tone /ə tṓn/ (**a·toned, a·ton·ing, a·tones**) *vi.* to make reparation for a sin or a mistake (*formal*) [Mid-16thC. From *at one* "in agreement," as in the phrase *(to set) at one* "to reconcile."] —**a·ton·a·ble** *adj.* —**a·ton·er** *n.*

a·tone·ment /ə tṓnmənt/ *n.* **1. MAKING OF AMENDS** the making of reparation for a sin or a mistake **2. a·tone·ment, A·tone·ment RECONCILIATION BETWEEN GOD AND HUMANS** in Christian belief, the reconciliation between God and human beings brought about by the death of Jesus Christ [Early 16thC. Formed from ATONE, partly modeled on medieval Latin *adunamentum*, from *adunare* "to unite," and partly on earlier English *onement* "unification."]

a·ton·ic /ay tónnik/ *adj.* **1.** LING **UNSTRESSED** used to describe a syllable or sound that is not accented or stressed **2.** MED **LACKING MUSCLE TONE** connected with, caused by, or showing a lack of muscle tone [Mid-18thC. Formed from TONIC and ATONY.] —**at·o·nic·i·ty** /àytə níssitee, àytō-, at'n íssitee/ *n.*

at·o·ny /átt'nee/ *n.* **1.** LING **ABSENCE OF STRESS** lack of stress or accent **2.** MED **ABSENCE OF MUSCLE TONE** lack of normal muscle tone [Late 17thC. Via French or late Latin *atonia* "weakness" from Greek, from *atonos*, literally "lacking tone," from *tonos* (see TONE).]

a·top /ə tóp/ *prep., adv.* on or at the top of something (*literary*)

a·top·ic /ay tóppik, ə-/ *adj.* used to describe a condition that is caused by a hereditary tendency to react to certain allergens, such as occurs in hay fever, some skin irritations, and asthma [Early 20thC. Formed from Greek *atopia* "unusualness," from *atopos*, literally "out of place," which itself was formed from *topos* "place" (see TOPIC).] —**at·o·py** /áttəpee/ *n.*

-ator *suffix.* something or somebody that acts in a given way ○ *demonstrator* —**-atory** *suffix.*

ATP *n.* a chemical compound (**nucleotide**) occurring in living organisms that provides most of the energy required by cells during its conversion to another nucleotide (**ADP**). Full form **adenosine triphosphate**

ATP·ase /ày tee peé ayss, -ayz/ *abbr.* adenosine triphosphatase

at·ra·bil·ious /àttrə bíllee əss, -bíllyəss/ *adj.* (*literary*) **1. GLOOMY** tending to feel very sad **2. PEEVISH** inclined to peevishness and irritability [Mid-17thC. Formed from Latin *atra bilis*, literally "black bile" (a translation of Greek *melankholia*), the bodily fluid thought to cause sadness and irritability.] —**at·ra·bil·ious·ness** *n.*

at·ra·zine /áttrə zeen/ *n.* a herbicide used to kill weeds, especially in agricultural crops. Formula: $C_8H_{14}N_5Cl$. [Mid-20thC. Coined from the Latin stem *atr-* "black" (because it prevents photosynthesis) + TRIAZINE.]

a·trem·ble /ə trémb'l/ *adj.* shaking or trembling from a strong emotion such as fear or excitement (*literary*)

a·tre·sia /ə treézhə/ *n.* the abnormal and usually congenital absence of a body opening such as the anus, ear canal, or intestine [Early 19thC. Formed from Greek *trēsis* "perforation." Ultimately from an Indo-European base meaning "to twist, drill," which is also the ancestor of English *drill.*]

A·treus /áy trooss, áytree əss/ *n.* in Greek mythology, king of Mycenae and father of Agamemnon and Menelaus

a·tri·a plural of **atrium**

a·tri·o·ven·tric·u·lar /àytree ō ven tríkyələr/ *adj.* relating to the upper and lower chambers, atria, and ventricles of the heart [Mid-19thC. Coined from ATRIUM + VENTRICULAR.]

at-risk *adj.* exposed to danger or harm of some kind, e.g., abuse or violence

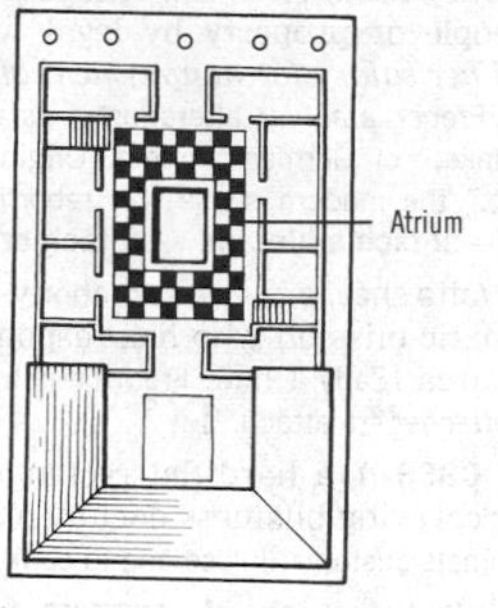

Atrium

a·tri·um /áytree əm/ (*plural* **-ums** *or* **-a** /-ə/) *n.* **1.** ARCHIT **CENTRAL HALL WITH SKYLIGHT** a central hall usually with a glass roof or skylight and extending the full height or several stories of a building **2.** ARCHIT, HIST **ROMAN COURTYARD** the open central courtyard of an ancient Roman house **3.** ANAT **BODY CHAMBER OR CAVITY** a cavity or chamber of the body, especially one of the upper chambers of the heart that takes blood from the veins and pumps it into a ventricle [Late 16thC. From Latin.]

a·tro·cious /ə trṓshəss/ *adj.* **1. VERY BAD** appallingly bad ○ *atrocious manners* **2. VERY CRUEL** extremely evil or cruel ○ *atrocious treatment of prisoners* **3. UGLY TO LOOK AT** so ugly in taste or appearance as to elicit revulsion ○ *an atrocious hat* [Mid-17thC. Formed from the Latin stem *atroc-*, from *atrox*, literally "dark in appearance," from *ater* "dark." Originally in English, "wantonly cruel."] —**a·tro·cious·ly** *adv.* —**a·tro·cious·ness** *n.*

a·troc·i·ty /ə tróssətee/ (*plural* **-ties**) *n.* **1. SHOCKINGLY CRUEL ACT** a shockingly cruel act, especially an act of wanton violence against an enemy in wartime ○ *to deplore the atrocities of war* **2. EXTREME CRUELTY** extreme evil or cruelty ○ *an act of atrocity* **3. SOMETHING VERY BAD** something repellent or extremely bad of its kind [Mid-16thC. Directly or via French from Latin *atrocitas*, from *atrox* (see ATROCIOUS).]

at·ro·phy /áttrəfee/ *n.* **1. WASTING AWAY** the shrinking in size of some part or organ of the body, usually caused by injury, disease, or lack of use **2. LESSENING OF ABILITY** weakening or lessening of some ability ■ *vi.* (**-phied, -phy·ing, -phies**) **WEAKEN** to weaken or waste away through disuse or the effects of disease [Early 17thC. Via late Latin *atrophia* from Greek, literally "lack of food," from *trophē* "food" (see -TROPHY).] —**a·troph·ic** /ə tróffik/ *adj.*

at·ro·pine /áttrə peen, -pin/, **at·ro·pin** /-pin/ *n.* a poisonous alkaloid obtained from belladonna or related plants, used medically to dilate the pupils of the eyes and to stop spasms. It is also used by the armed forces as an antidote for nerve-gas poisoning. Formula: $C_{17}H_{23}NO_3$. [Mid-19thC. Formed from modern Latin *Atropa*, genus name of the belladonna plant.]

At·ro·pos /áttrə pòss/ *n.* in Greek mythology, one of the Fates, who were three goddesses who influenced human destiny. Atropos was known as the Inexorable, and carried the shears that cut the thread of life. ◊ **Clotho, Lachesis**

ATS *abbr.* Applications Technology Satellite

att. *abbr.* **1.** attached **2.** attention **3.** attorney

at·ta·boy /áttə boy/ *interj.* **USED TO CHEER SOMEBODY ON** used to express enthusiastic encouragement or approval to a man or boy (*slang*) ■ *n.* **CONGRATULATIONS** an act or an instance of congratulating somebody on an achievement (*slang*) ○ *received several attaboys from top management after the sales presentation* [Early 20thC. Alteration of "That's the boy!".]

at·tach /ə tách/ (**-tached, -tach·ing, -ta·ches**) *v.* **1.** *vt.* **SECURE SOMETHING TO SOMETHING ELSE** to secure one thing to another ○ *attached the door to the frame* **2.** *vt.* **ADD SOMETHING TO SOMETHING ELSE** to append one thing to another as a separate piece, the two being held together ○ *attached copies of the contracts* **3.** *vi.* **BE ASSOCIATED WITH SOMETHING** to have a close innate relationship to something ○ *little prestige attached to this post* **4.** *vt.* **ASCRIBE SOMETHING** to assign a certain character or quality to something under consideration ○ *I attach no importance whatsoever to their claims.* **5.** *vt.* **BIND EMOTIONALLY** to bind somebody emotionally to somebody else or to something (*usually passive*) **6.** *vt.* MIL **PLACE SOMEBODY ON TEMP DUTY** to assign military personnel to a military group on a temporary basis **7.** *vt.* LAW **SEIZE SOMETHING LEGALLY** to seize people or property by legal writ ○ *They've attached her salary for nonpayment of taxes.* [14thC. From Old French *atachier,* alteration of *estachier* "to fasten with a stake," of Germanic origin. Originally in English, "to arrest," the modern sense was reborrowed later from French.] —**at·tach·a·ble** *adj.* —**at·tach·er** *n.*

at·ta·ché /àttə sháy, a tà-/ *n.* somebody on the staff of a diplomatic mission who has responsibilities in a specific area [Early 19thC. From French, the past participle of *attacher* "to attach."]

at·ta·ché case *n.* a hard flat rectangular briefcase used for carrying business documents [From the fact that diplomats customarily use one to carry documents]

at·tached /ə tácht/ *adj.* **1. ENCLOSED** fastened to or enclosed with something else ○ *Please see the attached documents and call with any questions.* **2. DEVOTED** devoted to or fond of somebody or something **3. COMMITTED EMOTIONALLY TO SOMEBODY** committed to an emotional relationship with somebody else (*informal*) **4.** ARCHIT **TOUCHING ANOTHER STRUCTURE** sharing a wall with another building, and thus not standing alone **5.** *Malaysia, Singapore* **EMPLOYED** having a permanent job with a person or organization ○ *My brother is attached to the Ministry.*

at·tach·ment /ə táchmənt/ *n.* **1. EMOTIONAL BOND** an emotional bond or tie to somebody or something. ◊ **bonding 2. ATTACHED TEXT** a document or file attached to another or to an e-mail message **3. ACT OF ATTACHING** the action of attaching one thing to another ○ *The attachment of that new printer took me two hours.* **4. PART ATTACHED** an accessory attached or to be attached to a machine **5. MEANS OF ATTACHING SOMETHING** a means by which something is attached to something else **6.** LAW **LEGAL SEIZURE** the legal seizure of people or property, especially to acquire jurisdiction over them or it

at·tach·ment of earn·ings *n.* a court order directing a third party, usually an employer, to withhold somebody's wages in order to satisfy unpaid debts

at·tack /ə ták/ *v.* (**-tacked, -tack·ing, -tacks**) **1.** *vti.* **HARM** to try to harm somebody by using violence or try to defeat an enemy or capture an enemy position **2.** *vt.* **CRITICIZE SOMEBODY OR SOMETHING** to subject somebody or something to strong or vehement criticism ○ *The press has repeatedly attacked his plan.* **3.** *vti.* **INFECT SOMEBODY OR DAMAGE SOMETHING** to cause an infection, illness, or damage in somebody or something ○ *The disease can attack at any age.* **4.** *vt.* **MAKE A VIGOROUS START ON SOMETHING** to begin something such as work with enthusiasm or determination and deal vigorously with it **5.** *vti.* SPORTS, GAMES **TRY TO WIN** to attempt to defeat, or score against, an opponent or an opposing team in a competitive game or team sport ○ *The chess game began sluggishly, with both sides slow to attack.* ■ *n.* **1. ACTION OF ATTACKING** the process or an instance of attacking **2. BOUT OF ILLNESS** an occurrence of something such as a medical disorder that is temporarily debilitating ○ *an attack of asthma* **3. ATTACKING MEMBERS OF TEAM** the offensive players on a team, especially the forwards on a soccer team (*takes a singular verb*) **4.** MUSIC **ENERGETIC WAY OF PLAYING** the decisive or energetic way in which a musician begins to play a piece or passage [Early 17thC. Via French *attaquer* from Italian *attacare battaglia* "to join battle." Ultimately from a prehistoric Germanic word meaning "to join," which is also the ancestor of English *attach.*]

at·tack·er /ə tákər/ *n.* **1. SOMEBODY WHO ASSAULTS** somebody who commits an assault on somebody else **2. CRITIC** somebody who criticizes somebody or something **3.** SPORTS **PLAYER WITH SCORING ROLE** a player whose role is to score or create scoring opportunities

at·tain /ə táyn/ (**-tained, -tain·ing, -tains**) *vt.* **1. ACCOMPLISH SOMETHING** to achieve a goal or desired state, usually with effort **2. REACH SPECIFIED STATE** to reach a specified age, speed, or size [13thC. Via Old French *ataindre* from Latin *attingere,* literally "to reach to," from *tangere* "to touch" (see TANGENT).] —**at·tain·a·bil·ity** /ə táynə bíllətee/ *n.* —**at·tain·a·ble** /-əb'l/ *adj.* —**at·tain·a·ble·ness** /-nəss/ *n.*

WORD KEY: SYNONYMS

See Synonyms at ***accomplish.***

at·tain·der /ə táyndər/ *n.* in former times, the removal of the rights or the confiscation of the property of somebody outlawed or sentenced to death for a serious crime, often treason [15thC. From Anglo-Norman, a variant of Old French *ataindre* "to affect, dishonor" (see ATTAIN).]

at·tain·ment /ə táynmənt/ *n.* **1. ACCOMPLISHMENT OF SOMETHING** the achievement of the goals that somebody has set **2. TALENT OR ABILITY** a skill, accomplishment, or distinction, especially one achieved through effort (*often used in the plural*)

at·taint /ə táynt/ *vt.* (**-taint·ed, -taint·ing, -taints**) **DEPRIVE SOMEBODY OF RIGHTS** in former times, to take away the civil rights of somebody outlawed or sentenced to death for committing a serious crime, often treason (*archaic*) (*often passive*) ■ *n.* **LOSS OF REPUTATION** loss of honor or good reputation (*archaic*) [14thC. From Old French *atainte,* the feminine past participle of *ataindre* "to affect" (see ATTAIN).]

at·tar /áttər, á taàr/, **at·ar** *n.* essential oil extracted from flowers, especially the oil extracted from rose petals [Mid-17thC. From Arabic dialect *aṭar.*]

at·tempt /ə témpt, ə témt/ *vti.* (**-tempt·ed, -tempt·ing, -tempts**) **TRY TO DO SOMETHING** to try to do something, especially without much expectation of success ■ *n.* **1. EFFORT TO DO SOMETHING** an act of trying to do something ○ *a successful attempt at cooking* **2. ATTACK** an attack or assault ○ *an attempt on his life* [14thC. Via Old French from Latin *attemptare,* literally "to try for," from *temptare* (see TEMPT).] —**at·tempt·a·ble** *adj.* —**at·tempt·er** *n.*

WORD KEY: SYNONYMS

See Synonyms at ***try.***

at·tempt·ed /ə témptəd, ə témtəd/ *adj.* used to describe something at which a failed attempt has been made, especially a crime or offense ○ *an attempted robbery*

at·tend /ə ténd/ (**-tend·ed, -tend·ing, -tends**) *v.* **1.** *vti.* **GO TO EVENT** to go to or be present at an event ○ *Hundreds attended the wedding.* **2.** *vti.* **REGULARLY GO TO SPECIFIC ESTABLISHMENT** to go regularly to an institution such as a school or church for instruction or worship **3.** *vi.* **LISTEN OR WATCH CAREFULLY** to listen or play close attention to somebody or something **4.** *vt.* **OCCUR ALONG WITH SOMETHING** to accompany something or be associated with it (*usually passive*) **5.** *vt.* **BE SOMEBODY'S ATTENDANT** to escort somebody or act as an attendant to somebody (*usually passive*) **6.** *vi.* **RESULT FROM SOMETHING** to be the consequence of something (*literary*) [14thC. Via Old French *atendre* from Latin *attendere,* literally "to reach toward," from *tendere* "to stretch" (see TEND).] —**at·tend·er** *n.*

attend to *vti.* to deal with or look after somebody or something ○ *patients to attend to* ○ *attend to business*

at·ten·dance /ə téndəns/ *n.* **1. PRESENCE AT EVENT OR INSTITUTION** an instance of being at an event or regularly going to a school, church, or other institution **2. NUMBER ATTENDING** the number of people who are present at an event or institution

at·ten·dant /ə téndənt/ *n.* **1. SOMEBODY SERVING IN A PUBLIC PLACE** somebody employed to serve or help members of the public in a public institution or place ○ *a museum attendant* **2. ESCORT** somebody who escorts or serves another, especially bridesmaids escorting a bride ■ *adj.* **OCCURRING ALONG WITH SOMETHING** associated with something, or resulting or following from it ○ *parenthood and its attendant anxieties*

at·ten·dee /ə tèn deé, à ten-/ *n.* any of the people attending something, especially a conference, course, or seminar

at·tend·ing /ə ténding/ *adj.* **WORKING IN TEACHING HOSPITAL** serving on the staff of a teaching hospital ○ *The attending physician made the rounds of all the wards every morning.* ■ *n.* **HOSPITAL DOCTOR** a physician who serves on the staff of a teaching hospital ○ *The orders for these medications were written by two attendings.*

at·ten·tion /ə ténsh'n/ *n.* **1. CONCENTRATION** mental focus, serious consideration, or concentration **2. INTEREST** notice or interest ○ *media attention* ○ *A letter for the attention of Mr. Brown.* **3. APPROPRIATE TREATMENT** care, tending, or appropriate treatment **4. AFFECTIONATE ACT** a polite, considerate, or affectionate act (*formal*) (*often used in the plural*) **5.** MIL **FORMAL MILITARY POSTURE** a formal standing attitude assumed by members of the armed forces in drill and often when receiving orders, with feet together, eyes forward, and arms at the sides ■ *interj.* MIL **MILITARY ORDER** a shouted military order to assume posture of attention [14thC. From Latin *attention-,* from the stem of *attendere* (see ATTEND).]

at·ten·tion def·i·cit dis·or·der, at·ten·tion def·i·cit hy·per·ac·tiv·i·ty dis·or·der *n.* a condition, occurring mainly in children, characterized by hyperactivity, inability to concentrate, and impulsive or inappropriate behavior

at·ten·tion line *n.* a line in a formally addressed letter or on an envelope addressed to an organization indicating for whom, especially for which employee or member of staff, the letter is intended

at·ten·tion span *n.* the length of time that somebody can concentrate effectively on a particular task or activity

at·ten·tive /ə téntiv/ *adj.* **1. CONSIDERATE OR RESPONSIVE** behaving toward somebody in a way that shows special regard or affection **2. PAYING ATTENTION** listening or watching carefully and with concentration [14thC. From French *attentif,* from *atendre* (see ATTEND).] —**at·ten·tive·ly** *adv.* —**at·ten·tive·ness** *n.*

at·ten·u·ate (**-at·ed, -at·ing, -ates**) *v.* /ə ténnyoo àyt/ **1.** *vti.* **MAKE OR BECOME WEAKER** to reduce the size, strength, or density of something, or to become thinner, weaker, or less dense **2.** *vt.* BIOL **MAKE PATHOGEN LESS VIRULENT** to reduce the virulence of a bacterium or virus, e.g., by exposing it to heat or producing a culture of it in a special medium. Attenuated bacteria or viruses are used in some vaccines. [Mid-16thC. From Latin *attenuat-,* the past participle stem of *attenuare,* literally "to make thin," from *tenuis* "thin" (see TENUOUS).]

at·ten·u·at·ed /ə ténnyə àytəd/ *adj.* long, narrow, and sometimes tapering

at·ten·u·a·tor *n.* a device for reducing the strength of a wave, especially an electrical signal

at·test /ə tést/ (**-test·ed, -test·ing, -tests**) *vti.* **1. BE EVIDENCE OF SOMETHING** to show that something exists or is true or valid **2. CONFIRM SOMETHING** to state that something is true, especially in a formal written statement [15thC. Via French *attester* from Latin *attestari,* literally "to witness to," from *testis* "witness" (see TESTAMENT).] —**at·test·ant** *n.* —**at·tes·ta·tion** /à te stáysh'n, àtte-/ *n.* —**at·tes·tor** /ə téstər/ *n.*

Att. Gen. *abbr.* Attorney General

at·tic /áttik/ *n.* a room or the area that occupies the space under a pitched roof ○ *boxes in the attic* [Late 17thC. Via French *attique* "Attic" from Latin *Atticus* (see ATTIC). The word originally described a decorative structure (in the Attic style) above the main façade of a building.]

At·tic /áttik/ *adj.* **1. OF ATTICA** relating to or typical of the ancient Greek territory of Attica or of the modern Greek department of Attica **2. ELEGANTLY WITTY** elegantly succinct or drily witty ■ *n.* **EXTINCT DIALECT OF ATTICA** a dialect of ancient Greek that was spoken in Athens and surrounding areas. Most of the literature of Classical Greece is written in Attic. [Late 16thC. Via Latin from Greek *Attikos,* from *Attikē* "Attica."]

At·ti·ca /áttikə/ **1.** department of east central Greece. Capital: Athens. Area: 5,466 sq. mi./14,257 sq. km. **2.** peninsula region of ancient Greece that was divided into 12 states

At·ti·cism /áttə sìzzəm/, **at·ti·cism** *n.* a witty or elegantly simple and concise turn of phrase [Late 16thC. From Greek *Attikismos,* from *Attikos* (see ATTIC.]

At·ti·la /ə tíllə, áttlə/ (406?–453?) Hunnish warrior king who led an army of Mongolian nomads and subdued lands from the Rhine to the frontiers of China.

at·tire /ə tír/ *n.* **CLOTHING** clothing, especially a garment or combination of garments, worn on a particular occasion (*formal*) ■ *vt.* (**-tired, -tir·ing, -tires**) **DRESS** to dress yourself or somebody else, especially in clothes of a particular type (*formal*) [13thC. From Old French *atirier* "to array," literally "to put in order," from *tire* "order" (see TIER).]

at·ti·tude /áttə tood/ *n.* **1. PERSONAL VIEW OF SOMETHING** an opinion or general feeling about something ○ *a positive attitude to change* **2. BODILY POSTURE** a physical posture, either conscious or unconsious, especially while interacting with others **3. CONSCIOUS AS-**

SERTIVENESS an arrogant or assertive manner or stance assumed as a challenge or for effect (*informal*) ○ *a streetwise teenager with an attitude* **4.** AEROSP ORIENTATION OF AIRCRAFT'S AXES the angle of an aircraft in relation to the direction of the airflow or to the horizontal plane **5.** SPACE TECH ORIENTATION OF SPACECRAFT the angle of a spacecraft in relation to its direction of movement [Late 17thC. Via French from, ultimately, late Latin *aptitudo* "disposition."]

at·ti·tu·di·nal /àtti to͝od'nəl/ *adj.* insisting strongly on your rights [Late 20thC. From ATTITUDE in the sense "contentiousness."]

at·ti·tu·di·nize /áttə tood'n ìz/ (**-nized, -niz·ing, -niz·es**) *vi.* to strike exaggerated or unspontaneous poses, or adopt extreme opinions, for effect

At·tle·bor·o /átt'l bùrr ō/ city in southeastern Massachusetts, northwest of Providence, Rhode Island. Population: 39,070 (1996).

Att·lee /áttlee/, **Clement, 1st Earl Attlee** (1883–1967) British politician who was prime minister (1945–51) and deputy prime minister in Churchill's wartime coalition government. His post-war government introduced the welfare state and granted independence to India.

attn. *abbr.* attention

at·tor·ney /ə túrnee/ (*plural* **-neys**) *n.* **1.** LAWYER a qualified lawyer, especially one who represents clients in court proceedings **2.** SOMEBODY GIVEN LEGAL POWER somebody legally empowered by a document (**power of attorney**) to make decisions and act on behalf of somebody else [14thC. From Old French *atorne*, the past participle of *atorner* "to appoint," literally "to turn over," from *torner* (see TURN).] —**at·tor·ney·ship** *n.*

WORD KEY: SYNONYMS

See Synonyms at ***lawyer***.

at·tor·ney at law (*plural* **at·tor·neys at law**) *n.* a lawyer qualified to appear in court to represent somebody who is a party to a legal action

at·tor·ney gen·er·al (*plural* **at·tor·ney gen·er·als** *or* **at·tor·neys gen·er·al**) *n.* **1.** COUNTRY'S CHIEF LEGAL OFFICER a country's chief legal officer, and its government's chief legal adviser. In the United States, the attorney general is a member of the President's cabinet. **2.** STATE'S CHIEF LEGAL OFFICER the chief law officer of a state, and its government's chief legal adviser **3.** CHIEF LAW OFFICER OF CANADA the chief law officer of a Canadian province, and its government's chief legal adviser

at·tract /ə trákt/ (**-tract·ed, -tract·ing, -tracts**) *v.* **1.** *vt.* DRAW CLOSER to draw objects nearer, e.g., as a magnet draws iron objects toward it **2.** *vt.* ENTICE to be appealing enough to make people visit a place or spend their money **3.** *vt.* GET A RESPONSE to win or elicit a response from people, especially support or encouragement **4.** *vt.* DRAW SOMEBODY'S ATTENTION to draw or secure somebody's attention, or become the focus of somebody's attention ○ *"It takes a big idea to attract the attention of consumers and get them to buy your product."* (David Ogilvy, *Ogilvy on Advertising*; 1985) **5.** *vt.* HAVE APPEAL to appeal to people or awaken a response in them **6.** *vti.* AROUSE SEXUAL FEELINGS to rouse or fascinate somebody sexually [15thC. From Latin *attract-*, the past participle stem of *attrahere*, literally "to draw toward," from *trahere* "to draw" (see TRACTION).] —**at·tract·a·ble** *adj.* —**at·tract·er** *n.*

at·trac·tion /ə trákshən/ *n.* **1.** POWER OF ATTRACTING the power of attracting or the feeling of being attracted ○ *"Our mutual attraction was immediate, and we enjoyed one another's company."* (Peter Ustinov, *Dear Me*; 1977) **2.** APPEALING QUALITY OR FEATURE a quality or feature that attracts somebody ○ *The idea has its attractions.* **3.** THING OR PLACE THAT DRAWS TOURISTS something, e.g., an historic site or building, that people, especially tourists, like to see or visit

at·trac·tive /ə tráktiv/ *adj.* **1.** AGREEABLE pleasing in appearance or manner **2.** GOOD-LOOKING good-looking or sexually desirable **3.** INTERESTING interesting or appealing because of the probable advantages ○ *an attractive proposition* —**at·trac·tive·ness** *n.*

WORD KEY: SYNONYMS

See Synonyms at ***good-looking***.

at·trac·tive·ly /ə tráktivlee/ *adv.* in a pleasing, appealing, or sexually interesting way ○ *attractively priced furnishings* ○ *attractively situated a few minutes from the beach*

at·tract·or /ə tráktər/ *n.* a fixed point or state of equilibrium that the behavior of a system is attracted to and tends to imitate

at·trib. *abbr.* attributive

at·trib·ut·a·ble /ə tríbbyətəb'l/ *adj.* caused or explained by something

at·trib·ute *vt.* /ə tríbbyoot/ (**-ut·ed, -ut·ing, -utes**) **1.** ASCRIBE A FEATURE to think of something as caused by a particular circumstance ○ *To what do you attribute your success?* **2.** GIVE CREDIT to give credit for a certain thing, such as a work of art or literature, or a saying, to a particular person, often wrongly ○ *It's a bon mot that is often wrongly attributed to Saki.* **3.** ASSIGN QUALITIES to regard somebody or something as having particular qualities ○ *the pigheadedness you attribute to your computer on bad days* ■ *n.* /áttri byo͞ot/ QUALITY OR PROPERTY a quality, property, or characteristic of somebody or something [14thC. Directly or via French from Latin *attribut-*, the past participle stem of *attribuere*, literally "to allot to," from *tribuere* (see TRIBUTE).] —**at·trib·ut·er** /ə tríbbyootər/ *n.*

at·tri·bu·tion /àttrə byo͞osh'n/ *n.* the ascribing of something to somebody or something, e.g., a work of art to a certain artist or circumstances to a particular cause

at·trib·u·tive /ə tríbbyətiv/ *adj.* forming part of a noun phrase and typically preceding the noun. For example, the adjective "tiny" in the noun phrase "one tiny problem" is in the attributive position. —**at·trib·u·tive·ly** *adv.* —**at·trib·u·tive·ness** *n.*

at·trit /ə trít/ (**-trit·ted, -trit·ting, -trits**) *vt.* to wear something down little by little, especially enemy forces by constant attacks (*informal*) [Mid-20thC. Back-formation from ATTRITION.]

at·tri·tion /ə trísh'n/ *n.* **1.** WEARING AWAY OF SURFACE the wearing away of a surface, typically by friction or abrasion **2.** WEAKENING BY PERSISTENT ATTACK the gradual wearing away of morale and the powers of resistance by persistent attacks **3.** LOSS OF PERSONNEL the gradual reduction of the size of a workforce by not replacing personnel lost through retirement or resignation **4.** SORROW FOR SIN remorse for sin typically engendered by the fear of damnation [15thC. Via French from, ultimately, Latin *attrit-*, the past participle stem of *atterere*, literally "to rub away," from *terere* "to rub" (see TRITE).]

At·tu /á to͞o/ most western of the Aleutian Islands, Alaska. It is rocky and barren, and during World War II it was taken by the Japanese in June 1942 and retaken by U.S. and Canadian forces in June 1943. Area: 390 sq. mi./1,010 sq. km.

At·tucks /áttəks/, **Crispus** (1723?–70) American patriot. He was a sailor, and perhaps a runaway slave, who was killed in the Boston Massacre.

at·tune /ə to͞on/ (**-tuned, -tun·ing, -tunes**) *vt.* to adjust or accustom something to become receptive or responsive to something else

atty. *abbr.* attorney

Atty. Gen. *abbr.* attorney general

ATV *abbr.* all-terrain vehicle

At·wa·ter /át wòttər, -wàwtər/ city in central California, east of San Jose. Population: 23,638 (1996).

a·twit·ter /ə twíttər/ *adj.* full of excited chatter about something

Margaret Atwood

At·wood /át wo͝od/, **Margaret** (*b.* 1939) Canadian writer whose works include poems and novels such as *"The Handmaid's Tale"* (1986).

at. wt. *abbr.* atomic weight

a·typ·i·cal /ay típpik'l/ *adj.* not conforming to the usual type or expected pattern

Au *symbol.* gold [From Latin *aurum* (see GOLD)]

A.U., a.u. *abbr.* angstrom unit

A.U. *abbr.* astronomical unit

au·bade /ō baád/ *n.* a song, poem, or piece of instrumental music celebrating or greeting the dawn (*literary*) [Late 17thC. Via French from Provençal *albada*, from *alba* "dawn," from Latin *albus* "white" (see ALB).]

au·ber·gine /ōbər zheèn/ *n. U.K.* = **eggplant** [Late 18thC. Via French, Catalan, and Arabic from Persian *bādingān*.]

Au·bert de Gaspé /ō bàir də gaásp/, **Philippe-Joseph** (1786–1871) Canadian novelist, author of *Les Anciens Canadiens* (1863).

au·burn /áw bùrn/ *adj.* dark coppery red or reddish brown in color ○ *auburn hair* [15thC. From Old French (influenced in sense by the similarity of the variant spelling *abrun* to *brun* "brown"), from medieval Latin *alburnus* "whitish," from Latin *albus* "white."] —**auburn** *n.*

Au·burn /áwbərn/ **1.** city northwest of Phenix City, in east-central Alabama. Population: 37,664 (1996). **2.** city in southwestern Maine, on the west bank of the Androscoggin River, north of Lewiston. Population: 22,997 (1996). **3.** city in central Massachusetts. It is a southeastern suburb of Worcester. Population: 15,002 (1996). **4.** city in central New York , north of Lake Owasco . It is a southwestern suburb of Syracuse. Population: 29,774 (1996). **5.** city in west-central Washington, south of Seattle. Population: 36,393 (1996).

A.U.C. *abbr.* ab urbe condita (*used by Roman classical writers to specify the dates of events in terms of the number of years since Rome's foundation in 753* B.C.)

Auck·land /áwklənd/ **1.** administrative region of New Zealand, located in northwestern North Island and including the city of Auckland. Population: 1,077,205 (1996). Area: 6,287 sq. mi./16,282 sq. km. **2.** the largest city in New Zealand, located in northwestern North Island. Founded in 1840, it is a commercial and industrial center and port. Population: 997,940 (1996).

au con·traire /ō kòn traír/ *adv.* indeed, the opposite is really the case [From French, literally "to the contrary"]

au cou·rant /ō ko͞o róN/ *adj.* abreast of the latest developments [From French, literally "in the current"]

auc·tion /áwksh'n/ *n.* **1.** SALE BY BIDDING a sale of goods or property at which intending buyers bid against one another for individual items. Each item is sold to the bidder offering the highest price. **2.** BRIDGE BIDDING IN GAME OF BRIDGE the bidding phase in a game of bridge, during which players contract to win a certain number of tricks if a certain suit is trumps ■ *vti.* (**-tioned, -tion·ing, -tions**) SELL AT AUCTION to sell goods by auction [Late 16thC. From the Latin stem *auction-*, literally "increase," from *augere* (see AUGMENT).] —**auc·tion·a·ble** *adj.*

auc·tion bridge *n.* a form of bridge in which all tricks won count toward the score, as distinct from contract bridge, in which only those tricks contracted to win count

auc·tion·eer /àwkshə neér/ *n.* somebody who is in charge of and announces the bids at an auction —**auc·tion·eer·ing** *n.*

AUD *abbr.* Australian dollar

aud. *abbr.* **1.** audit **2.** auditor

au·da·cious /aw dáyshəss/ *adj.* bold, daring, or fearless, especially in challenging assumptions or conventions [Mid-16thC. Formed from Latin *audac-*, the stem of *audax* "bold," from *audere* "to dare," from *avidus* (see AVIDITY).] —**au·da·cious·ness** *n.*

WORD KEY: SYNONYMS

See Synonyms at ***bold***.

au·da·cious·ly /aw dáyshəsslee/ *adv.* in a bold way that challenges assumptions or conventions

au·dac·i·ty /aw dássətee/ *n.* **1.** BOLDNESS OR DARING daring or willingness to challenge assumptions or conventions or tackle something difficult or dangerous **2.** IMPUDENCE lack of respect in somebody's behavior toward another

AKG London

W. H. Auden

Au·den /áwd'n/, **W. H.** (1907–73) British-born U.S. poet and dramatist. One of the most influential poets of his generation, he wrote numerous works including *"September 1939"* and *"Lullaby"*, and won the Pulitzer Prize for *The Age of Anxiety* (1947). Full name **Wystan Hugh Auden**

audi- *prefix.* = **-audio**

au·di·al /áwdiəl/ *adj.* relating to hearing or sounds [Mid-20thC. Formed from AUDIO.]

au·di·ble /áwdib'l/ *adj.* **CAPABLE OF BEING HEARD** loud or clear enough to be heard ○ *an audible gasp from the crowd* ■ *n.* **CALL FOR NEW TACTIC** in football, a new play called out in coded form by the quarterback at the line of scrimmage [15thC. From late Latin *audibilis,* from Latin *audire* "to hear." Ultimately from an Indo-European word meaning "to perceive," which is also the ancestor of English *audience, obey,* and *aesthetic.*] — **au·di·bil·i·ty** /àwdi bíllətee/ *n.* —**au·di·ble·ness** /áwdəb'lnəss/ *n.*

au·di·bly /áwdəblee/ *adv.* loudly enough to allow others to hear ○ *a man in the back row sobbing audibly*

au·di·ence /áwdee əns/ *n.* **1. PEOPLE WATCHING LIVE PERFORMANCE** a group of people who are watching and listening to a show, concert, or other live performance **2. PEOPLE WATCHING OR LISTENING TO BROADCAST** the viewers of a movie or a television program, or the listeners to a radio program, **3. AUTHOR'S READERSHIP** the people who read a particular writer's books **4. FORMAL INTERVIEW** a formal, usually prearranged, interview with somebody important [14thC. Via French from Latin *audientia,* literally "a hearing," from *audire* "to hear" (see AUDIBLE).]

au·dile /áw dīl/ *adj.* = **auditory** [Late 19thC. Formed from Latin *audire* "to hear" (see AUDIBLE).]

au·di·o /áwdee ō/ *n.* the recording and reproduction of sound [Early 20thC. The prefix AUDIO-, used as a word.]

audio-, **audi-** *prefix.* sound, hearing ○ *audiogram* [from Latin *audire* "to hear" (see AUDIBLE)]

au·di·o book *n.* a commercial recording, usually on a cassette tape, of somebody reading the text of a well-known book

au·dio·cas·sette /àwdee ō kə sét/ *n.* a cassette containing an audiotape, for use in a tape recorder

au·di·o clip *n.* an extract from a longer sound recording, e.g., from a movie soundtrack, that can be listened to on a personal computer

au·di·o fre·quen·cy *n.* a frequency that is audible to the human ear, between 20 and 20,000 hertz in people with normal hearing

au·dio·gram /áwdee ō gràm/ *n.* a tracing produced by an audiometer, recording the sharpness of somebody's hearing

au·di·ol·o·gy /àwdee óllәjee/ *n.* the scientific study of hearing, especially for diagnosing and treating hearing defects —**au·di·o·log·i·cal** /àwdee ə lójjik'l/ *adj.* —**au·di·ol·o·gist** /-óllәjist/ *n.*

au·di·om·e·ter /àwdee ómmətər/ *n.* an instrument for testing the ability of a human ear to detect sounds over a range of frequencies and intensities — **au·di·o·met·ric** /àwdee ō méttrik/ *adj.* —**au·di·om·e·try** /-ómmətree/ *n.*

au·di·o·phile /áwdee ō fīl/ *n.* somebody who has an enthusiasm for sound reproduction, especially high-fidelity recordings or broadcasts of music

au·di·o·tape /áwdee ō tàyp/ *n.* **1. SOUND-RECORDING TAPE** magnetic tape for recording sound, or a length of this, typically in a cassette **2. SOUND RECORDING ON TAPE** a sound recording on magnetic tape, especially an audiocassette for use in a tape recorder

au·di·o·vis·u·al /àwdi ō vízhoo əl/ *adj.* **1. OF SOUND AND VISION** relating to sound and vision, especially when combined, e.g., in a presentation using both film and sound recordings **2. OF HEARING AND SIGHT** relating to the faculties of hearing and seeing ■ *n.* **TEACHING AID USING SOUND AND VISION** a teaching or lecture aid that combines sound and vision, e.g., in the form of video equipment, software programs, or slides accompanied by sound recordings

au·di·o·vi·sual aid *n. U.K.* = **audiovisual**

au·dit /áwdət/ *n.* **1. CHECK OF ACCOUNTS** a formal examination, correction, and official endorsing of financial accounts, especially those of a business, undertaken annually by an accountant **2. EFFICIENCY CHECK** a systematic check or assessment, especially of the efficiency or effectiveness of an organization or department, typically carried out by an independent assessor ■ *vt.* **(-dit·ed, -dit·ing, -dits) 1. CARRY OUT AUDIT** to carry out an audit of the financial accounts of a business, department, or organization to establish accuracy or efficiency **2. SIT IN ON CLASS** to attend a class without asking for or receiving graduation credit for it, usually attending all the sessions but not doing the assignments [15thC. From Latin *auditus* "hearing," from *audit-,* the past participle stem of *audire* "to hear" (see AUDIBLE); so called because originally the accounts were read aloud.] —**au·dit·a·ble** *adj.*

au·di·tee /àwdi tée/ *n.* a person or organization that is being audited

au·di·tion /aw dísh'n/ *n.* **1. TEST PERFORMANCE BY CANDIDATE** a test in the form of a short performance, taken, e.g., by an actor applying for a role in a movie or play **2.** PHYSIOL **HEARING** the sense, faculty, or process of hearing ■ *vti.* **(-tioned, -tion·ing, -tions) DO OR GIVE AN AUDITION** to do an audition or give somebody an audition for a role [Late 16thC. From the Latin stem *audition-,* literally "hearing," from *audire* (see AUDIBLE).]

au·di·tive /áwdətiv/ *adj.* = **auditory** [Early 17thC. Via French from, ultimately, Latin *audire* "to hear" (see AUDIBLE).]

au·di·tor /áwdətər/ *n.* **1.** BUSINESS **SOMEBODY CHECKING ACCOUNTS OR SYSTEMS** somebody who is qualified to audit accounts or to conduct an audit of a department or organization **2. STUDENT SITTING IN ON CLASS** a student who attends a class without asking for or receiving graduation credit **3. HEARER** a hearer or listener, e.g., a member of an audience or somebody listening to somebody who is talking (*formal*) [14thC. Via Anglo-Norman from Latin *auditor* "hearer," from *audire* (see AUDIBLE).]

au·di·tor-gen·er·al (*plural* **au·di·tor-gen·er·als** *or* **au·di·tors-gen·er·al**) *n.* in Canada, an independent auditor who prepares annual reports on federal government spending, including the spending of some Crown corporations

au·di·to·ri·um /àwdi táwree əm/ (*plural* **-ums** *or* **-a** /-ə/) *n.* **1. HALL OR LECTURE ROOM** a hall or a building with a hall that is used for lectures, concerts, and other events **2. PART OF THEATER WHERE AUDIENCE SITS** the area of a theater or concert hall where the audience sits [Early 17thC. From Latin, literally "a place for hearing," formed from *audire* (see AUDIBLE).]

au·di·to·ry /áwdə tàwree/ *adj.* relating to the faculty, organs, or process of hearing [Late 16thC. From late Latin *auditorius,* from Latin *audire* (see AUDIBLE).]

au·dit trail *n.* a record kept, e.g., by a computer, of a sequence of events or transactions

Au·du·bon /áwdə bòn/, **John James** (1785–1851) Haitian-born U.S. ornithologist, naturalist, and artist who was known for co-authoring *The Ornithological Biography* (5 vols, (1831–39).

au fait /ō fáy/ *adj.* abreast of the latest developments in something, or supplied with the most recent facts about something [From French, literally "to the fact"]

aug. *abbr.* GRAM augmentative

Aug. *abbr.* August

Au·ge·an /aw jée ən/ *adj.* **1. FILTHY** disgustingly dirty, like the Augean stables **2. DIFFICULT** extremely difficult and unpleasant

Au·ge·an sta·bles *n.* in Greek mythology, the stables owned by King Augeas that had not been cleaned in 30 years. One of Hercules' tasks was to clean them in one day, which he achieved by diverting two rivers through them. ◇ **cleanse the Augean stables** to put something that is extremely chaotic and disorganized into a state of order

au·ger /áwgər/ *n.* a hand tool with a corkscrew-shaped bit for boring holes, or a larger tool, using the same principle, for boring holes in the ground [Old English *nafogār,* formed from NAVE[2] and *gār* "spear" (see GORE[1]). The initial "n" was lost in the 16thC by false division of "a nauger" as "an auger."]

aught /awt/ *pron.* anything whatever (*archaic literary*) [Old English *āwiht,* literally "ever a thing." Ultimately from a prehistoric Germanic word that was formed from the ancestors of English *aye*[2] and *wight.*]

au·gite /áw jīt, áwgīt/ *n.* a dark green mineral of the pyroxene group, containing aluminum, calcium, iron, and magnesium. It is found in igneous rock. [Early 19thC. Via Latin *augites,* a precious stone (possibly turquoise), from Greek *augitēs,* from *augē* "luster."]

aug·ment /awg mént/ *v.* **(-ment·ed, -ment·ing, -ments) 1.** *vti.* **INCREASE** to grow, or to increase something in number, amount, size, strength, or intensity (*formal*) **2.** *vt.* MUSIC **ENLARGE INTERVAL BY SEMITONE** in music, to enlarge a perfect or major interval by a semitone ■ *n.* GRAM **PREFIXED VOWEL** in Greek or Sanskrit grammar, a vowel prefixed to a verb, or added to its initial vowel so as to lengthen it into a diphthong, to form a past tense [14thC.Via French from, ultimately, Latin *augere* "to increase" (source also of English *auction*). Ultimately from an Indo-European word that is also the ancestor of English *wax, eke,* and *august.*] — **aug·ment·er** *n.*

WORD KEY: SYNONYMS

See Synonyms at ***increase***.

aug·men·ta·tion /àwgmən táysh'n, -men-/ *n.* **1. INCREASE** the increasing, or growth, of something in number, amount, size, strength, or intensity, or the amount by which something grows or is added to ○ *augmentation in costs* ○ *breast augmentation* **2.** MUSIC **INCREASING NOTE VALUES** the technique of varying a theme by increasing its note values proportionally

aug·men·ta·tive /awg méntətiv/ *adj.* **1. CAUSING AN INCREASE** tending to add to or increase something or to enable something to grow or increase (*formal*) **2.** GRAM **DENOTING GREAT SIZE OR IMPORTANCE** used to describe an affix, such as Spanish "-ote" or Italian "-one," that signifies great size or importance, or a word to which an affix of this kind has been added ■ *n.* GRAM **AUGMENTATIVE AFFIX OR WORD** an affix signifying great size or importance, or a word to which an affix of this kind has been added

aug·ment·ed /awg méntəd/ *adj.* in music, used to describe a perfect or major interval that has been enlarged by a semitone

au gra·tin /ō graát'n, ō grátt'n, ō graa taáN/ *adj.* sprinkled with breadcrumbs, sometimes mixed with grated cheese, and browned before serving [From French, literally "with a gratin crust"]

au·gur /áwgər/ *n.* **1. INTERPRETER OF MESSAGES FROM ROMAN GODS** a religious official in ancient Rome who interpreted natural phenomena, such as the flight of birds, as signs that the gods favored or disapproved of actions proposed by the city **2. SOOTHSAYER OR PROPHET** any soothsayer, prophet, or diviner ■ *vt.* **(-gured, -gur·ing, -gurs) INDICATE WHAT WILL HAPPEN** to suggest or indicate what will happen in the future [14thC. From Latin (source also of English inaugurate). Probably ultimately from an Indo-European word meaning "to increase," which in Latin developed the sense "divine favor" (see AUGMENT).] — **au·gu·ral** /áwgyərəl, -gə-/ *adj.*

au·gu·ry /áwgyəree, -gə-/ (*plural* **-ries**) *n.* **1. DIVINATION** the art, activity, prophecies, or pronouncements of an augur, soothsayer, or diviner **2. PORTENT OR OMEN** an indication of what will happen in the future

au·gust /aw gúst/ *adj.* full of solemn splendor and dignity (*formal*) [Mid-17thC. Directly or via French from Latin *augustus.* Ultimately from an Indo-European word meaning "to increase," which is also the ancestor of English *wax, eke,* and *augment.*]

Au·gust /áwgəst/ *n.* the eighth month of the year in the Gregorian calendar. It has 31 days. [Pre-12thC. From Latin *augustus,* named for the Roman emperor *Augustus* Caesar.]

Au·gus·ta /aw gústə, ə-/ **1.** city on the western bank of the Savannah River in east-central Georgia, previously known as Fort Cornwallis. Population: 41,783 (1996). **2.** capital of Maine and vacation resort, in the southwest of the state, on the Kennebec River. Population: 20,441 (1996).

Au·gus·tan /aw gústən/ *adj.* **1. OF AUGUSTUS CAESAR OR HIS TIME** relating to the Roman emperor Augustus Caesar, to his reign, or to the classical writers, including Virgil, Ovid, and Horace, who flourished during this period **2. CHARACTERIZED BY CLASSICAL WRITING** relating to any period or the writers or works of a period during which writing in the classical style flourished, especially during 17th-century France and 18th-century England ■ *n.* **AUGUSTAN WRITER OR STUDENT** a writer from an Augustan period, or somebody who studies Augustan literature

Au·gus·tine /áwgə steen, aw gústin/, **St.** (354–430) Roman priest and theologian. His masterpiece, *De Civitate Dei* (*The City of God*), greatly influenced the development of Christianity. He was bishop of Hippo, North Africa, from 396 until his death.

Au·gus·tine, St. (*d.* 604) Roman priest. Sent by Pope Gregory I to convert the Anglo-Saxons, he became the first Archbishop of Canterbury (597–604).

Au·gus·tin·i·an /àwgə stínnee ən/ *adj.* **OF ST . AUGUSTINE** relating to St . Augustine of Hippo, or to his teachings, or to any of the Christian religious orders living according to his rule or system of monastic life. ■ *n.* **FOLLOWER OF AUGUSTINE OR HIS RULE** a follower of St. Augustine, especially a member of one of the religious orders living according to his rule.

Au·gus·tus /aw gústəss/ (63 B.C.–A.D. 14) Roman emperor. The founder of the Roman Empire, he was the adopted son of Julius Caesar. He succeeded his adoptive father as absolute ruler in 27 B.C. after a period of civil war.

Auk

auk /awk/ *n.* a small black-and-white heavy-bodied sea bird that belongs to the puffin family. Auks are found in cool northern seas and are skilled divers for fish. Family: Alcidae. [Late 17thC. Via Norwegian *alk* from Old Norse *álka.*]

auk·let /áwklət/ *n.* a small auk found in the North Pacific that nests in burrows or rock slides. Family: Alcidae.

auld lang syne /áwld lang zín/ *n. Scotland* old times or times long gone (*archaic*) [Literally "old long since," "old long ago"]

au na·tu·rel /ō náchə rél/ *adv., adj.* **1. SIMPLY OR UNCOOKED** served simply and plainly, e.g., uncooked or without seasoning or salt **2. NAKED** wearing no clothes (*humorous*) [From French, literally "in the natural state"]

Aung San /awng sán/, **U** (1916?–47) Burmese nationalist leader. He became prime minister of British Burma after World War II and negotiated Burmese independence.

Aung San Suu Kyi /áwng san soo kí/, **Daw** (*b.* 1945) Burmese human rights activist who won the Nobel Peace Prize (1991) for establishing Burma's National League for Democracy (NLD) party.

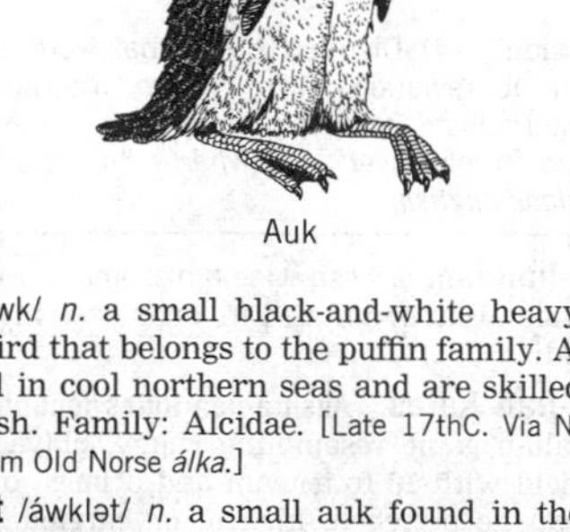

Aung San Suu Kyi

aunt /ant, aant/ *n.* somebody's mother's or father's sister, or somebody's uncle's wife, used before her first name as a title or form of address [13thC. Via Anglo-Norman from Latin *amita* "father's sister."] —**aunt·hood** *n.*

aunt·ie /ántee, áantee/, **aunt·y** (*plural* **-ies**) *n.* an aunt or close woman friend of a child's parents (*informal*)

aunt·y /ántee/ (*plural* **-ies**) *n.* = **auntie**

au pair /ō páir/ *n.* a young person from another country living with a family to learn the language, and helping with childcare and domestic work in return for room and board [From French, literally "on equal terms"]

au·ra /áwrə/ (*plural* **-ras** *or* **-rae** /-ree/) *n.* **1. DISTINCTIVE QUALITY** a characteristic or distinctive impression created by somebody or something ○ *an aura of mystery* **2.** PARANORMAL **FORCE EMANATING FROM SOMEBODY OR SOMETHING** a force that is said to surround all people and objects, discernible, often as a bright glow, only to people of unusual psychic sensitivity **3.** MED **WARNING SENSATION BEFORE EPILEPTIC SEIZURE** a distinctive sensation or visual disturbance that may signal the beginning of an epileptic seizure or a migraine [Mid-18thC. Via Latin, "gentle breeze," from Greek.]

au·ral /áwrəl/ *adj.* relating to the ear, hearing, or to receptiveness and response to speech or other sounds [Mid-19thC. Formed from Latin *auris* "ear." Ultimately from an Indo-European word meaning "ear," which is also the ancestor of English *ear* and *scout.*] —**au·ral·ly** *adv.*

WORD KEY: USAGE

aural or **oral**? These two words are often confused because they are pronounced in a similar way and have meanings that are close. Essentially ***aural*** has to do with hearing whereas ***oral*** has to do with speaking. An ***aural*** test is a medical examination of the ears, whereas an ***oral*** test is any kind of test in which the answers are spoken rather than written.

au·rar plural of **eyrir**

au·re·ate /áwree ət, -àyt/ *adj.* **1. GOLDEN** gold, gilded, golden, or gold-colored **2. ELABORATELY WORDED** expressed or written in a highly or excessively ornamented, florid, or elaborate style [15thC. From Latin *aureatus*, from *aureus* "golden," from *aurum* "gold."]

au·rei plural of **aureus**

au·re·ole /áwri ōl/, **au·re·o·la** /aw rée ələ/ *n.* **1. HALO** a painted or carved representation of a circle of light around the head of a divine being or a saint **2.** METEOROL = **corona** *n.* 2 [Mid-19thC. Via French from late Latin *corona aureola*, literally "golden crown."]

au·re·us /áwree əss/ (*plural* **-i** /-ī/) *n.* a gold coin that was a unit of currency in the Roman Empire between 30 B.C. and A.D. 310 [Early 17thC. From Latin, noun use of *aureus* "golden" (see AUREATE).]

au re·voir /àw rəv wáar, ō-/ *interj.* goodbye till we see each other again [From French, literally "until seeing again"]

auri-[1] *prefix.* ear, hearing ○ *auriform* [from Latin *auris* (see AURAL)]

auri-[2] *prefix.* gold ○ *auriferous* [from Latin *aurum* (see AURUM)]

au·ric /áwrik/ *adj.* containing gold with a valence of three ○ *auric oxide* [Early 19thC. Formed from Latin *aurum* "gold."]

au·ri·cle /áwrək'l/ *n.* **1. VISIBLE PART OF EAR** the part of the external ear that projects outward from the head **2. PART OF HEART CHAMBER** an ear-shaped muscular part that sticks out from the surface of each upper chamber **(atrium)** of the heart **3. ATRIUM** an atrium of the heart (*dated*) [Mid-17thC. From Latin *auricula*, literally "little ear," from *auris* "ear" (see AURAL).] —**au·ri·cled** *adj.*

au·ric·u·la /aw ríkyələ/ (*plural* **-las** *or* **-lae** /aw ríkyə lee, aw ríkyə lī/) *n.* a yellow-flowered alpine primrose with leaves shaped like a bear's ear. Latin name: *Primula auricula.* [Mid-17thC. From Latin (see AURICLE).]

au·ric·u·lar /aw ríkyələr/ *adj.* **1. EAR-SHAPED** shaped like an ear **2. RELATING TO HEARING ORGANS** relating to the ear or to the sense of hearing **3. RELATING TO HEART CHAMBERS** relating to the ear-shaped muscular part **(auricle)** on the surface of each upper chamber **(atrium)** of the heart

au·ric·u·late /aw ríkyələt, aw ríkyə làyt/ *adj.* **1. WITH EAR-SHAPED LEAF ATTACHMENT** used to describe leaves that have an attachment at the base that is shaped like an ear **2. WITH EARS** relating to an animal that has ears, auricles, or extensions that resemble earlobes

au·rif·er·ous /aw ríffərəss/ *adj.* used to describe rock or minerals that contain gold

Au·rig·na·cian /àwrig náysh'n, àwrin yáysh'n/ *adj.* belonging to a prehistoric culture associated with Cro-Magnon people in Europe around the period 30,000 to 22,000 B.C. [Early 20thC. Named for the village of *Aurignac* in southern France, where the first evidence of such a culture was discovered.]

au·rochs /ów ròks, áw-/ (*plural* **-rochs**) *n.* a long-horned wild ox, now extinct but thought to be an ancestor of modern domestic cattle. The aurochs once inhabited the forests of North Africa, Europe, and Southwest Asia. [Late 18thC. From German, variant of *Auerochs*, literally "original ox."]

au·ro·ra /àw ráwrə, ə-/ (*plural* **-ras** *or* **-rae** /-ree/) *n.* **1. NORTHERN OR SOUTHERN LIGHTS** a phenomenon occurring in the night sky around the polar regions, caused by atmospheric gases interacting with solar particles to create streamers, folds, or arches of colored light **2. au·ro·ra, Au·ro·ra DAWN** the dawn, usually personified or regarded, as in classical literature, as a goddess [15thC. From Latin, "dawn." Ultimately from an Indo-European word meaning "to shine," which is also the ancestor of English *east* and *Easter.*] —**au·ro·ral** *adj.*

Au·ro·ra /aw ráwrə, ə-/ **1.** city in northeastern Colorado. It is a northern suburb of Denver. Population: 252,341 (1996). **2.** city southwest of Chicago in northeastern Illinois, on the east bank of the Fox River. Population: 116,405 (1996).

au·ro·ra aus·tra·lis /-aw stráyliss/ *n.* the colored lights seen in the skies around the South Pole [From modern Latin, literally "southern aurora"]

au·ro·ra bo·re·al·is /-bawree álliss/ *n.* the colored lights seen in the skies around the North Pole [From modern Latin, literally "northern aurora"]

au·ro·ra trout (*plural* **au·ro·ra trout** *or* **au·ro·ra trouts**) *n.* a rare, brilliantly colored, unspotted brook trout found in northern Ontario. Latin name: *Salvelinus fontinalis.*

AUS *abbr.* Army of the United States

Aus. *abbr.* Australia ■ *abbr.* Australian ■ *abbr.* Austria ■ *abbr.* Austrian

Ausch·witz /ów shwits/ site of the largest Nazi concentration camp, where about 22 million people were murdered between 1941 and 1945. Situated in southern Poland, southeast of Katowice, it is now a museum and archive.

Ausch·witz Lie *n.* denial that the attempted extermination of the Jews by the Nazis ever took place

aus·cul·tate /áwskəl tàyt/ (**-tat·ed, -tat·ing, -tates**) *vt.* to listen to various sounds made by a patient's internal organs, usually with the help of a stethoscope, in order to make a diagnosis [Mid-19thC. Back-formation from AUSCULTATION.] —**aus·cul·ta·tive** /áwskəl tàytiv/ *adj.* —**aus·cul·ta·to·ry** /-skúltə tàwree/ *adj.*

aus·cul·ta·tion /àwskəl táysh'n/ *n.* listening to the sounds made by a patient's internal organs, especially the heart, lungs, and abdominal organs, usually with a stethoscope, in order to make a diagnosis [Mid-17thC. From the Latin stem *auscultation-*, from *auscultare* "to listen to."]

aus·land·er /óws làndər/ *n.* somebody from another country or area or who is an outsider [Mid-20thC. From German *Ausländer*, literally "outlander."]

aus·le·se /òwss láyzə/ *n.* a middle grade of high-quality German table wine, made from selected late-picked grapes and typically medium sweet to sweet [Mid-19thC. From German, literally "selection."]

aus·pice /áwspəss/ *n.* (*plural* **-pi·ces** /-eess/) **OMEN** a sign or token for the future, especially a happy or promising one ■ **aus·pi·ces** *npl.* **SUPPORT** the help or support of a person or organization ○ *a study conducted under the auspices of the United Nations* [Mid-17thC. Via French from Latin *auspicium* "taking omens," from *auspex* "soothsayer," originally literally "somebody who foretells the future by studying the flight pattern of birds," from *avis* "bird" + a stem of *specere* "to look."]

aus·pi·cious /aw spíshəss/ *adj.* marked by lucky signs or good omens, and therefore by the promise of success or happiness —**aus·pi·cious·ly** *adv.* —**aus·pi·cious·ness** *n.*

Aus·sie /áwsee/ *adj.* AUSTRALIAN Australian (*informal*) ■ *n.* AN AUSTRALIAN somebody who is Australian (*informal*) [Early 20thC. Shortening.]

Aust. *abbr.* Australia ■ *abbr.* Australian ■ *abbr.* Austria ■ *abbr.* Austrian

AKG London

Jane Austen

Aus·ten /áwstən/, **Jane** (1775–1817) British novelist, writer of elegant, satirical fiction, including *Pride and Prejudice* (1813).

aus·ten·ite /áwstə nìt/ *n.* a solid solution of carbon in iron that occurs as a component of steel at a certain stage of manufacture [Early 20thC. Named for the English metallurgist Sir William Roberts-*Austen* (1843–1902).] —**aus·ten·it·ic** /àwstə níttik/ *adj.*

aus·tere /aw steer/ *adj.* **1.** SUGGESTING PHYSICAL HARDSHIP imposing or suggesting physical hardship **2.** UNSMILING grimly unsmiling, humorless, or suggesting strict self-denial **3.** PLAIN AND WITHOUT LUXURY plain and simple, without luxury or self-indulgence **4.** PLAIN IN STYLE OR DESIGN severely plain in design or lines, without distractions or decoration [14thC. Via French and Latin from Greek *austēros*. Ultimately from an Indo-European word meaning "dry, harsh," which is also the ancestor of English *sere* and *sear*.] —**aus·tere·ly** *adv.* —**aus·tere·ness** *n.*

aus·ter·i·ty /aw stérrətee/ (*plural* **-ties**) *n.* **1.** SEVERITY OR PLAINNESS severity of discipline, regime, expression, or design **2.** ECONOMY MEASURE a saving, economy, or act of self-denial, especially in respect of something regarded as a luxury **3.** ECON ENFORCED THRIFT thrift imposed as government policy, with restricted access to or availability of consumer goods

Aus·ter·litz /áwstər lìts, ówstər-/ site of a major battle in 1805 in what is now the eastern Czech Republic, when Napoleon defeated Russian and Austrian forces

Aus·tin /áwstin/ capital of Texas and university town in the south of the state, on the Colorado River. Population: 541,278 (1996).

Aus·tin, Stephen Fuller (1793–1836) U.S. political leader. He encouraged the settlement of Texas and became Texas's first secretary of state.

aus·tral[1] /áwstrəl/ *adj.* relating to, belonging to, or coming from the south [15thC. From Latin *australis*, from *auster* "south," of unknown origin.]

aus·tral[2] /ówstrəl/ (*plural* **-trals** *or* **-tral·es**) *n.* **1.** UNIT OF CURRENCY IN ARGENTINA a subunit of currency in Argentina. See table at **currency 2.** COIN WORTH AN AUSTRAL a coin worth an austral [Late 20thC. Via Spanish from Latin *australis* (see AUSTRAL[1]).]

Aus·tral. *abbr.* **1.** Australasia **2.** Australia ■ *abbr.* Australian

Aus·tral·a·sia /àwstrəl áyzhə/ region consisting of Australia, New Zealand, New Guinea, and neighboring islands of the South Pacific —**Aus·tral·a·sian** *adj., n.*

Aus·tra·lia /aw stráylee ə/ country occupying the continent of Australia. Australia was founded in 1901. Language: English. Currency: Australian dollar. Capital: Canberra. Population: 18,311,000 (1996). Area: 2,966,200 sq. mi./7,682,300 sq. km.

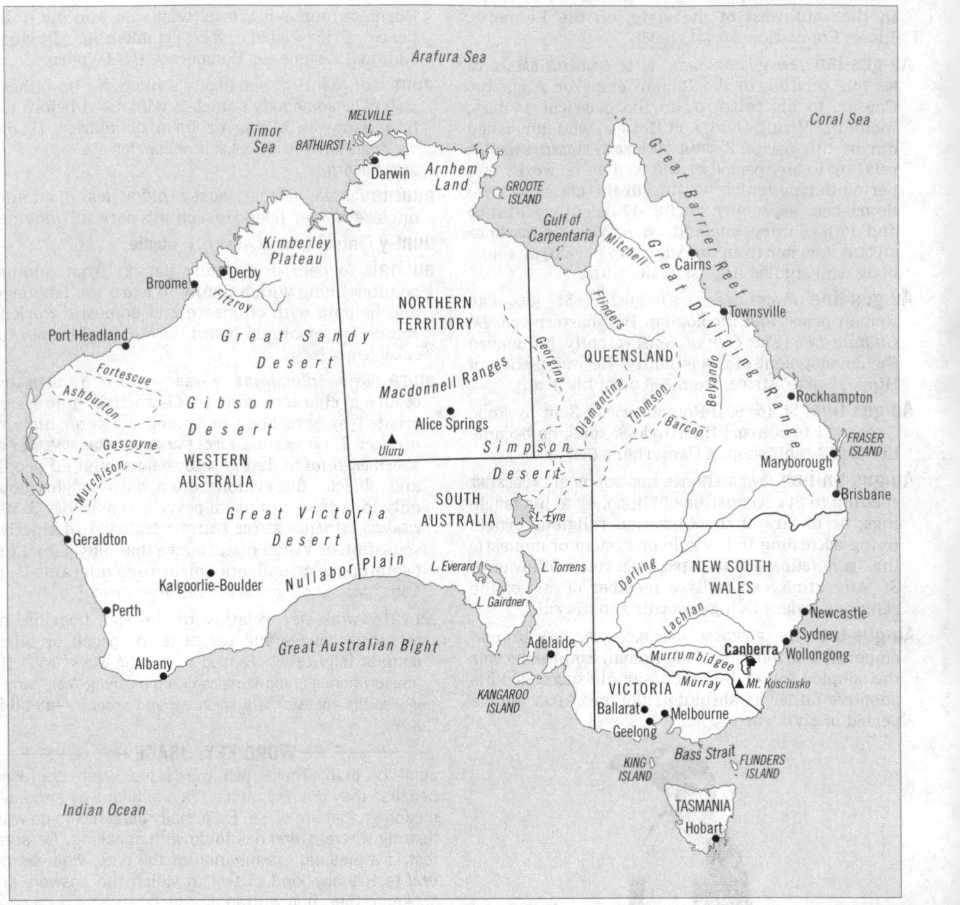

Australia

Aus·tra·lian /aw stráylee ən/ *adj.* **1.** OF AUSTRALIA relating to or typical of Australia, or its people or culture **2.** OF ABORIGINAL LANGUAGES OF AUSTRALIA relating to the family of languages spoken in Australia before European settlement. Most Australian languages are now extinct or approaching extinction. ■ *n.* **1.** SOMEBODY FROM AUSTRALIA somebody who was born in or who is a citizen of Australia **2.** AUSTRALIAN ENGLISH the form of English that is spoken in Australia

Aus·tra·lian bal·lot *n.* = **secret ballot**

Aus·tra·lian En·glish the form of English spoken in Australians as distinct from other forms of English such as American English or British English

WORD KEY: WORLD ENGLISH

Australian English is the English language as used in the Commonwealth of Australia, population 15 million, which is, with Canada, third in size and distinctness among the primary English-speaking countries. English has been used in Australia for about 200 years. Australian English, after the United States and the United Kingdom, is markedly homogeneous, with three kinds of accent: (1) *Cultivated Australian*, similar to Received Pronunciation in the United Kingdom, and formerly highly regarded; (2) *Broad Australian*, often compared with Cockney; and (3) *General Australian*, the majority variety, occupying the social middle ground. Australian English is "non-rhotic" (that is, *r* is not pronounced in words such as *art, door,* and *worker*), the vowel in *can't dance* is closer to that in "kent dense" than in "cahnt dahnce" or "kaynt daynce," and the Broad version of *I'm going there today* sounds to some ears like "I'm going there to die." Australian English and British English spelling are generally identical (with some ambivalence in the *-or/our* endings, most notably in U.S.-style *Labor*, the name of a political party). Grammar is comparable to general usage in both Britain and the United States, but Australian English has a large and distinctive home-grown vocabulary that includes: (1) Adoptions from Aboriginal languages, with a penchant for spelling with double letters (as in *corroboree* and *kookaburra*) and mainly relating to animals, plants, objects, and localities, for example, *billabong, boomerang, didgeridoo, dingo, koala, Murrumbidgee, Woomera*) a process similar to American English's adoption from Native American languages; (2) Extensions in meaning of everyday words, for example, *to feel crook* "to feel ill," *to farewell someone* "to give someone a farewell party," *mob* "a flock or group (of sheep, kangaroos, etc.)," *station* "a ranch," as in *sheep station*; (3) Extensions or shifts in the meaning of British dialect words, such as *cobber* (a friend, mate), *dinkum* "reliable, genuine," *dunny* "a lavatory," *wowser* "a spoil-sport, prude"; (4) Distinctive informal word endings, e.g., -o in abbreviations such as *arvo* "afternoon" and *journo* "journalist," and *-ie* in names for workers, such as *truckie* "truck-driver" and *wharfie* "stevedore." See ***New Zealand English***.

Aus·tra·lian·ism /aw sstráylee ə nìzzəm/ *n.* a word or expression that originated in, or is used mainly in, Australia

Aus·tra·lian Rules, Aus·tra·lian Rules foot·ball *n.* an Australian game resembling rugby, played on an oval field with 18 to a team and a large oval ball that can be punched, kicked, or carried (*takes a singular verb*)

Aus·tra·lian ter·ri·er *n.* a short stocky terrier with erect ears and a straight, wiry coat that is normally blue- or silver-gray with brown patches on the muzzle and feet

Aus·tra·loid /áwstrə lòyd/ *adj.* ABORIGINAL belonging or relating to the ethnic group that includes the Australian Aborigines and certain other southern Asian and Pacific peoples ■ *n.* AUSTRALOID PERSON a member of one of the Australoid peoples

aus·tra·lo·pith·e·cine /àwstrəlō píthə seen/ *adj.* OF PREHISTORIC AFRICAN PRIMATE relating to a prehistoric primate whose fossilized remains, resembling those of humans, have been found in southern and eastern Africa ■ *n.* PREHISTORIC PRIMATE an australopithecine primate. Genus: *Australopithecus.* [Mid-20thC. Formed from modern Latin *Australopithecus*, from Latin *australis* "southern" + Greek *pithēkos* "ape."]

Aus·tra·sia /aw stráyzhə/ eastern part of the medieval kingdom of the Franks, consisting of what are now parts of France, Germany, and the Netherlands

Aus·tri·a /áwstriə/ democratic federal republic in central Europe. Language: German. Currency: Schilling. Capital: Vienna. Population: 8,054,000 (1995). Area: 32,378 sq. mi./83,858 sq. km. —**Aus·tri·an** *adj., n.*

Aus·tri·an blind *n.* a type of fabric window blind that consists of parallel panels that can be gathered up vertically into loose billowing folds

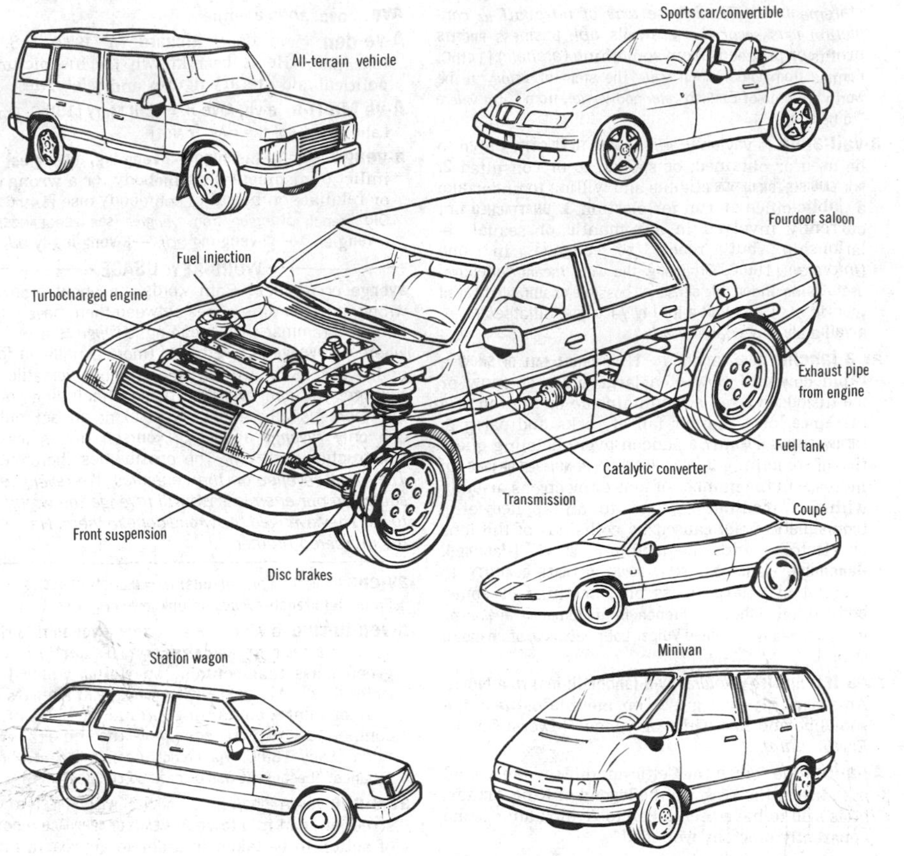

Automobile

au·to·mo·tive /áwtə mṓtiv/ *adj.* **1. OF MOTOR VEHICLES** relating to or involving motor vehicles **2. SELF-PROPELLED** propelled by its own motor or engine

au·to·nom·ic /àwtə nómmik/ *adj.* **1.** PHYSIOL **CONTROLLED BY AUTOMATIC RESPONSES** used to describe functions of the nervous system not under the voluntary control of the individual, e.g., the regulation of heartbeat or gland secretions **2.** PHYSIOL **WITHOUT THOUGHT** used to describe an action or response that occurs without conscious control **3.** BIOL **FROM INTERNAL STIMULI** produced or caused by internal stimuli —**au·to·nom·i·cal·ly** *adv.*

au·to·nom·ic nerv·ous sys·tem *n.* the part of the nervous system in humans and other vertebrates that controls involuntary activity, e.g., the action of the heart and glands, breathing, digestive processes, and reflex actions

au·ton·o·mous /aw tónnəməs/ *adj.* **1. SELF-GOVERNING** politically independent and self-governing **2. ABLE TO CHOOSE** able to make decisions and act on them as a free and independent moral agent **3. SELF-SUFFICIENT** existing, reacting, or developing as an independent, self-regulating organism —**au·ton·o·mous·ly** *adv.*

au·ton·o·my /aw tónnəmee/ *n.* **1.** POL **SELF-GOVERNMENT** political independence and self-government **2.** PHILOSOPHY **EXISTENCE AS INDEPENDENT MORAL AGENT** personal independence and the capacity to make moral decisions and act on them **3.** LITERAT **INDEPENDENCE OF A TEXT** the status of a text as an aesthetic object not to be judged or commented on in the light of external knowledge, e.g., of the biography of the author [Early 17thC. From Greek *autonomia*, from *autonomos* "having its own laws," from *nomos* "law."] —**au·ton·o·mist** *n.*

au·to·pi·lot /áwtō pīlət/ *n.* AEROSP, NAUT = **automatic pilot** *n.* 1 ◇ **on autopilot** without guidance, control, or proper attention (*informal*) ○ *The business has been on autopilot since she resigned.*

au·to·pis·ta /àwtə peéstə/ *n.* an expressway in a Spanish-speaking country or region [Mid-20thC. From Spanish, literally "automobile track."]

au·to·plas·ty /áwtə plàstee/ (*plural* **-ties**) *n.* the repair of a patient's body using tissue, e.g., skin, taken from another part of the patient's body —**au·to·plas·tic** /àwtə plástik/ *adj.* —**au·to·plas·ti·cal·ly** /-iklee/ *adv.*

au·top·sy /áwt opsee/ (*plural* **-sies**) *n.* **1.** MED **EXAMINATION TO FIND CAUSE OF DEATH** the medical examination of a dead body in order to establish the cause and circumstances of death **2. EXHAUSTIVE EXAMINATION** an exhaustive critical examination of something [Mid-17thC. Via French or modern Latin from Greek *autopsia* "seeing with your own eyes," from *autoptēs* "eye witness."]

au·to rac·ing *n.* racing in motor vehicles, especially in cars that are specially designed to travel at high speeds

au·to·ra·di·o·graph /àwtō ráydee ə graf/, **au·to·ra·di·o·gram** /-gram/ *n.* a photograph that reveals how radioactivity is distributed in a specimen or sample, made by exposing a photographic plate to the radiation —**au·to·ra·di·o·graph·ic** /àwtō raydee ə gráffik/ *adj.* —**au·to·ra·di·og·ra·phy** /-óggrəfee/ *n.*

au·to·rick·shaw /àwtō rík shaw/ *n.* a vehicle with three wheels, like a covered motor scooter with a back seat for passengers, that is used as a taxi on the Indian subcontinent

au·to·route /áwtō root/ *n.* an expressway in a French-speaking country or region [Mid-20thC. From French, literally "automobile route."]

au·to·save /áwtō sàyv/ *n.* a computer program feature in which data in an open file is saved automatically at intervals usually determinable by the user. This feature can minimize data loss in the event of a crash.

au·to·some /áwtə sōm/ *n.* a chromosome other than one that determines sex [Early 20thC. Coined from AUTO- + -SOME, on the model of CHROMOSOME.] —**au·to·so·mal** /àwtə sṓm'l/ *adj.* —**au·to·so·mal·ly** /-əlee/ *adv.*

au·to·stra·da /ówtō straadə, áwtō-/ *n.* an expressway in an Italian-speaking country or region [Early 20thC. From Italian, literally "automobile road."]

au·to·sug·ges·tion /àwtō sə jéschən/ *n.* the process by which somebody's perceptions, behavior, or physical condition may be altered by means of his or her power of suggestion —**au·to·sug·gest** *vt.* —**au·to·sug·gest·i·bil·i·ty** /àwtō sə jestə bíllətee/ *n.* —**au·to·sug·gest·i·ble** /-jéstəb'l/ *adj.* —**au·to·sug·ges·tive** /-jéstiv/ *adj.*

au·to·tel·ic /àwtō téllik/ *adj.* **1.** PHILOSOPHY **POSSESSING INTERNAL PURPOSE** concerning an entity or event that has within itself the purpose of its existence or occurrence **2.** LEISURE **DONE FOR ITS OWN SAKE** done for its own sake rather than to gain a material reward or avoid a punishment [Early 20thC. Formed from Greek *autotelēs*, from *autos* "self" + *telos* "end."] —**au·to·tel·ism** *n.*

au·to·tim·er /áwtō tìmər/ *n.* an automatic timing device, e.g., on a stove

au·tot·o·mize /aw tóttəm īz/ (**-mized, -miz·ing, -miz·es**) *vti.* to cast off a part of the body such as the tail or a leg in order to escape from an attacker or because it has become trapped. This is done, e.g., by lizards, snakes, worms, and crustaceans.

au·tot·o·my /aw tóttəmee/ *n.* the casting off of part of the body by an animal such as a lizard, snake, worm, or crustacean when it is caught or attacked by a predator [Late 19thC. Coined from AUTO- + -TOMY.] —**au·to·tom·ic** /àwtə tómmik/ *adj.*

au·to·tox·e·mi·a /àwtō tok seémee ə/ *n.* = **autointoxication**

au·to·tox·in /àwtə tóksən/ *n.* a substance that poisons the system within which it is formed

au·to·trans·form·er /àwtō trans fáwrmər/ *n.* a transformer in which the primary and secondary coils share all or some windings

au·to·trans·fu·sion /àwtō trans fyoózh'n/ *n.* a blood transfusion using the patient's own blood

au·to·troph·ic /àwtə troffik, -trṓfik/ *adj.* used to describe organisms, especially green plants, that are capable of making nutrients from inorganic materials [Late 19thC. Coined from AUTO- + -TROPHIC.] —**au·to·troph** /-trōf, -trof/ *n.* —**au·to·troph·i·cal·ly** /àwtə troffiklee, -trṓfiklee/ *adv.* —**au·tot·ro·phy** /aw tóttrəfee/ *n.*

au·to·wind·er /áwtō wìndər/ *n.* a device that automatically winds the film in a camera forward after a photograph is taken

au·tox·i·da·tion /àw tòksi dáysh'n/ *n.* **1. OXIDATION IN AIR** the oxidation of certain substances that occurs at normal temperatures as a result of contact with air **2. OXIDATION OF TWO SUBSTANCES** oxidation that occurs only when there is another substance present that also undergoes oxidation

au·tumn /áwtəm/ *n.* **1. SEASON AFTER SUMMER AND BEFORE WINTER** the season occurring between summer and winter. In the northern hemisphere it is the time when weather begins to become colder, many fruits ripen, and leaves change color and drop. Autumn traditionally lasts from September 22 to December 21 in the northern hemisphere, and from March 21 to June 21 in the southern hemisphere. **2. TIME OF LATE MATURITY** a time in the development of something that follows its most vigorous and successful phase, before its decline ○ *in the autumn of his career as a cellist* [14thC. From Latin *autumnus*, of uncertain origin. The word replaced HARVEST as the term for this time of year.]

au·tum·nal /aw túmn'l/ *adj.* occurring in or typical of autumn

au·tum·nal e·qui·nox *n.* **1.** CALENDAR **TIME WHEN SUN CROSSES EQUATORIAL PLANE** the first day of autumn, when the sun crosses the plane of the Earth's equator and makes day and night approximately of equal length. The day occurs about September 22 in the northern hemisphere and March 21 in the southern hemisphere. **2.** ASTRON **SUN'S PATH CROSSING CELESTIAL EQUATOR** the position of the sun during the autumnal equinox

au·tumn cro·cus (*plural* **au·tumn cro·cus·es** *or* **au·tumn cro·ci**) *n.* an autumn-flowering plant that has crocus-shaped purple or pink flowers growing directly from the ground after the leaves have died down. Latin name: *Colchicum autumnale.*

au·tun·ite /ṓtə nīt, áwtə nīt/ *n.* a yellow radioactive fluorescent mineral consisting of hydrated calcium uranium phosphate [Mid-19thC. Named for the town of *Autun* in eastern France, near where the mineral was first discovered.]

aux. *abbr.* auxiliary

aux·e·sis /awg zeéssiss, -seéssiss/ *n.* growth in animals or plants caused by an increase in the size of cells, not by cellular division [Mid-19thC. Via late Latin from Greek.] —**aux·et·ic** *adj.* —**aux·et·i·cal·ly** *adv.*

aux·il·ia·ry /awg zíllyəree, -zílləree/ *adj.* **1. GIVING SUPPORT** acting to support or supplement a group of people **2. HELD IN RESERVE** available as backup for a system, process, or piece of equipment **3. SECONDARY** secondary to something larger **4.** NAUT **WITH MOTOR AND SAILS** used to describe a boat with an engine to supplement or replace the sails ■ *n.* (*plural* **-ries**) **1.** HR **SUPPORTING PERSON OR THING** somebody who or something that acts in a supporting, backup, or supplementary role **2.** GRAM = **auxiliary verb 3.** MIL **MEMBER OF SUPPORTING TROOPS** a member of a foreign troop that fights with an army as allies or mercenaries and has its own command structure (*often used in the plural*) **4.** NAUT **SAILING SHIP WITH ENGINE** a sailing ship equipped with an engine **5.** NAVY **NAVAL SUPPORT VESSEL** a naval vessel, e.g., a tug or transport ship, that does not engage in combat [Early 17thC. From Latin *auxiliarius*, from *auxilium* "help, assistance."]

aux·il·ia·ry lan·guage *n.* a language, e.g., English, Esperanto, or Kiswahili, that is used by speakers of other languages in order to communicate

aux·il·ia·ry note *n.* MUSIC a note that falls between two adjacent notes of the same pitch and is not an overtone

aux·il·ia·ry ro·tor *n.* the tail rotor of a helicopter

aux·il·ia·ry verb *n.* a verb that is used with another verb to indicate person, number, mood, tense, or aspect. Some auxiliary verbs in English are "be," "have," "will," and "do."

WORD KEY: USAGE

Auxiliary verb The auxiliary verbs are *be, do,* and *have,* which together with the so-called modal (or modal auxiliary) verbs *can, may, shall, should, will,* and *would* are used with other verbs to form past and future tenses, negatives, questions, the passive voice, and other special functions. Most ordinary verbs cannot fulfill these functions by themselves; for example, you have to use the auxiliary verb *do* to form negatives and questions (*They don't like it. Do you want to leave?*), the auxiliary verbs *be* and *have* to form past tenses (*We were leaving. They haven't decided.*), and the modal verbs *shall* and *will* to form future tenses (*He will drive you to the station. Shall we go now?*). Sometimes more than one auxiliary verb is used to form a tense, as in *We will be going* and *They have been paid.* The verb *be* is used to form the passive voice: *The letter was posted last night.* See also the note at ***modal.***

aux·in /áwksən/ *n.* a natural plant hormone or synthetic substance that affects growth and the development of shoots, roots, fruit, and flowers [Mid-20thC. Coined from Greek *auxein* "to increase" + -IN.] —**aux·in·ic** /awk sínnik/ *adj.* —**aux·in·i·cal·ly** /-iklee/ *adv.*

aux·o·ton·ic /àwksə tónnik/ *adj.* occurring against increasing force as part of a muscle contraction [Coined from Greek *auxein* "to increase" + TONIC]

aux·o·troph /áwksə trof/ *n.* a mutant strain of an organism, e.g., a bacterium, that has lost the ability to synthesize a particular nutrient **(growth factor)** and must obtain it from its environment to survive. ◊ **prototroph** [Mid-20thC. Back-formation from AUXOTROPHIC.]

aux·o·troph·ic /àwksə tróffik/ *adj.* used to describe a mutant strain of an organism, e.g., a bacterium, that has lost the ability to synthesize a particular nutrient **(growth factor)** and must obtain it from its environment to survive [Mid-20thC. Coined from Greek *auxein* "to increase" + -TROPHIC.]

Au·yu·it·tuq Na·tion·al Park /áuyoo ée̱t-k-/ Canada's first national park north of the Arctic Circle, located on eastern Baffin Island in Nunavut Territory. Area: 8,289 sq. mi./21,469 sq. km.

Av /aav/, **Ab** /aab/ *n.* in the Jewish calendar, the eleventh month of the civil year and the fifth month of the religious year, falling in approximately July to August. It is thirty days long. [Late 18thC. From Hebrew *āḇ.*]

AV *abbr.* **1.** COMMUNICATION audiovisual **2. AV, A.V.** BIBLE Authorized Version

av. *abbr.* **1. av., Av.** avenue **2.** average **3.** MEASURE avoirdupois

A/V, a/v, a.v. *abbr.* FIN ad valorem

av·a·da·vat /àvədə vàt/ *n.* an Asian waxbill often kept as a cagebird. The male of one species is green and the male of the other species is red. Genus: *Estrilda.* [Late 17thC. Alteration of *Ahmadabad,* a city in western India where these birds were sold.]

a·vail /ə váyl/ *v.* (**a·vailed, a·vail·ing, a·vails**) **1.** *vr.* **USE SOMETHING** to make use of something useful or helpful while you have the opportunity **2.** *vti.* **HELP** to be helpful or useful to somebody or to help somebody succeed ■ *n.* **HELP OR ADVANTAGE** help, advantage, or success in achieving something (*used in negative statements*) ○ *His defense was of no avail, a conviction was secured.* ■ **a·vails** *npl.* BUSINESS **PROFITS** profits or proceeds from something (*archaic*) [14thC. Formed from Old French *vail-,* the stem of *valoir* "to be worth" (source of English *valor* and *value*), from Latin *valere* "to be strong."]

a·vail·a·ble /ə váyləb'l/ *adj.* **1. ABLE TO BE GOTTEN** able to be used or obtained, or spoken to or consulted **2.** POL **ELIGIBLE FOR OFFICE** eligible and willing to undertake a public office or run for election **3. UNATTACHED** not currently involved in a romantic or sexual relationship but ready to engage in one (*informal*) [15thC. Originally, the word meant "effective, useful"; the underlying sense is "possible or suitable to avail yourself of."] —**a·vail·a·bil·i·ty** /ə vàylə bíllətee/ *n.* —**a·vail·a·bly** /ə váylablee/ *adv.*

av·a·lanche /ávə lanch/ *n.* **1. DOWNHILL FALL OF SNOW** a rapid downhill flow of a large mass of snow or ice dislodged from a mountainside or the top of a precipice, or a similar fall of rocks and earth **2. OVERWHELMING QUANTITY** a sudden overwhelming quantity of something **3.** PHYS **INCREASE IN NUMBER OF IONS** an increase in the number of ions or electrons, usually within a medium exposed to an applied electromagnetic field, caused by collisions of the ions or electrons with the medium ■ *vti.* (**-lanched, -lanch·ing, -lanch·es**) **FLOW DOWN IN LARGE QUANTITY** to descend in a large mass on something or somebody [Late 18thC. Via French from Romansh *avalantze,* from, ultimately, assumed Vulgar Latin *labanca,* of unknown origin.]

av·a·lanche lil·y (*plural* **av·a·lanche lil·ies**) *n.* a North American lily that grows on mountains near the snowline and has white or yellow flowers. Genus: *Erythronium.*

Av·a·lon /ávə lon/ *n.* in Celtic mythology, an island paradise in the West. In the legend of King Arthur, he is said to have been taken to Avalon after being apparently mortally wounded.

a·vant-garde /àavaan gaárd/ *n.* **ARTISTS WITH NEW IDEAS AND METHODS** writers, artists, film makers, or musicians whose work is innovative, experimental, or unconventional ■ *adj.* **1. ARTISTICALLY NEW** artistically new, experimental, or unconventional **2. OF THE AVANT-GARDE** belonging to the artistically innovative [Early 20thC. From French, literally "before the guard" (see VANGUARD).] —**a·vant-gard·ism** *n.* —**a·vant-gard·ist** *n.*

Avar /aá vaar/ *n.* a language of the Caucasian family spoken in the Dagestan republic of Russia —**Avar** *adj.*

av·a·rice /ávvərəs/ *n.* an unreasonably strong desire to obtain and keep money [13thC. Via French from Latin *avaritia,* from *avarus* "greedy," from *avere* "to desire" (source of English *avid*).]

av·a·ri·cious /àvvə ríshəs/ *adj.* showing an unreasonably strong desire for money —**av·a·ri·cious·ly** *adv.* —**av·a·ri·cious·ness** *n.*

a·vas·cu·lar /ay váskyələr/ *adj.* lacking blood vessels in body tissue —**a·vas·cu·lar·i·ty** /ay vàskyə lérrətee/ *n.*

a·vast /ə vást/ *interj.* used by sailors as a command to stop doing something or to ignore a previous order [Early 17thC. Alteration of Dutch *hou'vast,* shortening of *houd vast,* literally "hold fast."]

av·a·tar /ávvə taar/ *n.* **1. INCARNATION OF HINDU GOD** an incarnation of a Hindu god in human or animal form, especially one of the incarnations of Vishnu such as Rama and Krishna **2. EMBODIMENT OF SOMETHING** somebody who embodies, personifies, or is the manifestation of an idea or concept **3.** COMPUT **IMAGE OF PERSON IN VIRTUAL REALITY** a movable three-dimensional image that can be used to represent somebody in cyberspace, e.g., an Internet user [Late 18thC. From Sanskrit *avatāra* "descent," referring to the descent of a god to earth.]

a·vaunt /ə váwnt/ *interj.* used as a command to go away, especially to an evil spirit (*archaic*) [14thC. From French *avant* "forward," from Latin *ante* "before."]

avdp. *abbr.* avoirdupois

a·ve /aá vày/, **A·ve** *interj., n.* = **Hail Mary** ■ *interj.* **GREETING OR FAREWELL** used as a greeting or farewell (*archaic*) ■ *n.* **1. TIME FOR PRAYER** the time when the Hail Mary is to be said, marked by the ringing of a bell **2. ROSARY BEAD** a small bead on a rosary, used for keeping track of how many times the Hail Mary has been said [13thC. From Latin, imperative of *avere* "to be or fare well."]

Ave., ave. *abbr.* avenue

A·ve·don /ávvə dòn/, **Richard** (*b.* 1923) U.S. photographer. He is best known for his pictures of political and literary figures and celebrities.

A·ve Ma·ri·a, a·ve, A·ve *n.* = **Hail Mary** [13thC. From the Latin original of the HAIL MARY.]

a·venge /ə vénj/ (**a·venged, a·veng·ing, a·veng·es**) *vt.* to inflict punishment on somebody for a wrong done, or retaliate on behalf of somebody else [14thC. From Old French *avengier,* from *vengier* (see VENGEANCE).] —**a·veng·er** *n.* —**a·veng·ing** *adj.* —**a·veng·ing·ly** *adv.*

WORD KEY: USAGE

avenge or **revenge**? Both words are about repaying a wrong, and the differences between them have more to do with grammar than meaning. ***Avenge*** is a verb only whereas ***revenge*** is a verb and (more usually, in fact) a noun. But as a verb ***avenge*** is more versatile than ***revenge***: you can ***avenge*** a person (including yourself but more usually somebody else) or an act but you can only ***revenge*** an act or yourself (in an awkward construction with *on*). The possibilities therefore are: *They took revenge on their enemies. We revenged ourselves on our enemies. We will revenge the wrong done to us. They avenged the wrong done to them. He avenged his murdered brother.*

av·ens /ávvənz/ (*plural* **-ens**) *n.* = **mountain avens** [12thC. From Old French *avence,* of unknown origin.]

a·ven·tu·rine /ə vénchə reen, -rin/, **a·ven·tu·rin** /-rin/ *n.* **1.** CRAFT **GLASS CONTAINING SHINY PARTICLES** dark brown or green glass that contains sparkling mineral particles **2.** MINERALS **MINERAL CONTAINING SHINY PARTICLES** feldspar or quartz containing minute particles of iron compounds or, in some of the quartz types, mica [Early 18thC. Via French from Italian *avventurino* "chance" (because it was discovered accidentally).]

av·e·nue /ávvə noo/ *n.* **1.** TRANSP **WIDE STREET** a wide street or road in a town **2. MEANS OF APPROACH** a course of action to be taken in order to approach, attain, or gain access to somebody or something ○ *need to explore all avenues* [Early 17thC. From French, literally "approach," feminine past participle of *avenir* "to arrive," from Latin *advenire* (see ADVENT).]

a·ver /ə vúr/ (**a·verred, a·verr·ing, a·vers**) *vt.* **1. ASSERT CONFIDENTLY** to assert or allege something confidently (*formal*) **2.** LAW **ALLEGE** to state or allege that something is true [14thC. Via French *avérer* from, ultimately, Latin *verus* "true" (source of English *veracity, verify,* and *very*).] —**a·ver·ment** *n.* —**a·ver·ra·ble** *adj.*

av·er·age /ávvərij, ávrij/ *n.* **1. TYPICAL AMOUNT** the level, amount, or degree of something that is typical of a group or class of people or things **2.** MATH **NUMBER CONSIDERED TYPICAL OF NUMBER GROUP** a number that can be regarded as typical of a group of numbers, calculated by adding the numbers together, then dividing the total by the amount of numbers **3.** SPORTS **MEASURE OF PLAYING PERFORMANCE** a measure of a player's or team's achievement, reached by dividing the number of opportunities for successful performances by how many times a successful performance was achieved **4.** STOCK EXCH **INTERMEDIATE PRICE** a measure of stock exchange performance, based on the total of prices for a group or class of securities, divided by the number of securities **5.** LAW **LOSS AT SEA** in maritime law, the loss or damage of a ship and its cargo, or the division of the costs of this loss or damage among the owner or partners involved ■ *adj.* **1. TYPICAL** without any extraordinary, untypical, or exceptional characteristic ○ *just an average guy* **2.** MATH **CALCULATED AS TOTAL DIVIDED BY MEMBERS** obtained by adding the numerical value for each member or part of a group or class and dividing the total by the number of members **3. NOT VERY GOOD** not terrible but not very good either ○ *The performance was no better than average.* ■ *vt.* (**-aged, -ag·ing, -ag·es**) **1.** MATH **CALCULATE NUMERICAL AVERAGE** to calculate a numerical average of something, by finding the total amount and dividing it by the number of members in the group **2. HAVE AS AVERAGE** to have or show as an average **3. ACHIEVE OR GET AS AVERAGE** to do, produce, or receive a particular amount of something as an average ○ *She averages one trip to Asia each year.* [15thC. Alteration, modeled on DAMAGE, of French *avarie,* from, ultimately, Arabic *'awār* "damage to goods."] —**av·er·age·ly** *adv.* —**av·er·age·ness** *n.*

average down *vi.* to purchase more shares of a stock when its price is falling, in the hope of reducing costs and increasing profits

average out *v.* **1.** *vi.* **HAVE AS AVERAGE** to have or show as an average **2.** *vt.* MATH **CALCULATE AVERAGE** to calculate the numerical average of something

average up *vi.* to purchase more shares of a stock when its price is rising, in the hope of increasing profits

av·er·age de·vi·a·tion *n.* STATS = **mean deviation**

a·verse /ə vúrs/ *adj.* **1.** **OPPOSED TO SOMETHING** strongly opposed to or disliking something (*formal*) ○ *The board is not averse to the idea of further talks.* ○ *risk-averse* **2.** BOT **TURNED AWAY FROM STEM** used to describe a leaf or flower that is turned away from the main stem or axis [Late 16thC. From Latin *aversus*, literally "turned away," past participle of *avertere* (see AVERT).] —**a·verse·ness** *n.*

WORD KEY: USAGE

See Usage note at ***adverse***.

WORD KEY: SYNONYMS

See Synonyms at ***unwilling***.

a·ver·sion /ə vúrzh'n/ *n.* **1.** **STRONG DISLIKE** a strong feeling of dislike or hatred of somebody or something (*formal*) **2.** **SOMEBODY OR SOMETHING DISLIKED** somebody or something strongly disliked

WORD KEY: SYNONYMS

See Synonyms at ***dislike***.

a·ver·sion ther·a·py *n.* **1.** **THERAPY GIVING CERTAIN BEHAVIOR UNPLEASANT CONSEQUENCES** a method of therapy that attempts to eliminate undesired behavior by associating it repeatedly with painful or unpleasant effects **2.** **THERAPY TO OVERCOME FEARS OR DISLIKES** therapy aimed at eliminating an irrational fear or dislike by making somebody experience the thing feared or disliked in remote or indirect ways that gradually become closer and more direct

a·ver·sive /ə vúrsiv/ *adj.* inducing dislike or loathing of something —**a·ver·sive·ly** *adv.* —**aver·sive·ness** *n.*

a·vert /ə vúrt/ (**a·vert·ed, a·vert·ing, a·verts**) *vt.* **1.** **PREVENT SOMETHING FROM HAPPENING** to prevent something from occurring, especially something harmful **2.** **LOOK AWAY** to turn your eyes away from something [14thC. Via Old French from Latin *avertere* "to turn away," from *vertere* "to turn" (see VERSE), evolving from "to turn someone away."] —**a·vert·i·ble** *adj.*

A·ver·y /áyvəree/, **Milton Clark** (1895–1965) U.S. artist. His work typically uses broad sections of color on large canvases.

A·ves·ta /ə véstə/ *n.* the sacred book of the Zoroastrian religion [Early 16thC. From Middle Persian *Avastāk*, literally "original text."]

A·ves·tan /ə véstən/, **A·ves·tic** /ə véstik/ *n.* an ancient language once spoken in various parts of the Middle East. It belongs to the Iranian group of languages. The sacred writings of the Zoroastrians are written in Avestan. [Mid-19thC. Formed from AVESTA.] —**A·ves·tan** *adj.*

avg. *abbr.* average

a·vi·an /áyvee ən/ *adj.* belonging to, relating to, or characteristic of birds [Late 19thC. Formed from Latin *avis* "bird" (source of English *augur* and *inaugurate*).]

a·vi·ar·y /áyvee erree/ (*plural* **-ies**) *n.* an enclosure or large cage where birds are kept [Late 16thC. From Latin *aviarium*, from *avis* (see AVIAN).]

a·vi·a·tion /àyvee áysh'n/ *n.* the design, manufacture, use, or operation of aircraft [Mid-19thC. From French, formed from Latin *avis* "bird" (see AVIAN).]

a·vi·a·tion med·i·cine *n.* the branch of medicine concerned with the physical and psychological effects of flying in aircraft

a·vi·a·tor /áyvee àytər/ *n.* the pilot of an aircraft

a·vi·a·tor glass·es *npl.* eyeglasses with oval tinted lenses and a metal frame

a·vi·cul·ture /áyvi kùlchər, ávvi kùlchər/ *n.* the care and rearing of birds in cages, aviaries, or enclosures [Late 19thC. Coined from Latin *avis* "bird" + CULTURE.] —**a·vi·cul·tur·ist** *n.*

av·id /ávvid/ *adj.* eager for, dedicated to, or enthusiastic about something [Mid-18thC. Back-formation from AVIDITY.] —**av·id·ly** *adv.*

av·i·din /ávvədən/ *n.* a protein found in egg white that inactivates the vitamin biotin by binding with it but that loses its ability to bind when subjected to heat [Mid-20thC. Formed from AVID, because of its "avidity" for BIOTIN.]

a·vid·i·ty /ə víddətee/ *n.* **1.** **EAGERNESS OR GREED** great eagerness or greed for something **2.** CHEM = **affinity** **3.** BIOL **STRENGTH OF ANTIGEN-ANTIBODY BINDING** a measure of the strength with which an antibody binds to an antigen [15thC. Via French from Latin *avidus*, from *avere* "to desire" (source of English *avarice*).]

a·vi·fau·na /áyvə fáwnə, àvvə-/ (*plural* **a·vi·fau·nas** *or* **a·fvi·fau·nae** /-fáwnee/) *n.* all the birds present in a region, environment, or period of time [Late 19thC. Coined from Latin *avis* "bird" + FAUNA.] —**a·vi·fau·nal** *adj.*

A·vi·gnon /àavi nyáwN/ capital of the Vaucluse Department in the Provence-Alpes-Côte d'Azur Region in southeastern France. Population: 89,440 (1990).

a·vi·on·ics /àyvee ónniks/ *n.* **TECHNOLOGY APPLIED TO AIRCRAFT AND SPACECRAFT** the development and use of electric and electronic equipment for aircraft and spacecraft (*takes a singular verb*) ■ *npl.* **PLANE OR SPACECRAFT TECHNOLOGICAL DEVICES** the electrical and electronic equipment of an aircraft or spacecraft (*takes a plural verb*) [Mid-20thC. A blend of AVIATION and ELECTRONICS.] —**a·vi·on·ic** *adj.*

a·vir·u·lent /ay vírrələnt, -ryələnt/ *adj.* used to describe microorganisms that are not likely to cause disease in another organism —**a·vir·u·lence** *n.*

a·vi·ta·min·o·sis /ày vītəmə nṓssəss/ (*plural* **-ses** /-seez/) *n.* a disease caused by deficiency of a particular vitamin —**a·vi·ta·min·ot·ic** /-nóttik/ *adj.*

A·viv /ə veév/ *n.* JUDAISM = **Nisan**

avn. *abbr.* aviation

a·vo /ávvoo/ (*plural* **a·vos**) *n.* a subunit of currency in Macao. See table at **currency** [Early 20thC. From Portuguese, shortened from *oitavo* "eighth," from Latin *octavus* (source of English *octave*), from *octo* "eight."]

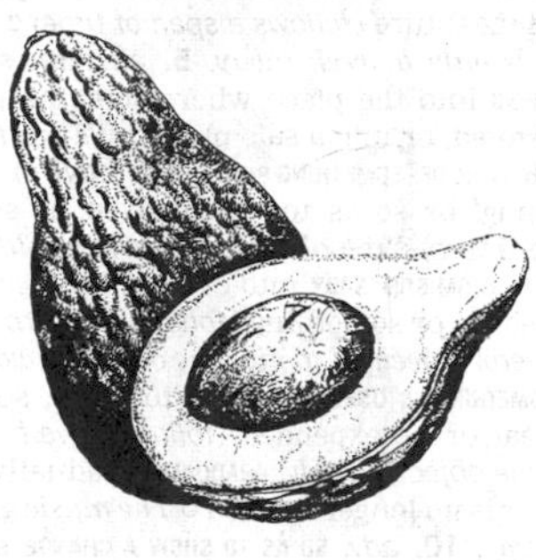

Avocado

av·o·ca·do /àvvə kaádō, aàvə-/ *n.* (*plural* **-dos**) **1.** **av·o·ca·do, av·o·ca·do pear** **GREEN-FLESHED EDIBLE FRUIT** a fruit with a leathery dark green or blackish skin with a soft, smooth-tasting, pale green flesh and a large stony seed, eaten raw in salads or dips **2.** **TREE ON WHICH AVOCADOS GROW** a tropical tree that bears avocados. Latin name: *Persea americana.* **3.** **CREAMY GREEN** a dull creamy green color, like that of the flesh of an avocado ■ *adj.* **OF CREAMY GREEN COLOR** of a dull creamy green color, like the flesh of an avocado [Mid-17thC. From Spanish, an alteration (influenced by *avocado* "lawyer") of *aguacate*, from Nahuatl *ahuacatl*, literally "testicle" (because of the shape of the fruit).]

av·o·ca·tion /àvvə káysh'n/ *n.* **1.** **OCCUPATION** a calling or occupation (*formal*) **2.** **HOBBY** a hobby or pastime (*formal*) **3.** **DISTRACTION** something that distracts or diverts somebody from what he or she is doing (*archaic*) [Early 17thC. From Latin, "distraction," from, ultimately *vocare* "to call" (see VOCATION).] —**av·o·ca·tion·al** *adj.* —**av·o·ca·tion·al·ly** *adv.*

av·o·cet /ávvə set/ *n.* a shore bird with black and white plumage, long legs, and a long slender upward-curving beak. Genus: *Recurvirostra.* [Late 17thC. Via French *avocette* from Italian *avosetta*.]

Avocet

A·vo·ga·dro /àavə gaá drō/, **Amedeo, Conte di Quaregna e Ceretto** (1776–1856) Italian physicist and chemist who formulated Avogadro's law. Full name **Lorenzo Romano Amedeo Carlo Avogadro**

A·vo·ga·dro's law *n.* a principle in physics stating that equal volumes of different gases at the same temperature and pressure contain the same number of molecules [Late 19thC. Named for Amedeo AVOGADRO.]

A·vo·ga·dro's num·ber, **A·vo·ga·dro's con·stant** *n.* the number of atoms or molecules, 6.023×10^{23}, contained in one mole of a substance. Symbol **N** [Late 19thC. Named for Amedeo AVOGADRO.]

a·void /ə vóyd/ (**a·void·ed, a·void·ing, a·voids**) *v.* **1.** *vt.* **NOT GO NEAR** to keep away from somebody or something ○ *a place to be avoided* **2.** *vti.* **NOT DO SOMETHING OR PREVENT SOMETHING** to manage not to do something or to stop something from happening ○ *I narrowly avoided colliding with it.* **3.** *vt.* LAW **STATE SOMETHING IS NOT VALID** to say that something is void or invalid [14thC. Via Anglo-Norman from, ultimately, Old French *vuide* "empty" (see VOID).] —**a·void·a·ble** *adj.* —**a·void·a·bly** *adv.* —**a·void·er** *n.*

WORD KEY: USAGE

avoid, evade, or **elude**? All three words involve keeping away from somebody or something or keeping somebody or something away from you. The main difference between ***avoid*** and ***evade*** is that ***avoid*** is neutral in tone whereas ***evade*** implies dishonesty or deception, or at least some sort of ulterior motive. If you avoid a responsibility, you take measures to prevent it being necessary, whereas if you evade a responsibility you get out of it in an underhand or deceitful way when the necessity is still there. ***Avoid*** can be followed by a verbal noun in *-ing*, whereas ***evade*** must be followed by an ordinary noun: *We avoided having to pay. We evaded payment.* ***Elude*** implies clever or ingenious avoidance without it being devious or wrong. It also has the special meaning of "escape," as in *Her name eludes me.*

WORD KEY: SYNONYMS

See Synonyms at ***escape***

a·void·ance /ə vóyd'ns/ *n.* **1.** **ACT OF KEEPING AWAY** the act of staying away from somebody or something **2.** **ACT OF NOT DOING SOMETHING** the act of refraining from doing something or preventing something from happening or applying **3.** LAW **ACT OF MAKING SOMETHING INVALID** the act of making something void or invalid

WORD KEY: USAGE

avoidance or **evasion**? The difference corresponds to the difference between ***avoid*** and ***evade***. In particular, **tax avoidance** means a legal method, whereas **tax evasion** means an illegal method, of reducing a liability to pay taxes.

av·oir·du·pois /àvvər də póyz/ *n.* **1.** MEASURE = **avoirdupois weight** **2.** **SOMEBODY'S WEIGHT** the amount that somebody weighs (*humorous*) [14thC. From Old French *aveir de peis*, literally "goods of weight." The word originally denoted merchandise sold by weight, hence the system used to weigh them.]

av·oir·du·pois weight, **av·oir·du·pois** *n.* a system for measuring weights based on the pound

A·von /áy vòn, -vən/ city in northcentral Connecticut. It lies on the Farmington River, northwest of Hartford. Population: 13,833 (1996).

a·vouch /ə vówch/ (**a·vouched, a·vouch·ing, a·vouch·es**) *vt.* to acknowledge, guarantee, or confirm that something is true (*archaic*) [15thC. Via Old French *avochier* from Latin *advocare* (see AVOW).]

a·vow /ə vów/ (**a·vowed, a·vow·ing, a·vows**) *vt.* to state or affirm that something is a fact (*formal*) [13thC. Via Old French *avouer* "to acknowledge" from Latin *advocare* "to summon" (see ADVOCATE).] —**a·vow·a·ble** *adj.* —**a·vow·a·bly** *adv.* —**a·vow·ed·ly** /ə vówədlee/ *adv.*

a·vow·al /ə vów əl/ *n.* a frank statement or admission (*formal*)

a·vul·sion /ə vúlsh'n/ *n.* **1.** MED **SEPARATION OF BODY PART** the tearing away or separation of part of the body, resulting from an accident or performed during surgery **2.** LAW **REMOVAL OF SOIL** the removal of soil from one person's land to another's, especially by a flood [Early 17thC. Directly or via French from the Latin stem *avulsion-*, from, ultimately, *vellere* "to pull" (source of English *convulse* and *svelte*).]

a·vun·cu·lar /ə vúng kyələr/ *adj.* **1. LIKE AN UNCLE** resembling an uncle, especially one who is friendly, helpful, or good-humored **2. OF AN UNCLE** relating to or deriving from an uncle (*formal or humorous*) [Mid-19thC. Formed from Latin *avunculus* "maternal uncle," literally "little uncle" (see UNCLE).] —**a·vun·cu·lar·i·ty** /ə vùng kyə lérratee/ *n.* —**a·vun·cu·lar·ly** /-kyələrlee/ *adv.*

a·vun·cu·late /ə vúng kyələt/ *n.* in some patrilineal societies, a special relationship similar to that of father and son that exists between a man and his sister's sons —**avunculate** *adj.*

aw /aw/ *interj. U.S. Scotland* used to express surprise, disappointment, or pity (*informal*) [Mid-19thC. Natural exclamation.]

a.w. *abbr.* **1. a.w., A/W** MEASURE actual weight **2.** MEASURE, PHYS atomic weight **3.** NAUT all water

AWACS /áy waks/ *n.* a radar and computer system carried in an aircraft to track large numbers of low-flying aircraft [Acronym formed from *airborne warning and control system*]

a·wait /ə wáyt/ (**a·wait·ed, a·wait·ing, a·waits**) *v.* **1.** *vti.* **WAIT FOR SOMETHING** to expect or be looking for somebody or something **2.** *vt.* **BE WAITING FOR SOMEBODY** to be going to happen or be given to somebody ○ *"Where we find a difficulty we may always expect that a discovery awaits us."* (C. S. Lewis, *Reflections on the Psalms*; 1961) [13thC. Via Anglo-Norman *awaitier*, from, ultimately, Old French *guaitier*, from a prehistoric Germanic base that is also the ancestor of English *wake*.]

a·wake /ə wáyk/ *adj.* **1. NOT ASLEEP** fully conscious and not asleep **2. ALERT** alert and vigilant about what is going on all around ○ *"The color had come back to his face, and his eyes were clear, and fully awake and aware."* (J. R. R. Tolkien, *The Fellowship of the Ring*; 1954) **3. AWARE OF SOMETHING** fully aware of something or alert to it ■ *vti.* (**a·woke** /ə wṓk/ *or* **a·waked, a·waked** *or* **a·wok·en** /ə wṓkən/, **a·wak·ing, a·wakes**) **1. EMERGE FROM SLEEP** to rouse somebody or be roused from sleep **2. BECOME OR MAKE SOMEBODY AWARE** to become or make somebody become alert to something **3. AROUSE SOMEBODY** to arouse yourself or somebody else from a dazed or dreamlike state **4. AROUSE FEELINGS** to arouse feelings or memories [Old English *āwæcnan*, from two Old English verbs, *wacian* "to be awake" and assumed *wacen* "to wake up," both ancestors of English *wake*[1]]

a·wak·en /ə wáyk'n/ (**-ened, -en·ing, -ens**) *vti.* to wake up from a state of sleep or a state likened to sleep [Old English *āwæcnian*, from *wæcnan* "to waken"] —**a·wak·en·er** *n.*

a·wak·en·ing /ə wáykəning/ *adj.* **JUST BEGINNING** just beginning or growing ■ *n.* **1. AROUSAL FROM SLEEP** the act or process of waking from sleep **2. RENEWED ATTENTION TO SOMETHING** a revival or renewal of interest in something, especially religion **3. SUDDEN AWARENESS** a sudden recognition or realization of something

a·ward /ə wáwrd/ *n.* **1. SOMETHING GIVEN FOR ACHIEVEMENT** something, e.g., a prize, that is given in recognition of somebody's merit or an achievement **2.** LAW **SOMETHING GRANTED BY LAW COURT** something bestowed, granted, or assigned to somebody by a court of law or by arbitration ■ *vt.* (**a·ward·ed, a·ward·ing, a·wards**) **1. GIVE SOMETHING FOR MERIT** to give somebody something in recognition of merit **2.** LAW **BESTOW AS RESULT OF COURT'S DECISION** to bestow or grant something by a judicial decision or by arbitration [14thC. Via Anglo-Norman, "to decide a legal case," from, ultimately, Old French *warder* "to judge," from a prehistoric Germanic base that is also the ancestor of English *warden*.] —**a·ward·a·ble** *adj.* —**a·ward·er** *n.*

a·ward·ee /ə wàwr dée/ *n.* somebody who receives an award by a judicial decision or by arbitration

a·ware /ə wáir/ *adj.* **1. KNOWING SOMETHING** having knowledge of something because you have observed it or somebody has told you about it ○ *We are already aware of the problem, and we are dealing with it.* **2. NOTICING OR REALIZING SOMETHING** mindful that something exists because you notice it or realize that it is happening ○ *He became aware of a pain in his left side.* **3. KNOWLEDGEABLE** well-informed about what is going on in the world or about the latest developments in a particular sphere of activity ○ *More financially aware investors were starting to sell their stock.* [Old English *gewær*, literally "very watchful," from *wær* "watchful" (source of English *wary* and *beware*)] —**a·ware·ness** *n.*

WORD KEY: SYNONYMS

aware, conscious, mindful, cognizant, sensible

CORE MEANING: having knowledge of the existence of something

aware the most wide-ranging term, indicating that somebody knows something either intellectually or intuitively; **conscious** having something in the forefront of the mind, often in a slightly troubling way; **mindful** actively attentive, or deliberately keeping something in mind; **cognizant** a formal term indicating that somebody has a special knowledge about something, sometimes because of having made a deliberate effort to find out; **sensible** a formal or literary term for *aware*.

a·wash /ə wósh, ə wáwsh/ *adj.* **1. COVERED IN WATER** covered in water or some other liquid **2. OVERSUPPLIED** having more of something than is desirable or manageable ○ *an office awash with letters of complaint* **3.** SHIPPING **WITH WATER RUNNING OVER THE SIDES** sunk so low that water is able to come in over the sides of the vessel

a·way /ə wáy/ CORE MEANING: an adverb used to indicate that something or somebody moves so as to leave a particular place ○ *I really need to go away for a while.* ○ *The truck drove away leaving us stranded.* ○ *The cat has run away.*

1. *adv.* **UNINVOLVED** separated or far from somebody or something ○ *I try to stay away from trouble.* **2.** *adv.* **IN A DIFFERENT DIRECTION** in a different direction from the one somebody was originally facing or looking in ○ *He turned his face away.* **3.** *adv.* **INTO THE DISTANCE** toward the distance ○ *pine groves stretching away toward the sea* **4.** *adv.* **IN THE FUTURE** at a particular time in the future (*follows a span of time*) ○ *Thanksgiving is only a week away.* **5.** *adv.* **INTO STORAGE OR SAFEKEEPING** into the place where something is normally stored, or into a safe place ○ *We put the silver away.* **6.** *adv.* **OFF SOMETHING** so as to remove or separate something, or so as to be removed or separated (*follows a verb*) ○ *a tool to chip away the old paint* **7.** *adv.* **TO OR FROM SOMEBODY** into or out of the possession of somebody or something (*follows the verb or object of the verb*) ○ *decided to give the old car away* **8.** *adv.* **UNTIL SOMETHING IS USED UP** so as to make something disappear or be expended (*follows a verb and precedes the object*) **9.** *adv.* **GRADUALLY** gradually until it ceases or is no longer noticed ○ *The music gradually died away.* **10.** *adv.* **SO AS TO SHOW A CHANGE** so that a perceptible change from one thing to another occurs ○ *a shift away from heavier taxation* **11.** *adv.* **WITHOUT STOPPING** continuously and usually energetically over a period of time ○ *hammering away in the garage* **12.** *adv.* **SO AS TO SET OUT** so as to be on a trip ○ *hope to get away after breakfast* **13.** *adv., adj.* **IN ANOTHER PLACE** not in the particular place or the place where somebody usually is, especially at home or at work ○ *I'll be away until Thursday.* ○ *She works away from the office.* **14.** *adv., adj.* **IN DISTANCE OR TIME** as measured in distance or time from here (*follows a measure or indication of distance or time*) ○ *He works about 10 minutes away.* ○ *The mountains are not far away.* **15.** *adv., adj.* SPORTS **ON OPPOSING TEAM'S FIELD** played on an opponent's home field ○ *Their next three games will be played away.* ○ *Their away record has been very poor this season.* **16.** *adj.* GOLF **FURTHEST FROM THE HOLE** placed furthest from the hole in a game of golf [Old English *aweg*, from *on weg* "on (your) way." The meaning evolved from "on" (as in "move on") to "from this (or that) place."]

awe /aw/ *n.* **1. MIXTURE OF WONDER AND DREAD** a feeling of amazement and respect mixed with fear that is often coupled with a feeling of personal insignificance or powerlessness ○ *Filled with awe, they gazed at the ruins of the massive temple.* **2. ABILITY TO INSPIRE DREAD** the ability to inspire dread or reverence (*archaic*) ■ *vt.* (**awed, aw·ing, awes**) **CAUSE AWE IN SOMEBODY** to make somebody feel awe (*usually passive*) ○ *The visiting ambassadors were awed by this display of military might.* [13thC. From Old Norse *agi*. Ultimately from an Indo-European word meaning "to be afraid," which is also the source of English *ail*.]

a·weath·er /ə wéthər/ *adv.* SAILING toward the windward side

a·weigh /ə wáy/ *adj.* SAILING hanging clear of the bottom of a body of water ○ *Anchors aweigh!*

awe-in·spir·ing *adj.* so impressive as to make a person feel humble or slightly afraid

aw·en·daw /áwin dàw/ *n. Southern U.S.* spoon bread made from hominy or cornmeal [Named for a South Carolina hamlet in upper Charleston County, inland from Bulls Bay, from a Native American name]

awe·some /áwsəm/ *adj.* **1. IMPRESSIVE AND FRIGHTENING** so impressive or overwhelming as to inspire a strong feeling of admiration or fear ○ *the awesome destructive power of a tornado* **2. EXCELLENT** used as a general term of enthusiastic approval (*hip slang*) ○ *The second track on this CD is totally awesome.* ○ *That's awesome skateboarding!* —**awe·some·ly** *adv.* —**awe·some·ness** *n.*

awe·struck /áw strùk/, **awe·strick·en** /-strìkən/ *adj.* filled with a feeling of awe

aw·ful /áwf'l/ *adj.* **1. EXTREMELY BAD** very bad or unpleasant ○ *an awful smell* **2. CAUSING SHOCK OR SADNESS** extremely shocking, saddening, or unpleasant ○ *an awful accident* **3. NOT VERY WELL** in very poor health ○ *I feel awful this morning.* **4. VERY GREAT** enormous in size, amount, number, or extent (*informal*) ○ *We spent an awful lot of money on furniture.* **5. AWE-INSPIRING** so impressive as to inspire awe (*literary*) ■ *adv.* **EXTREMELY** to an extreme degree or extent (*informal*) ○ *It's awful hot this morning.* [13thC. The original meaning was "awe-inspiring."] —**aw·ful·ness** *n.*

aw·ful·ly /áwflee, -fəlee/ *adv.* **1. VERY** to an extremely great degree ○ *I'm awfully grateful to you for helping me out.* **2. BADLY OR UNPLEASANTLY** in a very bad or unpleasant way ○ *treated them awfully*

a·while /ə hwíl/ *adv.* for a short time (*literary*)

WORD KEY: USAGE

awhile or **a while**? Both expressions are derived from the word **while**, but they have a different role in the sentence. ***Awhile*** is an adverb (*Let us wait awhile*), whereas ***a while*** written as two words is a noun phrase (and is normally preceded by *for*): *I'm going to be away for a while.* Sometimes, however, the word *for* is left out, making ***a while*** look more like an adverbial phrase, although it is still strictly a noun phrase: *We had to wait quite a while.* This use is fairly easy to identify because **while** is qualified in some way, for example, *quite a while* or *a long while.*

a·whirl /ə hwúrl/ *adj.* **1. IN A DIZZY STATE** in a dizzy state of excitement or confusion ○ *Her mind was awhirl with new ideas.* **2. AROUND AND AROUND** moving around and around (*literary*) ○ *red and golden leaves awhirl in the autumn breeze*

awk·ward /áwkwərd/ *adj.* **1. EMBARRASSING** embarrassing and requiring great tact or skill to resolve ○ *I find myself in an awkward situation.* **2. DIFFICULT OR UNCOMFORTABLE TO USE** difficult to use because you have to move your body into an uncomfortable position **3. PERFORMED GRACELESSLY** performed in a way that lacks grace and looks uncomfortable **4. WITHOUT GRACEFUL COORDINATION** lacking physical coordination and grace ○ *an awkward, gangling adolescent* **5. SHYLY UNCOMFORTABLE** shy, uncomfortable, and embarrassed ○ *He was always awkward around kids.* [Mid-16thC. Formed from obsolete *awke* "turned the wrong way" (from Old Norse *afugr* "turned backward") + -WARD.] —**awk·ward·ly** *adv.* —**awk·ward·ness** *n.*

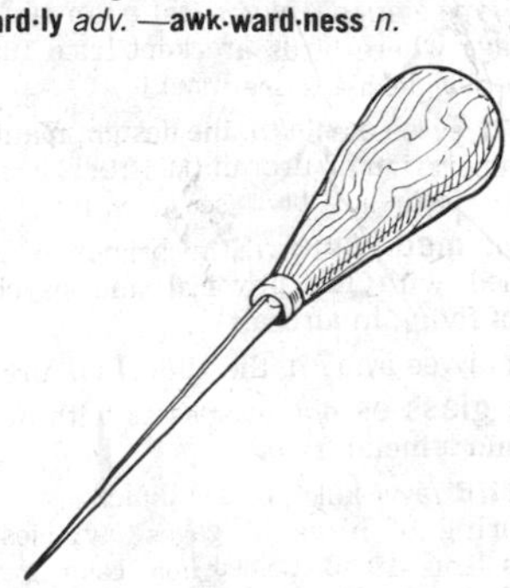

Awl

awl /awl/ *n.* a tool consisting of a handle and a slim metal shaft with a sharp point, used for punching small holes in leather or wood [Old English *æl*, of uncertain origin: perhaps from a non-Indo-European language in Anatolia (Asia Minor)]

awn /awn/ *n.* a stiff bristle projecting from the tip of a plant organ, e.g., from the sheath surrounding a cereal or grass seed [12thC. From the Old Norse stem *agn-* "chaff."] —**awned** *adj.* —**awn·less** /áwnləss/ *adj.*

awn·ing /áwning/ *n.* a plastic, canvas, or metal porch or shade supported by a frame and often foldable, that is placed over a storefront, doorway, window, or side of a recreational vehicle [Early 17thC. Origin uncertain.]

a·woke past tense of **awake**

a·wok·en past participle of **awake**

AWOL /áy wàwl/, **a.w.o.l.** *adj.* **AWAY FROM POSITION WITHOUT PERMISSION** absent from a post, especially a military position assigned, without official permission ■ *n.* MIL **DESERTER** a member of the armed forces who is absent from his or her place of assignment without official permission [From *a(bsent) w(ith)o(ut) l(eave)*]

a·wry /ə rī́/ *adj.* **1. CROOKED** not in the proper position but turned or twisted to one side ○ *The cushions were awry and there was mud on the carpet.* **2. AMISS** not in keeping with plans or expectations ○ *Our plans have gone awry.* [14thC. From the phrase *on wry*, literally "in a twist."]

aw-shucks *adj.* modest, self-conscious, and unsophisticated in a homespun manner (*informal*)

ax /aks/, **axe** *n.* (*plural* **ax·es**) **1. TOOL FOR CUTTING** a tool consisting of a flat heavy metal head with a sharpened edge attached to a long handle, used to chop wood or fell trees **2. JOB LOSS** dismissal from a job (*slang*) ○ *Her secretary got the ax yesterday.* **3. IMMEDIATE CLOSURE** the immediate closure of an institution or the sudden discontinuation of a project or funding (*slang*) ○ *The tractor plant is slated for the ax.* **4.** MUSIC **MUSICAL INSTRUMENT** a musical instrument, specifically a rock guitar or a jazz saxophone (*slang*) ■ *vt.* (**axed, ax·ing, ax·es; axed, ax·ing, ax·es**) **1. TERMINATE SOMETHING** to end something, e.g., a job, a service, or a television program usually without prior warning or discussion (*informal*) (*usually passive*) ○ *In July, the show was axed.* **2. FIRE SOMEBODY** to dismiss somebody from a job, especially abruptly (*informal*) **3. REDUCE SOMETHING DRASTICALLY** to cut something, e.g., expenditures or services, drastically ○ *Most of the welfare provisions were axed from the budget.* [Old English *æcs*. Ultimately from an Indo-European word denoting a cutting or hewing tool.] ◇ **an ax to grind** a personal consideration or motivation, especially one involving a grievance ○ *It was clear from their hostile questioning that certain reporters had an ax to grind on this issue.*

ax. *abbr.* axiom

axe *n.*, *vt.* = **ax**

ax·el /áks'l/ *n.* a figure-skating jump in which the skater takes off from the forward outside edge of one skate, turns in midair, and lands on the rear outside edge of the other skate [Mid-20thC. Named for *Axel* Rudolph Paulser (1885–1938), Norwegian skater.]

Ax·el Hei·berg Is·land /-hī́ burg-/ easternmost and largest Sverdrup Island, west of Ellesmere Island, in Nunavut Territory, Canada. Area: 16,671 sq. mi./43,178 sq. km.

a·xen·ic /ay zénnik, -zéen-/ *adj.* used to describe a culture of an organism that is free from contamination by other living organisms [Mid-20thC. Coined from Greek *a-* "not" + *xenikos* "alien, strange."]

ax·es plural of **axis**[1]

ax·i·al /áksee əl/ *adj.* **1.** GEOM **OF AXIS** relating to or forming an axis **2.** CRYSTALS **LOCATED ALONG PLANE OF AXIS** located on or in the plane of an axis of a crystal **3.** ANAT **OF AXIS OF ORGANISM** located in or relating to the axis of an organism —**ax·i·al·ly** *adv.*

ax·i·al skel·e·ton *n.* the bones that make up the vertebral column and skull

ax·il /áks'l/ *n.* the space between a leaf or branch and the stem to which it is attached [Late 18thC. From Latin *axilla* (see AXILLA).]

ax·ile /ák sīl/ *adj.* used to describe a plant structure that grows along an axis

ax·il·la /ak síllə/ (*plural* **-lae** /-síllee/) *n.* **1.** ANAT = **armpit** (*technical*) **2.** ZOOL **HOLLOW UNDER BIRD'S WING** the hollow underneath the wing of a bird [Early 17thC. From Latin, literally "little wing," from *ala* "wing, upper arm."]

ax·il·lar /ak síllər, áksələr/ *n.* ZOOL a feather growing from the hollow (**axilla**) under a bird's wing

ax·il·lar·y /áksə lérree/ *adj.* **1.** ANAT **OF ARMPIT** relating to or near the armpit **2.** BOT **BETWEEN LEAF OR BRANCH AND STEM** relating to or growing in the space (**axil**) between a leaf or branch and the stem ■ *n.* (*plural* **-ies**) ZOOL = **axillar**

ax·i·nite /áksi nīt/ *n.* a brilliant brown mineral consisting of wedge-shaped crystals of calcium and aluminum borosilicate with some iron and manganese [Early 19thC. Coined from Greek *axinē* "ax" + -ITE.]

ax·i·ol·o·gy /àksee óllәjee/ *n.* the study of the nature, types, and governing criteria of values and value judgments [Early 20thC. From French *axiologie*, from Greek *axia* "value" (see AXIOM).] —**ax·i·o·log·i·cal** /àksee ə lójjik'l/ *adj.* —**ax·i·o·log·i·cal·ly** /-lójjikəlee/ *adv.* —**ax·i·ol·o·gist** /-óllәjist/ *n.*

ax·i·om /áksee əm/ *n.* **1. GENERALLY ACCEPTED TRUTH** a statement or idea that people accept as self-evidently true **2.** MATH, LOGIC **BASIC PROPOSITION ASSUMED TO BE TRUE** a basic proposition of a system that, although unproven, is used to prove the other propositions in the system [15thC. Directly or via French from Latin *axioma*, from Greek *axiōma*, literally "something worthy," from, ultimately, *axios* "weighty, worthy."]

ax·i·o·mat·ic /àksee ə máttik/ *adj.* **1. SELF-EVIDENT** self-evidently true, or universally accepted as being true **2.** MATH, LOGIC **BASED ON AXIOMS** consisting of or based on axioms [Late 18thC. From Greek *axiōmatikos*, from the stem of *axiōma* (see AXIOM).]

ax·is[1] /áksiss/ (*plural* **-es** /ák seez/) *n.* **1.** SCI **LINE AROUND WHICH OBJECT ROTATES** an imaginary straight line around which an object, such as the earth, rotates **2.** GEOM **LINE AROUND WHICH SHAPE IS SYMMETRICAL** a straight line around which a geometric figure or three-dimensional object is symmetrical **3.** GEOM one of two or more lines on which coordinates are measured. Often on a graph two axes form its left and lower margins. **4. ALLIANCE** an alliance or association between two or more people, organizations, or countries that is thought of as forming a center of power or influence ○ *the Paris-Bonn axis* **5.** AIR **LINE DEFINING DIRECTION OF AIRCRAFT** any one of the three mutually perpendicular lines in an aircraft that define its orientation **6.** ANAT **SECOND VERTEBRA IN NECK** the second vertebra in the neck, which acts as the pivot on which the head and first vertebra turn **7.** BOT **CENTRAL PART OF PLANT** the main part of a plant, usually the stem and the root, from which all subsidiary parts develop **8.** OPTICS **LINE PERPENDICULAR TO LENS OR MIRROR** the axis of symmetry of an optical system, especially a line perpendicular to the surface of a lens or mirror **9.** GEOL **LINE AT MAXIMUM CURVATURE** an imaginary line along the crest of an anticline or the trough of a syncline at the point of maximum curvature **10.** CRYSTALS **LINE PASSING THROUGH CRYSTAL** an imaginary line, one of three or four that pass through the center of a crystal and are used to define its symmetry and the arrangement of its atoms [14thC. From Latin, "axle, pivot." Ultimately from an Indo-European word meaning "axis," which is also the ancestor of English *axle*.]

ax·is[2] *n.* = **axis deer** [Early 17thC. From Latin *axis*, an unidentified wild animal in India, of unknown origin.]

Ax·is *n.* the military and political alliance of Germany, Italy, and, later, Japan that fought the Allies in World War II [Mid-20thC. From Mussolini's idea of "an axis around which all European states animated by the will to collaboration and peace can also assemble."]

ax·is deer (*plural* **ax·is deer**), **ax·is** *n.* a deer with a reddish brown, white-spotted coat that lives in India and central Asia. Latin name: *Axis axis.*

ax·i·sym·met·ric /àksi sə méttrik/, **ax·i·sym·met·ri·cal** /-méttrik'l/ *adj.* symmetrical with respect to an axis —**ax·i·sym·met·ri·cal·ly** *adv.*

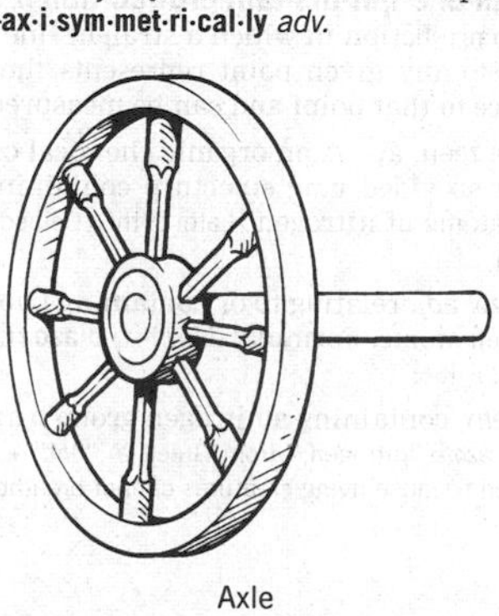

Axle

ax·le /áks'l/ *n.* **1. SHAFT ON WHICH WHEEL TURNS** a shaft on which a wheel or set of wheels revolves, especially a shaft under the body of a vehicle that connects a pair of wheels **2. SPINDLE ON WHICH WHEEL TURNS** the spindle on which one or more wheels revolve [Late 16thC. Shortening of AXLETREE.]

ax·le·tree /áks'l trèe/ *n.* a shaft that runs underneath the body of a vehicle such as a cart or carriage and connects a pair of wheels [13thC. From Old Norse *öxultré*, from *öxull* "axle" + *tré* "tree, beam."]

ax·man /áks màn, -mən/ (*plural* **-men** /-mèn/) *n.* **1. MAN WITH AX** a man who carries or uses an ax as either a tool or a weapon **2.** MUSIC **ROCK OR JAZZ MUSICIAN** a rock guitarist or a jazz saxophone player (*slang*)

Ax·min·ster /áks mìnstər/ *n.* a high-quality carpet with a cut pile that is usually woven into a colorful pattern [Early 19thC. Named for *Axminster*, a town in Devon, southwestern England, where they were originally made.]

ax·o·lem·ma /áksə lémmə/ *n.* the membranous sheath that encloses the long thin extension of a nerve cell (**axon**) [Late 19thC. Coined from Greek *axōn* "axis" + *lemma* "skin, husk."]

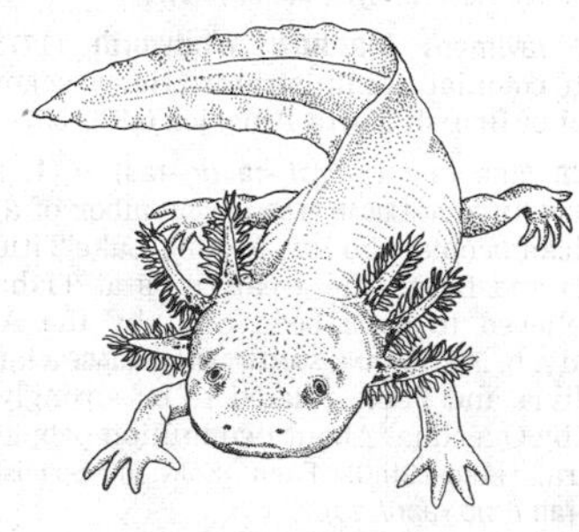

Axolotl

ax·o·lotl /áksə làwt'l/ (*plural* **-lotls** *or* **-lotl**) *n.* an aquatic salamander native to Mexico and the western United States that often retains its external gills as an adult. Genus: *Ambystoma.* [Late 18thC. From Nahuatl, from *atl* "water" + *xolotl* "servant."]

ax·on /ák son/ *n.* an extension of a nerve cell, similar in shape to a thread, that transmits impulses outward from the cell body [Late 19thC. From Greek *axōn* "axis."]

ax·o·neme /áksə neem/ *n.* BIOL a bundle of fibrils that form the central core of a cilium or flagellum. It consists of nine pairs of microtubules surrounding a central pair. [Early 20thC. Coined from Greek *axōn* "axis" + *nēma* "thread."]

ax·o·no·met·ric /àksənə méttrik, àksənō-/ *adj.* used to describe a method of drawing a three-dimensional object so that the vertical and horizontal axes are drawn to scale but the curves and diagonals appear distorted

ax·o·plasm /áksə plàzzəm/ *n.* the cytoplasm of a nerve cell extension (**axon**) —**ax·o·plas·mic** /àksə plázmik/ *adj.*

ay[1] *interj.*, *n.* = **aye**[1]

ay[2] *adv.* = **aye**[2]

a·yah /ī́ ə/ *n.* *S Asia* a maid whose duties include the care of children [Late 18thC. Via Portuguese *aia* "female tutor" from Latin *avia* "grandmother."]

a·ya·tol·lah /ī ə tṓlə/ *n.* a Shiite religious leader in Iran, often one who takes an important political as well as religious role [Mid-20thC. Via Persian from Arabic *'āyatu-llāh* "miraculous sign of God," from *'āya* "sign, miracle" + *allāh* "God."]

aye[1] /ī/, **ay** *interj.* **YES** used to say yes (*regional*) ■ *n.* (*plural* **ayes**) **VOTE OR VOTER IN FAVOR** a vote in favor of a motion, or somebody who casts a vote in favor [Late 16thC. Origin uncertain: perhaps from the pronoun I (at first it was always written as I), or perhaps from AYE[2].]

aye[2] /ī/, **ay** *adv.* always or forever (*archaic or regional*) [13thC. From Old Norse *ei*, *ey*; probably related to English *ever*.]

aye-aye /ī́ ī/ *n.* a small nocturnal primate that lives in trees and is found in Madagascar, and has a long bushy tail, long bony fingers, and teeth resembling those of a rodent. Latin name: *Daubentonia madagascariensis.* [Late 18thC. Via French from Malagasy *aiay*; probably an imitation of its cry.]

Ayers Rock /áyərz-/ former name for **Uluru**

Aye-aye

AYH *abbr.* American Youth Hostels

a·yin /aa yin/ *n.* the 16th letter of the Hebrew alphabet, written as an apostrophe and pronounced approximately like an "o." See table at **alphabet** [Early 19thC. From Hebrew *'ayin,* literally "eye."]

Ayl·mer /áylmər/, **Matthew Whitworth** (1775–1850) British colonial administrator. He was governor general of British North America (1830–35).

Ay·ma·ra /īmə raá/ (*plural* **-ra** *or* **-ras**) *n.* **1.** PEOPLES **MEMBER OF NATIVE AMERICAN PEOPLE** a member of a South American people who live around Lake Titicaca in Bolivia and Peru. The great ruins at Tiahuanaco are believed to have been built by the Aymara around A.D. 500. **2.** LANG **S AMERICAN LANGUAGE** a language of Bolivia and Peru, related to or strongly influenced by Quechua. About two million people speak Aymara. [Mid-19thC. From Bolivian Spanish.] —**Ay·ma·ran** /īmə raán/ *adj.*

A·yur·ved·a /àayər váydə, -véedə/ *n.* an ancient Hindu treatise on the art of healing and prolonging life [Early 20thC. From Sanskrit *āyur-veda* "medicine," literally "science of life," from *āyur-* "life, vital power" + *veda* "knowledge."] —**A·yur·ved·ic** *adj.*

AZ *abbr.* Arizona

az. *abbr.* **1.** ASTRON azimuth **2.** HERALDRY azure

Azalea

a·zal·ea /ə záylyə/ (*plural* **-eas** *or* **-ea**) *n.* a flowering shrub that is widely grown for its large pink, purple, white, yellow, or orange flowers. Some azaleas lose their leaves, while the small varieties of Japanese origin are evergreen. Genus: *Rhododendron.* [Mid-18thC. Via modern Latin from Greek, from *azaleos* "dry" (related to English *ardent, arid,* and *ash*). From the dry soil in which it flourishes, or from its dry brittle wood.]

a·zan /aa zaán/ *n.* the Islamic call to prayer that the muezzin repeats five times a day from the minaret of a mosque [Mid-19thC. From Arabic *"adān"* "announcement."]

A·za·po /ə záppō/ *n.* a Socialist political movement in South Africa [Late 20thC. Acronym formed from *Azanian People's Organization.*]

az·a·thi·o·prine /àzə thī́ ə preen/ *n.* a synthetic drug that suppresses the body's immune responses and is widely used during and after transplant surgery to prevent rejection of the transplanted organ [Mid-20thC. Coined from AZA- + THI- + PURINE.]

a·ze·o·trope /áy zee ə trōp/ *n.* a mixture of liquids that has a different boiling point from any of its components and retains its composition when it is a vapor [Early 20thC. Coined from A- "not" + Greek *zeo-*, the combining form of *zein* "to boil" (source of English *eczema*)+ Greek *-tropos* "turning, changing."] —**a·ze·o·trop·ic** /àyzee ə tróppik/ *adj.* —**a·ze·ot·ro·py** /àyzee óttrəpee/ *n.*

Azerbaijan

A·zer·bai·jan /àzzər bī jaán, -zhaán/ country of southwestern Asia bisected by Armenia. It is surrounded by the Caspian Sea, Russia, Georgia, and Iran. Language: Azeri. Currency: manat. Capital: Baku. Population: 7,797,476 (1997). Area: 33,436 sq. mi./86,600 sq. km. —**A·zer·bai·ja·ni** /àzzər bī jaánee/ *n., adj.*

A·ze·ri /ə záiree/ *n., adj.* LANG the official language of independent Azerbaijan, also spoken in the province of Azerbaijan in northwestern Iran. A Turkic language of the Altaic family, it is spoken by about 14 million people.

az·er·ty /ə zúrtee/, **AZ·ER·TY** *adj.* using the commonest type of computer or typewriter keyboard layout in continental Europe, where the top row of letters, beginning from the left, runs A, Z, E, R, T, Y. ◊ **qwerty**

az·ide /á zīd, áy-/ *n.* any chemical compound containing a group of three adjacent nitrogen atoms. Formula: N_3. [Early 20thC. Coined from AZO- + -IDE.]

a·zi·do·thy·mi·dine /ə zīddō thī́mə deen/ *n.* full form of **AZT**

A·zil·ian /ə zíllee ən/ *n.* a prehistoric culture that existed in Spain and southwestern France from around 10,000 to 8,000 B.C. The distinctive artifacts produced by this culture include flat bone harpoons and painted pebbles. [Late 19thC. Named for Mas d' *Azil* in the French Pyrenees, where a cave containing bone and flint implements was found.]

az·i·muth /ázzəməth/ *n.* **1.** ASTRON **EASTWARD ANGLE TO OBJECT FROM NORTH** the angle measured from north, eastward along the horizon to the point where a vertical circle through a celestial object intersects the horizon **2.** NAVIG **HORIZONTAL ANGLE OF BEARING** the angular distance along the horizon between a point of reference, usually the observer's bearing, and another object [Early 17thC. Via French *azimut* from Arabic *as-samūt*, plural of *as-samt*, literally "the way," from *samt* "way, direction" (see ZENITH).] —**az·i·muth·al** /àzzə múth'l/ *adj.* —**az·i·muth·al·ly** /-múthəlee/ *adv.*

az·i·muth·al e·qui·dis·tant pro·jec·tion *n.* a method of map projection in which a straight line from the center to any given point represents the shortest distance to that point and can be measured to scale

az·ine /á zeen, áy-/ *n.* an organic chemical compound with a six-sided ring structure containing one or more atoms of nitrogen [Late 19thC. Coined from AZO- + -INE.]

az·o /ázzō/ *adj.* relating to or containing two adjacent nitrogen atoms. Formula: -N=N-. ◊ **diazo** [Late 19thC. From AZO-.]

azo- *prefix.* containing a nitrogen group ○ *azole* [From French *azote* "nitrogen," from Greek *a-* "not" + *zōē* "life," so called because living creatures cannot breathe it]

az·o·ben·zene /àzzō bén zeen, àyzō bén zeen/ *n.* a yellow or orange crystalline solid that is used mainly for making dyes. Formula: $C_6H_5N{=}NC_6H_5$.

az·o com·pound *n.* any compound containing two adjacent nitrogen atoms attached to aromatic groups

az·o dye *n.* an artificial dye containing an azo group. Azo dyes, usually orange, yellow, or brown, are derived from amines.

a·zo·ic /ay zṓ ik, ə-/ *adj.* **1.** GEOL, PALEONT **BEFORE THERE WAS LIFE ON EARTH** belonging to a geologic period before the appearance of living organisms on Earth **2.** GEOL **WITHOUT ANY LIFE** without any trace of life or organic remains [Mid-19thC. Formed from Greek *azōos,* literally "without life," from *zōē* "life."]

az·ole /á zōl, áy-/ *n.* an organic chemical compound with a ring structure comprising five linked atoms, of which at least one is nitrogen [Late 19thC. Coined from AZO- + -OLE.]

a·zon·al /ay zṓn'l/ *adj.* **1.** **WITH NO ZONES** not divided into zones **2.** **NOT RESTRICTED TO AN AREA** not restricted to a specific zone or geographic area

a·zon·al soil *n.* a soil with characteristics that are not determined by the climate and vegetation of the area in which it is found, e.g., glacial or volcanic soil

a·zon·ic /ay zónnik, ay zṓnik/ *adj.* = **azonal** *adj.* 2

A·zores /áy zàwrz/ archipelago in the North Atlantic Ocean, west of Portugal, of which it is an autonomous region. There are nine main islands. Capital: Ponta Delgada. Population: 239,900 (1992). Area: 868 sq. mi./2,247 sq. km.

az·o·te·mi·a /àzzə teémee ə/ *n.* = **uremia** [Early 20thC. Coined from obsolete *azote* "nitrogen" (see AZO-) + -EMIA.] —**az·o·te·mic** /àzzə témmik, -teémik/ *adj.*

az·ot·ic /ə zóttik, ə-/ *adj.* relating to or containing nitrogen [Late 18thC. Formed from obsolete *azote* "nitrogen" (see AZO-).]

a·zo·to·bac·ter /ə zṓtə bàktər, ə-/ *n.* a rod-shaped or spherical bacterium found in soil and water that fixes atmospheric nitrogen. Family: Azotobacter. [Early 20thC. From modern Latin, family name, coined from French *azote* "nitrogen" (see AZO-) + *bacterium.*]

AZT *n.* an antiviral drug used in the treatment of AIDS. It works by inhibiting the enzyme reverse transcriptase, which the AIDS virus requires in order to reproduce. Full form **azidothymidine**

Az·tec /áz tèk/ *n.* **1.** PEOPLES **MEMBER OF NATIVE AMERICAN PEOPLE OF MEXICO** a member of a Middle American people whose powerful empire dominated central Mexico during the 14th and 15th centuries. The Spanish, under Cortés, defeated them around 1520. As well as having highly developed artistic, musical, astronomical, and mathematical skills, the Aztecs were excellent engineers and architects. **2.** LANG = **Nahuatl** ■ *adj.* **Az·tec, Az·tec·an** PEOPLES **OF AZTECS** relating to the Aztecs or their culture and civilization [Late 18thC. Via French *Aztèque* or Spanish *Azteca* from Nahuatl *aztecatl* "somebody from Aztlan."]

a·zu·ki bean *n.* = **adzuki bean**

az·ure /ázhər/ *adj.* **1.** **DEEP BLUE IN HUE** deep blue, like the color of a clear sky (*literary*) ○ *the azure depths of the ocean* **2.** HERALDRY **BLUE** colored blue on a coat of arms ■ *n.* (*literary*) **1.** **BLUE SKY** a clear blue sky **2.** **DEEP BLUE HUE** a deep blue color, like that of a clear sky ○ *the azure of her eyes* [13thC. Via Old French *azur* from medieval Latin *azzurum,* from Arabic *al-lāzaward,* literally "the lapis lazuli," from Persian *lāžward* "lapis lazuli" (source of "lazuli" in English *lapis lazuli*).]

az·ur·ite /ázhə rīt/ *n.* a deep blue mineral consisting of a hydrated carbonate of copper. It is a source of copper, and some forms are used as gemstones.

A·zu·sa /ə zóossə/ city in southwestern California. It lies east of Los Angeles, near San Gabriel Canyon. Population: 41,203 (1996).

a·zy·gos /ázzəgəss/ *adj.* occurring as a single muscle or vein rather than as a pair [Mid-17thC. Formed from Greek *azugos,* literally "without yoke," from *zugon* "yoke" (see ZYGOTE).]

Bb

b[1] /bee/ (*plural* **b's**), **B** (*plural* **B's** *or* **Bs**) *n.* **1. 2ND LETTER IN ENGLISH ALPHABET** the second letter and first consonant in the alphabet in modern English, and in other languages that also use the Latin alphabet **2. SOUND OF "B"** the speech sound represented by the letter "b" **3. LETTER "B" WRITTEN** a written representation of the letter "b"

b[2] *abbr.* PHYS **1.** barn **2. b, B** bel

B[1] *n.* **1.** MUSIC **7TH NOTE OF SCALE IN C** the seventh note of a scale in C major **2.** MUSIC **SOMETHING THAT PRODUCES A B** a string, key, or pipe tuned to produce the note B **3.** MUSIC **SCALE BEGINNING ON B** a scale or key that starts on the note B **4.** MUSIC **WRITTEN SYMBOL OF B** a graphic representation of the note B **5.** EDUC **SECOND HIGHEST GRADE** the second highest grade in a series, e.g., an above-average grade for academic work **6.** ANAT **BLOOD TYPE** a type of human blood in the ABO group

B[2] *symbol.* **1.** boron **2.** eleven (*used in hexadecimal notation*) **3.** PHYS magnetic flux density **4.** PHYS baryon number

B[3] *abbr.* bishop

b. *abbr.* **1.** baseman **2. b., B.** MUSIC bass[1] **3. b., B.** MUSIC basso **4.** base **5. b., B.** book **6.** born **7. b., B.** breadth

B. *abbr.* **1.** EDUC bachelor (*used in degree titles*) **2.** FIN baht **3.** FIN balboa **4.** MICROBIOL bacillus **5.** Baumé scale **6.** GEOG Bay (*used on maps*) **7.** MUSIC basso **8.** Bible **9.** FIN bolivar

Ba *symbol.* barium

BA, B.A. *abbr.* **1.** EDUC Bachelor of Arts **2.** BASEBALL batting average

baa /ba, baa/ *vi.* (**baaed, baa·ing, baas**) **BLEAT LIKE SHEEP** to make the long wavering cry characteristic of a sheep or lamb ■ *n.* (*plural* **baas**) **CRY OF SHEEP** the long wavering cry characteristic of a sheep or lamb [Early 16thC. An imitation of the sound.]

Ba·al /báyəl, baal/ (*plural* **-al·im** /báyəlim, baálim/ *or* **-als**) *n.* **1. ANCIENT SEMITIC GOD** any of the fertility or nature gods worshiped by the Canaanites and the Phoenicians, and considered false idols by the ancient Hebrews **2. Ba·al, ba·al FALSE GOD** an idol or false god

Baal·bek /baál bèk, báyəl bèk/ town in eastern Lebanon between the Litani and Asi rivers. It is the site of the ancient ruins of Heliopolis. Population: 15,600 (1995).

baal tesh·u·vah /-tə shoóvə, -choóvə/ (*plural* **baa·lei tesh·u·vah** /bàyə lay-/), **baal tsh·u·va** (*plural* **baa·lei tsh·u·va**) *n.* somebody who returns to Orthodox Jewish practice after having previously abandoned it [From Hebrew, literally "master of return"]

Bab /baab, bab/ *n.* the title of a Persian religious leader, Mirza Ali Muhammad (1819–50), who founded Babism and was executed as a heretic to Islam [Mid-19thC. Via Persian, from Arabic *bāb* "intermediary," literally "gate."]

ba·ba /baábə/ (*plural* **-bas**) *n.* a dessert made of leavened dough soaked in a rum-flavored syrup and baked in a pan [Early 19thC. Via French, from Polish, literally "married (peasant) woman, old woman."]

Ba·bang·i·da /bə báng geedə/, **Ibrahim** (*b.* 1941) Nigerian soldier and politician. He was president of Nigeria from 1985 to 1993.

ba·bas·su /baàbə soó/ (*plural* **-sus** *or* **-su**) *n.* a tall Brazilian palm tree that produces nuts whose oil is used in the manufacture of soap, margarine, cosmetics, and cooking oil. Genus: *Orbignya.* [Early 20thC. From Brazilian Portuguese *babaçú*, from Tupi *ybá* "fruit" + *guasu* "large."]

bab·bitt /bábbit/ *n.* **BEARING** a bearing made of babbitt metal ■ *vt.* (**-bit·ted, -bit·ting, -bitts**) **COVER SURFACE WITH BABBITT METAL** to cover or line a surface with babbitt metal or a similar alloy [Late 19thC. Named for Isaac *Babbitt* (1799–1862), U.S. inventor of the alloy.]

Bab·bitt /bábbit/ *n.* a self-satisfied narrow-minded man who cannot see beyond his own business and social interests ○ *"His name was ... Babbitt, and ... he was nimble in the calling of selling houses for more than people could afford to pay"* (Sinclair Lewis, *Babbitt*; 1922) [Early 20thC. Named for George F. *Babbitt*, the main character in the satirical novel *Babbitt* (1922) by Sinclair Lewis.] —**Bab·bitt·ry** *n.*

Bab·bitt /bábbit/, **Irving** (1865–1933) U.S. humanist and scholar. He was a leader of the New Humanism movement, influential in literary studies in the first decades of the 20th century.

Bab·bitt, Milton (*b.* 1916) U.S. composer. He was a leader in the development of serialism and electronic music. Full name **Milton Byron Babbitt**

bab·bitt met·al *n.* a soft alloy used especially in the manufacture of antifriction bearings. It originally consisted of tin, copper, and antimony, but now often contains lead. [Named for its U.S. inventor, Isaac *Babbitt* (1799–1862)]

bab·ble /bább'l/ *v.* (**-bled, -bling, -bles**) **1.** *vti.* **SPEAK INCOHERENTLY** to say something rapidly and incoherently without pausing, usually because of excitement or fear ○ *He babbled something about leaving a deposit and then dashed out.* **2.** *vi.* **SPEAK IN AN IRRELEVANT WAY** to talk rapidly or at length in a way people find irrelevant ○ *He babbled on about the importance of some new gadget.* **3.** *vi.* **MURMUR** to make a continuous low murmuring or bubbling sound ○ *a brook babbling through the pasture* **4.** *vti.* **BLURT SOMETHING OUT** to reveal something thoughtlessly or impulsively that is supposed to be secret or confidential ○ *immediately babbled the whole story to the neighbors* ■ *n.* **1. SOUND OF LOUD UNINTELLIGIBLE VOICES** the sound of voices speaking too excitedly and rapidly to be heard properly ○ *the babble of guests in the hallway* **2. FOOLISH TALK** irrelevant chatter **3. SOUND OF RUNNING WATER** the low continuous murmuring or bubbling sound made by water as it flows along [13thC. Origin uncertain; probably from Middle Low German or Middle Dutch *babbelen*, an imitation of the sound, or from a similar formation in English.] —**bab·ble·ment** *n.* —**bab·bler** *n.*

babe /bayb/ *n.* **1. LOVER** used as an affectionate term of address to a lover or somebody you love (*slang*) **2. YOUNG WOMAN CONSIDERED GOOD-LOOKING** an young woman who is considered good-looking (*slang*) **3. BABY** a baby or small child (*literary or archaic*) **4. HANDSOME YOUTH** an attractive young man (*slang*) [14thC. Origin uncertain, probably from obsolete *baban* "baby," ultimately an imitation of childish utterances.] ◇ **a babe in arms** somebody who is innocent and inexperienced ◇ **a babe in the woods** somebody who is naive and trusts other people too easily

ba·bel /bább'l, báyb'l/ *n.* (*literary*) **1. CONFUSED NOISE** a confused noise, especially the noise of loud unintelligible voices all talking at once **2. NOISY PLACE** a scene or place of noisy confusion [Early 16thC. From the TOWER OF BABEL.]

Ba·bel /báyb'l, bább'l/ ➧ **Tower of Babel**

ba·be·si·o·sis /bə beèzee óssiss/, **bab·e·si·a·sis** /bábbi zī́ə siss/ *n.* a disease of humans and animals caused by protozoan infection of red blood cells and transmitted by a tick bite

Ba·bi /baábee/ (*plural* **-bis**) *n.* EASTERN RELIG a follower of the Bab or of Babism [Mid-19thC. Via Persian, from Arabic, formed from *bāb* (see BAB).]

Ba·bin·ski re·flex /bə bìnskee-/, **Ba·bin·ski's re·flex** *n.* a curling upward of the big toe when the sole of the foot is stroked, which is a normal reflex in children up to two years old but indicates disease of the brain or spinal cord in older people [Early 20thC. Named for J. F. F. *Babinski* (1857–1932), French neurologist.]

bab·i·ru·sa /bàbbə roóssə, baàbə-/ (*plural* **-sas** *or* **-sa**), **bab·i·rus·sa** (*plural* **-sas** *or* **-sa**), **bab·i·rou·sa** (*plural* **-sas** *or* **-sa**) *n.* a wild boar living in the forests of Indonesia and Malaysia that has almost hairless skin and very large curved tusks. Latin name: *Babyrousa babyrussa.* [Late 17thC. From Malay, from *babi* "pig" + *rusa* "deer," from its horns, which suggest a deer's antlers.]

Ba·bism /baá bìzzəm/ *n.* a pantheistic religion founded in Persia by the Bab, Mirza Ali Muhammad (1819–50), that forbade polygamy, begging, slave-trading, and the use of alcohol or drugs

bab·ka /baábkə/ *n.* a sweet cake made with candied citrus peel, raisins, almonds, and sometimes rum [Late 20thC. From Polish, literally "little old woman," formed from *baba* (see BABA).]

ba·boo *n.* = **babu**

Baboon

ba·boon /ba boón/ *n.* **1. LARGE MONKEY** a large ground-dwelling monkey native to Africa and Asia with a prominent snout resembling a dog's muzzle, large teeth, and bare pink patches on the buttocks. Genus: *Papio.* **2. RUDE CLUMSY PERSON** somebody who is thought of as rude or oafishly clumsy (*insult*) [15thC. From French *babuin* "gaping figure, baboon" or medieval Latin *babewynus*, both of uncertain origin: possibly from French *baboue* "muzzle, grimace."]

Bab·son /bábsən/, **Roger** (1875–1967) U.S. statistician. He lectured and wrote about statistics as applied to investments, and founded Babson College, Massachusetts, in 1919. Full name **Roger Ward Babson**

ba·bu /baá boo/, **ba·boo** *n.* a courtesy title or form of address in Hindi equivalent to "Mr" [Late 18thC. From Hindi *bābū*, literally "father."]

ba·bul /bə boól/ (*plural* **-buls** *or* **-bul**) *n.* an acacia tree found in North Africa and India that is a source of gum arabic, tannin, and hardwood. Latin name: *Acacia nilotica.* [Early 19thC. Via Hindi *babūl*, Bengali *bābul* from Sanskrit *babbūla*.]

ba·bush·ka /bə boóshkə/ *n.* **1. SCARF** a headscarf folded and tied under the chin in the style of Russian peasant women **2. RUSSIAN GRANDMOTHER** a traditional Russian grandmother figure [Mid-20thC. From

Russian, "grandmother," literally "little old woman," formed from *baba* (see BABA).]

ba·by /báybee/ *n.* (*plural* **-bies**) **1. VERY YOUNG CHILD** a very young child who is not yet able to walk or talk **2. UNBORN CHILD** a child that is still in the womb **3. CHILDISH PERSON** somebody who behaves childishly or is overly dependent on others ○ *told him not to be such a baby* **4. YOUNGEST MEMBER** the youngest member of a family or group ○ *the baby of the team* **5. IMMATURE ANIMAL** a very young animal **6. TERM OF ENDEARMENT** an affectionate term of endearment, especially for a woman (*slang*) **7. SOMETHING REGARDED WITH AFFECTION OR PRIDE** something or somebody regarded with affection, pride, or admiration (*slang*) ○ *That baby can go at speeds of up to 150!* ■ *adj.* **SMALLER AND YOUNGER** smaller and younger than usual, as are certain vegetables served as delicacies ■ *vt.* (**-bied, -by·ing, -bies**) **TREAT SOMEBODY WITH GREAT CARE** to show a great or inordinate amount of care to something or somebody [14thC. Pet form of BABE.] ◇ **throw out the baby with the bathwater** to reject something in its entirety without discriminating between what is bad and what is good or would be useful to retain

WORD KEY: ORIGIN

In Old English, the term for what we would now call a ***baby*** was *child*, and it seems only to have been from about the 11th century that *child* began to extend its range to the slightly more mature age that it now covers. Then when the word ***baby*** came into the language in the 14th century, it was also used in this developed sense of "child," and only gradually came to refer to infants not yet capable of speech or walking.

ba·by blue *n.* a pale pastel blue color [Origin uncertain, perhaps from the lightness of the color] —**baby-blue** *adj.*

ba·by-blue-eyes (*plural* **ba·by-blue-eyes**) *n.* a spreading annual plant that has serrated gray-green leaves and small bowl-shaped blue flowers with white centers. Latin name: *Nemophila menziesii.* (*takes a singular or plural verb*) [From the fancied resemblance of its spots to eyes]

ba·by blues *npl.* the depression experienced by some women after giving birth (*informal*) (*used with a singular or plural verb*)

ba·by bond *n.* a bond issued for an amount lower than $1,000, usually between $25 and $500

ba·by bo·nus *n. Can* = **child tax benefit**

ba·by boom *n.* a sudden large increase in the birthrate over a particular period, especially the 15 years after World War II

ba·by boom·er *n.* somebody born during a baby boom, especially the one following the end of World War II

ba·by bug·gy *n.* a baby's or young child's stroller (*regional*)

ba·by bust *n.* a sudden large decrease in the birthrate over a particular period

ba·by car·riage *n.* a small carriage, usually consisting of a rectangular body on four wheels with a folding hood and a handle, designed for pushing an infant, especially outdoors

ba·by-dolls *npl.* women's nightwear consisting of a loose top and loose shorts, popularized by the short pajamas worn in the movie *Baby Doll* in 1956

ba·by face *n.* **1. FACE LIKE A BABY'S** a smooth round face that gives somebody a childlike innocent look **2. SOMEBODY WITH CHILDLIKE FACE** somebody who has a baby face

ba·by grand *n.* a small grand piano about 5 ft./1.5 m. long

ba·by·hood /báybi ho͝od/ *n.* the period during which a child is considered to be a baby, usually from birth to two or three years

ba·by·ish /báybee ish/ *adj.* **1. LIKE A BABY** like a baby in appearance or behavior **2. SUITABLE FOR A BABY** suitable for a baby or for a younger child ○ *Clothes like these are too babyish for a child his age.*

Bab·y·lon[1] /bábbə lən, -lòn/ the capital of ancient Babylonia, sited on the Euphrates River in modern Iraq. It was known for its opulence, and the Hanging Gardens there were one of the Seven Wonders of the World.

Bab·y·lon[2] town and vacation spot on Long Island, New York. Population: 202,889 (1990).

Bab·y·lon[3] /bábbə lòn/ *n.* **1. PLACE OF IMMORALITY** a place of great luxury or immorality (*disapproving*) **2. PLACE OF EXILE** a place of exile or captivity

Bab·y·lo·ni·a /bàbbə lṓnee ə, -lṓnyə/ *n.* an empire in Mesopotamia that flourished from the first half of the second millennium B.C. until its conquest by Persia in 539 B.C.

Bab·y·lo·ni·an /bàbbə lṓnee ən/ *n.* **1.** HIST, PEOPLES **SOMEBODY FROM BABYLON** somebody who lived in ancient Babylon or Babylonia **2.** LANG **DIALECT OF AKKADIAN** the Akkadian language, particularly the form of it that is recorded in cuneiform texts from Babylonia —**Bab·y·lo·ni·an** *adj.*

Bab·y·lo·ni·an cap·tiv·i·ty *n.* the period of time that the Jews spent in exile in Babylonia in the sixth century B.C.

ba·by's breath (*plural* **ba·by's breath** *or* **ba·by's breaths**) *n.* **1. PLANT WITH SPRAYS OF SMALL FLOWERS** a flowering plant that has a mass of delicate branched stems bearing small fragrant white or pink flowers, often used in bouquets and floral arrangements. Latin name: *Gypsophila paniculata.* **2. BEDSTRAW PLANT** a perennial plant that has many flowers on the end of delicate stems, especially a bedstraw [From its delicate scent]

ba·by-sit (**ba·by-sat, ba·by-sit·ting, ba·by-sits**), **ba·by·sit** (**-sat, -sit·ting, -sits**) *v.* **1.** *vti.* **TAKE CARE OF CHILD** to take care of a child or children in the child's home while the parents are out **2.** *vt.* **TAKE CARE OF SOMEBODY OR SOMETHING** to take care of somebody or something unable to be left unsupervised or needing constant attention (*informal*) ○ *Would you babysit my plants next week?* [Mid-20thC. Back-formation from BABYSITTER.]

ba·by-sit·ter /báybi sìtər/, **ba·by·sit·ter** *n.* somebody who takes care of children in their own home while their parents are out

ba·by's tears (*plural* **ba·by's tears**) *n.* an evergreen plant that has many small roundish leaves and tiny flowers. It is native to Corsica and Sardinia. Latin name: *Soleirolia solerolii.* (*takes a singular or plural verb*) [From the small size of the flowers]

ba·by talk *n.* **1. BABIES' SPEECH** the sounds and words used by babies when they are learning to talk **2. LANGUAGE USED BY ADULTS TO CHILDREN** the simplified or specially modified language and exaggerated intonation that adults use to show affection when talking to very small children

ba·by tooth *n.* = **milk tooth**

BAC, **B.A.C.** *abbr.* blood-alcohol concentration

Ba·call /bə káwl/, **Lauren** (*b.* 1924) U.S. actor. She starred in musicals and movies including *To Have and Have Not* (1944) and *The Big Sleep* (1946). Her first husband was Humphrey Bogart. Real name **Betty Joan Perske**

Ba·cău city in eastern Romania. It is the capital of Bacău County, and a major rail hub. Population: 204,495 (1992).

bac·ca·lau·re·ate /bàkə láwree ət/ *n.* a bachelor's degree (*formal*) [Mid-17thC. Directly or via French, from medieval Latin *baccalaureatus*, from *baccalaureus* "bachelor."]

bac·ca·lau·re·ate ser·mon *n.* a farewell sermon delivered to a graduating class, usually at a high school, college, or university

bac·ca·rat /bàakə ráa, bàkə-/ *n.* a card game, similar to chemin de fer, in which three hands are dealt and players bet against the banker. The winning hand is the one that totals nine points or is closest to nine points without exceeding it. [Mid-19thC. From French *baccara*, of unknown origin.]

bac·cate /bák àyt/ *adj.* similar to a berry in shape or texture [Early 19thC. From Latin *baccatus*, from *bacca* "berry," of uncertain origin.]

Bac·chae /bák ee/ *npl.* in Greek and Roman mythology, the priestesses and women who participated in the orgiastic rites of Bacchus [Early 20thC. Via Latin, from Greek *Bakkhai*, plural of *Bakkhē* "priest of Bacchus," from *Bakkhos* "Bacchus."]

bac·cha·nal /bàkə nál, -náal, bákə nəl/ *n.* **1. PARTICIPANT IN ORGIASTIC RITES** somebody who took part in the orgiastic rites of the god Bacchus **2. LOUD DRUNK** a riotous drunken reveler (*literary*) **3. DRUNKEN PARTY** a noisy drunken celebration or spree (*literary*) ■ *adj.* **RELATING TO BACCHUS** relating to Bacchus or the worship of Bacchus [Mid-16thC. From Latin *bacchanalis* "of Bacchus," from *Bacchus* "Bacchus."]

bac·cha·na·lia /bàkə náylyə, -náylee ə/ *n.* riotous drunken revels (*literary*) (*takes a singular or plural verb*) [Late 16thC. From Latin *bacchanalia*, plural of *bacchanalis* (see BACCHANAL).] —**bac·cha·na·lian** *adj.*

Bac·cha·na·lia /bàkə náylyə, -lee ə/ *n.* HIST, RELIG ancient Roman festivities in honor of Bacchus that involved orgiastic rites (*takes a singular or plural verb*) —**Bac·cha·na·lian** *adj.*

bac·chant /bə kánt, bə kaánt, bákənt/ *n.* a priest, priestess, or other devotee of Bacchus [Late 16thC. Via French *bacchante* from Latin *baccant-*, the present participle stem of *bacchari* "to celebrate the feast of Bacchus," from *Bacchus* "Bacchus."]

bac·chan·te /bə kántee, -kaántee, -kánt, -kaánt/ *n.* a priestess or female devotee of Bacchus [Late 18thC. From French *bacchante* (see BACCHANT).]

bac·chan·tic /bə kántik, -kaán-/ *adj.* relating to the worship of Bacchus and the orgiastic rites associated with it

bac·chic /bákik/ *adj.* characterized by riotous drunkenness (*literary*)

Bac·chic /bákik/ *adj.* MYTHOL relating to Bacchus

Bac·chus /bákəss, baákəss/ *n.* in classical mythology, the god of wine, identified with the Greek god Dionysus and the Roman god Liber. He was worshiped with orgiastic and ecstatic rites. [Via Latin, from Greek *Bakkhos*]

bach /bach/ (**bached, bach·ing, bach·es**), **batch** (**batched, batch·ing, batch·es**) *vi. U.S., ANZ* to live alone as a single man and keep house for yourself (*informal*) [Mid-19thC. Shortening of BACHELOR.]

Bach /baakh, baak/, **C.P.E.** (1714–88) German composer. The son of Johann Sebastian Bach, he composed numerous concertos and sonatas as well as chamber and church music. He also wrote *The True Art of Clavier Playing* (1753). Full name **Carl Philipp Emanuel Bach**. Known as **Berlin Bach, Hamburg Bach**

Bach, J.C. (1735–82) German composer. The youngest son of Johann Sebastian Bach and a composer of church music and operas, he settled in London (1762) and was musician to Queen Charlotte. Full name **Johann Christian Bach**. Known as **London Bach, English Bach**

AKG London

Johann Sebastian Bach

Bach, Johann Sebastian (1685–1750) German composer and organist. Known as a supreme master of counterpoint, he wrote many organ works, chamber and keyboard works, and oratorios, and over 295 cantatas. His works include the *"Brandenburg" Concertos* (1721) and *St. Matthew Passion* (1727).

Bach, W.F. (1710–84) German composer. He led a dissolute life despite being a gifted organist and composer. He was the eldest son of Johann Sebastian Bach. Full name **Wilhelm Friedemann Bach**. Known as **Halle Bach**

bach·e·lor /báchələr, báchlər/ *n.* **1. UNMARRIED MAN** a man who is not married, or one who has never been married **2. YOUNG KNIGHT** a young knight in feudal times who served under the banner of another knight or a great lord **3. UNMATED YOUNG MALE SEAL** a young male seal, especially a fur seal, that older male seals keep from having access to breeding grounds **4.** *Can* = **bachelor apartment** [13thC. Via Old French *bacheler* "young man aspiring to knighthood" from assumed Vulgar Latin *baccalaris*, of uncertain origin.] —**bach·e·lor·dom** *n.* —**bach·e·lor·hood** *n.* —**bach·e·lor·ship** *n.*

bach·e·lor a·part·ment *n. Can* an apartment consisting of a large single room, a small kitchen, and a bathroom

Bach·e·lor of Arts *n.* a college or university degree awarded to somebody who has successfully completed an undergraduate course in an aspect of the arts or humanities

Bach·e·lor of Sci·ence *n.* a college or university degree awarded to somebody who has successfully completed an undergraduate course in an aspect of the sciences or technology

bach·e·lor par·ty *n.* = **stag party**

bach·e·lor's but·ton *n.* a plant with small round flowers, e.g., a cornflower [From the resemblance of the flowers to buttons]

bach·e·lor's de·gree *n.* a degree awarded on the successful completion of an undergraduate course at a college or university

bac·il·lar·y /bássə lèrree, bəsí ləree/ *adj.* **1.** OF BACILLI relating to or caused by rod-shaped bacteria **(bacilli) 2.** ROD-SHAPED shaped like a small rod or consisting of small rod-shaped parts

ba·cil·lus /bə sílləss/ (*plural* **-li** /-sílli/) *n.* **1.** ROD-SHAPED BACTERIUM an aerobic, rod-shaped, spore-producing bacterium. Bacilli occur mainly in chains and include many saprophytes, some parasites, and the bacterium that causes anthrax. Genus: *Bacillus.* **2.** ROD-SHAPED BACTERIUM a rod-shaped bacterium [Late 19thC. From late Latin, literally "little rod," formed from *baculus* "rod, stick" (source of English *baguette* and *imbecile*).]

bac·i·tra·cin /bàssi tráys'n/ *n.* an antibiotic that is used mainly in the treatment of skin infections caused by gram-positive bacteria [Mid-20thC. Coined from BACILLUS + Margaret *Tracy,* name of a U.S. child in whom the substance was discovered in a wound + -IN.]

back /bak/ *n.* **1.** ANAT REAR PART OF BODY the rear part of the human body between the neck and the pelvis **2.** ANAT SPINE the spinal column **3.** ZOOL BACK OF AN ANIMAL the area of a vertebrate animal's body on either side of the backbone **4.** CLOTHES PART OF GARMENT the part of a garment designed to cover the wearer's back **5.** PART AT THE REAR the part that is at the rear of something or is farthest from the front ○ *Someone at the back of the crowd called out.* **6.** SIDE NOT USUALLY SEEN the side of something such as a sheet of paper or a photo that carries less information or is away from the viewer **7.** FURNITURE PART OF PIECE OF FURNITURE the part of a seat designed to support somebody's spine **8.** SPORTS DEFENSIVE PLAYER a player in games such as soccer or hockey whose role is mainly to prevent the other team from scoring **9.** FOOTBALL PLAYER BEHIND LINE a player positioned behind the offensive or defensive line, especially in football **10.** PUBL PART OF BOOK OR PERIODICAL the part of a book, magazine, or newspaper that is located toward the last page ○ *the index at the back of the book* **11.** PRINTING PART TO WHICH PAGES ARE FIXED the part of the book where the pages are glued or stitched to the binding ■ *adv.* **1.** IN A REVERSE DIRECTION in the opposite direction from the one somebody or something was previously facing or moving ○ *He looked back at us over his shoulder.* **2.** AT A DISTANCE at a distance from where something is situated or taking place ○ *Stay back; the dog might bite you.* **3.** IN RESERVE as a reserve or supply kept for future use ○ *I kept back part of the proceeds.* **4.** SO AS TO UNCOVER SOMETHING away from something so as to leave something else uncovered or revealed ○ *roll back the carpet* **5.** SO AS TO RECLINE in or into a reclining position ○ *Sit back and relax.* **6.** IN OR INTO THE PAST used to indicate a time in the past ○ *It happened about three weeks back.* ◊ **ago 7.** TO THE ORIGINAL OWNER to or into the keeping of the original or former owner or possessor ○ *You can have it back now, because I've finished with it.* **8.** IN RETURN as a reaction or reponse to something ○ *She called me while I was out, so I called her back.* **9.** INDICATES DIRECTION AND DISTANCE in the distance behind something, especially somebody's present position ○ *We passed it about two miles back.* **10.** RETURNED TO CONDITION OR TOPIC used to indicate a return to a state, situation, or subject of discussion ○ *to get back to your point* **11.** POPULAR AGAIN into fashion or popularity again ○ *The 70s are back.* ○ *Do you think Depression glass will ever come back?* ■ *adj.* **1.** LOCATED AT THE REAR located at the rear of something or at the part farthest from the front ○ *Use the back entrance.* **2.** PUBL ISSUED EARLIER published or issued at an earlier date ○ *a back issue* **3.** DUE EARLIER due at or owed from an earlier date ○ *paid the back taxes in full* **4.** LOCATED AWAY FROM MAIN ROADS located away from the main roads or the center of a town ○ *a quiet back street* **5.** REMOTE situated away from the main centers of population or activity ○ *explored the back areas of the huge canyon* **6.** REVERSE moving in an opposite direction from the usual one **7.** LING FORMED AT REAR OF MOUTH formed at or toward the rear of the mouth, as the vowel in "ball" is ○ *a back vowel* ■ *v.* **(backed, back·ing, backs) 1.** *vti.* MOVE BACKWARD to move backward, or make somebody or something move backward ○ *The vehicle in front backed into me.* **2.** *vt.* SUPPORT PERSON OR CAUSE to give a person or cause financial, political, or moral support **3.** *vt.* GAMBLING BET ON OUTCOME OF RACE to bet money on the person, team, or horse thought likely to win a race or competition **4.** *vt.* PROVIDE PROOF TO SUPPORT SOMETHING to provide evidence or proof in support a statement ○ *But can they back their allegations?* **5.** *vt.* REINFORCE SOMETHING to reinforce something by adding a support or backing ○ *colored paper backed with cardboard* **6.** *vt.* BE BEHIND SOMETHING to be situated behind something (*usually passive*) ○ *a lake backed by a range of mountains* **7.** *vt.* MUSIC PROVIDE MUSICAL ACCOMPANIMENT FOR SOMEBODY to provide an instrumental or vocal accompaniment to somebody or something **8.** *vi.* SAILING CHANGE DIRECTION to change direction, moving in an counterclockwise direction (*refers to wind*) **9.** *vt.* ADDRESS AN ENVELOPE to write an address on an envelope or letter (*regional*) [Old English *bæc,* from prehistoric Germanic] ◇ **back and fill 1.** to dither or vacillate in actions or decision-making **2.** SAILING to adjust the sails of a vessel in order to allow the wind to move in and out of them in an alternating manner as the boat is maneuvered in a narrow channel ◇ **back of** at the back of or behind something (*informal*) ◇ **behind somebody's back** when somebody is not present ◇ **be** *or* **get on somebody's back** to criticize or pressurize somebody (*slang*) ◇ **get off somebody's back** to stop criticizing or pressurizing somebody (*slang*) ◇ **have your back to the wall** to be in a very difficult situation, with little chance of getting out of it ◇ **in back of** behind something ◇ **put your back intosth** to put effort and especially physical strength into doing something ◇ **turn your back on somebody** *or* **something** to ignore or reject somebody or something ◇ **you scratch my back and I'll scratch yours** if you help me, I will help you in return (*often refers to unofficial or dishonest business dealings*)

WORD KEY: USAGE

Movement in time: ***back*** as it applies to the past refers to a change to an earlier time. *They have moved the estimate of its date of origin back a hundred years* would mean a change from, say, A.D. 1000 to A.D. 900. As the word applies to the future, however, it usually signifies a change to a later time: *The forecast is for rain, so let's move the picnic back a week.* What the two uses have in common is movement in time away from the present. *Up* is the opposite of ***back*** in this sense: *Let's move the date up* means moving the date closer to the present, and thus in future contexts changing it to an earlier one. *Forward* in future contexts is used less consistently than either ***back*** or *up*; it is best avoided. All these words become particularly confusing when the subject is, e.g., a decision, now in the past, about what was at the time the future: *Last month she told me she wanted to move my appointment back.* In a context like this, *make earlier* or *make later* is clearer.

WORD KEY: USAGE

back of and **in back of** The phrase ***back of*** is standard and ***in back of*** is its informal variant. Both mean "behind," and ***in back of*** is formed on the direct analogy of ***in front of***: *There was a swimming pool (in) back of the house.*

WORD KEY: REGIONAL NOTE

In the sense "to address an envelope or letter," ***back*** is a mainly Southern and South Midland term, being found from Tennessee and Georgia to Texas, with scattered instances in New England, the Midwest, and the West.

back away *vi.* **1.** MOVE AWAY BACKWARD to walk backward away from somebody or something, usually because of fear **2.** RETREAT FROM A SITUATION to withdraw from a situation or previous position ○ *We think they'll back away from any direct confrontation over sanctions.*

back down *vi.* to abandon a claim, opinion, or commitment because of the degree of opposition it arouses

back off *vi.* **1.** MOVE BACK to move away backward **2.** WITHDRAW to withdraw from a previous commitment, claim, or position **3.** EASE PRESSURE ON SOMEBODY to stop putting pressure on somebody to do something

back out *v.* **1.** *vi.* WITHDRAW to withdraw from a previous commitment ○ *The buyer backed out before the papers were signed.* **2.** *vti.* GO BACKWARD to move out backward, or cause something to move out backward

back up *v.* **1.** *vt.* TO SUPPORT SOMEBODY to provide support for a person or idea ○ *I'm sure you'll back me up on this.* **2.** *vt.* COMPUT COPY COMPUTER FILES to make a copy or copies of computer data to keep in case anything goes wrong with the original **3.** *vti.* GO BACKWARD to go or move something backward **4.** *vti.* ACCUMULATE to build up, or cause something to build up, especially because normal flow is obstructed ○ *Traffic was backed up three miles from the accident.* **5.** *vt.* PROVE STATEMENT to supply proof that a statement is true ○ *Evidence of growth is backed up by recent economic statistics.*

Back /bak/, **Sir George** (1796–1878) British-born Canadian explorer. He helped map the North American coastline, accompanied Sir John Franklin's Arctic expeditions, and searched for Sir John Ross.

back·ache /bák àyk/ *n.* an ache or pain affecting the back, most commonly the lower back

back ba·con *n. Can* relatively fat-free bacon from the loin or rib-end of a pig

back·beat /bák bèet/ *n.* MUSIC a loud rhythmic beat occurring on the offbeats of the bar, used especially in rock music

back·bench /bák bènch/ *n.* **1.** *U.K., Can, ANZ* AREA FOR MPS NOT IN GOVERNMENT a rear bench in a legislative assembly reserved for junior members of Parliament (*usually plural*) ○ *on the back benches* **2.** NEW MEMBERS OF CONGRESS new members of Congress, or members of Congress who have low seniority

back·bench·er /bák bènchər/ *n.* **1.** NEW MEMBER OF CONGRESS a new member of Congress, or one who has low seniority **2.** *U.K., Can, ANZ* MP NOT IN GOVERNMENT a junior member of the lower house of a legislative assembly who is not a government minister or an official Opposition spokesperson

back·bend /bák bènd/ *n.* an exercise in gymnastics in which somebody bends over backward from a standing position until the hands touch the floor

back·bite /bák bìt/ (**-bit** /-bìt/, **-bit·ten** /-bìtt'n/, **-bit·ing, -bites**) *vti.* to make spiteful or slanderous comments about somebody who is not present [12thC. From the idea of an animal biting another (usually of the same species) on the back, often in play.] —**back·bit·er** *n.*

back·board /bák bàwrd, -bōrd/ *n.* **1.** BASKETBALL BOARD BEHIND THE BASKET the board situated behind the basket that serves to rebound the ball onto the court **2.** MED BOARD USED TO SUPPORT INJURED BACK a board that is used to support the back after injury or as aid to recovery after surgery **3.** BOARD FORMING BACK OF SOMETHING a board that forms the back of something, e.g., a cart or boat

back·bone /bák bōn/ *n.* **1.** = **spinal column 2.** SOMETHING SIMILAR TO SPINAL COLUMN something that is similar in shape or position to a spinal colomn ○ *the Andes, the backbone of South America* **3.** CENTRAL SUPPORTING PART the part of an organization or system that is its strongest unifying factor and main support ○ *People like her form the backbone of this nation.* **4.** FORTITUDE strength of character and determination ○ *He doesn't have the backbone to stand up to his critics.* **5.** COMPUT HIGH-SPEED RELAY a high-speed relay, e.g., over fiber-optic cables or satellites, that feeds smaller channels in corporate networks and the Internet

back·break·er /bák bràykər/ *n.* **1.** WRESTLING HOLD a wrestling hold in which somebody's back is bent backward over the opponent's knee or shoulder **2.** BACKBREAKING TASK an exhausting task, or one that demands a tremendous physical effort (*informal*)

back·break·ing /bák bràyking/ *adj.* involving enormous physical effort

back burn·er ◇ **put something on the back burner** to assign something a lower priority or give something less prominence ○ *The project has been put on the back burner.*

back chan·nel *n.* a covert way of exchanging sensitive information in politics or diplomacy that circumvents the usual procedures

back·chat /bák chàt/ *n. U.K.* = **back talk** (*informal*)

back·cloth /bák klawth, -kloth/ (*plural* **-cloths**) *n.* THEATER = **backdrop** *n.* 1

back con·ces·sion *n. Can* a concession that is sparsely populated or remote from well-traveled roads

back coun·try *n. U.S., Can, ANZ* a remote, sparsely populated rural area, often used for various forms of outdoor recreation, including backpacking and camping ○ *backpacking in rugged back country*

back·court /bák kàwrt, -kŏrt/ *n.* **1.** RACKET GAMES **REAR OF COURT** the area between the baseline and the service line on a tennis court or the area of the court nearest the back boundary line or back wall in similar games **2.** BASKETBALL **DEFENDED HALF OF BASKETBALL COURT** the half of the court where the basket being defended is located **3.** BASKETBALL **DEFENSIVE PLAYERS** the players who defend the backcourt

back·cross /bák kràwss, -kròss/ *vt.* (**-crossed, -cross·ing, -cross·es**) **CROSS HYBRID WITH PARENT** to cross an organism, especially a hybrid, with one of its parents or an individual genetically identical to that parent ■ *n.* **1. HYBRID OBTAINED BY BACKCROSSING** a hybrid obtained by backcrossing **2. ACT OF BACKCROSSING** the act or the process of backcrossing organisms

back·date /bák dàyt/ (**-dat·ed, -dat·ing, -dates**) *vt.* to put a date on a document that is earlier than the actual date of its writing or signing

back dive *n.* a dive made when the diver's back is facing the water

back door *n.* **1. REAR DOOR** a door or entrance at the rear of a building **2. DISHONEST ADVANTAGE** an underhand or indirect way that gives somebody an unfair advantage

back·door /bák dàwr, -dŏr/ *adj.* carried out in secrecy or in a surreptitious way ○ *There's been a lot of backdoor pressure on her to step down.*

back·down /bák dòwn/ *n.* the abandonment of a course of action or an opinion in the face of opposition from other people

back·drop /bák dròp/ *n.* **1.** THEATER **PAINTED CLOTH AT BACK OF STAGE** a large painted cloth hung at the back of the stage that usually depicts the setting in which the action of a scene takes place **2. SETTING FOR SOMETHING** the setting for something, e.g., the scenery or colors behind it ○ *The ski-jumping took place against a backdrop of jagged mountain peaks.*

back end *n. N England* autumn

back end load *n.* a mutual fund sales charge paid when shares are sold

back·er /bákər/ *n.* **1. SUPPORTER** somebody who gives moral or financial support to somebody or something **2. GAMBLER** somebody who bets on somebody or something

WORD KEY: SYNONYMS

backer, angel, guarantor, patron, sponsor

CORE MEANING: somebody who provides financial support

backer the most general term of the group, indicating support of either a financial or nonfinancial nature; **angel** a person who provides financial support for an enterprise, for example, a theatrical venture; **guarantor** somebody who gives a legal undertaking to make good any financial losses incurred in a venture; **patron** a person who provides an artist or writer with the financial means to pursue his or her art, or who contributes money to an institution, such as a theater or art gallery, or cause; **sponsor** a person who contributes money to somebody participating in some kind of fundraising event, such as a marathon race, or a company that provides financial support for an activity such as a sports or musical event, usually in return for publicity for the company and its products.

back·field /bák fèeld/ *n.* FOOTBALL **1. AREA OF FIELD** in football, the area of the playing field behind the line of scrimmage **2. PLAYERS** the players who line up behind the line of scrimmage **3. POSITIONS** the positions of the players who line up behind the line of scrimmage

back·fill /bák fìl/ *vt.* (**-filled, -fill·ing, -fills**) **REFILL A TRENCH** to refill a trench or other excavation with the soil dug out of it ■ *n.* **SOIL** the soil used to refill a trench

back·fire /bák fìr/ *vi.* (**-fired, -fir·ing, -fires**) **1. HAVE OPPOSITE EFFECT** to have an effect opposite to the one intended ○ *The policy of mandatory testing may well backfire and do more harm than good.* **2.** AUTOMOT **MAKE EXPLOSION IN EXHAUST PIPE** to produce an explosion of prematurely ignited fuel in an internal-combustion engine or of unburned exhaust gases in the exhaust pipe **3.** FORESTRY **START FIRE TO CREATE FIREBREAK** to start a fire in the path of an advancing wildfire in order to halt its advance ■ *n.* **1.** AUTOMOT **EXPLOSION IN CAR EXHAUST** an explosion of prematurely ignited fuel in an internal-combustion engine or of unburned exhaust gases in the exhaust pipe **2.** FORESTRY **FIRE STARTED TO CREATE FIREBREAK** a fire deliberately started in order to clear the ground in front of an advancing wildfire so as to halt it

back·flow /bák flō/ *n.* the flowing back of something toward the source

back-for·ma·tion *n.* **1. PROCESS OF WORD FORMATION** a process of word formation in which a new word is coined by removing a real or imagined affix from an existing word **2. NEW WORD FORMED BY AFFIX REMOVAL** a word formed by back-formation, e.g., "greed" from "greedy," or "televise" from "television"

back for·ty *n.* a remote, usually unused part of a farm or ranch

back four *n.* a defensive formation in soccer that consists of two wing backs and two center backs deployed in a straight line across the field

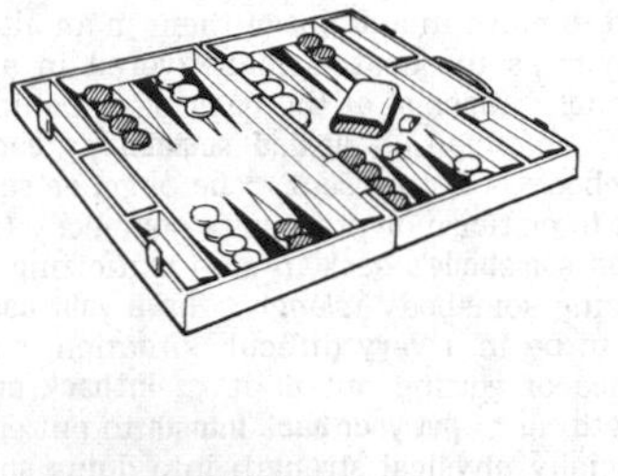

Backgammon

back·gam·mon /bák gàmmən/ *n.* **1. BOARD GAME INVOLVING DICE** a board game for two players who each move their 15 pieces around the board according to the throw of a pair of dice. The object of the game is to be the first to gather all your pieces in one corner and remove them from the board. **2. COMPLETE VICTORY IN BACKGAMMON** the most complete form of victory in backgammon, when a player succeeds in removing all 15 pieces while the other still has a piece furthest from the point at which he or she can remove pieces from the board [Mid-17thC. From BACK + obsolete *gamen*, an early form of GAME; probably from the pieces sometimes being put "back" on the table.]

back·ground /bák gròwnd/ *n.* **1. PERSONAL CIRCUMSTANCES AND EXPERIENCES** the personal circumstances and experiences that shape somebody's life, e.g., ethnic and social origins, upbringing, education, and work experience ○ *a group of people from very different backgrounds* **2. CAUSES OF AN EVENT** the circumstances leading up to an event that explain its cause ○ *The meeting takes place against a background of rising tension.* **3. SCENERY BEHIND SOMETHING** the setting for a scene, e.g., the scenery behind it ○ *A silvery lake shone against a background of tall dark firs.* **4.** ARTS **PART OF PICTURE** the part of a picture or pattern that appears to be in the distance or behind the most important part **5. INFORMATION** information that helps to explain what somebody or something is like or why something is happening **6. INCONSPICUOUS POSITION** a position of relative inconspicuousness or unimportance ○ *working tirelessly in the background* **7.** NUCLEAR PHYS = **background radiation** **8.** ELECTRON ENG, PHYS **SIGNAL CAUSING DISTORTION OR INTERFERENCE** an extraneous signal, often in the form of electronic or acoustic noise, that can cause distortion or affect an instrument reading (*often used before a noun*) ○ *background interference* **9.** COMPUT **LOW-PRIORITY ENVIRONMENT IN COMPUTERS** the low-priority environment in computers that can perform more than one task at a time ■ *adj.* **1. AS PART OF THE BACKGROUND** situated or depicted in, or forming part of, the background to something **2. ACCOMPANYING** functioning or suitable as an accompaniment to something else ◇ **on background** on conditions of anonymity and in an effort to provide the press with nonattributable information, usually sensitive in nature ○ *addressed the sensitive issue on background only*

back·ground·er /bák gròwndər/ *n.* an informal meeting or press conference in which a government spokesperson provides journalists with background information on condition that the informant is not identified as the source

back·ground mu·sic *n.* music used as a suitable accompaniment to action or dialog in a movie, or to create a pleasant atmosphere for an activity or in a public place

back·ground pro·cess·ing *n.* COMPUT execution of computer programs and tasks either while the user works with an interactive application in the foreground or during pauses in the execution of a foreground program or task. Once started, background tasks such as printing or copying data execute without user input.

back·ground ra·di·a·tion *n.* low-level radiation occurring naturally as a result of radioactivity present in the air, soil, and buildings and other structures

back·hand /bák hànd/ *n.* **1.** RACKET GAMES **BACKHANDED STROKE** in tennis and similar games, a stroke made with the back of the hand turned toward the ball as the arm moves outward from a position across the body **2.** RACKET GAMES **BACKHAND SIDE** the side of a tennis court, or of the body, on which a player would naturally play a backhand stroke. It is the left-hand side for a right-handed player. **3.** BASEBALL **CATCH MADE ON BACKHAND SIDE** a catch made with the catcher's hand, in a mitt, held across his or her body **4. HANDWRITING SLOPING LEFTWARD** a style of handwriting in which the letters slope to the left ■ *adj.* **WITH BACK OF HAND TOWARD BALL** carried out with the back of the hand facing in the direction in which the stroke, movement, or blow is made ■ *adv.* **BACKHANDEDLY** with a backhand stroke ■ *vt.* (**-hand·ed, -hand·ing, -hands**) **1. CONTACT BALL WITH BACKHAND** to strike a ball with a backhand stroke, or to catch it with the hand held across the body ○ *She backhanded the ball just over the net.* **2. HIT SOMEBODY WITH BACK OF HAND** to hit somebody or something with the back of the hand ○ *accidentally backhanded an opponent*

back·hand·ed /bák hàndəd/ *adj.* **1. PLAYED BACKHAND** carried out with the back of the hand facing in the direction in which the stroke, movement, or blow is made ○ *a backhanded return* **2. WITH DOUBLE MEANING** with a doubtful or double meaning, especially one that can be understood equally as a compliment or as an insult ○ *a backhanded compliment* **3. WRITTEN WITH LETTERS SLOPING LEFTWARD** written in a style of handwriting in which the letters slope to the left ■ *adv.* **WITH BACKHANDED STROKE** with the back of the hand facing in the direction in which a stroke, movement, or blow is made —**back·hand·ed·ly** *adv.* —**back·hand·ed·ness** *n.*

back·hoe /bák hō/ *n.* a digging machine or attachment consisting of a hinged scoop attached to a jointed mechanical arm that drags the scoop back toward the cab from which it is operated

back·ing /báking/ *n.* **1. SUPPORT OR HELP** active approval, support, or help, often in financial form, given to an individual, organization, or cause **2. SUPPORTERS** the people or organizations giving support to a person or cause **3. REAR SURFACE** material forming or covering the back of something, especially to strengthen, stiffen, or protect it **4.** MUSIC **MUSICAL ACCOMPANIMENT** the music or singing that accompanies the playing or singing of the main performer of a piece of popular music or jazz

back is·sue *n.* PUBL a previous issue of a magazine or newspaper

back judge *n.* in football, a referee stationed behind the line of scrimmage who keeps the time in a game and determines players eligible to receive a pass [From the fact that this referee is responsible for calls in the backfield]

back·lash /bák làsh/ (*plural* **-lash·es**) *n.* **1. STRONG REACTION** a strong adverse reaction among a group of people to an event, development, or trend, especially one that benefits another group **2. VIOLENT BACKWARD MOVEMENT** a sudden violent backward jerking movement, e.g., when a cable breaks under strain **3.** MECH ENG **RECOIL BETWEEN MACHINE PARTS** a jarring recoil that sometimes occurs when worn or badly fitting parts of a mechanism come together **4.** MECH ENG **PLAY BETWEEN MACHINE PARTS** excessive play between adjacent parts in a mechanism such as a set of gears, usually as a result of the parts being worn or badly fitted

5. ANGLING **FISHING LINE TANGLE** a tangle in the part of a fishing line that is wound on the reel

back·less /bákləss/ *adj.* with the back cut very low ○ *a backless dress*

back·light /bák lìt/ *n.* **LIGHT FROM BEHIND** light that illuminates the subject of a photograph or painting from behind ■ *vt.* (**-light·ed** *or* **-lit** /-lìt/, **-light·ed** *or* **-lit, -light·ing, -lights**) **ILLUMINATE FROM BEHIND** to illuminate a subject from behind —**back·light·ing** *n.*

back·list /bák lìst/ *n.* PUBL the range of books already published by a publisher that are still in print ○ *The departing editor had built up a highly respectable backlist.*

back·lit past tense, past participle of **backlight**

back·log /bák lōg, -làwg/ *n.* **1. THINGS STILL TO BE DONE** a quantity of unfinished business or work that has built up over a period of time and must be dealt with before progress can be made ○ *She faced a backlog of work when she came back from the Bahamas.* **2. LARGE LOG ON A FIRE** a large log placed at the back of an open fire ■ *vti.* (**-logged, -log·ging, -logs**) **ACCUMULATE** to accumulate and need to be dealt with, or to accumulate work or material that needs to be dealt with ○ *Order fulfillment got backlogged when nearly everyone in the department came down with the flu.*

back mat·ter *n.* PUBL the parts of a book that appear after the main text, e.g. , the index or an appendix

back mu·ta·tion *n.* the reversion of a mutated gene to its original form

back num·ber *n.* PUBL = **back issue**

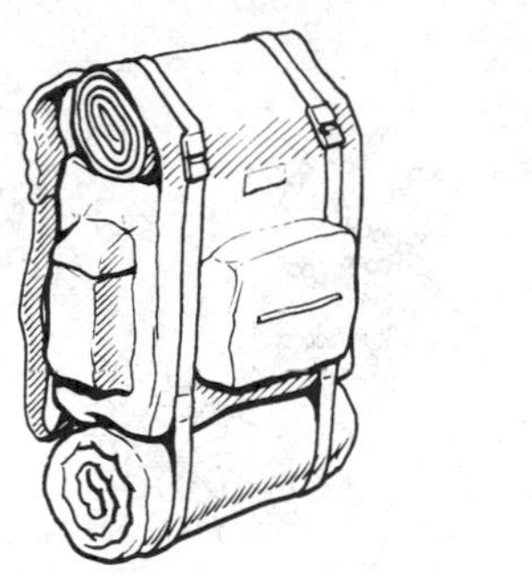

Backpack

back·pack /bák pàk/ *n.* **1.** LEISURE **RUCKSACK** a large straight-sided sturdy fabric bag, often attached to a metal frame, worn strapped to the back and used by hikers and travelers for carrying their belongings, equipment, and supplies **2. EQUIPMENT CARRIED ON THE BACK** a pack or carrier for a piece of equipment, such as an astronaut's personal life-support system, that is designed to be strapped on the user's back ■ *v.* (**-packed, -pack·ing, -packs**) **1.** *vi.* LEISURE **HIKE WITH BACKPACK** to travel, especially hike, carrying belongings or supplies in a backpack ○ *She spent a month backpacking in the Rockies.* **2.** *vt.* **CARRY SOMETHING ON THE BACK** to transport something, usually equipment or supplies, in a pack on the back ○ *astronauts backpacking oxygen during a spacewalk* —**back·pack·er** *n.*

back pass *n.* SOCCER a pass from an outfield player back to the goalkeeper, in soccer. Goalkeepers are forbidden to handle back passes with their hands.

back pay *n.* pay that is owed to an employee for work done before the current payment period and is either overdue or results from a backdated pay increase

back·ped·al /bák pèdd'l/ (**-aled, -al·ing, -als**) *v.* **1.** *vti.* CYCLING **PEDAL BACKWARD** to turn the pedals of a bicycle backward, e.g., in order to operate a brake **2.** *vi.* SPORTS **MOVE BACKWARD** to move quickly backward, e.g., in order to get away from an opponent or to catch a ball **3.** *vi.* **RETREAT** to try to escape the consequences of a statement or action by retracting it, modifying it, or toning it down

back·plate /bák plàyt/ *n.* a piece of armor protecting the back

back pres·sure *n.* **1.** ENG **RESISTANT PRESSURE** resistant pressure exerted by any solid, liquid, or gas to the forward motion of a system, especially the pressure opposing the exhaust stroke of a piston in an internal-combustion engine **2.** INDUST **OIL OR GAS PRESSURE** the pressure exerted by fluids in the bore of an oil well on the oil and gas in the reservoir. Careful control of this pressure ensures an even supply of oil. **3.** MED **PRESSURE DUE TO OBSTRUCTION** pressure within a blood vessel or the urinary system that builds up when there is an obstruction to the flow of fluid

back pro·jec·tion *n.* the cinematic technique of projecting a film onto a translucent screen from behind, usually to provide a moving background against which other action can be filmed

back·rest /bák rèst/ *n.* a part of a seat designed to support the user's back

back·room /bák ròom, -ròom/, **back room** *n.* **1. ROOM AT THE BACK** a room at or toward the back of a building **2. MEETING PLACE OF POWER ELITE** the supposed meeting place of a group that exercises a powerful behind-the-scenes influence on events or an organization ■ *adj.* **back·room, back-room UNOBTRUSIVE OR CLANDESTINE** taking place away from the center of activity or attention, but usually important or influential nonetheless ○ *The tax law was hammered out in a back-room deal between Republicans and Democrats.*

back·saw /bák sàw/ *n.* a small saw stiffened and strengthened by a strip of metal on its noncutting edge

back·scat·ter /bák skàttər/ *n.* **1. DEFLECTION OF RADIATION OR PARTICLES** the deflection of radiation or particles through angles of greater than 90 degrees measured with respect to the original direction of travel through a medium **2. DEFLECTED RADIATION OR PARTICLES** radiation or particles deflected more than 90 degrees while passing through a medium

back·scratch·er /bák skràchər/ *n.* **1. TOOL FOR SCRATCHING THE BACK** a long-handled implement, often ending in a claw or hand shape, for scratching your own back **2. SOMEBODY WHO EXCHANGES FAVORS** somebody who does favors for others in order to receive similar favors from them (*informal*)

back·scratch·ing /bák skràching/ *n.* the doing of favors for other people in return for similar favors from them (*informal*) —**backscratch** *vi.*

back seat *n.* **1. SEAT IN THE BACK** a seat at the back of a vehicle **2. LESS IMPORTANT ROLE** a less important or active role ◇ **take a back seat (to somebody)** to allow somebody else to direct or control something while taking on a relatively less important role yourself

back-seat driv·er *n.* (*informal*) **1. PASSENGER WHO PESTERS A DRIVER** a passenger in a vehicle who continually pesters the driver with unwanted advice or criticism **2. SOMEBODY GIVING UNWANTED ADVICE** somebody who gives unwanted advice or criticism while somebody else carries out a task, or who attempts to control something for which he or she has no responsibility

back·set /bák sèt/ *n.* an eddy or a current flowing against the direction of the main current in a body of water

back·shore /bák shàwr, -shòr/ *n.* the area of the shore that is above the high-water mark except in very severe weather [Early 20thC. Coined from SHORE, on the model of *foreshore*.]

back·side /bák sìd/ *n.* a person's buttocks (*informal*)

back·sight /bák sìt/ *n.* **1.** ARMS **REAR SIGHT ON GUN** a sight on the part of a firearm nearest to the aimer's eye **2.** CIV ENG **SURVEYING SIGHT TAKEN BACKWARD** a sight or reading taken by a surveyor back toward a position from which a previous sight has been made

back slang *n.* a type of slang in which words are disguised by being pronounced as if spelled backward

back·slap /bák slàp/ (**-slapped, -slap·ping, -slaps**) *vti.* to treat somebody, or treat each other, in a hearty, jovial, and enthusiastically complimentary way, with or without physical slaps on the back ○ *a political candidate who backslapped his way across the country* —**back·slap·per** *n.*

back·slash /bák slàsh/ (*plural* **-slash·es**) *n.* a keyboard character (\) with various uses in computing and programming

back·slide /bák slìd/ (**-slid** /-slìd/, **-slid, -slid·ing, -slides**) *vi.* to fall back into wrongdoing or a bad habit after having attempted to change your behavior or to lose faith in a religion after being a believer —**back·slid·er** *n.*

back·space /bák spàyss/ *vi.* (**-spaced, -spac·ing, -spac·es**) **MOVE BACK ONE SPACE** to move the cursor of a computer or the carriage of a typewriter back one or more spaces using the key designed for this purpose ■ *n.* **KEY FOR MOVING BACK ONE SPACE** a key on a computer or typewriter keyboard that moves the cursor or carriage back one space at a time

back·spin /bák spìn/ *n.* spin that makes a ball rotate in the opposite direction to its line of movement so that when it lands or strikes something its forward momentum will be reduced

back·splash /bák splàsh/ *n.* a vertical waterproof surface, usually tiled, that protects the area above a sink or bath from splashes

back·stab /bák stàb/ (**-stabbed, -stab·bing, -stabs**) *vt.* to do or say something harmful to somebody after pretending to be a friend [Early 20thC. From the expression *to stab somebody in the back*.] —**back·stab·ber** *n.* —**back·stab·bing** *n.*

back·stage *adv.* /bàk stáyj/ **1.** THEATER **BEHIND THE SCENES** behind the area of a theater stage that is visible to an audience, e.g., in the areas where stage technicians work or in the dressing rooms ○ *Journalists were allowed backstage to interview the star.* **2. IN PRIVATE** in private or out of the view of the general public ■ *adj.* /bák stàyj/ **1.** THEATER **SITUATED OR WORKING BEHIND THE SCENES** situated or working in the area of a stage not visible to an audience **2. NOT VISIBLE TO PUBLIC** taking place in private or out of the view of the general public

back·stairs /bák stàirz/ *npl.* **PRIVATE STAIRS** a set of stairs in a private part of a house, often originally for the use of servants ■ *adj.* **SECRET** carried on secretly or furtively [Mid-17thC. The sense "secret" derives from the backstairs in royal palaces, which were inaccessible to state visitors.]

back·stay /bák stày/ *n.* **1.** SAILING **SUPPORTING ROPE** a rope leading backward from the top of a mast to the side or stern and giving support to the mast **2. BACK SUPPORT** a thing that supports or strengthens the back of something else, e.g., a piece of leather covering the back seam of a shoe

back·stick /bák stìk/ *n.* a large log at the back of a fire or campfire (*regional*)

WORD KEY: REGIONAL NOTE

The term ***backstick*** is most common today in Tennessee, Mississippi, Arkansas, and Upper Alabama. It is now essentially an upcountry folk term.

back·stitch /bák stìch/ *n.* **REINFORCED STITCH** a method of stitching in which each new stitch starts from the middle of the previous stitch ■ *vti.* (**-stitched, -stitch·ing, -stitch·es**) **STITCH STRONGLY** to sew fabric using backstitches

back·stop /bák stòp/ *n.* **1.** SPORTS **SCREEN TO STOP A BALL** a screen or barrier to stop the ball traveling out of the playing area, especially behind the home plate at a baseball field **2.** BASEBALL = **catcher** *n.* 1 **3.** MECH ENG **CATCH STOPPING BACKWARD MOVEMENT** a catch on a mechanism designed to prevent it from moving back too far **4. ADDITIONAL SUPPORT** somebody or something providing additional support or protection in case somebody or something else fails ■ *vt.* (**-stopped, -stop·ping, -stops**) **GIVE SUPPORT TO SOMEBODY** to give support or backing to somebody or something, or to reinforce somebody or something

back·sto·ry (*plural* **back·sto·ries**) *n.* **1. BACKGROUND TO STORY** the events that are supposed to have taken place before the action of a movie, television program, or novel begins (*informal*) **2.** = **prequel**

back·street /bák strèet/ *n.* **back·street, back street MINOR STREET** a small unimportant street off the main highways in a city or town ■ *adj.* **1. back·street, back-street IN A BACKSTREET** situated or taking place in a backstreet **2. back·street ILLICIT** carried out furtively or illicitly in a place where it is unlikely to attract public attention

back stretch *n.* the straight section of a racing circuit opposite the home stretch

back·stroke /bák stròk/ *n.* **1.** SWIMMING **SWIMMING ON THE BACK** a method of swimming on the back in which the swimmer makes circular backward movements with each arm alternately while kicking the legs rhythmically up and down **2. RETURN STROKE** a stroke or movement in the opposite direction to that of the original or forward one **3.** SPORTS **BACKHAND STROKE** a backhand stroke ■ *vi.* (**-stroked, -strok·ing, -strokes**) SWIMMING **SWIM BACKSTROKE** to swim using the backstroke —**back·strok·er** *n.*

back·swept /bák swèpt/ *adj.* angled, slanting, or brushed backward ○ *a backswept hairstyle*

back·swim·mer /bák swìmmər/ *n.* a North American water bug that swims lying on its back and propelled by its broad hindlegs. Family: Notonectidae.

back·swing /bák swìng/ *n.* SPORTS the backward movement of a player's club, bat, or racket away from the eventual point of contact with the ball in preparation for making the actual stroke

back·sword /bák sàwrd, -sòrd/ *n.* **1.** ARMS **ONE-EDGED SWORD** a sword with a cutting edge on one side of the blade only **2.** FENCING **FENCING STICK** a stick with a basket-shaped hilt used in fencing practice

back talk *n.* rude or impertinent answers or comments

back-to-back *adj.* **1. WITH BACKS TO EACH OTHER** standing or sitting with backs turned to, and sometimes touching, one another **2. CONSECUTIVE** following immediately one after the other ○ *We had back-to-back meetings prior to the product launch.* —**back-to-back** *adv.*

back·track /bák tràk/ (**-tracked, -track·ing, -tracks**) *vi.* **1. GO BACK** to go back in the direction from which you have come **2. CHANGE YOUR MIND** to change, or distance yourself from, a previous action, opinion, statement, or policy, especially as a result of other people's opposition to it ○ *After enormous public outrage, the government backtracked on its proposed ban.*

back·up /bák ùp/ *n.* **1. SUPPORT** support or assistance from other people, e.g., from the supplier of a product when it breaks down **2. REINFORCEMENTS** reinforcements to help personnel already committed, especially police officers ○ *The officers at the scene are calling for a backup.* **3. SUBSTITUTE OR RESERVE** a substitute or reserve that can be used if the thing normally used fails **4.** COMPUT **SECURITY COPY** a separate copy of data with which somebody is working that is stored, e.g., on a floppy disk **5.** COMPUT **COPYING** the procedure for making a separate copy or copies of data with which somebody is working ○ *The backup is done automatically every morning.* **6. OVERFLOW** an overflow from a pipe caused by a blockage ○ *a backup of water* **7. TRAFFIC HOLDUP** a buildup or stoppage of traffic caused by an obstruction, e.g., an accident or road construction **8.** MUSIC **ACCOMPANIMENT** instrumental music or singing forming an accompaniment to the main performer of a piece of popular music or jazz ■ *adj.* **1. SUPPORTING** acting as a support, reserve, or reinforcement ○ *The field commander radioed for backup troops.* **2.** COMPUT **COPIED** made or kept in case something goes wrong with the original ○ *Check the condition of your backup disk.* **3.** MUSIC **PROVIDING MUSICAL ACCOMPANIMENT** providing instrumental or vocal accompaniment for a pop or jazz performer, usually a singer [Mid-20thC. From the phrase *back up.*]

back·up light *n.* a light on the back of a motor vehicle that comes on when the vehicle is in reverse

back·ward /bákwərd/ *adj.* **1. TO THE REAR** in the opposite direction to the one in which somebody or something is facing **2. REVERSED** positioned the opposite way around, arranged in the opposite order, or proceeding in the opposite direction to the normal one **3. NOT ACHIEVING USUAL OR EXPECTED STANDARD** lagging behind the progress and development of others of comparable status ○ *a backward economy* **4. RETROGRADE** causing or representing a return to a previous or less advanced, and usually less satisfactory, state ○ *a backward step developmentally* **5. TOWARD THE PAST** directed toward the past ○ *a backward look over the city's progress during the last century* **6. SHY** shy or lacking in self-confidence ■ *adv.* **back·ward, back·wards 1. BACK FIRST** with your or something's back facing in the direction in which you move or it moves ○ *She walked backward out of the room.* **2. TOWARD THE REAR** behind somebody or in a direction away from the front of something ○ *I reached backward until I felt my fingers touch the wall.* **3. WRONG WAY AROUND** the opposite way around, or in the reverse order or direction from the usual ○ *You've got your shirt on backward.* **4. TOWARD THE PAST** toward or into the past ○ *travel backward in time* **5. INTO A WORSE CONDITION** into a state that is worse or less advanced than the previous or original one ○ *Everything's gone backward since the new committee took over.* —**back·ward·ness** *n.* ◇ **bend or lean over backward** to make an exceptional effort to do something, especially to help somebody ○ *I felt uncomfortable although everybody bent over backward to make me feel welcome.*

WORD KEY: USAGE

backward or **backwards**? ***Backward*** is the only form available for the adjective: *A backward glance.* ***Backward*** is more common in adverbial use as well, but in other parts of the English-speaking world ***backwards*** is more usual for the adverb. *The vehicle moved slowly backward/backwards.*

back·ward-look·ing *adj.* more concerned with or relevant to a past state of affairs than the present

back·wards *adv.* = **backward**

back·wash /bák wòsh, -wàwsh/ *n.* **1. RETREATING WAVE** the movement of water back down a beach after a wave has broken **2.** NAUT **WATER PUSHED BACKWARD** a backward movement or flow in water produced by a ship's propeller or by oars **3.** AIR **AIR PUSHED BACKWARD** a backward rush of air produced by an aircraft propeller or jet engine **4. CONSEQUENCES** the consequential effects of an event or action, especially unpleasant or unsettling ones

back·wa·ter /bák wàwtər, -wòttər/ *n.* **1. SMALL STAGNANT BRANCH OF RIVER** a still body of water connected to a river but not affected by its current **2. STILL WATER** a still body of water held back by a dam, obstruction, or prevailing countercurrent **3. DULL PLACE** a place or situation regarded as cut off from the mainstream of activity or development and consequently seen as quiet and uneventful or unimportant and dull

back·woods /bák wo͝odz/ *n.* (*takes a singular or plural verb*) **1. REMOTE WOODED AREAS** a sparsely inhabited forested area distant from the main centers of population **2. UNSOPHISTICATED AREA** an area regarded as remote, rustic, and culturally unsophisticated ■ *adj.* **1. IN OR FROM REMOTE AREA** situated in, coming from, or typical of a sparsely settled area **2. UNSOPHISTICATED** rustic, uncouth, or culturally unsophisticated

back·woods·man /bák wo͝odzmən/ (*plural* **-men** /-mən/) *n.* somebody who lives in the backwoods

back yard *n.* **1. YARD BEHIND A HOUSE** a yard or a garden behind a house **2. GARDEN** a back garden **3. SOMEBODY'S NEIGHBORHOOD** somebody's immediate neighborhood or the area considered as somebody's home ground ○ *The gangs know better than to cause trouble in each other's back yard.*

back·yard /bák yaàrd/ *adj.* situated or happening in a back yard ○ *good weather for backyard barbecues*

ba·con /báykən/ *n.* meat from the back and sides of a hog that has been salted, dried, and often smoked [14thC. Via Old French, from a prehistoric Germanic word meaning literally "back meat," which is also the ancestor of English *back.*] ◇ **bring home the bacon** to earn the money on which a family lives (*informal*) ◇ **save somebody's bacon** to save somebody from serious trouble, punishment, injury, or danger (*informal*)

Ba·con /báykən/, **Sir Francis, 1st Baron Verulam and Viscount St. Albans** (1561–1626) English philosopher, lawyer, and statesman. A pioneer of modern scientific thought, he wrote *The Advancement of Learning* (1605) and *Essayes* (1597–1625). He was Lord Chancellor (1618–21), but was dismissed for bribery.

Ba·con, Francis (1909–92) Irish-born British painter. A major late-20th century painter, he often used gory and shocking imagery, as in *Head Surrounded by Sides of Beef (Study After Velázquez)* (1954).

Ba·co·ni·an /bay kṓnee ən/ *adj.* **OF WORKS OF SIR FRANCIS BACON** typical of or similar to the philosophy of Sir Francis Bacon, particularly his method of inductive reasoning in which the emphasis is placed on collecting instances rather than testing theories ■ *n.* **1.** PHILOS **FOLLOWER OF SIR FRANCIS BACON** somebody who studies the philosophy of Sir Francis Bacon or whose own philosophy or philosophical method is strongly influenced by him **2.** LITERAT **BELIEVER IN BACON AS AUTHOR OF SHAKESPEARE'S PLAYS** somebody who believes that the plays usually attributed to Shakespeare were actually written by Sir Francis Bacon

bact. *abbr.* **1.** bacteria **2.** bacteriology

bac·te·re·mi·a /bàktə reémee ə/ *n.* the presence of bacteria in the blood —**bac·te·re·mic** /-reémik/ *adj.* —**bac·te·re·mi·cal·ly** /-reémiklee/ *adv.*

bacteri- *prefix.* = **bacterio-**

bac·te·ri·a plural of **bacterium**

bac·te·ri·al /bak teéree əl/ *adj.* consisting of, caused by, or connected with bacteria —**bac·te·ri·al·ly** *adv.*

bac·te·ri·cide /bak teéri sīd/ *n.* a substance or agent that destroys bacteria —**bac·te·ri·cid·al** /bak teéri sīd'l/ *adj.*

bacterio- *prefix.* **1.** bacteria, bacterial ○ *bacteriostat* **2.** pressure, weight ○ *barometer* [From modern Latin *bacterium* "BACTERIUM"]

bacteriol. *abbr.* **1.** bacteriological **2.** bacteriology

bac·te·ri·ol·o·gy /bak teéree óllәjee/ *n.* the scientific study of bacteria, especially in relation to medicine and agriculture —**bac·te·ri·o·log·i·cal** /bak teéree ə lójjik'l/ *adj.* —**bac·te·ri·o·log·i·cal·ly** *adv.* —**bac·te·ri·ol·o·gist** /bak teéree óllәjist/ *n.*

bac·te·ri·ol·y·sis /bak teéree óllississ/ (*plural* **-ses** /-seèz/) *n.* the dissolution or destruction of a bacterial cell, e.g., as a result of the use of a bactericidal agent during disinfection —**bac·te·ri·o·lyt·ic** /bak teéree ə líttik/ *adj.*

bac·te·ri·o·phage /bak teéree ə fàyj/ *n.* a virus that infects bacteria and may integrate into the genetic material of its host cell. Bacteriophages are used as vectors in gene cloning and have other biotechnological uses. —**bac·te·ri·o·phag·ic** /bak teéree ə fájjik/ *adj.* —**bac·te·ri·oph·a·gous** /-óffəgəss/ *adj.* —**bac·te·ri·oph·a·gy** /-óffəjee/ *n.*

bac·te·ri·o·sta·sis /bak teéree ō stáyssiss/ *n.* inhibition of bacterial growth and multiplication by a chemical agent

bac·te·ri·o·stat /bak teéree ə stàt/ *n.* a substance that restricts the growth and activity of bacteria without killing them —**bac·te·ri·o·stat·ic** /bak teéri ō státtik/ *adj.* —**bac·te·ri·o·stat·i·cal·ly** /-státtiklee/ *adv.*

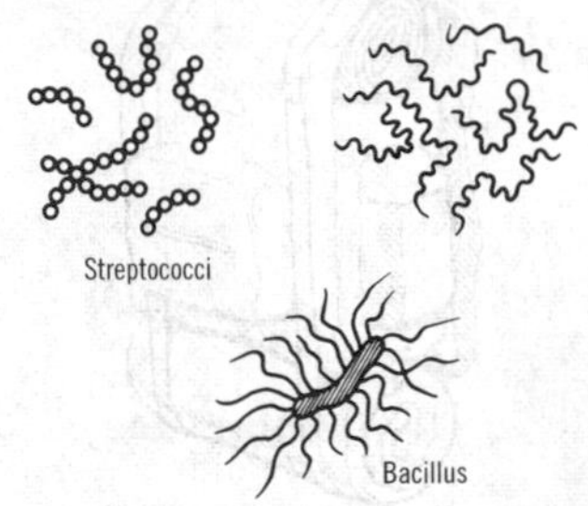

Bacteria

bac·te·ri·um /bak teéree əm/ (*plural* **-a** /-ree ə/) *n.* a single-celled, often parasitic microorganism without distinct nuclei or organized cell structures. Various species are responsible for decay, fermentation, nitrogen fixation, and many plant and animal diseases. Kingdom: *Eubacteria.* [Mid-19thC. From, ultimately, Greek *baktērion* "little rod" (because the first ones discovered were rod-shaped), from *baktron* "rod."]

bac·te·ri·u·ri·a /bak teéri yo͝oree ə/ *n.* the presence of bacteria in urine

bac·te·roid /báktə ròyd/ *n.* **BACTERIUM IN HUMAN MOUTH AND GUT** a bacterium that can grow only in the absence of air, found in the human mouth and intestinal tract, in the rumen of ruminant animals, and in sewage. Genus: *Bacteroides.* ■ *adj.* **RESEMBLING A BACTERIUM** resembling a bacterium in structure or behavior

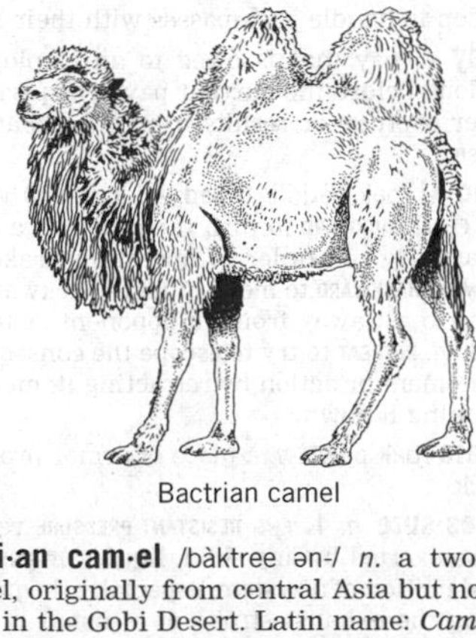
Bactrian camel

Bac·tri·an cam·el /bàktree ən-/ *n.* a two-humped camel, originally from central Asia but now found only in the Gobi Desert. Latin name: *Camelus bactrianus.* [Early 17thC. *Bactrian* from, ultimately, Latin *Bactrianus,* from *Bactria,* an ancient country in central Asia.]

bac·u·li·form /bákyələ fàwrm, bə kyóōlə-/ *adj.* shaped like a rod [Coined from Latin *baculum* "rod" (see BACULUM) + -FORM]

bad /bad/ *adj.* (**worse** /wurss/, **worst** /wurst/) **1. OF POOR QUALITY** below an acceptable standard in quality or performance ○ *bad driving* **2. UNSKILLFUL** lacking the skill or competence to perform a task adequately ○ *I've always been bad at remembering dates.* **3. NOT FUNCTIONING PROPERLY** not functioning properly because of a fault ○ *bad TV reception* **4. INCORRECT** incorrect according to the normal rules, especially those governing the use of language ○ *used bad grammar in the essay* **5. WICKED** morally evil, blameworthy, or unacceptable ○ *It's how you tell the good guys from the bad guys.* **6. MISBEHAVING AND DISOBEDIENT** troublesome or annoying to other, especially older, people, usually through rudeness, disobedience, or mischievousness ○ *Go to your room, you bad child!* **7. ANGRY AND UNPLEASANT TOWARD OTHERS** characterized by anger and unpleasantness toward other people ○ *in a bad mood* **8. OFFENSIVE** likely to cause offense to other people because it deals with a taboo subject or expresses violent feelings ○ *swearing and other bad language* **9. HARMFUL** liable to damage health or cause injury ○ *Reading in a dim light is bad for the eyes.* **10. ROTTEN** rotted or deteriorated in quality to the point of being unfit to eat or drink ○ *This milk is bad.* **11. INJURED OR DISEASED** affected by an injury or disease, or not functioning properly, and often causing pain ○ *She's got a bad tooth.* **12. UNWELL** unwell or in pain ○ *I've been feeling bad for a couple of days.* **13. UNEASY** uneasy or regretful about something, or causing somebody to feel this way ○ *I feel really bad about having had to reprimand you.* **14. MORE UNPLEASANT THAN USUAL** possessing an unpleasant, painful, or troublesome quality to a higher degree than usual ○ *Was the pain very bad?* **15. DISTRESSING** likely to cause unhappiness or disappointment ○ *I'm afraid the news is bad.* **16. UNFAVORABLE** containing or indicating an unfavorable assessment of somebody's performance, work, or character ○ *received a bad job evaluation* **17.** (*comparative* **bad·der**, *superlative* **bad·dest**) **VERY GOOD** extremely good (*slang*) ○ *the baddest outfit at the party* ■ *n.* **1. EVIL** wrong or immoral behavior ○ *You're old enough to know good from bad.* **2. UNSATISFACTORY OR UNPLEASANT THINGS** things or events that are unsatisfactory or unpleasant ○ *You've got to take the good with the bad.* ■ *adv.* (*informal*) **1. BADLY** in an unsatisfactory manner ○ *We didn't do too bad.* **2. VERY MUCH** to an intense or extreme degree ○ *He's got it bad!* [13thC. Origin uncertain, possibly from Old English *bæddel* "effeminate man."] —**bad·ness** *n.* ◇ **go bad** to become rotten or unfit to eat ◇ **go from bad to worse** to become even more unpleasant, unsatisfactory, or morally unacceptable than before ◇ **not (half** *or* **so** *or* **that** *or* **too) bad** fairly good or of a standard that is admitted to be satisfactory, sometimes grudgingly or cautiously, but often in a positive or definitely approving way ○ *That's not bad for a first attempt.*

WORD KEY: SYNONYMS

bad, criminal, delinquent, mischievous, naughty

CORE MEANING: indicating wrongdoing

bad the most general and widely used term, applying to a whole range of wrongdoing from the most trivial to the most immoral or evil; **criminal** specifically used in connection with wrongdoing that constitutes a criminal offense, but also used informally to indicate strong disapproval; **delinquent** a formal word, literally meaning neglectful of duty, for wrongdoing of a criminal or socially unacceptable nature; **mischievous** applied to children or their actions to suggest wrongdoing of a minor and often playful kind, but, when used of adults, suggesting more harmful wrongdoing designed to cause trouble; **naughty** used of children or their actions to describe both relatively trivial misdeeds and more major ones.

bad ac·tor *n.* a persistent wrongdoer, or somebody or something that causes trouble or has a harmful effect

bad ap·ple *n.* somebody who is thought to be the source of a bad influence on others, especially a source of moral corruption (*informal*) [From the idea that one bad apple can spoil a whole bunch]

bad·ass /bád àss/ *n.* (*plural* **-ass·es**) **BAD-TEMPERED PERSON** somebody who is bad-tempered or aggressive (*slang*) ■ *adj.* (*slang*) **1. BAD-TEMPERED** bad-tempered or aggressive ○ *badass talk* **2. EXTREMELY GOOD** extremely good and impressive, or having a very powerful effect [Mid-20thC. Expressive alteration of BAD.]

bad blood *n.* an intense and usually long-lasting feeling of hatred, anger, or resentment [From blood in the sense of "feelings, emotions"]

bad breath *n.* unpleasant-smelling breath

bad check *n.* a check that is invalid because there are insufficient funds in the account to cover it

bad debt *n.* a sum of money owed that is unlikely to be repaid

bad·die /báddee/, **bad·dy** (*plural* **-dies**) *n.* somebody, especially a character in a movie or a novel, who does evil or criminal things (*informal*)

bade past tense of **bid**

Ba·den-Pow·ell /bàyd'n pṓəl/, **Robert, 1st Baron Baden-Powell of Gilwell** (1857–1941) British soldier and founder of the Boy Scout movement (1908). Full name **Robert Stephenson Smyth Baden-Powell**

bad faith *n.* insincerity, especially as evidenced by actions that do not accord with somebody's stated intentions

badge /baj/ *n.* **1. EMBLEM** a small distinctively shaped or marked piece of fabric, metal, or plastic worn on clothing as a sign of rank, membership, or achievement **2. IDENTIFYING FEATURE** a characteristic or identifying mark of a particular quality or of a particular type of person ■ *vt.* (**badged, badg·ing, badg·es**) **1. PUT IDENTIFYING MARK ON SOMETHING** to put a badge or a distinctive identifying mark on something **2. SELL WITH BADGE ON** to market a product under different badges or brand names [14thC. From Old French *bage*, of unknown origin.]

Badger

badg·er /bájjər/ *n.* **BURROWING MAMMAL** a medium-sized burrowing animal that is related to the weasel and has short legs, strong claws, and a thick coat. It usually has black and white stripes on the sides of its head. Subfamily: Melinae. ■ *vt.* (**-ered, -er·ing, -ers**) **PESTER SOMEBODY** to pester or annoy somebody continually ○ *kept badgering me to go shopping* [Early 16thC. Origin uncertain, perhaps from BADGE, because of the markings on its head.]

Badg·er /bájjər/ *n.* somebody who was born in or who lives in Wisconsin [From the fact that the badger is the state animal of Wisconsin]

bad hair day *n.* a day during which somebody feels bad, looks bad, and experiences a series of difficulties or annoyances (*slang*)

bad·i·nage /bàdd'n áazh/ *n.* the exchange of playful or joking remarks between people in conversation [Mid-17thC. From French, via *badin* "fool, joker" from, ultimately, assumed Vulgar Latin *badare* "to yawn, gape" (source of English *bay* and *abash*).]

bad·lands /bád lándz/ *npl.* a barren area of gullies and bare mountain peaks or mesas formed by erosion

Bad·lands Na·tion·al Park national park in South Dakota and Nebraska that contains an arid region where wind erosion has caused unusual rock formations

bad·ly /báddlee/ *adv.* **1. POORLY** in an unsatisfactory, incompetent, or incorrect way ○ *The paint job had been badly done.* **2. UNHAPPILY** in such a way as to cause suffering, sorrow, or disappointment to the people involved ○ *felt badly let down* **3. SEVERELY** to a degree that causes serious concern for the person or thing involved ○ *Two of the survivors were very badly burned.* **4. VERY MUCH** very much, or to an extreme degree ○ *We're badly in need of new ideas.* **5. WICKEDLY** in a way that is immoral, or that causes trouble, offense, or annoyance to other people ○ *had been behaving badly* **6. REMORSEFUL** full of remorse or regret ○ *feel badly about it*

bad man, Bad Man *n.* the Devil (*regional*)

WORD KEY: REGIONAL NOTE

The bad man is a euphemism for the Devil that is often capitalized, suggesting importance to religion or superstition. The term is most common in Tennessee and the Lower South, with scattered occurrences from New York to California.

bad·min·ton /bád mìntən/ *n.* SPORTS a game similar to tennis, using rackets to strike a shuttlecock back and forth across a high net [Mid-19thC. Named for *Badminton*, a village in southwestern England that is the seat of the Duke of Beaufort.]

bad·mouth /bád mowth, -mowth/ (**-mouthed, -mouth·ing, -mouths**) *vt.* to make sharply critical or disparaging remarks about somebody to other people (*slang*)

bad news *n.* somebody or something that is likely to cause trouble and should be avoided (*slang*) ○ *Something tells me this guy's bad news.*

bad-talk (**bad-talked, bad-talk·ing, bad-talks**) *vt.* *Carib* to speak ill of somebody (*informal*)

bad-tem·pered *adj.* characterized by anger and unpleasantness toward other people —**bad-tem·pered·ly** *adv.*

Bae·de·ker /báydəkər/, **bae·de·ker** *n.* any guidebook for travelers [Mid-19thC. From Karl *Baedeker*, German publisher of a series of guidebooks.]

Bae·ke·land /báykələnd, báykə lànd/, **Leo** (1863–1944) Belgian-born U.S. chemist. He invented bakelite, a plastic resin (1909), and was a founder of the modern plastics industry. Full name **Leo Hendrik Baekeland**

Ba·ez /bī éz, bī èz/, **Joan** (*b.* 1941) U.S. folksinger and activist. From the 1960s, she was widely known for her folk and protest songs and for her human rights campaigning.

Baf·fin /báffin/, **William** (1584–1622) English navigator. While trying to find the Northwest Passage (1612–16), he explored the Hudson Strait and Baffin Island.

Baff·in Is·land Canada's largest island, located in the northeast of the country, forming part of Nunavut. Area: 183,810 sq. mi./476,070 sq. km.

baf·fle /báff'l/ *vt.* (**-fled, -fling, -fles**) **1. PUZZLE SOMEBODY** to prove too difficult or complicated for somebody to understand, solve, or deal with, and cause a feeling of confusion or helplessness **2. FRUSTRATE SOMETHING** to hinder or thwart an action or intention (*formal*) **3.** TECH **CONTROL SOMETHING** to impede or control the movement of a fluid or gas or the emission of sound or light waves ■ *n.* **1.** TECH **RESTRAINING DEVICE** a device used to control or impede the flow or emission of something and reduce its force **2.** ACOUSTICS **PARTITION IN LOUDSPEAKER** a partition in a loudspeaker or microphone intended to prevent sound waves of different frequencies from interfering with one another [Mid-16thC. Perhaps a blend of French *bafouer* "to ridicule" and Scots *bauchle* "to revile," both of unknown origin. Its earliest meaning was "to disgrace publicly."] —**baf·fle·ment** *n.*

baf·fle·gab /báff'l gàb/ *n.* pretentious and obscure talk full of technical terminology or circumlocutions (*slang*) [Mid-20thC. From BAFFLE + GAB.]

baf·fling /báffling/ *adj.* impossible for the mind to understand, and causing a feeling of confusion or helplessness ○ *I find the new technology baffling.*

bag /bag/ *n.* **1. FLEXIBLE CONTAINER** a nonrigid portable container made of fabric, leather, paper, or plastic in a wide variety of sizes, opening at one end and used mainly for packaging or carrying merchandise **2. AMOUNT IN FLEXIBLE CONTAINER** the amount that can be contained in a bag, often used as a measure **3. PORTABLE CONTAINER FOR EQUIPMENT OR BELONGINGS** a portable container made of strong flexible material for carrying somebody's belongings or equipment ○ *I threw everything into a bag and rushed out.* **4. ITEM OF BAGGAGE** an item of traveler's baggage, e.g., a suitcase, that can be carried by hand (*often used in the plural*) ○ *Did you check the bags before coming to the departure gate?* **5. PURSE** a woman's purse **6.** HUNT **NUMBER OF ANIMALS SHOT** the number of animals shot or captured by an individual hunter or party **7. OFFENSIVE TERM** an offensive term deliberately insulting a woman's age and appearance (*slang insult*) **8. SOMEBODY'S SPECIALTY** something that somebody is particularly interested in or good at (*slang dated*) **9.** BASEBALL = **base**[1] *n.* 21 **10.** DRUGS **SMALL QUANTITY OF ILLEGAL DRUG** a small quantity of an illegal drug, e.g., heroin or marijuana, in a piece of folded paper, a plastic bag, or a similar container (*slang*) ■ *v.* (**bagged, bag·ging, bags**) **1.** *vt.* **PUT INTO BAG** to put something into a bag ○ *He spent the afternoon bagging groceries at the local supermarket.* **2.** *vti.* **BULGE** to bulge or become baggy, or cause something to do this **3.** *vt.* HUNT **SHOOT OR CAPTURE ANIMAL** to shoot or capture a game animal or bird ○ *He bagged a six-point buck.* **4.** *vt.* **OBTAIN SOMETHING** to take, catch, seize, or steal something, usually in an opportunistic way (*informal*) ○ *They've gotten hold of our mailing list and are using it to bag some of our customers.* [13thC. From Old Norse *baggi.*] —**bag·ger** *n.* ◇ **bag and baggage** with all your belongings ◇ **bag of tricks 1.** everything, especially all the equipment necessary to do something (*informal*) ○ *They picked up the whole bag of tricks and slung it onto the back of a truck.* **2.** a magician's collection of equipment and props ◇ **bags of** a huge amount or number of something (*informal*) ◇ **be left holding the bag** to be left in a situation where you are solely responsible for something because other people have abdicated their own responsibility ◇ **in the bag** certain to be achieved or obtained (*informal*)

Ba·gan·da /bə gaándə/ *npl.* an ethnic group living in East Africa, mainly in Uganda, and representing about 30 percent of the population [Late 19thC. From Bantu.]

ba·gasse /bə gáss/ *n.* **1.** AGRIC **PULP** the pulp or dry refuse left after the juice has been extracted from sugar cane, grapes, or sugar beets, and used as fuel, in making paper, and as cattle feed **2.** PAPER **PAPER** paper made from bagasse [Early 19thC. Via French, from Spanish *bagazo* "dregs," from Latin *baca* "berry."]

bag·a·telle /bàggə tél/ *n.* **1.** MUSIC **SHORT PLAYFUL PIECE OF MUSIC** a short piece of classical music, usually for piano, written in a playful style **2.** GAME **BOARD GAME** a game played on a board or table, in which balls have to be propelled by a cue or spring-loaded launcher past obstacles and into numbered holes **3. SOMETHING UNIMPORTANT** a thing of little importance (*formal*) ○ *a mere bagatelle* [Mid-17thC. Via French, from Italian *bagatella*, of unknown origin.]

ba·gel /báyg'l/ *n.* a glazed ring-shaped bread roll made from dough that is dropped in boiling water and then baked, which gives a slightly chewy texture to the crust [Early 20thC. Via Yiddish *beygl* from, ultimately, Old High German *boug* "ring."]

bag·ful /bág fòol/ *n.* the amount a bag holds

bag·gage /bággij/ *n.* **1. PACKED SUITCASES AND BAGS** suitcases and other containers holding the belongings of people who are traveling **2. PRECONCEIVED IDEAS** ideas, beliefs, or practices retained from somebody's previous life experiences, especially insofar as they affect a new situation where they may be no longer relevant or appropriate (*informal*) ○ *emotional baggage* **3.** MIL **PORTABLE EQUIPMENT** the equipment and supplies that a military force carries with it on campaign **4. IMPUDENT GIRL OR WOMAN** a girl or woman who is thought of as impudent or obstinate (*insult dated*) **5. PROSTITUTE** an immoral woman, especially a prostitute (*insult dated*) [15thC. Via French, from Old French *bague* "bundle," of uncertain origin: probably from Germanic.]

bag·gage car *n.* a car on a train reserved for transporting passengers' baggage

bag·gage check *n.* a room in a train or bus station where you can temporarily deposit baggage

bag·gage han·dler *n.* somebody whose job it is to load and unload baggage onto and off airplanes

bag·ga·ta·way /bə gátə way/ *n.* an early from of lacrosse played by the Native American peoples of eastern North America [Early 19thC. From Ojibwa *paka'towe* "(he) plays lacrosse."]

bag·gies /bággeez/ *npl.* clothing that is cut extra large for the size of the wearer and hangs loosely on the body (*informal*)

Bag·gies /bággeez/ *tdmk.* a trademark for a brand of small plastic storage bags

bag·ging /bágging/ *n.* coarse material used for making bags

bag·gy /bággee/ (**-gi·er, -gi·est**) *adj.* hanging loosely, puffed out, or bulging, either as a deliberate style or as a result of being too big for the wearer or having stretched while being worn —**bag·gi·ly** *adv.* —**bag·gi·ness** *n.*

Bagh·dad /bág dàd/, **Bag·dad, Bagh·dād** capital of Iraq in the eastern part of the country, on the Tigris River, northwest of Basra. Population: 4,478,000 (1995).

bag job *n.* = **black bag job** (*slang*)

bag la·dy *n.* a homeless woman who carries her possessions in shopping bags (*informal*)

bag·man /bágmən/ (*plural* **-men** /-mən/) *n.* **1.** *U.S., ANZ* **SOMEBODY HANDLING ILLICIT MONEY** somebody who makes deliveries or collections of money on behalf of somebody else involved in criminal activities (*slang*) **2.** *Can* POL **FUNDRAISER** somebody who raises funds for a political party

ba·gnio /bánnyō, baán-/ (*plural* **-gnios**) *n.* **1. BROTHEL** a house of prostitution (*literary*) **2. PRISON** a prison, especially a prison in Asia (*archaic*) **3. BATHHOUSE** a bathhouse in Italy or Turkey (*archaic*) [Late 16thC. Via Italian *bagno* "bath" from Latin *balneus*, because public baths were often the site of illicit encounters and prostitution.]

Bag·nold /bág nōld/, **Enid** (1889–1981) British author and playwright. She is best known as the author of *National Velvet* (1935).

bag of wa·ters *n.* = **amnion**

bag per·son *n.* a homeless person who carries his or her possessions in shopping bags (*informal*)

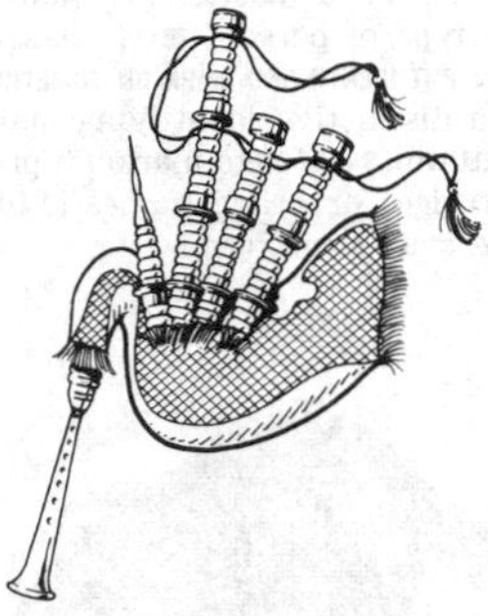

Bagpipes

bag·pipes /bág pīps/ *npl.* a wind instrument consisting of an inflatable bag with an inlet pipe and one or more outlet pipes that produce either a fixed or a variable note. The player squeezes the inflated bag under his or her arm, forcing the air out through the speaking pipes and using finger holes to control the pitch of the note. (*sometimes singular*) —**bag·pip·er** *n.*

bags *npl.* prominent folds of skin beneath the eyes, often caused by fatigue

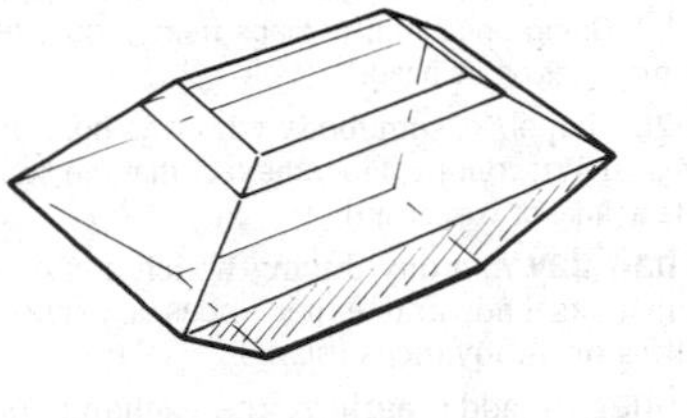

Baguette

ba·guette /ba gét/ *n.* **1.** FOOD **STICK-SHAPED LOAF** a long thin loaf of French bread **2. RECTANGULAR GEM** a gem cut into a long rectangular shape **3. SHAPE OF BAGUETTE GEM** the long narrow rectangular shape that a baguette gem is cut into **4.** ARCHIT **CONVEX MOLDING** a small narrow rounded convex molding on a wall or column [Early 18thC. Via French from, ultimately, Latin *baculum* "stick" (see BACULUM).]

bag·wig /bág wìg/ *n.* an 18th-century wig with the back hair gathered in a decorative bag

bah /baa, ba/ *interj.* used to express scornful irritation, disgust, or contempt

Ba·ha'i /baa haá ee, bə hī/ *n.* (*plural* **-ha'is**) **1. RELIGION EMPHASIZING SPIRITUAL UNITY OF HUMANKIND** a religion founded in Iran in 1863 that maintains that the teachings of all religions are of value and humankind is spiritually one, and advocates world peace **2. BELIEVER IN BAHA'I** somebody who believes in and follows the teachings of Baha'i ■ *adj.* **CONNECTED WITH BAHA'I** connected with or characteristic of Baha'i [Late 19thC. Via Persian *bahā'ī* from Arabic *bahā'* "splendor."] —**Ba·ha'ism** *n.* —**Ba·ha'ist** *n.*

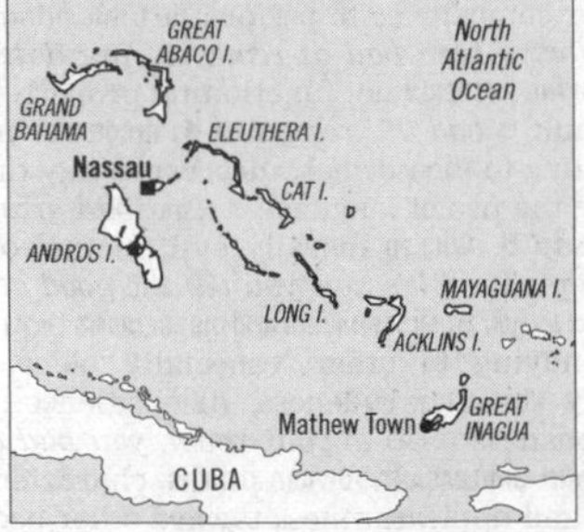

Bahamas

Ba·ha·mas /bə haáməz, -háyməz/ nation consisting of hundreds of islands, islets, and keys in the Atlantic Ocean southeast of Florida and north of Cuba. It was settled by the British in the 17th century and became independent in 1973. Language: English. Currency: Bahamian dollar. Capital: Nassau. Population: 259,367 (1996). Area: 5,380 sq. mi./13,940 sq. km. —**Ba·ha·mi·an** /bə háymee ən, bə h-mee ən/ *n., adj.*

Ba·ha·sa In·do·ne·sia /baa haássə-/ *n.* the form of Malay that is the official language of Indonesia [From Malay, "language of Indonesia"]

Ba·ha·sa Ma·lay·sia /baa haássə-/ *n.* the form of Malay that is the official language of Malaysia [From Malay, "language of Malaysia"]

Ba·hi·a /bə heé ə, baa eé ə/ **1.** state in eastern Brazil on the Atlantic coast. Capital: Salvador. Population: 12,531,895 (1996). Area: 218,850 sq. mi./566,970 sq. km. **2.** former name for **Salvador**

Ba·hi·a grass *n.* a perennial tropical American grass, grown in the southern United States for lawns, to stabilize soil, and as forage. Latin name: *Paspalum notatum.* [Early 20thC. Named after BAHIA.]

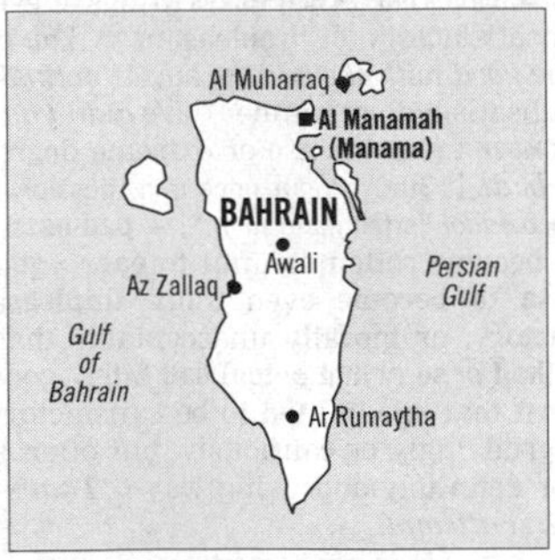

Bahrain

Bah·rain /baa ráyn/, **Bah·rein** independent island state on the Persian Gulf off the coast of Saudi Arabia, northwest of Qatar. Language: Arabic, English, Farsi, Urdu. Currency: Bahraini dinar. Capital: Manama. Population: 603,318 (1997). Area: 273 sq. mi./707 sq. km. —**Bah·rain·i** /baa ráynee/ (*plural* **-is**) *n., adj.*

baht /baat/ (*plural* **bahts** *or* **baht**) *n.* **1.** see table at **currency 2. SOMETHING WORTH A BAHT** a bill or coin worth one baht [Early 19thC. From Thai *bāt.*]

baigan *n. Carib* = **bhaigan**

Bai·kal, Lake /bī kaál/ the world's deepest lake and the largest freshwater lake on the Eurasian continent, in southern Siberia, Russia. Area: 12,200 sq. mi./31,500 sq. km. Depth: 5,371 ft./1,637 m.

bail[1] /bayl/ *n.* **1. SECURITY FOR APPEARANCE IN COURT** a sum of money deposited to secure an accused person's temporary release from custody and to guarantee that person's appearance in court at a later date. If the person fails to appear in court on the date set, the money is forfeited. **2. SOMEBODY WHO PAYS BAIL** somebody who deposits money as bail for somebody else **3. RELEASE UNDER SECURITY** temporary release from custody after bail has been paid ○ *Her brother was out on bail.* ■ *vt.* (**bailed, bail·ing, bails**) **FREE SOMEBODY BY PAYING BAIL** to release an accused person from custody after bail has been paid (*usually passive*) [14thC. Via Old French, "temporary custody," from, ultimately, Latin *bajulus* "somebody who carries (responsibility)," of unknown origin.] ◇ **jump** *or* **skip bail** to fail to appear in court as promised at the end of a bail period (*informal*)

bail out *vt.* to secure somebody's release from legal custody by paying bail, or posting bond

bail[2] /bayl/ (**bailed, bail·ing, bails**) *vti.* to empty water out of a boat, using a bucket or similar container ○ *We bailed the sinking boat for an hour.* [Early 17thC. From earlier *baille* "bucket," via Old French, from an assumed Vulgar Latin *bajula* "water carrier."] —**bail·er** *n.*

bail out *v.* **1.** *vti.* EMPTY WATER OUT OF BOAT to empty water out of a boat, using a bucket or similar container ○ *bailing water out as the boat slowly sank* **2.** *vi.* PARACHUTE FROM PLANE to escape from a plane that is in danger of crashing by making a parachute jump **3.** *vi.* ESCAPE FROM DIFFICULT SITUATION to abandon hurriedly and unceremoniously a situation that is dangerous or difficult ○ *When the company hit the skids, she was the first to bail out.* **4.** *vt.* HELP SOMEBODY OUT OF TROUBLE to help somebody out of a difficult situation

bail[3] /bayl/ *n.* in cricket, either of the two short pieces of wood laid on top of the stumps to make the wicket [Mid-18thC. Origin uncertain, possibly via Old French from, ultimately, Latin *baculum* "stick" (see BACULUM). Originally "outer wall of a castle."]

bail[4] /bayl/ *n.* **1.** HINGED BAR a hinged bar on a typewriter or printer that holds the paper against the platen **2.** SEMICIRCULAR HANDLE a semicircular handle, e.g., on a bucket **3.** SEMICIRCULAR SUPPORT a semicircular support, e.g., to hold up the canopy on a covered wagon [15thC. Origin uncertain, probably from assumed Old English *bēgel* or a Scandinavian word meaning "ring."]

bail·a·ble /báyləb'l/ *adj.* **1.** ELIGIBLE FOR BAIL eligible to be released on bail ○ *a bailable prisoner* **2.** ALLOWING BAIL for which bail is allowable ○ *a bailable offense*

bail bar *n.* = **bail**[4] *n.* 1

bail bond *n.* a document in which the prisoner released on bail and the person who pays the bail money promise that the prisoner will appear in court at a set time

bail bonds·man (*plural* **bail bonds·men**) *n.* somebody engaged in the business of providing bail money, or acting as surety, for an accused person

bai·ley /báylee/ (*plural* **-leys**) *n.* **1.** OUTER WALL OF A CASTLE the outermost wall surrounding a castle **2.** COURT INSIDE A CASTLE WALL a courtyard inside the walls, especially the outermost walls, of a castle [13thC. Origin uncertain, probably an alteration of BAIL[3], under the influence of medieval Latin *ballium*.]

Bai·ley bridge *n.* a temporary steel bridge made of prefabricated parts and designed for quick construction [Mid-20thC. Named for the English engineer Sir D. Coleman *Bailey* (1901–85), who designed it.]

bail·iff /báylif/ *n.* **1.** LAW COURT OFFICIAL a court official whose tasks include supervising prisoners and keeping order in court during a trial **2.** *U.K.* LAW SHERIFF'S OFFICER a legal officer who serves under a sheriff and is empowered to take possession of a debtor's property, forcibly if necessary, to serve writs, and to make arrests **3.** *U.K.* STEWARD a steward or agent of a landowner or landlord [13thC. Via the Old French stem *baillif-* "overseer" from assumed medieval Latin *bajulivus*, from Latin *bajulus* (see BAIL[1]).]

bail·i·wick /báyli wìk/ *n.* an area of activity in which somebody has particular responsibility, or in which he or she has specialized knowledge or ability ○ *Export permits are her bailiwick.* [15thC. From BAILIFF + *wik* "town" (via Old English *wīc* from Latin *vicus*; see VICINITY).]

bail·ment /báylmənt/ *n.* the granting of bail to somebody in custody

bail·out /báyl òwt/ *n.* an intervention by a person or company to help another person or company out of financial difficulties

bails·man /báylzmən/ (*plural* **-men** /-mən/) *n.* LAW = **bail bondsman**

Bai·ly's beads /bàyleez-/ *npl.* bright points of sunlight that briefly appear around the Moon immediately before and after a total eclipse of the Sun. They are caused by sunlight shining through valleys on the Moon. [Mid-19thC. Named for the English astronomer Francis *Baily* (1774–1844).]

Bain-marie

bain-ma·rie /bàN mə rée/ (*plural* **bain-ma·ries**) *n.* a cooking utensil containing heated water into which another container is placed to be kept warm or cooked gently [Early 19thC. From French, translation of medieval Latin *balneum Mariae*, translation of Greek *kaminos Marias* "alchemist's apparatus," literally "furnace of Maria," alchemist and sister of Moses.]

Bai·ram /bī ráam/ *n.* either of two Islamic festivals, the Lesser Bairam celebrated at the end of Ramadan or the Greater Bairam seventy days later, at the end of the Islamic year [Late 16thC. Via Turkish *bayram* from, ultimately, Persian *bazrām*.]

Baird /baird/, **John Logie** (1888–1946) British inventor. He demonstrated the first television system in 1926. He also researched radar.

Bai·ri·ki /bī réekee/ administrative center of Kiribati, situated on Tarawa atoll in the western Pacific Ocean. Population: 1,956.

bairn /bairn/ *n. Scotland, N England* a young child [Old English *bearn*. Ultimately from an Indo-European word meaning "to carry, bear children," which is also the ancestor of English *bear, bring, suffer,* and *metaphor*.]

Bai·sak·hi /bī sáakee/ *n.* the Sikh New Year festival, usually celebrated on April 13. It commemorates the founding in 1699 of the Khalsa order by Gobind Singh.

bait[1] /bayt/ *n.* **1.** ANGLING, HUNT FOOD FOR ATTRACTING ANIMALS a piece of food attached to the end of a hook or thrown into water to entice a fish into biting it, or placed in a trap to lure an animal in ○ *fishing with live bait* **2.** ENTICEMENT something used to attract somebody or something else into being caught, or used to tempt somebody to do something ■ *vt.* (**bait·ed, bait·ing, baits**) **1.** ANGLING, HUNT PUT FOOD ON HOOK to put a food attractant on a hook or in a trap ○ *This line's baited with a minnow.* **2.** HARASS SOMEBODY to persecute, tease, or harass somebody ○ *Stop baiting your little brother!* **3.** ATTACK ANIMAL WITH DOGS to set dogs onto a chained animal, usually a bear or bull, for sport [13thC. Noun: from Old Norse *beit* "food"; verb: from *beita* "to hunt with dogs," from *bíta* "to bite."] —**bait·er** *n.* ◇ **fish** *or* **cut bait** to do what needs to be done or else step aside and allow somebody else to do it ◇ **rise to the bait** to react to something, especially to temptation or provocation, in precisely the way that somebody wants you to, e.g., by getting angry when somebody teases you

bait[2] /bayt/ *vi.* = **bate**[2]

bait and switch *n.* a tactic used in sales in which buyers are tempted by an advertised bargain but then persuaded to buy a more expensive item instead (*slang*)

bai·za /bī zaa/ (*plural* **-zas** *or* **-za**) *n.* see table at **currency** [Late 20thC. Via Arabic from Hindi *paisā*.]

baize /bayz/ *n.* a green woolen cloth, similar to felt, used chiefly for covering the tops of pool tables or card tables [Late 16thC. From French *baies*, the plural of *bai* "bay-colored" (see BAY[4]), probably because of its original color.]

Ba·ja Cal·i·for·nia /baa haa-/ peninsula in northwestern Mexico between the Gulf of California and the Pacific Ocean, divided into the states of Baja California and Baja California Sur. Length: 760 mi./1,220 km.

ba·jee *n.* FOOD = **bhaji**

bake /bayk/ *v.* (**baked, bak·ing, bakes**) **1.** *vti.* COOK FOOD IN OVEN to cook something such as bread, a cake, or a pie in an oven by dry heat, or be cooked in this way **2.** *vti.* HARDEN BY HEAT to become hardened, or harden something, by exposing it to dry heat **3.** *vi.* BE VERY HOT to be or feel very hot (*informal*) ○ *You must be baking in that heavy coat.* ■ *n.* **1.** AMOUNT BAKED a number of things baked at the same time **2.** PARTY WITH BAKED FOOD a party at which baked food is served (*informal*) (*often used in combination*) ○ *an oyster bake on the shore* [Old English *bacan* (source of English *batch*). Ultimately from an Indo-European base meaning "to warm," which is also the ancestor of English *bath*.]

baked A·las·ka *n.* a dessert consisting of a cooked cake base that is cooled, topped with ice cream, covered with meringue, and then quickly browned in a very hot oven

Ba·ke·lite *tdmk.* a trademark for any of various synthetic resins used in many manufacturing applications

Bake-Off a service mark for a cooking contest during which contestants prepare their own recipes, especially of baked goods, with the winners receiving prizes

bak·er /báykər/ *n.* **1.** SOMEBODY WHO MAKES BREAD AND CAKES somebody who makes bread, cakes, and other baked foods, especially somebody who makes them for sale **2.** PORTABLE OVEN a portable oven

Bak·er /báykər/, **Dame Janet** (*b.* 1933) British mezzo-soprano. After performing as a soloist for Sir John Barbirolli in the 1960s, she moved on to opera, and is associated especially with English music. Born **Janet Abbott**

AKG London

Josephine Baker

Bak·er, Josephine (1906–75) U.S.-born French dancer and entertainer. She performed as a singer and dancer in New York before settling in Paris in 1925. Highly popular in Europe, she campaigned for racial equality in the United States in the 1950s and 1960s. Born **Freda Josephine McDonald**

bak·er's doz·en *n.* a set of thirteen items [From the fact that retailers of bread formerly received an extra loaf with each dozen from the baker, which they were entitled to keep as profit]

Ba·kers·field /báykərzfeeld/ city in south central California in the valley of the San Joaquin River. Population: 205,508 (1996).

bak·er·sheet /báykər shèet/ *n. New England* a drip pan used in cooking

bak·er·y /báykəree/ (*plural* **-ies**) *n.* **1.** PLACE WHERE THINGS ARE BAKED a building or part of a building where items of food, especially bread and cakes, are baked **2.** STORE SELLING BAKED FOOD a store or part of a store where items of baked food, especially bread and cakes, are sold [Mid-19thC. Its earliest meaning was "the work of a baker."]

bake·shop /báyk shòp/ *n.* a small bakery, especially one forming part of a larger store such as a supermarket

bak·ing /báyking/ *n.* **1.** COOKING OF BREAD AND CAKES the cooking of bread, cakes, and other foods by dry heat in an oven ○ *did the baking early in the morning* **2.** AMOUNT BAKED AT ONE TIME a quantity of items baked at one time ○ *a baking of 46 rolls* ■ *adj.* VERY HOT very hot and dry ○ *a baking sun*

bak·ing pow·der *n.* a mixture containing sodium bicarbonate, starch, and acids, used to make cakes and some light doughs rise. The acids react with bicarbonate of soda when liquid is added, releasing carbon dioxide that aerates the mixture.

bak·ing sheet *n.* a flat metal tray used for cooking, especially baking, food in an oven

bak·ing so·da *n.* sodium bicarbonate used as a raising agent in baking

ba·kla·va /baáklə vaà, baáklə vaá/ *n.* a dessert, originally from Turkey, made of paper-thin pastry brushed with butter, layered with nuts and baked, with syrup or honey poured over it after cooking [Mid-17thC. From Turkish.]

bak·ra /bákrə/ *n. Carib* a white person, particularly one from Britain [Mid-18thC. From Ibibio and Efik *(m)bakara* "European, master."]

bak·sheesh /bák sheèsh, bak sheésh/ *n.* in the Middle East, money given as a tip or bribe, or as charity [Mid-18thC. From Persian *bakšīš*. Ultimately from an Indo-European word meaning "to share out," which is also the ancestor of English *pagoda* and *nebbish*.]

Ba·ku /baa kóo/ capital of Azerbaijan, on the shores of the Caspian Sea, in the center of an oil-producing region in the eastern part of the country. Population: 1,780,000 (1990).

Ba·ku·nin /bə kóonin, -kóonyin/, **Mikhail** (1814–76) Russian-born anarchist. Born an aristocrat, he was sent in exile to Siberia in 1857, but escaped to England in 1861 to become Europe's leading anarchist. Full name **Mikhail Aleksandrovich Bakunin**

BAL *n.* = **dimercaprol** [An acronym of *British anti-lewisite*]

bal. *abbr.* balance

Ba·laam /báyləm/ *n.* in the Bible, a Mesopotamian seer who, when called on to curse the Israelites, instead praised them after being reproached by his donkey (Numbers 22–24)

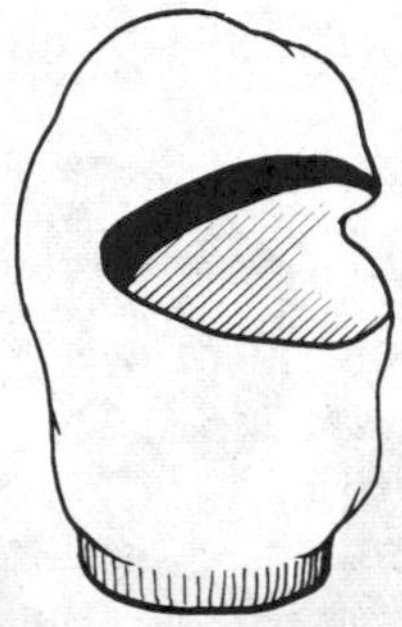

Balaclava

bal·a·cla·va /bàllə klaávə/ *n.* a close-fitting knitted covering for the head and neck, leaving only the face, or parts of it, exposed [Late 19thC. Named for the village of *Balaklava* in the Crimea, probably because the cap was worn by infantry involved in the campaign there.]

Bal·a·guer /baàlə gáir/, **Joaquín** (*b.* 1907) Dominican political leader. He was president of the Dominican Republic (1960–62, 1966–78, and 1986–96). Full name **Joaquín Vidella Balaguer**

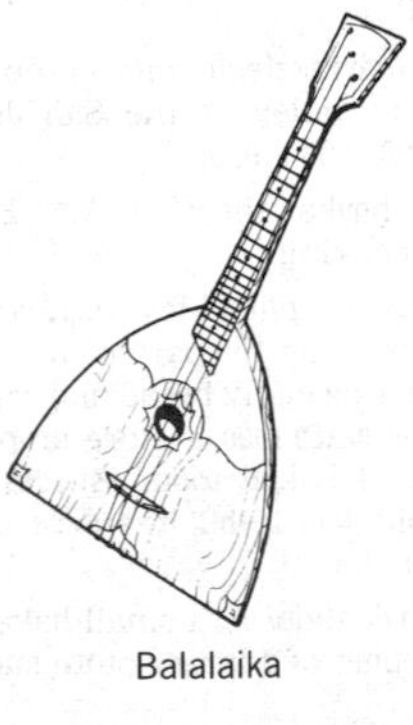

Balalaika

bal·a·lai·ka /bàllə líkə/ *n.* a Russian musical instrument with a triangular sound box and three strings that produces sounds similar to a mandolin when plucked or strummed [Late 18thC. From Russian, of Turkic origin.]

bal·ance /bálləns/ *n.* **1. STEADY STATE ON A NARROW BASE** a state in which a body or object remains reasonably steady in a particular position while resting on a base that is narrow or small relative to its other dimensions. For human beings, this most commonly involves remaining upright and steady on the feet. ○ *He lost his balance and fell from the beam.* **2. OPPOSITION OF EQUAL FORCES** a state in which two opposing forces or factors are of equal strength or importance so that they effectively cancel each other out and stability is maintained **3. HARMONY** a

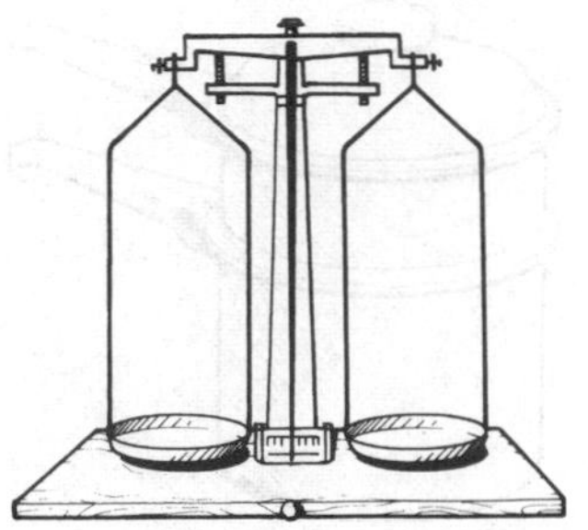

Balance

state in which various elements form a satisfying and harmonious whole and nothing is out of proportion or unduly emphasized at the expense of the rest **4. EMOTIONAL STABILITY** a state of emotional and mental stability in which somebody is calm and able to make rational decisions and judgments **5.** TECH **WEIGHING MACHINE** a simple mechanical device for weighing objects or samples, often consisting of a pivoted horizontal beam with a pan suspended from each end. Material to be weighed is put in one pan and weights of a fixed value are gradually added to the other until the beam returns to the horizontal. **6. COUNTERWEIGHT** something that offsets or counters the weight or influence of another element ○ *a system of checks and balances* **7. GREATER PART** the greater, more significant, or more influential part of something, such as evidence or opinion that is likely to sway a decision **8. REMAINDER** a remaining or outstanding amount, e.g., the amount remaining in a bank account after a withdrawal or the amount still to be paid to settle a bill **9.** ACCT **EQUAL DEBIT AND CREDIT** a position where the amounts on the debit and credit sides of an account are equal and cancel each other out **10.** ACCT **DIFFERENCE BETWEEN DEBIT AND CREDIT** the amount by which the debit and credit sides of an account differ **11.** CHEM **EQUALITY OF ELEMENTS IN AN EQUATION** a state of a chemical equation where the number of the atoms of each chemical element are equal on both sides of the equation ■ *v.* **(-anced, -anc·ing, -anc·es) 1.** *vti.* **REMAIN IN OR GIVE SOMETHING EQUILIBRIUM** to achieve or maintain, or cause somebody or something to achieve or maintain, a position of steadiness while resting on a narrow base ○ *balanced precariously on a branch* **2.** *vti.* **PLACE IN PRECARIOUS POSITION** to place an object in a position where it is or seems to be in imminent danger of falling over or of falling off something (*often passive*) **3.** *vt.* **ASSESS SOMETHING** to assess and compare the relative importance of different factors or alternatives before making a choice or decision ○ *balanced the pros and cons of the plan before moving ahead with it* **4.** *vt.* **WEIGH IN BALANCE** to weigh something in a balance or by an action or method that resembles the working of a balance **5.** *vti.* **EQUAL OR CANCEL OUT** to be equal to something in force, weight, or importance, or cancel it out **6.** *vt.* ARTS **BRING ELEMENTS INTO HARMONY** to arrange the different elements of something so that they form a harmonious and well-proportioned whole **7.** *vt.* MATH, CHEM **BRING EQUATION INTO EQUALITY** to bring the elements of a chemical or mathematical equation into a state of equality **8.** *vt.* ACCT **ASSESS ACCOUNT** to assess the relative positions of the debit and credit sides of an account **9.** *vt.* ACCT **EQUALIZE ACCOUNT** to make the debit and credit sides of an account equal [13thC. Via Old French from, ultimately, Latin *(libra) bilanx*, literally "(scales) with two pans," from *lanx* "plate, pan."] —**bal·ance·a·ble** *adj.* ◇ **hang in the balance** to be in a dramatic and tense situation where two diametrically opposed outcomes are possible and the possibility of an unfavorable one is real and greatly feared ◇ **hold the balance 1.** to have the power to decide in which way a situation will develop or which of two opposing sides will prevail **2.** to control the key to maintaining an existing state of equilibrium between two opposing forces ◇ **on (the) balance** having taken all the relevant factors into consideration and assessed their relative significance ○ *The situation, on balance, is relatively hopeful.* ◇ **strike a balance** to reach a compromise between two extremes ◇ **throw somebody off balance** to surprise or confuse somebody

balance out *v.* **1.** *vti.* **CANCEL SOMETHING OUT** to act as an equal and opposing weight, force, or value to something and either neutralize or complement its effect ○ *This gain balances out last month's losses.* **2.** *vi.* **WORK OUT EVENLY** to arrive at a state of equality or harmony, usually through one thing offsetting the other over a period of time ○ *These things tend to balance out in the end.*

Bal·ance *n.* ZODIAC = **Libra**

bal·ance beam *n.* a narrow horizontal wooden bar on legs that women gymnasts stand on to perform balancing exercises, or the event involving this

bal·anced /bállənst/ *adj.* **1. EVEN-HANDED** taking account of all sides on their merits without prejudice or favoritism ○ *a balanced assessment* **2. HEALTHY** containing different elements in suitable quantities or suitably arranged to produce a satisfying and effective whole ○ *a balanced diet* **3. MENTALLY STABLE** in a state of mental and emotional stability and able to make rational judgments

bal·ance of pay·ments *n.* the difference between the amount paid by a national government to other countries and the amount it receives from them

bal·ance of pow·er *n.* **1. EQUILIBRIUM OF POWER BETWEEN NATIONS** the distribution of power among two or more nations, where the pattern of force and dominance among them is balanced such that no single nation has dominance over the others **2. POWER TO AFFECT SITUATION DECISIVELY** the power of a single country, group, or individual to affect a situation decisively by supporting either of two opposing sides whose powers are equally balanced

bal·ance of ter·ror *n.* a situation in which two potentially hostile nations or groups have the military capability to inflict roughly equal destruction on each other and war is thus prevented

bal·ance of trade *n.* the difference between the value of the total imports and total exports of a country as assessed over a fixed period

bal·ance sheet *n.* a statement showing the assets and liabilities of a company or institution at a particular time

bal·ance weight *n.* a weight used to counterbalance a moving part in a machine

bal·ance wheel *n.* a wheel in a machine, especially in a clock, that regulates the rate of movement of the main mechanism

Bal·an·chine /bállən cheèn, bàllən cheén/, **George** (1904–83) Russian-born U.S. dancer and choreographer. Cofounder of the New York City Ballet (1948), he revolutionized classical ballet with his innovative choreography. Born **Georgy Melitonovich Balanchivadze**

bal·anc·ing act *n.* **1. ATTEMPT TO DEAL WITH MANY THINGS** a skillful or precarious attempt to deal with or survive a situation where you have to conciliate opposing groups, reconcile opposing views, or perform a large variety of tasks (*informal*) **2.** ARTS **PERFORMANCE OF BALANCING THINGS** an entertainment in which the performer keeps objects balanced in precarious positions, or balances himself or herself on an unstable object, such as an upended chair

bal·an·i·tis /bàllə nítiss/ *n.* inflammation of the head of the penis, usually caused by an infection [Mid-19thC. Formed from Greek *balanos* "acorn, glans penis."]

bal·as /bálləss/, **bal·as ru·by** *n.* a red form of the mineral spinel, used as a gemstone [15thC. Via Old French *balais* and Spanish *balax* from, ultimately, Arabic *balakš*, from Persian *Badakšān*, the region of Afghanistan where it is found.]

ba·la·ta /bə laátə/ *n.* a gum resembling and used as a substitute for rubber, made from the sap of a tropical tree. It is used for making gaskets and chewing gum, and as a substitute for gutta percha. [Early 17thC. From Carib *balatá*.]

bal·bo·a /bal bó ə/ *n.* **1.** see table at **currency 2. SOMETHING WORTH A BALBOA** a coin worth one balboa [Early 20thC. Named for Vasco Núñez de BALBOA.]

Bal·bo·a /bal bó ə/ town and port in Panama where the Panama Canal flows into the Gulf of Panama. Population: 1,214 (1990).

Bal·bo·a, Vasco Núñez de (1475?–1519) Spanish explorer. He was the first European to reach the Pacific Ocean (1513).

bal·co·ny /bálkənee/ (*plural* **-nies**) *n.* **1.** ARCHIT **PLATFORM ON WALL OF BUILDING** a platform projecting from the interior or exterior wall of a building, usually enclosed by a rail or parapet **2.** THEATER **THEATER GALLERY** one of the separate areas of seating raised entirely above the ground level in a theater, movie theater, or concert hall [Early 17thC. Via Italian *balcone* from Old Italian, "scaffold," from a prehistoric Germanic word that is also the ancestor of English *balk* "wooden beam."] —**bal·co·nied** *adj.*

bald /bawld/ *adj.* **1. WITH HAIRLESS HEAD** having little or no hair on the head **2. WITHOUT NATURAL COVERING** with little or no hair, fur, grass, or other natural covering, and with the bare skin or surface showing ○ *a bald patch on the grass* **3.** AUTOMOT **WORN** having a very worn-down tread ○ *Bald tires are dangerous on wet roads.* **4. PLAIN** plain and direct, with no attempt to elaborate or explain ○ *a bald statement of the facts* **5.** *Can* **TREELESS** treeless or nearly treeless ○ *a bald prairie* **6. UNORNAMENTED** plain, bare, and without ornamentation, often to the point of seeming dull or prosaic **7.** ZOOL **WITH WHITE MARKINGS** used to describe birds and mammals that have white markings on the face or head [14thC. Origin uncertain, possibly formed from an earlier *bal* "white spot or streak, especially on a horse's face."] —**bald·ness** *n.*

bal·da·chin /báwldəkin, báld-/ *n.* **1.** ARCHIT, CHR **CANOPY** a canopy made of cloth or stone erected over an altar, shrine, or throne in a Christian church **2.** CHR **PORTABLE CANOPY** a canopy carried above a priest or venerated object during a religious procession **3.** TEXTILES **BROCADE** a rich silk and gold brocade [Late 16thC. From Italian *baldacchino*, from *Baldacco* "Baghdad," where it was made.]

bald cy·press *n.* **1. SOUTHERN U.S. CONIFER** a deciduous coniferous tree, related to sequoias, found in the southern United States. Latin name: *Taxodium distichum.* **2. WOOD OF BALD CYPRESS** the hard wood of a bald cypress tree, used in boat building and for making shingles [*Bald* from the fact that it sheds its needles, unlike most members of its family]

Bald eagle

bald ea·gle *n.* a large North American eagle found mainly near lakes and rivers, the adult of which has a white head and tail. An image of it is used as an emblem of the United States. Latin name: *Haliaeetus leucocephalus.*

Bal·der /báwldər/ *n.* in Norse mythology, one of Odin's sons, who was god of the summer sun. He was vulnerable only to mistletoe, by which he was killed.

bal·der·dash /báwldər dàsh/ *n.* senseless or pointless talk or writing [Late 16thC. Origin unknown.]

bald-faced *adj.* = **barefaced** *adj.* 1

bald·head /báwld hèd/ *n.* somebody with a bald head (*informal offensive*)

bald·ing /báwlding/ *adj.* partly bald, or in the process of losing the hair on the head

bald·ly /báwldlee/ *adv.* in a simple and blunt way ○ *To put it baldly, she did a lousy job.*

bald·pate /báwld pàyt/ *n.* = **widgeon**

bal·dric /báwldrik/ *n.* a sash or belt worn from one shoulder to the opposite hip, used to support a sword [13thC. Directly and via Old French *baudre* from Middle High German *balderich*, of unknown origin.]

Bald·win /báldwin/ borough in southwestern Pennsylvania on the Monongahela River. It is a southeastern suburb of Pittsburgh. Population: 21,923 (1990).

Bald·win, James (1924–87) U.S. writer. His novels and essays addressed racism in the United States, and include *Go Tell It on the Mountain* (1953) and *Notes of a Native Son* (1955). Full name **James Arthur Baldwin**

Bald·win, Robert (1804–58) Canadian statesman. He

Bob Adelman

James Baldwin

was joint prime minister of the united Province of Canada (1842–43, 1848–51).

Bald·win, Stanley, 1st Earl Baldwin of Bewdley (1867–1947) British statesman. Conservative party leader and prime minister (1923–24, 1924–29, 1935–37), he retired from politics in 1937 amid criticism that he had ignored Germany's preparations for World War II.

Bald·win Park city in southwestern California, in the San Gabriel Valley. It is an eastern suburb of Los Angeles. Population: 71,414 (1996).

bald·y /báwldee/ (*plural* **baldi·es**) *n.* somebody who is bald or balding (*informal offensive*)

bale[1] /bayl/ *n.* **LARGE BUNDLE OR PACKAGE** a large bundle or package of hay or a raw material such as cotton, tightly bound with string or wire to keep it in shape during transportation or storage ■ *vti.* (**baled, bal·ing, bales**) **MAKE INTO BUNDLES** to gather and fasten material or goods into bales ○ *baling hay* [14thC. From Old French, from a prehistoric Germanic word that is also the ancestor of English *ball* and *balloon*. The underlying meaning is "rolled-up bundle."] —**bal·er** *n.*

bale[2] /bayl/ *n.* evil or suffering (*archaic or literary*) [Old English *bealu*]

Bal·e·ar·ic /bàllee árrik/ *adj.* belonging to or typical of the Balearic Islands

Balearic Islands

Bal·e·ar·ic Is·lands /bàllee árrik-/ island group in the western Mediterranean that includes Mallorca, Menorca, and Ibiza. It is a province and autonomous region of Spain. Population: 736,865 (1991). Area: 1,935 sq. mi./5,012 sq. km.

ba·leen /bə léen/ *n.* a horny substance that grows as fringed plates from the upper jaws of certain whales, acting to strain food, especially small crustaceans, from the water [14thC. Via Old French *balaine* from Latin *balaena* "whale," from Greek *phalaina.*]

ba·leen whale *n.* a large whale that has two blowholes and a set of horny fringed plates (**baleen**) instead of teeth. Right, gray, and blue whales are baleen whales. Suborder: Mysticeti.

bale·ful /báylfəl/ *adj.* **1. THREATENING** threatening, or seeming to threaten, harm, or misfortune ○ *a baleful stare* **2. HARMFUL** causing or threatening to cause harm —**bale·ful·ly** *adv.* —**bale·ful·ness** *n.*

WORD KEY: USAGE

baleful or **baneful**? ***Baleful***, meaning "harmful," is a much more common term than ***baneful***, meaning "destructive," which is largely confined to literary use.

Ba·li /baálee/ mountainous island east of Java, Indonesia, that is a popular vacation destination. Capital: Denpasar. Population: 2,895,600 (1995). Area: 2,171 sq. mi./5,623 sq. km.

bal·i·bun·tal /bàlli búnt'l/ *n.* **1. WOVEN STRAW** fine straw woven into material, used especially for making hats in the Philippines **2. STRAW HAT** a hat made from balibuntal [Early 20thC. From *Baliuag* in the Philippines, where it was made, + Tagalog *buntal* "straw from the talipot palm tree."]

Ba·lik·pa·pan /baàlik paá paan/ city and port in Indonesia, situated on the island of Borneo, on the Makassar Strait. Population: 368,729 (1990).

Ba·li·nese /baàlə néez, -néess/ (*plural* **-nese**) *n.* **1. SOMEBODY FROM BALI** somebody who was born or raised on the Indonesian island of Bali **2. AUSTRONESIAN LANGUAGE** a language spoken on Bali that is a member of the Austronesian language family. Balinese is spoken by between two and three million people. [Early 19thC. From Dutch *Balinees*, from *Bali* (see BALI).] —**Ba·li·nese** *adj.*

Ba·li·nese cat *n.* a domestic cat belonging to a breed resembling Siamese cats but with long hair

bal·i·si·er /bə léezee ày/ *n.* a small bushy shrub bearing a distinctive flower ranging in color from yellow to bright red. The flower is the symbol of the People's National Movement, one of the major political parties of Trinidad. Family: Heliconia.

balk /bawk/, **baulk** *v.* (**balked, balk·ing, balks; baulked, baulk·ing, baulks**) **1.** *vi.* **STOP SHORT** to stop suddenly and refuse to go on, especially when faced with an obstacle ○ *The horse balked and refused the jump.* **2.** *vi.* **TURN AWAY** to hesitate or be unwilling to do something, usually because of a natural revulsion or moral scruples ○ *I balked at getting down on my hands and knees to wipe the floor.* **3.** *vti.* **REFUSE TO DEAL WITH SOMETHING** to refuse to deal with something that presents a difficulty **4.** *vt.* **FOIL SOMEBODY** to prevent somebody from carrying out a plan or intention (*often passive*) ○ *acted like a lion balked of its prey* **5.** *vi.* BASEBALL **MAKE ILLEGAL PITCHING MOTION** to make an illegal motion in baseball, by pretending to pitch but not actually pitching ■ *n.* **1.** BUILDING **LARGE PIECE OF WOOD** a large squared piece of wood **2.** BUILDING **WOODEN BEAM IN HOUSE ROOF** a wooden tie beam in the roof of a house **3.** AGRIC **UNPLOWED RIDGE** a ridge of land left unplowed to serve as a boundary or to counter erosion **4.** BASEBALL **ILLEGAL PITCHING MOVE** an illegal motion by the pitcher when there are runners on base, in which the pitcher pretends to throw the ball toward the plate or to a base but does not release it **5. OBSTACLE** something that hinders or frustrates ○ *a balk to further progress in the peace negotiations* **6.** CUE GAMES **AREA BEHIND BALKLINE** the area between the balkline and the bottom cushion on a billiard table, or in balkline billiards between any balkline and the cushion [From Old English *balca* "ridge" and Old Norse *bálkr* "beam, bar," both ultimately from an Indo-European word meaning "beam," which is also the ancestor of English *balcony, fulcrum,* and *debauch*] —**balk·er** *n.*

Bal·kan /báwlkən/ *adj.* relating to the states of the Balkan Peninsula, or their peoples or cultures [Mid-19thC. From Turkish, name of a mountain chain.]

Bal·kan·i·za·tion /bàwlkəni záysh'n/, **bal·kan·i·za·tion** *n.* division of an area, region, or group into smaller and often mutually hostile units [Early 20thC. From the political fragmentation of the Balkan states between the Treaty of Berlin (1878) and the Balkan Wars (1912–13).] —**Bal·kan·ize** *vt.*

Bal·kan Moun·tains extension of the Alpine mountain system, running across central Bulgaria. The highest point is Botev Peak7,795 ft./2,376 m.

Bal·kan Pen·in·su·la mountainous peninsula in southeastern Europe between the Adriatic and Ionian seas in the west and the Aegean and Black seas in the east. It includes Albania, Bosnia and Herzegovina, Bulgaria, mainland Greece, Macedonia, European Turkey, and parts of Croatia, Slovenia, and Yugoslavia. The Sava and Danube rivers are considered to be the northern borders.

Bal·kans = **Balkan States**

Bal·kan States, Bal·kans the countries in the Balkan Peninsula, including Albania, Bosnia-Herzegovina, Bulgaria, Croatia, Greece, Macedonia, the European part of Turkey, and the Federal Republic of Yugoslavia

balk·line /báwk lìn/, **balk line** *n.* **1. LINE ON BILLIARD TABLE** a straight line parallel to the end of a billiard table, from behind which opening shots with the cue ball are made **2. DIVIDING LINE ON BILLIARD TABLE** one of four lines parallel to the edges of a billiard table that divide it into the central area and eight smaller compartments that are used in a particular variety of billiards **3.** VARIETY OF BILLIARDS the variety of billiards in which balklines are used —**balk-line** *adj.*

balk·y /báwkee/ (**-i·er, -i·est**) *adj.* difficult and uncooperative ○ *a balky mule that stopped dead in its tracks* —**balk·i·ly** *adv.* —**balk·i·ness** *n.*

ball[1] /bawl/ *n.* **1.** ROUND OBJECT PLAYED WITH an object, usually round in shape and often hollow and flexible, central to many games and sports in which it is thrown, struck, or kicked **2.** ROUND OR ROUNDISH THING something spherical or almost spherical, especially a spherical mass or arrangement of material ○ *a ball of wool* **3.** A GAME WITH BALL a game, especially one played by children, in which a ball is used and, e.g., is thrown from one player to another ○ *Who's coming out to play ball?* **4.** SPORTS BALL PLAYED IN A PARTICULAR WAY a particular use, movement, or way of transferring the ball to another player in the course of a game ○ *a long ball into the end zone* **5.** BASEBALL PITCH THAT IS NOT A STRIKE in baseball, any single pitch of the ball that does not pass through the strike zone and at which the batter does not swing **6.** ARMS SOLID PROJECTILE a solid nonexploding and usually round projectile shot from an old-fashioned pistol, musket, or cannon **7.** ARMS SOLID PROJECTILES COLLECTIVELY a collective term for the solid projectiles fired from old-fashioned guns ○ *The gunners were ordered to change from ball to case-shot.* **8.** ROUNDED BODY PART a rounded part of the body, e.g., at the base of the thumb or just behind the toes ○ *the ball of the foot* **9.** ANAT TESTICLE a testicle (*slang offensive*) ■ *vti.* (**balled, ball·ing, balls**) **1.** MAKE INTO OR FORM BALL to mold, gather, or wind something into a ball, or become a ball-shaped mass ○ *She balled her fists.* **2.** OFFENSIVE TERM an offensive term meaning to have sexual intercourse (*taboo offensive*) [13thC. From Old Norse *böllr* or assumed Old English *beall*, from a prehistoric Germanic word that is also the ancestor of English *balloon, bale*[1], and *ballot*.] ◇ **carry the ball** to be in charge of getting something done (*slang*) ○ *We're looking for a fundraiser, and so we need a good organizer to carry the ball.* ◇ **drop the ball** to abandon responsibility for or botch something suddenly (*slang*) ○ *The project was going ahead full speed until he dropped the ball.* ◇ **get** *or* **set** *or* **start the ball rolling** to start something off, especially a conversation or project ◇ **on the ball** aware of what is going on and quick to respond and take action (*informal*) ◇ **have something on the ball** to have a particular level of knowledge, competence, or skill to offer in a certain situation (*informal*) ○ *She has a lot on the ball; let's give her the opportunity to chair the committee.* ◇ **play ball (with somebody)** to cooperate together or with somebody (*slang*) ◇ **the ball is in somebody's court** used to say that it is somebody's turn to take action (*slang*) ◇ **the whole ball of wax** the whole affair (*slang*) ○ *We only wanted a plane ticket, but the travel agent wanted to sell us the whole ball of wax.*

balls up *vt. U.K.* = **ball up** (*slang*) [From *balls* "muddle," from the sense of "testicles"]

ball up *vt.* to make a complete mess of something by mistake or through lack of skill (*slang offensive*) [From BALL "to become clogged" (as if with a ball)]

ball[2] /bawl/ *n.* a large-scale formal social event at which the main activity is dancing [Early 17thC. Via French *bal* from, ultimately, late Latin *ballare* "to dance," from Greek *ballizein*.] ◇ **have a ball** to enjoy yourself very much (*dated slang*) ○ *It was a great party; we really had a ball!*

Ball /bawl/, **Lucille** (1911–89) U.S. actor. A gifted comedian, she appeared with her husband Desi Arnaz in the television comedy *I Love Lucy* (1951–57), the first of several popular series. She was also a successful television producer. Full name **Lucille Désirée Ball**

bal·lad /bállәd/ *n.* **1.** MUSIC, LITERAT NARRATIVE SONG a song or poem, especially a traditional one or one in a traditional style, telling a story in a number of short regular stanzas, often with a refrain ○ *the Ballad of Bonnie and Clyde* **2.** MUSIC SLOW ROMANTIC SONG a slow romantic popular song ○ *two up-tempo numbers followed by a ballad* [Late 15thC. Via French *ballade* from, ultimately, late Latin *ballare* (see BALL[2]).] —**bal·lad·ic** /bә láddik, ba-/ *adj.* —**bal·lad·ist** /bállә dist/ *n.*

bal·lade /bә laád, ba-/ *n.* **1.** LITERAT POEM WITH REFRAIN a poem consisting of three stanzas of eight or ten lines and a short concluding explanatory stanza (**envoy**), all of which end with the same refrain **2.** INSTRUMENTAL PIECE SUGGESTING A STORY an instrumental piece, usually for piano, intended to suggest the telling of a story as in a ballad. The best-known ballades in the classical repertoire are by Chopin and Brahms. [14thC. Variant of BALLAD.]

bal·lad·eer /bàllә deér/ *n.* somebody who sings ballads

bal·lad op·er·a *n.* a form of opera with spoken dialogue and popular tunes made into songs. The most famous example is John Gay's *The Beggar's Opera.*

bal·lad·ry /bállәdree/ *n.* **1.** BALLADS COLLECTIVELY ballads considered collectively **2.** WRITING OR PERFORMING BALLADS the composing or performing of ballads

bal·lad stan·za *n.* a stanza form frequently used in ballads that has four lines, the first and third with four stresses and unrhymed, the second and fourth with three stresses and rhyming

ball and chain *n.* **1.** IRON BALL ON A CHAIN a type of restraint formerly used for prisoners consisting of an iron ball on a chain that is attached at its other end to the prisoner's ankle **2.** GREAT HINDRANCE something considered to be a great hindrance or restraint ○ *Censorship is the ball and chain fettering artistic freedom of expression.* **3.** OFFENSIVE TERM an offensive term deliberately insulting a man's wife (*dated slang insult*)

ball-and-claw *adj.* having a foot or another part modeled in the shape of an animal's claw holding a ball ○ *a ball-and-claw bathtub*

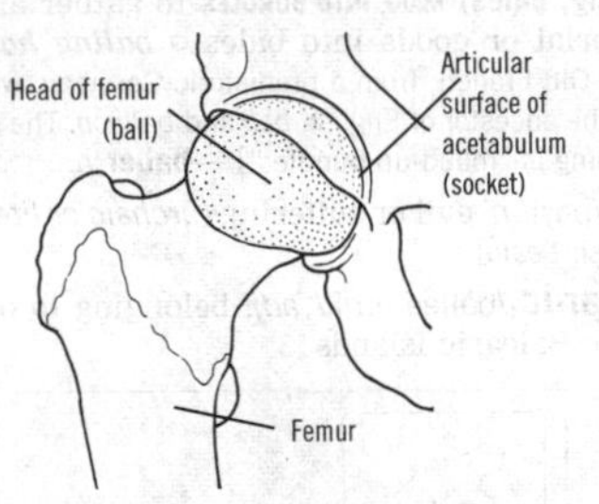

Ball and socket joint

ball and sock·et joint, ball joint *n.* **1.** ANAT JOINT LIKE HIP JOINT a joint such as the hip joint, in which a bone with a rounded end fits into a concave area of the adjoining bone, allowing a wide range of movement **2.** MECH ENG JUNCTION BETWEEN MOVING PARTS a junction between two moving parts of a mechanism in which the rounded end of one part fits into a cup-shaped socket on the other

bal·last /bállәst/ *n.* **1.** NAUT STABILIZING HEAVY WEIGHTS heavy material carried in the hold of a ship, especially one that has no cargo, or in the gondola of a balloon, to give the craft increased stability **2.** SOMETHING THAT GIVES BULK OR STABILITY anything that serves no particular purpose except to give bulk or weight to something or that provides additional stability **3.** TRANSP FOUNDATION MATERIAL stones or gravel used as a foundation for a road or a railroad track **4.** BUILDING GRAVEL USED IN MAKING CONCRETE gravel used in making concrete and in earthworks ■ *vt.* (**-last·ed, -last·ing, -lasts**) **1.** LOAD SOMETHING WITH BALLAST to load ballast onto something **2.** STABILIZE SOMETHING to give stability to something [Mid-16thC. Origin uncertain, probably from Old Danish, literally "mere weight," from *bar* "bare, mere" + *last* "load."]

ball bear·ing *n.* **1.** FRICTION-REDUCING METAL BALL a metal ball used to reduce friction between moving parts **2.** TYPE OF BEARING a bearing containing a number of metal balls that rotate freely to reduce friction between moving parts

ball boy *n.* **1.** TENNIS COLLECTOR OF TENNIS BALLS a boy who retrieves balls during a tennis match at the end of each point and delivers them to the server when required **2.** BASEBALL KEEPER OF BASEBALLS a boy who takes care of the balls that are out of play during a baseball game or practice

ball·break·er /báwl bràykәr/ *n.* a deliberately offensive term for a woman who is regarded as aggressive toward men (*slang taboo*)

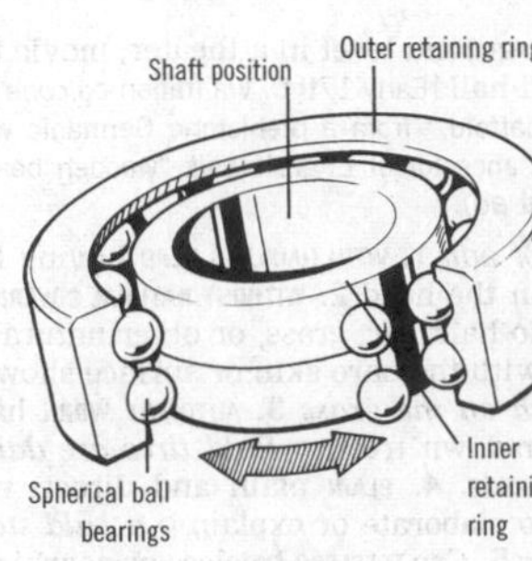

Ball bearing

ball·bust·er /báwl bùstәr/ *n.* (*slang taboo*) **1.** DIFFICULT JOB a difficult and unpleasant job **2.** = **ballbreaker**

ball car·ri·er *n.* in football, a player who carries the ball toward or across the opposing team's goal line

ball clay *n.* a sedimentary clay containing kaolin, mica, other minerals, and organic matter, used in ceramics [*Ball* from an obsolete mining process in which clay was handled as rounded cubes (balls)]

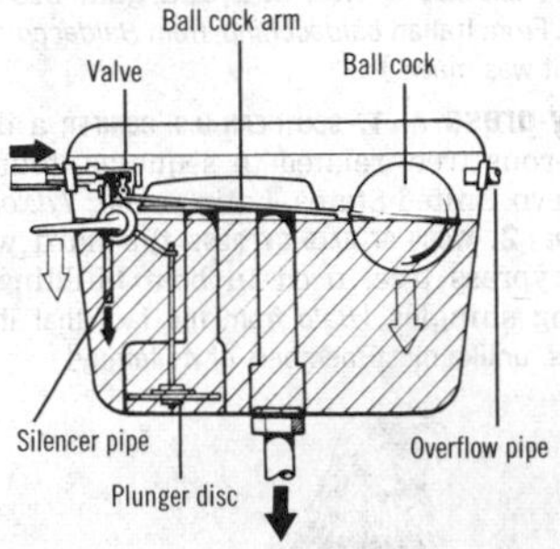

Ball cock

ball cock *n.* a floating ball on the end of an arm that is connected to a valve controlling the water level in a cistern or tank. The valve opens as the ball falls and closes as it rises.

bal·le·ri·na /bàllә reénә/ *n.* **1.** WOMAN DANCER a woman ballet dancer **2.** PRINCIPAL WOMAN BALLET DANCER a woman dancer in a ballet company who is regularly given principal parts [Late 18thC. From the feminine form of Italian *ballerino* "dancing master" from *ballare* "to dance," ultimately from the same Greek source as BALL[2].]

Balles·teros /bàllә stérrōss/, **Severiano** (*b.* 1957) Spanish golfer. The youngest golfer to win the British Open (1979), he won that tournament twice more as well as the Masters and the World Match-play.

Ballet: Darcy Bussell performing in the Royal Ballet's *Laurencia* (1990)

bal·let /ba láy, bállày/ *n.* **1.** FORM OF DANCE a form of dance characterized by conventional steps, poses, and graceful movements including leaps and spins. Women ballet dancers often wear pointe shoes to perform steps balancing on the tips of their toes. **2.** STORY PERFORMED BY DANCERS a choreographed presentation of a story or theme performed to music by ballet dancers, or the musical score written for this **3.** GROUP OF DANCERS a company of ballet dancers who perform together [Mid-17thC. Via French, from Italian *balletto* (see BALL[2]).]

bal·let·ic /ba léttik, bə-/ *adj.* with the grace of somebody dancing in a ballet

bal·let·o·mane /bə léttə màyn/ *n.* somebody who passionately loves ballet [Mid-20thC. Coined from BALLET + -MANE.] —**bal·let·o·ma·ni·a** /ba lèttə máynee ə, -máynyə/ *n.*

bal·let shoe *n.* 1. **BALLET DANCER'S SHOE** a flat light flexible slipper made of silk or leather, worn by ballet dancers for performing and practice 2. = **toe shoe** 3. **LIGHT FLAT SHOE** a flat shoe resembling one worn by a ballet dancer

ball game /báw gàym/, **ball·game** *n.* 1. **BASEBALL** a game of baseball 2. **ANCIENT NATIVE AMERICAN GAME** a team game with religious significance, played with a ball on walled courts by the Mayan and other Mesoamerican peoples ◇ **a whole new ball game** a completely new or different set of circumstances (*slang*)

ball girl *n.* 1. TENNIS **COLLECTOR OF TENNIS BALLS** a girl who retrieves balls during a tennis match at the end of each point and delivers them to the server when required 2. BASEBALL **KEEPER OF BASEBALLS** a girl who takes care of balls that are out of play during a baseball game or practice

ball gown, ball·gown *n.* a full-length formal dress suitable for wearing to a ball

bal·lis·ta /bə lístə/ (*plural* **-tae** /-tee/) *n.* a piece of military equipment that was used in ancient times to hurl stones and other missiles over a distance [Early 16thC. Via Latin, from, ultimately, Greek *ballein* "to throw."]

bal·lis·tic /bə lístik/ *adj.* relating to the movements of objects propelled through the air [Mid-18thC. Formed from BALLISTA.] —**bal·lis·ti·cal·ly** *adv.* ◇ **go ballistic** to become extremely angry (*slang*)

bal·lis·tic mis·sile *n.* a missile that maintains a course determined by its initial orientation and engine thrust, rather than one calculated by guidance systems during flight

bal·lis·tics /bə lístiks/ *n.* 1. **STUDY OF PROJECTILES** the study of the movements and forces involved in the propulsion of objects through the air (*takes a singular verb*) 2. **STUDY OF FIREARMS** the study of firearms and ammunition (*takes a singular verb*) 3. **FIRING CHARACTERISTICS OF WEAPON** the characteristics of a firearm that affect the way missiles are fired (*takes a singular or plural verb*)

ball joint *n.* = **ball and socket joint** *n.* 2

ball light·ning *n.* a rare form of lightning that takes the shape of a moving glowing ball, typically disappearing without explosion

ball of fire *n.* an extremely energetic and dynamic person (*informal*)

bal·loon /bə lóon/ *n.* 1. **GAS-FILLED BAG USED AS TOY** a small colored bag made of thin rubber or plastic that is inflated with air or helium and used as a toy or decoration 2. AIR **GAS-FILLED BAG USED IN AIR TRANSPORT** an extremely large bag filled with a lighter-than-air gas and used as a form of air transport, carrying passengers or equipment in a suspended basket or gondola 3. **SPEECH CIRCLE IN CARTOON** a rounded outline with a point directed toward a character in a cartoon that encloses the text of the character's speech or thought 4. **BRANDY GLASS** a glass with a large rounded bowl, used for drinking brandy ■ *vi.* (**-looned, -loon·ing, -loons**) 1. **SWELL** to form a large round swollen shape 2. **INCREASE IN AMOUNT** to increase in amount suddenly and rapidly [Late 16thC. Via French *ballon* or Italian *ballone* "large ball" (see BALL[1]).] ◇ **go over** *or* **down like a lead balloon** to be completely unsuccessful (*slang*)

bal·loon an·gi·o·plas·ty *n.* the use of a balloon catheter to widen a narrowed artery

bal·loon cath·e·ter *n.* a tube that can be inserted into a blood vessel or other body part and inflated while inside, e.g., to widen a narrowed artery

bal·loon·ing /bə lóoning/ *n.* the sport of riding in or piloting a balloon

bal·loon·ist /bə lóonəst/ *n.* somebody who pilots a balloon for sport

bal·loon loan *n.* a loan that is repaid with a series of regular payments and one much larger payment at the end

bal·loon mort·gage *n.* a mortgage that is paid back in a series of regular payments with one much larger payment at the end

bal·loon sail *n.* a large balloon-shaped foresail, used to replace or assist the jib in light winds

bal·loon tire *n.* a pneumatic tire with a wide tread inflated to a low pressure, used to drive on soft surfaces such as deep sand

bal·loon vine *n.* a tropical vine with small flowers and ornamental pods shaped like balloons. Latin name: *Cardiospermum halicacabum.*

bal·loon whisk *n.* a hand-held whisk made of stiff wires that form a loop at one end and are gathered into a covered handle at the other

bal·lot /bállət/ *n.* 1. **VOTING SYSTEM** a system in which eligible people vote, usually in secret, to determine the outcome of an election or make some other collective decision 2. = **ballot paper** 3. **TOTAL VOTES** the total number of votes that have been cast in an election ■ *v.* (**-lot·ed, -lot·ing, -lots**) 1. *vt.* **ASK PEOPLE TO VOTE** to carry out a ballot on members of an organization or an electorate 2. *vi.* **VOTE** to vote in a ballot [Mid-16thC. From Italian *ballotta* "little ball," from *balla* "ball" (see BALL[1]). From the small balls that were used for casting votes.] —**bal·lot·er** *n.*

bal·lot box *n.* 1. **BOX FOR VOTES** a box in which voters put their ballot papers after marking them 2. **ELECTION BY BALLOT** the system in which leaders are elected or decisions are made using a ballot ○ *The people will decide at the ballot box.*

bal·lot pa·per *n.* a piece of paper or card on which somebody can record a vote

bal·lot rig·ging *n.* the use of dishonest or illegal methods of voting to ensure victory for a particular candidate or party in an election

ball·park /báwl paark/ *n.* 1. SPORT **PARK FOR PLAYING BALL GAMES** a stadium or area of land for playing ball games, especially baseball 2. AEROSP **TOUCHDOWN AREA FOR SPACECRAFT** the approximate area within which a spacecraft is intended to touch down ■ *adj.* **APPROXIMATE** rough or approximate (*informal*) ○ *a ballpark figure* ◇ **in the right ballpark** within the right general range or scope (*slang*)

ball play·er, ball·play·er *n.* somebody who plays baseball, softball, football, or basketball

ball·point /báwl pòynt/, **ball·point pen** *n.* a pen with a small rotating ball at its tip that transfers the ink from an inner tube onto the writing surface

ball·room /báwl ròom, -ròom/ *n.* a very large room with a smooth floor and a high ceiling, used for formal dances

ball·room danc·ing *n.* formal dancing with a partner in dances that use a set pattern of steps, e.g., the foxtrot, quickstep, and waltz (*formal*)

Balls·ton Spa /bàwlstən-/ village southwest of Saratoga Springs in eastern New York, noted for its mineral springs. Population: 5,512 (1996).

balls·y /báwlzee/ (**-i·er, -i·est**) *adj.* unusually tough, courageous, or determined (*slang taboo*) [Mid-20thC. From BALL[1].]

ball valve *n.* a nonreturn valve in which a ball moves in and out of an aperture in response to changes in fluid or mechanical pressure

Ball·win /báwlwin/ city in eastern Missouri, a western suburb of St. Louis. Population: 20,853 (1996).

bal·ly·hoo /bálleehoo/ *n.* (*plural* **-hoos**) 1. **SENSATIONAL ADVERTISING** sensational, loud, or sustained advertising 2. **UPROAR** a noisy argument or disturbance ■ *vt.* (**-hooed, -hoo·ing, -hoos**) **ADVERTISE SOMETHING LOUDLY** to advertise or publicize something loudly and insistently [Mid-19thC. Origin unknown.]

bal·ly·rag *vt.* = **bullyrag** [Late 18thC. Origin unknown.]

balm /baam, baalm/ *n.* 1. **SOOTHING OIL** a fragrant oily substance obtained as a resin from various plants such as evergreen trees, used in soothing ointments or other preparations 2. **SOMETHING THAT SOOTHES** something that has the effect of calming, soothing, or comforting ○ *balm to his wounded ego* 3. **PLANT OF MINT FAMILY** a plant of the mint family, e.g., bee balm or horse balm 4. **NICE SMELL** a pleasant scent (*literary*) 5. BOT = **lemon balm** [13thC. Via French *bame* from Latin *balsamum* (see BALSAM). The "l" found its way into the English spelling from the Latin form.]

Bal·mer se·ries /báImər-/ *n.* a series of lines in the visible part of the atomic spectrum of hydrogen [Early 20thC. Named for the Swiss physicist J. J. *Balmer* (1825–98), who discovered it.]

balm of Gil·e·ad /-gíllee əd, -àd/ *n.* 1. = **balsam fir** 2. **POPLAR TREE** a hybrid poplar tree that has heart-shaped leaves and resinous buds. Genus: *Populus.* 3. **FRAGRANT RESIN** the fragrant resin produced by the balm of Gilead tree [Mid-18thC. Named for the *balm of Gilead* in Coverdale's Bible.]

Bal·mor·al /bal máwrəl/, **bal·mor·al** *n.* 1. **LACED WALKING SHOE** a strong walking shoe that is fastened with laces 2. **WOOLEN CAP** a traditional Scottish flat woolen cap [Mid-19thC. Named for the royal estate of *Balmoral* in Scotland. Because of Queen Victoria's fondness for this estate, Scottish items became fashionable during her reign.]

balm·y /baamee, baalm-/ (**-i·er, -i·est**) *adj.* 1. **PLEASANTLY MILD** used to describe weather that is pleasantly mild ○ *a balmy summer evening* 2. = **barmy** (*informal*) —**balm·i·ly** *adv.* —**balm·i·ness** *n.*

bal·ne·ol·o·gy /bàlnee óllə jee/ *n.* a branch of medicine concerned with therapeutic bathing, especially in natural mineral spring water —**bal·ne·o·log·i·cal** /-ə láwjək'l/ *adj.* —**bal·ne·ol·o·gist** /-óllajəst/ *n.*

bal·ne·o·ther·a·py /bàlnee ə thérrəpee/ *n.* the medical practice of treatment by immersion in baths, especially those in spas containing water with a high mineral content [Late 19thC. Coined from Latin *balneum* "bath" + THERAPY.]

Ba·lo·chi *n., adj.* = **Baluchi**

ba·lo·ney /bə lónee/ *n.* (*informal*) 1. FOOD = **bologna** *n.* 1 2. **NONSENSE** any silly or stupid talk ○ *Don't talk baloney.* [Early 20thC. Origin uncertain: perhaps an alteration of *Bologna* in BOLOGNA SAUSAGE.]

Bal·qash, Lake /baal kaash, bal kásh/ shallow lake in southeastern Kazakhstan into which the Ili River flows. Area: 7,030 sq. mi./18,200 sq. km.

bal·sa /báwlsə, baal-/ (*plural* **-sas** *or* **-sa**) *n.* 1. **TREE WITH LIGHTWEIGHT WOOD** a South American tree that yields a lightweight softwood. Genus: *Ochroma.* 2. **bal·sa, bal·sa wood LIGHTWEIGHT WOOD** a lightweight wood obtained from the balsa tree, used in making rafts and toy models and as insulation [Early 17thC. From Spanish, "raft," because the tree was useful for making rafts.]

bal·sam /báwlsəm, baal-/ *n.* 1. **OILY RESINOUS PLANT SUBSTANCE** an oily resinous substance (**oleoresin**) obtained from plants, especially one containing benzoic acid or cinnamic acid, that is used in making perfume and medicine 2. **PREPARATION CONTAINING BALSAM** a preparation containing or resembling balsam 3. **FLOWERING PLANT** a plant of the family that includes impatiens and garden balsam. Family: Balsaminaceae. [Pre-12thC. Via Latin, from Greek *balsamon*, of uncertain origin: perhaps from Hebrew *bāsām* "spice."] —**bal·sam·ic** /bawl sámmik, baal-/ *adj.*

bal·sam ap·ple *n.* a tropical vine related to the gourd and naturalized in North America that is grown ornamentally for its yellow flowers and orange fruit. Latin name: *Mormordica balsamina.*

bal·sam fir (*plural* **bal·sam firs** *or* **bal·sam fir**) *n.* a pyramid-shaped North American fir tree, used for pulpwood and popular as a Christmas tree. It is the source of Canada balsam. Latin name: *Abies balsamea.*

bal·sam·ic vin·e·gar /bawl sàmmik-, baal-/ *n.* an expensive Italian vinegar made from the juice of white grapes. It is matured in wood for 10 to 50 years, giving it a characteristic dark color and rich sweet-sour taste.

bal·sam of Pe·ru *n.* 1. **TREE PRODUCING TIMBER AND RESINOUS EXTRACT** a South American tree that produces high-quality timber. It is also the source of a balsam used medicinally, in making chocolate, and in perfumery. Latin name: *Myroxylon balsamum var. pareirae.* 2. **BALSAM FROM TREE** the balsam obtained from the balsam of Peru tree

bal·sam pop·lar *n.* a North American poplar tree with broad leaves and sticky resinous buds. Latin name: *Populus balsamifera.*

Balt /bawlt/ *n.* 1. **SOMEBODY FROM ONE OF BALTIC STATES** somebody who lives in or was born or raised in Lithuania, Latvia, or Estonia 2. **SPEAKER OF BALTIC STATES LANGUAGE** somebody whose native language is Lithuanian, Latvian, or Estonian [Late 19thC. From late Latin *balthae.*]

Bal·tha·zar /bal tháyzzər, bàl thə zaar/, **Bal·tha·sar** *n.* one of the three wise men who, according to the Bible, brought gifts to Bethlehem to honor the birth of Jesus (Matthew 2:1–12)

bal·ti /báwltee, baál-, bál-/ *n.* a spicy dish originally from Pakistan that is traditionally served in the bowl-shaped pan it is cooked in

Bal·ti /báwltee, baál-, bál-/ *n.* a language spoken in northern Kashmir that may be counted as a dialect of Tibetan [Early 20thC. From a Ladakhi dialect name.] —**Bal·ti** *adj.*

Bal·tic[1] /báwltik/ *n.* a group of northeastern European languages that includes Latvian, Lithuanian, and the extinct Old Prussian. It is a branch of the Indo-European family, closely linked with the Slavic group. About five million people speak a Baltic language. [Late 16thC. From late Latin *Balticus.*] —**Bal·tic** *adj.*

Bal·tic[2] *n.* **1.** = **Baltic Sea 2.** = **Baltic States** —**Bal·tic** *adj.*

Bal·tic Sea, Bal·tic sea in northwestern Europe. Nearly landlocked, it borders Sweden, Finland, Russia, Estonia, Latvia, Lithuania, Poland, Germany, and Denmark. Area: 160,000 sq. mi./ 414,000 sq. km.

Bal·tic States, Bal·tic the nations of Estonia, Latvia, and Lithuania, considered as a group

Bal·ti·more /báwltə màwr, -mŏr/ the largest city in Maryland, near the Chesapeake Bay. This port town is home to the Johns Hopkins University. Population: 702,979 (1994).

Bal·ti·more o·ri·ole *n.* a North American bird, the male of which has a black head and upper body with orange underside and tail. The female has olive-brown plumage. Latin name: *Icterus galbula.* [Late 17thC. Named for George Calvert, Lord *Baltimore* (1580?-1632), the English proprietor of Maryland, whose coat of arms has the same colors as the male bird.]

Bal·to-Sla·vic /bàwl tō-/, **Bal·to-Sla·von·ic** *n.* the Baltic and Slavic branches of the Indo-European language family, sometimes considered to form a unified grouping —**Bal·to-Sla·vic** *adj.*

Ba·lu·chi /bə lóochee/ (*plural* **-chis** *or* **-chi**), **Ba·lo·chi** (*plural* **-chis** *or* **-chi**) *n.* **1.** SOMEBODY FROM BALUCHISTAN somebody who lives in or was born or raised in the region of Baluchistan **2.** IRANIAN LANGUAGE a language spoken in Baluchistan belonging to the Eastern Iranian group of languages. Baluchi is spoken by about five million people. [Early 17thC. From Persian *Balučī.*] —**Ba·lu·chi** *adj.*

Ba·lu·chi·stan /bə lóochi stán/ mountainous desert region in southwestern Pakistan and southeastern Iran

bal·us·ter /bállәstәr/ *n.* **1.** POST SUPPORTING HANDRAIL an upright post supporting a handrail, e.g., in the banister of a staircase **2.** VASE-SHAPED LEG OR STEM a support, e.g., a chair leg or the stem of a glass, that is shaped like a long narrow vase [Early 17thC. Via French *balustre* from Italian *balaustro,* from, ultimately, Greek *balaustion* "blossom of the wild pomegranate," because early balusters resembled its shape.]

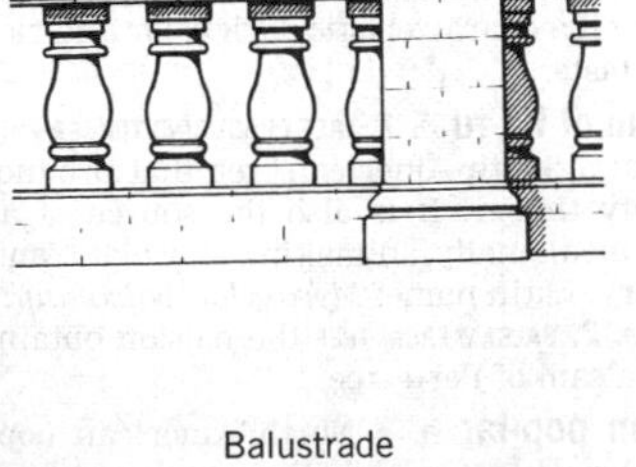

Balustrade

bal·us·trade /bállə strayd/ *n.* a decorative railing together with its supporting balusters, often used at the front of a parapet or gallery [Mid-17thC. Via French from either Spanish *balastrada* or Italian *balaustrata* from *balaustro* (see BALUSTER).]

Bal·zac /báwl zàk, bál-, baal zaák/, **Honoré de** (1799–1850) French novelist. He wrote 90 novels that provide a panoramic social history of France from 1789 to 1830, and arranged them under the collective title *The Human Comedy.* —**Bal·zac·i·an** /bal zákee ən, -záysh'n/ *adj.*

bam /bam/ *vti.* (**bammed, bam·ming, bams**) MAKE LOUD NOISE to make a loud hammering or thudding noise ○ *The police bammed on the door with a battering ram.* ■ *n.* LOUD NOISE a loud thudding or hammering noise ○ *The dictionary fell to the floor with a bam.* ■ *interj.* USED TO INDICATE SUDDEN IMPACT used to indicate sudden impact, the result of such impact, or the sudden occurrence of an event of great significance (*informal*) ○ *All of a sudden, bam! I was 30!*

Ba·ma·ko /baámə kṓ/ capital and largest city of Mali, situated on the Niger River. Population: 800,000 (1993).

Bam·ba·ra /baam baáraa/ (*plural* **-ra** *or* **-ras**) *n.* **1.** MEMBER OF W AFRICAN PEOPLE a member of an African people living mainly in Mali, western Africa **2.** MANDE LANGUAGE a language spoken in Mali, Senegal, Burkina Faso, and the Ivory Coast. It belongs to the Mande group of Niger-Congo languages and is spoken by between one and two million people. [Late 19thC. From Bambara.] —**Bam·ba·ra** *adj.*

bam·bi·no /bam beénō, baam beénō/ (*plural* **-nos** *or* **-ni** /-beénee/) *n.* **1.** BABY a baby or young child (*informal*) **2.** IMAGE OF INFANT JESUS CHRIST a representation of Jesus Christ as a baby [Early 18thC. From Italian, "baby," literally "silly little one," formed from *bambo* "silly."]

bam·boo /bam bóo/ (*plural* **-boos**) *n.* **1.** TALL STIFF-STEMMED PLANT a plant with long woody, often hollow, stems that grows in dense clumps in tropical and semitropical regions. Family: Bambusaceae. **2.** BAMBOO STEM the strong hollow stems of bamboo plants, used to make furniture, for building, and as canes and fishing rods [Late 16thC. Via Dutch *bamboes* from modern Latin *bambusa* from, ultimately, Malay *mambu.* The "s" of the Dutch form was later assumed to be a plural and dropped.]

bam·boo cur·tain *n.* the political, military, and ideological barrier that effectively isolated China from Western countries from the Communist revolution of 1949 until China's relaxation of trade barriers in 1979 [Coined on the model of IRON CURTAIN]

bam·boo shoot *n.* an edible young shoot of the bamboo plant that is eaten sliced and cooked in Asian dishes

bam·boo·zle /bam bóoz'l/ (**-zled, -zling, -zles**) *vt.* (*informal*) **1.** CHEAT SOMEBODY to trick or deceive somebody through misleading statements or falsehoods **2.** PERPLEX SOMEBODY to make somebody confused [Early 18thC. Of obscure origin.] —**bam·boo·zler** *n.*

ban[1] /ban/ *vt.* (**banned, ban·ning, bans**) **1.** FORBID SOMETHING to forbid something officially or legally so that it cannot be done, used, seen, or read **2.** STOP SOMEBODY FROM DOING SOMETHING to forbid somebody from doing something or going somewhere **3.** HIST RESTRICT RIGHTS IN SOUTH AFRICA during the apartheid era in South Africa, to punish somebody suspected of breaking the apartheid laws by preventing the person from moving around freely and having contact with other people ■ *n.* **1.** ORDER FORBIDDING SOMETHING an order officially or legally forbidding something so that it cannot be done, used, seen, or read **2.** PUBLIC REVILEMENT public condemnation of somebody or something (*archaic*) **3.** CURSE a powerful curse on somebody (*archaic*) [Old English *bannan* "to summon, proclaim"; the noun came via Old French *ban* "summons for military duty, proclamation"]

ban[2] /baan/ (*plural* **ba·ni** /baánnee/) *n.* see table at **currency** [Late 19thC. Via Romanian, from Serbo-Croat *bān* "lord" from Turkic *bayan* "very rich person," formed from *bay* "rich gentleman."]

Ba·na·ba /baa naábə/ one of the 33 islands of Kiribati in the western Pacific Ocean. Population: 284 (1990). Area: 2 sq. mi./5 sq. km. Former name **Ocean Island**

ba·nal /bə nál, báyn'l, bə naál/ *adj.* boringly ordinary and lacking in originality [Mid-19thC. From French, from *ban* (see BAN[1]), which developed in French from "compulsory military service" via "(something) common to all" to "commonplace."] —**ba·nal·ly** *adv.*

ba·nal·i·ty /bə nállətee, bay-/ (*plural* **-ties**) *n.* **1.** BORING ORDINARINESS conventional or dull ordinariness **2.** UNREMARKABLE COMMENT OR FEATURE an ordinary remark or feature that lacks originality

ba·nan·a /bə nánə/ (*plural* **-as** *or* **-a**) *n.* **1.** LONG CURVED YELLOW FRUIT a long and slightly curved fruit with a skin that turns from green to yellow when ripe. The edible part inside has a creamy color and soft texture. ◊ **plantain 2.** PLANT ON WHICH BANANAS GROW a tropical plant with large leaves and hanging

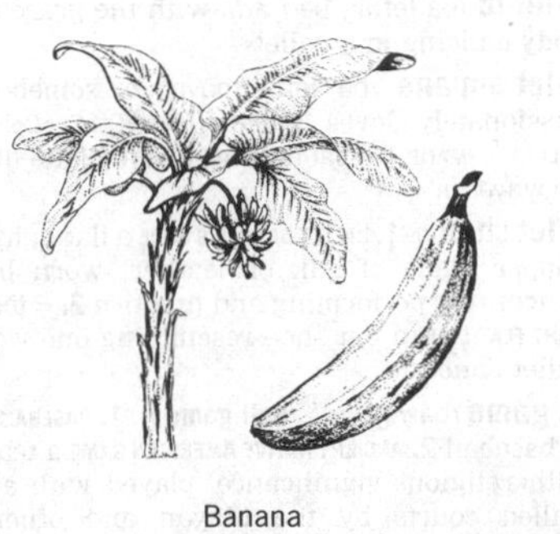

Banana

clusters of long curved fruits. Genus: *Musa.* [Late 16thC. Via Spanish and Portuguese, from Mande.] ◇ **go bananas** to become uncontrollably or unreasonably angry or excited (*informal*)

ba·nan·a·quit /bə nánə kwìt/ *n.* a bird found in Central and South America that resembles a warbler with a downturned bill. Latin name: *Coereba flaveola.*

ba·nan·a re·pub·lic *n.* a small country with an unstable government, typically a military dictatorship, and an economy dependent on the export of a single product or on outside financial help (*disapproving*)

ba·nan·a split *n.* a dessert made from a peeled banana cut in half lengthwise, typically topped with three scoops of ice cream, three types of syrup, chopped nuts, pieces of fruit, and whipped cream

ba·nau·sic /bə náwsik, -zik/ *adj.* **1.** UNCREATIVE with no art, creativity, or imagination **2.** PRACTICAL OR MATERIALISTIC practical or materialistic rather than uplifting or inspiring [Mid-19thC. Formed from Greek *banausikos* "of or for artisans."]

banc /bangk/ *n.* a meeting held by all the judges of a court [Early 18thC. From Anglo-French *banc* "bench," deriving from Latin *in banco,* literally "on the bench," which referred to full court sittings of a Superior Court of Common Law.]

ban·co /báng kō, baáng-/ *interj.* USED FOR BETTING AGAINST THE BANK used in baccarat and chemin de fer to declare that a player wishes to place a bet equivalent to the total worth of the bank ■ *n.* (*plural* **-cos**) BET AGAINST THE BANK in baccarat and chemin de fer, a bet placed equivalent to to the total worth of the bank [Late 18thC. Via French, from Italian (see BANK[1]).]

Ban·croft /bán kràwft, -kròft, báng-/, **Anne** (*b.* 1931) U.S. actor. She won an Academy Award for her part in the movie *The Miracle Worker* (1962) and gained fame as Mrs. Robinson in *The Graduate* (1967). Real name **Anna Maria Louise Italiano**

Ban·croft, George (1800–91) U.S. statesman and historian. He founded the U.S. Naval Academy at Annapolis (1845), was ambassador to several nations, and wrote the 10-volume *History of the United States* (1834–40, 1852–74).

band[1] /band/ *n.* **1.** MUSIC MUSICIANS PLAYING TOGETHER a group of musicians who play together, particularly a group playing popular or rock music. ◊ **pop group 2.** MUSIC, HIST INSTRUMENTAL ENSEMBLE in pre-18th-century Europe, an instrumental ensemble (*archaic*) **3.** GROUP WITH SAME BELIEFS OR PURPOSE a group of people who have the same ideas or beliefs or who are pursuing the same activity together ○ *a growing band of supporters* **4.** ANTHROP SMALL SIMPLY-STRUCTURED GROUP a small group of people with a relatively simple social structure **5.** ANIMALS TOGETHER a group of animals [15thC. From French *bande,* of uncertain origin: probably from the same prehistoric Germanic ancestor as English *banner.*] ◇ **to beat the band** to a very great extent or degree (*dated*)

band together *vi.* to form a group in order to achieve a goal

band[2] /band/ *n.* **1.** STRIP OR LOOP OF MATERIAL a strip of fabric, metal, elastic, or other material placed around something to strengthen it or around several things to hold them together **2.** CONTRASTING STRIPE a long narrow area that is different in material, color, or texture from the adjacent parts **3.** CLOTHES STRIP OR CIRCLE OF MATERIAL a strip or circle of fabric or elastic used for such purposes as decoration, identification, strengthening parts of clothing, or absorbing sweat on the forehead or hands

4. ACCESSORIES **RING** a plain ring worn on a finger ○ *a wedding band* **5.** MECH ENG **MOVING BELT** a moving belt in a piece of machinery **6.** RADIO **RANGE OF RADIO FREQUENCIES** a range of frequencies or wavelengths assigned to a radio station or radio broadcaster **7.** PHYS **RANGE OF ENERGIES** the range of energies possessed by electrons in a solid **8.** GEOL **ORE OR MINERAL LAYER** a layer of rock with a different composition or texture from the adjacent layers ■ *vt.* **(band·ed, band·ing, bands) PUT BAND ON OR AROUND SOMETHING** to put a strip on or around something to decorate or identify it or to hold a number of things together [13thC. From Old Norse, later reinforced by French *bande*, both, ultimately, from a prehistoric Germanic ancestor that was also the source of English *bind*, *bend*, and *bond*.]

band·age /bándij/ *n.* **CLOTH STRIP FOR COVERING INJURY** a long narrow strip of thin or elasticized fabric that can be wrapped and fastened around a wound or injured part of the body to protect or support it ■ *vt.* **(-aged, -ag·ing, -ag·es) APPLY BANDAGE** to protect a wound or support an injured body part by applying a bandage [Late 16thC. From French, from *bande* (see BAND[2]).] —**band·ag·er** *n.*

Band-Aid *tdmk.* a trademark for an adhesive bandage with a central gauze pad

ban·dan·na /ban dánnə/, **ban·dan·a** *n.* a large square of brightly colored cotton or silk cloth worn over the hair or around the neck [Mid-18thC. Probably via Portuguese, from Hindi *bāndhnū*, the name of a method of tie-dyeing, from *bāndhnā* "to tie."]

Ban·dar·an·aike /baàn draa neé keé/, **Chandrika** (*b.* 1945) Sri Lankan politician. The daughter of S.W.R.D. Bandaranaike, she was elected president of Sri Lanka in 1994 and appointed her mother, Sirimavo Bandaranaike, prime minister. Full name **Chandrika Bandaranaike Kumaratunga**

Ban·dar·an·aike, Sirimavo (*b.* 1916) Sri Lankan politician. The succeeded her husband S.W.R.D. Bandaranaike to become the world's first woman prime minister (1960–65, 1970–77, 1994 -). She nationalized schools and foreign-owned plantations in Sri Lanka. Born **Sirimavo Ratwatte**

Ban·dar·an·aike, S.W.R.D. (1899–1959) Sri Lankan statesman. Prime minister of Sri Lanka (1956–59), he was assassinated by a Buddhist monk. Full name **Solomon West Ridgeway Dias Bandaranaike**

Ban·dar Se·ri Be·ga·wan /bùn dər sèrri bə gaá wən/ capital of Brunei, in the northern part of the country, on Brunei Bay. Population: 50,000 (1995).

Ban·da Sea /bándə-, baándə-/ sea in the Pacific Ocean in eastern Indonesia, north of the island of Timor and southeast of Celebes Island. Area: 285,000 sq. mi./738,150 sq. km.

B & B *abbr.* bed and breakfast (*informal*)

band·box /bánd bòks/ *n.* a round lightweight box for carrying accessories such as hats [Mid-17thC. Formed from BAND[2] + BOX, so called because they were originally used to carry neckbands.]

band coun·cil *n. Can* POL a unit of Aboriginal local government that consists of a chief and a group of elected councilors

ban·deau /bàn dṓ/ (*plural* **-deaux** /ban dṓz/ *or* **-deaus**) *n.* **1. BAND FOR HAIR** a ribbon or band of material worn around the head to keep the hair in place **2. BAND OF MATERIAL WORN OVER BREASTS** a piece of material worn around the chest to cover the breasts [Early 18thC. From French, from Old French *bandel* "little band," from *bande* (see BAND[2]).]

band·ed /bándəd/ *adj.* marked with bands of different or contrasting colors ○ *banded agate*

ban·de·ri·lla /bàndə reé ə, -reél yə/ *n.* in a bullfight, a long decorated barbed dart that is thrust into the neck or shoulder of a bull by a bullfighter's assistant [Late 18thC. From Spanish "a little banner," from *bandera* "banner."]

ban·de·ri·lle·ro /bàndə ree érrō, -reel yáirō/ (*plural* **-ros**) *n.* a bullfighter's assistant who sticks a banderilla into the bull during a bullfight [Late 18thC. From Spanish, from *banderilla* (see BANDERILLA).]

ban·de·role /bándə rṑl/, **ban·de·rol, ban·ner·ol** /bánnə rṑl/ *n.* **1.** NAUT **FLAG ON MASTHEAD** a long narrow flag with a divided end that is flown on a ship's masthead **2. FLAG AT FUNERAL** a flag that is carried at a funeral or used to cover a tomb **3.** ARCHIT **INSCRIBED BAND** a sculpted scroll or band bearing an inscription **4.** HIST **RIBBON ON KNIGHT'S LANCE** a ribbon or streamer hanging from a knight's lance [Mid-16thC. Via French, from Italian

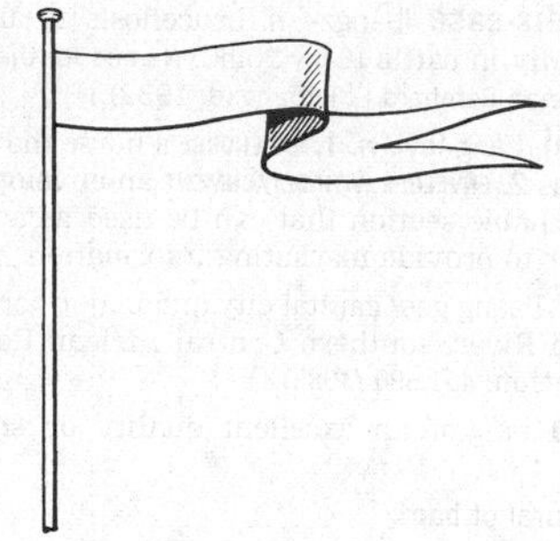

Banderole

banderuola "small banner," from *bandiera* "banner." Ultimately from the same prehistoric Germanic ancestor as English *band*[2].]

Bandicoot

ban·di·coot /bándi koòt/ *n.* a marsupial with a long nose, strong hind legs, and a long tail. Bandicoots eat mainly insects and plants and are found in Australia, Tasmania, and New Guinea. Family: Peramelidae. [Late 18thC. From Telugu *pandikokku*, literally "pig-rat."]

ban·di·coot rat *n.* a large rodent found in southern Asia that is a serious pest to farmers. Latin name: *Bandicota indica*.

band·ing /bánding/ *n. U.K.* = **tracking**

ban·dit /bándit/ *n.* **1. ARMED ROBBER** an armed robber who steals from travelers and other people, usually at gunpoint **2. GANGSTER** a member of a gang of violent criminals **3. EXPLOITATIVE PERSON** somebody who cheats or swindles other people **4.** AIR FORCE **ENEMY AIRCRAFT** an enemy aircraft sighted by a crew while flying (*informal*) ○ *Bandits at twelve o'clock high!* [Late 16thC. From Italian *bandito*, from *bandire* "to ban." Ultimately from the same prehistoric Germanic ancestor as English *ban*[1].] ◇ **make out like a bandit** *or* **bandits** to be extremely successful, especially by making a lot of money in a short period of time (*informal*)

ban·dit·ry /bánditree/ *n.* the occurrence or prevalence of armed robbery and violent crime

band·lead·er /bánd leèdər/ *n.* the conductor of a band, especially of a dance band

band list *n. Can* a list of members of an Aboriginal community **(band)** that is recognized by the federal government

band·mas·ter /bánd màstər/ *n.* the conductor of a band, especially of a brass band or a military band

ban·dog /bán dòg/ *n.* an aggressive dog produced by cross-breeding a pit bull terrier with a mastiff, rottweiler, or Rhodesian ridgeback [15thC. A blend of BAND[2] and DOG, because it originally referred to a dog that was chained up or bound.]

ban·do·leer /bàndə leér/, **ban·do·lier** *n.* a soldier's belt with loops or small pockets for storing cartridges, worn over the shoulder and across the chest [Late 16thC. From French, perhaps from Spanish *bandolera*, from *banda* "sash," or from Catalan *bandolera*, from *bandoler* "bandit."]

ban·do·ne·on /ban dṓnee òn/ *n.* a square concertina, used especially in Argentina [Early 20thC. Via Spanish *bandonéon* from German *Bandonion*, which was named for its 19thC German inventor Heinrich *Band*.] —**ban·do·ne·on·ist** /ban dṓnee ənəst/ *n.*

ban·dore /bán dàwr, -dṑr/ *n.* a musical instrument similar to a large guitar or lute that was played in the 16th and 17th centuries [Mid-16thC. Of uncertain origin. Forms of the word are found in many European languages and appear to go back to Latin *pandura*, from Greek *pandoura* "three-stringed lute."]

band-pass fil·ter *n.* **1. FREQUENCY FILTER** an electronic filter that passes only those frequencies within a specified range **2. DEVICE TRANSMITTING LIGHT OF PARTICULAR WAVELENGTHS** a device transmitting electromagnetic radiation, especially visible light, within a restricted wavelength range

band saw *n.* a stationary power saw with a continuous vertically mounted blade

band shell *n.* a bandstand with a curved wall at the back that is designed to reflect the sound toward the audience

bands·man /bándzmən/ (*plural* **-men** /-mən/) *n.* a player in a brass band or military band

band·stand /bánd stànd/ *n.* a platform for a band or small orchestra to perform on, especially outdoors

band the·o·ry *n.* a theory that explains the electrical conductivity of solids in terms of energy bands containing electrons

Ban·dung /baán dòong/ city in southern Indonesia, on western Java Island, southeast of Jakarta. Population: 2,056,915 (1990).

B & W, **b & w** *abbr.* PHOTOGRAPHY black-and-white

band·wag·on /bánd wàgən/ *n.* **1. INCREASINGLY POPULAR MOVEMENT** a cause or movement that is gaining popularity and support **2. WAGON FOR MUSICIANS** an ornately decorated wagon that musicians perform on during a parade ◇ **jump** *or* **climb on the bandwagon** to join in something only because it is fashionable or likely to be profitable

band·width /bánd wìdth/ *n.* **1.** RADIO, TELECOM **RANGE OF RADIO FREQUENCIES** a range of radio frequencies used in radio or telecommunications transmission and reception **2.** COMPUT **COMMUNICATIONS CAPACITY** the capacity of a communications channel, e.g., a connection to the Internet, often measured in bits per second

ban·dy /bándee/ *vt.* **(-died, -dy·ing, -dies) CASUALLY EXCHANGE WORDS** to toss words back and forth casually, often without caring whether they are true or what effect they may have ○ *I've heard the name being bandied about.* ■ *adj.* **(-di·er, -di·est) CURVED SO KNEES CANNOT MEET** used to describe legs that curve outward so that the knees cannot meet [Late 16thC. Origin uncertain, perhaps from French *bander* "to take sides at tennis," which probably goes back to the same ancestor as BAND[1].] ◇ **bandy words with somebody** to have an argument or discussion with somebody, often one that is unnecessary or a waste of time

ban·dy-ban·dy (*plural* **ban·dy-ban·dies**) *n. ANZ* a small, mildly venomous Australian snake marked with black-and-white bands. Latin name: *Vermicella annulata.* [Early 20thC. From an Aboriginal language.]

ban·dy-leg·ged *adj.* having legs that curve outward, so that the knees do not touch

bane /bayn/ *n.* **1. SOMETHING THAT CAUSES MISERY** something that continually causes problems or misery ○ *It's the bane of my life.* **2. SOMETHING THAT CAUSES RUIN** something that causes death, destruction, or ruin (*literary or archaic*) **3. DEADLY POISON** a fatal poison (*often used in combination in the names of poisonous plants*) [Old English *bana*, ultimately from a prehistoric Germanic word]

bane·ful /báynfòol/ *adj.* causing ruin or destruction (literary) —**bane·ful·ly** *adv.* —**bane·ful·ness** *n.*

WORD KEY: USAGE

See usage note at ***baleful.***

Banff Na·tion·al Park national park in the Rocky Mountains, southwestern Alberta, Canada. Area: 2,564 sq. mi./6,641 sq. km.

bang[1] /bang/ *n.* **1. SUDDEN LOUD NOISE** a sudden loud noise, e.g., the sound of a gun firing or a door slamming shut **2. SHARP HIT** a sharp blow or hit ○ *a nasty bang on the head* **3. PLEASURE** a great deal of pleasure (*informal*) ○ *I got a real bang out of the musical.* **4. ENERGY BURST** a burst of energy or activity (*informal*) ○ *The party started with a bang.* **5.** DRUGS **INJECTION OF DRUG** an injection of an illegal drug such as heroin (*slang*) **6.** COMPUT **CHARACTER IN TYPESETTING** the character (!) in typesetting ■ **bangs** *npl.* **FRINGE OF HAIR ACROSS FOREHEAD** the hair falling over the forehead when it is cut square above the eyes ■ *v.* **(banged, bang·ing, bangs) 1.** *vti.* **HIT** to hit something hard, or slam something against a surface ○ *He banged his fist on* *the table.* **2.** *vti.* **HIT ACCIDENTALLY** to hit something unintentionally ○ *She banged her knee.* **3.** *vti.* **CLOSE HARD AND NOISILY** to close suddenly and loudly, or make something close, with a sudden loud noise ○ *The door banged shut.* **4.** *vi.* **MAKE LOUD NOISE** to make a sudden loud noise ○ *children banging on pots and pans* **5.** *vi.* **MOVE AROUND NOISILY** to move around making a lot of noise ○ *bang sulkily around the house* **6.** *vti.* **OFFENSIVE TERM** an offensive term meaning to have sexual intercourse with somebody (*slang offensive*) **7.** *vi.* DRUGS **INJECT A DRUG** to inject an illegal drug such as heroin (*slang*) ■ *adv.* **SUDDENLY** suddenly and unexpectedly ○ *I turned around and bang, there he was!* ■ *interj.* **IMITATING EXPLOSIVE SOUND** used especially by children to imitate the sound of a gun firing (*informal*) ○ *Bang! You're dead!* [Mid-16thC. An imitation of the sound.] ◇ **bang for your buck** value for money spent or effort expended (*slang*) ◇ **bang on** *U.K., Can* exactly right ◇ **go out with a bang** to end or finish something in a dramatic way (*informal*) ◇ **go over with a bang** to be very successful (*informal*) ○ *The new novel went over with a bang, selling over two million copies.*

bang away *vi.* to keep doing something persistently and determinedly

bang out *vt.* (*informal*) **1.** **PRODUCE SOMETHING QUICKLY** to produce something speedily ○ *bang out a term paper overnight* **2.** **PLAY A TUNE LOUDLY** to play a tune on a musical instrument loudly and without sensitivity to the music

bang up *vt.* to damage something badly, or be damaged badly (*informal*) ○ *I banged up my car on the icy road.*

bang[2] /bang/ *n.* = **bhang**

Ban·ga·lore /bánggəlōr/ capital of Karnataka State in south central India. Population: 2,651,000 (1991).

ban·ga·lore tor·pe·do (*plural* **ban·ga·lore tor·pe·does**) *n.* an explosive device in a metal tube, used to blow holes in barbed-wire fences or to detonate land mines [Early 20thC. Named for BANGALORE where it was invented.]

Ban·ga·si = **Banghazi**

bang·bel·ly /báng bèlee/ *n. Can* a piece of dough that has been fried, baked, or stewed

Bang·ka /baáng kaa/, **Ban·ka** island in western Indonesia forming part of the Malay Archipelago. Pangkalpinang is the largest town. Area: 4,609 sq. mi./11,937 sq. km.

Bang·kok /báng kòk/ capital city and port on the Chao Phraya River, just north of the Gulf of Thailand, southern Thailand. Population: 5,562,141 (1992).

Bang·la /baáng glə/ *n.* LANG = **Bengali**

Bangladesh

Bang·la·desh /baànglə désh/ republic in south central Asia, formerly part of India and then, from 1947 to 1971, Pakistan. It became a separate nation following a civil war in 1971. Language: Bengali. Currency: taka. Capital: Dhaka. Population: 125,340,261 (1997). Area: 56,977 sq. mi./147,570 sq. km. Official name **People's Republic of Bangladesh** —**Bang·la·desh·i** /baàng glə déshee/ *n., adj.*

ban·gle /báng g'l/ *n.* **1.** **RIGID BRACELET** a stiff metal, plastic, or wooden bracelet that is worn around the arm, wrist, or ankle **2.** **DISK ATTACHED TO BRACELET** a decorative disk, charm, or other ornament that hangs from a bracelet [Late 18thC. From Hindi *bangrī* "colored glass bracelet."]

Ban·gor /bángər/ city and port on the Penobscot River, northeast of Belfast, in south central Maine. Population: 31,649 (1996).

Bang's dis·ease /bángz-/ *n.* brucellosis in animals, especially in cattle [Early 20thC. Named for the Danish veterinarian Bernhard L. F. *Bang* (d. 1932).]

bang·tail /báng tayl/ *n.* **1.** **RACEHORSE** a horse that is run in races **2.** **ENVELOPE WITH DETACHMENT** an envelope with a detachable section that can be used as an order form or to provide marketing information

Ban·gui /baang gée/ capital city and major port of the Ubangi River, southern Central African Republic. Population: 451,690 (1988).

bang-up *adj.* of an excellent quality or standard (*slang*)

ba·ni plural of **ban**[2]

ban·ish /bánnish/ (**-ished, -ish·ing, -ish·es**) *vt.* **1.** **SEND SOMEBODY AWAY** to exile somebody from a place, or send somebody to another place officially as a punishment **2.** **GET RID OF SOMETHING** to forbid or expel something, or put it out of your mind ○ *Let us banish from our minds all dark thoughts.* [14thC. From French *baniss-*, the stem of *banir* "to proclaim," from assumed Vulgar Latin *bannire*. Ultimately from a prehistoric Germanic word, the ancestor of English *ban*[1] and *bandit*.] —**ban·ish·er** *n.*

ban·ish·ment /bánnishmənt/ *n.* **1.** **EXPULSION** the forcible expulsion or exile of somebody or something **2.** **PERIOD OF EXILE** a period of time spent in exile

ban·is·ter /bánnəstər/, **ban·nis·ter** *n.* **1.** **HANDRAIL ON STAIRCASE** a handrail supported by posts running up the outside edge of a staircase **2.** **POST SUPPORTING HANDRAIL** any one of the posts supporting a handrail on a staircase [Mid-17thC. Alteration of BALUSTER.]

Ban·ja Lu·ka /bànyə lóokə/ city on the Vrbas River in northern Bosnia-Herzegovina. Population: 142,644 (1991).

Ban·jar·ma·sin /baànjər maá s'n/, **Band·jar·ma·sin** city in southeastern Borneo, Indonesiaeo. It is the capital of South Kalimantan Province. Population: 480,737 (1990).

ban·jo /bán jō/ (*plural* **-jos** *or* **-joes**) *n.* a musical instrument that has a round sound box covered with parchment, five strings, and a long neck. Plucked or strummed, it is popular in North American folk music. [Mid-18thC. Related to Jamaican English *banja* "fiddle," of uncertain origin, probably from an African language, and related to Kimbundu *mbanza* "stringed musical instrument."]

Ban·jul /baànjool/ capital and largest city of the Gambia. It is situated at the mouth of the Gambia River. Population: 42,407 (1993).

bank[1] /bangk/ *n.* **1.** **BUSINESS OFFERING FINANCIAL SERVICES** a business that keeps money for individuals or companies, exchanges currencies, makes loans, and offers other financial services **2.** **BANK'S LOCAL OFFICE** a local office of a bank **3.** GAMBLING **FUND OF MONEY OR TOKENS** the fund of money, tokens, chips, or other pieces that players can draw out in certain games, or the player who holds the fund **4.** **STORE OF SOMETHING** a supply of something stored, ready for immediate use, e.g., data, food, or blood ■ *v.* (**banked, bank·ing, banks**) **1.** *vt.* **DEPOSIT MONEY IN BANK** to pay money into a bank ○ *banked the check immediately* **2.** *vi.* **HAVE ACCOUNT WITH FINANCIAL INSTITUTION** to have an account with or use a particular bank ○ *bank with a local institution* [15thC. Directly or via French *banque* from Italian *banca* "bank, bench, table." The sense bank developed in the source language from the table on which banking was transacted.] ◇ **break the bank 1.** GAMBLING to win more money than is available **2.** to leave somebody very short of or without money (*informal*)

bank on *vi.* to count on something happening ○ *We're banking on your support.*

bank[2] /bangk/ *n.* **1.** **SIDE OF WATERWAY** the steep side of a river, stream, lake, or canal **2.** **RAISED AREA OF LAND BELOW WATER** a ridge of sand or other sedimentary deposit in a river or coastal sea that decreases the depth of the water above it and may become visible at low tide **3.** **EARTH OR SNOW WITH SLOPING SIDE** a pile of earth, snow, or sand, or a raised area of ground with a sloping side **4.** METEOROL **MASS OF CLOUD** a large dense area of cloud or fog **5.** MOTOR SPORTS **SLOPE AT BEND IN RACETRACK** an upward slope at a bend in a road or racetrack, designed to reduce the likelihood of drivers going off the road or track when traveling around the bend at speed **6.** AIR **TURNING ANGLE OF AIRCRAFT** the angle made by an airplane as it turns **7.** CUE GAMES **CUSHION OF POOL TABLE** the cushion of a billiard or pool table **8.** MINING **MOUTH OF MINE SHAFT** the area around the mouth of a mine shaft **9.** *U.K.* RAIL **LONG TRACK GRADIENT** a long gradient or slope on a railway **10.** AGRIC **PILE OF VEGETABLES** a heap of vegetables, usually potatoes, covered with earth and mulch and sometimes stored in a shed (*regional*) ■ *v.* **1.** *vti.* **FORM INTO PILE** to make something into a pile or a large heap or form a pile or heap ○ *snow banked against the fence* **2.** *vt.* **COVER FIRE** to cover a fire with ashes or fuel so that it will continue to burn slowly for a long time **3.** *vti.* AIR **TILT WHILE TURNING PLANE** to tilt an airplane with one wing higher than the other while turning, or turn an airplane so that it tilts **4.** *vti.* MOTOR SPORTS **TILT WHILE DRIVING** to tilt a vehicle, especially a motorcycle while traveling around a bend at speed, or travel around a bend like this **5.** *vt.* MOTOR SPORTS **BUILD SLOPE INTO ROAD OR RACETRACK** to build a slope into a road or racetrack at a bend **6.** *vt.* CUE GAMES **HIT BILLIARD BALL INTO CUSHION** to hit a billiard ball into the cushion [12thC. From assumed Old Norse *banki* "ridge, bank." Ultimately from a prehistoric Germanic ancestor that is also the ancestor of English *bench* and *bank*[1].]

WORD KEY: REGIONAL NOTE

In the sense "a heap of potatoes" ***bank*** is most common in the Lower South, where it competes with potato *bunk*, potato *hill*, potato *hole*, potato *house*, potato *kiln*, and potato *pump*.

bank[3] /bangk/ *n.* **1.** **ROW OF SIMILAR THINGS** a row or several rows of things of one type ○ *a bank of switches* **2.** NAUT **GALLEY ROWERS' BENCH** a bench for rowers in a galley **3.** NAUT **GALLEY OARS** a row of oars in a galley **4.** **SECONDARY PART OF HEADLINE** a secondary part of a headline running below the main headline in smaller type ■ *vt.* (**banked, bank·ing, banks**) **PUT THINGS INTO ROWS** to arrange things in rows or tiers [13thC. From French *banc* "bench." Ultimately from a prehistoric Germanic word that is also the ancestor of English *bank*[2] and *bench*.]

bank·a·ble /bángkəb'l/ *adj.* **1.** **LIKELY TO BRING IN MONEY** likely to become financially profitable ○ *a bankable movie star* **2.** **ACCEPTABLE TO A BANK** readily and legally acceptable to a bank —**bank·a·bil·i·ty** /bàngkə bíllətee/ *n.*

bank ac·count *n.* an arrangement according to which a bank accepts deposits of money and keeps that money available for withdrawal by the named account holder or holders

bank bal·ance *n.* the amount of money in a bank account at any given time

bank barn *n.* in the United States or Canada, a two-story barn built into a hillside that has an entrance to the first story at the front and an entrance to the second story at the back

bank bill *n.* = **banknote**

bank·book /bángk bòok/ *n.* = **passbook**

bank card *n.* = **ATM card**

bank dis·count *n.* the interest on a loan that is deducted from the amount borrowed at the time the loan is taken out

bank draft *n.* a bill of exchange drawn by one bank on another

bank·er /bángkər/ *n.* **1.** **SOMEBODY SENIOR IN BANKING** somebody who owns or works at a senior level in a bank **2.** GAMBLING **PLAYER IN CHARGE OF BANK** the player in charge of the bank in a gambling game [Mid-16thC. From BANK[1].] —**bank·er·ly** *adj.*

bank·ers' hours, bank·er's hours *npl.* a short working day (*informal*)

Bank·head /bángk hèd/, **Tallulah** (1902–68) U.S. actor. She was famous for the husky voice and extravagant acting style on stage in such plays as Lillian Hellman's *The Little Foxes* (1939) and in films including *Lifeboat* (1944). Born **Tallulah Brockman**

bank·ing[1] /bángking/ *n.* the work carried out by banks or bankers

bank·ing[2] /bángking/ *n. New England, Can* in rural areas of New England and the Maritime Provinces, seaweed or hay piled against the side of a house as a form of insulation

bank man·ag·er *n.* somebody who is in charge of a branch of a bank

bank·note /bángk nōt/ *n.* a piece of paper money issued by a bank that may be freely exchanged for goods or services

Bank of Can·a·da *n.* the federal central bank of Canada

Bank of Eng·land *n.* the central bank of England and Wales

bank·roll /bángk rōl/ *n.* **1.** ROLL OF PAPER MONEY a roll of banknotes **2.** FUND OF MONEY a fund of money used to finance a project ■ *vt.* (**-rolled, -roll·ing, -rolls**) FINANCE SOMETHING to provide the money needed to finance a project on a continuing basis (*informal*) —**bank·roll·er** *n.*

bank·rupt /bángk rùpt/ *adj.* **1.** UNABLE TO PAY DEBTS judged legally to be unable to pay off personal debts **2.** WITHOUT RESOURCES completely lacking in a particular quality, especially in good or ethical qualities ○ *morally bankrupt* ■ *n.* **1.** SOMEBODY WHO CANNOT PAY DEBTS somebody who has been declared legally unable to pay his or her outstanding debts **2.** SOMEBODY WITHOUT RESOURCES somebody who is completely lacking a particular quality, especially good or ethical qualities ■ *vt.* (**-rupt·ed, -rupt·ing, -rupts**) DEPLETE SOMEBODY'S FUNDS to cost so much that a person or business will have hardly any money left or will be declared bankrupt [Mid-16thC. From Italian *banca rotta*, literally "broken table," from *banca* (see BANK[1]) + *rotto*, from Latin *ruptus* "broken." Formerly a symbol for a bankrupt moneylender.]

bank·rupt·cy /bángk ruptsee/ (*plural* **-cies**) *n.* **1.** LEGAL INABILITY TO PAY DEBTS the state of having been legally declared bankrupt **2.** LACK OF RESOURCES the complete lack of a particular quality, especially good or ethical qualities ○ *moral bankruptcy*

Banks /bangks/, **Sir Joseph** (1743–1820) British naturalist. A member of Captain Cook's expedition around the world (1768–71), he helped to establish botany as a science and was instrumental in developing Kew Gardens in London.

bank·si·a /bángksee ə/ (*plural* **-as** *or* **-a**) *n.* a small Australian evergreen tree or shrub with leathery narrow leaves and cylindrical flowers. Family: Proteaceae. [Early 19thC. Modern Latin, named for Joseph BANKS.]

Banks Is·land /bángks-/ island in the Inuvik Region, Northwest Territories, Canada. It has a predominantly Inuit population. Area: 27,038 sq. mi./70,028 sq. km.

bank state·ment *n.* a document showing all the transactions in a bank account over a specific period of time

Ban·ne·ker /bánnəkər/, **Benjamin** (1731–1806) U.S. mathematician and astronomer. He published an annual almanac (1792–1802) and helped plan the District of Columbia (1791–93).

ban·ner /bánnər/ *n.* **1.** CLOTH SUSPENDED BETWEEN TWO POLES a long piece of cloth, often bearing a symbol or slogan, and attached at each end to a pole or hanging from the top of a pole **2.** GUIDING PRINCIPLE a guiding principle, cause, or philosophy ○ *under the banner of the labor union movement* **3.** COMPUT WEB SITE ADVERTISEMENT an advertisement in the form of a rectangular logo or headline spread across the width of a Web page **4.** NATION'S OR ARMY'S FLAG the flag of a country or army **5.** HIST FLAG OF KING, EMPEROR, OR KNIGHT a flag used by a king, emperor, or knight when going into battle **6.** PRESS = **banner headline** ■ *adj.* ESPECIALLY GOOD especially good or successful ○ *a banner year for sales* ■ *vt.* (**-ner·ing, -ners**) PRESS HEAD ARTICLE WITH BIG HEADLINE to give a newspaper article a banner headline ○ *We bannered the piece on the storm in huge black type.* [13thC. Via Anglo-Norman *banere* from Old French *banière* from, ultimately, medieval Latin *bandum* "standard." Ultimately from the same prehistoric Germanic word that is also the ancestor of English *band*[1].]

WORD KEY: CULTURAL NOTE

The Star-Spangled Banner, a patriotic song with lyrics by writer Francis Scott Key set to music by English composer John Stafford Smith (1814). Penned by Key after he had witnessed the successful defense of the city of Baltimore by U.S. troops against a British attack in 1814, it soon became a popular patriotic song. It was adopted as the national anthem of the United States on March 3, 1931.

ban·ner·et /bánnərət, -ret, -rét/ *n.* **1.** KNIGHT WITH OWN ARMY a knight who was entitled to lead his own men into battle and was thus of a higher rank than other knights **2.** HISTORICAL TITLE FOR BRAVERY in former times, a title given by a king or queen for bravery in battle [13thC. From Old French *baneret*, literally "bannered," from *banière* (see BANNER).]

ban·ner head·line *n.* a headline in large letters that runs across an entire page of a newspaper

ban·ner·ol *n.* = **banderole**

ban·nis·ter *n.* = **banister**

Ban·nis·ter /bánnistər/, **Sir Roger** (*b.* 1929) British athlete. He was the first man to run the mile in under four minutes (1954). Full name **Sir Roger Gilbert Bannister**

ban·nock /bánnək/ *n.* **1.** *New England* CORNBREAD GRIDDLE CAKE cornbread baked on a griddle **2.** *Can* ASH LEAVENED BREAD COOKED ON GRIDDLE a dough of flour, water, lard, and sometimes baking powder cooked on a griddle or in a frying pan, often over a campfire [Old English *bannuc*, from an earlier word meaning "drop"]

banns /banz/ *npl.* an announcement of a forthcoming marriage, proclaimed in the church of the engaged couple on three successive Sundays [14thC. From BAN[1].]

ban·quet /bángkwit/ *n.* **1.** CEREMONIAL MEAL an elaborate formal meal attended by many guests, often held in honor of a particular person or occasion and followed by speeches **2.** BIG MEAL an elaborate or lavish meal of many courses ■ *vi.* (**-quet·ed, -quet·ing, -quets**) EXPERIENCE A BANQUET to eat or drink as a guest at a banquet [15thC. From French, literally "little bank" (see BANK[3]). Originally, this referred to a small snack eaten while seated on a bench, not at a table.] —**ban·quet·er** *n.*

ban·quet hall *n.* a room large enough to accommodate a banquet, usually in a palace, castle, or stately home

ban·quet room *n.* a room large enough to accommodate a banquet in a hotel, resort, or restaurant

ban·quette /bàng két/ *n.* **1.** UPHOLSTERED BENCH an upholstered bench along a wall, especially in a restaurant **2.** RAISED STEP FOR GUNNER a raised step in a trench or behind a parapet on which a soldier may stand to fire or a gun may be mounted **3.** *Southern U.S.* = **sidewalk 4.** RAISED BUFFET SHELF a raised ledge at the back of a buffet, used as a shelf for dishes and utensils [Early 17thC. Via French, from Italian *banchetta* "little bench," formed from *banca* "bench, shelf" (see BANK[1]).]

ban·shee /bán shee/ *n.* **1.** SPIRIT WHO WARNS OF DEATH in Gaelic folklore, a spirit of a woman who appears, wailing, to signal that somebody in the household is going to die **2.** *Ireland* FEMALE FAIRY a female fairy [Late 17thC. Via Irish *bean sidhe* from Old Irish *ben* "woman" + *side* "of the fairy world."]

ban·tam /bántəm/ *n.* **1.** SMALL DOMESTIC FOWL a bird belonging to a breed of small domestic fowl **2.** = **bantamweight 3.** *Can* HOCKEY, SOFTBALL JUNIOR PLAYER in hockey and softball, a category of players from 13 to 15 years of age, or a player in this category ■ *adj.* **1.** MINIATURE small in size **2.** OVERCONFIDENT overconfident and slightly aggressive [Mid-18thC. Named for the town of *Bantam* in Java from where the birds are supposed to have been imported, although they are not native there.]

ban·tam·weight /bántəm wàyt/, **ban·tam** *n.* **1.** BOXER WEIGHING LESS THAN FEATHERWEIGHT a professional boxer weighing 112–118 lb./51–53.5 kg, or an amateur weighing 112–119 lb./51–54 kg **2.** LIGHTWEIGHT WRESTLER a wrestler weighing 115–126 lb./52–57 kg

ban·ter /bántər/ *n.* LIGHT TEASING REMARKS lighthearted teasing or amusing remarks that are exchanged between people ■ *vi.* (**-tered, -ter·ing, -ters**) EXCHANGE TEASING REMARKS to exchange lighthearted teasing remarks [Late 17thC. Origin unknown.] —**ban·ter·er** *n.*

Ban·ting /bánting/, **Sir Frederick Grant** (1891–1941) Canadian physician. He co-discovered insulin with Charles Best (1922), for which he shared the Nobel Prize in physiology or medicine (1923).

Ban·tu /bán too/ (*plural* **-tu** *or* **-tus**) *n.* **1.** LANG AFRICAN LANGUAGE GROUP a group of over 500 languages, including Kiswahili, Xhosa, and Zulu, spoken in central, eastern, and southern Africa. It belongs to the Benue-Congo subfamily of Niger-Congo languages and has over 150 million speakers. **2.** PEOPLES MEMBER OF AFRICAN PEOPLE a member of a large group of peoples living in equatorial and southern Africa [Mid-19thC. In some Bantu languages the plural of *-ntu* "person."] —**Ban·tu** *adj.*

WORD KEY: USAGE

Sensitivity trap In post-apartheid South Africa, ***Bantu*** is considered highly offensive when used with reference to Black people, especially in the singular to refer to one person, and ***Black*** or ***African*** are the normally accepted terms. In technical contexts outside South Africa, for example, academic discussions of anthropology and language, the term continues in use.

Banyan

ban·yan /bánnyən, -yan/ *n.* a tree grown in the Indian subcontinent and East Indies for shade or ornament. The roots grow down from the branches into the ground to form new secondary trunks. Latin name: *Ficus benghalensis.* [Late 16thC. Via Portuguese, from Gujarati *vāṇiyo* "man of the trading class," from Sanskrit *nāṇija* "merchant." Applied to a tree under which some traders had built a pagoda.]

ban·zai /ban zī, bán zī/ *interj.* PATRIOTIC JAPANESE SHOUT a patriotic Japanese battle cry or shout ■ *adj.* RECKLESS AND FEROCIOUS IN BATTLE reckless and utterly ferocious in a military attack [Late 19thC. From Japanese, literally "(may you live) ten thousand years."]

ba·o·bab /b-ōbab, baáō-/ *n.* a tropical tree native to southern Africa and northwestern Australia that has a very thick trunk, and bears fruit with a hard rind and edible pulp. Latin name: *Adansonia digitata.* [Mid-17thC. Origin uncertain: perhaps from North African Arabic *bū ḥibab* "fruit of many seeds."]

Bao Dai /bòw dī/, **Emperor of Annam** (*b.* 1913). The last emperor of the Nguyen dynasty (1926–45) in Indochina, he renounced his title and headed Vietnam under French rule (1949–55) before being deposed and forced into exile. Born **Nguyen Vinh Duy**

bap·tism /báptizzəm/ *n.* **1.** RITE OF PURIFICATION a religious ceremony in which somebody is sprinkled with or immersed in water to symbolize purification. In Christian baptisms, the person is often named and accepted into the Christian faith. **2.** INITIATION OR NAMING CEREMONY a ceremony that serves as an initiation or naming ritual —**bap·tis·mal** /bap tízməl/ *adj.* —**bap·tis·mal·ly** *adv.*

bap·tism of fire *n.* **1.** INITIAL ORDEAL a difficult or dangerous first experience in a new situation **2.** SOLDIER'S FIRST BATTLE a soldier's first experience of battle

Bap·tist /báptəst/ *n.* a member of a Protestant denomination that baptizes people by total immersion when they are old enough to understand and declare their faith —**Bap·tist** *adj.*

bap·tis·ter·y /báptəstree/ (*plural* **-ies**), **bap·tis·try** (*plural* **-tries**) *n.* **1.** PART OF CHRISTIAN CHURCH a part of a Christian church used for baptisms **2.** POOL IN CHURCH FOR BAPTISMS a tank or pool in a Baptist church used for baptisms by total immersion

bap·tize /bap tīz, báp tīz/ (**-tized, -tiz·ing, -tiz·es**) *v.* **1.** *vti.* PERFORM CEREMONY OF BAPTISM to sprinkle somebody with or immerse somebody in water as a sign that the person has been accepted into the Christian faith **2.** *vt.* NAME SOMEBODY IN BAPTISM to give a personal name to somebody during the Christian ceremony of baptism [13thC. Via French *baptiser* and ecclesiastical Latin *baptisare* from Greek *baptizein* "to baptize," from *baptein* "to dip."] —**bap·tiz·er** *n.*

bar[1] /baar/ *n.* **1.** LENGTH OF SOLID MATERIAL a length of metal, wood, or other solid material used as a barrier, or as part of a structure **2.** SMALL BLOCK a small, solid, usually rectangular, block of some substance ○ *a bar of soap* **3.** BARRIER something that blocks or hinders progress ○ *Aloofness is a bar to making friends easily.* **4.** PLACE FOR DRINKING a place where alcoholic drinks can be bought and drunk **5.** DRINKS COUNTER a counter where alcoholic drinks are served

6. PLACE PROVIDING PRODUCT OR SERVICE a commercial establishment, or a counter inside one, where a product or service is provided ○ *a juice bar* **7.** NARROW BAND a narrow stripe or band of color or light **8.** SOMETHING USED AS A STANDARD something referred to as an authority or standard ○ *We need to raise the bar of academic courses for all our students.* **9.** LAW PART OF LAW COURT the railing in a law court that separates the judge, jury, lawyers, people on trial, and witnesses from the public **10.** LAW LAWYERS OR THEIR PROFESSION lawyers considered collectively, or the profession of a lawyer **11.** *U.K.* LAW PLACE FOR DEFENDANT IN COURT the place in a British law court where somebody on trial stands or sits **12.** LAW TRIBUNAL a tribunal or court of law **13.** LAW DEFEAT OF LEGAL ACTION the defeat, prevention, or nullification of an action or claim, or the process by which this is achieved **14.** MUSIC UNIT OF TIME IN MUSIC a fundamental unit of time into which all music is divided, according to the number of beats **15.** MUSIC VERTICAL LINE SEPARATING MUSICAL UNITS any one of the vertical lines on a sheet of music that separates each unit of musical time **16.** MIL METAL STRIP SHOWING RANK a metal strip worn on a military uniform to show rank or a service distinction **17.** SPORTS = **crossbar** **18.** GYMNASTICS = **horizontal bar** **19.** BALLET = **barre** **20.** HERALDRY LINE ACROSS SHIELD a horizontal line on a shield, usually one of two or three parallel lines **21.** GEOG RIDGE OF SAND a low ridge of sand or shingle in the shallow part of the bed of a body of water **22.** GEOG RIVER'S CRESCENT-SHAPED SAND DEPOSIT a crescent-shaped area of alluvium deposited on the convex bend of a river bed **23.** BACKGAMMON STRIP IN BACKGAMMON BOARD the central dividing strip on a backgammon board ■ *vt.* (**barred, bar·ring, bars**) **1.** FASTEN WITH BAR to fasten something with a bar ○ *barred the door* **2.** BLOCK SOMETHING to block something by means of bars or barriers **3.** NOT ALLOW SOMEBODY ENTRY to refuse somebody entry to a place ○ *He was barred from the club.* **4.** NOT ALLOW SOMEBODY TO DO SOMETHING to prevent somebody or forbid somebody to do something **5.** MARK SOMETHING WITH BARS to mark something with stripes or bands of color (*usually passive*) **6.** LAW HALT COURT CASE to prevent a court case from going ahead by making a legal objection to it ■ *prep.* EXCLUDING except for ○ *The fight was all over, bar the shouting.* [12thC. Via Old French *barre* from Vulgar Latin *barra*, of unknown origin.] ◇ **behind bars** in prison ○ *a convicted felon who spent 20 years behind bars*

bar[2] /baar/ *n.* a unit of pressure that can be used in combination with SI units and prefixes, equal to 10^5 newtons per square meter [Early 20thC. From Greek *baros* "weight."]

Bar *n.* LAW lawyers considered collectively, or the profession of a lawyer ○ *the federal and state Bars*

BAR *abbr.* Browning automatic rifle

bar. *abbr.* **1.** barometer **2.** barometric **3.** barrel

Bar. *abbr.* BIBLE Baruch

B.Ar., **B.Arch.** *abbr.* Bachelor of Architecture

Bar·a /bàrrə/, **Theda** (1890–1955) U.S. actor. One of the first women to become a movie star, she was known for her allure, and is best remembered for the line "Kiss me, my fool!" Born **Theodosia Goodman**. Known as **Vamp**

Ba·rab·bas /bə rábəs/ *n.* in the Bible, a condemned thief who was freed by Pilate on Passover instead of Jesus Christ (Matthew 27)

ba·ra·chois /bárə shwàw/ *n. Can* a tidal pond separated from a beach by a sandbar [From Canadian French]

Ba·ra·nof Is·land /bérrə nàwf-, -nòf-/ island off southeastern Alaska, part of the Alexander Archipelago. It is named for the first governor of the Russian colony of Alaska, Aleksandr Baranov (1746–1819). Area: 1,607 sq. mi./4,162 sq. km.

ba·ra·sing·ha /baàrə síng gə/ (*plural* **-ha**) *n.* = **swamp deer** [Mid-19thC. From Hindi *barah-singā*, literally "twelve-tined."]

bar·a·the·a /bàrrə theé ə/ *n.* a type of fabric made from a combination of silk, cotton, wool, or synthetic material, often used for making coats [Mid-19thC. Origin unknown.]

ba·ra·za /bə raázə/ *n.* a public meeting or a place where meetings are held in eastern Africa [Late 19thC. From Kiswahili.]

Barb

barb[1] /baarb/ *n.* **1.** REVERSE POINT OF ARROW a sharp point facing away from the head of an arrow, fishhook, or harpoon, designed to make it difficult to remove **2.** WOUNDING REMARK a pointed or wounding remark **3.** (*plural* **barbs** *or* **barb**) ZOOL AQUARIUM FISH a small fish often kept in aquariums. Genera: *Barbus* and *Puntius*. **4.** CLOTHES MEDIEVAL HEADDRESS a white cloth headdress covering the chin and throat, worn by women in the Middle Ages **5.** ZOOL PART OF FEATHER a stiff filament that forms the framework of a feather. The barbs stick out on each side of the main shaft. **6.** ZOOL WHISKER ON ANIMAL'S HEAD a growth on an animal's head like a beard or whisker **7.** BOT BRISTLE OF A PLANT a hooked projection on some plants and fruits ■ *vt.* (**barbed, barb·ing, barbs**) FIT WITH BARB to provide something with a barb or barbs [14thC. Via Old French *barbe* "beard, appendage like a beard," from Latin *barba* "beard."]

barb[2] /baarb/ (*plural* **barbs** *or* **barb**) *n.* a horse belonging to a breed originally from North Africa, noted for speed and stamina [Mid-17thC. Via French *barbe* from Italian *barbero* "of Barbary."]

barb[3] /baarb/ *n.* a barbiturate (*slang*) [Mid-20thC. Shortening.]

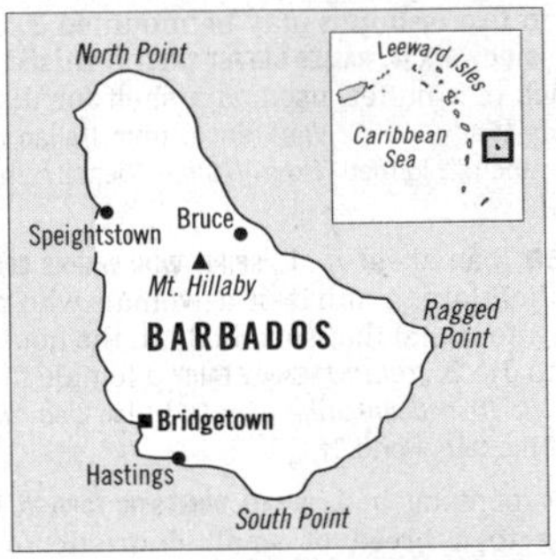

Barbados

Bar·ba·dos /baar báydəss, baar báydòss/ island nation in the West Indies off northeastern South America. Settled by the British in the 17th century, it has been an independent state within the British Commonwealth since 1966. Language: English. Currency: Barbados dollar. Capital: Bridgetown. Population: 258,756 (1997). Area: 166 sq. mi./430 sq. km. —**Bar·ba·di·an** /baar báydee ən/ *n., adj.*

Bar·ba·dos al·mond *n.* = **Indian almond**

Bar·ba·dos cher·ry (*plural* **Bar·ba·dos cher·ries**) *n.* **1.** TROPICAL TREE WITH EDIBLE FRUIT a tropical American evergreen tree with red flowers and edible fruits resembling cherries. Latin name: *Malpighia glabra.* **2.** EDIBLE FRUIT the edible fruit of the Barbados cherry, often used in jellies and desserts

Bar·ba·dos goose·ber·ry (*plural* **Bar·ba·dos goose·ber·ries**) *n.* **1.** CACTUS WITH EDIBLE FRUIT a broad-leafed tropical American cactus with spiny, climbing or trailing shoots, fragrant flowers, and edible fruits. Latin name: *Pereskia aculeata.* **2.** CACTUS FRUIT the edible yellow fruit of the Barbados gooseberry, often used in preserves

bar·bar·i·an /baar báiree ən/ *n.* **1.** PERSON FROM PRIMITIVE CULTURE especially in ancient times, a member of a people whose culture and behavior was considered primitive and uncivilized **2.** UNCULTURED PERSON somebody who is considered to have no interest in culture **3.** AGGRESSIVE PERSON an extremely aggressive or violent person [14thC. From Old French *barbarien* or Latin *barbarianus*, from *barbarus* (see BARBAROUS).] —**bar·bar·i·an·ism** *n.*

bar·bar·ic /baar bàrrik/ *adj.* **1.** CRUEL cruel or extremely brutal **2.** OF PRIMITIVE CULTURES typical of peoples and cultures seen as primitive and unsophisticated [14thC. Directly or via Old French *barbarique* from Latin *barbaricus*, from Greek *barbarikos*, from *barbaros* (see BARBAROUS).] —**bar·bar·i·cal·ly** *adv.*

bar·ba·rism /baárbə rìzzəm/ *n.* **1.** CRUEL ACT a cruel or brutal act **2.** PRIMITIVE QUALITY the primitive nature of a culture or civilization **3.** GRAM UNGRAMMATICAL WORD a word or expression considered to be grammatically incorrect **4.** UNCONVENTIONAL OR UNACCEPTABLE THING something that breaks rules of convention or good taste [15thC. Via French *barbarisme* from Latin *barbarismus*, from Greek *barbarismos*, from *barbarizein* (see BARBARIZE).]

bar·bar·i·ty /baar bérrətee/ (*plural* **-ties**) *n.* **1.** CRUEL ACT a cruel act **2.** PRIMITIVE STATE a primitive or uncivilized state [Mid-16thC. From Latin *barbarus* (see BARBAROUS).]

bar·ba·rize /baárbə rìz/ (**-rized, -riz·ing, -riz·es**) *vti.* **1.** MAKE OR BECOME CRUEL to become, or make somebody, cruel or brutal **2.** MAKE OR BECOME MORE PRIMITIVE to become more primitive, or less cultured, or reduce something to this state [15thC. From Greek *barbarizein* "to act or speak like a foreigner, to speak gibberish," from *barbaros* (see BARBAROUS).] —**bar·ba·ri·za·tion** /baárbərə záysh'n/ *n.*

Bar·ba·ros·sa (1483?–1546) Greek-born Ottoman admiral and pirate. Admiral of the Ottoman fleet after 1533, he was feared as a pirate on the Barbary coast. He defeated Holy Roman Emperor Charles V (1538) and sacked Gibraltar (1540). Born **Khair ad-Din**

bar·ba·rous /baárbərəs/ *adj.* **1.** EXTREMELY CRUEL showing extreme cruelty **2.** PRIMITIVE OR UNCIVILIZED characterized by a primitive or uncivilized culture **3.** NOT SOPHISTICATED lacking sophistication or refinement **4.** GRAM UNGRAMMATICAL using ungrammatical language [15thC. Via Latin *barbarus* from Greek *barbaros* "non-Greek, foreign, ignorant, uncivilized."] —**bar·ba·rous·ly** *adv.* —**bar·ba·rous·ness** *n.*

Barbary /baárbəree/ former region of North Africa stretching from the Atlantic coast to western Egypt. It included the Barbary States of Morocco, Algeria, Tripolitania, Tunisia, and Moorish Spain.

Bar·ba·ry ape *n.* a tailless monkey that lives in caves and cliffs on Gibraltar and in northwestern Africa. Latin name: *Macaca sylvana.*

Barbary Coast **1.** formerly, the Mediterranean coast of North Africa. It was an important base for pirates between the 16th and 19th centuries. **2.** the waterfront area of San Francisco, California, between the 1849 gold rush and the 1906 earthquake. It was notorious for its gambling dens, brothels, and saloons.

Bar·ba·ry sheep (*plural* **Bar·ba·ry sheep**) *n.* = **aoudad**

Bar·beau /baar bő/, **Charles Marius** (1883–1969) Canadian anthropologist and folklorist. He collected folk traditions and pioneered professional folklore studies in Canada.

bar·be·cue /baárbə kyoò/, **bar·be·que** *n.* **1.** EQUIPMENT FOR COOKING OUTDOORS an apparatus, including a grill and fuel, used for cooking food outdoors **2.** OUTDOOR PARTY WITH FOOD COOKED OUTDOORS an outdoor party where people eat food cooked on a grill **3.** FOOD COOKED ON GRILL food, especially meat, poultry, and fish, cooked on a grill ■ *vt.* (**-cued, -cu·ing, -cues**) COOK FOOD ON GRILL OUTDOORS to cook food on a grill outdoors [Mid-17thC. From American Spanish *barbacoa*, of uncertain origin, probably from Arawak *barbakoa* "frame of sticks." Current senses evolved from the practice of drying or smoking meat on a wooden frame.]

bar·be·cue sauce *n.* a sweet-sour and spicy sauce, sometimes with chili, used to marinate meat or served as an accompaniment to meat

barbed /baarbd/ *adj.* **1.** WITH BARBS with one or more backward-facing points **2.** SPITEFUL critical or biting ○ *a barbed comment*

barbed wire *n.* strong wire with pointed projections along its length, used to make fences and barriers

bar·bel /baárb'l/ *n.* **1.** FEELER ON MOUTH OF FISH a slender feeler resembling a whisker on the lips or jaws of some fishes **2.** FISH WITH BARBELS a toothless European fish with barbels that resembles the carp. Genus: *Barbus.* [From Latin *barba* "beard"]

bar·bell /baár bèl/ *n.* a metal bar with removable weights at either end, used in weightlifting [Late 19thC. Blend of BAR[1] and DUMBELL.] —**bar·bel·ler** *n.*

bar·bel·late /baárbə làyt, baar béllət/ *adj.* with short barbs or bristles [Mid-19thC. From modern Latin *barbella* "very small beard," from Latin *barbula* (see BARBULE).]

bar·ber /baárbər/ *n.* SOMEBODY WHO CUTS HAIR somebody whose profession it is to cut men's hair and shave their beards ■ *v.* **(-bered, -ber·ing, -bers) 1.** *vt.* CUT SOMEBODY'S HAIR to cut or shave somebody's hair, especially a man's **2.** *vi.* WORK AS BARBER to work as a barber [13thC. From Anglo-Norman *barbour,* which was formed from French *barbe* (see BARB[1]).]

WORD KEY: CULTURAL NOTE

The Barber of Seville, an opera by Italian composer Gioacchino Antonio Rossini (1816). A comedy based on a play by Beaumarchais (1775), it tells of the attempts of Count Almaviva, disguised as a poor student called Lindoro, to woo Rosina, ward of Doctor Bartolo. Almaviva is assisted in his eventful courtship by the wily local barber, Figaro.

Bar·ber /baárbər/, **Samuel** (1910–81) U.S. composer. His neo-Romantic works, which include *Adagio for Strings* (1936), won two Pulitzer Prizes.

bar·ber·ry /baár bèrree/ (*plural* **-ries**) *n.* a thorny flowering shrub native to Asia but widely grown as a garden or hedge plant, especially a yellow-flowered variety that has orange or red berries. Genus: *Berberis.* [14thC. From Old French *berberis* (see BERBERIS), influenced by BERRY.]

bar·ber·shop /baárbər shòp/ *n.* **1.** BARBER'S BUSINESS PLACE the business place of a barber **2.** MUSIC MUSIC FOR MEN SINGING IN HARMONY a style of popular music for unaccompanied single-sex voices in close harmony, originally for four male voices. There are now many female barbershop groups and larger barbershop choirs.

bar·ber's itch *n.* any rash or skin eruption on the face and neck, especially around the beard, caused by a fungal infection

bar·ber's pole *n.* a short pole with red and white stripes found outside a barber's shop

bar·ber's rash *n.* = **barber's itch**

Bar·ber·ton /baárbərtən/ city in northeastern Ohio, a southeastern suburb of Akron. Population: 27,623 (1990).

bar·bet /baárbət/ *n.* a small brightly colored tropical bird related to the toucan, with a large head, a thick hairy bill, short rounded wings, and a short tail. Family: Capitonidae. [Late 16thC. From French, literally "small beard," formed from *barbe* (see BARB[1]).]

bar·bette /baar bét/ *n.* **1.** WARSHIP ARMOR a metal cylinder giving armored protection to a gun turret on a warship **2.** GUN PLATFORM a mound of earth inside a fortress used as a platform for cannons [Late 18thC. From French, literally "small beard" (perhaps from the idea of cannon sticking over the parapet like a line of bristles), formed from *barbe* (see BARB[1]).]

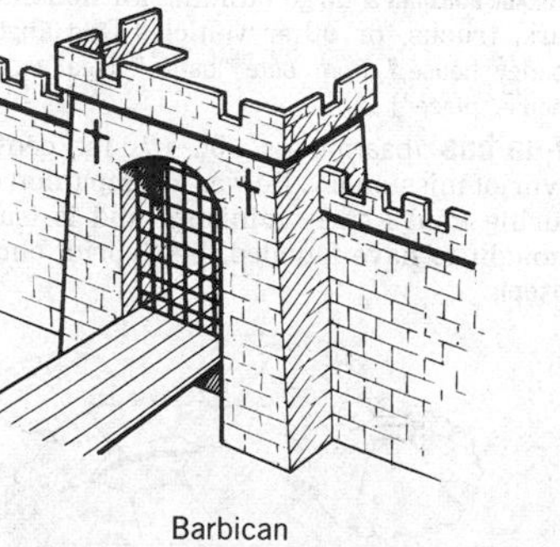

Barbican

bar·bi·can /baárbikən/ *n.* a strong defensive tower at the entrance to a town or fortress [13thC. Via Old French *barbacane* from, ultimately, Persian *barbarkhana* "guard house."]

bar·bi·cel /baárbi sèl/ *n.* a tiny projection on the filaments (**barbules**) of feathers, linking them together [Mid-19thC. From Italian or modern Latin *barbicella* "small beard," formed from Latin *barba* "beard."]

bar·bie /baárbee/ *n.* *Aus* a barbecue (*informal*) [Late 20thC. Shortening.]

Bar·bie /baárbee/, **Klaus** (1913–91) German SS officer. In occupied France during World War II, he deported thousands of Jews to Auschwitz and killed French Resistance workers. He was tried in France after extradition from Bolivia (1983) and imprisoned for life. Known as **Butcher of Lyons** (the)

bar·bi·tal /baárbi tòl, -tàwl/ *n.* a barbiturate with a long-lasting sedative or hypnotic effect, usually prescribed in the form of a white soluble powder. Formula: $C_8H_{12}N_2O_3$. [Early 20thC. From BARBITURIC ACID.]

bar·bi·tu·rate /baar bíchərət, -bíchə ràyt/ *n.* one of a class of barbituric acid derivatives with sedative and hypnotic properties [Late 19thC. From BARBITURIC ACID.]

bar·bi·tu·ric ac·id /baárbə choorik-/ *n.* a white crystalline solid used for making barbiturates. Formula: $C_4H_4N_2O$. [*Barbituric* from French *acide barbiturique*, used to translate German *Barbitursäure*, coined in 1863 by Adolf von Baeyer, a German chemist, from the name Barbara]

Bar·bi·zon School /baárbə zòn-/ *n.* a group of mid-19th-century French painters, which included Corot, Millet, Daubigny, and Rousseau, noted for their realistic depictions of landscapes [Late 19thC. Named for the village of *Barbizon* in France, where the artists met.]

Bar·bu·da /baar bóodə/ coral island of the independent state of Antigua and Barbuda, in the Caribbean Sea. Population: 1,280 (1995). Area: 62 sq. mi./161 sq. km. ◊ **Antigua and Barbuda** —**Bar·bu·dan** /baar bóod'n/ *n., adj.*

bar·bule /baár byool/ *n.* a slender filament attached to the thicker spines (**barbs**) on a feather's central shaft that interlocks with others [Mid-19thC. From Latin *barbula* "little beard," from *barba* "beard."]

barb·wire /baárb wìr/ *n.* = **barbed wire**

bar·ca·role /baárkə rōl/, **bar·ca·rolle** *n.* **1.** GONDOLIERS' SONG a song traditionally sung by Venetian gondoliers **2.** INSTRUMENTAL PIECE IMITATING BARCAROLE a piece of instrumental music that imitates a gondolier's song, made popular especially by Chopin and Mendelssohn [Early 17thC. Via French, from Venetian Italian *barcaruola*, from *barcarolo* "gondolier,"from late Latin *barca* "bark."]

Bar·ce·lo·na /baàrssə lṓnə/ second largest city of Spain and a major seaport on the northern Mediterranean coast. It is capital of Barcelona Province and the autonomous region of Catalonia. Population: 1,630,867 (1994).

bar chart *n.* = **bar graph**

bar code *n.* a sequence of numbers and vertical lines identifying an item and often its price when interpreted by an optical scanner

bar code read·er *n.* an optical scanner used to read bar codes

bard[1] /baard/ *n.* **1.** ANCIENT CELTIC POET in ancient Celtic culture, a poet who composed and recited epic poems describing important events **2.** POET a poet, especially one of national importance (*literary* or *humorous*) [15thC. Via Gaelic *bàrd* from Celtic. Originally a Scottish term for an itinerant minstrel-poet; the elevated sense of "poet" dates from the 17thC.] —**bard·ic** *adj.*

bard[2] /baard/ *n.* ARMOR FOR HORSE a piece of armor for a horse ■ *vt.* **(bard·ed, bard·ing, bards) 1.** DECORATE HORSE WITH BARD to put a bard on a horse **2.** COOK COVER MEAT WITH FAT to cover meat with fat before roasting it to prevent it from drying out [15thC. Via French *barde* from, ultimately, Arabic *barda'a* "saddle cloth, padded saddle."]

Bar·deen /baar deén/, **John** (1908–91) U.S. physicist. He shared two Nobel Prizes in physics, for developing the transistor (1956) and for his research in superconductivity (1972).

Bar·dot /baar dṓ/, **Brigitte** (*b.* 1934) French actor and activist. She became an international symbol for movies including *And God Created Woman* (1956). She retired from movies in 1973 to devote herself to campaigning for animal welfare. Real name **Camille Javal**

bare /bair/ *adj.* **(bar·er, bar·est) 1.** NOT COVERED not covered by clothing ○ *bare legs* **2.** WITHOUT PLANTS without vegetation ○ *a bare hillside* **3.** WITHOUT DECORATION without the usual furnishings or decorations ○ *the room was bare except for an iron bedstead* **4.** BASIC simple or essential ○ *the bare facts* **5.** EMPHASIZING SMALLNESS used to emphasize how small something is ○ *the bare minimum of supplies* **6.** MINIMUM only just sufficient ○ *the bare essentials* ■ *vt.* **(bared, bar·ing, bares)** EXPOSE SOMETHING to reveal or expose something ○ *The dog bared its teeth.* ○ *an investigative report that bared the details of the conspiracy* [Old English *baer*, ultimately from a prehistoric Germanic word] —**bare·ness** *n.*

WORD KEY: SYNONYMS

See Synonyms at ***naked.***

bare·back /báir bàk/, **bare·backed** /-bàkt/ *adv., adj.* on the bare back of a horse that is usually saddled

bare bones *npl.* the essential elements or structure of something, without any elaboration (*informal*)

bare·bones /bàir bṓnz/ *adj.* containing only the basic elements or components ○ *the cost of a barebones computing system*

bare·faced /bàir fáyst/ *adj.* **1.** UNDISGUISED shamelessly undisguised ○ *a barefaced lie* **2.** WITH BARE FACE with an uncovered or clean-shaven face —**bare·fac·ed·ly** /bàir fáystlee, -fáysəd-/ *adv.* —**bare·fac·ed·ness** /-fáystnəs, -fáysədnəs/ *n.*

bare·foot /báir fòot/, **bare·foot·ed** /-fòotəd, -fòotəd/ *adj., adv.* wearing nothing on the feet

bare·foot doc·tor *n.* an auxiliary healthcare worker who is trained to carry out various activities, e.g., dispensing of medications, first aid, and delivering babies, especially one working in rural areas of China

bare·hand·ed /bàir hándəd/ *adj., adv.* without weapons, or with ungloved hands —**bare·hand·ed·ness** *n.*

bare·head·ed /bàir hédəd/ *adj., adv.* wearing nothing on the head —**bare·head·ed·ness** *n.*

bare·knuck·le /báir nùkl/, **bare·knuck·led** /-nùkl'd/ *adv.* BOXING WITHOUT BOXING GLOVES not wearing boxing gloves ■ *adj.* **1.** BOXING USING BARE HANDS using ungloved hands ○ *He was a great bareknuckle champion in his time.* **2.** AGGRESSIVE AND COMPETITIVE characterized by open aggression or competitiveness ○ *a bareknuckle exchange on the Senate floor*

bare·leg·ged /bàir légd, -léggəd/ *adj., adv.* with nothing covering the legs —**bare·leg·ged·ness** /bàir léggədnəs/ *n.*

bare·ly /báirlee/ *adv.* **1.** TO A VERY LIMITED EXTENT almost not, or for a very inadequate amount of time ○ *They had barely enough money to pay the rent.* ○ *She had barely sat down when the phone rang.* ◊ **hardly 2.** SIMPLY AND WITHOUT DECORATION sparsely or simply, with no adornments ○ *a barely furnished office*

WORD KEY: USAGE

See Usage note at ***hardly.***

Bar·en·boim /bàrrən bòym/, **Daniel** (*b.* 1942) Argentinean-born Israeli pianist and conductor. A noted performer of the classical repertoire, he was musical director and conductor of orchestras including the English Chamber Orchestra, the Orchestre de Paris, and the Chicago Symphony Orchestra.

Ba·rents /baárənts/, **Ba·rentz, Willem** (1550?–97) Dutch explorer. In his search for a Northeast Passage to Asia, he discovered Spitsbergen. Barents Sea is named for him.

Ba·rents Sea /bérrənts-/ shallow part of the Arctic Ocean, north of Norway, Finland, and Russia and south of Franz Josef Land. Area: 529,000 sq. mi./ 1,370,100 sq. km.

barf /baarf/ *vti.* **(barfed, barf·ing, barfs)** VOMIT to vomit the contents of the stomach (*informal*) ■ *n.* (*informal*) **1.** ACT OF VOMITING an act of vomiting the contents of the stomach **2.** SOMETHING VOMITED vomited food [Mid-20thC. Probably an imitation of the sound.] —**barf·y** *adj.*

bar·fly /baár flì/ (*plural* **-flies**) *n.* somebody who spends large amounts of time in bars (*slang*) [Early 20thC. Formed by analogy with "house fly" and "fruit fly," the barfly being regarded as a similar pest.]

bar·gain /baárgən/ *n.* **1.** CHEAP PURCHASE something offered or bought at less than the normal price **2.** MUTUAL PACT an agreement between two people or parties in which each side promises to carry out an obligation **3.** PRICE AGREEMENT a commercial agreement between two parties that fixes the price of something **4.** THINGS RECEIVED BY AGREEMENT goods or services obtained by a commercial agreement ■ *v.* **(-gained, -gain·ing, -gains) 1.** *vi.* NEGOTIATE WITH SOMEBODY to negotiate the terms of an agreement with somebody **2.** *vt.* EXCHANGE SOMETHING to exchange one thing for another [14thC. From Old French *bargaignier* "to trade, negotiate, dispute," of uncertain origin, probably ultimately from a prehistoric Germanic word.] —**bar·gain·er** *n.* ◇ **in** *or* **into the bargain** as well ○ *hardworking and very intelligent in the bargain*

bargain away *vt.* to lose something by giving it away as part of an agreement that is ultimately disadvantageous

bargain for *vi.* to expect or believe something to be of a certain nature, and prepare for it ○ *The bill was a lot more than we'd bargained for.*

bargain on *vi.* expect or believe something will happen, and prepare for it ○ *We hadn't bargained on the train arriving early.*

bar·gain base·ment *n.* PART OF STORE SELLING CHEAP GOODS an area of a store, often in the basement, selling merchandise cheaply ■ *adj.* **bar·gain-base·ment** lower than normal ○ *at bargain-basement prices*

bar·gain hunt·er *n.* somebody who enjoys seeking out bargains —**bar·gain hunt·ing** *n.*

bar·gain·ing /baárgəning/ *n.* negotiations to reach an agreement, especially between employers and employees

bar·gain·ing chip *n.* something that can be used as leverage in negotiations

barge /baarj/ *n.* **1.** FREIGHT BOAT a long narrow flat-bottomed boat used for transporting freight on rivers or canals **2.** OPEN BOAT USED CEREMONIALLY a large open boat used during ceremonies **3.** SMALL NAVAL BOAT a motorboat used by a high-ranking naval officer for ceremonial occasions ○ *an admiral's barge* ■ *v.* **(barged, barg·ing, barg·es) 1.** *vti.* MOVE ROUGHLY to move roughly, colliding with other people **2.** *vti.* PUSH to push somebody or something roughly **3.** *vt.* TRANSPORT BY BARGE to transport freight by barge [13thC. From Old French *barge* or medieval Latin *bargia*, of uncertain origin, perhaps from late Latin *barca* (source of English *barque*), or from Greek *baris* "Nile boat."]

barge in *vi.* to enter or intrude suddenly or rudely ○ *Don't just barge in here without knocking.*

barge in on *vi.* to interrupt somebody in a clumsy or rude manner ○ *Don't barge in on them; they are having a private meeting.*

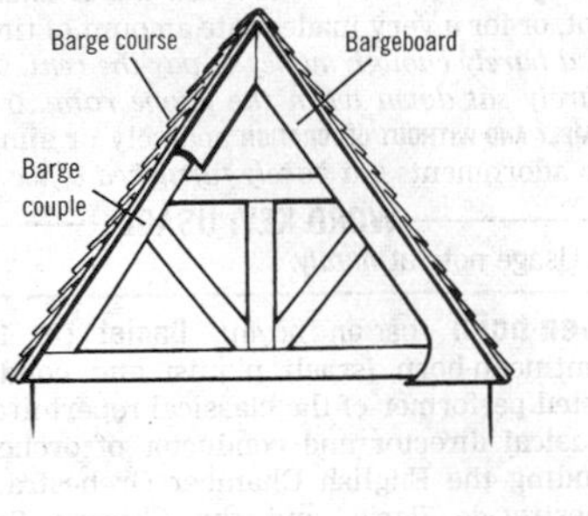

Bargeboard

barge·board /baárj bàwrd/ *n.* an ornamental board attached to the gable end of a roof [Mid-19thC. *Barge* from medieval Latin *bargus*, a kind of gallows.]

barge course *n.* **1.** ROOF'S OVERHANG the overhang of a roof at its gable end **2.** WALL'S TOP LAYER OF BRICKS bricks laid on their edge as the top layer of a brick wall [*Barge* from medieval Latin *bargus*, a kind of gallows]

barg·ee /baar jeé/ *n. U.K.* = **bargeman**

bar·gel·lo /baar jéllō/ (*plural* **-los**) *n.* a straight needle-point stitch that is worked in zigzag waves across the canvas to create chevron or scallop patterns [Mid-20thC. Named for the *Bargello* Palace in Florence, Italy, where there are several examples.]

barge·man /baárjmən/ (*plural* **-men** /-mən/) *n.* a person who works on a freight-carrying barge, either as the captain or a crew member

barge·pole /baárj pōl/ *n.* a long pole used to propel barges

bar·ghest /-gèst/, **bar·guest** *n.* a spirit that takes the form of a black dog or other animal, believed to portend death or tragedy to anyone who sees it [Mid-18thC. From *bar* of uncertain origin (possibly from BARROW²) + ghest, a dialectal variant of GHOST.]

bar girl *n.* = **B-girl**

bar graph *n.* a graph consisting of a series of vertical or horizontal bars representing statistical data

bar·guest *n.* = **barghest**

Bar Har·bor /baár-/ town and tourist spot on Mount Desert Island, southeastern Maine. It is near Acadia National Park. Population: 4,571 (1996).

bar·hop /baár hòp/ (**-hopped, -hop·ping, -hops**) *vi.* to visit a number of different bars during an evening (*informal*)

bar·i·at·rics /bàrree áttriks/ *n.* the branch of medicine concerned with the treatment of obesity (*takes a singular verb*) [Mid-20thC. Coined from BARO- + -IATRICS.] —**bar·i·at·ric** *adj.*

bar·ic /báirik/ *adj.* **1.** OF BARIUM relating to or containing barium **2.** OF BAROMETRIC PRESSURE relating to barometric pressure

ba·ril·la /bə ríllə/ *n.* **1.** PLANT BURNED FOR SODIUM CARBONATE a European plant once burned to produce a form of sodium carbonate. Latin name: *Salsola kali* and *Salsola soda.* **2.** ASH FROM BARILLA PLANT a sodium carbonate and sodium sulfate alkali ash obtained from burning the barilla plant, formerly used in making soap [Early 17thC. From Spanish *barilla* "small bar," from *barra* "bar."]

barit. *abbr.* baritone

bar·ite /bái rìt/ *n.* barium sulfate in the form of a yellow, white, or colorless mineral, the main ore from which barium is obtained. Formula: $BaSO_4$. [Mid-19thC. From BARIUM and -ITE.]

bar·i·tone /bàrrə tōn/, **bar·y·tone** *n.* **1.** MALE SINGER OR VOICE a male singing voice with a range lower than a tenor and higher than a bass, or a singer with this voice **2.** WIND INSTRUMENT a wind instrument with the second lowest range in its family [Early 17thC. Via Italian *baritono* from Greek *barutonos*, "deep-sounding, baritone."]

bar·i·um /báiree əm/ *n.* a soft silver-white toxic chemical element used in alloys. Symbol **Ba** [Early 19thC. From BARYTA + -IUM.]

bar·i·um en·e·ma *n.* the introduction of a barium salt suspension into the rectum and colon before an X-ray is taken

bar·i·um sul·fate *n.* a white or yellowish odorless powder, useful in medicine because it cannot be penetrated by X-rays. Formula: $BaSO_4$.

bark¹ /baark/ *n.* **1.** DOG'S NOISE the natural loud abrupt sound made by a dog or fox **2.** SOUND RESEMBLING DOG'S NOISE a sound similar to the bark of a dog ○ *the bark of guns in the distance* ■ *v.* **(barked, bark·ing, barks) 1.** *vi.* MAKE DOG'S SOUND to make the loud abrupt sound of a dog or fox **2.** *vi.* MAKE SOUND SIMILAR TO DOG'S to make a sound similar to a dog's bark **3.** *vti.* SPEAK AGGRESSIVELY to say something in a loud or aggressive manner ○ *He barked out an order.*

bark² /baark/ *n.* OUTER LAYER OF TREE the rough outer covering of the woody stems of trees or other plants ■ *vt.* **(barked, bark·ing, barks) 1.** GRAZE SKIN to have the skin rubbed off a part of the body through abrasive contact with another object ○ *I barked my shins climbing the fence.* **2.** STRIP BARK FROM TREE to remove the bark from a tree or log **3.** MANUF TAN LEATHER USING BARK to tan leather using tannins derived from some kinds of bark [13thC. From Old Norse *börkr.*] —**bark·y** *adj.*

bark³ /baark/, **barque** *n.* **1.** SMALL SHIP WITH SAILS RUNNING BREADTHWAYS a small sailing ship with masts whose sails are fixed breadthways **(square)** except for the last mast, which has its sail running lengthwise **(fore-and-aft) 2.** SMALL BOAT any small sailing ship or boat

bark bee·tle *n.* a beetle that burrows under the bark of trees. Family: Scolytidae.

bar·keep /baár keèp/ *n.* = **bartender**

bar·keep·er /baár keèpər/ *n.* **1.** PERSON RUNNING BAR somebody who owns or runs a bar **2.** = **bartender**

bark·er¹ /baárkər/ *n.* **1.** ADVERTISER OF FAIRGROUND ATTRACTIONS somebody who stands outside the entrance to a fair, carnival, or other place of entertainment and shouts out its attractions **2.** BARKING DOG a dog that barks, especially one that barks a lot

bark·er² /baárkər/ *n.* a person or machine that strips bark off trees and logs or prepares bark for tanning

Bar·kley /baárklee/, **Alben W., 35th vice president of the United States** (1877–1956). He was a member of the U.S. Senate and was Truman's vice president (1949–53). Full name **Alben William Barkley**

bark man·tis (*plural* **bark man·tis·es** *or* **bark man·tes**) *n.* an insect whose shape and color blends in well with tree bark. Latin name: *Gonatista grisea.*

bar·le·duc /baàr lə dóok/ *n.* a preserve made from gooseberries or white and red currants [Named for the town of *Bar-le-Duc* in northeastern France]

bar·ley /baárlee/ *n.* **1.** GRAIN CROP a cereal plant with a long head of whiskered grains, widely grown for food, malt production, and livestock feed. Latin name: *Hordeum vulgare.* **2.** GRAIN the grain from a barley plant [Old English *bærlic* "barley-like," formed from *bære, bere* "barley," (source of English *barn*). Ultimately from an Indo-European base that is also the ancestor of English *farina* and *farrago.*]

bar·ley·corn /baárli kàwrn/ *n.* a single grain of barley (*archaic*)

bar·ley sug·ar *n.* a clear hard candy made from boiled-down sugar,

Bar·low /baárlō/, **Joel** (1754–1812) U.S. politician and poet. A diplomat, he is best known for his poem 'Hasty Pudding' (1796).

Bar·low knife /baárlō-/ (*plural* **Bar·low knives**) *n.* a pocketknife with one blade for cutting and another for poking or gouging [Late 18thC. Named for the original makers, the *Barlow* family, cutlers in Sheffield, England.]

barm /baarm/ *n.* the foam that rises to the surface during the fermentation of malt liquor [Old English *beorma*. Ultimately from a prehistoric Germanic word that is also the ancestor of English *brew, bread,* and *broth.*]

bar·maid /baár mảyd/ *n.* a woman who serves in a bar

bar·man /baármən/ (*plural* **-men** /-mən/) *n. U.K.* a man who serves in a bar

Bar·me·cid·al /baàrmə síd'l/, **Bar·me·cide** /-sìd/ *adj.* abundant or lavish only in appearance and not in reality (*literary*) [Mid-18thC. From *Barmecide*, a prince in *The Arabian Nights* who served a series of empty dishes to a hungry beggar to test his sense of humor.]

bar mitz·vah /baar mítsvə/ *n.* **1.** JEWISH RITE OF PASSAGE the ritual ceremony that marks the 13th birthday of a Jewish boy, after which he takes full responsibility for his moral and spiritual conduct **2.** JEWISH BOY REACHING 13 a Jewish boy who has reached the age of 13, the age of religious responsibility [Early 19thC. From Hebrew *bar miṣwāh*, literally "son of the commandment."]

barm·y /baármee/ (**-i·er, -i·est**), **balm·y** (**-i·er, -i·est**) *adj. U.K.* (*informal*) **1.** SLIGHTLY IRRATIONAL unconventional or slightly irrational in behavior **2.** NONSENSICAL completely lacking in good sense or reason ○ *That's a barmy idea and you know it.* [15thC. Literally "frothy," formed from barm.]

barn /baarn/ *n.* **1.** LARGE FARM OUTBUILDING a large outbuilding on a farm used to store grain or shelter livestock **2.** LARGE BUILDING any large building, especially one that is plain and functional **3.** VEHICLE STORAGE BUILDING a large building for housing railroad cars, trucks, or other vehicles [Old English *ber(e)n* "barley house," from *bere* "barley" (see BARLEY) + *ærn* "house, place"]

Bar·na·bas /baárnəbəss/, **St.** (*fl.* 1st century A.D.) Cypriot missionary. He was a companion of St. Paul during Paul's early ministry, and is traditionally thought to have founded the Cypriot church. Born **Joseph**

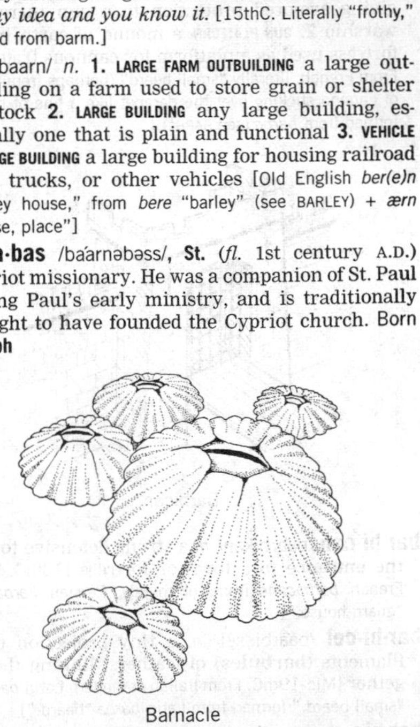

Barnacle

bar·na·cle /baárnək'l/ *n.* **1.** MARINE BIOL CLINGING MARINE ORGANISM a small marine organism with a shell that clings to rocks and ships and draws food by using slender hairs **(cirri)**. Subclass: Cirripedia. **2.** ZOOL =

barnacle goose 3. **SOMEBODY WHO CLINGS** a clinging or dependent person or thing [12thC. From medieval Latin *berneca*, of unknown origin.]

bar·na·cle goose (*plural* **bar·na·cle geese**) *n.* a wild goose found in northern Europe and Greenland that has gray wings and a black-and-white head and body. Latin name: *Branta leucopsis.*

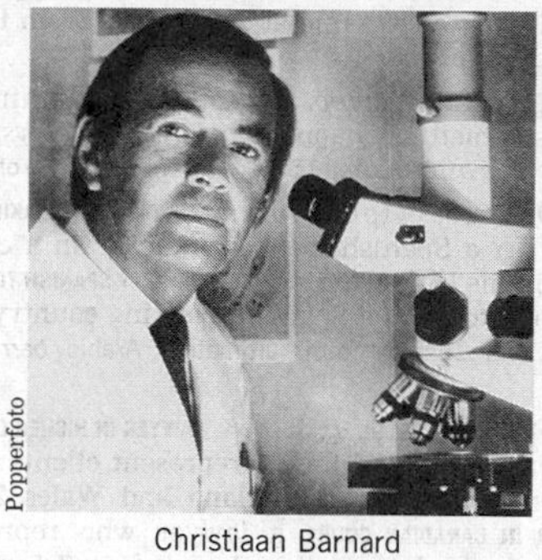

Popperfoto

Christiaan Barnard

Bar·nard /baárnaard/, **Christiaan** (*b.* 1922) South African surgeon. He performed the world's first successful human heart transplant operation in 1967. Full name **Christiaan Neethling Barnard**

Bar·nard /baárnərd/, **Edward** (1857–1923) U.S. astronomer. He discovered comets, stars and moons, including Amalthea, a moon of Jupiter, (1892) and Barnard's star (1916). He was also a pioneering astrophotographer. Full name **Edward Emerson Barnard**

Bar·nard /baárnaard/, **Henry** (1811–1900) U.S. educator and legislator. A tireless reformer of public education, he was the first U.S. commissioner of education (1867–70).

Bar·nard's star /baár naardz-, baárnərdz-/ *n.* a red dwarf star in the constellation Ophiuchus [Early 20thC. Named for Edward Emerson *Barnard*.]

barn·burn·er /baárn bùrnər/ *n.* an event or occasion memorable for being impressive or successful (*informal*) [Mid-19thC. Supposedly from a story of a man who burned down his barn to rid it of rats.]

barn dance *n.* a party, originally held in a barn, with square dancing

Bar·ne·gat Bay /baárnə gat-, -nəgət-/ inlet on the coast of New Jersey, separated from the Atlantic Ocean by Long Beach Island and Island Beach Peninsula

barn owl *n.* an owl with white and pale brown feathers that often nests in barns

barn rais·ing *n.* the building of a wooden barn by a team of people, traditionally a small rural community, often presented as a symbol of bygone community fellowship

Barn·sta·ble /baárnstəb'l/ city and tourist resort in southeastern Massachusetts on an inlet of Cape Cod Bay. Population: 43,699 (1996).

barn·storm /baárn stàwrm/ (**-stormed, -storm·ing, -storms**) *v.* **1.** *vti.* **MAKE PERFORMING TOUR OF RURAL AREAS** to travel from place to place giving performances **2.** *vi.* **DO FLYING STUNTS** to perform exhibitions of aerial acrobatics at shows and fairs **3.** *vti.* **TOUR RURAL AREAS MAKING POLITICAL SPEECHES** to go on a whistlestop tour of rural areas making political speeches as part of an election campaign —**barn·storm·er** *n.* —**barn·storm·ing** /baárn stàwrming/ *adj.*

barn swal·low *n.* a common swallow, that has long pointed wings, a forked tail, a navy blue back, and light brown underparts. Latin name: *Hirundo rustica.*

Bar·num /baárnəm/, **P. T.** (1810–91) U.S. showman, known for his spectacular circuses, including "The Greatest Show on Earth" (1871). With James Bailey (1847–1906) he originated the Barnum and Bailey Circus (1881). Full name **Phineas Taylor Barnum**

barn·yard /baárn yaàrd/ *n.* **AREA OF FARM AROUND BARN** the area around a barn, where small farm animals roam ■ *adj.* **CRUDE** crude or vulgar (*informal*) ○ *barnyard humor*

barn·yard grass *n.* a coarse weedy grass with spiky clusters of flowers, sometimes grown as forage. Latin name: *Echinochloa crusgalli.*

bar·o·cep·tor /bárrə sèptər/ = **baroreceptor**

bar·o·gram /bárrə gràm/ *n.* a record of atmospheric pressure produced by a barograph or other meteorological instrument

bar·o·graph /bárrə gràf/ *n.* a barometer that gives a continuous printed record of variations in atmospheric pressure —**bar·o·graph·ic** /bàrrə gráffik/ *adj.*

Ba·ro·lo /bə rṓllo, ba-/ *n.* a full-bodied red wine made in the area around Barolo in northwestern Italy

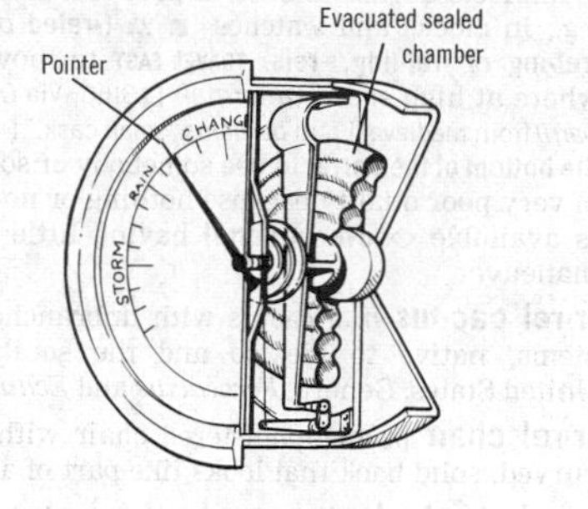

Barometer

ba·rom·e·ter /bə rómmətər/ *n.* **1.** **INSTRUMENT MEASURING ATMOSPHERIC PRESSURE** an instrument measuring changes in atmospheric pressure, used in weather forecasting **2.** **INDICATOR OF MOOD** something that indicates an atmosphere or mood ○ *the barometer of public opinion* —**bar·o·met·ric** /bàrrə méttrik/ *adj.* —**bar·o·met·ri·cal** /-méttrik'l/ *adj.* —**bar·o·met·ri·cal·ly** /-méttrikəlee/ *adv.* —**ba·rom·e·try** /bə rómmətree/ *n.*

bar·o·met·ric pres·sure *n.* atmospheric pressure as recorded by a barometer

bar·on /bárrən/ *n.* **1.** **NOBLEMAN** a male member of the lowest rank of British or Japanese nobility, or a nobleman of various ranks in some European countries **2.** **POWERFUL PERSON** somebody who has power or influence ○ *an oil baron* **3.** **MEDIEVAL NOBLEMAN** a nobleman in the Middle Ages who was given land in return for loyal service **4.** a cut of beef consisting of a double sirloin, joined at the backbone [12thC. Via Anglo-Norman *barun* and Old French *baron* from medieval Latin *baron-* "man, warrior." Probably ultimately from a prehistoric Germanic word that is also the ancestor of English *bairn*.]

bar·on·age /bérrənij/ *n.* **1.** **BARONS AS A GROUP** barons considered collectively **2.** **RANK OF BARON** a baron's rank or position

bar·on·ess /bérrənəs, bérrə nès/ *n.* **1.** **MINOR NOBLEWOMAN** a woman who belongs to the lowest rank of British or Japanese nobility, or to any of various ranks of the nobility in some European countries **2.** **BARON'S WIFE OR WIDOW** a baron's wife or widow

bar·on·et /bérrənət, bérrə nèt/ *n.* a British man who holds the lowest hereditary rank of honor

bar·on·et·age /bérrənətij/ *n.* **1.** **BARONETS AS A GROUP** baronets collectively **2.** = **baronetcy**

bar·on·et·cy /bérrənətsee/ *n.* a baronet's rank or position

ba·rong /bə ráwng, bə róng/ *n.* a large knife with a broad blade, used by the Moro people of the Philippines [Late 19thC. From Malayo-Polynesian.]

ba·ro·ni·al /bə rṓnee əl/ *adj.* **1.** **RELATING TO BARONS** relating to or associated with barons **2.** **LARGE AND IMPRESSIVE** large, imposing, or sumptuous ○ *a baronial fireplace*

bar·o·ny /bàrrənee/ (*plural* **-nies**) *n.* **1.** **BARON'S RANK OR LAND** a baron's rank or position, or the land held by a baron **2.** **INFLUENTIAL PERSON'S TERRITORY** a powerful businessperson's area of influence ○ *a newspaper tycoon zealously guarding his barony*

bar·o·phil·ic /bàrrə fíllik/ *adj.* used to describe an organism that can tolerate high atmospheric pressure —**bar·o·phile** /bàrrə fìl/ *n.*

ba·ro·pho·bic /bàrrə fṓbik/ *adj.* used to describe an organism that cannot tolerate conditions of high atmospheric pressure —**ba·ro·phobe** /bàrrə fṓb/ *n.* —**ba·ro·pho·bi·a** *n.*

ba·roque /bə rṓk, bə rók/ *adj.* **1.** **IN VERY ORNAMENTAL STYLE** bizarre or highly exaggerated in style **2.** **IN 17THC STYLE** in the Baroque style of art or architecture [Mid-18thC. Via French, applied to ornate architecture, from Italian *barocco* and Portuguese *barroco* "irregularly shaped pearl," of unknown origin.] —**ba·roque·ly** *adv.*

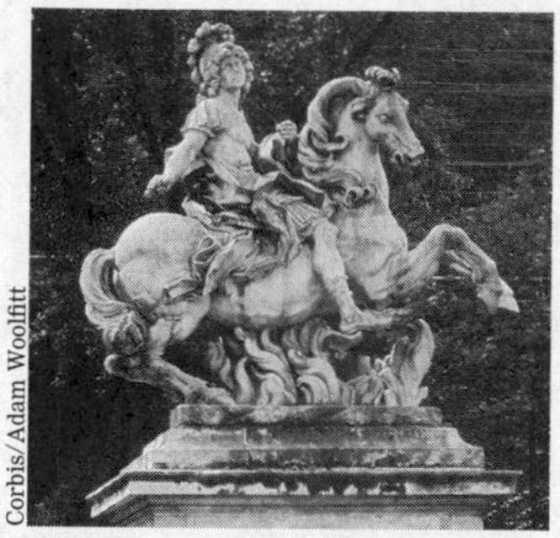

Corbis/Adam Woolfitt

Baroque: Statue of Louis XIV (17th century) by Gianlorenzo Bernini at Versailles, France

Ba·roque *n.* **1.** **FLAMBOYANT STYLE OF EUROPEAN ARCHITECTURE AND ART** a highly ornamental style of European architecture and art that lasted from the mid-16th to the early 18th centuries, or this period in European history **2.** **17THC CLASSICAL MUSIC** classical music of the 17th century, the period of such composers as Purcell, Vivaldi, and Telemann —**Ba·roque** *adj.*

bar·o·re·cep·tor /bárrō ri sèptər/ *n.* a nerve ending that is sensitive to blood pressure changes

bar·o·ther·mo·graph /bàrrə thérmə gràf/ *n.* an instrument that records atmospheric pressure and temperature simultaneously

bar·o·ti·tis *n.* pain in the ear caused by pressure differences, e.g., during air travel (*informal*)

baro·trauma /bárrō trawmə/ *n.* MED pain in and possible damage to an organ occurring as a result of changes in atmospheric pressure

ba·rouche /bə ro͞osh/ *n.* a four-wheeled horse-drawn carriage, widely used in the 19th century, with two facing double seats, a retractable hood, and a box seat at the front for the driver [Early 19thC. Via German dialect *Barutsche* from Italian *baroccio* "two-wheeled," from, ultimately, Latin *birotus*, from *rota* "wheel."]

bar·per·son /baár pùrs'n/ (*plural* **-peo·ple** /-peèp'l/) *n.* somebody who serves in a bar

bar point *n.* the seventh point on a large backgammon board, near the bar

barque /baark/ *n.* = **bark**[3]

Bar·qui·si·me·to /baàr kə sə máytō/ city in northwestern Venezuela and the capital of Lara State, on the Turbio River. Population: 602,662 (1991).

bar·ra /bárrə/ (*plural* **-ras** or **-ra**) *n.* = **barramundi** *n.*

bar·rack[1] /bárrək/ *n.* = **barracks** ■ *vt.* (**-racked, -rack·ing, -racks**) **1.** **PUT SOLDIERS IN BARRACKS** to house soldiers in a barracks **2.** **PUT SOMEBODY IN TEMPORARY ACCOMMODATION** to house people in any kind of temporary accommodation (*often passive*) [Late 17thC. From BARRACKS.]

bar·rack[2] /bárrək/ (**-racked, -rack·ing, -racks**) *vti.* (*informal*) **1.** *U.K.* **SHOUT AT SOMEBODY IN PROTEST** to shout at somebody in criticism or protest **2.** *Aus* **SHOUT IN SUPPORT OF SOMEBODY** to shout support for somebody, especially a player or team [Late 19thC. Origin uncertain, possibly from Northern Irish dialect *barrack* "brag." Originally Australian.] —**bar·rack·er** /bérrəkər/ *n.*

bar·racks /bárrəks/ *n.* (*takes a singular or plural verb*) **1.** **SOLDIERS' QUARTERS** a building used to accommodate military personnel **2.** **TEMPORARY ACCOMMODATION** any temporary accommodation [Late 17thC. Via French *baraque* from Italian *baracca* or Spanish *barraca* "soldier's tent," also called "barrack," of unknown origin.]

bar·ra·coon /bàrrə ko͞on, -ko͝on/ *n.* in former times, a large building used to confine slaves or convicts in temporarily [Mid-19thC. From Spanish *barracon* "large barracks," from *barraca* "barracks."]

bar·ra·cou·ta /bàrrə ko͞otə/ (*plural* **-tas** or **-ta**) *n.* a large predatory sea fish with strong teeth and a projecting lower jaw, found only in the Pacific Ocean. It has teeth like a barracuda, but is not related to it. Family: Gempylidae. [Late 17thC. Alteration of BARRACUDA.]

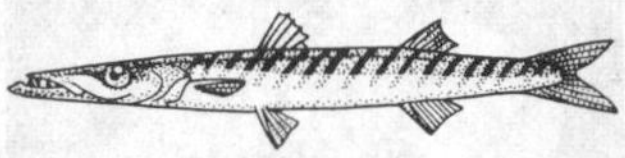

Barracuda

bar·ra·cu·da /bàrrə kóodə/ (*plural* **-das** *or* **-da**) *n.* a predatory sea fish with a long body and protruding jaws and teeth, found in tropical seas. Genus: *Sphyraena.* [Late 17thC. Via American Spanish, from Spanish dialect *barraco* "overlapping tooth," of unknown origin.]

bar·rage /bə raázh/ *n.* **1. MILITARY BOMBARDMENT** a long continuous burst of gunfire **2. ATTACKING FLOW OF SOMETHING** a rapid attacking outpouring of something ○ *a barrage of criticism* **3. RIVER BARRIER** an artificial barrier built across a river or canal to provide water or prevent flooding ■ *vt.* (**-raged, -rag·ing, -rag·es**) **1. FIRE CONTINUOUSLY ON ENEMY** to attack an enemy with rapid and continuous gunfire **2. ATTACK SOMEBODY CONTINUOUSLY** to subject somebody to a relentless onslaught ○ *Those two have been barraging me with questions all morning.* [Mid-19thC. From French, "barrier," from *barrer* "to block," from *barre* "bar" (see BAR[1]).]

bar·rage bal·loon *n.* any one of a set of large balloons anchored to the ground in wartime to deter enemy aircraft

bar·ra·mun·di /bàrrə múndee/ (*plural* **-dis** *or* **-dies** *or* **-di**), **bar·ra·mun·da** /-múndə/ (*plural* **-das** *or* **-da**) *n.* an edible Australian fish of the perch family. Latin name: *Lates calcarifer.* [Late 19thC. Origin uncertain, probably from a Queensland Aboriginal word.]

bar·ran·ca /bə ráng kə/, **bar·ran·co** /bə ráng kō/ (*plural* **-cos**) *n. Southwest U.S.* a ravine or steep bank [Late 17thC. From Spanish, of unknown origin.]

Bar·ran·quil·la /baá raan keé yə/ river port and capital of Atlántico Department, northern Colombia. It is situated on the Magdalena River, about 8 mi./13 km inland from the Caribbean Sea. Population: 1,064,255 (1995).

bar·ra·try /bàrrətree/ *n.* **1.** LAW **BRINGING OF UNREASONABLE LAWSUITS** the illegal action of persistently bringing lawsuits for little or no reason **2. ILLEGAL SHIPPING PRACTICE** any unlawful practice committed by a ship's master or crew that harms its owner or charterer **3. BUYING OF CHURCH OR GOVERNMENT POSITION** the sale or purchase of a position in government or the church [15thC. From French *baraterie* "combat, deceit," from *barater* "to fight, cheat," ultimately from Greek *prattein* "to do" (source of English *practice*).] —**bar·ra·tor** *n.* —**bar·ra·trous** *adj.* —**bar·ra·trous·ly** *adv.*

Barr bod·y /baár bòdee/ (*plural* **Barr bod·ies**) *n.* an inactive X chromosome present in the cells of females, used in a test to determine sex [Mid-20thC. Named for the Canadian anatomist Murray L. *Barr,* born 1908, who first reported its existence.]

barre /baar/ *n.* a rail attached to a wall, at about hip height, used by ballet dancers when exercising [Mid-20thC. From French (see BAR[1]).]

bar·ré /baa ráy/ *n.* **1. USING FINGER TO RAISE GUITAR'S PITCH** the placing of the index finger over all the strings of a guitar or similar string instrument to raise the pitch of each string simultaneously **2. CHORD PLAYED IN BARRÉ FASHION** a chord played on a guitar or similar string instrument in a barré fashion [Late 19thC. From French *barre,* past participle of *barrer* (see BARRAGE).]

Barre /bárree/ city in east central Vermont noted for its granite quarries. Population: 9,206 (1996).

barred /baard/ *adj.* **1. WITH STRIPES** having strips of color **2. WITH BARS FITTED** fitted with or made of bars **3. CLOSED** closed off

barred owl *n.* a large North American owl with dark eyes, broad brownish stripes across its breast, and streaked underparts. Latin name: *Strix varia.*

barred spi·ral gal·ax·y (*plural* **barred spi·ral gal·ax·ies**) *n.* a galaxy in which the stars form a spiral with a bright bar across the center

bar·rel /bàrrəl/ *n.* **1. LARGE CASK** a cylindrical container with a flat top and bottom, used to store liquids **2. AMOUNT HELD BY BARREL** the amount held by a barrel **3. UNIT OF VOLUME IN OIL INDUSTRY** a unit of liquid volume used in the oil industry, usually taken to be 42 U.S. gallons (approximately 159 liters) **4. UNIT OF VOLUME IN BREWING INDUSTRY** a unit of liquid volume used in the brewing industry, equal to 31 U.S. gallons (approximately 164 liters) **5. TUBELIKE PART OF A GUN** the tube-shaped part of gun through which bullets are fired **6. CYLINDRICAL PART** any one of various hollow cylindrical devices that form part of a mechanism, e.g., in clocks and watches ■ *vi.* (**-reled** *or* **-relled, -rel·ing** *or* **-rel·ling, -rels**) **TRAVEL FAST** to move somewhere at high speed (*informal*) [13thC. Via Old French *barril* from medieval Latin *barriclus* "small cask."] ◇ **scrape the bottom of the barrel** to use somebody or something of very poor quality because nothing or no one else is available ◇ **over a barrel** having little room to maneuver

bar·rel cac·tus *n.* a cactus with unbranched spiny stems, native to Mexico and the southwestern United States. Genera: *Ferocactus* and *Echinocactus.*

bar·rel chair *n.* an upholstered chair with a high, curved, solid back that looks like part of a barrel

bar·rel-chest·ed *adj.* with a large rounded chest

bar·rel·ful /bérrəl fòol/ *n.* = **barrel** *n.* 2

bar·rel·head /bérrəl hèd/ *n.* the flat circular top of a barrel

bar·rel·house /bàrrəl hòws/ (*plural* **-houses** /-hòwzəz/) *n.* **1. SEEDY BAR** a cheap disreputable bar, especially one where there is music and dancing (*dated*) **2. STYLE OF JAZZ** a loud rough style of jazz characterized by a heavy two-beat rhythm [Late 19thC. So called from the barrels of liquor along the walls.]

bar·rel or·gan *n.* a mechanical musical instrument consisting of a cylinder turned with a handle, which allows air to pass through a set of pipes [So called from the internal cylinder or *barrel*]

bar·rel roll (**bar·rel rolled, bar·rel rol·ling, bar·rel rolls**) *n.* a flight maneuver in which an aircraft makes one complete sideways revolution

bar·rel vault *n.* a ceiling in the shape of a half cylinder

bar·ren /bàrrən/ *adj.* **1. BARE OF VEGETATION** with no trees or other plants growing **2. NOT FRUITING** producing no fruit or seed **3. UNABLE TO HAVE CHILDREN** not able to bear children (*archaic or literary*) **4. WITH NO USEFUL RESULT** not producing valuable results or interesting effects ○ *It was a barren period in her career.* **5. LACKING IN SOMETHING** lacking in a particular thing (*literary*) ○ *Our writers seem somewhat barren of new ideas.* ■ *n.* **FLAT SCRUBLAND** an area of flat, scrubby, unproductive land (*often used in the plural*) [12thC. From Old French *baraigne,* of unknown origin.] —**bar·ren·ly** *adv.* —**bar·ren·ness** *n.*

bar·ret /bárrət/ *n.* a flat hat similar in shape to the biretta worn by Roman Catholic clergy [Early 19thC. Via French *barrette* from Italian *berretta* "biretta" (see BIRETTA).]

bar·rette /bə rét/ *n.* a metal or plastic clasp used by women and girls to keep their hair in place [Early 20thC. From French, literally "small bar," formed from *barre* "bar" (see BAR[1]).]

bar·ri·cade /bárri kàyd, -káyd/ *n.* **DEFENSIVE BARRIER** a barrier that protects defenders or blocks a route ■ *vt.* (**-cad·ed, -cad·ing, -cades**) **OBSTRUCT SOMETHING WITH BARRICADES** to obstruct or protect something, or protect yourself, using barricades [Late 16thC. From French, formed from *barrique* "barrel." So called because the earliest barricades were made of barrels filled with earth, rock, and debris.]

Bar·rie /bàrree/, **Sir J. M.** (1860–1937) British author. He wrote *Peter Pan* (1904) and numerous other plays including *The Admirable Crichton* (1902). Full name **Sir James Matthew Barrie**

bar·ri·er /bàrree ər/ *n.* **1. THING THAT OBSTRUCTS** something that obstructs or separates, often by emphasizing differences **2. STRUCTURE BLOCKING ACCESS** a structure, e.g., a fence, intended to prevent access or keep one place separate from another **3. LIMIT OR STANDARD** something considered to be a limit, standard, or boundary **4.** GEOG **ICE SHELF** the part of the Antarctic ice shelf that extends over the sea and partly rests on the ocean floor [14thC. Via Old French *barriere* from, ultimately, Vulgar Latin *barra* "bar" (see BAR[1]).]

bar·ri·er is·land *n.* a long sandy island that runs parallel to a coastline and serves to protect the shore from erosion

bar·ri·er meth·od *n.* a method of contraception in which the access of sperm to the womb is blocked, e.g., by use of a condom or diaphragm

bar·ri·er reef *n.* a narrow ridge of coral lying parallel and close to a coastline and separated from it by a wide deep lagoon

bar·ring /baáring/ *prep.* except for something, or unless something happens ○ *Barring delays, we'll arrive this afternoon.* [15thC. Present participle of BAR[1].]

bar·ri·o /baáree ō/ (*plural* **-os**) *n.* **1. SPANISH-SPEAKING PART OF U.S. CITY** a Spanish-speaking quarter in a city or town in the United States **2. DISTRICT OF SPANISH TOWN** an area of a town in a Spanish-speaking country [Mid-19thC. Via Spanish from, ultimately, Arabic *barr* "open area,."]

bar·ris·ter /bárrəstər/ *n.* **1.** *U.K.* **LAWYER IN HIGHER COURT** a lawyer who is qualified to represent clients in the higher law courts in England and Wales **2.** *Can* **LAWYER IN CANADIAN COURT** a lawyer who represents clients in any law court in Canada [15thC. From BAR[1], perhaps modeled on words such as *minister* and *chorister.*]

WORD KEY: SYNONYMS

See Synonyms at *lawyer.*

bar·room /baár ròom, -ròom/ *n.* a bar for serving drinks, especially one inside a larger establishment such as a hotel or club

bar·row[1] /bárrō/ *n.* **1.** *U.K.* **HAND CART** a two-wheeled cart used by street vendors to sell their wares. ◊ **pushcart 2.** = **wheelbarrow** [Old English *bearwe* "stretcher, bier." Ultimately from a prehistoric Germanic word meaning "to bear," which is also the ancestor of English *bear* and *bier.*]

bar·row[2] /bárrō/ *n.* a large mound of earth above a prehistoric tomb [Old English *beorg* "hill, tumulus," from a prehistoric Germanic word meaning "to hide or protect," which is also the ancestor of English *borough* and *belfry*]

bar·row[3] /bárrō/ *n.* a pig that has been castrated before sexual maturity [Old English *b(e)arg,* from prehistoric Germanic]

Bar·row /bárrō/ village in northwestern Alaska with a predominantly Inuit population. It is southwest of Point Barrow, the northernmost point of the United States. Population: 4,080 (1996).

Bar·row, Clyde (1909–34) U.S. outlaw. He and Bonnie Parker robbed banks and killed 12 people (1932–34) before being killed by Louisiana police.

Bar·ry /bárree/, **Philip James** (1896–1949) U.S. playwright. He is known for sophisticated comedies such as *The Philadelphia Story* (1939).

Bar·ry·more /bárri màwr/, **Ethel** (1879–1959) U.S. actor. The sister of John and Lionel Barrymore, she had a long stage career and won an Academy Award for *None but the Lonely Heart* (1944).

Bar·ry·more, John (1882–1942) U.S. actor. A handsome leading man, he made numerous films, but was most famous for his performance of Hamlet. He was the brother of Ethel and Lionel Barrymore.

Bar·ry·more, Lionel (1878–1954) U.S. actor. The brother of Ethel and John Barrymore, he won an Academy Award for *Free Soul* (1931) and appeared in the original *Dr Kildare* films.

Bar·sac /baár sàk/ *n.* a sweet white Bordeaux wine from the area around the town of Barsac, France

bar sin·is·ter (*plural* **bars sin·is·ter**) *n.* **1.** HERALDRY = **bend sinister 2. EVIDENCE OF SOMEBODY'S ILLEGITIMACY** evidence suggesting that somebody is of illegitimate birth

bar tack *n.* a straight stitch that crosses a piece of cloth at a right angle to a slit, e.g., at the end of a buttonhole

bar·tend·er /baár tèndər/ *n.* somebody who serves in a bar

bar·ter /baártər/ *v.* (**-tered, -ter·ing, -ters**) **1.** *vti.* **EXCHANGE GOODS OR SERVICES** to exchange goods or services in return for other goods or services **2.** *vi.* **NEGOTIATE TERMS OF AGREEMENT** to negotiate or argue over the terms of a transaction ■ *n.* **1. BARTERING** the practice or system of bartering **2. THINGS BARTERED** goods or services that are bartered [15thC. Origin uncertain, probably from Old French *barater* (see BARRATRY).] —**bar·ter·er** *n.*

Barth /baarth/, **John** (*b.* 1930) U.S. writer and educator. He is known for his formal experimentation in fictional works such as *Giles Goat-Boy* (1966) and *Tidewater Tales* (1987). Full name **John Simmons Barth**

Barthes /baart/, **Roland** (1915–80) French philosopher and writer. He was a leading proponent of structuralism and author of the seminal critical work *Writing Degree Zero* (1953). He formulated the literary theory that the "meaning" of a text lies not in its author's intentions but in its underlying semiotic structure. Full name **Roland Gérard Barthes**

Bar·tho·lin's gland /baártəlinz-/ *n.* either of two small glands on either side of the lower vagina that secrete a lubricating mucus during sexual stimulation. ◊ **Cowper's gland** [Early 20thC. Named for Kaspar *Bartholin* (1655–1738), the Danish anatomist who described them.]

Bartizan

bar·ti·zan /baártizən, baártə zàn/ *n.* a small turret that projects from a tower or wall of a fortress or castle, used as a lookout or a defensive position [Mid-16thC. From *bartisane*, a Scots variant of *bratticing* "timberwork," from BRATTICE.] —**bar·ti·zaned** *adj.*

Bar·tles·ville /baárt'lz vìl/ city in northeastern Oklahoma, on the Caney River, in an agricultural and oil-producing region. Population: 34,256 (1990).

Bart·lett /baártlət/ city in southwestern Tennessee, a northeastern suburb of Memphis. Population: 35,735 (1996).

Bart·lett, John (1820–1905) U.S. publisher and compiler. Best known for his *Bartlett's Familiar Quotations* (1855), for many years he owned the University Book Store at Harvard (1849–63).

Bart·lett, Josiah (1729–95) American politician. A physician and delegate to the Continental Congress, he signed the Declaration of Independence and was New Hampshire's first governor (1793–94).

Bar·tók /baár tòk, -tàwk/, **Béla** (1881–1945) Hungarian composer. Influenced by Hungarian folk music, he wrote piano concertos, string quartets, and the opera *Duke Bluebeard's Castle* (1911).

bar·ton /baárt'n/ *n.* a farmyard (*archaic*) [Old English *beretun* "threshing floor," from *bere* BARLEY + *tun* "place, farm, town" (see TOWN)]

Bar·ton /baárt'n/, **Clara** (1821–1912) U.S. humanitarian. She founded the American Red Cross and was its first president (1881–1904). Full name **Clarissa Harlowe Barton**

Bar·tram /baártrəm/, **John** (1699–1777) American botanist. He collected plants native to North America, made plant maps, and experimented with hybrids.

Bar·uch /bə ro͝ok/ *n.* a book in the Roman Catholic Old Testament and the Protestant Apocrypha traditionally ascribed to Baruch, a disciple of the prophet Jeremiah. See table at **Bible**

Bar·uch /bə ro͝ok/, **Bernard** (1870–1965) U.S. financier and statesman. An adviser to U.S. presidents from Wilson through Kennedy, he participated in the Paris Peace Conference (1919). Full name **Bernard Mannes Baruch**

bar·ware /baár wàir/ *n.* glassware and other items used to prepare and serve drinks

bar·y·cen·ter /bárri sèntər/ *n.* the center of the mass of a system, especially a system of celestial bodies [Late 19thC. From Greek *barus* "heavy" + CENTER.] —**bar·y·cen·tric** /bàrri séntrik/ *adj.*

bar·y·on /bárree òn/ *n.* a subatomic particle belonging to a group that undergo strong interactions, have a mass greater than or equal to that of the proton, and consist of three quarks [Mid-20thC. From Greek *barus* "heavy" + -ON.] —**bar·y·on·ic** /bàrree ónnik/ *adj.*

Popperfoto

Mikhail Baryshnikov

Ba·rysh·ni·kov /bə ríshni kàwf/, **Mikhail** (*b.* 1948) Russian-born U.S. dancer and choreographer. He defected from the Soviet Union (1974) and danced for and directed (1980–89) the American Ballet Theatre. Full name **Mikhail Nikolayevich Baryshnikov**

bar·y·sphere /bárri sfeer/ *n.* the Earth's core (*dated*) [Early 20thC. From Greek *barus* "heavy" + SPHERE.]

ba·ry·ta /bə rítə/ *n.* any one of various barium compounds [Early 19thC. From BARYTES with ending *-a* from SODA.] —**ba·ry·tic** /bə ríttik/ *adj.*

ba·ry·tes /bə ríteez, bárrə teez/ *n.* = **barite** [Late 18thC. From Greek *barutēs* "weight."]

bar·y·tone *n.* = **baritone**

Bar·zun /baárzən/, **Jacques** (*b.* 1907) French-born U.S. historian and educator. A distinguished language and literary critic, he worked as a teacher and administrator at Columbia University (1955–75). Full name **Jacques Martin Barzun**

bas·al /báyss'l/ *adj.* **1. AT THE BASE OR BOTTOM** at or forming the bottom of something **2. BASIC** basic or fundamental —**bas·al·ly** *adv.*

bas·al bod·y *n.* a structure found near the base of cells that have projecting threads (**cilia**)

bas·al cell *n.* a cell forming the deepest layer of the skin

bas·al cell car·ci·no·ma *n.* a slow-growing malignant tumor that typically affects the facial skin of older persons. It rarely spreads to other parts, and is generally curable by surgery or radiotherapy.

bas·al gan·gli·on *n.* a mass of gray matter that lies in the white matter near the base of each cerebral hemisphere of the brain. The basal ganglia help to regulate the body's voluntary movements.

bas·al met·a·bol·ic rate *n.* the rate at which an organism consumes oxygen while awake but at rest, measured in kilocalories per square meter of body surface per hour

bas·al me·tab·o·lism *n.* the amount of energy consumed by a resting organism simply in maintaining its basic functions

ba·salt /bə sáwlt, báy sàwlt/ *n.* **1. BLACK SHINY VOLCANIC ROCK** a hard black, often glassy, volcanic rock. It covers more than half the Earth's surface and was produced by the partial melting of the Earth's mantle. **2. BLACK UNGLAZED POTTERY** a hard black unglazed pottery [Early 17thC. Via Latin *basaltes*, a variant of *basanites*, from Greek *basanitēs* "very hard stone, touchstone," from Egyptian *bakhan* "slate."] —**ba·sal·tic** /bə sáwltik/ *adj.*

ba·salt·ware /bə sáwlt wàir, bá sàwlt-, báy-/ *n.* a hard black stoneware pottery made in England and parts of continental Europe in the 18th century

ba·san·ite /bássə nìt/ *n.* volcanic basaltic rock containing olivine and additional alkaline minerals [Mid-18thC. From Latin *basanites* (see BASALT).]

bas·cule /bás kyo͞ol/ *n.* **1. PIVOTING DEVICE** a counterbalanced device that pivots on a central axis so that the unweighted end rises as the weighted end is allowed to fall **2. bas·cule, bas·cule bridge BRIDGE WITH LIFTING ROADWAY** a bridge with a roadway that can be raised to allow tall boats and ships to pass through [Late 17thC. From French, "see- saw," ultimately from *battre* "to batter" (see BATTER) + cul "buttocks."]

base[1] /bayss/ *n.* **1. LOWEST PART** the lowest, bottom, or supporting part or layer of something **2. LOWER PART OF BUILT STRUCTURE** the lower part of a built structure, e.g. , a wall, pillar, or column, regarded as a separate feature **3. MAIN SUPPORTING ELEMENT** the main source of an important component in an economy or sphere of influence ○ *improve our customer base* **4. FUNDAMENTAL PRINCIPLE** the main principle or starting point of a system or theory **5. CENTER FROM WHICH ACTIVITIES START** a center from which activities start or are coordinated **6. MILITARY CENTER** a coordinating or supply center for military operations **7. MAIN INGREDIENT** a main ingredient to which others are added **8. SOLVENT** a medium in which ingredients or constituents may be dissolved or carried **9. ATTACHING PART OF ORGAN** the part of an organ or body part by which it is attached to a more central structure of an organism **10. LOWER PART OF HERALDIC SHIELD** the lower part of a heraldic shield **11.** GRAM **STEM OF WORD** in morphology, any part of a word regarded as a unit to which affixes or other bases may be added to form a derived word. For example, "paint" is the base of "painter" and "repaint." **12.** MATH **REFERENCE NUMBER** the number that is the basis for a system of calculation, represented by the total countable digits in the system. The base 10 system contains the ten digits 0–9. **13.** MATH **LOGARITHM REFERENCE** a number raised to a power denoted by a superscript. In the equation $10^2 = 100$, 10 is the base. Natural logarithms have a base e (= 2.718). **14.** GEOM **LOWER SIDE OF FIGURE** the lower side or face of a geometric figure **15.** MEASURE = **baseline** *n.* 1 **16. LOWEST STOCK PRICE** the lowest recorded price level of a tradable commodity or security **17.** CHEM **CHEMICAL COMPOUND** a chemical compound having a pH value between 8 and 14 that reacts with acids to form salts **18.** CHEM **CHEMICAL COMPOUND FORMING COVALENT BOND** a chemical compound that can accept a proton or donate a pair of electrons to form a covalent bond with an acid **19.** PHOTOGRAPHY **FILM FOUNDATION** an inert medium supporting the photographic emulsion of films **20.** ELEC ENG **MIDDLE REGION OF TRANSISTOR** the middle region of a transistor between the emitter and the collector **21.** BASEBALL **FIELD MARKER** any one of the four corners of the diamond-shaped infield that a batter must touch in order to score a run ■ *vt.* (**based, bas·ing, bas·es**) **1. MAKE A BASE** to create or provide a base for something **2. ASSIGN SOMEBODY TO BASE** to station, post, or assign somebody to a base **3. USE SOMETHING AS A BASIS** to use something as a base or basis for something else [14thC. Directly or via Old French from Latin *basis*, from Greek *basis* (see BASIS).] —**base·ness** *n.* ◇ **have all bases covered** to have made preparations to insure that you can deal with whatever happens ◇ **off base** wrong or inexact ○ *Your calculations are all off base* ◇ **touch base (with somebody)** to communicate briefly with somebody, e.g., to carry a project forward or exchange current information

WORD KEY: SYNONYMS

See Synonyms at *mean*.

base[2] /bayss/ *adj.* **1. LACKING MORALS** lacking proper social values or moral principles **2. OF POOR QUALITY** inferior in value or quality **3. COUNTERFEIT** containing a higher proportion of base metals than usual **4. ILLEGITIMATE** of humble or illegitimate birth (*archaic*) **5.** HIST **RELATING TO PEASANT** relating to a peasant (**villein**) renting land from a feudal lord (*archaic*) [14thC. Via French *bas* from medieval Latin *bassus* "short, low," which is found in classical Latin only as part of somebody's name.] —**base·ly** *adv.* —**base·ness** *n.*

Popperfoto

Baseball: A batter swings at the ball

base·ball /báyss bàwl/ *n.* **1. BAT AND BALL GAME** a game played with a bat and ball by two teams of nine players, on a field that has four bases arranged in a diamond pattern to mark the course a batter must take to score a run. Each team fields and bats alternately, and the goal is to score the most runs. **2.** BALL USED IN BASEBALL a hard leather-covered ball, about 9 in./23 cm in circumference, used in the game of baseball

base·ball cap *n.* a close-fitting cap with a visor, originally worn by baseball players

base·board /báyss bàwrd/ *n.* **1.** BOARD SERVING AS BASE a board that serves as the base of something **2.** BOARD COVERING WALL AND FLOOR JOINT a narrow board, attached to the base of an interior wall, that covers the joint between the wall and the floor

base·born /báyss bàwrn/ *adj.* (*archaic*) **1.** OF HUMBLE BIRTH born of poor or disgraced parents **2.** ILLEGITIMATE born of unmarried parents **3.** IGNOBLE dishonorable or unworthy

base burn·er *n.* a stove into which fuel is fed automatically from a hopper as needed

Bas·e·dow's dis·ease /bázzədōz-/ *n.* = **Graves' disease** [Late 19thC. Named for Karl Adolph von *Basedow* (1799–1854), German physician.]

Base Ex·change a service mark for stores on U.S. Air Force and U.S. Navy bases that sell merchandise to military personnel, their dependents, and authorized civilians

base hit *n.* BASEBALL a hit that enables the batter to reach a base safely without causing an error, a force play, or a fielder's choice

base house (*plural* **base hous·es**) *n.* a place where people go to smoke (**freebase**) illegal drugs such as cocaine or crack (*slang*)

Ba·sel /báas'l/, **Bas·le** city in northwestern Switzerland, situated on the highest navigation point of the Rhine. It is the capital of the half canton of Basel-Stadt. Population: 179,639 (1994).

base·less /báyssləss/ *adj.* **1.** UNTRUE without grounds or a factual basis **2.** LACKING SUPPORTING PART lacking a base or foundation —**base·less·ly** *adv.* — **base·less·ness** *n.*

base lev·el *n.* the lowest level to which moving water can erode a land surface, e.g., the bed of a stream, lake, or sea

base·line /báyss lìn/ *n.* **1.** MEASURE MEASURING LINE a line used as a basis for measurement, calculation, or location, e.g., in surveying or navigation **2.** STANDARD OF VALUE a standard of value to which other similar things are compared **3.** REFERENCE DATA the data used as a reference with which to compare future observations or results **4.** SPORTS BOUNDARY LINE AT END OF COURT a boundary line at each end of a court that marks the limit of play in tennis, badminton, or basketball **5.** BASEBALL LINE BETWEEN BASES a line running from home plate to first base and from home plate to third base, and extending into the outfield as foul lines **6.** BASEBALL RUNNER'S REFERENCE LINE in baseball, the area within which a base runner must stay when running between bases

base·lin·er /báyss lìnər/ *n.* a tennis player who prefers to play on or near the baseline, and who only occasionally moves to the net

base load *n.* the average demand placed on an electrical power supply system

base·man /báyssmən/ (*plural* **-men** /-mən/) *n.* BASEBALL any of the three fielders positioned near first, second, and third base

base·ment /báysmənt/ *n.* **1.** UNDERGROUND STORY OF BUILDING a story of a building that is wholly or partly below ground level **2.** ARCHIT LOWEST PART OF WALL OR BUILDING the foundation, substructure, or lowest part of a wall or building **3.** GEOL PART OF EARTH'S CRUST the highly folded igneous or metamorphic layer of rocks that lies beneath more recent, softer sedimentary rocks **4.** *New England* TOILET OR WASHROOM a toilet or washroom, especially in a school [Mid-18thC. Origin uncertain: possibly via obsolete Dutch *basement* from Italian *basamento* "base of a column," from *basare* "to base."]

base met·al *n.* a common inexpensive metal, e.g., copper, iron, lead, tin, or zinc, as distinguished from the precious metals of gold, silver, and platinum

ba·sen·ji /bə sénjee/ *n.* a dog belonging to a small curly-tailed African breed that rarely barks and has a short smooth coat varying from black to chestnut [Mid-20thC. From Bantu.]

base on balls *n.* BASEBALL an advance to first base awarded to a batter who receives four pitches outside the strike zone at which the batter does not swing

base pair *n.* a chemical unit that forms the bridge linking the complementary strands of DNA or RNA. It consists of a purine linked to a pyrimidine by hydrogen bonds.

base pair·ing *n.* the hydrogen bonding between complementary purine and pyrimidine bases, specifically adenine with thymine, and guanine with cytosine, that forms the double-stranded structure of DNA, RNA, and DNA/RNA hybrid molecules

base path *n.* BASEBALL = **baseline** *n.* **6**

base pay *n.* the pay for a job or position excluding any additional payments or allowances

base rate *n.* **1.** PAY PER UNIT the rate of pay set for a unit of work before anything extra is added **2.** *U.K.* INTEREST RATE USED BY CENTRAL BANKS the rate of interest used by U.K. clearing banks as a basis for calculating their lending rates

base run·ner *n.* BASEBALL a player on the team at bat who is on a base or is trying to get to one safely

ba·ses plural of **basis**

base u·nit *n.* a fundamental unit within a system of measurement from which other units in the system are derived

bash /bash/ *v.* (**bashed, bash·ing, bash·es**) (*informal*) **1.** *vt.* STRIKE WITH HEAVY BLOW to strike something or somebody with a heavy blow **2.** *vt.* SMASH to smash or strike something violently or damagingly **3.** *vt.* MAKE DENT to make a dent in something **4.** *vi.* COLLIDE WITH to crash into or collide with something **5.** *vt.* CRITICIZE to criticize harshly ■ *n.* **1.** CELEBRATION a party or celebration **2.** BLOW a strong blow (*informal*) **3.** DENT a dent (*informal*) [Mid-17thC. Probably an imitation of the sound of hitting; perhaps a blend of BANG[1] and either SMASH or DASH.]

bash up *vt.* to attack and injure somebody (*informal*)

bash·ful /báshfəl/ *adj.* shy, self-conscious, or modest [15thC. Formed from a shortened form of ABASH.] —**bash·ful·ly** *adv.* —**bash·ful·ness** *n.*

Bash·kor·to·stan /baash kàwrtə stán/ autonomous republic in central Russia, west of the Urals, bordering the republic of Tatarstan to the northwest and the republic of Udmurtia to the north. Capital: Ufa. Population: 4,055,300 (1994). Area: 55,444 sq. mi./143,600 sq. km. Former name **Bashkiria** (until 1992)

bash·o /baá shō, baa shố/ (*plural* **-os**) *n.* a sumo wrestling tournament [Late 20thC. From Japanese.]

Ba·sho /baá shō/, **Ba·shō** (1644–94) Japanese poet. He is closely identified with the haiku form. His work was strongly influenced by Zen Buddhism. Pseudonym of **Matsuo Munefusa**

basi- *prefix.* = **baso-**

ba·sic /báyssik/ *adj.* **1.** MOST IMPORTANT most important or essential ○ *a few basic guidelines* **2.** ELEMENTARY serving as a starting point or minimum **3.** WITHOUT EXTRA without anything extra ○ *a basic salary* **4.** PLAIN plain and utilitarian rather than luxurious or fancy (*informal*) **5.** CHEM RELATING TO CHEMICAL BASE containing, relating to, or being a chemical base **6.** CHEM ALKALINE having an alkaline reaction **7.** CHEM CONTAINING HYDROXIDE OR OXIDE GROUPS used to describe a salt that contains hydroxide or oxide groups in addition to other anions, e.g., the carbonate ion **8.** GEOL LOW IN SILICA used to describe rock that contains 45–53 percent total silica by weight, e.g., basalt **9.** METALL USING A BASE IN STEELMAKING used to describe a steelmaking process in which the furnace is lined with a base that combines with acidic impurities in the ore to produce basic slag ■ *n.* = **basic training** ■ **ba·sics** *npl.* MOST IMPORTANT THINGS the most important or fundamental elements of something —**ba·sic·i·ty** /bay síssətee/ *n.*

BA·SIC /báyssik/, **Ba·sic** *n.* a high-level computer programming language that uses a combination of common English terms and algebra [Acronym for Beginners All-purpose Symbolic Instruction Code]

ba·si·cal·ly /báysikəlee/ *adv.* **1.** ESSENTIALLY used to emphasize the most important aspect of something, or to give a simplified account of something more complicated **2.** IN GENERAL generally or in most respects **3.** SIMPLY in a simple way, using only essentials

WORD KEY: USAGE

Basically as a sentence adverb This use, in which ***basically*** is reduced to adding emphasis, is common in informal conversation but should be avoided otherwise. So too should the meaning "to speak generally rather than in detail," as in *It is basically the case that fats can cause heart disease.*

ba·sic ed·u·ca·tion *n.* the formal education deemed necessary for somebody to function properly in society

ba·sic rate *n.* COMM the standard cost or rate of pay excluding any discounts or additions

ba·sic slag *n.* the slag from steelmaking using a basic process. It is rich in phosphates and is used as a fertilizer.

ba·sic train·ing *n.* the initial training of a military recruit

ba·sid·i·o·my·cete /bə síddi ō mī seet, bə síddi ō mī séet/ *n.* a fungus that produces spores in a specialized structure (**basidium**). Mushrooms, puffballs, rusts, shelf fungi, and smuts are basidiomycetes. Class: Basidiomycetes. [Late 19thC. From modern Latin *Basidiomycetes*, class name, from *basidium* "basidium" (see BASIDIUM) + Greek *mukētes* "fungi."] —**ba·sid·i·o·my·ce·tous** /bə sìddi ō mī séetəss/ *adj.*

ba·sid·i·um /bə síddee əm/ (*plural* **-a** /-ə/) *n.* a cell or organ found in certain fungi from which external sexual spores are produced [Mid-19thC. From modern Latin, literally "small base," from Greek *basis* "step, base."] —**ba·sid·i·al** *adj.*

Ba·sie /báyzee/, **Count** (1904–84) U.S. composer and bandleader. He was one of the most enduring popular American musicians as the leader of his own big-band swing ensembles from 1935 until his death, and composed numbers including "One O'Clock Jump." Real name **William Basie**

ba·si·fy /báyssi fī/ (**-fied, -fy·ing, -fies**) *vt.* CHEM **1.** MAKE INTO BASE to change a chemical into a base **2.** MAKE ALKALINE to make something alkaline —**ba·si·fi·ca·tion** /bàyssifi káysh'n/ *n.*

bas·il /báyzz'l, bá-/ *n.* a herb with aromatic leaves used for seasoning. Sweet basil and purple basil are two common types. Latin name: *Ocimum basilicum.* [15thC. Via Old French *basile* from Latin *basilicum*, from Greek *basilikon (phuton)* "royal (herb)," from its usefulness in cooking and medicine.]

Bas·il /bázz'l, báy-/, **St.** (329?–379 A.D.) Greek prelate and scholar. He studied at Byzantium and Athens, became Bishop of Caesarea (370), and defended Christian philosophy againt heresies such as Arianism. Known as **Basil the Great**

bas·i·lar /bássələr/ *adj.* relating to or situated at the base of something, e.g.,the skull [Mid-16thC. From modern Latin *basilaris*, from Latin *basis* (see BASIS).]

ba·sil·i·ca /bə síllikə, -zíllikə/ *n.* **1.** PRIVILEGED ROMAN CATHOLIC CHURCH a Roman Catholic church or cathedral given ceremonial privileges by the Pope **2.** ARCHIT ANCIENT ROMAN BUILDING a type of ancient Roman building that had a central nave with an aisle on each side formed by two rows of columns, and typically a terminal semicircular apse. It was used as a court of justice, an assembly hall, or an exchange. **3.** LARGE CHRISTIAN CHURCH a Christian church building formed out of a Roman basilica or built to a similar design [Mid-16thC. Via Latin, "royal palace" from Greek *basilikē*, from *basilikos* "royal," from *basileus* "king" (source of English *basil* and *basilisk*).] —**ba·sil·i·can** *adj.*

Basilisk

bas·i·lisk /bássəlisk, bázz-/ *n.* **1.** MYTHOL LEGENDARY REPTILE a legendary reptile whose look or breath was supposed to be fatal. It was said to have been hatched by a serpent from a rooster's egg. **2.** ZOOL LIZARD RELATED TO IGUANA a tropical American lizard, related to the iguana, that is able to run upright on its long hind legs. The males have an inflatable crest at the back of the head. Genus: *Basiliscus.* [14thC. Via Latin from Greek *basilikos*, literally "kinglet," also "kind of serpent," formed from *basileus* "king" (source of English *basil* and *basilica*).]

ba·sin /báyss'n/ *n.* **1. OPEN CONTAINER FOR WASHING** an open metal, ceramic, or plastic container with sloping sides, typically used for holding water or washing **2. BASIN CONTENTS** the contents of or amount contained in a basin **3.** GEOG **LAND DRAINING INTO RIVER OR LAKE** a broad area of land drained by a single river and its tributaries, or draining into a lake **4. DOCK NEAR SEA** a dock built in a harbor or river that opens to the sea **5. DEPRESSION IN LAND FILLED WITH WATER** any depression in the Earth's surface that contains water **6.** GEOL **BOWL-SHAPED DEPRESSION** a bowl-shaped depression on land or on the ocean floor into which sediments may be deposited **7.** GEOL **CIRCULAR FORMATION OF SLOPING ROCK STRATA** a large circular outcrop of rock in which strata dip inward toward the center [13thC. Via Old French from medieval Latin *ba(s)cinus*, from *bacca* "water container," a word probably borrowed from Gaulish.]

bas·i·net /bàssə nét, -nèt/ *n.* a lightweight steel helmet, sometimes with a visor, worn in medieval times [14thC. From Old French *bacinet*, literally "little basin," from its shape.]

bas·in·ful /báyss'n fòol/ *n.* the quantity that a basin holds

ba·sip·e·tal /bay síppit'l/ *adj.* developing from the top of a stem toward the base so that the oldest leaves or flowers are at the top —**ba·sip·e·tal·ly** *adv.*

ba·sis /báyssiss/ (*plural* **-ses** /-seez/) *n.* **1. FOUNDATION** something that acts as a support or foundation, especially of an idea or argument **2. STARTING POINT** the point from which something, e.g., a discussion, starts or is developed **3. WAY OF PROCEEDING** the basic method or system according to which something is done or organized ○ *work on a part-time basis* **4. MAIN COMPONENT** the main component or ingredient of something **5.** MATH **SET OF VECTORS** in a vector space, the minimal set of vectors necessary to define all other vectors in the space [Late 16thC. Via Latin *basis* (source of English *base*) from Greek *basis* "step, base,"from *bainen* "to go."]

WORD KEY: USAGE

Basis ***Basis*** **does a number of jobs that other words can do better or that need not be done at all. Expressions such as** *on a continuing basis, on a daily basis,* **and** *on a regular basis,* **are only wordier ways of saying** *continually,daily,* **and** *regularly.* **By the same token,** *providing expert resources on a global basis* **means providing them anywhere; and** *we can help develop your basis for facilities design* **means, essentially,** *we can help you plan.* **Careful writers should avoid the unnecessary use of** ***basis.***

ba·sis point *n.* FIN one hundredth of one percent, used to express interest rates and bond yields

bask /bask/ (**basked, bask·ing, basks**) *vi.* **1. EXPOSE YOURSELF TO WARMTH** to lie in or expose yourself to enjoyable warmth, especially from the sun **2. GET PLEASURE FROM SOMETHING** to derive great satisfaction or pleasure from something [14thC. Origin uncertain: probably from Old Norse *bathask* "to bathe yourself," ultimately from the same prehistoric Germanic source as English *bath.*]

Bas·ker·ville /báskər vìl/ *n.* a typeface characterised by serifs [Early 19thC. Named for John *Baskerville* (1706–79), the British typefounder and printer who designed it.]

bas·ket /báskət/ *n.* **1. WOVEN CONTAINER** a container made of woven strips of material such as cane, wire, wood, or plastic, often with a handle or handles **2. BASKET CONTENTS** the contents of, or amount contained in a basket **3. SOMETHING LIKE A BASKET** something that looks like or is used like a basket, e.g. , the open gondola attached to a hot-air balloon **4.** BASKETBALL **GOAL** a mounted horizontal metal hoop with a hanging open net, through which a basketball player must throw the ball in order to score **5.** BASKETBALL **GOAL SCORED** a goal scored in basketball by throwing the ball through the basket. It is worth 1, 2, or 3 points depending on circumstances. **6. GROUP OF RELATED ITEMS** a group or collection of similar or related things or ideas [14thC. Origin unknown, found earlier in Old French.]

bas·ket·ball /báskət bàwl/ *n.* **1. BALL GAME PLAYED ON COURT** a game played by two teams of five players, who score points by throwing a ball through a basket mounted at the opponent's end of a rectangular

Basketball: Two players attempt to block a pass

court **2. BALL USED IN BASKETBALL** a ball of the type used in the game of basketball

bas·ket case *n.* **1. OFFENSIVE TERM** an offensive term for somebody who is suffering from severe nervous strain (*offensive*) **2. SOMEBODY INCAPACITATED** somebody who is completely incapacitated or ineffective (*informal*)

bas·ket chair *n.* a deep chair made of wicker or cane

bas·ket·ful /báskət fòol/ *n.* the quantity that a basket holds

bas·ket hilt *n.* a sword hilt with a guard made of interwoven strips —**bas·ket-hilt·ed** *adj.*

Bas·ket Mak·er *n.* a member of an ancient Native American culture of southwestern North America, preceding the Pueblo periods. The culture is noted for skill in basketmaking and for farming with little water.

bas·ket of cur·ren·cies *n.* a group of currencies of which the average value is used as a basis for comparison with another currency

bas·ket-of-gold *n.* a European perennial plant with oval hairy gray-green leaves and bright yellow flowers. Latin name: *Aurinia saxatilis.*

bas·ket·ry /báskətree/ *n.* **1.** CRAFT **BASKETMAKING** the art or craft of making baskets **2. BASKETS** baskets collectively

bas·ket star *n.* a marine organism that has thin branching interlaced arms and is related to the starfish. Genus: *Gorgonocephalus.*

bas·ket weave *n.* a textile weave that resembles the checkered pattern of a woven basket

bas·ket·work /báskət wùrk/ *n.* CRAFT = **basketry** *n.* 1

bask·ing shark *n.* a large plankton-eating shark measuring up to 40 ft./12 m that often floats on the surface of the sea. Latin name: *Cetorhinus maximus.*

bas·ma·ti /ba smaátee, baa-/ *n.* a long-grained aromatic brown or white rice originally grown in northern India and Pakistan [Mid-19thC. From Hindi *bāsmatī* "fragrant."]

bas mitz·vah /baas mítsvə/, **Bas Miz·vah** *n.* = **bat mitzvah**

baso- *prefix.* bottom, base ○ *basipetal* ■ chemical base ○ *basophil* [From Latin *basis* (see BASE)]

ba·so·phil /báysə fìl, -zə-/, **ba·so·phile** *n.* a white blood cell with granules that are readily stained by basic dyes, occurring in some blood diseases

ba·so·phil·i·a /bàyssə fíllee ə/, **ba·si·phil·i·a** *n.* **1.** BIOL **AFFINITY FOR BASIC DYES** the property of microorganisms and white blood cells of being stained with basic dyes **2.** MED **INCREASE IN STAINED CELLS** an abnormal increase in the blood of the type of cells that stain with basic dyes, occurring in a variety of blood diseases

ba·so·phil·ic /bàyssə fíllik/, **ba·soph·i·lous** /bə sóffələss/ *adj.* used to describe cells or cell components that are readily stained by basic dyes

Ba·sot·ho /bə sṓ tō, bə sōō tōō/ *npl.* an African Sotho people who live in Lesotho [Mid-19thC. From Sesotho.]

basque /bask/ *n.* **1. LONG CORSET** a woman's tight-fitting corset that covers the area from the breasts to the top of the thighs **2. JACKET EXTENSION** a part of the bodice of a woman's jacket that extends below the waist [Mid-19thC. Origin uncertain: perhaps from some perceived similarity to the Basque national costume.]

Basque /bask/ *n.* **1.** PEOPLES **MEMBER OF EUROPEAN PEOPLE** a member of a people of unknown origin living in the western Pyrenees, in northeastern Spain and southwestern France **2.** LANG **LANGUAGE OF BASQUES** the language spoken by the Basque people. It has no known relationship with any other languages and is spoken by about 700,000 people. [Early 19thC. Via French from Latin *Vasco*, the Romans' name for these people, which also developed into *Gascon.*] —**Basque** *adj.*

Basque Coun·try autonomous region of northern Spain, consisting of the provinces of Álava, Guipúzcoa, and Vizcaya. The regional capital is Vitoria. Population: 2,130,783 (1995). Area: 2,803 sq. mi./7,261 sq. km. Spanish **Pais Vasco.** Basque **Euskadi**

Bas·ra /baássrə/ city and port in southeastern Iraq, at the northern end of the Shatt al Arab waterway. Population: 872,176 (1987).

bas-re·lief /baa-/ *n.* **1. FLAT SCULPTURE** a type of sculpture in which the design projects slightly from a flat background, but without any part being totally detached from the background. ◊ **high relief 2. PIECE OF BAS-RELIEF** an example or piece of bas-relief sculpture [Early 17thC. From the earlier BASSO RILIEVO, altered to match the French form of the word.]

bass[1] /bayss/ *n.* **1.** MUSIC **LOWEST SINGING VOICE** a voice of the lowest range, or somebody with that voice **2.** MUSIC **LOWEST PITCHES** the lower half of the total range of pitches produced by a voice or an instrument **3.** MUSIC **LOWEST MUSICAL PART** the lowest part in instrumental or vocal part music **4.** MUSIC **LOWEST INSTRUMENT IN FAMILY** the instrument that has the lowest range in a family of musical instruments **5.** MUSIC **LOW FREQUENCY IN AUDIO REPRODUCTION** the low-frequency part of the sound output from an electric amplifier **6. BASS CONTROL** a knob on a record player, CD player, or cassette player that controls the low-frequency part of its sound output ■ *adj.* **1. DEEP IN TONE** deep or grave in tone **2. LOW IN PITCH** low in pitch **3. RELATING TO BASS** relating to a bass [15thC. Via French *bas* from medieval Latin *bassus*, influenced by Italian *basso* "basso" (see BASSO).]

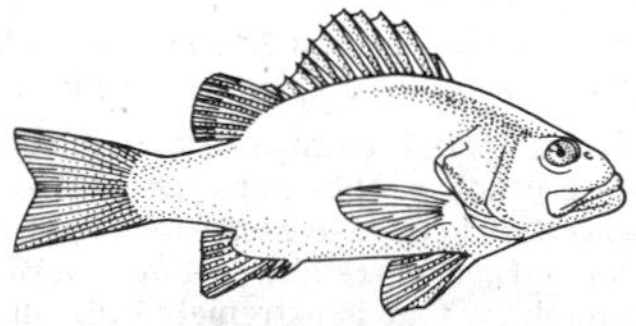

Bass

bass[2] /bass/ (*plural* **bass** *or* **bass·es**) *n.* a spiny-finned fish found in rivers, lakes, and seas that is caught for food. Families: Centrarchidae and Percichthyidae and Serranidae. [15thC. Alteration of Old English *bærs, bears*, of prehistoric Germanic origin.]

bass[3] /bass/ *n.* **1.** = **bast fiber 2.** INDUST = **basswood** *n.* 1 [Late 17thC. Alteration of BAST.]

Bass /bass/, **Sam** (1851–78) U.S. outlaw. He robbed trains and stagecoaches with organized gangs, and was shot dead in Texas (1878).

bass-bar·i·tone *n.* a singing voice between baritone and bass, or somebody with that voice

bass clef *n.* **1. MUSICAL SYMBOL** a symbol on a musical staff indicating that a note on the fourth line from the bottom represents the F a fifth below middle C **2. MUSICAL STAFF FOR BASS** the musical staff on which the bass part of a composition is written. It is identified by a bass clef symbol.

bass drum *n.* a large drum that has a cylindrical body, two drumheads, and a low indefinite pitch

Bas·sein /bə sáyn/ city in southern Myanmar (Burma), about 85 mi./137 km west of the capital, Yangon. Population: 144,092 (1983).

bas·set /bássət/ *n.* = **basset hound**

Basse·terre /bass táir, baass-/ capital of St. Kitts and Nevis, in the Leeward Islands. It is situated on the southwestern coast of St. Kitts island. Population: 12,600 (1994).

bas·set horn /bássət-/ *n.* an alto clarinet in F, used in classical music [Mid-19thC. From German, itself a translation of French *cor de basset*, from Italian *corno di* *bassetto,* literally "cello-horn," from its sharing the cello's range.]

bas·set hound *n.* a dog of a breed with short legs, long ears, and a short-haired, white, black, and tan coat, originally bred for hunting [Early 17thC. From French, formed from *bas* "low," from its short legs.]

bass gui·tar *n.* a four-string guitar, usually electric, that has the same pitch and tuning as a double bass

bas·si·net /bàssə nét, -nèt/ *n.* a baby's bed in the shape of a basket, commonly made of wood or wicker [Mid-19thC. From French, literally "little basin," from *bassin* (see BASIN).]

bass·ist /báyssist/ *n.* a player of a bass guitar or a double bass

bas·so /bássō, ba͡assō/ (*plural* **-sos** *or* **-si** /ba͡asee/) *n.* a bass singer, especially of opera [Early 18thC. Via Italian from medieval Latin *bassus* (see BASE[2]).]

bas·so con·tin·u·o /bàssō kən tínnyoo ō, ba͡assō-/ *n.* = **continuo**

bas·soon /bə so͡on, ba-/ *n.* a low-pitched double-reed instrument of the oboe family. Its wooden body is a long U-shaped tube, attached to the mouthpiece by means of a thin metal pipe. [Early 18thC. Via French from Italian *bassone,* literally "large bass," from *basso* "basso" (see BASSO).]

bas·so pro·fun·do /-prə fúndō, -prə fo͡on-/ (*plural* **bas·so pro·fun·dos**) *n.* a bass singer with an exceptionally low range [Mid-19thC. From Italian, literally "deep bass."]

bas·so-re·lie·vo (*plural* **bas·so-re·lie·vos**), **bas·so-ri·lie·vo** (*plural* **bas·so-ri·lie·vos**) *n.* = **bas-relief** [Mid-17thC. From Italian *basso-rilievo,* literally "low relief."]

bass vi·ol *n.* **1.** = **viola da gamba 2.** = **double bass**

bass·wood /báss wo͝od/ *n.* **1.** TREES **N AMERICAN LINDEN TREE** a North American linden tree, commonly used as a shade tree. Latin name: *Tilia americana.* **2.** INDUST **WOOD OF BASSWOOD TREE** the soft light-colored wood of the basswood tree, used for making boxes and crates and for carving [From BASS[3]]

bast /bast/ *n.* **1.** BOT = **phloem 2.** *U.K.* INDUST = **bast fiber 3.** = **raffia** [Old English *bæst,* of unknown origin]

bas·tard /bástərd/ *n.* **1. OFFENSIVE TERM** an offensive term for a disagreeable or obnoxious person (*slang insult*) **2. OFFENSIVE TERM** an offensive term for somebody born to unmarried parents (*archaic or offensive*) **3. DIFFICULT THING** something that is extremely difficult, trying, or unpleasant (*slang*) **4. ABNORMAL THING** something that is abnormal, inferior, or of questionable or mixed origin ■ *adj.* **1. WITH UNMARRIED PARENTS** born to unmarried parents (*archaic or offensive*) **2. NOT GENUINE** not the real thing **3. OF INFERIOR OR MIXED ORIGIN** of an inferior, ill-conceived, or mixed origin **4.** ZOOL **SIMILAR** used to describe plants and animals that are similar but not identical to, and usually slightly inferior to, a particular kind or species **5. ABNORMAL** abnormal or irregular in shape, size, or appearance [14thC. Via Old French *bastart* from medieval Latin *bastardus,* probably from *bastum* "pack saddle," the idea probably being of a child produced from a relationship with a traveler.] — **bas·tard·ly** *adj.*

bas·tard·ize /bástər dìz/ (**-ized, -iz·ing, -iz·es**) *vt.* **1. DEBASE** to lower the value or quality of something by combining it with something else **2. DECLARE SOMEBODY ILLEGITIMATE** to prove or declare somebody to be illegitimate (*archaic*) —**bas·tard·i·za·tion** /bàstərdi záysh'n/ *n.*

bas·tard ti·tle *n.* PUBL = **half title**

bas·tard wing *n.* the part of a bird's wing that corresponds to a thumb and contains a few short feathers

bas·tard·y /bástərdee/ *n.* the state of being a child with unmarried parents (*archaic*)

baste[1] /bayst/ (**bast·ed, bast·ing, bastes**) *vt.* COOK to moisten meat or fish at intervals during cooking with a liquid such as melted fat or cooking juices [14thC. Via Old French *bastir* from, ultimately, a prehistoric Germanic word meaning "to join together with bast."]

baste[2] /bayst/ (**bast·ed, bast·ing, bastes**) *vt.* **1.** SEW **SEW LOOSELY** to sew fabric with long loose stitches in order to hold pieces of material together temporarily **2. SEW DIAGONALLY** to sew fabric with rows of long diagonal stitches [Mid-16thC. Origin uncertain: perhaps from BASTE[3].]

baste[3] /bayst/ (**bast·ed, bast·ing, bastes**) *vt.* **1. BEAT** to beat somebody severely **2. SCOLD** to scold somebody vigorously [15thC. Origin unknown.]

bast·er /báystər/ *n.* a cooking utensil consisting of a long tube with a rubber bulb attached at one end, with which you draw up cooking juices from the pot and release them over the food

bast fi·ber *n.* a strong woody fibrous material obtained chiefly from the phloem of plants such as flax, hemp, and jute, and used for making ropes, mats, and textiles

bas·tille /ba stee͡l/ *n.* a fortress or fortified tower [14thC. From French, an alteration of *bastide,* ultimately from Provençal *bastir* "to build."]

Bas·tille Day *n.* a French national holiday observed on July 14, commemorating the storming of the Bastille in 1789 at the beginning of the French Revolution

bas·ti·na·do /bàsti náydō, -na͡a-/ *n.* (*plural* **-does**) **1. PUNISHMENT BY BEATING FEET** a punishment or torture in which the soles of the victim's feet are beaten with a stick **2. THRASHING** a beating or a blow with a club **3. CLUB** a stick or club ■ *vt.* (**-doed, -do·ing, -does**) **BEAT WITH STICK** to beat somebody with a stick, especially on the soles of the feet [Late 16thC. From Spanish *bastonada,* from *bastón* "cudgel."]

bast·ing /báysting/ *n.* **1.** SEW **LOOSE STITCHES** loose or temporary stitches **2. MOISTENING DURING COOKING** the process of moistening meat or fish during cooking

bas·tion /báschən, bástee ən/ *n.* **1. STRONG SUPPORTER** somebody or something regarded as providing strong defense or support, especially for a belief or cause, or a place where there are such people ○ *The northeastern part of the state is a liberal bastion.* **2. FORTIFICATION** a fortified place **3. PROJECTING PART** a projecting part of a wall, rampart, or other fortification [Mid-16thC. Via French from Italian *bastione,* from *bastire* "to build."]

bast·naes·ite /bástnə sīt/, **bast·na·site** *n.* a rare yellow to reddish brown mineral, a fluorocarbonate of lanthanum and cerium, that is a source of rare-earth elements [Late 19thC. Named for *Bastnäs* in Sweden, where it was found.]

bat[1] /bat/ *n.* **1.** SPORTS **CLUB USED IN SPORTS** a club used to strike the ball in sports such as baseball and cricket, usually wooden but sometimes made of metal or plastic **2. HEAVY STICK OR CLUB** a heavy stick or wooden club **3.** BASEBALL **BATTER** a batter in baseball **4. BLOW FROM STICK** a blow from a stout stick or club **5.** *U.K.* AIR = **paddle** ■ *v.* (**bat·ted, bat·ting, bats**) **1.** *vi.* BASEBALL **HAVE TURN AT BATTING** to come to bat in sports such as baseball and cricket **2.** *vt.* BASEBALL **HOLD STATED BATTING AVERAGE** in baseball, to have a particular batting average **3.** *vt.* BASEBALL **ADVANCE A RUNNER** in baseball, to advance a runner to the next base by making a base hit **4.** *vt.* **STRIKE WITH BAT** to strike somebody or something with a bat [Old English *batt,* of uncertain origin, possibly influenced by Old French *batte*] ◇ **be at bat** to be the person on whom success or failure depends (*informal*) ◇ **go to bat for somebody** to support or assist somebody (*informal*) ◇ **right off the bat** immediately (*informal*)

bat around *v.* **1.** *vt.* **DISCUSS** to discuss or consider something at length (*informal*) **2. HAVE ALL BATTERS UP** in baseball, to have all nine batters up, especially in one inning

bat out *vt.* to produce or compose something, especially in a casual or rushed manner (*informal*) ○ *bat out three news items in an hour*

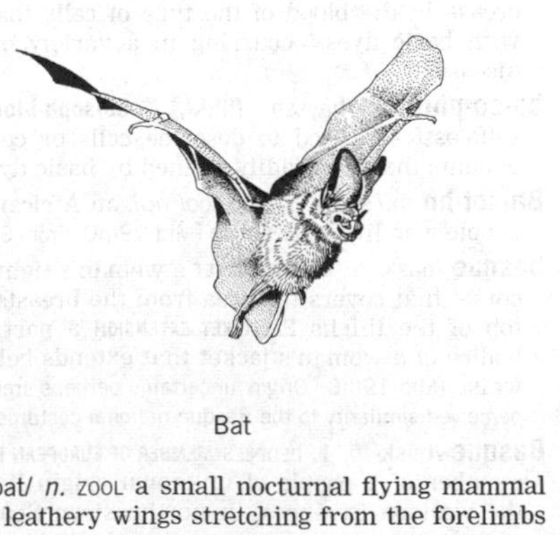

Bat

bat[2] /bat/ *n.* ZOOL a small nocturnal flying mammal with leathery wings stretching from the forelimbs to the rear legs and tail. Bats eat fruit or insects, usually hang upside down when resting, and often use echolocation to detect prey and to navigate. Order: *Chiroptera.* [Late 16thC. Alteration of Middle English *backe,* from a Scandinavian word such as Old Swedish *natbakka* "night bat" or Old Norse *le-erblaka* "leather flapper."] ◇ **have bats in the belfry** to be slightly but harmlessly eccentric (*informal*) ◇ **like a bat out of hell** extremely fast (*informal*)

bat[3] /bat/ (**bat·ted, bat·ting, bats**) *vt.* to wink or flutter something, especially the eyes or eyelids [Early 19thC. Variant of BATE[2].]

bat. /bat/ *abbr.* **1.** battalion **2.** COMPUT batch

Ba·taan /bə tán, -ta͡an/ peninsula of Luzon Island in the Philippines, the scene of intense Japanese-American World War II combat. Area: 530 sq. mi./1,373 sq. km.

Ba·tak /bə ta͡ak, ba͡a ta͡ak/ *n.* a group of Austronesian languages spoken by about three million people in Sumatra, Indonesia. Toba Batak is the best known of the Batak languages. [Early 19thC. From Batak.] — **Ba·tak** *adj.*

Ba·tan·gas /bə ta͡ang ga͡ass/ city and port on Luzon Island in the Philippines. It is the capital of Batangas Province. Population: 185,000 (1990).

Ba·ta·vi·a /bə táyvee ə/ city in western New York. It is the site of the Tonawanda Indian Reservation. Population: 16,310 (1990). ■ former name for **Jakarta**

bat·boy /bát bòy/ *n.* a boy employed to look after the equipment, especially the bats, of a baseball team

batch[1] /bach/ *n.* **1. QUANTITY REGARDED AS GROUP** a quantity of people or things treated or regarded as a group, especially when subdivided from a larger group **2.** COOK **AMOUNT BAKED** the amount of something baked at one time or produced at one baking **3. AMOUNT FOR ONE OPERATION** the amount of material prepared or needed for, or produced in, one operation **4.** COMPUT **PROGRAMS PROCESSED TOGETHER** a set of programs or jobs submitted for processing on a computer at one time ■ *vt.* (**batched, batch·ing, batch·es**) **PROCESS ITEMS AS BATCH** to process or assemble items as a batch or in batches [15thC. From assumed Old English *bæcce* "something baked," from *bacan* "to bake" (see BAKE).]

batch[2] /bách/ *vi.* = **bach**

bat chay·il /baat kha͡ayil/, **bat hay·ill** *n.* = **bat mitzvah** *n.* **2** [Late 20thC. From Hebrew, literally "daughter of valor."]

batch file *n.* a computer file containing a series of commands to be processed by a computer, as if they were entered from the keyboard consecutively. Most personal computers execute a batch file called AUTOEXEC.BAT at the start of each operating session to prepare the system for use.

batch proc·ess·ing *n.* a mode of computer operation in which programs are executed without the user being able to influence processing while it is in progress

bate[1] /bayt/ (**bat·ed, bat·ing, bates**) *vt.* (*archaic*) **1. HOLD SOMETHING BACK** to hold back or moderate something **2. SUBTRACT** to subtract something, or take something away [14thC. Shortened form of ABATE.]

bate[2] /bayt/ (**bat·ed, bat·ing, bates**), **bait** (**bait·ed, bait·ing, baits**) *vi.* to beat the wings wildly or impatiently in an attempt to fly off something, e.g., a perch or a falconer's fist, when still attached by a leash (*refers to a falcon or other hunting bird*) [13thC. From Old French *batre* (see BATTER[1]).]

bat-eared fox *n.* a yellowish gray fox with large ears, found in eastern and southern Africa. Latin name: *Otocyon megalotis.*

ba·teau /ba tō/ (*plural* **-teaux** /ba tōz, -tō/) *n.* a light flat-bottomed riverboat with sharply tapering stern and bow [Early 18thC. From French, "boat."]

ba·teau bridge *n.* = **pontoon bridge**

Ba·tei Din /ba͡a tay dín/ *n.* plural of **Beth Din**

ba·te·leur /bàtt'lər/, **ba·te·leur ea·gle** *n.* a crested African eagle that has a short tail and long broad wings. It feeds mainly on carrion. Latin name: *Terathopius ecaudatus.* [Mid-19thC. From French, literally "juggler, rogue."]

Bates /bayts/, **Katherine Lee** (1859–1929) U.S. educator and writer. She wrote *America the Beautiful* (1893).

Bates·i·an mim·ic·ry /bàytsee ən-/ *n.* a type of mimicry in which a harmless species is protected from predators by its resemblance to a species that is harmful or unpalatable to them [Late 19thC. Named for H.W. Bates (1825–92), who discovered it.]

bat·fish /bát fish/ (*plural* **-fish** *or* **-fish·es**) *n.* a marine angler fish that has a flattened head and body and waddles on the sea bottom using pectoral and pelvic fins. Family: Ogcocephalidae.

bat·fowl /bát fòwl/ (**-fowled, -fowl·ing, -fowls**) *vi.* to catch roosting birds at night by temporarily blinding them with a light and netting or hitting them

bat·girl /bát gùrl/ *n.* a girl employed to look after the equipment, especially the bats, of a baseball team

bath /bath/ *n.* (*plural* **baths** /baths, bat͟hz/) **1.** IMMERSION OF BODY the act of immersing all or part of the body in a bathtub in order to wash it **2.** WATER IN TUB water used for bathing **3.** = **bathtub 4.** = **bathroom** *n.* 1 **5.** BODY TREATMENT the act of immersing all or part of the body in an enveloping substance, e.g., mud, usually for therapeutic reasons **6.** CHEM LIQUID a liquid, or a liquid and its container, used for a particular purpose such as developing photographs or maintaining something at a constant temperature ■ **baths** *npl.* BATHHOUSE a building with facilities for people to have baths ■ *vi.* **(bathed, bath·ing, baths** /bath/) *U.K.* = **bathe** [Old English *bæþ*, from prehistoric Germanic] ◇ **take a bath** to suffer a severe financial setback (*slang*)

Bath /bath/ city on the Avon River in Somerset, England. It is the site of the only natural hot springs in England and has been a spa since Roman times. Population: 85,202 (1991).

bath chair *n.* an old-fashioned type of wheelchair, often with a hood [From its being first used in BATH, England]

bathe /bayt͟h/ **(bathed, bath·ing, bathes)** *v.* **1.** *vti.* WASH IN BATH to wash yourself or somebody else in a bath **2.** *vt.* CLEANSE WOUND to apply water or another liquid to a wound or part of the body in order to cleanse, heal, or soothe it **3.** *vt.* DIP SOMETHING IN LIQUID to immerse something in liquid **4.** *vt.* COVER SOMETHING to cover or surround something with light, color, or a substance ○ *bathed in a golden glow* **5.** *vt.* FLOW ALONG EDGE OF SOMETHING to flow along the edge of something **6.** *vi.* SWIM OR PADDLE IN OPEN WATER to swim or paddle, especially for pleasure, in an area of open water such as the sea or a river [Old English *bæþ*, from prehistoric Germanic]

bath·er /báyt͟hər/ *n.* somebody who is swimming

ba·thet·ic /bə thétik/ *adj.* **1.** SHOWING BATHOS showing or characterized by bathos **2.** TRITE trite, commonplace, or absurdly sentimental [Late 18thC. Formed from BATHOS, on the model of *pathos, pathetic.*] —**ba·thet·i·cal·ly** *adv.*

bath·house /báth hòws/ (*plural* **-houses** /-hòwzəz/) *n.* **1.** BUILDING EQUIPPED WITH BATHS a building equipped with baths, especially for public use **2.** BUILDING FOR CHANGING a building near a swimming pool, equipped with showers and locker rooms

bath·ing /báyt͟hing/ *n.* the activity of swimming in an area of open water, e.g., the sea or a river (*dated*)

bath·ing cap *n.* a tight-fitting rubber cap that swimmers wear to keep their hair dry (*dated*)

bath·ing suit *n.* a swimsuit

bath·ing trunks *npl.* a pair of swimming trunks (*dated*)

bath·mat /báth màt/ *n.* **1.** MAT BESIDE BATHTUB a mat that is placed beside a bathtub or shower for somebody to step out onto **2.** MAT INSIDE BATHTUB a mat, often made of rubber, that is placed in a bathtub or shower to prevent somebody from slipping

batho- deep, depth ○ *bathometer* [From Greek *bathos* "depth"]

bath·o·chrom·ic /bàthə krṓmik/ *adj.* used to describe a move to a longer wavelength in a compound's absorption spectrum

bath oil *n.* a scented oil used to add fragrance to bathwater

bath·o·lith /báthə lìth/, **bath·o·lite** /-lìt/ *n.* a large mass of igneous rock, composed of granite or gabbro, formed deep in the Earth's crust and intruded in a molten state —**bath·o·lith·ic** /bàthə líthik/ *adj.*

ba·thom·e·ter /bə thómmətər/ *n.* an instrument for measuring the depth of a body of water —**bath·o·met·ric** /bàthə méttrik/ *adj.* —**ba·thom·e·try** /bə thómmətree/ *n.*

bath·o·phi·lous /bə thóffiləss/ *adj.* used to describe organisms that are adapted to living in very deep water

ba·thos /báy thòss, -thàwss/ *n.* **1.** EXCESSIVE PATHOS insincere and excessively sentimental pathos **2.** ABRUPT CHANGE TO ORDINARY STYLE in writing or speech, a sudden descent in style or manner from the elevated or sublime to the commonplace, producing a ludicrous effect **3.** = **anticlimax** [Early 18thC. From Greek, "depth," from *bathus* "deep" (source of English *bathy-*). The English meaning seems to have been created by the English poet Alexander POPE (1688–1744).]

bath·robe /báth rōb/ *n.* a loose-fitting garment with a belt worn before or after bathing, or for lounging

bath·room /báth ròom, -rŏŏm/ *n.* **1.** TOILET a room with a toilet **2.** ROOM CONTAINING BATHTUB a room containing a bathtub or shower and, usually, a sink and a toilet

bath·room scale *n.* a step-on device for people to weigh themselves on at home, usually kept in a bathroom

bath salts *npl.* soluble mineral salts used to perfume and soften bathwater

Bath·she·ba /bath sheébə, báth shəbə/ in the Bible, the wife of Uriah and later of David, by whom she became the mother of Solomon (II Samuel 11–12)

bath tow·el *n.* a large towel used to dry the body after a bath or shower

bath·tub /báth tùb/ *n.* a large container, often oblong in shape and usually made of enameled metal or plastic, in which you sit to wash your body

bath·tub gin *n.* homemade spirits consisting of alcohol mixed with flavoring (*slang*)

bath·tub ring *n.* a ring of grime deposited on the inside of a bathtub at the high-water mark of bathwater

Bath·urst[1] *n.* former name for **Banjul**

Bath·urst[2] /báthərst/ summer resort city in northeastern New Brunswick, Canada. Population: 13,815 (1996).

bath·wa·ter /báth wàwtər/ *n.* the water used for a bath

bathy- deep, depth ○ *bathysphere* [From Greek *bathus* "deep"]

bath·y·al /báthee əl/ *adj.* relating to or living in ocean depths between 650 and 6,550 ft./200 and 2,000 m

bath·y·lim·net·ic /bàthə lim néttik/ *adj.* used to describe organisms that live deep in lakes and marshes [Early 20thC. Coined from BATHY- + Greek *limnon* "pool" + -ETIC.]

ba·thym·e·try /bə thímmətree/ *n.* **1.** MEASUREMENT OF WATER DEPTH the measurement of the depth of large bodies of water, e.g., lakes, oceans, and seas **2.** DEPTH MEASUREMENTS the data obtained by the use of bathymetry —**bath·y·met·ric** /bàthə méttrik/ *adj.* —**bath·y·met·ri·cal·ly** *adv.*

bath·y·pe·lag·ic /bàthəpə lájjik/ *adj.* relating to or living in the depths of the ocean, especially between 2,000 and 12,000 ft./600 and 3,600 m

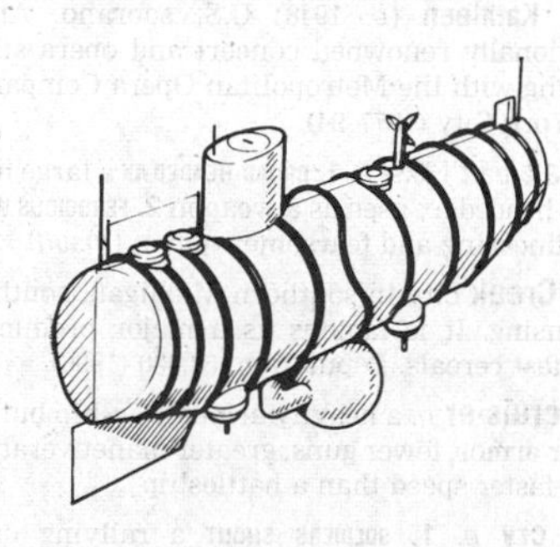

Bathyscaphe

bath·y·scaphe /báthə skàf, -skàyf/, **bath·y·scaph** *n.* a deep-sea research vessel that has a large flotation hull and an observation cabin attached to its underside, and can dive to depths over 6.2 mi./10,000 m [Mid-20thC. Coined from BATHY- + Greek *skaphos* "ship."]

bath·y·sphere /báthə sfeer/ *n.* a strong steel diving sphere that can be lowered by cable to depths of 3,000 ft./900 m

ba·tik /bə teék/, **bat·tik** *n.* **1.** FABRIC PRINTING TECHNIQUE a method of hand-printing a fabric by covering with removable wax the parts that will not be dyed **2.** HAND-DYED FABRIC fabric that has been hand-dyed by the batik method **3.** DESIGN PRODUCED BY BATIK METHOD a design produced by batik [Late 19thC. From Javanese, literally "painted."]

Ba·tis·ta y Zal·dí·var /bə teéstə ee zaal deé vaar/, **Fulgencio** (1901–73) Cuban soldier and political leader. His presidency of Cuba (1940–44, 1952–59) was ended by Fidel Castro's revolution (1959).

ba·tiste /bə teést, ba-/ *n.* a fine soft plain-woven fabric made of cotton or linen, used especially for clothing [Early 19thC. From French, possibly from the name of *Baptiste* of Cambrai, a 13th-century cloth maker.]

Bat·lle y Or·dó·ñez /baatye ee awr t͟háwn yàyss/, **José** (1856–1929) Uruguayan statesman. As president (1903–07, 1911–15), he helped to modernize Uruguay's society, economy, and government.

bat mitz·vah /baat mítsvə/, **bath mitz·vah** /-/, **bas mitz·vah** /baass-/ *n.* **1.** JEWISH RITE OF PASSAGE the ritual that marks the 13th birthday of a Jewish girl, after which she takes full responsibility for her moral and spiritual conduct **2.** JEWISH GIRL REACHING 13 a Jewish girl who has reached the age of about 13, the age of religious responsibility [From Hebrew *bat miṣwāh* "daughter of commandment"]

ba·ton /bə tón, bátt'n/ *n.* **1.** MUSIC CONDUCTING STICK a short thin stick used by a conductor to direct musical performers **2.** PUBLIC ADMIN POLICE STICK a short thick stick used as a weapon, e.g., by police **3.** SPORTS RELAY TEAM STICK a short stick or hollow cylinder passed by each runner in a relay team to the next runner **4.** DRUM MAJOR'S STICK a long stick with a knob at one or both ends, carried and twirled by a drum major or majorette **5.** OFFICIAL STAFF a staff carried by an official, e.g., a field marshal, as a symbol of office **6.** HERALDRY DIAGONAL LINE ON COAT OF ARMS a shortened narrow diagonal line on a coat of arms, especially one signifying bastardy [Early 16thC. Via French from, ultimately, late Latin *bastum* "stick."]

bâ·ton de com·man·de·ment /ba tàwn də kə maánd maán/ (*plural* **bâ·tons de com·man·de·ment** /ba tàwn də kə maánd maán/) *n.* an antler fragment from prehistoric times, often marked with carving and thought to have been used as a tool [From French, literally "baton of command," which was originally thought to be its purpose]

Bat·on Rouge /bátt'n roozh/ capital of Louisiana, situated on the Mississippi River in the southeastern part of the state. Population: 227,482 (1994).

ba·tra·chi·an /bə tráykee ən/ *n.* TAILLESS AMPHIBIAN a tailless amphibian, e.g., a frog or toad ■ *adj.* RELATING TO TAILLESS AMPHIBIANS relating to amphibians without tails, e.g., frogs or toads [Mid-19thC. Formed from modern Latin *Batrachia*, former order name, from Greek *batrakhos* "frog."]

bats /bats/ *adj.* harmlessly eccentric (*informal*) [Early 20thC. From the phrase *have bats in the belfry.*]

bats·man /bátsmən/ (*plural* **-men** /-mən/) *n.* a baseball player who bats or is batting. ◊ **hit batsman**

batt /bat/ *n.* TEXTILES = **batting**[2] [Late 19thC. shortening.]

batt. *abbr.* battalion

bat·tal·ion /bə tállyən/ *n.* **1.** MILITARY UNIT a military unit typically consisting of a headquarters and three or more companies, batteries, or other subunits of similar size **2.** LARGE BODY OF SOLDIERS a large body of soldiers organized to act together **3.** LARGE NUMBER a large group or number (*often used in the plural*) [Late 16thC. Via French from Italian *bataglione*, literally "great battle," ultimately from late Latin *bat(t)uere* "to beat" (source of English *batter* and *battle*).]

batte·ment /bat maán, -mənt/ *n.* a ballet movement in which one leg is extended, either once or repeatedly, to the front, side, or back, and then beat against the supporting foot [Mid-19thC. From French, literally "beating."]

bat·ten /bátt'n/ *n.* **1.** SAILING STRIP FOR KEEPING SAILS IN SHAPE a thin flexible strip of wood or plastic inserted in pockets at the edge of a sail to keep it taut and flat **2.** NAUT SLAT FOR FASTENING DOWN TARPAULIN a narrow metal or wooden slat used to fasten down the edges of a tarpaulin covering a ship's raised hatch in poor weather **3.** THEATER LIGHTS IN THEATER a row of lights in a theater, or the strip or bar that holds it ■ *vt.* **(-tened, -ten·ing, -tens)** PROVIDE WITH BATTENS to provide, strengthen, or secure something with battens [Late 16thC. From Old Norse *batna* "to improve, get better," ultimately from the same prehistoric Germanic source as English *better* and *best*.]

bat·ter[1] /báttər/ *vt.* (**-tered, -ter·ing, -ters**) **1. HIT REPEATEDLY** to hit or beat something repeatedly using heavy blows in order to break, bruise, or damage it **2. SUBJECT TO ATTACK** to subject somebody to persistent attack or violence **3. DAMAGE BY HEAVY BLOWS OR WEAR** to damage or injure something by hard blows or heavy wear (*often passive*) ■ *n.* PRINTING **1. DAMAGED TYPE** a damaged or worn printing type or plate **2. FAULTY IMPRESSION** a defective impression resulting from a printing batter [14thC. Via Old French *batre* from, ultimately, late Latin *bat(t)uere* "to beat" (source of English *batten* and *battle*).] —**bat·ter·er** *n.*

bat·ter[2] /báttər/ *n.* COOK **MIXTURE OF FLOUR, MILK, AND EGGS** a liquid mixture of flour, milk, and eggs used in making cakes and pancakes, and for coating foods before frying ■ *vt.* (**-tered, -ter·ing, -ters**) COOK **COAT FOOD IN BATTER** to cover food with batter before frying [Mid-16thC. Origin unknown.]

bat·ter[3] /báttər/ *n.* SPORTS a player who bats, especially in baseball

bat·ter[4] /báttər/ *vt.* (**-tered, -ter·ing, -ters**) **BUILD IN RECEDING SLOPE** to build something, e.g., a wall or similar structure, in a way that forms an upwardly receding slope ■ *n.* **RECEDING UPWARD SLOPE** a receding upward slope of the outer face of a wall, hedge, or similar structure [14thC. From Old French *bateüre* "act of beating," from *batre* (see BATTER[1]); from the idea of beating the mixture.]

bat·ter bread *n. Southern U.S.* corn bread made with eggs and milk

WORD KEY: REGIONAL NOTE

Batter bread, also called *baby bread*, is a Virginian term for corn bread that competes with *awendo, egg bread, spoon bread*, and dozens of other terms across the Southern states.

bat·ter·cake /báttər kàyk/ *n. Southern U.S.* **1.** = **pancake** *n.* 1 **2.** = **johnnycake**

bat·tered /báttərd/ *adj.* **1. MALTREATED** subjected to persistent physical assault, especially by a spouse, partner, or caregiver **2. SHOWING SIGNS OF WEAR** marked by dents, scratches, and other signs of heavy wear

bat·ter·ie /báttəree, bat rée/ *n.* a ballet movement in which the dancer beats the feet or calves together during a leap [Early 18thC. From French, literally "battery."]

bat·ter·ie de cui·sine /bat rée də kwi zéen/ (*plural* **bat·ter·ies de cui·sine** /bat rée də kwi zéen/) *n.* a set of cooking utensils, pots, and pans [Late 18thC. From French, literally "set (of implements) for cooking."]

bat·ter·ing ram *n.* **1. HEAVY BEAM** a large heavy beam used in ancient times to break down the walls and doors of a fortification under siege **2. DOOR BREAKER** a heavy metal bar used by police officers and firefighters to break down doors

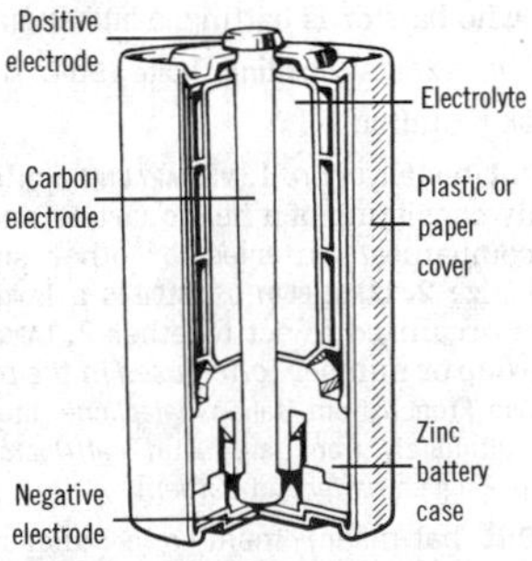

Battery: Cutaway view of a simple battery

bat·ter·y /báttəree/ (*plural* **-ies**) *n.* **1.** ELEC **POWER SOURCE** a number of connected electric cells that produce a direct current through the conversion of chemical energy into electrical energy **2.** LAW **UNLAWFUL USE OF FORCE ON SOMEBODY** the unlawful use of any physical force on another person, including beating or offensive touching without the person's consent **3.** BASEBALL **PITCHER AND CATCHER OF BASEBALL TEAM** the pitcher and catcher of a baseball team **4.** MIL **GROUPING OF ARTILLERY** a grouping of similar artillery pieces, e.g., guns or missile launchers, that function as a single tactical unit **5.** MIL **GUN EMPLACEMENT** a prepared position for artillery **6.** MIL **ARMY ARTILLERY UNIT** an army artillery unit corresponding to a company in an infantry regiment **7. GROUPING OF SIMILAR THINGS USED TOGETHER** an array or grouping of similar things intended to be used together **8. SIMILAR THINGS TOGETHER** a cluster of similar things or ideas taken, used, or considered together **9. ACT OF BATTERING** the act of battering, beating, or pounding something **10.** MUSIC **PERCUSSION SECTION** the percussion section of an orchestra [Mid-16thC. Via Old French *baterie* from, ultimately, late Latin *bat(t)uere* "to hit" (source of English *battle*). "Group of guns" comes from the idea of "beating" a target down.] ◇ **recharge your batteries** to restore your level of energy and strength (*informal*)

bat·ter·y charg·er *n.* a device for restoring power to electrical batteries

bat·tik *n.* = **batik**

bat·ting[1] /bátting/ *n.* SPORTS the action or ability of a player or team that hits with a bat, especially in baseball or cricket

bat·ting[2] /bátting/ *n.* TEXTILES bulky material made from fabric or other fibers, used for padding and stuffing [Early 19thC. Formed from BAT[1] "to hit," from the beating out of impurities from cotton.]

bat·ting av·er·age *n.* SPORTS a measure of a baseball batter's performance, calculated by dividing the total of base hits gained in a given period by the number of times at bat

bat·tle /bátt'l/ *n.* **1.** MIL **ARMED FIGHT** a large-scale fight between armed forces involving combat between armies, warships, or aircraft **2. STRUGGLE** a drawn-out conflict between adversaries, or against powerful forces ○ *the battle against malaria* ■ *v.* (**-tled, -tling, -tles**) **1.** *vti.* **FIGHT** to fight in a battle **2.** *vi.* **STRIVE** to strive or contend in order to overcome or achieve something [13thC. Via French *bataille* from, ultimately, late Latin *battualia* "military or gladatorial exercises," from *bat(t)uere* "to beat" (source of English *battery* and *batten*).] —**bat·tler** *n.* ◇ **fight a losing battle** to try hard with no prospect of success ◇ **be half the battle** to be an important first part of a difficult task ○ *Shipping the books on time is only half the battle; we have to sell them too* ◇ **do battle with somebody or something** to fight or struggle against somebody or something

WORD KEY: USAGE

The people of South Carolina have been battling a hurricane. This transitive use of ***battle*** (with a direct object, instead of *battle against* or *battle with*) is a feature of American usage that has begun to enter other Englishes also. This is partly a revival of an older use that died out in the 19th century.

WORD KEY: SYNONYMS

See Synonyms at ***fight***.

WORD KEY: ORIGIN

The Latin word *bat(t)uere* from which ***battle*** is derived is also the source of English *abate, battalion, battery, battlements, combat, debate,* and *rebate*.

Bat·tle, Kathleen (*b.* 1948) U.S. soprano. An internationally renowned concert and opera singer, she sang with the Metropolitan Opera Company in New York City (1977–94).

bat·tle-ax /bátt'l àks/ *n.* **1. BROAD-HEADED AX** a large heavy broad-headed ax used as a weapon **2. FEROCIOUS WOMAN** a domineering and fearsome woman (*insult*)

Bat·tle Creek city in southern Michigan, southwest of Lansing. It is famous as a major producer of breakfast cereals. Population: 53,430 (1996).

bat·tle cruis·er *n.* a heavily armed warship but with lighter armor, fewer guns, greater maneuverability, and a faster speed than a battleship

bat·tle cry *n.* **1. SOLDIERS' SHOUT** a rallying or encouraging shout that soldiers make when going into battle **2. SUPPORTERS' SLOGAN** a slogan used by supporters of a cause to rally fellow supporters

bat·tle·dore /bátt'l dàwr/ *n.* **1. EARLY RACKET GAME** an early racket game played by two people with flat wooden rackets and a shuttlecock. It is the ancestor of badminton. **2. LIGHT RACKET USED IN BATTLEDORE** a light racket, smaller than a tennis racket, used for hitting the shuttlecock in battledore **3. WOODEN BAT** a wooden bat used in the past to beat clothes when washing them [15thC. Origin uncertain: probably from Provençal *batedor* "beater," from *batre* "to beat," from late Latin *bat(t)uere* (see BATTLE).]

bat·tle dress *n.* the ordinary uniform worn by a soldier

bat·tle fa·tigue *n.* = **combat fatigue**

bat·tle·field /bátt'l fèeld/ *n.* **1. PLACE OF BATTLE** the place where a battle is fought **2. AREA OF CONFLICT** an area of conflict or contention

bat·tle group *n.* **1. ARMY UNIT** a U.S. army unit that usually consists of five companies **2. GROUP OF WARSHIPS** a naval force made up of warships and other vessels

bat·tle line *n.* a position along which a battle takes place ◇ **draw (up) the battle lines** to prepare for a fight, quarrel, or contest

bat·tle·ments /bátt'lmənts/ *npl.* a defensive or decorative parapet with indentations [14thC. Formed from French *bateiller* "to fortify."]

bat·tle plan *n.* **1. FIGHTING STRATEGY** a strategy for fighting a battle **2. OPERATION STRATEGY** a strategy for any operation or contest

bat·tler /bátt'lər/ *n.* somebody who fights, especially in a courageous or indomitable way

bat·tle roy·al (*plural* **bat·tles roy·al** *or* **bat·tle roy·als**) *n.* **1. BATTLE INVOLVING MANY COMBATANTS** a battle involving many combatants, especially a fight to the finish **2. GREAT CONFLICT** a passionate conflict, especially one that unfolds in public

bat·tle·ship /bátt'l shìp/ *n.* the largest type of warship that carries the heaviest armor

bat·tle·ship gray *adj.* of a medium gray color tinged with blue, like the color in which battleships are commonly painted —**bat·tle·ship gray** *n.*

bat·tle·wag·on /bátt'l wàggən/, **bat·tle wag·on** *n.* = **battleship** (*informal*)

bat·tue /ba tóo/ *n.* **1. DRIVING OF GAME IN HUNT** the beating of bushes, brush, and underbrush in order to drive game toward hunters **2. HUNT USING BATTUE** a hunt in which battue is used **3. SLAUGHTER** a wholesale massacre or indiscriminate slaughter [Early 19thC. From French, literally "beaten," from the past participle of *battre* (see BATTER[1]).]

bat·ty /báttee/ (**-ti·er, -ti·est**) *adj.* slightly eccentric (*informal*) [Early 20thC. From the phrase *have bats in the belfry*.] —**bat·ti·ness** *n.*

Ba·tu·mi /bə tóomee/, **Ba·tum** city and port in southwestern Georgia on the Black Sea, and the capital of Ajaria autonomous region. Population: 137,500 (1991).

bat·wing sleeve /bát wing-/ *n.* a sleeve that is wide at the armhole and tight at the wrist

bau·ble /báwb'l/ *n.* **1. TRINKET** something that is small and decorative but of little real value **2. MOCK SCEPTER** a mock scepter of office carried by a court jester (*archaic*) [14thC. From Old French, "plaything," of unknown origin.]

baud /bawd/ *n.* a unit for measuring data transmission speed, equal to one unit element per second [Mid-20thC. Named for the French engineer J M E *Baudot* (1845–1903), who invented a method of transmitting information using binary digits.]

Baude·laire /bōd láir/, **Charles** (1821–67) French critic and poet. His symbolist verse, notably *Les fleurs du mal* (1857), explored his sense of melancholy, isolation, and the attractions of evil and vice. Full name **Charles Pierre Baudelaire**

Bau·douin I /bō dwáN/, **King of the Belgians** (1930–93). He spent five years in voluntary exile in Switzerland before ascending the throne on the abdication of his father, Leopold III, in 1951. Full name **Baudouin Albert Charles Leopold Axel Marie Gustave**

Bau·haus /bów hòwss/ *n.* an influential German school of architecture and design, founded in 1919 by Walter Gropius. It attempted to synthesize technology, craftsmanship, design, and art, and was noted for a style of functional architecture. [Early 20thC. From German, coined by Gropius from *Bau* "building" + *Haus* "house."]

bau·hin·i·a /baw hínnee ə, bō-/ *n.* a tropical or subtropical climbing plant of the pea family that has flattened stems and is cultivated for its flowers of various colors. Genus: *Bauhinia*. [Late 18thC. From modern Latin, named for the Swiss botanist brothers *Bauhin* (Jean (1541–1613) and Gaspard (1560–1624).]

baulk *n., v.* = **balk**

Baum /bawm, baam/, **L. Frank** (1856–1919) U.S. writer. He wrote about the fairytale land of Oz in 14 volumes starting with *The Wonderful Wizard of Oz* (1900). Full name **Lyman Frank Baum**

Bau·mé scale /bō máy-, bŏ may-/ *n.* a scale for calibrating hydrometers that are used to ascertain the relative density of liquids [Mid-19thC. Named for its inventor, the French chemist Antoine *Baumé* (1728–1804).]

baux·ite /báwk sìt/ *n.* an impure amorphous mixture of aluminum hydroxides that is the principal ore of aluminum [Mid-19thC. Named for the southern French village of Les *Baux*, where the first sample described in the scientific press came from.]

Ba·var·i·a /bə váireeə/ the largest state of Germany. It is situated in the southeastern part of Germany and has borders with Baden-Württemberg, Hessen, Thüringen and Saxony states, and the Czech Republic and Austria. Capital: Munich. Population: 11,922,000 (1994). Area: 27,238 sq. mi./70,546 sq. km.

Ba·var·i·an /bə váiree ən/ *n.* **1.** SOMEBODY FROM BAVARIA somebody who lives in or was born or raised in the German state of Bavaria **2.** GERMAN DIALECT a group of High German dialects spoken in Bavaria and parts of Austria —**Ba·var·i·an** *adj.*

bawd /bawd/ *n.* **1.** MADAM OF BROTHEL a woman who runs a brothel **2.** PROSTITUTE a prostitute [14thC. Origin uncertain: probably from Old French *baude* "bold, lively," of prehistoric Germanic origin.]

bawd·ry /báwdree/ *n.* (*archaic*) **1.** PROCURING OF PROSTITUTES the supplying of prostitutes for men **2.** VULGARITY coarse or obscene language

bawd·y /báwdee/ (**-i·er, -i·est**) *adj.* ribald in a frank, humorous, and often crude way —**bawd·i·ly** *adv.* —**bawd·i·ness** *n.*

bawd·y·house /báwdi hòwss/ (*plural* **-hous·es** /-hòwzəz/) *n.* a house of prostitution (*archaic*)

bawl /báwl/ *vti.* (**bawled, bawl·ing, bawls**) **1.** SHOUT to shout something in a loud and usually aggressive voice **2.** CRY NOISILY to cry very loudly and energetically (*informal*) ■ *n.* LOUD SHOUT a loud cry or shout [15thC. Origin uncertain: perhaps from Old Norse *baula* "to low," but ultimately an imitation of the sound.] —**bawl·er** *n.*

bawl out *v.* **1.** *vti.* SHOUT SOMETHING LOUDLY to shout or cry something out loudly **2.** *vt.* TELL OFF to tell somebody off loudly and angrily (*informal*)

bay[1] /bay/ *n.* **1.** CURVED INLET OF SEA an area of sea enclosed by a wide inward-curving stretch of coastline **2.** LAND WITH CURVING HILLS AROUND a lowland area with curving hills partly surrounding it [14thC. Via French *baie* from Spanish *bahía*, of Iberian origin.]

bay[2] /bay/ *n.* **1.** SPECIAL AREA OR COMPARTMENT an area, e.g., in a building, bus station, or aircraft, that is divided off and used for a particular purpose **2.** SPACE BETWEEN TWO PILLARS a section of a wall or building between two vertical structures such as pillars or buttresses **3.** RECESS a recess or alcove in a wall **4.** = **bay window** *n.* 1 [14thC. From French *baie* "opening," from *bayer* "to gape, stand open," from assumed Vulgar Latin *batare* "to yawn, gape."]

bay[3] /bay/ *n.* **1.** TREE WITH AROMATIC LEAVES a small evergreen Mediterranean tree of the laurel family with stiff dark green aromatic leaves that are used dried as a flavoring in cooking. Latin name: *Laurus nobilis.* **2.** = **laurel** *n.* 2 **3.** TREE LIKE THE LAUREL a shrub or tree resembling the laurel, such as the bayberry ■ **bays** *npl.* WREATH FOR POET OR VICTOR a wreath woven out of laurel leaves, classically presented to poets and victors, or the honor conferred by this (*literary*) [14thC. Via Old French *baie* from Latin *baca* "berry."]

bay[4] /bay/ *n.* **1.** REDDISH-BROWN COLORED ANIMAL an animal with a reddish-brown coat, especially a horse **2.** REDDISH BROWN a reddish-brown color ■ *adj.* BAY-COLORED of a reddish-brown color (*refers to horses*) ○ *a bay mare* [14thC. Via Old French *bai* from Latin *badius* "chestnut-colored" (used only of horses).]

bay[5] /bay/ *v.* (**bayed, bay·ing, bays**) **1.** *vi.* HOWL to make the howling sound of a hunting dog on the trail of an animal **2.** *vi.* MAKE LOUD OUTCRY FOR SOMETHING to call noisily and aggressively for something bad to happen to somebody **3.** *vt.* CORNER HUNTED ANIMAL to corner or exhaust a hunted animal so that it must turn and face its hunters ■ *n.* POSITION OF NO ESCAPE the position in which a hunted animal or a person being pursued has to face the hunters or pursuers [13thC. Via Old French *(a)baier* from assumed Vulgar Latin *abbaiare*; ultimately an imitation of the sound.] ◇ **keep somebody** *or* **something at bay** to keep somebody or something unpleasant at a distance to avoid difficulty or harm ○ *Take these drops twice a day and you'll keep colds and flu at bay.*

ba·ya·dere /bí ə deér, -dáir/ *n.* fabric with horizontal stripes of bold contrasting colors [Mid-19thC. Via French from Portuguese *bailladeira* "woman dancer," from *bailar* "to dance"; from the fabric of the dancers' costumes.]

Ba·ya·món /bí aa mṓn/ city in northeastern Puerto Rico, west of the Bayamón River, and west of San Juan. Population: 231,845 (1996).

Bay·a·zid I /bí əzid/, **Bay·ez·it I, Ba·ja·zet, Bay·a·zid, Sultan of the Ottoman Empire** (1360?–1403?). He reigned from 1389 to 1402. He conquered much of the Balkans and Asia Minor, but was eventually defeated in 1402 by the Tatar Timur. Known as **Yilderim "Lightning"**

Bay·a·zid II, Sultan of the Ottoman Empire (1448–1512). He ruled from 1481 to 1512, and constructed the Mosque of Bayazid in Constantinople (1505).

bay·ber·ry /báy bèrree/ (*plural* **-ries**) *n.* **1.** N AMERICAN SHRUB a shrub of the eastern coast of North America that has aromatic leaves and fruits covered with a waxy substance used in making candles. Genus: *Myrica.* **2.** = **bay rum tree 3.** FRUIT OF BAYBERRY SHRUB the fruit of the North American bayberry shrub

Bay Cit·y 1. city and port in eastern Michigan, situated where the Saginaw River flows into Saginaw Bay. Population: 36,548 (1996). **2.** city in southeastern Texas, near the Colorado River, southwest of Houston. Population: 18,705 (1996).

Bayes' the·o·rem /báyz-/ *n.* a theorem of conditional probability that allows estimates of probability to be revised continually based on observations of occurrences of events [Mid-19thC. Named for Thomas *Bayes* (1702–61), British mathematician.]

Ba·yeux /bay ǒo, baa yǒo/ town in Calvados Department, northern France. The Bayeux Tapestry, and 11th-century embroidery depicting the Norman conquest of 1066, is housed in the town's museum. Population: 15,106 (1990).

Ba·yeux tap·es·try *n.* a linen embroidery from the 11th century that hangs in Bayeux, France, and depicts the Norman conquest of England

bay lau·rel *n.* = **bay**[3] *n.* 1

bay leaf *n.* the aromatic leaf of the Mediterranean bay tree, used for flavoring in cooking

bay lynx *n.* = **bobcat** [From BAY[4]]

Bay of Pigs bay on the southwestern coast of Cuba that was the site of an abortive attempt by U.S.-backed Cuban exiles to overthrow the government of Fidel Castro in 1961

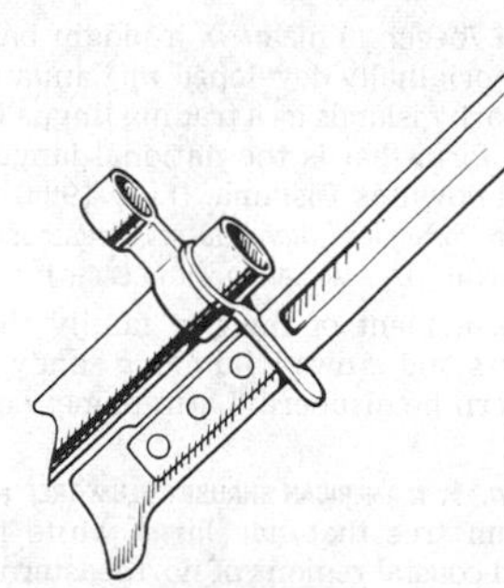

Bayonet

bay·o·net /báyənət, bàyə nét/ *n.* BLADE FITTED TO RIFLE a blade that can be attached to the end of a rifle and used for stabbing ■ *vt.* (**-net·ed** *or* **-net·ted, -net·ing** *or* **-net·ting, -nets**) STAB WITH BAYONET to stab or kill somebody with a bayonet [Early 17thC. From French *baïonnette*, named for BAYONNE where it was first made.]

Ba·yonne /bay ṓn/ city in northeastern New Jersey, on a peninsula connected to Staten Island by a bridge. Population: 60,499 (1996).

bay·ou /bí òo, bí ō/ (*plural* **-ous**) *n.* in the southern United States, an area of slow-moving water, often overgrown with reeds, leading from a river or lake [Mid-18thC. Via Louisiana French from Choctaw *bayuk* "small river forming part of a delta."]

Bay·reuth /bī róyt/ city in Bavaria, southern Germany, northeast of Nuremberg. It is the site of an annual Wagner opera festival. Population: 73,100 (1992).

bay rum *n.* a liquid used in men's cosmetics made by dissolving the oil of the leaves of the bay rum tree and other fragrant oils in alcohol and water. It was originally made by distilling the oil with rum.

bay rum tree *n.* a tropical American tree whose leaves produce an oil used to make bay rum and in perfumes and soaps. Latin name: *Pimenta racemosa.*

Bay Shore one of approximately 20 communities comprising the town of Islip, on Long Island, New York

Bay Street *n.* **1.** TORONTO FINANCIAL DISTRICT the street in Toronto on which Canada's largest stock exchange is located **2.** TORONTO FINANCIAL MARKETS the controlling financial interests of Toronto, Canada

Bay·town /báy town/ city and port in southeastern Texas, on the northern shore of Galveston Bay, north of Galveston. Population: 68,156 (1996).

bay win·dow *n.* **1.** PROTRUDING WINDOW a rounded or three-sided window that sticks out from an outside wall and forms a recess on the inside **2.** BULGING BELLY a large bulging belly (*slang*)

bay·wood /báy wòŏd/ *n.* a light variety of mahogany from southern Mexico [Named for the *Bay* of Campeche, Mexico]

ba·zaar /bə za̋ar/ *n.* **1.** CHARITABLE SALE a sale of goods to raise money for charity, often held outdoors **2.** VARIETY STORE a retail store that sells a wide variety of items **3.** MIDDLE EASTERN MARKET a street market in Middle Eastern countries [Late 16thC. Via Italian and Turkish from Persian *bāzār* "market."]

ba·zo·dee /bə zṓ deé/ *adj.* *Carib* unable to think clearly, either because of psychological turmoil or because of some physical condition or effect (*slang*) [Via French Creole from French *abasourdi* "stunned, bewildered"]

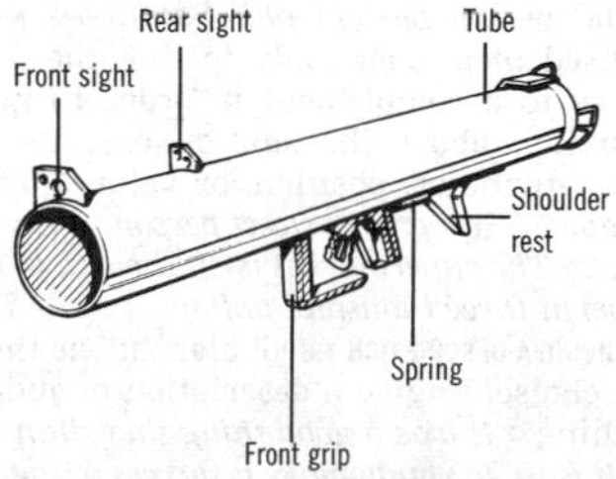

Bazooka

ba·zoo·ka /bə zóokə/ *n.* a tube-shaped weapon, fired from the shoulder, that launches a missile that can disable a tank [Mid-20thC. Origin uncertain: originally applied to a crude musical instrument similar to a trombone, and perhaps coined from earlier slang *bazoo* "kazoo," of unknown origin.]

bb, b.b. *abbr.* ball bearing

BB[1] *n.* a pellet fired from a shotgun or air rifle [Late 19thC. From the official designation of shot that is 0.18 in. (0.46 cm) in diameter.]

BB[2] *abbr.* **1.** BASEBALL base on balls **2. BB, B.B.** JUDAISM B'nai B'rith

B.B.A. *abbr.* Bachelor of Business Administration

BBB *abbr.* Better Business Bureau

BBC *abbr.* British Broadcasting Corporation

BB gun *n.* an air rifle that has a spring-loaded plunger rather than a lever for compressing air inside the barrel [From BB[1]]

bbl, bbl. *abbr.* barrel

BBQ *abbr.* barbecue

BBS *abbr.* COMPUT Bulletin Board System

B.C.[1], B.C. *adv.* used to indicate a date that is a specified number of years before the birth of Jesus Christ (*used after a date*) Full form **before Christ**

B.C.[2] *abbr.* British Columbia

bcc, b.c.c. *abbr.* blind carbon copy

BCD *abbr.* binary coded decimal

B.C.E.[1] *abbr.* **1.** Bachelor of Chemical Engineering **2.** Bachelor of Civil Engineering

B.C.E.[2] *abbr.* B.C.E. Before the Common Era

B cell *n.* a type of white blood cell **(lymphocyte)**, formed in bone marrow in mammals and present in blood and lymph, that creates antibodies in response to a specific antigen

BCG *n.* an anti-tuberculosis vaccine made from a weakened strain of the tubercle bacillus. Full form **bacillus Calmette-Guérin (vaccine)**

B com·plex *n.* = **vitamin B complex**

BC soil *n.* soil made up of two distinct layers

bd *abbr.* bundle

BD *abbr.* **1.** bank draft **2.** bomb disposal **3. BD, B.D.** bills discounted

bd. *abbr.* **1.** board **2.** bond **3.** PUBL bound

B.D. *abbr.* Bachelor of Divinity

b/d *abbr.* ACCT brought down

B/D, b/d *abbr.* **1.** bank draft **2.** bills discounted

bdel·li·um /déllee əm/ *n.* **1. RESINOUS TREE** a tropical tree of Africa and western Asia that produces a resin similar to myrrh. Genus: *Commiphora.* **2. VALUABLE RESIN** the transparent yellowish resin of the bdellium tree, valued for its perfume [14thC. Via Latin and Greek from, ultimately, a Semitic language.]

bd. ft. *abbr.* board foot

bdl *abbr.* bundle

Bdr *abbr.* Bombadier

bdrm. *abbr.* bedroom

bds. *abbr.* PUBL bound in boards

be *(stressed)* /bee/; *(unstressed)* /bee/ (*1st person singular past indicative* **was,** *2nd person singular past indicative* **were,** *3rd person singular past indicative* **was,** *1st person plural past indicative* **were,** *2nd person plural past indicative* **were,** *3rd person plural past indicative* **were,** *past subjunctive* **were,** *past participle* **been,** *present subjunctive* **be,** *1st person present singular* **am,** *2nd person present singular* **are,** *3rd person present singular* **is,** *1st person present plural* **are,** *2nd person present plural* **are**) CORE MEANING: a verb used most commonly to link the subject of a clause to a complement in order to give more information about the subject, e.g., its identity, nature, attributes, position, or value ○ *This is my colleague.* ○ *He's a very sweet person.* ○ *Her new car is blue.* ○ *The supermarket is on the left.* ○ *The clock was worth three thousand dollars.*

vi. **1. GIVING A DESCRIPTION** used after "it" as the subject of the clause, to give a description or judgment of something ○ *It was a good thing they didn't go after all.* ○ *It is up to you to make a success of the business.* **2. EXIST OR BE TRUE** used after "there" to indicate that something exists or is true ○ *There was nothing in the news today about the resignation.* ○ *There are too many people in here.* **3. EXIST** to exist, have presence, or live ○ *I think, therefore I am.* ○ *Our cat has ceased to be.* **4. HAPPEN** to happen or take place ○ *The meeting will be at 2 o'clock in the conference room.* **5. STAY** to stay or visit ○ *He wanted nothing but to be with the family.* ○ *Have you ever been to Italy?* **6. HAVE PARTICULAR QUALITY** to have a particular quality or attribute ○ *To be really precise, you must state the exact time at which the accident happened.* **7. REMAIN** used to indicate that a certain situation remains ○ *The fact of the matter is, I just don't want to stay here any more.* **8. EXPRESSING CONTINUATION** used as an auxiliary verb with the present participles of other verbs to express continuation ○ *The firm will be instituting more training programs next year.* **9. FORMING THE PASSIVE** used as an auxiliary verb with the past participles of transitive verbs to form the passive voice ○ *She was sent on the mission.* **10. FORMING PERFECT TENSE** used as an auxiliary verb with the past participles of some intransitive verbs to form a perfect tense (*archaic*) ○ *She is gone.* **11. EXPRESSING THE FUTURE** used as an auxiliary verb to indicate that something is planned, expected, intended, or supposed to happen in the future (*used with an infinitive*) ○ *The meeting is to take place tomorrow.* ○ *What am I to do?* **12. EXPRESSING UNPLANNED ACTION IN THE PAST** used as an auxiliary verb when reporting past events to indicate that something happened later than the time reported and was unplanned or uncertain at the time (*used with an infinitive*) ○ *He kissed her goodbye; it was to be the last time he ever saw her.* [Old English *bēon*, via a prehistoric Germanic base meaning "exist, dwell" from an Indo-European base meaning "exist, grow"] ◇ **be that as it may** even if that is the case ○ *"I don't even like camping vacations."–"Be that as it may, you're still going with us."* ◇ **be off** go away ○ *It's already seven o'clock; I'm off.*

WORD KEY: ORIGIN

The prehistoric Germanic word that is the ancestor of the verb ***be*** is also the source of English *boor, booth, bower, build, bylaw, husband,* and *neighbor.*

Be *symbol.* beryllium

BE, B.E. *abbr.* Board of Education

B.E. *abbr.* **1.** Bachelor of Education **2.** Bachelor of Engineering

be- *prefix.* **1.** thoroughly, excessively ○ *bedazzle* ○ *bespatter* **2.** on, over, about ○ *bewail* **3.** to surround or cover with ○ *befog* ○ *bedew* **4.** to furnish with ○ *befriend* **5.** to make ○ *belittle* [ETYMOLOGY: Old English *be-, bi-.* Ultimately from an Indo-European base meaning "around," which is also the ancestor of English *ambi-, amphi-,* and *by.*]

B/E *abbr.* bill of exchange

beach /beech/ *n.* **COASTAL SAND** a strip of sand or pebbles at the point where land meets the sea or a lake ■ *vti.* **(beached, beach·ing, beach·es) HAUL BOAT ASHORE** to pull or run a boat onto a beach, or be pulled onto a beach [Mid-16thC. Origin uncertain: perhaps from Old English *bæce* "brook." Originally in the meaning of "shingle."]

beach ball *n.* a large light easily inflated ball, often brightly colored, for playing with on a beach

beach bug·gy *n. U.K.* = **dune buggy**

beach bum *n.* a person with no serious occupation who spends time lazing around on beaches (*informal*)

beach·comb·er /beéch kōmər/ *n.* **1. SOMEBODY SALVAGING THINGS FROM BEACH** somebody who wanders along beaches looking through debris for useful or valuable things **2.** *U.K.* = **comber**

beached /beecht/ *adj.* stranded on a beach or out of the water

beach flea *n.* = **sand flea**

beach·front /beéch frùnt/ *n.* a strip of land that adjoins a beach

beach grass *n.* a thick grass with strong roots that grows along sandy shores in North America. It is often planted to stop beach erosion. Genus: *Ammophila.*

beach·head /beéch hèd/ *n.* **1. CAPTURED ENEMY BEACH** a part of an enemy shoreline that troops have captured and are using as a base for launching an attack **2. BASE FOR ACHIEVING SOMETHING** an initial success that lays the groundwork for achieving an objective [Modeled on BRIDGEHEAD]

Beach-la-Mar /beéch lə maár/ *n.* a pidgin based on English that originally developed in Vanuatu, Fiji, and other nearby islands as a trading lingua franca. The modern form that is the national language of Vanuatu is known as Bislama. [Early 19thC. By folk etymology from Portuguese *bicho do mar* "sea cucumber," literally "sea worm," by association with BEACH.]

beach pea *n.* a plant of the pea family that has purple flowers and grows wild along sandy shores of the northern hemisphere. Latin name: *Lathyrus japonicus.*

beach plum *n.* **1. N AMERICAN SHRUBBY PLUM TREE** a small shrubby plum tree that has large white flowers and grows in coastal regions of northeastern North America. Latin name: *Prunus maritima.* **2. EDIBLE PURPLE FRUIT** the dark purple edible fruit of the beach plum tree

beach·scape /beéch skàyp/ *n.* a view of a beach, either in reality or in a painting or photograph

beach·side /beéch sìd/ *adj.* on or next to a beach

beach·wear /beéch wàir/ *n.* casual clothing designed to be worn on a beach

Beach·y Head /beéchee-/ chalk headland on the English Channel near Eastbourne, East Sussex, southern England. Height: 570 ft./171 m.

bea·con /beékən/ **(-coned, -con·ing, -cons)** *n.* **1.** SHIPPING **FLASHING LIGHT FOR SHIPS** a lighthouse or signaling buoy that produces a flashing light to warn or guide ships **2.** NAVIG **RADIO TRANSMITTER PRODUCING NAVIGATION SIGNAL** a radio transmitter that continuously broadcasts a signal that aircraft use for guidance **3. SIGNALING FIRE ON HILL** a fire lit on a hilltop or tower in former times as a signal, e.g., to warn of invasion **4. HILL SUITABLE FOR SIGNALING FIRES** a prominent hill on which fires were formerly lit as a signal (*often used in place names*) **5. SOURCE OF INSPIRATION** somebody or something that inspires or guides others (*literary*) [Old English *bēacen* "signal, sign." Ultimately from a prehistoric Germanic word that also produced English *beckon.*]

Bea·con /beékən/ city in southeastern New York, on the Hudson River. Population: 13,275 (1996).

bead /beed/ *n.* **1. BALL FOR A NECKLACE** a small gemstone or sphere of glass, plastic, or wood, pierced for stringing on a necklace or for sewing onto fabric **2. DROP OF MOISTURE** a drop of moisture, especially of sweat **3.** ARCHIT, FURNITURE **BUILDING OR FURNITURE TRIM** an edge or rim that sticks out on a building or a piece of furniture, traditionally with a pattern of rounded knobs **4.** ARMS **GUN SIGHT** a knob sticking up on the end of the barrel of a gun, forming the front part of the gun's sight **5.** AUTOMOT **SEAL ON A TIRE** a projecting lip on the tire of a motor vehicle that seals to the wheel rim **6.** METALL **DEPOSIT OF METAL** a deposit of metal used in welding ■ **beads** *npl.* **1.** RELIG **ROSARY** a rosary **2. NECKLACE** a necklace made of beads ■ *v.* **(bead·ed, bead·ing, beads) 1.** *vt.* **DECORATE WITH BEADS** to trim or ornament something with beads **2.** *vi.* **FORM INTO BEADS** to form drops of moisture [Old English *gebed* "prayer." The meaning "small ball" evolved in the 14thC via "prayer said on a rosary" and "rosary bead."] ◇ **draw a bead on somebody** *or* **something 1.** to take careful aim at somebody or something **2.** to single out somebody or something for special consideration ◇ **tell** *or* **say** *or* **count your beads** to say prayers recited in sequence and counted using a rosary

bead·ing /beéding/ *n.* **1. BUILDING OR FURNITURE TRIM** an edge or rim that sticks out on a building or a piece of furniture, traditionally with a pattern of rounded knobs **2. CARVED WOOD FOR EDGING** a rounded piece of molding, e.g., on a door

bea·dle /beéd'l/ *n.* **1.** JUDAISM **CARETAKER OF A SYNAGOGUE** an official who acts as caretaker of a synagogue and oversees the running of the service **2.** CHR **MINOR CHURCH OFFICIAL** a minor parish official once employed in the Church of England to usher and keep order [13thC. From Old French *bedel*, literally "proclaimer, messenger," from a prehistoric Germanic word that is also the ancestor of English *bid.*]

Bea·dle /beéd'l/, **George Wells** (1903–89) U.S. geneticist. He won a Nobel Prize (1958) for his pioneering research into the role of genes in synthesis of cellular substances. Full name **George Wells Beadle**

bead·work /beéd wùrk/ *n.* **1. WOODEN EDGING** decorative wooden edging, e.g., on a door or window frame **2. PATTERN OF BEADS** decoration using beads to form a design, e.g., on furniture or knitwear

bead·y /beédee/ **(-i·er, -i·est)** *adj.* **1. LIKE BEADS** small, round, and shiny like glass beads **2. COVERED WITH BEADS** covered or ornamented with beads —**bead·i·ly** *adv.* —**bead·i·ness** *n.* ◇ **keep a** *or* **your beady eye on somebody** *or* **something** to watch somebody or something very carefully (*informal*)

bea·gle /beég'l/ *n.* a small smooth-haired dog belonging to a breed with a white, tan, and black coat and long drooping ears, often used for hunting [15thC. Origin uncertain: perhaps from Old French *beegueule* "noisy person," from *beer,* "to gape" (source of English *bay*[2]) + *gueule* "throat" (see GULLET).]

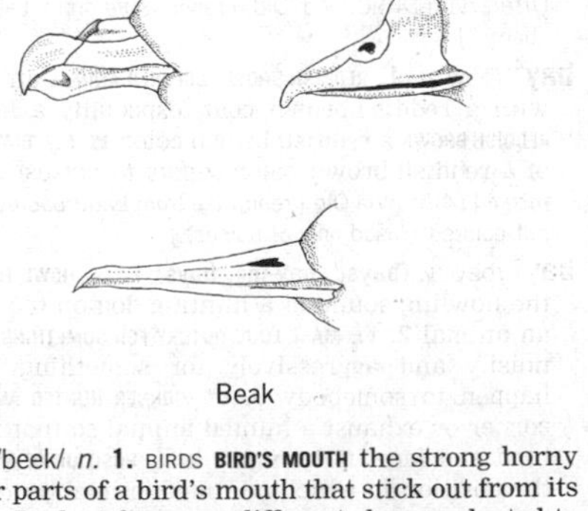

Beak

beak /beek/ *n.* **1.** BIRDS **BIRD'S MOUTH** the strong horny outer parts of a bird's mouth that stick out from its head. Beaks take many different shapes adapted to the eating habits of individual bird species. **2.** ZOOL **PROTRUDING PART OF ANIMAL'S MOUTH** a projecting part of the mouth or jaw of animals other than birds, e.g., the sucking mouthpart of an insect or the bony jaw projection of a fish **3.** ZOOL **PART OF MOLLUSK'S SHELL** the oldest part of the shell of a mollusk with a hinged shell, found nearest the hinge **4. SOMEBODY'S NOSE** somebody's nose, especially when it is long or hooked (*slang*) **5. PROJECTING PART** a part that sticks out, e.g., the lip of a container **6.** ARCHIT **CURVED CORNICE OR MOLDING** a cornice or molding with a downward-curving edge [13thC. Via Old French *bec* from Latin *beccus*, of Gaulish origin.] —**beak·less** *adj.*

beaked /beekt/ *adj.* having a beak or some part resembling a beak

beaked whale *n.* a widely found, medium-sized, toothed whale with a long snout. Family: Ziphiidae.

beak·er /beékər/ *n.* **1. LABORATORY CONTAINER** a flat-bottomed glass container used in laboratories **2. WIDE CUP** a wide-mouthed cup, especially a plastic one without a handle [14thC. Via Old Norse *bikarr* from assumed Vulgar Latin *bicarium*, perhaps ultimately from Greek *bikos* "wine jar, earthen vessel."]

Beak·er folk *npl.* a prehistoric people who lived throughout Central Europe during the period 2000 to 1000 B.C. The remains of pottery beakers are often found in areas where they are known to have lived.

be-all ◇ **the be-all and end-all** the thing that is most important

beam /beem/ *n.* **1.** CONSTR **HORIZONTAL STRUCTURAL SUPPORT** a horizontal structural member that carries the load by bending, e.g., a long piece of timber, metal, or concrete spanning a room and supporting the story or roof above **2. LINE OF LIGHT** a narrow line of light, e.g., from a flashlight **3.** PHYS **FLOW OF RADIATION** a narrow stream of radiation or particles flowing in one direction **4.** NAVIG **GUIDING SIGNAL** a radio or radar signal intended to guide a ship or aircraft, or the direction indicated by this **5. BROAD SMILE** a broad smile of happiness or satisfaction **6.** NAUT **STRUCTURAL CROSSPIECE IN SHIP** a structural member of a ship or boat that joins the sides and supports the deck **7.** NAUT **SHIP'S BREADTH** the full breadth of a ship **8.** NAUT **SIDE OF SHIP** either of the sides of a ship **9. HORIZONTAL PART OF BALANCE** the pivoted horizontal bar of a balance on which the two scales hang **10. MAIN SUPPORTING SHAFT** a main bar or shaft, e.g., either of the main stems of a deer's antlers or the central shaft of a plow **11.** MECH ENG **CONNECTING LEVER IN ENGINE** a lever connecting the piston rod and crankshaft in an engine **12.** MANUF **ROLLER IN LOOM** a cylinder in a loom on which either the warp or the cloth is wound ■ *v.* **(beamed, beam·ing, beams) 1.** *vti.* **SMILE BROADLY** to smile broadly with happiness or satisfaction, or express feelings by smiling broadly **2.** *vt.* BROADCAST **SEND AS RADIO OR TV SIGNAL** to send or transmit a program to a distant place in the form of a radio or television signal **3.** *vti.* **SHINE** to shine in a particular direction **4.** *vti.* **CHANGE CIRCUMSTANCES SUDDENLY** to move between completely different places or situations in a sudden and disorienting way (*slang*) (*used with "up" or "down"*) [Old English *bēam* "tree, piece of timber, column, ray," from a prehistoric Germanic word that is also the ancestor of English *boom*] ◇ **off the beam, off beam** missing the point or relevance ◇ **on the beam 1.** using a beam for guidance **2.** on track or working effectively

beam an·ten·na *n.* a radio or television antenna designed to transmit or receive signals in or from a particular direction

beam com·pass *n.* a tool for drawing very large circles or arcs, consisting of a horizontal bar with sliding legs

beam-ends *npl.* the ends of the beams supporting the deck of a vessel ◇ **on her** *or* **its beam-ends** used to describe a ship leaning so far to one side that its deck is vertical

Bea·mon /beémən/, **Bob** (*b.* 1946) U.S. athlete. He set a world long jump record of 29 ft. 2.5 in./8.9 m at the 1968 Olympic Games in Mexico City; it lasted for 23 years. Full name **Robert Beamon**

beam split·ter *n.* a device used in holography to divide a laser light into two beams by means of a prism and mirror so as to produce a three-dimensional image

beam·y /beémee/ (**-i·er, -i·est**) *adj.* **1. SHINING BRIGHTLY** sending out beams of light (*literary*) **2. WITH BROAD BEAM** having a broad beam, or broad in the beam (*refers to a ship*)

bean /been/ *n.* **1. PLANT WITH EDIBLE PODS AND SEEDS** a climbing or short bushy plant that is cultivated for its edible, usually green, pods and seeds. Genus: *Phaseolus.* ◊ **French bean 2. EDIBLE GREEN POD** a long thin usually green seedpod of a bean plant eaten cooked as a vegetable **3. SMALL ROUND VEGETABLE** a small round or kidney-shaped seed of various colors that is eaten as a vegetable and can be dried to preserve it **4.** = **soybean 5.** = **broad bean 6. SEED USED IN FOOD OR DRINK** a coffee, cocoa, or carob seed that is processed and used in food or drink **7. HEAD** a person's head or brain (*slang*) ■ **beans** *npl.* **NOTHING** nothing at all (*informal*) ■ *vt.* **(beaned, bean·ing, beans) HIT ON HEAD** to hit somebody on the head (*slang*) [Old English *bēan*, from prehistoric Germanic] ◇ **full of beans 1.** bright and energetic (*informal*) **2.** full of incorrect information or nonsense (*informal*) ◇ **not know beans about something** to have no knowledge or understanding of something (*informal*) ◇ **spill the beans** to reveal secret information (*informal*)

bean·bag /beén bàg/ *n.* **1.** GAME **BEAN-FILLED BAG USED IN GAMES** a small cloth bag filled with dried beans or something similar, thrown or otherwise used in children's games **2.** FURNITURE **LARGE CUSHION USED AS SEAT** an oversized cushion filled with tiny polystyrene balls, laid on the floor and used as a chair

bean ball *n.* in baseball, a ball deliberately pitched at the batter's head (*informal*) [From BEAN in the sense of "head"]

bean bee·tle *n.* = **Mexican bean beetle**

bean count·er *n.* an accountant as contrasted with the creative staff of an organization (*slang insult*)

bean curd *n.* tofu, especially as used in Chinese cookery

bean·er·y /beénəree/ (*plural* **-ies**) *n.* a cheap restaurant (*informal*)

Bean·head /beén hed/ *n.* a first-year cadet at the United States Military Academy at West Point (*slang*)

bean·ie /beénee/ *n.* a round tight-fitting hat like a skullcap, formerly worn by schoolboys and young college students [Formed from BEAN in the sense of "head"]

bean·o /beénō/ *n.* the game of bingo, sometimes played with beans as markers, and often considered illegal gambling (*informal*)

bean·pole /beén pōl/ *n.* **1. STICK SUPPORTING BEAN PLANT** a stick or pole for supporting a climbing bean plant **2. TALL THIN PERSON** somebody who is very tall and thin (*informal*)

bean sprouts *npl.* long pale shoots of sprouted bean seeds, particularly of the mung bean, harvested while crisp and used raw or very lightly cooked

bear[1] /bair/ *n.* **1.** ZOOL **LARGE FURRY ANIMAL** a large strong omnivorous four-legged mammal that has thick shaggy fur and sharp claws and walks on the flat of its paws. Family: Ursidae. **2.** ZOOL **MEDIUM-SIZED FURRY ANIMAL** an animal that resembles but is unrelated to the true bear, e.g., the koala **3.** = **teddy bear 4. BAD-TEMPERED PERSON** somebody who is surly or ill-tempered (*informal*) **5. DIFFICULT THING** something difficult to experience or endure (*slang*) **6.** STOCK EXCH **SOMEBODY WHO ANTICIPATES FALLING PRICES** somebody who sells stocks or commodities in anticipation of falling prices. ◊ **bull**[1] *n.* 4 **7.** FIN **SOMEBODY ANTICIPATING BAD BUSINESS CONDITIONS** somebody who anticipates unfavorable business conditions [Old English *bera*, from a prehistoric Germanic word meaning "the brown one." In the financial sense, probably from the expression "to sell the bear's skin before you have caught the bear."]

WORD KEY: ORIGIN

The prehistoric Germanic word from which ***bear*** is derived is also the ancestor of English *amphora, barrow, berth, bier, birth, born, burden, fertile, paraphernalia,* and *suffer.*

bear[2] /bair/ (**bore** /bawr/, **borne** /bawrn/ *or* **born** /bawrn/, **bear·ing, bears**) *v.* **1.** *vti.* **TOLERATE** to be able to endure something without great distress or annoyance (*used with a negative*) ○ *couldn't bear to see them unhappy* **2.** *vt.* **SUPPORT SOMETHING** to hold or support a weight or something heavy **3.** *vti.* **BE FIT FOR SOMETHING** to withstand being subjected to a particular action ○ *Will her theories bear scrutiny?* **4.** *vt.* **MERIT SOMETHING** to be worthy of an action ○ *These allegations bear further investigation.* **5.** *vt.* **ACCEPT AS RESPONSIBILITY** to accept something as a duty or responsibility **6.** *vt.* **BE CHARACTERIZED BY SOMETHING** to have something as a quality, characteristic, or permanent attribute ○ *The description bore no relation to reality.* **7.** *vt.* **BE MARKED BY SOMETHING** to show physical signs of something **8.** *vt.* **CARRY** to hold or support and transport somebody or something **9.** *vt.* **PRODUCE SOMETHING** to yield something by a natural process, or produce something desirable or valuable ○ *the tree bore fruit* **10.** *vt.* **GIVE BIRTH** to give birth to a child or young. ◊ **born 11.** *vt.* **THINK SOMETHING** to hold a particular thought, feeling, or idea in the mind ○ *I bore him no ill will.* **12.** *vt.* **TRANSMIT** to hold something in mind and communicate it to others (*formal*) **13.** *vi.* **HEAD IN A CERTAIN DIRECTION** to move or turn in a particular direction ○ *Bear right when the road divides.* **14.** *vt.* **BEHAVE IN A CERTAIN WAY** to conduct or carry yourself in a particular way [Old English *beran*] ◇ **bring something to bear (on something)** to use something to force a desired outcome

bear down *vi.* to push with the vaginal muscles during childbirth

bear down on *vi.* **1. APPROACH** to move quickly and menacingly toward somebody or something **2. PRESS DOWN** to exert downward pressure on something

bear on, bear up·on *vi.* **1. BE RELEVANT** to relate to or affect something **2. CAUSE DIFFICULTY** to be a problem for, or a burden to, somebody or something

bear out *vt.* to prove something or somebody to be true or justified ○ *This bears out my theory.*

bear up *vi.* **1. WITHSTAND EXAMINATION** to remain true or undamaged after being examined or criticized **2. STAY CHEERFUL IN DIFFICULTIES** to remain cheerful and determined in spite of problems

bear upon *vi.* = **bear on**

bear with *vi.* to be patient with somebody trying to do something

Bear /bair/ river that rises in Utah and flows through Wyoming and Idaho before entering Utah and emptying into the Great Salt Lake. Length: 350 mi./563 km.

bear·a·ble /báirəb'l/ *adj.* not too unpleasant to put up with or accept

bear·bait·ing /báir bàyting/ *n.* the setting of fierce dogs onto a chained bear, once a popular form of public entertainment

bear·ber·ry /báir bèrree/ (*plural* **-ries**) *n.* a trailing evergreen shrub of North America, Europe, and Asia that has small pinkish flowers and red berries. Latin name: *Arctostaphylos uva-ursi.* [Early 17thC. From BEAR[1].]

bear·cat /báir kàt/ *n.* = **red panda**

beard /beerd/ *n.* **1. HAIR GROWING ON MAN'S CHIN** the hair on a man's chin and, often, his neck and cheeks **2.** ZOOL **TUFTS GROWING ON PLANTS AND ANIMALS** a growth of longer hair on an animal, e.g., on a goat's chin, or a long slender growth on plants, e.g., on barley and wheat heads **3. ATTENTION-DIVERTING PERSON OR THING** somebody or something that diverts attention or suspicion from another ■ *vt.* **(beard·ed, beard·ing, beards) STAND UP TO SOMEBODY OPENLY** to oppose or confront something or somebody confidently or disrespectfully ○ *bearded the senator in the cloak room and took him to task for his position on taxes* [Old English. Ultimately from an Indo-European word meaning "beard," which is also the ancestor of English *barber.*] —**beard·less** *adj.*

beard·ed /beérdəd/ *adj.* having a beard —**beard·ed·ness** *n.*

beard·ed col·lie *n.* a medium-sized gray or brown-and-white dog with a long coat, drooping ears, and a tuft of hair on its chin, belonging to a breed used for herding animals

beard·ed drag·on, beard·ed liz·ard *n.* a large Australian lizard with a pouch under its chin, that inflates to ward off attackers. Latin name: *Amphibolus barbatus.*

beard·ed i·ris *n.* an iris growing from a rhizome that has numerous hairs, often colored, along the center of each drooping lower petal

beard·ed tit *n.* = **reedling**

beard·ed vul·ture *n.* = **lammergeier**

Beards·ley /beérdzlee/, **Aubrey** (1872–98) British artist and illustrator. One of the "Decadents" in the 1890s, he produced art nouveau illustrations in a distinctive black-and-white style, including series for *Morte d'Arthur* (1893) and *Salomé* (1894). Full name **Aubrey Vincent Beardsley**

beard·tongue /béerd tùng/ *n.* BOT = **penstemon** [Early 19thC. From the tufts resembling hair on one of its stamens.]

bear·er /báirər/ *n.* **1.** **BRINGER** somebody who brings or carries something **2.** FIN **HOLDER OF REDEEMABLE NOTE** somebody possessing a document redeemable for payment **3.** = **pallbearer** **4.** **PORTER** a local person employed to carry equipment on an expedition

bear·er bond *n.* a bond payable only to the party that presents it

bear gar·den *n.* a noisy or unruly place or occasion

bear hug *n.* **1.** **TIGHT EMBRACE** an enthusiastic or energetic embrace **2.** WRESTLING **SQUEEZING HOLD IN WRESTLING** in wrestling, a tight, squeezing hold around an opponent's chest and arms **3.** COMM **WARNING OF INTENDED TAKEOVER** one company's warning to another of its intention to assume control

bear·ing /báiring/ *n.* **1.** **RELEVANCE** an effect on something, or a connection with something ○ *This has no bearing on the matter under discussion.* **2.** **WAY OF MOVING OR STANDING** somebody's way of moving, standing, or behaving generally ○ *her dignified bearing* **3.** NAVIG **CALCULATION OF DIRECTION OR GEOGRAPHIC POSITION** somebody's location or direction of movement calculated using a map or compass **4.** MECH ENG **HOUSING FOR A MOVING PART** the part of a machine that supports a sliding or rotating part **5.** BUILDING **SUPPORT FOR BEAM** a support for a beam or girder **6.** HERALDRY **HERALDIC DEVICE** a heraldic device or charge ◇ **find** *or* **get your bearings** **1.** to learn exactly where you are and in which direction you should proceed **2.** to become familiar with a new environment ◇ **lose your bearings** **1.** to become uncertain about where you are and in which direction you should proceed **2.** to become unable to react in a normal manner

bear·ing pile *n.* a column of concrete, steel, or timber driven vertically into the ground to transfer the weight of a structure built above onto firm soil below

bear·ing rein *n. U.K.* = **checkrein**

bear·ish /báirish/ *adj.* **1.** **CLUMSY** moving or behaving roughly or clumsily **2.** **BAD-TEMPERED** surly or ill-tempered toward people **3.** STOCK EXCH **ANTICIPATING FALLING PRICES** conducive to or characterized by selling rather than buying stocks or commodities in anticipation of falling prices **4.** FIN **ANTICIPATING BAD BUSINESS CONDITIONS** anticipating unfavorable business conditions

bear mar·ket *n.* STOCK EXCH a situation in a stock or commodity market in which stockholders are selling in anticipation of falling prices

Bear Mount·ain /báir-/ mountain in southeastern New York State on the western bank of the Hudson River. Height: 1,305 ft./398 m.

bé·ar·naise sauce /bàir nayz-, bày aar-/ *n.* a savory sauce served with steak, chicken, or fish, made from egg yolks, butter, shallots, tarragon, and sometimes other herbs, and vinegar or lemon juice [Late 19thC. *Béarnaise* from French, formed from *Béarn*, name of a district in southwestern France.]

bear raid *n.* STOCK EXCH an attempt to lower a stock or commodity price by selling large numbers of shares, usually in order to buy them back at a lowered price

bear's breech *n.* a large garden plant with spiky leaves and whitish purple-streaked flowers. Latin name: *Acanthus mollis.*

bear's ear *n.* BOT = **auricula**

bear·skin /báir skìn/ *n.* **1.** **BEAR'S PELT** a bear's skin with the fur still attached, stripped from the animal **2.** TEXTILES **SHAGGY WOOLEN CLOTH** coarse woolen fabric, often used to make overcoats **3.** MIL **SOLDIER'S TALL FUR HAT** a tall fur hat worn as part of the ceremonial uniform of soldiers in some British army regiments and by drum majors

Barnaby's

Bearskin: Two British soldiers wearing bearskins

bear trout *n.* the lake trout of Lake Superior, most frequently observed in the Upper Peninsula of Michigan (*regional*)

beast /beest/ *n.* **1.** **LARGE ANIMAL** an animal, especially a large four-footed mammal **2.** **IRRATIONAL SIDE OF SOMEBODY'S PERSONALITY** the instinctive, irrational, or aggressive part of somebody's personality **3.** **BRUTAL PERSON** a cruel or aggressive person **4.** **SOMETHING UNPLEASANT** a thing or situation that is difficult or unpleasant (*informal*) ○ *This is truly a beast of a job!* [12thC. Via Old French *beste* from Latin *bestia*, of unknown origin.]

beast fa·ble *n.* a story that teaches a moral lesson using the exploits of animals that speak and act like human beings

beast·ie /béestee/ *n. U.S., Scotland* a small animal, especially an insect or small crawling creature (*informal*)

beast·ly /béestlee/ *adj.* thoroughly unpleasant or objectionable —**beast·li·ness** *n.*

beast of bur·den *n.* an animal, e.g., a donkey or an ox, used to carry or pull things or do other heavy work

beast of prey *n.* a mammal that hunts other animals for food

beat /beet/ *v.* (**beat, beat·en** /béet'n/, **beat·ing, beats**) **1.** *vt.* **DEFEAT** to defeat somebody in a contest ○ *She was beaten in the semifinal.* **2.** *vt.* **HIT REPEATEDLY** to hit somebody or something with repeated heavy blows ○ *beaten nearly to death.* **3.** *vi.* **KNOCK AGAINST REPEATEDLY** to knock or strike against something repeatedly ○ *waves beating against the rocks* **4.** *vt.* **FLOG** to inflict physical punishment or injury on somebody using an instrument such as a whip, stick, or belt ○ *He was beaten with a strap.* **5.** *vi.* **PULSATE** to make natural short rhythmical movements (*refers to the heart or pulse*) **6.** *vti.* MUSIC **HIT DRUM** to hit a drum repeatedly to produce a musical rhythm or a signal **7.** *vt.* MUSIC **SET MUSICAL RHYTHM** to show or establish a musical rhythm, e.g., with a conductor's baton or by clapping hands **8.** *vt.* COOK **STIR VIGOROUSLY** to mix moist ingredients vigorously to combine them, make them smooth, or incorporate air into them ○ *Now, beat the eggs.* **9.** *vt.* **OVERCOME OBSTACLES IN SOMETHING** to overcome the difficulties or obstacles created by something ○ *You can't beat the system.* **10.** *vt.* **ARRIVE AHEAD OF SOMEBODY** to arrive or finish something sooner than somebody else or than a time limit ○ *She beat me to the office.* **11.** *vt.* **AVOID LATER DELAYS** to take early action to avoid being prevented or delayed by something ○ *Order now and beat the rush!* **12.** *vt.* **SURPASS** to surpass a previous best performance ○ *beat the long jump record* **13.** *vti.* **BE BETTER** to be or do better than a particular thing, activity, or quality (*informal*) ○ *Sitting by the pool sure beats working.* **14.** *vt.* **MAKE BY BLOWS** to shape or make something by pounding or trampling ○ *beat silver into jewelry* **15.** *vti.* BIRDS **FLAP WINGS** to move the wings up and down in flight or an attempt at flight, or be moved in this way ○ *The vulture beat its wings.* **16.** *vt.* **FORCE TO WITHDRAW** to force somebody to retreat or accept a weaker position ○ *they beat back the enemy* **17.** *vti.* HUNT **DRIVE GAME FROM BRUSH** to move through or disturb cover in order to frighten animals and birds for hunting **18.** *vi.* NAUT **SAIL INTO WIND** to sail a boat or ship as nearly as possible in the direction from which the wind is blowing ■ *n.* **1.** **STEADY THROBBING** a rhythmical sound or movement made by something throbbing or pulsating (*often used in combination*) ○ *a fast heartbeat* **2.** **STROKE** an act of striking one thing against another, or the sound of one thing striking against another, especially repeatedly and rhythmically ○ *a drum beat* **3.** MUSIC **SET RHYTHM** a single element of measured time in a musical piece or poem. Beats occur at regular intervals and are the rhythmic and metrical foundations of music. **4.** MUSIC **CONDUCTOR'S SIGNAL** a movement made by a conductor's baton or hand to indicate a musical beat **5.** MUSIC **DOMINANT RHYTHM** the dominant rhythm in a piece of music, especially a strong rhythm in rock music **6.** **USUAL ROUTE** a regular route followed or area covered while working, e.g., by a police officer ○ *the local police officer on the beat* **7.** **AREA SOMEBODY USUALLY GOES TO** the places somebody usually frequents, especially somebody's usual hunting or fishing area ■ *adj.* **1.** **TIRED OUT** completely exhausted (*slang*) **2.** **PUZZLED** unable to understand or think how to proceed (*informal*) ○ *It has me beat.* **3.** **beat, Beat** **OF THE BEAT GENERATION** typical of or produced by members of the Beat Generation [Old English *bēatan*. Via a prehistoric Germanic base that also produced (via French) English *button* and *buttress*, from an Indo-European base meaning "strike," which also produced English *confute* and *refute*.] ◇ **beat it!** used to tell somebody to go away (*slang*) ◇ **beat somebody to it** *or* **something** to succeed in doing something before somebody else can do it (*informal*) ◇ **it beats me** used to indicate you have no answer (*informal*) ◇ **not miss a beat** to show no sign of surprise or upset

WORD KEY: SYNONYMS

See Synonyms at ***defeat***.

beat down *v.* **1.** *vi.* **COME DOWN STRONGLY** to shine intensely or fall heavily from the sky (*refers to sun or rain*) **2.** *vt.* **PERSUADE SOMEBODY TO SELL FOR LESS** to persuade somebody to charge less than the intended selling price (*informal*)

beat off *v.* **1.** *vt.* **REPEL ATTACK** to stop an attack or challenge by vigorous action **2.** *vi.* **MASTURBATE** to masturbate (*slang taboo*)

beat up *vt.* to injure somebody badly by repeated punches or kicks (*informal*)

beat upon *v.* = **beat up**

beat·box *n.* MUSIC an electronic drum used mainly in hip-hop and rap music to provide accompanying rhythm and sounds (*informal*)

beat·en past participle of **beat**

beat·er /béetər/ *n.* **1.** **TOOL FOR BEATING** a tool for beating something, e.g., a shaped stick for beating the dust out of carpets, or an electric food mixer attachment for beating eggs (*often used in combination*) **2.** HUNT **HUNTER'S ASSISTANT FOR DRIVING BIRDS OUT** somebody who scares game from hiding, usually by hitting trees and bushes with a stick, so that hunters can shoot them **3.** **SOMEBODY WHO BEATS METAL** somebody who beats or hammers metal **4.** **OLD CAR** an old rusty automobile in poor running condition (*informal*)

Beat Gen·er·a·tion *n.* **1.** **YOUTH MOVEMENT IN 1950S AMERICA** young people in the 1950s who rejected the traditional values, customs, and dress of Western society and experimented with Eastern philosophies, communal living, and illegal drugs **2.** **1950S WRITERS** a group of writers associated with the attitudes of the Beat Generation, including Jack Kerouac, Allen Ginsberg, and Laurence Ferlinghetti

be·a·tif·ic /bèe ə tíffik/ *adj.* (*literary*) **1.** **BLISSFUL** expressing or radiating great happiness and serenity **2.** **OF HEAVENLY HAPPINESS** bringing or expressing the perfect happiness and inner peace supposed to be enjoyed by the soul in heaven [Mid-17thC. Directly or via French *béatifique* from Latin *beatificus*, from *beatus* "blessed."] —**be·a·tif·i·cal·ly** *adv.*

be·at·i·fy /bee átti fì/ (**-fied, -fy·ing, -fies**) *vt.* **1.** CHR **DECLARE SOMEBODY TO BE HOLY** in the Roman Catholic Church, to state officially that a dead person lived a holy life, usually as the first step toward sainthood **2.** **MAKE SOMEBODY HAPPY** to make somebody extremely happy (*literary*) [Mid-16thC. Directly or via French *béatifer* from ecclesiastical Latin *beatificare*, from Latin *beatificus* (see BEATIFIC).] —**be·at·i·fi·ca·tion** /bee àttifi káysh'n/ *n.*

beat·ing /béeting/ *n.* **1.** **REPEATED HITTING** an attack or punishment in which somebody is repeatedly hit **2.** **DEFEAT** a severe defeat or setback, e.g., in a competition or in business ◇ **take some beating** to be difficult to improve on because of its excellence ○ *Her speech on the Senate floor will take some beating.*

beat·ing reed *n.* a reed in woodwind instruments that vibrates as air passes over it

be·at·i·tude /bee áttə tood/ *n.* (*literary*) **1.** **HEAVENLY HAPPINESS** the perfect happiness and inner peace supposed to be enjoyed by the soul in heaven **2.** **BLISS** extreme happiness and serenity [15thC. Directly or via French from the Latin stem *beatitud-*, from *beatus* "blessed."]

Be·at·i·tude *n.* **1.** BIBLE **STATEMENT OF THOSE WHO ARE BLESSED** each of the sayings of Jesus Christ in the Sermon on the Mount about the eight groups of people who will receive blessing in heaven (Matthew 5:3–11) **2.** CHR **TITLE OF NON-ORTHODOX BISHOP** a title given to a senior bishop in non-Orthodox churches of the eastern Mediterranean

Beatles

Beat·les /bē'tlz/ (1959–70) British pop music group. This group of musicians from Liverpool, Paul McCartney, John Lennon, George Harrison, and Ringo Starr, revolutionized popular music in the 1960s.

beat·nik /bē'tnik/ *n.* a member of the Beat Generation of the 1950s

Bea·ton /bē't'n/, **Sir Cecil** (1904–80) British photographer and designer. He was a fashion and high-society photographer. He also designed scenery and costumes for *My Fair Lady*, *Gigi*, and other productions. Full name **Sir Cecil Walter Hardy Beaton**

Be·a·trix /báyə triks, bēe ə-/, **Queen of the Netherlands** (*b.* 1938). She acceded to the throne on the abdication of her mother, Queen Juliana, in 1980. Full name **Beatrix Wilhelmina Armgard**

Beat·tie /bēetee/, **Ann** (*b.* 1947) U.S. writer. She is author of the novel *Chilly Scenes of Winter* (1976) and the short-story collection *Where You'll Find Me* (1986).

beat-up *adj.* in bad condition because of overuse (*informal*)

beau /bō/ (*plural* **beaus** *or* **beaux** /bōz/) *n.* **1. BOYFRIEND** a boyfriend or male admirer (*dated*) **2. FASHIONABLY DRESSED MAN** a man always smartly dressed in the most fashionable clothes (*archaic*) [Late 17thC. From French, from *beau* "beautiful," from Latin *bellus* (see BEAUTY).]

beau·coup /bō kōō/ *adj.* very many or very much (*slang*) ○ *His new suit cost beaucoup dollars.* [Early 20thC. From French.]

Beau·fort scale /bṓfərt-/ *n.* an international scale of wind speeds indicated by numbers ranging from 0 for calm to 12 for hurricane. Each force is recognized by its effects on things such as flags and trees and on people and the surface of the sea. [Mid-19thC. Named for Sir Francis *Beaufort* (1774–1857), British admiral who devised the scale.]

Beau·fort Sea section of the Arctic Ocean northwest of Canada and north of Alaska. Area: 170,000 sq. mi./450,000 sq.km. Depth: 15,360 ft./4,682 m.

beau geste /bō zhést/ (*plural* **beaux gestes** /bō zhést/) *n.* a kind or magnanimous act (*literary*) [Early 20thC. From French, literally "fine gesture."]

beau i·de·al /bō ī dēe əl/ *n.* somebody's idea of perfection or beauty, or a perfect example of something (*literary*) [Early 19thC. From French, literally "ideal beauty" (but usually taken as meaning "beautiful ideal").]

Beau·jo·lais /bōzhə láy/ (*plural* **-lais** /bōzhə láy/) *n.* a fruity fairly light red or white wine produced in the Beaujolais district of the Burgundy region in central France

Beau·jo·lais nou·veau *n.* Beaujolais sold from November in the year of its production

beau monde /bō mónd, bō máwnd/ *n.* the part of society made up of the richest and most fashionable people [Late 17thC. From French, literally "beautiful world."]

Beau·mont /bṓ mont/ city and port in southeastern Texas connected to the Gulf of Mexico by the Neches River ship canal. Population: 111,224 (1996).

Beau·re·gard /bō rə gaard/, **P.G.T.** (1818–93) U.S. Confederate general. He led troops from the first engagement at Charleston, South Carolina (1861), throughout the Civil War. Full name **Pierre Gustave Toutant Beauregard**

beaut /byoot/ *n.* ANZ, U.S. a fine or impressive thing (*slang*) [Mid-19thC. Shortening of BEAUTY or BEAUTIFUL.]

beau·te·ous /byōōtee əss/ *adj.* beautiful to look at (*literary*) —**beau·te·ous·ly** *adv.* —**beau·te·ous·ness** *n.*

beau·ti·cian /byoo tísh'n/ *n.* somebody trained to give beauty treatments, e.g., application of makeup and facial treatments

beau·ti·ful /byōōtif'l/ *adj.* **1. PLEASING TO THE SENSES** very pleasing and impressive to listen to, touch, or especially to look at **2. EXCELLENT** very good or enjoyable —**beau·ti·ful·ly** *adv.* —**beau·ti·ful·ness** *n.*

WORD KEY: SYNONYMS

See Synonyms at ***good-looking***.

beau·ti·ful peo·ple *npl.* **1. HIGH SOCIETY** rich fashionable people **2.** in the 1960s, hippies collectively

beau·ti·fy /byōōti fī/ (**-fied, -fy·ing, -fies**) *vt.* to make something pleasing and impressive to look at —**beau·ti·fi·ca·tion** /byootifi káysh'n/ *n.* —**beau·ti·fi·er** /byōōti fīr/ *n.*

beau·ty /byōōtee/ (*plural* **-ties**) *n.* **1. PLEASING AND IMPRESSIVE QUALITIES** the combination of qualities that make something pleasing and impressive to listen to or touch, or especially to look at **2. PLEASING PERSONAL APPEARANCE** personal physical attractiveness, especially with regard to the use of cosmetics and other methods of enhancing it **3. BEAUTIFUL WOMAN** a beautiful woman or girl ○ *her reputation as a great beauty* **4. FINE EXAMPLE** something very good, attractive, or impressive of its kind **5. EXCELLENT ASPECT** an attractive, useful, or satisfying feature ○ *Great fuel economy is one of the beauties of this vehicle.* [13thC. Via Old French *bealte* from the Vulgar Latin stem *bellitat-*, from Latin *bellus* "handsome, fine," from *bonus* "good."]

WORD KEY: CULTURAL NOTE

Sleeping Beauty, a ballet by Russian composer Peter Ilich Tchaikovsky (1889). Based on Charles Perrault's fairy tale *La belle au bois dormant*, it tells the story of Princess Aurora, who is condemned to death by the wicked fairy Carabosse. Her sentence is commuted to a hundred years' sleep, from which she is eventually awakened by the handsome Prince Florimund.

beau·ty·bush /byōōti bōōsh/ *n.* a Chinese shrub of the honeysuckle family, grown for its pink flowers and fruit with hairy knobby skin. Latin name: *Kolkwitzia amabilis*.

beau·ty mark *n.* = **beauty spot** *n.* **2**

beau·ty par·lor *n.* a business where beauty treatments are provided, e.g., hair styling, facials, and manicures

beau·ty quark *n.* = **bottom quark**

beau·ty queen *n.* a woman judged to be the most beautiful of all the candidates in a competition for beautiful women

beau·ty sa·lon *n.* = **beauty parlor**

beau·ty shop *n.* = **beauty parlor**

beau·ty sleep *n.* deep restful sleep, especially before midnight, supposed to preserve youthful good looks (*informal*)

beau·ty spot *n.* **1. POPULAR SCENIC PLACE** a place that people often visit because of its attractive scenery **2. SMALL NATURAL MARK ON FACE** a mole or other small round blemish on somebody's face **3. DOT WORN ON THE FACE** a small black or brown dot of silk or makeup on somebody's face used to emphasize the skin's paleness or hide a blemish. Beauty spots were especially popular among aristocratic women in 18th-century Europe.

Beau·voir /bō vwaar/, **Simone de** (1908–86) French writer. She wrote the feminist classic, *The Second Sex* (1949) and the novel *The Mandarins* (1954). She was the lifelong companion of Jean-Paul Sartre.

AKG London

Simone de Beauvoir

beaux plural of **beau**

Beaver

bea·ver[1] /bēevər/ *n.* **1.** (*plural* **-vers** *or* **-ver**) ZOOL **FURRY FLAT-TAILED WATER ANIMAL** a semiaquatic rodent that lives in North America, Europe, and Asia and has a broad flat tail and webbed hind feet. Beavers are noted for felling trees to build dams and partially submerged dens called lodges. Genus: *Castor*. **2.** INDUST **FUR FROM BEAVER** the valuable fur of the beaver **3.** CLOTHES **MAN'S FUR HAT** a man's hat made of beaver fur, felt, or a fabric imitating beaver fur **4.** TEXTILES **THICK FABRIC** thick woolen or cotton fabric **5. OFFENSIVE TERM** a woman's outer sex organs and pubic hair (*slang taboo*) ■ *vi.* (**-vered, -ver·ing, -vers**) **WORK HARD AND CONTINUOUSLY** to work hard with unflagging energy and attention (*informal*) [Old English *beofor*. Ultimately from an Indo-European word meaning "brown animal."]

bea·ver[2] /bēevər/ *n.* the guard for the lower part of the face on a medieval helmet [15thC. From French *baviere*, originally "child's bib," from *baver* "to slaver."]

bea·ver·board /bēevər bàwrd/ *n.* a thick board made of compressed wood fibers, used to make the ceilings and inner walls of buildings

Bea·ver·ton /bēevərtən/ city in northwestern Oregon. It is a western suburb of Portland. Population: 63,224 (1996).

be·bee·ru /bə bēeroo/ *n.* = **greenheart** [Mid-19thC. Via Spanish *bibirú* from Carib.]

be·bop /bēe bòp/ *n.* fast jazz music with complex harmonies and melodies. Charlie Parker was the most famous exponent of the style. [Mid-20thC. An imitation of either the two-beat phrase of such music or the nonsense syllables of scat singing.] —**be·bop·per** *n.*

be·calm /bi kaam/ (**-calmed, -calm·ing, -calms**) *vt.* **1.** SAILING **STOP A SAILBOAT** to cause a sailing boat or sailing ship to stop moving because of lack of wind (*usually passive*) **2. SOOTHE SOMEBODY** to bring peace and quiet to somebody

be·came past tense of **become**

be·cause /bi káwz, -kúz/ *conj.* for the reason that follows [14thC. From the phrase *by cause* "for the reason (that)," which was modeled on Old French *par chance.*] ◇ **because of** indicating the reason or cause

WORD KEY: USAGE

because, as, for, or **since**? ***As*** and ***since*** are used more often at the beginning of a sentence than ***because***, and tend to be used when the reason is already well known or when the reason is considered not as important as the main statement: *As you're only staying a little while, we'd better eat now. He refrained from comment, since he knew it might annoy his companions.* ***Because*** puts a greater emphasis on the cause: *He liked her because she was witty and lively.* ***Because*** and ***for*** are both used to introduce reasons that justify a statement as distinct from giving a reason for it: *You must have forgotten to invite them, because/for they didn't turn up.* ***For*** is never used at the beginning of a sentence. ***As*** can sometimes be understood to mean "while" as well as "because": *As Luisa went back to work, Tony stayed behind to look after the baby.* In these cases, it is better to avoid ambiguity and use either ***because*** or ***while*** as appropriate.

bec·ca·fi·co /bekə fēekō/ (*plural* **-cos**) *n.* = **Orphean warbler** [Mid-17thC. From Italian, literally "figpecker," from *beccare* "to peck" (from, ultimately, late Latin *beccus* "beak," source of English *beak*) + *fico* "fig."]

bé·cha·mel sauce /bàyshə mel-/ *n.* a sauce made from milk thickened and made rich with butter and flour, flavored with onion, bay, and mace, and served hot with meat or fish [Late 18thC. Named for its inventor, Louis, Marquis de *Béchamel* (1630–1703), steward to Louis XIV of France.]

bêche-de-mer /bèsh də máir/ (*plural* **bêches-de-mer** /bèsh də máir/ *or* **bêche-de-mer**) *n.* ZOOL = **trepang** [Early 19thC. A pseudo-French word based on Portuguese *bicho do mar* (see BEACH-LA-MAR).]

Bech·u·a·na·land /bech waánə lànd/ former name for **Botswana** (until 1966)

beck /bek/ *n.* a nod, wave, or similar gesture to attract attention (*literary*) [14thC. From the obsolete verb *beck* "to beckon, bow," a shortening of BECKON.] ◇ **at somebody's beck and call** always available and ready to carry out somebody's wishes

Beck·er /békər/, **Boris** (*b.* 1967) German tennis player. The youngest ever men's singles champion at Wimbledon (1985), he won again in 1986 and 1989.

beck·et /békət/ *n.* a rope with a knot at one end and a small loop or hook at the other, used for tying down loose equipment on a ship or boat [Mid-18thC. Origin unknown.]

Beck·et /békət/, **Thomas à, St.** (1118?–70) English saint and martyr. He became Archbishop of Canterbury in 1162 and was assassinated by knights of Henry II. In 1155 he became the first Englishman to hold the office of Chancellor since the Norman Conquest. His strong views on religious prerogative brought him into conflict with Henry II.

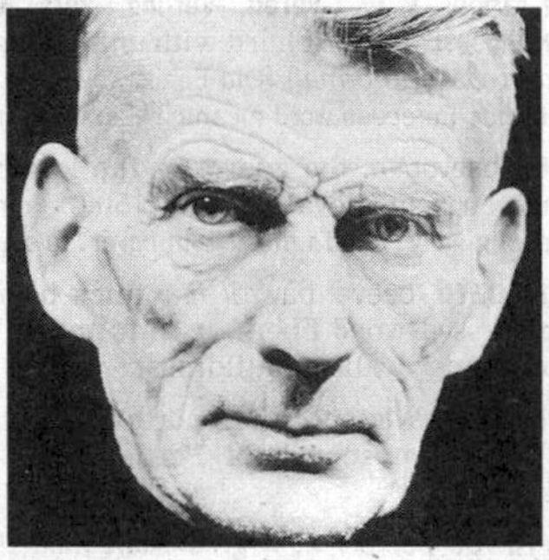

Samuel Beckett

Beck·ett /békit/, **Samuel** (1906–89) Irish writer. His bleak dramas of the absurd include *Waiting for Godot* (1954) and *Not I* (1973). He won a Nobel Prize in literature (1969). Beckett settled in Paris in 1937, and produced novels, plays, and poems in both English and French. Full name **Samuel Barclay Beckett**

beck·on /békən/ (**-oned, -on·ing, -ons**) *vti.* **1.** GESTURE TO SOMEBODY TO COME to signal to somebody to approach with a movement of the hand or head **2.** ATTRACT OR TEMPT to be an attraction or temptation to somebody (*literary*) [Old English *bēcnan*. Ultimately from the same prehistoric Germanic base as *beacon*.] —**beck·on·er** *n.* —**beck·on·ing·ly** *adv.*

be·cloud /bi klówd/ (**-cloud·ed, -cloud·ing, -clouds**) *vt.* (*literary*) **1.** COVER WITH CLOUD to cover or conceal something with cloud or mist **2.** CONFUSE OR OBSCURE to make something confused or difficult to understand

be·come /bi kúm/ (**-came** /-káym/, **-come, -com·ing, -comes**) *v.* **1.** *vi.* COME TO BE SOMETHING to change or develop into something ○ *The caterpillar will soon become a moth.* **2.** *vt.* SUIT to suit the appearance or personality of somebody ○ *That color really becomes you.* **3.** *vt.* BE APPROPRIATE to be an appropriate or socially acceptable thing for somebody to do or say (*formal*) [Old English *becuman*]

become of *vi.* to happen to somebody or something ○ *What will become of us?*

be·com·ing /bi kúmming/ *adj.* **1.** SHOWING SOMEBODY TO ADVANTAGE attractively suitable for somebody's appearance **2.** BEFITTING appropriate or fitting for somebody —**be·com·ing·ly** *adv.* —**be·com·ing·ness** *n.*

bec·que·rel /be krél, békə rèl/ *n.* the SI unit for measuring radioactivity, equal to the activity resulting from the decay of one nucleus of radioactive matter in one second. Symbol **Bq** [Late 19thC. Named for Alexandre Edmond *Becquerel* (1852–1908), French physicist.]

bed /bed/ *n.* **1.** FURNITURE ON WHICH TO SLEEP a piece of furniture on which to sleep, usually consisting of a rectangular frame with a mattress on top **2.** MATTRESS a mattress, especially with its coverings **3.** PLACE FOR SLEEPING a place in which to sleep, or an object on which to sleep ○ *looking for a bed for the night* **4.** ACCOMMODATIONS FOR GUEST OR PATIENT a place for one person to stay or sleep as a guest in a hotel or a patient in a hospital **5.** SLEEP sleep or rest in bed, or the time for this **6.** STATE OF INTIMACY the state of sexual intimacy associated with being in bed with somebody ○ *the marriage bed* **7.** GARDENING PATCH OF SOIL an area of soil prepared for plants, especially flowers, or an area where particular plants are growing ○ *a rose bed* **8.** GEOG GROUND UNDER WATER the ground at the bottom of the sea, a river, or a lake **9.** AREA OF SEA WITH SHELLFISH an area of the sea, a river, or a lake, where a particular kind of shellfish is found or cultivated ○ *oyster beds* **10.** SURFACE ON WHICH TO BUILD a prepared surface on which something is built or laid, e.g., the foundation of a road or a railroad track **11.** COOK LAYER OF FOOD a layer of food on which another item of food is placed for serving **12.** GEOL LAYER OF ROCK a layer of rock, normally sedimentary, that is generally homogeneous and was deposited more or less continuously without erosion ■ *v.* (**bed·ded, bed·ding, beds**) **1.** *vt.* FIX INTO SURROUNDING SURFACE to embed something firmly in a surrounding mass of a substance such as rock or concrete **2.** *vt.* HAVE SEXUAL INTERCOURSE WITH SOMEBODY to have sexual intercourse with somebody (*informal*) **3.** *vti.* FORM LAYER to arrange something, or be arranged, in a layer or stratum [Old English *bedd*, from a prehistoric Germanic word meaning "dig"] ◇ **a bed of nails** an extremely difficult situation or existence ◇ **go to bed with somebody** to have sexual intercourse with somebody ◇ **put something to bed** to finish something, such as a project ◇ **get up on the wrong side of the bed** to be in an irritable or angry mood right from the start of the day

WORD KEY: ORIGIN

Bed meant both "sleeping place" and "garden plot" in Old English, and if the latter is the original sense, it could mean that the word comes ultimately from a prehistoric Germanic ancestor meaning "dig" (which is also the ancestor of English *fossil*), and that the underlying notion of a bed was originally of a sleeping place dug or scraped in the ground, like an animal's lair.

bed down *v.* **1.** *vi.* GO TO BED to settle down somewhere, not usually in a bed, ready for sleep **2.** *vt.* PUT TO BED to put a person to bed or an animal in a place with bedding for the night

bed in *vti.* to settle something firmly into place, or fit firmly into place

bed out *vt.* to put young plants raised indoors into their final growing position outside

B.Ed. *abbr.* Bachelor of Education

bed and board *n.* accommodation and meals provided for somebody

bed and break·fast *n.* **1.** GUESTHOUSE a small hotel or, more often, a private home that offers overnight accommodations and breakfast for paying guests **2.** ROOM AND BREAKFAST overnight accommodations and breakfast provided for paying guests

be·daub /bi dáwb/ (**-daubed, -daub·ing, -daubs**) *vt.* to smear a surface thickly or carelessly with something that spoils it or makes it dirty (*literary*)

be·daz·zle /bi dázz'l/ (**-zled, -zling, -zles**) *vt.* (*literary*) **1.** IMPRESS SOMEBODY GREATLY to astonish somebody by being immediately impressive (*usually passive*) **2.** BLIND WITH LIGHT to make somebody temporarily unable to see by shining a bright light

bed bath *n. U.K.* = **sponge bath**

bed·bug /béd bug/ *n.* a small wingless bloodsucking insect that infests the bedding and furnishings of dirty houses and the nests of mammals. Family: Cimicidae.

bed check *n.* an inspection to see if all the members of a group of people under supervision, e.g., students or soldiers are in bed after lights out

bed·clothes /béd klōthz, -klōz/ *npl.* the sheets, blankets, and any other similar coverings on a bed

bed·da·ble /béddəb'l/ *adj.* considered attractive enough to make a good sexual partner (*informal*)

bed·der /béddər/ *n.* GARDENING = **bedding plant**

bed·ding /bédding/ *n.* **1.** BED COVERINGS the coverings, e.g., sheets, quilts, and blankets, and the mattress and pillows used to prepare a bed **2.** SOMETHING USED AS BED something used to make a bed **3.** BED FOR ANIMALS material such as straw put down for animals to lie on **4.** BUILDING UNDER LAYER a layer of material put down under something else, especially to serve as a foundation **5.** GEOL ARRANGEMENT OF ROCK STRATA the arrangement of a group of rock strata, or beds, in a particular area or outcrop

bed·ding plant *n.* a plant suitable for planting in a flower bed for one season's display

Bede /beed/, **Bae·da** /beédə/, **St.** (673?–735) English theologian and historian. He wrote many grammatical and historical works, including his *Ecclesiastical History of the English People* (completed in 731). Known as **the Venerable Bede**

be·deck /bi dék/ (**-decked, -deck·ing, -decks**) *vt.* to make something look pretty or festive, especially by decorating it with colorful flags, ribbons, or streamers (*literary*)

be·dev·il /bi dévv'l/ (**-iled, -il·ing, -ils**) *vt.* to be a continual source of problems or irritation to something or somebody —**be·dev·il·ment** *n.*

be·dew /bi dōō, -dyōō/ (**-dewed, -dew·ing, -dews**) *vt.* to wet or cover something with dew or drops of liquid (*literary*)

bed·fel·low /béd felō/ *n.* **1.** ASSOCIATE somebody who or something that becomes paired or allied with somebody or something else **2.** SOMEBODY WHO SHARES BED somebody who sleeps in the same bed as somebody else (*archaic*)

Bed·ford /bédfərd/ city in northeastern Texas situated between Fort Worth and Dallas. Population: 49,431 (1996).

Bed·ford cord *n.* a heavy ribbed fabric resembling corduroy

bed·head /béd hed/ *n.* the upper end of a bed, often with a headboard or rail

bed-hop·ping *n.* casual sex with successive partners (*informal*)

be·dim /bi dím/ (**-dimmed, -dim·ming, -dims**) *vt.* (*literary*) **1.** MAKE LESS PERCEPTIVE to make the eyes or mind less able to perceive things clearly **2.** MAKE INDISTINCT to make something appear less bright or distinct

be·di·zen /bi dīz'n, -dizz'n/ (**-zened, -zen·ing, -zens**) *vt.* to dress or decorate somebody or something in a way that seems exaggeratedly or vulgarly conspicuous and showy (*literary*) [Mid-17thC. Formed from earlier *dizen* "to put flax on to a rod."] —**be·di·zen·ment** *n.*

bed jack·et *n.* a woman's short light jacket worn over a nightgown when sitting up in bed

bed·lam /bédləm/ *n.* **1.** CHAOS a place or situation full of noise, frenzied activity, and confusion **2.** PSYCHIATRIC HOSPITAL a psychiatric hospital (*archaic*) [15thC. Alteration of BETHLEHEM.]

bed lin·en *n.* any one or all of the sheets, pillowcases, and other fabric coverings that go on a bed

Bed·ling·ton ter·ri·er /bèdlingtən-/, **Bed·ling·ton** *n.* a dog belonging to a breed of English terriers that have a tapering head and fleecy coat that makes them look similar to lambs [Mid-19thC. Named for the Northern English town of *Bedlington*, where this breed was developed in the early 19thC.]

bed mold·ing *n.* in classical architecture, the lowest section of a cornice, protruding less than the topmost part

Bed·ou·in /béddoo ən, bédwin/ (*plural* **-ins** *or* **-in**), **Bed·u·in** (*plural* **-ins** *or* **-in**) *n.* a nomadic Arab of the desert regions of Arabia and North Africa [15thC. Via Old French *beduin* from, ultimately, Arabic *badw* "desert, nomadic desert people."] —**Bed·ou·in** *adj.*

bed·pan /béd pàn/ *n.* a shallow container into which a sick or frail person can urinate or defecate while lying in bed

bed·plate /béd playt/ *n.* a heavy metal base or platform to which the frame of an engine or machine is attached

bed·post /béd pōst/ *n.* one of the posts at the corners of a bed, especially a four-poster bed

be·drag·gled /bi drágg'ld/ *adj.* wet, dirty, and unkempt, or with hair or clothes in this state

bed·rail /béd rayl/ *n.* a rail at the head, foot, or side of a bed

bed rest *n.* staying in bed to rest and recover when not well

bed·rid·den /béd rìd'n/ *adj.* forced to remain in bed because of illness, weakness, or injury [Old English *bedrida,* literally "bed-rider," hence "somebody who is carried about in a bed"]

bed·rock /béd ròk/ *n.* **1.** GEOL **UNDERLYING ROCK** the solid rock beneath a layer of soil, rock fragments, or gravel **2. UNDERLYING FACTS OR PRINCIPLES** the facts or principles on which something is based **3. LOWEST POINT** the lowest point, especially in a time of hardship or unhappiness

bed·roll /béd rōl/ *n.* a roll of bedding carried by somebody who is hiking or camping

bed·room /béd ròom, -ròom/ *n.* **ROOM FOR SLEEPING** a room that has a bed in it and is used mainly for sleeping ■ *adj.* **FEATURING SEX** involving, depicting, or suggesting sexual activity ○ *a bedroom comedy*

bed·room com·mu·ni·ty *n.* a town or suburb inhabited mainly by people who travel to work in a nearby city

bed·room sub·urb *n.* = **bedroom community**

beds. *abbr.* bedrooms (*used in advertisements*)

bed·side /béd sīd/ *n.* the side of a bed, or the space next to it —**bed·side** *adj.*

bed·side man·ner *n.* a doctor's way of talking to and dealing with patients

bed·sit·ter /béd sìttər/ *n. U.K.* a combined bedroom and living room, especially one that is rented and serves as somebody's residence [*Sitter* formed from SITTING ROOM + -ER]

bed·sore /béd sàwr/ *n.* an ulcer on the skin caused by pressure and friction from bedding when somebody is confined to bed for a long time

bed·spread /béd spred/ *n.* a decorative covering placed on top of bedding

bed·stead /béd sted/ *n.* the structural framework of a bed, excluding the mattress and coverings [*Stead* because it originally denoted the place where the bed stood]

bed·time /béd tīm/ *n.* the time when somebody normally goes to bed

Bed·u·in *n., adj.* = **Bedouin**

bed·warm·er /béd wàwrmər/ *n.* a covered metal container for hot coals, formerly used to warm a bed

bed·wet·ting *n.* accidental urination in bed during sleep (*especially of children*) —**bed·wet·ter** *n.*

Bee (life size ×2)

bee /bee/ *n.* **1. HONEY-MAKING INSECT** a flying insect with a furry body that makes a buzzing sound as it flies. Some species of bees have stingers, and some live in hives and produce honey. Superfamily: Apoidea. ◊ **bumblebee, honeybee 2. GATHERING FOR ACTIVITY AND SOCIALIZING** a gathering at which people combine working together at a particular activity or having a friendly competition with socializing ○ *a sewing bee* ○ *a quilting bee* [Old English *bēo* from a prehistoric Germanic word]

bee balm *n.* a North American plant of the mint family with aromatic leaves and variously colored spikes of flowers. Genus: *Monarda.*

bee·bread /beé bred/ *n.* a yellow-brown pollen stored by bees and mixed with honey as food for their larvae

beech /beech/ *n.* **1.** TREES **DECIDUOUS TREE** a tall tree found in temperate regions that has smooth gray bark, glossy leaves, and nuts enclosed in spiny cases. Genus: *Fagus.* **2.** INDUST **BEECH WOOD** the wood of the beech tree, used especially for furniture [Old English *bēce* from a prehistoric Germanic word]

beech·drops /beéch drops/ *n.* a low-growing, brownish-colored plant of the broomrape family that has white, tube-shaped flowers and lives as a parasite on the roots of beech trees. Latin name: *Epifagus virginiana.* (*takes a singular or plural verb*)

Bee·cher /beéchər/, **Henry Ward** (1813–87) U.S. clergyman and orator. The son of Lyman Beecher, he was a popular revivalist preacher, abolitionist, and supporter of women's suffrage. He was acquitted of an adultery charge after a sensational trial (1874).

Bee·cher, Lyman (1775–63) U.S. Presbyterian clergyman. A popular Presbyterian preacher in New England, he was the first president of Lane Theological Seminary near Cincinnati (1832–50). He was the father of Henry Ward Beecher and Harriet Beecher Stowe.

beech mar·ten *n.* = **stone marten**

beech mast *n.* the fruits and seeds of beech trees

beech·nut /beéch nut/ *n.* the small triangular hard edible fruit of the beech tree

bee-eat·er *n.* a small brightly colored bird found in Europe and Asia that preys on insects. Family: *Meropidae.*

beef /beef/ *n.* **1.** FOOD **MEAT FROM CATTLE** meat from a cow, heifer, bull, or steer **2.** (*plural* **beeves** *or* **beef**) AGRIC **ANIMAL GIVING BEEF** a cow, heifer, bull, or steer being reared for meat **3. STRENGTH** muscular strength or effort (*informal*) **4. COMPLAINT** a complaint (*slang*) ■ *vi.* (**beefed, beef·ing, beefs**) **COMPLAIN** to complain about something (*slang*) [12thC. Via Anglo-Norman *boef* from the stem of Latin *bos* "ox" (source of English *bovine*).]

beef up *vt.* to make something stronger or more effective (*informal*) [From the idea of adding muscle in the same way as fattening up cattle for meat] —**beefed-up** *adj.*

beef·a·lo /beéfə lō/ (*plural* **-lo** *or* **-loes**) *n.* a cross between the North American bison and domestic cattle that is raised for its resistance to disease and its lean meat [Late 20thC. Blend of BEEF and BUFFALO.]

beef bour·gui·gnon /-bòor geen yáwn, -yawn/ *n.* a rich French stew consisting of chunks of beef braised in red wine, with carrots, onions, mushrooms, and sometimes bacon [*Bourguignon* from French, "of Burgundy"]

beef·burg·er /beéf bùrgər/ *n.* = **hamburger**

beef·cake /beéf kayk/ *n.* muscular men or pictures of them, considered from the point of view of their physical appearance (*informal*) [Modeled on CHEESECAKE]

Barnaby's

Beefeater: A Yeoman of the Guard at the Tower of London, with Tower Bridge in the background

beef·eat·er /beéf eètər/ *n.* one of the Yeomen of the Guard of a British monarch, a group who act as warders of the Tower of London wearing a uniform of Tudor dress

bee fly *n.* a fly that resembles a bee, eats pollen and nectar, and whose larvae develop as parasites on insect larvae. Family: Bombyliidae.

beef·steak /beéf stayk/ *n.* a slice of lean, tender beef that can be broiled or fried

beef·steak fun·gus, beef·steak mush·room *n.* an edible bracket fungus with a large reddish cap that grows especially on oak and ash trees. Latin name: *Fistulina hepatica.* [Because its cap resembles a beefsteak]

beef·steak to·ma·to *n.* a large, firm-fleshed tomato [From its color and density]

beef stro·ga·noff /beéf strógə nawf/ *n.* a dish consisting of thin strips of sautéed beef cooked with onions and mushrooms in a sour cream sauce [Named in honor of Count Paul *Stroganoff,* a 19thC Russian diplomat]

beef to·ma·to *n. U.K.* = **beefsteak tomato**

beef Wel·ling·ton *n.* a dish consisting of a fillet of beef, covered in pâté de foie gras, wrapped in pastry, and baked

beef·wood /beéf wòod/ *n.* **1.** INDUST **HARD REDDISH WOOD** a hard red-colored wood used in construction and cabinetmaking **2.** TREES **AUSTRALIAN EVERGREEN TREE** an Australian tree that produces beefwood. Genus: *Casuarina.*

beef·y /beéfee/ (**-i·er, -i·est**) *adj.* **1. MUSCULAR** strong and muscular **2. POWERFUL** having strength, power, or substance (*informal*) ○ *a novel with a really beefy plot* **3. LIKE BEEF** containing, produced by, or resembling beef —**beef·i·ly** *adv.* —**beef·i·ness** *n.*

bee glue *n.* = **propolis**

bee gum *n. Southern U.S., Midwest* a beehive, especially in a hollow tree or log [*gum* because it originally denoted a hive in a gum tree]

bee·hive /beé hīv/ *n.* **1. HIVE FOR BEES** a structure housing a colony of bees **2. TALL HAIRSTYLE** a hairstyle for women, popular around 1960, in which the hair is arranged in a high rounded shape on top of the head ■ *adj.* **BEEHIVE-SHAPED** shaped like a beehive, with a round base rising in a cone to a domed top

Bee·hive /beé hīv/ *n. NZ* the dome-shaped Parliament building in Wellington, New Zealand

bee·hive house *n.* a type of round prehistoric house with a domed roof

bee·keep·er /beé keèpər/ *n.* somebody who keeps bees in hives for the purpose of producing honey or pollinating crops —**bee·keep·ing** *n.*

bee kill·er *n.* = **robber fly**

bee·line /beé līn/ *n.* a very direct line, path, or other course from one point to another [From the belief that bees return to their hives in a straight line]

Be·el·ze·bub /bee élzə bùb/ *n.* the Devil, or one of the chief devils in hell [Pre-12thC. Via Latin from Hebrew *ba'al zĕbūb,* literally "Lord of Flies," a Philistine god.]

been past participle of **be** ◇ **been there, done that (bought the tee shirt)** used to indicate somebody's blasé attitude (*slang*)

bee or·chid *n.* a European orchid with a flower that looks like a bee. Latin name: *Ophrys apiphera.*

beep /beep/ *n.* **SHORT HIGH NOISE** a short high-pitched noise emitted as a signal by a piece of electronic equipment or the horn of a vehicle ■ *v.* **1.** *vti.* **MAKE BEEP** to make a beep, or cause a vehicle horn or other device to make a beep **2.** *vt.* to page somebody using a beeper [Early 20thC. An imitation of the sound.]

beep·er /beépər/ *n.* = **pager** (*informal*)

bee plant *n.* any plant that is particularly attractive to bees

beer /beer/ *n.* **1. DRINK BREWED FROM MALT** a typically bitter-tasting alcoholic drink brewed by fermenting malt with sugar and yeast and flavoring it with hops **2. DRINK OF BEER** a drink or glass of beer **3. HERBAL DRINK** a carbonated or slightly fermented drink made from, or flavored with, the roots, leaves, or seeds of a plant [Old English *bēor.* Ultimately from late Latin *biber* "drink," from *bibere* "to drink" (source of English *imbibe* and *beverage*).]

beer bel·ly *n.* an extended stomach often associated with having drunk too much beer (*slang*)

beer gar·den *n.* an open space or garden, often attached to a tavern, where beer and other alcoholic drinks can be purchased and drunk in the open air

beer gut *n.* = **beer belly** (*slang*)

beer par·lour *n. Can* a bar where beer is served

Beer·she·ba /beer sheébə, bər sheébə/ city on the edge of the Ivegev Desert, southwest of Jerusalem, Israel. In biblical times it was in the extreme southern part of Palestine. Population: 156,500 (1997).

beer·y /beéree/ (**-i·er, -i·est**) *adj.* **1. SLIGHTLY INEBRIATED** typical of somebody who is slightly inebriated from having drunk too much beer **2. LIKE BEER** smelling or tasting of beer —**beer·i·ly** *adv.* —**beer·i·ness** *n.*

bee's knees *npl.* somebody or something considered outstanding and wonderful (*dated informal*) [Modeled on CAT'S WHISKERS]

bee·stings /bée̱stingz/, **bea·stings** *n. U.K.* the first milk secreted by a mammal, especially a cow or goat, after it has given birth [Old English *bȳsting*. Ultimately from a prehistoric Germanic word of unknown origin.]

bee-stung *adj.* full and rounded, as if stung by a bee ○ *bee-stung lips*

bees·wax /béez wàks/ *n.* 1. **WAX MADE BY BEES** the dark yellow substance secreted by honeybees and used for building honeycombs 2. **COMMERCIALLY PROCESSED BEESWAX** wax produced by bees that has been commercially processed for use in furniture polishes, candles, and crayons ■ *vt.* (**-waxed, -wax·ing, -wax·es**) **POLISH WITH BEESWAX** to polish something with beeswax

bees·wing /béez wìng/ *n.* a thin shiny sediment that forms in port and some other wines when they are kept for a long time after bottling

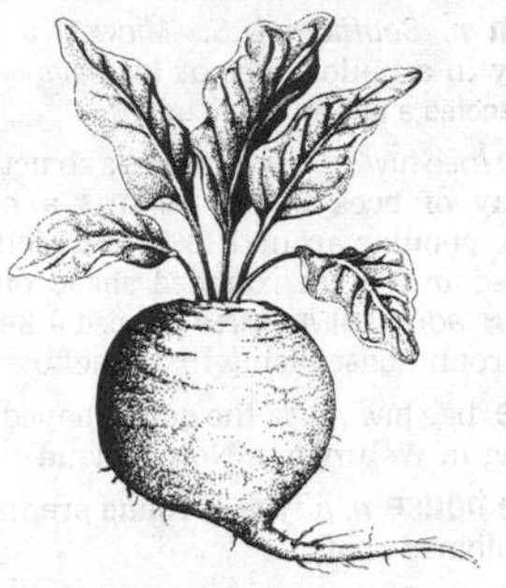

Beet

beet /beet/ *n.* 1. **PLANT WITH SWOLLEN ROOT** a plant with a large swollen root. Some types are eaten cooked, others are fed to animals, and one type yields sugar. Genus: *Beta*. ◊ **spinach beet, sugar beet, mangelwurzel** 2. **ROOT OF BEET PLANT AS VEGETABLE** the red-colored root of a variety of beet plant, eaten as a vegetable (*usually plural*) [Old English *bēte*, related to German *Bete*. Ultimately from Latin *beta*, perhaps of Celtic origin.]

AKG London

Ludwig van Beethoven

Bee·tho·ven /báy tōvən/, **Ludwig van** (1770–1827) German composer. His symphonies and chamber pieces reached new levels of expressivity, inspiring the Romantics. He composed nine symphonies, 32 piano sonatas, and 16 string quartets, among many other works.

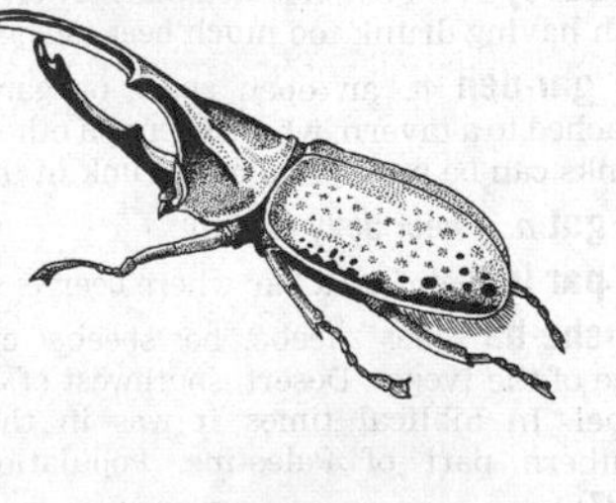

Beetle

bee·tle[1] /béet'l/ *n.* 1. INSECTS **HARD-BACKED INSECT** an insect belonging to a large order characterized by a modified outer pair of wings that forms a hard covering for the inner pair. Order: Coleoptera. 2. **INSECT RESEMBLING A BEETLE** a insect with an appearance similar to a beetle ■ *vi.* (**-tled, -tling, -tles**) *U.K.* **GO QUICKLY** to go somewhere quickly (*informal*) [Old English *bitula, bitela*, from *bītan* "to bite," from its biting mouthparts]

bee·tle[2] /béet'l/ *n.* 1. BUILDING **LARGE MALLET** a large tool with a long handle and a heavy wooden head, used for driving in stakes, ramming, and pounding 2. TEXTILES **TEXTILE-FINISHING MACHINE** a machine that beats cloth to give it a smooth finish ■ *vt.* (**-tled, -tling, -tles**) TEXTILES **FINISH CLOTH** to give a finishing treatment to cloth with a beetle [Old English *bētel, bīetel*. Ultimately from a prehistoric Germanic word.]

bee·tle[3] /béet'l/ *vi.* (**-tled, -tling, -tles**) **OVERHANG** to overhang or jut out (*literary*) ■ *adj.* **JUTTING OUT** jutting out and shaggy (*literary*) ○ *beetle brows* [14thC. Of unknown origin: perhaps from the resemblance of a beetle's antennae to eyebrows.] —**bee·tling** *adj.*

bee·tle-browed *adj.* having eyebrows that are thick and bushy, or that jut out over the eyes

bee·tle·weed /béet'l wèed/ *n.* = **galax**

bee tree *n.* any tree that seems particularly attractive to bees

beet·root /béetròot/ *n. U.K.* 1. = **beet** *n.* 2 2. = **beet**

beet sug·ar *n.* sugar that has been extracted from sugar beets

beeves plural of **beef** *n.* 2

be·fall /bi fáwl/ (**-fell** /bi fél/, **-fall·en** /bi fáwlən/, **-fall·ing, -falls**) *vti.* to happen, or happen to somebody, especially through the unexpected workings of chance or fate (*archaic or literary*)

be·fit /bi fít/ (**-fit·ted, -fit·ting, -fits**) *vt.* to be suitable or appropriate for somebody or something —**be·fit·ting** *adj.* —**be·fit·ting·ly** *adv.*

be·fog /bi fóg/ (**-fogged, -fog·ging, -fogs**) *vt.* (*literary*) 1. **CONFUSE** to make somebody or something vague or confused 2. **COVER WITH FOG** to make something difficult to see or see through because it is covered with fog

be·fore /bi fáwr/ CORE MEANING: a grammatical word indicating that a point in time, event, or situation precedes another in a sequence ○ (prep) *We try all of the products before deciding to stock them.* ○ (conj) *We lost a lot of manufacturing jobs in the 12 years before I became president.* ○ (conj) *She died at the hospital before her parents could reach her side.* ○ (adv) *They had left the subway terminal perhaps twenty minutes before.* ○ (adv) *He has had this nightmare before.*

1. *prep.* **IN THE PRESENCE OF** in the presence of a person or body of people ○ *spoke before a huge crowd* 2. *prep.* **WITH MORE IMPORTANCE THAN** indicating that one thing is preferable to or more important than another ○ *Their needs come before yours.* 3. *prep.* **INDICATES LOCATION** located close to something but just ahead of it 4. *prep.* **AHEAD OF** stretching ahead of somebody 5. *prep., conj., adv.* **EARLIER** earlier than a particular date, time, or event 6. *prep., conj.* **INDICATES SEQUENCE** used to indicate a sequence of actions, one preceding the other and closely connected with it 7. *adv.* **PREVIOUSLY** on a previous occasion 8. *conj.* **RATHER THAN** used to indicate that somebody would prefer to do one thing rather than what they consider to be a worse thing ○ *I'll die before I tell you anything about it.* [Old English *beforan*. Ultimately from a prehistoric Germanic word that is also the ancestor of English *for*, which originally meant "before."]

be·fore·hand /bi fáwr hànd/ *adv.* used to indicate that a situation, action, or event happens ahead of time or in advance of something

be·fore·men·tioned /bi fáwr mènsh'nd/ *adj.* that has been mentioned before (*formal*)

be·foul /bi fówl/ (**-fouled, -foul·ing, -fouls**) *vt.* to make something dirty or impure, or diminish somebody or something's moral purity or reputation (*archaic or literary*) —**be·foul·ment** *n.*

be·friend /bi frénd/ (**-friend·ed, -friend·ing, -friends**) *vt.* to be friendly to somebody, especially to somebody who has no friends and needs help —**be·friend·er** *n.*

be·fud·dle /bi fúdd'l/ (**-dled, -dling, -dles**) *vt.* 1. **CONFUSE** to make somebody confused or perplexed 2. **TO INEBRIATE** to make somebody inebriated and unable to think clearly —**be·fud·dled** *adj.* —**be·fud·dle·ment** *n.*

beg /beg/ (**begged, beg·ging, begs**) *v.* 1. *vti.* **ASK WITH EMOTION** to ask somebody for something in a very intense, humble, or even humiliating way 2. *vti.* **ASK FOR CHARITY** to ask people for gifts of money or food, especially in the street 3. *vi.* **SIT UP AND ASK FOR FOOD** to ask for food by performing an action that has been previously taught, especially, for a dog, by sitting up and holding out the front legs 4. *vt.* **EVADE** to avoid answering or dealing with a point, especially by assuming that it has already been dealt with ○ *beg the question* [Probably from Old English *bedecian*, ultimately from a prehistoric Germanic base that is also the ancestor of English *bid*]

WORD KEY: USAGE

Begging the question To ***beg the question*** is often used to mean "to raise the question" or "to avoid a direct answer," since both meanings are consistent with the form of the idiom. The basic meaning of this idiom relates to the validity of a proposition that is used as a basis of argument. For example, in an argument about the effect on the environment of gas emissions from road traffic, the proposition that a higher tax on vehicles would contribute to cleaner air begs the question, because it needs to be proved that raising taxes would result in fewer road users. The fallacy implied by the notion of begging the question usually involves the omission of one stage in an argument, or a questionable assumption of its validity.

beg off *vi.* to ask to be excused from doing something

be·gad /bi gád/ *interj.* used to add emphasis to something that is said (*archaic*) [Late 16thC. Alteration of "by God" to avoid offense.]

be·gan past tense of **begin**

be·get /bi gét/ (**-got, -got·ten** /-gótt'n/ *or* **-got** /-gót/, **-get·ting, -gets**) *vt.* 1. **FATHER** to be the father of a child (*archaic*) 2. **CAUSE** to be the cause of something [Old English *begietan* "to get"] —**be·get·ter** *n.*

beg·gar /béggər/ *n.* 1. **SOMEBODY WHO BEGS** somebody who begs for money or food from strangers 2. **VERY POOR PERSON** somebody who is very poor ■ *vt.* (**-gared, -gar·ing, -gars**) 1. **MAKE POOR** to make somebody poor (*literary*) 2. **BE BEYOND SCOPE OF** to be so extraordinary as to make description or belief impossible

beg·gar·ly /béggərlee/ *adj.* insufficient and showing stinginess —**beg·gar·li·ness** *n.*

beg·gar's lice, beg·gar ticks (*plural* **beg·gar ticks**) *n.* 1. **PLANT WITH STICKY BURS** a plant that has burs that stick to clothes and fur. Genus: *Bidens*. (*takes a singular or plural verb*) 2. the burs of a beggar's lice plant

beg·gar·y /béggəree/ *n.* a state of extreme poverty

beg·ging bowl *n.* a bowl carried by somebody who begs to collect gifts of food or money

be·gin /bi gín/ (**-gan** /-gán/, **-gun** /-gún/, **-gin·ning, -gins**) *v.* 1. *vti.* **START** to do something that was not being done before ○ *People began to leave.* 2. *vti.* **HAVE AS ITS STARTING POINT** to have as its starting point, first action, or first part, or be the starting point or first part of something ○ *The story begins with a birthday party.* 3. *vti.* **COME OR BRING INTO BEING** to come into existence, or cause something to come into existence or take place ○ *The business began as a two-person operation.* 4. *vt.* **UNDERTAKE FOR FIRST TIME** to undertake, use, or give attention to something for the first time 5. *vti.* **START TO SPEAK** to start to say something, or start by saying something 6. *vt.* **BE CAPABLE OF** to be able to succeed in accomplishing a particular task (*used in negative statements*) ○ *The salary doesn't even begin to meet her expectations* ○ *I couldn't begin to explain how awful it was* [Old English *beginnan*. Ultimately from a prehistoric Germanic word that is also the ancestor of German and Dutch *beginnen*.]

Be·gin /báygin/, **Menachem** (1913–92) Russian-born Israeli statesman. As prime minister of Israel (1977–83), he shared the 1978 Nobel Peace Prize with Egyptian president Anwar al-Sadat and signed the first-ever Israeli treaty with an Arab state (1979). Full name **Menachem Wolfovitch Begin**

be·gin·ner /bi gínnər/ *n.* somebody who has just started to do or learn something

WORD KEY: SYNONYMS

beginner, apprentice, greenhorn, novice, trainee, tyro

CORE MEANING: a person who has not acquired the necessary experience or skills to do something

beginner the most general term and one of the most informal, without the negative connotations of some of the other terms; **apprentice** a somewhat technical term, usually without negative connotations, indicating somebody who is being taught the skills of a trade by somebody fully trained; **greenhorn** a derogatory term used to emphasize the lack of experience and gullibility of somebody who has just started something; **novice** a derogatory term that emphasizes the general ineptness of somebody who has just started something; **trainee** a more general term than "apprentice" but one that also suggests that somebody has started on a training program of some kind to learn the skills of a job; **tyro** a more derogatory word than "beginner," used to emphasize the rawness and inexperience of somebody.

---

be·gin·ner's luck *n.* early success that seems inconsistent with somebody's lack of experience

be·gin·ning /bi gínning/ *n.* **1. FIRST PART** the first part or early stages of something **2. START** the point in time or space at which something starts, comes into existence, or is first encountered ■ **be·gin·nings** *npl.* **EARLY CONDITIONS** the conditions in which something or somebody starts

be·gone /bi gáwn, be gón/ *interj.* used to tell somebody to go away (*archaic*)

be·go·nia /bi gṓnyə/ *n.* a widely grown houseplant and garden plant that has round brightly colored flowers and ragged-edged leaves. Genus: *Begonia.* [Mid-18thC. From Modern Latin, named for Michel *Bégon*, (1638–1710), Governor of French Canada and patron of botany.]

be·gor·ra /bi gáwrə, -górə/ *interj. Ireland* used as an exclamation or a mild oath (*archaic*) [Mid-19thC. Alteration of "by God" to avoid offense.]

be·got past tense, past participle of **beget**

be·got·ten past participle of **beget**

be·grime /bi grī́m/ (**-grimed, -grim·ing, -grimes**) *vt.* to cover something with grime (*literary*)

be·grudge /bi grúj/ (**-grudged, -grudg·ing, -grudg·es**) *vt.* **1. RESENT SOMETHING SOMEBODY HAS** to resent the fact that somebody has something ○ *begrudged me my success* **2. NOT WANT TO GIVE** to be unwilling to give or pay something

be·grudg·ing /bi grújjing/ *adj.* showing unwillingness to give somebody something or to let somebody be admired or praised —**be·grudg·ing·ly** *adv.*

be·guile /bi gī́l/ (**-guiled, -guil·ing, -guiles**) *vt.* **1. CHARM** to win and hold somebody's attention, interest, or devotion **2. DECEIVE** to mislead or deceive somebody (*literary*) **3. CHEAT** to rob somebody of something (*literary*) **4. PASS** to pass time in a pleasant way (*literary*) [13thC. *guile* in the obsolete sense "to trick."] —**be·guile·ment** *n.* —**be·guil·er** *n.*

be·guil·ing /bi gī́ling/ *adj.* having the power to gain people's interest or devotion —**be·guil·ing·ly** *adv.*

be·guine /bi geén/ *n.* a ballroom dance similar to the rumba, originating in the West Indies [Early 20thC. Via French *béguine* from *béguin* "flirtation," originally "hood," from *beguine* "lay sister in the Netherlands," from, ultimately, Middle Dutch *beggaert*, literally "somebody who rattles off prayers."]

be·gum /báygəm, beé-/ *n.* **1. WOMAN'S TITLE** a title of respect for a woman in some Islamic communities **2. IMPORTANT WOMAN** a woman of high rank in some Islamic communities [Mid-17thC. Via Urdu from East Turkic, literally "my mistress."]

be·gun past participle of **begin**

be·have /bi háyv/ (**-haved, -hav·ing, -haves**) *vi.* **1. ACT** to act in a particular way that expresses general character, state of mind, or response to a situation or other people ○ *He's been behaving oddly.* **2. BEHAVE WELL** to act in an acceptable way, especially by being polite, good-tempered, and self-controlled **3. PERFORM** to perform in or react to particular conditions, or operate in accordance with natural laws [15thC. Formed from HAVE in the obsolete sense "to hold, comport."]

be·hav·ior /bi háyvyər/ *n.* **1. THE WAY SOMEBODY BEHAVES** the way in which somebody behaves **2.** PSYCHOL **RESPONSE** the way in which a person, organism, or group responds to a certain set of conditions **3. WHAT SOMETHING DOES** the way that a machine operates or a substance reacts under a certain set of conditions [15thC. Modeled on earlier *haviour* "possession," from, ultimately, Old French *aveir* "to have."] —**be·hav·ior·al** *adj.* —**be·hav·ior·al·ly** *adv.*

be·hav·ior·al con·ta·gion *n.* the spread of a type of behavior first exhibited by a few people in a group to the group as a whole

be·hav·ior·al med·i·cine *n.* = **behavior medicine**

be·hav·ior·al psy·chol·o·gy *n.* a branch of psychology based on the observation and modification of the way that people behave

be·hav·ior·al sci·ence *n.* **1. SCIENCE STUDYING BEHAVIOR** a science such as sociology, psychology, or anthropology that is concerned with the ways in which people or animals behave **2. STUDY OF BEHAVIOR** the use of scientific methods to study the behavior of living creatures —**be·hav·ior·al sci·en·tist** *n.*

be·hav·ior·al ther·a·py *n.* = **behavior therapy**

be·hav·ior·ism /bi háyvyərìz'm, bə-/ *n.* **1.** PSYCHOL **NON-ANALYTICAL PSYCHOLOGY** an approach to the study of psychology that concentrates exclusively on observing, measuring, and modifying behavior **2.** PHILOS **MATERIALIST PHILOSOPHICAL THEORY** the theory that statements about the mind and mental states are really about actual or potential behavior —**be·hav·ior·ist** *adj., n.* —**be·hav·ior·is·tic** /-rístik/ *adj.*

be·hav·ior med·i·cine, be·hav·ior·al med·i·cine *n.* the use of behavior modification to treat or prevent medical or psychological conditions

be·hav·ior mod·i·fi·ca·tion *n.* psychological treatment that attempts to change somebody's behavior by rewarding new and desirable responses and making accustomed undesirable ones less attractive

be·hav·ior ther·a·py *n.* a form of psychotherapy, the goal of which is observable changes in problem behaviors rather than changes in mental state

be·hav·iour *n.* U.K. = **behavior**

be·head /bi héd/ (**-head·ed, -head·ing, -heads**) *vt.* to cut the head off somebody or something, especially as a form of execution

be·held past tense, past participle of **behold**

be·he·moth /bi heé məth, beé əməth/ *n.* **1. be·he·moth, Be·he·moth** BIBLE **HUGE ANIMAL** a huge beast referred to in the Bible, usually thought to be a hippopotamus (Job 40:15) **2. SOMETHING HUGE** something that is enormously big or powerful [14thC. From Hebrew *bĕhēmōṯ*, from *bĕhēmāh* "beast."]

be·hest /bi hést, bə-/ *n.* an order or request (*formal*) ○ *arrived at the conference only at her behest* [Alteration of Old English *behǣs*. Ultimately from a prehistoric Germanic base meaning "to bid, call."]

be·hind /bi hī́nd, bə-/ CORE MEANING: a grammatical word indicating that somebody or something is in or is going toward a position at the back or rear of something ○ (prep) *From behind the door we heard country music.* ○ (prep) *She was behind the wheel, and I was in the back*. ○ (adv) *their car was hit from behind* ○ (adv) *She had to go back because she'd left her money behind.*

1. *prep., adv.* **AT THE BACK OF** in or toward a position further back or at the rear of something **2.** *prep., adv.* **FOLLOWING** following somebody or something **3.** *adv.* **IN DEBT** in debt or in arrears on a payment ○ *months behind on the payments* **4.** *adv.* **REMAINING** used to indicate that somebody or something is left after another's departure **5.** *prep.* **IN THE PAST** indicates that an achievement or experience happened in the past ○ *My best days are behind me.* **6.** *prep.* **LATE** indicates that something is not as far advanced as it should be ○ *seven weeks behind schedule* **7.** *prep.* **CAUSING SOMETHING** causing or being responsible for something ○ *the reason behind it* **8.** *prep.* **SUPPORTING SOMEBODY** backing or supporting somebody ○ *I'm behind you all the way on this issue.* **9.** *prep.* **UNDERNEATH** underneath the external appearance of somebody or something ○ *Behind his calm exterior, he was very confused* **10.** *n.* **BUTTOCKS** somebody's buttocks (*informal*) [Old English *behindan*, literally "by from behind," from *hindan* "from behind," of prehistoric Germanic origin]

be·hind·hand /bi hī́nd hànd, bə-/ *adj.* **1. BEHIND SCHEDULE** behind schedule **2. LAGGING BEHIND** behind in development or achievement **3.** FIN **IN ARREARS** in arrears for payment of a debt [Mid-16thC. Modeled on BEFOREHAND.]

be·hind-the-scenes *adj.* carried out privately or secretly ○ *a lot of frantic behind-the-scenes negotiation*

be·hold /bi hṓld, bə-/ (**-held** /bi héld/, **-held, -hold·ing, -holds**) *v.* **1.** *vt.* **SEE** to see something or somebody (*archaic or literary*) **2.** *vi.* **TAKE NOTE** used to tell somebody to look at something or listen to something, especially something amazing or unexpected (*used as a command*) ○ *Behold the fellow who didn't listen to his lawyer; he's now in jail.* [Old English *bihaldan*. Ultimately from a prehistoric Germanic word meaning "to watch, guard."] —**be·hold·er** *n.*

be·hold·en /bi hṓld'n, bə-/ *adj.* under an obligation to somebody because of something helpful that person has done [14thC. Originally the past participle of BEHOLD, in the obsolete sense "to hold under obligation."]

be·hoove /bi hoóv, bə-/ (**-hooved, -hoov·ing, -hooves**) *vt.* to be right and proper or appropriate for somebody (*formal*) ○ *It ill behooves him to complain.* [Old English *behōfian* "to need"]

be·hove /bi hṓv/ (**-hoved, -hov·ing, -hoves**) *vt.* U.K. = **behoove**

Behr·man /báirmən/, **S. N.** (1893–1973) U.S. playwright. His 21 Broadway plays include sophisticated, witty comedies of manners such as *No Time for Comedy* (1939). Full name **Samuel Nathaniel Behrman**

Bei·der·becke /bī́dər bèk/, **Bix** (1903–31) U.S. musician. He was one of the major jazz musicians of his generation. Real name **Leon Bismarke Beiderbecke**

beige /bayzh/ *adj.* COLORS **VERY PALE BROWN** of a very pale brown color with a tinge of yellow or pink ■ *n.* **1.** COLORS **PALE BROWN** a very pale brown hue with a tinge of yellow or pink **2.** TEXTILES **UNDYED WOOLEN CLOTH** cloth made of wool that has not been dyed or bleached [Mid-19thC. Via French, perhaps from, ultimately, late Latin *bombax* "cotton" (source of English *bombastic*).]

bei·gnet /ben yáy/ *n.* **1. FRITTER** a small piece of seafood, covered in batter and then deep-fat fried **2.** *Southern U.S.* **SQUARE HOLELESS DOUGHNUT** in southern Louisiana, a square doughnut that has no hole in its center [Mid-19thC. From French, from *beigne* "a bump caused by a blow," from its shape.]

Bei·jing /bay jíng/, **Pe·king** /peè kíng, pày-/ national capital of China as well as a cultural, administrative, and educational center. It is situated in the northeastern part of the country, northwest of Bo Hai gulf. Population: 7,000,000 (1991).

be·ing /beé ing/ *n.* **1. EXISTENCE** the state of existing **2. ESSENTIAL NATURE** somebody's essential nature or character **3. LIVING THING** a living thing, especially one conceived of as supernatural or not living on earth **4. PERSON** a human individual

Bei·rut /bay róot/ capital, port, and largest city in Lebanon, situated on the Mediterranean Sea. Population: 1,500,000 (1998).

Bé·jart /bay zhaár/, **Maurice** (*b.* 1928) French dancer and choreographer. He founded the Ballet of the 20th Century and was known for his expressionist fusion of modern dance, ballet, and acrobatics. Real name **Maurice Jean de Berger**

be·je·sus /bi jeézəss, -jáy-/ *n. Ireland* used to emphasize a statement or question (*slang*) [Early 20thC. Alteration of "by Jesus" to avoid offense.]

be·jew·el /bi jóo əl, bə-/ (**-eled, -el·ing, -els**) *vt.* to decorate something lavishly with jewels or colorful decorative objects (*literary*)

Be·kaa Val·ley /bə kaá/, **Be·káa Val·ley** valley in Lebanon, east of Beirut, running down the center of the country between the Lebanon and Anti-Lebanon Mountains. Length: 75 mi./120 km.

bel /bel/ *n.* a logarithmic unit for comparing the loudness or strength of signals, equal to an intensity ratio of 10 to 1 [Early 20thC. Named for the Scottish-born scientist Alexander Graham *Bell* (1847–1922), the inventor of the telephone.]

be·la·bor /bi láybər/ (**-bored, -bor·ing, -bors**) *vt.* **1. HARP ON** to repeat something unnecessarily, or discuss it at too great a length or in too much detail **2. CRITICIZE** to subject somebody to a sustained verbal or literary attack (*literary*) **3. BEAT** to hit somebody hard and repeatedly with something (*literary or humorous*)

be·la·bour (**-boured, -bour·ing, -bours**) *vt.* U.K. = **belabor**

Be·la·rus /béllə rooss/ republic in eastern Europe. It

Belarus

became an independent nation after the dissolution of the former Soviet Union in 1991. Language: Belarusian, Russian. Currency: Belarusian ruble. Capital: Minsk. Population: 10,412,219 (1997). Area: 80,153 sq. mi./207,595 sq. km. Official name **Republic of Belarus**

Be·la·ru·sian /bèllə rúsh'n/ *n.* **1.** PEOPLES **SOMEBODY FROM BELARUS** somebody who was born or raised in Belarus, or who is a citizen of Belarus **2.** LANG **SLAVIC LANGUAGE** the official language of the Republic of Belarus, belonging to the East Slavic group of Indo-European languages. Belarusian is spoken by about 11 million people. —**Be·la·ru·sian** *adj.*

Be·las·co /bə láskō/, **David** (1859–1931) U.S. producer and playwright. The naturalistic productions he staged at his New York City theater greatly influenced the American stage.

be·lat·ed /bi láytid, bə-/ *adj.* occurring after the appropriate or expected time, especially too late to be effective or useful [Early 17thC. Formed from earlier *belate* "to make late, delay."] —**be·lat·ed·ly** *adv.* —**be·lat·ed·ness** *n.*

Be·lau = **Palau**

Be·laún·de Ter·ry /bèlaa oon day térree/, **Fernando** (*b.* 1912) Peruvian statesman. He was president of Peru (1963–68, 1980–85).

be·lay /bi láy, bə-/ *vti.* (**-layed, -lay·ing, -lays**) **1.** NAUT **FASTEN LINE ON SHIP** to fasten a rope or line to a securing point on a ship or boat **2.** CLIMBING **SECURE ROPE** to fasten or control the rope to which a climber is attached by wrapping it around a metal device or another person **3.** NAUT **STOP** to tell somebody to stop doing something or to cancel an earlier instruction (*used as a command*) ■ *n.* CLIMBING **1. SECURING OF CLIMBER'S ROPE** the fastening or controlling of a climber's rope by wrapping it around a metal device or another person, or the method by which this is done **2. FASTENING POINT** the point to which a climber's rope is fastened [Old English *belecgan* "to surround." Ultimately from a prehistoric Germanic word that is also the ancestor of Dutch *beleggen*. Reintroduced from Dutch in the 16thC in nautical senses.]

be·lay·ing pin /bi láying-/ *n.* a large wooden or metal pin that fits into a hole in a rail on a ship or boat and to which a rope can be fastened

bel can·to /bel kaántō/ *n.* **1. STYLE OF SINGING** a style of operatic singing that concentrates on producing a pure and even tone. It was developed in Italy in the 17th and 18th centuries. **2. INSTRUMENTAL STYLE** a style of expressive melodic instrumental playing that uses the principles of bel canto singing [Late 19thC. From Italian, literally "fine song."]

belch /belch/ *vti.* (**belched, belch·ing, belch·es**) **1. RELEASE GAS FROM MOUTH NOISILY** to let gas from the stomach out through the mouth, making a loud noise in the throat **2. SEND OR COME OUT VISIBLY** to send out large amounts of steam, smoke, or gas, or come out of something in a thick cloud ■ *n.* **BURPING** an act or the noise of burping [Old English *bealcettan, bælcan*. Perhaps ultimately from a prehistoric Germanic word that is also the ancestor of German *bölken* "to bleat, belch."]

be·lea·guer /bi léegər, bə-/ (**-guered, -guer·ing, -guers**) *vt.* (*usually passive*) **1. ANNOY** to make somebody feel harassed, hemmed in, or under severe pressure **2. BESIEGE** to surround somebody or something with an army [Late 16thC. From Dutch *belegeren*, literally "to camp around," hence "to besiege."] —**be·lea·guer·ment** *n.*

Be·lém /bə lém/ port and capital of Pará State on the Pará River in northern Brazil. Population: 1,244,690 (1992).

bel·em·nite /bélləm nìt/ *n.* any of the fossilized cylinder-shaped internal shells of an extinct order of cephalopods that were common in the Mesozoic era [Early 17thC. From Modern Latin, from Greek *belemon* "a dart," from its shape.]

bel es·prit /bèl es prée, -əs-/ (*plural* **beaux es·prits** /bōz-/) *n.* a witty, intelligent, and cultured person [Mid-17thC. From French, literally "fine mind."]

Bel·fast /bél fàst, bel fást/ port and capital of Northern Ireland, located at the head of Belfast Lough on the Lagan River. Population: 296,700 (1995).

bel·fry /bélfree/ (*plural* **-fries**) *n.* **1. SPACE FOR BELLS** the part of a church steeple or a tower in which bells are hung **2. BELL TOWER** a tower on a building, in which a bell or bells are hung [13thC. By folk etymology from Old French *berfrei* "movable siege tower" (from

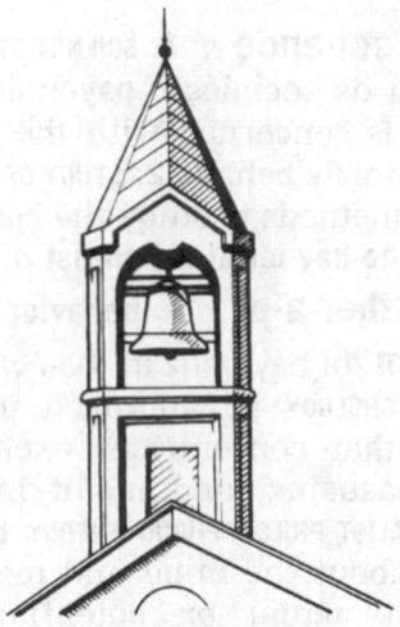

Belfry

assumed Frankish, literally "to protect peace"), by association with BELL.] —**bel·fried** *adj.*

Bel·gae /bél gì, bél jee/ *n.* an ancient Celtic people who lived in northern Gaul and parts of southern England

Bel·gian /bélj'n/ *n.* **SOMEBODY FROM BELGIUM** somebody who was born or raised in Belgium, or who is a citizen of Belgium ■ *adj.* **1. OF BELGIUM** relating to or typical of Belgium, or its people or culture **2. OF FLEMISH OR WALLOON** relating to the Flemish or Walloon French languages

Bel·gian hare *n.* a breed of slender reddish brown domestic rabbit with long legs and ears, or any member of the breed

Bel·gian Ma·li·nois /-màlənwaá/ (*plural* **Bel·gian Ma·li·noises**) *n.* a sturdy dog with a short dense coat and black mask, belonging to a breed used for herding animals that is related to the Belgian sheepdog

Bel·gian sheep·dog *n.* a dog with a long black coat, bred in Belgium for herding sheep

Bel·gian Ter·vu·ren /ter vyŏŏrən, tər-/ *n.* a sturdy dog with a long brown coat with black tips belonging to a breed related to the Belgian sheepdog [Mid-20thC. *Tervuren* from the name of a commune in Belgium.]

Belgium

Bel·gium /béljəm/ kingdom in northwestern Europe that became independent in 1830. Language: Flemish, French, German. Currency: Belgian franc. Capital: Brussels. Population: 10,165,059 (1997). Area: 11,787 sq. mi./30,528 sq. km. Official name **Kingdom of Belgium**

Bel·grade /bél grayd/ capital of Yugoslavia and the Republic of Serbia that forms part of Yugoslavia. It is situated at the junction of the Danube and Sava rivers. Population: 1,136,786 (1991).

Bel·gra·no /bel graánō/, **Manuel** (1770–1820) Argentine general and statesman. He led Argentine troops in revolt against Spanish rule, winning major battles (1812 and 1813) and was later a diplomat.

Be·li·al /béelee əl/ *n.* a personification of evil or worthlessness, mentioned in the Bible and often thought of as a devil or demon [13thC. From Hebrew *bĕliyya'al* "worthlessness."]

be·lie /bi lí, bə-/ (**-lied, -ly·ing, -lies**) *vt.* **1. GIVE FALSE IMPRESSION** to disguise the true nature of something **2. SHOW TO BE FALSE** to show that something is not true or real ○ *The evidence belies the testimony of the witness* [Old English *belēogan*. Ultimately from a prehistoric Germanic word that is also the ancestor of German *belügen*.]

be·lief /bi léef/ *n.* **1. ACCEPTANCE OF TRUTH OF SOMETHING** acceptance by the mind that something is true or real, often underpinned by an emotional or spiritual sense of certainty ○ *belief in an afterlife* **2. TRUST** confidence that somebody or something is good or will be effective ○ *belief in democracy* **3. SOMETHING THAT SOMEBODY BELIEVES IN** a statement, principle, or doctrine that a person or group accepts as true **4. OPINION** an opinion, especially a firm and considered one **5.** RELIG **RELIGIOUS FAITH** religious faith [12thC. Alteration of Old English *gelēafa* on the model of BELIEVE.]

be·lief sys·tem *n.* **1. SET OF BELIEFS** a set of beliefs, e.g., in religion or politics, that form a unified system **2. ORGANIZED SOCIETAL BELIEFS** a collection and organization of beliefs prevalent in a community or society

be·liev·a·ble /bi léevəb'l, bə-/ *adj.* seeming to be true or authentic, and capable of being believed or believed in —**be·liev·a·bil·i·ty** /bi léevə bíllətee, bə-/ *n.* —**be·liev·a·bly** *adv.*

be·lieve /bi léev/ (**-lieved, -liev·ing, -lieves**) *v.* **1.** *vt.* **ACCEPT AS TRUE** to accept that something is true or real ○ *I don't know which story to believe.* **2.** *vt.* **ACCEPT AS TRUTHFUL** to accept that somebody is telling the truth ○ *Nobody will believe you!* **3.** *vt.* **CREDIT WITH SOMETHING** to accept that somebody or something has a particular quality or ability ○ *No one believed her capable of such a malicious remark.* **4.** *vi.* **THINK THAT SOMETHING EXISTS** to be of the opinion that something exists or is a reality, especially when there is no absolute proof of its existence or reality ○ *believe in reincarnation* **5.** *vi.* **TRUST** to be confident that somebody or something is good, or will be effective ○ *We all believe in you.* **6.** *vi.* **THINK SOMETHING IS GOOD** to be of the opinion that something is right or beneficial, and, usually, to act in accordance with that belief ○ *believe strongly in freedom of expression* **7.** *vi.* RELIG **HAVE RELIGIOUS FAITH** to have a religious belief [Old English *belyfan*, an alteration of earlier *gelēfan*. Ultimately from a prehistoric Germanic word meaning "to love, trust."]

be·liev·er /bi léevər/ *n.* **1. SOMEBODY WITH RELIGIOUS FAITH** somebody who believes in God and in the teachings of a particular religious faith **2. SUPPORTER OF AN IDEA** somebody who holds a belief and usually acts in accordance with it ○ *a great believer in discipline*

be·like /bi lík, bə-/ *adv.* probably (*archaic*) [Mid-16thC. From an earlier form of BY + LIKE.]

Bel·in·da /bə líndə/ *n.* a small natural satellite of Uranus, discovered in 1986 by the Voyager 2 planetary probe

be·lit·tle /bi lítt'l, bə-/ (**-tled, -tling, -tles**) *vt.* to make something seem less good or important than it is —**be·lit·tle·ment** *n.* —**be·lit·tler** *n.*

Be·li·veau /bélli vō/, **Jean** (*b.* 1931) Canadian hockey player. A center for the Montreal Canadiens, he was the National Hockey League's most valuable player in 1956 and 1964.

Belize

Be·lize /bə léez/ country in Central America on the Caribbean Sea, bordered to the west by Mexico and Guatemala. It became a British crown colony in 1862 and became an independent Commonwealth state in 1981. Language: English, Spanish. Currency: Belizean dollar. Capital: Belmopan. Population: 224,663 (1997). Area: 8,867 sq. mi./22,965 sq. km. Former name **British Honduras** —**Be·li·ze·an** *n.*, *adj.*

Be·lize Cit·y city and the main port of Belize on the Caribbean Sea. It was the capital of British Honduras between 1884 and 1972. Population: 50,000 (1990).

bell[1] /bel/ *n.* **1. OBJECT WITH RINGING SOUND** a hollow open-ended metal instrument with a rounded top that produces a ringing sound when struck. Bells are traditionally used as summonses and signals. **2. ELECTRICAL DEVICE PRODUCING SOUND** a device activated by electricity that produces a ringing or buzzing signal **3.** SOMETHING BELL-SHAPED something with the curved and open-ended shape of a bell, especially a flower **4.** MUSIC FLARED END OF WIND INSTRUMENT the flared end of a wind instrument, from which the sound emerges **5.** NAUT DURATION OF SHIP'S WATCH the time during a watch on a ship, indicated by rings on a bell, one ring for each half hour that has passed ■ **bells** *npl.* MUSIC PERCUSSION INSTRUMENT a percussion instrument consisting of metal tubes or bars hung from a frame that give out a ringing sound when struck ■ *vti.* (**belled, bell·ing, bells**) BECOME OR MAKE WIDER to open out, or open something out, into a curved or flared shape similar to that of a bell [Old English *belle*, from prehistoric Germanic] ◇ **ring a bell** to evoke a vague memory of something or somebody ○ *Her name doesn't ring a bell*

WORD KEY: CULTURAL NOTE

For Whom the Bell Tolls, a novel by U.S. writer Ernest Hemingway (1940). Widely viewed as Hemingway's most ambitious work, it is set during the Spanish Civil War and tells the story of Robert Jordan, a U.S. volunteer fighting for the Republicans, who falls in love with a fellow volunteer called Maria. It was made into a movie by Sam Woods in 1943.

bell[2] /bel/ *n.* BELLOW a bellowing sound made by a rutting stag or by a hunting dog during the chase ■ *vi.* (**belled, bell·ing, bells**) BELLOW to make a bellowing sound [Old English *bellan*, from prehistoric Germanic]

Bell /bel/ city in southwestern California, and a southern suburb of Los Angeles. Population: 35,077 (1996).

Bell, Alexander Graham (1847–1922) Scottish-born U.S. inventor and educator. He made the first intelligible telephonic transmission (1876), patented the telephone (1876), and founded Bell Telephone Company (1877). Among his numerous other inventions were wax cylinder recordings (1886) and the hydrofoil (1917).

Bel·la Coo·la /bèlə kōōlə/ *n.* a member of an aboriginal People of Canada living along the Bella Coola River in British Columbia

bel·la·don·na /bèllə dónnə/ *n.* **1.** PLANTS BUSH WITH POISONOUS BLACK BERRIES an extremely poisonous Eurasian plant with drooping purplish flowers and small black berries. Latin name: *Atropa belladonna.* **2.** PHARM DRUG FROM BELLADONNA a drug, e.g., atropine or hyoscyamine, that is made from belladonna [Mid-18thC. Via Modern Latin from Italian, literally "beautiful lady," from the use of belladonna to dilate the pupils, making the eyes look larger and brighter.]

bel·la·don·na lil·y *n.* = **amaryllis**

Bel·la·my /béllәmee/, **Edward** (1850–98) U.S. writer. His utopian novel *Looking Backward* (1888) achieved widespread popularity and spread socialist ideas.

bel·lar·mine /béll aar meèn, béllər-/ *n.* a large earthenware or stoneware jug decorated with a bearded face [Mid-17thC. Named for St. Robert *Bellarmin*, 1542–1621, Jesuit cardinal lampooned by the original jugs.]

bell·bird /bél bùrd/ *n.* a tropical American or Australasian bird with a call that sounds like a bell. The members of the cotinga and honey-eater families are bellbirds.

bell-bot·tom pants, **bell-bot·toms** *npl.* pants that widen below the knees into a bell shape

bell·boy /bél bòy/ *n.* = **bellhop**

bell buoy *n.* a floating buoy with a bell on top that is rung by the movement of the waves and gives a warning or positional signal to ships

bell cap·tain *n.* somebody in charge of the bellhops in a hotel

bell crank *n.* a lever with two arms that share a fulcrum at the point where they join

belle /bel/ *n.* **1.** BEAUTIFUL WOMAN a beautiful girl or woman **2.** MOST BEAUTIFUL WOMAN a woman considered to be the most conspicuously attractive of all those living in a particular place or attending a particular social event [Early 17thC. From French "beautiful."]

Bel·leek ware /bə leék-/, **Bel·leek** *n.* a type of very thin, typically cream-colored porcelain with a lustrous glaze [Mid-19thC. Named for the town in Northern Ireland where it was made.]

belle é·poque /bel ay púk/ *n.* an era of cultural refinement, social elegance, and general prosperity and security, especially the last decades of the 19th century and the early years of the 20th prior to World War I [Mid-20thC. French, literally "fine period."]

Belle Fourche /bèl fōōsh/ river that rises in northeastern Wyoming and flows eastward to join the Cheyenne River in western South Dakota. Length: 350 mi./563 km.

Belle Isle, Strait of channel separating Newfoundland from Labrador, Canada, connecting the Gulf of St. Lawrence with the Atlantic. Length: 90 mi./145 km.

Bel·ler·o·phon /bə lérrəfən, -fon/ *n.* in Greek mythology, a hero who tamed the winged horse Pegasus and slew the fire-breathing monster Chimera

belles-let·tres /bel léttrə/ *n.* writings that are valued for their elegance and aesthetic qualities rather than for any human interest or moral or instructive content (*takes a singular or plural verb*) [Mid-17thC. French, literally "fine letters."] —**bel·let·rism** *n.* — **bel·let·rist** *n.*

Belle·ville /bélvìl/ city in southwestern Illinois, an eastern suburb of St. Louis. Population: 41,608 (1996).

Belle·vue /bélvyōō/ **1.** city in eastern Nebraska, on the west bank of the Missouri River, a southern suburb of Omaha. Population: 42,807 (1996). **2.** city in west central Washington, beside Lake Washington. It is a suburb of Seattle. Population: 92,267 (1996).

bell·flow·er /bél flowər/ *n.* = **campanula**

bell·found·ry /bél fowndree/ (*plural* **-ries**) *n.* a foundry that specializes in making bells

bell glass *n.* = **bell jar** *n.* **2**

bell·hop /bél hòp/ *n.* an employee in a hotel who helps guests by carrying their luggage and running errands

bel·li·cose /bélli kòss/ *adj.* ready or inclined to quarrel, fight, or go to war [15thC. From Latin *bellicosus*, from *bellum* "war" (source of English *rebel*).] —**bel·li·cose·ly** *adv.* —**bel·li·cose·ness** *n.* —**bel·li·cos·i·ty** /belli kóssitee/ *n.*

bel·lig·er·ence /bə líjjərəns/ *n.* the quality of being hostile, ready to start a fight, or ready to go to war

bel·lig·er·en·cy /bə líjjərənsee/ *n.* **1.** = **belligerence 2.** STATE OF WAR the state of being at war

bel·lig·er·ent /bə líjjərənt/ *adj.* **1.** HOSTILE OR AGGRESSIVE hostile, ready to start a fight, or ready to go to war **2.** ENGAGED IN WAR taking part in warfare, especially in a war recognized by the law of nations **3.** RELATING TO BELLIGERENT NATION relating to or characteristic of a participant in war or a fight ■ *n.* PARTICIPANT IN WAR a participant in a war or fight, especially a nation engaged in a war recognized by the law of nations [Late 16thC. From Latin *belligerare* "to wage war," from *belliger*, literally "carrying on war," from *bellum* "war" + *gerere* "to carry on."] —**bel·lig·er·ent·ly** *adv.*

Bel·ling·ham /bélling hàm/ city and port in northwestern Washington, just south of the Canadian border, at the head of Bellingham Bay. Population: 61,043 (1996).

Bel·lings·hau·sen /béllingz hòwz'n/, **Fabian Gottlieb von** (1778–1852) Russian explorer. He explored an area of the Antarctic Sea (1819–21) that was later named for him.

Bel·lings·hau·sen Sea predominantly ice-covered sea constituting part of the southern Pacific Ocean, off the coast of Antarctica

Bel·li·ni /bə leénee/, **Giovanni** (1430?–1516) Italian painter. The son of Jacopo Bellini, he produced calm yet sensuous religious pictures, combining figures and landscape in naturalistic light.

Bel·li·ni, Jacopo (1400?–70?) Italian painter. He produced stylized paintings and drawings with strong architectural elements.

bell jar *n.* **1.** GLASS COVER FOR DISPLAYED OBJECTS a glass cover, shaped like a bell, used to protect and display delicate items **2.** CHEM GLASS COVER FOR EXPERIMENTS a glass cover shaped like a bell used in laboratories to enclose equipment in experiments, especially to prevent gases from escaping or entering

bell·man /bélmən/ (*plural* **-men** /-mən/) *n.* **1.** = **bellhop 2.** MAN WHO RINGS BELL a man who rings a bell, especially a town crier (*archaic*)

bell met·al *n.* an alloy of copper with 20 to 25 percent tin, used to cast bells and plain bearings

Bel·loc /béllòk, -ək/, **Hilaire** (1870–1953) French-born British writer. He wrote *Cautionary Tales for Children* (1907) and biographies of historical figures including *Napoleon* (1932). Full name **Joseph Hilaire Pierre Belloc**

bel·low /béllō/ *v.* (**-lowed, -low·ing, -lows**) **1.** *vi.* UTTER ROAR LIKE BULL to give a bull's loud deep roar or a roar like that of a bull **2.** *vti.* SHOUT LOUDLY to shout something in a loud deep voice ■ *n.* **1.** ROAR LIKE BULL'S a bull's loud deep roar, or a roar like that of a bull **2.** LOUD SHOUT a loud deep shout or cry [Origin uncertain: perhaps from Old English *bylgan*, or from *belgan* "to be enraged"] —**bel·low·er** *n.*

Bel·low /béllō/, **Saul** (*b.* 1915) Canadian-born U.S. writer. He won the Nobel Prize in literature (1976). His novels include the Pulitzer prize-winning *Humboldt's Gift* (1975).

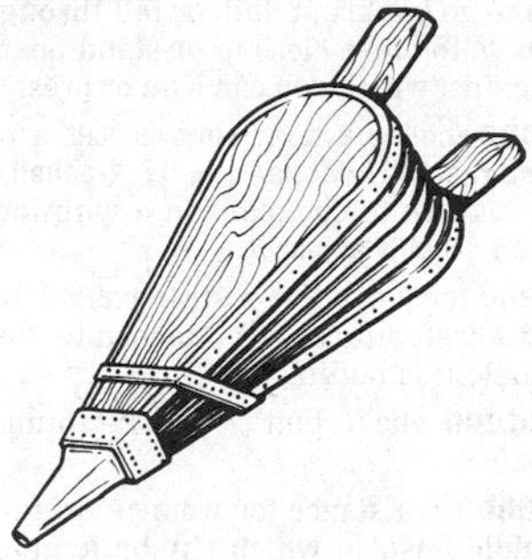

Bellows

bel·lows /béllōz/ (*plural* **-lows**) *n.* (*takes a singular or plural verb*) **1.** COMPRESSIBLE CHAMBER FOR PUMPING AIR a device or piece of equipment with a chamber with flexible sides that can be expanded to draw air in and compressed to force the air out **2.** PLEATED EXPANDABLE PART something constructed of a pleated material and, like a bellows, able to be expanded and contracted, e.g., the part enclosing the lenses on some cameras or photographic enlargers [12thC. Origin uncertain: probably from Old English *belga*, a shortening of *blæstbelig*, literally "blowing bag," from *blæst* "blowing" (source of *blast*) + *belig* "bag" (source of *belly*).]

Bel·lows /béllōz/, **George Wesley** (1882–1925) U.S. artist. He was a realist painter who depicted urban scenes and boxing matches, as in *Stag at Sharkey's* (1909).

bell pep·per *n.* = **sweet pepper** [From its shape]

bell·pull /bél pōōl/ *n.* a handle or cord that when pulled makes a bell ring

bell push *n.* a button that when pressed causes an electric bell to ring

bell-ring·er *n.* **1.** SOMEBODY RINGING CHURCH BELLS somebody who rings church bells, whether as an ecclesiastical function or as a hobby **2.** SOMEBODY PLAYING HANDBELLS a musician who plays handbells —**bell-ring·ing** *n.*

bells and whis·tles *npl.* special features that are not necessary but are incorporated in a product to make it appear more desirable or useful (*informal*)

bells of Ire·land *n.* an annual plant with small flowers surrounded by green cup-shaped sepals. Latin name: *Moluccella laevis.*

Bell's pal·sy *n.* paralysis of the muscles on one side of the face, causing a distorted facial expression. It results from injury to the facial nerve and is usually temporary. [Mid-19thC. Named for the Scottish anatomist Sir Charles *Bell*, 1774–1842, who described it.]

bell tow·er *n.* a tower with a bell or bells housed in it

bell·weth·er /bél wethər/ *n.* **1.** INDICATOR OF FUTURE DEVELOPMENTS somebody who or something that acts as an indicator of future developments or trends **2.** LEADER somebody who takes the initiative or leads others **3.** SHEEP LEADING FLOCK a sheep that leads the rest of the flock, usually wearing a bell around its neck (*archaic*)

Bell·wood /bélwŏŏd/ town in northeastern Illinois, a western suburb of Chicago. Population: 20,122 (1996).

bell·wort /bél wùrt, -wàwrt/ (*plural* **-worts** *or* **-wort**) *n.* a North American plant of the lily family with yellow bell-shaped flowers. Genus: *Uvularia.*

bel·ly /béllee/ *n.* (*plural* **-lies**) **1.** MIDDLE PART OF BODY the part of the body of a vertebrate that contains the stomach, intestines, and other organs **2.** FRONT OF BODY AROUND STOMACH the surface of the body of a vertebrate around the stomach **3.** STOMACH the stomach (*informal*) **4.** APPETITE the desire or need for food and drink **5.** DESIRE OR PERSISTENCE the courage or desire to have or do something ○ *They haven't got the belly for a fight.* **6.** BULGING PART a part of something that bulges out, e.g., a sail **7.** INTERIOR CAVITY the interior cavity of a structure, especially a ship **8.** MUSIC UPPER SURFACE OF STRINGED INSTRUMENT the top or front surface of the body of a stringed instrument, over which the strings are stretched ■ *vti.* (**-lied, -ly·ing, -lies**) BULGE to bulge or make something bulge ○ *The wind bellied out the sail.* [Old English *belig* "bag." Ultimately from an Indo-European word meaning "to swell" that is also the ancestor of English *billow* and *bolster.*] ◇ **go** *or* **turn belly up** to go bankrupt, fail, or fall through

belly up to *vi.* to move close to or stand next to something against which you can lean or press (*informal*)

bel·ly·ache /béllee àyk/ *n.* STOMACH ACHE a painful or upset stomach (*informal*) ■ *vi.* (**-ached, -ach·ing, -aches**) COMPLAIN to complain in a whining manner (*informal*) —**bel·ly·ach·er** *n.*

bel·ly·band /bélli bànd/ *n.* a strap passed around the belly of a draft animal and attached to the shafts of the vehicle it is pulling

bel·ly·but·ton /bélli bùtt'n/ *n.* the human navel (*informal*)

bel·ly dance *n.* a dance for women, originally from the Middle East, in which rhythmic movement of the hips and abdomen is emphasized —**bel·ly danc·er** *n.* —**bel·ly danc·ing** *n.*

bel·ly flop *n.* **1.** SWIMMING DIVE IN WHICH STOMACH SMACKS WATER an almost horizontal dive where the front of the diver's body hits the water first **2.** AIR = **belly landing** —**bel·ly-flop** *vi.*

bel·ly·ful /bélli fool/ *n.* (*informal*) **1.** ALL SOMEBODY CAN EAT all the food that somebody wants or is able to eat **2.** EXCESS an undesirable or excessive amount of something

bel·ly land·ing *n.* an emergency landing of an aircraft with the wheels not extended —**belly-land** *vti.*

bel·ly laugh *n.* a deep and unrestrained laugh

Bel·mont /bél mònt/ **1.** city on the San Mateo Peninsula, south of San Francisco, western California. Population: 25,562 (1996). **2.** town in northeastern Massachusetts. It is a northwestern suburb of Boston and Cambridge. Population: 24,044 (1996).

Bel·mo·pan /bèlmō pán/ capital of Belize, located on the Belize River in the eastern part of the country. Population: 6,500 (1996).

Be·lo Ho·ri·zon·te /béllō hàwri zàwntee/ city and capital of Minas Gerais State in eastern Brazil. Population: 2,091,770 (1996).

Be·loit /bə lóyt/ city in southern Wisconsin, on the Rock River, south of Madison. Population: 35,836 (1996).

be·long /bi láwng, -lóng/ (**-longed, -long·ing, -longs**) *vi.* **1.** BE SOMEBODY'S PROPERTY to be the property of a person or organization ○ *Who does this coat belong to?* **2.** BE PERSONALLY LINKED to be linked to a particular place or person by a relationship such as birth, affection, or membership **3.** BE CLASSIFIED to be part of a class or group ○ *Tulips belong to the lily family.* **4.** BE PART OF to be a part or component of something else **5.** BE IN RIGHT PLACE to be in an appropriate or usual place ○ *He belongs in jail.* **6.** BE ACCEPTED to be accepted or made welcome in a place or group ○ *feeling that I didn't belong* [14th C. Formed from obsolete English *long* "to relate to," with the literal sense of "to relate to thoroughly."]

Be·long·er /bi láwngər, -lóng-/ *n. Carib* somebody of African descent who was born and lives on a Caribbean island

be·long·ing /bi láwnging, -lóng-/ *n.* FEELING AT HOME the state of being comfortable and accepted in a place or community ■ **be·long·ings** *npl.* PERSONAL POSSESSIONS the things somebody owns or has with him or her

Be·lo·rus·sia /bèllō rúshə/ = **Belarus**

Bel·o·rus·sian /bèllō rúsh'n/ *adj.*, *n.* Belarusian (*dated*)

be·lov·ed /bi lúvvid/; (*predicatively*) /-lúvd/ *adj.* ADORED loved very much ■ *n.* LOVED PERSON somebody who is loved very much

be·low /bi lṓ/ CORE MEANING: a grammatical word indicating something situated or placed beneath something else or lower than something else ○ (prep) *a river below the town* ○ (adv) *on the shelf below*

1. *prep., adv.* IN LOWER GRADE at or to a level, standard, or grade that is lower than that specified or understood ○ *animals ranked below humans* ○ *below average* ○ *30 degrees below* **2.** *adv.* FURTHER DOWN lower down or later on in a text, especially on the same page ○ *see below* ○ *on page 29 below* **3.** *adv.* NAUT LOWER THAN THE DECK on or to a level of a ship or boat that is lower than the deck **4.** *adv.* RELIG ON EARTH on earth or in hell, as opposed to in heaven (*archaic*) [14thC. Formed from an earlier form of *by* + LOW, possibly modeled on *beneath.*]

be·low·ground /bi lṓ grównd/ *adj.* UNDERGROUND situated under the ground ■ *adv.* UNDER THE GROUND into or under the ground

Bel·sen /bélzən/ village in northwestern Germany, about 10 mi./16 km north of Celle. It is the site of the Bergen-Belsen Nazi concentration camp (1943–45).

Bel·shaz·zar /bel shάzzər/ *n.* a king of Babylon in the sixth century B.C. The Bible tells of the foretelling of his death in an inscription that mysteriously appears on the wall of his palace during a feast (Daniel 5).

belt /belt/ *n.* **1.** ACCESSORIES STRIP OF MATERIAL AROUND WAIST a strip of material worn around the waist, used to hold up clothing for the lower body, as decoration, or to carry tools or weapons **2.** INDUST BAND AS PART OF MACHINE a band of strong flexible material used in machinery to transmit motion or power or to move articles **3.** TRANSP = **seat belt** **4.** BLOW a hard blow (*informal*) **5.** DRINK a drink of liquor (*slang*) **6.** SPECIFIC AREA an area or region where a particular item or quality is characteristic ○ *a wheat belt* **7.** STRIP OF SOMETHING DIFFERENT a band or stripe of a different color, texture, or substance from what it encircles or crosses **8.** SPORTS BELT GIVEN FOR ACHIEVEMENT a belt awarded to a sports competitor, especially in boxing or the martial arts, as a trophy or a sign of having attained a particular grade **9.** SPORTS SOMEBODY HOLDING BELT FOR SPORTING ACHIEVEMENT somebody awarded a particular belt for a sporting achievement, usually in boxing or one of the martial arts **10.** BELT AS SIGN OF RANK a belt worn as a sign of a particular rank, e.g., by a knight or an earl **11.** a sudden strong emotional reaction (*slang*) ○ *Read this! It'll give you a belt.* **12.** = **beltway** ■ *v.* (**belt·ed, belt·ing, belts**) **1.** *vt.* FASTEN WITH BELT to fasten or attach something with a belt **2.** *vt.* HIT HARD to strike somebody or something with a hard blow (*informal*) **3.** *vi.* MOVE FAST to move very quickly (*informal*) **4.** *vt.* HIT WITH BELT to strike somebody with a belt [Old English. Ultimately from Latin *balteus* "girdle," of, perhaps, Etruscan origin.] ◇ **below the belt** unfair and often hurtful ◇ **have something under your belt** to have done or acquired something that will be of benefit to you in the future ○ *She has 12 computer science courses under her belt.* ◇ **tighten your belt** to reduce your expenditures

belt out *vt.* to sing or play something loudly and enthusiastically (*informal*)

belt up *vti.* to fasten a safety belt, or secure somebody with a safety belt

Bel·tane /bél tàyn, -tèn/ *n.* an ancient Celtic festival at the beginning of May, marked by the lighting of bonfires [15thC. Via Gaelic *bealltainn* from Old Irish.]

belt·course /bélt kàwrs/ *n.* = **stringcourse**

belt drive *n.* a system for transmitting power from one shaft to another by means of an endless flexible belt looped over pulleys mounted on the shafts

belt high·way *n.* = **beltway**

belt·ing /bélting/ *n.* **1.** MATERIAL FOR BELTS material used for making belts **2.** BELTS COLLECTIVELY belts considered collectively

Bel·ton /bélt'n/ **1.** city in western Missouri, a southern suburb of Kansas City. Population: 20,862 (1996). **2.** city in central Texas, northeast of Austin and southwest of Waco. Population: 14,800 (1996).

belt sand·er *n.* a sander that uses a continuous belt coated with an abrasive

belt·way /bélt wày/ *n.* a highway that surrounds or skirts an urban area

be·lu·ga /bə lóogə/ (*plural* **-gas** *or* **-ga**) *n.* **1.** RUSSIAN STURGEON a large white sturgeon found in the Black Sea and the Caspian Sea. Its eggs are used in caviar, and isinglass was traditionally made from its air bladders. Latin name: *Huso huso* and *Acipenser huso.* **2. be·lu·ga, be·lu·ga cav·i·ar** CAVIAR caviar made from the eggs of the beluga sturgeon **3.** = **white whale** [Late 16thC. From Russian, literally "large white," from *belyĭ* "white."]

bel·ve·dere /bélvi deer/ *n.* a building or part of a building positioned to offer a fine view of the surrounding area [Late 16thC. From Italian, literally "beautiful to see."]

be·ma /beémə/ *n.* **1. be·ma, bi·ma, bi·mah** JUDAISM PLATFORM FOR SCRIPTURE READINGS in a synagogue, the raised platform where the scriptures are read **2.** CHR PLATFORM THAT ALTAR IS ON in an Orthodox church, the raised area where the altar is located [Late 17thC. From Greek *bēma* "step, platform."]

Bem·ba /bémbə/ (*plural* **-ba** *or* **-bas**) *n.* **1.** PEOPLES MEMBER OF AFRICAN PEOPLE a member of an African people chiefly located in Zambia **2.** LANG AFRICAN LANGUAGE a Bantu language spoken in east central Africa and belonging to the Benue-Congo group of languages. Bemba is spoken by more than two million people. [Mid-20thC. From Bantu.] —**Bem·ba** *adj.*

Be·mel·mans /beém'lmənz, bémm'l-/, **Ludwig** (1898–1962) Austrian-born U.S. writer and illustrator. He is known for his classic children's book, *Madeline* (1939).

be·mire /bi mír/ (**-mired, -mir·ing, -mires**) *vt.* **1.** SOIL to soil something or somebody with mud or dirt (*archaic*) **2.** CAUSE TO STICK IN MUD to cause somebody or something to become stuck in mud (*archaic or literary*) (*usually passive*)

be·moan /bi mṓn/ (**-moaned, -moan·ing, -moans**) *vt.* to express grief or disappointment about something

be·muse /bi myóoz/ (**-mused, -mus·ing, -mus·es**) *vt.* to cause somebody to be confused or puzzled —**be·muse·ment** /bi myóozmənt/ *n.*

be·mused /bi myóozd/ *adj.* confused, puzzled, and unable to understand or think clearly —**be·mus·ed·ly** /bi myóozidlee/ *adv.*

Be·na·dryl /bénnədril/ *tdmk.* a trademark for allergy, sinus, cold, and headache medication

Be·na·res /bə náarəz, -eez/ former name for **Varanasi**

bench /bench/ *n.* **1.** FURNITURE LONG BACKLESS SEAT a long seat for two or more people, usually made without a back or arms **2.** NAUT SEAT IN BOAT a seat for a rower in a boat **3.** WORK TABLE a long strong work table **4.** LAW JUDGE'S SEAT the seat where a judge sits in a court **5.** LAW JUDGE a judge or magistrate presiding over a court **6.** LAW JUDGES the judges of a court system **7.** LAW JUDGESHIP the office or position of a judge **8.** SPORTS SEAT FOR NONPLAYING ATHLETES in team sports, the seat for players not on the field or court during play **9.** SPORTS SUBSTITUTE PLAYERS ON SPORTS TEAM the substitute players of a sports team **10.** GEOL LEDGE OF LAND a narrow flat ledge of land, often the remnant of a former shoreline **11.** MINING LEDGE IN MINE a ledge formed by excavation in a mine **12.** PLATFORM FOR SHOWING ANIMALS a platform used for displaying dogs, cats, or other animals at a show ■ *vt.* (**benched, bench·ing, bench·es**) **1.** SPORTS PUT ON NONPLAYERS' BENCH to exclude or remove a member of a sports team from play **2.** DISPLAY ANIMAL AT SHOW to display a dog, cat, or other animal at a show on a bench **3.** PROVIDE WITH BENCHES to provide something with benches [Old English *benc.* Ultimately from a prehistoric Germanic word that was also the ancestor of German *Bank* and English *bank* "riverbank," the underlying idea being of a "raised ridge."]

Bench·ley /bénchlee/, **Peter** (*b.* 1940) U.S. writer. The son of Robert Benchley, he is the author of *Jaws* (1974) and other thrillers.

Bench·ley, Robert (1889–1945) U.S. humorist, screenwriter, and actor. Known for his wit, he was theater critic of the *New Yorker* and wrote humorous short movies. Full name **Robert Charles Benchley**

bench·mark /bénch maark/ *n.* **1.** STANDARD a standard against which something can be measured or assessed **2.** COMPUT TEST OF COMPUTER PERFORMANCE a test or set of tests used to measure the performance of computer hardware or software ■ *adj.* USED AS STANDARD used as a standard for measuring or assessing something ■ *vt.* (**-marked, -mark·ing, -marks**) **1.** PROVIDE STANDARD to provide a standard against which something can be measured or assessed **2.** COMPUT TEST COMPUTER PERFORMANCE to test the performance of computer hardware or software for the purpose of comparison with similar products

bench mark *n.* a mark made by a surveyor on a permanent object that shows an established position and elevation and is used as a reference point

bench press *n.* in weightlifting, a lift where somebody lies on a bench with the feet on the floor and raises a weight from chest level to arm's length —**bench-press** *vti.*

bench seat *n.* in a motor vehicle, a seat that extends across the full width of the vehicle

bench test *n.* a trial of a machine or part in the laboratory or workshop to confirm that it works properly before it is installed —**bench-test** *vti.*

bench·warm·er /bénch wàrmər/ *n.* a substitute player on a sports team who spends most of the game on the bench

bend[1] /bend/ *v.* (**bent** /bent/, **bend·ing, bends**) **1.** *vti.* **BECOME OR MAKE CURVED** to take on or cause something to take on a curved or angled shape ○ *The wooden struts bent under pressure.* **2.** *vti.* **STOOP** to make or cause somebody to make a stooping or inclined movement ○ *I bent to pick up the ball.* **3.** *vti.* **YIELD OR FORCE TO YIELD** to yield in response to a strong will or force, or force somebody or something to yield **4.** *vti.* **CHANGE OR CAUSE TO CHANGE DIRECTION** to change or cause something to change direction or course ○ *The path bends to the right.* **5.** *vt.* **DISTORT FOR SOMEBODY'S BENEFIT** to adapt or interpret something in a way that was not originally intended, especially for personal benefit or to help somebody else ○ *bend the rules* **6.** *vti.* **CONCENTRATE ON DOING SOMETHING** to concentrate on doing something ○ *bent her mind to the task in hand* **7.** *vt.* NAUT **ATTACH** to attach or fasten something, especially a pair of lines or ropes ■ *n.* **1. CURVE** a curved part of something, especially a sharp curve in a road **2. ACT OF BENDING** an act of bending **3.** NAUT **KNOT JOINING TWO ROPES** a knot that joins one line to another [Old English *bendan* "to tie, curve" (because if you tie something it becomes curved). Ultimately from a prehistoric Germanic word that was also the ancestor of English *bind, bond,* and *bundle.*] —**bend·a·bil·i·ty** *n.* —**bend·a·ble** *adj.* ◇ **around the bend** wild or distracted (*slang*)

WORD KEY: ORIGIN

The prehistoric Germanic word from which ***bend*** comes is also the ancestor of English *band, bind, bond,* and *bundle.*

bend[2] /bend/ *n.* HERALDRY a band that crosses a heraldic shield diagonally from top right to bottom left [Old English, "band," originally a sense of BEND[1] and, later, from Old French *bende*]

Bend /bend/ city in central Oregon, east of Eugene, on the eastern bank of the Deschutes River. Population: 31,733 (1996).

ben·day /ben dáy/, **Ben Day** *adj.* used to describe a printing process of adding tone to an image by overlaying a transparent sheet patterned with dots before the image is reproduced to make a plate [Early 20thC. Named for the U.S. printer *Benjamin Day* Jr. (1838–1916), who invented the process.]

bend·ed /béndəd/ *adj.* in a position so as to be curved or bent (*dated*) ○ *on bended knee*

bend·er /béndər/ *n.* a prolonged bout of drinking (*slang*)

ben·dro·flu·a·zide /bèndrō floó ə zīd/ *n. U.K.* = **bendroflumethiazide**

ben·dro·flu·me·thi·a·zide /bendrō floō methī̀ə zīd/ *n.* a diuretic drug used in the treatment of edema and hypertension. It acts on a part of the kidneys to promote the excretion of salt and water.

bends /bendz/ *n.* decompression sickness, especially in divers (*informal*) (*takes a singular or plural verb*)

bend sin·is·ter (*plural* **bends sin·is·ter**) *n.* a band that crosses a heraldic shield diagonally from top left to bottom right, used to indicate a bastard line of descent [From SINISTER "on the left"]

be·neath /bi neéth/ CORE MEANING: a grammatical word indicating a position underneath or lower than something

1. *prep., adv.* **UNDERNEATH** in, at, or to a lower position or less superficial level than that specified or understood ○ *kept in a box beneath the bed* ○ *a door giving access to the cellar beneath* ○ *Beneath his veneer of politeness lay hostility.* **2.** *prep., adv.* **LOWER** in, at, or to a lower level, grade, or standard than that specified or understood ○ *She always supported those beneath her.* **3.** *prep.* **TOO LOW FOR** too low in status or character for ○ *beneath contempt* ○ *Telling tales should be beneath you.* [Old English *binithan, bineothan,* literally "by or from below." Ultimately from a prehistoric Germanic word that is also the ancestor of English *nether.*]

ben·e·dic·ite /bènni díssətee, báy nay díchi tày/ *n.* a blessing or grace used in some Christian religious communities [13thC. From Latin, "bless you!," a form of *benedicere,* literally "to say well to," from *bene* "well" + *dicere* "to say."]

Ben·e·dic·ite /bènni díssətee, báy nay díchi tày/ *n.* a Latin hymn beginning "Benedicite omnia opera Domini Domino," traditionally translated as "O all ye works of the Lord, bless ye the Lord"

Ben·e·dict XV /bénnidìkt/, **Pope** (1854–1922). As pope (1914–22) he was active in organizing war relief during World War I. Born **Giacomo della Chiesa**

Ben·e·dict, Ruth (1887–1948) U.S. anthropologist. She studied Native American peoples. Her writings include *Patterns of Culture* (1934). Born **Ruth Fulton**

Ben·e·dic·tine /bènni díktin, -teen/ *n.* **MONK OR NUN** a monk or nun belonging to a religious order founded by St. Benedict or following his rule. ■ *adj.* **OF ST. BENEDICT** relating to or characteristic of St. Benedict, his rule, or the monastic order that he founded.

ben·e·dic·tion /bènni díksh'n/ *n.* **1. EXPRESSION OF APPROVAL** an expression of approval or good wishes **2. PRAYER ASKING FOR GOD'S BLESSING** a prayer asking for God's blessing, usually at the end of a service **3. Ben·e·dic·tion, ben·e·dic·tion CATHOLIC DEVOTIONAL SERVICE** in the Roman Catholic Church, a devotional service during which the congregation is blessed with the Host **4. BLESSEDNESS** the state of being blessed [15thC. Directly or via French *bénédiction* from the Latin stem *benediction-* from, ultimately, *benedicere,* literally "to say well to," from *bene* "well" + *dicere* "to say."] —**ben·e·dic·tive** *adj.* —**ben·e·dic·to·ry** /bènni díktəree/ *adj.*

Ben·e·dict's so·lu·tion /bénni dìkts-/, **Ben·e·dict's re·a·gent** *n.* a solution of copper sulfate, sodium citrate, and sodium carbonate that turns red in the presence of glucose and other sugars that are reducing agents. It is used in urine tests for diabetes. [Early 20thC. Named for the U.S. chemist Stanley Rossiter *Benedict,* 1884–1936.]

Ben·e·dic·tus /bènni díktəss/ *n.* **1. LATIN HYMN FROM LUKE** a Latin hymn from Luke, beginning "Benedictus qui venit in nomine Domini" ("Blessed is he that cometh in the name of the Lord") **2. LATIN HYMN FROM MATTHEW** a Latin hymn from Matthew, beginning "Benedictus Dominus Deus Israel" ("Blessed be the Lord God of Israel") [Mid-16thC. From Latin *benedicere* (see BENEDICTION).]

ben·e·fac·tion /bénnə fàksh'n, bènnə fáksh'n/ *n.* **1. DOING GOOD** an act of doing good **2. GOOD DEED** a good deed, especially an act of charity **3. DONATION** a donation given to a charity [Mid-17thC. From Late Latin *benefaction-,* formed from *bene facere,* literally "to do well to," from *bene* "well" + *fact-,* the past participle stem of Latin *facere* "to do."]

ben·e·fac·tor /bénnə fàktər/ *n.* somebody who aids a cause, institution, or individual, especially with a gift of money

ben·e·fac·tress /bénnə fàktriss/ *n.* a woman who aids a cause, institution, or individual, especially with a gift of money

be·nef·ic /bə néffik/ *adj.* doing good or charitable acts (*literary*) [Early 17thC. From Latin *beneficus,* from *bene facere* (see BENEFACTION).]

ben·e·fice /bénnəfiss/ *n.* **1.** CHR **ENDOWED CHURCH LIVING** a church office that provides a living for its holder through an endowment attached to it **2.** CHR **REVENUE FOR CHURCH LIVING** the revenue or property that provides the living of the holder of a church benefice **3.** HIST **FORM OF FEUDAL TENURE** a form of feudal tenure in which a vassal held land from a superior, especially in return for military service ■ *vt.* (**-ficed, -fic·ing, -fic·es**) CHR **PROVIDE WITH BENEFICE** to provide a member of the clergy with a church office that will yield a living [14thC. Via Old French from Latin *beneficium,* literally "doing well," from *bene* "well" + *fic-,* a variant of the stem of *facere* "to do."]

be·nef·i·cence /bə néffissəns/ *n.* **1. GENEROSITY** generosity or charity **2. GENEROUS GIFT** a good or charitable act, especially a generous gift **3. BENEFICIAL EFFECT** the beneficial nature or effect that something has

be·nef·i·cent /bə néffissənt/ *adj.* **1. DOING GOOD** doing good or charitable acts **2. PRODUCING BENEFIT** producing benefits or advantages [Early 17thC. From Latin *beneficent-,* the stem of *beneficentior,* literally "more beneficent," from *beneficus,* from *bene facere* (see BENEFACTION).] —**be·nef·i·cent·ly** *adv.*

ben·e·fi·cial /bènnə físh'l/ *adj.* **1. HAVING GOOD EFFECT** producing a good or advantageous effect ○ *The exercise should prove beneficial to his health.* **2.** LAW **PROFITABLE** entitling somebody to or entitled to profits or property [15thC. Directly or via French *bénéficial* from Late Latin *beneficialis,* from Latin *beneficium* (see BENEFICE).] —**ben·e·fi·cial·ly** *adv.* —**ben·e·fi·cial·ness** *n.*

ben·e·fi·ci·ar·y /bènnə físhee èrree, -físhəree/ *n.* (*plural* **-ies**) **1. SOMEBODY BENEFITING** somebody who receives a benefit from something **2.** LAW **LEGAL RECIPIENT OF MONEY** somebody who is entitled by a will, trust, or insurance policy to receive money or property **3.** CHR **HOLDER OF BENEFICE** a member of the clergy who holds an office that provides a living (**benefice**) ■ *adj.* CHR **RELATING TO BENEFICE** relating to a church office that provides a living (**benefice**) or the member of the clergy who holds it [Early 17thC. From Latin *beneficarius,* from *beneficium* (see BENEFICE).]

ben·e·fit /bénnəfit/ *n.* **1. ADVANTAGE** something that has a good effect or promotes wellbeing ○ *They eventually reaped the benefits of all their hard work.* **2.** SOC WELFARE **GOVERNMENT ASSISTANCE** a regular payment made by a government agency, such as Social Security, to somebody qualified to receive it or in need of financial assistance (*often used in the plural*) **3. MONEY PAID TO CLAIMANT** a payment made to a claimant or entitled person by an employer, insurance company, or other institution (*often used in the plural*) **4. PERFORMANCE FOR CHARITY** a performance by entertainers, athletes, or others to raise money for somebody or something, especially a charity ■ *vti.* (**-fit·ed** *or* **-fit·ted, -fit·ing** *or* **-fit·ting, -fits**) **GIVE OR RECEIVE BENEFIT** to give or receive help, an advantage, or another benefit [14thC. Via Anglo-Norman *benfet* and Old French *bienfait* from, ultimately, Latin *benefactum* "good deed," from *bene facere* (see BENEFACTION).] ◇ **give somebody the benefit of the doubt** to assume that somebody is telling the truth about something or is innocent of something because there is not enough evidence that the person is lying or guilty

ben·e·fit of cler·gy *n.* **1.** CHR **CHURCH BLESSING** the official approval or ministration of the church ○ *married without benefit of clergy* **2.** LAW, HISTORY **CLERICAL EXEMPTION FROM CIVIL TRIAL** the privilege held by the clergy in the Middle Ages that entitled them to trial by an ecclesiastical court and exemption from trial by secular authorities

Be·ne·lux /bénnə lùks/ *n.* the countries of Belgium the Netherlands and Luxembourg as a group. The three countries formed a customs union in 1948 that was replaced by the Benelux Economic Union in 1960. [Mid-20thC. Acronym of "Belgium," "Netherlands," and "Luxembourg."]

Be·nét /bi náy/, **Stephen Vincent** (1898–1943) U.S. author and poet. He wrote *John Brown's Body* (1928), which won a Pulitzer Prize.

Be·nét, William Rose (1886–1950) U.S. poet, critic, and editor. The brother of Stephen Vincent Benét, he cofounded *The Saturday Review of Literature* in 1924.

be·nev·o·lence /bə névvələns/ *n.* **1. TENDENCY TO BE KIND** an inclination to be kind and helpful or generous **2. GENEROUS ACT** something done or given out of kindness **3.** HIST **FORCED LOAN IMPOSED BY ENGLISH KING** a compulsory loan or gift of money imposed by English kings of the late Middle Ages on their subjects [15thC. Via French *bénévolence* from Latin *benevolentia,* from *benevolent-* (see BENEVOLENT).]

be·nev·o·lent /bə névvələnt/ *adj.* **1. KIND** showing kindness or goodwill **2. CHARITABLE** performing good or charitable acts and not seeking to make a profit [15thC. Via Old French *benivolent* from Latin *benevolent-,* the present participle stem of *bene velle* "to wish well."] —**be·nev·o·lent·ly** *adv.*

Ben·gal /ben gáwl, beng-, bén gəl, béng-/ former province of northeastern India. In 1947 it was divided into the Indian state of West Bengal and East Bengal, now Bangladesh. Area: 87,700 sq. mi./ 224,500 sq. km. —**Ben·ga·lese** *n.*

Ben·gal, Bay of northeastern section of the Indian Ocean bordered by India, Bangladesh, and

Myanmar (Burma). Area: 839,000 sq. mi./2,172,000 sq. km.

Ben·ga·li /ben gáwlee, bèng-/ *n.* **1.** PEOPLES **SOMEBODY FROM BANGLADESH OR WEST BENGAL** somebody who lives in or was born or raised in Bangladesh or the state of West Bengal in India **2.** LANG **INDIC LANGUAGE** the national language of Bangladesh and state language of West Bengal, India. It is an Indic language of the Indo-European family. There are Bengali-speaking communities in many parts of the world, and the language is spoken by at least 170 million people. [Late 18thC. Formed from Hindi *baṅgālī*.] — **Ben·ga·li** *adj.*

ben·ga·line /béng gə leen/ *n.* a heavyweight ribbed fabric, usually of cotton and silk or wool [Late 19thC. From French, because of its similarity to cloth made in Bengal.]

Ben·gha·zi /ben gaázee, beng-/, **Ben·ga·si, Ban·ghā·zī** city and port in northeastern Libya on the gulf of Sidra. It is near the site of the ancient Greek colony of Euhesperides. Population: 446,250 (1988).

David Ben-Gurion

Ben-Gur·i·on /ben gŏŏree ən/, **David** (1886–1973) Polish-born Israeli statesman. He was the first prime minister of Israel (1948–53, 1955–63). Born **David Gruen**

be·night·ed /bi nítid/ *adj.* **1. UNENLIGHTENED** unenlightened intellectually, socially, or morally **2. OVERTAKEN BY NIGHT** overtaken by night or the dark — **be·night·ed·ly** *adv.* —**be·night·ed·ness** *n.*

be·nign /bi nín/ *adj.* **1. KINDLY** having a kind and gentle disposition or appearance **2. NOT LIFE-THREATENING** not a threat to life or long-term health, especially by being noncancerous **3. HARMLESS** neutral or harmless in its effect or influence **4. FAVORABLE** mild or favorable in effect ○ *a benign climate* [14thC. Via French *bénigne* from Latin *benignus* of uncertain origin: probably from, ultimately, *bene genus*, literally "well born," from *bene* "well" + *-genus* "born."] —**be·nign·ly** *adv.*

be·nig·nant /bi nígnənt/ *adj.* kind and gracious in behavior or appearance, especially toward social inferiors —**be·nig·nan·cy** *n.*

be·nig·ni·ty /bi nígnitee/ (*plural* **-ties**) *n.* **1. KINDLINESS** kindness and gentleness of disposition or appearance **2. KIND ACT** a kind or gracious act

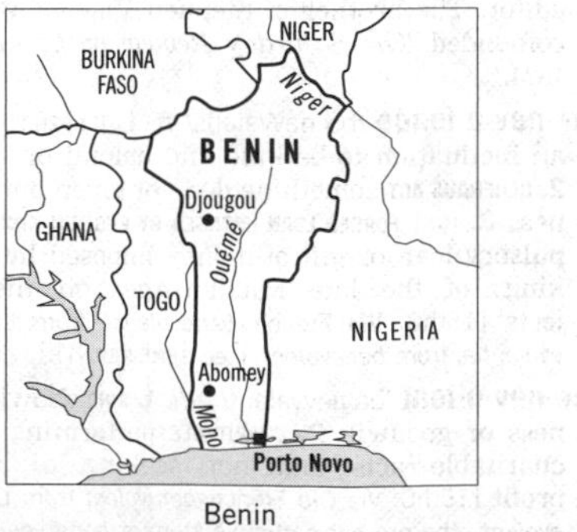

Benin

Be·nin /bə nín, be neen/ republic in western Africa between Togo and Nigeria, with a short coastline on the Bight of Benin. It became independent from France in 1960. Language: French. Currency: CFA franc. Capital: Porto-Novo. Population: 5,902,178 (1997). Area: 43,484 sq. mi./112,622 sq. km. Official name **Republic of Benin**. Former name **Dahomey** (until 1975) —**Be·nin·ese** /bènnə neez/ *adj., n.*

Be·nin, Bight of wide bay in West Africa, the western section of the Gulf of Guinea. It stretches from the mouth of the Volta River to the mouth of the Niger River, with Lagos as one of its principal ports. Length: approximately 450 mi./720 km.

Be·nin Cit·y capital of Edo State in southern Nigeria. It was the capital of the Kingdom of Benin that flourished in the 15th and 16th centuries, producing magnificent brass, bronze, and ivory sculptures. Population: 223,900 (1995).

ben·i·son /bennizən, bennissən/ *n.* a blessing or benediction (*archaic*) [12thC. Via Old French *benisson* from the Latin stem *benediction-* (see BENEDICTION).]

ben·ja·min /bénjəmən/ *n.* = **benzoin** [Mid-16thC. Alteration of an earlier form of BENZOIN by association with the male forename "Benjamin."]

Ben·ja·min /bénjəmən/ *n.* in the Bible, the youngest son of Jacob and Rachel and father of the smallest tribe of Israel

Ben·ja·min /bénjəmən/, **Judah** (1811–84) U.S. politician and lawyer. Secretary of war in Jefferson Davis's cabinet, he fled to England after the Civil War and made a career as a lawyer. Full name **Judah Philip Benjamin**

ben·ne /bénnee/ *n.* **bene, ben·ni** *n.* = **sesame** [Mid-18thC. From Mande.]

ben·net /bénnit/ *n.* = **herb bennet** [15thC. Via French *herbe benëite* from Medieval Latin *herba benedicta* "blessed plant," because it was said to frighten off the Devil.]

Ben·nett, James Gordon (1841–1918) U.S. newspaper owner and editor. As editor of the *New York Herald*, he financed H.M. Stanley's African expeditions.

Ben·nett, Richard Bedford, 1st Viscount (1870–1947) Canadian statesman and business executive. He was Conservative prime minister of Canada (1930–35). Known as **Iron Heel Bennett**

Ben·ning·ton /bénningtən/ town and ski resort in southwestern Vermont, the site of Bennington College. Population: 16,328 (1996).

ben·ny /bénnee/ (*plural* **-nies**) *n.* an amphetamine tablet, especially Benzedrine™ (*dated slang*) [Mid-20thC. Shortening of BENZEDRINE™.]

Ben·ny /bénnee/, **Jack** (1894–1974) U.S. comedian. He is known for his miserly self-caricature in the *Jack Benny Show* on radio and television (1932–65). Real name **Benjamin Kubelsky**

bensh /bench/ (**benshed, bensh·ing, bensh·es**), **bentsh** (**bent·shed, bent·shing, bent·shes**) *vi.* to say a Jewish benediction after eating a meal [Via Yiddish *bentshen* from Latin *benedicere* "to bless"]

bent[1] past tense, past participle of **bend**[1]

WORD KEY: SYNONYMS

See Synonyms at ***talent***.

bent[2] /bent/ *adj.* **1. CURVED** having a curved, twisted, or angled shape **2. DETERMINED** having a fixed desire to do or accomplish something ○ *bent on making a name for herself* **3.** *U.K.* **CORRUPT** dishonest or corrupt in behavior (*slang*) ○ *a bent cop* ■ *n.* **1. NATURAL INCLINATION** a strong natural inclination or talent for something **2.** CIV ENG **CROSSWISE SUPPORT** a crosswise framework or member used to strengthen a structure

bent[3] /bent/ *n.* **1. GRASS OF TEMPERATE REGIONS** a perennial grass of temperate regions, grown for hay and planted for lawns or putting greens. Genus: *Agrostis*. **2. REEDY GRASS** a stiff reedy grass (*archaic*) **3. GRASS STALK** a flower stalk of a stiff grass (*archaic*) [Old English *beonet*. Ultimately from a prehistoric Germanic word that is also the ancestor of German *Binse*.]

Ben·tham /bénthəm/, **Jeremy** (1748–1832) British philosopher, jurist, and social reformer. The chief proponent of utilitarianism, he wrote *Introduction to the Principles of Morals and Legislation* (1789). He helped found University College London.

Ben·tham·ism /bénthə mìzzəm/ *n.* the utilitarian philosophy of Jeremy Bentham, which argues that the highest good is the happiness of the greatest number. ◊ **consequentialism, deontology** —**Ben·tham·ite** *n., adj.*

ben·thic /bénthik/, **ben·thon·ic** /ben thónnik/ *adj.* relating to or characteristic of the bottom of a sea, lake, or deep river, or the animals and plants that live there

ben·thos /bén thòss/ *n.* the animals and plants that live on or in the sediment at the bottom of a sea, lake, or deep river [Late 19thC. From Greek, "depth of the sea."]

ben·to /béntō/ (*plural* **-tos**) *n.* FOOD = **obento**

Ben·ton /béntən/, **Thomas Hart** (1889–1975) U.S. artist. Known for his naturalistic populist panels and murals, he is credited with founding the Regionalist school of painting.

Ben·ton Har·bor city on the southeastern shore of Lake Michigan, in southwestern Michigan. Population: 11,824 (1996).

ben·ton·ite /bént'n ìt/ *n.* a light-colored valuable clay that expands with the addition of water and is used as oil-well drilling mud and as a filler in the building, paper, soap, and pharmaceutical industries [Late 19thC. Named for Fort *Benton*, Montana, where it was first identified.] —**ben·ton·it·ic** /bènt'n íttik/ *adj.*

bentsh *vi.* = **bensh**

bent-wing moth *n.* a large Australian ghost moth whose larvae, up to 6 in./15 cm long, bore into and are harmful to eucalyptus trees. Latin name: *Leto staceyi*.

bent·wood /bént wŏŏd/ *n.* wood that has been bent into a curved shape by being steamed and then put into a mold. It is used to make furniture.

Be·nue-Con·go /bàyn way-/ *n.* a group of about 700 languages spoken across central and southern Africa and belonging to the Niger-Congo family of languages. Bantu languages form the largest subgroup of Benue-Congo. —**Be·nue-Con·go** *adj.*

be·numb /bi núm/ (**-numbed, -numb·ing, -numbs**) *vt.* **1. MAKE UNABLE TO FEEL** to remove the sense of feeling from a faculty or part of the body, especially by exposure to extreme cold **2. MAKE INACTIVE** to make somebody incapable of activity or thought (*usually passive*) — **be·numb·ment** *n.*

benz- /bents/ *prefix.* = **benzo-** (*used before vowels*)

benz·al·de·hyde /ben záldə hìd/ *n.* a colorless volatile liquid with the odor of, and occurring naturally in, almonds. It is used in the manufacture of dyes, flavorings, and perfumes. Formula: C_6H_5CHO.

Ben·ze·drine /bénzə dreen/ *tdmk.* a trademark for a preparation of amphetamine, a medical stimulant

ben·zene /bén zeen, ben zeen/ *n.* a colorless volatile toxic liquid with a distinctive odor, obtained from petroleum and used in the manufacture of dyes, polymers, and industrial chemicals such as phenol. Formula: C_6H_6. Former name **benzol** [Mid-19thC. Formed from BENZOIC.]

ben·zene ring *n.* a molecular structure common to benzene and its derivatives in which six carbon atoms are bonded in a hexagon by alternating single and double bonds

ben·zine /bén zeen, ben zeen/, **ben·zin** /-zin/ *n.* a liquid that is obtained from crude oil and has a carefully selected boiling point range. It is used widely as an industrial solvent, e.g., to extract oils from seeds. [Mid-19thC. Formed from BENZOIC.]

benzo- *prefix.* benzene, benzoic acid ○ *benzopyrene* [From BENZOIN]

ben·zo·di·az·e·pine /bènzō dī ázzə peen, -ázzəpin/ *n.* a compound belonging to a group used as minor tranquilizers and as a short-term treatment for sleeping difficulties

ben·zo·ic ac·id /ben zō ik-/ *n.* a colorless crystalline solid found in some natural resins and manufactured synthetically. It is used as a food preservative and in the manufacture of pharmaceuticals and cosmetics. Formula: C_6H_5COOH.

ben·zo·in /bénzō in, -zòyn/ *n.* a toxic white crystalline solid occurring in natural resins or manufactured synthetically. It is used in medications, perfumes, and incense. Formula: $C_{14}H_{12}O_2$. [Mid-16thC. Via French *benjoin* from, ultimately Arabic *lubānjāwī* "incense from Sumatra."]

ben·zol /bén zàwl, -zōl, -zòl/ *n.* = **benzene** [Mid-19thC. Formed from *benzoic*.]

ben·zo·py·rene /bènzō pí reen, -pī reen/ *n.* a yellow carcinogenic crystalline solid that is one of the most harmful constituents of cigarette smoke. Formula: $C_{20}H_{12}$.

ben·zo·quin·one /bènzōkwi nōn, bènzō kwee nōn/ *n.* a yellow crystalline solid with an unpleasant odor. It is used in the manufacture of dyes, antioxidants, and as a photographic developer. Formula: $C_6H_4O_2$.

ben·zo·yl /bénzō ìl/ *adj.* relating to or containing a particular group of carbon and hydrogen atoms. Formula: C_6H_5CO–. [Mid-19thC. From German, from *Benzoësäure* "benzoic acid" + Greek *hylē* "wood, matter."]

benz·py·rene *n.* = **benzopyrene**

Ben-Zvi /ben zvì/, **Itzhak** (1884–1963) Polish-born Israeli statesman. A leading Zionist, he moved to Palestine in 1907. He was the second president of Israel (1952–63).

ben·zyl /bénzil, -zeel/ *adj.* relating to or containing a particular group of carbon and hydrogen atoms. Formula: $C_6H_5CH_2$–.

Be·o·wulf /báy ə wòòlf/ *n.* an anonymous Old English epic poem of the eighth century A.D. describing the exploits of the hero Beowulf, in particular his slaying of the monster Grendel and its mother

be·queath /bi kweeth, -kweeth/ (**-queathed, -queath·ing, -queaths**) *vt.* **1. LEAVE SOMEBODY SOMETHING IN WILL** to leave personal or other property to somebody after death by means of a will **2. HAND DOWN TO POSTERITY** to hand something, e.g., knowledge or a practice, down to future generations [Old English *becwe-an*, literally "to speak about," from *cwe-an* "to speak." The underlying idea is of expressing your will.] —**be·queath·al** *n.* —**be·queath·er** *n.* —**be·queath·ment** *n.*

be·quest /bi kwést/ *n.* **1. SOMETHING LEFT IN WILL** something disposed of in a will **2. SOMETHING HANDED DOWN TO POSTERITY** something passed down to future generations **3. ACT OF BEQUEATHING** an act of bequeathing something [14thC. Formed from BEQUEATH.]

Bé·ran·ger /bày raaN zháy/, **Pierre Jean de** (1780–1857) French poet. His witty political poems were very popular, though they earned him several spells in jail.

be·rate /bi ráyt/ (**-rat·ed, -rat·ing, -rates**) *vt.* to scold somebody vigorously and lengthily [Mid-16thC. Formed from RATE "to berate."]

Ber·ber /búrbər/ (*plural* **-bers** *or* **-ber**) *n.* **1.** PEOPLES **MEMBER OF N AFRICAN PEOPLE** a member of a people living in northern Africa **2.** LANG **GROUP OF AFRO-ASIATIC LANGUAGES** a group of about twenty languages spoken across northern Africa, especially in Algeria and Morocco, and constituting a branch of the Afro-Asiatic languages. Berber is sometimes regarded as a single language with very divergent dialects. About 12 million people speak a Berber language. [Mid-18thC. From Arabic *barbar* (source also of English *barbary*).] —**Ber·ber** *adj.*

ber·ber·ine /búrbə reen, búrbərin/, **ber·ber·in** /búrbərin/ *n.* a pale yellow toxic crystalline solid obtained from the roots of barberry and other plants, used formerly as an amebicide and in the treatment of cholera. Formula: $C_{20}H_{19}NO_5$. [Mid-19thC. Formed from BERBERIS.]

ber·be·ris /búrbəriss/ *n.* BOT = **barberry** [Late 16thC. Via Modern Latin or Old French from Medieval Latin *barbaris* (source of English *barberry*).]

ber·ceuse /bùr s-z/ *n.* **1. LULLABY** a lullaby or cradlesong **2.** MUSIC **PIECE OF MUSIC RESEMBLING LULLABY** an instrumental piece of music, usually in $\frac{6}{8}$ time, meant to sound like a lullaby [Late 19thC. From French, from *bercer* "to rock."]

Berch·tes·ga·den /báirkhtəss gaad'n/ town in southeastern Bavaria, Germany, a popular ski resort. Adolf Hitler's fortified retreat, the Berghof, was nearby. Population: 7,979 (1991).

Ber·czy /búrkzee/, **William von Moll** (1744–1813) German-born Canadian painter and architect. One of his most famous paintings is *The Woolsey Family* (1809).

ber·dache /bər dásh/ *n.* among some Native American peoples, somebody, usually a man, who takes on the dress, role, and status of the opposite sex [Early 19thC. Via French, "catamite," from, ultimately, Arabic *bardaj* "slave."]

Be·re·a /bə réeə/ city in northeastern Ohio, northwest of Akron and southwest of Cleveland. Population: 18,909 (1996).

be·reave /bi reev/ (**-reaved** *or* **-reft** /bi réft/, **-reav·ing, -reaves**) *vt.* to deprive somebody of a beloved person or a treasured thing, especially through death (*often passive*) [Old English *bereafian* "to deprive, rob." Ultimately from a prehistoric Germanic word that is also the ancestor of Dutch *beroven*, German *berauben* and English *rob*.] —**be·reave·ment** *n.* —**be·reav·er** *n.*

be·reaved /bi reevd/ *adj.* **DEPRIVED OF LOVED ONE BY DEATH** having lost a loved one through death ■ *n.* (*plural* **-reaved**) **SOMEBODY BEREAVED** somebody who has suffered the loss by death of a loved one

be·reft /bi réft/ (**-reft**) *adj.* **1. DEPRIVED** deprived of somebody or something loved or valued **2. LACKING** lacking in something desirable or necessary ○ *"Lively as the Tabloid Decade* (the 1990s) *has been, it wouldn't be the worst thing if it uncharacteristically just dribbled out, bereft of new material"* (David Kamp *Vanity Fair*; February 1999) **3. FEELING SENSE OF LOSS** filled with a sense of loss **4.** = **bereaved**

Ber·e·ni·ce's Hair /berrə nìssiz-/ *n.* = **Coma Berenices** [Mid-16thC. Named for a third century B.C. Egyptian queen whose hair, cut off and dedicated as an offering for her husband's safe return from war, is said to have been placed in the stars.]

Ber·en·son /bérrənssən/, **Bernard** (1865–1959) Lithuanian-born U.S. art critic and collector. He wrote extensively about Renaissance painting, and was an influential authenticator, collector, and dealer of art. Born **Bernard Valvrojenski**

be·ret /bérrày/ *n.* a flat round soft hat, usually woolen, with a tight-fitting headband [Early 19thC. Via French from, ultimately, late Latin *birrus* "hooded cloak" (source also of English *biretta*), possibly of Celtic origin.]

be·ret·ta *n.* CHR = **biretta**

berg /burg/ *n.* an iceberg [Early 19thC. Shortening.]

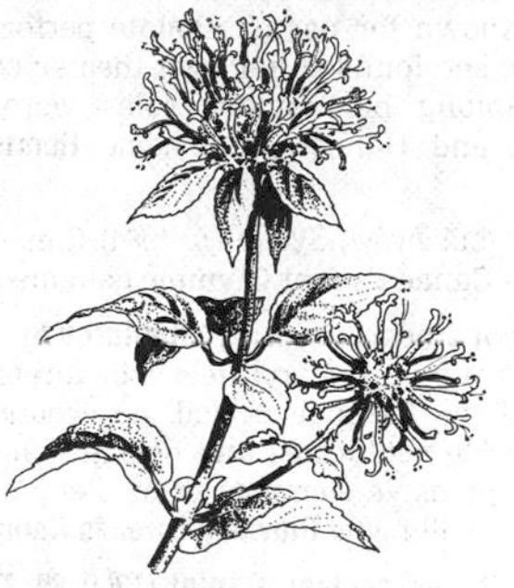

Bergamot

ber·ga·mot /búrgə mòt/ (*plural* **-mots** *or* **-mot**) *n.* **1. ber·ga·mot, ber·ga·mot or·ange SPINY ASIAN CITRUS TREE** a spiny Asian citrus tree that bears sour pear-shaped fruit. Latin name: *Citrus bergamia.* **2. ber·ga·mot, ber·ga·mot oil OIL FROM FRUIT OF BERGAMOT TREE** a fragrant yellow-green essential oil extracted from the rind of the fruits of bergamot trees, used in making perfumes **3. MEDITERRANEAN MINT PLANT** a Mediterranean mint plant that is the source of a fragrant oil similar to bergamot oil. Latin name: *Mentha citrata.* **4.** = **bee balm 5.** = **wild bergamot** [Late 17thC. Named for BERGAMO.]

Ber·gen /búrgən, bér-/ city and port in southwestern Norway and the administrative capital of Hordaland County. Population: 221,717 (1995).

Ber·gen-Bel·sen, **Bel·sen** ➧ **Belsen**

Ber·gen·field /búrgən feeld/ borough in northeastern New Jersey, north of Jersey City and east of Paterson. Population: 24,625 (1996).

ber·gen·ia /bùr geenee ə/ (*plural* **-ias** *or* **-ia**) *n.* a perennial plant with large leathery leaves, grown in gardens for its early, usually red, purple, or pink, flowers. Genus: *Bergenia*. [Mid-19thC. Named for the German botanist and physician Karl August von *Bergen*, 1704–60.]

ber·gère /bùr zháir/ (*plural* **-gères**) *n.* a type of chair or sofa with sides and back made of woven cane [Mid-18thC. From French, literally "shepherdess."]

Berg·man /búrgmən/, **Ingmar** (*b.* 1918) Swedish movie director. His many movies include dark, brooding movie classics such as *Wild Strawberries* (1957) and *The Seventh Seal* (1957). Full name **Ernst Ingmar Bergman**

Berg·man, Ingrid (1915–82) Swedish-born U.S. movie actor. Best known for her role in the movie *Casablanca* (1942), she acted in numerous U.S. and European movies, and won three Academy Awards.

berg·schrund /búrk shròònt/ (*plural* **-schrunds** *or* **-schrunde** /-ndə/) *n.* a crevasse formed at the head of a glacier [Mid-19thC. From German, literally "mountain cleft."]

Berg·son /búrgs'n/, **Henri** (1859–1941) French philosopher. One of his most influential ideas was the central role that creative energy plays in human development. He won the Nobel Prize in literature in 1927. Full name **Henri Louis Bergson** —**Berg·so·ni·an** /bèrg sōnee ən/ *n., adj.*

Berg·son·ism /búrgsənizzəm/ *n.* the philosophy of Henri Bergson, which posits the existence of a universal life-giving force (**élan vital**)

ber·i·ber·i /bèrri bérree/ *n.* a degenerative disease of the nerves caused by a deficiency of the vitamin thiamine and marked by pain, paralysis, and swelling [Early 18thC. From Sinhalese, "weakness."]

Ber·ing /beering, báiring, báring, báyring/, **Vitus** (1681–1741) Danish-born Russian explorer. He investigated the theory that Asia and North America were once connected. The Bering Sea and Bering Strait are named for him. Full name **Vitus Jonassen Bering**

Ber·ing land bridge *n.* a link between Alaska and Siberia that was above sea level during the Ice Age between 13,000 and 10,000 years ago and provided a route for prehistoric man and animals into the Americas

Ber·ing Sea part of the North Pacific Ocean surrounded by the Aleutian Islands, Siberia, and Alaska. Area: 873,000 sq. mi./2,261,000 sq. km. Depth: 15,659 ft./4,773 m.

Be·ring Strait narrow stretch of sea connecting the Bering Sea to the Arctic Ocean, and separating Russia from Alaska. At its narrowest point it is 51 mi./82 km wide.

Be·ri·o, Luciano (*b.* 1925) Italian-born composer. His experimental compositions combined prerecorded and electronic sounds, and spoken words.

Berke·le·ian·ism /baarklee ə nìzzəm, búrk-/ *n.* the philosophy of George Berkeley, particularly his view that the material world is an idea in God's mind and that an object's existence consists in its being perceived [Early 19thC. Named for Bishop *Berkeley*.] —**Berke·le·ian** *adj., n.*

Berke·ley /búrklee/ city in western California on San Francisco Bay, home to the University of California. Population: 103,243 (1996).

Berke·ley, Busby (1895–1976) U.S. movie director and choreographer. He is famous for his work in Broadway and Hollywood musicals including *42nd Street* (1933). Real name **William Berkeley Enos**

Berke·ley /búrklee, baarklee/, **Sir William** (1606–77) English-born U.S. administrator of the colony of Virginia (1641–51, 1660–76).

ber·ke·li·um /bər keelee əm, búrklee əm/ *n.* a synthetic radioactive element produced by bombarding the element americium-241 with helium ions. Symbol **Bk** [Mid-20thC. Named for BERKELEY, California, where it was first made.]

Berk·shire Hills /búrksheer-, -shər-/, **Berk·shires** low forested mountains in western Massachusetts, part of the Appalachian Mountains and a major resort area. The highest point is Mount Greylock 3,491 ft./1,064 m.

Berle /burl/, **Milton** (*b.* 1908) U.S. comedian. After a career in vaudeville, he became a fixture on television in the 1940s and 50s. Born **Milton Berlinger**. Known as **Mr. Television, Uncle Miltie**

ber·lin /bər lín/ *n.* **ber·lin, ber·line 1. FOUR-WHEELED COVERED CARRIAGE** a four-wheeled covered carriage popular in the 18th century **2. LIMOUSINE** a large and luxurious automobile with a glass partition between the driver and the passengers [Late 17thC. Named for the city of *Berlin*.]

Ber·lin /bur lín/ capital and the largest city of Germany. At the end of World War II (1945), the city was divided into East and West Berlin. It became the national capital again following the reunification of East and West Germany in 1990. Population: 3,472,000 (1997). ➧ **Berlin Wall** —**Ber·lin·er** *n.*

Express Newspapers

Irving Berlin

Ber·lin, Irving (1888–1989) Russian-born U.S. songwriter. One of the all-time great writers of American popular songs, including *White Christmas*, he also wrote numerous musicals, including *Annie Get Your Gun* (1946). Born **Israel Baline**

Ber·lin, Sir Isaiah (1909–97) Latvian-born British philosopher and historian. He espoused liberal humanism in works such as *Two Concepts of Liberty* (1959), *Vico and Herder* (1976), and *The Crooked Timber of Humanity* (1990).

ber·line /bər lín/ *n.* = **berlin** *n.* 1, **berlin** *n.* 2 [Mid-18thC. French form of BERLIN.]

Ber·lin Wall *n.* a fortified wall surrounding West Berlin, Germany, built in 1961 to prevent East German citizens traveling to the West. Its demolition in 1989 marked the end of the Cold War.

Ber·lin wool *n.* a fine wool yarn used for making clothes and in tapestry

Ber·lin wool·work *n.* needlepoint embroidery stitched with Berlin wools from handpainted colored charts, popular especially in the second half of the 19th century

Ber·li·oz /bérlee ōz, -ōs/, **Hector** (1803–69) French composer. He was a seminal figure in 19th-century romanticism. Major works among his symphonies, operas, and masses include *Symphonie Fantastique* (1831) and the opera *The Trojans* (1856–58). Full name **Louis Hector Berlioz**

berm /burm/, **berme** *n.* 1. NARROW PATH a ledge or narrow path along the top or bottom of a slope, at the edge of a road, or along a canal 2. EARTHEN EMBANKMENT an earthen embankment or wall, usually erected to provide protection from the weather or act as a landscaping screen 3. RIDGE ABOVE HIGH TIDE MARK a natural ridge or flat platform formed at the rear of a beach, above the high tide mark 4. MIL LEDGE BETWEEN MOAT AND RAMPART a ledge or narrow path between a moat or ditch and a rampart 5. MINING ROADWAY IN STRIP MINE a narrow roadway cut in the slope of a strip mine [Early 18thC. Via French from Dutch, of uncertain origin.]

Ber·mu·da /bər myoódə/ self-governing British dependency in the western North Atlantic Ocean. It contains more than 150 islands, 20 of which are inhabited. Language: English. Currency: Bermuda dollar. Capital: Hamilton. Population: 61,600 (1995). Area: 21 sq. mi./53 sq. km. —**Ber·mu·dan** *n., adj.*

Ber·mu·da bag *n.* an oval-shaped handbag with wooden handles and removable covers

Ber·mu·da grass *n.* a creeping grass with wiry roots, native to southern Europe but now widespread. It is used for lawns and pastures and to stabilize sand dunes. Latin name: *Cynodon dactylon.*

Ber·mu·da on·ion *n.* any one of various mild-flavored onions with a round flattened shape

Ber·mu·da rig *n.* a fore-and-aft arrangement of a boat's mast and sails that has a tall pointed mainsail on a sharply raked mast

Ber·mu·da shorts /bər myoódəz/, **Ber·mu·das** *npl.* tailored shorts whose legs extend almost to the knee

Ber·mu·da Tri·an·gle *n.* an area in the western Atlantic Ocean, between Bermuda, Florida, and Puerto Rico, where many ships and aircraft are believed to have disappeared in mysterious circumstances

Bern /burn, bern/, **Berne** capital of Switzerland since 1848. Situated on the Aar River in western Switzerland, it is also capital of Bern Canton. Population: 134,129 (1994).

Ber·na·dette of Lourdes /bùrnə dét əv lo͝ord, -lo͝ordz/, **St.** (1844–79) French nun and visionary. She claimed (1858) to have received apparitions of the Virgin Mary near her birthplace, Lourdes, which became a popular place of Roman Catholic pilgrimage. Born **Marie Bernarde Soubirous**

Ber·nar·dine /búrnə deen/ *n.* 1. CISTERCIAN MONK a monk belonging to a stricter branch of the Cistercian order 2. NUN a nun belonging to a non-Cistercian order that follows a rule based on the original Cistercian rule ■ *adj.* 1. OF THE BERNARDINES relating to or characteristic of a Bernardine 2. OF ST. BERNARD relating to or characteristic of St. Bernard of Clairvaux or his monastic reforms.

Berne = **Bern**

Barnaby's

Sarah Bernhardt

Bern·hardt /búrn haart/, **Sarah** (1844–1923) French actor. Known for her passionate performances in tragedy, she founded her own theater company in 1899. Among her famous roles were Cordelia, Phèdre, and Hamlet. Real name **Henriette Rosine Bernard**

Ber·ni·er /bur nyáy/, **Sylvie** (*b.* 1964) Canadian diver. She was Canada's first Olympic gold medal winner.

Ber·ni·ni /bərnéenee, ber-/, **Gianlorenzo** (1598–1680) Italian sculptor and architect. The foremost Italian artist of the Baroque period, he produced bronze and marble sculptures and designed many of the most impressive elements of St. Peter's Cathedral in Rome. Full name **Giovanni Lorenzo Bernini**

Ber·noul·li /bər nóolee/, **Daniel** (1700–82) Dutch-born Swiss mathematician and physicist. The son of Johann Bernoulli, he formulated the Bernoulli effect governing the conservation of energy in fluid dynamics.

Ber·noul·li, Jakob (1654–1705) Swiss mathematician. The brother of Johann Bernoulli, he wrote *Ars conjectandi* (1713) on the theory of probability and made theoretical advances in geometry and calculus.

Ber·noul·li, Johann *or* **Jean** (1667–1748) Swiss mathematician. He helped write the first textbook on differential calculus. He was the brother of Jakob Bernoulli and the father of Daniel Bernoulli.

Ber·noul·li dis·tri·bu·tion *n.* = **binomial distribution** [Mid-20thC. Named for Jakob BERNOULLI.]

Ber·noul·li's prin·ci·ple, Ber·noul·li's law *n.* the physical law that the sum of the pressure, potential energy, and kinetic energy is constant at any point in a tube through which a liquid is flowing steadily [Mid-20thC. Named for Jakob BERNOULLI.]

Library of Congress

Leonard Bernstein

Bern·stein /búrn stīn, -steen/, **Leonard** (1918–90) U.S. conductor, composer, and pianist. He composed classical works and the musicals *Candide* (1956) and *West Side Story* (1957).

Ber·ra /bérrə/, **Yogi** (*b.* 1925) U.S. baseball player and manager. He had an 18 year career as catcher with the New York Yankees, then managed the New York Mets and Yankees. He was celebrated for his humorous malapropisms. Real name **Lawrence Peter Berra**

ber·ried /bérreed/ *adj.* 1. BOT WITH BERRIES bearing berries or small fruits resembling berries 2. ZOOL CARRYING EGGS used to describe a lobster that is carrying eggs

ber·ry /bérree/ *n.* (*plural* **-ries**) 1. BOT SMALL JUICY FRUIT any small juicy or fleshy fruit. Berries are usually round and may be edible or inedible. 2. BOT FLESHY SEED-CONTAINING FRUIT a soft fleshy fruit that contains many seeds. Tomato, grape, and banana fruits are berries. (*technical*) 3. BOT KERNEL a seed or kernel, e.g., a coffee bean 4. ZOOL LOBSTER EGG an egg of a lobster or other egg-carrying crustacean ■ *vi.* (**-ried, -ry·ing, -ries**) 1. SEARCH FOR EDIBLE BERRIES to gather or hunt for berries to eat 2. BEAR BERRIES to produce berries (*refers to bushes*) [Old English *beri(g)e.* Ultimately from a prehistoric Germanic word that is also the ancestor of Dutch *bes* and German *Beere.*]

Ber·ry /bérree/, **Martha McChesney** (1866–1942) U.S. educator. She founded schools in Appalachia that taught practical skills and became a model for other schools across the South.

Ber·ry·man /bérreemən/, **John** (1914–72) U.S. poet, writer, and critic. In collections such as the Pulitzer Prize-winning *77 Dream Songs* (1964) he revealed his own emotional struggles. Full name **John McAlpin Berryman**

ber·seem /bər seem/ *n.* a Mediterranean clover grown for forage for grazing livestock and to improve soil quality, especially in the southern United States and the Nile Valley. Latin name: *Trifolium alexandrinum.* [Early 20thC. Via Arabic *birsīm* from Coptic *bersīm.*]

ber·serk /bər súrk, -zúrk/ *adj.* extremely aggressive or angry ○ *go berserk* [Early 19thC. From Old Norse *berserk* "wild warrior," probably from the stem of *bjorn* "bear" + *serkr* "shirt," because either they wore bearskins or were fierce like bears.] —**ber·serk·ly** *adv.*

ber·serk·er /bər súrkər, -zúr-/ *n.* a member of a group of Norse warriors who fought with wild unrestrained aggression

berth /burth/ *n.* 1. BED ON SHIP OR TRAIN a bed, usually built-in, on a ship or a train 2. NAUT DOCK FOR SHIP a place, usually alongside a quay or dock, where a ship ties up or anchors 3. NAUT ROOM TO MANEUVER AT SEA sufficient room between a ship and the shore or between a ship and another vessel or object to allow the ship to maneuver safely 4. PARKING PLACE a place for a motor vehicle to park or be loaded or unloaded 5. NAUT JOB ON SHIP a position as a member of a ship's crew 6. JOB a job or position of employment (*informal*) ■ *v.* (**berthed, berth·ing, berths**) 1. *vti.* NAUT DOCK A SHIP to dock or moor a vessel, or be docked or moored 2. *vt.* NAUT ASSIGN MOORING TO VESSEL to assign a vessel a place to dock or moor 3. *vt.* ASSIGN BERTH TO SOMEBODY to assign somebody a berth on a ship or train [Early 17thC. Formed from BEAR "to carry." Originally in the sense "enough room to steer in," probably influenced by BEAR in the sense "to steer in a particular direction."] ◇ **give somebody** *or* **something a wide berth** to keep well away from somebody or something

ber·tha /búrthə/ *n.* a wide long collar around the shoulders of a woman's low-necked dress [Mid-19thC. From French *berthe,* named for the Carolingian Queen *Bertha,* died A.D. 783, wife of Pepin the Short.]

Ber·thon /bair thóN/, **George Theodore** (1806–92) Austrian-born Canadian portraitist. He is noted for his portraits of the business and judicial elite of Upper Canada.

Ber·til·lon sys·tem /búrt'l òn-, berti yáwN-/ *n.* a former method of identifying people, especially criminals, on the basis of detailed records of their physical measurements and characteristics [Late 19thC. Named for the French criminologist Alphonse *Bertillon,* 1853–1914, who invented it.]

Ber·ton /búrt'n/, **Pierre** (*b.* 1920) Canadian journalist, historian, and media personality. He wrote works of popular history, including *Klondike* (1958).

Ber·wyn /búrwin/ city in northeastern Illinois. It is

a residential suburb west of Chicago. Population: 43,735 (1996).

ber·yl /bérrəl/ *n.* a hard mineral, beryllium aluminum silicate, that occurs in white, yellow, pink, green, or blue forms. The green form is emerald, the blue is aquamarine, and the other forms are also valued as gems. Formula: $Be_3Al_2Si_6O_{18}$. [12thC. Via French and Latin *beryllus* from Greek *bērullos*, probably from, ultimately, Pali *veḷuriya*, perhaps meaning "white, pale."] —**ber·yl·line** /bèrrə lín, -līn/ *adj.*

be·ryl·li·um /bə rílee əm/ *n.* a metallic gray-white chemical element that is light, hard, brittle, and resists corrosion. It is used in alloys, as a lightweight construction material, and in windows in X-ray tubes. Symbol **Be** [Mid-19thC. Formed from BERYL, which is a major source.]

be·seech /bi séech/ (**-sought** /bi sáwt/ *or* **-seeched, -seech·ing, -seech·es**) *vt.* (*literary*) **1. BEG SOMEBODY** to ask earnestly or beg somebody to do something **2. BEG FOR SOMETHING** to ask urgently for something [12thC. Formed from SEEK.] —**be·seech·er** *n.* —**be·seech·ing·ly** *adv.*

be·set /bi sét/ (**-set, -set·ting, -sets**) *vt.* (*usually passive*) **1. HARASS** to harass or trouble somebody or something continually ○ *beset by nasty rumors.* **2. SURROUND** to attack somebody or something on all sides (*formal*) **3. SET WITH JEWELS** to surround or set something with jewels or other ornaments (*literary*) [Old English *besettan*, literally "to set about"] —**be·set·ment** *n.* —**be·set·ter** *n.*

be·set·ting /bi sétting/ *adj.* harassing or troubling somebody continually

be·shrew /bi shróo/ (**-shrewed, -shrew·ing, -shrews**) *vt.* to curse or wish evil upon somebody (*archaic; usually used in mild oaths*) [13thC. Formed from SHREW in its obsolete sense "to nag."]

be·side /bi sīd/ *prep.* **1. AT THE SIDE OF** in a position next to or alongside ○ *Sit beside me.* **2. COMPARED WITH** in comparison with ○ *handsome beside his brother* **3. AS WELL AS** in addition to ○ *in another dictionary beside this one* [Old English *be sīdan*, literally "by the side of"] ◇ **beside yourself** in a very excited or agitated state

WORD KEY: USAGE

beside or **besides**? ***Beside*** is used with reference to physical position: *Come and sit beside me.* It is also used in the idiomatic expression ***to be beside yourself***: *They were beside themselves with worry.* ***Besides*** is an adverb meaning "moreover": *it's late and besides, the weather's too cold*, and a preposition meaning "in addition to": *They've already paid a lot for the house besides what they'll need for improvements.* Note that ***besides*** is inclusive, whereas ***except*** is exclusive, so that *they are all friends of mine besides Larry* means that Larry is also a friend whereas *they are all friends of mine except Larry* means that Larry is not a friend.

be·sides /bi sīdz/ *prep., adv.* **AS WELL** in addition to something or somebody specified or understood ○ *Besides fruit, we will also need cheese, and crackers.* ■ *adv.* **MOREOVER** what is more ○ *He's my cousin. Besides, he's good company.*

be·siege /bi séej/ (**-sieged, -sieg·ing, -sieg·es**) *vt.* **1. SURROUND WITH ARMY** to surround a city or stronghold with armed forces in order to bring about its surrender or capture **2. CROWD AROUND SOMEBODY** to crowd around somebody in an oppressive way (*usually passive*) ○ *the newlyweds were besieged by reporters outside their hotel* **3. HARASS** to harass a person or organization with insistent demands or complaints (*usually passive*) ○ *The box office was besieged by fans wanting tickets.* [13thC. Formed from earlier *assiege*, via Old French *asegier* from, ultimately, Latin *sedere* (see SIEGE).] —**be·siege·ment** *n.* —**be·sieg·er** *n.*

be·smear /bi sméer/ (**-smeared, -smear·ing, -smears**) *vt.* **1. SMEAR WITH SUBSTANCE** to smear somebody or something with mud, dirt, or some greasy or sticky substance **2. SULLY** to bring shame or disgrace on somebody or something

be·smirch /bi smúrch/ (**-smirched, -smirch·ing, -smirch·es**) *vt.* **1. SULLY** to bring shame or disgrace on somebody's reputation **2. MAKE DIRTY** to make something dirty (*literary*) —**be·smirch·er** *n.* —**be·smirch·ment** *n.*

be·som /béezəm, bízzəm/ *n.* **1. BROOM MADE FROM TWIGS** a broom, especially one made from a bundle of twigs **2.** SPORTS **BROOM USED IN CURLING** a broom used in curling to sweep the ice in front of a moving stone in order to help it slide ■ *vt.* (**-somed, -som·ing, -soms**) **SWEEP WITH BROOM** to sweep something with a broom [Old English *bes(e)ma*. Ultimately from a prehistoric Germanic word that is also the ancestor of Dutch *bezem* and German *Besen*.]

be·sot·ted /bi sóttəd/ *adj.* **1. INFATUATED** made confused through affection for or attraction to somebody **2. MUDDLED** in a confused mental state, especially through having drunk too much alcohol (*archaic*) [Late 16thC. Formed from earlier *sot* "to stupefy," from Old French, "fool."]

be·sought past tense, past participle of **beseech**

be·span·gle /bi spáng g'l/ (**-gled, -gling, -gles**) *vt.* to ornament something with something bright, especially spangles

be·spat·ter /bi spáttər/ (**-tered, -ter·ing, -ters**) *vt.* to splash something with mud, paint, or some other substance

be·speak /bi spéek/ (**-spoke** /-spṓk/, **-spo·ken** /-spṓkən/, **-speak·ing, -speaks**) *vt.* **1. SIGNIFY** to be a sign or indication of something **2. ASK FOR POLITELY** to ask politely for something, e.g., a favor (*formal*) **3. ADDRESS SOMEBODY** to speak to somebody (*literary*) **4. PORTEND** to foretell something (*archaic*) [Old English *bisprecan*, literally "to speak about," from *sprecan* "to speak" (see SPEAK)]

be·spec·ta·cled /bi spéktək'ld/ *adj.* wearing eyeglasses

be·spoke past tense of **bespeak**

be·spo·ken past participle of **bespeak**

be·sprin·kle /bi spríngk'l/ (**-kled, -kling, -kles**) *vt.* to sprinkle small quantities of liquid or something light over the surface of something (*often passive*)

Bes·sa·ra·bi·a /bèssə ráybee ə/ Historic region in southeastern Europe, between the Prut and Dniester Rivers, corresponding rougly to present-day Moldova and part of Ukraine. A much-contested area, it was a province of Romania between 1918 and 1940.

Bes·sel /béssəl/, **Friedrich Wilhelm** (1784–1846) German mathematician and astronomer. He identified and determined the distance of the nearest stars, and predicted the existence of a planet beyond Uranus.

Bes·se·mer /béssəmər/ city south of Birmingham, central Alabama, named for Sir Henry Bessemer. Population: 31,234 (1996).

Bes·se·mer proc·ess *n.* a largely obsolete method for making steel from impure iron by forcing air through the molten metal in a specialized furnace (**Bessemer converter**) [Late 19thC. Named for Sir Henry *Bessemer*, who patented it.]

Bes·sette /be sét/, **Gerard** (*b.* 1920) Canadian novelist and critic. The author of *L'incubation* (1965), he was a leader in Canadian psychoanalytic literary criticism.

best /best/ CORE MEANING: better than anybody or anything else

1. *adj.* **BETTER THAN ALL OTHERS** of the highest quality or standard or the most excellent type ○ *the best days of your life* ○ *wearing her best dress* ○ *the best sprinter of the decade* **2.** *adj.* **MOST LIKELY TO SUCCEED** most likely to have or come near to the desired outcome ○ *the best thing to do in the circumstances* **3.** *adj.* **MOST INTIMATE** liked, trusted, and confided in more than anybody else ○ *my best friends* **4.** *adv.* **MORE THAN ALL OTHERS** in the highest degree or to the greatest extent ○ *likes me best* **5.** *adv.* **MOST SUCCESSFULLY** in a way that is most likely to have or come near to the desired outcome ○ *It works best if you warm it up first.* **6.** *adv.* **TO THE HIGHEST STANDARD** to a higher standard than anybody or anything else ○ *the best trained horse in the competition* **7.** *n.* **WHAT IS BEST** the best possible things or circumstances ○ *want the best for their family* ○ *will only buy the best* **8.** *n.* **SOMEBODY OR SOMETHING BETTER THAN OTHERS** somebody or something of the highest quality or standard ○ *is the best at hockey* **9.** *n.* **TOP QUALITY** the highest quality or standard that somebody or something is capable of ○ *do your best* ○ *past its best* **10.** *n.* SPORTS **TOP ACHIEVEMENT** the best time or score that somebody has achieved in a sport or game ○ *trying to beat her personal best in the marathon* **11.** *n.* **ENDORSEMENT** used as an enthusiastic endorsement of something (*slang*) ○ *How is your hotel? – It's the best!* [Old English *betest*; superlative of GOOD and WELL. Ultimately from a prehistoric Germanic word that is also the ancestor of German and Dutch *best*.] ◇ **at best** according to the most favorable interpretation ◇ **at the best of times** even when circumstances are at their most favorable ◇ **at your** *or* **its best** performing at the peak of ability or effectiveness ◇ **make the best of something** to do what is required to deal with an unfavorable situation

Best /best/, **Charles H.** (1899–1978) U.S.-born Canadian physiologist. He was the codiscoverer of insulin with Frederick Banting (1922). Full name **Charles Herbert Best**

best-ball *adj.* using a scoring method in which a golfer competes against a team of two or three other golfers, with the team recording only the best individual score for each hole

best boy *n.* the chief assistant to the electrician in charge of lighting (**gaffer**) on a movie or television set

bes·tial /béschəl, bées-/ *adj.* **1. INHUMAN** lacking normal human feelings of pity or remorse ○ *bestial cruelty* **2. SEXUALLY DEPRAVED** sexual in a depraved or purely physical manner **3. BRUTISH** lacking intellect, reason, or culture **4. RELATING TO BEASTS** relating to or characteristic of a beast [14thC. Via Old French from, ultimately, Latin *bestia* (see BEAST).] —**bes·tial·ly** *adv.*

bes·ti·al·i·ty /bèschee állitee, bèes-/ *n.* **1. SEX WITH ANIMAL** sexual intercourse or other sexual activity between a human being and an animal **2. INHUMAN BEHAVIOR** an act, behavior, or condition more appropriate for an animal than a human being

bes·tial·ize /béschə līz, bées-/ (**-ized, -iz·ing, -iz·es**) *vt.* **1. REDUCE TO LEVEL OF ANIMAL** to make somebody behave or live like an animal **2. MAKE INHUMAN** to make somebody inhuman or savage

bes·ti·ar·y /béschee èrree, bées-/ (*plural* **-ies**) *n.* a medieval book containing pictures and moralizing stories about real and imaginary animals [Mid-19thC. From medieval Latin *bestiarium*, from Latin *bestia* "beast."]

be·stir /bi stúr/ (**-stirred, -stir·ring, -stirs**) *vr.* to begin to do something after a period of inactivity (*formal*) ○ *After a long afternoon nap, they finally bestirred themselves to start the supper preparations.* [14thC. Coined from BE- "all over, thoroughly" + STIR.]

best man (*plural* **best men**) *n.* a male attendant of a bridegroom, who carries out important duties during the wedding celebrations

be·stow /bi stṓ/ (**-stowed, -stow·ing, -stows**) *vt.* **1. GIVE OR PRESENT SOMETHING** to present something to somebody (*formal*) **2. PUT SOMEWHERE** to put something somewhere (*archaic*) ○ *"Alonso hence, and bestow your luggage where you found it."* (William Shakespeare, *The Tempest*; 1611) —**be·stow·ment** *n.*

WORD KEY: SYNONYMS

See Synonyms at ***give***.

be·strew /bi stróo/ (**-strewed, -strewed** *or* **-strewn** /-stróon/, **-strew·ing, -strews**) *vt.* (*literary*) **1. SCATTER THINGS** to scatter things over something ○ *a church aisle bestrewn with flowers* **2. BE SCATTERED OVER SOMETHING** to be scattered over something ○ *the rice that bestrewed the church steps after the wedding*

be·stride /bi strīd/ (**-strode** /-strṓd/, **-strid·den** /-strídd'n/, **-strid·ing, -strides**) *vt.* to sit or stand with one leg on each side of something ○ *He bestrode the courtroom entranceway, holding forth on the merits of the case to the assembled press.*

best·sell·er /bèst séllər/ *n.* **1. POPULAR PRODUCT** something, especially a book, that is commercially very successful **2. AUTHOR OF POPULAR BOOKS** an author who writes bestsellers

best·sell·ing /bèst sélling/ *adj.* far more popular and successful than other products on sale at the same time ○ *his bestselling account of life in the wilderness*

bet /bet/ *n.* **1. ACT OF BETTING** an agreement that the person who incorrectly predicts the outcome of a future event will forfeit something, usually money, to another **2. AMOUNT WAGERED** the amount of money that somebody agrees to pay as a bet ○ *She placed a bet of $5, and won $500.* **3. WHAT SOMEBODY EXPECTS OR THINKS** what somebody expects to happen or thinks is true ○ *My bet is they'll decide to overlook the whole thing.* **4. SOMEBODY OR SOMETHING LIKELY TO WIN** somebody or something likely to be successful ○ *She's a good bet for a vice-presidency.* ■ *vti.* (**bet** *or* **bet·ted, bet·ting, bets**) **1. RISK SOMETHING OF VALUE** to agree with somebody that something specified, usually money, will be forfeited by the person who incorrectly predicts the outcome of a future event to the other **2. THINK**

SOMETHING IS TRUE to express certainty that something will happen, has happened, or is true (*informal*) ○ *I bet he's forgotten to bring the keys.* [Late 16thC. Origin uncertain: perhaps a shortening of ABET; the underlying idea would be of support for what you think may happen.] ◇ **your best** *or* **safest bet** the course of action most likely to be productive ◇ **you bet!** used to show emphatic agreement (*informal*)

be·ta /báytə, beétə/ *n.* **1. 2ND LETTER OF GREEK ALPHABET** the second letter of the Greek alphabet, represented in English as "b." See table at **alphabet 2.** FIN **MEASURE OF PRICE SENSITIVITY** a measure of the relative price sensitivity of a security to that of the overall market **3.** COMPUT **TEST** a beta test (*informal*) ■ *adj.* **1.** NUCLEAR PHYS **RELATING TO ELECTRONS PRODUCED BY RADIOACTIVITY** used to describe electrons, especially those formed by the splitting of a neutron into a proton and an electron **2.** CHEM **SECOND NEAREST TO DESIGNATED ATOM** used to describe the second nearest atom to a designated atom or group of atoms in an organic molecule **3. DESCRIBING MINOR FORM OF ELEMENT** used to describe a minor form of a chemical element with more than one form (**allotrope**) [14thC. Via Latin and Greek from Canaanite *bet* "house" (see BETH).]

Be·ta /báytə, beétə/ *n.* the second brightest star in a constellation (*followed by the Latin genitive*) ○ *Beta Centauri*

be·ta-block·er *n.* a drug belonging to a group used to regulate the activity of the heart, especially in the treatment of high blood pressure, by suppressing the activity of beta-receptors

be·ta-car·o·tene *n.* = **carotene**

be·ta de·cay *n.* the radioactive transformation of an atomic nucleus during which an electron or positron is produced, although the mass number remains unchanged

be·ta·ine /beétə een, -in/ *n.* a sweet-tasting organic compound that occurs naturally in plants and animals, especially in sugar beets. It has been used as a treatment for muscular degeneration. Formula: $C_5H_{11}NO_2$. [Mid-19thC. Formed from Latin *beta* "beet" (see BEET.]

be·take /bi táyk/ (**-took** /-to͝ok/, **-tak·en** /-táykən/, **-tak·ing, -takes**) *vr.* to go somewhere (*archaic or literary*)

Be·tan·court /bétt'n ko͝or, bé taan ko͝ort/, **Rómulo** (1908–81) Venezuelan statesman. He helped to found Democratic Action (1941) and spent periods in exile. As president of Venezuela (1959–64) he instituted reforms that paved the way for democracy.

be·ta-ox·i·da·tion *n.* BIOCHEM the breakdown of fatty acids that occurs during cellular metabolism, characterized by the successive removal from one end of the molecule of segments that contain two carbon atoms

be·ta par·ti·cle *n.* a high-speed electron emitted from the nucleus of an atom during radioactive decay and created by the splitting of a neutron into a proton and an electron

be·ta proc·ess *n.* = **beta decay**

be·ta ray *n.* a stream of beta particles

be·ta-re·cep·tor *n.* a site on cells in the autonomic nervous system that responds to hormones such as epinephrine and operates to control blood pressure, regulate the heartbeat, and contract muscles

be·ta rhythm *n.* a pattern of electrical waves in the brain of somebody who is awake and active (**beta waves**), registering on an electroencephalogram at a reading between 18 and 30 hertz

be·ta test *vt.* (**be·ta test·ed, be·ta test·ing, be·ta tests**) **GIVE TO USERS TO TRY** to test a product, especially computer software, by giving it to customers to try out before the final version is put on sale ■ *n.* **TEST BY CUSTOMERS** a test of a product, especially computer software, by giving it to a few customers to try out, before the final version is put on sale

be·ta trans·for·ma·tion *n.* = **beta decay**

be·ta·tron /báytə tròn, beétə-/ *n.* a device that accelerates electrons in a circular orbit by means of a rapidly alternating magnetic field. In this way, electrons can reach energies of 340 MeV and may be used to strike a metal target to produce a continuous stream of gamma rays. [Mid-20thC. Coined from BETA+ -TRON.]

be·ta·ware /báytə wair, beétə-/ *n.* a version of computer software that is to be tested by giving it to customers before the final version is put on sale

be·ta wave *n.* a high-frequency electrical wave produced in the human brain and associated with normal wakefulness. ◊ **beta rhythm**

bet·cha /béchə/ *contr.* a form of "bet you" used mainly in conversation (*nonstandard*) ○ *Betcha the Lions win by 20 points.*

be·tel /beét'l/ (*plural* **-tels** *or* **-tel**) *n.* an evergreen Asian climbing plant with wide leaves that people in Asia chew as a mild stimulant and digestive aid. Latin name: *Piper betle.* [Mid-16thC. Via Portuguese from Malayalam *verrila*, from Tamil *vrrilai*.]

Be·tel·geuse /beét'l jo͞oz, beét'l jŏz/ *n.* a bright red variable supergiant star that is the second brightest star in the constellation Orion and the twelfth brightest in the night sky

be·tel nut *n.* one of the dark red seeds of the betel palm that is wrapped in betel leaves with lime and chewed by people in Asia as a mild stimulant

be·tel palm *n.* a tropical Asian palm tree that has orange fruit and dark red seeds. Latin name: *Areca catechu.*

bete noire /bet nwaár/ (*plural* **betes noires** /bèt-/), **bête noire** (*plural* **bête noires**) *n.* somebody or something you particularly dislike (*literary*) [Mid-19thC. From French, literally "black beast."]

beth /bet/ *n.* the second letter of the Hebrew alphabet, represented as "b" in English. See table at **alphabet** [Early 19thC. From Hebrew, from *bayith* "house."]

Beth Din /bet deén/ (*plural* **Ba·tei Din** /baá tay deén/) *n.* a Jewish religious court regulating matters of Jewish law such as dietary laws, divorce, and conversion [Late 18thC. From Hebrew *bēṯ dīn* "house of judgment."]

Be·the /báytə/, **Hans** (*b.* 1906) German-born U.S. physicist. He helped develop the atomic bomb (1943–46). His work on stellar nuclear energy won him the Nobel Prize in physics (1967). Full name **Hans Albrecht Bethe**

beth·el /béthəl/ *n.* (*archaic*) **1. HOLY PLACE** a place that is regarded as sacred or holy **2. SAILORS' CHAPEL** a chapel for sailors and other seafarers [Early 17thC. From Hebrew *bēṯ- 'ēl*, literally "house of God."]

Beth·el Park /bèthəl-/ borough in southwestern Pennsylvania in a former coal-mining region south of Pittsburgh. Population: 33,661 (1996).

Be·thes·da /bə thézdə/ town northwest of Washington, D.C., in Montgomery County, Maryland. It is home to the National Institutes of Health and two large army and navy medical centers. Population: 62,936 (1990).

be·think /bi thíngk/ (**-thought** /-tháwt/, **-thought, -think·ing, -thinks**) *vr.* to think of or remember something (*archaic*)

Beth·le·hem /béthli hèm, -lee əm/ **1.** town in the West Bank near Jerusalem. Part of Israel since 1967, it has been administered by the Palestinian Authority since 1995. Thought to be the birthplace of King David and Jesus, it is regarded as a holy city by Christians. Population: 34,100 (1987). **2.** city in eastern Pennsylvania on the Lehigh River. It is a major steel-manufacturing center. Population: 70,245 (1996).

be·thought past tense, past participle of **bethink**

Corbis/Library of Congress

Mary McLeod Bethune

Be·thune /bə tho͞on, -thyo͞on/, **Mary McLeod** (1875–1955) U.S. educator and activist. The child of slaves, she founded and was president of what became Bethune-Cookman College, Daytona Beach, Florida. She promoted education for African Americans and founded the National Council of Negro Women (1935).

be·tide /bi tíd/ (**-tides**) *vti.* to happen, or happen to somebody (*archaic*) ○ *Whether good or ill betide you, trust in God.*

be·times /bi tímz/ *adv.* (*archaic*) **1. EARLY** early, or in good time **2. SOON** in a short time [13thC. From BY + TIME.]

bê·tise /bay teéz/ (*plural* **-tis·es** /bay teéz/) *n.* mildly ridiculous action or remark (*literary*) [Early 19thC. From French, from *bête* "foolish," from Old French *beste* "beast."]

be·to·ken /bi tókən/ (**-kened, -ken·ing, -kens**) *vt.* to be a sign that something exists or will happen (*literary*)

bet·o·ny /bétt'nee/ (*plural* **-nies**) *n.* **1. PLANT WITH PURPLISH FLOWERS** a plant of the mint family that grows in Europe and Asia and has purplish flowers, formerly used in medicine. Latin name: *Stachys officinalis.* **2. PLANT LIKE TRUE BETONY** any plant resembling betony proper **3.** = **lousewort** [14thC. From, ultimately, Latin *betonica*, variant of *Vettonica*, of uncertain origin: perhaps formed from *Vettones* (plural), an Iberian people.]

be·took past tense of **betake**

be·tray /bi tráy/ (**-trayed, -tray·ing, -trays**) *vt.* **1. HELP AN ENEMY** to harm or be disloyal to your own country or another person by helping or giving information to an enemy **2. SURRENDER SOMEBODY OR SOMETHING TREACHEROUSLY** to deliver somebody or something to an enemy ○ *He betrayed his own brother to the secret police.* **3. GO AGAINST A PROMISE** to act in a way that is contrary to a promise made ○ *"If an intelligent person is betrayed repeatedly, and humiliated publicly, yet chooses to remain in that situation, one must ask: what are the rewards?"* (Gail Sheehy, *Vanity Fair*; February 1999) **4. REVEAL SOMETHING** to show something, often unintentionally ○ *She said nothing, but her bright eyes betrayed her excitement.* **5. DECEIVE SOMEBODY** to deceive somebody, or lead somebody into doing something wrong (*dated*) [13thC. Formed from Old French *trair*, from Latin *tradere* "to hand over."] —**be·tray·er** *n.*

be·tray·al /bi tráy əl/ *n.* the act or an instance of betraying somebody or something

be·troth /bi tróth, -tráwth/ (**-trothed, -troth·ing, -troths**) *vt.* to promise to marry somebody, or promise that somebody will marry somebody (*formal*) [14thC. Coined from BE- + TRUTH.]

be·troth·al /bi tróthəl, -tráwthəl/ *n.* the act of becoming engaged to marry somebody, or the state of being engaged to somebody (*formal*)

be·trothed /bi tróthd, -tráwtht/ (*plural* **-trotheds** *or* **-trothed**) *n.* the person to whom somebody is engaged to be married (*formal*) —**betrothed** *adj.*

Bet·tel·heim /bétt'l hìm/, **Bruno** (1903–90) Austrian-born U.S. psychologist. A member of the University of Chicago faculty, he was best known for his treatment of autistic children and for his study of the meaning of fairy tales, *The Uses of Enchantment* (1976).

Bet·ten·dorf /bétt'n dàwrf/ city in eastern Iowa, on the Mississippi River, in Scott County. Population: 31,015 (1996).

bet·ter[1] /béttər/ (**-tered, -ter·ing, -ters**) CORE MEANING: indicating that a thing or an action is superior in some way to something else or is an improvement upon a situation ○ (adj) *Concentrated laundry detergent is better because it requires a smaller box or bottle.* ○ (adj) *She is gradually getting better, albeit slowly.* ○ (adv) *Treatment programs may get the job done better.*

1. *adj.* **MORE LIKABLE** more attractive or likable than something else ○ *That hairsyle is far better than the one you had before.* **2.** *adj.* **OF GREATER QUALITY** of greater quality, usefulness, or suitability than something else ○ *Economic security helps ensure a better future for our children.* ○ *It is better to light a candle than to curse the darkness.* **3.** *adj.* **IMPROVED IN HEALTH** in an improved state of health, after not being well ○ *I'm feeling much better today, thank you.* **4.** *adv.* **MORE OR TO A HIGHER STANDARD** more, or in a more skillful or effective way ○ *He plays tennis much better than I do.* ○ *I liked her much better after I got to know her.* **5.** *adv.* **PREFERABLY** in a way that is preferable or more advantageous ○ *Such things are better left unsaid.* **6.** *adv.* **OUGHT TO OR MUST DO SOMETHING** indicates that it would be more advantageous for somebody to act in a particular way (*nonstandard*) ○ *You better listen* *to me!* **7.** *vt.* SURPASS SOMETHING to improve on something ○ *She hopes to better the record that she set at last year's championships.* ○ *He summed the whole thing up in a way that I couldn't possibly better.* **8.** *vt.* IMPROVE SELF OR THING to improve yourself or something (*formal*) ○ *They tried to better themselves by attaining a good education.* ○ *attempts to better the lot of the refugees* **9.** *n.* SUPERIOR PERSON a person who is superior to another in some way (*often used in the plural*) ○ *You should listen to the advice of your elders and betters.* [13thC. From Old English *bettra*, from the comparative of a prehistoric Germanic word meaning "advantageous," which is also the ancestor of English *best* and *boot* "remedy."] ◇ **for better or worse** whatever the outcome may be ◇ **get the better of somebody 1.** to defeat somebody in some way **2.** to be too strong for somebody to control ◇ **go one better** to do something that has been done before but in a superior or preferable way ◇ **had better do something** ought to or must do something ○ *You'd better tell them soon.* ◇ **think better of something** to change your mind and decide not to do something ○ *After seeing the ice on the streets we thought better of making the trip.*

bet·ter² /béttər/ *n.* GAMBLING = **bettor**

bet·ter half (*plural* **bet·ter halves**) *n.* somebody's wife or husband (*informal*)

bet·ter·ment /béttərmənt/ *n.* **1.** CHANGE FOR BETTER a change that improves something, especially somebody's financial or social condition (*formal*) **2.** PROPERTY IMPROVEMENT improvement of a building or land that increases its value

bet·ting /bétting/ *n.* the activity of placing bets

bet·tor /béttər/, **bet·ter** *n.* somebody who bets

be·tween /bi twéen/ CORE MEANING: a grammatical word indicating an intermediate point between two places or times ○ (prep) *I was standing between two other women.* ○ (prep) *I intend to pay off my mortgage between now and 2010.* ○ (adv) *He worked two shifts, with an hour off between.*

prep. **1.** TO AND FROM from one place to another ○ *She travels between Los Angeles and Santa Monica most days.* **2.** TOGETHER together or in combination with ○ *Between us we should have enough money to pay for the trip.* **3.** INDICATES COMPARISON indicates a comparison, discussion, or relationship involving two people or groups ○ *Reconciliation was hampered by personality conflicts between company executives.* **4.** INDICATES CHOICES indicates two or more possible courses of action ○ *Police offer them a choice between school, a stiff fine, or community service.* [13thC. From Old English *betwēonum*, literally "by two each," from *twēonum* "two each" (related to *twā* "two" (see TWO).] ◇ **(just) between you and me** used to indicate that something is very confidential

WORD KEY: USAGE

between or **among**? Although some people insist on using ***among*** and not ***between*** when more than two items are involved, it is established usage to use ***between*** in this meaning as well, especially when ***among*** might sound too formal: *There is still no agreement on this topic between the NATO countries.*

be·tween·times /bi twéen tīmz/ *adv.* in the intervals between doing other things

be·twixt /bi twíkst/ *adv., prep.* between (*archaic*) [14thC. From Old English *betweox*, from *tweox* "for two" (see TWO). The final "t" began to be used widely in the 16thC.] ◇ **betwixt and between** between two groups or categories, without belonging to one or the other

BeV *abbr.* billion (10^9) electron volts

bev·el /bévv'l/ *n.* **1.** SLANTING EDGE a surface that joins another surface at an angle that is not a right angle **2.** ANGLE the angle at which one surface joins another, when this is not a right angle **3.** TOOL a tool with two legs that can be adjusted to make various angles, and used to measure or mark an angle on something ■ *vt.* (**-eled, -el·ing, -els**) MAKE SLANTING EDGE to shape the edge of something so that it forms an angle other than a right angle with the main surface ○ *a mirror with beveled edges* [Late 17thC. From assumed Old French, of uncertain origin: perhaps formed from *baif* "gaping."]

bev·el gear *n.* either of a pair of gear wheels, one conical and the other flat or conical, connecting and transmitting power between shafts that are not parallel

bev·el square *n.* = **bevel** *n.* 3

bev·er·age /bévvərij, bévvrij/ *n.* a drink other than water (*formal*) (*used mainly in commercial contexts*) [14thC. From Old French *bevrage*, from *bevre*, variant of *boire*, from Latin *bibere* "to drink" (source of English *bib* and *imbibe*).]

Bev·er·ly /bévvərlee/ city on Massachuetts Bay in northeastern Massachusetts. It was home to America's first successful cotton mill. Population: 38,195 (1990).

Bev·er·ly Hills wealthy residential and commercial city in southwestern California, a western suburb of Los Angeles. Population: 32,367 (1996).

bev·y /bévvee/ (*plural* **-ies**) *n.* **1.** GROUP OF PEOPLE a group of people **2.** GROUP OF ANIMALS a group of animals, especially quail, larks, or roe deer [15thC. Origin uncertain: perhaps from Old French *bevee* "drink."]

be·wail /bi wáyl/ (**-wailed, -wail·ing, -wails**) *vt.* to express great sadness about something (*formal*)

be·ware /bi wáir/ *vti.* to be on guard against somebody or something (*used only as a command and in the infinitive*) [13thC. From the phrase *be ware* "be careful" (see AWARE).]

be·whis·kered /bi wískərd/ *adj.* sporting whiskers or a beard ○ *bewhiskered gentlemen drinking port in their club*

Be·wick's swan /byóo iks/ *n.* a small swan belonging to the race of tundra swans that lives mainly in marshy and swampy Arctic regions of Europe and Asia. Latin name: *Cygnus bewickii.*

be·wigged /bi wígd/ *adj.* wearing a wig

be·wil·der /bi wíldər/ (**-dered, -der·ing, -ders**) *vt.* to confuse or puzzle somebody completely [Late 17thC. Back-formation from BEWILDERED.] —**be·wil·der·ment** *n.*

be·wil·dered /bi wíldərd/ *adj.* extremely confused [Late 17thC. Coined from BE + archaic *wilder*, of uncertain origin: probably a back-formation from WILDERNESS on the model of WANDER.] —**be·wil·dered·ly** *adv.* —**be·wil·dered·ness** *n.*

be·wil·der·ing /bi wíldəring/ *adj.* extremely confusing —**be·wil·der·ing·ly** *adv.*

be·witch /bi wích/ (**-witched, -witch·ing, -witch·es**) *vt.* **1.** ENCHANT SOMEBODY to fascinate or be very attractive to somebody (*often passive*) **2.** CAST SPELL ON SOMEBODY OR SOMETHING to affect somebody or something using a magic spell [13thC. Coined from BE- + *wicchen* "to enchant," from, ultimately, an earlier form of WITCH.] —**be·witch·er** *n.* —**be·witch·ment** *n.*

be·witch·ing /bi wíching/ *adj.* fascinating, charming, or very attractive —**be·witch·ing·ly** *adv.*

bey /bay/ (*plural* **beys**) *n.* **1.** GOVERNOR a title used for various high-ranking officials in the Ottoman Empire, especially governors of a province **2.** TITLE a respectful form of address for men used in Turkey and Egypt [Late 16thC. From Turkish, from Old Turkish *beg* "prince."]

be·yond /bee ónd, bi yónd/ CORE MEANING: a grammatical word indicating that something is on the other side of something else, either physically or in the abstract ○ (prep) *They are expanding environmental protection programs beyond the border area.* ○ (prep) *The gift of laughter is beyond price.*

1. *prep., adv.* AFTER A STATED TIME indicates that something continues after a particular time ○ *will remain the world's leading economy in the next decade and beyond* **2.** *prep.* PAST past a particular stage or situation ○ *Don't attempt to live beyond your income.* **3.** *prep.* FARTHER THAN further than a particular state of mind or emotion ○ *The site has proved to be popular beyond anyone's wildest dreams.* **4.** *prep.* EXCEPT indicates an exception ○ *He was incapable of any emotion beyond a certain rueful irony.* **5.** *prep.* IMPOSSIBLE FOR indicates that something is impossible for somebody to do ○ *It is beyond me to describe the complexities of this problem.* **6.** *n.* THE HEREAFTER the form of existence that some people believe the spirit reaches after death ○ *Our loved ones may speak to us from the beyond.* **7.** *n.* WHAT IS OUT THERE an area that lies outside what is known ○ *Humanity stands at the edge of the solar system, contemplating the beyond.* [14thC. From Old English *begeondan*, from *geond* "yonder" + *-an* "from."]

bez·el /bézz'l/ *n.* **1.** SLOPING EDGE OF TOOL the face of a cutting tool, especially a chisel, that slopes toward the cutting edge **2.** GROOVE TO HOLD WATCH GLASS the groove that holds the glass of a watch, light, or instrument dial in position [Late 16thC. From Old French, of uncertain origin.]

be·zique /bə zéek/ *n.* **1.** CARD GAME a card game like pinochle, played with the highest 64 cards from two decks **2.** HAND AT CARDS the combination of the queen of spades and the jack of diamonds, which gains a high score in the game of bezique [Mid-19thC. From French *besigue*, of uncertain origin: perhaps from Persian *bazigar* "acrobat" or *bazi* "game."]

be·zoar /bée zàwr, -zŏr/ *n.* a hard mass of material such as fruit or hair found in the intestines of a ruminant animal and believed in the past to be an antidote to poison [15thC. Via French *bezourd* from Arabic *badhizahr*, from Persian *padzahr*, from *pad* "protection (against)" + *zahr* "poison."]

bf, b.f., B/F, b/f *abbr.* **1.** ACCT brought forward **2.** PRINTING boldface

BF *symbol.* Belgian franc

bg. *abbr.* bags

BG/B.G. *abbr.* brigadier general

B-girl *n.* **1.** WOMAN EMPLOYED BY BAR a woman employed by a bar to entertain and encourage customers to spend money freely (*slang dated*) **2.** FEMALE FAN OF HIP-HOP AND RAP a female devotee of hip-hop and rap music culture (*slang*) [Origin uncertain: probably from *bar girl*]

BH *abbr.* Belize (*international vehicle registration*)

BHA *abbr.* butylated hydroanisole

Bha·dra·pa·da /baádrə paádə/ *n.* in the Hindu calendar, the sixth month of the year, made up of 29 or 30 days and falling in approximately August to September

Bha·ga·vad·gi·ta /baágə vaad géetə/, **Bha·ga·vad-Gi·ta** *n.* a Hindu religious text in which the god Krishna teaches the importance of detachment from personal aims, fulfillment of religious duties, and devotion to God [Late 18thC. From Sanskrit *Bhagavadgītā*, literally "song of the blessed one" (referring to Krishna), from *bhagavant-* "blessed" + *gītā* "song."]

Bhai *n.* a title of respect that is used after a Sikh man's name to indicate distinction

bhai·gan /bī́ gan/, **bai·gan** (*plural* **bhai·gans** *or* **bai·gans**) *n. Carib* an eggplant

bha·ji /baájee/ (*plural* **-jis**), **bha·jee, ba·jee** *n.* an Indian dish consisting of vegetable fritters, often made with gram flour or chickpea flour

bhak·ti /baáktee/ *n.* the Hindu practice of loving devotion to God as the means of salvation [Mid-19thC. From Sanskrit, "devotion."]

bhang /bang/, **bang** *n.* a drug made from the Indian hemp or cannabis plant [Late 16thC. Via Portuguese *bangue* from Persian and Urdu *bang* and Hindustani *bhan*, from Sanskrit *bhanga*.]

bhar·al /baárəl/ *n.* a wild sheep from the Himalayas with a bluish-gray coat and curved-back horns. Latin name: *Pseudois nayaur.* [Mid-19thC. From Hindustani.]

BHC *abbr.* benzene hexachloride

Bho·pal /bō paál/, **Bhō·pal** city and capital of Madhya Pradesh State, central India. It was the site of the world's worst industrial accident when a gas leak at a chemical plant killed more than 3,300 people in 1984. Population: 1,063,662 (1991).

bhp, b.hp. *abbr.* brake horsepower

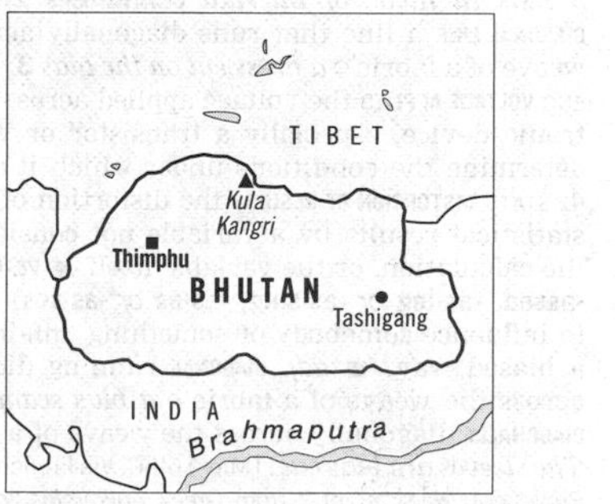

Bhutan

Bhu·tan /boo tán, -taán/ landlocked kingdom in the eastern Himalayas between India and the Tibet region of China. It is an absolute monarchy and one of the world's least developed countries. Language: Dzongkha. Currency: ngultrum. Capital: Thimphu.

Population: 842,000 (1996). Area: 18,100 sq. mi./47,000 sq. km. Official name **Kingdom of Bhutan** —**Bhu·tan·ese** *n., adj.*

Benazir Bhutto

Bhut·to /bŏotō/, **Benazir** (*b.* 1953) Pakistani politician. The daughter of Prime Minister Zulfikar Ali Bhutto (1928–79), she led the Pakistan People's Party and was herself elected prime minister (1988–90, 1993–96).

bi /bī/ *adj.* BISEXUAL bisexual (*slang*) ■ *n.* (*plural* **bi's**) BISEXUAL PERSON somebody who is bisexual (*slang*)

Bi *symbol.* bismuth

bi- *prefix.* two, twice, both ○ *biaxial* ○ *bimonthly* [From Latin *bi-*, the stem of *bis* "twice," and *bini* "two by two." Ultimately from the Indo-European word for "two," which is also the ancestor of English *two, dual*, and *binary*.]

BIA *abbr.* Bureau of Indian Affairs

Bi·a·fra /bee áffrə, -áaffrə/ region of eastern Nigeria that was declared a secessionist state by the majority Ibo people between 1967 and 1970. Official name **Republic of Biafra** —**Bi·a·fran** *n., adj.*

bi·a·ly /bee áalee/ (*plural* **-lys**) *n.* a flat, round, baked roll with small pieces of baked onion on top [Mid-20thC. Shortening of *bialystoker*, literally "of Bialystok," the city in Poland where this bread was made.]

Bi·an·ca /biángkə/ *n.* a small natural satellite of Uranus, discovered in 1986 by the Voyager 2 planetary probe

bi-and-bi *n. Can* Canada's French- and English-language cultures (*informal*)

bi·an·nu·al /bī ánnyoo əl/ *adj.* happening twice in a year

WORD KEY: USAGE

biannual or **biennial**? ***Biannual*** means "twice a year" whereas ***biennial*** means "every two years." Because many people are unsure about which is which, it is often advisable to use the more straightforward expressions ***twice-yearly*** and ***two-yearly***: *Interest is paid on a twice-yearly basis.* (or, less formally, *Interest is paid twice a year.*) *They met at a series of two-yearly conferences on the environment.*

Biar·ritz /bée̩ə rits, bée̩ə ríts/ tourist resort on the Bay of Biscay in the Pyrénées-Atlantiques Department, southwestern France. Population: 28,887 (1990).

bi·as /bī əss/ *n.* (*plural* **-as·es** *or* **-as·ses**) **1.** PREFERENCE an unfair preference for or dislike of something ○ *a bias in favor of internal candidates* **2.** TEXTILES DIAGONAL LINE a line that runs diagonally across the weave of a fabric ○ *a dress cut on the bias* **3.** ELECTRON ENG VOLTAGE APPLIED the voltage applied across an electronic device, especially a transistor or valve, to determine the conditions under which it operates **4.** STATS DISTORTION OF RESULTS the distortion of a set of statistical results by a variable not considered in the calculation, or the variable itself ■ *vt.* (**-ased** *or* **-assed, -as·ing** *or* **-as·sing, -as·es** *or* **-as·ses**) INFLUENCE to influence somebody or something unfairly or in a biased way ■ *adj.* DIAGONAL running diagonally across the weave of a fabric ○ *a bias seam* ■ *adv.* DIAGONALLY diagonally across the weave of a fabric ○ *The sleeves are bias cut*. [Mid-16thC. Via French from Old Provençal *biais* "slant," from Greek *epikarsios* "oblique."]

bi·as bind·ing *n. U.K.* = **bias tape**

bi·ased /bī əst/, **bi·assed** *adj.* **1.** PREJUDICED unable or unwilling to form a fair or objective opinion about somebody or something ○ *a biased opinion* **2.** UNFAIR unfair or partial because of a preference for or dislike of something ○ *a biased sample*

bi·as-ply tire *n.* a tire that has layers of fiber running diagonally to the line of the tread

bi·as tape *n.* a long narrow strip of material, cut on the bias, and used to form the edge of a hem or to bind the edges of a garment

bi·as volt·age *n.* = **bias** *n.* 3

bi·ath·lon /bī áth lən, -lòn/ *n.* a competition that combines cross-country skiing with rifle shooting at targets along the course [Mid-20thC. Coined from BI- + Greek *athlon* "prize from a contest."] —**bi·ath·lete** *n.*

bi·ax·i·al /bī áksee əl/ *adj.* having two axes —**bi·ax·i·al·ly** *adv.*

Bia·y·stok /bee áali stàwk/ capital of Bialystok Province in northeastern Poland. It is an industrial city in a predominantly agricultural region. Population: 277,800 (1995).

bib /bib/ *n.* **1.** PROTECTIVE CLOTHING a small piece of material fastened under a child's chin to protect the clothing while eating **2.** PART OF GARMENT the front part of a pinafore, apron, or pair of overalls that covers the chest [Late 16thC. Origin uncertain: probably from Latin *bibere* "to drink" (source of English *imbibe*).] ◇ **somebody's best bib and tucker** somebody's finest clothes (*informal*)

Bib. *abbr.* **1.** Bible **2.** biblical

bibb /bib/ *n.* a part attached to the mast of a sailing ship to support the trestletrees [Late 18thC. Variant of BIB.]

bib·ber /bíbbər/ *n.* somebody who regularly drinks alcohol (*archaic*) [Mid-16thC. Formed from *bib* "to drink frequently" (see BIB).]

Bibb let·tuce /bib-/ *n.* a variety of lettuce that forms a small loose head of dark green leaves [Mid-20thC. Named for the U.S. horticulturist Major John *Bibb*.]

bib·cock /bíb kòk/ *n.* a faucet with a nozzle that is bent downward [Late 18thC. Origin uncertain: perhaps from BIB + COCK.]

bi·be·lot /béebə lō, bi bló/ *n.* a small and attractive ornament or piece of jewelry [Late 19thC. From French, a variant by doubling of *bel* "beautiful."]

bibl. *abbr.* **1.** bibliography **2.** bibliographical

Bi·ble /bīb'l/ *n.* **1.** CHRISTIAN HOLY BOOK the sacred book of the Christian religion, consisting of the Old Testament, the New Testament, and, for some Christians, the Apocrypha **2.** BIBLE JEWISH HOLY BOOK the Hebrew scriptures, consisting of the Torah or Law, the Prophets, and the Hagiographa or Writings **3.** **Bi·ble, bi·ble** RELIGION'S HOLY BOOK the holy book of any religion **4.** **Bi·ble, bible** COPY OF BIBLE a copy or edition of the Bible **5.** ESSENTIAL BOOK a book that is considered an authority on a particular subject ○ *a bible for amateur renovaters* [14thC. From, ultimately, Latin *biblia (sacra)* (plural) "(sacred) books," from Greek, plural of *biblion* "book," from *biblos* "papyrus, scroll."]

Bi·ble belt *n.* those areas of the southern and Midwestern United States that are characterized by strong Protestant beliefs and strict interpretation of the Bible

Bi·ble pa·per *n.* thin strong paper often used for Bibles and reference books

Bi·ble-thump·er *n.* a committed Christian whose outspoken evangelizing is regarded by some as extreme (*slang*)

bib·li·cal /bíbblikəl/, **Bib·li·cal** *adj.* **1.** OF THE BIBLE relating to the Bible, or written about in the Bible **2.** LIKE THE BIBLE like the Bible, especially in style of language —**bib·li·cal·ly** *adv.*

Bib·li·cist /bíbblissist/, **bib·li·cist** *n.* **1.** BIBLICAL SCHOLAR a scholar who studies the Bible **2.** STRICT CONSTRUCTIONIST OF BIBLE somebody who interprets the Bible in a strict or literal way —**Bib·li·cism** *n.*

biblio- *prefix.* book ○ *bibliomania* [From Greek *biblion*, literally "small book," from *biblos* "papyrus, scroll," from *Bublos*, Phoenician city from which papyrus was imported]

bib·li·og·ra·phy /bìbblee óggrəfee/ (*plural* **-phies**) *n.* **1.** BOOK SOURCES a list of books and articles consulted, appearing at the end of a book or other text **2.** BOOKS ON SUBJECT a list of books and articles on a particular subject **3.** LIST OF PUBLICATIONS a list of the books and articles written by a particular author or issued by a particular publisher **4.** BOOK HISTORY the history of books and other publications, and the work of classifying and describing them —**bib·li·og·ra·pher** *n.* —**bib·li·o·graph·ic** /bìbblee ə gráffik/ *adj.* —**bib·li·o·graph·i·cal** *adj.* —**bib·li·o·graph·i·cal·ly** *adv.*

bib·li·o·man·cy /bíbblee ə mànsee/ *n.* an attempt to foretell the future or answer a question by picking a passage at random from a book, especially the Bible

bib·li·o·ma·ni·a /bìbblee ə máynee ə, -máynyə/ *n.* an extreme fondness for books, or an obsessive urge to collect them —**bib·li·o·ma·ni·ac** *n.*

bib·li·o·phile /bíbblee ə fīl/ *n.* somebody who loves or collects books

bib·u·lous /bíbbyələss/ *adj.* tending to drink too much alcohol (*literary or humorous*) [Late 17thC. From Latin *bibulus* from *bibere* "to drink."] —**bib·u·lous·ly** *adv.* —**bib·u·lous·ness** *n.*

WORD KEY: ORIGIN

The Latin word *bibere* from which ***bibulous*** is derived is also the source of English *beer, beverage*, and *imbibe*.

bi·cam·er·al /bī kámmərəl/ *adj.* having two separate and distinct lawmaking assemblies, e.g., the Senate and the House of Representatives in the United States [Mid-19thC. Formed from Latin *camera* "chamber" (see CAMERA).] —**bi·cam·er·al·ism** *n.* —**bi·cam·er·al·ist** *n.*

bi·carb /bī kaarb/ *n.* sodium bicarbonate (*informal*) [Early 20thC. Shortening of BICARBONATE.]

bi·car·bon·ate /bī kaárbənàyt, -it/ *n.* = **hydrogen carbonate**

bi·car·bon·ate of so·da *n.* **1.** PHARM ANTACID sodium bicarbonate taken medicinally to counter the effects of excess acid in the stomach **2.** COOK = **baking soda**

bice /bīss/ *n.* a dull blue or color pigment [14thC. From French *bis* "dark gray," of unknown origin.]

bice blue *n.* a deep sky-blue color

bice green *n.* a bright leaf-green color

bi·cen·ten·a·ry /bī sen ténnəree, bī sen tənnèree/ *n.* (*plural* **-ries**) *U.K.* = **bicentennial** ■ *adj. U.K.* = **bicentennial**

bi·cen·ten·ni·al /bī sen ténnee əl/ *n.* 200TH ANNIVERSARY an anniversary on which something is 200 years old ■ *adj.* CELEBRATING 200 YEARS marking or celebrating a 200th anniversary —**bi·cen·ten·ni·al·ly** *adv.*

bi·ceph·a·lous /bī séffələss/ *adj.* having two heads, or two parts resembling heads [Early 19thC. Coined from BI- + Greek *kephalē* "head" + -OUS.]

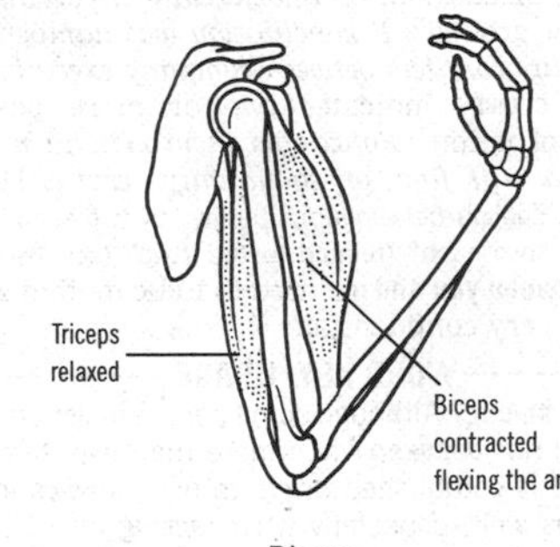

Biceps

bi·ceps /bī sèps/ (*plural* **-ceps** *or* **-ceps·es**) *n.* **1.** ARM MUSCLE a large muscle in the upper arm that contracts to bend the elbow **2.** MUSCLE WITH TWO ATTACHMENT POINTS a muscle that has two points of attachment at one end, especially one (**biceps brachii**) in the upper arm and one (**biceps femoris**) in the back of the thigh [Mid-17thC. Via French from Latin, "two-headed," from *caput* "head."]

bi·cip·i·tal /bī síppit'l/ *adj.* relating to or typical of a biceps muscle [Mid-17thC. Formed from Latin *bicipit-*, stem of *biceps* (see BICEPS).]

bick·er /bíkər/ (**-ered, -er·ing, -ers**) *vi.* to argue in a bad-tempered way about something unimportant [13thC. Coined from Middle Dutch *bicken* "to stab, attack" + English *-er* "repeatedly."]

bick·er·ing /bíkəring/ *n.* bad-tempered arguing about something unimportant

bi·coas·tal /bī kōst'l/ *adj.* OF TWO COASTS traveling between two coasts, occurring on each of two coasts, or extending between two coasts. It is used especially with reference to the East and West coasts of North America. ○ *a bicoastal marriage – he, in Hollywood; she, on Broadway* ■ *n.* EAST-WEST COAST RESIDENT OR TRAVELER somebody regularly traveling between the East and West coasts of North America or living at least part of the time on each coast

BOOKS OF THE BIBLE

There is no straightforward explanation of the origin of either the Jewish or the Christian canon of scripture. The Jewish scriptures listed represent the Hebrew Bible as it came to be fixed probably at some time in the 2nd century AD. There existed, however, an alternative version in Greek, known as the Septuagint, which contained seven books that are now found in the Roman Catholic and Eastern Orthodox canons. These are usually known collectively as the Apocrypha, though modern biblical scholars prefer the term Deuterocanonical.

The Old Testament canon was formally fixed for western Christians in the 16th century, when Protestant denominations for the most part adopted the shorter Jewish canon. Roman Catholicism formally embraced the Septuagint as the basis for its Bible at the Council of Trent in 1546. The Orthodox Churches accepted effectively the same canon as the Roman Catholic one in 1672 at the Synod of Jerusalem, though the Russian Orthodox Church remained ambivalent, and at least down to the mid-20th century tended to omit the Deuterocanonical texts from its canon.

**indicates Deuterocanonical books*

	Jewish Scriptures	Old Testament: Roman Catholicism and Eastern Orthodoxy	Old Testament: Protestant Churches
The Law	Genesis	Genesis	Genesis
	Exodus	Exodus	Exodus
	Leviticus	Leviticus	Leviticus
	Numbers	Numbers	Numbers
	Deuteronomy	Deuteronomy	Deuteronomy
The Prophets	Joshua	Joshua	Joshua
	Judges	Judges	Judges
		Ruth	Ruth
	1 Samuel	1 Samuel	1 Samuel
	2 Samuel	2 Samuel	2 Samuel
	1 Kings	1 Kings	1 Kings
	2 Kings	2 Kings	2 Kings
		1 Chronicles	1 Chronicles
		2 Chronicles	2 Chronicles
		Ezra	Ezra
		Nehemiah	Nehemiah
		Tobit*	
		Judith*	
		Esther	Esther
		1 Maccabees*	
		2 Maccabees*	
		Job	Job
		Psalms	Psalms
		Proverbs	Proverbs
		Ecclesiastes	Ecclesiastes
		Wisdom*	
		Ecclesiasticus*	
		Song of Songs	Song of Solomon
	Isaiah	Isaiah	Isaiah
	Jeremiah	Jeremiah	Jeremiah

	Jewish Scriptures	Old Testament: Roman Catholicism and Eastern Orthodoxy	Old Testament: Protestant Churches
Prophets (continued)		Lamentations	Lamentations
		Baruch*	
	Ezekiel	Ezekiel	Ezekiel
	Hosea	Daniel	Daniel
		Hosea	Hosea
	Joel	Joel	Joel
	Amos	Amos	Amos
	Obadiah	Obadiah	Obadiah
	Jonah	Jonah	Jonah
	Micah	Micah	Micah
	Nahum	Nahum	Nahum
	Habakkuk	Habakkuk	Habakkuk
	Zephaniah	Zephaniah	Zephaniah
	Haggai	Haggai	Haggai
	Zechariah	Zechariah	Zechariah
	Malachi	Malachi	Malachi
The Writings	Psalms		
	Proverbs		
	Job		
	Song of Songs		
	Ruth		
	Lamentations		
	Ecclesiastes		
	Esther		
	Daniel		
	Ezra		
	Nehemiah		
	1 Chronicles		
	2 Chronicles		

New Testament
Matthew
Mark
Luke
John
Acts of the Apostles
Romans
1 Corinthians
2 Corinthians
Galatians
Ephesians
Philippians
Colossians
1 Thessalonians
2 Thessalonians
1 Timothy
2 Timothy
Titus
Philemon
Hebrews
James
1 Peter
2 Peter
1 John
2 John
3 John
Jude
Revelation

○ *bicoastals who take the red-eye out of LAX every Sunday for New York*

bi·col·or /bī kùllər/, **bi·col·ored** /bī kùllərd/ *adj.* having two colors

bi·con·cave /bī kon káyv, bī kón kàyv/ *adj.* OPTICS used to describe a lens with two faces that are concave

bi·con·di·tion·al /bī kən dísh'n'l/ *n.* a proposition in logic involving two statements, one of which is true if, and only if, the other is true

bi·con·vex /bī kon véks, bī kón vèks/ *adj.* OPTICS used to describe a lens with two faces that are convex

bi·cul·tur·al /bī kúlchərəl/ *adj.* **1. WITH TWO CULTURES** relating to or containing two cultures ○ *a bicultural society* **2. OF FRENCH AND ENGLISH CULTURES** relating to or typical of both English and French culture in Canada —**bi·cul·tur·al·ism** *n.*

bi·cus·pid /bī kúspid/ *adj.* BIOL **WITH TWO POINTS** with two cusps or points ○ *a bicuspid tooth* ■ *n.* **PREMOLAR TOOTH** a tooth with two points, especially one of the eight teeth **(premolars)** that come between the canines and the molars in adult humans [Mid-19thC. Coined from BI- + Latin *cuspid-*, stem of *cuspis* (see CUSP).]

bi·cus·pid valve *n.* ANAT = **mitral valve**

Bicycle

bi·cy·cle /bī sik'l, -sik'l, -sĭk'l/ *n.* **TWO-WHEELED VEHICLE** a vehicle with two wheels and a seat that is moved by pushing pedals with the feet, and steered by handlebars at the front wheel ■ *vi.* **(-cled, -cling, -cles) RIDE A BICYCLE** to travel by bicycle [Mid-19thC. Coined from BI- + CYCLE on the model of TRICYCLE.] —**bi·cy·cler** *n.*

bi·cy·cle mo·to·cross *n.* full form of **BMX**

bi·cy·clic /bī sīklik, -sík-/ *adj.* **1. WITH TWO CIRCLES OR RINGS** consisting of or arranged in two circles, rings, or cycles **2.** CHEM **WITH TWO RINGS OF ATOMS** used to describe a molecule containing atoms arranged in two rings

bid /bid/ *v.* **(bade** *or* **bid, bid·den** /bídd'n/ *or* **bid** *or* **bade** /bad, bayd/, **bid·ding, bids) 1.** (*past and past participle* **bid**) *vti.* **OFFER MONEY AT AUCTION** to offer a particular amount of money for something at an auction **2.** (*past and past participle* **bid**) *vi.* **OFFER PRICE FOR WORK** to offer to do a piece of work for a particular price **3.** *vt.* **SAY TO SOMEBODY** to say something to somebody as a greeting or farewell ○ *She called in on her way to the airport to bid us goodbye.* **4.** (*past and past participle* **bid**) *vti.* CARDS **STATE NUMBER OF TRICKS** to declare the number of card tricks to be taken **5.** *vt.* **ORDER** to tell somebody to do something (*archaic*) ○ *We were bidden to sit quietly, and so we did.* **6.** *vt.* **INVITE** to invite somebody somewhere (*archaic*) **7.** (*past and past participle* **bid**) *vi.* **TRY TO ACHIEVE SOMETHING** to make an attempt to achieve a particular goal ○ *He hasn't decided whether or not he'll bid for the Presidency.* ■ *n.* **1. OFFER MADE TO PAY** an offer of money for something at an auction **2. OFFER** an offer to do a piece of work for a particular price ○ *bids were invited for the contract* **3. ATTEMPT** an attempt to do something or get something ○ *in a desperate bid to save the situation.* ◊ **takeover bid 4.** CARDS **STATEMENT OF TRICKS** a statement of the number of tricks that a player will take in a card game [12thC. Partly from Old English *biddan* "to request," and partly from Old English *beodan* "to offer."]

bid in *vt.* to bid at an auction for something already owned, in order to increase its final selling price

bid up *vt.* to make bids at an auction or similar sale that are intended to increase the price of something, not to obtain it

b.i.d. *adv.* twice a day (*used in prescriptions*) [Abbreviation of Latin *bis in die* "twice a day"]

bid·da·ble /bíddəb'l/ *adj.* likely to do as asked or ordered —**bid·da·bil·i·ty** /bìddə bíllətee/ *n.* —**bid·da·ble·ness** /bíddəb'lnəss/ *n.*

Bid·de·ford /bíddəfərd/ city in southwestern Maine, on the south bank of the Saco River, southwest of Portland. Population: 20,788 (1996).

bid·der /bíddər/ *n.* somebody who makes a bid, especially at an auction

bid·ding /bídding/ *n.* **1. MAKING OF BIDS** the making of bids at an auction or in a card game **2. SOMEBODY'S ORDERS** somebody's orders or instructions ○ *lots of paperwork to do at the boss's bidding*

Bid·dle /bídd'l/, **Nicholas** (1786–1844) U.S. financier. A lawyer and editor, he was president of the Second Bank of the United States (1822–39).

bid·dy /bíddee/ (*plural* **-dies**) *n.* **1. OFFENSIVE TERM** an offensive term that insults a woman's behavior as fussing or interfering (*slang insult*) **2. CHICKEN** a chicken (*regional*) [Early 17thC. Origin unknown.]

bide /bīd/ **(bode** /bōd/ *or* **bid·ed** *archaic*, **bid·ed, bid·ing, bides)** *v.* (*archaic*) **1.** *vi.* **STAY** to stay, remain, or wait ○ *Bide here with us a while.* **2.** *vt.* **ENDURE** to bear or endure something ○ *We must bide the king's displeasure.* [Old English *bīden*. Ultimately from an Indo-European word that is also the ancestor of English *beetle*, *boat*, and *fission*.] ◇ **bide your time** to wait for a good opportunity to do something

bi·det /bee dáy/ *n.* a low bathroom plumbing fixture resembling a toilet and equipped with a spray or jet of water, used for washing the genital and anal areas [Mid-17thC. From French, literally "pony," from *bider* "to trot," of unknown origin.]

bid price *n.* the price that a dealer on the stock exchange will pay for a security

Bie·der·mei·er /beédər mī ər/ *adj.* belonging to or typical of a highly conventional neoclassical style of home decoration and furnishing that was popular among the middle class in 19th-century Germany [Early 20thC. Named for the fictional poet Gottlieb *Biedermeier*, created in 1854 by Ludwig Eichrodt (1827–92).]

Bien·court /byaaN kóor/, **Charles de, Baron de Saint-Just** (1591?–1623) French-born Canadian colonist. He was the administrator of the original French colony of Acadia in present-day Nova Scotia.

Bi·en Ho·a /biən hố ə/ city in southern Vietnam east of Ho Chi Minh City, on the Dong Nai River. Population: 273,953 (1989).

bi·en·ni·al /bī énnee əl/ *adj.* **1. BIANNUAL** happening every two years **2. FLOWERING IN SECOND YEAR** used to describe a plant that lives for two years and produces flowers and fruit in the second year ■ *n.* **1. PLANT THAT LIVES TWO YEARS** a plant that lives for two years and produces fruit and flowers in the second year **2. EVENT** an event that happens every two years [Early 17thC. From, ultimately, Latin *biennium* "two-year period."] —**bi·en·ni·al·ly** *adv.*

WORD KEY: USAGE

See Usage note at *biannual*.

bier /beer/ *n.* **1. STAND FOR CASKET** a table on which a casket or a corpse is placed **2. FRAME FOR CARRYING COFFIN** a wooden frame on which a corpse or a coffin is carried to where it will be buried (*literary*) [Old English *bǣr*, from a prehistoric Germanic word that is also the ancestor of English *bear* "to carry"]

Bierce /beers/, **Ambrose** (1842–1914?) U.S. writer. Known for his satirical political articles and short stories, he wrote *The Devil's Dictionary* (1906). He disappeared in Mexico in 1913. Full name **Ambrose Gwinett Bierce**

Bier·stadt /beér stàt, -shtaat/, **Albert** (1830–1902) German-born U.S. artist. He was associated with the Hudson River School of painters. His romantic landscapes include *Rocky Mountains* (1863).

bi·fa·cial /bī fáysh'l/ *adj.* **1.** BOT **WITH DIFFERENT SURFACES** used to describe leaves with upper and lower surfaces that are different from each other **2. TWO-SIDED** having two sides or surfaces

bi·far·i·ous /bī férree əss/ *adj.* used to describe plant parts that are arranged in two rows, one on either side of an axis [Mid-17thC. Formed from Latin *bifarius*, literally "doing twice," from *-farius* "doing."] —**bi·far·i·ous·ly** *adv.*

biff /bif/ **(biffed, biff·ing, biffs)** *vt.* to hit somebody with the fist (*informal*) [Mid-19thC. An imitation of the sound caused.] —**biff** *n.*

bif·fy /bíffee/ (*plural* **-fies** *informal*) *n. Midwest* a toilet, especially an outhouse (*informal*) [Origin uncertain: probably a variant of PRIVY]

bi·fid /bīfid/ *adj.* BOT, ZOOL divided at one end into two equal parts [Mid-17thC. From Latin *bifidus*, literally "twice divided," from *findere* "to divide."] —**bi·fid·i·ty** /bī fídditee/ *n.* —**bi·fid·ly** /bīfidlee/ *adv.*

bi·fi·lar /bī fīlər/ *adj.* used to describe a part suspended on two parallel wires or threads, especially the moving part of an electrical measuring instrument [Mid-19thC. Coined from BI- + Latin *filum* "thread."]

bi·flag·el·late /bī flájjəlit, -làyt/ *adj.* used to describe a cell that has two slender appendages **(flagella)**

bi·fo·cal /bī fṓk'l, bī fṓk'l/ *adj.* **WITH TWO FOCAL LENGTHS** used to describe lenses with sections that have different focal lengths, especially in glasses for near and distant vision ■ **bi·fo·cals** *npl.* **GLASSES FOR NEAR AND DISTANT VISION** a pair of glasses with bifocal lenses [Late 19thC. Benjamin Franklin developed bifocals under the name "double spectacles" 100 years before the term was coined.]

bi·fur·cate *vti.* /bī fər kàyt, bī fúr-/ **(-cat·ed, -cat·ing, -cates) DIVIDE IN TWO** to split or branch off into two parts, or split something into two parts ■ *adj.* /bī fur kàyt, bī fúr kàyt, bī furkət, bī fúrkət/ **DIVIDING IN TWO** separating or branching off into two parts [Early 17thC. From, ultimately, Latin *bifurcare*, literally "to fork twice," from *furca* "fork" (see FORK).] —**bi·fur·ca·tion** /bīfər káysh'n/ *n.*

big /big/ *adj.* **(big·ger, big·gest) 1. OF GREAT SIZE** of great size, number, or amount ○ *a big crowd* **2. OF GREAT POWER** of great power or volume ○ *A big cheer went up.* **3. SIGNIFICANT** significant or important to somebody ○ *your big moment* **4. SIGNIFICANTLY GREAT** significantly or surprisingly great ○ *You're making a big mistake.* **5. OLDER** older or grown-up (*usually used by or to children*) ○ *When I'm big, I'll be rich and famous.* **6. IMPORTANT** important and powerful ○ *one of the big fashion houses* **7. ENTHUSIASTIC** enthusiastic about something or somebody (*informal*) ○ *I'm a big baseball fan.* **8. GREAT** used to make a word convey greater dislike or disapproval (*informal*) ○ *It's all a big con, really.* **9. MAGNANIMOUS** generous or noble ○ *She's a woman with a big heart.* **10. AMBITIOUS** full of boastful or unrealistic ambition ○ *She's not likely to fall for his big talk.* **11. FILLED** filled with or swollen by something (*literary*) ○ *eyes big with tears* **12. PREGNANT** in an obvious state of pregnancy (*archaic*) ○ *She was big with child.* **13.** WINE **FULL-BODIED** full-bodied and full of flavor ○ *The best accompaniment to this dish would be a big Chianti.* ■ *adv.* **1. AMBITIOUSLY** in a way that is ambitious, and often boastful or unrealistic ○ *You have to think big if you want to get anywhere.* **2. SUCCESSFULLY** in a highly successful way (*informal*) ○ *This approach should go over big at the convention.* [14thC. Origin uncertain: perhaps from Scandinavian.] ◇ **big on** enthusiastic about something or recognizing its importance (*informal*) ◇ **too big for your britches** *or* **boots** over confident (*informal*) ○ *Now that she's won the talent contest, she's gotten too big for her britches.* ◇ **in a big way** to a great degree or with great enthusiasm (*informal*) ○ *They fell for each other in a big way.* ○ *They're going into antiques in a big way.* ◇ **make it big** to be extremely successful (*informal*)

big·a·mist /bíggəməst/ *n.* somebody who is married illegally to two people simultaneously

big·a·mous /bíggəməss/ *adj.* involved in or constituting an illegal marriage made when an existing marriage is still valid [Late 19thC. Formed from Latin *bigamus* (see BIGAMY).] —**big·a·mous·ly** *adv.*

big·a·my /bíggəmee/ *n.* the crime of marrying somebody while being legally married to somebody else [13thC. From, ultimately, Latin *bigamus*, literally "marriage twice," from Greek *gamos* "marriage."]

Big Ap·ple *n.* an informal name for New York City [From APPLE, used by jazz musicians to mean "job," and the fact that New York was the most sought-after place to have a job or engagement]

big band *n.* a large jazz or dance band, especially one that was popular in the 1930s and 1940s ○ *the big band sound of Tommy Dorsey*

big bang *n.* the explosion of a single extremely dense

mass of matter that started the universe according to the big bang theory

big bang the·o·ry *n.* the theory that the universe started with the explosion of a small amount of extremely dense matter. The theory is supported by evidence that the universe is still expanding.

big beat *n.* a type of blues with a heavy backbeat, a precursor of rock and roll

Big Ben *n.* **1. CLOCK ABOVE PARLIAMENT BUILDING** the large clock above the Houses of Parliament in London, or the tower in which it stands **2. LARGE BELL** the large bell that chimes the hours in the clock tower of the Houses of Parliament in London [Named for Sir *Benjamin* Hall, the Chief Commissioner of Works when the bell was cast in 1856]

Big Bend Na·tion·al Park /bìg bénd-/ national park in southwestern Texas, known for its scenery and wildlife, and bounded by the Río Grande. Area: 324,219 acres/801,163 hectares.

Big Ber·tha *n.* a type of long-range gun used by Germany in World War I [Early 20thC. Named for *Bertha* Krupp, daughter of the armaments manufacturer Alfred Krupp.]

Big Black river in western Mississippi that flows southwestward to join the Mississippi River near Vicksburg. Length: 330 mi./531 km.

Big Board *n.* an informal name for the New York Stock Exchange (*informal*)

Big Broth·er *n.* a person or group who exerts dictatorial control and maintains a constant watch over others, often while presenting a caring image [Coined by the English author George Orwell in his novel *Nineteen Eighty-Four* (1949)] —**Big Broth·er·ism** *n.*

big bucks *npl.* a large amount of money (*slang*)

big busi·ness *n.* the activity of large commercial organizations, or these organizations considered as a group

big cat *n.* any large carnivorous wild mammal related to the domestic cat. Lions, tigers, leopards, lynxes, and mountain lions are types of big cats. Family: Felidae.

big cheese *n.* somebody who is important, especially the head of an organization (*slang dated*)

Big Chief *n.* = **big cheese** (*slang dated*)

Big Chill *n.* death, a near-death experience, or a state of perilous misery (*slang*) ○ *When the deck crane's cable snapped, that seaman came very close to the Big Chill.* [From the film *The Big Chill* (1983)]

big cit·y (*plural* **big cit·ies**) *n.* the largest city in an area ○ *the lure of the big city*

big-cit·y *adj.* typical of life in a large metropolitan area ○ *the fast-paced big-city lifestyle*

big-cone pine *n.* = **coulter pine**

big dad·dy *n.* (*slang*) **1. SOMEBODY OR SOMETHING REGARDED WITH RESPECT** somebody who or something that is respected, powerful, or well known for something in particular ○ *the big daddy of the blues guitar* **2. PATERNALISTIC HEAD** the head of an organization, especially one who exerts paternalistic control

big deal *interj.* **IS THAT ALL?** used to counter that something is less impressive or important than somebody thinks it is (*informal*) ○ *So he's head of a department. Big deal.* ■ *n.* **SOMETHING IMPORTANT** something that is very important (*informal*) ○ *Let's not make a big deal out of a minor misunderstanding.*

Big Dip·per *n.* the seven brightest stars in the constellation Ursa Major

Big Eas·y *n.* an informal name for New Orleans, Louisiana ○ *a night on the town in the Big Easy* [From *The Big Easy* (1970), a novel by James Conaway]

big en·chi·la·da, **Big En·chi·lada** *n.* (*slang*) **1. BOSS** somebody who is in charge **2. BIG PRIZE** the top prize or award in a competition [Origin unknown. First used in the Watergate tapes to describe the U.S. Attorney General.]

bi·ge·ner·ic /bī jə nérik/ *adj.* BOT used to describe a hybrid produced from two different genera

big·eye /bíggī/ (*plural* **-eyes** *or* **-eye**) *n.* a small tropical or subtropical sea fish with rough reddish or silvery scales and very large eyes. Family: Priacanthidae.

big fish *n.* = **big shot** (*slang*)

Big·foot /bíg fòot/, **big·foot** *n.* a large hairy humanoid creature supposed to live in the wilderness areas of northwestern North America, and described as standing 7–10 ft./2–3 m tall [Mid-20thC. From the size of the footprints it is said to leave.]

big game *n.* **1. LARGE ANIMALS HUNTED FOR SPORT** large wild animals hunted for sport, especially the larger African mammals **2. MAIN OBJECTIVE** the main purpose of a complex or risky set of actions

big·gie /bíggee/ *n.* (*informal*) **1. LARGE THING** something that is big **2. SOMETHING OR SOMEBODY IMPORTANT** somebody or something that is very significant, important, powerful, or successful [Mid-20thC. Formed from BIG.]

big·gish /bíggish/ *adj.* fairly large, although not extremely large ○ *The house is really nice, and it's got a biggish backyard.*

big·gi·ty /bíggi tee/, **big·ge·ty** *adj.* conceitedly impudent or cocky, or behaving and speaking in a manner indicating this (*regional*) [Late 19thC. Origin uncertain: possibly formed from BIG on the model of "uppity."]

big gov·ern·ment *n.* government perceived as being excessively big-spending and attempting to control too many aspects of people's lives

big gun *n.* a powerful or influential person (*informal*) [From the earlier meaning "heavy artillery"]

big guy *n.* = **big shot** (*slang*)

big hair *n.* hair that is rather long with a lot of body, often teased or sprayed so that it stands away from the head (*informal*)

big·head /bíg hèd/ *n.* (*informal*) **1. CONCEITED PERSON** somebody who is too proud of his or her own abilities, achievements, or appearance **2. TOO MUCH PRIDE** too much conceit —**big·head·ed** *adj.*

big-heart·ed *adj.* showing kindness and willingness to help and support others

big·horn /bíg hàwrn/ (*plural* **-horns** *or* **-horn**) *n.* a large wild sheep of western North America and northeastern Asia that has a long coarse brown coat and very large curving horns. It is well adapted for living in mountainous regions and can leap over rocky terrain with great agility and speed. Genus: *Ovis.* ◊ **mountain sheep**

Big·horn /bíg hàwrn/ river flowing from Wyoming into Montana. It is a major tributary of the Yellowstone. Length: 336 mi./541 km.

Big·horn Moun·tains mountain range of north central Wyoming and southern Montana, part of the Rocky Mountains. The highest point is Cloud Peak 13,187 ft/4,019 m. Bighorn National Forest lies in the range.

big house (*plural* **big hous·es**) *n.* a large penitentiary (*slang*)

bight /bīt/ *n.* **1. CURVE OF COASTLINE** a wide curving bend in a shoreline, forming a bay **2. ROPE LOOP** a loop or slack curve in a rope [Old English *byht*. Ultimately from an Indo-European word meaning "to bend," also the ancestor of English *bow* and *bagel*.]

big league *n.* **1.** SPORTS **MAJOR LEAGUE IN SPORTS** a major sports league, especially in baseball **2. HIGHEST LEVEL IN ENDEAVOR** the highest level of achievement in any field, or the people who occupy the top positions in it (*informal*)

big-league *adj.* among the most successful or influential in a particular field

big lie, **Big Lie** *n.* a gross misrepresentation of the facts concerning a major issue, especially for political purposes

Big Man *n.* in some cultures, including prehistoric cultures, a male leader whose leadership is based on influence, not official or formally recognized authority

big·mouth /bíg mòwth/ (*plural* **-mouths** /-mowths, -mowthz/) *n.* (*informal*) **1. BOASTFUL PERSON** a noisy, vulgar, or boastful person **2. INDISCREET PERSON** somebody who cannot keep a secret

big name *n.* a well-known and successful person, organization, or product —**big-name** *adj.*

big noise *n.* = **big shot** (*informal*)

big·no·ni·a /big nṓnee ə/ *n.* a climbing woody evergreen shrub grown for its trumpet-shaped red, orange, or yellow flowers. Genus: *Bignonia.* [Late 18thC. From modern Latin, genus name after the French librarian Abbé J. P. *Bignon* 1662–1743.]

big·ot /bíggət/ *n.* somebody who has very strong opinions, especially on matters of politics, religion, or ethnicity and refuses to accept different views [Late 16thC. From French, of unknown origin.]

big·ot·ed /bíggətid/ *adj.* holding very strong opinions, especially on matters of politics, religion, or ethnicity and unwilling to accept different views —**big·ot·ed·ly** *adv.* —**big·ot·ed·ness** *n.*

big·ot·ry /bíggə tree/ *n.* intolerance toward people who hold different views, especially on matters of politics, religion, or ethnicity [Late 17thC. Formed from BIGOT, on the model of French *bigoterie*.]

big sci·ence *n.* any area of scientific research that needs major capital investment

big screen *n.* the movie industry and films made for the movie industry, as opposed to television or video

big shot *n.* an important person with a great deal of power or influence (*informal*)

Big Sioux /-sōō/ river that rises in South Dakota and empties into the Missouri River in Iowa. Length: 400 mi./650 km.

Big Spring city and major oil-refining center in western Texas, northeast of Midland and Odessa. Population: 23,248 (1996).

big stick *n.* a threat of force or severe penalties [From "speak softly and carry a big stick," an adage made popular by President Theodore Roosevelt]

big-tick·et *adj.* costing a lot of money (*informal*)

big time *n.* **TOP LEVEL OF ACHIEVEMENT** the highest level of achievement and success in a profession or other activity (*slang*) ○ *Now that you've appeared on Broadway, you've hit the big time.* ■ *adv.* **GREATLY** on a grand scale or to a significant degree (*slang*) ○ *He had messed up his life big time.* —**big tim·er** *n.*

big top *n.* **1. CIRCUS TENT** a large round tent, especially the main tent, used for circus performances **2. CIRCUS** the circus, or the life of a circus performer

big tree *n.* = **giant sequoia**

big wheel *n.* = **big shot** (*informal*)

big·wig /bíg wìg/ *n.* = **big shot** (*informal*) [Early 18thC. From the fact that important people once wore full-length wigs, whereas ordinary people wore short ones.]

Bi·har /bi haár/, **Bi·hār** state in northeastern India that is crossed by the Ganges River and shares a border with Nepal. Capital: Patna. Population: 93,080,000 (1994). Area: 67,134 sq. mi./173,876 sq. km.

Bi·ha·ri /bi haáree/ (*plural* **-ri** *or* **-ris**) *n.* **1.** PEOPLES **MEMBER OF PEOPLE IN INDIAN SUBCONTINENT** a member of a people who live mostly in the Indian state of Bihar, but also in Bangladesh and Pakistan **2.** LANG **HINDI AREA LANGUAGE** a language of the state of Bihar, in India, belonging to the Indic group and closely related to Hindi [Late 19thC. From Hindi *bihārī*.] —**Bi·ha·ri** *adj.*

bi·jec·tion /bī jékshən/ *n.* a mathematical mapping between two spaces in which every element in each space corresponds to only one element of the other space for mapping in either direction [Mid-20thC. Formed from BI-, on the model of INJECTION.] —**bi·jec·tive** *adj.*

bi·jou /beé zhoo/ (*plural* **-jous** /beé zhooz/ *or* **-joux** /beé zhoo/) *n.* a small delicate jewel or ornamental object [Mid-17thC. Via French, "trinket," from Breton *bizoù* "jeweled ring," from *biz* "finger," of unknown origin.]

Bi·ka·ner /bikə náir/, **Bī·kā·ner** walled city in Rajasthan State, northwestern India. It was founded in 1488 and was formerly capital of the princely state of Bikaner. Population: 415,355 (1991).

bike /bīk/ *n.* **BICYCLE OR MOTORCYCLE** a bicycle or a motorcycle (*informal*) ■ *vi.* (**biked, bik·ing, bikes**) **GO BY BIKE** to ride somewhere on a bicycle or motorcycle (*informal*) [Late 19thC. Shortening of BICYCLE.]

bik·er /bīkər/ *n.* somebody who rides a motorcycle, especially somebody who belongs to a gang of riders

bike·way /bīk wày/ *n.* a route or traffic lane for bicycles

bi·ki·ni /bi keénee/ *n.* **1. WOMAN'S TWO-PIECE BATHING SUIT** a woman's or girl's two-piece bathing suit consisting of a bra-style top and panties-style bottoms **2. bi·ki·ni, bi·ki·nis BRIEFS** very scanty briefs for women or men [Mid-20thC. Named for BIKINI ATOLL, where an atom bomb was tested in 1946. The impact of the swimsuit was supposed to be similar.] —**bi·ki·nied** *adj.*

Bi·ki·ni /bə keénee/ atoll consisting of 36 islets in the Marshall Islands, the western Pacific Ocean. It was used as a nuclear testing site by the United States between 1946 and 1958. Area: 2 sq. mi./5 sq. km.

bi·ki·ni line *n.* the area where the top of a woman's thighs meets the lower edge of her bikini or underwear

Bik·o /be'ekō/, **Steve** (1946–77) South African political activist. He founded and led the Black Consciousness Movement. He was beaten to death in police custody. Full name **Stephen Bantu Biko**

bi·la·bi·al /bī láybee əl/ *adj.* USING BOTH LIPS used to describe a consonant pronounced by closing or rounding both lips ■ *n.* CONSONANT PRONOUNCED USING BOTH LIPS a consonant pronounced by bringing both lips into contact with each other or by rounding them. In English, the bilabials are "b," "p," "m," and "w." —**bi·la·bi·al·ly** *adv.*

bi·lat·er·al /bī láttərəl/ *adj.* **1.** POL INVOLVING TWO GROUPS involving or carried out by two groups, especially the political representatives of two countries ○ *bilateral talks* **2.** ON BOTH SIDES relating to or affecting both of two sides ○ *bilateral kidney failure* — **bi·lat·er·al·ism** /bī láttərəl ìzzəm/ *n.* —**bi·lat·er·al·ly** *adv.*

bi·lat·er·al sym·me·try *n.* symmetry in which an imaginary plane divides an object into right and left halves, each side being a mirror image of the other. Most animals exhibit this symmetry.

bi·lay·er /bī layər/ *n.* **1.** BIOCHEM TWO-MOLECULE LAYER a membrane that consists of two layers of molecules **2.** BIOL = **lipid bilayer**

Bil·ba·o /bil ba'aō, -bów/ industrial city and Spain's leading port in the Basque Country, northern Spain. It is the site of the Guggenheim Museum Bilbao that was opened in 1997. Population: 370,997 (1995).

bil·ber·ry /bíll bèree/ (*plural* **-ries**) *n.* **1.** BLUE-BLACK BERRY a small edible blue-black berry from a hardy shrub that grows wild in northern Europe **2.** FRUIT BUSH the shrub that produces bilberries. Genus: *Vaccinium.* [Late 16thC. Bil- of uncertain origin: probably from Scandinavian.]

bil·by /bíll bee/ (*plural* **-bies**) *n.* an Australasian marsupial resembling a rat with large ears, a pointed nose, and a long tail. It lives in a burrow and eats small mammals and lizards. Genus: *Macrotis.* [Late 19thC. From Yuwaalaraay *bilbi* (an Aboriginal language).]

bil·dungs·ro·man /bíll dōōngz rō ma'an/ *n.* a novel about the early years of somebody's life, exploring the development of his or her character and personality [Early 20thC. From German, literally "education-novel."]

bile /bīl/ *n.* **1.** PHYSIOL DIGESTIVE FLUID a yellowish-green fluid produced in the liver, stored in the gallbladder, and passed through ducts to the small intestine, where it plays an essential role in emulsifying fats **2.** BITTERNESS feelings of bitterness and irritability (*literary*) **3.** HIST BODILY HUMOR according to medieval medicine, one of the four basic fluids of the body (**humors**), an excess of which was thought to make somebody prone to anger [Mid-16thC. Via French from Latin *bilis*; probably ultimately of Celtic origin.]

bile duct *n.* a tube that carries bile from the liver or gallbladder to the small intestine. The (**hepatic**) and (**cystic**) ducts merge to form the common bile duct.

bi·lev·el *adj.* **1.** TWO-LEVEL with two levels for cargo or passengers **2.** HAVING TWO GROUND-FLOOR LEVELS having two ground-floor levels divided by a vertical partition ■ *n.* a bi-level house

bilge /bilj/ *n.* **1.** LOWER HULL OF BOAT the part of a boat below the water where the sides curve inward to the keel **2.** LOWER HULL'S INSIDES the area inside the bottom of a boat, beneath the lowest floorboards **3.** DIRTY WATER IN BOAT BOTTOM dirty water that collects inside the bottom of a boat **4.** BARREL'S WIDEST PART the widest part of a barrel or cask **5.** PAP ridiculous silly talk or ideas (*informal*) ○ *a load of bilge* ■ *vti.* (**bilged, bilg·ing, bilg·es**) SPRING A LEAK to be, or cause a boat to be, damaged in the lower part of the hull and start leaking [15thC. Origin uncertain: probably an alteration of BULGE.]

bilge keel *n.* either of two fin-shaped underwater projections on either side of a boat's hull, designed to control rolling

bilge wa·ter *n.* = **bilge** *n.* 3

bil·har·zi·a /bil ha'ar zee ə/ *n.* **1.** ZOOL = **schistosome 2.** MED = **schistosomiasis** [Mid-19thC. From modern Latin, genus name, after the German physician Theodor *Bilharz*, 1825–62, who first identified the parasite.]

bil·har·zi·a·sis /bìl haar zī́ əssiss/ *n.* = **schistosomiasis**

bil·i·ar·y /bíllee èrree/ *adj.* **1.** ANAT RELATING TO BILE relating to bile or the transporting of bile **2.** MED AFFECTING A BILE DUCT affecting a bile duct or the system of ducts in the liver ○ *biliary cirrhosis* [Mid-18thC. Formed from Latin *bilis* "bile."]

bi·lin·e·ar /bī línnee ər/ *adj.* relating to or representing a mathematical expression with two variables, such as x + y, neither of which is squared, cubed, or raised to another power or exponent

bi·lin·gual /bī líng gwəl, bī líng gyōō əl/ *adj.* **1.** SPEAKING TWO LANGUAGES able to speak two languages easily and naturally **2.** IN TWO LANGUAGES written, expressed, or conducted in two languages ○ *a bilingual dictionary* ■ *n.* BILINGUAL SPEAKER somebody who speaks two languages easily and naturally [Mid-19thC. Formed from Latin *bilinguis*, from *bi-* "two" + *lingua* "tongue, speech."] —**bi·lin·gual·ly** *adv.*

bi·lin·gual·ism /bī líng gwə lìzzəm, bī líng gyōō əlizzəm/ *n.* **1.** FLUENCY IN TWO LANGUAGES the ability to speak two languages easily and naturally **2.** USE OF TWO LANGUAGES the regular use of two languages in everyday communication

bil·ious /bíllyəss/ *adj.* **1.** NAUSEATED unsettled in the stomach, as if about to vomit **2.** NAUSEATINGLY UNPLEASANT extremely unpleasant to look at ○ *The walls were painted bilious green.* **3.** SHOWING BAD MOOD bad-tempered and irritable, or indicating this ○ *a bilious stare* [Mid-16thC. From Latin *biliosus*, from *bilis* "bile" (see BILE).] —**bil·ious·ly** *adv.* —**bil·ious·ness** *n.*

bil·i·ru·bin /bìlli rōōbin/ *n.* a reddish-yellow bile pigment that is an intermediate product of the breakdown of hemoglobin in the liver. Too much bilirubin in the blood causes jaundice. [Late 19thC. From German, from Latin *bilis* "bile" + *ruber* "red."]

bil·i·ver·din /bìlli vúrdin/ *n.* a greenish bile pigment that is an intermediate product of the breakdown of hemoglobin in the liver and that in turn can break down to produce bilirubin [Mid-19thC. From German, from Latin *bilis* "bile" + French *vert* "green."]

bilk /bilk/ (**bilked, bilk·ing, bilks**) *vt.* **1.** CHEAT to cheat somebody, especially by swindling him or her out of money (*informal*) **2.** AVOID PAYING to avoid paying a debt or the person to whom money is owed (*informal*) **3.** AVOID OR EVADE to escape from somebody, or manage to lose a pursuer [Mid-17thC. Origin uncertain: perhaps an alteration of BALK.] —**bilk·er** *n.*

bill[1] /bil/ *n.* **1.** STATEMENT OF MONEY OWED a written statement of how much money has to be paid for items that have been bought or for services provided ○ *I'll send you the bill.* **2.** AMOUNT OWED the amount of money owed for items or services provided, as shown on a statement ○ *The bill for the meal came to $150!* **3.** POL LAW PROPOSAL a written proposal for a new law, discussed and voted upon by the members of a legislative body **4.** ADVERTISING NOTICE a notice, poster, or leaflet advertising something **5.** LIST OF ITEMS a list, especially of entertainment features or acts in a show, or the program of entertainment itself ○ *We've got a brilliant new comedian on the bill tonight.* **6.** a piece of paper money **7.** $100 one hundred, or a piece of paper money worth one hundred (*slang*) ■ *vt.* **1.** SEND REQUEST FOR PAYMENT to send somebody a statement of how much money is owed for items bought or services provided ○ *Bill me for the cost of dry-cleaning.* **2.** ADVERTISE to advertise an event or performance, especially using posters ○ *It's billed as the biggest ice show on the East Coast.* **3.** DESCRIBE to describe an emerging or forthcoming thing in a particular way ○ *billed as the technological advance of the decade* [14thC. Via Anglo-Norman *bille* from, ultimately, medieval Latin *bulla* "seal on a document."] —**bill·a·ble** *adj.* —**bill·er** *n.* ◇ **fill** *or* **fit the bill** to be suitable for a particular purpose

bill[2] /bil/ *n.* **1.** BIRDS BIRD'S BEAK the beak of a bird, consisting of two pointed jaws protected by a horny covering **2.** ZOOL MOUTHPART OF ANIMAL the mouthparts of a platypus or other animal **3.** NAUT POINT OF AN ANCHOR the point at the very end of one of the arms of an anchor [Old English *bile*, of unknown origin] ◇ **bill and coo** to kiss and whisper intimately, as young lovers do, in a way thought to be reminiscent of the affectionate behavior of doves

bil·la·bong /bíllə bawng, bíllə bong/ *n.* *Aus* a pool or waterhole formed by a side channel of a river during the wet season [Mid-19thC. From Wiradhuri (an Aboriginal language), from *bila* "river" + *bang* "watercourse that only runs after rain."]

bill·board[1] /bíl bàwrd/ *n.* **1.** ADVERTISING BOARD a very large board erected by the roadside or attached to a building, used for displaying advertisements **2.** INTRODUCTORY SELECTION OF HIGHLIGHTS a selection of the highlights of sthsuch as a television show or a program of sports events, presented as an introduction to it ■ *vt.* PROMOTE SOMETHING to promote or advertise something (*often passive*) ○ *a political program billboarded as "the people's right to reply"*

bill·board[2] /bíl bàwrd/ *n.* a ledge on the front of a boat or ship to which the anchor is secured

bill·bug /bíl bùg/ *n.* a weevil whose larvae feed on the roots of cereal grasses. Genus: *Calendra* and *Sitophilus.* [Mid-19thC. Formed from BILL[2]; so called because of its pointed snout.]

Bille·ric·a /bil ríkə, bèlə ríkə/ town in northeastern Massachusetts, northwest of Boston, on the Concord River. Population: 38,861 (1996).

bil·let[1] /bíllit/ *n.* **1.** MIL ACCOMMODATIONS FOR SERVICE PEOPLE a private home or a guest house providing temporary accommodations for people in the armed forces **2.** MIL ORDER TO PROVIDE ACCOMMODATION an official order stating that a householder has to provide temporary accommodations for a member of the armed forces **3.** EMPLOYMENT POSITION a position of employment together with its tasks (*informal*) **4.** BRIEF LETTER a short letter or a note to somebody (*archaic*) ■ *v.* (**-let·ed, -let·ing, -lets**) MIL **1.** *vti.* ASSIGN SOLDIER TO TEMPORARY ACCOMMODATIONS to arrange for a member of the armed forces have temporary accommodations in a particular house, or to have such temporary accommodations somewhere **2.** *vt.* PROVIDE TEMPORARY ACCOMMODATIONS FOR SOLDIER to provide temporary accommodations in your home for a member of the armed forces [15thC. From Anglo-Norman *billette* "written orders," literally "small document," from Old French *bulle.*]

bil·let[2] /bíllit/ *n.* **1.** CHUNK OF WOOD a short thick piece of wood, especially firewood **2.** METALL METAL BAR IN SEMIFINISHED STATE a metal bar or block with a simple shape that requires further working **3.** ARCHIT DECORATIVE MOLDING any one of a series of short, evenly spaced blocks or cylinders forming part of a decorative molding [15thC. From Old French *billette*, literally "small log," from *bille* "log," from assumed Vulgar Latin *bilia*; probably ultimately of Celtic origin.]

bil·let-doux /bìllay dōō/ (*plural* **bil·lets-doux** /-dōō, -dōōz/) *n.* a letter expressing affectionate and romantic thoughts (*literary*) [Late 17thC. From French, literally "sweet note."]

bill·fish /bíl fish/ (*plural* **-fish** *or* **-fish·es**) *n.* a large fish with jaws resembling spears that lives near the surface of tropical and semitropical waters and is hunted for sport. Marlin, sailfish, and swordfish are billfish. Family: Xiphiidae. [Formed from BILL[2]]

bill·fold /bíl fōld/ *n.* a pocket-sized folding container for paper money, credit cards, stamps, and photographs, sometimes with a compartment for loose change [Formed from BILL[1]]

bill·hook /bíl hōōk/ *n.* a woodcutting tool with a wooden handle and a large broad curved blade, used especially to lop branches off trees [Formed from obsolete *bill* "a bladed or pointed weapon"]

bil·liard /bíllyərd/ *adj.* relating to or used in the cue game billiards ○ *a billiard table*

bil·liards /bíllyərdz/ *n.* an indoor game in which a felt-tipped stick (**cue**) is used to hit three colored balls across a cloth-covered table into pockets (*takes a singular verb*) [Late 16thC. From French *billard*, from *bille* "log" (see BILLET[2]).]

bill·ing /bílling/ *n.* **1.** POSITION IN TERMS OF ADVERTISING the particular importance or prominence given to a performer or event in advertisements ○ *an exciting young band currently getting top billing* **2.** ADVERTISING the advertising or promoting of a performance, event, or product **3. bill·ing, bill·ings** TOTAL BUSINESS TRANSACTED the total amount of business transacted in a given period, especially in advertising, insurance, or law, or the value of that business ○ *The law firm's billings are up this month.* ○ *She charged 1,000 billing hours to that case.* [Formed from BILL[1]]

Bil·lings /bíllingz/ city on the Yellowstone River in southern Montana northeast of Yellowstone National Park. Population: 91,195 (1996).

Bil·lings, Josh (1818–85) U.S. humorist. He is known for his deliberately misspelled sketches of rural life. Pseudonym of **Henry Wheeler Shaw**

bil·lion /bíllyən/ (*plural* **-lions** *or* **-lion**) *n.* **1.** ONE THOUSAND MILLION one thousand million, written as 1 followed by nine zeros **2.** *U.K.* ONE MILLION MILLION one million million, written as 1 followed by 12 zeros (*dated*) **3.** LARGE NUMBER an extremely large but unspecified number of people or things (*informal*) (*often plural*) **4.** BILLION DOLLARS a billion dollars [Late 17thC. From French, "a million million," from *bis* "twice" + *million* "MILLION."] —**bil·lionth** *n., adj.*

bil·lion·aire /bìllyə náir/ *n.* a very rich person, literally somebody who has money and property worth more than a billion dollars [Late 19thC. Modeled on MILLIONAIRE.]

bill of en·try *n.* a list of goods to be imported or exported, presented to officials at a customhouse

bill of ex·change *n.* a document setting out an instruction to pay a named person a fixed sum of money on a specified date or when the person requests payment

bill of fare *n.* **1.** MENU a menu of food available in a restaurant or served at a special function **2.** LIST OF ITEMS a list of items of any kind, especially events in a program of entertainment (*informal*)

bill of goods *n.* **1.** CONSIGNMENT OF GOODS a quantity of goods to be delivered **2.** FAKE OR WORTHLESS THING something fake or something not worth having (*informal*) ○ *What kind of bill of goods have they dumped on you this time?*

bill of health *n.* a certificate stating that the crew of a ship is healthy and is not affected by infectious diseases ◇ **a clean bill of health** a good report on somebody's health, or a good report about the state of something, e.g., an organization's efficiency or profitability

bill of in·dict·ment *n.* a document setting out the criminal charges against somebody, presented to a grand jury

bill of lad·ing *n.* a list of merchandise being transported, especially by ship, together with the conditions that apply to their transportation

bill of par·tic·u·lars *n.* a list of the charges, claims, or counterclaims made in a legal action

bill of rights *n.* a list of basic human rights as guaranteed by the laws of a country

Bill of Rights *n.* the first ten amendments to the U.S. Constitution, which protect people's basic human rights

bill of sale *n.* a document stating that something has been sold or transferred to the ownership of another party

bil·lon /bíllən/ *n.* **1.** ALLOY USED FOR COINS an alloy consisting of a small amount of silver or gold mixed with a base metal such as copper, used especially for making coins **2.** SILVER-COPPER ALLOY USED FOR MEDALS an alloy of silver with copper in high proportion, used especially for making medals [Early 18thC. From French, "ingot, bronze money," from *bille* "log" (see BILLET[2]).]

bil·low /bíllō/ *v.* **1.** *vt.* SWELL WITH AIR to fill with air, or cause something made of fabric to fill with air, and swell outward ○ *the wind billowing their dresses* **2.** *vi.* FLOW IN CURLING MASS to flow upward or along in a curling mass ■ *n.* FLOWING CURLING MASS a curling or rolling mass of something, e.g., waves or clouds of smoke [Mid-16thC. From Old Norse *bylgja* "wave." Ultimately from an Indo-European word meaning "to swell," which is also the ancestor of English *bellows, belly,* and *bulge.*]

bil·low·y /bíllōwee/ *adj.* moving in a large curling or rolling mass

bill·post·er /bíl pōstər/ *n.* somebody who puts up advertising notices in public places ○ *Billposters will be prosecuted.* [Formed from BILL[1]] —**bill·post·ing** *n.*

bil·ly[1] /bíllee/ (*plural* **-lies**) *n.* = **billy club** (*informal*) [Mid-19thC. Origin uncertain: perhaps an alteration of BILLET[2], or from the man's nickname *Billy.*]

bil·ly[2] /bíllee/ (*plural* **-lies**) *n. U.K., ANZ* a light metal cooking pot, used for boiling water or cooking food on a campfire [Mid-19thC. Origin uncertain: perhaps from Scottish dialect *billy-pot* "cooking utensil," or of Australian Aboriginal origin.]

billy[3] /bíllee/ (*plural* **bil·lies**) *n.* = **billy goat**

bil·ly·can /bílli kàn/ *n.* = **billy[2]** *n.*

bil·ly club *n.* a short stick or club used as a weapon by a police officer [From BILLY[1]]

bil·ly goat *n.* a male goat [From *Billy,* a nickname for William]

Bil·ly the Kid /bìllee-/ (1859–81) U.S. outlaw. A notorious robber and cattle rustler on the Western frontier, he claimed to have killed at least 21 people. He used numerous aliases, and the facts of his life are not clearly known. Real name **Henry McCarty**

bi·lo·bate /bī lṓ bàyt/, **bi·lobed** /bī́ lṑbd/ *adj.* having or in the form of two lobes ○ *a bilobate leaf*

Bi·lox·i /bə lúksee, -lók-/ city and port in southeastern Mississippi, midway between New Orleans, Louisiana and Mobile, Alabama. Population: 48,414 (1996).

bil·tong /bíl tòng, -tàwng/ *n. S Africa* strips of lean meat dried in the sun [Early 19thC. From Afrikaans, from Dutch *bil* "buttock, rump" + *tong* "tongue." So called because the meat is usually taken from the hind quarter, and is said to taste like smoked tongue.]

Bim /bim/ *n.* somebody who lives in, or comes from, Barbados (*informal*) [Mid-19thC. Origin unknown.]

bi·ma, bi·mah *n.* JUDAISM = **bema** *n.* 1

bi·man·u·al /bī mányoo əl/ *adj.* done with two hands, or needing the use of two hands —**bi·man·u·al·ly** *adv.*

bim·bo /bím bō/ (*plural* **-bos**) *n.* (*slang insult*) **1.** OFFENSIVE TERM an offensive term that deliberately insults a woman's intelligence while implying that she is good-looking **2.** OFFENSIVE TERM an offensive term for a man or woman who is regarded as being unintelligent or superficial [Early 20thC. Origin uncertain: probably from Italian, "baby, small child."]

bi·me·tal·lic /bī mə tállik/ *adj.* containing or consisting of two metals

bi·me·tal·lic strip *n.* a strip composed of two metals with different coefficients of expansion fixed together that bend at different rates when heated. Bimetallic strips are used in thermostats, thermal switches, and some thermometers.

bi·mil·le·nar·y /bī míllə nèrree, bī̀mə lénnə ree/ *adj.* RELATING TO 2,000TH ANNIVERSARY relating to or celebrating a 2,000th anniversary ■ *n.* (*plural* **-ies**) 2,000TH ANNIVERSARY the 2,000th anniversary of something. Also called **bimillennial**

bi·mod·al /bī mṓd'l/ *adj.* STATS relating to or consisting of a set of observations with two peaks, representing two values that occur with equal frequency and more often than any other value ○ *bimodal distribution* —**bi·mo·dal·i·ty** /bī mō dállitee/ *n.*

bi·mo·lec·u·lar /bī̀mə lékyələr/ *adj.* relating to, consisting of, or formed from two molecules

bi·month·ly /bī múnnthlee/ *adj.* OCCURING EVERY TWO MONTHS produced or held every two months ■ *adj., adv.* OCCURRING TWICE A MONTH produced or held twice a month ■ *n.* (*plural* **-lies**) PUBL PUBLICATION ISSUED BIMONTHLY a publication, e.g., a magazine or journal, that appears every two months or twice a month

bi·mor·phe·mic /bī mawr féemik/ *adj.* consisting of two of the smallest units of meaning in language (**morphemes**). The word "fallen" is bimorphemic, comprising the free morpheme "fall" and the bound past participle morpheme "-en."

bin /bin/ *n.* **1.** LARGE STORAGE CONTAINER a large storage container, e.g., an industrial container for grain or coal or an open container holding merchandise in a store **2.** *U.K.* TRASH CONTAINER a container for trash or wastepaper (*often used in combination*) **3.** WINE STORAGE SHELVES FOR WINE a set of shelves with compartments for storing bottles of wine in a cellar ■ *vt.* (**binned, bin·ning, bins**) STORE IN BIN to put something in a storage bin [Old English *binn,* of Celtic origin]

bi·na·ry /bī́nəree/ *adj.* **1.** IN TWO PARTS consisting of two parts or two separate elements **2.** MATH RELATING TO NUMBER SYSTEM BASED ON TWO used to describe a number system, or a number belonging to it, that has 2 rather than 10 as its base **3.** CHEM HAVING ONLY TWO CHEMICAL ELEMENTS consisting of two different chemical elements only **4.** CHEM HAVING TWO CHEMICALS MIXING TOXICALLY consisting of or using two harmless components that, when combined, become extremely toxic **5.** MUSIC = **duple** ■ *n.* (*plural* **-ries**) **1.** MATH BINARY NUMBER SYSTEM the binary number system ○ *written in binary* **2.** MATH BINARY DIGIT a binary number or digit **3.** ASTRON = **binary star** **4.** ARMS = **binary weapon** [15thC. From late Latin *binarius,* from Latin *bini* "two by two."]

bi·na·ry code *n.* a computer code that uses the binary number system. Numbers and letters are translated into signals that a computer reads as sequences of ones and zeros called binary digits (**bits**).

bi·na·ry cod·ed dec·i·mal *n.* a numbering system in which each digit of a decimal is converted into a binary number

bi·na·ry dig·it *n.* either of the digits 0 and 1, used in the binary system. ◊ **bit**

bi·na·ry file *n.* a computer file that contains data in a raw or nontext state made up of characters that only a computer can read. Executable programs are stored and transmitted in binary files, as are most numeric data files. ◊ **ASCII file**

bi·na·ry fis·sion *n.* the reproduction of a cell or a one-celled organism by division into two nearly equal parts

bi·na·ry form *n.* a musical form that has two complementary parts, both usually repeated

bi·na·ry no·ta·tion *n.* = **binary system**

bi·na·ry star *n.* a pair of stars that revolve around their common center of mass under mutual gravitational attraction

bi·na·ry sys·tem *n.* the number system with 2 as its base, decimal numbers being expressed as sequences of the digits 0 and 1. For example, the number 5 breaks down as one 1, no 2s, and one 4, written as 101 read from right to left.

bi·na·ry weap·on *n.* a chemical weapon, e.g., a bomb or artillery shell, containing two chemicals that are harmless in isolation but combine to form a toxic compound before reaching the target

bi·na·tion·al /bī náshənəl, -náshnəl/ *adj.* relating to two nations, or with two nations taking part

bin·au·ral /bī náwrəl, bi-/ *adj.* **1.** INVOLVING BOTH EARS relating to both ears, or the perception of sound by both ears **2.** IN STEREO recorded onto two separate channels using two microphones, so as to sound realistic when heard through headphones

bind /bīnd/ *v.* (**bound** /bownd/, **bound, bind·ing, binds**) **1.** *vt.* TIE FIRMLY TO SOMETHING to tie something firmly to something else by winding a cord tightly around both things **2.** *vt.* WRAP RIBBON OR BANDAGE AROUND to wind a cord, tape, or bandage firmly around something to protect it or hold it together ○ *You have to bind the wound firmly.* **3.** *vt.* TIE SOMEBODY'S HANDS OR FEET TOGETHER to tie somebody's hands or feet together to make it difficult to escape (*often passive*) ○ *bound hand and foot* **4.** *vt.* SEW PROTECT EDGE OF FABRIC to protect or decorate the edge of a piece of material by stitching over it or attaching a strip of fabric to it **5.** *vti.* CAUSE FEELINGS OF LOYALTY OR CLOSENESS to form a link or relationship based on loyalty, affection, or a shared experience ○ *the natural instinct that binds mother and child* **6.** *vt.* FORCE TO DO SOMETHING to oblige or compel somebody to do something, e.g., by invoking a law or a promise that has been made (*often passive*) ○ *priests who are bound by their vow of celibacy* **7.** *vt.* PUBL PUT BOOK TOGETHER to attach pages to one another and put them in a cover to form a book, leaflet, or other publication **8.** *vti.* STICK TOGETHER to stick together, or cause elements or ingredients to stick together, so as to form a solid mass ○ *The water, sand, and cement bind to form workable mortar.* **9.** *vti.* CHEM FORM CHEMICAL BOND to form a chemical bond **10.** *vt.* MED MAKE FECES FIRMER to make the feces firmer and more solid, especially to curb diarrhea ○ *White rice is said to bind you.* **11.** *vi.* ENG BECOME STIFF OR STUCK to become stiff, stuck, or unable to move freely (*refers to mechanical parts*) ○ *The brakes are binding.* **12.** *vt.* EMPLOY AS APPRENTICE in former times, to employ somebody as an apprentice under the terms of an agreement that obliged the apprentice to work for a fixed period, often several years ■ *n.* **1.** NUISANCE something that is annoying or causes inconvenience ○ *I have to go to the hospital every two weeks: it's a real bind.* **2.** FENCING FENCING MOVEMENT a fencing movement that pushes an opponent's blade out of line **3.** CHESS DOMINANT POSITION IN CHESS in chess, a position of dominance in the center of the board that restricts an opponent's moves [Old English *bindan.* Ultimately from an Indo-European word that is also the ancestor of English *band, bend, bond,* and *bundle.*] ◇ **in a bind** in a difficult or unpleasant situation, especially a situation in which every option leads to difficulties

bind off *vti.* KNITTING to remove stitches from a knitting needle and finish them off so that they will not unravel. Stitches are bound off to shape the sides of a piece of knitting, or at the end when it is completed.

bind over *vt.* LAW to accept bail from an accused person, obligating the accused to appear at trial ○ *The accused was bound over for trial.*

bind·er /bíndər/ *n.* **1.** **HARD COVER FOR PAPERS** a stiff cover with clips inside for holding loose sheets of paper or magazines **2.** **MACHINE FOR BINDING BOOKS OR PAPERS** a machine for holding sheets of paper together to form a book or booklet **3.** **BOOKBINDER** somebody whose job is to make books by assembling the pages and putting on the cover **4.** **CORD OR TIE** a length of cord, string, or tape that is used to tie things together **5.** **SOMETHING THAT STICKS THINGS** a substance added to form dry ingredients into a solid mass or to maintain an even consistency throughout a liquid or semiliquid substance **6.** AGRIC **MACHINE FOR MAKING SHEAVES** an attachment on a reaping machine for bundling cut grain into sheaves, or a reaping machine with this attachment **7.** COMM **STATEMENT BINDING SOMEBODY TO AGREEMENT** a formal statement together with the payment of a deposit, showing that somebody has serious intentions of going ahead with an agreement, especially an agreement to purchase insurance

bind·er·y /bíndəree/ (*plural* **-ies**) *n.* a place where the pages and covers of books are put together

bind·ing /bín ding/ *n.* **1.** PUBL **BOOK COVERING** the cover of a book, or the material used to cover books **2.** PUBL **SOMETHING HOLDING BOOK'S PAGES TOGETHER** the glue, strip of plastic, or other material that holds the pages of a book or booklet together **3.** **CORD USED FOR TYING** something that is used to tie or protect things, especially a cord or tape that is wound around something **4.** SEW **FABRIC EDGING** a strip of fabric or tape attached to the edge of a piece of material to prevent it from fraying **5.** SKIING **SKI FASTENING** one of the fastenings on a ski that hold the ski to the boot ■ *adj.* **OBLIGING SOMEBODY TO DO SOMETHING** creating a legal or moral obligation to do something, with no possibility of withdrawal or avoidance

bind·ing en·er·gy *n.* PHYS **1.** **ENERGY TO REMOVE PARTICLE FROM SYSTEM** the energy required to remove a particle from a system, e.g., an electron from an atom **2.** **ENERGY TO SEPARATE SYSTEM INTO COMPONENTS** the energy required to separate a system into its individual particles or components

bin·dle·stiff /bínd'l stìf/ *n.* somebody who is homeless, has no job, and travels around with a small bundle of possessions (*informal*) [Early 20thC. From *bindle* "bundle" (probably from German dialect *bindel*) + *stiff* in the sense "hobo."]

bind·weed /bínd wèed/ *n.* a plant with long twining stems, especially a wild plant with large white funnel-shaped flowers, generally regarded as a weed. Genera: *Convolvulus* and *Calystegia.*

bin end *n.* one of the last bottles remaining from a single quantity of wine, often sold at a reduced price

binge /binj/ *n.* **1.** **HEAVY DRINKING OR EATING SESSION** a short period when somebody drinks or eats far too much, especially a period of uncontrolled drinking or eating caused by a disorder such as alcoholism or bulimia **2.** **SPREE** a short period of time when something enjoyable is done in an unrestrained way ○ *a shopping binge* ■ *vi.* (**binged, binge·ing** *or* **bing·ing, bing·es**) **1.** **EAT TOO MUCH** to eat far too much food very quickly, sometimes as a symptom of an eating disorder such as bulimia **2.** **BE SELF-INDULGENT WITH SOMETHING** to do or consume something in an unrestrained self-indulgent way ○ *stay in all day and binge on old movies* [Early 19thC. From a dialect word meaning "to soak," of unknown origin.] —**bing·er** *n.*

binge eat·ing *n.* uncontrolled eating, especially when caused by bulimia

Bing·ham /bíngəm/, **George Caleb** (1811–79) U.S. artist. He is known for his paintings depicting quiet landscapes and U.S. pioneer life.

Bing·ham, Hiram (1789–1869) U.S. clergyman. He founded the first Protestant mission in Hawaii and translated the Bible into Hawaiian.

Bing·ham·ton /bíngəmtən/ city in New York where the Susquehanna and Chenango rivers meet, southeast of Ithaca. Population: 48,294 (1996).

bin·go /bíng gō/ *n.* **LOTTERY GAME WITH NUMBERED CARDS** a game played communally with numbered cards in which numbers are selected at random and the first person to cover all or specified numbered slots on his or her card wins ■ *interj.* **1.** **CALL IN BINGO** a shout of success, called by a player who has won a game of bingo **2.** **EXCLAMATION OF SUCCESS** used to express satisfaction at sudden success or achievement [Early 20thC. Origin uncertain: perhaps from *bing,* the sound of a bell ringing or a target being hit.]

bin·na·cle /bínnək'l/ *n.* a support or mounting for a ship's compass [15thC. Alteration of Spanish *bitácula,* from Latin *habitaculum* "housing," from *habitare* "to inhabit."]

bin·oc·u·lar /bə nókyələr, bī-/ *adj.* involving or using both eyes, or relating to vision using both eyes. ◊ **monocular** [Mid-18thC. Coined from Latin *bini* "two together" + *oculus* "eye."] —**bin·oc·u·lar·i·ty** /bə nòkyə lárritee, bī-/ *n.*

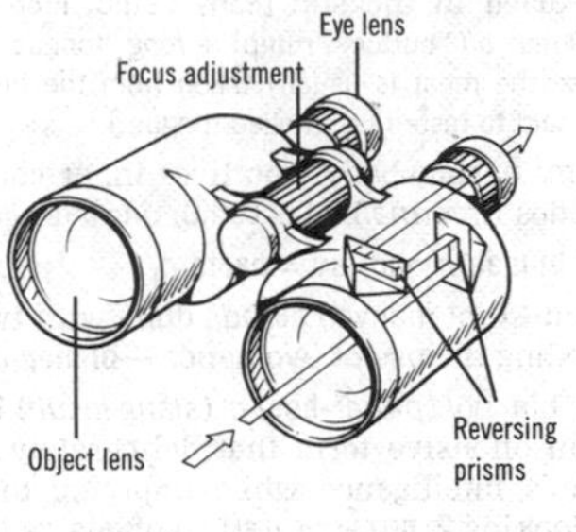

Binoculars

bin·oc·u·lars /bə nókyələrz, bī-/ *npl.* a device for looking at distant objects that magnifies what is seen using a lens for each eye

bi·no·mi·al /bī nómee əl/ *n.* **1.** MATH **EXPRESSION WITH TWO TERMS** a mathematical expression made up of two terms and a plus or minus sign **2.** BIOL **ORGANISM'S TWO-PART NAME** a pair of Latin or Latinized words forming a scientific name in the classification of plants, animals, and microorganisms. The first word represents the genus and the second the species. ■ *adj.* **HAVING TWO NAMES OR TERMS** relating to or consisting of two names, especially the two elements of a scientific name, or two terms, e.g., the terms of a mathematical expression [Mid-16thC. Formed from modern Latin *binomius,* from Latin *bi-* "two" + Greek *nomos* "part."] —**bi·no·mi·al·ly** *adv.*

bi·no·mi·al co·ef·fi·cient *n.* a number that multiplies the variables in a two-part mathematical expression, e.g., the numbers 3 and 4 in the expression 3x-4y

bi·no·mi·al dis·tri·bu·tion *n.* a formula that indicates the probability of achieving a given number of successful outcomes in a predetermined number of statistical trials when the probability of success is the same for each trial

bi·no·mi·al no·men·cla·ture *n.* the system of assigning two-part Latin or Latinized scientific names to plants, animals, and microorganisms, with the first word denoting the genus and the second the species

bi·no·mi·al the·o·rem *n.* a mathematical formula used to calculate the value of a two-part mathematical expression that is squared, cubed, or raised to another power or exponent, e.g., $(x+y)^n$, without explicitly multiplying the parts themselves

bin·tu·rong /bin to͝or awng, -òn/ *n.* a Southeast Asian mammal resembling a cat, with a thick black coat, a long tail, and tufts on its ears. The largest of the civet family, it lives in dense forests, uses its tail for grasping branches when climbing, and can also swim to catch fish. Latin name: *Arctictus binturong.* [Early 19thC. From Malay.]

bi·nu·cle·ar /bī no͞oklee ər, -nyo͞oklee-/ *adj.* = **binucleate**

bi·nu·cle·ate /bī no͞oklee it, -àyt, -nyo͞o-/, **bi·nu·cle·at·ed** /-àytid/, **bi·nu·cle·ar** /-ər/ *adj.* BIOL having two distinct cell nuclei

bi·o /bī ō/ (*plural* **-os**) *n.* a biographical work (*informal*) ○ *mostly fiction and celebrity bios* [Mid-20th C. Shortening of BIOGRAPHY.]

bio- *prefix.* BIOL life, biology ○ *bioengineering* [From Greek *bios* "life, way of living." Ultimately from an Indo-European base meaning "to live," which is also the ancestor of English *quick, vital, zoo-,* and *hygiene.*]

bi·o·ac·cu·mu·la·tion /bī ō ə kyo͞omyə láysh'n/ *n.* the accumulation of a harmful substance such as a radioactive element, a heavy metal, or an organochlorine in a biological organism, especially one that forms part of the food chain —**bi·o·ac·cu·mu·la·tive** /bī ō ə kyo͞omyə làytiv/ *adj.*

bi·o·ac·tive /bī ō áktiv/ *adj.* capable of producing an effect or reaction in living tissue

bi·o·ac·tiv·i·ty /bī ō ak tívvitee/ *n.* the effect that a substance or agent has on living tissue or an organism

bi·o·as·say /bī ō ássày, bī ō a sáy/ *n.* a technique for determining the concentration or potency of a substance such as a drug by measuring its effect on a living organism —**bi·o·as·say** *vt.*

bi·o·as·tro·nau·tics /bī ō àstrə náw tiks/ *n.* the study of the effects of space flight on living things, especially the biological and medical effects (*takes a singular verb*) —**bi·o·as·tro·nau·ti·cal** *adj.*

bi·o·as·tron·o·my /bī ō ə strónəmee/ *n.* the study of the possibility of life in the universe other than on Earth

bi·o·a·vail·a·bil·i·ty /bī ō ə vàylə bíllitee/ *n.* the degree to which a drug or other substance can be absorbed and utilized by those parts of the body on which it is intended to have an effect

bi·o·ce·no·sis /bī ō si nóssiss/ (*plural* **-nos·es**) *n.* a diverse group of species or organisms with its own distinct habitat, interacting to form an ecological community [Late 19thC. From modern Latin, from Greek *bios* "life" + *koinōsis* "sharing," from *koinos* "common."]

bi·o·chem·i·cal /bī ō kémmik'l/ *adj.* relating to the chemical substances present in living organisms and the reactions and methods used to identify or characterize them —**bi·o·chem·i·cal·ly** *adv.*

bi·o·chem·i·cal en·gi·neer·ing *n.* the branch of chemical engineering that is concerned with the large-scale culture of living cells in fermentation processes

bi·o·chem·i·cal ox·y·gen de·mand *n.* a measure of the pollution present in water, obtained by measuring the amount of oxygen absorbed from the water by the microorganisms present in it

bi·o·chem·is·try /bī ō kémmi stree/ *n.* **1.** **CHEMISTRY OF LIVING ORGANISMS** the scientific study of the chemical substances, processes, and reactions that occur in living organisms **2.** **CHEMICAL NATURE OF ORGANISM OR SYSTEM** the chemistry or composition of a particular organism or system —**bi·o·chem·ist** *n.*

bi·o·cide /bī ə sīd/ *n.* = **pesticide** —**bi·o·cid·al** /bī ə sīd'l/ *adj.*

bi·o·cli·mat·ic /bī ō klī máttik/ *adj.* relating to the relationship between climate and living organisms, or to the study of bioclimatology

bi·o·cli·ma·tol·o·gy /bī ō klīmə tólləjee/ *n.* the study of how climate affects living things —**bi·o·cli·ma·tol·o·gist** *n.*

bi·o·com·pat·i·bil·i·ty /bī ō kəm patə bíllitee/ *n.* the compatibility of a donated organ or artificial limb with the living tissue into which it is implanted or with which it is brought into contact. Incompatibility leads to toxic reactions or immunological rejection. —**bi·o·com·pat·i·ble** /bī ō kəm pátəb'l/ *adj.*

bi·o·com·put·er /bī ō kəm pyo͞otər/ *n.* a very fast computer made from biochemical substances instead of conventional materials. Its calculations are performed using biological processes instead of semiconductor technology. [Late 20thC]

bi·o·con·trol /bī ō kən trṓl/ *n.* = **biological control**

bio·con·ver·sion /bī ō kən vúrzhən, -shən/ *n.* the conversion of organic material into a source of energy, using biological processes or organisms

bi·o·da·ta /bī ō dàytə, -dàtə/ *n.* S Asia somebody's résumé (*takes a singular or plural noun*)

bi·o·de·grad·a·ble /bī ō di gráydəb'l/ *adj.* made of substances that will decay relatively quickly as a result of the action of bacteria and break down into elements such as carbon that are recycled naturally —**bi·o·de·grad·a·bil·i·ty** /bī ō di gràydə bíllitee/ *n.*

bi·o·de·grade /bī ō di gráyd/ (**-grad·ed, -grad·ing, -grades**) *vi.* to decay naturally as the result of the action of bacteria —**bi·o·de·gra·da·tion** /bī ō dè grə dáysh'n/ *n.*

bi·o·die·sel /bī ō deez'l, -s'l/ *n.* a substitute for diesel fuel made wholly or partly from organic products, especially processed vegetable oils such as soybean oil and groundnut oil

bi·o·di·ver·si·ty /bī ō dī vúrssitee/ *n.* the range of organisms present in a given ecological community or system. It can be measured by the numbers and types of different species, or the genetic variations within and between species.

bi·o·dy·nam·ics /bī ō dī námmiks/ *n.* the study of how energy, motion, and other forces affect living things (*takes a singular verb*) —**bi·o·dy·nam·ic** *adj.*

bio·e·lec·tric·i·ty /bī ō ilek tríssitee, -eelek-/ *n.* electric current generated by living tissue —**bi·o·e·lec·tric** *adj.*

bi·o·en·er·get·ics /bī ō enər jéttiks/ *n.* (*takes a singular verb*) **1.** BIOL **STUDY OF ENERGY IN LIVING THINGS** the study of the conversion of energy in organisms and biological systems, e.g., in photosynthesis **2.** ALTERN MED **THERAPIES DESIGNED TO RELEASE ENERGY** a combination of therapies, including breathing and body exercise and the free expression of feelings and impulses, designed to relieve tension and release physical and emotional energy **3.** PSYCHOL **REICHIAN THERAPY** a therapy, devised by Wilhelm Reich in the 1940s, that uses an analysis of somebody's physical posture and movements to enhance emotional wellbeing —**bi·o·en·er·get·ic** *adj.*

bi·o·en·gi·neer·ing /bī ō énjə neering/ *n.* the use of engineering principles and techniques to solve medical problems, e.g., in the design of artificial limbs or in organ replacement —**bi·o·en·gi·neer** *n.*

bi·o·eth·ics /bī ō éthiks/ *n.* the study of the moral and ethical choices faced in medical research and in the treatment of patients, especially when the application of advanced technology is involved (*takes a singular verb*) —**bi·o·eth·i·cal** *adj.* —**bi·o·eth·i·cist** *n.*

bi·o·feed·back /bī ō feed bàk/ *n.* the use of monitoring devices that display information about the operation of a bodily function, e.g., heart rate or blood pressure, that is not normally consciously controlled. This helps a patient to learn to control the function consciously.

bi·o·fla·vo·noid /bī ō fláyvənoyd/ *n.* a biologically active compound found in the rinds of citrus fruits and some other plants

bi·o·fu·el /bī ō fyoo əl/ *n.* a renewable fuel, e.g., biodiesel, biogas, and methane, that is derived from biological matter

biog. *abbr.* **1.** biographer **2.** biographical **3.** biography

bi·o·gas /bī ō gàs/ *n.* a mixture of carbon dioxide and methane formed by the decay of organic waste matter and used as a fuel

bi·o·gen·e·sis /bī ō jénnississ/ *n.* **1. DEVELOPMENT OF LIVING THINGS** the generation of living things from other preexisting life forms **2. ORIGINS OF LIFE** the theory that living things can arise only from other living things and cannot be spontaneously created **3.** BIOL = **recapitulation** *n.* 2 —**bi·o·ge·net·ic** /bī ō jə néttik/ *adj.*

bio·gen·ic /bī ō jénik/ *adj.* resulting from biological activity or from living things ○ *a biogenic amine*

bi·o·ge·o·chem·is·try /bī ō jee ō kémmistree/ *n.* the study of the chemical relationships between organisms and their physical environment —**bi·o·ge·o·chem·i·cal** /bī ō jee ō kémmikəl/ *adj.*

bi·o·ge·og·ra·phy /bī ō jee ógrəfee/ *n.* the study of the geographical distribution of plants and animals —**bi·o·ge·og·ra·pher** *n.* —**bi·o·ge·o·graph·ic** /bī ō jee ə gráffik/ *adj.* —**bi·o·ge·o·graph·i·cal** /-gráffikəl/ *adj.*

bi·og·ra·phee /bī ògrəfee, bee-/ *n.* somebody whose life is described in a biography

bi·o·graph·i·cal /bī ə gráffikəl/ *adj.* **1. RELATING TO SOMEBODY'S LIFE STORY** relating to, containing, or consisting of a description of somebody's life, written by another person ○ *a biographical dictionary* **2. RELATING TO WRITING OF BIOGRAPHIES** relating to biography as a form of writing —**bi·o·graph·i·cal·ly** *adv.*

bi·og·ra·phy /bī ógrəfee, bee-/ (*plural* **-phies**) *n.* **1. ACCOUNT OF SOMEBODY'S LIFE** an account of somebody's life, e.g., in the form of a book, movie, or television program, written or produced by another person **2. BIOGRAPHIES IN GENERAL** books about people's lives, considered as a whole or as a type of literature [Late 17thC. Via French and Latin from medieval Greek *biographia* "writing about lives," from Greek *bios* "life" (see BIO-) + *graphein* "to write" (see GRAPHIC).] —**bi·o·graph·er** *n.*

bi·o·haz·ard /bī ō hàzzərd/ *n.* a risk to human beings or their environment, especially one presented by a toxic or infectious agent —**bi·o·haz·ard·ous** /bī ō házzər dəss/ *adj.*

bi·o·in·stru·men·ta·tion /bī ō ìnstrə men táyshən/ *n.* instruments used to record and display information about the body's functions

Bi·o·ko /bee ókō/ island in the Gulf of Guinea that forms part of Equatorial Guinea. It contains the national capital, Malabo. Population: 57,190 (1983). Area: 779 sq. mi./2,017 sq. km. Former name **Fernando Póo** (until 1973). Former name **Macias Nguema**

biol. *abbr.* **1.** biological **2.** biology

bi·o·log·i·cal /bī ə lójjik'l/ *adj.* **1. CONCERNING LIVING THINGS** relating to living organisms ○ *biological diversity* **2. RELATING TO BIOLOGY** relating to the science of biology **3. CONTAINING ENZYMES** containing enzymes that are intended to digest stains caused by natural substances ○ *biological detergent* **4. GENETICALLY RELATED** related by birth rather than by adoption ○ *my biological mother* ■ *n.* **MEDICATION OR VACCINE FROM LIVING ORGANISMS** a drug or other compound such as an antibiotic or a vaccine that is produced by living organisms. It is often a commercially important product of genetic engineering. —**bi·o·log·i·cal·ly** *adv.*

bi·o·log·i·cal clock *n.* the set of mechanisms within living organisms that link physiological processes with daily, monthly, or seasonal cycles or with stages of development and aging

bi·o·log·i·cal con·trol *n.* a method of reducing or eliminating plant pests by introducing predators or microorganisms that attack the targeted pests but spare other species in the area

bi·o·log·i·cal ox·y·gen de·mand *n.* = **biochemical oxygen demand**

bi·o·log·i·cal shield *n.* a massive structure, usually made of concrete and steel, built around the core of a nuclear reactor to protect operating personnel from radiation

bi·o·log·i·cal war·fare *n.* the use of microorganisms and toxic biological products to cause death or injury to plants and animals, including humans

bi·o·log·i·cal weap·on *n.* a missile, bomb, or other device used to deliver and disseminate biological agents that are designed to cause disease, death, or damage to the environment and to humans

bi·ol·o·gy /bī óllәjee/ *n.* **1. SCIENCE OF LIFE** the science that deals with all forms of life, including their classification, physiology, chemistry, and interactions **2. LIFE IN ONE PLACE** the forms of life in a particular environment and their behavior, development, and history ○ *the biology of desert regions* **3. PLANT'S OR ANIMAL'S MAKEUP** the physical makeup and functioning of a particular plant or animal ○ *the biology of the fruit fly* [Early 19thC. Via French *biologie* from German, from Greek *bios* "life" (see BIO-).] —**bi·ol·o·gist** *n.*

bi·o·lu·mi·nes·cence /bī ō loomə néssənss/ *n.* the generation and emission of light by living organisms such as fireflies, some bacteria and fungi, and many marine animals —**bi·o·lu·mi·nes·cent** *adj.*

bi·o·mag·ni·fi·ca·tion /bī ō mágnəfi káysh'n/ *n.* = **bioaccumulation**

bi·o·mass /bī ō màs/ *n.* **1. MASS OF ORGANISMS IN ECOSYSTEM** the mass of living organisms within a given environment, measured in terms of weight per unit of area **2. PLANT AND ANIMAL WASTE AS FUEL** plant and animal material, e.g., agricultural waste products, used as a source of fuel **3. ORGANISM'S DRY WEIGHT** the mass of material in a living organism, or in a community of organisms, usually measured in terms of dry weight

bi·o·ma·te·ri·al /bī ō mə teeree əl/ *n.* material that can safely be implanted into the human body and left there without causing an adverse reaction

bi·o·math·e·mat·ics /bī ō màthə máttiks/ *n.* the application of mathematical methods and formulas to medical or biological phenomena (*takes a singular verb*) —**bi·o·math·e·mat·i·cal** *adj.* —**bi·o·math·e·ma·ti·cian** /bī ō màthəmə tíshən/ *n.*

bi·ome /bī ōm/ *n.* a division of the world's vegetation that corresponds to a particular climate and is characterized by certain types of plants and animals, e.g., tropical rain forest or desert. The world's lakes and oceans may also be considered biomes, although they are less susceptible to climatic influences than terrestrial biomes. [Early 20thC. Coined from BIO- and -OME.]

bi·o·me·chan·ics /bī ō mi kánniks/ *n.* MED **MOTION STUDY** the study of body movements and of the forces acting on the musculoskeletal system (*takes a singular verb*) ■ *npl.* **MECHANICAL FORCES ACTING ON BODY** the mechanical forces at work in a particular body or organ (*takes a plural verb*) —**bi·o·me·chan·i·cal** *adj.* —**bi·o·me·chan·i·cal·ly** *adv.*

bi·o·med·i·cal en·gi·neer·ing *n.* = **bioengineering**

bi·o·med·i·cine /bī ō médisin/ *n.* **1. BASIC SCIENCE APPLIED TO MEDICINE** the employing of the principles of biology, biochemistry, physiology, and other basic sciences to solve problems in clinical medicine **2. STUDY OF BODY IN EXTREME CONDITIONS** the study of the body's ability to withstand the stresses of unusual environments, e.g., outer space —**bi·o·med·i·cal** /bī ō méddikəl/ *adj.*

bi·o·me·te·or·ol·o·gy /bī ō meetee ə rólə jee/ *n.* the study of how weather conditions affect living things

bi·om·e·try /bī ómitree/ *n.* the application of statistical techniques to biological studies —**bi·o·met·rist** *n.*

bi·o·mol·e·cule /bī ō móli kyool/ *n.* **1. MOLECULE THAT ORGANISMS ARE MADE OF** one of the molecules from which living organisms are made **2. MOLECULE OF BIOLOGICAL COMPOUND** a molecule of a compound produced by or important to a biological organism —**bi·o·mo·lec·u·lar** /bī o mə lékyələr/ *adj.*

bi·on·ic /bī ónik/ *adj.* **1. HAVING ELECTRONICALLY POWERED ORGANS** having many or most ordinary human organs or functions replaced or enhanced by electronically powered parts that give superhuman capabilities, in the realm of science fiction **2. HAVING SUPERHUMAN QUALITIES** having superhuman strength, speed, or intensity (*informal*) ○ *a bionic appetite* **3.** BIOL **INVOLVING BIONICS** involving or relating to bionics [Early 20thC. Coined from BIO- + ELECTRONIC.]

bi·on·ics /bī óniks/ *n.* (*takes a singular verb*) **1. APPLICATION OF BIOLOGICAL INFORMATION TO MACHINES** the study of biological function and mechanics, and the application of them to machine design **2. USE OF ELECTRONICALLY OPERATED REPLACEMENT ORGANS** the use of electronic devices to replace damaged limbs and organs

-biont *suffix.* an organism that lives under particular conditions ○ *halobiont* [From SYMBIONT]

bi·o·or·gan·ic /bī ō awr gánnik/ *adj.* used to describe a carbon-based (**organic**) compound produced by a living organism or of biological importance

bi·o·phys·ics /bī ō fízziks/ *n.* the science that applies the laws and methods of physics to the study of biological processes (*takes a singular verb*) —**bi·o·phys·i·cal** *adj.* —**bi·o·phys·i·cal·ly** *adv.* —**bi·o·phys·i·cist** *n.*

bi·o·pol·y·mer /bī ō póllәmәr/ *n.* a substance that is composed of molecules joined in long chains (**polymers**) and is produced in living organisms. Proteins and DNA are biopolymers.

bi·o·proc·ess /bī ō pròssess, -pròssess/ *n.* any method for producing commercially useful biological material

bi·op·sy /bī òpsee/ (*plural* **-sies**) *n.* the removal of a sample of tissue from a living person for laboratory examination [Late 19thC. Coined from BIO- + Greek *opsis* "a viewing," from *ōps* "eye"; modeled on NECROPSY.] —**bi·op·sic** /bī ópsik/ *adj.* —**bi·op·tic** /bī óptik/ *adj.*

bi·o·psy·chol·o·gy /bī ō sī kóllәjee/ *n.* = **psychobiology**

bi·o·re·ac·tor /bī ō ree àktər/ *n.* **1. MICROORGANISM USED IN INDUSTRIAL PROCESSES** a microorganism that, through its biochemical reactions, can produce medically or commercially useful materials, e.g., beer from fermentation of yeast or insulin from genetically altered bacteria **2. TANK FOR GROWING MICROORGANISMS** a large tank for growing microorganisms used in industrial production

bi·o·re·me·di·a·tion /bī ō ri meedee áysh'n/ *n.* the use of biological means to restore or clean up contaminated land, e.g., by adding bacteria and other organisms that consume or neutralize contaminants in the soil

bi·o·rhythm /bī ō rìthəm/ *n.* a cyclical change, e.g., sleeping, waking, or the reproductive cycle, that takes place within living organisms. Some people believe that biorhythms affect behavior, mood, and sense of well-being. (*often used in the plural*) —

bi·o·rhyth·mic /bī ō rīthmik/ *adj.* —**bi·o·rhyth·mi·cal·ly** /-rīthmiklee/ *adv.*

bi·o·rhyth·mics /bī ō rīthmiks/ *n.* a branch of science dealing with biorhythms (*takes a singular verb*)

BIOS *abbr.* COMPUT Basic Input-Output System

bi·o·sat·el·lite /bī ō sàtt'l īt/ *n.* a satellite designed for living beings, including humans, to live in

bi·o·sci·ence /bī ō sī əns/ *n.* a science, e.g., biology, ecology, physiology, or molecular biology that studies structures, functions, interactions, or other aspects of living organisms

bi·o·sci·en·tist /bī ō sī əntist/ *n.* a specialist in any of the life sciences, e.g., biology, ecology, physiology, or molecular biology

bi·o·sen·sor /bī ō sènsər, -sawr/ *n.* an apparatus for detecting chemical or physical signals that provide information about specific biological activities. Blood pressure or heart monitors and systems that use live organisms are types of biosensors.

-biosis *suffix.* a particular mode of life ○ *necrobiosis* [From Greek *biōsis* "way of living," from *bioun* "to live," from *bios* "life" (see BIO-)] —**-biotic** *suffix.*

bi·o·sphere /bī ə sfeer/ *n.* the whole area of the Earth's surface, atmosphere, and sea that is inhabited by living things —**bi·o·spher·ic** /bīə sfeerik, -sférik/ *adj.*

bi·o·sphere re·serve *n.* a type of nationally or internationally protected area managed primarily to preserve natural ecological processes. Biosphere reserves are often open to tourists.

bi·o·spher·ic cy·cles *npl.* the natural recycling processes essential to life on Earth, involving the principal elements that make up the biosphere. They include the oxygen cycle, carbon cycle, nitrogen cycle, and water cycle.

bi·o·stat·ics /bī ō státtiks/ *n.* a branch of science dealing with the relationship between the structure and the function of an organism (*takes a singular verb*) —**bi·o·stat·ic** *adj.* —**bi·o·stat·i·cal·ly** *adv.*

bi·o·stra·tig·ra·phy /bī ō strə tíggrəfee/ *n.* the branch of science that uses animal and plant fossils to date and correlate sequences of sedimentary rocks

bi·o·strome /bī ə strōm/ *n.* a thin layer in a rock formation that consists of organic material such as fossils, deposited at the site where they lived [Early 20thC. From modern Latin, formed from Greek *strōma* "bed, covering."]

bi·o·syn·the·sis /bī ō sínthississ/ *n.* the synthesis of chemical substances as the result of biological activity —**bi·o·syn·thet·ic** /bī ō sin théttik/ *adj.* —**bi·o·syn·thet·i·cal·ly** /-théttiklee/ *adv.*

bi·o·sys·tem·at·ics /bī ō sìstə máttiks/ *n.* the study of the relationships among groups of species using criteria such as morphology, biochemistry, and DNA comparisons, especially to determine the evolutionary history of a species (*takes a singular verb*) —**bi·o·sys·tem·at·ic** *adj.*

bi·o·ta /bī ōtə/ *n.* the total complement of animals and plants in a particular area ○ *The biotas of tropical forests are the richest of all.* [Early 20thC. Via modern Latin from Greek *biotē* "life," from *bios* "life" (see BIO-).]

bi·o·tech /bī ō ték/ *n.* = **biotechnology** [Late 20thC. Shortening.]

bi·o·tech·ni·cal /bī ō téknik'l/ *adj.* relating to or involving biotechnology

bi·o·tech·nol·o·gy /bī ō tek nólləjee/ *n.* PRACTICAL USE OF BIOLOGICAL PROCESSES the use of biological processes or living microorganisms in industrial production. Early examples of biotechnology include the making of cheese, wine, and beer, while later developments include vaccine and insulin production. ■ = **ergonomics** —**bi·o·tech·no·log·i·cal** /bī ō teknə lójjik'l/ *adj.* —**bi·o·tech·no·log·i·cal·ly** /-lójjiklee/ *adv.* —**bi·o·tech·nol·o·gist** /-nólləjist/ *n.*

bi·o·te·lem·e·try /bī ō tə lémmitree/ *n.* the remote monitoring of vital processes, e.g., by attaching a signaling device to an animal

bi·o·ther·a·py /bī ō thèrrəpee/ (*plural* **-pies**) *n.* the treatment of disease with substances produced through the activity of living organisms, such as serums, vaccines, or antibiotics

bi·ot·ic /bī óttik/ *adj.* used to describe the features of a natural system that are living [Early 17thC. Via late Latin from Greek *biōtikos* "of life, lively," ultimately from *bios* "life" (see BIO-). In modern use from French *biotique*.]

bi·ot·ic po·ten·tial *n.* the optimal ability of an organism or a species to survive and reproduce successfully

bi·o·tin /bī ətin/ *n.* a vitamin in the B complex that is found in egg yolk, cereals, milk, and liver and is used by the body in metabolizing fat and carbohydrates. Deficiency can lead to dermatitis, loss of appetite, hair loss, and anemia. Formula: $C_{10}H_{16}N_2O_3S$. [Mid-20thC. Coined from Greek *biōtos* "life, sustenance," from *bios* "life" (see BIO-) + -IN.]

bi·o·tite /bī ə tīt/ *n.* a black, dark brown, or green silicate mineral found in igneous and metamorphic rocks. It is a member of the mica group of minerals and shares a similar crystal structure. [Mid-19thC. Named for the French physicist J.-B. *Biot* (1774–1862).]

bi·o·tope /bī ətōp/ *n.* a small area with a distinct set of environmental conditions that supports a particular ecological community of plants and animals [Early 20thC. From German *Biotop*, formed from Greek *topos* "place."]

bi·o·tron /bī ə tròn/ *n.* a place in a laboratory in which temperature and other environmental conditions can be controlled

bi·o·troph /bī ə trōf/ *n.* a parasite that feeds on the living tissue of its host

bi·o·type /bī ə tīp/ *n.* a naturally occurring group of individuals with the same genetic makeup (**genotype**) —**bi·o·typ·ic** /bī ə típpik/ *adj.*

bi·pa·ren·tal /bī pə rént'l/ *adj.* descended from two parents, male and female, as opposed to being the product of asexual reproduction

bi·pa·ri·e·tal /bī pə rī it'l/ *adj.* relating to or involving both parietal bones of the skull, particularly with respect to the measurement of the distance between their rounded projections

bip·a·rous /bíppərəss/ *adj.* **1.** ZOOL BEARING YOUNG IN PAIRS giving birth to two offspring at one time **2.** BOT PRODUCING TWO BRANCHES producing two branches from a single stem [Mid-18thC. Coined from BI- + -PAROUS.]

bi·par·ti·san /bī paártizz'n, -tiss'n/ *adj.* relating to, undertaken by, or including two political parties ○ *bipartisan support* —**bi·par·ti·san·ism** *n.* —**bi·par·ti·san·ship** *n.*

bi·par·tite /bī paár tīt/ *adj.* **1.** POL TWO-PART made or shared by two groups of people ○ *a bipartite agreement* **2.** BOT DIVIDED IN TWO used to describe leaves that are almost completely divided into two parts —**bi·par·tite·ly** *adv.* —**bi·par·ti·tion** /bī paar tísh'n/ *n.*

bi·ped /bī pèd/ *n.* an animal, e.g., a human, with only two legs for locomotion [Mid-17thC. Directly or via French *bipède* from the Latin stem *biped-* "two-footed," from *ped-* "foot."]

bi·ped·al /bī pédd'l, -peéd'l/ *adj.* used to describe an animal that has two legs or feet [15thC. From Latin *bipedalis*, from the stem *biped-* (see BIPED).]

bi·ped·al·ism /bī pédd'l ìzz'm/ *n.* walking upright on two feet as opposed to moving on all four limbs

bi·pha·sic /bī fáyzik/ *adj.* having two phases

bi·phen·yl /bī fénn'l, -feén'l/ *n.* a white crystalline substance used as a fungicide, in organic synthesis, and as a heat transfer agent. Formula: $C_{12}H_{10}$.

bi·pin·nate /bī pínn àyt/ *adj.* used to describe leaves divided into leaflets that are themselves subdivided —**bi·pin·nate·ly** *adv.*

bi·plane /bī plàyn/ *n.* an airplane with two sets of wings, one above the other. The type was built and flown mainly in the early part of the 20th century.

bi·pod /bī pòd/ *n.* a stand or support that has two legs

bi·po·lar /bī pōlər/ *adj.* **1.** TWO-POLED with two poles **2.** HAVING TWO DIFFERENT IDEAS having two quite different opinions, attitudes, or natures **3.** GEOG RELATING TO N AND S POLES involving, found at, or relating to both the North and South Poles **4.** PSYCHIAT HAVING MANIC AND DEPRESSED PERIODS characterized by shifts between episodes of mania and depression **5.** ELECTRON ENG USING NEGATIVE AND POSITIVE CHARGE CARRIERS used to describe electronic devices, especially transistors, in which both negative and positive charge carriers are utilized —**bi·po·lar·i·ty** /bī pō lárritee/ *n.*

bi·po·lar dis·or·der *n.* a psychiatric disorder characterized by extreme mood swings, ranging between episodes of acute euphoria (**mania**) and severe depression

bi·po·ten·ti·al·i·ty /bīpə tenshee állitee/ *n.* the potential early in embryological development for a cell or organ to differentiate in one of two ways, especially for a gonad to become either an ovary or a testis

bi·prism /bī prizz'm/ *n.* a glass prism that produces a double image of a single object

bi·pro·pel·lant /bīprə péllənt/ *n.* a substance made up of two elements, usually a fuel and an oxidizer, that is used to propel a rocket

bi·quad·rat·ic /bī kwo dráttik/ *adj.* OF THE SQUARE OF A SQUARE relating to the fourth power of a number ○ *a biquadratic equation* ■ *n.* EQUATION INVOLVING SQUARE OF SQUARE an equation that involves the fourth power of a number

bi·ra·di·al /bī ráydee əl/ *adj.* MARINE BIOL with both bilateral and radial symmetry, as found in some primitive marine animals

bi·ra·mous /bī ráyməss/ *adj.* BIOL divided into or forming two branches ○ *a biramous appendage*

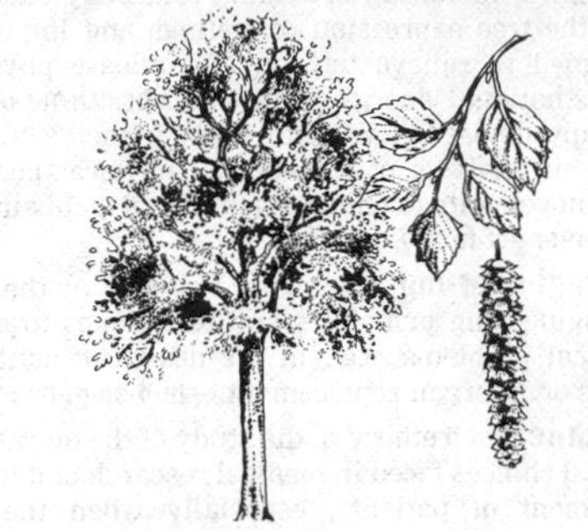

Birch

birch /burch/ *n.* **1.** TALL TREE WITH PEELING BARK a tall tree that grows in the northern hemisphere and has thin, papery, peeling bark. Genus: *Betula.* **2.** WOOD OF A BIRCH the wood that comes from the birch tree **3.** ROD FOR FLOGGING SOMEBODY a birch rod or bundle of twigs, especially one formerly used to beat people as a punishment ■ *vt.* (**birched, birch·ing, birch·es**) PUNISH BY BEATING to beat somebody with a birch rod as a punishment [Old English *birce*, from a prehistoric Germanic word that also produced Dutch *berk* and German *Birke*. Ultimately from an Indo-European word that is also the ancestor of English *bright*.]

Birch·er /búrchər/ *n.* a member of the John Birch Society, a right-wing political organization in the United States with the prime mission of fighting Communism [Mid-20thC. Named for John *Birch*, a U.S. Baptist missionary killed in 1945 by Chinese Communists.]

birch-leaf min·er *n.* a sawfly of the eastern United States, the larvae of which feed on birch leaves. Latin name: *Fenusa pumila.*

bird /burd/ *n.* **1.** TWO-LEGGED WINGED ANIMAL a two-legged warm-blooded animal that has wings, a hard beak, and a body covered with feathers. Birds lay eggs from which their young hatch, and most species can fly. Class: Aves. **2.** FOWL EATEN AS FOOD a fowl, e.g., a turkey, chicken, duck, goose, or game hen, cooked and eaten as food **3.** KIND OF PERSON somebody of a particular type (*informal*) ○ *he's a wise old bird* **4.** AIRPLANE OR SPACECRAFT an aircraft, satellite, or rocket (*slang*) **5.** RACKET GAMES = **shuttlecock** **6.** SPORTS = **clay pigeon** [Old English *brid* "young bird," of unknown origin] ◇ **give** *or* **flip** *or* **shoot somebody the bird** to hold the middle finger erect with the back of the hand toward somebody, as an insult (*slang*) ◇ **kill two birds with one stone** to achieve two goals with one action ◇ **(strictly) for the birds** worthless or unacceptable (*informal*) ◇ **the birds and the bees** the facts about sexual reproduction in humans (*informal humorous*)

Bird /burd/, **Larry** (*b.* 1956) U.S. basketball player. As the Boston Celtics' star forward (1979–92), he led them to three NBA championships and was three times the NBA's most valuable player. Full name **Larry Joe Bird**

bird·bath /búrd bàth/ (*plural* **-baths** /-bathz/) *n.* a small shallow basin containing water that is placed outside a house for birds to bathe in

bird·brain /búrd bràyn/ *n.* somebody who is silly or mildly unintelligent (*informal*) —**bird·brained** *adj.*

bird·cage /búrd kàyj/ *n.* a cage with wire or bamboo bars used to keep birds in captivity

bird·call /búrd kàwl/ *n.* **1. BIRD'S CRY** the sound or cry of a bird, especially a warning cry **2. INSTRUMENT IMITATING BIRD'S SOUND** a device that imitates a bird's call, used especially in trying to hunt or catch birds

bird colo·nel *n.* a full colonel in the United States Army, Air Force, or Marine Corps, as opposed to a lieutenant colonel (*informal*) [From the insignia of an eagle worn by a U.S. colonel]

bird dog *n.* a dog used to bring back game birds after they have been shot

bird-dog (**bird-dogged, bird-dog·ged, bird-dog·ging, bird-dogs**) *vti.* to watch somebody or something carefully and persistently (*informal*)

bird·er /búrdər/ *n.* = **birdwatcher**

bird feed·er *n.* a device containing food such as nuts that allows birds to feed at will

bird·house /búrd hòwss/ (*plural* **-hous·es** /-hòwzez/) *n.* **1. SHELTER FOR BIRDS** a small box or shelter that is specially built for birds to nest in **2. LARGE BIRDCAGE** a large cage in which birds are kept in captivity

bird·ie /búrdee/ *n.* **1.** GOLF **GOLF SCORE** a score in golf in which the ball is hit into the hole using one stroke fewer than the accepted standard number of strokes (**par**) for that hole **2.** RACKET GAMES = **shuttlecock** ■ *vt.* (**-ied, -ie·ing, -ies**) GOLF **PLAY HOLE ONE STROKE UNDER PAR** to play a hole in golf in one stroke less than the accepted standard number (**par**) [Late 18thC. In the sense "golf score," perhaps from slang *bird* "exceptionally smart or accomplished person."]

bird·life /búrd lìf/ *n.* all the birds that live in a particular area or region

bird·lime /búrd lìm/ *n.* **STICKY SUBSTANCE FOR TRAPPING BIRDS** a sticky substance made from plants that is spread on trees to catch birds ■ *vt.* (**-limed, -lim·ing, -limes**) **TRAP BIRDS WITH STICKY SUBSTANCE** to spread a sticky substance on trees in order to catch birds

bird louse (*plural* **bird lice**) *n.* a wingless insect with a flattened body that is not truly parasitic but lives on the feathers and skin debris of birds, often causing skin irritation. Suborder: Mallophaga.

bird of par·a·dise *n.* **1.** BIRDS **BIRD WITH BRIGHT FEATHERS** a bird from New Guinea and Australia, the male of which has bright feathers used in spectacular mating displays. Family: Paradisaeidae. **2.** PLANTS **PLANT WITH FLOWERS LIKE BIRD'S HEAD** a South African or South American plant that has flowers containing erect orange and blue petals resembling a bird's head and crest in shape. Genus: *Strelitzia.*

bird of pas·sage *n.* **1. MIGRATORY BIRD** a bird that migrates from one region or country to another according to the season **2. TRANSIENT** somebody who travels around a lot, rarely staying in the same place for long

bird of prey *n.* a bird that kills other birds and animals for food and has excellent eyesight, sharp talons, and a sharp curved beak. Owls, eagles, and hawks are birds of prey.

bird pep·per *n.* **1.** PLANTS **PEPPER PLANT** a tropical plant that has a thin hot-tasting fruit. The bird pepper is thought to be the ancestor of the sweet pepper and many hot peppers. Latin name: *Capsicum frutescens.* **2.** FOOD **HOT-TASTING PEPPER** the small pod-shaped hot-tasting fruit of the bird pepper plant

bird sanc·tu·ar·y (*plural* **bird sanc·tu·ar·ies**), **bird reserve** *n.* a natural area where birds are kept under protection so that they can live and breed in safety and under observation

bird·seed /búrd seed/ *n.* seed or a mixture of seeds, usually used for feeding caged or wild birds

Birds·eye /búrdz ì/, **Clarence** (1886–1956) U.S. inventor and business executive. He pioneered the retailing of quick-frozen and dehydrated foods.

bird's-eye *n.* **1. FABRIC PATTERN** a pattern for fabric that is composed of diamond shapes with a dot in the middle of each **2. PATTERNED FABRIC** fabric with a bird's-eye pattern ■ *adj.* **MARKED WITH SPOTS** marked with round dark spots resembling the eyes of birds ○ *bird's-eye maple*

bird's-eye view *n.* **1. VIEW FROM HIGH UP** a view that is seen from somewhere very high up **2. GENERAL IMPRESSION** an overall impression or summary of something without details

bird's-foot tre·foil *n.* a creeping wild plant that has yellow flowers with red tips and seedpods in the shape of a bird's foot. Latin name: *Lotus corniculatus.*

bird·shot /búrd shòt/ *n.* small lead shot designed to be fired from a shotgun

bird's nest *n.* a food delicacy obtained from high cliffs in Southeast Asia, believed to be swifts' nests built with the birds' saliva. Bird's nest, usually used in soups, is believed by the Chinese to be good for the skin and lungs. (*hyphenated when used before a noun*) ○ *bird's-nest soup*

bird's-nest fern *n.* a fern with long green fronds shaped like a bird's nest that grows on the ground or on trees in parts of Australia, India, and the South Pacific islands. Latin name: *Asplenium nidus.*

bird·song /búrd sòng/ *n.* the sounds made by a bird to attract a mate or defend territory

bird spi·der *n.* a large hairy spider from tropical America that eats birds. Family: Aviculariidae.

bird strike *n.* a collision between a bird and an aircraft in flight

bird·watch·er /búrd wòchər/ *n.* somebody who as a hobby observes birds in their natural habitats, usually from a distance using binoculars — **bird·watch·ing** *n.*

bi·re·frin·gence /bì ri frínjənss/ *n.* the splitting of one ray of light into two in an anisotropic medium — **bi·re·frin·gent** *adj.*

bi·reme /bì reem/ *n.* an ancient warship that had two ranks of oars on each side [Late 16thC. From Latin *biremis*, literally "two-oared," from *remus* "oar."]

bi·ret·ta /bə réttə/, **be·ret·ta** *n.* a stiff hat worn by Roman Catholic clerics that has three upright sections meeting at the center on top. Priests wear black birettas, bishops purple ones, and cardinals red ones. [Late 16thC. From Italian *berretta* or Spanish *birreta*, from late Latin *birrus, birrum* "hooded cape or cloak" (source of English *beret*), perhaps ultimately of Celtic origin.]

bi·ri·a·ni *n.* = **biryani**

Birkenstock *tdmk.* a trademark for a brand of footwear that includes sandals and clogs

birl /burl/ (**birled, birl·ing, birls**) *vt.* to cause a floating log to spin around in water [Early 18thC. Thought to be an imitation of the sound of something rotating rapidly.] — **birl·er** *n.*

birl·ing /búrling/ *n.* a game played by lumberjacks in which players have to balance on spinning floating logs [Late 16thC. From Gaelic *birlinn, beirlinn.*]

Bir·ming·ham /búrmingham, -əm/ **1.** the second largest city in central England and a major industrial center. Located in the west Midlands, it has three universities, two cathedrals, and the National Exhibition Centre, built in 1976. Population: 1,017,500 (1995). **2.** city in northern Alabama. Just south of the Appalachian Mountains, it is the largest city in the state. Population: 258,543 (1996). **3.** city in southeastern Michigan, just southeast of Pontiac. It is a northwestern suburb of Detroit. Population: 19,794 (1996).

Bir·ney /búrnee/, **Earle** (*b.* 1904) Canadian poet. He wrote experimental poetry in the 1960s. Full name **Alfred Earle Birney**

Bir·ney, James (1792–1857) U.S. abolitionist. He advocated the emancipation of slaves and twice ran as the Liberty Party candidate for president (1840, 1844). Full name **James Gillespie Birney**

birr[1] /bur/ *vti.* (**birred, bir·ring, birrs**) *U.S., Scotland* **MAKE WHIR** to make a whirring sound, or cause something to make a whirring sound ■ *n. U.S., Scotland* **WHIR** a whirring sound [14thC. From Old Norse *byrr* "favorable wind," of uncertain origin: perhaps literally "thing carried," and ultimately from an Indo-European word that also produced English *burden.*]

birr[2] /beer/ *n.* **1. ETHIOPIAN UNIT OF CURRENCY.** See table at **currency 2. BILL AND COIN WORTH A BIRR** a bill and coin worth one birr [Late 20thC. From Amharic.]

birth /burth/ *n.* **1. EVENT OF BEING BORN** the emergence of the young of a human or animal from the mother's womb into the outside world ○ *The father was present at the birth.* **2. PROCESS OF BEING BORN** the process of bringing forth young from a mother's womb ○ *the growing number of home births* **3. TIME OR PLACE OF BIRTH** the time or place of birth **4. SOMEBODY'S HERITAGE** somebody's social or national origins ○ *a man of noble birth* ○ *Italian by birth* **5. ORIGIN OF SOMETHING** the origin, beginning, or formation of something ○ *the birth of jazz* **6. SOMEBODY'S CHILD** the child of a particular mother born at a particular time (*archaic*) ■ *adj.* **BIOLOGICALLY RELATED AS A PARENT** biologically related to somebody, especially as a parent, rather than related by adoption ■ *vt. Southern U.S.* **HAVE OR DELIVER INFANT** to have or deliver a baby [13thC. From Old Norse *byr-*, ultimately from an Indo-European word that also produced English *bear* "to carry."] ◇ **give birth 1.** to produce a child or young from the womb **2.** to originate or be responsible for creating something ○ *a revolution that gave birth to a free nation*

birth ca·nal *n.* the passageway including the cervix and vagina through which a fetus emerges from the womb into the outside world

birth cer·tif·i·cate *n.* an official document that states when and where somebody was born and the parents' names

birth con·trol *n.* the deliberate limiting, usually by contraceptive means, of the number of children born

birth con·trol pill *n.* = **oral contraceptive**

birth·day /búrth dày/ *n.* **1. ANNIVERSARY OF DAY OF BIRTH** the day in each year that is the anniversary of the day somebody was born (*often used before a noun*) **2. DAY SOMEBODY IS BORN** the day on which somebody is born

WORD KEY: CULTURAL NOTE

The Birthday Party, a play by English dramatist Harold Pinter (1958). It tells the story of a young man called Stanley whose comfortable life in a seaside boarding house is disrupted by the arrival of two mysterious intimidating strangers, Goldberg and McCann. Noted for its sinisterly formal dialogue, the play creates a disturbing atmosphere of paranoia and fear.

birth·day suit *n.* a state of nakedness (*slang humorous*)

birth fa·ther *n.* somebody's biological father, especially in the case of an adopted child

birth·ing /búrthing/ *n.* **GIVING BIRTH** the process of giving birth, especially when using natural childbirth methods ■ *adj.* **FOR FACILITATING CHILDBIRTH** designed to facilitate childbirth ○ *a birthing pool*

birth·ing cen·ter *n.* a clinic or hospital that provides medical care during labor and childbirth in a friendly environment resembling the mother's own home

birth·ing chair *n.* a chair designed to support a woman and ease the process of childbirth by enabling gravity to act on the fetus as it moves through the birth canal

birth·ing room *n.* an area with nonclinical-looking surroundings in a hospital or other building set up for childbirth

birth·mark /búrth maark/ *n.* a reddish or brown marking seen on the skin of some newborn babies that typically remains visible for life

birth moth·er *n.* somebody's biological mother, especially in the case of an adopted child

birth pangs *n.* = **contraction** ■ *npl.* **INITIAL DIFFICULTIES** a difficult or troubled period at the start of something

birth par·ent *n.* somebody's biological mother or father, especially in the case of an adopted child

birth·place /búrth plàyss/ *n.* a place where somebody was born or where something first started ○ *Shakespeare's birthplace* ○ *the birthplace of classical philosophy*

birth·rate /búrth ràyt/ *n.* the number of live births per 1,000 members of the population in a year ○ *a declining birthrate*

birth·right /búrth rìt/ *n.* **1. BASIC ENTITLEMENT** a basic right that somebody has or is thought to be entitled to from birth ○ *Freedom of speech is our birthright.* **2. FAMILY PROPERTY SOMEBODY EXPECTS TO OWN** property or money that somebody feels entitled to because it belongs in the family

birth·root /búrth root, -ròot/ (*plural* **-roots** *or* **-root**) *n.* a North American plant whose roots were once used by Native Americans to help ease childbirth. Genus: *Trillium.* ◊ **trillium**

birth·stone /búrth stòn/ *n.* a precious or semiprecious stone such as an amethyst or garnet that is popularly associated with the month in which somebody was born. A birthstone is believed by some people to bring luck.

birth·wort /búrth wùrt, -wàwrt/ *n.* a European climbing plant that was formerly used to help ease pain during childbirth. Latin name: *Aristolochia clematitis.*

bi·ry·a·ni /bìrree áanee/, **bi·ri·a·ni** *n.* an Indian dish containing spicy colored rice mixed with meat, fish, or vegetables ○ *chicken biryani* [Mid-20thC. Via Hindi from Persian *biriyān*, literally "fried, grilled."]

bis /biss/ *adv.* **TO BE REPEATED** to be played or sung again (*used as a musical direction*) ■ *interj.* **CALLING FOR ENCORE** used by members of an audience to call for an encore [Early 17thC. Via French and Italian from Latin, "twice," ultimately from an Indo-European word meaning "two," which is also the ancestor of English *two*.]

Bis·cay, Bay of /bis káy/ arm of the North Atlantic Ocean between western France and northern Spain. Area: 86,000 sq. mi./223,000 sq. km.

Bis·cayne Bay /bis káyn-, bís kàyn-/ shallow inlet of the Atlantic Ocean on the East Coast of southern Florida. The city of Miami is on the northern shore, and Biscayne Bay National Park is to the east. Length: 40 mi./64 km.

bis·cot·to /bi skóttō/ (*plural* **-ti** /-ee/) *n.* a hard oblong cookie often containing nuts and usually flavored with anise [Via Italian from medieval Latin *bis coctus* "twice cooked" (see BISCUIT)]

bis·cuit /bískit/ *n.* **1.** FOOD **SMALL ROUND PIECE OF BREAD** a small round plain piece of bread that rises with baking powder or soda and is then baked in an oven **2.** *U.K.* FOOD = **cookie 3.** COLORS **LIGHT BROWN** a light brown color **4.** CERAMICS **UNGLAZED POTTERY** pottery that has been fired but not glazed ■ *adj.* COLORS **LIGHT BROWN** of a light brown color [14thC. From Old French *bescuit*, literally "twice-cooked," ultimately from Latin *bis* "twice" + *coctus*, past participle of *coquere* "to cook" (source of English *cook*).]

bis·cuit fir·ing *n.* the first firing of something made of clay, at a relatively low temperature

bis·cuit ware *n.* pots or pottery that have been through a first firing at a relatively low temperature

bi·sect /bī sèkt, bī sékt/ (**-sect·ed, -sect·ing, -sects**) *vt.* **1.** **SPLIT INTO TWO** to split something into two parts ○ *The river bisects the town.* **2.** MATH **HALVE** to divide something into two exactly equal parts [Mid-17thC. Coined from BI- + Latin *sect-*, the past participle stem of *secare* "to cut" (see SECTION).] —**bi·sec·tion** /bī séksh'n/ *n.* —**bi·sec·tion·al** *adj.* —**bi·sec·tion·al·ly** *adv.*

bi·sec·tor /bī sèktər, bī séktər/ *n.* a straight line or plane that divides an angle or another line into two exactly equal parts

bi·sex·u·al /bī sékshooəl, bī sékshəl/ *adj.* **1.** **ATTRACTED TO BOTH SEXES** sexually attracted to both men and women, or engaging in both heterosexual and homosexual activity **2.** **BOTH MALE AND FEMALE IN CHARACTERISTICS** having both male and female characteristics **3.** BIOL **WITH MALE AND FEMALE REPRODUCTIVE ORGANS** used to describe something such as a flower that has both male and female reproductive organs ■ *n.* **SOMEBODY SEXUALLY ATTRACTED TO BOTH SEXES** somebody who is sexually attracted to both men and women, or who engages in both heterosexual and homosexual activity —**bi·sex·u·al·i·ty** /bī sekshoo állətee/ *n.* —**bi·sex·u·al·ly** *adv.*

Bish·kek /bish kék/ capital of Kyrgyzstan, in the northern part of the country, on the Chu River, just south of the border with Kazakhstan. Population: 630,000 (1994).

bish·op /bíshəp/ *n.* **1.** CHR **SENIOR CHRISTIAN CLERIC** a senior Christian cleric, especially in the Roman Catholic, Episcopal, and Orthodox churches, who is in charge of the spiritual life and administration of a particular region (**diocese**) **2.** CHESS **CHESS PIECE** a chess piece that can be moved diagonally across the board over any number of squares of the same color [Pre-12thC. Via Latin *episcopus* "bishop, overseer" from Greek *episkopos* "overseer," from *skopos* "watcher" (source of English *scope*).]

Bish·op /bíshəp/, **Elizabeth** (1911–79) U.S. poet. Known for her personal, reflective poetry, she won the Pulitzer Prize for her collections *North and South: A Cold Spring* (1955).

bish·op·ric /bíshəprik/ *n.* **1.** **BISHOP'S DIOCESE** an area that a bishop is in charge of **2.** **BISHOP'S SEE** a place where a bishop's cathedral is situated **3.** **RANK OF BISHOP** the rank or office of a bishop [Pre-12thC. Formed from BISHOP + Old English *rīce* "realm, power."]

bish·op's cap *n.* = **miterwort**

bish·op's weed *n.* = **goutweed**

Bis·la·ma /bis láamə/ *n.* the national language of Vanuatu in the Pacific, a modern form of the English-based pidgin language known as Beach-la-Mar. Approximately 128,000 people speak Bislama. [Late 20thC. Local pronunciation and official spelling of BEACH-LA-MAR.]

Bis·marck /bíz maàrk/ capital of North Dakota, on the eastern bank of the Missouri River. Population: 53,514 (1996).

Bis·marck, Otto Edward Leopold von, Prince (1815–98) German statesman. As Prussian prime minister after 1862, he embarked on the European wars that unified the German states. He was the most powerful statesman in Europe as chancellor of the new German Empire from 1871 to 1890. Known as **the Iron Chancellor**

Bis·marck Ar·chi·pel·a·go group of over 200 islands, part of Papua New Guinea, in the western Pacific Ocean, off New Guinea. Area: 20,720 sq. mi./51,800 sq. km.

bis·muth /bízməth/ *n.* a heavy reddish-white crystalline metallic element that breaks easily and is widely used in alloys. The compounds of bismuth are used in medicines. Symbol **Bi** [Mid-17thC. From obsolete German *Bismut* and modern Latin *bisemutum* from Middle High German *wise* "meadow" + *muth* "claim to a mine."]

Bison

bi·son /bíss'n/ (*plural* **-son**) *n.* a large hairy animal resembling an ox, but with massive head and shoulders and a humped back. Bison were once common in North America and Europe, but are now mainly found only in protected areas. Genus: *Bison.* ◊ **buffalo, wisent** [Early 17thC. Directly or via French from Latin *bison*, which came from a prehistoric Germanic source that also produced English *wisent*.]

bisque[1] /bisk/ *n.* a rich soup made from shellfish ○ *lobster bisque* [Mid-17thC. From French, of unknown origin: perhaps an alteration of *Biscaye* "Biscay."]

bisque[2] /bisk/ *n.* **1.** CERAMICS = **biscuit** *n.* 4 **2.** COLORS **PINKISH BROWN** a pinkish-brown color ■ *adj.* **PINKISH-BROWN** pinkish-brown in color [Mid-17thC. Alteration of BISCUIT, perhaps in order to seem fashionably French.]

bisque[3] /bisk/ *n.* an extra turn, stroke, or point that is given as an advantage to a weaker player in a game of tennis, golf, or croquet [Mid-17thC. From French, of unknown origin.]

Bis·sau /bi sów/ city on the northern shore of the Geba River estuary and capital of Guinea-Bissau since 1941. Population: 200,000 (1994).

bis·sex·tile /bī sékstil, -stīl, bi-/ *adj.* **MAKING A LEAP YEAR** having the extra day in a year that makes it a leap year ○ *bissextile month* ■ *n.* **LEAP YEAR** a leap year [Late 16thC. From late Latin *bis(s)extilus*, from Latin *bi(s)sextus (dies)*, literally "twice-sixth (day)" (February 24, counted twice in a leap year; the sixth day before March 1), in the ancient Roman calendar from *sextus* "sixth."]

bis·tort /bís tàwrt/ *n.* a plant found in Europe and Asia with an S-shaped underground stem (**rhizome**) that was dried and used in traditional medicine. Latin name: *Polygonum bistorta.* [Early 16thC. Directly or via French from assumed medieval Latin *bistorta*, from *bis* "twice" + *torta*, feminine past participle of *torquere* "to twist" (see TORQUE); from its twisted roots.]

bis·tou·ry /bístəree/ (*plural* **-ries**) *n.* a thin surgical knife designed to cut from the inside outward, formerly used to cut open abscesses or enlarge fistulas [Mid-18thC. From French, of uncertain origin: perhaps from Italian dialectal *bistori* "dagger," which evolved from *pistorino* "of Pistoia," a city in northern Italy famous for the manufacture of knives.]

bis·tro /béestrō, bís-/ (*plural* **-tros**) *n.* a small restaurant or bar [Early 20thC. From French, originally "little restaurant," of uncertain origin, perhaps related to *bistouille* "raw spirits," or from dialect *bistraud* "little shepherd."]

bi·sul·fate /bī súl fàyt/ *n.* = **hydrogen sulfate**

bi·sul·fide /bī súl fīd/ *n.* = **disulfide**

bi·sul·fite /bī súl fīt/ *n.* = **hydrogen sulfite**

bit[1] /bit/ *n.* **1.** **PIECE** a small piece of something ○ *There were bits of paper everywhere.* **2.** **SHORT AMOUNT OF TIME** a very short period of time or distance ○ *I'll do it in a bit.* **3.** **TWELVE-AND-ONE-HALF CENTS** an eighth of a dollar (*slang dated*) (*used in the plural*) ○ *two bits* **4.** MONEY **SMALL COIN** a small coin of a particular value (*informal dated*) ○ *a threepenny bit* **5.** ARTS **SHORT PERFORMANCE** a short routine, joke, or skit in a performance **6.** CINEMA **SMALL ACTING PART** a small part in a movie or play (*often used before a noun*) ○ *I had a bit part in one of her movies.* **7.** **EVERYTHING ABOUT A ROLE** all the aspects of a particular role in life (*informal*) ○ *did the whole two-career marriage bit* [Old English *bita*, formed from *bītan* "to bite" (see BITE). Originally "piece bitten off, morsel"; the more general meaning "piece" dates from the 13thC.] ◇ **a bit** somewhat (*informal*) ◇ **bit by bit** gradually ◇ **bits and pieces** miscellaneous small objects (*informal*) ○ *I collected up my bits and pieces and left.* ◇ **do your bit** to contribute your share to work that needs to be done ◇ **every bit** in every way ○ *She is every bit as skilled as he is.* ◇ **to bits** very much or to the greatest degree possible (*informal*) ○ *I just love the kids to bits!*

bit[2] /bit/ *n.* **1.** **MOUTHPIECE OF BRIDLE** a part of a bridle, that consists of a metal mouthpiece held in a horse's mouth by the reins and used to control the horse **2.** **DETACHABLE PART OF DRILL** a small metal tool that is inserted into a drill or brace and used for boring or drilling **3.** **TOOL BLADE** the part of a plane that is used for cutting **4.** **PART OF KEY** the part of a key that moves the tumblers or bolt of a lock **5.** **PART OF PINCERS** the gripping part of a pair of pincers ■ *vt.* (**bit·ted, bit·ting, bits**) **1.** **INSERT BRIDLE BIT** to put a bit into the mouth of a horse **2.** **RESTRAIN** to restrain somebody, or hold somebody back [Old English *bite*, from, ultimately, an Indo-European base that is also the ancestor of English *bitter* and *bite*. The original meaning was "a bite."] ◇ **champ** *or* **chafe at the bit** to be impatient for something to happen, or impatient because no action is possible ◇ **get** *or* **take** *or* **have the bit between your teeth** to start something and refuse stubbornly to stop

bit[3] /bit/ *n.* **1.** **DIGIT IN BINARY NOTATION** in binary notation, either of the digits 0 or 1 used to represent one of only two outcomes, e.g., on or off **2.** **UNIT OF INFORMATION IN COMPUTER** the smallest unit of information storable in a computer or a peripheral device, expressed as 0 or 1. Eight bits make a byte, the common measure of memory or storage capacity. [Mid-20thC. Blend of BINARY and DIGIT.]

bit[4] /bit/ past tense, past participle of **bite**

bitch /bich/ *n.* **1.** ZOOL **FEMALE DOG** a female dog, or the female of another related animal, e.g., the fox, or another carnivore, e.g., the ferret **2.** **OFFENSIVE TERM** a highly offensive term that deliberately insults a woman's temperament (*taboo insult*) **3.** **WOMAN OR GIRL** a woman or girl or a girlfriend (*slang*) (*used especially in Black English*) **4.** **COMPLAINT** a querulous nagging complaint (*slang*) **5.** **SOMETHING DIFFICULT** a difficult thing or situation (*slang*) ○ *That lock's a real bitch to open.* ■ *vi.* (**bitched, bitch·ing, bitch·es**) **1.** **BE NASTY ABOUT SOMEBODY** to talk about somebody who is not present in an unpleasant or malicious way (*slang*) **2.** **COMPLAIN CONTINUALLY** to complain or grumble about something continually [Old English *bicce*, perhaps from an Old Norse word]

bitch·in /bíchən/ *adj.* **GREAT** particularly or extremely good (*slang*) ■ *adv.* **VERY** extremely (*slang*) [Mid-20th C. Alteration of bitching, shortening of sonofabitching, from SON OF A BITCH.]

bitch·y /bíchee/ (**-i·er, -i·est**) *adj.* malicious or unpleasant in speaking to, talking about, or behaving toward somebody (*slang*) —**bitch·i·ly** *adv.* —**bitch·i·ness** *n.*

bite /bīt/ *v.* (**bit, bit·ten** /bítt'n/ *or* **bit** /bit/, **bit·ing, bites**) **1.** *vti.* **GRIP WITH THE TEETH** to hold something tightly, tear something off, or cut through something using the teeth ○ *I bit into the fruit.* **2.** *vt.* **STING** to puncture or tear the skin of a person or animal using fangs or teeth ○ *got bitten by a wasp* **3.** *vti.* **GRIP SOMETHING FIRMLY** to make firm or secure contact with something ○ *This stripped screw isn't biting.* **4.** *vi.* **CORRODE SOMETHING** to eat into something with a corrosive action

○ *The acid had bitten into the metal surface.* **5.** *vi.* **CUT INTO SOMEBODY OR SOMETHING** to penetrate somebody or something sharply, as if with a honed blade **6.** *vi.* **TAKE BAIT** to attempt to take the bait that has been placed on the end of a fishing line (*refers to fish*) **7.** *vi.* **RISE TO SOMEBODY ELSE'S BAIT** to respond when somebody else tries to get you involved in a scheme or an argument (*informal*) ○ *Even though baited by the opposing attorney in court, she refused to bite.* **8.** *vi.* **BE EFFECTIVE** to have an effect or influence ○ *The trade sanctions are at last beginning to bite.* ■ *n.* **1. SEIZURE OF SOMETHING WITH TEETH** the action of taking something between the teeth and tearing it off **2. MOUTHFUL** a piece of food torn off with the teeth **3. INJURY FROM TEETH OR INSECT** an injury that has been caused by an animal or insect puncturing or tearing the skin with teeth or fangs ○ *a mosquito bite* **4. ATTEMPT BY FISH TO TAKE BAIT** an attempt by a fish to eat the bait that has been put on the end of a fishing line **5. PIQUANCY** a pleasantly sharp taste **6. WIT AND INTELLIGENCE** a penetrating and intelligent quality **7. COLDNESS** a cold sharp sensation that is quite painful ○ *There's a bite in the air today.* **8.** MECH ENG **DEPTH OF MACHINE TOOL'S BLADE** the depth to which a machine tool can cut **9. GRIP** the grip that something such as a tool has on something else **10.** DENT **FIT BETWEEN TEETH** the way the upper and lower teeth meet and fit together when the jaw is closed **11. CORROSIVE EFFECT** the corrosive effect of acid on a surface **12. PERIOD WHEN FISH EAT** a time when fish usually feed ○ *The catfish bite is usually the heaviest and best in the evening.* [Old English *bītan*, from, ultimately, an Indo-European base that also produced English *beetle* and *fission*] —**bit·a·ble** *adj.* —**bit·er** *n.* ◇ **bite off more than you can chew** to take on more than you can deal with (*informal*)

bite back *v.* **1.** *vt.* **STOP FROM EXPRESSING** to hold back from saying something or openly crying ○ *I bit back my tears.* **2.** *vti.* **GIVE SHARP RETORT** to retort sharply, or say something in a very sharp manner in response to somebody else

bite·plate /bīt plàyt/ *n.* a removable acrylic dental device that sticks to the roof of the mouth and is worn to encourage the back teeth to come through or to correct an overbite

bite-sized, **bite-size** *adj.* small enough to be eaten as a single mouthful ○ *cut the meat into bite-sized pieces*

Bite·wing-Pro *tdmk.* a trademark for a dental X-ray device used for examining the crowns of the upper and lower teeth

Bi·thyn·i·a /bi thínnee ə/ ancient country of northwestern Asia Minor, on the Black Sea in present-day Turkey

bit·ing /bíting/ *adj.* **1. VERY COLD** cold enough to cause discomfort or pain ○ *a biting north wind* **2. CLEVERLY SARCASTIC** sarcastic and clever

bit·ing louse (*plural* **bit·ing lice**) *n.* a wingless insect that spends its entire life cycle as a parasite on the body of a bird or mammal and feeds on skin flakes, feathers, glandular secretions, and blood. Suborder: Mallophaga.

bit·ing midge, **bit·ing gnat** *n.* = **punkie**

bit map *n.* **COMPUTER IMAGE REPRESENTED AS BITS** a representation of a graphic image in computer memory consisting of rows and columns of dots, each corresponding to a pixel. For monochrome images one bit is sufficient to represent each dot, while colors and shades of gray require more than one bit of data for each dot. ■ *vt.* (**bit-mapped, bit-map·ping, bit-maps**) **REPRESENT COMPUTER IMAGE AS BITS** to represent a graphic image in computer memory as a matrix of dots or to recreate the image on a computer screen from such a bit map [From BIT³]

bi·tok /beetok/ *n.* fried ground beef patties served with a sour cream sauce [Via Russian from French *bifteck (haché)*, "(ground) beef," from English *beefsteak*]

bitt /bit/ *n.* **POST ON SHIP** either of a pair of posts on a ship's deck for fastening cables (*often used in the plural*) ■ *vt.* (**bitt·ed, bitt·ing, bitts**) **TIE TO A BITT** to fasten something around a bitt [15thC. Origin uncertain: perhaps from Old Norse *biti* "beam," from, ultimately, an Indo-European base that is also the ancestor of English *bite*.]

bit·ten past participle of **bite**

bit·ter /bíttər/ (**-tered, -ter·ing, -ters**) *adj.* **1. STRONG AND SHARP IN TASTE** having a sharp strong unpleasant taste, e.g., like that of orange peel **2. RESENTFUL** angry and resentful ○ *a bitter smile* **3. DIFFICULT TO ACCEPT** painful or very hard to accept ○ *a bitter blow* **4. HOSTILE** expressing intense hostility ○ *bitter fighting.* **5. VERY COLD** penetratingly and unpleasantly cold ○ *a bitter wind* [Old English *biter*, from, ultimately, an Indo-European base that also produced English *bite*, *beetle*, and *fission*] —**bit·ter·ness** *n.*

bit·ter al·mond *n.* a type of almond tree that produces nuts containing hydrogen cyanide. When detoxified, the almond oil can be used as a flavoring.

bit·ter al·oes *n.* = **aloes**

bit·ter·brush /bíttər brùsh/ *n.* a shrub with yellow flowers that grows in western North America. Latin name: *Purshia tridentata.*

bit·ter cress *n.* a plant belonging to the mustard family that has clusters of typically white flowers and often grows in damp places. Genus: *Cardamine.*

bit·ter end *n.* the very end of something, however unpleasant it is ○ *They held out to the bitter end.* [Originally "end of a ship's cable or mooring rope secured on board the ship"; *bitter* perhaps from BITT, but now interpreted as "painful"]

bit·ter·en·der /bìttər éndər/ *n.* a highly obstinate, inflexible, recalcitrant person who takes a stand, refusing to budge until he or she is forced by adverse circumstances to do so ○ *The senior advisors in the administration, bitterenders refusing to divulge information to the courts, were eventually forced to resign in disgrace.*

bit·ter·ling /bíttərling/ *n.* a small brightly colored freshwater fish from central Europe that is often kept in aquariums. Latin name: *Rhodeus sericeus.* [Late 19thC. From German, literally "small bitter (fish)."]

bit·ter·ly /bíttərlee/ *adv.* **1. RESENTFULLY AND ANGRILY** with feelings of anger, injustice, and resentment ○ *wept bitterly* **2. INTENSELY AND NEGATIVELY** intensely or profoundly, in reaction to an unpleasant situation ○ *a bitterly fought divorce case* **3. EXTREMELY AND PENETRATINGLY** to an extreme and penetrating degree ○ *bitterly cold*

bit·tern¹ /bíttərn/ *n.* a wading bird of the heron family, similar to the herons but with mottled brownish plumage, shorter legs and neck, and a booming call. Family: Ardeidae. [Early 16thC. Alteration of *bitore*, probably from, ultimately, Anglo-Latin *butorius* or Old French *butor*, both ultimately from Latin *butio* "bittern" + *taurus* "bull," from its booming voice.]

bit·tern² /bíttərn/ *n.* the bitter liquid that is left after common salt has crystallized from sea water [Late 17thC. Formed from BITTER, but the origin of the final *-n* is not known.]

bit·ter·nut /bíttər nùt/ *n.* **1. HICKORY TREE** a type of hickory tree, native to eastern North America, that bears thin-shelled nuts with a bitter kernel. Latin name: *Carya cordiformis.* **2. THIN-SHELLED NUT** the nut that grows on the bitternut tree

bit·ter or·ange *n.* **1. ORANGE TREE WITH BITTER FRUIT** an orange tree that produces bitter fruit used for making marmalade. Latin name: *Citrus aurantium.* **2. ORANGE USED FOR MARMALADE** the bitter-tasting fruit of the bitter orange, used for making marmalade

bit·ter pill *n.* something unpleasant that nonetheless must be accepted ○ *Not getting the job was a bitter pill for him to swallow.*

bit·ter·root /bíttər ro͞ot, -ro͝ot/ *n.* a western North American plant of the purslane family that has edible starchy roots and is able to grow and live in dry surroundings. Latin name: *Lewisia redivia.*

Bit·ter·root Range /bíttər ro͞ot ràynj/ mountain range of the northern Rocky Mountains, extending about 435 mi./700 km along the Idaho-Montana border. Its highest peak is Scott Peak 11,393 ft./3,473 m.

bit·ters /bíttərz/ *n.* **ALCOHOLIC LIQUID** a slightly alcoholic liquid flavored with plant extracts and used as a mixer with certain cocktails (*takes a singular verb*) ■ *npl.* **DIGESTIVE AID** a bitter-tasting liquid used as a digestive aid

bit·ter·sweet /bíttər swe͞et/ *adj.* **1. BOTH BITTER AND SWEET** smelling or tasting both bitter and sweet at the same time **2. BOTH HAPPY AND SAD** causing feelings of happiness and sadness at the same time ■ *n.* PLANTS **1. PLANT WITH BRIGHT CAPSULES AND SEEDS** a poisonous climbing plant found in North America that has orange capsules containing bright red seeds. Genus: *Celastus.* **2. NIGHTSHADE** a sprawling plant with purple flowers and poisonous red fruits resembling berries, and stems that taste bitter then sweet when chewed. Latin name: *Solanum dulcamara.*

bit·ter·weed /bíttər we͞ed/ *n.* an American plant, such as sneezeweed or some species of ragweed, that contains a bitter-tasting substance

bit·ty /bíttee/ (**-ti·er, -ti·est**) *adj.* extremely small in size or physical stature (*informal*) ○ *a little bitty kid riding a tricycle*

bi·tu·men /bi to͞omən, -tyo͞omən, bī-/ *n.* a sticky mixture of hydrocarbons derived from petroleum and found in substances such as asphalt and tar that are used for road surfacing and roofing [15thC. From Latin, "asphalt," probably from a Celtic source.] —**bi·tu·mi·noid** *adj.*

bi·tu·mi·nize /bi to͞omə nīz, -tyo͞omə-, bī-/ (**-nized, -niz·ing, -niz·es**) *vt.* to cover or treat something with bitumen or to convert something into bitumen —**bi·tu·mi·ni·za·tion** /bi to͞oməni záysh'n/ *n.*

bi·tu·mi·nous /bi to͞omənəss, -tyo͞omənəss, bī-/ *adj.* relating to or containing bitumen

bi·tu·mi·nous coal *n.* a type of soft coal that burns with a smoky flame

bi·va·lence /bī váyləns/ *n.* the property that a proposition has in classical systems of logic of being either true or false

bi·va·lent /bī váylənt/ *adj.* **1.** CHEM = **divalent 2.** GENETICS **PAIRED** used to describe structurally identical (**homologous**) chromosomes that come together during cell division (**meiosis**) ■ *n.* GENETICS **PAIR OF CHROMOSOMES** a pair of structurally identical (**homologous**) chromosomes that come together during cell division (**meiosis**)

bi·valve /bī vàlv/ *n.* a marine or freshwater mollusk that has its body contained within two shells joined by a hinge. Oysters, mussels, and clams are bivalves. —**bi·valved** *adj.* —**bi·val·vu·lar** /bī válvyələr/ *adj.*

bi·var·i·ate /bī váiree it, -ayt/ *adj.* relating to or involving two variables

biv·ou·ac /bívvoo àk, bívwàk/ *n.* **1. MILITARY OR MOUNTAINEERING CAMP** a very simple temporary camp that is set up and used by soldiers or mountaineers **2.** MOUNTAINEERING **BRIEF OVERNIGHT STAY** a short stay, usually overnight, often with minimum equipment ■ *vi.* (**-acked, -ack·ing, -acs**) **MAKE CAMP** to set up and stay in a very simple temporary camp [Early 18thC. Via French from, probably, Low German *bīwake*, from *bi-* "by" + *wake* "watch, vigil."]

bi·week·ly /bī we͞eklee/ *adj.* **1. COMING OUT EVERY TWO WEEKS** produced or appearing every two weeks **2. COMING OUT TWICE A WEEK** produced or appearing twice a week ■ *adv.* **1. ONCE EVERY TWO WEEKS** at two-week intervals **2. TWICE A WEEK** twice during a one-week period ■ *n.* (*plural* **-lies**) **TWICE-WEEKLY PUBLICATION** a publication that appears every two weeks

WORD KEY: USAGE

How many times is **biweekly**? Confusion is caused by the fact that ***biweekly*** and ***bimonthly*** can mean either "once every two weeks (or months)" or "twice a week (or month)." If you want to avoid doubt it is better to rephrase: *The talks are held twice a week at the local school, The talks are held every two weeks at the local school.*

bi·year·ly /bī yéerlee/ *adj.* **1. COMING OUT EVERY TWO YEARS** produced or appearing every two years **2. COMING OUT TWICE A YEAR** produced or appearing twice a year ■ *adv.* **1. ONCE EVERY TWO YEARS** at two-year intervals **2. TWICE A YEAR** twice during a one-year period

biz /biz/ *n.* a business of a particular type, typically involving fashion, entertainment, or the media (*slang*) [Mid-19thC. Shortened from BUSINESS.]

bi·zarre /bi zaár/ *adj.* amusingly or grotesquely strange or unusual [Mid-17thC. Via French, "odd," formerly "brave, handsome," from Spanish *bizarro* "brave" (perhaps influenced by Basque *bizar* "beard," taken as a symbol of vigor), from, ultimately, Italian *bizzarro* "angry."] —**bi·zarre·ly** *adv.* —**bi·zarre·ness** *n.*

bi·zar·re·rie /bi zaáraree/ *n.* amusing or grotesque strangeness or oddity [Mid-18thC. From French.]

Bi·zet /bee záy/, **Georges** (1838–75) French composer. He completed the opera *Carmen* just before his death. Born **Alexandre César Léopold Bizet**

bi·zon·al /bī zōn'l/ *adj.* made up of two zones

Bk *symbol.* berkelium

bk. *abbr.* 1. bank 2. book

bkcy. *abbr.* bankruptcy

bkg. *abbr.* banking

bkgd. *abbr.* background

bkpt. *abbr.* bankrupt

bks. *abbr.* 1. barracks 2. books

bl. *abbr.* 1. barrel 2. black 3. blue 4. bale

B.L. *abbr.* 1. Bachelor of Laws 2. Bachelor of Letters

B/L *abbr.* bill of lading

blab /blab/ *vi.* **(blabbed, blab·bing, blabs)** *(informal)* **1.** TELL SECRETS to talk indiscreetly about something that is supposed to be secret **2.** CHATTER to chatter in a mildly incoherent way ■ *n.* = **blabbermouth** [13thC. Origin uncertain, but ultimately probably from a prehistoric Germanic word imitating the sound of vacuous talking (compare Danish *blabbre* "to gabble").]

blab·ber /blábbər/ *vi.* **(-bered, -ber·ing, -bers)** CHATTER to chatter in a mildly incoherent way ■ *n.* **1.** = **blabbermouth 2.** NOISE OF CHATTER the sound made by people talking loudly and incoherently [14thC. Origin uncertain, but probably formed from BLAB.]

blab·ber·mouth /blábbər mòwth/ *(plural* **-mouths** /-mòwthz/) *n.* somebody who in unable to keep from talking too much or from revealing secrets *(informal)*

black /blak/ *adj.* **1.** COLORS OF THE DARKEST COLOR being the color of coal or carbon **2.** DEVOID OF LIGHT completely dark, with no light **3. black, Black** DARK-SKINNED belonging to an African ethnic group, or to any other ethnic group with very dark skin **4. black, Black** RELATING TO AFRICAN AMERICAN PEOPLE relating to a U.S. ethnic group descended from dark-skinned African peoples **5.** FULL OF ANGER filled with anger or hostility **6.** HOPELESS so depressing as to end all hope **7.** EVIL evil, or associated with evil **8.** DIRTY covered with mud, soil, or any other dark substance **9.** BEVERAGES WITHOUT MILK served without adding milk or cream **10.** FUNNY AND MACABRE dealing with very serious things in a humorous and often macabre way **11.** SERIOUSLY BAD OR UNFORTUNATE causing or associated with severely bad conditions or misfortune **12.** DISHONORABLE extremely dishonorable and deserving the most serious criticism **13.** MIL CLANDESTINE carried out in the utmost secrecy ■ *n.* **1.** COLORS DARKEST COLOR a color value that has no hue as a result of the absorption of nearly all light from all visible wavelengths **2.** COLORS COAL-COLORED DYE OR PIGMENT a pigment or dye that is the color of carbon or coal **3. black, Black** PEOPLES MEMBER OF DARK SKINNED PEOPLE a member of an African ethnic group or any other ethnic group with very dark skin **4. black, Black** PEOPLES AFRICAN AMERICAN PERSON a member of a U.S. ethnic group descended from dark-skinned African peoples **5.** BLACK MATERIAL OR CLOTHES fabric or clothing that is black in color **6.** TOTAL DARKNESS complete darkness **7.** BOARD GAMES BLACK PIECE a black piece in a game such as chess or checkers **8.** BOARD GAMES PLAYER WITH BLACK PIECES a player in games such as chess or checkers who is playing with the black pieces **9.** CUE GAMES BLACK BALL a black ball in snooker, which is the last ball to be sunk **10.** ARCHERY BLACK RING ON ARCHERY TARGET a black ring on a target in archery, which gives a player a score of three **11.** GAMBLING BLACK COLOR BETS ARE PLACED ON one of the colors on which players can lay their bets when gambling at such games as roulette ■ *vt.* **(blacked, black·ing, blacks) 1.** MAKE BLACK to make something black, or cover something in black **2.** USE BLACK POLISH to cover something, e.g., shoes or boots, with black polish **3.** BRUISE THE EYE to hit somebody's eye so that it becomes very bruised and turns a purplish-black color [Old English *blæc*, of uncertain origin: perhaps ultimately from an Indo-European base meaning "shine, burn," which also produced English *flame*; the underlying sense would be "scorch" and, hence, "make dark"] —**black·ish** *adj.* —**black·ness** *n.* ◇ **in the black 1.** having or making money or a profit **2.** not in debt or overdrawn

WORD KEY: USAGE

Sensitivity trap The word ***black*** is standard in current usage for a dark-skinned person of African origin or descent. However, many Americans of African descent prefer the more formal term *African American*, used both as noun and adjective. See also the note at colored.

Black /blak/, **Davidson** (1884–1934) Canadian anthropologist. He identified "Peking Man" *(Sinanthropus pekinensis)*, a prehistoric human species later called *Homo Erectus*, in China in the late 1920s.

Black, Hugo (1886–1971) U.S. Supreme Court justice. On the U.S. Supreme Court (1937–71), he was known for upholding a literal interpretation of the First Amendment of the Constitution. Full name **Hugo LaFayette Black**

Black, Samuel (1780–1841) Scottish-born Canadian explorer and fur trader. He kept a journal of his discoveries.

Black, Shirley (*b.* 1927) U.S. actor and former ambassador. She is arguably the most popular child actress starring in "The Littlest Rebel" and "Bright Eyes" (1934).

black al·der *n.* = **winterberry**

black-and-blue *adj.* covered with bruises, or feeling very bruised (*not hyphenated after a verb*)

Black and Tan *n.* a member of the armed force that was sent by the British to Ireland in 1921 to fight Sinn Fein. Their uniform was khaki, with a black beret and armband.

black and white *n.* **1.** PRINTED OR WRITTEN MATTER material either handwritten or printed **2.** VISUAL MEDIUM WITHOUT COLORED IMAGES a visual medium without colors, and in hues of black, white, and shades of gray

black-and-white *adj.* **1.** NOT IN COLOR representing an image in which colors have been converted to black, white, and shades of gray ○ *a black-and-white photograph* **2.** REPRODUCING IMAGES NOT IN COLOR reproducing images in which colors have been converted to black, white, and shades of gray ○ *a black-and-white television* **3.** CLEARCUT clearcut and straightforward, allowing no room for compromise or doubt (*not hyphenated after a verb*) ○ *Everything is black and white as far as she's concerned.*

Black An·gus *n.* = **Angus** [*Angus* from the name of an administrative region of northeastern Scotland]

black arts *npl.* magic that is used for evil purposes, calling upon the help of the Devil

black-backed gull *n.* either of two species of common gull with a black back and wings and white underparts, found in North Atlantic coastal waters. Latin name: *Larus marinus* and *Larus fuscus.*

black bag job *n.* an illegal clandestine entry into somebody's premises by a law enforcement agency or a private detective (*slang*)

black·ball /blák bawl/ *vt.* **(-balled, -ball·ing, -balls) 1.** KEEP FROM JOINING to prevent somebody from becoming a member of a club by voting against the person **2.** EXCLUDE FROM GROUP to exclude somebody from a group or profession ■ *n.* **1.** NEGATIVE VOTE a vote against somebody, especially somebody wanting to join a group **2.** VOTING TOKEN a black ball used to show a negative vote (*archaic*)

black bass *(plural* **black bass**) *n.* a large freshwater bass of North America that is popular as a game fish. Genus: *Micropterus.*

black bean *n.* **1.** PLANTS BEAN PLANT any bean plant with small black seeds that are dried and used in cooking **2.** FOOD DRIED BEAN a dried seed from a black bean plant, used in cooking, often as an accompaniment to rice **3.** TREES BEAN TREE a tree found in the rain forests of eastern Australia that has smooth bark, dark green leaves, and yellow or red flowers. It is used in furniture-making. Latin name: *Castanospermum australe.* **4.** FOOD FERMENTED SOYBEAN a soybean used fermented in Asian cooking ○ *black bean sauce*

black bear *n.* **1.** N AMERICAN BEAR a bear that lives in the forests of North America and ranges from brownish yellow to black in color. Latin name: *Euarctos americanus.* **2.** ASIATIC BEAR a bear that lives in central and eastern Asia and has a black coat with a whitish V-shaped mark on its chest. Latin name: *Selenarctos thibetanus.*

black belt *n.* **1.** BELT SHOWING SKILL IN MARTIAL ARTS a belt that is worn by somebody who has reached the highest level of skill in a martial art such as judo or karate **2.** SOMEBODY WITH BLACK BELT somebody who has reached the highest level of skill in a martial art such as judo or karate, and who is entitled to wear a belt that is black **3. black belt, Black Belt** FERTILE AGRICULTURAL REGION a region in the southern United States, stretching from Georgia across Alabama and Mississippi, with extremely fertile dark soil

Blackberry

black·ber·ry /blák bèrree/ *(plural* **-ries**) *n.* **1.** PLANTS THORNY BUSH WITH SMALL PURPLE FRUITS a thorny European bush of the rose family that has pink or white flowers and purple edible fruit made up of a cluster of small round sections. Latin name: *Rubus fruticosus.* **2.** FOOD FRUIT OF BLACKBERRY the fruit of the blackberry bush

black·ber·ry lil·y *n.* an ornamental plant from China that has orange flowers with small red spots and clusters of blackish seeds that look like blackberries. Latin name: *Belamcanda chinensis.*

black bile *n.* one of the four humors that were once believed to be the base of somebody's character, associated with a melancholy temperament. It was characterized as cold and dry. (*archaic*)

black birch *n.* = **sweet birch**

Blackbird

black·bird /blák bùrd/ *n.* **1.** BIRD WITH BLACK FEATHERS a bird belonging to a family widespread throughout North and South America, with black feathers showing a metallic sheen or bold patterns of yellow, orange, or red. Family: Icteridae. **2.** COMMON EUROPEAN BIRD WITH BLACK FEATHERS a common European bird, the male of which has black feathers and a yellow beak. The female has brown feathers. Latin name: *Turdus merula.*

black·board /blák bàwrd/ *n.* a board of either a dark color or white that is written on with contrasting chalk or erasible markers, used especially in classrooms. ◊ **whiteboard**

black·bod·y *(plural* **-ies**) *n.* PHYS an ideal object that would absorb all of the radiation incident on it without reflecting any

black book *n.* **1.** BOOK OF PHONE NUMBERS a book in which somebody keeps the names and telephone numbers of private friends, especially boyfriends or girlfriends (*informal*) **2.** BOOK OF BLACKLISTED PEOPLE a book in which the names of people who are to be punished or blacklisted are kept

black bot·tom pie *n.* a dessert with a layer of chocolate on the bottom and vanilla pudding on top

black box *n.* **1.** AIR = **flight recorder 2.** COMPUT COMPONENT OF UNKNOWN CONSTRUCTION an electronic component whose constituents or circuitry are unknown or irrelevant, but whose function is understood

black bread *n.* a very dark rye bread that is particularly popular in Germany and Slavic countries

black·buck /blák bùk/ *(plural* **-bucks** *or* **-buck**) *n.* a small antelope, the male of which has a black back, white underbelly, and spiral horns. It was once abundant in India but is now rare. Latin name: *Antilope cervicapra.*

black·cap /blák kàp/ *n.* **1. SMALL SONGBIRD** a small brown-gray warbler of Eurasia and Africa, the male of which has a black-topped head. Latin name: *Sylvia atricapilla*. **2. BIRD WITH BLACK CROWN** any bird similar to the blackcap warbler that has a black-topped head, e.g., a chickadee **3.** BOT = **black raspberry**

black cher·ry *n.* **1. WILD N AMERICAN CHERRY TREE** a large wild North American cherry tree that has dark bark, white flowers, and black fruits. Latin name: *Prunus serotina*. **2. WOOD OF BLACK CHERRY TREE** the wood of the black cherry tree, used for furniture, cabinets, and musical instruments **3. DARK-COLORED CHERRY** a dark-skinned cherry, especially one from the black cherry tree

black·cock /blák kòk/ (*plural* **-cocks** *or* **-cock**) *n.* the male of the black grouse

black cod *n.* = **sablefish**

black com·e·dy *n.* comedy containing bitter jokes about unpleasant aspects of life

black cow *n. Midwest* a root beer float made with vanilla ice cream

black crap·pie *n.* a medium-sized edible sunfish with black-spotted skin, found in lakes and rivers of eastern North America. Latin name: *Pomoxis nigromaculatus*. [*Crappie*, origin unknown]

black·damp /blák damp/ *n.* atmospheric conditions in a mine that prevent normal breathing because insufficient oxygen remains after an explosion

Black Death *n.* the bubonic plague epidemic that killed over 50 million people throughout Asia and Europe in the 14th century [*Black* probably from the color of the buboes]

black di·a·mond *n.* **1.** = **carbonado 2. BLACK HEMATITE** the black variety of hematite, the principal ore of iron ■ **black di·a·monds** *npl.* **COAL** coal (*informal*)

black duck *n.* a brownish duck of northeastern North America. Latin name: *Anas rubripes*.

black e·con·o·my *n.* the part of an economy that consists of unofficial or illegal, and therefore untaxed, earnings

black·en /blákən/ (**-ened, -en·ing, -ens**) *v.* **1.** *vti.* **TURN BLACK** to become, or cause something to become, darker or black **2.** *vt.* **SLANDER** to harm or damage somebody's reputation (*formal*)

Black Eng·lish *n.* any one of the varieties of English that have developed in Black communities worldwide, many of which share features of grammar and vocabulary. ◆ **African American Vernacular English**

black eye *n.* an area of bruising around somebody's eye

black-eyed bean *n. U.K.* = **black-eyed pea**

black-eyed pea *n.* **1. EDIBLE LEGUME** a legume widely cultivated in the southern United States for forage and for its seeds. Latin name: *Vigna unguiculata*. **2. SMALL BEAN WITH BLACK SPOT** a small beige bean with a black spot. Black-eyed peas are traditionally eaten on New Year's Day in some parts of the United States.

black-eyed Su·san *n.* **1. FLOWER WITH DARK CENTER** a North American plant that has yellowish-orange flowers with a dark conical center. Genus: *Rudbeckia*. **2. CLIMBING PLANT WITH YELLOW FLOWERS** a tropical African climbing plant that has yellow flowers with purple centers. Latin name: *Thunbergia alata*.

black·fish /blák fìsh/ (*plural* **-fish** *or* **-fish·es**) *n.* **1. SMALL ARCTIC FISH** a small freshwater fish that is very abundant in Arctic North America and Siberia. Latin name: *Dallia pectoralis*. **2. SALMON AFTER SPAWNING** a female salmon that has spawned **3.** = **pilot whale**

black flag *n.* = **Jolly Roger** ■ *vt.* (**black-flagged, black-flag·ging, black-flags**) **CALL RACING DRIVER INTO PITS** to signal to a racing driver to pull into the pits by waving a black flag

black fly /blák flì/ (*plural* **black flies** *or* **black fly**) *n.* a small dark biting gnat that causes painful itchy welts in people and animals. Family: Simuliidae.

black·fly (*plural* **-flies** *or* **-fly**) *n.* a black aphid that infests many types of plant. Genus: *Aphis*.

Black·foot /blák fòot/ (*plural* **-feet** /-fèet/ *or* **-foot**) *n.* **1.** PEOPLES **NATIVE AMERICAN** a member of a group of Native American peoples living in Alberta, Saskatchewan, and Montana **2.** LANG **ALGONQUIAN LANGUAGE** an Algonquian language spoken in Alberta and in Montana. Blackfoot is spoken by about 8,000 people. [Late 18thC. Translation of Blackfoot *Siksika*, said to be from the blackening of the soles of their moccasins when they walked across burned prairies.] —**Black·foot** *adj.*

black-foot·ed al·ba·tross *n.* a dark albatross of the Pacific that spends most of its time at sea. Latin name: *Diomedea nigripes*.

black-foot·ed fer·ret *n.* a North American weasel that has a light-colored coat and blackish patches on its face, tail, and feet. Latin name: *Mustela nigripes*.

Black For·est wooded highland region in Baden-Württemberg State, southwestern Germany that contains the sources of the Danube and Neckar rivers. Area: about 2,000 sq. mi./5,180 sq. km.

Black For·est cake *n.* a rich chocolate cake that is topped and filled with cherries and whipped cream [Probably from the cake's dark color]

Black For·est ga·teau *n. U.K.* = **Black Forest cake**

Black Fri·ar *n.* a member of the Dominican order of monks

black grouse (*plural* **black grouse**) *n.* a large grouse of Europe and western Asia with a lyre-shaped tail. The male is black with white patches on its wings. Latin name: *Lyrurus tetrix*.

black guil·le·mot *n.* a small seabird of northeastern North America that belongs to the auk family and has black plumage with white wing patches in summer. Latin name: *Cepphus grylle*.

Black Hand *n.* an early 20th-century criminal organization of Sicilian immigrants in the United States that practiced blackmail and violence (*informal*) [Translation of Italian *La Mano Negra*, the name of a Sicilian and Italian-American criminal society of the late 19th and 20th centuries]

black haw, black·haw *n.* **1. WILD PLANT** a shrub or small tree of the honeysuckle family, native to the eastern United States, with white flowers and bluish-black fruits. Latin name: *Viburnum prunifolium*. **2.** = **sheepberry**

Black Hawk (1767–1838) U.S. Native American leader. A leader of the Sauk people, he fought against Native Americans' westward displacement by Europeans in what became known as the Black Hawk War (1832).

black·head /blák hed/ *n.* **1. DARK BLOCKED PORE** a small plug of dark fatty matter blocking a follicle on the skin, especially on the face **2.** VET **FOWL DISEASE** an infectious disease of turkeys and related fowl resulting in darkened head skin. It is caused by a protozoan. **3.** BIRDS **BIRD WITH BLACK HEAD** a bird with a dark-colored head, especially a duck or gull

Black Hills mountainous region in western South Dakota and northeastern Wyoming, a mining area famous for the granite sculptures of Mount Rushmore National Memorial. The highest point is Harney Peak. Height: 7,242 ft./2,207 m. Area: 6,000 sq. mi./15,000 sq. km.

black hole *n.* **1. OBJECT IN SPACE** an object in space thought to contain a celestial object with such a strong gravitational pull that no matter or energy can escape from it. Black holes are believed to form when stars collapse in upon themselves. **2. PLACE WHERE THINGS GET LOST** a place or thing into which objects disappear and are not expected to be seen again (*humorous*)

black hu·mor *n.* humor that deals with unpleasant aspects of life in a bitter or ironic way —**black hu·mor·ist** *n.*

black ice *n.* a thin, almost invisible, layer of ice formed when rain falls on a surface that is below freezing [*Black* from the typical color of the underlying road surface]

black·ing /bláking/ *n.* polish used, especially formerly, to make shoes and stoves black

black·jack /blák jak/ *n.* **1.** CARDS **CARD GAME** a card game in which the winner is the player holding cards of a total value closest to, but not more than, 21 points **2.** CARDS **WINNING COMBINATION OF CARDS** a combination of an ace and a face card, which is a winning hand in blackjack **3.** MINERALS **BLACK MINERAL** a black variety of the mineral sphalerite or zinc blende **4.** ARMS **SHORT CLUB** a weapon in the form of a short leather-covered club ■ *interj.* CARDS **INDICATING A WIN AT BLACKJACK** used to indicate to other players that a blackjack has been dealt ■ *vt.* (**-jacks, -jacked, -jack·ing, -jacks**) **1. HIT WITH CLUB** to hit somebody with a short club **2. FORCE** to force somebody to do something [*Jack* from *jack* "knave in a pack of cards"]

black·jack oak *n.* a small oak tree with blackish bark that is common in the southeastern United States. Latin name: *Quercus marilandica*.

Black Ket·tle (c. 1803–68) U.S. Native American leader. He led the Southern Cheyenne, many of whom were massacred by U.S. forces in 1864, and was himself killed in a massacre.

black knight *n.* a company that makes an unwelcome attempt to take over another

black lead *n.* a commercial form of graphite

black·leg /blák lèg/ *n.* **1.** VET **DISEASE OF FARM ANIMALS** an infectious bacterial disease of farm animals that causes swellings on the legs **2.** BOT **POTATO DISEASE** a disease of potato plants caused by the bacterium *Erwinia carotovora* that makes the lower stems rot **3.** BOT **DISEASE OF OILSEED RAPE** a fungal disease of cabbage, oilseed rape, and similar plants that causes the stems to rot. It is caused by the bacterium *Leptosphaeria maculans*. **4.** GAMBLING **GAMBLER WHO CHEATS** a cheat at cards or horseracing (*informal*) **5.** *U.K.* **SOMEBODY WHO WORKS DURING STRIKE** a worker who is criticized and despised by striking colleagues for working during a strike (*slang*) = **scab**

black let·ter *n.* PRINTING = **Gothic**

black light *n.* **1. INVISIBLE LIGHT** any invisible electromagnetic radiation, e.g., ultraviolet or infrared light **2. DEVICE EMITTING BLACK LIGHT** a bulb, tube, or other device that emits black light when stimulated with electrical current

black·list /blák list/ *n.* **LIST OF DISAPPROVED PEOPLE** a list of people or groups who are under suspicion or excluded from something ○ *a credit blacklist* ■ *vt.* (**-list·ed, -list·ing, -lists**) **1. PUT ON BLACKLIST** to add somebody's name to a blacklist **2. CONDEMN** to shun or condemn somebody for behavior that breaks implicit or explicit rules

black lo·cust *n.* **1. TALL WHITE-FLOWERED TREE** a tall North American tree with compound leaves, fragrant white flowers in spring, and hard wood. Latin name: *Robinia pseudoacacia*. **2. HARD WOOD** the hard, light-colored wood of the black locust

black lung *n.* MED = **anthracosis**

black·ly /bláklee/ *adv.* **1. ANGRILY** in an angry or threatening way **2. WITH A BLACK APPEARANCE** showing or making use of the color black

black mag·ic *n.* magic that involves evil forces and spirits

black·mail /blák mayl/ *n.* **1. USE OF SECRETS TO COMPEL** the act of forcing somebody to pay money or do something by threatening to reveal shameful or incriminating facts about him or her. ◊ **greenmail, graymail 2. COERCION** unfair threatening or incriminating of somebody, as a way of achieving a result ■ *vt.* (**-mailed, -mailing, -mails**) **USE SECRETS TO COMPEL SOMEBODY** to force somebody to pay money or do something by threatening to reveal shameful or incriminating facts about him or her [Mid-16thC. *Mail* from obsolete *mail* "tribute, tax," from Old Norse *mál* "speech, agreement"; the word originally referred to protection money extorted by Scottish border bandits.] —**black·mail·er** *n.*

black mark *n.* a record of something that somebody has done that gives people a bad opinion of him or her ○ *Avoiding the family reunion counted as a blackmark against me.*

black mar·ket *n.* a system of buying and selling officially controlled goods illegally —**black mar·ket·eer** *n.* —**black mar·ket·eer·ing** *n.* —**black mar·ket·er** *n.*

black mass *n.* an imitation of a Christian Mass said to be conducted by worshipers of the Devil

black mea·sles *n.* a severe form of measles, with bleeding under the skin causing dark spots or patches (*takes a singular or plural verb*)

black mon·ey *n.* money earned unofficially or illegally

Black Monk *n.* a member of the Benedictine order of monks, who wear black cloaks over their white habits

Black Moun·tains mountain range in western North Carolina, part of the Blue Ridge and the highest range in the Appalachians. Its highest point is Mount Mitchell, 6,684 ft./2,037 m, the highest peak in the United States east of the Mississippi River.

Black·mun /blákmən/, **Harry** (1908–99) U.S. Supreme Court justice. On the Supreme Court (1970–94), he became identified with his decision supporting abortion rights in *Roe v. Wade* (1973). Full name **Harry Andrew Blackmun**

Black Mus·lim *n.* a member of the Nation of Islam, an almost exclusively Black Islamic denomination based in the United States

black mus·tard *n.* a yellow-flowered plant of Europe and Asia with strong-tasting seeds used to make mustard. Latin name: *Brassica nigra.*

Black na·tion·al·ist *n.* a member of any political organization that promotes separate self-governing communities or states for Black people —**Black na·tion·al·ism** *n.*

black night·shade *n.* a widely found plant of the nightshade family that has poisonous leaves, white star-shaped flowers, and black berries. Latin name: *Solanum nigrum.*

black·out /blák owt/ *n.* **1.** MED **LOSS OF CONSCIOUSNESS** a temporary loss of consciousness, sight, or memory **2.** BROADCAST **WITHDRAWAL OF BROADCASTING** a refusal to broadcast radio or television programs, or a sports event for which tickets are still available **3.** COMMUNICATION **WITHHOLDING OF INFORMATION** the withholding of news or information about a subject, especially by official sources **4.** ELEC **LOSS OF ELECTRIC LIGHT** a failure of an electrical supply **5.** MIL **PERIOD OF EXTINGUISHING OR HIDING LIGHTS** a period during wartime in which all lights are to be turned off or covered up at night to prevent towns from being seen from enemy aircraft **6.** RADIO **LOSS OF RADIO COMMUNICATION** a loss of radio communication between an aircraft or ship and headquarters

Black Pan·ther *n.* a member of a militant Black political organization opposed to white domination that was active in the United States especially in the late 1960s and early 1970s [*Panther* from the emblem used by certain Black Power electoral candidates in Alabama in the mid-1960s]

black pep·per *n.* dark brown seasoning made by grinding pepper seeds that have not had their black outer covering removed

black·poll /blák pōl/, **black·poll war·bler** *n.* a small bird found in northern North America that has streaky plumage and is abundant in conifer forests. Latin name: *Dendroica striata.* [Poll from obsolete *poll* "head"]

black pow·der *n.* gunpowder, especially the kind formerly used in mines and quarries. It contains saltpeter, sulfur, and charcoal and is now mainly used in fireworks and muzzleloading firearms.

Black Pow·er *n.* a movement formed by Black people to engender social equality and emphasize pride in their racial identity via Black cultural and political institutions and organizations

black pud·ding *n. U.K., Southern U.S.* = **blood sausage**

black rac·er *n.* a dark-colored nonpoisonous snake of the eastern United States. Latin name: *Coluber constrictor.*

black rasp·ber·ry (*plural* **black rasp·ber·ries**) *n.* **1. TYPE OF RASPBERRY PLANT** a prickly North American shrub that produces edible berries. Latin name: *Rubus occidentalis.* **2. DARK-COLORED RASPBERRY** the fruit of the black raspberry, generally smaller and darker-colored than the cultivated raspberry

black rat *n.* a common dark brown rat that is a household pest and disease carrier. It was originally from Eurasia but was imported to coastal cities throughout the world, and is an important carrier of plague. Latin name: *Rattus rattus.*

black rot *n.* any plant disease that causes blackening as well as decay

Blacks·burg /bláksbərg/ town in southwestern Virginia, southwest of Salem, on the west side of the Allegheny Mountains. Population: 34,294 (1996).

Black Sea large inland sea linked to the Mediterranean by the Bosporus, the Sea of Marmara, and the Dardanelles. It is bordered by Bulgaria, Romania, Ukraine, Russia, Georgia, and Turkey. Area: 168,500 sq. mi./436,400 sq. km.

black shale *n.* a mudstone that contains organic carbon, e.g., an oil-bearing shale

black sheep *n.* somebody regarded with shame or contempt by the other members of a family or group [From black sheep's wool being less valuable to the shepherd than white]

Black·shirt /blák shùrt/, **black·shirt** *n.* a member of any European fascist movement active before and during World War II, especially a member of the Italian Fascist Party [From the distinctive item of the party's uniform]

black skim·mer *n.* a black-and-white seabird of coastal North America that has a black-tipped red bill with the lower mandible longer than the upper. Latin name: *Rhynchops niger.*

black·smith /blák smith/ *n.* somebody whose job is making and repairing iron and metal objects, including horseshoes. Blacksmiths originally worked by hand with a hammer and anvil, but now more often use electrically powered tools. [*Black* from their working with iron or black metal (as opposed to tin or white metal)]

black·snake /blák snayk/ *n.* **1. DARK NONVENOMOUS SNAKE** a dark-colored, chiefly nonvenomous, snake, such as the black racer. Genera: *Coluber* and *Elaphe.* **2. WHIP OF BRAIDED LEATHER** a long tapering whip made of braided strips of leather or hide

black spot *n.* BOT a plant disease that causes black patches to form on leaves, particularly on roses

black spruce *n.* a dark green conifer found in marshy areas in northern North America. Latin name: *Picea mariana.*

Black Stone *n.* the sacred stone in the Kaaba in the great mosque in Mecca, said to have been given by God. It is reddish black in color.

black·strap /blàk strap/, **black·strap mo·las·ses** *n.* molasses from which all refinable sugar has been removed [From *blackstrap* "strong dark port," drink made from rum and molasses]

Black Stud·ies *npl.* an academic subject or curriculum that deals with the history, culture, and literature of Black communities worldwide, often with an emphasis on African American culture

black stump *n. Aus* an imaginary stump marking the farthest edge of civilization (*informal*) ○ *I grew up beyond the black stump and didn't see a city until I was 25.* [Perhaps from the frequency with which fire-blackened tree stumps were mentioned in direction-giving in the Australian outback]

black swal·low·tail *n.* a common North American swallowtail butterfly with black, blue, and white markings and two small red eyespots on the trailing edge of its hind wing. Latin name: *Papilio polyxenes.*

black swan *n.* a large swan with black plumage and a red beak found throughout Australia and in New Zealand, where it is an introduced species. Latin name: *Cygnus atratus.*

black-tailed deer *n.* a mule deer with a tail that is black on top, found west of the North American Continental Divide. Latin name: *Odocoileus hemionus columbianus.*

black tea *n.* dark-colored tea leaves that have been fermented before being dried. ◊ **green tea**

black·thorn /blák thawrn/ *n.* **1. THORNY BUSH** a thorny black-stemmed bush of Europe and Asia that has white flowers and small blue-black berries called sloes. Latin name: *Prunus spinosa.* **2. HARDWOOD WALKING STICK** a walking stick made from the hard wood of the blackthorn

black tie *n.* **1. BLACK BOW TIE** a black bow tie worn on formal occasions **2. FORMAL STYLE OF DRESS FOR MEN** a formal style in men's dress that includes a black bow tie and a tuxedo —**black-tie** *adj.*

black·top /blák top/ *n.* **1. ROAD-SURFACING MATERIAL** a road-surfacing material bound together with a tarry substance such as asphalt **2. ROAD MADE WITH BLACKTOP** a road or other area with a blacktop surface ■ *vti.* (**-topped, -top·ping, -tops**) **COAT SURFACE WITH BLACKTOP** to cover a road or other surface with blacktop

black vul·ture *n.* **1. AMERICAN VULTURE** a common vulture native to North and South America that has black plumage and a bald black head. Latin name: *Coragyps atratus.* **2. LARGE VULTURE** a large dark vulture native to southern Europe and the Middle East. Latin name: *Aegypius monachus.*

black wal·nut *n.* **1.** TREES **N AMERICAN WALNUT TREE** a North American walnut tree with hard dark wood and edible nuts in very hard shells. Latin name: *Juglans nigra.* **2.** INDUST **N AMERICAN WALNUT WOOD** the hard wood of the black walnut tree, used especially for veneer and cabinets **3.** FOOD **EDIBLE NUT** an edible nut from the black walnut tree

black·wa·ter fe·ver *n.* a serious condition, developing from malaria, that causes a rapid and massive loss of red blood cells and turns the urine dark red or blackish

Black·well /blák wèl, -wəl/, **Antoinette Louisa** (1825–1921) U.S. minister and feminist. She was the first woman formally ordained as a minister of a Protestant church in the United States (1853), and wrote on women's rights.

Black·well, Elizabeth (1821–1910) British-born doctor. The first woman to earn a medical degree in the United States (1849), she founded a women's medical college in New York (1869) and later practiced in England. Emily Blackwell was her sister.

Black·well, Emily (1826–1910) British-born U.S. doctor. She was a pioneering woman physician who with her sister Elizabeth Blackwell developed the New York Infirmary for Women and Children (1857). She was dean of its medical school (1869–99).

Black widow

black wid·ow *n.* a highly poisonous spider of temperate North America and the Far East. The female has a black body with an hourglass-shaped red marking on the abdomen. Latin name: *Latrodectus mactans.* [*Widow* from the female's habit of eating her mate]

blad·der /bláddər/ *n.* **1.** ANAT **BODILY SAC FOR LIQUID OR GAS** an organ or other body part for storing a liquid or gas, especially the sac that stores urine (**urinary bladder**) or the sac that stores bile (**gall bladder**) **2. INFLATABLE INNER BAG** an inflatable part of something, especially a football, that resembles a bag **3.** BOT **SAC IN PLANT** a sac found in some plants, e.g., in bladder wrack to store air allowing the plant to float, or in bladderwort to trap insects **4.** MED **FLUID-FILLED BLISTER** a blister or small sac filled with fluid [Old English *blædre, blæddre.* Ultimately from an Indo-European base that is also the ancestor of English *blow* "to puff," *flatulent,* and *inflate.*] —**blad·der·y** /bláddəree/ *adj.*

blad·der cam·pi·on *n.* a wild European plant with a swollen calyx below the petals of its white flowers. Latin name: *Silene vulgaris.*

blad·der fern *n.* a small delicate fern that grows in rocks and walls and has a bulbous seed pod. Latin name: *Cystoperis fragilis.*

blad·der kelp *n.* any of various brown algae with inflated bladders from which leaflike streamers are suspended

blad·der·nose /bláddər nōz/ *n.* ZOOL = **hooded seal** [Bladder from the inflatable pouch near its nose]

blad·der·nut /bláddər nut/ *n.* **1. TREE WITH BULBOUS SEED POD** a small tree or shrub that produces clusters of small white flowers and bulbous seed pods. Genus: *Staphylea.* **2. SEED POD** the seed pod of a bladdernut tree or shrub

blad·der worm *n.* the larva of a tapeworm, shaped like a sac and armed with six hooks. Class: Cestoda.

blad·der·wort /bláddər wurt, bláddər wawrt/ *n.* an aquatic plant with floating leaves bearing small bladders that are used to trap insects. Genus: *Utricularia.*

blad·der wrack *n.* a brown seaweed that has bulbous air bladders on its fronds, allowing them to float. It grows between the high and low water line. Latin name: *Fucus vesiculosus.*

blade /blayd/ *n.* **1. CUTTING PART** the flat sharp-edged cutting part of a tool or weapon **2. LONG THIN FLAT PART** a long thin flat part of some tools or machines, e.g., a propeller **3. THIN LEAF** a long thin leaf, especially of grass **4.** FLAT STRIKING PART the flat striking part of something such as an oar or a golf club **5.** RAZOR BLADE a razor blade **6.** SPORTS PART OF ICE SKATE the metal part of an ice skate that glides on the ice **7.** PHON PART OF TONGUE the flat upper part of the tongue just behind the tip **8.** ARCHEOL STONE FRAGMENT a parallel-sided stone flake that is at least twice as long as it is wide **9.** SWORD a sword (*literary*) ○ *"And then dreams he of cutting foreign throats/ Of breaches, ambuscadoes, Spanish blades"* (William Shakespeare, *Romeo and Juliet*) **10.** SWORDSMAN a swordsman (*archaic*) **11.** DASHING MAN an energetic fun-loving man (*dated informal*) ■ **blades** *npl.* SPORTS in-line roller skates (*informal*) ■ *vi.* to skate on in-line roller skates (*informal*) [Old English *blæd.* Ultimately from a prehistoric Germanic stem that is also the ancestor of English *bloom, blossom, blow* "to blossom," and *flower.* The original meaning was "leaf."]

blad·ing /bláyding/ *n.* SPORTS the activity of skating on in-line skates

blah /blaa/ *n.* NONSENSE talk or writing that is inane or boring (*informal*) ■ **blahs** *npl.* MALAISE a condition of feeling bored, restless, and listlessl ○ *She's got the blahs today.* ■ *vi.* (**bla·hed, blahing, blahs**) TALK NONSENSE to talk in a meaningless way (*informal*) (*often repeated for emphasis*) ■ *adj.* DULL dull and uninteresting or uninterested (*informal*) ○ *feeling really blah today* [Early 20thC. An imitation of the sound of somebody talking vacuously.]

Blaine /blayn/ city in southeastern Minnesota. It is a northern suburb of St. Paul, and lies northeast of Minneapolis. Population: 43,241 (1996).

Blaine, James G. (1830–93) U.S. statesman. Speaker of the House of Representatives (1869–75) and secretary of state (1881, 1889–92), he was defeated in four presidential bids. Full name **James Gillespie Blaine**

Tony Blair

Blair /blair/, **Tony** (*b.* 1953) British politician. A member of Parliament from 1983, he was elected Labour Party leader in 1994, and became prime minister in 1997. Full name **Anthony Charles Lynton Blair** —**Blair·ite** *n., adj.*

Blake /blayk/, **Edward** (1833–1912) Canadian politician. He was the Liberal premier of Ontario (1871–72) and federal minister (1873–78).

Blake, Eubie (1883–1983) U.S. musician. He was an innovative composer of shows including the revue *Shuffle Along* (1921). Real name **James Herbert Blake**

Blake, William (1757–1827) British poet, painter, and engraver. He wrote *Songs of Innocence* (1789), *The Marriage of Heaven and Hell* (1790–93), and *Jerusalem* (1804–20), illustrating his poetry with highly original engravings and watercolors. He championed mystical wisdom and the unfettered imagination in the face of 18th-century rationalism. —**Blakeian** *adj.*

Blak·ey, Art (1919–90) U.S. jazz musician His innovations as a drummer led to the development of bebop and hard bop. His band, the Jazz Messengers (1954), introduced young musicians. Full name **Arthur Blakey**

blame /blaym/ *vt.* (**blamed, blam·ing, blames**) **1.** CONSIDER SOMEBODY RESPONSIBLE to consider somebody to be responsible for something wrong or unfortunate that has happened ○ *She blames me for what happened.* **2.** CRITICIZE to find fault with somebody (*used in negative statements and questions*) ○ *I don't blame you for wanting to know what happened.* ■ *n.* RESPONSIBILITY responsibility for something wrong or unfortunate that has happened ○ *It's still not clear where the blame lies.* [12thC. Via Old French *bla(s)mer* from Latin *blastemare,* an alteration of *blasphemare* "to reproach" (source of English *blaspheme*).] —**blam·a·ble** *adj.* ◇ **to blame** responsible for something wrong or unfortunate that has happened ○ *Who's to blame for the mixup?*

blame·less /bláymləss/ *adj.* **1.** NOT RESPONSIBLE not responsible for something wrong or unfortunate that has happened ○ *No one involved is entirely blameless.* **2.** INNOCENT doing nothing bad or wrong ○ *a blameless life* —**blame·less·ly** *adv.* —**blame·less·ness** *n.*

blame·wor·thy /bláym wurthee/ *adj.* deserving blame or criticism —**blame·wor·thi·ness** /bláym wurthinəss/ *n.*

Blam·ey /bláymee/, **Sir Thomas Albert** (1884–1951) Australian soldier. Commander of the World War II Allied Land Forces in the southwestern Pacific (1942–45), he later became Australia's first field marshal in 1950.

blanch /blanch/ (**blanched, blanch·ing, blanch·es**), **blench** /blench/ (**blenched, blench·ing, blench·es**) *v.* **1.** *vt.* PUT FOOD BRIEFLY IN BOILING WATER to put food in boiling water for a few seconds in order to loosen the skin or to kill enzymes **2.** *vi.* TURN PALE to become pale suddenly **3.** *vt.* WHITEN VEGETABLES BY GROWING IN DARK to grow vegetables, especially celery and endive, in dark conditions in order to whiten the stems and improve their flavor **4.** *vti.* REMOVE OR LOSE COLOR to lose color, or cause something to lose color [14thC. From French *blanchir* "to whiten," from *blanche,* feminine of *blanc* "white" (source of English *blank* and *blanket*).] —**blanch·er** *n.*

blanc·mange /blə maánj, -maánzh/ *n.* a dessert similar to pudding made with milk, sugar, flavorings, and cornstarch and eaten cold [14thC. From Old French *blanc mangier,* from *blanc* "white" (see BLANCH) + *mangier* "food," from *mangier* "to eat" (source of English *manger*), from Latin *manducare* "to chew."]

bland /bland/ *adj.* **1.** INSIPID lacking flavor, character, or interest ○ *a bland diet* **2.** FREE OF STRESS free from anything annoying or upsetting **3.** UNEMOTIONAL without emotion [Mid-17thC. From Latin *blandus* "smooth, flattering," of unknown origin.] —**bland·ly** /blándlee/ *adv.* —**bland·ness** *n.*

blan·dish /blándish/ (**-dished, -dish·ing, -dish·es**) *vti.* to persuade somebody by flattery (*formal*) [14thC. Via the Old French stem *blandiss-* from, ultimately, Latin *blandus* "smooth, flattering" (source of English *bland*).] —**blan·dish·er** *n.*

blan·dish·ment /blándishmənt/ *n.* **1.** FLATTERY the use of flattery and enticements to persuade somebody to do something **2.** PIECE OF FLATTERY a piece of flattery intended to persuade somebody to do something (*formal*) (*often used in the plural*) ○ *impervious to all blandishments*

blank /blank/ *adj.* **1.** NOT MARKED not written on, drawn on, or printed on ○ *a blank page* **2.** UNBROKEN plain and unvaried ○ *a blank wall* **3.** LACKING INTEREST having or showing no interest or awareness ○ *a blank expression* **4.** UNEVENTFUL OR UNPRODUCTIVE characterized by lack of useful action or result ○ *It was one of those blank periods when nothing particular was happening.* **5.** DOWNRIGHT complete or absolute ○ *She stared at me in blank amazement.* ■ *n.* **1.** EMPTINESS OF MIND a complete absence of awareness or memory ○ *I remember hearing a loud noise: the rest is a blank.* **2.** VOID a period about which nothing is known ○ *There are a lot of blanks in her account of the event.* **3.** SPACE IN WHICH TO WRITE a space left blank in which to write, in a form or document ○ *Fill in the blanks.* **4.** MARK INDICATING MISSING WORD a mark ( ) in writing or print indicating that a word or letter is missing ○ *a word meaning solitary, spelt a-l- - -e* **5.** DOCUMENT WITH BLANK SPACES a form or document with spaces for writing in **6.** ARMS = **blank cartridge** **7.** MANUF PIECE FROM WHICH ARTICLE IS MADE a piece of metal or other material that will be shaped to produce a finished article **8.** BULL'S-EYE the bull's-eye of a target ■ *v.* (**blanked, blank·ing, blanks**) **1.** *vt.* OBLITERATE to delete or block something out (*often used with out*) **2.** *vi.* FORGET TEMPORARILY to forget something suddenly and temporarily ○ *I tried to recall their names, but I just blanked.* **3.** *vt.* SPORTS PREVENT FROM SCORING to prevent an opponent from scoring [13thC. From French *blanc* "white" (see BLANCH). Originally in the sense "white."] —**blank·ness** /blángknəss/ *n.* ◇ **draw a blank** to be unsuccessful in a search or inquiry ◇ **fire** *or* **shoot blanks** to be unable to impregnate a woman because of a low sperm count (*slang*) ◇ **go blank** to be unable to think of or remember something

blank car·tridge *n.* a gun cartridge that contains explosive but no bullet

blank check *n.* **1.** CHECK WITH NO AMOUNT STATED a signed check that has not yet had the amount payable filled in **2.** PERMISSION complete freedom to act or decide (*informal*) ○ *They gave us a blank check in our negotiations.*

blank en·dorse·ment *n.* an endorsement on a bill of exchange that does not name a payee and so may benefit the bearer

blan·ket /blángkət/ *n.* **1.** LARGE PIECE OF THICK CLOTH a piece of thick cloth used as a cover for a bed or for spreading on the ground and sitting on **2.** COVERING LAYER a layer of something, covering an area completely ■ *adj.* APPLYING GENERALLY applying to all areas or situations ○ *We have blanket approval for our proposals.* ■ *n.* NUCLEAR PHYS LAYER AROUND CORE OF NUCLEAR REACTOR in a nuclear reactor, a layer of material surrounding the radioactive core used to reflect neutrons or to create more fissile material ■ *vt.* (**-ket·ed, -ket·ing, -kets**) **1.** COVER WITH LAYER to cover something with a thick layer ○ *The streets were blanketed with snow.* **2.** COVER TO SUPPRESS to cover something, especially a fire, in order to stop it or put it out ○ *Foam from the fire extinguisher quickly blanketed the flames.* **3.** APPLY UNIFORMLY to apply all over something in a uniform manner ○ *The county was blanketed with leaflets.* **4.** NAUT PREVENT WIND REACHING SAILS to take the wind from the sails of another boat by sailing to windward of it [14thC. From Old Northern French *blanquet,* "blanket," Old French *blanchet,* from *blanc* "white" (see BLANCH). The original meaning was "white cloth."]

blan·ket flow·er *n.* = **gaillardia**

blan·ket stitch *n.* looped stitching with wide gaps between stitches, used to reinforce the edge of a piece of fabric [From its use on the edges of blankets]

blank·ly /blánklee/ *adv.* **1.** IN A VACANT WAY in a way that suggests a complete lack of interest, understanding, or awareness ○ *She stared at me blankly.* **2.** DOWNRIGHT completely and without exception

blank verse *n.* unrhymed poetry that has a regular rhythm and line length, especially iambic pentameter

blare /blair/ *v.* (**blared, blar·ing, blares**) **1.** *vti.* MAKE LOUD SOUND to make a loud harsh noise **2.** *vt.* ANNOUNCE SOMETHING to proclaim something loudly ○ *"Heiress disappears," the headlines blared.* ■ *n.* LOUD STRIDENT SOUND a loud harsh noise that is intended to be heard [14thC. Origin uncertain: possibly from assumed Old English *blæren,* Middle Dutch *bleren* "to bleat, shout," or Middle Low German *blaren*; ultimately probably an imitation of the sound.]

blar·ney /blaárnee/ *n.* NONSENSE unintelligent or insincere talk (*informal*) ■ *vti.* (**-neyed, -ney·ing, -neys**) WHEEDLE to persuade somebody with flattery (*informal*) [Late 18thC. Named for the BLARNEY STONE.]

Blar·ney Stone *n.* a stone in Blarney Castle, near Cork in Ireland, that is said to give the power of persuasive talk to people who kiss it

bla·sé /blaa záy/ *adj.* not impressed or worried by something, usually because of having experienced it before [Early 19thC. From French, "satiated."]

blas·pheme /blas féem, blás feem/ (**-phemed, -phem·ing, -phemes**) *v.* **1.** SWEAR IMPIOUSLY to swear in a way that insults religion **2.** *vt.* INSULT RELIGION to treat God or sacred things disrespectfully through words or action [14thC. Via Old French *blasfemer* from ecclesiastical Latin *blasphemare* "to revile" (source of English *blame*), from Greek *blasphēmein,* formed from *blasphēmos* "evil-speaking."] —**blas·phem·er** /blas féemər, blásfəmər/ *n.*

blas·phe·mous /blásfəməss/ *adj.* expressing or involving disrespect for God or sacred things —**blas·phe·mous·ly** *adv.* —**blas·phe·mous·ness** *n.*

blas·phe·my /blásfəmee/ (*plural* **-mies**) *n.* **1.** DISRESPECT FOR RELIGION disrespect for God or sacred things **2.** SOMETHING SHOWING DISRESPECT FOR RELIGION something done or said that shows disrespect for God or sacred things

blast /blast/ *n.* **1.** EXPLOSION an explosion, or a sudden rush of air caused by an explosion ○ *Several homes were destroyed by the blast.* **2.** AIR OR GAS CURRENT a sudden strong current of air or wind **3.** LOUD EXPLOSIVE SOUND the sound made by an explosion ○ *We were almost deafened by the blasts.* **4.** INSTRUMENT'S LOUD SOUND a short loud sound made on an instrument, whistle, or car horn **5. OUTBURST** a loud or angry outburst ○ *a blast of criticism* **6. GOOD TIME** an enjoyable occasion of fun and laughter (*slang*) ○ *The party was a real blast!* ■ *v.* **(blast·ed, blast·ing, blasts) 1.** *vti.* **BLOW UP WITH EXPLOSIVES** to destroy or break open something using explosives ○ *Rescuers blasted a hole in the rock.* ○ *Road crews had to blast a way through the mountains.* **2.** *vt.* **HIT HARD** to strike something with great force (*informal*) ○ *She blasted the ball into the net* **3.** *vti.* **MAKE A LOUD NOISE** to come out with great force or volume or make something do this (*informal*) **4.** *vt.* **CRITICIZE** to subject somebody or something to severe criticism (*informal*) **5.** *vt.* BOT **BLIGHT** to affect a plant with a withering disease (*often passive*) [Old English *blǣst*. Ultimately from an Indo-European base that is also the ancestor of English *blaze* and *blow*.] —**blast·er** *n.* ◇ **(at) full blast** at maximum volume or speed

WORD KEY: SYNONYMS

See Synonyms at ***criticize***.

blast away *vi.* to fire a gun repeatedly (*informal*)
blast off *vti.* to launch a rocket, spacecraft, or astronaut into space, or be launched into space

-blast *suffix.* embryonic cell ○ *melanoblast* [From Greek *blastos* "bud"] —**blastic** *suffix.*

blast·ed /blástəd/ *adj., adv.* used to express mild irritation (*informal*) ○ *Then the blasted handle broke.*

blas·te·ma /bla steémə/ (*plural* **-mas** *or* **-ma·ta** /-mətə/) *n.* a group of unspecialized animal cells from which an organ or new tissue develops [Mid-19thC. From Greek, "sprout."] —**blas·te·mal** *adj.* —**blas·te·mat·ic** /blàstə máttik/ *adj.* —**blas·te·mic** /bla steémik/ *adj.*

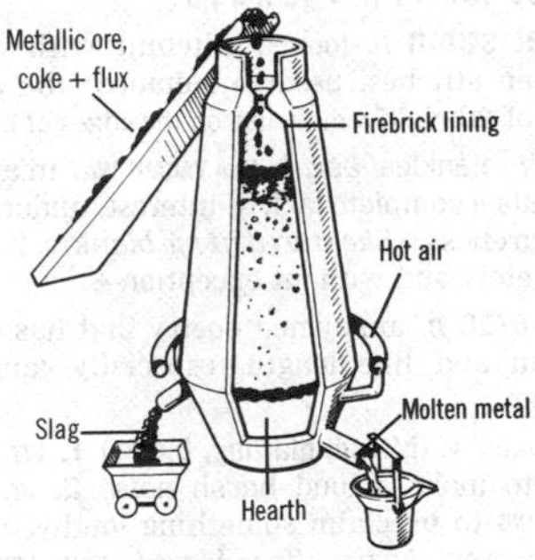

Blast furnace

blast fur·nace *n.* a vertical shaft furnace for smelting metals. Fuel, ores, and slag-forming rock are loaded from above, and air is blown in from the bottom to raise the temperature. The molten metal is tapped periodically from the base.

blast·ing /blásting/ *n.* **1. BLOWING UP ROCK** the blowing up of rock in a quarry, or mine, or road-building operation ○ *"Danger! Blasting."* **2. CURSING** swearing in annoyance (*informal*)

blast·ing pow·der *n.* a form of gunpowder containing sodium nitrate instead of potassium nitrate that is used in blasting rock and ores

blasto- *prefix.* bud, germ ○ *blastomycete* [From Greek *blastos* "bud"]

blas·to·coel /blástə seel/, **blas·to·coele** *n.* the cavity that forms within the mass of cells (**blastula**) in a developing embryo and that fills with fluid [Late 19thC. Coined from BLASTO- + Greek *koilos* "hollow."] —**blas·to·coe·lic** /blàstə seélik/ *adj.*

blas·to·cyst /blástə sist/ *n.* a mammalian embryo at the stage where it is implanted in the wall of the womb —**blas·to·cys·tic** /blàstə sístik/ *adj.*

blas·to·derm /blástə durm/ *n.* a layer of cells arising from the repeated division of a fertilized mammalian egg that develops into an embryo [Mid-19thC. Coined from BLASTO- + *-derm*, formed from Greek *derma* "skin."] —**blas·to·der·mat·ic** /blàstədər máttik/ *adj.* —**blas·to·der·mic** /blàstə dúrmik/ *adj.*

blast·off /blást of/ *n.* a launch of a rocket, spacecraft, or missile

blas·to·gen·e·sis /blàstə jénnəsiss/ *n.* asexual reproduction by budding —**blas·to·ge·net·ic** /blàstə jə néttik/ *adj.* —**blas·to·gen·ic** /blàstə jénnik/ *adj.*

blas·to·my·co·sis /blà stō mī kóssiss/ *n.* a fungal infection causing lesions on the lungs, skin, or mucous membranes

blas·to·pore /blástə pawr/ *n.* an opening in a young embryo that develops into the anus in some mammals —**blas·to·por·al** *adj.* —**blasto·por·ic** /blàstə páwrik/ *adj.*

blas·to·sphere /blástə sfeer/ *n.* = **blastula**

blas·to·spore /blástə spawr/ *n.* a fungal spore produced by budding

blas·tu·la /bláschələ/ (*plural* **-las** *or* **-lae** /-lee/) *n.* an embryo at an early stage of development, consisting of a hollow ball of cells [Late 19thC. From modern Latin, formed from Greek *blastos* "sprout, germ."] —**blas·tu·lar** *adj.* —**blas·tu·la·tion** /blàschə láysh'n/ *n.*

blat[1] /blat/ *vi.* **(blat·ted, blat·ting, blats),** *n.* **BLEAT** a bleating sound (*regional*) ■ *vti.* **(blat·ted, blat·ting, blats)** = **blab** *v.* 1 (*informal*) [Mid-19thC. An imitation of the sound.]

blat[2] /blat/, **blatt** *n.* a popular newspaper (*slang*) [Mid-20thC. From German *Blatt* "leaf, sheet (of paper)."]

bla·tant /bláyt'nt/ *adj.* **1. VERY OBVIOUS** so obvious or conspicuous as to be impossible to hide ○ *blatant falsehoods* **2. NOISY** excessively or offensively noisy (*literary*) [Late 16thC. Origin uncertain: possibly an alteration of Scottish *blatand* "bleating," or from Latin *blatire* "to babble."] —**bla·tan·cy** *n.* —**bla·tant·ly** *adv.*

WORD KEY: USAGE

blatant or **flagrant**? Both words describe openly offensive behavior, but there is a difference. ***Blatant*** emphasizes the obviousness of the offense, whereas ***flagrant*** emphasizes the shocking effect that the offense has. A ***blatant*** lie is one that is easily discerned, whereas a ***flagrant*** lie is one that is particularly shameless or outrageous.

blath·er /bláthər/, **bleth·er** /bléthər/, **blith·er** *vi.* **(-ered, -er·ing, -ers) TALK INANELY** to talk in an unintelligent or inane manner, especially at length (*informal*) ■ *n.* **FOOLISH TALK** foolish and prolonged talk (*informal*) [Early 16thC. Originally a Scottish and northern English dialect word. From Old Norse *bla-ra* "to chatter, babble."] —**blath·er·er** *n.*

blath·er·skite /bláthər skīt/, **bleth·er·skite** *n.* (*dated informal*) **1. TALKATIVE PERSON** somebody who likes to chat about silly or unimportant things **2. INANE TALK** chat about silly or unimportant things [Mid-17thC. From BLATHER + Scottish dialect *skate* "contemptible person."]

blatt *n.* = **blat**

Blax·ploi·ta·tion /blàk sploy táysh'n/ *n.* depiction of Blacks in movies or other media in a way that appeals to people's popular and often inaccurate or negative notions of their experiences and qualities (*informal*) [Late 20thC. Blend of *Blacks* (plural of BLACK) and EXPLOITATION.]

blaze[1] /blayz/ *vi.* **(blazed, blaz·ing, blaz·es) 1. BURN BRIGHTLY** to burn brightly and fiercely **2. SHINE** to shine or appear to shine brightly **3. EXPERIENCE STRONG EMOTION** to be affected by a strong emotion (*informal*) ○ *blazing with indignation* **4. FIRE GUN** to fire a gun repeatedly ■ *n.* **1. BRIGHT FIRE** a bright flame or fire **2. CONSPICUOUS DISPLAY** a display that attracts attention ○ *a blaze of glory.* [Old English *blæse* "torch, bright flame"]

WORD KEY: SYNONYMS

See Synonyms at ***fire***.

blaze[2] /blayz/ *n.* **1. WHITE MARK ON ANIMAL'S FACE** a white streak on the face of a horse or other animal **2. MARK SHOWING THE WAY** a mark indicating a path, originally a cut made in a tree trunk ■ *vt.* **(blazed, blaz·ing, blaz·es) 1. MARK PATH** to indicate a new path by making marks **2. DO SOMETHING NEW** to lead the way in doing something new ○ *He blazed the way to the understanding of DNA's structure.* [Mid-17thC. Origin uncertain: possibly from Old Norse *blesi*, Middle High German *blasse*, or Middle Low German *bles* "white mark."]

blaze[3] /blayz/ **(blazed, blaz·ing, blaz·es)** *vt.* to spread news or information loudly and clearly (*archaic*) [14thC. Via Middle Dutch *blāzen* "to swell" from, ultimately, an Indo-European base that is also the ancestor of English *blow* and *blast*.]

blaz·er /bláyzər/ *n.* a sports jacket for men or women, sometimes in a bright color or pattern [Mid-17thC. From the typically bright color, in particular that of the red jackets once worn by members of a Cambridge University, England, boat club.]

blaz·es /bláyzəz/ *npl.* used to add emphasis (*informal*) ○ *What in blazes did you do that for?* ○ *run like blazes*

blaz·ing /bláyzing/ *adj.* **1. INTENSE** intense and impassioned ○ *a blazing row* **2. HOT** very hot ○ *sitting in the blazing sun* ■ *adv.* **EXTREMELY** extremely or intensely ○ *blazing hot* —**blaz·ing·ly** *adv.*

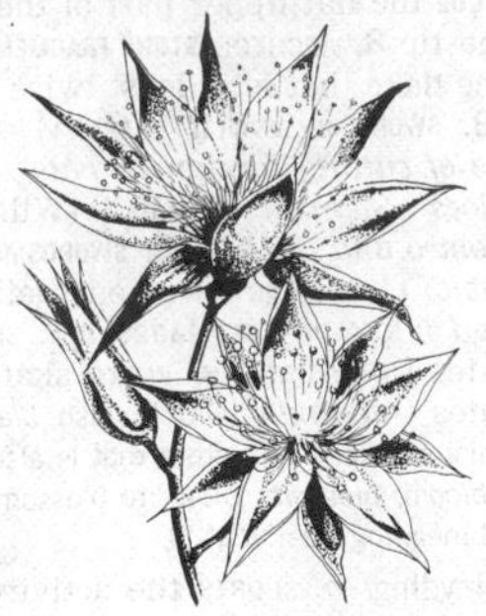
Blazing star

blaz·ing star *n.* **1. PLANT WITH WHITE FLOWERS** a North American plant of the lily family that has a long head of white flowers. Latin name: *Chamaelirium luteum.* **2. PLANT WITH WHITE OR PURPLE FLOWERS** a North American flower of the daisy family with long heads of white or purplish flowers. Genus: *Liatris.* **3. PLANT WITH CLUSTERS OF FLOWERS** a North American plant with rough leaves and red or purple flowers. Genus: *Laevicaulis.*

bla·zon /bláyz'n/ *vt.* **(-zoned, -zon·ing, -zons) 1. PROCLAIM WIDELY** to announce something widely or ostentatiously **2.** HERALDRY **DEPICT COAT OF ARMS** to create or describe a coat of arms using the traditional symbols ■ *n.* HERALDRY **COAT OF ARMS** a coat of arms, or a technical description of one [13thC. From French *blason* "shield," of unknown origin.] —**bla·zon·er** *n.*— **bla·zon·ment** *n.*

bla·zon·ry /bláyz'nree/ *n.* **1.** HERALDRY **MAKING OR EXPLAINING COATS OF ARMS** the art of creating or explaining coats of arms **2.** HERALDRY **COATS OF ARMS** coats of arms individually or collectively **3. BRILLIANT DISPLAY** a bright or showy display (*literary*)

bldg. *abbr.* building

bleach /bleech/ *n.* **1. COLOR-REMOVING SUBSTANCE** a chemical substance that removes color and stains and is also used as a cleansing agent and disinfectant **2. APPLICATION OF BLEACH** an act of using bleach on something ■ *v.* **(bleached, bleach·ing, bleach·es) 1.** *vt.* **USE BLEACH ON** to clean or whiten something using bleach **2.** *vti.* **LIGHTEN IN COLOR** to make something whiter or lighter, or become lighter or whiter [Old English *blǣcan* "to make white," from *blǣc* "pale, shining," from a prehistoric Germanic base that is also the ancestor of English *bleak*] —**bleach·er** *n.*

bleach·ers /bleéchərz/ *npl.* (*sometimes used in the singular*) **1. STADIUM SEATS** seats in an uncovered area of a sports stadium **2. INDOOR SEATS IN SPORTS ARENA** retractable tiered benches for spectators in a gymnasium, at a swimming pool, or in some other indoor sports arena [Late 19thC. From the sun's bleaching of the exposed benches.]

bleach·ing pow·der *n.* a white powder, obtained from calcium hydroxide and chlorine, that is used as a disinfectant and a bleaching agent. Formula: $CaCl(OCl)$.

bleak /bleek/ *adj.* **1. UNWELCOMING** providing little comfort or shelter ○ *a cabin on a bleak hilltop* **2. DISCOURAGING** without hope or expectation of success or improvement ○ *The company's future looks bleak.* **3. COLD AND CLOUDY** unpleasantly cold, dull, and windy ○ *bleak winter days* [14thC. From Old Norse *bleikr* "pale, white, shining."] —**bleak·ly** /bleéklee/ *adv.* —**bleak·ness** /bleéknəss/ *n.*

blear /bleer/ *vt.* **(bleared, blearing, blears)** to make eyes misty or eyesight dim, e.g., with tears (*usually passive*) [14thC. Origin unknown.]

blear·y /bleéree/ **(-i·er, -i·est)** *adj.* **1. SEEING DIMLY** not seeing clearly owing to mistiness or blurring, especially that associated with sleepiness ○ *a bleary gaze* **2. OBSCURED** obscured and not easy to see — **blear·i·ly** /bleéreelee/ *adv.* —**blear·i·ness** *n.*

blear·y-eyed *adj.* seeing unclearly, especially because of sleepiness or drunkenness

bleat /bleet/ *v.* **(bleat·ed, bleat·ing, bleats) 1.** *vi.* **MAKE SHEEP'S NOISE** to make the wavering cry of a sheep, goat, or calf **2.** *vti.* **COMPLAIN ANNOYINGLY** to complain about something in an irritating way (*informal*) ■ *n.* **SHEEP'S SOUND** the wavering cry of a sheep, goat, or calf [Old English *blǣtan.* Ultimately from a prehistoric Germanic word that is also the ancestor of Dutch *blaten*; an imitation of the sound.] —**bleat·er** *n.*

bleb /bleb/ *n.* **1.** MED **BLISTER** a small blister on the skin **2. BUBBLE** a small bubble, e.g., in glass [Early 17thC. An alteration of BLOB.] —**bleb·by** /blébbee/ *adj.*

bleed /bleed/ *v.* (**bled** /bled/, **bled, bleed·ing, bleeds**) **1.** *vi.* **LOSE BLOOD** to lose blood from the body, through a wound or because of illness ○ *The wound was bleeding heavily.* **2.** *vt.* **TAKE BLOOD FROM** to take blood from a person or animal, especially in order to treat a disease **3.** *vi.* **FEEL SORROW** to feel sadness or pity ○ *My heart bleeds for her in her loss.* **4.** *vi.* **EXUDE SAP** to exude sap from a plant's wound **5.** *vi.* **RELEASE COLOR** to release color when wet or being washed (*refers to fabrics*) **6.** *vt.* **TAKE MONEY OR RESOURCES FROM** to use up large amounts of money or resources from an individual or organization, especially dishonestly (*informal*) ○ *bleeding public funds.* **7.** *vt.* **DRAW OFF LIQUID OR GAS** to draw liquid or gas out of a container or pressurized system ○ *bleed a radiator* **8.** *vti.* PRINTING **OVERRUN PAGE** to print something, or to be printed, so that part of something is cut off by the edge of the page **9.** *vti.* PRINTING **MAKE COLORS OF ILLUSTRATION RUN** to print something, or to be printed, so that colors run into other colors or over the edge of an illustration ■ *n.* **1. INSTANCE OF BLEEDING** an instance of losing blood **2.** PRINTING **SOMETHING THAT OVERRUNS PRINTED PAGE** an illustration or piece of text printed in such a way that part of it is cut off the page [Old English *blēdan.* Ultimately from a prehistoric Germanic base that is also the ancestor of English *blood* and *bless.*]

bleed·er /bléedər/ *n.* MED a blood vessel that is bleeding during surgery and requires clamping or other measures to stop it

bleed·ing /bléeding/ *adj., adv. U.K.* used for emphasis, as a milder form of "bloody" (*slang*)

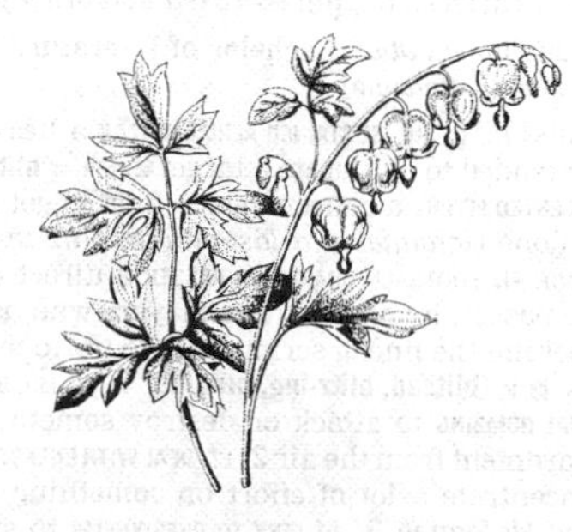

Bleeding heart

bleed·ing heart *n.* **1. PLANT WITH HEART-SHAPED FLOWERS** a plant with drooping pink, red, or white heart-shaped flowers. Genus: *Dicentra.* **2. FOOLISHLY SOFT-HEARTED PERSON** somebody regarded as naively kind or sympathetic (*informal*)

bleed·ing heart lib·er·al *n.* a political liberal who is thought too sympathetic or sentimental (*informal*)

bleep /bleep/ *n.* **ELECTRONIC SOUND** a short high-pitched electronic noise, intended as a signal and repeated intermittently ■ *v.* (**bleeped, bleep·ing, bleeps**) **1.** *vi.* **MAKE ELECTRONIC SOUND** to make a short high-pitched electronic noise **2. bleep, bleep out** *vt.* **REMOVE OFFENSIVE LANGUAGE** to remove offensive material from a broadcast, and replace it with a short high-pitched electronic sound ○ *They bleeped most of his comments.* [Mid-20thC. An imitation of the sound.]

bleep out *vt.* = **bleep**

bleep·ing /bléeping/ *adj.* used in place of a swearword to indicate mild irritation ○ *Where are the bleeping car keys?* [Mid-20thC]

blem·ish /blémish/ *n.* **1. SPOILING MARK OR FLAW** a mark or imperfection that spoils the appearance of something ○ *a cream that hides skin blemishes* **2. SPOILING FAULT** something that spoils a person's reputation or good record ■ *vt.* (**-ished, -ish·ing, -ish·es**) **MAR** to spoil the appearance or reputation of something [14thC. From the Old French stem *ble(s)miss-* "to make pale, injure."] —**blem·ish·er** *n.*

WORD KEY: SYNONYMS

See Synonyms at ***flaw.***

blench[1] /blench/ (**blenched, blench·ing, blench·es**) *vi.* to move back or away in fear (*literary*) [Old English *blencan* "to deceive, cheat," of unknown origin. The modern meaning probably developed via "to evade, dodge" and "to move suddenly."] —**blench·er** *n.*

blench[2] *vi.* = **blanch** [Early 19thC. An alteration of BLANCH, by association with BLENCH[1].]

blend /blend/ *v.* (**blend·ed, blend·ing, blends**) **1.** *vti.* **MIX INGREDIENTS** to mix different substances together so that they do not readily separate ○ *blend the butter and sugar together* **2.** *vt.* **CREATE PRODUCT BY MIXING INGREDIENTS** to create food or beverages by mixing different types of ingredients (*often passive*) **3.** *vti.* **INTERMINGLE** to mix with other people or things without being conspicuous, or mix something in this way ○ *blend fact and fiction* **4.** *vti.* **MAKE PLEASING COMBINATION** to combine things or qualities to create a pleasing effect, or be combined in this way ○ *instruments blending harmoniously* **5.** *vi.* **SHADE IMPERCEPTIBLY INTO EACH OTHER** to shade from one color to another without obvious transitions and boundaries ■ *n.* **1. MIXTURE** a mixture or combination ○ *an interesting blend of traditional styles and modern materials* **2. FOOD OR DRINK MIXTURE** a food or beverage created by mixing different types of ingredient ○ *an expensive coffee blend* **3. WORD MADE BY JOINING TWO WORDS** a new word made by joining parts of other words, as in "telex," formed from "teleprinter" and "exchange" [14thC. Probably from the Old Norse present stem *blend-* "to mix."]

WORD KEY: SYNONYMS

See Synonyms at ***mixture.***

blend in *vi.* **1. FIT IN** to have personal qualities that suit a situation well ○ *He's a likable boy who blends in well.* **2. BE DIFFICULT TO PICK OUT** to be difficult to see or distinguish from similar things around

blende /blend/ *n.* **1.** = **sphalerite 2. SULFIDE ORE** metallic sulfide ore that has a bright luster [Late 17thC. From German *blenden* "to deceive"; so called because sphalerite, despite resembling galena ore, does not yield lead.]

blend·ed whis·key *n.* whiskey made by blending two or more whiskeys, or whiskey and neutral spirits

blend·er /bléndər/ *n.* **1. APPLIANCE FOR MIXING FOOD** an electrical kitchen appliance used to liquidize and blend foods **2. SOMEBODY OR SOMETHING THAT BLENDS** somebody or something that blends things, especially a person or company that blends foods or drinks

blen·ny /blénnee/ (*plural* **-nies** *or* **-ny**) *n.* a small scaleless long-bodied fish found in rocky coastal areas and coral reefs. Family: Blenniidae. [Mid-18thC. From Latin *blennius*, formed from Greek *blennos* "slime" from the fish's covering of mucus.]

blephar- *prefix.* = **blepharo-**

bleph·a·ri·tis /bléffə rítiss/ *n.* inflammation of one or both eyelids [Formed from Greek *blepharon* "eyelid"+-ITIS]

blepharo- *prefix.* **1.** eyelid ○ *blepharospasm* **2.** cilium, flagella ○ *blepharoplast* [From Greek *blepharon* "eyelid," of unknown origin]

Blesbok

bles·bok /blés bok/ (*plural* **-boks** *or* **-bok**) *n.* a reddish brown southern African antelope that has a white streak on its nose. Latin name: *Damaliscus dorcas.* [Early 19thC. From Afrikaans, from Dutch *bles* "white facial streak" + *bok* "buck."]

bless /bles/ (**blessed, blest** /blest/, **bless·ing, bless·es**) *vt.* **1.** RELIG **MAKE HOLY** to bestow holiness on somebody or something in a religious ceremony ○ *The bishop blessed the new chapel.* **2. PROTECT** to watch over somebody or something protectively ○ *We prayed for God to bless our marriage.* **3. WISH WELL** to declare approval and support for somebody or something ○ *The governor has blessed the new plan.* **4. CONFER PERSONAL BENEFIT ON** to give somebody a desirable quality or talent (*usually passive*) ○ *blessed with brains as well as good looks* **5. THANK** to express heartfelt thanks to somebody (*often expressing a wish*) ○ *Bless you for speaking up for my child!* [Old English *blētsian*, from a prehistoric Germanic base that also produced English *bleed* and *blood*; the original sense seems to have been "to mark with blood"] —**bless·er** *n.*

bless·ed /bléssəd/ *adj.* **1.** RELIG **HOLY** made holy **2.** CHR **BEATIFIED** declared holy by the pope, usually as the first stage toward being declared a saint **3. BESTOWING JOY** bringing happiness or good luck ○ *The rain has brought farmers blessed relief from the long drought.* ■ *adj., adv.* **USED FOR EMPHASIS** used to add emphasis in an expression of annoyance (*informal*) ○ *She wouldn't say a blessed thing about it.* —**bless·ed·ly** *adv.* —**bless·ed·ness** *n.*

Bless·ed Sac·ra·ment *n.* in various Christian churches, the bread and wine that has been blessed for use in Holy Communion

bless·ing /blέssing/ *n.* **1.** RELIG **GOD'S HELP** help from God or another deity **2.** RELIG **RELIGIOUS ACT** a ceremony in which an ordained person invokes or bestows divine help **3.** RELIG **PRAYER BEFORE MEAL** a prayer of thanks before a meal **4. EXPRESSION OF APPROVAL** approval or good wishes **5. SOMETHING FORTUNATE** something to be glad or relieved about ○ *It's a blessing that the rescuers arrived in time to save the air crash victims*

blest past participle of **bless**

bleth·er *vi., n.* = **blather**

bleth·er·skite *n.* = **blatherskite** (*informal*)

blew 1. past tense of **blow**[1] **2.** past tense of **blow**[3]

ble·wit /blóo it/ *n.* an edible fungus with a brown cap and a bluish stem. Genus: *Lepista.* [Early 19thC. Probably formed from *blue*, reflecting the color of its stem.]

Bligh /blī/, **William** (1754–1817) British naval officer. Cast adrift in the Pacific by mutineers of the HMS *Bounty* (1789), he navigated nearly 4,000 miles in an open boat to reach Timor. He was promoted to rear admiral in 1811 and vice admiral in 1814.

blight /blīt/ *n.* **1. DESTRUCTIVE FORCE** something that spoils or damages things severely **2. RUINED STATE** a severely spoiled or ruined state, especially of an urban area ○ *urban blight* **3.** BOT **PLANT DISEASE** a plant disease, caused by bacteria, fungi, or viruses, in which symptoms range from brownish blotches on the foliage to withering of the entire plant without rotting **4.** *U.K.* BOT = **potato blight 5. CAUSE OF BLIGHT IN PLANTS** a bacterium, fungus, or virus that causes blight in plants ■ *vt.* **1. RUIN** to spoil or damage something severely ○ *a football career blighted by injury* **2.** PLANTS **AFFECT PLANT WITH BLIGHT** to cause a plant to wither without rotting [Mid-16thC. Origin uncertain.]

Bligh·ty /blītee/, **bligh·ty** *n. U.K.* England or Britain (*dated humorous slang*) [Early 20thC. Anglicization of Hindi *bilāyatī*, literally "foreign, European," originally used by British soldiers serving in India for "home."]

bli·mey /blīmee/ *interj. U.K.* used to express amazement or shock (*informal*) ○ *Blimey, that's expensive!* ◊ **cor blimey** [Late 19thC. Alteration of "*blind me!*" or "*blame me!*"]

blimp[1] /blimp/ *n.* a nonrigid airship that nowadays uses helium rather than hydrogen to remain buoyant [Early 20thC. Origin uncertain: perhaps from "Type B-limp," an airship without a rigid internal structure, as opposed to the "Type A-rigid" with a rigid framework.]

blimp[2] /blimp/, **Colo·nel Blimp** *n. U.K.* somebody who is stubborn, pompous, or very conservative (*humorous*) [Mid-20thC. Named for a cartoon character invented by the cartoonist David Low (1891–1963).]

blind /blīnd/ *adj.* **1. UNABLE TO SEE** unable to see, permanently or temporarily **2. UNABLE TO RECOGNIZE** unwilling or unable to understand something ○ *blind to the consequences* **3. UNCONTROLLABLE** so extreme and uncontrollable as to make somebody behave irrationally ○ *blind rage* ○ *blind fear* **4. UNQUESTIONING** not based on fact and usually total and unquestioning ○ *blind prejudice* **5.** lacking awareness ○ *a blind stupor* **6.** NOT GIVING A CLEAR VIEW not giving a clear view and possibly dangerous ○ *a blind corner* **7.** SEW MADE ON UNDERSIDE OF FABRIC hidden from sight on the underside of a fabric **8.** WITHOUT DOORS OR WINDOWS without doors or windows, or not enclosing an open space **9.** CLOSED AT ONE END closed off at one end ○ *a blind unused tunnel* **10.** DONE WITHOUT LOOKING done without looking or while unable to see ○ *blind taste tests* **11.** DONE UNPREPARED done without preparation or the relevant information ○ *a blind presentation* **12.** WITH INFORMATION CONCEALED FOR UNPREJUDICED RESULT used to describe scientific experiments or similar evaluations in which information is withheld in order to obtain an unprejudiced result **13.** BOT WITHOUT A GROWING POINT used to describe a plant in which growth stops because the growing point is damaged. It may be caused by pests, nutrient deficiency, waterlogging of the soil, or drought. ■ *adv.* **1.** WITHOUT PRIOR EXAMINATION OR PREPARATION without previously thinking about or preparing for something ○ *You shouldn't buy livestock blind.* **2.** AIR USING INSTRUMENTS using information from aircraft instruments, without being able to see **3.** TOTALLY totally or utterly (*informal*) ○ *an unscrupulous lawyer who robbed his clients blind* ■ *vt.* (**blind·ed, blind·ing, blinds**) **1.** MAKE PERMANENTLY BLIND to make somebody permanently unable to see **2.** MAKE TEMPORARILY BLIND to make somebody temporarily unable to see ○ *blinded by the lights* **3.** MAKE UNABLE TO JUDGE PROPERLY to make somebody unable to judge or act rationally ○ *blinded by rage* **4.** CONFUSE to make it difficult for somebody to understand something ○ *Stop trying to blind us with statistics.* ■ *n.* **1.** WINDOW COVERING a device that is pulled down to shut out the light from a window **2.** COVER OR SUBTERFUGE something that is intended to conceal the true nature of somebody's activities **3.** PROXY a person or organization whose public activities conceal a secret purpose **4.** OBSTRUCTION anything that blocks the free passage of light, sight, or air ○ *The trees act as a blind to sunlight.* **5.** HUNT HIDING PLACE FOR HUNTERS a place, e.g., a bush or undergrowth, in which shooters can hide, especially when hunting fowl [Old English *blind.* Ultimately from an Indo-European word meaning "confusion, obscurity," which is also the ancestor of English *blunder.* The underlying idea is of someone wandering around in darkness.] —**blind·ly** *adv.* —**blind·ness** *n.*

blind al·ley *n.* **1.** CLOSED-OFF PASSAGE a narrow alley or passage that is closed off at one end **2.** UNPRODUCTIVE UNDERTAKING something that produces no worthwhile results

blind date *n.* **1.** DATE WITH SOMEBODY UNKNOWN a date arranged between people who have not seen or met each other before **2.** SOMEBODY MET ON BLIND DATE somebody whom you meet on a blind date

blind·er /blɪ̄ndər/ *n.* SOMETHING THAT OBSCURES VISION something that prevents clear vision or understanding ■ **blind·ers** *npl.* EYE COVERS FOR HORSE a pair of flaps attached to a horse's bridle, one beside each eye, to keep the horse looking straight ahead

blind·fold /blɪ̄nd fōld/ *n.* BANDAGE TIED OVER EYES a piece of cloth tied over the eyes to prevent the wearer from seeing ■ *vt.* (**-fold·ed, -fold·ing, -folds**) **1.** PUT BANDAGE ON EYES to prevent somebody from seeing by putting a bandage or other material over the person's eyes **2.** PREVENT FROM UNDERSTANDING to prevent somebody from understanding clearly [Early 16thC. By folk etymology (from FOLD, with the idea of "folding" something around the eyes) from the past tense of obsolete *blindfell* "to strike blind."]

blind·fold·ed /blɪ̄nd fōldəd/ *adj.* wearing a blindfold ○ *heavily blindfolded*

blind gut *n.* = **cecum** [From BLIND *adj.* 9 "closed at one end."]

blind·ing /blɪ̄nding/ *adj.* causing blindness, especially temporarily, by being bright ○ *a blinding flash of light* —**blind·ing·ly** *adv.*

blind·man's buff *n.* a children's game in which one player is blindfolded and has to catch and identify other players by touch [*Buff* a shortening of BUFFET "stroke with the hand"]

blind pig *n.* = **blind tiger** (*regional*) [From the custom of exhibiting stuffed animals in speakeasies]

blind side /blɪ̄ndsɪ̄d/ *n.* the area that is out of your field of vision ○ *The cyclist came up on my blind side.*

blind-side, **blind·side** *vt.* **1.** ATTACK FROM BLIND SIDE to attack somebody from the blind side, especially in sports **2.** ATTACK WHEN VULNERABLE to put somebody at a disadvantage

blind snake *n.* a small tropical nonvenomous snake with scales over its eyes, adapted for burrowing and eating small soil invertebrates. Families: Typhlopidae and Anomalepididae.

blind spot *n.* **1.** ANAT = **optic disk** **2.** AREA OF IGNORANCE a subject that somebody is ignorant about ○ *have a blind spot for math* **3.** DIRECTION IN WHICH VISION IS OBSCURED an area or direction, especially on a road, in which somebody's vision is obscured **4.** ACOUSTICS ACOUSTICALLY IMPAIRED AREA an area in an auditorium where things cannot be clearly heard **5.** BROADCAST PLACE WITH POOR RADIO RECEPTION an area within the normal range of a radio transmitter where reception is poor

blind stag·gers *n.* VET the symptoms of a form of plant poisoning that affects the nervous system of cattle, horses, and other domestic animals, causing them to lose their coordination, stagger, and often fall (*takes a singular verb*) [From the stumbling around]

blind ti·ger *n.* a place where liquor is sold or served illegally (*regional*) [From the custom of exhibiting stuffed animals in speakeasies]

blind·worm /blɪ̄nd wurm/ *n.* = **slowworm** [15thC. *Blind* from the animal's small eyes.]

bli·ni /blínnee/ (*plural* **-nis** *or* **-ni**) *n.* a small pancake made with yeast and buckwheat flour, traditional in Russia and other parts of Eastern Europe [Late 20thC. From Russian *bliný,* plural of *blin.*]

blink /blingk/ *v.* (**blinked, blink·ing, blinks**) **1.** *vti.* CLOSE AND REOPEN EYES to close and reopen both eyes rapidly **2.** *vti.* LOOK WHILE BLINKING to look at somebody or something while blinking **3.** *vt.* HIDE OR REMOVE BY BLINKING to open and shut the eyes rapidly to remove something from them ○ *He blinked away his tears.* **4.** *vti.* FLASH to flash on and off, especially as a signal **5.** *vt.* TRANSMIT MESSAGE BY BLINKING LIGHT to transmit a message by making a light flash on and off **6.** *vi.* WAVER to waver or lose your nerve ○ *After a ten-week strike, it was management that finally blinked.* ■ *n.* **1.** ACT OF BLINKING EYES a rapid closing and reopening of both eyes **2.** METEOROL = **iceblink, snowblink** [13thC. Partly from a variant of BLENCH "to flinch," and partly from Middle Dutch *blinken* "to glitter," of unknown origin. The underlying idea is of "flashing," hence "sudden movement."] ◇ **on the blink** not working properly (*informal*) ○ *The television's on the blink.*

blink·er /blíngkər/ *n.* FLASHING LIGHT a light that flashes in order to give a message or warning, especially on a motor vehicle. Blinkers were used to send coded messages, especially between ships, to avoid interception of radio signals during World Wars I and II. ■ **blink·ers** *npl. U.K.* = **blinders** ■ *vt.* (**-ered, -er·ing, -ers**) FIT HORSE WITH BLINKERS to put blinders on a horse

blink·ered /blíngkərd/ *adj.* unable or unwilling to understand anything outside a very narrow range (*disapproving*) ○ *took a very blinkered attitude toward the reduction of trade barriers*

blip /blip/ *n.* **1.** SPOT ON DISPLAY SCREEN a spot of light, often accompanied by a high-pitched sound, indicating the position of something on a screen ○ *The submarine shows up as a series of faint blips on the screen.* **2.** = **bleep** **3.** SUDDEN DEVIATION a sudden temporary problem in the normal progress of something ■ *vi.* (**blipped, blip·ping, blips**) MAKE A BLIP to produce a blip [Late 19thC. An imitation of the sound.]

bliss /bliss/ *n.* **1.** PERFECT HAPPINESS perfect untroubled happiness ○ *It was bliss to have a day at home.* **2.** SPIRITUAL JOY a state of spiritual joy [Old English *bliss,* an alteration of *blīþs,* from a prehistoric Germanic word meaning "gentle, kind," which is also the ancestor of English *blithe*]

WORD KEY: CULTURAL NOTE

Bliss, a novel by Australian writer Peter Carey (1981). A fable about the battle between good and evil, it tells the story of advertising executive Harry Joy who, after a successful heart bypass operation, becomes convinced that he has woken up in Hell. It was made into a movie by Ray Lawrence in 1985.

bliss out (**blissed out, blissing out, blisses out**) *vi.* to go into a state of extreme happiness or euphoria (*slang*) ○ *bliss out on chocolates*

bliss·ful /blísf'l/ *adj.* **1.** PERFECTLY HAPPY characterized by perfect happiness ○ *a look of blissful contentment* **2.** HAPPY BECAUSE UNAWARE serenely happy because of being unaware of something ○ *blissful ignorance* —**bliss·ful·ly** *adv.* —**bliss·ful·ness** *n.*

blis·ter /blístər/ *n.* **1.** MED PAINFUL SWELLING a painful swelling on the skin containing fluid (**serum**) **2.** PLANTS PLANT DISEASE a swelling in a leaf or other plant part indicating disease **3.** BUBBLE ON PAINT a bubble containing liquid or air on paintwork or rubber **4.** AEROSP AIRCRAFT DOME a rounded, usually transparent dome on the fuselage of an aircraft, used for observation ■ *vti.* (**-tered, -ter·ing, -ters**) FORM BLISTERS to be raised in a blister or blisters, or to cause blisters to form [14thC. Origin uncertain: perhaps via Old French *blestre* "swelling" from Middle Dutch *bluyster,* of unknown origin.] —**blis·ter·y** *adj.*

blis·ter bee·tle *n.* a soft-bodied beetle that secretes for its own defense a substance that raises burning blisters on the skin of vertebrates. Family: Meloidae.

blis·ter·ing /blístəring/ *adj.* **1.** VERY HOT extremely hot **2.** SCORNFUL extremely scornful or critical ○ *a blistering attack on the governor's failures* —**blis·ter·ing·ly** *adv.*

blis·ter pack *n.* a package in which small items are contained in raised domes of plastic

B.Lit. /bēe lít/ *n., abbr.* Bachelor of Literature [Latin, *Baccalaureus Litterarum*]

blithe /blīth, blīth/ *adj.* **1.** CHEERFUL AND CAREFREE happy, cheerful, and carefree (*literary*) **2.** CASUAL casually indifferent ○ *with a blithe disregard for anyone's feelings* [Old English *blīþe,* from a prehistoric Germanic word meaning "gentle" (see BLISS)] —**blithe·ly** *adv.* —**blithe·ness** *n.*

blith·er *vi.* = **blather** (*informal*) [Mid-19thC. Variant of BLATHER.]

blith·er·ing /blíthəring/ *adj.* used to express annoyance and contempt for somebody or something (*informal insult*)

blithe spir·it *n.* somebody whose characteristic mood is one of carefree happiness (*used approvingly*)

B.Litt. /bēe lít/ *n., abbr.* Bachelor of Literature [Latin, *Baccalaureus Litterarum*]

blitz /blits/ *n.* **1.** MIL SUSTAINED AERIAL ATTACK a heavy air raid intended to obliterate a target **2.** MIL = **blitzkrieg** **3.** CONCERTED EFFORT a concentrated effort to get something done (*informal*) ○ *a last-minute blitz to finish the book* **4.** FOOTBALL CHARGE ON PASSER a direct attack on the passer, by one or more players who usually stay behind the line of scrimmage, to try to prevent a pass ■ *v.* (**blitzed, blitz·ing, blitz·es**) **1.** *vt.* MIL DESTROY BY AERIAL BOMBING to attack or destroy something by bombardment from the air **2.** *vt.* DEAL WITH ENERGETICALLY to concentrate a lot of effort on something to get it done (*informal*) **3.** *vt.* TRY TO OVERWHELM to subject somebody to an overwhelming amount of something, often in order to force him or her into agreement or submission (*informal*) ○ *blitzed with a stream of facts* **4.** *vti.* FOOTBALL CHARGE PASSER to charge the passer in order to prevent a pass [Mid-20thC. Shortening of BLITZKRIEG.]

blitz·krieg /blíts kreeg/ *n.* a swift military offensive using ground and air forces [Mid-20thC. From German, literally "lightning war."]

bliv·et, **bliv·it** *n.* **1.** LIQUID CARRIER a collapsible rubberized bladder used to transport and store fuel and water in forward areas of a battlefield **2.** something useless, pointless, or annoying (*slang*) **3.** SOMETHING DIFFICULT TO NAME something whose name you do not know or cannot remember (*slang*) [Mid-20thC. Origin unknown.]

blivit /blívvət/ *n.* **1.** = **blivet** **2.** PROBLEM DIFFICULT TO SOLVE an intractable problem, especially in computing (*slang*) **3.** POINTLESS SOURCE OF ANNOYANCE a source of annoyance that is pointless (*slang*)

Blix·en /blíksən/, **Karen, Baroness** (1885–1962) Danish writer. A much-traveled author, she is best known for her semiautobiographical *Out of Africa* (1937). ➧ **Isak Dinesen**

bliz·zard /blízzərd/ *n.* a severe snowstorm with strong winds and poor visibility. For a snowstorm to be classified as a blizzard, winds must exceed 35 mi./56 km per hour and the temperature must be 20°F/-7°C or lower. [Early 19thC. Origin uncertain: perhaps coined from dialectal *blizz* "violent rainstorm" + -ARD; or thought to suggest the sound of the wind or the falling of the snow.]

blk. *abbr.* 1. block 2. bulk

B.LL. *abbr.* Bachelor of Laws [Latin, Baccalaureus Legum]

BLM *abbr.* Bureau of Land Management

bloat /blōt/ *vti.* (**bloat·ed, bloat·ing, bloats**) **1. SWELL** to become swollen or inflated, or to make something do this **2. EXCESSIVELY EXPAND** to increase excessively or to make something do this **3. SWELL WITH PRIDE** to become or cause to become unpleasantly proud or conceited ■ *n.* **1. EXCESSIVE INCREASE** an excessive amount or excessive increase in something ○ *corporate bloat* **2.** VET **CATTLE DISEASE** a disease affecting cattle and sheep, characterized by excessive gas in the main stomach compartment **(rumen)** [Early 17thC. Origin uncertain: probably from Old Norse *blautr* "soft, wet." The modern meaning "to swell" apparently evolved from the obsolete meaning "flabby" via "swollen."]

bloat·ed /blṓtəd/ *adj.* **1. SWOLLEN** swollen with liquid, air, or gas **2. OVERFULL AFTER OVEREATING** overfull after eating too much **3. TOO LARGE** excessively large (*disapproving*) ○ *a bloated expense account* — **bloat·ed·ness** *n.*

bloat·er /blṓtər/ **FISH CURED BY SOAKING AND SMOKING** a large herring that has been soaked in brine and smoked ■ *n.* **FRESHWATER FISH** a common freshwater cisco native to the Great Lakes. Latin name: *Coregonus hoyi.* [Mid-19thC. From obsolete *bloat herring, bloat* of uncertain origin: perhaps from BLOAT, because herrings preserved by smoking are plumper than those fully dried.]

bloat·ware /blṓt wair/ *n.* COMPUT a computer program with many, often superfluous features that take up so much memory that the computer's performance is impaired (*informal*)

blob /blob/ *n.* **1. SOFT MASS** a soft lump or drop of something such as paint or glue **2. SMALL SPOT OF COLOR** a small rounded spot of color **3. INDISTINCT FORM** an indistinct or shapeless form or object ■ *vt.* (**blobbed, blob·bing, blobs**) **PUT BLOBS ON SOMETHING** to apply blobs of color or a soft substance to something [15thC. Origin uncertain: perhaps from obsolete *blober* "bubble, bubbling"; or an imitation of the sound made by the lips in producing a bubble.]

bloc /blok/, **block** *n.* **1. UNITED GROUP OF COUNTRIES** a group of countries with a shared aim ○ *former Eastern bloc countries* **2. LOOSE COALITION IN LEGISLATURE** a usually temporary grouping within a legislature, made up of diverse members acting together for a common interest or purpose ○ *the environmental bloc in Congress* [Early 20thC. From French, from Old French (see BLOCK).]

Bloch /blok/, **Ernest** (1880–1959) Swiss-born U.S. composer. He incorporated themes from Jewish music in such works as his symphony *Israel* (1912–16).

block /blok/ *n.* **1. SOLID LUMP** a large solid piece of a hard substance, usually with flat sides **2.** CONSTR **BUILDING UNIT** a large flat-sided piece of hard material such as stone or wood, used in building **3.** = **building block 4. CHOPPING BASE** a large piece of wood used for chopping things on **5. PLACE FOR BEHEADING PEOPLE** a large piece of wood or stone on which people were beheaded in former times **6. AUCTIONEER'S PLATFORM** a stand on which articles in an auction are displayed **7.** PRINTING **PRINTING DEVICE** a piece of wood, metal, or stone with a design engraved on it used for printing **8.** SPORTS = **starting block 9. STREET SECTION** the section of a street between two parallel streets ○ *The post office is in the middle of the next block.* **10. GROUP OF BUILDINGS** a group of buildings in a town or city bounded on each side by a street ○ *I'm just taking the dog for a walk around the block.* **11. SPECIAL-PURPOSE BUILDING** a building or part of a building designed for a particular purpose ○ *the new science block* **12.** *U.K.* **LARGE BUILDING** a building divided into offices or apartments ○ *an apartment block* **13. LAND AREA** an area of land marked for division or development **14. UNBROKEN EXPANSE OR AREA** a uniform expanse of something such as color **15. SET OF SIMILAR ITEMS** a set of similar items sold as a unit ○ *a block of tickets* **16. GROUP OF POSTAGE STAMPS** a group of four or more postage stamps forming a rectangle **17.** RAIL **LENGTH OF TRACK** a length of railroad track on which only one train is permitted at a time **18.** COMPUT **UNIT OF DATA** a set of contiguous data that performs some action together ○ *a block of text* **19.** POL = **bloc 20. OBSTRUCTION** something that obstructs or prevents progress **21.** SPORTS **OBSTRUCTION OF PLAY** an act of deliberately preventing a ball or another player from moving forward **22.** FOOTBALL **OBSTRUCTING PLAYERS** the act of preventing defensive players from interfering with movement toward the goal **23.** MED **OBSTRUCTION OF PHYSIOLOGICAL FUNCTION** an interruption of the normal functioning of an organ of the body **24. DISRUPTION OF PSYCHOLOGICAL PROCESSES** an inability to begin or continue a psychological process, often attributed to emotional stress **25.** = **engine block 26.** *ANZ* **LARGE AREA OF SETTLED LAND** an extensive area of land used for a particular purpose, e.g., housing or farming. ■ *v.* (**blocked, block·ing, blocks**) **1.** *vt.* **OBSTRUCT** to prevent or hinder movement through, into, or out of something ○ *The drains are blocked with leaves.* ○ *He stood in front of me, blocking my way.* **2.** *vt.* **HINDER SOMEBODY'S OR SOMETHING'S MOVEMENT OR PROGRESS** to prevent something from moving or developing ○ *Her promotion was blocked by the senior vice-president* **3.** *vt.* **OBSTRUCT SIGHT OF SOMETHING** to obstruct somebody's line of sight **4.** *vti.* SPORTS **OBSTRUCT PLAYER OR BALL** to prevent a ball or another player from moving forward **5.** *vti.* FOOTBALL **OBSTRUCT PLAYER** to prevent a defensive player from interfering with movement toward the goal **6.** *vti.* MED **PREVENT NORMAL FUNCTIONING** to prevent the normal functioning of a physiological process ○ *a blocked tear duct* **7.** *vti.* **FAIL TO REMEMBER** to fail to remember something or to have a psychological block ○ *block a memory* **8.** *vt.* **MAKE INTO BLOCK** to shape something into a block **9.** *vt.* **SUPPORT WITH BLOCK** to support or strengthen something using a block **10.** *vt.* **SHAPE ON BLOCK** to mold something with or on a block **11.** *vt.* PRINTING **STAMP USING BLOCK** to stamp a surface with a title or using an engraved block **12.** *vti.* THEATER **REHEARSE BASIC MOVEMENTS FOR SCENE** to plan and rehearse the basic movements and positions for the actors in a scene **13.** *vt.* = **blockade** (*archaic*) [14thC. Via Old French *bloc* from Middle Dutch *blok* "tree trunk."] ◇ **block and level** to level a portable structure by placing blocks of various heights under its corners ◇ **on the block** for sale at an auction

WORD KEY: SYNONYMS

See Synonyms at *hinder.*

block in *vt.* **1. PREVENT FROM MOVING** to prevent somebody or something moving from a place by being, or placing something, in the way ○ *Two double-parked cars have blocked us in.* **2. FILL SOMETHING IN** to fill in something hollow so that it becomes solid **3. SKETCH SOMETHING IN OUTLINE** to make a quick, rough sketch showing the general outlines or idea of a place or plan **4. SHADE EMPTY SPACES** to fill in the blank spaces on an outline design with color

block off *vt.* **1. PHYSICALLY OBSTRUCT** to put up or form a barrier in order to prevent anybody or anything from entering ○ *Police blocked off the street.* **2. OBSTRUCT SIGHT OF** to put up or form a barrier that prevents something from being seen

block out *vt.* **1. PUT OUT OF MIND** to prevent a disturbing thought from entering the mind **2. DESCRIBE WITHOUT DETAIL** to describe something in a general fashion, without great detail ○ *block out a proposal* **3.** PHOTOGRAPHY **COVER PART OF NEGATIVE** to cover part of a negative or stencil when printing from it to prevent that part from appearing

block up *vti.* to prevent movement through something by filling all the space in, or to become completely obstructed

block·ade /blo káyd/ *n.* **1. PREVENTION OF ACCESS** an organized action to prevent people or goods entering or leaving a place **2. FORCES FORMING BLOCKADE** the ships or forces used to maintain a blockade **3. OBSTACLE OR OBSTRUCTION** something that prevents access to a place ■ *vt.* (**-ad·ed, -ad·ing, -ades**) **1. SUBJECT PLACE TO BLOCKADE** to impose a blockade on a place **2. BLOCK ACCESS TO PLACE** to obstruct access to a place [Late 17thC. Perhaps modeled on AMBUSCADE.] —**block·ad·er** *n.*

block·age /blókij/ *n.* **1. PHYSICAL OBSTRUCTION** something that obstructs movement through a pipe or channel ○ *a blockage in an artery* **2. ACT OF BLOCKING** the act of blocking something

block and tack·le (*plural* **blocks and tack·les**) *n.* a system of two pulley blocks, each with at least one pulley with rope or cable threaded through them, used for hoisting or hauling. The greater the number of pulleys, the greater the weight that can be raised by the same force on the rope or cable.

block·bust·er /blók bustər/ *n.* **1. POPULAR SUCCESS** something such as a book, play or film that is either very large or achieves enormous commercial success (*informal*) **2.** MIL **HUGE DESTRUCTIVE BOMB** a large high-explosive bomb designed to demolish buildings over a large area (*dated*) **3.** BUSINESS **PERSON WHO PRACTICES BLOCKBUSTING** somebody who attempts to persuade people to sell their houses by instilling fear of declining property values (*informal*)

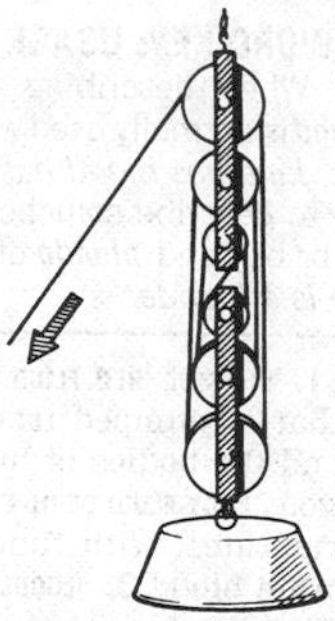

Block and tackle

block·bust·ing /blók busting/ *n.* **EXPLOITATION TECHNIQUE** the practice of persuading homeowners to sell low for fear of declining property values (*informal*) ■ *adj.* **SUCCESSFUL** sensational and enormously successful commercially ○ *a blockbusting novel*

block cap·i·tal *n.* a plain capital letter that is not joined to other letters ○ *Fill out the form in block capitals.*

block di·a·gram *n.* a diagram in which the essential parts of a system or process are represented by labeled rectangles

block·er /blókər/ *n.* **1.** PHARM **CHEMICAL AGENT** a drug that prevents a physiological function **2.** FOOTBALL **OFFENSIVE PLAYER** in football, an offensive player who tries to keep the defense from reaching the ball, kicker, or passer

block grant *n.* money from the federal budget granted to state or local governments to spend on local services

block·head /blók hed/ *n.* a person regarded as very unintelligent (*dated insult*) [Mid-16thC. The meaning "stupid" evolved from the wooden heads used to display hats and wigs.]

block·house /blók hows/ (*plural* **-hous·es**) *n.* **1. SMALL, EASILY DEFENDED BUILDING** a small military building with apertures to fire through, used as part of a defensive system or an observation post **2. WOODEN FORT** a fort of former times constructed from heavy wooden beams

Block Is·land /blók ìlənd/ island in the Atlantic Ocean at the northern end of Long Island Sound in southern Rhode Island. A resort and fishing center, it is named for the Dutch sailor Adriaen Block, who landed there in 1614. Population: 836 (1991). Area: 11 sq. mi./28 sq. km.

block let·ter *n.* **1.** = **block capital 2.** PRINTING **SANS SERIF FONT OR LETTER** a compressed sans serif typeface or individual letter

block par·ty (*plural* **block par·ties**) *n.* a party for all the people who live on the same block or street

block plane *n.* a small carpenter's plane with the blade at a low pitch, used to cut across the grain of the wood

block print·ing *n.* printing from hand-carved or engraved blocks

block·y /blókee/ (**-i·er, -i·est**) *adj.* three-dimensional, boxy in shape, and seemingly solid

Bloc Qué·bé·cois /-káy bay kwáa/ *n.* POL a Canadian federal political party consisting of members from Quebec and espousing that province's interests, especially sovereignty or separation from Canada

bloke /blōk/ *n. U.K., ANZ* a man (*informal*) [Mid-19thC. From Shelta, a secret jargon used by Romany people in Britain and Ireland.]

blond /blaand/, **blonde** *adj.* **1. FAIR** yellowish or golden in color **2. FAIR-HAIRED AND LIGHT-SKINNED** with fair hair and a light-colored skin ○ *a blond little boy* ○ *a blond little girl* **3. LIGHT COLORED** light-colored, ranging from light yellowish brown to grayish yellow ○ *blond wood* **4. BLEACHED** used to describe wood that is light-colored, usually through bleaching ○ *blonde walnut* ■ *n.* **FAIR-HAIRED PERSON** a person with blond hair [15thC. Via French from, ultimately, medieval Latin *blundus* "yellow," of uncertain origin: perhaps ultimately from a prehistoric Germanic word meaning "clouded," which is also the ancestor of English *blend.*] —**blond·ness** *n.*

WORD KEY: USAGE

blond or **blonde**? When describing the color of somebody's hair, ***blond*** is normally used whether the person is male or female. *Jane has blond hair.* When used as a noun or adjective to describe somebody directly, ***blond*** is used of a man or boy and ***blonde*** of a woman or girl. *He is blond. Jane is a blonde.*

blood /blud/ *n.* **1.** PHYSIOL **RED FLUID CIRCULATING IN BODY** the red fluid that is pumped from the heart and circulates around the bodies of humans and other vertebrates **2.** ZOOL **BODY FLUID OF INVERTEBRATES** a liquid found in invertebrates, with functions similar to those of vertebrate blood **3. BLOODSHED** bloodshed or killing **4. VITAL LIFE FORCE** blood considered as a vital life force **5. FAMILY OR KINSHIP** family background or descent from a particular ancestor, especially when viewed as determining a person's character or appearance **6. PURE BREEDING** pure breeding in animals, especially horses **7. MEMBERS OF GROUP** people considered for their potential to strengthen and improve an organization (*informal*) **8. BLACK MALE** a Black male (*slang*) (*used primarily among Black people*) ■ *vt.* (**blood·ed, blood·ing, bloods**) **1.** MIL **INITIATE TROOPS IN BATTLE** to subject troops to their first experience of battle **2.** HUNT **LET DOG TASTE BLOOD** to give a dog its first taste of the blood of a freshly killed animal in order to make it eager to hunt [Old English *blōd*, from a prehistoric Germanic word that is also the ancestor of English *bleed*] ◇ **be out for** *or* **after somebody's blood** to be intending to punish somebody ◇ **blood is thicker than water** family ties and loyalties take precedence over other relationships ◇ **blood on somebody's hands** responsibility for somebody's death ◇ **in cold blood** deliberately, and in a way that shows a complete lack of emotion ○ *was murdered in cold blood* ◇ **make somebody's blood boil** to make somebody extremely angry ◇ **make somebody's blood run cold** to frighten or horrify somebody ◇ **sweat blood** to make a great effort

blood bank *n.* **1. STORE FOR BLOOD** a place where blood or blood plasma is stored for transfusion **2. BLOOD SUPPLY** the blood or blood plasma stored in a blood bank

blood·bath /blúd bath/ (*plural* **-baths** /blúd bathez/) *n.* a battle or fight characterized by mass killing

blood broth·er *n.* either one of two men or boys who have sworn mutual loyalty and friendship

blood clot *n.* a thick mass of coagulated blood

blood count *n.* **1. DETERMINATION OF BLOOD CELL NUMBER** a counting of the number of red and white blood cells and platelets in a given volume of blood **2. NUMBER OF CELLS** the actual number of cells and platelets found in a blood count

blood·cur·dling /blúd kurdling/ *adj.* arousing extreme fear ○ *bloodcurdling screams*

blood do·nor *n.* somebody who gives some of his or her own blood for use in transfusions

blood dop·ing *n.* the practice of reinjecting an athlete with his or her own red blood cells shortly before a competition in order to enhance performance. The practice is illegal in most organized competitions.

blood·ed /blúddəd/ *adj.* belonging to a superior breed ○ *blooded mares*

blood feud *n.* a long-lasting feud between families or clans involving murder

blood·fin /blúd fin/ *n.* a small red-finned freshwater fish native to Argentina, popular in aquariums. Latin name: *Aphyocharax rubripinnis.*

blood fluke *n.* a parasitic flatworm that is common in tropical Asia and Africa and is found in human blood. It relies on two hosts, humans and some types of snails, to complete its life cycle. Genus: *Schistosoma.*

blood group *n.* any class into which human blood is divided for transfusion purposes according to the presence or absence of genetically determined antigens that determine its immunological compatibility. The ABO system is the most commonly known set of blood groups.

blood·hound /blúd hownd/ *n.* **1. TRACKING DOG** a large powerful dog with drooping ears, sagging jowls, and a keen sense of smell, formerly used for tracking **2. SLEUTH** a detective who is relentless in pursuing people or things (*informal*) [14thC. From the dog's skill in following the scent of people and animals.]

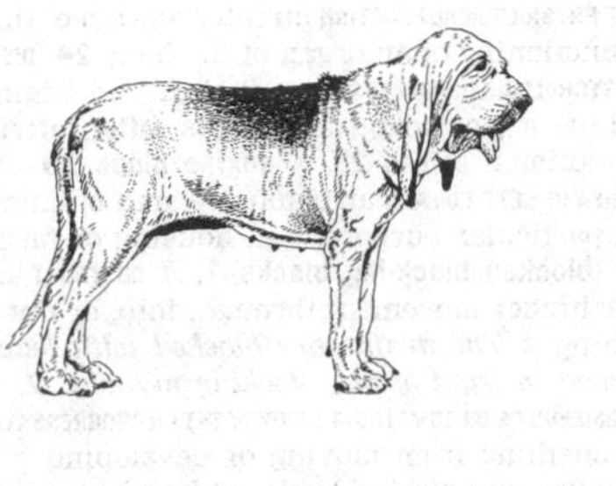

Bloodhound

blood·less /blúddləss/ *adj.* **1. WITHOUT KILLING OR VIOLENCE** conducted without killing or great violence ○ *a bloodless coup* **2. PALE AND ANEMIC** pale and anemic-looking **3. LACKING LIVELINESS** dull and lacking liveliness ○ *a bloodless performance* **4. LACKING EMOTION** cold and lacking in human emotion ○ *bloodless statistics* **5. LACKING BLOOD** lacking blood, or the expected amount of blood ○ *bloodless surgery* —**blood·less·ly** *adv.* —**blood·less·ness** *n.*

blood·let·ting /blúd letting/ *n.* **1.** MED = **phlebotomy 2. BITTER QUARRELING** bitter violent fighting between rival groups **3. EJECTION AS OF PEOPLE** the large-scale ejection, or laying off, of human resources in a corporation (*formal*) ○ *corporate bloodletting in which a number of senior managers were let go* —**blood·let·ter** *n.*

blood·line /blúd līn/ *n.* a direct line of descent from a particular human or animal ancestor, especially with respect to the common characteristics shared by that ancestor's descendants

blood lust *n.* a strong desire for killing or violence

blood mon·ey *n.* **1. COMPENSATION PAID FOR KILLING** in some cultures, compensation paid to the relatives of somebody who has been killed or murdered **2. FEE FOR HIRED KILLER** the fee paid to a hired killer or to somebody who reveals where the victim of a murder is to be found **3. REWARD FOR FINDING KILLER** the reward paid to somebody for giving information about a criminal, especially a murderer

blood or·ange *n.* an orange that has deep red flesh

blood plas·ma *n.* = **plasma**

blood poi·son·ing *n.* infection of the blood, generally caused either by the presence in the blood of microorganisms (**septicemia**) or of toxins produced by body cells (**toxemia**)

blood pres·sure *n.* the pressure exerted by the blood against the walls of blood vessels. Blood pressure depends on the strength of the heartbeat, thickness and volume of the blood, the elasticity of the artery walls, and the healthiness of the individual.

blood pro·file *n.* = **complete blood count**

blood red *n.* **BRIGHT RED** a deep vivid red color ■ *adj.* **DEEP RED** of a deep vivid red color, like that of blood (*hyphenated when used before a noun*) [Old English *blōdrēad*]

blood re·la·tion, blood rel·a·tive *n.* a person who is related to another person by birth rather than marriage

blood·root /blúd root/ (*plural* **-roots** *or* **-root**) *n.* a plant of eastern North America that produces a single white flower and has poisonous, deep red sap in its roots. Latin name: *Sanguinaria canadensis.*

blood sau·sage *n.* a dark-colored sausage whose main ingredient is pig's blood

blood·shed /blúd shed/ *n.* activity resulting in killings or injuries

blood·shot /blúd shot/ *adj.* inflamed and red as a result of the widening of small blood vessels in the white of the eye ○ *bloodshot eyes* [Mid-16thC. *Shot* the past participle of SHOOT.]

blood sport *n.* a sport in which animals are killed. Hunting and bullfighting are blood sports.

blood·stain /blúd stayn/ *n.* a dark stain left by dried blood —**blood·stained** *adj.*

blood·stone /blúd stōn/ *n.* a semiprecious mineral that is a deep green variety of chalcedony with small red spots or streaks of red jasper in it

blood·stream /blúd streem/ *n.* the flow of blood circulating through the blood vessels of a person or animal

blood·suck·er /blúd sukər/ *n.* **1. PARASITE THAT SUCKS BLOOD** a parasite that sucks blood from its host, e.g., leeches and mosquitoes **2. EXPLOITER** somebody who exploits somebody else, especially by extortion or blackmail (*informal disapproving*) —**blood·suck·ing** *n., adj.*

blood sug·ar *n.* the concentration of glucose in the blood

blood test *n.* a scientific analysis of a sample of blood

blood·thirst·y /blúd thurstee/ (**bloodthirst·i·er, bloodthirst·i·est**) *adj.* **1. EAGER FOR VIOLENCE** eager to take part in or witness violence and bloodshed **2. VIOLENT** full of intentional violence or killing [Mid-16thC. From BLOOD + THIRSTY, modeled on German *blutdürstig*, coined by Martin Luther.] —**blood·thirst·i·ly** *adv.* —**blood·thirst·i·ness** *n.*

blood type *n.* = **blood group**

blood ves·sel *n.* any of the arteries, veins, or capillaries through which blood flows

blood·worm /blúd wurm/ *n.* **1. AQUATIC MIDGE LARVA** the red aquatic larva of a freshwater midge. Genus: *Chironomus.* **2. REDDISH WORM USED AS FISHING BAIT** a reddish segmented worm that is often used as fishing bait. Genera: *Tubifex* and *Polycirrus.* (*regional*)

WORD KEY: REGIONAL NOTE

Although recorded from Canada throughout the Middle Atlantic states, ***bloodworm*** recurs most frequently in New Jersey.

blood·y /blúddee/ *adj.* (**-i·er, -i·est**) **1. BLOODSTAINED** covered or smeared with blood ○ *Her hands were bloody and shaking.* **2. RELATING TO BLOOD** resembling or containing blood **3. INVOLVING MUCH BLOODSHED** involving a great deal of killing and bloodshed **4. SWEARWORD** used as a swearword or to add emphasis (*slang*) ○ *a bloody nuisance* ■ *adv. U.K.* **SWEARWORD** used as a swearword or to add emphasis (*slang*) ○ *a bloody good job too!* ■ *vt.* (**-ied, -y·ing, -ies**) **STAIN WITH BLOOD** to stain or smear something with blood [In the emphatic sense, perhaps originally a reference to the habits of the "bloods," or wealthy young men, in phrases such as "*bloody drunk*," literally "as drunk as a blood"] —**blood·i·ly** *adv.* —**blood·i·ness** *n.*

blood·y mar·y (*plural* **blood·y mar·ys**), **Blood·y Mar·y** *n.* a cocktail consisting of vodka, tomato juice, and other spices

blood·y-mind·ed *adj. U.K.* intentionally uncooperative and obstructive (*informal*) [From earlier sense "inclined to violence, cruel"] —**blood·y-mind·ed·ly** *adv.* —**blood·y-mind·ed·ness** *n.*

bloom[1] /bloom/ *n.* **1.** PLANTS **FLOWER** a flower, especially on a plant cultivated chiefly for its flowers **2.** PLANTS **MASS OF FLOWERS** the mass of flowers on a single plant **3.** PLANTS **FLOWERING** the state of being in flower ○ *roses in full bloom* **4. PRIME** the condition of greatest freshness or health (*literary*) ○ *in the bloom of youth* **5.** BOT **HEALTHY APPEARANCE OR COMPLEXION** a fresh, youthful, healthy complexion **6. WHITE COATING ON LEAVES OR FRUIT** a thin white coating on the leaves of some plants and on fruits **7. WHITE POWDER ON COINS** a fine white powder sometimes found on newly minted coins **8.** COOK **COATING ON CHOCOLATE** a mottled white coating on chocolate, usually caused by incorrect temperature during storage **9.** ECOL = **algal bloom** ■ *vi.* (**bloomed, bloom·ing, blooms**) **1.** PLANTS **TO FLOWER** to open into flower ○ *The roses bloomed early this year.* **2.** PLANTS **PRODUCE PLANTS** to produce abundant plant life, especially unexpectedly ○ *make the desert bloom* **3. PROSPER OR FLOURISH** to reach the fullest stage of development or maturity (*literary*) **4. APPEAR HEALTHY** to appear healthy and vigorous (*literary*) **5. APPEAR SUDDENLY** to appear suddenly, usually in a cloud ○ *A cloud of smoke bloomed under the rocket.* **6.** ECOL **BECOME COVERED WITH ALGAE** to become discolored on the surface because of an excessive growth of algae or phytoplankton (*refers to bodies of water*) [13thC. From Old Norse *blóm*, from, ultimately, an Indo-European word that is also the ancestor of English *flower*.] —**bloom·y** *adj.*

bloom[2] /bloom/ *n.* METALL **BAR OF SEMIFINISHED METAL** a bar of steel or wrought iron hammered or rolled from an ingot ■ *vt.* (**bloomed, bloom·ing, blooms**) **FLATTEN AN INGOT** to convert an ingot of iron or steel into a bloom [Pre-12thC. From Old Norse *blóm* (see BLOOM[1]).]

bloom·er /bloŏmər/ *n.* **1.** PLANTS **PLANT THAT FLOWERS** a flowering plant, especially considered with respect to the time of its flowering ○ *an early bloomer* **2.** *U.K.* **EMBARRASSING MISTAKE** a mildly embarrassing mistake (*informal humorous*) [Mid-18thC. "Mistake" a shortening and alteration of *blooming error*.]

Bloom·er /blo͞omər/, **Amelia** (1818–94) U.S. feminist and reformer. She was founding editor of the feminist journal *The Lily* (1849–55), and fashioned a pants-like garment for women that was nicknamed "bloomers." Born **Amelia Jenks**

bloom·ers /blo͞omərs/ *npl.* (*dated*) **1. BAGGY UNDERWEAR** baggy underwear for women or girls, especially garments that reach down to just above the knee **2. WOMEN'S LOOSE SPORTS PANTS** loose pants gathered at the knee, worn by women for cycling or swimming in the late 19th century **3. LONG LOOSE WOMEN'S PANTS** long loose pants gathered at the ankle and formerly worn by women and girls under a shorter skirt [Mid-19thC. Named for Amelia BLOOMER.]

Bloom·field /blo͞om fēēld/ town in Essex County, northeastern New Jersey, just north of Newark. Population: 45,061 (1990).

bloom·ing /blo͞oming/ *adj.* **FLOURISHING** flourishing and in exceptionally good health or condition ■ *adj., adv. U.K.* **USED FOR EMPHASIS** used as a euphemistic alternative for "bloody" (*dated informal*) ○ *a blooming idiot* ○ *not blooming likely*

Bloo·ming·ton /blo͞omingtən/ **1.** city in central Illinois, directly north of Decatur. Population: 57,365 (1996). **2.** city in southern Indiana, southwest of Indianapolis. It is home to Indiana University. Population: 66,479 (1996). **3.** city on the Minnesota River in southeastern Minnesota, a southern suburb of Minneapolis. Population: 86,664 (1996).

Blooms·bur·y Group /blo͞omz berri-, blo͞omzbəree-/ *n.* a group of artists and writers who congregated in Bloomsbury in London after World War I. They shared political views and an experimental approach to their respective fields. [Early 20thC. Named for *Bloomsbury*, a district in west central London.]

bloop /bloop/ *vt.* (**blooped, bloop·ing, bloops**) BASEBALL **HIT BASEBALL** to hit a baseball just over the infield ■ *n.* BASEBALL = **blooper** *n.* 2 [Early 20thC. An imitation of the sound.]

bloop·er /blo͞opər/ *n.* **1. EMBARRASSING MISTAKE** a mildly embarrassing mistake (*informal humorous*) **2.** BASEBALL **HIT** a hit just beyond the infield **3.** BASEBALL **PITCH** a lobbed underhand pitch [Early 20thC. Formed from BLOOP.]

Blo·quiste /blo kéest/ *n. Can* POL a member of the Bloc Québécois [Late 20thC. From Canadian French, where it was formed from *Bloc*.]

blos·som /blóssəm/ *n.* **1. MASS OF FLOWERS ON TREE** a mass of flowers appearing on a tree or bush **2. SINGLE FLOWER** a single flower **3. FLOWERING** the state of flowering ○ *cherry trees in blossom* ■ *vi.* (**-somed, -som·ing, -soms**) **1. COME INTO FLOWER** to open into flower **2. DEVELOP WELL** to develop in a pleasing or promising way **3. blos·som, blos·som out STOP BEING SHY** to stop being shy and reserved [Old English *blōstm*. Ultimately from an Indo-European base that is related to Latin *flos* (source of English *flower*).] —**blos·som·y** *adj.*

blot[1] /blot/ *n.* **1. STAIN** a stain or spot caused by a drop of liquid **2. EYESORE** something ugly that spoils the appearance of something ○ *a blot on the landscape* **3. BLEMISH** something that spoils somebody or something's good name or reputation ■ *v.* (**blot·ted, blot·ting, blots**) **1.** *vti.* **CREATE BLOT** to make a blot on paper **2.** *vt.* **BRING DISREPUTE** to bring dishonor on somebody's reputation **3.** *vt.* **DRY WITH ABSORBENT MATERIAL** to soak up liquid from the surface of something using absorbent material [14thC. Origin uncertain: probably from Scandinavian.]

blot out *vt.* **1. OBSCURE** to cover something so that it can no longer be seen **2. OBLITERATE FROM MEMORY** to remove something painful from the mind

blot[2] /blot/ *n.* **1.** BACKGAMMON **EXPOSED PIECE** a piece placed alone on a point and therefore exposed to capture by the opposing player **2. WEAK POINT** a weak or exposed point (*archaic*) [Late 16thC. Origin uncertain: probably from Dutch *bloot* "exposed, naked."]

blotch /bloch/ *n.* **1. SPOT OR MARK** an irregularly shaped spot or mark **2. BLEMISH ON SKIN** a reddish patch on the skin **3.** PLANTS **PLANT DISEASE** any fungal disease of plants marked by discolored areas on leaves and stems ■ *vti.* (**blotched, blotch·ing, blotch·es**) **MARK WITH BLOTCHES** to mark or become marked with blotches [Early 17thC. Blend of BLOT and BOTCH.] —**blotch·i·ly** *adv.* —**blotch·i·ness** *n.* —**blotch·y** *adj.*

blot·ter /blóttər/ *n.* **1. PIECE OF BLOTTING PAPER** a sheet of blotting paper that absorbs ink or water **2. LOGBOOK** a book used for recording daily events and transactions ○ *a police blotter*

blot·ting pa·per *n.* soft paper used for soaking up ink from paper

blot·to /blóttō/ *adj.* extremely inebriated (*slang*) [Early 20thC. Formed obscurely from BLOT, noun or verb.]

blouse /blowss, blowz/ (**bloused, blous·ing, blous·es,** *plural* **blous·es**) *n.* **1. WOMAN'S SHIRT** a woman's loose-fitting shirt **2. PEASANT SMOCK** a loose-fitting shirt or smock, often part of peasant dress **3. CADET'S OR SOLDIER'S TUNIC** a tunic, sometimes loose and sometimes very snug, that is a part of some military uniforms [Early 19thC. From French, of unknown origin.]

blou·son /blówsson, -ss'n, -zon, -z'n/ *n.* **1. GARMENT LIKE A SHIRT** a woman's garment resembling a shirt that is gathered at the waist **2. SHORT JACKET** a short jacket that fits closely at the waist and becomes looser over the upper body [Early 20thC. From French.]

blow[1] /blō/ *v.* (**blew** /bloo/, **blown** /blōn/, **blow·ing, blows**) **1.** *vi.* **BE MOVING AS AIR** to be moving as a current of air ○ *It blew all night.* **2.** *vti.* **MOVE WITH AIR CURRENT** to move something with a current of air, especially air exhaled through the mouth ○ *I blew the dust off the shelf.* **3.** *vti.* **EXHALE** to send a stream of air out from the mouth ○ *She blew on her soup* **4.** *vt.* **MAKE BY BLOWING** to make bubbles or smoke rings by sending a stream of air out from the mouth **5.** *vt.* **CLEAR NOSE** to clear the nose by forcing air through it **6.** *vt.* CRAFT **SHAPE HOT GLASS** to give shape to molten glass by forcing air into it **7.** *vti.* MUSIC **SOUND BY BLOWING** to make a sound from a musical instrument by blowing air into it, or to emit a sound when blown **8.** *vt.* **SEND A KISS** to send somebody a symbolic kiss by kissing your hand and then blowing across it **9.** *vi.* ZOOL **EXPEL MOIST AIR** to expel moist air from the lungs up through the blowhole (*refers to whales, dolphins, and other cetaceans*) **10.** *vi.* **BREATHE HARD** to breathe hard or pant through exertion **11.** *vt.* **EXHAUST HORSE** to cause a horse to breathe hard through overexertion **12.** *vti.* **DESTROY OR MOVE BY EXPLOSION** to destroy or displace something or somebody violently ○ *The blast blew the roof off.* **13.** *vt.* **OPEN BY FORCE** to break open something that is firmly shut using explosives **14.** *vti.* CARS **PUNCTURE** to cause or experience a blowout (*informal*) **15.** *vti.* ELEC **CAUSE FUSE TO BURN OUT** to burn out and break an electrical circuit, or to cause a piece of equipment to do this ○ *The toaster blew when I plugged it in.* **16.** *vti.* **BREAK BECAUSE OF PRESSURE** to cause something to rupture under excess pressure, or to undergo this process **17.** *vt.* **MISS AN OPPORTUNITY** to fail to take advantage of an opportunity (*slang*) **18.** *vt.* **WASTE MONEY** to spend money wastefully (*slang*) ○ *blew a bundle of dough on fast cars* **19.** *vt.* **EXPOSE** to expose something secret (*slang*) ○ *blew his cover* **20.** *vt.* **DISREGARD** to disregard something as trivial (*slang dated*) (*usually used as a command*) ○ *Blow the expense!* **21.** *vti.* **LEAVE A PLACE SUDDENLY** to leave a place suddenly (*slang*) ○ *When the cops arrived, the thieves blew* **22.** *vti.* MUSIC **PLAY MUSIC INFORMALLY** to play music, especially informally or with other musicians (*slang*) **23.** *vt.* **INHALE DRUG** to inhale a drug (*slang*) **24.** *vt.* **FELLATE** to fellate (*slang offensive*) **25.** (*past participle* **blowed**) *vt. U.K.* **EXPRESSING SURPRISE** used to express surprise (*dated informal*) ○ *Blow me down, look who's here!* ■ *n.* **1. ACT OF BLOWING** an act of blowing **2.** MUSIC **SOUND PRODUCED BY BLOWING** the sound produced by blowing on a musical instrument or the like **3. STRONG WIND** a strong wind (*informal*) **4.** *U.S., ANZ* **BOAST** an act of boasting (*informal*) **5. COCAINE** the drug cocaine (*slang*) [Old English *blāwan*. Ultimately from an Indo-European word that is also the ancestor of English *bladder*, *flatulent*, and *inflate*.]
◇ **blow a fuse** *or* **gasket** to lose your temper (*informal*)
◇ **blow it** to spoil your chances of success (*slang*)

blow away *v.* **1.** *vti.* **MOVE BY WIND** to move something from its place, or to be moved, by the force of a current of air or the wind **2.** *vt.* **KILL** to shoot somebody dead (*slang*) **3.** *vt.* **DEFEAT DECISIVELY** to subject somebody to an overwhelming defeat (*slang*) **4.** *vt.* **OVERWHELM** to affect somebody emotionally (*slang*) ○ *an epic movie that just blew me away*

blow in *vi.* **1. ARRIVE** to arrive or enter a place in a casual way (*slang*) ○ *blew in at midnight from Toronto* **2. START PRODUCING** to start producing oil (*refers to oil wells*)

blow off *v.* **1.** *vti.* TECH, ENG **RELEASE GAS** to release a gas or liquid under pressure. ◊ **blow out 2.** *vt.* **FAIL TO MEET** to disregard an obligation to meet somebody (*slang*) ○ *Lee blew me off, so I'm free for lunch.*

blow out *v.* **1.** *vti.* **EXTINGUISH** to extinguish a flame with a blast of air or wind **2.** *vr.* METEOROL **DIE DOWN** to return to a state of calm after a storm (*refers to storms and winds*) **3.** *vi.* CARS **PUNCTURE** to puncture suddenly and at high speed (*refers to tires*) **4.** *vi.* TECH, INDUST **EMIT UNCONTROLLABLY** to release oil or gas explosively (*refers to gas or oil wells*)

blow over *vi.* **1. DIE DOWN** to become less violent (*refers to storms*) **2. BE FORGOTTEN** to no longer excite strong feelings (*informal*) ○ *It was quite a scandal but it all blew over.*

blow up *v.* **1.** *vti.* **DESTROY BY EXPLOSION** to destroy something or kill somebody by causing an explosion, or to be destroyed in this way **2.** *vti.* **EXPLODE OR DETONATE** to detonate an explosive, or to explode **3.** *vti.* **INFLATE** to blow air into something so that it becomes swollen, or to swell as a result of being filled with air **4.** *vt.* PHOTOGRAPHY **ENLARGE IMAGE** to enlarge a photograph **5.** *vi.* **BECOME ANGRY** to lose your temper suddenly (*informal*) **6.** *vi.* **BEGIN TO BLOW** to begin to develop or gather force (*refers to winds or storms*) **7.** *vt.* **EXAGGERATE** exaggerate the value or importance of something (*informal*) **8.** *vt.* CINEMA, PHOTOGRAPHY **EXPAND IMAGES** to expand the images of a motion picture from a smaller gauge of film to a larger or to expand a small portion of an image so that it becomes the subject of another

blow[2] /blō/ *n.* **1. HARD HIT** a hard hit with a fist or weapon ○ *a nasty blow on the head* **2. ACTION HELPING CAUSE** an important action that helps a cause or belief ○ *They struck an important blow for civil rights.* **3. SETBACK** a sudden setback ○ *a blow to his confidence* [15thC. Originally northern English and Scottish dialect *blaw*, of uncertain origin: perhaps ultimately from a prehistoric Germanic word meaning "to strike."]

blow[3] /blō/ (**blew** /bloo/, **blown** /blōn/, **blow·ing, blows**) *vti.* to blossom or to cause something to blossom [Old English *blōwan*. Ultimately from a prehistoric Germanic word that is also the ancestor of English *bloom*.]

blow·back /blṓ bak/ *n.* **1. FIREARM POWER RESIDUE** the powdery residue that is released or ejected upon firing bullets or shells from a weapon **2. REACTION** a reaction or effect resulting from an action or cause, usually a negative reaction (*informal*) ○ *The blowback from the press revelations was terrific.* **3. SYSTEM FOR RELOADING AUTOMATIC WEAPONS** the escape to the rear of gases formed during the firing of a weapon. The gases activate a piston that forces back the bolt, allowing the spent casing to be ejected and a fresh cartridge inserted.

blow-by-blow *adj.* describing something in great detail ○ *a blow-by-blow account* [From the idea of commenting on the sequence of punches at a boxing match]

blow-dry *vt.* **STYLE HAIR WITH HAIRDRYER** to dry and style hair using a hair dryer ■ *n.* **BLOW-DRIED HAIRSTYLE** a hairstyle produced by blow-drying

blow·er /blṓ ər/ *n.* **1. BLOWING MACHINE** a machine that produces a current of air or gas ○ *a leaf blower* **2. LOW-PRESSURE COMPRESSOR** an air compressor that produces air at low pressure **3.** = **supercharger 4. BRAGGART** a boastful person (*informal*)

blow·fish /blṓ fish/ (*plural* **-fish** *or* **-fish·es**) *n.* = **puffer**

blow·fly /blṓ flī/ (*plural* **-flies**) *n.* a large fly such as a bluebottle that lays its eggs in rotting meat, in dung, or in open wounds. Family: Calliphoridae. [Early 19thC. "*Blow*" from BLOW, in the sense "to deposit eggs."]

blow·gun /blṓ gun/ *n.* a long narrow tube through which darts or pellets are shot by blowing

blow·hard /blṓ haard/ *n.* somebody who boasts but is considered ineffectual [Mid-19thC. "*Blow*" from BLOW, in the sense "to boast."]

blow·hole /blṓ hōl/ *n.* **1.** MARINE BIOL **NOSTRIL OF WHALE OR SIMILAR MAMMAL** a nostril in the top of the head of a whale, dolphin, or similar sea mammal that allows the exchange of air from the lungs **2.** MARINE BIOL **BREATHING HOLE IN ICE** a hole in ice where aquatic mammals come to the surface to breathe **3.** CIV ENG **AIR VENT** a vent to permit the escape of air or gas from a tunnel or passage **4.** METALL **BUBBLE IN INGOT** a gas pocket formed in a metal as it solidifies

blow job *n.* the act of fellatio (*slang offensive*)

blow·lamp /blṓ lamp/ *n. U.K.* = **blowtorch**

blown[1] /blōn/ *adj.* **1. SWOLLEN** swollen or inflated **2.** = **flyblown 3. OUT OF BREATH** out of breath and panting **4.**

MADE BY BLOWING made or shaped by blowing ○ *blown glass*

blown[2] past participle of **blow**[1]

blow·off /blṓ of/ *n.* TECH, INDUST **1.** DISCHARGE OF SURPLUS STEAM a discharge of surplus gas or fluid under pressure **2.** VENT FOR GAS OR LIQUID a device through which surplus gas or liquid under pressure is released

blow·out /blṓ owt/ *n.* **1.** TIRE PUNCTURE a sudden puncture of a tire **2.** GUSH OF OIL OR GAS a sudden rush of oil or gas from an oil well to the surface **3.** BIG PARTY a big party with ample food and drink (*slang*)

blow·pipe /blṓ pīp/ *n.* **1.** ARMS = **blowgun 2.** CHEM TUBE FOR CONCENTRATING HEAT a small tube that leads a jet of air into a flame to increase its heat **3.** CRAFT GLASSBLOWER'S TUBE a long narrow iron tube used in glassblowing to shape molten glass

blow·sy *adj.* = **blowzy**

blow·torch /blṓ tawrch/ *n.* a small, usually portable, gas burner that intensifies the heat of its flame by a blast of air or oxygen

blow·up /blṓ up/ *n.* **1.** PHOTOGRAPHY PHOTOGRAPHIC ENLARGEMENT an enlargement of a photograph or picture **2.** OUTBURST OF TEMPER a sudden outburst of temper (*informal*) **3.** EXPLOSION an explosion caused by a bomb or similar device **4.** CINEMA, PHOTOGRAPHY EXPANDED FILM a motion picture on a larger gauge of film that has been expanded in size from a smaller gauge, e.g., from 16 mm to 35 mm

blow·y /blṓ ee/ (**-i·er, -i·est**) *adj.* windy or breezy (*informal*)

blow·zy /blówzee/ (**-zi·er, -zi·est**), **blow·sy** (**-si·er, -si·est**) *adj.* **1.** RED-FACED with a reddish face and coarse complexion (*disapproving*) **2.** SLOVENLY slovenly and careless in appearance [Early 17thC. Formed from obsolete *blowze* "wench."] —**blow·zi·ly** *adv.* —**blow·zi·ness** *n.*

BLS *abbr.* Bureau of Labor Statistics

BLT (*plural* **BLTs** *or* **BLT's**) *n.* a sandwich with a filling of bacon, lettuce, and tomato

blub·ber /blúbbər/ *v.* (**-bered, -ber·ing, -bers**) (*informal*) **1.** *vi.* SOB LOUDLY to sob in a loud and unattractive manner **2.** *vt.* SAY WHILE SOBBING to say something while blubbering ■ *n.* **1.** FAT OF MARINE MAMMALS the insulating fat of whales and other large sea mammals, used as a source of oil and food **2.** UNSIGHTLY FAT unsightly body fat (*informal*) [14thC. Origin uncertain: perhaps an imitation of the sound of bubbling water. "Fat" may come from the sense "fish's entrails," from their bubbling appearance when ripped open.] —**blub·ber·er** *n.* —**blub·ber·y** *adj.*

bludg·eon /blújjən/ *n.* SHORT CLUB a short stout club used as a weapon ■ *vt.* (**-eoned, -eon·ing, -eons**) **1.** HIT WITH HEAVY OBJECT to hit somebody repeatedly with a heavy object ○ *bludgeoned to death* **2.** COERCE OR BULLY to coerce or bully somebody into doing something [Mid-18thC. Origin unknown.] —**bludg·eon·er** *n.*

blue /bloo/ *adj.* (**blu·er, blu·est**) **1.** OF THE COLOR OF THE SKY having the color of the sky on a cloudless day, or any similar shade **2.** SLIGHTLY PURPLE IN SKIN COLOR with the skin appearing slightly purple because of cold, bruising, or exertion **3.** BIOL BLUISH used to describe animals and plants that are bluish or blue-gray in color ○ *a blue whale* ○ *a blue spruce* **4.** DEPRESSED depressed, or accompanied by feelings of depression (*informal*) ○ *feeling blue* ○ *a blue day* **5.** EXPLICIT depicting or referring to sex in an explicit or offensive way (*informal*) **6.** PURITANICAL rigidly conservative in moral and social views (*dated*) ■ *n.* **1.** COLOR OF THE SKY the color of the sky on a cloudless day. Blue lies toward one end of the visible spectrum and is one of the three primary colors of light and pigment. **2.** BLUE PIGMENT a blue dye or pigment **3.** THE DISTANCE the far distance (*informal*) ○ *disappeared off into the blue* **4.** ARCHERY BLUE RING ON TARGET the blue ring on the target in archery **5. blue, Blue** MEMBER OF UNION ARMY a member of the Union Army in the Civil War. ◊ **gray**[1] *n.* 4 **6. blue, Blue** UNION ARMY the Union Army in the Civil War. ◊ **gray**[1] *n.* 5 **7.** ZOOL SMALL-WINGED BLUE BUTTERFLY a common blue small-winged butterfly. Subfamily: Plebeiinae. ■ *v.* (**blued, blue·ing** *or* **blu·ing, blues**) **1.** *vti.* MAKE OR BECOME BLUE to make something blue or to become blue **2.** *vt.* TREAT WITH BLUING to treat something with bluing [13thC. From Old French *bleu*. Ultimately from an Indo-European word whose meaning evolved from "yellow" via "white" and "pale" to "livid, the color of bruised skin." In the sense "to squander" perhaps an alteration of BLOW.] —**blue·ness** *n.* ◇ **out of the blue** unexpectedly ○ *The offer came out of the blue.*

blue ba·by *n.* a baby born with a bluish skin color (**cyanosis**) as a result of a congenital heart defect that causes the mixing of venous and arterial blood

blue·beard /bloŏ beerd/, **Blue·beard** *n.* a man who marries and then kills successive wives [Early 19thC. Named for *Blue Beard*, a translation of French *Barbe Bleue*, a character in a story by Charles Perrault (1628–1703).]

Bluebell

blue·bell /bloŏ bel/ *n.* **1.** EUROPEAN WOODLAND PLANT a woodland plant of the lily family that has long thin leaves and small blue bell-shaped flowers. Genus: *Endymion.* **2.** = **harebell 3.** PLANT OF EASTERN N AMERICA a plant of the borage family, native to eastern North America, that has showy blue flowers. Genus: *Mertenia.*

blue·ber·ry /bloŏ berree/ (*plural* **-ries**) *n.* **1.** SHRUB WITH EDIBLE BERRIES a shrub of the heath family that has tubular flowers and bears small edible bluish black berries. Genus: *Vaccinium.* **2.** BERRY the edible dark blue berry of the blueberry plant, popular in pies and muffins

blue·bill /bloŏ bil/ *n.* **1.** = **scaup 2.** HEAVY-BILLED BIRD any African waxbill with a heavy metallic blue bill. Genus: *Spermophaga.*

blue·bird /bloŏ burd/ *n.* **1.** N AMERICAN SONGBIRD a North American thrush that has bright blue plumage with a bluish or reddish-brown breast. Genus: *Sialia.* **2.** BLUE BIRD any bird with blue feathers

blue-black *adj.* black tinged with blue or with a blue sheen when caught by the light —**blue-black** *n.*

blue blood, **blue·blood** *n.* **1.** NOBLE DESCENT the quality of being royal or aristocratic by birth **2.** ARISTOCRAT an aristocrat, or a noble, or a person born into a respectable and very wealthy family —**blue-blood·ed** *adj.*

blue·bon·net /bloŏ bonnət/ *n.* **1.** PLANT WITH SPIKES OF BLUE FLOWERS either of two low-growing lupines, native to Texas, with spikes of light blue flowers. Latin name: *Lupinus texensis* and *Lupinus subcarnosus.* **2.** SCOTTISH WOOLEN CAP a wide round flat cap of blue wool, formerly worn in Scotland

blue book *n.* **1.** U.S. SCHOOL EXAM BOOK a thin blank notebook with blue covers, used in schools for writing examination answers **2.** GOVERNMENT REPORT an official government report bound in a blue cover, especially one published by the British or Canadian government

blue·bot·tle /bloŏ bott'l/ *n.* **1.** INSECTS LARGE BUZZING FLY a large buzzing blowfly with an iridescent blue body that lays its eggs in decaying plant and animal material. Genus: *Calliphora.* **2.** PLANTS BLUE-FLOWERED PLANT a blue-flowered plant, especially the cornflower or grape hyacinth

blue cat *n.* a large bluish freshwater catfish of the Mississippi valley that is a popular food and game fish. It may grow to over 100 lbs/450 kg. Latin name: *Ictalurus furcatus.*

blue cheese *n.* any whitish cheese with veins of blue mold

blue chip *n.* **1.** STOCK EXCH VALUABLE STOCK IN RELIABLE COMPANY a stock selling for a high price because it belongs to a company that is considered to be well-established, highly successful, and reliable **2.** BUSINESS VALUABLE ASSET OR COMPANY an extremely valuable asset, especially a well-established, reliable, and successful company **3.** GAMBLING POKER CHIP a blue-colored gambling chip of high value —**blue-chip** *adj.*

blue-chip·per *n.* BUSINESS a blue-chip company

blue·coat /bloŏ kōt/ *n.* somebody who wears a blue coat, especially a police officer (*archaic*)

blue co·hosh *n.* a North American perennial plant of the barberry family with large blue berries. The root is sometimes used to induce labor in childbirth. Latin name: *Caulophyllum thalictroides.*

blue-col·lar *adj.* relating to, typical of, or belonging to workers who do manual or industrial work, and who often require work clothes or protective clothing. ◊ **white-collar, pink-collar** [Mid-20thC. From the clothing typically worn by such workers.] —**blue-col·lar** *n.*

blue crab *n.* an edible bluish crab found on the Atlantic and Gulf coasts of North America. Latin name: *Callinectes sapidus.*

blue·curls /bloŏ kùrlz/ *n.* a North American plant of the mint family that has curled blue stamens in blue flowers. Genus: *Trichostema.* (*takes a singular or plural verb*)

blue dev·il *n.* BARBITURATE CAPSULE a capsule containing the barbiturate amobarbital (*slang*) ■ **blue dev·ils** *npl.* DEPRESSION depression or low spirits (*dated slang*)

blue-eyed boy *n. U.K.* = **fair-haired boy** (*informal*)

blue-eyed Mar·y *n.* a North American plant of the snapdragon family that has blue and white flowers. Latin name: *Collinsia verna.*

blue·fin /bloŏ fin/, **blue·fin tu·na** *n.* a large tuna that lives in temperate seas and is caught for sport and food. Latin name: *Thunnus thynnus.*

blue·fish /bloŏ fish/ (*plural* **-fish** *or* **-fish·es**) *n.* **1.** BLUISH SEA FISH a bluish fish with a silver underside, caught for sport and food in temperate and tropical regions of the Atlantic and Indian oceans. Latin name: *Pomatomus saltatrix.* **2.** ANY BLUISH FISH any fish with bluish coloring

blue flag *n.* any North American iris with large blue-violet flowers. The root of one variety has been used medicinally as a purgative, emetic, and liver stimulant. Latin name: *Iris versicolor.*

blue fox *n.* **1.** ARCTIC FOX an Arctic fox with a tawny-brown coat that turns pale blue-gray in winter. Latin name: *Alopex lagopus.* **2.** BLUE FOX FUR the fur of a blue fox

blue funk *n.* a state of depression (*dated informal*)

blue·gill /bloŏ gil/ (*plural* **-gills** *or* **-gill**) *n.* a freshwater sunfish common in eastern and central North America. Latin name: *Lepomis macrochirus.*

blue·grass /bloŏ gràss/ *n.* **1.** MUSIC STYLE OF COUNTRY MUSIC a style of country music from the southern United States, usually played on fiddle, banjo, guitar, and mandolin and featuring close harmony and instrumental solos (*often used before a noun*) **2.** BOT BLUE-GREEN GRASS a blue-green grass found in North America and Europe, used for fodder and as a lawn grass. Kentucky bluegrass is one species of bluegrass. Genus: *Poa.* [Mid-18thC. Originally referring to a species of grass indigenous to Kentucky and Virginia, the word came to refer to the folk music associated with these areas.]

Blue·grass State *n.* the state of Kentucky (*informal*)

blue-green al·gae *npl.* BIOL = **cyanobacteria**

blue grouse *n.* a species of grouse that lives in western North America and produces a deep booming sound from air sacs on its neck. The male has gray-blue plumage. Latin name: *Dendragapus obscurus.* (*regional*)

WORD KEY: REGIONAL NOTE

The term ***blue grouse*** occurs in the Pacific Northwest, especially in Oregon.

blue gum *n.* **1.** HARD-TIMBERED AUSTRALIAN EUCALYPTUS a tall Australian eucalyptus tree, native to Tasmania, with hard timber and aromatic leaves from which a medicinal oil is extracted. Latin name: *Eucalyptus globulus.* **2.** AUSTRALIAN EUCALYPTUS an Australian eucalyptus tree that has smooth blue-gray bark. Genus: *Eucalyptus.*

blue heav·en *n.* = **blue devil** (*slang*)

blue her·on *n.* a North American heron with bluish gray plumage, such as the great blue heron

blue·ing *n.* = **bluing**

blue·ish *adj.* = **bluish**

blue·jack·et /blóo jàkət/ *n.* an enlisted man in the navy (*slang*)

blue jay *n.* a North American bird that belongs to the jay family and has blue plumage, a crested head, and a white underside. Latin name: *Cyanocitta cristata.*

blue jeans *npl.* a pair of jeans made of blue denim

blue law *n.* **1. MORAL LAW** a law regulating moral conduct, e.g., a law prohibiting the sale of alcohol on Sundays **2. OLD LAW GOVERNING MORAL CONDUCT** a law intended to govern moral conduct in colonial New England [*Blue* in the sense of "puritanical"]

blue line *n.* either of two blue lines that divide an ice hockey rink into the defensive, neutral, and offensive zones

blue moon *n.* **1. LONG TIME** a long period of time (*informal*) ○ *once in a blue moon* **2. 2ND FULL MOON IN A MONTH** a second full moon in a calendar month. As there is a full moon every 29.5 days, a blue moon is a comparatively rare event. [From the notion of the moon appearing blue, a rare if not unheard of event. Sense 2 from the rarity of the phenomenon.]

Blue Moun·tains plateau region about 47 mi./65 km west of Sydney, Australia, part of the Great Dividing Range. Its highest point is Bird Rock, 3,871 ft./1,134 m. Area: 540 sq. mi./1,400 sq. km.

Blue Nile /-nīl/ river in northeastern Africa that rises in Ethiopia and supplies about 70 percent of the water that reaches Khartoum, where it joins the White Nile to form the Nile proper. Length: 850 mi./1,370 km.

blue·nose /blóo nōz/ *n.* somebody who is excessively concerned with morals (*dated informal*) [In the sense "puritanical person," compare BLUE LAW]

blue note *n.* a musical note played or sung slightly lower than usual, especially in blues and jazz

blue-pen·cil (**blue-pen·ciled** *or* **blue-pen·cilled, blue-pen·cil·ing** *or* **blue-pen·cil·ling, blue-pen·cils**) *vt.* to edit a piece of writing by marking it, in order to shorten, censor, or delete it [From the use of a blue pencil in the editing process]

Blue Pe·ter *n.* a blue flag with a white square in the middle, used by ships to signal that they are ready to sail [*Peter* from *Peter*, personal name, from the fact that the pattern on the flag represents the letter P in the International Code of Symbols]

blue-plate *adj.* used to describe a main course offered by a restaurant at a lower price than usual ○ *We had the blue-plate special.* [Origin uncertain: probably from the fact that specially priced meals were often served on cheap, blue-patterned plates]

blue·point /blóo pòynt/ (*plural* **-point** *or* **-points**) *n.* a small oyster of the northeastern coastal waters of the United States, usually eaten raw. Latin name: *Crassostrea virginica.* [Late 18thC. Named for *Blue Point*, Long Island, because many of the oysters are from the oyster beds near there.]

blue point *n.* a domestic cat, especially a Siamese, that has a bluish-cream coat and dark gray markings on its extremities (**points**). ◊ **seal point**

blue·print /blóo prìnt/ *n.* **1. PRINT OF PLAN** a photographic print of a technical drawing with white lines printed on a blue background, usually used as a reference before and during the building process **2. PLAN OR GUIDE** a plan of action, or something already done that can be used as a guide to doing something in the future ○ *His administration's policies became a blueprint for those that followed.* ■ *vt.* (**-print·ed, -print·ing, -prints**) **1. MAKE BLUEPRINT OF** to make a blueprint of something, especially a technical drawing **2. MAKE PLAN FOR** to make or be a plan for something

blue rac·er *n.* a blue-green subspecies of the blacksnake that is found in the United States from Michigan to Texas. Latin name: *Coluber constrictor flaviventris.*

blue rib·and *n. U.K.* = **blue ribbon**

blue rib·bon *n.* **1. BADGE MADE OF BLUE RIBBON** an emblem or badge made of blue ribbon and awarded for first prize in a competition **2. HIGHEST DISTINCTION** the highest distinction or first prize in a particular field —**blue-rib·bon** *adj.*

blue-rib·bon ju·ry (*plural* **blue-rib·bon ju·ries**) *n.* a jury of well-educated people chosen by the court for a case involving issues that are difficult to follow

Blue Ridge, Blue Ridge Moun·tains mountain range in the United States, extending from northern Georgia across western North Carolina and into West Virginia. It is the easternmost range of the Appalachian Mountains, with its highest point at Mount Mitchell 6,684 ft./2,037 m.

blue run·ner *n.* ZOOL = **runner** *n.* **16**

blues /blooz/ *n.* (*plural* **blues**) MUSIC **PIECE OF MUSIC** a song or instrumental piece of music in the style of a type of popular music that developed from Black American folk songs in the early 20th century, consisting mainly of slow sad songs often performed over a repeating harmonic pattern (*takes a singular or plural verb*) ■ *npl.* **FEELING OF SADNESS** a feeling of unhappiness or low spirits (*informal*) [Mid-18thC. From BLUE DEVILS.]

blue shark *n.* a shark that has a dark blue back and white underside and lives in tropical and temperate seas. Latin name: *Prionace glauca.*

blue sheep *n.* = **bharal**

blue·shift /blóo shìft/ *n.* a displacement in the wavelengths of spectral lines toward the blue end of the visible spectrum, indicating that the radiation source and observer are approaching each other. ◊ **Doppler effect, redshift**

blue-sky *adj.* (*informal*) **1. CREATIVE OR IMPRACTICAL** idealistic or visionary and not practical **2. THEORETICAL** purely theoretical and having no concrete goal **3. CHEAP OR WORTHLESS** not worth very much money ○ *blue-sky stocks* —**blue-sky** *vi.*

blue-sky law *n.* a state law regulating the sale of securities, designed to protect investors from being sold stocks or bonds with no real value

blues·man /blóozmən/ (*plural* **-men** /-mən/) *n.* somebody who plays or sings the blues

Blue Springs city in western Missouri, southeast of Independence and Kansas City. Population: 44,667 (1996).

blue spruce *n.* a common North American evergreen tree of the Rocky Mountains with short sharp blue-gray needles. Latin name: *Picea pungens.*

blue·stem /blóo stèm/ *n.* a North American grass that has smooth bluish leaf sheaths and slender spikes in pairs or clusters, used for hay in the western United States. Big bluestem and little bluestem are two different species. Latin name: *Andropogon gerardii* and *Schizachyrium scoparium.*

blue·stock·ing /blóo stòking/ *n.* a woman who is highly educated or has scholarly or literary interests (*offensive*)

WORD KEY: ORIGIN

At the literary gatherings held at the houses of fashionable mid-18th-century hostesses, it became the custom to wear casual rather than full formal dress. In the case of gentlemen's stockings, this meant gray worsted (conventionally called "blue" at that time) rather than black silk. This lack of decorum was disapproved of in some quarters, and one Admiral Boscowan dubbed the participants the "Blue Stocking Society." Women who attended their highbrow meetings thus became known as "Blue Stocking Ladies" (even though it was men who had originally worn the stockings).

blue·stone /blóo stōn/ *n.* BUILDING a blue-gray sandstone used in the construction industry or for paving, especially a sandstone quarried from near the Hudson River in North America

blue streak *n.* a fast-moving person or thing (*informal humorous*) ◇ **talk a blue streak** to talk very quickly and without pausing (*informal*)

blues·y /blóozee/ (**blue·si·er, blue·si·est**) *adj.* composed or performed in or like the style of the blues (*informal*) ○ *a bluesy ballad*

blue·tongue /blóo tùng/ (*plural* **-tongues** *or* **-tongue**) *n.* a viral disease of sheep, goats, and cattle transmitted by biting insects, especially mosquitoes, that involves fever, inflammation, ulceration, and death of tissue around the mouth and tongue

blu·ets /blóo əts/ (*plural* **-ets**) *n.* a North American plant of the madder family with small, pale blue to white, four-petaled flowers with yellow centers. Genus: *Hedyotis.* (*takes a singular or plural verb*) [Early 18thC. Plural of *bluet*, from French *bl(e)uet*, literally "small blue," from *bleu* "blue" (see BLUE).]

blue vit·ri·ol *n.* copper sulfate (*archaic*)

blue wa·ter *n.* the ocean far away from the shore (*literary*)

blue-water *adj.* operating on or traveling over the oceans ○ *a blue-water sailor*

blue·weed /blóo wèed/ (*plural* **-weeds** *or* **-weed**) *n.* **1.** = **viper's bugloss 2. SUNFLOWER WITH BLUE-GRAY LEAVES** a weedy sunflower plant with blue-gray leaves that grows in the southwestern United States. Latin name: *Helianthus ciliaris.*

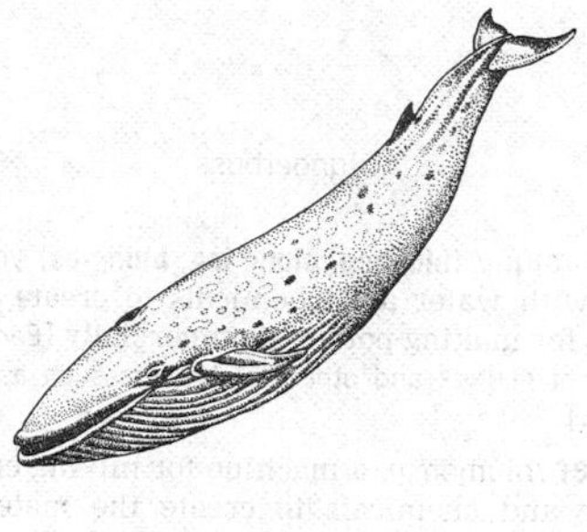

Blue whale

blue whale (*plural* **blue whales** *or* **blue whale**) *n.* a slate-blue whale with grooves along the throat that migrates between polar and equatorial seas. It is the world's largest living animal. Latin name: *Balaenoptera musculus.*

bluff[1] /bluf/ *v.* (**bluffed, bluff·ing, bluffs**) **1.** *vti.* **PRETEND TO BE CONFIDENT** to pretend to have strength, confidence, or the intention of doing something, in order to deceive somebody **2.** *vti.* CARDS **DECEIVE PLAYERS ABOUT CARDS** to try to deceive other players in a card game about the true value of your hand **3.** *vt. Malaysia, Singapore* **DECEIVE SOMEBODY IN MINOR WAY** to try to mislead somebody about something relatively unimportant (*informal*) ■ *n.* **1. FEIGNED CONFIDENCE** a pretense of strength, confidence, or of the intention of doing something **2. SOMEBODY WHO BLUFFS** somebody who pretends to be stronger or more confident than he or she really is [Late 17thC. From Dutch *bluffen* "to brag" or *bluf* "bragging."] —**bluff·a·ble** *adj.* —**bluff·er** *n.*

bluff[2] /bluf/ *n.* **CLIFF WITH BROAD FACE** a high steep bank, cliff, or headland, especially one with a broad face ■ *adj.* **1. STEEP AND BROAD** having a broad, flattened, or rounded steep front **2. BLUNT BUT KIND IN MANNER** cheerful and friendly but outspoken and often insensitive to others' feelings [Early 17thC. From Dutch *blaf* "flat."] —**bluff·ly** *adv.* —**bluff·ness** *n.*

blu·ing /blóo ing/, **blue·ing** *n.* a substance used in laundering to prevent white materials from turning yellow

blu·ish /blóo ish/, **blue·ish** *adj.* of a color that is near to blue or contains some blue

Blum·berg, Baruch S. (*b.* 1925) U.S. biochemist His reasearch led to the development of a vaccine against hepatitis B and won him a shared Nobel Prize in physiology or medicine (1976). Full name **Baruch Samuel Blumberg**

Blume /bloom/, **Judy** (*b.* 1938) U.S. writer. Her fiction for young people dealt openly with contemporary issues such as divorce and attracted a large readership.

blun·der /blúndər/ *n.* **STUPID MISTAKE** a serious or embarrassing mistake, usually the result of carelessness or ignorance ■ *v.* (**-dered, -der·ing, -ders**) **1.** *vi.* **MAKE A SERIOUS MISTAKE** to make a serious or embarrassing mistake as a result of carelessness or ignorance **2.** *vi.* **MOVE CLUMSILY** to stumble or move clumsily **3.** *vti.* **ACT IN A CONFUSED WAY** to act in a manner that is clumsy, ignorant, or thoughtless **4.** *vti.* **SPEAK IN CLUMSY MANNER** to say or write something in a clumsy or thoughtless way [14thC. Via a Scandinavian language from, ultimately, an Indo-European base that is also the ancestor of English *blind.*] —**blun·der·er** *n.* —**blun·der·ing·ly** *adv.*

WORD KEY: SYNONYMS

See Synonyms at ***mistake.***

blun·der·buss /blúndər bùss/ *n.* **1. WIDE-MOUTHED GUN** a short, wide-muzzled firearm of the 17th century, used to fire shot with a scattering effect at close range **2. BLUNDERING PERSON** somebody who behaves or speaks clumsily (*informal*) [Mid-17thC. Alteration of Dutch *donderbus*, from *donder* "thunder" + *bus* "gun."]

Blunderbuss

blunge /blunj/ (**blunged, blung·ing, blung·es**) *vt.* to mix clay with water and chemicals to create the material for making pottery commercially [Early 19thC. Blend of PLUNGE and other "bl-" words such as BLOW or BLEND.]

blung·er /blúnjər/ *n.* a machine for mixing clay with water and chemicals to create the material for making pottery commercially

blunt /blunt/ *adj.* **1. NOT SHARP** having a cutting edge or point that is not sharp **2. FRANK OR HONEST WITHOUT SENSITIVITY** very frank or straightforward and showing no delicacy or consideration ■ *v.* (**blunt·ed, blunt·ing, blunts**) **1.** *vti.* **MAKE SOMETHING LESS SHARP** to make the point or cutting edge of something dull rather than sharp **2.** *vt.* **LESSEN OR WEAKEN** to make something such as a sense or an emotion less effective or less intense [13thC. Origin uncertain: possibly from Old Norse *blundr* "dozing." Ultimately from the same Indo-European base that is the ancestor of English *blind* and *blunder.*] —**blunt·ly** *adv.* —**blunt·ness** *n.*

blur /blur/ *n.* **1. FUZZY OR INDISTINCT IMAGE** something that cannot be seen clearly, e.g., because it moves too quickly or because it is not distinctly remembered **2. SMEAR OR SMEARED AREA** a mark on something that makes it unclear, or an area of something that is unclear ■ *vti.* (**blurred, blur·ring, blurs**) **1. MAKE OR BECOME VAGUE** to become less clear or distinct, or to make something such as an idea less clear or distinct **2. MAKE OR BECOME FUZZY** to become fuzzy or unclear, or to make something such as somebody's vision or an image on paper fuzzy or unclear ■ *adj.* *Malaysia, Singapore* **CONFUSED** confused or uncertain about something (*informal*) ○ *I am very blur about linguistics.* [Mid-16thC. Probably a variant of BLEAR.] —**blur·ri·ness** *n.* —**blur·ry** *adj.*

blurb /blurb/ *n.* a short piece of writing that praises and promotes something, especially a paragraph on the cover of a book (*slang*) [Early 20thC. A slang term coined by Gelett Burgess, a U.S. humorist.] —**blurb** *vt.*

blurt /blurt/ (**blurt·ed, blurt·ing, blurts**) *vti.* to say something suddenly or impulsively, as if by accident ○ *blurted out an apology* [Late 16thC. Probably an imitation of the sound of letting out breath suddenly, modeled on BLOW and SQUIRT.]

blush /blush/ *vi.* (**blushed, blush·ing, blush·es**) **1. BECOME RED IN FACE** to turn red in the face because of emotion, especially embarrassment, shame, modesty, or pleasure **2. BECOME EMBARRASSED** to feel embarrassed or ashamed (*formal*) **3. TURN RED OR PINK** to become red or pink (*literary*) ■ *n.* **1. REDDENING OF FACE** a reddening of the face caused by emotion, especially embarrassment, shame, modesty, or pleasure **2. RED OR PINK** a red color or rosy glow **3.** COSMETICS **PINK MAKEUP FOR CHEEKS** a pink or reddish powder or cream applied to the face, especially to accent the cheekbones [Old English *blyscan.* Ultimately from an Indo-European base that is also the ancestor of English *flame, blaze,* and *blue.*] —**blush·ful** *adj.* —**blush·ing** *adj.* —**blush·ing·ly** *adv.*

blush·er /blúshər/ *n.* = **blush**

blush wine *n.* wine with a slight pink tinge

blus·ter /blústər/ *v.* (**-tered, -ter·ing, -ters**) **1.** *vti.* **SPEAK OR UTTER LOUDLY OR ARROGANTLY** to speak loudly, boisterously, or arrogantly, or to say something in this way **2.** *vti.* **BEHAVE IN BULLYING WAY** to behave or do something in a bullying or threatening way **3.** *vi.* **BLOW LOUDLY IN GUSTS** to blow in loud gusts (*refers to wind*) ■ *n.* **1. LOUD BULLYING OR BRAGGING SPEECH** loud arrogant or threatening speech or behavior **2. SUDDEN LOUD GUST OF WIND** a loud gust of wind **3. LOUD FUSS** a loud or angry commotion [Early 15thC. From Middle Low German *blustern* "to blow violently."] —**blus·ter·er** *n.* —**blus·ter·ing·ly** *adv.* —**blus·ter·y** *adj.*

Blvd. *abbr.* Boulevard

Bly /blī/, **Nellie** (1867–1922) U.S. journalist. She used her platform as a *New York World* journalist to campaign for social issues, and gained notoriety for her 72-day round-the-world trip (1889–90). Pseudonym of **Elizabeth Cochrane Seaman.** Born **Elizabeth Cochrane**

Blythe·ville /blīth vìl/ city in northeastern Arkansas, south of the Missouri border and west of the Mississippi River. Population: 18,743 (1996).

b.m. *abbr.* **1.** board measure **2.** bowel movement

BMEWS *abbr.* ballistic missile early warning system

BMI *abbr.* body mass index

B.M.O.C. *n.* a student whom others respect or who holds an important position in a student organization. Full form **big man on campus**

B mov·ie *n.* a low-budget movie that was formerly shown in addition to the main feature [*B* from its lesser importance than the main feature] —**B-mov·ie** *adj.*

bmp, BMP *suffix.* used after the period in a DOS-based computer file to show that the file is an image stored as a series of pixels

B.Mus. *abbr.* Bachelor of Music

BMX *n.* the riding of bicycles over rough terrain and open country or a racing course. Full form **bicycle motocross** [Representing an abbreviation of *bicycle motocross*]

bn. *abbr.* **1.** billion **2. bn., Bn.** battalion

Bn. *abbr.* **1.** baron **2.** battalion

B'nai B'rith /bə này bríth/ *n.* an international Jewish social service organization founded in New York in 1843 [From Hebrew, "Sons of the Covenant"]

BO *n.* an unpleasant smell that comes from a person because of sweat, lack of hygiene, or physical disorder (*informal*) Full form **body odor**

b.o. *abbr.* **1.** branch office **2.** broker's order **3.** FIN buyer's option

B/O *abbr.* ACCT brought over

bo·a /bṓ ə/ *n.* **1. TROPICAL SNAKE THAT SQUEEZES PREY** a nonvenomous, often large, snake that kills by winding its body around its prey and crushing it. Family: Boidae. **2. LONG FLUFFY SCARF** a long fluffy scarf of feathers or fur worn by women around the neck [14thC. From Latin "large water snake."]

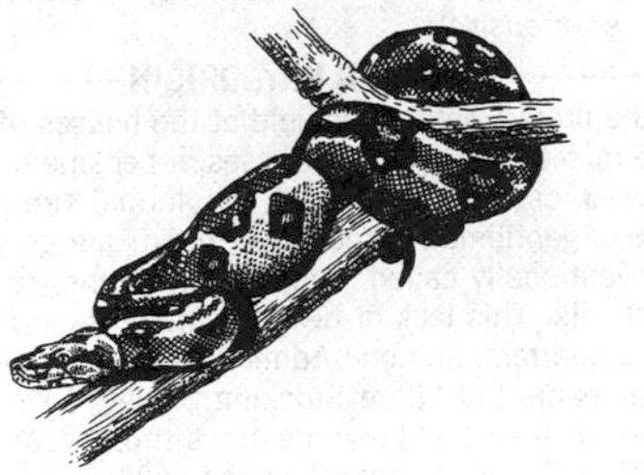

Boa constrictor

bo·a con·stric·tor *n.* a large snake of the boa family that lives in tropical America and the West Indies and kills by winding its body around its prey and crushing it. Latin name: *Boa constrictor.*

boar /bawr, bōr/ (*plural* **boars** *or* **boar**) *n.* **1. UNCASTRATED HOG** a male hog that has not been castrated **2. MALE MAMMAL** a male mammal, e.g., a male badger, beaver, or raccoon **3. WILD BOAR** a wild boar [Old English *bār*]

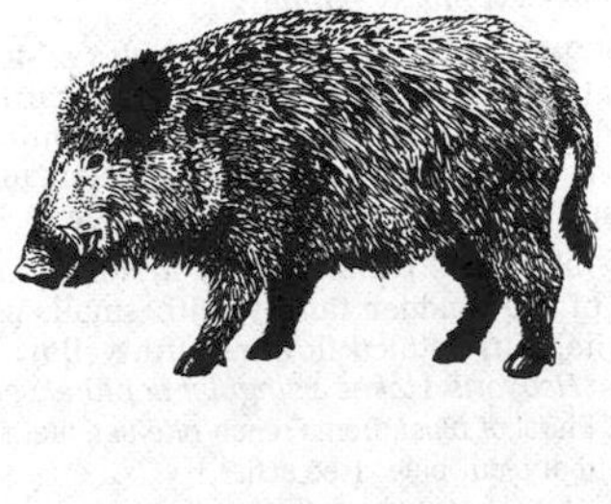

Boar

board /bawrd, bōrd/ *n.* **1. FLAT PIECE OF WOOD** a piece of wood cut into a flat rectangular shape, especially a long and narrow piece used for building **2. FLAT SURFACE FOR PARTICULAR PURPOSE** a flat piece of wood, plastic, or other rigid material, used for a particular purpose, e.g., chopping food **3.** BOARD GAMES **FLAT SURFACE FOR GAME** a flat surface on which a game is played, especially a piece of wood or cardboard marked with colored areas for a particular game such as chess **4. COMPOSITE MATERIAL PRESSED INTO A SHEET** a rigid sheet material made by compressing layers of other materials, e.g., plywood **5. CONTROL PANEL** a panel on which the controls of a piece of electrical equipment are mounted **6.** EDUC = **chalkboard 7. NOTICE BOARD** a notice board **8.** NAUT **SHIP'S SIDE** the side of a ship **9.** ELEC ENG **CIRCUIT BOARD** a printed circuit board **10.** SWIMMING = **diving board 11.** SPORTS = **surfboard 12.** SPORTS = **scoreboard 13.** SPORTS **SNOWBOARD** a snowboard **14.** BASKETBALL = **backboard** *n.* 1 **15.** PUBL **BOOK COVER** either of the pair of pieces of stiff cardboard that together form the front and back covers of a book **16. GROUP CHOSEN TO MAKE DECISIONS** a group of people chosen to make executive or managerial decisions for an organization **17. DAILY MEALS** daily meals provided at the place where somebody lives, usually for money or in return for work **18. TABLE WITH FOOD** a table used for meals, especially one spread with food (*archaic*) **19.** SAILING **DISTANCE SAILED INTO WIND** the distance covered by a sailing vessel in one period of sailing as near as possible into the wind ■ **boards** *npl.* SPORTS **ICE HOCKEY RINK ENCLOSURE** the wooden wall that surrounds an ice hockey rink ■ *v.* (**board·ed, board·ing, boards**) **1.** *vti.* **GET ONTO VEHICLE AS PASSENGER** to get onto a vehicle, especially a ship, train, or aircraft, as a passenger **2.** *vti.* **TAKE PASSENGERS ON FOR JOURNEY** to take passengers onto a ship, plane, or other vehicle ○ *This flight is now boarding.* **3.** *vt.* NAUT **ATTACK OR INSPECT SHIP** to come alongside of a ship in order for people to go from one ship to another for the purposes of attack or inspection **4.** *vti.* **COVER SOMETHING WITH BOARDS** to attach boards to something, especially to cover any openings **5.** *vti.* **BE PROVIDED WITH ROOM AND MEALS** to be provided with accommodations and meals, e.g., in a school or guest house, in return for money or work, or to arrange for this to happen [Old English *bord,* from two related prehistoric Germanic words with the meanings "board, plank" and "border, ship's side"] ◇ **bring** *or* **get** *or* **take somebody on board** to bring or accept somebody, e.g., a new employee, into an existing group or project (*informal*) ◇ **go by the board** to be neglected, no longer used, cast aside, or destroyed ◇ **take something on board** to understand or realize something fully

board bridge *n.* BOARD GAMES = **duplicate bridge**

board cer·ti·fi·ca·tion *n.* official and documented recognition from an official panel of experts in a particular field, e.g., medicine, that somebody is highly qualified in that field

board-cer·ti·fied *adj.* officially certified as expert in a particular field after passing an exam and meeting strict standards

board·er /báwrdər, bórdər/ *n.* **1. SOMEBODY PAYING FOR FOOD AND BED** somebody who pays for a room, and usually for daily meals, in a private home or a boarding house **2.** NAUT **SOMEBODY TRYING TO CAPTURE SHIP** somebody who attempts to get onto a ship in order to capture or inspect it

board foot (*plural* **board feet**) *n.* a unit of volume for measuring lumber, equal to the volume of a board that is one foot square and one inch thick

board game *n.* a game that involves moving pieces around on a board marked with colored areas for a particular game, e.g., chess or backgammon

board·ing house /báwrding-, bṓrding-/ *n.* a private home that provides a room and meals to paying guests who are usually long-term residents. ◊ **bed and breakfast**

board·ing pass *n.* an additional ticket, or part of a ticket, that somebody must have in order to be allowed onto an aircraft or ship as a passenger

board·ing school *n.* a school that provides some or all students with a place to live and daily meals

board meas·ure *n.* a system for measuring lumber volume based on the board foot

board of ed·u·ca·tion *n.* a group of people elected or appointed in each county or local school system in the United States to make decisions about education in public schools

board of trade *n.* an organization of business and banks that have the goal of promoting commercial interest in a state, city, or other area

board·room /báwrd ro͝om, -ro͞om, bőrd ro͝om, -ro͞om/ *n.* a room where the members of a board meet

board·sail·ing /báwrd sàyling, bőrd-/ *n.* = **windsurfing** —**board·sail·or** *n.*

board·walk /báwrd wàwk, bőrd-/ *n.* a raised walkway made of boards, often built along beaches at beach resorts

boar·ish /báwrish, bőrish/ *adj.* brutal or crude ○ *boarish behavior* —**boar·ish·ly** *adv.* —**boar·ish·ness** *n.*

Bo·as /bő àz/, **Franz** (1858–1942) German-born U.S. anthropologist. He helped establish anthropology as an academic discipline. He advocated a scientific approach to anthropological investigation and supported the theory of cultural relativism.

boast[1] /bōst/ *v.* (**boast·ed, boast·ing, boasts**) **1.** *vti.* SPEAK PROUDLY ABOUT POSSESSIONS OR ACCOMPLISHMENTS to praise yourself, or speak arrogantly about things you possess or have achieved **2.** *vt.* POSSESS SOMETHING DESIRABLE to possess something, especially something that is very desirable ○ *Our town boasts the world's biggest roller coaster.* ■ *n.* **1.** EXCESSIVELY PROUD STATEMENT something you say or write that praises yourself, or arrogantly refers to your possessions or achievements **2.** DESIRABLE POSSESSION something possessed that is very desirable [13thC. Via Anglo-Norman *bost* "boasting" from, ultimately, the Scandinavian base that was also the source of German *böse* "wicked."] —**boast·er** *n.* —**boast·ful** *adj.* —**boast·ful·ly** *adv.* —**boast·ful·ness** *n.*

boast[2] /bōst/ (**boast·ed, boast·ing, boasts**) *vt.* SCULPTURE to shape stone roughly using a chisel [Early 19thC. Origin unknown.]

boat /bōt/ *n.* **1.** SMALL VESSEL FOR TRAVELING ON WATER a small, often open vessel for traveling on water **2.** SHIP OR SUBMARINE any water vessel, including a ship or submarine **3.** SOMETHING SHAPED LIKE A BOAT an open container shaped like a boat, e.g., one for holding gravy or incense ■ *v.* (**boat·ed, boat·ing, boats**) **1.** *vi.* TRAVEL BY BOAT to travel by boat or ride in a boat for pleasure **2.** *vt.* CARRY BY BOAT to move or transport something by boat **3.** *vt.* ANGLING PULL FISH TO BOAT to bring a caught fish to a boat [Old English *bāt*] ◇ **in the same boat** in the same situation or having the same problems as somebody else ◇ **miss the boat** to fail to seize an opportunity ◇ **rock the boat** to cause trouble, especially by questioning an accepted situation (*informal*)

boat deck *n.* a deck on a ship where the lifeboats are carried

boa·tel /bō tél/, **bo·tel** *n.* **1.** HOTEL FOR BOAT OWNERS a waterside hotel where people traveling in boats can stay and moor their boats **2.** SHIP USED AS HOTEL a ship that functions as a hotel [Mid-20thC. Blend of BOAT and HOTEL.]

boat·er /bőtər/ *n.* **1.** SOMEBODY USING BOAT somebody who travels by boat or rides in a boat for pleasure **2.** STRAW HAT WITH FLAT TOP a straw hat with a flat brim, a flat crown, and a hat band [12thC. Formed from BOAT; the hat was originally associated with boating.]

boat hook *n.* a long pole with a hook on one end, used for pulling or pushing boats, rafts, or logs

boat·house /bőt hòwss/ (*plural* **-hous·es** /-hòwziz/) *n.* a small building beside water, in which boats are kept

boat·load /bőt lōd/ *n.* **1.** AMOUNT THAT FILLS BOAT an amount of something or a number of people that fills a boat **2.** LARGE AMOUNT OR NUMBER a large amount of something or a large number of people (*informal*)

boat·man /bőtmən/ (*plural* **-men** /-mən/) *n.* somebody who operates or works on a boat, especially a man who takes people for rides on a boat or who rents boats out to others

boat·man·ship /bőtmən shìp/ *n.* the skill of sailing a boat

boat neck *n.* a wide shallow neckline that runs from shoulder to shoulder and is equally deep at the front and back, similar to the neckline of a traditional sailor's blouse

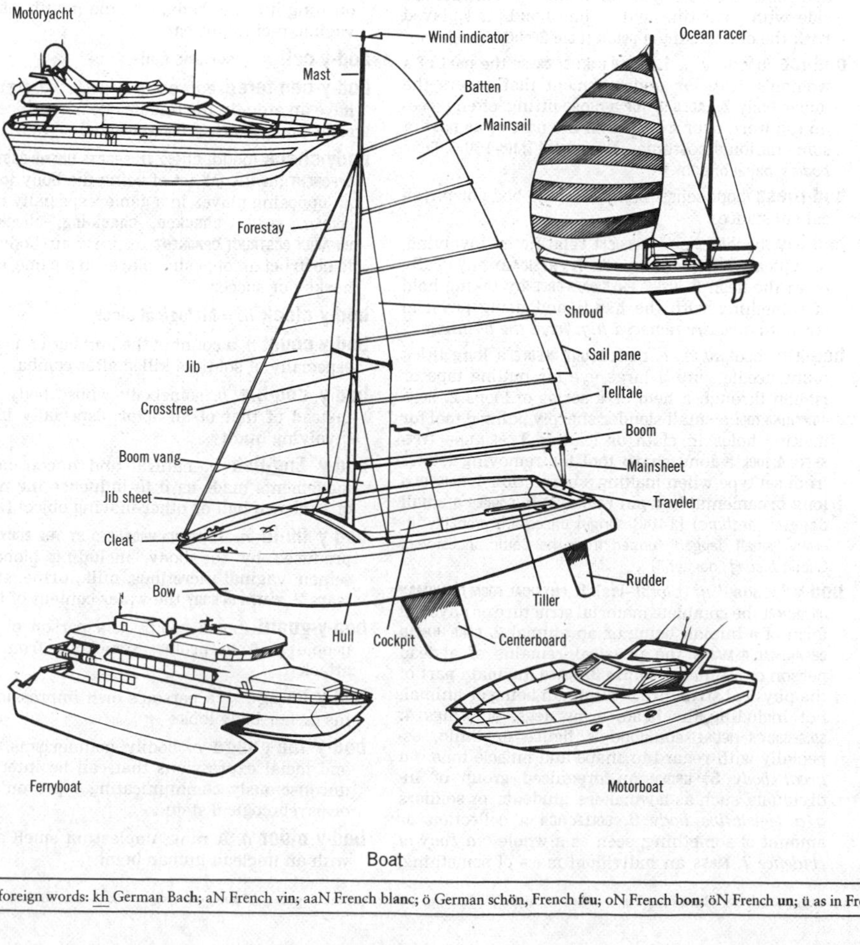

Boat

boat peo·ple *npl.* refugees who leave their country by boat

boat·swain /bőss'n/, **bo's'n, bo·sun** *n.* a noncommissioned officer or a warrant officer on a ship in charge of the maintenance of the vessel, its boats, and other equipment [Old English *bātswegen*, from *bāt*, an earlier form of BOAT + Old Norse *sveinn* "boy" (see SWAIN)]

boat·swain's chair *n.* a board supported by ropes, slung over the side of a ship or up in the rigging so that somebody can sit on it while working

boat train *n.* a train that takes people between a dockside and a town, usually timed to coincide with the arrival or departure of a ferry or liner

bob[1] /bob/ *v.* (**bobbed, bob·bing, bobs**) **1.** *vi.* BOUNCE to bounce up and down quickly and repeatedly, especially in and out of the water while floating **2.** *vi.* MAKE CURTSY, BOW, OR NOD to make a quick movement, especially a curtsy, bow, or nod (*archaic*) **3.** *vti.* TAP OR CAUSE TO TAP to tap lightly and quickly or to cause something to tap in this way (*archaic*) ■ *n.* **1.** SMALL HANGING OR BOUNCING OBJECT a small hanging or bouncing object, e.g., a curl of hair, a weight on a plumb line, or a fishing bobber **2.** CURTSY, BOW, OR NOD a quick movement such as a curtsy, bow, or nod (*archaic*) [14thC. Origin uncertain: probably from earlier *bobben* "to strike, beat," an imitation of the sound. The meaning was extended to cover a variety of short, quick movements.]

bob[2] /bob/ *n.* **1.** WOMAN'S SHORT HAIRCUT a woman's short haircut, especially a straight cut at chin length **2.** SOMETHING CUT SHORT something that has been cut short, e.g., a horse's tail when docked, a dog's ears when clipped, or a short line of poetry at the end of a stanza **3.** OPERATION ON NOSE a surgical shortening or reshaping of the nose (*informal*) **4.** = **bobsled** (*informal*) ■ *vt.* (**bobbed, bob·bing, bobs**) CUT HAIR SHORT to cut a person's hair or a horse's tail short so that it is all one length [14thC. From earlier *bobbe* "bunch, cluster," possibly from a Celtic language (compare Gaelic *bab* "tassel, cluster") The meaning "short haircut" arose in the early 20thC.]

bob[3] /bob/ (*plural* **bob**) *n. U.K.* a shilling in the former British currency system (*informal*) [Late 18thC. Origin unknown.]

bob[4] /bob/ *n.* POLISHING WHEEL a small polishing wheel of felt or leather ■ *vt.* (**bobbed, bob·bing, bobs**) POLISH WITH BOB to polish something with a small polishing wheel of felt or leather

bob·ber /bóbbər/ *n.* a light object attached to a fishing line that floats on the surface of the water to keep the bait at the proper depth [Late 18thC. Formed from BOB[1].]

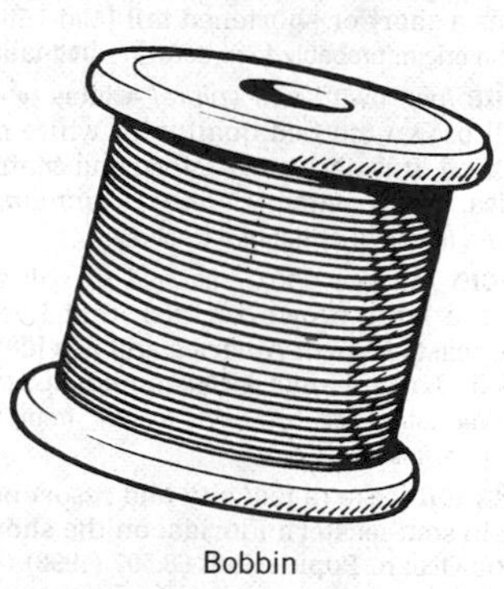

Bobbin

bob·bin /bóbbin/ *n.* **1.** CYLINDER WOUND WITH THREAD OR WIRE a cylinder on which thread, yarn, or wire is wound, to be unwound as it is used, especially for sewing, spinning, weaving, knitting, or making lace. ◊ **spindle, reel 2.** CORD USED AS TRIM a narrow cotton cord, often braided, formerly used as a trimming or binding in dressmaking [Mid-16thC. Via French *bobine* "sewing instrument" from Old French *balbiner*, probably an alteration of *balbier* "to stutter," from, ultimately, Latin *balbus* "stuttering."]

bob·bi·net /bòbbə nét/ *n.* a machine-made net fabric with a hexagonal mesh

bob·bin lace *n.* a lace made by winding thread by hand around bobbins or pins stuck into a pillow

bob·ble /bóbb'l/ *n.* MISTAKE a mistake or blunder (*informal*) ■ *v.* (**-bled, -bling, -bles**) **1.** *vti.* MOVE UP AND DOWN to move, or to cause something to move, quickly and repeatedly up and down **2.** *vt.* HANDLE

CLUMSILY to handle something clumsily, such as a ball in a game, or to do something ineptly (*informal*) [Early 19thC. Probably formed from BOB[1].]

bob·by /bóbbee/ (*plural* **-bies**) *n. U.K.* a policeman (*dated informal*) [Mid-19thC. From the diminutive of the personal name "Robert," after Sir Robert Peel, who introduced the 1828 Police Act.]

bob·by pin *n. U.S., Can, ANZ* a hair clip made of a tightly folded piece of wire that slides into the hair and holds it in place [Probably from the use of BOB[2] to denote a hairstyle]

bob·by socks, bob·by sox *npl.* ankle socks that fold over at the top, popular among teenage girls in the 1940s and 1950s [*Bobby* "small, short," of uncertain origin: probably formed from BOB[2]]

bob·by·sox·er /bóbbi sòksər/ *n.* a teenage girl of the 1940s and 1950s (*informal*) [Because they wore BOBBY SOCKS]

bob·cat /bób kàt/ *n.* a medium-sized North American wild cat that is related to the lynx and has reddish-brown fur with black markings, tufted ears, and a short tail. Latin name: *Lynx rufus*. [Late 19thC. *Bob* from BOB[2], from its short tail.]

Bob·cat *tdmk.* a trademark for hydraulic excavating machinery and loaders

bob·o·link /bóbbə lingk/ (*plural* **-links** *or* **-link**) *n.* a songbird with a distinctive bubbly song that nests in North America and migrates to South America. The male is white and yellow above and black underneath. Latin name: *Dolichonyx oryzivorus*. [Late 18thC. An imitation of the bird's call.]

bob skate *n.* an ice skate that has two parallel blades, usually used by children [*Bob* from BOB[2] in the sense "short"]

bob·sled /bób slèd/ *vi.* (**-sled·ded, -sled·ding, -sleds**) **RIDE IN BOBSLED** to ride or race in a bobsled ■ *n.* **1. RACING SLED** a long racing sled with steering, brakes, a seat for two or more, and two pairs of runners, one in front and one in back **2. SLED MADE OF TWO SHORT SLEDS** a long sled made of two short sleds attached one behind the other, used for recreation or for carrying things over snow [*Bob* from BOB[1] in the sense "short"]

bob·sleigh /bób slày/ *n. U.K.* = **bobsled** ■ *vi.* (**-sleighed, -sleigh·ing, -sleighs**) *U.K.* = **bobsled** [Bob from BOB[1] in the sense "short"]

bob·stay /bób stày/ *n.* a rope used to hold down a ship's bowsprit [*Bob* of uncertain origin: probably from BOB[1] *v.* 1.]

bob·tail /bób tàyl/ *n.* **1. SHORT TAIL** an animal's tail that is naturally short or has been cut short **2. ANIMAL WITH SHORT TAIL** an animal, especially a horse or dog, that has a short or shortened tail [Mid-16thC. *Bob* of uncertain origin: probably from BOB[2].] —**bob·tailed** *adj.*

bob·white /bób hwìt, -wìt/ (*plural* **-whites** *or* **-white**) *n.* a small brown mottled quail with white markings on its head. It is native to eastern and central North America. Latin name: *Colinus virginianus*. [Early 19thC. An imitation of the bird's call.]

bo·cac·cio /bə kaá chō, -kaáchee ō/ (*plural* **-cio** *or* **-cios**) *n.* a large brown rockfish that lives off the Pacific coast of North America and is widely caught for food. Latin name: *Sebastes paucispinis*. [Late 19thC. Via Italian *bocaccio* "ugly mouth" from, ultimately, Latin *bucca* "mouth."]

Bo·ca Ra·ton /bōkə rə tṓn/ city and resort near Palm Beach in southeastern Florida, on the shores of the Atlantic Ocean. Population: 68,507 (1996).

Boc·cac·cio /bō kaáchee ō, -chō/, **Giovanni** (1313–75) Italian writer and humanist. He wrote the *Decameron* (1348–58), a collection of 100 tales told by refugees from the Florentine plague of 1348. A classic of world literature, it profoundly influenced English writers such as Shakespeare.

boc·ce /bóchee/, **boc·ci** *n.* an Italian game similar to lawn bowling, usually played on a long earth-floored court [Early 20thC. Via Italian *bocce*, the plural of *boccia* "ball," from Vulgar Latin *bottia* "boss."]

Boc·che·ri·ni /bòkə reénee, bòkə-, báwke-/, **Luigi** (1743–1805) Italian composer and cellist. A prolific writer of chamber music, he composed for the Spanish and Prussian courts. Full name **Luigi Rodolfo Boccherini**

Boche /bosh, bawsh/, **boche** *n.* (*plural* **Boches** *or* **Boche;** *plural* **boches** *or* **boche**) *U.K.* **OFFENSIVE TERM** an offensive term for a German, especially a German soldier of World War I (*slang dated offensive*) ■ **Boche, boche** *npl. U.K.* **OFFENSIVE TERM FOR GERMANS** an offensive term used for the Germans collectively, especially the German soldiers of World War I (*dated slang insult*) [Early 20thC. Shortening of French *alboche*, a blend of *allemand* "German" and *caboche* "cabbage, blockhead."]

bock beer /bók-/ *n.* a dark rich beer [Mid-19thC. From German *Bockbier*, an alteration of *Einbecker Bier*, named after *Einbeck*, a German town.]

bod /bod/ *n.* (*slang*) **1. SOMEBODY'S BODY** somebody's body or figure **2. PERSON** a person [Late 18thC. Shortening.]

B.O.D. *abbr.* biochemical oxygen demand

bo·da·cious /bō dáyshəss/, **bow·da·cious** *adj. Southern U.S., Midwest* (*informal humorous*) **1. BOLD** outrageously arrogant or uninhibited ○ *a bodacious lie* **2. IMPRESSIVE** remarkable or excellent ○ *That's one bodacious boat!* ■ *adv. Southern U.S., Midwest* **VERY** extremely (*informal humorous*) ○ *I'm bodacious hungry* [Mid-19thC. Possibly an alteration of dialect *boldacious*, a blend of BOLD and AUDACIOUS.] —**bo·da·cious·ly** *adv.*

bode[1] /bōd/ (**bod·ed, bod·ing, bodes**) *vti.* to be an indication of something particular that is about to happen ○ *This does not bode well for the future of the organization.* [Old English *bodian* "to announce, foretell," formed from *boda* "messenger"]

bode[2] *v.* past tense of **bide**

bo·de·ga /bō dáygə/ *n.* **1. SMALL GROCERY STORE** a small grocery store, often selling wine, in a Spanish-speaking neighborhood **2. WINE SHOP** a wine shop or warehouse for the storage of wine in a Spanish-speaking country [Mid-19thC. Via Spanish from Latin *apotheca* "storehouse."]

Bod·en·heim /bṓd'n hìm/, **Maxwell** (1893–1954) U.S. writer. A bohemian in Greenwich Village, New York City, he published poems and novels including a volume of *Selected Poems* (1946). Born **Maxwell Bodenheimer**

Bod·hid·harma /bōdi dúrmə/ (*fl.* 6th century) Indian monk He was the semilegendary founder of the Zen school of Buddhism.

bo·dhi·satt·va /bòdi sútvə/ *n.* a god or being that has attained enlightenment worthy of nirvana but remains in the human world to help others [Early 19thC. From Sanskrit *bodhi* "perfect knowledge" (from the stem *budh-* "to know"; see BUDDHA) + *sattva* "being, reality."]

bod·hrán /bówraan/ *n.* a shallow drum used in Irish and sometimes Scottish folk music, covered on one side with goatskin, held in one hand, and played with the other using a stick [Late 20thC. From Irish.]

bod·ice /bóddiss/ *n.* **1. UPPER PART OF DRESS** the part of a woman's dress or undergarment that covers the upper body **2. LACED-UP TOP** a close-fitting, often laced-up top worn over a blouse in the past or as part of some national costumes **3.** = **corset** [Mid-16thC. From *bodies*, plural of BODY.]

bod·i·less /bóddeeliss/ *adj.* having no body or physical substance

bod·i·ly /bóddlee/ *adj.* **PHYSICAL** relating to, involving, or typical of the body ■ *adv.* **1. PHYSICALLY** physically or in the flesh **2. USING PHYSICAL FORCE** by taking hold of something with the hands and using physical strength ○ *bodily removed him from the building*

bod·kin /bódkin/ *n.* **1. LARGE BLUNT NEEDLE** a long thick blunt needle with a large eye for pulling tape or ribbon through a hem or a series of loops **2. HOLE-PUNCHING TOOL** a small slender sharply pointed tool for making holes in cloth or leather **3.** PRINTING **TYPE-SETTING TOOL** a long sharp tool for removing letters from set type when making a correction **4. HAIRPIN** a long ornamental hairpin (*archaic*) **5. DAGGER** a small dagger (*archaic*) [14thC. Origin uncertain: probably literally "small dagger" formed from the Celtic ancestor of Gaelic *biodag* "dagger."]

bod·y /bóddee/ *n.* (*plural* **-ies**) **1. PHYSICAL FORM OF HUMAN OR ANIMAL** the complete material structure or physical form of a human being or an animal **2. DEAD HUMAN OR ANIMAL REMAINS** the physical remains of a dead person or animal. ◊ **corpse 3. TORSO** the main part of the physical structure of a human being or animal, not including the head, arms, legs, or wings **4. SOMEBODY'S FIGURE** somebody's figure or build, especially with regard to shape and muscle tone ○ *a great body* **5. GROUP** an organized group of individuals, such as lawmakers, students, or soldiers ○ *a legislative body* **6. COLLECTION** a collection or amount of something, seen as a whole ○ *a body of evidence* **7. MASS** an individual mass of something, especially water or land ○ *a large body of water* **8. MAIN PART** the main or central part of something, e.g., the majority of a quantity **9.** ARCHIT **NAVE** the nave or central part of a church **10. MAIN PART OF VEHICLE** the main part of a vehicle, e.g., the fuselage of an aircraft or the outer shell of a car. ◊ **bodywork 11.** MUSIC **MAIN PART OF MUSICAL INSTRUMENT** the largest part of a musical instrument, especially the sound box of a stringed instrument **12. MAIN PART OF SOMETHING WRITTEN** the main part of a piece of writing ○ *in the body of the text.* **13. FULLNESS OF FLAVOR IN WINE** the extent to which a wine seems full when tasted. Body increases with alcohol content and density. ○ *a French red with plenty of body* **14. THICKNESS OF LIQUID** the thickness or opacity of a liquid such as paint or soup **15. FULLNESS OF TEXTURE** a fullness and bounciness in texture or appearance ○ *designed to give hair more body* **16. FIRMNESS OF FABRIC** the firmness or substantial feel of a type of cloth **17.** *U.K.* = **body suit 18. UPPER PART OF GARMENT** the part of a garment that covers a person's torso **19. PERSON** used to refer to a person or yourself in an impersonal way (*informal*) ○ *This treatment could make a body feel unwelcome!* **20.** CERAMICS **MATERIAL FOR MAKING CERAMICS** the blend of clay and other raw materials used in a ceramic piece **21.** PHYS **PHYSICAL OBJECT** a distinguishable physical object **22.** MATH **OBJECT REPRESENTED MATHEMATICALLY** a physical object represented mathematically ■ *vt.* (**-ied, -y·ing, -ies**) **TO GIVE SHAPE** to give shape or substance to something (*literary*) [Old English *bodig*]

bod·y ar·mor *n.* a protective covering for the upper part of the torso

bod·y bag *n.* a bag designed to hold a dead body, usually made of plastic and fitted with a zipper

bod·y blow *n.* **1. SERIOUS SETBACK OR DISAPPOINTMENT** something that causes great physical, financial, or emotional damage to somebody or something **2.** BOXING **BODY PUNCH** a punch that lands between the neck and the waist

bod·y board *n.* a short polystyrene surfboard on which a surfer lies rather than stands

bod·y·build·ing /bóddi bilding/ *n.* the practice of developing the muscles of the body through weight-lifting and diet —**bod·y·build·er** *n.*

bod·y bun·ker *n.* a small shield attached to the arm for fending off stones and other light projectiles

bod·y cav·i·ty *n.* **1.** = **coelom 2. OPENING INTO THE BODY** an opening into the body, e.g., the mouth, esophagus, vagina, rectum, or ear

bod·y cell *n.* = **somatic cell**

bod·y-cen·tered *adj.* used to describe crystals that have an atom in the middle of each unit cell as well as at the corners. ◊ **face-centered**

body·check /bóddi chèk/ *n.* SPORTS **UNFAIR OBSTRUCTION OF OPPONENT** an illegal act of using the body to obstruct an opposing player in a game, especially hockey or soccer ■ *vt.* (**-checked, -check·ing, -checks**) SPORTS **UNFAIRLY OBSTRUCT OPPONENT** to use your body illegally to obstruct an opposing player in a game, especially hockey or soccer

bod·y clock *n.* = **biological clock**

bod·y count *n.* a count of the number of dead bodies, especially of soldiers killed after combat

bod·y dou·ble *n.* somebody whose body is filmed instead of that of an actor, especially in a scene involving nudity

bod·y Eng·lish *n.* natural and unconscious body movements made as if to influence the movement of a thrown ball or other moving object (*informal*)

bod·y flu·id *n.* **1. LIQUID PRODUCED BY THE BODY** a liquid produced by the body, including blood, saliva, semen, vaginal secretions, milk, urine, sweat, and tears **2. WATER IN BODY** the water content of the body

bod·y·guard /bóddi gaard/ *n.* a person or group of people paid to protect somebody from physical attack

bod·y im·age *n.* a person's own impression of how his or her body looks

bod·y lan·guage *n.* bodily mannerisms, postures, and facial expressions that can be interpreted as unconsciously communicating a person's feelings or psychological state

bod·y o·dor *n.* A rank, unpleasant smell associated with an unclean human being

bod·y pack·er *n.* somebody who smuggles illegal narcotics inside his or her body by swallowing them (*slang*)

bod·y pol·i·tic *n.* the people of a nation or any politically organized state, considered as a group

bod·y pop·ping *n.* a type of dancing, popular especially in the 1980s, involving convulsive, sinuous, or robotic movements (*slang*) —**bod·y pop·per** *n.*

bod·y search *n.* a detailed physical examination of somebody suspected of hiding something such as weapons or narcotics on his or her person

bod·y shield *n.* = **body bunker**

bod·y shirt *n.* a shirt that fits closely to the body, often worn under other clothing and sometimes with a snapped crotch

bod·y shop *n.* a workshop where car bodies are repaired (*informal*)

bod·y snatch·er *n.* somebody who steals corpses from graves, usually to sell for medical study —**bod·y·snatch·ing** *n.*

bod·y stock·ing *n.* a close-fitting, usually sheer, one-piece garment that covers the body and sometimes the arms and legs

bod·y suit *n.* a woman's close-fitting, one-piece garment that covers the torso and is fastened at the crotch by snaps

bod·y·surf /bóddi sùrf/ (**-surfed, -surf·ing, -surfs**) *vi.* to surf without a board by lying on a wave and using the body as a surfboard —**bod·y·surf·er** *n.*

bod·y wall *n.* the part of an animal's body that forms its external surface, encloses the body cavity, and consists of layers of skin and muscle

bod·y·work /bóddi wùrk/ *n.* **1.** CARS **AUTO BODY** the outer frame of a car or other motor vehicle **2. REPAIR OF MOTOR VEHICLE BODY** the work of repairing the outer frame of a car or other motor vehicle **3. MASSAGE OR PHYSICAL MANIPULATION OF BODY** physical manipulation of the human body, including all types of massage, to improve general health or posture or to treat injuries

boehm·ite /báy mìt, bő-/ *n.* a mineral found in bauxite and consisting of hydrous aluminum oxide that ranges in color from light gray to dark reddish brown [Early 20thC. Named for Johann Böhm, a German chemist (1895–1952).]

Boer /bōr, bawr, bŏŏr/ *n.* somebody of Dutch descent who settled in South Africa [Mid-19thC. From Dutch *boer* "farmer."] —**Boer** *adj.*

Boer War *n.* a war fought in South Africa from 1899 to 1902 between the British and the descendants of the Dutch, ending eventually in a British victory

BOF *abbr.* COMPUT beginning of file

boff /bof/ *n.* **1. FUNNY JOKE** a joke that gets a big laugh (*informal dated*) **2. BIG LAUGH** a big hearty laugh (*informal dated*) **3. SUCCESS** something that is a conspicuous success, especially a hit show (*informal dated*) **4. PUNCH OR SLAP** a blow with the fist or open hand (*informal*) **5. INTERCOURSE** sexual intercourse (*slang*) ■ *v.* (**boffed, boff·ing, boffs**) **1.** *vt.* **PUNCH OR SLAP SOMEBODY** to hit somebody with the fist or open hand (*informal*) **2.** *vti.* **HAVE SEX** to have sexual intercourse with somebody (*slang*) [Mid-20thC. Probably a blend of the first elements of the two words in BOX-OFFICE, indicating a box-office success.]

bof·fin /bóffin/ *n.* *U.K.* a scientific expert, especially one involved in research and who appears unconventional or absent-minded (*informal*) [Mid-20thC. Origin unknown.]

bof·fo /bóffō/ *adj.* **EXCELLENT** excellent or extremely successful (*informal dated*) ■ *n.* (*plural* **-fos**) = **boff** *n.* 3 (*informal dated*) [Mid-20thC. Shortening of *boffola* (see BOFFOLA) Formed from *boff* "great commercial success, especially in the theater," of uncertain origin: perhaps from *box office*.]

bof·fo·la /bo fólə/ *n.* = **boff** *n.* 3 (*informal dated*) [Mid-20thC. Extension of BOFF.]

Bo·fors gun /bő fàwrz-, bŏŏ-/ *n.* a 40 mm antiaircraft gun with one or two barrels, developed in Sweden and used by U.S. and British forces in World War II [Mid-20thC]

bog /bawg, bog/ *n.* an area of wet marshy ground, largely consisting of accumulated decomposing plant material. It supports vegetation such as cranberries and moss and may ultimately turn into peat. [14thC. From Gaelic *bognach* "marsh," formed from *bog* "soft."]

bog down (**bogged down, bogging down, bogs down**) *vt.* to slow somebody's general progress (*informal*) ○ *got bogged down in unimportant details*

Bo·ga·lu·sa /bōgə lŏŏssə/ city in eastern Louisiana, just west of the Mississippi River, north of New Orleans. Population: 13,877 (1996).

Bo·gan, **Louise** /bőgən/, (1897–1970) U.S. poet and critic. In addition to publishing her own poetry and reviews, she was poetry editor of *The New Yorker* (1931–69).

bo·gart /bő gaart/ (**-gart·ed, -gart·ing, -garts**) *v.* **1.** *vt.* **HOG SOMETHING** to take more than your share of something (*slang dated*) ○ *Don't bogart the beer!* **2.** *vti.* **BULLY OR GET SOMETHING BY BULLYING** to behave in a hostile belligerent way, or to get something by intimidation (*slang*) ○ *He's trying to bogart his way in.* [Mid-20thC. Probably for the actor, Humphrey *Bogart*.]

Humphrey Bogart

Bo·gart, **Humphrey** /bő gaart/, (1899–1957) U.S. movie actor. The classic American "tough-but-tender" leading man, his many movies include *Casablanca* (1942) and *The African Queen* (1951). Full name **Humphrey DeForest Bogart**

bog as·pho·del *n.* a plant of the lily family that is common in boggy areas and has grassy leaves and clusters of small yellow flowers. Latin name: *Narthecium ossifragum* and *Narthecium americanum*.

bo·gey /bőgee/ *n.* **1. CAUSE OF TROUBLE** something that troubles, annoys, or frightens somebody **2.** GOLF **ONE OVER PAR** a golf score of one over par for a particular hole **3.** AIR FORCE **UNIDENTIFIED FLYING AIRCRAFT** an aircraft in flight that cannot be identified, especially one assumed to be hostile (*slang*) **4.** = **bogeyman** *n.* 1 **5.** *U.K.* = **booger** *n.* 2 (*slang*) **6. POLICE OFFICER** a police officer or detective (*slang dated*) ■ *vt.* (**-geyed, -gey·ing, -geys**) GOLF **SCORE ONE OVER PAR FOR HOLE** to score one over par for a particular hole in golf [Mid-19thC. Alteration of BOGLE.]

bog·ey·man /bŏŏggi màn, bőgee-, bŏŏgee-/ (*plural* **-men**), **bo·gy·man** (*plural* **-men** /-mèn/), **boog·ey·man** (*plural* **-men**) *n.* **1. FEAR-INDUCING PERSON** a real or imaginary person or monster that causes fear or is invoked to cause fear, especially in children **2. SOMEBODY BELIEVED TO BE EVIL** somebody considered to be especially hateful, evil, or frightening ○ *The press treated him as a left-wing bogeyman.*

bog·gle /bógg'l/ (**-gled, -gling, -gles**) *v.* **1.** *vti.* **BAFFLE OR BECOME BAFFLED** to astonish or confuse somebody, or to become astonished or confused (*informal*) ◊ **mind-boggling** **2.** *vi.* **HESITATE WITH SECOND THOUGHTS** to hesitate before doing something, usually because of being overwhelmed, afraid, or concerned **3.** *vti.* **MAKE A TRIVIAL MISTAKE** to make a trivial mistake or mismanage something (*informal*) [Late 16thC. Origin uncertain: probably related to BOGLE.] —**bog·gler** *n.*

bog·gy /bóggee/ (**-gi·er, -gi·est**) *adj.* used to describe an area of land that is always or is usually wet or muddy

bog·hop·per /báwg hòppər, bóg-/ *n.* = **bogtrotter** (*slang offensive*)

bo·gie /bőgee/ *n.* a framework mounted on a set of wheels on the undercarriage of a vehicle. Railroad vehicles have one at each end and they swivel to allow the vehicle to go round a curve. [Mid-19thC. Origin unknown.]

Bo·gor /bő gàwr/ city in Indonesia, near Jakarta, on western Java island. It is known for its botanical gardens. Population: 271,711 (1990).

Bo·go·tá /bògə taá/ capital of Colombia situated on a plateau in the eastern Andes. It is Colombia's largest city and its commercial, cultural, and political center. Population: 5,237,635 (1995).

bog rose·mar·y *n.* an evergreen shrub of the heath family that has pink or white urn-shaped flowers. Latin name: *Andromeda polifolia*.

bog spav·in *n.* a chronic puffy inflammation of the soft tissue of the hock joint of horses

bog·trot·ter /báwg tròtter, bóg-/ *n.* a highly offensive term for an Irish or Irish-American person (*slang offensive*)

bogue /bōg/ *adj.* = **bogus** *adj.* 2 (*slang*) ■ *n.* **CIGARETTE** a cigarette (*slang*) ■ *vti.* (**bogued, bogu·ing, bogues**) **SMOKE** to smoke a cigarette (*slang*)

bogue out *vi.* to become useless (*slang*) (*refers to computer technology*)

bo·gus /bógəss/ *adj.* **1. FAKE OR DECEITFUL** false, dishonest, or fraudulently imitating something **2. BAD OR USELESS** not good, pleasant, or acceptable (*slang*) [Early 19thC. After *bogus*, a machine for producing counterfeit money. The ultimate origin is uncertain.] —**bo·gus·ly** *adv.* —**bo·gus·ness** *n.*

WORD KEY: ORIGIN

The word ***bogus*** is first recorded in American usage in the 1820s, referring to a machine for producing counterfeit money; its modern uses seem to have developed from there. Its ultimate origins remain unclear, but one suggestion is that it comes from *tantrabogus*, a word reportedly in use in New England in the early 19th century for "a sinister-looking object" (which itself may have been based on *bogy*, meaning "devil"). Another theory is that it may be related to Hausa *boko*, meaning "deceit, fraud," and have crossed the Atlantic with transported slaves.

bo·gy·man *n.* = **bogeyman**

bo·hea /bō heé/ *n.* a low-quality black Chinese tea [Early 18thC. From Chinese dialect *Bu-yi*, a variant of *Wu-yi*, after the Wu-Yi hills in southeastern China.]

bo·he·mi·a /bō heémee ə/ *n.* **1. UNCONVENTIONAL COMMUNITY** a community of artists and other people who live unconventional lives **2. UNCONVENTIONAL LIFESTYLE** the unconventional lifestyle characteristic of bohemians

Bo·he·mi·a /bō heémee ə/ historic region in the western Czech Republic. A former kingdom, it was the westernmost province of Czechoslovakia from 1918 to 1939 and from 1945 to 1949, but it was then divided into several new districts. Area: 20,100 sq. mi./52,060 sq. km.

bo·he·mi·an /bō heémee ən/ *n.* somebody, often a writer or an artist, who does not live according to the conventions of society [Mid-19th C. From the medieval association with members of the Romany people with Bohemia.] —**bo·he·mi·an** *adj.* —**bo·he·mi·an·ism** *n.*

Bo·he·mi·an /bō heémee ən/ *n.* **1.** PEOPLES **SOMEBODY FROM BOHEMIA** somebody who was born or raised in Bohemia **2.** LANG **CZECH LANGUAGE** the Czech language (*dated*) ■ *adj.* **OF BOHEMIA** belonging to or typical of Bohemia, or its people or culture

Bo·he·mi·an Breth·ren *npl.* a Protestant Christian society founded by the Hussites in Bohemia in 1467. It became the Moravian Church in 1722.

bo·ho /bőhō/ *n., adj. U.S., U.K., Can* bohemian (*slang*)

Bohr, **Niels** /bawr, bōr/, (1885–1962) Danish physicist. He won the Nobel Prize in physics (1922) for his work on quantum theory. He participated in U.S. atomic bomb delvelopment during World War II, and later worked for peaceful application of nuclear technology. Full name **Niels Henrik David Bohr**

Bohr ef·fect *n.* the effect that carbon dioxide has on the oxygen equilibrium of hemoglobin. Increased carbon dioxide concentrations reduce hemoglobin's ability to bind to oxygen atoms. [Mid-20thC. Named for Christian *Bohr* (1855–1911), Danish physiologist.]

Bohr the·o·ry *n.* a theory of atomic structure postulating that electrons move around a nucleus in distinct orbits and a jump between orbits is accompanied by the absorption or emission of a photon. It was the earliest important attempt to apply quantum theory to atomic structure. [Named for Niels BOHR]

bo·hunk /bő hungk/ *n.* an offensive term for a person from central or southeastern Europe (*slang* *offensive*) [Early 20thC. Blend of BOHEMIAN and "hunk," a shortening of "Hungarian."]

boil[1] /boyl/ *v.* (**boiled, boil·ing, boils**) **1.** *vti.* **REACH BOILING POINT** to cause a liquid to reach the temperature at which it turns to gas, when bubbles may be seen to form, or to reach this state **2.** *vti.* **CONTAIN OR CAUSE TO CONTAIN BOILING LIQUID** to contain liquid that has reached boiling point, or to cause the liquid in a container to boil **3.** *vti.* COOK **COOK IN BOILING LIQUID** to cook something by submerging it in boiling liquid for a certain amount of time, or to be cooked in this way. ◊ **simmer 4.** *vti.* **PLACE IN BOILING WATER** to put something such as clothing in boiling water, e.g., to clean or sterilize it, or to be put in boiling water for these purposes **5.** *vi.* **GET VERY HOT** to be or become extremely hot (*informal*) ○ *It's boiling in there!* **6.** *vi.* **BUBBLE ON SURFACE** to be stirred up and have bubbles breaking on the surface **7.** *vi.* **GET VERY ANGRY** to be or become very angry ○ *boiling with rage* ■ *n.* **1. STATE OF BUBBLING AT HIGH TEMPERATURE** the point at which a liquid bubbles because of having reached the temperature at which it turns to gas, or the state of bubbling at this temperature **2.** *Southern U.S.* **OUTDOOR PICNIC** an outdoor picnic at which shellfish, such as crabs, shrimp, oysters, or crayfish, are boiled and eaten (*informal*) ○ *a Low Country crab boil* [13thC. Via Old French *boillir* from Latin *bullire* "to bubble," from *bulla* "a bubble."]

boil away *vti.* to turn completely into steam, or turn all of a quantity of liquid into steam by boiling it

boil down *v.* **1.** *vti.* **REDUCE LIQUID IN MIXTURE** to make a liquid mixture thicker and reduce its volume by heating it rapidly until much of the liquid turns to steam, or to be made thicker in this way **2.** *vt.* **SUMMARIZE** to condense or summarize something such as information or text (*informal*)

boil down to *vi.* to mean or amount to something in essence (*informal*) ○ *It all boils down to the single question: Is he telling the truth?*

boil off *vti.* to remove something from a mixture by heating the mixture rapidly until it turns to steam, or to be removed in this way

boil over *v.* **1.** *vti.* **FROTH UP AND OVERFLOW** to reach or to cause a liquid to reach boiling point and be so full of bubbles that some of it spills from the container **2.** *vi.* **OVERFLOW WITH AN EMOTION** to become too intense or out of control ○ *her anger boiled over*

boil[2] /boyl/ *n.* MED a painful pus-filled abscess on the skin caused by bacterial infection of a hair follicle [Old English *byl* "inflammation"]

boil·er /bóylər/ *n.* **1. WATER HEATING TANK** a large tank in which water is heated and stored, either as hot water or as steam, and used for heating or generating power **2.** COOK **COOKING CHICKEN** a chicken suitable for boiling ○ *boilers, fryers and roasters on sale today*

boil·er·mak·er /bóylər màykər/ *n.* **1. WHISKEY WITH BEER CHASER** a drink of whiskey followed by a beer **2. SOMEBODY MAKING BOILERS** somebody who works in heavy industry making or repairing large metal objects, especially boilers

boil·er·plate /bóylər plàyt/ *n.* **1. PLATE USED FOR MAKING BOILERS** steel plate used for making boilers **2. CLICHÉD WRITING** writing that says nothing new, informative, or interesting **3. FORMULAIC LANGUAGE** stock or formulaic language, such as that used in legal forms and documents like powers of attorney and authors' contracts

boil·er room *n.* an area or room that houses one or more boilers

boil·er-room *adj.* **1. SHADY TELEPHONE SALES** used to describe high-pressure sales tactics, usually by telephone and often illegal, to sell stock or real estate of questionable value (*slang*) **2. OF POLITICAL CAMPAIGN WORKERS** relating to or being political campaign workers who perform administrative support tasks and make polling phone calls for the candidate

boil·ing /bóyling/ *adj.* **1. HOT** extremely hot **2. FURIOUS** extremely angry

boil·ing point *n.* **1. TEMPERATURE AT WHICH LIQUID BOILS** the temperature at which a liquid turns to gas. Water turns to steam at 212°F or 100°C at sea level. **2. CRISIS POINT** the point at which people lose their tempers or a situation becomes critical

boing /boyng/ *n.* the sound made by something that bounces [Mid-20thC. An imitation of the sound.]

Boi·se /bóyssee, bóyzee/ **1.** capital and largest city of Idaho, on the Boise River. Population: 152,737 (1996). **2.** river in southwestern Idaho that rises in the Sawtooth Mountains and empties into the Snake River. Length: 95 mi./153 km.

bois·ter·ous /bóystərəss, -strəss/ *adj.* **1. NOISY, ENERGETIC, AND ROWDY** full of noisy enthusiasm and energy, and often roughness or wildness **2. TURBULENT** wild, rough, or stormy [13thC. Alteration of earlier *boistous*, which came via Old French *boistos* "clumsy, rough" from Latin *buxus* "made from box-tree wood."] —**bois·ter·ous·ly** *adv.* —**bois·ter·ous·ness** *n.*

Bok /bok/, **Edward** (1863–1930) Dutch-born U.S. editor. He edited *The Ladies' Home Journal* (1889–1919) and won a Pulitzer Prize for *The Americanization of Edward Bok* (1920). Full name **Edward William Bok**

bok choy /bòk chóy/ *n.* a Chinese cabbage with long white stalks and narrow green leaves. Latin name: *Brassica chinensis.* [Mid-20thC. From Chinese Guangdang dialect *baahk-choi*, literally "white vegetable."]

Bol. *abbr.* Bolivia ■ *abbr.* Bolivian

bo·la /bṓlə/, **bo·las** /-ləss/ *n.* a strong cord with weights attached to the ends, used for catching cows by South American cowhands (**gauchos**) who throw it to entangle the cows' legs [Early 19thC. Via Spanish, "ball," from, ultimately, Latin *bulla* "bubble."]

bold /bōld/ *adj.* **1. FEARLESS AND ADVENTUROUS** willing and eager to face danger or adventure with a sense of confidence and fearlessness **2. REQUIRING OR SHOWING A DARING PERSONALITY** requiring or showing fearlessness, daring, and often originality **3. IMPUDENT OR PRESUMPTUOUS** lacking in modesty, or so assertive as to be impolite **4. CLEAR AND CONSPICUOUS** standing out and therefore easily noticed ○ *bold colors* **5. STEEP** rising abruptly and steeply from the surroundings ○ *a bold cliff* **6.** PRINTING **DARKER THAN STANDARD** having darker thicker lines than standard type, fonts, or lettering ■ *n.* PRINTING **TYPE DARKER THAN STANDARD** type, fonts, or lettering with darker thicker lines than is standard ■ *vt.* to set, print, or display text in boldface type [Old English *bald.* Ultimately from the Indo-European base that was also the source of English *fool, bull, boulder,* and *phallus.*] —**bold·ly** *adv.* —**bold·ness** *n.*

bold·face /bṓld fàyss/ *adj.* PRINTING = **bold** *adj.* **6** ■ *n.* = **bold** ■ *vt.* (**-faced, -fac·ing, -fac·es**) PRINTING **DARKEN LETTERS** to make letters darker and thicker for emphasis

bold-faced /bṓld fàyst/, **bold·faced** *adj.* **1. BRAZEN** showing impudence or lack of shame or modesty **2.** PRINTING = **bold** *adj.* **6**

bole[1] /bōl/ *n.* the trunk of a tree [14thC. From Old Norse *bolr.*]

bole[2] /bōl/ *n.* a reddish brown clay used as a pigment [14thC. From late Latin *bolus* "clod of earth" (see BOLUS).]

bo·lec·tion /bō lékshən/ *n.* a molding covering an architectural joint and projecting beyond it. A bolection molding is usually S-shaped in cross section. [Mid-17thC. Origin unknown.]

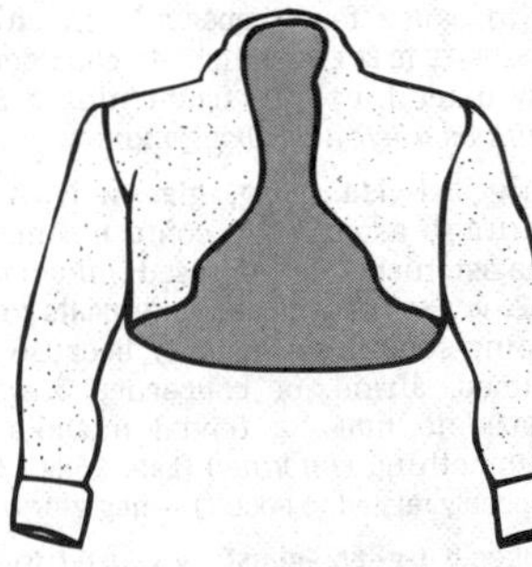

Bolero

bo·le·ro /bō láirō, bə-/ (*plural* **-ros**) *n.* **1. SPANISH DANCE** a Spanish dance in triple time that involves much foot-stamping and dramatic posing **2. SPANISH DANCE MUSIC** a piece of music for a bolero, or written in the rhythm of a bolero **3. SHORT OPEN JACKET** a short jacket, with or without sleeves, worn open over a blouse or shirt [Late 18thC. From Spanish, from *bola* "ball" (see BOLA).]

bo·le·tus /bō leétəss/ (*plural* **-tus·es** *or* **-ti** /-tī/) *n.* a fungus that has a rounded cap with pores rather than gills on the underside. Cep mushrooms are an edible species of boletus. Genus: *Boletus.* [Early 16thC. From Latin, of uncertain origin.]

Bol·eyn /bŏŏlin, bŏŏ lín/, **Anne, Queen of England and Ireland** (1507?–36). She was the second wife of Henry VIII (1533–36) and the mother of Elizabeth I. Henry VIII accused her of adultery and had her beheaded.

bo·lide /bṓ līd, -lid/ *n.* a bright meteor that explodes [Early 19thC. Via French from, ultimately, Greek *bolis* "missile."]

Bo·ling·brook /bṓling brŏŏk, bŏŏling-/ village in northeastern Illinois, a southwestern suburb of Chicago. Population: 51,312 (1996).

bo·li·var /bōlleévaar, bóllə vər/ *n.* **1.** see table at **currency 2. COIN OR BILL WORTH ONE BOLIVAR** a coin or bill worth one bolivar [Late 19thC. Named for Simón BOLÍVAR.]

Bo·lí·var /bóllə vaàr, bóllə-, bōlleé vaar/, **Simón** (1783–1830) South American revolutionary. He was the leader of the independence movement that drove the Spanish from Venezuela, Colombia, Ecuador, Peru, and Bolivia (1812–24). Known as **the Liberator**

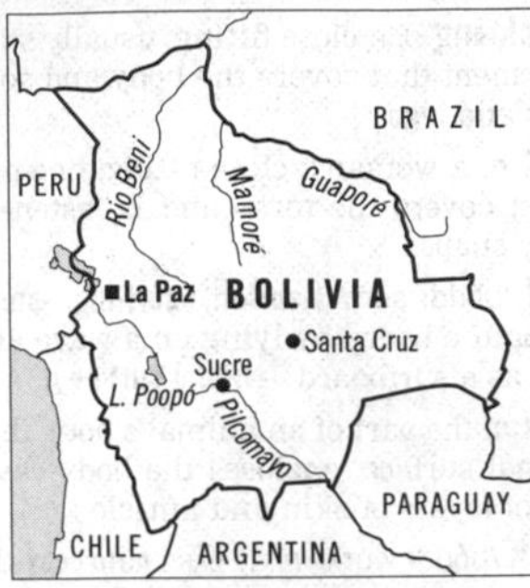

Bolivia

Bo·liv·i·a /bə lívvee ə, bō-/ landlocked republic in west central South America. Part of the Inca empire, it was conquered by the Spanish in 1538 and became independent in 1825. Language: Spanish. Currency: Boliviano. Capital: Sucre. Population: 7,669,868 (1997). Area: 424,164 sq. mi./1,098,581 sq. km. —**Bo·liv·i·an** *n., adj.*

bo·li·vi·a·no /bə livvee aánō, bō-/ (*plural* **-nos**) *n.* see table at **currency** [Late 19thC. From Spanish, "Bolivian."]

boll /bōl/ *n.* a rounded seedpod or capsule, especially of cotton [15thC. From Middle Dutch *bolle* "round object."]

bol·lard /bóllərd/ *n.* **1.** NAUT **POST FOR MOORING SHIPS** a strong post on a wharf, or on the deck of a ship, used for securing ropes **2.** MOUNTAINEERING **ROCK SUITABLE FOR SECURING ROPE** a spike of rock or a pillar of ice around which a rope can be secured [Mid-19thC. Origin uncertain; probably formed from BOLE[1].]

bol·lix /bólliks/ *n.* **CONFUSED SITUATION** a mess or muddle, especially one caused by bungling (*slang*) ■ *vt.* (**-lixed, -lix·ing, -lix·es**) **SPOIL OR CONFUSE SOMETHING** to make a mess or muddle of something (*slang*) ○ *bollix a job* ○ *They got my travel arrangements totally bollixed up.* [Mid-20thC. Alteration of BOLLOCKS.]

boll wee·vil *n.* a weevil found in the southern United States and Mexico whose larvae infest and destroy cotton bolls. Latin name: *Anthonomus grandis.*

boll·worm /bṓl wùrm/ *n.* a moth caterpillar, especially the corn earworm or pink bollworm, that feeds on and destroys cotton and other crops

bo·lo /bṓlō/ (*plural* **-los**) *n.* a machete from the Philippines with a single-edged blade [Early 20thC. From Philippine Spanish.]

bo·lo·gna /bə lōnee, -nə, -nyə/ *n.* **1.** FOOD **SMOKED SAUSAGE MADE OF MIXED MEATS** a large smoked sausage made with a variety of finely ground seasoned meats, usually including beef and pork **2. CHICKEN OR TURKEY SAUSAGE** a sausage similar to a smoked beef or pork bologna, made with finely ground chicken or turkey [Mid-19thC. Named for the Italian city of *Bologna*, where it was originally made.]

Bo·lo·gna /bə lṓnyə/ capital of Bologna Province and Emilia-Romagna Region, in northern Italy. It was an important cultural center in the Middle Ages and Renaissance. Population: 404,378 (1991).

bo·lo·gnese /bōlə náyz/, **Bo·lo·gnese** *adj.* used to describe an Italian sauce for pasta, made with ground meat and tomato [Early 19thC. From Italian, "(in the style) of Bologna."]

bo·lom·e·ter /bō lómmətər/ *n.* an instrument for measuring radiant energy by determining the changes of resistance in an electrical conductor [Late 19thC. Coined from Greek *bolē* "ray" + -METER.] —**bo·lo·met·ric** /bōlə méttrik/ *adj.* —**bo·lom·e·try** /bō lómmətree/ *n.*

bo·lo punch *n.* in boxing, a long powerful swinging uppercut [Origin unknown]

bo·lo tie, **bo·la tie** *n.* a thin necktie of cord fastened in front by a clasp [Alteration of BOLA, from its similarity to South American bolas]

Bol·she·vik /bṓlshəvìk, ból-/ *n.* **1.** **RUSSIAN COMMUNIST** a member of the radical group within the Russian Socialist party that became the Communist Party in 1918 **2.** **Bol·she·vik, bol·she·vik** **COMMUNIST OR COMMUNIST SYMPATHIZER** somebody who is a Communist or is sympathetic to Communism (*informal dated*) **3.** **Bol·she·vik, bol·she·vik** **POLITICAL RADICAL** any revolutionary or radical socialist (*disapproving*) [Early 20thC. From Russian *bol'shevik*, from *bol'she* "more"; from the fact that the radicals were in the majority.]

Bol·she·vism /bṓlshə vìzzəm, ból-/, **bol·she·vism** *n.* **1.** **BOLSHEVIK IDEOLOGY** the ideology and policies of the Bolsheviks, especially advocacy of the forcible overthrow of capitalism **2.** **COMMUNISM** Communism or revolutionary socialism (*dated*)

bol·shie /bólshee/, **bol·shy** *n.* (*plural* **-shies**) **BOLSHEVIK** a Bolshevik (*informal dated*) ■ *adj. U.K., Can* (*informal*) **1.** **UNCOOPERATIVE** tending to be argumentative or uncooperative **2.** **POLITICALLY RADICAL** politically radical or subversive [Early 20thC. Formed from BOLSHEVIK.]

bol·son /bōl sṓn/ *n.* in the deserts of the southwestern United States and Mexico, a flat-bottomed depression surrounded by mountains, typically containing a salt pan or lake [Mid-19thC. From American Spanish *bolsón*, literally "big purse" (from its shape), via Spanish *bolsa* "purse, pouch" from late Latin *bursa* (see BURSA).]

bol·ster[1] /bṓlstər/ *vt.* (**-stered, -ster·ing, -sters**) **1.** **ENCOURAGE THROUGH SUPPORT** to strengthen something through support or encouragement **2.** **KEEP RAISED** to prop something up ■ *n.* **1.** **LONG CYLINDRICAL PILLOW** a long firm cylindrical pillow placed under other pillows to support them **2.** MECH ENG **PAD PREVENTING FRICTION** a pad or cushion fitted to machinery to prevent friction or give support **3.** BUILDING **HORIZONTAL SUPPORTING TIMBER** a short horizontal timber positioned between the top of a post and the beam it supports, to spread the load of the post [Old English, "cushion." Ultimately from an Indo-European word meaning "to swell," which is also the ancestor of English *bulge*, *billow*, *belly*, and *bellows*.] —**bol·ster·er** *n.*

bol·ster[2] /bṓlstər/ *n.* a chisel with a wide cutting edge, used for cutting stone [Early 20thC. Alteration of *boaster*, from *boast* "to cut with a chisel," of unknown origin.]

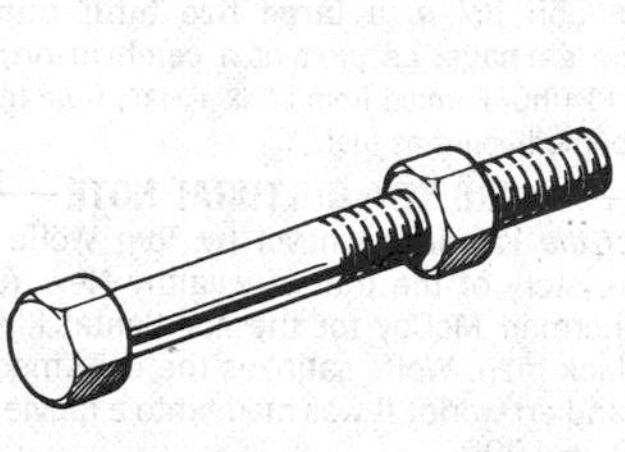

Bolt

bolt[1] /bōlt/ *n.* **1.** **BAR FOR FASTENING DOOR** a sliding bar that fits into a socket and secures a door or gate **2.** BUILDING **SHORT SCREW** a short cylindrical metal bar with a screw thread, used with a nut **3.** METEOROL **LIGHTNING FLASH** a flash of lightning **4.** TEXTILES **ROLL OF FABRIC** a rolled length of woven goods or wallpaper **5.** ARMS **ARROW FOR CROSSBOW** a short arrow for use with a crossbow **6.** ARMS **PART OF GUN** in a breech-loading firearm, a sliding rod, bar, or plate that ejects a used cartridge and closes the breech **7.** POL **REFUSAL OF SUPPORT** a refusal to support a political party, candidate, or policy **8.** MOUNTAINEERING **METAL PIN** a nail-like metal shaft used to provide an anchor in rock faces ■ *v.* (**bolt·ed, bolt·ing, bolts**) **1.** *vt.* **LOCK WITH BOLT** to fasten a door by sliding a bolt into a socket **2.** *vi.* **RUSH AWAY** to move suddenly and quickly, especially out of fright **3.** *vt.* **EXPEL FROM HIDING PLACE** to flush out a wild animal that is hidden or concealed **4.** *vt.* **DEVOUR HURRIEDLY** to swallow food hurriedly without chewing **5.** *vi.* BOT **PREMATURELY PRODUCE SEEDS** to flower and produce seeds earlier than expected or wanted **6.** *vt.* TEXTILES **ROLL INTO BOLT** to roll fabric or wallpaper into a bolt **7.** *vt.* POL **REFUSE TO SUPPORT** to refuse to support a political party, candidate, or policy [Old English, "crossbow bolt"] ◇ **like a bolt from the blue** very suddenly and unexpectedly ◇ **make a bolt for something** to make a sudden rush toward something

bolt[2] /bōlt/ (**bolt·ed, bolt·ing, bolts**) *vt.* to filter a substance through a cloth or sieve, especially flour [12thC. From Old French *buleter*, of Germanic origin.]

bolt-ac·tion *adj.* used to describe a gun with a sliding bolt that replaces the used cartridge and closes the breech

bolt·er /bṓltər/ *n.* **1.** **HORSE LIKELY TO BOLT** a horse that is liable to frighten easily and run **2.** POL **SOMEBODY WHO ABANDONS POLITICAL PARTY** somebody who refuses to support a political party, candidate, or policy **3.** NAVY **FAILED CARRIER LANDING** a failed landing on an aircraft carrier that results in the pilot to have to fly off and try again ■ *vi.* (**-ered, -er·ing, -ers**) NAVY **ABORT CARRIER LANDING** to be forced to fly off and try again after failing to engage the arresting gear while landing an airplane on an aircraft carrier

bolt·hole /bṓlt hṑl/ *n.* a place of escape, especially for an animal fleeing from danger ○ *The rabbit ran down a bolthole*

bol·to·ni·a /bōl tṓnee ə/ (*plural* **-as** *or* **-a**) *n.* a perennial North American flower of the daisy family, with white, pink, or violet-colored flowers. Genus: *Boltonia*. [Late 18thC. From modern Latin, genus name, named for the 18th-century English botanist James *Bolton*.]

bolt·rope /bṓlt rṑp/ *n.* a rope sewn along the lower edge or leading edge of a sail to strengthen it

Boltz·mann con·stant /bòltsmən-/ *n.* the ratio of the universal gas constant to Avogadro's number. Symbol *k* [Named for the Austrian physicist Ludwig *Boltzmann* (1844–1906)]

bo·lus /bṓləss/ *n.* **1.** **INTRAVENOUS INJECTION OF DRUG** a dose of a drug given quickly by intravenous injection **2.** **LARGE PILL** a very large pill **3.** **ROUND MASS** a soft rounded ball, especially of chewed food [Mid-16thC. Via late Latin from Greek *bōlos* "clod of earth," of unknown origin.]

bomb /bom/ *n.* **1.** ARMS **EXPLOSIVE PROJECTILE** a missile containing explosive or other destructive material **2.** ARMS **SPECIALIZED EXPLOSIVE DEVICE** a device that contains explosive material, especially one designed to explode after some time **3.** **bomb, Bomb** ARMS **ATOMIC BOMB** the atomic bomb considered as the absolute weapon of mass destruction ○ *lived in dread of the Bomb during the Cold War* **4.** *U.S., Can, ANZ* ARTS **ARTISTIC FAILURE** a performance that is a commercial or artistic failure (*informal*) **5.** FOOTBALL **LONG HIGH PASS** a long high forward pass, especially one that results in a touchdown (*informal*) **6.** **CONTAINER FOR AEROSOL** a container holding a compressed gas **7.** *U.K.* **LOT OF MONEY** a great deal of money (*informal*) ○ *it cost a bomb* **8.** MED **DEVICE FOR DIRECTING RADIATION** a device that contains radioactive material and is used to beam therapeutic radiation at a patient **9.** GEOL **SOLIDIFIED LAVA** a solidified rounded or teardrop-shaped mass of lava from a volcano **10.** **SOMETHING OR SOMEBODY GOOD** something or somebody extremely good or exciting (*slang*) ○ *Their lead singer is the bomb.* ■ *v.* (**bombed, bomb·ing, bombs**) **1.** *vti.* MIL **ATTACK PEOPLE AND PLACES WITH BOMBS** to drop bombs on people or places, or attack or destroy them with bombs ○ *bombing enemy territory* **2.** *vt.* ARMS **DAMAGE BUILDING WITH EXPLOSION** to destroy or damage a building by placing an explosive device there (*often used with "out"*) ○ *the wreckage of bombed-out homes* **3.** *vi.* **FAIL MISERABLY** to fail badly as a performance (*informal*) **4.** *vt.* SPORTS **DEFEAT OVERWHELMINGLY** to defeat somebody or something overwhelmingly (*informal*) **5.** *vi.* **MOVE VERY FAST** to move exceptionally fast, especially in a vehicle (*informal*) **6.** *vi.* COMPUT **CRASH** to fail suddenly (*informal*) [Late 17thC. Via French, Italian, and Latin from, ultimately, Greek *bombos* "booming sound" (source of English *bombard*), ultimately an imitation of the sound.]

bom·bard /bom baárd, bóm baàrd/ *vt.* (**-bard·ed, -bard·ing, -bards**) **1.** MIL **ATTACK WITH MISSILES** to attack an enemy or enemy territory intensively with sustained artillery fire or bombs **2.** **HIT REPEATEDLY** to attack somebody persistently and vigorously **3.** **OVERWHELM** to overwhelm somebody with something, e.g., questions **4.** PHYS **HIT WITH HIGH-ENERGY PARTICLES** to direct high-energy particles against atoms or nuclei ■ *n.* HIST, ARMS **MEDIEVAL CANNON** a cannon used in medieval times to throw large stones [15thC. From French *bombarder*, from *bombarde* "cannon," via medieval Latin *bombarda* from Latin *bombus*, from Greek *bombos* (see BOMB).] —**bom·bard·er** *n.*

bom·bar·dier /bòmbər deér/ *n.* **1.** **SOMEBODY WHO RELEASES BOMBS** a member of a military aircraft crew who releases bombs **2.** **ARTILLERY SOLDIER** a member of the artillery (*archaic*) [Mid-16thC. From French, from *bombarde* "cannon" (see BOMBARD).]

bom·bar·dier bee·tle *n.* a beetle that squirts volatile acrid liquid when attacked. Latin name: *Brachinus crepitans*.

bom·bard·ment /bom baárdmənt/ *n.* **1.** **ATTACK BY BOMBS OR ARTILLERY** an intensive and sustained attack by bombs or artillery fire **2.** **CONSTANT STREAM OF SOMETHING** a large number of things, e.g., questions, aggressively directed at somebody or something

bom·bar·don /bómbərdòn, bom baárd'n/ *n.* **1.** **BASS TUBA** a brass wind instrument of the tuba family **2.** **REED STOP ON ORGAN** a bass reed stop on an organ [Mid-19thC. Via Italian *bombardone* from, ultimately, medieval Latin *bombarda* "bombard" (see BOMBARD).]

bom·ba·sine *n.* TEXTILES = **bombazine**

bom·bast /bóm bàst/ *n.* language that is full of long or pretentious words, used to impress others [Late 16thC. Alteration of Old French *bombace* "cotton stuffing," which came via medieval Latin *bombax* "cotton" from Greek *bombux* "silk, silkworm."] —**bom·bas·tic** /bom bástik/ *adj.* —**bom·bas·ti·cal·ly** /-bástiklee/ *adv.*

Bom·bay /bom báy/ former name for **Mumbai**

Bom·bay duck (*plural* **Bom·bay ducks** *or* **Bom·bay duck**) *n.* **1.** **DRIED FISH** a fish, especially the bummalo, dried, salted, grilled, and served as a pungent accompaniment to Indian foods **2.** = **bummalo** [Mid-19thC. Marathi *bombīla* "bummalo," by folk eytmology from "Bombay," by association with BOMBAY, from where the fish were exported.]

bom·ba·zine /bòmbə zeén/, **bom·ba·sine** *n.* a twilled material made from silk or cotton and worsted, usually dyed black. Black bombazine was used formerly to make mourning clothes. [Late 16thC. Via French *bombasin* from, ultimately, medieval Latin *bombycinus* "silken," from Latin *bombyx* "silk, silkworm," from Greek *bombux* (source of English *bombast*).]

bomb bay *n.* the compartment on board a bomber aircraft in which the bombs are carried

bomb cal·o·rim·e·ter *n.* a device for measuring calorific values in which substances are burned inside a sealed vessel

bomb dis·pos·al *n.* the task or process of rendering bombs harmless by defusing, removing, or detonating them in a controlled explosion (*hyphenated when used before a noun*) ○ *a bomb-disposal expert*

bombe /bom, bawNb/ *n.* a dome-shaped frozen or set dessert [Late 19thC. From French, literally "bomb," from the shape of the metal mold it is made in.]

bom·bé /bom báy/ *adj.* used to describe furniture with a bulging convex shape. This style is typical of French rococo furniture of the 18th century. [Early 20thC. From French, literally "swollen."]

bombed /bomd/ *adj.* **1.** **DAMAGED BY BOMBING** severely damaged or destroyed by bombing **2.** **INTOXICATED** drunk, or intoxicated by drugs (*slang*)

bomb·er /bómmər/ *n.* **1.** AIR FORCE **AIRCRAFT THAT DROPS BOMBS** an aircraft designed for carrying and dropping bombs **2.** CRIMINOL **SOMEBODY WHO PLANTS BOMBS** somebody who hides, places, or sets bombs

bomb·er jack·et *n.* a short jacket, usually leather, with an elastic waist and usually a zipper at the front [From the wearing of such jackets by the crew of U.S. bomber aircraft]

bom·bi·nate /bómbə nàyt/ (**-nat·ed, -nat·ing, -nates**), **bom·bi·late** /-làyt/ (**-lat·ed, -lat·ing, -lates**) *vi.* to make a humming or buzzing noise [Late 19thC. From medieval Latin *bombinat-*, the past participle stem of *bombinare*, from Latin *bombus* "buzzing, booming," from Greek *bombos* (see BOMB).] —**bom·bi·na·tion** /bòmbə náyshən/ *n.*

bomb·ing /bómming/ *n.* AIR FORCE the act or process of dropping bombs from aircraft

bomb·let /bómlət/ *n.* a small bomb or explosive device packed into a larger bomb

bomb·proof /bóm pro͞of/ *adj.* constructed to withstand the impact of bombs

bomb·shell /bóm shèl/ *n.* **1.** ARMS **ARTILLERY SHELL OR BOMB** an artillery shell or a bomb **2. SURPRISING NEWS** an unexpected and shocking piece of news (*informal*) **3. STUNNING WOMAN** an exceedingly attractive and glamorous woman (*dated informal*)

bomb·sight /bóm sìt/ *n.* a device in an aircraft for aiming bombs

bomb site *n.* an area devastated by bombs

bom·by·cid /bómbissid/ *adj.* belonging to the family of moths that includes the silkworm moths. Family: Bombycidae. [From modern Latin *Bombycidae*, family name, from Latin *bombyx* "silkworm" (see BOMBAZINE)] —**bom·by·cid** *n.*

Bo·na, Mount /bṓnə/ the highest peak in the Wrangell Mountains, southern Alaska. Height: 16,500 ft./5,032 m.

bo·na fide /bṓnə fìd, bònə fídee, bónə fìd, bònə fídee/ *adj.* **1. AUTHENTIC** authentic and genuine in nature ○ *a bona fide offer* **2. SINCERE AND HONEST** without any intention to deceive [From Latin, literally "with good faith"]

bo·na fi·des /-fídeez, -fìdz/ *npl.* a sincere statement or evidence of good intentions

Bo·naire Is·land /baw náir-/ island in the Netherlands Antilles off the coast of Venezuela. It is a popular tourist destination. Population: 12,533 (1994). Area: 112 sq. mi./290 sq. km.

bo·nan·za /bə nánzə/ *n.* **1. SOURCE OF WEALTH** a source that yields great riches or success **2. VALUABLE MINERAL DEPOSIT** an extremely valuable mineral deposit [Early 19thC. Via Spanish from medieval Latin *bonacia* "calm seas," an alteration of *malacia*, "calm seas" influenced by Latin *bonus* "good."]

Bo·na·parte ➧ **Napoleon I**

Bo·na·part·ism /bṓnə paàr tìzzəm/ *n.* **1. NAPOLEONIC RULE** government by or on the pattern of Napoleon I **2. LOYALTY TO NAPOLEONIC TRADITION** support for Napoleon I and Napoleon III of France or their dynasty [Early 19thC. Named for the emperor NAPOLEON Bonaparte.] —**Bo·na·part·ist** *n.*

Bon·a·ven·tu·re /bònnə ven cho͞orə, -to͞orə, -tyo͞orə/, **Bon·a·ven·tu·ra, St.** (1221?–74) Italian monk and theologian. He was minister general of the Franciscan order (1257) and wrote the official biography of St. Francis (1263). Born **Giovanni di Fidanza**. Known as **the Seraphic Doctor**

bon·bon /bón bòn/ *n.* **1. CANDY** a candy confection **2. SOMETHING SWEET** something that is sweet and unsubstantial [Late 18thC. From French, literally "good-good," from Latin *bonus* "good" (see BONUS).]

bon·bon·nière /bònbon yáir/ *n.* an ornamental bowl or box for candy [Early 19thC. From French, from *bonbon* "BONBON."]

bond /bond/ *n.* **1. ADHESION** the way in which one surface sticks to another **2. ADHESIVE SUBSTANCE** a substance that makes objects adhere **3. LINK BINDING PEOPLE TOGETHER** a link that binds people together in a relationship **4. RESTRAINT** a situation that limits somebody socially, psychologically, or emotionally **5.** LAW **SOLEMN PROMISE** a solemn agreement promising to do something **6.** FIN **CERTIFICATE PROMISING REPAYMENT OF DEBT** a certificate issued by the government or a company promising to pay back borrowed money at a fixed rate of interest on a specified date **7.** LAW **PROMISE TO PAY** a document that legally obliges one party to pay money to another **8.** LAW **PAYMENT SECURING BAIL** a sum of money paid to secure the release from prison of somebody awaiting trial, on the condition that the person appears on the date of the trial **9. SOMETHING THAT BINDS** an object such as a rope, band, or chain that binds somebody or something **10. INSURANCE POLICY AGAINST FINANCIAL LOSSES** an insurance policy held by an employer or contractor that protects clients' or customers' money as a safeguard against unforeseen financial loss by a third party **11.** CHEM **ATTRACTIVE FORCE** a fundamental attractive force that binds atoms and ions in a molecule. There are different types of bond. **12.** COMM **SECURE STORAGE** secure storage of goods before payment of duty **13.** CONSTR **TECHNIQUE FOR OVERLAPPING BRICKS** an overlapping pattern in which bricks or tiles can be laid **14.** = **bond paper 15.** = **bonded whiskey** ■ **bonds** *npl.* **IMPRISONMENT** the state of imprisonment (*archaic*) ■ *v.* **(bond·ed, bond·ing, bonds) 1.** *vt.* CHEM **LINK WITH CHEMICAL BOND** to link atoms or ions with a chemical bond **2.** *vti.* **ADHERE OR MAKE ADHERE** to stick together or make two surfaces stick together **3.** *vt.* COMM **STORE SECURELY** store goods securely until duty is paid **4.** *vti.* PSYCHOL **LINK EMOTIONALLY** to link together, or cause people to be linked together, emotionally or psychologically **5.** *vti.* FIN **CONVERT INTO DEBT UNDER BOND** to convert something or be converted into a debt with a bond as security **6.** *vt.* CONSTR **OVERLAP** to lay bricks or tiles so that they overlap in a pattern **7.** *vt.* SEW **FUSE TOGETHER** to fuse two fabrics together [13thC. Variant of BAND[2].] —**bond·a·ble** *adj.* —**bond·er** *n.*

bond·age /bóndij/ *n.* **1. SLAVERY** the condition of being a slave or serf **2. PHYSICAL RESTRAINT** the practice of being tied up or restrained physically during sexual intercourse **3. CONTROL BY SOMETHING** the condition of being controlled by something that limits freedom [14thC. Via Anglo-Norman from, ultimately, Old Norse *bóndi* "husbandman," from the present participle of *búa* "to dwell" (source of English *husband*).]

bond·ed /bóndəd/ *adj.* **1. PROTECTED BY INSURANCE** protected by insurance against financial losses caused by a third party **2.** COMM **STORED BEFORE TAXATION** stored securely until duty or tax is paid **3.** INDUST **MADE TO ADHERE IN LAYERS** chemically attached or fused together in layers

bond·ed ware·house *n.* a warehouse that holds goods awaiting duty or tax to be paid on them

bond·ed whis·key *n.* a whiskey that has been aged at least four years in a bonded warehouse before use

bond·hold·er /bónd hòldər/ *n.* somebody who owns bonds issued by a government or company

bond·ing /bónding/ *n.* **1.** PSYCHOL **FORMATION OF EMOTIONAL BONDS** the formation of a close emotional tie between people, e.g., between a mother and her newly born infant. ◊ **attachment 2.** DENT **COATING A TOOTH** the process of coating a tooth with a durable resinous substance **3. PROCESS OF BONDING SOMETHING** the process by which something is bonded

bond·man /bóndmən/ (*plural* **-men** /bóndmən/) *n.* a male slave or serf [13thC. Coined from earlier *bond* "bound in servitude" + MAN.]

bond pa·per *n.* a strong, white, high-quality paper

bond·ser·vant /bónd sùrvənt/ *n.* a slave or serf [15thC. Formed from earlier *bond* "bound in servitude" + SERVANT.]

bonds·man /bóndzmən/ (*plural* **-men** /-mən/) *n.* **1. SOMEBODY RESPONSIBLE FOR A LEGAL BOND** somebody who assumes responsibility for a legal bond **2.** HIST = **bondman**

bond·stone /bónd stṑn/ *n.* a stone that extends into the interior of a wall in order to strengthen it

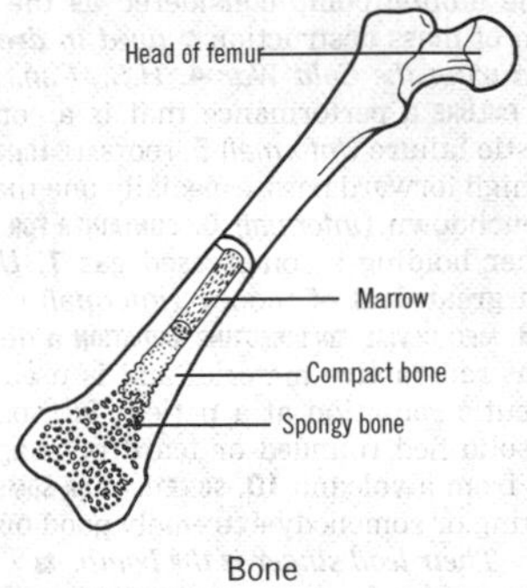

Bone

bone /bṑn/ *n.* **1.** ANAT **SECTION OF THE SKELETON** any one of the hard parts forming the skeleton in vertebrate animals **2.** ANAT **MATERIAL MAKING UP BONES** the main material that makes up a vertebrate skeleton, formed principally from collagen fibers and calcium phosphate **3.** INDUST **SUBSTANCE RESEMBLING BONE** something hard that resembles the bone of the vertebrate skeleton, e.g., whalebone or ivory **4. SOMETHING GIVEN AS SUBSTITUTE** something intended solely to soothe or placate somebody (*slang*) ○ *Throw him a bone in the form of a bonus and he'll calm down* **5.** COLORS **IVORY COLOR** the ivory or off-white color of bone **6.** CLOTHES **STRIP USED AS STIFFENING** a flat strip of hard material, e.g., whalebone or plastic, used to stiffen a garment ■ **bones** *npl.* **1. LIVING BODY** somebody's living body (*humorous*) ○ *I must rest my weary bones.* **2. DEAD BODY** the skeleton or corpse of a dead person or animal **3.** MUSIC **PAIR OF RHYTHMICALLY CLACKING BARS** a pair of bars or strips of wood, metal, or bone, that are struck together sharply to make musical rhythms **4. STRUCTURE OF SOMETHING** the structure or framework of something **5. DICE** a pair of dice (*informal*) ■ *vt.* **(boned, bon·ing, bones) 1.** COOKING **REMOVE BONES FROM** to remove the bones from fish, meat, or poultry when preparing it for cooking or eating **2.** CLOTHES **STIFFEN** to add flat strips to stiffen a garment **3. OFFENSIVE TERM** to have sexual intercourse (*slang offensive*) ■ *adv.* **VERY** extremely or totally ○ *bone idle* [Old English *bān*. Ultimately from a prehistoric Germanic word meaning "long bone."] ◇ **have a bone to pick with somebody** to have cause for disagreement with somebody ◇ **in your bones** without having to think or reason ◇ **make no bones about something** to say something openly and frankly

bone up *vi.* to review or study something intensely (*informal*)

bone chi·na *n.* **1. FINE WHITE PORCELAIN** a fine white porcelain made from a mixture of clay and bone ash **2. ARTICLES MADE OF BONE CHINA** articles made of bone china

bone·fish /bṓn fìsh/ (*plural* **-fish** *or* **-fish·es**) *n.* a large game fish found in warm shallow waters. Latin name: *Albula vulpes.*

bone·head /bṓn hèd/ *n.* an offensive term that deliberately insults somebody's intelligence (*informal insult*) —**bone·head·ed** *adj.* —**bone·head·ed·ness** *n.*

bone mar·row *n.* a soft reddish substance inside some bones that is involved in the production of blood cells. New white and red blood cells are formed only in the marrow of the flat bones such as the ribs, breastbone, or pelvis in adults.

bone meal *n.* ground animal bones, used as a fertilizer or in animal feed [*Meal* from MEAL[2]]

bone of con·ten·tion *n.* a subject of constant argument or disagreement between people [From the fighting of dogs over possession of a bone]

bon·er /bṓnər/ *n.* **1. EMBARRASSING MISTAKE** an embarrassing mistake (*informal*) **2. ERECTION** an erect penis (*slang*) **3. DEVICE THAT BONES** something that is designed for boning something, or somebody who bones something ○ *a fish boner*

bone·set /bṓn sèt/ (*plural* **-set** *or* **-sets**) *n.* a North American plant of the daisy family believed to have healing properties. Genus: *Eupatorium.*

bone·shak·er /bṓn shàykər/ *n.* an early type of bicycle with solid tires and no springs

bone spav·in *n.* an inflammation of the bones in a horse's hock, resulting in swelling and lameness

Bon·e·var·di /bònə vaárdee/, **Marcelo** (*b.* 1929) Argentine artist. He is best known for his geometric figures on relief constructions.

bone·yard /bṓn yaàrd/ *n.* (*informal*) **1. CEMETERY** a cemetery **2. PLACE FOR DISCARDED OBJECTS** a place where discarded metal objects are collected before being recycled

bon·fire /bón fìr/ *n.* a large fire built outside for burning garbage, as part of a celebration, or as a signal [14thC. Formed from BONE + FIRE, from the original use of burned bones as fuel.]

WORD KEY: CULTURAL NOTE

Bonfire of the Vanities, a novel by Tom Wolfe (1988). Using the story of the trial of wealthy New York bond trader Sherman McCoy for the accidental killing of a young Black man, Wolfe satirizes the U.S. media, legal system, and art world. It was made into a movie by Brian de Palma in 1990.

Bon·fire Night *n.* November 5, the anniversary of the day on which Guy Fawkes' plot to blow up the British parliament (**the Gunpowder Plot**) was discovered in 1605. In the United Kingdom and other Commonwealth countries it is celebrated with fireworks and bonfires.

bong[1] /bong, bawng/ *n.*, *interj.* **REVERBERATING SOUND** a deep resonant sound, especially from a bell ■ *vi.* **(bonged, bong·ing, bongs) MAKE A REVERBERATING SOUND** to make a deep resonant sound [Mid-19thC. An imitation of the sound.]

bong[2] /bong, bawng/ *n.* **1.** DRUGS **DRUG-USER'S WATER PIPE** a water pipe for smoking marijuana or other drugs (*slang*) **2.** MOUNTAINEERING **METAL DEVICE FOR PROTECTING CLIMBERS** a large metal device resembling a tube, used in providing protection for climbers [Late 20thC. Origin uncertain: probably from Thai *baung*.]

bon·go /bóng gṑ, báwng/ (*plural* **-gos** *or* **-goes** *or* **-go**) *n.* a forest-dwelling antelope found in central Africa that has a reddish coat with vertical white stripes and spiralling horns. Latin name: *Boocercus euryceros.* [Mid-19thC. From Kikongo.]

bon·go drums, bon·gos *npl.* a set of two small deep-bodied drums that are held between the knees and beaten with the fingers [From American Spanish *bongó*]

bon·ho·mie /bònnə meé/ *n.* easy good-humored friendliness [Late 18thC. From French *bonhomme*, literally "good man."] —**bon·ho·mous** *adj.*

Bon·i·face /bónnə fàyss/, **St.** (675?–754?) Saxon missionary. Commissioned to preach to the German peoples in 718, he became a bishop in 723. He was killed by non-Christians in Friesia. Born **Wynfrith.** Known as **the Apostle of Germany**

bo·ni·to /bə neétō/ (*plural* **-tos** *or* **-to**) *n.* **1. FISH OF MACKEREL FAMILY** a striped edible fish found in Atlantic and Pacific waters. Genus: *Sarda.* **2. FISH RESEMBLING TRUE BONITO** a fish such as the skipjack that resembles or is related to the bonito [Late 16thC. Origin uncertain: probably via Spanish, literally "pretty," from Latin *bonus* "good" (see BONUS).]

bonk /bonk/ *vt.* (**bonked, bonk·ing, bonks**) **BANG** to bang or hit something or somebody (*informal*) ■ *n.* **SHARP BLOW** a sharp blow, typically on the head [Early 20thC. An imitation of the sound.]

bon mot /bàwN mṓ/ (*plural* **bons mots** /bàwN mṓ, -mṓz/) *n.* a witty comment [From French, literally "good word"]

Bonn /bon, bawn/ city on the Rhine in North Rhine-Westphalia state, west central Germany. It was the capital of West Germany from 1949 to 1990. Population: 297,400 (1992).

Bonnet

bon·net /bónnət/ *n.* **1. WOMAN'S HAT** a hat framing the face and usually tied under the chin, worn by a woman or girl **2.** *U.K., Carib* AUTOMOT = **hood 3. NATIVE AMERICAN HEADDRESS** a ceremonial feathered headdress traditionally worn by some Native Americans **4. CHIMNEY COWL** a wire cover fitted over a chimney pot **5.** ENG **PROTECTIVE COVER** a protective cap or cover fitting over a machine part **6.** SAILING **EXTRA PIECE OF SAIL** an extra strip of canvas laced to the base of a foresail, used to extend it when the wind is light [14thC. Via Old French from medieval Latin *abonnis* "headgear," possibly of Germanic origin.] —**bon·net·ed** *adj.*

bon·net·head /bónnət hed/ (*plural* **-heads** *or* **-head**), **bon·net·head shark** *n.* a shark with a spade-shaped head, found in shallow Atlantic waters. Latin name: *Sphyrna tiburo.*

Bon·ne·ville Salt Flats /bònnəvìl-/ barren salt plain in northwestern Utah, the bed of a prehistoric lake. It has been used for setting world land speed records since the 1930s. Area: 100 sq. mi./260 sq. km.

bon·ny /bónnee/ (**-ni·er, -ni·est**), **bon·nie** (**-ni·er, -ni·est**) *adj. Scotland, N England* **1. ATTRACTIVE** pleasing to look at **2. SUBSTANTIAL** fairly large **3. EXCELLENT** extremely good [15thC. Origin uncertain: perhaps via French *bon* "good" from Latin *bonus.*] —**bon·ni·ly** *adv.* —**bon·ni·ness** *n.*

bon·ny·clab·ber /bónni klàbbər/ *n. Ireland, U.S.* sour milk that has curdled (*regional*) [Early 17thC. From Irish *bainne clabair* "thick milk for churning."]

WORD KEY: REGIONAL NOTE

Though also used in Ireland, this is a New England term that extends as far south as Maryland and as far west as Indiana. In the South, the term is replaced with such regionalisms as *blinky, clabber milk,* and *sour milk.*

Bonsai

bon·sai /bón sī, bon sī́, -zī/ (*plural* **-sai** *or* **-sais**) *n.* **1.** GARDENING **ART OF GROWING MINIATURE TREES** the art of growing miniaturized forms of trees and shrubs by rigorous pruning of roots and branches **2.** TREES **MINIATURIZED TREE** a tree or shrub miniaturized using bonsai techniques [Early 20thC. From Japanese, literally "tray planting."]

bon·spiel /bón speel, -shpeel/ *n.* SPORTS a curling match or tournament [Mid-16thC. Origin uncertain: probably from Dutch or Low German.]

bon·te·bok /bóntə bòk/ (*plural* **-boks** *or* **-bok**) *n.* a southern African antelope with a reddish coat, white markings on the face and rump, and white legs. Latin name: *Damaliscus pygargus.* [Late 18thC. From Afrikaans, literally "pied buck."]

bon ton /bàwN táwN, bon tón/ *n.* (*literary*) **1. GOOD TASTE** good taste, style, or manners ○ *People thought it bon ton to be seen attending such an occasion.* **2. FASHIONABLE SOCIETY** fashionable society [From French, literally "good tone"]

bo·nus /bṓnəss/ *n.* **1. UNEXPECTED EXTRA** an extra unexpected advantage **2. EXTRA MONEY** an amount of money given in addition to normal pay, especially as a reward **3. PREMIUM PAID TO SOMEBODY** an extra dividend or premium paid to the purchaser, holder, promoter, or vendor of a stock or insurance policy **4. SPECIAL GOVERNMENT PAYMENT TO INDIVIDUALS** a special payment by a government to an individual **5. PREMIUM PAID FOR AGREEING TO SOMETHING** a premium paid for signing a contract or taking out a loan [Late 18thC. From Latin, "good" (source of English *bounty*). Ultimately from an Indo-European base meaning "to show favor," which is also the ancestor of English *benevolent, embellish,* and *beauty.*]

bon vi·vant /bòN veevaáN/ (*plural* **bons vi·vants** /bòN veevaáN/), **bon vi·veur** /-vee vúr/ (*plural* **bons vi·veurs** /-vúrz/) *n.* somebody who enjoys the luxuries in life, e.g., good food and wine (*literary*) [*Bon vivant* from French, literally "one who lives well"; *bon viveur* formed in English on the model of *bon vivant* and French *viveur* "living person"]

bon voy·age /bòN vwaayaázh/ *interj.* used to wish somebody an enjoyable and safe trip [From French, literally "good journey"]

bon·y /bṓnee/ (**-i·er, -i·est**) *adj.* **1. HAVING PROMINENT BONES** extremely thin and with prominent bones **2.** FOOD **CONTAINING MANY BONES** containing a lot of bones, and often difficult to eat **3.** ANAT **OF OR LIKE BONE** consisting of or like bone **4.** ZOOL **WITH A BACKBONE** used to describe fish that have a skeleton of bone, as distinct from cartilaginous fish such as sharks. The great majority of fish are bony. Class: Osteichthyes. —**bon·i·ness** *n.*

bonze /bonz/ *n.* a Buddhist monk in Southeast Asia, China, or Japan [Late 16thC. Via French from, ultimately, Japanese *bonsō.*]

boo /boo/ *interj.* **1. EXPRESSING DISAPPROVAL** used to express dissatisfaction or contempt, especially at a speaker or performer **2. USED TO STARTLE SOMEBODY** used to surprise or startle somebody ■ *n.* **SOUND "BOO!"** an utterance of "boo!" ■ *vti.* (**booed, boo·ing, boos**) **EXPRESS DISAPPROVAL** to shout "boo!" in order to express disapproval or contempt of somebody, especially a speaker or performer [Early 19thC. Originally an imitation of a cow's lowing.] ◇ **not say boo** to be silent or reticent (*informal*)

boob[1] /boob/, **boo·by** /bóobee/ (*plural* **-bies**) *n.* a woman's breast (*slang*) (*considered offensive by many people; often used in the plural*) [Mid-20thC. From earlier *bubby,* of uncertain origin: perhaps from Low German.]

boob[2] /boob/ *n.* **1. UNINTELLIGENT PERSON** somebody who is considered unintelligent or ignorant **2.** *U.K.* **UNFORTUNATE MISTAKE** an unfortunate and embarrassing mistake (*informal*) ■ *vi.* (**boobed, boob·ing, boobs**) *U.K., Can* **MAKE AN UNFORTUNATE MISTAKE** to make an unfortunate and embarrassing mistake (*informal*) [Early 20thC. Shortening of BOOBY[1].]

boo-boo *n.* **1. MISTAKE** a mistake or tactless remark (*informal*) **2. SLIGHT DAMAGE TO SOMEBODY'S BODY** a cut, injury, or sore place on the body (*babytalk*) [Mid-20thC. Origin uncertain.]

boo·book /boó bòok/ (*plural* **-books** *or* **-book**) *n.* a small brown owl, native to Australia and New Zealand. Genus: *Ninox.* [Early 19thC. From an Australian Aboriginal language, ultimately an imitation of the bird's call.]

boob tube[1] *n. U.K.* = **tube top** (*slang*)

boob tube[2] *n.* television (*informal*)

boo·by[1] /bóobee/ (*plural* **-bies**) *n.* **1. UNINTELLIGENT PERSON** somebody who is silly or unintelligent (*dated informal*) **2.** BIRDS **LARGE TROPICAL SEABIRD** a large tropical seabird with white plumage and dark markings, often with a brightly colored bill and feet. There are many species, including pelicans and cormorants. Family: Sulidae. [Early 17thC. Origin uncertain: probably an alteration of Spanish *bobo,* from Latin *balbus* "stammering."]

boo·by[2] /bóobee/ *n.* = **boob**[1]

boo·by hatch *n.* **1. OFFENSIVE TERM** an offensive term for a a mental health facility (*slang offensive*) **2. HATCHWAY COVER** a cover for a small hatchway on a sailing ship [*Booby* from *booby* "bird," because these hatches are a favorite haunt for these birds]

boo·by prize *n.* a prize given as a joke to the person or team coming last in a competition

boo·by trap *n.* **1. HIDDEN EXPLOSIVE DEVICE** a bomb that is hidden or disguised and is designed to explode when touched or moved **2. TRAP LAID AS JOKE** a trap set as a practical joke

boo·by-trap (**boo·by-trapped, boo·by-trap·ping, boo·by-traps**) *vt.* to place a booby trap in a place, or attach one to something (*often passive*)

boo·dle /bóod'l/ *n.* **1. DISHONESTLY ACQUIRED MONEY** a large amount of money that has been acquired or used in a corrupt way (*slang*) **2.** = **caboodle** (*informal*) [Early 17thC. From Dutch *boedel* "estate, possessions."]

boog·er /bóoggər/ *n.* **1.** = **bogeyman** *n.* 1 (*informal*) **2. NASAL MUCUS** a lump of mucus in or from somebody's nose (*slang*) [Mid-19thC. Origin uncertain: probably an alteration of BUGGER.]

boog·ie /bóoggee/ *vi.* (**-ied, -ie·ing, -ies**) **1.** DANCING **DANCE TO ROCK MUSIC** to dance to fast rock music (*informal*) **2. GO SOMEWHERE** to go somewhere specified, on foot or by vehicle (*slang*) ○ *Let's boogie along to the French Quarter* ○ *Get your coat; it's time to boogie out of here* **3. HAVE SEX** to have sexual intercourse (*dated slang*) ■ *n.* MUSIC = **boogie-woogie** [Mid-20thC. Of West African origin see BOOGIE-WOOGIE.]

boogie on down *vi.* to go off somewhere (*slang*)

Boogie *tdmk.* a trademark for a short flexible surfboard on which a surfer lies prone

boog·ie-woog·ie /bòogi wóoggee/ *n.* a jazz piano style derived from the blues [Origin uncertain: perhaps an alteration of Black West African English *bogi-bogi* "to dance," from Hausa *buga* "to beat drums"]

boo·hoo /boo hóo/ *n., interj.* **SOUND OF COPIOUS WEEPING** used to represent the sound of noisy weeping ■ *vi.* (**-hooed, -hoo·ing, -hoos**) **SOB** to cry noisily [Mid-19thC. An imitation of the sound.]

book /bòok/ *n.* **1. BOUND COLLECTION OF PAGES** a collection of printed or manuscript pages sewn or glued together along one side and bound between rigid boards or flexible covers **2. PUBLISHED WORK** a published work of literature, science, or reference, or one intended for publication **3. BOUND SET OF BLANK SHEETS** a bound set of blank sheets of paper, e.g. for writing in **4. SET OF THINGS BOUND TOGETHER** a set of objects, e.g., matches or fabric samples, that are bound or otherwise fixed together **5. DIVISION OF LITERARY WORK** each of several major divisions of a literary work, or of the Bible **6. SET OF RULES** the body of rules or procedures relevant to a situation ○ *likes to do things by the book* **7. BOOKMAKER'S RECORD** a record kept by a bookmaker of the bets made and of the money paid out **8. SCRIPT OR LIBRETTO** the script of a play, or the libretto of an opera **9.** CARDS **NUMBER OF TRICKS NEEDED IN SCORING** the number of tricks that need to be won by a player or side in order to be scored **10. IMAGINARY RECORD** any imaginary record, archive, or repository of knowledge **11.** SPORTS **RECORD ABOUT SPORTS OPPONENTS** in sports, a record of facts and information about the strengths and weaknesses of a player or team **12.** = **promptbook 13. book, Book BIBLE** the Christian Bible ■ **books** *npl.* **1.** ACCT **FINANCIAL ACCOUNTS** the financial records and accounts of an organization **2. LEARNING** academic study ■ *v.* **(booked, book·ing, books) 1.** *vti.* **MAKE RESERVATION** to arrange for somebody to keep a place available at a specified time, e.g., at the theater or in a restaurant **2.** *vt.* **ENGAGE TO DO SOMETHING** to engage somebody in advance to do something or be somewhere, especially as a performer (*often passive*) **3.** *vi.* **LEAVE A PLACE** to leave a place (*hip slang*) ○ *Yo man, let's book!* **4.** *vt. U.K.* SPORTS **TAKE NAME OF OFFENDING PLAYER** officially to take the name of a player who has committed an offense (*often passive*) **5.** *vt.* LAW **CHARGE WITH OFFENSE** to charge somebody with a criminal offense, pending legal proceedings (*often passive*) [Old English *bōc* "written document." Ultimately from an Indo-European word meaning "beech," which is also the ancestor of English *beech*; the early Germanic peoples carved runic inscriptions on beechwood tablets.] ◇ **a closed book** somebody about whom or something about which little if anything is known or understood ◇ **an open book** something or somebody fully comprehended ◇ **bring somebody to book** to admonish somebody ◇ **cook the books** to alter records, especially financial accounts, to conceal irregularities or wrongdoing (*slang*) ◇ **in somebody's book** in somebody's opinion ◇ **in somebody's good** *or* **bad books** in *or* out of favor with somebody ◇ **make book on something** to accept bets on the likelihood of something happening ◇ **throw the book at somebody** to charge somebody with all the offenses he or she may be guilty of, or punish somebody with the maximum penalty

book up *vi.* to sell out something in advance (*usually passive*)

book·a·ble /bŏŏkəb'l/ *adj.* able to be applied for in advance and reserved

book·bind·er /bŏŏk bìndər/ *n.* somebody who binds books, especially as a profession —**book·bind·er·y** *n.* —**book·bind·ing** *n.*

book·case /bŏŏk kàyss/ *n.* a set of shelves, either fixed to a wall or free-standing, used for holding books

book club *n.* **1. FIRM SELLING BOOKS AT REDUCED PRICES** an organization that offers its members books at reduced prices **2. DISCUSSION GROUP ABOUT BOOKS** a small informal group that meets to discuss books and related topics

book·end /bŏŏk ènd/ *n.* **1. SUPPORT FOR ROW OF BOOKS** either of a pair of supports placed at each end of a row of books **2.** SPORTS **DEFENSIVE PLAYER IN FOOTBALL** in football, a player positioned at one of the ends of the defensive line (*informal*) ■ *vt.* **OCCUR EITHER SIDE OF** to occur on both sides or at the beginning and end of something (*informal*) ○ *bookend a speech with anecdotes*

book·ie /bŏŏkee/ *n.* = **bookmaker** *n.* 1 (*informal*) [Late 19thC. Formed from BOOKMAKER.]

book·ing /bŏŏking/ *n.* **1. ADVANCE RESERVATION** an arrangement by which something such as a theater seat or hotel room is kept for somebody's use at a specified time **2. ARRANGEMENT TO PERFORM** a contract or arrangement for an entertainer to perform somewhere

book·ish /bŏŏkish/ *adj.* devoted to reading, especially to the exclusion of other things —**book·ish·ly** *adv.* —**book·ish·ness** *n.*

book·keep·ing /bŏŏk keeping/, **book-keep·ing** *n.* the activity or profession of recording the money received and spent by an individual, business, or organization —**book·keep·er** *n.*

book learn·ing *n.* knowledge obtained from books rather than from experience

book·let /bŏŏklət/ *n.* a small book with a paper cover and few pages, usually containing information about a particular subject

book·louse /bŏŏk lòwss/ (*plural* **-lice** /-lìss/) *n.* a small wingless insect that destroys books by feeding on the paste used in the binding. Order: Psocoptera.

book lung *n.* the breathing organ in spiders and other arachnids, with membranous tissue arranged in folds that resemble the leaves of a book

book·mak·er /bŏŏk màykər/ *n.* **1. SOMEBODY WHO RECEIVES BETS** somebody who takes bets and pays out money to people who win **2. SOMEBODY WHO MAKES BOOKS** somebody who designs, prints, or binds books —**book·mak·ing** *n.*

book·man /bŏŏkmən/ (*plural* **-men** /-mən/) *n.* somebody who is interested in and knowledgable about books, especially as collector's items

book·mark /bŏŏk maark/ *n.* **1. PLACE MARKER IN BOOK** a strip of leather or other material inserted between the pages of a book to mark a place in it **2.** COMPUT **PLACE MARKER IN ELECTRONIC TEXT** an electronic marker inserted in a word processed document, identifying it for later reference or retrieval **3.** COMPUT **ADDRESS OF INTERNET SITE** the address of a user's favorite Internet site electronically listed for easy access ■ *vt.* **(-marked, -mark·ing, -marks)** COMPUT **LIST AN INTERNET ADDRESS** to list the address of an Internet site

book·mo·bile /bŏŏk mō beel/ *n.* a large motor vehicle equipped as a small lending library, used for taking books to people, especially in rural areas

Book of Chang·es *n.* = **I Ching**

Book of Com·mon Prayer *n.* the official book giving the order and content of services in the Episcopal Church. Since 1980 the Alternative Service Book has also been in use.

book of hours *n.* a medieval service book, used especially in monasteries, containing the offices, prayers, and services prescribed for the various canonical hours

Book of Kells /-kélz/ *n.* an illuminated manuscript of the Christian Gospels, produced at Kells in Ireland in the 8th century A.D. and now kept in Trinity College, Dublin

Book of Life *n.* CHR the Bible

Book of Mor·mon *n.* a book believed by Mormons to have been revealed by the prophet Mormon to Joseph Smith. It contains the history of an ancient American people to whom Jesus Christ appeared.

book·plate /bŏŏk plàyt/ *n.* a label for sticking into the front of a book, bearing the name of the owner and sometimes a coat of arms or personal design

book·rest /bŏŏk rèst/ *n.* a support, often angled, for an open book

book·sell·er /bŏŏk sèllər/ *n.* somebody who buys and sells books

book·shelf /bŏŏk shèlf/ (*plural* **-shelves** /-shèlvz/) *n.* a shelf designed for holding books

book·shop /bŏŏk shòp/ *n.* a store, especially a small one, that specializes in selling books

book·stall /bŏŏk stàwl/ *n.* a stall where books are sold

book·stand /bŏŏk stànd/ *n.* **1.** = **bookstall 2. SUPPORT FOR OPEN BOOK** a support for an open book, often adjustable and made of wood, metal, or plastic

book·store /bŏŏk stàwr, -stòr/ *n.* a store that sells books

book val·ue *n.* **1. VALUE ACCORDING TO ACCOUNTING RECORDS** the value of a commodity or asset according to the accounting records of the firm owning it **2. NET VALUE OF BUSINESS ENTERPRISE** the net value of a business after liabilities have been deducted from assets

book·worm /bŏŏk wùrm/ *n.* **1. ENTHUSIASTIC READER** somebody who reads a great deal (*informal*) **2. INSECT EATING BOOKS** any insect whose larvae eat the binding paste or paper in books

Bool·e·an /bŏŏlee ən/ *adj.* using or characterized by a system of symbolic logic that uses combinations of such logical operators as "AND," "OR," and "NOT" to determine relationships between entities. Boolean operations are extensively used in writing computer programs and in computer searches using keywords. [Mid-19thC. Named for the English mathematician George *Boole* (1815–64), who devised the system.]

Bool·e·an al·ge·bra *n.* a form of algebra concerned with the logical functions of variables that are restricted to two values, true or false. Boolean algebra is fundamental to circuit design and to the design, function, and operation of computers.

boom[1] /boom/ *v.* **(boomed, boom·ing, booms) 1.** *vi.* **MAKE A LOUD DEEP SOUND** to make a loud deep reverberating sound **2.** *vt.* **UTTER WITH DEEP SOUND** to utter something, e.g., a warning, in a loud deep voice **3.** *vt.* **CAMPAIGN FOR SOMEBODY** to campaign vigorously for somebody ■ *n.* **1. LOUD DEEP SOUND** a loud deep reverberating sound **2.** ECON **SIGNIFICANT INCREASE IN TRADE** a significant expansion of business and investment, either across an economy or in a specific market **3. SIGNIFICANT INCREASE** a significant increase in the amount of something, e.g., in a population level or in the public interest in something **4.** ZOOL **DEEP LOUD BIRD OR ANIMAL NOISE** a deep loud cry made by some birds and animals, e.g., bitterns or grouse [15thC. Origin uncertain: possibly from Dutch *bommen* "to hum, buzz"; ultimately an imitation of the sound.] —**boom·y** *adj.*

boom[2] /boom/ *n.* **1.** CINEMA, TV **EXTENDABLE OVERHEAD POLE** an extendable pole carrying overhead equipment, such as a camera, for positioning over a television or movie set **2.** SAILING **BEAM HOLDING SAIL AT ANGLE** a beam to which the bottom edge of a sail is attached in order to hold the sail at an advantageous angle to the wind **3.** MIL, INDUST **FLOATING BARRIER** a floating barrier used to confine or restrict something, e.g., a barrier to protect a harbor from attack or to confine an oil spill **4.** SHIPPING **POLE USED TO MOVE CARGO** a long pole extending from the mast of a derrick to lift or lower cargo **5.** AIR **CONNECTING SPAR FOR AIRCRAFT** a spar that connects the tail and the fuselage in some aircraft [Mid-16thC. From Dutch, "beam, pole." Ultimately from a prehistoric Germanic word meaning "tree," which is also the ancestor of English *beam* and *bumpkin*.] ◇ **lower the boom** to initiate action to prevent something or punish somebody (*informal*)

boom and bust, boom or bust *n.* the alternation in an economy or market between immoderate growth and collapse and recession

boom box *n.* = **ghetto blaster**

boom·er /bŏŏmər/ *n.* **1.** = **baby boomer** (*informal*) **2. SOMEBODY WHO MOVES TO PROSPEROUS PLACE** somebody who moves to a place that is undergoing an economic boom **3.** NAVY **SUBMARINE** a nuclear-powered submarine armed with ballistic missiles (*slang*)

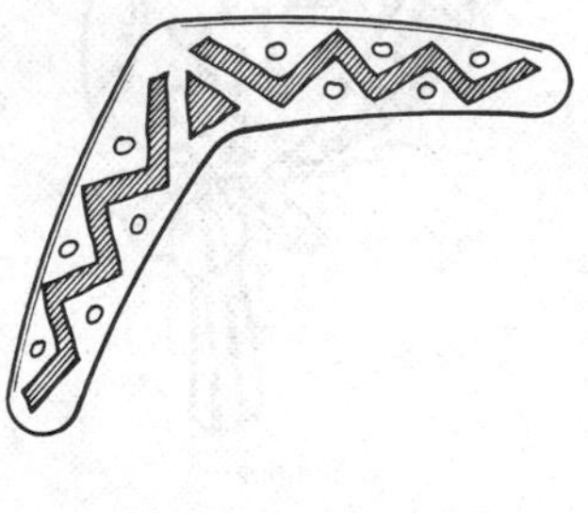

Boomerang

boo·mer·ang /bŏŏmə ràng/ *n.* **1.** SOC SCI, ARMS **CURVED MISSILE** a flat bent or curved piece of wood used as a weapon by Australian Aborigines. It is designed to return to the person who throws it. **2. SOMETHING HARMFUL TO INITIATOR** something that does harm to its initiator ■ *vi.* **(-anged, -ang·ing, -angs) BACKFIRE ON INITIATOR** to backfire on an initiator of an action, causing harm [Late 18thC. From Aboriginal.]

boom·kin *n.* = **bumpkin**[2]

boom·let /bŏŏmlət/ *n.* a short period of sudden and intense economic growth

boom town *n.* a town that significantly increases in size and wealth, often as the result of new and profitable industry

boon /boon/ *n.* **1. GREAT BENEFIT** something that functions as a blessing or benefit to somebody **2. GIFT OR FAVOR** a gift or favor from somebody (*archaic or literary*) [From Old Norse *bón* "prayer, petition." Ultimately from an Indo-European word meaning "to speak," which is also the ancestor of English *ban, banish,* and *fame.*]

boon com·pan·ion *n.* an intimate and inseparable friend [*Boon* via French *bon* from Latin *bonus* "good" (see BONUS)]

boon·docks /bŏŏn dòks/ *npl.* anywhere far from civilization, used as an archetype of a provincial way of life and lack of sophistication (*informal*) [Mid-20thC. From Tagalog *bundok* "mountain."]

boon·dog·gle /bŏŏn dàwgg'l, -dògg'l/ *n.* (*informal*) **1. INSIGNIFICANT PURSUIT** an activity or project that is trivial and wasteful of time or money **2. POLITICALLY MOTIVATED GOVERNMENT PROJECT** a government project of little practical value funded to gain political favor ■ *vi.* **(-gled, -gling, -gles)** (*informal*) **1. DO SOMETHING IMPRACTICAL** to do something unimportant or impractical **2.** DECEIVE OR MISLEAD SOMEBODY to deceive or attempt to deceive somebody [Mid-20thC. Coined by the U.S. scoutmaster R. H. Link for a braided leather cord made by Scouts.] —**boon·dog·gler** *n.* —**boon·dog·gling** *n.*

Boone /boon/, **Daniel** (1734–1820) U.S. pioneer. He lived on the frontier from age 16 and was instrumental in exploring and settling Kentucky in the 1770s. He founded Boonesboro (1775).

boon·ga·ry /bóong gərèe/ (*plural* **-ries** *or* **-ry**) *n.* a kangaroo, native to northern Australia, that lives in trees. Latin name: *Dendrolagus lumholtzi.* [Late 19thC. From Aboriginal.]

boon·ies /bóoneez/ *npl.* = **boondocks** (*informal*) [Mid-20thC. Shortening.]

boor /boor/ *n.* somebody who behaves in a crass, insensitive, or ill-mannered way [Mid-16thC. From Dutch *boer* "peasant" (source of English *Boer*). Ultimately from a prehistoric Germanic word that is also the ancestor of English *neighbor.*] —**boor·ish** *adj.* —**boor·ish·ly** *adv.* —**boor·ish·ness** *n.*

boost /boost/ *vt.* (**boost·ed, boost·ing, boosts**) **1.** IMPROVE SOMETHING to improve or strengthen something **2.** INCREASE SOMETHING to cause something to increase ○ *measures to boost productivity* **3.** ASSIST BY PUSHING OR LIFTING to assist somebody or something to get up or over something by giving a push or lift from below **4.** ELEC RAISE VOLTAGE IN SOMETHING to increase the voltage in an electrical circuit **5.** COMM VIGOROUSLY PROMOTE SOMETHING to promote something widely and intensively so that people will buy it **6.** SHOPLIFT to shoplift an article (*informal*) ■ *n.* **1.** ENCOURAGEMENT something that helps to encourage or improve somebody or something in some way **2.** INCREASE IN SOMETHING an increase in something ○ *a boost in income* **3.** PUSH OR LIFT FROM BELOW a push from below to help somebody up or over something **4.** ADVERTISING CAMPAIGN a campaign advertising or promoting something [Early 19thC. Origin uncertain.]

boost·er /bóostər/ *n.* **1.** VIGOROUS PROMOTER OF SOMETHING OR SOMEBODY an enthusiastic promoter or supporter of something or somebody, e.g., a team **2.** ELECTRON ENG RADIO-FREQUENCY AMPLIFIER a radio-frequency amplifier that amplifies weak television or radio signals and retransmits them so that they can be received by viewers or listeners **3.** SPACE TECH = **booster rocket 4.** SOMEBODY OR SOMETHING THAT IMPROVES CONFIDENCE somebody or something that encourages or improves something such as confidence (*usually used in combination*) ○ *a morale-booster* **5.** DEVICE THAT ASSISTS SOMETHING a device used to increase the effectiveness of some piece of equipment **6.** MED SUPPLEMENTARY DOSE OF VACCINE a repeat dose of a vaccine given some years after the initial course to maintain the level of immunity provided by the previous dose **7.** SHOPLIFTER a shoplifter (*slang*)

boost·er ca·bles *npl.* ELEC ENG = **jumper cables**

boost·er·ism /bóostə rìzzəm/ *n.* the practice or habit of publicizing and promoting something, especially a place, product, or enterprise (*informal*)

boost·er rock·et *n.* an engine in a space vehicle that is used to give thrust during the launch and extra thrust during another stage of the flight

boost·er seat *n.* a seat that can be placed over another seat in a motor vehicle or at a table to raise a child into a higher position

boot[1] /boot/ *n.* **1.** STRONG SHOE EXTENDING UP LOWER LEG a strong item of footwear that covers part of the lower leg (*often used in combination*) ○ *an ankle boot* **2.** HARD KICK the act of kicking something hard **3.** = **Denver boot 4.** DISMISSAL FROM JOB dismissal from employment or from a personal relationship (*informal*) **5.** MECH ENG PROTECTIVE COVERING a protective covering, e.g., a rubber sheath for protecting a coupling between two shafts **6.** EQU COVERING FOR HORSE'S LEG a protective covering for the lower part of a horse's leg **7.** MILITARY RECRUIT a naval or marine corps recruit (*informal*) **8.** BASEBALL FUMBLE OF INFIELD GROUND BALL a fumble of a ground ball hit to an infielder **9.** HIST INSTRUMENT OF TORTURE a bootlike instrument of torture that was used to enclose and crush the victim's foot **10.** *U.K.* AUTOMOT = **trunk** ■ *vt.* (**boot·ed, boot·ing, boots**) **1.** MAKE ERROR to make a fumble or error (*informal*) **2.** KICK A HORSE WHILE RIDING IT to urge a horse on by kicking or digging in with the heels while it is being ridden in a race **3.** KICK SOMEBODY OR SOMETHING HARD to kick somebody or something hard **4.** PUT BOOT ON CAR to fix a boot to the wheel of an illegally parked car to prevent it being driven away [14thC. From Old French *bote,* of unknown origin. The sense "luggage compartment" evolved from the meaning "outside step for attendants on a coach."] ◇ **get too big for your boots** to start to think too highly of yourself ◇ **lick somebody's boots** to be extremely obsequious to somebody

boot out *vt.* to force somebody to leave a place, group of people, or job (*informal*)

boot[2] /boot/ *n.* COMPUTER STARTUP PROCEDURE the process of starting or restarting a computer and loading the operating system ■ *vi.* (**boot·ed, boot·ing, boot·ing, boots**) COMPUT START UP to start or become ready to start operating [Late 20thC. Shortening of BOOTSTRAP, from *bootstrap loader,* a simple program that enables a computer to start up and load its full operating system.]

boot up *vt.* to start or restart a computer

boot[3] /boot/ [Old English *bōt* "remedy." Ultimately from an Indo-European word meaning "good," which is also the ancestor of English *better.*] ◇ **to boot** in addition

boot·black /bóot blàk/ *n.* a person who cleans people's shoes in the street

boot camp *n.* **1.** MIL CAMP FOR MILITARY RECRUITS a training camp for recruits to the U.S. military (*informal*) **2.** SOC SCI CAMP FOR DELINQUENTS a disciplinary camp in some jurisdictions to which juvenile delinquents are sent [*Boot* from BOOT[1] in the sense of "navy or marine corps recruit"]

boo·tee /bóo tee/, **boo·tie** *n.* **1.** BABY'S KNITTED BOOT a soft woolen boot for a baby **2.** ANKLE BOOT an ankle boot for a woman or child

Bo·ö·tes /bō ṓteez/ *n.* a constellation of the northern hemisphere lying between Ursa Major and Virgo. It is dominated by the bright star Arcturus.

booth /booth/ (*plural* **booths** /booth̲z, booths/) *n.* **1.** SMALL PARTITIONED ENCLOSURE a partitioned enclosure or small room shaped like a box that offers privacy, e.g., when telephoning, selling tickets, or voting **2.** SMALL TENT OR STALL a tent, stall, or other light structure at a fair or exhibition, offering some form of entertainment or goods for sale **3.** RESTAURANT COMPARTMENT a small, partly enclosed area in a restaurant with a table and highbacked seats **4.** SMALL ROOM USED IN BROADCASTING a small soundproof room used for recording sound or for broadcasting [12thC. Of Scandinavian origin. Ultimately from an Indo-European base meaning "to live, dwell," which is also the ancestor of English *bustle, husband, build,* and *neighbor.*]

Booth /booth/, **Edwin** (1833–93) U.S. actor. A leading actor of tragic theatrical roles, he was best known for his portrayal of Hamlet. He was the brother of John Wilkes Booth. Full name **Edwin Thomas Booth**

Booth, John Wilkes (1838–65) U.S. actor and assassin of Abraham Lincoln. He was the brother of Edwin Booth. A partisan of the Confederacy during the Civil War, he shot Abraham Lincoln at Ford's Theatre in Washington, D.C., on April 14, 1865, and was himself killed soon afterward.

Booth, Shirley (1907–92) U.S. actor. She won an Academy Award for *Come Back Little Sheba* (1952).

Boo·thi·a Pen·in·su·la the northernmost tip of mainland North America, in Northwest Territories, Canada, directly west of Baffin Island. Area: 12,483 sq. mi./32,331 sq. km.

boot hill, Boot Hill *n.* a cemetery in a settlement on the U.S. frontier, especially one for gunfighters killed in action

Betty Boothroyd

Booth·royd /bóoth ròyd/, **Betty** (*b.* 1929) British politician. She became speaker of the House of Commons in 1992.

boo·tie *n.* = **bootee**

boot·jack /bóot jàk/ *n.* a device similar to a yoke, used for gripping the back of a boot when removing it

boot·lace /bóot làyss/ *n.* a long shoelace, traditionally a narrow cord or a leather thong, for lacing up boots

boot·leg /bóot lèg/ *v.* (**-legged, -leg·ging, -legs**) **1.** *vti.* DEAL IN ILLEGAL GOODS to make, transport, or sell illegal goods, especially illegally copied or recorded material **2.** *vi.* FOOTBALL FAKE A PASS in football, to pretend to pass the ball to another player while running with the ball concealed against the hip ■ *n.* **1.** SOMETHING ILLEGALLY MADE an illegally made product, especially an illegal recording **2.** ILLEGAL ALCOHOL alcohol or an alcoholic beverage that has been smuggled or illegally distilled **3.** FOOTBALL FAKED PASS in football, a move in which a player fakes a pass, but runs on with the ball concealed next to the hip [Early 20thC. Back-formation from BOOTLEGGER.]

boot·leg·ger /bóot lèggər/ *n.* somebody who illegally sells smuggled or pirated goods [Late 19thC. From liquor smugglers carrying bottles in their boots.]

boot·less /bóotləss/ *adj.* having little or no success [Old English *bōtlēas* "irremediable," from BOOT[3]] —**boot·less·ly** *adv.* —**boot·less·ness** *n.*

boot·lick /bóot lìk/ (**bootlicked, boot·lick·ing, boot·licks**) *vti.* to flatter somebody in a position of authority in order to gain an advantage (*informal disapproving*) —**boot·lick·er** *n.* —**boot·lick·ing** *n., adj.*

boot·strap /bóot stràp/ *n.* LOOP ATTACHED TO BOOT a loop of leather or fabric attached to the back or side of a boot to help pull it on ■ *adj.* SELF-RELIANT AND SELF-SUSTAINING relying solely on somebody's or something's own efforts and resources ■ *vt.* (**-strapped, -strap·ping, -straps**) HELP YOURSELF to help yourself unaided ◇ **pull yourself up by your (own) bootstraps** to improve your situation in life by your own efforts

boot tree *n.* **1.** DEVICE FOR KEEPING BOOTS IN SHAPE a wooden or metal device shaped like a foot and lower leg, placed inside a boot to preserve its shape **2.** DEVICE FOR KEEPING BOOTS IN PLACE a foot-shaped support for making or repairing boots

boo·ty /bóotee/ *n.* money or valuables seized or stolen, especially by soldiers in war [15thC. Directly or via Old French *butin* from Middle Low German *būte* "exchange."]

booze /booz/ *vi.* (**boozed, booz·ing, booz·es**) OVERINDULGE IN ALCOHOL to drink alcoholic beverages, especially to excess (*slang*) ■ *n.* (*slang*) **1.** ALCOHOL alcoholic drink **2.** SESSION OF HEAVY DRINKING a period of time spent overindulging in alcohol [13thC. From Middle Dutch *būsen* "to drink to excess," of unknown origin.]

booze·hound /bóoz hòwnd/ *n.* somebody who drinks alcohol to excess (*slang*)

booz·er /bóozər/ *n.* (*slang*) **1.** *U.K., ANZ* BAR a public house or bar **2.** EXCESSIVE DRINKER somebody who drinks alcohol to excess

booz·y /bóozee/ (**-i·er, -i·est**) *adj.* (*slang*) **1.** WITH EXCESSIVE DRINKING featuring the drinking of alcohol to excess **2.** CONTAINING ALCOHOL containing or flavored with alcohol **3.** DRINKING EXCESSIVELY tending to drink alcohol excessively **4.** SHOWING EFFECTS OF EXCESSIVE DRINKING showing the effects of prolonged excessive drinking —**booz·i·ly** *adv.*

bop[1] /bop/ *vi.* (**bopped, bop·ping, bops**) **1.** GO CASUALLY to go somewhere on the spur of the moment (*informal*) **2.** DANCE to dance to pop music, especially in a disco (*dated informal*) ■ *n.* **1.** A SPELL OF DANCING a session of dancing to pop music (*informal*) ○ *We had one quick bop and left.* **2.** DANCE a social event organized for the purpose of dancing to pop music (*dated informal*) **3.** MUSIC = **bebop** [Mid-20thC. Shortening of BEBOP.]

bop[2] /bop/ *vt.* (**bopped, bop·ping, bops**) HIT to hit somebody, especially on the head (*informal*) ■ *n.* BLOW DELIVERED a blow, especially a hit on the head (*informal*) [Late 19thC. An imitation of the sound.]

bop·per /bóppər/ *n.* **1.** MUSIC JAZZ MUSICIAN a jazz musician who plays bebop **2.** = **teenybopper** (*dated*)

BOQ *abbr.* Bachelor Officers' Quarters

bo·ra /báwrə, bṓrə/, **Bo·ra** *n.* a cold, dry, strong northeasterly wind that blows down the mountains of Central Europe and along the shores of the Adriatic [Mid-19thC. From a dialect variant of Italian *borea,* from Latin *boreas* "north wind."]

Bo·ra-Bo·ra /bàwrə báwrə, bṑrə bṓrə/ island and tourist resort in the Southern Pacific. One of the Leeward Island of French Polynesia, it was used as a U.S. air base in World War II. Population: 4,225 (1988). Area: 15 sq. mi./39 sq. km.

bo·rac·ic /bə rássik/ *adj.* = **boric** [Late 18thC. Formed from medieval Latin *borac-*, stem of *borax* (see BORAX).]

bor·age /báwrij, bórij/ *n.* a hairy Mediterranean plant with large star-shaped blue flowers and thick oval leaves that taste of cucumber and are sometimes used in salads. It also produces oil with pharmaceutical uses. Latin name: *Borago officinalis.* [13thC. Via French *bourrache* from Latin *bor(r)ago,* of uncertain origin: perhaps from Arabic *abūḥurāš,* literally "father of roughness" (from its rough leaves).]

bo·rane /báw ràyn, bṓ ràyn/ *n.* a compound containing only boron and hydrogen. Some compounds are used in the manufacture of fuels for rockets and jet engines. [Early 20thC. Coined from BORON + -ANE.]

bo·rate /báw ràyt, bṓ ràyt/ *n.* a salt or ester of boric acid [Late 18thC. Coined from BORAX + -ATE.]

bo·rax /báw ràks, báwrəks, bṓr-/ *n.* a white crystalline solid that occurs in alkaline soils and salt deposits and is an ore of boron. It is used in cleaning products, as a water softener, and as a preservative. Formula: $Na_2B_4O_7.10H_2O$. [14thC. Via medieval Latin and colloquial Arabic from Pahlavi *būrak.*]

bor·bo·ryg·mus /bàwrbə rígməss/ *n.* the rumbling sounds made by the movement of gases in the stomach and intestine (*technical*) [Early 18thC. From Greek *borborugmos,* from *borboruzein* "to have a rumbling in the bowels."] —**bor·bo·ryg·mic** *adj.*

Bor·deaux[1] /bawr dṓ/ city on the Garonne River and capital of Gironde Department in the Aquitaine Region, southwestern France. It is an important center for the wine trade. Population: 213,274 (1990).

Bor·deaux[2] /bawr dṓ/ (*plural* **-deaux**) *n.* red or white wine produced in the region around Bordeaux, France

Bor·deaux mix·ture *n.* a solution of copper sulfate and calcium hydroxide that is sprayed on trees and other plants as a fungicide

bor·del·lo /bawr déllō/ (*plural* **-los**) *n.* a house of prostitution (*literary*) [Late 16thC. Via Italian from French *bordel,* literally "cabin, small hut," of uncertain origin: perhaps ultimately from Germanic.]

Bor·den /báwrd'n/, **Sir Robert** (1854–1937) Canadian statesman. He was prime minister of Canada (1911–20), and campaigned for dominion status. Full name **Sir Robert Laird Borden**

bor·der /báwrdər/ *n.* **1. STRIP AROUND EDGE** a band that runs along the edge of something, e.g., a printed page or a framed painting, often decorated or itself added for decoration ○ *a handkerchief with a patterned border* **2. LINE DIVIDING TWO AREAS** the line that officially separates two countries or regions, or the land on either side of it (*often used before a noun*) ○ *across the border* ○ *border country* **3. LAND AT EDGE** the edge of an area of land, or the ground near the edge ○ *a shy animal that rarely comes nearer than the border of the field* **4. NARROW FLOWERBED** a narrow flowerbed along a wall or at the edge of a lawn or path ■ *vti.* (**-dered, -der·ing, -ders**) **1. FORM FRONTIER WITH PLACE** to form the frontier with another country or the boundary between two regions ○ *Italy borders Austria in the Alps.* **2. BE NEXT TO SOMETHING** to form a line along the edge of something ○ *a field bordered by willow trees* [14thC. From Old French *bordeüre,* ultimately from a Germanic word that is also one of the ancestors of English *board.*]

border on *vi.* to be almost the same as something ○ *an admissions policy bordering on the ridiculous*

Bor·der col·lie *n.* a dog with a long silky black-and-white coat, belonging to a breed often kept as sheepdogs [So called because it was originally bred in the Borders, between England and Scotland]

bor·der·land /báwrdər lànd/ *n.* **1. AREA AT TERRITORY'S EDGE** the area near the edge of a country or region, especially a remote area **2. POINT WHERE THINGS OVERLAP** the indeterminate area between two conditions, categories, or activities that is hard to define because it contains features or qualities of both

bor·der·line /báwrdər līn/ *n.* **SEPARATING LINE** the notional line that separates one state or quality from another very similar one ○ *the borderline between frankness and rudeness* ■ *adj.* **1. AT CATEGORY'S EDGE** not clearly belonging to one or other of two categories ○ *Borderline applicants will be reinterviewed.* **2.** PSYCHOL **PSYCHOLOGICALLY UNSTABLE** used to describe a psychological condition characterized by emotional instability and marked by self-destructive, manipulative, and erratic behavior **3.** MED **ALMOST DEVELOPED** used to describe a medical condition that a patient is likely to develop unless preventive steps are taken ○ *borderline hypertension*

Bor·der ter·ri·er *n.* a small short dog belonging to a breed of terriers with rough coats that are kept as pets [So called because it was originally bred in the Borders, between England and Scotland]

Bor·du·as /bàwrdoo àà/, **Paul Émile** (1905–60) Canadian painter. His exploration of spontaneous painting (**automism**) led to abstract works such as *L'Étoile noir* (1957).

bor·dure /báwrjər/ *n.* the decorated edge running around the edge of the shield on a coat of arms, signifying that the bearer is not the chief of the family [14thC. An earlier spelling of BORDER.]

bore[1] /bawr, bōr/ *vt.* (**bored, bor·ing, bores**) **MAKE SOMEBODY UNINTERESTED** to make somebody lose interest and so feel tired and annoyed ○ *He bored us stiff with a detailed explanation of the itinerary for his vacation.* ■ *n.* **SOMETHING THAT BORES** somebody or something regarded as wholly uninteresting or tiresome ○ *Peeling potatoes is a bore!* [Mid-18thC. Origin unknown.]

bore[2] /bawr, bōr/ *vti.* (**bored, bor·ing, bores**) **1. MAKE HOLE IN SOMETHING** to make a deep hole in something, such as that made by a drill, a bullet, or a boring insect **2. PENETRATE** to penetrate into the inner or hidden parts of somebody or something ○ *questioning that bores deep into their private affairs* ■ *n.* **SIZE OF PIPE** the internal diameter of a pipe, gun barrel, or any other hollow cylindrical part [Old English *borian.* Ultimately from an Indo-European word that is also the ancestor of English *perforate.*]

bore[3] /bawr, bōr/ *n.* a large powerful wave that the tide causes to move up a river or narrow estuary [Early 17thC. Origin uncertain: perhaps from Old Norse *bára* "wave."]

bore[4] /bawr, bōr/ *v.* past participle of **bear**[2]

bo·re·al /báwree əl, bōree-/ *adj.* used to describe a region that has a northern temperate climate, with cold winters and warm summers [15thC. Directly or via French from late Latin *borealis,* from Latin *Boreas* (see BOREAS).]

Bo·re·as /báwree əss, bōree-/ *n.* **1. GOD OF NORTH WIND** in Greek mythology, the god who personifies the north wind. ◊ **Zephyrus 2. Bo·re·as, bo·re·as NORTH WIND** a wind blowing from the north (*literary*) [14thC. Via Latin from Greek.]

bored /bawrd, bōrd/ *adj.* feeling tired and irritable, either because of being exposed to something uninteresting or because of having nothing to do

bore·dom /báwrdəm, bṓr-/ *n.* the feeling of being bored ○ *I nearly died of boredom.*

bore·hole /báwr hōl, bṓr-/ *n.* a deep hole drilled into the ground to obtain samples for geological study or to release or extract water or oil

bor·er /báwrər, bṓr-/ *n.* **1.** MECH ENG **TOOL FOR BORING HOLES** a machine or hand tool used for boring holes **2.** ZOOL **ANIMAL THAT BORES** an organism, especially an insect or a mollusk, that bores into a plant or into wood or rock

Borg /bawrg, bōrg/, **Björn** (*b.* 1956) Swedish tennis player. He was the Wimbledon men's singles champion from 1976 to 1980 and won the French singles title six times. Full name **Björn Rune Borg**

Bor·ge /báwrgə, bṓrgə/, **Victor** (*b.* 1909) Danish-born U.S. musician. He became famous for his solo comedy shows performed at the piano.

Bor·ges /báwr hess/, **Jacobo** (*b.* 1931) Venezuelan artist. He is noted for his paintings portraying social themes.

Bor·ges, Jorge Luis (1899–1986) Argentine writer. An avant-garde poet and essayist, he is famous for his short stories, of which *Fictions* (1945) and *The Aleph* (1949) are outstanding collections. He was director of Venezuela's National Library from 1955 to 1973.

Bor·gia /báwrjə, -zhə/, **Cesare, Duke of the Romagna** (1476?–1507) Italian soldier. The illegitimate son of Pope Alexander VI and the brother of Lucrezia Borgia, he conquered several central Italian city-states in an attempt to found his own kingdom.

Bor·gia, Lucrezia (1480–1519) Italian art patron. During her third marriage to the Duke of Este, she attracted Italy's foremost painters and writers to her court in Ferrara. She was the sister of Cesare Borgia.

Bor·glum /báwrgləm/, **Gutzon** (1867–1941) U.S. sculptor. He spent his last fourteen years carving the giant sculptures of four U.S. presidents into the rock face of Mount Rushmore. Full name **John Gutzon de la Mothe Borglum**

bo·ric /báwrik, bṓrik/ *adj.* containing or relating to boron [Mid-19thC. Coined from BORON + -IC.]

bo·ric ac·id *n.* a weak acidic white crystalline solid used in the manufacture of glass and porcelain, as a fire retardant, and as an antiseptic. Formula: H_3BO_3.

bor·ing[1] /báwring, bṓring/ *adj.* stimulating no interest or enthusiasm —**bor·ing·ly** *adv.* —**bor·ing·ness** *n.*

WORD KEY: SYNONYMS

boring, dull, monotonous, tedious, uninteresting

CORE MEANING: causing a state of impatience and weariness

boring the most general term in this group, it can be used as a substitute for both "dull" and "monotonous" and simply indicates that somebody or something is lacking in interest, stimulation, or variety; **dull** uninteresting because of a lack of liveliness, humor, or variety; **monotonous** suggesting that the cause is too much uniformity and a lack of variation; **tedious** suggesting weariness to the point of physical as well mental discomfort; **uninteresting** suggesting simply that something is not engaging somebody's interest rather than it is arousing actual impatience or weariness.

bor·ing[2] /báwring, bṓring/ *adj.* used to describe animals or tools that make holes in things

Bor·laug /báwr làwg/, **Norman** (*b.* 1914) U.S. agronomist. He received the Nobel Peace Prize in 1970 for developing the high-yield wheat that launched the "green revolution" in the developing world. Full name **Norman Ernest Borlaug**

Bor·mann /báwr maan/, **Martin** (1900–45?) German Nazi politician. A close and loyal adviser of Adolf Hitler, he stayed with Hitler to the end of World War II, when he is thought to have been killed by a sniper.

born[1] /bawrn/ *adj.* **1. BROUGHT INTO LIFE** brought into existence as a baby from a mother's womb ○ *a child born in Birmingham.* ◊ **bear 2. BEGUN** developed from a particular source or root cause ○ *a realization born of long experience* **3. NATURALLY PREDISPOSED** having the particular natural talent or innate character trait ○ *describes the young Napoleon as a born leader* **4. WITH SPECIFIED ORIGINAL STATUS** given a particular status or condition by or at birth (*often used in combination*) ○ *the Canadian-born singer-songwriter* [Old English *boren,* past participle of *beran* "bear" (see BEAR)] ◇ **born and bred** coming from a particular place or background and usually having the qualities or character regarded as typical it

WORD KEY: USAGE

See Usage note at ***born.***

born[2] /bawrn/ past participle of **bear**[2]

born-a·gain *adj.* with all the enthusiasm of somebody who has been recently converted to a cause or an idea [Originally in BORN-AGAIN CHRISTIAN]

born-a·gain Chris·tian *n.* somebody with a new and passionately felt and expressed Christian faith [From John 3:3 "Except a man be born again, he cannot see the kingdom of God" (referring to a spiritual rebirth)]

borne past participle of **bear**[2]

WORD KEY: USAGE

born or **borne**? ***Borne*** is the primary past participle of the verb *bear: They had borne enough pain. The following points should be borne in mind. His account is simply not borne out by the facts.* In meanings relating to birth, ***borne*** is used when the mother is the subject of the verb, or when the verb is passive followed by the preposition "by": *Maria had already borne six children. The twins were borne by an Italian mother.* But when the subject is the child, ***born*** is the past participle of choice: *He was not born in a hospital.* ***Born*** is also the adjective of choice, used in a combination, to indicate condition, location, or status of birth: *newly born pups* and *a southern-born poet.*

Bor·ne·o /báwrnee ō/ island of the Malay Archipelago in the Pacific Ocean, near Southeast Asia and the Philippines. Population: 12,500,000 1991. Area: 290,000 sq. mi./751,100 sq. km. —**Bor·ne·an** *n., adj.*

Born·holm dis·ease /báwrn hōm-, -hōlm-/ *n.* an acute epidemic viral infection whose symptoms include fever and pain around the base of the chest [Because the disease was first identified on the Danish island of *Bornholm*]

born·ite /báwr nīt/ *n.* a brown mineral with a metallic sheen that is an ore of copper [Early 19thC. Named for the Austrian mineralogist Ignatius von *Born* (1742–91).]

boro-[1] *prefix.* = **boro-** (*used before vowels*)

boro-[2] *prefix.* boron ○ *borosilicate* [From BORON]

Bo·ro·din /báwrədin/, **Aleksander Porfiryevich** (1833–87) Russian composer and chemist. A professor of chemistry in St. Petersburg, he wrote the opera *Prince Igor* and other orchestral works.

Bo·ro·di·no /bàwrrə dēenō/ village in Russia about 70 mi./110 km west of Moscow. It was the site in 1812 of an important Napoleon victory.

bo·ron /báw ròn/ *n.* a yellow-brown chemical element that is hard and brittle, with properties intermediate between a metal and nonmetal. It is used in alloys, glass, and ceramics, and in nuclear reactors to absorb radiation. Symbol **B** [Early 19thC. Formed from BORAX, modeled on CARBON, which it resembles in some respects.]

bo·ro·sil·i·cate /bàwrō síllikət, -sílli kàyt/ *n.* a salt of boric and silicic acids. Borosilicates are used in the manufacture of heat- and chemical-resistant glass.

bor·ough /búrō, búrrō/ *n.* **1. DISTRICT OF CITY** an administrative division of a large city, responsible for running local services such as housing and education **2. SELF-GOVERNING TOWN** in some states, a town that has formed itself into a legal corporation and governs itself **3. ENGLISH TOWN** in England a town that once had special privileges granted to it by royal charter [Old English *burg* "fortress, fortified town," from a prehistoric Germanic word meaning "to protect," which is also the ancestor of English *bury, barrow, belfry,* and *borrow*]

Bor·ro·mi·ni /bàwrə mēenee/, **Francesco** (1599–1667) Italian architect. He designed the church of San Carlo alle Quattro Fontane in Rome (1637–41). Born **Francesco Castelli**

bor·row /báwrō, bórō/ *v.* (**-rowed, -row·ing, -rows**) **1.** *vti.* **RECEIVE MONEY AS LOAN** to arrange to be given money by somebody or by a bank or other financial institution for a fixed period of time. The money is normally paid back in installments, with interest. ○ *We've already borrowed heavily this year.* **2.** *vt.* **USE SOMEBODY ELSE'S PROPERTY** to get temporary possession or use of something belonging to somebody else, usually after asking permission ○ *Dad, can I borrow the car?* **3.** *vt.* **TAKE FROM LIBRARY** to take out a book or other item from a library **4.** *vt.* **COPY FROM SOMEBODY'S WORK** to copy something from somebody else's work, especially a work of art of some kind ○ *some shots clearly borrowed from a famous director* **5.** *vt.* LANGUAGE **TAKE FROM ANOTHER LANGUAGE** to adopt a word from another language **6.** *vi.* GOLF **PUTT ALLOWING FOR SLOPE** to putt to the left or right of a straight line on a green to allow for the effect of the slope **7.** *vi.* GOLF **VEER LEFT OR RIGHT** to veer to the left or right as a result of the slope on a green (*refers to a golf ball*) ■ *n.* GOLF **EXTENT OF VEERING** the degree to which a golf ball veers to the left or right as a result of the slope of a green [Old English *borgian* "to borrow against security," from a prehistoric Germanic word meaning "to protect"] —**bor·row·er** *n.*

bor·row·ing /báwrō ing, bórō ing/ *n.* **1. LOAN OF MONEY** the borrowing of money or the amount of money borrowed, especially from a bank or other financial institution **2.** LANGUAGE **ADOPTED WORD** a word that has been adopted from another language **3. COPIED IDEA** an idea copied from somebody else's work, especially a work of art of some kind

bor·row pit *n.* a hole left where stones or other materials have been dug up for use in construction work elsewhere

borscht /bawrsht/ *n.* a Russian or Polish soup whose main ingredient is beets [Early 19thC. From Russian *borshch.*]

borscht belt *n.* a showbusiness circuit based on the many Jewish hotels formerly in the Catskill Mountains (*informal*) [Early 20thC. From the idea that borscht was a favorite dish of Jewish people, many of whom were immigrants, or descended from immigrants, from Eastern Europe or Russia.]

bort /bawrt/ *n.* a diamond of inferior quality that is used industrially on grinding wheels and other abrasive devices [Early 17thC. Origin uncertain: perhaps from Dutch *boort,* or from Old French *bort* "bastard."]

bor·zoi /báwr zòy/ (*plural* **-zois**) *n.* a tall graceful domestic dog with a long silky coat, belonging to a breed formerly used in Russia to hunt wolves [Late 19thC. From Russian, formed from *borzyǐ* "swift."]

Bosc /bosk/ *n.* a variety of pear that has a long neck, a reddish-yellow skin, and juicy sweet flesh [Named for the 19th-century Belgian horticulturalist Louis *Bosc*]

bos·cage /bóskij/ *n.* densely growing trees and bushes (*literary*) [14thC. From Old French, ultimately from a Germanic word that is also the ancestor of English *bush.*]

Hieronymus Bosch

Bosch /bosh, bawsh/, **Hieronymus** (1450?–1516) Dutch painter. His allegorical paintings teeming with demons and monsters include *The Seven Deadly Sins* and *The Garden of Earthly Delights.* Real name **Jerome van Aken**

Bosch, Juan Domingo (1909–63) Dominican writer and statesman. He lived in exile from 1937 to 1961 during the dictatorship of Rafael Trujillo. He was elected president of the Dominican Republic (1962), but was overthrown in 1963 and never regained office.

bosh /bosh/ *interj.* used to dismiss as nonsense what has just been said (*dated informal*) [Mid-19thC. From Turkish *boş* "empty, worthless."]

bosk /bosk/, **bosque** *n.* a small forest made up of densely growing small trees or bushes (*literary*) [Early 19thC. Back-formation from BOSKY.]

bosk·y /bóskee/ (**-i·er, -i·est**) *adj.* covered with small trees or bushes growing densely (*literary*) [Late 16thC. Formed from Middle English *bosk,* a variant of BUSH.]

bo's'n *n.* = **boatswain**

Bos·ni·a /bózneeə/ *n.* the northern region of Bosnia-Herzegovina —**Bos·ni·an** *adj., n.*

Bosnia-Herzegovina

Bos·ni·a-Her·ze·go·vi·na /bóznee ə hèrtsə gōveenə/, **Bos·ni·a** a republic in the former Federal People's Republic of Yugoslavia that declared its independence in 1992. In 1995, following civil war between Bosnian Muslims, Serbs, and Croats, it was divided into two self-governing provinces: a Muslim-Croat Federation and a Serb Republic. Language: Serbo-Croatian. Currency: Dinar. Capital: Sarajevo. Population: 3,222,584 (1997). Area: 19,745 sq. mi./51,129 sq. km. Official name **Republic of Bosnia Herzegovina**

bos·om /bŏŏzzəm, bŏŏzzəm/ *n.* **1. WOMAN'S BREASTS** a woman's breasts or chest **2. CLOTHES COVERING BREASTS** a part of a garment, e.g., a dress, that covers the chest **3. PROTECTIVE PLACE** a familiar source of protection, security, or affection (*literary*) ○ *back in the bosom of her family* **4. SEAT OF EMOTION** the place where emotions are felt (*literary*) ■ *adj.* **CLOSE IN FRIENDSHIP** used to describe a friend to whom somebody is very close (*informal*) ○ *a bosom buddy* [Old English *bōsm,* of uncertain origin: perhaps ultimately from an Indo-European word that is also the ancestor of English *bough* and *bow* (of a ship)]

bo·som·y /bŏŏzzəmee/ (**-i·er, -i·est**) *adj.* with large breasts

bo·son /bōson/ *n.* an elementary particle that has zero or integral spin and obeys statistical rules that place no restriction on the number of identical particles that may be in the same state. Photons and alpha particles are bosons. [Mid-20thC. Named for the Indian physicist S. N. *Bose* (1894–1974), who, with Albert Einstein, stated the statistical relations that describe the behavior of these particles.]

Bos·po·rus /bóspərəss/, **Bos·pho·rus** /-fərəss/ strait linking the Black Sea and the Sea of Marmara. It separates European and Asian Turkey. Length: 20 mi./32 km.

bosque *n.* = **bosk** (*literary*)

boss[1] /bawss, boss/ *n.* **1. SOMEBODY IN CHARGE** somebody who is in charge of others, especially in a work environment ○ *asked the boss for some time off* **2. DOMINANT PERSON** the person who is the dominant partner in a relationship or the dominant member of a group, who tends to make decisions and give instructions (*informal*) (*often used ironically*) **3. POWERFUL POLITICIAN** a politician who exerts a controlling influence, e.g., by applying pressure on others to vote in a particular way (*informal*) ■ *vt.* (**bossed, boss·ing, boss·es**) **GIVE ORDERS** to give others orders in a way that seeks to demonstrate or establish authority and is often resisted or resented ○ *You find the big kids trying to boss the little kids around.* ■ *adj.* **EXCELLENT** so good as to dominate in a group (*slang*) ○ *a boss drummer* [Early 19thC. From Dutch *baas* "master," of unknown origin.] ◇ **be your own boss 1.** to work under your own authority, e.g., with freelance or self-employed status **2.** to make decisions relating to your own life, rather than have them dictated by others

boss[2] /bawss, boss/ *n.* **1. KNOB** a round raised part that sticks out from a surface, e.g., a stud at the center of a shield **2.** ARCHIT **CEILING DECORATION** a decorative knob on a vaulted ceiling at points where the ribs meet **3.** BIOL **SWELLING** a round swelling on a plant or the horn of an animal **4.** MECH ENG **SHAFT PART** a thicker part of a shaft at a point where another part is attached to it **5.** GEOL **VOLCANIC ROCK MASS** a mass of volcanic rock with a roughly circular cross section and vertical sides [14thC. From Old French *boce,* of unknown origin.]

bos·sa no·va /bòssə nōvə, bàwssə-/ *n.* **1. DANCE** a lively ballroom dance similar to the samba. It originated in Brazil in the early 1960s. **2. MUSIC FOR DANCE** a piece of music for the bossa nova [Mid-20thC. From Portuguese, literally "new trend."]

bos·set /bóssit/ *n.* a rudimentary antler that grows on each side of a young deer's head [Mid-19thC. From French, literally "little boss knob."]

Bos·sier Cit·y /bōzhər-/ city in northwestern Louisiana on the Red River, on the northwestern outskirts of Shreveport. Population: 55,686 (1996).

boss·ism /báw sizzəm, bó sizzəm/ *n.* political control, especially the control of a big city's political machine, by one person who is usually not an officeholder and whose methods are usually corrupt

boss·y /báwssee, bóssee/ (**-i·er, -i·est**) *adj.* fond of giving people orders ○ *The other children don't like it when you're bossy.* —**boss·i·ly** *adv.* —**boss·i·ness** *n.*

bos·ton /báwstən, bós-/ *n.* a version of whist in which two decks of cards are used and players bid for the right to name trumps [Early 19thC. From French, said to have been devised by French naval officers involved in the Siege of BOSTON (Massachusetts) in the American Revolution.]

Bos·ton /báwstən, bós-/ capital and largest city of Massachusetts. Situated at the mouth of the Charles River on Boston Bay, it is home to Boston and Northeastern universities. Population: 558,394 (1996). —**Bos·to·ni·an** /baw stōnee ən, bos-/ *n., adj.*

Bos·ton bull, Bos·ton bull·dog *n.* = **Boston terrier**

Bos·ton crab *n.* a wrestling hold in which a wrestler is grabbed by the legs, turned face down, and sat on

Bos·ton cream pie *n.* a round sandwich cake filled with cream or custard and covered with chocolate sauce

Bos·ton fern *n.* a fern with delicate, crested fronds. It is a popular houseplant. Latin name: *Nephrolepis exaltata* var. *bostoniensis.*

Bos·ton i·vy (*plural* **Bos·ton i·vies**) *n.* a climbing plant with leaves having three black lobes that turn red in the fall. It is a popular garden plant. Latin name: *Parthenocissus tricuspidata.*

Bos·ton let·tuce *n.* a variety of lettuce with a round head and soft, yellow and green leaves

Bos·ton rock·er *n.* a rocking chair with a seat that curves up to meet a high back

Bos·ton Tea Par·ty *n.* a protest against British taxes made by the citizens of Boston in 1773, leading to the American Revolution. The protesters boarded three British ships and threw their cargoes of tea overboard.

Bos·ton ter·ri·er *n.* a stocky dog with a smooth, brindled, or black coat with white markings, belonging to a breed that is a cross between a bulldog and a terrier

bo·sun /bṓs'n/ *n.* an officer on a ship whose job is to supervise the maintenance of the ship and its equipment [Mid-17thC. Representing a pronunciation of BOATSWAIN.]

Bos·well /bóz wèl, -wəl/, **James** (1740–95) Scottish lawyer and biographer. He met the writer Samuel Johnson in 1973 and after two decades of close association wrote *Life of Samuel Johnson* (1791), one of the masterpieces of English biography.

Bos·worth Field /bòz wərth-/ site of a decisive battle in 1485 when Henry Tudor defeated Richard III and claimed the English throne. It is near the town of Market Bosworth, central Leicestershire.

bot[1] /bot/ *n.* a larva of the botfly. It lives as a parasite inside the human body and the bodies of horses, sheep, and cattle. [Early 16thC. Origin uncertain: probably from Low Dutch.]

bot[2] /bot/ *n.* a computer program that performs routine or time-consuming tasks, e.g., searching Web sites on the Internet, automatically or semi-independently (*usually used in combination*) [Late 20thC. Shortening of ROBOT.]

BOT *abbr.* COMPUT beginning of tape

bot. *abbr.* **1.** botanical **2.** botany

bo·tan·i·cal /bə tánnik'l/, **bo·tan·ic** /bə tánnik/ *adj.* **OF PLANTS** relating to plants, especially to the scientific study of plants ■ *n.* **PLANT-BASED DRUG** a drug or other medicinal or cosmetic product that is made from plants (*often used in the plural*) [Mid-17thC. Directly or via French *botanique* from late Latin *botanicus,* from Greek *botanikos,* from *botanē* "plant."] —**bo·tan·i·cal·ly** *adv.*

bo·tan·i·cal gar·den, bo·tan·ic gar·den *n.* an area, often open to the public, in which exotic, rare, or scientifically interesting plants are grown and studied

bot·a·nist /bótt'nist/ *n.* somebody with an expert scientific knowledge of, or a strong interest in, plants [Mid-17thC. From French *botaniste,* from *botanique* (see BOTANICAL.]

bot·a·nize /bótt'n ìz/ (**-nized, -niz·ing, -niz·es**) *vti.* to collect or study plants (*informal*) [Mid-18thC. Via modern Latin *botanizare* from Greek *botanizein* "to gather plants," from *botanē* "plant."] —**bot·a·niz·er** *n.*

bot·a·ny /bótt'nee/ (*plural* **-nies**) *n.* **1. STUDY OF PLANTS** the scientific study of plants **2. PLANT LIFE OF SPECIFIC AREA** the plant life that exists within a particular area **3. BIOLOGICAL CHARACTERISTICS OF PLANT** the biological description of a single plant or group of plants [Late 17thC. Formed from BOTANIC.]

Bot·a·ny Bay bay south of Sydney, New South Wales, Australia. It was Captain Cook's first landing site on the continent in 1770.

Bot·a·ny wool *n.* a fine grade of merino wool used in the manufacture of yarns and fabrics [Named for BOTANY BAY]

botch /boch/ *vt.* (**botched, botch·ing, botch·es**) **DO SOMETHING BADLY** to do something very badly out of clumsiness or lack of care ○ *managed to botch a simple repair job* ○ *botched the piano concerto up* ■ *n.* **botch BADLY DONE JOB** a job or task that has been done very badly (*informal*) [14thC. Origin unknown.] —**botch·er** *n.* —**botch·i·ly** *adv.* —**botch·i·ness** *n.* —**botch·y** *adj.*

bot·fly /bót flì/ (*plural* **-flies**) *n.* a two-winged hairy parasitic fly that lays its eggs under the skin or in the digestive tract, sometimes causing serious illness. Botflies live as parasites on people, horses, sheep, and cattle. Families: Oestridae and Gasterophilidae.

both /bōth/ *adj.* **TWO** relating to or being two people or things considered together ○ *For the first time I find that I like both candidates.* ○ *There are only two licensed check cashers in Monmouth and Ocean counties, and both are in Asbury Park.* ■ *conj.* **NOT JUST ONE** used with two facts or alternatives joined by "and" to indicate that not just one but also the other one is included ○ *Truancy is now treated as both a law-enforcement and an educational issue.* [13thC. From Old Norse *bá-ir.* Ultimately from two Indo-European words meaning "both the."]

WORD KEY: USAGE

A flexible word, ***both*** has many roles, as a pronoun (*I like both*), adjective (or determiner) (*I like both boys*), and adverb (or conjunction) (*They are both pleasant and cheerful*). Its mobility in a sentence is so great that its meaning can become ambiguous. In the last example, it is not immediately clear whether ***both*** belongs with "they" or with the complement of the sentence, "pleasant and cheerful"; in speech, intonation will normally clarify the intention. However, when writing, you need to ensure that you are not leaving the reader in doubt. The principal restriction that applies to ***both*** is that it should refer to two people or things and no more; if three or more are meant it is necessary to use ***each***, which behaves grammatically in ways quite similar to ***both***. (However, ***each*** is regarded as singular while ***both*** is plural, and ***both*** alone allows the construction *I saw them both.*) When pairing ***both*** with ***and***, it is important to retain a balance between the two parts of the construction, with regard to the position of ***both*** and the types of words linked. Examples of poor balance are *She is both charming and an intellectual* (better: *She is both charming and intelligent*) and *He is both a fine singer and likes to paint* (better: *He both sings well and likes to paint*). In terms of possession, *of* + ***both*** is preferred, as in *the parents of both,* as opposed to *both their parents* and *both their responsibility* or *both their responsibilities.*

Bo·tha /bṓtə, bṓ taá/, **P. W.** (*b.* 1916) South African statesman. He was prime minister (1978–84) and first state president (1984–89) of South Africa. Full name **Pieter Willem Botha**

both·er /bóthər/ *v.* (**-ered, -er·ing, -ers**) **1.** *vi.* **MAKE EFFORT** to take the time or trouble to do something (*often used in negative statements*) ○ *He didn't even bother to get out of the car.* **2.** *vti.* **WORRY SOMEBODY** to make somebody feel worried, anxious, or upset ○ *It bothers me to think of you all on your own.* **3.** *vt.* **DISTURB SOMEBODY** to annoy or disturb somebody, e.g., by interrupting or by making unwelcome advances ○ *Is the music bothering you?* **4.** *vt.* **GIVE PAIN** to make somebody feel physical discomfort or pain ○ *My back is bothering me again.* ■ *n.* **1. EFFORT** trouble or effort to do something ○ *Don't go to all that bother for me.* **2. SOURCE OF ANNOYANCE** somebody or something that causes annoyance, e.g., by making noise [Late 17thC. Origin uncertain.]

WORD KEY: SYNONYMS

bother, annoy, bug, disturb, irk, trouble, worry

CORE MEANING: to interfere with somebody's composure

bother suggesting a range of interference with composure, both mental and physical, from interrupting somebody's concentration to causing discomfort or pain; **annoy** to interfere with somebody's composure in such a way as to affect the nerves and cause irritation or anger; **bug** a slang word meaning much the same as *annoy*; **disturb** either to interrupt somebody in the process of doing something or seriously to interfere with somebody's peace of mind; **irk** a less common word meaning much the same as *annoy* but sometimes suggesting a greater degree of intolerance; **trouble** a more formal word for *disturb* in both its senses given above; **worry** to cause anxiety in somebody and so interfere with his/her composure, the cause of the discomposure being often less clear-cut than in the case of *disturb* or *trouble.*

both·er·a·tion /bòthə ráysh'n/ *interj.* used as an expression of mild annoyance (*dated informal*)

both·er·some /bóthərsəm/ *adj.* causing annoyance and inconvenience

bo tree /bṓ-/ *n.* an tree found in India that belongs to the fig family, regarded as sacred by Buddhists. The Buddha is said to have achieved enlightenment while sitting under a bo tree. Latin name: *Ficus religiosa.* [Mid-19thC. Partial translation of Sinhalese *bōgaha,* from *bō* (from Pali and Sanskrit *bodhi* "perfect knowledge") + *gaha* "tree."]

bot·ry·oid·al /bòttree óyd'l/ *adj.* used to describe minerals and plant parts shaped like a bunch of grapes [Late 18thC. Formed from Greek *botruoeidēs,* from *botrus* "bunch of grapes."]

bots /bots/ *n.* an intestinal disease of horses, sheep, and cattle, caused by infection with botfly larvae (*takes a singular or plural verb*)

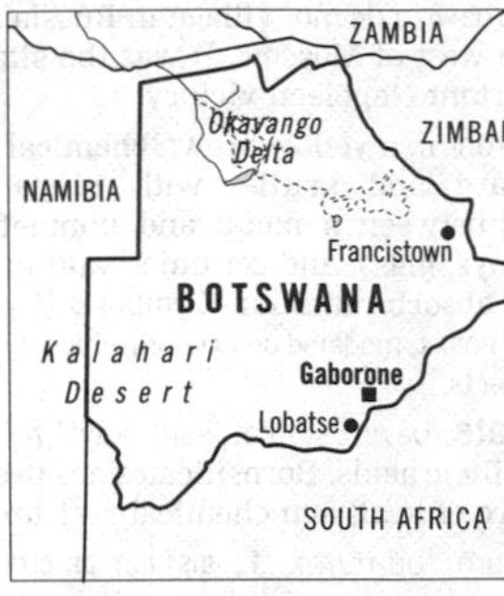

Botswana

Bot·swa·na /bot swaánə/ landlocked country in southern Africa, that shares borders with Namibia, Zambia, Zimbabwe, and South Africa. It became independent from Britain in 1966. Language: English, Setswana. Currency: Pula. Capital: Gaborone. Population: 1,431,981 (1997). Area: 224,607 sq. mi./581,730 sq. km. Official name **Republic of Botswana**. Former name **Bechuanaland** (until 1966) —**Bot·swa·nan** *n., adj.*

bot·te /bótə/ *n.* a thrust or hit in fencing [14thC. From Old French *bot(te)* "blow, hit."]

Sandro Botticelli: *The Birth of Venus* (after 1482)

Bot·ti·cel·li /bòtti chéllee/, **Sandro** (1445–1510) Italian painter. He specialized in classical themes, exemplified in paintings such as *The Birth of Venus* and *Primavera.* Real name **Alessandro di Mariano Filipepi**

bot·tle /bótt'l/ *n.* **1. CONTAINER FOR LIQUIDS** a container for liquids, usually made of glass or plastic, with a narrow neck and no handle **2. AMOUNT IN BOTTLE** the amount of liquid contained in a bottle **3. CONTAINER FOR BABY'S MILK** a plastic or glass container with a rubber nipple used for feeding a baby, or an amount of milk given by using one of these ○ *Has he had his bottle yet?* **4. ALCOHOL** alcohol, or the habit of drinking it to excess (*informal*) ■ *vt.* (**-tled, -tling, -tles**) **1. PUT IN BOTTLE** to put a liquid, e.g., wine, beer, or milk, in a bottle for storage or sale **2.** *U.K.* **PRESERVE IN JARS** to store fruit or vegetables in a preserving liquid in a glass container [14thC. Via Old French *boteille* from medieval Latin *butticula* "little cask," from late Latin *buttis* "cask, barrel" (source of English *butt*).]

bottle up *vt.* **1. ENTRAP** to contain, hold, or entrap something or somebody, especially a group of people **2. CONTAIN FEELINGS** to conceal or repress strong feelings ○ *all the resentment she's been bottling up for years*

bot·tle bank *n. U.K.* a large container or group of containers in which members of the public can deposit used glass bottles and jars for recycling

bot·tle·brush /bótt'l brùsh/ *n.* an Australian shrub or small tree that has a mass of spiky red flowers with large stamens. Genera: *Callistemon* and *Melaleuca.* [From the plant's resemblance to a cylindrical brush for cleaning bottles]

bot·tled /bótt'ld/ *adj.* stored or sold in bottles

bot·tle-feed (**bot·tle-fed, bot·tle-feed·ing, bot·tle-feeds**) *vt.* to feed a baby or a young animal formula milk from a bottle, as distinct from breast-feeding or suckling it

bot·tle gourd *n.* a European climbing plant that produces bottle-shaped fruits. The dried shells of the fruits can be used as containers for liquids. Latin name: *Lagenaria siceraria.*

bot·tle green *adj.* of a dark-green color, like certain types of wine bottles —**bot·tle green** *n.*

bot·tle·neck /bótt'l nèk/ *n.* **1. TRAFFIC CONSTRICTION** a junction or a narrow section of a road that slows traffic or causes traffic jams **2. DELAY IN PROGRESS** a delay caused when one part of a process or activity is slower than the others and so hinders overall progress

bot·tle-nosed dol·phin, bot·tlenose dol·phin *n.* a dolphin with a long snout, found in warm waters. Latin name: *Tursiops truncatus.*

bot·tler /bótt'lər/ *n.* a company that bottles beverages as part of a manufacturing process

bot·tle tree *n.* an Australian tree that has a swollen bottle-shaped trunk and gives off an unpleasant smell. Genus: *Brachychiton.*

bot·tom /bóttəm/ *n.* **1. LOWEST PART** the lowest or deepest part of something ○ *From the bottom of the hill it seems a long way up.* **2. UNDERSIDE** the underneath side or surface of something ○ *rust on the bottom of the boat* **3. FARTHEST POINT** the part of something that is farthest away ○ *ponies grazing at the bottom of the field* **4. LAND UNDER WATER** the ground underneath a sea, lake, or river ○ *Can you dive down and touch the bottom?* **5. END OF LIST** the end of a list or series, especially the lowest level of excellence or achievement ○ *teams at the bottom of the league* **6. ROOT CAUSE** the fundamental, often hidden, cause or origin of something ○ *get to the bottom of the problem* **7. LOWEST RANK** the lowest level in a hierarchy ○ *worked her way up from the bottom* **8. BUTTOCKS** somebody's buttocks, or, particularly when speaking to children, any body part in this general area (*informal*) **9. PART COVERING LOWER BODY** the part of a two-piece garment, e.g., a tracksuit or bikini, that covers the lower body (*often used in the plural*) **10. VALLEY** a dry valley or hollow (*often used in place names*) ○ *Six Mile Bottom* ■ *adj.* **1. LOWEST** in the lower or lowest position ○ *Look on the bottom shelf.* **2. LEAST SUCCESSFUL** in the position of least excellence or achievement ○ *the bottom five teams* ■ *v.* (**-tomed, -tom·ing, -toms**) **1.** *vi.* **HIT SEA FLOOR** to scrape the underside against the floor of the sea or a river, because the water is too shallow (*refers to ships*) **2.** *vt.* ELEC ENG **OVERLOAD TRANSISTOR** to overload a transistor to the point where additional input produces no additional output **3.** *vt.* **ESTABLISH NATURE OF** to discover the true nature, cause, or origin of something (*archaic*) [Old English *botm.* Ultimately from an Indo-European word that is also the ancestor of English *found* and *fundamental.*] ◇ **at bottom** in reality, when external appearances are stripped away ◇ **bottoms up** used as a drinking toast ◇ **hit (rock) bottom** to reach the lowest point in your personal, professional, or emotional life

bottom out *vi.* after a decline, to stop falling any lower and stabilize at a low level ○ *After plummeting 200 points, the stock market finally bottomed out*

bot·tom drawer *n. U.K.* = **hope chest** [Beacuse items were taditionally kept in the bottom drawer of a young woman's chest of drawers]

bot·tom feed·er *n.* **1. WATER ORGANISM EATING OFF BOTTOM** a fresh- or saltwater animal, especially a fish that feeds on material drifting to the bottom of a body of water **2. CONTEMPTIBLE PERSON** a person regarded with contempt (*slang insult*)

bot·tom·land /bóttəm lànd/ *n.* low-lying fertile land bordering a river

bot·tom·less /bóttəmliss/ *adj.* **1. VERY DEEP** so deep that what is specified appears to have no bottom **2. PLENTIFUL** with unlimited or seemingly unlimited resources, especially of money ○ *a bottomless fund* **3. UNFATHOMABLE** too well hidden to be discovered or too mysterious to be understood

bot·tom line *n.* **1.** FIN **PROFIT OR LOSS** the final profit or loss that a company makes at the end of a given period of time **2. UNAVOIDABLE FACTOR** the most important factor that must be accepted, however reluctantly ○ *The bottom line is that the sponsors want a French driver on the team.* **3.** FIN **LOWEST ACCEPTABLE AMOUNT** the least amount of money regarded as acceptable, e.g., in a business deal

bot·tom·most /bóttəm mȯst/ *adj.* at the very lowest level ○ *the bottommost rung of the ladder*

bot·tom round *n.* a cut of beef from the outer part of a round

bot·toms /bóttəmz/ *n.* = **bottom** *n.* 9

bot·tom·set bed /bóttəm set-/ *n.* a layer of sediment deposited by a river at the base of an accumulating delta

bot·u·lin /bóchəlin/ *n.* a toxin produced by the bacterium *Clostridium botulinum* that causes botulism [Early 20thC. From modern Latin *botulinus* (see BOTULINUM).]

bot·u·li·num /bòchə lī́nəm/, **bot·u·li·nus** /-lī́nəss/ *n.* a bacterium that causes botulism when it is present in food. It is an anaerobic bacterium, requiring the absence of free oxygen. Latin name: *Clostridium botulinum.* [Early 20thC. From modern Latin, neuter of *botulinus,* formed from Latin *botulus* "sausage."] —**bot·u·li·nal** *adj.*

bot·u·lism /bóchə lìzzəm/ *n.* a serious form of food poisoning caused by eating preserved food that has been contaminated with botulinum organisms [Late 19thC. From German *Botulismus,* literally "sausage poisoning," formed from Latin *botulus* "sausage."]

bou·bou /bóoboo/ *n.* an African bird, a type of shrike, that is black with a white slash on each wing. It is known for singing in pairs. Genus: *Lanarius.* [Late 20thC. From an African language.]

bou·chée /boo sháy/ *n.* a small bite-sized pastry case filled with a savory mixture [Mid-19thC. From French, literally "mouthful," formed from *bouche* "mouth," from Latin *bucca* "cheek."]

Bou·cher /boo sháy/, **François** (1703–70) French painter. He worked at the court of Louis XV, painting mythological and pastoral scenes in the Rococo style.

Bou·cher, Pierre (1622?–1717) French-born Canadian soldier and landowner. He recorded his experiences of life in New France.

bou·clé /boo kláy/ *n.* a yarn with loops or bumps along its length that give a bumpy effect when knit or woven (*often used before a noun*) [Late 19thC. From French, past participle of *boucler* "to curl" (source of English *buckle*), ultimately from Latin *buccula* "cheek strap of a helmet," from *bucca* "cheek."]

bou·din /boo dán, -dáN/ *n.* a spicy sausage made of pork, pork liver, and rice. It is a popular ingredient in Louisiana Creole cuisine. [Mid-19thC. From French, from, ultimately, Latin *botellus* "pudding, small intestine," diminutive of *botulus* "sausage" (source of English *botulism* and *pudding*).]

bou·doir /bóo dwàwr/ *n.* a woman's bedroom or private sitting room [Late 18thC. From French, literally "a place to sulk in," from *bouder* "to pout or sulk."]

bouf·fant /boo fáant/ *adj.* **BACKCOMBED INTO FULL SHAPE** used to describe a woman's hairstyle in which hair is backcombed or teased to give fullness and height ■ *n.* **HAIRSTYLE** a full, high hairstyle for women [Early 19thC. From French, present participle of *bouffer* "to swell or puff up," ultimately an imitation of the sound.]

bouffe /boof/ *n.* = **opéra bouffe** [Via French from Italian *buffa,* feminine of *buffo* "comic" (see BUFFOON)]

Bou·gain·ville /bóogən vìl, boo gaN véel/ The largest island of the Solomon Island group in eastern Papua New Guinea, in the southwestern Pacific Ocean. Area: approximately3,492 sq. mi./8,730 sq. km.

Bou·gain·ville /bóogən vìl, boo gaN véel/, **Louis Antoine, comte de** (1729–1811) French navigator. He made the first French circumnavigation of the world (1766–69).

bou·gain·vil·le·a /bòogən víllee ə, -víllyə, -vée ə, bō-/, **bou·gain·vil·lae·a** *n.* a climbing woody plant with insignificant flowers that have attractive red, purple, or pink surrounding leaves (**bracts**). It is native to South America and is popular in warm climates elsewhere. Genus: *Bougainvillea.* [Mid-19thC. From modern Latin, named for Louis Antoine de BOUGAINVILLE, who led the expedition on which the plant was discovered.]

bough /bow/ *n.* a large main branch of a tree, from which smaller branches grow [Old English *bōg* "bough, shoulder." Ultimately from an Indo-European word meaning "arm," which is also the ancestor of English *bow* (of a ship).]

WORD KEY: CULTURAL NOTE

The Golden Bough, a book by Scottish anthropologist Sir James Frazer (1890). An encyclopedic, rationalistic survey of mythology and religion that suggests that civilizations generally progress from a belief in magic to faith in religion and thence to an acceptance of science. Hugely influential, it notably provided T. S. Eliot with several striking images for his poem *The Waste Land* (1922).

bought[1] *v.* past tense, past participle of **buy**

bought[2] /bawt/ *adj.* commercially made rather than homemade

bought·en /báwt'n/ *adj.* commercially made rather than homemade (*regional*) ○ *"Better to go down dignified/ With boughten friendship at your side."* (Robert Frost, *Provide, Provide*) [Late 18thC. Formed from BOUGHT on the model of *foughten,* an archaic form of FOUGHT.]

WORD KEY: REGIONAL NOTE

Spreading westward out of New England, across the Northern states to the Pacific and virtually unused in the South Midland and Southern states, the term ***boughten*** endures as a Northern folk term, commonly still heard in the compound *store-boughten,* as in *I don't like store-boughten bread.*

bou·gie /bóozhee, -jee/ *n.* a medical instrument in the form of a flexible tube, inserted into a body passage such as the rectum to open it to allow medicines or instruments to be introduced [Mid-18thC. From French, named for the town of *Bougie* (Arabic *Bijāya*) in Algeria, which traded in wax. The word originally denoted a wax candle.]

bouil·la·baisse /bòoyə báyss, bóolyə bàyss/ *n.* a rich soup made with fish, shellfish, vegetables, herbs, and saffron. It originated in the south of France. [Mid-19thC. Via French from modern Provençal *bouiabaisso.*]

bouil·lon /bóol yòn, -yən, bóo yòn/ *n.* a clear liquid that is traditionally made by boiling meat, bones, and vegetables together [Mid-17thC. From French, formed from *bouillir* (see BOIL).]

bouil·lon cube *n.* a small cube of dried and concentrated food extracts that, when added to hot water, makes a stock for use in soups, stews, and sauces

Boul. *abbr.* Boulevard

Bou·lan·ger /boo laaN zháy/, **Nadia** (1887–1979) French composer and music teacher. She composed noble and instrumental music until 1918. During many years of teaching in Paris, her students included Elliott Carter, Aaron Copland, Walter Piston, and Virgil Thomson. Full name **Nadia Juliette Boulanger**

boul·der /bṓldər/ *n.* **1. LARGE ROCK** a large round rock **2.** GEOL **ROCK FRAGMENT** a large fragment of rock greater than 8 in./200 mm in diameter [15thC. Shortening of *boulderstone,* a partial translation of a Scandinavian word.]

Boul·der /bṓldər/ resort city in northern Colorado, northwest of Denver, southeast of Rocky Mountain National Park, original home to University of Colorado, opened in 1877. Population: 90,928 (1996).

boul·der clay *n.* = **till**[4] *n.*

bould·er·ing /bṓldəring/ *n.* rock climbing that involves climbing short and extremely difficult slopes —**bould·er·er** *n.*

Boul·ding /bṓlding/, **Kenneth** (1910–93) British-born U.S. economist. His *Meaning of the Twentieth Century* (1964) concerns ethical aspects of socioeconomic issues during peacetime. Full name **Kenneth Ewart Boulding**

boule /bool/ *n.* a pear-shaped imitation gemstone made in a furnace from synthetic aluminum oxide (**corundum**) [Early 20thC. From French (see BOWL[2]).]

boules /boolz/ *n.* an outdoor game of French origin, similar to bowling. It is traditionally played on open dusty ground in public places with heavy metal balls that are tossed backhand. (*takes a singu-*

lar verb) [Early 20thC. From French, plural of *boule* (see BOWL[2]).]

boul·e·vard /bŏŏlə vaàrd, bŏŏlə-/ *n.* **1.** WIDE STREET a wide street, especially one lined by trees (*often used in place names*) **2.** *Midwest* MEDIAN STRIP a median strip, or a strip of planted ground between the lands of a divided highway [Mid-18thC. From French (originally "rampart," later a promenade on the site of one), from Middle Low German and Middle Dutch *bolwerk* "bulwark" (see BULWARK).]

bou·le·vard·ier /bŏŏlə vaard yáy, -eér/ *n.* a fashionable, sophisticated man who treats life with light-hearted cynicism (*dated*) [Late 19thC. From French, formed from *boulevard* (see BOULEVARD).]

boul·e·vard strip *n. Midwest, Can* a median strip or a strip of planted ground between the lanes of a divided highway, sometimes also denoting the strip of ground between a sidewalk and a street

bou·le·ver·se·ment /bŏŏlə vèrsə maàN/ *n.* a scene of shouting and anger (*formal*) [Late 17thC. From French, literally "upset, upheaval," formed from *bouleverser* "to turn over like a ball," from *boule* (see BOWL[2]).]

Bou·lez /boo léz/, **Pierre** (*b.* 1925) French composer and conductor. He conducted major orchestras in Europe and the United States and championed new music.

boulle /bool/ *n.* elaborate inlay work on furniture, using tortoiseshell, ivory, or brass in scroll shapes. It was popular in France in the 17th century. (*often used before a noun*) [Early 19thC. From French, named for the French cabinetmaker André Charles Boule (1642–1732), who first used it.]

Bou·logne-sur-Mer /boo lōn sur mèr, -láwnyə-/, **Bou·logne** city and port on the English Channel in Pas-de-Calais Department, northwestern France. Population: 44,244 (1990).

bounce /bowns/ *v.* (**bounced, bounc·ing, bounc·es**) **1.** *vti.* SPRING AWAY FROM SURFACE to move away quickly after hitting a surface, or throw something so that it hits a surface and moves away ○ *bouncing a tennis ball against a wall* ○ *Onlookers saw the car bounce off a tree.* **2.** *vi.* JUMP UP AND DOWN to jump up and down repeatedly on a soft surface ○ *children bouncing on trampolines* **3.** *vt.* LIFT REPEATEDLY ON KNEE to lift a baby or child up and down on your knee for fun **4.** *vti.* REFLECT FROM SURFACE to strike a surface, or cause something to strike a surface, and be reflected back ○ *the use of a fixed orbiting satellite to bounce the transmission signal back to earth* **5.** *vi.* MOVE SWINGINGLY to move in an up-and-down or swinging way ○ *with her long blonde hair bouncing as she walked* **6.** *vi.* GO ENERGETICALLY to walk quickly and energetically ○ *She bounced up to the guests and breezily said hello.* **7.** *vti.* REFUSE TO PAY to refuse payment of a check, or be refused by a bank, because there is insufficient money in the account on which it is drawn **8.** *vt.* WRITE BAD CHECK to write a check that the bank will not honor **9.** *vt.* MENTION IN ORDER TO RECEIVE OPINIONS to mention something, especially an idea or suggestion, to somebody in order to get reactions or opinions (*slang*) ○ *She bounced a couple of theories off of the students.* **10.** *vt.* THROW OUT to eject somebody from a place or expel somebody from a club or other organization (*slang*) ○ *managed to get themselves bounced out of the restaurant* **11.** *vi.* COMPUT COME BACK to be returned undelivered to a sender of an electronic mail message ○ *My last e-mail to you bounced.* ■ *n.* **1.** ACT OF REBOUNDING a springing away from a surface after hitting it ○ *hit the ball before the second bounce* **2.** SPRINGINESS the capacity of a ball or other object to bounce, or of a surface to cause objects hitting it to bounce **3.** BOBBING MOVEMENT swinging or bobbing movement, or the capacity to swing or bob up and down ○ *a conditioner guaranteed to give your hair added bounce* **4.** ENERGY lively energy **5.** POL POSITIVE REBOUND a positive rebound in the polls sustained by a party or candidate (*informal*) ○ *a post-convention bounce* [13thC. Originally "to beat, thump," of uncertain origin: perhaps it suggests the action.]

bounce back *vi.* to recover quickly and completely after a bad experience

bounc·er /bównsər/ *n.* **1.** GUARD AT NIGHTCLUB a security guard who usually stands at the door of a nightclub or other place of entertainment and is responsible for preventing undesirable people from entering and for ejecting troublemakers **2.** BASEBALL STRUCK BALL THAT BOUNCES a ball that bounces along the ground after being hit

bounc·ing /bównsing/ *adj.* used to describe a healthy active baby ○ *the proud parents of a beautiful bouncing baby boy*

bounc·ing Bet *n.* a low-growing perennial plant with pink or white flowers. In the past, its leaves were used as a soap substitute. Latin name: *Saponaria officinalis.* Also called **soapwort** [*Bet* is a nickname for *Elizabeth*]

bounc·y /bównsee/ (**-i·er, -i·est**) *adj.* **1.** LIVELY lively and energetic **2.** BOUNCING WELL tending to bounce or capable of bouncing well ○ *bouncy material used in making tennis balls* **3.** SPRINGY tending to bounce objects hitting it or resting on it —**bounc·i·ly** *adv.* —**bounc·i·ness** *n.*

bound[1] /bownd/ *v.* past participle, past tense of **bind**

bound[2] /bownd/ *adj.* **1.** CERTAIN TO DO SOMETHING certain to happen or do something because custom, experience, or common sense dictates it ○ *If you play music late at night, people are bound to complain.* **2.** OBLIGATED obliged to do something or behave in a certain way, e.g., for legal or moral reasons **3.** DETERMINED firmly resolved ○ *She was bound on becoming the best in the business.* [14thC. Shortening of BOUNDEN.] ◇ **bound up with somebody** *or* **something** to be closely involved with or connected to somebody or something

bound[3] /bownd/ *vi.* (**bound·ed, bound·ing, bounds**) GO ENERGETICALLY to move quickly and energetically, with large strides or jumps ○ *A puppy came bounding across the lawn.* ■ *n.* ENERGETIC LEAP an energetic long or high jump [Early 16thC. Via French *bondir* "to resound," later "to rebound," from, ultimately, Latin *bombire* "to buzz," from *bombus* "humming, booming" (source of English *bomb*), from Greek.]

bound[4] /bownd/ *adj.* **1.** ON THE WAY SOMEWHERE traveling toward a particular place (*often used in combination*) ○ *a Spanish trawler bound for the Irish Sea* ○ *homeward bound* **2.** DESTINED certain to reach or achieve something ○ *young performers bound for international stardom* [Late 16thC. Originally *boun*, from Old Norse *búinn*, past participle of *búa* "to prepare"; probably influenced by BOUND[1].]

bound[5] /bownd/ *vt.* (**bound·ed, bound·ing, bounds**) **1.** SURROUND to form the boundary to an area or site ○ *grounds bounded on three sides by the river* **2.** RESTRICT to impose limits on something ○ *political views not bounded by moral convictions* ■ *n.* MATH LIMITING NUMBER a number that represents the upper or lower end of a range of possible values ■ *adj.* **1.** LING NOT ABLE TO BE USED ALONE used to describe a unit of meaning (**morpheme**) that cannot be used on its own as a word. ◊ **free** *adj.* 20 **2.** GRAM NOT ABLE TO BE USED ALONE used to describe a grammatical element such as a clause that can only be used with another element [14thC. Originally "boundary marker," from Anglo-Norman *bounde* and Old French *bodne*, ultimately from medieval Latin *butina*, of uncertain origin: probably from Celtic.]

bound·a·ry /bówndəree, -dree/ (*plural* **-ries**) *n.* **1.** BORDER the official line that divides one area of land from another ○ *Multinational companies operate across national boundaries.* **2.** LIMIT the point at which something ends or beyond which it becomes something else ○ *pushing back the boundaries of human knowledge* [Early 17thC. Alteration of *bounder*, from BOUND[4].]

bound·a·ry con·di·tion *n.* the set of requirements that must be met in order for the solution to a set of differential equations to be found

bound·a·ry lay·er *n.* the region of a viscous fluid, e.g., air or water, closest to the surface of a solid that is in motion relative to the fluid

bound·ed /bówndəd/ *adj.* used to describe a mathematical set that has an upper and lower limiting number (**bound**[4])

bound·en[1] /bównd'n/ *v.* past participle of **bind** (*archaic*)

boun·den[2] /bównd'n/ *adj.* relating to that which binds somebody morally ○ *It is your bounden duty to consider the honor of the family.*

bound·er /bówndər/ *n.* (*insult*) **1.** DISHONORABLE PERSON somebody, especially a man, who behaves in a dishonorable or morally unacceptable way **2.** PARVENU an ill-bred, social-climbing man [16thC. Formed from BOUND[2].]

bound form *n.* a linguistic unit that can only occur as part of a word and not as a separate word itself, e.g., "-ly" in "quickly"

bound·less /bówndliss/ *adj.* seeming to have no end or limit —**bound·less·ly** *adv.* —**bound·less·ness** *n.*

bounds /bowndz/ *npl.* limits, especially restrictions on what can happen or what can be done ○ *a joke that goes beyond the bounds of good taste* ◇ **know no bounds** to be very great, strong, or intense ○ *an ego that knows no bounds* ◇ **out of bounds 1.** outside the area where somebody is allowed to go ○ *a basketball that is out of bounds* **2.** not open or available ○ *Discussion of the candidate's private life is out of bounds.*

boun·te·ous /bówntee əss/ *adj.* (*literary*) **1.** GENEROUS giving generously **2.** ABUNDANT given in generous measure [14thC. Alteration of Old French *bontif* (on the model of PLENTEOUS), from *bonté* (see BOUNTY).] —**boun·te·ous·ly** *adv.* —**boun·te·ous·ness** *n.*

boun·ti·ful /bówntəf'l/ *adj.* (*literary*) **1.** GENEROUS giving generously **2.** ABUNDANT in plentiful supply [Early 16thC. Formed from BOUNTY, in the sense "goodness, generosity."] —**boun·ti·ful·ly** *adv.* —**boun·ti·ful·ness** *n.*

WORD KEY: SYNONYMS

See Synonyms at ***generous.***

Boun·ti·ful /bówntəf'l/ city in northern Utah, north of Salt Lake City. It was founded by a Mormon pioneer in 1847. Population: 39,595 (1996).

boun·ty /bówntee/ (*plural* **-ties**) *n.* **1.** REWARD a reward of money offered for finding a criminal or other wanted person, or for killing a person or a predator **2.** GENEROSITY generosity in giving (*literary*) ○ *"a trifling additional claim upon your bounty and good nature"* (Sir Walter Scott, *Waverley*; 1814) **3.** ABUNDANT SUPPLY a plentiful or generous supply (*literary*) ○ *"As a grand mansion, "The Broadway Estate" is home to a bounty of rooms, each with a distinct personality."* (Patti Martinhome, *Living Page, Asbury Park Press; 1997*) [14thC. Via French *bonté* from Latin *bonitas* "goodness," from *bonus* "good" (source of English *bonus* and *bonanza*).]

Boun·ty /bówntee/ *n.* the British naval ship commanded by Captain William Bligh on a scientific voyage to Tahiti in 1789. Bligh's cruelty provoked a mutiny led by Fletcher Christian.

boun·ty hunt·er *n.* **1.** SEEKER OF REWARDS somebody who pursues wanted criminals or fugitives for financial reward **2.** HUNTER OF ANIMALS somebody who hunts animals whose capture attracts a reward, e.g., because they are dangerous or are pests

Boun·ty Is·lands /bòwntee-/ group of 13 uninhabited islands in the southwestern Pacific Ocean, 415 mi./668 km east of New Zealand. The islands are part of New Zealand. Area: 0.5 sq. mi./1.4 sq. km.

bou·quet /bō káy, boo-/ *n.* **1.** BUNCH OF FLOWERS a bunch of cut flowers that have been specially chosen or arranged **2.** SCENT OF WINE a wine's characteristic scent **3.** PRAISE an expression of congratulation or praise (*literary*) [Early 18thC. From French, "thicket," literally "small forest," from Old French *bois* "forest," ultimately from a Germanic word that is also the ancestor of English *bush*.]

WORD KEY: SYNONYMS

See Synonyms at ***smell.***

bou·quet gar·ni /-gaar neé/ (*plural* **bou·quets gar·nis** /boo kày gaar neé/) *n.* a bunch of mixed herbs, or an equivalent dried herb mixture in a small bag, that is used to add flavor to stews, soups, sauces, and other dishes [Mid-19thC. From French, literally "garnished bouquet."]

bou·quet·ier /bŏŏkə tyér, -teér/ *n.* a small trumpet-shaped container used to hold the flowers in a bouquet

Bou·ras·sa /boo raássa/, **Henri** (1868–1952) Canadian politician and journalist. A member of the Canadian House of Commons (1896–99, 1900–07, 1925–35), he was a leading French Canadian nationalist. He was founding editor of the nationalist daily *Le Devoir* (1910–32).

bour·bon /búrbən/ *n.* a type of whiskey distilled mainly in the United States from a fermented mixture of hot water and grain (**mash**) containing at least 51% corn [Mid-19thC. Named for *Bourbon* County, Kentucky, where it was first distilled.]

bour·don /bŏŏrd'n/ *n.* **1.** BAGPIPE PIPE OR NOTE the bass pipe on a set of bagpipes, or the bass note it produces **2.** ORGAN STOP the bass stop on an organ, especially on a 16-foot pipe [Mid-19thC. From French, literally "drone." An imitation of the sound.]

Bour·don gauge /bŏŏrd'n-/ *n.* a pressure gauge with a flattened curved tube that straightens under pressure, allowing the force to be measured [Named for the French hydraulic engineer Eugène *Bourdon*, who invented it]

bourg /bŏŏrg/ a town or village, especially a medieval French market town [12thC. Via French from Latin *burgus* "castle," later "borough," ultimately from a Germanic word that is also the ancestor of English *borough.*]

bour·geois /bŏŏr zhwaá, bŏŏr zhwaá/ *adj.* **1. MIDDLE-CLASS AND CONVENTIONAL** typical of affluent middle-class people, who are often characterized as conventional, conservative, or materialistic in outlook **2.** POL **MIDDLE-CLASS** according to Marxist theory, relating to the social class that owns most of the wealth and is regarded as exploiting the working class ■ *n.* (*plural* **-geois**) **1. CONVENTIONAL PERSON** somebody with a bourgeois outlook **2.** POL **CAPITALIST** in Marxist analysis, a member of the bourgeois social class [Mid-16thC. From French, literally "citizen of a city or borough," ultimately from Latin *burgus* (see BOURG).]

bour·geoi·sie /bŏŏr zhwaa zeé/ *n.* **1. EXPLOITATIVE MIDDLE CLASS** the social class that, according to Marxist theory, owns the means of producing wealth and exploits the working class **2. MIDDLE-CLASS PEOPLE** affluent middle-class people characterized as conventional, conservative, or materialistic in outlook [Early 18thC. From French, formed from *bourgeois* (see BOURGEOIS).]

bour·geoi·si·fy /bŏŏr zhwaázə fī/ (**-fied, -fy·ing, -fies**) *vt.* to impose bourgeois values on somebody or something, or make somebody or something bourgeois in character —**bour·geoi·si·fi·ca·tion** /boor zhwaázifi káysh'n/ *n.*

Bour·geoys /bŏŏr zhwaá/, **Marguerite** (1620–1700) French-born Canadian nun. She founded the Congregation de Nôtre-Dame de Montréal.

bour·guig·nonne /bŏŏr geen yṓN/ *adj.* cooked in a red wine sauce with mushrooms and small whole onions, in a style that originated in the Burgundy region of France [Early 20thC. From French, formed from *Bourgogne* "Burgundy."]

Bourke-White /bùrk hwít, -wít/, **Margaret** (1906–71) U.S. photographer and writer. She was a leading photojournalist who was closely identified with *Life.* She was the magazine's staff photographer from 1936 to 1969.

bourn[1] /bawrn, bōrn/, **bourne** *n.* a small stream that only flows in the winter months [14thC. A southern English variant of BURN.]

bourn[2] /bawrn, bŏŏrn/ *n.* (*archaic*) **1. BOUNDARY** a boundary between one place or one thing and another ○ *"I'll set a bourn how far to be beloved."* (William Shakespeare, *Antony & Cleopatra*; 1606) **2. GOAL** something that is aimed for or aspired to [Early 16thC. From French *borne*, from Old French *bodne* (see BOUND[4]).]

bourse /bŏŏrs/, **Bourse** *n.* a European stock exchange, especially the one in Paris [Late 16thC. Via French from medieval Latin *bursa* "bag, purse" from, ultimately, Greek *bursa* "leather" (source of English *purse*).]

bouse /bowz/ (**boused, bous·ing, bous·es**) *vt.* to hoist something with a tackle [Late 16thC. Origin unknown.]

bou·stro·phe·don /bŏŏstrə feéd'n, -feé dòn/ *n.* an ancient method of inscribing and writing in which lines are written alternately from right to left and from left to right [Early 17thC. From Greek, literally "as the ox turns in plowing," from *bous* "ox" + *-strophos* "turning," from *strephein* "to turn."] —**bou·stroph·e·don·ic** /boo strŏffi dónnik/ *adj.*

bout /bowt/ *n.* **1. ATTACK OF ILLNESS** a temporary or short-lived attack of illness, usually a common and not very serious illness ○ *a recent bout of the flu* **2. SHORT PERIOD OF ACTIVITY** a short time spent doing something, often something considered distasteful **3. FIGHT** a boxing or wrestling match [Mid-16thC. Variant of archaic *bought* "curve," of uncertain origin: probably from Low German *bucht.* The meaning developed via "turn of a plow" to "turn of work."]

bou·tique /boo teék/ *n.* **1. SMALL CLOTHES STORE** a small store that sells fashionable clothes **2. SMALL SPECIALIST STORE** a small store selling specialist goods or services of any kind, e.g., imported foods and wines (*often used before a noun*) [Mid-18thC. Via French from, ultimately, Greek *apothēkē* "storehouse" (source of English *apothecary*).]

bou·tique brew·er·y (*plural* **bou·tique brew·er·ies**) *n.* = **microbrewery**

bou·ton /boo táwN/ *n.* the knob or swelling on a nerve-cell extension **(axon)** at the point where it forms a junction **(synapse)** with a neuron [Mid-19thC. From French (see BUTTON).]

bou·ton·niere /bŏŏt'n eér, -yáir/, **bou·ton·nière** *n.* a small flower worn in a buttonhole (*formal*) [Late 19thC. From French, formed from *bouton* (see BUTTON).]

Bou·tros -Gha·li /bōōtrōss gaálee/, **Boutros** (*b.* 1922) Egyptian diplomat He was the sixth general secretary of the UN (1992–96).

bou·var·di·a /boo vaár dee ə/ *n.* a shrub with thin straight leaves and tubular flowers in various bright colors. It is native to Mexico and Central America. Genus: *Bouvardia.* [Late 18thC. From modern Latin, named for Charles *Bouvard* (1572–1658), superintendent of the Jardin du Roi (King's Garden), Paris.]

bou·vier /boo vyáy/ *n.* a large powerful dog with a rough fawn or black coat, originally bred in Belgium to herd cattle [Early 20thC. From French, shortened from *bouvier des Flandres*, literally "cowherd of Flanders."]

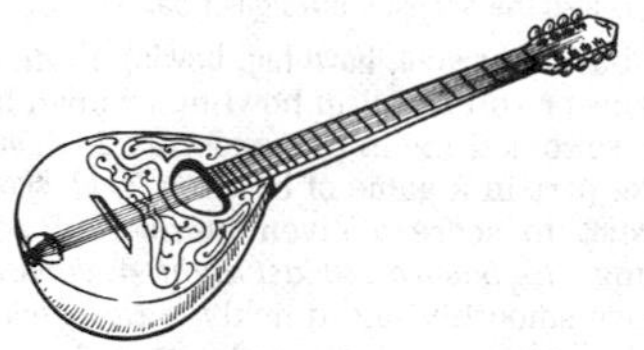

Bouzouki

bou·zou·ki /bŏŏ zŏŏkee, bə-/ (*plural* **-kis**) *n.* a long-necked stringed musical instrument of Greek origin. It is similar in appearance and sound to a mandolin. [Mid-20thC. From modern Greek *mpouzouki*, of uncertain origin: perhaps from Turkish *bozuk* "spoiled" (used of roughly made instruments).]

bo·vid /bṓvid/ *adj.* relating or belonging to the family of hollow-horned, hoofed, ruminant animals that includes cattle, sheep, and antelopes. Family: Bovidae. [Late 19thC. Formed from Latin *bov-* (see BOVINE).] —**bo·vid** *n.*

bo·vine /bṓ vīn, -veen/ *adj.* **1. OF CATTLE GENUS** relating or belonging to the genus of ruminant animals that includes cattle, oxen, and buffalo. Genus: *Bos.* **2. SLOW** displaying the slowness regarded as typical of cattle and related animals (*literary*) ■ *n.* **BOVINE ANIMAL** an animal belonging to the same genus as cattle [Early 19thC. From late Latin *bovinus*, from Latin *bov-*, stem of *bos* "ox" (source of English *beef*).]

bo·vine so·mat·o·trop·in *n.* a hormone in cattle that regulates growth and milk production. It can also be produced artificially by genetic engineering and used to increase milk yields.

bo·vine spon·gi·form en·ceph·a·lop·a·thy /-spùnjəfawrm en sèffə lòpa thee/ *n.* full form of **BSE**

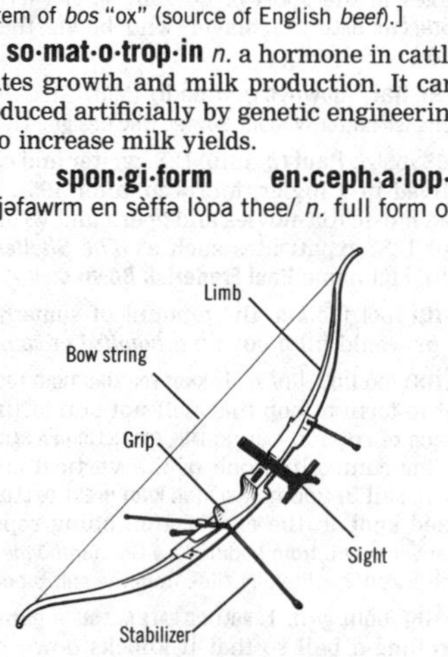

Bow

bow[1] /bō/ *n.* **1. LOOPED KNOT** a knot in which the loops remain visible, e.g., in tied shoelaces or in ribbons used for decorating gifts or hair. ◊ **bow tie 2.** SPORTS, ARMS **WEAPON FOR FIRING ARROWS** a weapon used to fire arrows, consisting of a curved, flexible piece of wood and a taut string fastened to the two ends **3.** MUSIC **ROD FOR PLAYING STRINGED INSTRUMENTS** a rod with horsehair tightly stretched between the two ends, used for playing stringed instruments **4. CURVED SHAPE OR PART** a rounded or semicircular shape, e.g., a part of a building or a loop in a river **5. FRAME OF GLASSES** the frame for a pair of glasses, or the part of the frame that curls around the ear **6.** ARCHERY, HIST = **bowman**[1] (*literary*) **7.** = **rainbow** ■ **bows** *npl.* ARCHERY, HIST **ARCHERS** bowmen or archers considered as a group (*literary*) ■ *v.* (**bowed, bow·ing, bows**) **1.** *vti.* **BEND SOMETHING INTO BOW SHAPE** to bend, or bend something, into a rounded or bow shape **2.** *vti.* MUSIC **DRAW BOW ACROSS STRINGED INSTRUMENT** to draw a bow across the strings of a stringed instrument **3.** *vt.* MUSIC **INDICATE BOWING FOR MUSIC** to mark a piece of music to indicate which notes are to be played with the bow moving in one direction across the strings and which are to be played with it moving in the opposite direction [Old English *boga.* Ultimately from a prehistoric Germanic word meaning "to bend," which is also the ancestor of English *bow*[2], *bight*, and *bagel.*]

bow[2] /bow/ *v.* (**bowed, bow·ing, bows**) **1.** *vti.* **BEND HEAD OR BODY FORWARD** to bend the head forward, or to bend forward from the waist, as a signal of respect, greeting, consent, submission, or acknowledgment ○ *bowing her head in shame* **2.** *vti.* **BEND SOMETHING OR DROOP** to bend something over so that it droops, or to be bent in this way ○ *branches bowed down with fruit.* **3.** *vi.* **YIELD TO SOMETHING OR SOMEBODY** to accept something and yield to it, often unwillingly ○ *bowed to the demands of pressure groups* ■ *n.* **BENDING FORWARD OF UPPER BODY** a bending forward of the upper part of the body to show respect, acknowledgment, subservience, courtesy, or greeting [Old English *būgan* (source also of English *buxom*). Ultimately from an Indo-European word meaning "to bend," which is also the ancestor of English *bow*[1].] ◇ **bow and scrape** to be excessively polite or attentive in an attempt to ingratiate yourself with somebody

bow[3] /bow/ *n.* **1.** SHIPPING **FRONT PART OF VESSEL** the front section of a boat or other vessel **2.** ROWING **PERSON IN BOW** the rower or oar closest to the front of a boat [Early 17thC. From Low German *boog* or Middle Dutch *boeg.*]

Bow /bō/, **Clara** (1905–65) U.S. actor. She enjoyed a brief career in the late 1920s as the most popular female movie star in the country, but spent her last three decades in retirement. Known as **the It Girl**

bow·da·cious *adj., adv. Southern U.S.* = **bodacious**

Bow·ditch /bówdich/, **Nathaniel** (1773–1838) U.S. mathematician and astronomer. His *New American Practical Navigator* (1802) became the standard sailors' navigation guide.

bowd·ler·ize /bódlə rīz, bówd-/ (**-ized, -iz·ing, -iz·es**) *vti.* to remove parts of a work of literature that are considered indecent [Mid-19thC. Formed from the name of the English editor Thomas *Bowdler* (1754–1825), who published an edition of Shakespeare omitting scenes that he considered unsuitable.] —**bowd·ler·ism** *n.* —**bowd·ler·i·za·tion** /bowdlə rī záyshən/ *n.* —**bowd·ler·iz·er** /-rīzər/ *n.*

bow·el /bów əl, bowl/ *n.* **1. INTESTINE** the intestine **2. PART OF THE INTESTINE** a section or part of the intestines, especially the part of the intestine that connects to the anus ■ **bow·els** *npl.* **DEPTHS OF SOMETHING** the deepest or innermost part of something ○ *the bowels of the ship* [13thC. Via Anglo-Norman *buel* and Old French *boël* from Latin *botellus*, literally "small sausage" (from its shape), from *botulus* "sausage" (source of English *botulism*).]

Bow·ell /bṓ əl/, **Sir Mackenzie** (1823–1917) British-born Canadian politician. He was prime minister of Canada (1894–96).

bow·el move·ment *n.* **1. EXPULSION OF FECES** the passing of feces out of the body through the anus **2. FECES** feces passed through the anus

Bow·en ther·a·py /bṓən-/ *n.* a technique that balances the body and initiates healing and encourages emotional stability using gentle manipulation of muscles and connective tissues [Mid-20thC. Named for Tom *Bowen* of Victoria, Australia (1916–82), its originator.]

bow·er[1] /bówər/ *n.* **1. SHADY SHELTER** a shady, leafy shelter or recess, especially in a garden or wood **2. WOMAN'S BEDROOM OR APARTMENTS** a woman's bedroom or private apartments, especially in a medieval castle **3. PICTURESQUE COTTAGE** a picturesque country cottage, especially one that is used as a retreat (*literary*) [Old

English *būr* "dwelling." Ultimately from an Indo-European base meaning "to be, live," which is also the ancestor of English *be.*] —**bow·er·y** *adj.*

bow·er[2] /bówər/ *n.* the anchor at a ship's bow

Bowerbird

bow·er·bird /bówər bùrd/ *n.* a bird native to New Guinea and Australia that is noted for the elaborate structures that the male builds for courtship. Family: Ptilonorynchidae.

Bow·er·y /bówə ree, bówree/ *n.* a street and area in lower Manhattan, New York City, that was a famous theatrical district in the 19th century

bow·fin /bṓ fìn/ (*plural* **-fins** *or* **-fin**) *n.* a freshwater fish of eastern North America, with a mottled greenish brown body and a long dorsal fin. It is the only member of its family that survives from the Paleocene epoch. Latin name: *Amia calva.*

bow·front /bṓ frùnt/ *adj.* **1. CURVING OUT** used to describe a piece of furniture with a front that curves outward ○ *a bowfront desk* **2.** ARCHIT **WITH BOW WINDOW** designed or constructed with a bow window at the front

bow·head /bṓ hèd/ (*plural* **-heads** *or* **-head**) *n.* a baleen whale that lives in the Arctic seas and has an arched upper jaw. Latin name: *Balaena mysticetus.*

Bow·ie /bóoee/ city in west central Maryland, west of Annapolis and northeast of Washington, D.C. Population: 40,181 (1996).

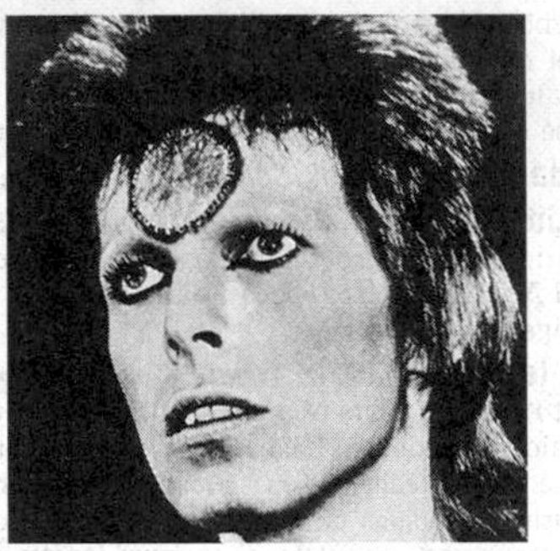

David Bowie

Bow·ie /bṓee, bówee/, **David** (*b.* 1947) British pop singer and actor. He pioneered glam rock in the 1970s. His albums include *The Rise and Fall of Ziggy Stardust and the Spiders From Mars* (1972). Born **David Robert James**

Bow·ie /bóoee, bṓee/, **Jim** (1796?–1836) U.S. pioneer. A colonel in the Texas army, he died at the Battle of the Alamo. Full name **James Bowie**

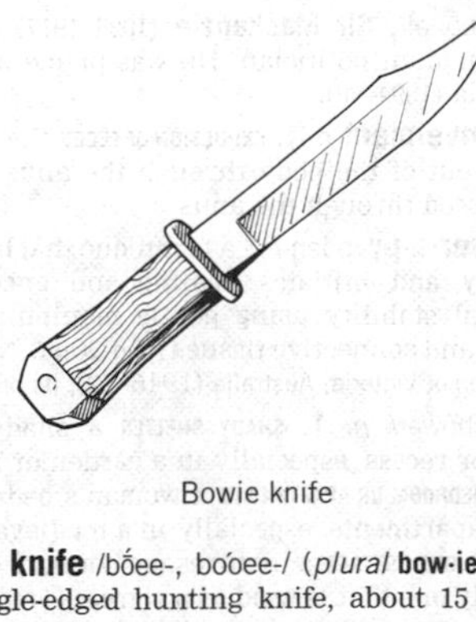

Bowie knife

bow·ie knife /bṓee-, bóoee-/ (*plural* **bow·ie knives**) *n.* a single-edged hunting knife, about 15 in./38 cm long and curved near the point, with a short hilt and a guard for the hand [Mid-19thC. Named after James Bowie, who popularized it.]

bow·ing /bṓing/ *n.* **1. PLAYING STRINGED INSTRUMENT WITH BOW** the use of a bow to play a stringed instrument such as the violin or cello **2. DIRECTION OF BOW** the way a specific piece should be played on a stringed instrument, with respect to the direction in which the bow is moved for successive notes

bow·knot /bṓ nòt/ *n.* a decorative knot in the form of a bow

bowl[1] /bōl/ *n.* **1. ROUND CONTAINER** an open container, usually round in shape and wider than it is deep, and typically used for holding food and liquids **2. AMOUNT IN BOWL** the amount a bowl can hold ○ *two bowls of cereal* **3. PART LIKE BOWL** a bowl-shaped part of something ○ *a toilet bowl* **4.** GEOG **DEPRESSION IN GROUND** a round depression in the surface of the land. ◊ **dust bowl 5. bowl, Bowl STADIUM** a bowl-shaped stadium or amphitheater **6. FOOTBALL GAME** a postseason game played between champion or high-ranking football teams. The Super Bowl is the professional championship game, and the Rose Bowl is the oldest college postseason game. **7. MILDLY ALCOHOLIC DRINK** a mildly alcoholic beverage or the type of cup used for drinking it (*literary*) [Old English *bolla.* Ultimately from an Indo-European word meaning "to swell, be round," which is also the ancestor of English *ball.*]

bowl[2] /bōl/ *v.* (**bowled, bowl·ing, bowls**) **1.** *vti.* **ROLL BALL** to throw or roll a ball in bowling or lawn bowling, or cause something to roll smoothly **2.** *vi.* **GO BOWLING** to take part in a game of bowling **3.** *vt.* **SCORE POINTS IN BOWLING** to score a given number of points in bowling ○ *He bowled 250 last night.* **4.** *vi.* **MOVE QUICKLY** to move smoothly and quickly ○ *He bowled down the highway on his motorcycle.* ■ *n.* **1. WOODEN BALL USED IN LAWN BOWLING** a wooden ball used in the game of lawn bowling, which has slightly flattened sides in order to make it roll in a curve **2. ROLL OF THE BALL** one roll of the ball in bowling or lawn bowling **3.** TECH **REVOLVING DRUM** a rotating cylinder or drum in a machine ■ *vti.* (**bowled, bowl·ing, bowls**) CRICKET **SEND BALL TO BATSMAN OR BATSWOMAN** to send a ball, usually overarm, to a batsman or batswoman [15thC. Via French *boule* from Latin *bulla* "bubble."]

bowl over *vt.* **1. ASTONISH SOMEBODY** to amaze or delight somebody ○ *I was completely bowled over by their generous offer.* **2. KNOCK SOMETHING OR SOMEBODY DOWN ACCIDENTALLY** to knock something or somebody down, especially accidentally during a headlong rush ○ *The dog bowled three chairs over in its excitement.*

bow·leg·ged /bṓ léggid, -lègd/ *adj.* having legs that curve outward around or below the knee area [Mid-16thC. From BOW[1].]

bow·legs /bṓ lègz/ *n.* a condition in which the legs curve outward around the knee area (*takes a singular verb*) —**bow·leg** *n.*

bowl·er /bṓlər/ *n.* **1. PLAYER IN BOWLING** somebody who engages in the sport of bowling **2.** CRICKET **SOMEBODY WHO THROWS BALL** the player who bowls the ball in cricket

bowl·er hat, bowl·er *n.* = **derby** [Mid-19thC. Named for the English hatter William *Bowler,* who designed it in 1850.]

Bowles /bōlz/, **Paul** (*b.* 1910) U.S. writer and composer He lived in Tangier, Morocco, after 1952. He composed music for movies and opera and wrote novels about U.S. expatriates such as *The Sheltering Sky* (1949). Full name **Paul Frederick Bowles**

bowl·ful /bṓl fòol/ *n.* the amount of something that fills or would fill a bowl ○ *a bowlful of soup*

bow·line /bṓ lin, -lìn/ *n.* **1. KNOT FORMING TIGHT LOOP** a knot used to form a loop that will not slip at the end of a piece of rope **2.** SAILING **LINE FOR HOLDING A SAIL STEADY** a line for controlling one of the vertical edges of a square sail **3.** MOUNTAINEERING **KNOT IN END OF CLIMBING ROPE** a fixed knot in the end of a climbing rope [14thC. Origin uncertain: from Middle Low German *bōlīne* or Middle Dutch *boechline,* literally "line from the ship's bow."]

bowl·ing /bṓling/ *n.* **1. ROLLING BALL AT PINS** a game played by rolling a ball so that it knocks down pins **2.** = **lawn bowling 3.** CRICKET **THROWING BALL TO BATSMAN OR BATSWOMAN** the throwing of the ball, usually overarm, to a batsman or batswoman in cricket

bowl·ing al·ley *n.* **1. BUILDING FOR BOWLING** a building where people go to bowl **2. SMOOTH LANE USED IN BOWLING** the long, narrow, smooth expanse of floor down which a ball is rolled in bowling

bowl·ing ball *n.* the heavy ball used in the game of bowling, with holes in it for the bowler's thumb and two fingers

bowl·ing green *n.* a piece of natural grass outdoors or a piece of artificial grass indoors for playing lawn bowling

Bowl·ing Green 1. city in south central Kentucky, on the western bank of the Barren River, southwest of Louisville. Population: 44,208 (1996). **2.** city in northwestern Ohio, south of Toledo. Bowling Green State University was founded here in 1910. Population: 23,307 (1996).

bowls /bōlz/ *n. U.K.* = **lawn bowling** (*takes a singular verb*)

bow·man[1] /bṓmən/ (*plural* **-men** /-mən/) *n.* somebody who uses a bow and arrows, or a crossbow

bow·man[2] /bówmən/ (*plural* **-men** /-mən/) *n.* a man or boy who rows at the bow of a boat

Bow·man's cap·sule /bṓmənz-/ *n.* a cup-shaped part of the kidney that extracts waste and water from the blood and produces urine [Late 19thC. Named for the English surgeon Sir William *Bowman* (1816–92), who discovered its function.]

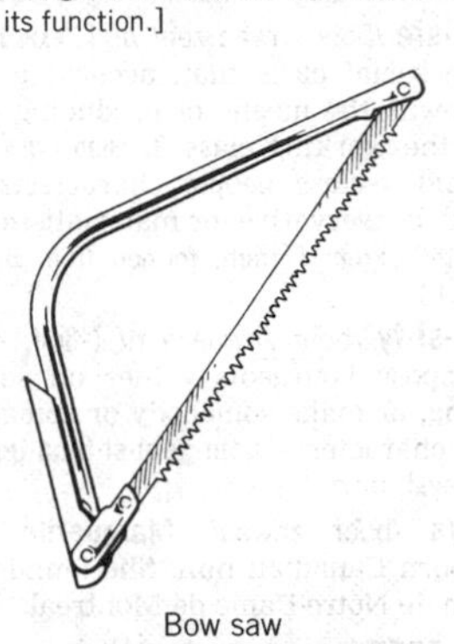

Bow saw

bow saw /bṓ-/ *n.* a saw with a thin blade held in a bow-shaped frame with a narrow handle at each end, used for cutting curves

Bow·ser /bówzər/ *tdmk.* a trademark for a mobile tanker with a pumping apparatus, containing fuel for aircraft or military vehicles

bow·shot /bṓ shòt/ *n.* the distance that an arrow travels when it has been shot from a bow

bow·sprit /bów sprìt, bṓ-/ *n.* a spar that projects forward from the stem of a ship, to which the stays of the foremast are fastened [14thC. From Low German *bōgsprēt* or Middle Dutch *boechspriet,* literally "pole at the bow."]

bow·string /bṓ strìng/ *n.* the taut string on an archer's bow, usually made of strands of hemp

bow·string hemp (*plural* **bow·string hemps** *or* **bow·string hemp**) *n.* **1.** PLANTS **TROPICAL PLANT** a tropical African or Asian perennial plant with thick leaves that are grouped in rosettes, cultivated for its fibers. Genus: *Sansevieria.* **2.** INDUST **FIBERS OF HEMP** the fibers of bowstring hemp plants, used to make bowstrings, mats, and nets

bow tie /bō tī, bṓ tī/ *n.* a short tie, knotted in a bow at the neck

bow weight /bṓ-/ *n.* the amount of force needed to pull a bowstring back to its fullest extent

bow win·dow /bṓ-/ *n.* a bay window that is curved

bow-wow /bów wow/ *interj.* **IMITATION OF BARKING** used to imitate the bark of a dog ■ *n.* **NOISY PUBLIC OUTCRY** a public clamor about something or somebody (*slang*) ○ *All the bow-wow over the trial eventually died down.* ■ *vi.* (**bow-wowed, bow-wow·ing, bow-wows**) **BARK OR IMITATE BARKING** to bark, or imitate the sound of barking [Late 16thC. An imitation of the sound.]

bow·yer /bṓyər/ *n.* **1. MAKER OR SELLER OF BOWS** somebody who makes or sells bows for archery **2. ARCHER** an archer or bowman (*archaic*) [13thC. From BOW + -IER.]

box[1] /boks/ *n.* **1. CONTAINER** a container for objects or dry goods, often with a removable or hinged lid, and usually square or rectangular **2. AMOUNT BOX HOLDS** the amount of something a box holds or could hold **3. RECTANGULAR SHAPE** a square or rectangular shape printed on paper, or on a computer screen, usually containing information or requiring information to be entered in it ○ *Check the boxes if the following items apply to you.* **4. AREA OR STRUCTURE WITH BEST SEATS**

an enclosed area in a public building or at a sports venue, especially a theater, stadium, or racetrack, that contains the best and most luxurious seats. ◊ **skybox 5.** ENCLOSED AREA IN COURTROOM the enclosed area in a courtroom that is reserved for certain specified participants in a court case **6.** SMALL BUILDING PROVIDING SHELTER a small building that is used as a shelter, especially by military personnel **7.** BOX THAT HOUSES EQUIPMENT a box, usually affixed to a wall or on a stand, that houses equipment such as a fire extinguisher, emergency telephone, or first-aid materials **8.** MAIL POST OFFICE BOX a post office box or similar private mailbox, used as a mailing address either because it is convenient or in order to protect the privacy of the addressee. ◊ **box number 9.** BASEBALL BATTER'S BOX the rectangular area on either side of home plate on a baseball diamond, in which the batter stands **10.** SPORTS PART OF PLAYING AREA a marked-off part of the playing area in certain sports, e.g., baseball and soccer, used for a specific purpose, or subject to special rules **11.** DRIVER'S SEAT IN HORSE-DRAWN COACH raised seat for the driver in a horse-drawn coach **12.** AGRIC COMPARTMENT FOR LIVESTOCK a compartment for horses or other farm animals, either in a building or in a vehicle. ◊ **box stall, horsebox 13.** TELEVISION the television set (*slang*) ○ *What's on the box tonight?* **14.** COFFIN a casket for a corpse (*informal*) **15.** *Aus, U.S.* OFFENSIVE TERM an offensive term for a woman's vulva and vagina (*taboo slang*) **16.** AGRIC HOLE IN TREE TO COLLECT SAP a hole or hollow cut into the base of a tree in order to collect sap ■ *vt.* **(boxed, box·ing, box·es) 1.** PACK IN BOXES to pack individual items into boxes ○ *There are 300 pieces waiting to be boxed before shipping.* **2.** OUTLINE SOMETHING WITH BOX to enclose something on a page or on a computer screen in a box ○ *Box the title to make it stand out more.* **3.** AGRIC CUT HOLE IN TREE FOR SAP to cut a box in the base of a tree to collect the sap [Pre-12thC. Via late Latin *buxis* from Greek *puxis* "wooden container," from *puxos* "boxwood" (source of English *box*³).]

box in *vt.* to surround somebody or something by or with something else, so that it is impossible to move ○ *My car is compelely boxed in by those trucks.*

box² /boks/ **(boxed, box·ing, box·es)** *vti.* to fight using the techniques of boxing, or fight somebody in a boxing match ○ *He boxed in exhibition bouts to entertain the crowds.* [14thC. Origin unknown.]

box on *vi.* to continue with a boxing match. It is usually a command, given by the referee after a fight has been stopped, e.g., for a count.

box³ /boks/ (*plural* **box** *or* **box·es**) *n.* **1.** TREES EVERGREEN SHRUB a dense evergreen tree or shrub with shiny dark green oval leaves, often cultivated as a hedge. Genus: *Buxus.* **2.** INDUST = **boxwood** [Pre-12thC. Via Latin *buxus* from Greek *puxos* (source of English *box*¹), of unknown origin.]

box⁴ /boks/ *vti.* SAILING = **boxhaul** [Mid-18thC. Origin uncertain: perhaps via Spanish *bojar* "to sail around," from Middle Low German *bōgen* "to bend."]

box beam *n.* = **box girder**

box bed *n.* an old-fashioned bed, enclosed on three sides and the top by a wooden structure resembling a box

box·board /bóks bàwrd, -bōrd/ *n.* a tough cardboard made from wood and wastepaper pulp, used for making boxes

box calf *n.* black calfskin leather that has been tanned with chromium salts [Early 20thC. Named for Joseph *Box*, a 19th-century London bootmaker.]

box cam·er·a *n.* a camera shaped like a box, with a simple lens that has a fixed focus and a single shutter speed

box can·yon *n.* a canyon with steep walls that can be entered readily only from the downstream direction

box·car /bóks kaar/ *n.* a fully enclosed railroad car, usually with sliding doors, which is used to transport freight

box coat *n.* **1.** LOOSE COAT a coat that hangs loosely from the shoulders **2.** HEAVY COAT WORN BY COACHMEN a heavy coat, worn in the past by a coachman when sitting on the box, or by anyone riding outside a carriage

box el·der (*plural* **box el·ders** *or* **box el·der**) *n.* a fast-growing North American maple tree. Latin name: *Acer negundo.* [From BOX³]

box·er¹ /bóksər/ *n.* somebody who fights in boxing matches

box·er² /bóksər/ *n.* a person or machine whose task it is to pack things into boxes

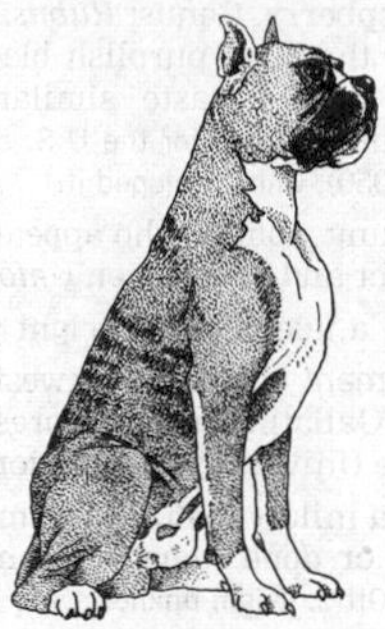
Boxer

box·er³ /bóksər/ *n.* a medium-sized smooth-haired dog belonging to a breed developed in Germany. Its characteristics are a flat face with a black mask and a short-brownish tan coat. [Early 20thC. Via German from English *boxer*, so called because of its wide flattened nose.]

Box·er /bóksər/ *n.* a member of a secret society in China that launched an unsuccessful rebellion in 1900 **(the Boxer Rebellion)** [Early 20thC. Translation of Mandarin *yì hé quán*, literally "righteous harmonious fists."]

Box·er Re·bel·lion *n.* an unsuccessful rebellion in China in 1900, the aim of which was to drive out all foreigners, remove all foreign influence, and compel Christian Chinese people to give up that religion

box·er shorts, box·ers *npl.* underpants with a gathered waistband and loose-fitting short legs [So called because they resemble the trunks worn by boxers]

box·fish /bóks fish/ (*plural* **-fish** *or* **-fish·es**) *n.* = **trunkfish**

box·ful /bóks fo͝ol/ *n.* the amount a box holds or can hold

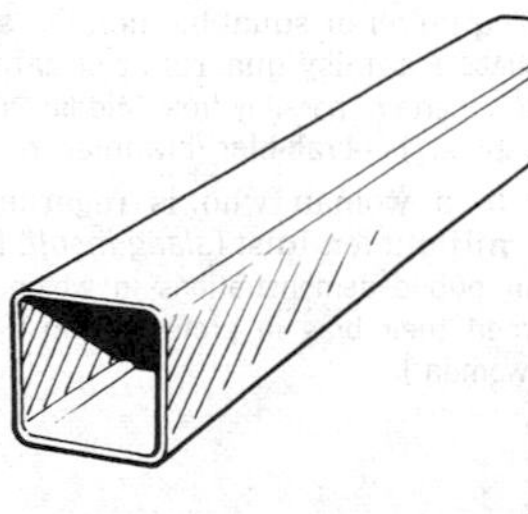
Box girder

box gird·er *n.* a hollow girder or beam that is square or rectangular in section

box·haul /bóks hàwl/ **(-hauled, -haul·ing, -hauls)** *vti.* to turn a square-rigged ship onto a new tack by backwinding the foresails and steering hard around [Mid-18thC. From BOX¹ + HAUL.]

box·ing /bóksing/ *n.* the sport of fighting with the fists, with the aim of knocking out the opposing boxer, or inflicting enough punishment to cause the other boxer to quit or be judged defeated

Box·ing Day *n.* December 26, the day after Christmas Day, observed as a public holiday in England, Wales, and certain Commonwealth countries [So called because it was the day on which Christmas gifts were traditionally given to service workers]

box·ing glove *n.* a thick padded glove tied at the wrist, worn by boxers for fighting

box·ing ring *n.* the square raised platform with roped-in sides, used as the fighting arena in boxing matches. Each fighter has a corner diagonally opposite the other, sometimes referred to as "the red and blue corners."

box kite *n.* a kite without a tail, consisting of two open-ended boxes joined by thin sticks

box lunch *n.* **1.** LUNCH PACKED IN SMALL BOX a lunch for one person, packed in a small box **2.** = **obento**

box lyre *n.* a plucked stringed instrument, formed from a hollow wooden box with strings running across the soundboard, which are attached to arms

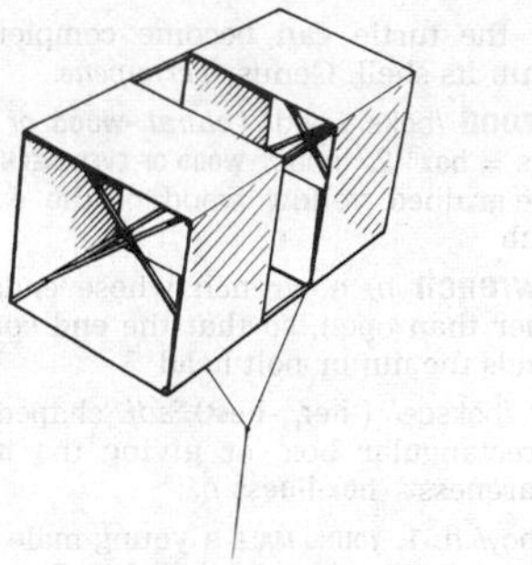
Box kite

jutting out to form a crossbar. Box lyres were known in ancient Sumer in 2800 B.C. and were widely played in Europe until A.D. 1000. One type of box lyre played by professional musicians was a cithara.

box num·ber *n.* the number assigned to an anonymous address for mail, either at a post office or as a reference for a reply to a newspaper advertisement

box of·fice *n.* **1.** PLACE WHERE TICKETS ARE BOUGHT the place where tickets are bought for entertainments such as movies, plays, or concerts (*often used before a noun*) ○ *box office receipts* **2.** MONEY FROM TICKET SALES ticket sales for a piece of theatrical and cinematic entertainment, or the income from these sales (*informal*) (*often used before a noun*) **3.** AUDIENCE POPULARITY drawing power to attract an audience to a theater (*informal*) ○ *The show makes great box office.* [So called because it was originally where a box in the theater could be reserved]

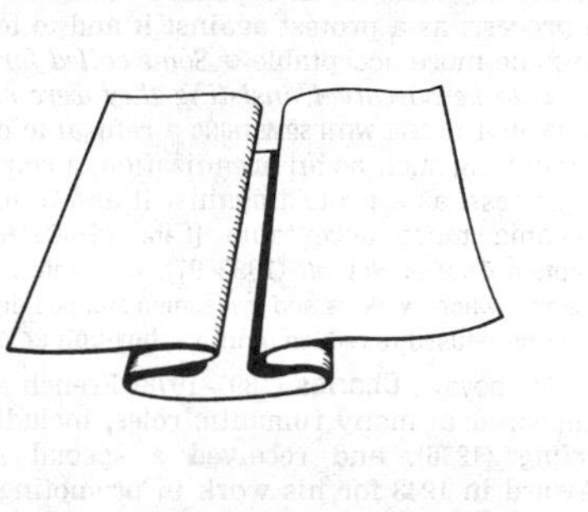
Box pleat

box pleat *n.* a pleat in which fabric is folded under and then back again on both the right and left, and pressed so as to lie flat

box score *n.* a printed summary of a game, especially a baseball game, in table form, listing the players and their positions and performance in the game

box seat *n.* **1.** THEATER, SPORTS SEAT IN THEATER OR STADIUM BOX a seat in a box in a theater or a sports stadium **2.** TRANSP BOX WHERE CARRIAGE DRIVER SITS the box on a horse-drawn carriage on which the driver sits

box set *n.* **1.** THEATER TRADITIONAL STAGE SET a stage set with a ceiling and three walls **2. box set, boxed set** SET OF SIMILAR ITEMS a set of similar items, e.g., recordings of music, that are packaged together in a box and sold as a single unit ○ *a four-CD box set*

box so·cial *n.* an event in which donated box lunches are auctioned off to raise money

box span·ner *n. U.K.* = **box wrench**

box spring *n.* a set of coiled springs contained in a frame, which is covered with fabric and used as a base for a mattress

box stall *n.* a large enclosed stall within a building in which a large untethered farm animal, such as a bull or stallion, may move around freely

box step *n.* the basic step in ballroom dancing, in which the feet are moved in a pattern forming the shape of a square

box·thorn /bóks thàwrn/ (*plural* **-thorns** *or* **-thorns**) *n.* = **matrimony vine** [From BOX³]

box tor·toise *n.* = **box turtle**

box tree *n.* = **box**³ *n.* 1

box tur·tle *n.* a North American land turtle that has the part of the shell over the abdomen hinged so that the turtle can become completely enclosed within its shell. Genus: *Terrapene.*

box·wood /bóks wŏŏd/ (*plural* **-wood** *or* **-woods**) *n.* **1.** TREES = **box**[3] **2.** INDUST **WOOD OF EVERGREEN BOX** the hard close-grained yellow wood of the evergreen box shrub

box wrench *n.* a wrench whose ends are closed, rather than open, so that the end completely surrounds the nut or bolt head

box·y /bóksee/ (**-i·er, -i·est**) *adj.* shaped like a cube or rectangular box, or giving the impression of squareness —**box·i·ness** *n.*

boy /boy/ *n.* **1. YOUNG MALE** a young male person ○ *I've had this hobby since I was a boy.* **2. SON** somebody's male child ○ *I'm very proud of that boy of mine.* **3. IMMATURE MAN** a man who is regarded as immature or inexperienced, especially a young man ○ *This should separate the men from the boys!* **4. MALE FROM CERTAIN AREA** a youth or man who comes from or was raised in a particular area **5. WAY OF ADDRESSING MALE ANIMAL** a way of addressing a male animal, especially a dog or a horse ○ *Get down, boy!* ■ **boys** *npl.* **A GROUP OF MALE FRIENDS** a group of men of any age who often socialize together ○ *a night out with the boys* ■ *interj.* **EXCLAMATION OF SURPRISE** used to express surprise, pleasure, or disgust ○ *Oh boy! Would you just take a look at that!* [13thC. Origin uncertain: perhaps from assumed Old French *embuié* "servant," the past participle of *embuier* "to fetter."]

bo·yar /bō yaár, bóyər/ *n.* from the 12th century to the early 18th century, a member of a class of the higher Russian nobility ranking below a prince [Late 16thC. From Russian *boyarin* "grandee."]

boy·cott /bóy kòt/ *vt.* (**-cott·ed, -cott·ing, -cotts**) **REFUSE TO DEAL WITH SOMETHING** to cease or refuse to deal with something such as an organization, a company, or a process, as a protest against it and to force it to become more acceptable ○ *Some called for the elections to be boycotted, insisting they were rigged.* ■ *n.* **REFUSAL TO DEAL WITH SOMETHING** a refusal to deal with something such as an organization, a company, or a process, as a protest against it and to force it to become more acceptable [Late 19thC. Named for Captain Charles *Boycott* (1832–97), an estate manager in Ireland, whom workers and tradesmen stopped dealing with after he refused to reduce rents.] —**boy·cott·er** *n.*

Boy·er /boyáy/, **Charles** (1897–1978) French actor. He appeared in many romantic roles, including *Mayerling* (1936), and received a special Academy Award in 1943 for his work in promoting Franco-American cultural relations.

Boy·er, Jean Pierre (1776–1850) Haitian politician. A freeborn mulatto, he played a major role in gaining independence for Haiti, and served as president of the new republic (1826–43).

boy·friend /bóy fr-nd/ *n.* a man with whom somebody has a romantic or sexual relationship

boy·hood /bóy hŏŏd/ *n.* the time in a male person's life when he is a boy

boy·ish /bóy ish/ *adj.* resembling a very young man's fresh looks or youthful behavior in a way that is pleasing or attractive —**boy·ish·ly** *adv.* —**boy·ish·ness** *n.*

Boyle's law /boylz-/ *n.* the principle that the volume of a confined gas at constant temperature varies inversely with its pressure [Named for the Irish-born scientist Robert *Boyle* (1627–91), who formulated it]

boy-meets-girl *adj.* based on a developing romance between a young man and a young woman, and treated in a predictable or hackneyed way in film or print ○ *It's a typical boy-meets-girl story where they live happily ever after.*

Boyn·ton Beach /bòyntən-/ city and vacation spot in southeastern Florida, north of Fort Lauderdale. Population: 50,742 (1996).

boy·o /bóyō/ *n.* used as a form of address for a boy or man, chiefly among Irish-Americans, one to another (*slang*) ○ *Relax, boyo. This job is going to be a snap.* [Late 19thC. Formed from BOY.]

Boy Scout *n.* **1.** LEISURE **MEMBER OF U.S. BOYS' ORGANIZATION** a member of the Boy Scouts of America, an organization whose objectives are to develop character, physical fitness, and citizenship, often through community and outdoor activities. ◊ **Scout 2. boy scout, Boy Scout A NAIVE OR OVERZEALOUS MAN** a man who is considered to be naive or overzealous (*insult*)

boy·sen·ber·ry /bóyz'n bèrree/ (*plural* **-ries**) *n.* **1.** PLANTS **TYPE OF BRAMBLE** a hybrid of the loganberry, blackberry, and raspberry. Genus: *Rubus.* **2.** FOOD **FRUIT OF THE BOYSENBERRY** the large purplish black fruit of the boysenberry, with a taste similar to a loganberry [Mid-20thC. Named for the U.S. botanist Rudolph *Boysen* (1895–1950), who developed it.]

boy toy *n.* a young woman who appears deliberately to try to attract and please men (*informal insult*)

boy won·der *n.* a talented and bright young man

Boze·man /bṓzmən/ city in southwestern Montana, on the edge of Gallatin National Forest. It is home to Montana State University. Population: 28,522 (1996).

bo·zo /bṓzō/ *n.* a mildly insulting term for somebody who has said or done something unwise (*informal insult*) [Early 20thC. Origin unknown.]

BP, **B.P.** *abbr.* blood pressure

bp. *abbr.* **1.** baptized **2.** base pair **3.** bills payable **4.** birthplace **5.** CHESS bishop

B/P *abbr.* bills payable

B.Pharm. /bèe faárm/ *abbr.* Bachelor of Pharmacy

B.Phil. *abbr.* Bachelor of Philosophy

B pic·ture *n.* a B movie (*dated*)

bpl., **bpl** *abbr.* birthplace

B.P.O.E., **BPOE** *abbr.* Benevolent and Protective Order of Elks

bps *n.* a measurement of data transfer speed, e.g., in modems and serial ports. Abbr of **bits per second**

Bq *symbol.* becquerel

Br *symbol.* bromine

BR *abbr.* **1.** bedroom **2. BR, B/R** bills receivable

br. *abbr.* **1.** branch **2.** brass **3.** brief **4.** bronze **5.** brother **6.** brown

Br. *abbr.* Britain ■ *abbr.* **1.** British **2.** Brother

bra /braa/ *n.* an undergarment designed to support and shape a woman's breasts [Mid-20thC. Shortening of *brassiere*, from French, "bodice," from *bras* "arm," from Latin *brachium* (see BRACHIUM).]

brab·ble /brább'l/ *vi.* (**-bled, -bling, -bles**) **QUARREL NOISILY OR SQUABBLE** to quarrel or squabble noisily ■ *n.* **NOISY QUARREL OR SQUABBLE** a noisy quarrel or squabble [Early 16thC. Origin uncertain: possibly from Middle Dutch *brabbelen* "to squabble."] —**brab·bler** /brábblər/ *n.*

bra burn·er *n.* a woman who is regarded as an aggressive, militant feminist (*slang insult*) [Mid-20th Century. From public demonstrations in which feminists allegedly burned their bras in protest against social restrictions on women.]

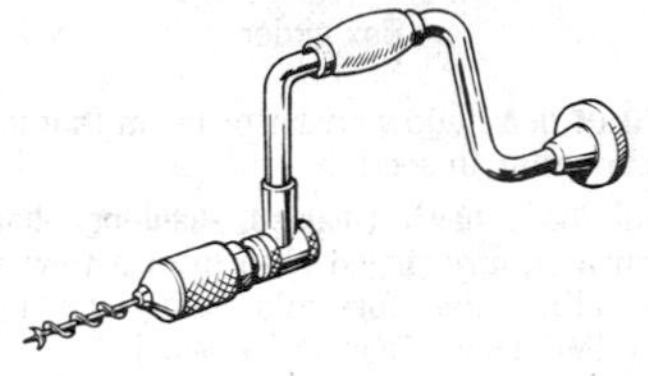

Brace

brace[1] /brayss/ *n.* **1.** MED **SUPPORT FOR PART OF BODY** an orthopedic appliance that holds or supports part of the body **2. CLAMP** a device that keeps something steady or holds two things together **3.** BUILDING **A SUPPORT FOR SOMETHING CONSTRUCTED** a device used in the building trade to hold a structure or part steady or upright, e.g., a beam, or wooden framework **4. brace** (*plural* **brace**) **PAIR** a pair of similar things, e.g., wild game, hunting dogs, or pistols ○ *two brace of pheasants* **5.** CONSTR **TOOL FOR HOLDING DRILL BIT** a tool with an adjustable socket at one end for holding a drill bit, and a handle like a crank at the other for turning the bit **6.** PRINTING **EITHER SYMBOL** { } either of a pair of symbols, { }, used in printing or writing **7.** MUSIC **ADJUSTER FOR DRUM TENSION** a sliding loop on the cords of a drum, used to change its tension **8.** MUSIC **BRACKET CONNECTING LINES OF MUSIC** a thick line or bracket connecting a group of the staves in a piece of music, e.g., all the choral parts, or the accompaniment **9.** MATH **SYMBOL OF MATHEMATICAL GROUPING** either of a pair of symbols { }, for additional grouping of mathematical quantities after parentheses and square brackets have been used **10.** MIL **STIFF MILITARY POSTURE** a very erect, stiff posture with the chest thrust out, hands at the sides, feet together, and chin tucked in, taught to military recruits and cadets **11.** ARCHERY, FENCING = **bracer**[2] *n.* ■ **brac·es** *npl.* **1.** DENT **APPLIANCE AFFIXED TO TEETH** a dental appliance that is wired or otherwise affixed to the teeth, and that can be tightened in order to straighten them (*sometimes used in the singular*) **2.** *U.K.* = **suspenders** ■ *v.* (**braced, brac·ing, brac·es**) **1.** *vt.* **SUPPORT OR STRENGTHEN SOMETHING** to support or strengthen something, especially part of a building, with a brace ○ *Anchor bolts cannot be used to brace these shelves.* **2.** *vi.* **PREPARE FOR SOMETHING** to prepare, or prepare yourself, for something dangerous or unpleasant that is likely to happen or about to happen, especially some sort of impact or difficulty ○ *Coastal residents are bracing for the hurricane.* [From Old French, literally "two outstretched arms, fathom," from Latin *bracchia*, plural of *brachium* "arm" (see BRACHIUM)]

brace up *vi.* to be strong and resolute in facing difficulty ○ *Brace up and face the facts.*

brace[2] /brayss/ *n.* SAILING on a square-rigged ship, a rope used to control the spar that extends a sail [Early 17thC. Origin uncertain: possibly an alteration of French *bras de vergue*, literally "yard arm," under the influence of "brace."]

brace·let /bráysslit/ *n.* **JEWELRY WORN AROUND WRIST OR ARM** a piece of jewelry, e.g., a chain or a bangle, that is worn around the wrist or arm ■ **brace·lets** *npl.* **HANDCUFFS** a pair of handcuffs (*slang*) [15thC. Via French from, ultimately, Latin *bracchiale* "armlet," from *brachium* "arm" (see BRACHIUM).]

brace po·si·tion *n.* a protective position that somebody adopts before impact in a crash, protecting the head with the arms and bringing the legs up underneath the chest

brac·er[1] /bráyssər/ *n.* **1. SUPPORT** somebody or something that braces **2.** BEVERAGES **INVIGORATING DRINK** an invigorating often alcoholic drink [Mid-16thC. Formed from BRACE[1].]

bra·cer[2] /bráyssər/, **brace** /brayss/ *n.* ARCHERY, FENCING a leather guard worn by fencers and archers to protect the arm [14thC. From Old French *bracière*, from *bras* "arm," from Latin *brachium* (see BRACHIUM).]

bra·ce·ro /brə sáirō/ (*plural* **-ros**) *n.* a Mexican worker who is allowed entry into the United States to work for a limited time, typically on a farm [Early 20thC. From Spanish, "laborer," from *brazo* "arm," from Latin *brachium* (see BRACHIUM).]

brace root *n.* = **prop root**

bra·chi·a *n.* plural of **brachium**

bra·chi·al /bráykee əl, brákee-/ *adj.* relating to or situated in the arm, foreleg, or wing [Late 16thC. From Latin *brachialis*, from *brachium* (see BRACHIUM).]

bra·chi·ate /bráykee it, -àyt, brák ee-/ *adj.* **WITH ARMS** having arms or appendages like arms ■ *vi.* (**-at·ed, -at·ing, -ates**) **MOVE BY SWINGING FROM ARMS** to move along by swinging from one hold to the next with the arms (*refers to tree-dwelling animals*) [Mid-18thC. From Latin *brachiatus*, from *brachium* (see BRACHIUM).] —**bra·chi·a·tion** /bràykee áysh'n/ *n.* —**bra·chi·a·tor** *n.*

brachio- *prefix.* arm ○ *brachiocephalic* [From Latin *brachium* (see BRACHIUM)]

bra·chi·o·ce·phal·ic /bràykee ō sə fállik, bràkee-/ *adj.* relating to or supplying the arms and the head

bra·chi·o·pod /bráykee ə pòd, brákee-/ *n.* a marine invertebrate animal with hinged shells enclosing tentacles. Phylum: Brachiopoda. [Mid-19thC. From modern Latin *Brachiopoda*, phylum name, from Latin *brachium* "arm" and -POD.] —**brach·i·o·pod** *adj.*

bra·chi·o·sau·rus /bràykee ə sáwrəss, bràkee-/ (*plural* **-rus·es** *or* **-ri** /-rī/), **bra·chi·o·saur** /-sáwr/ *n.* a dinosaur with a massive sloping body up to 100 ft./30 m long. Genus: *Brachiosaurus.* [Early 20thC. From modern Latin, genus name, which was coined from BRACHIUM (from the unusual length of the animal's humerus bones) + Greek *sauros* "lizard."]

bra·chi·um /bráykee əm/ (*plural* **-a** /-kee ə/) *n.* **1.** ANAT **ARM** an arm, especially the upper arm (*technical*) **2.** ZOOL **ANIMAL LIMB CORRESPONDING TO ARM** a structure, e.g., a wing, that corresponds to an arm [Mid-18thC. Via Latin from Greek *brakhiōn* "upper arm," literally "shorter" from *brakhus* "short" (see BRACHY-).]

brachy- *prefix.* short ○ *brachyodont* [From Greek *brakhus.* Ultimately from an Indo-European word meaning "short," which is also the ancestor of English *brief, abbreviate,* and *brace.*]

brach·y·ce·phal·ic /bràki səffállik/, **brach·y·ceph·a·lous** /-séffələss/ *adj.* with a short, broad, and almost spherical head —**brach·y·ceph·a·lism** /bràki séffə lìzzəm/ *n.* —**brach·y·ceph·a·ly** /-séffəlee/ *n.*

brach·y·dac·tyl·ic /bràki dak tíllik/, **brach·y·dac·ty·lous** /-dáktələss/ *adj.* with abnormally short fingers or toes —**brach·y·dac·tyl·i·a** /bràki dak tílleeə/ *n.* —**brach·y·dac·ty·ly** /-dáktəlee/ *n.*

bra·chyl·o·gy /bra kíllәjee/ *n.* **1.** **BREVITY IN WORD USE** brevity in speech or writing, or an instance of such brevity **2.** **SHORTENED FORM OF TERM** a shortened form of an expression, used in informal speech [Mid-16thC. Via late Latin from Greek *brakhulogia,* literally "shortness of speech."] —**bra·chyl·o·gous** *adj.*

bra·chyp·ter·ous /bra kíptərəss/ *adj.* used to describe insects and some species of diving birds with short or not fully developed wings —**bra·chyp·ter·ism** /bra kíptə rìzzəm, brə-/ *n.*

brac·ing /bráyssing/ *adj.* **REFRESHINGLY INVIGORATING** refreshing or invigorating ○ *a bracing cold shower* ■ *n.* **BRACES SUPPORTING SOMETHING** a system of braces that are used to support or strengthen a structure —**brac·ing·ly** *adv.*

bra·ci·o·la /braachee ólə, braach ólə/ (*plural* **-o·las** *or* **-ole** /-lay, -lè/) *n.* a thin slice of meat that is usually wrapped around a stuffing and cooked in wine [Mid-20thC. From Italian, literally "something cooked over coals," from *brace* "live coals," probably of Germanic origin.]

Bracken

brack·en /brákən/ (*plural* **-en** *or* **-ens**) *n.* a large fern, common in most temperate and tropical regions, with extensive underground stems and large triangular fronds. Latin name: *Pteridium aquilinum.* [14thC. From assumed Old Norse *brakni.*]

brack·et /brákit/ *n.* **1.** **L-SHAPED STRUCTURE ON WALL** an L-shaped structure that is attached to a wall to hold up something, e.g., a shelf or speaker **2.** **TYPE OF SHELF** a shelf that usually has an integral part that attaches to the wall as its support and can sometimes be swiveled **3.** PRINTING **EITHER OF THE SYMBOLS [ ]** either one of a pair of symbols, [ ], used in keying or printing to indicate the insertion of special commentary, such as that made by an editor **4.** *U.K.* PRINTING = **parenthesis** (*often used in plural*) **5.** **GROUP WITHIN CERTAIN LIMITS** a section of a population or group that falls within specific defined limits ○ *taxpayers in the $50,000 to $70,000 bracket* ■ *vt.* (**-et·ed, -et·ing, -ets**) **1.** **SUPPORT SOMETHING WITH BRACKETS** to attach brackets to something, especially a wall, or to support something with brackets **2.** **PUT SOMETHING INSIDE BRACKETS** to put something, especially text or a mathematical equation, inside brackets **3.** **GROUP THINGS OR PEOPLE TOGETHER** to group or class things or people together, usually because they are similar in some way ○ *Rail and bus can be bracketed together under public transportation.* [Late 16thC. Origin uncertain: possibly via French *braguette* "codpiece" (because of its shape) from, ultimately, Latin *bracae* "breeches."] —**brack·et·ing** *n.*

brack·et creep *n.* movement into a higher tax bracket due to a slow increase in income, especially as a result of cost-of-living pay increases

brack·et fun·gus (*plural* **brack·et fun·gi** *or* **brack·et fun·gus·es**) *n.* a fungus that forms growths that look somewhat like shelves. The growths generally appear on tree trunks and other wooden structures.

brack·ish /brákish/ *adj.* somewhat salty, especially from being a mixture of fresh and salt water [Mid-16thC. Formed from Dutch *brak* "salty water," of unknown origin.] —**brack·ish·ness** *n.*

brac·o·nid /brákənid/ *n.* a fly whose larvae are parasitic on other insects. Family: Braconidae. [Late 19thC. From modern Latin *Braconidae,* family name, from Greek *brakhus* "short" (see BRACHY-).]

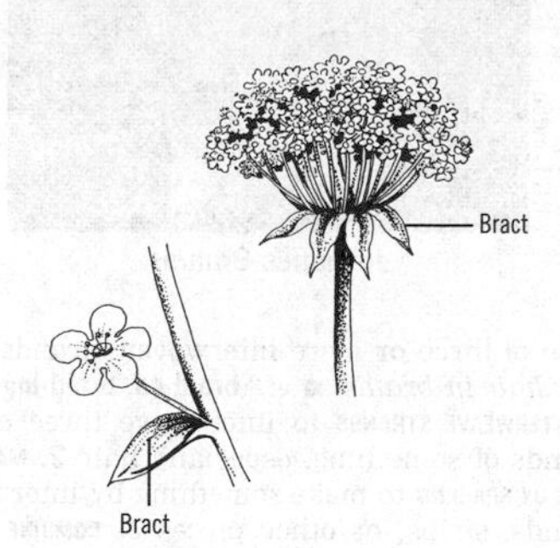

Bract

bract /brakt/ *n.* BOT a modified leaf that arises from the stem at the point where the flower or flower cluster develops [Late 18thC. From Latin *bractea* "thin metal plate, gold leaf," of uncertain origin.] —**brac·te·al** /bráktee əl/ *adj.*

brac·te·ate /bráktee it, -àyt/ *adj.* BOT **WITH BRACTS** used to describe a plant that has bracts ■ *n.* ARCHEOL **DECORATED DISH** a decorated dish or plate made of precious metal [Early 19thC. From Latin *bracteatus,* from *bractea* (see BRACT).]

brac·te·ole /bráktee òl/ *n.* an organ resembling a leaf or scale that arises from a branch of a flower cluster where the flowers develop, and where the entire cluster itself develops above a bract [Early 19thC. From Latin *bracteola,* literally "small bract," from *bractea* (see BRACT).] —**brac·te·o·late** /bráktee ə lit, -làyt/ *adj.*

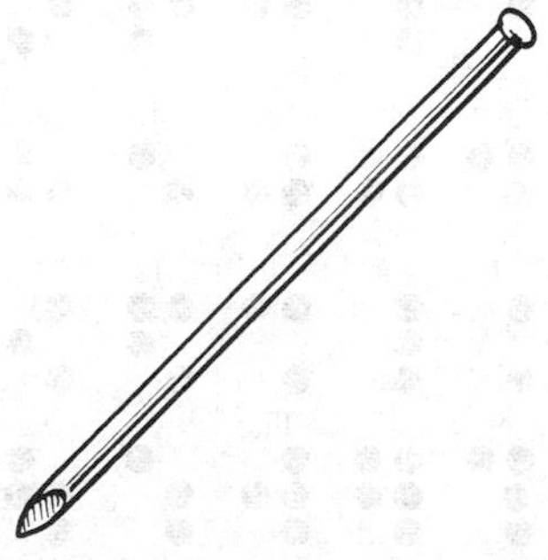

Brad

brad /brad/ *n.* a thin tapered nail with a small head that is either symmetrical or formed on one side only [13thC. From Old Norse *broddr* "spike."]

brad·awl /brád àwl/ *n.* a hand tool with a pointed tip, used for making holes in wood, leather, and other materials, to allow screws and nails to be inserted

Brad·dock /bráddək/, **Edward** (1695–1755) British general. He led British forces in North America (1755) during the French and Indian War, and was killed in an ambush at Fort Duquesne, near present-day Pittsburgh, from which George Washington escaped.

Bra·den·ton /bráyd'ntən/ city in western Florida, northwest of Sarasota, on the south side of Tampa Bay. Population: 47,219 (1996).

Brad·ford /brádfərd/, **William** (1590–1657) English-born Puritan leader and New England colonist. He sailed to North America on the *Mayflower* (1620) and was governor of Plymouth colony almost continuously from 1621 through 1656. He wrote the *History of Plimouth Plantation* (1620–47), published in 1856 and still a major historical source.

Brad·ley /brádlee/, **Bill** (*b.* 1943) U.S. politician. He was a long-serving Democrat in the U.S. Senate (1979–97) after a ten-year career as a professional basketball star with the New York Knicks. Full name **William Warren Bradley**

Brad·ley, Omar (1893–1981) U.S. general. During World War II he was responsible for Allied campaigns in Tunisia, Sicily, and France, where he commanded 1.4 million U.S. troops. He was famous for his concern for the ordinary soldier. Full name **Omar Nelson Bradley**. Known as **the GI General**

Brad·ley, Thomas (*b.* 1917) U.S. politician. A former police officer, he was elected the first African American mayor of Los Angeles in 1973.

Sir Don Bradman

Brad·man /brádmən/, **Sir Don** (*b.* 1908) Australian cricketer. He was Australian Test captain (1936–48), and one of the highest-scoring batsmen of all time, with a Test average of 99.94 runs. Full name **Sir Donald George Bradman**

Brad·street /brád street/, **Anne** (1612?–72) English-born American New England poet. An early settler (1630) and the wife of a governor of the Massachusetts Bay Colony, she is regarded as the first English poet in America. Her verse was first published in England in 1650. Born **Ann Dudley**

Bra·dy /bráydee/, **Mathew B.** (1823?–1896) U.S. photographer. His photographs of prominent personalities, including Abraham Lincoln, and of the Civil War have fixed the popular image of the United States in the mid-19th century.

brady- /bráydee/ *prefix.* slow ○ *bradycardia* [From Greek *bradus,* of unknown origin]

brad·y·car·di·a /bràddi kaárdee ə/ *n.* slowness of the heart rate, usually measured as fewer than 60 beats per minute in an adult human [Late 19thC. Coined from BRADY- + Greek *kardia* "heart" + -IA, literally "slow-heart condition."] —**brad·y·car·dic** /bràddi kaárdik/ *adj.*

brad·y·ki·nin /bráddi kínin, -kínin/ *n.* a chemical (**peptide**) derived from plasma protein that forms at the site of injured tissue. It plays a role in producing inflammation, dilates blood vessels, and contracts smooth muscle. [Mid-20thC. Coined from BRADY- + Greek *kinein* "to move" + -IN.]

brae /bray/ *n. Scotland* in Scotland, a hill or slope (*often used in place names*) [14thC. From Old Norse *brá* "eyelash." The underlying meaning is "brow of a hill."]

brag /brag/ *vi.* (**bragged, brag·ging, brags**) **TALK WITH TOO MUCH PRIDE** to talk shamelessly or with excessive pride about achievements or possessions ○ *The police arrested him after he bragged about the bank robbery to his friends.* ■ *n.* **1.** **BOASTFUL REMARK** a boastful statement or display of arrogant behavior **2.** **SUBJECT OF BOAST** something bragged or boasted about **3.** **SOMEBODY WHO BRAGS** a boastful person **4.** CARDS **CARD GAME** a card game similar to poker [14thC. Origin unknown.] —**brag·ger** *n.* —**brag·ging** *n., adj.* —**brag·ging·ly** *adv.*

Brage *n.* = **Bragi**

Bragg /brag/, **Braxton** (1817–76) U.S. Confederate general. He was defeated in the Civil War Chattanooga Campaign (1863).

Bragg, Sir Lawrence (1890–1971) Australian-born British physicist. He collaborated with his father, Sir William Bragg, in developing an X-ray technique for examining crystals. They shared the Nobel Prize in physics in 1915. Full name **Sir William Lawrence Bragg**

brag·ga·do·ci·o /bràggə dóssee ò, -shee ò, -shō/ (*plural* **-os**) *n.* **1.** **OVERBLOWN, EMPTY BOASTING** empty boasting and swaggering self-aggrandizement **2.** **BRAGGART** somebody who makes overblown claims or empty boasts [Late 16thC. Alteration of *Braggadocchio,* the personification of boastfulness in Spenser's *Faerie Queen.*]

brag·gart /brággərt/ *n.* somebody who talks immodestly, shamelessly, or with excessive pride about his or her achievements or possessions [Late

16thC. From French *bragard*, from *braguer* "to brag," of uncertain origin: possibly from English *brag*.]

Bragg's law /brágz-/ *n.* a law stating the directions in which X-rays reflected from a crystal are most intense [Early 20thC. Named for Sir William Henry BRAGG and his son, Sir William Lawrence *Bragg* (1890–1971), English physicists.]

Bra·gi /bráagee/, **Bra·ge** /-gə/ *n.* in Nordic mythology, the god of poetry, eloquence, and music

Bra·he /braa, bráahee, bráa ə/, **Tycho** (1546–1601) Danish astronomer. He employed extremely precise observations of stars and planets to correct inaccuracies in existing astronomical tables.

Brah·ma[1] /bráamə/ *n.* **1.** HINDU GOD a Hindu god, the source of knowledge and understanding, regarded as the protector of the world and in later tradition called the creator **2.** = **Brahman** *n.* 1 [From Sanskrit *brāhmaṇa-*, from *brahman-* (see BRAHMIN)]

Brah·ma[2] /bráamə, bráy-/ *n.* BIRDS a large domestic fowl with heavily feathered legs and feet and a small tail and wings [Mid-19thC. Shortening of *Brahmaputra fowl*, so called because it was first imported from a town on the Brahmaputra river in India.]

Brah·man /bráamən/ *n.* **1.** ULTIMATE POWER UNDERLYING THE UNIVERSE in Hinduism, the ultimate impersonal reality underlying everything in the universe, from which everything comes and to which it returns **2.** = **Brahma**[1] *n.* 1 **3.** = **Brahmin** *n.* 1, **Brahmin** *n.* 2 [Late 18thC. From Sanskrit (see BRAHMIN).] —**Brah·man·ic** /braamánik/ *adj.* —**Brah·man·i·cal** *adj.*

Brah·ma·na /bráamənə/ *n.* a sacred Hindu text, belonging to a group of commentaries on the Vedas [From Sanskrit *brāhmaṇam*, from *brāhmaṇa-* (see BRAHMIN)]

Brah·ma·ni /bráamənee/, **brah·ma·ni** *n.* a woman of the Brahmin caste [Late 18thC. From Sanskrit *brāhmaṇī*, feminine of *brāhmaṇa-* (see BRAHMIN).]

Brah·man·ism, **brah·man·ism** *n.* = **Brahminism** — **Brah·man·ist** *n.*

Brahmin

Brah·min /bráamin/ (*plural* **-mins** *or* **-min**), **brah·min** (*plural* **-mins** *or* **-min**) *n.* **1.** INDIAN RELIG HIGHEST HINDU CASTE the first of the four Hindu castes, the members of which are priests and scholars of Vedic literature **2.** INDIAN RELIG MEMBER OF BRAHMIN CASTE a member of the Brahmin caste **3.** MEMBER OF CULTURAL ELITE a member of the cultural, social, or intellectual elite, especially formerly in New England [15thC. From Sanskrit *brāhmaṇa-*, from *brahman-* "priest." Ultimately from an Indo-European word meaning "priest."] —**Brah·min·ic** /braamínik/ *adj.* —**Brah·min·i·cal** /-mínnik'l/ *adj.*

Brah·min·ism /bráamə nìzzəm/, **brah·min·ism, Brah·man·ism, brah·man·ism** *n.* the traditional social and religious system of Vedic Hinduism — **Brah·min·ist** /bráamənist/ *n.*

Brahms /braamz/, **Johannes** (1833–97) German composer. His works includes four symphonies, two piano concertos, and *A German Requiem* (1868).

Bra·hu·i /braa hòo ee/ (*plural* **-is** *or* **-i**) *n.* **1.** DRAVIDIAN LANGUAGE a Dravidian language spoken in southwestern Pakistan. Brahui is spoken by about two million people, many of whom are bilingual in Baluchi or Sindhi. **2.** MEMBER OF ASIAN PEOPLE a member of an Asian Brahui-speaking people who live in southwestern Pakistan [Early 19thC. From Brahui.] — **Bra·hu·i** *adj.*

braid /brayd/ *n.* **1.** INDUST, CLOTHES DECORATIVE SILKY CORD decorative and often silky cord or interwoven thread, used especially to trim and bind, in decorating uniforms, and as edging for soft furnishings **2.** SOMETHING INTERWOVEN something that is

Johannes Brahms

made of three or more interwoven strands ○ *wear your hair in braids* ■ *vt.* (**braid·ed, braid·ing, braids**) **1.** INTERWEAVE STRANDS to interweave three or more strands of something, especially hair **2.** MAKE SOMETHING BY BRAIDING to make something by interweaving strands, strips, or other pieces **3.** COMBINE SEPARATE THINGS to combine or intermingle several separate things into something complex ○ *Elements from several different cultures were braided into the performance piece.* **4.** DECORATE SOMETHING WITH BRAID to decorate uniforms or edge furnishings with braid [Old English *bregdan* "to weave, lay hold of" (source also of English *upbraid*)]

braid·ed /bráydid/ *adj.* **1.** INTERWOVEN interwoven from three or more strands **2.** EDGED WITH CORD decorated or edged with silky, especially gold, cord **3.** CONSISTING OF INTERCONNECTED TRACKS OR CHANNELS composed of several interconnected tracks or channels that divide and reunite ○ *a braided river*

braid·ing /bráyding/ *n.* **1.** INDUST SILKY THREAD OR CORD decorative silky thread or cord, used especially to decorate uniforms and furnishings **2.** SEW EMBROIDERY embroidery worked in decorative silky thread

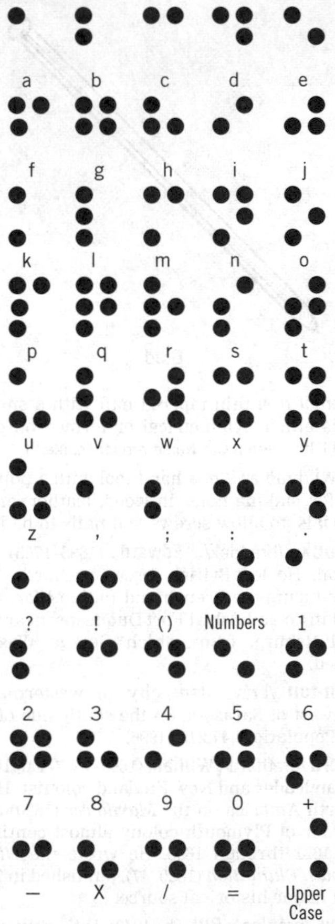

Braille

Braille /brayl/ *n.* a writing system for visually impaired or sightless people, consisting of patterns of raised dots that are read by touch [Mid-19thC. Named after Louis BRAILLE.]

Braille /brayl/, **Louis** (1809–52) French educator. He was blind from early childhood and in 1829 he invented the Braille system of raised dots to enable visually impaired people to read and write.

Braill·er /bráylər/, **Braille·writ·er** /bráyl rìtər/ *n.* a machine similar to a typewriter that prints Braille

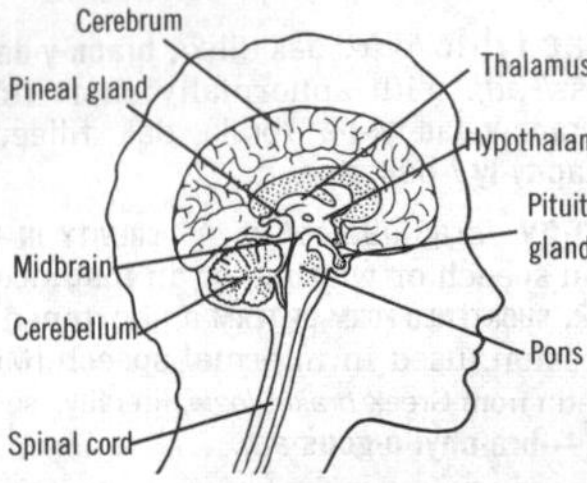

Brain: Cross section of human brain

brain /brayn/ *n.* **1.** ANAT ORGAN OF THOUGHT AND FEELING the controlling center of the nervous system in vertebrates, connected to the spinal cord and enclosed in the cranium. It consists of a mass of nerve tissue and nerve-supporting and nourishing tissue (**neuroglia**), is the center of thought and emotions, and regulates bodily activities. **2.** ZOOL CENTER OF NERVOUS-SYSTEM IN INVERTEBRATES a nervous-system center in some invertebrates that is functionally similar to the brain in vertebrates **3.** INTELLECT somebody's intellectual abilities or intellectual center ○ *His heart was beating violently and his brain was in a turmoil.* **4.** BRAINY PERSON a very intelligent person, especially the most intelligent person in a certain group (*informal*) ○ *Lee's the brain of the family.* ■ *vt.* (**brained, brain·ing, brains**) HIT SOMEBODY ON HEAD to hit somebody violently on the head (*slang*) [Old English *brægen*] ◇ **have something on the brain** to be obsessed with something ○ *She has making money on the brain.* ◇ **pick somebody's brains** to ask questions of somebody, in order to learn what he or she knows about something ○ *Let me pick your brains about how to market this new book.* ◇ **rack your brains** to try to remember something or solve a problem by thinking very hard ○ *I racked my brains but still could not recall her address.*

brain·case /bráyn kàyss/ *n.* the part of the skull enclosing the brain

brain·child /bráyn chìld/ (*plural* **-chil·dren**) *n.* an original plan or idea attributed to a single person or to a group of people

brain cor·al (*plural* **brain cor·al** *or* **brain cor·als**) *n.* coral that forms rounded colonies resembling the convex folds of the human brain. Genus: *Meandrina.*

brain dam·age *n.* injury to the brain tissue that can impair normal functioning

brain-dead *adj.* **1.** MED WITH NONFUNCTIONING BRAIN lacking functions of the brain and central nervous system as measured by brainwave activity on an electroencephalogram over a set period of time **2.** OFFENSIVE TERM an offensive term for somebody considered to have extremely low intellectual ability (*slang offensive*)

brain death *n.* the end of all functions of the brain and central nervous system as measured by brainwave activity on an electroencephalogram over a set period of time. There are strict legal criteria for determining brain death, since its occurrence can allow cessation of life support or removal of organs for transplantation.

brain drain *n.* the movement of highly skilled people, especially scientists and technical workers, to a country offering better opportunities

Brain·erd /bráynərd/ city in central Minnesota, on the bank of the Mississippi River, north of St. Cloud. Population: 13,285 (1996).

brain fe·ver *n.* a term for inflammation of the brain or its covering membranes (*archaic*)

brain·less /bráynliss/ *adj.* lacking intelligence — **brain·less·ly** *adv.* —**brain·less·ness** *n.*

brain·pan /bráyn pàn/ *n.* = **braincase**

brain·pow·er /bráyn pòwər/ *n.* somebody's intellectual capability

brain scan *n.* **1.** IMAGE OF BRAIN SHOWING ABNORMALITIES a series of two-dimensional cross sections of the brain produced by means of computerized imaging techniques and showing the presence of tumors or other abnormalities. Information presented in three dimensions can be derived from the combined cross sections. **2.** PROCEDURE FOR SCANNING THE BRAIN the procedure involved in producing this image

brain·stem /bráyn stèm/ *n.* the part of the brain between the spinal column and the cerebral hemispheres. It consists of the midbrain, pons, and medulla oblongata.

brain·storm /bráyn stàwrm/ *n.* **1.** BRILLIANT IDEA a sudden, exciting idea (*informal*) ○ *I just had a brainstorm! I'll tell you how we can do it.* **2.** BRIEF PSYCHOLOGICAL DISTURBANCE a momentary psychological disturbance ■ *vti.* **(-stormed, -storm·ing, -storms)** THINK QUICKLY AND CREATIVELY to generate creative ideas spontaneously, usually for problem-solving, and especially in an intensive group discussion that does not allow time for reflection —**brain·storm·er** *n.* —**brain·storm·ing** *n.*

brain sur·geon *n.* a very intelligent person (*informal*) ○ *It doesn't take a brain surgeon to understand this software.*

brain·teas·er /bráyn teezər/ *n.* a difficult or complex problem that requires careful thought in order to solve it, often done for amusement

Brain·tree /bráyn tree/ town in eastern Massachusetts. It is a southern suburb of Boston, and directly south of Quincy. Population: 34,708 (1996).

brain trust *n.* **1.** HIGH-LEVEL ADVISERS a group of high-level advisers, usually unofficial, to a government or administration **2.** INEPT PEOPLE a group of people regarded as self-important, inept, and operating at a level of authority beyond their competence (*slang*) ○ *The inventory control fiasco is the product of the brain trust called "Corporate Operations."* **3. brain trust, Brain Trust** HIST ADVISERS TO ROOSEVELT a group of high-level academics who helped President Franklin Delano Roosevelt, especially prior to his taking office, formulate the New Deal —**brain trust·er** *n.*

brain·wash /bráyn wòsh, -wàwsh/ **(-washed, -wash·ing, -wash·es)** *vt.* **1.** IMPOSE BELIEFS ON SOMEBODY to impose a set of usually political or religious beliefs on somebody by the use of various coercive methods of indoctrination, including destruction of the victim's prior beliefs **2.** CONDITION SOMEBODY TO BEHAVE DIFFERENTLY to induce somebody to believe or do something, e.g., to buy a new product, especially by constant repetition or advertising

brain·wash·ing /bráyn wòshing, -wàwshing/ *n.* inducing somebody to believe or do something, such as buy a new product, especially by means of constant repetition or advertising

brain wave *n.* **1.** WAVE OF VOLTAGE IN BRAIN one of the rhythmic waves of voltage arising from electrical activity within brain tissue **2.** = **brainstorm** *n.* 1 (*informal*)

brain·work /bráyn wùrk/ *n.* concentrated intellectual activity, especially that required to do a job —**brain·work·er** *n.*

brain·y /bráynee/ **(-i·er, -i·est)** *adj.* extremely intelligent (*informal*) —**brain·i·ly** *adv.* —**brain·i·ness** *n.*

braise /brayz/ **(braised, brais·ing, brais·es)** *vt.* to cook food, especially meat or vegetables, by browning briefly in hot fat, adding a little liquid, and cooking at a low temperature in a covered pot [Mid-18thC. From French *braiser*, from *braise* "live coals" (source of English *brazier*).]

brake[1] /brayk/ *n.* **1.** DEVICE THAT SLOWS OR STOPS MACHINE the part of a machine or vehicle that slows it down or stops it (*often used in the plural*) **2.** RESTRAINT ON SOMETHING a slowing down or stopping of something such as expenditure or development, or something that causes this ○ *The brake on investment is largely a result of political factors.* ■ *v.* **(braked, brak·ing, brakes) 1.** *vti.* SLOW OR STOP MACHINE to slow down or stop, or to make something such as a vehicle or a machine go more slowly or stop ○ *The driver braked hard .* **2.** *vt.* SLOW OR HALT DEVELOPMENT to slow down or halt the progress of something or an increase in something [Late 18thC. Origin uncertain: possibly from an earlier sense "bridle, curb," from Middle Dutch or Low German, "nose ring, flax brake" (see BRAKE[4]).]

brake[2] /brayk/ (*plural* **brake** *or* **brakes**) *n.* **1.** FERN a fern with compound leaves resembling feathers, popular as a houseplant. Genus: *Pteris*. **2.** = **bracken** [14thC. Origin uncertain: possibly a back-formation from BRACKEN, the "-en" being mistaken for a plural ending.]

brake[3] /brayk/ *n.* an area of dense undergrowth, shrubs, and brush [Old English *bracu*, of uncertain origin]

brake[4] /brayk/ *n.* **1.** FIBER-SEPARATING MACHINE a tool or machine for crushing and separating the fibers of flax or hemp **2.** METAL-FOLDING MACHINE a machine, frequently hydraulically powered, for precision bending and folding of sheet metal [15thC. Origin uncertain: from Middle Low German or Middle Dutch. Ultimately from a prehistoric Germanic base meaning "to break."]

brake[5] /brayk/ *n.* a lever or handle on a pump or other machine [Early 17thC. Origin uncertain.]

brake chute *n.* = **brake parachute**

brake drum *n.* the metal cylinder attached to the wheel of a vehicle that slows the rotation of the wheel when pressure is applied

brake fade *n.* a decrease in braking efficiency of a motor vehicle, caused by the brakes overheating

brake flu·id *n.* the oily liquid used in hydraulic brake system to transmit pressure from the brake pedal to the brakes

brake horse·pow·er *n.* a measure of the work produced by an engine, calibrated in horsepower and determined by the force exerted on a friction brake

brake light *n.* a rear light on a motor vehicle that lights up when the driver brakes.

brake lin·ing *n.* the thin, replaceable strip of material attached to a brake shoe

brake·man /bráykmən/ (*plural* **-men** /-mən/) *n.* a member of a train crew or other railroad employee who operates, inspects, or repairs brakes

brake pad *n.* a replaceable block of material that presses against the surface of a disk brake

brake par·a·chute, brake chute *n.* a parachute that is attached to the back of a vehicle and acts as a brake

brake shoe *n.* a curved block that presses against a wheel or brake drum to slow it down

brak·ing dis·tance /bráyking-/ *n.* the distance a vehicle needs to come to a complete stop when the brakes have been applied

bra·less /braáliss/ *adj.* not wearing a bra

Bra·man·te /brə maán tay, braa maán te/, **Donato** (1444–1514) Italian architect and painter. He rebuilt and renovated the Vatican and St. Peter's in Rome (1505–6). Real name **Donato di Pascuccio d'Antonio**

bram·ble /brámb'l/ **(-bled, -bling, -bles)** *n.* **1.** PRICKLY SHRUB WITH EDIBLE FRUIT a prickly shrub of the rose family, especially blackberry or raspberry canes. Genus: *Rubus*. **2.** PRICKLY SHRUB a prickly shrub or bush similar to, or related to, the blackberry, e.g., a sweetbriar **3.** BLACKBERRY a blackberry [Old English *bræmbel*. Ultimately from a prehistoric Germanic word meaning "thorny bush," which is also the ancestor of English *broom*.]

bram·bling /brámbling/ *n.* a bird of northern Europe and Asia related to the chaffinch, with a speckled head and back and rusty brown breast. Latin name: *Fringilla montifringilla*. [Mid-16thC. Origin uncertain: possibly formed from BRAMBLE and -LING.]

bram·bly /brámblee/ **(-bli·er, -bli·est)** *adj.* covered in or containing prickly shrubs, especially blackberries or wild roses ○ *a brambly garden*

Bramp·ton /brámptən/ city and industrial center in southeastern Ontario, Canada. Population: 268,251 (1996).

bran /bran/ *n.* the husks of cereal grain that are partly or completely removed during the milling process and used as a supplementary source of dietary fiber [13thC. From French, of unknown origin.]

Bran /bran/ *n.* in Celtic mythology, a giant god who ruled Britain and installed his son, Gwern, as king of Ireland

Bran·agh /brannə/, **Kenneth** (*b.* 1960) Irish-born U.K. actor and director. He directed and acted in movies including *Henry V* (1989). Full name **Kenneth Charles Branagh**

branch /branch/ *n.* **1.** BOT PART OF TREE GROWING FROM TRUNK a woody limb of a tree that grows out from a larger limb or from the trunk **2.** BOT PART OF PLANT STEM OR ROOT a subdivision of the stem, root, or flower cluster of a plant **3.** SOMETHING LIKE TREE BRANCH something that resembles a branch of a tree in structure **4.** LOCAL UNIT IN ORGANIZATION a store, bank, or other organization that is part of a larger group and is located in a different part of a geographical area from the parent organization ○ *The account is held at the bank's Elm Street branch.* **5.** DISTINCT PART OF LARGE ORGANIZATION a subdivision of a large organization, usually with a specialized mission ○ *Each branch of the military has a distinctive history and reputation.* **6.** PART OF SUBJECT AREA one part of a large area of study or subject ○ *Ethics is a branch of philosophy.* **7.** FAMILY LINE one line of a family that is descended from a common ancestor ○ *the Peruvian branch of the family* **8.** GEOG TRIBUTARY STREAM a river or stream flowing into another river ○ *a branch of the Colorado River* **9.** *Southern U.S.* GEOG CREEK a small stream or a creek ○ *A branch runs through our lower pasture.* **10.** MATH PART OF CURVE a distinctive part of a curve that is separated from the rest of the curve, e.g., by discontinuities or extreme points **11. branch, branch wa·ter** *Southern U.S.* BEVERAGES DRINKING WATER drinking water, especially from a clean spring or stream, and used particularly for mixing with bourbon **12.** COMPUT ALTERNATIVE SEQUENCE OF COMPUTER INSTRUCTIONS any one of several alternative sequences of computer program instructions that are activated according to certain specific conditions, e.g., the value of a variable ■ *v.* **(branched, branch·ing, branch·es) 1.** *vti.* DIVIDE INTO SMALLER PARTS to divide or cause something to divide into lesser parts ○ *Part of the path branches off toward the river.* **2.** *vi.* BOT HAVE BRANCHES to grow branches **3.** *vi.* EXPAND ACTIVITIES OR INTERESTS to become involved in something new, especially as a way of extending or expanding personal interests or business activities ○ *The company has branched into the multimedia market.* **4.** *vi.* COMPUT JUMP TO ALTERNATE PROGRAM PATH to execute an alternative sequence of computer program instructions as a result of the detection of a specific condition [13thC. Via French *branche* from late Latin *branca* "paw," possibly of Celtic origin. The underlying meaning was "limb."]

branch out *vi.* to do something different, often involving an element of risk

-branch *suffix.* gills ○ *opisthobranch* [From Latin *branchia* "gills" (see BRANCHIA)]

bran·chi·a /brángkee ə/ (*plural* **-ae** /-kee ee/) *n.* a gill in aquatic animals or a similar structure found in the embryos of higher animals, including humans [Late 17thC. Via Latin from Greek *bragkhia*, "gills," of unknown origin.] —**bran·chi·al** /brángkee əl/ *adj.* —**bran·chi·ate** /bránkeeit/ *adj.*

bran·chi·al cleft, bran·chi·al groove *n.* a gill slit (*technical*)

bran·chi·o·pod /brángkee ə pòd/ *n.* a small, usually freshwater, crustacean with a segmented body and flat gill-bearing appendages. Subclass: Branchiopoda. [Early 19thC. From modern Latin *Branchiopoda*, subclass name, coined from Latin *branchia* "gills" + -POD.] —**bran·chi·o·pod** *adj.* —**bran·chi·op·o·dous** /brànkee aápədəss/ *adj.*

branch·let /bránchlit/ *n.* a small branch, usually forming the outermost part of a larger branch

branch line *n.* part of a railroad system that is routed to smaller towns and villages that are not served by a main line, particularly in Europe. ◊ **main line**

branch of·fi·cer *n.* the person in charge of a branch of an organization, especially a bank

branch plant *n.* *Can* a subsidiary business owned and controlled by a company based in another country

branch wa·ter *n.* *Southern U.S.* = **branch** *n.* 11

Bran·cu·si /bran koózee, braang koósh/, **Constantin** (1876–1957) Romanian sculptor. He was a pioneer of 20th-century European sculpture and was particularly concerned with the inner form of his subject.

brand /brand/ *n.* **1.** COMM PRODUCT OR MANUFACTURER a name, usually a trademark, of a manufacturer or product, or the product identified by this name ○ *What brand of shampoo do you use?* **2.** PARTICULAR TYPE OF SOMETHING a distinctive type or kind of something **3.** AGRIC MARK BURNED ON ANIMAL a mark burned into the hide of a range animal to identify it as the property of a particular ranch, farm, or owner ○ *The Triple S is the brand on all our steers.* ◊ **branding iron 4.** HIST MARK ON CRIMINAL OR SLAVE in the past, a mark made on the skin of a criminal or a slave, especially to identify the owner **5.** SIGN OR MARK OF DISGRACE a sign or mark of disgrace, infamy, or notoriety ○ *He bore the brand of disloyalty.* **6.** BURNED OR BURNING PIECE OF WOOD a piece of wood that is burned or smoldering (*archaic*) **7.** TORCH a flaming torch (*literary*) ◊ **firebrand** **8.** ARMS SWORD a sword (*literary*) **9.** FUNGI FUNGAL DISEASE OF PLANTS a fungal disease that affects garden plants by causing brown spots to appear on leaves ■ *vt.* **(brand·ed, brand·ing, brands)** **1.** MARK SKIN OR HIDE to mark an animal's skin or hide with a hot iron, especially as a means of identification ○ *All the cattle have been branded.* **2.** DESCRIBE SOMEBODY OR SOMETHING AS BAD to class somebody or something as bad, illegal, or undesirable, often arbitrarily ○ *branded as a cheat* **3.** MAKE INDELIBLE MARK ON SOMEBODY to make an indelible mark or impression on somebody or something ○ *The words "Duty, Honor, Country" are branded into the hearts of all West Pointers.* [Old English, "burning stick." Ultimately from an Indo-European word meaning "to be hot," which was also the ancestor of English *burn, brimstone, brandish,* and *brandy.*] —**brand·er** *n.*

brand·ed /brándəd/ *adj.* bearing a company name or trademark, usually considered a mark of prestige or quality

Bran·deis /brán diss/, **Louis** (1856–1941) U.S. supreme court justice He was an important legal theoretician and a liberal member of the Supreme Court (1916–39). Full name **Louis Dembitz Brandeis**

AKG London

Brandenburg Gate, Berlin, Germany

Bran·den·burg Gate *n.* **Brandenburg Gate** a large neoclassical stone gateway in central Berlin, Germany, completed in 1781. It has long served as a symbol of the city and a focal point for public gatherings.

bran·died /brándeed/ *adj.* cooked or preserved in brandy

brand·ing i·ron *n.* an iron tool that is heated and pressed onto a surface, especially an animal's hide, in order to leave a permanent identifying mark. ◊ **brand** *n.* 3

bran·dish /brándish/ **(-dished, -dish·ing, -dish·es)** *vt.* to wave something about, especially a weapon, in a menacing, theatrical, or triumphant way [14thC. From French *brandiss-*, the stem of *brandir,* from *brand* "sword." Ultimately of Germanic origin.] —**bran·dish·er** *n.*

brand lead·er *n.* the best-selling product in a particular category

brand·ling /brándling/ *n.* a small, reddish brown earthworm that is often used as bait by anglers. Latin name: *Eisenia foetida.* [Mid-17thC. So called because of its bright coloring, like a burning brand.]

brand loy·al·ty (*plural* **brand loy·al·ties**) *n.* the tendency to buy a particular brand of a product

brand name *n.* a trade name for a product or service produced by a particular company. It may or may not be a registered trademark. ○ *A computer with a brand name can cost 10 percent more.*

brand-new *adj.* completely new and unused [From the idea of something glowing as if newly made in a furnace]

Bran·do /brándō/, **Marlon** (*b.* 1924) U.S. actor. He has appeared in numerous Hollywood movies, including *The Wild One* (1954) and *The Godfather* (1972).

Brand·on /brándən/ the second largest city in Manitoba Province, Canada. Population: 39,175 (1996).

Brandt /brant, braant/, **Willy** (1913–92) German statesman. He was mayor of West Berlin (1957–66) and was elected Chancellor of the Federal Republic of Germany in 1969. His pursuit of reconciliation between East and West earned him the Nobel Peace Prize in 1971. Real name **Herbert Ernst Karl Frahm**

Marlon Brando

bran·dy /brándee/ (*plural* **-dies**) *n.* a liquor that is distilled from the fermented juice of grapes or other fruit [Early 17thC. Shortening of *brandy-wine,* from Dutch *brandewijn,* literally "burned (i.e. distilled) wine."]

bran·dy Al·ex·an·der *n.* a cocktail with a base of brandy

bran·dy but·ter *n. U.K.* = **hard sauce**

bran·dy snif·ter *n.* = **snifter** *n.* 1

Bran·dy·wine Creek /brándi wīn-/ *n.* the site near Philadelphia, Pennsylvania, of an important defeat of the Continental Army by the British forces in 1777

branks /brangks/ *npl.* a device consisting of a metal frame for the head and a bit to restrain the tongue, used in the past to restrain and punish quarrelsome or nagging women [Mid-16thC. Origin uncertain: perhaps from Dutch *branken* "branches, legs," from late Latin *branca* "paw" (source of English *branch*).]

bran·ni·gan /bránnigən/ *n.* **1.** SQUABBLE a loud quarrel or brawl **2.** BINGE a drinking binge [Early 20thC. Origin uncertain: probably from the Irish surname Brannigan.]

Bran·son /bránsən/, **Richard** (*b.* 1950) British entrepreneur. He started a chain of record stores (1971), founded an airline (1984), and launched a radio station (1993). Full name **Richard Charles Nicholas Branson**

brant /brant/ (*plural* **brants** *or* **brant**) *n.* a small, dark-colored wild goose found in Arctic regions. Genus: *Branta.* [14thC. Variant of BRENT GOOSE.]

Brant /brant/, **Joseph** (1742–1807) Native American leader. He was a Mohawk chief who allied his people with the British during the Revolutionary War. Born **Thayendanega**

Brant·ford /brántfərd/ city in southeastern Ontario, Canada, on the Grand River directly north of the Niagara Falls. Population: 84,764 (1996).

brash[1] /brash/ *adj.* **1.** AGGRESSIVELY SELF-ASSERTIVE self-assertive in an aggressive or rude way **2.** HASTY acting or made in a hasty or impulsive fashion ○ *The candidates are realistic about their chances on Tuesday and are not making any brash predictions.* [Early 19thC. Origin uncertain: perhaps an alteration of RASH.] —**brash·ly** *adv.* —**brash·ness** *n.*

brash[2] /brash/ *adj.* easily cracked or broken [Mid-16thC. Origin unknown.]

brash[3] /brash/ *n.* a pile of loose trash, e.g., broken rocks or garden refuse [Late 18thC. Origin uncertain: perhaps an alteration of French *brèche* "breach in a wall, rubble," from Italian *breccia.*]

brash·y /bráshee/ (**-i·er, -i·est**) *adj.* **1.** IN PIECES loosely broken or fragmented ○ *soft, brashy ice* **2.** BRITTLE easily cracked or broken

Bra·sí·lia /brə zíllyə/ city and capital of Brazil. A relatively new city, laid out on an uninhabited site in 1957, it is in the Federal District, east central Brazil. Population: 1,817,001 (1996).

brass /brass/ *n.* **1.** INDUST YELLOW ALLOY a hard yellow shiny metal that is an alloy of zinc and copper, frequently with the addition of other metallic elements to impart specific properties **2.** ITEMS MADE OF BRASS a collection of ornaments or items made of brass ○ *a collection of brass* **3.** ITEM MADE OF BRASS an individual ornament or item made of brass (*usually used in the plural*) **4.** MUSIC BRASS MUSICAL INSTRUMENTS the musical instruments made of brass, such as the trumpet and trombone **5.** MUSIC PLAYERS OF BRASS INSTRUMENTS the players of brass instruments, especially when considered as one of the four main

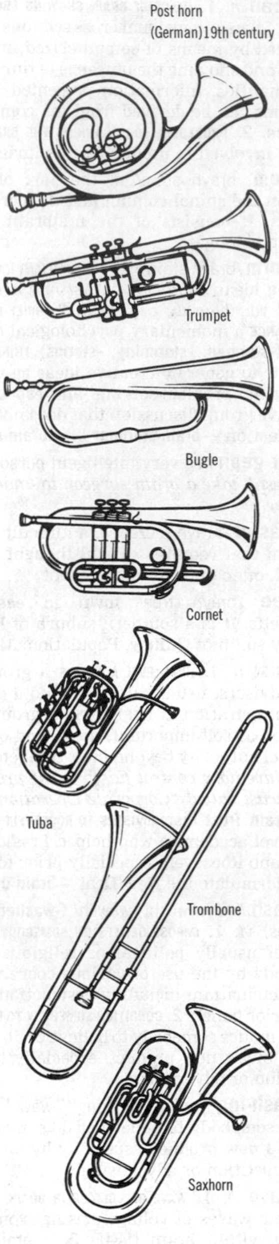

Brass: Brass musical instruments

sections of an orchestra **6.** MIL HIGH-RANKING OFFICERS high-ranking officers, especially in the military (*informal*) **7.** EXCESSIVE SELF-ASSURANCE extreme, and usually excessive, self-confidence (*informal*) ○ *He had the brass to lie about every aspect of his background.* **8.** *N England* MONEY money or cash (*informal*) **9.** MECH ENG REPLACEABLE BRASS LINER FOR BEARING a replaceable brass or bronze liner for a bearing ■ **brass·es** *npl.* MUSIC BRASS MUSICAL INSTRUMENT GROUP OR PLAYERS the musical instruments made of brass, such as the trumpet and trombone, as a group, or their players [Old English *bræs,* of unknown origin (source of English *brazen*)]

brass band *n.* a band consisting of brass wind instruments and sometimes percussion instruments

brass·bound /bráss bòwnd/ *adj.* **1.** TRIMMED OR BANDED WITH BRASS trimmed or banded with brass or similar metal **2.** UNBENDING AND IRON-WILLED unreasonably inflexible in manner or character

brass-col·lar *adj.* never abandoning a particular political party and always voting a straight ticket ○ *brass-collar Democrats*

bras·se·rie /brássə reé, brass reé/ *n.* a type of restaurant that will serve customers drinks with or without food [Mid-19thC. From French, literally "brewery," from Old French *bracier* "to brew," via Vulgar Latin from, ultimately, Latin *brace* "malt," of Celtic origin.]

brass hat *n.* a high-ranking military officer (*slang*) (*often used in the plural*) [From the gold braid on officers' uniform caps]

bras·si·ca /brássikə/ *n.* a plant of the mustard family. Cabbage, kale, broccoli, cauliflower, rutabaga, turnip, oilseed rape, and mustard are brassicas. Genus: *Brassica.* [Early 19thC. From modern Latin, genus name from Latin, "cabbage."]

brass·ie /brássee/ *n.* a former name for a golf club (a 2 wood), which had a brass-plated sole (*archaic*)

bras·siere /brə zeér/ *n.* = **bra** [Early 20thC. From French.]

brass knuck·les *npl.* a metal chain or a set of rings attached to a bar that can be put over the fingers to serve as a weapon

brass ring *n.* the opportunity for success, or hard-earned success (*informal*) ○ *to have a shot at the brass ring at last* [From the custom of giving a free ride to any child who grabbed one of the rings hung around a carousel]

brass rub·bing *n.* a copy of an engraved plaque or tablet, especially one set into the floor or wall of a church. It is made by putting a piece of paper over the engraving and rubbing it with something soft such as chalk or graphite.

brass tacks *npl.* the most basic or fundamental parts of a situation or issue [Perhaps from their use as a medium of exchange when even iron nails were unavailable] ◇ **get down to brass tacks** to begin to deal with the most basic or important issues of a situation ○ *It's time we got down to brass tacks.*

brass·ware /bráss wair/ *n.* items such as plates and ornaments made from brass

brass·y /brássee/ (**-i·er, -i·est**) *adj.* **1. FLASHY AND VULGAR** brightly dressed in a cheap and showy way, and behaving too confidently or noisily (*insult*) **2. SOUNDING LIKE BRASS INSTRUMENTS** dominated by or resembling the sounds of brass musical instruments, and therefore typically short, harsh, and high-pitched ○ *a brassy mixture of reggae, funk, calypso, and jazz* **3. BRAZENLY OVERBEARING** brazen or strident in style ○ *Their brassy management approach failed utterly.* **4. OF BRASS** made of or containing brass **5. OF GOLDEN YELLOW COLOR** golden yellow in color or hue —**brass·i·ly** *adv.* —**brass·i·ness** *n.*

brat /brat/ *n.* **1. DEMANDING AND SELFISH PERSON** somebody, either a child or an adult, who is tiresomely demanding and selfish, like a spoiled child **2. CHILD FROM MILITARY FAMILY** the son or daughter of a serving member of the army or the air force (*informal*) [Mid-16thC. Origin uncertain: perhaps from an obsolete word meaning "rag," from Old English *bratt* "cloak," of Celtic origin.] —**brat·ty** *adj.* —**brat·tish** *adj.*

Bra·ti·sla·va /bràti slaávə, braáti-/ capital and largest city of Slovakia. It lies on the Danube River in the southwest of the country, about 35 mi./56 km east of Vienna. Population: 441,453 (1994).

brat pack *n.* a group of successful or affluent young people, especially actors [Coined from BRAT, on the model of "rat pack"]

Bratsk /braatsk/ town in Siberia, eastern Russia, developed as a home for employees of the Bratsk Dam hydroelectric plant on the Angara River. Population: 257,000 (1995).

Brat·tain /brátt'n/, **Walter H.** (1902–87) Chinese-born U.S. physicist. He shared a Nobel Prize in physics (1956) for his research on transistors and semiconductors. Full name **Walter Houser Brattain**

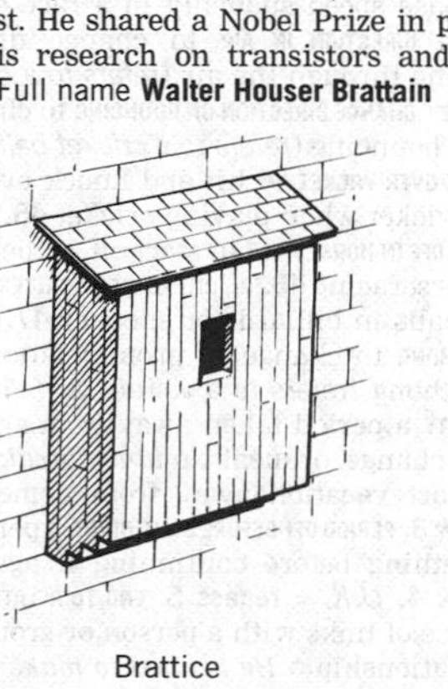

Brattice

brat·tice /bráttiss/ *n.* **1. MINING PARTITION FOR MINE VENTILATION** a partition used to assist ventilation in a mine **2. MIL, HIST TEMPORARY PARAPET** in medieval times, a temporary wooden parapet or gallery erected on the battlement of a fortress and used during a siege [13thC. Via Anglo-Norman and Old French *bretesche* from medieval Latin *bretescha turris* "British tower," from Old English *brittisc* (see BRITISH).]

Brat·tle·bo·ro /brátt'lbərō/ city in southeastern Vermont, on the western bank of the Connecticut River, east of Bennington. Population: 12,136 (1996).

brat·ty /bráttee/ (**-ti·er, -ti·est**) *adj.* tiresomely demanding or selfish, like a spoiled child ○ *a bratty, know-it-all child.* —**brat·ti·ness** *n.*

brat·wurst /brát wùrst, braát-, brát vòorst, braát-/ *n.* a highly seasoned fresh German sausage made of pork or of pork and veal [Early 20thC. From German, literally "frying sausage."]

Braun /brown/, **Wernher von** (1912–77) German-born U.S. rocket engineer. He moved to the United States during World War II and was a major contributor to the U.S. atomic bomb and space programs.

Braun·schwei·ger /brówn shwìgər/ *n.* a type of spicy smoked liver sausage [Early 20thC. From German, named for the city of *Braunschweig* (Brunswick).]

bra·va /braá vaá, braa vaá/ *interj., n.* a shout of approval for a woman or girl performer. ◊ **bravo** [Early 19thC. From Italian, feminine of *bravo* (see BRAVE).]

bra·va·do /brə vaá dō/ *n.* a real or pretended display of courage or boldness ○ *a breathtaking act of bravado* [Late 16thC. Alteration of Spanish *bravada*, from *bravo* (see BRAVE).]

brave /brayv/ *adj.* (**brav·er, brav·est**) **HAVING OR SHOWING COURAGE** having or showing courage, especially when facing danger, difficulty, or pain ■ *n.* **1. BRAVE PEOPLE** those people who are courageous **2. NATIVE AMERICAN WARRIOR** a Native American warrior ■ *vt.* (**braved, brav·ing, braves**) **1. FACE ONSLAUGHT OF SOMETHING** to face the onslaught of something unpleasant with courage and resolution **2. CHALLENGE SOMETHING** to defy something despite there being only a small chance of being victorious [15thC. Via French from Italian *bravo* "bold" or Spanish *bravo* "brave, savage," both ultimately from Latin *barbarus* (see BARBAROUS).] —**brave·ly** *adv.* —**brave·ness** *n.*

WORD KEY: SYNONYMS

See Synonyms at ***bold***.

brave out *vt.* to live through something that is difficult or unpleasant

brave new world *n.* the world of the future, usually either a technology-based utopia or a sinister totalitarian world devoid of human values (*often used ironically*) [Mid-20th Century. From *Brave New World* (1932), a novel by Aldous HUXLEY. Huxley took the expression from Shakespeare's *The Tempest*: "O brave new world/ That has such people in it!".]

WORD KEY: CULTURAL NOTE

Brave New World, a novel by English writer Aldous Huxley (1932). Written partly as a response to more utopian writers of the day, it depicts a bleak and sterile future civilization in which feelings are stimulated by drugs, and babies are bred in factories.

brav·er·y /bráyvəree, bráyvree/ *n.* extreme courage in the face of danger or difficulty, or an example of extreme courage [Mid-16thC. From French *braverie* or Italian *braveria*, both ultimately from Italian *bravo* "bold" (source of English *brave*).]

WORD KEY: SYNONYMS

See Synonyms at ***courage***.

bra·vis·si·mo /braa víssəmō/ *interj.* used as a cry of great and enthusiastic approval by members of a theatre audience [Mid-18thC. From Italian, "most excellent," the strongest form of *bravo* (see BRAVO).]

bra·vo /braávō, braa vó/ *interj.* **AUDIENCE'S SHOUT OF APPROVAL** used as a cry of approval by members of a theatre audience ■ *n.* (*plural* **-vos**) **1. CRY OF "BRAVO"** a shout of "bravo" to express admiration **2. HIRED ASSASSIN** a hired assassin (*archaic*) [Mid-18thC. From Italian, "excellent" (source of English *brave*). The underlying idea is an acknowledgment of showmanship.]

Bra·vo /braávō/ *n.* the code word for the letter "b" in the NATO phonetic alphabet, used in international radio communications

bra·vu·ra /brə vòorə, -vyòorə/ *n.* **1. DAZZLING ARTISTIC FLAIR** great skill that is shown when something artistic is done in an exciting or innovative way ○ *a bravura performance* **2. SHOWY DISPLAY** showy style or behavior ■ *adj.* **WITH OR REQUIRING FLAIR** displaying or requiring great artistic skill and style ○ *the bravura vividness of her versatile performance* [Mid-18thC. From Italian, "courage, spirit," from *bravo* "bold" (source of English *brave*).]

braw /braw/ *adj. Scotland* attractive or pleasant [Late 16thC. Variant of BRAVE.]

brawl /brawl/ *n.* **1. NOISY FIGHT** a rough and noisy fight, usually in a public place and one involving a large number of people **2. LOUD NOISE** a loud deep noise, especially the noise of rushing water **3. LOUD PARTY** a noisy boisterous party (*slang*) ■ *vi.* (**brawled, brawl·ing, brawls**) **1. FIGHT NOISILY** to fight or wrestle noisily, especially in a public place **2. MAKE DEEP LOUD SOUND** to make a deep loud roaring sound, especially the sound of rushing water [14thC. Origin uncertain.] —**brawl·er** *n.* —**brawl·ing** *n.*

brawl·y /bráwlee/ (**-i·er, -i·est**) *adj.* involved in a fight, or always ready to become involved in one (*informal*) [Mid-17thC. Formed from BRAWL.]

brawn /brawn/ *n.* **1. STRONG MUSCLES** very strong muscles, especially on the arms and legs **2. BODILY STRENGTH** physical strength, especially as opposed to intellectual power **3. FOOD** = **headcheese** [14thC. From Anglo-Norman *braun* "fleshy part of the leg," from, ultimately, prehistoric Germanic, and related to German *Braten* "roast meat."]

brawn·y /bráwnee/ (**-i·er, -i·est**) *adj.* **1. MUSCULAR** muscular and strong-looking **2. CALLUSED** with the skin hardened by calluses —**brawn·i·ly** *adv.* —**brawni·ness** *n.*

bray[1] /bray/ *n.* **1. DONKEY'S CRY** the sound a donkey makes **2. HARSH VOICE OR LAUGH** a harsh high-pitched rasping voice or laugh ■ *v.* (**brayed, bray·ing, brays**) **1.** *vi.* **MAKE DONKEY'S SOUND** to make the sound a donkey makes **2.** *vti.* **SPEAK WITH HARSH VOICE** to speak, laugh, or say something in a harsh high-pitched rasping voice [13thC. From Old French *braire* "to cry," which may, ultimately, be of Celtic origin.] —**bray·er** *n.*

bray[2] /bray/ (**brayed, bray·ing, brays**) *vt.* **1. GRIND SOMETHING FINELY** to crush something to a fine powder or consistency **2. PRINTING INK THINLY** to spread ink in a thin layer on a surface [14thC. From Anglo-Norman *braier* and Old French *breier*, ultimately from a prehistoric Germanic word that also produced English *break*.]

Braz. *abbr.* Brazil ■ *abbr.* Brazilian

braze[1] /brayz/ (**brazed, braz·ing, braz·es**) *vt.* **1. MAKE SOMETHING WITH BRASS** to make something out of brass or decorate something with brass **2. MAKE SOMETHING HARD LIKE BRASS** to give something a hardness like that of brass [Old English *brasian*. Formed from *bræs* "brass," subsequently reinforced by the parallel GLASS and GLAZE.] —**braz·er** *n.*

braze[2] /brayz/ (**brazed, braz·ing, braz·es**) *vt.* to join two pieces of metal together with a solder that has a high melting point [Mid-16thC. From Old French *braser* "to burn."] —**braz·er** *n.*

bra·zen /bráyz'n/ *adj.* **1. BOLD AND UNASHAMED** showing or expressing boldness and complete lack of shame **2. HARSH-SOUNDING** with an unpleasantly loud and resonant sound **3. OF OR LIKE BRASS** made of brass or resembling it, especially in color or hardness (*literary*) [Old English *bræsen* "made of brass," from *bræs* "brass." The meaning "bold" evolved from the idea of the hardness of brass.] —**bra·zen·ness** *n.*

brazen out, bra·zen through *vt.* to face a difficult situation confidently, without showing shame or embarrassment

bra·zen·faced /bráyz'n fàyst/ *adj.* shameless and audacious

bra·zen·ly /bráyz'nlee/ *adv.* in a bold or shameless way

bra·zier[1] /bráyzhər/ *n.* somebody who makes and repairs brass articles [14thC. Probably from BRASS + -IER, on the model of GLASS and GLAZIER.]

bra·zier[2] /bráyzhər/ *n.* a metal container used outdoors for burning coal or charcoal, either for cooking or to keep people warm [Late 17thC. From French *brasier*, from *braise* "hot coals" (source of English *braise*).]

bra·zil /brəzíl/ *n.* **1.** = **brazilwood 2.** *U.K.* = **Brazil nut** [14thC. From medieval Latin *brasilium*, of uncertain origin; perhaps from French *braise* "hot coals" (source of English *braise*), from the color of the wood.]

Brazil

Bra·zil /brəzíl/ republic and the largest country in South America. Colonized by the Portuguese from 1500 onwards, it became an independent republic in 1889. Language: Portuguese. Currency: real. Capital: Brasília. Population: 167,660,687 (1997). Area: 3,300,171 sq. mi./8,547,404 sq. km. —**Bra·zil·i·an** *n., adj.*

Bra·zil Ba·sin basin of the Atlantic Ocean on the American side of the Mid-Atlantic Ridge. Depth: 16,400 ft./5,000 m.

Bra·zil nut *n.* **1.** FOOD **EDIBLE SEED WITH TRIANGULAR SHELL** the long thick edible seed of a tropical South American tree, with a hard shell that is nearly triangular in cross-section **2.** TREES **TROPICAL SOUTH AMERICAN TREE** the tropical South American evergreen tree that bears Brazil nuts in clusters inside large round capsules. Latin name: *Bertholletia excelsa.*

bra·zil·wood /brəzíl wo͝od/, **brazil** *n.* a kind of red wood obtained from various tropical and North American trees, especially one native to Brazil. It is used in the manufacture of red dyes and violin bows.

Braz·os /brázzōss/ river that flows from northern Texas southeastward into the Gulf of Mexico near Freeport. Length: 1,280 mi./2,060 km.

Braz·za·ville /brázə vil/ capital city of the Republic of Congo and a major port on the Congo River. It was founded in 1880 by the french explorer Pierre Savorgnan de Brazza (1852–1905). Population: 937,579 (1995).

breach /breech/ *v.* (**breached, breach·ing, breach·es**) **1.** *vt.* **MAKE OPENING THROUGH SOMETHING** to break down an obstruction to allow something to pass through it **2.** *vt.* **SURPASS LIMIT** to go beyond a target or limit **3.** *vt.* **BREAK LAW OR PROMISE** to fail to obey, keep, or preserve something, e.g., a law or trust **4.** *vi.* **LEAP OUT** to leap above the surface of the water (*refers to whales*) ■ *n.* **1. HOLE** a hole in something that is caused by something else forcing its way through **2. GAP** a gap that results when something or somebody leaves **3. FAILURE TO MAINTAIN SOMETHING** a failure to obey, keep, or preserve something, e.g., a law, a trust or a promise **4. ESTRANGEMENT** a breakdown in friendly relations **5. WHALE'S LEAP** a leap out of the water by a whale [13thC. From Old French *breche,* ultimately from a prehistoric Germanic base that is also the ancestor of English *break.*]

breach of prom·ise *n.* failure in fulfilling a promise, especially in former times the breaking of a promise to marry somebody

bread /bred/ *n.* **1. FOOD MADE FROM FLOUR AND WATER** a food typically made by mixing flour, water, and yeast and allowing it to rise before baking it **2. MEANS OF SURVIVAL** food, sustenance, or a means of survival or support **3. MONEY** money to live on (*dated slang*) [Old English *brēad,* of uncertain origin: probably ultimately "something broken off," and related to BRITTLE] ◇ **cast your bread upon the waters** to spend time and effort, especially to help others, without expecting any immediate advantage for yourself (*formal*) ◇ **know which side your bread is buttered (on)** to know what is to your advantage (*informal*)

bread and but·ter *n.* **1. SUSTAINING INCOME** a dependable source of income **2. MAINSTAY** something that is the essential or sustaining part of something else

bread-and-but·ter let·ter, **bread-and-but·ter note** *n.* a letter or note expressing thanks for somebody's hospitality

bread-and-but·ter pud·ding (*plural* **bread-and-but·ter pud·dings**) *n. U.K.* = **bread pudding**

bread and cir·cus·es *npl.* something done or given to keep people happy, especially something provided or encouraged by governments to win popular appeal or avert public unrest [A translation of Latin *panis et circenses* (Juvenal, *Satires*), referring to the food and entertainment provided by the authorities in ancient Rome]

bread·bas·ket /bréd bàskit/ *n.* **1. BASKET FOR BREAD** a basket in which bread is served **2. CEREAL-GROWING REGION** a region that is an important grower of grain **3. BELLY** the stomach or abdomen (*slang dated*)

bread bin *n. U.K.* = **breadbox**

bread·board /bréd bawrd/ *n.* **1. BOARD FOR CUTTING BREAD ON** a board for kneading or cutting bread on **2.** ELEC ENG **TEST VERSION OF ELECTRICAL CIRCUIT** a preliminary version of an electrical or electronic circuit put together for test purposes ■ *vt.* (**-board·ed, -board·ing, -boards**) ELEC ENG **MAKE TEST VERSION OF CIRCUIT** to make a preliminary version of an electrical or electronic circuit for test purposes —**bread·board·ing** *n.*

bread·box /bréd bòks/ *n.* a box at home for storing bread in to keep it fresh

bread·crumb /bréd krùm/ *n.* a tiny piece of bread, either soft or hard (*often used in the plural*)

bread·fruit /bréd froot/ (*plural* **-fruit** *or* **-fruits**) *n.* **1.** FOOD **FRUIT WITH BREADY TEXTURE WHEN COOKED** a large round seedless tropical fruit that is usually eaten baked or roasted, when it takes on the texture of bread **2.** TREES **EVERGREEN PACIFIC TREE** the evergreen tree that bears breadfruit. It is native to the Pacific Islands, and belongs to the fig family. Latin name: *Artocarpus altilis.*

bread·line /bréd līn/ *n.* **1. PEOPLE WAITING FOR FOOD HANDOUTS** a line of people waiting for handouts of free food **2.** *U.K.* **LOW LIVING STANDARD** a very low standard of living, with only just enough food and money to survive [Late 19thC. From the original sense, "line of needy people outside a bakery that was giving away unsold bread."]

bread mold *n.* a fungus that grows on decaying bread and other foods, forming a dense cottony growth. Latin name: *Rhizopus nigricans.*

bread·nut /bréd nut/ *n.* **1.** TREES **LARGE TROPICAL TREE** a large tree native to Central America, Mexico, and the West Indies, with yellow fruits containing edible seeds. Latin name: *Brosimum alicastrum.* **2.** FOOD **SEED FROM TROPICAL FRUIT** the edible seed of the breadnut tree, sometimes ground into flour

bread pud·ding *n.* a dessert made with buttered bread that is layered in a dish, sometimes with raisins, covered in a mixture of egg, sugar, milk, and spices and then baked

bread·root /bréd ro͞ot, -ro͝ot/ *n.* a perennial plant of the pea family that is native to North America and has a starchy edible root. It was once an important source of food among the Native American population. Latin name: *Psoralea esculenta.*

bread·stuff /bréd stùf/ *n.* bread in any form, or the flour, meal, or grain used to make it

breadth /bredth/ *n.* **1. DISTANCE FROM SIDE TO SIDE** the distance or measurement of something from one side to the other **2. PIECE OF FABRIC IN STANDARD WIDTH** a standardized width that something, especially fabric, is produced or available in, or a piece of fabric in a standardized width **3. GREAT EXTENT** the extent of something, especially when it is impressively great **4. BROADMINDEDNESS** an open and tolerant view of life and the world [Early 16thC. Formed from obsolete English *brede* "breadth" (which came from the same prehistoric Germanic base as English *broad*), on the model of *length.*] —**breadth·wise** *adj., adv.*

bread·win·ner /bréd wìnnər/ *n.* somebody who earns money to support a family, especially somebody whose earnings are the family's main income

break /brayk/ *v.* (**broke** /brōk/, **bro·ken** /brṓkən/, **break·ing, breaks**) **1.** *vti.* **SEPARATE SOMETHING INTO PIECES** to become damaged or damage something so that it separates into pieces ○ *it broke in two* **2.** *vt.* MED **DAMAGE BODY** to damage a body part, e.g., a bone ○ *She broke her leg.* **3.** *vti.* **DAMAGE PART OF MACHINE** to damage a part of a tool or machine so that it stops functioning properly, or become damaged and stop functioning properly ○ *The washing machine is broken.* **4.** *vti.* **TEAR SURFACE** to become torn, or make a tear or hole in a surface or seal, allowing the possibility of a leak or spill ○ *Store in the refrigerator after breaking the seal on the bottle.* **5.** *vt.* **DISOBEY RULE** to disobey a rule or law ○ *He's broken the law.* **6.** *vt.* **GO BACK ON WORD** to renege on a promise or agreement **7.** *vt.* **END BAD SITUATION** to end, change, or rectify a difficult or disadvantageous situation ○ *break the deadlock between rival factions* **8.** *vt.* **END SILENCE** to end a period of silence **9.** *vti.* **FINISH RELATIONSHIP** to end an involvement with an individual or group ○ *They broke their links with the terrorists.* **10.** *vt.* **END SOMETHING** to finish something, bring it to an end, or stop somebody doing it ○ *break the coffee-drinking habit* **11.** *vt.* **INTERRUPT SOMETHING** to interrupt something temporarily ○ *The distraction broke her train of thought.* **12.** *vt.* **RUIN SOMEBODY'S LIFE** to destroy somebody's career, resolve, courage, or hope of success ○ *The media can make or break her.* **13.** *vti.* **ESCAPE** to escape from a restraint ○ *break free* **14.** *vi.* **TAKE PERIOD FOR REST** to take a period of leisure ○ *break for lunch* **15.** *vt.* **STAND BETWEEN PERSON AND SOMETHING** to stand in the way of or weaken the effect of something, e.g., a fall or blow ○ *He tried to break her fall.* **16.** *vt.* **BEAT RECORD** to beat a previous record **17.** *vt.* **EXCEED LIMIT** to exceed a limit or constraint ○ *break the speed limit* **18.** *vti.* **REVEAL OR BE REVEALED** to reveal something personally, or to be revealed, particularly by the media ○ *She broke it to me gently.* ○ *Panic ensued when the news broke.* **19.** *vi.* **BECOME DEEPER** to settle into an adult man's register (*refers to a boy's voice*) **20.** *vi.* **STOP SPEAKING FROM EMOTION** to stop speaking and hesitate when overcome with emotion ○ *Her voice broke and tears slid down her face.* **21.** *vi.* MUSIC **CHANGE TONE WITH REGISTER** to change in tone or quality when changing register (*refers to a voice or musical instrument*) **22.** *vi.* **BECOME DAYLIGHT** to become light at sunrise **23.** *vi.* METEOROL **CHANGE WEATHER PATTERN** to change after a settled period **24.** *vi.* METEOROL **SUDDENLY START** to suddenly begin to rain, snow, or hail ○ *The storm broke.* **25.** *vi.* OCEANOG **TURN TO SURF** to start collapsing into surf when close to shore or hitting rocks or similar objects (*refers to a wave*) **26.** *vt.* **INTERPRET A CODE** to understand a code and be able to translate it accurately **27.** *vt.* **PROVE UNTRUE** to prove that something is untrue or wrong **28.** *vt.* LAW **INVALIDATE WILL** to use legal means to declare a will invalid **29.** *vt.* **BLOW OPEN SAFE** to open a safe using explosives **30.** *vt.* EQU **TRAIN HORSE TO ACCEPT HARNESS** to train a horse to become accustomed to a saddle, bit, and rider **31.** *vt.* MONEY **SWAP NOTE FOR CHANGE** to exchange a note of money for smaller units of money, either coins or smaller notes and coins ○ *break a $20 bill* **32.** *vi.* MED **FLOW OUT IN CHILDBIRTH** to flow out when the amniotic sac around an unborn baby breaks during the first stage of labor (*refers to amniotic fluid*) ○ *Her waters have broken.* **33.** *vi.* **TURN OUT** to happen or turn out in a particular way ○ *Things are breaking well.* **34.** *vt.* **REDUCE TO POVERTY** to cause somebody to be extremely poor or bankrupt **35.** *vti.* ZOOL **EMERGE OUT OF WATER** to emerge or erupt above the surface of a body of water **36.** *vt.* MIL **DEMOTE** to demote somebody to a lower rank **37.** *vt.* ELEC **INTERRUPT FLOW OF ELECTRIC CURRENT** to interrupt the flow of electricity in an electrical circuit **38.** *vi.* STOCK EXCH **FALL SHARPLY** to fall in price (*refers to stock exchange quotations*) **39.** *vti.* TENNIS **WIN GAME OFF OPPONENT'S SERVICE** to win a game in tennis in which the other player is serving **40.** *vi.* BOXING, WRESTLING **SEPARATE FROM CLINCH** to separate after being in a boxing or wrestling clinch **41.** *vi.* SPORTS **SPEED UP IN RACE** to increase speed suddenly in a race **42.** *vi.* BASEBALL **CHANGE DIRECTION IN AIR** to change direction while moving through the air (*refers to a baseball*) **43.** *vi.* CRICKET **CHANGE DIRECTION ON BOUNCING** to change direction after bouncing (*refers to a cricket ball*) **44.** *vt.* CRICKET **KNOCK OVER WICKET** to hit and knock over a bail from the wicket when playing cricket **45.** *vi.* HORSERACING **START OFF IN HORSE RACE** to start off at the start of a race in horseracing **46.** *vi.* CUE GAMES **SCATTER BALLS** to scatter the balls in billiards or snooker **47.** *vi.* PHON **BECOME DIPHTHONG** to change in pronunciation, becoming a diphthong (*refers to a vowel*) ■ *n.* **1. PERIOD OFF FROM ACTIVITY** a period taken away from an activity for a rest, change, or meal ○ *a lunch break* **2. BRIEF VACATION** a short vacation away from home ○ *a weekend break* **3. PERIOD OFF BEFORE CONTINUING** a period away from something before continuing it again ○ *a career break* **4.** *U.K.* = **recess 5. END TO RELATIONSHIP** the severance of links with a person or group or an end to a relationship ○ *He wanted to make the break with his partner.* **6. END** an end to something ○ *a break with tradition* **7.** TV **PERIOD IN PROGRAM FOR COMMERCIALS** a period during a television program or between programs when commercials are shown **8.** SPORTS

INTERVAL IN MATCH an interval in a sports match **9.** PAUSE IN SPEECH a pause when speaking ○ *a break in the conversation* **10.** MED FRACTURE a fracture in a bone **11.** CRACK a crack in something **12.** METEOROL CHANGE IN WEATHER a change in the weather **13.** LUCKY OPPORTUNITY FOR SUCCESS an unexpected opportunity that allows somebody to achieve something or become successful (*informal*) ○ *He got his first break when he was spotted playing for his college.* **14.** a piece of good luck or bad luck ○ *a lucky break* **15.** FIN ADVANTAGEOUS FINANCIAL SITUATION an advantageous financial situation in which somebody is repaid or makes a reduced payment ○ *a tax break* **16.** ESCAPE ATTEMPT a sudden attempt to escape ○ *make a break for it* **17.** DISCONTINUITY a discontinuity in something, by which it changes in quality or level **18.** SUNRISE the time when the sun first rises (*literary*) ○ *at the break of day* **19.** TENNIS WINNING OF GAME OFF OPPONENT'S SERVICE the winning of a game in tennis in which the other player is serving **20.** HORSERACING START OF HORSE RACE the start of a horse race **21.** ELEC INTERRUPTION IN FLOW OF ELECTRICITY an interruption in the flow of electricity in an electrical circuit **22.** MUSIC INSTRUMENTAL PART IN SONG an instrumental part in a piece of pop music **23.** MUSIC IMPROVISED JAZZ SOLO an improvised solo part in a piece of jazz music **24.** MUSIC CHANGE IN REGISTER a change in register in a voice or musical instrument **25.** POETRY = **caesura** **26.** STOCK EXCH FALL IN PRICES a sudden fall in prices, particularly in a stock market **27.** CUE GAMES SERIES OF SUCCESSFUL SHOTS a sequence of successful shots in one player's turn in billiards or snooker, or the points scored from them **28.** CUE GAMES FIRST SHOT THAT SCATTERS BALLS an opening shot in billiards or snooker, which scatters the balls **29.** BOWLING FAILURE TO KNOCK DOWN ALL PINS a failure to knock down all the pins in bowling after the second throw **30.** RADIO ACCESS TO CB RADIO CHANNEL access for a CB radio operator to a radio channel ■ *interj.* BOXING, WRESTLING USED TO SEPARATE FIGHTERS used to command boxers or wrestlers to separate from a clinch [Old English *brecan*. Ultimately from an Indo-European root that also produced Latin *frangere* "to break" (source of English *fracture*).] ◇ **break even** to make neither a profit nor a loss from a venture ◇ **give somebody a break** to stop nagging or criticizing somebody or to start treating somebody fairly (*informal*) ◇ **make a clean break** to end a relationship or association completely and for good

WORD KEY: SYNONYMS

See Synonyms at ***holiday***.

break away *vi.* **1.** LEAVE OR GET AWAY to sever relations with or detach from a person or group **2.** DEPART FROM CUSTOM to change or depart from established customs or procedures **3.** PULL AWAY QUICKLY to depart or pull away from somebody or something, usually at high speed

break down TEAR DOWN to destroy something or cause something to fall or collapse ■ *v.* **1.** *vti.* BECOME OR MAKE EMOTIONAL to become upset emotionally, or to cause somebody to become upset emotionally **2.** *vti.* EXPERIENCE OR CAUSE HEALTH COLLAPSE to experience, or cause somebody to experience, a physical or psychological collapse **3.** *vti.* STOP RESISTING to yield or end any resistance, or to cause somebody to yield or somebody's resistance to end **4.** *vi.* FAIL TO FUNCTION PROPERLY to stop working, or to stop working properly, effectively, or usefully **5.** *vti.* WEAKEN to become or cause somebody or something to become weak and ineffective **6.** *vt.* ANALYZE BY DIVIDING INTO PARTS to analyze or examine something by reducing it to its simplest terms or component parts **7.** *vi.* BE DIVISIBLE INTO ELEMENTS to divide into or be reducible to separate parts when analyzed **8.** *vti.* DECOMPOSE CHEMICALLY to decompose chemically, or to cause something to undergo chemical decomposition **9.** *vi.* ELEC ENG EXPERIENCE ELECTRICAL INSULATION FAILURE to experience a sudden failure of an insulating material to halt the current flow

break in BEGIN USING SOMEBODY OR SOMETHING NEW to begin to employ somebody new or use something new, supplying the training or modifications needed for good performance ■ *vi.* **1.** ENTER FORCIBLY to enter a place or building forcibly and usually illegally **2.** START TALKING to interrupt a conversation or discussion

break into *vt.* **1.** ENTER BUILDING FORCIBLY AND ILLEGALLY to enter a building or place forcibly and usually illegally **2.** BEGIN SPEAKING to interrupt something that is being said or discussed **3.** DO SOMETHING SUDDENLY to begin doing something suddenly, e.g., runnning or singing **4.** START WORK IN NEW FIELD to begin working in a profession or field, often after having tried to do so for some time without success

break off *v.* **1.** *vt.* TAKE OFF PIECE OF SOMETHING to separate a piece from a solid mass or the main part of something **2.** *vti.* END BEING OR DOING SOMETHING TOGETHER to discontinue a relationship or interaction with somebody or a group **3.** *vi.* STOP SPEAKING to stop talking, usually abruptly

break out *v.* **1.** *vi.* HAVE SKIN RASH to develop a case of acne or a rash, especially suddenly **2.** *vi.* BEGIN ABRUPTLY to happen or begin suddenly and strongly (*refers to wars and violence*) **3.** *vi.* BECOME FREE FROM SOMETHING to escape or emerge from something that confines, restrains, or traps, such as a prison cell **4.** *vt.* PREPARE SOMETHING FOR USE to open something or get something ready for use or action **5.** *vt.* CLASSIFY DATA ITEMS to classify, summarize, outline, or separate data items in order to analyze, explain, or identify something

break through *vti.* to burst or advance quickly and suddenly through an obstruction or opposition, e.g., from an enemy

break up *v.* DIVIDE OR INTERRUPT SOMETHING to divide or separate something into pieces or sections, or interrupt the continuity of something ■ *v.* **1.** *vi.* DISPERSE to separate, or have members separate, and go in different directions **2.** *vti.* END to cause a relationship, interaction, or gathering to end, or to come to an end **3.** *vti.* CAUSE EMOTIONAL RESPONSE to cause somebody to burst into tears or laughter

break with *vt.* to separate from somebody or from a tradition, rule, or trend

break·a·ble /bráykəbəl/ *adj.* EASILY BROKEN likely to be broken if not handled carefully ■ *n.* FRAGILE OBJECT something that is easily broken if not handled carefully (*usually used in the plural*) —**break·a·bil·i·ty** /bràykə bíllitee/ *n.* —**break·a·ble·ness** /-əbəlnəss/ *n.*

break·age /bráykij/ *n.* **1.** SOMETHING BROKEN something that has been broken, usually accidentally (*usually used in the plural*) ○ *All breakages must be paid for.* **2.** BREAKING the breaking of something **3.** DAMAGE damage as a result of breaking something

break·a·way /bráykə wày/ *n.* **1.** SOMETHING BREAKING OFF somebody or something that breaks or has broken away **2.** SOMETHING MADE TO BREAK OFF something that is designed to break away or break apart from the whole **3.** BREAKING AWAY the breaking away of somebody or something ■ *adj.* **1.** MADE TO BREAK OFF designed to break away or apart, either as a safety mechanism or to create an illusion, e.g., a theater prop **2.** HAVING SEVERED TIES WITH SOMETHING having broken ties or connections to somebody or a group

break·beat /bráyk bèet/ *n.* a drum pattern with a syncopated beat that is electronically looped, used mostly in jungle, drum and bass, and hardcore music

break·bone fe·ver /bràyk bōn-/ *n.* = **dengue** [From the pains in the joints that are one of its symptoms]

break·danc·ing /bráyk dànsing/ *n.* a highly energetic, fast, and acrobatic style of solo dancing to rap music, typically involving spinning of the body on the ground. Breakdancing started in the United States in the 1980s. [*Break* of uncertain meaning: perhaps related to BREAKDOWN in the sense of "fast dance"] —**break·dance** *n., vi.* —**break·danc·er** *n.*

break·down /bráyk dòwn/ *n.* **1.** FAILURE TO WORK a failure to operate or an interruption of the operation of a machine or vehicle **2.** FAILURE TO COMMUNICATE a disruption of the understanding and interaction between people or groups ○ *breakdown in the talks* **3.** ELEC ENG SUDDEN PASSAGE OF CURRENT THROUGH INSULATOR the sudden passage of electrical current through an insulator **4.** PERSONAL HEALTH CRISIS a sudden physical or psychological collapse **5.** DATA SUMMARY OR EXPLANATION a summary, explanation, analysis, or outline of data items collected **6.** DECOMPOSITION INTO PARTS a breaking down of something into its essential components, parts, or elements **7.** DANCE FOLK DANCE a fast energetic U.S. folk dance

break·down lor·ry, **break·down truck** *n. U.K.* = **wrecker**

break·er[1] /bráykər/ *n.* **1.** ELEC ENG = **circuit breaker** **2.** LARGE WHITE-CAPPED WAVE a large, usually white-capped, wave that is cresting or breaking, especially onto the shore **3.** DANCE BREAKDANCER somebody who does breakdancing (*slang*) **4.** BREAKING MACHINE something, e.g., a machine, that is used to crush or break up rocks, fibers, or other substances **5.** HORSE TRAINER somebody who trains horses so that they can be ridden ■ *interj.* RADIO OPENING MESSAGE used by CB radio operators to announce that they are beginning to transmit on a channel

brea·ker[2] /bráykər/ *n.* a small cask for water, used especially on lifeboats [Mid-19thC. From Spanish *barrica* "cask" (see BARRICADE).]

break-e·ven /bràyk éevən/, **break-e·ven point** *n.* the point or level of financial activity at which expenditure equals income or the value of an investment equals its cost, and the result is neither a profit nor loss

break·fast /brékfəst/ *n.* DAY'S FIRST MEAL the first meal of the day, usually eaten in the morning (*often used before a noun*) ■ *vi.* (**-fast·ed, -fast·ing, -fasts**) HAVE BREAKFAST to eat breakfast, usually in the morning [15thC. From FAST "period without food," from the idea of being without food while asleep.] —**break·fast·er** *n.*

break·front /bráyk frùnt/ *adj.* used to describe a piece of furniture, e.g., a cabinet or bookcase, with a central section that juts forward slightly —**break·front** *n.*

break-in *n.* **1.** FORCED ENTRY an illegal forced entry into a building or place **2.** INITIAL PERIOD OF WORK OR USE a trial run or an initial period of employment or operation during which somebody's or something's performance is evaluated and training or troubleshooting is done

break·ing[1] /bráyking/ *n.* LING the changing of a simple vowel into a diphthong when certain other speech sounds come before or after it. For example, the vowel in "feet" becomes a diphthong in "feel."

break·ing[2] /bráyking/ *n.* DANCE breakdancing (*slang*)

break·ing and en·ter·ing *n.* the crime of forcibly entering property, usually in order to steal from it

break·ing point *n.* **1.** POINT WHEN COPING BECOMES IMPOSSIBLE the point at which somebody loses the ability to deal physically, psychologically, or emotionally with a stressful situation **2.** CRITICAL MOMENT the point at which a condition or situation reaches a crisis

break·neck /bráyk nèk/ *adj.* so fast or quick as to be hazardous or reckless ○ *at breakneck speed*

break of day *n.* the time when the sun rises in the morning

break·off /bráyk àwf/ *n.* a discontinuation of something, especially when this is abrupt ○ *the breakoff of negotiations*

break·out /bráyk owt/ *n.* **1.** FORCEFUL ESCAPE a forceful escape or emergence from being confined, restrained, or trapped **2.** DATA ANALYSIS a summary or breakdown of data that has been collected [Early 19thC]

break·point /bráyk pòynt/ *n.* **1.** COMPUT PAUSE ALLOWING REVIEW OF COMPUTER PROGRAM a pause inserted into a computer program under development or being serviced so that the contents of registers and memory locations can be examined to correct a programming logic error **2.** POINT WHERE STOP OR CHANGE OCCURS a point where something stops, pauses, changes, or breaks apart

break point *n.* a point in tennis which, if won, results in the player who is not serving winning the game

break·through /bráyk thròo/ *n.* **1.** IMPORTANT DISCOVERY an important new discovery, especially in science, medicine, or technology, that has a dramatic and far-reaching effect **2.** REMOVAL OF BARRIER TO PROGRESS an event that causes or marks the breaking down of a barrier to progress, e.g., in negotiations **3.** MIL PENETRATION OF ENEMY LINE an attacking army's advance through and beyond an enemy's line of defense ■ *adj.* BRINGING PUBLIC RECOGNITION bringing public attention and fame to a performer

break through bleed·ing *n.* bleeding from the womb that occurs between menstrual periods

break·up /bráyk ùp/ *n.* **1.** BREAKING APART OR UP a breaking into separate pieces or sections that are not connected or continuous **2.** END OF RELATIONSHIP the breaking off or discontinuation of a personal relationship **3.** SPRING THAW OF LODGED ICE the melting or breaking apart of lodged ice in rivers and harbors in the spring **4.** EMOTIONAL BREAKDOWN a loss of control over the emotions

break·wa·ter /bráyk wàwtər, -wòtər/ *n.* an offshore barrier that protects a harbor or other coastal area from the full force of the sea

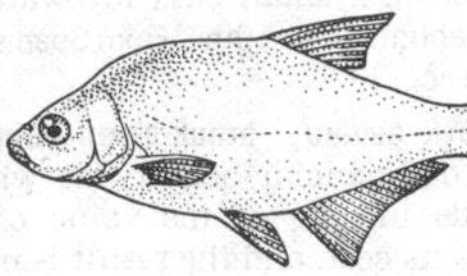

Bream

bream[1] /breem, brim/ (*plural* **bream** *or* **breams**) *n.* **1.** **EURASIAN FRESHWATER FISH** a freshwater fish native to Europe and Asia that has a deep thin body and is yellowish in color. Latin name: *Abramis brama.* **2.** **FRESHWATER FISH LIKE BREAM** a freshwater fish that resembles the bream, introduced into Europe and Asia from North America. Freshwater sunfishes and bluegills are breams. Genus: *Lepomis.* **3.** = **sea bream** [14thC. From Old French *bre(s)me,* ultimately of Germanic origin.]

bream[2] /breem/ (**breamed, bream·ing, breams**) *vt.* to clear the shells, seaweed, and mud off the bottom of a ship by heating it to soften the pitch and then scraping away the debris (*archaic*) [Early 17thC. Probably from Middle Dutch *bremme* "broom, furze"; from the burning of broom as part of the process.]

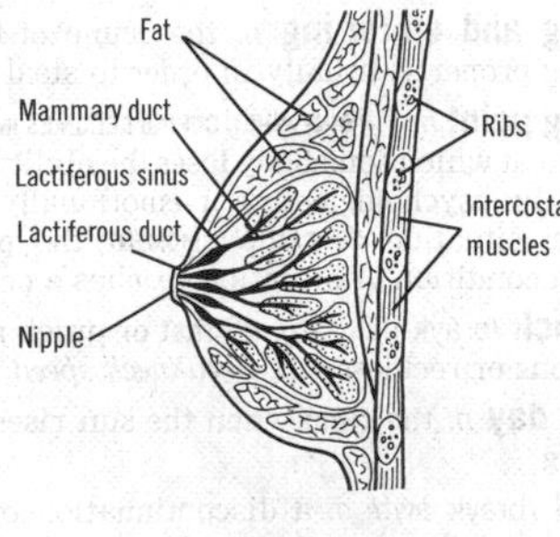

Breast: Cross section of female breast

breast /brest/ *n.* **1.** ANAT **ORGAN ON HUMAN CHEST** soft rounded organs on each side of the chest in women and men. In women the organs are more prominent and produce milk after childbirth. **2.** ZOOL **ANIMAL MILK GLAND** a gland in mammals corresponding to the human breast **3.** **SOMEBODY'S CHEST** the front of the human chest **4.** CLOTHES **GARMENT SECTION** the part or section of clothing covering the front of the chest **5.** **SEAT OF EMOTIONS** the chest regarded as the place where human emotions reside (*literary*) ○ *to beat your breast* **6.** **ANIMAL'S CHEST** the chest of an animal, especially a mammal or bird **7.** **MEAT FROM ANIMAL'S CHEST** meat from the chest of an animal, especially from a chicken or other poultry **8.** **FONT OF NOURISHMENT** a source of sustenance or protection (*literary*) **9.** **PART STICKING OUT OR UP** a part that is rounded, projects, or in some way resembles a breast ■ *vt.* (**breast·ed, breast·ing, breasts**) **1.** **REACH HILLTOP** to reach the summit of a hill **2.** **FACE SOMETHING BOLDLY** to confront a difficulty squarely and boldly and deal with it in a determined way **3.** **PUSH SOMETHING WITH CHEST** to touch or push against something with the chest ○ *managed to breast the tape ahead of her rival* [Old English *brēost.* Ultimately, perhaps, from an Indo-European base denoting swelling.] ◇ **make a clean breast of something** to confess or admit to something, especially something previously denied or withheld

breast·bone /brést bōn/ *n.* a long bone running down the front of the chest, flat in many animals but ridged in most birds. In humans, the top seven pairs of ribs are connected to it.

breast-feed (**breast-fed, breast-feed·ing, breast-feeds**) *vti.* to feed a baby with milk from the breast

breast·plate /brést plàyt/ *n.* **1.** **ARMOR COVERING CHEST** a piece of armor that covers the chest **2.** JUDAISM **JEWISH PRIESTLY GARMENT** a garment worn over the breast by Jewish high priests in ancient times, set with twelve precious stones representing the twelve tribes of Israel

breast·stroke /brést strōk/ *n.* a swimming stroke in which the arms are extended and pulled back together in a circular motion while the legs are thrust out and pulled together —**breast·stroke** *vi.* —**breast·strok·er** *n.*

breast·work /brést wùrk/ *n.* in former times, an earth wall built at chest height as a temporary barrier for defense

breath /breth/ *n.* **1.** **AIR BREATHED IN AND OUT** the air that a person or animal inhales and exhales **2.** **AIR EXHALED** the air that somebody exhales, especially with reference to how it feels or smells to somebody nearby **3.** **BREATHING OF AIR** an inhaling or exhaling of air, or the entire process of inhaling and exhaling ○ *take a deep breath* **4.** **HINT** a faint hint of something ○ *a breath of scandal* **5.** **LIFE** the vital force or spirit of a living person or animal **6.** **SHORT PAUSE** a momentary pause or respite **7.** **WAFT** a fleeting or slight fragrance or movement of air ○ *not a breath of wind* **8.** **SOFT SOUND** a sound or whispering that is soft and almost inaudible [Old English *bræþ* "odor, especially of something burning or cooking." Ultimately from an Indo-European base denoting heat. The modern meaning evolved via the notion of exhalation.] ◇ **a breath of fresh air** somebody or something that is refreshingly new and exciting ◇ **catch your breath 1.** to stop breathing for an instant, e.g., from shock or physical pain **2.** to regain a normal breathing rhythm after exertion ◇ **don't hold your breath!** used to indicate that it is extremely unlikely that something will happen (*informal*) ◇ **in the same breath** at almost the same moment or shortly afterward ◇ **out of breath** breathing heavily because of physical exertion ◇ **take somebody's breath away** to astonish or greatly impress somebody ◇ **under your breath** in a whispering or muttering voice ◇ **with bated breath** full of anxious anticipation

breath·a·ble /bree̱thəb'l/ *adj.* **1.** **SUITABLE FOR BREATHING** suitable or possible for people to breathe **2.** TEXTILES **LETTING AIR IN AND MOISTURE OUT** allowing air in and body moisture out, keeping the wearer cooler and drier than other fabrics or clothes do (*refers to fabric*) —**breath·a·bil·i·ty** /bree̱thə bíllətee/ *n.*

breath·a·lyze /bréthə līz/ (**-lyzed, -lyz·ing, -lyz·es**) *vt.* to test somebody, especially a driver, for drunkenness by making him or her breathe into a Breathalyzer™ [Mid-20thC. Back-formation from BREATHALYZER.]

Breath·a·lyz·er /bréthə līzər/ *tdmk.* a trademark for an apparatus that measures a subject's blood alcohol concentration

breathe /bree̱th/ (**breathed, breath·ing, breathes**) *v.* **1.** *vti.* **TAKE IN AIR** to repeatedly and alternately take in and blow out air in order to stay alive ○ *breathe in deeply* **2.** *vti.* **EXPEL SUBSTANCE WITH BREATH** to expel a substance, e.g., cigarette smoke, from the mouth or nose along with the breath, or to be exhaled in this way **3.** *vt.* **SMELL SOMETHING** to take in the aroma of something **4.** *vti.* **TAKE IN AIR** to take in air, e.g., for combustion or in order to equalize internal and external pressure (*refers to machines*) **5.** *vi.* TEXTILES **ALLOW AIR THROUGH** to allow air and moisture to pass through fabric or clothing **6.** *vt.* **SAY SOMETHING SECRETIVELY** to say something in a soft voice or secretively **7.** *vt.* **GIVE SOMEBODY OR SOMETHING A QUALITY** to instill a particular quality in somebody or something ○ *breathed new life into the group* **8.** *vti.* **EXUDE QUALITY** to suggest a particular quality in abundance, or to be suggested or displayed noticeably **9.** *vi.* **LIVE** to be alive **10.** *vi.* **DEVELOP FLAVOR THROUGH EXPOSURE TO AIR** to be exposed to air in order to develop flavor (*refers to wine*) **11.** *vti.* **PAUSE TO REST** to allow a person or animal, e.g., a horse, to pause to rest or catch a breath **12.** *vi.* **WAFT** to blow softly or move gently [13thC. Formed from BREATH.] ◇ **breathe easy** *or* **freely** *or* **easily** to relax and stop worrying about something or things in general ◇ **breathe your last** to die (*literary*)

breathed /brétht/ /breht, bree̱thd/ *adj.* **1.** PHON **UNVOICED** pronounced without vibrating the vocal cords **2.** **BREATHING** with a particular type of breathing (*usually used in combination*)

breath·er /bree̱thər/ *n.* **1.** **BREATHING PERSON** somebody who breathes in a particular way (*used in combination*) ○ *a heavy breather* **2.** **PAUSE TO REST** a short rest while in the middle of doing something (*informal*) **3.** **VENT** a vent in an area or enclosure that is otherwise sealed [Early 20thC. From the idea of stopping for breath.]

breath·ing /bree̱thing/ *n.* **1.** **INHALING AND EXHALING** the process of taking air into the lungs and pushing it out again **2.** PHON **PRONUNCIATION OF VOWELS IN ANCIENT GREEK** in ancient Greek, the pronouncing of an initial vowel with an "h" sound before it (**rough breathing**), or without an "h"sound (**smooth breathing**), or either of the symbols indicating these pronunciations

breath·ing space, **breath·ing room** *n.* time to relax or sort out problems without pressures, constraints, interruptions, or interference. ◊ **breathing spell**

breath·ing spell *n.* an opportunity to relax or sort out problems without pressures, constraints, interruptions, or interference

breath·less /bréthləss/ *adj.* **1.** **UNABLE TO BREATHE PROPERLY** experiencing difficulty in breathing, or breathing faster than normal, because of physical exertion or illness **2.** **WITH SHALLOW BREATHING** breathing very shallowly because of intense emotion, e.g., fear or excitement **3.** **EXCITING OR INTENSE** capable of causing difficulties in breathing because of intense excitement, emotion, or speed **4.** **HOT AND WITHOUT BREEZE** lacking any air movement or breeze **5.** **NOT ALIVE** dead and no longer breathing (*literary*) —**breath·less·ly** *adv.* —**breath·less·ness** *n.*

breath·tak·ing /bréth tàyking/ *adj.* evoking strong emotions, especially excitement, awe, or shock [Mid-20thC] —**breath·tak·ing·ly** *adv.*

breath test *n.* a test using a device that a person breathes into to determine the level of alcohol in the breath, especially one conducted by police on the driver of a road vehicle

breath·y /bréthee/ (**-i·er, -i·est**) *adj.* **1.** **WITH SOUND OF BREATHING** with a discernible sound of breathing accompanying spoken words **2.** MUSIC **LACKING GOOD BREATH CONTROL** without proper control of the breath, which creates an uneven or weak vocal or instrumental sound —**breath·i·ly** *adv.* —**breath·i·ness** *n.*

Bré·beuf /bráy bo͝of/, **Jean de, St.** (1593–1649) French-born Canadian missionary. He worked as a Jesuit missionary among the Huron people in Canada after 1625.

brec·ci·a /bréchee ə, bréchə, bréshee ə, bréshə/ *n.* a coarse-grained sedimentary rock made of sharp fragments of rock and stone cemented together by finer material. Breccia is produced by volcanic activity or erosion, including frost shattering. [Late 18thC. Via Italian, "gravel," from, ultimately, an Indo-European base that also produced English *break.* The underlying sense is "broken rock."] —**brec·ci·al** *adj.* —**brec·ci·ate** /bréchee ayt, -shee-/ *vti.* —**brec·ci·a·tion** /-aysh'n/ *n.*

Brecht /brekt, brekht/, **Bertolt** (1898–1956) German playwright and director. One of the most influential dramatists of the 20th century, he was the author of *The Threepenny Opera* (1928) in collaboration with Kurt Weill, *Mother Courage* (1941), and *The Caucasian Chalk Circle* (1945). After 1948 he worked with the Berliner Ensemble in East Berlin. Full name **Eugene Bertolt Friedrich Brecht**

Breck·in·ridge /brékən rìj/, **John C.** (1821–75) statesman and vice president of the United States. He was James Buchanan's vice president (1857–61). During the civil war he was a Confederate general and secretary of war. Full name **John Cabell Breckinridge**

bred[1] /bred/ past tense, past participle of **breed**

bred[2] /bred/ *adj.* raised in a particular manner (*used in combination*) ○ *city-bred*

brede /breed/ *n.* decorative embroidery or braiding (*archaic*) [Mid-17thC. A variant of BRAID.]

bred-in-the-bone *adj.* **1.** **INGRAINED** deeply instilled or firmly established **2.** **HABITUAL** used to describe a habit, especially a bad habit, that has become deeply ingrained over time

breech /breech/ *n.* **1.** ARMS **BACK OF GUN BARREL** the rear part of the barrel of a rifle or shotgun, near the stock **2.** **PART OF PULLEY** the lower part of a pulley block, to which the rope, cable, or chain is fixed **3.** ANAT **BUTTOCKS** the back lower portion of the trunk of the body [Old English *brēc,* plural of *brōc* "garment covering the thighs and lower trunk." The modern meanings evolved from the notion of "lower part."]

WORD KEY: USAGE

See Usage note at *breach.*

breech birth (*plural* **breech births**) *n.* MED the delivery of a baby with its buttocks, rather than its head, emerging first

breech·block /breech blòk/ *n.* the part of a breech-loading gun that is detached from the barrel to allow cartridges to be loaded into the back of the barrel

breech·cloth /breech klòth/ (*plural* **-cloths**) *n.* = **loincloth**

breech de·liv·er·y *n.* = **breech birth**

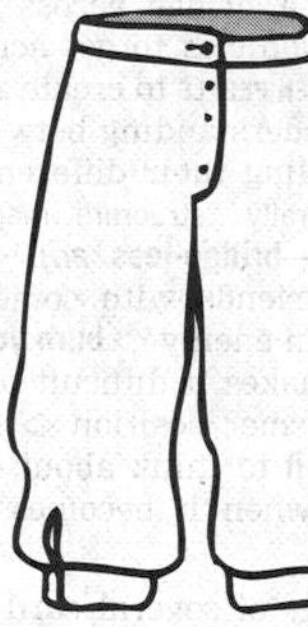

Breeches

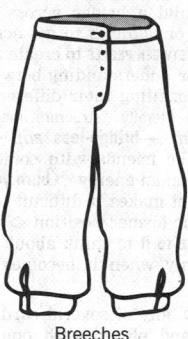

breech·es /bríchiz, breé-/, **britch·es** /bríchiz/ *npl.* **1.** **KNEE-LENGTH PANTS** pants with legs that come down to the knee **2.** **TROUSERS** trousers of any kind (*informal*) [13thC. Plural of BREECH.]

breech·es buoy *n.* a piece of equipment used for transferring people between moving ships, consisting of a canvas harness suspended from a pulley and line that links both ships

breech·ing /breéching, brích-/ *n.* **1.** EQU **STRAP ON HORSE'S HARNESS** the strap of a harness that passes behind the hindquarters of a horse or donkey **2.** ZOOL **HAIR ON ANIMAL'S HINDQUARTERS** the short hair or wool on the rump and hind legs of an animal, e.g., a sheep, goat, or dog **3.** ARMS **GUN'S BREECH PARTS** parts of a gun that form or make up the breech **4.** NAVY **ROPE SECURING SHIP'S GUN** in former times, ropes used to secure guns to the side of a ship to control the recoil

breech·load·er /breech lòdər/ *n.* a gun that is loaded by inserting cartridges through the back of the barrel —**breech·load·ing** *adj.*

breed /breed/ *n.* **1.** BIOL **DISTINCT ANIMAL OR PLANT** a strain of an animal or plant with identifiable characteristics that distinguish it from other members of its species, especially one whose characteristics are preserved by controlled mating or propagating **2.** **SOMEBODY OR SOMETHING OF PARTICULAR TYPE** a particular type of thing or person, especially one that can be easily distinguished from other similar things or people ○ *a new breed of managers* ■ *v.* (**bred** /bred/, **bred, breed·ing, breeds**) **1.** *vti.* BIOL **MATE AND PRODUCE YOUNG** to mate and give birth to offspring **2.** *vt.* AGRIC **RAISE ANIMALS OR PLANTS** to reproduce and raise animals or plants, especially for commercial purposes or for shows and competitions **3.** *vt.* GENETICS **SELECT ANIMALS OR PLANTS** to select animals or plants as part of a process of improving or preserving their special characteristics **4.** *vti.* **PRODUCE OR BE PRODUCED** to produce or create something, or be produced or created ○ *Experience breeds confidence.* **5.** *vt.* PHYS **PRODUCE NUCLEAR FUEL** to make fissionable substances using a breeder reactor [Old English *brēdan* "to produce or nurture offspring." Ultimately from an Indo-European base denoting "heat"; the underlying sense is "incubation."]

breed·er /breédər/ *n.* **1.** **SOMEBODY WHO BREEDS ANIMALS OR PLANTS** somebody who raises animals or propagates and grows plants, either to maintain an existing breed or produce a new one **2.** **ANIMAL OR PLANT USED FOR BREEDING** an animal or plant kept to produce offspring **3.** **CAUSAL FACTOR** a cause or a source of something **4.** **HETEROSEXUAL** an insulting term for somebody who is heterosexual (*slang insult*) **5.** PHYS = **breeder reactor**

breed·er re·ac·tor, **breed·er** *n.* a nuclear reactor that produces more fuel than it consumes. This kind of reactor is used mainly to produce plutonium.

breed·ing /breéding/ *n.* **1.** **UPBRINGING** somebody's upbringing, education, and training in manners and other social skills, especially an upbringing that produces polished manners and self-assurance **2.** **ANCESTRY** somebody's family or ancestry **3.** **REPRODUCTION** the mating and producing of young (*often used before a noun*) ○ *prime breeding stock* **4.** GENETICS **DEVELOPMENT OF IMPROVED ANIMALS AND PLANTS** the development of new types of plants or animals with improved characteristics **5.** PHYS **REACTOR'S FUEL PRODUCTION EXCEEDING CONSUMPTION** production of fissionable material in a breeder reactor in quantities in excess of the fuel it consumes

breed·ing ground *n.* **1.** **ANIMAL'S MATING AREA** an area where animals mate and produce young **2.** **ENVIRONMENT ENCOURAGING SOMETHING** an environment or situation that is likely to produce or encourage a particular phenomenon ○ *The festival is a breeding ground for new comedy talent.*

breeze /breez/ *n.* **1.** METEOROL **LIGHT TO MODERATE WIND** a wind ranging in strength from light to moderate, with a speed of 4 to 31 mph/6 to 50 kph **2.** **SOMETHING EASY** a task or object that is easily achieved (*informal*) ■ *vi.* (**breezed, breez·ing, breez·es**) **1.** **GO SOMEWHERE BRISKLY** to move quickly and confidently or cheerfully, e.g., into a meeting **2.** **ACCOMPLISH EASILY** to progress through something easily and with little difficulty or effort ○ *He breezed through his certification test with no trouble.* [Mid-16thC. Probably from Spanish *brisa* and Portuguese *briza* "northeast wind," of unknown origin.] ◇ **shoot the breeze** to spend time chatting (*slang*)

breeze block *n. U.K.* = **cinder block** [*Breeze* from French *braise* "hot coals" (source of English *braise* and *brazier*)]

breeze·way /breez wày/ *n.* a roofed passageway with open sides that connects two buildings, e.g., a house and garage

breez·i·ly /breézəlee/ *adv.* in a lively, cheerful, and relaxed way

breez·y /breézee/ (**-i·er, -i·est**) *adj.* **1.** METEOROL **SLIGHTLY WINDY** with a light to moderate wind **2.** **LIVELY AND CHEERFUL** lively, cheerful, and relaxed —**breez·i·ness** *n.*

breg·ma /brégmə/ (*plural* **-ma·ta** /-mətə/) *n.* the place on the skull at the top of the forehead where the frontal bone and the two parietal bones meet, used as a reference point when measuring skulls [Late 16thC. From Greek, "front of the head."] —**breg·mat·ic** /breg máttik/ *adj.*

Bre·men /brémən/ city, major port, and capital of the state of Bremen in northwestern Germany. It is situated on the Weser River, about 43 mi./69 km from the North Sea. Population: 551,000 (1994).

brems·strah·lung /brémsshtraàləng, brémz-/ *n.* the electromagnetic radiation that is produced by an electrically charged subatomic particle, such as an electron, when it is suddenly slowed down by the electric field of an atomic nucleus [Mid-20thC. From German, from *bremsen* "to brake" + *Strahlung* "radiation."]

Bren·dan /bréndən/, **St.** (484–577) Irish Saint and traveller. He founded the monastery of Clonfert in Co. Galway (561). Known as **the Navigator**

Bren·nan /brénnən/, **Walter** (1894–1974) U.S. actor. A three-time Academy Award winner, he was a character actor best remembered as Amos McCoy on television's *The Real McCoys* (1957–63).

Bren·nan, William J., Jr. (1906–97) U.S. Supreme Court justice. During his long Supreme Court Tenure (1956–90) he was known for his dedication to maintaining freedom of speech.

Bren·ner Pass /brénnər-/ Alpine mountain pass linking Innsbruck, Austria and Bolzano, Italy. With a maximum elevation of 4,497 ft./1,371 m, it has been an important route between Austria and Italysince antiquity.

brent goose /brént-/, **brent** *n. U.K.* = **brant** [Origin unknown]

Brent·wood /brént wood/ community forming part of Islip, a town situated on Long Island, New York. Population: 45,218 (1990).

Br'er /brair, brur/ *n. Southern U.S.* a written representation of the way African Americans in the Southern United States supposedly once pronounced the word "brother" when using it as a form of address

bre·sao·la /bre sṓlə, bri zṓlə/ *n.* slices of salt-cured air-dried beef served with a dressing of olive oil, lemon juice, and black pepper [Late 20thC. From Italian, from *brasare* "to cook slowly."]

Brest /brést/ port and largest city in Finistère Department in the Bretagne Region, western France. Population: 153,099 (1990).

breth·ren /bréthrən/ plural of **brother** (*archaic*) ■ *npl.* **1.** **MEMBERS OF SAME GROUP** members of the same family, group, class, or community (*literary or humorous*) ○ *the weaker brethren among us* **2.** **MEMBERS OF CHURCH** the members, especially male members, of a particular church or other religious group, especially a Protestant Christian denomination (*archaic or literary*) [12thC. From *brōeþre, breþre*, a plural of Old English *brōþor* "brother." *Brethren* remained the standard plural of *brother* until the 17thC, when it was superseded by *brothers*.]

Bret·on /brét'n/ *n.* **1.** **SOMEBODY FROM BRITTANY** somebody who lives in or was born or raised in the region of Brittany in northwestern France **2.** **CELTIC LANGUAGE OF BRITTANY** a Celtic language spoken in mostly rural areas of Brittany, and most closely related to Cornish. It is spoken by a little over half a million people. —**Bret·on** *adj.*

Bret·ton Woods /brétt'n-/ tourist resort in New Hampshire. In 1944, it hosted the United Nations Bretton Woods Conference where The International Monetary Fund and the International Bank for Reconstruction and Development were set up. Area: 10,000 acres/4,050 hectares.

Breu·er /bróyər/, **Marcel** (1902–81) Hungarian-born U.S. architect. He designed the Whitney Museum of American Art (1966) and other modernist buildings, and is regarded as the designer of the tubular steel-framed chair. Full name **Marcel Lajos Breuer**

brev. *abbr.* brevet

breve /brev, breev/ *n.* **1.** PHON **MARK OVER SHORT VOWEL** a mark ˘ placed over a vowel to show that it has a short sound **2.** POETRY **MARK OVER UNSTRESSED POETIC SYLLABLE** a mark ˘ that is used to show a short or unstressed syllable in poetry **3.** MUSIC **LONG MUSICAL NOTE** a musical note that is equal in length to two whole notes [14thC. A variant of BRIEF.]

bre·vet /brə vét, brévit/ *n.* (*plural* **-vets**) **MILITARY PROMOTION** a temporary promotion of a military officer without an increase in pay ■ *vt.* (**-vet·ed, -vet·ing, -vets**) **PROMOTE IN RANK BUT NOT PAY** to promote a military officer by brevet [14thC. From French, literally "little letter," from Old French *brief* "letter" (source of English *brief*). The modern meaning evolved from the earlier sense "official letter."] —**bre·vet·cy** *n.*

bre·vi·ar·y /breévee èree/ (*plural* **-ies**) *n.* in the Roman Catholic Church, a book that contains the hymns, psalms, and prayers prescribed for each day [15thC. From Latin *breviarium* "summary, abridgment," from *breviare* "to shorten" (source of English *abbreviate* and *abridge*). Originally an abridged version of the psalms.]

brev·i·ty /brévitee/ *n.* **1.** **BRIEFNESS** shortness in time **2.** **USE OF FEW WORDS** the economical use of words in speech or writing [15thC. Via Old French *brievete* from the Latin stem *brevitat-*, from *brevis* "short" (source of English *brief*).]

brew /broo/ *vti.* (**brewed, brew·ing, brews**) **1.** **MAKE BEER** to make beer or similar alcoholic drinks by a process of steeping, boiling, and fermenting grain with hops, sugar, and other ingredients **2.** **MAKE TEA OR COFFEE** to prepare a drink of tea or coffee, or to develop the full flavor that tea or coffee should have before being ready to drink **3.** **DEVELOP THREATENINGLY** to form, concoct, or develop ominously or threateningly ○ *a scandal was brewing* ■ *n.* **1.** **KIND OF BEER** a type of beer, e.g., a lager or ale **2.** **BREWED BEVERAGE** a drink such as coffee or tea or a serving of such a drink (*informal*) **3.** **MIXTURE** a combination of ingredients or elements of any kind [Old English *breowan*] —**brew·er** *n.* —**brew·ing** *n.*

brew·er's yeast /bróoərz-/ *n.* the yeast that is used in brewing beer, also used as a dietary source of vitamins, especially vitamin B. Latin name: *Saccharomyces cerevisiae.*

brew·er·y /broo əree, brooree/ (*plural* **-ies**) *n.* a company that brews beer or a building where beer or a similar drink is brewed

brew·is /broo iss, brooz/ *n.* broth thickened with bread, or a dish of bread soaked in milk, broth, or gravy (*regional*) [13thC. From Old French *bro(u)ez* (plural) and *bro(u)et* (singular), from *breu*, from a prehistoric Germanic word that also produced English *broth.*]

brew·pub /broopùb/ *n.* a restaurant or bar where the beer is made on the premises

Brew·ster /broo stər/, **William** (1567–1644) English-born U.S. settler. He led the pilgrims who reached

America on the *Mayflower* (1620) and established Plymouth Colony.

Brey·er /brī́ər/, **Stephen** (*b.* 1938) U.S. Supreme Court justice. Appointed to the Supreme Court in 1994, he was known for his carefully reasoned opinions. Full name **Stephen Gerald Breyer**

Brezh·nev /brézh nef, -nyif/, **Leonid Ilyich** (1906–82) Soviet statesman. Leader of the Soviet Communist Party (1964–82), he exerted strong control over Warsaw Pact countries.

bri·ar[1] /brī́ ər/ (*plural* **-ars** *or* **-ar**), **bri·er** (*plural* **-ers** *or* **-er**) *n.* **1.** PLANTS **SHRUB OF SOUTHERN EUROPE** a shrub that belongs to the heather family and is native to southern Europe. Its hard woody roots are used to make tobacco pipes. Latin name: *Erica arborea.* **2. KIND OF TOBACCO PIPE** a tobacco pipe made from the wood of the roots of the briar [Mid-19thC. From French *bruyère* "wild heather," ultimately of Gaulish origin. The English spelling was based on that of the unrelated BRIAR[2], with which it is often confused.]

WORD KEY: ORIGIN

English has two words *briar.* Both can also be spelled *brier*, and their meanings are similar, so they tend to get confused. One goes back to Old English, when it was applied to any prickly bush, especially the blackberry; in modern usage it is applied to a type of wild rose. The other is much more recent. It means "wild heather," and it was borrowed from French *bruyère.* At first it was spelled *bruyer* in English, but because of its similarity to ***briar*** in the "wild rose" sense, it too came to be spelled ***briar.*** It is the root of this second type of briar that is used to make pipes.

bri·ar[2] /brī́ ər/ *n.* = **brier**[2]

bri·ard /bree áar, bree áard/ *n.* a dog belonging to an ancient French breed of strong sheepdogs with stiff and slightly wavy coats of a single color, usually black [Mid-20thC. From French, literally "of Brie," an area of northern France where the dog originated.]

bri·ar·wood /brī́ər wòod/ *n.* wood from the root of the European briar, used for making tobacco pipes

bribe /brīb/ *vti.* (**bribed, brib·ing, bribes**) **PERSUADE SOMEBODY WITH ENTICEMENT** to give somebody money or some other incentive to do something, especially something illegal or dishonest ■ *n.* **INCENTIVE TO PERSUADE SOMEBODY** money or some other incentive that is given to persuade somebody to do something, especially something illegal or dishonest [14thC. From Old French *briber* or *brimber* "to beg," from *bribe* "morsel of food given to a beggar," of unknown origin.] —**brib·er** *n.* —**brib·a·ble** *adj.*

brib·er·y /brībəree/ (*plural* **-ies**) *n.* the offering of money or other incentives to persuade somebody to do something, especially something dishonest or illegal

bric-a-brac /bríkə bràk/ *n.* small, ornamental objects that are of interest or sentimental value but of little monetary value [Mid-19thC. From French, from the obsolete phrase *à bric et à brac* "at random" (in which *brac* is a fanciful alteration of *bric* "piece").]

Brice /brīss/, **Fannie** (1891–1951) U.S. entertainer. She appeared in various revues, movies and radio programs. Her life inspired the musical *Funny Girl* (1964). Real name **Fannie Borach**

brick /brik/ *n.* **1.** BUILDING **HARD BLOCK USED FOR CONSTRUCTION** a rectangular block of clay or a similar material that is baked until it is hard and is used for building houses, walls, and other large permanent structures **2.** INDUST **BRICKS OR THEIR MATERIAL** bricks collectively, or the material they are made of **3. CHILD'S BUILDING BLOCK** a child's wooden or plastic block used with others to make shapes or structures **4. BLOCK OF SOMETHING** a rectangular block of something, e.g., ice cream or coffee **5. RELIABLE SUPPORTIVE PERSON** somebody who is helpful or supportive in times of difficulty (*informal dated*) ■ *vt.* (**bricked, brick·ing, bricks**) **1. MAKE SOMETHING WITH BRICKS** to use bricks to build something or as a liner or paving material for something **2. CLOSE UP WITH BRICKS** to close something up or wall something off with bricks and mortar ○ *the window had been bricked up* [15thC. From Middle Dutch *bricke*, later reinforced by French *brique* (perhaps borrowed from Middle Dutch). Ultimate origin uncertain: perhaps literally "fragment."] ◇ **hit the bricks 1.** to go out and actively look for something, e.g., a job or housing (*informal*) **2.** to go on strike (*informal*)

brick·bat /brík bàt/ *n.* **1. CRITICISM** harshly unfavorable criticism **2. PIECE OF SOMETHING HARD** a broken fragment of something hard, e.g., a piece of a brick, used as a missile [Mid-16thC. *Bat* from *bat* "piece (of brick)," which is probably the same word as BAT.]

brick·lay·er /brík lày ər/ *n.* somebody trained to construct houses, walls, and other large permanent structures by cementing bricks together with mortar —**brick·lay·ing** *n.*

brick-red *adj.* of a warm brownish-red color similar to that of red clay bricks —**brick red** *n.*

brick·work /brík wùrk/ *n.* **1. STRUCTURE BUILT FROM BRICK** something, e.g., a wall, building, or walk that is made up of bricks **2. BRICKLAYER'S TECHNIQUE** the technique or skill of laying bricks

brick·yard /brík yaàrd/ *n.* a place where bricks are made, stored, or sold

bri·co·lage /brèe kō láazh, brìkō-/ *n.* something that is made or put together with whatever materials happen to be available [Mid-20thC. From French, from *bricoler* "to do odd jobs," from *bricole* (see BRICOLE).]

bri·cole /bri kṓl, brík'l/ *n.* **1.** CUE GAMES **TYPE OF BILLIARDS SHOT** in billiards, a shot where the cue ball touches the cushion after hitting the target ball and before hitting another ball **2.** ARMS **ANCIENT MILITARY CATAPULT** a catapult that ancient and medieval soldiers used to launch stones **3.** MIL **SOLDIER'S HARNESS FOR HAULING GUNS** in former times, a harness worn by soldiers for hauling guns [Early 16thC. Via French from Provençal *bricola* or Italian *briccola*, of unknown origin.]

bri·dal /brī́d'l/ *adj.* **OF BRIDES OR WEDDINGS** for or associated with brides or weddings ■ *n.* **WEDDING** a wedding or marriage ceremony [By folk etymology (from BRIDE and -AL) from Old English *bryd-ealu* "wedding festival at which much ale is drunk," literally "bride-ale"]

bri·dal wreath *n.* a shrub with arching branches that produces a mass of small white flowers in spring. Genus: *Spiraea.*

bride /brīd/ *n.* a woman who is about to marry or has just married [Old English *bryd*]

bride·groom /brī́d gròom, -gròom/ *n.* a man who is about to marry or has just married [By folk etymology (from GROOM) from Old English *brȳdguma*, literally "bride-man," from *guma* "man," ultimately from an Indo-European word meaning "earth," which also produced English *hominid*]

bride price *n.* in some societies, a payment in the form of money or property made by the groom to the bride or her family

brides·maid /brī́dz màyd/ *n.* a girl or woman who helps the bride on her wedding day

bridge[1] /brij/ *n.* **1.** CIV ENG **STRUCTURE ALLOWING PASSAGE ACROSS OBSTACLE** a structure that is built above and across a river, road, or other obstacle to allow people or vehicles to cross it **2. LINK OR MEANS OF APPROACH** something that provides a link, connection, or means of coming together **3.** SHIPPING **SHIP'S CONTROL ROOM OR PLATFORM** the platform or room on a ship or other vessel from which the captain controls its course **4.** DENT **PARTIAL FALSE TEETH** a set of one or more false teeth that act as a replacement for missing natural teeth. It can be permanently anchored to natural teeth (**fixed bridge**), or set into a metal appliance and temporarily clipped on to natural teeth (**removable bridge**). **5.** ANAT **TOP OF NOSE** the top part of the nose between the eyes **6.** OPHTHALMOL **PART OF EYEGLASSES** the part of a pair of eyeglasses that connects the two lenses together at the front and rests on the nose **7.** MUSIC **PART OF STRINGED INSTRUMENT** the part of a stringed instrument that keeps the strings away from the body. It is high and curved on a violin but shallow and straight on a guitar. **8.** MUSIC **CONNECTING PASSAGE** a transitional or connecting section in a musical work **9.** CUE GAMES **CUE REST WITH HIGH END** a long-handled support for a player's cue in billiards, with a high arching end **10.** CUE GAMES **HAND USED AS REST** the player's hand used as a rest for the cue in billiards **11.** ELEC ENG **PART OF ELECTRICAL CIRCUIT** a part of an electrical circuit fitted with a device that measures electrical resistance or capacitance ■ *vt.* (**bridged, bridg·ing, bridg·es**) **1.** CIV ENG **BUILD BRIDGE ACROSS OBSTACLE** to build a bridge across an obstacle to allow people or vehicles to get across it **2. CREATE UNDERSTANDING BETWEEN PEOPLE** to create a means of communication or understanding between people or a means of reconciling their differences [Old English *brycg*, perhaps literally "structure made of logs"] —**bridge·a·ble** *adj.* —**bridge·less** *adj.* ◇ **build bridges** to try to make friends with somebody who has previously been an enemy ◇ **burn your bridges** to do something that makes it difficult or impossible to return to your former position ◇ **cross that bridge when you come to it** to think about or worry about something only when it becomes a reality or a priority

bridge[2] /brij/ *n.* any of several card games derived from whist and played with one deck of cards divided between four players who play in two pairs. The term is generally used to refer to contract bridge, which is the most popular form of the game. [Late 19thC. Origin uncertain: perhaps from assumed Turkish *bir-üç*, literally "one three," since in the game of bridge one hand is exposed and three are hidden.]

bridge·board /bríj bàwrd, -bōrd/ *n.* a notched board at either side of a staircase, supporting the horizontal and vertical boards that form the steps

bridge·head /bríj hèd/ *n.* **1.** MIL **ARMY'S POSITION SEIZED IN ENEMY TERRITORY** a forward position seized by advancing troops in enemy territory and serving as a basis for further advances **2.** MIL **DEFENSIVE MILITARY POSITION** a fortified position from which troops defend the end of a bridge that is nearest to the enemy **3. PIONEERING FOOTHOLD** any position from which further advancement can be attained **4. END OF BRIDGE** the area immediately surrounding the end of a bridge

bridge loan *n.* money borrowed to finance something until permanent financing can be obtained, especially a loan to finance the purchase of a new building or property until an old one is sold

Bridge of Sighs *n.* a covered canal bridge of carved stone in Venice, Italy, built in the late 16th century between the Doge's Palace and the prison. Its name is believed to come from the sighs of prisoners crossing the bridge to be tried or executed.

Bridge·port /bríj pàwrt, -pōrt/ city in southwestern Connecticut where the Pequonnock River empties into Long Island Sound. Population: 137,990 (1996).

Brid·ger /bríjjər/, **James** (1804–81) U.S. pioneer. He guided many expeditions in the American West and led a federal military campaign against the Mormons (1857–58).

Bridge·town /bríj tòwn/ capital, main port, and tourist center of Barbados in the West Indies. Population: 6,720 (1990).

bridge·work /bríj wùrk/ *n.* **1. WORK OF FITTING FALSE TEETH** provision of false teeth to replace missing or removed natural teeth **2.** = **bridge**[1]

bridg·ing loan /bríjjing-/ *n. U.K.* = **bridge loan**

Bridg·man /bríjmən/, **P.W.** (1882–1961) U.S. physicist. He won the Nobel Prize in physics in 1946 in rec-

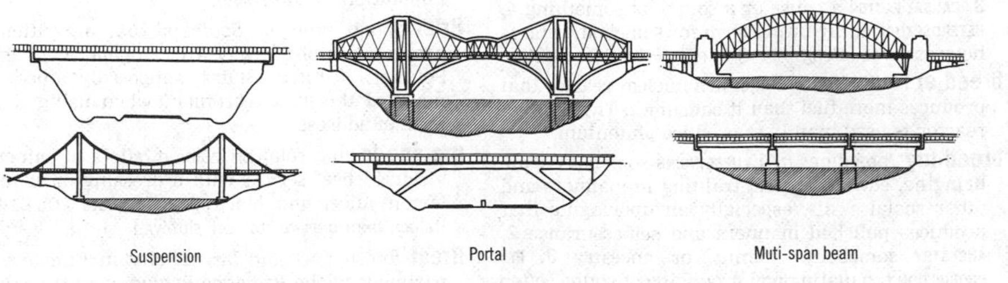

Bridge

ognition of his work on thermodynamics. Full name **Percy Williams Bridgman**

bri·dle /brī́d'l/ *n.* **1.** EQU **HARNESS FOR HORSE'S HEAD** a set of leather straps fitted to a horse's head and incorporating the bit and the reins **2. RESTRAINING THING** something that acts as a control or restraint ■ *v.* **(-dled, -dling, -dles) 1.** *vt.* EQU **PUT BRIDLE ON HORSE** to provide a horse with a bridle **2.** *vi.* **SHOW ANGER OR INDIGNATION** to react with slight anger or indignation, sometimes by rearing the head **3.** *vt.* **EXERCISE CONTROL OR RESTRAINT** to show restraint in expressing a feeling or control or in curbing something [Old English *brīdel*, ultimately from a prehistoric Germanic base meaning "to move jerkily from side to side," which is also the ancestor of English *braid*]

Brie /bree/ *n.* a type of soft cow's-milk cheese with a whitish rind, originally made in Brie in northeastern France. It is similar to Camembert, but milder in flavor.

brief /breef/ *adj.* **1. NOT LENGTHY** lasting for only a short time ○ *a brief conversation* **2. CONCISE** containing only the necessary information without any extra details **3.** CLOTHES **SCANTY** leaving much of the wearer's body exposed **4. CURT** curt or abrupt speech or conversation ■ *n.* **1. SYNOPSIS OF DOCUMENTS** a digest or synopsis of a larger document or group of documents **2. BRIEFING** a briefing, or the information conveyed during one **3. SUMMARY** an outline or summary, e.g., of a book **4.** LAW **ATTORNEY'S CASE SUBMITTED TO COURT BEFOREHAND** an outline of how a legal case will be argued, together with evidence and supporting statements, submitted by an attorney to a court prior to a trial **5.** LAW **OUTLINE OF LEGAL CASE FOR ATTORNEY** an outline of one side of a legal case for an attorney, containing the evidence and points of law pertinent to the argument of the case **6.** CHR **PAPAL LETTER** a letter from the Pope, less formal than a papal bull ■ **briefs** *npl.* **SNUG UNDERWEAR FOR LOWER BODY** men's or women's close-fitting underwear that covers the buttocks and genital area entirely ■ *vt.* **(briefed, brief·ing, briefs) 1. GIVE INFORMATION TO PREPARE SOMEBODY** to give somebody all the necessary information about something in preparation for a discussion or decision. ◊ **debrief 2. SUMMARIZE SOMETHING** to make a summary of something, especially a written summary [13thC. Via Old French from Latin *brevis* "short" (source also of English *abbreviate*, *abridge*, and *brevity*).] —**brief·er** *n.* —**brief·ly** *adv.* —**brief·ness** *n.*

Briefcase

brief·case /breéf kàyss/ *n.* a small rectangular case with a handle, used for carrying books and papers

brief·ing /breéfing/ *n.* **1. MEETING TO CONVEY INFORMATION** a meeting held to provide information about the main facts of an issue or a situation **2. INFORMATION FROM MEETING** the information conveyed at a briefing

bri·er[1] *n.* = **briar**[1]

bri·er[2] /brī́ ər/, **bri·ar** *n.* a thorny wild plant, especially a trailing rose [Old English *brēr*, of unknown origin] —**bri·er·y** *adj.*

brig /brig/ *n.* **1. SAILING SHIP** a two-masted sailing ship with square-rigged sails on both masts **2. SHIP'S PRISON** a secure area in a ship of the U.S. Navy, which can be used as a prison while the ship is at sea **3. MILITARY PRISON** a building or part of a building that is used as a prison in a U.S. military installation [Early 18thC. Shortening of BRIGANTINE.]

Brig. *abbr.* **1.** brigadier **2.** brigade

bri·gade /bri gáyd/ *n.* **1. MILITARY UNIT** a military unit consisting of two or more combat battalions or regiments and associated support units. It is smaller than a division and is commanded by a brigadier general or a colonel. **2. GROUP WITH COMMON GOAL OR CHARACTERISTIC** a group of people organized to achieve a particular goal, or characterized by a common trait such as attitude, background, appearance, or activities ■ *vt.* **(-gad·ed, -gad·ing, -gades) ORGANIZE INTO A TASK FORCE** to organize a group of people in order to achieve a particular goal [Mid-17thC. Via French from Italian *brigata* "military company," from *brigare* "to contend, brawl," from *briga* "strife," of unknown origin.]

brig·a·dier gen·er·al /brìggə deér/ (*plural* **brig·a·diers gen·er·al**), **brig·a·dier** (*plural* **-diers**) *n.* in the United States and Canada, an officer in the Army, Air Force, or Marines who ranks above a colonel and below a major general

brig·and /bríggənd/ *n.* a bandit operating in wild or isolated terrain, usually as a member of a roving band (*dated*) [14thC. Via Old French from Italian *brigante*, originally "foot-soldier," from the present participle of *brigare* (see BRIGADE).] —**brig·and·age** *n.* —**brig·and·ism** *n.* —**brig·and·ry** *n.*

brig·an·dine /bríggən deèn/ *n.* a coat of flexible medieval body armor consisting of metal links or sheets attached to fabric or leather [15thC. Directly or via Old French from Italian *brigantina*, from *brigante* (see BRIGAND).]

brig·an·tine /bríggən teèn/ *n.* a two-masted sailing ship with square-rigged sails on the foremast and fore-and-aft sails on the mainmast [Early 16thC. Directly or via Old French *brigandine* from Italian *brigantino* "fighting ship," from *brigante* (see BRIGAND).]

Brig. Gen. *abbr.* brigadier general

bright /brīt/ *adj.* **1. SHOWING LIGHT** reflecting or giving off strong light ○ *It was a bright moonlit night.* **2. ILLUMINATED** illuminated with strong natural or artificial light **3. INTENSELY COLORED** intense in color, or decorated with intense colors ○ *bright blue* **4. INTELLIGENT** showing an ability to think, learn, or respond quickly ○ *she was brighter than other children of her age.* **5. CHEERFUL** cheerful and lively ○ *he seems much brighter this morning* **6. PROMISING SUCCESS** promising a successful outcome **7. ADMIRABLE** deserving admiration and glory ○ *one of the brightest stars of the theater* **8. CLEAR SOUNDING** used to describe sounds with a clear crisp quality and little harmonic resonance **9. BEAUTIFUL** remarkably beautiful or handsome (*archaic*) ■ *adv.* **WITH LIGHT** with a great deal of light ■ **brights** *npl.* **HEADLIGHTS** the headlights on a motor vehicle when set to high beam [Old English *beorht*. Ultimately from an Indo-European word meaning "shine."] —**bright·ish** *adj.*

WORD KEY: SYNONYMS

See Synonyms at ***intelligent***.

WORD KEY: CULTURAL NOTE

Bright Lights, Big City, a novel by Jay McInerney (1984). This is a leading example of a type of hip urban fiction that flourished in the 1980s. The hectic yuppy milieu in New York City that it describes, its inhabitants apparently having it all—glamorous careers, easy money, and easier sex—turns out to be unexpectedly fragile, however, and the novel is at heart a chronicle of loss and redemption.

bright·en /brī́t'n/ **(-ened, -en·ing, -ens)** *v.* **1.** *vi.* **LOOK HAPPY** to become enthusiastic, lively, or happy ○ *She brightened visibly at the suggestion.* **2.** *vt.* **ADD INTEREST** to add color or interest to something ○ *their visit brightened the day for us.* **3.** *vi.* **BECOME CLEARER** to become less overcast or rainy ○ *It's going to brighten this afternoon.* **4.** *vti.* **ILLUMINATE OR GET LIGHTER** to increase the amount of light emitted or reflected, or to be filled with an increasing amount of light **5.** *vti.* **MAKE OR BECOME MORE PROMISING** to make something seem more promising or to appear more likely to be successful [Old English *gebeorhtnan*]

brighten up *vti.* to make somebody or something that is dark, colorless, or gloomy become brighter, or to become lighter, more colorful, or livelier

bright·en·er /brī́t'nər/ *n.* *U.K.* a chemical compound added to some soaps and detergents to make white and light-colored fabrics appear brighter by converting some of the ultraviolet radiation into visible light

bright lights *npl.* the entertainment and activities of a big city (*informal*)

bright·ly /brī́tlee/ *adv.* **1. WITH A LOT OF LIGHT** in a way that reflects or gives out a great deal of light **2. CHEERFULLY** in a way that appears happy, alert, and animated ○ *"Shall we go?" said Sam brightly.* **3. VIVIDLY** in vivid and intense colors **4. WITH A CLEAR SOUND** with a clear and crisp sound quality [Old English *beorhtlīce*]

bright neb·u·la *n.* a cloud of material in space that appears bright because it is illuminated by the stars around it

bright·ness /brī́tnəss/ *n.* **1. STRONG LIGHT** the intensity of light reflected or given off by something **2. SMARTNESS** the ability to think, learn, or respond quickly **3. CHEERFUL MANNER** a happy or animated attitude or manner **4. PROMISE OF SUCCESS** the promise of a successful outcome **5. CLARITY** a clear crisp sound quality **6. LIGHT EMITTED IN PARTICULAR DIRECTION** the intensity of light (**luminance**) emitted by an object in a particular direction, used by an observer to compare the luminance of other visible objects **7.** PHYS **ATTRIBUTE OF A COLOR** the attribute of a color that makes its appearance comparable to a standard neutral, such as black, gray, or white [Old English *beorhtnes*]

Brigh·ton /brī́tən/ seaside resort on the English Channel in East Sussex, southern England. Population: 133,400 (1991).

Bright's dis·ease /brī́ts-/ *n.* an inflammatory disease of the kidneys, such as glomerulonephritis (*dated*) [Mid-19thC. Named for the English physician Richard *Bright* (1789–1858), who first diagnosed it.]

bright·work /brī́t wùrk/ *n.* fittings or trimmings of polished metal or varnished wood, e.g., on a vehicle or boat

brill /bril/ (*plural* **brill** *or* **brills**) *n.* an edible European flatfish that is closely related to the turbot. Latin name: *Scophthalmus rhombus.* [15thC. Origin unknown.]

Brill /bril/, **Abraham Arden** (1874–1948) Austrian-born U.S. psychiatrist. He practiced Freudian psychology and advocated using psychoanalysis to treat patients with psychiatric disorders.

Bril·lat-Sa·va·rin /bree yaà saa vaa ráN/, **Anthelme** (1755–1826) French politician and writer. His *Physiology of Taste* (1825) is a classic of gastronomic literature. Full name **Jean Anthelme Brillat-Savarin**

bril·liance /brílyəns/, **bril·lian·cy** /-ənsee/ *n.* **1. BRIGHTNESS** dazzling brightness **2. GREAT ABILITY OR SKILL** exceptional ability, skill, or success ○ *the technical brilliance of the pianist's performance* **3. SPLENDOR** imposing splendor

bril·liant /brílyənt/ *adj.* **1. EXTREMELY BRIGHT OR RADIANT** extremely bright or radiant ○ *brilliant sunshine* **2. VIVID** vividly colored ○ *a brilliant shade of green* **3. INTELLIGENT OR TALENTED** showing exceptional intelligence, skill, or talent ○ *a brilliant mathematician* **4. EXCELLENT** distinguished by excellence **5. MAGNIFICENT** imposing in splendor and magnificence ■ *adj., interj.* **GREAT** used to express great satisfaction with somebody or something (*informal*) ■ *n.* **BRILLIANT-CUT GEMSTONE** a diamond or other gemstone cut with many facets to maximize brilliance [Late 17thC. From French *brillant*, the present participle of *briller* "to shine," from Italian *brillare*, of uncertain origin: perhaps from, ultimately, Latin *berillus* "precious stone" (source of English *beryl*).] —**bril·liant·ly** *adv.* —**bril·liant·ness** *n.*

bril·liant-cut *adj.* used to describe a gemstone that is cut into a multifaceted shape intended to maximize brilliance while minimizing loss of weight. A brilliant-cut gemstone is shaped like two polygonal pyramids joined base to base, with the point of the upper pyramid cut off to form a large flat facet. ○ *a brilliant-cut diamond*

bril·lian·tine /brílyən teèn/ *n.* **1. HAIR OIL** an oily hair cream used by men to keep their hair in place and make it look glossy **2. FABRIC** a lightweight fabric with a lustrous sheen, often made from cotton woven with mohair or worsted [Late 19thC. From French *brillantine*, from *brillant* (see BRILLIANT).]

brim /brim/ *n.* **1. HAT EDGE** the rim around the edge of a hat, shaped to stand out from the head **2. TOP EDGE** the top edge of a container such as a cup or bowl ■ *v.* **(brimmed, brim·ming, brims) 1.** *vti.* **BE FULL TO THE TOP** to fill something or to be full to the top edge ○ *The cup was brimming with hot coffee.* **2.** *vi.* **BURST** to have an apparently boundless supply of something ○ *She was brimming with ideas.* **3.** *vi.* **OVERFLOW** to be so full as to be overflowing ○ *eyes brimming with tears* [13thC. Origin uncertain: perhaps from a prehistoric Germanic base that also produced English *bear* "to carry." It originally meant "edge"; "hat edge" first appears in Shakespeare.] —**brim·less** *adj.*

brim·ful /brím fo͝ol/ *adj.* 1. FULL TO THE TOP full to the top edge of something 2. FULLY SUPPLIED WITH with an apparently boundless supply of something ○ *brimful of energy*

brim·stone /brím stōn/ *n.* sulfur (*archaic*) [12thC. Literally "burning stone," formed from Old English *byrne* "burning," from *birnan* (see BURN).]

brin·dle /brínd'l/ *adj.* = **brindled** ■ *n.* BRINDLED COLORING brindled coloring [Late 17thC. Back-formation from BRINDLED.]

brin·dled /brínd'ld/, **brin·dle** /-d'l/ *adj.* tawny brown or gray marked with darker streaks or patches [Late 17thC. Alteration of earlier *brinded* (influenced by GRIZZLED or SPECKLED), of uncertain origin: probably from a Scandinavian word meaning "marked as by burning."]

brine /brīn/ *n.* 1. SALT WATER FOR PRESERVING water containing a significant amount of salt, used for curing, preserving, and developing flavor in food 2. SEA WATER the salt water of the sea (*literary*) 3. STRONG SALT SOLUTION a strong salt solution ■ *vt.* (**brined, brin·ing, brines**) TREAT SOMETHING WITH SALT WATER to preserve, can, pickle, or soak something in salt water [Old English *brīne*, of unknown origin] —**brin·er** *n.* —**brin·ish** *adj.*

Bri·nell hard·ness /bri nél-/ *n.* the hardness of a metal or alloy, determined by pressing a steel ball into its surface under standard pressure and measuring the surface area of the resulting indentation [Early 20thC. Named for the Swedish engineer Johan A. *Brinell* (1849–1925), who devised the method.]

Bri·nell hard·ness num·ber *n.* a number expressing the hardness of a metal or alloy. It is the ratio of the pressure applied to a steel ball forced into the surface of the metal to the surface area of the resulting indentation.

brine shrimp *n.* a small crustacean that lives in salt lakes and brine pools. Brine shrimp are used as food for aquarium fish. Genus: *Artemia*.

bring /bring/ (**brought** /brawt/, **bring·ing, brings**) *v.* 1. *vt.* TAKE SOMEBODY OR SOMETHING ALONG to come from one place to another with somebody or something ○ *Please bring me a glass of water.* 2. *vt.* ATTRACT SOMETHING to draw something to yourself or another person ○ *This charm is supposed to bring luck.* 3. *vt.* MAKE SOMETHING HAPPEN to cause something to take place ○ *The heavy rain brought flooding.* 4. *vt.* CAUSE TO BE IN A PARTICULAR STATE to force something or somebody to arrive at a particular situation or condition ○ *The scandal brought his career to a halt.* 5. *vt.* CAUSE TO ENTER MIND to cause something to enter somebody's mind ○ *Seeing you brings memories of good times.* 6. *vr.* MAKE YOURSELF DO SOMETHING to persuade or force yourself to do something (*usually with negatives or in questions*) ○ *She still can't bring herself to think about the tragedy.* 7. *vt.* SELL FOR PARTICULAR PRICE to be sold for a particular price 8. *vt.* LAW BEGIN LEGAL ACTION to begin a legal action 9. *vt.* LAW PRESENT EVIDENCE to present evidence before a court [Old English *bringan*. Ultimately from an Indo-European word that also produced English *bier*, *offer*, and *paraphernalia*.] —**bring·er** *n.*

bring about *vt.* to make something happen

bring around, bring *vt.* 1. ALTER OPINION to sway somebody's opinion or thinking ○ *We'll bring them around eventually* 2. REVIVE to revive a person who has lost consciousness

bring back *vt.* 1. EVOKE MEMORIES to evoke memories of something forgotten 2. RESTORE to restore something that has been discontinued ○ *widespread support for bringing back on-the-spot fines*

bring down *vt.* 1. TOPPLE SOMETHING to cause the downfall of an authority or institution 2. KILL OR WOUND to make a person or animal fall by wounding or killing it 3. *Can, ANZ* POL PRESENT A BILL to present a bill or other piece of legislation in a parliament

bring forth *vt.* 1. GIVE BIRTH to bear young 2. PRODUCE FRUIT to produce fruit or flowers

bring forward *vt.* 1. BRING CLOSER IN TIME to move something, e.g., an appointment, to an earlier date or time 2. SUGGEST FOR DISCUSSION OR CONSIDERATION to offer something for discussion or consideration 3. ACCT CARRY AMOUNT TO NEXT PAGE to carry a sum from one column or page to the next

bring in *vt.* 1. INTRODUCE SOMETHING to introduce something, e.g., a new policy or law 2. EARN OR ACQUIRE SOMETHING to acquire money as profits, pay, or interest ○ *She barely brings in enough to live on.* 3. LAW PRESENT SOMETHING IN COURT to present something in a court of law 4. GET OIL WELL TO PRODUCE to cause an oil well to begin producing oil 5. INTRODUCE FOR CONSIDERATION to introduce something for consideration

bring off *vt.* 1. COMPLETE SOMETHING to succeed in doing something difficult 2. to cause somebody to have an orgasm (*slang taboo*)

bring on *vt.* 1. CAUSE to be the cause of something happening or appearing ○ *exhaustion brought on by overwork* 2. ENCOURAGE DEVELOPMENT to further the development of a quality, or of the person having it 3. MAKE SOMEBODY OR SOMETHING APPEAR to cause somebody or something to appear

bring out *vt.* 1. MAKE KNOWN to make something known 2. CALL ATTENTION TO to emphasize a quality in somebody or something ○ *That outfit brings out the red in your hair.* 3. INTRODUCE FOR SALE to produce or issue something for sale to the public ○ *The company has just brought out a new version.* 4. INTRODUCE TO SOCIETY to introduce a debutante to society

bring to *vt.* 1. REVIVE to restore somebody to consciousness 2. NAUT TURN SHIP INTO WIND to head a boat or ship into the wind in order to slow it down or stop it

bring up *vt.* 1. RAISE SUBJECT to raise a subject for discussion 2. REAR A CHILD to provide care, training, and education for a child until maturity 3. MAKE SOMETHING STOP SUDDENLY to cause somebody or something to come to a standstill 4. VOMIT to cough something up or to expel it from the stomach through the mouth

brink /bringk/ *n.* 1. VERGE OF SOMETHING CRUCIAL the crucial point in a situation when something disastrous or momentous is about to happen ○ *teetering on the brink of bankruptcy* 2. EDGE OF SOMETHING the very edge of something, e.g., a steep drop or a riverbank [13thC. From Old Norse *brekka*, literally "slope."]

brink·man·ship /bríngkmən shìp/, **brinks·man·ship** /bríngksmən-/ *n.* the practice, especially in international relations, of taking a dispute to the verge of conflict in the hope of forcing the opposition to make concessions

brin·y /brínee/ *adj.* (**-i·er, -i·est**) OF SEA WATER relating to, containing, or tasting like sea water ■ *n. U.K.* SEA the sea —**brin·i·ness** *n.*

bri·o /brée ō/ *n.* energy or vigor (*literary*) [Mid-18thC. From Italian.]

bri·oche /bree ósh/ *n.* a sweet French bread roll made from a dough enriched with eggs and butter [Early 19thC. From French, formed from Old French *brier* "to knead."]

bri·o·lette /brée ə lét/ *n.* a gem in the shape of a teardrop or oval that is cut with long triangular facets over its entire surface [Mid-19thC. From French, of uncertain origin: perhaps, in allusion to its shape, an alteration of *brignolette* "little dried plum," named for the French city *Brignoles*, where the plums are produced.]

bri·quette /bri két/, **bri·quet** *n.* a small block of compressed material, e.g., charcoal, sawdust, or coal dust, that is burned as fuel for cooking or heating [Late 19thC. From French, literally "little brick," formed from *brique* (see BRICK).]

bris /briss/, **brith** /brith, brit/ *n.* the religious circumcision ceremony for Jewish males [Early 20thC. From Hebrew *berīṯ (mīlāh)*, literally "covenant (of circumcision)."]

Bris·bane /brízbən/ city on the Brisbane River and the capital of Queensland, eastern Australia. Population: 1,291,117 (1996).

brisk /brisk/ *adj.* 1. QUICK done quickly and energetically ○ *a brisk walk* 2. HURRIED speaking or behaving in an abrupt way ○ *a brisk reply* 3. BUSY showing or experiencing much activity ○ *business was brisk* 4. INVIGORATING refreshingly cool ○ *brisk autumn days* [Late 16thC. Origin uncertain: probably from French *brusque* (see BRUSQUE).] —**brisk·ly** *adv.* —**brisk·ness** *n.*

bris·ket /brískit/ *n.* 1. BREAST OF ANIMAL the breast of a four-legged animal 2. BREAST MEAT a cut of meat, especially of beef, taken from an animal's breast [14thC. Origin uncertain: perhaps formed from Old Norse *brjósk* "cartilage, gristle."]

bris·ling /brízzling, bríss-/ (*plural* **-ling** *or* **-lings**) *n.* a small edible fish of the herring family that is smoked and canned in oil or tomato sauce. Latin name: *Clupea sprattus*. [Early 20thC. From Norwegian or Danish.]

bris·tle /bríss'l/ *n.* 1. STIFF HAIR a short stiff hair on an animal or plant or a mass of short stiff hairs growing, e.g., on a hog's back or a man's face 2. HAIR ON BRUSH the short stiff natural or synthetic hair on a brush ■ *v.* (**-tled, -tling, -tles**) 1. *vti.* HAVE OR SET HAIR ON END to make the hair or fur stand upright in response to fear or anger, or to show such a response 2. *vi.* BECOME OFFENDED BY SOMETHING to react somewhat angrily or indignantly to something or somebody ○ *He bristled at the suggestion.* 3. *vi.* HAVE LARGE AMOUNT to have an abundance of something ○ *a mighty battleship bristling with guns* 4. *vt.* GIVE SOMETHING BRISTLES to provide or cover something with bristles [13thC. Formed from Old English *byrst* "bristle." Ultimately from an Indo-European word that also produced German *Borste* "bristle."]

bris·tle·cone pine /bríss'l kōn-/ *n.* a small pine tree with bristly cones, native to California. Bristlecone pines are the longest-living trees in the world. Genus: *Pinus*. [Late 19thC. From the prickles on its cones.]

bris·tle·tail /bríss'l tàyl/ (*plural* **-tails** *or* **-tail**) *n.* a wingless insect that has a long segmented abdomen with two or three long bristles at the end. Order: Thysanura.

bris·tling /bríssling/ *adj.* 1. WITH MANY BRISTLES thick with stiff hairs 2. ANGRY OR INDIGNANT reacting with anger and indignation

bris·tly /brísslee/ (**-tli·er, -tli·est**) *adj.* 1. ROUGH WITH BRISTLES prickly and rough with bristles 2. EASILY ANGERED quick to anger —**bris·tli·ness** *n.*

Bris·tol /bríst'l/ 1. city in central Connecticut, northeast of Waterbury and southwest of Hartford. Population: 59,619 (1996). 2. town and port in eastern Rhode Island, on a peninsula reaching into Narragansett Bay. Population: 21,958 (1996). 3. city in northeastern Tennessee, on the Tennessee-Virginia border, northeast of Johnson City. Population: 23,275 (1996). 4. city in Virginia, southwest of Abington, opposite Bristol, Tennessee. Population: 17,957 (1996). 5. university city and seaport on the Avon River in southwestern England. Population: 400,700 (1995).

Bris·tol board *n.* a type of fine smooth lightweight cardboard used in design and drawing [Early 19thC. Named after the English city and port *Bristol*, where it was first manufactured.]

brit /brit/ (*plural* **brits** *or* **brit**) *n.* 1. YOUNG HERRING the young form of some fish including the herring and the sprat 2. WHALE FOOD a mass of tiny marine organisms, especially crustaceans, that is a source of food for whalebone whales and some fish [Early 17thC. Origin unknown.]

Brit /brit/ *n.* a British person (*informal*) [Early 20thC. Shortening.]

Brit. *abbr.* Britain ■ *abbr.* British

Brit·ain /brítt'n/ 1. island in the Atlantic Ocean off the northwestern coast of Europe, including England, Scotland, and Wales. Area: 244,101 sq. km/94,248 sq. mi. 2. = **Great Britain, United Kingdom**

Bri·tan·nia /bri tánnyə/ *n.* 1. SYMBOL OF BRITAIN the personification and symbol of Britain, shown as a seated woman wearing a helmet and holding a trident 2. SOUTHERN ANCIENT BRITAIN the name given by the Romans to the southern part of Great Britain at the time of the Roman Empire 3. **Bri·tan·nia, bri·tan·nia** = **Britannia metal** [Pre-12thC. From Latin *Brit(t)annia*.]

Bri·tan·nia met·al, bri·tan·nia met·al *n.* an alloy of tin, antimony, and copper that is similar to pewter and is used for decorative items and for bearings

Bri·tan·nic /bri tánnik/ *adj.* belonging to Britain ○ *Her Britannic Majesty*

britch·es /bríchəz/ *npl.* = **breeches** ◇ **too big for your britches** behaving in a self-important manner

brith *n.* JUDAISM = **bris**

Brit·i·cism /brítti sìzzəm/ *n.* something, e.g., a word or custom, that is characteristic of the British or of Britain [Mid-19thC. Formed from BRITISH, on the model of SCOTTICISM or GALLICISM.]

Brit·ish /bríttish/ *n.* 1. PEOPLE OF UNITED KINGDOM the people of the United Kingdom of Great Britain and Northern Ireland 2. = **British English** 3. LANGUAGE OF ANCIENT BRITONS the language spoken by the ancient Celtic people who lived in southern Britain ■ *adj.* 1. OF UNITED KINGDOM relating to or typical of the United Kingdom of Great Britain and Northern Ireland, or its peoples or cultures 2. RELATING TO ANCIENT BRITONS relating to or typical of the ancient Britons or their culture [Pre-12thC. Originally *Brettisc*, from *Bret* "ancient Briton," directly or via Latin *Britto* from a Celtic word.]

British Columbia

Brit·ish Co·lum·bi·a westernmost province of Canada, situated on the Pacific coast, north of the U.S. border, west of Alberta, and south of Yukon Territory and the Northwest Territories. Capital: Victoria. Population: 3,724,500 (1996). Area: 365,946 sq. mi./947,800 sq. km.

Brit·ish Com·mon·wealth of Na·tions *n.* = **Commonwealth of Nations**

Brit·ish Em·pire *n.* a group of colonies, protectorates, and other territories brought under British rule after the late 16th century, and by the 19th century comprising more than one-quarter of the world's population. Most of Britain's former colonies became independent after World War II, and as sovereign states, many joined the Commonwealth.

Brit·ish Eng·lish *n.* the form of English used by people in Great Britain, as opposed to the form used in other English-speaking countries

WORD KEY: WORLD ENGLISH

British English is the English language as used in the United Kingdom of Great Britain (England, Scotland, and Wales) and Northern Ireland. With a population of over 57 million, the United Kingdom is the second largest primary English-speaking country after the United States, and it continues to have prestige as the place of origin of the English language. The term British English is not, however, precise, being variously used to refer to: all varieties of English in the U.K. as a whole; all varieties in Britain as a whole; all varieties in England alone; the forms of only the standard language in the U.K. as a whole; those forms in Britain as a whole; those forms in England alone; and, notably, that variety of the standard language based on upper- and middle-class usage (especially at the turn of the 20th century in southeastern England). See also ***American English, Australian English.***

Brit·ish·er /bríttishər/ *n.* a British subject or a person from Britain (*informal*)

Brit·ish Gui·a·na former name for **Guyana**

Brit·ish Hon·du·ras former name for **Belize**

Brit·ish In·di·a *n.* The part of the Indian subcontinent under British administration from 1765 to 1947, when the independent states of India and Pakistan were created

Brit·ish In·di·an O·cean Ter·ri·to·ry a British overseas territory in the Indian Ocean, consisting of five uninhabited coral islands, the largest of which is Diego Garcia. Area: 23 sq. mi./60 sq. km.

Brit·ish Isles group of islands in the northeastern Atlantic separated from mainland Europe by the North Sea and English Channel. It consists of the large islands of Great Britain and Ireland and almost 5,000 surrounding smaller islands and islets.

Brit·ish Li·brar·y *n.* the United Kingdom's national library in London that contains books, sound recordings, and manuscripts brought together from various national collections, e.g., the British Museum

Brit·ish So·ma·li·land /-/ former British protectorate in East Africa from 1884 until 1960, when it united with Italian Somaliland to form the republic of Somalia

Brit·ish ther·mal u·nit *n.* the amount of heat needed to raise the temperature of one pound of water by one degree Fahrenheit, equal to approximately 1055 joules

Brit·on /brítt'n/ *n.* **1. BRITISH PERSON** somebody who was born or raised in Great Britain, or who is a citizen of Great Britain **2. INHABITANT OF ANCIENT BRITAIN** a member of the ancient Celtic people who once lived in southern Britain [13thC. Via French *Breton* from the Latin stem *Britton-*, ultimately of Celtic origin.]

brit·ska *n.* = **britzka**

Brit·tain /brítt'n/, **Vera** (1893–1970) British writer. Her World War I memoir *Testament of Youth* (1933) speaks for a generation of young people whose lives were forever changed by the experience of war. Full name **Vera Mary Brittain**

Brit·ta·ny /brítt'nee/ peninsular region in northwestern France, between the Bay of Biscay and the English Channel. The region's capital is Rennes. Population: 2,795,600 (1990). Area: 10,505 sq. mi./27,208 sq. km.

Brit·ten /brítt'n/, **Benjamin** (1913–76) British composer. Regarded as one of the finest of British composers of the 20th century, he wrote major choral works including the operas *Peter Grimes* (1945) and *Billy Budd* (1951) and the *War Requiem* (1962). Full name **Edward Benjamin Britten**

brit·tle /brítt'l/ *adj.* **1. HARD AND BREAKABLE** hard and likely to break or crack ○ *plastic that has become brittle with age.* **2. SHARP-SOUNDING** having a sharp, unnerving quality or tone **3. NOT LASTING** lacking durability or permanence **4. NOT FRIENDLY** lacking personal warmth ○ *a brittle quality to her that I didn't like* **5. IRRITABLE** easily irritated or annoyed ■ *n.* **TOFFEE NUT CANDY** a crunchy candy made from caramel and nuts [14thC. Formed from Old English *gebryttan* "to shatter."] — **brit·tle·ly** *adv.* —**brit·tle·ness** *n.*

brit·tle-bone dis·ease *n. U.K.* **1.** = **osteoporosis 2.** = **osteogenesis imperfecta**

brit·tle·bush /brítt'l bòosh/ (*plural* **-bush·es** *or* **-bush**) *n.* a shrub of North American deserts, with brittle gray leaves and yellow flowers. Latin name: *Encelia farinosa.*

brit·tle star *n.* a marine animal similar to a starfish but with thinner, longer, and more flexible arms that can be regenerated if broken off. Class: Ophiuroidea. [From its brittle arms]

Brit·ton·ic *adj., n.* = **Brythonic** [Early 20thC. Formed from the Latin stem *Britton-* (see BRITON).]

brit·zka /brítskə/, **brit·ska** *n.* a horse-drawn carriage with a rear-facing front seat and a folding top over the back seat [Early 19thC. From Polish *bryczka.*]

Brix scale /bríks-/ *n.* a scale used in a hydrometer for measuring the sugar content of a solution at a particular temperature [Late 19thC. Named for its inventor, the German scientist Adolf S. *Brix* (1798–1890).]

bro /brō/ *n.* a brother (*informal*)

bro., **Bro.** *abbr.* brother

broach /brōch/ *v.* (**broached, broach·ing, broach·es**) **1.** *vt.* **BRING UP DIFFICULT SUBJECT** to introduce a subject for discussion, usually one that is awkward ○ *He finally broached the question of the loan* **2.** *vt.* **OPEN SOMETHING** to open a container for the first time ○ *broach a bottle of wine* **3.** *vt.* **PIERCE CASK** to make a hole in a cask to draw off liquid **4.** *vt.* **BORE HOLE** to make or enlarge a hole in something **5.** *vi.* NAVY **COME UP THROUGH SURFACE OF WATER** to break the surface of water from below without completely emerging (*refers to a submarine*) **6.** *vi.* NAUT **TURN SIDEWAYS TO THE WIND** to be turned broadside to the wind, e.g., by heavy seas, with a risk of capsizing ■ *n.* **1. TOOL FOR ENLARGING HOLES** a tool for enlarging holes **2. ROASTING SPIT** a roasting spit **3. TOOL FOR PIERCING CASKS** a tool used for making holes in casks **4.** = **brooch** [14thC. From Old French *brocher* "to stitch," from *broche* "skewer, long needle." The meaning "introduce a subject" evolved from "pierce" via "tap a barrel."] —**broach·er** *n.*

broad /brawd/ *adj.* **1. VERY WIDE** large from one side to the other ○ *a broad forehead* **2. LARGE AND SPACIOUS** extending a great distance in all directions ○ *the broad plains of the Steppes* **3. MEASURED ACROSS** measured from side to side ○ *as broad as it is long* **4. FULL AND CLEAR** full and clear to see ○ *a broad grin* ○ *broad daylight* **5. COVERING A WIDE RANGE** comprehensive in content, knowledge, experience, ability, or application ○ *She has very broad interests.* **6. NOT DETAILED** general, rather than detailed ○ *I'll give you a broad outline of the project.* **7. WIDESPREAD OR GENERALIZED** widespread or generalized throughout a large and diverse group of people ○ *a broad feeling of disillusionment in the party* **8. OBVIOUS** meant to be easily understood ○ *dropping broad hints about their plans* **9. UNOBSTRUCTED** with nothing blocking the way **10. TOLERANT** tending to tolerate or accept rather than to condemn the ideas and conduct of other people ○ *I think I have fairly broad views on the whole.* **11. POTENTIALLY OFFENSIVE** potentially offensive to accepted standards of propriety **12.** LING **STRONGLY REGIONAL** used to describe a regional accent that is very strong or pronounced **13.** PHON used to describe a phonetic transcription that gives only major differences **14.** LING **PRONOUNCED WITH THE TONGUE DOWN** used to describe a vowel pronounced with the tongue low and flat and the mouth open wide ■ *n.* **1. WIDE PART** the wide part of something ○ *He slapped Jack across the broad of his back.* **2. OFFENSIVE TERM** an offensive term for a woman (*slang offensive*) ■ *adv.* **COMPLETELY** to the fullest extent [Old English *brād.* Ultimately from a prehistoric Germanic word that is also the ancestor of German *breit* "broad."] —**broad·ness** *n.* ◇ **in broad daylight** in open daylight for all to see

broad ar·row *n.* an arrow with a wide barbed head

broad·ax /bráwd àks/ *n.* a heavy battleax with a wide blade

broad·band /bráwd bànd/ *adj.* **1.** PHYS **COVERING MANY FREQUENCIES** using a wide range of electromagnetic frequencies **2.** COMPUT **TRANSFERRING DATA FAST** capable of transferring large amounts of data at high speed

broad bean *n.* **1. BEAN PLANT** a plant grown worldwide for its large flat edible seeds. Latin name: *Vicia faba.* **2. LARGE EDIBLE BEAN SEED** the large green seed of the broad bean plant, cooked and eaten as a vegetable

broad·bill /bráwd bìl/ (*plural* **-bills** *or* **-bill**) *n.* a tropical African or Asian bird with brightly colored feathers and a short broad bill. Family: Eurylaemidae.

broad-brush *adj.* attempting to cover all conditions and instances ○ *a broad-brush approach*

broad·cast /bráwd kàst/ *v.* (**-cast** *or* **-cast·ed, -cast·ing, -casts**) **1.** *vti.* **TRANSMIT RADIO SIGNALS** to transmit a program or information on television or radio **2.** *vi.* **BE ON TELEVISION OR RADIO** to take part in a radio or television program **3.** *vt.* **MAKE SOMETHING WIDELY KNOWN** to make something widely known ○ *They broadcast the rumors all over town.* **4.** *vt.* **SCATTER SEED** to sow seed by scattering it ■ *n.* **1. PROGRAM** a television or radio program **2. TRANSMISSION** a transmission of radio or television signals **3. SCATTERING SEED** a sowing of seed by scattering it ■ *adj.* **1. FOR BROADCASTING ON TELEVISION OR RADIO** relating to, suitable for, or transmitted by radio or television **2. SCATTERED WIDELY** scattered widely ■ *adv.* **WIDELY** over a wide area [Mid-18thC. The meaning "to transmit" evolved from the idea of scattering seeds widely.]

WORD KEY: SYNONYMS

See Synonyms at ***scatter.***

broad·cast·er /bráwd kàstər/ *n.* a person who regularly takes part in television or radio programs, especially news or talk shows

broad·cast·ing /bráwd kàsting/ *n.* the making and transmission of television and radio programs

broad·cloth /bráwd klàwth/ *n.* **1. FINE WOVEN CLOTH** a fine, closely woven cloth of wool, cotton, or silk with a shiny finish, used for clothing **2. PLAIN-WEAVE WOOL FABRIC** a woolen fabric with a plain weave, smooth finish, and dense texture, originally of double width [15thC. From the specification of cloth 2 yds. (1.8 m) wide as "broad cloth" in an English Act of Parliament of 1482.]

broad·en /bráwd'n/ (**-ened, -en·ing, -ens**) *vti.* **1. WIDEN SOMETHING** to make something wider or to become wider **2. ENLARGE RANGE OF SOMETHING** to enlarge the range or magnitude of something, or to become more wide-ranging

broad gauge *n.* a railroad track that has a distance between the rails that is greater than the standard 56.5 in./143.5 cm. Broad gauge allows greater passenger comfort and carrying capacity but increases the cost of construction.

broad-gauge *adj.* **1. FOR BROAD GAUGE** relating to or designed for a railroad using broad gauge **2. WIDE-RANGING** wide in application or range

broad jump *n.* a long jump in track-and-field sports (*dated*)

broad·leaf /bráwd leef/ *n.* (*plural* **-leaves** /-leevz/ *or* **-leaf**) **TOBACCO PLANT WITH BROAD LEAVES** a tobacco plant that has broad leaves suitable for making cigars ■ *adj.* = **broad-leaved**

broad-leaved, **broad·leaf, broad-leafed** *adj.* used to describe trees that have wide leaves rather than leaves that are like pine needles. Broad-leaved plants can be evergreen, such as holly, or deciduous, such as maple.

broad·loom /bráwd lòom/ *adj.* **WOVEN ON WIDE LOOM** used to describe carpet that is woven on a wide loom ■ *n.* **WIDE SEAMLESS CARPET** a carpet woven on a wide loom that can be laid with few or no seams

broad·ly /bráwdlee/ *adv.* **1. GENERALLY** in general terms, not allowing for exceptions ○ *Broadly speaking, there are two types of tourists.* **2. MOSTLY** for the most part ○ *It is broadly based on the German prototype.* **3. WITH AN ENTHUSIASTIC SMILE** with a smile that shows great enthusiasm or friendliness ○ *smiling broadly*

broad-mind·ed *adj.* willing to tolerate a wide range of ideas and behavior —**broad-mind·ed·ly** *adv.* —**broad-mind·ed·ness** *n.*

broad·sheet /bráwd sheet/ *n.* = **broadside** *n.* 5

broad·side /bráwd sīd/ *vt.* **(-sid·ed, -sid·ing, -sides) HIT SIDE OF SOMETHING** to collide with the side of something ○ *The car was broadsided by the train.* ■ *n.* **1. LARGE FLAT SURFACE** a large flat and usually vertical surface ○ *the broadside of the barn* **2.** NAUT **SHIP'S SIDE** the side of a ship above the waterline from bow to quarter **3.** NAVY **SHIP'S GUNS AND GUNFIRE** all the guns on one side of a ship or the simultaneous firing of them **4. STRONG VERBAL OR WRITTEN ATTACK** a strong verbal or written attack on somebody ○ *a vicious broadside on the President* **5.** PRINTING **LARGE PAPER FOR PRINTING** a large sheet of paper that is printed on one side, or something, such as an advertisement, that is printed on one side of a large sheet of paper ■ *adv.* **1. FROM THE SIDE** with the side facing toward something ○ *The ship hit the rocks broadside on.* **2. WITH NO APPARENT OBJECTIVE** with no apparent objective ○ *Her proposals were attacked broadside.*

broad-spec·trum *adj.* used to describe antibiotics and other chemicals that destroy a wide range of organisms, e.g., bacteria and agricultural pests

broad·sword /bráwd sàwrd/ *n.* a sword with a wide flat blade designed for cutting rather than for thrusting [Old English]

broad·tail /bráwd tàyl/ *n.* **1. BLACK WAVY LAMBSWOOL** the black wavy fur or pelt of a prematurely born karakul lamb **2.** = **karakul** *n.* 1

Broad·way /bráwd wày/ *n.* **1. AVENUE IN NEW YORK CITY** a long avenue extending north and south through the borough of Manhattan in New York City. Part of it is the main thoroughfare of the city's theater district. **2.** **U.S. THEATER** used to refer to the commercial theater business in the United States ○ *This is not Broadway material.*

broad-winged hawk *n.* a common woodland hawk of eastern North America with broad wings that are white on the underside and a broadly banded tail. Latin name: *Buteo platypterus.*

Brob·ding·nag·i·an /bròbding nággee ən/ *adj.* extraordinarily large (*literary*) [Early 18thC. Formed from *Brobdingnag*, name of a fictitious land of giants in Jonathan Swift's *Gulliver's Travels* (1726).]

bro·cade /brō káyd/ *n.* **FABRIC WITH RAISED DESIGN** a heavy fabric of silk, cotton, or wool woven with a raised design, often using metallic threads. A true brocade is based on one or two basic colors with additional colored threads brought from the back to the front to produce the raised design. ■ *vt.* **(-cad·ed, -cad·ing, -cades) WEAVE FABRIC WITH RAISED DESIGN** to weave fabric with a raised design [Late 16thC. Via Spanish or Portuguese *brocado* from Italian *broccato*, from *brocco* "twisted thread, shoot," from, ultimately, Latin *brocchus* (see BROACH).] —**bro·cad·ed** *adj.*

broc·a·tel /bròkə tél/ *n.* a heavy fabric with raised designs, used chiefly in upholstery [Mid-17thC. Via French from Italian *broccatello* "gold tinsel," literally "small brocade," from *broccato* (see BROCADE).]

broc·co·li /brókəlee/ *n.* **1. PLANT WITH EDIBLE FLOWER HEAD** a plant of the cabbage family with green, purple, or white flower heads that are cooked and eaten as a vegetable. Heading broccoli has green flower heads like cauliflowers and sprouting broccoli has multiple small purple or white flowering shoots. Latin name: *Brassica oleracea italica.* **2. EDIBLE FLOWER HEAD** the flower head of the broccoli plant, eaten as a vegetable before the flowers have opened [Mid-17thC. From Italian, the plural of *broccolo* "cabbage sprout," from

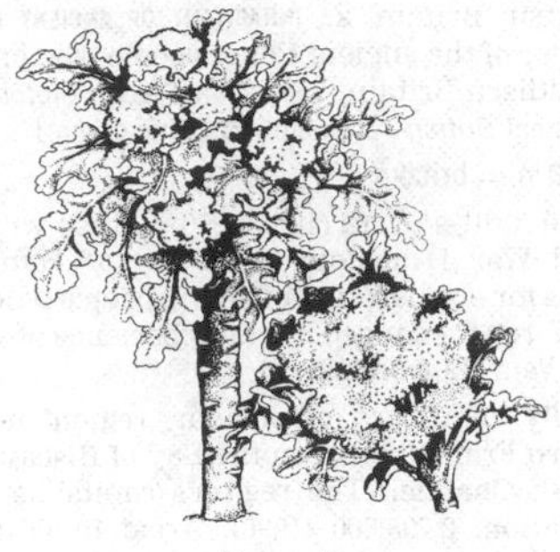

Broccoli

brocco "shoot," from, ultimately, Latin *brocchus* (see BROACH).]

bro·ché /brō sháy/ *adj.* woven with a raised pattern [Late 19thC. From French, the past participle of *brocher* (see BROACH).]

bro·chette /brō shét/ *n.* **1. KEBAB SKEWER** a small skewer on which chunks of food are broiled or roasted **2. SKEWERED FOOD** food, e.g., meat or fish, that has been cooked on a brochette [15thC. From French, literally "little skewer," formed from *broche* (see BROACH).]

bro·chure /brō shóor/ *n.* a booklet or pamphlet that contains descriptive information or advertising [Mid-18thC. From French, literally "something stitched together," formed from *brocher* (see BROACH).]

Brock /brok/, **Sir Isaac** (1769–1812) British-born Canadian soldier. He was a military commander during the War of 1812.

Brock·ton /bráaktən/ city in southeastern Massachusetts, a southern suburb of Boston, northeast of Taunton. Population: 92,234 (1996).

bro·der·ie ang·laise /brōdəree ong gláyz/ *n.* embroidery in the form of an ornamental pattern of small holes with stitched edges [Mid-19thC. From French, literally "English embroidery."]

Brod·sky /bródskee/, **Joseph** (1940–96) Soviet-born U.S. poet and essayist. He won the Nobel Prize in literature (1987) and was U.S. poet laureate (1991–92).

bro·gan /brṓgən/ *n.* a heavy ankle-high work boot [Mid-19thC. From Irish or Scots Gaelic *brōgan*, literally "little shoe," from *brōg* (see BROGUE[2]).]

brogue[1] /brōg/ *n.* a regional accent, especially the accent of Irish people speaking English [Early 18thC. Origin uncertain: perhaps from BROGUE[2], in allusion to the footwear of Irish or Scottish speakers.]

brogue[2] /brōg/ *n.* **1.** = **wing tip 2. IRISH OR SCOTTISH SHOE** a simple heavy untanned shoe formerly worn in Ireland and Scotland [Late 16thC. Via Irish and Scots Gaelic *brōg* from Old Norse *brók* "leg covering."]

broi·der /bróydər/ **(-dered, -der·ing, -ders)** *vti.* to embroider (*archaic*) [14thC. From Old French *brosder*; ultimately from a prehistoric Germanic word.]

broil[1] /broyl/ *v.* **(broiled, broil·ing, broils) 1.** *vt.* **COOK USING DIRECT HEAT** to cook food by using direct heat **2.** *vti.* **BE VERY HOT** to make somebody or something extremely hot or to be extremely hot ○ *We had been broiling in the sun all morning.* **3.** *vi.* **BE VERY ANGRY** to be extremely angry ■ *n.* **1. USE OF DIRECT HEAT** a use of direct heat to cook something **2. BROILED FOOD** a food cooked using direct heat [14thC. From Old French *bruler*, of uncertain origin: perhaps based ultimately on Latin *ustulare* "to burn up," from the past participle of *urere* "to burn."]

broil[2] /broyl/ *n.* **BRAWL** a brawl (*archaic*) ■ *vi.* **(broiled, broil·ing, broils) TAKE PART IN BRAWL** to engage in a brawl (*archaic*) [15thC. Via Anglo-Norman *broiller* "to mix up, confuse" from Old French *brōoillier*, from *breu* "broth."]

broil·er /bróylər/ *n.* **1. ROASTING CHICKEN** a young chicken for roasting **2. GRATE FOR BROILING FOOD** a pan or grate on which to broil food **3. STOVE COMPARTMENT FOR BROILING** a part of a stove or oven in which to broil food **4. HOT DAY** a very hot day (*informal*)

broke[1] past tense of **break**

broke[2] /brōk/ *adj.* (*informal*) **1. HAVING NO MONEY** without any money to spend **2. BANKRUPT** totally bankrupt [Early 18thC. Alteration of BROKEN.] ◇ **go for broke** to risk everything to achieve a goal (*informal*)

bro·ken[1] past participle of **break**

bro·ken[2] /brṓkən/ *adj.* **1. NO LONGER WHOLE** in two or more pieces, e.g., after having been dropped or struck with something hard **2. OUT OF ORDER** no longer in working condition ○ *The CD player is broken.* **3. NOT KEPT** not honored or fulfilled ○ *a broken promise* **4. NOT CONTINUOUS** lacking continuity **5. UNEVEN** having an uneven surface ○ *We traveled over broken terrain.* **6. WEAK** physically weakened ○ *his health was broken* **7. DESTROYED BY ADVERSITY** destroyed or badly hurt by grief or misfortune **8. SPLIT APART** split apart by divorce, separation, or desertion **9. INCOMPLETE** lacking parts necessary to be complete ○ *a broken set of books* **10. DISORGANIZED** lacking order or harmony ○ *escaping in broken ranks* **11.** LANGUAGE **IMPERFECTLY SPOKEN** spoken in an imperfect or halting manner [Old English *brocen*]

Bro·ken Ar·row city in northeastern Oklahoma, a southeastern suburb of Tulsa. Population: 69,175 (1996).

bro·ken chord *n.* a chord played as a quick succession of notes (**arpeggio**) rather than simultaneously

bro·ken con·sort *n.* a musical ensemble made up of instruments of different types, used especially in music of the Renaissance

bro·ken-down *adj.* **1. NOT WORKING** damaged or not working ○ *a broken-down old machine* **2. DILAPIDATED** in very poor condition

bro·ken-field *adj.* FOOTBALL making quick changes in direction while carrying the ball downfield in order to avoid widely scattered opposing players ○ *broken-field running* [From the discontinuous defense line]

bro·ken·heart·ed /brṓkən haártəd/ *adj.* extremely sad, e.g., after bereavement, great disappointment, or the end of a love affair —**bro·ken·heart·ed·ly** *adv.* —**bro·ken·heart·ed·ness** *n.*

bro·ken-wind·ed *adj.* used to describe a horse that is suffering from the lung disease COPD

bro·ker /brṓkər/ *n.* **1. COMMERCIAL AGENT** a person who is paid to act as an agent for others, e.g., in negotiating contracts or buying and selling goods and services **2.** = **stockbroker 3.** = **power broker** ■ *vt.* **(-kered, -ker·ing, -kers) ARRANGE DEAL OR SALE** to act as an agent in arranging a deal, sale, or contract [14thC. From Anglo-Norman *brocour* "small trader," of uncertain origin: perhaps via Portuguese *alborcar* "to barter" from, ultimately, Arabic; alternatively, formed from Old French *brocher* (see BROACH).]

bro·ker·age /brṓkərij/ *n.* **1. PAYMENT TO A BROKER** a fee paid to somebody who acts as a financial agent for somebody else **2. BROKER'S BUSINESS** the business of being a broker **3. STOCKBROKER'S BUSINESS** a company whose business is buying and selling stocks and bonds for its clients

brom- *prefix.* bromine, bromic ○ *bromate* [From BROMINE and BROMIDE]

bro·mate /brṓ màyt/ *n.* **CHEMICAL COMPOUND OF BROMIC ACID** a salt, ester, or ion of bromic acid ■ *vt.* **(-mat·ed, -mat·ing, -mates)** = **brominate** [Mid-19thC. Coined from BROMIC + -ATE.]

brome·grass /brṓm gràss/, **brome** *n.* a tall grass with small drooping flower spikes that grows in temperate regions. Some types of bromegrass are cultivated for hay, while others are weeds. Genus: *Bromus.*

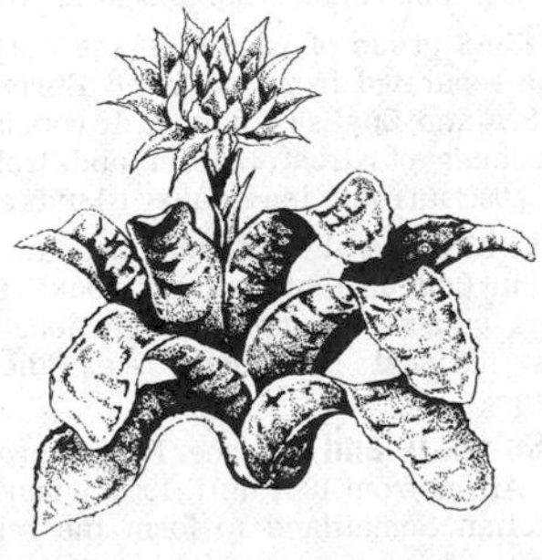

Bromeliad

bro·me·li·ad /brō méelee àd/ *n.* a tropical American plant with fleshy leaves forming a funnel that holds water. Many bromeliads grow on other plants for physical support. Family: Bromeliaceae. [Mid-19thC. Named for the Swedish botanist Olaf *Bromel* (1639–1705).]

bro·mic /brṓmik/ *adj.* relating to or containing bromine with a valence of five

bro·mic ac·id *n.* an unstable colorless acid that is a strong oxidizing agent and is used in the manufacture of pharmaceuticals and dyes. Formula: $HBrO_3$.

bro·mide /brṓ mīd/ *n.* **1.** CHEM **BROMINE COMPOUND** a chemical compound that contains bromine and another element or group, e.g., silver bromide **2.** CHEM **POTASSIUM BROMIDE** potassium bromide, especially when used as a sedative **3. UNORIGINAL SAYING** a saying that lacks originality or significance (*dated*) **4. UNINTERESTING PERSON** a tedious or uninteresting person

bro·mide pa·per *n.* a light-sensitive photographic paper that is coated with silver bromide emulsion

bro·mid·ic /brō míddik/ *adj.* without originality or interest

bro·mi·nate /brṓmi nàyt/ (**-nat·ed, -nat·ing, -nates**) *vt.* to treat or combine a substance with bromine or a bromine compound —**bro·mi·na·tion** /brṓmi náysh'n/ *n.*

bro·mine /brṓ meen/ *n.* a pungent dark red volatile liquid that is a nonmetallic chemical element of the halogen series and is used in sedatives and photographic materials. Symbol **Br** [Early 19thC. Coined from French *brome* (from Greek *brōmos* "stench") + -INE.]

bro·mism /brṓ mizzəm/ *n.* a condition caused by overuse of bromide medications and marked by memory problems, dullness, drowsiness, and loss of muscular coordination

bronc /brongk/ *n.* a bronco (*informal*) [Late 19thC. Shortening.]

bronch- *prefix.* = **broncho-**

bron·chi plural of **bronchus**

bron·chi·al /bróngkee əl/ *adj.* relating to or affecting the tubes (**bronchi**) that carry air from the windpipe into the lungs ○ *a bronchial infection* —**bron·chi·al·ly** *adv.*

bron·chi·al pneu·mo·nia *n.* = **bronchopneumonia**

bron·chi·al tube *n.* a tubular passage forming part of a network of airways to and within the lungs. Two main tubes (**bronchi**) lead from the windpipe to each lung, dividing into smaller bronchi and subsequently bronchioles.

bron·chi·ec·ta·sis /bròngkee éktəssiss/ *n.* chronic dilation of the airways to and within the lungs, causing coughing and excessive mucus production [Late 19thC. Coined from late Latin *bronchia* (see BRONCHIOLE) + Greek *ektasis* "dilation."]

bron·chi·ole /bróngki ōl/ *n.* a narrow tube inside the lungs that branches off the main air passages (**bronchi**) [Mid-19thC. From modern Latin *bronchiolus*, literally "little bronchium," from late Latin *bronchia*, from, ultimately, Greek *brogkhos* (see BRONCHUS).] —**bron·chi·o·lar** /bròngki ṓlər/ *adj.*

bron·chi·tis /brong kítiss/ *n.* inflammation of the mucous membrane in the airways (**bronchial tubes**) of the lungs, resulting from infection or irritation and causing breathing problems and severe coughing —**bron·chit·ic** /brong kíttik/ *adj.*

bron·cho /bróngkō/ *n.* = **bronco**

broncho- *prefix.* bronchus, bronchial ○ *bronchoscope* [Via late Latin from, ultimately, Greek *brogkhos* (see BRONCHUS)]

bron·cho·di·la·tor /bròngkō dī láytər, bròngkō dí làytər/ *n.* a drug, often used in the treatment of asthma, that eases breathing by widening and relaxing the air passages to the lungs

bron·cho·pneu·mon·ia /bròngkō noo mṓnee ə/ *n.* inflammation of the lungs caused by an infection in the air passages (**bronchioles**)

bron·cho·scope /bróngkə skōp/ *n.* a thin instrument with a light on the end, used for looking inside the air passages (**bronchi**) leading to the lungs —**bron·cho·scop·ic** /bròngkə skóppik/ *adj.* —**bron·cho·scop·i·cal·ly** *adv.* —**bron·chos·co·pist** /brong kóskəpist/ *n.* —**bron·chos·co·py** /-kóskəpee/ *n.*

bron·chus /bróngkəss/ (*plural* **-chi** /-kī, -kee/) *n.* a tube leading from the windpipe to a lung, which provides for the passage of air. = **bronchial tube** [Late 17thC. Via modern Latin from, ultimately, Greek *brogkhos* "windpipe." Ultimately from an Indo-European word that is also the ancestor of English *devour* and *gorge*.]

bron·co /bróng kō/, **bron·cho** *n.* a wild or partly broken horse of the western United States, used in rodeos [Mid-19thC. From Spanish, literally "rough, wild," of uncertain origin: perhaps from Latin *brocchus* (see BROACH).]

bron·co·bust·er /bróngkō bùstər/ *n.* a person who breaks wild horses (*informal*)

Bronf·man /brónfmən/, **Samuel Leonard** (1891?–1971) Canadian business executive. He was the founder and chief operating officer of the distilling company Seagrams.

Bron·të /bróntee/, **Anne** (1820–49) British novelist and poet. The sister of Charlotte Brontë and Emily Brontë, she wrote the novels *Agnes Grey* (1845) and *The Tenant of Wildfell Hall* (1847).

Barnaby's

Charlotte Brontë

Bron·të, Charlotte (1816–55) British novelist. Elder sister of Emily Brontë and Anne Brontë, she wrote novels including *Jane Eyre* (1847).

Bron·të, Emily (1818–48) British poet and novelist. Sister of Charlotte Brontë and Anne Brontë, she wrote *Wuthering Heights* (1847).

bron·to·sau·rus /bròntə sáwrəss/, **bron·to·saur** /bróntə sàwr/ (*plural* **-saurs**) *n.* a large vegetarian dinosaur that lived in North America during the Jurassic period and had a small head, short front legs, and a long neck and tail. Genus: *Apatosaurus*. [Late 19thC. From modern Latin *brontosaurus*, alternate genus name, which was coined from Greek *brontē* "thunder" + *sauros* "lizard."]

Bronx /braanks/ the northernmost of the five boroughs of New York City, located on the mainland with the Harlem and Hudson rivers to the west, Westchester County to the north, Long Island Sound to the east, and the East River to the south. Population: 1,203,789 (1990).

Bronx cheer *n.* a loud sound showing disapproval that is made by sticking the tongue out between closed lips and blowing (*informal*) [Named for the BRONX]

bronze /bronz/ *n.* **1. COPPER AND TIN ALLOY** a hard yellowish-brown alloy of copper and tin, sometimes containing small amounts of other metals. Bronze is harder than copper and is often cast to make statues. **2. COPPER-BASED ALLOY** an alloy of copper with a substance other than tin, e.g., aluminum or silicon **3.** SCULPTURE **BRONZE WORK OF ART** an object that is made from bronze, especially a statue or other piece of cast sculpture **4.** SPORTS **BRONZE MEDAL** a bronze medal ○ *She was hoping for at least a bronze.* **5.** COLORS **DEEP YELLOWISH BROWN COLOR** a deep yellowish brown color, like that of bronze ■ *adj.* **1. MADE OF BRONZE** made of bronze **2.** COLORS **DEEP YELLOWISH BROWN** of a deep yellowish brown color, like bronze ■ *v.* (**bronzed, bronz·ing, bronz·es**) **1.** *vt.* **MAKE SOMETHING LOOK LIKE BRONZE** to give something the yellowish-brown sheen or weathered patina of bronze **2.** *vti.* **TAN SKIN** to make somebody's skin suntanned or to become suntanned (*informal*) ○ *bronzed by the sun.* [Early 18thC. Via French from Italian *bronzo*, of uncertain origin: probably from Persian *birinj* "brass"; alternatively, named for the Italian city *Brindisi*, where in antiquity bronze mirrors were made.] —**bronz·er** *n.* —**bronz·y** *adj.*

Bronze Age *n.* a period of cultural history, approximately between 3500 and 1500 B.C., that succeeded the Stone Age and was characterized by the use of tools made of bronze

bronze med·al *n.* a medal that is awarded to a person who places third in a competition, especially a sporting event —**bronze med·al·ist** *n.*

Bronze Star *n.* a U.S. military award given for heroism or meritorious service in nonaerial combat

Bron·zi·no /bron zeeno/, **Il** (1503–72) Italian painter. Known as a portraitist of the Medici family, Dante, and Boccaccio, he also painted religious pictures. Real name **Agnoli Tori di Cosimo di Mariano**

bronz·ite /brón zīt/ *n.* an iron-containing form of orthopyroxine with a metallic sheen

brooch /brōch, brooch/, **broach** *n.* a piece of jewelry that is fastened to a garment by a hinged pin and catch. Brooches are usually worn by women, e.g., on the upper part of a dress, on the lapel of a jacket, or at the neck of a blouse. [13thC. From Old French *broche* (see BROACH).]

brood /brood/ *n.* **1. YOUNG OF BIRDS OR ANIMALS** the young of an animal, especially young birds, that are born and reared together **2. FAMILY'S CHILDREN** the children of one family (*informal humorous*) ○ *that brood of noisy brats* **3. GROUP OF SIMILAR PEOPLE** a group whose members share a common origin or background ○ *the latest brood of avant-garde artists* ■ *adj.* **KEPT FOR BREEDING** used to describe a female farm animal that is kept for the purpose of producing young ■ *v.* (**brood·ed, brood·ing, broods**) **1.** *vi.* **BE WORRIED** to be preoccupied with a troublesome or unwelcome thought **2.** *vi.* **THINK UNPLEASANT THOUGHTS** to think resentful, dark, or miserable thoughts **3.** *vti.* **KEEP EGGS WARM** to sit on or hatch eggs, or to cover young birds for warmth **4.** *vi.* **BE HEAVY OR OMINOUS** to loom or hang heavily and ominously (*literary*) ○ *the dark clouds brooding overhead* [Old English *brōd*. Ultimately from an Indo-European base meaning "heat." The underlying idea is of nursing young (or emotions) by keeping them warm.]

brood·er /bróodər/ *n.* **1. HEATED PLACE FOR YOUNG ANIMAL** a heated area or enclosure for raising young animals, especially young fowl, with or without the presence of their mother. It provides an optimum environment in which heat, light, food, and water can be carefully controlled. **2. HEN THAT BROODS EGGS** a hen that sits on eggs to keep them warm before they hatch **3. PERSON WHO WORRIES** a person who worries persistently over things

brood·mare /bróod màir/ *n.* a mare that is kept specially for breeding

brood·y /bróodee/ (**-i·er, -i·est**) *adj.* **1. READY TO INCUBATE EGGS** used to describe a hen that is ready to sit on eggs to keep them warm before they hatch, especially a hen that is no longer able to lay eggs **2. THOUGHTFUL OR SULLEN** showing deep thought, anxiety, or resentment ○ *His long broody silences were hard to bear.* —**brood·i·ly** *adv.* —**brood·i·ness** *n.*

brook[1] /brŏŏk/ *n.* a small freshwater stream [Old English *brōc*. From a prehistoric Germanic word that is also the ancestor of German *Bruch* "marsh."]

brook[2] /brŏŏk/ (**brooked, brook·ing, brooks**) *vt.* to put up with something (*formal*) (*used in the negative*) ○ *I will brook no interference in this matter.* [Old English *brūcan*. Ultimately from an Indo-European base that also produced English *fruit*. The meaning "to tolerate" evolved from "to use (as food)" via "to stomach."]

Brook /brŏŏk/, **Peter** (*b.* 1925) British-born director. He was associated with the Royal Shakespeare Company from 1962. Full name **Peter Stephen Paul Brook**

Brook·er /brŏŏkər/, **Bertram** (1888–1955) British-born Canadian artist and writer. He painted *Sounds Assembling* (1928) and wrote *Think of the Earth* (1937).

Brook Farm *n.* an experimental cooperative community established by a group of writers and scholars on a farm in West Roxbury, Massachusetts. It lasted from 1841 to 1846.

Brook·field /brŏŏk feeld/ city in southeastern Wisconsin, a northwestern suburb of Milwaukee, near the shore of Lake Michigan. Population: 37,729 (1996). ■ suburb of Chicago, Illinois, west of the Des Plaines River. The Brookfield Zoo, established in 1934, is a major tourist attraction. Population: 18,876 (1990).

brook·ite /brŏŏ kīt/ *n.* a translucent or reddish brown to black mineral composed of titanium dioxide in the form of orthorhombic crystals. Formula: TiO_2. [Early 19thC. Named for the English mineralogist Henry J. *Brook* (1771–1857).]

Brook·line /brŏŏk līn/ town in eastern Massachusetts, a southwestern suburb of Boston. It was the birthplace of President John F. Kennedy. Population: 54,137 (1996).

Brook·lyn /broŏklin/ one of the five boroughs of New York City, located on the western tip of Long Island with Staten Island and Manhattan to the west and Queens to the north and east. Population: 2,273,966 (1996).

Brook·lyn Cen·ter city in southeastern Minnesota, a northwestern suburb of Minneapolis. Population: 28,132 (1996).

Brook·lyn Park city in southeastern Minnesota, north of Minneapolis, on the Mississippi River. Population: 56,381 (1990).

Brook·ner /broŏknər/, **Anita** (*b.* 1928) British writer. Her novels included the Booker Prize-winning *Hotel du Lac* (1984).

Brook Park city in northeastern Ohio, a southwestern suburb of Cleveland. Population: 22,646 (1996).

Brooks /broŏks/, **Gwendolyn** (*b.* 1917) U.S. poet. Her *Annie Allen* (1949) won a Pulitzer Prize. Other works include *Children Coming Home* (1992). Full name **Gwendolyn Elizabeth Brooks**

Brooks, Mel (*b.* 1926) U.S. movie actor and director. His films include *The Producers* (1968), *Blazing Saddles* (1974), and *Spaceballs* (1987). Born **Melvin Kaminsky**

Brooks, Van Wyck (1886–1963) U.S. critic and biographer. He wrote *The Flowering of New England, 1815–65* (1936).

Brooks Range mountain range of northern Alaska, stretching from Kotzebue Sound eastward to the Canadian border, separating the North Slope from the Yukon Basin. Its highest point is Mount Chamberlin 9,239 ft./2,816 m.

brook trout *n.* a freshwater fish of the salmon family, originally from eastern North America and introduced throughout North America and into Europe. It is a popular food and game fish. Latin name: *Salvelinus fontinalis.*

broom /broom/ *n.* **1. BRUSH FOR SWEEPING** a brush with a head of twigs or bristles attached to a long thin handle, used for sweeping indoors or outdoors **2.** PLANTS **PLANT WITH BRIGHT YELLOW FLOWERS** a leguminous shrub that grows wild in Europe and Asia and is widely cultivated for its bright yellow flowers. Latin name: *Cytisus scoparius.* **3.** PLANTS **PLANT RESEMBLING BROOM** a shrub with yellow flowers that resembles broom and grows in Europe and Asia. Genera: *Genista* and *Spartium.* ■ *vt.* **(broomed, broom·ing, brooms) SWEEP SOMETHING** to sweep something with a broom or brush [Old English *brōm.* From a prehistoric Germanic word that also produced English *bramble.* Originally only a plant name, the word acquired the meaning "brush" because brushes were made from broom twigs.]

broom·corn /broŏm kàwrn, broŏm-/ *n.* a variety of sorghum with long stiff stalks that are sometimes used for making brooms. Latin name: *Sorghum bicolor.*

Broom·field /broŏm feeld/ city in northern Colorado, southeast of Boulder and northwest of Denver. Population: 31,743 (1996).

broom·rape /broŏm ràyp/ *n.* a plant that has small flowers and tiny leaves resembling scales and lacking chlorophyll. It lives on the roots of other plants, including crops. Genus: *Orobanche.* [Late 16thC. "Rape" from medieval Latin *rapum* "tuber."]

broom·stick /broŏm stìk/ *n.* the long handle of a broom

Broonzy /broŏnzee/, **Big Bill** (1893–1953) U.S. musician. He incorporated a wide range of influences as a master composer and performer of blues. Born **William Lee Conley**

bros., Bros. *abbr.* COMM brothers

broth /brawth, broth/ *n.* a liquid made by cooking vegetables, meat, seafood, or poultry in water for a long time, used as a base for soups and sauces [Old English *broþ.* Ultimately from an Indo-European base meaning "heat, boil," which also produced English *brew* and *fervent.*]

broth·el /bróth'l/ *n.* a place where people pay to have sexual intercourse with prostitutes [14thC. Shortening of earlier *brothel-house,* from Old English *broþen* "ruined," which was used for "worthless person," and came to denote a prostitute in the 15thC.]

broth·er /brúthər/ *n.* **1. MALE SIBLING** a boy or man who has the same father and mother as another person **2.** (*plural* **broth·ers** *or* **breth·ren**) **FELLOW MEMBER** a man who belongs to the same race, religion, profession, trade, or organization as another man ○ *fraternity brothers* **3. CLOSE MALE FRIEND** used to address a close male friend **4.** (*plural* **broth·ers** *or* **breth·ren**) CHR **LAY MEMBER** a lay member of a religious order for men **5.** (*plural* **broth·ers** *or* **breth·ren**) CHR **DEVOTED RELIGIOUS WORKER** a man who devotes himself to the work of a men's religious order without having been ordained ■ *interj.* **EXPRESSING SURPRISE OR ANNOYANCE** used to express surprise, annoyance, or disappointment (*informal*) ○ *Oh brother! What happened here today?* [Old English *brōþor.* Ultimately from an Indo-European word that also produced Latin *frater* "brother" (source of English *fraternal*), Greek *phratēr,* Sanskrit *bhrātṛ,* and German *Bruder.*]

broth·er·hood /brúthər hoŏd/ *n.* **1. HAVING SAME PARENTS** the relationship of brothers **2. GROUP OF MEN** an organization of men, e.g., a labor union, that is united for a common purpose **3. ALL THE MEMBERS** all the members of a particular profession or trade **4. GOODWILL** a feeling of fellowship and sympathy for other people

broth·er-in-law (*plural* **broth·ers-in-law**) *n.* **1. SISTER'S HUSBAND** the husband of somebody's sister **2. SPOUSE'S BROTHER** the brother of somebody's husband or wife **3. SPOUSE'S SISTER'S HUSBAND** the husband of the sister of somebody's husband or wife

broth·er·ly /brúthərlee/ *adj.* the showing feelings that a brother might be expected to have toward his sister or brother [Old English *brōþorlic*]

brougham /broom, broŏ əm, brōm, brō əm/ *n.* a one-horse carriage with an open seat at the front for the driver and a closed compartment at the back for passengers, used in the 19th century [Mid-19thC. Named for the English politician and educational reformer Henry Peter, Lord *Brougham* (1778–1868), who designed the original brougham.]

brought *v.* past tense, past participle of **bring**

brou·ha·ha /broŏ haa haa/ *n.* a noisy commotion or uproar (*formal*) [Late 19thC. From French, of uncertain origin: perhaps from Hebrew *bāruḵ habbā,* literally "blessed is the comer, welcome!"; in allusion to the loud prayers at a traditional Jewish synagogue.]

Broun /broon/, **Heywood** (1888–1939) U.S. journalist and novelist. He was co-founder of the Newspaper Guild and a social campaigner. Full name **Heywood Campbell Broun**

brow /brow/ *n.* **1. FOREHEAD** the area on somebody's face above the eyes and below the hairline **2.** = **eyebrow 3. TOP OF HILL** the top edge of a hill [Old English *brū.* Ultimately from an Indo-European word that is also the ancestor of German *Braue* "eyebrow." Originally in the meaning "eyelash."]

bro·wal·li·a /brə wólee ə/ (*plural* **-a** *or* **-as**) *n.* a tropical American plant of the nightshade family cultivated for its blue, white, or violet flowers. Genus: *Browallia.* [Late 18thC. From modern Latin, genus name, named for the Swedish botanist Johann *Browall* (1707–55).]

brow·band /brów bànd/ *n.* a strap that is part of a horse's bridle and goes across its forehead

brow·beat /brów beet/ (**-beat, -beat·en** /-beet'n/, **-beat·ing, -beats**) *vt.* to bully or intimidate somebody sternly ○ *His father browbeat him into joining.* [Late 16thC. Origin uncertain: perhaps the underlying idea is of intimidating somebody by furrowing the brows.] — **brow·beat·er** *n.*

brown /brown/ *n.* **1. COLOR BETWEEN RED AND YELLOW** a color that varies between red and yellow and ranges from light to dark, such as the color of wood or soil **2. BROWN CLOTHING** fabric or clothing that is brown in color ○ *We had to wear brown for school.* **3. BROWN PIGMENT OR DYE** a pigment or dye that is formed from a combination of red, yellow, and black and has or is near to the color of wood or soil **4. BROWN OBJECT** a brown object ○ *She decided to take the brown.* **5. FLOCK OF GAME BIRDS** a flock of game birds flying closely together ■ *adj.* **1. BETWEEN RED AND YELLOW IN COLOR** having a color that varies between red and yellow, and can range from light to dark, such as that of wood or soil ○ *the fruit was brown and rotten* **2. SUNTANNED** deeply suntanned or sunburned **3. PARTIALLY OR WHOLLY UNPROCESSED** used to describe foodstuffs that are partially or wholly unprocessed so that their natural brown color remains ■ *vti.* **(browned, brown·ing, browns) MAKE OR BECOME BROWN** to make something brown or to become brown, e.g., in cooking or sunbathing [Old English *brūn* . Ultimately from an Indo-European word meaning "bright, brown," which also produced English *bear*[1], *bruin, beaver,* and *burnish.*] — **brown·ish** *adj.* —**brown·ness** *n.*

Brown /brown/, **Capability** (1715–83) British landscape gardener. He landscaped the grounds of many English country houses, including Blenheim Palace in Oxfordshire and Chatsworth in Derbyshire, and created a naturalistic style of landscape design. Real name **Lancelot Brown**

Brown, Charles Brockden (1771–1810) U.S. writer. Considered by many to have been the first American novelist, he wrote the gothic novel *Wieland* (1798).

Brown, George (1818–80) Scottish-born Canadian journalist and politician. He founded the Toronto *Globe* and was prime minister for two days in 1858.

Brown, Jim (*b.* 1936) U.S. football player. He was an outstanding fullback with the Cleveland Browns (1966–75) and later acted in movies including *The Dirty Dozen* (1967). Full name **James Nathaniel Brown**

Brown, John (1800–59) U.S. abolitionist. Convicted of treason after a failed attempt to launch a slave rebellion, he was hanged in Virginia. The song *"John Brown's Body"* commemorates his actions.

Brown, Moses (1738–1836) U.S. philanthropist. He helped eradicate slavery in Rhode Island and started the first U.S. cotton factory (1789).

brown ad·i·pose tis·sue *n.* = **brown fat**

brown al·ga *n.* a marine alga that has chlorophyll masked by brown pigment. The kelps and wracks are brown algae. Division: *Phaeophyta.*

brown-bag (**brown-bagged, brown-bag·ging, brown-bags**) *vti.* to bring a lunch to work from home, typically in a brown paper bag or other similar container

brown bag·ging *n.* **1. TAKING PACKED LUNCH TO WORK** the practice of taking a packed lunch from home to work, typically in a brown paper bag or other similar container **2. TAKING ALCOHOLIC DRINK TO PUBLIC ESTABLISHMENT** the practice of taking your own alcoholic drink into a public establishment, such as a restaurant or a club, that does not have a license to sell alcohol (*informal*)

brown bear *n.* a bear that is mainly brown in color, found in western North America and northern Europe and Asia. The most widely distributed of all bears, brown bears vary in size from the small Syrian variety to the giant Kodiak bear and include the North American grizzlies. Latin name: *Ursus arctos.*

Brown Bet·ty /-béttee/ (*plural* **Brown Bet·ties**) *n.* a baked apple dessert made from apples, breadcrumbs, sugar, spices, butter, and sometimes raisins

brown bread *n.* **1. WHOLEWHEAT BREAD** bread made using wholewheat flour **2. TRADITIONAL MOLASSES BREAD** an old-fashioned bread containing molasses, risen with baking soda, and either steamed or baked

brown coal *n.* a soft, brown-black fossil fuel with visible plant remains and a high moisture content

brown dwarf *n.* a star that is smaller than a planet and has a mass equivalent to less than one-tenth of the Sun's mass

brown earth *n.* a type of soil formed in temperate humid regions under deciduous forests and characterized by a dark brown layer rich in organic material

brown fat *n.* a dark-colored fatty tissue in many mammals, especially hibernating animals and human babies, that produces heat in order to control body temperature

Brown·i·an move·ment /brównee ən-/, **Brown·i·an mo·tion** *n.* the random movement of microscopic particles suspended in a liquid or gas that occurs as a result of collisions with molecules of the surrounding medium [Named for the English botanist Robert *Brown* 1773–1858, who first described it in connection with the motions of pollen grains]

brown·ie /brównee/ *n.* **1. RICH FLAT CHOCOLATE CAKE** a piece of flat rich chocolate cake baked in a square or rectangular pan and sometimes containing chopped nuts **2. HELPFUL ELF OR GOBLIN** in folklore, a small supernatural being believed to do helpful work at night [Early 16thC, with the sense "elf." The term was first used of a chocolate cake in late 19thC.]

Brown·ie[1] *n.* a member of the Girl Scouts of the United States of America, aged from six to eight years of age [Early 20thC. So called because of their brown uniform.]

Brown·ie^2 *tdmk.* a trademark for a make of box camera

brown·ie point, **Brown·ie point** *n.* a credit earned for doing something helpful, especially in order to please (*informal*) [From the points used by Brownies for advancement]

Brown·ing /brówning/, **Elizabeth Barrett** (1806–61) British poet. Her works include *Sonnets from the Portuguese* (1850), *Aurora Leigh* (1856), and *Poems Before Congress* (1860). She married Robert Browning in 1846 and lived with him in Italy. Born **Elizabeth Barrett**

Brown·ing, Robert (1812–89) British poet. His works include *Men and Women* (1855), *Dramatis Personae* (1864), and *The Ring and the Book* (1868–69). He married Elizabeth Barrett in 1846.

Brown·ing au·to·mat·ic ri·fle *n.* an air-cooled, gas-operated, magazine-fed rifle with a .30 caliber barrel, capable of firing between 200 and 350 rounds per minute with an effective range of 2,000 ft./600 m [Named for the U.S. arms designer John M. *Browning* 1855–1926.]

Brown·ing ma·chine gun *n.* an air- or water-cooled, belt-fed, automatic machine gun with either a .30 or .50 caliber barrel, capable of firing over 500 rounds per minute [Named for the U.S. arms designer John M. *Browning* 1855–1926.]

brown lace·wing *n.* an insect with brownish wings that often feeds on agricultural pests. Family: Hemerobiidae.

brown lung dis·ease, **brown lung** *n.* = **byssinosis**

brown mus·tard *n.* **1. PLANT OF MUSTARD FAMILY** an annual plant of the mustard family with pale yellow flowers, irregularly lobed leaves, and dark reddish brown oil-rich seeds used in cooking. Latin name: *Brassica juncea.* **2. GROUND SEEDS USED IN COOKING** the ground seeds of the brown mustard plant, used as a cooking spice

brown·nose /brówn nōz/ (**-nosed, -nos·ing, -noses**) *vti.* to be unnaturally subservient or obsequious to somebody in authority (*slang*) (*considered offensive by some speakers*) ○ *He brownnosed his way to the top of the firm.* [So called with relation to its synonym: "kiss-ass"] —**brown·nose** *n.* —**brown·nos·er** *n.*

brown·out /brówn òwt/ *n.* **1. DIMMING OF LIGHTS** a dimming or reduction in the use of electric lights in a city, town, or region, especially as an economy measure **2. POWER REDUCTION** a temporary reduction in electrical power caused by high consumer demand or by technical malfunction **3. LAPSE OF CONCENTRATION** a temporary lapse of concentration or focus [Mid-20thC. Modeled on "blackout."]

brown owl *n.* = **tawny owl**

brown pa·per *n.* thick strong brown-colored paper used for wrapping packages and for making paper bags

brown patch *n.* a soil-borne fungal disease of grass that produces round dead patches

brown rat *n.* an extremely destructive rat, originally from Europe and Asia, that is found worldwide in populated areas. Latin name: *Rattus norvegicus.*

brown re·cluse spi·der *n.* a pale brown poisonous spider found in the United States and South America that has a violin-shaped mark on the head area. Latin name: *Loxosceles reclusa.*

brown rice *n.* unpolished rice in which the yellowish brown outer layer containing the bran remains intact. This type of rice retains its B vitamins, thus making it more nutritious than white rice. ◊ **white rice**

brown rot *n.* a disease of ripe tree fruits such as apples and peaches, caused by fungi. The infected fruit turns brown, and concentric yellow rings appear on the plant. Genus: *Rhizoctonia.*

brown sauce *n.* a sauce made from a dark meat stock, thickened with flour that has been browned in fat

Brown Shirt *n.* a Nazi storm trooper [Translation of German *Braunhemd*, from the brown uniform shirts of the Nazi storm troopers]

brown·stone /brówn stōn/ *n.* **1. SANDSTONE** a reddish brown sandstone used as a building material **2. SANDSTONE BUILDING** a house or building made from or faced with reddish brown sandstone, especially an apartment building in New York City

WORD KEY: SYNONYMS

See Synonyms at *house*.

brown stud·y *n.* a state of deep thought or serious absorption (*dated*) [Origin uncertain: probably from BROWN in the sense "gloomy"]

brown sug·ar *n.* **1. REFINED SUGAR WITH MOLASSES** a soft refined sugar that is light or dark brown in color. It is made from refined white sugar combined with a mild refined molasses and is used in cooking. **2. UNREFINED SUGAR** unrefined or partially refined sugar **3. HEROIN** the drug heroin (*slang*)

Browns·ville /brównzvil/ city and port in southern Texas, on the bank of the Río Grande, opposite Matamoros, Mexico. Population: 132,091 (1996).

Brown Swiss *n.* a large brown dairy cow belonging to a hardy breed originating in Switzerland

brown-tail moth (*plural* **brown-tail moths**) *n.* a white and brown moth, native to Europe and also found in the eastern United States, whose caterpillars destroy the leaves of trees and produce a poison that causes breathing problems and a rash in humans. Latin name: *Euproctis chrysorrhoea.*

brown thrash·er *n.* a bird that is related to the mockingbird and has a long tail, long curving beak, reddish brown back, and white breast with black spots. It is found in the eastern and central United States and in the rain forests of Dominica and the Lesser Antilles. Latin name: *Toxostoma rufum.*

brown trout *n.* a common freshwater fish that is brownish in color and is caught for food or sport. It is native to Europe and also found in North America. Latin name: *Salmo trutta.*

browse /browz/ *v.* (**browsed, brows·ing, brows·es**) **1.** *vti.* **READ CASUALLY** to read through something quickly or superficially **2.** *vi.* **LOOK THROUGH OR OVER CASUALLY** to look through or over something, especially merchandise in a store, in a leisurely manner with the hope of finding something of interest **3.** *vti.* COMPUT **SCAN COMPUTER FILES** to scan and view files in a computer database or on the Internet, especially on the World Wide Web **4.** *vti.* ZOOL **FEED ON VEGETATION** to feed or graze on tender vegetation such as the shoots, leaves, or twigs of shrubs or trees ■ *n.* **1. SESSION OF BROWSING** a superficial read through something, e.g., a newspaper, or a leisurely look over something, e.g., the merchandise in a store **2.** ZOOL **FEEDING PERIOD** a session of feeding on tender shoots or twigs of shrubs and trees **3. TENDER VEGETATION USED AS FOOD** the tender shoots, leaves, or twigs of shrubs and trees used as food by animals such as deer and cattle [Early 16thC. Via obsolete French *broust* from Old French *brost*, of Germanic origin.]

brows·er /brówzər/ *n.* **1.** COMPUT **SOFTWARE FOR SEARCHING INTERNET** a piece of computer software that allows an Internet user to search for information on the World Wide Web **2. SOMEBODY WHO BROWSES** somebody who reads or looks over something, e.g., a reference book or the merchandise in a store, in a leisurely or superficial manner [Mid-16thC]

Bru·beck /broō bèk/, **Dave** (*b.* 1920) U.S. pianist and composer. He is known for his progressive jazz compositions such as *Blue Rondo a la Turk*1957. Full name **David William Brubeck**

Bruce, Robert, King of Scots (1274–1329). Leader of the Scottish War of Independence.

bru·cel·lo·sis /broōssi lṓssiss/ *n.* a chronic infectious disease of some domestic animals, e.g., cattle, dogs, goats, and pigs, that is caused by bacteria and may lead to spontaneous abortion. It can be transmitted to human beings through contaminated milk, causing symptoms such as fever, headache, painful joints, aches, and weakness. Genus: *Brucella.* ◊ **Bang's disease** [Mid-20thC. Coined from *Brucella* (the name of the genus of bacteria that causes the disease), from the name of Sir David *Bruce* (1855–1931), a Scottish physician.]

bru·cine /broō sseen/ *n.* a poisonous white crystalline alkaloid derived from the seeds of the nux vomica tree and used to render alcohol unfit for human consumption. Formula: $C_{23}H_{26}N_2O_4$. [Early 19thC. From modern Latin *Brucea*, name of a tree thought to bear the false angostura bark the substance is derived from.]

bru·cite /broōss ìt/ *n.* a mineral form of magnesium hydroxide that occurs in hydrothermal deposits and in metamorphized limestone [Early 19thC. Named for the U.S. mineralogist Archibald *Bruce* (1777–1818).]

Bruck·ner /broōknər/, **Anton** (1824–96) Austrian composer. He wrote nine symphonies and four masses. His music was influenced by Wagner and Schubert.

Brue·ghel /broygəl, broo-/, **Brue·gel, Breu·ghel, Jan** (1568–1625) Flemish painter. The son of Pieter Brueghel the Elder, he produced still lifes and landscape paintings.

Brue·ghel, Brue·gel, Breu·ghel, Pieter (1520–69) Flemish painter. He produced religious and moral allegories in contemporary landscapes, depicting peasant life in works such as *Peasant Wedding* (1568). Known as **Pieter Brueghel the Elder**

Bruges /broozh/ capital of West Flanders Province, western Belgium. It is famous for its traditional lace industries. Population: 115,815 (1996).

bru·in /broō in/, **Bruin** *n.* used as a name for a bear in folklore, fables, and children's stories [15thC. From Middle Dutch, literally "brown."]

bruise /brooz/ *n.* (*plural* **bruis·es**) **1. SKIN DISCOLORATION CAUSED BY INJURY** a tender area of skin discoloration caused by blood leaking from blood vessels damaged by pressure or impact **2. DAMAGE TO PLANT TISSUE** damage to underlying plant or fruit tissue, visible as a soft discolored area on the unbroken surface and caused by pressure or impact **3. EMOTIONAL INJURY** an injury that is not physical, e.g., hurt feelings or damaged self-esteem ■ *v.* (**bruised, bruis·ing, bruis·es**) **1.** *vti.* **INJURE CAUSING SKIN DISCOLORATION** to injure, or sustain an injury to, a part of the body resulting in discoloration caused by blood leaking from damaged blood vessels **2.** *vti.* **DAMAGE PLANT TISSUE** to damage plant tissue or to sustain damage by pressure or impact, leaving a softened and discolored surface area **3.** *vt.* COOK **CRUSH FOOD** to crush or pound food, especially to extract juice from it or bring out its flavor **4.** *vt.* **UPSET SOMEBODY** to injure somebody's feelings or harm somebody's self-esteem ○ *I was bruised by the criticism* [Partly from Old English *brȳsan* "to crush," and partly from Anglo-Norman *bruser* "to break," of prehistoric Germanic origin]

bruis·er /broōzər/ *n.* a large strong man or youth, e.g., a boxer, bodyguard, bar bouncer, or football player (*informal*)

bruis·ing /broōzing/ *n.* **DISCOLORATION OF SKIN SURFACE** bruises or the dark patches left on the surface of bruised skin ■ *adj.* **PAINFUL** causing emotional, psychological, or physical pain

bruit /broot/ *n.* **1.** MED **ABNORMAL SOUND INSIDE BODY** an abnormal sound heard inside the body, usually with the aid of a stethoscope, and caused by turbulent blood flow within the heart or blood vessels **2. A RUMOR OR REPORT** a story, true or untrue, that is passed around among people (*archaic*) **3. NOISE OR DIN** loud sounds or the noise made by them (*archaic*) ■ *vt.* (**bruit·ed, bruit·ing, bruits**) **SPREAD STORY** to circulate stories, whether true or untrue [From Old French, from the past participle of *bruire* "to roar," from assumed Vulgar Latin *brugire*, a blend of assumed *brager* and Latin *rugire*]

Bru·lé /broo láy/, **Étienne** (1592?–1632) French-born Canadian explorer. He lived among Native Americans and was perhaps the first European to see the Great Lakes.

Bru·maire /bri mér/ *n.* the second month of the year in the French Revolutionary calendar, corresponding to the period from October 23 to November 21 in the Gregorian calendar [Early 19thC. From French, formed from *brume* "brume."]

brume /broom/ *n.* a weather condition in which fog or mist is present, or the fog or mist itself (*literary*) [Early 18thC. Via French, literally "fog," from Latin *bruma* "winter" (see BRUMAL).] —**bru·mous** *adj.*

brum·ma·gem /brúmməjəm/, **Brum·ma·gem** *n.* **SOMETHING CHEAP AND SHOWY** something, especially imitation jewelry, that is cheap and gaudy ■ *adj.* **CHEAPLY SHOWY** cheap and shoddy [Mid-17thC. From *Brummagem*, alteration of Birmingham, England, originally referring to counterfeit coins made there.]

Brum·mie /brúmmee/, **Brum·my** (*plural* **-mies**) *adj.* relating to or typical of the English city of Birmingham (*informal*)

brunch /brunch/ (*plural* **brunch·es**) *n.* a meal that combines breakfast and lunch, eaten late in the morning [Late 19thC. Blend of BREAKFAST and LUNCH.]

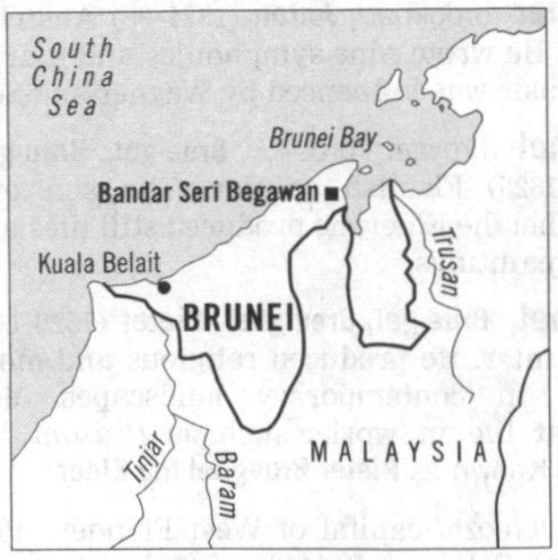

Brunei

Bru·nei /broo nī́/ island sultanate bisected by Malaysia in northwestern Borneo, eastern Asia. Language: Malay. Currency: Brunei dollar. Capital: Bandar Seri Begawan. Population: 307,612 (1997). Area: 2,226 sq. mi./5,765 sq. km. Official name **Negara Brunei Darussalam**

Isambard Kingdom Brunel

Bru·nel /broo nél/, **Isambard Kingdom** (1806–59) British engineer. He designed the Clifton Suspension Bridge and constructed the *Great Western* (1837), the first steamship designed to cross the Atlantic.

Bru·nel·le·schi /broŏnə léskee/, **Filippo** (1377–1446) Italian architect and sculptor. One of the greatest Renaissance architects, he designed the dome of the cathedral in Florence (1420–61) and built several churches in Florence. Real name **Filippo di Ser Brunellesco**

bru·net /broo nét/ *n.* SOMEBODY WITH DARK HAIR somebody with dark or brown hair ■ *adj.* WITH DARK HAIR with dark or brown hair [Mid-16thC. From French, formed from *brun*, of Germanic origin.]

bru·nette /broo nét/ *n.* WOMAN WITH DARK-HAIR a girl or woman with dark brown hair ■ *adj.* **1.** DARK BROWN used to describe hair that is dark brown **2.** WITH DARK HAIR used to describe a girl or woman with dark brown hair [Early 17thC. From French, the feminine form of *brunet* "BRUNET."]

Brun·hild /broŏn híld/, **Brünn·hil·de** /-híldə/ *n.* in medieval Germanic mythology, the queen of Iceland who promises to marry whoever can defeat her in battle. Siegfried does so on behalf of King Gunther.

Bru·no /broŏnō/, **St.** (1030?–1101) German monk in the French mountains at Chartreuse. He founded a monastery of hermit monks (1084), which later became the Carthusian contemplative order. Known as **Bruno the Carthusian**

Bruns·wick /brúnzwik/ **1.** city in southeastern Georgia, on the northern shore of St. Simons Sound, southwest of Savannah. Population: 15,525 (1996). **2.** town in southeastern Maine, on the Androscoggin River, southeast of Lewiston and northeast of Portland. Population: 20,827 (1996). **3.** city in northern Ohio, southwest of Cleveland. Population: 31,641 (1996).

Bruns·wick stew *n.* a stew that contains vegetables and usually wild game meat, such as squirrel or rabbit [Named for *Brunswick* County in southern Virginia, where it was supposedly first made]

brunt /brunt/ *n.* **1.** MAIN FORCE OF SOMETHING the main force or effect of something, e.g., a blow or an attack **2.** GREATER BURDEN OF SOMETHING the greater part or the main burden **3.** FORCEFUL ATTACK a forceful blow or attack (*archaic*) [14thC. Origin unknown.]

Brush

brush[1] /brush/ *n.* **1.** TOOL WITH BRISTLES ATTACHED TO HANDLE an implement consisting of bristles set into a handle, used especially for grooming the hair or for painting, polishing, scrubbing, or sweeping **2.** USE OF BRUSH the use of a brush, e.g., to groom the hair or to sweep a surface **3.** LIGHT CONTACT a light stroke or momentary contact **4.** SHORT UNPLEASANT ENCOUNTER a brief unpleasant encounter ○ *a brush with evil* **5.** BUSHY TAIL OF FOX a bushy tail, especially the tail of a fox as a hunting trophy **6.** ELEC ELECTRICAL CONDUCTOR an electrical conductor that makes sliding contact between a stationary and a moving part of a generator or motor while completing a circuit and conveying a current **7.** = **brush discharge** ■ *v.* **(brushed, brush·ing, brush·es) 1.** *vti.* USE BRUSH ON SOMETHING to use a brush to clean, groom, paint, polish, or scrub **2.** *vt.* APPLY WITH BRUSH to apply something such as paint or varnish to a surface using a brush **3.** *vt.* REMOVE SOMETHING WITH BRUSH remove with a brush or sweeping motion **4.** *vt.* REJECT SOMETHING to dismiss, ignore, or rebuff something or somebody in an abrupt or curt manner ○ *They brushed aside the suggestion.* **5.** *vti.* GRAZE AGAINST SOMETHING to touch something lightly and briefly in passing **6.** *vi.* MOVE PAST SOMETHING CLOSELY AND QUICKLY to move past something or somebody very fast so as to come into brief contact [14thC. From Old French *broisse*, probably a variant of *broce* "brushwood" (see BRUSH[2]), suggesting that cut branches were used to make brooms or brushes.] —**brush·er** *n.* —**brush·y** *adj.* ◇ **tar somebody with the same brush** to attribute unfairly the faults and deficits of somebody to another

brush off *vt.* to dismiss or disregard somebody or something in an abrupt manner

brush up *vt.* to refresh or renew knowledge of or skill in something

brush[2] /brush/ *n.* **1.** = **brushwood** *n.* 1 **2.** TWIGS AND BRANCHES cut or broken branches and twigs **3.** BACKWOODS wild and sparsely populated woodland [14thC. Via Anglo-Norman *brousse*, a variant of Old French *broce* "broken branches": possibly from Latin *bruscum* "knot on a maple tree."]

brush bor·der *n.* a dense layer of tiny protuberances that lines certain absorbing cells, e.g., in the intestine and kidney

brush cut *n.* a hairstyle with the hair cropped close to the head so that it stands up like a brush

brush dis·charge, **brush** *n.* a luminous electric discharge between two conductors, consisting of a flow of ionized particles with less intensity than a spark [Late 18thC. From its brushlike appearance.]

brushed /brusht/ *adj.* **1.** FINISHED WITH SOFT AND FUZZY SURFACE used to describe a knitted or woven fabric that has a nap produced by a brushing process during manufacture **2.** NONREFLECTIVE a metallic surface with a nonreflective sheen

brush·fire *n.* **1.** FIRE IN DRY BRUSH a fire in dry brush and scrub that usually spreads quickly **2.** SMALL CRISIS a minor crisis, often one of many **3.** A SMALL WAR a localized but often intensely fought war ■ *adj.* INVOLVING LOCAL MILITARY involving only small-scale and local military mobilization

brush·mark /brúsh maark/ *n.* a mark or line left by the bristles of a brush on a painted or varnished surface

brush·off /brúsh ôf/ *n.* an abrupt dismissal, rejection, or snub (*informal*)

brush·stroke /brúsh strōk/ *n.* a movement of a paintbrush that produces a particular look or mark on a painted surface, or the mark itself

brush·wood /brúsh wŏŏd/ *n.* **1.** THICKET a dense undergrowth of small trees and bushes **2.** = **brush**[2] *n.* 2

brush·work /brúsh wùrk/ *n.* **1.** ARTIST'S CHARACTERISTIC WAY OF APPLYING PAINT the characteristic manner in which an artist applies paint with a brush **2.** WORK DONE WITH BRUSH the product of an artist's use of a brush in painting

brusque /brusk/ *adj.* abrupt, blunt, or curt in manner or speech [Early 17thC. Via French from, ultimately, late Latin *bruscum* "coarse, rough," of uncertain origin.] —**brusque·ly** *adv.* —**brusque·ness** *n.*

brus·que·rie /broŏskəree, broŏs-/ *n.* bluntness or abruptness of manner [Mid-18thC. From French, formed from *brusque* (see BRUSQUE).]

Brus·sels /brúss'lz/ the largest city and capital of Belgium. It is situated in the center of Belgium and is the headquarters of the European Union and the North Atlantic Treaty Organisation (NATO). Population: 948,122 (1996).

Brus·sels car·pet *n.* a carpet with a heavy patterned pile formed by small woolen loops attached to a linen base

Brus·sels grif·fon *n.* = **griffon** [So called because the breed originated in Belgium]

Brus·sels lace *n.* **1.** FINE LACE a fine lace with a floral design, made with bobbins or with needle and thread, that originated in or near Brussels **2.** MACHINE-MADE NET LACE a machine-made net lace with an appliqué design

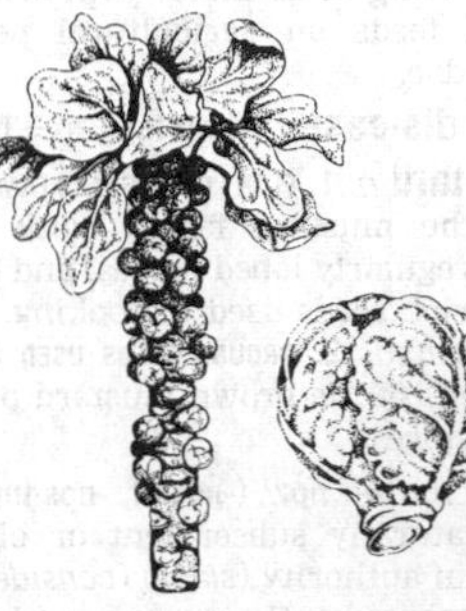

Brussels sprout

Brus·sels sprout *n.* **1.** PLANT PRODUCING EDIBLE GREEN BUDS a plant related to the cabbage that has a thick stalk lined with edible swollen green buds resembling small cabbages. Latin name: *Brassica oleracea*. **2.** GREEN VEGETABLE LIKE TINY CABBAGE a small green swollen bud like a tiny cabbage that is produced by the Brussels sprout plant and is eaten as a vegetable [First grown near Brussels, the capital of Belgium]

brut /broot/ *adj.* used to describe wine, especially sparkling white wine, that is extremely dry in taste [Late 19thC. Via French, "unsweetened," literally "rough, unrefined," from Latin *brutus* (see BRUTE).]

bru·tal /broŏtəl/ *adj.* **1.** RUTHLESS AND CRUEL extremely ruthless or cruel **2.** HARSH AND SEVERE unrelentingly harsh and severe ○ *a brutal regime* **3.** DIRECT IN MANNER direct or insensitive in manner or speech ○ *with brutal frankness* **4.** LIKE AN ANIMAL relating to or typical of beasts or lower animals (*archaic*) [15thC. Directly or via French from medieval Latin *brutalis*, from Latin *brutus* (see BRUTE).] —**bru·tal·ness** *n.*

bru·tal·ism /broŏtəlizzəm/ *n.* a style of modern architecture characterized by massiveness, a lack of exterior decoration, harsh lines, and the use of structural materials such as exposed concrete and service pipes [Early 19thC. Ultimately from French *beton brut* "rough (concrete)."] —**bru·tal·ist** *n., adj.*

bru·tal·i·ty /broo tálətee/ (*plural* **-ties**) *n.* **1.** BEING CRUEL cruel, harsh, or ruthless behavior or treatment **2.** ACT OF CRUELTY a cruel, harsh, or ruthless act

bru·tal·ize /broŏtə līz/ (**-ized, -iz·ing, -iz·es**) *vt.* **1.** MAKE SOMEBODY BRUTAL to make somebody brutal, inhuman, or unfeeling **2.** TREAT SOMEBODY CRUELLY to treat somebody brutally, cruelly, or harshly —**bru·tal·i·za·tion** /broŏtələ záyshən/ *n.*

bru·tal·ly /broŏtəlee/ *adv.* **1.** CRUELLY OR HARSHLY in a cruel or harsh manner **2.** VERY FRANKLY OR CALLOUSLY in an unpleasantly or insensitively forthright or severe manner ○ *brutally honest*

brute /broot/ *n.* **1.** SOMEBODY BRUTAL somebody who is very cruel, ruthless, or insensitive **2.** ANIMAL an animal other than a human being (*literary*) ■ *adj.* **1.** PURELY PHYSICAL purely physical or instinctive, rather than intellectual or reasoned **2.** CRUEL OR SAVAGE displaying extreme cruelty and savagery **3. STARK** unremittingly harsh or severe **4. CRUDE OR BARBARIC** used to describe behavior, actions, or instincts that are considered crude, especially those prompted by physical desire and hunger **5. OF BEASTS** relating or belonging to lower animals, as opposed to human beings [15thC. Via French *brut* from Latin *brutus* "stupid, animal-like." Ultimately from an Indo-European word meaning "heavy," which is also the ancestor of English *gravity, baritone,* and *guru.*] —**brut·ism** *n.*

brut·ish /bróotish/ *adj.* **1. RELATING TO BEASTS** relating to or characteristic of lower animals **2. CRUEL** cruel, ruthless, or insensitive **3. COARSELY UNINTELLIGENT** coarse, crude, unintelligent, or lacking sensitivity **4. CARNAL** animalistically carnal or sensual —**brut·ish·ly** *adv.* —**brut·ish·ness** *n.*

Bru·tus, Marcus Junius (85?–42 B.C.) Roman general and politician. He sided with Pompey against Caesar during the civil war 49 B.C.), and was a principal conspirator in Caesar's assassination (44 B.C.). He was defeated by Mark Antony and Octavian at Philippi (42 B.C.), and committed suicide.

brux·ism /brúksìzzəm/ *n.* the unconscious habit of grinding or gritting the teeth that occurs during sleep or in stressful situations and can lead to excessive wear of the teeth [Mid-20thC. Formed from Greek *brukein* "to gnash the teeth."]

Bry·an /brī́ən/ city in eastern Texas, northeast of Austin and northwest of Houston. Population: 58,247 (1996).

Bry·an /brī́ ən/, **William Jennings** (1860–1925) U.S. reformer, orator, and lawyer. Three times the losing Democratic candidate for president, he advocated bimetallism, notably in his famous "Cross of Gold" speech (1896). As the winning prosecutor in the Scopes trial (1925), he upheld the right of the states to ban the teaching of evolution.

Bry·ant /brī́ ənt/, **William Cullen** (1794–1878) U.S. poet, critic, and editor. His work included the nature poems *"Thanatopsis"* (1817) and *"To a Waterfowl"* (1821).

Bryce Can·yon Na·tion·al Park /brīs-/ national park in southwestern Utah, established in 1928 and noted for its highly colored, unusually eroded rock formations. Area: 35,835 acres/14,502 hectares.

Brym·ner /brímmnər/, **William** (1855–1925) Scottish-born Canadian painter. He was an influential art teacher and painted *Early Morning in September* (1899).

Bryn·hild /brínhìld/ *n.* in Norse mythology, a Valkyrie who is woken from an enchanted sleep by Sigurd and later tricked into marrying his brother-in-law, Gunnar

Bryn·ner /brínnər/, **Yul** (1915–85) Mongolian-Romani-born U.S. actor. He came to the U.S. (1940) and made a career on stage, television and in the movies. He was closely identified with his role as the king in *The King and I* in both stage (1951) movie (1956) versions.

bryo- *prefix.* moss ○ *bryophyte* [From Greek *bruon*; related to *bruein* "to teem" (source of English *embryo*)]

bry·ol·o·gy /brī áaləjee/ *n.* the branch of botany concerned with the study of hornworts, mosses, and liverworts —**bry·o·log·i·cal** /brīə láajikəl/ *adj.* —**bry·ol·o·gist** /brī áaləjist/ *n.*

bry·o·ny /brī́ ənee/ (*plural* **-nies**) *n.* a climbing plant that belongs to the marrow family, has large leaves, tendrils, and red or black berries, and is found in Europe and North Africa. Genus: *Bryonia.* [Pre-12thC. Via Latin from Greek *bruonia*, from *bruein* "to teem" (source of English *embryo*).]

bry·o·phyte /brī́ə fīt/ *n.* a nonflowering plant, often growing in damp places, that has separate gamete-bearing and spore-bearing forms. Mosses are bryophytes. Division: *Bryophyta.* —**bry·o·phyt·ic** /brīə fíttik/ *adj.*

bry·o·phyte lay·er *n.* = **moss layer**

bry·o·zo·an /brīə zṓən/ *n.* an aquatic invertebrate animal that reproduces by budding. Bryozoans often form colonies on the sea bottom or attached to seaweed. Phylum: Bryozoa. [Late 19thC. From modern Latin *Bryozoa*, which was coined from Greek *bruon* "moss" + *zoion* "animal."] —**bry·o·zo·an** *adj.*

Bryth·on /bríth'n, brithón/ *n.* somebody who speaks Breton, Welsh, or Cornish [Late 19thC. From Welsh.]

Bry·thon·ic /bri thónik/, **Brit·ton·ic** /-tónik/ *n.* **GROUP OF CELTIC LANGUAGES** a group of languages, comprising Breton, Welsh, and Cornish, that belongs to the Celtic branch of Indo-European languages. About one million people speak a Brythonic language. ■ *adj.* **OF BRYTHONS** relating to or typical of the Brythons, or their language or culture [Late 19thC. Formed from Welsh *Brython.*]

B.S. *abbr.* **1.** Bachelor of Science **2.** balance sheet **3.** bill of sale **4.** bullshit (*slang taboo*)

BSA *abbr.* Boy Scouts of America

BSc. *abbr.* Bachelor of Science

BSE *n.* a disease that affects the nervous system of cattle, believed to be caused by an abnormal transmissable protein (**prion**) and related to Creutzfeldt-Jakob disease in humans. Full form **bovine spongiform encephalopathy**

bsh. *abbr.* bushel

B share *n.* a type of unit trust investment in which the main charges are levied toward the end of the investment period

Bs/L *abbr.* bills of lading

B.S.N. *abbr.* Bachelor of Science in Nursing

BST *abbr.* bovine somatotropin

Bt. *abbr.* baronet

btl. *abbr.* bottle

btry. *abbr.* MIL battery

btu, **BTU** *abbr.* British thermal unit

BTW, **btw** *abbr.* by the way (*used in e-mail messages*)

bty. *abbr.* MIL battery

bu. *abbr.* **1.** bureau **2.** bushel

buaya /bwá yə/ *n. Malaysia, Singapore* a man who tends to flirt (*informal*) [From Malay, literally "crocodile"]

bub /bub/ *n.* used as a term of address to an unnamed male person, especially one encountered and spoken to casually (*slang*) [Mid-19thC. Shortening and alteration of BROTHER.]

bu·bal /byóo bəl/ (*plural* **-bal** *or* **-bals**) *n.* a large hartebeest of northern Africa. Latin name: *Alcephalus boselaphus.* [Late 18thC. Via French from Latin *bubalus* from Greek *boubalos* "gazelle."]

bub·ba /búbbə/ *n. Southern U.S.* **1. CONSERVATIVE SOUTHERNER** a typically rural white Southern man with traditional or conservative values and political opinions **2. BROTHER** a brother or friend who is close enough to regard as a brother (*often used as a term of address between male friends or brothers*) [Mid-19thC. Alteration of BROTHER.]

bub·ble /búbbəl/ *n.* **1. THIN GLOBE-SHAPED FILM** a thin film of something, usually spherical or dome-shaped and filled with air or a gas **2. SOMETHING LIKE A BUBBLE** something spherical or dome-shaped like a bubble **3. GLOBULE WITHIN LIQUID OR SOLID** a globule of air or a gas within a liquid or a solid, e.g., in a soft drink or in glass **4. GURGLING SOUND** a gurgling sound made by a boiling or effervescent liquid **5. SOUND OF MANY BUBBLES BURSTING** a sound produced by bubbles forming and bursting **6. DOME** a dome, usually made of transparent glass or plastic **7. PROTECTED AREA** a protected, isolated, or exempted area **8. FALSE CONFIDENCE** a false feeling of confidence or security ○ *The rocketing housing market is a bubble that will surely burst.* **9. RISKY PLAN** a risky or unreliable business enterprise or speculative plan, especially one proving to be fraudulent or unsuccessful ■ *v.* (**-bled, -bling, -bles**) **1.** *vi.* **EFFERVESCE OR BOIL UP** to form or produce spherical or dome-shaped pockets of air or gas in a liquid **2.** *vi.* **GURGLE** to move or flow with a gurgling sound **3.** *vi.* **EMERGE OR APPEAR** to emerge or rise to the surface **4.** *vi.* **BE ESPECIALLY LIVELY WITH EMOTION** to be animated with or display an emotion such as excitement, happiness, or anger ○ *bubbling with mirth* **5.** *vt.* **EXPRESS SOMETHING ENTHUSIASTICALLY** to say something with great animation and friendly enthusiasm **6.** *vt.* **MAKE SOMETHING BUBBLE** to cause something to form bubbles or to move in bubbles through a liquid [14thC. Origin uncertain: probably an imitation of the sound of bubbling water.]

bub·ble bath *n.* **1. FOAM BATH PREPARATION** a usually perfumed and colored preparation in liquid or crystal form that is added to bath water in order to make it foam **2. BATH CONTAINING FOAM** a bath to which a preparation has been added to make the bath water foam

bub·ble cham·ber *n.* a chamber containing a liquid, usually liquid hydrogen just above its boiling point, in which the trail of a particle can be observed as a line of bubbles created by the particle

bub·ble gum *n.* a type of chewing gum that can be blown from the mouth into large bubbles

bub·ble-jet print·er *n.* a printer in which ink is heated to form bubbles that burst onto the paper

bub·ble mem·o·ry *n.* a type of computer memory in which data is stored in the form of binary digits represented by the presence or absence of minute areas of magnetization in a semiconductor

bub·ble pack *n.* = **blister pack**

bub·ble point *n.* the temperature at which vapor bubbles start to appear when a liquid mixture is heated

bub·bler /búbblər/ *n.* **1.** *U.S., Aus* **DRINKING FOUNTAIN** a drinking fountain, especially one that spouts water from a vertical nozzle (*regional*) **2. DEVICE THAT BUBBLES GAS THROUGH LIQUID** a device for bubbling gas through a liquid **3. SOMETHING THAT BUBBLES** something that emits bubbles, e.g., a mountain spring [Early 18thC, when the sense was usually "swindler"]

bub·ble top *n.* **1. TRANSPARENT DOME** a transparent glass or plastic dome used in building, e.g., one forming a roof over a swimming pool **2. TRANSPARENT DOME USED AS VEHICLE TOP** a transparent dome, usually made of bulletproof plastic or glass, that forms the top or roof of a motor vehicle, e.g., one in which a head of state rides **3. VEHICLE WITH TRANSPARENT DOME AS ROOF** a motor vehicle that has a top or roof consisting of a transparent dome, usually made of bulletproof plastic or glass —**bub·ble·top** *adj.*

bub·bly /búblee/ *adj.* (**-bli·er, -bli·est**) **1. FOAMY OR EFFERVESCENT** full of or producing bubbles **2. LIKE BUBBLES** resembling a bubble or bubbles **3. CHEERFULLY EXCITED** feeling and exhibiting cheerful excitement ■ *n.* **CHAMPAGNE** sparkling wine, especially champagne (*informal*) —**bub·bli·ness** *n.*

Bu·ber /bóobər/, **Martin** (1878–1965) Austrian-born Israeli theologian and philosopher. He was an intellectual leader of German Jews before World War II and expounded his influential religious philosophy of dialogue in his best-known work, *I and Thou* (1922).

bu·bo /byóobō/ (*plural* **-boes**) *n.* swelling and inflammation of a lymph node, especially in the area of the armpit or groin [14thC. Via Latin from Greek *boubōn* "swelling in the groin."]

bu·bon·ic /boo bónnik/ *adj.* used to describe a swelling (**bubo**) of the lymph nodes

bu·bon·ic plague *n.* an infectious fatal epidemic disease caused by a bacterium transmitted by fleas that have bitten an infected host, and characterized by fever, chills, and the formation of swellings (**buboes**). In the 14th century, an extensive epidemic of it occurred known as the Black Death. In modern times, infection is limited and sporadic and can be treated successfully with antibiotics. Latin name: *Yersinia pestis.* [Formed from Latin *bubon-*, the stem of *bubo* BUBO]

bu·bon·o·cele /boo bónə seel/ *n.* an incomplete hernia of the groin accompanied by swelling [Early 17thC. Via modern Latin from Greek *boubōnokēlē*, literally "groin rupture."]

buc·cal /bóokəl/ *adj.* **1. OF CHEEKS** relating to or forming part of the cheek ○ *the buccal surface of a tooth* **2. OF THE MOUTH** relating to the mouth [Early 19thC. Formed from Latin *bucca* "cheek" (source also of English *buckle* and *embouchure*).]

buc·ca·neer /bùkə néer/ *n.* **1. PIRATE** a pirate, especially one who preyed on Spanish colonies and shipping in the West Indies in the 17th century **2. UNSCRUPULOUS ADVENTURER OR BUSINESSPERSON** a ruthless or unscrupulous adventurer, businessperson, or politician ■ *vi.* (**-neered, -neer·ing, -neers**) **ACT LIKE BUCCANEER** to be or behave like a buccaneer [Mid-17thC. From French *boucanier*, from *boucaner* "to cook over an open fire." The underlying meaning is "a hunter who cooks or cures meat outdoors."] —**buc·ca·neer·ish** *adj.* —**buc·ca·neer·ing** *adj., n.*

buc·ci·na·tor /búksə náytər/ *n.* a flat thin muscle that compresses the cheek and is used in blowing and chewing [Late 17thC. From Latin, formed from *buccinare* "to blow the trumpet," from *buccina*, a kind of trumpet.]

Bu·ceph·a·lus /byoo sséffələss/ *n.* the favorite war horse of Alexander the Great, which he tamed when still a boy

Bu·chan·an /byoō kánnən, bə kánnən/, **James** (1791–1868) U.S. statesman and 15th president of the United States. A Federalist turned Democrat, he was a U.S. Representative (1821–23), Senator (1834–45), and secretary of state (1845–49). During his presidency (1857–61) he was unable to avert the Civil War (1861–65).

Bu·cha·rest /bōōkə rèst/ the largest city and capital of Romania. It is situated on a plain in the southeastern part of the country, north of the Danube River. Population: 2,339,156 (1994).

Bu·chen·wald /bóokk ən wàwld, bōōkk ən-/ village near Weimar, central Germany that was the site of a World War II Nazi concentration camp (1937–45)

Buch·ner fun·nel /b-knər-/, **Büch·ner fun·nel** *n.* a cylindrical funnel, usually made of porcelain, with a flat perforated base through which liquids are drawn and filtered under reduced pressure [Named for the German chemist Eduard *Büchner* 1860–1917]

bu·chu /bōō koo/ (*plural* **-chus** *or* **-chu**), **bu·cku** (*plural* **-ckus** *or* **-cku**) *n.* a southern African shrub with leaves that are used as a mild diuretic and urinary antiseptic. Genus: *Agathosma.* [Mid-18thC. Via Afrikaans from Nama.]

Buch·wald /búk wàwld/, **Art** (*b.* 1925) U.S. journalist His popular column, first appearing in the *International Herald Tribune* and later widely syndicated in the United States, offered a satirical view of American life and politics. Full name **Arthur Buchwald**

buck[1] /buk/ *n.* **1. MALE ANIMAL** a male animal of some species, including antelope, deer, goat, kangaroo, and rabbit **2.** (*plural* **buck** *or* **bucks**) *S Africa* **ANTELOPE OR DEER** an antelope or deer of either sex **3.** = **buckskin** *n.* 1 **4. ARTICLE MADE OF BUCKSKIN** an article made of buckskin, e.g. a shoe **5. VIRILE YOUNG MAN** a man, especially a strong, virile, impetuous, or spirited young man (*informal dated*) **6. DANDY OR FOP** a young man who takes elaborate care to be neat and stylish (*archaic*) ■ *adj.* **OF LOWEST GRADE** of the lowest grade within a particular military category [Old English *buc* "male deer" and *bucca* "male goat"]

buck up *v.* **1.** *vti.* **MAKE OR BECOME MORE CHEERFUL** to raise the morale or spirits of somebody or to become more cheerful, confident, or encouraged (*informal*) **2.** *vi.* **HURRY UP** to hurry or act more quickly (*informal dated*)

buck[2] /buk/ *v.* (**bucked, buck·ing, bucks**) **1.** *vi.* **JUMP UPWARD** to jump or rear upward with the back arched and the legs stiff **2.** *vt.* **THROW RIDER** to throw a rider by rearing or jumping upward on the hindlegs or forelegs **3.** *vi.* **MAKE JOLTING MOTION** to move in a jerky or erratic manner **4.** *vti.* **STAND IN OPPOSITION** to oppose or resist something obstinately (*informal*) **5.** *vi.* **STRIVE WITH DETERMINATION FOR SOMETHING** to use grit and determination in striving for something, typically over the long term (*informal*) **6.** *vt.* **GAMBLE AGAINST SOMETHING** to take a risk against something ○ *buck the odds* **7.** *vti.* **BUTT WITH LOWERED HEAD** to charge against somebody or something with the head lowered **8.** *vt.* FOOTBALL **CHARGE INTO SOMEBODY** to charge into an opposing teammate or into an opposing line ■ *n.* **ACT OF BUCKING** the movement or action of bucking [Mid-19thC. From BUCK[1]. Originally, it referred to the motions of a copulating male rabbit.]

buck[3] /buk/ *n. U.S., Can, ANZ* (*informal*) **1. DOLLAR** a United States, Canadian, Australian, or New Zealand dollar **2. AMOUNT OF MONEY** a specified or unspecified amount of money [Mid-19thC. Shortening of BUCKSKIN, used as a unit of exchange on the American frontier.]

buck[4] /buk/ *n.* **1. VAULTING HORSE** a covered block used as a vaulting horse **2.** = **sawhorse** [Early 19thC. From BUCK[1].]

buck[5] /buk/ (**bucked, buck·ing, bucks**) *n.* a counter or marker formerly used in poker and passed from one player to another to indicate some obligation, especially somebody's turn to deal [Mid-19thC. Origin uncertain.] ◇ **pass the buck** to shift responsibility to somebody else (*informal*)

Buck /buk/, **Pearl S.** (1892–1973) U.S. writer. Best known for novels depicting Chinese life, such as the Pulitzer Prize-winning *The Good Earth* (1931). She won the Nobel Prize in literature in 1938. Born **Pearl Sydenstricker**

buck·a·roo /bùkə rōō/ (*plural* **-roos**), **buck·er·oo** (*plural* **-oos**) *n.* **1. COWBOY** a cowhand in the southwestern United States (*informal*) **2. BRONCOBUSTER** a cowhand who breaks wild horses [Early 19thC. Alteration of Spanish *vaquero* "cowboy," under the influence of BUCK[2].]

buck·bean /búk bēen/ *n.* a marsh plant of the gentian family that has white, pink, or purplish flowers and is native to the northern hemisphere. Latin name: *Menyanthes trifoliata.* [Late 16thC. Translation of Flemish *boks boonen* "goat's beans."]

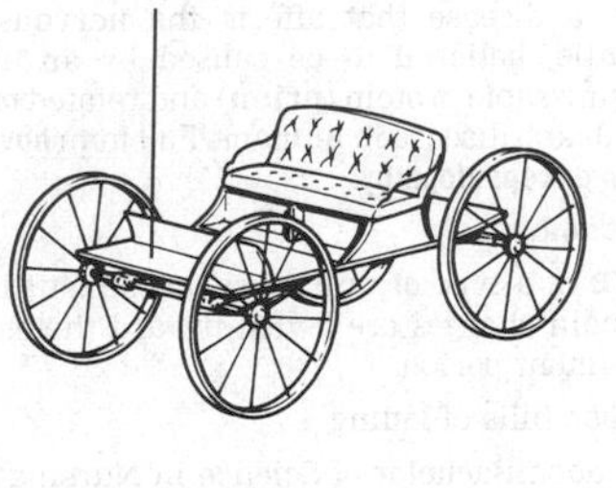

Buck board

buck board /búk bàwrd/ *n.* an open four-wheeled horse-drawn carriage with the seat or seats mounted on a flexible board between the front and rear axles [Late 17thC. Buck from an obsolete word meaning "belly, body (of a wagon)."]

buck·er·oo *n.* = **buckaroo**

buck·et /búkit/ *n.* **1. CYLINDRICAL CONTAINER** a container, usually cylindrical in shape with an open top and a semicircular handle, used for catching or holding liquids or solids **2. BUCKETFUL** the contents of a bucket or the amount that a bucket will hold **3. LARGE QUANTITY** a very large quantity or amount of something (*informal*) (*often used in the plural*) **4. SOMETHING LIKE A BUCKET** something resembling or suggesting a bucket in shape or function, e.g., a compartment on the outer edge of a waterwheel **5. MACHINE PART** any of various machine parts that resemble a bucket, e.g., the scoop on a front-end loader **6. FOOD CONTAINER** a large plastic or paper container for food, e.g., fried chicken or ice cream **7.** TRANSP = **bucket seat 8.** BASKETBALL = **basket** *n.* 4 ■ *v.* (**-et·ed, -et·ing, -ets**) **1.** *vt.* **CARRY OR PUT SOMETHING IN BUCKET** to carry, hold, lift, or put something in a bucket **2.** *vi.* **MOVE FAST** to move or drive fast, jerkily, haphazardly, or recklessly (*informal*) ○ *We went bucketing down the freeway.* [13thC. From Anglo-Norman *buket*, of Germanic origin.] ◇ **kick the bucket** to die (*slang*)

buck·et bri·gade *n.* a line of people formed to pass buckets of water from hand to hand, especially to put out a fire

buck·et·ful /búkitfōōl/ *n.* **1. AMOUNT IN BUCKET** the contents of a bucket or the amount that a bucket will hold **2. HUGE QUANTITY** a very large quantity or amount of something (*usually plural*)

buck·et lad·der *n.* a continuous chain of buckets used for excavating land or dredging riverbeds (*hyphenated when used before a noun*) ○ *bucket-ladder dredger*

buck·et seat *n.* an individual seat with a rounded back in a vehicle or aircraft

buck·et shop *n.* a dishonest unregistered stock-brokerage that speculates and gambles on stocks and commodities using its client's capital [Originally referring to saloons selling small amounts of liquor in buckets]

buck·eye /búk ī/ *n.* **1.** (*plural* **-eyes** *or* **-eye**) **POISONOUS HORSE-CHESTNUT TREE** a poisonous tree or shrub of the horse-chestnut family that is native to North America and has large shiny brown seeds encased in a prickly or smooth covering. Genus: *Aesculus.* **2. FRUIT OR POISONOUS SEED OF BUCKEYE** a prickly or smooth fruit of the buckeye tree or the large brown poisonous seed it contains [Mid-18thC. Formed from BUCK[1] + EYE, because of the seed's resemblance to a deer's eye.]

Buck·eye /búk ī/ *n.* a native or resident of Ohio (*informal*)

buck fe·ver *n.* (*informal*) **1. NERVOUS EXCITEMENT OF NOVICE HUNTER** nervous excitement felt by an inexperienced hunter at the sight of game **2. NERVOUS EXCITEMENT** nervous excitement felt by somebody faced with a new situation, experience, or responsibility

buck·horn /búk hàwrn/ *n.* **1. HORN OF BUCK** the horn of a male deer or antelope **2. MATERIAL FROM A BUCK'S HORN** the material from the horn of a male deer or antelope, used to make handles for knives and tools **3.** (*plural* **-horns** *or* **-horn**) **PLANT WITH LEAVES RESEMBLING ANIMAL'S HORN** a plant of Europe and Asia with leaves shaped like the horn of a deer or antelope. Latin name: *Plantago coronopus.*

buck·hound /búk hòwnd/ *n.* a hound used for chasing game, especially deer

Buck·ing·ham Pal·ace /bùkingəm pálləss, -ham-/ *n.* the official London residence of the British monarch. It was built in 1703 for John Sheffield, Duke of Buckingham and Normandy, and rebuilt by John Nash in the early 19th century.

buck·le /búkəl/ *n.* **1. METAL FASTENER** a clasp, typically consisting of a metal frame with a hinged prong, for fastening two loose ends, especially of a belt, shoe, or strap **2. ORNAMENT RESEMBLING BUCKLE** an ornament that resembles a buckle, e.g., on a shoe or a hat **3. A BULGE, BEND, OR KINK** a bend or kink in something, e.g., a rope, or a bulge in something, e.g., a piece of wood ■ *v.* (**-led, -ling, -les**) **1.** *vti.* **FASTEN SOMETHING WITH BUCKLE** to fasten something, e.g., a shoe or seatbelt, with a buckle, or to be fastened with such a device **2.** *vti.* **BEND OR CAUSE SOMETHING TO BEND** to bend out of shape, warp, or crumple, usually because of heat or pressure, or to distort something in this way **3.** *vi.* **COLLAPSE** to collapse or lose strength completely, sometimes as a result of a structural defect or weakness **4.** *vi.* **GIVE IN** to succumb or yield to pressure, especially emotional strain or fear [14thC. Via Anglo-Norman *bucle* and Old French *bocle* from Latin *buccula* "cheek strap of a helmet," from *bucca* "cheek."]

buckle down *vi.* to set out to accomplish something with vigor or determination (*informal*)

buckle under *vi.* to give in under pressure or stress

buckle up *vti.* to fasten the buckle on a seatbelt, e.g., in a motor vehicle or an aircraft

buck·ler /búklər/ *n.* **1. SHIELD** a small round shield either worn on the forearm or held by a short handle at arm's length **2. MEANS OF PROTECTION** a defense or means of protection (*literary*) ■ *vt.* (**-lered, -ler·ing, -lers**) **PROTECT SOMEBODY OR SOMETHING** to shield or defend somebody or something with a buckler (*archaic*) [13thC. From Old French *bocler*, from *bocle* "boss of a shield" (see BUCKLE).]

buck·ler fern *n.* a perennial deciduous or semi-evergreen fern that grows to about 3 ft./1 m in height. There is a broad buckler fern and a narrow buckler fern. Genus: *Dryopteris.* [So called because of the kidney-shaped flap of tissue covering the receptacle in which its spores are formed]

Buck·ley /búklee/, **William F. Jr.** (*b.* 1925) U.S. writer and editor. A conservative political commentator, he was founding editor of the *National Review* (1955) and hosted the television program "Firing Line" (1966). His books include *The Culture of Liberty* (1993). Full name **William Frank Jr. Buckley**

buck·min·ster·ful·ler·ene /bùkminstər fōōlərēen/ *n.* a stable form of carbon containing 60 carbon atoms that occurs naturally in certain minerals [Late 20thC. From the molecule's resemblance to the geodesic dome structure invented by the U.S. architect R. *Buckminster Fuller* (1895–1983).]

buck-na·ked, **buck na·ked** *adj.* wearing no clothes at all (*regional*)

buck·o /búkō/ (*plural* **-os**) *n.* **1. SWAGGERING BULLY** a swaggering bully or bossy person (*slang*) **2.** *Ireland, U.S.* **MALE PERSON** a boy or man (*informal*) [Late 19thC. Formed from BUCK[1].]

buck-pass·ing *n.* the shifting of blame or responsibility to somebody else (*informal*) [From BUCK[5]] —**buck-pass·er** *n.*

buck·ram /búkrəm/ *n.* **STIFF FABRIC** a coarse cotton or linen fabric that has been stiffened with starch, gum, or latex. It is used in bookbinding and for stiffening garments. ■ *adj.* **LIKE BUCKRAM** resembling buckram in rigidity ■ *vt.* (**-ramed, -ram·ing, -rams**) **STIFFEN SOMETHING WITH BUCKRAM** to stiffen or strengthen something with buckram [14thC. From Old French *boquerant* "cloth from Bukhara."]

bucks /buks/ *npl.* buckskin breeches or shoes, especially casual oxford shoes

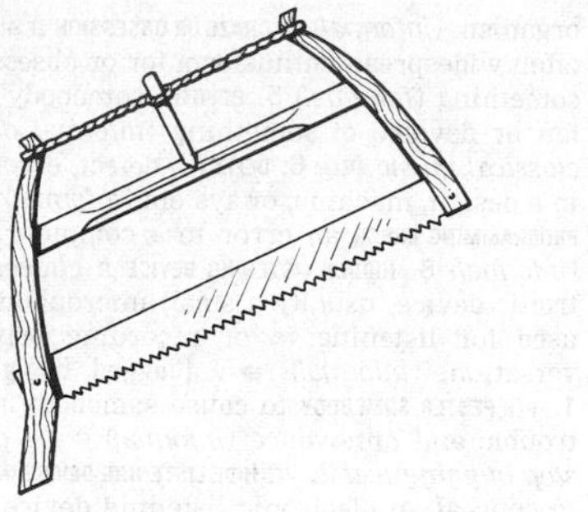

Bucksaw

buck·saw /búk sò/ *n.* a woodcutting saw in which the blade is set in an H-shaped frame [Mid-19thC. From BUCK[4].]

buck·shot /búk shòt/ *n.* a large size of lead shot used in shotgun shells, especially for hunting game

buck·skin /búk skìn/ *n.* **1. DEERSKIN** the skin of a male deer **2. SOFT LEATHER** a soft pliable grayish yellow leather, usually with a suede finish, originally made from deerskin and now usually from sheepskin **3. SOMEBODY WEARING BUCKSKIN** somebody wearing clothes made of buckskin, especially an early American living in the backwoods or an early frontier soldier (*archaic*) **4. GRAYISH YELLOW HORSE** a horse of a grayish yellow color ■ **buck·skins** *npl.* **BUCKSKIN GARMENTS** clothing made from buckskin leather, especially jackets, chaps, hats, and moccasins ■ *adj.* **GRAYISH YELLOW** grayish yellow in color

buck·thorn /búk thàwrn/ (*plural* **-thorns** *or* **-thorn**) *n.* a thorny shrub or small tree with greenish flowers and black berries that were formerly used as a purgative. Genus: *Rhamnus.* [Late 16thC. Translation of modern Latin *cervi spina* "stag's thorn."]

buck·tooth /bùk to͞oth/ (*plural* **-teeth**) *n.* a protruding upper front tooth (*informal*) —**buck·toothed** *adj.*

buck·u *n.* = **buchu**

buck·wheat /búk wèet, -hwèet/ *n.* **1. PLANT WITH EDIBLE SEED** an Asian plant grown for its edible triangular seeds. Latin name: *Fagopyrum esculentum.* **2. EDIBLE SEED** the seed produced by the buckwheat plant. It is cooked as a cereal, ground into flour, or used as animal fodder. [Mid-16thC. Anglicization of Middle Dutch *boecweite*, literally "beech wheat," so called because its grains resemble beech nuts.]

buck·y·ball /búki bàwl/ *n.* a ball-shaped carbon molecule found in stable forms of carbon (**fullerenes**), especially the molecule containing 60 carbon atoms (**buckminsterfullerene**). It sometimes occurs naturally but is usually synthesized. (*informal*) [Late 20thC. Coined from *Bucky*, the nickname of R. Buckminster Fuller (see BUCKMINSTERFULLERENE) + BALL.]

bu·col·ic /byoo kólik/ *adj.* **1. OF THE COUNTRYSIDE** relating to or characteristic of the countryside, country people, or country life ○ *a writer of bucolic poems* **2. OF SHEPHERDS** relating to or characteristic of shepherds, herdsmen, or flocks ■ *n.* **1.** LITERAT **PASTORAL POEM** a poem about the countryside or country life **2. COUNTRY PERSON** a farmer, shepherd, or other person from the country [Early 16thC. Via Latin from, ultimately, Greek *boukolos*, literally "cowherd."] —**bu·col·i·cal·ly** *adv.*

bud[1] /bud/ *n.* **1. OUTGROWTH ON PLANT STEM** an outgrowth on a stem or branch consisting of a shortened stem and immature leaves or flowers, often enclosed by protective scales **2. UNOPENED FLOWER** a flower that has not yet opened **3.** ZOOL **REPRODUCTIVE OUTGROWTH OF SIMPLE ORGANISM** an asexually produced outgrowth of a simple organism, e.g., an invertebrate or a yeast, that breaks away from the parent and develops into a new individual **4. SOMETHING RESEMBLING PLANT BUD** something shaped like a plant bud **5. SOMEBODY OR SOMETHING IMMATURE** somebody or something that is small, immature, or not yet fully developed ■ *v.* (**bud·ded, bud·ding, buds**) **1.** *vi.* **PRODUCE PLANT BUDS** to produce outgrowths that develop into flowers or leaves **2.** *vi.* **START TO GROW** to start to develop or grow from a plant bud **3.** *vi.* **BEGIN TO DEVELOP** to begin to develop or grow from something small into another, usually larger, thing ○ *Seeds of dissent are budding in the heartland.* **4.** *vi.* ZOOL **REPRODUCE ASEXUALLY** to reproduce asexually by producing an outgrowth that eventually separates to form a new individual, as occurs in invertebrates and yeasts **5.** *vt.* GARDENING **GRAFT BUD INTO ANOTHER PLANT** to insert a bud from one plant into the bark of another, usually one of a different variety, in order to propagate a plant from the bud [14thC. Origin uncertain.] —**bud·der** *n.* —**bud·less** *adj.* ◇ **nip something in the bud** to put an end to a plan or idea before it can be developed (*informal*)

bud[2] /bud/ *n.* = **buddy** (*informal*) [Mid-19thC. Shortening.]

Bu·da·pest /bo͞odə pèst, -pèsht/ capital and largest city of Hungary. It is situated on the Danube River in northern Hungary near the Slovak border. Population: 1,930,000 (1995).

Barnaby's

Buddha: Daibutsu (Great Buddha), Kamakura, Japan

bud·dha /bo͝oddə/, **Bud·dha** *n.* **1. SOMEBODY ENLIGHTENED** somebody who has achieved a state of perfect enlightenment, in accord with the teachings of the Buddha **2. IMAGE OF BUDDHA** a statue, picture, or other representation of the Buddha [Late 17thC. From Sanskrit, the past participle of *budh-* "to wake up, be enlightened."]

Bud·dha /bo͝oddə/ (563–483 B.C.) Nepalese-born Indian philosopher, he renounced his life as a prince. He attained Enlightenment about 528 B.C. and developed and taught the doctrines of Buddhism. Born **Siddharta Gautama**. Known as **Sakyamuni**

Bud·dha·hood /bo͝oddəho͝od/ *n.* the state of spiritual enlightenment attained by the Buddha

Bud·dhism /bo͝oddìzzəm/ *n.* a world religion or philosophy based on the teaching of the Buddha and holding that a state of enlightenment can be attained by suppressing worldly desires

Bud·dhist /bo͝oddist/ *n.* **BELIEVER IN BUDDHISM** somebody who believes in and practices Buddhism ■ *adj.* **OF BUDDHISM** relating to, associated with, or practicing Buddhism —**Bud·dhis·tic** /boo dístik/ *adj.*

bud·ding /búdding/ *adj.* **PROMISING** beginning to show a particular talent ○ *a budding actor* ■ *n.* **1.** BOT **DEVELOPMENT OF BUDS** the formation and growth of buds on a plant stem **2.** GARDENING **GRAFTING A BUD** artificial propagation, especially of woody plants, by grafting a bud from one variety onto the stem of another **3.** ZOOL **ASEXUAL REPRODUCTION** a form of asexual reproduction in which an outgrowth of the parent becomes constricted and eventually separates to form a new individual, as occurs in invertebrates and yeasts

bud·dle /búddəl/ *n.* a sloping trough in which crushed ore is separated from waste by washing with water [Mid-16thC. Origin unknown.]

bud·dle·ia (*plural* **-ias** *or* **-ia**) *n.* a deciduous ornamental shrub or small tree that is native to warm regions and has tapering heads of small, scented, purple flowers that attract butterflies. Latin name: *Buddleja davidii.* [Late 18thC. From modern Latin, genus name, after the English botanist Adam *Buddle* (d. 1715).]

bud·dy /búddee/ *n.* (*plural* **-dies**) **1. FRIEND** a good friend, colleague, companion, or partner (*informal*) **2. TERM OF ADDRESS FOR MALE** a form of address to a man or boy (*informal*) ○ *Hey, buddy!* **3. HELPER TO AIDS PATIENT** a volunteer who gives help and support to someone who has AIDS ■ *vi.* (**-died, -dy·ing, -dies**) **ACT AS AIDS HELPER** to act as a helper to someone with AIDS [Mid-19thC. Origin uncertain: possibly an alteration of BROTHER.]

buddy up *vi.* to become friends with or work closely with somebody else (*informal*)

bud·dy-bud·dy *adj.* appearing to enjoy a close friendship (*informal*)

bud·dy stores *npl.* fuel tanks on a host aircraft from which fuel can be transferred to another plane during flight

bud·dy sys·tem *n.* an arrangement by which individuals are paired for mutual safety, e.g., in mountain climbing

budge[1] /buj/ (**budged, budg·ing, budg·es**) *vti.* **1. MOVE** to move, or to alter the position of something by movement (*usually with negatives*) ○ *I tried moving the machine, but it wouldn't budge.* **2. CHANGE OPINION** to change or make somebody change an attitude, decision, or opinion ○ *Once she's made up her mind, no amount of persuasion will budge her.* [Late 16thC. Via French *bouger* from assumed Vulgar Latin *bullicare*, literally "to keep bubbling up," from Latin *bullire* (see BOIL[1]).]

budge[2] /buj/ *n.* **FUR** a type of fur, usually made of lambskin, worn with the wool outward and formerly used as a trimming on academic or official gowns ■ *adj.* **1. WITH FUR** made from, trimmed with, or lined with budge **2. FORMAL OR STIFF** formal, pompous, solemn, or stiff (*archaic*) [Origin uncertain]

Budge /buj/, **Don** (*b.* 1915) U.S. tennis player. One of the greatest players of his generation, he was the first tennis player ever to win a grand slam (1938). Full name **John Donald Budge**

budg·er·i·gar /bújəri ghaàr/ *n.* a small bright green parrot with a yellow head, found in flocks in arid areas of central Australia. It is a popular domestic pet around the world and is bred in captivity for its bright plumage. Latin name: *Melopsittacus undulatus.* [Mid-19thC. Alteration of Yuwaalaraay *gijirigaa*.]

budg·et /bújət/ *n.* **1. SUMMARY OF INCOME AND SPENDING** an often itemized estimate of income and spending, e.g., of a country or company, during a specified period. It sometimes includes systematic proposals as to how expenses will be met. **2. PLAN FOR ALLOCATING RESOURCES** a plan specifying how resources, e.g., time or money, will be spent or allocated during a particular period **3. MONEY FOR SPECIFIC PURPOSE** the total amount of money allocated or needed for a specific purpose or period of time **4. QUANTITY OR SUPPLY** a specified quantity, stock, or supply **5. BAG OR POUCH** a bag, pouch, or wallet (*regional*) ■ *adj.* **CHEAP OR ECONOMICAL** suitable for people with a limited amount of money to spend ■ *v.* (**-et·ed, -et·ing, -ets**) **1.** *vti.* **PLAN SPENDING** to plan the allocation, expenditure, or use of resources, especially money or time **2.** *vt.* **ENTER IN BUDGET** to make provision for something or enter something in a budget **3.** *vi.* **LIVE WITHIN SPENDING LIMITS** to live within a budget ○ *Having budgeted well all their lives, they can afford to retire early.* [15thC. Via Old French *bougette* "leather pouch, purse" from, ultimately, Latin *bulga* "leather sack" (see BULGE).]

budg·et·ar·y /bújətèree/ *adj.* relating to budgets

budg·et def·i·cit *n.* the amount of government expenditure that exceeds revenue

budg·et·er /bújətər/ *n.* **1. MAKER OF BUDGET** somebody who draws up a budget **2. SOMEBODY CONFINED BY BUDGET** somebody who is limited to a budget

budg·ie /bújee/ *n.* a budgerigar, especially one kept as a domestic pet (*informal*) [Early 20thC. Shortening.]

bud scale *n.* any of the scaly leaves that form a protective sheath around a plant bud and are sometimes hairy or resinous

bud·worm /búd wùrm/ *n.* a moth larva that feeds on conifer buds and is one of the most destructive pests in North America. Latin name: *Harmolga fumiferana.*

Bue·na Park /bwàynə-/ city in southern California, southeast of Los Angeles. Population: 71,999 (1996).

Bue·na Vis·ta /bwàynə vístə, bwènaa vèestaa/ village in Coahuila State, Mexico, the site of an important American victory in the Mexican War in 1847

Bue·no /bwáynō/, **Maria** (*b.* 1940) Brazilian tennis player. She won singles titles at the U.S. championships (1959, 1963, 1964, 1966) and at Wimbledon (1959, 1960, and 1964). Full name **Marie Ester Audion Bueno**

Bue·nos Ai·res /bwàynəss íreez, -áareez/ capital and largest city of Argentina, situated in the eastern part of the country. It is a port on the Río de la Plata and the nation's commercial and cultural center. Population: 2,988,006 (1995).

buff[1] /buf/ *vt.* (**buffed, buff·ing, buffs**) **1. POLISH SOMETHING** to clean or polish something with a piece of soft material **2. MAKE SURFACE SOFT** to make the surface of something, especially of leather, soft and velvety like buff by raising a nap ■ *n.* **1.** COLORS **PALE YELLOWISH BROWN** a dull yellowish beige color **2.** INDUST **SOFT**

LEATHER a soft thick undyed leather that is made chiefly from the skins of buffalo, elk, or oxen and has a light yellow color 3. POLISHING CLOTH a cloth of soft material such as leather or velvet, used for polishing, often mounted on a block 4. ENG POLISHING DISK a revolving disk consisting of layers of cloth impregnated with abrasive powders, used for polishing metal or other hard bright surfaces 5. CLOTHES LEATHER GARMENT a garment made of buff leather, e.g., a military uniform coat ■ *adj.* 1. COLORS PALE YELLOWISH BROWN of a dull yellowish brown color 2. OF BUFF LEATHER made of buff leather [Late 16thC. Alteration of French *buffle* "buffalo," from late Latin *bufalus* (see BUFFALO).] ◇ **in the buff** naked (*informal*)

buff[2] /buf/ *n.* somebody who is enthusiastic about and has a wide knowledge of a particular subject ○ *a movie buff* ○ *an opera buff* [Early 19thC. From the overcoats made of buff leather formerly worn by volunteer firemen in New York City, who were known as "fire buffs."]

buff[3] /buf/ *vt.* (**buffed, buff·ing, buffs**) DEADEN FORCE OF SOMETHING to deaden or reduce the force of something ■ *n.* BLOW OR SLAP a blow, buffet, or slap (*archaic*) [15thC. From Old French *bufe* (see BUFFET[2]).]

buff[4] /buf/ *adj.* having a handsome or beautiful face and physique (*slang*) [Late 20thC. Origin uncertain: probably from BUFF[1].]

buf·fa·lo /búffəlō/ *n.* (*plural* **-loes** *or* **-los** *or* **-lo**) 1. TYPE OF HORNED CATTLE a type of horned cattle belonging to various species, including the African buffalo and domesticated breeds of the Asian water buffalo. Family: Bovidae. 2. N AMERICAN BISON the North American bison. ◊ **bison** 3. = **buffalo fish** ■ *vt.* (**-loed, -lo·ing, -loes**) (*informal*) 1. BAFFLE SOMEBODY to throw somebody into a state of confusion and puzzled bewilderment 2. *Can* INTIMIDATE SOMEBODY to coerce or inhibit somebody aggressively [Mid-16thC. Via Portuguese or Italian from late Latin *bufalus*, from Greek *boubalos* "gazelle."]

Buf·fa·lo /búffəlō/ city and port in northeastern New York beside Lake Erie and on the Niagara River. Population: 310,548 (1996).

buf·fa·lo ber·ry *n.* 1. SHRUB WITH BERRIES a North American shrub of the oleaster family with silvery foliage and edible berries. Genus: *Shepherdia.* 2. EDIBLE BERRY the edible fruit of the buffalo berry shrub

Buf·fa·lo Bill /bùffəlō bíl/ (1846–1917) U.S. scout and statesman. He sometimes worked as an army scout in the western territories, and earned his nickname by killing thousands of buffalo to feed railway workers in the 1860s. From 1883 to 1913 he toured with his own "Wild West Show." Real name **William Frederick Cody**

buf·fa·lo bug *n.* = **carpet beetle**

buf·fa·lo chips *npl.* dried buffalo dung used as fuel (*informal*)

buf·fa·lo fish *n.* a large freshwater fish of the sucker family that resembles the carp. Buffalo fish have a humped back and are found mostly in the Mississippi Valley. Genus: *Ictiobus.*

buf·fa·lo grass *n.* a short gray-green grass of the plains of central North America that is used as forage and for lawns. Latin name: *Buchloë dactyloides.*

Buf·fa·lo Grove village in northeastern Illinois, a northwestern suburb of Chicago. Population: 41,169 (1996).

buf·fa·lo jump *n.* a cliff over which buffalo were stampeded by the Native American peoples of the North American plains in order to provide a source of food

buf·fa·lo robe *n.* the skin of the American bison, prepared with the hair left on and used as a blanket, coat, or rug

buf·fa·lo sol·dier, Buf·fa·lo Sol·dier *n.* a Black soldier in the U.S. Army during the period between the Civil War and World War I (*informal*)

Buf·fa·lo wings *npl.* chicken wings, typically in barbecue sauce, served as an appetizer [So called because they were supposedly first served in a restaurant in or named for Buffalo, New York]

buff·er[1] /búffər/ *n.* 1. PROTECTOR AGAINST IMPACT somebody or something that reduces shock or impact or protects against other harm, usually by interception 2. RAIL DEVICE ON TRAIN OR TRACK either of a pair of spring-loaded or hydraulic pads attached to both ends of rolling stock or at the end of a railroad track. They stop the train running off the end of the track and may also absorb impact. 3. CHEM SUBSTANCE MAINTAINING PH a substance that minimizes a change in pH of a solution by neutralizing added acids and bases, or a solution containing such a substance 4. COMPUT MEMORY AREA a temporary storage area used for data being transmitted between two devices to compensate for differences in the rate at which each device functions or the availability of the receiving device. A buffer enables the faster device, such as a computer, to complete sending the data and begin another task without waiting for the slower device, such as a printer. ■ *vt.* (**-ered, -er·ing, -ers**) 1. CUSHION SOMETHING AGAINST SHOCK to protect something against impact or reduce the shock of an impact on something 2. CHEM ADD BUFFER TO SOLUTION to add to a solution a substance that will keep its pH constant [Mid-19thC. Formed from an obsolete word meaning "to hit something softly," possibly from French (see BUFFET[2]).]

buff·er[2] /búffər/ *n.* 1. USER OF BUFFER somebody who polishes something with a buffer 2. = **buff**[1] *n.* 2 [Mid-19thC. Formed from BUFF[1].]

buff·er state *n.* a small neutral state that lies between two potentially hostile powers and reduces the risk of conflict between them

buff·er stock *n.* a stock of a basic commodity accumulated by a government, e.g., when supplies are plentiful and prices low, and held for use when supplies are short to stabilize the price

buff·er zone *n.* 1. NEUTRAL TERRITORY a neutral area that lies between hostile forces and reduces the risk of conflict between them 2. SEPARATING AREA any area designed to form a barrier that prevents potential conflict or harmful contact

buf·fet[1] /bə fáy, boo-/ *n.* 1. SELF-SERVICE MEAL a meal at which people serve themselves from various dishes set out on a table, sideboard, or counter 2. TABLE WITH REFRESHMENTS a serving counter or table on which the meals or refreshments are displayed 3. DINING-ROOM SERVING TABLE a piece of dining-room furniture with drawers for tableware, used for storing table items and for serving dishes [Early 18thC. From French, "footstool, sideboard," of unknown origin.]

buf·fet[2] /búffət/ *n.* 1. BLOW WITH HAND a blow struck with the fist or hand 2. REPEATED BLOW a heavy or repeated blow or stroke 3. AIR = **buffeting** ■ *v.* (**-fet·ed, -fet·ing, -fets**) 1. *vt.* BATTER SOMETHING to knock or strike against something forcefully or repeatedly 2. *vt.* HIT SOMETHING SHARPLY to hit something sharply, especially with the hand 3. *vi.* STRUGGLE TO PROGRESS to proceed under difficult conditions [Pre-12thC. From Old French, literally "small blow," from *bufe* "blow," originally an imitation of the sound.] —**buf·fet·er** *n.*

buf·fet·ing /búffəting/ *n.* an irregular shaking of a part or the whole of an aircraft during flight, typically caused by strong winds

buf·fi plural of **buffo**

buff·ing wheel *n.* a wheel covered with a soft material such as lamb's wool, leather, or velvet and used to shine or polish something, especially metal

buf·fle·head /búffəl hèd/ (*plural* **-heads** *or* **-head**) *n.* a small North American diving duck, the male of which has black and white plumage and a large fluffy head, while the female is dark brown. Latin name: *Bucephala albeola.* [Mid-17thC. Formed from obsolete *buffle* "buffalo" (from French; see BUFF[1]), so called because of its large head.]

buf·fo /bóofō/ *n.* (*plural* **-fi** /-fee/ *or* **-fos**) MALE OPERA SINGER a male singer of comic roles in opera ■ *adj.* FUNNY comic in a manner that is characteristic of a buffo [Mid-18thC. From Italian, formed from *buffare* "to puff, act the clown" (source of English *buffoon*).]

buf·foon /bə fóon/ *n.* 1. CLOWN somebody who amuses others by clowning, by joking, or by ridiculous behavior 2. BUMBLING PERSON somebody who is regarded as behaving in a mildly inappropriate way [Mid-16thC. Via French *bouffon* from, ultimately, Italian *buffare* "to clown," literally "to puff," originally an imitation of the sound.]

buf·foon·er·y /bə fóonəree/ *n.* silly behavior

buff wheel *n.* = **buffing wheel**

bug /bug/ *n.* 1. INSECTS TYPE OF INSECT an insect with thickened forewings and mouthparts adapted for piercing and sucking. Order: Hemiptera. 2. INSECTS ANY INSECT any insect or similar organism, especially one considered to be a pest, e.g., an aphid, bed bug, or cockroach 3. AILMENT CAUSED BY GERM any mild ailment that is caused by an unspecified micro-organism (*informal*) 4. CRAZE OR OBSESSION a strong and often widespread enthusiasm for or obsession with something (*informal*) 5. DEVOTEE somebody who is a fan or devotee of something (*informal dated*) ○ *a classical music bug* 6. DEFECT a defect, error, or flaw in a design, machine, or system (*informal*) 7. COMPUT PROGRAMMING ERROR an error in a computer program (*informal*) 8. HIDDEN LISTENING DEVICE a concealed electronic device, usually a small microphone, that is used for listening to or recording private conversations (*informal*) ■ *v.* (**bugged, bug·ging, bugs**) 1. *vt.* PESTER SOMEBODY to cause somebody persistent trouble and annoyance (*informal*) ○ *Go away and stop bugging me!* 2. *vt.* HIDE LISTENING DEVICE IN SOMETHING to conceal an electronic listening device in something ○ *She suspected her phone had been bugged.* 3. *vt.* LISTEN TO SOMETHING SECRETLY to listen to or eavesdrop on a conversation using an electronic surveillance device ○ *He thinks someone is bugging his phone conversations.* 4. *vi.* BULGE OUTWARD to grow large, especially in bulging outward, as the eyes do when somebody is surprised or scared (*informal*) [14thC. Origin unknown.]

WORD KEY: SYNONYMS

See Synonyms at *bother.*

bug off *vi.* to go away quickly, usually as a result of being ordered to do so (*slang*) ○ *We just told him to bug off and leave us alone.*

bug out *vi.* (*slang*) 1. BEHAVE IN IRRATIONAL WAY suddenly to become very angry or upset, or start behaving in an irrational way 2. RUSH OFF IN FRIGHT to hurry away, especially from a military post, in fear or panic or to avoid duty ○ *They had contempt for certain soldiers who just wanted to bug out.*

bug·a·boo /búggəbōo/ (*plural* **-boos**) *n.* something that causes fear, annoyance, or trouble, especially an imagined threat or problem [Mid-18thC. Origin uncertain.]

Bu·gan·da /boo gaánda/ kingdom in the area north of Lake Victoria, southern Uganda. It became part of Uganda in 1962 and the kingdom was dissolved in 1967.

Bu·gat·ti /boo gaátee/, **Ettore** (1882–1947) Italian automobile designer and manufacturer. He is best known for the racing cars he produced in the 1930s. Full name **Ettore Arco Isidoro Bugatti**

bug·bane /búg bàyn/ *n.* a European plant whose small white flowers are reputed to repel insects. Latin name: *Cimicifuga foetida.*

bug·bear /búg bàyr/ *n.* 1. CONTINUING PROBLEM a continuing source of annoyance or difficulty 2. SOURCE OF FEAR a source of obsessive or groundless fear 3. MONSTER a monster invented to frighten children, traditionally in the form of a bear that eats those who misbehave [Late 16thC. From an obsolete word meaning "hobgoblin" + BEAR[1].]

bug-eyed *adj.* (*informal*) 1. WITH BULGING EYES having protruding eyes 2. AGOG wide-eyed with amazement or fear

bug·ger[1] /búggər/ *n.* OFFENSIVE TERM a highly offensive term for somebody who practices sodomy (*slang offensive*) ■ *vti.* (**-gered, -ger·ing, -gers**) OFFENSIVE TERM to practic sodomy (*taboo offensive*) [Mid-16thC. Via French *bougre* "heretic" from Latin *Bulgarus*, literally "Bulgarian," from Western Christian association of heresy with sodomy.]

bug·ger[2] /búggər/ *n.* somebody who conceals listening devices in something, such as a room or telephone

bug·ger·y /búggəree/ *n.* = **sodomy** [14thC. From Middle Dutch *buggerie* (formed from *bugger*) or Old French *bougrerie*, formed from *bougre* (see BUGGER).]

bug·gy[1] /búggee/ (*plural* **-gies**) *n.* 1. HORSE-DRAWN VEHICLE a lightweight horse-drawn carriage 2. BATTERY-POWERED VEHICLE a small battery-powered vehicle used for a special purpose ○ *a golf buggy* 3. BABY CARRIAGE a light baby carriage 4. *U.K.* STROLLER a lightweight stroller for young children [Mid-18thC. Origin unknown.]

bug·gy[2] /búggee/ (**-gi·er, -gi·est**) *adj.* 1. INSECT-RIDDEN infested with insects 2. NUTTY eccentric (*slang*) [Early 18thC. Formed from BUG.] —**bug·gi·ness** *n.*

bug·house /búg hòws/ *n.* an offensive term for a mental health facility (*slang offensive*) [Late 19thC. From BUG, in the sense "obsession, an obsessive person."]

bug juice *n.* (*slang*) 1. SWEET DRINK any sugary brightly colored beverage 2. INSECT REPELLANT a spray, liquid, or lotion used to repel insects [From the unpleasant color and flavor of the drink]

bu·gle[1] /byóog'l/ *n.* **BRASS INSTRUMENT** a brass instrument like a short trumpet without valves, used for military signals ■ *vi.* **(-gled, -gling, -gles) PLAY BUGLE** to play the bugle [14thC. Via Old French from Latin *buculus*, diminutive of *bos* "ox." The original term was "bugle horn," denoting the horn of an ox used as a hunting horn.] —**bu·gler** *n.*

bu·gle[2] /byóog'l/ *n.* = **bugleweed** [13thC. Directly or via Old French from late Latin *bugula.*]

bu·gle bead, bu·gle *n.* a tube-shaped bead made of glass or plastic used in embroidery or bead trimmings

bu·gle·weed /byóog'l wèed/ *n.* an aromatic plant related to mint, with blue or white flowers. Genus: *Lycopus* and *Ajuga.*

bu·gloss /byóo glòss/ *n.* a hairy plant related to borage, with clusters of drooping blue flowers. Genus: *Lycopsis.* [14thC. From, ultimately, Latin *buglossus*, from Greek *buglōssus*, literally "ox-tongued" (from the shape and roughness of the leaves).]

buhl *n.* = **boulle** [Early 19thC. Via German from French *boule* (see BOULE).]

buhr·stone /búr stṑn/, **bur·stone, burr·stone** *n.* **1. ROUGH HARD ROCK** rough hard quartz rock, formerly used to make millstones and grindstones **2. STONE FOR MILLING OR GRINDING** a millstone or grindstone made from buhrstone [Mid-17thC. *Buhr* is a variant of BURR[1] (because of the stone's roughness).]

build /bild/ *v.* **(built** /bilt/, **build·ing, builds) 1.** *vt.* **MAKE SOMETHING BY JOINING PARTS** to make a structure by putting the parts of it together ○ *to build a wall* **2.** *vt.* **HAVE SOMETHING BUILT** to have a building or other structure made ○ *The emperor built a number of these pavilions.* **3.** *vti.* **TO FORM OR DEVELOP** to form or develop an enterprise or circumstance ○ *building a solid business relationship* **4.** *vi.* **INCREASE** to increase or mount steadily ○ *Tension is starting to build.* **5.** *vt.* **COLLECT A SET OF PLAYING CARDS** in card games, to form a set by gathering related cards ■ *n.* **1. BODY STRUCTURE** the physical structure, shape, and size of a person ○ *the wrestler's heavy build* **2.** COMPUT **STAGE OF SOFTWARE DEVELOPMENT** a stage in the development of computer software in which two or more independently developed software components are linked so that they can be tested in conjunction with one another ○ *testing the first build of the software* **3. STANDARD OF CONSTRUCTION** the standard of construction of something, e.g., a vehicle [Old English *byldan* "to construct a house," from *bold* "dwelling," from a prehistoric Germanic word meaning "to dwell," which is also the source of English *bower*]

build in *vt.* **1. INCORPORATE IN STRUCTURE** to construct a piece of furniture so that it becomes part of the structure of a room, or to add an object so that it becomes part of another structure **2. INCLUDE** to create or add something to a system or organization ○ *They built in the shelves.*

build into *vt.* to create or add something as a permanent feature ○ *These safeguards will be built into the system.*

build on *v.* **1.** *vt.* **DEVELOP OR IMPROVE FURTHER** to use something as a basis for further development or improvement ○ *hoping to build on the success of their first CD* **2.** *vi.* **ATTACH NEW PART TO BUILDING** to add something as an extra part joined to an existing building ○ *The sun porch was built on about ten years later.*

build up *v.* **1.** *vti.* **DEVELOP** to increase or develop gradually ○ *Traffic is building up on the interstate.* **2.** *vt.* **PRAISE EXCESSIVELY** to emphasize or exaggerate the good qualities of somebody or something ○ *I expected someone more impressive after the way she built him up.* **3.** *vt.* **MAKE SOMEBODY STRONGER AND HEALTHIER** to make somebody stronger and healthier, especially by feeding

build up to *vi.* to develop toward a point or climax

build·a·ble /bíldəb'l/ *adj.* used to describe land that is suitable for building on

build·er /bíldər/ *n.* **1. SOMEBODY WHO BUILDS** a person or company engaged in building or repairing houses or other large structures **2. DETERGENT ADDITIVE** a substance added to detergents to improve their cleaning properties

WORD KEY: CULTURAL NOTE

The Master Builder, a play by Norwegian dramatist Henrik Ibsen (1845). Typical of Ibsen's more symbolic later works, it is the story of a successful architect, Halvard Solness, who is disturbed by his continued good fortune and fearful that he will eventually have to pay a price for it. His search for redemption eventually leads to his own death.

build·ing /bílding/ *n.* **1. WALLED ROOFED STRUCTURE** a structure with walls and a roof, e.g., a house or factory **2. MAKING LARGE STRUCTURES** the business or task of constructing houses, factories, bridges, and other large structures (*often used before a noun*)

build·ing and loan as·so·ci·a·tion *n.* = **savings and loan association**

build·ing block *n.* **1. BRICK-SHAPED CONSTRUCTION BLOCK** a large block of concrete or similar hard material, used for building houses and other large structures **2. CHILD'S TOY BLOCK** one of a set of children's wooden or plastic bricks **3. COMPONENT** an element or component regarded as contributing to the growth of an organization, plan, or system ○ *He acquired companies as building blocks for his financial empire.*

build·ing line *n.* a line on a property beyond which no building is allowed

build·ing pa·per *n.* a damp-proofing and insulating material consisting of a bitumen and fiber mix sandwiched between heavy-duty paper

build·up /bíld ùp/ *n.* **1. ACCUMULATION** a large amount of something or a number of things gradually accumulated or developed ○ *prevents the buildup of plaque* **2. IMPRESSIVE DESCRIPTION** a description that emphasizes or exaggerates the good qualities of somebody or something

built[1] past tense and past participle of **build**

built[2] /bilt/ *adj.* attractively well-proportioned in body shape (*informal*) ○ *Her new boyfriend's really built.*

built-in *adj.* **1. INTEGRAL** designed or fitted as a fixed or permanent part **2. NATURAL** forming a natural feature or characteristic ○ *She has a built-in optimism that she brings to each job.*

built-in ob·so·les·cence *n.* = **planned obsolescence**

built-up *adj.* **1. WITH MANY BUILDINGS** used to describe an area that has many buildings **2. MADE HIGHER OR THICKER** having several layers or added thickness ○ *built-up heels*

Bu·jold /boó zhṑld/, **Genevieve** (*b.* 1942) French-Canadian-U.S. movie actress. She played Anne Boleyn in the movie *Anne of the Thousand Days* (1969).

Bu·jum·bu·ra /boòjəm bóorrə/ capital and largest city of Burundi. It is situated in the western part of the country, on Lake Tanganyika. Population: 300,000 (1996).

Bu·ka·vu /boo kaá voò/ capital of Sud-Kivu Region in the eastern Democratic Republic of Congo. It is situated on Lake Kivu, close to the border with Rwanda. Population: 201,569 (1994).

Bu·kha·ra /boo kaárə, -kh-/ city in southern Uzbekistan, in the Amu Darya valley, west of Samarqand. Population: 236,000 (1994).

Bu·kha·ri /boo kaá ree/ (810–870) Arabian scholar. He traveled throughout the Muslim world and compiled the oral traditions of the Prophet Muhammad into the Sunni foundation text, *al-Sahih* ("The Genuine"). Full name **Muhammad Ibn-Ismail al-Bukhari**

bul. *abbr.* bulletin

Bu·la·wa·yo /boòllə waá yṑ/ industrial city on the Matsheumlope River, southwestern Zimbabwe. Population: 620,936 (1992).

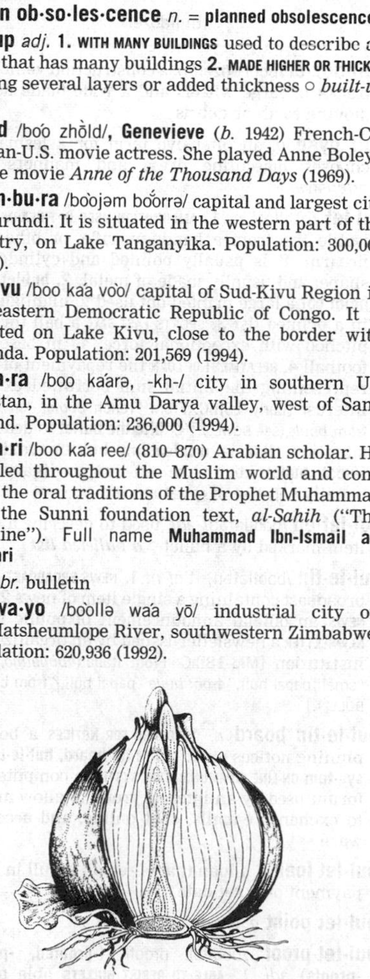

Bulb

bulb /bulb/ *n.* **1.** = **light bulb 2. UNDERGROUND PLANT PART** any underground plant storage organ, e.g., a corm, tuber, or rhizome, from which a new plant grows every year **3. PLANT GROWING FROM BULB** a plant that develops from a bulb or other underground storage organ, e.g., a tulip or crocus **4. ROUNDED PART** a rounded part of something, e.g., the mercury reservoir of a thermometer or the squeezable rubber ball on a dropper **5. ROUNDED PART OF BODY ORGAN** a rounded or enlarged section of a cylindrical body part [Mid-16thC. Via Latin *bulbus* from Greek *bolbos* "bulbous root, onion."]

bul·bar /búlbər/ *adj.* used to describe any bulb-shaped organ of the body

bul·bel *n.* = **bulbil**

bulb fly *n.* a fly similar to a wasp, whose larvae live in and eat bulbs. Family: Syrphidae.

bul·bif·er·ous /bul bíffərəs/ *adj.* used to describe plants that produce bulbs

bul·bil /búlb'l, búl bìl/, **bul·bel** /búlb'l, búl bèl/ *n.* a new bulb growing like a bud on a plant or leaf stem [Mid-19thC. From modern Latin *bulbillus*, diminutive of Latin *bulbus* (see BULB).]

bul·bo·u·re·thral gland /bùlbō yoò reéthrəl-/ *n.* = **Cowper's gland** [*Bulbourethral* from Latin *bulbus* (see BULB) + URETHRAL]

bul·bous /búlbəss/ *adj.* **1. ROUNDED** rounded and swollen-looking **2. BOT GROWING FROM BULB** growing from a plant bulb [Late 16thC. From Latin *bulbosus*, from bulbus (see BULB), or directly formed from BULB.] —**bul·bous·ly** *adv.* —**bul·bous·ness** *n.*

bul·bul /bóol bóol/ *n.* **1. TROPICAL BIRD** a grayish or brownish songbird of tropical Africa and Asia, also introduced into Australia. Family: Pycnonotidae. **2. BIRD IN PERSIAN POETRY** a songbird frequently mentioned in Persian poetry, taken to be the nightingale [Mid-17thC. From Persian, an imitation of its song.]

Bul·gar /búl gaàr/ *n.* a member of an ancient Slavic people that settled in areas of present-day Bulgaria around the 7th century A.D. [Mid-18thC. From medieval Latin *Bulgarus*, from Old Church Slavonic *Blŭgary* (plural) "Bulgars."]

Bulgaria

Bul·gar·i·a /bul gáiree ə/ republic in southeastern Europe, on the western shores of the Black Sea. Part of the Ottoman Empire from the 14th to the late 19th centuries, it gained independence in 1908. Language: Bulgarian. Currency: Lev. Capital: Sofia. Population: 8,290,988 (1997). Area: 42,855 sq. mi./110,994 sq. km. Official name **People's Republic of Bulgaria**

Bul·gar·i·an /bul gáireeən/ *n.* **1. SOMEBODY FROM BULGARIA** somebody who was born or raised in, or who is a citizen of, Bulgaria **2. SOUTH SLAVIC LANGUAGE** the official language of Bulgaria, one of the South Slavic group of Indo-European languages. Bulgarian is spoken by about nine million people. [Mid-16thC. Formed from medieval Latin *Bulgaria*, from *Bulgar* "Bulgar" (see BULGAR).] —**Bul·gar·i·an** *adj.*

bulge /bulj/ *vi.* **(bulged, bulg·ing, bulg·es) 1. SWELL** to expand or swell **2. BE OVERFILLED** to contain so much that the sides expand outward (*informal*) ■ *n.* **1. PART THAT EXPANDS OUTWARD** an area or part that curves or has expanded outward **2. INCREASE** a sudden temporary increase ○ *a bulge in the population figures* [12thC. Via Old French *boulge* "leather sack, bag," from Latin *bulga* (source of English *budget*), from Gaulish. Originally "bag, pouch," hence "something rounded."] —**bulg·ing** *adj.* —**bulg·y** *adj.*

bul·gur /búlgər, bóol-/, **bul·ghar, bul·gar, bul·gur wheat** *n.* wheat that has been parboiled, dried, and broken or cracked into small pieces. It is a common ingredient in Middle Eastern and vegetarian cooking. [Mid-20thC. Via Turkish from Persian *bulġūr*, literally "bruised grain."]

bu·lim·i·a /byoo límmee ə/ *n.* a condition in which bouts of overeating are followed by undereating, use of laxatives, or self-induced vomiting. It is associated with depression and anxiety about putting on weight. [14thC. From modern Latin, from, ultimately, Greek *boulimia*, literally "hunger of an ox," from *bous* "ox" + *limos* "hunger."] —**bu·lim·ic** *adj., n.*

bulk /bulk/ *n.* **1. LARGE SIZE** large size or mass **2. LARGE BODY** a large or overweight person's body **3. FIBER IN FOOD** the indigestible fiber that is a constituent of some food **4. THE GREATER PART** the greater part of something **5. CARGO** a ship's cargo **6. PART OF SHIP** the part of a ship where cargo is stored ■ *adj.* **IN LARGE QUANTITY** in or of a large quantity [15thC. Partly from Old Norse *búlki* "heap" (ultimately from an Indo-European word meaning "to swell," which is also the ancestor of English *bowl*); partly from Old English *būc* "belly."]

bulk up *vti.* to increase in size or volume (*informal*)

bulk buy *n.* a large amount or number of something bought at one time, usually at a reduced rate —**bulk buy·ing** *n.*

bulk car·ri·er *n.* a ship that carries loose unpackaged cargo, e.g., coal or grain

bulk·head /búlk hèd/ *n.* **1. PARTITION INSIDE VEHICLE** a partition inside a ship, aircraft, or large vehicle **2. RETAINING WALL** a wall built to hold back something, e.g., water or soil [15thC. *Bulk* from Old Norse *bálkr* "partition" (source of English *balk*).]

bulk·ing /búlking/ *n.* the increase in the volume of sand, cement, and other building materials when they become damp

bulk mail *n.* material, typically advertising, that is sent through the mail in very large quantities at a reduced unit cost

bulk·y /búlkee/ (**-i·er, -i·est**) *adj.* **1. AWKWARDLY LARGE** large and awkward to carry or move **2. BROAD** heavily built, or broad and muscular —**bulk·i·ly** *adv.* —**bulk·i·ness** *n.*

bull[1] /bool/ *n.* **1. MALE OF CATTLE** an uncastrated adult male of any breed of domestic cattle or other bovine animal **2. MALE MAMMAL** a sexually mature male of any of various large mammals, including whales, seals, moose, and elephants **3.** = **bullshit** *n.* (*slang offensive*) **4.** STOCK EXCH **BUYER OF RISING SECURITIES** an investor who buys securities in anticipation of rising prices, intending to resell them soon for profit. ◊ **bear**[1] *n.* 6 **5. BIG MAN** a hefty or aggressive man ■ *v.* (**bulled, bull·ing, bulls**) **1.** *vti.* **PUSH** to push forcefully or energetically ○ *He bulled his way into the reception.* **2.** *vt.* STOCK EXCH **RAISE PRICES WITH SPECULATIVE BUYING** to attempt to raise prices in a particular commodity or market by buying large quantities and thus reducing availability and increasing demand [Pre-12thC. From Old Norse *boli* "bull."] ◇ **shoot the bull** to chatter idly (*slang*) ◇ **take the bull by the horns** to deal with a difficult situation forcefully and decisively

bull[2] /bool/ *n.* a written statement formally issued by the Pope and bearing an official seal [13thC. Via French *bulle* from Latin *bulla* "bubble," later "seal," hence "sealed document" (source of English *boil* and *budge*).]

Bull /bool/ *n.* ASTRON, ZODIAC = **Taurus** [Early 16thC. Translation of Latin *Taurus*.]

bull. *abbr.* bulletin

bul·la /boollə/ (*plural* **-lae** /-lee/) *n.* **1. BLISTER** a blister (*technical*) **2. BONY PART** any rounded, bony, and protruding part of the body **3. POPE'S SEAL** the Pope's official seal [14thC. From, ultimately, Latin (see BULL[2]).]

bull·bait·ing /bool bàyting/ *n.* the former entertainment of setting fierce dogs to attack a bull, popular in medieval times

bull bars *npl.* a metal framework mounted on the front of a vehicle to protect it against impact

bull·bat /bool bàt/ *n.* = **nighthawk** *n.* 1 [Mid-19thC. From the roaring sound the animal makes when flying.]

bull·dog /bool dòg/ *n.* **1. SMOOTH-HAIRED DOG** a smooth-haired muscular dog belonging to a breed developed in England for contests with bulls **2.** ARMS **PISTOL** a short-barreled revolver ■ *vt.* (**-dogged, -dog·ging, -dogs**) **1. ATTACK** to attack like an angry bulldog **2. FORCE A STEER TO THE GROUND** to force a steer to the ground by pulling on its horns and twisting its neck [15thC. Formed from BULL[1].] —**bull·dog·ger** *n.*

Bulldog

bull·doze /bool dōz/ (**-dozed, -doz·ing, -doz·es**) *v.* **1.** *vt.* **DEMOLISH WITH BULLDOZERS** to demolish a building or clear debris using bulldozers **2.** *vti.* **FORCE A WAY** to force way past or through an obstruction (*informal*) **3.** *vt.* **FORCE ACTION** to force somebody to do something or to insist on a course of action stubbornly or ruthlessly (*informal*) [Late 19thC. Origin uncertain; perhaps from BULL + DOSE: "to give a 'dose' (treatment) fit for a bull."]

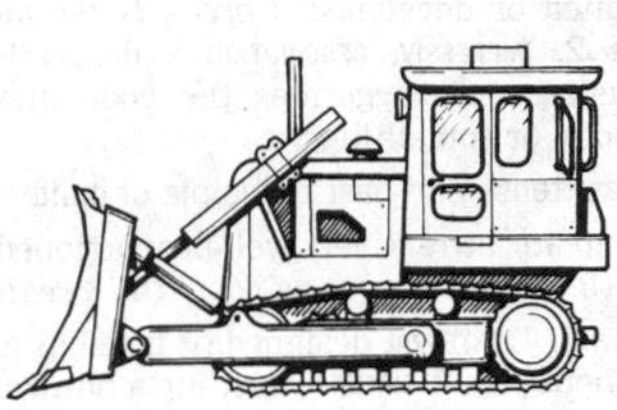

Bulldozer

bull·doz·er /bool dōzər/ *n.* a construction vehicle with tracks or large wheels and a wide blade used for moving earth or debris

bull dyke *n.* an offensive term for a lesbian who chooses masculine dress and manners (*slang offensive*)

bul·let /boollət/ *n.* **1. AMMUNITION USED IN FIREARM** a projectile fire from a handgun, rifle, or other small firearm. It is usually pointed and cylindrical in shape, and usually made of metal. **2. bul·let, bul·let point DOT** a large printed dot used to highlight items in a printed list **3.** SPORTS **FAST BALL** a ball thrown or pitched with exceptional force, as in baseball or football **4. REPAYMENT OF LOAN** the repayment of a loan, representing the initial sum borrowed excluding interest [Early 16thC. From French *boulet* "small ball," from *boule* (see BOWL[2]).] ◇ **bite the bullet** to deal with a situation that is unpleasant but unavoidable ◇ **sweat bullets** to make an extraordinary effort, usually because of great anxiety

bul·let·ed /boollətəd/ *adj.* used to describe a printed item marked by a bullet ○ *a bulleted list*

bul·le·tin /boollətən, -t'n/ *n.* **1. NEWS BROADCAST** a short broadcast containing a single item of news **2. OFFICIAL NEWS** an official announcement of public news **3. NEWSLETTER** a newsletter issued by an organization or institution [Mid-18thC. From Italian *bulletino*, literally "small papal bull," from *bulla* "papal bull," from Latin (see BULL[2]).]

bul·le·tin board *n.* **1. BOARD FOR NOTICES** a board for pinning notices on **2. bul·le·tin board, bul·le·tin board sys·tem ON-LINE COMMUNICATION SYSTEM** a computer-based forum used by an interest group to allow members to exchange e-mails, chat online, and access software

bul·let loan *n.* a loan that is repaid in full in a single payment on a set date

bul·let point *n.* PRINTING = **bullet** *n.* 2

bul·let·proof /boollət proof/ (**-proofed, -proof·ing, -proofs**) *adj.* **1. ABLE TO RESIST BULLETS** able to resist the penetration of bullets ○ *bulletproof glass* **2. INVULNERABLE TO ATTACK** invulnerable to attack or criticism (*informal*) ○ *Nobody's bulletproof in this company.*

bul·let train *n.* a high-speed passenger train in Japan

bul·let·wood /boollət wood/ *n.* **1. TROPICAL AMERICAN TREE** a tropical American tree grown for its tough durable wood. Latin name: *Manilkara bidentata.* **2. HARD WOOD** the tough durable wood of the bulletwood tree

bull fid·dle *n.* a double bass (*informal*)

bull·fight /bool fīt/ *n.* a traditional public entertainment, especially in Spain and Mexico, in which a bull is baited and killed —**bull·fight·er** *n.* —**bull·fight·ing** *n.*

bull·finch /bool finch/ *n.* a small Eurasian bird with a short thick beak, a black head, and a pink to red breast. Latin name: *Pyrrhula pyrrhula.* [Late 16thC. Said to be from the bird's thick "bull-like" neck.]

bull·frog /bool fràwg, -fròg/ *n.* a large frog of eastern North America with a deep croak. Genus: *Rana.* [Mid-18thC. So called because of its strong croak, said to sound like a bull bellowing.]

bull·head /bool hèd/ *n.* **1. N AMERICAN CATFISH** a common catfish found in North American rivers and lakes. Genus: *Ictalurus.* **2. LARGE-HEADED FRESHWATER FISH** a large-headed fish such as the freshwater sculpin. Genus: *Cottus.* [15thC. Originally denoting a small freshwater fish with a large head.]

bull·head·ed /bool hèddəd/ *adj.* stubborn and uncooperative (*informal*) —**bull·head·ed·ly** *adv.* —**bull·head·ed·ness** *n.*

bull·horn /bool hàwrn/ *n.* a device that consists of a hand-held microphone with a cone-shaped speaker attached, used for amplifying the voice

bul·lion /boollyən/ *n.* **1. BARS OF GOLD OR SILVER** gold or silver in the form of bars or ingots **2. MASS OF METAL** any metal in the form of an unshaped mass **3.** TEXTILES **GOLD OR SILVER BRAID** ornamental fringing or braid made of twisted gold or silver thread and used, e.g., to edge curtains [15thC. From Anglo-Norman, literally "mint," ultimately from Latin *bullire* "to boil," from *bulla* (see BULL[2]). The underlying idea is of metal being melted.]

bull·ish /boollish/ *adj.* **1. EXPECTING GOOD STOCK MARKET FIGURES** expecting or producing good results, especially rising stock market prices **2. OPTIMISTIC** confident and optimistic (*informal*) **3. BRAWNY** broad and strong —**bull·ish·ly** *adv.* —**bull·ish·ness** *n.*

bull mar·ket *n.* a stock market in which prices are rising and are expected to continue rising. ◊ **bear market**

bull mas·tiff *n.* a dog belonging to a large muscular smooth-haired breed developed by crossing the bulldog and the mastiff

bull·necked /bool nèkt/ *adj.* having a short thick neck [Middle English]

bull·nose /bool nōz/ *n.* a disease of hogs that causes the snout to swell

bull·nosed /bool nōzd/ *adj.* having a rounded protruding front part

bul·lock /boollək/ *n.* **1. YOUNG BULL** a young domestic bull **2. CASTRATED BULL** a castrated domestic bull [Old English *bulluc* "young bull," diminutive of *bula* "bull"]

bul·lock's heart *n.* = **custard apple**

bull·pen /bool pèn/ *n.* **1. BASEBALL WARM-UP AREA** the part of a baseball field where the relief pitchers warm up **2. RELIEF PITCHERS** a baseball team's relief pitchers **3. TEMPORARY CELL** a cell for prisoners waiting to be brought into court (*informal*) **4. AREA FOR CLERICAL WORKERS** an area containing the desks of many white-collar workers, often separated by movable partitions of limited height [Early 19thC. Originally "pen for bulls," hence "any enclosure."]

bull·ring /bool rìng/ *n.* an arena where bullfights are held

bull ses·sion *n.* an informal discussion, especially between men

bull's eye *n.* **1.** SPORTS **MIDDLE OF TARGET** the center of a target, which usually carries the highest score ○ *She hit the the bull's eye perfectly.* **2.** SPORTS **TOP-SCORING SHOT** a shot that hits the center of a target **3. ROUND WINDOW** a small round window, especially a disk of thick glass in a ship's deck for letting in light below deck **4. HARD CANDY** a hard round peppermint candy, usually striped **5. THICK LENS** a small thick lens for intensifying light **6. TYPE OF LAMP** a lamp fitted with a bull's-eye lens ■ *n., interj.* **PRECISE ACHIEVEMENT** a precise or highly effective achievement (*informal*)

bull·shit /bŏŏl shìt/ *n.* OFFENSIVE TERM an offensive term for talk or writing dismissed as foolish or inaccurate (*slang offensive*) ■ *vti.* (**-shit·ted, -shit·ting, -shits**) (*slang offensive*) **1.** OFFENSIVE TERM an offensive term meaning to say things that are completely untrue or very foolish **2.** OFFENSIVE TERM an offensive term meaning to try to intimidate, deceive, or persuade somebody with deceitful or foolish talk — **bull·shit·ter** *n.*

bull snake *n.* a large, burrowing, nonpoisonous snake of North America that has yellow and brown markings and feeds mainly on rodents. Genus: *Pituophis.*

bull ter·ri·er *n.* a smooth-haired muscular dog belonging to a breed developed in England by crossing the bulldog with a breed of terrier

bull this·tle *n.* a European thistle, widely distributed in temperate areas, with a large flowering head. Latin name: *Cirsium vulgare.*

bull·whip /bŏŏl wìp, -hwìp/ *n.* LARGE WHIP a long heavy whip made of braided strips of hide, knotted at the end ■ *vt.* (**-whipped, -whip·ping, -whips**) BEAT to beat somebody with a bullwhip

bul·ly[1] /bŏŏllee/ *n.* (*plural* **-lies**) AGGRESSIVE PERSON an aggressive person who intimidates or mistreats weaker people ■ *vt.* (**-lied, -ly·ing, -lies**) INTIMIDATE to intimidate or mistreat weaker people [Mid-16thC. Origin uncertain; probably from Middle Dutch *boele* "lover." Originally "sweetheart," then "fine fellow," "blusterer."]

bul·ly[2] /bŏŏllee/ (*plural* **-lies**) *n.* a small New Zealand river fish. Genera: *Gobiomorphus* and *Phylinodon.* [Mid-19thC. Origin uncertain: probably shortened from BULLHEAD.]

bul·ly·boy /bŏŏlli bòy/ *n.* an aggressive bully or thug

bul·ly pul·pit *n.* a position of prominent authority, such as political office, that gives the holder a wide audience

bul·ly·rag /bŏŏlli ràg/ (**-ragged, -rag·ging, -rags**), **bal·ly·rag** (**-ragged, -rag·ging, -rags**) *vt.* to persecute somebody with insults or cruel practical jokes (*informal*) [Late 18thC. Alteration of *ballyrag*, of unknown origin.]

bul·ly tree *n.* a tropical American tree that yields a sap from which a hard rubber substance (**balata**) is made. Latin name: *Manilkara bidentata.*

bul·rush /bŏŏl rùsh/ *n.* **1.** WATERSIDE PLANT a plant that grows in wet conditions, with leaves like grass and clusters of drooping brown flowers. Genus: *Scirpus.* **2.** *U.K.* TALL MARSH PLANT WITH BROWN HEADS a tall marsh plant with brown furry flower spikes. Genus: *Typha.* **3.** = **papyrus** [Middle English. Origin uncertain: probably a blend of BULL and RUSH.]

bul·wark /bŏŏlwərk/ *n.* **1.** DEFENSIVE WALL a wall-like structure built to keep out attackers **2.** PROTECTION a person or thing that gives protection or support **3.** HARBOR WALL a wall built in the sea to shelter a harbor ■ **bul·warks** *npl.* SHIP'S SIDES the sides of a ship projecting above the deck ■ *vt.* (**-warked, -wark·ing, -warks**) **1.** PROTECT WITH WALLS to fortify or protect a place by building walls around it **2.** SAFEGUARD to defend or support somebody or something strongly [15thC. From Middle Low German *bolwerk* "rampart made of tree trunks" (source of English *boulevard*), from *bole* "tree trunk" + *werk* "work."]

bum[1] /bum/ *n.* (*informal*) **1.** GOOD-FOR-NOTHING somebody considered to be irresponsible or worthless **2.** HOBO a homeless person living on the street **3.** DEVOTEE a person excessively devoted to a particular activity or place ○ *a ski bum* ■ *vt.* (**bummed, bum·ming, bums**) BEG to get something by asking or begging (*informal*) ■ *adj.* USELESS useless, worthless, or of poor quality (*informal*) ○ *gave me some pretty bum advice* [Mid-19thC. Shortening of BUMMER, in the earlier sense "lazy, irresponsible person."] ◇ **give somebody the bum's rush** to order or force somebody abruptly to leave a place (*slang*)

bum[2] /bum/ *n.* *U.K.* the buttocks (*informal*) [14thC. Origin unknown.]

bum bag *n.* *U.K.* = **fanny pack**

bum·ber·shoot /búmbər shòot/ *n.* an umbrella (*humorous*) [Late 19thC. From *bumber* (alteration of *umbre-* in *umbrella*) + *shoot* representing *chute* as in *parachute.*]

bum·ble[1] /búmb'l/ *vti.* (**-bled, -bling, -bles**) SPEAK CLUMSILY to speak in a hesitant or muddled way ■ *n.*, *vt.* (**-bled, -bling, -bles**) MOVE CLUMSILY to move or proceed clumsily ■ *vt.* (**-bled, -bling, -bles**) = **bungle** (*informal*) [Mid-16thC. Origin uncertain: perhaps a blend of BUNGLE and STUMBLE.] —**bum·bler** *n.*

bum·ble[2] /búmb'l/ (**-bled, -bling, -bles**) *vi.* to make a humming sound [14thC. An imitation of the sound.]

bum·ble·bee /búmb'l bèe/ *n.* a large hairy bee of North America and Eurasia that nests in burrows and makes a loud droning noise in flight. Genus: *Bombus.* [Mid-16thC. From the droning sound it makes when flying.]

bum·ble·dom /búmb'ldəm/ *n.* pompous self-importance and officiousness in a minor official (*humorous*) [Mid-19thC. Named for Mr. *Bumble*, an officious beadle in Dickens' novel *Oliver Twist.*]

bum·ble-pup·py *n.* *U.K.* = **tetherball** [Early 19thC. Origin unknown.]

bum·bling /búmbling/ *adj.* speaking or behaving in a clumsy or confused way (*informal*)

bum·boat /búm bòt/ *n.* a small boat that is used for selling goods to ships at anchor [Late 17thC. *Bum* from BUM[1]. Originally "boat collecting rubbish and filth from moored ships."]

bum·fuz·zle /búm fùzz'l, -fúzz'l/ (**-zled, -zling, -zles**) *vt.* *Southern U.S.* to confuse somebody (*informal*) [Early 20thC. Alteration of BAMBOOZLE, in the manner of confuse.]

bum·ma·lo /búmməlō/ (*plural* **-lo**) *n.* a small bluntnosed edible fish found in brackish Indian waters. Latin name: *Harpadon nehereus.* [Late 17thC. Origin uncertain: probably an alteration of Marathi *bombīl.*]

bummed /bumd/ *adj.* depressed as a result of an unpleasant experience (*slang*)

bum·mer /búmmər/ *n.* (*slang*) **1.** ANNOYING THING something annoying or unpleasant **2.** FLOP a failure **3.** BAD REACTION TO DRUG a bad reaction to a hallucinogenic drug [Mid-19thC. Origin uncertain: probably from German *Bummler* "idler, layabout," from *bummeln* "to stroll or loaf around."]

bump /bump/ *v.* (**bumped, bump·ing, bumps**) **1.** *vti.* KNOCK to hit or knock something **2.** *vti.* MOVE UNSTEADILY to move in a jolting or bouncing way ○ *We bumped along the dirt track.* **3.** *vt.* TURN AWAY A PASSENGER to turn away an airline passenger with a reserved seat because the flight has been overbooked (*informal*) ■ *n.* **1.** ACCIDENTAL KNOCK a light blow or impact ○ *that bump dented the bodywork* **2.** LUMP ON SURFACE a raised area on a flat surface ○ *a bump in the road* **3.** SWELLING ON BODY a swelling on the body caused by an impact ○ *a bump on the elbow* **4.** SOUND OF IMPACT the dull sound of one thing hitting another **5.** RAISED AREA ON SKULL any of numerous raised areas on the skull, formerly thought to indicate intelligence or personality type [Mid-16thC. An imitation of the sound.] ◇ **bump and grind** to dance erotically, thrusting and rotating the pelvis (*slang*)

bump into *vi.* **1.** MEET BY CHANCE to meet somebody by chance **2.** COLLIDE ACCIDENTALLY to knock against or hit somebody or something accidentally

bump off *vt.* to murder somebody (*slang*)

bump up *vt.* to increase prices suddenly and sharply (*informal*)

bump up against *vi.* **1.** COME INTO CONTACT WITH to come into contact with something, usually with a sound **2.** CONFRONT to come into conflict with somebody

bump·er /búmpər/ *n.* PROTECTING BAR ON VEHICLE a projecting rim or bar on the front or back of a vehicle, designed to protect it from damage ■ *adj.* LARGE unusually large ○ *a bumper crop*

bump·er car *n.* a small electric car used as part of a fairground entertainment. The cars are designed to be bumped into each other in a raised enclosure.

bump·er stick·er *n.* a small adhesive sign, typically mounted on a car bumper or window

bump·er-to-bump·er *adj.*, *adv.* forming a line of close slow-moving vehicles ○ *bumper-to-bumper traffic* ○ *drive bumper-to-bumper*

bump·kin[1] /búmpkin, búm-/ *n.* a country person regarded as unsophisticated (*informal*) [Late 16thC. Origin uncertain: perhaps from Dutch *boomken* or Middle Dutch *bommekijn* "short rotund person," literally "little tree."]

bump·kin[2] /búmpkin, búm-/, **bum·kin** /búm-/ *n.* a pole at the back of a ship or boat to which a sail is attached by a rope [Mid-17thC. Anglicization of Dutch *boomken.*]

bump·tious /búmpshəss/ *adj.* stating opinions aggressively or self-importantly [Early 19thC. A playful blend of BUMP and FRACTIOUS.] —**bump·tious·ly** *adv.* — **bump·tious·ness** *n.*

bump·y /búmpee/ (**-i·er, -i·est**) *adj.* **1.** UNEVEN having a rough or uneven surface ○ *a bumpy road* **2.** BOUNCY uncomfortably bouncy or rough ○ *a bumpy ride* **3.** DIFFICULT with setbacks from time to time (*informal*) ○ *Things seemed to be going well, but it looks like this project's going to be bumpy after all.* —**bump·i·ly** *adv.* —**bump·i·ness** *n.*

bum rap *n.* a false or fraudulent accusation or appraisal (*slang*)

bum steer *n.* a piece of misleading information or bad advice (*slang*)

bun /bun/ *n.* **1.** ROUND BREAD ROLL a small round bread roll, sometimes sweetened and with added fruit or spice **2.** HAIR COILED AT BACK OF HEAD hair gathered in a tight round coil on the back or top of the head ■ **buns** *npl.* BUTTOCKS the buttocks (*slang*) [14thC. Origin unknown.]

bunch /bunch/ *n.* **1.** COLLECTION OF THINGS a number of things grouped or joined together **2.** CLUSTER OF FRUITS a cluster of fruits growing on a stem **3.** GROUP OF PEOPLE a group of people, especially friends or associates (*informal*) ■ *vti.* (**bunched, bunch·ing, bunch·es**) GATHER to gather things or people into a cluster or close group [14thC. Origin unknown.] —**bunch·i·ness** *n.* — **bunch·y** *adj.*

bunch·ber·ry /búnch bèrree/ (*plural* **-ries**) *n.* a creeping plant of the dogwood family that bears red berries. Latin name: *Cornus canadensis.*

Bunche /bunch/, **Ralph** (1904–71) U.S. diplomat. He received the Nobel Peace Prize in 1950 for in his work as a U.N. mediator resolving Arab-Israeli conflicts. Full name **Ralph Johnson Bunche**

bunch·flow·er /búnch flòwr/ *n.* a perennial plant of the lilac family with leaves like grass and clusters of pale green flowers, found in the eastern United States. Latin name: *Melanthium virginicum.*

bunch grass *n.* any grass that grows in clumps or tufts

Bun·cho Ta·ni /bùnchō táanee/ (1763–1840) Japanese artist. A noted book illustrator, he was responsible for introducing the Western style to Japanese painting.

bun·co /búngkō/, **bun·ko** *n.* (*plural* **-coes**; *plural* **-koes**) SWINDLE a trick or scheme that deceives people into parting with money (*slang*) ■ *vt.* (**-coed, -co·ing, -cos; -koed, -ko·ing, -kos**) DEFRAUD to trick somebody into giving money (*slang*) [Late 19thC. Of uncertain origin; perhaps from Spanish *banca*, a kind of card game.]

bund[1] /bund/ *n.* *S Asia* an embankment or dyke surrounding rice fields or acting as a breakwater to prevent flooding. ◊ **levee** [Early 19thC. From Urdu *band*, from Persian.]

bund[2] /bund/, **Bund** *n.* a political organization, especially a socialist Jewish labor movement in Tsarist Russia or a German-American group of Nazi sympathizers in the United States in the 1930s and 1940s [Late 19thC. From German, literally "association."]

bun·dle /búnd'l/ *n.* **1.** A COLLECTION OF THINGS HELD TOGETHER a number of things tied, wrapped, or held together **2.** A LOT OF MONEY a large sum of money (*slang*) **3.** BIOL BAND OF PARALLEL TISSUES a band of tissues running parallel to each other, e.g., muscle or nerve fibers, or vascular tissue in plants **4.** COMPUT SET OF COMPUTER EQUIPMENT: computer hardware and software supplied as a package at an inclusive price ■ *vt.* (**-dled, -dling, -dles**) **1.** COMPUT SUPPLY COMPUTER EQUIPMENT to package computer hardware and software together at an inclusive price **2.** SHOVE SOMEBODY OR SOMETHING to push somebody or something roughly and hurriedly (*informal*) [14thC. Origin uncertain, perhaps from Old English *byndelle* "binding" or Dutch *bundel*, both related to English *bind.*] —**bun·dler** *n.*

bundle off *vt.* to send somebody away hurriedly (*informal*) ○ *We bundled the children off to school.*

bundle up *v.* **1.** *vt.* GATHER INTO BUNDLE to gather things into a bundle **2.** *vti.* DRESS WARMLY to dress in warm clothes, or to dress somebody in warm clothes (*informal*) ○ *Bundle up, it's cold outside.*

bun·dle of nerves *n.* somebody who is feeling nervous, especially before an event (*informal*)

bung /bung/ *n.* **1.** STOPPER a stopper or plug, especially one made of cork or rubber **2.** *U.K.* PAYOFF an illicit fee paid to a soccer player, manager, or agent to facilitate a player transfer (*slang*) ■ *vt.* (**bunged, bung·ing, bungs**) STOP SOMETHING UP to plug or seal a hole with a bung [15thC. From Middle Dutch *bonghe*, of uncertain origin, probably from late Latin *puncta* "puncture," from Latin *pungere* "to prick" (source of English *pungent*).]

bun·ga·low /búng gəlō/ *n.* **1. SINGLE-STORY HOUSE** a single-story house **2. LIGHTWEIGHT TROPICAL HOUSE** a simply-built one-story house with a veranda and a wide, gently sloping roof in Southeast Asia and the South Pacific ■ *Malaysia, Singapore* **HOUSE** a house, usually of two or more stories [Late 17thC. From Hindi *banglā* "of Bengal."]

bun·gee /bún jèe/ *n.* a cord or rope made from elastic material [Early 20thC. Origin unknown.]

bun·gee jump (*unmarked inflection* **bun·gee jumps**) *n.* a dive from a high place using an elastic cord tied to the ankles as a restraint —**bun·gee jump·ing** *n.*

bung·hole /búng hōl/ *n.* a hole in a barrel or vat, used for drawing off the contents and closed with a bung

bun·gle /búng g'l/ *vt.* (**-gled, -gling, -gles**) **SPOIL SOMETHING** to cause something to fail through carelessness or incompetence (*informal*) ■ *n.* **MISTAKE** a careless or clumsy action or mistake (*informal*) [Mid-16thC. Thought to suggest the action.] —**bun·gling** *adj.* —**bun·gling·ly** *adv.*

bun·gler /búng glər/ *n.* a person whose carelessness or incompetence causes failure (*informal*)

bun·ion /búnyən/ *n.* inflammation of the sac (**bursa**) around the first joint of the big toe, accompanied by swelling and sideways displacement of the joint [Early 18thC. Directly or via English dialect *bunny* "lump, swelling" from Old French *buigne* "bump on the head," probably ultimately of Germanic origin.]

bunk[1] /bungk/ *n.* **1. SIMPLE BED** a simple narrow bed built on a shelf or in a recess **2.** = **bunk bed 3. SLEEPING PLACE** any bed or place to sleep (*informal*) ■ *vi.* (**bunked, bunk·ing, bunks**) **SLEEP** to sleep in a place away from home (*informal*) ○ *"You may as well bunk at the YMCA and get in on their recreation programs."* (Garrison Keillor, *We Are Still Married*; 1989) [Mid-18thC. Origin uncertain, perhaps shortened from BUNKER.]

bunk[2] /bungk/ *n.* talk or writing dismissed as nonsensical or inaccurate (*slang*) [Early 20thC. Shortened from BUNKUM.]

bunk bed *n.* either of a pair of single beds fitted one on top of the other

bun·ker /bùngkər/ *n.* **1. UNDERGROUND SHELTER** an undergound shelter, especially one built for troops, with a fortified gun position above ground **2. SAND HAZARD** a sand-filled hollow on a golf course, built as a hazard **3. FUEL STORAGE CONTAINER** a fuel-storage container on a ship **4. LARGE OUTDOOR CONTAINER** a large outdoor bin or chest ■ *vt.* (**-kered, -ker·ing, -kers**) **1. SEND GOLF BALL INTO BUNKER** to hit a golf ball into a bunker **2. PUT SOMETHING IN OUTDOOR BIN** to put or store something in a large outdoor bin or chest [Mid-16thC. Origin unknown.]

Bun·ker Hill /búngkər-/ hill in Boston, Massachusetts, the site of the first battle of the American Revolution in 1775. Height: 110 ft./34 m.

bunk·house /búnk hòws/ (*plural* **-hous·es** /-hòwziz/) *n.* a building providing simple sleeping facilities

bun·ko *n., vt.* = **bunco**

bun·kum /búngkəm/ *n.* talk or writing dismissed as nonsensical or inaccurate (*informal*) [Mid-19thC. Alteration of *Buncombe* County in North Carolina, whose congressman defended a dull and irrelevant speech by saying he made it to impress the people of Buncombe.]

bun·ny /búnnee/ (*plural* **-nies**) *n.* a child's word for a rabbit [Early 17thC. From English dialect *bun* "rabbit's tail, rabbit," from Gaelic *bun* "stump, bottom."]

bun·ny hug *n.* a lively ballroom dance popular in the United States in the early 20th century

bun·ny slopes *npl.* the gentlest slopes in a ski resort or complex, designed for beginners to use [Bunny of uncertain origin]

bun·o·dont /byóonə dònt/ *adj.* having molars with separate rounded ridges (**cusps**), typical of omnivores [Late 19thC. From Greek *bounos* "mound" + -ODONT.]

Bun·ra·ku /bóon ràa kóo, bóon ràa-/ *n.* traditional Japanese puppetry using large wooden puppets, each worked by several puppeteers who are visible to the audience and with a separate narrator offstage [Early 20thC. From Japanese, named for the *Bunraku-za* theater, built in the early 19thC by the puppeteer *Bunraku-ken* Oemurea (died 1810).]

Bun·sen /búnsən/, **Robert Wilhelm** (1811–99) German chemist and physicist. One of the discoverers of spectrum analysis (1859), he also invented a galvanic battery. He popularized the laboratory gas burner that bears his name.

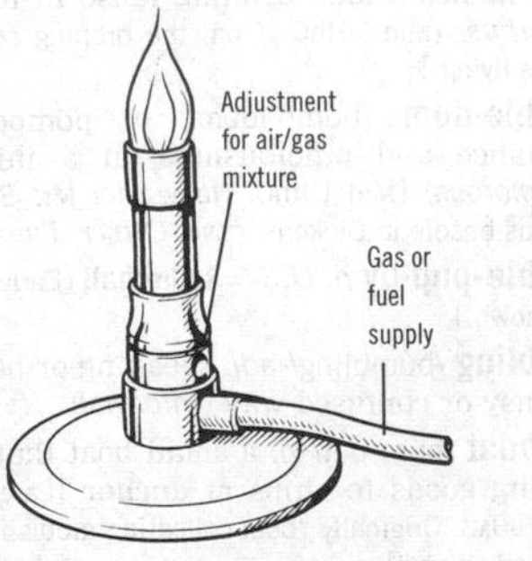

Bunsen burner

Bun·sen burn·er /bùnsən-/ *n.* a portable tube-shaped gas burner with an adjustable hole to control air intake and flame type, used in laboratories [Late 19thC. Named for Robert W. BUNSEN, who popularized it.]

Bun·shaft /bún shàft/, **Gordon** (1909–90) U.S. architect. His innovations in designing public and corporate buildings included the use of sloping facades.

bunt[1] /bunt/ *vt.* (**bunt·ed, bunt·ing, bunts**) **HIT A BALL GENTLY** in baseball, to hit a pitched ball very gently, holding the bat horizontally with both hands ■ *n.* **GENTLE HIT OF BALL** an instance of bunting a baseball ■ *n., vt.* (**bunt·ed, bunt·ing, bunts**) = **butt**[1] *v.* 1 [Mid-18thC. An imitation of the sound.] —**bun·ter** *n.*

bunt[2] /bunt/ *n.* the baggy pouch-like middle part of a sail [Late 16thC. Origin uncertain: perhaps ultimately from Low German *bunt* "bundle."]

bun·tal /búnt'l/ *n.* straw from the large leaves of the talipot palm tree of Southeast Asia [Early 20thC. From Tagalog.]

bunt·ing[1] /búnting/ *n.* a small seed-eating songbird related to the finch, with a short stout bill and usually brown or gray feathers. Family: Emberizidae. [13thC. Origin unknown.]

bunt·ing[2] /búnting/ *n.* strings of cloth or paper decorations for hanging outdoors [Early 18thC. Origin uncertain, perhaps from German *bunt* "colored."]

bunt·line /búnt lìn/ *n.* a rope attached to the bottom of a square sail, used to roll up the sail

Luis Buñuel

Bu·ñu·el /bóonyoo él/, **Luis** (1900–83) Spanish movie director. One of the greatest masters of filmmaking, he incorporated uncompromising social criticisms in works such as *The Discreet Charm of the Bourgeoisie* (1972).

bun·ya /búnyə/, **bun·ya-bun·ya, bun·ya pine** *n.* a tall Australian tree with cones containing edible seeds that are eaten raw or roasted and are ground into flour. Latin name: *Araucaria bidwillii.* [Mid-19thC. From Yagara *bunya-bunya.*]

Bun·yan /búnnyən/, **John** (1628–88) English preacher and writer. A Puritan preacher, he was jailed for 12 years for his religious beliefs. He wrote the autobiographical *Grace Abounding to the Chief of Sinners* (1666) and the great spiritual allegory *Pilgrim's Progress* (1678).

Bun·yan, Paul /búnnyən/ *n.* LEGEND In U.S. folklore, a giant lumberjack who performs superhuman feats with his blue ox, Babe

Bun·yan·esque /bùnyə nésk/ *adj.* **1. ALLEGORICAL** richly allegorical, like the writings of John Bunyan **2. GIGANTIC** supernaturally large, like the legendary giant lumberjack Paul Bunyan

Buo·nar·ro·ti /bwàw naa rṓ tee/, **Michelangelo** ♦ **Michelangelo**

buoy[1] /bóo ee, boy/ *n.* **1. FLOATING SIGNAL** a large anchored float, often equipped with lights or bells, that serves as a guide or warning to ships **2.** = **lifebuoy** ■ *vt.* (**buoyed, buoy·ing, buoys**) **MARK WITH BUOY** to use a buoy to mark the location of something in water, e.g., a hazard or channel [13thC. Origin uncertain: perhaps from Middle Dutch *bo(e)ye* or Old French *boie* "chain" (with which a buoy is tethered), both ultimately from a Germanic word meaning "signal."]

buoy[2] /bóo ee, boy/ (**buoyed, buoy·ing, buoys**) *vt.* to keep something from falling or sinking ○ *steps to buoy the country's currency* [Late 16thC. From Spanish *boyar* "to float," from *boya* "buoy."]

buoy up *vt.* **1. KEEP SOMEBODY'S SPIRITS UP** to keep somebody cheerful or optimistic in spite of difficulties ○ *The arrival of the children has buoyed us all up.* **2. ENCOURAGE** to give support or encouragement to somebody ○ *Buoyed up by a few wise investments, the company went on to prosper the following year.*

buoy·an·cy /bóy ənsee/, **buoy·ance** /-əns/ *n.* **1. FORCE CAUSING FLOATING** the tendency of a liquid or gas to cause less dense objects to float or rise to the surface **2. TENDENCY TO FLOAT** the tendency of an object to float **3. POWER TO RECOVER EMOTIONALLY** the ability to recover quickly from a disappointment or failure **4. CHEERFULNESS** cheerfulness or optimism

buoy·ant /bóy ənt/ *adj.* **1. PUSHING UPWARD** causing immersed objects to float or rise to the surface of a liquid, or upward in a gas **2. ABLE TO FLOAT** tending to float or rise to the surface of a liquid, or upward in a gas **3. QUICK TO RECOVER EMOTIONALLY** tending to recover quickly from a disappointment or failure **4. CHEERFUL** cheerful or optimistic [Late 16thC. From Old French, or from Spanish *boyante*, present participle of *boyar* "to float," from *boya* (see BUOY).] —**buoy·ant·ly** *adv.*

bu·pi·va·caine /byoo pívvə kayn/ *n.* a powerful local anesthetic used especially in epidural anesthesia [Origin uncertain: perhaps from BUTYL + *pipecoloxylidide* + *-vacaine* (from *procaine*)]

bu·pres·tid /byoo préstid/ *n.* a metallic-colored tropical beetle found worldwide that bores into wood during the larva stage. Family: Buprestidae. [Mid-19thC. From modern Latin *Buprestidae* (plural), family name, ultimately from Greek *bouprēstis*, literally "ox-sweller," from *bous* "ox."]

bur[1] /bur/, **burr** *n.* **1.** BOT **PRICKLY SEED HUSK** a prickly husk covering the seeds of plants such as burdock **2.** BOT **TREE GROWTH** a lumpy outgrowth of wood on a tree **3.** SURG **BONE DRILL** an instrument for drilling holes in bone, especially into the skull [14thC. Of uncertain origin: probably from Scandinavian, related to Danish *burre* "burdock."]

bur[2] *n.* = **burr**[1]

bur. *abbr.* bureau

Bur. *abbr.* Burma ■ *abbr.* Burmese

Bu·ra·ku·min /bóo rákoo mìn/ *npl.* members of the lowest Japanese caste [Mid-20thC. From Japanese, literally "hamlet people."]

bu·ran /boo ràan/ *n.* a strong wind in central Asia, bringing dust storms in summer and blizzards in winter [Mid-19thC. Via Russian from Turkic *boran.*]

burb /burb/ *n.* a suburb (*slang*) [Shortening]

Bur·bank /búr bàngk/ **1.** city in southwestern California, in the San Fernando Valley, a northern suburb of Los Angeles. Population: 96,579 (1996). **2.** city in northeastern Illinois, a suburb of Chicago. Population: 27,714 (1996).

Bur·bank, Luther (1849–1926) U.S. horticulturalist and botanist. He developed many different varieties of fruits, vegetables, and flowers.

Bur·ber·ry /búrbərree/ *tdmk.* a trademark for a brand of outerwear, especially waterproof cloth raincoats and accessories

bur·ble /búrb'l/ *v.* (**-bled, -bling, -bles**) **1.** *vi.* **MAKE BUBBLING SOUND** to make a gentle bubbling sound, like the sound of running water **2.** *vti.* **SPEAK EXCITEDLY** to speak or say something in a fast excited way (*informal*) **3.**

vi. **BECOME TURBULENT** to become turbulent (*refers to the airflow around an aircraft's wing*) ■ *n.* **1. GENTLE SOUND** a gentle bubbling or gurgling sound **2. STREAM OF TALK** a flow of fast excited talking (*informal*) **3. BREAK IN AIRFLOW** a break in the flow of air around an aircraft's wing, which causes turbulence [14thC. An imitation of the sound.] —**bur·bler** *n.* —**bur·bly** *adv.*

bur·bot /búrbət/ (*plural* **-bot** *or* **-bots**) *n.* a freshwater fish of the cod family found in North America, northern Europe, and Asia. Latin name: *Lota lota.* [14thC. From Old French *borbette*, of uncertain origin: probably formed from *borbe* "mud, slime."]

bur·den[1] /búrd'n/ *n.* **1. SOMETHING CARRIED** a load being carried ○ *carrying a heavy burden on his back* **2. WORRYING RESPONSIBILITY** a difficult or worrying responsibility or duty ○ *the burdens of parenthood* **3. SHIP'S CAPACITY** the maximum weight of cargo that a ship can carry ■ *vt.* (**-dened, -den·ing, -dens**) **1. GIVE RESPONSIBILITY TO SOMEBODY** to give somebody a task that is difficult to deal with or something worrying to think about **2. IMPOSE BURDEN ON SOMEBODY** to cause somebody or something to carry a burden [Old English *byrthen.* Ultimately from an Indo-European word meaning "to bear," which is also the ancestor of English *birth, fertile,* and *suffer.*]

WORD KEY: SYNONYMS

See Synonyms at ***subject.***

bur·den[2] /búrd'n/ *n.* **1. CHORUS** a chorus in a song **2. THEME** a main or recurring theme in music or literature (*literary*) [Late 16thC. Alteration of Middle English *bourdon* "bass part underlying a melody," from French, literally "bass, drone."]

bur·den of proof *n.* the responsibility of proving a case or argument, especially in a court of law

bur·den·some /búrd'nsəm/ *adj.* difficult or worrying to bear or deal with

bur·dock /búr dòk/ *n.* a tall biennial plant found wild in temperate areas, with a long taproot and small prickly purple flower heads. Genus: *Arctium.* [Late 16thC. From BURR + DOCK[1].]

bu·reau /byŏŏrō/ (*plural* **bureaus** *or* **bu·reaux**) *n.* **1. ORGANIZATION** an organization, or one of its branches **2. GOVERNMENT DEPARTMENT** a government department, or one of its branches **3. CHEST OF DRAWERS** a chest of drawers, especially a low one **4. WRITING DESK** a narrow desk with a writing surface and drawers [Late 17thC. From French, literally "baize" (used for desks), of uncertain origin: probably formed from *buire* "dark brown," from, ultimately, Greek *purros* "red," from *pur* "fire."]

bu·reauc·ra·cy /byoo rókrəsee/ (*plural* **-cies**) *n.* **1. ADMINISTRATIVE SYSTEM** an administrative system, especially in a government, that divides work into specific categories carried out by special departments of nonelected officials **2. OFFICIALS COLLECTIVELY** the nonelected officials of an organization or department **3. STATE OR ORGANIZATION** a state or organization operated by a hierarchy of paid officials **4. FRUSTRATING RULES** complex rules and regulations applied rigidly [Early 19thC. From French *bureaucratie*, from *bureau* "office" + *cracy* "rule."]

bu·reau·crat /byŏŏrə kràt/ *n.* **1. ADMINISTRATIVE OFFICIAL** an administrative or government official **2. INFLEXIBLE OFFICIAL** an official who applies rules rigidly —**bu·reau·cra·tism** /byoo rókrə tìzzəm/ *n.*

bu·reau·crat·ese /byoo ròkrəteéz/ *n.* over-formal, jargon-filled language often used by earnest officials

bu·reau·crat·ic /byŏŏrə kráttik/ *adj.* **1. ADMINISTRATIVE** relating to the way administrative systems are organized ○ *the bureaucratic structure* **2. TOO RIGID** used to describe an administrative system or official that applies rules rigidly —**bu·reau·crat·i·cal·ly** *adv.*

bu·reau·cra·tize /byoo rókrə tìz/ (**-tized, -tiz·ing, -tiz·es**) *vt.* **1. MAKE SOMETHING INTO BUREAUCRACY** to change a system into a bureaucracy **2. MAKE SOMETHING TOO RIGID OR COMPLEX** to make a system or procedure rigid or complex —**bu·reau·cra·ti·za·tion** /byoo ròkrətə záyshən/ *n.*

bu·reau de change /byŏŏrō də shaáNzh/ (*plural* **bu·reaus de change** /byŏŏrō-/ *or* **bu·reaux de change** /byŏŏrō-/) *n. U.K.* an office or part of a bank where foreign currency is exchanged [From French, literally "office of exchange"]

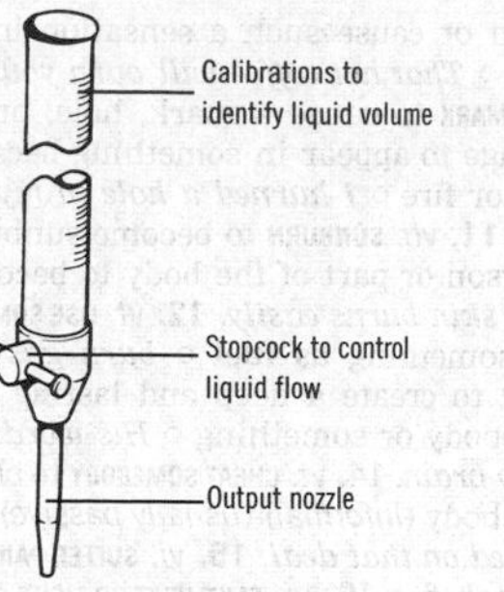

Burette

bu·rette /byoo rét/ *n.* a glass tube with measurements marked on the side and a stopcock at the bottom, used in laboratories to release an accurately measured quantity of liquid [Mid-19thC. From French, diminutive of *buire* "jug," probably ultimately of Germanic origin.]

burg /burg/ *n.* **1. TOWN** a city or town (*informal*) **2. ANCIENT FORTRESS** an ancient fortress or walled town [Mid-18thC. *Enclosure* from late Latin *burgus* "town," from German *Burg*; both ultimately from an ancient Germanic word that is also the ancestor of English *borough.*]

bur·gee /bùr jeé, búr jeè/ *n.* a light identification flag flown from the top of a mast [Mid-18thC. Origin uncertain: perhaps from French *bourgeois* in the sense "master, owner," from late Latin *burgus* (see BOURG).]

bur·geon /búrjən/ (**-geoned, -geon·ing, -geons**) *vi.* (*literary*) **1. PRODUCE NEW GROWTH** to produce new buds and leaves or to swell and develop into leaves and flowers **2. FLOURISH** to flourish or develop rapidly [14thC. From French *bourgeonner*, from *bourgeon* "a shoot or bud," from, ultimately, late Latin *burra* "wool."]

bur·geon·ing /búrjəning/ *adj.* growing or expanding rapidly ○ *burgeoning wealth*

burg·er /búrgər/ *n.* **1. MEAT SNACK** a flat round patty of cooked ground meat, usually served in a bun **2. SAVORY SNACK** a round flat patty made of chicken, fish, vegetables, or nuts, usually served in a bun [Mid-20thC. Back-formation from HAMBURGER.]

Bur·ger /búrgər/, **Warren** (1907–95) U.S. chief justice of the U.S. Supreme Court. Appointed by President Nixon on the strength of his reputation as a judicial conservative, he sat on the U.S. Supreme Court from 1969 to 1986. Full name **Warren Earl Burger**

-burger /búrgər/ *suffix.* Resembling ground beef or a hamburger ○ *veggieburger* [From HAMBURGER]

bur·gess /búrjəss/ *n.* a member of the lower legislative house in Maryland or Virginia before the American Revolution

Bur·gess /búrjəss/, **Anthony** (1917–93) British writer and critic. His books include *A Clockwork Orange* (1962) and *A Dead Man in Deptford* (1993). Born **John Anthony Burgess Wilson**

Bur·gess, John William (1844–1931) U.S. political scientist and educator. In addition to scholarly publications and teaching, he established political science as an academic discipline and helped make Columbia a major university by founding the School of Political Science there in 1880.

burgh·er /búrgər/ *n.* **1. MEDIEVAL MERCHANT** a merchant in a medieval European town **2. CITIZEN** a citizen, especially a prosperous or conservative member of the middle class (*humorous*) **3. PRE-19THC PARLIAMENTARY REPRESENTATIVE** a parliamentary representative from a corporate town, borough, or university before 19th-century reforms [Late 16thC. Partly formed from BURGH, partly from German or Dutch *burger*, from *burg* (see BURG).]

bur·glar /búrglər/ *n.* somebody who enters or remains in a building to commit a felony, usually in order to steal something [Mid-16thC. From obsolete legal French *burgier*, from the assumed Latin stem *burg-* "to plunder."]

bur·glar a·larm *n.* an electronic device designed to make a loud noise when somebody enters a building in any way other than that intended by the resident or owner

bur·glar·ize /búrglə rìz/ (**-ized, -iz·ing, -iz·es**) *vt.* to enter a building intending to commit a felony, usually to steal something (*often passive*)

bur·glar·proof /búrglər pròof/ *adj.* secured with locks, alarms, or other devices so as to discourage or prevent unauthorized entry

bur·gla·ry /búrgləree/ (*plural* **-ries**) *n.* the crime of entering a building to commit a felony, usually theft, or an instance of such a crime —**bur·glar·i·ous** /bur gláiree əss/ *adj.* —**bur·glar·i·ous·ly** *adv.*

WORD KEY: SYNONYMS

See Synonyms at ***theft.***

bur·gle /búrg'l/ (**-gled, -gling, -gles**) *vt.* = **burglarize** (*often passive*) [Late 19thC. Back-formation from BURGLAR.]

bur·go·mas·ter /búrgə màstər/ *n.* the mayor or chief magistrate in some northern European towns [Late 16thC. From Dutch *burgomeester*, literally "town master."]

bur·goo /búr gòo, búr góo/ (*plural* **-goos**) *n. Southern U.S.* **1. STEW** a spicy meat stew cooked outdoors **2. OUTDOOR PARTY** an outdoor party where burgoo is cooked and eaten [Late 17thC. Via Arabic *burğul* from Persian *burğūl*, variant of *burğūr*, literally "bruised grain" (source of English *bulgur*).]

Bur·goyne /bur góyn, búr gòyn/, **John** (1722–92) British general. His attempt to lead a British invasion into New York from Canada was thwarted at Saratoga (1777). He also wrote plays, including *The Heiress* (1786).

bur·gun·dy /búrgəndee/, **Bur·gun·dy** *n.* (*plural* **-dies**) **1. KIND OF WINE** red or white wine produced in the Burgundy region of central France **2. DEEP RED COLOR** a deep red color, like that of red Burgundy wine ■ *adj.* **OF DEEP RED COLOR** of a deep red color, like red Burgundy wine

bur·i·al /bérreeəl/ *n.* the act or ceremony of putting a dead body into the ground or into the sea [Old English *byrgels*, from *byrgan* (see BURY)]

bur·i·al ground *n.* an area of land where dead bodies are buried, especially an ancient site

Bur·i·at *n.* = **Buryat**

Bur·i·dan's ass /byŏŏrəd'nz-/ *n.* a situation used to demonstrate the impracticality of making choices according to a formal system of reasoning [Named for Jean *Buridan* (1300–58), French philosopher who wrote of an ass that starves to death because it cannot choose between two identical piles of food]

bur·ied treas·ure *n.* valuable items buried or thought to be buried in the ground for safekeeping

bu·rin /byŏŏrin/ *n.* **1. CHISEL** an engraver's chisel for making grooves **2. PREHISTORIC TOOL** a prehistoric chisellike flint tool, used for cutting and engraving during the Upper Palaeolithic period [Mid-17thC. From French.]

bur·ka /búrkə/ *n.* an all-over garment with veiled eyeholes, worn by some Muslim women [Mid-19thC. Via Urdu or Persian *burka'* from Arabic *burku'.*]

burke /burk/ (**burked, burk·ing, burkes**) *vt.* **1. KEEP SOMETHING QUIET** to prevent information from becoming known **2. KEEP SOMEBODY QUIET** to prevent somebody from revealing information **3. EVADE** to evade an issue or question **4. MURDER DISCREETLY** to murder somebody silently and without leaving marks or wounds, especially by suffocation [Early 19thC. Named for William *Burke* (1792–1829), hanged in Edinburgh for killing people in order to sell their bodies for dissection.]

Burke /burk/, **Edmund** (1729–97) Irish-born British political philosopher and statesman. As a Whig member of Parliament (1765–94), he was one of the greatest orators of the age. He played a leading role in the impeachment of Warren Hastings (1788–95). His *Reflections on the Revolution in France* (1790) condemned the French Revolution and reached a wide European audience.

Bur·ki·na Fa·so /bərkeènə fássō/ landlocked republic in western Africa. A former French territory, it became independent in 1960. Language: French. Currency: CFA franc. Capital: Ouagadougou. Population: 10,963,300 (1997). Area: 105,900 sq. mi./274,200 sq. km. Former name **Upper Volta** (until 1984)

Bur·kitt's lym·pho·ma /búrkits-/ *n.* a rare malignant tumor attacking white blood cells, associated with a virus spread by insects. It is found mainly in children in Central Africa. [Mid-20thC. Named for the British surgeon Denis *Burkitt* (1911–93), who mapped its geographical distribution in Africa.]

burl /burl/ *n.* **1. KNOT ON TREE** a knotty growth on a tree trunk **2. KNOTTY WOOD** knotty wood or a decorative

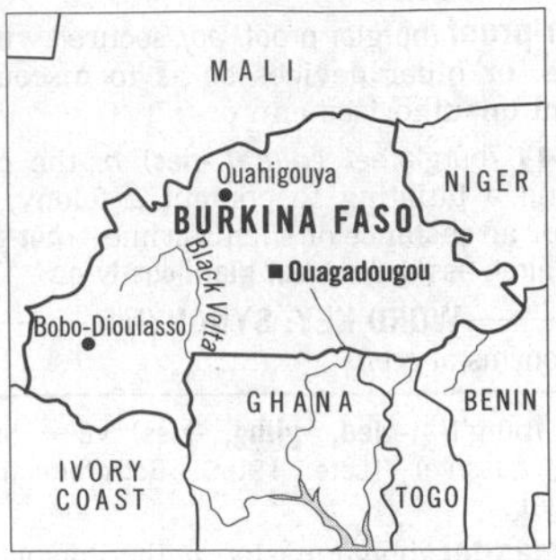

Burkina Faso

veneer made from it **3.** **KNOT IN CLOTH** a knot in thread or cloth ■ *vt.* **(burled, burl·ing, burls)** **REMOVE KNOTS FROM CLOTH** to pick knots off newly woven cloth [15thC. Via Old French *bourle* "tuft of wool" from, ultimately, late Latin *burra* "wool" (source of English *burgeon*).] —**burl·er** *n.*

bur·lap /búr làp/ *n.* coarse cloth woven from jute, hemp, or a similar rough thread [Late 17thC. Origin unknown.]

bur·lesque /bur lésk/ *n.* **1.** **MOCKERY BY LUDICROUS IMITATION** the mocking of a serious matter or style by imitating it in an incongruous way **2.** **WORK USING BURLESQUE** a literary or dramatic work that uses burlesque **3.** **LUDICROUS IMITATION** an incongruous imitation of something **4.** **VARIETY SHOW** a variety show of a type that often includes striptease ■ *vt.* **(burlesqued, burlesquing, burlesques)** **MOCK BY LUDICROUS IMITATION** to mock something serious by imitating it in an incongruous way [Mid-17thC. Via French from Italian *burlesco*, from *burla* "mockery, fun."] —**burlesquer** *n.*

bur·ley /búrlee/ *n.* a light-colored, thin-leaved tobacco grown mainly in Kentucky [Late 19thC. Origin uncertain, perhaps from the personal name *Burley*.]

Bur·lin·game /búrling gàym/ city in western California, on the San Mateo peninsula, a southern suburb of San Francisco. Population: 27,716 (1996).

Bur·ling·ton /búrlingtən/ **1.** city and port in the southeastern corner of Iowa, southwest of Davenport, on the western bank of the Mississippi River. Population: 26,853 (1996). **2.** city in northwestern Vermont, on Lake Champlain. It is home to the University of Vermont. Population: 39,004 (1996).

bur·ly /búrlee/ **(-li·er, -li·est)** *adj.* **1.** **STOUT AND STRONG** strong and with a broad sturdy frame ○ *flanked by two burly bodyguards* **2.** **ROBUST** rough and robust ○ *a burly laugh* [14thC. Origin uncertain: probably from assumed Old English *borlic* "excellent," ultimately from an Indo-European word meaning "to carry," which is also the ancestor of English *bear* "to carry."] —**bur·li·ness** *n.*

Bur·ma /búrmə/ former name for **Myanmar** (until 1989)

bur mar·i·gold *n.* = **beggar's lice**

Bur·mese /bur méez/ *npl.* **PEOPLE OF MYANMAR** the people of Myanmar, formerly Burma ■ *n.* **SINO-TIBETAN LANGUAGE** the official language of Myanmar, formerly Burma, one of the Tibeto-Burman group of Sino-Tibetan languages. Burmese is spoken by between 20 and 27 million people. ■ *adj.* **OF MYANMAR** relating to or typical of Myanmar, its people, language, or culture

Bur·mese cat *n.* a domestic cat with a chocolate-colored or silvery-brown coat and yellow eyes, similar in build to the Siamese cat

burn /burn/ *v.* **(burned** *or* **burnt, burned** /burnd/ *or* **burnt** /burnt/, **burn·ing, burns)** **1.** *vti.* **BE OR SET ON FIRE** to be on fire or cause something to be on fire **2.** *vti.* **DESTROY SOMETHING BY FIRE** to destroy something or be destroyed by fire ○ *The house was burned to the ground.* **3.** *vt.* **DAMAGE SOMETHING BY FIRE** to injure, damage, or affect somebody or something with fire or extreme heat ○ *I burned my hand on the iron.* **4.** *vt.* **OVERCOOK SOMETHING** to spoil food or a cooking pan by subjecting it to too much heat **5.** *vi.* **BE OVERCOOKED** to be spoiled because of being subjected to too intense a heat or being cooked for too long **6.** *vt.* **USE SOMETHING UP** to use up or consume something ○ *You won't burn many calories watching TV.* **7.** *vi.* **FEEL FEVERISH** to feel or look extremely hot or feverish because of illness or embarrassment ○ *Her cheeks were burning.* **8.** *vti.* **KILL OR DIE BY FIRE** to kill somebody with fire or die by fire, usually as a form of execution **9.** *vti.* **CAUSE OR FEEL STINGING** to feel an intense stinging or smarting sensation or cause such a sensation in a part of the body ○ *That hot coffee will burn your throat* **10.** *vt.* **MAKE MARK** to cause a mark, hole, or other sign of damage to appear in something because of intense heat or fire ○ *I burned a hole in my shirt with the iron.* **11.** *vti.* **SUNBURN** to become sunburned or cause a person or part of the body to become sunburned ○ *My skin burns easily.* **12.** *vt.* **USE SOMETHING AS FUEL** to use something as fuel ○ *burn gas* **13.** *vi.* **IMPRESS DEEPLY** to create a deep and lasting impression on somebody or something ○ *His words were burning in my brain.* **14.** *vt.* **CHEAT SOMEBODY** to cheat or swindle somebody (*informal*) (*usually passive*) ○ *We really got burned on that deal.* **15.** *vi.* **SUFFER PAIN** to suffer pain through fire **16.** *vi.* **EMIT HEAT OR LIGHT** to emit heat or light ○ *A light was burning outside the front porch.* **17.** *vi.* **CONTAIN A FIRE** to contain a fire or operate by means of fire ○ *a fireplace burning bright* **18.** *vi.* **FEEL STRONG EMOTION** to feel an emotion such as anger or shame very intensely ○ *burning with shame* **19.** *vti.* **ELECTROCUTE** to electrocute somebody or be electrocuted (*informal*) **20.** *vi.* **YEARN** to yearn to do or acquire something ○ *burning to succeed* **21.** *vti.* CHEM **COMBUST** to undergo combustion, thus taking in oxygen, or to cause something to undergo combustion ■ *n.* **1.** SPACE TECH **ROCKET ENGINE ADJUSTMENT** a controlled firing of a rocket's engine for adjusting course and position **2.** **STINGING** a stinging sensation or feeling of intense heat ○ *the burn of the iodine on my skin* **3.** MED **HEAT INJURY** an injury caused by fire, heat, radiation, chemical action, electricity, or friction, resulting in redness and blistering of the skin and often causing damage to underlying tissues. ◊ **first-degree burn, second-degree burn, third-degree burn** **4.** **FIRE OR HEAT MARK** a mark or hole left on or in something such as fabric, wood, or plastic as a result of burning **5.** **STATE OF ANGER** a state of anger ○ *He's been in a slow burn all morning.* **6.** **SKIN BURN** sunburn or windburn **7.** FITNESS **SENSATION OF BURNING** a sensation of burning that occurs during strenuous exercise, and the positive psychological sensation associated with it ○ *You can feel the burn after an hour of aerobics* [Old English *birnan* "to be on fire" and *bærnan* "to cause to burn," from a prehistoric Germanic word that is also the ancestor of English *brand*]

burn down *vti.* to catch fire and burn until virtually nothing remains, or to burn something such as a building in order to destroy it

burn in *vt.* **1.** COMPUT **TEST SOMETHING BY RUNNING IT CONTINUOUSLY** to operate a semiconductor-based device or piece of software for a continuous period as a test for defects or failure **2.** PHOTOGRAPHY **EXPOSE PART OF PICTURE** to expose a specific part of an image on photographic paper while masking other areas so that they are not exposed any further

burn off *v.* **1.** *vt.* **GET RID OF EXCESS FAT** to use up energy or get rid of unwanted fat by exercising ○ *burn off a few extra calories* **2.** *vt.* AGRIC **REMOVE VEGETATION** to remove vegetation by fire or with chemicals, either to clear the land or in preparation for harvesting a root crop **3.** *vt.* ENERGY **GET RID OF EXCESS GAS** to get rid of unwanted gas, e.g., at an oil-well head, by burning it **4.** *vti.* METEOROL **DISSIPATE** to dissipate fog or clouds by the heat of the sun, or to be dissipated in this way

burn out *v.* **1.** *vi.* **FINISH BURNING** to stop burning when reduced to nothing **2.** *vti.* **WEAR OUT THROUGH HEAT** to stop working or to cause something to stop working because of too much heat or friction ○ *The motor must have burned out* **3.** *vti.* **BECOME EXHAUSTED** to become or make somebody exhausted or unwell through too much hard work, stress, or reckless living (*informal*) ○ *You'll burn yourself out if you don't slow down.*

burn up *v.* **1.** *vti.* **DESTROY BY FIRE** to destroy something or be destroyed by intense heat or fire **2.** *vi.* **BE VERY HOT** to be very hot or overheated ○ *burning up with fever* **3.** *vt.* **ANNOY** to annoy somebody or make somebody angry (*informal*)

burn bag *n.* a bag for putting secret or politically sensitive documents in before burning them

burned-out, **burnt-out** *adj.* **1.** **COMPLETELY EXHAUSTED** exhausted physically or emotionally through too much hard work, stress, or reckless living **2.** **DESTROYED BY FIRE** destroyed on the inside by fire

Burne-Jones /búrn jōnz/, **Sir Edward** (1833–98) British designer. A leading member of the pre-Raphaelite school, he painted classical and mythological subjects in a dreamlike style. His book illustrations and designs for stained glass and tapestries showed the strong influence of medieval art. Born **Edward Coley Jones**

burn·er /búrnər/ *n.* **1.** **PART OF STOVE OR LAMP** the part of a fuel-burning stove, lamp, or heater that produces a flame when lit **2.** **RING ON RANGE** one of the circular rings or plates on a gas or electric range that produces heat or a flame **3.** **FURNACE** an incinerator or furnace that burns fuel, waste products, or trash **4.** **LARGE GRAFFITI** a large, complex mural or graffiti painted by a graffiti artist, usually on the outside wall of a building (*slang*)

bur·net /bər nét/ (*plural* **-nets** *or* **-net**) *n.* a plant of the rose family with flowers of various colors. The most common variety, the salad burnet, is cultivated and used in salads and herbal teas. Genus: *Sanguisorba.* [14thC. From Old French *brunet* and *brunete*, literally "small brown," which were formed from *brun* "brown," from a prehistoric Germanic word that is also the ancestor of English *brown*.]

Bur·nett /bər nét/, **Frances Hodgson** (1849–1924) British-born U.S. writer. She wrote children's books, including the classical novel *The Secret Garden* (1911). Born **Frances Eliza Hodgson**

Burn·ham /búrnəm/, **Forbes** (1923–85) Guyanan statesman. He was prime minister (1964–80) and president (1980–85) of Guyana. Full name **Linden Forbes Sampson Burnham**

burn-in *n.* COMPUT a final stage in the manufacture of semiconductor-based devices or software in which they are operated for a prescribed period to test for defects or failures and thus improve their reliability

burn·ing /búrning/ *adj.* **1.** **VERY HOT** extremely hot **2.** **ON FIRE** producing flames or on fire **3.** **ARDENT** emotionally intense or strong ○ *he spoke with a burning passion* **4.** **IMPORTANT** of immediate or urgent importance ○ *one of the burning issues of the day* ■ *adv.* **EXTREMELY** extremely ○ *a burning hot day* [Old English]

burn·ing bush *n.* **1.** **SHRUB WITH RED BERRIES OR FOLIAGE** a shrub that produces bright red berries or foliage. Genus: *Euonymus.* **2.** = **gas plant** **3.** **BUSHY PLANT WITH RED AUTUMN COLOR** a bushy annual plant with narrow light green leaves that turn red in fall, such as the summer cypress [Alludes to the burning bush of Exodus 3. In the sense of "gas plant," from its leaves' secretion of flammable oil.]

burn·ing glass *n.* a convex lens that can concentrate the sun's rays to produce an intense spot of heat or fire at the focus

bur·nish /búrnish/ *vt.* **(-nished, -nish·ing, -nish·es)** **1.** **POLISH SOMETHING** to polish metal until it shines **2.** **MAKE SOMETHING SHINY** to produce a glossy finish on something such as pottery or fabric by rubbing it with a smooth instrument ■ *n.* **SHINY SURFACE** a smooth shiny finish ○ *a bowl with a bright burnish* [14thC. From the Old French stem *burniss-* of *burnir*, variant of *brunir* "to make bright or brown," from *brun* (see BURNET).] —**bur·nish·er** *n.*

bur·nished /búrnisht/ *adj.* **1.** **SHINY** polished until shiny **2.** **LUSTROUS** brown and lustrous or smooth (*literary*) ○ *the burnished coat of the chestnut mare*

bur·noose /bur nóos/, **bur·nous, burn·ouse** *n.* a long hooded cloak worn by some Arabs, or a fashionable imitation of this [Late 16thC. Via French *burnous* from Arabic *burnus*, from Greek *birros* "hooded cloak."]

burn·out /búrn òwt/ *n.* **1.** **EXHAUSTION** psychological exhaustion and diminished efficiency resulting from overwork or prolonged exposure to stress ○ *reported a high rate of burnout among nurses* **2.** **EXTREMELY EXHAUSTED PERSON** somebody affected by psychological exhaustion (*informal*) **3.** MECH ENG **MACHINE FAILURE THROUGH HEAT** failure of a machine or part of a machine to work because of overuse or excessive heat or friction **4.** AEROSP **ROCKET FAILURE** failure of a rocket or jet engine to work because the fuel supply has been exhausted or cut off

Burns /burnz/, **George** (1896–1996) U.S. comedian and actor. He conducted one of the longest-running acts in show business, encompassing vaudeville, radio, movies, and television, and won an Academy Award for *The Sunshine Boys* (1975).

Burns, Robert (1759–96) Scottish poet. The author of *Poems, Chiefly in the Scottish Dialect* (1786) and hundreds of songs, he is regarded as Scotland's national poet. His many songs include "Auld Lang Syne," "Scots Wha Hae" and the narrative poem "Tam O'Shanter."

Robert Burns

Burns, Tommy (1881–1955) Canadian boxer. He was Canada's only world heavyweight boxing champion (1906–08).

Burn·side /búrn sīd/, **Ambrose** (1824–81) U.S. general. He fought in campaigns against the Native Americans on the frontier and served as a general in the Union Army in the Civil War. His spectacular side whiskers inspired the creation of the term "sideburns." Full name **Ambrose Everett Burnside**

burn·sides /búrn sīdz/ *npl.* heavy side whiskers and a mustache worn with a clean-shaven chin [Late 19thC. Named for Ambrose E. BURNSIDE (1824–81), a Union general during the American Civil War who was known for his side whiskers.]

burnt[1] /burnt/ past tense, past participle of **burn**

burnt[2] /burnt/ *adj.* **1. AFFECTED BY BURNING** affected or spoiled by burning, especially by overcooking **2.** PAINTING **DARKENED BY HEAT** used to describe a pigment or dye that has been darkened through a heating process ○ *burnt umber*

burnt al·mond *n.* candy with an almond in the center and a coating of burnt sugar

burnt of·fer·ing *n.* **1. SACRIFICE** an animal or other offering that is burned on an altar as a sacrifice in some religions **2. BURNT FOOD** burnt or overcooked food that is nevertheless served up (*humorous*)

burnt-out *adj.* = **burned-out**

burnt si·en·na *n.* **1.** PAINTING **BROWN PIGMENT** a reddish brown pigment or dye originally obtained by roasting raw sienna **2.** COLORS **DARK REDDISH BROWN** a dark reddish brown color

burnt um·ber *n.* **1.** PAINTING **DARK BROWN PIGMENT** a dark brown pigment or dye originally obtained by roasting raw umber **2.** COLORS **DEEP BROWN** a deep brown color

burp /burp/ *n.* **NOISE MADE THROUGH MOUTH** a noise made through the mouth when air is suddenly forced up through the windpipe from the stomach ■ *v.* **(burped, burp·ing, burps) 1.** *vi.* **BELCH** to make a noise through the mouth when air is suddenly forced up through the windpipe from the stomach **2.** *vt.* **MAKE BABY BRING UP GAS** to make a baby expel air from its stomach through its windpipe after feeding by rubbing or patting its back [Mid-20thC. An imitation of the sound.]

burp gun *n.* a lightweight submachine gun (*informal*)

burr[1] /bur/ *n.* **burr, bur** ENG **1. ROUGH EDGE** a rough edge on material such as metal after it has been cut or drilled **2. TOOL FOR REMOVING BURRS** a tool used for removing the rough edges from metal that has been cut or drilled ■ *vt.* **(burred, burr·ing, burrs) 1. CREATE ROUGH EDGE** to create a rough edge on a piece of metal or other piece of work by cutting or drilling **2. REMOVE ROUGH EDGE** to remove a rough edge from a piece of metal or other workpiece [Early 17thC. A variant of BUR.]

burr[2] /bur/ *n.* **1. WHIRRING SOUND** a whirring or buzzing sound ○ *the steady burr of the machines downstairs* **2. ROLLED "R"** a way of speaking the letter "r" in some regional accents of English, in which the sound is rolled or trilled ■ *v.* **(burred, burr·ing, burrs) 1.** *vi.* **MAKE WHIRRING SOUND** to make a whirring or buzzing sound ○ *The sewing machine burred away quietly* **2.** *vti.* **SPEAK WITH BURR** to speak with or pronounce words with a burr [Mid-18thC. Origin uncertain: perhaps an imitation of the sound, or from BURR[1] in the sense of a "rough" sound.]

burr[3] /bur/ *n.* a washer that fits around the end of a rivet [14thC. Shortening of Old English *burg* "stronghold, fortified enclosure"; hence "circle," later "washer."]

Burr /bur/, **Aaron** (1756–1836) U.S. statesman and Vice President of the United States. He was Thomas Jefferson's first vice president (1801–05). He killed Alexander Hamilton in a duel after a long public feud (1804).

bur·ri·to /bə reétō/ (*plural* **-tos**) *n.* in Mexican cooking, a flour tortilla wrapped around a filling of meat, beans, or cheese [Mid-20thC. From American Spanish, literally "small burro," from Spanish *burro* (see BURRO).]

bur·ro /búrrō/ (*plural* **-ros**) *n.* a small donkey, especially one that is used as a pack animal [Early 19thC. From Spanish, a back-formation from *borrico* "donkey," from late Latin *burricus* "small horse," of uncertain origin: perhaps from Germanic.]

bur·ro's tail *n.* a Mexican plant popular as a house plant for its hanging stems and thick, succulent leaves that resemble tails. Latin name: *Sedum morganianum.*

Bur·roughs /búrrōz/, **Edgar Rice** (1875–1950) U.S. writer. He created the character Tarzan in a series of popular novels starting in 1914.

Bur·roughs, John (1837–1921) U.S. naturalist, essayist, and poet. He wrote essays on nature and possessed extensive natural history collections.

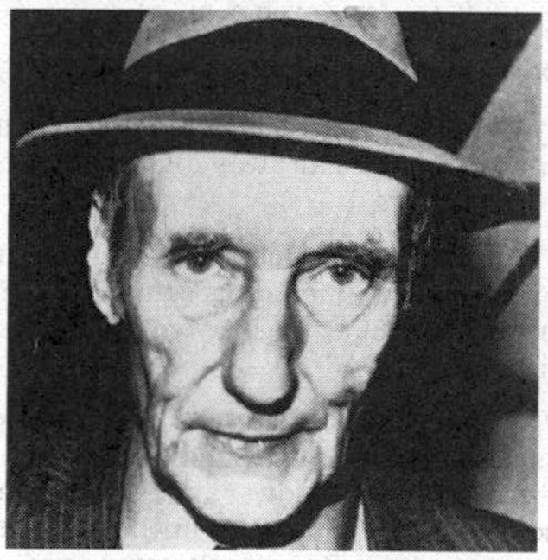
William S. Burroughs

Bur·roughs, William S. (1914–97) U.S. writer. A leading figure of the Beat Generation, he wrote *Naked Lunch* (1959) and *The Soft Machine* (1961). Full name **William Seward Burroughs**

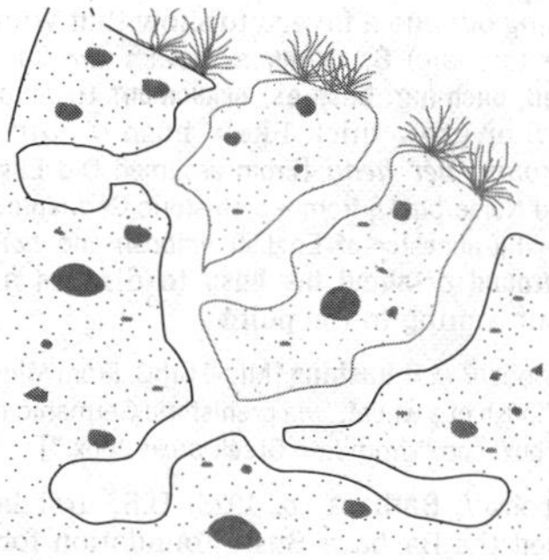
Burrow

bur·row /búrrō/ *n.* **1. RABBIT'S HOME** a hole or tunnel dug as a living space by a small animal such as a rabbit **2. SNUG PLACE** a small snug place created by digging or hollowing ■ *v.* **(-rowed, -row·ing, -rows) 1.** *vti.* **DIG HOLE OR TUNNEL** to make a hole or tunnel by digging **2.** *vi.* **SEARCH BY DIGGING** to look for something by groping or digging ○ *She burrowed in her handbag for her lipstick* **3.** *vi.* **MOVE BY DIGGING** to move through something solid by digging or by creating a space ○ *He burrowed through the undergrowth.* **4.** *vi.* **HIDE OR LIVE IN BURROW** to hide or live in a burrow **5.** *vi.* **LOOK INTO THOROUGHLY** to research or investigate something very thoroughly ○ *had spent years burrowing into the history of the era* [13thC. A variant of BOROUGH.] — **bur·row·er** *n.*

bur·row·ing owl *n.* a small owl that lives in the prairies of North and South America and nests in abandoned burrows of other animals such as prairie dogs or rabbits. Latin name: *Athene cunicularia.*

bur·ry[1] /búree/ **(-ri·er, -ri·est)** *adj.* **1. COVERED IN BURS** covered in burs **2. LIKE A BUR** resembling a bur or burs

bur·ry[2] /búree/ **(-ri·er, -ri·est)** *adj.* characterized by or spoken with a burr

bur·sa /búrssə/ (*plural* **-sas** *or* **-sae** /-seé/) *n.* ANAT a fluid-filled body sac that reduces friction around joints or between other parts that rub against one another [Early 19thC. Via modern Latin from medieval Latin, "bag, purse," from Greek, "wineskin" (source of English *purse*).] —**bur·sal** *adj.*

Bur·sa /búr saá/ city in northwestern Turkey, south of the Sea of Marmara, south of Istanbul, and west of Ankara. It was the capital of the Ottoman Empire from 1326 to 1402. Population: 996,600 (1994).

bur·sa of Fa·bri·ci·us /bùrsə əv fə breéshəss/ *n.* an organ in immature birds that produces B lymphocytes. It resembles a sac and is situated in part of the lower pelvic region **(cloaca)**. [Named for Girolamo *Fabrici* (Latinized form *Fabricius*) (1533–1619), an Italian anatomist]

bur·sar /búrsər/ *n.* an official who has charge of funds, particularly in a university, college, school, or monastery [13thC. From either French *boursier* or medieval Latin *bursarius*, ultimately from *bursa* (see BURSA).] — **bur·sar·ship** *n.*

bur·sa·ry /búrsəree/ (*plural* **-ries**) *n.* **1. STUDENT'S GRANT** a grant or scholarship offered to a student at a school, college, or university in some countries, e.g., Canada and Scotland **2. BURSAR'S OFFICE** the office or room where a bursar works [Late 17thC. From medieval Latin *bursaria* "bursar's office," from *bursa* (see BURSA).] — **bur·sar·i·al** /bur sáirree əl/ *adj.*

burse /burs/ *n.* **1. CONTAINER USED IN CHURCH RITUAL** in the Roman Catholic Church, a flat case that is used for carrying a special linen cloth **(corporal)** when celebrating Mass **2. PURSE** a purse (*archaic*) [13thC. Directly or via French *bourse* from medieval Latin *bursa* (see BURSA).]

bur·si·con /búr sə kòn/ *n.* a hormone secreted in the brain of insects and released by ganglia in the thorax and abdomen that affects processes that follow molting, such as the hardening of the cuticle [Mid-20thC. Coined from BURSA "sac, sac-like bodily cavity."]

bur·si·tis /bur sítiss/ *n.* inflammation of a fluid-filled sac **(bursa)** of the body, particularly at the elbow, knee, or shoulder joint

burst /burst/ *v.* **(burst, burst·ing, bursts) 1.** *vi.* **SPLIT OR BREAK** to split or break apart suddenly and violently because of excess internal pressure ○ *the suitcase had burst open* **2.** *vt.* **MAKE SOMETHING SPLIT** to cause something to split open suddenly and disgorge its contents, e.g., by piercing it or applying external pressure **3.** *vi.* **VERY FULL** to be so full as to appear close to splitting open or overflowing ○ *Every hotel in town was bursting with tourists.* **4.** *vt.* **RUPTURE** to rupture an internal organ or blood vessel **5.** *vt.* **FLOW OVER SOMETHING** to overflow the normal limit of containment ○ *The river burst its banks.* **6.** *vi.* **MOVE SUDDENLY** to go, come, or move suddenly and with great energy and speed ○ *He burst into the room.* **7.** *vi.* **BE OVERWHELMED** to feel an emotion so intensely that it is almost overwhelming ○ *I thought I would burst with excitement.* **8.** *vi.* **BECOME SUDDENLY NOTICED** to appear suddenly and become noticed and prominent at a particular time and in a particular situation ○ *an exciting new product about to burst onto the market* **9.** *vt.* **DIVIDE PAPER** to separate continuous stationery, e.g., computer printout, into individual sheets ■ *n.* **1. EXPLOSION OR RUPTURE** a sudden and often noisy splitting or breaking open of something **2. SHORT, INTENSE PERIOD** a short, sudden, and intense period of some activity or phenomenon ○ *a burst of publicity* **3. SUSTAINED ACTIVITY** a period of sustained activity ○ *I read it in two short bursts.* ○ *a burst of speed* **4. GUNFIRE** a short, sudden, and noisy volley of gunfire [Old English *berstan*, from prehistoric Germanic] — **burst·er** *n.*

burst into *vi.* **1. CHANGE STATE SUDDENLY** to start to happen or appear suddenly and often dramatically ○ *The truck crashed and burst into flames.* ○ *Spring saw the landscape burst into life.* **2. START TO EXPRESS SOMETHING** to give sudden and full expression to a strong emotion such as laughter or tears

burst out *v.* **1.** *vi.* **SUDDENLY START** to start expressing something suddenly and fully ○ *burst out laughing* **2.** *vt.* **EXCLAIM** to say something suddenly, as if a suppressed emotion or opinion had been welling up inside

burst·ing disk *n.* a disk, usually made of thin metal, that is designed to protect equipment by rupturing under abnormal pressure to form a safe outlet for the process fluid

bur·then /búrthən/ *n.* **BURDEN** a burden (*archaic*) ■ *vt.* (**-thened, -then·ing, -thens**) **BURDEN** to burden (*archaic*) [Variant of BURDEN]

bur·ton /búrt'n/ *n.* a kind of light tackle with double or single blocks used for hoisting [Early 18thC. Alteration of obsolete *Breton (tackle)*, of uncertain origin: probably so called because it was characteristic of Brittany.]

Bur·ton /búrt'n/ city in eastern Michigan, on the Thread River. It is a suburb of Flint. Population: 27,617 (1990).

Bur·ton, Harold (1888–1964) U.S. Supreme Court justice. He was appointed by President Truman to the U.S. Supreme Court (1945–58). Full name **Harold Hitz Burton**

Bur·ton, Richard (1925–84) Welsh-born British actor. His movies included *Look Back in Anger* (1959) and *Cleopatra* (1963).

Bur·ton, Tim (*b.* 1960) U.S. movie director. He directed *Batman* (1989) and *Edward Scissorhands* (1990).

Burundi

Bu·run·di /bŏŏ rŏŏndee/ landlocked republic in east central Africa. It is surrounded by Rwanda to the north, Tanzania to the east and south, and the Democratic Republic of the Congo to the west. Formerly part of the Belgian territory of Ruanda-Urundi, it became independent in 1962. Language: Kirundi, French. Currency: Burundi franc. Capital: Bujumbura. Population: 5,397,107 (1997). Area: 10,747 sq. mi./27,834 sq. km. Official name **Republic of Burundi**. Former name **Ruanda-Urundi** (until 1962) —**Bu·run·di·an** *n., adj.*

bur·weed /búr wēed/ *n.* a weed with burs

bur·y /bérree/ (**-ied, -y·ing, -ies**) *v.* **1.** *vt.* **PUT SOMETHING IN HOLE** to dig a hole, put something in it, and replace the soil or other material removed ○ *a dog burying its bone* **2.** *vt.* **INTER DEAD BODY** to put a dead body in a grave dug in the ground, or sometimes under water, usually as part of a religious ritual ○ *He asked to be buried at sea.* **3.** *vt.* **LOSE SOMEBODY THROUGH DEATH** to lose somebody, e.g., a spouse or a close relative, through death ○ *She has buried four husbands.* **4.** *vt.* **HIDE SOMETHING BY COVERING** to hide something by covering it with a lot of things so it cannot be seen ○ *He buried the letter under a pile of books.* **5.** *vt.* **COVER SOMETHING UP** to cover something or somebody completely with something ○ *buried alive under the rubble* **6.** *vt.* **OBSCURE SOMETHING** to make something difficult to find or distinguish ○ *The announcement was buried at the end of the program.* **7.** *vt.* **SINK SOMETHING DEEPLY** to sink deep into something so that it is difficult to see or retrieve ○ *The splinter had buried itself under his nail.* **8.** *vt.* **HIDE SOMETHING FROM SIGHT** to put the face or head somewhere, usually on or under a soft and yielding surface ○ *She buried her face in her hands.* **9.** *vt.* **MOVE CARD** to move a playing card from the top to another location in the deck **10.** *vr.* **CONCENTRATE INTENSELY ON SOMETHING** to concentrate exclusively and intensely on something ○ *She tended to bury herself in her work.* **11.** *vt.* **SUPPRESS OR FORGET SOMETHING** to suppress and forget something unpleasant or undesirable ○ *their efforts to bury the past* [Old English *byrgan*, from a prehistoric Germanic base meaning "protection, shelter" (hence "to shelter a corpse"), which is also the ancestor of English *borough* and *burrow*]

Bur·y·at /bŏŏr yaát/, **Bur·i·at** *n.* **1.** **MONGOL FROM BURYATIA** a member of a Mongoloid people living in Buryatia, in Siberia in southeastern Russia **2.** **MONGOLIAN LANGUAGE** a language spoken by the Buryats. It is regarded as a dialect of Mongolian and belongs to the Altaic language family. Buryat is spoken by about 300,000 people. [Mid-19thC. From Mongolian *Buriyad*.] —**Bur·y·at** *adj.*

bus /bus/ *n.* (*plural* **bus·es** *or* **bus·ses**) **1.** **LARGE PASSENGER VEHICLE** a long motor vehicle with many seats, usually divided by a central aisle. Buses transport fare-paying passengers along a specific route. **2.** **OLD CAR OR PLANE** a vehicle, especially a car or plane (*informal*) ○ *I can't get this old bus to start!* **3.** COMPUT **DATA CHANNEL** a channel or path for transferring data electronically in a computer system, particularly the path between the central processing unit and a peripheral device **4.** **HAND TRUCK** a four-wheeled cart or hand truck used for carrying things such as dishes in restaurants **5.** ARMS **ROCKET WARHEAD** the final stage of a multistage rocket, containing the warhead **6.** SPACE TECH **SPACECRAFT COMPONENT** the part of a space exploration vehicle that contains the atmospheric re-entry probes ■ *v.* (**bused** *or* **bussed, bus·ing** *or* **bus·sing, bus·es** *or* **bus·ses**) **1.** *vti.* **TRAVEL OR CARRY PASSENGERS BY BUS** to travel or transport passengers to a particular destination by bus **2.** *vi.* **TRANSPORT SCHOOLCHILDREN** to transport schoolchildren by bus to another school distant from their homes, especially in an effort to achieve racial balance in the school population **3.** *vi.* **WORK AS BUSBOY** to work as a busboy **4.** *vt.* **REMOVE DISHES** to remove dirty dishes and other meal debris from tables in a public restaurant or café ○ *a fast food place where they expect you to bus your own dishes* [Early 19thC. Shortening of OMNIBUS.]

bus. *abbr.* business

bus·boy /búss bòy/ *n.* somebody employed in a restaurant or café to clear away dishes, set tables, and assist the servers

bus·by /búzbee/ (*plural* **-bies**) *n.* a tall fur helmet worn by some soldiers, including some British guards regiments [Mid-18thC. Origin uncertain: perhaps from the surname *Busby*.]

bush[1] /bŏŏsh/ *n.* **1.** **WOODY BRANCHED PLANT** a woody plant that is smaller than a tree and has many branches growing up from the lower part of the main stem **2.** **THICKET** a thick clump of bushes **3.** **UNCULTIVATED AND UNSETTLED LAND** wild, uncultivated, and sparsely populated areas of land covered with natural vegetation, especially in Africa and Australia ○ *living in the bush* **4.** **DENSE MASS** a dense large mass of something, especially hair or beard ○ *a great bush of black hair* **5.** *Can* = **wood lot** **6.** **BUSHY TAIL** a bushy tail, especially of a fox **7.** **VINTNER'S SIGN** a bunch of ivy hung outside a tavern to show that wine is sold inside (*archaic*) **8.** **TAVERN** a tavern (*archaic*) ■ *vi.* (**bushed, bush·ing, bush·es**) **BRANCH OUT** to branch out, spread, or grow thick like a bush ○ *hair bushing out around her head* [From assumed Old English *bysc* and Old Norse *buski*, from a prehistoric Germanic base that is also the ancestor of English *ambush* and *bouquet*] ◇ **beat around** *or* **about the bush** to discuss a subject without coming to the point

bush[2] /bŏŏsh/ *n.* = **bushing** [Mid-16thC. From Middle Dutch *busse* "bush of a wheel," via prehistoric Germanic from Latin *pyxis* "box, cap," from late Greek *puxis* "box."]

Bush /bŏŏsh/, **Barbara** (*b.* 1925) U.S. first lady. She founded the Barbara Bush Foundation for Family Literacy (1989) to promote literacy in the United States.

Library of Congress

George Bush

Bush, George (*b.* 1924) U.S. statesman and 41st President of the United States. A Republican, he was Ronald Reagan's vice president (1981–88) before his own election to the presidency (1989–93). His presidency was notable for the passage of the Americans with Disabillities Act (1990) and, in foreign policy, the end of the Cold War and the fighting of the Gulf War (1990). Full name **George Herbert Walker Bush**

Bush, George, Jr. (*b.* 1946) U.S. politician. The son of President George Bush, he was elected Republican governor of Texas in 1996. Full name **George Herbert Walker Bush**

Bush, Jack (1909–77) Canadian painter. A radical abstract artist, he painted the series *Flags* and *Sashes* (1962–63).

Bush, Vannevar (1890–1974) U.S. inventor and engineer. He invented a differential analyzer (1930), the forerunner of the analog computer.

bush ba·by *n.* a small nocturnal primate that lives in trees in Africa and has big round eyes, large ears, and a long tail. Family: Galagidae.

bush bean *n.* a bean that grows in bush form and does not require support for climbing. Latin name: *Phaseolus vulgaris*.

bush·buck /bŏŏsh bùk/ (*plural* **-bucks** *or* **-buck**) *n.* a small African antelope that has a reddish-brown coat, usually with white stripes, and twisted horns. It lives in the bush in sub-Saharan Africa. Latin name: *Tragelaphus scriptus*. [Mid-19thC. Translation of Afrikaans *bosbok*, from Dutch *bosch* "bush" + *bok* "buck."]

bush clo·ver *n.* a plant with three-leafed compound leaves and small flowers, typically grown for forage, erosion control, or decoration. Genus: *Lespedeza*.

bush dog *n.* a wild dog of South America that lives in dense undergrowth, usually near rivers. It is sometimes kept as a pet. Latin name: *Speothos venaticus*.

bushed /bŏŏsht/ *adj.* exhausted from overwork or lack of sleep (*informal*) [Late 19thC. From the state typical of one who wanders in the bush.]

bush·el[1] /bŏŏsh'l/ *n.* **1.** **U.S. UNIT OF VOLUME** a unit of measure in the U.S. Customary system used for measuring dry goods, equal to 64 U.S. pints (35.24 liters) **2.** **FORMER U.K. UNIT OF VOLUME** a unit of dry or liquid measure in the British Imperial system, equal to 8 imperial gallons (36.37 liters), formerly used for measuring items such as wheat, fruit, and liquids **3.** **CONTAINER** a container that has a capacity of one bushel **4.** **LARGE AMOUNT** a large amount (*dated informal*) [15thC. From Old French *boisell*, of uncertain origin: probably formed from assumed *boisse* "measure of grain," from assumed Gallo-Romance *bostia* "handful," from Gaulish.]

bush·el[2] /bŏŏsh'l/ (**-eled, -el·ing, -els**) *vt.* to mend or alter an article of clothing (*regional regional or archaic*) —**bush·el·er** /bŏŏsh'lər/ *n.* —**bush·el·man** /bŏŏsh'lmən, bŏŏsh'l màn/ *n.*

bush·fire /bŏŏsh fīr/ *n.* a fire in the bush or in a forest area that spreads quickly and easily goes out of control

bush grass *n.* a type of grass with leaves that grow tall like reeds in the damp clay soils of Europe and Asia. Latin name: *Calamagrostis epigejos*.

bush·ham·mer /bŏŏsh hàmmər/ *n.* a powered hammer with small pyramidal points cut into the working surface, used to form a rough surface on stonework [Late 19thC. Origin uncertain: probably a translation of German *Boszhammer*; *Bosz-* from *boszen* "to beat."]

bush hon·ey·suck·le *n.* a shrub of eastern North America with deciduous leaves and small clusters of yellow flowers. Genus: *Diervilla*.

Bu·shi·do /bŏŏshi dō, bŏŏshí dō/ *n.* the code of honor and behavior of the Japanese warrior class (**samurai**), emphasizing self-discipline, courage, and loyalty [Late 19thC. From Japanese, literally "military knight's way, warrior's doctrine."]

bush·ing /bŏŏshing/ *n.* **1.** **METAL SLEEVE** a cylindrical metal sleeve used to prevent abrasion, as a bearing, or as a guide for certain tool parts such as valve rods **2.** **INSULATION** a layer of electrical insulation that allows a live conductor to pass through a grounded wall **3.** **PIPE ADAPTOR** an adaptor or screw-piece for connecting two different sizes of pipe [Mid-19thC. Formed from BUSH[2].]

Bu·shire /boo sheer/ = **Bushehr**

bush jack·et *n.* a lightweight cotton jacket resembling a shirt, with patch pockets and a belt

bush league *n.* **1.** BASEBALL **BASEBALL MINOR LEAGUE** a minor league in baseball **2.** **SECOND-RATE ACTIVITY** a sphere of activity for those who cannot compete with the best ○ *a lawyer in the bush leagues* —**bush-league** *adj.* —**bush-leagu·er** *n.*

bush line *n. Can* a small airline that serves remote setlements, especially in the north of Canada

bush lot *n. Can* = **wood lot**

bush·man /bo͝oshmən/ (*plural* **-men** /-mən/) *n. ANZ* somebody who has long experience of living, working, or traveling in remote country areas

Bush·man /bo͝oshmən/ (*plural* **-men** /-mən/) *n.* an offensive term for a member of the San people [Late 18thC. Modeled on Dutch *boschjesman*.]

bush·mas·ter /bo͝osh màstər/ *n.* a large venomous snake with grayish-brown markings, the longest snake found in Central and South America, growing up to 12 ft./3.6 m in length. Latin name: *Lachesis mutus.*

Bush·nell /bo͝oshnəl/, **David** (1742–1824) U.S. inventor. He is credited with the invention of the *Turtle*, an early submarine (1775).

Bush·nell, Horace (1802–76) U.S. minister. His liberal religious writings included *God in Christ* (1849).

bush pig *n.* a black or brown wild pig of southern Africa that has small tusks and long tufts of hair on the face and ears. Latin name: *Potamochoerus porcus.*

bush pi·lot *n.* a pilot who flies a small plane into and out of areas that are difficult to reach with other means of transportation

bush·rang·er /bo͝osh ràynjər/ *n.* **1. BACKWOODSMAN** somebody who lives an isolated life in the wilderness **2.** *ANZ* **ESCAPED CONVICT** in former times, an escaped convict living on the run in the bush **3.** *ANZ* **RURAL CRIMINAL** in former times, a criminal who lived in the bush and survived by robbing passersby or local people

bush shrike *n.* a bird of the shrike family, typically olive-backed with a bright yellow or red breast. It chases its prey on foot in the forests of Africa. Genus: *Malaconotus.*

bush tel·e·graph *n.* **1. METHOD OF SPREADING GOSSIP SWIFTLY** a method of communicating information or rumors swiftly and unofficially by word of mouth or other means (*informal*) = **grapevine 2. PRIMITIVE METHOD OF COMMUNICATION** a method of communicating over distances, e.g., with drumbeats

bush·tit /bo͝osh tìt/ *n.* a small gray North American bird of the titmouse family, known for building hanging nests. Genus: *Psaltriparus.*

bush·whack /bo͝osh wàk, -hwàk/ (**-whacked, -whack·ing, -whacks**) *v.* **1.** *vt.* **AMBUSH SOMEBODY** to ambush somebody (*informal*) **2.** *vi. U.S., Can, Aus* **CUT THROUGH WOODS** to cut a way through thick woods or forest **3.** *vi. U.S., Can, Aus* **TRAVEL THROUGH WOODS** to travel through woods, forest, or the bush **4.** *vi.* **FIGHT AS GUERRILLA** to fight as a guerrilla [Mid-19thC. Back-formation from BUSHWHACKER.]

bush·whack·er /bo͝osh hwàkər/ *n.* **1.** *U.S., Can, Aus* **SOMEBODY WHO LIVES IN THE BUSH** somebody who travels around or lives in the bush or in wooded, isolated regions **2. CLEARER OF BUSH** somebody who clears away bush or undergrowth **3.** HIST **CONFEDERATE GUERRILLA IN CIVIL WAR** a confederate guerrilla in the Civil War **4. RURAL GUERRILLA** a guerrilla who fights in remote or rural areas **5. CLEARING TOOL** a tool for clearing or cutting a way through bush, trees, or undergrowth [Early 19thC. From BUSH + WHACKER; possibly modeled on Dutch *boschwachter* "forest keeper."]

bush·y /bo͝oshee/ (**-i·er, -i·est**) *adj.* **1. THICK AND FULL** very thick and full **2. DENSE AND WOODY** with many branches growing up together, producing a rounded shape like a bush **3. COVERED WITH BUSHES** covered or overgrown with bushes —**bush·i·ly** *adv.* —**bush·i·ness** *n.*

bus·i·ly /bízzilee/ *adv.* in an active, energetic, and concentrated way ○ *busily cleaning the house*

busi·ness /bíznəss/ *n.* **1. LINE OF WORK** a particular trade or profession ○ *the retail business* **2. COMMERCIAL ORGANIZATION** a company or other organization that buys and sells goods, makes products, or provides services ○ *take over an ailing business* **3. COMMERCIAL ACTIVITY** commercial activity involving the exchange of money for goods or services ○ *a good person to do business with* **4. LEVEL OF COMMERCE** the amount of commercial activity or patronage that exists at a particular time ○ *Business is poor right now.* **5. COMMERCIAL PRACTICE** commercial practice or procedure ○ *It's bad business to neglect smaller clients.* **6. PATRONAGE** the commercial dealings that a person or organization has with another company or individual ○ *If this goes on, I shall take my business elsewhere!* **7. IMPORTANT MATTERS** tasks or important things that a person has to do or deal with ○ *We have important business to discuss.* **8. PRIVATE MATTERS** personal responsibilities and concerns ○ *What business is it of yours?* **9. AFFAIR** a situation or event that is characterized by difficulty, fuss, or unpleasantness ○ *that business about the tickets* **10. UNSPECIFIED ACTIVITIES** activities or things that are not clearly described or defined ○ *designing, measuring, and all that kind of business* **11.** THEATER **ACTOR'S SMALL ACTIONS** an action or series of actions performed by an actor for dramatic or comic effect, or to fill in a pause when little is happening on stage **12. SOMETHING EXCELLENT** something very impressive or excellent (*informal*) ○ *He thinks his new car is really the business.* ■ *adj.* **OF COMMERCE** relating to, belonging to, or involving commerce and the world of professional workers ○ *good business practice* [Old English *bisignis* "anxiety, distress," from *bisig* "anxious, busy"] ◇ **do your business** to defecate (*informal*) (*used euphemistically*) ◇ **get down to business** to deal with important matters, leaving extraneous ones behind ◇ **have no business doing something** to have no right to do something ◇ **like nobody's business** very hard or strongly ◇ **mean business** to have sincere and forthright intentions ◇ **not be in the business of doing something** to consider something inappropriate or outside the usual area of responsibility

busi·ness ad·min·is·tra·tion *n.* a course of study at a university, college, or other institute of higher education that teaches the basic principles of business and business practices

busi·ness card *n.* a small card printed with a person's name, job title, business address, and contact numbers

busi·ness class *n.* **AIR-TRAVEL CATEGORY** a superior level of service in air travel that is less expensive than first class and caters for business travelers (*hyphenated when used before a noun*) ■ *adv.* **IN BUSINESS-CLASS SECTION** in the business-class section of an airplane

busi·ness cy·cle *n.* a recurrent cycle of growth, decline, recession, and recovery in the economic activity of a capitalist country

busi·ness dis·trict *n.* an area reserved for, or composed mainly of, retail businesses or offices

busi·ness end *n.* the part of a tool or device that does the work, as opposed to the body or handle (*informal*) ○ *the business end of a gun*

busi·ness en·ve·lope *n.* a standard envelope used for business mail that holds letter-size paper folded in thirds

busi·ness hours *npl.* **1. HOURS OF OPERATION** the hours during which business is conducted **2. NORMAL OFFICE HOURS** the normal hours that most offices are open, usually between about 9 AM and 5:30 PM

busi·ness·like /bíznəss lìk/ *adj.* **1. EFFICIENT AND PRACTICAL** showing qualities or attributes that are useful and desirable in a business context, e.g., efficiency, practicality, and methodicalness ○ *a very businesslike operation* **2. UNEMOTIONAL** practical and unemotional

busi·ness·man /bíznəss màn/ (*plural* **-men** /-mèn/) *n.* a man who works in business, especially at a senior level

busi·ness·per·son /bíznəss pùrs'n/ (*plural* **-peo·ple** /-peèp'l/) *n.* a person who works in business, especially at a senior level

busi·ness plan *n.* a plan that sets out the future strategy and financial development of a business, usually covering a period of several years

busi·ness school *n.* a graduate school that offers MBAs and related courses of study

busi·ness suit *n.* a suit consisting of a coat and pants, or a coat and skirt, made from the same cloth

busi·ness·wom·an /bíznəss wo͝omən/ (*plural* **-en** /-wìmmin/) *n.* a woman who works in business, especially at a senior level

bus·ing /bússing/, **bus·sing** *n.* the transportation of children by bus to another school distant from their homes in an effort to achieve racial balance in school populations

busk /busk/ *n.* a strip of wood, steel, or whalebone used to stiffen the front of a corset [Late 16thC. Via French *busc* from Italian *busco* "splinter," from Germanic.]

busk·er /búskər/ *n. U.K.* somebody who entertains in the street or a public place in the hope of receiving money from passers-by

bus·kin /búskin/ *n.* **1. ATHENIAN ACTOR'S BOOT** a thick-soled laced boot worn by tragic actors in ancient Greece to give them extra height **2. GREEK DRAMA** tragic drama, particularly in the ancient Greek style (*archaic*) **3. MEDIEVAL SANDAL** a calf-length laced boot worn in the Middle Ages [Early 16thC. Origin uncertain: probably via Old French *bousequin* (a variant of *brousequin*) from Middle Dutch *broseken*, of unknown origin.]

bus lane *n.* a lane on a road in some cities or towns that during certain hours of the day can only be used by buses

bus·load /bús lòd/ *n.* the number of passengers that a bus carries or can carry ○ *demonstrators arriving in busloads*

bus·man /búsmən/ (*plural* **-men** /-mən/) *n.* somebody who drives a bus (*archaic*)

bus·man's hol·i·day *n.* a vacation or leisure activity that is similar to the work somebody normally engages in (*informal*) [Origin uncertain: probably from drivers of horse-drawn buses taking a vacation being driven around on their own bus, perhaps so as to check on the treatment of their horses]

Bu·son /bo͞o sàwn/ (1716–84) Japanese poet and artist. He is noted for his haiku and was regarded as one of the finest painters of his time.

buss /bus/ *n.* **KISS** a kiss (*regional dated*) ■ *vti.* (**bussed, bus·sing, buss·es**) **KISS SOMEBODY** to kiss somebody or something (*regional dated*) [Late 16thC. Origin uncertain: probably an alteration of obsolete *bass* "to kiss," via French *baiser* from Latin *basiare*.]

bus·sing /bússing/ *n.* = **busing**

bus stop *n.* a designated place along a specific route where a bus stops to pick up or let off passengers

bust[1] /bust/ *n.* **1. WOMAN'S BREASTS** a woman's breasts, or the measurement around this part of her upper body **2.** SCULPTURE **SCULPTURE OF HEAD AND SHOULDERS** a sculpture of the head and shoulders of a person [Mid-17thC. Via French from Italian *busto*, of uncertain origin: probably from Latin *bustum* "tomb," from, ultimately, *ambuere*, literally "to burn around," from *urere* "to burn."]

bust[2] /bust/ *v.* (**bust·ed** *or* **bust, bust·ing, busts**) **1.** *vti.* **MAKE OR BECOME USELESS** to break something mechanical or electrical, or to cease operating properly (*informal*) ○ *Your brother just busted our TV!* **2.** *vti.* **BREAK OR GET BROKEN** to break or damage something by hitting it or by subjecting it to a powerful impact, or to break in this way (*informal*) ○ *I busted my leg skiing.* **3.** *vti.* **BURST** to burst something or to undergo bursting **4.** *vt.* **RAID PLACE OR ARREST PERSON** to mount a police raid, especially in connection with illegal drugs (*slang*) **5.** *vti.* FIN **MAKE OR BECOME BANKRUPT** to make somebody bankrupt or to become bankrupt (*informal*) **6.** *vt.* MIL **DEMOTE SOMEBODY** to demote a member of the armed forces (*informal*) **7.** *vt.* RIDING **BREAK IN HORSE** to break in a horse (*informal*) **8.** *vt.* **BREAK UP ORGANIZATION** to break up an organization when it has become too powerful (*informal*) **9.** *vt.* **HIT SOMEBODY** to hit or punch somebody (*informal*) ○ *I busted him over the head.* **10.** *vi.* CARDS **GO OVER LIMIT** in blackjack, to have cards totaling more than 21 points **11.** *vi.* CARDS **FAIL TO COMPLETE HAND** in poker, to fail to complete a flush or straight ■ *n.* **1. POLICE RAID** a police raid or arrest, especially in connection with illegal drugs (*slang*) **2. FAILURE** somebody or something that fails completely (*informal*) ○ *The plan seemed perfect in theory, but it was a bust in reality.* **3.** FIN **BANKRUPTCY** bankruptcy or financial failure (*informal*) ○ *periods of boom and bust* **4. PUNCH** a punch or blow (*informal*) **5. PARTY** a disorganized party or celebration (*informal*) [Mid-18thC. Alteration of BURST.]

Bus·ta·man·te /bo͝ostə maán tày/, **Sir Alexander** (1884–1977) Jamaican statesman. He served as independent Jamaica's first prime minister (1962–67). Born **Sir William Alexander Clarke**

bus·tard /bústərd/ (*plural* **-tards** *or* **-tard**) *n.* a bird with long legs, a rotund body, and a long neck that lives on open grassy land in southern Eurasia, Africa, and Australia. Family: Otididae. [15thC. Origin uncertain: probably from assumed Anglo-Norman *bustarde*, blend of *bistarde* and *oustarde*, both from Latin *avis tarda* "slow bird"; from its slow walk.]

bust·er /bústər/ *n.* **1. FORM OF ADDRESS** used as a jocular or mildly threatening term of address, usually for a man or boy (*informal*) **2.** = **broncobuster 3. BREAKER**

somebody or something that breaks up or destroys something (*informal*) (*usually in combination*) [Mid-19thC. Either formed from BUST[1], or an alteration of *burster*, in which sense ("person or thing that bursts") the word is first attested.]

bus·tier /boos tyáy/ *n.* a close-fitting sleeveless and usually strapless bodice worn by women as lingerie or evening wear [Late 20thC. From French, where it was formed from *buste* (see BUST[1]).]

bus·tle[1] /búss'l/ *vi.* (**-tled, -tling, -tles**) **GO HURRIEDLY AND SHOWILY** to work or do something in an ostentatiously hurried and energetic way ○ *He bustled around in preparation for their arrival.* ■ *n.* **ENERGETIC ACTIVITY** energetic, busy, and noisy activity ○ *a great bustle surrounding the arriving guests* [14thC. Origin uncertain: perhaps an alteration of obsolete *buskle*, from dialect *busk*, from Old Norse *búask* "to prepare yourself."] —**bus·tler** *n.*

bus·tle[2] /búss'l/ *n.* a pad or frame worn in the 19th century under the top of a woman's long skirt to fill it out at the back [Late 18thC. Origin uncertain; perhaps a use of the noun BUSTLE in the sense "something that makes a stir."]

bus·tling /búss'ling, bússling/ *adj.* full of or characterized by energetic and noisy activity —**bus·tling·ly** *adv.*

bust·y /bústee/ (**-i·er, -i·est**) *adj.* used to describe a woman with conspicuously large breasts (*informal*) [Mid-20thC. Formed from BUST[1].]

bu·sul·fan /byoo súlfən/ *n.* a drug used to treat certain kinds of chronic leukemia. Formula: $C_6H_{14}O_6S_2$. = **busulphan** [Mid-20thC. Blend of BUTANE and SULFONYL.]

bu·sul·phan *n.* = **busulfan**

bus·y /bízzee/ *adj.* (**-i·er, -i·est**) **1. OCCUPIED** fully occupied in a particular activity, especially work ○ *She seemed too busy even to talk to me.* ○ *He was busy writing letters all morning.* **2. FULL OF BUSTLE** full of activity, with a large number of people moving around ○ *the busy city streets* **3. NOT FREE** committed to something that has previously been planned or arranged and so unable to undertake another activity ○ *I'm sorry but I'm busy tomorrow night.* **4.** UTIL **UNAVAILABLE TO USE** used to describe a telephone line that is in use and so unavailable ○ *The line's busy, will you hold?* **5. ACTIVE** engaged in or characterized by constant, and usually purposeful, activity ○ *busy people who lead busy lives* **6. ELABORATE** characterized by overcomplex detail, colors, or patterns ○ *a very busy painting* ■ *v.* (**-ied, -y·ing, -ies**) **1.** *vr.* **OCCUPY YOURSELF** to start doing something that will keep you occupied and working for a period of time **2.** *vt.* **OCCUPY SOMEBODY** to occupy somebody ○ *The work busied him all afternoon.* [Old English *bisig* "busy, anxious"] —**bus·y·ness** *n.*

bus·y·bod·y /bízzi bòddee/ (*plural* **-ies**) *n.* somebody who tends to meddle with other people's business (*informal*)

Bus·y Liz·zie /bìzzi lízzee/ (*plural* **Bus·y Liz·zie** *or* **Bus·y Liz·zies**) *n. U.K.* = **impatiens** [Origin uncertain: probably a rhyming phrase modeled on the plant's Latin name *impatiens* "impatient"]

bus·y sig·nal *n.* a repeating burst of sound on a telephone line that indicates the line is in use

bus·y·work /bízzi wurk/ *n.* activities assigned or undertaken that take up time but do not necessarily yield productive results

but /but/ CORE MEANING: a grammatical word used in the middle of or at the beginning of a sentence to introduce something that is true in spite of either being or seeming contrary to what has just been said ○ *I thought it was late, but it was only 9 o'clock.* ○ *Not one, but two offers were received.* ○ *Yes, but not now.* ○ *It's true her name is Spanish, but she's actually Greek.* ○ *I'm a blonde, but both my mother and father have dark hair.*

1. *conj.* **INTRODUCING AN OPPOSING PROPOSITION** used to introduce a statement that disagrees with something just said, or that expresses an emotion such as surprise or disbelief at what was just said ○ *"I don't think you're suitable for the job." "But I have all the right qualifications!"* **2.** *conj.* **INTRODUCING FURTHER INFORMATION** used to introduce a clause or a new sentence that adds information such as background or reasoning ○ *Jeff isn't coming with us. But he doesn't like horror movies anyway.* **3.** *conj.* **EXCEPT THAT** used to introduce a dependent clause, e.g., a reason for doing or not doing something ○ *I would have called, but I couldn't find a phone.* **4.** *conj.* **WITHOUT SOMETHING HAPPENING** used to indicate that something does not happen without something else happening or being the case (*formal*) (*usually used after a negative*) ○ *She never leaves home but she forgets her keys.* **5.** *conj.* **THAT** used to introduce a subordinate clause (*regional*) ○ *It's not so difficult, but I can't understand it.* **6.** *conj.* **WHEN** than or when (*informal*) **7.** *conj., prep.* **EXCEPT** used to indicate the exception to a statement just made ○ *He could do nothing but stand and watch her leave.* ○ *There was nothing but a lump of moldy bread in the cupboard.* **8.** *adv.* **ONLY, JUST, OR MERELY** used to indicate that something happens or is true just to the extent mentioned and not more ○ *This is but one of the breadmaking techniques used.* ○ *He arrived but a minute ago.* ○ *We can but try.* **9.** *adv.* **FOR EMPHASIS** used to emphasize a statement (*slang*) ○ *Man, but he's fast!* **10.** *n.* **OBJECTIONS** objections to something (*informal*) ○ *Allow time to consider all the if's and but's from the children.* [Old English *būtan* "outside, without, except, but," from a prehistoric Germanic word that is also the ancestor of English *by* and *without*] ◇ **all but** almost ○ *I was all but asleep when the phone rang.* ◇ **but for** if not for, or if it had not been for ◇ **but that 1.** except that ○ *Nothing is important but that I see you again.* **2.** used as a subordinating conjunction equivalent to "that" following negative words such as "doubt" and "deny" (*archaic*) (*follows a negative*)

WORD KEY: USAGE

Can **but** begin a sentence? Some people object to the use of ***but***, like ***and***, at the beginning of a sentence, regarding it as a joining word that has to have words on either side of it. However, this is a mistaken notion that has no foundation in English structure and usage. It is, however, advisable to reserve this use for occasions when the special effect that initial position affords is needed, otherwise it can become an awkward affectation.

But is usually not followed by a comma; a comma may or may not precede ***but***, depending on the individual sentence structure and context; thus, *I wanted to leave early*[,] *but the rest of the group did not*, not *I wanted to leave early, but, the rest of the group did not.*

Avoid unnecessary redundancy in using ***but*** and other terms such as *however* together. Write *However,* [or *but*] *the State Department has lodged a formal protest* not *But the State Department has, however, lodged a formal protest.*

When ***but*** is used to indicate an exception, as in *No one but me* (or *I*) *has* (or *have*) *seen the document*, either wording can be used, based on your interpretation of the function of ***but***: is it a preposition, as in the first variation, or is it a conjunction, as in the second, parenthetic, variation? Though strong cases have been made for both wordings, the prepositional wording does carry slightly more weight, as you can recast the sentence to *No one has seen the document but me*, placing the ***but*** phrase at the end, where its prepositional function is quite clear.

WORD KEY: USAGE

See Usage note at ***help***.

but- *prefix.* Containing a group of four carbon atoms ○ *butene* [From BUTYRIC]

bu·ta·di·ene /byoōtə dí een/ *n.* a colorless flammable gas that is important in the manufacture of polymers. It is used in the production of synthetic rubber, nylon, and latex paints. Formula: $CH_2{=}CHCH{=}CH_2$. [Early 20thC. Coined from BUTANE + DI-.]

bu·ta·nal /byoōt'nəl/ *n.* CHEM a colorless, flammable liquid that has two different molecular structures (**isomers**). It is used in the manufacture of solvents, resins, and plasticizers. Formula: C_4H_8O. [Late 20thC. Coined from BUTANOL.]

bu·tane /byoō tàyn/ *n.* a colorless, highly flammable gas that is compressed for use in lighter fluids and for household and industrial purposes. It is found in natural gas and has two different molecular structures (**isomers**). Formula: C_4H_{10}. [Late 19thC. Coined from BUTYL + -ANE.]

bu·ta·no·ic ac·id /byoōtənō ik-/ *n.* a thick colorless liquid that is the cause of the smell in rancid butter. The ester produced from it is used in flavorings and scents. Formula: C_3H_7COOH. [*Butanoic* formed from BUTANE]

bu·ta·nol /byoōtə nòl, byoōt'n òl/ *n.* a colorless toxic liquid with four different molecular structures (**isomers**). It is used as a solvent in such items as paint remover, and also in the manufacture of other organic substances. Formula: C_4H_9OH.

butch /bŏŏch/ *adj.* **1. MASCULINE AND STRONG** used to describe a man who is extremely masculine and strong **2. OFFENSIVE TERM** an offensive term insulting a woman's appearance and sexuality (*slang offensive*) ■ *n.* **1. OFFENSIVE TERM** an offensive term that insults a woman's appearance and sexuality (*slang offensive*) **2.** HAIR = **crew cut** [Mid-20thC. Origin uncertain; probably from the male nickname *Butch*.]

butch·er /bŏŏchər/ *n.* **1. MEAT SELLER** somebody who cuts up, prepares, and sells meat at retail **2. SLAUGHTERER** somebody who slaughters animals in preparation for selling their meat as food **3. BRUTAL KILLER** somebody who kills, or is responsible for the killing of, large numbers of people in a brutal manner **4. BOTCHER** somebody who does something badly and produces unattractive results ○ *a butcher of the sonnet form* ■ *vt.* (**-ered, -er·ing, -ers**) **1. KILL ANIMAL FOR FOOD** to slaughter and prepare the meat of an animal for food **2. KILL PEOPLE BRUTALLY** to kill people in a brutal way **3. BOTCH SOMETHING** to do, perform, or make something very incompetently (*informal*) ○ *The original script had been butchered.* [13thC. Via Anglo-Norman from Old French *bo(u)chier* "slaughterer of he-goats," from *boc* "he-goat," of uncertain origin: probably from Celtic.] —**butch·er·er** *n.*

butch·er·bird /bŏŏchər bùrd/ *n.* **1. AUSTRALASIAN SONGBIRD** an Australasian songbird of the magpie family, usually with black or black-and-white plumage. It impales insects and other prey on thorns. Genus: *Cracticus.* **2. BIRD OF SHRIKE FAMILY** a bird of the shrike family that impales its prey on thorns and barbed wire. Genus: *Lanius.*

butch·er-block *adj.* made from or resembling blocks or strips of wood glued together and planed, similar to a block that a butcher chops meat on ○ *butcher-block countertops*

butch·er knife *n.* a large heavy-duty knife for use in the kitchen or for butchering

butch·er's broom *n.* an evergreen Mediterranean shrub with stiff stems that were formerly used for making brooms. Latin name: *Ruscus aculeatus.*

butch·er's knife *n.* U.K. = **butcher knife**

butch·er·y /bŏŏcharee/ (*plural* **-ies**) *n.* **1. MASS KILLING** brutal, senseless, and cruel slaughter of people, usually in large numbers ○ *an act of appalling butchery* **2. USE OF KNIVES ON CARCASS** the use of knives or other tools to remove meat from an animal's carcass ○ *"The tools are often found in association with broken animal bones, which sometimes show signs of butchery." ("Ape at the Brink," Discover Magazine*; 1994) **3. BUTCHER'S WORK OR TRADE** the work or trade of a butcher **4. INCOMPETENCE** an incompetent attempt at a job, performance, or activity (*informal*) ○ *the singer's butchery of the melody* [14thC. From French *boucherie*, ultimately from Old French *bo(u)chier* (see BUTCHER).]

butch hair·cut *n.* = **crew cut**

bu·tene /byoō teen/ *n.* a colorless, flammable, and easily liquefiable gas with three different molecular structures (**isomers**). The butenes provide the basic molecule for manufacturing a variety of polymers. Formula: C_4H_8. [Late 19thC. Coined from BUTYL + -ENE.]

bu·te·o /byoōtee ō/ (*plural* **-os**) *n.* a large, broad-winged, soaring hawk or buzzard from North America and Eurasia. Genus: *Buteo.* [Mid-20thC. Via modern Latin (genus name) from Latin "(kind of) hawk or falcon."]

Bu·the·le·zi /bootə láyzee/, **Mangosuthu Gatsha** (*b.* 1928) South African political leader. He was chief minister of KwaZulu, a black South African homeland (1976–94), and founded Inkatha, a Zulu nationalist organization. Known as **Chief Buthelezi**

but·ler /búttlər/ *n.* the male head servant in a large or important household, with responsibilities that include overseeing the other staff, taking care of the wine and silverware, and sometimes receiving guests [13thC. From Anglo-Norman *buteler* and French *bouteillier* "cup-bearer," formed from *bouteille* "wine vessel, bottle" (see BOTTLE.)]

But·ler /búttlər/ city and manufacturing center in western Pennsylvania, north of Pittsburgh. Population: 17,026 (1991).

But·ler, Nicholas Murray (1862–1947) U.S. educator. President of Columbia College (1902–12) and the newly formed Columbia University (1912–45), he shared the Nobel Peace Prize in 1931 for his role as president of the Carnegie Endowment for International Peace (1925–45).

But·ler, Samuel (1612–80) English satirist. He wrote "Hudibras," a poetic satire on the Puritans (1663–78).

but·ler's pan·try /bútləree/, **but·ler·y** *n.* a room situated between a kitchen and dining room, used for serving food and for storage

butt[1] /but/ *v.* **(butt·ed, butt·ing, butts) 1.** *vt.* **RAM SOMEBODY OR SOMETHING** to hit or push against somebody or something with the head or horns **2.** *vi.* **STICK OUT** to project or jut out ■ *n.* **A PUSH** a push with the head or horns [15thC. Via Anglo-Norman *buter* and Old French *bo(u)ter* from, ultimately, a prehistoric Germanic base that is also the ancestor of English *button*.] —**but·ter** *n.*

butt in *vi.* to interrupt and attempt to join in a conversation or activity without being invited

butt out *vi. U.S., ANZ* to keep out of other people's business or conversation (*slang*)

butt[2] /but/ *n.* **1. OBJECT OF RIDICULE OR CONTEMPT** somebody or something that is an object of ridicule or contempt for other people ○ *He became the butt of their satire.* **2. GOAL** a goal or aim (*archaic*) **3. HINGE** a butt hinge, or either of its two parts **4.** = **butt joint** ■ **butts** *npl.* **1.** ARCHERY, RIFLE SHOOTING **MOUND BEHIND TARGET** in archery and rifle shooting, a mound of earth behind the target, designed to stop any stray bullets or arrows **2.** ARCHERY **TARGET RANGE** a target range **3.** ARCHERY, RIFLE SHOOTING **TARGET** a target at a shooting or archery range ■ *vti.* **(butt·ed, butt·ing, butts) ABUT** to lie with one flat end against the flat end of something else, or to place something in such a position ○ *The beam butts against the wall.* [14thC. From French *but* "goal," of uncertain origin: probably from prehistoric Germanic; perhaps influenced by French *butte* "rising ground, target."]

butt[3] /but/ *n.* **1. BUTTOCKS** a person's or animal's buttocks (*informal*) (*considered offensive by some people*) **2. THICK END** the thicker or larger end of something, such as the part of a rifle held against the shoulder **3. CIGARETTE END** the part of a cigarette that remains after the rest has been smoked [15thC. Origin uncertain.]

butt[4] /but/ *n.* **1. CASK** a large cask for holding wine or ale **2. UNIT FOR MEASURING LIQUID VOLUME** a unit for measuring liquid volume equal to 126 U.S. gallons (approximately 477 liters) [15thC. Via Anglo-Norman *but* and Old French *bot* from late Latin *buttis* (source of English *butler*).]

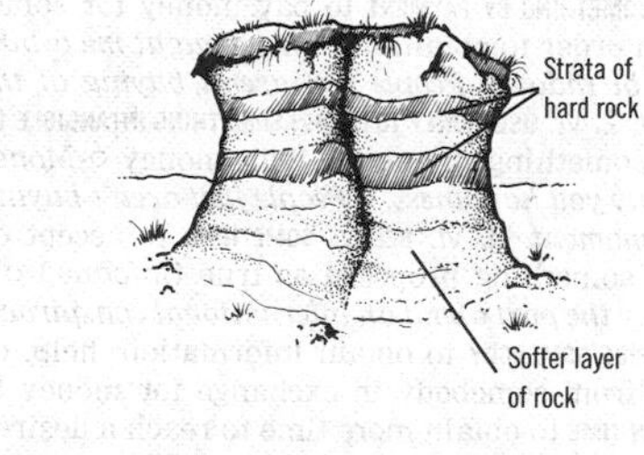

Butte

butte /byoot/ *n.* in the western United States and Canada, a hill that rises abruptly from a flat area of land, with steep sides and a flat top. ◊ **mesa** [Mid-19thC. From French, "mound, hillock" (possible source of English *butt*[2]).]

Butte /byoot/ city in southwestern Montana, situated more than 1 mi./1.7 km above sea level in the Rocky Mountains. It was settled by gold prospectors in the 1860s and is still a mining center. Population: 34,051 (1996). Full name **Butte-Silver Bow**

but·ter /búttər/ *n.* **1. SOFT CREAMY SPREAD** a soft, pale yellow, fatty food made by churning cream and used for cooking or spreading on food ○ *butter sauce* **2. SUBSTANCE RESEMBLING BUTTER** any substance that is similar to butter in consistency or appearance ○ *apple butter* ■ *vt.* **(-tered, -ter·ing, -ters) PUT BUTTER ON SOMETHING** to spread butter on something or add butter to something [Old English *butere*, via prehistoric Germanic from Latin *butyrum*, from Greek *bouturon*, of uncertain origin: perhaps originally "cow's milk curds," formed from *bous* "ox"] ◇ **look as if butter wouldn't melt in your mouth** to look more innocent than you really are

butter up *vt.* to flatter somebody in the hope of winning favor or cooperation (*informal*)

but·ter-and-eggs *n.* = **toadflax** (*used with a singular or plural verb*)

but·ter·ball /búttər bàwl/ *n.* **1. CHUBBY PERSON** somebody who is chubby (*informal insult*) **2.** BIRDS = **bufflehead**

but·ter bean *n.* (*regional*) **1. DRIED LIMA BEAN** a lima bean that is cream-colored because it is cooked from the dried form **2.** = **wax bean**

but·ter·bur /búttər bùr/ (*plural* **-burs** *or* **-bur**) *n.* a waterside plant that has purple flowers and large soft leaves in which butter was formerly wrapped. Genus: *Petasites.*

but·ter clam *n.* a large clam found off the Pacific coast of North America with a delicate flavor and a shell that was formerly used for barter by Native Americans. Genus: *Saxidomus.*

but·ter·cup /búttər kùp/ *n.* a plant with yellow cup-shaped flowers that grows in grassland in cold or temperate regions. Genus: *Ranunculus.* [Early 16thC. From the color and shape of its flowers.]

but·ter·cup squash *n.* a small winter squash with a flattish top, dark green skin, and yellow-orange flesh. Latin name: *Cucurbita maxima.*

but·ter·fat /búttər fàt/ *n.* the natural fats found in dairy products

but·ter·fin·gers /búttər fìngərz/ (*plural* **-gers**) *n.* somebody who has a tendency to drop things accidentally out of clumsiness or poor coordination (*informal*) (*takes a singular verb*) [Early 17thC. From butter's slippery smoothness, as if the person's hands were greased with butter.] —**but·ter·fin·gered** *adj.*

but·ter·fish /búttər fìsh/ (*plural* **-fish** *or* **-fish·es**) *n.* a small inshore fish, found worldwide, that is a popular food because of its high lipid content and fine flavor. Family: Stromateidae. [Late 17thC. From the slipperiness of its mucous coating, likened to butter.]

but·ter·flies /búttər flìz/ *npl.* a fluttering feeling in the stomach caused by nervousness (*informal*)

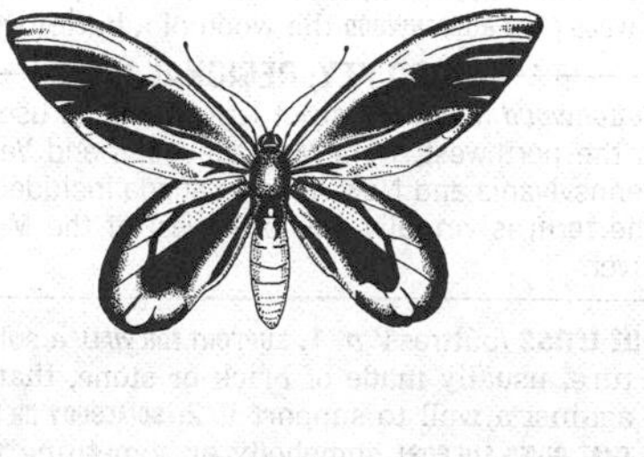

Butterfly

but·ter·fly /búttər flì/ *n.* (*plural* **-flies**) **1. INSECT WITH BIG COLORFUL WINGS** an insect with two pairs of often brightly colored wings and knobbed antennae. It develops from a caterpillar and lives for only a short time. Order: Lepidoptera. **2. butterfly, butterfly stroke SWIMMING STROKE** a swimming stroke in which both arms are lifted simultaneously above and over the head while both the feet are kicked up and down **3. SWIMMING COMPETITION** a race in which swimmers do the butterfly stroke **4. PERSON LACKING CONCENTRATION** somebody who is unable to concentrate on any one activity or occupation for very long **5.** STOCK EXCH **TYPE OF DEAL ON STOCK MARKET** the buying and selling of options on the stock market on the same day but at different prices or with different expiry dates ■ *vt.* **(-flied, -fly·ing, -flies)** COOK **SPLIT FOOD** to split a piece of food, such as meat or fish, along its length, separating it into halves [Old English *buttorflēoge*: *buttor-* "butter" perhaps from the color of some butterflies' wings or excrement, or from the belief that butterflies consume butter]

WORD KEY: CULTURAL NOTE

Madame Butterfly, an opera by Italian composer Giacomo Puccini (1904). Set in Nagasaki, Japan, it tells of the love of a young Japanese woman, Cio-Cio San, for a U.S. naval officer, Pinkerton, who half-heartedly agrees to an arranged marriage with her. When Pinkerton later returns from a three-year sojourn in the United States with another wife, a heartbroken San commits suicide.

but·ter·fly bush *n.* = **buddleia** [From the butterflies attracted to its flowers]

but·ter·fly chair *n.* a chair made from a continuous folded metal rod with four upward-pointing corners on which a fitted canvas seat rests

but·ter·fly di·a·gram *n.* a graphical representation of the appearance of sunspots over an 11-year cycle [From its butterfly shape]

but·ter·fly ef·fect *n.* the supposed influence exerted on a dynamic system by a small change in initial conditions. ◊ **chaos theory** [Named for a 1979 paper by the U.S. meterologist Edward N. Lorenz, (b. 1917), entitled "Does the flap of a butterfly's wings in Brazil set off a tornado in Texas?".]

but·ter·fly fish *n.* a small boldly patterned tropical fish with a flattish body and a tapered snout. Family: Chaetodontidae. [From its shape or color, likened to a butterfly]

but·ter·fly nut *n.* = **wing nut** [From its winglike projections, likened to a butterfly's wings]

but·ter·fly stroke *n.* = **butterfly** *n.* **2**

but·ter·fly valve *n.* **1. VALVE IN PIPE** a valve consisting of a disk that turns inside a pipe, especially one used as a throttle valve in a carburetor **2. ONE-WAY VALVE** a valve consisting of two semicircular plates that are hinged around a central spindle, used to allow flow in one direction only [From its shape, likened to a butterfly's wings]

but·ter·fly weed *n.* a North American plant that has clusters of bright orange flowers and a root that was once used in the treatment of pleurisy. Latin name: *Asclepias tuberosa.* [From the fact that it is attractive to butterflies]

but·ter knife *n.* a small knife with a broad blunt blade used for spreading butter

but·ter·milk /búttər mìlk/ *n.* **1. CULTURED MILK** a sour-tasting drink made by adding certain microorganisms to milk **2. BY-PRODUCT OF CHURNING** the sour-tasting liquid that is left over after milk or cream has been churned to make butter. It is used in baking.

but·ter·milk sky *n.* = **mackerel sky** (*regional*) [From its appearance, likened to the texture of cultured buttermilk]

but·ter·nut /búttər nùt/ *n.* **1. N AMERICAN WALNUT TREE** a North American walnut tree that has hard light-brown wood and edible nuts enclosed in a sticky husk. Latin name: *Juglans cinerea.* **2. NUT OF BUTTERNUT TREE** the oily edible nut of the butternut tree, similar in appearance to a walnut and with a sweetish taste **3. WOOD OF BUTTERNUT TREE** the hard light-brown wood of the butternut tree, used for making furniture **4. BUTTERNUT BARK** the bark of the butternut tree, formerly used as a laxative **5. BROWN DYE** a brown dye obtained from the husks of the nuts of the butternut tree **6. CONFEDERATE SOLDIER** a Confederate soldier in the Civil War (*informal*) ■ **but·ter·nuts** *npl.* **CONFEDERATE SOLDIERS' UNIFORMS** clothes that have been dyed with butternut dye, especially the clothes of Confederate soldiers in the Civil War

but·ter·nut squash *n.* a beige-colored winter squash shaped like a club with a bulbous end and with firm yellow-orange flesh

but·ter·scotch /búttər skòch/ *n.* **1. BRITTLE SUGAR CANDY** a brittle brown-colored candy made from butter, brown sugar, corn syrup, water, and flavorings, with a taste similar to that of toffee **2. BUTTERSCOTCH FLAVORING** a kind of flavoring made from the ingredients used in butterscotch **3.** COLORS **LIGHT BROWN** a light brown color ■ *adj.* **1. FLAVORED WITH BUTTERSCOTCH** flavored with butterscotch ○ *butterscotch ice cream* **2.** COLORS **LIGHT-BROWN** light-brown in color [Mid-19thC. Origin uncertain: probably formed from BUTTER + SCOTCH "having been first made in Scotland"; or perhaps an alteration of dialect *butterscot.*]

but·ter tart *n. Can* a tart filled with butter, sugar or syrup, and usually raisins

but·ter·weed /búttər wèed/ *n.* a wild plant with yellow flowers. Family: Compositae. [Mid-19thC. *Butter* from its yellow flowers or smooth foliage, likened to butter.]

but·ter·wort /búttər wùrt, búttər wàwrt/ (*plural* **-worts** *or* **-wort**) *n.* a carnivorous bog plant with violet flowers and a rosette of sticky fleshy leaves that trap and digest insects. Genus: *Pinguicula.*

but·ter·y[1] /búttəree/ **(-i·er, -i·est)** *adj.* **1. LIKE OR OF BUTTER** resembling, tasting like, or containing butter ○ *a* *smooth, buttery taste* 2. ADULATORY tending or serving to flatter and praise —**but·ter·i·ness** *n.*

but·ter·y[2] /búttəree/ (*plural* **-ies**) *n.* a room in which food or drinks are stored [14thC. From Anglo-Norman *boterie*, of uncertain origin: perhaps formed from *but* "cask" (see BUTT[4]), or ultimately from Old French *botele* "bottle" (see BOTTLE).]

butt hinge *n.* a hinge consisting of two parts, one of which is attached to a door jamb, the other to the door itself, allowing the door to swing open and shut [From BUTT[2]]

butt·in·sky /but ínskee/ (*plural* **-skies**) *n.* somebody who has a tendency to intrude on other people's affairs or conversations or to meddle and pry (*informal*) [Early 20thC. Formed from BUTT IN + *-sky* (common Slavic noun ending).]

butt joint, **butt** *n.* a joint consisting of two parts of wood or other material that are placed squarely together rather than overlapping or interlocking [From BUTT[2]]

but·tock /búttək/ *n.* 1. PART OF BOTTOM in humans, either of the two fleshy mounds above the legs and below the hollow of the back (*often used in the plural*) 2. ANIMAL RUMP the rump of an animal [Old English *buttuc* "end ridge of land" (literally "small butt"), from assumed *butt* "ridge," of uncertain origin]

but·ton /bútt'n/ *n.* 1. DISK FOR HOLDING CLOTHES TOGETHER a flat and usually round piece of plastic or other material on a piece of clothing that fits into a slit or loop on another part and holds the two parts together 2. ELEC ELECTRICAL SWITCH a small disk fitted in an electrical appliance or attached to a surface that activates an electrical connection when pressed 3. SMALL ROUND OBJECT a small round object that resembles a button 4. *U.S., Aus* SMALL SIGN WORN ON CLOTHES a small round flat metal or plastic object with an image or words printed on it, worn attached to clothes 5. BIOL ROUNDED PART a rounded knob-shaped part or organ, such as the head of an unripe mushroom 6. COMPUT SMALL ACTIVATING ICON ON COMPUTER SCREEN a small oblong image in a dialog box of a computer-screen display, activated to perform a task by clicking with the mouse or pressing the "Enter" key 7. COMPUT ACTIVATING PART OF COMPUTER MOUSE the part of a computer mouse that when pressed or clicked performs a function, e.g., inserting the cursor at a specific point 8. FENCING PROTECTIVE COVERING ON FOIL a small rounded plastic or rubber covering placed on the tip of a fencing foil to protect participants from injury 9. ZOOL END OF RATTLESNAKE'S TAIL the terminal section of a rattlesnake's tail ■ *v.* (**-toned, -ton·ing, -tons**) 1. *vt.* FASTEN WITH BUTTONS to fasten something with a button or buttons 2. *vi.* to have buttons that can be fastened on a particular side of a garment opening or in a particular place on the garment ○ *The dress buttons at the back.* 3. *vt.* PUT BUTTON IN HOLE to put a button through a slit or loop designed to receive it ○ *I never button the top button of my shirt.* 4. *vt.* SHUT MOUTH to close the mouth or lips and be quiet (*informal*) ○ *Just button your mouth.* [14thC. Via French *bouton* "bud, knob," from assumed Vulgar Latin *bottare*, from a prehistoric Germanic word that is also the ancestor of English *buttress*.] —**but·ton·er** *n.* ◇ **on the button** exactly right (*informal*) ◇ **push somebody's buttons** to provoke a reaction in somebody deliberately

button up *v.* 1. *vt.* DO UP BUTTONS to fasten something with buttons 2. *vi.* STOP TALKING to stop talking or refuse to talk (*informal*) 3. *vt.* CLOSE SOMETHING TIGHTLY to close or seal something tightly

but·ton·ball /bútt'n bàwl/ *n.* 1. = **sycamore** 2. = **buttonbush** [Early 19thC. From the shape of its fruit, likened to buttons.]

but·ton blan·ket *n.* *Can* a blanket decorated with buttons and usually bearing a family crest that is part of the traditional regalia of some Pacific Coast Aboriginal peoples

but·ton·bush /bútt'n bòosh/ *n.* a North American deciduous shrub with clusters of small white flowers and leaves that grow in pairs on either side of the stem. Latin name: *Cephalanthus occidentalis.* [Mid-18thC. From its globular flower heads, likened to buttons.]

but·ton-down *adj.* 1. FASTENED DOWN AT ENDS WITH BUTTONS used to describe a collar that has a buttonhole at the end of each flap to fasten it to the front of a shirt 2. = **buttoned-down**

but·toned-down, **but·ton-down** *adj.* conservative and narrow-minded (*informal*)

but·ton·hole /bútt'n hòl/ *n.* 1. HOLE FOR BUTTON a slit in a garment or other article of clothing through which a button is passed to fasten two pieces of material together 2. *U.K.* = **boutonniere** ■ *vt.* (**-holed, -hol·ing, -holes**) 1. ACCOST SOMEBODY to compel somebody to listen, allowing no avenue of escape (*informal*) ○ *He buttonholed me outside my office.* 2. GIVE SOMETHING BUTTONHOLES to make buttonholes in something 3. SEW WITH BUTTONHOLE STITCH to sew something with buttonhole stitch —**but·ton·hol·er** *n.*

but·ton·hole stitch *n.* a tightly worked looped stitch used for reinforcing buttonholes

but·ton·hook /bútt'n hòok/ *n.* 1. CLOTHES HOOK FOR PULLING BUTTONS a small hook formerly used for pulling small buttons through buttonholes on tight boots or gloves 2. SPORTS OFFENSIVE PLAY in football, an offensive play in which the pass receiver approaches the goal and then cuts back toward the line of scrimmage

but·ton·mold /bútt'n mòld/ *n.* a small piece of plastic, metal, or wood that forms the base of a button covered in fabric or leather

but·ton mush·room *n.* 1. UNOPENED MUSHROOM an immature unopened mushroom, typically sold canned or bottled 2. SMALL EDIBLE MUSHROOM a small mushroom cultivated for food. Latin name: *Agaricus bisporus.* [See BUTTON]

but·ton quail *n.* a small terrestrial bird of South Eurasia, Africa, and Australia that has no hind toes. It resembles a quail, but is related to the crane. Family: Turnicidae.

but·ton snake·root *n.* 1. = **blazing star** *n.* 2 2. PLANT USED TO TREAT SNAKEBITE a wild plant of the southeastern United States with whitish flowers that is sometimes used to treat snakebite. Latin name: *Eryngium yuccifolium.* [So called from its small discoid flower heads]

but·ton tow *n.* *U.K.* a ski lift in which the occupant straddles a disk attached to a metal pole suspended from a moving cable

but·ton·wood /bútt'n wòod/ *n.* 1. = **sycamore** (*regional*) 2. MANGROVE TREE a mangrove tree of the American and African tropics. Latin name: *Conocarpus erectus.* 3. WOOD FROM BUTTONWOOD the wood of a buttonwood tree

WORD KEY: REGIONAL NOTE

Buttonwood in the sense of "sycamore" is used chiefly in the northwest, from Massachusetts and Vermont to Pennsylvania and New Jersey, Canada included as well. The term is virtually unknown west of the Mississippi River.

but·tress /búttrəss/ *n.* 1. SUPPORT FOR WALL a solid structure, usually made of brick or stone, that is built against a wall to support it 2. SOMEBODY OR SOMETHING THAT GIVES SUPPORT somebody or something that acts as a source of support, help, and reinforcement ○ *The constitution is a buttress of our civil rights.* 3. PROJECTING ROCK a large projecting rock mass that appears to support the rock above it 4. HOOF PART the pointed horny rear part of a horse's hoof ■ *vt.* (**-tressed, -tress·ing, -tress·es**) 1. SUPPORT WALL to support a wall with a buttress 2. SUPPORT OR REINFORCE SOMETHING to support or reinforce something, especially an argument, piece of analysis, or point of view ○ *He buttressed his views with lengthy quotations from the scriptures.* [14thC. From Old French *(ars) bouterez* "thrusting (arch)," from *bouter* "to butt, thrust against" (see BUTT[1]).]

butt shaft *n.* a blunt-headed arrow used for archery practice [From BUTT[3]]

butt-weld (**butt-weld·ed, butt-weld·ing, butt-welds**) *vt.* to weld a joint in which the two pieces are placed end to end rather than overlapped —**butt weld** *n.*

bu·tut /bòo tòot/ *n.* 1. see table at **currency** 2. GAMBIAN COIN a coin worth one butut [Late 20thC. From Wolof.]

bu·tyl /byòot'l, byòo tìl/ *n.* a carbon and hydrogen group that can exist with any of four molecular structures (**isomers**). Formula: C_4H_9-. [Mid-19thC. Coined from BUTYRIC + -YL.]

bu·tyl ac·e·tate *n.* = **butyl ethanoate**

bu·tyl al·co·hol *n.* = **butanol**

bu·tyl·ate /byòot'l àyt/ (**-at·ed, -at·ing, -ates**) *vt.* to introduce a butyl group or groups into a chemical compound —**bu·tyl·a·tion** /byòot'l áysh'n/ *n.*

bu·tyl·at·ed hy·drox·y·tol·u·ene *n.* a crystalline solid that is used in petroleum products and as an antioxidant for use in food products. Formula: $[(CH_3)_3C]_2C_6H_2OH(CH_3)$. [Mid-20thC. "Hydroxytoluene" coined from HYDROXY- + TOLUENE.]

bu·tyl·ene /byòot'l èen/ *n.* = **butene**

bu·tyl eth·a·no·ate *n.* a colorless flammable toxic liquid with a fruity odor that has three different molecular structures (**isomers**). It is used as a solvent for lacquers. Formula: $CH_3COOC_4H_9$.

bu·tyl rub·ber *n.* a synthetic rubber that is extremely resistant to abrasion, tearing, sunlight, and chemical attack. Butyl rubber is produced by a reaction between isobutylene and a small amount of isoprene. It is used in inner tubes and hose, for insulation, and as seals for food jars.

bu·ty·ra·ceous /byòotə ráyshəss/ *adj.* containing, resembling, or producing butter (*technical*) [Mid-17thC. Coined from BUTYRIC + -ACEOUS.]

bu·tyr·al·de·hyde /byòotə ráldə hìd/ *n.* a clear colorless flammable liquid used in manufacturing solvents, resins, and plasticizers. Formula: C_4H_8O.

bu·ty·rate /byòotə ràyt/ *n.* a chemical compound that is a salt or ester of butanoic acid [Mid-19thC. Coined from BUTYRIC + -ATE.]

bu·tyr·ic /byoo téerik/ *adj.* 1. RELATING TO BUTYRIC ACID relating to or containing butyric acid 2. RELATING TO BUTTER relating to or containing butter (*technical*) [Early 19thC. Coined from Latin *butyrum* (see BUTTER) + -IC.]

bu·tyr·ic ac·id *n.* = **butanoic acid**

bu·ty·rin /byòotərin/ *n.* a colorless liquid or oil found in butter and formed from butanoic acid and glycerol. It can exist with any one of three molecular structures (**isomers**). [Early 19thC. From BUTYRIC + GLYCERIN.]

bu·ty·ro·phe·none /byoo tìrō fə nōn, byòotərō fə nōn/ *n.* a drug belonging a class of drugs similar to the phenothiazines, used to treat severe psychiatric disorders [Early 20thC. From BUTYRIC + PHENO-.]

bux·om /búksəm/ *adj.* 1. WITH LARGE BREASTS used to describe a woman with a full figure and large breasts (*dated*) 2. PLUMP AND HEALTHY-LOOKING used to describe a woman who is plump, attractive, and healthy-looking (*archaic*) [Assumed Old English *(ge)būhsum*, literally "pliable" (hence "compliant," "lively," "comely," "large-breasted"), from *(ge)būgan* "to bend" (source of English *bow*)] —**bux·om·ly** *adv.* —**bux·om·ness** *n.*

buy /bī/ *v.* (**bought** /bawt/, **bought, buy·ing, buys**) 1. *vti.* ACQUIRE SOMETHING BY PAYMENT to pay money for something in order to obtain it ○ *They bought me a bike for my birthday* ○ *People just aren't buying at the moment.* 2. *vt.* USE MONEY TO OBTAIN SOMETHING INTANGIBLE to obtain something intangible with money ○ *Money won't buy you happiness.* ○ *People just aren't buying at the moment.* 3. *vt.* BELIEVE SOMETHING to accept or believe something proposed as true (*informal*) ○ *I don't buy the part about an international conspiracy.* 4. *vt.* BRIBE SOMEBODY to obtain information, help, or loyalty from somebody in exchange for money 5. *vt.* OBTAIN TIME to obtain more time to reach a desired end by taking strategic action ○ *a maneuver that should buy us another week* 6. *vt.* OBTAIN SOMETHING BY SACRIFICE to obtain something by sacrificing a thing of equivalent value ○ *buy peace with land* 7. *vi.* BE BUYER FOR COMPANY OR INDIVIDUAL to purchase goods on behalf of a company or another individual ○ *She buys for Macy's.* ■ *n.* 1. SOMETHING BOUGHT something that you pay money for, considered relative to its worth ○ *a good buy* 2. EXCHANGE OF MONEY FOR GOODS an exchange of money for goods or services [Old English *bycgan* "to buy, pay for," from a prehistoric Germanic base] —**buy·a·ble** *adj.*

buy in *v.* 1. *vi.* PAY TO TAKE PART IN SOMETHING to pay in order to take part in or have a share of something 2. *vi.* BUY STOCK IN COMPANY to buy stock in a company as the controlling interest 3. *vt.* WITHDRAW ITEM FROM AUCTION to withdraw an item from sale at an auction because it has failed to reach its upset price

buy into *vi.* 1. ACCEPT SOMETHING to accept or believe in a proposition or idea (*informal*) ○ *I don't buy into that "greed is good" attitude.* 2. PAY TO PARTICIPATE IN SOMETHING to pay money in order to take part in something ○ *buy into a timeshare* 3. BUY STOCK IN COMPANY to buy stock in a company

buy off *vt.* to bribe somebody in order to prevent

something happening or ensure cooperation ○ *They tried to buy off the entire jury.*

buy out *vt.* **1.** PAY SOMEBODY TO RELINQUISH INTEREST to pay somebody to relinquish interest in a property or other enterprise ○ *She was bought out by her partners.* **2.** COMM PURCHASE ENTIRE STOCK OF COMPANY to purchase the entire stock of or controlling financial interest in a company or business **3.** MIL RELEASE SOMEBODY FROM MILITARY SERVICE to pay money to release somebody from military service

buy up *vt.* **1.** BUY ALL OF A COMMODITY to buy everything, or everything that is available, of a commodity ○ *They've been buying up property in the area.* **2.** BUY SOMETHING IN QUANTITY to buy something in great quantity without regard to expense ○ *buying up modern paintings*

buy-back *n.* the repurchase by a company or an individual of something, e.g., stock or goods, according to a previously made contractual agreement

buy·er /bī́r/ *n.* **1.** SOMEBODY BUYING SOMETHING somebody who is in the process of buying something or who intends to buy something **2.** SOMEBODY WHO BUYS GOODS FOR COMPANY a person whose job is to choose and buy goods or merchandise for a company, factory, or store

buy·er's mar·ket *n.* a situation in which supply exceeds demand, prices are relatively low, and buyers therefore have an advantage. ◊ **seller's market**

buy·out /bī́ òwt/ *n.* **1.** BUYING ENTIRE AMOUNT OF SOMETHING the purchase of an entire amount or quantity of something **2.** PURCHASE OF CONTROLLING INTEREST IN COMPANY the purchase of a controlling interest in a company ○ *a management buyout*

buzz /buz/ *n.* **1.** STEADY HUMMING SOUND a steady low humming sound like that of a bee ○ *the low buzz of insects flitting over the flowers* **2.** HUM OF TALK a low murmur of conversation made by a group of people, especially when they are excited or interested in something ○ *a buzz of voices emerging from the living room* **3.** SOUND the sound made by a buzzer **4.** FEELING OF EXCITEMENT a feeling of excitement or satisfaction often linked with a sense of achievement (*informal*) ○ *It gives me a tremendous buzz to hear someone saying the lines that I've written.* **5.** INTOXICATION a feeling of intoxication (*slang*) **6.** TELEPHONE CALL a telephone call (*informal*) **7.** LATEST GOSSIP the latest gossip or information within a particular industry or locale (*informal*) ○ *The buzz at the festival was that he'd pick up an award for best director.* **8.** FAD a short-lived interest or enthusiasm (*informal*) **9.** publicity, or interest generated by publicity (*informal*) ■ *v.* (**buzzed, buzz·ing, buzz·es**) **1.** *vi.* MAKE STEADY HUMMING SOUND to make a steady low humming sound like that of a bee **2.** *vi.* BE ANIMATED BY SOMETHING to be animated by the talk or activity of people ○ *The room was buzzing with excitement.* **3.** *vi.* MOVE SPEEDILY to move around speedily and busily ○ *buzzing around in small cars that dodged through traffic* **4.** *vti.* WORK BUZZER to activate a buzzer **5.** *vt.* LET SOMEBODY INTO BUILDING ELECTRONICALLY to admit somebody to a building by activating an electronic system that controls a door ○ *waiting for them to buzz me in* **6.** *vi.* MAKING ELECTRONIC HUMMING SOUND to make an electronic humming noise when activated ○ *When the timer buzzes, turn the oven down.* **7.** *vi.* BE EXCITED to be filled with anxious or excited thoughts ○ *My head was buzzing with all the things I'd heard that night.* **8.** *vi.* BE RINGING to be filled with a continuous ringing sound, e.g., after being exposed to loud noise ○ *My ears were buzzing after the concert.* **9.** *vt.* TELEPHONE SOMEBODY to call somebody on the telephone (*informal*) **10.** *vt.* FLY LOW OVER PEOPLE OR PLACE to fly an aircraft low over people or buildings, or across the path of other aircraft (*informal*) [14thC. An imitation of the sound.]

buzz off *vi.* to go away (*informal*)

buz·zard /búzzərd/ (*plural* **-zards** *or* **-zard**) *n.* **1.** VULTURE any North American vulture, e.g., the turkey vulture **2.** *U.K.* = **buteo 3.** BAD-TEMPERED PERSON a mean, bad-tempered, or unpleasant person (*dated*) [14thC. From Old French *busard*, of uncertain origin: probably formed from Latin *buteo(n-)* "(kind of) falcon or hawk," of unknown origin.]

buzz bomb *n.* = **robot bomb**

buzz cut *n.* a hairstyle in which the hair is cut very close to the skull with a razor

buzz·er /búzzər/ *n.* an electronic device that makes a humming or buzzing sound when activated [Early 17thC. An early sense of the word is "buzzing insect."]

buzz saw *n.* = **circular saw**

buzz·word /búz wùrd/ *n.* a fashionable word or concept, often associated with a particular group of people and not understood by outsiders (*informal*) ○ *the latest media buzzword*

b.v. *abbr.* ACCT book value

B vi·ta·min *n.* a water-soluble vitamin that acts as a coenzyme in biochemical reactions, including those concerned with the production of energy from foods. The B vitamins are B1 thiamine, B2 riboflavin, B6 pyridoxine, B12 cobalamine, B5 pantothenic acid, folic acid, and biotin.

BVM *abbr.* Blessed Virgin Mary [Latin, Beata Virgo Maria]

bvt *abbr.* **1.** brevet **2.** brevetted

BW *abbr.* **1.** biological warfare **2.** bacteriological warfare **3. BW, B/W, b/w** black-and-white

bwa·na /bwáanə/ *n.* used as a respectful term of address for a man in East Africa [Late 19thC. From Kiswahili.]

B.W.I. *abbr.* British West Indies

BWR *abbr.* PHYS boiling-water reactor

BWV *abbr.* Bach Werke-Verzeichnis (*used before a number to indicate one of the works by J. S. Bach in the catalog compiled by Wolfgang Schmieder*)

BX *abbr.* Base Exchange

bx. *abbr.* box

by[1] /bī/ CORE MEANING: a grammatical word expressing a spatial relationship, indicating that somebody or something is beside or close to somebody or something else ○ (prep) *standing by the window* ○ (adv) *A large crowd of shoppers stood by watching.*

1. *prep., adv.* PAST SOMEBODY OR SOMETHING IN SPACE indicates movement past somebody or something, sometimes including a brief stop (*used following a verb expressing movement*) ○ *He drove by his apartment building.* ○ *The server came by, pouring us some more coffee.* **2.** *prep., adv.* AT THAT PLACE at the place specified or understood, usually for a short visit ○ *We stopped by Jan's place.* ○ *Drop by any time.* **3.** *prep.* THROUGH passing through something ○ *entering by the back door* **4.** *prep.* BEFORE THAT TIME happening or required at or before the time stated ○ *reservations required by Sunday* **5.** *prep.* DURING happening during a particular time period ○ *By day he worked in a canning factory.* **6.** *prep.* IN MEASURES OF at a rate based on a particular measure, such as time, weight, or volume ○ *These vegetables are sold by weight.* **7.** *prep.* ARITH INDICATING FACTOR OR DIVISOR used in multiplication and division to indicate any number or quantity being multiplied, or to indicate the number or quantity that divides another ○ *What is 144 divided by 12?* **8.** *prep.* MEASURE INDICATES DIMENSIONS used between the measurements of the dimensions of an object, expressing area or volume **9.** *prep.* MEASURE DIFFERING IN THE AMOUNT OF used to indicate an amount, extent, or rate at which something increases, decreases, or differs ○ *Tax rates are to be cut by 0.25%.* **10.** *prep.* MEASURE used to indicate a direction ○ *north by northwest* **11.** *prep.* IN AMOUNTS OF PARTICULAR SIZE in groups or amounts of a particular size ○ *Visitors arrived by the truckload.* **12.** *prep.* GRADUALLY used to link two identical words to indicate a progression or sequence ○ *One by one we told our stories.* ○ *You can see an improvement day by day.* **13.** *prep.* INDICATES CAUSE used to indicate the person or thing causing an action, situation, or reaction (*used following a passive verb*) ○ *He was hit by a ball.* **14.** *prep.* INDICATES CREATOR, AUTHOR, OR ARTIST used to indicate the person who wrote or created something such as a written piece or work of art ○ *written by A.A. Milne* **15.** *prep.* USING A METHOD OR MEDIUM used to indicate the particular mode, method, or action through which something occurs or is done ○ *traveling by ocean liner* ○ *She earns a living by playing the harp.* **16.** *prep.* INDICATING MEANS indicating the action used to achieve something (*followed by a gerund*) ○ *The key to attracting banks back to inner cities is by attracting business.* **17.** *prep.* THROUGH A PARTICULAR MANNER with, in, or through a particular manner of doing something ○ *used by permission of the author* **18.** *prep.* ACCORDING TO AN UNCHANGING QUALITY in terms of a particular attribute or function ○ *a teacher by profession and a learner by nature* **19.** *prep.* IN COMPLIANCE WITH in order to comply with something, especially the law ○ *By law, patients must have access to their records.* **20.** *prep.* AT A PARTICULAR PART at a particular part of something, such as a hand or corner ○ *held the dancer by the waist* **21.** *adv.* IN THE NAME OF SOMETHING SACRED used to indicate something considered holy when making a solemn oath or promise ○ *By all that is sacred, I ask you to stop.* **22.** *adv.* PAST IN TIME indicates the passage of the stated amount of time (*when following a verb expressing movement*) ○ *as time goes by* **23.** *adv.* AWAY OR ASIDE in a place for safekeeping for use later ○ *I spent some of the money and put some by for hard times.* [Old English *bī*, from a prehistoric Germanic word (also the ancestor of English *be-*) of uncertain origin: ultimately probably from an Indo-European word meaning "near"] ◇ **by and by** after a while (*literary*) ◇ **by the by, by the bye** incidentally or by the way

by[2] *n.* = **bye**[2]

b.y. *abbr.* billion years

by- *prefix.* **1.** secondary ○ *byroad* ○ *byproduct* **2.** past ○ *bygone* [From BY]

by·bid·der *n.* somebody who bids at an auction in order to raise the price for a seller —**by-bidding** *n.*

Byb·los /bíbbləss/ an ancient Phoenician city, near modern-day Beirut, Lebanon, on the Mediterranean Sea. It was the principal city of Phoenicia in the second millennium B.C., and an important source of papyrus.

by-blow *n.* **1.** CHANCE BLOW a blow that hits somebody or something by chance or in passing **2.** ILLEGITIMATE CHILD a man's illegitimate child (*archaic*)

by-catch *n.* ANGLING fish that are caught unintentionally in addition to the required species. ◊ **rough fish**

bye[1] /bī/ *n.* SPORTS the right to proceed to the next round of a competition without contesting the present round, often through nonappearance of an opponent [Mid-16thC. From *by.*]

bye[2] /bī/ *interj.* used to say goodbye (*informal*) [Early 18thC. Shortening of GOODBYE.]

bye- *prefix.* = **by-**

bye-bye *interj.* GOODBYE used to say goodbye (*informal*) ■ *adv.* OUT out somewhere, e.g., for a walk (*babytalk*) ○ *points to the buggy when he wants to go bye-bye* ■ *n.* BED OR SLEEP bed or sleep (*babytalk*) [Child's variation of GOODBYE]

bye-byes *n. U.K.* = **bye-bye** (*babytalk*) [From a refrain used in lullabies]

by-e·lec·tion, bye-e·lec·tion *n.* an election held between official general or local elections to fill a vacant seat, e.g., to replace a member of parliament or local councilor who has died or resigned

Bye·lo·rus·sia /byèllō rúshə/ *n.* former name for **Belarus** —**Bye·lo·rus·sian** *n., adj.*

by·gone /bī́ gòn/ *adj.* PAST existing or having happened a long time ago ○ *reminders of a bygone age* ■ *n.* SOMETHING FROM LONG AGO something that happened, existed, or was manufactured a long time ago (*often used in the plural*) ◇ **let bygones be bygones** to forgive past offenses or resentments

by·law /bī́ làw/ *n.* **1.** INTERNAL RULE a law or regulation that governs the internal affairs of a company or other organization **2.** LAW SECONDARY LAW a secondary law [13thC. Origin uncertain: probably from Old Norse *býlagu* "town law" from *býr* "town" + *lagu* "law."]

by·line /bī́ līn/ *n.* **1.** REPORTER'S NAME the name of the author of an article in a newspaper or magazine, printed at the head of the article **2.** SOCCER = **goal line** ■ *vt.* (**-lined, -lin·ing, -lines**) WRITE ARTICLE to write an article that will include a byline [Early 20thC. Because the article would be headed with the word BY, followed by the author's name.]

by-name /bī́ nàym/ *n.* **1.** NICKNAME somebody's nickname **2.** SURNAME somebody's surname [Late 16thC]

BYOB *abbr.* bring your own bottle (*used on party invitations*)

by·pass /bī́ pàss/ *n.* **1.** TRANSP ROAD AROUND TOWN a road built around a town or city to keep through traffic away from the center **2.** MED OPERATION TO REROUTE BLOOD a surgical operation to redirect the blood, usually via a grafted blood vessel, carried out when the existing blood vessel has become blocked ○ *a heart bypass* **3.** MED NEW ROUTE FOR BLOOD a new route for the blood, created by a bypass operation **4.** ELEC ENG = **shunt 5.** EMERGENCY CHANNEL a channel, e.g., a pipe carrying gas or water, brought into use when the main channel is blocked ■ *vt.* (**-passed, -pass·ing, -pass·es**) **1.** GO AROUND A PLACE to avoid a place by traveling around it **2.** TRANSP BUILD BYPASS to build a bypass around a place **3.** AVOID SOMETHING to avoid an obstacle, obstruction, or problem by using an alternative route or method **4.** AVOID STANDARD PROCEDURE to ignore or avoid a standard procedure for doing something, or ignore somebody who is usually consulted

by·path /bī pàth/ *n.* a rarely used path, especially in the country

by-play *n.* matters of subsidiary importance or interest that take place while the main action is going on, e.g., in a stage play

by·prod·uct /bī pròddəkt/ *n.* **1.** INCIDENTAL PRODUCT something produced as a secondary result of the manufacture or production of something else, often something useful or commercially valuable **2.** SECONDARY RESULT something that happens as an incidental result of something else

Byrd /burd/, **Richard** (1888–1957) U.S. explorer. He claimed to be the first person to fly over the North Pole (1926) and led five expeditions to Antarctica (1928–56). Full name **Richard Evelyn Byrd**

Byrnes /burnz/, **James Francis** (1879–1972) U.S. statesman. He held various legal and government positions (1911–55), including secretary of state (1945–47).

by·road /bī rōd/ *n.* a side road carrying a small volume of traffic

By·ron, George Gordon Noel, 6th Baron Byron (1788–1824) British poet. An influential figure of the romantic movement, his major works include "Childe Harold's Pilgrimage" (1812–18) and the long satirical poem "Don Juan" (1819–24). After scandalizing London with his promiscuity, Lord Byron lived abroad, largely in Italy, and died aiding the Greeks in their revolt against the Turks.

Byronic /bī rónnik/ *adj.* **1.** LITERAT OF BYRON relating to or characteristic of Lord Byron or his poetry **2.** MOODY used to describe a brooding and solitary man who seems capable of great passion and suffering

AKG London

Lord Byron

bys·si·no·sis /bìssi nṓssiss/ *n.* a respiratory disease caused by prolonged inhalation of dust from textile fibers, marked by coughing, wheezing, shortness of breath, and permanent lung damage [Late 19thC. Coined from Latin *byssinus* "of fine linen," from *byssus* (see BYSSUS) + -OSIS.]

bys·sus /bíssəss/ (*plural* **-sus·es** *or* **-si** /-sī/) *n.* **1.** MUSSEL'S MEANS OF CLINGING a mass of strong silky threads that mollusks such as mussels use to attach themselves to rocks and other hard surfaces **2.** ARCHEOL CLOTH FOR WRAPPING MUMMY a type of fine linen used by the ancient Egyptians to wrap mummies [14thC. Via Latin, "fine linen," from Greek *bussos*, of, ultimately, Semitic origin.]

by·stand·er /bī stàndər/ *n.* somebody who observes an activity but is not involved in it

by·stand·er ef·fect *n.* the reluctance of members of a crowd to intervene in an incident they are witnessing

by·street /bī street/ *n.* a side street that is not regularly used by people or traffic

byte /bīt/ *n.* **1.** UNIT OF COMPUTER INFORMATION a set of adjacent bits, now commonly a group of eight, used in computing to represent a unit of data such as a number or letter **2.** COMPUTER STORAGE UNIT a unit of computer memory equal to that needed to store a single character [Mid-20thC. Origin uncertain: probably an alteration of BIT "unit of computer information" by association with BITE "morsel," or an acronym formed from "binary digit eight."]

by·way /bī wày/ *n.* **1.** SIDE ROAD a small side road not regularly used by people or traffic **2.** MINOR ASPECTS the less important aspects of a particular pursuit or field of knowledge ○ *the byways of numismatics*

by·word /bī wùrd/ *n.* **1.** WELL-KNOWN EXAMPLE somebody or something that is well known for a particular quality ○ *The magazine became a byword for cutting-edge style.* **2.** CATCHPHRASE a word or phrase that is in common use at a particular time **3.** PROVERB a proverb common to a particular place, group, or time **4.** SOMETHING SCORNED an object of notoriety or scorn [Old English *bīwyrde* "proverb," a translation of Latin *proverbium* (source of English *proverb*)]

Byz·an·tine /bízz'n teen, -tīn, bi zántin/ *adj.* **1.** HIST OF BYZANTIUM relating to or typical of the ancient city of Byzantium, or its people or culture **2.** HIST OF BYZANTINE EMPIRE relating to the Byzantine Empire, the eastern part of the late Roman Empire **3.** ARTS, ARCHIT OF BYZANTINE ART OR ARCHITECTURE relating to or typical of the colorful style of religious art or the ornate style of architecture developed under the Byzantine Empire, which was characterized by great use of marble and mosaic **4.** CHR OF ORTHODOX CHURCH relating to or typical of the Orthodox Church and its traditions **5. Byz·an·tine, byz·an·tine** VERY COMPLEX extremely complex or intricate **6. Byz·an·tine, byz·an·tine** DEVIOUS marked by deviousness or scheming ■ *n.* HIST SOMEBODY FROM BYZANTIUM somebody who lived in the ancient city of Byzantium or the Byzantine Empire [Late 16thC. From Latin *Byzantinus*, from *Byzantium*, from Greek *Buzantion*.]

Byz·an·tine Church *n.* = **Orthodox Church**

Byz·an·tine Em·pire *n.* the eastern part of the late Roman Empire, dating from A.D. 330, when Constantine I rebuilt Byzantium and renamed it Constantinople, to 1453, when it fell to the Ottoman Turks. It was the center of Orthodox Christianity.

By·zan·ti·um /bi zánshee əm, -zántee-/ *n.* an ancient Greek city on the site of modern-day Istanbul, conquered by the Romans in A.D. 196, and rebuilt in A.D. 330 by Constantine I, who renamed it Constantinople. As the capital of the Byzantine Empire (until 1453), it was the largest city in the Christian world.

C c

c[1] /see/ (*plural* **c's**), **C** (*plural* **C's** *or* **Cs**) *n.* **1.** **3RD LETTER IN ENGLISH ALPHABET** the third letter and second consonant of the alphabet in modern English, and in other languages that also use the Latin alphabet **2.** **SOUND OF** any speech sound represented by the letter "c" **3.** **LETTER WRITTEN** a written representation of the letter ◇ **the big C** cancer (*informal*)

c[2] *symbol.* PHYS speed of light in a vacuum

c[3] *abbr.* **1.** canceled **2.** PHYS candle **3.** MEASURE carat **4.** MATH constant **5.** MEASURE cubic

C[1] (*plural* **Cs** *or* **C's**) *n.* **1.** EDUC **3RD HIGHEST GRADE** the third highest grade in a series, e.g., an average grade for academic work **2.** MUSIC **1ST NOTE OF SCALE IN C** the first note of a scale in C major **3.** MUSIC **SOMETHING THAT PRODUCES A C** a string, key, or pipe tuned to produce the note C **4.** MUSIC **SCALE BEGINNING ON C** a scale or key that starts on the note C **5.** MUSIC **WRITTEN SYMBOL OF C** a graphic representation of the tone of C **6.** COMPUT **PROGRAMMING LANGUAGE** a high-level computer programming language

C[2] *symbol.* **1.** CHEM ELEM carbon **2.** ELEC ENG capacitance **3.** 100 (*used in Roman numerals*) **4.** MEASURE Celsius **5.** MEASURE centigrade **6.** BIOCHEM cytosine

C[3] *abbr.* **1.** MEASURE Celsius **2.** MEASURE centigrade **3.** PHYS charm **4.** DRUGS cocaine (*slang*) **5.** ELEC coulomb **6.** College **7.** POL Congress

C++ /see pluss plúss/ *n.* COMPUT an object-oriented version of the programming language C, developed in the 1980s

c. *abbr.* **1.** MEASURE capacity **2.** GEOG cape **3.** carton **4.** case **5.** BASEBALL catcher **6.** MONEY cent **7.** MONEY centavo **8.** MONEY centime **9.** century **10.** chapter **11.** RELIG church **12.** circa (*used before dates*) **13.** consul **14.** copy **15.** PUBL copyright **16.** MIL corps **17.** SPORTS cup **18.** MEASURE gallon

C. *abbr.* **1.** capacity **2.** GEOG cape **3.** carton **4.** case **5.** BASEBALL catcher **6.** Catholic **7.** Celtic **8.** MONEY cent **9.** MONEY centavo **10.** MONEY centime **11.** century **12.** chancellor **13.** chapter **14.** chief **15.** RELIG church **16.** circa **17.** city **18.** companion **19.** congress **20.** conservative **21.** consul **22.** copy **23.** PUBL copyright **24.** MIL corps **25.** court **26.** SPORTS cup

C3I /see three í/ *n.* command, control, communications, and intelligence, which are the operational aspects of military science, as opposed to training or logistics

Ca *symbol.* calcium

CA *abbr.* **1.** California **2.** chronological age

ca. *abbr.* circa (*used before dates*)

c.a. *abbr.* chartered accountant

C.A. *abbr.* Central America ■ *abbr.* **1.** Central American **2.** ACCT chartered accountant **3.** chronological age

C/A *abbr.* FIN **1.** capital account **2.** credit account

CAA, **C.A.A.** *abbr.* Civil Aeronautics Administration

cab /kab/ *n.* **1.** = **taxi** **2.** **DRIVER'S COMPARTMENT** the part of a large vehicle, e.g., a truck, a locomotive, or a large crane, where the driver or operator sits **3.** **HORSE-DRAWN VEHICLE FOR HIRE** a lightweight horse-drawn carriage formerly used for public hire ■ *v.* (**cab·bed, cab·bing, cabs**) **1.** *vi.* **DRIVE TAXI** to drive a taxi as a job **2.** *vi.* **RIDE IN TAXI** to go somewhere by taxi **3.** *vt.* **TAKE SOMETHING BY TAXI** to transport something or somebody by taxi ○ *cab a package downtown* [Early 19thC. Shortening of CABRIOLET.]

CAB *abbr.* Civil Aeronautics Board

ca·bal /kə bál/ *n.* **1.** **GROUP OF PLOTTERS** a group of conspirators or plotters, particularly one formed for political purposes **2.** **SECRET PLOT** a secret plot or conspiracy, especially a political one **3.** **CLIQUE** an exclusive group of people ■ *vi.* (**-balled, -bal·ling, -bals**) **CONSPIRE AS GROUP** to form a group and plot together against somebody or something [Early 17thC. Via French *cabale* from medieval Latin *cab(b)ala* "secret teaching" (see CABALA).]

cab·a·la /kábbələ, kə baálə/, **kab·ba·lah, cab·ba·la, kab·a·la, kab·ba·la** *n.* **1.** **MYSTICAL JEWISH TEACHINGS** a body of mystical Jewish teachings based on an interpretation of hidden meanings in the Hebrew Scriptures **2.** **SET OF MYSTICAL BELIEFS** a set of secret or mystical beliefs [Early 16thC. Via medieval Latin from, ultimately, rabbinical Hebrew *qabbalah* "tradition," from *qibbel* "to receive, accept." The underlying idea is "something received or handed down."] —**cab·a·lism** /kábbə lìzzəm/ *n.* —**cab·a·list** *n.* —**cab·a·lis·tic** /kàbbə lístik/ *adj.* —**cab·ba·lis·ti·cal·ly** /-lístiklee/ *adv.*

ca·bal·et·ta /kàbbə léttə, kaàbə léttə/ *n.* **1.** **SIMPLE ARIA** a short simple aria of 19th-century Italian opera, usually found in conjunction with a preceding cavatina **2.** **LAST SECTION OF ARIA** the final section of an aria or duet, which typically has a lively rhythm [Mid-19thC. From Italian, literally "little stanza," ultimately from Latin *copula* "link" (see COPULA).]

cab·a·lis·tic /kàbbə lístik/, **cab·ba·lis·tic, ka·ba·lis·tic, kab·ba·lis·tic** *adj.* **1.** **OF THE CABALA** relating to the teachings of the cabala **2.** **MYSTERIOUS** mysterious or esoteric ○ *the cabalistic teachings of the alchemists* —**cab·a·lis·ti·cal·ly** *adv.*

cab·al·le·ro /kàbbə láirō, kaàbb'l yáirō/ (*plural* **-ros**) *n.* **1.** **SPANISH KNIGHT OR GENTLEMAN** a Spanish knight, cavalier, or gentleman **2.** *Southwest U.S.* **HORSEMAN** a horseman, especially of Spanish-speaking regions [Mid-19thC. Via Spanish from late Latin *caballarius*, from Latin *caballus* "horse" (source of English *cavalier* and *chivalry*).]

ca·ban·a /kə bánnə, kə bányə/ *n.* a shelter in which swimmers or sunbathers can change their clothes, on a beach or by a swimming pool [Late 19thC. Via Spanish from late Latin *capanna* (see CABIN).]

cab·a·ret /kàbbə ráy/ *n.* **1.** **FLOOR SHOW** a floor show consisting of singing, dancing, and comic acts performed in a restaurant, club, or bar **2.** **RESTAURANT OR BAR WITH CABARET** a restaurant, club, or bar offering a cabaret [Mid-17thC. Via French from, ultimately, Old French dialect *camberet* "little room," ultimately from Latin *camera* "room" (see CAMERA).]

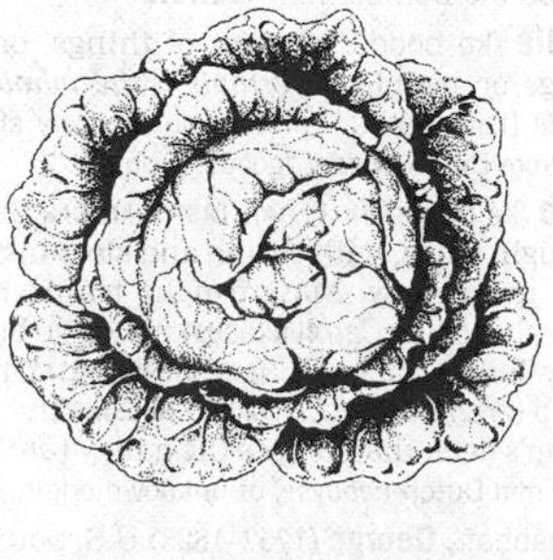

Cabbage

cab·bage /kábbij/ *n.* **1.** **LEAFY VEGETABLE** a plant with a short stem and a roundish head of closely layered green, white, or red leaves that is eaten as a vegetable. Latin name: *Brassica oleracea* var. *capitata.* **2.** **LEAVES OF CABBAGE AS FOOD** the leaves or head of a cabbage prepared as food, either raw or cooked **3.** **PLANT RELATED TO CABBAGE** a plant related to cabbage proper, e.g., Chinese cabbage **4.** **EDIBLE PALM BUD** the bud of a number of species of palm, eaten as a vegetable **5.** **PAPER MONEY** money, especially in the form of banknotes (*dated slang*) [15thC. From Old French *caboche* (source of BOCHE), a variant of *caboce* "head," perhaps ultimately from Latin *caput* (see CAPITAL).] —**cab·bag·y** *adj.*

cab·bage but·ter·fly *n.* any light-colored butterfly whose larvae (**cabbageworms**) feed on the leaves of cabbages and related plants. Family: Pieridae.

cab·bage let·tuce *n.* a variety of lettuce that has a rounded head like a cabbage

cab·bage palm *n.* **1.** **PALM WITH EDIBLE BUDS** a palm tree whose leaf buds resemble cabbages and are eaten as a vegetable. Latin name: *Roystonea oleracea.* **2.** **PLANT RESEMBLING CABBAGE** any palm or similar plant resembling a cabbage

cab·bage pal·met·to *n.* a tropical palm tree native to the southeastern United States and the Bahamas, with edible leaf buds and fan-shaped leaves that are used in Christian celebrations on Palm Sunday. Latin name: *Sabal palmetto.*

cab·bage rose *n.* a shrub rose of hybrid origin that is grown in gardens for its fragrant double flowers. Latin name: *Rosa centifolia.*

cab·bage salad *n.* a salad of shredded raw cabbage and carrots in mayonnaise (*regional*)

WORD KEY: CULTURAL NOTE

Cabbage salad *is essentially a Northern term, belonging especially to New York state, Michigan, and Wisconsin. It is rare in the Middle, Southern, Rocky Mountain, and Pacific states.*

cab·bage white *n. U.K.* = **cabbage butterfly**

cab·bage·worm /kábbij wùrm/ *n.* a larva that feeds on cabbage and related plants, especially the larva of the cabbage butterfly

cab·ba·la *n.* = **cabala**

cab·by /kábbee/ (*plural* **-bies**), **cab·bie** *n.* a taxi driver (*informal*)

cab·driv·er /káb drìvər/ *n.* a taxi driver

Cab·ell /kább'l/, **James Branch** (1879–1958) U.S. writer and essayist. Known for his satirical and controversial novel *Jurgen, or Comedy of Justice* (1919), which was temporarily suppressed as immoral, he became popular in the 1920s.

ca·ber /káybər/ *n.* a long thick wooden pole used in Scottish Highland Games in an event known as "tossing the caber," in which contestants have to throw a caber end over end [Early 16thC. From Gaelic *cabar* "pole."]

cab·er·net sau·vi·gnon /kàbbər náy sōveen yṓn/ *n.* **1.** **BLACK GRAPE USED FOR RED WINE** a variety of black grape that is used to make red wine **2.** WINE **DRY RED WINE** dry red wine made from the cabernet sauvignon grape [From French]

Ca·be·za de Va·ca /kə bàyzə də vaákə/, **Álvar Núñez** (1490?–1557?) Spanish explorer. He led European expeditions to various regions in the Americas.

cab·e·zon /kábbə zŏn, kàbbə zṓn/ (*plural* **-zons** *or* **-zon**) *n.* a spiny striped and mottled fish found in northern Pacific waters, popular as a food fish. Latin name: *Scorpaenichthys marmoratus.*

cab·in /kábbin/ *n.* **1.** BUILDING **WOODEN HUT** a small, simple house, especially one made of wood in forest or mountain areas **2.** NAUT **SMALL ROOM ON SHIP** a small room on a boat or ship, where people live or sleep **3.** NAUT **SHELTER ON SMALL BOAT** a covered compartment that houses the wheel on a small boat, used for shelter in bad weather and often as a living space **4.** AIR **AIRPLANE INTERIOR** the part of a passenger airplane where the passengers sit, or the part of a cargo airplane where the cargo is carried **5.** SPACE TECH **CREW QUARTERS ON SPACECRAFT** the part of a spacecraft where the crew work, live, or sleep **6.** NAVY **ROOM ON SHIP** the commanding officer's room on a warship ■ *vti.* **(-ined, -in·ing, -ins) KEEP SOMEBODY OR SELF CONFINED** to confine somebody, or live confined, in a small enclosed space (*literary*) (*usually passive*) [14thC. Via Old French *cabane* from, ultimately, late Latin *capanna, cavanna* "hut."]

WORD KEY: CULTURAL NOTE

Uncle Tom's Cabin, a novel by Harriet Beecher Stowe (1852). Set in the American South, it is the story of a Black slave, Uncle Tom, who is sold by his kindly owners and eventually dies at the hands of a vicious Yankee master. Such was this antislavery abolitionist novel's influence that it was described as one of the causes of the Civil War.

cab·in boy *n.* a boy who acted as a servant on board a sailing ship, waiting on officers and passengers

cab·in class *n.* **INTERMEDIATE CLASS ON PASSENGER SHIPS** a class of accommodation on some passenger ships that is lower than first class and higher than tourist class ■ *adj., adv.* **IN CABIN CLASS** in cabin class on a passenger ship

cab·in cruis·er *n.* a large, powerful, and luxurious motorboat with generous living space

cab·i·net /kábbinət/ *n.* **1.** FURNITURE **PIECE OF FURNITURE** an upright piece of furniture usually made of wood and consisting of drawers, shelves, and compartments for storing or displaying objects **2.** TV OR RADIO **COVERING** the outer casing of a television or hi-fi system, especially the wooden casing of an old-fashioned model **3. cab·i·net, Cab·i·net GOVERNMENT LEADER'S ADVISERS** a group of senior officials appointed by a president, prime minister, or other government leader to advise on policy **4. PRIVATE ROOM** a small private room (*archaic*) ■ *adj.* **FOR DISPLAY IN CABINET** small or decorative enough to be displayed in a cabinet [Mid-16thC. From French, literally "small room" (the original sense in English), from Old Picard *cabine* "room for gambling."]

cab·i·net·mak·er /kábbinət màykər/ *n.* a skilled woodworker who specializes in making furniture — **cab·i·net·mak·ing** *n.*

cab·i·net·ry /kábbinətree/, **cab·i·net·work** /kábbinət wùrk/ *n.* articles, especially fine furniture, made by a skilled woodworker

cab·in fe·ver *n.* an emotional condition, marked by irritability, distress, or depression, caused by prolonged isolation or confined living quarters

ca·ble /káyb'l/ *n.* **1. STRONG ROPE OR WIRE** a strong thick rope or steel wire used for lifting, pulling, towing, or securing things **2.** ELEC **BUNDLE OF ELECTRICAL WIRES** a group of wires for transmitting electrical signals that are bound together and usually have shared or common insulation. ◊ **coaxial cable 3.** NAUT **MOORING ROPE OR CHAIN** a rope or chain attached to an anchor or used for mooring a ship **4.** TELECOM **OVERSEAS TELEGRAM** a telegram, originally sent by underseas cable, now usually by telephone, radio, or satellite **5.** TV = **cable television 6.** KNITTING = **cable stitch** ■ *v.* **(-bled, -bling, -bles) 1.** *vti.* **SEND TELEGRAM** to send somebody a telegram **2.** *vt.* TELECOM **SEND SOMETHING VIA TELEGRAM** to send something, e.g., money or information, to somebody in a distant place by sending a telegram **3.** *vt.* **FASTEN OR FIT SOMETHING WITH CABLES** to fasten something with cables, or fit cables to something **4.** *vt.* TV **SUPPLY PLACE WITH CABLE TV** to connect a building or area to a cable television network [Pre-12thC. Via Old French dialect from late Latin *capulum* "halter," from Latin *capere* "to seize" (see CAPTURE).] —**ca·bler** *n.* —**ca·bling** *n.*

Ca·ble /káyb'l/, **George Washington** (1844–1925) U.S. writer, known for his novels and short stories set in New Orleans.

ca·ble-ac·cess *adj.* TV showing programs that are made locally, often of local interest only, as opposed to commercially produced material ○ *cable-access television*

Cable car

ca·ble car *n.* **1. CAR SUSPENDED FROM OVERHEAD CABLE** a car suspended from an overhead cable, used to transport passengers up and down steep hills or across valleys **2. CABLE RAILROAD CAR** a car on a cable railroad

ca·ble·cast /káyb'l kàst/ *n.* a broadcast over a cable television network [Late 20thC. Coined from CABLE + "-cast" from BROADCAST.] —**ca·ble·cast·er** *n.* —**ca·ble·cast·ing** *n.*

ca·ble·gram /káyb'l gràm/ *n.* = **cable**

ca·ble-laid *adj.* used to describe thick ropes made of three thinner ropes, each with three strands, twisted together counterclockwise

ca·ble mo·dem *n.* a modem that connects a computer with the cable television network for high-speed data communications

ca·ble rail·way *n.* a hillside railway consisting of a track along which cars are pulled by a moving cable that is operated by a stationary engine

ca·ble re·lease *n.* a cable fitted with a control button and attached to a camera in order to take photographs without shaking the camera, e.g., during long exposures

ca·ble-stayed bridge *n.* a suspension bridge with the cables that support the deck connected directly to the bridge's piers rather than to suspenders

ca·ble stitch *n.* a knitting stitch that produces a pattern resembling twisted rope

ca·blet /káyblət/ *n.* a cable-laid rope that has a circumference of less than 10 in./25 cm

ca·ble tel·e·vi·sion /kàyb'l télevizh'n/, **ca·ble·vi·sion** /káyb'l vìzh'n/, **ca·ble TV** *n.* a television system in which signals are sent to a central antenna and then transmitted by cable to subscribers

ca·ble·way /káyb'l wày/ *n.* any transportation system consisting of an overhead cable used for transporting suspended cars or containers

cab·o·chon /kábbə shòn/ *n.* **1. ROUND GEM** a highly polished rounded unfaceted gem **2. ROUNDED GEM-CUTTING** the gem-cutting style that results in a cabochon ■ *adj., adv.* **ROUND** in the cabochon style [Mid-16thC. From French, literally "little head," from Old French *caboche* "head" (source of English *cabbage*); from the size and shape of such gems.]

Ca·bo·clo /kə bó klòo, kə bó klò/, **ca·bo·clo** *n.* somebody, especially a Brazilian, who is partially or entirely descended from the peoples who were the original inhabitants of Brazil [Early 19thC. Via Brazilian Portuguese from, perhaps, Tupi *Kaa-boc* "copper-colored one."]

ca·bom·ba /kə bómbə/ *n.* = **fanwort**

ca·boo·dle /kə bóod'l/ *n.* a lot of things, or a group of things or people (*informal*) ○ *the whole kit and caboodle* [Late 19thC. Probably an arbitrary alteration of BOODLE from Dutch *boedel* "goods, property."]

ca·boose /kə bóoss/ *n.* **1.** RAIL **LAST TRAIN CAR** the last car on a freight train, with eating and sleeping facilities for the train crew. Most freight trains no longer have a caboose. **2.** *Can* **BUNKHOUSE** a mobile bunkhouse used by lumberjacks **3.** NAUT **SHIP'S GALLEY** the galley of a ship (*archaic*) **4.** *U.K.* **GALLEY HOUSING** the structure on a ship's deck that houses the galley (*archaic*) [Mid-18thC. From Dutch *cabuyse*, of unknown origin.]

Ca·bot /kábbət/, **George** (1752–1823) U.S. politician. He was a U.S. senator (1791–96) and headed the Hartford Convention (1814).

Ca·bot, John (1450?–99?) Italian explorer. He made the first recorded contact (1497) with North America after the Vikings. Born **Giovanni Caboto**

Ca·bot, Sebastian (1476?–1557) Italian-born British navigator and cartographer. He made expeditions to North and South America (1508–09, 1525–28) for Spain and England and published a world map (1544).

cab·o·tage /kábbə taázh/ *n.* **1.** SHIPPING **NATIONAL SHIPPING** trade, shipping, or navigation that takes place in coastal waters within the boundaries of a single country **2.** AIR **INTERNAL AIR TRAFFIC** the right of a country to operate internal traffic, especially air traffic, using its own carriers and not those of other countries [Mid-19thC. From French, from *caboter* "to coast along," from Spanish *cabo* "cape, headland," from, ultimately, Latin *caput* "head" (source of English *cape*).]

Ca·bral /kə braál/, **Pedro Álvares** (1460?–1526?) Portuguese explorer. He was the first European to visit Bahia, Brazil, and declared it a Portuguese territory.

ca·bret·ta /kə bréttə/ *n.* a type of soft leather obtained from the skins of certain South American and African sheep and used mainly for making gloves and shoes [Early 20thC. Coined from Spanish *cabra* "female goat" (from Latin *capra*) + Italian *-etta* "little."]

ca·bril·la /kə breéyə, kə bríllə/ (*plural* **-las** *or* **-la**) *n.* a sea bass that lives in warm coastal waters, especially in the Mediterranean and off the California coast. Genera: *Epinephelus* and *Paralabrax*. [Mid-19thC. From Spanish, literally "little female goat," from *cabra* (see CABRETTA).]

Ca·bril·lo /kə breé lō, kə breé yō/, **Juan Rodríguez** (*d.* 1543) Portuguese-born Spanish explorer. He joined forces with Cortés in Mexico from 1520 and explored the western coast of North America (1542), reaching northern California.

Ca·bri·ni /kə breénee/, **Frances Xavier St.** (1850–1917) Italian-born U.S. social-welfare worker. She was the first Roman Catholic American saint (1946). Known as **Saint of the Immigrants, Mother Cabrini**

cab·ri·ole /kábbri ōl/ *n.* **1.** FURNITURE **FURNITURE LEG** a curving furniture leg tapering into a decorative foot that is often carved to look like an animal's paw, popular in the early 18th century **2.** BALLET **BALLET MOVEMENT** a ballet movement in which the dancer leaps into the air with one leg outstretched sideways and the other beating against it [Late 18thC. From French "leap," from *cabrioler*, a variant of *caprioler* "to caper."]

cab·ri·o·let /kàbbree ə láy/ *n.* **1.** CARS **CONVERTIBLE AUTOMOBILE** a two-door convertible automobile ○ *She bought a new red cabriolet last week.* **2.** TRANSP **TWO-SEATER CARRIAGE** a two-wheeled, two-seater, horse-drawn carriage with a folding roof [Mid-18thC. From French, from *cabrioler* (see CABRIOLE), because of the bouncing motion of a horse-drawn vehicle.]

cab·stand /káb stànd/ *n.* = **taxi stand**

cac- *prefix.* = **caco-** (*used before vowels*)

ca·ca·o /kə ków, kə káy ō, kə kaá ō/ (*plural* **-os** *or* **-o**) *n.* **1. COCOA TREE** a tropical American evergreen tree with small yellowish flowers and fleshy pods containing seeds that are the source of cocoa and chocolate. Latin name: *Theobroma cacao*. **2. SEEDS OF CACAO TREE** the dried fatty seeds of the cacao tree, from which cocoa, chocolate, and other foods and products are derived **3.** = **cocoa bean 4. ca·ca·o, ca·ca·o but·ter** = **cocoa butter** [Mid-16thC. Via Spanish from Nahuatl *cacauatl*, from *uatl* "tree."]

ca·ca·o bean *n.* = **cocoa bean**

cac·cia·tore /kaachə táwree/ *adj.* cooked with mushrooms, tomatoes, and herbs (*usually used after a noun*) ○ *chicken cacciatore* [Mid-20thC. From Italian, literally "hunter"; from its original use as a sauce for game.]

Cá·ce·res /kássə ràyss/, **Andres Avelino** (1836–1923?) Peruvian soldier and politician. He was president of Peru (1886–90 and 1894–95).

ca·cha·ca /kə shaássə/ *n.* a Brazilian rum made from sugarcane

cach·a·lot /káshə lòt, káshə lō/ *n.* = **sperm whale** [Mid-18thC. Via French from Spanish or Portuguese *cachalote*, perhaps from *cachola* "big head."]

cache /kash/ *n.* **1. HIDDEN SUPPLY** a hidden store of things, especially weapons or valuables **2. SECRET PLACE FOR HIDING THINGS** a secret place where a store of things is kept hidden **3.** COMPUT **MEMORY FOR FREQUENTLY USED DATA** an area of high-speed computer memory used for the temporary storage of frequently used data to allow faster access ■ *vt.* **(cached, cach·ing, cach·es)**

1. HIDE SUPPLY OF THINGS to store a hidden supply of things, especially weapons or valuables, in a secret place **2.** COMPUT **HOLD DATA IN CACHE** to store data in a cache [Late 18thC. From French, from *cacher* (see CACHET).]

ca·chec·tic /kə kéktik/ *adj.* MED affected by or relating to cachexia [Early 17thC. Via French *cachectique* or Latin *cachecticus* from Greek *kakhektikos* (see CACHEXIA).]

cache mem·o·ry *n.* = **cache**

cache·pot /kásh pòt, kásh pō/ *n.* a decorative container for a flowerpot [Late 19thC. From French, literally "hide pot."]

ca·chet /ka sháy/ *n.* **1. QUALITY THAT ATTRACTS ADMIRATION** a quality of distinction and style that people admire and approve of **2. OFFICIAL MARK** an official seal or stamp on a letter or other document **3.** STAMPS **COMMEMORATIVE POSTMARK** a commemorative mark stamped on mail to mark a particular event **4.** STAMPS **COLLECTOR'S MARK** a small mark made on the back of a postage stamp by a stamp collector **5.** PHARM **EDIBLE MEDICINE CAPSULE** an edible hollow case formerly used by pharmacists to enclose unpleasant-tasting medicine in order to make it more palatable [Early 17thC. From French, "stamp, distinguishing mark," from Old French *cacher* "to press" (see CACHE).]

ca·chex·i·a /kə kéksee ə/ *n.* a condition marked by loss of appetite, weight loss, muscular wasting, and general mental and physical debilitation, caused by chronic disease [Mid-16thC. Via French *cachexie* or late Latin *cachexia* from Greek *kakhexia*, from *kakos* "bad" + *hexis* "habit."]

cach·in·nate /kákə nàyt/ (**-nat·ed, -nat·ing, -nates**) *vi.* to laugh convulsively and loudly (*literary*) [Early 19thC. From Latin *cacchinat-*, past participle stem of *cachinnare*, an imitation of the sound.] —**cach·in·na·tion** *n.* —**cach·in·na·tor** *n.*

ca·chou /ka shoō, ká shoō/ *n.* **1. BREATH LOZENGE** a perfumed pastille or lozenge taken to sweeten the breath **2.** = **catechu** [Late 16thC. Via French from, ultimately, Malayalam *kaccu*.]

ca·chu·cha /kə choōchə/ *n.* **1.** DANCE **CASTANET DANCE** a lively Andalusian dance for a solo dancer with castanets **2.** MUSIC **MUSIC FOR CACHUCHA** a piece of music that accompanies the cachucha, in 3/4 time [Mid-19thC. From Spanish.]

ca·cique /kə seēk/ *n.* **1.** HIST **NATIVE AMERICAN CHIEF** a Native American chief in Latin America during colonial times **2.** POL **POLITICAL LEADER** a local political boss, especially in Latin America or Spain **3.** BIRDS **TROPICAL AMERICAN SONGBIRD** a boldly colored tropical blackbird of Central and South America that feeds on fruit and insects. It is gregarious and nests, roosts, and feeds in colonies. Genus: *Cacicus.* [Mid-16thC. Via Spanish or French from Taino.]

cack-hand·ed /kak hándəd/ *adj. U.K.* **1. CLUMSY** clumsy (*informal*) **2. LEFT-HANDED** naturally left-handed (*regional offensive*) [Mid-19thC. Origin uncertain: perhaps from Old Norse *keikr* "bent backwards."] —**cack-hand·ed·ness** *n.*

cack·le /kák'l/ *v.* (**-led, -ling, -les**) **1.** *vi.* **LAUGH HARSHLY AND SHRILLY** to laugh a harsh high-pitched malicious laugh, often suggesting pleasure at others' misfortune or glee in your own good fortune **2.** *vt.* **SAY SOMETHING WITH HARSH SHRILL LAUGH** to say something with a malicious high-pitched laugh **3.** *vi.* **MAKE SQUAWKING NOISE** to squawk shrilly, especially after laying an egg (*refers to hens*) ■ *n.* **MALICIOUS LAUGH** a high-pitched malicious laugh or tone of voice [12thC. From Middle Low German or Middle Dutch *kākel(e)n*, of imitative origin.] —**cack·ler** *n.*

caco- *prefix.* bad ○ *cacology* [From Greek *kakos* (source of English *cacophony*)]

cac·o·de·mon /kàkə deēmən/, **cac·o·dae·mon** *n.* an evil spirit (*archaic*) [Late 16thC. From Greek *kakodaimōn*.]

cac·o·dyl /kákə dìl/ *n.* a poisonous oily flammable liquid that contains arsenic and has an unpleasant garlicky smell. Formula: $C_4H_{12}As_2$. [Mid-19thC. Coined from Greek *kakodes*, literally "bad smelling" + -YL.] —**cac·o·dyl·ic** /kàkə díllik/ *adj.*

ca·cog·ra·phy /kə kóggrəfee/ *n.* (*formal*) **1. BAD HANDWRITING** poor handwriting **2. MISSPELLING** incorrect spelling —**ca·co·graph·ic** /kàkə gráffik/ *adj.* —**ca·co·graph·i·cal** /-gráffik'l/ *adj.*

cac·o·mis·tle /kákə mìss'l/, **cac·o·mix·le** /kákə mìks'l/ *n.* a carnivorous mammal resembling the cat, found in the southwestern United States and Mexico, with brown fur and a long black-banded tail. It is related to but smaller than the raccoon. Latin name: *Bassariscus astutus.* [Mid-19thC. Via American Spanish *cacomixtle* from Nahuatl *tlacomiztli*, literally "half mountain lion."]

cac·o·nym /kákənim/ *n.* the wrong name for something, especially in the classification of plants and animals (*formal*) [Late 19thC. Coined from CACO- "bad" + -ONYM "name."] —**ca·con·y·my** /kə kónnəmee/ *n.*

ca·coph·o·nous /kə kóffənəss/ *adj.* sounding loud, jarring, and unpleasant [Late 18thC. Formed from Greek *kakophōnos* "bad-sounding."] —**ca·coph·o·nous·ly** *adv.*

ca·coph·o·ny /kə kóffənee/ (*plural* **-nies**) *n.* **1. UNPLEASANT NOISE** an unpleasant combination of loud, often jarring, sounds **2. USE OF JARRING SOUNDS** the use of harsh unpleasant sounds in language, e.g., for literary effect [Mid-17thC. Via French from Greek *kakophōnia*, from *kakophōnos* (see CACOPHONOUS).]

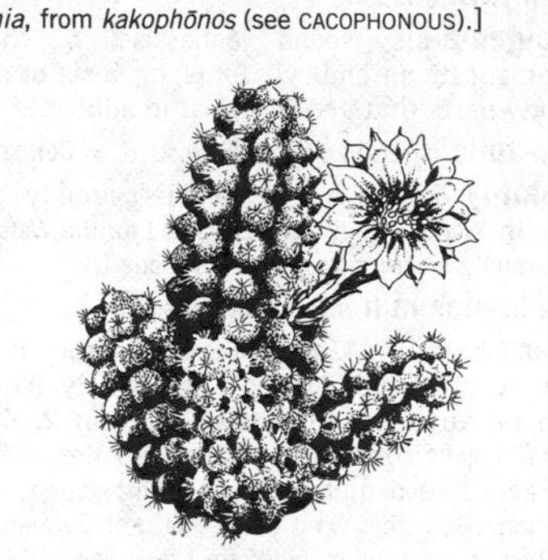

Cactus

cac·tus /káktəss/ (*plural* **-ti** /kák tì/ *or* **-tus·es** *or* **-tus**) *n.* a plant belonging to a large family of spiny leafless plants with fleshy stems and branches, found in dry desert regions of the Americas. Many varieties produce brightly colored flowers. Family: Cactaceae. [Mid-18thC. Via Latin, "cardoon," from Greek *kaktos*, of unknown origin.]

ca·cu·mi·nal /kə kyoōmən'l/ *n., adj.* = **retroflex** [Mid-19thC. Formed from Latin *cacuminare* "to make pointed," from *cacumen* "point, summit."]

cad /kad/ *n.* a man who does not behave as a gentleman should, especially toward a woman (*dated*) [Mid-19thC. Shortening of CADDIE "errand-boy." The meaning apparently evolved from the word's use at Oxford University for "townsperson," via "a man of inferior social and moral stature."] —**cad·dish** *adj.* —**cad·dish·ly** *adv.* —**cad·dish·ness** *n.*

CAD /kad/ *abbr.* computer-aided design

ca·das·tre /kə dástər/, **ca·das·ter** *n.* an official register containing information on the value, extent, and ownership of land for the purposes of taxation [Late 18thC. Via French from, ultimately, Italian *catastico*, from Greek *katastikhon* "list," from *kata stikhan* "line by line."] —**ca·das·tral** /kə dástrəl/ *adj.*

ca·dav·er /kə dávvər/ *n.* a dead body, especially one that is to be dissected [14thC. From Latin, from *cadere* "to fall, die" (source of English *cadence* and *accident*).] —**ca·dav·er·ic** *adj.*

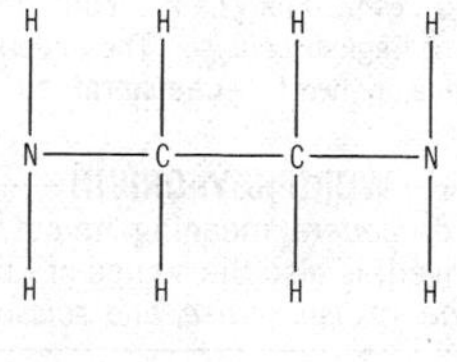

Cadaverine

ca·dav·er·ine /kə dávvə reēn/ *n.* a thick toxic colorless liquid with an extremely unpleasant smell, produced when flesh rots

ca·dav·er·ous /kə dávvərəss/ *adj.* **1. OF CORPSES** suggesting death or corpses (*formal or literary*) **2. PALE** deathly pale (*literary*) **3. EXTREMELY THIN** thin to the point of resembling a skeleton or corpse —**ca·dav·er·ous·ly** *adv.* —**ca·dav·er·ous·ness** *n.*

CAD/CAM /kád kàm/ *abbr.* computer-aided design and manufacturing

cad·dice *n.* TEXTILES = **caddis**

cad·dice fly *n.* = **caddis fly**

cad·dice worm *n.* = **caddis worm**

cad·die /káddee/, **cad·dy** *n.* (*plural* **-dies**) **GOLFER'S ASSISTANT** somebody who carries a golfer's bag of clubs and assists in other ways, e.g., in judging distances and choosing clubs ■ *vi.* (**-died, -dy·ing, -dies; -died**) **BE GOLFER'S CADDIE** to act as a caddie for a golfer [Late 18thC. Originally a Scots form of CADET. The main modern meaning "golfer's porter" evolved from "young member of the gentry who joins the army" via "messenger boy."]

cad·dis /káddiss/, **cad·dice** *n.* a type of coarse woolen fabric, braid, or yarn [Mid-16thC. Via Old French from Provençal, of unknown origin.]

cad·dis fly (*plural* **cad·dis flies**), **cad·dice fly** (*plural* **cad·dice flies**) *n.* an insect with four membranous wings, multijointed antennae, and larvae (**caddis worms**) that live in water. Order: Trichoptera. [*Caddis* perhaps after CADDIS "fabric," because the larva makes a protective case from coarse silken material]

cad·dis worm, **cad·dice worm** *n.* a larva of a caddis fly. It lives in water inside a protective silken case that is covered with sand and debris. [See CADDIS FLY]

Cad·do /káddō/ (*plural* **-do** *or* **-dos**) *n.* a member of a confederacy of Native Americans in central Oklahoma who formerly lived in the Red River area of Arkansas, Louisiana, and East Texas [Via American French from Caddo *kaduhdā·čuˀ*] —**Cad·do** *adj.*

cad·dy[1] *n.*, *vi.* = **caddie**

cad·dy[2] /káddee/ (*plural* **-dies**) *n.* a small box or tin used for storing something, especially tea [Late 18thC. Alteration of *catty*, from Malay *kati*, a standard measure for tea set by the East India Company.]

-cade *suffix.* procession ○ *motorcade* [From CAVALCADE]

ca·delle /kə dél/ *n.* a small black beetle that feeds on grain and other stored foods, found throughout the world. Latin name: *Tenebroides mauritanicus.* [Mid-19thC. Via French from, ultimately, Latin *cadellus* "little dog."]

ca·dence /káyd'ns/ *n.* **1. RHYTHM** the beat or measure of something that follows a set rhythm, e.g., a dance or a march **2. FALLING TONE** a drop in the pitch of the voice, e.g., at the end of a sentence **3. INTONATION** the way in which the voice rises and falls in pitch when somebody is speaking **4. RHYTHM IN LANGUAGE** the way in which poetry or prose flows according to a rhythm **5.** MUSIC **MUSICAL SEQUENCE** a short sequence of notes that marks the end of a piece or passage of music. In tonal music, a cadence brings about a harmonic resolution. [14thC. Via Old French, "rhythm" from Italian *cadenza*, literally "falling away." Ultimately from Latin *cadent-*, the present participle stem of *cadere* "to fall" *accident, cadaver,* and *case*).] —**ca·denced** *adj.*

WORD KEY: ORIGIN

The Latin word *cadere*, from which ***cadence*** is derived, meaning "to fall," is also the source of English *accident, cadaver, case, cheat, coincide, decay, deciduous, incident, occasion,* and *Occident.*

ca·dent /káyd'nt/ *adj.* with a noticeable rhythm or cadence (*literary*) [Early 17thC. From Latin *cadent-*; "falling," the present participle stem of *cadere* (see CADENCE).]

ca·den·tial /kə dénsh'l/ *adj.* **1. OF RHYTHM** relating to rhythm or a rhythmical cadence **2.** MUSIC **OF CADENZAS** relating to cadenzas or a musical cadence

ca·den·za /kə dénzə/ *n.* an elaborate solo passage of virtuoso singing or playing near the end of a section or piece of music, sometimes improvised by the soloist [Mid-18thC. From Italian (see CADENCE).]

ca·det /kə dét/ *n.* **1. MILITARY TRAINEE** a young man or woman who is training to become a full member of the armed forces or the police force, especially a student at a military or naval academy **2. YOUNG PERSON IN UNIFORMED ORGANIZATION** somebody of school age who who attends a military school or is a member of a uniformed organization with a military theme **3. YOUNGER SON** a younger son or brother (*dated*) **4. PIMP** a pimp (*slang*) [Early 17thC. From French, originally Gascon dialect *capdet* "younger son" (because noble Gascon families traditionally sent these into the army), literally "chief," from, ultimately, Latin *caput* "head" (see CAPITAL).] —**ca·det·ship** *n.*

Ca·dette /kə dét/ *n.* a member of a division of the

Girl Scouts of America for girls between 11 and 14 years [Mid-20thC. Formed from CADET.]

cadge /kaj/ (**cadged, cadg·ing, cadg·es**) *vti.* to scrounge or beg something from somebody (*informal*) [Early 17thC. Back-formation from CADGER.] —**cadg·er** *n.*

cadg·er /kájjər/ *n.* somebody who habitually takes or borrows things or asks for favors from people (*informal*) [15thC. Origin unknown. Originally in the sense "itinerant peddler," the modern meaning evolved via "beggar, opportunist."]

ca·di /káadee/, **qa·di** *n.* a minor judge in a Muslim community where Islamic law is followed [Late 16thC. From Arabic *ḳāḍī*.]

Cad·il·lac /kədd'làk/ city in Michigan, southeast of Traverse City, situated on Lake Cadillac in a forested region. Population: 10,498 (1996).

Cá·diz /kə díz, káydiz/ capital of Cádiz Province and a major port in the autonomous region of Andalusia in southwestern Spain. Population: 154,511 (1995).

cad·mi·um /kádmee əm/ *n.* a soft malleable toxic bluish-white metallic chemical element found in zinc, copper, and lead ores. The metal is used in alloys, in electroplating, in nuclear reactors, and in dental amalgams, and its compounds are used as pigments and in electronics. Symbol **Cd** [Early 19thC. Formed from Latin *cadmia* "calamine, zinc ore" (source of English *calamine*), from Greek *kadm(e)ia gē* "earth of Cadmus" see CADMUS, so-called because the substance came originally from Thebes.]

cad·mi·um sul·fide *n.* an orange or yellowish-brown poisonous salt used in paints as a pigment, in medicine, and in electronic parts. Formula: CdS.

cad·mi·um yel·low *n.* an bright yellow pigment that contains cadmium sulfide, or paint prepared with this pigment

Cad·mus /kádməss/ *n.* in Greek mythology, a prince who slew a dragon and planted its teeth in the ground, from which armed men sprouted and fought each other. With the five survivors Cadmus founded Thebes.

cad·re /káddree, kaá dràyl/ *n.* **1.** MIL **MILITARY UNIT** a group of experienced professionals at the core of a military organization who are able to train new recruits and expand the operations of the unit **2.** POL **CORE OF ACTIVISTS** a core group of political activists or revolutionaries **3. CORE GROUP** a controlling or representative group at the center of an organization **4. SMALL GROUP OF TEAM-SPIRITED PEOPLE** a tightly knit, highly trained group of people **5. MEMBER OF CADRE** a member of a cadre [Mid-19thC. Via French, "frame" from Italian *quadro* "framework," from Latin *quadrum* "square."]

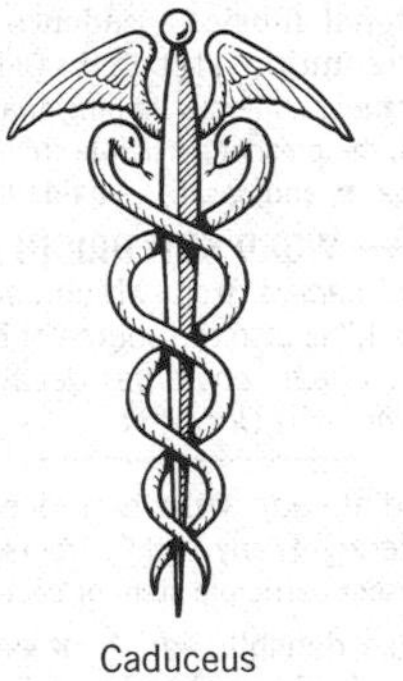

Caduceus

ca·du·ce·us /kə dóossee əss, kə dóoshəss/ (*plural* **-i** /kə dóossi ī/) *n.* **1.** MYTHOL **HERMES' STAFF** in classical mythology, a winged staff entwined with two serpents, the symbol of Hermes or Mercury. It is also associated with the Greek god of healing, Asclepius. **2.** MED **MEDICAL INSIGNIA** a symbol of the U.S. Army Medical Corps and various other medical organizations that is modeled on Hermes' caduceus. ◊ **staff of Aesculapius** [Late 16thC. Via Latin from Doric Greek *karuk(e)ion*, from *kērux* "herald."] —**ca·du·ce·an** *adj.*

ca·du·ci·ty /kə dóossətee/ *n.* (*literary*) **1. INFIRMITY** the frailty or senility that sometimes characterizes old age **2. PERISHABLENESS** the quality of being perishable or impermanent [Mid-18thC. From French *caducité*, from *caduc* "transitory," from Latin *caducus* (see CADUCOUS).]

ca·du·cous /kə dóokəss/ *adj.* used to describe a plant or animal part that drops off or is shed in the early stages of development, as certain leaves or flower parts do [Late-18thC. Formed from Latin *caducus* "liable to fall"(see CADUCITY).]

CAE *abbr.* computer-aided engineering

cae·cil·ian /sə síllyən, sə síllee ən/ *n.* a limbless tropical amphibian that looks like an earthworm, has small or no eyes, and burrows in the soil. Order: Gymnophiona. [Late 19thC. Formed from modern Latin *Caecilia*, genus name, from Latin *caecilia* "slow-worm."]

cae·cum /séekəm/ *n.* = **cecum**

Cae·lum /séeləm/ *n.* a constellation in the sky of the southern hemisphere near Columba and Eridanus [From Latin *caelum* "chisel," from its shape]

Caen /kaaN/ capital of Calvados Department in the Basse-Normandie Region, in northwestern France. It was largely rebuilt after World War II. Population: 115,624 (1990).

cae·no·gen·e·sis /seenō jénnəssiss/ *n.* the development by an embryo, fetus, or larva of organs or body parts that are later lost in adult life

Cae·no·zo·ic /seenō zṓ ik/ *adj., n.* U.K. = **Cenozoic**

caer·phil·ly /kaar fíllee/ *n.* a pale crumbly cheese made in Wales [Early 20thC. Named for the Welsh town of Caerphilly, where it was originally made.]

cae·ru·lo·plas·min *n.* = **ceruloplasmin**

Cae·sar /séezər/ *n.* **1. TITLE OF ROMAN EMPERORS** the title given to a Roman emperor, especially from the reign of Augustus to that of Hadrian **2. Caesar, cae·sar TYRANT** somebody such as a ruler or leader who acts like a dictator [Old English *casere*. From a prehistoric Germanic word (source also of German *Kaiser* and Russian *tsar*), ultimately from Latin *Caesar*, the family name of Julius Caesar, of Etruscan origin.]

Cae·sar /séezər/, **Gaius Julius** (100–44 B.C.) Roman general and statesman who emerged from civil war as dictator of Rome and was assassinated by republican conspirators. Full name **Gaius Julius Caesar**

Cae·sa·rea /sèezə rée ə/ ancient seaport on the coast of Samaria, and the Roman capital of Palestine, situated approximately 22 mi./35 km south of present-day Haifa, Israel

cae·sar·e·an *adj., n.* = **cesarean**

Cae·sar·ism /séezə rìzzəm/ *n.* dictatorial or tyrannical government —**Cae·sar·ist** *n.* —**Cae·sar·is·tic** /sèezə rístik/ *adj.*

cae·sar sal·ad *n.* a salad made with lettuce, croutons, parmesan cheese, and anchovies, with an egg-based dressing [Named for *Caesar* Gardini, a restaurant proprietor in Tijuana, Mexico, who is said to have invented it]

cae·si·um *n.* = **cesium**

caes·pi·tose /séspi tōss/ *adj.* used to describe a plant that grows in tufts or clumps. U.K. = **cespitose** [Late 18thC. Formed from the Latin stem *caespit-* "turf."]

cae·su·ra /si zóorə, si zhóorə/ (*plural* **-ras** *or* **-rae** /-ree/), **ce·su·ra** (*plural* **-ras** *or* **-rae**) *n.* **1.** POETRY **PAUSE IN LINE OF VERSE** a pause in a line of poetry, especially to allow its sense to be made clear or to follow the rhythms of natural speech, often near the middle of the line **2.** POETRY **BREAK IN LINE OF VERSE** in classical poetry, especially Greek, a break between two words that are part of the same unit of rhythm (**foot**), usually near the middle of the line **3.** MUSIC **MUSICAL INTERRUPTION** a brief interruption in a musical phrase **4. PAUSE** a pause or break in speech or conversation (*formal*) [Mid-16thC. From Latin, "cut," from *caedere* "to cut" (source of English *concise*). The underlying idea is of cutting the line in two.] —**cae·su·ral** *adj.* —**cae·su·ric** *adj.*

WORD KEY: ORIGIN

The Latin word *caedere*, meaning "to cut," from which ***caesura*** is derived, is also the source of English, *chisel*, *concise*, *decide*, *excise*, *incise*, and *scissors*.

C.A.F. *abbr.* cost and freight

ca·fé /ka fáy, kə fáy/ *n.* a small informal restaurant serving drinks, snacks, and often light meals [Early 19thC. Via French, "coffee(-house)," from, ultimately, Turkish *kahveh* "coffee" or Arabic *qahwah* "coffee, wine" (source of English *coffee*).]

CAFE /ká fày/ *n.* a federally mandated average fuel-consumption rate for the vehicles produced by a manufacturer. Full form **corporate average fuel economy**

ca·fé au lait /ka fày ō láy/ *n.* (*plural* **ca·fé au laits** /ka fày ō láy/ *or* **ca·fés au lait**) **1. COFFEE WITH MILK** strong coffee with hot milk **2.** COLORS **PALE BROWN COLOR** a pale brown color, like that of milky coffee ■ *adj.* COLORS **OF PALE BROWN COLOR** of a pale brown color, like milky coffee [Mid-18thC. From French, literally "coffee with milk."]

ca·fé lat·te /kaá fe laá tè, kà fay laá tè/ *n.* = **latte**

ca·fé noir /ka fày nwaár/ (*plural* **ca·fés noirs** /ka fày nwaár/) *n.* coffee without milk or cream [From French, literally "black coffee"]

ca·fé so·ci·e·ty *n.* people such as celebrities and media people who attend fashionable events and visit fashionable restaurants, clubs, and resorts

caf·e·te·ri·a /kàffə téeree ə/ *n.* a self-service restaurant or coffee shop, especially one in a workplace or school [Mid-19thC. From American Spanish, formed from *café* "coffee."]

caf·e·te·ri·a ben·e·fit *n.* an employee benefit, such as health insurance coverage, that is selected from a range of choices that are designed to meet different needs

caf·e·te·ri·a-style *adj.* allowing people to choose from a variety of different things

ca·fe·tière /kàffə tyáir, -téer/ *n.* U.K. = **French press pot** [Mid-19thC. From French, formed from *café* (see CAFÉ).]

caf·e·to·ri·um /kàffə táwree əm/ (*plural* **-ri·ums** /kàffə táwree əz/ *or* **-ria**) *n.* a large room, usually in school, that doubles as a cafeteria and an auditorium [Mid-20thC. Blend of CAFETERIA and AUDITORIUM.]

caf·fein·at·ed /káffə nàytəd/ *adj.* containing caffeine

caf·feine /ka féen, ká fèen/, **caf·fein** *n.* a stimulant found in coffee, tea, the cola nuts used to make soft drinks, and cocoa. It is widely used in medicine, e.g., in tonic medicines and painkillers. [Mid-19thC. From French, formed from *café* "coffee."]

caf·fein·ism /káffi nìzzəm, káffee ə nìzzəm/ *n.* a condition caused by an excessive amount of caffeine in the body, resulting in symptoms of high blood pressure, diarrhea, palpitations, accelerated breathing, and insomnia

caf·fé lat·te /kaá fe laá tè, ká fay laá tè/ *n.* = **latte**

caf·tan /káf tàn, káftən, kaf tán/, **kaf·tan** *n.* **1. MEN'S TUNIC** a full-length tunic or robe for men, usually made of rich fabric, worn chiefly in eastern Mediterranean countries **2. WESTERN GARMENT** a western imitation of the caftan, often brightly colored and worn by men and women. It was popular in the 1970s and is still associated with hippy culture. [Late 16thC. Via Turkish *kaftan* from Persian *kaftān*.]

cage /kayj/ *n.* **1. ANIMAL ENCLOSURE** an enclosure, usually made from bars or wire, in which to keep animals or birds **2. ENCLOSING OR PROTECTING WIRE-MESH STRUCTURE** a wire-mesh structure used to protect or enclose something **3. ELEVATOR PLATFORM** the part of an elevator that people stand in, particularly one in an elevator that goes down a mine shaft **4.** BASEBALL **SCREEN TO STOP BALLS** in baseball, a screen behind home plate that stops thrown or fouled balls **5.** BASKETBALL **BASKET** the basket in the game of basketball (*informal*) **6.** HOCKEY **HOCKEY GOAL** the goal in ice hockey (*informal*) **7. TEMPORARY PRISON CELL** a barred room or strong mesh enclosure for confining prisoners temporarily, e.g., in a police station ■ *vt.* (**caged, cag·ing, cag·es**) **1. PUT PERSON OR ANIMAL IN CAGE** to place or keep a person or animal in a cage **2. PUT IN CONFINING CONDITIONS** to confine a person or animal in conditions resembling those of a cage [12thC. Via Old French from Latin *cavea* "enclosure, dungeon" (source also of English *jail*).] —**caged** *adj.* ◇ **rattle somebody's cage** to annoy or upset somebody deliberately ○ *"We kept after him and kept after him and finally rattled his cage a little bit, he said."* (*Cincinnati Post*; 1997)

Cage, John (1912–92) U.S. composer. His avant-garde music includes *4'33"* (1952), in which musicians sit silently with their instruments. Full name **John Milton Cage, Jr.**

Cage, Nicholas (*b.* 1964) U.S. actor. He frequently plays offbeat movie characters such as his Academy Award-winning role in *Leaving Las Vegas* (1995).

cage·ling /káyjling/ *n.* a bird that is kept as a pet in a cage (*archaic or literary*)

ca·gey /káyjee/ (**-gi·er, -gi·est**), **ca·gy** (**-gi·er, -gi·est**) *adj.* cautious and secretive rather than open, honest, or direct (*informal*) [Late 19thC. Origin uncertain: perhaps formed from CAGE, the underlying idea being of keeping your intentions "locked away" in secret.] —**ca·gi·ly** *adv.* —**ca·gi·ness** *n.*

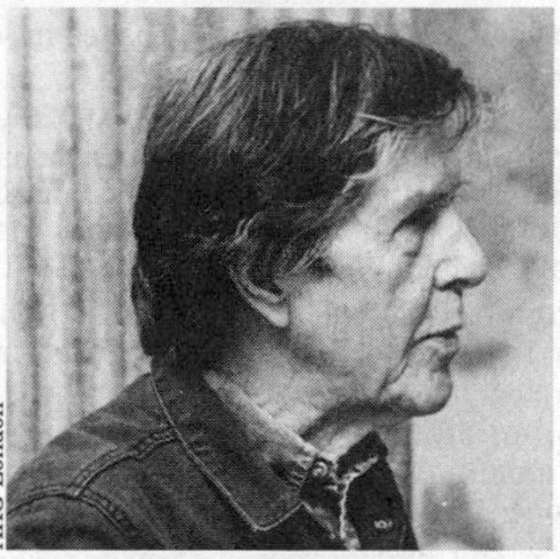

AKG London

John Cage

James Cagney

Cag·ney /kágnee/, **James** (1904–86) U.S. movie actor, known for both comic and tough gangster roles. Full name **James Francis Cagney**

Ca·guas /kaá gwaáss/ city in eastern Puerto Rico, south of San Juan and southeast of Bayamon. Population: 140,114 (1996).

Ca·ho·kia Mounds /kə hṓkee ə-/ group of prehistoric Native American mounds, including the largest prehistoric earthwork in the United States, situated 8 mi./13 km northeast of East St. Louis, Missouri.

ca·how /kə hów/ *n.* a large brown-and-white bird that burrows into the ground. It was formerly abundant in Bermuda, where it is still found, now near extinction. Latin name: *Pterodroma cahow.* [Early 17thC. An imitation of the sound of its call.]

CAI *abbr.* computer-aided instruction

Cai·a·phas /káy əfess kī́-/ (*fl.* A.D.18–37) Jewish high priest. He presided over the trial of Jesus Christ.

Cai·cos Is·lands /kī́kōss-/ ➧ **Turks and Caicos Islands**

cai·man /káymən/, **cay·man** *n.* a Central and South American reptile of the alligator family that looks like a much smaller slimmer version of the alligator with a proportionally longer tail. Genus: *Caiman.*

cai·man /káymən/ (*plural* **-mans** *or* **-man**), **cay·man** (*plural* **-mans** *or* **-man**) *n.* a tropical American reptile related to the alligator. It looks like a much smaller, slimmer version of the alligator with a proportionally longer tail. Genus: *Caiman.* [Late 16thC. Via Spanish *caimán* from Carib *caymán.*]

Cain /kayn/ *n.* in the Bible, the elder son of Adam and Eve, who killed his brother Abel (Genesis 4) ◇ **raise Cain** to cause a noisy disturbance

Caine, Michael (*b.* 1933) British actor. His films include *Zulu* (1963) and *Hannah and her Sisters* (1986), for which he won an Oscar. Real name **Maurice Joseph Micklewhite**

-caine *suffix.* a synthetic alkaloid anesthetic ○ *phenacaine* [From COCAINE]

ca·ïque /kaa eek, kīk/ *n.* **1.** TURKISH ROWBOAT a long narrow rowboat used in the waters around Turkey **2.** SMALL GREEK BOAT any small rowboat, sailboat, or motorboat used in the Greek Islands and the eastern Mediterranean [Early 17thC. Via French from, ultimately, Turkish *kayik.*]

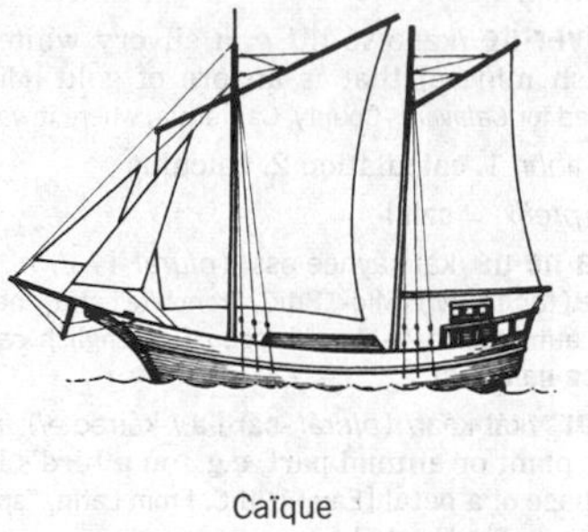

Caïque

caird /kaird/ *n.* *Scotland* a vagrant or a traveling tinker (*archaic*) [Mid-17thC. From Gaelic *ceard* "metal-worker."]

cairn /kairn/ *n.* **1.** PILE OF STONES USED AS MARKER a pile of stones set on a hill or mountain to mark a spot for walkers and climbers, or as a memorial to somebody who died there **2.** = **Cairn terrier** [Mid-16thC. From Gaelic *carn* "heap of stones." Ultimately from an Indo-European base that is also the ancestor of English *cornet* and *horn.*] —**cairned** *adj.*

cairn·gorm /káirn gàwrm/, **cairn·gorm stone** *n.* a variety of quartz, usually smoky yellow, gray, or brown in color, found in Scotland and used in making jewelry [Late 18thC. Named for the Cairngorm Mountains, in northeastern Scotland, where it is found.]

Cairn ter·ri·er /káirn-/ *n.* a small terrier with a shaggy coat of rough hair, originally bred in Scotland

Cai·ro /kī́ rō/ capital of Egypt and Africa's largest city. It is situated on the Nile River, at the southern end of the Nile delta. Population: 6,800,000 (1992).

caisse pop·u·laire /kèss poppyoŏ láir/ (*plural* **caisses pop·u·laires** /kèss poppyoŏ láir/) *n.* *Quebec* in Quebec and other French-speaking parts of Canada, a financial institution resembling a credit union [From French]

cais·son /káy sòn, káyss'n/ *n.* **1.** CONSTR UNDERWATER WORK CHAMBER a bottomless watertight chamber filled with compressed air, used as a base from which construction work is carried out underwater **2.** INSUR FLOAT TO RAISE SHIPS a hollow structure attached to a sunken object, e.g., a wrecked ship, then pumped full of air until it acts as a float, raising the object to the surface **3.** CIV ENG, INSUR WATER BLOCK a floating watertight structure used to keep water from entering a dry dock, canal lock, or basin **4.** ARMS AMMUNITION BOX a large container for ammunition **5.** MIL HORSE-DRAWN VEHICLE a two-wheeled horse-drawn vehicle, formerly used to carry ammunition but now often used to carry coffins at state or military funerals **6.** ARCHIT = **coffer** [Late 17thC. Via French from, ultimately, Italian *cassone* "large box," from *cassa* "box," from Latin *capsa* (source of English *case* and *capsule*).]

cais·son dis·ease *n.* = **decompression sickness**

cai·tiff /káytif/ *n.* COWARD a coward (*archaic*) ■ *adj.* COWARDLY cowardly and despicable (*archaic*) [13thC. Via Old French *caitif* "captive, wretched person" from Latin *captivus* (source of English *captive*) from, ultimately, *capere* "to take."]

ca·je·put /kájjə poŏt/ *n.* **1.** TREES FLOWERING TREE a small flowering tree or shrub of the myrtle family, native to the East Indies and Australia but now also naturalized in Florida. It yields a valuable oil. Latin name: *Melaleuca leucadendron.* **2.** PHARM MEDICINAL OIL a greenish oil obtained from the cajeput tree, with various medicinal uses [Late 18thC. From Malay *kayuputih*, literally "white tree."]

ca·jole /kə jṓl/ (**-joled, -jol·ing, -joles**) *vti.* to persuade somebody to do something by flattery or gentle but persistent argument [Mid-17thC. From French *cajoler*, of uncertain origin: perhaps a blend of Old French *cageoler* "to chatter like a jay" and *gaioler* "to lure into a cage."] —**ca·jole·ment** *n.* —**ca·jol·er** *n.* —**ca·jol·er·y** *n.*

Ca·jun /káyjən/ *n.* **1.** PEOPLES LOUISIANAN OF FRENCH DESCENT a native of Louisiana who is descended from the French colonists exiled from Acadia, Canada, in the 18th century **2.** LANG FRENCH DIALECT a dialect of French spoken in Louisiana that developed from the French spoken by 18th-century settlers who were expelled from Acadia, Canada [Mid-19thC. Alteration of *Acadian* "(inhabitant) of Acadia," a former French colony in North America.] —**Ca·jun** *adj.*

cake /kayk/ *n.* **1.** BAKED SWEET FLOUR-BASED FOOD a baked sweet food usually made from flour, sugar, eggs, and other ingredients **2.** SHAPED PORTION OF SAVORY FOOD an individual portion of savory food, shaped into a small round piece and cooked, often by frying or broiling **3.** BLOCK OF SOMETHING a solid block of something, e.g., soap, ice, or chocolate **4.** THICK LAYER a thick layer of something that has collected over a period of time **5.** THING DIVIDED UP something, e.g., an amount of money, that is to be shared or divided up ○ *Everyone wants a slice of the cake.* ■ *v.* (**caked, cak·ing, cakes**) **1.** *vti.* FORM CRUST ON SOMETHING to form, or cover an object with, a thick layer of something, especially dirt, grease, or grime ○ *My boots were caked with mud after I walked through the field.* **2.** *vi.* FORM INTO A CAKE to form into a solid mass [12thC. From Old Norse *kaka* "flat round loaf."] —**cak·ey** *adj.* ◇ **have your cake and eat it (too)** to try to enjoy the advantages of two things, each of which tends to make the other impossible ◇ **take the cake 1.** to be even worse than all the other bad or annoying things that went before (*informal*) **2.** to be outstandingly good or successful (*informal*)

cake·walk /káyk wàwk/ *n.* **1.** COMPETITION BASED ON WALKING an informal contest to music, with a cake as a prize for executing the most elaborate or amusing walking steps, popular among African Americans in the United States in the 19th century **2.** SOMETHING VERY EASY something that is very easy to do or to achieve (*informal*) **3.** DANCE STRUTTING DANCE any kind of popular dancing with exaggeratedly elaborate or strutting steps **4.** MUSIC MUSIC FOR CAKEWALK a piece of music suitable for any kind of elaborate strutting dance ■ *vi.* (**-walked, -walk·ing, -walks**) DANCE DANCE WITH STRUTTING STEPS to dance with exaggeratedly fancy strutting steps —**cake·walk·er** *n.*

cal, Cal *abbr.* MEASURE mean calorie

CAL[1] *abbr.* **1.** TIME calendar **2.** MEASURE caliber

CAL[2] *abbr.* computer-assisted learning

Cal. *abbr.* California

Cal·a·bar bean /kállə baar-/ *n.* the dark brown poisonous seed, used as a source of the drug physostigmine, of a tropical African climbing plant. Latin name: *Physostigma venenosum.* [Named for *Calabar*, a town and province in Nigeria]

cal·a·bash /kállə bàsh/ *n.* **1.** TROPICAL AMERICAN EVERGREEN TREE a tropical American evergreen tree with bell-shaped flowers and large round fruit. Latin name: *Crescentia cujete.* **2.** = **bottle gourd 3.** FRUIT OF CALABASH PLANT the large ball-shaped fruit of the calabash tree, or of the bottle gourd or some other gourd **4.** GOURD USED AS CONTAINER the hollowed-out dried shell of the calabash fruit or of the bottle gourd or some other gourd, used as a container [Mid-17thC. Via French *calabasse* from, ultimately, Persian *karbuz* "melon."]

Cal·a·bash /kállə bàsh/ *n.* a way of preparing food in the southeastern United States that involves deep-frying seafoods and piling them up on serving plates [Origin uncertain: perhaps from *Calabash*, name of a town in North Carolina where the style was developed]

cal·a·boose /kállə bōoss/ *n.* *Southwest U.S.* a jail (*informal*) [Late 18thC. From Louisiana French *calabouse*, via Spanish *calabozo* "dungeon" from assumed Vulgar Latin *calafodium*, from assumed *cala* "protected place" + Latin *fodere* "to dig."]

WORD KEY: CULTURAL NOTE

Calaboose in the sense of a local jail is common across the South and West, with a few instances in the Northeast.

cal·a·bre·se /kàllə bráyzee/ *n.* a variety of green broccoli [Mid-20thC. From Italian, "of Calabria," where it was developed.]

Ca·la·bri·a /kə láybree ə, kə laábree ə/ region in southern Italy forming the "toe" of the Italian peninsula. It includes the provinces of Cataranzo, Cosenza, and Reggio di Calabria. Capital: Catanzaro. Population: 2,076,128 (1995). Area: 5,822 sq. mi./15,080 sq. km.

ca·la·di·um /kə láydee əm/ *n.* tropical American plant with white, green, red, or pink variegated leaves, widely grown as a potted plant. Genus: *Caladium.* [Mid-19thC. From modern Latin, formed from Malay *keladi.*]

Ca·lais /ká lày, ka láy/ seaport on the English Channel in the Pas-de-Calais Department, Nord-Pas-de-Calais region, in northwestern France. The Calais-Dover route is the shortest crossing between France and the United Kingdom. Population: 101,768 (1990).

ca·la·lu /kállə lōo/, **ca·la·loo** *n.* *Carib* the leaves of various plants when used as salad, in soups, or cooked as greens [Mid-18thC. From American Spanish *calalú*, perhaps from, ultimately, an African source.]

cal·a·man·co /kàllə mángkō/ *n.* a glossy woolen fabric with a checked pattern on one side [Late 16thC. Origin unknown.]

cal·a·man·der /kállə màndər/ *n.* the hard black-and-brown striped wood of a number of Asian trees, used for making furniture [Early 19thC. From Sinhalese *kalumādirriya,* perhaps from *kalu* "black" + English *coromandel* "ebony."]

ca·la·ma·ri /kaàlə maàree, kàllə maàree/ *npl.* squid served as food, especially in Mediterranean cuisine [Late 20thC. From Italian, plural of *calamaro* "squid," via medieval Latin *calamarium* "pen-case" (so called from the shape of the squid's internal shell) from Latin *calamus* "reed pen" (see CALAMUS).]

cal·a·mi plural of **calamus**

cal·a·mine /kállə mīn, kálləmin/ *n.* **1. SOOTHING PINK POWDER** a pink powder made from zinc oxide and ferric oxide, used medicinally in lotions and creams to soothe irritated skin **2.** = **smithsonite** [Late 16thC. Via Old French from medieval Latin *calamina,* an alteration of Latin *cadmia* "zinc ore" (see CADMIUM).]

cal·a·mint /kállə mìnt/ (*plural* **-mints** *or* **-mint**) *n.* a mint plant grown for its drooping white, pink, or purple flowers. Genera: *Satureja* and *Calamintha.* [14thC. Via Old French *calament* (perhaps influenced by English *mint*) from, ultimately, Greek *kalaminthē.*]

cal·a·mite /kállə mīt/ *n.* a prehistoric plant that grew in the Paleozoic era, related to the horsetail. Genus: *Calamites.* [Mid-19thC. From modern Latin *calamites,* genus name, from Latin *calamus* (see CALAMUS).]

ca·lam·i·tous /kə lámmitəss/ *adj.* causing great trouble, tragedy, or disaster [Mid-16thC. Directly or via French *calamiteux* from Latin *calamitosus,* from *calamitas* (see CALAMITY).] —**ca·lam·i·tous·ly** *adv.*

ca·lam·i·ty /kə lámmitee/ (*plural* **-ties**) *n.* **1. DISASTER** a disastrous situation or event (*often used ironically*) **2. DISTRESS** misery or distress resulting from a disastrous event (*archaic*) [14thC. Via Old French *calamité* from Latin *calamitas* "disaster, defeat." Originally used in English with the meaning "adversity."]

Library of Congress
Calamity Jane

Ca·lam·i·ty Jane /kə làmmiti jáyn/ (1852?–1903) U.S. frontierswoman. She worked as a scout in the American West. Real name **Martha Jane Canary**

cal·a·mon·din /kállə móndin/ *n.* **1. SMALL CITRUS TREE OF PHILIPPINES** a hybrid citrus tree native to the Philippines. Latin name: *Citrofortunella mitis.* **2. FRUIT OF CALAMONDIN** the small tart orange-yellow fruit of a calamondin tree [Early 20thC. From Tagalog *kalamunding.*]

cal·a·mus /kálləməss/ (*plural* **-mi** /-mī/) *n.* **1. ASIAN PALM** a tropical Asian palm tree, some species of which are used for rattan. Genus: *Calamus.* **2.** = **sweet flag 3. ROOT OF SWEET FLAG** the aromatic root of the sweet flag plant, the source of an aromatic oil used in perfumery **4. FEATHER SHAFT** the hollow shaft of a feather [14thC. Via Latin from Greek *kalamos* "reed, pen."]

ca·lan·do /kə laàndō/ *adv., adj.* played with gradually decreasing volume and slowing tempo (*used as a musical direction*) [Early 19thC. From Italian, literally "slackening."]

ca·lan·dri·a /kə lándree ə/ *n.* the cylindrical core of a nuclear reactor with vertical holes [Early 20thC. From Spanish, formed from Greek *kylindros* "cylinder" (source of English *cylinder*).]

cal·a·the·a /kàllə theé ə/ *n.* a tropical South American evergreen plant with showy variegated leaves, widely grown as a greenhouse and potted plant. Genus: *Calathea.* [From modern Latin, formed from Greek *kalathos* (see CALATHUS)]

cal·a·thus /kálləthəss/ (*plural* **-thi** /-thī/) *n.* a vase-shaped basket full of fruit that often appears in ancient Greek and Egyptian art as a symbol of fruitfulness [Mid-18thC. Via Latin from Greek *kalathos* "basket."]

cal·a·ver·ite /kàllə vé rīt/ *n.* a silvery white or yellowish mineral that is an ore of gold [Mid-19thC. Named for *Calaveras* County, California, where it was found.]

calc. *abbr.* **1.** calculation **2.** calculus

calc- *prefix.* = **calci-**

cal·ca·ne·us /kal káynee əss/ (*plural* **-i** /-ī/) *n.* the heel bone (*technical*) [Mid-18thC. From late Latin, "heel," from the Latin stem *calc-* "heel" (source of English *caulk*).] —**cal·ca·ne·al** *adj.*

cal·car[1] /kál kaàr/ (*plural* **-car·i·a** /-káiree ə/) *n.* a spur on a plant or animal part, e.g., on a bird's leg or at the base of a petal [Early 19thC. From Latin, "spur," from the stem *calc-* "heel."]

cal·car[2] /kál kaàr/ *n.* a furnace formerly used in glassmaking for burning materials to make frit, the viscous substance from which glass is subsequently made [Mid-17thC. From Italian *calcara.*]

cal·car·e·ous /kal káiree əss/ *adj.* **1. OF CALCIUM CARBONATE** containing or characteristic of calcium carbonate **2.** BOT **GROWING IN LIMESTONE CONDITIONS** growing on limestone or in earth containing limestone ○ *calcareous algae* [Late 17thC. Formed from Latin *calcarius* "of lime," from the stem *calc-* "lime" (source of English *chalk*).] —**cal·car·e·ous·ly** *adv.*

cal·car·i·a plural of **calcar**

cal·car·if·er·ous /kàlkə ríffərəss/ *adj.* used to describe a plant or animal part that has a spur on it [Mid-19thC. Coined from Latin *calcar* (see CALCAR[1]) + -IFEROUS.]

cal·ce·o·lar·i·a /kàlsee ə láiree ə/ *n.* a tropical American plant with speckled slipper-shaped flowers. Genus: *Calceolaria.* [Late 18thC. From modern Latin, genus name, from Latin *calceolus* "little shoe."]

Cal·chas /kál kàss/ *n.* in Greek mythology, a soothsayer who accompanied the Greeks during the Trojan War, advising them, among other things, to build the Trojan Horse

calci- *prefix.* CHEM calcium, calcium salt, lime ○ *calcific* [From Latin *calc-,* the stem of *calx* "lime" (see CALX)]

cal·cic /kálsik/ *adj.* containing, derived from, or relating to calcium or lime

cal·cif·er·ol /kal síffə rōl, kal síffə ròl/ *n.* = **vitamin** D_2 (*technical*) [Mid-20thC. Coined from CALCIFEROUS + -OL.]

cal·cif·er·ous /kal síffərəss/ *adj.* producing or containing calcium carbonate or other calcium salts [Late 18thC. Coined from CALCI- + -FEROUS.]

cal·cif·ic /kal síffik/ *adj.* producing lime salts, or involved in their production [Mid-19thC. Coined from CALCI- + -FIC.]

cal·ci·fi·ca·tion /kàlsəfi káysh'n/ *n.* **1.** CHEM **CONVERSION INTO LIME** the conversion of a substance into lime **2.** MED **ABNORMAL HARDENING** the abnormal hardening or stiffening of a body part caused by deposits of calcium salts **3.** MED **HARD BODY PART** a body part that has become hardened or stiffened by calcification **4. LACK OF CHANGE** a condition in which improvement, change, or progress ceases (*formal*)

cal·ci·fuge /kálsə fyooj/ *n.* plant that prefers an acidic soil, or will not grow in chalky soil [Mid-19thC. Coined from CALCI- + -FUGE.] —**cal·cif·u·gal** /kal síffyəg'l/ *adj.* —**cal·cif·u·gous** /-gəss/ *adj.*

cal·ci·fy /kálsə fī/ (**-fied, -fy·ing, -fies**) *vti.* **1.** CHEM **TURN INTO LIME** to convert a substance into lime, or be converted into lime **2.** MED **TURN HARD WITH CALCIUM** to become, or cause a body part to become, abnormally hard or stiff as a result of the deposit of calcium salts **3. BECOME RIGID AND UNCHANGING** to become, or cause something to become, rigid and unchanging (*formal*)

cal·ci·mine /kálsə mīn/ *n.* **COATING FOR INTERIOR WALLS** a mixture of zinc oxide, water, and glue, sometimes with a coloring added, brushed onto interior walls as a decorative and sealing finish ■ *vt.* (**-mined, -min·ing, -mines**) **COAT WALL WITH CALCIMINE** to cover a wall with calcimine [Mid-19thC. Alteration of KALSOMINE, influenced by *calci-.*]

cal·cine /kal sín, kál sīn/ (**-cined, -cin·ing, -cines**) *vti.* to heat a solid to a high temperature, converting it to a powdery residue by drying, decomposing, or oxidizing it, or to undergo this process [14thC. From medieval Latin *calcinare* "to burn until like lime," from, ultimately, the Latin stem *calc-* "lime" (see CALCIUM).] —**cal·ci·na·tion** /kàlsə náysh'n/ *n.*

cal·ci·no·sis /kàlsə nṓssiss/ *n.* a medical condition in which nodules of calcium are deposited in soft body tissues

cal·cite /kál sīt/ *n.* a colorless or white crystalline mineral that is a form of calcium carbonate. It is the main constituent of limestone, marble, and chalk and is used in cement, plaster, glass, and paints. Formula: $CaCO_3$. —**cal·cit·ic** /kal síttik/ *adj.*

cal·ci·to·nin /kàlsi tṓnin/ *n.* a hormone, produced by the thyroid and parathyroid glands, that increases the deposition of calcium in bones

cal·cit·ri·ol[1] /kálsə treé òl/ *n.* BIOCHEM the active form of Vitamin D that functions as a steroid hormone [Late 20thC. Origin uncertain; probably formed from CALCIUM + TRIOL.]

cal·cit·ri·ol[2] /kálsə treé òl/ *n.* PHARM a drug used to control or reverse bone loss from diseases such as rickets and kidney dysfunction

cal·ci·um /kálsee əm/ *n.* a soft silver-white element that is an alkaline earth metal constituting about three percent of the earth's crust. It is essential to the formation of bones and teeth. Symbol **Ca** [Early 19thC. Coined from Latin *calc-,* the stem of *calx* "lime" (see CALX) + -IUM.]

cal·ci·um a·cet·y·lide *n.* = **calcium carbide**

cal·ci·um an·tag·o·nist *n.* a drug used to treat angina by widening the arteries and slowing the heart. The drug restricts the normal movement of calcium ions through the muscle tissue of the artery walls and heart.

cal·ci·um car·bide *n.* a colorless or grayish-black powdery compound used in the generation of acetylene gas for welding. Formula: CaC_2.

cal·ci·um car·bon·ate *n.* a white crystalline solid that is one of the most common natural substances, forming chalk, limestone, and marble, and occurs in animal shells and bones. It is a constituent of antacids for indigestion, paint, cement, and toothpaste. Formula: $CaCO_3$.

cal·ci·um chan·nel block·er *n.* = **calcium antagonist**

cal·ci·um chlo·ride *n.* a white salt that absorbs moisture easily and quickly, and is used for drying gases, deicing roads, and also in pulp and paper treatment. Formula: $CaCl_2$.

cal·ci·um cy·an·am·ide *n.* a white or grayish-black crystalline compound that releases ammonia slowly in the presence of water and is used as a fertilizer. Formula: $CaCN_2$.

cal·ci·um cy·a·nide *n.* a white or grayish-black powder that decomposes in humid conditions to give hydrogen cyanide and was formerly used as an insecticide and rodent poison and in fumigation. Formula: $Ca(CN)_2$.

cal·ci·um cy·cla·mate *n.* a sweet-tasting salt of cyclamic acid formerly used as a sugar substitute. Formula: $Ca(C_6H_{11}NHSO_3)_2.2H_2O$.

cal·ci·um fluo·ride *n.* a colorless or white substance occurring naturally as fluorite. Formula: CaF_2.

cal·ci·um glu·co·nate *n.* a calcium salt used as a medication in cases of calcium deficiency and osteoporosis and as a mineral supplement. Formula: $CaC_{12}H_{22}O_{14}$.

cal·ci·um hy·drox·ide *n.* a white alkaline powder derived from the action of water on calcium oxide, used to treat acid soil and in the manufacture of cement, plaster, and glass. Formula: $Ca(OH)_2$.

cal·ci·um hy·po·chlo·rite *n.* a white crystalline solid, soluble in water, that is a stable chlorine carrier used as a bleaching agent, disinfectant, and bactericide. Formula: $Ca(OCl)_2$.

cal·ci·um light *n.* = **limelight**

cal·ci·um ni·trate *n.* a white solid that absorbs moisture very quickly, is a strong oxidizer, and is used as a fertilizer and in some explosives. Formula: $Ca(NO_3)_2.4H_2O$.

cal·ci·um ox·ide *n.* a white crystalline powder used in the manufacture of steel and glass, the refining of aluminum, copper, and zinc, and sewage treatment. Formula: CaO.

cal·ci·um phos·phate *n.* any of several phosphates of calcium that occur naturally in rocks and animal bones and are used, in the form of bone ash, as a fertilizer

cal·crete /kál kreet/ *n.* an accumulation in the soil of a layer of calcium carbonate and other alkaline minerals just below the surface [Early 20thC. Coined from CALC- + *(con)crete*.]

calc·spar /kálk spaàr/ *n.* = **calcite** [Early 19thC. Coined from the Latin stem *calc-* "lime" (see CALCIUM) + SPAR.]

calc·tu·fa *n.* = **tufa** [Early 19thC. Coined from the Latin stem *calc-* "lime" (see CALCIUM) + TUFA.]

cal·cu·la·ble /kálkyələb'l/ *adj.* **1. ABLE TO BE CALCULATED** able to be worked out or estimated, using mathematics **2. PREDICTABLE** likely to behave in the way that is expected —**cal·cu·la·bil·i·ty** /kàlkyələ bíllətee/ *n.*

cal·cu·late /kálkyə làyt/ (**-lat·ed, -lat·ing, -lates**) *v.* **1.** *vti.* MATH **WORK OUT MATHEMATICALLY** to figure out or estimate a figure using mathematics **2.** *vti.* **DECIDE** to consider a situation carefully and decide what is likely to happen **3.** *vt.* **THINK OR SUPPOSE SOMETHING** to think or suppose that a particular thing is the case (*regional*) ○ *I calculate he'll never make a farmer.* **4.** *vi.* **INTEND** to be planning or intending to do a particular thing (*regional*) ○ *We were calculating on going home around midnight.* [Late 16thC. From late Latin *calculat-* "to calculate," past participle stem of *calulare* from, ultimately, Latin *calculus* "pebble" (see CALCULUS).]

cal·cu·lat·ed /kálkyə làytəd/ *adj.* **1. CAREFULLY CONSIDERED** done or accepted after careful consideration of the possible results **2. DELIBERATE** planned or deliberate —**cal·cu·lat·ed·ly** *adv.* —**cal·cu·lat·ed·ness** *n.*

cal·cu·lat·ing /kálkyə làyting/ *adj.* **1. SCHEMING** determined to gain the greatest personal advantage **2. SHOWING SOMEBODY'S SCHEMING NATURE** indicative of somebody's scheming nature **3.** making careful assessments before acting ○ *a calculating candidate who carefully preplanned all statements to the media* —**cal·cu·lat·ing·ly** *adv.*

cal·cu·la·tion /kàlkyə láysh'n/ *n.* **1.** MATH **PROCESS OF CALCULATING SOMETHING** the process, or a step in the process, of working out the answer to a mathematical problem **2. ESTIMATE** an estimate or answer obtained by calculating **3. DELIBERATENESS** consideration of something, especially when thinking of personal advantage —**cal·cu·la·tion·al** *adj.* —**cal·cu·la·tive** *adj.*

Calculator

cal·cu·la·tor /kálkyə làytər/ *n.* a device used to compute arithmetic operations, especially a small hand-held electronic device

cal·cu·lous /kálkyələss/ *adj.* relating to abnormal hard formations of minerals (**calculi**) in the body

cal·cu·lus /kálkyələss/ *n.* (*plural* **-li** /kálkyə lī/ *or* **-lus·es**) **1.** MATH **BRANCH OF MATHEMATICS** a branch of mathematics dealing with the way that relations between certain sets (**functions**) are affected by very small changes in one of their variables (**independent variable**) as they approach zero. It is used to find slopes of curves, rates of change, and volumes of curved figures. ◊ **differential calculus, integral calculus 2.** MATH, LOGIC **METHOD OF CALCULATION** a method or system of calculation using symbols or symbolic logic **3.** MED **STONE** a stone or concretion, especially one in the kidney, gallbladder, or urinary bladder (*technical*) **4.** DENT = **tartar** ■ **NONMATHEMATICAL DECISION-MAKING CRITERIA** a nonmathematical evaluation, estimation or computation, e.g., in short- or long-term decision-making or strategy formulation ○ *"Democrats win points in this calculus."* (*U.S. News and World Report*; 1998) [Mid-17thC. From Latin, "pebble," a diminutive of *calx* "lime, limestone" (see CALX).]

Cal·cut·ta /kal kúttə/ capital of West Bengal state and one of India's largest cities. It is a major commercial and industrial city and port, situated on the Hoogly River, an arm of the Ganges about 60 mi./100 km from its mouth at the Bay of Bengal. Population: 11,021,915 (metropolitan area) (1991).

cal·da·ri·um /kal dáiree əm/ (*plural* **-a** /-ə/) *n.* the hot room in an ancient Roman bathhouse [Mid-18thC. Via Latin from, ultimately, *calere* "to be warm" (source of English *calorie*).]

AKG London

Alexander Young Calder

Cal·der /káwldər/, **Alexander Young** (1898–1976) U.S. painter and sculptor, known for his abstract sculptures, especially mobiles and stabiles.

cal·de·ra /kal dáirə/ (*plural* **-ras**) *n.* a large crater in a volcano, caused by a major eruption followed by the collapse of the volcanic pipe walls that form the volcano's cone. It may later contain a lake. [Late 17thC. Via Spanish from late Latin *caldaria* "cooking pot," formed from Latin *caldus* "warm."]

Cal·der·dale /káwldər dàyl/ local government unitary authority in northern England, established 1997. Capital: Halifax is the administrative center. Population: 193,200 (1995).

Cal·dey Is·land /káwldi-/ island off the coast of Pembrokeshire, Wales, and location of a Cistercian monastery. Welsh **Ynys Pyr**

cal·dron /káwldrən/, **caul·dron** *n.* **1. POT FOR BOILING** a large metal pot in which liquids are boiled **2. DANGEROUS AND TENSE SITUATION** a situation of great tension, unrest, and stressfulness ○ *"He is heading into a caldron in the House of Representatives."* (*U.S. News & World Report*; 1998) [13thC. Via Anglo-Norman and Old Norman French *caudron* from late Latin *calderia* "cooking pot," from, ultimately, Latin *calidus* "hot."]

Cald·well /káwld wèl, -wəl/ city in southwestern Idaho, on the southern bank of the Boise River, west of Boise. Population: 21,089 (1996).

Cald·well, Erskine (1903–87) U.S. writer. His novels about rural poverty include *Tobacco Road* (1932). Full name **Erskine Preston Caldwell**

Cald·well, Janet Taylor (1900–85) British-born U.S. writer. She is known for her novels about family dynasties, including *Dynasty of Death* (1938).

Cald·well, Sarah (*b.* 1928) U.S. conductor and opera producer, associated with the Boston Opera Company, and known for unusual opera productions.

Cal·e·do·ni·a /kàllə dṓnee ə/ Roman name for the northern part of Britain and poetic name for Scotland

Cal·e·do·ni·an /kàllə dṓnee ən/ *adj.* **1. OF SCOTLAND** relating to or typical of Scotland or its people or culture (*literary*) **2. OF PALEOZOIC EUROPE** relating to the Paleozoic era in northwestern Europe, when many mountains were formed ■ *n.* **SCOT** a Scottish person (*literary*)

cal·en·dar /kálləndər/ *n.* **1. SYSTEM OF CALCULATING YEAR** a system of calculating the days and months of the year and when the year begins and ends **2. CHART OF YEAR** a chart showing the days and months of the year, especially a particular year **3. TIMETABLE** a timetable of events, usually covering a period of a year **4. LIST** an official list of things to be done or considered ■ *vt.* (**-dared, -dar·ing, -dars**) **SCHEDULE** to enter something in a calendar or diary [12thC. Via Anglo-Norman *calender* from Latin *calendarium* "moneylender's account book," from *calendae* "first day of the month."] —**ca·len·dri·cal** /kə léndrik'l/ *adj.*

cal·en·dar day *n.* the period of 24 hours from midnight to midnight

cal·en·dar month *n.* **1.** = **month** *n.* 1 **2.** = **month** *n.* 3

cal·en·dar year *n.* **1. JANUARY 1 TO DECEMBER 31** the period of 365 or 366 days from January 1 to December 31 **2. UNTIL SAME DATE NEXT YEAR** the period of time between a date in one year and the same date in the next

cal·en·der /kálləndər/ *n.* **ROLLERS FOR TREATING PAPER, CLOTH, ETC** a machine with rollers used to form thin sheets from paper, plastic, or other material, or to impart a desired surface finish ■ *vt.* (**-dered, -der·ing, -ders**) **PASS THROUGH CALENDER** to give the required thickness or surface finish to a material by pulling it through a calender [Early 16thC. Via French *calendre* from assumed Vulgar Latin *colondra*, an alteration (influenced by Latin *columna* "column") of Latin *cylindrus* "roller" (source of English *cylinder*).] —**cal·en·der·er** *n.*

ca·len·dri·cal /kə léndrik'l/ *adj.* relating to a calendar, or to calendars

cal·ends /kálləndz, káyləndz/, **kal·ends** *npl.* the first day of the month in the ancient Roman calendar [14thC. Via French *calendes* from Latin *calendae* "first day of the month."]

ca·len·du·la /kə lénjələ/ (*plural* **-las** *or* **-la**) *n.* a garden plant of the daisy family with bright orange or yellow flowers that have traditionally been used in cooking or for medical purposes. Latin name: *Calendula officinalis.* [Late 16thC. From modern Latin, formed from Latin *calendae* "first day of the month" (see CALENDS). From its use in treating menstrual disorders.]

cal·en·ture /kállən choor/ *n.* a fever occurring in tropical regions, formerly believed to be caused by heat [Late 16thC. Via French from Spanish *calentura*, from, ultimately, Latin *calere* "to be warm" (source of English *calorie*).]

calf[1] /kaf/ (*plural* **calves** /kavz/) *n.* **1. YOUNG COW OR BULL** a very young cow or bull of domestic cattle **2. YOUNG ANIMAL** the young of some other animals besides the cow, including the elephant, whale, giraffe, and buffalo **3.** = **calfskin 4. PIECE OF ICEBERG** a large piece of ice that has broken away from an iceberg [Old English *cælf*. Ultimately from a prehistoric Germanic word that is also the ancestor of German *Kalb* and Old Norse *kalfr.*] ◇ **kill the fatted calf** to have a great celebration in honor of somebody, usually a family member who has been absent for some time

calf[2] /kaf/ (*plural* **calves** /kavz/) *n.* the fleshy part at the back of the leg below the knee [14thC. From Old Norse *kálfi*, of uncertain origin.]

calf·skin /káf skìn/ *n.* **1. LEATHER** fine leather made from the skin of calves **2. SKIN OF CALF** the skin of a calf

Cal·ga·ry /kálgəree/ city in southern Alberta, Canada. It is an important center for transportation, finance, and the petroleum industry. Population: 821,628 (1996).

Cal·houn /kal hoón/, **John Caldwell** (1782–1850) U.S. Vice President. He served (1825–32) under John Quincy Adams and Andrew Jackson.

Ca·li /kaàlee/ capital of Valle de Cauca Department and second largest city in Colombia. It is situated on the Cali River in western Colombia. Population: 1,718,871 (1995).

cal·i·ber /kállibər/ *n.* **1. ABILITY** a person's ability, intelligence, or character ○ *We don't often get candidates of her caliber.* **2.** ARMS **BORE OF FIREARM** the inner diameter of a pipe or cylinder, especially the barrel of a firearm **3.** ARMS **SIZE OF BULLET** the external diameter of a projectile, e.g., a bullet or a shell [Mid-16thC. Via French *calibre* from, ultimately, Arabic *ḳālib* "mold," which is in turn ultimately from Greek *kalapous* "shoemaker's last."]

cal·i·brate /kálli bràyt/ (**-brat·ed, -brat·ing, -brates**) *vt.* **1.** MEASURE **MARK SCALE ON SOMETHING** to establish and mark the units shown on a measuring instrument **2.** MEASURE **ENSURE ACCURACY OF SOMETHING** to test and adjust the accuracy of a measuring instrument or process **3.** ARMS **MEASURE BORE OF SOMETHING** to measure the internal diameter of a gun or cylinder —**cal·i·bra·tor** *n.*

cal·i·bra·tion /kàlli bráysh'n/ *n.* **1. STANDARDIZATION OF MEASURING INSTRUMENT** the checking of a measuring instrument against an accurate standard to determine any deviation and correct for errors **2. MARK ON SCALE** a mark showing one of the units of measurement on a measuring instrument

cal·i·bre *n.* U.K. = **caliber**

ca·li·ces plural of **calix**

ca·li·che /kə leéchee/ *n.* **1. LAYER OF CLAY OR SAND** a layer of clay or sand containing minerals, e.g., sodium nitrate and sodium chloride, found in arid regions

CALENDARS AND FESTIVALS

The Gregorian calendar was introduced in 1582 by Pope Gregory XIII, replacing the Julian calendar, and is based on a solar year of 365 days plus an extra day every four years (the leap year) and in centenary years evenly divisible by 400. The other calendars shown are based on lunar months. Each Hindu month is divided in two equal parts: krsna-paksa and sukla-paksa. Both the Hindu and the Jewish calendars are adjusted at intervals to the solar year. The Islamic calendar is not adjusted to the solar year so advances through the solar year on a 32.5 year cycle. The first month of each calendar is marked with a 1.

Gregorian calendar	Jewish calendar	Hindu calendar	Islamic calendar
	Tevet *29 days*	Pausa	
1 January *31 days*	Shevat *30 days*	Magha	1 Muharram *30 days*
February *28 days* [1]	Adar *29 days* [2]	1 Phalguna	Safar *29 days*
March *31 days*	Nisan *30 days*	Caitra	Rabi I *30 days*
April *30 days*	Iyar *29 days*	Vaisakha	Rabi II *29 days*
May *31 days*	Sivan *30 days*	Jyaistha	Jumada I *30 days*
June *30 days*	Tammuz *29 days*	Asadha	Jumada II *29 days*
July *31 days*	Av *30 days*	Sravana	Rajab *30 days*
August *31 days*	1 Elul *29 days*	Bhadrapada	Shaban *29 days*
September *30 days*	Tishri *30 days*	Asvina	Ramadan *30 days*
October *31 days*	Heshvan *29 days* [3]	Kartika	Shawwal *29 days*
November *30 days*	Kislev *29 days* [4]	Margasirsa	Dhu'l-Qadah *30 days*
December *31 days*	Tevet	Pausa	Dhu'l-Hijjah *29 days* [5]

Christian festivals	Jewish festivals	Hindu festivals	Islamic festivals
Annunciation *25 March*	Hanukkah *25 Kislev for eight days*	Dassera *First half of Asvina*	Ashura *10 Muharram*
Ascension *40 days after Easter*	Passover *14 Nisan for seven days*	Diwali *Second half of Asvina*	Id al-Adha *10 Dhu'l-Qadah to 1 Dhu'l-Hijjah*
Christmas *25 December: Roman Catholic and Protestant churches* *6 January: Eastern Orthodox churches*	Purim *14 Adar*	Ganesa caturthi *4 sukla paksa of Bhadrapada*	Id al-Fitr *1 Shawwal*
Easter *First Sunday after the full moon of the vernal equinox*	Rosh Hashanah *1 and 2 Tishri*	Holi *Sukla-paksa of Phalguna*	Isra wa al-Miraj *27 Rajab*
Epiphany *6 January*	Shabuoth *6 Sivan*	Krsna-jayanti *8 krsna-paksa of Sravana*	Laylat al-Baraah *15 Shaban*
Pentecost *50 days after Easter*	Sukkot *15 Tishri for eight or nine days*	Rakhi bandham *Full moon of Sravana*	Laylat al-Qadr *27 Ramadan*
Transfiguration *6 August*	Yom Kippur *10 Tishri*	Siva-ratri *13 krsna-paksa of Magha*	Mawlid al-Nabi *12 Rabi I*
Trinity *First Sunday after Pentecost*			Ras al-Am *1 Muharram*
			Ramadan

Notes

1. February has 29 days in a leap year.
2. The intercalary month Adar Sheni (29 days) is added every 3 years to adjust the Jewish calendar to the solar year.
3. The month Heshvan has 30 days in some years.
4. The month Kislev has 30 days in some years.
5. The month Dhu'l-Hijjah has 30 days in some years.

Calendar

of South America **2.** = **calcrete** [Mid-19thC. From American Spanish.]

cal·i·co /kálli kō/ (*plural* **-coes**) *n.* **1. BRIGHT COTTON CLOTH** a coarse cotton cloth with a bright printed pattern **2.** *U.K.* **WHITE COTTON CLOTH** a white or unbleached cotton cloth **3. ANIMAL WITH BLOTCHED COAT** an animal with a blotched coat, usually white with black and reddish patches [Mid-16thC. Alteration of *Calicut*, former name of a city and port on the southwestern coast of India (now Kozhikode), from which such cloth was exported.]

cal·i·co bass *n.* = **black crappie**

cal·i·co bush *n.* = **mountain laurel**

cal·i·co moth *n.* a with orange and white markings, sometimes seen migrating in large swarms. Genus: *Utetheisa.*

ca·lif *n.* = **caliph**

Calif. *abbr.* California

ca·lif·ate *n.* = **caliphate**

Cal·i·for·nia /kàlli fáwrnyə/ the most populous U.S. state, bordered by the Pacific Ocean, Oregon, Nevada, Arizona, and Mexico. Capital: Sacramento. Population: 32,268,301 (1997). Area: 158,869 sq. mi./411,469 sq. km. —**Cal·i·for·nian** *n., adj.*

Cal·i·for·ni·a, Gulf of arm of the Pacific Ocean that extends northward between mainland Mexico and Baja California. Area: 59,000 sq. mi./152,810 sq. km. Alternate name **Sea of Cortes**

Cal·i·for·nia bay *n.* = **California laurel**

Cal·i·for·nia con·dor *n.* a large dark gray or brown vulture of the southeastern United States, with a wingspan of about 10 ft./3 m and a naked head and neck. It is being rescued from extinction by a captive breeding program. Latin name: *Gymnogyps californianus.*

Cal·i·for·ni·a Cur·rent current in northern Pacific Ocean. It flows from north to south along the western coast of North America before turning west.

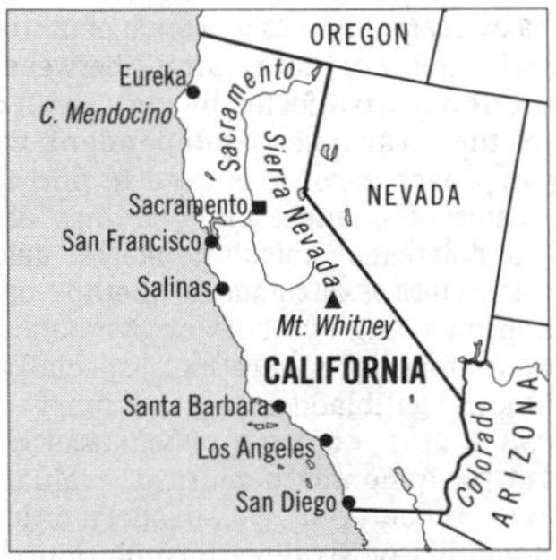

California

Cal·i·for·nia lau·rel *n.* an evergreen tree of the laurel family native to the West Coast of the United States, with clusters of small greenish flowers and small green or purple fruits. Latin name: *Umbellularia californica.*

Cal·i·for·nia pop·py, **Cal·i·for·nian pop·py** *n.* an annual plant with bluish divided leaves, commonly cultivated for its bright red to yellow flowers. It is the California state flower. Latin name: *Eschscholzia californica.*

cal·i·for·nite /kàlli fáwr nīt/ *n.* a compact form of green vesuvianite found in California, that resembles jade and is used as an ornamental stone

cal·i·for·ni·um /kàlli fáwrnee əm/ *n.* a synthetic radioactive metallic chemical element produced by bombarding curium or americium with neutrons. It is used as a neutron source. Symbol **Cf** [Mid-20thC. The element is so named because it was first synthesized at the University of California.]

Ca·lig·u·la /kə líggyələ/ (A.D. 12–41) Roman emperor. A despotic ruler (37–41), he bankrupted the state with his extravagance and was assassinated. Full name **Gaius Julius Caesar Germanicus**

cal·i·pash /kállə pàsh, kàllə pásh/ *n.* a thick green fat obtained from beneath the upper shell of turtles [Late 17thC. Origin uncertain: perhaps an alteration of Spanish *carapacho* "carapace" (source of English *carapace*), or perhaps from a Caribbean language.]

cal·i·pee /kállə pee, kállə pée/ *n.* a thick yellow fat obtained from beneath the lower shells of turtles, considered to be a delicacy [Mid-17thC. Origin uncertain: perhaps from a Caribbean language.]

cal·i·per /kállipər/ *n.* **1.** MEASURE **MEASURING INSTRUMENT** an instrument used to measure the internal or external dimensions of objects and consisting of two curved hinged legs joined at one end **2. MEASURING INSTRUMENT FOR LARGE OBJECTS** a measuring instrument with a fixed arm and an arm that moves along a graduated scale, used for measuring the diameter of large cylindrical objects such as logs **3.** *U.K.* MED **LEG BRACE** a leg splint consisting of metal rods and straps, that enables the hip bone, rather than the foot, to support weight when walking ■ *vt.* **(-pered, -per·ing, -pers)** MEASURE **MEASURE WITH CALIPERS** to measure something using a caliper [Late 16thC. Origin uncertain: perhaps an alteration of CALIBRE.]

cal·i·pers /kállipərz/ *npl.* TECH a measuring instrument with two hinged legs

ca·liph /káylif, kállif/, **ca·lif, ka·lif, kha·lif** *n.* a title taken by Muslim rulers, e.g., the Turkish sultans, that asserts religious authority to rule derived from that of Muhammad [14thC. Via French *caliphe* from Arabic *kalīfa* "successor, deputy," from *kalafa* "to succeed."]

ca·liph·ate /káyli fàyt, kálli fàyt/, **ca·lif·ate, ka·lif·ate, kha·lif·ate** *n.* the territory over which a caliph's rule extends, or the time for which it lasts

cal·is·then·ics /kàlliss thénniks/ *n.* **PERFORMANCE OF CALISTHENICS** the practice of performing calisthenics (*takes a singular verb*) ■ *npl.* **PHYSICAL EXERCISE ROUTINE** vigorous physical exercises for improving fitness and muscle tone, including pushups, sit-ups, and jumping jacks (*takes a plural verb*) [Early 19thC. Coined from the Greek stem *kalli-* "beauty" + Greek *sthenos* "strength" + -ICS.] —**cal·is·then·ic** *adj.*

ca·lix /káyliks, káll-/ (*plural* **-li·ces** /-li seez/) *n.* **1. CUP** a chalice or cup **2.** ANAT = **calyx** [Early 18thC. From Latin, "cup" (see CHALICE).]

calk[1] /kawk/ *n.* **1. HORSESHOE SPIKE** a metal spike on a horseshoe to prevent slipping **2. SPIKED PLATE PROTECTING SOLES** a spiked plate attached to the bottom of a boot or shoe to prevent slipping and preserve the sole ■ *vt.* **(calked, calk·ing, calks) FIT CALK ON SOMETHING** to put a calk on a horseshoe, boot, or shoe [Late 16thC. Origin uncertain: perhaps from Latin *calcaneum* "heel."]

calk[2] *vt.* = **caulk**

call /kawl/ *v.* **(called, call·ing, calls) 1.** *vti.* **SAY LOUDLY** to say something in a loud voice ○ *"Supper's ready," he called from the kitchen.* **2.** *vt.* **DESCRIBE AS SOMETHING** to describe or think of somebody or something in a particular way ○ *I'd call him a fool.* **3.** *vt.* **REFER TO** to use a particular term to address or refer to somebody ○ *He always called his father "Sir."* **4.** *vt.* **SUMMON** to summon or alert somebody or something by means of a formal request ○ *I'll call a cab.* **5.** *vt.* **READ OUT** to read names or numbers from a list **6.** *vti.* **TELEPHONE** to contact somebody by telephone or radio **7.** *vt.* **NAME SOMEBODY OR SOMETHING** to give somebody or something a name ○ *What are you going to call the baby?* **8.** *vi.* **CRY** to give a cry (*refers to birds or animals*) **9.** *vi.* **VISIT SOMEBODY** to visit somebody, or the place where somebody lives or works ○ *I called to see her yesterday.* **10.** *vti.* **REQUEST SOMETHING TO HAPPEN** to make an official order or request for something, e.g., a meeting ○ *An emergency meeting has been called for July 15th.* **11.** *vt.* **PREDICT** to predict what is going to happen, especially in politics ○ *It's a very hard result to call.* **12.** *vti.* DANCE **INSTRUCT DANCERS** to give directions to people who are dancing, e.g., in a square dance **13.** *vt.* FIN **DEMAND REPAYMENT OF SOMETHING** to demand payment of a loan or bond issue **14.** *vt.* **CHALLENGE SOMEBODY** to challenge somebody to prove something, especially to demand to see somebody's hand in a game of poker **15.** *vti.* **DECLARE CHOICE IN GAME** to make a declaration in a game, e.g., to choose heads or tails, or choose trumps in a card game ○ *I'll toss, you call.* **16.** *vt.* SPORTS **OFFICIALLY DECIDE IN GAME** to make an official decision in a sports event or a game **17.** *vt.* **POSTPONE A GAME** to postpone or stop a sports event due to bad weather or other unsuitable conditions ○ *The game was called when it got too dark to play anymore.* ■ *n.* **1. SHOUT** a shout or cry **2. BIRD OR ANIMAL CRY** the sound made by a bird or animal **3. SIGNAL** a signal given by a sound, e.g., on a horn or whistle **4. TELEPHONE MESSAGE** a telephone conversation, or an attempt to get in touch with somebody by telephone **5. REQUEST TO COME** a request for somebody to come ○ *The rescue squads answer thousands of calls a year.* **6. EXPRESSED WISH** a demand or request for something to be done ○ *There have been calls for him to resign.* **7. FEELING OF DUTY** a feeling that a particular job or way of life is a personal duty **8. STRONG APPEAL OF PLACE OR LIFESTYLE** the feeling of strong attraction exerted by a particular place or way of life ○ *the call of the wild* **9. VISIT** a short visit to somebody at his or her house or place of work ○ *made a few calls on the way home.* **10.** SPORTS **REFEREE'S DECISION** a decision made by a referee **11.** GAME **DECLARATION IN GAME** a declaration made during a game, e.g., the choice of heads or tails when a coin is tossed ○ *It's your call.* **12. PREDICTION** a prediction of what is about to happen, especially in politics ○ *In terms of changing policy at election time, it's a difficult call to make.* **13. DEMAND OR OBLIGATION** a demand or obligation that somebody has to fulfill ○ *I'd like to help, but I have a great many calls on my time.* **14. REMINDER** a reminder, given electronically, by telephone, or in person, that somebody should wake up or that something is about to happen **15. HUNTER'S DEVICE TO ATTRACT GAME** a device that imitates the cry of a bird or other animal, used as a lure in hunting [12thC. From Old Norse *kalla.*] ◇ **there's no call for something** *or* **to do something 1.** used to say that a particular remark or action is not welcome or necessary ○ *There's no call to get angry.* **2.** people do not want something, especially a specified commercial product ○ *There's no call for bathing suits at this time of year.* ◇ **it's somebody's call** a decision is entirely up to somebody ○ *It's your call whether we drive or fly.* ◇ **be on call** to be on duty away from the workplace, available to be summoned

WORD KEY: CULTURAL NOTE

The Call of the Wild, a novel by Jack London (1903). Noted for its unsentimental portrayal of pioneer life, it is the tale of a dog, "Buck," who is sent to the Yukon to work as a sled dog. After demonstrating his strength and courage in the service of humans, he takes to the wild with a pack of wolves.

call back *v.* **1.** *vti.* **TELEPHONE SOMEBODY AGAIN** to contact somebody by telephone again **2.** *vt.* **ASK TO RETURN** to recall somebody, e.g., for a second audition or to return to a job **3.** *vi. U.K.* **VISIT SOMEBODY AGAIN** to visit somebody again

call down *vt.* **1. INVOKE SOMETHING** to pray or appeal for good or bad things to happen to somebody **2. REPRIMAND** to rebuke somebody who has done something wrong ○ *The judge called the lawyers down for their unseemly courtroom antics.*

call for *vt.* **1. REQUEST FOR SOMETHING TO HAPPEN** to make a demand or request for some action to take place **2. NEED** to need or require a particular thing or quality **3. ARRIVE AND PICK UP** to arrive and pick up somebody **4. SUGGEST AS LIKELY** to suggest that something is likely to happen (*refers to a weather forecast*) ○ *The weathercasters are calling for thunderstorms in the late afternoon.*

call forth *vt.* to inspire an emotion, energy, or courage

call in *v.* **1.** *vt.* **ASK HELP FROM** to ask somebody to come and give advice or help **2.** *vi.* **TELEPHONE PLACE OF WORK** to telephone a place of work in order to get or leave a message **3.** *vt.* **ASK FOR SOMETHING TO BE REPAID** to ask for a debt or loan to be repaid **4.** *vt.* **ARRANGE RETURN OF SOMETHING** to arrange or request for something to be returned, e.g. outdated currency or defective goods

call off *vt.* **1. CANCEL EVENT** to cancel or stop an event **2. STOP FROM ATTACKING** to order a dog or a person to stop attacking somebody

call on *vt.* **1. ASK TO DO SOMETHING** to ask or tell somebody to do something **2. VISIT** to visit somebody, often in a formal manner

call out *vt.* **1. SUMMON PEOPLE TO HELP** to summon somebody or an organization to come and help **2. ORDER TO STRIKE** to tell workers to stop work and go on strike **3. CHALLENGE TO A FIGHT** to challenge somebody to a duel or fight

call up *vt.* **1.** = **draft 2. SUMMON** to summon somebody who or something that is available in reserve ○ *The governor called up the National Guard.* **3.** COMPUT **DISPLAY ON COMPUTER SCREEN** to instruct a computer to find and display a particular piece of information ○ *call up last month's sales figures* **4. EVOKE** to bring back memories of something

call upon *vt.* **1. ASK FORMALLY** to ask somebody in a formal way to do something **2. MAKE DEMANDS ON** to make demands on somebody or on somebody's abilities

cal·la /kállə/ *n.* = **calla lily**

call·a·ble /káwləb'l/ *adj.* **1. REPAYABLE ON DEMAND** used to describe a loan that is repayable on demand **2. CONVERTIBLE BEFORE MATURING** used to describe a stock or bond that is convertible before reaching maturity

Cal·la·ghan /kálləhən, -hàn/, **Morley Edward** (1903–90) Canadian writer. His novels, known for their hard-hitting realism, include *They Shall Inherit the Earth* (1935) and *The Loved and the Lost* (1955).

cal·lais /kállee iss/ *n.* a green stone used by Stone Age and Bronze Age people of Europe to make beads and ornaments [Late 19thC. From Greek *kallais.*]

cal·la lil·y /kállə-/, **cal·la** *n.* **1. WHITE ORNAMENTAL LILY** an ornamental lily, originally from southern Africa, that has a white funnel-shaped cone around a long yellow spike bearing the flowers themselves. Latin name: *Zantedeschia aethiopica.* **2. ORNAMENTAL LILY** an ornamental lily of the arum type, with a large, brightly colored, funnel-shaped cone around a long flower spike. Genus: *Zantedeschia.*

cal·la·loo /kàllə lóo, kàllə lóo/ (*plural* **-loos**) *n. Carib* **1. CARIBBEAN SOUP** a thick soup like sauce made of the leaves of the dasheen plant **(callalloo bush)**, with okra, a hot pepper, coconut milk, onions, herbs, and often crabs **2.** a complex mixture or confusion [Mid-18thC. From American Spanish *calalu.*]

Ca·llao /kaa yów/ city and chief seaport of Peru, situated on Callao Bay 8 mi./13 km west of Lima. Population: 637,755 (1993).

Maria Callas

Cal·las /kálləss, kál ass/, **Maria** (1923–77) U.S.-born opera soprano. One of the leading opera singers of the mid-20th century, she was known for her incisive portrayals of such characters as Norma and Tosca. Born **Maria Anna Sofia Cecilia Kalogeropoulos**

call·back /káwl bàk/ *n.* **1. RETURN CALL** a telephone call made back to somebody who has recently phoned **2. RECALLING OF SOMEBODY** an act of asking somebody to return **3. PRODUCT RECALL** the recalling of a faulty product by a manufacturer

call·board /káwl bàwrd/ *n.* a board backstage in a theater, giving information to actors and other people involved in a production

call·boy /káwl bòy/ *n.* **1. GIVER OF ACTORS' GET-READY CALL** somebody in a theater who tells the actors when the time for them to go on stage is approaching **2.** = **bellhop 3.** a male prostitute

call cen·ter *n.* TELECOM, BUSINESS a place that handles high-volume incoming telephone calls on behalf of a large organization

call·er /káwlər/ *n.* **1.** SOMEBODY PHONING OR VISITING somebody who makes a telephone call or who visits somebody **2.** ANNOUNCER somebody who announces something, e.g., the moves in a square dance or the numbers in a game of bingo

call·er ID *n.* an electronic device attached to a telephone that, on a small screen, shows the name and telephone number of somebody who is calling or has called

Cal·les /kaá yèss/, **Plutarco Elías** (1877–1945) Mexican statesman. He was secretary of the interior (1920–23) and president of Mexico (1924–28).

call girl *n.* a prostitute who makes appointments with clients by telephone

calli- *prefix.* beautiful ○ *calliopsis* [From Greek *kallos* "beauty"]

cal·lig·ra·phy /kə líggrəfee/ *n.* **1.** SKILL OF HANDWRITING the art or skill of producing beautiful handwriting **2.** HANDWRITING beautiful or artistic handwriting [Early 17thC. From Greek *kalligraphia*, literally "beautiful writing," from *kallos* "beauty" + *graphein* "to write."] —**cal·lig·ra·pher** *n.* —**cal·li·graph·ic** /kàlli gráffik/ *adj.* —**cal·li·graph·i·cal·ly** /-gráffikəlee/ *adv.* —**cal·lig·ra·phist** /kəlíggrəfist/ *n.*

call-in *n.* **1.** SHOW WHERE AUDIENCE PHONES IN OPINIONS a radio or television show in which the listeners or viewers phone and express their opinions **2.** LISTENER OR VIEWER'S CALL a telephone call from a radio listener or a television viewer to a talk show ○ *You will be interviewed live for 30 minutes on a show with call-ins.*

call·ing /káwling/ *n.* **1.** IMPULSE TO FOLLOW PARTICULAR JOB a strong urge to follow a particular career or do a particular type of work **2.** JOB a job or profession

call·ing card *n.* a small card with information such as name, address, and telephone number on it, that can be given to people met socially or in business

cal·li·o·pe /kə lī́ əpee, kálli ōp/ *n.* an organ that generates sound by the release of steam or compressed air through pipes, with tunes often played mechanically, as on a player piano. They are usually found in fairgrounds or circuses. [Mid-19thC. Formed from Latin *Calliope* "CALLIOPE."]

Cal·li·o·pe /kə lī́ əpee/ *n.* the Muse of epic poetry, one of the nine Muses believed to inspire and nurture the arts in Greek mythology. ◊ **Muse** [Via Latin from Greek *Kalliopē*, literally "beautiful-voiced"]

cal·li·per *n.*, *vt.* U.K. = **caliper**

cal·li·pers *npl.* U.K. = **calipers**

cal·li·pyg·i·an /kàllə píjjee ən/, **cal·li·py·gous** /kàllə pī́gəss/ *adj.* having well-shaped buttocks (*literary*) [Late 18thC. Formed from Greek *kallipūgos*, literally "beautiful buttocks," a term applied to a statue of the goddess Aphrodite, from *kalli-* "BEAUTY-" + *pūgē* "buttocks."]

Cal·lis·to /kə lístō/ *n.* **1.** GREEK NYMPH in Greek mythology, a nymph who was changed into a bear by Hera and later became the constellation of the Great Bear **2.** LARGE SATELLITE OF JUPITER a large satellite of Jupiter that was discovered in 1610 [Via Latin from Greek *Kallistô* from, ultimately, *kalos* "beautiful"]

call let·ters *npl.* a signal, usually a group of letters and numbers, used for identification by a radio transmitting station or a unit or operator in radio communication with others

call loan *n.* a loan that must be repaid on demand

call mon·ey *n.* money that has been borrowed and that is repayable on demand

call num·ber *n.* a number that identifies a library book and its position in a library classification system

call of na·ture *n.* a need to urinate or defecate (*humorous*)

cal·lose /ká lōss/ *n.* an insoluble substance found in plant cell walls and formed in flowering plants in response to injury. It consists of chains of linked glucose units. [Mid-19thC. Formed from Latin *callosus* "callous" (see CALLOUS).]

cal·los·i·ty /kə lóssətee/ (*plural* **-ties**) *n.* a local thickening of the outer layer of the skin caused by repeated friction or pressure

cal·lous /kálləss/ *adj.* showing no concern if other people are hurt or upset [14thC. Either via French *calleux* or directly from its source Latin *callosus*, from *callus* "hard skin."] —**cal·lous·ly** *adv.* —**cal·lous·ness** *n.*

cal·loused /kálləst/ *adj.* having an area of hard thickened skin

cal·low /kállō/ *adj.* young or immature, and lacking the experience of life that comes with adulthood [Old English *calu*, from a prehistoric Germanic base of uncertain origin: possibly from Latin *calvus* "bald" (source of English *Calvary*)] —**cal·low·ness** *n.*

Cal·lo·way /kállə wày/, **Cab** (1907–94) U.S. jazz musician, known for his exuberant performances, catchphrase "hi-de-ho," and scat singing. Full name **Cabel Calloway**

call sign *n.* = **call letters**

call slip *n.* a form for requesting a library book that is not kept on the shelves used by the public

call to quar·ters *n.* **1.** SIGNAL TO RETURN TO BARRACKS a signal requiring army personnel to return to barracks **2.** TIME OF CONFINEMENT TO BARRACKS a period of time during which army personnel must remain in barracks

call-up *n.* *U.K.* MIL = **draft**

cal·lus /kálləss/ *n.* **1.** PATCH OF THICKENED SKIN a hard thickened area of skin, especially on the palm of the hand or the sole of the foot, caused by repeated pressure or friction **2.** MED MASS FORMED IN HEALING BONE a mass of fibrous tissue, calcium, cartilage, and bone that forms progressively during the healing of a bone fracture **3.** BOT PLANT TISSUE plant tissue that forms at the site of a wound, or that develops during tissue culture of plant parts, giving rise to new plantlets [Mid-16thC. From Latin. Ultimately from an Indo-European base meaning "hard" that is also the ancestor of English *Excalibur*.]

calm /kaam/ *adj.* **1.** NOT ANXIOUS without anxiety or strong emotion **2.** NOT WINDY without wind or storms **3.** AT LOWEST POINT OF BEAUFORT SCALE relating to or having a wind speed of not more than 1 mi./1.6 km per hour **4.** NOT STORMY smooth and without any large waves ○ *smooth sailing on calm seas* ■ *n.* **1.** PEACE AND QUIET a situation of complete peace and quiet, with no noise, trouble, or anxiety **2.** ABSENCE OF WIND still weather, without wind or waves caused by wind ■ *vt.* (**calmed, calm·ing, calms**) MAKE LESS TENSE to make somebody less anxious or upset [14thC. Origin uncertain: probably via French *calme* or directly from late Latin *cauma* from Greek *kauma* "heat of the day."]

WORD KEY: SYNONYMS

calm, unruffled, serene, peaceful, tranquil, placid, composed, still

CORE MEANING: free from agitation or disturbance

calm the most general term; **unruffled** an informal term for "calm"; **serene** a term describing a state of total calmness, often with a spiritual or philosophical quality; **peaceful** quiet and undisturbed; **tranquil** a slightly formal or literary term suggesting a lasting calmness; **placid** a term suggesting that somebody is not temperamentally excitable; **still** calm by an effort of will; **composed** a term suggesting an absence of movement and noise.

calm down *vti.* to become or make somebody become less excited, anxious, or upset

calm·a·tive /kaámətiv, kálmətiv/ *adj.* CALMING having a calming or quieting effect ■ *n.* CALMING DRUG a drug or treatment that has a calming or quieting effect

calm·ly *adv.* in a relaxed, unemotional way without any excitement or anxiety ○ *She took the bad news calmly enough.*

calm·ness /kaámnəs/ *n.* stillness and tranquility, without wind ○ *the exceptional calmness of the weather*

cal·mod·u·lin /kal mójjəlin/ *n.* a protein found in the cells of most living organisms that plays a crucial role in maintaining stable calcium concentration in the cell cytoplasm [Late 20thC. Contraction of CALCIUM + MODULATE + -IN.]

cal·o·mel /kállə mèl, -məl/ *n.* a white or colorless tasteless compound used as a fungicide and insecticide and, formerly, in medicine as a purgative. Formula: Hg_2Cl_2. [Late 17thC. From modern Latin, of uncertain origin: probably formed from Greek *kalos* "beautiful" + *melas* "black."]

ca·lor·ic /kə láwrik/ *adj.* relating to calories or heat transfer —**ca·lor·i·cal·ly** *adv.*

cal·o·rie /kálləree/ *n.* **1.** UNIT OF ENERGY a unit of energy equal to 4.1855 joules, originally defined as the quantity of heat required to raise the temperature of 1 g of pure water by 1° C. It has now been superseded by the joule. **2.** LARGER UNIT OF ENERGY a unit of energy equal to the heat required to raise the temperature of 1 kg of pure water by 1° C **3.** UNIT OF FOOD ENERGY a unit of energy-producing potential in food, equal to one large calorie [Mid-19thC. From French, formed from Latin *calor* "heat," from *calere* "to be warm or hot."]

cal·o·rif·ic /kàllə ríffik/ *adj.* relating to or generating heat or calories

cal·o·rif·ic val·ue *n.* the amount of heat generated by the complete combustion of a unit mass of fuel, now expressed in joules per kilogram

cal·o·rim·e·ter /kàllə rímmitər/ *n.* an apparatus for measuring the amount of heat given out or taken in during a process such as combustion or change of state. The measurements are often made by observing the amount of solid liquefied, or liquid vaporized, under set conditions. —**ca·lor·i·met·ric** /kàlləri méttrik, kə làwrə méttrik/ *adj.* —**ca·lor·i·met·ri·cal·ly** /-méttrikəlee/ *adv.* —**cal·o·rim·e·try** /kàllə rímmətree/ *n.*

cal·o·rize /kállə rīz/ (**-rized, -riz·ing, -riz·es**) *v.* to treat the surface of steel or iron with aluminum powder and heat to 800–1,000° C to prevent or reduce rusting [Mid-20thC. Formed from Latin *calor* "heat" (source of English *calorie*).]

ca·lo·type /kállə tīp/ *n.* **1.** EARLY PHOTOGRAPHIC PROCESS a 19th-century photographic process producing a negative on a plate that was wetted with silver iodide **2.** EARLY PHOTOGRAPH a photograph produced by the calotype process [Mid-19thC. Coined from Greek *kalos* "beautiful" + -TYPE.]

calque /kalk/ *n.* = **loan translation** [Mid-20thC. Via French, "copy," from, ultimately, Latin *calcare* "to tread" (see CALK[1]).]

cal·trop /káltrəp, káwltrəp/ *n.* **1.** (*plural* **-trops** *or* **-trop**) SPINY PLANT a spiny European plant formally naturalized in California as a serious weed, harmful to livestock. Latin name: *Tribulus terrestris*. **2.** = **water chestnut 3.** = **star thistle 4.** MIL SPIKES TO CATCH HOOVES OR TIRES a military device with four spikes arranged so that one will always point upward, scattered on the ground to lame horses or puncture tires [Pre-12thC. Variant of obsolete *calcatrippe* "thistle," from medieval Latin *calcatrippa*, of uncertain origin: probably formed from Latin *calcare* "to tread" (see CALK[1]).]

cal·u·met /kállyə mèt, kállyəmət/ *n.* a long-stemmed ceremonial pipe used by some Native American peoples [Late 17thC. Via French, "pipe," a dialect variant of *chalumeau*, from, ultimately, Latin *calamus* "reed."]

Cal·u·met Cit·y city in northeastern Illinois, situated 20 mi./32 km south of Chicago, on the Illinois-Indiana border. Population: 37,242 (1996).

ca·lum·ni·ate /kə lúmnee àyt/ (**-at·ed, -at·ing, -ates**) *vt.* to accuse somebody falsely or slander somebody (*formal*) [Mid-16thC. Via the Latin stem *calumniat-* from, ultimately, *calumnia* "false accusation" (see CALUMNY).] —**ca·lum·ni·a·ble** *adj.* —**ca·lum·ni·a·tion** *n.* —**ca·lum·ni·a·tor** *n.*

cal·um·ny /kálləmnee/ (*plural* **-nies**) *n.* (*formal*) **1.** DEFAMATION the making of false statements about somebody with malicious intent **2.** DEFAMATORY STATEMENT a slanderous statement or false accusation [15thC. From Latin *calumnia* "false accusation" (also the source of English *challenge*), from *calvi* "to deceive."] —**ca·lum·ni·ous** /kə lúmnee əss/ *adj.* —**ca·lum·ni·ous·ly** /-əsslee/ *adv.*

cal·va·dos /kálvə dōss, kálvə dòss/ *n.* apple brandy distilled from cider, made in the Normandy Region of France [Early 20thC. Named for *Calvados*, a department of Normandy, France, where the drink is made.]

cal·var·i·um /kal váiree əm/ (*plural* **-a** /-ə/) *n.* the upper domed portion of the skull (*technical*) [Late 19thC. Alteration of Latin *calvaria* "skull" from, ultimately, *calvus* "bald."]

cal·va·ry /kálvəree/ (*plural* **-ries**) *n.* **1.** a time of great suffering (*literary*) **2.** SCULPTURE OF CRUCIFIXION a sculpture representing Jesus Christ's crucifixion

Cal·va·ry /kálvəree, kálvree/ *n.* the hill just outside the city walls of ancient Jerusalem where the crucifixion of Jesus Christ took place [Pre-12thC. Formed from Latin *calvaria* "skull" (see CALVARIUM), a translation of Greek *golgotha*, from Aramaic *gōgoltā*; so called from the shape of the hill.]

Cal·va·ry cross *n.* a Christian cross mounted on three symmetrical steps

calve /kav, kaav/ (**calved, calv·ing, calves**) *vti.* **1.** ZOOL **GIVE BIRTH TO CALF** to give birth to a calf **2.** GEOG **SPLIT** to release a mass of ice that breaks away [Old English *calfian.* Formed from *cælf* "calf."]

Cal·vert /kálvərt/, **Cecelius, 2nd Baron Baltimore** (1605–75) British-born U.S. colonial administrator. He inherited Maryland (1632), settled the colony, and implemented the policies written into its charter.

Cal·vert, Charles, 3rd Baron Baltimore (1637–1715) British-born U.S. colonial administrator. He governed the Maryland colony (1661–89).

Cal·vert, George, 1st Baron Baltimore (1580?–1632) British-born U.S. absentee colonial administrator. He governed present-day Maryland (1632) and advocated religious tolerance.

calves plural of **calf**[1], **calf**[2]

Cal·vin /kálvin/, **John** (1509–64) French-born Swiss Protestant reformer. He founded a Presbyterian government in Switzerland and developed the doctrine of the Protestant Reformation in *Institutes of the Christian Religion* (1536).

Cal·vin cy·cle *n.* a series of chemical reactions, occurring in all photosynthesizing plants, by which carbon dioxide is converted to glucose [Named for Melvin *Calvin* (1911–97), U.S. chemist who discovered it]

Cal·vin·ism /kálvi nìzzəm/ *n.* the religious doctrine of John Calvin, which emphasizes that salvation comes through faith in God, and also that God has already chosen those who will believe and be saved —**Cal·vin·ist** *n., adj.* —**Cal·vin·is·ti·cal·ly** /-nístiklee/ *adv.*

cal·vi·ties /kal víshee èez, kal víshiz/ *n.* baldness (*technical*) [Early 17thC. From Latin, formed from *calvus* "bald."]

Cal·vo /kálvō, kaálvō/, **Carlos** (1824–1906) Argentine statesman and lawyer. He formulated the Calvo Doctrine (1869), which set new guidelines regarding national debt.

calx /kalks/ (*plural* **calx·es** *or* **cal·ces** /kál sèez/) *n.* **1.** CHEM **METAL OXIDE** the powdery oxide of a metal formed when an ore or a mineral is roasted **2.** ANAT **BACK OF HEEL** the rounded part at the back of the heel [15thC. From Latin, "lime, limestone" (source of English *calcium* and *chalk*), from Greek *khalix* "pebble."]

ca·ly·ces plural of **calyx**

ca·lyc·u·lus /kə líkyələss/ (*plural* **-li** /-lī/), **ca·ly·cle** /káylik'l, kállik'l/, **cal·i·cle** *n.* a small cup-shaped structure, e.g., the depression at the top of a coral skeleton [Late 19thC. From Latin, "calyx of a flower," a diminutive of *calyx* "husk" (see CALYX).] —**ca·lyc·u·lar** *adj.* —**ca·lyc·u·late** /kə líkyə làyt, kə líkyələt/ *adj.*

Ca·ly·do·ni·an boar /kalli dṓnee ən báwr/ *n.* in Greek mythology, a gigantic wild boar sent by the goddess Artemis to destroy the city of Calydon, that is killed by Meleager, the son of the city's king

ca·lyp·so /kə lípsō/ (*plural* **-sos**) *n.* **1.** **CARIBBEAN SONG** a Caribbean, especially Trinidadian, ballad with a lively dance rhythm, that deals satirically with social and political topics **2.** **CARIBBEAN DANCE MUSIC** Caribbean dance music that has syncopated rhythms, is usually improvised, and is often played by a steel band [Early 20thC. Origin unknown.]

Ca·lyp·so /kə lípsō/ *n.* in Greek mythology, a nymph who kept Odysseus on her island for seven years

ca·lyx /káyliks, kálliks/ (*plural* **ca·lyx·es** *or* **cal·y·ces** /-li sèez/) *n.* **1.** **FLOWER SEPALS** the group of sepals, usually green, around the outside of a flower that encloses and protects the flower bud **2.** ANAT **PART OF KIDNEY** one of the funnel-shaped hollows in the pelvis of the kidney, through which urine passes to the ureter [Late 17thC. Via Latin from Greek *kalux* "husk, shell," from *kaluptein* "to conceal."]

cal·zo·ne /kal zṓnee/ (*plural* **-nes** /-neez/ *or* **-ni** /-nee/) *n.* a semicircular Italian turnover made from pizza dough with a savory filling [Late 20thC. From Italian, literally "trouser leg" from, ultimately, Latin *calceus* "shoe," from *calx* "heel."]

cam /kam/ *n.* an irregularly-shaped projection on a rotating shaft that changes rotary motion into a reciprocating up-and-down motion in another machine part (**cam follower**) that touches it [Late 18thC. From Dutch *kam* "comb."]

CAM /kam/ *abbr.* computer-aided manufacturing

Ca·ma·güey Ar·chi·pel·a·go /kámmə gwày-/ group of coral islands situated off east central Cuba, including the islands of Romano, Sabinal, and Coco, and extending approximately 150 mi./241 km from northwest to southeast

ca·ma·ra·der·ie /kaàmə raádəree, kàmmə ráddəree/ *n.* a feeling of close friendship and trust among a particular group of people [Mid-19thC. From French, formed from *camarade* "comrade" (see COMRADE).]

cam·a·ril·la /kàmmə ríllə, kàmmə reéyə/ *n.* a group of advisers, especially a secretive group advising an important person [Mid-19thC. From Spanish, literally "small room," formed from *camara* "room."]

Cam·a·ril·lo /kàmmə ríllō/ city in southwestern California, east of Santa Barbara and northwest of Los Angeles. Population: 57,090 (1996).

cam·as /kámməss/ (*plural* **ca·mass·es** *or* **cam·as**), **cam·ass** (*plural* **ca·mass·es** *or* **cam·ass**) *n.* **1.** **PLANT WITH EDIBLE BULB** a North American plant with grassy leaves, a cluster of blue and white flowers, and an edible bulb. Latin name: *Camassia quamash.* **2.** = **death camas** [Early 19thC. From Chinook Jargon *qamaš.*]

cam·ber /kámbər/ *n.* **1.** **UPWARD CURVE IN ROAD** a slight upward curve in a structure, especially the curve in the surface of a road **2.** **SLANT OF VEHICLE'S WHEELS** a slant in the steerable wheels on a vehicle that makes them slightly closer together at the bottom than at the top ■ *vti.* (**-bered, -ber·ing, -bers**) **MAKE CURVED SHAPE** to form something or be formed with a camber [Early 17thC. Via French *cambre* "arched" from Latin *camur* "curved inwards," of uncertain origin: perhaps from Greek *kamara* "vault."] —**cam·bered** *adj.*

cam·bist /kámbist/ *n.* a dealer in foreign exchange [Early 19thC. Via French from Italian *cambista,* from medieval Latin *cambium* "exchange" (see CAMBIUM).]

cam·bi·um /kámbee əm/ (*plural* **-bi·ums** *or* **-b·ia** /-bee ə/) *n.* a cylindrical layer of cells in plant roots and stems that produces the new tissue responsible for increased girth, particularly sap-conducting tissues, xylem and phloem, and bark [Late 17thC. From medieval Latin *cambium* "exchange," from Latin *cambire* "to exchange" (source of English *change*).] —**cam·bi·al** *adj.*

Cambodia

Cam·bo·di·a /kam bṓdee ə/ republic in southeastern Asia, in the southern part of Indochina, bordered by Thailand, Laos, Vietnam, and the Gulf of Thailand. Language: Khmer and French. Currency: riel. Capital: Phnom Penh. Population: 11,163,861 (1997). Area: 69,898 sq. mi./181,035 sq. km. Official name **Kingdom of Cambodia**

Cam·bo·di·an /kam bṓdee ən/ *n.* **1.** PEOPLES **SOMEBODY FROM CAMBODIA** somebody who was born in or who lives in Cambodia **2.** LANG **KHMER** the Khmer language (*dated*) —**Cam·bo·di·an** *adj.*

cam·bo·gia /kam bṓjə/ *n.* = **gamboge**

Cam·bri·an /kámbree ən/ *adj.* **1.** **RELATING TO PREHISTORIC ERA** relating to the earliest part of the Paleozoic era, in which invertebrate animal life, including trilobites, appeared, and marine algae developed **2.** **WELSH** relating to or from Wales [Mid-17thC. Formed from medieval Latin *Cambria* "Wales," from Welsh *Cymry.*]

cam·bric /káymbrik/ *n.* a thin white linen or cotton fabric [14thC. Named for *Kamerijk* "Cambrai," where the fabric was originally made.]

cam·bric tea *n.* a hot drink of very weak, sweet tea, made with a lot of milk. Cambric tea is typically a children's drink.

Cam·bridge /káym brìj/ **1.** university city in eastern England. It lies on the Cam River, and is the administrative headquarters of Cambridgeshire and a local government district. Population: city, 95,682 (1991); district, 114,800 (1995). **2.** city in Massachusetts. It is home to Harvard University, Radcliffe College, and the Massachusetts Institute of Technology. Population: 93,707 (1996).

Cam·by·ses I /kam bī́ sèez/ (*fl.* 6th century B.C.) Persian king. The son of Cyrus, he reigned as king of the Achaemenid dynasty around 600–559 B.C.

Cam·by·ses II (*d.* 523? B.C.) Persian king. He reigned from 529 B.C. to 522 B.C., and conquered Egypt (525 B.C.) to expand the Persian Empire.

Camcorder

cam·cord·er /kám kàwrdər/ *n.* a portable video camera and recorder [Late 20thC. A blend of CAMERA + RECORDER.]

Cam·den /kámdən/ **1.** city and port in southwestern New Jersey, on the eastern bank of the Delaware River. Population: 84,844 (1996). **2.** borough in North London, England. Population: 184,900 (1995).

came past tense of **come**

cam·el /kámm'l/ *n.* **1.** (*plural* **-els** *or* **-el**) **DESERT ANIMAL** a ruminant animal of southern Eurasia that has either one or two humps on its back and is adapted to an arid climate. The Arabian camel or dromedary has one hump, the Bactrian camel has two. Genus: *Camelus.* **2.** = **caisson** ■ *adj.* COLORS **LIGHT BROWN** a light sandy brown [Pre-12thC. Via Latin from Greek *kamēlos,* of Semitic origin.]

cam·el·back /kámm'l bàk/ *adj.* shaped like an arch or a camel's hump

cam·el·eer /kàmm'l eér/ *n.* somebody who controls or rides a camel (*dated*)

cam·el hair, cam·el's hair *n.* **1.** **HAIR OF CAMEL** hair from the camel, used in making clothing and rugs **2.** TEXTILES **FABRIC** soft fabric containing camel hair or a similar fiber, often used for making coats **3.** PAINTING **PAINTBRUSH** a paintbrush used primarily for watercolors, normally made of squirrel hair

cam·e·lid /kámm'lid, kə méllid/ *n.* a member of the family that includes camels, llamas, and their relatives, all of which have feet with two toes and thick leathery soles. Family: Camelidae.

ca·mel·lia /kə meélyə, kə meélee ə/ (*plural* **-lias** *or* **-lia**) *n.* **1.** **SHRUB WITH ROSE-SHAPED FLOWERS** a shrub of the tea family, often grown as an ornamental for its glossy evergreen leaves and rose-shaped flowers. Latin name: *Camellia japonica.* **2.** **TREE OR SHRUB RESEMBLING CAMELLIA** any tree or shrub of the tea family that resembles the camellia. Genus: *Camellia.* [Mid-18thC. From modern Latin, formed from *Camellus,* the Latinized name of Joseph *Kamel* (1661–1706), Moravian Jesuit missionary and botanist who first described the plant.]

ca·mel·o·pard /kə méllə paàrd/ *n.* **1.** **GIRAFFE** a giraffe (*archaic*) = **giraffe 2.** ASTRON = **Camelopardalis** [14thC. Formed from Latin from Greek *kamēlopardalis,* from *kamēlos* "camel" + *pardalis* "pard" (as the animal has a camel like head with spots like a leopard).]

Ca·mel·o·par·da·lis /kə mèllə paàrd'liss, kə mèllō paàrd'liss/, **Ca·mel·o·par·dus** /-paàrdəss/ *n.* a large and faint constellation in the northern hemisphere, known as the Giraffe [From Latin (see CAMELOPARD).]

Cam·e·lot /kámmə lòt/ *n.* **1.** **ARTHURIAN CITY** the legendary city of King Arthur **2.** **IDEALIZED PLACE OR SITUATION** a place or situation regarded as very enlightened, cultured, beautiful, and peaceful

WORD KEY: CULTURAL NOTE

Camelot, the 1960 musical by Alan Jay Lerner and Frederick Loewe, takes its title from the site of King Arthur's legendary sixth-century English court, and its tragic yet lavishly produced story centers on Arthur, his queen, Guinevere, and Lancelot. The word "Camelot" soon came to be associated in the U.S. public mind with the youthful stylishness, sophistication, and optimism of the John F. Kennedy administration (1961–63), chiefly because the musical's popularity coincided in time with the period of John and Jacqueline Kennedy's occupation of the White House. Further, the media reported that the First Couple enjoyed listening to recordings of this musical. As a result "Camelot" eventually took on the generic meaning of "a period, time, or place regarded as idyllic, peaceful, idealistic, youthful, enlightened, and optimistic." And so the mythology enveloping a sixth-century English king was conferred via the theater and politics to the grandson of Irish immigrants – a 20th-century U.S. president – whose "one brief shining moment" was cut short by assassination on November 22, 1963.

cam·el's hair *n.* = **camel hair**

Cam·em·bert /kámməm bàir/ *n.* a small round soft French cheese with an edible white rind that becomes more intense in flavor and softer in the center as it ripens [Late 19thC. Named for *Camembert*, a town in Normandy, France, where the cheese was first made.]

cam·e·o /kámmi ò/ *n.* **1.** CARVED STONE a semiprecious stone carved to give a raised design in one color against a background of another, especially a pale head against a darker background **2.** BRIEF APPEARANCE BY FAMOUS ACTOR a single brief appearance by a distinguished actor in a movie or play [15thC. From Italian, of unknown origin.]

cam·e·o ware *n.* chinaware that has pale figures in relief on a colored background

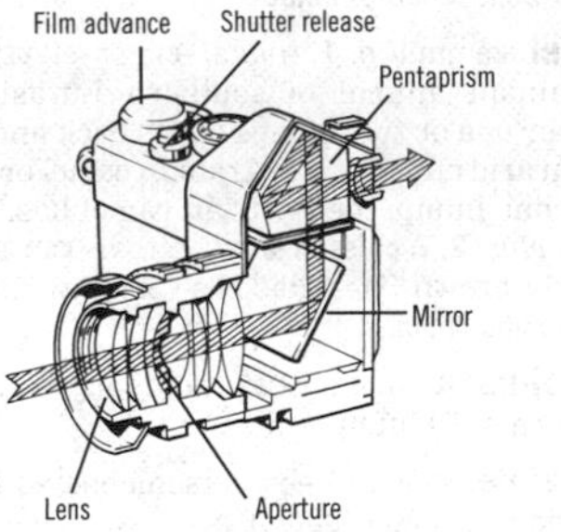

Camera

cam·er·a /kámmərə, kámmrə/ *n.* **1.** DEVICE FOR TAKING PHOTOGRAPHS a device for taking photographs by letting light from an image fall briefly onto sensitized film, usually by means of a lens and shutter mechanism. ◊ **movie camera 2.** DEVICE FOR MAKING PICTURES a device that converts images into electrical signals for television transmission, video recording, or digital storage [Early 18thC. Via Latin, "vault" (source of English *chamber*), from Greek *kamara*.]

cam·er·a lu·ci·da /kàmmərə lóossidə, kàmmrə-/ (*plural* **cam·er·a lu·ci·das**) *n.* a box or chamber that allows images to be projected onto a surface so they can be traced [Early 18thC. From Latin, "bright chamber."]

cam·er·a·man /kámmrə màn, kámmərə-, -mən/ (*plural* **-men** /-mèn, -mən/) *n.* somebody who operates a movie or television camera, especially, but not always, a man

cam·er·a ob·scu·ra /-əb skyóorə, -ob skyóorə/ *n.* a box or small darkened room into which a moving image of what is outside is projected using a simple lens and a small hole in one of the sides of the box or room [Early 18thC. From Latin, literally "dark chamber," because the room is darkened.]

cam·er·a·per·son /kámmrə pùrs'n, kámmərə-/ *n.* somebody who operates a movie or television camera

cam·er·a-read·y *adj.* used to describe or relating to material in its final publishable format, ready to be photographed or electronically scanned for the purpose of preparing printing plates

cam·er·a-shy *adj.* with a dislike of being photographed or filmed

cam·er·a·wo·man /kámmrə wòommən, kámmərə wòommən/ (*plural* **-women** /-wìmmin/) *n.* a woman who operates a movie or television camera

cam·er·a·work /kámmrə wùrk, kámmərə-/ *n.* the ways in which cameras are used in movies and television, especially their positioning and movement

cam·er·lin·go /kàmmər líng gō/ (*plural* **-gos**), **cam·er·len·go** /-léng gō/ (*plural* **-gos**) *n.* in the Roman Catholic Church, a cardinal who deals with the Pope's financial and other secular affairs [Early 17thC. Via Italian from a Frankish word that is also the source of English *chamberlain*.]

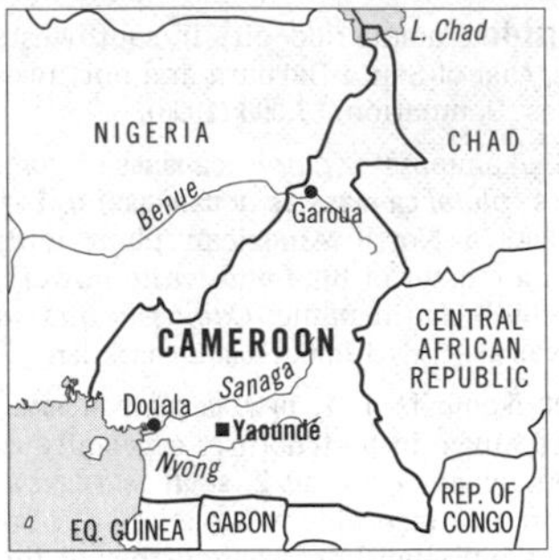

Cameroon

Cam·e·roon[1] /kàmmə róon/ country in west central Africa. It became a German protectorate in 1884. After World War I it was divided into French and British Cameroon. French Cameroon became independent in 1960. In 1961, part of British Cameroon joined Nigeria, while the rest joined French Cameroon in a federal republic. Cameroon became a unitary state in 1972. Language: French, English. Currency: CFA franc. Capital: Yaoundé. Population: 14,611,357 (1997). Area: 183,569 sq. mi./475,442 sq. km. Official name **Republic of Cameroon**

Cam·e·roon[2] active volcano in southwestern Cameroon that had a major eruption in 1982. It is also the highest mountain in West Africa. Height: 13,435 ft./4,095 m.

cam·i /kámmee/ *n.* a camisole (*informal*) [Early 20thC. Shortening.]

cam·i·knick·ers /kámmi nìkərz/ *npl.* loose knee-length knickers for women, usually made of silky fabric and decorated with ruffles

cam·i·sa·do /kàmmə sáydō, -saádō/ (*plural* **-does**) *n.* a surprise attack at night [Mid-16thC. From Spanish *camisada*, literally "attack in your shirt" (because attackers wore shirts over their armor in order to recognize each other), from *camisa* "shirt."]

ca·mise /kə meéz, -meéss/ *n.* a style of loose shirt or tunic worn in former times [Early 19thC. Via Arabic *ḳamīṣ* from, perhaps, late Latin *camisia* "linen shirt, nightgown" (source of English *camisole* and *chemise*).]

cam·i·sole /kámmi sòl/ *n.* **1.** WOMAN'S TOP GARMENT a woman's sleeveless top with thin shoulder straps and a straight neckline ○ *a camisole top* **2.** WOMAN'S UNDERGARMENT a woman's sleeveless undergarment covering the upper torso [Early 19thC. Via French from, ultimately, late Latin *camisia* "linen shirt, nightgown" (source of English *chemise*).]

Cam·lan /kámlən/ *n.* in Arthurian legend, the battlefield in Southwest England where King Arthur was mortally wounded by his traitorous nephew Mordred before being carried away to Avalon

cam·let /kámlət/ *n.* **1.** TEXTILES MEDIEVAL CLOTH a luxurious cloth of Asian origin used in the Middle Ages. It was a blend of goat's hair and silk, possibly originally camel hair and silk. **2.** CLOTHES GARMENT MADE FROM CAMLET a piece of clothing made from camlet [14thC. Via Old French *chamelot* from, ultimately, Arabic *ḵamla(t)* "nap, pile, fibers," and popularly associated with CAMEL, hence the possibly erroneous belief that the cloth was made from camel hair.]

cam·o /kámmō/ *n.* camouflage clothes or material used by military personnel (*slang*) [Shortening of CAMOUFLAGE]

cam·o·gie /kə mōgee/ *n.* an Irish stick-and-ball game that is a form of hurling played by women. Camogie was developed in 1900 by women in Dublin, Ireland, and the game has become increasingly popular with more than 400 clubs affiliated with the Camogie League. [Early 20thC. From Irish Gaelic *camógaíocht*, from *camóg* "crooked stick."]

cam·o·mile *n.* = **chamomile**

ca·moo·di /kə móodee/ (*plural* **-dis**) *n.* = **anaconda** [Early 19thC. From Arawak *kamudu*.]

Ca·mor·ra /kə máwrə/ *n.* a secret society formed in Italy in the early 1800s that was involved in criminal and terrorist activities. The Camorra allied itself with Garibaldi and helped to eject the ruling Bourbons, then declined in the early 20th century and was suppressed in 1922 by Mussolini's Fascist government. [Mid-19thC. Via Italian from, possibly, Spanish *camorra* "dispute."]

cam·ou·flage /kámmə flaàzh, -flaàj/ *n.* **1.** CONCEALING OF THINGS the concealing of things, especially troops and military equipment, by disguising them to look like their surroundings, e.g., by covering them with branches or leaf-clad netting **2.** CONCEALING DEVICES devices designed to conceal by imitating the colors and textures of the surrounding environment, e.g., battledress made from fabric in irregular patches of browns and greens ○ *a camouflage jacket* **3.** PROTECTIVE COLORATION IN ANIMALS the devices that animals use to blend into their environment in order to avoid being seen by predators or prey, especially coloration **4.** DISGUISE something that is intended to hide, disguise, or mislead ■ *vt.* (**-flaged, -flag·ing, -flag·es**) **1.** HIDE SOMETHING to conceal something by making it match its surroundings, especially in appearance **2.** DISGUISE SOMETHING to disguise something in order to mislead somebody, often somebody perceived as a threat [Early 20thC. From French, from *camoufler* "to disguise," from Italian *camuffare* "to disguise, deceive."] —**cam·ou·flag·er** *n.*

camp[1] /kamp/ *n.* **1.** PLACE WITH REMOVABLE ACCOMMODATIONS a place where short-term accommodations have been temporarily erected or sited, in the form, e.g., of tents or camper vehicles for vacationers **2.** PLACE FOR TEMPORARY STAY a set of buildings where people are housed temporarily, e.g., as prisoners, refugees, or troops **3.** RUSTIC SHACK a small, very rustic house in an isolated place, used for weekend fishing or hunting trips (*regional*) ○ *a fishing camp on one of the Great Lakes* **4.** GROUP a group of people who share the same ideas, beliefs, or aims, or who form one of the sides in a debate ○ *the President's camp* ○ *members of the environmentalist camp* ■ *vi.* (**camped, camp·ing, camps**) **1.** STAY TEMPORARILY to stay in temporary accommodations, especially in a tent ○ *We camped by a stream.* **2.** TAKE TEMPORARY POSITION to take up a temporary position somewhere, e.g., as a protester or in alternative accommodations ○ *We will camp on his doorstep until we get some action.* [Early 16thC. Via French from, ultimately, Latin *campus* "level field, site for military exercises or sports" (source of English *campagna, campaign, champaign,* and *champion*).]

camp out *vi.* **1.** LIVE OUTDOORS to live or sleep outdoors, with or without a tent ○ *We would be camping out under the stars for the next three nights.* **2.** STAY SOMEWHERE TEMPORARILY to take up a temporary position somewhere, e.g., as a protester or in alternative accommodations ○ *Hordes of journalists camped out in the palace grounds.*

camp[2] /kamp/ *adj.* **1.** OVER-FEMININE exaggeratedly or affectedly feminine, especially in a man **2.** AMUSINGLY BRASH deliberately and exaggeratedly brash or vulgar in an amusing, often self-parodying way ■ *n.* **1.** EXAGGERATED FEMININITY exaggeratedly or affectedly feminine behavior, especially in men **2.** DELIBERATE OUTRAGEOUSNESS deliberate outrageousness for humorous effect ○ *The performance is high camp.* ■ *vi.* (**camped, camp·ing, camps**) BEHAVE IN CAMP WAY to behave in an outrageously exaggerated, dramatic, feminine, or vulgar way [Early 20thC. Origin unknown, though derivation from French *camper* "to pose" or English dialect *kemp* "uncouth" has been suggested.] ◇ **camp it up 1.** to behave in a deliberately outrageous way for humorous effect (*informal*) **2.** to behave in an exaggeratedly or affectedly feminine way, especially as a flaunting of male gayness (*informal*) **3.** to overact in a stage or musical production (*informal*)

Camp /kamp/, **Walter Chauncey** (1859–1925) U.S. football coach. He invented many of the current rules of the game at Yale University (1888–92).

cam·paign /kam páyn/ *n.* **1.** PLANNED ACTIONS a planned and organized series of actions intended to achieve a specific goal, especially fighting for or against something or raising people's awareness of something ○ *a national TV advertising campaign* **2.** POL **VOTE-SEEKING ACTIVITIES** a series of events, including rallies and speeches, that are intended to persuade voters to vote for a particular politician or party ○ *kept her campaign promises to the electorate* ○ *ran an expensive nationwide campaign* **3.** MIL **MILITARY OPERATIONS** a series of military or terrorist operations taking place in one area over a particular period, intended to achieve a specific objective ■ *vi.* **(-paigned, -paign·ing, -paigns) 1. PARTICIPATE IN CAMPAIGN** to take part in a campaign to achieve a specific aim ○ *parents campaigning to get the school re-opened* **2. PARTICIPATE IN POLITICAL CAMPAIGN** to take part in a political campaign ○ *We campaigned particularly strongly in the south.* [Early 17thC. Via French *campagne* "open country" from, ultimately, Latin *campus* "field" (source of English *camp*); the modern sense "military operations" derives from the fighting of battles in open countryside.]

cam·paign·er /kam páynər/ *n.* **1. SOMEBODY WHO CAMPAIGNS** somebody involved in a campaign for social or political change ○ *human rights campaigners* **2.** POL **POLITICIAN OR POLITICAL WORKER** a politician working to be elected, or a worker in an election campaign **3. VETERAN** somebody with experience of many conflicts or struggles ○ *They left the floor debate to their most seasoned campaigner.*

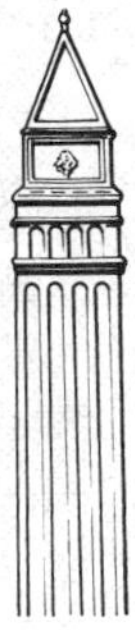
Campanile

cam·pa·ni·le /kàmpə neélee/ (*plural* **-les** *or* **-li**) *n.* a bell tower, especially a freestanding bell tower of the kind found in Italy [Mid-17thC. From Italian *campanile*, from *campana* "bell," from late Latin *campana* (see CAMPANOLOGY).]

cam·pa·nol·o·gy /kàmpə nóləjee/ *n.* the study or practice of bell ringing [Mid-19thC. From modern Latin *campanologia*, from late Latin *campana* "bell" (source of English *campanile*), from Latin *campanus* "of Campania" (southern Italy), a former source of bronze for making bells.] —**cam·pa·nol·o·gist** /kàmpə nólləjist/ *n.*

cam·pan·u·la /kam pánnyələ/ *n.* an annual or perennial plant, native to northern temperate regions, that bears bell-shaped blue, white, or pink flowers. Some species are widely grown as garden plants. Genus: *Campanula.* [Early 17thC. From modern Latin, literally "little bell," from late Latin *campana* (see CAMPANOLOGY).]

camp bed *n.* = **cot**

Camp·bell /kámb'l/ city in western California, southeast of San Francisco and southwest of San Jose. Population: 38,380 (1996).

Camp·bell, Wilfred (1858?–1918) Canadian writer. His works include the poetry collection *Lake Lyrics* (1889) and the novel *Ian of the Orcades* (1906).

Camp·bell, William Wallace (1862–1938) U.S. astronomer. He was a pioneer in using spectroscopy to determine the velocity of stars. His published works include *Stellar Motions* (1913).

Cam·pe·che /kam peéchee/ capital of Campeche state, on the western coast of the Yucatan peninsula in southeastern Mexico. Population: 172,200 (1990).

camp·er /kámpər/ *n.* **1. SOMEBODY WHO CAMPS** somebody who goes camping ○ *accessories for campers and hikers* **2. RECREATIONAL VEHICLE** a motor vehicle equipped as a self-contained traveling home, smaller than a motor home. It has basic facilities for cooking, washing, and sleeping. **3. TRAILER FOR LIVING IN** a trailer equipped as a self-contained traveling home, hauled by a car

cam·pe·si·no /kàmpə seénō, kaàmpə seénō/ (*plural* **-nos**) *n.* a farmer or agricultural worker in Latin American countries [Mid-20thC. Via Spanish, from, ultimately, Latin *campus* (see CAMPUS).]

camp·fire /kámp fìr/ *n.* a wood fire built outside by campers, for cooking on or for warmth

Camp Fire Girl *n.* a member of an organization for girls aged 7 through 18 that aims to teach sound moral values and practical skills

camp fol·low·er *n.* **1. SOMEBODY UNOFFICIALLY SUPPLYING THE MILITARY** a civilian who follows a military unit from place to place in order to earn money by supplying products or services, e.g., services as a prostitute **2. UNCOMMITTED OR TEMPORARY SUPPORTER** somebody who supports a group or an organization but does not belong to it, often somebody who becomes temporarily associated with a political party for selfish reasons

camp·ground /kámp grὸwnd/ *n.* an outdoor area designed for camping, usually providing campers with some facilities, e.g., showers, toilets, and a store

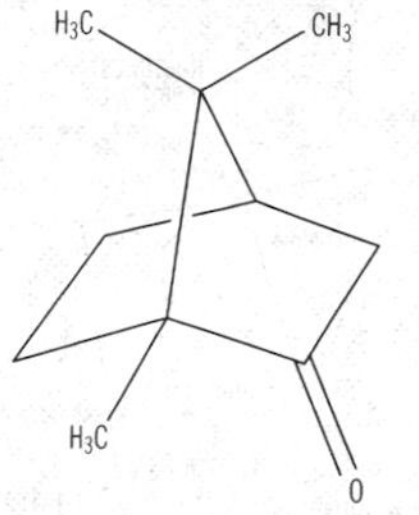

Camphor

cam·phor /kámfər/ *n.* a strong-smelling compound, used in medicinal creams for its mild antiseptic and anti-itching properties, and to make celluloid, plastics, and explosives. [14thC. Directly or via Old French *camphore* from medieval Latin *camphora*, which came via Arabic and Malay from Sanskrit *karpūra*.] —**cam·phor·ic** /kam fáwrik/ *adj.*

cam·phor·ate /kámfə ràyt/ (**-at·ed, -at·ing, -ates**) *vt.* to treat or impregnate something with camphor

cam·phor ice *n.* an ointment used to relieve minor skin ailments, made of camphor mixed with white wax and castor oil

cam·phor oil *n.* the oil that is distilled from the steamed bark and wood of the camphor tree

cam·phor tree *n.* an evergreen tree, native to eastern Asia, whose wood and bark are a source of camphor. The tree is also cultivated in the southern United States as an ornamental. Latin name: *Cinnamomum camphora.*

cam·phor·weed /kámfər weéd/ *n.* either of two North American flowering plants, with clusters of small flowerheads. Latin name: *Heterotheca subaxillaris* and *Pluchea camphorata.*

cam·pim·e·try /kam pímmətree/ *n.* the measuring of the field of vision or the sensitivity of the retina to color and space [Early 20thC. Coined from Latin *campus* "field" + -METRY.]

camp·ing /kámping/ *n.* living outdoors in a tent or trailer while on vacation or as a recreational activity ○ *camping equipment*

cam·pi·on /kámpee ən/ *n.* a flowering plant of the pink family, native to the northern hemisphere, and producing pink, red, or white flowers. Genera: *Lychnis* and *Silene.* [Mid-16thC. Origin uncertain: perhaps originally a variant of CHAMPION, from the former use of a type of campion for making garlands for athletics champions.]

Cam·pi·on /kámpee ən/, **Jane** (*b.* 1954) New Zealand movie director. She directed the Oscar-winning *The Piano* (1993).

camp meet·ing *n.* a religious rally held outdoors, especially one lasting several days with participants camping nearby

cam·po /kámpō, kaámpō/ (*plural* **-pos**) *n.* a large grassy plain in South America, with scattered bushes and small stunted trees [Mid-19thC. Via either American Spanish or Portuguese, "field," from Latin *campus* (source of English *camp* and *scamper*).]

Cam·po·bel·lo /kàmpə béllō/ island off the southwestern coast of New Brunswick, Canada, a favorite summer vacation spot of Franklin D. Roosevelt. Area: 27 sq. mi./70 sq. km. Population: 1,317 (1991).

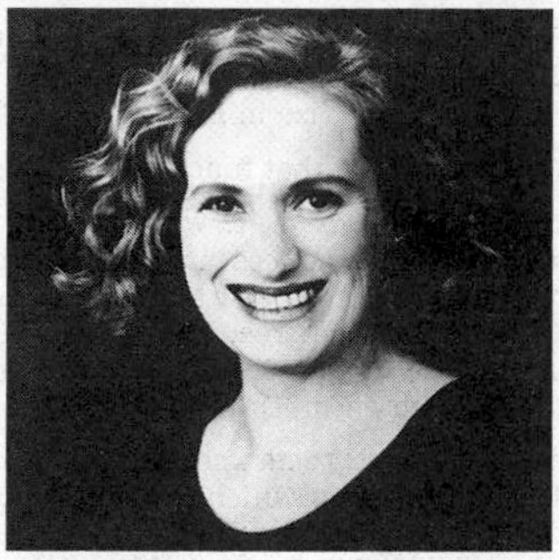
Jane Campion

camp·o·ree /kàmpə reé/ *n.* a gathering of Boy Scouts or Girl Scouts from a particular area [Early 20thC. Probably a blend of CAMP and JAMBOREE.]

camp rob·ber *n.* a bird, especially the gray jay, that visits campgrounds to steal food (*regional*)

WORD KEY: REGIONAL NOTE

Camp robber is common in the Upper Rocky Mountain states and the Pacific Northwest. The bird is also called *camp robin, camp thief, Rock Mountain magpie,* and *Canadian camp robber.*

camp·site /kámp sìt/ *n.* **1.** *U.K.* = **campground 2. INDIVIDUAL CAMPING AREA** a single unit of land within a campground, for a camper to pitch a tent on or park a trailer or camper on

camp·stool /kámp stòol/ *n.* a stool that folds up for easy storage and carriage, designed for use when camping

cam·pus /kámpəss/ *n.* **1. COLLEGE OR UNIVERSITY SITE** an area of land that contains the main buildings and grounds of a university or college, or one of the sites on which such buildings are located ○ *accommodations on campus* **2. SCHOOL SITE** an area of land that contains the buildings and grounds of a public school **3. SITE** a site on which the buildings of an organization or institution are located ○ *a dormitory for nursing students on the hospital campus* [Late 18thC. From Latin, "level field, plain" (source of English *camp* and *champion*).]

cam·pus nov·el *n.* a novel that satirizes university life. The genre appeared in Britain in the late 1970s and early 1980s.

camp·y /kámpee/ (**-i·er, -i·est**) *adj.* (*informal*) **1. OVERLY FEMININE** exaggeratedly or affectedly feminine, especially in a man **2. DELIBERATELY OUTRAGEOUS** deliberately and humorously outrageous —**camp·i·ly** *adv.* —**camp·i·ness** *n.*

cam·py·lo·bac·ter /kámpəlō bàktər/ *n.* a rod- or spiral-shaped bacterium that is a common cause of food poisoning in humans and of spontaneous abortion in farm animals [Late 20thC. Coined from *campylo-* (from Greek *kampulos* "bent") + *-bacter* (from *bacterium*), literally "bent bacterium"; so called because of the genus *Campylobacter*'s curved and spiral-shaped bacteria.]

Cam Ranh Bay /kàm raan báy/ inlet of the South China Sea, situated on the southeastern coast of Vietnam between Phan Rang and Nha Trang

Cam·rose /kám rōz/ city in east central Alberta, Canada. Population: 13,728 (1996).

cam·shaft /kám shàft/ *n.* a shaft that has one or more cams attached, especially one that operates the valves in a vehicle's internal combustion engine

Ca·mus /ká mōō/, **Albert** (1913–60) Algerian-born

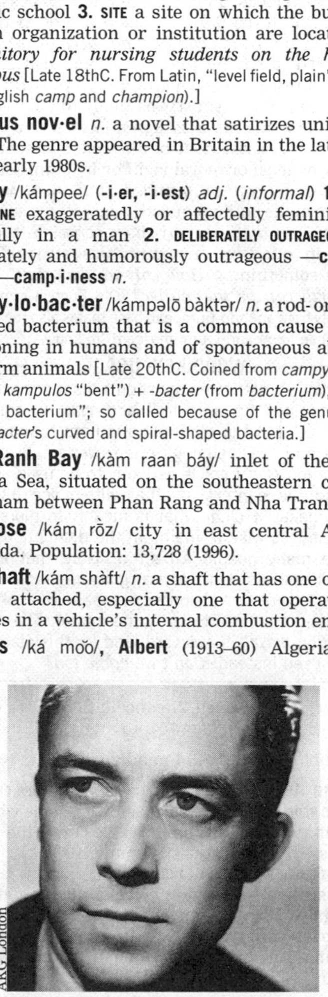

Albert Camus

French novelist, essayist, and dramatist. Author of *The Outsider* (1942) and *The Plague* (1947), he was awarded the Nobel Prize in literature (1957).

cam wheel *n.* a wheel that functions as a cam

cam·wood /kám wŏŏd/ *n.* **1. W AFRICAN TREE** a West African tree that produces hard red wood. Latin name: *Baphia nitida.* **2. HARD RED WOOD** the hard red wood of the camwood tree, formerly used in cabinetmaking and as the source of a red dye [Late 17thC. *Cam* probably from Temne *k'am.*]

can[1] /kan/ *n.* **1. FOOD CONTAINER** a sealed metal container, usually cylindrical, in which food or drink is preserved or packaged and sold **2. METAL CONTAINER** any metal container with a removable lid or cap, especially one for storing or packaging liquids, e.g., chemicals and paint **3. CONTENTS OF CAN** the contents of a metal container ○ *I drank two cans of beer.* ○ *We used up three cans of paint.* **4. PRESSURIZED CONTAINER** a metal container that holds liquid under pressure so that it can be released as a spray ○ *a can of hairspray* **5. PRISON** prison (*slang*) ○ *in the can* **6. TOILET** a toilet (*slang*) **7. BUTTOCKS** the buttocks (*slang*) ○ *When a guy falls on his can, everybody laughs.* **8.** NAVY **SHIP** a ship (*slang*) **9.** SHIPPING = **can buoy** ■ *vt.* (**canned, can·ning, cans**) **1. PUT IN METAL CONTAINERS** to package or preserve food or drink by putting it in sealed metal containers **2. DISMISS FROM JOB** to dismiss somebody from a job (*slang*) **3. STOP SOMETHING** to stop something regarded as inappropriate under the circumstances, e.g., laughter, tears, or jokes (*slang*) ○ *Just can the giggling, please.* [Old English *canne.* Either from a prehistoric Germanic word or from late Latin *canna.*] —**can·ful** *n.* —**can·ner** *n.* ◇ **in the can 1.** in the final edited form ready for broadcasting or distribution (*informal*) ○ *There's a lot more to do before the movie's in the can.* **2.** having been successfully completed or negotiated (*informal*) ○ *At last, after three weeks of tough negotiations, the contract was in the can.*

can[2] (*stressed*) /kan/; (*unstressed*) /kən/ CORE MEANING: a modal verb used to indicate that it is possible for something to be done or made use of in the way mentioned ○ *Loans can be made over the phone.*
vi. **1. ABLE TO** having the ability, knowledge, or the opportunity to do something ○ *If you can keep a secret, so can I.* **2. BE LIKELY** be likely to be true or the case ○ *Truancy can also signal more severe, isolated problems.* **3. BE ALLOWED TO** be allowed to do something, either by legal or moral right or by permission ○ *In Britain, you can get married at 16.* **4. BE ACCEPTABLE** used to make polite requests, suggestions, and offers ○ *Can I get anybody any more coffee?* **5. BE POSSIBLE** used in questions to emphasize strong feelings about something ○ *How can you say that?* ○ *What on earth can be the matter?* [Old English *cunnan.* Ultimately from an Indo-European base that is also the ancestor of English *know* and Latin *gnoscere* "to know."]

WORD KEY: USAGE

can or **may**? Purists often insist on a distinction between ***can***, meaning "be able to," and ***may***, meaning "be allowed to," but the distinction is hard to maintain in practice and the meanings often overlap. In everyday conversation *Can I go?* is as likely to be used as *May I go?*, and the context together with voice intonation usually makes it clear what is meant. In more formal situations it is wise to maintain the distinction, if only because many people expect it. Note that ***may*** has ambiguities of its own. *He may go* can mean either "he is allowed to go" or "it is possible that he will go"; again, intonation and context clarify the matter. The negative contraction ***mayn't*** is awkward, and for this reason ***can't*** is often used instead: *Can't we come too?*

can. *abbr.* **1.** canceled **2.** cancellation **3.** MIL cannon **4.** MUSIC canon **5.** POETRY canto

Can. *abbr.* **1.** Canada **2.** Canadian

Ca·naan·ite /káynə nīt/ *n.* **1.** PEOPLES **MEMBER OF ANCIENT SEMITIC PEOPLE** a member of a Semitic people who lived in Canaan from around 3000 B.C. until the time of the Israelites' conquest around 1000 B.C. **2.** LANG **EXTINCT MIDDLE EASTERN LANGUAGE** an extinct language once spoken in a region between the Jordan River and the Mediterranean Sea. It belongs to the Semitic group of Afro-Asiatic languages. ■ *adj.* **OF CANAAN** relating to or typical of Canaan, its people, or its culture —**Ca·naan·ite** *adj.*

Canad. *abbr.* Canadian

Canada

Ca·na·da /kánnədə/ federation occupying the northern half of North America and the second largest country in the world. Language: English, French. Currency: Canadian dollar. Capital: Ottawa. Population: 31,000,000 (1997). Area: 3,849,674 sq. mi./9,970,610 sq. km.

Can·a·da bal·sam *n.* thick resin secreted from the bark of the balsam fir. The resin is yellowish when liquid but becomes transparent when it dries. It is used for mounting specimens on microscopic slides.

Can·a·da Day *n.* in Canada, an annual holiday held on July 1 to commemorate the day in 1867 when Canada was the first British colony to become a dominion. The new dominion of Canada was a federation of Nova Scotia, New Brunswick, Quebec, and Ontario, with Prince Edward Island and Newfoundland joining later. Former name **Dominion Day**

Ca·na·da East former name for **Quebec** (1841–67)

Can·a·da goose (*plural* **Can·a·da geese**) *n.* a large North American goose with a brownish body, a black head and neck, and a white patch on its throat, also introduced into Europe. Latin name: *Branta canadensis.*

Can·a·da jay *n.* = **gray jay**

Can·a·da lil·y *n.* a North American lily with small orange funnel-shaped flowers. Latin name: *Lilium canadense.*

Can·a·da lynx *n.* a dark gray lynx that is native to Canada and the northern United States. Latin name: *Lynx canadensis.*

Can·a·da this·tle *n.* a lilac- or white-flowered variety of thistle native to Europe and Asia, now also found in North America, where it has become a fast-spreading weed. Latin name: *Cirsium arvense.*

Ca·na·da West former name for **Ontario** (1841–67)

Ca·na·di·an[1] /kə náydee ən/ *adj.* **OF CANADA** relating to or typical of Canada, or its people or culture ■ *n.* **SOMEBODY FROM CANADA** somebody who was born in or is a citizen of Canada

Ca·na·di·an[2] /kə náydee ən/ river in the southwestern United States that flows from southern Colorado across New Mexico and Texas into Oklahoma. Length: 906 mi./1,458 km.

Ca·na·di·an ba·con *n.* relatively fat-free bacon from the loin or rib end of a hog

Ca·na·di·an Eng·lish *n.* the variety of English spoken in Canada

WORD KEY: WORLD ENGLISH

Canadian English is the English language as it is used in the federation of Canada, which is geographically the largest English-speaking country in the world. However, in demographic terms (with a population of over 29 million, of which over 7 million are French-speaking, mainly in the province of Quebec), it is third equal with Australia. ***Canadian English*** has coexisted for about 230 years with Canadian French, which predates it by a century, as the French were Canada's first main European settlers. English and French are co-official languages in a nation whose linguistic mosaic includes indigenous languages (including Cree, Inuktitut, Iroquois, and Ojibwa) and immigrant languages (including Cantonese, Italian, and Ukrainian). There are at least three regional varieties of spoken ***Canadian English***: (1) the Atlantic provinces, in which the Newfoundland dialect is the most distinctive; (2) Quebec, whose English-speakers are influenced by French, and whose French-speakers, when using English, range from native-speaker fluency to varying mixtures of the two languages; (3) the rest of Canada, whose educated variety (focused on Ontario) is generally taken as the national norm. Written and printed ***Canadian English*** blends, to an increasing degree, the conventions of the United Kingdom (decreasingly influential) and, increasingly, those of the United States. U.S. spelling now predominates. Official federal bilingualism often leads to hybrid formulas such as *Jeux Canada Games* (blending French *Jeux Canada* and English *Canada Games*). ***Canadian English*** is "rhotic", i.e., *r* is pronounced in such words as *art, door, worker.* A feature of ***Canadian English*** is the use of the particle *eh* with a rising tone at the end of a sentence, as in "It's nice, eh?" Distinctively ***Canadian English*** vocabulary includes: (1) adoptions from indigenous languages, as in *anorak* and *kayak* (both international), *mackinaw* (a bush jacket), *muskeg* (mossy, swampy land); (2) adoptions from French, as in *anglophone* and *francophone* (both in the French style, without a capital), *caboteur* (a coastal trading vessel); (3) British English usages adapted for local purposes include *riding* (originally one of three divisions of Yorkshire, England, which in Canada means a political constituency), and *prime minister* (the federal first minister) contrasted with *premier* (the first minister of a provincial government).

Ca·na·di·an foot·ball *n.* a form of football that is similar to U.S. football but takes place on a larger field, has 12 players on each team, and uses three rather than four plays to advance at least ten yards or score

Ca·na·di·an hem·lock *n.* a coniferous evergreen tree that is native to Canada and is a valuable source of lumber and pulpwood. Latin name: *Tsuga canadensis.*

Cana·di·an·ism /kə náydee ə nìzzəm/ *n.* a word or other expression originating in or restricted in use to Canada

Ca·na·di·an·ize /kə náydee ə nīz/ (**-ized, -iz·ing, -iz·es**) *vti.* to make something Canadian in form, content, or status, or become Canadian —**Ca·na·di·an·iza·tion** /kə nàydee ənə záysh'n/ *n.*

Ca·na·di·an jay *n.* = **gray jay**

Ca·na·di·an lynx *n.* = **Canada lynx**

Ca·na·di·an Shield plateau region of eastern Canada extending southward and eastward from Hudson Bay. Area: 1,775,000 sq. mi./4,600,000 sq. km.

Ca·na·di·an whis·key *n. Can* blended whiskey made mainly from rye

ca·naille /kə náyl, kə nī/ *n.* the lowest class of people (*literary disapproving*) [Late 16thC. Via French from Italian *canaglia* "pack of dogs," from, ultimately, Latin *canis* "dog" (source of English *canine* and *canary*).]

ca·nal /kə nál/ *n.* **1. WATERWAY** an artificial waterway constructed for use by shipping, for irrigation, or for recreational use. It may take in parts of natural rivers along its course. **2.** ANAT **TUBE IN BODY** a tube-shaped passage in the body, carrying air, liquids, or semisolid material **3.** ASTRON **FEATURE ON SURFACE OF MARS** an apparent surface marking on Mars, formerly thought to be part of a system of water channels, a view discredited by more recent data [15thC. From French, an alteration (based on Italian *canale* or Latin *canalis*) of earlier *chanel* (source of English *channel*), from Latin *canalis* "pipe, canal," from *canna* (see CANE).]

ca·nal boat *n.* a long boat that is used on canals to carry freight or for recreational boating

Ca·na·let·to /kànnə léttō/, **Antonio** (1697–1768) Italian artist, known especially for his views of Venice and London.

can·a·lic·u·late /kànnə líkyələt, -làyt/ *adj.* with one or more grooves or hollows running lengthwise

can·a·lic·u·lus /kànnə líkyələss/ (*plural* **-li** /-lī/) *n.* a minute canal or duct in the body, especially one of the four narrow tubes that carry tears from behind the eyelids to the lacrimal sac [Mid-16thC. From Latin, literally "little pipe," from *canalis* (see CANAL).] —**can·a·lic·u·lar** *adj.*

can·a·li·za·tion /kànn'lə záysh'n/ *n.* **1. CANAL BUILDING** the building of canals, either from scratch or by converting existing waterways into canals **2. SYSTEM OF CANALS** a system of artificial waterways **3. DIRECTING OF SOMETHING** the directing or focusing of something, e.g., energy, in a particular direction (*formal*)

can·a·lize /kánn'l īz/ (**-lized, -liz·ing, -liz·es**) *v.* **1.** *vt.* **BUILD CANALS** to provide an area with canals, or convert existing waterways into canals **2.** *vt.* **DIRECT SOMETHING** to direct or focus something, e.g., energy or enthusiasm, in a particular direction (*formal*) **3.** *vi.* **FLOW INTO CHANNEL** to flow into or form a new channel **4.** *vt.* MIL **PUSH ENEMY FORCES** to drive enemy forces into a narrow space, either by firing on them or by erecting obstacles in their way

Can·an·dai·gua /kànnən dáygwə/ city in northwestern New York, at the northern end of Lake Canandaigua. Population: 10,736 (1996).

can·a·pé /kánnə pày, kánnəpee/ *n.* a bite-sized base of bread, cracker, or pastry with a topping, usually highly garnished, and served as an appetizer or to accompany drinks [Late 19thC. Via French, literally "sofa," from medieval Latin *canopeum* "mosquito net (over a bed)" (see CANOPY); the underlying idea is of a seat on which the topping sits.]

ca·nard /kə naárd/ *n.* **1. HOAX** a deliberately false report or rumor, especially something silly intended as a joke (*literary*) **2. AIRCRAFT PART LIKE WING** a small projection like a wing near the nose of an aircraft, attached in order to create extra horizontal stability **3. AIRCRAFT** an aircraft fitted with a canard [Mid-19thC. From French "duck," ultimately of imitative origin.]

ca·nar·y /kə náiree/ (*plural* **-ies**) *n.* **1.** BIRDS **YELLOW FINCH** a small yellow finch, native to the Canaries and adjacent islands, that has been domesticated as a songbird pet and as a show bird. In the past, these birds were used to detect gas in coal mines. Latin name: *Serinus canarius.* **2.** WINE **WINE** a sweet wine from the Canary Islands, similar to Madeira **3.** COLORS = **canary yellow 4.** DANCE, HIST **DANCE** a lively court dance popular in the 16th century **5. WOMAN SINGER** a female singer, especially in a dance band (*dated slang*) **6. POLICE INFORMER** a police informer (*dated slang*) [Late 16thC. Via French *Canarie*, the chief island of the Canary Islands, from, ultimately, Latin *Canaria Insula* "Isle of Dogs," from the large dogs that inhabited it in Roman times.]

ca·nar·y creep·er *n.* a climbing plant with small yellow flowers, native to Peru. Latin name: *Tropaeolum peregrinum.*

Ca·nar·y Cur·rent cold current of the Atlantic Ocean, flowing south from Spain down the western coast of northern Africa, joining the westward-flowing North Equatorial Current west of Mauritania-Senegal

ca·nar·y grass *n.* an annual grass plant native to northwestern Africa and the Canary Islands, and cultivated for its seeds that are sold as birdseed. Latin name: *Phalaris canariensis.*

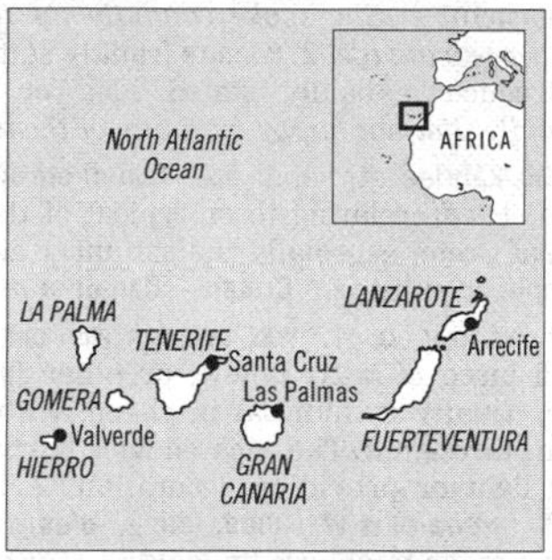

Canary Islands

Ca·nar·y Is·lands, Ca·nar·ies autonomous region of Spain, comprising the provinces of Las Palmas and Santa Cruz de Tenerife. Situated off the northwestern coast of Africa, they consist of seven large islands and various islets. The climate is subtropical and tourism is important, especially on the islands of Gran Canaria and Tenerife. Population: 1,631,498 (1995). Area: 2,808 sq. mi./7,273 sq. km. Spanish **Islas Canarias**

ca·nar·y yel·low, ca·nar·y *adj.* of a bright yellow color, like the plumage of certain varieties of canary —**ca·nar·y yel·low** *n.*

ca·nas·ta /kə nástə/ *n.* **1. VARIANT OF RUMMY** a variant of the card game rummy played with two 52-card packs. Players are dealt 15 cards, the goal being to collect groups of seven similar cards. **2. SET OF CARDS** a point-scoring set of cards in canasta [Mid-20thC. Via Spanish, literally "basket," from Latin *canistrum* (source of English *canister*), because two packs of cards (a "basketful") are used.]

Can·ber·ra /kán bèrrə, -bərə/ capital city of Australia, located in the Australian Capital Territory in southeastern Australia. Construction of this purpose-built capital began in 1912. Population: 322,723 (1996).

can buoy *n.* an unlighted marker buoy for shipping, cylindrical or cone-shaped above the water

canc. *abbr.* **1.** canceled **2.** cancellation

can·can /kán kàn/ *n.* a dance danced by a chorus line of women who perform high kicks to reveal their underwear. It originated in the 1840s in the music halls in Paris. [Mid-19thC. From French, possibly from *canard* "duck," originally "noise, uproar."]

can·can skirt *n.* a skirt with layers of ruffles and attached underwear that is shown by cancan dancers when the skirt is lifted during the dance

can·cel /kánss'l/ *v.* (**-celed, -cel·ing, -cels**) **1.** *vti.* **STOP SOMETHING FROM HAPPENING** to stop a previously arranged event from happening ○ *We had to cancel five classes because nobody showed up.* ○ *The guest speaker is ill and has had to cancel.* **2.** *vti.* **END CONTRACT** to withdraw officially or legally from a contract ○ *Members are free to cancel at any time.* **3.** *vt.* **MARK AS USED** to invalidate a legal or official document to show that it has been used and cannot be reused ○ *machines that cancel postage stamps* **4.** *vt.* **REVERSE INSTRUCTION** to reverse an instruction to a machine, especially a computer, or bring a machine's operation to an end ○ *Cancel the download from the Internet.* **5.** *vt.* **DELETE** to mark something for deletion, usually by drawing a line through it **6.** *vti.* MATH **REMOVE COMMON FACTOR** to remove a common factor from the numerator and denominator of a fraction or the common terms from the two sides of an equation ○ *The twelves cancel and you end up with 8 by 6 again.* ■ *n.* **1.** PRINTING **INSERTED PAGE** a new page or section of a book inserted to replace a missing original or an original that contained errors **2.** PRINTING **PAGE TO BE REPLACED** a faulty page or section of a book replaced by another **3.** = **cancellation** [14thC. Via French *canceller* from Latin *cancellare* "to cross out (writing)" (literally "to make like a lattice"), from *cancelli* "lattice" (source of English *chancel*), from *cancer* "grating, lattice."] —**can·cel·a·ble** *adj.* —**can·cel·er** *n.*

cancel out *vt.* to combine two opposite or equally powerful things with the result that their strengths, qualities, or effects are neutralized

can·ce·la·tion *n.* = **cancellation**

can·cel·bot /kánss'l bòt/ *n.* a computer program that finds and cancels unwanted articles sent to an Internet newsgroup by a specific user [Late 20thC. Blend of CANCEL and ROBOT.]

can·cel·late /kánss'l àyt, kánss'lət/, **can·cel·lat·ed** /kánss'l àytəd/ *adj.* **1.** ANAT = **cancellous 2.** BOT **FORMING A MESH** forming a mesh or network

can·cel·la·tion /kànss'l áysh'n/, **can·ce·la·tion** *n.* **1. CANCELING OF SOMETHING** the canceling of something, e.g., an appointment or order ○ *We had one cancellation for two o'clock, so we can fit you in then.* ○ *There is a cancellation charge if you withdraw your order at the last minute.* **2. THING MADE AVAILABLE** something, e.g., a seat in a theater, that has become available because the person who reserved it has canceled **3. CANCELING MARK** a mark that officially or legally invalidates something, especially a postage stamp [Mid-16thC. Formed from Latin *cancellat-*, the past participle stem of *cancellare* (see CANCEL).]

can·cel·lous /kánss'ləss, kan sélləss/ *adj.* ANAT used to describe bone that has a mesh of hollows on the inside, as opposed to being compact or dense [Mid-19thC. Formed from Latin *cancelli* (see CANCEL).]

can·cer /kánssər/ *n.* **1. MALIGNANT TUMOR** a malignant tumor or growth caused when cells multiply uncontrollably, destroying healthy tissue. The different forms are sarcomas, carcinomas, leukemias, and lymphomas. **2. ILLNESS CAUSED BY TUMOR** the illness or condition that is caused by the presence of a malignant tumor **3. FAST-SPREADING BAD PHENOMENON** something, usually something negative, that develops or spreads quickly and usually destructively [Pre-12thC. From Latin, literally "crab" (source of English *canker*), translated from Greek *karkinos* (source of English *carcinoma*); the sense "tumor" evolved because of the swollen veins, thought to resemble crabs.]

Can·cer /kánssər/ *n.* **1.** ASTRON **CONSTELLATION BETWEEN GEMINI AND LEO** a constellation in the northern hemisphere between Gemini and Leo **2.** ZODIAC **4TH SIGN OF THE ZODIAC** the fourth sign of the zodiac, represented by a crab and lasting from approximately June 21 to July 22. Cancer is classified as a water sign, and its ruling planet is the Moon. **3.** ZODIAC **SOMEBODY BORN UNDER CANCER SIGN** somebody whose birthday falls between June 21 and July 22 [Pre-12thC. From Latin (see CANCER); from the constellation's sideways movement across the sky.]

Can·cer·i·an /kan sáiree ən/ *n., adj.* = **Cancer** *n.* 3

can·cer·o·pho·bi·a /kànsərə fṓbee ə/ *n.* an obsessive fear of developing cancer

can·cer·ous /kánssərəss/ *adj.* **1. AFFECTED BY CANCER** used to describe a body part affected by cancer, or a malignant tumor ○ *cancerous cells that were detected early* **2. CAUSING HARM** developing rapidly to cause widespread harm

can·cer stick *n.* a cigarette (*slang*)

can·croid /káng krȯyd/ *adj.* CRABLIKE like a crab in shape, structure, or movement ■ *n.* = **squamous cell carcinoma** [Early 19thC. Formed from Latin *cancr-*, the stem of *cancer* "crab, cancer" (see CANCER).]

Can·cún /kàn ko͝on/ island resort on the northeastern coast of Quintana Roo state, Mexico. Population: 27,500 (1980).

can·del·a /kan déllə/ *n.* the SI unit of luminous intensity, based on a standard for blackbody radiation. Symbol **cd** [Mid-20thC. From Latin, "candle, taper" (see CANDLE).]

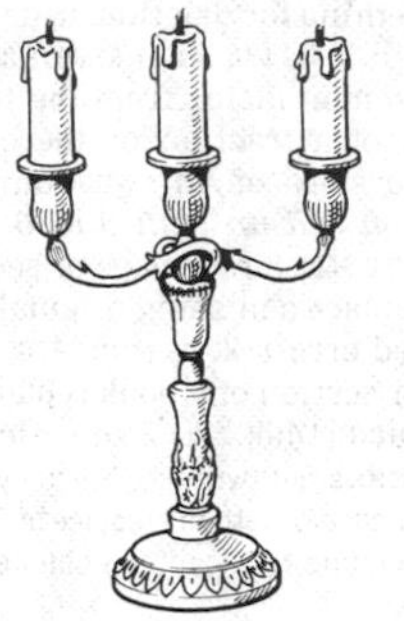

Candelabrum

can·de·la·brum /kànd'l aábrəm, -ábbrəm/ (*plural* **-bra** /-aábrə, -ábbrə/ *or* **-brums**) *n.* a large decorative candleholder with several arms or branches, or a similarly shaped electric light fixture [Early 19thC. From Latin, the plural of *candelabrum* "candlestick," from *candela* "candle, taper" (see CANDLE).]

can·des·cence /kan déss'nss/ *n.* the brightness or dazzle of white light or white heat (*literary*) ○ *the candescence of snow on a cloudless morning* [Late 19thC. Formed from Latin *candescere* "to begin to glow," from *candere* (see CANDESCENT).]

can·des·cent /kan déss'nt/ *adj.* shining or glowing with an intense white light (*literary*) [Early 19thC. Formed from Latin *candere* "to be white, glow" (source of English *candid, candle,* and *incense*).] —**can·des·cence** *n.* —**can·des·cent·ly** *adv.*

c & i *abbr.* cost and insurance

can·did /kándid/ *adj.* 1. HONEST honest or direct in a way that people find either refreshing or distasteful ○ *a surprisingly candid admission* 2. PHOTOGRAPHED INFORMALLY photographed or filmed without the subject knowing or having the opportunity to prepare or pose ○ *a candid documentary* 3. UNBIASED free from prejudice or bias (*archaic*) ○ *with candid hearts and minds* 4. KIND with innocence or purity of heart untainted by malicious thoughts and feelings (*archaic*) 5. WHITE white, especially with the whiteness of innocence or purity (*archaic*) ○ *"kissing her candid brow, and feeling that heaven had vouchsafed him a blessing"* (George Eliot, *Middlemarch*; 1872) ■ *n.* UNPOSED PHOTOGRAPH a photograph that is taken, unposed and informally, of a person or group ○ *hired a professional photographer to do the wedding candids* [Mid-17thC. Directly or via French *candide* "guileless" from Latin *candidus* "white, shining," from *candere* "to be white, glisten"; the current sense evolved via "pure" and "impartial."] —**can·did·ly** *adv.* —**can·did·ness** *n.*

can·di·da /kándidə/ *n.* MED 1. FUNGUS THAT CAUSES YEAST INFECTION a fungus that can cause yeast infection, especially in the mouth and vagina. Latin name: *Candida albicans.* 2. = **yeast infection** [Mid-20thC. From Latin, feminine of *candidus* "white" (see CANDID), because of its color.]

can·di·da·cy /kándidəssee/ *n.* somebody's offering of himself or herself as a candidate ○ *She isn't expected to declare her candidacy for re-election.*

can·di·date /kándi dàyt, kándidət/ *n.* 1. APPLICANT FOR OFFICE somebody who runs for election to a political office or an official position ○ *names of candidates for the leadership of the party* 2. APPLICANT FOR JOB somebody who applies for a new job or is being considered for a new job ○ *The successful candidate will have had experience with market research.* 3. LIKELY OR SUITABLE PERSON somebody who seems suitable for something, e.g., a surgical operation or a new treatment protocol, or who seems likely to be affected by a particular disease ○ *Men in this group are prime candidates for a heart attack.* 4. EXAM TAKER somebody who sits for an exam, especially somebody who is scheduled to receive a degree upon passing exams ○ *She is a candidate for a juris doctor degree in May.* 5. COMPETITOR somebody competing with others for a prize or award ○ *Candidates for Oscars include two Canadians and two Americans.* [Early 17thC. Directly or via French *candidat* from Latin *candidatus*, literally "clothed in white"; from the white togas worn by candidates for election in ancient Rome.]

WORD KEY: SYNONYMS

candidate, contender, contestant, aspirant, applicant, entrant

CORE MEANING: somebody who is seeking to be chosen for something or to win something

candidate the most general term for somebody who is being considered for a job, grant, or prize, running for election to a position, or taking part in an examination; **contender** somebody who competes with others to win something such as a sporting title or a high honor; **contestant** somebody who takes part in a contest or competitive event; **aspirant** somebody aspiring to distinction or advancement; **applicant** somebody who has asked or applied to be a candidate for something; **entrant** a term similar to "contestant," often used of somebody who enters an examination or contest.

can·did cam·er·a *n.* the use of hidden cameras to film subjects unawares, often in stage-managed situations intended to elicit amusing responses (*hyphenated when used before a noun*)

can·di·di·a·sis /kàndə dí əssiss/ (*plural* **-didi·as·es** /-seez/) *n.* yeast infection (*technical*) [Mid-20thC. Coined from CANDIDA + -IASIS.]

can·did·ly /kándidlee/ *adv.* 1. FRANKLY in an honest or direct way that people might find either refreshing or distasteful ○ *She spoke candidly on television about her private life.* 2. IN TRUTH frankly stated, used to introduce a baldly stated idea or opinion ○ *Candidly, I'm not happy with any of them.*

Can·di·ot /kándee ət, kándi òt/, **Can·di·ote** /kándi ōt, kándee ət/ *adj.* relating to or typical of the Greek island of Crete, especially the capital, Iráklion, or its people or culture. ◊ **Cretan** —**Can·di·ot** *n.*

can·dle /kánd'l/ *n.* 1. WAX CYLINDER PROVIDING LIGHT a molded piece of wax, tallow, or other fatty substance, usually cylindrical in shape, with a wick running through it. The encased wick burns slowly, giving light or providing decoration. 2. CANDELA a candela (*archaic*) ■ *vt.* (**-dled, -dling, -dles**) TEST EGG to test an egg for freshness by looking at it against a bright light [Pre-12thC. From Latin *candella*, earlier *candela* (source of English *candela* and *candelabra*), from *candere* "to be white, glisten" (source of English *candid, incendiary,* and *incense*).] ◇ **burn the candle at both ends** to get up very early and go to bed very late, allowing for very little rest ◇ **not hold a candle to somebody** to be not nearly as good at something as somebody ○ *As a writer, he does not hold a candle to his mother.*

can·dle·ber·ry /kánd'l bèrree/ (*plural* **-ries**) *n.* any shrub or tree that has berries that can be used for making candles

can·dle·fish /kánd'l fish/ (*plural* **-fish·es** *or* **-fish**) *n.* an oily saltwater fish found in the northern Pacific Ocean. Latin name: *Thaleichthys pacificus.* [From the former use of the dried fish as a lamp by pushing a piece of bark through it as a wick]

can·dle·hold·er /kánd'l hōldər/ *n.* a holder for a candle, often a decorative one. Candleholders can be of many shapes but are not necessarily tall and thin like candlesticks.

can·dle·light /kánd'l līt/ *n.* 1. LIGHT FROM CANDLES the light that a burning candle provides ○ *reading by candlelight* 2. DUSK twilight, the time when candles are lit (*literary*)

can·dle·lit /kánd'l lìt/ *adj.* lit by candles, or done by candlelight ○ *a silent, candlelit march through the streets*

Can·dle·mas /kánd'lməss/ *n.* a Christian feast held on February 2, commemorating the purification of the Virgin Mary and the presentation of the infant Jesus in the Temple. This is also the time when church candles are blessed. [Pre-12thC. *-Mas* from ecclesiastical Latin *missa* "the mass" (source of English *mass*).]

can·dle·nut /kánd'l nùt/ *n.* 1. TROPICAL TREE a tropical tree of the spurge family, native to Asia and Polynesia. Latin name: *Aleurites moluccana.* 2. OILY NUT the seed of the candlenut tree, used as a source of oil in paints and varnishes, and, in Asia and Polynesia, threaded with a wick for use as a candle

can·dle·pin /kánd'l pìn/ *n.* a slim pin used in the bowling game candlepins [*Candle* from its shape and comparative slenderness]

can·dle·pins /kánd'l pìnz/ *n.* a bowling game using slender pins and a ball smaller than that used in tenpins (*takes a singular verb*)

can·dle·pow·er /kánd'l pòwr/ *n.* the intensity of light measured in candelas

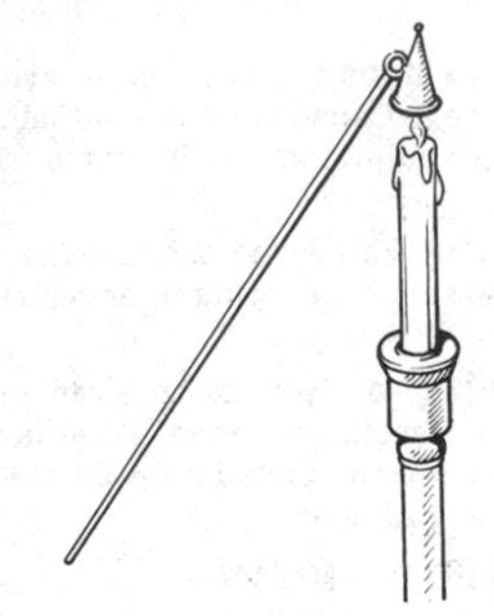

Candlesnuffer

can·dle·snuff·er /kánd'l snùffər/ *n.* a device, usually made of metal, consisting of a small cone on the end of a long thin handle, placed over the flame of a candle to put it out

can·dle·stick /kánd'l stìk/ *n.* a tall thin holder for a candle

can·dle·wick /kánd'l wìk/ *n.* 1. THICK STRING thick string used for candle wicks 2. COTTON FABRIC tufted cotton fabric used for bedcovers, dressing gowns, and other garments 3. EMBROIDERY YARN soft cotton yarn used for embroidery

can·dle·wood /kánd'l wo͝od/ *n.* 1. RESINOUS TREE any tree or shrub that produces resinous wood that can be burned for light and fuel 2. RESINOUS WOOD the resinous wood of a candlewood tree

C and M, C&M *abbr.* care and maintenance

can-do *adj.* eager to take on a job or challenge and confident of success (*informal*) ○ *We're only looking at can-do executives with proven track records.*

can·dor /kándər/ *n.* 1. CANDID QUALITY honesty or directness, whether refreshing or distasteful ○ *He spoke of their conspicuous candor and bravery.* 2. FREEDOM FROM PREJUDICE freedom from prejudice or bias (*archaic*) 3. KINDNESS innocence or purity of heart arising from a complete absence of malicious thoughts and feelings (*archaic*) ○ *"But the gentleness and candor of Rebecca's nature imputed no fault to Ivanhoe for sharing in the universal prejudices of his age and religion."* (Walter Scott, *Ivanhoe*; 1819) 4. WHITENESS whiteness, especially the whiteness of innocence or purity (*archaic*) [14thC. From Latin *candor* "glossy whiteness, sincerity," from *cand-*, the base *candidus* "dazzling white" (source of English *candid*) and *candere* "to be white, glisten" (source of English *candle*).]

can·dour *n.* U.K. = **candor**

CAN·DU re·ac·tor /kán doo-, kan do͝o-/ *n.* a form of nuclear reactor designed and built in Canada that uses replaceable fuel bundles and heavy water to moderate fission and cool the reactor core [*CANDU* from the first letters of CANADA + DEUTERIUM + URANIUM]

C&W *abbr.* MUSIC country and western

can·dy /kándee/ *n.* (*plural* **-dies**) 1. SMALL CONFECTION small sweet food items such as chocolate bars, mints, and toffee, usually eaten for pleasure and not as part of a meal 2. PIECE OF CONFECTIONERY a small hard, chewy, or soft piece of food made from sugar and other ingredients or flavorings such as chocolate, nuts, fruit, or peppermint ○ *Our store sells the finest chocolate candy in the country.* 3. HARD DRUGS heroin, cocaine, or any other hard drug (*slang*) ■ *v.* (**-died, -dy·ing, -dies**) 1. *vti.* TURN SUGAR SOLUTION INTO CRYSTALS to turn a sugar solution into crystals, especially by boiling it, or be converted into sugar crystals 2. *vt.* STEEP IN SUGAR to dress a food by impregnating it with sugar, in order either to preserve it or to make it more pleasant to eat 3. *vt.* COAT WITH SUGAR SYRUP to coat food with sugar or sugar syrup, or be coated with sugar or sugar syrup [13thC. Via Old French *candi* from Arabic *qandī* "crystalized into sugar," from *qand* "cane sugar."]

can·dy ap·ple *n.* an apple on a stick coated with a mixture of toffee or melted cinnamon candy

can·dy-ass *n.* a weak or cowardly person, especially a man (*slang offensive*) —**can·dy-ass** *adj.*

can·dy·floss /kándi flòss/ *n. U.K.* = **cotton candy**

can·dy man *n.* **1. CANDY SELLER** in former times, a roving seller of candy **2. DRUG PUSHER** somebody who sells drugs, especially heroin, cocaine, and other hard drugs (*slang*)

can·dy-striped *adj.* with a pattern of narrow stripes in a single color, usually red or pink, on a white background

can·dy strip·er *n.* a volunteer worker in a hospital, especially a young person [From the volunteers' red-and-white striped uniform]

can·dy·tuft /kándi tùft/ *n.* a flowering plant with thin leaves and clusters of white, red, or purple flowers. There are annual and perennial types, and the genus is native to Europe and the Mediterranean. Genus: *Iberis.* [Early 17thC. *Candy* an obsolete form of *Candia*, a former name for Crete.]

cane /kayn/ *n.* **1. WALKING STICK** a stick that people use to help them walk **2. STICK FOR PUNISHMENT BEATINGS** a long flexible stick for administering beatings, especially one formerly used to punish schoolchildren **3. BAMBOO STEM** a hollow lightweight stem of a tropical plant, especially bamboo, used in various ways in the house and garden, e.g., as a growing support for plants **4. WOVEN STEMS** the stems of various palms and grass plants, e.g., rattan, woven together to make furniture, baskets, and other household items **5. STEM OF FRUIT PLANT** the long woody stem of various fruit-bearing plants such as the raspberry or blackberry **6. LONG-STEMMED PLANT** a coarse grass or reed with long stiff stems, e.g., sugarcane or sorghum ■ *vt.* **(caned, can·ing, canes) BEAT SOMEBODY** to beat somebody, especially, formerly, a schoolchild, with a cane [14thC. Via Old French *cane* and Latin *canna* from Greek *kanna* "reed" (source also of English *canal* and *cannon*), ultimately of Semitic origin.]

cane·brake /káyn bràyk/ *n.* an area of land planted or overgrown with cane

ca·ne·pho·ra /kə néffərə/ (*plural* **-rae** /-reè, -rī/) *n.* an ancient Greek sculpture representing a human figure carrying a basket on its head [Early 17thC. Via Latin from Greek *kanēphoros*, literally "basket-carrying."]

cane piece *n.* in the Caribbean, a field of sugarcane, especially one that is isolated and belongs to a small farmer

can·er /káynər/ *n.* somebody who makes or repairs furniture and other items made of cane

cane rat *n.* a large rat native to sub-Saharan areas of Africa, measuring up to 2 ft./60 cm without the tail, and eaten locally as a delicacy. Genus: *Thryonomys.* [Because it eats sugarcane]

ca·nes·cent /kə néss'nt/ *adj.* **1. WHITE AND HAIRY** used to describe plant parts that have a white or whitish-gray covering of fine hairs **2. BECOMING WHITE OR GRAYISH** becoming white or grayish [Mid-19thC. From the present participle stem of Latin *canescere* "to grow white," from *canus* "white, hoary."] —**ca·nes·cence** *n.*

cane sug·ar *n.* sucrose obtained from sugarcane or sugar beets

Ca·nes Ve·nat·i·ci /kàyneez və náttə seè/ *n.* a constellation of stars visible in the northern hemisphere near Ursa Major and Boötes, under the handle of the Big Dipper [From Latin, literally "hunting dogs"]

cane toad *n.* a large South American toad introduced into Australia to control pests in sugarcane. A spectacular failure as a pest control, it has now become a major pest itself. Latin name: *Bufo marinus.*

can·field /kán feèld/ *n.* a gambling game developed from the card game solitaire [Early 20thC. Named for the U.S. gambler Richard Albert *Canfield* (1855–1914), who devised the game and turned it into a form of gambling.]

cangue /kang/, **cang** *n.* a heavy wooden yoke worn on the shoulders and enclosing the neck and arms, formerly used in China for punishing petty criminals [Late 17thC. Via French from Portuguese *canga* "yoke," from Vietnamese *gong.*]

Ca·nic·u·la /kə níkyələ/ *n.* = **Sirius** [12thC. From Latin, literally "little dog" (see CANICULAR).]

ca·nic·u·lar /kə níkyələr/ *adj.* relating to the star Sirius [14thC. From late Latin *canicularis*, from *canicula*, literally "little dog" (denoting the "dog star"), from *canis* "dog" (source of English *canine* and *kennel*).]

can·id /kánnid, káy-/ *n.* any carnivorous mammal of the dog family, which includes the foxes, wolves, jackals, dingos, coyotes, and domestic breeds [Late 19thC. From modern Latin *Canidae*, the family name, from Latin *canis* "dog" (source of English *canine, canary*, and *kennel*).]

ca·nine /káy nīn/ *adj.* **OF DOGS** relating to dogs ○ *a canine trainer* ○ *members of the canine family* ■ *n.* **1.** DENT **POINTED TOOTH** a pointed tooth between the incisors and the first bicuspids. Most mammals have two in each jaw. **2. DOG** a dog (*often used humorously*) [15thC. Directly or via French *canin(e)* from Latin *caninus*, from *canis* "dog" (source of English *kennel*).]

ca·nine dis·tem·per *n.* = **distemper**

ca·nine tooth *n.* = **canine** *n.* 1

can·ing /káyning/ *n.* a punishment beating with a cane, especially the beatings formerly administered to schoolchildren

Ca·nis Ma·jor /kàyniss-, kànniss-/ *n.* a constellation of stars containing the star Sirius, situated southeast of Orion. Canis Major and Canis Minor represent dogs following at the heels of Orion the Hunter. ◊ **Canis Minor** [From Latin, literally "greater dog"]

Ca·nis Mi·nor /kàyniss-, kànniss-/ *n.* a constellation of stars containing the star Procyon, situated east of Orion. ◊ **Canis Major** [From Latin, literally "lesser dog"]

can·is·tel /kánni stèl, kánni stél/ *n.* **1. SUBTROPICAL TREE** a tree that bears a sweet egg-shaped fruit with a strong musky smell. It is native to Mexico, Central America, and the Caribbean. Latin name: *Pouteria campechiana.* **2. FRUIT OF CANISTEL TREE** the fruit of the canistel tree [From American Spanish]

can·is·ter /kánnistər/ *n.* **1. PRESSURIZED CONTAINER** a pressurized metal container holding a substance released as a spray **2. SEALED CONTAINER** a strong sealed metal container for hazardous chemicals **3. FOOD CONTAINER** a metal container with a lid, for storing tea, coffee, or other dry foods **4.** ARMS **EXPLOSIVE** a weapon used in former times consisting of a metal shell filled with gas and shot or shrapnel, designed to explode when thrown or fired from a cannon [Late 15thC. Via Latin *canistrum* (source of English *canasta*) from Greek *kanastron* "wicker basket," from *kanna* "reed" (source of English *cane*).]

can·ker /kángkər/ *n.* **1.** BOT **PLANT DISEASE** any disease that creates open wounds on the trunks and branches of woody plants. Cankers can be caused by bacteria, fungi, or pests. **2.** VET **ANIMAL DISEASE** any of several diseases of animals, e.g., a disease of horses that makes their hooves become soft and spongy, a disease that can cause ulcers in the outer ears of some animals, or a throat infection of some birds **3. EVIL** an evil or corrupting influence that spreads and is difficult to wipe out ○ *"This canker that eats up Love's tender spring"* (William Shakespeare, *Venus and Adonis*; 1593) ■ *vti.* **(-kered, -ker·ing, -kers) 1.** BOT **DEVELOP CANKER** to develop canker, or cause the trunks and branches of woody plants to develop canker **2. MAKE OR BECOME CORRUPT** to become a source of spreading corruption or evil, or cause something to decay as a result of spreading corruption or evil [14thC. Via Old Northern French *cancre* from the Latin stem *cancr-* "crab, cancer" (see CANCER).] —**can·ker·ous** *adj.*

can·ker brake *n.* = **Christmas fern** [*Brake* perhaps a shortening of BRACKEN]

can·ker·root /kángkər ro͝ot, kángkər ro͞ot/ *n.* = **goldthread**

can·ker sore *n.* an ulcer on the lips or inside the mouth

can·ker·worm /kángkər wòrm/ *n.* the larva of either of two types of moth that destroys the leaves and fruit of trees in North America. Latin name: *Paleacrita vernata* and *Alsophila pometaria.*

can·na /kánnə/ *n.* a perennial tropical plant native to the West Indies and Central America that is cultivated for its clusters of red or yellow flowers and luxuriant foliage. Genus: *Canna.* [Mid-18thC. Via modern Latin *Canna*, genus name, from Latin *canna* "reed, cane" (see CANE).]

can·na·bi·di·ol /kànnəbi deè òl, kànnəbi dī òl/ *n.* one of the chemical constituents of cannabis. Formula: $C_{21}H_{28}(OH)_2$. [Mid-20thC. Coined from CANNABIS + DI- + -OL.]

can·na·bis /kánnəbiss/ *n.* **1. DRUG** a mild intoxicant and hallucinogen produced in various forms from the dried leaves and flowers of the hemp plant, smoked or chewed to induce relaxation and mild euphoria. Its recreational use is illegal in most countries. **2. HEMP PLANT** the hemp plant, especially when grown as a source of cannabis. Latin name: *Cannabis sativa.* [Early 18thC. Via Latin (source of English *canvas*) from Greek *kannabis.*]

can·na·bis res·in *n.* the drug cannabis in the form of a greenish-black resin

canned /kand/ *adj.* **1. PRESERVED IN A CAN** preserved by being sealed into airtight metal containers **2. PRERECORDED** prerecorded in a standardized form for general use, rather than recorded for a specific broadcast or performance ○ *The actors learn to leave pauses where the canned laughter is to be inserted.* **3. UNVARYING** used repeatedly with little or no variation, and therefore lacking freshness or originality ○ *gave the usual canned spiel about not wanting to raise taxes* **4. DRUNK** extremely inebriated (*slang*)

Canned Heat *tdmk.* a trademark for fuel consisting of solid alcohol or paraffin packed into small cans and used to heat food

can·nel /kánn'l/, **can·nel coal** *n.* a bituminous coal that burns brightly and creates a lot of smoke [Mid-16thC. From northern English dialect *cannel* "candle," from its bright flame.]

can·nel·lo·ni /kànn'l ṓnee/ *n.* wide tubes or rolls of pasta that are stuffed with a filling, e.g., meat or cheese, topped with sauce, often tomato, then baked [Mid-20thC. From Italian, the plural of *cannellone* "tubular noodle," from, ultimately, Latin *canna* "cane, reed" (see CANE).]

can·ne·lure /kánn'l o͝or/ *n.* a groove around the cylindrical part of a bullet [Mid-18thC. From French, from *canneler* "to make a groove in," from *canne* "reed" (see CANE).]

can·ner·y /kánnəree/ (*plural* **-ies**) *n.* a factory where food is packaged into cans

Cannes /kan, kanz/ resort and seaport on the French Riviera that is the site of an annual international film festival. It is situated in the Alpes-Maritimes Department in the Provence-Alpes-Côtes-d'Azur administrative region of southern France. Population: 335,647 (1990).

can·ni·bal /kánnib'l/ *n.* **1. SOMEBODY WHO EATS HUMAN FLESH** somebody who eats human flesh, whether as food or as part of a religious ritual **2. ANIMAL THAT EATS ITS OWN SPECIES** an animal that eats the flesh of other animals of the same species [Mid-16thC. From Spanish *Canibales*, a variant (used by the explorer Columbus) of *Caribes*, the name of a cannibalistic people of Cuba and Haiti (see CARIB).]

can·ni·bal·ism /kánnib'l ìzzəm/ *n.* **1. HUMANS EATING HUMANS** the eating of human flesh by other human beings, whether for food or as a religious ritual **2. ANIMALS EATING OWN SPECIES** the eating of animal flesh by animals of the same species

can·ni·bal·is·tic /kànnib'l ístik/ *adj.* relating to, involving, or practicing cannibalism —**can·ni·bal·is·ti·cal·ly** *adv.*

can·ni·bal·ize /kánnib'l ìz/ (**-ized, -iz·ing, -iz·es**) *vt.* **1. STEAL PARTS** to take parts from something, especially a machine, in order to use them elsewhere ○ *The troops, hard-pressed for spare parts, cannibalized the tracks from a wrecked tank to repair their own damaged vehicle.* **2. EAT MEMBER OF OWN SPECIES** to eat the flesh of another human being or of an animal of the same species —**can·ni·bal·i·za·tion** /kànnib'lə záysh'n/ *n.*

can·ni·kin /kánnikin/ *n.* a small can, especially one used for drinking from [Late 16thC. From Dutch *kanneken*, literally "little can," from Middle Dutch *canne* "can."]

can·no·li /kə nṓlee/ (*plural* **-li**) *n.* a deep-fried sweet Italian pastry with a soft cheese and candied fruit filling. It originated in Sicily. [Mid-20thC. Via Italian, the plural of *cannolo*, literally "little tube," from, ultimately, Latin *canna* "reed, pipe" (see CANE).]

can·non /kánnən/ *n.* **1.** (*plural* **-nons** *or* **-non**) **FORMER WEAPON** a weapon used in former times, now used only ceremonially, consisting of a simple iron tube mounted on wheels. It fires heavy iron balls and other projectiles. ○ *The cannon fired a 21-gun salute.* **2. MODERN WEAPON** a modern heavy artillery weapon large enough to need to be mounted for firing, e.g., one mounted on a warship or on a tracked vehicle **3. AIRCRAFT GUN** a rapid-firing gun mounted on an aircraft **4.** *U.K.* CUE GAMES = **carom 5. BELL LOOP** the loop at the top of a bell from which it is suspended ■ *v.* **(-noned, -non·ing, -nons) 1.** *vt.* = **cannonade 2.** *vi.* **COLLIDE** to collide with something or bounce off it at great speed and with a lot of force ○ *The car, out of control on the icy road, cannoned into the bridge abutment and burst into flames.* **3.** *vi. U.K.* CUE GAMES **MAKE A CAROM** in cue games, to make a carom [14thC. Via French *canon* from Italian *cannone*, literally "large tube," from, ultimately, Latin *canna* "reed, tube" (see CANE).]

Can·non /kánnən/, **Joseph Gurney** (1836–1926) U.S. political leader. He was a powerful Republican Speaker of the House of Representatives (1903–11) during a long congressional career (1873–1923). Known as **Uncle Joe**

can·non·ade /kànnə náyd/ *n.* **1.** MIL **BOMBARDMENT** a sustained bombardment with heavy artillery **2. SOMETHING LIKE A BOMBARDMENT** something that sounds or feels like an artillery bombardment ○ *"The deep cannonade of roaring thunder belched forth its fearsome challenge."* (Edgar Rice Burroughs, *Tarzan of the Apes*; 1914) ■ *v.* **(-ad·ed, -ad·ing, -ades) 1.** *vti.* **BOMBARD** to subject an enemy to a cannonade **2.** *vt.* **ATTACK SOMEBODY** to subject somebody to a sustained attack, e.g., with words of criticism or reproach [Mid-16thC. Via French from Italian *cannonata*, from *cannone* (see CANNON).]

can·non·ball /kánnən bàwl/ *n.* **1. BALL FIRED FROM CANNON** a heavy metal or stone ball fired from an old-fashioned cannon **2. JUMP INTO WATER** a jump into water with the body tucked into a ball, usually with head down and knees drawn up to the chest ■ *vi.* **(-balled, -ball·ing, -balls) TRAVEL QUICKLY** to travel at great speed (*informal*) ○ *The fast freight train cannonballed through the dark tunnel.*

can·non·ball tree *n.* a South American tree that produces round fruits with woody husks that are used to make containers and utensils. Latin name: *Couroupita guianensis.*

can·non bone *n.* a bone in the lower limbs of some hoofed animals, evolved from the fusing of the metatarsals or metacarpals [*Cannon* because of the bone's tubular shape]

can·non·eer /kànnə neér/ *n.* in former times, a soldier who fired a cannon [Mid-16thC. Via French *canonnier* from Italian *cannoniere*, from *cannone* (see CANNON).]

can·non fod·der *n.* (*informal*) **1. LOW-RANKING MILITARY PERSONNEL** members of the lowest ranks of the military, regarded as an expendable resource in wartime **2. EXPENDABLE PERSON** any person or group regarded as a resource to be exploited or sacrificed ○ *Our team ended up as cannon fodder for the opponents in the first championship game.*

can·non·ry /kánnənree/ (*plural* **-ries**) *n.* **1. BURST OF ARTILLERY FIRE** a burst of artillery fire **2. ARTILLERY** artillery in general

can·not /ká nòt, kə nót/ *v.* an alternative way of writing "can not"

WORD KEY: USAGE

See Usage note at ***help.***

can·nu·la /kánnyələ/ (*plural* **-las** *or* **-lae** /-lee/), **can·u·la** (*plural* **-las** *or* **-lae**) *n.* a flexible tube with a sharp-pointed part at one end that is inserted into a duct, vein, or cavity in order to drain away fluid or to administer drugs [Late 17thC. From Latin, literally "little tube," from *canna* "reed, pipe" (see CANE).]

can·nu·late /kánnyə làyt/, **can·u·late** *vt.* **(-lat·ed, -lat·ing, -lates) INSERT TUBE INTO BODY** to insert a tube (**cannula**) into a vein or cavity in order to drain away fluid or to administer drugs ■ *adj.* **TUBULAR** tubular in shape (*technical*) —**can·nu·la·tion** /kànnyə láysh'n/ *n.*

can·ny /kánnee/ **(-ni·er, -ni·est)** *adj.* shrewd enough not to be easily deceived ○ *a canny negotiator* [Late 16thC. Originally a Scots dialect form of CAN in its original meaning "to know, come to know" (hence "to be able").] —**can·ni·ly** *adv.* —**can·ni·ness** *n.*

ca·noe /kə nóo/ *n.* **LIGHT NARROW POINTED BOAT** a lightweight boat identically pointed at each end. It can be paddled by one or two people and sometimes can carry other people as passengers. Canoes were originally made from natural materials, but modern canoes are made of aluminum or of molded plastic and fiberglass. ■ *vi.* **(-noed, -noe·ing, -noes) TRAVEL IN CANOE** to travel or paddle in a canoe, often as a sport or hobby [Mid-16thC. Alteration (influenced by French *canoë*) of Spanish *canoa* from, ultimately, Carib *canaoua*.] —**ca·noe·a·ble** *adj.* ◇ **paddle your own canoe** to take control of and responsibility for your own life and affairs (*informal*)

ca·noe birch *n.* = **paper birch**

ca·noe·ing /kə nóo ing/ *n.* the sport, hobby, or activity of paddling a canoe

ca·noe·ist /kə nóo ist/ *n.* somebody who canoes, especially as a hobby or a sport

can of worms *n.* a complicated situation that results from unforeseen problems, especially an issue that seems likely to create conflicts (*informal*)

ca·no·la /kə nólə/ *n.* **1.** PLANTS **TYPE OF RAPESEED PLANT** a type of rapeseed plant that yields oil with high nutritional quality **2.** FOOD = **canola oil** [Late 20thC. Coined from CANADA + -OLA (influenced by Latin *oleum* "oil").]

ca·no·la oil *n.* a kind of rapeseed oil that has a high level of monounsaturated fatty acids, used as a cooking oil

can·on[1] /kánnən/ *n.* **1. GENERAL RULE** a general rule, principle, or standard ○ *one of the fundamental canons of free-market economics* **2. RELIGIOUS DECREE** a decree issued by a religious authority, especially one ruling on religious practices **3. BODY OF RELIGIOUS WRITINGS** a set of religious writings regarded as authentic and definitive and forming a religion's body of scripture **4. LIST OF SAINTS** in the Roman Catholic Church, the complete list of all the saints **5. PART OF MASS** in the Roman Catholic Mass, the prayer during which the bread and wine are consecrated **6. SET OF ARTISTIC WORKS** a set of artistic works established as genuine and complete, e.g., the works of a particular writer, painter, or moviemaker ○ *It's not one of the best-known pictures in the Welles canon.* **7.** MUSIC **STAGGERED SINGING OR PLAYING** a musical technique in which different instruments or voices enter one after the other, each playing or singing exactly the same sequence of notes, resulting in often complex counterpoint [Pre-12thC. Via Latin from Greek *kanōn* "rule."]

can·on[2] /kánnən/ *n.* **1. MEMBER OF CLERGY ATTACHED TO CATHEDRAL** a member of the Christian clergy who is on the permanent staff of a cathedral and has specific duties in relation to the running of it **2.** = **canon regular** [12thC. Via Old French *canonie* from ecclesiastical Latin *canonicus* "(somebody living) according to a rule," from Latin *canon* "rule" (see CANON[1]).]

cañ·on *n.* = **canyon**

can·on·ess /kánnənəss/ *n.* in the Roman Catholic Church, a woman who belongs to one of several religious orders in which members live under a rule, not a vow

ca·non·ic *adj.* = **canonical** [15thC. Directly or via French *canonique* from Latin *canonicus*, from, ultimately, Greek *kanōn* "rule" (source also of *canon*[1]).]

ca·non·i·cal /kə nónnik'l/, **ca·non·i·c** *adj.* **1. OF A CANON OF WORKS** relating or belonging to the biblical canon or a canon of artistic works established as genuine and complete **2. FOLLOWING CANON LAW** conforming to or authorized by canon law **3. CONFORMING TO GENERAL PRINCIPLES** conforming to accepted principles or standard practice **4. OF CATHEDRAL OR REGULAR CANONS** relating to members of the clergy who are canons **5.** MUSIC **OF MUSICAL CANON** relating to musical canons, or sung or played in a canon [15thC. From medieval Latin *canonicalis*, from Greek *kanōn* "rule" (source also of *canon*[1]).] —**ca·non·i·cal·ly** *adv.*

ca·non·i·cal hour *n.* **1. PRAYER TIME** in the Roman Catholic Church, any of the daily prayer times when specific prayers are said. These times are the matins with lauds, prime, tierce, sext, nones, vespers, and compline. **2. TIME FOR MARRIAGE** in the Church of England, any time between 8 A.M and 6 P.M when marriages can be officially celebrated

ca·non·i·cals /kə nónnik'lz/ *npl.* ceremonial robes worn by members of the clergy during a religious ceremony

can·on·ic·i·ty /kànnə nìssətee/ *n.* inclusion in a religious or secular canon, or status as an included item

can·on·ist /kánnənist/ *n.* = **canon lawyer** [Mid-16thC. Directly or via French *canoniste* from medieval Latin *canonista*, from, ultimately, Greek *kanōn* "rule" (source also of *canon*[1]).] —**can·on·is·tic** /kànnə nístik/ *adj.* —**can·on·is·ti·cal** *adj.*

can·on·i·za·tion /kànnəni záysh'n/ *n.* **1. NOMINATION AS A SAINT** the formal process or decree by which a deceased person is declared by the Roman Catholic Church to be a saint **2. RELIGIOUS APPROVAL** the official sanctioning of something by a religious authority **3. IDOLIZATION** the idolizing of somebody, or the glorifying of somebody or something ○ *the canonization of a young president who was merely human like the rest of us* [14thC. From the medieval Latin stem *canonization-*, from *canonizare* (see CANONIZE).]

can·on·ize /kánnə nìz/ **(-ized, -iz·ing, -iz·es)** *vt.* **1. DECLARE AS SAINT** in the Roman Catholic Church, to declare a deceased person to be a saint **2. GIVE RELIGIOUS APPROVAL TO** to declare something to be acceptable or valid according to canon law **3. GLORIFY** to idolize somebody or glorify something ○ *"And fame in time to come canonize us"* (William Shakespeare, *Troilus and Cressida*; 1601) [14thC. Via medieval Latin *canonizare*, from, ultimately, Greek *kanōn* "rule" (source also of *canon*[1]).] —**can·on·iz·er** *n.*

can·on law *n.* the body of laws that governs the affairs of the Christian church or a particular branch of it

can·on law·yer *n.* a specialist in or practitioner of canon law

can·on reg·u·lar (*plural* **can·ons reg·u·lar**) *n.* a member of any of several Roman Catholic orders of monks living in communities that follow Augustinian rules

can·on·ry /kánnənree/ (*plural* **-ries**) *n.* **1. CANON'S STATUS** the status or position of a religious canon **2. CANON'S SALARY** the salary that a religious canon receives

ca·noo·dle /kə nóod'l/ **(-noo·dled, -nood·ling, -noo·dles)** *vti.* to kiss and cuddle somebody in a mildly romantic or sexual way (*informal*) ○ *couples canoodling on the back row of the dark theater* [Mid-19thC. Origin unknown.]

can o·pen·er *n.* a device, either electric-powered or operated by hand, used for opening cans, especially cans of food

Canopic jar

ca·no·pic jar /kə nòppik-/, **Ca·no·pic jar** *n.* a jar used in ancient Egypt to hold the embalmed entrails of a mummy [Late 19thC. *Canopic* from Latin *Canopicus*, from *Canopus*, port in ancient Egypt and site of ancient monuments.]

Ca·no·pus /kə nópəss, kə nóppəss/ *n.* the second brightest star in the sky after Sirius, 98 light-years away from Earth and situated in the Argo constellation. Because it is so bright, spacecraft often take Canopus as a reference point for orientation.

can·o·py /kánnəpee/ (*plural* **-pies**) *n.* **1. COVERING FOR SHELTER** a covering put above something else to provide shelter or for decoration, especially a fabric covering designed to be removed or folded away **2.** BOT **TREETOPS** the uppermost layer of vegetation in a forest, consisting of the tops of trees forming a kind of ceiling **3. SKY** the sky as a covering or ceiling (*literary*) ○ *the vast canopy of stars* **4.** ARCHIT **ROOFED STRUCTURE** a roofed structure that covers an area, especially one that shelters a passageway between two buildings **5.** AIR **PART OF PARACHUTE** the part of a parachute that opens and fills with air **6.** AIR **COCKPIT COVER** the transparent cover of an aircraft's cockpit [14thC. Via medieval Latin *canopeum* "canopy above an altar" from, ultimately, Greek *kōnōpeion* "bed with a mosquito net," from *kōnōps* "mosquito."] —**can·o·pied** *adj.*

Ca·no·va /kə nṓvə/, **Antonio, Marquis of Ischia** (1757–1822) Italian sculptor. His neoclassical works include figures of Napoleon I and George Washington.

canst *(stressed)* /kanst/; *(unstressed)* /kənst/ *v.* an archaic form of the verb "can" used with "thou"

cant[1] /kant/ *n.* **1. CLICHÉD TALK** boring talk filled with clichés and platitudes **2. HYPOCRITICAL TALK** insincere talk, especially where morals and religion are concerned **3. JARGON** the special language or vocabulary of a particular group, especially a group whom some people look down on ■ *vi.* **(cant·ed, cant·ing, cants) SPEAK CANT** to use cant, especially to speak or lecture others hypocritically on matters of religion or morals [Mid-16thC. Probably from Latin *cantare* "to sing"; perhaps from an ironic comparison between a church choir's singing and the speech of beggars and criminals.] —**can·ter** *n.* —**cant·ing** *adj.* —**cant·ing·ly** *adv.*

WORD KEY: ORIGIN

The Latin word *cantare*, meaning "to sing," from which *cant* is derived, is also the source of English *accent, cantabile, cantata, canto, cantor,* and *chant.*

cant[2] /kant/ *n.* **1. SLOPE** slope, degree of slope, or a sloping surface **2. JOLT** a jolt that knocks something out of its straight or level position **3. SLOPING EDGE** a sloping edge, e.g., the bevel on the blade of a cutting tool ■ *v.* **(cant·ed, cant·ing, cants) 1.** *vt.* **JOLT SOMETHING** to knock something out of its straight or level position **2.** *vti.* **PUT AT AN ANGLE** to lie, or set something, at an angle [14thC. Via Middle Low German *kante* or Middle Dutch *cant* "edge" from assumed Vulgar Latin *canto* (source of English *decant*), from Latin *cantus* "wheel rim, tire," probably of Celtic origin.]

can't /kant/ *contr.* cannot

Cant. *abbr.* Canticle of Canticles

can·ta·bi·le /kaan taábi lày/ *adv.* **FLOWING** in a smooth, flowing, and melodious style (*used as a musical direction*) ■ *n.* **CANTABILE PIECE** a cantabile passage or piece of music [Early 18thC. Via Italian, "that can be sung."] —**can·ta·bi·le** *adj.*

Can·ta·brig·i·an /kàntə bríjjee ən/ *n.* **1. CAMBRIDGE STUDENT** a student or graduate of the University of Cambridge in England **2. SOMEBODY FROM CAMBRIDGE** somebody from Cambridge in England or Cambridge in Massachusetts [Mid-16thC. From Latin *Cantabrigia* "Cambridge (England)."] —**Can·ta·brig·i·an** *adj.*

can·ta·la /kan taálə/ *n.* **1.** PLANTS **TROPICAL PLANT GROWN FOR FIBER** a tropical American plant that is a species of agave. It is grown for its leaf fibers. Latin name: *Agave cantala.* **2. TOUGH PLANT FIBER** a coarse strong fiber from the leaves of the cantala plant, used to make nets, rope, and twine [Early 20thC. Origin unknown.]

can·ta·loupe /kánt'l òp/, **can·ta·loup** *n.* **1. ORANGE-FLESHED MELON** a round melon with a netted, often ridged rind and aromatic orange flesh. Latin name: *Cucumis melo reticulatus.* **2. ANY ORANGE MELON** any orange-fleshed melon [Late 18thC. Via French from Italian *Cantaluppi*, a papal villa near Rome where a similar melon was introduced from Armenia.]

can·tan·ker·ous /kan tángkərəss/ *adj.* **1. GROUCHY** easily angered and difficult to get along with **2. AWKWARD TO USE** difficult to work with or use (*informal*) [Mid-18thC. Origin uncertain: probably a blend of RANCOROUS and an unknown element (or perhaps via Middle English *contekour* "brawler" from assumed Anglo-Norman *contek* "strife").] —**can·tan·ker·ous·ly** *adv.* —**can·tan·ker·ous·ness** *n.*

can·ta·ta /kən taátə/ *n.* a musical composition for voices and instruments, usually on a religious theme, containing arias, choruses, and recitatives [Early 18thC. Via Italian from Latin, the feminine past participle of *cantare* "to sing"(source of English *cant, chant,* and *incantation*), from *canere* "to sing."]

can·ta·trice /kaàntə treè chày, -treèss/ *n.* a female singer, especially of opera [Early 19thC. Directly or via Italian from French, from Latin *cantatrix*, from *cantare* (see CANTATA).]

cant dog *n.* = **cant hook** [From CANT[2] + DOG in the sense of "mechanical device"]

can·teen /kan teén/ *n.* **1. CAFETERIA** a place where food is served, especially at a military base or workplace **2. PORTABLE DRINKING FLASK** a small container used by campers or soldiers for carrying liquids such as drinking water **3.** *U.K.* **SOLDIERS' SHOP** a store selling food, toiletries, and other items on a military base **4. TEMPORARY FOOD STAND** a mobile or temporary food stand **5. RECREATION CENTER** a recreation center or social club, especially for soldiers or teenagers (*dated*) **6. PORTABLE BOWLS AND EATING UTENSILS** a portable set of cooking and eating utensils used by soldiers or campers (*dated*) **7.** *U.K.* **FLATWARE BOX** a box or chest with compartments for storing flatware [Mid-18thC. Via French *cantine* from Italian *cantina* "cellar," perhaps via *canto* "corner (for storage)" from assumed Vulgar Latin *canthus* "corner, edge," from Latin, "iron tire."]

can·ter /kántər/ *n.* **1. HORSE'S MEDIUM PACE** a smooth easy gait of a horse or donkey, slower than a gallop but faster than a trot **2. HORSE RIDE AT CANTER** a horse ride at a canter ■ *v.* **(-tered, -ter·ing, -ters) 1.** *vi.* **MOVE AT CANTER** to move or ride at a canter **2.** *vt.* **MAKE HORSE CANTER** to make a horse go at a canter [Early 18thC. Shortening of *Canterbury gallop*, referring to the pace of medieval pilgrims who rode to the shrine of St. Thomas à Becket in Canterbury, England.]

Can·ter·bur·y /kántər bèrree/ historic city in Kent, England. Its cathedral is the mother church of the Church of England. Population: 36,464 (1991).

Can·ter·bur·y bells *n.* a European plant cultivated for its bell-shaped flowers. Latin name: *Campanula medium.* (*takes a singular or plural verb*) [Perhaps from a fanciful association of the bell-shaped flowers with the bells worn by pilgrims' horses, referring to the pilgrimage destination of *Canterbury*, England (see CANTER)]

can·tha·ris /kánthəriss/ (*plural* **-thar·i·des** /-thérri deèz/) *n.* = **Spanish fly** [14thC. Via Latin from Greek *kantharis*, of unknown origin.]

can·thi plural of **canthus**

cant hook *n.* a wooden pole with a pivoting metal hook at one end, used in forestry for handling logs [From CANT[2]]

can·thus /kánthəss/ (*plural* **-thi** /-thī/) *n.* the corner or angle at either side of the eye [Mid-17thC. Via Latin from Greek *kanthos* (source of English *decant*).]

can·ti·cle /kántik'l/ *n.* a song or chant, especially a hymn containing words derived from the Bible, used in the Christian liturgy [13thC. From Latin *canticulum*, literally "little song," from *canticum* "song," from *cantus* "song" (see CANTO).]

Can·ti·cle of Can·ti·cles *n.* = **Song of Solomon**

can·ti·le·na /kànt'l eénə/ *n.* a smooth-flowing melodious line in vocal or instrumental music [Mid-18thC. Directly or via Italian from Latin, "song," from *cantus* "song" (see CANTO).]

can·ti·le·ver /kánt'l eèvər/ *n.* **1.** CIV ENG **PROJECTION SUPPORTED AT ONE END** a projecting structure that is attached or supported at only one end **2.** BUILDING **SUPPORTING BRACKET** a bracket that supports a balcony or a cornice **3.** AEROSP **WING WITH NO EXTERNAL BRACE** an aircraft wing constructed without external braces ■ *v.* **(-vered, -ver·ing, -vers) 1.** *vt.* CIV ENG **ATTACH SOMETHING AT ONE END** to construct something in such a way that it is attached or supported at only one end **2.** *vi.* **EXTEND LIKE CANTILEVER** to project outward like a cantilever [Mid-17thC. Origin unknown.]

can·ti·le·ver bridge *n.* a bridge consisting of arms projecting outward from supporting piers and meeting in the middle of each span

can·til·late /kánt'l àyt/ **(-lat·ed, -lat·ing, -lates)** *vti.* to chant or intone something, especially passages of the Hebrew Scriptures [Mid-19thC. From Latin *cantillat-*, the past participle stem of *cantillare* "to sing low, hum," from *cantare* (see CANTATA).] —**can·til·la·tion** /kànt'l áysh'n/ *n.*

can·ti·na /kan teénə/ *n.* a bar or wine shop, especially in a Spanish-speaking country or region [Late 19thC. Via Spanish, "bar, wine cellar," from Italian, "(wine)cellar" (see CANTEEN).]

Can·tin·flas /kántin flàss/ (1911–93) Mexican movie actor. He was known for his comic characters and, off-screen, for his campaigning for social justice. Real name **Mario Moreno**

can·tle /kánt'l/ *n.* **1. BACK OF SADDLE** the raised back part of a saddle for a horse **2. PIECE** a corner, portion, segment, or broken-off piece of something (*archaic*) [14thC. Via Anglo-Norman *cantel* from medieval Latin *cantellus* "small corner," from assumed Vulgar Latin *cant(h)us* (see CANTEEN).]

can·to /kántō/ (*plural* **-tos**) *n.* POETRY any of the main divisions of a long poem [Late 16thC. Via Italian from Latin *cantus* "song" (source of English *accent* and *descant*), from *cantare* (see CANTATA).]

can·ton /kántən, kán tòn/ *n.* **1. PART OF COUNTRY** division of a country, especially one of the states into which Switzerland is divided **2. PART OF FRENCH ARRONDISSEMENT** a division of a French arrondissement **3. PART OF FLAG** a rectangular division in the top corner of a flag, next to the staff **4.** HERALDRY **PART OF SHIELD** a small square or oblong division of a shield, usually in the top left corner [Early 16thC. Via French from Italian dialect *cantone*, literally "large corner, large part," from *canto* "corner" (see CANTEEN).] —**can·ton·al** /kántən'l, kan tónn'l/ *adj.*

Can·ton /kántən, kán tòn/ **1.** = **Guangzhou 2.** city in Mississippi, northeast of Jackson, between the Big Black River and the Pearl River. Population: 10,328 (1996). **3.** city in northeastern Ohio, southeast of Akron; home of the Football Hall of Fame. Population: 81,079 (1996).

Can·ton crêpe *n.* a fine soft crinkled dress fabric of silk or rayon, slightly heavier than crêpe de Chine [Mid-19thC. Named for CANTON, where it was first made.]

Can·ton·ese /kàntə neéz, -neéss/ *n.* (*plural* **-ese**) **1.** LANG **CHINESE LANGUAGE** a regional language of Guangzhou (Canton) and the province of Guangdong, China. It is a Chinese language of the Sino-Tibetan family, and the most widely spoken language in Chinese communities elsewhere in the world. It is spoken by about 70 million people. **2.** PEOPLES **SOMEBODY FROM GUANGDONG** somebody who was born or lives in the Chinese city of Guangzhou or the surrounding province of Guangdong ■ *adj.* **1. OF GUANGDONG** relating to or typical of Guangzhou, Guangdong, or their people or culture **2. OF A CHINESE LANGUAGE** relating to the Cantonese language **3.** COOK **TYPE OF CHINESE CUISINE** typical of or constituting the style and food of the southern Chinese city of Guangzhou and the surrounding province of Guangdong

can·ton·ment /kan tṓnmənt, kan tónmənt/ *n.* **1. TEMPORARY TROOP ACCOMMODATIONS** temporary accommodations for troops, especially the winter quarters of an army **2. ASSIGNMENT TO QUARTERS** the assignment of troops to temporary quarters **3. MILITARY CAMP IN BRITISH INDIA** a permanent military station in India during the time of British imperial rule [Mid-18thC. From French *cantonnement*, from *cantonner* "to quarter, billet," from *canton* (see CANTON).]

Can·ton ware *n.* Chinese porcelain and other ceramic ware of types exported during the 18th and 19th centuries [Early 20thC. So named because, particularly during the 18th and 19th centuries, such pottery was exported from China by way of CANTON.]

can·tor /kántər/ *n.* **1.** JUDAISM **CHIEF SINGER IN SYNAGOGUE** a Jewish religious official who is the chief singer of the liturgy in a synagogue **2.** CHR **LEAD SINGER IN CHOIR** somebody who leads the singing in a church choir or congregation [Mid-16thC. From Latin, "singer," from *cantere* (see CANTATA).] —**can·to·ri·al** /kan táwree əl/ *adj.*

Can·tor /kántər/, **Eddie** (1892–1964) U.S. stage performer. He was known for his song *"Banjo Eyes"* and energetic performances in vaudeville and on Broadway.

can·tus /kántəss/ (*plural* **-tus**) *n.* **1.** MUSIC = **cantus firmus 2. MEDIEVAL ECCLESIASTICAL CHANT** a melody or style of singing used in the medieval church [Late 16thC. From Latin, "song" (see CANTO).]

can·tus fir·mus /-fúrməss/ (*plural* **can·tus fir·mi**) *n.* a melody, often derived from chant, that forms the basis of a composition to which other melodic lines are added [From Latin, literally "firm song, fixed song"]

can·ty /kántee/ **(-ti·er, -ti·est)** *adj. N England, Scotland* cheerful, lively, or sprightly [Early 18thC. From Scottish (formerly) and northern English dialect *cant* "bold, brisk," perhaps from Dutch *kant* "side, edge."] —**can·ti·ly** *adv.* —**can·ti·ness** *n.*

Ca·nuck /kə núk/ *n.* **1. CANADIAN** somebody from Canada (*slang*) **2. OFFENSIVE TERM** an offensive term used to refer to a French-Canadian person (*slang offensive*) [Mid-19thC. Probably from (a Native American pronunciation of) CANADA.]

can·u·la *n.* = **cannula**

can·u·lar *adj.* = **cannular**

can·u·late *v.* = **cannulate**

can·vas /kánvəss/ *n.* **1.** TEXTILES **HEAVY FABRIC** a strong heavy closely woven fabric of cotton, hemp, or jute **2.** PAINTING **FABRIC FOR PAINTING ON** a piece of canvas on which a painting is done, especially in oils **3.** PAINTING **PAINTING** a painting that has been done on a canvas

4. **BACKGROUND** the background against which events happen 5. SEW **CLOTH FOR NEEDLEWORK** a fabric with a coarse loose weave, used for embroidery or tapestry 6. NAUT **FABRIC FOR SAILS** any fabric used to make sails 7. NAUT **SAIL** a vessel's sail or sails 8. **TENT** a tent or group of tents 9. BOXING, WRESTLING **FLOOR OF RING** the floor of a boxing or wrestling ring when covered with canvas ■ *vt.* (**-vased, -vas·ing, -vas·es**) **COVER SOMETHING WITH CANVAS** to cover or line something with canvas [14thC. Via Old Northern French *canevas* from, ultimately, Latin *cannabis* "cannabis, hemp" (source of English *cannabis*), canvas being originally a cloth made from hemp.] ◇ **under canvas** living in a tent

Canvasback

can·vas·back /kánvəss bàk/ *n.* a North American wild duck, the male of which has a white back and a reddish-brown head and neck. Latin name: *Aythya valisineria.* [So called on account of the male's white back]

can·vass /kánvəss/, **can·vas** *v.* (**-vassed, -vass·ing, -vass·es**) 1. *vti.* **VISIT SOMEBODY TO SOLICIT SOMETHING** to travel around an area asking people for something, e.g., sale orders, opinions, or votes 2. *vt.* **DEBATE SOMETHING** to debate or discuss something thoroughly 3. *vt.* **LOOK AT SOMETHING CAREFULLY** to examine something in detail ○ *The ballots were thoroughly canvassed to confirm their authenticity.* ■ *n.* 1. **OPINION POLL** a survey of public opinion, especially before an election 2. **SALE OFFER TO MEMBERS OF GROUP** an offer of something, especially something for sale, to people in a particular area or group 3. **CAREFUL INSPECTION** a close inspection or examination [Early 16thC. From CANVAS; possibly the original sense "to toss in a canvas sheet (in sport or punishment)" evolved via "to criticize roughly" into "to debate," then "to solicit votes."]

can·vass·er /kánvəssər/ *n.* somebody who canvasses, especially for a political party

can·yon /kányən/, **ca·ñon** *n.* a deep narrow valley with steep sides, often with a stream running through it [Mid-19thC. Via Mexican Spanish *cañón* from Spanish, literally "large tube, pipe, or conduit," from *caña* "pipe," from Latin *canna* "reed, pipe" (see CANE).]

WORD KEY: REGIONAL NOTE

Canyon is a Western term, originally from Texas and extending through the Rocky Mountain states to the Pacific coast. It is rare in the East and Midwest and absent from the Midlands and the South.

Can·yon·lands Na·tion·al Park /kànyən lándz-/ U.S. National Park in southeastern Utah, established in 1964 and noted for its rock formations. Area: 337,570 acres/136,610 hectares.

can·zo·na /kan zṓnə, kaant sṓnə/ *n.* 1. MUSIC **SONGLIKE MADRIGAL** a song resembling a madrigal but simpler and less serious in form and content 2. MUSIC **INSTRUMENTAL PIECE** an instrumental piece in the style of a canzona 3. POETRY = **canzone** *n.* 1 [Late 19thC. From Italian, formed from *canzone* "song" (see CANZONE).]

can·zo·ne /kan zṓnee, kaant sṓ này/ (*plural* **-nes** *or* **-ni** /-zṓnee, -sṓnee/) *n.* 1. POETRY **MEDIEVAL LOVE POEM** a love poem written by the troubadours of medieval Italy and Provence 2. MUSIC = **canzona** *n.* 1, **canzona** *n.* 2 [Late 16thC. Via Italian from, ultimately, Latin *cant-*, the past participle stem of *canere* "to sing" (source of English *cantata* and *shanty*).]

can·zo·net /kànzə nét/, **can·zo·net·ta** /-néttə/ *n.* 1. **LIGHT ENGLISH SONG** a short light English song of the 17th or 18th century, originally intended for a group of singers or for a soloist with accompaniment 2. **SONG RESEMBLING MADRIGAL** a Renaissance song with different parts for different singers, similar to the madrigal [Late 16thC. From Italian *canzonetta*, literally "small canzone," from *canzone* (see CANZONE).]

can·zo·ni plural of **canzone**

cap /kap/ *n.* 1. CLOTHES **HAT** a covering for the head, usually soft and close-fitting and often with a visor and no brim 2. CLOTHES **UNIFORM HAT** a head covering, usually part of a uniform, worn to identify the wearer's occupation or rank 3. CLOTHES **PROTECTIVE COVERING FOR HAIR** a head covering worn to protect the hair, usually close-fitting or elasticized around the edge 4. CLOTHES **HAT WORN AT GRADUATION** an academic mortarboard, worn with a gown on a ceremonial occasion 5. **COVER** a removable cover or lid that closes the end of something when it is not in use 6. **COVERING AT TIP** something that covers the top or tip of something, especially as protection 7. **TOP PART** the top part of something, e.g., a hill or mountain 8. **UPPER LIMIT** an upper limit on something, e.g., the amount that may be spent on an item 9. ARMS = **percussion cap** 10. **EXPLOSIVE FOR TOY GUN** a small quantity of explosive enclosed in paper for use in a toy gun 11. DENT **COVERING FOR TOOTH** a covering to preserve or replace the crown of a tooth 12. ARCHIT **TOP OF COLUMN** the upper part of a column or pedestal 13. FUNGI **TOP OF MUSHROOM** the dome-shaped upper part of certain fungi, e.g. mushrooms 14. BOT **SPORE-CAPSULE COVERING** the hood that covers the spore-bearing capsule of mosses and liverworts 15. BIRDS **PATCH ON BIRD'S HEAD** a patch of feathers of a different color on the top of a bird's head 16. GEOL = **cap rock** 17. PAPER **PAPER SIZE** any of various sizes of paper (*dated*) 18. AUTOMOT **NEW SURFACE FOR TIRE** a new layer of rubber applied to the surface of a worn tire 19. CELL BIOL **MOLECULE CLUSTER** an aggregation of molecules at one end of something such as a cell or virus 20. MATH **SET INTERSECTION SYMBOL** a mathematical symbol ($\cap$) representing the intersection of two sets ■ *v.* (**capped, cap·ping, caps**) 1. *vt.* **COVER SOMETHING WITH CAP** to put a cap over something 2. *vt.* **LIE ON TOP OF SOMETHING** to cover the top or tip of something 3. *vt.* **SURPASS SOMETHING** to improve on something that has already happened or been done 4. *vt.* **COMPLETE SOMETHING** to add the finishing touch to something, e.g., an effort or a process 5. *vt.* **IMPOSE LIMIT ON SOMETHING** to put an upper limit on something, e.g., the amount of money to be charged or spent 6. *vt.* **AWARD SPECIAL HAT** to give somebody a special cap as a symbol of achievement or as an honor 7. *vt. NZ, Scotland* UNIV **GIVE SOMEBODY DEGREE** to award an academic degree to somebody 8. *vti.* CHEM **FORM CLUSTER OF MOLECULES** to form a cluster of molecules on something [Pre-12thC. From late Latin *cappa* "hood, hooded cloak" (source of English *cape* and Italian *cappuccino*).] ◇ **cap in hand** with a humble or apologetic attitude ◇ **set your cap for** *or* **at somebody** to try to attract somebody, especially with a view to marriage (*dated*)

cap. *abbr.* 1. capacity 2. capital 3. capitalize 4. capital letter 5. ANAT caput

C.A.P. *abbr.* 1. Civil Air Patrol 2. computer-aided production

Ca·pa /káppə/, **Robert** (1913–54) Hungarian-born U.S. photographer. He covered combat from the Spanish Civil War to Vietnam, where he was killed by a land mine.

ca·pa·bil·i·ty /kàypə bíllətee/ (*plural* **-ties**) *n.* 1. **COMPETENCY** the ability necessary to do something 2. **TALENT THAT COULD BE DEVELOPED** an ability or characteristic that has potential for development ○ *a man of immense capabilities* 3. **POTENTIAL FOR USE** the potential to be used for a particular purpose or treated in a particular manner

WORD KEY: SYNONYMS

See Synonyms at ***ability***.

Ca·pa·blan·ca /kàppə blángkə/, **José Raúl** (1888–1942) Cuban chess grandmaster. He was the world champion between 1921 and 1927.

ca·pa·ble /káypəb'l/ *adj.* 1. **DOING SOMETHING WELL** good at a particular task or job or at a number of different things ○ *a very capable hotel manager* 2. **ABLE TO DO PARTICULAR THING** possessing the qualities needed to do a particular thing 3. **LIABLE TO** permitting or susceptible to something ○ *an action capable of being misinterpreted* 4. LAW **LEGALLY COMPETENT** the ability or the legal power to do something [Mid-16thC. Via French from late Latin *capabilis*, from Latin *capere* "to take." Originally "able to take in."] —**ca·pa·ble·ness** *n.*

ca·pa·bly /káypəblee/ *adv.* in a competent or efficient way

ca·pa·cious /kə páyshəss/ *adj.* big enough to contain a large quantity [Early 17thC. From Latin *capac-*, stem of *capax* "able to hold," from *capere* (see CAPABLE).] —**ca·pa·cious·ly** *adv.* —**ca·pa·cious·ness** *n.*

ca·pac·i·tance /kə pássitənss/ *n.* 1. **ABILITY TO STORE ELECTRIC CHARGE** the ability of a substance to store electric charge 2. **MEASURE OF ELECTRIC CHARGE STORAGE** a measure of the capacitance of a substance, equal to the surface charge divided by the electric potential. Symbol *C* 3. **PART OF ELECTRIC CIRCUIT** the part of an electric circuit that has capacitance

ca·pac·i·tate /kə pássi tàyt/ (**-tat·ed, -tat·ing, -tates**) *vt.* 1. **MAKE SOMEBODY CAPABLE** to make somebody able, fit, or qualified to do something (*formal*) 2. LAW **GIVE SOMEBODY LEGAL POWER** to make somebody legally able to do something 3. BIOL **CAUSE CHANGE IN SPERM COATING** to cause the coatings on a sperm to be able to interact with proteins on the ovum

ca·pac·i·ta·tion /kə pàssi táysh'n/ *n.* physical changes in the coatings of a sperm to permit penetration and fertilization of an egg

ca·pac·i·tive /kə pássitiv/ *adj.* relating to electrical capacitance —**ca·pac·i·tive·ly** *adv.*

ca·pac·i·tor /kə pássitər/ *n.* an electrical component, used to store a charge temporarily, consisting of two conducting surfaces separated by a nonconductor (**dielectric**)

ca·pac·i·ty /kə pássitee/ (*plural* **-ties**) *n.* 1. **VOLUME** the room to hold or take in something 2. **MENTAL OR PHYSICAL ABILITY** the ability to do or experience something 3. **MAXIMUM VOLUME** the maximum amount that can be held or taken in ○ *The theater was filled to capacity.* 4. **MAXIMUM PRODUCTIVITY** the maximum amount of output or productivity ○ *a factory operating at less than full capacity* 5. **OFFICIAL ROLE** an official function or position that somebody has 6. ELEC **MEASURE OF ELECTRIC OUTPUT** a measure of the electric output of a battery or generator 7. COMPUT **COMPUTER STORAGE SPACE** the amount of data that can be stored by a specific computer device 8. LAW **LEGAL COMPETENCE** the legal ability or qualification to do something, e.g., make an arrest or a will [15thC. Via French *capacité* from, ultimately, Latin *capac-* (see CAPACIOUS).]

WORD KEY: SYNONYMS

See Synonyms at ***ability***.

cap and bells *npl.* a cap with bells attached to it, traditionally worn by a court jester, or the outfit of a court jester

cap-a-pie /kàppə peé/, **cap-à-pie** *adv.* from head to foot (*archaic*) [From Old French *cap a pie* "from head to foot"]

ca·par·i·son /kə pérris'n/ *n.* 1. **FANCY COVERING FOR HORSE** an ornamental covering for a horse, especially for a warhorse in former times 2. **HARNESS OR SADDLE DECORATIONS** a decorative harness for a horse or decorations for its saddle or other fittings 3. **ELABORATE CLOTHING OR ORNAMENTS** elaborate or rich clothing and ornaments ■ *vt.* (**-soned, -son·ing, -sons**) 1. **PUT CAPARISON ON HORSE** to provide a horse with a caparison 2. **DRESS SOMEBODY ELABORATELY** to dress somebody or yourself in finery [Early 16thC. Via obsolete French *caparasson* from, ultimately, perhaps late Latin *cappa* (see CAP).]

cape[1] /kayp/ *n.* 1. **LOOSE OUTER GARMENT** a sleeveless outer garment that is fastened at the neck and hangs loosely from the shoulders 2. **COAT PART LIKE CAPE** a piece of material like a cape that forms part of a coat or other garment 3. BIRDS **FEATHERS ON BIRD'S SHOULDER** a covering of short feathers on the shoulders of certain birds, especially fowl [Mid-16thC. Via French from, ultimately, late Latin *cappa* (see CAP).]

cape[2] /kayp/ *n.* a point of land that juts out into water, especially a headland significant for navigation [14thC. Via French *cap* from, ultimately, Latin *caput* "head."]

Cape Bret·on High·lands Na·tion·al Park Canadian National Park, situated on northern Cape Breton Island, Nova Scotia, and established in 1936. Area: 234,880 acres/95,126 hectares.

Cape Bret·on Is·land northern island in Nova Scotia, Canada, separated from the mainland by the Strait of Canso. Area: 3,980 sq. mi./10,311 sq. km.

Cape Ca·nav·er·al /-kə návvərəl/ cape in Brevard County, Florida, situated on the eastern coast of the Canaveral peninsula. Also known as **Cape Kennedy**

Cape Cod[1], **Cape Cod cot·tage** *n.* a colonial style of house usually one and a half stories high, with clapboard siding, a compact rectangular floor plan, central chimney, steep gable roof, and dormer windows [Early 20thC. So called because such houses are characteristic of CAPE COD, Massachusetts.]

Cape Cod[2] peninsula in southeastern Massachusetts

Cape Cod Na·tion·al Sea·shore park on Cape Cod, Massachusetts, authorized in 1961 and noted for its beaches, sand dunes, and marshes. Area: 43,569 acres/17,632 hectares.

Cape Col·ored (*plural* **Cape Col·ored** *or* **Cape Col·oreds**) *n.* somebody of mixed ethnic descent in the Western Cape Province who speaks Afrikaans or English [*Cape* from the CAPE of Good Hope]

Cape Cor·al city in southwestern Florida, on the Caloosahatchee River near the Gulf of Mexico. Population: 88,053 (1996).

Cape Dutch *n.* LANG the form of Dutch that developed into Afrikaans [*Cape* from the CAPE of Good Hope; *Dutch* from the early Dutch settlers or from the viewing of Afrikaans as a dialect of its parent language, Dutch]

Cape Fear river in North Carolina, flows southeast from confluence of Haw and Deep rivers to the Atlantic Ocean below Wilmington. Length: about 202 mi./325 km.

Cape Gi·rar·deau /-je raárdō/ city in southeastern Missouri, on the Mississippi River, southeast of St. Louis. Population: 35,464 (1996).

Cape goose·ber·ry *n.* BOT a tropical plant of the nightshade family that is native to the Americas and bears edible yellow berries. Latin name: *Physalis peruviana.* [*Cape* from its cultivation in the CAPE of Good Hope]

Cape Hat·ter·as Na·tion·al Sea·shore /kayp háttərəss-/ park in eastern North Carolina, authorized in 1937 and noted for its beaches and wildlife. It includes Pea Island National Wildlife Refuge. Area: 30,319 acres/12,270 hectares.

Cape Horn cape at the southern extremity of South America. Height: 1,391 ft./424 m. Spanish **Cabo de Hornos**

Cape jas·mine *n.* = **gardenia**

cap·e·lin /káppəlin, kápplin/, **cap·lin** /kápplin/ *n.* a small edible marine fish of the smelt family, found in the northern and Arctic seas. Latin name: *Mallotus villosus.* [Early 17thC. Via French from, ultimately, medieval Latin *cappellanus* "custodian of St. Martin's cloak," from late Latin *cappa* "hooded cloak" (see CAP).]

Ca·pel·la /kə péllə/ *n.* a double star that is the brightest star in the constellation Auriga, approximately 46 light-years from Earth

cap·el·li·ni /kàppə leénee/ *n.* long and fine noodles, resembling thin spaghetti [From Italian, literally "little hairs"]

ca·pell·meis·ter *n.* = **kapellmeister**

Cape Look·out Na·tion·al Sea·shore park on eastern North Carolina's Outer Banks. Authorized in 1966, it was named a Biosphere Reserve in 1986. Area: 28,243 acres/11,430 hectares.

Cape of Good Hope tip of the Cape Peninsula, South Africa. It is situated about 30 mi./48 km south of Cape Town and was rounded by the Portuguese navigator Bartolomeu Dias in 1488.

Cape prim·rose *n.* BOT = **streptocarpus** [Origin uncertain: probably named for the CAPE of Good Hope or CAPE Province]

Cape Prov·ince former province of South Africa that was abolished in 1994. The region is now divided into the three provinces of Eastern Cape, Northern Cape, and Western Cape.

ca·per[1] /káypər/ *n.* **1. PLAYFUL JUMP** a playful leap or dancing step **2. PLAYFUL ACT OR TRICK** a light-hearted adventurous act or prank **3. QUESTIONABLE ACTIVITY** a dangerous or illegal activity, especially one involving robbery (*informal*) ■ *vi.* **(-pered, -per·ing, -pers) PRANCE HAPPILY** to leap or dance around in a happy playful manner [Late 16thC. Shortening of CAPRIOLE.]

Caper

ca·per[2] /káypər/ *n.* **1. PICKLED FLOWER BUD** an edible flower bud of a Mediterranean shrub, pickled or salted and used as a flavoring or garnish (*often used in the plural*) **2. PLANT WITH EDIBLE BUDS** a Mediterranean shrub with spiny trailing stems, cultivated for its edible buds. Latin name: *Capparis spinosa.* **3. PLANT RELATED TO CAPER** any of various plants in the same family as the caper. Family: Capparidaceae. [14thC. Back-formation from earlier *caperis* (taken as plural), directly or via French *câpres* from Latin *capparis*, from Greek *kapparis*, of unknown origin.]

cap·er·cail·lie /kàppər káylee, -káylyee/ (*plural* **-lie** *or* **-lies**), **cap·er·cail·zie** /-káylzee/ (*plural* **-zie** *or* **-zies**) *n.* a large woodland bird of the grouse family, native to Europe and Asia, with dark gray plumage. Latin name: *Tetrao urogallus.* [Mid-16thC. From Gaelic *capull coille*, literally "horse of the wood."]

Ca·per·naum /kə púrnee əm/ city of ancient Palestine, situated on the northwestern shore of the Sea of Galilee

cap·er spurge *n.* a European plant of the spurge family that produces a milky fluid (**latex**). Latin name: *Euphorbia lathyris.* [From CAPER[2]]

cape·skin /káyp skìn/ *n.* a soft light leather made from South African sheepskin [*Cape* from the CAPE of Good Hope]

Ca·pe·tian /kə peésh'n/ *n.* **MEDIEVAL FRENCH RULER** a member of the royal dynasty founded by Hugh Capet that ruled France from A.D. 987 to 1328 ■ *adj.* **OF THE CAPETIANS** relating to the Capetians or the period of their rule

Cape Town legislative capital of South Africa and capital of Western Cape Province. It is situated at the northern end of the Cape Peninsula at the foot of Table Mountain. Population: 854,616 (1991). Afrikaans **Kaapstad**

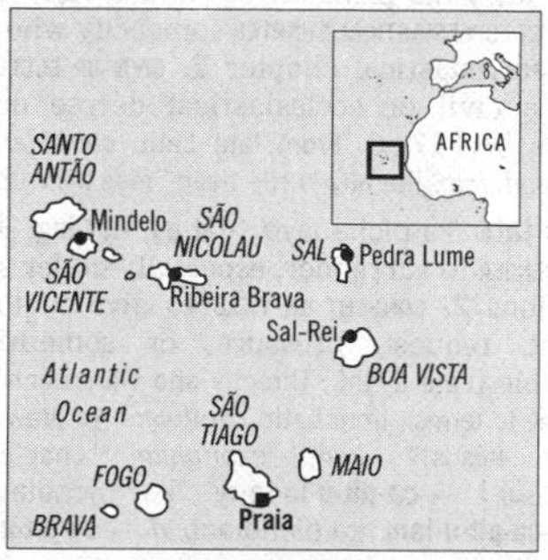

Cape Verde

Cape Verd·e /-vúrd/ island republic lying about 400 mi./644 km off the coast of Senegal in West Africa. A former Portuguese colony, it became independent in 1975. Language: Portuguese. Currency: escudo. Capital: Praia. Population: 393,843 (1997). Area: 1,557 sq. mi./4,033 sq. km. Official name **Republic of Cape Verde.** Portuguese **Cabo Verde**

cape·work /káyp wùrk/ *n.* the skill of a bullfighter in using a cape to control the movements of a bull

cap·ful /káp fòol/ *n.* the amount held by the cap of a container when used to measure the contents

cap gun *n.* a toy gun that can be loaded with a small quantity of explosive enclosed in paper (**cap**)

Cap-Hai·tien /kàp háyshən/ seaport in northern Haiti. Population: 68,000 (1994).

ca·pi·as /káypee əss/ *n.* LAW a warrant authorizing an officer of the law to arrest a named person [From Latin, "you are to seize," part of *capere* "to take" (source of English *capable, capacious, capture,* and *chase*)]

cap·il·la·ceous /kàppə láyshəss/ *adj.* **1. LIKE A HAIR** resembling a hair **2.** BIOL **WITH MANY FILAMENTS** having many filaments that resemble a hair or thread [Early 18thC. Formed from Latin *capillaceus*, from *capillus* "hair" (see CAPILLARY).]

cap·il·lar·i·ty /kàppə lérrətee/ *n.* **1.** PHYS = **capillary action 2.** BIOL, PHYS **CAPILLARY STATE** the state of being capillary [Mid-19thC. Via French *capillarité* from, ultimately, Latin *capillus* "hair" (see CAPILLARY).]

cap·il·lar·y /káppə lèrree/ *n.* (*plural* **-ies**) **1.** ANAT **THIN BLOOD VESSEL** an extremely narrow thin-walled blood vessel that connects small arteries (**arterioles**) with small veins (**venules**) to form a network throughout the body **2.** = **capillary tube** ■ *adj.* **1.** PHYS **RELATING TO CAPILLARY ACTION** involving or relating to capillary action **2.** ANAT **OF BLOOD CAPILLARIES** relating to the capillaries of the blood system **3. RESEMBLING HAIR** as fine and slender as a hair **4. SMALL IN DIAMETER** with a very small internal diameter [Mid-17thC. From Latin *capillaris*, from *capillus* "hair" (source of English *disheveled*); modeled on French *capillaire* "capillary."]

cap·il·lar·y ac·tion *n.* a phenomenon in which a liquid's surface rises, falls, or becomes distorted in shape where it is in contact with a solid. It is caused by the difference between the relative attraction of the molecules of the liquid for each other and for those of the solid.

cap·il·lar·y bed *n.* the collective mass of capillaries in the body or in any particular site

cap·il·lar·y tube, cap·il·lar·y *n.* a tube with a very small internal diameter, especially a glass tube with a fine bore and thick walls used in thermometers and similar pieces of equipment

cap·i·ta 1. plural of **caput 2.** ◊ **per capita**

cap·i·tal[1] /káppit'l/ *n.* **1.** GEOG, POL **SEAT OF GOVERNMENT** a city that is the seat of government of a country, state, or province **2. CENTER OF ACTIVITY** a city that is the center of a specified activity **3.** ECON **MATERIAL WEALTH** material wealth in the form of money or property **4.** FIN **CASH FOR INVESTMENT** money that can be used to produce further wealth **5. ADVANTAGE** advantage derived from or useful in a particular situation ○ *a powerful senator's seemingly endless political capital* **6.** ECON **ECONOMIC RESOURCE** any resource or resources that can be used to generate economic wealth ○ *a waste of human capital* **7. WEALTHY PEOPLE** the capitalist class considered as a group ○ *capital's influence on government policy* **8.** ACCT **NET WORTH** the assets of a business that remain after its debts and other liabilities are paid or deducted **9.** LING = **capital letter** (*often used in the plural*) ■ *adj.* **1.** LING **UPPERCASE** used to describe the form of letters used at the beginning of sentences and names, e.g., A, B, and C as distinct from a, b, and c **2.** CRIMINOL **RELATING TO DEATH PENALTY** involving or incurring punishment by death **3.** GEOG, POL **GOVERNMENT** functioning as or relating to a seat of government **4.** FIN **OF FINANCIAL CAPITAL** involving or relating to financial capital **5. GRAVE** having extremely serious consequences ○ *a capital blunder that sealed their fate* **6. PRINCIPAL** constituting the highest category, or among those in the highest category ○ *a national issue of capital importance* **7.** *U.K.* **EXCELLENT** used to indicate that somebody thinks something is excellent (*dated*) [12thC. Via French from Latin *capitalis* "of the head," from *caput* "head."]

WORD KEY: USAGE

capital or **capitol**? A ***capital*** is a town or city that is a seat of government; a capitol is the building in which the legislature meets. Thus *During their two-day visit to the capital, the class toured the capitol and met their district's representative.*

cap·i·tal[2] /káppit'l/ *n.* the upper part of an architectural pillar or column, on top of the shaft and supporting the entablature [Via Old French *capitel* from late Latin *capitellum*, literally "little head" (see CAPITELLUM)]

cap·i·tal ac·count *n.* **1. RECORD OF CAPITAL INVESTED** a business account that records how much the owners or stockholders have invested in a company **2.** ACCT **STATEMENT ABOUT NET WORTH** a statement of a company's or individual's net worth at a given time

cap·i·tal al·low·ance *n.* money spent by a company on fixed assets and deducted from its profits before taxes are calculated

cap·i·tal as·set *n.* = **fixed asset**

cap·i·tal ex·pen·di·ture *n.* an expenditure on long-term business assets **(fixed assets)** such as buildings

cap·i·tal gain *n.* a profit made from the sale of a financial asset such as stock or a house (*often used in the plural*)

cap·i·tal gains tax *n.* a tax on profit above a fixed level made from the sale of financial assets

cap·i·tal goods *npl.* goods that are used in the production of other goods rather than being sold to consumers. ◊ **consumer goods**

cap·i·tal-in·ten·sive *adj.* using or requiring a proportionately large financial expenditure relative to the amount of labor involved

cap·i·tal·ism /káppit'l ìzzəm/ *n.* an economic system based on the private ownership of the means of production and distribution of goods, characterized by a free competitive market and motivation by profit

cap·i·tal·ist /káppit'list/ *n.* **1.** **INVESTOR** somebody who invests money in a business **2.** **BELIEVER IN CAPITALISM** a supporter of capitalism or a participant in a capitalist economy **3.** **RICH PERSON** a wealthy person, especially somebody made rich by capitalism and considered to be greedy (*informal*) ■ *adj.* **cap·i·tal·ist, cap·i·tal·is·tic 1.** **OF CAPITALISM** involving or relating to capitalism or capitalists **2.** **FAVORING CAPITALISM** practicing or supporting capitalism —**cap·i·tal·is·ti·cal·ly** /-ístikəlee/ *adv.*

cap·i·tal·i·za·tion /kàppit'li záysh'n/ *n.* **1.** **RAISING OF CAPITAL** the supplying of financial capital to a business **2.** LING **USE OF CAPITAL LETTERS** the use of or conversion to capital letters **3.** **CAPITAL IN COMPANY** the money that is invested in a business or the value of a company's stocks and bonds **4.** ACCT **TREATING SOMETHING AS CAPITAL** the treatment of debt or an expenditure as capital

cap·i·tal·ize /káppit'l ìz/ (**-ized, -iz·ing, -iz·es**) *v.* **1.** *vti.* LING **USE CAPITAL LETTERS** to write or print something with capital letters or an initial capital letter **2.** *vi.* **BENEFIT FROM SOMETHING** to profit by or take advantage of something ○ *to capitalize on an opponent's mistake* **3.** *vt.* **USE SOMETHING AS CAPITAL** to use debt or budgeted expenditure as capital for development **4.** *vt.* **AUTHORIZE ISSUE OF CAPITAL STOCK** to authorize a business enterprise to issue a specified amount of capital stock **5.** *vt.* **FINANCE SOMETHING** to supply capital for a business enterprise **6.** *vt.* **EXCHANGE DEBT FOR STOCK** to convert a corporation's debt into shares of stock **7.** *vt.* ACCT **TREAT EXPENSES AS ASSETS** to treat an expenditure as an asset in a business account instead of as an expense **8.** *vt.* **VALUE FUTURE INCOME** to determine the current value of a future cash flow, earnings, or other income —**cap·i·tal·iz·a·ble** *adj.*

cap·i·tal let·ter *n.* a letter of the alphabet in the form used at the beginning of sentences and names, e.g., A, B, and C as distinct from a, b, and c

cap·i·tal lev·y *n.* a tax on fixed assets or property

cap·i·tal·ly /káppitəlee/ *adv.* in a way that arouses admiration (*dated*)

cap·i·tal mar·ket *n.* a financial market involving institutions that deal with securities with a life of more than one year

cap·i·tal pun·ish·ment *n.* execution as a punishment for a person convicted of committing a crime

cap·i·tal ship *n.* a ship that belongs to the largest and most heavily armed class of warships

cap·i·tal stock *n.* the amount of stock that a company issues or the value of that stock

cap·i·tate /káppi tàyt/ *adj.* **1.** BOT **DENSELY CLUSTERED** used to describe a flower head composed of small flowers arranged in a dense cluster **2.** ANAT, ZOOL **ENLARGED AT END** used to describe a body part that is enlarged and rounded [Mid-17thC. From Latin *capitatus* "having a head," from *caput* "head."]

cap·i·tat·ed /káppi tàytəd/ *adj.* based on the number of individuals involved, or per person ○ *capitated payments* [Late 20thC. Formed from CAPITATION.]

cap·i·ta·tion /kàppi táysh'n/ *n.* **1.** **FIXED TAX PER PERSON** a form of taxation in which each person pays the same fixed amount **2.** **FIXED FEE PER PERSON** a payment or fee charged at an equal amount per person **3.** **COUNTING HEADS** a method of assessing the number of individuals by counting heads (*formal*) [Early 17thC. Directly or via French from the late Latin stem *captitation-* "poll tax," ultimately from the Latin stem *capit-* of *caput* "head."] —**cap·i·ta·tive** /káppi tàytiv/ *adj.*

cap·i·tel·lum /kàppi télləm/ (*plural* **-la** /-lə/) *n.* a rounded enlarged part at the end of a bone, especially that of the upper arm bone **(humerus)** that forms the elbow joint with one of the lower bones **(radius)** [Early 18thC. From Latin, literally "little head," from *caput* "head."]

cap·i·tol /káppit'l/ *n.* a building or group of buildings in which a state legislature meets and where other state government offices may be housed [14thC. From Old French *capitolie*, later remodeled on its source, Latin *Capitolium*, the temple of Jupiter in Rome, from *caput* "head."]

WORD KEY: USAGE

See Usage note at ***capital.***

CORBIS

Capitol, Washington, D.C.

Cap·i·tol /káppit'l/ *n.* the white marble domed building in Washington, D.C., where the United States Congress meets

Cap·i·tol Hill *n.* the United States Congress (*informal*)

Cap·i·tol Reef Na·tion·al Park U.S. National Park in southcentral Utah. Established as a national monument in 1937, it became a national park in 1971. Area: 241,904 acres/97,895 hectares.

ca·pit·u·la plural of **capitulum**

ca·pit·u·lar /kə píchələr/ *adj.* **1.** CHR **OF AN ECCLESIASTICAL CHAPTER** belonging or relating to a cathedral or other ecclesiastical chapter **2.** BOT **DENSELY CLUSTERED** used to describe a flower head **(capitulum)** consisting of many small flowers **3.** ANAT, ZOOL **ROUNDED** used to describe the rounded end **(capitulum)** of a bone [Early 16thC. From late Latin *capitularis*, from *capitulum*, literally "little head" (see CAPITULUM).] —**ca·pit·u·lar·ly** *adv.*

ca·pit·u·lar·y /kə píchə lèrree/ (*plural* **-ies**) *n.* **1.** CHR **MEMBER OF ECCLESIASTICAL CHAPTER** somebody who belongs to an ecclesiastical chapter **2.** **CIVIL OR ECCLESIASTICAL DECREE** a civil or ecclesiastical decree or set of decrees [Mid-17thC. From late Latin *capitularius*, from Latin *capitulum*, literally "little head" (see CAPITULUM).]

ca·pit·u·late /kə píchə làyt/ (**-lat·ed, -lat·ing, -lates**) *vi.* **1.** **SURRENDER** to surrender, especially under specified conditions **2.** **CONSENT OR YIELD** to give in to an argument, request, pressure, or something unavoidable [Late 17thC. Directly and via French *capituler* "to come to terms" from Latin *capitulare* "to draw up under distinct heads," from *capitulum* "chapter" (see CAPITULUM).] —**ca·pit·u·la·to·ry** /kə píchələ tàwree/ *adj.* —**ca·pit·u·lant** /kə píchələnt/ *n.* —**ca·pit·u·la·tor** *n.*

ca·pit·u·la·tion /kə pìchə láysh'n/ *n.* (*formal*) **1.** **GIVING UP** surrender or a giving up of resistance **2.** **TERMS OF SURRENDER** a document that sets out the agreed terms of surrender **3.** **SUMMARY** an outline or summary in document form

ca·pit·u·lum /kə píchələm/ (*plural* **-la** /kə píchələ/) *n.* **1.** BOT **TYPE OF FLOWER HEAD** a flower head that looks like a large single flower but consists of numerous tiny flowers clustered together on a disk **2.** ANAT, ZOOL **ROUNDED PART** a rounded enlarged body part, e.g., at the end of a bone or at the tips of an insect's antennae [Early 18thC. From Latin, literally "little head," from *caput* "head."]

ca·piz /kəpízz, káppiz/ *n.* **1.** **MOLLUSK WITH HINGED SHELL** a small mollusk with a hinged shell that is chiefly found in the Philippines. Latin name: *Placuna placenta.* **2. capiz, capiz shell** the shell of the capiz. It has a shiny translucent lining and is used in making jewelry, lampshades, and ornaments. [From a language in the Philippines]

cap·let /kápplət/ *n.* a small smooth oval medicinal tablet for oral use

cap·lin *n.* = **capelin**

ca·po·ei·ra /kàpoo áyrə/ *n.* **FORM OF MARTIAL ART** a martial art and dance form, originally from Brazil, that is used to promote physical fitness and grace of movement [Late 20thC. From Portuguese]

ca·po[1] /káypō/ (*plural* **-pos**) *n.* a small movable bar fitted across all the strings of a guitar or similar instrument to raise the pitch [Mid-20thC. Shortening of *capo tasto*, from Italian, literally "head stop."]

ca·po[2] /kaápō, káppō/ (*plural* **-pos**) *n.* the title of a leader in the Mafia or a similar criminal organization [Mid-20thC. Via Italian from Latin *caput* "head."]

ca·pon /káy pòn, -pən/ *n.* a male chicken castrated to improve its growth and the quality of its flesh for eating [Pre-12thC. Via Anglo-Norman *capun* from, ultimately, the Latin stem *capon* "capon."]

ca·po·na·ta /kaàpə naátə/ *n.* a dish made from chopped eggplant and other vegetables [Mid-20thC. Via Italian from, ultimately, the Latin stem *capon-* "capon."]

Library of Congress

Al Capone

Ca·pone /kə pṓn/, **Al** (1899–1947) Italian-born U.S. gangster and racketeer. Active in Chicago during the Prohibition era, he was imprisoned in 1931 for tax evasion. Full name **Alphonse Capone**. Known as **Scarface**

cap·o·ral /káppərəl, kàppə rál/ *n.* a strong dark coarse tobacco [Mid-19thC. From French *tabac du caporal* "corporal's tobacco" (being superior to *tabac du soldat* "soldier's tobacco").]

ca·pote /kə pṓtee/ *n.* a long coat or cloak, usually with a hood [Early 19thC. From French *capote*, "little cape," from *cape* "cape, cloak," from late Latin *cappa* (see CAP).]

AKG London

Truman Capote

Ca·po·te /kə pṓtee/, **Truman** (1924–84) U.S. writer. He was known for technically complex novels such as *Other Voices, Other Rooms* (1948).

Capp /kap/, **Al** (1909–79) U.S. cartoonist, known for his comic strip *L'il Abner* (1934–77). Full name **Alfred Gerald Chaplin**

cap·pel·let·ti /kàppə léttee/ *n.* small pieces of pasta shaped like pointed hats, filled with a seasoned mixture of cheese or meat (*takes a singular or plural verb*) [Mid-20thC. From Italian, literally "little hats," from *capella* "hat," from medieval Latin *capellus*, literally "little hat," from Latin *cappa* (see CAP).]

cap·per /káppər/ *n.* **1.** **CAP-FITTING MACHINE** a machine that fits caps on bottles **2.** **FINISHING TOUCH OR FINAL STRAW** something good or bad that is the last in a string of such events (*informal*) **3.** **CAPMAKER** somebody who or something that makes caps (*archaic*) **4.** **DECOY FOR CRIME**

a decoy or lure, especially somebody who acts as a shill in a con game (*archaic slang*) [13thC. Originally "somebody who makes caps as headwear." The present-day meanings did not appear before the late 16thC.]

cap pis·tol *n.* = **cap gun**

cap·puc·ci·no /kàppə chéé nō, aàpə chéé nō/ (*plural* **-nos**) *n.* a drink made with espresso coffee and frothed hot milk, sometimes topped with powdered chocolate or cinnamon [Mid-20thC. From Italian, originally "Capuchin (friar)," from *cappuccio* "hood, cowl," ultimately from late Latin *cappa* (see CAP) ; from the resemblance in color to a Capuchin friar's habit.]

Ca·pri /káa preé, ká preé, kə preé/ island resort in Napoli Province, Campania Region, southern Italy. It is situated near the southern entrance to the Bay of Naples. Population: 7,400 (1990). Area: 4 sq. mi./10.4 sq. km.

cap·ric ac·id /kàpprik-/ *n.* an acid obtained from animal fats and oils and used in the manufacture of artificial fruit flavors, perfumes, plasticizers, and resins. Formula: $C_{10}H_{20}O_2$. [*Capric* from the Latin stem *capr-* "goat"; (see CAPRINE, because of the acid's smell]

ca·pric·cio /kə preéchō, kə preéchi ō/ (*plural* **-ci·os**) *n.* **1.** MUSIC **LIVELY INSTRUMENTAL WORK** a piece of instrumental music with a free form, an improvisatory style, and usually a lively tempo **2. PRANK** a lighthearted act or prank **3. WHIM** a sudden idea, impulsive decision, or change of mind [Early 17thC. From Italian, literally "head with hair standing on end" (see CAPRICE).]

ca·pric·cio·so /kə preéchi óssō, kaàpri chóssō/ *adv.* in a lively and fanciful manner (*used as a musical direction*) [Mid-18thC. From Italian, from *capriccio*, literally "head with hair standing on end" (see CAPRICE).] — **ca·pric·ci·o·so** *adj.*

ca·price /kə preéss/ *n.* **1. IMPULSIVE TENDENCY** a tendency to sudden impulsive decisions or changes of mind **2. SUDDEN CHANGE OR ACTION** a sudden unexpected action or change of mind **3. WHIM** a sudden idea, impulsive decision, or change of mind **4.** MUSIC = **capriccio** [Mid-17thC. Via French from Italian *capriccio*, literally "head with hair standing on end," from *capo* "head" (from Latin *caput*) and *riccio* "hedgehog" (from Latin *(h)ericius*); influenced by Italian *capra* "goat."]

ca·pri·cious /kə príshəss, kə preéshəss/ *adj.* tending to make sudden and unpredictable changes — **ca·pri·cious·ly** *adv.* —**ca·pri·cious·ness** *n.*

Cap·ri·corn /kápprì kàwrn/ *n.* **1.** ASTROL **TENTH SIGN OF ZODIAC** the tenth sign of the zodiac, represented by a goat with a fish's tail and extending from December 22 to January 19. Capricorn is classified as an earth sign, and its ruling planet is Saturn. **2. Cap·ri·corn, Cap·ri·corn·i·an, Cap·ri·corn·e·an** ASTROL **SOMEBODY BORN IN CAPRICORN** somebody whose birthday falls between December 22 and January 19 **3.** ASTRON **CONSTELLATION** a faint zodiacal constellation in the equatorial region of the southern hemisphere, lying between Aquarius and Sagittarius **4.** GEOG = **tropic of Capricorn** [Pre-12thC. From Latin *capricornus*, literally "goat's horn," from *caper* "goat" (source of English *caper*[1]) + *cornu* "horn" (source of English *cornet*).] —**Cap·ri·corn** *adj.*

cap·ri·fig /kápprə fig/ *n.* **1. WILD FIG TREE** a wild fig tree of southern Europe and Asia Minor used in the pollination of certain edible figs. Latin name: *Ficus carica sylvestris.* **2. FIG** the fig borne by the caprifig tree [15thC. A partial translation of Latin *caprificus.*]

cap·rine /ká prīn/ *adj.* relating to or resembling a goat [15thC. From Latin *caprinus*, from *caper* "goat" (source of English *cab, cabriole, caper*[1], and *capriole*).]

cap·ri·ole /káppri ōl/ *n.* **1.** DRESSAGE **VERTICAL LEAP BY HORSE** in dressage, a vertical leap in which all four of the horse's feet leave the ground and then its hind legs are kicked out **2.** BALLET **BALLET LEAP** a playful leap or jump performed in ballet ■ *vi.* (**-oled, -ol·ing, -oles**) BALLET, DRESSAGE **PERFORM CAPRIOLE** to perform a capriole [Late 16thC. Via French from, ultimately, Latin *capreolus*, literally "little goat," from *caper* (see CAPRINE).]

ca·pri pants /kə preé-/, **Ca·pri pants, ca·pris** /kə preéz/, **Ca·pris** *npl.* close-fitting women's pants that end above the ankle [Mid-20thC. Named for the island of *Capri.*]

ca·pris /kə preéz/, **Ca·pris** *npl.* = **capri pants**

cap rock *n.* GEOL **1. ROCK COVERING SALT** a layer of rock that lies above a salt dome and consists of anhydrite, gypsum, or limestone **2. ROCK COVERING FOSSIL FUEL** an impermeable layer of rock that lies above a deposit of gas or oil and prevents it from percolating upward

ca·pro·ic ac·id /kə prō ik-/ *n.* a liquid fatty acid that occurs in fats and oils or is made synthetically, used in flavorings and in medicine. Formula: $C_6H_{12}O_2$. [*Caproic* from the Latin stem *capr-* "goat" (see CAPRINE), because of the acid's smell]

ca·pryl·ic ac·id /kə prillik-/ *n.* an oily fatty acid with an unpleasant taste and smell, found in animal fats and used in dyes and perfumes. Formula: $C_8H_{16}O_2$. [*Caprylic* from the Latin stem *capr-* "goat" (see CAPRINE), because of the acid's smell]

caps. *abbr.* **1.** capsule **2.** capital letters

cap·sa·i·cin /kap sáy əssin/ *n.* a colorless compound obtained from hot peppers, used medicinally and as a flavoring. Formula: $C_{18}H_{27}NO_3$. [Late 19thC. An alteration of *capsicine*, from *capsicum.*]

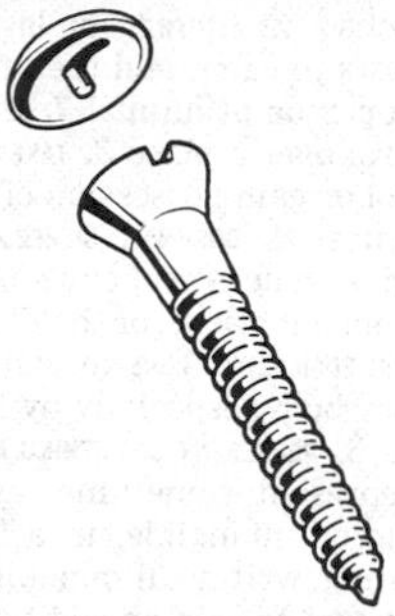

Cap screw

cap screw *n.* a long-threaded bolt with a head that may be square, hexagonal, slotted, or socketed

Cap·si·an /kápsee ən/ *adj.* belonging to a late Paleolithic culture of northern Africa and southern Europe, characterized by the use of geometrically shaped tools and distinctive art forms such as engraved limestone slabs [Early 20thC. From French *capsien*, from Latin *Capsa* "Gafsa," a town in central Tunisia where Paleolithic remains were found.]

cap·si·cum /kápsikəm/ *n.* **1.** = **pepper.** ◊ **chili 2. FRUIT** the fruit of the capsicum plant, especially a dried hot red pepper [Late 16thC. From modern Latin *capsicum*, perhaps from Latin *capsa* "repository, box" (source of English *capsule, case,* and *chassis*) because, of the podlike fruit.]

cap·sid /kápsid/ *n.* the outer coat of protein that surrounds a virus particle [Mid-20thC. Formed from Latin *capsa* "repository, box" (source of English *capsule, case,* and *chassis*).]

cap·size /káp sīz, kap sīz/ (**-sized, -siz·ing, -siz·es**) *vti.* to overturn on the surface of the water or cause a boat to overturn [Late 18thC. Of uncertain origin: perhaps, ultimately, from Spanish *capuzar* "to sink a ship by the head."] —**cap·siz·al** *n.*

Cap sleeve

cap sleeve *n.* a very short sleeve that hangs over the shoulder but does not extend beyond the armhole on the underside

caps lock *n.* a key on a computer keyboard or typewriter that, if pressed once, causes all subsequent letters to be typed as capital letters

cap·so·mere /kápsə meér/ *n.* any of the individual protein units that make up the outer coat (**capsid**) of a virus [Mid-20thC. Coined from CAPSID + -MERE, probably modeled on French *capsomère.*]

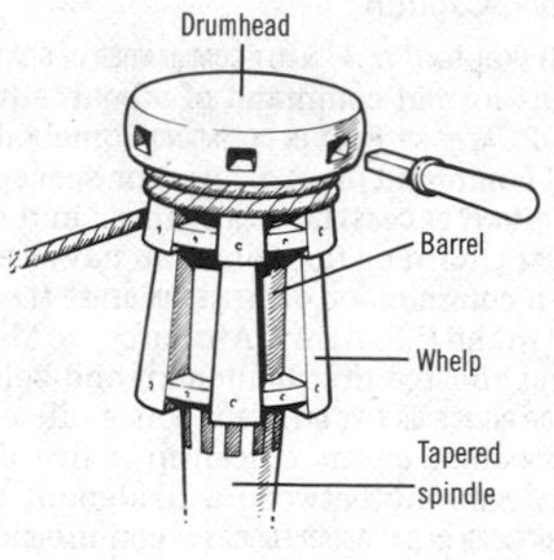

Capstan

cap·stan /kápstən/ *n.* **1.** NAUT **ROTATING CYLINDER** a device consisting of a vertical rotatable drum around which a cable is wound, used to move heavy weights or to haul in ropes on a ship **2.** HOUSEHOLD **ROTATING SHAFT IN TAPE RECORDER** a rotating shaft in a tape recorder, used to pull the magnetic tape past the head [14thC. Via Provençal *cabestan* from, ultimately, Latin *capistrum* "halter," from *capere* "to seize" (see CAPABLE).]

cap·stan bar *n.* NAUT a long lever used to turn a capstan by hand

cap·stone /káp stōn/ *n.* **1.** BUILDING **TOP STONE** a stone used at the top of a wall or another structure **2. HIGH POINT** something considered the highest achievement or most important action in a series of actions

cap·su·lar /kápsələr, kápsyələr/ *adj.* **1. OF OR LIKE CAPSULE** relating to or resembling a capsule **2. IN OR AS CAPSULE** enclosed in or in the form of a capsule

cap·su·late /kápsə làyt, kápsyə làyt/, **cap·su·lat·ed** /kápsə làytəd, kápsyə làytəd/ *adj.* enclosed in or made into a capsule (*formal*) —**cap·su·la·tion** /kàpsə láysh'n, kàpsyə láysh'n/ *n.*

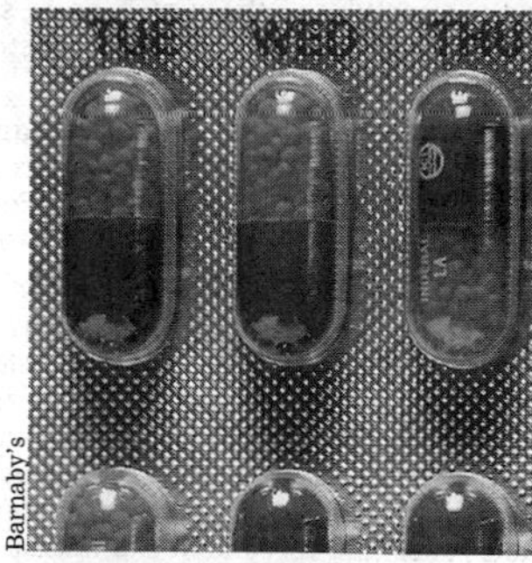

Capsule

cap·sule /káps'l, káp sool/, **cap·sule** *n.* **1.** PHARM **PILL OR CASING** a pill consisting of a small cylindrical container made of a soluble substance such as gelatin, enclosing a dose of medicine or a nutritional supplement, or the container itself **2.** BOT **SEED CASE** a fruit containing seeds that it releases by splitting open when it is dry and mature **3.** BOT **SPORE SAC** a sac containing the spores of a moss or a liverwort **4.** MICROBIOL **GELATINOUS COVERING OF MICROORGANISM** a gelatinous covering that surrounds certain microorganisms **5.** ANAT **MEMBRANE SURROUNDING BODY PART** a membrane or sac enclosing an organ or body part **6.** ANAT **WHITE MATTER IN BRAIN** a layer of white fibers in the forebrain **7.** SPACE TECH = **space capsule 8.** AIR **EJECTABLE COCKPIT** a sealed cockpit in an aircraft that can be ejected in an emergency **9. SEAL ON CONTAINER** a protective seal such as the metal, plastic, or wax covering that protects the cork of a wine bottle **10. SHORT SUMMARY** a very brief summary ■ *adj.* **1. VERY BRIEF** expressed in an extremely brief or highly condensed way **2. COMPACT** very small or compact ■ *vt.* (**-suled, -sul·ing, -sules**) = **capsulize** [Mid-17thC. Via French from Latin *capsula*, literally "little box," from *capsa* "repository, box" (source of English *case*), from *capere* "to take" (see CAPABLE).]

cap·sul·ize /kápsə līz, kápsyə līz/ (**-ized, -iz·ing, -iz·es**) *vt.* **1. PUT SOMETHING CONCISELY** to express something in a very brief or condensed way **2. MAKE A CAPSULE WITH SOMETHING** to put something into a capsule or into the form of a capsule

cap·su·lot·o·my /kàpsə lóttəmee/ (*plural* **-mies**) *n.* a surgical procedure involving cutting into the capsule surrounding a body part, e.g., that of the lens of the eye in the removal of a cataract

Capt. *abbr.* Captain

cap·tain /káptən/ *n.* **1.** NAUT **COMMANDER OF BOAT** somebody who has formal command of a boat, ship, or other vessel **2.** AEROSP **PILOT IN COMMAND** somebody who has formal command of an aircraft or spacecraft **3.** NAVY **OFFICER IN NAVY OR COAST GUARD** an officer in the U.S. Navy or Coast Guard or the Canadian navy ranking next above a commander **4. OFFICER IN OTHER ARMED FORCES** an officer in the U.S. Army, Air Force, or Marine Corps ranking above a first lieutenant and below a major **5. SENIOR POLICE OR FIRE OFFICER** a police officer in charge of a precinct or an officer in a fire department, usually ranking between a lieutenant and a chief **6.** MIL **OFFICER IN CANADIAN FORCES** a commissioned officer in the Canadian army or air force, ranking above a lieutenant and below a major **7.** MIL **RANK** the rank of captain **8.** SPORTS **TEAM LEADER** a leader of a team in a sport or game **9. IMPORTANT PERSON** an influential leader in a field or organization **10. SUPERVISOR** a title sometimes given to somebody who supervises others, such as somebody in charge of bellhops or waiters or a local division of a political party ■ *vt.* **(-tained, -tain·ing, -tains) COMMAND SOMETHING** to be the captain of something [14thC. Via late Old French *capitain* from late Latin *capitaneus* "chief," from *caput* "head," from the captain's position as the "head" of a team or other group.]

cap·tain·cy /káptənsee/ (*plural* **-cies** *or* **-ships**) *n.* **1. CAPTAIN'S RANK** the position or rank that a captain holds **2. TERM AS CAPTAIN** the period or time that a captain holds that rank or position **3. CAPTAIN'S RESPONSIBILITY** an area of authority belonging to a captain **4. CAPTAIN'S QUALITIES** the ability or leadership of a captain

cap·tain's chair *n.* a wooden chair with a saddle seat and a low curved back and arms supported on vertical spindles

cap·tain's mast *n.* a disciplinary hearing at which a captain or commanding officer of a navy ship or force hears and acts on cases against enlisted personnel

cap·tan /káptən, káp tàn/ *n.* an agricultural fungicide in the form of a white powder, used on fruits, flowers, and vegetables. Formula: $C_9H_8Cl_3NO_2S$. [Mid-20thC. Shortening of MERCAPTAN.]

cap·tion /kápshən/ *n.* **1. COMMENT WITH ILLUSTRATION** a short description or title accompanying an illustration in a printed text **2.** PRINTING, PUBL **HEADING OR SUBHEADING** a heading or subheading in a document or article **3.** CINEMA **MOVIE OR TELEVISION SUBTITLE** a printed explanation in a motion picture or on television, especially a translation of dialogue accompanying a scene or an explanation preceding a scene **4.** LAW **HEADING OF LEGAL DOCUMENT** an attachment to or heading of a legal document that identifies the circumstances of its production and the sources of its authority ■ *vt.* **(-tioned, -tion·ing, -tions) GIVE SOMETHING CAPTION** to provide something with a caption [14thC. From the Latin stem *caption-* "act of taking," from *capt-*, the past participle stem of *capere* "to take" (see CAPABLE); influenced by Latin *caput* "head."] —**cap·tion·less** *adj.*

cap·tious /kápshəss/ *adj.* **1. OVERLY CRITICAL** tending to find fault and make trivial and excessive criticisms **2. ENTRAPPING** intended to confuse or entrap an opponent in an argument [Directly or via French *captieux* from Latin *captiosus*, from the Latin stem *caption-* "act of taking (in), deceptive argument" (see CAPTION)] —**cap·tious·ly** *adv.* —**cap·tious·ness** *n.*

cap·ti·vate /káptə vàyt/ **(-vat·ed, -vat·ing, -vates)** *vt.* **1. ENCHANT SOMEBODY** to attract and hold somebody's attention by charm or other pleasing or irresistible features **2. CAPTURE SOMEBODY** to take somebody or something captive (*archaic*) [Early 16thC. From late Latin *captivat-*, the past participle stem of *captivare* "to capture," from Latin *captivus* (see CAPTIVE).] —**cap·ti·va·tion** /kàptə váysh'n/ *n.* —**cap·ti·va·tor** /-vàytər/ *n.*

cap·ti·vat·ing /káptə vàyting/ *adj.* attracting and holding somebody's attention by charm or other pleasing or irresistible features —**cap·ti·vat·ing·ly** *adv.*

cap·tive /káptiv/ *n.* **1. PRISONER** a person or animal that is forcibly confined or restrained, especially somebody held prisoner **2. SOMEBODY DOMINATED BY EMOTION** somebody who is enslaved by a strong emotion such as love or anger ■ *adj.* **1. UNABLE TO ESCAPE** prevented from escaping **2. VERY ATTRACTED** irresistibly attracted to somebody or something **3. FORCED TO USE OR ACCEPT SOMETHING** forced by circumstances to buy, accept, or pay attention to something, usually because there is other option or no means of escape [15thC. From Latin *captivus*, from Latin *capt-*, the past participle stem of *capere* "to seize, take" (see CAPABLE).]

cap·tiv·i·ty /kap tívvətee/ *n.* the state of being a prisoner or a period of time that somebody is held prisoner

cap·to·pril /káptə prìl/ *n.* a drug used in the treatment of high blood pressure that blocks the action of a substance **(angiotensin)** that causes blood vessels to constrict. Formula: $C_9H_{15}NO_3S$. [Late 20thC. Coined from MERCAPTAN + -O- + PROLINE + *-il* (an alteration of -YL).]

cap·tor /káptər, káp tàwr/ *n.* a person who or animal that takes or holds another person or animal prisoner [Mid-16thC. From Latin, from the stem *capt-* (see CAPTIVE).]

cap·ture /kápchər/ *vt.* **(-tured, -tur·ing, -tures) 1. TAKE SOMEBODY PRISONER** to catch and then forcibly lock up or restrain a person or animal **2. SEIZE PLACE** to seize or gain control over a place **3. TAKE SOMETHING IN GAME** to win control or gain possession of something in a game or contest **4. DOMINATE SOMEBODY'S THOUGHTS** to enchant or dominate somebody's mind, especially somebody's imagination, or hold somebody's attention **5. WIN SOMEBODY'S LOVE** to win the love or affection of somebody, especially by being charming or attractive **6. REPRESENT SOMETHING ACCURATELY** to describe or represent something, especially something fleeting or intangible, in a lasting medium such as painting, writing, filmmaking, or sculpture **7.** PHYS **GAIN PARTICLE** to gain an additional elementary particle **8.** COMPUT **RECORD DATA ON COMPUTER** to record data being processed or displayed and store it in the memory of a computer or as a file in a computer ■ *n.* **1. BEING TAKEN OR TAKING PRISONER** the act of being captured or of capturing somebody or something **2. SOMEBODY OR SOMETHING CAPTURED** somebody or something that has been captured and held in captivity **3.** PHYS **GAIN OF PARTICLE** a process in which an atom, ion, molecule, or nucleus gains an additional elementary particle, often followed by an emission of radiation **4.** COMPUT **RECORDING OF DATA** the recording of data being processed or displayed and storage of it in the memory of a computer or as a file in a computer **5.** GEOG **DIVERSION OF RIVER OVER TIME** the diversion of the headwaters of one river into the channel of another, brought about by erosion over a long period of time [Mid-16thC. Via French from Latin *captura* "seizure," from the stem *capt-* (see CAPTIVE).] —**cap·tur·er** *n.*

ca·puche /kə po͞och, -po͞osh/ *n.* a large hood on a cloak, especially the cowl worn by a Capuchin monk [Late 16thC. Via French (now *capuce*) from Italian *cappuccio* (see CAPUCHIN).]

Capuchin

cap·u·chin /káppyəchin, kə pyo͞ochin, káppyəshin, kə pyo͞oshin/ *n.* **1. cap·u·chin, cap·u·chin mon·key LONG-TAILED MONKEY** an agile and intelligent long-tailed monkey with a tuft of hair on its head that resembles a monk's cowl, found in the forests of Central and South America. Latin name: *Cebus capucinus*. **2. CLOAK WITH HOOD** a hooded cloak worn by women (*archaic*) [Mid-18thC. From CAPUCHIN.]

Cap·u·chin /káppyəchin, kə pyo͞ochin, káppyəshin, kə pyo͞oshin/ *n.* a member of an independent order of Franciscan friars founded in 1525 in Italy [Late 16thC. Via French from Italian *cappuccino* (see CAPPUCCINO).]

cap·u·chin mon·key *n.* ZOOL = **capuchin** *n.* 1

ca·put /káypət, káppət/ (*plural* **-pi·ta** /káppitə/) *n.* ANAT **1. HEAD** the head (*technical*) **2. PROMINENT PART** the most prominent part of something such as a bodily organ [From Latin]

Capybara

cap·y·ba·ra /kàppi baárə, kàppi bérrə/ (*plural* **-ras** *or* **-ra**) *n.* the largest living rodent, resembling a large guinea pig. It lives along rivers in Central and South America and can grow to a length of more than 4 ft./1.2 m. Latin name: *Hydrochoerus hydrochaeris*. [Early 17thC. Via either Spanish *capibara* or Portuguese *capivara* from Tupi *capiuára*, from *capī* "grass" + *uára* "eater."]

car /kaar/ *n.* **1. PASSENGER-CARRYING ROAD VEHICLE** a road vehicle, usually with four wheels and powered by an internal-combustion engine, designed to carry a small number of passengers **2. VEHICLE ON RAILS** a vehicle designed to run on rails, e.g., a streetcar or a railroad car **3. TRAVELING COMPARTMENT FOR PEOPLE OR THINGS** the part of an airship, balloon, or cable car for carrying passengers and cargo **4. ELEVATOR** the box-shaped container of an elevator in which people or goods are carried up or down **5. CHARIOT** a chariot (*archaic or literary*) [14thC. Via Anglo-Norman and Old Northern French *carre* from, ultimately, Latin *carrum* (source of English *career* and *chariot*), from Celtic, the underlying meaning being "to move swiftly."]

car. *abbr.* carat

car·a·bao /kérrə bòw, kaárə bòw/ (*plural* **-bao** *or* **-baos**) *n.* ZOOL = **water buffalo** [Early 20thC. Via Spanish from Visayan *karabáw*, from Malay *kĕrbau*.]

car·a·bid /kérrəbid, kə rábbid/ *n.* a beetle that lives in the soil. Many species feed on other insects. Family: Carabidae. [Late 19thC. From modern Latin *Carabidae* (family name), from Latin *carabus* "(a kind of) seacrab," from Greek *karabos* "horned beetle."]

car·a·bi·neer /kèrrəbi neér/, **car·a·bi·nier** *n.* a soldier armed with a lightweight short-barreled rifle **(carbine)** [Mid-17thC. From French *carabinier*, from *carabine* "carbine," see CARBINE.]

car·a·bi·ner /kèrrə beénər/, **kar·a·bi·ner** *n.* an oblong metal ring with an openable spring-hinged side, used in rock and mountain climbing for such purposes as clipping a freely running rope to a piton [Mid-20thC. From German *Karabiner-haken* "spring-hook," from its use for attaching a carbine rifle to a belt.]

car·a·bin·e·ro /kèrrəbi nérrō/ (*plural* **-ros**) *n.* **1. SPANISH POLICE OFFICER** a member of the national police force of Spain **2. FILIPINO CUSTOMS OR COAST GUARD OFFICER** a customs, coast guard, or revenue officer in the Philippines [Mid-19thC. From Spanish, from *carabina* "carbine," from French *carabine* (source of English *carbine*).]

car·a·bi·nier *n.* = **carabineer**

ca·ra·bi·nie·re /kèrrəbi nyáiree, kaárəbi nyáir e/ (*plural* **cara·binieri** /kèrrəbi nyáiree/) *n.* a member of the national police force of Italy [Mid-19thC. Via Italian from French *carabinier* (source of English *carabineer*).]

car·a·cal /kérrə kàl/ (*plural* **-cals** *or* **-cal**) *n.* **1. WILDCAT OF AFRICA AND ASIA** a medium-sized wildcat with long legs, a smooth reddish-brown coat, a short tail, and long tufted ears, found in the dry savannas of Africa and southern Asia. Latin name: *Lynx caracal*. **2. CARACAL'S FUR** the fur of the caracal [Mid-18thC. Via either French or Spanish from Turkish *karakulak*, literally "black ear," from *kara* "black" + *kulak* "ear."]

car·a·car·a /kèrrə kérrə, kèrrə kə raá/ *n.* a large long-legged carrion-eating or predatory bird of the falcon family, native to Central, and South America. Genus: *Polyborus*. [Mid-19thC. Via Spanish or Portuguese *caracará* from Tupi-Guarani; ultimately an imitation of the sound the bird makes.]

Caracal

Ca·ra·cas /kə rákəss/ city and capital of Venezuela, situated at an altitude of approximately 3,000 ft./900 m. Population: 1,964,846 (1992).

car·a·cole /kérrə kōl/, **car·a·col** *n.* **HALF TURN** in dressage, a half turn to the left or right performed by a horse and rider ■ *vti.* (**-coled, -col·ing, -coles; -coled, -col·ing, -cols**) **MAKE CARACOLE** to perform or cause a horse to perform a caracole [Early 17thC. From French *caracoler*, from *caracol(e)* "snail's shell, spiral."]

Ca·rac·ta·cus /kə ráktəkəss/ (*fl.* A.D. 50) British tribal ruler. He was defeated by the Romans.

car·a·cul *n.* = **karakul**

ca·rafe /kə ráf/ *n.* **1. CONTAINER FOR SERVING DRINKS** a container with a wide cylindrical base, a narrow neck, and a flared open top, usually made of glass and used to serve liquids, especially wine or water at the table **2. CONTAINER FOR COFFEE** a glass pot with a lip molded to form a spout and a handle, used especially with a drip coffeemaker to brew and serve coffee **3. QUANTITY IN CARAFE** the contents or capacity of a carafe [Late 18thC. Via French from Italian *caraffa*, of unknown origin.]

car a·larm *n.* an electronically operated device fitted to a car, designed to make a loud noise if somebody attempts to break into or tamper with the vehicle

ca·ram·ba *interj.* used to express surprise, amazement, or dismay (*slang*) [Spanish]

car·am·bo·la /kèrrəm bṓlə/ *n.* **1. TROPICAL FRUIT TREE** an evergreen tree cultivated in tropical regions, especially Southeast Asia, for its edible fruit. Latin name: *Averrhoa carambola*. **2. STAR-SHAPED FRUIT** the smooth-skinned yellow fruit of the carambola tree, with lengthwise ridges that give it a star-shaped cross section. The thin skin is edible, and the juicy, slightly crisp fruit has a delicate flavor. [Late 16thC. Via Portuguese from, probably, Marathi *karambal*.]

car·a·mel /kérrəməl, -mèl, kaármәl/ *n.* **1. BURNT SUGAR** sugar melted or dissolved in a small amount of water and heated until it turns golden or dark brown. It is used as a flavoring and coloring. **2. CHEWY CANDY** a chewy candy that can be soft or firm, made with butter, milk, and sugar ■ *adj.* **OF YELLOWISH-BROWN COLOR** yellowish-brown in color ■ *n.* **YELLOWISH-BROWN COLOR** a yellowish-brown color [Early 18thC. Via French from Spanish *caramelo*, an alteration of Provençal *canamel* "sugar cane," ultimately from Latin *canna* "cane" + *mel* "honey."]

car·a·mel·ize /kérrəmə līz, kaármə līz/ (**-ized, -iz·ing, -iz·es**) *vti.* to heat sugar or boil dissolved sugar until it turns dark brown, as when broiling dry sugar on top of a dessert or to undergo this process [Mid-19thC. From French *caraméliser*, from *caramel* "burned sugar, caramel" (see CARAMEL).] —**car·a·mel·i·za·tion** /kèrrəməli záysh'n, kaárməli záysh'n/ *n.*

ca·ran·gid /kə ránjid, kə ráng gid/ *n.* any spiny-finned marine fish of a family that includes the jack and pompano. Family: Carangidae. [Late 19thC. From modern Latin *Carangidae*, family name, from *Caranx*, genus name, which came, ultimately, from Spanish *caranga* "shad, horse mackerel," of unknown origin.]

car·a·pace /kérrə pàyss/ *n.* **1.** ZOOL **ANIMAL SHELL** a thick hard case or shell made of bone or chitin that covers part of the body, especially the back, of an animal such as a crab or turtle **2. SELF-PROTECTIVENESS** self-protection or a disguise that shelters somebody as a shell does a turtle, e.g., shy or arrogant behavior [Mid-19thC. Via French from Spanish *carapacho*, of unknown origin.]

car·at /kérrət/ *n.* **1. WEIGHT USED FOR GEMS** a unit of weight for precious stones, especially diamonds, equal to 200 milligrams **2.** = **karat** [15thC. Via French from, ultimately, Greek *keration* "fruit of the carob" , from *keras* "horn"; because carob beans were used as standard weights for small quantities.]

Ca·ra·vag·gi·o /kèrrə vaájee ō, kèrrə vaájō/, **Michelangelo Merisi da** (1573–1610) Italian painter. He was an exponent of the Baroque style, and his tempestuous life is reflected in his realistic and dramatically lit works.

car·a·van /kérrə vàn/ *n.* **1. GROUP OF DESERT MERCHANTS WITH CAMELS** a group of traders, especially in Africa and Asia, crossing the desert together for safety, usually with a train of camels **2. GROUP OF TRAVELERS** a group of people, vehicles, or supervised animals that are traveling together for security **3. ROMANY PEOPLE'S VAN** a large covered vehicle or van used as a traveling home, particularly by Romany people or circus performers **4.** *U.K.* = **trailer** ■ *vi.* (**-vanned** *or* **-vaned, -van·ning** *or* **-van·ing, -vans**) **1.** to travel in a group **2.** *U.K.* **SPEND TIME IN CAMPER** to vacation or travel around in a camper [Late 16thC. Via French *caravane* from Persian *kārvān* "group of desert travelers" (source of English *van*).]

car·a·van·ner /kérrə vànnər/, **car·a·van·er** *n.* **1. SOMEBODY TRAVELING IN GROUP** somebody traveling in a group for security **2.** *U.K.* **SOMEBODY SPENDING TIME IN CAMPER** somebody who vacations in or travels around with a camper

car·a·van·se·rai /kàrrə vánsə rày, -vánsə rī/ (*plural* **-rais**), **car·a·van·sa·ry** *n.* **1. DESERT INN FOR TRAVELING CARAVANS** a large inn with a central courtyard, found in some eastern countries and used by caravans crossing the desert **2.** = **caravan** *n.* 1 [Late 16thC. From Persian *kārwānsarāī*, from *kārwān* (see CARAVAN) + *sarāī* "inn" (see SERAI).]

car·a·vel /kérrə vèl/, **car·a·velle, car·vel** /kaárv'l, kaár vèl/ *n.* a light sailing ship with two or three masts, used in the Mediterranean from the 14th to 17th century [Early 16thC. From French *caravelle*.]

car·a·way /kérrə wày/ *n.* **1. ANNUAL HERB** a European and Asian plant with finely divided leaves, clusters of small white or pinkish flowers, and aromatic fruits that look like seeds and are used to flavor food. Latin name: *Carum carvi*. **2.** = **caraway seed** *n.* [13thC. Directly or via Old French *carvi* from medieval Latin *carui*, of uncertain origin: probably ultimately from Greek *karon* "cumin" (which has similar seeds).]

car·a·way seed *n.* the aromatic dried ripe fruit of the caraway plant, used as a spice for flavoring a variety of foods

carb[1] /kaarb/ *n.* a carburetor (*informal*) [Mid-20thC. shortening.]

carb[2] /kaarb/ *n.* a carbohydrate or a high-carbohydrate food (*slang*) [Mid-20thC. Shortening of CARBOHYDRATE.]

carb- *prefix.* CHEM = **carbo-** (*used before vowels*)

car·ba·mate /kaárbə màyt, kaar bá màyt/ *n.* any salt or ester of carbamic acid, used especially as a pesticide [Mid-19thC. Coined from CARBO- + AMIDE + -ATE.]

car·ba·maz·e·pine /kaàrbə mázzə peen/ *n.* an analgesic and anticonvulsant drug used to treat epilepsy, pain, and manic-depressive psychosis [Rearrangement of *dibenzazepinecarboxamide*, chemical name]

car·bam·ic ac·id /kaar bàmmik-/ *n.* an acid that exists only in the form of its salt or ester. Formula: NH_2COOH. [*Carbamic* coined from CARBO- + AMIDE + -IC]

car·ba·mide /kaárbə mīd, kaar bámmid/ *n.* = **urea** [Mid-19thC. Coined from CARBO- + AMIDE.]

car·ban·i·on /kaar bá nī ən, kaár bánnī òn/ *n.* an organic ion that has a carbon atom with a negative charge [Mid-20thC. Coined from CARB- + ANION.]

car·barn /kaár baarn/ *n.* a building where buses or streetcars are stored

car·ba·ryl /kaárbə rìl/ *n.* an insecticide used as a substitute for DDT in a broad range of applications [Mid-20thC. Blend of CARBAMATE and ARYL.]

car·bene /kaár been/ *n.* any molecule containing a carbon atom with only three bonds. Carbenes are highly reactive and only exist fleetingly in certain chemical reactions.

car·bide /kaár bīd/ *n.* **1. COMPOUND CONTAINING CARBON AND ANOTHER ELEMENT** a compound containing carbon and one other element, especially a metal **2.** = **calcium carbide** [Mid-19thC. Coined from CARBON + -IDE.]

car·bine /kaár been, kaár bīn/ *n.* a lightweight rifle with a short barrel [Early 17thC. From French *carabine*, from *carabin* "mounted musketeer," of unknown origin.]

car·bi·neer /kaárbi neér/ *n.* = **carabineer**

car·bi·nol /kaárbə nòl, kaárbə nàwl/ *n.* = **methanol** [Mid-19thC. Coined from CARBON + -INE + -OL.]

car·bo /kaárbō/ (*plural* **-bos**) *n.* a carbohydrate (*slang*) ○ *pasta is a good source of carbo* [Shortening]

carbo- *prefix.* CHEM carbon, carbonic ○ *carbocyclic* [From French, from *carbone* (see CARBON)]

car·bo·cy·clic /kaárbō síklik, -síklik/ *adj.* used to describe a chemical compound containing a closed ring of carbon atoms

car·bo·hy·drase /kaárbō hí drayss, -drayz/ *n.* any enzyme that aids the breakdown of a carbohydrate. Amylase is a carbohydrase. [Early 20thC. Coined from CARBOHYDRATE + -ASE.]

car·bo·hy·drate /kaárbō hí dràyt/ *n.* **1. ENERGY COMPONENT OF DIET** an organic compound derived from carbon, hydrogen, and oxygen that is an important source of food and energy for humans and animals. Sugar, starch, and cellulose are carbohydrates. **2. FOOD CONTAINING CARBOHYDRATES** any food containing carbohydrates, e.g., bread, pasta, or potatoes [Mid-19thC. Coined from CARBO- + HYDRATE.]

car·bo·hy·drate load·ing *n.* a controversial practice of first starving the body of carbohydrates, then following a high-carbohydrate diet just before an athletic event in an attempt to increase performance

car·bol·ic /kaar bóllik/ *n.* = **phenol** [Mid-19thC. Coined from CARBO- + -OL + -IC.]

car·bol·ic ac·id *n.* = **phenol**

car·bo-load·ing *n.* carbohydrate loading (*slang*)

car bomb *n.* an explosive device concealed inside or under a vehicle and detonated by remote control or when the engine is started

car-bomb (**car-bombed, car-bomb·ing, car-bombs**) *vt.* to place a car bomb in or under a vehicle, or use such an explosive-laden vehicle against a target

car·bon /kaárbən/ *n.* **1.** CHEM ELEM **NONMETALLIC CHEMICAL ELEMENT** a nonmetallic chemical element that exists in two main forms, diamond and graphite. Its ability to form large numbers of organic compounds allowed living organisms to evolve. Symbol **C** **2. CARBON COPY** a carbon copy of a document (*informal*) **3. CARBON PAPER** carbon paper (*informal*) **4. ELECTRICAL COMPONENT MADE OF CARBON** something made of carbon, especially an electrode or a lamp filament [Late 18thC. Via French *carbone* from the Latin stem *carbon-* "coal" (source of English *carbuncle*), of uncertain origin; perhaps ultimately from an Indo-European word meaning "fire."] —**car·bon·ous** *adj.*

car·bon 12 /kaárbən twélv/ *n.* an isotope of carbon with relative atomic mass of 12. It is used as the standard in determining the relative atomic mass of other elements.

car·bon 14 /kaárbən fawr teén/ *n.* a naturally radioactive isotope of carbon with atomic mass of 14 and a half-life of 5,780 years, used as a tracer element and in carbon dating

car·bon-14 dat·ing, **car·bon-14 method** *n.* = **carbon dating**

car·bo·na·ceous /kaárbə náyshəss/ *adj.* relating to, containing, or resembling carbon

car·bo·na·do[1] /kaárbə náydō, -naádō/ *n.* (*plural* **-dos**) **SCORED AND GRILLED MEAT OR FISH** a piece of scored and grilled meat or fish (*archaic*) ■ *vt.* (**-doed, -do·ing, -does**) (*archaic*) **1. SCORE AND GRILL MEAT OR FISH** to prepare meat or fish by scoring and grilling it **2. CUT OR SLASH** to cut or slash somebody or something [Late 16thC. Via Spanish *carbonada* from, ultimately, the Latin stem *carbon-* "coal" (source of English *carbon*), because it is broiled on coals.]

car·bo·na·do[2] /kaárbə náydō, -naádō/ (*plural* **-dos** *or* **-does**) *n.* a dark-colored diamond or an aggregate of diamond particles that is extremely hard and is used industrially, e.g., for drilling and polishing [Mid-19thC. From Portuguese.]

car·bo·na·ra /kaárbə naárə/ *n.* a hot pasta dish prepared with eggs, chopped ham or bacon, and cheese ○ *spaghetti carbonara* [Mid-20thC. From Italian *(alla) carbonara*, literally "on the charcoal grill," from *carbone* "charcoal," from Latin *carbon-* (see CARBON).]

car·bon arc *n.* an electric discharge between two carbon electrodes or between an electrode and a metal to be welded, characterized by bright light and intense heat

Car·bo·na·ri /kaàbə naáree/ *npl.* members of a secret society in early 19th-century Italy that aimed to establish a unified liberal republican government [Early 19thC. From Italian, plural of *carbonaro* "charcoal burner," from, ultimately, Latin *carbon-* (see CARBON); from their use of symbols from the charcoal-burning trade.]

car·bon·ate *n.* /kaárbə nàyt, kaárbənət/ **1. SALT OR ESTER OF CARBONIC ACID** any salt or ester of carbonic acid **2. MINERAL COMPOSED OF CRYSTALLIZED CARBONATES** a mineral composed of calcium, magnesium, and other carbonates in various crystal forms ■ *vt.* /kaárbə nàyt/ **(-at·ed, -at·ing, -ates) 1. CONVERT TO CARBONATE** to convert a chemical compound into a carbonate **2. MAKE LIQUID BUBBLY AND GASEOUS** to make a liquid bubbly and gaseous by introducing carbon dioxide into it **3.** = **carbonize** —**car·bon·a·tor** *n.*

car·bon·at·ed wa·ter *n.* = **soda water**

car·bon·a·tion /kaárbə náysh'n/ *n.* **1. REACTION WITH CARBON DIOXIDE** permeation or reaction with carbon dioxide **2.** = **carbonization**

car·bon·a·tite /kaar bónnə tīt/ *n.* an unusual alkaline igneous rock high in carbonate materials, found in eastern Africa and thought to derive from the Earth's mantle [Early 20thC. Coined from CARBONATE + -ITE.]

car·bon bi·sul·fide *n.* = **carbon disulfide**

car·bon black *n.* any form of finely divided carbon produced by partial combustion of petroleum or natural gas, used in making pigment, ink, and rubber

car·bon brush *n.* a block of carbon in an engine or generator that conveys current between the moving and the stationary parts

car·bon cop·y *n.* **1. DUPLICATE MADE WITH CARBON PAPER** a duplicate of written or drawn material that is made by using carbon paper **2. SOMEBODY OR SOMETHING IDENTICAL** somebody or something that is identical to or very much like somebody or something else (*informal*) ○ *This situation is a carbon copy of last year's crisis.*

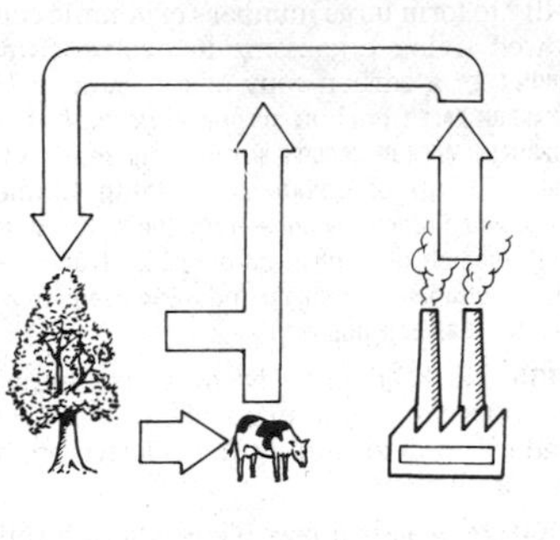

Carbon cycle

car·bon cy·cle *n.* **1. CARBON FLOW BETWEEN ORGANISMS AND ENVIRONMENT** the series of interlinked processes, including photosynthesis and respiration, through which carbon, mainly in the form of carbon compounds, is exchanged between living organisms and the nonliving environment. Carbon dioxide is taken from the atmosphere by photosynthesizing plants and returned by the respiration of plants and animals and by the combustion of fossil fuels. **2. SOURCE OF ENERGY IN STARS** a chain reaction believed to generate significant energy in some stars, in which carbon is used as a catalyst to fuse four hydrogen nuclei into one helium nucleus

Car·bon·dale /kaárbən dàyl/ **1.** city in southwestern Illinois, southeast of Belleville. Population: 26,676 (1996). **2.** city in northeastern Pennsylvania, northeast of Scranton, once an important coal-mining center. Population: 9,953 (1996).

car·bon dat·ing *n.* a method of dating organic remains based on their content of carbon-14

car·bon di·ox·ide *n.* a heavy colorless odorless atmospheric gas produced during respiration and used by plants during photosynthesis. It is also formed by combustion, and increasing atmospheric levels may alter the Earth's climate. It is used in refrigeration, carbonated drinks, and fire extinguishers. Formula: CO_2.

car·bon di·sul·fide *n.* a colorless poisonous flammable liquid containing impurities that give it a rotten-egg smell. It is used in making cellophane and rayon and as a solvent and fumigant.

car·bon fi·ber *n.* a very strong light thread manufactured from carbonized acrylic, used to reinforce resins, metal, and ceramics. Articles made with carbon fiber include turbine blades and poles for pole vaulting.

car·bon fix·a·tion *n.* the process by which plants synthesize carbon dioxide into organic compounds

car·bon·ic /kaar bónnik/ *adj.* containing carbon

car·bon·ic ac·id *n.* a weak acid formed when carbon dioxide is dissolved in water. Formula: H_2CO_3.

car·bon·ic an·hy·drase /-an hīdràyss, -dràyz/ *n.* an enzyme in living tissue, e.g., blood cells, that contains zinc and aids the transfer of carbon dioxide from the tissues to the lungs

car·bon·if·er·ous /kaárbə níffərəss/ *adj.* containing or yielding coal or carbon

Car·bon·if·er·ous *n.* the period of geologic time when true reptiles first appeared and when much of the Earth's surface was covered by forests, 362.5 million to 290 million years ago. [Because numerous coal deposits were formed during this time] —**Car·bon·if·er·ous** *adj.*

car·bo·ni·um i·on *n.* an organic ion that has a carbon atom bearing a positive charge

car·bon·i·za·tion /kaárbəni záysh'n/ *n.* **1. TREATMENT TO TURN SOMETHING INTO CARBON** the burning, fossilization, or chemical treatment of something that turns it into carbon **2. COATING WITH CARBON** the process of covering or coating something with carbon **3.** = **destructive distillation**

car·bon·ize /kaárbə nīz/ **(-ized, -iz·ing, -iz·es)** *v.* **1.** *vti.* **TURN INTO CARBON** to turn into carbon, or turn something into carbon, by partial burning, by fossilization, or through chemical treatment **2.** *vt.* **COVER OR COAT WITH CARBON** to cover or coat the surface of something with carbon —**car·bon·iz·er** *n.*

car·bon·less /kaárbənləss/ *adj.* chemically treated to make duplicate copies without the use of carbon paper

car·bon mi·cro·phone *n.* a microphone containing carbon granules that change resistance according to the vibrating pressure of sound waves, thereby modulating the frequency of the sound waves

car·bon mon·ox·ide *n.* a colorless odorless toxic gas formed when carbon-containing compounds or fuels are burned with insufficient air. Formula: CO.

car·bon·nade /kaárbə nàyd/, **car·bonade** *n.* a stew made with beef and onions cooked in beer [Mid-17thC. From French, from *carbone* (see CARBON).]

car·bon-ni·tro·gen cy·cle *n.* = **carbon cycle** *n.* 2

car·bon pa·per *n.* paper used for making copies, coated on one side with a waxy pigment that often contains carbon

car·bon proc·ess, car·bon print·ing *n.* a printing process that uses sensitized carbon tissue to produce positive prints

car·bon star *n.* a star that has a lower temperature and proportionately more carbon in relation to nitrogen than other stars

car·bon steel *n.* steel containing carbon with properties that vary according to the carbon content

car·bon val·ue *n.* a measurement of the extent to which a lubricant forms carbon when in use

car·bon·yl /kaárbənil, kaárbə neél/ *adj.* relating to or containing the group of atoms found in certain organic and inorganic compounds. Formula: =C=O. ■ *n.* **METAL COMPOUND** a compound that has a metal bound to a carbonyl group —**car·bon·yl·ic** /kaárbə níllik/ *adj.*

car·bon·yl chlo·ride *n.* = **phosgene**

car boot sale *n. U.K.* a sale of second-hand and new merchandise from the trunks of people's cars, usually taking place on an open-air site rented for the purpose

car·borne /kaár bàwrn/ *adj.* in a car or traveling by automobile ○ *roads jammed with carborne commuters* [Late 20thC]

Car·bo·run·dum /kaárbə rúndəm/ *tdmk.* a trademark for abrasives composed of silicon carbide

carboxy- *prefix.* CHEM carboxyl ○ *carboxypeptidase* [From CARBOXYL]

car·box·y·he·mo·glo·bin /kaar bòksi heemə glṓbin/ *n.* a stable compound formed in the blood when inhaled carbon monoxide binds with hemoglobin, thus preventing it from binding with oxygen

car·box·yl·ase /kaar bóksə làyss, -làyz/ *n.* an enzyme that aids the absorption or release of carbon dioxide from, e.g., certain acids

car·box·y·late *n.* /kaar bóksə làyt, kaar bóksələt/ **SALT OR ESTER OF CARBOXYLIC ACID** any salt or ester of a carboxylic acid ■ *vt.* /kaar bóksə làyt/ **(-lat·ed, -lat·ing, -lates) FORM CARBOXYLIC ACID** to form carboxylic acid by introducing a carboxyl group or carbon dioxide into a compound —**car·box·yl·a·tion** /kaar bòksə láysh'n/ *n.*

car·box·yl·ic ac·id /kaar bok sillik-/ *n.* any organic acid that contains the carboxyl group

car·box·y·meth·yl·cel·lu·lose /kaar bòksi meth'l séllyə lōss/ *n.* a derivative of cellulose used in paper production, as a stabilizer and emulsifier in foods, as an antacid, and as bulk in laxatives

car·box·y·pep·ti·dase /kaar bòksi pépti dàyss, -dàyz/ *n.* a protein-digesting enzyme secreted into the duodenum as a component of pancreatic juice

car·boy /kaár bòy/ *n.* a large container made of plastic or glass, usually protected by a wooden casing, used to hold corrosive liquids such as acids [Mid-18thC. Ultimately from Persian *karāba* "large glass flagon."]

car bra *n.* a cover fastened around the front of an automobile to protect the grille (*informal*)

car·bun·cle /kaár bùngk'l/ *n.* **1.** MED **INFLAMED SWELLING** a multiple-headed boil **2. ROUNDED RED GEMSTONE** a red gemstone, especially a garnet, that is smoothly rounded and polished [13thC. Via Old French *charbu(n)cle* from Latin *carbunculus* "red gemstone, inflamed spot" (literally "small coal"), from *carbon-* (see CARBON).] —**car·bun·cled** *adj.* —**car·bun·cu·lar** /kaar búngkyələr/ *adj.*

car·bu·ra·tion /kaárbə ráysh'n/, **car·bu·re·tion** *n.* the process of mixing the correct proportions of liquid fuel with air to achieve combustion [Late 19thC. Formed from CARBURET.]

car·bu·ret /kaárbə ráyt, kaárbə rèt/ **(-ret·ed, -ret·ing, -rets)** *vt.* to mix a gas with hydrocarbons in order to increase fuel energy [Early 19thC. From obsolete *carburet* "carbide."]

car·bu·ret·ed /kaárbə ràytəd, kaárbə rèttəd/ *adj.* equipped with a carburetor

car·bu·re·tion *n.* = **carburation**

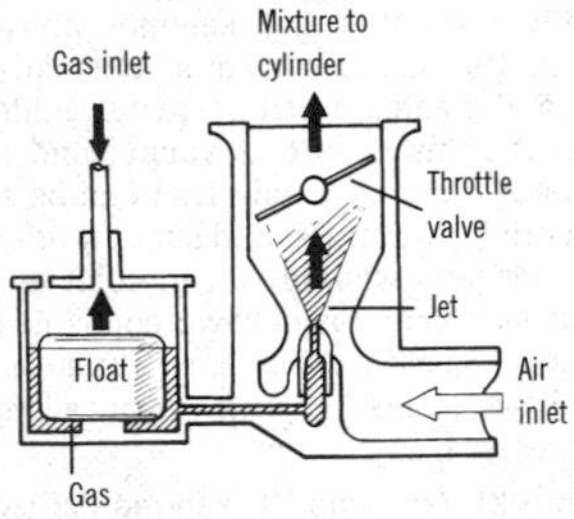

Carburetor

car·bu·re·tor /kaárbə ràytər/ *n.* a device in an internal combustion engine that mixes liquid fuel and air in the correct proportions, vaporizes them, and transfers the mixture to the cylinders [Mid-19thC. Formed from CARBURET.]

car·bu·ret·tor *n.* U.K. = **carburetor**

car·bu·rize /kaárbə rīz/ **(-rized, -riz·ing, -riz·es)** *vt.* = **carbonize** [Mid-19thC. Formed from CARBURET.] —**car·bu·ri·za·tion** /kaárbəri záysh'n/ *n.*

car·ca·jou /kaárkə jōō, kaárkə zhōō/ (*plural* **-jous** *or* **-jou**) *n.* = **wolverine** [Early 18thC. Via Canadian French from Montagnais *kwa:hkwa:če:w.*]

car·cass /kaárkəss/ *n.* **1. DEAD BODY OF ANIMAL** the dead body of an animal, especially one slaughtered and prepared for use as meat **2. PERSON** a living person's body (*humorous*) ○ *Move your carcass!* **3. REMAINS OF SOMETHING** the remains of something decayed or almost totally destroyed **4. BASIC STRUCTURE** the basic structure or framework of something [14thC. From Anglo-Norman *carcois* and French *carcasse*; ultimately of unknown origin.]

Car·cas·sonne /kaárkə són/ city and capital of Aude Department, southern France, situated on the Aude River 57 mi./92 km southeast of Toulouse. Population: 44,991 (1990).

Car·che·mish /kaár kə mìsh/ ancient city on the Euphrates River, northeast of Aleppo in present-day northern Syria

carcin- *prefix.* MED = **carcino-** (*used before vowels*)

carcino- *prefix.* MED cancer ○ *carcinogenic* [From Greek *karkinos* "crab, cancer"; ultimately related to Latin *cancer* (source of English *cancer* and *canker*)]

car·cin·o·gen /kaar sínnəjən, kaárs'nə jèn/ *n.* a substance or agent that can cause cancer. Radiation and some chemicals and viruses are carcinogens. [Mid-19thC. Blend of CARCINOMA and -GEN.]

car·ci·no·gen·e·sis /kaárs'nə jénnəsiss/ *n.* the production of cancerous cells [Early 20thC. Blend of CARCINOMA and GENESIS.]

car·cin·o·gen·ic /kaárs'nə jénnik/ *adj.* capable of causing cancer [Early 20thC. Blend of CARCINOMA and -GENIC.] —**car·ci·no·ge·nic·i·ty** /kaárs'nōjə nìssətee/ *n.*

car·ci·noid /kaárs'n òyd/ *n.* a small benign or malignant tumor on the walls of the small intestine that sometimes produces physiologically active compounds such as serotonin or prostaglandins that are normally deactivated by the liver. In carcinoid syndrome excessive amounts of such compounds are released from the infected liver into the circulation and cause flushing, headache, diarrhea, and asthma. [Early 20thC. Blend of CARCINOMA and -OID.]

car·ci·no·ma /kaárs'n ṓmə/ *n.* **1.** MALIGNANT TUMOR a malignant tumor that starts in the surface layer (**epithelium**) of an organ or body part and may spread to other parts of the body **2.** = **cancer** [Early 18thC. Via Latin from Greek *karkinōma* (stem *karkinōmat-*), from *karkinos* "crab" (source of English *cancer*); from the crablike pattern of the surrounding swollen blood vessels.] —**car·ci·no·ma·toid** *adj.* —**car·ci·nom·a·tous** /-ómmətəss/ *adj.*

car·ci·no·ma·to·sis /kaárs'n ōmə tṓssiss/ *n.* a condition in which cancer has spread widely throughout the body

car·ci·no·sar·co·ma /kaárs'nō saar kṓmə/ (*plural* **-mas** *or* **-ma·ta** /-kṓmətə/) *n.* a malignant tumor containing elements of both a carcinoma and a sarcoma

car·ci·no·sis /kaárs'n ṓssiss/ *n.* = **carcinomatosis**

car coat *n.* an overcoat that ends at mid-thigh

card[1] /kaard/ *n.* **1.** PAPER WITH PICTURES AND GREETINGS a piece of stiff paper, usually folded in half and with designs or illustrations, used to send greetings of various kinds, especially on birthdays and holidays **2.** GAME PRINTED STIFF PAPER FOR GAMES a small piece of stiff paper, part of a set, that is printed with symbols or figures and used to play games or tell fortunes **3.** STIFF PAPER SHOWING IDENTITY a small piece of stiff paper or plastic that shows somebody's identity, business position, or membership in a club or organization **4.** PLASTIC CARD HOLDING INFORMATION a small piece of plastic that holds information in a magnetic strip or microprocessor, used in financial activities such as getting cash from ATMs or making phone calls **5.** = **postcard 6.** SPORTS = **racecard 7.** = **index card 8.** AMUSING PERSON an amusing or eccentric person (*dated informal*) **9.** COLLECTABLE STIFF PAPER WITH PICTURE a piece of stiff paper with a picture on one side, collected as part of a set of such items **10.** COLORED CARD SHOWN TO SOCCER PLAYER a small piece of red or yellow stiff paper that is shown to a soccer player who has violated the rules during a game **11.** COMPUT PUNCH CARD = **punchcard 12.** ELEC ENG PRINTED CIRCUIT BOARD a printed circuit board **13.** COMPUT= **expansion card 14.** NAVIG = **compass card 15.** WINE LIST a wine list in a restaurant **16.** MENU a restaurant menu ○ *We ate our way through the entire card.* **17.** PORTION OF DRUGS a portion of a narcotic, especially heroin (*slang*) **18. cards** GAME USING CARDS any game played using playing cards ■ *vt.* (**card·ed, card·ing, cards**) (*informal*) **1.** ASK FOR IDENTIFICATION to ask somebody to show identification, usually to check that the person is of legal age to drink alcohol or be admitted somewhere **2.** GOLF RECORD A GOLF SCORE to record a score after playing a hole or round of golf [15thC. Via French *carte* from Latin *c(h)arta* "papyrus leaf, paper," from Greek *khartēs* "papyrus leaf" (source of English *chart* and

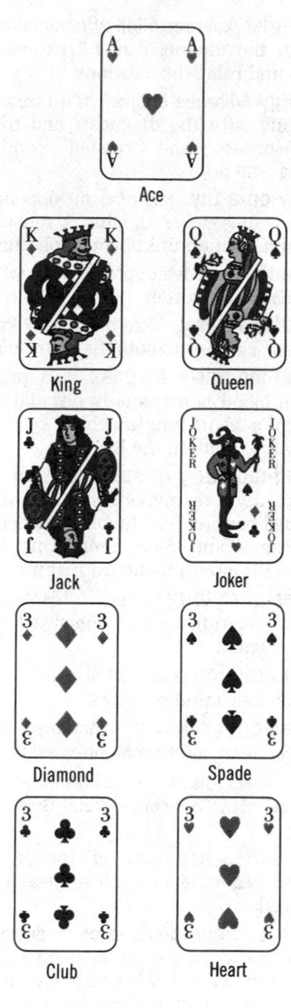

Card: Playing cards

cartoon), of uncertain origin: probably from Egyptian.] ◇ **have** *or* **keep a card up your sleeve** to have a secret plan or tactic ready to be used if necessary (*informal*) ◇ **a few cards short of a (full) deck** not very intelligent (*informal*) ◇ **have the cards stacked against you** to be in a situation that is extremely disadvantageous to you and that may prevent you from achieving your goals (*informal*) ◇ **hold all the cards** to be in complete control of a situation (*informal*) ◇ **in the cards** likely to happen (*informal*) ○ *The stock market took the collapse of the banking giant in its stride, as it had been in the cards for some time.* ◇ **play your cards right** to take the fullest possible advantage of your chances of success (*informal*) ◇ **put** *or* **lay your cards on the table** to reveal openly what your intentions and plans are (*informal*)

card in *vi.* to sign into a place, usually the place of work, by using a magnetic card

card out *vi.* to sign out of a place, usually from the place of work, by using a magnetic card. ◊ **clock out**

card[2] /kaard/ *vt.* (**card·ed, card·ing, cards**) COMB AND CLEAN WOOL OR COTTON to comb out and clean wool, cotton, or other fibers before spinning ■ *n.* **1.** TOOL OR MACHINE FOR CARDING a tool or machine with wire teeth used to comb out or clean wool, cotton, or other fibers before spinning **2.** DEVICE TO MAKE CLOTH NAPPED a device for raising the nap on cloth [14thC. Via French from late Latin *cardus* "thistle," from Latin *carduus* "thistle, artichoke" (source of English *chard* and *cardoon*).] —**card·er** *n.*

Card. *abbr.* Cardinal

card- *prefix.* MED = **cardio-**

car·da·mom /kaárdəməm/, **car·da·mon** /-mən/, **car·da·mum** /-məm/ *n.* **1.** PLANTS TROPICAL PLANT a perennial tropical plant that has large hairy leaves, clusters of small white flowers, and aromatic pods and seeds. Latin name: *Elettaria cardamomum.* **2.** COOK SPICE FROM CARDAMOM PLANT the pods and seeds of the cardamom plant, used whole or crushed as a spice or flavoring [14thC. Directly or via French *cardamome* from Latin *cardamomum*, from Greek *kardamōmon*, from *kardamon* "cress" + *amōmon* "amomum."]

car·dan joint /kaárd'n-/ *n.* a type of universal joint that can rotate when out of alignment [Early 20thC. Named for Gerolamo *Cardano* (1501–76), Italian mathematician who invented it.]

car·dan shaft *n.* part of the transmission system in some vehicles [See CARDAN JOINT]

card·board /kaárd bàwrd/ *n.* LIGHTWEIGHT PAPER BOARD a stiff light material made from wastepaper pulp, often used for making containers or packaging for goods ■ *adj.* two-dimensional or lacking in depth ○ *gave a cardboard rendition of the sonata*

card-car·ry·ing *adj.* **1.** BEING OFFICIAL MEMBER OF ORGANIZATION officially listed as belonging to an organization and subscribing to its beliefs **2.** COMMITTED TO CAUSE deeply committed to a cause or movement (*informal*) [From the membership card typically held by such members; first applied to members of the Communist Party]

card cat·a·log *n.* an alphabetical listing of items such as names and addresses or books in a library, with each item formerly on a separate card now most often computerized

card·ed /kaárdəd/ *adj.* **1.** shown a red or yellow card as a warning that a player has violated a rule in soccer. **2.** SPORTS *Can.* used to describe an amateur athlete who is being funded by a government grant to enable him or her to pursue training

Cár·de·nas, Lázaro (1895–1970) Mexican politician and soldier. He served in various Mexican military and government posts before serving as president (1934–40).

card·hold·er /kaárd hṑldər/ *n.* somebody who possesses a card that carries information, especially a credit, debit, bank, or phone card

cardi- *prefix.* MED = **cardio-**

car·di·a /kaárdee ə/ (*plural* **-ae** /-èe/ *or* **-as**) *n.* the opening of the esophagus into the stomach, or the upper part of the stomach where it is connected to the esophagus [Late 18thC. From Greek *kardia* (see CARDIAC).]

car·di·ac /kaárdee àk/ *adj.* **1.** HEART-RELATED relating to or affecting the heart **2.** OF THE UPPER PART OF STOMACH relating to the upper part of the stomach, where it is connected to the esophagus [Early 17thC. Via French from Latin *cardiacus*, from Greek *kardia* "heart, cardia." Ultimately from an Indo-European word that is also the ancestor of English *courage, concord*, and *heart*.]

car·di·ac ar·rest *n.* the sudden stopping of the heartbeat and therefore of the pumping action of the heart. Cardiac arrest requires immediate treatment to prevent brain damage and death.

car·di·ac com·pres·sion, car·di·ac mass·age *n.* rhythmic compression of somebody's heart in order to restore or maintain blood circulation after the person has had a heart attack. ◊ **CPR**

car·di·al·gia /kaárdee áljə, kaárdee áljee ə/ *n.* **1.** HEARTBURN heartburn (*technical*) **2.** HEART PAIN pain in or near the heart [Mid-17thC. Via modern Latin from Greek *kardialgia*, from *kardia* (see CARDIAC).]

Car·diff /kaárdif/ capital and largest city of Wales. It is the home of the Welsh Assembly and is an important industrial center. Population: 315,000 (1996). Welsh **Caerdydd**

Cardigan

car·di·gan /kaárdigən/ *n.* a long-sleeved sweater that fastens up the front [Mid-19thC. Named for the 7th Earl of *Cardigan*, James Thomas Brudenell (1797–1868), who led the charge of the Light Brigade during the Crimean War (1854).]

Car·di·gan Welsh cor·gi *n.* a dog belonging to the larger of two breeds of corgi with a long tail [Named for CARDIGANSHIRE, former county in Wales]

Cardinal

car·di·nal /kaárd'nəl/ *n.* **1.** CHR **ROMAN CATHOLIC DIGNITARY** in the Roman Catholic Church, one of the group of clergy, next in rank to the Pope, who elect the Pope from their own number and act as his advisers **2.** COLORS **DEEP RED** a deep strong red color, the same as that of the robes worn by a cardinal **3.** BIRDS **BRIGHT RED BIRD** a North American crested finch, the male of which has bright red plumage with a black face. Latin name: *Cardinalis cardinalis.* **4.** MATH = **cardinal number 5.** CLOTHES **WOMAN'S HOODED CAPE** a woman's short cape with a hood, originally scarlet in color, that was worn in the 17th and 18th centuries ■ *adj.* **1. IMPORTANT** fundamentally important **2.** COLORS **BRIGHT RED** bright red in color [12thC. Via French from medieval Latin *cardinalis,* from the Latin stem *cardin-* "hinge." The underlying idea is of a hinge upon which everything hangs.] —**car·di·nal·ly** *adv.*

car·di·nal·ate /kaárd'nələt, -làyt/, **car·di·nal·ship** /-shìp/ *n.* **1. ALL CARDINALS** the cardinals of the Roman Catholic Church regarded collectively **2. TERM OF OFFICE OF CARDINAL** the term of office of a Roman Catholic cardinal **3. OFFICE OF CARDINAL** the rank or office of a Roman Catholic cardinal

car·di·nal fish *n.* a small tropical marine fish, usually red or brown, often abundant on coral reefs. Family: Apogonidae.

car·di·nal flow·er *n.* a perennial lobelia native to central and eastern North America that has a cluster of brilliantly colored, usually red, flowers. Latin name: *Lobelia cardinalis.*

car·di·nal num·ber *n.* a number, such as 4 or 42, used to denote quantity but not order

car·di·nal point *n.* any of the four principal points of the compass, North, South, East, or West

car·di·nal·ship *n.* = **cardinalate**

car·di·nal vir·tue *n.* any one of the principal virtues in the classical or Christian traditions. In the classical tradition they are justice, prudence, temperance, and fortitude, and in the Christian tradition they are justice, prudence, temperance, and fortitude together with faith, hope, and charity.

car·di·nal vow·els *npl.* a fixed set of vowel sounds, based on the position of the tongue and the shape of the mouth cavity, and spaced at approximately equal acoustic intervals. They are used in describing the vowel sounds of a language.

card in·dex *n. U.K.* = **card catalog**

cardio- *prefix.* MED heart ○ *cardiopulmonary* [From Greek *kardia* (see CARDIAC)]

car·di·o·ac·cel·er·a·tor /kaárdi ō ək séllə ràytər/ *n.* a drug or other agent that increases the heart rate [Late 20thC] —**car·di·o·ac·cel·er·a·tion** /-sellə ráysh'n/ *n.*

car·di·o·gen·ic /kaárdi ō jénnik/ *adj.* resulting from activity or disease of the heart

car·di·o·gram /kaárdee ə gràm/ *n.* a graphic record made by a cardiograph, especially an electrocardiogram

car·di·o·graph /kaárdee ə gràf/ *n.* **1. INSTRUMENT FOR RECORDING HEART ACTIVITY** an instrument for recording heart activity, used in the diagnosis of heart disorders **2.** = **electrocardiograph** —**car·di·o·graph·ic** /kaárdee ə gráffik/ *adj.* —**car·di·o·graph·i·cal** /-gráffik'l/ *adj.* —**car·di·o·graph·i·cal·ly** /-gráffiklee/ *adv.* —**car·di·og·ra·phy** /kaárdee óggrəfee/ *n.*

car·di·og·raph·er /kaárdee óggrəfər/ *n.* a medical technician trained in using a cardiograph, especially an electrocardiograph

car·di·ol·o·gist /kaárdee óllәjist/ *n.* a doctor who specializes in the diagnosis and treatment of heart disorders and related conditions

car·di·ol·o·gy /kaárdee óllәjee/ *n.* a branch of medicine dealing with the diagnosis and treatment of heart disorders and related conditions — **car·di·o·log·i·cal** *adj.*

car·di·o·my·op·a·thy /kaárdi ō mī óppəthee/ (*plural* **-thies**) *n.* a disease of the heart muscle, usually chronic and with an unknown or obscure cause

car·di·op·a·thy /kaárdee óppəthee/ (*plural* **-thies**) *n.* a heart disease or disorder

car·di·o·pul·mo·nar·y /kaárdi ō poólmə nèrree, -púlmə-/ *adj.* relating to both the heart and the lungs

car·di·o·pul·mo·nar·y by·pass *n.* a procedure by which the blood is artificially circulated and oxygenated by a heart-lung machine so that surgery may be carried out on the heart

car·di·o·pul·mo·nar·y re·sus·ci·ta·tion *n.* an emergency technique to revive somebody whose heart has stopped beating that involves clearing the person's airways and then alternating heart compression with mouth-to-mouth respiration

car·di·o·res·pi·ra·to·ry /kaárdi ō réspərə tàwree, -ri spírə-/ *adj.* relating to both the heart and the respiratory system

car·di·o·tho·rac·ic /kaárdi ō thə rássik/ *adj.* relating to both the heart and the chest

car·di·o·vas·cu·lar /kaárdi ō váskyələr/ *adj.* relating to both the heart and the blood vessels

car·di·tis /kaar dítiss/ *n.* inflammation of the heart [Late 18thC. Formed from Greek *kardia* (see CARDIAC).]

-cardium *suffix.* MED part of the heart ○ *endocardium* [Via modern Latin from Greek *kardia* "heart" (see CARDIAC)]

car·doon /kaar doón/ (*plural* **-doon** *or* **-doons**) *n.* a large southern European perennial plant related to the artichoke that has spiny leaves and edible roots and leafstalks. Latin name: *Cynara cardunculus.* [Early 17thC. Via French *cardon* from, ultimately, Latin *carduus* "thistle, artichoke" (see CARD[2]).]

Car·do·so /kaar dóssō/, **Fernando Henrique** (*b.* 1931) Brazilian sociologist and political leader. He was elected president in 1995 after serving in various government posts.

Car·do·zo /kaar dózō/, **Benjamin Nathan** (1870–1938) U.S. Supreme Court justice. He served on the U.S. Supreme Court from 1932 until his death.

card·phone /kaárd fōn/ *n. U.K.* a payphone operated by a phonecard

card·sharp /kaárd shaàrp/, **card·sharp·er** /-ər/ *n.* somebody who regularly cheats when playing cards — **card·sharp·ing** *n.*

card ta·ble *n.* a small table, usually folding, used for playing card games

care /kair/ *v.* (**cared, car·ing, cares**) **1.** *vti.* **BE CONCERNED** to be interested or concerned ○ *I said I couldn't care less if he did leave.* **2.** *vi.* **FEEL AFFECTION AND CONCERN** to feel affection or love and concern for somebody **3.** *vi.* **TEND SOMEBODY OR SOMETHING** to tend or supervise somebody or something **4.** *vi.* **LIKE OR WANT SOMETHING** to like or be in favor of something (*formal*) ○ *Would you care for dessert, sir?* ■ *n.* **1. UPKEEP** the process of maintaining something in good condition ○ *a skin care treatment* **2. CAREFUL ATTENTION** careful attention to avoid damage or error ○ *take care crossing the road* **3. WORRY** a worry or cause for anxiety ○ *without a care in the world* **4. ATTENTIVE TREATMENT OF SOMEBODY** the providing of whatever is needed for somebody's well-being, e.g., somebody dependent or physically or mentally challenged ○ *responsible for the 20 children in her care* ○ *residential care* **5. LEGAL OVERSIGHT OF SOMEBODY** legal oversight of and responsibility for somebody such as a minor ○ *was put into the care of temporary foster parents* [Old English *caru* "sorrow." Ultimately from an Indo-European word that is also the ancestor of English *chary, slogan,* and *garrulous.*] ◇ **in care of** into the temporary possession of an addressee who will ensure that the specified item will be delivered to the intended recipient ○ *sent the letter to her in care of her parents*

WORD KEY: USAGE

could care less or **couldn't care less?** In informal English ***I could care less*** is all but synonymous with ***I couldn't care less,*** except that it carries overtones of irony. However it should be pointed out that many people strongly oppose this usage.

CARE /kair/ *abbr.* Cooperative for American Relief Everywhere

ca·reen /kə reén/ (**-reened, -reen·ing, -reens**) *v.* **1.** *vi.* **SWAY OR SWERVE WHILE MOVING** to move forwards at high speed, swaying, lurching, or swerving from one side to the other ○ *a motorcycle careening around sharp curves* **2.** *vi.* **RUSH** to rush pell-mell ○ *He seemed to careen through life in a happy-go-lucky manner.* **3.** *vti.* SHIPPING **TURN BOAT ON SIDE** to turn over onto the side, or turn a boat over on its side, especially for repairs or cleaning **4.** *vi.* NAUT **HEEL IN THE WIND** to heel over to one side while sailing [Late 16thC. Via French *carène* from, ultimately, Latin *carina* "keel," originally "nutshell" (source of English *carina*).] —**ca·reen·er** *n.*

ca·reer /kə reér/ *n.* **1. LONG-TERM OR LIFELONG JOB** a job or occupation regarded as a long-term or lifelong activity **2. PROFESSIONAL PROGRESS** somebody's progress in a chosen profession or during that person's working life **3. GENERAL PROGRESS** the general path or progress taken by somebody or something ○ *a piece of legislation whose career is rich with conflicting amendments* **4. RAPID FORWARD LURCHING MOTION** a rushing onward while lurching or swaying ■ *adj.* **1. PROFESSIONAL FOR LIFE** trained for and expecting to work in a particular occupation for an entire working life rather than briefly ○ *a career diplomat* **2. DOING ILLEGAL ACTS THROUGH LIFETIME** committing illegal acts throughout a lifetime, without apparent remorse or desire for self-improvement ○ *a career criminal, who, after 25 years of armed robbery, was imprisoned* ■ *vi.* (**-reered, -reer·ing, -reers**) **LURCH RAPIDLY ONWARD** to rush forward while lurching or swaying [Mid-16thC. Via French *carrière* from, ultimately, Latin *carrus* "two-wheeled wagon" (see CAR). Originally "racecourse," then "swift course."]

WORD KEY: CULTURAL NOTE

My Brilliant Career, a novel by Australian writer Miles Franklin (1901). It is an account of a young girl's struggle to choose between an independent career and a comfortable life as the wife of a wealthy landowner. It was made into a movie directed by Gillian Armstrong in 1979.

ca·reer coun·sel·or *n.* somebody whose job is to advise high-school students on possible careers and jobs as they approach graduation

ca·reer·ism /kə reér ìzzəm/ *n.* the behavior of somebody whose principal motivation is career advancement —**ca·reer·ist** *n.*

ca·reer wom·an *n.* a woman who has a career or who takes her working life seriously

care·free /káir freè/ *adj.* having no worries or responsibilities —**care·free·ness** *n.*

care·ful /káirf'l/ *adj.* **1. CAUTIOUS** acting with caution and attention **2. PAINSTAKING** showing close attention to accuracy and detail **3.** *U.K.* **NOT OVERSPENDING OR BEING WASTEFUL** making sure that money or resources are not spent or used wastefully or without thought **4. WATCHFUL** watchful and protective about something **5. ANXIOUS** full of anxious cares (*archaic*)

WORD KEY: SYNONYMS

careful, conscientious, scrupulous, thorough, meticulous, painstaking, assiduous, punctilious, finicky, fussy

CORE MEANING: exercising care and attention in doing something

careful a wide-ranging term, suggesting attention to detail and implying cautiousness in avoiding errors or inaccuracies; **conscientious** a term suggesting great care, attention, and industriousness toward work, especially as part of somebody's personal ethic; **scrupulous** conscientious, particularly with respect to ethical or moral behavior; **thorough** attentive to detail; **meticulous** a formal term suggesting a high degree of thoroughness; **painstaking** a term emphasizing that somebody is expending unusual effort; **assiduous** a formal term implying that somebody is working very hard or doggedly; **punctilious** a formal term suggesting a rigorous, sometimes excessive attention to fine detail, especially in the observance of rules; **finicky** an informal word suggesting an irritating and unnecessary degree of carefulness; **fussy** a disapproving term similar to "finicky".

care·ful·ly /káirfəlee/ *adv.* **1. PAINSTAKINGLY** with painstaking attention to detail **2. WITH CAUTION AND ATTENTION** with caution and attention so as to avoid damage or potential problems

care·ful·ness /káirf'lnəss/ *n.* **1. CAUTION AND ATTENTION GIVEN TO SOMETHING** caution and attention given to something so as to avoid damage or potential problems **2. ATTENTION TO DETAIL** painstaking attention to detail

care·giv·er /káir gìvvər/ *n.* **1. INDIVIDUAL WHO LOOKS AFTER SOMEBODY** the individual who has the principal responsibility for caring for a child or dependent adult, especially in the home **2. SOMEBODY ASSISTING IN MANAGEMENT OF ILLNESS** a medical or other professional who assists in the management of an illness or disability —**care·giv·ing** *n.*

care la·bel *n.* a label, sewn onto a piece of clothing or other item, that gives cleaning instructions for the item

care·less /káirləss/ *adj.* **1. NOT GIVING CAREFUL ATTENTION** not giving enough careful attention to the details of something **2. SHOWING NO CONCERN** disregarding or showing no concern about something **3. NOT CAREFULLY WORKED ON** not carefully worked on or practiced, but done or assumed easily and naturally **4. WITHOUT ANXIETIES** without cares or worries **5.** not giving or receiving any care —**care·less·ly** *adv.*

care·less·ness /káirləssnəss/ *n.* **1. LACK OF ATTENTION** lack of careful attention to the details of something **2. EXAMPLE OF NEGLIGENCE** an example of negligence or of a failure to take enough trouble with something **3. LACK OF CONCERN** lack of concern about something

care pack·age *n.* a package of food or personal items for somebody far from home, e.g., a member of the armed forces or a student boarding at a school (*informal*)

car·er /káirər/ *n. U.K.* = **caregiver**

ca·ress /kə réss/ *vt.* (**-ressed, -ress·ing, -ress·es**) **1. TOUCH OR STROKE AFFECTIONATELY** to touch or stroke somebody or something affectionately **2. AFFECT IN SOOTHING WAY** to touch, pass over, or affect somebody in a soothing or pleasant way ■ *n.* **GENTLE TOUCH** a gentle affectionate touch or embrace [Mid-17thC. Via French *caresse* from, ultimately, Latin *carus* "dear" (source of English *charity* and *cherish*).] —**ca·ress·er** *n.* —**ca·res·sive** *adj.* —**ca·res·sive·ly** *adv.*

ca·ress·ing /kə réssing/ *adj.* gentle and soothing —**ca·ress·ing·ly** *adv.*

car·et /kérrət/ *n.* a mark (ʎ) made on printed or manuscript material to show where something such as a letter or word should be inserted [Late 17thC. From Latin *caret*, literally "there is lacking," a form of *carere* "to be without, lack."]

care·tak·er /káir tàykər/ *n.* **1. TEMPORARY OFFICEHOLDER** somebody who holds an office temporarily, especially when it has unexpectedly been vacated **2.** = **caregiver 3. SOMEBODY OFFERING EMOTIONAL SUPPORT** somebody giving care or emotional support to another **4.** *U.K.* = **janitor**

care·tak·er gov·ern·ment *n.* a government that is in power temporarily, e.g., until an election is held

care·tak·ing /káir tàyking/ *n.* the occupation of looking after a property such as an office building or a school and supervising its maintenance and cleaning

care work·er *n.* somebody employed to look after people who are physically or mentally challenged and who live in residential accommodations

care·worn /káir wàwrn/ *adj.* exhausted or otherwise badly affected by anxiety or worry

car·fare /kaár fàir/ *n.* the amount charged for a ride on a bus or streetcar or in a taxicab

car·ful /kaár fòol/ *n.* = **carload** *n.* 1

car·go /kaárgō/ (*plural* **-goes** *or* **-gos**) *n.* **1. GOODS CARRIED AS FREIGHT** goods carried as freight by sea, road, or air **2. LOAD** a load of something [Mid-17thC. Via Spanish, from, ultimately, late Latin *car(ri)care* "to load," from Latin *carrus* "two-wheeled wagon" (see CAR).]

car·go cult *n.* a religion in some southwestern Pacific islands whose devotees believe that ancestral spirits will return to the island bringing modern consumer goods and wealth

car·go pock·et *n.* a large pocket with a pleat and a flap

car·hop /kaár hòp/ *n.* **1. SERVER AT DRIVE-IN RESTAURANT** somebody who serves food to people in parked cars at a drive-in restaurant **2. SOMEBODY WHO LOOKS AFTER CUSTOMERS' CARS** somebody who takes care of the vehicles of guests staying at a resort or large hotel (*dated*) [Mid-20thC. From CAR + *hop* (from BELLHOP).]

Car·ib /kérrib/ (*plural* **-ibs** *or* **-ib**) *n.* **1.** PEOPLES **NATIVE AMERICAN** a member of a group of Native American people who inhabit part of Central America, northeastern South America, and the Lesser Antilles **2.** LANG **S AMERICAN LANGUAGE** a language of the Cariban family spoken in Venezuela and neighboring countries. Carib is spoken by 20,000 people. [Mid-16thC. Via Spanish *caribe* from Arawak *carib* (source of English *cannibal*).] —**Car·ib** *adj.*

Carib. *abbr.* Caribbean

Car·i·ban /kérrəbən, kə reébən/ (*plural* **-bans** *or* **-ban**) *n.* **1.** PEOPLES, LANG = **Carib 2.** LANG, PEOPLES **GROUP OF S AMERICAN LANGUAGES** a group of about 30 languages spoken in northern South America. About 40,000 people speak a Cariban language. —**Car·i·ban** *adj.*

Car·ib·be·an /kèrrə beé ən, kə ríbbee ən/ *n.* **1. REGION INCLUDING THE WEST INDIES** region comprising the states and islands of the Caribbean Sea, including the West Indies **2. SOMEBODY FROM CARIBBEAN** somebody who was born in or is a citizen of any of the Caribbean islands ■ *adj.* **1. OF CARIBBEAN** relating to or typical of any of the countries of the Caribbean or their people or culture **2. OF THE CARIBS** relating to or typical of the Caribs or their culture

Car·ib·be·an Eng·lish *n.* the variety of English spoken in the Caribbean islands

WORD KEY: WORLD ENGLISH

The English language as used in the Caribbean region, also called *West Indian English*. The islands and coasts of the Caribbean, since their discovery by Columbus in 1492, have, since that time, been claimed, disputed, settled, and governed by the Spanish, Portuguese, French, British, Dutch, Danish, and Americans with obvious, long-term, varied effects on the languages spoken there. In the second half of the 20th century, most of the territories are independent, but colonization has created a complex inheritance. In such mainland areas as Belize and Guyana, indigenous languages survive, but not on the islands, and in all territories there is a complex continuum between the standard forms of English (American and British), Dutch, French, and Spanish on the one side and their creole varieties on the other. In general terms, the creoles mix European lexical items with varying degrees of African structural features. In most Anglo-Caribbean territories, although school-based standard English is the official language it is a minority form and, in states like Belize and Guyana, English mixes with a range of other languages. Apart from Barbados and Guyana, ***Caribbean English*** is usually non-rhotic (i.e., r is not pronounced in such words as art, door, worker).

Ca·rib·be·an Sea arm of the Atlantic Ocean, surrounded by the West Indies, northern South America, and eastern Central America. Area: 750,000 sq. mi./1,940,000 sq. km. Depth: Cayman Trench 24,720 ft./7,535 m.

ca·ri·be /kə reébee/ *n.* ZOOL = **piranha** [Mid-19thC. From Spanish (see CARIB).]

Car·i·boo Moun·tains section of Canada's Rocky Mountains. The highest peak is Mount Sir Wilfrid Laurier. Height: 11,499 ft./3,505 m.

Caribou

car·i·bou /kérrə bòo/ (*plural* **-bou** *or* **-bous**) *n.* a large deer that lives in large herds in northern regions and is characterized by large branched antlers present on both sexes. Reindeer are domesticated caribou. Genus: *Rangifer*. [Mid-17thC. Via Canadian French from Micmac *ʔalipu*, literally "snow shoveler," from the animal's removal of snow to find grass.]

Car·i·bou In·u·it *n.* somebody belonging to any of the Inuit peoples who inhabit the Barren Grounds in northern Canada. They depend upon caribou for survival.

car·i·ca·ture /kérrəkə chòor, -chər/ *n.* **1. COMIC EXAGGERATION** a drawing, description, or performance that exaggerates somebody's or something's characteristics, e.g., somebody's physical features, for humorous or satirical effect **2. TRAVESTY** a ridiculously inappropriate or unsuccessful version of or attempt at something **3. OF CARICATURES** the art of creating caricatures ■ *vt.* (**-tured, -tur·ing, -tures**) **REPRESENT WITH COMIC EXAGGERATION** to represent somebody or something with a caricature [Mid-18thC. From, ultimately, Italian *caricatura*, from *caricare* "to exaggerate, load," from late Latin *carricare*, from Latin *carrus* "wagon" (see CAR).] —**car·i·ca·tur·al** *adj.*

car·i·ca·tur·ist /kérrəkə chòorist/ *n.* somebody who creates caricatures, especially an artist

CARI·COM /kérrə kòm/ *abbr.* Caribbean Community and Common Market

car·ies /káiriz/ *n.* progressive decay of a tooth or, less commonly, a bone [Late 16thC. From Latin.]

CAR·IF·TA /ka ríftə/ *abbr.* Caribbean Free Trade Association

car·il·lon /kérrə lòn, -lən/ *n.* **1. SET OF STATIONARY BELLS** a set of chromatically tuned stationary bells, usually hung in a tower and played from a keyboard **2. TUNE PLAYED ON SET OF BELLS** a tune played on a keyboard connected to a set of stationary bells **3. ORGAN STOP IMITATING BELLS** an organ stop that imitates the sound of a carillon ■ *vi.* (**-onned, -lon·ning, -lons**) **PLAY STATIONARY BELLS** to play a set of stationary bells, using a keyboard [Late 18thC. Via French from an assumed Proto-Romance word meaning "peal of four bells."]

car·il·lon·neur /kèrrələ núr/ *n.* somebody who plays a carillon [Late 18thC. From French.]

ca·ri·na /kə rínə, -reénə/ *n.* **1.** ZOOL **PROJECTING PART OF BIRD'S BREASTBONE** the prominent keel-shaped projection of the breastbone of a bird to which the flight muscles are anchored **2.** BOT **BOAT-SHAPED FUSED PETALS** the boat-shaped part of a pea flower, formed by the two fused lower petals **3.** ANAT **KEEL-SHAPED BODY PART** a keel-shaped body part, e.g., the ridge at the base of the windpipe where it divides to form the bronchi [Early 18thC. From Latin, "keel" (source of English *careen*).] —**ca·ri·nate** /kérrə nàyt/ *adj.*

Ca·ri·na /kə rínə, -reénə/ *n.* a constellation in the sky of the southern hemisphere near the Southern Cross that contains Canopus, the second brightest star in the sky

car·ing /káiring/ *adj.* **1. SHOWING CONCERN** compassionate or showing concern for others **2. RELATING TO PROFESSION LOOKING AFTER PEOPLE** belonging or relating to a profession such as nursing or social work that involves looking after people's physical, medical, or general welfare ■ *n.* **PROVISION OF MEDICAL OR SIMILAR CARE** provision of medical or other types of care, either professionally or in general —**car·ingly** *adv.*

car·i·o·ca /kèrri ṓkə/ *n.* **1. BRAZILIAN DANCE** a Brazilian dance similar to the samba **2. MUSIC FOR CARIOCA** a piece of music or a tune to which the carioca is danced [Mid-20thC. From Portuguese, ultimately from Tupian.]

Car·i·o·can /kèrri ṓkən/, **Car·i·o·ca** /-ṓkə/ *n.* **SOMEBODY FROM RIO DE JANEIRO** somebody who was born in or lives in Rio de Janeiro, Brazil ■ *adj.* **OF RIO DE JANEIRO** relating to or typical of Rio de Janeiro or its people or culture

car·i·o·gen·ic /kàiri ō jénnik, kàiree ə-/ *adj.* causing caries in the teeth [Mid-20thC. Coined from CARIES + -GENIC.]

car·i·ole /kàiri ōl/, **car·ri·ole** *n.* a small open carriage or covered cart, the former drawn by one horse [Mid-18thC. Via French from Italian *carriuola*, literally "little car," from *carro* "car," from Latin *carrus* "wagon" (see CAR).]

car·i·ous /kéree əss/, **car·i·ose** /-ōss/ *adj.* having caries in the teeth or bone [Mid-16thC. From Latin *cariosus*, from *caries*.] —**car·i·os·i·ty** /kèrree óssətee/ *n.* —**car·i·ous·ness** /káiree əssnəss/ *n.*

car·jack·ing /kaár jàking/ *n.* the crime of holding up a car and either stealing it, robbing the driver, or forcing the driver to drive somewhere for criminal purposes [Late 20thC. Blend of CAR and HIJACKER.] —**car·jack** *vti.* —**car·jack·er** *n.*

Carle·ton /kaárltən/, **Guy, 1st Baron Dorchester** (1724–1808) Irish-born Canadian soldier and governor of

Quebec. He advocated French-Canadian culture and opposed elected assemblies.

car·line /kaárlin, kaár līn/ (*plural* **-line** *or* **-lines**) *n.* a plant of Europe and Asia that resembles a thistle in appearance, with spiny leaves and yellow flower heads. Latin name: *Carlina vulgaris.* [Late 16thC, via French, from medieval Latin *carlina,* of uncertain origin: perhaps ultimately from Latin *carduus* "thistle" (see CARD[2]), by folk etymology from *Carolus* Magnus (Charlemagne)]

car·ling /kaárling, -lin/ *n.* a fore-and-aft wooden beam that supports a boat's deck, especially around an opening in the deck such as a hatchway [14thC. From Old Norse.]

Car·lisle /kaar līl, kaár līl/ borough in southern Pennsylvania, southwest of Harrisburg. Population: 18,039 (1996).

Car·list /kaárlist/ *n.* a supporter of Don Carlos or his descendants as rightful monarchs of Spain during the 19th century [Mid-19thC. From Spanish *carlista,* from the name of Don CARLOS.]

car·load /kaár lōd/ *n.* **1.** FULL COMPLEMENT OF PASSENGERS a full complement of people able to get into and ride in an automobile **2.** MINIMUM WEIGHT FOR SENDING FREIGHT the minimum weight at which freight qualifies for a reduced rate

car·load rate *n.* a reduced rate for shipping freight

Car·lo·vin·gi·an /kaàrlə vínjən, kaàrlə vínjee ən/ *adj.* = **Carolingian**

Carls·bad /kaárlz bàd/ **1.** city in southeastern New Mexico, southeast of Roswell and southwest of Hobbs. Population: 26,535 (1996). **2.** city and resort in southwestern California, north of San Diego, on the Pacific Ocean. Population: 69,069 (1996).

Carls·bad Cav·erns Na·tion·al Park park in southeastern New Mexico, established in 1930, and noted for its chain of caverns with unusual geologic formations. Area: 46,766 acres/18,926 hectares.

Carl·son /kaárlsən/, **Chester Floyd** (1906–68) U.S. inventor. He patented the process that led to the introduction in 1959 of the first photocopying machine.

Carl XVI Gus·taf /kaárl gústàf/, **King of Sweden** (*b.* 1946) Swedish monarch. He succeeded his grandfather, Gustaf VI, in 1973.

car·mag·nole /kaàrmən yṓl, -yṓl/ *n.* **1.** FRENCH REVOLUTIONARY TUNE AND DANCE a dance and a popular song of the French Revolution **2.** FRENCH REVOLUTIONARY'S CLOTHING the typical costume of many of the French Revolutionaries, consisting of a short jacket with a broad collar, black trousers with a tricolored sash, and a red liberty cap [Late 18thC. From French; of uncertain origin: ultimately probably from *Carmagnola,* town in Piedmont, northwestern Italy.]

car·mak·er /kaár màykər/ *n.* a manufacturer of motor vehicles, specifically automobiles

car·man /kaármən/ (*plural* **-men**) *n.* a streetcar or subway driver (*dated*)

Car·man, Bliss (1861–1929) Canadian poet and essayist. He became poet laureate of Canada in 1928. Full name **William Bliss Carman**

Car·me /kaármee/ *n.* **1.** MYTHOL GREEK NYMPH in Greek mythology, a nymph and mother of the Cretan goddess Britomaris **2.** ASTRON SATELLITE OF JUPITER a small satellite of Jupiter that was discovered in 1938

Car·mel /kaárm'l/ city and artists' colony in western California, southwest of San Jose, on the Pacific Ocean. Population: 4,084 (1996).

Car·mel, Mount mountain in northern Israel, near the Mediterranean Sea, with many biblical associations. Height: 1,789 ft./545 m.

Car·mel·ite /kaármə līt/ *n.* **1.** MEMBER OF ORDER OF FRIARS a member of an order of mendicant friars, founded around 1155 and called Our Lady of Mount Carmel **2.** MEMBER OF ORDER OF NUNS a member of the order of nuns of Our Lady of Mount Carmel, founded in 1452 and noted for the strictness of its rule ■ *adj.* BELONGING TO ORDER OF CARMELITES belonging or relating to either of the orders of Our Lady of Mount Carmel [15thC. Directly or via French *carmélite* from medieval Latin *Carmelita,* named for Mount CARMEL, where the order was founded.]

Car·mi·chael /kaár mīk'l/ unincorporated settlement in Sacramento County, central California, near Sacramento. Population: 48,702 (1990).

Car·mi·chael, Hoagy (1899–1981) U.S. singer and songwriter. He wrote the music for the song *Stardust* (1929). Full name **Hoagland Howard Carmichael**

car·mine /kaármin, -mīn/ *n.* **1.** DEEP RED COLOR a deep red color tinged with purple **2.** RED PIGMENT a bright red pigment made from cochineal ■ *adj.* DEEP RED of a deep red tinged with purple [Early 18thC. Via French *carmin* from, ultimately, Arabic *ḳirmiz* "kermes" (source of English *crimson* and *kermes*).]

Car·na·by Street /kaárnəbi-/ a street in Soho in central London notable in the 1960s as the heart of the new youth-centered fashion trade

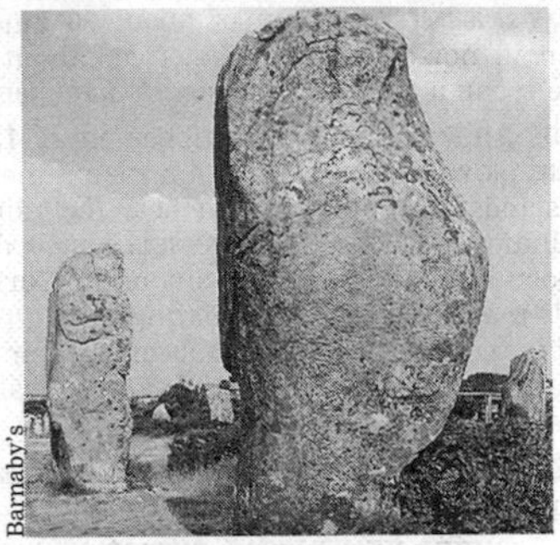

Prehistoric stone monuments at Carnac, France

Car·nac /kaár nàk/ village in Morbihan Department, Bretagne Region, in western France. It is famous for its prehistoric stone monuments, which number more than 3,000.

car·nage /kaárnij/ *n.* widespread and indiscriminate slaughter or massacre, especially of human beings [Early 17thC. From, ultimately, medieval Latin *carnaticum* "flesh (especially as tribute to a feudal lord)," from the Latin stem *carn-* "flesh."]

car·nal /kaárn'l/ *adj.* **1.** RELATING TO PHYSICAL NEEDS relating to somebody's physical needs or appetites, especially as contrasted with spiritual or intellectual qualities (*formal*) **2.** SENSUAL sensual or sexual **3.** RELATING TO BODY relating to or consisting of the body (*formal*) [15thC. From Christian Latin *carnalis,* from the Latin stem *carn-* "flesh" (source of English *carnage, carnival,* and *charnel*).] —**car·nal·ist** *n.* —**car·nal·i·ty** /kaar nállətee/ *n.* —**car·nal·ly** /kaárn'lee/ *adv.*

car·nal knowl·edge *n.* sexual intercourse, especially involving penetration (*formal*)

car·nall·ite /kaárn'l īt/ *n.* a white or light-colored mineral that is a hydrous chloride of magnesium and potassium and an important source of potassium used in fertilizers [Mid-19thC. Named for Rudolf von *Carnall,* a German mining engineer (1804–74).]

Car·nap /kaár nàp/, **Rudolf** (1891–1970) German-born U.S. philosopher and logician. He used mathematics and probability statistics to arrive at a system of inductive logic.

car·nap·per /kaár nàppər/, **car·naper** *n.* somebody who steals a car (*informal*) [Late 20thC. Blend of CAR and KIDNAPPER.]

car·nas·si·al /kaar nássee əl/ *adj.* used to describe the larger sharp cheek teeth in the upper and lower jaw of a carnivore that are adapted for cutting flesh [Mid-19thC. Via French *carnassier* "carnivorous," from, ultimately, the Latin stem *carn-* (see CARNAL).]

Car·nat·ic /kaar náttik/ linguistic region in south central India between the Eastern Ghats and the Coromandel coast. It is now part of Madras state.

car·na·tion /kaar náysh'n/ *n.* **1.** PLANTS FLOWER WITH CLOVE SCENT a perennial plant of the Pink family with fringed petals, widely grown for its fragrant white, pink, or red flowers often smelling of cloves. Latin name: *Dianthus caryophyllus.* **2.** PINKISH COLOR a pale reddish-pink color ■ *adj.* of the color carnation [Mid-16thC. Via French from the late Latin stem *carnation-* "fleshiness," from Latin *carn-* (see CARNAL), because of its color.]

Carnation

car·nau·ba /kaar náwbə, -nówbə/ (*plural* **-ba** *or* **-bas**) *n.* **1.** PALM TREE a fan palm native to Brazil with an edible root and leaves that yield a hard wax used, e.g., in polish and floor wax. Latin name: *Copernicia prunifera.* **2.** = **carnauba wax** [Mid-19thC. Via Portuguese from Tupi.]

car·nau·ba wax *n.* wax obtained from the young leaves of the carnauba tree and used in the manufacture of polish and candles

Car·ne·gie /kaárnəgee, kaar náygee, -néggee, -neégee/, **Andrew** (1835–1919) Scottish-born U.S. industrialist and philanthropist who made a fortune in the steel industry. His philanthropic gifts endowed numerous public libraries in the United States.

Car·ne·gie, Dale (1888–1955) U.S. writer. His works on public speaking and self-esteem include *How to Win Friends and Influence People* (1936). Real name **Dale Carnegey**

car·nel·ian /kaar neélyən/, **cor·nel·ian** *n.* a hard reddish translucent mineral, a form of chalcedony, used as a gemstone [Late 17thC. Alteration of *cornelian* (influenced by the Latin stem *carn-* "flesh"), from obsolete French *corneline,* of uncertain origin: perhaps from Latin *cornu* "horn" or *cornum* "cornelian cherry."]

car·net /kaar náy/ *n.* **1.** BOOK OF TRAVEL TICKETS a book of travel tickets or coupons costing less than the individual tickets purchased separately **2.** CUSTOMS DOCUMENT FOR CAR a customs document for a car that allows it to be taken across national borders without payment of duty [Early 19thC. From French.]

car·ney, **carnie** *n.* = **carny**[1]

car·ni·tine /kaárni teen/ *n.* a chemical compound found in muscle and the liver that aids in the transport of fatty acids across cell membranes. Formula: $C_7H_{15}NO_3$. [Early 20thC. Formed from the Latin stem *carn-* (see CARNAL).]

car·ni·val /kaárnəvəl/ *n.* **1.** PUBLIC CELEBRATION a public festive occasion or period, often with street processions, costumes, music, and dancing **2.** OUTDOOR SHOW a traveling outdoor amusement show with rides and sideshows **3.** ENTERTAINMENT WITH GAMES AND PRIZES an organized event with a program of games, competitions, and prizes **4.** CARNIVAL BEFORE LENT the period just before Lent begins, celebrated with a carnival in some Roman Catholic areas, e.g., Mardi Gras in New Orleans [Mid-16thC. Via Italian *carnevale* from medieval Latin *carnelevamen* "Shrovetide" (literally "cessation of meat eating"), from Latin *carn-* (see CARNAL).]

car·ni·vore /kaárnə vàwr/ *n.* **1.** FLESH-EATING ANIMAL an animal that eats other animals. ◊ **herbivore, omnivore** **2.** BOT, ZOOL a carnivorous plant **3.** SOMEBODY WHO ENJOYS MEAT somebody who is not a vegetarian and likes eating meat (*humorous*) [Mid-19thC. Via French from Latin *carnivorus* "carnivorous" (see CARNIVOROUS).]

car·niv·o·rous /kaar nívvərəss/ *adj.* **1.** ZOOL MEAT-EATING feeding mainly on the flesh of other animals **2.** BOT ABLE TO DIGEST ANIMALS AS FOOD able to catch and digest animals such as insects and small invertebrates ○ *a carnivorous plant* [Late 16thC. Formed from Latin *carnivorus,* literally "meat-eating," from the stem *carn-* (see CARNAL).] —**car·niv·o·rous·ly** *adv.* —**car·niv·o·rous·ness** *n.*

Car·not cy·cle /kaar nṓ-/ *n.* a theoretical reversible heat-engine cycle that gives maximum efficiency

car·no·tite /kaárnə tīt/ *n.* a yellow radioactive mineral that is a source of radium and uranium [Late 19thC. Named for Marie Adolphe *Carnot* (1839–1920), a French inspector of mines.]

Car·not prin·ci·ple *n.* the principle that the efficiency of a reversible heat engine depends on the maximum and minimum temperatures of the working fluid during the operating cycle

car·ny[1] /kaárnee/ (*plural* **-nies**), **car·nie, car·ney** *n.* (*informal*) **1.** CARNIVAL a carnival **2.** SOMEBODY WHO WORKS IN CARNIVAL somebody who works in a fairground or carnival, or a member of that person's family [Mid-20thC. Shortening of CARNIVAL.]

car·ny[2] /kaárnee/ (**-nied, -ny·ing, -nies**) *vt. U.K.* to try to persuade or coax somebody into doing something (*informal*) [Early 19thC. Origin unknown.]

Car·o /kaárō/, **Miguel Antonio** (1843–1909) Colombian politician, writer, and poet. President of Colombia (1894–98), he was also a noted writer.

car·ob /kérrəb/ (*plural* **-obs** *or* **-ob**) *n.* **1.** EVERGREEN TREE WITH EDIBLE PODS an evergreen tree that is native to the Mediterranean and has red flowers and edible pods. Latin name: *Ceratonia siliqua.* **2.** POD OF CAROB TREE the long dark-colored edible pod of the carob tree that contains a sweet-tasting pulp **3.** EDIBLE POWDER LIKE CHOCOLATE an edible powder with a taste similar to that of chocolate, made from the seeds and pods of the carob tree [Mid-16thC. Via obsolete French *car(r)obe* from, ultimately, Arabic *karrūb(a)* (source of English *algarroba*).]

ca·roche /kə rṓch, -sh/ *n.* a grand horse-drawn carriage used on ceremonial occasions [Late 16thC. Via obsolete French *carroche* from Italian *carraccio* "large chariot," from, ultimately, Latin *carrum* (see CAR).]

car·ol /kérrəl/ *n.* **1.** JOYFUL HYMN a joyful religious song or hymn, especially a Christian song celebrating Christmas **2.** DANCE a dance in a circle, or the music accompanying it (*archaic*) ■ *v.* (**-oled, -ol·ing, -ols**) **1.** *vi.* SING CHRISTMAS SONGS to sing hymns that celebrate Christmas, especially as a group going from house to house **2.** *vti.* SING to sing or call out something in a joyful and lively way (*literary*) ○ *The sun shone, and the birds were caroling.* **3.** *vt.* CELEBRATE to celebrate something, originally in song (*literary*) ○ *All the children caroled the good tidings.* [13thC. From Old French *carole*, of uncertain origin: probably via late Latin *choraula* "choral song" from Greek *khoraulēs*, literally "flute player who accompanies the chorus."] —**car·ol·er** *n.*

WORD KEY: CULTURAL NOTE

A Christmas Carol, a novella by Charles Dickens (1843). It recounts the story of an avaricious merchant, Ebenezer Scrooge, who is visited by the ghosts of Christmas Past, Christmas Present, and Christmas Future. Confronted by the effects of his miserly behavior on others, Scrooge resolves to become a more generous and charitable person. Over time, the name *Scrooge* has come to mean a petty malicious miser.

Car·o·le·an /kèrrə leé ən/ *adj.* = **Caroline**

ca·ro·li /kérrə lī/ plural of **carolus**

Ca·ro·li·na /kèrrə línə/ city in northeastern Puerto Rico. It is a southeastern suburb of San Juan. Population: 188,427 (1996).

Ca·ro·li·na all·spice *n.* a deciduous shrub of the southeastern United States, with large fragrant flowers. Latin name: *Calycanthus floridus.* [Named for the former British colony of *Carolina* (now North Carolina and South Carolina)]

Ca·ro·li·na jas·mine, **Ca·ro·li·na yel·low jas·mine** *n.* a poisonous evergreen climbing plant of the southeastern United States, with fragrant yellow trumpet-shaped flowers. Latin name: *Gelsemium sempervirens.* [See CAROLINA ALLSPICE]

Car·o·line /kérrə līn, kérrlin/ *adj.* **1.** OF CHARLES I AND II relating to the English kings Charles I and Charles II or their reigns **2.** OF MONARCH NAMED CHARLES relating to any king or emperor called Charles [Early 17thC. From medieval Latin *Carolinus*, from *Carolus* "Charles."]

Car·o·line Is·lands archipelago consisting of more than 600 islands, north of New Guinea in the western Pacific Ocean. Area: 450 sq. mi./1,165 sq. km.

Car·o·lin·gi·an /kèrrə línjee ən, kèrrə línjən/ *adj.* RELATING TO EARLY EUROPEAN KINGS relating to the dynasty of Frankish kings descended from the emperor Charlemagne that ruled France and Germany from the 8th to the 10th century ■ *n.* FRANKISH KING any of the Frankish kings who ruled France and Germany from the 8th to the 10th century

Car·o·lin·i·an /kèrrə línnyən/ *adj.* **1.** OF NORTH, OR SOUTH CAROLINA relating to or typical of North or South Carolina, or their inhabitants or culture **2.** HIST = **Caroline 3.** HIST = **Carolingian**

car·o·lus /kérrələss/ (*plural* **car·o·lus·es** *or* **ca·ro·li** /-lī/) *n.* a gold coin named for any of the kings or emperors called Charles who issued it, especially one issued by Charles I of England [Early 16thC. From medieval Latin *Carolus* "Charles."]

car·om /kérrəm/ *n.* **1.** CUE GAMES BILLIARDS SHOT a shot in billiards in which the cue ball hits one object ball and rebounds to hit another **2.** CUE GAMES POOL SHOT a shot in pool in which the object ball is rebounded off another ball and into a pocket **3.** A REBOUND FOLLOWING A COLLISION a collision that is followed by one of the objects rebounding off at an angle ■ *vi.* (**-omed, -om·ing, -oms**) **1.** REBOUND OFF A BALL to rebound off another ball in pool or billiards **2.** REBOUND OFF SOMETHING OR CAUSE REBOUND to rebound off another object or series of objects or cause this to happen ○ *The car swerved and caromed off the railing.* [Late 18thC. Shortening of CARAMBOLE.]

car·om bil·liards *n.* a type of billiards played on a table with no pockets

car·o·tene /kérrə teén/, **car·o·tin** /-t'n/ *n.* an organic chemical compound occurring in several forms in plants and producing an orange or red color. Carotene is a source of vitamin A. [Mid-19thC. Formed from Latin *carota* (see CARROT).]

ca·rot·e·noid /kə rótt'n òyd/, **ca·rot·i·noid** *n.* an organic chemical compound belonging to a group including the carotenes that gives a yellow, orange, or red color to plants —**ca·rot·e·noid** *adj.*

Ca·roth·ers /kə róthərz/, **Wallace Hume** (1896–1937) U.S. chemist. He invented the synthetic fibers neoprene and nylon while working for the DuPont Company.

ca·rot·id /kə róttid/, **ca·rot·id ar·ter·y** *n.* a large artery on either side of the neck that supplies blood to the head. Each carotid branches into an internal and an external carotid. [Early 17thC. Via French *carotide* or modern Latin *carotides* from Greek *karōtides*, from, ultimately, *karoun* "to stupefy." From the belief that pressure on the arteries causes stupor.]

ca·rot·id bod·y (*plural* **ca·rot·id bod·ies**) *n.* a cluster of cells and nerve fibers in each carotid artery that is sensitive to oxygen and acidity levels in the blood and is part of the system that regulates them

ca·rot·id si·nus *n.* a slight bulge in each carotid artery that contains pressure-sensitive nerve endings and forms part of the system that monitors and controls blood pressure

car·o·tin *n.* = **carotene**

ca·rot·i·noid *n.* = **carotenoid**

ca·rous·al /kə rówz'l/ *n.* a noisy and boisterous drinking party (*literary*)

ca·rouse /kə rówz/ *vi.* (**-roused, -rous·ing, -rous·es**) DRINK AND BECOME NOISY to drink and become noisy, especially in a group (*literary*) ■ *n.* NOISY PARTY a noisy and boisterous drinking party (*archaic*) [Mid-16thC. From German *gar aus (trinken)*, literally "(to drink) right up."] —**ca·rous·er** *n.*

car·ou·sel /kèrrə sél, kérrə sèl/ *n.* **1.** = **merry-go-round** *n.* **2.** CONVEYOR BELT a circular conveyor belt, especially one at an airport displaying baggage for arriving passengers to pick up **3.** HOLDER FOR PHOTOGRAPHIC SLIDES a circular rotating holder that loads photographic slides into a projector one at a time [Mid-17thC. Via French *carrousel* from Italian *carosello* "tilting match."]

carp[1] /kaarp/ (**carped, carp·ing, carps**) *vi.* to keep complaining or finding fault ○ *I wish you'd stop carping, I'm doing my best.* [13thC. From Old Norse *karpa* "to brag." The current meaning evolved from "to talk" under the influence of Latin *carpere* "to pluck," also "to slander" (source of English *carpet*).] —**carp·er** *n.*

WORD KEY: SYNONYMS

See Synonyms at ***complain.***

carp[2] /kaarp/ (*plural* **carp** *or* **carps**) *n.* **1.** LARGE FRESHWATER FISH a large fish with a single fin on its back, originally from Asia and now found worldwide in lakes and slow-moving rivers. It is widely bred for food. Latin name: *Cyprinus carpio.* **2.** FISH OF CARP FAMILY any fish of the carp family, which includes goldfish and koi. Family: Cyprinidae. [14thC. Via French *carpe* from, ultimately, late Latin *carpa*.]

-carp *suffix.* part of a fruit ○ *pericarp* [Via modern Latin *-carpium* from, ultimately, Greek *karpos* "fruit" (see CARPO-)] —**-carpous** *suffix.*

car·pac·cio /kaar paáchō, -i ō/ *n.* a dish of raw beef or tuna sliced thinly, moistened with olive oil and lemon juice, and seasoned [Mid-20thC. Named for the Italian painter Vittore *Carpaccio* circa 1460–1525, who favored red pigments. From its red color.]

car·pal /kaárp'l/ *adj.* OF THE WRIST relating to the bones in the wrist ■ *n.* WRIST BONE a bone in the wrist [Mid-18thC. Formed from CARPUS.]

car·pal tun·nel syn·drome *n.* a condition of pain and weakness in the hand caused by repetitive compression of a nerve that passes through the wrist into the hand

car park *n. U.K.* an enclosure or building where cars can be parked temporarily

Car·pa·thi·an Moun·tains /kaar páythee ən-/ mountain system in eastern Europe, situated along the border between Slovakia and Poland and extending southward through the Ukraine and eastern Romania. Its highest peak is Gerlachovka 8,711 ft./2,655 m.

car·pe di·em /kaárpə deé èm/ *interj.* LIVE IN THE PRESENT used as an invocation to enjoy the present and not worry about the future ■ *n.* ACT OF LIVING FOR THE PRESENT the act of living for the moment and enjoying the present [From Latin, literally "seize the day"]

car·pel /kaárp'l/ *n.* a female reproductive organ in a flower, enclosing the fertilized ovules that are developing into seeds. It consists of the stigma and usually a style. [Mid-19thC. From French *carpelle* or modern Latin *carpellum*, literally "little fruit," both formed from Greek *karpos* "fruit."] —**car·pel·lar·y** /kaárp'l èrree/ *adj.*

car·pel·late /kaárp'l àyt, -ət/ *adj.* used to describe a flower or plant that has carpels

car·pen·ter /kaárpəntər/ *n.* BUILDER OF WOODEN STRUCTURES OR OBJECTS somebody who builds and repairs wooden structures, e.g., houses and boats, or the wooden parts of them ■ *v.* (**-tered, -ter·ing, -ters**) **1.** *vi.* BUILD WOODEN STRUCTURES to build and repair wooden structures, or the wooden parts of them (*technical*) **2.** *vt.* MAKE SOMETHING WOODEN to make something by cutting and joining pieces of wood ○ *He had carpentered a series of perfectly fitting dovetail joints.* **3.** *vt.* MAKE SOMETHING IN EFFICIENT WAY to make or devise something efficiently and systematically ○ *They met every day, in the vain attempt to carpenter an agreement that would be acceptable to both sides.* [12thC. Via Anglo-Norman and Old French *carpentier* from late Latin *carpentarius (artifex)* "carriage(maker)," from *carpentum* "two-wheeled carriage."]

car·pen·ter ant *n.* a large ant that bores into wood to make its nest. It usually bores into old or rotten wood, but it can also attack lumber in homes and cause much damage. Genus: *Camponotus.*

car·pen·ter bee *n.* a bee that bores tunnels into wood to lay its eggs. Families: Xylocopidae and Ceratinidae.

Car·pen·ters·ville /kaárpəntərz vìl/ village in northeastern Illinois, southeast of Rockford, on the western bank of the Fox River. Population: 24,629 (1996).

car·pen·try /kaárpəntree/ *n.* **1.** THE BUILDING OF WOODEN STRUCTURES the work or occupation of building and repairing things made of wood, e.g., houses and boats, or the wooden parts of them ○ *a career in carpentry* **2.** THINGS MADE OUT OF WOOD the work or objects produced by a carpenter ○ *fine carpentry for sale*

car·pet /kaárpət/ *n.* **1.** FLOOR COVERING thick fabric for covering a floor **2.** PIECE OF FLOOR COVERING a piece of thick, heavy fabric covering the floor of a room or area **3.** LAYER OR COVERING a layer or covering (*literary*) ○ *a carpet of snow* ■ *vt.* (**-pet·ed, -pet·ing, -pets**) **1.** COVER FLOOR WITH CARPET to cover a floor, or the floor of a room, with a carpet ○ *We could carpet every room in the house with the money she spent on that rug.* **2.** COVER to cover something in a layer (*literary*) ○ *The valley was carpeted with flowers.* [14thC. Via Old French *carpite* or medieval Latin *carpita* from, ultimately, Latin *carpere* "to pluck." The underlying idea is of a cloth made from plucked or unraveled fabric.] ◇ **roll out the red carpet** to give a special welcome to a distinguished visitor ◇ **sweep something under the carpet** to conceal or ignore something that needs attention

car·pet·bag /kaárpət bàg/ *n.* TRAVELING BAG a medium-sized traveling bag originally made of a thick fabric such as carpet ■ *adj.* relating to or consisting of carpetbaggers

car·pet·bag·ger /kaárpət bàggər/ *n.* **1.** POST-CIVIL WAR OPPORTUNIST an opportunistic Northerner who moved to the Southern United States after the Civil War, especially one seeking political or commercial advantage **2.** POL OUTSIDER SEEKING LOCAL VOTE an outsider whose only interest in coming to a place is to win it as a political seat —**car·pet·bag·ger·y** *n.*

car·pet bee·tle *n.* a small beetle whose larvae feed on fabric, furs, or animal remains. Genera: *Anthrenus* and *Attagenus.*

car·pet-bomb *vt.* (**car·pet-bombed, car·pet-bomb·ing, car·pet-bombs**) **DESTROY AREA WITH INTENSIVE BOMBING** to bomb an area intensively ■ *n.* **CAMPAIGN TO INFLUENCE PUBLIC OPINION** to conduct an intensive campaign, especially in the media, to sway public opinion or to destroy somebody's reputation [*Carpet* from the idea that the bombing covers an area as completely as a carpet covers a floor]

car·pet grass *n.* a coarse grass that forms a tight matted growth and is widely used in warm humid areas for turf and pasture. Genus: *Axonopus.*

car·pet·ing /kaárpəting/ *n.* **1. FABRIC FOR FLOORS** thick fabric used for covering floors **2. CARPETS** carpets regarded collectively ○ *How much do you want to spend on carpeting?*

car·pet·lay·er /kaárpət làyr/ *n.* a person who cuts and fits wall-to-wall carpet

car·pet shark *n.* a shark with a mottled back resembling the pattern of a carpet. Family: Larentidae.

car·pet slip·per *n.* a slipper with an upper side made of a thick fabric that resembles carpet

car·pet snake *n.* a large python found throughout southern Australia with a pattern of scales on its back resembling a traditional carpet. Latin name: *Morelia variegata.*

car·pet·sweep·er /kaárpət swéepər/ *n.* a device for lifting dirt off carpets, with a long handle and revolving brushes in a wheeled casing

car·pet tile *n.* a square of carpeting laid together with others to cover a floor

car·pet·weed /kaárpət wéed/ *n.* a low, close-growing North American weed with tiny greenish-white flowers. Latin name: *Mollugo verticillata.*

car phone *n.* a mobile phone designed for use in a car

car·pi plural of **carpus**

carp·ing /kaárping/ *adj.* complaining or finding fault, or tending to ○ *his usual carping comments* —**carp·ing·ly** *adv.*

carpo- *prefix.* fruit ○ *carpophagous* [From Greek *karpos.* Ultimately from an Indo-European base meaning "to gather, pick," which is also the ancestor of English *harvest* and *excerpt.*]

car·pol·o·gy /kaar póllәjee/ *n.* the branch of botany that deals with the study of fruits and seeds [Early 19thC] —**car·po·log·i·cal** /kaárpə lójjik'l/ *adj.* —**car·pol·o·gist** /kaar póllәjist/ *n.*

car pool *n.* **1. GROUP USING OWN CARS IN TURN** a group of associated people sharing the use of their cars, each in turn driving the others **2. SHARED DRIVING ARRANGEMENTS** the actual arrangement made by a group of people, such as coworkers or parents, to share the duty of driving to and from somewhere **3.** = **motor pool**

car-pool (**car-pooled, car-pool·ing, car-pools**) *vi.* to drive or be driven regularly from one place to another as a small group, with each member sharing driving responsibilities

car·poph·a·gous /kaar póffəgəss/ *adj.* ZOOL = **frugivorous**

car·po·phore /kaárpə fàwr/ *n.* **1. STAMEN-BEARING PART OF FLOWER** the part of a flower that bears the carpels and stamens **2. SPORE-BEARING PART OF FUNGUS** the part of some fungi that contains the spores or supports the part that contains them

car·port /kaár pàwrt/ *n.* an open-sided shelter for a parked car, attached to a house or other building

car·po·spore /kaárpə spàwr/ *n.* a spore that forms in some red algae after fertilization

car·pus /kaárpəss/ (*plural* **-pi** /-pī/) *n.* **1. BONE IN WRIST JOINT** any bone in the set of eight that form the wrist joint **2. BONE IN ANIMAL'S FRONT LEG JOINT** any bone in the set that form the joint between the forelimb of a vertebrate animal and its foot or paw, corresponding to the wrist [Late 17thC. Via modern Latin from Greek *karpos.*]

Carr /kaar/, **Emily** (1871–1945) Canadian painter and writer. She was noted for painting Native Americans and wrote *Klee Wyck* (1941).

car·rack /kérrək/, **car·ack** *n.* a large Mediterranean trading ship of the 14th, 15th, and 16th centuries [14thC. From French *caraque,* of uncertain origin: probably via Spanish *carraca* from, ultimately, Arabic *ḳurḳūra* "large merchant ship."]

car·ra·geen /kèrrə géen, kérrə géen/, **car·ra·gheen** *n.* **1.** = **Irish moss 2.** FOOD TECH = **carrageenan** [Early 19thC. From Irish *carraigín.*]

car·ra·geen·an /kèrrə géenən, kérrə géenən/, **car·ra·geen·in** *n.* a complex carbohydrate obtained from edible red seaweeds, especially the seaweed Irish moss, used in the commercial preparation of several kinds of food and drink [Late 19thC. From CARRAGEEN.]

car·ra·gheen *n.* = **carrageen**

Car·ran·za /kə ránzə, -raánzə/, **Venustiano** (1859–1920) Mexican revolutionary and politician. He was the Mexican Republic's first president (1914–20).

Car·ra·ra /kə raárə/ city in Massa-Carrara Province, Tuscany Region, in north central Italy. It is famous for its quarry, which produces some of the world's finest marble. Population: 68,480 (1991).

car·re·four /kérrə fàwr/ *n.* (*archaic*) **1. CROSSROADS** a crossroads **2. PUBLIC SQUARE** a public square at a place where several roads meet [15thC. Via French from, ultimately, Latin *quadrifurcus* "four-forked."]

car·rel /kə rél, kérrəl/, **car·rell** *n.* a bay, cubicle, or small room where one person can study in private, e.g., in a library [Late 16thC. Alteration of CAROL (from its earlier use for "circle").]

Car·rel /kə rél, kérrəl/, **Alexis** (1873–1944) French biologist and surgeon. He won the Nobel Prize in medicine in 1912 for developing the vascular surgical technique that led to organ transplants.

Car·re·ra /kə rérrə/, **Andrade Jorge** (1903–78) Ecuadorian poet. Often considered one of the greatest Spanish-language poets of the 20th century, he was also a diplomat.

Car·re·ra, Rafael (1814–65) Guatemalan revolutionary and politician. He served as elected president of Guatemala (1844–48) and was declared president for life (1851). Full name **José Rafael Carrera**

Car·rer·as /kə rérrəz/, **José** (*b.* 1946) Spanish singer. An operatic tenor, he became an international star in the 1970s.

Car·rey /káiree/, **Jim** (*b.* 1962) Canadian-born U.S. actor and comedian, known for his comic and serious performances in movies including *The Truman Show* (1998).

car·riage /kérrij/ *n.* **1. HORSE-DRAWN VEHICLE** a four-wheeled horse-drawn private passenger vehicle, especially one that is large and comfortable **2. WHEELED PLATFORM** a wheeled platform on which something is carried or supported **3. WAY OF HOLDING THE BODY** the way somebody holds his or her head and body when walking (*formal*) ○ *She was a tall woman with a beautiful upright carriage.* **4. TAKING AND DELIVERING GOODS** the transporting and delivering of goods **5. CHARGE FOR TAKING AND DELIVERING GOODS** a charge made for transporting and delivering goods **6.** *U.K.* **RAILROAD COACH** a railroad passenger coach **7. MOVING PART OF MACHINE** a part of a machine that holds and moves another part, e.g., the rotating and sliding paper holder on a typewriter **8.** = **baby carriage**

car·riage bolt *n.* a large square-necked threaded bolt that has a snaphead and is used in building

car·riage clock *n.* a small clock set in a case with a handle on top, originally used as travel clocks but now ornamental

car·riage dog *n.* a dalmatian (*archaic*) [So called because it was trained to run behind a carriage as an ornamental guard dog]

car·riage horse *n.* a horse used to pull carriages

car·riage re·turn *n.* the key or lever on a typewriter that sends the paper-holding carriage back and rotates it to move the paper upward, ready to begin a new line

car·riage trade *n.* the most wealthy and prestigious of possible customers ○ *They carry only the highest quality goods, catering to the carriage trade.*

car·riage·way /kérrij wày/ *n. U.K.* the part of a main road used for vehicles, especially one side of a major two-way road, carrying traffic in one direction only

car·rick bend /kàrrik-/ *n.* an intertwining knot similar to a granny knot, used for tying ropes together [*Carrick* probably an earlier variant of CARRACK]

car·rick bitt *n.* one of the two posts that support a ship's windlass [See CARRICK BEND]

car·ri·er /kérree ər/ *n.* **1.** TRANSP **TRANSPORTER OF PEOPLE OR GOODS** a person or company whose function or business is to transport things or people from one place to another ○ *These airlines are among the world's most popular carriers.* **2.** MED **TRANSMITTER OF DISEASE** a living creature that is infected with a disease and can pass it to others but does not itself display any of the symptoms **3.** GENETICS **TRANSMITTER OF GENETIC DEFECT** an individual carrying a gene for a particular genetic trait or disorder without being affected by it, because two copies of the gene, one from each parent, are usually necessary for the disorder to show itself **4.** ENG **PART OF MACHINE CONVEYING MOTION** a part of a machine that carries and moves something or transmits motion to another part **5. LUGGAGE RACK** a metal frame on which luggage can be tied to a road vehicle or bicycle **6.** NAVY **AIRCRAFT CARRIER** an aircraft carrier **7.** CHEM **MEANS OF TRANSMITTING ACTIVE SUBSTANCE** a neutral substance to which an active ingredient or agent is added as a way of applying or transferring the ingredient or agent ○ *Mix the dye and the carrier in equal proportions.* **8.** PHYS **BEARER OF ELECTRIC CHARGE** something that carries electric current, e.g. , an electron or ion **9.** TELECOM **RADIO WAVE CARRYING INFORMATION** an electromagnetic wave that is modulated to carry a signal in radio or television transmission **10. SOMEBODY WHO DELIVERS MAIL** somebody who is employed by the Postal Service to deliver and pick up mail **11. COMMUNICATIONS COMPANY** a telephone, television, or radio company **12. INSURANCE COMPANY** a company that provides insurance

car·ri·er air wing *n.* a squadron of aircraft operating from an aircraft carrier

car·ri·er bag *n. U.K.* a large plastic or paper shopping bag with handles, especially one supplied by a store

car·ri·er pi·geon *n.* **1. PIGEON TAKING MESSAGES** a domestic pigeon trained to deliver messages and return home **2. SHOW PIGEON** a large domestic pigeon bred for showing

car·ri·er wave *n.* TELECOM = **carrier** *n.* **9**

car·ri·ole *n.* = **cariole**

car·ri·on /kéree ən/ *n.* **1. ROTTING ANIMAL FLESH** the rotting flesh of a dead animal **2. SOMETHING DECAYING** something that is decaying or disgusting (*literary*) ■ *adj.* **OF DECOMPOSING FLESH** relating to rotting flesh or the eating of such an item [13thC. Via Anglo-Norman and Old Northern French *caroi(g)ne* from, ultimately, Latin *caro* "flesh" (source of English *carnal*).]

car·ri·on crow *n.* a medium-sized European crow, similar to the rook but with a greenish tinge to its black plumage. Latin name: *Corvus corone.*

car·ri·on flow·er *n.* **1. CLIMBING PLANT WITH FOUL-SMELLING FLOWERS** a North American climbing plant with small greenish flowers that smell like rotting flesh. Genus: *Smilax.* **2. TROPICAL PLANT WITH FOUL-SMELLING FLOWERS** a tropical succulent plant with foul-smelling star-shaped flowers. Genus: *Stapelia.*

Car·roll /kérrəl/, **Charles** (1737–1832) U.S. political leader. A leader of the Revolution, he signed the Declaration of Independence (1776) and was a U.S. senator (1789–92) from South Carolina. Known as **Charles Carroll of Carrollton**

Car·roll, Lewis (1832–98) British writer. Author of *Alice's Adventures in Wonderland* (1865) and other children's books. Under his real name, he was also a distinguished geometrician and photographer. Pseudonym of **Charles Lutwidge Dodgson**

Car·roll·ton /kárrəltən/ city in northeastern Texas. Population: 96,757 (1996).

car·ron·ade /kèrrə nàyd, kèrrə náyd/ *n.* a lightweight iron cannon formerly used on ships [Late 18thC. Named for *Carron,* a district in Falkirk, Scotland, where they were made.]

car·ron oil *n.* a mixture of limewater and linseed oil formerly used to soothe burns [Named for *Carron* (see CARRONADE). From its use at the ironworks there.]

car·rot /kérrət/ *n.* **1.** PLANTS **PLANT WITH EDIBLE ORANGE-COLORED ROOT** a biennial plant of the parsley family with delicate green feathery leaves that is grown for its edible orange roots. Latin name: *Daucus carota.* **2.** FOOD **THIN ORANGE ROOT VEGETABLE** the thin, tapering orange-colored root of the carrot plant that is eaten raw or cooked as a vegetable **3.** = **Queen Anne's lace** **4.** INCENTIVE something tempting, offered in order to persuade somebody to do something ○ *They offered us the carrot of a year's free gasoline if we'd buy the sports car right then.* [15thC. Via French *carotte* and Latin *carota* from Greek *karōton*.]

car·rot-and-stick *adj.* relating to or characterized by the use of persuasion involving a combination of rewards and punishments ○ *During the fast-paced negotiations, the diplomats employed a carrot-and-stick strategy.*

car·rot cake *n.* a cake made with finely grated carrots that give it a moist texture and delicate flavor

car·rot·y /kérrətee/ *adj.* **1.** TASTING LIKE CARROTS like carrots in taste **2.** RED used to describe hair that is red or auburn **3.** OF BRIGHT ORANGE COLOR of a bright reddish-orange color

car·ry /kérree/ *v.* (**-ried, -ry·ing, -ries**) **1.** *vt.* HOLD AND TRANSPORT SOMEBODY OR SOMETHING to take somebody or something that you are holding or supporting to another place ○ *The suitcase was too heavy for her to carry.* **2.** *vt.* BE CHANNEL OR ROUTE FOR SOMETHING to be the means by which something passes or is transmitted from one place to another ○ *The pipeline will carry oil to the coast.* **3.** *vt.* TELL OR CONTAIN to communicate or convey information, an idea, or a feeling by way of content or in an indirect manner ○ *The article carries wider implications than you may think.* **4.** *vt.* TAKE TO ANOTHER PLACE to take somebody or something to another place ○ *a truck carrying farm produce* **5.** *vt.* MOVE SOMEBODY, SOMETHING ALONG to take and move somebody or something by a flow or impetus ○ *The current carried them swiftly downstream.* ○ *She could hear children's voices, carried on the light breeze.* **6.** *vt.* HAVE TRANSMISSIBLE DISEASE to be infected with a disease and capable of infecting others ○ *You may be carrying a virus without knowing it.* **7.** *vt.* HAVE SOMETHING WITH YOU to have something with you, e.g., in your pocket or in a purse ○ *Staff should carry identification at all times.* **8.** *vt.* to hold, contain, or support something ○ *How much does the tanker carry?* ○ *a high roof carried on slender pillars* **9.** *vt. Southern U.S.* DRIVE SOMEBODY IN VEHICLE to transport somebody in a motor vehicle from one location to another ○ *Call me when you arrive; I'll carry you home from the airport.* **10.** *vt.* HOLD UP UNDER VEHICULAR TRAFFIC to be able to withstand a particular degree or amount of vehicular traffic ○ *a freeway that can carry hundreds of thousands of vehicles a day* **11.** *vt.* YIELD ENOUGH FORAGE to yield enough forage or grazing crops for animals to survive ○ *fields that can carry llamas as well as cattle* **12.** *vt.* BE RESPONSIBLE FOR to bear the responsibility for something ○ *The president carries heavy duties.* **13.** *vt.* MAKE SOMEBODY SUCCEED OR ENDURE to give somebody the incentive, impetus, or encouragement to achieve or deal with something ○ *Their exhilaration at this success may carry them further up in the league standings.* ○ *The audience cheered, carried along on a wave of enthusiasm.* **14.** *vt.* PUBLISH, BROADCAST, OR DISPLAY to feature or include an article, picture, item of news, or piece of information ○ *That evening, all the major networks carried the story.* ○ *Every pack carries a government health warning.* **15.** *vt.* INCLUDE OR RESULT IN SOMETHING to have something as a quality, feature, or consequence ○ *Reckless driving carries a heavy penalty.* **16.** *vti.* BE PREGNANT to be pregnant with a child ○ *She carried the child to term, and it was born on Saturday.* **17.** *vt.* DEVELOP AN IDEA to develop an idea in discussion or action ○ *If you carry that argument to its logical conclusion, no one should get married at all.* **18.** *vt.* MOVE OR BEHAVE to move or behave in a particular way, especially with confidence or dignity ○ *He was a handsome man who carried himself with dignity.* ○ *She carried her head high, and looked her accusers in the eye.* **19.** *vt.* COMM KEEP SOMETHING FOR SALE to keep something as stock in a store ○ *We don't carry household goods.* **20.** *vi.* BE HEARD AT A DISTANCE to be audible at a distance ○ *Sound carries a long way over water.* **21.** *vt.* SUPPORT WEAKER ELEMENT to support or compensate for a weaker element or participant ○ *The rest of the department has to carry him.* **22.** *vti.* VOTE FOR SOMETHING to accept a proposal by voting for it ○ *The nomination was carried, 40–29.* **23.** *vt.* GAIN SOMEBODY'S SUPPORT to win the support or sympathy of a person or group, especially by making a speech or appeal ○ *It looked for a moment as if he would carry the crowd.* **24.** *vt.* POL WIN VOTES OF AREA to win support from somebody ○ *Because the incumbent senator carried all the cities in her district, she won the election.* **25.** *vt.* MIL CAPTURE A PLACE to capture a place in battle ○ *Their charge carried the hill.* **26.** *vt.* MUSIC STAY IN TUNE WHEN SINGING to be able to sing and stay in tune ○ *Can you carry a tune?* **27.** *vt.* ACCT TRANSFER ITEM IN ACCOUNT OR CALCULATION to transfer a figure from one group or column to another in accounts or in a calculation **28.** *vt.* LIST SOMEONE AS A DEBTOR to continue to keep somebody as a debtor in the records ○ *We've carried him for two quarters; enough is enough.* **29.** *vi.* SPORTS BE HIT A CERTAIN DISTANCE to reach a certain distance after being struck ○ *Her approach shot didn't carry to the green.* **30.** *vt.* SPORTS MOVE WITH BALL IN SPORT to bring a ball forward a certain distance in a sport such as football ○ *Their first rush carried the ball well into the defenders' half.* **31.** *vt.* ARMS HAVE FIREPOWER RANGE to have a particular range of fire ○ *an artillery shell that carried for miles* **32.** *vi.* HAVE WEAPON to have a weapon, especially a gun, in your possession (*slang*) ○ *We knew his goons would be carrying too.* **33.** *vt.* PALM BALL IN BASKETBALL to keep a hand in illegal contact with the ball in basketball ■ *n.* (*plural* **-ries**) **1.** PICKING UP, HOLDING, AND TRANSPORTING SOMETHING the act of carrying something or how it is done ○ *It was a long, hard carry of all that luggage from the parking lot to the departures terminal.* **2.** DISTANCE COVERED the distance covered by something struck, thrown, launched, or fired, or the reach of something, e.g., a voice **3.** ACT OF RUNNING WITH BALL a sprint with the ball in football ○ *a 50-yard carry that won the game* **4.** PLACE WHERE BOAT IS CARRIED the land over which a canoe must be carried at a portage [14thC. Directly or via Anglo-Norman from Old North French *carier*, from *car* (see CAR).]

carry away *vt.* to make somebody become less controlled, reasonable, or attentive by arousing his or her emotion or interest (*usually passive*) ○ *I was completely carried away by the beauty of it.*

carry back *vt.* to transfer something such as a tax credit so that it is calculated against the previous year's income

carry forward *vt.* **1.** TRANSFER ITEM IN ACCOUNT OR CALCULATION to transfer an item to the next section or column in accounts or in a calculation **2.** TRANSFER SOMETHING TO NEXT YEAR to transfer something, such as a tax credit or liability, so that it is calculated against the next year's income

carry off *vt.* **1.** REMOVE SOMEBODY OR SOMETHING to take something or somebody away with determination or purpose, or by force ○ *carried him off, kicking and screaming, to his crib* **2.** WIN to win a prize (*informal*) ○ *She carried off the award for best newcomer.* **3.** DO SOMETHING SUCCESSFULLY OR WELL to succeed in doing something well or producing a good effect ○ *He was nervous about chairing the meeting, but carried it off in style.* ○ *It's a very sophisticated outfit, but she can't quite carry it off.* **4.** KILL SOMEBODY to kill somebody (*usually passive*) ○ *Half the settlers were carried off by smallpox.*

carry on *v.* **1.** *vti.* KEEP DOING SOMETHING to continue to do something ○ *Please just carry on with your work and pretend we're not here.* ○ *She carried on the business after her father retired.* **2.** *vt.* BE INVOLVED IN SOMETHING to engage in or be engaged in something ○ *They were carrying on an intense conversation in a corner of the bar.* **3.** *vi.* BEHAVE FOOLISHLY OR IMPROPERLY to behave or talk in a way that is socially awkward or improper (*informal*) ○ *I'm ashamed of the way he's been carrying on in public.* **4.** *vi.* HAVE AN AFFAIR to have a casual affair with somebody (*informal disapproving*)

carry out *vt.* **1.** DO OR PERFORM to perform or accomplish something ○ *carry out research* **2.** DO WHAT WAS ORDERED OR PLANNED to do something that has been ordered, planned, or stated as a goal ○ *We will carry out your instructions to the letter.*

carry over *v.* **1.** *vti.* LEAVE SOMETHING TO BE FINISHED LATER to leave the last part of something to be done at a later date ○ *There were so many candidates that the ceremonies were carried over to the next morning.* **2.** *vt.* ACCT, ARITH TRANSFER ITEM IN ACCOUNT OR CALCULATION to transfer an item to the next group or column in accounts or in a calculation **3.** *vt.* TRANSFER SOMETHING TO NEXT YEAR to transfer an allowance or entitlement from one year or part of a year to the next **4.** *vi.* CONTINUE TO EXIST to continue to exist or produce an effect in changed circumstances ○ *The dislike he always felt for me has obviously carried over into our relationship at work.*

carry through *v.* **1.** *vt.* DO WHAT WAS PLANNED to complete or accomplish something planned ○ *We outlined our policy before the election, and we are determined to carry it through.* **2.** *vt.* HELP SOMEBODY SURVIVE to give somebody the support or strength needed to overcome a difficulty ○ *It was my family's support that carried me through.* ○ *Only his determination not to be humiliated carried him through the next five hours.* **3.** *vi.* SURVIVE to continue to exist ○ *It is an old tradition that has carried through into the information age.*

car·ry·all /kérree àwl/ *n.* **1.** LARGE SOFT TRAVEL BAG a container or soft-sided bag for carrying belongings **2.** PASSENGER VEHICLE WITH FACING BENCHES a large passenger vehicle with two facing benches **3.** HORSE-DRAWN CARRIAGE a covered horse-drawn carriage for four people [Early 18thC. Alteration of CARIOLE, by association with *carry all*.]

car·ry·back /kérri bàk/ *n.* an amount of money, e.g., a tax credit, that is transferred to the accounts for the previous year

car·ry·cot /kérri kòt/ *n. U.K.* a lightweight portable bed for a baby, often detachable from a wheeled base

car·ry·ing ca·pac·i·ty (*plural* **car·ry·ing ca·pac·i·ties**) *n.* **1.** NUMBER OF THINGS OR PEOPLE ALLOWED the amount of things or people a vehicle or container can hold **2.** NUMBER OF ANIMALS LAND SUPPORTS the number of animals a region can support **3.** NUMBER OF PEOPLE AREA SUPPORTS the number of individuals a region can support in terms of its resources

car·ry·ing charge *n.* **1.** COST OF HOLDING ASSETS the cost to a business of holding or storing assets from which it currently earns no income **2.** INTEREST ON UNPAID BALANCE interest charged on the unpaid balance of a sum of borrowed money, especially the price of something that is being paid for in installments

car·ry·ing-on (*plural* **car·ry·ings-on**) *n.* behavior regarded as immature or improper (*informal*) ○ *I won't have that kind of carrying-on in my house.*

car·ry·on /kérri òn/ *n.* PASSENGER'S HAND LUGGAGE a piece of luggage suitable for taking in the cabin of an aircraft ■ *adj.* CARRIED ABOARD AN AIRCRAFT used to describe or relating to luggage small enough to be carried and stowed aboard the cabin of an aircraft

car·ry·out /kérri òwt/ *n. U.S., Scotland* an item of ready-to-eat food bought in a store or restaurant and taken elsewhere to eat (*often used as a modifier*) ○ *a carryout pizza*

car·ry·o·ver /kérri òvər/ *n.* **1.** SOMETHING CONTINUED INTO THE NEXT PERIOD something left over that is continued on, extended, or transferred to the next period ○ *This policy is a carryover from the previous administration.* **2.** ACCT, ARITH ITEM TRANSFERRED IN ACCOUNT OR CALCULATION an item transferred to the next group or column in accounts or in a calculation

car seat *n.* **1.** CHILD'S SEAT IN CAR a small seat for children, strapped inside a car **2.** SEAT IN CAR a driver's or passenger's seat in a car

car·sick /kaár sìk/ *adj.* made nauseated from the motion of a vehicle you are traveling in — **car·sick·ness** *n.*

Car·son /kaárzən/, **Johnny** (*b.* 1925) U.S. entertainer. He hosted *The Tonight Show* (1962–92).

Car·son, Kit (1809–68) U.S. hunter and scout. He accompanied the western expeditions of John Charles Frémont (1842–46) and helped Union forces in the Civil War. Full name **Christopher Carson**

UPI/Corbis-Bettmann

Rachel Carson

Car·son, Rachel (1907–64) U.S. ecologist. In *Silent Spring* (1962) she argued that agricultural pesticides damage the food chain.

Car·son Cit·y capital of Nevada, in western Nevada just east of Lake Tahoe and south of Reno. Population: 47,237 (1996).

cart /kaart/ *n.* **1. HORSE-DRAWN VEHICLE CARRYING GOODS** an open horse-drawn vehicle, especially one with only two wheels, used for carrying goods or as a farm vehicle **2. VEHICLE PUSHED BY HAND** a light vehicle or barrow pushed by hand **3. WHEELED CARRIER FOR MERCHANDISE OR BAGGAGE** a container or platform on small wheels on which things are pushed along, e.g., supermarket items or airport baggage **4. HORSE-DRAWN CARRIAGE** a light horse-drawn carriage with two wheels **5. SMALL MOTORIZED VEHICLE** a lightweight motorized vehicle, e.g., one ridden by golfers on a course **6. WHEELED TABLE** a small table on wheels, used for taking food and drinks to the table ■ *vt.* **(cart·ed, cart·ing, carts) 1. CARRY SOMETHING ROUGHLY** to take or pull somebody or something roughly or with difficulty (*informal*) ○ *I had to cart the Christmas tree home myself.* ○ *Do you have to cart all those books around?* **2. CARRY OR TRANSPORT SOMETHING OR SOMEBODY** to carry or transport something or somebody, especially in a cart ○ *carting the produce to market* ○ *We seem to spend half of Saturday carting the kids everywhere.* [12thC. From Old Norse *kartr.*] —**cart·a·ble** *adj.* ◇ **put the cart before the horse** to do or say things in the wrong order

cart·age /kaártij/ *n.* the cost of transporting or delivering goods by cart

Car·ta·ge·na /kaàrtə gáynə, -jeénə, -háynə/ capital of Bolívar Department in northwestern Colombia, a port on the Caribbean Sea's Bay of Cartagena. Population: 745,689 (1995).

carte *n.* = **quarte**

carte blanche /kaart blaánch, -blaáNsh/ *n.* permission or authority given to somebody to act with freedom or discretion ○ *She's been given carte blanche to make whatever changes she thinks necessary.* [From French, literally "white card." The underlying idea is of signing a blank sheet of paper on which anything might then be written.]

car·tel /kaar tél/ *n.* **1. GROUP OF BUSINESSES CONTROLLING MARKET** an alliance of business companies, formed to control production, competition, and prices **2. ALLIANCE OF LIKE-MINDED POLITICAL GROUPS** a political alliance among parties or groups having common goals [Mid-16thC. Via German *Kartell* and French *cartel* from Italian *cartello* "placard," from, ultimately, Latin *c(h)arta* (see CARD[1]). The underlying idea is of a written agreement.]

car·tel·ize /kaárt'l ìz/ **(-ized, -iz·ing, -iz·es)** *vti.* to form a cartel of business companies or political groups ○ *The market leaders had every incentive to cartelize.*

car·ter /kaártər/ *n.* somebody who uses a cart for transporting goods or for farm work

Car·ter, Angela (1940–92) English writer. Her novels include *The Magic Toyshop* (1967), *Nights at the Circus* (1984), and *Wise Children* (1991).

Jimmy Carter

Car·ter, Jimmy (*b.* 1924) U.S. statesman and 39th president of the United States. As president (1977–81) he negotiated the Panama Canal Treaty (1978) and the Camp David accords between Israel and Egypt (1978–79). Full name **James Earl Carter , Jr.**

Car·ter·et /kaártərət/, **Sir George** (1610?–80) British-born U.S. absentee colonial administrator. He was granted part of present-day New Jersey (1664) by King Charles II.

Car·te·sian /kaar teézh'n/ *adj.* **RELATING TO DESCARTES** relating to the 17th-century French philosopher René Descartes, or his philosophical or mathematical writings or theories ■ *n.* **BELIEVER IN DESCARTES'S WORK** a supporter of Descartes's philosophical or mathematical theories and systems [Mid-17thC. From modern Latin *Cartesianus*, from *Cartesius*, the Latinized form of DESCARTES.]

Car·te·sian co·or·di·nate *n.* **1. NUMBER SHOWING POSITION OF POINT ON PLANE** one of a pair of coordinates giving the location of a point on a plane, relative to an origin and two perpendicular axes **2. NUMBER SHOWING POSITION OF POINT IN SPACE** one of three coordinates giving the location of a point in space, relative to an origin and three mutually perpendicular planes

Car·te·sian·ism /kaar teézh'n ìzzəm/ *n.* the philosophy of René Descartes, especially his belief in a distinction between the observing mind and the observed world

Car·te·sian plane *n.* a plane having all points defined by Cartesian coordinates

Car·te·sian prod·uct *n.* a set of all the pairs of elements from two sets that have their first element from the first set and the second from the second set

Car·thage /kaárthij/ site of an ancient city, founded by the Phoenicians on the northern coast of Africa in 814 B.C. The site is now in a suburb of Tunis, capital of Tunisia. —**Car·tha·gin·i·an** /kaàrthə jínnee ən/ *n., adj.*

Car·thu·sian /kaar thoózh'n/ *n.* **MEMBER OF AUSTERE RELIGIOUS ORDER** a member of a Catholic order of monks and nuns founded in Roman France early in the 11th century, who live by strict rules and in great austerity ■ *adj.* **OF CARTHUSIANS** relating to the order of Carthusians [Mid-16thC. From medieval Latin *Carthusianus*, from *Carthusia*, the Latin name of *Chartreuse* in southern France, where the order's first monastery was built.]

Car·tier /kaárt yáy, kaártee àyl/, **Sir George-Étienne** (1814–73) Canadian politician and railway magnate. He was prime minister of Canada (1858–62).

Car·tier, Jacques (1491–1557) French navigator. He was the first European to explore and chart the St. Lawrence River (1534).

Car·tier Is·land /kaártee áy-/ small uninhabited island off the northern coast of Western Australia

car·ti·lage /kaárt'lij/ *n.* the tough elastic tissue that is found in the nose, throat, and ear and in other parts of the body and forms most of the skeleton in infancy, changing to bone during growth [15thC. Via French from Latin *cartilago.*]

car·ti·lage of San·tor·i·ni *n.* = **corniculate cartilage**

car·ti·lag·i·nous /kaàrt'l ájjinəss/ *adj.* **1. OF OR LIKE CARTILAGE** resembling, made of, or relating to cartilage **2. WITH MORE CARTILAGE THAN BONE** having a skeleton composed mostly of cartilage

car·ti·lag·i·nous fish (*plural* **car·ti·lag·i·nous fish** *or* **car·ti·lag·i·nous fish·es**) *n.* a fish with a skeleton made entirely of cartilage. Shark, rays, and ratfish are cartilaginous fish. Class: Chondrichthyes.

Cart·land /kaártlənd/, **Dame Barbara** (*b.* 1901) English novelist. She has written more than 400 books, mostly popular romances. Born **Mary Barbara Hamilton**

cart·load /kaárt lòd/ *n.* the amount that a cart can carry

car·to·gram /kaártə gràm/ *n.* a diagrammatic map showing the population and other statistics of a region [Late 19thC. From French *cartogramme*, from *carte* "map."]

car·tog·ra·pher /kaar tóggrəfər/ *n.* somebody who makes maps

car·to·graph·ic /kaàrtə gráffik/, **car·to·graph·i·cal** /-k'l/ *adj.* **1. OF MAPS** relating to maps ○ *cartographic design* **2. IN MAP FORM** in the form of a map ○ *cartographic representation* —**car·to·graph·i·cal·ly** /-kəlee/ *adv.*

car·tog·ra·phy /kaar tóggrəfee/ *n.* the science, skill, or work of making maps [Mid-19thC. From French *cartographie*, from *carte* "map."]

car·to·man·cy /kaártə mànsee/ *n.* fortune telling by using playing cards [Late 19thC. From French *cartomancie*, from *carte* "card" (see CARD[1]).]

car·ton /kaárt'n/ *n.* **1. CARDBOARD BOX** a cardboard box in which something, e.g., merchandise, movable property, or mail, is packaged **2. PLASTIC OR CARDBOARD CONTAINER** a container made of plastic or waxed cardboard in which food or drink is sold **3. CONTENTS OF CONTAINER** the various contents, e.g., juice or milk, contained in a carton ■ *vt.* **(-toned, -ton·ing, -tons) PUT SOMETHING IN CARTON** to put something in a carton ○ *Most of our milk is sold cartoned.* [Early 19thC. Via French from Italian *cartone* (see CARTOON).]

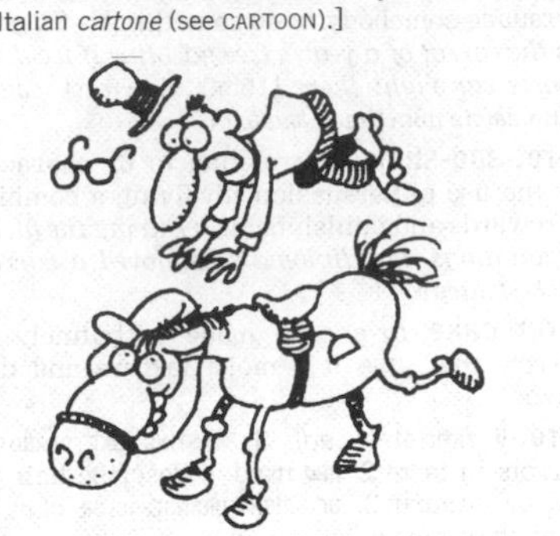
Cartoon

car·toon /kaar toón/ *n.* **1. ANIMATED FILM FROM DRAWINGS** an animated film made up of drawings that are photographed and projected in sequence so that the figures in them appear to move, especially a humorous film intended primarily for children **2. SEQUENCE OF DRAWINGS** a sequence of drawings that tell a short story, published in a newspaper or magazine **3. SATIRICAL DRAWING** a humorous drawing published in a newspaper or magazine and commenting on a topical event or theme **4. HUMOROUS DRAWING** a humorous drawing published in a newspaper or magazine, intended to entertain and often accompanied by a caption **5. PREPARATORY DRAWING** a drawing done, often in great detail, as a preliminary version of a painting or other art [Late 16thC. Via Italian *cartone*, literally "pasteboard"(on which artists' preparatory drawings were made), from, ultimately, Latin *c(h)arta* (see CARD[1]).]

car·toon·ish /kaar toónish/, **car·toon·y** /-toónee/ *adj.* resembling a humorous or animated cartoon —**car·toon·ish·ly** *adv.*

car·toon·ist /kaar toónist/ *n.* somebody who draws cartoons for animated films or for newspapers or magazines

car·toon·y *adj.* = **cartoonish**

car·top /kaár tòp/ *adj.* attached to or designed to be carried on a car's roof

car·toph·i·ly /kaar tóffilee/ *n.* collecting cigarette cards as a hobby [Mid-20thC. Coined from French *carte* "card" or Italian *carta* + -PHILY.] —**car·toph·i·list** *n.*

Cartouche: Gold signet ring with cartouche of Tutankhamun (1346–37 B.C.)

car·touche /kaar toósh/ *n.* **1. CASING FOR GUNPOWDER** the paper casing of a firework or cartridge **2. DECORATIVE PANEL** a decorative panel in the form of a frame or unrolled scroll, sometimes containing writing forming an artistic or architectural feature **3. FRAME FOR NAME** an oval or oblong shape containing writing, especially one containing a king's name in Egyptian hieroglyphics [Early 17thC. Via French from Italian *cartoccio* "paper cornet," from *carta* "paper."]

car·tridge /kaártrij/ *n.* **1. BULLET'S CASE** a cylindrical case holding an explosive charge and a bullet or shot, which is put into a gun **2. CONTAINER WITH HIGH EXPLOSIVES** a container used in blasting that contains high explosives **3. CONTAINER FOR LIQUID OR POWDER** a container of liquid or powder that is loaded into a device, e.g., a removable ink container for a pen or printer ○ *toner cartridges* **4. CASE FOR LOADING SOMETHING INTO MACHINE** a plastic case containing something that is loaded into a device, e.g., photographic film, a typewriter ribbon, a cassette, or a set of computer disks **5.** PART OF HI-FI PICKUP the part of the arm of a record player that holds the needle [Late 16thC. Anglicization of French *cartouche* (see CARTOUCHE).]

car·tridge belt *n.* a belt that holds gun cartridges or cartridge clips

car·tridge case *n.* the casing of a gun cartridge

car·tridge clip *n.* a container for bullets, loaded directly into an automatic weapon

car·tridge pen *n.* a pen that holds a replaceable ink cartridge

cart track *n. U.K.* a rough track or narrow unsurfaced road used by farm vehicles

car·tu·lar·y /kaárchə lèrree/ (*plural* **-ies**) *n.* **1.** SET OF OFFICIAL RECORDS a collection of official records, especially those relating to a large estate or a religious community **2.** PLACE FOR RECORDS a room or building where official records are kept [Mid-16thC. From medieval Latin *c(h)artularium*, from Latin *c(h)artula* "document," from *c(h)arta* (see CARD[1]).]

cart·wheel /kaárt hweel/ *n.* **1.** ACROBATIC MOVEMENT an acrobatic movement in which the body is turned sideways onto the hands, then over onto the feet again **2.** *U.K.* WOODEN WHEEL OF CART a large wooden spoked wheel for a cart **3.** LARGE COIN a large coin, especially a silver dollar (*dated*) ■ *vi.* (**cartwheeled, cartwheel·ing, cart·wheels**) DO CARTWHEEL to perform a cartwheel ○ *The motorcycle, struck from behind, cartwheeled into the median strip.*

cart·wright /kaárt rìt/ *n.* somebody who makes carts

Cart·wright, John (1740–1824) British politician and reformer. He campaigned for the abolition of slavery and against British taxation in North America.

Cart·wright, Peter (1785–1872) U.S. preacher. A Methodist Episcopal clergyman, he delivered lively sermons throughout the Midwest.

ca·run·cle /kə rúngk'l/ *n.* **1.** ZOOL FLESHY GROWTH a fleshy growth on the head or body, e.g., a rooster's comb **2.** BOT GROWTH ON PLANT a colored outgrowth of tissue in some types of seed near the point of attachment to the plant [Late 16thC. Via obsolete French from Latin *caruncula* "small piece of flesh," from *caro* (see CARRION).] —**ca·run·cu·lar** *adj.* —**ca·run·cu·late** *adj.* —**ca·run·cu·lat·ed** *adj.* —**ca·run·cu·lous** *adj.*

Ca·ru·so /kə róozzō/, **Enrico** (1873–1921) Italian operatic tenor. A powerful singer and actor, he appeared in the operas of Verdi and Puccini.

car·va·crol /kaárvə kròl/ *n.* an oily liquid with the smell of mint obtained from herbs such as savory, oregano, and thyme, used in flavorings, perfumes, and as a disinfectant [Mid-19thC. Coined from modern Latin *(Carum) carvi* "caraway" + Latin *acer* "sharp" + -OL.]

carve /kaarv/ (**carved, carv·ing, carves**) *v.* **1.** *vti.* MAKE SOMETHING BY CUTTING AND SHAPING to make an object or design by cutting and shaping a hard material such as wood or stone ○ *statues carved from marble* ○ *I remembered carving her name on a tree, years ago.* **2.** *vt.* CUT SUBSTANCE TO MAKE SOMETHING to cut and shape a material such as wood or stone in order to make an object or design **3.** *vti.* CUT MEAT to cut cooked meat into slices **4.** *vti.* MAKE SHAPE BY NATURAL FORCE to make a shape by an eroding action ○ *dunes carved into strange shapes by the wind* [Old English *ceorfan*. Ultimately from a prehistoric Germanic word meaning "to scratch."]

carve out *vt.* to make or achieve something through sustained hard work ○ *With unrelenting energy and ambition she had carved out a niche for herself in the world of investigative journalism.*

carve up *vt.* **1.** DIVIDE SOMETHING UP to divide something, or ownership of something, into rough or crude parts (*informal*) ○ *Their intention was to invade and carve up the kingdom among themselves.* **2.** INJURE SOMEBODY WITH KNIFE to wound somebody with a blade (*slang*)

car·vel *n.* = **caravel**

car·vel-built /kaárv'l-, -vel-/ *adj.* used to describe a boat or ship made of planks of wood with their edges flush, not overlapping [Late 18thC. Via French *caravelle* and Portuguese *caravela* "small ship" from, ultimately, Greek *karabos* "light ship, crayfish."]

carv·en /kaárv'n/ *adj.* carved (*archaic or literary*) ○ *thrones of carven onyx* ○ *Let the decree be carven in stone.* [14thC. Old past participle of CARVE, revived in the 19thC.]

carv·er /kaárvər/ *n.* **1.** MEAT KNIFE a knife for slicing cooked meat **2.** SOMEBODY OR SOMETHING THAT CARVES a person or device that carves meat **3.** FURNITURE DINING CHAIR WITH ARMS a dining chair with arms designed to stand at the head of the table

Car·ver, George Washington (1864–1943) U.S. botanist. He was noted for his research into the industrial uses of the peanut, soybean, and sweet potato. He invented "Carver's hybrid" cotton.

carv·ers /kaárvər/ *npl.* a large knife and fork for carving meat

carv·ing /kaárving/ *n.* **1.** SOMETHING MADE BY CUTTING WOOD an object or design formed by cutting and shaping a material, e.g., wood or stone ○ *The walls were covered with carvings depicting gods and heroes.* **2.** ACT OF CARVING SOMETHING the work or act of carving something ○ *The carving of the panels was exquisite.*

carv·ing knife *n.* a large knife for slicing meat

car wash *n.* **1.** PLACE WHERE VEHICLES ARE WASHED a site, often a tunnel-like building with drive-through conveyors, where motor vehicles are washed automatically by machine or can be washed manually **2.** EQUIPMENT FOR WASHING VEHICLES a shed or structure for washing motor vehicles automatically with revolving brushes and jets of water

Caryatid

car·y·at·id /kèrree áttid, kérree ə tìd/ (*plural* **-ids** *or* **-i·des** /-átti deez/) *n.* a column in the shape of a draped female figure supporting a structure such as the frieze or porch of a classical Greek temple [Mid-16thC. Via French *caryatide* and Latin *caryatides* from Greek *karuatides*, literally "maidens of Karuai"(now Caryae in southern Greece), the name given to the priestesses of Artemis there.] —**car·y·at·i·dal** *adj.* —**car·y·at·i·de·an** /-atti deé ən, -ə tíddee ən/ *adj.* —**car·y·a·tid·ic** /-ə tíddik/ *adj.*

car·y·op·sis /kèrree ópsiss/ (*plural* **-ses** /-seez/ *or* **-si·des** /-si deez/) *n.* a dry fruit that looks like a seed, borne by grasses and cereal crops such as wheat [Early 19thC. From modern Latin, formed from Greek *karuon* "nut" + *opsis* "appearance."]

CAS *abbr.* Certificate of Advanced Study

CASA *abbr.* Court-Appointed Special Advocate

ca·sa·ba /kə saábə/ *n.* a winter melon similar to the honeydew and cantaloupe, with whitish flesh. Latin name: *Cucumis melo* var. *inodorus.* [Late 19thC. Named after *Kasaba* (now Turgutlu), a city in western Turkey.]

Cas·a·blan·ca /kàssə blángkə, kaàssə blaángkə/ largest city and chief port in Morocco. It is situated on the Atlantic coast, about 50 mi./80 km southwest of Rabat. Population: 2,943,000 (1993). Arabic **Dar el-Beida**

Ca·sa Gran·de /kaàssə graándee, -day, kàssə grándee/ city in southern Arizona, south of Mesa, near the Santa Cruz River. Population: 21,314 (1996).

Ca·sals /kə zálz/, **Pablo** (1876–1973) Spanish cellist and composer. He was widely regarded as the greatest cellist of his generation.

Cas·a·no·va /kàssə nṓvə/ *n.* a charming seducer of women who moves quickly from one casual relationship to another, or who constantly pesters women in his pursuits [Early 20thC. Named after the Italian adventurer Giovanni Jacopo CASANOVA.]

Ca·sa·no·va, Giovanni Jacopo, Chevalier de Seingalt (1725–98) Italian adventurer and author. He was a soldier, diplomat, and spy whose amorous reputation rests on his 12-volume *History of My Life* (1826–38). Full name **Giovanni Giacomo Casanova, Chevalier de Seingalt**

cas·bah /káz baà/, **kas·bah** *n.* **1.** N AFRICAN FORTRESS a fortress or palace in any of various N African cities or towns **2.** OLDER DISTRICT the older part of a city or town in North Africa or the Middle East, which is often where the markets are situated [French, from Arabic *qaṣbah* "fortress"]

cas·cade /ka skáyd/ *n.* **1.** WATERFALL a small waterfall or series of waterfalls **2.** FLOWING LIQUID a fast downward flow of liquid or small objects **3.** HANGING MASS a flowing mass of something that hangs down or lies along a surface ○ *The bride carried a cascade of roses and baby's breath.* **4.** ELECTRON ENG, PHYS SUCCESSION a succession of things, e.g., chemical reactions or elements in an electrical circuit, each of which activates, affects, or determines the next ■ *v.* (**-cad·ed, -cad·ing, -cades**) **1.** *vti.* FLOW to flow fast and in large amounts, or to cause something to flow this way **2.** *vi.* HANG OR LIE to hang or lie in a flowing mass (*literary*) ○ *Fine lace ruffles cascaded from his throat and sleeves.* **3.** *vt.* COMPUT ARRANGE WINDOWS TO OVERLAP to arrange the windows on a computer screen so that they overlap, with the title bar of each visible [Mid-17thC. Via French from Italian *cascata*, from, ultimately, Latin *cadere* (see CASE[1]).]

Cas·cade Range range of mountains in the western United States, and the northern continuation of the Sierra Nevada range. Its highest peak is Mount Rainier. Height: 14,410 ft./4,392 m. Length: 700 mi./1,130 km.

cas·cad·ing men·u *n.* COMPUT a menu in a computer program that opens when you select a choice from another menu

cas·ca·du·ra /kàskə dóorə/ (*plural* **-ras** *or* **-ra**), **cas·ca·doo** /kàskə doó/ (*plural* **-doos** *or* **-doo**) *n. Carib* a small bony edible freshwater fish with thick scales that is considered a delicacy. According to a local legend, those who eat the cascadura will always return to Trinidad. [From Spanish *casca* "shell" + Spanish *dura* "hard"]

cas·car·a /ka skérrə/, **cas·car·a buck·thorn** *n.* **1.** N AMERICAN SHRUB a shrub or small tree of the northwestern United States. Latin name: *Rhamnus purshiana.* **2.** = **cascara sagrada** [Late 19thC. Shortening of CASCARA SAGRADA.]

cas·car·a sa·gra·da /-sə graádə/ *n.* the dried bark of the cascara shrub or tree, formerly used as a strong laxative but no longer prescribed medically [From Spanish, literally "sacred bark"]

cas·ca·ril·la /kàskə ríllə, -reé ə/ *n.* **1.** AROMATIC BARK an aromatic bark formerly used in medicine **2.** W INDIAN SHRUB a West Indian shrub from which cascarilla is obtained. Latin name: *Croton eluteria.* [Late 17thC. From Spanish, literally "small cascara" (see CASCARA SAGRADA).]

case[1] /kayss/ *n.* **1.** CIRCUMSTANCE a situation or set of circumstances ○ *I don't think the usual rules apply in this case.* ○ *Sometimes anxiety causes weight loss, but that's not the case here.* **2.** INSTANCE an instance or example of something ○ *This is nothing more than a case of mistaken identity.* **3.** SOMETHING EXAMINED OR INVESTIGATED a subject of investigation or scrutiny by a professional person, e.g., a doctor or police officer **4.** ACTUAL FACT what happens in reality or fact ○ *The case is that the witness has lied under oath.* **5.** PROBLEM a matter in question or a problem ○ *The case here is simply a matter of excessive expenditures, isn't it?* **6.** LAW SOMETHING EXAMINED IN LAW COURT a matter examined or judged in a court of law ○ *It'll be some weeks before your case comes to trial.* **7.** LAW ARGUMENTS a set of arguments and evidence that supports a legal claim in court ○ *He presented his case calmly and with skill.* **8.** ARGUMENT FOR OR AGAINST an argument for or against something ○ *You can make a good case for holding a referendum.* **9.** GRAM GRAMMATICAL FORM OF WORD a form of a noun, pronoun, or adjective that indicates its syntactical relation to surrounding words **10.** KIND OF PERSON somebody of a particular kind or in a particular condition, especially an unfortunate one (*informal*) ○ *He's a hopeless case.* **11.** ODD PERSON an odd or eccentric person (*informal*) ■ *vt.* (**cased, cas·ing, cas·es**) INSPECT PLACE to assess or survey a place with a view to robbing it (*slang*) [13thC. Via Old French *cas* "event" from Latin *casus*, from *cadere* "to fall" (source also of English *cadence* and *cascade*).] ◇ **a case in point** a relevant example ○ *A case in point for our discussion is the steady drop in unit sales.* ◇ **be on somebody's case** to persist in pestering somebody to do something (*slang*) ◇ **get off somebody's case** to stop pestering somebody to do something (*slang*) ○ *Please get off my case! I'll finish mowing the lawn later.* ◇ **in any case 1.** taking into account everything said or done before **2.** regardless of that ◇ **in case of something** if something happens ○ *In case of fire, leave by the nearest exit.* ◇ **(just) in case 1.** in preparation for an event that may possibly happen ○ *Take your umbrella, just in case.* **2.** used to introduce a piece of information and to explain your reason for giving it ○ *In case you're unaware of the fact, this is a nonsmoking area.*

case[2] /kayss/ *n.* **1.** HOLDER OR OUTER COVERING something that serves as a container or covering **2.** CONTAINER a container with its contents ○ *bought a case of soft drinks* **3.** PIECE OF BAGGAGE an item of baggage, especially a suitcase **4.** PRINTING KIND OF PRINTED CHARACTER the function of a printed character as a capital or small letter **5.** PRINTING TRAY HOLDING PRINTING TYPE in hot-metal printing, a tray with compartments into which individual printing blocks are slotted **6.** PAIR a pair, especially of pistols **7.** = **casing** *n.* **3** ■ *vt.* **(cased, cas·ing, cas·es)** PUT COVERING AROUND SOMETHING to enclose something in a covering [13thC. Via Old French dialect *casse* from Latin *capsa* "box," from *capere* "to hold" (source of English *capacious, capable,* and *occupy*).]

CASE /kayss/ *abbr.* **1.** computer-aided software engineering **2.** computer-aided systems engineering

ca·se·ase /káyssee àyss, -àyz/ *n.* an enzyme formed by certain bacteria that aids the breakdown of casein and is used in cheese ripening [20thC. From CASEIN + -ASE.]

ca·se·ate /káyssee àyt/ **(-at·ed, -at·ing, -ates)** *vi.* to undergo caseation [Late 19thC. Back-formation from CASEATION.]

ca·se·a·tion /kàyssee áysh'n/ *n.* the process by which dead tissue decays into a firm and dry mass, characteristic of tuberculosis [Mid-19thC. From medieval Latin *caseatio*, from Latin *caseus* "cheese."]

case·bear·er /káyss bàirər/ *n.* an insect whose larvae form a protective case around themselves

case·book /káyss bòok/ *n.* **1.** RECORD OF CASES DEALT WITH a record of legal or medical cases and their conduct **2.** SCHOLARLY COLLECTION a collection of academic writings on a subject

cased glass, case glass *n.* decorative glass consisting of several colored layers with some areas cut away in different patterns

ca·se·fy /káyssi fì/ **(-fied, -fy·ing, -fies)** *vti.* to develop, or cause something to develop, a soft consistency like that of cheese [20thC. Formed from Latin *caseus* "cheese."]

case glass *n.* = **cased glass**

case goods *npl.* **1.** MERCHANDISE SOLD IN BULK merchandise often sold in multiple packs, e.g., beer or fruit juice **2.** BOXLIKE FURNITURE types of furniture that have a boxlike structure, e.g., bureaus, and that provide storage space ■ *n.* FURNITURE SOLD AS SETS bedroom or dining-room furniture that is sold as sets

case gram·mar *n.* a system of grammar that analyzes sentences in terms of the semantic relation of the noun or noun phrase and other elements to the main verb

case·hard·en /káyss haàrd'n/ **(-ened, -en·ing, -ens)** *vt.* **1.** HARDEN IRON to harden the surface of an iron alloy by heating and then cooling in water **2.** HARDEN SOMEBODY'S ATTITUDE to make somebody unsympathetic or unfeeling as a result of extended dealing with difficult and distressing problems

case his·to·ry *n.* **1.** RECORD OF TREATMENT a record of somebody's medical or social history kept by a doctor or social worker **2.** RECORD OF WHAT HAPPENED a record of how an issue or problem has been dealt with, consulted as a guide to how to handle it or similar events in the future ○ *He researched the case histories of earlier attempts at farming on that river.*

ca·sein /kay séen, káysee in/ *n.* a protein formed in milk by the action of rennin or another agent, which is the main constituent of cheese. It is also used in plastics, adhesives, and paints. [Mid-19thC. Formed from Latin *caseus* "cheese."]

ca·sein·ate /kay sée nàyt, káyssee ə-/ *n.* a casein salt formed by compounding casein with a metal such as calcium or sodium

ca·sein·o·gen /kay séenəjən, kàyssee ínnəjən/ *n.* the main protein in milk, from which casein is formed

case knife *n.* **1.** TABLE KNIFE a table knife **2.** SHEATH KNIFE a sheath knife (*archaic*)

case law *n.* law established on the basis of previous verdicts, rather than law established by legislation

case·load /káyss lòd/ *n.* the number of cases to be dealt with, e.g., by a doctor or a lawyer, at a particular time

case·mate /káyss màyt/ *n.* a fortified compartment on an old sailing ship or a rampart, where a cannon was mounted [Mid-16thC. Directly or via French from Italian *casamatta*, of unknown origin.]

Casement

case·ment /káyssmənt/ *n.* **1.** HINGED WINDOW a window that opens on hinges, as distinct from one that slides up and down **2.** an encasement or covering [15thC. Via Anglo-Latin *cassimentum*, from, ultimately, Latin *capsa* (see CASE[2]). Originally in the meaning "hollow molding."]

ca·se·ose /káyssi òss/ *n.* a chemical produced in the digestion of cheese [20thC. Formed from Latin *caseus* "cheese."]

ca·se·ous /káyssee əss/ *adj.* used to describe firm, dry diseased tissue that has undergone caseation [Mid-17thC. Formed from Latin *caseus* "cheese."]

ca·sern /kə zúrn/, **ca·serne** *n.* a barracks, especially a temporary one [Late 17thC. Via French *caserne* from, ultimately, Latin *quarterna* "hut for four."]

case shot *n.* an old kind of cannon shell containing shrapnel

case stud·y *n.* **1.** STUDY OF SITUATION an analysis of a particular case or situation used as a basis for drawing conclusions in similar situations **2.** RECORD OF TREATMENT a record of somebody's problems and how they were dealt with, especially by a doctor or social worker

case sys·tem *n.* the teaching of law through the study of important and representative cases rather than by studying theory

case·work /káyss wùrk/ *n.* a system of making a social worker responsible for particular clients on a long-term basis

case·work·er /káyss wùrkər/ *n.* a professional social worker who is assigned a number of clients on a long-term basis

cash[1] /kash/ *n.* **1.** COINS AND BILLS money in the form of coins and bills as distinct from money orders or credit **2.** CURRENCY OR CHECKS money used as immediate payment in any form, e.g., currency or checks (*informal*) ■ *vt.* **(cashed, cash·ing, cash·es)** EXCHANGE SOMETHING FOR CURRENCY to exchange a check or money order for coins and bills ○ *You can cash your paycheck at the bank.* [Late 16thC. Directly or via obsolete French *casse* from Italian *cassa* "money-box, money," from Latin *capsa* (see CASE[2]).] —**cash·able** *adj.* ◇ **cash on the barrelhead** *or* **barrel** money paid at the time something is purchased ○ *You could buy the furniture on credit but it would be cheaper to pay cash on the barrelhead.*

cash in *v.* **1.** *vt.* TAKE WHAT IS OWED to withdraw from a business investment such as an insurance policy and take the money that is due **2.** *vi.* MAKE A LOT OF MONEY to make large amounts of money (*slang*) ○ *When the stock was sold, she really cashed in.* ◇ **cash in your chips 1.** to exit a gambling game (*slang*) **2.** to stop what you are doing, e.g., a task, and leave the site (*slang*) ○ *It's almost midnight; I'm cashing in my chips and going to bed.* **3.** to die (*slang*) **4.** to commit suicide (*slang*)

cash in on *vt.* to exploit a situation in order to get personal benefit, especially money ○ *It seemed that everyone who knew him wanted to cash in on his rise to fame.*

cash out *v.* **1.** *vti.* SELL ASSET TO PROFIT to sell off an asset that has been held for a long time, e.g., land, in order to profit ○ *He finally decided to cash out and sell the land that had been in his family for three generations.* **2.** *vi.* COMMIT SUICIDE to commit suicide (*slang*)

cash[2] /kash/ (*plural* **cash**) *n.* any of several former small Asian coins of low value [Late 16thC. Via Portuguese *caixa* from Tamil *kāçu*.]

cash-and-car·ry *n.* (*plural* **cash-and-car·ries**) **1.** INEXPENSIVE STORE a store selling inexpensive goods that are paid for in cash and taken away by the buyer **2.** POLICY OF SELLING WITHOUT DELIVERY SERVICE a policy of selling items for cash with no delivery service to customers ■ *adj.* CASH-ONLY AND WITHOUT DELIVERY sold, or operating, on a basis of cash-only payments by buyers who take their goods away at the time of purchase

cash bar *n.* a bar at a large party or reception at which drinks have to be paid for individually

cash·book /kásh bòok/ *n.* a book for keeping a record of money spent and received

cash box *n.* a lockable box for cash, especially one holding the daily takings of a small business

cash cow *n.* a profitable business or product with low overheads often used to fund other businesses or investments (*slang*) ○ *The grocery chain has been their cash cow for years.*

cash crop *n.* a crop grown for direct sale rather than personal consumption

cash dis·count *n.* a reduction in price offered to a buyer who can pay in cash or pay immediately

cash·ew /ká shòo/ *n.* **1.** TREES TROPICAL TREE BEARING EDIBLE NUTS a tropical American evergreen tree grown for its edible nuts. Latin name: *Anacardium occidentale.* **2.** FOOD = **cashew nut** [Late 16thC. Via Portuguese from Tupi *acajú*.]

cash·ew ap·ple *n.* the edible swollen stalk by which a cashew nut is attached to its stem, used to make preserves

cash·ew nut *n.* a kidney-shaped nut that grows on the tropical American cashew tree and is edible when roasted

cash flow *n.* **1.** MOVEMENT OF MONEY RECEIVED AND SPENT the pattern of income and expenses, and its consequences for how much money is available at a given time **2.** COMPANY'S MONEY RECEIVED AND SPENT the prediction or assessment of a company's income and expenditure over a period of time

cashier[1] /ka shéer/ *n.* **1.** BANK WORKER TAKING AND PAYING MONEY somebody in a bank who deals directly with customers and handles routine account transactions **2.** SOMEBODY RESPONSIBLE FOR FINANCIAL TRANSACTIONS an official in an organization who is responsible for receiving and paying out money and keeping financial records ■ *vi.* **(cashiered, cashier·ing, cash·iers)** WORK AS CASHIER to work as a cashier, especially in a place of business such as a restaurant or bar ○ *Who's cashiering tonight?* = **checker** [Late 16thC. Directly or via Dutch *cassier* from French *caissier*, from *casse* (see CASH[1]).]

cash·ier[2] /ka shéer/ **(-iered, cash·iered, -ier·ing, -iers)** *vt.* to dismiss somebody from the armed forces because of misconduct [Early 16thC. Via Middle Dutch *kasseren* "to disband (soldiers)" and French *casser* "to break, dismiss" from Latin *quassare* (see QUASH).]

cash·ier's check *n.* a guaranteed check issued by a bank against money taken from a customer's account or against cash provided for this purpose

cash·less /káshləss/ *adj.* using an electronic means of exchanging money instead of dealing in cash

cash ma·chine *n.* = **ATM**

cash·mere /kázh meer, kásh-/ *n.* **1.** GOAT'S SOFT WOOL the soft wool from a Himalayan goat **2.** FABRIC MADE FROM GOAT'S WOOL a woolen fabric made from cashmere **3.** IMITATION OF GOAT'S WOOL FABRIC a soft woolen fabric resembling the fabric made from cashmere [Late 17thC. An early spelling of KASHMIR.]

cash·mere goat *n.* a Himalayan goat reared for the soft wool that grows under its coarse outer coat

cash on de·liv·er·y *adv.* with full payment for ordered merchandise to be made by the buyer to the one delivering the goods ○ *bought the coat cash on delivery*

cash-poor *adj.* financially sound but having little readily available cash

cash ra·tio *n.* the ratio that a bank must maintain between available cash and total deposits

cash reg·is·ter *n.* a machine in a store that records sales, calculates totals, and has a drawer for money

cash-starved *adj.* having very little money or financial support

cash-strapped *adj.* having insufficient money (*informal*)

cas·i·mere *n.* = **cassimere**

Ca·si·mir III, the Great, King of Poland (1310–70). His reign (1333–70) as the "Peasants' King" saw the introduction of fairer laws and peace through diplomacy. He founded Cracow University (1354).

cas·ing /káyssing/ *n.* **1. OUTER COVERING** an outer covering, e.g., the sheath of an electrical cable or the skin of a sausage **2. FRAME FOR DOOR OR WINDOW** a frame containing a door, window, or stairway **3. LINER PIPE IN WELL** a liner pipe or tube in water, oil, or gas wells

ca·si·no /kə seénō/ (*plural* **-nos**) *n.* **1. GAMBLING ESTABLISHMENT** a private club, or a room in a club, hotel, or other establishment, where gambling takes place **2. ca·si·no, cas·si·no** CARDS **POINT-SCORING CARD GAME** a point-scoring card game in which players combine cards exposed on the table with cards in their hands, with the 10 of diamonds being the highest-valued card [Mid-18thC. From Italian, literally "small house," from, ultimately, Latin *casa* "house."]

cask /kask/ *n.* **1. BARREL CONTAINING ALCOHOL** a wooden barrel containing alcoholic drink **2. CONTAINER LIKE A BARREL** any barrel-like container, whether or not of wood **3. CONTENTS OF BARREL** the contents of a barrel or similar container **4.** = **flask** *n.* 6 [Early 16thC. Via French *casque* or Spanish *casco* "helmet, skull" from, ultimately, Latin *quassare* (see QUASH).]

cas·ket /káskət/ *n.* **1.** alternative for coffin **2. FANCY BOX** a decorative box for valuables [15thC. Origin uncertain: perhaps an alteration of French *cassette* (see CASSETTE).]

Cas·per /káspər/ city in east central Wyoming, on the northern bank of the North Platte river. Population: 48,800 (1996).

Cas·pi·an Sea /kàspee ən-/ large landlocked salt lake lying between southeastern Europe and Asia. It is the world's largest inland body of water. Area: 143,000 sq. mi./370,000 sq. km.

casque /kask/ *n.* **1. KNIGHT'S HELMET** a helmet from a suit of armor (*archaic*) **2.** ZOOL **GROWTH ON ANIMAL'S HEAD** a horny growth on the head of a bird, fish or reptile, resembling a helmet [Late 17thC. Via French from Spanish *casco* (see CASK).] —**casqued** *adj.*

Cass /kass/, **Lewis** (1782–1866) U.S. politician. He was secretary of war (1831–36) during the Seminole and Black Hawk wars and ran unsuccessfully for U.S. president (1848).

Cas·san·dra /kə sándrə/ *n.* somebody whose warnings of impending disaster are ignored [Early 17thC. Named after *Cassandra*, the daughter of Priam, king of Troy, who was granted the gift of prophecy by Apollo but was condemned never to be believed.]

cas·sa·ta /kə saátə/ *n.* **1. ICE CREAM WITH CANDIED FRUIT** brightly colored Italian ice cream containing nuts and candied fruit and layers or streaks of different flavors **2. SICILIAN CAKE WITH SOFT CHEESE** a Sicilian sponge cake, layered and coated with sweet ricotta, flavored with candied fruit and chopped chocolate, decorated with candied fruit, and eaten as a celebration cake or dessert [Early 20thC. From Italian.]

cas·sa·tion /kə sáysh'n, ka-/ *n.* **1. COURT OF APPEAL** a court of appeal in countries that follow the Napoleonic code of civil law **2.** MUSIC **SERENADE FOR INSTRUMENTS** an 18th-century instrumental work similar in form to a divertimento [15thC. Formed from Latin *cassare* "to annul."]

Cas·satt, Mary (1845–1926) U.S. artist. She is known for intimate impressionist portraits of mothers with their children, such as *The Bath* (1891–92).

cas·sa·va /kə saávə/ *n.* **1. TROPICAL PLANT WITH EDIBLE ROOT** a tropical plant with roots that are edible after processing. Latin name: *Manihot esculenta.* **2. EDIBLE ROOT OF PLANT** the root of the cassava plant, a large thick-skinned tuber like the potato when boiled, that is eaten in many tropical countries and is the source of tapioca. It is poisonous when raw and untreated. [Mid-16thC. From Taino *casávi.*]

Cas·se·grain·ian tel·e·scope /kassə gràynee ən-/ *n.* an astronomical telescope that uses a large concave mirror and a small convex mirror to form an image [Late 19thC. Named for its inventor, the French astronomer Giovanni *Cassegrain* (1625–1712).]

cas·se·role /kássə rōl/ *n.* **1. COOKED DISH** a stew or other moist food dish, cooked slowly at a low heat in a covered pot or dish **2. COOKING POT** a deep, heavy cooking pot suitable for use in an oven **3.** SCI **LABORATORY CONTAINER** a porcelain container used for heating substances in a laboratory ■ *vt.* (**-roled, -rol·ing, -roles**) **COOK FOOD IN LIQUID** to cook food slowly at a low heat with liquid in a covered pot [Early 18thC. From French, literally "small pan," from *casse* "pan," from, ultimately, Greek *kuathos* "cup."]

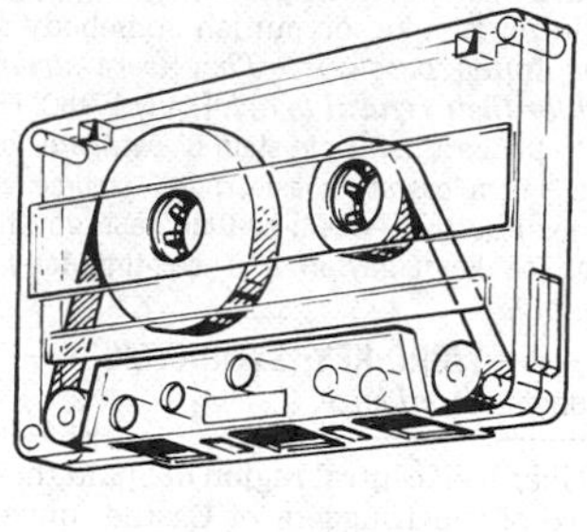

Cassette

cas·sette /kə sét/ *n.* **1. CASE CONTAINING MAGNETIC TAPE** a sealed plastic case containing a length of audio or video tape wound around spools ready for use **2. SEALED PLASTIC CASE** a sealed plastic case containing material for use in a machine, e.g., photographic film or ribbon for a printer [Late 18thC. From French, literally "small box," from *casse* (see CASH[1]).]

cas·sette deck *n.* a tape deck that plays or records audio cassettes

cas·sette play·er *n.* a machine that plays cassettes, but does not record audio

cas·sette re·cord·er *n.* a machine, especially a portable one, that plays and records audio cassettes

cas·sia /káshə/ *n.* **1. TREE WITH SCENTED BARK** an evergreen Asian tree with an aromatic bark. Latin name: *Cinnamomum aromaticum.* **2. AROMATIC BARK** the bark of the cassia tree [Pre-12thC. Via Latin from, ultimately, Hebrew *qĕṣī'āh.*]

cas·si·mere /kázzə meèr, kássə meèr/, **cas·i·mere** *n.* a plain or twill woolen fabric used for making suits [Mid-18thC. Alteration of CASHMERE.]

Cas·si·ni di·vi·sion /kə seéni di vìzh'n, kaa seéni di vìzh'n/, **Cas·si·ni's di·vi·sion** *n.* the dark area between the two brightest rings, the middle and outermost, of Saturn [Early 20thC. Named for its discoverer Giovanni Domenico *Cassini* (1625–1712), Italian-born French astronomer.]

cas·si·no *n.* = **casino** *n.* 2

Cas·si·o·pe·ia /kàssee ə peé ə/ *n.* a constellation shaped like the letter "W" in the sky of the northern hemisphere near Polaris

cas·sis /kə seéss, ka seéss/ *n.* a syrupy, usually alcoholic, cordial made in France from black currants, often mixed with white wine to make kir [Late 19thC. Via French, "black currant," from, probably, Latin *cassia* CASSIA.]

cas·sit·er·ite /kə síttə rìt/ *n.* a dark-colored mineral found in igneous rocks that is an important ore of tin. Formula: SnO_2. [Mid-19thC. Coined from Greek *kassiteros* "tin" + -ITE.]

cas·sock /kássək/ *n.* a full-length, usually black, robe worn by priests, their assistants, and singers in church choirs [Mid-16thC. Via French *casaque* "long coat" from Italian *casacca* "riding coat," perhaps from, ultimately, Turkic *kazak* "vagabond, adventurer" (source of English *Cossack*).] —**cas·socked** *adj.*

cas·sou·let /kàssə láy/ *n.* a French stew consisting of white beans cooked in a casserole with pork, ham, sausage, or other meats and topped with a browned crust of breadcrumbs [Mid-20thC. From French, literally "small stew pan, tureen," from, ultimately, Greek *kuathos* "cup, ladle" (source of English *casserole*).]

cas·so·war·y /kássoo èrree/ (*plural* **-ies**) *n.* a large black flightless bird of northeastern Australia and New Guinea that resembles an ostrich or emu. It has colorful wattles and a large bony head shield. Genus: *Casuarius.* [Early 17thC. From Malay *kesuari.*]

cast /kast/ *v.* (**cast, cast·ing, casts**) **1.** *vt.* **THROW SOMETHING OR SOMEBODY** to throw something or somebody, especially something that or somebody who is light in weight **2.** *vt.* **THROW SOMETHING ASHORE** to throw something up on the seashore ○ *pieces of driftwood that had been cast up by the incoming tide* **3.** *vt.* **FLING SOMETHING DOWN OR AWAY** to throw something away from yourself, usually with force **4.** *vt.* ANGLING **THROW BAIT, HOOK, OR LINE** to throw a line, baited hook, or fishing net into the water **5.** *vt.* **CAUSE SOMETHING TO APPEAR SOMEWHERE** to make something, e.g., light or shadow, appear in a place ○ *The bulb cast an eerie green glow over everything.* **6.** *vt.* **HAVE DISPIRITING EFFECT** to introduce something that reduces the enthusiasm, joy, or happiness of somebody or something ○ *Her mother's absence cast a shadow over the wedding plans.* **7.** *vt.* **CREATE MISTRUST** to generate a sense of uncertainty, distrust, or suspicion about something ○ *an accident that has cast doubt over the whole future of the project* **8.** *vt.* **DIRECT A LOOK** to direct the eyes or a look toward somebody or something, often in a surreptitious, disapproving, or anxious manner ○ *casting a discreet glance at his watch* **9.** *vt.* **DISMISS SOMETHING FROM THE MIND** to remove or banish something from your mind deliberately, decisively, and often with difficulty (*formal*) **10.** *vt.* **PUT SOMEBODY SOMEWHERE ROUGHLY** to put or throw somebody or something somewhere, especially in a rough or brutal way (*formal*) ○ *cast into the dungeon* **11.** *vti.* ARTS **SELECT PARTICIPANTS FOR PERFORMANCE** to choose somebody for a particular role in a drama, dance, or other performance, or choose people for all the roles in a production ○ *He was badly cast as Othello.* **12.** *vt.* **DESCRIBE SOMEBODY** to classify or describe somebody in a particular way ○ *I seem to have been cast as the villain in this affair.* **13.** *vt.* MANUF **FORM SOMETHING USING MOLD** to pour something such as molten metal or plaster into a mold and allow it to solidify, or make an object in this way **14.** *vt.* **SHED SOMETHING** to shed something, e.g., a skin ○ *a snake that had cast its skin* **15.** *vt.* **DROP SOMETHING** to drop or lose something **16.** *vt.* ACCT **CALCULATE SOMETHING** to add something up or calculate something ■ *n.* **1. ACT OF THROWING** the flinging, hurling, or throwing of something, or an instance of that **2. LENGTH OF THROW** the distance that something is thrown ○ *a 20-yard cast of a harpoon* **3.** ARTS **PERFORMERS** the actors or other performers who play the parts in a drama, dance, or other production **4.** MANUF **MOLDED OBJECT** an object that is made by pouring a molten substance, especially metal, into a mold and leaving it to solidify so that it takes on the shape of the mold **5.** MANUF **MOLD** a container of a particular shape into which a molten substance, especially metal, is poured and left to solidify **6.** MED **SUPPORT FOR BROKEN BONE** a stiff casing made from plaster of Paris or fiberglass that is used to hold a broken bone in place while it is healing ○ *He came back with his leg in a cast.* ◊ **plaster cast** **7.** MANUF, ARTS **MOLTEN IMPRESSION** an impression formed by pressing soft or molten material over or inside something and letting it harden or dry ○ *a cast of the pianist's hands* **8.** GEOL, PALEONT **PRESERVED SEDIMENT** preserved sediment made by the infilling of an impression such as a footprint **9. EMOTIONAL OR PSYCHOLOGICAL TYPE** the nature or quality of somebody's character or mind **10. PHYSICAL TYPE** the nature or quality of somebody's appearance ○ *I did not trust the sly cast of his face.* **11. STRABISMUS** a defect that causes one eye to look permanently sideways **12. OVERSPREADING OF ONE THING ONTO ANOTHER** the overspreading of something, especially an added color, that results in modification of the hue or general appearance of something else **13. TINGE** a general suggestion of something, e.g., a color ○ *The mud gave a brown cast to the water.* **14.** ANGLING **THROW OF LINE OR NET** the throwing of a fishing line or net into the water **15.** ANGLING **THROWN LINE OR NET** a fishing line or net that is thrown into the water **16.** GAMBLING, GAME **DICE THROW** a throw of a die, or the number that has been thrown **17.** BIOL **SOMETHING SHED BY ORGANISM** a part of an organism, e.g., an insect casing, a snake skin, or worm feces, that has been shed in a natural recurring process [12thC. From Old Norse *kasta* "to throw," of unknown origin. The theatrical senses are 17th-century developments, apparently based on the earlier meanings "a plan, design" and "to arrange, shape."] —**cas·ta·bil·i·ty** /kàstə bíllətee/ *n.* —**cast·a·ble** /kástəb'l/ *adj.*

cast around, cast a·bout *vi.* to search for something or try to devise a solution to a problem

cast aside *vt.* **1. ABANDON SOMEBODY OR SOMETHING** to reject and abandon somebody or something regarded as no longer interesting or useful ○ *You can't just cast him aside like that!* **2.** REJECT THOUGHT to abandon something, e.g., a feeling or belief (*formal*) ○ *You must cast your doubts aside and trust in me.*

cast off *v.* **1.** *vt.* GET RID OF SOMEBODY OR SOMETHING to reject or abandon something or somebody regarded as no longer useful or attractive ○ *cast off that old coat years ago.* **2.** *vti.* NAUT UNTIE MOORING LINES to untie the ropes securing a boat to its mooring so that it can move away **3.** *vti.* FINISH KNITTING to make the last row of stitches in a piece of knitting by looping each stitch over the next and removing it from the needle **4.** *vti.* PUBL FIT TEXT to calculate the amount of space a piece of text will take up when it has been typeset

cast on *vti.* to make the first row of stitches in a piece of knitting

cast out *vt.* to reject, abandon, or eject somebody or something (*formal*)

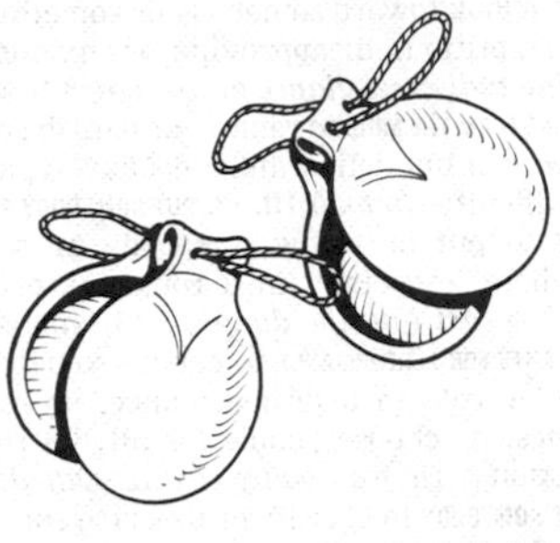

Castanet

cas·ta·net /kàstə nét/ *n.* either of a pair of small curved pieces of hard wood or plastic that are joined at the top and used to make a rhythmic clicking sound. They are held in the palm of the hand and tapped together, traditionally by Spanish flamenco dancers and musicians. [Early 17thC. From Spanish *castañeta*, literally "small chestnut," from *castaña* "chestnut" from Latin *castanea* (source of English *chestnut*); from their likeness to chestnut shells.]

cast·a·way /kástə wày/ *n.* SHIPWRECKED PERSON somebody who has been shipwrecked ■ *adj.* SHIPWRECKED shipwrecked or set adrift

caste /kast/ *n.* **1.** SOC SCI HINDU SOCIAL CLASS any of the four main hereditary classes (**varnas**) into which Hindu society is divided and that dictate the social position and status of people according to their professions **2.** SOC SCI HINDU CLASS SYSTEM the Hindu system of organizing society into hereditary classes **3.** SOC SCI CLASS SYSTEM any system that divides people into classes according to their rank, wealth, or profession, or that of the family into which they were born **4.** SOCIAL CLASS the class and rank or position of somebody in a society, based on birth, occupation, or some other criterion **5.** INSECTS INSECT RANK a rank within a colony or hive of social insects such as ants or bees. Members of a caste have a specialized role, e.g., as a soldier or worker. [Mid-16thC. Via Spanish and Portuguese *casta* "unmixed, pure race" from Latin *castus* "pure, chaste" (source of English *chaste* and *incest*), the underlying idea being "racial purity."]

Cas·tel Gan·dol·fo village in Rome province, Lazio Region, just south of Rome, Italy. It contains a palace that is the summer residence of the pope. Population: 6,952 (1993).

cas·tel·lan /kástələn/ *n.* in former times, somebody who governed or managed a castle [14thC. Via Old Northern French *castelain* from medieval Latin *castellanus*, from Latin *castellum* (see CASTLE).]

cas·tel·lat·ed /kástə làytəd/ *adj.* **1.** ARCHIT WITH BATTLEMENTS OR SERRATED TOP EDGE with battlements or a serrated top edge like the walls of a castle **2.** INDENTED OR SERRATED LIKE BATTLEMENTS with indented or serrated edges resembling the top of a castle wall ○ *an ornate tablecloth with a castellated edge* **3.** WITH CASTLE OR CASTLES with a castle or castles as part of the surroundings or landscape (*literary*) ○ *the castellated French countryside* [Late 17thC. Formed from medieval Latin *castellatus* "having a castle," from Latin *castellum* (see CASTLE).]

Cas·tel·o Bran·co /kə stèllō brángkō/, **Humberto** (1900–67) Brazilian soldier and statesman. He established himself as dictator of Brazil (1964) until his death.

caste mark *n.* a mark, usually a painted dot on the forehead, that shows a Hindu person's caste

cast·er /kástər/ *n.* **1.** SOMEBODY WHO CASTS somebody or something that casts something else **2. cast·er, cas·tor** COOK SMALL CONDIMENT CONTAINER a small container with a perforated top or open mouth for sprinkling sugar, salt, or other condiments **3. cast·er, cas·tor** FURNITURE SMALL WHEEL UNDER FURNITURE a small wheel on a mount that allows it to turn in all directions, attached under the corners of furniture and other heavy objects to make them easier to move **4. cast·er, cas·tor** COOK CONDIMENT STAND a small stand that holds condiment containers

cas·ti·gate /kásti gàyt/ (**-gat·ed, -gat·ing, -gates**) *vt.* to criticize, rebuke, or punish somebody severely (*formal*) (*often passive*) ○ *They were strongly castigated for their refusal to act.* [Early 17thC. From Latin *castigat-*, the past participle stem of *castigare* "to correct, chastise," from *castus* "chaste, pure" (source of English *chaste* and *incest*).] —**cas·ti·ga·tion** /kàsti gáysh'n/ *n.* —**cas·ti·ga·tor** /kásti gàytər/ *n.* —**cas·ti·ga·tor·y** /kástigə tàwree/ *adj.*

WORD KEY: SYNONYMS

See Synonyms at ***criticize***.

Cas·tile /kaz teél/ central region of Spain that formed the core of the Kingdom of Castile, under which Spain was united in the 15th and 16th centuries

Cas·tile soap *n.* a type of hard white unperfumed soap made from olive oil and lye [Named for CASTILE, where it was first made]

Cas·til·ian /ka stíllyən/, **Cas·til·lian** *n.* **1.** LANG SPANISH DIALECT the dialect of the Spanish language that is spoken in the province of Castile **2.** LANG SPANISH LANGUAGE official, standard, and literary Spanish, based on the dialect spoken in the province of Castile **3.** PEOPLES SOMEBODY FROM CASTILE somebody who lives or was born or raised in the province of Castile in Spain —**Cas·til·ian** *adj.*

Cas·til·la /kə stíllə/, **Ramón** (1797–1867) Peruvian army officer and statesman. He was the president of Peru (1845–51 and 1855–62) and abolished slavery in his country.

cast·ing /kásting/ *n.* **1.** MANUF, ARTS MAKING OF OBJECTS USING MOLDS the making of a solid object by pouring molten metal, glass, or plastic into a mold and allowing it to cool **2.** MANUF, ARTS OBJECT MADE WITH MOLD an object made using a mold **3.** ANGLING THROW OF FISHING LINE the throwing out of a fishing line or net **4.** SOMETHING THROWN something that is thrown out or thrown off **5.** ARTS SELECTION PROCESS FOR PERFORMERS the choosing of actors or other performers for a drama, dance, or other production, usually by audition, interview, or screen test **6.** ARTS CHOICE OF PERFORMERS the choice of actors or other performers for roles in a drama, dance, or other production ○ *The script was very sharp but the casting was terrible.*

cast·ing couch *n.* the granting of usually sexual favors in return for work in a film, television, or other production (*informal*) [From the idea of the sexual activity taking place on a couch in the office of somebody with power over casting]

cast·ing vote *n.* the deciding vote in a ballot or debate, cast by the chairperson or presiding officer when votes for and against something are equally divided

cast i·ron *n.* iron with a high carbon content, making it hard but brittle, so that it must be shaped by casting rather than hammering or beating

cast-i·ron *adj.* **1.** METALL OF CAST IRON made from cast iron **2.** VERY STRONG extremely strong or resistant **3.** ALLOWING NO CHANGE not permitting any alteration of its terms ○ *a cast-iron agreement*

cas·tle /káss'l/ *n.* **1.** ARCHIT FORTRESS a large fortified building or complex of buildings, usually with tall solid walls, battlements, and a permanent garrison, built especially during the Middle Ages **2.** ARCHIT MANOR HOUSE a large magnificent house built, especially in the 18th and 19th centuries, to resemble the fortified castles of the past **3.** PRIVATE REFUGE the building, property, or place to which somebody, especially the owner, turns for privacy or refuge **4.** CHESS = **rook** ■ *vti.* (**-tled, -tling, -tles**) CHESS MOVE KING AND ROOK in chess, to move the king two squares to the left or right and move the nearest rook over the king to the adjacent square on the opposite side [Pre-12thC. From Latin *castellum* "fortified village" (source of English *castellated* and *chateau*), from *castrum* "fortified place." Later reborrowed from Anglo-Norman *castel* "fortress" (also from Latin *castellum*).] ◇ **build castles in the air** to have dreams or plans that are extremely unlikely to succeed or be realized

Cas·tle /káss'l/, **Irene Foote** (1893–1969) U.S. dancer. She and her husband, Vernon Castle, were innovators in ballroom dance.

cas·tled /káss'ld/ *adj.* ARCHIT = **castellated** *adj.* 1

Cast·le Peak 1. mountain in the Sierra Nevada range, eastern Fresno County, central California. Height: 10,668 ft./3,252 m. **2.** mountain in Gunnison and Pitkin counties, central Colorado. Height: 14,265 ft./4,348 m. **3.** mountain in southwestern Custer County, central Idaho. Height: 11,820 ft./3,603 m.

cast·off /kást ɔ̀f, kást àwf/ *n.* **1.** REJECTED THING OR PERSON something that or somebody who has been rejected or abandoned because no longer considered useful or attractive (*often used in the plural*) ○ *I don't want your old castoffs!* **2.** PUBL CALCULATION OF TEXT LENGTH a calculation of the length of a piece of text made before fitting copy into available space

cas·tor /kástər/ *n.* **1.** INDUST BEAVER OIL a brown oily aromatic substance secreted from glands in a beaver's groin and used in medicine and perfumes **2.** INDUST BEAVER FUR the fur of a beaver **3.** CLOTHES BEAVER HAT a hat made of beaver fur or imitation beaver fur **4.** TEXTILES HEAVY FABRIC a heavy cloth made of wool [14thC. Via French or Latin from Greek *kastōr* "beaver."]

Cas·tor /kástər/ *n.* **1.** ASTRON BRIGHT STAR IN CONSTELLATION GEMINI the second brightest star in the constellation Gemini **2.** MYTHOL ➧ **Castor and Pollux**

Cas·tor and Pol·lux *npl.* in classical mythology, the twin sons of Leda and the brothers of Helen of Troy and Clytemnestra

cas·tor bean *n.* **1.** = **castor-oil plant 2.** CASTOR-OIL PLANT SEED the poisonous seed of the castor-oil plant, from which castor oil is produced

cas·tor oil *n.* a thin yellowish oil obtained from the seeds of the castor-oil plant, used medicinally as a laxative and industrially as a lubricant [*Castor* of uncertain origin: perhaps the same word as CASTOR, possibly because the oil has medical properties and a bitter taste similar to that of the beaver's secretion]

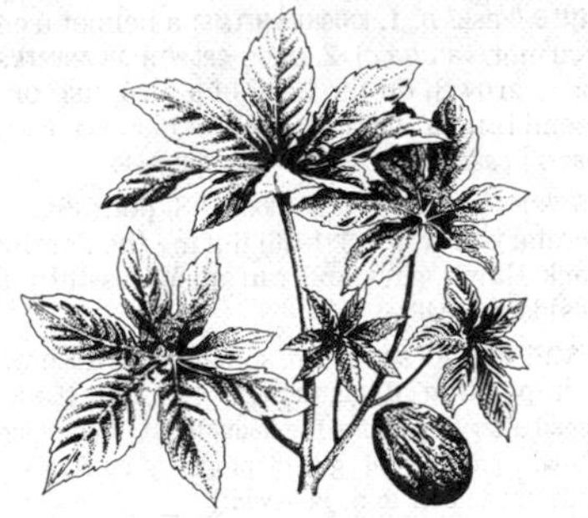

Castor-oil plant

cas·tor-oil plant *n.* a tall tropical plant with large lobed leaves that is cultivated for ornament and for its seeds, from which castor oil is produced. Latin name: *Ricinus communis.*

cas·tra·men·ta·tion /kàstrəmə táysh'n/ *n.* the creation and laying out of a military encampment [Late 17thC. From French *castramétation*, from Latin *castra metari* "to measure or mark out a camp."]

cas·trate /ká stràyt/ (**-trat·ed, -trat·ing, -trates**) *vt.* **1.** VET, MED REMOVE TESTICLES FROM MALE to remove the testicles of a man or male animal, making reproduction impossible. Animals are sometimes castrated to make them more docile and to prevent disease. **2.** WEAKEN SOMEBODY OR SOMETHING to take away the strength, power, force, or vigor of somebody or something ○ *The department was castrated through heavy budget cuts.* **3.** VET, MED REMOVE OVARIES FROM FEMALE to remove the ovaries of a woman or female animal, making reproduction impossible [15thC. From Latin *castrat-*, the past participle stem of *castrare* "to cut off, castrate," from, perhaps, assumed *castrum* "knife."] —**cas·trat·er** *n.* —**cas·tra·tion** /ka stráysh'n/ *n.*

ca·stra·to /ka straátō, kə-/ (*plural* **cas·tra·ti** /-tee/ *or* **cas·tra·tos**) *n.* a male singer who was castrated before puberty in order to retain a soprano or alto voice, a practice that ceased when it became illegal in the 19th century [Mid-18thC. From Italian, literally "castrated one," from the past participle of Latin *castrare* (see CASTRATE).]

Cas·tries /kaá streéz, -ss/ capital city of St. Lucia in the West Indies. Population: 11,147 (1991).

Cas·tro /kástrō/, **Cipriano** (1858–1924) Venezuelan military leader. He served as president after a coup until he himself was deposed (1899–1908).

Popperfoto

Fidel Castro

Cas·tro, Fidel (*b.* 1926) Cuban statesman. He led the revolution that overthrew Fulgencio Batista and headed a Communist government as prime minister (1959–76) and president (from 1976).

Cas·tro·ism /kástrō ìzzəm/ *n.* the Communist political, social, and economic policies of Fidel Castro and his supporters [Mid-20thC. Named for Fidel CASTRO.] —**Cas·tro·ist** *n., adj.* —**Cas·tro·ite** *n., adj.*

Cas·tro Val·ley town in Alameda County, western California, situated north of Hayward. Population: 48,619 (1990).

ca·su·al /kázhoo əl/ *adj.* **1. CHANCE OR UNPREMEDITATED** happening or done by chance or without prior thought or planning **2. OCCASIONAL OR TEMPORARY** relating to or taking on work that is available at irregular intervals or seasonally, with no security, benefits, or prospects of permanent employment **3. KNOWN ONLY SLIGHTLY** relating to somebody or something known only slightly ○ *a casual acquaintance whom I had met at work* **4. SUPERFICIAL** not involving emotional commitment or promises of loyalty, or lacking in thoroughness or seriousness **5. LENIENT** possessing a permissive or lenient approach to things ○ *very casual about enforcing the rules* **6. INDIFFERENT** showing little interest or enthusiasm **7. NONCHALANT** cool, calm, or nonchalant in manner **8. NOT FORMAL** informal and relaxed **9.** CLOTHES **COMFORTABLE** comfortable and suitable for wearing on informal occasions **10.** BIOL = **adventive** ■ *n.* **1. TEMPORARY WORKER** somebody who is employed on a temporary or seasonal basis to do a job **2.** MIL **SOLDIER ON TEMPORARY ASSIGNMENT** a soldier who is temporarily attached to a unit while waiting to be assigned to a permanent unit **3.** BIOL = **adventive** [14thC. Directly or via French *casuel* from Latin *casualis*, from *casus* "chance, event, accident" (source of English *case* and *casuist*).] —**ca·su·al·ly** *adv.* —**ca·su·al·ness** *n.*

ca·su·al·ty /kázhoo əltee/ (*plural* **-ties**) *n.* **1. ACCIDENT VICTIM** somebody who is seriously injured or killed in an accident **2.** MIL **INJURED OR DEAD SOLDIER** a member of the armed forces who is killed or injured during combat **3. VICTIM** something or somebody destroyed or suffering as an indirect result of a particular event or circumstances **4.** *U.K.* = **emergency room** (*informal*) (*often used before a noun*) ○ *rushed to casualty with multiple fractures* [15thC. Alteration (on the model of words like PENALTY) of medieval Latin *casualitas* "chance," from *casualis* (see CASUAL); the underlying idea is "somebody killed by accident."]

ca·su·a·ri·na /kàzhoo ə reénə, kàzhoo ə rīnə/ (*plural* **-nas** *or* **-na**) *n.* a tree found mainly in Australia and some parts of Asia with needle-shaped leaves that form whorls at the end of short branches. Genus: *Casuarina.* [Late 18thC. From modern Latin, formed from *casuarius* "cassowary" from the similarity of its branches to the bird's feathers.]

ca·su·ist /kázhoo ist/ *n.* **1.** PHILOS, RELIG **SOMEBODY CONSIDERING ETHICS AND MORALS** somebody, especially a theologian, who tries to settle questions of ethics and morals by applying general rules and principles to them **2. SOMEBODY USING MISLEADINGLY SUBTLE REASONING** somebody who uses subtle and sophisticated reasoning, especially on moral issues, in order to justify something or to mislead somebody (*disapproving*) [Early 17thC. Via French from, ultimately, modern Latin, formed from Latin *casus* "chance, event" (source of English *case* and *casual*).] —**ca·su·is·tic** /kàzhoo ístik/ *adj.* —**ca·su·is·ti·cal** *adj.* —**ca·su·is·ti·cal·ly** *adv.*

ca·su·ist·ry /kázhoo istree/ *n.* **1.** PHILOS, RELIG **APPLICATION OF PRINCIPLES TO MORAL QUESTIONS** the application of general rules and principles to questions of ethics and morals in order to resolve them **2. MISLEADINGLY SUBTLE REASONING** the use of sophisticated and subtle argument and reasoning, especially on moral issues, in order to justify something or mislead somebody (*disapproving*)

ca·sus bel·li /kàssəss béllī, káyssəss bé lī/ (*plural* **ca·sus bel·li**) *n.* a situation or event that causes, or is the pretext for starting, a war or other conflict (*formal*) [From modern Latin, literally "occasion of war"]

cat /kat/ *n.* **1.** ZOOL **FURRY ANIMAL THAT PURRS AND MEOWS** a small domesticated mammal that has soft fur, sharp claws, pointed ears, and, usually, a long furry tail. Cats are widely kept as pets or to catch mice. Latin name: *Felis catus.* **2.** ZOOL = **big cat 3. BAD-TEMPERED WOMAN** a spiteful or malicious woman (*informal insult*) **4. MAN** a man (*dated slang*) ○ *He's a real cool cat.* **5.** MUSIC **JAZZ PLAYER** a musician who plays jazz (*dated slang*) **6.** NAUT **ANCHOR TACKLE OR CATHEAD** a set of heavy tackle used for raising an anchor to the cathead, or the cathead itself **7.** = **cat-o'-nine-tails 8.** ZOOL = **catfish 9.** SAILING **CATAMARAN** a catamaran (*informal*) **10.** SAILING **CATBOAT** a catboat (*informal*) **11.** AUTOMOT **CATALYTIC CONVERTER** a catalytic converter (*informal*) ■ *v.* (**cat·ted, cat·ting, cats**) **1.** *vt.* NAUT **RAISE ANCHOR** to raise the anchor to the cathead **2.** *vi.* **SEARCH FOR PARTNER** to travel or wander around in search of a sexual partner (*slang*) [Old English *catt, catte*, from prehistoric Germanic, perhaps ultimately from Egyptian; later reinforced by Anglo-Norman *cat* (probably ultimately from the same ancestor)] ◇ **be raining cats and dogs** to be raining very heavily ◇ **has the cat got your tongue?** used, often to a child, to prompt somebody to speak and to ask the reason for his or her silence ◇ **let the cat out of the bag** to disclose secret or confidential information ◇ **like a cat on a hot tin roof** *or* **hot bricks** extremely nervous or agitated ◇ **play cat and mouse with somebody** to treat somebody who is in your power in such a way that he or she does not know what you are going to do next ◇ **think that you are the cat's pajamas** *or* **whiskers** to have an extremely high opinion of yourself ◇ **when the cat's away the mice will play** when somebody in authority is absent, those he or she is in charge of will misbehave

CAT *abbr.* **1.** AIR clear-air turbulence **2.** MED computerized axial tomography **3.** STOCK EXCH computer-aided trading

cat. *abbr.* catalog

cata- *prefix.* down, apart ○ *catabolism* ○ *catalysis* [From Greek *kata* "down, back, apart"]

ca·tab·o·lism /kə tábbə lìzzəm/ *n.* a metabolic process in which energy is released through the conversion of complex molecules into simpler ones [Late 19thC. Formed (probably on the model of METABOLISM) from Greek *katabolē* "throwing down," from *ballein* "to throw."] —**cat·a·bol·ic** /kàttə bóllik/ *adj.* —**cat·a·bol·i·cal·ly** *adv.*

ca·tab·o·lite /kə tábbə līt/ *n.* a product of catabolism, especially a waste product

cat·a·chre·sis /kàttə kreéssiss/ (*plural* **-ses** /-seéz/) *n.* the incorrect use of words, e.g., by mixing metaphors or applying terminology wrongly [Mid-16thC. Via Latin from Greek *katakhrēsis*, from *katakhrēsthai* "to misuse."] —**cat·a·chres·tic** /kàttə kréstik/ *adj.* —**cat·a·chres·ti·cal** *adj.* —**cat·a·chres·ti·cal·ly** /-ikəlee/ *adv.*

cat·a·clysm /káttə klìzzəm/ *n.* **1. DISASTER** a sudden and violent upheaval or disaster that causes great changes in society, e.g., a war, earthquake, or drought ○ *one of the greatest cataclysms of the 20th century* **2. FLOOD** a terrible and devastating flood [Early 17thC. Via French from, ultimately, Greek *kataklusmos* "deluge," from *kluzein* "to wash."] —**cat·a·clys·mal** /kàttə klízməl/ *adj.* —**cat·a·clys·mic** /-mik/ *adj.* —**cat·a·clys·mi·cal·ly** /-mikəlee/ *adv.*

cat·a·comb /káttə kōm/ *n.* (*often used in the plural*) **1. UNDERGROUND CEMETERY** an underground cemetery consisting of passages or tunnels with rooms and recesses leading off them for burial chambers. In ancient Rome, Christians used catacombs for burial. **2. NETWORK OF TUNNELS BELOW GROUND** any underground network of passages or tunnels [Pre-12thC. Via Old French from late Latin *catacumbas*, the name of the subterranean cemetery of St. Sebastian in Rome, which reputedly housed the bodies of St. Peter and St. Paul.]

ca·tad·ro·mous /kə táddrəməss/ *adj.* used to describe fish that spend most of their lives in fresh water but migrate to salt water to breed, as eels do. ◊ **anadromous** [Late 19thC. Coined (on the model of ANADROMOUS) from CATA- "down" + -DROMOUS "running," in reference to migration from upper to lower water.]

cat·a·falque /káttə fàlk, káttə fàwlk/ *n.* **1. PLATFORM FOR COFFIN** a raised and decorated platform on which the coffin of a distinguished person lies in state before or during a funeral **2. REPRESENTATION OF COFFIN** in the Roman Catholic Church, a structure resembling a coffin that is used to represent a dead person at a requiem mass given after the person's funeral [Mid-17thC. Via French from Italian *catafalco*, probably from assumed Vulgar Latin *catafal(i)cum* (source of English *scaffold*), perhaps formed from *cata-* "down" + *fala* "scaffolding."]

Cat·a·lan /kátt'l àn, kátt'l án/ *n.* **1.** LANG **ROMANCE LANGUAGE** the regional language of Catalonia and the Balearic Islands, Spain, also spoken in Andorra and the French region of Roussillon. It belongs to the Romance group of Indo-European languages and is spoken by about seven million people. **2.** PEOPLES **SOMEBODY FROM CATALONIA** somebody who lives in or was born or raised in the autonomous region of Catalonia, Spain —**Cat·a·lan** *adj.*

cat·a·lase /kátt'l àyss, -àyz/ *n.* an enzyme in living cells that aids the breakdown of hydrogen peroxide to oxygen and water [Early 20thC. Coined from CATALYSIS + -ASE.] —**cat·a·lat·ic** /kàtt'l áttik/ *adj.*

cat·a·lep·sy /kátt'l èpsee/ *n.* actual or apparent unconsciousness while muscles become rigid and remain in any position in which they are placed. The condition occurs naturally in diseases such as schizophrenia or epilepsy and can be induced by hypnosis or drugs. [14thC. Directly or via French from late Latin, from Greek *katalēpsis* "seizure," from *katalambanein*, literally "to seize upon," from *lambanein* "to seize."] —**cat·a·lep·tic** /kàtt'l éptik/ *adj.* —**cat·a·lep·ti·cal·ly** /-éptikəlee/ *adv.*

cat·a·lex·is /kàtt'l éksiss/ *n.* the lack of one syllable in the final foot of a line of verse [Mid-19thC. From Greek *katalēxis* "termination," from *katalēgein*, literally "to leave off," from *legein* "to cease."] —**cat·a·lec·tic** /-éktik/ *adj.*

cat·a·log /kátt'l òg/, **cat·a·logue** *n.* (*plural* **-logues**) **1.** COMM **LIST OF GOODS FOR SALE** a list of goods for sale, with prices and illustrations, presented in book form or sometimes in other formats including CD-ROM or video, and often used for mail order **2.** ARTS **EXHIBITION GUIDE** a booklet that lists and often illustrates the objects on show at an exhibition **3.** LIBRARIES **LIST OF BOOKS** a list of the books and periodicals in a library, usually arranged according to subject, title, or author **4. SERIES OF THINGS** a long list of different things or events that all relate to a particular issue or person, especially things or events that are unpleasant or undesirable ○ *a catalog of disorders* **5. A-Z CARD FILE** an alphabetical card file **6.** UNIV **COURSE LIST** a list of all the courses offered at a college or university, together with other information about the faculty or campus ■ *v.* (**-loged, -log·ing, -logs; -logued, -logu·ing, -logues**) **1.** *vti.* **MAKE A CATALOG** to classify and list items to form a catalog **2.** *vt.* **ENTER SOMETHING IN CATALOG** to enter something in a catalog ○ *I have cataloged all the new additions to the collection.* **3.** *vi.* **BE LISTED** to be listed in a catalog, especially with a price or value specified ○ *a diamond ring that catalogs at a vastly inflated price* **4.** *vt.* **LIST SERIES OF THINGS OR EVENTS** to list or describe a series of related events, items, or characteristics ○ *a history of the twentieth century that catalogs many examples of human ingenuity* [15thC. Via French from, ultimately, Greek *katalogos* "list," from *katalegein*, literally "to pick out," from *legein* "to choose."] —**cat·a·log·er** *n.*

cat·a·logue rai·son·né /kátt'l og rayzə náy, -rezzə-/ (*plural* **cat·a·logues rai·son·nés**) *n.* a detailed list of works by a particular artist, especially one produced to accompany an exhibition or collection [From French, literally "reasoned catalog"]

Cat·a·lo·nia /kàtt'l ṓnyə/ autonomous region in northeastern Spain. It contains the provinces of Barcelona, Girona, Lléida, and Tarragona. Capital: Barcelona. Population: 6,226,869 (1995). Area: 12,328 sq. mi./31,930 sq. km. Catalan **Catalunya**. Spanish **Cataluña** —**Cat·al·o·nian** *adj., n.*

ca·tal·y·sis /kə tálləssiss/ (*plural* **-ses** /-seez/) *n.* the increase in the rate of a chemical reaction by the introduction of a catalyst [Mid-17thC. Via modern Latin, "dissolution" (the original sense in English), from Greek *katalusis*, from *kataluein* "to dissolve," from *luein* "to set free."]

cat·a·lyst /kátt'list/ *n.* **1.** CHEM **CHEMICAL THAT ACCELERATES CHEMICAL REACTION** a substance that increases the rate of a chemical reaction without itself undergoing any change **2. STIMULUS TO CHANGE** somebody or something that makes a change happen or brings about an event ○ *The quarrel acted as a catalyst for the breakup of their partnership.* [Early 20thC. Formed from CATALYSIS, on the model of ANALYST.]

cat·a·lyt·ic /kàtt'l íttik/ *adj.* involving or causing an increase in the rate of a chemical reaction by the use of a catalyst [Mid-19thC. From Greek *katalutikos* "able to dissolve," from *katalusis* (see CATALYSIS).] —**cat·a·lyt·i·cal·ly** *adv.*

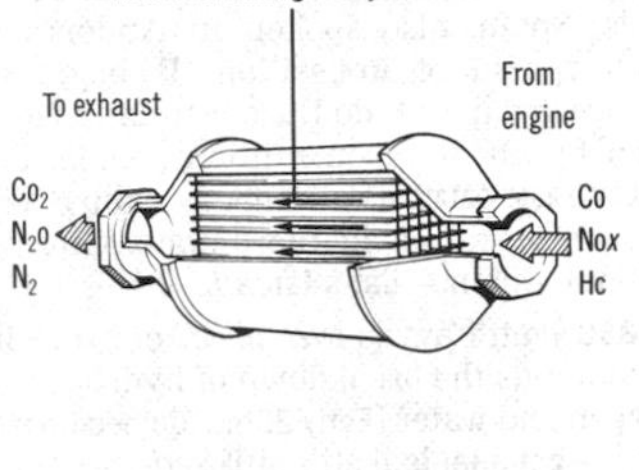

Catalytic converter

cat·a·lyt·ic con·vert·er *n.* in the exhaust system of a motor vehicle, a chamber in which gases mix with air so that pollutants such as carbon monoxide can be oxidized. The chamber contains a platinum-iridium catalyst.

cat·a·lyt·ic crack·er *n.* an oil-refinery device that breaks down large molecules from crude oil into smaller ones that are useful as fuel, using heat and a catalyst to lower the required temperature

cat·a·lyze /kátt'l ìz/ (**-lyzed, -lyz·ing, -lyz·es**) *vt.* **1.** CHEM **INCREASE CHEMICAL REACTION RATE** to increase the rate of a chemical reaction by the action or use of a catalyst **2. BRING SOMETHING ABOUT** to cause a particular thing to happen or bring about a particular state of affairs ○ *The hearings have catalyzed the passage of financial reforms.* **3. TRANSFORM SOMETHING** to cause something to undergo basic change ○ *Passage of the new anticrime bill has catalyzed local law-enforcement.* [Late 19thC. Formed from CATALYSIS, on the model of ANALYZE.] —**cat·a·lyz·er** *n.*

cat·a·ma·ran /kàttəmə rán/ *n.* **1. DOUBLE-HULLED CRAFT** a sailboat or engine-powered boat that has two identical hulls fixed together by a rigid framework **2. LOG RAFT** a simple raft made from logs or floats tied together [Early 17thC. From Tamil *kaṭṭumaram*, literally "tied wood."]

cat·a·mite /káttə mìt/ *n.* a boy or youth with whom a man has homosexual intercourse (*literary*) [Late 16thC. Via Latin *catamitus* from Greek *Ganumēdēs* GANYMEDE, a handsome youth in Greek mythology.]

cat·a·mount /káttə mòwnt/, **cat·a·moun·tain** /kàttə mównt'n/ *n.* = **mountain lion** [Mid-17thC. From *cat of the mountain*.]

cat and mouse *n.* the game of ticktacktoe (*regional*) (*takes a singular verb*) [From German *Katz und Maus*]

cat-and-mouse *adj.* cruel or sadistic, especially in exploiting, compounding, and enjoying somebody else's suffering or fear

ca·taph·o·ra /kə táffərə/ *n.* the use of a word or phrase, usually a pronoun, that refers to something mentioned later, as does "it" in "It's easy to make mistakes" [Late 20thC. Coined from CATA- + ANAPHORA.] —**cat·a·phor·ic** /kàttə fáwrik/ *adj.*

cat·a·pho·re·sis /kàttəfə reéssiss/ (*plural* **-ses** /-seez/) *n.* = **electrophoresis** [Late 19thC. Coined from CATA- + Greek *phorēsis* "being carried."] —**cat·a·pho·ret·ic** /kàttəfə réttik/ *adj.* —**cat·a·pho·ret·i·cal·ly** /-réttikəlee/ *adv.*

cat·a·pla·sia /kàttə pláyzhə, -zhee ə/ *n.* the degeneration of cells or tissue to a more primitive or embryonic form —**cat·a·plas·tic** /-plástik/ *adj.*

cat·a·plasm /káttə plàzzəm/ *n.* a poultice (*archaic*) [Mid-16thC. Via French *cataplasme* from, ultimately, Greek *kataplasma*, from *kataplassein*, literally "to plaster over," from *plassein* "to plaster, mold."]

cat·a·plex·y /káttə plèksee/ *n.* sudden temporary paralysis caused by shock, fear, or ecstasy [Late 19thC. Formed from Greek *kataplēxis* "stupefaction," from *kataplēssein*, literally "to strike down," from *plēssein* "to strike."] —**cat·a·plec·tic** /kàttə pléktik/ *adj.*

cat·a·pult /káttə pùlt, káttə pŏŏlt/ *n.* **1.** ARMS, HIST **MEDIEVAL LAUNCHING WEAPON** a large heavy war machine consisting of a wooden frame and a throwing device operated by levers, used in medieval times to hurl large stones at an enemy **2.** MIL **PLANE OR MISSILE LAUNCHER** a launching mechanism on an aircraft carrier or warship, used to propel planes or missiles at a speed sufficient for them to take off **3.** *U.K.* = **slingshot** ■ *v.* (**-pult·ed, -pult·ing, -pults**) **1.** *vt.* **HURL SOMETHING** to throw something with great force from a catapult (*often passive*) ○ *The fighters were catapulted from the carrier at 30-second intervals.* **2.** *vti.* **FLING OR BE FLUNG** to throw somebody or something violently into the air by collision, impact, or a force that has an effect like a catapult, or be thrown in this way ○ *They were catapulted out of their seats by the force of the impact.* **3.** *vt.* **MAKE SOMEBODY FAMOUS SUDDENLY** to thrust somebody unexpectedly and suddenly into a particular situation ○ *the hit that catapulted her to fame at the tender age of fifteen* [Late 16thC. Directly or via French from Latin *catapulta*, from Greek *katapeltēs*, from, ultimately, *pallein* "to hurl."]

cat·a·ract /káttə ràkt/ *n.* **1.** OPHTHALMOL **EYE DISEASE** an eye disease in which the lens becomes covered in an opaque film that affects sight, eventually causing total blindness. The condition usually affects older people and is generally found in both eyes to varying degrees. It can be treated surgically by replacing the lens with an artificial implant. **2.** OPHTHALMOL **FILM OVER EYE LENS** the lens of the eye or the membrane surrounding it (**capsule**) that has become opaque as a result of disease **3.** GEOG **WATERFALL** a series of river rapids and small waterfalls with only moderate vertical drop (*literary*) **4. FLOOD** a heavy downpour of rain or a great flood (*literary*) ○ *Spring cataracts have flooded the low-lying farmlands.* [15thC. Via Latin *cataracta* "waterfall, portcullis" (hence, "something that obstructs"), from Greek *kataraktēs* "down-dashing," from *katarassein*, literally "to dash down," from *arassein* "to strike."]

ca·tarrh /kə taár/ *n.* inflammation of a mucous membrane, especially in the nose and throat, causing an increase in the production of mucus, as happens in the common cold [15thC. Via French *catarrhe* from, ultimately, Greek *katarrhous*, from *katarrhein*, literally "to flow down," from *rhein* "to flow" (see RHEUM).] —**ca·tarrh·al** *adj.* —**ca·tarrh·ous** *adj.*

ca·tarrh·ine /káttə rìn/ *adj.* **WITH CLOSELY-SET NOSTRILS** used to describe animals that have nostrils set close together and directed downward. Humans, apes, and some monkeys are catarrhine. ■ *n.* **PRIMATE WITH CLOSELY-SET NOSTRILS** an animal with a catarrhine nose structure, e.g., a human or ape. Suborder: Catarrhini. [Mid-19thC. Coined from CATA- + Greek *rhinos* "nose" (see RHINO-).]

ca·tas·ta·sis /kə tástəssiss/ *n.* the intense part of the action in a classical tragedy, immediately preceding the tragic climax [Mid-16thC. From Greek *katastasis* "settling, appointment," from *stasis* "STASIS."]

ca·tas·tro·phe /kə tástrəfee/ *n.* **1. DISASTER** a terrible disaster or accident, especially one that leads to great loss of life **2. HUMILIATING TOTAL FAILURE** an absolute failure, often in humiliating or embarrassing circumstances **3.** THEATER **RESOLUTION OF PLOT** the concluding part of the action in a drama, especially a classical tragedy, when the plot is resolved **4.** GEOL **VIOLENT SEISMIC CHANGE** a sudden and violent change in the earth's crust caused by an earthquake, flood, or any other natural process [Mid-16thC. Via Latin *catastropha* from Greek *katastrophē* "overturning, sudden turn," from *katastrephein*, literally "to overturn," from *strephein* "to turn."]

cat·a·stroph·ic /kàttə stróffik/ *adj.* **1. DISASTROUS** causing or liable to cause widespread damage or death ○ *the uncontrolled spread of an infection that has had a catastrophic effect on livestock* **2. AWFUL** completely unsuccessful or very bad ○ *The party was a catastrophic affair, ending in a riot.* **3.** MED **LIFE-THREATENING AND REQUIRING EXPENSIVE TREATMENT** so serious in nature as to require extensive, long-term, and expensive medical treatment ○ *cancer, AIDS, and other catastrophic illnesses requiring excellent insurance coverage* **4.** INSUR **PROVIDING EXTENSIVE COVERAGE FOR HIGH EXPENSES** used to describe insurance plans, policies, or coverage appropriate to protect the insured party against expenses incurred in the event of a life-threatening condition requiring extensive medical intervention —**cat·a·stroph·i·cal·ly** *adv.*

ca·tas·tro·phism /kə tástrə fizzəm/ *n.* **1.** GEOL **THEORY OF GEOLOGICAL VIOLENCE** a theory, now discredited, that the geological features of the earth were formed by a series of sudden violent catastrophes rather than a gradual evolutionary process. A more recent version of this theory holds that the evolutionary process of geological development has on occasions been supplemented by such catastrophes. **2. PESSIMISM** an outlook or attitude that foresees disaster as the only possible outcome of any action or situation —**ca·tas·tro·phist** *n.*

cat·a·to·ni·a /kàttə tṓnee ə/ *n.* a condition, often associated with schizophrenia, characterized by periods of inertia or apparent stupor and rigidity of the muscles [Late 19thC. Coined from CATA- + Greek *tonos* "tone, tension" (source of English *tone*) + -IA.]

cat·a·ton·ic /kàttə tónnik/ *adj.* **1. IN STATE RESEMBLING TRANCE** in a state of inertia or apparent stupor often associated with schizophrenia and characterized by rigidity of the muscles **2. IN DRUNKEN STUPOR** in a stupefied or unconscious state, especially one caused by drunkenness (*informal*) —**cat·a·ton·i·cal·ly** *adv.*

Ca·taw·ba /kə táwbə/ (*plural* **-ba** *or* **-bas**) *n.* **1.** PEOPLES **MEMBER OF NATIVE AMERICAN PEOPLE** a member of a Native American people who originally occupied lands along the Carolinian Catawba and Wateree Rivers and whose few surviving members now live mainly in South Carolina **2.** PLANTS, FOOD **VARIETY OF BLACK GRAPE** a reddish-colored variety of the North American fox grape **3.** WINE **RED WINE** a red wine made from the Catawba grape [Early 18thC. Named for the *Catawba* river in the Carolinas.]

cat·bird /kát bùrd/ *n.* a North American songbird of the mockingbird family with a call resembling the cry of a cat. It has dark-gray plumage and a black cap. Latin name: *Dumetella carolinensis.*

cat·bird seat *n.* a position or situation that gives somebody power and an edge over others, especially competitors or opponents (*informal*) [Origin uncertain: perhaps from the perception of catbirds as clever and masterful or from the fact that they sit on high perches]

Catboat

cat·boat /kát bṓt/ *n.* a sailboat that is broad across the beam and has a single sail on a forward-stepped mast [Late 19thC. *Cat* of uncertain origin: perhaps from obsolete *cat* "merchant sailing vessel," from medieval Latin *catta* "ship" or Old French *chat* "merchant ship."]

cat bur·glar *n.* a burglar who, using stealth and agility, breaks into properties, especially through high windows or small openings [From the burglar's catlike agility]

cat·call /kát kàwl/ *n.* **JEER** a whistle or shout expressing disapproval or dislike, especially at a sporting event or live performance ■ *vti.* (**-called, -call·ing, -calls**) **UTTER JEERS** to shout or whistle at somebody as an expression of disapproval or dislike [Mid-17thC. From the resemblance to cats' nocturnal cries.]

catch /kach, kech/ *v.* (**caught, catch·ing, catch·es**) **1.** *vti.* **STOP SOMETHING WITH THE HANDS** to take hold of or stop something that is traveling through the air **2.** *vt.* **COLLECT FALLING OBJECTS FROM BELOW** to collect something falling, e.g., rain, from below **3.** *vt.* **GRASP SOMEBODY OR**

SOMETHING to take tight hold of somebody or something suddenly ○ *He caught me by the shoulder.* **4.** *vt.* HUNT **CAPTURE ANIMAL** to capture or trap an animal, bird, fish, or other living thing **5.** *vt.* CRIMINOL **CAPTURE CRIMINAL** to capture somebody, especially a criminal or somebody suspected of wrongdoing, after a search or chase ○ *Have they caught the culprit?* **6.** *vt.* **REACH SOMEBODY OR SOMETHING** to reach or get alongside a person or vehicle moving ahead, usually while moving quickly ○ *trying to catch the car in front* **7.** *vt.* TRANSP **GET ON BOARD PUBLIC TRANSPORTATION** to arrive in time to board a bus, train, or other form of public transportation ○ *I have a plane to catch.* **8.** *vti.* MED **GET DISEASE** to become infected with a disease **9.** *vt.* **SURPRISE SOMEBODY DOING WRONG** to surprise or stop somebody who is in the act of doing something illegal or forbidden ○ *He caught her taking money from the till.* **10.** *vt.* **SURPRISE SOMEBODY DOING SOMETHING EMBARRASSING** to surprise or observe somebody who is doing something considered embarrassing, impolite, or private ○ *I caught him gazing at himself in the mirror.* **11.** *vt.* **ATTRACT SOMEBODY'S ATTENTION** to attract the interest or attention of others ○ *a campaign that had caught the nation's imagination* **12.** *vti.* **MANAGE TO HEAR SOMETHING** to manage to hear what is being said ○ *I'm sorry, I didn't quite catch that.* **13.** *vt.* **UNDERSTAND SOMETHING** to understand the right meaning of something **14.** *vt.* **NOTICE SOMETHING SUBTLE OR FLEETING** to notice something subtle or fleeting, e.g., something in the way somebody is speaking that tells you how that person really feels ○ *I caught a note of sarcasm in his voice.* **15.** *vt.* ARTS **SEE PERFORMER OR PRODUCTION** to see a particular television program, a movie, or a play, or see a particular person performing in something (*informal*) ○ *If you get the chance, try and catch the new production of "Hamlet."* **16.** *vt.* **MANAGE TO MEET SOMEBODY** to manage to meet or talk to somebody, especially somebody who is very busy (*informal*) ○ *I was hoping to catch the doctor before she left.* **17.** *vt.* **GET SOMETHING YOU NEED** to get food, drink, or rest only hurriedly or in small amounts (*informal*) ○ *We can stop and catch a bite to eat.* **18.** *vt.* **STRIKE SOMEBODY** to strike somebody with a blow ○ *a blow that caught him on the side of the head* **19.** *vt.* **TAKE IMPACT OF SOMETHING** to receive the impact or force from something such as a blow or the force of somebody's anger or emotions ○ *He caught the full impact of the blast.* **20.** *vti.* **ENTANGLE SOMETHING** to entangle or hook something such as clothing on something sharp, or become entangled or hooked, sometimes resulting in damage ○ *She caught her blouse on a nail.* **21.** *vti.* **TRAP SOMETHING** to trap something in an opening or door, or become trapped ○ *I caught my fingers in the mailbox.* **22.** *vt.* **DELAY SOMEBODY** to delay somebody or hold somebody up (*usually passive*) **23.** *vr.* **STOP YOURSELF FROM DOING SOMETHING** to stop yourself from saying or doing something ○ *He was about to make a sarcastic remark but caught himself just in time.* **24.** *vt.* **SURPRISE SOMEBODY** to take somebody by surprise (*usually passive*) ○ *She got caught in the rain and was absolutely soaked.* **25.** *vt.* **TRICK SOMEBODY** to trick or deceive somebody **26.** *vt.* **REPRODUCE ASPECTS OF SOMETHING OR SOMEBODY** to reproduce successfully the most typical aspects of somebody or something ○ *a novel that catches the mood of prewar Berlin* **27.** *vt.* CINEMA, TV, RECORDING **RECORD SOMETHING ON FILM** to record somebody or something on film or tape ○ *the very first time this elusive bird has been caught on film* **28.** *vti.* **BE CARRIED BY EMOTION** to be eager to do something, or get caught up in the emotion of the moment **29.** *vi.* **BEGIN TO BURN** to ignite, become alight, or begin to burn **30.** *vi.* BASEBALL **PLAY AS CATCHER** to act as catcher on a team ○ *Clevenger will be catching again in the second game of the World Series.* ■ *n.* **1. ACT OF CATCHING SOMETHING** the catching of something, such as a ball **2. SOMEBODY WHO CAN CATCH** somebody who has a particular ability to catch things ○ *He missed the ball again! He's such a lousy catch!* **3.** SPORTS **BALL GAME** a game in which people throw a ball to each other and catch it **4.** SPORTS **MOVE IN BALL GAMES** a move in which a player in baseball, basketball, or football catches the ball **5. NUMBER OF THINGS CAUGHT** the amount or number of things caught, e.g., when fishing ○ *Not much of a catch today, I'm afraid.* **6. IDEAL OR DESIRABLE PERSON** somebody or something regarded as ideal or particularly desirable, especially as a marriage partner (*informal*) ○ *Her friends regarded Tom as quite a catch.* **7. DEVICE THAT CLOSES OR FASTENS** a device for fastening something, e.g., a door, window, or piece of jewelry **8. SNAG** a hidden or unexpected problem, especially one suspected to exist because everything seems too good to be true (*informal*) ○ *Okay, it sounds great: where's the catch?* **9. BREAK IN VOICE** a brief moment when somebody's voice becomes husky or unclear because of intense emotion ○ *There was a slight catch in his voice as he read the letter out loud.* **10.** MUSIC **HUMOROUS SONG** a type of round or canon with humorous, often risqué, words, popular in the 17th and 18th centuries [12thC. Via Anglo-Norman or Old French *cachier* "to chase," variant of *chacier*, from, ultimately, Latin *captare* "to try to catch," from *capere* "to take."] —**catch·a·ble** *adj.* ◇ **catch it** to get into trouble (*informal*) ◇ **catch somebody with his or her pants down 1.** to expose somebody in a very embarrassing situation, especially one that suggests hypocrisy or incompetence **2.** to surprise somebody in a state of unpreparedness at a time when alertness is required

catch on *vi.* (*informal*) **1. BECOME POPULAR OR WIDESPREAD** to become popular or widely used **2. GET THE IDEA** to understand a new idea, task, or process ○ *pretty slow to catch on*

catch out *vt.* **1. DEVISE WAY TO SHOW SOMEBODY'S MISTAKES** to find ways of exposing errors or ignorance in order to embarrass somebody or show superiority (*informal*) ○ *He would try to catch me out by asking awkward questions during safety inspections.* **2. EXPOSE WRONGDOER** to catch somebody doing something wrong or illegal, especially when deliberately setting out to do so (*informal*) **3.** BASEBALL **CATCH BALL HIT BY SOMEBODY** to catch a ball hit by a player in baseball while it is still in the air, forcing the player or the player's team to retire

catch up *v.* **1.** *vti.* **REACH SOMEBODY OR SOMETHING TRAVELING AHEAD** to reach or get alongside a person who or vehicle that was moving or had gone ahead **2.** *vt.* **PICK SOMETHING UP** to quickly pick something or somebody up in the hands or arms ○ *He caught up all the papers and strode off.* **3.** *vi.* **GET UP TO DATE** to make up for lost time by working harder, to bring something closer to a completion, or to be brought up to date or briefed on current conditions ○ *I really must make time to catch up on my reading.* **4.** *vt.* **ENGROSS SOMEBODY** to absorb somebody's attention completely (*usually passive*) ○ *I was so caught up in my work that I didn't have time for lunch.* **5.** *vt.* **BECOME INVOLVED UNHAPPILY** to become involved in something undesirable (*usually passive*) ○ *They were caught up in the whole messy affair even though they tried to stay out of it.*

catch up with *vt.* **1. FIND WRONGDOER** to find somebody who has committed a crime or done something wrong, especially after a search or chase ○ *By the time the police caught up with him, he had changed his name and moved to Brazil.* **2. FINALLY AFFECT SOMEBODY** to finally have an effect after a period during which somebody seemed free from the usual consequences of a particular way of behaving ○ *All those late nights will catch up with you eventually.*

Catch-22 (*plural* **Catch-22's** *or* **Catch-22s**), **catch-22** *n.* a situation in which whatever outcome somebody desires is impossible to attain because the rules always work against it [Named for the 1955 novel *Catch-22* by Joseph Heller, in which the "catch" was that an airman wishing to stop flying missions must be sane and therefore must continue]

WORD KEY: CULTURAL NOTE

Catch-22, a novel by Joseph Heller (1961). The title of this dark satire relates to the skewed military logic that entraps the protagonist, Yossarian, a pilot serving in Italy during World War II. Although he has flown sufficient missions to be sent home, he is also obliged to obey orders, and his orders are to keep flying. The term ***Catch-22*** eventually took on the following meanings of its own: "a situation or problem from which extrication is impossible because of built-in illogical rules and regulations," "an absurd situation," "a snag or catch," and "a self-defeating course of action.".

catch·all /kách àwl, kéch-/ *n.* **1. SOMETHING ENCOMPASSING RANGE OF POSSIBILITIES** something that covers a wide range of possibilities, meanings, ideas, or situations (*often used before a noun*) ○ *one of those catchall phrases that doesn't really mean very much at all* **2. STORAGE CONTAINER** a container or storage area for holding a wide variety of miscellaneous items

catch and re·lease *n.* a conservation policy adopted by some anglers whereby they release some or all of the fish they catch in order to sustain fish populations

catch-as-catch-can *n.* **NO-HOLDS-BARRED WRESTLING** a style of wrestling in which most holds are permitted, including many that are not allowed in other wrestling styles ■ *adj.* **MAKING DO** making do with whatever is available ○ *We took a catch-as-catch-can approach to our summer vacation.* ■ *adv.* **USING WHAT COMES TO HAND** using whatever happens to be available ○ *The press conference was arranged catch-as-catch-can at very short notice.*

catch ba·sin *n.* **1. SEWER FILTER** a device or receptacle at the entrance of a sewer designed to prevent obstructive material from entering and blocking the sewer **2. DRAINAGE COLLECTION AREA OR RESERVOIR** an area or reservoir for catching drainage water or runoff

catch colt *n. Midwest* = **old-field colt**

catch crop *n.* a fast-growing crop grown between harvest and planting of two main crops, between the rows of a main crop, or as a substitute after a crop failure [From the idea of catching an opportunity to grow it]

catch·er /káchər, kéchər/ *n.* **1.** BASEBALL **PLAYER POSITIONED BEHIND BATTER** the baseball player who stands behind home plate, signals for pitches, and catches pitched balls that have not been hit by the batter **2. SOMETHING OR SOMEBODY THAT CATCHES** a person, animal, or device that catches things

catch·fly /kách flī, kéch-/ (*plural* **-flies** *or* **-fly**) *n.* a plant related to the campion and ragged robin that exudes a sticky substance on the stem beneath each pair of leaves. Genus: *Silene* and *Lychnis.*

catch·ing /káching, kéch-/ *adj.* **1.** MED **INFECTIOUS** used to describe an illness that can be transmitted to other people because it is contagious or infectious ○ *Don't worry: it's not catching!* **2. ATTRACTIVE** so attractive as to be memorable **3. AFFECTING ONE PERSON AFTER ANOTHER** passed from one person to another like an infection ○ *a pessimism that seemed to be catching*

catch·ment /káchmənt, kéch-/ *n.* **1. RAINWATER RECEPTACLE** a structure, reservoir, or container for collecting rainwater **2. COLLECTED RAINWATER** the rainwater that collects in a catchment **3. COLLECTING OF RAINWATER** the collecting or catching of rainwater

catch·ment ar·e·a *n.* **1.** GEOG **DRAINAGE AREA** the area of land that drains rainfall into a river or lake **2.** EDUC, HEALTH **AREA COVERED BY SERVICE** the area from which a particular school or hospital will accept pupils or patients

catch·pen·ny /kách pènnee, kéch-/ *adj.* **FAST-SELLING AND SHODDY** cheap and made to be sold quickly and easily without much regard for quality (*dated*) ■ *n.* (*plural* **-nies**) **FAST-SELLING SHODDY ITEM** a cheap shoddy item made to be sold quickly and easily (*dated*)

catch phrase *n.* a phrase that is used so frequently by a particular person or group that it becomes identified with it

catch·pole /kách pōl, kéch-/ *n.* in England in former times, a sheriff's officer who collected money from debtors [Pre-12thC. From either assumed Anglo-Norman or Old French *cachepol* or Anglo-Latin *cacepollus*, both literally "chicken-catcher."]

catch·up /kách ùp, kéch-/ *n.* = **ketchup**

catch-up *n.* an increase in the amount or quality of something to bring it up to a desired or established standard ○ *a budgetary catch-up that managed at the last minute to fund the agency through the fourth quarter*

catch·wa·ter drain /kách wottər-, kéch-/ *n.* a drain cut along the edge of high ground to catch water from it and divert it so that it does not fall onto low-lying ground

catch·weight /kách wāyt, kéch-/ *adj.* used to describe a a sports contest, e.g., in wrestling or horse-racing, that has no weight restrictions [Early 19thC. Origin uncertain: perhaps from the idea of catching whichever weight you could.]

catch·word /kách wùrd, kéch-/ *n.* **1. POPULAR WORD** a word or phrase that is so frequently used, often over a short period of time, that it comes to be identified with a particular feeling, quality, or idea ○ *catchwords of the 1980s such as "upwardly mobile" and "yuppie"* **2.** *U.K.* PUBL = **guideword 3.** PRINTING **BINDER'S CUE** the first word of a page of printed text repeated at the bottom right-hand corner of the previous page, originally placed there to draw the binder's attention to it **4.** THEATER **ACTOR'S CUE** a cue for an actor to come on stage or to speak

catch·y /káchee, kéchee/ (**-i·er, -i·est**) *adj.* **1. MEMORABLE** easy to remember because of having a simple and effective melody or wording **2. ATTRACTING ATTENTION** tending to attract interest or attention because of a notable, unique, or pleasing character or quality ○ *an attempt to come up with a catchy name for a new soft drink* **3. TRICKY** designed to catch people out or trip them up ○ *There were some catchy questions on the English test.* **4. FITFUL** coming in spasmodic or irregular bursts ○ *light rain with catchy squalls of wind* —**catch·i·ness** *n.*

cat·e·che·sis /kàttə kéessiss/ (*plural* **-ses** /-seez/) *n.* oral religious instruction given in advance of baptism or confirmation [Early 17thC. Via ecclesiastical Latin from Greek *katēkhēsis* "instruction by word of mouth," from *katēkhein* (see CATECHIZE).] —**cat·e·chet·i·cal** /kàttə kéttik'l/ *adj.*

cat·e·chin /kátti kìn/ *n.* a yellow crystalline substance used in tanning and dyeing [Mid-19thC. Coined from CATECHU + -IN.]

cat·e·chism /káttə kìzzəm/ *n.* **1.** CHR **QUESTION-AND-ANSWER TEACHING** instruction in the principles of Christianity using set questions and answers **2.** CHR **RELIGIOUS QUESTIONS AND ANSWERS** the series of questions and answers that are used to test people's religious knowledge in advance of Christian baptism or confirmation **3.** CHR **QUESTION-AND-ANSWER BOOK** a book containing questions and answers used to test the religious knowledge of people preparing for Christian baptism or confirmation **4. BOOK FOR ROTE LEARNING** a handbook that teaches the basic principles of a subject, especially by repetition **5. BODY OF PRINCIPLES FOLLOWED UNTHINKINGLY** a body of basic beliefs and principles followed slavishly or unthinkingly **6. INTERROGATION** a close and intense session of questioning on a particular subject, especially forming part of an examination or an interrogation [Early 16thC. Via ecclesiastical Latin *catechismus* from ecclesiastical Greek, from *katēkhizein* (see CATECHIZE).] —**cat·e·chis·mal** /kàttə kízm'l/ *adj.*

cat·e·chist /káttəkist/ *n.* somebody who instructs people in the basic principles of the Christian religion, especially people preparing for baptism or confirmation —**cat·e·chis·tic** /kàttə kístik/ *adj.* —**cat·e·chis·ti·cal** /-kístik'l/ *adj.*

cat·e·chize /káttə kīz/ (**-chized, -chiz·ing, -chiz·es**) *vt.* **1.** CHR **TEACH SOMEBODY ABOUT CHRISTIANITY** to instruct somebody in the basic principles of the Christian religion using questions and answers **2. INTERROGATE SOMEBODY** to question somebody closely, e.g., in an examination or interrogation [15thC. Via ecclesiastical Latin *catechizare* from ecclesiastical Greek *katēkhizein*, from *katēkhein* "to instruct orally" (literally "to sound through"), from, ultimately, *ēkhē* "sound."] —**cat·e·chi·za·tion** /kàttəki záysh'n/ *n.* —**cat·e·chiz·er** /káttə kīzər/ *n.*

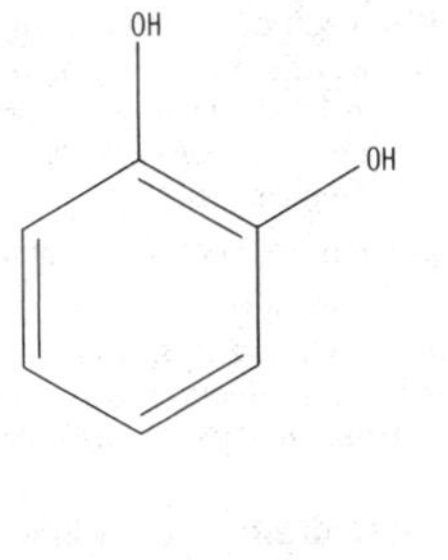

Catechol

cat·e·chol /káttə kòl, -kàwl/ *n.* a colorless crystalline solid used as a photographic developer, as an antioxidant, and in the manufacture of dyes and pharmaceuticals. Formula: $C_6H_6O_2$. [Late 19thC. Coined from CATECHU + -OL.]

cat·e·cho·la·mine /kàttə kṓlə meen, -káwlə-/ *n.* an organic compound (**amine**) that affects the sympathetic nervous system. Dopamine and epinephrine are catecholamines.

cat·e·chu /káttə choo/ *n.* an astringent water-soluble substance obtained especially from an Asian acacia tree and used in medicine and dyeing [Late 17thC. From modern Latin, formed from Malay *kacu* (source of English *cachou*).]

cat·e·chu·men /kàttə kyóomən/ *n.* somebody who is receiving religious instruction in preparation for Christian baptism or confirmation [14thC. Directly or via French *catéchumène* from ecclesiastical Latin *catechumenus*, from Greek *katēkhoumenos* "being instructed," the present participle passive of *katēkhein* (see CATECHIZE).] —**cat·e·chu·men·ism** /kàttə kyóomə nìzzəm/ *n.*

cat·e·gor·i·cal /kàttə gáwrik'l/, **cat·e·gor·ic** /-gáwrik/ *adj.* **1. ABSOLUTE AND EXPLICIT** absolute, certain, and unconditional, with no room for doubt, question, or contradiction ○ *The press office has issued a categorical denial of these allegations.* **2. INVOLVING CATEGORIES** involving or relating to the use of categories or categorization —**cat·e·gor·i·cal·ly** *adv.* —**cat·e·gor·i·cal·ness** *n.*

cat·e·gor·i·cal im·per·a·tive *n.* according to the moral philosophy of Immanuel Kant, an unconditional moral law applying to all rational beings. It is also independent of all personal desires and motives.

cat·e·go·ri·za·tion /kàttəgəri záysh'n/ *n.* **1. SORTING INTO CATEGORIES** the defining and grouping of people or things into categories **2. CATEGORY** a group of people or things regarded as being in or forming a particular category

cat·e·go·rize /káttəgə rīz/ (**-rized, -riz·ing, -riz·es**) *vt.* to place somebody or something in a particular category and define or judge the person or thing accordingly ○ *It was originally categorized as a cactus, but it's actually a succulent.* —**cat·e·go·riz·a·ble** *adj.*

cat·e·go·ry /káttə gàwree/ (*plural* **-ries**) *n.* a group or set of things, people, or actions that are classified together because of common characteristics ○ *There are choices available in the following categories: leisure, fitness, health.* [15thC. Ultimately via late Latin from Greek *katēgoria* "statement, accusation," from *katēgorein* "to speak against"; the meaning developed from "accusation" via "assertion, naming" to "list."]

ca·te·na /kə teénə/ (*plural* **-nae** /-nee/ *or* **-nas**) *n.* a series of connected commentaries on or excerpts of writings, especially comments on the Bible written by early Christian theologians [Mid-17thC. From Latin, "chain" (source also of English *concatenation*).]

cat·e·nac·ci·o /kàttə náchi ō/ *n.* a strongly defensive formation in soccer, involving one free defender positioned behind his or her teammates [Late 20thC. From Italian, "door bolt" from, ultimately, Latin *catena* (see CATENA).]

cat·e·nar·y /kátt'n èrree, kə teénəree/ (*plural* **-ies**) *n.* the curve adopted by a length of heavy cable, rope, or chain of uniform density, hanging between two points, or something with this shape [Mid-18thC. From modern Latin *catenaria*, from Latin *catena* (see CATENA).] —**cat·e·nar·y** *adj.*

cat·e·nate /kátt'n àyt/ (**-nat·ed, -nat·ing, -nates**) *vt.* **1. MAKE SOMETHING INTO CHAIN** to form something into a chain or a series of chains **2.** CHEM **FORM CHAIN OF ATOMS** to form a chain of atoms of the same element held together by chemical bonds [Early 17thC. From Latin *catenat-*, the past participle stem of *catenare* "to chain, bind together," from *catena* (see CATENA).]

ca·ter /káytər/ (**-tered, -ter·ing, -ters**) *vti.* **1. PROVIDE WHAT IS WANTED** to provide what is wanted or needed in a particular situation or by a particular group of people ○ *We try to cater to all tastes in our bookshop.* **2. SUPPLY FOOD** to provide food and drink for a number of people, e.g., at a party or meeting ○ *We can cater up to a hundred people here.* [Late 16thC. Shortening of obsolete *acater* "caterer" (the original sense in English), from Anglo-Norman *acateor*, from *ac(h)ater* "to buy" from, ultimately, Latin *capere* "to take."]

cat·er·cor·nered, **cat·er·cor·ner**, **cat·ty·cor·nered**, **cat·ty·cor·ner** *adj.* **DIAGONAL** positioned or arranged diagonally ■ *adv.* **1. DIAGONALLY** in a diagonal position or arrangement ○ *He sits cater-cornered from me in history class.* **2. OPPOSITE** diagonally opposite something or somebody else ○ *Their office is cater-cornered from the bank.* [Mid-19thC. *Cater* originally a dialect adverb meaning "diagonally," from French *quatre* "four."]

ca·ter·er /káytərər/ *n.* a person who or company that provides and sometimes serves the food and drink for a social or business function, e.g., a wedding, party, or meeting —**ca·ter·ing** *n.*

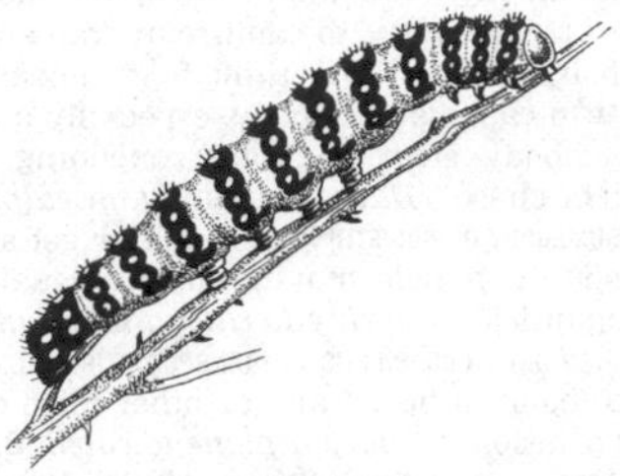
Caterpillar

cat·er·pil·lar /káttər pìllər/ *n.* the larva of a butterfly or moth. It has a long soft body, many short legs, and often brightly colored or spiny skin. [15thC. Alteration (probably influenced by obsolete *piller* "plunderer") of assumed Old Northern French *catepelose*, from assumed late Latin *catta pilosa* "hairy cat."]

Cat·er·pil·lar /káttər pìllər/ *tdmk.* a trademark for tractors that have continuous treads composed of chain

cat·er·waul /káttər wàwl/ *vi.* (**-wauled, -waul·ing, -wauls**) **YOWL OR ARGUE LOUDLY** to make a loud howling noise like a cat in heat, or have a noisy argument ○ *a street musician caterwauling in the background while we tried to talk* ■ *n.* **YOWL** a loud howl or cry that sounds like a cat in heat [14thC. Origin uncertain: perhaps from Low German *katerwaulen*, or from an earlier form of CAT + a Middle English word meaning "to yowl" of imitative origin.]

cat·fight /kát fīt/ *n.* **1. FIGHT AMONG CATS** a fight that takes place among cats **2. FIGHT ESPECIALLY BETWEEN WOMEN** a vicious argument or fight, especially between women (*informal*)

cat·fish /kát fish/ (*plural* **-fish** *or* **-fish·es**) *n.* a scaleless, usually freshwater, fish with long whiskers (**barbels**) around its mouth that are sensitive to touch, taste, and smell. Order: Siluriformes. [From its barbels, likened to a cat's whiskers]

cat·gut /kát gùt/ *n.* a tough thin cord made from the dried intestines of sheep and other animals, used for stringing tennis rackets and musical instruments, and as surgical thread [Late 16thC. Origin uncertain: probably from CAT (for unknown reasons), or perhaps a contraction of "cattle-gut."]

cath. *abbr.* cathode

Cath. *abbr.* **1.** Cathedral **2.** Catholic

Cath·ar /ká thaar/ (*plural* **-ars** *or* **-a·ri** /káthəree/) *n.* a member of a 12th- and 13th-century European heretical sect who believed the earth was ruled by Satan. They also believed that salvation lay in the renunciation of materialism and the adoption of a spiritual way of life. [Late 16thC. Via medieval Latin *Cathari* "Cathars," from Greek *katharoi* "the pure," from *katharos* "pure" (see CATHARSIS).] —**Cath·a·rism** /káthə rìzzəm/ *n.* —**Cath·a·rist** /-rist/ *n.* —**Cath·a·rist·ic** /káthə rístik/ *adj.*

ca·thar·sis /kə thaársiss/ (*plural* **-ses** /-seez/) *n.* **1. EMOTIONAL RELEASE** an experience or feeling of spiritual release and purification brought about by an intense emotional experience **2.** THEATER **EMOTIONAL PURGING THROUGH GREEK TRAGEDY** according to Aristotle, a purifying of the emotions that is brought about in the audience of a tragic drama through the evocation of intense fear and pity **3.** PSYCHIAT **PURGING OF COMPLEXES** the process of bringing to the surface repressed emotions, complexes, and feelings in an effort to identify and relieve them, or the result of this process **4.** MED **PURGING OF BOWELS** cleansing or purging of the bowels [Early 19thC. Via modern Latin from Greek *katharsis*, from *kathairein* "to purge, cleanse," from *katharos* "pure, clean."]

ca·thar·tic /kə thaártik/ *adj.* **1. PURIFYING** producing a feeling of being purified emotionally, spiritually, or psychologically as a result of an intense emotional experience or therapeutic technique ○ *a film that had a truly cathartic effect on me* **2.** MED **HAVING PURGATIVE EFFECT ON BOWELS** used to describe a medicine that causes emptying of the bowels ■ *n.* PHARM **PURGATIVE MEDICINE** a medicine that causes emptying of the bowels —**ca·thar·ti·cal·ly** *adv.*

Ca·thay /ka tháy/ *n.* a medieval name for China (*archaic or literary*)

cat·head /kát hèd/ *n.* a horizontal wooden or iron beam projecting from a ship's bow, where the anchor is carried and hoisted [From CAT "to raise the anchor"]

ca·thect /kə thékt, ka-/ (**-thect·ed, -thect·ing, -thects**) *vt.* PSYCHOANAL to concentrate emotional or psychic energy on something, e.g., an object, a person, or an idea [Mid-20thC. Back-formation from *cathectic*, formed from CATHEXIS.] —**ca·thec·tic** *adj.*

ca·the·dra /kə theédrə/ (*plural* **-dras** *or* **-drae** /-dree/) *n.* **1.** BISHOP'S THRONE a bishop's official seat or throne. ◊ **ex cathedra 2.** BISHOP'S RANK OR OFFICE the official rank, office, or jurisdiction of a bishop **3.** OFFICIAL CHAIR an official chair of an office or position, used by an authority figure [15thC. Via Latin from Greek *kathedra*, from *kata* "down" + *hedra* "seat."]

ca·the·dral /kə theédr'l/ *n.* **1.** BISHOP'S CHURCH a church that contains a bishop's throne and is the most important church in the bishop's diocese **2.** LARGE CHURCH a large, important church ■ *adj.* **1.** OF BISHOP OR CATHEDRAL relating to, belonging to, or having a bishop or cathedral **2.** BY CHAIR OF AUTHORITY related to or coming from a chair of authority **3.** LIKE A CATHEDRAL resembling or appropriate to a cathedral **4.** MADE BY BISHOP used to describe an official religious announcement made by a bishop or pope [13thC. Via Old French from late Latin *cathedralis*, from Latin *cathedra* "bishop's throne" (source of English *chair*; see CATHEDRA).]

ca·the·dral ceil·ing *n.* a high ceiling that is slanted toward a central ridge or point, or that takes in two levels, e.g., in a living room with an overhanging balcony

Ca·the·dral Cit·y city in southern California, southeast of Palm Springs, southwest of Joshua Tree National Park. Population: 36,327 (1996).

ca·thep·sin /kə thépsən/ *n.* an enzyme that breaks down proteins after cell death or in some diseased conditions [Early 20thC. From German *Kathepsin*, from Greek *kathepsein* "to digest," literally "to boil down," from *hepsein* "to boil."]

Willa Cather

Cath·er, Willa (1873–1947) U.S. writer. Her novels include the Pulitzer Prize-winning *One of Ours* (1922). Full name **Willa Sibert Cather**

Cath·er·ine de Méd·i·cis /káthərin də méddi cheè, káthrin-, kaatreén də maydeesseèss/, **Cath·er·ine de 'Med·i·ci, Queen of France** (1519–89) Italian-born widow of the French king Henry II. She was regent of France (1560–63) and may have instigated the St. Bartholomew's Day Massacre (1572).

Cath·er·ine of Ar·a·gon, Cath·er·ine of Ar·a·gón (1485–1536) Spanish-born English queen consort. The annulment of her marriage to King Henry VIII in 1533 precipitated the English Reformation.

Cath·er·ine the Great (1729–96) German-born Russian monarch. Empress from 1762 after deposing her husband, she extended and consolidated Russian power and culture.

Catherine the Great

Cath·er·ine wheel *n.* **1.** *U.K.* = **pinwheel 2.** ARCHIT CIRCULAR WINDOW a circular window divided by ribs radiating from the center [Late 16thC. Named for Saint *Catherine* of Alexandria, who was sentenced to be executed on a spiked wheel.]

cath·e·ter /káthətər/ *n.* a thin flexible tube that is inserted into a part of the body to inject or drain away fluid, or to keep a passage open. Catheters also have many diagnostic and surgical applications. [Early 17thC. Via late Latin from Greek *kathetēr*, from *kathienai* "to send down," from *hienai* "to send."]

cath·e·ter·ize /káthətə rīz/ (**-ized, -iz·ing, -iz·es**) *vt.* to insert a catheter into a patient or a specific part of the body —**cath·e·ter·i·za·tion** /kàthətəri záysh'n/ *n.*

ca·thex·is /kə théksiss, ka-/ (*plural* **-es** /-seez, ka-/) *n.* PSYCHOANAL the concentration of a great deal of psychological and emotional energy on one particular person, thing, or idea [Early 20thC. From Greek *kathexis* "holding" from *katekhein* "to hold fast," from *ekhein* "to hold." Translation of German *Besetzung*.]

ca·thi·o·der·mie /kàthi ō dúrmee/ *n.* a beauty treatment in which an electric current is passed over the skin, through a special gel with which the skin is covered [Late 20thC. From CATION + French *-dermie* "-dermy."]

cath·ode /ká thōd/ *n.* **1.** NEGATIVE ELECTRODE the negative electrode of an electrolytic cell **2.** ELECTRON SOURCE the negatively charged source of electrons in an electron tube **3.** POSITIVE TERMINAL the positive terminal of a cell that is producing electrical energy by a chemical process that cannot be reversed [Mid-19thC. From Greek *kathodos*, literally "way down," from *kata* "down" + *hodos* "way."] —**ca·tho·dal** /ka thōd'l/ *adj.* —**ca·tho·dal·ly** /-dəlee/ *adv.*

cath·ode ray *n.* a stream of electrons that is emitted from a cathode in a vacuum tube

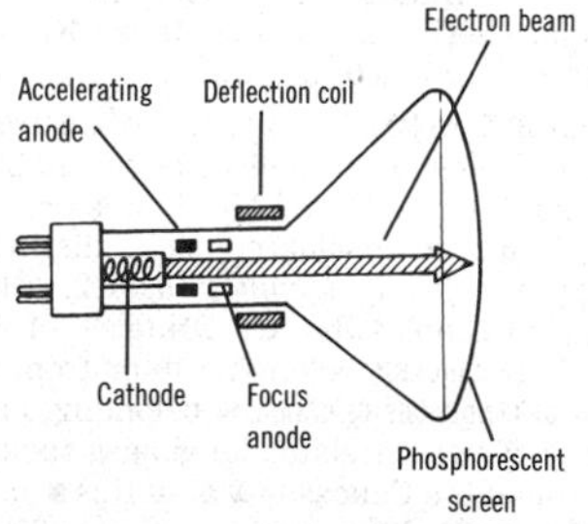

Cathode-ray tube

cath·ode-ray tube *n.* a vacuum tube in which a stream of electrons is produced and directed onto a fluorescent screen, e.g., in a television or visual display unit, creating images and text

ca·thod·ic /ka thóddik/ *adj.* relating to or involving a cathode —**ca·thod·i·cal·ly** *adv.*

ca·thod·ic pro·tec·tion *n.* the prevention of electrolytic corrosion in something metallic, e.g., an underground pipe or a ship, by making it the cathode in an electrolytic cell

cat hole *n.* either of two holes at the stern of a ship through which large ropes are passed

cath·o·lic /káthlik, káthəlik/ *adj.* **1.** ALL-INCLUSIVE including or concerned with all people **2.** USEFUL TO ALL useful or interesting to a wide range of people **3.** ALL-EMBRACING interested in or sympathetic to a wide range of things [14thC. Via Latin *catholicus* from, ultimately, Greek *katholikos* "universal," from *katholou* "in general," from *kata* "in regard to" + *holos* "whole."] —**ca·thol·i·cal·ly** /kə thóllikəlee/ *adv.*

Cath·o·lic *adj.* **1.** ROMAN CATHOLIC belonging to or characteristic of the Roman Catholic Church **2.** CHRISTIAN belonging to the community of all Christian churches **3.** OF THE HISTORICAL UNITED CHURCH belonging to the united Christian church that existed before its separation into different churches, or to any church that regards itself as continuing the traditions of that united church ■ *n.* CHURCH MEMBER a member of the Roman Catholic Church [14thC. Via Christian Latin from Greek *katholikē (ekklēsia)* "universal church," from *katholikos* (see CATHOLIC).]

Cath·o·lic Church *n.* **1.** = **Roman Catholic Church 2.** CHURCH DESCENDED FROM ANCIENT CHRISTIAN CHURCH any church that regards itself as continuing the traditions of the Christian church before it was divided into separate churches

Cath·o·lic E·pis·tles *npl.* the New Testament Epistles of James I and II, Peter, John, and Jude, addressed to the Christian churches as a whole rather than to a local church

Ca·thol·i·cism /kə thóllə sìzzəm/ *n.* **1.** CATHOLIC BELIEFS the beliefs, doctrines, and rituals of a Catholic church, especially those of the Roman Catholic Church **2.** MEMBERSHIP OF CATHOLIC CHURCH membership of a Catholic church, especially of the Roman Catholic Church

cath·o·lic·i·ty /kàthə líssətee/ *n.* **1.** WIDENESS OF RANGE wideness of range of tastes or interests **2.** INCLUSIVENESS the quality of including or applying to everyone or everything

Cath·o·lic·i·ty *n.* = **Catholicism**

ca·thol·i·cize /kə thóllə sīz/ (**-cized, -ciz·ing, -ciz·es**) *vti.* to broaden something, e.g., an idea, classification, or range of things, to include or apply to many or all things or people, or become broader in this way

Ca·thol·i·cize (**-cized, -ciz·ing, -ciz·es**) *vti.* to convert somebody to Catholicism, or be converted to Catholicism

ca·thol·i·con /kə thólli kòn/ *n.* a remedy that is supposed to cure every ailment (*archaic*) [Early 17thC. Via French from modern Latin *catholicum (remedium)* "universal (remedy)," from Greek *katholikos* (see CATHOLIC).]

cat·house /kát hòwss/ *n.* a brothel (*slang*) [Mid-20thC. From CAT in the obsolete sense "prostitute."]

Cat·i·line /kátt'lìn/ (108?–62 B.C.) Roman conspirator. His plan to foment revolution by assassinating Marcus Cicero failed, and he was killed in battle with republican forces. Full name **Lucius Sergius Catilina**

cat·i·on /kát ī ən/ *n.* an ion that has a positive electric charge and is attracted toward the cathode in electrolysis [Mid-19thC. Coined from Greek *kata* "down" + ION.] —**cat·i·on·ic** /kàt ī ónnik/ *adj.*

cat·kin /kátkən/ *n.* a long hanging furry cluster of tiny leaves and petalless flowers, produced by trees such as willows, birches, alders, and poplars [Late 16thC. From obsolete Dutch *katteken* "kitten."]

Cat·lin /káttlin/, **George** (1796–1872) U.S. artist and writer. His paintings are records of Native American life. His books include *My Life Among the Indians* (1867).

cat·mint /kátmint/ *n.* = **catnip**

cat·nap /kát nàp/ *vi.* (**-napped, -nap·ping, -naps**) TAKE A SHORT SLEEP to take a short, light sleep, or several short light sleeps ■ *n.* SHORT SLEEP a short, light sleep [From the cat's habit of sleeping lightly during the day] —**cat·nap·per** *n.*

cat·nip /kátnip/ *n.* a plant of the mint family that has grayish leaves, blue or white flowers, and a strong smell that attracts cats. Genus: *Nepeta*. [Early 18thC. *Nip*, variant of obsolete *nep* "catmint," via Old English *nepta* from Latin *nepeta*, of uncertain origin.]

cat-o'-nine-tails (*plural* **cat-o'-nine-tails**) *n.* a whip with several, usually nine, strands of knotted rope, used in the past for flogging in the navy

Ca·tons·ville village in Baltimore County, Maryland, situated southwest of the city of Baltimore. Population: 35,233 (1990).

ca·top·tric /kə tóptrik/, **ca·top·tri·cal** /-trik'l/ *adj.* relating to or involving a mirror or reflection [Mid-16thC. From Greek *katoptrikos*, from *katoptron* "mirror," literally "something that looks back"; related to *optos* "seen" (see OPTIC).]

ca·top·trics /kə tóptriks/ *n.* the branch of optics that deals with mirrors and reflection (*takes a singular verb*)

Ca·to the El·der /kày tō-/, **Marcus Portius** (234–149 B.C.) Roman general and statesman. As censor he fought against Greek cultural influence and against the luxury and immorality of Rome. Known as **the Censor**

cat rig *n.* the rig of a catboat, usually with a gaff

CAT scan *n.* **1.** DIAGNOSTIC X-RAY SCAN a diagnostic, medical, radiological scan in which cross-sectional images of a part of the body are formed through computerized axial tomography and shown on a computer screen **2.** = **CAT scanner**

CAT scan·ner *n.* the radiological, diagnostic scanning equipment used to make a CAT scan

cat's cra·dle *n.* a children's game in which a loop of string is threaded between the fingers of both hands in variable complex patterns [Origin uncertain: perhaps an alteration of "cratch cradle," the manger in which the infant Jesus was laid, from an alteration of French *crèche* "CRECHE"]

cat scratch dis·ease, **cat scratch fe·ver** *n.* an illness marked by fever and swollen lymph glands, thought to be caused by a bacterium transmitted to humans by the scratch of a cat

cat's-eye *n.* **1.** SEMIPRECIOUS STONE any of various gemstones, especially chrysoberyl and chalcedony, that when cut in a rounded shape reflect a narrow silvery band of light that seems to come from within **2.** REFLECTIVE ROAD MARKER a small reflecting device that is set into a road surface, curb, or post to assist drivers at night in staying on the road or within lanes **3.** GLASS MARBLE a clear glass marble with a core or swirl of color at the center

Cats·kill Moun·tains /káts kil-/ group of mountains in the Appalachian system, southeastern New York, situated along the western bank of the Hudson River. Its highest peak is Slide Mountain, 4,204 ft./1,281 m.

cat's me·ow *n.* = **cat's pajamas** (*dated slang*)

cat's pa·ja·mas *n.* an excellent or special person or thing (*dated slang*)

cat's-paw *n.* **1.** SOMEBODY USED AS A TOOL somebody who is tricked or manipulated into doing something for another person, without understanding what is happening, as in the fable of the fox and the cat **2.** LOOPED KNOT a knot with two loops, for attaching a rope to a hook

cat squir·rel *n.* the eastern gray squirrel (*regional*)

WORD KEY: REGIONAL NOTE

Cat squirrel is used to refer to the gray squirrel in an area that extends from South Carolina, south and west, to Texas. It is also common in the Ozarks of Missouri and Arkansas, but is primarily a Gulf States term.

cat·suit /kát so͞ot/ *n.* a close-fitting one-piece pantsuit [So called because it gives a sleek outline]

cat·sup *n.* = **ketchup**

Catt /kat/, **Carrie Chapman** (1859–1947) U.S. suffragist. She was president of the International Woman Suffrage Alliance (1904–23). Born **Carrie Lane Chapman**

cat·ta·lo /káttəlō/ (*plural* **-loes** *or* **-los**) *n.* = **beefalo** [Late 19thC. Blend of CATTLE and BUFFALO.]

cat·ter·y /káttəree/ (*plural* **-ies**) *n.* a place where cats are bred or cared for

cat·tish /káttish/ *adj.* = **catty** —**cat·tish·ly** *adv.* —**cat·tish·ness** *n.*

cat·tle /kátt'l/ *npl.* (*takes a plural verb*) **1.** FARM ANIMALS OF THE OX FAMILY large domesticated mammals kept for the production of milk, meat, and hides, and also as draft animals. Cows and oxen are common types of cattle. Genus: *Bos.* **2.** PEOPLE REGARDED AS ANIMALS people who are regarded as belonging to a low order, especially a crowd of people regarded as an unthinking mass (*disapproving*) [13thC. Via Anglo-Norman *catel* from, ultimately, Latin *capitale* "funds."]

cat·tle call *n.* an audition in which large numbers of often inexperienced actors try for various minor parts

cat·tle e·gret *n.* a small, white, yellow-billed egret that often feeds on insects stirred up by cattle, native to Africa, southern Europe, and Asia and now widespread in the southeastern United States. Latin name: *Bubulus ibis.*

cat·tle grid *n. U.K.* = **cattle guard**

cat·tle grub *n.* a parasitic larva of the warble fly, which causes a swelling under the skin of cattle and horses

cat·tle guard *n.* a grid of metal bars over a shallow pit in a road, designed to stop animals, but not people or vehicles, from leaving an enclosed area

cat·tle·man /kátt'lmən, -màn/ (*plural* **-men** /-mèn, -mèn/) *n.* somebody who works with cattle, or who owns and raises cattle

cat·tle plague *n.* = **rinderpest**

cat·tle prod *n.* an electrified rod designed for driving and controlling cattle by giving them mild shocks

cat·tle tick *n.* a brown tick that transmits the protozoan that causes Texas fever in cattle, found especially in the southern United States and South America. Genus: *Boophilus.*

cat·tle truck *n. U.K.* = **stock car**

cat·tle·ya /káttlee ə, kat láy ə, kat lée ə/ (*plural* **-yas**) *n.* an orchid with decorative purple, pink, or white flowers that grows mainly as an epiphyte in tropical America and is also a popular greenhouse plant. Genus: *Cattleya.* [Early 19thC. From modern Latin, genus name, named for William *Cattley* (died 1832), English patron of botany.]

Cat·ton /kátt'n/, **Bruce** (1899–1978) U.S. historian. He wrote many volumes on the Civil War. Full name **Charles Bruce Catton**

cat train *n. Canadian* in northern regions of Canada, a series of linked sled s mounted on runners that is pulled over snow by a tractor with Caterpillar™ treads

cat·ty /káttee/ (**-ti·er, -ti·est**) *adj.* **1.** SLYLY MEAN spiteful or malicious, especially in a subtle way **2.** RESEMBLING CAT like a cat, especially in being cautious or secretive —**cat·ti·ly** *adv.* —**cat·ti·ness** *n.*

cat·ty-corn·ered, **cat·ty-corn·er** *adj.* = **cater-cornered**

Ca·tul·lus, Gaius Valerius (84?–54? B.C.) Roman poet. He wrote love poems addressed to "Lesbia" and satirical attacks on Julius Caesar. —**Ca·tul·lan** *adj.*

CATV *abbr.* community antenna television

cat·walk /kát wàwk/ *n.* **1.** RAISED PLATFORM a long narrow raised platform along which the models walk in a fashion show **2.** HIGH WALKWAY a narrow walkway high above the ground, e.g., along the side of a building or behind the stage in a theater [So named because cats can walk safely along something narrow]

Cau·ca·sia /kaw káyzhə/ region of southeastern Europe and southwestern Asia, divided by the Caucasian Mountains and containing Georgia, Armenia, Azerbaijan, and southern Russia. Area: 150,000 sq. mi./400,000 sq. km.

Cau·ca·sian /kaw káyzh'n/ *adj.* **1.** ETHNOL OF FORMER ETHNIC GROUP belonging to or typical of the light-skinned peoples of Europe, North Africa, western Asia, and India, formerly considered as a distinct ethnic group (*no longer in technical use*) **2.** WHITE-SKINNED relating to people who are white or of European origin **3.** OF CAUCASIA belonging to or from Caucasia **4.** LANG OF LANGUAGES OF CAUCASIA belonging or relating to either of two unrelated languages spoken in the area around the Caucasus Mountains ■ *n.* **1.** ETHNOL MEMBER OF FORMER ETHNIC GROUP a member of the former Caucasian ethnic group (*no longer in technical use*) **2.** WHITE PERSON somebody white or of European origin **3.** PEOPLES SOMEBODY FROM CAUCASIA somebody who lives in or comes from Caucasia **4.** LANG LANGUAGES OF CAUCASIA either of two unrelated language families spoken in the area around the Caucasus Mountains, Kartvelian or South Caucasian, and North Caucasian [Early 17thC. Named for CAUCASIA, where the group of people was mistakenly thought to have originated.]

Cau·ca·soid /káwkə zòyd, -sòyd/ *adj.*, *n.* = **Caucasian** *adj.* 1 ■ *n.* = **Caucasian** *n.* 1

Cau·ca·sus Moun·tains /káwkəssəss-/ mountain range that is considered a boundary between Europe and Asia, extending through Georgia, Armenia, Azerbaijan, and southwestern Russia. Its highest peak is El'brus 18,510 ft./5,642 m.

cau·cus /káwkəss/ *n.* **1.** POLITICAL MEETING a closed meeting of people from one political party, especially a local meeting to select delegates or candidates **2.** SPECIAL-INTEREST GROUP a group of people, often within a larger group, e.g., a legislative assembly, who unite to promote a particular policy or particular interests ○ *the Congressional Black Caucus* ■ *vi.* (**-cused, -cus·ing, -cus·es**) FORM A CAUCUS to hold or meet in a caucus [Mid-18thC. Origin uncertain: perhaps from Algonquian *cau'-cau'-as'u* "elder, adviser."]

cau·dal /káwd'l/ *adj.* **1.** OF A TAIL relating to, involving, typical of, or like a tail **2.** IN HIND PART OF BODY situated in or extending toward the hind part of the body [Mid-17thC. From modern Latin *caudalis*, from Latin *cauda* "tail."] —**cau·dal·ly** *adv.*

cau·date /káw dàyt/, **cau·dat·ed** /-dàytəd/ *adj.* with a tail or an appendage like a tail [Early 17thC. From medieval Latin *caudatus*, from Latin *cauda* "tail."] —**cau·da·tion** /kaw dáysh'n/ *n.*

cau·dex /káw dèks/ (*plural* **-di·ces** /káwdi sèez/ *or* **-dex·es**) *n.* **1.** STEM a trunk of a tree that bears leaves only at its apex, as in a palm or tree fern **2.** STEM BASE the swollen stem base of certain nonwoody perennial plants that survives over the winter and from which new growth is produced [Late 18thC. From Latin, "tree trunk," a variant of *codex* (source of English *codex*), of unknown origin.]

cau·dil·lis·mo /kòwdeel yéezmō, kòwdi-/ *n.* government by a dictator or caudillo [Mid-19thC. From Spanish, formed from *caudillo* "CAUDILLO."]

cau·dil·lo /kow dée yō, -déel yō/ (*plural* **-los**) *n.* a military or political leader, especially a dictator, in a Spanish-speaking country [Mid-19thC. Via Spanish, "leader," from late Latin *capitellum* "little head," from *caput* "head."]

cau·dle /káwd'l/ *n.* a drink made of hot ale or wine, with bread or oatmeal, sugar, and spices [13thC. Via Old Northern French from, ultimately, Latin *caldum* "hot drink," from *calidus* "hot."]

caught past tense, past participle of **catch**

caul /kawl/ *n.* **1.** MEMBRANE IN THE WOMB the membrane surrounding the amniotic fluid, a part of which sometimes covers a baby's head when it is born **2.** = **omentum** [14thC. Origin uncertain.]

caul·dron /káwldrən/ *n.* = **caldron**

Cauliflower

cau·li·flow·er /káwli flòwr/ *n.* **1.** PLANTS VEGETABLE PLANT a plant that is related to the cabbage and has green leaves surrounding a large solid head of edible white or light-green flowers. Latin name: *Brassica oleracea* var. *botrytis.* **2.** FOOD FLOWER HEAD EATEN AS VEGETABLE the flower head of the cauliflower plant, eaten as a vegetable [Late 16thC. Alteration of modern Latin *cauliflora*, from Latin *caulis* "stem" + *flor-*, the stem of *flos* "flower."]

cau·li·flow·er ear *n.* an ear that is permanently swollen and deformed as a result of bleeding into the ear tissues after being repeatedly struck, usually in boxing

caulk /kawk/, **calk** *vt.* (**caulked, caulk·ing, caulks; calked, calk·ing, calks**) **1.** MAKE BOAT WATERTIGHT to make a boat or the seams between its planks watertight by filling the seams with waterproof material, e.g., pitch **2.** FILL SOMETHING IN to fill in the cracks or gaps in something, e.g., a pipe or a window frame, with a waterproof material ■ *n.* = **caulking** [15thC. Via Old Northern French *cauquer* "to tread, stamp down" from Latin *calcare*, from *calc-*, the stem of *calx* "heel" (source of English *inculcate*).] —**caulk·er** *n.*

caulk·ing /káwking/ *n.* material used to make a boat watertight by filling in its seams or to stop up the cracks or gaps in something

caus. *abbr.* GRAM causative

caus·al /káwz'l/ *adj.* **1.** BEING OR INVOLVING THE CAUSE involving or being the cause of something else or the relationship of cause and effect **2.** GRAM EXPRESSING A CAUSE expressing or indicating a cause or the relationship of cause and effect ■ *n.* GRAM WORD EXPRESSING CAUSE a word or other grammatical element that expresses the reason or cause of something, or a relationship of cause and effect —**caus·al·ly** *adv.*

cau·sal·gia /kaw zálјə, -zálјee ə/ *n.* a persistent burning sensation of the skin, caused usually by injury to a peripheral nerve [Mid-19thC. Coined from Greek *kausos* "burning" + -ALGIA.] —**cau·sal·gic** *adj.*

cau·sal·i·ty /kaw zállətee/ *n.* **1.** PRINCIPLE OF CAUSE AND EFFECT the principle that everything that happens must have a cause **2.** QUALITY OF CAUSING EFFECT the action that causes an effect, or the ability to cause an effect

cau·sa·tion /kaw záysh'n/ *n.* **1. CAUSE OR ACT OF CAUSING** the fact that something causes an effect, or the action of causing an effect **2. CAUSE-AND-EFFECT RELATIONSHIP** the relationship between a cause and its effect

caus·a·tive /káwzətiv/ *adj.* **1. INVOLVING CAUSE AND EFFECT** involving being the cause of something or the relationship of the cause and effect **2.** GRAM **EXPRESSING CAUSE** used to describe verbs that express the action of something causing something else ■ *n.* GRAM **CAUSATIVE VERB** a causative verb, or a form or class of causative verbs —**caus·a·tive·ly** *adv.* —**caus·a·tive·ness** *n.*

cause /kawz/ *n.* **1. WHAT MAKES SOMETHING HAPPEN** something that or somebody who makes something happen or exist or is responsible for a certain result ○ *the cause of all the uproar* **2. REASON** a reason or grounds for doing or feeling something ○ *no cause for complaint* **3. PRINCIPLE** a principle or idea that people believe in and work for **4. INTEREST** the interests and goals of a group of people **5.** LAW **LEGAL CASE** a lawsuit, or the reason that a suit is brought in a court of law **6. DISCUSSION SUBJECT** something under discussion or to be decided ■ *vt.* **(caused, caus·ing, caus·es) BE THE REASON FOR SOMETHING** to make something happen or exist or be the reason that somebody does something or something happens [13thC. Via Old French from Latin *causa* "reason, motive, lawsuit" (source of English *accuse* and *excuse*), of unknown origin.] —**caus·a·bil·i·ty** /kàwzə bíllətee/ *n.* —**caus·a·ble** /káwzəb'l/ *adj.* —**cause·less** /-ləss/ *adj.* —**caus·er** /-ər/ *n.*

WORD KEY: ORIGIN

Cause is derived from the Latin word *causa*, meaning "reason," "motive," or "lawsuit," which is also the source of English *accuse* and *excuse*.

WORD KEY: CULTURAL NOTE

Rebel Without a Cause, a movie by U.S. director Nicholas Ray (1955). The movie that made actor James Dean a symbol of an alienated generation, it is the story of Jim, a youth who seems unable to stay out of trouble. His attempts to win the affections of a local girl, Judy, lead to conflict with her boyfriend and, ultimately, tragedy.

'cause /kəz, kawz/ *conj.* because (*informal*) [15thC. Shortening.]

cause cé·lè·bre /kàwz sə lébbrə/ (*plural* **caus·es cé·lè·bres**) *n.* a legal case or public controversy that arouses great interest and becomes famous, because of the issues or the people involved [From French, literally "celebrated case"]

cau·se·rie /kṓzəree, kṓzree/ *n.* **1. CHAT** an informal conversation (*literary*) **2.** LITERAT **INFORMAL PIECE OF WRITING** a short piece of writing in a light informal style [Early 19thC. From French, via *causer* "to chat" from Latin *causari* "to discuss," from *causa* "case, subject."]

cause·way /káwz wày/ *n.* **1. RAISED PATH** a raised path or road over a marsh or water or across land that is sometimes covered by water **2. PAVED ROAD** a road or path with a paved or cobbled surface [15thC. Formed from CAUSEY + WAY.]

caus·ey /káwzee/ (*plural* **-eys**) *n.* a causeway (*archaic*) [12thC. Via Anglo-Norman *caucie* from medieval Latin *calciata (via)* "paved (road)," from Latin *calx* "limestone."]

caus·tic /káwstik/ *adj.* **1.** CHEM **CORRODING** corrosive or burning by chemical action **2. SARCASTIC** very sarcastic, in a way that is particularly bitter or cutting or causes intensely bad emotions ■ *n.* **1.** CHEM **SUBSTANCE THAT CORRODES** a substance that can corrode or burn away other substances by chemical action, especially a strong alkali **2.** OPTICS **CURVE FORMED BY REFLECTIONS** a peaked curve formed on a plane by parallel light rays reflected or refracted from a cylindrical or spherical surface. Caustics can sometimes be seen on the surface of drinks in glazed mugs or cups, or on the base of the mug or cup when empty. [14thC. Via Latin from Greek *kaustikos*, from *kaustos* "combustible," from *kaiein* "to burn" (see CAUTERY).] —**caus·ti·cal** *adj.* —**caus·ti·cal·ly** /-əlee/ *adv.* —**caus·tic·ness** /-nəss/ *n.*

caus·tic pot·ash *n.* = **potassium hydroxide**

caus·tic so·da *n.* = **sodium hydroxide**

cau·ter·ize /káwtə rīz/ (**-ized, -iz·ing, -iz·es**) *vt.* to seal a wound, or destroy abnormal or infected tissue, with a heated instrument, a laser, an electric current, or a caustic substance [14thC. Via French *cautériser* from, ultimately, late Latin *cauterium* (see CAUTERY).] —**cau·ter·i·za·tion** /kàwtəri záysh'n/ *n.*

cau·ter·y /káwtəree/ (*plural* **-ies**) *n.* **1. SOMETHING USED TO CAUTERIZE TISSUE** an instrument or substance used to seal a wound or to destroy abnormal or infected tissue by burning **2. CAUTERIZATION** the process or action of sealing a wound or destroying abnormal or infected tissue by burning [14thC. Via Latin from Greek *kautērion* "branding iron," from *kaiein* "to burn" (source of English *caustic, holocaust*, and *calm*).]

cau·tion /káwsh'n/ *n.* **1. CAREFULNESS** care, thoughtfulness, lack of haste, and close attention that enable somebody to avoid any risks involved in a task or procedure **2. WARNING** a warning to somebody to be careful about something or in doing something **3. UNUSUAL PERSON** a surprising or amusing person or thing (*dated*) ■ *vt.* **(-tioned, -tion·ing, -tions) 1. WARN** to warn or advise somebody that something is risky or dangerous **2.** *U.K.* LAW **GIVE WARNING ABOUT EVIDENCE** to give a formal warning to somebody who has been arrested that anything he or she says may be used in evidence [Late 16thC. Via French from the Latin stem *caution-*, from *caut-*, the past participle stem of *cavere* "to take heed" (source also of English *caveat*).] —**cau·tion·er** *n.* ◇ **throw caution to the wind(s)** to be reckless

cau·tion·ar·y /káwsh'n èrree/ *adj.* involving, giving, or being a warning

cau·tious /káwshəss/ *adj.* having or showing care, thoughtfulness, restraint, and lack of haste [Mid-17thC. From CAUTION, on the model of *ambitious*.] —**cau·tious·ly** *adv.* —**cau·tious·ness** *n.*

WORD KEY: SYNONYMS

cautious, careful, chary, circumspect, prudent, vigilant, wary, guarded, cagey

CORE MEANING: attentive to risk or danger

cautious a general term for being aware of potential risk and modifying your behavior accordingly; **careful** taking reasonable care to avoid risks; **chary** extremely cautious, often to the extent of being reluctant to act; **circumspect** taking into consideration all possible circumstances and consequences before acting; **prudent** a term suggesting cautiousness arising from good judgment or shrewdness; **vigilant** extremely alert and conscious of possible dangers; **wary** combining vigilance with feelings of suspicion; **guarded** cautious about sharing information with others; **cagey** an informal term for "guarded," suggesting an element of craftiness.

Cav., **cav.** *abbr.* cavalry

cav·al·cade /kàvv'l káyd, kávv'l kàyd/ *n.* **1. PROCESSION** a procession, especially one of people on horses, in carriages, or in cars **2. SERIES** a series or procession of things or people, especially a spectacular or dramatic one [Late 16thC. Via French from Italian *cavalcata*, from *cavalcare* "to ride on horseback," via medieval Latin *caballicare* from Latin *caballus* "horse."]

cav·a·lier /kàvv'l éer/ *adj.* **CARELESS** showing an arrogant or jaunty disregard or lack of respect for something or somebody ■ *n.* **1. GENTLEMAN** a gallant or chivalrous gentleman, especially one escorting a lady (*formal*) **2. MOUNTED SOLDIER** a knight or soldier who fought on horseback (*archaic*) [Mid-16thC. Via French from Italian *cavaliere* "knight" from medieval Latin *caballarius* "horseman," from Latin *caballus* "horse," of unknown origin.] —**cav·a·lier·ly** *adv.*

Cav·a·lier *n.* a supporter of King Charles I in the English Civil War. ◊ **Roundhead**

ca·val·la /kə vállə/ (*plural* **-la** *or* **-las**) *n.* **1. TROPICAL FISH** a tropical marine fish with a flattened body and forked tail. Family: Carangidae. **2.** = **king mackerel** [Early 17thC. From Spanish *caballa* "horse mackerel," via late Latin from Latin *caballus* "horse."]

cav·al·ry /kávv'lree/ (*plural* **-ries**) *n.* **1. SOLDIERS ON HORSEBACK** the part of an army made up of soldiers trained to fight on horseback **2. MOBILE TROOPS** the more mobile part of a modern army, using armored vehicles and helicopters [Mid-16thC. Via French from Italian *cavalleria* "mounted militia," from *cavallo* "horse," from Latin *caballus*, of unknown origin.]

cav·al·ry·man /kávv'lrimən/ (*plural* **-men** /-mən/) *n.* a soldier belonging to a regiment of cavalry

ca·va·ti·na /kàvvə téenə, kaa-/ (*plural* **-nas** *or* **-ne** /-téenee/) *n.* a short and simple operatic song, especially a slow aria of 18th- and 19th-century Italian opera, usually followed by a livelier cabaletta [Early 19thC. From Italian.]

cave /kayv/ *n.* **LARGE UNDERGROUND HOLLOW** a large, naturally hollowed-out place in the ground, or in rock above ground, that can be reached from the surface or from water ■ *vt.* **(caved, cav·ing, caves) HOLLOW SOMETHING OUT** to hollow out or undermine something [13thC. Via Old French from, ultimately, Latin *cavus* "hollow" (source also of English *cavern, cavity, concave*, and *excavate*).]

cave in *v.* **1.** *vti.* **COLLAPSE** to collapse or cause something to collapse because of pressure or because of being undermined **2.** *vi.* **YIELD** to yield to persuasion or threats, after trying to resist

ca·ve·at /káyvee àt, kàvvee àt/ *n.* **1. WARNING OR PROVISO** something said as a warning, caution, or qualification **2.** LAW **REQUEST TO A COURT** an official request to a court not to proceed with a case without notice to the person making the request [Mid-16thC. From Latin, literally "let him or her beware," from *cavere* "to heed" (source of English *caution*).]

ca·ve·at emp·tor /-émp tawr/ *n.* the commercial principle that the buyer is responsible for making sure that goods bought are of a reasonable quality, unless the seller is offering a guarantee of their quality [Early 16thC. From Latin, "let the buyer beware."]

cave·fish /káyv fìsh/ (*plural* **-fish** *or* **-fish·es**) *n.* a small North American freshwater fish that lives in subterranean waters and has underdeveloped eyes. Family: Amblyopsidae.

cave-in *n.* **1. COLLAPSE** a collapse of something caused by pressure or undermining **2. ROOF FALL** a place where something has collapsed because of pressure or being undermined **3. YIELDING** a yielding to persuasion or threats, after trying to resist

cave·man /káyv màn/ (*plural* **-men** /-mèn/) *n.* **1. STONE AGE MAN** somebody living in a cave, especially a prehistoric human being of the Paleolithic period **2. BRUTE** a man who behaves in a brutish or uncivilized way (*informal*)

cave paint·ing *n.* any of the paintings made on the walls of caves by Paleolithic peoples in different parts of the world

cav·er /káyvər/ *n.* somebody who explores and climbs in underground caves and passages for sport

cav·ern /kávvərn/ *n.* **LARGE CAVE** a large underground cave, or a large chamber in an underground series of caves ■ *vt.* **(-erned, -ern·ing, -erns) 1. MAKE SOMETHING HOLLOW** to make a mountain, cliff, or area of ground hollow **2. ENCLOSE** to enclose something in a cave or cavern (*literary*) [14thC. Directly or via French *caverne* from Latin *caverna*, from *cavus* "hollow" (see CAVE).]

cav·ern·ous /kávvərnəss/ *adj.* **1. LIKE CAVERN** like or suggestive of a cavern, especially in being large, dark, deep, and hollow **2. HOLLOW-SOUNDING** with a hollow, resonating sound —**cav·ern·ous·ly** *adv.*

caves·son /kávvəssən/ *n.* a stiff noseband used in breaking horses [Late 16thC. Via French *caveçon* from, ultimately, medieval Latin *capitium* "head covering," from Latin *capit-*, the stem of *caput* "head."]

ca·vet·to /kə véttō/ (*plural* **-ti** /-tee/) *n.* a concave architectural molding with a curve that is roughly a quarter circle [Mid-17thC. From Italian, a diminutive of *cavo* "hollow," from Latin *cavus* (see CAVE).]

cav·i·ar /kávvee aar, kaavee aar/, **cav·i·are** *n.* the salted roe of a large fish, particularly the sturgeon, eaten as a delicacy [Mid-16thC. Via French from Italian *caviaro* from Turkish *havyar*, from Persian dialect *khāvyār*.]

cav·il /kávv'l/ *vi.* **(-iled** *or* **-illed, -il·ing** *or* **-il·ling, -ils) OBJECT FOR NO GOOD REASON** to make objections about something on small and unimportant points ■ *n.* **CARPING CRITICISM** a trivial and unreasonable objection [Mid-16thC. Via French *caviller* from Latin *cavillari*, from *cavilla* "scoffing, mockery."] —**cav·il·er** *n.*

cav·ing /káyving/ *n.* the activity of exploring and climbing in underground caves and passages for sport

ca·vi·tand /kávvitənd/ *n.* CHEM a molecule, especially a synthetic receptor, that is hollow and has one open end [Late 20thC. Formed from CAVITY.]

cav·i·tate /kávvi tàyt/ **(-tat·ed, -tat·ing, -tates)** *vt.* to form bubbles or cavities in a substance [Early 20thC. Back-formation from CAVITATION.]

cav·i·ta·tion /kàvvi táysh'n/ *n.* **1.** PHYS **DISTURBANCE OF LIQUID** the rapid formation and collapse of bubbles in a liquid, caused by the movement of something in the liquid, e.g., a propeller, or by waves of high-frequency sound **2. PITTING OF SURFACE** the pitting of a solid surface as a result of the forces of repeated cavitation in a surrounding liquid **3.** MED **FORMATION OF CAVITIES IN TISSUE** the formation of cavities in body tissue caused by a disease, e.g., as an effect of tuberculosis on the lungs [Late 19thC. From CAVITY + -ATION.]

cav·i·ty /kávvitee/ (*plural* **-ties**) *n.* **1. HOLLOW PLACE** a hole or hollow space in something **2.** DENT **HOLE IN TOOTH** a hole in a tooth, caused by decay **3.** ANAT **HOLLOW WITHIN THE BODY** a hollow area inside the body [Mid-16thC. Via French *cavité* from late Latin *cavitas*, from Latin *cavus* "hollow" (see CAVE).]

ca·vo-re·lie·vo /kaávō ri leévō, kày-/ (*plural* **ca·vo-re·lie·vos** *or* **ca·vo-re·lie·vi** /kaávō ri leévee, káy-/) *n.* a relief sculpture in which even the highest part lies below the level of the original surface, or this style of relief sculpture [Late 19thC. From Italian, "hollow relief."]

ca·vort /kə vávrt/ (**-vort·ed, -vort·ing, -vorts**) *vi.* to behave in a physically lively and uninhibited way [Late 18thC. Origin uncertain: perhaps an alteration of CURVET.]

Ca·vour /kə voór/, **Camillo Benso, Conte di** (1810–61) Italian statesman. He was prime minister of Piedmont (1852–59, 1860–61) and chief architect of the unification of Italy (1861). Full name **Camilo Benso, Conte di Cavour**

ca·vy /káyvee/ (*plural* **-vies**) *n.* a short-tailed ground-living South American rodent of the family that includes the guinea pig. Family: Caviidae. [Late 18thC. Via modern Latin *Cavia*, genus name, from Galibi *cabiai*.]

caw /kaw/ *vi.* (**cawed, caw·ing, caws**) **MAKE BIRD CALL** to make the loud harsh cry of a crow or a related bird, or make a sound like this ■ *n.* **BIRD'S CRY** the loud harsh cry of a crow or a related bird, or a sound like this [Late 16thC. An imitation of the sound.]

Cax·ton /kákstən/, **William** (1422?–91) English printer. He established the first printing press in England (1477) and printed over 100 books, including *The Canterbury Tales.*

cay /kee, kay/ *n.* a small low island or reef in the sea, made of coral or sand, especially in the Caribbean [Late 17thC. Via Spanish *cayo* "shoal," of uncertain origin: probably from Taino.]

Cay·enne /kī én, kay én/ city and capital of French Guiana, situated in the northern coast of Cayenne Island. Population: 41,667 (1990).

cay·enne pep·per, cay·enne *n.* a very hot-tasting red powder made of the dried and ground fruit and seeds of several kinds of chili. It is used in cooking and as a gastric astringent. [Early 18thC. Alteration of earlier *kian* (from Tupi *kyynha*), by association with CAYENNE.]

Cay·man Is·lands /káymən-/ group of three islands, situated in the northwestern Caribbean Sea, approximately 200 mi./320 km northwest of Jamaica. Capital: George Town. Population: 25,355 (1990). Area: 118 sq. mi./306 sq. km.

Ca·yu·ga /kay yoógə, kī yoógə/ (*plural* **-ga** *or* **-gas**) *n.* a member of a Native American people who originally occupied lands along Cayuga Lake, and whose members now live mainly in western New York State, Wisconsin, Ontario, and Oklahoma. The Cayuga were one of the five peoples who formed the Iroquois Confederacy, later known as the Six Nations. [Mid-18thC. From the Cayuga language, literally "the place where locusts were taken out."] —**Ca·yu·ga** *adj.*

Ca·yu·ga Lake one of the Finger Lakes, situated in Cayuga and Seneca counties, central New York State. Area: 66 sq. mi./171 sq. km.

cay·use /kī yoóss, kī yoóss/ *n. Northwest U.S.* a small pony of a western North American breed [Mid-19thC. Shortening of *Cayuse pony*, named for the *Cayuse*, a Native American people of the Pacific Northwest.]

CB *abbr.* RADIO Citizens Band

CBA *abbr.* cost-benefit analysis

CBC *abbr.* Canadian Broadcasting Corporation

C.B.D. *abbr.* **1. C.B.D., cbd** cash before delivery **2.** central business district

CB·er /si beé ər/ *n.* somebody who communicates by radio on the Citizens Band

CBI *abbr.* computer-based instruction

CBO *abbr.* Congressional Budget Office

CBR *abbr.* ARMS, MIL chemical, bacteriological, and radiation

CBS *abbr.* Columbia Broadcasting System

CBT *abbr.* computer-based training

CBW *abbr.* chemical and biological warfare

cc, c.c. *abbr.* **1.** BUSINESS (carbon) copy **2.** cubic centimeter **3.** AUTOMOT, MEASURE cubic capacity (*used after a number to indicate the power of an internal-combustion engine*)

CC *abbr.* **1.** City Council **2.** closed caption (*used in television guides to indicate that a program is available with captions for hearing-impaired people*)

cc. *abbr.* chapters

CCA *abbr.* current-cost accounting

CCC *abbr.* Civilian Conservation Corps

CCD *abbr.* **1.** Confraternity of Christian Doctrine **2.** COMPUT charge-coupled device

CCK *abbr.* cholecystokinin

cckw. *abbr.* counterclockwise

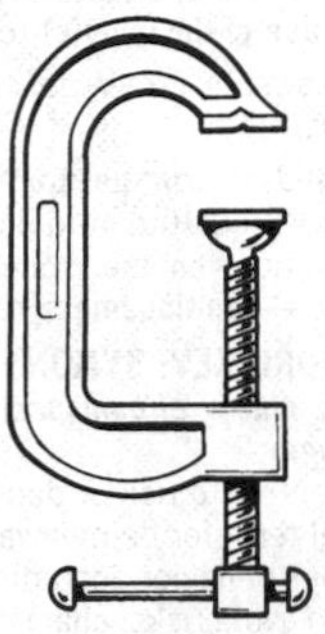

C-clamp

C-clamp *n.* a metal clamp shaped like a letter C, with horizontal flat pieces at the ends, that can be adjusted by a screw

C clef *n.* a symbol on a musical staff that shows the position of middle C. The alto and tenor clefs are the only commonly used C clefs today, and are used mostly in viola, cello, and bassoon music.

CCS *abbr.* Combined Chiefs of Staff

CCTV *abbr.* closed-circuit television

CCU *abbr.* coronary care unit

cd *symbol.* candela

Cd *symbol.* cadmium

CD *abbr.* **1.** compact disk **2.** certificate of deposit **3.** Civil Defense **4.** Corps Diplomatique (*often displayed on the backs of cars that belong to embassies*)

cd. *abbr.* cord

c.d. *abbr.* cash discount

c/d *abbr.* **1.** ACCT carried down **2.** cum dividend

C/D *abbr.* certificate of deposit

CDC *abbr.* Centers for Disease Control

CDD *abbr.* MIL certificate of disability for discharge

CDE *n.* a compact disk that can have its contents erased and something else recorded onto it. Full form **compact disk erasable.** ◊ **CDR**

cdf *abbr.* STATS cumulative distribution function

CDI, CD-I *n.* an interactive compact disk containing text, video, and audio and accessed using a self-contained player plugged into a television set. Full form **compact disk interactive**

CDN *abbr.* Canada (*international vehicle registration*)

Cdn. *abbr.* Canadian

CDR *n.* a compact disk that can be used to record something but cannot be erased. Full form **compact disk recordable.** ◊ **CDE**

Cdr., CDR. *abbr.* Commander

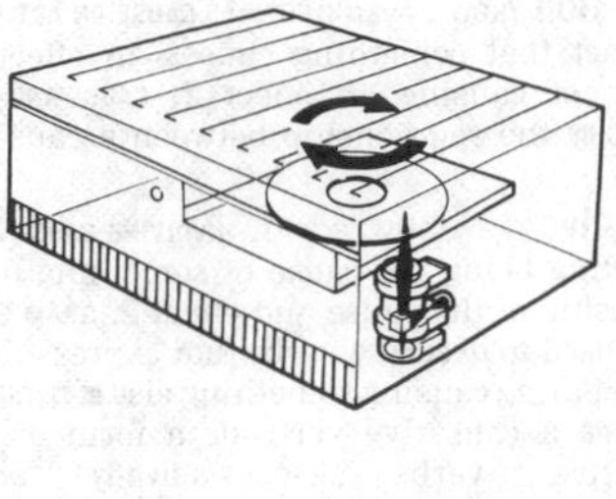

CD-ROM: CD-ROM within a disk drive

CD-ROM /seé dee róm/ *n.* a compact disk containing a large amount of data, including text and images, that can be viewed using a computer but cannot be altered or erased. Full form **compact disk read-only memory**

CDT *abbr.* Central Daylight Time

CDV *abbr.* **1.** CD-video **2.** compact video disk

CD-vid·e·o *n.* **1. COMPACT DISK WITH VIDEO IMAGES** a compact disk used to store and play back video images **2. PLAYER FOR CD-VIDEOS** a player for compact disks that stores and plays back video images

CDW *abbr.* INSUR collision damage waiver

Ce *symbol.* cerium

CE *abbr.* **1.** Common Era **2.** civil engineer

C.E. *abbr.* **1.** chemical engineer **2.** chief engineer **3.** civil engineer **4.** Common Era

CEA *abbr.* Council of Economic Advisors

ce·a·no·thus /seé ə nṓthəss/ *n.* a North American shrub that has dark green leaves and tiny clusters of blue, white, or pink flowers. Genus: *Ceanothus.* [Late 18thC. Via modern Latin, genus name, from Greek *keanōthos*, a kind of thistle.]

cease /seess/ *v.* (**ceased, ceas·ing, ceas·es**) **1.** *vi.* **STOP HAPPENING** to come to an end **2.** *vti.* **END** to bring something to an end ■ *n.* **ENDING** an end or pause (*archaic*) [14thC. Via French *cesser* from Latin *cessare*, from *cedere* (see CEDE).] ◇ **without cease** without stopping, or without a break

cease·fire /seéss fīr/ *n.* **1. AGREEMENT TO STOP FIGHTING** an agreement between opposing sides in a conflict that they will stop fighting, usually for a limited time during which they will try to reach a more permanent peace agreement **2. ORDER TO STOP FIRING** a military order to stop firing

cease·less /seéssləss/ *adj.* without pause or end —**cease·less·ly** *adv.* —**cease·less·ness** *n.*

Ceau·şes·cu /chow shéskoo/, **Nicolae** (1918–89) Romanian former head of state. The Communist president of Romania (1967–89), he was overthrown and executed in a popular revolution.

Ce·bu /say boó/ island of the Philippines, in the Pacific Ocean, near the islands of Negros and Mindanao. Population: 2,646,000 (1990). Area: 1,707 sq. mi./4,422 sq. km.

Ce·cil·ia /se seélyə/, **St.** (?–230?) Roman Christian martyr. She is regarded as the patron saint of music.

ce·cro·pi·a moth /si krṓpee ə-/ *n.* a large North American moth with red, white, and black wings that has a silkworm caterpillar. Latin name: *Hyalophora cecropia.* [Mid-19thC. Via modern Latin, species name, named for CECROPS.]

Ce·crops /seé krops/ *n.* in Greek mythology, the first king of Attica and founder of Athens

ce·cum /seékəm/ (*plural* **-ca**), **cae·cum** (*plural* **-ca** /seékə/) *n.* the pouch in which the large intestine begins, which is open at one end [Early 18thC. From Latin *(intestinum) caecum* "blind (gut)," from *caecus* "blind."] —**ce·cal** *adj.* —**ce·cal·ly** *adv.*

CED *abbr.* Committee for Economic Development

ce·dar /seédər/ *n.* **1. TALL EVERGREEN TREE** a tall evergreen tree of Europe, Asia, and Africa, with spreading branches, needles, and large rounded upright cones. Genus: *Cedrus.* **2. TREE LIKE TRUE CEDAR** an evergreen tree that resembles a true cedar, e.g., a red cedar **3. WOOD FROM CEDAR** the durable fragrant wood of a cedar tree [Pre-12thC. Via Old French *cedre* from, ultimately, Greek *kedros* "cedar, juniper," of unknown origin.]

Ce·dar river that flows southeastward from southeastern Minnesota to southeastern Iowa, where it joins the Iowa River. Length: 300 mi./483 km.

ce·dar-ap·ple rust *n.* a disease that develops first on red cedars and then on apple trees in its progress through its life cycle and is caused by a rust fungus. Latin name: *Gymnosporangium juniperi-virginianae.*

Ce·dar Cit·y city in southwestern Utah, north of Zion National Park and northeast of Saint George. Population: 17,811 (1996).

Ce·dar Falls city in northeastern Iowa, on the Cedar River, northwest of Waterloo and Cedar Rapids. Population: 34,884 (1996).

Cedar of Lebanon

ce·dar of Leb·a·non *n.* a tall long-lived cedar with horizontally spreading branches that grows in Lebanon and Turkey. Latin name: *Cedrus libari.*

Ce·dar Rap·ids city in eastern Iowa, on the Cedar River, northwest of Davenport. Population: 113,482 (1996).

ce·dar wax·wing *n.* a brown North American bird that has a crested head, bright red waxy drops at the end of some wing feathers, and a yellow-tipped tail. It eats the berries of red cedar trees. Latin name: *Bombycilla cedrorum.*

cede /seed/ (**ced·ed, ced·ing, cedes**) *vt.* to surrender or give up something, e.g., land, rights, or power, to another country, group, or person (*formal*) [Early 16thC. Via French *céder* from Latin *cedere* "to give way" (source of English *concede, precede, excess,* and *ancestor*).]

WORD KEY: ORIGIN

Cede *is derived from the Latin word* cedere, *meaning "to give way," which is also the source of English* abscess, accede, ancestor, concede, decease, exceed, precede, predecessor, proceed, procession, recede, *and* succeed.

ce·di /sáydee/ (*plural* **-di**) *n.* **1.** see table at **currency 2.** **COIN OR BILL WORTH A CEDI** a coin or bill worth a cedi [Mid-20thC. Origin uncertain: possibly from Akan (Fanti) *sedī* "small shell, cowrie."]

ce·dil·la /sə díllə/ (*plural* **-las**) *n.* a mark placed beneath the letters c (ç) and s (ş) in some languages. In French and Portuguese, it shows that c is pronounced like s, not k. In modern Turkish it shows whether c and s are voiced or voiceless. [Late 16thC. Via obsolete Spanish, literally "little z," from Latin *zeta.*]

CEEB *abbr.* College Entry Examination Board

CEGEP /sáy zhèp/, **cegep** *n.* in Quebec, a post-secondary institution offering two-year programs leading to university and three-year programs qualifying students in a variety of professions and trades. Full form **Collège d'Enseignement Général et Professionel**

cei·ba /sáybə/ (*plural* **-bas**) *n.* = **silk-cotton tree** [Early 17thC. Via Spanish from Arawak, literally "giant tree."]

ceil /seel/ (**ceiled, ceil·ing, ceils**) *vt.* **1.** **PROVIDE WITH CEILING** to construct a ceiling for a room **2.** **LINE A CEILING** to line a ceiling with a material, e.g., plaster or wood [Early 16thC. Origin uncertain: perhaps via Old French, "canopy," from Latin *caelum* "heaven"; or via assumed Old French *celer* from Latin *caelare* "to carve," from *caelum* "chisel."]

cei·lidh /káylee/ *n.* a social event with singing and dancing to Scottish or Irish traditional music and storytelling [Late 19thC. Via Irish *céilidhe* and Scots Gaelic *ceilidh* from Old Irish *célide* "visit," from *céle* "companion."]

ceil·ing /seéling/ *n.* **1.** BUILDING **INSIDE TOP OF ROOM** the overhead surface of a room, or the material used to line this surface **2.** **UPPER LIMIT** a level above which something is not allowed to rise, e.g., prices, rents, or wages **3.** AIR **FLYING HEIGHT** the maximum height at which an aircraft can fly **4.** METEOROL **CLOUD LEVEL** the highest point, usually the base of a layer of clouds, from which the surface of the Earth can be seen [Mid-16thC. Formed from CEIL.] —**ceil·inged** *adj.* ◇ **hit the ceiling** to become very angry

ceil·om·e·ter /see lómmətər/ *n.* an instrument for measuring the height of a cloud ceiling [Mid-20thC. Formed from CEILING.]

cel·a·don /-dòn, séllədʼn/ *n.* **1.** COLORS **PALE GREEN COLOR** a pale green color tinged with gray **2.** CERAMICS **GRAY-GREEN PORCELAIN** a type of Chinese porcelain with a grayish-green glaze [Mid-18thC. From French *céladon,* from the name of a character in D'Urfé's romance *L'Astrée.*] —**cel·a·don** *adj.*

Ce·lae·no /se leénō/ *n.* in Greek mythology, one of the Pleiades

cel·an·dine /séllən dìn, -deèn/ *n.* **1.** **YELLOW FLOWER** a tall plant of the poppy family that has yellow flowers in summer and bright orange, poisonous sap. Latin name: *Cheladonium majus.* **2.** = **lesser celandine** [Pre-12thC. Via Old French *celidoine* from, ultimately, Greek *khelidonion,* from *khelidōn* "swallow"; so called because the plant flowered in spring, when swallows returned from migration.]

cel·an·dine pop·py *n.* a North American plant that resembles the greater celandine. Latin name: *Stylophorum diphyllum.*

-cele *suffix.* tumor, swelling ○ *varicocele* [From Greek *kēlē,* of unknown origin]

ce·leb /sə léb/ *n.* somebody who is a celebrity (*informal*) [Early 20thC. Shortening.]

Cel·e·bes /séllə beèz, sə leé beèz/ island in Indonesia, situated in the Malay Archipelago east of Borneo. Population: 13,732,500 (1995). Area: 72,989 sq. mi./189,040 sq. km.

Cel·e·bes Sea part of the Pacific Ocean, surrounded by the Philippines, Borneo, Celebes, the Sulu Archipelago, and the Sangihe Islands. Area: 165,000 sq. mi./427,000 km.

cel·e·brant /sélləbrənt/ *n.* **1.** **OFFICIATING PRIEST** a priest who is officiating at the Eucharist **2.** **WORSHIPER** somebody who takes part in a religious ceremony **3.** **SOMEBODY CELEBRATING** somebody who takes part in a celebration [Mid-19thC. From Latin *celebrare* (see CELEBRATE).]

cel·e·brate /séllə bràyt/ (**-brat·ed, -brat·ing, -brates**) *v.* **1.** *vti.* **SHOW HAPPINESS** to show happiness that something good or special has happened, by doing such things as eating and drinking together or playing music ○ *I told them about my promotion, and we went out to celebrate.* ○ *a noisy crowd of fans celebrating the victory* **2.** *vt.* **MARK AN OCCASION** to mark a special occasion or day by ceremonies or festivities **3.** *vti.* **PERFORM A RELIGIOUS CEREMONY** to perform a religious ceremony according to the prescribed forms **4.** *vt.* **PRAISE SOMETHING** to praise something publicly or make it famous [Mid-16thC. From Latin *celebrare* "to attend a festival," from *celeber* "frequented, famous" (source of English *celebrity*).] —**cel·e·bra·tion** /sèllə bráysh'n/ *n.* —**cel·e·bra·tive** /séllə bràytiv, -brətiv/ *adj.* —**cel·e·bra·tor** /-bràytər/ *n.* —**cel·e·bra·to·ry** /sélləbrə tàwree, sə lébbrə-/ *adj.*

cel·e·brat·ed /séllə bràytəd/ *adj.* famous and admired

ce·leb·ri·ty /sə lébbritee/ (*plural* **-ties**) *n.* **1.** **FAMOUS PERSON** somebody who is famous during his or her own lifetime **2.** **FAME** the state of being famous [14thC. Directly or via French *célébrité* from Latin *celebritas,* from *celeber* "frequented, famous" (source of English *celebrate*).]

ce·le·ri·ac /sə lérree àk/ *n.* a vegetable that is a type of celery with an edible root that looks like an irregularly shaped turnip and is eaten cooked or raw. Latin name: *Apium graveolens* var. *rapaceum.* [Mid-18thC. Alteration of CELERY.]

ce·ler·i·ty /sə lérrətee/ *n.* quickness in movement or in doing something (*formal*) [15thC. Via French *célérité* from Latin *celeritas,* from *celer* "swift" (source of English *accelerate*).]

cel·er·y /séllәree/ *n.* **1.** **LONG-STEMMED VEGETABLE** a vegetable plant with long, crisp flattish stems that are eaten raw or cooked. Latin name: *Apium graveolens* var. *dulce.* **2.** **CELERY STALKS** celery stalks eaten as a vegetable **3.** **SEASONING** the seeds of the celery plant, which are used as a seasoning [Mid-17thC. Via French *céleri* from, ultimately, Greek *selinon* "parsley."]

Celery

cel·er·y cab·bage *n.* = **Chinese cabbage** [So called because the long stalks topped with leaves resemble celery]

cel·er·y pine *n.* a New Zealand tree that has shoots resembling celery and yields timber. Latin name: *Phyllocladus trichomanoides.*

cel·er·y root *n.* = **celeriac**

ce·les·ta /sə léstə/ (*plural* **-tas**), **ce·leste** *n.* a musical instrument with keys that are played to make hammers strike metal plates, making a soft tinkling sound [Late 19thC. Alteration of French *céleste,* literally "celestial," from Latin *caelestis* (see CELESTIAL).]

ce·les·tial /sə léschəl/ *adj.* **1.** **HEAVENLY** belonging to, suitable for, in, or typical of heaven **2.** **OF THE SKY** relating to, involving, or observed in the sky or outer space [14thC. Via French from, ultimately, Latin *caelestis,* from *caelum* "sky, heaven."] —**ce·les·tial·ly** *adv.*

ce·les·tial bod·y *n.* any of the objects that are permanently present in the sky, e.g., a star or a planet

Ce·les·tial Em·pire *n.* a name for the former Chinese Empire (*archaic or literary*) [Translation of a Chinese term that stresses the divinity of the emperor and his importance in the universal scheme of things]

ce·les·tial e·qua·tor *n.* the great circle in which the plane of the Earth's equator intersects the celestial sphere

ce·les·tial globe *n.* a globe showing the positions of the celestial bodies

ce·les·tial ho·ri·zon *n.* = **horizon** *n.* **3**

ce·les·tial me·chan·ics *n.* the branch of astronomy concerned with the motions and positions of celestial bodies in gravitational fields (*takes a singular verb*)

ce·les·tial nav·i·ga·tion *n.* the steering of a ship or aircraft by observing the positions of the stars by means of triangulation

ce·les·tial pole *n.* either of the two points where a line in continuation of the earth's axis intersects the celestial sphere

ce·les·tial sphere *n.* the imaginary sphere around the Earth on which the Sun, Moon, stars, and planets appear to be placed

cel·es·tite /séllə stìt, sə lé stìt/, **cel·es·tine** /séllə steèn, -stìn/ *n.* a mineral, consisting of strontium sulfate, that is the chief ore of strontium. It is usually white but occasionally brown, orange, red, or blue. Formula: $SrSO_4$. [Early 19thC. Formed from Latin *caelestis* "of the sky" (see CELESTIAL).]

ce·li·ac /seélee àk/, **coe·li·ac** *adj.* relating to, involving, or contained in the abdomen [Mid-17thC. Via Latin from Greek *koiliakos,* from *koilia* "abdomen," from *koilos* "hollow."]

ce·li·ac dis·ease *n.* a disorder caused by a sensitivity to gluten that makes the digestive system unable to deal with fat. Symptoms include diarrhea and anemia.

cel·i·ba·cy /séllibəssee/ *n.* **1.** **SEXUAL ABSTINENCE** a state of sexual abstinence for religious reasons or as a personal choice **2.** **LIFE WITHOUT MARRIAGE** the condition of being unmarried [Mid-17thC. Formed from Latin *caelibatus* (see CELIBATE).]

cel·i·bate /sélləbət/ *adj.* **1.** **ABSTAINING** abstaining from sex **2.** **UNMARRIED** unmarried, especially because of a religious vow ■ *n.* **1.** **SOMEBODY WHO ABSTAINS FROM SEX** an adult who abstains from sex for religious reasons or as a personal choice **2.** **SOMEBODY UNMARRIED** an unmarried person, especially one who has taken a vow of celibacy [Early 19thC. From Latin *caelibatus,* from *caelebs* "unmarried," of unknown origin.] —**cel·i·bate·ly** *adv.*

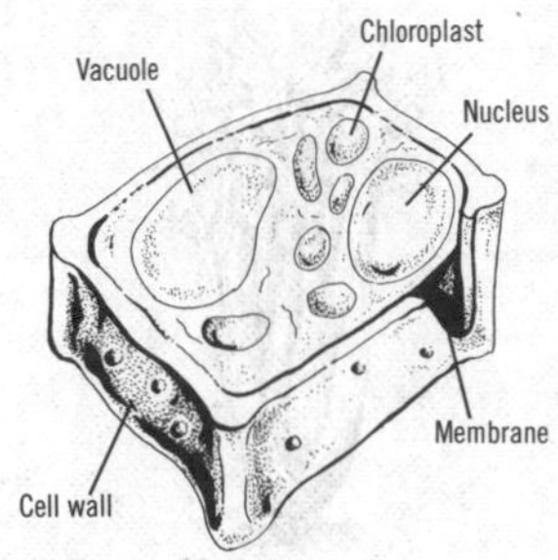

Cell: Structure of a plant cell

cell /sel/ *n.* **1.** ROOM FOR HOLDING PRISONER a room in a prison, in which one or more prisoners are confined, or a small room in a police station, used to confine somebody who has been arrested **2.** SMALL ROOM a very small and simple room, especially in a monastery or convent **3.** BIOL BASIC UNIT OF LIVING THING the smallest independently functioning unit in the structure of an organism, usually consisting of one or more nuclei surrounded by cytoplasm and enclosed by a membrane. Cells also contain organelles, e.g., mitochondria, lysosomes, and ribosomes. **4.** SMALL ENCLOSED STRUCTURE a small contained or hollow unit in a structure, e.g., a compartment in a honeycomb or the reproductive organs of a plant, or an area on an insect's wing **5.** ELEC, ENG SOMETHING THAT PRODUCES ELECTRICITY a device that produces electrical energy by the chemical action of electrodes in an electrolyte **6.** = **solar cell 7.** POL ACTIVIST GROUP a small group of people who work together and are part of a larger organization, especially members of a political organization who work in secret **8.** TELECOM RANGE OF MOBILE PHONE TRANSMITTER the area covered by one of the transmitters in a mobile telephone system that automatically switches a traveling user between short-range radio stations **9.** COMPUT SPACE IN TABLE a space for information in a table, e.g., in a computer spreadsheet, formed where a row and a column intersect **10.** CHR DEPENDENT RELIGIOUS HOUSE a small religious house that is dependent on a larger religious community [Pre-12thC. Via Old French *celle* from Latin *cella* "small chamber" (see CELLA).]

cel·la /séllə/ (*plural* **-lae** /-lee/) *n.* the inner room of a classical Greek or Roman temple, which contained the shrine or statue of the god [Late 17thC. From Latin, "small chamber." Ultimately from an Indo-European base meaning "to cover, conceal," which is also the ancestor of *hole, hell, helmet,* and *conceal.*]

cel·lar /séllər/ *n.* **1.** UNDERGROUND ROOM a room wholly or partly below ground level that is not suitable as living space and is usually used for storage **2.** BASEMENT a room on the lowest level of a building, usually underground, that can be used for storage but can also be living, working, or recreational space **3.** = **storm cellar 4.** PLACE FOR STORING WINE a room where wine is stored **5.** STOCK OF WINE a stock of wine **6.** LOWEST STANDING the lowest standing, grade, or rank, e.g., for an athlete ■ *vt.* (**-lared, -lar·ing, -lars**) STORE WINE to store something, especially wine, in a cellar [13thC. Via Anglo-Norman *celer* from late Latin *cellarium* "group of storage chambers," from Latin *cella* (see CELLA).]

cel·lar·age /séllərij/ *n.* **1.** STORAGE CHARGE a fee charged for storing something in a cellar **2.** CELLAR SPACE a cellar or cellars, or the amount of space in a cellar

cel·lar dwel·ler *n.* SPORTS a team habitually at the bottom of its league

cel·lar·er /séllərər/ *n.* somebody who is in charge of stores of food and drink, especially in a monastery

cel·lar·ette /sèllə rét/, **cel·lar·et** *n.* a cabinet or sideboard for storing bottles of wine and glasses

cel·lar·man /séllərmən/ (*plural* **-men** /séllərmən/) *n.* a man who is in charge of the cellar in a bar or restaurant and is responsible for maintaining good storage conditions

cell·block /sél blòk/ *n.* a group of cells forming a unit in a prison

cell di·vi·sion *n.* the process by which a cell divides to form two new cells, either to produce identical cells (**mitosis**) or to produce cells with half the number of chromosomes (**meiosis**)

Cel·li·ni /che léenee/, **Benvenuto** (1500–71) Italian sculptor and goldsmith. He wrote an autobiography considered a classic work of Renaissance literature.

cel·list /chéllist/ *n.* a musician who plays the cello

cell·mate /sél màyt/ *n.* a prisoner who shares a cell with another

cell mem·brane *n.* the membrane that surrounds the cytoplasm, through which substances pass in and out of the cell

cel·lo /chéllō/ (*plural* **-los**) *n.* a large stringed instrument of the violin family that is held upright between a seated player's knees and played with a bow. The cello has a full deep sound. [Late 19thC. Shortening of VIOLONCELLO.]

cel·lo·bi·ose /sèllə bī ōss, -ōz/ *n.* a sugar obtained by the breakdown of cellulose. Formula: $C_{12}H_{22}O_{11}$. [Early 20thC. Coined from CELLULOSE + BI- + -OSE.]

cel·lo·phane /séllə fàyn/ *n.* a thin, transparent waterproof material made from wood pulp and used for wrapping and covering [Early 20thC. A blend of CELLULOSE and -PHANE.]

Cellphone

cell·phone /sél fòn/ *n.* a mobile telephone operated through a cellular radio network [Late 20thC. Contraction of *cellular telephone.*]

cel·lu·lar /séllyələr/ *adj.* **1.** BIOL INVOLVING LIVING CELLS relating to or consisting of living cells **2.** CONTAINING SMALL PARTS OR GROUPS relating to small parts or groups making up a whole **3.** TELECOM ORGANIZED INTO CELLS organized as a system of cells, especially for radio communication **4.** INDUST, GEOL POROUS porous in texture and containing many small cavities **5.** TEXTILES OPEN-TEXTURED woven or knitted in a way that gives thickness of cloth and openness of texture [Mid-18thC. Via French *cellulaire* from modern Latin *cellularis,* from Latin *cellula* (see CELLULE).] —**cel·lu·lar·i·ty** /sèllyə lérrətee/ *n.* —**cel·lu·lar·ly** /séllyələrlee/ *adv.*

cel·lu·lar phone *n.* = **cellphone**

cel·lu·lar ra·di·o *n.* the type of radio communication used for mobile phones that consists of a network of transmitters, each covering a small area. The traveling user is automatically switched between radio stations.

cel·lu·lar tel·e·phone *n.* = **cellphone**

cel·lu·lase /séllyə làys, -làyz/ *n.* an enzyme found in certain microorganisms that converts cellulose to cellobiose [Early 20thC. Formed from CELLULOSE.]

cel·lule /sél yōōl/ *n.* a small cell in a living organism [Mid-19thC. Via French from Latin *cellula,* literally "small cell," from *cella* (see CELLA).]

cel·lu·lite /séllyə līt/ *n.* fatty deposits beneath the skin of the body that give a lumpy or grainy appearance to the skin surface, e.g., on the thighs and buttocks [Mid-20thC. From French, from *cellule* "CELLULE."]

cel·lu·li·tis /sèllyə lítiss/ *n.* infection and inflammation of the tissues beneath the skin

cel·lu·loid /séllyə lòyd/ *n.* **1.** INDUST COLORLESS PLASTIC a type of flammable transparent plastic, made from nitrocellulose and a plasticizer such as camphor **2.** CINEMA FILM the photographic film used for making movies **3.** CINEMA MOVIES the movies as a medium or art form ■ *adj.* INDUST OF OR WITH CELLULOID made of or treated with celluloid [Mid-19thC. Coined from CELLULOSE + -OID.]

cel·lu·lo·lyt·ic /sèllyəlō líttik/ *adj.* used to describe a process or an organism that breaks down the plant material cellulose, e.g., in the stomachs of cows and other ruminants [Mid-20thC. Coined from CELLULOSE and -LYTIC.]

cel·lu·lose /séllyə lòss, -lòz/ *n.* the main constituent of the cell walls of plants and algae. Its derivatives are used for making plastics, lacquers, explosives, and synthetic fibers. [Mid-19thC. From French, from Latin *cellula,* literally "small cell," from *cella* "cell" (see CELL).] —**cel·lu·lo·sic** /sèllyə lóssik/ *adj.*

cel·lu·lose ac·e·tate *n.* a chemical compound produced by the reaction of acetic or sulfuric acid on cellulose, used for making photographic film, plastics, textile fibers, and varnishes

cel·lu·lose ni·trate *n.* nitrocellulose (*dated*)

cell wall *n.* the outermost layer of a cell in plants and certain fungi, algae, and bacteria, providing a supporting framework

ce·lom *n.* = **coelom**

ce·lo·sia /si lṓzhə/ (*plural* **-sias** *or* **-sia**) *n.* a plant with feathery yellow to purplish-red flowers belonging to a genus that includes cockscomb. Genus: *Celosia.* [Early 19thC. From modern Latin, genus name, from Greek *kēlos* "burnt, dry," from the appearance of the flowers of some species.]

Cel·si·us /sélsee əss, sélshəss/ *adj.* using or measured on a metric temperature scale where water freezes at 0°C and boils at 100°C. The term "Celsius" is usually preferred to "centigrade," especially in technical contexts. ◊ **Fahrenheit, kelvin.** Symbol **C** [Mid-19thC. Named for its inventor Anders *Celsius* (1701–44), a Swedish astronomer.]

celt /selt/ *n.* a prehistoric chisel or ax that has a metal or stone head with a beveled edge [Early 18thC. From medieval Latin *celtis* "chisel."]

Celt /selt, kelt/, **Kelt** *n.* **1.** SOMEBODY WHO SPEAKS CELTIC LANGUAGE somebody who speaks or whose ancestors spoke a Celtic language **2.** MEMBER OF ANCIENT PEOPLE somebody who belonged to an ancient Indo-European people who, in pre-Roman times, lived in central and western Europe. They were driven to the western fringes of the continent by the Romans and certain Germanic peoples, especially the Angles and Saxons. [Mid-16thC. Via Latin *Celtae* "Celts" from Greek *Keltoi.* "Descendant of ancient Celts, speaker of Celtic" came from French *Celte* "Breton" (presumed representative of the ancient Gauls).]

Celt. *abbr.* Celtic

Celt·i·ber·i·an /sèlti bérree ən, kèlt-/ *n.* somebody who belonged to a Celtic people who inhabited the Iberian peninsula during classical times [Early 17thC. Formed from Latin *Celtiberia* "ancient province of Iberia," from *Celtae* "Celts" (see CELT) + *Iberia* (see IBERIAN).] —**Celt·i·ber·i·an** *adj.*

Celt·ic /séltik, kéltik/ *adj.* OF CELTS relating to or typical of the Celts or their cultures or languages ■ *n.* INDO-EUROPEAN LANGUAGE GROUP a group of languages that includes Irish, Scottish Gaelic, Welsh, and Breton. Part of the Indo-European family of languages, it has Brythonic and Goidelic subgroups. About one and a half million people speak a Celtic language.

Celt·ic cross *n.* a cross that has a broad ring around the intersection of the upright and crossbar

Celt·i·cism /sélti sìzzəm, kélt-/ *n.* **1.** LANGUAGE CELTIC WORD a word or idiom of Celtic origin that has become naturalized in another language. In English, examples include "plaid" from Scottish Gaelic and "leprechaun" from Irish Gaelic. **2.** CELTIC TRADITION a custom or belief of Celtic origin

Celt·i·cist /séltissist, kélt-/, **Kelt·i·cist** /kéltissist/ *n.* somebody who studies the Celts or their languages

cem·ba·lo /chémbə lō/ (*plural* **-li** /chémbə lee/ *or* **-los**) *n.* = **harpsichord** [Mid-19thC. From Italian, contraction of *clavicembalo,* from medieval Latin *clavicymbalum,* from Latin *clavis* "key" (see CLAVICLE) + *cymbalum* "cymbal" (see CYMBAL).] —**cem·ba·list** *n.*

ce·ment /sə mént/ *n.* **1.** POWDER FOR CONCRETE a fine gray powder of calcined limestone and clay. It is mixed with water and sand to make mortar, or with water, sand, and aggregate to make concrete. **2.** CONCRETE a building material that sets hard, made by mixing cement with water, sand, and aggregate **3.** GLUE a glue or similar bonding substance **4.** HUMAN BOND something that unites people or groups **5.** DENT SUBSTANCE USED IN DENTISTRY a substance used in dentistry for filling cavities and anchoring bridgework or crowns. ◊ **amalgam 6.** ANAT = **cementum 7.** GEOL MATERIAL BINDING ROCK a substance that binds together the particles in sedimentary rocks and fills the spaces ■ *vti.* (**-ment·ed, -ment·ing, -ments**) **1.** FIX OR BECOME FIXED WITH CEMENT to fix something in place with cement or a similar substance, or become fixed in this way **2. APPLY CEMENT TO SOMETHING** to cover or fill something with cement or a similar substance **3. MAKE OR BECOME CLOSE FRIENDS** to make a relationship between people very strong or permanent, or become very strong or permanent [14thC. Via French *ciment* from Latin *caementum* "quarry stone," (in plural) "stone chips (for making mortar)," from assumed *caedmentum*, from *caedere* "to hew" (see CHISEL).] —**ce·ment·er** *n.* ◇ **set in cement** firmly established and without any likelihood of change

ce·men·ta·tion /seè men táysh'n/ *n.* **1. CEMENTING** the application of cement or a similar substance to something, or the result of this **2.** CIV ENG **CEMENTING OF ROCKS** the injecting of cement into holes or fissures in rocks to make them watertight or strong **3.** METALL **HEATING METAL WITH POWDER** the modification of a solid, especially a metal, by heating it with one or more other substances that will diffuse into the surface, e.g., the production of steel by heating it with charcoal **4.** GEOL **SEDIMENTARY ROCK FORMATION** the process in which percolating groundwater deposits a cementing material to form a sedimentary rock

ce·ment·ite /sə mén tīt/ *n.* a hard brittle compound of iron and carbon that forms in some types of cast iron, in carbon steels, and in alloys of carbon and iron. Formula: Fe_3C.

ce·ment mix·er *n.* **1. MACHINE FOR MAKING CONCRETE** a transportable machine with a revolving drum in which cement powder, water, sand, and other materials can be mixed to make concrete, mortar, or stucco **2. CONCRETE TRUCK** a truck with a large revolving drum for mixing, transporting, and pouring concrete

ce·men·tum /sə méntəm/ *n.* the thin layer of bony tissue that covers the dentin of the roots and neck of a tooth [Mid-19thC. From Latin *caementum* (see CEMENT).]

cem·e·ter·y /sémmə tèrree/ (*plural* **-ies**) *n.* an area of ground in which the dead are buried [14thC. Via late Latin *coemeterium* from Greek *koimētērion* "dormitory," from *koiman* "to put to sleep." Originally "Roman catacombs."]

CEMF *abbr.* counter-electromotive force

cen. *abbr.* **1.** central **2.** century

-cene *suffix.* HIST recent ○ *Pliocene* [From Greek *kainos* "new." Ultimately related to Latin *recens*, the source of English *recent*.]

ceno- *prefix.* = **coeno-**

cen·o·bite /sénnə bīt/, **coen·o·bite** *n.* somebody who belongs to a convent, monastery, or other religious community [15thC. Via French *cénobite* or ecclesiastical Latin *coenobita*, from, ultimately, Greek *koinobion*, literally "common life."]

ce·no·gen·e·sis /seènə jénnəssiss, sènnə-/, **coen·o·gen·e·sis, caen·o·gen·e·sis** *n.* BIOL the development by an embryo, fetus, or larva of organs or body parts that are lost in adult life

cen·o·taph /sénnə tàf/ *n.* a monument erected as a memorial to a dead person or dead people buried elsewhere, especially people killed fighting a war [Early 17thC. From, ultimately, Greek *kenotaphion*, literally "empty tomb," from *kenos* "empty" (see KENOSIS) + *taphos* "tomb" (see EPITAPH).] —**cen·o·taph·ic** /sènnə táffik/ *adj.*

ce·no·te /si nṓtee/ *n.* a deep natural hole found in limestone, especially in Yucatán, Mexico. Cenotes were holy for the Mayans, who used them as places of sacrifice. [Mid-19thC. Via Yucatán Spanish from Maya *tzonot*.]

Ce·no·zo·ic /seènə zṓ ik, -zṓ ik/ *adj.* **OF MOST RECENT GEOLOGICAL ERA** belonging or relating to the most recent era of geological time, covering the period from the present to about 65 million years ago, during which modern plants and animals evolved ■ *n.* **MOST RECENT GEOLOGICAL ERA** the era of geological time that covers the period from the present day to about 65 million years ago [Mid-19thC. Coined from Greek *kainos* (source of English *-cene*) + -ZOIC.]

cense /sens/ (**censed, cens·ing, cens·es**) *vt.* **1. BURN INCENSE TO DEITY** to burn incense to a deity at an altar or shrine **2. PERFUME SOMETHING WITH INCENSE** to perfume a place or worshipers with incense [14thC. Shortening of French *encenser*, ultimately from Latin *incendere* "to set fire to," from *candere* "to glow" (source of English *candle*).]

Censer

cen·ser /sénsər/ *n.* a container used for burning incense, especially one that is swung in a religious procession or ceremony [13thC. From, ultimately, Old French *censier*, shortening of *encensier*, from *encens* "incense," from ecclesiastical Latin *incensum*, from the past participle of Latin *incendere* (see CENSE).]

cen·sor /sénsər/ *n.* **1. OFFICIAL REMOVING OBJECTIONABLE MATERIAL** an official who examines plays, films, letters, and publications with a view to removing or banning content considered to be offensive or a threat to security **2. SOMEBODY THAT SUPPRESSES SOMETHING** somebody or something that exercises suppressive control **3.** HISTORY **ANCIENT ROMAN OFFICIAL** either of two elected magistrates of ancient Rome who were responsible for holding the census, overseeing public morals, and controlling aspects of finance and taxation **4.** PSYCHIAT **INHIBITING FORCE IN MIND** a mechanism believed to be responsible for what can and cannot emerge from the subconscious to the conscious mind. It is thought to prevent harmful memories, ideas, and desires from reaching the conscious level. ■ *vt.* (**-sored, -sor·ing, -sors**) **1. REMOVE OFFENSIVE PARTS FROM SOMETHING** to remove or change any part of a publication, play, or film considered offensive or a threat to security **2. EXERCISE CONTROL OVER SOMETHING** to suppress or control something that may offend or harm others [Mid-16thC. From Latin *censere* (see CENSUS).] —**cen·sor·a·ble** *adj.* —**cen·so·ri·al** /sen sáwree əl/ *adj.*

cen·so·ri·ous /sen sáwree əss/ *adj.* **1. HIGHLY CRITICAL** inclined or eager to criticize people or things **2. CONVEYING CRITICISM** expressing strong disapproval or harsh criticism —**cen·so·ri·ous·ly** *adv.* —**cen·so·ri·ous·ness** *n.*

cen·sor·ship /sénsər shìp/ *n.* **1. SUPPRESSION OF PUBLISHED OR BROADCAST MATERIAL** the suppression of all or part of a publication, play, or film considered offensive or a threat to security **2. ANY SUPPRESSION** the suppression or attempted suppression of something regarded as objectionable **3.** HISTORY **ANCIENT ROMAN OFFICE** the office, authority, or term of an ancient Roman censor **4.** PSYCHIAT **SUPPRESSION OF MEMORIES** the suppression of potentially harmful memories, ideas, or desires from the conscious mind

cen·sur·a·ble /sénshərəb'l/ *adj.* deserving severe criticism, or likely to be severely criticized —**cen·sur·a·bil·i·ty** /sènshərə bíllətee/ *n.* —**cen·sur·a·ble·ness** /sénshərəb'lnəss/ *n.* —**cen·sur·a·bly** /-əblee/ *adv.*

cen·sure /sénshər/ *n.* **1. DISAPPROVAL** severe criticism **2. OFFICIAL CONDEMNATION** official expression of disapproval or condemnation, e.g., of a legislator by the legislature ■ *vt.* (**-sured, -sur·ing, -sures**) **1. CRITICIZE SOMEBODY OR SOMETHING** to subject somebody or something to severe criticism **2. CONDEMN SOMEBODY OR SOMETHING** to express official disapproval or condemnation of somebody or something, e.g., by a vote of a legislature [14thC. From, ultimately, Latin *censura* "judgment," from *censere* (see CENSUS).] —**cen·sur·er** *n.*

WORD KEY: SYNONYMS

See Synonyms at ***criticize***.

cen·sus /sénsəss/ (*plural* **-sus·es**) *n.* **1. COUNT OF POPULATION** an official count of a population carried out at set intervals **2. ANY COUNT** any systematic count or survey **3.** HISTORY **REGISTRATION OF ROMANS FOR TAXATION** in ancient Rome, a registration of the population and their property that was used for assessing taxes [Early 17thC. From Latin *censere* "to appraise, assess" (source of English *censor* and *censure*). Originally "tax."]

cent /sent/ *n.* **1. UNIT OF CURRENCY IN THE U.S., ETC.** a subunit of currency in countries such as the United States, Canada, Australia, New Zealand or South Africa where the main currency is the dollar or, in the case of the Netherlands, the guilder. It is worth one hundredth of the main unit. See table at **currency 2. COIN WORTH ONE CENT** a coin worth one cent [14thC. Directly or via French, cent "hundred," or Italian *cento*, "hundred," from Latin *centum* "hundred" (source of English *century*). Originally "hundred" (still in PERCENT).] ◇ **not worth a red cent** worthless

cent. *abbr.* **1.** centigrade **2.** central **3.** century

cent- *prefix.* = **centi-**. symbol **c**

cen·tal /sént'l/ *n.* = **hundredweight** *n.* 1 [Late 19thC. Formed from Latin *centum* (see CENT); perhaps modeled on QUINTAL.]

cen·tas /sén taàss/ (*plural* **-tas**) *n.* **1.** see table at **currency 2. COIN WORTH ONE CENTAS** a coin worth one centas

Centaur

cen·taur /sén tàwr/ *n.* in Greek mythology, a wild creature with the head, arms, and torso of a man joined to the body of a horse at its neck. Most centaurs were depicted as drunken womanizers. [14thC. From, ultimately, Latin *centaurus*, from Greek *kentauros*, of unknown origin. Originally, in Greek, "a wild people of Thessaly," supposedly very fine horse riders.]

Cen·tau·rus /sen táwrəss/ *n.* a large conspicuous constellation in the southern hemisphere. It contains Alpha Centauri and Beta Centauri, two very bright stars.

cen·tau·ry /sén tàwree/ (*plural* **-ries**) *n.* a plant of the gentian family, with pink or purple flowers. It has been used in herbal medicine for centuries. Latin name: *Centaurium erythaea*. [14thC. From late Latin *centaurea*, from its having been, according to legend, discovered by the centaur Chiron.]

cen·ta·vo /sen taávō/ (*plural* **-vos**) *n.* **1.** see table at **currency 2. COIN WORTH A CENTAVO** a coin worth one centavo [Late 19thC. From Spanish and Portuguese, literally "hundredth," both formed from Latin *centum* (see CENT).]

cen·te·nar·i·an /sènt'n áiree ən/ *n.* **100-YEAR-OLD PERSON** somebody who has reached or passed the age of a hundred ■ *adj.* **1. 100 YEARS OLD** at least a hundred years of age **2. OF CENTENARIANS** relating to or characteristic of a 100-year-old person

cen·ten·a·ry /sen tènnəri, sént'n èrree/ *adj.* **1. OF A CENTURY** relating to or involving a period of one hundred years **2. ONCE-A-CENTURY** occurring every 100 years **3.** *U.K.* = **centennial** ■ *n.* (*plural* **-ries**) **1. CENTURY** a period of one hundred years **2.** *U.K.* = **centennial** [Early 17thC. From Latin *centenarius* "containing a hundred," from *centeni* "hundred each," from *centum* (see CENT).]

cen·ten·ni·al /sen ténnee əl/ *adj.* **OF CENTURY** relating to or involving a period of a hundred years ■ *n.* **100TH ANNIVERSARY** the hundredth anniversary of something, or a celebration held to mark the anniversary ■ *adj.* **1. ONCE A CENTURY** occurring every hundred years **2. OF 100TH ANNIVERSARY** marking an anniversary of one hundred years [Late 18thC. Formed from Latin *centum* (see CENT); modeled on BIENNIAL.] —**cen·ten·ni·al·ly** *adv.*

Cen·ten·ni·al State *n.* Colorado (*informal*)

cen·ter /séntər/ *n.* **1. MIDDLE POINT OR AREA** the middle point, area, or part of something that is the same distance from all edges or opposite sides **2.** MATH **MIDDLE OF CIRCLE OR SPHERE** the interior point that is the same distance from all points on the circumference of a circle or the surface of a sphere or the vertices of a polygon **3.** MATH **MIDDLE OF LINE** the point on a line that is the same distance from both ends **4.** FOOD **FOOD FILLING** the filling of a chocolate, doughnut, or other food **5. MAIN PART OF TOWN** the part of a town or city where the main stores, offices, and other facilities are situated **6. PLACE FOR PARTICULAR ACTIVITY** a place where a particular activity is carried on ○ *a sports center* **7. FOCUS OF ATTENTION** the point that is the focus of attention or interest ○ *the issue at the center of the controversy* **8. INFLUENTIAL PLACE OR ORGANIZATION** a place, area, or group of people exerting control or influence over something or somebody else ○ *a center of design innovation* **9. CLUSTER OR CONCENTRATION** a place or part where something is concentrated or focused ○ *a population center* **10. cen·ter, Cen·ter** POL **POLITICAL MODERATES** those political parties or the section of a party holding views that are neither left-wing nor right-wing **11.** SPORTS **MIDDLE PLAYER OR POSITION** a player or position in the middle of the field or court, usually responsible for initiating play **12. PIVOTAL POINT OR AXIS** the point or line around which something rotates **13.** BASEBALL = **center field 14.** PHYS **POINT WHERE FORCE ACTS** the point at or through which a force is considered to act **15.** ANAT **GROUP OF NERVE CELLS REGULATING FUNCTION** a group of nerve cells, especially within the central nervous system, that controls a particular function of the body **16.** MECH ENG **CONICAL PART OF LATHE** a part of a lathe that supports the work to be turned **17.** MECH ENG **MARK TO GUIDE DRILL** a dimple made in metal with a pointed tool (**center punch**) to mark the center of a larger hole to be drilled ■ *v.* (**-tered, -ter·ing, -ters**) **1.** *vt.* **PUT SOMETHING IN MIDDLE** to position something in the middle of something **2.** *vti.* **FOCUS ON THEME** to have, or cause something to have its focus on a theme or topic ○ *the debate centers on the possible health risks involved* **3.** *vti.* **CONCENTRATE OR FOCUS** to be concentrated, or cause something to be concentrated, in a particular place or on a particular thing **4.** *vt.* FOOTBALL **PASS BALL BACK BETWEEN LEGS** to pass the football back between the legs at the beginning of a down **5.** *vt.* SPORTS **PASS BALL TOWARD MIDDLE** to pass, hit, or kick a ball or puck from the edge of the playing area toward the middle [14thC. From, ultimately, Greek *kentron* "point," from *kentein* "to prick" (source of English *eccentric*). "Middle" came from "stationary point of a compass."]

cen·ter back *n.* a player or position in the middle of the back line in various sports

cen·ter bit *n.* a drill attachment or tool for boring or cutting with a pointed projection in the middle and cutters at the sides

cen·ter·board /séntər bàwrd/ *n.* a keel in a sailboat that can be retracted upward in shallow water

Cen·te·reach /séntər reech/ town in Suffolk County, New York, situated on Long Island southeast of Stony Brook. Population: 26,720 (1990).

cen·tered /séntərd/ *adj.* **1. PLACED IN THE MIDDLE** positioned at the same distance from all edges or opposite sides **2. WELL-BALANCED** exhibiting confidence, self-awareness, and often a sense of determination — **cen·tered·ness** *n.*

cen·ter field, cen·ter *n.* **1. MIDDLE THIRD OF OUTFIELD** in baseball, the part of the outfield behind second base **2. POSITION OF CENTER FIELDER** the position of the baseball player who plays center field —**cen·ter field·er** *n.*

cen·ter·fold /séntər fōld/ *n.* **1. PICTURE OR FEATURE ON CENTER SPREAD** a single illustration, advertisement, or feature that covers the two facing pages in the middle of a magazine or newspaper, especially a photograph of a nude model **2. SOMEBODY POSING IN CENTERFOLD** somebody who is photographed, especially naked or nearly naked, for a centerfold **3.** = **center spread**

cen·ter for·ward *n.* the player or position in the middle of the forward attacking line in games such as soccer and hockey

cen·ter half·back *n.* the player or position in the middle of the halfback-line in soccer and field hockey

cen·ter·line /séntər līn/ *n.* **1. LINE DOWN MIDDLE OF ROAD** a solid or dashed line on a road that marks where traffic should flow, either separating lanes going in opposite directions or multiple lanes going the same way **2. LINE DOWN MIDDLE** a real or imaginary line through or along the middle of something

cen·ter of cur·va·ture *n.* the center of a circle whose radius is perpendicular to a line tangent to any point on the concave side of a smooth curve. ◊ **radius of curvature**

cen·ter of ex·cel·lence *n.* a place where the highest standards of achievement are aimed for in a given sphere of activity

cen·ter of grav·i·ty *n.* **1. FOCUS OF GRAVITATIONAL FORCES** the point through which the sum of gravitational forces on a body can be considered to act **2.** = **center of mass**

cen·ter of mass *n.* the point at which the total mass of a body or system is assumed to be centered and upon which the sum of external forces can be considered to act

cen·ter·piece /séntər pèess/ *n.* **1. SOMETHING IN CENTRAL POSITION** an object placed in the middle of something as decoration or to attract attention **2. MAIN FEATURE** the most important part or feature

cen·ter punch *n.* a pointed tool used in metalworking for making a dimple to guide a drill bit prior to drilling a hole

cen·ter spread *n.* **1. FACING MIDDLE PAGES** the two pages that face each other in the middle of a magazine or newspaper **2. ARTICLE ON MIDDLE PAGES** a magazine or newspaper article featured in the middle to give it prominence

cen·ter stage *n.* **1. MIDDLE OF STAGE** the middle area of a theater stage **2. FOCUS OF INTEREST** the center of people's attention or interest ■ *adv.* **1. IN MIDDLE OF STAGE** in or to the middle area of a theater stage **2. TO CENTER OF ATTENTION** at or to the center of people's attention or interest

Cen·ter·ville /séntər vìl/ **1.** city in northern Utah east of the Great Salt Lake and north of Salt Lake City. Population: 14,382 (1996). **2.** city in southwestern Ohio, a southeastern suburb of Dayton. Population: 22,456 (1996).

cen·tes·i·mal /sen téssəməl/ *adj.* **1. IN 100THS** divided into hundredths **2. 100TH** constituting one-hundredth of something **3. USING BASE OF 100** used to describe a number system that uses a base of 100 ■ *n.* **100TH PART** one hundredth of something [Late 17thC. Formed from Latin *centesimus* "hundredth," from *centum* "hundred" (see CENT).] —**cen·tes·i·mal·ly** /sen téssəməlee/ *adv.*

cen·tes·i·mo /sen téssəmō/ (*plural* **-mos** *or* **-mi** /-mee/) *n.* **1.** see table at **currency 2. COIN WORTH ONE CENTESIMO** a coin worth one centesimo [Mid-19thC. From Italian, from Latin *centesimus* (see CENTESIMAL).]

centi- *prefix.* **1.** hundredth ○ *centipoise* **2.** hundred ○ *centipede* [Via French from, ultimately, Latin *centum* "one hundred" (see CENT)]

cen·ti·grade /sénti gràyd/ *adj.* = **Celsius.** symbol **C** (*not used in scientific contexts*) [Early 19thC. From French, from earlier forms of CENTI- + -GRADE.]

cen·ti·gram /sénti gràm/ *n.* one hundredth of a gram

cen·ti·li·ter /sénti leètər/ *n.* a unit of liquid measure equal to one hundredth of a liter

cen·til·lion /sen tíllee ən/ (*plural* **-lions** *or* **-lion**) *n.* **1. ONE FOLLOWED BY 303 ZEROS** in the United States, Canada, and France, the number represented by the figure 1 followed by 303 zeros **2.** *U.K.* **ONE FOLLOWED BY 600 ZEROS** in the United Kingdom and Germany, the number represented by the figure 1 followed by 600 zeros [Mid-19thC. Formed from CENTI-, the second element being modeled on words such as MILLION and BILLION.]

cen·time /saán teèm, saan teèm/ *n.* **1.** see table at **currency 2. COIN WORTH ONE CENTIME** a coin worth one centime [Early 19thC. Via French from, ultimately, Latin *centesimus* (see CENTESIMAL).]

cen·ti·me·ter /sénti meètər/ *n.* a unit of length equal to one hundredth of a meter

cen·ti·me·ter-gram-sec·ond *adj.* using or relating to a measurement system that uses the centimeter as the unit for length, the gram for weight, and the second for time. In scientific contexts this has been replaced by the SI system.

cen·ti·mo /séntəmō/ (*plural* **-mos**) *n.* **1.** see table at **currency 2. COIN WORTH ONE CENTIMO** a coin worth one centimo [Late 19thC. Via Spanish from French *centime*, ultimately from Latin *centesimus* (see CENTESIMAL).]

cen·ti·mor·gan /sénti màwrgən/ *n.* a unit of measurement used to indicate how closely genes are linked together on the same chromosome [Mid-20thC. Coined from CENTI-+MORGAN, from the geneticist Thomas Hunt *Morgan*.]

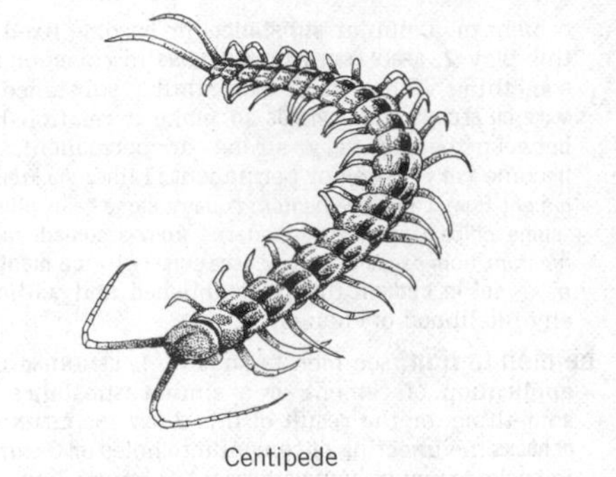

Centipede

cen·ti·pede /séntə peèd/ *n.* a small, fast-moving invertebrate animal with a long slender body divided into many segments, most of which bear one pair of legs. Centipedes eat other arthropods, e.g., small insects. Class: Chilopoda. [Mid-17thC. From, ultimately, Latin *centipeda*, literally "with a hundred feet," from earlier forms of CENTI- + -PEDE, from its many legs.]

cen·ti·pede grass *n.* a low-growing grass of Asian origin that grows in dense mats. It is used in the southern states of the United States as a lawn grass. Latin name: *Eremochloa ophiuroides.*

cen·ti·poise /sénti pòyz/ *n.* a unit of measurement for viscosity equal to one hundredth of a poise [Early 20thC. From CENTI- and POISE.]

cent·ner /séntnər/ *n.* **1. 50 KG** a unit of weight used in some European countries equivalent to 110.23 lb./50 kg **2. 100 KG** a unit of weight equivalent to 220.46 lb./100 kg [Mid-16thC. Via obsolete German from Latin *centenarius* (see CENTENARY).]

centr- *prefix.* = **centro-** (*used before a vowel*)

cen·tra plural of **centrum**

cen·tral /séntrəl/ *adj.* **1. IN THE MIDDLE** in, near, or forming the middle of something **2. EQUIDISTANT FROM OTHER POINTS** at approximately the same distance from a number of different points or places **3. IN MAIN PART OF TOWN** in the part of a town or city where the main stores, offices, and other facilities are situated **4. HAVING CONTROL OVER PARTS** controlling the activities of connected, subordinate, or subsidiary parts ○ *a central authority* **5. HAVING LINKED COMPONENTS** used to describe a system of linked devices controlled by a single unit or at a single point **6. CRUCIAL** of critical importance or great influence ○ *the notion is central to their thinking on the subject* **7. DOMINANT** with a major or the principal role **8.** ANAT **RELATING TO CENTRUM** relating to the centrum of a vertebra **9.** PHON **SAID WITH TONGUE IN MIDDLE POSITION** used to describe a vowel articulated with the tongue at or near the middle of the hard palate, as is the final vowel in "cola" ■ *n.* **1.** UTIL **TELEPHONE OPERATOR** a telephone exchange or an operator working there (*dated*) ○ *Hello, central. Get me the police!* **2. SUPERVISORY OFFICE** a main office or location that coordinates the work of several branches or a group of ndividuals ○ *fundraising central for the pledge drive* [Mid-17thC. From, ultimately, Latin *centralis*, from *centrum* (see CENTER).] — **cen·tral·ly** *adv.*

Cen·tral Af·ri·can Fed·er·a·tion federation from 1953 to 1963 of Nyasaland, Northern Rhodesia, and Southern Rhodesia, present-day Malawi, Zambia, and Zimbabwe

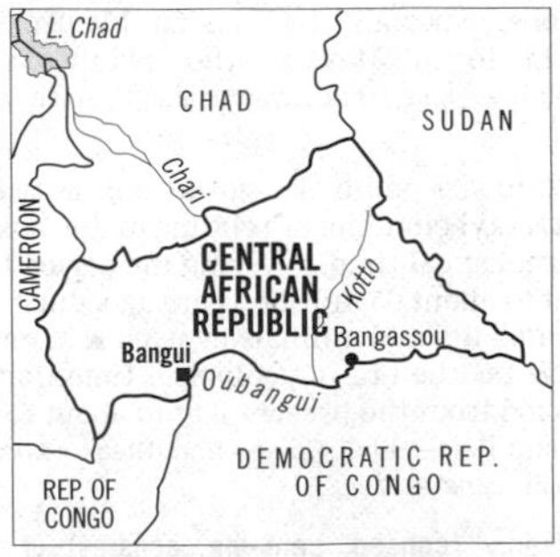

Central African Republic

Cen·tral Af·ri·can Re·pub·lic landlocked country in central Africa. Formerly part of French Equatorial Africa, it became independent in 1960. It is bordered on the north by Chad, on the east by Sudan, on the south by the Democratic Republic of Congo, and on the west by Cameroon. Language: French. Currency: C.F.A. franc. Capital: Bangui. Population: 3,308,198 (1997). Area: 240,324 sq. mi./622,436 sq. km. Former name **Ubangi-Shari** (until 1958)

Cen·tral A·mer·i·ca the southern part of North America, extending from the southern border of Mexico to northwestern Colombia, South America. It includes the countries of Guatemala, Belize, Honduras, El Salvador, Nicaragua, Costa Rica, and Panama. Population: 31,300,000 (1993). Area: 201,930 sq. mi./523,000 sq. km.

cen·tral an·gle *n.* an angle formed in the center of a circle by the meeting of two radii

cen·tral bank *n.* a financial institution, e.g., the U.S. Federal Reserve Bank, whose function is to regulate state fiscal and monetary activities. It is responsible for the issue of bills and for controlling the flow of currency. —**cen·tral bank·er** *n.*

cen·tral cast·ing *n.* the department in a film or theater production company whose function is to select appropriate actors to audition for specified parts

cen·tral city *n.* a densely populated city at the heart of a metropolitan area

Cen·tral Com·mit·tee *n.* in a Communist party, the part of the bureaucracy responsible for party policy. ◊ **Politburo**

Cen·tral Day·light Time *n.* a variation of Central Standard Time from early April to late October, when clocks are set an hour ahead

Cen·tral Eur·o·pe·an Time *n.* the standard time adopted by most Western European countries, one hour ahead of Greenwich Mean Time

cen·tral gov·ern·ment *n.* the area of government that is concerned with national issues such as taxation, defense, international relations, and trade

cen·tral heat·ing *n.* a system designed to heat a whole building from a single source of heat by pumping hot water or air to room radiators or vents —**cen·tral·ly heat·ed** *adj.*

Cen·tral·ia /sen tráylyə/ city in southwestern Washington, south of Olympia, in a major lumbering area. Population: 13,281 (1996).

Cen·tral In·tel·li·gence Agency *n.* full form of **CIA**

Cen·tral Is·lip town in Suffolk County, New York, situated on Long Island just east of Brentwood. Population: 26,028 (1990).

cen·tral·ism /séntrə lìzzəm/ *n.* the concentration of control, especially political control, in a single authority —**cen·tral·ist** *n., adj.* —**cen·tral·is·tic** /sèntrə lístik/ *adj.*

cen·tral·i·ty /sen trállətee/ *n.* **1.** CRITICAL ROLE the crucial importance of somebody or something **2.** POSITION IN MIDDLE the location of somebody or something in or near the middle of something **3.** LOCATION IN MAIN PART OF TOWN the location of something in the part of a town or city where the main shops, offices, and other facilities are situated

cen·tral·i·za·tion /sèntrəli záysh'n/ *n.* **1.** CONCENTRATION OF POWER IN FEW HANDS the concentration of political or administrative power in a central authority with a resulting lack of power at local or subordinate levels **2.** APPROACHING MIDDLE OF SOMETHING the coming or bringing of something to or toward the middle of something

cen·tral·ize /séntrə lìz/ (**-ized, -iz·ing, -iz·es**) *vti.* **1.** MOVE POWER TO A FEW HANDS to remove political or administrative power from local or subordinate levels and concentrate it in a central authority **2.** CONCENTRATE AT SINGLE PLACE to concentrate or collect something at a single point —**cen·tral·iz·er** *n.*

Cen·tral Mount Stu·art mountain in central Australia, considered the geographical center of the continent. Height: 2,772 ft./845 m.

cen·tral nerv·ous sys·tem *n.* the part of the nervous system, consisting of the brain and spinal cord, that controls and coordinates most functions of the body and mind. Impulses from sense organs travel to the central nervous system and impulses to muscles and glands travel from it. ◊ **spinal cord, brain**

Cen·tral Park *n.* a large park in Manhattan in New York City. It was the first urban park to be developed in the United States and served as a model for subsequent city parks.

cen·tral pro·cess·ing u·nit *n.* the part of a computer that performs operations and executes software commands

cen·tral res·er·va·tion *n. U.K.* = **median strip**

Cen·tral Stan·dard Time, **Cen·tral Time** *n.* **1.** STANDARD TIME IN CENTRAL NORTH AMERICA the standard time in the zone that includes the central states of the United States and the central provinces of Canada. Central Standard Time is six hours behind Greenwich Mean Time. **2.** STANDARD TIME IN CENTRAL AUSTRALIA the standard time in the time zone centered on longitude 135° E, which includes the central part of Australia. It is nine-and-a-half hours behind Greenwich Mean Time.

cen·tral sul·cus *n.* a deep groove in each of the hemispheres of the brain, separating the frontal and parietal lobes

Cen·tral Time *n.* = **Central Standard Time**

Cen·tral Val·ley irrigated valley situated between the Sacramento and San Joaquin rivers in California, and between the Sierra Nevada and Coastal mountain ranges

cen·tre /séntər/ *n., vti.* (**-tred, -tring, -tres**) U.K. = **center**

centri- *prefix.* = **centro-**

cen·tric /séntrik/, **cen·tri·cal** /-trik'l/ *adj.* **1.** AT OR AS THE MIDDLE at or constituting the middle of something **2.** ANAT OF OR FROM NERVE CENTER issuing from or relating to a nerve center **3.** BOT WITH CONCENTRIC LAYERS OF TISSUE used to describe a plant's vascular bundles in which one type of sap-conducting tissue is surrounded by another **4.** BOT TAPERING AND CYLINDRICAL used to describe leaves that are tapering and cylindrical. ◊ **terete 5.** BIOL OF A CLASS OF DIATOMS relating to a class of diatoms that have radial symmetry. Class: Centrales. —**cen·tri·cal·ly** *adv.* —**cen·tric·i·ty** /sen tríssəteé/ *n.*

-centric *suffix.* **1.** having a particular number or kind of centers ○ *hexcentric* ○ *acentric* **2.** having as its center ○ *egocentric* [From medieval Latin *-centricus*, from Latin *centrum* (see CENTER)]

cen·trif·u·gal /sen tríffyəg'l, -tríffəg'l/ *adj.* **1.** PHYS AWAY FROM CENTER acting, moving, or pulling away from a center or axis. ◊ **centripetal 2.** TECH EMPLOYING CENTRIFUGAL FORCE using or operated by centrifugal force **3.** PHYSIOL = **efferent 4.** BOT DEVELOPING OUTWARD used to describe a plant part or tissue that develops from the center outward **5.** POL DECENTRALIZING POWER tending to disperse political or administrative power away from a central authority ■ *n.* TECH APPARATUS USING CENTRIFUGAL FORCE an apparatus that uses centrifugal force, or a rotating drum in such an apparatus —**cen·trif·u·gal·ism** *n.* —**cen·trif·u·gal·ly** *adv.*

cen·trif·u·gal force *n.* an apparent force that seems to pull a rotating or spinning object away from a center

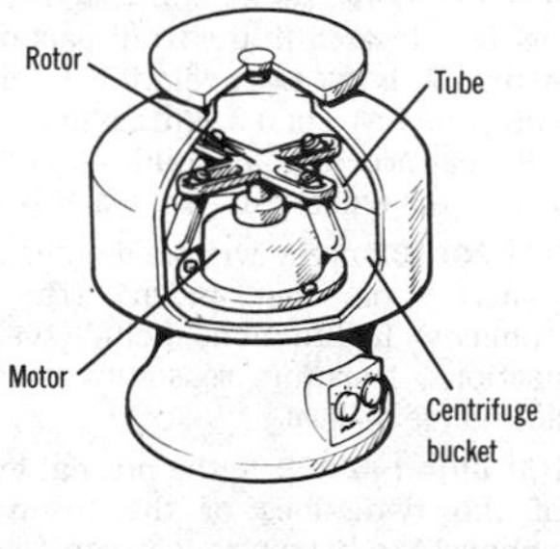

Centrifuge

cen·tri·fuge /séntrə fyoōj/ *n.* **1.** SEPARATION EQUIPMENT a device that rotates rapidly and uses centrifugal force to separate substances of different densities **2.** ROTATING DEVICE a rotating apparatus used to simulate the effects of gravity or acceleration on humans or animals ■ *vt.* (**-fuged, -fug·ing, -fug·es**) SUBJECT SOMETHING TO CENTRIFUGAL ACTION to subject something to the force of a centrifuge, especially in order to separate different substances [Early 18thC. From, ultimately, Latin *centrifugus* "centrifugal," literally "fleeing the center," from *fugere* "to flee" (see FUGITIVE).] —**cen·trif·u·ga·tion** /sàntrəfyə gáysh'n/ *n.*

cen·tri·ole /séntri ōl/ *n.* BIOL a two-part rod-shaped structure with the parts lying at right angles to each other, located in pairs near the nucleus of an animal cell. During cell division, centrioles move to opposite ends of the cell and form the poles of the spindle fibers that pull the chromosomes apart. [Late 19thC. From modern Latin *centriolum*, literally "small center," from *centrum* "center" (see CENTER).]

cen·trip·e·tal /sen tríppət'l/ *adj.* **1.** PHYS TOWARD CENTER acting, moving, or pulling toward a center or axis. ◊ **centrifugal 2.** TECH EMPLOYING CENTRIPETAL FORCE using or operated by centripetal force **3.** PHYSIOL = **afferent 4.** BOT DEVELOPING INWARD used to describe a plant part or tissue that develops from the perimeter inward **5.** CENTRALIZING POWER tending to concentrate political or administrative power in a central authority [Early 18thC. Formed from modern Latin *centripetus*, literally "seeking the center," from Latin *petere* "to seek" (see PETITION).] —**cen·trip·e·tal·ly** *adv.*

cen·trip·e·tal force *n.* a force that pulls a rotating or spinning object toward a center or axis

cen·trism /sén trìzzəm/ *n.* the holding or advocating of moderate political or other views —**cen·trist** *n., adj.*

centro- *prefix.* center ○ *centrosome* [From Latin *centrum* and Greek *kentron* (see CENTER)]

cen·tro·bar·ic /sàntrə bérrik/ *adj.* relating to a center of gravity [Early 18thC. From Greek *kentrobarikē*, literally "center-weight," from *baros* "weight" (see BARO-).]

cen·troid /sén tròyd/ *n.* PHYS = **center of mass** [Late 19thC. Coined from CENTRO- + -OID.]

cen·tro·lec·i·thal /sèntrə léssəthəl/ *adj.* used to describe an egg with the yolk in the middle. ◊ **isolecithal** [Late 19thC. Coined from CENTRO- + LECITHIN + -AL.]

cen·tro·mere /séntrə meér/ *n.* BIOL the point at which two parts (**chromatids**) of a chromosome join and at which the spindle fibers are attached during cell division (**mitosis**) —**cen·tro·mer·ic** /sèntrə mérrik, sèntrə meérik/ *adj.*

cen·tro·some /séntrə sōm/ *n.* BIOL a small region of cytoplasm near the nucleus of a cell, containing rod-shaped structures (**centrioles**) —**cen·tro·so·mic** /sèntrə sómmik/ *adj.*

cen·trum /séntrəm/ (*plural* **-trums** *or* **-tra** /-trə/) *n.* a thick mass of bone in a vertebra that is the point of attachment to the vertebrae above and below [Mid-19thC. From Latin (see CENTER).]

cen·tum /kéntəm/ *adj.* used to describe those ancient Indo-European language groups in which the /k/ sound, when preceding a front vowel, did not palatalize. ◊ **satem** [Early 20thC. From Latin "hundred" (see CENT). The Latin and Sanskrit words for "hundred," *centum* /k-/ and *satem* /s-/, exemplify the division and have given their names to the groupings.]

cen·tu·ri·on /sen tōōree ən, sen chōōree ən/ *n.* in ancient Rome, an officer in charge of a unit of foot soldiers (**century**) [14thC. From the Latin stem *centurion-*, from *centuria* "century," from *centum* "hundred" (see CENT).] —**cen·tu·ri·al** *adj.*

cen·tu·ry /sénchəree/ (*plural* **-ries**) *n.* **1.** 100 YEARS any period of a hundred years **2.** TIME 100-YEAR PERIOD IN DATING SYSTEM a period of a hundred years in a dating system, from a year numbered 1 or 00, e.g., 1901 or 2000, to one ending in 00 or 99, e.g., 2000 or 2099. Centuries are counted forward or backward from a significant event, e.g., the birth of Jesus Christ. **3.** 100 THINGS any group or total of a hundred similar things **4.** LONG TIME a very long time (*informal*) (*usually used in the plural*) **5.** HIST UNIT OF ROMAN SOLDIERS a group of foot soldiers in ancient Rome, originally comprising a hundred men but later between sixty and eighty. ◊ **maniple 6.** HIST GROUP OF ROMAN VOTERS a division of citizens in ancient Rome for voting purposes [14thC. From Latin *centuria*, literally "group of a hundred," from *centum* (see CENT).]

cen·tu·ry plant *n.* a plant found in Mexico and the southern United States, with grayish-green leaves and flowers on a tall stalk. It takes ten to thirty years to mature and flowers just once before dying. Latin name: *Agave americana*. [From the length of its maturation, likened to a hundred years]

C.E.O. (*plural* **C.E.O'.s**) *abbr.* chief executive officer

ce·orl /churl/, **churl** *n.* in Anglo-Saxon England, a freeman of the lowest class [Old English, from a prehistoric Germanic word that is also the ancestor of English *carl*]

cep /sep/, **cèpe** /sep, seep/ *n.* an edible woodland mushroom with a shiny brown cap and a creamy-colored underside. It has a rich nutty flavor. Latin name: *Boletus edulis*. [Mid-19thC. Via French *cèpe* from Gascon *cep* "tree trunk, mushroom," from Latin *cippus* "stake."]

cephal- *prefix*. = **cephalo-** (*used before vowels*)

ce·phal·ic /sə fállik/ *adj*. relating to the head, or in the region of the head [15thC. From, ultimately, Greek *kephalikos*, from *kephalē* (see CEPHALO-).] — **ce·phal·i·cal·ly** *adv*.

-cephalic *suffix*. having a particular number or kind of heads ○ *monocephalic* ○ *brachycephalic* [Via Latin *cephalicus* from, ultimately, Greek *kephalē* "head" (see CEPHALO-)]

ce·phal·ic in·dex *n*. the ratio of the width to the length of a human skull, measured at the widest and longest points, and multiplied by 100

ceph·a·lin /séffəlin/, **keph·a·lin** /kéffə lin/ *n*. a chemical found especially in the nervous tissue of the brain and spinal column and involved in controlling bleeding

ceph·a·li·za·tion /sèffəli záysh'n/ *n*. the tendency for sensory, neural, and feeding organs to be concentrated at the front end of the body, leading to the development of a head in many organisms

cephalo- *prefix*. head, skull ○ *cephalometry* [Via modern Latin from, ultimately, Greek *kephalē*. Ultimately from an Indo-European word that is also the ancestor of English *gable*.]

ceph·a·lo·me·ter /sèffə lómmətər/ *n*. an instrument used to measure the size of the human head

ceph·a·lom·e·try /sèffə lómmətree/ *n*. the measurement of human heads, especially using X-rays or ultrasound. It is practiced in dentistry to determine if the mouth can accommodate new teeth and in obstetrics to gauge if a fetal head can pass through the birth canal. —**ceph·a·lo·met·ric** /sèffəlō méttrik/ *adj*.

ceph·a·lo·pod /séffələ pòd/ *n*. a marine animal with a large head and tentacles. Octopus, squid, and cuttlefish are cephalopods. Class: Cephalopoda. [Early 19thC. From modern Latin, class name, from, ultimately, earlier forms of CEPHALO- + -POD.] — **ceph·a·lo·pod** *adj*. —**ceph·a·lop·o·dan** /sèffə lóppəd'n/ *adj*., *n*. —**ceph·a·lo·pod·ic** /-lə póddik/ *adj*. —**ceph·a·lo·po·dous** /-lóppədəss/ *adj*.

ceph·a·lo·spo·rin /sèffələ spáwrin/ *n*. an antibiotic derived from fungi, effective against a wide range of bacteria. ◊ **penicillin** [Mid-20thC. Formed from modern Latin *Cephalosporium*, from earlier forms of CEPHALO- + SPORE.]

ceph·a·lo·tho·rax /sèffələ tháw ràks/ (*plural* **-rax·es** *or* **-rac·es** /-rə seez/) *n*. the fused head and thorax typical of spiders and other arachnids and many crustaceans

-cephalous *suffix*. having a particular number or kind of heads ○ *dicephalous* ○ *autocephalous* [Formed from Greek *-kephalos*, from *kephalē* "head" (see CEPHALO-)]

-cephaly *suffix*. a particular condition of the head or skull ○ *microcephaly* [Formed from Greek *kephalē* "head"]

Ce·phe·id /seéfee id, séffee id/, **Ce·phe·id var·i·a·ble** *n*. a star that has regular periods of varying brightness, usually lasting from one to fifty days [Early 20thC. Coined from CEPHEUS + -ID.]

Ce·pheus /seéfee əss/ *n*. a constellation located in the northern hemisphere close to Draco and Cassiopeia

ce·ra·ceous /sə ráyshəss/ *adj*. like wax in appearance or texture (*technical*) [Mid-18thC. Formed from Latin *cera* "wax" (see CERE).]

ce·ram·al /sə rámm'l/ *n*. = **cermet** [Mid-20thC. Blend of CERAMIC and ALLOY.]

ce·ram·ic /sə rámmik/ *n*. **1. HARD FIRED CLAY** a hard brittle heat-resistant material made by firing a mixture of clay and chemicals at high temperature **2. FIRED CLAY OBJECT** an object made from ceramic ■ *adj*. **1. OF CERAMIC** made of ceramic **2. RELATING TO PRODUCTION OF CERAMICS** relating to or involving the production of ceramic objects [Early 19thC. From Greek *keramikos* "of pottery," from *keramos* "potter's earth, pottery."]

ce·ram·i·cist /sə rámməssist/ *n*. = **ceramist**

ce·ram·ics /sə rámmiks/ *n*. the art, technology, or process of making ceramic objects (*takes a singular verb*)

ce·ram·ist /sə rámmist/, **ce·ram·i·cist** /sə rámməssist/ *n*. somebody who makes ceramic objects

Ce·ram Sea /sáy raam-/ sea in the western Pacific Ocean, in central Moluccas, Indonesia, west of New Guinea. Area: 20,000 sq. mi./51,800 sq. km.

ce·ras·tes /sə ráss teez/ (*plural* **-tes**) *n*. a poisonous snake of northern Africa and southwestern Asia that has a projection like a horn above each eye. Genus: *Cerastes*. ◊ **horned viper** [14thC. From, ultimately, Greek *kerastēs*, literally "horned," from *keras* "horn" (source of English *keratin*).]

cer·a·toid /sérrə toyd/ *adj*. resembling the horn of an animal in appearance or substance [From Greek *keratoeidēs* "hornlike," from earlier forms of CERAT- + -OID]

Cer·ber·us /súrbərəss/ *n*. in Greek mythology, the fierce dog that guards the entrance to Hades, usually represented as having three heads — **Cer·ber·e·an** /sùrbə reé ən/ *adj*.

-cercal *suffix*. having a particular kind of tail ○ *diphycercal* [Formed from French *-cerque*, from Greek *kerkos* "tail"]

cer·car·i·a /sər káiree ə/ (*plural* **-ae** /-ee/ *or* **-as**) *n*. the tadpole-shaped larva of various parasitic worms (**flukes**) [Mid-19thC. From modern Latin, from Greek *kerkos* "tail" (see CERCUS).] —**cer·car·i·al** *adj*.

cer·cus /súrkəss/ (*plural* **-ci** /-see/) *n*. either of two sensory appendages at the end of the abdomen of the female mosquito and other insects [Early 19thC. Via modern Latin from Greek *kerkos* "tail."] —**cer·cal** *adj*.

cere /seer/ *n*. the thick skin at the base of the upper beak of some birds, e.g., parrots. The cere contains the bird's nostrils. [15thC. From Latin *cera* "wax" (source of English *cerumen*), of uncertain origin: probably from Greek *kēros*.]

ce·re·al /seéree əl/ *n*. **1. CROP PLANT WITH EDIBLE GRAIN** a plant belonging to the grass family that is cultivated for its nutritious grains. Cereals include oats, barley, rye, wheat, rice, and corn. **2. GRAIN** the grain produced by a cereal plant **3. BREAKFAST FOOD** food made from cereal grain and eaten especially at breakfast, usually with milk [Early 19thC. Directly or via French *céréale* from Latin *cerealis* "relating to the cultivation of grain," from CERES, the name of the Roman goddess of agriculture.]

ce·re·al leaf bee·tle *n*. a small reddish-brown beetle that feeds on the leaves of cereal plants, causing a significant problem for farmers. Latin name: *Oulema melanopus*.

cer·e·bel·lum /sèrrə béllәm/ (*plural* **-lums** *or* **-la** /-lə/) *n*. the part of the brain located directly behind the front part (**cerebrum**), typically consisting of two hemispheres connected by a thin central region. Its main function is to control and coordinate muscular activity and maintain balance. [Mid-16thC. From Latin, literally "small brain," from *cerebrum* (see CEREBRUM).] —**cer·e·bel·lar** *adj*.

cer·e·bra *n*. plural of **cerebrum**

cer·e·bral /sə reébrəl, sérrə-/ *adj*. **1. OF THE FRONT OF BRAIN** relating to or located in the front part of the brain (**cerebrum**) **2. OF THE BRAIN** relating to or involving the brain or any part of it **3. INTELLECTUAL** involving the psychological processes of thinking and reasoning rather than the emotions —**cer·e·bral·ly** *adv*.

cer·e·bral cor·tex *n*. the wrinkled outer layer of the front parts of the brain (**the cerebral hemispheres**). Its functions include the perception of sensations, learning, reasoning, and memory. Technical name **pallium**

cer·e·bral dom·i·nance *n*. the normal tendency for one of the two sides of the brain (**cerebral hemispheres**) to have stronger control over some functions of the mind and body. When the left hemisphere is dominant somebody is likely to be right-handed, and vice versa.

cer·e·bral hem·i·sphere *n*. either of the two symmetrical halves of the front part of the brain (**cerebrum**)

cer·e·bral pal·sy *n*. a condition caused by brain damage around the time of birth and marked by lack of muscle control, especially in the limbs — **cer·e·bral-pal·sied** *adj*.

cer·e·brate /sérrə bràyt/ (**-brat·ed, -brat·ing, -brates**) *vi*. to use the mind to think or reason (*formal*) [Early 20thC. Origin uncertain: either formed directly from Latin *cerebrum* "brain" (see CEREBRUM), or a back-formation from *cerebration*.] —**cer·e·bra·tion** /sèrrə bráysh'n/ *n*.

cerebro- *prefix*. brain, cerebrum ○ *cerebrovascular* [From CEREBRUM]

cer·e·bro·side /sérrəbrō sīd/ *n*. a chemical substance (**lipid**) found in the brain and the covering (**myelin sheath**) of some nerves [Late 19thC. Coined from CEREBRO- + -OSE + -IDE.]

cer·e·bro·spi·nal /sèrrəbrō spīn'l, sə reébrə-/ *adj*. relating to or involving the brain and spinal cord

cer·e·bro·spi·nal flu·id *n*. the colorless fluid in and around the brain and spinal cord that absorbs shocks and maintains uniform pressure

cer·e·bro·spi·nal men·in·gi·tis *n*. inflammation of the membranes (**meninges**) surrounding the brain and spinal cord, causing high fever and sometimes unconsciousness

cer·e·bro·vas·cu·lar /sèrrəbrō váskyələr, sə reébrə-/ *adj*. relating to or involving the blood vessels that supply the brain

cer·e·bro·vas·cu·lar ac·ci·dent *n*. any physical event, e.g., cerebral hemorrhage, that may lead to a stroke

cer·e·brum /sə reébrəm, sérrə-/ (*plural* **-brums** *or* **-bra** /-brə/) *n*. the front part of the brain, divided into two symmetrical halves (**cerebral hemispheres**). In humans, it is where activities including reasoning, learning, sensory perception, and emotional responses take place. [Early 17thC. From Latin, "brain" (source of English *cerebellum*, *cerebral*, and *cerebrate*). Ultimately from an Indo-European base meaning "head."]

cere·cloth /seér klàwth/ *n*. fabric that has been coated with melted wax to make it waterproof [Mid-16thC. Alteration of *cered cloth*, literally "waxed cloth," *cered* the past participle of *cere* "to wax," from Latin *cerare*, from *cera* "wax" (see CERE).]

cer·e·ment /sérrəmənt, seérmənt/ *n*. = **cerecloth** ■ **cer·e·ments** *npl*. **BURIAL GARMENTS** a burial shroud or clothes [Early 17thC. Formed from *cere* "to wax" (see CERECLOTH).]

cer·e·mo·ni·al /sèrrə mṓnee əl/ *adj*. **1. RELATING TO FORMAL OCCASIONS** used on a formal occasion or at a ceremony **2. INVOLVING CEREMONY** involving or done as part of a ceremony ■ *n*. **1. FORMAL ETIQUETTE** the correct way to behave on formal occasions **2. RITUAL** a ceremony or set of ceremonies for an occasion **3.** CHR **ORDER OF SERVICE** the set order of rites or ceremonies in a Christian church, or a book containing this — **cer·e·mo·ni·al·ism** *n*. —**cer·e·mo·ni·al·ist** *n*. —**cer·e·mo·ni·al·ly** *adv*.

cer·e·mo·ni·ous /sèrrə mṓnee əss/ *adj*. **1. VERY FORMAL** excessively polite or formal **2. ADHERING TO CONVENTION** always careful to observe formalities and behave correctly **3. INVOLVING CEREMONY** involving ceremony or consisting of ceremony —**cer·e·mo·ni·ous·ly** *adv*. —**cer·e·mo·ni·ous·ness** *n*.

WORD KEY: USAGE

ceremonial or **ceremonious**? ***Ceremonial*** is the more neutral word, describing things that have to do with ceremony or are a part of it, e.g., *ceremonial occasions*. It is not now used of people. ***Ceremonious*** is more judgmental, and is used of people: a *ceremonious person*, or somebody with a *ceremonious manner*, is somebody who likes and adheres to formalities, perhaps even overly so.

cer·e·mo·ny /sérrə mṓnee/ (*plural* **-nies**) *n*. **1. RITUAL FOR FORMAL OCCASION** a formal event to celebrate or solemnize something such as a wedding, an official opening, or an anniversary **2. FORMAL ETIQUETTE** the forms of behavior that are expected or observed on a formal occasion **3. SOCIAL GESTURE** a polite social gesture or ritual performed for the sake of convention [14thC. From, ultimately, Latin *caerimonia* "sacred rite, religious worship, ceremony," of unknown origin.] ◇ **stand on ceremony** to behave in a formal manner or insist on formality

Ce·ren·kov ef·fect /chə réng kof-, -kawv-/, **Che·ren·kov ef·fect** *n*. the emission of light by a charged particle as it passes through a transparent medium at a speed greater than that of light in the same medium [Mid-20thC. Named for Pavel A. *Cherenkov* (1904–90), a Soviet physicist.]

Ce·ren·kov ra·di·a·tion /chə réng kof-, chə réng kawv-/, **Che·ren·kov ra·di·a·tion** *n*. light emitted by a charged particle as it passes through a transparent medium at a speed greater than that of light in the same medium [Mid-20thC. See CERENKOV EFFECT.]

Cer·es[1] /seér eez/ *n*. **1.** MYTHOL **GODDESS OF AGRICULTURE** the Roman goddess of agriculture. Greek equivalent **Demeter 2.** ASTRON **LARGEST ASTEROID** the largest asteroid and the first to be discovered, in 1801, orbiting between Mars and Saturn [From Latin]

Ce·res[2] city in central California, south of Stockton and northeast of San Jose. Population: 31,146 (1996).

ce·re·us /séeree əss/ *n.* **1.** SPINY RIBBED CACTUS any of several cacti with spiny ribbed stems, especially a Brazilian species that can reach a height of 40 ft./13 m. Genus: *Cereus.* **2.** CACTUS RELATED TO CEREUS any of several cacti related to the true cereus, e.g., the night-blooming cereus [Late 17thC. From modern Latin, genus name, from Latin, "wax taper, candle," from *cera* "wax" (see CERE); from its shape, likened to a candle.]

ce·ri·a /séeree ə/ *n.* = **ceric oxide** [From modern Latin, plural of *cerium* (see CERIUM)]

ce·ric /séerik, sérrik/ *adj.* relating to or containing cerium with a valence of 4 [Mid-19thC. Coined from CERIUM + -IC.]

ce·ric ox·ide *n.* a white crystalline powder used in the manufacture of ceramics and to polish glass. Formula: CeO_2.

cer·iph *n.* = **serif**

ce·rise /sə rées, -z/ *n.* a deep, vivid red color with a tinge of pink [Mid-19thC. Via French, "cherry," from assumed Vulgar Latin *ceresia*, ultimately from Greek *kerasos* "cherry tree" (source of English *cherry*).] —**ce·rise** *adj.*

ce·ri·um /séeree əm/ *n.* a gray malleable metallic chemical element that is the most abundant of the rare-earth group. It is used in metallurgy, in the manufacture of glass and ceramics, and to make cigarette-lighter flints. Symbol **Ce** [Early 19thC. From modern Latin, from *Ceres* (the asteroid that was discovered just before this element; see CERES).]

cer·met /súr mèt/ *n.* a durable substance that can withstand high temperatures, formed by bonding ceramic particles with metal [Mid-20thC. Blend of CERAMIC and METAL.]

cer·nu·ous /súrnyoo əss/ *adj.* used to describe flowers and buds that droop naturally [Mid-17thC. Formed from Latin *cernuus* "inclined forward."]

ce·ro /séerō, sérrō/ (*plural* **-ro** *or* **-ros**) *n.* a large edible marine fish found in warm western Atlantic waters that has silvery sides and large spiny fins. Latin name: *Scomberomorus regalis.* [Late 19thC. Alteration of Spanish *sierra* "saw, sawfish," from Latin *serra* "saw."]

ce·ro·tic ac·id /sə rōttik-, sə ròttik-/ *n.* a white fatty acid found in natural waxes such as beeswax and carnauba wax. Formula: $CH_3(CH_2)_{24}COOH$. [Mid-19thC. *Cerotic* formed from Latin *cerotum* "wax salve," from Greek *kērōton* "waxed."]

ce·rous /séerəss/ *adj.* relating to or containing cerium with a valence of 3 [Mid-19thC. Coined from CERIUM + -OUS.]

Cer·ri·tos /sə réetəs/ city in southwestern California, a southeastern suburb of Los Angeles. Population: 53,645 (1996).

cert. /surt/ *abbr.* **1.** certificate **2.** certification **3.** certified

cer·tain /súrt'n/ *adj.* **1.** WITHOUT DOUBT having no doubts about something ○ *I'm certain he's the man I saw.* **2.** KNOWN OR SET definitely known, fixed, or settled **3.** INEVITABLE guaranteed to happen or to do something ○ *they're certain to lose* **4.** RELIABLE able to be relied on **5.** NOT DEFINED undeniable but difficult to define, quantify, or express ○ *a certain hesitation in his manner* **6.** NOT NAMED able to be identified but not named ○ *A certain selfish person has used up all the milk.* **7.** UNKNOWN OR UNFAMILIAR used to indicate that only the name of the person, thing, or place mentioned is known ○ *A certain Mr. Esposito was involved.* ■ *pron.* SOME of an imprecise but limited number (*formal*) [13thC. From, ultimately, assumed Vulgar Latin *certanus*, from Latin *certus* "determined," originally a past participle of *cernere* "to separate, decide."] ◇ **certain of** some but not all of (*formal*) ◇ **for certain** without any doubt ◇ **make certain 1.** to check that something has been done or is the case **2.** to take action to achieve something

WORD KEY: ORIGIN

Certain is derived form the Latin word *cernere*, meaning "to separate" or "to decide," which is also the source of English *crime, decree, discern, discrete, discriminate, excrement, secret,* and *secretary.*

cer·tain·ly /súrt'nlee/ *adv.* **1.** DEFINITELY without any doubt or qualification on the part of the speaker ○ *It's certainly a big problem.* **2.** USED TO CONCEDE POINT used to concede a point that has been made ○ *That's certainly an area we could improve upon.* **3.** YES used to indicate unreserved assent ◇ **certainly not** used to indicate emphatic denial or refusal

cer·tain·ty /súrt'ntee/ (*plural* **-ties**) *n.* **1.** SOMETHING INEVITABLE a conclusion or outcome that is beyond doubt **2.** SOMEBODY OR SOMETHING CERTAIN OF SUCCESS somebody who or something that is strongly expected to win or achieve something **3.** CONFIDENCE a complete lack of doubt about something ◇ **for a certainty** without any doubt

certif. *n., abbr.* certificate

cer·ti·fi·a·ble /súrtə fì əb'l/ *adj.* **1.** WORTHY OF CERTIFICATION capable of being certified, e.g., as authentic, valid, or qualified **2.** REQUIRING PSYCHIATRIC TREATMENT legally or medically declared to be affected by a psychiatric disorder (*dated*) —**cer·ti·fi·a·bly** *adv.*

cer·tif·i·cate *n.* /sər tíffikət/ **1.** DOCUMENT PROVIDING OFFICIAL EVIDENCE an official document that gives proof and details of something, e.g., personal status, educational achievements, ownership, or authenticity **2.** DOCUMENT SHOWING CONFORMITY TO STANDARD an official document awarded to somebody who or something that has passed a test or examination or conforms to a required standard **3.** DOCUMENT SHOWING QUALIFICATION an official document awarded to somebody who has completed a course of study or training ■ *vt.* /sər tíffi kàyt/ (**-cat·ed, -cat·ing, -cates**) **1.** GIVE CERTIFICATE TO SOMEBODY OR SOMETHING to award a certificate to somebody or something **2.** AUTHORIZE OR PROVE SOMETHING WITH CERTIFICATE to authorize or provide evidence of something with a certificate [15thC. From, ultimately, medieval Latin *certificatum*, from the past participle of late Latin *certificare* "to certify" (see CERTIFY). The underlying idea is of a document that makes something certain.] —**cer·ti·fi·ca·tion** *n.* —**cer·tif·i·ca·to·ry** /sər tíffikə tàwree/ *adj.*

cer·tif·i·cate of or·i·gin *n.* an official document stating what country a consignment of goods has come from

cer·ti·fied check *n.* a check that the issuing bank guarantees to honor because sufficient funds have been set aside to cover the check

cer·ti·fied mail *n.* mail that must be signed for on delivery but that carries no insurance to cover the value of the contents. ◊ **registered mail**

cer·ti·fied pub·lic ac·count·ant *n.* a public accountant who has met the requirements of a particular U.S. state and is therefore allowed to practice there

cer·ti·fy /súrtə fì/ (**-fied, -fy·ing, -fies**) *v.* **1.** *vti.* CONFIRM TRUTH OR ACCURACY OF SOMETHING to state or confirm that something is true or correct **2.** *vt.* PROVE QUALITY OF SOMEBODY OR SOMETHING to declare that somebody or something has passed a test or achieved a certain standard **3.** *vt.* BANKING GUARANTEE PAYMENT OF CHECK to indicate on a check that there are sufficient funds to guarantee payment **4.** *vt.* ISSUE WITH A CERTIFICATE to award a certificate to somebody or something **5.** *vt.* DECLARE SOMEBODY TO HAVE PSYCHIATRIC DISORDER to declare somebody officially or legally to have a psychiatric disorder and require confinement in a mental health facility (*dated*) [14thC. Via French *certifier* from late Latin *certificare*, literally "to make certain," from Latin *certus* (see CERTAIN).] —**cer·ti·fi·er** *n.*

cer·ti·o·rar·i /sùrshee ə ráiree, sùrshee ə ráaree/ *n.* LAW a writ issued by a higher court to obtain records on a case from a lower court so that the case can be reviewed. ◊ **mandamus** [15thC. From late Latin, literally "to be informed," the passive of Latin *certiorare* "to inform," from, ultimately, *certus* "sure"; the word occurs in the Latin version of the writ.]

cer·ti·tude /súrti tòod/ *n.* **1.** FEELING OF CERTAINTY the feeling of conviction about something, especially an opinion or religious faith **2.** SOMETHING THAT IS CERTAIN something that is certain to happen or about which somebody can feel sure [15thC. From late Latin *certitudo*, from Latin *certus* (see CERTAIN).]

ce·ru·le·an /sə ròolee ən/ *adj.* of a deep blue color, like the sky on a clear day (*literary*) [Mid-17thC. Formed from Latin *caeruleus* "sky-blue, sea-blue," from *caelum* "sky" (source of English *celestial*), of unknown origin.] —**ce·ru·le·an** *n.*

ce·ru·lo·plas·min /sə ròolō plázmin/ *n.* a protein that helps the blood to store and transport copper [Mid-20thC. Coined from modern Latin *cerulo-* (from Latin *caeruleus*; see CERULEAN) + PLASMA + -IN. From its blue color.]

ce·ru·men /sə ròomən/ *n.* the waxy secretion of glands lining the canal of the external ear (*technical*) [Late 17thC. From modern Latin, formed from Latin *cera* "wax."] —**ce·ru·mi·nous** /sə ròomənəss/ *adj.*

ce·ruse /sə ròoss, séer òoss/ *n.* **1.** WHITE LEAD USED AS PIGMENT white lead used as a pigment and formerly in cosmetics **2.** COSMETIC CONTAINING WHITE LEAD a cosmetic containing white lead. Lead is now known to damage the skin and is no longer used in cosmetics. [14thC. Via French from Latin *cerussa*, of uncertain origin: perhaps ultimately from Greek *kēros* "wax."]

ce·rus·site /sə rú sìt/ *n.* a brittle colorless mineral, occurring mainly as crystals or granular aggregates in white to yellow and brown to black transparent or translucent forms. It is composed of lead carbonate and is used as a lead ore. [Mid-19thC. Coined from Latin *cerussa* (see CERUSE) + -ITE.]

Cer·van·tes /sur vánt t'èez/, **Miguel de** (1547–1616) Spanish novelist and dramatist. His novel *Don Quixote* (1605–15) greatly influenced the development of the novel. Full name **Miguel de Cervantes Saavedra**

cer·ve·lat /súrvə làt, súrvə làa/ *n.* a German cured sausage made from pork and beef, usually smoked, with a mild flavor and a fine texture [Early 17thC. Via French from Italian *cervellata*, from *cervello* "brain," from Latin *cerebellum* (see CEREBELLUM); from the fact that the sausage was originally made from brains.]

cer·vi·cal /súrvik'l/ *adj.* relating or belonging to the neck or any part of the body that resembles a neck, e.g., the cervix of the womb [Mid-19thC. Via French from Latin *cervic-*, the stem of *cervix* "neck."]

cer·vi·cal cap *n.* = **diaphragm**

cer·vi·cal smear *n. U.K.* = **Pap smear.** ◊ **smear test**

cer·vi·ces /súrvi séez/ plural of **cervix**

cer·vi·ci·tis /sùrvi sítiss/ *n.* inflammation of the cervix of the womb [Late 19thC. Coined from the Latin stem *cervic-* (see CERVIX) + -ITIS.]

cer·vid /súrvid/ *n.* any ruminant mammal, e.g., a deer, elk, or reindeer, characterized by the presence of antlers in the male or sometimes in both sexes. Family: Cervidae. [Late 19thC. From modern Latin *Cervidae* (plural), family name, from Latin *cervus* (see CERVINE).] —**cer·vid** *adj.*

cer·vine /súr vìn/ *adj.* relating to, resembling, or typical of a deer [Mid-19thC. From Latin *cervinus*, from *cervus* "deer." Ultimately from an Indo-European word meaning "horn, head."]

cer·vix /súrviks/ (*plural* **-vix·es** *or* **-vi·ces** /-vi séez/) *n.* **1.** NECK OF WOMB the neck of the womb, consisting of a narrow passage leading to the vagina. The cervix widens greatly during childbirth to permit delivery of the baby. **2.** NECK the neck (*technical*) **3.** PART RESEMBLING NECK any part of the body that resembles a neck in shape or function [15thC. From Latin, "neck."]

ce·sar·e·an, ce·sar·e·an sec·tion *n.* an operation to deliver a baby by cuttting through the mother's abdomen and womb [From the belief that Julius CAESAR was born this way]

ce·si·um clock *n.* TIME a type of clock in which cesium atoms are stimulated by an alternating magnetic field. A precise time is determined when the frequencies of atoms and the field match.

ces·sa·tion /se sáysh'n/ *n.* a stop, pause, or interruption, especially a permanent discontinuation [15thC. From the Latin stem *cessation-*, from *cessat-*, the past participle stem of *cessare* "to hold back, stop."]

ces·sion /sésh'n/ *n.* (*formal*) **1.** GIVING UP OR YIELDING the ceding or giving up of something, especially land, property, or a right **2.** SOMETHING GIVEN UP something ceded or given up, especially land, property, or a right [14thC. Directly or via French from the Latin stem *cession-*, from *cess-*, the past participle stem of *cedere* "to yield" (see CEDE).]

cess·pit /séss pìt/ *n.* a pit for the collection of waste matter and water, especially sewage [Mid-19thC. *Cess* from CESSPOOL.]

cess·pool /sess pòol/ *n.* **1.** UNDERGROUND CONTAINER FOR WASTE MATTER a covered underground tank or well for the collection of waste matter and water, especially sewage. ◊ **sink 2.** FILTHY OR IMMORAL PLACE a foul and putrid place or situation, especially one linked with moral depravity [Late 17thC. Origin uncertain: probably by folk etymology (from POOL) from earlier *cesperalle*, variant of *suspiral* "cesspool," earlier "drainpipe," from Old French *suspirail* "breathing hole," from *souspirer* "to breathe."]

ces·ta /séssta/ *n.* a curved wicker basket for catching and throwing the ball in the game of jai alai [Early 20thC. Via Spanish, literally "basket," from Latin *cista* "chest" (see CHEST).]

c'est la vie /sè laa vée/ *interj.* used to express philosophical acceptance of the way things are [Mid-20thC. From French, literally "that's life."]

ces·tode /séss tōd/ *n.* a tapeworm (*technical*) [Mid-19thC. From modern Latin *Cestoda* (plural), class name, from Latin *cestus* "belt," from Greek *kestos*, originally "stitched."]

ces·tus /séstəss/ (*plural* **-ti** /-tī/) *n.* a girdle or belt, especially one worn by women in ancient Greece [Mid-16thC. Via Latin from Greek *kestos* "belt," originally "stitched."]

ce·su·ra *n.* = **caesura**

C.E.T. *abbr.* Central European Time

ce·ta·cean /si táysh'n/ *n.* a large aquatic mammal, e.g., a whale or a dolphin, that has a streamlined body with forelimbs modified as flippers, no hind limbs, and a blowhole on the back. Order: Cetacea. [Mid-19thC. Formed from modern Latin *Cetacea* (plural), order name, from Latin *cetus* "whale," from Greek *kētos* "sea-monster, huge fish, whale," of unknown origin.] —**ce·ta·ceous** *adj.*

ce·tane /sée tàyn/ *n.* a colorless oily hydrocarbon found in petroleum. It is used in measuring the ignition quality of diesel fuels and as a solvent. Formula: $C_{16}H_{34}$. [Late 19thC. Coined from *cetyl* (see CETYL ALCOHOL) + -ANE.]

ce·tane num·ber, ce·tane rat·ing *n.* the performance rating of a diesel fuel expressed as the percentage of cetane in a mixture with 1-methylnaphthalene that shows the same ignition properties. The higher the cetane number, the better the performance.

cete /seet/ *n.* a group or company of badgers [15thC. Origin uncertain: perhaps from Latin *coetus* "assembly, company," a variant of *coitus* "combination."]

ce·ter·is par·i·bus /káytəriss páaribəss, sèttəriss pérrəbəss/ *adv.* used to indicate that something would be the case if everything else under consideration remains the same [Early 17thC. From modern Latin, literally "other things being equal."]

ce·tol·o·gy /si tólləjee/ *n.* the branch of zoology concerned with the study of whales, dolphins, and related mammals [Mid-19thC. Coined from Latin *cetus* "whale" + -OLOGY.] —**ce·to·log·i·cal** /seet'l ójjik'l/ *adj.* —**ce·tol·o·gist** /si tólləjist/ *n.*

Ce·tus /seetəss/ *n.* a constellation in the sky of the southern hemisphere near Aquarius and Eridanus that contains the bright star Mira

ce·tyl al·co·hol /seet'l-/ *n.* a white waxy crystalline solid used in making cosmetics, pharmaceuticals, and detergents. Formula: $C_{16}H_{34}O$. [*Cetyl* coined from Latin *cetus* "whale" + -YL. From the fact that the first compounds were isolated from spermaceti.]

Cé·vennes /say vén/ mountain range in France extending from the northern Ardèche Department to the southwestern Hérault Department. The highest peak is Mont Mézenc 5,755 ft./1,754 m.

ce·vi·che /se vée chày/, **se·vi·che** *n.* a Latin American dish of raw fish marinated in lemon or lime juice and served as a type of salad with chopped onions and tomatoes [Mid-20thC. From American Spanish *seviche, ceviche*, from, apparently, Spanish *cebo* "fodder, fish pieces used for bait," from Latin *cibus* "food."]

Cey·lon /sə lón, say-/ former name for **Sri Lanka** (until 1972) —**Cey·lo·nese** *adj., n.*

Cey·lon moss *n.* a red seaweed of the East Indian Ocean that is a source of the gelatinous material agar. Latin name: *Gracilaria lichenoides.* [Because it grows in CEYLON]

Ce·yx /sée iks/ *n.* In Greek mythology, a king of Trachis in Thessaly who died in a shipwreck and whose wife, Alcyone, drowned herself in grief

Cé·zanne /say zán, -zaán/, **Paul** (1839–1906) French painter. His post-impressionist representation of nature in such paintings as *Rocky Landscape in Aix* (1887?) inspired cubism.

Cf *symbol.* californium

CF *abbr.* **1.** BASEBALL center field **2.** BASEBALL center fielder **3.** cystic fibrosis

Paul Cézanne: Self-portrait

cf. *abbr.* **1.** compare **2.** calfskin

C.F., **c.f.** *abbr.* cost and freight

C/F *abbr.* carried forward

CFA franc *n.* the unit of currency used in some African countries. See table at **currency** [*CFA* abbreviation of French *Communauté financière africaine* "African financial community"]

CFB *abbr.* Canadian Forces Base

CFC *n.* a gas containing carbon, hydrogen, chlorine, and fluorine, used as a refrigerant and aerosol propellant. Some forms of CFC damage the ozone layer in the Earth's atmosphere. Full form **chlorofluorocarbon**

CFE *abbr.* Conventional Forces in Europe

C.F.I., **c.f.i.** *abbr.* cost, freight, and insurance. ◊ **c.i.f.**

CFL *abbr.* Canadian Football League

cfm, **c.f.m.** *abbr.* cubic feet per minute

CFO *abbr.* chief financial officer

cfs, **c.f.s.** *abbr.* cubic feet per second

CFTC *abbr.* Commodity Futures Trading Commission

cg *abbr.* **cg** centigram

CG *abbr.* captain general

c.g. *abbr.* center of gravity

C.G. *abbr.* **1.** Coast Guard **2.** MIL commanding general **3.** RELIG consul general

cge. *abbr.* **1.** BANKING charge **2.** FREIGHT carriage

cgm *abbr.* centigram

cgs u·nits *npl.* a metric system of measurement based on the centimeter, gram, and second as the fundamental units of length, mass, and time. Cgs units have been replaced in science and technology by SI units. [*Cgs* from *centimeter-gram-second*]

ch. *abbr.* **1.** chapter **2.** church **3.** children **4.** child **5.** BANKING check **6. ch., Ch.** chief **7. ch., Ch.** chaplain

Ch. *abbr.* **1.** China **2.** BROADCAST channel

C.H., **c.h.** *abbr.* **1.** courthouse **2.** BANKING clearing house **3.** customhouse

cha·ba·zite /kábbə zīt/ *n.* a pink, yellow, white, or colorless mineral of the zeolite group, found in cavities in igneous rocks and as a deposit in hot springs. Chabazite is a hydrated silicate of calcium and aluminum. [Early 19thC. Formed from earlier *chabazie*, from Greek *khabazie*, a misspelling of *khalazie*, from, ultimately, *khalaza* "hail" (see CHALAZA), from its form and color.]

Cha·blis /sha blée, shə-, shábblee/, **cha·blis** *n.* **1.** WHITE WINE FROM CENTRAL FRANCE a very dry white Burgundy wine made in the region around Chablis in central France **2.** WHITE WINE LIKE CHABLIS a semidry white wine, similar to French Chablis, that is made in California or elsewhere

cha-cha /cháa chaa/, **cha-cha-cha** *n.* **1.** RHYTHMIC LATIN AMERICAN DANCE a fast rhythmic ballroom dance of Latin American origin consisting of three steps and a hip-swaying shuffle **2.** DANCE MUSIC music written for the cha-cha ■ *vi.* (**cha-chaed, cha-cha·ing, cha-chas; cha-cha-chaed, cha-cha-cha·ing, cha-cha-chas** /cháa chaa cháa/) DANCE to dance the cha-cha [From American Spanish (Cuban) *cha-cha-cha*, probably an imitation of the musical accompaniment]

chach·ka /cháachkə/ *n.* a inexpensive trinket or souvenir [Mid-20thC. Via Yiddish *tshatshke* from Polish *czaczko*.]

chac·ma /chákmə/ (*plural* **-mas**) *n.* a ground-dwelling baboon of southern Africa that has a dark-gray coat and naked face with a long muzzle. Some authorities regard the chacma as a variety of savanna baboon rather than a distinct species. Latin name: *Papio ursinus.* [Mid-19thC. From Khoikhoi.]

Cha·co /chaákō/ province of northern Argentina. Capital: Resistencia. Population: 799,302 (1991). Area: 38,468 sq. mi./99,632 sq. km.

cha·co·ni·a /chə kṓnee ə/ (*plural* **-as** *or* **-a**) *n.* a red flower with large, conspicuous sepals that is the national flower of Trinidad and Tobago. Latin name: *Warszewiczia coccinea.*

cha·conne /sha kón, shaa kón/ (*plural* **-connes**) *n.* **1.** DANCE ANCIENT DANCE an ancient, moderately slow dance that probably originated in Spain **2.** MUSIC MUSICAL FORM a musical composition consisting of variations on a fixed bass line continually repeated (**ground bass**) [Late 17thC. Via French from Spanish *chacona*, probably from Basque *chucun* "pretty."]

cha·cun à son gout /shaa kō naa son góo/ used to express the individuality or peculiarity of somebody's taste or choice [From French, literally "each to his or her own taste"]

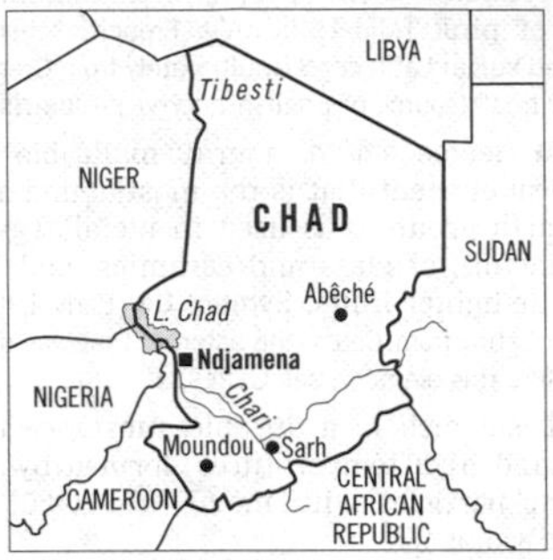

Chad

Chad /chad/ landlocked republic in northcentral Africa, bordered on the north by Libya, on the east by Sudan, on the south by the Central African Republic, and on the west by Cameroon, Nigeria, and Niger. A former French territory, it became independent in 1960. Language: French. Currency: C.F.A. franc. Capital: Ndjamena. Population: 7,166,023 (1997). Area: 495,800 sq. mi./1,284,000 sq. km. Official name **Republic of Chad** —**Chad·i·an** *adj., n.*

Chad, Lake lake in central Africa, situated at the junction of Nigeria, Niger, and Chad. Area: approximately 4,000 to 10,000 sq. mi./10,360 to 25,900 sq. km.

cha·dar /cháadər/ *n.* = **chador**

Chad·ic /cháddik/ *n.* a group of more than 100 languages spoken in west-central Africa. It is a branch of the Afro-Asiatic family of languages. There are about 25 million native speakers of Chadic languages, the most widespread being Hausa. —**Chadic** *adj.*

cha·dor /chúddər/, **cha·dar, chud·dar** *n.* **1.** DARK ROBE WORN BY MUSLIMS a dark traditional garment worn by Muslim and sometimes by Hindu women that covers almost all of the head and body **2.** CLOTH FOR MUSLIM TOMB a cloth that is used to cover a Muslim tomb [Early 17thC. Directly or via Urdu from Persian *čādar*, literally "sheet, veil."]

chae·ta /kéetə/ (*plural* **-tae** /-tee/) *n.* a bristle that occurs singly or in clusters in certain worms, e.g., earthworms and ragworms, and helps them to move [Mid-19thC. Via modern Latin from Greek *khaitē* "long hair."]

chae·tog·nath /kée tog nàth, kéetəg nàth/ *n.* a torpedo-shaped invertebrate marine animal with an almost transparent body and fins running horizontally down both sides of the trunk and tail. Phylum: Chaetognatha. [Late 19thC. From modern Latin *Chaetognatha*, phylum name, from Greek *khaitē* (see CHAETA) + *gnathos* "jaw"; from the spines on its head.] —**chae·tog·na·thous** /kee tógnəthəss/ *adj.*

chafe /chayf/ *v.* (**chafed, chaf·ing, chafes**) **1.** *vti.* BECOME WORN OR MAKE SOMETHING WORN to become sore or worn by rubbing or make something sore or worn in this way **2.** *vi.* CAUSE FRICTION to rub something, causing friction **3.** *vt.* RUB SOMETHING TO WARM IT to warm something, especially the hands or other parts of the body, by rubbing **4.** *vti.* BECOME ANNOYED OR ANNOY SOME-

BODY to be or make somebody irritated, annoyed, or impatient ■ *n.* 1. SORENESS OR WEAR soreness or wear caused by rubbing 2. FEELING OF IRRITATION a feeling of irritation, annoyance, or impatience [13thC. Via Old French *chaufer* from Latin *calefacere* "to make warm," from *calere* "to be warm" (source of English *nonchalant*) + *facere* "to make."]

cha·fer /cháyfər/ *n.* a large slow-moving scarab beetle, e.g., the cockchafer [Old English *ceafor.* Probably ultimately from an Indo-European word meaning "jaw, mouth." Related to German *Käfer* "beetle."]

chaff[1] /chaf/ *n.* 1. SEED COVERINGS REMOVED BY THRESHING the dry coverings **(bracts)** of grains and other grass seeds, which are separated by the process of threshing. When cereal crops are harvested mechanically, chaff is removed by the combine harvester and deposited with the straw in the field. 2. MIL STRIPS OF METAL TO OBSTRUCT RADAR glass fibers or silvered nylon filaments dispersed into the air as an antiradar measure 3. WORTHLESS THING something that is worthless or irrelevant [Old English *ceaf,* of uncertain origin: probably from a prehistoric Germanic base meaning "chew"] —**chaf·fy** *adj.*

chaff[2] /chaf/ *v.* **(chaffed, chaff·ing, chaffs)** 1. *vt.* TEASE SOMEBODY LIGHTHEARTEDLY to tease somebody in fun 2. *vi.* BANTER to exchange light-hearted teasing or joking remarks ■ *n.* JOKING light-hearted joking or teasing [Early 19thC. Origin uncertain: perhaps an alteration of CHAFE.] —**chaff·er** *n.*

chaf·fer /cháffər/ *vi.* **(-fered, -fer·ing, -fers)** 1. HAGGLE to haggle or bargain about something 2. BANDY WORDS to chatter idly ■ *n.* BARGAINING OR HAGGLING bargaining or haggling about something [12thC. From Old English *ceap* "bargain, sale" + *faru* "faring, going," perhaps modeled on Old Norse *kaupför* "trading-journey."] —**chaf·fer·er** *n.*

chaf·finch /chá finch/ *n.* a finch, common in gardens and farmland of Europe and western Asia, that has white wing bars and a bluish hood, the males being more colorful. Latin name: *Fringilla coelebs.* [Old English *ceaffinc.* Because it pecks among farmyard chaff.]

chaf·ing dish *n.* a shallow pan with a source of heat beneath it, used for cooking food or keeping food warm at the table

Cha·gall /shaa gáal/, **Marc** (1887–1985) Russian-born French painter and designer. His colorful fantasies, anticipating surrealism, stem largely from eastern European Jewish folklore.

Cha·gas' dis·ease /shaágəss-/, **Cha·gas's dis·ease** *n.* an often fatal disease, occurring in South and Central America, that affects the heart and nervous system and is caused by a protozoan parasite transmitted by blood-sucking insects. ◊ **sleeping sickness** [Early 20thC. Named for Carlos *Chagas* (1879–1934), Brazilian physician, who first described it.]

cha·grin /shə grín/ *n.* ANGER AT BEING LET DOWN a feeling of vexation or humiliation due to disappointment about something ■ *vt.* **(-grined, -grin·ing, -grins)** VEX THROUGH FRUSTRATION to frustrate or annoy somebody through disappointed hopes [Early 18thC. From French, "sad, vexed," the original sense in English.]

cha·grined *adj.* frustrated, annoyed, or embarrassed through disappointed hopes

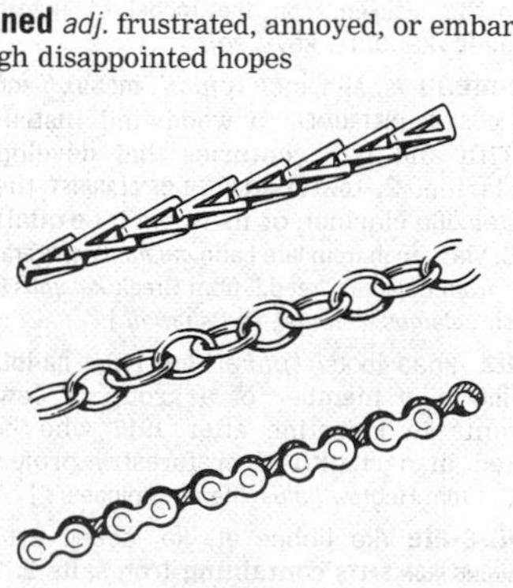

Chain

chain /chayn/ *n.* 1. SERIES OF JOINED METAL RINGS a flexible interlinked series of usually metal links that may be used to support or restrain something, as an ornament or decoration, or to drive or move something 2. ACCESSORIES SERIES OF LINKS USED AS ACCESSORY a series of rings, links, or disks used as a necklace, bracelet, or other piece of jewelry 3. COMM BUSINESSES UNDER ONE MANAGEMENT OR OWNERSHIP a number of stores, hotels, restaurants, or other businesses that are owned by the same company and offer similar goods or services but are found in different locations 4. GEOG SERIES OF GEOGRAPHICAL FORMATIONS a series of associated geographical features or formations, e.g., mountains, lakes, or islands 5. SOMETHING RESEMBLING A CHAIN a series of things or people linked or joined together for some purpose ○ *They stood hand in hand to form a human chain round the perimeter.* 6. SEQUENCE OF RELATED EVENTS OR FACTS a sequence of facts or events that happen one after the other and are connected in some way 7. CHEM SERIES OF ATOMS a series of atoms, usually of a single element such as carbon, that are joined in a line or ring within a molecule 8. BADGE OF OFFICE a chain worn round the neck as a badge of office 9. ENG ENGINEERING MEASUREMENT OR DEVICE a unit of length measuring 100 ft./about 30 m, or a device to measure such lengths 10. = **Gunter's chain** (*dated*) ■ **chains** *npl.* RESTRAINING CIRCUMSTANCES feelings or circumstances that restrain or confine somebody (*literary*) ■ *vt.* **(chained, chain·ing, chains)** 1. FASTEN SOMETHING WITH A CHAIN to fasten, tie, or restrain something or somebody with a chain or chains 2. RESTRICT SOMEBODY'S MOBILITY to restrict or confine somebody's freedom of movement or action ○ *She was chained to the computer all day.* 3. MEASURE WITH A CHAIN to use a chain or tape to measure something [13thC. Via Old French *chaeine* from Latin *catena* (source of English *concatenate*), of unknown origin.] —**chain·less** *adj.*
◇ **yank somebody's chain** to say something that is untrue in order to tease or annoy somebody (*informal*)

chain drive *n.* an endless linked chain that meshes with the teeth of two sprocket wheels to transfer energy and motion from one to the other —**chain-driv·en** *adj.*

chaî·né /shə náy/ (*plural* **-nés** /shə náy/) *n.* a series of short, usually fast turns made by a ballet dancer moving in a straight line across a floor or stage [Mid-20thC. From French *chaîné,* literally "chained, linked," the past participle of *chaîner* "to chain," from, ultimately, Old French *chaeine* (see CHAIN).]

chained /chaynd/ *adj.* 1. FASTENED WITH CHAIN tied up or fastened with a chain 2. LINKED forming a chain

chain gang *n.* a group of prisoners who work away from the prison and are shackled together, usually with leg irons and a series of chains

chain grate, chain grate stoker *n.* a mechanism that stokes a large industrial furnace mechanically by supplying fuel on a conveyor that is driven by a chain

chain·let /cháynlət/ *n.* a small chain

chain let·ter *n.* a letter sent to a number of people, each of whom is asked to send copies to the same number of new people, sometimes requesting and promising money to recipients

chain light·ning *n.* lightning that appears as a jagged line of light splitting into two or more branches near the ground

chain-link fence /chàynlingk-/ *n.* a fence formed from lengths of strong wire that are interwoven in a diamond pattern —**chain-link fenc·ing** *n.*

chain mail *n.* interlinked rings of metal forming a flexible piece of armor, worn by knights in medieval times

chain·man /cháynmən/ (*plural* **-men**) *n.* somebody who measures with a chain or tape in surveying something

chain of com·mand *n.* a hierarchy of officials in the armed forces or in business, each reporting to and taking orders from the next most senior person

chain pick·er·el *n.* a large slender greenish black freshwater fish of eastern North America that resembles a young pike and has chain-shaped markings along each flank. Latin name: *Esox niger.*

chain re·ac·tion *n.* 1. CONNECTED SEQUENCE OF EVENTS a series of events following quickly from each other, each of which causes the next one 2. NUCLEAR PHYS SELF-SUSTAINING NUCLEAR FISSION a self-sustaining nuclear reaction in which each fission of an atomic nucleus causes neutrons and energy to be emitted, each collision of neutrons with other nuclei causing a further fission 3. CHEM SERIES OF CHEMICAL REACTIONS a series of chemical reactions in which the product from one reaction helps to create the next one —**chain-re·act** *vi.*

chain saw *n.* a portable motor-driven saw with cutting teeth made of links that form a continuous chain, used for cutting wood

chain shot *n.* two cannonballs or half-balls connected by a chain, formerly used to destroy a ship's rigging

chain-smoke **(chain-smoked, chain-smok·ing, chain-smokes)** *vti.* to smoke cigarettes continuously, often lighting the next from the previous one as it is finished —**chain-smok·er** *n.*

chain stitch *n.* a hand, machine, or crochet stitch in which each stitch forms a loop through the forward end of the previous one to resemble the links of a chain —**chain-stitch** *vti.*

chain store *n.* one of a series of retail stores, especially department stores or supermarkets, owned by the same company

chair /chair/ *n.* 1. SEAT WITH BACK AND SOMETIMES ARMRESTS a seat with a back support, usually for one person. Most chairs have four legs or feet and some have rests for the arms. 2. ELECTRIC CHAIR the electric chair (*informal*) 3. CHAIRPERSON somebody presiding over something such as a committee, board, or meeting, or the position of such a person 4. UNIV SOMEBODY WHO HOLDS AN ENDOWED PROFESSORSHIP somebody who holds an endowed professorship at a university 5. MUSIC RANKED POSITION OF ORCHESTRAL MUSICIAN the ranked position of a musician in an orchestra 6. BUILDING SUPPORTING DEVICE DURING POURING OF CONCRETE a device to keep reinforcing rods in place during the pouring of concrete 7. SEDAN CHAIR a sedan chair (*archaic*) ■ *vt.* **(chaired, chair·ing, chairs)** 1. PRESIDE OVER SOMETHING to preside over something such as a committee, board, or meeting 2. *U.K.* CARRY WINNER ON SHOULDERS to carry a victor or champion on the shoulders in triumph [13thC. Via Old French *chaiere* from Latin *cathedra* "seat."]

WORD KEY: USAGE

Chair has long been used to mean "the authority or position of chairman," and has been extended to mean, more concretely, "somebody presiding over a meeting or committee," in order to avoid having to use the gender-specific terms *chairman* and *chairwoman.* An alternative is *chairperson.*

chair·borne /cháir bàwrn/ *adj.* working at a desk in an office job in the armed forces, especially the air force, rather than having combat or field duties (*informal*)

chair car *n.* 1. RAILROAD CAR WITH CHAIRS a railroad car with individual adjustable chairs instead of compartments with long seats 2. = **parlor car**

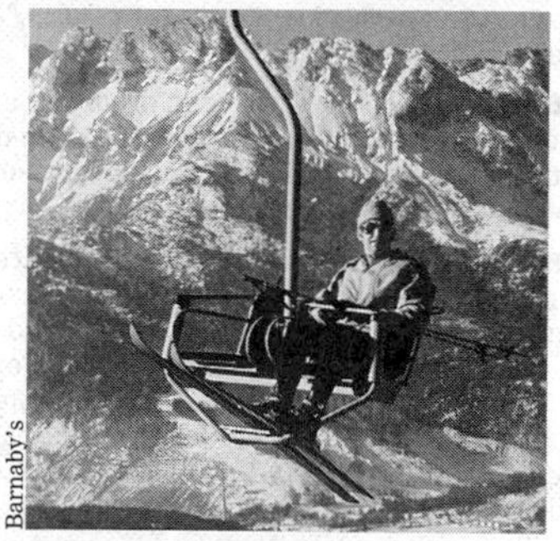

Chair lift

chair lift *n.* a series of seats suspended from a moving cable, used to carry passengers up or down a mountain or other slope

chair·man /cháirmən/ (*plural* **-men**) *n.* 1. SOMEBODY WHO PRESIDES OVER SOMETHING the presiding officer of something such as a committee or meeting 2. **chair·man, chair·man of the board** CHIEF PRESIDING OFFICER OF A COMPANY the chief presiding officer of a business corporation, elected by its board of directors and responsible for corporate policy and supervision of upper management —**chair·man·ship** *n.*

WORD KEY: USAGE

See Usage note at *chair.*

chair·per·son /cháir pùrs'n/ (*plural* **-sons**) *n.* the presiding officer of something such as a committee, board, or meeting

WORD KEY: USAGE

See Usage note at ***chair.***

chair·wom·an /cháir wŏŏmmən/ (*plural* **-en** /cháir wìmmin/) *n.* a woman who is the presiding officer of something such as a committee, board, or meeting

WORD KEY: USAGE

See Usage note at ***chair.***

chaise /shayz/ (*plural* **chaises** /shayz/) *n.* **1.** = **chaise longue 2.** SMALL OPEN HORSE-DRAWN CARRIAGE a light open two-wheeled carriage for one or more people, usually hooded and drawn by one horse **3.** = **post chaise** [Mid-17thC. From French, a variant of *chaire.*]

Chaise longue

chaise longue /shayz láwng/ (*plural* **chaise longues** *or* **chaises longues** /shayz láwng/) *n.* **1.** FOLDABLE CHAIR WITH ADJUSTABLE BACK a long low foldable chair with an adjustable back, used on a patio or beach **2.** CHAIR FOR LYING ON a chair with an elongated seat, one armrest, and sometimes an adjustable back, designed for lying on [From French, literally "long chair"]

chak·ra /chaákrə, chúkrə/ (*plural* **-ras**) *n.* in yoga, any one of the centers of spiritual power in the body. Each chakra is associated with a different god in Hinduism. [Late 18thC. From Sanskrit *cakra*, literally "wheel."]

cha·la·za /kə láyzə, kə lázzə/ (*plural* **-zas** *or* **-zae** /-zee/) *n.* **1.** ZOOL STRAND HOLDING EGG YOLK IN PLACE a spiral chord of albumen that is attached at each end of the yolk to the lining membrane inside a bird's egg, holding it in position **2.** BOT BASE OF IMMATURE SEED the base of the immature seed of a plant [Early 18thC. Via modern Latin from Greek *khalaza* "hail, small lump or knot like a hailstone" (source of English *chabazite*).] —**cha·la·zal** *adj.*

cha·la·zi·on /kə láyzee ən/ *n.* = **meibomian cyst** [Early 18thC. From Greek *khalazion*, literally "small lump," formed from *khalaza* (see CHALAZA).]

Chal·ce·don /kálsə dòn, kal sédd'n/ *n.* an ancient Greek city on the Bosporus near modern-day Istanbul that was founded in 685 B.C. —**Chal·ce·do·ni·an** /kàlsə dṓnyən, kàlsə dṓnee ən/ *adj., n.*

chal·ced·o·ny /kal sédd'nee/ *n.* a translucent or grayish form of quartz in which the microscopic crystals are packed together in parallel bands, used as a gemstone and in ornaments. Formula: SiO_2. [13thC. Via Latin *c(h)alcedonius* from Greek *khalkēdōn*, a mystical stone, of uncertain origin: perhaps from *Khalkēdōn* (see CHALCEDON).] —**chal·ce·don·ic** /kàlsə dónnik/ *adj.*

chal·cid /kálsid/ *n.* a small wasp with bright metallic coloration whose larvae are often parasites of other insects in various stages of life. Superfamily: Chalcidoidea. [Late 19thC. Via modern Latin *Chalcid-*, the stem of *Chalcis*, genus name, from Greek *khalkos* "copper," from its metallic color and sheen.]

chalco- *prefix.* copper ○ *chalcopyrite* [From Greek *khalkos*]

chal·co·cite /kálkə sìt/ *n.* a gray to black brittle copper sulfide that is an important ore of copper. Formula: Cu_2S.

chal·cog·ra·phy /kal kóggrəfee/ *n.* engraving on copper or brass —**chal·cog·ra·pher** *n.* —**chal·cog·ra·phist** *n.* —**chal·co·graph·ic** /kàlkə gráffik/ *adj.* —**chal·co·graph·i·cal** /-gráffik'l/ *adj.*

chal·co·lith·ic /kàlkə líthik/ *adj.* belonging or relating to the transitional period between the Neolithic and Bronze ages, beginning around 400 B.C., when the use of copper became more prevalent

chal·co·py·rite /kàlkə pí rìt/ *n.* a brassy yellow sulfide of copper and iron that is the commonest ore of copper. Formula: $CuFeS_2$.

Chal·de·a /kal dée ə/ ancient region of Mesopotamia, between the Euphrates and the Persian Gulf, in modern-day southern Iraq

Chal·de·an /kal dée ən/, **Chal·dae·an** *n.* **1.** PEOPLES MEMBER OF ANCIENT SEMITIC PEOPLE a member of an ancient Semitic people who lived in Chaldea in southern Babylonia, where they were the dominant ethnic group during the 8th and 7th centuries B.C. **2.** LANG ARAMAIC DIALECT a dialect of the modern Aramaic language, spoken in Iraq and by communities now settled in the United States **3.** SOOTHSAYER an astrologer, fortune-teller, or enchanter (*archaic*) [Late 16thC. Formed from Latin *Chaldaeus*, from, ultimately, Assyrian *kaldū.*] —**Chal·da·ic** /kal dáy ik/ *n., adj.* —**Chal·de·an** /-dée ən/ *adj.*

Chal·dee /káldee, kal dée/ *n.* **1.** LANG ARAMAIC the Aramaic language (*dated*) **2.** PEOPLES = **Chaldean** *n.* 1 [14thC. Via Old French from Latin *Chaldaeus* (see CHALDEAN).]

chal·dron /cháwldrən/ *n.* a former unit of capacity, especially a U.S. unit equivalent to 1.268 m^3 used to measure solids or a British unit equivalent to 1.309 m^3 used to measure solids and liquids [Mid-16thC. Via Old French *chauderon* "kettle," from, ultimately, Latin *caldarium* "vessel containing warm water for bathing."]

cha·let /sha láy, shá lày/ *n.* a house or cottage traditionally made of wood with wide overhanging eaves, originally built in Switzerland [Late 18thC. From Swiss French, of uncertain origin: possibly formed from Old French *chasel* "farmstead," from, ultimately, Latin *casa* "hut, cottage."]

chal·ice /chálliss/ *n.* **1.** METAL CUP a metal drinking cup or goblet (*literary*) **2.** CHR CUP USED AT COMMUNION OR MASS a gold or silver cup used in a church for serving the wine at Communion or Mass [14thC. Directly or via French from Latin *calic-*, the stem of *calix* "cup" (source of English *calix*).]

chal·i·co·there /kállikə theer/ *n.* an extinct mammal resembling a horse with clawed feet and forelimbs slightly longer than the hind limbs. It lived from about 55 million to about 10,000 years ago. Suborder: Chalicotheriidae. [Early 20thC. From modern Latin *Chalicotherium*, genus name, literally "animal found in gravel," from the Greek stem *khalik-* "pebble, gravel" + *thērion*, literally "small animal," from *thēr* "animal."]

chalk /chawk/ *n.* **1.** GEOL POWDERY WHITE ROCK a soft white or gray fine-grained sedimentary rock consisting of nearly pure calcium carbonate that contains minute fossil fragments of marine organisms **2.** SOFT MARKER MADE FROM CHALK a piece of chalk or a similar substance, sometimes colored, used for writing or drawing, e.g., on a blackboard **3.** CUE GAMES CUBE OF CHALK FOR RUBBING CUE a small cube of chalk or similar substance used for rubbing the tip of a pool or billiard cue to increase friction between the cue and the ball ■ *v.* (**chalked, chalk·ing, chalks**) **1.** *vti.* DRAW OR MARK SOMETHING WITH CHALK to draw, write, or mark something with chalk **2.** *vi.* BECOME POWDERY to become powdery **3.** *vt.* CUE GAMES RUB CHALK ON A CUE to treat a pool or billiard cue with chalk [Old English *cealc* "lime(stone), chalk," via prehistoric Germanic from the Latin stem *calc-* "lime(stone)," from Greek *khalix* "small stone, pebble" (source of English *calcium* and *calculate*)]

chalk up *vt.* **1.** SCORE OR KEEP SCORE OF SOMETHING to score or achieve something, or record a score or victory **2.** *U.K.* CHARGE SOMETHING TO SOMEBODY to record the cost of something and charge it to somebody or somebody's account **3.** ATTRIBUTE TO SOMETHING to credit or ascribe something to something or somebody [From the British custom at pubs or bars of writing up with chalk an account of credit given]

chalk·board /cháwk b'awrd/ *n.* = **blackboard**

chalk·stone /cháwk stṑn/ *n.* a piece of chalk taken straight from the ground

chalk talk *n.* an informal lecture during which illustrations or examples are given on a blackboard

chalk·y /cháwkee/ (**-i·er, -i·est**) *adj.* containing chalk, or resembling chalk in color or texture —**chalk·i·ness** *n.*

chal·lah /khaálə, haálə/ (*plural* **-lahs** *or* **-loth**), **hal·lah** (*plural* **-lahs** *or* **-loth**) *n.* white bread enriched with eggs, usually in a braided loaf, traditionally eaten by Jews on Friday evening at the Sabbath meal [Early 20thC. From Hebrew *ḥallāh*, from, probably, *ḥll* "to pierce," from its original shape.]

chal·lenge /chállənj/ *vt.* (**-lenged, -leng·ing, -leng·es**) **1.** INVITE SOMEBODY TO CONTEST SOMETHING to invite somebody to participate in a fight, contest, or competition **2.** DARE to dare somebody to do something **3.** CALL SOMETHING INTO QUESTION to call something into question by demanding an explanation, justification, or proof **4.** STIMULATE to stimulate somebody by making demands on the intellect **5.** ORDER SOMEBODY TO PRODUCE IDENTIFICATION to order somebody to stop and produce identification or a password **6.** LAW OBJECT TO INCLUSION OF JUROR to make a formal objection against the inclusion of a prospective juror on a jury **7.** IMMUNOL TEST WHETHER SOMETHING PRODUCES ALLERGY to expose a person or animal to a substance in order to determine whether an allergy or other adverse reaction will occur ■ *n.* **1.** INVITATION TO TAKE PART IN CONTEST an invitation to somebody to compete in a fight, contest, or competition **2.** STIMULATING TEST OF ABILITIES a test of somebody's abilities or a situation that tests somebody's abilities in a stimulating way **3.** QUESTIONING OF SOMETHING a questioning of something by demanding an explanation, justification, or proof **4.** DEMAND FOR IDENTIFICATION an order to somebody to stop and produce identification or a password **5.** LAW OBJECTION AGAINST JUROR an objection against the inclusion of somebody on a jury **6.** CLAIM AGAINST VOTING ELIGIBILITY a claim that somebody is not entitled to a vote, or that a vote is invalid **7.** IMMUNOL TESTING FOR ALLERGY exposure of a person or animal to a substance in order to determine whether an allergy or other adverse reaction will occur [13thC. Via Old French *c(h)alengier* "to accuse" from Latin *calumniare* "to accuse falsely," from *calumnia* "false accusation" (source of English *calumny*).] —**chal·lenge·a·ble** *adj.*

chal·lenged /chállənjd/ *adj.* **1.** WITH SPECIFIED PROBLEM having a specified handicap **2.** LACKING IN SOMETHING lacking in a specified quality or characteristic (*humorous*) ○ *vertically challenged*

chal·leng·er /chállənjər/ *n.* **1.** SOMEBODY WHO SEEKS A FIGHT somebody who issues an invitation to a fight, contest, or competition **2.** SOMEBODY WHO OPPOSES CHAMPION somebody who competes for a championship against the champion, especially in boxing

chal·leng·ing /chállənjing/ *adj.* demanding physical or psychological effort of a stimulating kind —**chal·leng·ing·ly** *adv.*

chal·lis /shállee/, **chal·lie** *n.* a soft lightweight fabric for clothes, often patterned with a small print and made of wool, cotton, or synthetic fibers [Mid-19thC. Origin uncertain: perhaps from the surname *Challis.*]

Chal·mette /shal mét/ unincorporated settlement and county seat of St. Bernard parish, southeastern Louisiana, situated on the Mississippi River downstream from New Orleans. Population: 31,860 (1990).

cha·lone /káy lṑn, ká-/ *n.* a substance produced by cells that inhibits the division of cells of a similar type. Chalones are usually glycoproteins. [Early 20thC. Formed from Greek *khalōn*, the present participle of *khalan* "to slacken," on the model of HORMONE.] —**cha·lon·ic** /ka lṓnik, kay-/ *adj.*

chal·u·meau /shàllə mṓ/ (*plural* **-meaux** /-mṓ/) *n.* **1.** EARLY MUSICAL INSTRUMENT a woodwind instrument of the 17th and 18th centuries that developed into the clarinet **2.** LOWEST REGISTER OF CLARINET the lowest register of a clarinet, or its warm tone quality [Early 18thC. Via French from late Latin *calamellus*, literally "small reed," from *calamus* "reed," from Greek *kalamos* (source of English *calamus*, *caramel*, and *shawm*).]

cha·lutz /khaa lŏŏts/ (*plural* **-lutz·im**), **ha·lutz** (*plural* **-lutz·im**) *n.* a member of a group of Jewish immigrants to Palestine after 1917 who began or worked in agricultural or forestry projects [Early 20thC. From Hebrew *ḥaluṣ*, literally "pioneer."]

cha·lyb·e·ate /kə líbbee ət, kə léebee àyt/ *adj.* **1.** CONTAINING IRON SALTS containing iron salts **2.** TASTING OF IRON having a taste like iron [Mid-17thC. From modern Latin *chalybeatus*, from Latin *chalybs* "steel," from Greek *khalups.*]

cha·ly·bite /kálli bìt/ *n.* = **siderite** [Mid-19thC. Coined from Greek *khalyb-*, the stem of *khalyps* "steel" + -ITE.]

cham /kam/ *n.* a Tartar or Mogul khan (*archaic*) [15thC. Via French from Turkic *kān* "lord, prince."]

Cham /kam/ (*plural* **Chams** *or* **Cham**) *n.* **1.** MEMBER OF VIETNAMESE PEOPLE a member of a people who originally lived in Champa, a former kingdom in present-day Vietnam. After the Annamese invaded in the 17th century, many Chams fled to Cambodia. **2.** LANG **AUSTRONESIAN LANGUAGE** a language spoken in parts of Vietnam and Cambodia. It belongs to the Austronesian family of languages. Cham is spoken by about 230,000 people. —**Cham** *adj.*

Cha·mae·leon /kə méelee ən, -lyən/, **Cha·me·leon** *n.* a faint constellation lying near the south celestial pole

cham·ae·phyte /kámmi fìt/ *n.* a perennial plant that produces buds on or close to the ground. The buds remain dormant during the winter. [Early 20thC. Coined from Greek *khamai* "low, on the ground" (see CHAMELEON) + -PHYTE.]

cham·ber /cháymbər/ *n.* **1. ROOM FOR SPECIFIC PURPOSE** a room used for a designated purpose **2.** ARMS **PLACE IN GUN FOR AMMUNITION** the compartment for a cartridge in a revolver or rifle, or for a shell in a cannon **3. OFFICIAL ASSEMBLY OR MEETING PLACE** a legislative or judicial assembly, or the place where such a body meets **4. ORGANIZED BODY OF PEOPLE** a body of people organized into a group for a specific purpose **5. COMPARTMENT IN SOMETHING** an enclosed space, compartment, or cavity, e.g., one inside a machine, the body, or a plant **6. BEDROOM** a bedroom or other room in somebody's home (*archaic or literary*) **7. OFFICIAL RECEPTION ROOM** a reception room in an official residence or a palace **8.** = **chamber pot 9.** FIN **TREASURY** a treasury, especially for government funds (*archaic*) ■ **cham·bers** *npl.* **JUDGE'S PRIVATE OFFICE** a judge's private office for discussing cases or legal matters not taken up in open court ■ *adj.* **OF CHAMBER MUSIC** relating to, written as, or performing chamber music ■ *vt.* **(-bered, -ber·ing, -bers) 1.** ARMS **PUT AMMUNITION IN WEAPON** to insert a round of ammunition in the breech of a weapon **2. ENCLOSE IN OR PROVIDE WITH CHAMBERS** to put something in or provide something with a chamber or chambers [12thC. Via French *chambre* from Latin *camera* "vault, arch, room" (source of English *camera*), from Greek *kamara* "vault, something with an arched cover."]

cham·bered /cháymbərd/ *adj.* **1. WITH CAVITIES** containing a chamber or chambers **2. ENCLOSED** enclosed or confined in a chamber or something similar

cham·bered nau·ti·lus *n.* = **pearly nautilus.** ◊ **paper nautilus**

cham·ber·lain /cháymbərlin/ *n.* **1. MANAGER OF ROYAL OR NOBLE HOUSEHOLD** an official who manages the household of a monarch or member of the nobility **2. TREASURER OF MUNICIPALITY** the treasurer of a municipality **3.** CHR **PRIEST WHO IS PAPAL ATTENDANT** a priest who is an attendant to the Pope, often an honorary position [12thC. Via Old French from assumed Frankish *kamarling*, literally "little room," from, ultimately, Greek, "vaulted room, vault." The underlying meaning is "bedchamber attendant."]

Cham·ber·lain /cháymbərlin/, **Owen** (*b.* 1920) U.S. physicist. He shared a Nobel Prize in physics (1959) for his research into atomic nuclei, and discovered the antiproton.

Cham·ber·lain, Wilt (*b.* 1936) U.S. basketball player. He dominated the National Basketball Association during his career (1960–73), winning seven scoring titles. Full name **Wilton Norman Chamberlain**

cham·ber·maid /cháymbər màyd/ *n.* a woman employed to tidy and clean bedrooms in hotels or guest houses

cham·ber mu·sic *n.* classical instrumental music written for a small group e.g., a quartet or trio, and often originally intended for performance in a large room or a small concert hall

cham·ber of com·merce *n.* an organization of local business people who work together to promote and protect common interests in trade

cham·ber of hor·rors *n.* an exhibition depicting macabre or gruesome objects and incidents [From the name given to a room in Madame Tussaud's waxwork exhibition in London, England, containing effigies of noted criminals]

cham·ber or·ches·tra *n.* a small orchestra, usually of fewer than 40 players, that performs classical music. A chamber orchestra can play at more modest-sized venues than a full symphony orchestra.

cham·ber pot *n.* a large bowl used in a bedroom for urination and defecation

Cham·bers·burg /cháymbərz bùrg/ borough in Pennsylvania, southwest of Harrisburg. It was burned down by Confederate troops during the Civil War. Population: 17,202 (1996).

cham·bray /shám bràỳ/ *n.* a fine lightweight cotton or linen fabric with colored lengthwise fibers interlaced with white [Early 19thC. Alteration of the name of *Cambrai*, a city in northern France where the cloth was originally made.]

Chameleon

cha·me·leon /kə méelee ən, -lyən/ *n.* **1. LIZARD THAT CHANGES COLOR** a tree-dwelling lizard found chiefly in Africa and Madagascar, with long thin legs, a strong curled tail, a long sticky tongue, and the ability to change color. Family: Chamaeleonidae. **2.** = **anole 3. SOMEBODY WHO IS CHANGEABLE** somebody who easily and frequently changes personality or appearance [14thC. Via Latin from Greek *khamaileōn*, literally "ground lion," from *khamai* "low, on the ground" + *leōn* "lion."] —**cha·me·le·on·ic** /kə méelee ónnik/ *adj.*

Cha·me·leon *n.* ASTRON = **Chamaeleon**

cha·metz /khaa méts, kháwməts/, **cho·metz, ha·metz, ho·metz** *n.* leavened bread or other food that may not be eaten by Jews during Passover [Mid-19thC. From Hebrew *hāmēs*.]

cham·fer /chámfər/ *n.* **SHALLOW ANGLED CUT** a shallow cut, edge, or groove made in wood, usually at an angle of 45 degrees to a corner ■ *vt.* **(-fered, -fer·ing, -fers) MAKE SHALLOW CUT IN WOOD** to make a shallow cut, edge, or groove in wood, usually at an angle of 45 degrees to a corner [Mid-16thC. Back-formation from *chamfering* "grooving," from French *chanfrein* "beveled edge," variant of *chanfreint*, past participle of *chanfraindre* "to bevel," from *chant* "edge" (from Latin *canthus* "iron tire") + *fraindre* "to break."] —**cham·fered** *adj.*

cham·fron /chámfrən/ *n.* a piece of armor used in medieval times to protect a horse's head in battle [15thC. From French *chanfrain*, of uncertain origin: perhaps from Old French *chafrener* "to harness a horse," literally "to put a bridle on," from *chief* "head" + *frener* "to bridle."]

cha·mi·so /cha méesō/, **cha·mi·se** /chə méez/ *n.* an evergreen shrub of the rose family that is native to southern California and has small needle-shaped leaves and small white flowers. Latin name: *Adenostoma fasciculatum*. [Mid-19thC. Via Mexican Spanish from Spanish *chamizo* "burned stick," from, ultimately, Latin *flamma* "flame"; from its dry appearance.]

Chamois

cham·ois /shámmee/ *n.* (*plural* **-ois** /-mee/ *or* **-oix**) **1. EURASIAN GOAT ANTELOPE** an agile goat antelope found in mountainous regions of Europe and southwestern Asia that has slender backward-curving horns and a tawny coat that darkens in winter. Latin name: *Rupicapra rupicapra*. **2. cham·ois, cham·ois leather SOFT PLIABLE LEATHER** soft pliable leather used for cleaning and polishing. Originally made from the hide of the chamois, it is now usually made from that of sheep or goats. **3. CHAMOIS LEATHER CLOTH FOR POLISHING** a piece of chamois leather, or a natural or synthetic substitute, used for cleaning and polishing **4.** COLORS **GRAYISH YELLOW** a grayish-yellow color, like that of chamois leather ■ *adj.* COLORS **GRAYISH-YELLOW** of a grayish-yellow color ■ *vt.* **(-oised, -ois·ing, -ois·es) CLEAN OR POLISH SOMETHING WITH CHAMOIS** to clean or polish something with a chamois [Mid-16thC. Via French from late Latin *camox*, of uncertain origin: probably from a language spoken in the Alps before the Romans penetrated northward.]

Cha·mor·ro /chaa máwrō/, **Violeta Barrios de** (*b.* 1929) Nicaraguan political leader. The manager of the opposition newspaper *La Prensa*, she became president of Nicaragua (1990–97).

champ[1] /champ/ *n.* **BITING, CHEWING, OR GRINDING SOMETHING** the process of biting, chewing, or grinding something vigorously, noisily, or impatiently, or the sound that this makes ■ *v.* **(champed, champ·ing, champs) 1.** *vti.* **BITE SOMETHING VIGOROUSLY** to bite, chew, or grind something vigorously, noisily, or impatiently **2.** *vt. Scotland* **MASH FOOD** to mash something, e.g., potatoes (*informal*) [Mid-16thC. Origin uncertain: probably an imitation of the sound.] —**cham·per** *n.*

champ[2] /champ/ *n.* a champion (*informal*) [Mid-19thC. Shortening.]

cham·pac *n.* = **champak**

cham·pagne /sham páyn/ *n.* **1.** WINE **DRY WHITE SPARKLING WINE FROM CHAMPAGNE** a dry white sparkling wine produced in the Champagne region of northeastern France, often drunk at special occasions **2.** WINE **WHITE WINE RESEMBLING CHAMPAGNE** any dry or semisweet white wine resembling champagne and made by a similar process **3.** COLORS **PALE BROWNISH GOLD** a very pale brownish-gold color ■ *adj.* **1. EXTRAVAGANT** involving luxury and indulgence ○ *a champagne lifestyle* **2. PALE BROWNISH-GOLD** of a very pale brownish-gold color [Mid-17thC]

cham·paign /sham páyn/ *n.* a wide expanse of open countryside (*literary*) [14thC. Via French *champagne* from late Latin *campania* "level country," from Latin, *Campania*, a province in Middle Italy (source of English *campaign*).]

Cham·paign /sham páyn/ city in eastern Illinois, west of Urbana. It shares the University of Illinois with Urbana. Population: 64,002 (1996).

cham·pak /chám pàk, chúm pùk/ (*plural* **-paks** *or* **-pak**), **cham·pac** (*plural* **-pacs** *or* **-pac**) *n.* an Asian evergreen tree whose wood is used for furniture. It has fragrant orange-yellow flowers whose oil is used in perfumery and is sacred to Hindus and Buddhists. Latin name: *Michelia champaca*. [Late 18thC. Via Hindi from Sanskrit *cāmpākā*, from Dravidian (a non-Indo-European language family).]

cham·per·ty /chámpərtee/ (*plural* **-ties**) *n.* LAW an agreement between a litigant and somebody who aids or finances litigation in return for a share of the proceeds following a successful outcome [15thC. From Anglo-Norman *champartie*, from Old French *champart* "field rent (a portion received by a feudal lord of the produce from land leased)," from *champ* "field" + *part* "portion."] —**cham·per·tous** *adj.*

cham·pi·gnon /sham pínnyən, shaaNpin yáwN/ *n.* a mushroom, especially one cultivated for eating [Late 16thC. From French, literally "little country," formed from *champagne*, from late Latin *campania* "level country." The underlying idea is of something that grows in the countryside.]

cham·pi·on /chámpee ən/ *n.* **1. SUPREME VICTOR IN CONTEST** a person who or team that competes in and wins a contest, competition, or tournament **2. SHOW WINNER** something, e.g., an animal or plant, that wins first place in a show **3. DEFENDER** somebody who defends, supports, or promotes a person or cause **4. REMARKABLE PERSON** somebody who exemplifies excellence or achievement **5. HERO OR WARRIOR** a hero or warrior, especially a knight who fights in behalf or or in defense of a monarch (*archaic or literary*) ■ *vt.* **(-oned, -on·ing, -ons) DEFEND** to defend, support, or promote a cause or person [12thC. Via Old French, "combatant," from the late Latin stem *campion-* "combatant in the arena or athletic field," from Latin *campus* "field."]

cham·pi·on·ship /chámpee ən shìp/ *n.* **1. CONTEST TO DECIDE A CHAMPION** a contest, competition, or tournament that is held to decide who will be the overall winner **2.** TITLE OR TIME OF BEING CHAMPION the designation or period of being a champion **3.** DEFENDING OR SUPPORTING SOMEBODY OR SOMETHING the defense, support, or promotion of a person or cause

Cham·plain, Lake /sham pláyn/ lake situated between Vermont and New York, extending approximately 6 mi./10 km into Canada. Area: 430 s. mi./1,100 sq. km. Depth: 399 ft./122 m.

Cham·plain /sham pláyn, shaáN plán/, **Samuel de** (1567?–1635) French explorer. His North American expeditions (1603–08) led to the establishment of New France (Canada).

champ·le·vé /shaàNlə váy/ *n.* enamel work in which colored enamels are used to fill channels cut into a metal base [Mid-19thC. From French, literally "raised field," from *champ* "field" + *levé* "raised."] —**champ·le·vé** *adj.*

Chanc. *abbr.* **1.** chancellor **2.** chancery

chance /chanss/ *n.* **1.** LIKELIHOOD THAT SOMETHING WILL HAPPEN the degree of probability that something will happen (*often used in the plural*) ○ *There's a strong chance we'll win.* **2.** OPPORTUNITY OR OPPORTUNE TIME FOR SOMETHING an opportunity or a set of circumstances that makes it possible for something to happen ○ *I was given no chance to explain.* **3.** SUPPOSED FORCE THAT MAKES THINGS HAPPEN the supposed force that makes things happen in a particular way without any apparent cause **4.** BASEBALL OPPORTUNITY TO MAKE PUTOUT OR ASSIST in baseball, an opportunity to field a ball and make a putout or assist **5.** RAFFLE OR LOTTERY TICKET a ticket in a raffle or lottery **6.** UNEXPECTED HAPPENING an unexpected event **7.** SOMETHING CAUSED BY LUCK something caused by luck or fortune ■ *v.* (**chanced, chanc·ing, chanc·es**) **1.** *vt.* DO SOMETHING RISKY to do something knowing that it is risky **2.** *vi.* DO SOMETHING UNPLANNED to do something or happen without a cause or plan [13thC. Via Anglo-Norman from, ultimately, late Latin *cadentia* "falling," from the present participle of Latin *cadere* "to fall."] —**chance·less** *adj.* ◇ **by any chance** used to inquire if there is any possibility of something ○ *Is there a copy you could lend me, by any chance?* ◇ **by chance** unexpectedly or without plan ◇ **fat chance** something that is highly unlikely (*informal*)

chance on, chance u·pon *vt.* to find or encounter somebody or something unexpectedly

Chance /chanss/, **Frank** (1877–1924) U.S. baseball player. Playing for the Chicago Cubs, he formed a double-play combination with Joseph Tinker and John Evers.

chan·cel /chánss'l/ *n.* an area of a church near the altar for the use of clergy and choir, often separated from the nave by a screen or steps [14thC. Via Old French from Latin *cancelli*, literally "little lattices" (source also of *chancellor*), from *cancer* "lattice." The underlying idea is of a place enclosed by a grating.]

chan·cel·ler·y /chánsələree, chánsləree/ (*plural* **-ies**), **chan·cel·lor·y** (*plural* **-ies**) *n.* **1.** CHANCELLOR'S RESIDENCE the official residence of a chancellor **2.** CHANCELLOR'S RANK the position or rank of a chancellor **3.** OFFICES OF EMBASSY OR CONSULATE the offices of an embassy or a consulate

chan·cel·lor /chánsələr, chánsslər/, **Chan·cel·lor** *n.* **1.** HEAD OF GOVERNMENT IN PARLIAMENTARY DEMOCRACY the chief minister of government in some parliamentary democracies **2.** CHIEF ADMINISTRATIVE OFFICER OF UNIVERSITY the chief administrative officer of some universities **3.** *U.K., Can* HONORARY HEAD OF UNIVERSITY the honorary head of a university **4.** JUDGE IN SOME U.S. COURTS in some U.S. states, the presiding judge of a court of equity or chancery **5.** SECRETARY TO MONARCH OR NOBLE a secretary to a monarch or noble (*archaic*) [Pre-12thC. Via Anglo-Norman *c(h)anceler* from Latin *cancellarius* "court secretary" (originally the attendant at the grating that separated the public from the judges), from *cancelli* "grating" (see CHANCEL).] —**chan·cel·lor·ship** *n.*

Chan·cel·lor of the Ex·che·quer *n.* a member of the British government who is the chief minister of finance

chan·cel·lor·y *n.* = **chancellery**

chance-med·ley *n.* **1.** LAW KILLING IN SELF-DEFENSE the killing of an assailant in self-defense during an unexpected brawl **2.** SOMETHING HAPPENING BY CHANCE a haphazard event or action, or the randomness of chance [15thC. From Anglo-Norman *chance medlee*, literally "mixed chance"; from the idea of being only partly accidental.]

chan·cer·y /chánsəree/ (*plural* **-ies**), **Chan·cer·y** (*plural* **-ies**) *n.* **1.** RELIG = **chancellery 2.** = **chancellery 3.** LAW = **court of chancery 4.** LAW LORD CHANCELLOR'S COURT the Lord Chancellor's court, one of the five divisions of the High Court of Justice in England [14thC. Contraction of CHANCELLERY.]

chan·cre /shángkər/ *n.* **1.** ULCER INDICATING SYPHILIS AND OTHER DISEASES a small painless highly infectious ulcer or sore that is the first sign of syphilis and certain other infectious diseases **2.** ULCER a sore or ulcer at the point where a disease-causing organism (**pathogen**) enters the body [Late 16thC. Via French from Latin *cancer* "ulcer."] —**chan·crous** *adj.*

chan·croid /sháng kròyd/ *n.* **1.** SEXUALLY TRANSMITTED DISEASE a sexually transmitted disease that causes a painful ragged ulcer at the site of infection and is treated with antibiotics. It is caused by infection with a bacterium *Haemophilus ducreyi.* **2.** ULCER a painful ragged ulcer that is characteristic of the sexually transmitted disease chancroid —**chan·croid·al** /shang króyd'l/ *adj.*

chanc·y /chánsee/ (**-i·er, -i·est**) *adj.* **1.** RISKY involving risks or danger **2.** RANDOM OR HAPHAZARD occurring in a random or haphazard way —**chanc·i·ly** *adv.* —**chanc·i·ness** *n.*

Chandelier

chan·de·lier /shànd'l éer/ *n.* a decorative hanging light with several branches and holders for candles or light bulbs [Mid-18thC. From French, formed from *chandelle* "candle" (originally the light in a chandelier), from Latin *candela* "candle."] —**chan·de·liered** *adj.*

chan·delle /shan dél, shaaN-/ *n.* STEEP CLIMBING TURN OF AIRCRAFT a steep climbing turn in which an aircraft almost stalls as it uses momentum to increase the rate of climb ■ *vi.* (**-delled, -del·ling, -delles**) EXECUTE CHANDELLE to climb steeply in an aircraft, turning at the same time and almost stalling [Early 20thC. From French, literally "candle."]

chan·dler /chándlər/ *n.* **1.** SELLER OF SPECIFIED GOODS a seller of specified supplies and goods ○ *a ship's chandler* **2.** CANDLE MAKER AND SELLER a seller or maker of candles **3.** GROCER somebody who sells groceries and provisions (*archaic*) [14thC. From Anglo-Norman *chaundeler*, Old French *chandelier*, formed from Old French *c(h)andelle* "candle," from Latin *candela*.]

Raymond Chandler

Chan·dler /chándlər/, **Raymond** (1888–1959) U.S. writer. He wrote gritty mystery and crime novels such as *The Big Sleep* (1939) and *Strangers on a Train* (1951). Full name **Raymond Thornton Chandler**

chan·dler·y /chándləree/ (*plural* **-ies**) *n.* the goods that a chandler deals in, or the place where they are stored or sold

Chan·dra·sek·har lim·it /shàndrə say kaar-/ *n.* the upper limit for the mass of a white dwarf star. A star above the limit, having exhausted its nuclear energy, would collapse to a neutron star or a black hole. [Named for Subrahmanyan *Chandrasekhar* (b. 1910), Pakistan astrophysicist, who formulated it]

Coco Chanel

Cha·nel /shə nél/, **Coco** (1883–1971) French couturier. Her name became synonymous with a distinctively elegant style of women's suit. Full name **Gabrielle Bonheur Chanel**

Cha·ney /cháynee/, **Lon** (1883–1930) U.S. silent movie actor. He specialized in horror roles, especially in *The Hunchback of Notre Dame* (1923) and *The Phantom of the Opera* (1925). Full name **Alonso Chaney**

Chang·chun /chaàng chóon/ transportation center and capital city of Jilin province in northeastern China. Population: 2,110,000 (1991).

change /chaynj/ *v.* (**changed, chang·ing, chang·es**) **1.** *vti.* BECOME OR MAKE SOMETHING DIFFERENT to become different, or make something or somebody different **2.** *vt.* SUBSTITUTE OR REPLACE SOMETHING to exchange, substitute, or replace something ○ *We changed the batteries regularly.* **3.** *vti.* PASS FROM ONE STATE TO ANOTHER to pass or make something pass from one state or stage to another ○ *Water changes to ice when it freezes.* **4.** *vti.* REMOVE CLOTHES AND PUT ON OTHERS to remove one or more articles of clothing and replace them with something else ○ *Are you going to change for dinner?* **5.** *vt.* FIN EXCHANGE MONEY FOR SMALLER UNITS to exchange a unit of money for an equal amount of money in lower denominations ○ *Can you change a $10 bill for two fives?* **6.** *vti.* MOVE FROM ONE VEHICLE TO ANOTHER to get out of one vehicle or means of transportation and continue the journey in another **7.** *vt.* REMOVE AND REPLACE SOMETHING to remove something dirty or used and replace it with another that is clean or unused **8.** *vi.* BECOME DEEPER to become deeper in register (*refers to a boy's voice*) **9.** *vt.* FIN CONVERT ONE CURRENCY INTO ANOTHER to replace money of one currency with an equivalent amount in another currency, calculated according to an exchange rate **10.** *vti. U.K.* OPERATE GEARS OF VEHICLE to put a car or other vehicle into a different gear ■ *n.* **1.** MAKING OR BECOMING DIFFERENT alteration, variation, or modification, or the result of this ○ *There's been a change of plan.* **2.** COINS coins collectively, especially coins of small denomination **3.** FIN MONEY GIVEN BACK the balance of money given back to a customer who has handed over a larger sum than the cost of the goods or services purchased **4.** FRESH SET OF SOMETHING a different, clean, or fresh set of something, especially clothes **5.** VARIANCE FROM ROUTINE a variance from a routine or pattern, especially a welcome one ○ *She could do with a change.* **6.** TRANSITION FROM SOMETHING a shift from one state, stage, or phase to another ○ *a change in attitude* **7.** MENOPAUSE the menopause (*dated informal*) **8.** EXCHANGE OR REPLACEMENT an exchange, substitution, or replacement of something or somebody **9.** FIN MONEY EXCHANGED FOR HIGHER DENOMINATION a sum of money given or received as an equivalent of a higher denomination **10.** MUSIC PROCEDURE FOR RINGING BELLS the order in which a set of tuned bells are rung. ◊ **change ringing** [12thC. Via Old French *changer* from late Latin *cambiare*, from Latin *cambire* "to exchange, barter," of uncertain origin: probably from Celtic.] —**chang·er** *n.* ◇ **ring the changes** to repeat something with variations

WORD KEY: SYNONYMS

change, alter, modify, convert, vary, shift, transform, transmute

CORE MEANING: to make or become different

change the most general term; **alter** a narrower term, often suggesting a change in an aspect of something rather than in its entirety; **modify** to make minor changes or alterations, especially in order to improve something; **convert** to change something concrete such as a building from one form or function to another; **vary** to change within a range of possibilities, or in connection with something else, with a suggestion of instability; **shift** to change from one position or direction to another; **transform** to make a radical and often very obvious change into a different form; **transmute** a more formal term for "transform".

---

change down *vi. U.K.* = **downshift**

change off *vi.* to alternate tasks, or tasks and work breaks, especially with somebody else

change over *vi.* **1. SUBSTITUTE SOMETHING FOR SOMETHING ELSE** to replace one system, method, or product with another **2.** *U.K.* SPORTS **EXCHANGE ENDS OF PLAYING FIELD** in team sports, to switch to opposite ends of a playing field, usually halfway through a game

change·a·ble /cháynjəbəl/ *adj.* **1. LIABLE TO CHANGE** capable of or liable to change ○ *his mood was changeable* **2. VARIABLE IN COLOR** variable in color according to viewpoint or lighting —**change·a·bil·i·ty** /chàynjə bíllətee/ *n.* —**change·a·ble·ness** /cháynjəb'lnəss/ *n.* —**change·a·bly** /-əblee/ *adv.*

change·ful /cháynjfəl/ *adj.* changing frequently —**change·ful·ly** *adv.* —**change·ful·ness** *n.*

change·less /cháynjləss/ *adj.* not liable to change —**change·less·ly** *adv.* —**change·less·ness** *n.*

change·ling /cháynjling/ *n.* in folklore, a child who is secretly substituted for another one by fairies

change of heart *n.* a profound change of attitude or opinion

change of life *n.* the menopause (*dated informal*)

change of pace *n.* **1. TEMPORARY CHANGE IN ROUTINE** a temporary change in pattern or routine **2.** BASEBALL = **changeup**

change of ven·ue *n.* **1.** LAW **MOVE OF TRIAL TO ANOTHER LOCATION** the movement of a trial to another jurisdiction **2. MOVE OF EVENT TO ANOTHER PLACE** a relocation of a public event, especially a play or concert

change·o·ver /cháynj òvər/ *n.* **1. COMPLETE CHANGE FROM SOMETHING** a conversion, reversal, or complete change from one position, situation, or system to another **2.** SPORTS **EXCHANGE OF ENDS IN PLAYING FIELD** in team sports, the switch of teams to opposite ends of a playing field

change purse *n.* a small receptacle for coins, often carried inside a larger purse

change ring·ing *n.* the ordered ringing of a peal of bells in various combinations so that none of the combinations is repeated and all possible permutations are rung

change·up /cháynj ùp/, **change-up** *n.* **1. CHANGE OF PITCH'S SPEED** in baseball, a ball thrown by a pitcher that resembles a fastball but moves more slowly, adversely affecting the batter's timing **2. CHANGE OF PACE OR MOOD** an unexpected shift in pace, rhythm, or feeling (*informal*)

chang·ing of the guard *n.* the action or ceremony in which one shift of guards takes up duty while another leaves, especially outside Buckingham Palace in London, England

chang·ing room *n. U.K.* an area in a sports or leisure center where clothes can be changed and showers taken

Chang Jiang /chaàng jee aáng/ = **Yangtze**

Chang·sha /cháng shaà/ capital of the Hunan Province, situated north of Guangzhou, in southeastern China. Population: 1,330,000 (1991).

Chang·zhou /chaàng jṓ/ city situated in the center of the Yangtze River Delta, 100 mi./162 km west of Shanghai. Population: 800,000 (1996).

chan·nel[1] /chánn'l/ *n.* **1.** BROADCAST **FREQUENCY SPECTRUM USED IN TRANSMISSION** the portion of a frequency spectrum that is set aside for a specific purpose, e.g., the broadcasting of a television or radio signal **2.** BROADCAST **TV OR RADIO STATION** a television or radio station broadcasting on a specified band of the frequency spectrum **3.** GEOG **STRIP OF WATER SEPARATING LAND** a wide passage of water between an island and a larger body of land **4.** NAUT **NAVIGABLE PASSAGE** a navigable route through a river or harbor, especially one that has been deepened by dredging **5. MEANS OF COMMUNICATION** a course or means of communication or expression (*often used in the plural*) ○ *the proper channels* **6.** GEOG **ROUTE OF WATERWAY** the course of a stream, river, canal, or other waterway **7.** PARANORMAL **SPIRIT MEDIUM WHO ACTS AS GUIDE** in spiritualism, somebody who acts as a medium for receiving messages from the spirit world **8.** COMPUT **PATH FOR COMPUTER ELECTRONIC SIGNALS** a path for electronic signals within a computer or between a computer and a peripheral device **9.** ELECTRON ENG **PATH FOR ELECTRICAL CURRENT** a path for an electrical current or signal **10. TUBULAR PASSAGE FOR LIQUID** a long narrow passage or tube along which a liquid can flow ○ *a drainage channel* **11. GROOVE OR TRENCH** a long narrow groove or furrow, e.g., in architecture or sculpture ■ *v.* **(-neled, -neling, -nels) 1.** *vt.* **DIRECT SOMETHING ALONG SPECIFIC ROUTE** to direct, guide, or convey something, e.g., money or information, through or along a specific route ○ *They channeled all their energies into the game.* **2.** *vti.* PARANORMAL **SPEAK WITH A SPIRIT** in spiritualism, to act as a medium for a spirit **3.** *vt.* **MAKE CHANNEL IN LAND OR WATER** to make a channel in land or water **4.** *vt.* **MAKE GROOVE OR FURROW IN SOMETHING** to cut a long narrow groove or furrow in a surface [14thC. Via Old French *chanel* from Latin *canalis* "groove, waterpipe, canal," from *canna* "pipe, reed," from Greek *kanna* "reed" (source of English *cane, cannister,* and *canyon*).] —**chan·nel·er** *n.*

chan·nel[2] /chánn'l/ *n.* a flat piece of wood or metal projecting horizontally from the side of a ship to increase the spread of the ropes or cables (**shrouds**) supporting the mast [Mid-18thC. Alteration of *chainwale,* from CHAIN + WALE.]

chan·nel bass *n.* a large reddish edible fish of the drum family that lives in the waters off the Atlantic coast of the U.S. Latin name: *Sciaenops ocellata.*

chan·nel-hop·ping *n. U.K.* = **channel-surfing** —**chan·nel-hop** *vi.* —**chan·nel-hop·per** *n.*

chan·nel·ing /chánnəling/ *n.* **1.** PARANORMAL **SPIRITUAL COMMUNICATION THROUGH A MEDIUM** in spiritualism, the practice of acting as a medium for receiving messages from the spirit world **2. CREATION OF CHANNEL** the making of a channel in or on something **3. TUBING THAT PROTECTS WIRES** a protective casing or container that carries one or more cables or wires inside or outside a building

chan·nel i·ron *n.* an iron or steel bar with a U-shaped cross section

Chan·nel Is·lands /chánn'l-/ group of islands in the English Channel, near the French coast. The islands Jersey, Guernsey, Alderney, and Sark are self-governing Crown dependencies. Language: English; Norman-French. Population: 143,534 (1991). Area: 75 sq. mi./195 sq. km.

Chan·nel Is·lands Na·tion·al Park park made up of five islands off the coast of southern California, a national park since 1980. Area: 249,354 acres/100,914 hectares.

chan·nel·ize /chánn'l ìz/ **(-ized, -iz·ing, -iz·es)** *vt.* to make a channel for something, or direct something through a channel —**chan·nel·i·za·tion** /chànn'li záysh'n/ *n.*

chan·nel·ling *n.* U.K. = **channeling**

chan·nel-surf *vi.* to use of a remote control device to move rapidly through many different television channels, either to see whether there is anything worth watching or without searching for anything in particular —**chan·nel-surf·er** *n.*

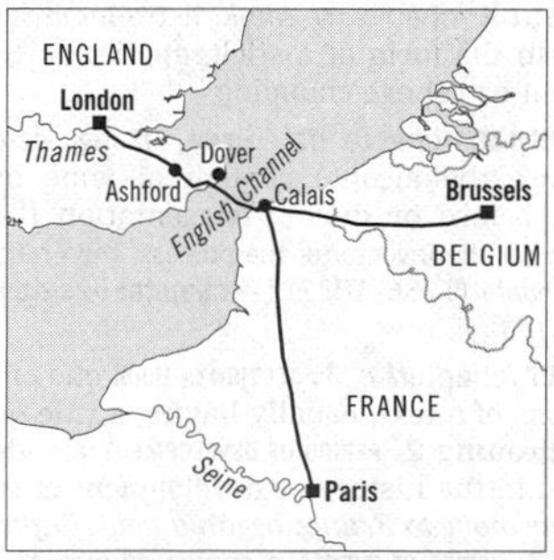

Channel Tunnel: Map showing railroad routes using the Channel Tunnel

Chan·nel Tun·nel *n.* a railroad tunnel, opened in 1994, that runs underneath the English Channel and links Folkestone in England with Coquelles near Calais in France. ◊ **Chunnel**

Chan·ning /chánning/, **Edward** (1856–31) U.S. historian. A professor of history at Harvard (1883–1929), he wrote the six-volume *History of the United States* (1905–25).

Chan·ning, William Ellery (1780–1842) U.S. minister. His writings, sermons, and influence on transcendentalism helped to spread Unitarianism throughout New England.

cha·no·yu /chaà naw yóo/ *n.* a Japanese ceremony in which tea is ritually prepared, served, and consumed [Late 20thC. From Japanese, literally "hot water for tea."]

chan·son /shaaN sáwN/ *n.* a French song, e.g., a satirical cabaret song of the 20th century or a Renaissance song similar to the madrigal [15thC. Via French, "song," from the Latin stem *cantion-,* from *cantare* "to sing."]

chan·son de geste /shaaN sàwN də zhést/ (*plural* **chan·sons de geste** /shaaN sàwN də zhést/) *n.* a French epic poem written between the 11th and 14th centuries, usually celebrating the exploits of legendary events and figures [From French, literally "song of heroic deeds"]

chan·son·nier /shaàNsən yáy/ *n.* a cabaret performer or writer of chansons [Late 19thC. From French, from *chanson* (see CHANSON).]

chant /chant/ *n.* **1. PHRASE SPOKEN REPEATEDLY BY CROWD** a phrase or slogan repeatedly and rhythmically spoken, often with a simple singsong intonation, especially in unison by a crowd or group **2.** MUSIC **MUSIC FOR RELIGIOUS PASSAGE** a musical passage in which words or syllables are sung on the same note, or a single word or syllable is sung on a series of notes. Chants are used in psalms, canticles, and other parts of a religious service. **3.** CHR **HYMN OR PRAYER SUNG TO CHANT** a psalm, hymn, or prayer sung to a chant **4. SOMETHING SPOKEN MONOTONOUSLY OR REPETITIOUSLY** a monotonous or repetitive song or intonation of the voice ■ *vti.* **(chant·ed, chant·ing, chants) 1. REPEAT SLOGAN CONTINUALLY** to speak a slogan repeatedly and rhythmically with a simple singsong intonation **2.** CHR **SING HYMN OR PRAYER AS CHANT** to sing or intone part of a religious service as a chant **3. UTTER MONOTONOUSLY** to speak or sing something monotonously [14thC. Via French, "song," from Latin *cantus,* from the past participle of *canere* "to sing" (source of English *accent* and *incentive*).] —**chant·ing·ly** *adv.*

chan·te·cler *n.* = **chanticleer**

chant·er /chántər/ *n.* **1. SOMEBODY CHANTING SLOGAN** somebody who chants a slogan **2.** MUSIC, CHR **SOMEBODY WHO CHANTS PSALM OR HYMN** somebody who chants a musical passage, e.g., a priest or chorister **3.** MUSIC **PIPE WITH FINGERHOLES ON BAGPIPE** on a bagpipe, a pipe with fingerholes on which the melody is played **4.** MUSIC **PIPE FOR PRACTICING BAGPIPE FINGERING** a pipe used to learn or practice bagpipe fingering

chan·te·relle /shàntə rél, shaàntə-/ *n.* an edible mushroom found in temperate woodlands that has a yellow-to-orange trumpet-shaped cap. Latin name: *Cantharellus cibarius.* [Late 18thC. Via French from modern Latin *cantharellus,* literally "little cup," from Latin *cantharus* "drinking vessel," from Greek *kantharos,* of unknown origin.]

chan·teuse /shaan tö̈z/ (*plural* **-teuses** /-tö̈z/) *n.* a woman singer, especially in a nightclub or cabaret [Mid-19thC. From French.]

chan·tey /chántee, shántee/ (*plural* **-teys**), **chan·ty** (*plural* **-ties**), **shan·ty** (*plural* **-ties**) *n.* a song chanted by sailors as they work [Mid-19thC. Origin uncertain: perhaps an anglicization of French *chantez* "sing!".]

chan·ti·cleer /chánti kleér, shánti-/, **chan·te·cler** *n.* a rooster, especially in fairy tales (*literary*) [13thC. From Old French *Chantecler,* from *chanter* "to sing" + *cler* "clear."]

Chan·til·ly /shàn tíllee, shaàNti yeé/ *n.* **1. Chan·tilly, Chan·tilly lace** TEXTILES **DELICATE LACE OFTEN USED FOR GOWNS** a delicate ornamental lace in black or white with an outlined design, often used for bridal and evening gowns **2. Chan·til·ly, Chan·til·ly cream** FOOD **TYPE OF WHIPPED CREAM** whipped cream, sweetened and often flavored with vanilla

chan·try /chántree/ (*plural* **-tries**) *n.* **1. ENDOWMENT FOR PERFORMANCE OF MASS** an endowment to pay for the saying of masses for the soul of the founder or somebody named by the founder **2. chantry, chantry chapel ENDOWED CHAPEL FOR CHANTRIES** a chapel or altar endowed for the performance of chantries [14thC. From Anglo-Norman *chaunterie,* Old French *chanterie,* formed from Old French *chanter* "to sing."]

Cha·nu·kah Cha·nuk·kah *n.* = Hanukkah

cha·ol·o·gy /kay óllәjee/ *n.* the study of chaos theory and chaotic systems —**cha·ol·o·gist** *n.*

cha·os /káy òss/ *n.* **1.** DISORDER a state of complete disorder and confusion **2. cha·os, Cha·os** EARLIEST CONDITION OF UNIVERSE the unbounded space and formless matter supposed to have existed before the creation of the universe **3.** PHYS APPARENT DISORDER the unpredictability inherent in a system such as the weather, in which apparently random changes occur as a result of the system's extreme sensitivity to small differences in initial conditions [15thC. Directly or via French from Latin, from Greek *khaos* "void, abyss," the original sense in English (source of English *gas*).]

cha·os the·o·ry *n.* a theory that complex natural systems obey certain rules but are so sensitive that small initial changes can cause unexpected final effects, thus giving an impression of randomness. ◊ **butterfly effect**

cha·ot·ic /kay óttik/ *adj.* **1.** DISORDERED completely disordered and out of control **2.** PHYS INHERENTLY UNPREDICTABLE used to describe the state of a system according to chaos theory [Early 18thC. Formed from CHAOS, modeled on words such as EROTIC and HYPNOTIC.] —**cha·ot·i·cal·ly** *adv.*

chap[1] /chap/ *vti.* (**chapped, chap·ping, chaps**) BECOME SORE AND ROUGHENED to become or make skin sore and cracked by exposure to wind or cold ■ *n.* **1.** AREA OF SORE SKIN a sore cracked area of skin, caused by exposure to wind or cold **2.** GEOL CRACK IN GROUND a crack or fissure in dry ground [14thC. Origin unknown.] —**chapped** *adj.*

chap[2] /chap/ *n. U.K.* a man or youth, especially somebody whose name is not known or not relevant (*informal*) [Late 16thC. Shortening of *chapman*. The word originally denoted a buyer or customer; the current meaning dates from the early 18thC.]

chap[3] /chap/ *n.* the lower exterior half of the jaw, especially the cheek [Mid-16thC. Origin unknown.]

chap. *abbr.* **1.** chapter **2.** chaplain

chap·ar·ral /shàppә rál/ *n.* a dense thicket of shrubs or small trees, especially of evergreen oaks in southern California [Mid-19thC. From Spanish, formed from *chaparra* "dwarf evergreen oak" (source of English *chaps*).]

chap·ar·ral bird *n.* = **roadrunner** [So called because it lives among dry brush and chaparral]

cha·pa·ti /chә paátee/ (*plural* **-tis** *or* **-ties**), **cha·pat·ti** (*plural* **-tis** *or* **-ties**) *n.* a thin round unleavened bread used in Indian cooking [Early 19thC. From Hindi *capātī*, from *capānā* "to flatten, roll out."]

chap·book /cháp bòòk/ *n.* a small booklet of poems, ballads, or stories, originally sold by traveling peddlers [Early 19thC. Blend of *chapman* and *book*.]

chape /chayp, chap/ *n.* **1.** TIP OF SCABBARD the metal tip of a scabbard **2.** TONGUE OF BUCKLE the tongue of a buckle [14thC. Via French, "cape, hood," from late Latin *cappa* (see CAP).]

cha·peau /sha pṓ/ (*plural* **-peaux** /-pṓ, -pṓz/ *or* **-peaus** /-pṓ, -pṓz/) *n.* a hat as an item of high fashion or ceremonial dress (*formal*) [15thC. Via French from late Latin *cappellum*, literally "small hooded cloak," from *cappa* (see CAP).]

chap·el /cháppʹl/ *n.* **1.** CHR ROOM FOR WORSHIP a place in a hospital, prison, or other institution, or in a large house, consecrated for Christian worship **2.** RELIG SEPARATE AREA OF CHURCH a separate area in a church, having its own altar and intended for private prayer **3.** CHR PROTESTANT CHURCH a place of worship used by a nonestablished Protestant denomination such as the Methodists or Baptists **4.** CHR SERVICE IN CHAPEL a service held in a chapel, especially in a nonestablished church **5.** PLACE FOR FUNERALS a funeral home, or a room in a funeral home where funeral services are held **6.** PUBL LABOR UNION BRANCH a branch of a labor union in printing and journalism **7.** PUBL MEETING OF PRINTERS' CHAPEL a meeting of a printers' or journalists' chapel [12thC. Via Old French *chapele* from medieval Latin *cappella*, literally "small hooded cloak," from late Latin *cappa* (see CAP).]

Chap·el Hill /chappʹl-/ town in north central North Carolina, home to the main campus of the University of North Carolina. Population: 44,244 (1996).

chap·el of ease *n.* a church built for people who live a long distance from a parish church

chap·er·on /sháppә rṑn/, **chap·er·one** *n.* **1.** SUPERVISOR OF YOUNG WOMAN somebody, especially an older or married woman, who accompanies and supervises a young single woman at social events **2.** GROUP SUPERVISOR somebody who accompanies and supervises a group of young people ■ *vti.* (**-oned, -on·ing, -ons; -oned, -on·ing, -ones**) ACT AS A CHAPERON to accompany a person or a group as a chaperon [12thC. Via French from late Latin *cappa* (see CAP). The word originally denoted a hood or cap.] —**chap·er·on·age** *n.*

chap·i·ter /cháppitәr/ *n.* = **capital**[2] [13thC. From French *chapitre* (see CHAPTER).]

chap·lain /chápplin/ *n.* a member of the clergy employed to give religious guidance, e.g., to members of the armed services, schoolchildren, or prisoners [12thC. Via Anglo-Norman and Old French *chapelain*, from medieval Latin *cappellanus*, originally "guardian of the cloak of St. Martin of Tours," from *cappella* (see CHAPEL).] —**chap·lain·ship** *n.*

chap·lain·cy /chápplinsee/ (*plural* **-cies**) *n.* **1.** JOB AS CHAPLAIN a post or position as chaplain **2.** CHAPLAIN'S PLACE OF WORK the place or building where a chaplain works

chap·let /chápplәt/ *n.* **1.** HEAD DECORATION a decorative circle of beads or flowers worn on the head **2.** CHR PRAYER BEADS a string of beads used by Roman Catholics for counting prayers. A chaplet has 55 beads, one third of the number on a rosary. **3.** ARCHIT BEADED MOLDING a small molding resembling a string of beads [14thC. Via French *chapelet* from, ultimately, late Latin *cappa* (see CAP).] —**chap·let·ed** *adj.*

Charlie Chaplin

Chap·lin /chápplin/, **Charlie** (1889–1977) British-born U.S. actor, director, and producer who is best known for the tramp character that he played in over seventy films. Full name **Sir Charles Spencer Chaplin**

chap·man /chápmәn/ (*plural* **-men**) *n. U.K.* a wandering peddler (*archaic*) [Old English *cēapman*, from *cēap* (see CHEAP)]

chaps /chaps, shaps/ *npl.* protective leather leggings, like a pair of pants with no seat or crotch, worn on horseback over ordinary pants by ranch workers, rodeo contestants, and cowboys [Late 19thC. Shortening of *chaparejos*, an alteration (probably influenced by Spanish *aparejo* "equipment") of *chaparreras*, from *chaparra* (see CHAPARRAL); because chaps were worn when riding through chaparral.]

Chap Stick /cháp stìk/ *tdmk.* a trademark for a lip balm in the form of a stick, applied to the lips to prevent or relieve chapping

chap·tal·ize /cháptә līz/ (**-ized, -iz·ing, -iz·es**) *vt.* to increase the alcohol content of wine by adding sugar before or during fermentation [Late 19thC. Named for the inventor of the process, the French chemist J. A. *Chaptal* (1756–1832).] —**chap·tal·i·za·tion** /chàptәli záyshʹn/ *n.*

chap·ter /cháptәr/ *n.* **1.** SECTION OF BOOK one of the main sections of a text, usually having a title or number as a heading **2.** PERIOD OF DEVELOPMENT an identifiable period in the history or development of something ○ *Their move to France began a new chapter in their lives.* **3.** SERIES OF EVENTS a series of events having a common characteristic ○ *a turbulent chapter in the movements of history* **4.** CHR GROUP OF CANONS the body of canons of a cathedral or collegiate church, or the body of members of an order of knighthood **5.** BRANCH OF A GROUP a branch of a society or organization **6.** RELIG ASSEMBLY OF A CHAPTER a meeting of a cathedral or church chapter [12thC. Via French *chapitre* from Latin *capitulum*, literally "small head," from *caput* "head" (source of English *capital*).] ◇ **give** *or* **quote chapter and verse** to give exact information and detailed references on a topic

Chap·ter 11 *n.* a section of the U.S. Federal Bankruptcy Code that allows an insolvent company to be reorganized, sometimes providing for repayment of debts or the creation of a new corporate entity

chap·ter house *n.* **1.** CHR BUILDING WHERE CHAPTER MEETS a building used for meetings by a religious chapter **2.** COLLEGE MEETING PLACE a building used by a fraternity or sorority

Cha·pul·te·pec /chә pòòltә pèk/ rocky hill in Mexico, fortified by Aztec rulers, situated 3 mi./5 km southwest of Mexico City

char[1] /chaar/ (**charred, char·ring, chars**) *v.* **1.** *vti.* BLACKEN BY BURNING to blacken something or become blackened by burning or scorching **2.** *vt.* MAKE INTO CHARCOAL to turn wood into charcoal by partial burning [Late 17thC. Back-formation from CHARCOAL.]

char[2] /chaar/ (*plural* **char** *or* **chars**), **charr** (*plural* **charr** *or* **charrs**) *n.* a trout that has light-colored spots, found in northern waters [Mid-17thC. Origin uncertain: perhaps from Celtic.]

char·a·cin /kérrәssin/ (*plural* **-cin** *or* **-cins**), **char·a·cid** /kérrәssid/ (*plural* **-cid** *or* **-cids**) *n.* a small brightly colored freshwater fish of Africa and South America, often kept in aquariums. Family: Characidae. [Late 19thC. Via modern Latin *Characinus*, genus name, from Greek *kharax* (see CHARACTER), used to denote a kind of fish.]

char·ac·ter /kérrәktәr/ *n.* **1.** DISTINCTIVE QUALITIES the set of qualities that make somebody or something distinctive, especially somebody's qualities of mind and feeling ○ *It's just not in my character to behave like that.* **2.** POSITIVE QUALITIES qualities that make somebody or something interesting or attractive ○ *an old house full of character* **3.** REPUTATION somebody's public reputation ○ *an attack on his good character that ended in court* **4.** LITERAT, CINEMA SOMEBODY IN BOOK OR MOVIE one of the people portrayed in a book, play, or movie ○ *None of the central characters are particularly important.* **5.** UNUSUAL PERSON somebody who has an unusual or eccentric personality **6.** INDIVIDUAL somebody considered in terms of personality, behavior, or appearance ○ *he was a flamboyant character* **7.** LETTER OR SYMBOL any written or printed letter, number, or other symbol **8.** COMPUT COMPUTER UNIT OF DATA a single letter, number, or symbol that can be displayed on a computer screen or printer and represents one byte of data **9.** GENETICS GENETICALLY CONTROLLED CHARACTERISTIC an attribute of a genetically determined organism, e.g., a structure or trait **10.** WRITTEN TESTIMONIAL a written summary of somebody's abilities and personality, written by an employer or other person who knows the person well **11.** CAPACITY OR POSITION a particular role, position, or function that somebody has in society or in an organization (*formal*) ○ *speaking in her character as chairperson* **12.** STYLE OF WRITING OR PRINTING style of handwriting or printing ■ *vt.* (**-tered, -ter·ing, -ters**) WRITE to write or carve words carefully and skillfully on paper, stone, or metal (*archaic*) [14thC. Via French *caractère* from, ultimately, Greek *kharaktēr* "tool for marking," from *kharassein* "to engrave," from *kharax* "pointed stake."] ◇ **in character** *or* **out of character 1.** typical (or untypical) of the behavior of a particular person or thing **2.** involved (or not involved) in the psychological preparations for acting out a particular role in a play, movie, or other dramatic work

char·ac·ter ac·tor *n.* an actor who specializes in playing the roles of unusual or distinctive characters

char·ac·ter as·sas·si·na·tion *n.* a deliberate and sustained attack on somebody's reputation

char·ac·ter·is·tic /kèrrәktә rístik/ *n.* **1.** DEFINING FEATURE a feature or quality that makes somebody or something recognizable **2.** MATH WHOLE NUMBER IN LOGARITHM the whole number (**integer**) found to the left of the decimal point in a common logarithm, e.g., the characteristic of 5.4321 is 5 ■ *adj.* TYPICAL distinguishing or typical of a particular person or thing —**char·ac·ter·is·ti·cal·ly** *adv.*

char·ac·ter·i·za·tion /kèrrәktәri záyshʹn/ *n.* **1.** PORTRAYAL OF FICTIONAL CHARACTER the way in which the writer portrays the characters in a book, play, or movie **2.** DESCRIPTION a description of the character or nature or somebody or something

char·ac·ter·ize /kérrəktə rīz/ (**-ized, -iz·ing, -iz·es**) *vt.* **1.** DESCRIBE SOMEBODY OR SOMETHING to describe the character or characteristics of somebody or something **2.** BE TYPICAL OF SOMEBODY OR SOMETHING to be typical of the way a particular person or thing behaves or looks —**char·ac·ter·iz·a·ble** *adj.* —**char·ac·ter·iz·er** *n.*

char·ac·ter·less /kérrəktərləss/ *adj.* without any interesting or distinctive features ○ *a characterless view* —**char·ac·ter·less·ly** *adv.* —**char·ac·ter·less·ness** *n.*

char·ac·ter rec·og·ni·tion *n.* a magnetic or optical process, by which written or printed letters, numbers, or symbols can be recognized and digitized for use in a computer

char·ac·ter set *n.* a set of letters, numbers, and symbols that can be coded for use by a computer or printer

char·ac·ter sketch *n.* a short description of somebody's character and behavior

char·ac·ter wit·ness *n.* a witness who gives evidence of somebody's good character in a court of law

cha·rade /shə ráyd/ *n.* **1.** RIDICULOUS PRETENSE an absurdly false or pointless act or situation **2.** CLUE IN CHARADES a clue in the game of charades [Late 18thC. Via French from, ultimately, modern Provençal *charra* "to chatter," perhaps an imitation of the sound.]

cha·rades /shə ráydz/ *n.* a game in which somebody provides a visual or acted clue for a word or phrase, often the title of a book, play, or movie, for others to guess (*takes a singular verb*)

char·broil /chaár brȯyl/ (**-broiled, -broil·ing, -broils**) *vt.* to broil food over charcoal on a barbecue or on a ridged pan that produces a similar visual effect [Mid-20thC. Blend of CHARCOAL and BROIL.] —**char·broil·er** *n.*

char·coal /chaár kōl/ *n.* **1.** CHEM CARBON a black or dark gray form of carbon, produced by heating wood or another organic substance in an enclosed space without air. Charcoal is used as a fuel, as an absorbent, in smelting, in explosives, and by artists for drawing. **2.** DRAWING DRAWING IMPLEMENT sticks of charcoal used for drawing **3.** DRAWING DRAWING USING CHARCOAL a drawing done with charcoal ■ *n., adj.* = **charcoal gray** [14thC. Origin of *char* uncertain: possibly from Old French *charbon* "charcoal"; or literally "turned (into charcoal)," from Old English *cierran* "to turn." *Coal* in the obsolete sense "charcoal."]

char·coal-gray *adj.* of a dark gray color —**char·coal gray** *n.*

char·cu·ter·ie /shaar kóotə rée, shaar kóotəree/ *n.* **1.** COLD COOKED MEATS cold cooked, cured, or processed meat and meat products **2.** STORE SELLING CHARCUTERIE a store that specializes in charcuterie [Mid-19thC. From French, formed from obsolete *char cuite* "cooked flesh."]

chard /chaard/ *n.* PLANTS = **Swiss chard** [Mid-17thC. Via French *carde* (possibly by association with *chardon* "thistle") from, ultimately, Latin *cardu(u)s* "thistle, artichoke" (source of English *cardoon*).]

Char·din /shaar dáN/, **Jean Baptiste Siméon** (1699–1779) French painter. He was a master of lower-middle-class domestic and genre scenes, e.g., *The Benediction* (1740), now in the Louvre, Paris, France.

char·don·nay, **Char·don·nay** *n.* **1.** WHITE GRAPE a white grape used for making wine **2.** WHITE WINE a dry white wine made from the chardonnay grape [Early 20thC. From French.]

charge /chaarj/ *v.* (**charged, charg·ing, charg·es**) **1.** *vti.* COMM ASK MONEY FOR SOMETHING to ask somebody for an amount as a price or fee **2.** *vt.* IMPOSE A FEE OR PENALTY to hold a person or organization financially liable for something **3.** *vti.* FIN DEBIT to allow, and enter a record of, a deferred payment for something **4.** *vt.* LAW ACCUSE SOMEBODY OF CRIME to accuse somebody formally of having committed a crime **5.** *vt.* CRITICIZE to criticize somebody for doing something wrong ○ *Her boss charged her with being lazy and incompetent.* **6.** *vt.* ORDER TO DO SOMETHING to order or instruct somebody formally to do something ○ *The judge charged the jury to consider all the facts.* **7.** *vti.* ATTACK IN A RUSH to attack somebody or something by rushing forward, especially in a battle ○ *Police in riot gear charged the lines of demonstrators.* **8.** *vi.* *U.K.* RUSH to run somewhere carelessly or clumsily ○ *He came charging in from the back yard.* **9.** *vti.* ELEC RESTORE POWER IN BATTERY to restore the power in a battery by connecting it to a supply of electricity **10.** *vt.* LOAD OR FILL SOMETHING to load or fill something, e.g., a gun with explosive, or a glass with drink (*formal*) **11.** *vt.* PERVADE A PLACE to give an atmosphere of intense interest, excitement, or other strong emotion to a place (*usually passive*) ○ *The concert hall was charged with anticipation.* **12.** *vt.* HERALDRY PUT HERALDIC DEVICE ON SOMETHING to put a heraldic device on something such as a shield or banner ■ *n.* **1.** COMM AMOUNT OF MONEY ASKED the price of something that is for sale, or the fee asked for a service or in payment of a financial liability such as a tax ○ *We had to pay several extra charges before getting the vehicle back.* **2.** RESPONSIBILITY the responsibility or duty of looking after somebody or something ○ *He took on the children's welfare as an extra charge.* **3.** SOMEBODY BEING TAKEN CARE OF somebody, especially a child or a member of a minister's congregation, for whom somebody else is responsible (*formal*) ○ *The nanny was keeping a close watch on her little charges.* **4.** LAW ACCUSATION an accusation of wrongdoing, especially an official statement accusing somebody of committing a crime **5.** RUSH TO ATTACK a rush forward to attack, especially in a battle, or the signal for this **6.** ELEC POWER IN BATTERY the power stored in a battery **7.** PHYS ELECTRIC PROPERTY OF MATTER a fundamental characteristic of matter, responsible for all electric and electromotive forces, expressed in two forms known as positive and negative **8.** PHYS EXCESS OR LACK OF ELECTRONS a quantity of electricity caused by an excess or lack of electrons **9.** ENOUGH EXPLOSIVE FOR DETONATION the amount of explosive used to detonate a shell or cartridge **10.** ENOUGH TO FILL SOMETHING the amount required to fill a container or to make a mechanism work **11.** AN ORDER TO DO SOMETHING a formal order or instruction to do something, e.g., a judge's instructions to a jury **12.** SUDDEN BURST OF EXCITEMENT a sudden burst of excitement or interest **13.** HERALDRY HERALDIC DESIGN a design or image used as part of a coat of arms [12thC. Via French *charger* "to load, charge" from late Latin *car(ri)care*, from Latin *carrus* "carriage." The underlying idea is of "loading, burdening."]

charge·a·ble /chaárjəb'l/ *adj.* **1.** ABLE TO BE CHARGED liable or able to be charged **2.** LAW SUBJECT TO A CHARGE used to describe property or land capable of being subject to a charge —**charge·a·bil·i·ty** /chaárjə billətee/ *n.*

charge ac·count *n.* COMM a system of accounts by which customers can buy goods or services and pay at a later date

charge card *n.* a card issued to customers by a store, bank, or other organization, used to charge purchases to an account for later payment

charge-coup·led de·vice *n.* a semiconductor device that converts light patterns into digital signals that can be read by a computer, used especially in digital cameras and optical scanners

char·gé d'af·faires /shaár zhay də fáir/ (*plural* **chargés d'af·faires** /shaár zhay də fáir/) *n.* a diplomat ranking immediately below an ambassador who deputizes in the ambassador's absence, or a diplomat who heads a minor diplomatic mission [Mid-18thC. From French, literally "somebody in charge of affairs."]

charge den·si·ty *n.* the amount of electric charge per unit of area or volume. Symbol **ρ**

charge of quar·ters *n.* an enlisted person who administers a military unit, especially at night or during holidays

charg·er[1] /chaárjər/ *n.* **1.** LARGE HORSE a large strong cavalry horse **2.** ELEC = **battery charger** **3.** SOMEBODY OR SOMETHING THAT CHARGES somebody or something that charges

charg·er[2] /chaárjər/ *n.* a large flat serving dish of a kind now mainly collected for display [14thC. From Anglo-Norman *chargeour*, literally "something that loads," from Old French *charger* (see CHARGE).]

char·grill /chaár grìl/ (**-grilled, -gril·ling, -grills**) *vt.* = **charbroil** [From *char(coal)* + *grill*, modeled on CHARBROIL]

char·i·ot /chérriət/ *n.* **1.** ANCIENT 2-WHEELED VEHICLE a two-wheeled horse-drawn vehicle used in ancient times in races, warfare, or processions **2.** CEREMONIAL CARRIAGE a four-wheeled horse-drawn carriage with rear seats only, used especially on ceremonial occasions [14thC. Via French from, ultimately, Latin *carrus* "carriage."]

char·i·o·teer /chèrriə téer/ *n.* a driver of a chariot

cha·ris·ma /kə rízmə/ *n.* **1.** MAGNETIC PERSONALITY the ability to inspire enthusiasm, interest, or affection in others by means of personal charm or influence **2.** **cha·ris·ma** (*plural* **-ma·ta**) CHR DIVINE GIFT a gift or power thought to be divinely bestowed [Mid-17thC. Via ecclesiastical Latin from Greek *kharisma*, from *kharis* "favor, grace."]

WORD KEY: USAGE

Charisma meaning "personal magnetism." In their generalized meanings, ***charisma*** and ***charismatic*** have moved a long way from their original meanings in theology, where they referred to supernatural gifts of speaking, healing, and so on. The modern meanings have developed from a use in sociology, in which the sense is "a power of leadership or authority," first used in translations of the German sociologist Max Weber (1864–1920).

char·is·mat·ic /kèrriz máttik/ *adj.* **1.** HAVING CHARISMA possessing great powers of charm or influence **2.** CHR SEEKING DIRECT SPIRITUAL EXPERIENCE used to describe Christian groups or worship characterized by a quest for spontaneous and ecstatic experiences such as healing, prophecy, and speaking in tongues ■ *n.* CHR MEMBER OF A CHARISMATIC GROUP a member of a charismatic group

char·i·ta·ble /chérritəb'l/ *adj.* **1.** GENEROUS generous to people in need **2.** SYMPATHETIC sympathetic, favorable, or tolerant in judging **3.** COLLECTIVELY DISPENSING HELP dispensing assistance to needy people by means of a group or organization —**char·i·ta·ble·ness** *n.* —**char·i·ta·bly** *adv.*

char·i·ty /chérritee/ (*plural* **-ties**) *n.* **1.** PROVISION OF HELP the voluntary provision of money, materials, or help to people in need **2.** MATERIAL HELP money, materials, or help voluntarily given to people in need **3.** ORGANIZATION PROVIDING CHARITY an organization that collects money and other voluntary contributions of help for people in need **4.** TOLERANT ATTITUDE the willingness to judge people in a tolerant or favorable way **5.** IMPARTIAL LOVE the impartial love of other people [12thC. Via French *charité* from Latin *caritas*, from *carus* "dear" (source of English *cherish*).]

cha·ri·va·ri /shìvvə rée, shívvə rée/ *n.* = **shivaree** [Mid-17thC. From French, of unknown origin.]

char·kha /chúr kaá/, **char·ka** *n.* a spinning wheel, especially for cotton, which is used in the Indian subcontinent [Late 19thC. Via Urdu *charḳa* from Persian *carḳ(a)*.]

char·la·dy /chaár làydee/ (*plural* **-dies**) *n.* = **charwoman** [Late 19thC. From the first element of CHARWOMAN + LADY.]

char·la·tan /shaárlət'n/ *n.* somebody who falsely claims a special skill or expertise [Early 17thC. Via French from Italian *ciarlatano*, from *ciarlare* "to babble, patter," an imitation of the sound of empty talk.] —**char·la·tan·ism** *n.* —**char·la·tan·ry** *n.*

Charle·magne /shaálə màyn/ (742–814) Frankish king and emperor. As emperor of the West (800–814), he inspired the "Carolingian Renaissance" of European culture.

Charles /chaarlz/, **Prince of Wales** (*b.* 1948) British heir apparent and son of Elizabeth II. He was married to Diana, Princess of Wales, from 1981 to 1996.

Charles I, King of England, Scotland, and Ireland (1600–49). He succeeded James I in 1625. His determination to rule without Parliament's authority led to the English Civil War (1642–48), which culminated in his execution.

Charles II, King of England, Scotland, and Ireland (1630–85). He was exiled during Oliver Cromwell's Protectorate (1653–59), but returned to England and formally ascended the throne after the restoration of the monarchy in 1660.

Charles V (1500–58) Belgian-born Spanish emperor. During his reign as Holy Roman Emperor (1519–58), he struggled to keep his Roman Catholic empire together and was finally forced to recognize Protestantism.

Charles, Ray (*b.* 1932) U.S. singer and pianist whose rhythm-and-blues style took its roots from country and western and gospel music. Real name **Ray Charles Robinson**

Charles's law /chaárlzəz-/ *n.* a law that holds that there is a direct relationship between the volume of a gas and its temperature, where its pressure is constant [Late 19thC. Named for the French physicist J. A. C. *Charles* (1746–1823), who discovered it.]

Charles·ton[1] /chaárlstən/ *n.* a lively North American dance, popular in the 1920s, characterized by kicking the feet out sideways while keeping the knees together [Early 20thC. Named for CHARLESTON in South Carolina.]

Charles·ton² /chaárlstən/ **1.** city and port in southeastern South Carolina where the Ashley, Cooper, and Wando rivers meet. Population: 71,052 (1996). **2.** capital of West Virginia and the largest city in the state. Population: 56,098 (1996).

char·ley horse /chaárli-/ *n.* a severe muscular cramp, especially in the upper leg (*informal*) [Origin unknown]

char·lie /chaárlee/ *n.* cocaine used as an illicit drug (*slang*)

Char·lie /chaárlee/ *n.* **1. CODE WORD FOR LETTER "C"** a code word for the letter "C," used in international radio communications **2. Char·lie, Char·ley** *U.S., Aus* **VIET CONG** used to refer to a member of the Viet Cong during the Vietnam War, or the Viet Cong collectively (*slang dated*)

char·lock /chaár lòk/ (*plural* **-lock** *or* **-locks**) *n.* a yellow-flowered Eurasian mustard plant that has hairy stems and leaves and is a common weed. Latin name: *Brassica kaber.* [Old English *cerlic*, of unknown origin]

char·lotte /shaárlət/ *n.* a sweet, cold or baked dish prepared in a deep straight-sided container and containing fruit surrounded by sponge cake, biscuits, or bread [Late 18thC. From French, probably from the name *Charlotte* (for unknown reasons).]

Char·lotte city in southern North Carolina, southwest of Winston-Salem and east of the Catawba River. Population: 441,297 (1996).

Char·lotte Am·a·lie /shaárlət ə maályə/ seaport and capital of St. Thomas Island and of the U.S. Virgin Islands. Population: 12,331 (1990).

char·lotte russe /shaárlət róoss/ (*plural* **char·lottes russes** /shaárlət róoss/) *n.* a cold set dessert made with cream or custard surrounded by sponge fingers [From French, literally "Russian charlotte"]

Char·lottes·ville /shaárləts vìl/ city in central Virginia on the western bank of the Rivanna River, northwest of Richmond. Population: 40,767 (1996).

Char·lotte·town /shaárlət tòwn/ capital city of Prince Edward Island, Canada, situated in the center of the island, on Hillsborough Bay. Population: 57,224 (1996).

charm /chaarm/ *n.* **1. ATTRACTIVENESS** the power to delight or attract people **2. ATTRACTIVE FEATURE** a feature or quality that delights or attracts (*often used in the plural*) **3. SOMETHING SUPPOSED TO BRING LUCK** something carried or worn because it is believed to bring good luck or ward off evil **4. TRINKET** a miniature metal animal, musical instrument, or similar trinket worn on a bracelet or around the neck **5. MAGIC SPELL** a special phrase or rhyme believed to have magical powers **6.** PHYS **CHARACTERISTIC OF ELEMENTARY PARTICLES** a quantum characteristic of elementary particles that accounts for the long lifetime of the J particle, lack of symmetry in hadron interactions, and failure of certain particles to react. Symbol **C** ■ *v.* (**charmed, charm·ing, charms**) **1.** *vti.* **DELIGHT** to delight or attract people **2.** *vt.* **INFLUENCE PEOPLE** to influence somebody or obtain something from somebody by using powers of persuasion and attraction **3.** *vti.* **CAST A SPELL** to affect somebody or something by, or as if by, the use of a supposed magic spell [13thC. Via French *charme* "charm, song" from Latin *carmen* "song, incantation," from *canere* "to sing, chant" (source of English *chant* and *incantation*).] —**charm·er** *n.*

charmed /chaarmd/ *adj.* **1. LUCKY** so pleasant or lucky as to suggest protection by a magic spell **2.** PHYS **HAVING CHARM** used to describe an elementary particle that has the property of charm

charmed cir·cle *n.* a privileged group or elite

charm·ing /chaárming/ *adj.* **DELIGHTFUL OR FASCINATING** having the power to delight or attract people ○ *a charming village* ○ *a charming young man* ■ *interj.* **EXPRESSING DISPLEASURE** used ironically to express disapproval or distaste at something just done or said (*informal*) —**charm·ing·ly** *adv.*

charm of·fen·sive *n.* a campaign, e.g., by a politician, to appear more pleasant, attractive, or reasonable, in order to gain popularity (*informal*)

char·nel /chaárn'l/ *n.* = **charnel house** ■ *adj.* **OF DEATH** suggestive of death or a tomb [14thC. Via Old French from medieval Latin *carnale*, from the Latin stem *carn-* "flesh" (source of English *carnage*).]

char·nel house *n.* a building or vault in which bones or dead bodies are placed

Cha·ro·lais /shèrrə láy/ (*plural* **-lais**), **Cha·rol·lais** (*plural* **-lais**) *n.* a large white cow belonging to a breed originating in France and bred for beef [Late 19thC. Named for Monts du *Charollais* in eastern France.]

Char·on /káirən/ *n.* **1.** MYTHOL **FERRYMAN IN GREEK UNDERWORLD** in Greek mythology, a ferryman who took the souls of the dead across the River Styx to Hades **2.** ASTRON **SATELLITE OF PLUTO** the only known satellite of Pluto, discovered in 1978

char·poy /chaár pòy/ *n.* a light bedstead of webbing stretched across a frame, commonly used in the Indian subcontinent [Mid-17thC. Via Urdu *chārpāī* from Persian.]

char·qui /chaárkee/ *n.* = **jerky** [Early 17thC. Via American Spanish (source of English *jerk*) from Quechua *cc'arki.*]

charr *n.* = **char**²

chart /chaart/ *n.* **1. DIAGRAM OR TABLE** a diagram or table displaying detailed information **2.** NAVIG **MAP TO NAVIGATE BY** a map for navigation by sea or air **3.** METEOROL **WEATHER MAP** an outline map that shows weather patterns **4.** ASTROL **BASIS FOR HOROSCOPE** a map that shows the relative positions of the planets at the time of somebody's birth on which his or her horoscope is based **5.** MUSIC **MUSICAL SCORE** a musical score (*technical*) **6.** SEW **STITCHING PLAN** a squared grid marked with symbols indicating the placement of stitches in embroidery ■ **charts** *npl.* **LIST OF POPULAR RECORDS** a list of the musical recordings that have sold most copies during a specific period ■ *v.* (**chart·ed, chart·ing, charts**) **1.** *vt.* **MAKE A CHART OF SOMETHING** to make a map, graph, or diagram of something **2.** *vt.* **MAKE A PLAN** to record or describe a plan **3.** *vi.* **BE IN THE CHARTS** to appear in the music charts [Late 16thC. Via French *charte* from Latin *charta* "paper, papyrus-leaf, card, map" (source of English *card*). The verb dates from the 19thC.] —**chart·a·ble** *adj.*

char·ter /chaártər/ *n.* **1. STATEMENT OF RIGHTS AND RESPONSIBILITIES** a formal written statement describing the rights and responsibilities of a state and its citizens **2.** LAW **FORMAL DOCUMENT OF INCORPORATION** a formal document incorporating an organization, company, or educational institution **3.** LAW **CONSTITUTION** a formal written statement of the aims, principles, and procedures of an organization **4.** LAW **DOCUMENT OF AUTHORIZATION** a document from an organization or society that authorizes the setting up of a new branch **5.** LAW **SPECIAL PRIVILEGE** a special privilege, immunity, or exemption, granted to a particular person or group **6.** TRANSP **RENT OR LEASE OF TRANSPORT** the renting or leasing of transport vehicles for personal or special use, or a contract or agreement for this purpose **7.** TRANSP **RENTED OR LEASED TRANSPORT** a vehicle chartered for personal or special use **8.** LAW = **charter party** ■ *vt.* (**-tered, -ter·ing, -ters**) **1.** TRANSP **RENT OR LEASE TRANSPORT** to rent or lease a vehicle for a personal or special purpose **2.** LAW **GRANT A CHARTER** to grant a charter of incorporation to a group or organization [12thC. Via French *chartre* from, ultimately, Latin *charta* (see CHART).] —**char·ter·er** *n.*

char·tered /chaártərd/ *adj.* **1. GRANTED A CHARTER** that has been granted a charter **2.** *U.K.* **FULLY QUALIFIED AS A PROFESSIONAL** having membership of a professional body that has been granted a royal charter

char·tered ac·count·ant *n. U.K.* an accountant who has passed the examinations of one of the governing professional bodies and has been granted a royal charter

char·ter flight *n.* a flight that has been chartered for a specific trip, especially as part of a vacation package

Char·ter·house /chaártər hòwss/ (*plural* **-hous·es** /-zəz/) *n.* a Carthusian monastery [14thC. Alteration (influenced by HOUSE) of Anglo-Norman *Chartrous* or French *Chartreuse* from, ultimately, medieval Latin *Cart(h)usia* "La Grande Chartreuse," a monastery near Grenoble, France.]

char·ter mem·ber *n.* a founding or original member of a society or organization

Char·ter of Rights *n.* a section of the Canadian Constitution stating the rights conferred by Canadian citizenship

char·ter par·ty *n.* a contractual arrangement by which the owner of a ship permits another person to use it to carry goods [Via French from medieval Latin *charta partita*, literally "divided charter"]

Char·ter School *n.* a publicly financed school run by parents, educators, and companies

Chart·ism /chaár tìzzəm/ *n.* the principles and practices of the movement advocating political and social reform in England between 1838 and 1848 [Mid-19thC. Named for the *People's Charter.*] —**Chart·ist** *n., adj.*

Char·tres /shaart, shaártrə/ capital of the Eure-et-Loir Department in northwestern France. It is situated about 50 mi./80 km southwest of Paris and is famous for its large Gothic cathedral. Population: 44,850 (1990).

char·treuse /shaar tróoz/ *adj.* **YELLOWISH-GREEN** having a bright yellowish-green color ■ *n.* **YELLOW OR GREEN LIQUEUR** a yellow or green aromatic liqueur, flavored with herbs and flowers [Early 19thC. From French (see CHARTERHOUSE).] —**char·treuse** *n.*

Char·treuse /shaar tróoz/ *tdmk.* a trademark for a yellow or green aromatic liqueur, flavored with herbs and flowers

char·wom·an /chaár wòommən/ (*plural* **-en** /-wìmmin/) *n.* a woman employed to clean a house or office [Late 16thC. *Char* ultimately from Old English *c(i)err* "turn," later "turn of work, chore."]

char·y /chérree/ (**-i·er, -i·est**) *adj.* **1. WARY** cautiously reluctant to do something **2. SPARING** reluctant to share, give, or use something **3. CONCERNED** fussily concerned **4. SHY** showing or characterized by shyness or modesty [Old English *cearig* "sorrowful, anxious." Ultimately from a prehistoric Germanic word that is also the ancestor of English *care.*] —**char·i·ly** *adv.* —**char·i·ness** *n.*

WORD KEY: SYNONYMS

See Synonyms at ***cautious***.

Cha·ryb·dis *n.* ♦ **Scylla and Charybdis**

chase¹ /chayss/ *v.* (**chased, chas·ing, chas·es**) **1.** *vti.* **PURSUE SOMEBODY OR SOMETHING** to try to catch or overtake somebody or something **2.** *vt.* **MAKE SOMEBODY RUN AWAY** to force a person or animal to run away ○ *The kids chased a black cat out of the garden.* **3.** *vi.* **RUSH AROUND** to rush around ○ *They chased around all day.* **4.** *vti.* **PAY PERSISTENT ATTENTION TO SOMEBODY** to seek the company of somebody for romantic or sexual purposes, especially in an obvious or unsubtle way ■ *n.* **1. PURSUIT** an act or situation in which something or somebody is being pursued **2.** HORSERACING = **steeplechase 3. SOMETHING PURSUED** somebody who or something, especially an animal, that is being pursued **4.** MUSIC **JAZZ DUET** a jazz duet in which the players play alternate phrases and try to outdo each other in virtuosity and invention [13thC. Via Old French *chacier* "to catch, seize" from, ultimately, Latin *captare* "to try to seize, chase," from *capere* "to seize, take."] ◇ **cut to the chase** to stop wasting time and get on with what needs to be dealt with (*informal*) ◇ **give chase** to pursue something or somebody forcefully (*formal*)

chase² /chayss/ *n.* **1. PART OF GUN BARREL** the external part of a gun barrel just behind the muzzle **2. GROOVE** a channel, groove, or trench for something such as a pipe to lie in or fit into ■ *vt.* (**chased, chas·ing, chas·es**) **1. CUT GROOVE IN SOMETHING** to cut or grind a channel, groove, or trench in something **2. CUT THREAD IN SCREW** to cut a metal screw thread with a machine tool (**chaser**) [Late 16thC. Via French *châsse* from Latin *capsa* "box, case" (source of English *capsule* and *case*). Early 17thC. Via French *chas* "enclosed space" from, ultimately, Latin *capsum* "thorax, church nave."]

chase³ /chayss/ (**chased, chas·ing, chas·es**) *vt.* to decorate metal or glass by engraving or embossing [15thC. Shortening of ENCHASE.]

chase⁴ /chayss/ (*plural* **chases**) *n.* PRINTING a rectangular frame into which metal type or blocks are fitted so that a page or plate can be printed or made [Late 16thC. Via French *châsse* from Latin *capsa* "box, case" (source of English *capsule* and *case*).]

Chase /chayss/, **Salmon Portland** (1808–73) U.S. politician and jurist. He held government posts including Chief Justice of the United States (1864–73).

Chase, Samuel (1741–1811) U.S. jurist. He was an associate justice of the U.S. Supreme Court (1796–1811).

chase plane *n.* an airplane that follows another aircraft carrying an important person such as a head of state

chas·er[1] /cháyssər/ *n.* **1.** SOMEBODY OR SOMETHING THAT CHASES somebody or something that forcefully pursues another person or thing **2.** BEVERAGES DIFFERENT DRINK a second drink, taken with or after one of a different kind, e.g., whiskey taken after beer **3.** ARMS NAVAL CANNON a cannon located at the bow or stern of a vessel and used in pursuing an enemy

chaser[2] /cháyssər/ *n.* **1.** ENGRAVER somebody who engraves metal or glass or who embosses metal **2.** MACHINE TOOL a machine tool for cutting screw threads

chasm /kázzəm/ *n.* **1.** DEEP HOLE IN THE EARTH a deep crack or hole in the ground **2.** WIDE DIFFERENCE a wide difference in feelings, ideas, or interests **3.** GAP OR BREAK a gap or break in the progress or continuity of something [Late 16thC. Via Latin *chasma* from Greek *khasma* "gaping hollow, gulf."]

chas·mog·a·mous /kaz móggəməss/ *adj.* used to describe flowers that open to allow pollination

chas·mog·a·my /kaz móggəmee/ *n.* the process by which a flower opens before it is pollinated [Early 20thC. Coined from CHASM and -GAMY.]

chas·sé /sha sáy/ *n.* GLIDING STEP a gliding step in dancing, especially in ballet or square dancing ■ *vi.* **(-séd, -sé·ing, -sés)** MAKE A CHASSÉ to make a chassé [Early 19thC. From French, literally "chasing, chase."]

chas·seur /sha súr/ *adj.* COOK IN WINE AND MUSHROOM SAUCE cooked in a rich white-wine and mushroom sauce ■ *n.* MIL FRENCH SOLDIER a soldier in a French special unit equipped and trained for rapid deployment [Mid-18thC. From French, literally "hunter."]

Chas·sid *n.* JUDAISM = **Hasid** —**Chas·si·dism** *n.*

chas·sis /shássee, chássee/ (*plural* **-sis** /-eez, -eez/) *n.* **1.** MAIN FRAME OF VEHICLE the frame and wheels that support the engine and body of a motor vehicle, or the frame and wheels of a carriage or wagon **2.** ELEC MOUNTING FOR ELECTRONIC DEVICE the mounting or supporting structure for the components of an electronic device, such as a television **3.** AIR AIRCRAFT LANDING GEAR the landing gear of an aircraft **4.** ARMS MOUNTING FOR GUN CARRIAGE a frame on which a gun carriage can move back and forth [Mid-17thC. Via French *châssis* from, ultimately, Latin *capsa* "box, case" (source of English *capsule* and *case*).]

chaste /chayst/ *adj.* **1.** ABSTAINING FROM SEX abstaining from sex on moral grounds **2.** SEXUALLY FAITHFUL not having extramarital sexual relations **3.** PURE IN THOUGHT AND DEED behaving in a pure way, with no immoral thoughts **4.** PLAIN plain, simple, and unadorned in style [13thC. Via French from Latin *castus* "pure" (source of English *caste, castigate,* and *incest*).] —**chaste·ly** *adv.* —**chaste·ness** *n.*

chas·ten /cháyss'n/ **(-tened, -ten·ing, -tens)** *vt.* **1.** DISCIPLINE SOMEBODY to subject somebody to discipline **2.** MAKE SOMEBODY SUBDUED to make somebody less self-satisfied or self-assertive and more subdued **3.** MODERATE INTENSITY OF SOMETHING to moderate the intensity of something [Early 16thC. Formed from obsolete *chaste* (see CHASTISE).] —**chas·tened** *adj.* —**chas·ten·er** *n.* —**chas·ten·ing** *adj.*

chaste tree *n.* a small ornamental Eurasian tree that has aromatic hairy leaves and fragrant clusters of light purplish flowers. Latin name: *Vitex agnus-castus.* [Translation of Latin *agnus castus* "chaste agnus," reputedly because certain ancient Greek women maintaining their state of chastity spread its leaves on the ground at the feast of Ceres]

chas·tise /chá stīz/ **(-tised, -tis·ing, -tis·es)** *vt.* to punish or scold somebody (*formal*) [14thC. Formed from obsolete English *chaste* "to chasten, reprove" (source of English *chasten*), via Old French *chastier* from Latin *castigare* (see CASTIGATE).] —**chas·tis·a·ble** *adj.* —**chas·tise·ment** *n.* —**chas·tis·er** *n.*

chas·ti·ty /chástətee/ *n.* **1.** SEXUAL ABSTINENCE the condition or practice of abstaining from sex on moral grounds **2.** PLAINNESS plainness or simplicity of style

chas·ti·ty belt *n.* a locking device passing around the waist and between the legs, used in medieval times to prevent a woman from having sexual intercourse

chas·u·ble /cházzəb'l, chássəb'l/ *n.* a loose sleeveless outer garment worn by a priest when celebrating Mass or the Eucharist [13thC. Via French from, ultimately, Latin *casula* "hooded cloak," literally "little house," from *casa* "house, hut."]

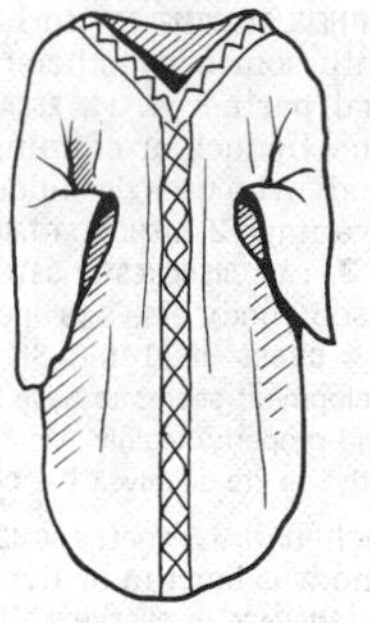

Chasuble

chat /chat/ *vi.* **(chat·ted, chat·ting, chats) 1.** TALK INFORMALLY to talk with somebody in a relaxed informal way **2.** COMPUT EXCHANGE MESSAGES BY COMPUTER to exchange messages in real time with one or more other computer users ■ *n.* **1.** INFORMAL TALK a relaxed informal conversation with somebody **2.** COMPUT EXCHANGE OF MESSAGES BY COMPUTER an informal exchange of messages in real time with one or more other computer users **3.** BIRDS SONGBIRD a small songbird related to the thrush with a harsh chattering cry. Subfamily: Turdinae. **4.** BIRDS = **yellow-breasted chat 5.** BIRDS AUSTRALIAN WREN any of several Australian wrens. Genus: *Ephthianura.* [15thC. Shortening of CHATTER.]

chat up *vt. U.K.* to talk to somebody flirtatiously or flatteringly (*informal*)

Chateau: Chenonceaux, France

cha·teau /sha tṓ/ (*plural* **-teaux** /-tṓ, -tṓz/ *or* **-teaus** /-tṓ, -tṓz/), **châ·teau** (*plural* **-teaux**) *n.* a castle or large house in France, often one that has a vineyard attached and gives its name to wine produced there [Mid-18thC. Via French from Latin *castellum* (see CASTLE).]

Cha·teau·bri·and /shàttōbrée aaN/ *n.* a thick beefsteak cut from the widest middle part of the filet [Late 19thC. Named for the French writer and statesman François René, Vicomte de *Chateaubriand* (1768–1848), whose chef is credited with creating a dish using the cut.]

chat·e·lain /shátt'l àyn/ *n.* in former times, a man who owned or controlled a castle or other large house [15thC. Via Old French *chastelain* (modern *châtelain*) from medieval Latin *castellanus* (see CASTELLAN).]

chat·e·laine /shátt'l àyn/ *n.* **1.** MISTRESS OF LARGE HOUSE in former times, a woman who owned or controlled a castle or other large house **2.** WOMAN'S CHAIN KEY a chain and clasp formerly worn at the waist by a woman to hold keys and other small items [Mid-19thC. From French *châtelaine*, the feminine of *châtelain* (see CHATELAIN).]

chat group *n.* COMPUT a group of people who exchange messages online, especially people who share a common interest

cha·toy·ant /shə tóyənt/ *adj.* IRIDESCENT having a changeable iridescent luster ■ *n.* IRIDESCENT GEMSTONE a chatoyant gemstone, e.g., a cat's eye [Late 18thC. From French, literally "shining like a cat's eyes."] —**cha·toy·an·cy** /shə tóyənsee/ *n.*

chat room *n.* a facility in a computer network, e.g., the Internet, in which participants exchange comments or information in real time

chat show *n. U.K.* = **talk show**

Chat·ta·hoo·chee /chàttə hóochee/ river that rises in northeastern Georgia and flows southwest and then southward to the Flint River. Length: 436 mi./702 km.

Chat·ta·noo·ga /chatt'n óogə/ city and port in southeastern Tennessee, on the Tennessee River, near the Tennessee-Georgia border. Population: 150,425 (1996).

chat·tel /chátt'l/ *n.* an item of personal property that is not freehold land and that is not intangible. Chattels are typically movable property (**chattels personal**), such as furniture or cars, but may also be interests in property (**chattels real**), such as leases. [13thC. Via Old French *chatel* "property" (source of English *cattle*) from, ultimately, Latin *capitalis* (see CAPITAL).]

chat·tel mort·gage *n.* a mortgage on personal possessions

chat·ter /cháttər/ *vi.* **(-tered, -ter·ing, -ters) 1.** TALK RAPIDLY to talk or converse rapidly and informally about unimportant things **2.** MAKE HIGH-PITCHED SOUNDS to make a rapid series of short high-pitched sounds that seem to resemble speech (*refers to animals or machinery*) **3.** CLICK TOGETHER to click together rapidly because of movement of the jaw caused by fear or cold (*refers to teeth*) **4.** VIBRATE DURING CUTTING to vibrate while cutting or being cut by a tool or machine, causing surface flaws (*refers to a sawblade or surface*) ■ *n.* **1.** TRIVIAL CONVERSATION rapid and informal talk or conversation, especially about unimportant things **2.** HIGH-PITCHED ANIMAL SOUNDS rapid short high-pitched sounds made by a bird, animal, or machine, that resemble human speech **3.** SURFACE FLAWS PRODUCED IN MACHINING imperfections in a surface, caused by vibration while being cut by a tool or machine [13thC. An imitation of the sound.]

chat·ter·box /cháttər bòks/ *n.* somebody who talks a lot, especially about unimportant things (*informal*)

chat·ter·er /cháttərər/ *n.* **1.** VERY TALKATIVE PERSON somebody who talks a lot, especially about unimportant matters **2.** BIRDS = **cotinga**

chat·ter mark *n.* **1.** GEOL MARK ON ROCK a crack or groove on the surface of rock, caused by the abrasive action of a glacier on bedrock or by the collision of fragments in water **2.** ENG VIBRATION MARK a mark left on something that has been machined, caused by vibration

chat·ty /cháttee/ **(-ti·er, -ti·est)** *adj.* **1.** FOND OF CHATTING fond of chatting about unimportant things **2.** FRIENDLY friendly and informal in tone —**chat·ti·ly** *adv.* —**chat·ti·ness** *n.*

Chau·cer /cháwssər/, **Geoffrey** (1343?–1400) English poet and author of *The Canterbury Tales* (1387–1400), one of the finest early works in English. —**Chau·cer·i·an** /chaw séeree ən/ *n., adj.*

chaud·froid /shō frwáa/ *n.* a hot béchamel sauce with aspic that sets when cold and is used to coat cold cooked savory foods [Late 19thC. From French, literally "hot-cold."]

chauf·feur /shṓfər, shō fúr/ *n.* HIRED DRIVER somebody employed to drive a car ■ *vti.* **(-feured, -feur·ing, -feurs)** DRIVE SOMEBODY to drive somebody from place to place in a car, or be employed to drive a car for somebody [Late 19thC. From French, literally "stoker, fireman," (used to denote the stoker and sometimes the driver of an early steam car), from *chauffer* "to heat."]

chaul·moo·gra /chawl móogrə/ *n.* a tropical tree of Southeast Asia with seeds that yield an oil once used to treat leprosy. Latin name: *Hydnocarpus kurzii.* [Early 19thC. From Bengali *cāul-mugrā.*]

chau·tau·qua /shə táwkwə/ *n.* an annual summer school or educational gathering, often held outdoors and offering lectures, concerts, and theatrical performances [Late 19thC. Named for *Chautauqua*, the southwestern New York State county and lake where such summer schools originated.]

Chau·tau·qua, Lake /shə táwk wə/ lake in southwestern New York, near Lake Erie. Length: 18 mi./29 km.

chau·vin·ism /shṓvə nìzzəm/ *n.* **1.** AGGRESSIVE PATRIOTISM unreasoning, overenthusiastic, and aggressive patriotism **2.** SENSE OF SUPERIORITY an excessive or prejudiced loyalty to a particular gender, group, or cause [Late 19thC. From French *chauvinisme*, which was coined from the name of Nicolas *Chauvin*, a French veteran of the Napoleonic wars.]

chau·vin·ist /shṓvənist/ *n.* **1.** SOMEBODY WITH SENSE OF SUPERIORITY somebody with an excessive or prejudiced loyalty to a particular gender, group, or cause **2.** UNREASONING PATRIOT an unreasoning, overenthusiastic, and aggressive patriot —

chau·vin·is·tic /shōvə nístik/ *adj.* —**chau·vin·is·ti·cal·ly** /-əlee/ *adv.*

Popperfoto
César Chàvez

Chá·vez /chaá vèz, shaá-/, **César** (1927–93) U.S. labor leader. He founded the National Farm Workers Association (1962) to help migrant farm workers.

chaw /chaw/ *vti.* (**chawed, chaw·ing, chaws**) **CHEW TOBACCO** to chew tobacco (*regional*) ■ *n.* **WAD OF CHEWING TOBACCO** a wad of chewing tobacco (*regional*) [Early 16thC. Variant of CHEW.]

Cha·yef·sky /chī éfskee/, **Paddy** (1923–81) U.S. playwright and screenwriter. He is known for his realist dramas, such as the movie *Marty* (1955). Real name **Sidney Chayefsky**

cha·yo·te /chaa yṓ tày/ *n.* **1.** PLANTS **TROPICAL CLIMBING PLANT** a tropical American climbing plant of the gourd family. Latin name: *Sechium edule.* **2.** FOOD **FRUIT OF CHAYOTE** the pear-shaped, furrowed green or white fruit of the chayote that is cooked and eaten as a vegetable [Late 19thC. Via Spanish from Nahuatl *chayotli.*]

cha·zan /khaázən/ (*plural* **-zan·im** *or* **-zans**), **haz·zan** (*plural* **-zan·im** /khə zaánim/ *or* **-zans**), **chaz·zen** (*plural* **-zens** *or* **-zen·im**) *n.* somebody who leads services in a synagogue, especially professionally

cha·ze·rai *n.* unattractive or unappetizing food or articles

chaz·zen *n.* = **chazan**

Ch.B. *abbr.* Bachelor of Surgery [Latin, *Chirurgiae Baccalaureus*]

cheap /cheep/ *adj.* **1. COSTING LITTLE** low in price or cost, or lower in price than might reasonably be expected **2. CHARGING LITTLE** charging low prices but offering good value **3. POOR QUALITY** inexpensive and of poor quality **4. WORTH LITTLE** worth little, or accorded little value ○ *In times of war, life is cheap.* **5. UNDESERVING OF RESPECT** not deserving of respect **6. OFFENSIVE** dishonorable, offensive, or unfair, especially in a way that seems obvious or calculated ○ *a cheap trick* **7. STINGY** stingy or unwilling to give freely ■ *adv.* **INEXPENSIVELY** at low cost [Old English *cēap* "trade, bargaining, a (good) bargain." Ultimately via a prehistoric Germanic word from Latin *caupo* "petty tradesman," "innkeeper."] —**cheap·ly** *adv.* —**cheap·ness** *n.* ◇ **on the cheap** at very low cost (*informal*)

cheap·en /cheépən/ (**-ened, -en·ing, -ens**) *vti.* **1. MAKE SOMETHING COST LESS** to make something less expensive, or become less expensive, especially in order to save money or increase profits, rather than to give better value **2. DEGRADE SOMEBODY OR SOMETHING** to lower the quality or reputation of somebody or something, or become lower in quality or reputation

cheap·ie /cheépee/, **cheap·y** (*plural* **-ies**) *n.* (*informal*) **1. SOMETHING CHEAP** something that is cheap **2. STINGY PERSON** somebody who is stingy or ungenerous

cheap·jack /cheép jàk/ *n.* **SELLER OF INFERIOR GOODS** somebody who sells inferior goods ■ *adj.* **INFERIOR** inferior in value or quality [From the name *Jack,* used as a general term for a man]

cheap·o /cheépō/ *adj.* cheap in price or cost (*informal*)

cheap shot *n.* an unfair or malicious attack on somebody or something, either in print or in speech

cheap·skate /cheép skàyt/ *n.* somebody who is stingy or ungenerous (*informal*)

cheap·y *n.* = **cheapie**

cheat /cheet/ *v.* (**cheat·ed, cheat·ing, cheats**) **1.** *vt.* **DECEIVE SOMEBODY** to deceive or mislead somebody, especially for personal advantage **2.** *vi.* **BREAK RULES TO GAIN ADVANTAGE** to break the rules in a game, examination, or contest, in an attempt to gain an unfair advantage **3.** *vi.* **BE UNFAITHFUL TO SOMEBODY** to have a sexual relationship with somebody other than a spouse or regular sexual partner **4.** *vt.* **ESCAPE HARM** to avoid harm or injury by luck or cunning ■ *n.* **1. DECEITFUL PERSON** somebody who uses deceit or trickery to gain an unfair advantage **2. DISHONEST TRICK** a dishonest or unfair trick **3.** LAW **DISHONESTLY OBTAINING PROPERTY** the obtaining of somebody else's property by dishonest means **4.** BOT = **chess**[3] *n.* [14thC. Shortening of ESCHEAT. The sense development seems to have been from "to confiscate (land and property) legally" via "to deprive of something dishonestly" to "to deceive."] —**cheat·er** *n.*

Che·chen /chéchən/ *n.* **1.** PEOPLES **SOMEBODY FROM CHECHNYA** somebody who was born in or lives in Chechnya **2.** LANG **MAJORITY LANGUAGE IN CHECHNYA** the majority language in Chechnya, belonging to the Nakh group of North Caucasian languages. Chechen is spoken by about one million people. —**Che·chen** *adj.*

Chech·ny·a /chech nyaá, chéchnee ə/ republic in southwestern Russia that formally separated from Ingushetia in 1992. In 1994, Russia refused to recognize Chechnya's independence, resulting in a conflict that ended formally in 1997. Capital: Grozny. Population: 1,500,000 (1994). Area: 5,800 sq. mi./ 15,000 sq. km.

check /chek/ *v.* (**checked, check·ing, checks**) **1.** *vti.* **EXAMINE SOMETHING** to examine something in order to establish its state or conditon ○ *Check the doors and windows to make sure they're locked.* **2.** *vti.* **CONFIRM TRUTH OR ACCURACY OF SOMETHING** to confirm or establish that something is true or accurate ○ *We need to check with the insurance company to find out whether we're covered.* **3.** *vi.* **BE CONSISTENT WITH SOMETHING ELSE** to be the same as, or consistent with something else ○ *What you're telling me now doesn't check with what you told me last week.* **4.** *vt.* **HALT OR SLOW SOMETHING** to stop or reduce the progress of some unwelcome process **5.** *vti.* **STOP SUDDENLY** to stop or pause suddenly, or make somebody or something stop suddenly ○ *In mid-sentence, he checked himself abruptly, looking terribly embarrassed.* **6.** *vt.* **PREVENT SOMETHING BEING EXPRESSED** to prevent something from being expressed, or control the urge to express something ○ *Checking the urge to laugh out loud, I buried my head in the newspaper.* **7.** *vt.* **MARK SOMETHING WITH CHECK MARK** to mark something with a check mark ○ *Check your preference.* ○ *Check here if the billing address is different from the shipping address.* **8.** *vt.* **REPRIMAND SOMEBODY** to criticize somebody for a fault or bad behavior **9.** *vt.* SPORTS **BLOCK OPPONENT** in sports such as ice hockey, to move directly into the path of an opponent, usually making physical contact, in order to block his or her progress **10.** *vt.* **HAND OVER BAGGAGE** to hand over something, especially baggage, so that it can be transported separately from passengers, usually in the same aircraft or vehicle ○ *You must check your luggage, sir.* **11.** *vt.* **HAND SOMETHING OVER FOR TEMPORARY KEEPING** to hand over something such as a coat in a restaurant, store, or museum, so that it can be looked after ○ *Do you want to check your coat, ma'am?* **12.** *vt.* CHESS **PUT OPPONENT'S KING IN THREATENING SITUATION** to put an opponent's king in a situation in which one of your pieces directly threatens it ■ *n.* **1. EXAMINATION** an examination or investigation of something, especially to verify its state or condition ○ *Routine checks should have revealed the cracks in the engine housing.* **2. SOMETHING THAT TESTS ACCURACY** something that can be used or referred to in order to test the accuracy, truth, or safety of something else ○ *Keep this list as a check for the things you have to do.* **3. MEANS OF CONTROLLING OR RESTRAINING SOMEBODY** a means of controlling or restraining somebody or something ○ *The United Nations was formed to act as a check on aggressive nations.* **4. PAPER MONEY SUBSTITUTE** a small printed form that, when filled out and signed, instructs a bank to pay a specified sum of money to the person named on it **5. RESTAURANT BILL** the bill in a restaurant or bar **6. NUMBERED TICKET FOR DEPOSITED ITEM** a numbered ticket or token given out when an item is left at a checkroom **7.** = **checkroom** **8. SYMBOL LIKE A V** a symbol like a V with a short left side and a long right side, used to indicate approval or preference ○ *Click on the left mouse button. A check will appear next to the category selected.* **9. PATTERN OF SQUARES** a pattern made up entirely of squares in at least two different colors that are arranged alternately **10. SQUARE IN CHECK PATTERN** a square in a pattern, in which at least two different colors are arranged alternately ○ *Every third check is red.* **11.** CHESS **MOVE ATTACKING KING** a move in chess by which a piece directly threatens the opposing king, or the position resulting from this move. The king must escape from this position to avoid checkmate. ○ *If you move your king there, you'll be in check.* **12.** SPORTS **BLOCKING MOVE** in sports, a move directly into the path of an attacking opponent ■ *adj.* = **checked** ■ *interj.* CHESS **WARNING THAT KING IS IN CHECK** used to announce that an opponent's king is in check [14thC. Via Old French *eschec* "check in chess," a warning that an opponent's king is under attack, from, ultimately, Persian *šāh* "king" (see SHAH).] —**check·a·ble** *adj.* ◇ **in check** restrained and under control ○ *managing to keep her anger in check*

check in *v.* **1.** *vti.* **REGISTER AT HOTEL** to register as a guest, or register a guest, on arrival at a hotel ○ *Has my colleague checked in yet?* **2.** *vti.* **ARRIVE FOR TRIP** to register and go through the necessary formalities before beginning a trip, especially by air ○ *All passengers should check in at least one hour before departure.* **3.** *vi.* **MAKE CONTACT** to make routine contact with a person or organization to exchange information ○ *The patrols are supposed to check in by radio at half-hourly intervals.*

check into *vt.* to investigate something in order to get more information about it, or to establish its truth or accuracy ○ *When we checked into his background, we found that he had several convictions for fraud.*

check off *vt.* to mark items on a list to show that they have been dealt with

check out *v.* **1.** *vi.* **LEAVE HOTEL** to pay the bill and leave a hotel or other place ○ *We'll be checking out later this morning.* **2.** *vi.* **LEAVE** to leave a particular place or a person (*informal*) **3.** *vi.* **DIE** to die (*slang*) **4.** *vt.* **INVESTIGATE SOMETHING** to establish that something is correct or valid ○ *The date is probably 1961. Check it out, will you?* **5.** *vt.* **EVALUATE AND QUALIFY PILOT** to instruct, evaluate the performance of, and then qualify a pilot to fly a certain type of aircraft ○ *She's been checked out to fly helicopters.* **6.** *vt.* **TAKE A LOOK AT SOMETHING** to visit a place briefly to get information about it (*informal*) ○ *Let's check out the new pizza place on 44th Street.* **7.** *vi.* **BE PROVED TRUE** to prove after investigation to be correct or valid ○ *If the DNA checks out, he's our man.* **8.** *vt.* **WITHDRAW** to withdraw an item from a place and register its withdrawal, especially to take a book or other item out of a library on loan ○ *A maximum of three books may be checked out.* **9.** *vti.* **PAY IN SUPERMARKET** to pay for something in a supermarket ○ *When I went to check out, I realized I'd left my purse in the car.* **10.** *vt.* **TAKE MONEY FOR GOODS AT SUPERMARKET** to calculate and take payment from a customer in a supermarket ○ *This person's in a hurry, so do you mind if I check her out first?*

check over *vt.* **1. EXAMINE SOMETHING** to examine something to make sure that it is correct or satisfactory ○ *Could you check my essay over to make sure there are no errors, please?* **2. EXAMINE SOMEBODY FOR HEALTH AND FITNESS** to examine somebody carefully to establish his or her state of health ○ *I've checked her over, and there are no broken bones.*

check through *vt.* **1. EXAMINE SOMETHING** to examine or review systematically all the parts of something to make sure that it is satisfactory **2. HAND IN BAGGAGE FOR TRANSPORTATION** to arrange for your baggage to be transferred automatically at interim stops on a trip or flight so that you do not get it back until you reach your destination ○ *Our bags are checked through to New Delhi.*

check up *vi.* to make inquiries to establish a point ○ *I checked up: no one by that name lives at that address.*

check up on *vt.* to make inquiries or obtain information about somebody or something, often secretly and usually because of suspicion or worry

check·book /chék bòòk/ *n.* a book of detachable checks

check·book jour·nal·ism *n.* the payment of large sums of money to people connected with an often sensational news event in order to obtain exclusive information for a newspaper

check box *n.* a small square on a computer screen that, when clicked on with a mouse, displays a small cross or check to show that an item has been selected

check dig·it *n.* in computing, a digit derived from and added to the other digits in a sequence, used to ensure that the sequence is correct

checked /chekt/ *adj.* having a pattern of small squares ○ *a red-and-white checked tablecloth*

check·er /chékər/ *n.* **1.** = **check** *n.* 9, **check** *n.* 10 **2. PIECE USED IN CHECKERS** a round flat piece used in the game of checkers ■ *vt.* (**-ered, -er·ing, -ers**) **1. MARK SOMETHING WITH CHECKER PATTERN** to mark something with a checker pattern or with alternating areas of light and shade **2. DISRUPT CONTINUOUS SUCCESS OF SOMETHING** to affect something adversely from time to time ○ *regrettable incidents that will checker his career* [12thC. Shortening of EXCHEQUER, which originally denoted the checked chessboard in English.]

check·er /chékər/ *n.* **1. SOMEBODY CHECKING SOMETHING** somebody who carries out a check on something **2. CASHIER** a cashier in a supermarket or large store **3.** BOARD GAMES **PIECE USED IN GAME OF CHECKERS** any one of the 24 pieces used in the game of checkers

check·er·bloom /chékər bloom/ *n.* a wild perennial mallow found in California with reddish-pink or purple flowers. Latin name: *Sidalcea malvaeflora.* [Early 20thC. Origin uncertain: probably from CHECKER + BLOOM.]

check·er·board /chékər bàwrd/ *n.* a game board patterned with two colors of squares, usually black and red, arranged alternately, that can be used for playing a variety of games including checkers

check·ered /chékərd/ *adj.* **1.** = **checked 2. UNEVEN OR INCONSISTENT** uneven or inconsistent, and characterized by periods of trouble or controversy as well as periods of success

check·ered flag *n.* a flag patterned with black and white squares that is waved as each participant in a car race crosses the finish line

check·ers /chékərz/ *n.* BOARD GAMES a board game played by two people, each using 12 pieces (**checkers**). The object is to jump over the opponent's pieces and remove them from the board. (*takes a singular verb*)

Check·ers speech /chékərz-/ *n.* POL a political speech dedicated to saving a politician's career by diverting attention from criticism rather than refuting it [From *Checkers*, the name of the family dog that U.S. vice-presidential candidate Richard M. Nixon referred to in a speech in 1952, defending himself against charges of campaign fund abuse.]

check-in *n.* **1. CHECKING IN AT HOTEL OR AIRPORT** the process of registering on arrival at a hotel or airport **2. REGISTRATION DESK** a place where people check in at a hotel or airport **3. SOMEBODY CHECKING IN** somebody who is checking in, e.g., a traveler at an airport, or a guest at a hotel ○ *Since the flight was overbooked, the five late check-ins had to wait.*

check·ing ac·count *n.* FIN a bank account that enables you to make withdrawals or payments to other people using checks

check·list /chék lìst/ *n.* a list of names, items, or points for consideration or action

check mark *n.* = **check** *n.* 8

check·mate /chék màyt/ *n.* **1. WINNING POSITION IN CHESS** a move or position in chess, in which a player's king cannot escape check and the other player wins the game **2. MOVE THAT PRODUCES CHECKMATE** a move in chess that produces checkmate, or a game that ends in checkmate ○ *The series was declared a draw with three checkmates apiece.* **3. COMPLETE DEFEAT** a situation of defeat or deadlock ■ *vt.* (**-mat·ed, -mat·ing, -mates**) **1. PUT KING IN CHECKMATE** in chess, to put an opponent's king in checkmate **2. THWART SOMEBODY** to make it impossible for somebody to succeed or proceed further ■ *interj.* **ANNOUNCEMENT OF CHECKMATE** used in chess to announce that an opponent's king is in checkmate [15thC. Via Old French *eschec mat* from, ultimately, Persian *šāh māt* "the king is dead."]

check·off /chék òf/ *n.* direct authorized deduction of union dues from the wages of employees

check·out /chék òwt/ *n.* **1. DEPARTURE FROM A HOTEL** the procedure involved in paying a hotel bill and leaving ○ *We'd like to arrange for a later checkout.* **2. SUPERMARKET PAY POINT** a point in a supermarket at which shoppers pay for their purchases and have them bagged ○ *Only three checkouts were open.* **3. SOMEBODY CHECKING OUT** somebody who is checking out, e.g., a traveler at an airport, or a guest at a hotel ○ *Apart from a couple of late checkouts, everyone seemed to be ready.* **4. INSPECTION OR TEST** an inspection or test carried out to make sure that something is working properly or is suitable for its purpose ○ *a preflight checkout of the plane*

check·point /chék pòynt/ *n.* a place where police or other officials stop and check vehicles

Check·point Char·lie *n.* a border crossing between East and West Berlin during the Cold War. Once situated on the Friedrichstrasse, it has now been demolished.

check·rail /chék ràyl/ *n.* *U.K.* = **guardrail** *n.* 2

check·rein /chék ràyn/ *n.* **1.** RIDING **SHORT REIN FOR A HORSE** a short rein designed to prevent a horse from lowering its head **2. REIN BETWEEN TWO HORSES** a rein used when driving a pair of horses, connecting the driving rein of one horse to the mouthpiece of the other

check·room /chék room, chék rŏom/ *n.* a room in a public building, e.g., a theater, restaurant, train or bus station where customers can leave belongings

check·sum /chék sùm/ *n.* COMPUT a value transmitted with a data stream, derived from the other elements in the data stream and used to check for transmission errors in the data. If the transmitted checksum differs from the one derived by the receiving computer, a transmission error has probably occurred and the transmission is repeated.

check·up /chék ùp/ *n.* a routine examination or inspection, especially one carried out by a doctor or dentist ○ *Regular checkups are required for all pilots.*

check valve *n.* a valve designed to allow liquids to flow in one direction only

ched·ar·im /kə daárim, khə daárim/ plural of **cheder**

ched·dar /chéddər/ *n.* a hard pale yellow or orange-red cheese with a flavor that ranges from mild to very sharp, depending on its maturity [Mid-17thC. Named for the village of *Cheddar*, England, where it was originally made.]

ched·er /káydər, kháydər/ (*plural* **-ar·im** /-daárim, -daárim/ *or* **-ers**) *n.* classes in Hebrew language and religious knowledge for younger Jewish children [Late 19thC. From Hebrew *ḥeder* "room."]

chee·cha·ko /chi chaákō, -chákō/ (*plural* **-kos**) *n.* *Northwest U.S., Can* in the late 19th century and early 20th century, an immigrant newly arrived in the mining areas of northwestern North America, including Alaska and the Yukon (*dated slang*) [Late 19thC. From Chinook jargon, literally "newcomer."]

cheek /cheek/ (**cheeked, cheek·ing, cheeks**) *n.* **1. SOFT PART OF FACE** the soft side area of the face between the nose and ear **2. BUTTOCK** either side of the buttocks (*informal*) **3. BAD MANNERS** impertinent or precocious words or behavior showing, or appearing to show, disregard for good manners or the feelings of others (*informal*) ○ *He had the cheek to ask me for a ride!* [Old English *cēoce* related to English *choke* and *cackle*] ◇ **cheek by jowl** side by side or very close together ○ *Antique dolls were crammed cheek by jowl onto the shelves.* ◇ **turn the other cheek** to accept injury or insults without resisting or retaliating

cheek·bone /cheek bōn/ *n.* an arch of bone in the face, below the eyes and above the cheeks

cheek·piece /cheek peess/ *n.* either of the two straps on a bridle that lie along the cheeks of a horse and join the bit to the crownpiece

cheek pouch *n.* a fold of skin in the mouth of some rodents and other mammals, e.g., squirrels and some monkeys, that acts as a pouch for storing food

cheek tooth *n.* a premolar or molar of a mammal, or any one of the teeth behind the canines

Cheek·to·wa·ga /cheektə waágə/ city in northwestern New York; an eastern suburb of Buffalo. Population: 99,561 (1996).

cheek·y /cheekee/ (**-i·er, -i·est**) *adj.* *U.K.* insolently or playfully rude or disrespectful (*informal*) — **cheek·i·ly** *adv.* —**cheek·i·ness** *n.*

cheep /cheep/ *n.* **SOUND MADE BY YOUNG BIRD** the high shrill sound made by a young bird ■ *vi.* (**cheeped, cheep·ing, cheeps**) **TO MAKE A HIGH SHRILL SOUND** to make a high shrill sound characteristic of young birds [Early 16thC. Originally from Scots dialect, as an imitation of the sound.]

cheer /cheer/ *n.* **1. SHOUT OF APPROVAL** a shout that expresses happiness, excitement, encouragement, or praise ○ *A huge cheer went up as the band walked onto the stage.* **2. WELL-BEING AND OPTIMISM** a sense of general well-being and optimism ○ *The latest sales figures will bring little cheer.* ■ *v.* (**cheered, cheer·ing, cheers**) **1.** *vti.* **SHOUT ENCOURAGEMENT OR SUPPORT** to shout encouragement, support, or appreciation, especially to people who are performing or competing **2.** *vt.* **MAKE SOMEBODY FEEL CHEERFUL** to make somebody feel more cheerful, confident, or optimistic (*often passive*) ○ *very cheering news* [13thC. Via Anglo-Norman *chere* "face, expression" from Latin *cara*, ultimately from Greek *kara* "head." The underlying meaning is "mood, as shown in the face."] —**cheer·er** *n.* —**cheer·ing·ly** *adv.*

cheer on *vt.* to give active or vocal support, especially at a sports event ○ *We went to cheer our team on in the championships.*

cheer up *vti.* **1. MAKE SOMEBODY FEEL LESS SAD** to become, or make somebody feel, less sad ○ *She cheered up a little when I suggested lunch.* **2. MAKE PLACE BRIGHTER OR MORE ATTRACTIVE** to become, or make something, brighter or more attractive and welcoming in appearance ○ *A coat of bright yellow paint will cheer up the dingiest of kitchens.*

cheer·ful /cheerfəl/ *adj.* **1. HAPPY AND OPTIMISTIC** in a happy and optimistic mood, or happy and optimistic by nature ○ *She remained her usual cheerful self despite recent setbacks.* **2. BRIGHT AND PLEASANT** causing people to feel cheerful ○ *a cheerful light blue* **3. WILLING AND UNRESENTFUL** showing willingness or good humor in complying ○ *They set to work cleaning up the mess with cheerful determination.* —**cheer·ful·ly** *adv.* —**cheer·ful·ness** *n.*

cheer·i·o /cheeri ó/ *interj.* *U.K.* used to say good-bye (*informal*) [Early 20thC. Alteration of CHEER.]

cheer·lead·er /cheer leedər/ *n.* **1. PERFORMER WHO MAKES CROWD CHEER** any of a group of uniformed performers who encourage the crowd to support a team at sports events **2. UNCRITICAL ENTHUSIAST** an uncritically enthusiastic supporter (*disapproving*)

cheer·less /cheerləss/ *adj.* lacking anything bright, pleasant, or encouraging ○ *a gloomy cheerless day* — **cheer·less·ly** *adv.* —**cheer·less·ness** *n.*

cheers /cheerz/ *interj.* **1. GOOD HEALTH** used to express good wishes just before drinking an alcoholic drink (*informal*) **2.** *U.K.* **GOOD BYE** good-bye or farewell (*spoken*) **3.** *U.K.* **THANKS** thank you ○ *Cheers, you've been a big help!*

cheer·y /cheeree/ (**-i·er, -i·est**) *adj.* happy or in good spirits —**cheer·i·ly** *adv.* —**cheer·i·ness** *n.*

cheese /cheez/ *n.* **1. SOLID FOOD MADE FROM MILK** a food made from the milk of cows, sheep, goats, and some other animals. Cheese ranges in texture form hard to semisoft, and in flavor from mildly acidic to sharp. **2. BLOCK OF CHEESE** an individual block of cheese [Old English *cēse*. Ultimately from a prehistoric Germanic word that was borrowed from Latin *caseus*, of unknown origin.]

cheese·burg·er /cheez bùrgər/ *n.* a hamburger covered with melted cheese, served on a bun

cheese·cake /cheez kàyk/ *n.* **1. DESSERT MADE WITH SWEETENED SOFT CHEESE** a dessert consisting of a layer of sweetened soft cheese mixed with cream and eggs on a cracker-crumb or pastry base **2. PHOTOGRAPHS OF ATTRACTIVE WOMEN** photographs of women that highlight their physical appearance, especially in a stereotypical way (*slang*) ◊ **beefcake**

cheese·cloth /cheez klàwth, cheez klòth/ *n.* a light woven cotton material, originally used for wrapping or straining cheese and now used as a material for lightweight clothes

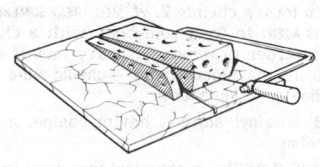

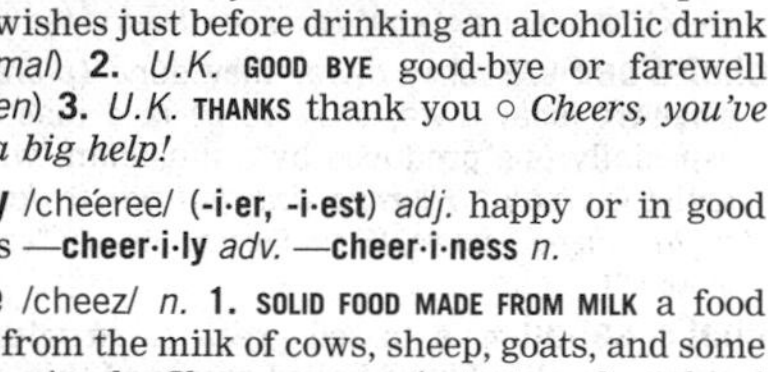

Cheese cutter

cheese cut·ter *n.* a board to which a piece of wire is attached for cutting cheese

cheese·par·ing /cheez pàiring/ *adj.* **STINGY** reluctant to spend money ■ *n.* **STINGINESS** reluctance to spend money [The word originally referred to "a paring of cheese rind," something only the most miserly would save]

cheese straw *n.* a long thin cracker of cheese-flavored pastry, served as a snack

chees·y /cheézee/ (**-i·er, -i·est**) *adj.* **1.** LIKE CHEESE having the flavor or smell of cheese **2.** TACKY cheap and tawdry (*informal*)

Cheetah

chee·tah /cheétə/ (*plural* **-tahs** *or* **-tah**) *n.* a large member of the cat family with a yellowish-brown, black-spotted coat, small head, slender body, and long legs, found mainly in Africa and southwestern Asia. It is the fastest land mammal, can reach speeds of up to 68 mph/110km/h while hunting, and is an endangered species. Latin name: *Acinonyx jubatus.* [Late 18thC. Via Hindi *cītā* from Sanskrit *citraka* "leopard, tiger" (literally "spotted, variegated"), from *citra-* "spotted."]

Chee·ver /cheévər/, **John** (1912–82) U.S. writer. His novels and short stories were frequently comedies of manners satirizing suburban life.

chef /shef/ *n.* a professional cook, especially the principal cook in a hotel or restaurant [Early 19thC. From French, shortening of *chef de cuisine* "head of the kitchen."]

chef-d'oeu·vre /shày d-vrə, shay dúrv/ (*plural* **chefs-d'oeu·vre** /shày d-vrə, shay dúrv/) *n.* a masterpiece, especially one produced by a musician, writer, or artist (*formal*) ○ *He regarded that particular speech as his chef-d'oeuvre.* [From French, literally "chief piece of work"]

chef's sal·ad *n.* a tossed green salad with added tomatoes, sliced hard-boiled eggs, and thin strips of meat and cheese

Che·khov /ché kawf, -kawv/, **Anton Pavlovich** (1860–1904) Russian writer. His plays and stories reveal the emotional depth of ordinary lives and include *The Seagull* (1896) and *The Cherry Orchard* (1904). —**Chek·ho·vi·an** /che kṓvee ən/ *n., adj.*

che·la[1] /keélə/ (*plural* **-lae** /-lee/) *n.* the opposable end joint that forms a claw on a limb of a lobster, crab, scorpion, or similar animal (**arthropod**) [Mid-17thC. Via modern Latin from Greek *khēlē* "claw," of unknown origin.]

che·la[2] /cháy laá/ *n.* the pupil or disciple of a Hindu religious teacher [Mid-19thC. From Hindi *celā.*]

che·late[1] /keé làyt/ *n.* COMPOUND OF METAL AND NONMETAL a chemical compound in which metallic and non-metallic, usually organic, atoms are combined. These compounds are characterized by a ring structure in which a metal ion is attached to two nonmetal ions by covalent bonds. ■ *adj.* RELATING TO CHELATES in the form of or typical of a chelate ■ *v.* (**-lat·ed, -lat·ing, -lates**) **1.** *vti.* CHEM COMBINE TO FORM CHELATE to combine, or combine something, with a metal to form a chelate **2.** *vt.* MED TREAT SOMEBODY WITH CHELATING AGENT to treat somebody with a chelating agent in order to remove a heavy metal, such as lead, from the bloodstream —**che·lat·a·ble** *adj.* —**che·la·tion** *n.* —**che·la·tor** *n.*

che·late[2] /keé làyt/ *adj.* ZOOL having chelae, or shaped like chelae

che·lat·ing a·gent *n.* a chemical that combines with a metal to form a chelate. Chelating agents are often used to remove unwanted heavy metal ions from the body, e.g., in cases of metal poisoning.

che·lic·er·a /kə líssərə/ (*plural* **-ae** /-ee/) *n.* either of the first mouthparts of horseshoe crabs and spiders, resembling fangs or pincers and used to grab or poison prey [Mid-19thC. From modern Latin, coined from *chela* "CHELA[1]" + Greek *keras* "horn."]

che·lic·er·ate /kə líssərət, -ràyt/ *n.* an invertebrate with feeding appendages shaped like pincers. Spiders and crabs are chelicerates. Phylum: Chelicerata. [Early 20thC. From modern Latin *chelicerata*, phylum name, formed from *chelicera* (see CHELICERA).]

che·li·form /keélə fàwrm/ *adj.* used to describe an appendage shaped like a pincer or chela [Late 18thC. Coined from modern Latin *chela* "CHELA[1]" + -FORM.]

Chelms·ford /chélmzfərd/ town in northeastern Massachusetts, southwest of Lowell and west of Billerica. Population: 33,484 (1996).

che·lo·ni·an /ki lṓnee ən/ *n.* a reptile, such as a turtle or tortoise, that has most of its body enclosed in a hard bony shell. Order: Chelonia. [Early 19thC. Via modern Latin *Chelonia*, order name, from Greek *khelōnē* "tortoise."] —**che·lo·ni·an** *adj.*

Chel·sea /chélsee/ city in eastern Massachusetts, just northeast of Boston, on the Mystic River. Population: 27,608 (1996).

Che·lya·binsk /chel yaábinsk/ city and capital of Chelyabinsk Oblast, in western Russia, situated 125 mi./201 km south of Yekaterinburg. Population: 1,143,000 (1992).

chem. *abbr.* **1.** chemical **2.** chemist **3.** chemistry

chem- *prefix.* = **chemo-**

chemi- *prefix.* = **chemo-**

chem·i·cal /kémmik'l/ *adj.* **1.** RELATING TO CHEMISTRY produced by or involved in the processes of chemistry **2.** COMPOSED OF CHEMICALS composed of or involving the use of chemicals ■ *n.* SUBSTANCE USED OR MADE BY CHEMISTRY a substance used in or produced by the processes of chemistry. A chemical has a defined atomic or molecular structure that results from, or takes part in, reactions involving changes in its structure, composition, and properties. [Late 16thC. Formed from modern Latin *chimicus* "alchemist," a shortening of medieval Latin *alchimicus*, from *alchimia* (see ALCHEMY).] —**chem·i·cal·ly** *adv.*

chem·i·cal a·buse *n.* = **substance abuse**

chem·i·cal bond *n.* a force resulting from the redistribution of energy contained by orbiting electrons, which tends to bind atoms together to form molecules

chem·i·cal de·pend·en·cy *n.* addiction to a chemical substance or drug

chem·i·cal en·gi·neer·ing *n.* a branch of engineering that deals with the industrial applications of chemistry and chemical processes —**chem·i·cal en·gi·neer** *n.*

chem·i·cal e·qua·tion *n.* a representation, using chemical symbols in a form resembling a mathematical equation, of the process involved in a chemical reaction

chemical free *adj.* not addicted to drugs or refraining from the use of drugs (*informal*)

Chem·i·cal Mace *tdmk.* a trademark for an aerosol used to immobilize an attacker for a brief time

chem·i·cal re·ac·tion *n.* a process that changes the molecular composition of a substance by redistributing atoms or groups of atoms without altering the structure of the nuclei of the atoms

chem·i·cal toi·let *n.* a portable toilet containing chemicals to neutralize human waste

chem·i·cal war·fare *n.* military operations involving the use of weapons containing substances such as nerve gas or poison

chem·i·cal weap·on *n.* a weapon containing a substance such as nerve gas or poison

chem·i·lu·mi·nes·cence /kèmmi loomi néss'ns/ *n.* emission of light as a result of a chemical reaction, without producing heat —**chem·i·lu·mi·nes·cent** *adj.*

che·min de fer /shə màN də fáir/ *n.* a gambling card game, similar to and derived from baccarat [From French, "railroad," in reference to the speed at which the game is played]

che·mise /shə meéz/ *n.* **1.** LONG LOOSE DRESS a type of long loose dress, sometimes loosely belted at the waist or hip **2.** LONG LOOSE UNDERGARMENT a long loose undergarment shaped like a dress [13thC. Via Old French from late Latin *camisia* "shirt, nightgown" (source of English *camisado*).]

chem·i·sette /shèmmi zét/ *n.* a decorative undergarment made of lace or other fine material, worn to fill space left at the neckline of a low-cut dress [Early 19thC. From French, literally "small chemise," from *chemise* (see CHEMISE).]

chem·i·sorb /kémmi sàwrb/ (**-sorbed, -sorb·ing, -sorbs**), **chem·o·sorb** /kémmə sàwrb/ (**-sorbed, -sorb·ing, -sorbs**) *vt.* to take up a substance by chemisorption [Mid-20thC. Back-formation from CHEMISORPTION.]

chem·i·sorp·tion /kemi sáwrpshən/ *n.* the process of coating the surface of a substance rather than being absorbed by it, accompanied by chemical bonding between the surface of the material and the adsorbed substance [Mid-20thC. Blend of CHEMI- and ADSORPTION.] —**chem·i·sorp·tive** *adj.*

chem·ist /kémmist/ *n.* **1.** SCIENTIST SPECIALIZING IN CHEMISTRY a scientist who works in the field of chemistry **2.** *U.K.* = **pharmacist 3.** *U.K.* = **drugstore** [Mid-16thC. Via French *chimiste* from modern Latin *chimista*, a shortening of medieval Latin *alchimista* "alchemist," from *alchimia* (see ALCHEMY).]

chem·is·try /kémmistree/ *n.* **1.** STUDY OF TRANSFORMATION OF MATTER a branch of science dealing with the structure, composition, properties, and reactive characteristics of substances, especially at the atomic and molecular levels. ◊ **inorganic chemistry, organic chemistry, physical chemistry 2.** CHEMICAL PROPERTIES OF SOMETHING the chemical composition, structure, and properties of a substance, or the chemical aspects of an activity ○ *the chemistry of wine-making* **3.** REACTION BETWEEN TWO PEOPLE the spontaneous reaction of individuals to each other, especially a mutual sense of attraction or understanding

che·mo /keémō/ *n.* chemotherapy (*informal*) [Mid-20thC. Shortening.]

chemo- *prefix.* chemical, chemistry ○ *chemoreceptor* [From CHEMICAL]

che·mo·ki·ne·sis /keémō ki neéssiss, -kī-/ *n.* increased activity of cells or organisms caused by the presence of a chemical agent

che·mo·lith·o·troph /keémō líthə tròf/ *n.* a bacterium that obtains its energy from inorganic compounds containing iron, nitrogen, or sulfur, and not from living on decaying organisms [Late 20thC] —**chem·o·lith·o·troph·ic** /keémō lithə trṓffik/ *adj.*

che·mo·pro·phy·lax·is /keémō prṓfə láksiss/ *n.* the use of chemical agents to prevent disease —**che·mo·pro·phy·lac·tic** *adj.*

che·mo·re·cep·tion /keémō ri sépsh'n/ *n.* the physiological response of an organism or sense organ to a chemical stimulus —**che·mo·re·cep·tive** *adj.* —**che·mo·re·cep·tiv·i·ty** /keémō ri sep tívvətee/ *n.*

che·mo·re·cep·tor /keémō ri séptər/ *n.* a sense organ, e.g., a taste bud, that responds to a chemical stimulus

che·mo·sen·so·ry /keémō sénsəree/ *adj.* involved in or relating to the perception of chemical agents, especially in the sense of smell

chem·o·sorb *vt.* = **chemisorb**

che·mo·sphere /keémə sfeer/ *n.* a variable region of the atmosphere, approximately 20 to 120 mi./30 to 190 km above the Earth's surface, where photochemical reactions take place —**che·mo·spher·ic** /keémə sférrik/ *adj.*

che·mo·stat /keémō stàt/ *n.* an apparatus designed to permit the growth of bacterial cultures at controlled rates [Mid-20thC. Coined from CHEMO-, on the model of *thermostat.*]

che·mo·sur·ger·y /keémō sùrjəree/ *n.* surgical removal of dead or diseased tissue by chemical means —**che·mo·sur·gi·cal** *adj.*

che·mo·syn·the·sis /keémō sínthəssiss/ *n.* the synthesis of organic molecules by an organism using energy derived from chemical reactions, e.g., the synthesis of carbohydrates by bacteria —**che·mo·syn·thet·ic** /keémō sin théttik/ *adj.* —**che·mo·syn·thet·i·cal·ly** /-əlee/ *adv.*

che·mo·tax·is /keémō táksiss/ *n.* movement or change in the position of a cell or organism in response to the presence of a chemical agent —**che·mo·tac·tic** *adj.* —**che·mo·tac·ti·cal·ly** *adv.*

che·mo·tax·on·o·my /keémō tak sónnəmee/ *n.* the identification and classification of plants and animals based on their biochemical composition —**che·mo·tax·o·nom·ic** /keémō taksə nómmik/ *adj.* —**che·mo·tax·o·nom·i·cal·ly** /-əlee/ *adv.* —**che·mo·tax·on·o·mist** /-tak sónnəmist/ *n.*

che·mo·ther·a·py /keémō thérrəpee/ (*plural* **-pies**) *n.* the use of chemical agents to treat diseases, infections, or other disorders, especially cancer —**che·mo·ther·a·peu·tic** /-therrə pyōōtik/ *adj.* —**che-**

mo·ther·a·peu·ti·cal·ly /-pyootikəlee/ *adv.* —**che·mo·ther·a·pist** /keemō thérrəpist/ *n.*

che·mot·ro·pism /ki móttrə pìzzəm/ *n.* the movement or growth of an organism or part of an organism in response to a chemical stimulus —**che·mo·trop·ic** /keemō tróppik/ *adj.* —**che·mo·trop·i·cal·ly** *adv.*

chem·ur·gy /kémmərjee/ *n.* a branch of applied chemistry dealing with the industrial application of organic substances, especially of agricultural origin [Mid-20thC. Coined from CHEMICAL, on the model of "metallurgy."] —**che·mur·gic** /kə múrjik/ *adj.* —**che·mur·gi·cal** *adj.*

chem·zyme /kém zīm/ *n.* a substance that is a chemical but acts like an enzyme, often used to increase the effectiveness of a drug by accelerating its action [Late 20thC. Blend of CHEMO- and ENZYME.]

Chen /chen/ *n.* a Chinese dynasty that ruled from A.D. 557 to 589

Cheng·de /chùng dú/, **Ch'eng-te** city and capital of the former Jehol Province, now Hebei Province, in northeastern China, situated on the Luan River, approximately 110 mi./177 km northeast of Beijing. Population: 365,519 (1990).

Cheng·du /chùng dóo/ provincial capital, situated northwest of Chungking, in Szechwan, China. Population: 2,810,000 (1991).

che·nille /shə neel/ *n.* **1. SOFT THICK COTTON OR SILK FABRIC** a soft thick fabric, usually made of cotton or silk with a raised pile, that is used to make furnishings and clothes **2. THICK SILK, COTTON, OR WORSTED CORD** a thick cord or yarn of silk, cotton, or worsted cord, used in embroidery and for fringes and trimmings [Mid-18thC. Via French, literally "hairy caterpillar," from Latin *canicula*, literally "little dog," from *canis* "dog" (see CANINE).]

Che·nin Blanc /shènnin blaángk/ *n.* a variety of white grape used for making light dry wine, especially in the Loire region of France [From French]

Chen·nault /shə náwlt/, **Claire Lee** (1890–1958) U.S. air force general. He retired from the U.S. Air Force in 1937 and formed the Flying Tigers.

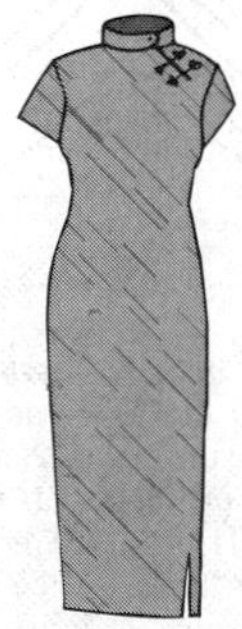

Cheongsam

che·ong·sam /chòng saám/ *n.* a straight dress with a small stand-up collar and a slit in the skirt, worn by Chinese women [Mid-20thC. From Chinese (Cantonese) (equivalent to Mandarin *chángshān*), literally "long gown."]

cheque /chek/ *n. U.K.* = **check** *n.* **4** [Early 18thC. Variant of CHECK, under the influence of *exchequer*.]

cheque·book *n.* U.K. = **checkbook**

che·quer·board *n. U.K.* = **checkerboard**

Cheq·uers /chékərz/ *n.* a country house in Buckinghamshire, in central southern England, that is the official country residence of the British Prime Minister

Cher /shair/ (*b.* 1946) U.S. entertainer. She turned to acting after a successful singing career and won an Academy Award for *Moonstruck* (1987). Full name **Cherilyn LaPierre**

Cher·bourg /sháir bòorg/ city and port on the English Channel in the Manche Department of the Basse-Normandie Region, in northwestern France. Population: 28,773 (1990).

che·rem /khérrəm, kháyrəm/, **he·rem** *n.* in former times, a form of Jewish excommunication involving the separation of an individual from the rest of the Jewish community for a limited period of time [Early 19thC. From Hebrew *ḥērem*, from *ḥāram* "to curse."]

Cher·em·is /chèrrə míss, chérrəmiss/ *n., adj.* LANG = **Mari**

cher·i·moy·a /chèrri móyə/ (*plural* **-as** *or* **-a**) *n.* **1.** TREES **TROPICAL TREE WITH HEART-SHAPED FRUIT** a tropical American tree of the custard apple family that has aromatic leaves, fragrant flowers, and edible fruit. Latin name: *Annona cherimola.* **2.** FOOD **FRUIT OF CHERIMOYA TREE** the heart-shaped fruit of the cherimoya tree, which has green skin turning purple-black when ripe and creamy-white scented flesh [Mid-18thC. Via Spanish from Quechua *chirimuya*, from *chiri* "cold, refreshing" + *muya* "circle."]

cher·ish /chérrish/ (**-ished, -ish·ing, -ish·es**) *vt.* **1. LOVE AND CARE FOR SOMEBODY** to feel or show great love or care for somebody ○ *He cherishes that girl.* **2. VALUE SOMETHING HIGHLY** to value something highly, e.g., as a right, freedom, or privilege ○ *I cherish my independence.* **3. RETAIN IN THE MIND** to retain a memory or wish in the mind as a source of pleasure or as an ambition [14thC. From French *chériss-*, the stem of *chérir* "to hold dear," from *cher* "dear," from Latin *carus* (see CHARITY).] —**cher·ish·a·ble** *adj.* —**cher·ish·er** *n.* —**cher·ish·ing·ly** *adv.*

Cher·nen·ko /chər nyéngkō/, **Konstantin** (1911–85) Soviet political leader. A long-time political ally of Leonid Brezhnev, he became general secretary of the Communist Party of the Soviet Union (1984–85).

Cher·no·byl /chər nṓb'l/ *n.* the site of a nuclear power plant near Kiev, in Ukraine, where there was a catastrophic accident in 1986

cher·no·zem /chùrnə zém/ *n.* fertile black or brown topsoil that is rich in humus and can support crops for long periods of time without the addition of fertilizers. It covers a large proportion of the Eurasian steppe, as well as a belt of land stretching from Saskatchewan in Canada through North Dakota into Texas. [Mid-19thC. From Russian, literally "black earth."] —**cher·no·zem·ic** *adj.*

Cher·o·kee /chérrəkee/ (*plural* **-kee** *or* **-kees**) *n.* **1. MEMBER OF NATIVE AMERICAN PEOPLE OF SOUTH** a member of a Native American people who originally occupied lands in southeastern parts of the United States and now live mainly in Oklahoma and North Carolina. The Cherokee were one of the Five Civilized Nations who, under the Removal Act of 1830, were sent to live on reservations in Oklahoma. **2. CHEROKEE LANGUAGE** the Iroquoian language of the Cherokee people. Cherokee is spoken by about 10,000 people. [Late 17thC. From Cherokee *tsalaki* (earlier *tsaraki*).] —**Cher·o·kee** *adj.*

Cher·o·kee rose *n.* a climbing evergreen rose with white flowers that is native to China and grows in the southeastern United States. Latin name: *Rosa laevigata.*

Cher·o·kee Strip *n.* an area of land in northern Oklahoma, purchased from the Cherokee people by the U.S. government in 1891 and made available for settlement in 1893

che·root /shə róot/ *n.* a cigar with two square-cut ends [Late 17thC. Via French *cheroute* from Tamil *curuṭṭu* "roll of tobacco."]

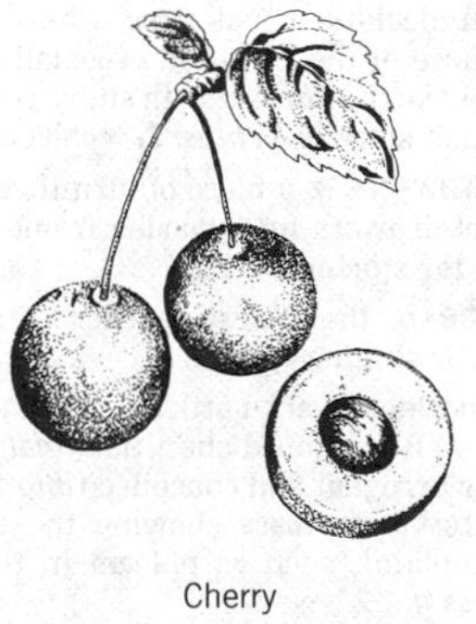

Cherry

cher·ry /chérree/ *n.* (*plural* **-ries**) **1.** TREES **FRUIT TREE** a common fruit tree or shrub that bears a small edible fruit in clusters with long thin stalks. Varieties include the sweet cherry, sour cherry, and chokecherry. Genus: *Prunus.* **2.** FOOD **FRUIT OF CHERRY TREE** the small round fruit of the cherry tree, which has a single hard pit and varies in color from bright red or yellow to dark purplish black **3.** INDUST **WOOD OF CHERRY TREE** the wood of the cherry tree, much valued as material for furniture and musical instruments **4. VIRGINITY** somebody's virginity, or the hymen as a symbol of a woman's virginity (*slang taboo*) ■ *adj.* **1.** *Midwest* **EXCELLENT** used to describe something that is an excellent example of its kind (*slang*) ○ *a totally cherry motorcycle* **2.** = **cherry red** [14thC. Via Old Northern French *cherise* (mistaken for a plural) from medieval Latin *ceresia*, ultimately from Greek *kerasos* "cherry tree."]

cher·ry bomb *n.* a powerful round red firecracker that explodes with a loud bang

Cher·ry Hill /chèrree-/ town in southwestern New Jersey, east of Camden and Philadelphia, Pennsylvania. Population: 68,982 (1996).

cher·ry lau·rel *n.* an evergreen Eurasian shrub cultivated for its white flowers and shiny leaves. Latin name: *Prunus laurocerasus.*

cher·ry-pick (**cher·ry-picked, cher·ry-pick·ing, cher·ry-picks**) *vti.* to select only the most lucrative or profitable opportunites, especially in business (*disapproving*)

Cherry picker

cher·ry pick·er *n.* a mobile crane with an enclosed platform that can be raised to allow somebody to work off the ground, e.g., on an overhead streetlight or wire

cher·ry plum *n.* a deciduous Eurasian plum tree that produces red or yellow fruit resembling cherries. Latin name: *Prunus cerasifera.*

cher·ry red *adj.* of a deep vivid red color tinged with pink —**cher·ry red** *n.*

cher·ry·stone /chérri stōn/ *n.* a half-grown quahog clam

cher·ry to·ma·to *n.* a small tomato with a strong sweet flavor. Latin name: *Lycopersicon esculentum.* [So called because of its size and sweetness]

cher·ry·wood /chérri wòod/ *n.* = **cherry** *n.* **3**

cher·so·nese /kúrsə neez, -neess/ *n.* a peninsula (*literary*) [Early 17thC. Via Latin *chersonesus* from Greek *khersonēsos*, from *khersos* "dry land" + *nēsos* "island."]

chert /churt/ *n.* a granular type of silica, usually found as bands of pebbles in sedimentary rock. It consists of microcrystalline quartz similar to flint, but more brittle. Formula: SiO_2. [Late 17thC. Origin unknown.] —**chert·y** *adj.*

Cherub: Garden sculptures at Wendens Ambo, Essex, England

cher·ub /chérrəb/ *n.* **1.** (*plural* **-u·bim** *or* **-ubs**) CHR **ANGEL OF SECOND ORDER** an angel, specifically one belonging to the second order of angels in the celestial hierarchy whose distinctive attribute is knowledge **2.** ARTS **DEPICTION OF ANGEL** an angel depicted as a chubby-faced child with wings, sometimes simply as a child's head above a pair of wings [Pre-12thC. Via Latin *cherub* and Greek *kheroub* from Hebrew *kĕrūḇ* probably of Akkadian origin, but later mistakenly connected with Aramaic *kĕ-rabyā* "like a child."]

che·ru·bic /chə ro͝obik/ *adj.* like a cherub in appearance or demeanor, especially in being sweet, innocent, often chubby-cheeked, and extremely well-behaved —**che·ru·bi·cal·ly** *adv.*

cher·vil /chúrvəl/ *n.* **1.** LEAFY HERB an herb cultivated for its leaves, which have a mild flavor of aniseed and resemble parsley. It is used to season and garnish food. Latin name: *Anthriscus cerefolium.* **2.** PLANT RELATED TO CHERVIL any plant related or similar to true chervil. Genera: *Anthriscus* and *Chaerophyllum.* [Pre-12thC. Via Latin *chaerephyllum* from Greek *khairephullon*, perhaps from *khairein* "to delight in" + *phullon* "leaf."]

Ches·a·peake /chéssa peek/ city in Virginia, south of Norfolk and Hampton, and east of the Great Dismal Swamp. Population: 192,342 (1996).

Ches·a·peake Bay largest inlet of the Atlantic Ocean on the East Coast of the United States, bounded by Virginia and Maryland. Area: 3,320 sq. mi./8,365 sq. km.

Ches·a·peake Bay re·triev·er *n.* a hunting dog belonging to a breed developed in the United States that has a thick short wavy coat from dark brown to tan in color. It is trained to retrieve game from water. [Late 19thC. Named for the CHESAPEAKE BAY, where the breed was developed.]

Chesh·ire[1] /chéshər/ *n.* a mild crumbly cheese that is usually white but sometimes red, originally made in Cheshire, England

Chesh·ire[2] /chéshər/ city in southern Connecticut, southeast of Waterbury. Population: 26,067 (1996).

Chesh·ire cat *n.* the cat in Lewis Carroll's *Alice's Adventures in Wonderland*, whose broad grin remained suspended in the air after the cat itself had disappeared

Chesh·van /késhvən, khéshvən/, **Hesh·van** *n.* in the Jewish calendar, the eighth month of the year, consisting of 29 or 30 days and roughly corresponding to the Gregorian October to November

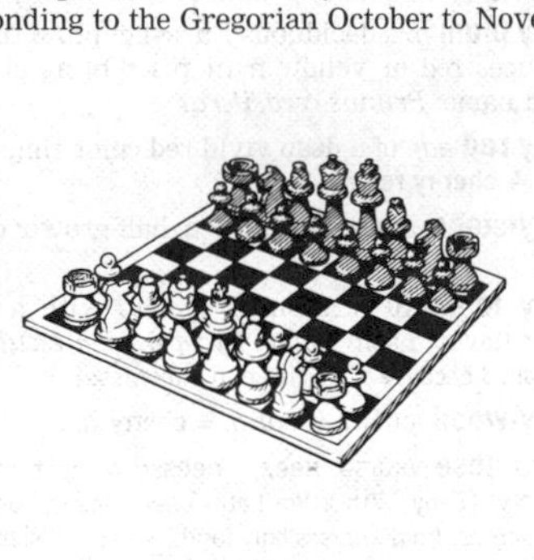

Chess

chess[1] /chess/ *n.* a game played on a checkered board by two players, each with 16 pieces representing a king and his attendants. The object is to capture **(checkmate)** the opponent's king. Each player begins with a king, a queen, two bishops, two knights, two rooks or castles, and eight pawns. [12thC. Shortening of Old French *esches*, plural of *eschec* "check!" (see CHECK).]

chess[2] /chess/ *n.* a deck board or floorboard of a pontoon bridge [Early 19thC. Origin uncertain: perhaps via Old French *chasse* "frame" from Latin *capsa* "box" (see CAPSULE).]

chess[3] /chess/ *n.* any one of several types of weedy bromegrass, especially an annual plant. Latin name: *Bromus secanilus.* [Mid-18thC. Origin unknown.]

chess·board /chéss bàwrd/ *n.* a square board divided into 64 alternate light and dark squares, used for playing chess or checkers. The eight vertical rows of squares are called files, the eight horizontal rows are called ranks, and the squares that stretch diagonally across the board are called diagonals.

chess·man /chéss màn/ (*plural* **-men** /-mèn/) *n.* any of the 32 pieces used in a game of chess

chess pie *n.* a pie filled with a rich mixture of eggs, butter, and sugar, often further flavored and baked [CHESS is perhaps an alteration of CHEST]

chess·piece /chéss peess/ *n.* = **chessman**

ches·sy·lite /chéssi lìt/ *n.* MINERALS = **azurite** [Mid-19thC. Named for the town of *Chessy*, near Lyons in France.]

chest /chest/ *n.* **1.** UPPER PART OF BODY the upper part of the body below the neck and above the stomach, covering the ribs and the organs that the ribs enclose **2.** FRONT PART OF BODY the front part of the body of a person or animal extending from the neck to the stomach ○ *the dog had a deep chest* **3.** STRONG RECTANGULAR BOX a strong rectangular box, usually with a lid and sometimes a lock, used for storage or transport [Old English *cest* (related to Dutch *kist* "coffin" and German *Kiste* "box"). From a prehistoric West Germanic word borrowed from Latin *cista*, from Greek *kistē* "basket."] —**chest·ful** /chéstfəl/ *n.* ◇ **get something off your chest** to talk openly about something that has been making you feel guilty, embarrassed, worried, or angry, especially when talking about it helps to reduce or remove those feelings

Ches·ter /chéstər/ city and port in southeastern Pennsylvania, south of Philadelphia, on the Delaware River. Population: 40,660 (1996).

ches·ter·field /chéstər feeld/ *n.* **1.** *Northwest U.S.* SOFA a large sofa with upright armrests at the same height as the back, usually upholstered in leather and with a rolled-over outward curve along the top **2.** *Can* COUCH any upholstered couch or sofa with back and arms **3.** OVERCOAT a style of overcoat, usually with concealed buttons and a velvet collar [Mid-19thC. Named for a 19thC earl of *Chesterfield.*]

Ches·ter·field /chéstər feeld/ city in eastern Missouri, on the Missouri River; a western suburb of St. Louis. Population: 45,490 (1996).

Ches·ter White *n.* a large white droop-eared hog belonging to a breed developed in Pennsylvania [Mid-19thC. Named for *Chester* County, Pennsylvania.]

chest·nut /chés nùt/ *n.* **1.** (*plural* **-nuts** *or* **-nut**) TREES TREE WITH PRICKLY FRUIT a tree or shrub with long toothed leaves, which bears edible nuts in a prickly burr and is found in North America, Europe, Japan, and China. Genus: *Castanea.* ◊ **water chestnut, American chestnut 2.** FOOD EDIBLE NUT the edible nut of the chestnut tree, which grows inside a prickly burr and has a glossy brown skin **3.** INDUST WOOD the coarse-grained durable wood of a chestnut tree **4.** REDDISH-BROWN HORSE a horse with a reddish-brown color **5.** ANAT CALLUS ON HORSE'S LEG a small hard callus found in several places on the inner surface of a horse's leg. Chestnuts are thought to be vestigial toes. **6.** DEEP BROWN COLOR a deep reddish-brown color **7.** STALE JOKE OR STORY a joke or story that has lost its impact through overuse (*informal*) ■ *adj.* COLORS OF DEEP BROWN COLOR of a deep reddish brown color [Early 16thC. Formed from earlier *chesten*, via Old French *chastaine* from Latin *castanea* (see CASTANET).]

chest·nut blight *n.* a disease with no known cure that kills chestnut trees and is especially destructive to North American chestnuts. It is caused by the fungus *Cryphonectria parasitica* and was probably imported from Asia into the United States in the early 20th century.

chest·nut oak *n.* **1.** N AMERICAN OAK TREE any North American deciduous oak tree whose leaves resemble those of the chestnut, especially one found in eastern North America with shiny yellow leaves. Latin name: *Quercus prinus.* **2.** = **chinquapin oak**

chest of draw·ers *n.* a piece of furniture consisting of a set of drawers in a wooden frame with a flat top, used for storing clothes

chest voice *n.* the lowest register of somebody's speaking or singing voice

chest·y /chéstee/ (**-i·er, -i·est**) *adj.* **1.** WITH LARGE CHEST having a well-developed chest (*informal*) **2.** CONCEITED extremely arrogant and conceited (*informal*) **3.** *U.K.* HAVING PHLEGM IN THE LUNGS showing the effects of a chest complaint, such as phlegm in the lungs —**chest·i·ness** *n.*

Chet·nik /chétnik/ (*plural* **Chet·niks** *or* **Cet·niks**) *n.* a Serbian nationalist who was part of a group who fought the Turks before World War I, and was involved in guerrilla warfare in World War I and World War II [Early 20thC. From Serbo-Croat *četnik*, from *četa* "band, troop."]

chet·rum /chét ro͝om/ (*plural* **-rum** *or* **-rums**) *n.* **1.** MINOR CURRENCY OF BHUTAN a subunit of currency in Bhutan. See table at **currency 2.** COIN WORTH ONE CHETRUM a coin worth one chetrum [Late 20thC. From Tibetan.]

che·val-de-frise /shə vàl də freez/ (*plural* **che·vaux-de-frise** /shə vō-/) *n.* **1.** OBSTACLE MADE OF BARBED WIRE an obstacle consisting of barbed wire or spikes attached to a wooden frame, used to block an advancing enemy force **2.** GLASS OR SPIKES TOPPING WALL a line of jagged glass, nails, or spikes set into masonry on top of a wall to deter intruders [From French, literally "horse of Friesland," in ironic reference to its use by the Friesians, who lacked cavalry, during the siege of Groningen in 1594]

che·val·et /shə vá lày, shèvvə láy/ *n.* the bridge of a bowed musical instrument [Late 19thC. From French, literally "small horse," from *cheval* "horse," from Latin *caballus* (source of English *cavalier* and *chivalry*).]

che·val glass /shə vál-/ *n.* a long mirror that is mounted in a frame so that it can be tilted [From French *cheval* "frame," literally "horse"]

chev·a·lier /shə vállee ày/ *n.* **1.** FRENCH TITLE OF HONOR used as the title of members of the French Legion of Honor and of other orders **2.** FRENCH KNIGHT OR NOBLEMAN a French knight or nobleman of the lowest rank [14thC. Via French from medieval Latin *caballarius*, from Latin *caballus* "horse" (source of English *cavalcade*, *cavalier*, and *cavalry*).]

che·vaux-de-frise plural of **cheval-de-frise**

che·vet /chə váy/ *n.* a complex of elaborate architectural structures at the eastern end of a church, especially a French Gothic church, usually consisting of a semicircular or polygonal apse with radiating chapels and many buttresses [Early 19thC. From French, literally "pillow."]

chèv·re /shévvrə/ *n.* any soft cheese made from goat's milk [Mid-20thC. Via French, "goat" from, ultimately, Latin *capra*, feminine of *caper* "goat" (source of English *caper*[2], *cabriolet*, and *chevron*).]

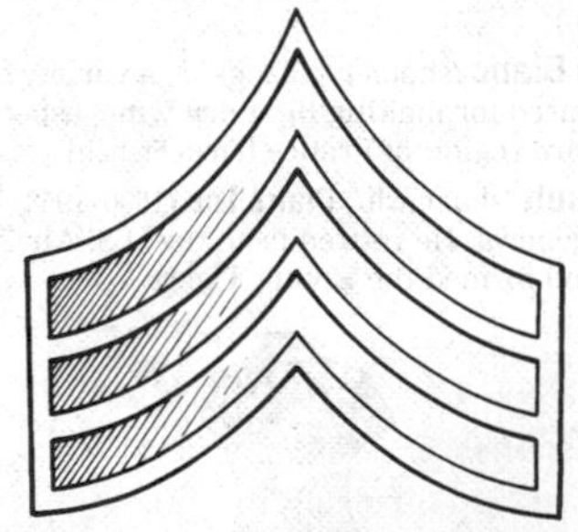

Chevron

chev·ron /shévvrən/ *n.* **1.** V-SHAPED SYMBOL a V-shaped symbol, especially one used as a sign of rank on military or police uniforms **2.** HERALDRY HERALDIC ORNAMENT a heraldic ornament in the form of a wide inverted V-shape [14thC. Via French, "rafter," from, ultimately, Latin *caper* "goat" (source of English *caper*[2] and *chèvre*).]

chev·ro·tain /shévvrə tàyn/ (*plural* **-tains** *or* **-tain**) *n.* a small ruminant animal similar to a deer, native to the rain forests of west central Africa and Southeast Asia. It is hornless and the male has projecting canine teeth. Family: Tragulidae. [Late 18thC. From French, literally "small goat, kid," from *chèvre* (see CHÈVRE).]

chev·y /chévvee/ *v.* = **chivvy**

Chev·y Chase /chèvvi cháyss/ town in Maryland, west of Washington, D.C., on the eastern bank of the Potomac River. Population: 2,218 (1996).

chew /choo/ *v.* (**chewed, chew·ing, chews**) **1.** *vti.* GRIND UP FOOD BEFORE SWALLOWING to grind up food or other material with the action of the teeth and jaws **2.** *vti.* DAMAGE SOMETHING BY BITING to gnaw at something repeatedly, usually causing damage ○ *chewing her nails* **3.** *vi.* CHEW TOBACCO to bite into and chew tobacco ■ *n.* **1.** CANDY a candy with a firm texture, which must be chewed before being swallowed ○ *chocolate chews* **2.** PIECE OF CHEWING TOBACCO a piece of dried tobacco for chewing [Old English *cēowan*, of prehistoric Germanic origin] —**chew·a·ble** *adj.* —**chew·er** *n.*

chew out *vt.* to tell somebody off for doing something wrong (*informal*) ○ *Dad chewed me out because I forgot to take out the garbage.*

chew over *vt.* to think about or discuss something over a period of time ○ *We chewed the problem over for a couple of days before coming to a decision.*

chew up *vt.* **1.** DAMAGE OR DESTROY SOMETHING to damage or destroy something, especially by passing it through machinery (*informal*) ○ *I'm afraid the machine* *chewed up your tape.* **2.** **DESTROY SOMETHING BY BITING** to destroy something by biting or chewing it

Che·wa /cháy waàl/ *n.* a language spoken in Malawi, Zambia, and Mozambique, and belonging to the Bantu group of Niger-Congo languages. There are over eight million Chewa speakers. ◊ **Nyanja** —**Che·wa** *adj.*

chew·ing gum *n.* a sweet flavored substance that is chewed but not swallowed. The elastic ingredient in chewing gum used to be chicle from the sapodilla tree, but synthetic equivalents are now commonly used. ○ *a stick of chewing gum.* ◊ **bubble gum**

chew·ing louse *n.* = **biting louse**

chew·y /chóoee/ (**-i·er, -i·est**) *adj.* having a consistency or texture that requires chewing —**chewi·ness** *n.*

Chey·enne[1] /shī án/ (*plural* **-enne** *or* **-ennes**) *n.* **1.** PEOPLES **MEMBER OF NATIVE AMERICAN PEOPLE** a member of a Native American people who originally occupied lands in western parts of the Great Plains and now live mainly in Oklahoma and Montana. The Cheyenne, along with the Sioux, were instrumental in the defeat of Custer and his forces at the Battle of Little Bighorn. **2.** LANG **CHEYENNE LANGUAGE** the Algonquian language of the Cheyenne people. Cheyenne is spoken by about 2,000 people. [Late 18thC. Via Canadian French from Dakota *šahíyena*.] —**Chey·enne** *adj.*

Chey·enne[2] /shī án/ **1.** river that rises in eastern Wyoming and flows eastward into South Dakota, where it joins the Missouri River. Length: 527 mi./848 km. **2.** city, capital of Wyoming, and county seat of Laramie County, situated in southeastern Wyoming 10 mi./16 km north of the border with Colorado. Population: 53,729 (1996).

Cheyne-Stokes res·pi·ra·tion /chàyn stṓks-/ *n.* an abnormal breathing pattern marked by shallow breathing alternating with periods of rapid heavy breathing, observed especially in comatose patients and often indicating impending death [Late 19thC. Named for the Scottish physician, John *Cheyne* (1777–1836) and the Irish physician, William *Stokes* (1804–78).]

chez /shay/ *prep.* at somebody's home or business premises, especially a restaurant [Mid-18thC. Via French from, ultimately, Latin *casa* "cottage" (source of *casino*, and *chasuble*).]

chg. *abbr.* **1.** change **2.** charge

chi[1] /kī/ (*plural* **chis**) *n.* the 22nd letter of the Greek alphabet, represented in English as "ch" or "kh." [15thC. From Greek *khi*.]

chi[2] /chee/, **ch'i, Chi, Ch'i, qi, Qi** *n.* in Chinese medicine and philosophy, the energy or life force of the universe, believed to flow round the body and to be present in all living things. The manipulation of chi is the basis of acupuncture and Chinese martial arts. [From Chinese *qì*]

Chiang Ching-kuo /chàng ching kwṓ/ (1910–88) Taiwanese political leader. He was president of Taiwan (1978–88) and initiated many economic, social, and political reforms.

Chiang Kai-shek

Chiang Kai-shek /chàng kī shék/ (1887–1975) Chinese military leader and statesman. He helped to overthrow the imperial government (1912) and developed Taiwan's economy as its president (1949–75).

Chi·an·ti /kee àantee/, **chi·an·ti** *n.* a light Italian red wine produced mainly from the Sangiovese grape in Tuscany in northwestern Italy [Mid-19thC. Named for the *Chianti* Mountains in Tuscany.]

Chi·a·pas /chee àapəss/ state in southeastern Mexico. Capital: Tuxtla Gutiérrez. Population: 3,654,000 (1993). Area: 28,528 sq. mi./73,887 sq. km.

chi·a·ro·scu·ro /kee àarə skóor ō/ *n.* the use of light and shade in paintings and drawings, or the effect produced by this [Mid-17thC. From Italian, literally "bright-dark," from *chiaro* "bright, clear" + *oscuro* "dark."] —**chi·a·ro·scu·rism** *n.* —**chi·a·ro·scu·rist** *n.*

chi·as·ma /kī ázmə/ (*plural* **-mas** *or* **-ma·ta** /-zmətə/) *n.* **1.** ANAT **CROSSING OVER OF BODY PARTS** any crossing over of biological tissue, e.g., the intersection of the optic nerves **2.** GENETICS **CROSSING POINT OF CHROMOSOME PARTS** the point at which two chromatids join during the fusion and exchange of genetic material (**crossing-over**) in cell division [Mid-19thC. Via modern Latin from Greek *khiasma* "crosspiece," from *khiazein* "to mark with an X," from *khi* "the letter chi."] —**chi·as·mal** *adj.* —**chi·as·mic** *adj.*

chi·as·mus /kī ázməss/ (*plural* **-mi** /-mī/) *n.* a rhetorical construction in which the order of the words in the second of two paired phrases is the reverse of the order in the first. An example is "gray was the morn, all things were gray." [Mid-17thC. Via modern Latin from Greek *khiasmos*, from *khiazein* (see CHIASMA).]

chi·as·to·lite /kī ástə līt/ *n.* a variety of the mineral andalusite that contains carbon impurities arranged in an X-shape [Early 19thC. Coined from Greek *khiastos* "marked with an X" (the past participle of *khiazein*; see CHIASMA) + -LITE.]

Chi·ba /chée baàl/ capital city of Chiba Prefecture, situated on the eastern shore of Tokyo Bay in Honshu, Japan. Population: 839,000 (1994).

Chib·cha /chíbchə/ (*plural* **-cha** *or* **-chas**) *n.* **1.** PEOPLES **MEMBER OF EXTINCT S AMERICAN PEOPLE** a member of an extinct Native South American people who lived in the Andes Mountains in the center of Colombia. The Chibcha died out following their defeat by the Spanish conquistador, Gonzalo Jeménez de Quesada, in the 1530s. **2.** LANG **LANGUAGE OF CHIBCHA** the extinct Chibchan language of the Chibcha [Early 19thC. Via American Spanish from Chibcha *zipa* "chief, hereditary leader."]

Chib·chan /chíbchən/ (*plural* **-chan** *or* **-chans**) *n.* **1.** **GROUP OF NATIVE CENTRAL AMERICAN LANGUAGES** a group of Native Central American languages spoken in Colombia and Panama. About 100,000 people speak a Chibchan language. **2.** **SOMEBODY WHO SPEAKS CHIBCHAN LANGUAGE** a member of any of the peoples who speak a language belonging to the Chibchan group —**Chib·chan** *adj.*

Chi·bou·gam·au /shi bóogə mṑ/ town in Abitibi County, southwestern Quebec, Canada, situated 150 mi./241 km northwest of Roberval. Population: 8,855 (1991).

chic /sheek/ *adj.* **STYLISH** stylish and elegant ■ *n.* **STYLE** fashionable style or elegance [Mid-19thC. From French, of uncertain origin: probably from German *Schick* "skill, elegance."] —**chic·ness** *n.*

Chi·ca·go /shi kaágō/ **1.** city and port in northeastern Illinois, situated on Lake Michigan. It is the third largest city in the United States. Population: 2,731,743 (1994). **2.** short river in Chicago, Illinois, formed in the city by the confluence of the South Branch. Length: 10 mi./16 km. —**Chi·ca·go·an** *n., adj.*

Chi·ca·go Board of Trade *n.* a major commodities exchange in Chicago that deals in grain and metal futures

Chi·ca·go Heights city in northeastern Illinois; a southern suburb of Chicago. Population: 31,899 (1996).

Chi·ca·na /chi kaánə/ (*plural* **-nas**) *n.* a North American woman or girl of Mexican descent [Mid-20thC. From Spanish, feminine of *Chicano* (see CHICANO).]

chi·cane[1] /shi káyn/ *n.* **1.** MOTOR SPORTS **SHARP BEND ON CAR RACING CIRCUIT** in car racing, a sharp double bend created by placing barriers on the circuit **2.** CARDS **HAND WITH NO TRUMPS** a bridge or whist hand without trumps or without cards of one suit [Late 19thC. From French, formed from *chicaner* see CHICANE[2].]

chi·cane[2] /shi káyn/ (**-caned, -can·ing, -canes**) *vi.* to practice chicanery [Late 17thC. From French *chicaner* "to quibble, pursue at law," of unknown origin.] —**chi·can·er** *n.*

chi·can·er·y /shi káynəree/ (*plural* **-ies**) *n.* deception or trickery, especially by the clever manipulation of language

Chi·ca·no /chi kaánō/ (*plural* **-nos**) *n.* a North American man or boy of Mexican descent [Mid-20thC. From American Spanish, a variant of Spanish *mexicano* "Mexican," from *México* "Mexico."]

Chi·che·wa /chi cháywə/ *n., adj.* = **Chewa**

chi·chi /sheeshee/ *adj.* trying too hard or too obviously to be chic or modish (*disapproving*) ○ *All this designer furniture – isn't it just a bit chichi?* [Mid-20thC. From French.]

chick /chik/ *n.* **1.** **BABY BIRD** a young bird, especially a young chicken **2.** **YOUNG WOMAN** an attractive girl or young woman (*slang*) (*considered offensive by some speakers*) [14thC. Shortening of CHICKEN.]

chick·a·dee /chíkə dee/ (*plural* **-dees** *or* **-dee**) *n.* a small North American titmouse with a distinctive call. It has gray plumage and a darker-colored crown on its head. Genus: *Parus.* [Mid-19thC. An imitation of the bird's call.]

Chick·a·hom·i·ny /chìkə hómmənee/ river in east central Virginia, rising northwest of Richmond. Length: 90 mi./145 km.

chick·a·ree /chíkə rèe/ (*plural* **-rees** *or* **-ree**) *n.* a squirrel of western North America, related to the red squirrel. Latin name: *Tamiascurus douglasi.* [Early 19thC. An imitation of the animal's cry.]

Chick·a·saw /chíkə sàw/ (*plural* **-saw** *or* **-saws**) *n.* **1.** PEOPLES **MEMBER OF NATIVE AMERICAN PEOPLE** a member of a Native American people who originally occupied lands in northeastern Mississippi and northwestern Alabama, and now live mainly in southern and central Oklahoma. The Chickasaw were one of the Five Civilized Nations who were sent to live on reservations in Oklahoma under the Removal Act of 1830. **2.** LANG **CHICKASAW LANGUAGE** the Muskogean language of the Chickasawpeople. Chickasaw is spoken by approximately 10,000 people. [Late 17thC. From Chickasaw *čikaša*.] —**Chick·a·saw** *adj.*

chick·en /chíkən/ *n.* **1.** **COMMON DOMESTIC FOWL** a domestic fowl, usually with brown or black feathers and a fleshy crest on its head, raised for its meat and eggs. Latin name: *Gallus domesticus.* ◊ **spring chicken** **2.** **MEAT FROM CHICKENS** meat obtained from chickens **3.** **COWARD** a cowardly or timid person (*informal*) ○ *You'll never do it – you're a chicken!* ■ *adj.* **COWARDLY** showing a lack of courage (*informal*) ○ *Are you too chicken to do a high dive?* [Old English *cīcen* (related to Dutch *kuiken*). Ultimately from a prehistoric Germanic word related to the ancestor of English *cock*.] ◇ **a chicken-and-egg situation** a situation in which it is impossible to know which of two related circumstances occurred first and caused the other ○ *Stress causes mistakes, and mistakes cause stress: it's a chicken-and-egg situation.*

WORD KEY: SYNONYMS

See Synonyms at ***cowardly.***

chicken out (chickened out, chickening out, chickens out) *vi.* to fail in or withdraw from something because of a lack of nerve (*slang*)

chick·en breast *n.* = **pigeon breast** —**chick·en-breasted** *adj.*

chick·en feed *n.* **1.** **FOOD FOR POULTRY** food for poultry **2.** **INSIGNIFICANT AMOUNT** an insignificant amount, especially an insignificant sum of money (*informal*)

chick·en-fried steak *n.* a cut of beef, usually round steak, that has been tenderized, dredged in flour, and then pan-fried

chick·en hawk *n.* **1.** **HAWK** a hawk that preys or is believed to prey on poultry **2.** **OFFENSIVE TERM** an offensive term for an older man who seeks young boys as sexual partners (*slang taboo*)

chick·en·head *n.* a protrusion from a rock face useful in providing a handhold for rock climbing

chick·en-heart·ed *adj.* easily frightened or lacking sufficient courage, boldness, or confidence (*insult*) —**chick·en-heart·ed·ness** *n.*

Chick·en Lit·tle *n.* somebody who constantly warns of impending danger that does not exist ○ *We won't get anywhere if we listen to the Chicken Littles among us.* [From the hen in the traditional story that told everyone the sky was falling, when she had been hit on the head by a falling acorn]

chick·en-liv·ered *adj.* = **chicken-hearted**

chick·en·pox /chíkən pòks/ *n.* a highly infectious viral disease, especially affecting children, characterized by a rash of small itching blisters on the skin and mild fever. Technical name **varicella** [Mid-18thC. Possibly so called because it is so much weaker than SMALLPOX.]

chick·en·shit /chíkən shìt/ *n.* **1.** PETTY DETAILS OR TASKS petty or tedious details or tasks (*slang offensive*) **2.** COWARD somebody who is cowardly or timid (*slang or offensive*) ■ *adj.* (*slang offensive*) **1.** PETTY petty or unimportant **2.** COWARDLY cowardly or frightened

chick·en snake *n.* = **rat snake**

chick·en wire *n.* a lightweight flexible galvanized wire fencing, usually made with a hexagonal mesh [From the use of the wire as a fence for enclosing chickens]

chick·pea /chík pèe/ *n.* **1.** YELLOW EDIBLE SEED an edible pale yellow seed about the size of a large pea. Chickpeas are the main ingredient of hummus. **2.** CHICKPEA PLANT an annual plant on which chickpeas grow, cultivated in Asia and Mediterranean regions. Latin name: *Cicer arietinum.* [Early 18thC. Alteration of earlier *chich pease*, via French *chiche* from Latin *cicer*, still the botanical Latin name for the plant.]

chick·weed /chík wèed/ *n.* a common European weed of cultivated land that produces small white flowers all year round. Latin name: *Stellaria media.* [*Chick* from the fact that chickens eat the plant]

chic·le /chík'l/ *n.* a gummy substance from the latex of the sapodilla tree, used as the main ingredient of chewing gum [Late 19thC. Via American Spanish from Nahuatl *tzictli*.] —**chic·ly** *adj.*

Chi·co /chéekō/ city in northern California, northwest of Sacramento, in the valley of the Sacramento River. Population: 45,965 (1996).

Chi·co·pee /chíkə pèe/ city in southwestern Massachusetts, at the junction of Chicopee River and the Connecticut River. Population: 54,532 (1996).

chic·o·ry /chíkəree/ (*plural* **-ries**) *n.* **1.** PLANT CULTIVATED FOR LEAVES AND ROOTS a perennial plant with blue flowers, native to Europe and northern Africa and naturalized in North America. It is cultivated for its leaves and roots. Latin name: *Cichorium intybus.* **2.** = **endive 3.** GROUND ROASTED ROOT OF CHICORY the dried, roasted, and ground root of the chicory plant, used as a coffee additive or substitute [15thC. Via obsolete French *cicoré* "endive."]

Chi·cou·ti·mi /she kóotə mèe/ river in Quebec, Canada, flowing from Laurentides Provincial Park to Lake Kenogami and the Saguenay. Length: 100 mi./160 km.

chide /chīd/ (**chid** /chid/ *or* **chid·ed, chid** /chid/ *or* **chid·den** /chídd'n/ *or* **chid·ed, chid·ing, chides**) *vti.* to reproach or scold somebody gently (*dated or literary*) [Old English *cidan*, of unknown origin] —**chid·er** *n.* —**chid·ing·ly** *adv.*

chief /cheef/ *n.* **1.** LEADER the person with the most authority or highest rank in a group or an organization, who ultimately controls or commands all the others **2.** ANTHROP CHIEFTAIN the leader or titular head of a people or group **3.** BOSS a supervisor, manager, or other person in authority, especially in the workplace (*informal*) **4.** NAUT CHIEF PETTY OFFICER a chief petty officer (*informal*) **5.** NAUT SHIP'S PRINCIPAL ENGINEER the principal engineer on a ship **6.** HERALDRY TOP SECTION OF HERALDIC SHIELD the upper third of the surface area of a heraldic shield ■ *adj.* **1.** MOST IMPORTANT most important, basic, or common **2.** HIGHEST IN AUTHORITY highest in authority, position, or rank [13thC. Via French *chef* from, ultimately, Latin *caput* "head" (source of English *achieve, capital* and *captain*).] —**chief·ship** *n.*

chief con·sta·ble *n. U.K.* in Britain, the police officer in overall command of a regional police force

chief·dom /chéefdəm/ *n.* **1.** STATE OF BEING CHIEF the position, rank, or status of a chief **2.** CHIEF'S PEOPLE OR TERRITORY the people or territory over which a chief rules **3.** POLITICAL SYSTEM a centralized political system with authority vested in formal, often hereditary, offices or titles

chief ex·ec·u·tive *n.* **1.** HEAD OF EXECUTIVE BODY the principal and highest-ranking member of an executive body, e.g., the head of a government or the governor of a U.S. state **2.** HIGHEST-RANKING EXECUTIVE the executive director of a business or similar organization who holds the highest rank and has overall responsibility for its day-to-day management **3.** U.S. PRESIDENT the president of the United States

chief ex·ec·u·tive of·fi·cer *n.* the highest-ranking executive officer within a company or corporation, who has responsibility for overall management of its day-to-day affairs under the supervision of the board of directors

chief jus·tice *n.* **1.** PRESIDING JUDGE a judge who presides over a court that has several judges, especially the Supreme Court of the United States **2.** SENIOR JUDGE the senior judge in the High Courts of Australia and other Commonwealth countries

chief·ly /chéeflee/ *adv.* **1.** ABOVE ALL above all, especially, or most importantly ○ *We moved to this area of the city chiefly because it's convenient for getting to work.* **2.** IN THE MAIN for the most part ○ *The human body consists chiefly of water.* ■ *adj.* RELATING TO CHIEFS belonging or relating to chiefs, or befitting a chief

chief mas·ter ser·geant *n.* a noncommissioned officer in the U.S. Air Force ranking below a chief warrant officer and above a senior master sergeant

chief of na·val op·er·a·tions *n.* a senior officer in the U.S. Navy who serves as the representative of that military organization to the Joint Chiefs of Staff

Chief of Smoke *n.* a noncommissioned officer in charge of laying and firing the guns in an artillery battery

chief of staff *n.* **1.** SENIOR RANKING OFFICER a high-ranking officer in the U.S. Army or Air Force who is a member of the U.S. Joint Chiefs of Staff **2.** SENIOR STAFF OFFICER the senior officer serving on a military staff, who has responsibility for managing it and for advising the commander

chief of state *n.* somebody who is the formal head of a nation, such as a president or monarch, as distinct from the head of a government

chief pet·ty of·fi·cer *n.* **1.** NONCOMMISSIONED OFFICER IN U.S. NAVY a noncommissioned officer ranking below senior chief petty officer in the U.S. Navy or Coast Guard **2.** NONCOMMISSIONED OFFICER IN CANADIAN NAVY the highest-ranking noncommissioned officer in the navy of Canada. The first class of chief petty officer is equivalent in rank to a chief warrant officer in the army or air force, the second class to a master warrant officer.

Chief Rab·bi *n.* the senior religious leader of the Jewish community in Great Britain and in some other countries

chief·tain /chéeftən/ *n.* the leader or titular head of a people or similar group [13thC. From Old French *chevetaine*, alteration (influenced by *chef* "leader") of late Latin *capitaneus*, from Latin *capt-*, stem of *caput* "head" (see CAPTAIN).] —**chief·tain·cy** *n.* —**chief·tain·ship** *n.*

chief war·rant of·fi·cer *n.* **1.** U.S. NAVY OFFICER a commissioned officer ranking immediately below an ensign or second lieutenant in the U.S. Navy or Coast Guard **2.** CANADIAN OFFICER the highest-ranking noncommissioned officer in the army or air force of Canada, equivalent in rank to a chief petty officer, first class, in the navy

chiff·chaff /chíf chàf/ *n.* a small grayish yellow Eurasian bird that has a characteristic repetitive song. Latin name: *Phylloscopus collybita.* [Late 18thC. An imitation of the bird's call.]

chif·fon /shi fón, shí fòn/ *n.* **1.** TEXTILES FABRIC a very light thin sheer plain-woven fabric of nylon, rayon, or silk **2.** ACCESSORIES CLOTHING ACCESSORIES decorative accessories for women, e.g., laces or ribbons (*often used in the plural*) ■ *adj.* **1.** TEXTILES MADE OF CHIFFON made of chiffon, or resembling it in lightness and fineness **2.** COOK HAVING A FLUFFY TEXTURE having a light fluffy texture, usually created by adding whipped egg whites or gelatin [Mid-18thC. From French, from *chiffe* "rag, flimsy stuff."]

chif·fon·ade /shìffə náyd, sh'iffə naád/ *n.* vegetables that have been shredded or finely chopped, often used as a garnish for other foods [Late 19thC. From French.]

chif·fo·nier /shìffə néer/ *n.* a relatively tall narrow chest of drawers that often has a mirror attached to the back [Mid-18thC. From French. Originally "rag-picker, collector of scraps," later "piece of furniture for storing sewing and offcuts of fabric."]

chif·fo·robe /shíffə rŏb/, **chif·fe·robe** /shíff rŏb/, **chiff·robe** *n.* a tall piece of furniture with drawers and a hanging space for clothes (*dated*) [Early 20thC. Blend of CHIFFONIER and WARDROBE.]

chi·ge·tai /chíggə tī/, **dzig·ge·tai** /zíggə-/ *n.* a wild ass related to the onager and native to Mongolia. Latin name: *Equus hemionus.* [Late 18thC. From Mongolian *chikitei*, literally "having ears," from *chiki* "ear."]

Chifforobe

chig·ger /chíggər/ *n.* **1.** PARASITIC LARVA a parasitic larva of a mite that sucks the blood of humans and other vertebrates, causing severe itching of the skin. It is widely known in the southern United States. Family: Trombiculidae. **2.** = **chigoe** *n.* 1 [Mid-18thC. From earlier CHIGOE.]

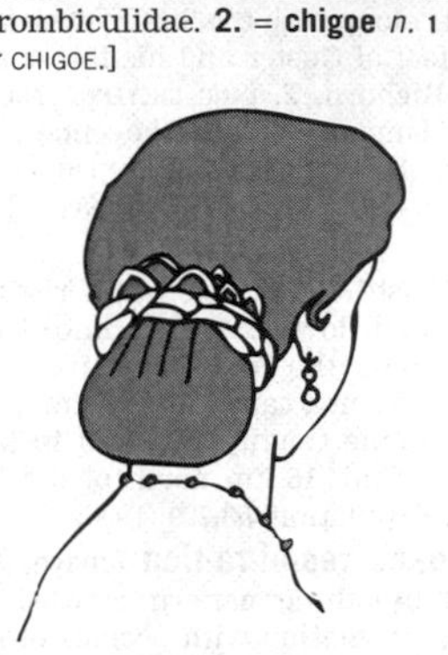

Chignon

chi·gnon /shéen yòn, sheen yón/ *n.* a knot or roll of hair, especially when worn at the nape of the neck [Late 18thC. From French, "nape of the neck, chain," from, ultimately, Latin *catena* "chain" (source of English *concatenation*).]

chig·oe /chíggō, chéegō/ *n.* **1.** TROPICAL FLEA THAT BURROWS INTO SKIN a small tropical flea, the fertilized female of which burrows under the skin causing painful itching sores that easily become infected. Latin name: *Tunga penetrans.* **2.** = **chigger** *n.* 1 [Mid-17thC. Via French *chique* from a West African language.]

chi·hua·hua /chə waá waá, chə waáwə/ *n.* a very small dog belonging to a breed originally from Mexico that has pointed ears, protruding eyes, and a tiny body with a disproportionately large head [Early 19thC. Named for CHIHUAHUA.]

Chi·hua·hua /chə waá waa, shə-/ *n.* **1.** state in northern Mexico. Capital: Chihuahua. Population: 2,792,989 (1995). Area: 95,401 sq. mi./247,087 sq. km. **2.** city and capital of Chihuahua state in northern Mexico. Population: 530,487 (1990).

Chi·hua·huan Des·ert /chə waá wən-, shə-/ the largest desert in North America, extending into parts of New Mexico, Texas, and sections of southeastern Arizona. Area: 200,000 sq. mi./518,000 sq. km.

Chi·ka·ma·tsu /chéekə maát sòo/, **Monzemon** (1653–1724) Japanese playwright. He is known for his historical romances and domestic tragedies written for the kabuki theater and *bunraku* puppet theater.

chil·blain /chíl blàyn/ *n.* a red itchy swelling on the ears, fingers, or toes, caused by exposure to damp and cold (*often used in the plural*) [Mid-16thC. From CHILL + BLAIN.] —**chil·blained** *adj.*

child /chīld/ (*plural* **chil·dren** /chíldrən/) *n.* **1.** YOUNG HUMAN BEING a young human being between birth and puberty **2.** HUMAN OFFSPRING a son or daughter of human parents **3.** SOMEBODY NOT YET OF AGE somebody under a legally specified age who is considered not to be legally responsible for his or her actions **4.** BABY a baby or infant **5.** UNBORN BABY an unborn baby **6.** IMMATURE PERSON an adult who behaves in a childish or childlike way **7.** PRODUCT OR RESULT somebody or something considered to be either produced or strongly influenced by a particular environment, period, or historical figure ○ *a child of nature* ○ *a child of the 1960s* **8.** DESCENDANT OR MEMBER OF A PEOPLE a descendant of somebody, or a member of a people founded by somebody (*often used in the plural*) [Old

English *cīld*, of uncertain origin] ◇ **with child** pregnant (*archaic or literary*)

Child /chīld/, **Lydia Maria** (1802–80) U.S. abolitionist, suffrage campaigner, and writer. She wrote *The History of the Condition of Women in Various Ages and Nations* (1835) and edited the *National Anti-Slavery Standard* (1840–49).

child a·buse *n.* severe mistreatment of a child by a parent, guardian, or other adult responsible for his or her welfare, including physical violence, neglect, sexual assault, or emotional cruelty —**child a·bus·er** *n.*

child·bear·ing /chīld bàiring/ *n.* the process of carrying a child in the womb and giving birth to it ○ *Her childbearing years are over.*

child·bed /chīld bèd/ *n.* the state of a woman in the process of giving birth to a child (*archaic*)

child·bed fe·ver *n.* MED puerperal sepsis (*archaic*)

child ben·e·fit *n. U.K.* in the U.K. and New Zealand, a regular payment made by the state to parents toward the maintenance of each child in a family below a certain age

child·birth /chīld bùrth/ *n.* the act or process of giving birth to a child ○ *natural childbirth methods*

child·care /chīld kàir/ *n.* the care and supervision of children by an adult, inside or outside the home and usually for pay, during times when the parents or guardians are at work

child-cen·tered *adj.* adapted to the needs and concerns of children as opposed to adults

childe /chīld/ (*plural* **childes**) *n.* a young person of noble birth (*archaic*) [Variant of CHILD]

Chil·der·mas /chíldərmass/ *n.* the religious holiday of Holy Innocents' Day (*archaic*) [Old English *cildramæsse*, from *childra* "of children" + *mæsse* "mass"]

child·hood /chīld hòod/ *n.* **1.** SOMEBODY'S EARLIEST YEARS the state of being a child, or the period of somebody's life when he or she is a child ○ *heard wonderful stories about her childhood.* **2.** EARLY STAGE an early period or stage in the development or existence of something ○ *Interplanetary travel is still in its childhood.*

child·ish /chīldish/ *adj.* **1.** IMMATURE showing a lack of emotional restraint, seriousness, good sense, maturity, or similar adult qualities ○ *I don't have time for your childish tantrums.* **2.** SOMEWHAT LIKE A CHILD like that of a child, or suitable for a child ○ *a childish voice* —**child·ish·ly** *adv.* —**child·ish·ness** *n.*

child la·bor *n.* the full-time employment of children, especially of those who are legally too young to work

child·less /chīldləss/ *adj.* not having had a child or children —**child·less·ness** *n.*

child·like /chīld līk/ *adj.* like a child, especially in having a sweet innocent unspoiled quality ○ *childlike innocence*

WORD KEY: USAGE

childish or **childlike**? Both words are used to describe people or behavior that have qualities associated with children. The difference is that ***childlike*** is complimentary and even affectionate, whereas **childish** is a dismissive and disapproving term. *She spoke with a childlike directness about her holiday. His reaction to the criticism was childish and resentful.*

child mind·er *n. U.K.* somebody who is employed to look after other people's children, especially when the parents or guardians are working —**child mind·ing** *n.*

child prod·i·gy *n.* a child who possesses extraordinary abilities or talents, often equal to those of adults

child·proof /chīld pròof/ *adj.* **1.** HARD FOR A CHILD TO OPEN designed to be difficult for children to open, tamper with, damage, or break **2.** MADE SAFE FOR CHILDREN made safe for young children to use or be in, e.g., through the removal of potential dangers and addition of extra safety devices ○ *Parents with toddlers should have at least one childproof room.* ■ *vt.* (**-proofed, -proof·ing, -proofs**) MAKE SOMETHING SAFE FOR CHILDREN to make something safe for children to use, or safe against damage or tampering by children ○ *You'll need to childproof your house before the baby is born.*

child pro·tec·tive serv·ic·es *npl.* a government agency charged with the supervision and protection of children at risk, specifically from abuse and neglect, or the supervision and protection administered by it

chil·dren plural of **child**

WORD KEY: CULTURAL NOTE

The Man Who Loved Children, a novel by Australian writer, Christina Stead (1891). Through the story of the stormy domestic life of Sam and Henny Pollitt and their six children, Stead examines the ways in which human beings attempt, and often fail, to communicate with one other.

child re·straint *n.* a seat belt or detachable seat designed to protect a child traveling in a vehicle or a plane

child seat *n.* a legally mandated detachable seat with a harness, attached to a car seat, used to protect a child too small to wear an adult seat belt

child's play *n.* something that is very straightforward for somebody to do ○ *Skiing these slopes will be child's play for her.*

child sup·port *n.* a sum of money paid regularly or in a lump sum by a divorced person to maintain the normal standard of living of his or her children

child tax ben·e·fit *n.* in Canada, an allowance or tax-free benefit given by the federal government or the province of Quebec to assist parents in the expense of rearing children below a specified age

chil·e /chíllee/ *n.* a chili pepper (*regional*) [Variant of CHILI]

Chile

Chil·e /chíllee, chee lày/ republic in southwestern South America bordered by Peru, Bolivia, Argentina, the Drake Passage, and the Pacific Ocean. Language: Spanish. Currency: peso. Capital: Santiago. Population: 14,508,131 (1997). Area: 292,135 sq. mi./756,626 sq. km. Official name **Republic of Chile** —**Chil·e·an** /chíllee ən/ *n., adj.*

Chil·e ni·ter *n.* CHEM = **Chile saltpeter**

Chil·e pine *n.* TREES = **monkey-puzzle**

Chil·e salt·pe·ter *n.* a form of sodium nitrate that occurs naturally in arid regions, especially in Chile and Peru. Formula: $NaNO_3$.

chil·i /chíllee/ (*plural* **-ies**) *n.* **1.** POD WITH STRONG FLAVOR a narrow, tapering, usually red or green pod, produced by various types of capsicum pepper plant. Chilies have a very hot taste and are used for flavoring sauces and relishes. **2.** = **chili powder 3.** = **chili sauce 4.** = **chili con carne** [Early 17thC. Via Spanish *chile* and *chili* from Nahuatl *chilli.*]

chil·i·asm /kíllee àzzəm/ *n.* = **millenarianism** [Early 17thC. From Greek *khiliasmos*, from *khilias* (stem *khiliad-*), from *khilioi* "one thousand."] —**chil·i·ast** *n.* —**chil·i·as·tic** /kìllee ástik/ *adj.*

chil·i·bur·ger /chílli bùrgər/ *n.* a hamburger served topped with chili con carne

chil·i con car·ne *n.* a highly spiced dish, originally a trail meal for Texas cowboys, made of chunks of meat, seasoned with chilies or chili powder [From American Spanish, literally "chili with meat"]

chil·i·dog /chílli dòg/ *n.* a hot dog topped with chili

chil·i pep·per *n.* = **chili** *n.* 1

chil·i pow·der *n.* a seasoning consisting of ground chilies blended with several other seasonings, such as cumin, garlic, and oregano, often added to a dish to give it a hot taste

chil·i sauce *n.* a highly spiced sauce made with tomatoes, ground dried chilies, and other seasonings

Chil·kat blan·ket /chíl kat-/ *n. Northwest U.S., Can* among Native American peoples of the Pacific Northwest coast of North America, a blanket woven from mountain goat hair with a warp of shredded cedar bark, worn on ceremonial occasions [*Chilkat* from the name of an Aboriginal people of Canada]

Chil·koot Pass /chílkoot-/ pass in the coastal range of the northern Rocky Mountains, Canada. Height: 3,502 ft./1,067 m.

chill /chil/ *n.* **1.** MODERATE COLDNESS a moderate but often unpleasant degree of coldness ○ *a chill in the air* **2.** MED SUDDEN SHORT FEVER a sudden short fever with shivering and a sensation of coldness **3.** COLDNESS CAUSED BY FEAR a sudden shuddering feeling of coldness caused by fear, anxiety, or excitement ○ *felt a chill run down my spine* **4.** DEPRESSING EFFECT a depressing or dampening effect on people or on an occasion ○ *The news cast a chill over the party.* **5.** LACK OF WARMTH an emotional coldness or unfriendliness in the atmosphere or in somebody's manner **6.** METALL MOLD USED IN CASTING METAL a mold made of a highly conductive material such as iron, used to achieve a rapid even cooling of the material being cast. The chill may be watercooled to accelerate the cooling. ■ **chills** *npl.* FEELING OF ATTRACTION a feeling of attraction to somebody ○ *That movie star just gives me chills!* ■ *adj.* **1.** MODERATELY COLD moderately cold, but usually cold enough to be unpleasant **2.** EMOTIONALLY COLD showing no friendliness or emotional warmth ■ *v.* (**chilled, chill·ing, chills**) **1.** *vt.* MAKE SOMEBODY OR SOMETHING COLD to make somebody or something become cold, usually unpleasantly cold ○ *I was sitting in a freezing draft that chilled me to the bone.* **2.** *vti.* COOL OR FREEZE FOOD to cool food or drink, or be left to cool, in a refrigerator **3.** *vt.* BE DISCOURAGING TO SOMEBODY OR SOMETHING to have a discouraging or dampening effect on somebody or something **4.** *vi.* = **chill out** (*slang*) **5.** *vti.* METALL HARDEN METAL OR BECOME HARD to harden a metal surface, or become hard, by rapid cooling [Old English *ciele*, from a prehistoric Germanic word that is also the ancestor of English *cold*] —**chill·ness** *n.*

chill out *vi.* (*slang*) **1.** CALM DOWN to stop being angry or tense **2.** RELAX to spend time relaxing

Chil·lán /chī yaán/ city in the Bío-Bío Region of central Chile, situated 56 mi./90 km northeast of Concepción. Population: 145,759 (1992).

chill·er /chíllər/ *n.* **1.** REFRIGERATED COMPARTMENT a refrigerated cooling or storage compartment **2.** FRIGHTENING MOVIE OR STORY a frightening movie or story (*slang*)

chill fac·tor *n.* METEOROL = **windchill factor**

chil·li *n.* U.K. = **chili**

Chil·li·cothe /chìllə kóthee, -káw-/ city in southern Ohio, directly south of Columbus, on the banks of the Scioto River. Population: 21,954 (1996).

chill·ing /chílling/ *adj.* causing a feeling of dread or horror ○ *a chilling account of his capture* —**chill·ing·ly** *adv.*

chil·lum /chílləm/ *n.* **1.** HASHISH PIPE a short straight pipe, usually made of clay, for smoking hashish, marijuana, or tobacco **2.** QUANTITY OF MARIJUANA OR TOBACCO a quantity of marijuana, hashish, or tobacco to be smoked [Late 18thC. From Hindi *chilam.*]

chill·y /chíllee/ (**-i·er, -i·est**) *adj.* **1.** MODERATELY COLD moderately or noticeably cold, usually enough to cause discomfort ○ *Bring a sweater to the park; it'll be chilly later.* **2.** FEELING COLD feeling cold enough to be uncomfortable **3.** UNFRIENDLY unfriendly or hostile ○ *a chilly reception* —**chill·i·ly** *adv.* —**chill·i·ness** *n.*

chi·lo·pod /kīlə pòd/ *n.* any of a group of arthropods that includes the centipedes (*technical*) [Mid-19thC. From modern Latin *Chilopoda*, from Greek *kheilos* "lip" + -POD.]

Chi·lung /jee lóong/ seaport in northern Taiwan, one of the two ports of the capital, Taipei. Population: 356,501 (1992). Former name **Kirun**

chi·mae·ra /kī meérə, ki-/ *n.* **1.** (*plural* **-ras** *or* **-ra**) DEEP-SEA FISH a deep-sea fish with a skeleton of cartilage, a smooth-skinned tapering body, and a tail that resembles a whip. Family: Chimaeridae. **2.** GENETICS = **chimera** [Early 19thC. From Latin (see CHIMERA).]

Chi·mae·ra /kī meérə, ki-/ *n.* = **Chimera**

Chim·bo·ra·zo /chìmbə raázō/ mountain peak in central Ecuador, and the highest point in the Cordillera Real. Height: 20,702 ft./6,310 m.

chime[1] /chīm/ *n.* **1.** SOUND OF BELL the musical ringing sound made by a bell or bells, or a similar sound made by some other object such as a doorbell **2.** DEVICE FOR STRIKING BELL a device for striking a bell or a set of bells in order to make a musical sound or play a tune (*often used in the plural*) **3.** MUSIC PERCUSSION INSTRUMENT one of a set of hanging bells, metal bars, or tubes tuned to a scale, used to produce a musical sound when struck **4.** NOTES SOUNDED BY A CLOCK a series of musical notes sounded by a clock before striking **5.** = **wind chime 6.** HARMONY an agreement or harmony among people or things (*literary*) ■ *v.* (**chimed, chim·ing, chimes**) **1.** *vi.* RING HARMONIOUSLY to make a harmonious ringing sound ○ *Did you hear the bells chiming?* **2.** *vt.* INDICATE SOMETHING BY CHIMING to indicate something, especially the time, by chiming ○ *The clock chimed three o'clock.* **3.** *vt.* PRODUCE MUSICAL SOUND to strike a bell or bells so as to produce a musical sound **4.** *vi.* HARMONIZE to harmonize or be in agreement with something else ○ *It was nice to find that her opinion chimed so perfectly with my own.* **5.** *vti.* SPEAK IN MUSICAL WAY to say or read something aloud in a rhythmical or musical way [13thC. Of uncertain origin: perhaps from Old French *chimbe*, from, ultimately, Latin *cymbalum* (see CYMBAL).] —**chim·er** *n.*

chime in *vi.* **1.** INTERRUPT OTHER PEOPLE'S CONVERSATION to interrupt or join in a conversation between other people, especially in order to voice an opinion **2.** COMBINE HARMONIOUSLY to agree or combine harmoniously with something else

chime[2] /chīm/ *n.* an edge or lip around the rim of a barrel or cask [14thC. Origin uncertain: probably from assumed Old English *cim*.]

chi·me·ra /kī meérə, ki-/, **chi·mae·ra** *n.* **1.** SOMETHING TOTALLY UNREALISTIC OR IMPRACTICAL a figment of the imagination, e.g., a wildly unrealistic idea or hope or a completely impractical plan **2.** GENETICS ORGANISM WITH GENETICALLY DIFFERENT TISSUES an organism, or part of one, with at least two genetically different tissues resulting from mutation, the grafting of plants, or the insertion of foreign cells into an embryo **3.** EMBRYOL ORGANISM WITH DNA FROM DIFFERENT SOURCES an organism that has genetic material from a variety of sources as a result of the insertion of unspecialized cells (**stem cells**) from other species into an embryo [See CHIMERA] —**chi·mer·ism** *n.*

Chi·me·ra /kī meérə, ki-/ *n.* **1.** FIRE-BREATHING MONSTER a female fire-breathing monster in Greek mythology, typically represented as a combination of a lion's head, goat's body, and serpent's tail **2.** IMAGINARY MONSTER any imaginary monster whose body is a grotesque combination of mismatched animal parts [14thC. Via Latin *chimaera* from Greek *khimaira* "she-goat."]

chi·mer·ic /kī mérrik, ki-/ *adj.* used to describe an organism that is composed of genetically different tissues, either naturally or as a result of a laboratory procedure

chi·mer·i·cal /kī meérik'l, ki-/ *adj.* **1.** IMAGINARY nonexistent, existing only in somebody's imagination, or wildly improbable or unrealistic **2.** PRONE TO FANTASIZING having a tendency to indulge in unrealistic fantasies (*literary*) —**chi·mer·i·cal·ly** *adv.* —**chi·mer·i·cal·ness** *n.*

chim·i·chan·ga /chìmmi chaáng gə/ *n.* a dish of the southwestern United States that consists of a deep-fried burrito containing a spicy filling of meat [Late 20thC. From Mexican Spanish, "trinket," of unknown origin.]

chim·ney /chímnee/ (*plural* **-neys**) *n.* **1.** STRUCTURE FOR VENTING GAS OR SMOKE a hollow vertical structure, usually made of brick or steel, that allows gas, smoke, or steam from a fire or furnace to escape into the atmosphere **2.** PART OF STRUCTURE RISING ABOVE ROOF the part of a chimney that rises above a roof **3.** SMOKE-VENTING PASSAGE INSIDE CHIMNEY a passage or pipe inside a chimney through which smoke or steam escapes **4.** GLASS TUBE PROTECTING LANTERN FLAME a tube, usually made of glass, used to enclose the flame of a lantern in order to promote burning and exclude drafts **5.** VOLCANIC VENT a part of a volcano or an oceanic ridge through which magma percolates, adding to the precipitated mineral matter that has accumulated **6.** MOUNTAINEERING CLEFT IN ROCK FACE a narrow vertical cleft in a rock face that is large enough for a climber to get inside and use as a means of ascending **7.** *U.K.* ENG = **smokestack** [13thC. From Old French *cheminée*, from late Latin *caminata*, from Latin *camera caminata* "room with a fireplace," from, ultimately, Greek *kaminos* "oven, furnace."]

chim·ney pot *n.* a short earthenware or metal pipe placed on the top of a chimney in order to increase the draft

chim·ney stack *n. U.K.* **1.** = **chimney** *n.* 2 **2.** TALL INDUSTRIAL CHIMNEY a tall, often cylindrical chimney attached to a factory or other large industrial building

chim·ney sweep *n.* somebody whose job is removing soot from chimneys

chim·ney swift *n.* a small dark North American swift that nests in chimneys. Latin name: *Chaetura pelagica.*

chimp /chimp/ *n.* a chimpanzee (*informal*)

Chimpanzee

chim·pan·zee /chìmpan zeé, chim pánzee/ *n.* a medium-sized ape from the forests of equatorial Africa that has long dark-brown hair covering its body except for its naked face and ears. Chimpanzees are sociable and intelligent and are considered to be the closest living relatives of human beings. Latin name: *Pan troglodytes* and *Pan paniscus.* [Mid-18thC. Via French *chimpanzé* from Kikongo.]

chin /chin/ *n.* PART OF FACE the part of the face below the lips, including the usually protruding front portion of the lower jaw ■ *v.* (**chinned, chin·ning, chins**) **1.** *vi.* MAKE CONVERSATION to talk casually with somebody about unimportant matters (*slang*) **2.** *vt.* PLACE VIOLIN UNDER CHIN to hold or place a violin under your chin ○ *He chinned his violin in readiness to begin playing.* **3.** *vti.* RAISE CHIN TO HIGH BAR to pull yourself up by the arms until your chin is level with the horizontal bar you are holding [Old English *cin*, from prehistoric Germanic] ◇ **keep your chin up** to remain cheerful and hopeful in spite of difficulties or hardships ◇ **take it on the chin** to accept misfortune staunchly, without flinching

Chin /chin/ (*plural* **Chin** *or* **Chins**) *n.* **1.** PEOPLES MEMBER OF PEOPLE OF SW MYANMAR a member of a people living in southwestern Myanmar and neighboring parts of India and Bangladesh **2.** LANG GROUP OF SINO-TIBETAN LANGUAGES a group of Sino-Tibetan languages spoken in southwestern Myanmar. About 800,000 people speak a Chin language. [Late 19thC. From Burmese, literally "hill-man."] —**Chin** *adj.*

Chin. *abbr.* Chinese

chi·na /chínə/ *n.* **1.** PORCELAIN porcelain or a similar high-quality translucent or white ceramic material **2.** ARTICLES MADE OF CHINA articles made of china, especially dishes and decorative objects [Late 16thC. From Persian *čīnī* "porcelain from China."]

China

Chi·na /chínə/ republic in eastern and central Asia. Language: Mandarin (official). Currency: renminbi (yuan). Capital: Beijing. Population: 1,226,274,731 (1997). Area: approximately 3,695,500 sq. mi./9,571,300 sq. km. Official name **People's Republic of China.** ◊ **Taiwan**

chi·na·ber·ry /chínə bèrree/ (*plural* **-ries**) *n.* **1.** TREE GROWN FOR SHADE a deciduous Asian tree of the mahogany family, widely grown in the United States for shade and its clusters of white or purple flowers. Latin name: *Melia azedarach.* **2.** = **soapberry 3.** FRUIT FROM CHINABERRY OR SOAPBERRY TREE a fruit produced by either the chinaberry or soapberry tree

chi·na clay *n.* = **kaolin**

chi·na clos·et *n.* a cabinet or cupboard used for storing or displaying china

Chi·na jute *n.* = **velvetleaf**

Chi·na·man /chínəmən/ (*plural* **-men** /-mən/) *n.* an offensive term for a man who was born in or who lives in China (*dated offensive*)

Chi·nan /jeé naán/ industrial city and capital of Shandong province in northeastern China. Population: 1,430,000 (1986).

Chi·na rose *n.* a rose that is native to China, has fragrant pink, red, or white flowers, and is the ancestor of many cultivated varieties. Latin name: *Rosa chinensis.*

Chi·na Sea part of the Pacific Ocean extending from Japan to the southern end of the Malay Peninsula. Area: East China Sea 290,000 sq. mi./752,000 sq. km. Depth: 8,913 ft./2,717 m.

Chi·na syn·drome *n.* a hypothetical accident in which the core of a nuclear reactor melts, allowing the radioactive fuel to burn through the floor of its container and straight down into the earth [From the idea of the molten core sinking through the earth and reaching China]

Chi·na·town /chínə tòwn/ *n.* an area of a city inhabited mainly by Chinese people, and containing businesses owned by them or selling Chinese products

Chi·na tree *n.* = **chinaberry** *n.* 1

chi·na·ware /chínə wàir/ *n.* plates, dishes, and other tableware made of china

chinch /chinch/ *n. Southern U.S.* a bedbug [Early 17thC. Via Spanish *chince* from the Latin stem *cimic-*.]

chinch bug, **cinch bug** *n.* **1.** SMALL INSECT THAT DESTROYS GRAIN a small black-and-white insect with short wings that causes serious damage to grain crops and grasses by sucking juices from them. Latin name: *Blissus leucopterus.* **2.** *Southern U.S.* = **chinch**

chin·che·rin·chee /chìnchə rínchee/ *n.* a South African plant of the lily family, with large fragrant flower heads that make it popular for use in flower arrangements. Latin name: *Ornithogalum thyrsoides.* [Early 20thC. An imitation of the sound created when stalks are rubbed together.]

Chinchilla

chin·chil·la /chin chíllə/ *n.* **1.** (*plural* **-las** *or* **-la**) SMALL RODENT a South American rodent that is the size of a squirrel, with a bushy tail and large round ears. It is bred in captivity for its soft silvery-gray fur. Latin name: *Chinchilla laniger.* **2.** FUR OF CHINCHILLA the fur of the chinchilla **3.** WOOLEN CLOTH a thick woolen fabric used to make overcoats [Early 17thC. Via Spanish from Aymara or Quechua.]

chinch·y /chínchee/ (**-i·er, -i·est**) *adj. Southern U.S.* cheap or miserly (*informal*) [Early 20thC. Formed from obsolete *chinch* "miser," earlier "miserly," from French *chiche.*]

Chin·co·teague po·ny /shìngkə teeg-, chìng-/ *n.* a small wild North American horse found on some islands off the Virginia coast

chine[1] /chīn/ *n.* **1.** FOOD **JOINT OF MEAT** a cut of meat that includes part of the backbone **2.** NAUT **BOTTOM CORNER OF BOAT** the join between the bottom and sides of some boats, especially those with a flat or V-shaped bottom ■ *vt.* **(chined, chin·ing, chines) CUT MEAT FROM BACKBONE** to cut meat along or across the backbone of the carcass [14thC. From Old French *eschine*, from a blend of the prehistoric Germanic ancestor of English *shin* and Latin *spina* "spine."]

chine[2] *n.* = **chime**[2]

Chi·nese /chī ne͞ez, -ne͞es/ *npl.* PEOPLES **PEOPLE OF CHINA** people born or living in China, or whose family came from China ■ *n.* (*plural* **-nese**) **1. GROUP OF LANGUAGES SPOKEN IN CHINA** a group of related languages spoken across most of China and Taiwan, and by large communities in many other countries. They constitute a branch of the Sino-Tibetan language family. **2. OFFICIAL LANGUAGE OF CHINA** the standard language of China and Taiwan and an official language of Singapore. It belongs to the Chinese group of Sino-Tibetan languages. Chinese has about 800 million native speakers, which is more than any other language. **3. FOOD, MEAL, OR RESTAURANT** a restaurant or takeout run by Chinese people and cooking food in styles from China, or food or a meal from one (*informal*) ■ *adj.* **1. OF CHINA** relating to or typical of China, its people, or culture **2. OF THE CHINESE LANGUAGE** relating to the language or language group Chinese

Chi·nese an·ise *n.* BOT = **star anise**

Chi·nese box·es *npl.* a set of matching boxes graduated in size so that each fits inside the next larger one, and as each opens it reveals another waiting to be opened

Chi·nese cab·bage *n.* PLANTS **1. VEGETABLE WITH WRINKLED LEAVES** a plant with a long head of overlapping wrinkled leaves and broad stalks, popular as a vegetable in Asian cooking. Latin name: *Brassica pekinensis.* **2.** = **bok choy**

Chi·nese cal·en·dar *n.* the traditional calendar used in China that divides the year into 24 fifteen-day periods and is based on both the lunar and solar cycles. It has five months containing 29 days, six months of 30 days, and one month of 20 or 30 days.

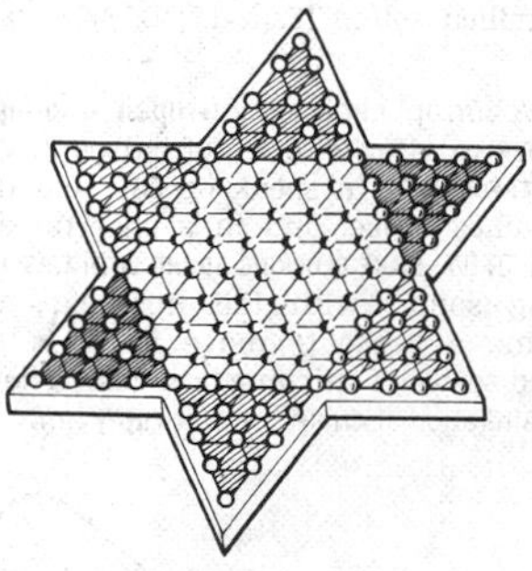

Chinese checkers

Chi·nese check·ers *n.* a game played on a board marked with a six-pointed star studded with small holes. Players move or jump marbles hole by hole toward an opposite point of the star. (*takes a singular verb*)

Chi·nese chest·nut *n.* a chestnut, originally native to China and Korea, that is resistant to a blight that affects other chestnuts. Latin name: *Castanea mollissima.*

Chi·nese cop·y *n.* an absolutely exact copy of an original, including any mistakes or defects it happens to contain

Chi·nese Em·pire *n.* China as a political entity and its form of government during the rule of the emperors. The Empire began with the Qin dynasty in the 5th century B.C. and lasted until the republic was established in the years 1911–12.

Chi·nese goose·ber·ry *n.* = **kiwi fruit**

Chi·nese lan·tern *n.* **1. PAPER COVERING FOR A LIGHT** a collapsible covering for a light made of thin brightly colored paper supported by thin wires **2.** *U.K.* = **winter cherry**

Chi·nese leaves *npl.* = **Chinese cabbage** *n.* **1**

Chi·nese New Year *n.* the first day of the Chinese month of Safar that falls between 21 Janunary and

Chinese lantern

19 February and marks the start of two weeks of celebrations

Chi·nese pars·ley *n.* = **coriander**

Chi·nese puz·zle *n.* a puzzle, either in the form of a game or a problem, that is extremely intricate, ingenious, and difficult to solve

Chi·nese rad·ish *n.* = **daikon**

Chi·nese red *n., adj.* = **vermilion**

Chi·nese res·tau·rant syn·drome *n.* a group of symptoms, including dizziness, headache, palpitations, and sweating, experienced by some people after eating food containing monosodium glutamate, an ingredient often used in preparing Chinese dishes

Chi·nese shar-pei *n.* ZOOL = **shar-pei**

Chi·nese wall *n.* **1. INSURMOUNTABLE BARRIER, ESPECIALLY TO COMMUNICATION** a strong or insurmountable barrier, especially one that obstructs the exchange of information **2.** STOCK EXCH **CONFIDENTIALITY BAR IN STOCK EXCHANGE BUSINESS** a set of strict rules preventing the exchange of confidential information between different departments of a stock exchange business, which might lead to its illegal use for gain

Chi·nese wa·ter tor·ture *n.* a method of psychological torture in which water is persistently dripped onto the victim's forehead

Chi·nese whis·pers *npl. U.K.* a game in which people in a circle pass a message by whispering it into the ear of the person next to them, the message becoming increasingly distorted on the way

Chi·nese wind·lass *n.* ENG = **differential windlass**

Chi·nese wood block *n.* a hollow slotted wooden block that, when struck, makes a sound similar to that of horses' hooves striking the ground

Chi·nese wood oil *n.* = **tung oil**

chink[1] /chingk/ *n.* **NARROW OPENING** a small narrow crack or slit ○ *Sunlight was coming through a chink in the curtains.* ■ *vt.* **(chinked, chink·ing, chinks) 1. FILL CRACKS IN SOMETHING** to fill up cracks or holes in something **2. FILL SOMETHING WITH CALK** to fill a gap or hole with calk **3. MAKE CRACKS IN SOMETHING** to make cracks in something ○ *A flying pebble chinked my car's windshield.* [Early 16thC. Origin uncertain.] —**chink·y** *adj.*

chink[2] /chingk/ *n.* **SHARP RINGING SOUND** a short sharp ringing sound such as that made when coins or glasses knock against each other ■ *vti.* **(chinked, chink·ing, chinks) MAKE OR CAUSE METALLIC SOUND** to make, or cause glass or metallic objects to make, a short sharp ringing sound ○ *We chinked glasses and said a toast.* [Late 16thC. An imitation of the sound.]

Chink /chingk/, **Chink·y** /chíngkee/ (*plural* **-ies**) *n.* an offensive term used to refer to a Chinese person (*slang offensive*) [Late 19thC. Formed from CHINA.]

chin·less /chínləss/ *adj.* **1. LACKING A PROJECTING CHIN** having a lower jaw that recedes under the mouth instead of projecting in front of it **2. WEAK** lacking strength of character

chin·less won·der *n.* somebody, especially an upper-class British man, who is considered weak, or inadequate (*informal insult*)

chi·no /chee̋nō/ *n.* **COTTON TWILL FABRIC** a durable coarse cotton twill fabric, often khaki-colored, that is used to make military uniforms, but is also popular for making casual pants ■ **chi·nos** *npl.* **CLOTHING MADE OF CHINO** men's trousers or women's pants made of chino [Mid-20thC. From American Spanish, literally "toasted," from the original color of the cloth.]

Chi·no /chēenō/ city in southwestern California, a suburb of Los Angeles. Population: 64,723 (1996).

Chi·no Hills city in southwestern California, an eastern suburb of Los Angeles, situated southwest of Chino. Population: 42,071 (1996).

chi·noi·se·rie /sheen waazə re̋e, sheen wa̋azəree/ *n.* **1. ART STYLE WITH CHINESE INFLUENCE** a style of art and interior design that reflects Chinese influence **2. OBJECT IN CHINOISERIE STYLE** an object or decoration in a style reflecting Chinese influence, or such objects and decorations collectively [Late 19thC. From French, from *chinois* "Chinese."]

Chi·no-La·ti·no /chee̋nō la te̋enō/ *adj.* combining elements of both Chinese and Latin culture, e.g., in cooking

chi·nook /shi no͝ok, chi no͝ok/ *n.* **1. WIND BLOWING ON NW U.S. COAST** a moist warm wind from the sea that affects weather along the northwestern coast of the United States **2. WIND OFF ROCKY MOUNTAINS** a dry warm wind that blows down the eastern slopes of the Rocky Mountains

Chi·nook /shi no͝ok, chi no͝ok/ (*plural* **-nook** *or* **-nooks**) *n.* **1.** PEOPLES **MEMBER OF NATIVE AMERICAN PEOPLE** a member of a Native American people who originally occupied coastal lands around the estuary of the Columbia River in Oregon, but who now live in western Washington State **2.** LANG **LANGUAGE OF CHINOOK PEOPLE** the extinct language of the Chinook people that was possibly a separate branch of the Penutian group of languages [Early 19thC. From Salish *tsinúk.*] —**Chi·nook** *adj.*

Chi·nook Jar·gon *n.* a pidgin language, once used for trading along the western coast of North America, made up of words borrowed from Chinook, Nootka, various Salashian languages, French, and English

Chi·nook salm·on *n.* a large salmon found in the northern Pacific Ocean that spawns in northern rivers of North America and North Asia. Its reddish flesh is highly prized. Latin name: *Oncorhyncus tshawytscha.*

chin·qua·pin /chíngkəpin/, **chin·ca·pin, chin·ka·pin** *n.* **1. SMALL TREE OF EASTERN U.S.** a small deciduous tree found in the eastern United States. Latin name: *Castanea pumila.* **2. LARGE EVERGREEN TREE** a large evergreen tree found in western North America. Latin name: *Castanopsis chrysophylla.* **3. EDIBLE NUT** the edible nut of either of the chinquapin trees [Early 17thC. From Virginian Algonquian.]

chin·qua·pin oak *n.* an oak tree with toothed leaves belonging to either of two species found in the eastern and central United States. Latin name: *Quercus prinoides* and *Quercus muhlenbergii.*

chin·strap /chín stràp/ *n.* a strap attached to a helmet or a hat that passes under the chin and is intended to keep the helmet or hat from falling off

chintz /chints/ *n.* **1. BRIGHTLY COLORED GLAZED FABRIC** a glazed fabric made of cotton and usually printed with a brightly colored pattern **2. PRINTED COTTON FABRIC FROM INDIA** a printed or stained calico fabric made in India [Early 17thC. Earlier *chints*, from *chint* "calico cloth," from Hindi *chīṭ* "stain," from Sanskrit *citra* "variegated."]

chintz·y /chíntsee/ (**-i·er, -i·est**) *adj.* **1. PENNY-PINCHING** mean and miserly ○ *He's so chintzy about money.* **2. TRASHY** cheap and gaudy ○ *Don't buy that chintzy suit; it'll fall apart the first time you have it cleaned.* **3.** *U.K.* **FUSSY OR QUAINT** used to describe a fussy, quaint, or would-be genteel style of decor (*informal disapproving*)

chin-up *n.* an exercise performed by hanging from a horizontal bar and pulling the body up until the chin has been raised above the bar

chin·wag /chín wàg/ (**-wagged, -wag·ging, -wags**) *vi.* to engage in casual conversation about events or other people's lives —**chin·wag·ger** *n.* —**chin·wag·ging** *n.*

chi·on·o·dox·a /kī ənō dóksə, kī ònnə dóksə/ *n.* (*plural* **chion·o·dox·as** *or* **chion·o·dox·a**) a hardy plant, native to Europe and Asia, that grows from a bulb and flowers in early spring. Genus: *Chionodoxa.* [Late 19thC. From modern Latin, from Greek *khiōn* "snow" + *doxa* "glory."]

chip /chip/ *n.* **1. SMALL PIECE BROKEN OR CUT OFF** a small piece that has been broken, chopped, or cut off something hard or brittle **2. CRACK** a space or crack left in something hard or brittle after a small piece has been broken off or out of it ○ *This cup has a chip in it.* **3.** FOOD **PIECE OF THIN CRISP SNACK FOOD** a very thin crunchy slice made from a starchy food, usually potato or corn, that has been fried until it is crisp ○ *corn chips* **4.** ELECTRON ENG **WAFER OF SEMICONDUCTOR MATERIAL** a small wafer of semiconductor material, usually silicon, forming the base on which an integrated circuit is laid out, or such a wafer together with its integrated circuit **5.** GAMBLING **TOKEN USED AS MONEY** a token, often a small round plastic disk, used to represent money in poker and other gambling games **6. DRIED DUNG** a piece of dried animal dung, sometimes used for fuel **7.** *U.K.* FOOD **LONG PIECE OF FRIED POTATO** a long finger-shaped wedge of potato traditionally fried in deep fat ○ *fish and chips* **8.** CRAFT **WOOD CUT AS WEAVING MATERIAL** wood, straw, or other material that has been dried and cut for use in weaving ■ *v.* **(chipped, chip·ping, chips) 1.** *vt.* **BREAK OFF SMALL PIECE FROM SOMETHING** to break one or more small pieces from something hard or brittle **2.** *vi.* **LOSE SMALL PIECES** to become damaged by having a small piece or small pieces break off ○ *paint that will not chip easily* **3.** *vt.* SPORTS **HIT SOMETHING IN HIGH ARC** to hit or kick a ball or puck so that it travels a short distance in a high arc ○ *The batter chipped the ball over the first baseman's head into right field.* **4.** *vi.* GOLF **PLAY A CHIP SHOT** in golf, to play a chip shot **5.** *vt.* **CARVE SOMETHING BY REMOVING SMALL PIECES** to carve or shape something by cutting small pieces off or out of it **6.** *vt.* **CHOP SOMETHING INTO CHIPS** to chop or cut up something, e.g., a potato, to form chips ○ *Will you chip the ice for drinks?* [Pre-12thC. From Latin *cippus* "stake."] —**chip·per** *n.* ◇ **cash in your chips** to die (*informal*) ◇ **a chip off the old block** somebody who looks and behaves very like one of his or her parents (*informal*) ◇ **have a chip on your shoulder** to feel inferior or badly treated and so act in an oversensitive and resentful manner (*informal*) ◇ **let the chips fall where they may** used to say that you are ready for whatever may be about to happen (*informal*) ◇ **when the chips are down** at a time of crisis or when vital matters are at stake (*informal*)

chip in *v.* **1.** *vti.* **CONTRIBUTE** to contribute something to a common fund or resource (*informal*) **2.** *vi.* **INTERRUPT** to interrupt a conversation in order to make a comment (*informal*) **3.** *vi.* **PUT MONEY INTO POOL IN POKER** in poker and other games, to put chips or money into the pool in order to play

chip·board /chíp bàwrd/ *n.* a construction material made from compressed wood chips held together by a synthetic resin and produced in the form of hard flat boards

Chip·e·wy·an /chìppə wī́ ən/ (*plural* **-an** *or* **-ans**) *n.* **1.** PEOPLES **MEMBER OF NATIVE AMERICAN PEOPLE** a member of a Native American people in Canada whose traditional territories are in northern Saskatchewan, Manitoba, and the Northwest Territories. In the 18th century, they abandoned their nomadic life to settle and become fur traders. **2.** LANG **CHIPEWYAN LANGUAGE** the Athabaskan language of the Chipewyan people. Chipewyan is spoken by about 8,000 people. [Late 18thC. From Cree *ci:pwaya:n*, literally "(wearing) pointed-skin (clothes)."] —**Chip·e·wy·an** *adj.*

chip·head /chíp hèd/ *n.* somebody who is very interested in, and highly skilled at, computer use (*slang*)

Chipmunk

chip·munk /chíp mùngk/ (*plural* **-munks** *or* **-munk**) *n.* a striped rodent of the squirrel family, native to North America and Asia. It lives on the ground, collects nuts and fruit, and stores food in cheek pouches. Genera: *Tamias* and *Eutamias.* [Mid-19thC. From Ojibwa *ajidamoon*? "squirrel," literally "one that comes down trees headlong."]

chip·o·lata /chìppə láatə/ *n. U.K.* a small thin sausage, usually made of finely ground pork [Late 19thC. Via French from Italian *cipollata*, literally "with onions," from *cipolla* "onion," from Latin *cepa* (source of English *chive*).]

chipped beef *n.* thin slices of dried smoked beef, often served in a cream sauce over rice or toast

Chip·pen·dale /chíppən dàyl/ *adj.* **18THC ENGLISH FURNITURE STYLE** used to describe furniture made by, or in the style of, Thomas Chippendale, characterized by graceful flowing lines, cabriole legs, and elaborate ornamentation ■ *n.* **PIECE OF FURNITURE IN CHIPPENDALE STYLE** a piece of furniture in the Chippendale style [Named for Thomas CHIPPENDALE]

Chip·pen·dale /chíppən dàyl/, **Thomas** (1718–79) British furniture designer. The influence of his neoclassical, increasingly eclectic style was spread through *The Gentleman and Cabinet Maker's Director* (1754).

chip·per[1] /chíppər/ *adj.* cheerful and full of vitality (*informal*) [Mid-19thC. Origin uncertain: perhaps a blend of dialect *kipper* and chipper, alteration of CHIRRUP.]

chip·per[2] **(-pered, -per·ing, -pers)** *vi.* **1. CHIRP LIKE BIRD** to chirp or twitter like a bird **2. BABBLE OR CHATTER** to babble or chatter [Early 18thC. Origin uncertain: probably an imitation of the sound, influenced by CHIRRUP.]

Chip·pe·wa /chíppə wàa, chíppəwə/ (*plural* **-was** *or* **-wa**) *adj.* = **Ojibwa** [Mid-18thC. Alteration of OJIBWA.]

Chip·pe·wa Falls city in western Wisconsin on the west bank of the Chippewa River, northeast of Eau Claire. Population: 12,784 (1996).

chip·ping /chípping/ *n.* = **chip** *n.* 1

chip·ping spar·row *n.* a small North American sparrow with a gray breast, reddish-brown crown, and black-and-white stripes near its eyes. Latin name: *Spizella passerina.* [*Chipping* from *chipper*, alteration of CHIRRUP]

chip·py[1] /chíppee/ (*plural* **-pies**), **chip·pie** *n.* a promiscuous woman or prostitute (*dated slang*) [Late 19thC. Formed from *chip* "to cheep like a bird," an imitation of the sound.]

chip·py[2] /chíppee/ **(-pier, -pi·est)** *adj. Can* behaving in an aggressive or belligerent way [From *have a chip on your shoulder*]

CHIPS /chips/ *abbr.* Clearing House Interbank Payments System

chip·set /chíp sèt/, **chip set** *n.* a group of microchips designed to perform one or more related functions as a unit, e.g., to update a computer screen display

chip shot *n.* **1. SHORT HIGH HIT OR KICK** a short-range kick or shot in which the ball or puck rises sharply into the air **2. APPROACH SHOT** a short approach shot in golf, used to loft the ball onto the green

Chi·rac /sheè rak/, **Jacques** (*b.* 1932) French politician. He was prime minister (1974–76 and 1986–88) and, after two unsuccessful attempts, was elected president in 1995. Full name **Jacques René Chirac**

chi·ral /kī́rəl/ *adj.* used to describe a molecule whose arrangement of atoms is such that it cannot be superimposed on its mirror image [Late 19thC. Formed from Greek *kheir* "hand."] —**chi·ral·i·ty** /kī rállətee/ *n.*

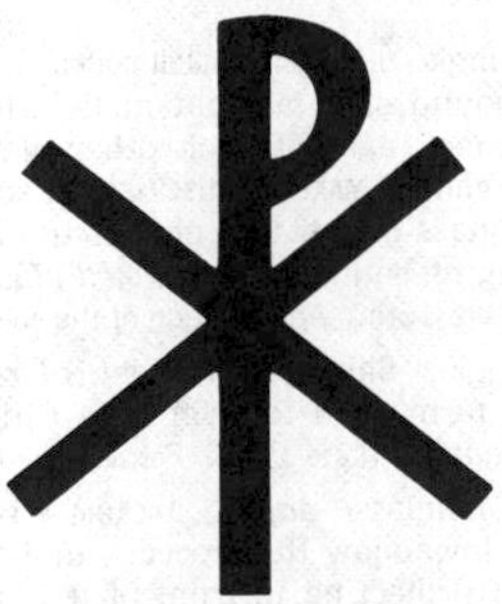

Chi-Rho

Chi-Rho /kī rṓ/ (*plural* **Chi-Rhos**) *n.* a monogram and symbol for Jesus Christ, formed by superimposing the Greek letters *chi* (X) and *rho* (P) [From the first two letters of Jesus Christ's name in Greek]

Chir·i·ca·hua /chèeri kàawə/ (*plural* **-hua** *or* **-huas**) *n.* a member of an Apache people that formerly roamed the southern parts of New Mexico and Arizona and the northern region of Mexico, and now primarily live in Oklahoma and New Mexico

Chir·i·ca·hua Na·tion·al Mon·u·ment park in southeastern Arizona, established in 1924 and noted for its unusual rock formations. Area: 11,985 acres/4,850 hectares.

chiro- *prefix.* hand ○ *chiromancy* [Via Latin from Greek *kheir* (source also of English *surgery*)]

chi·rog·ra·phy /kī róggrəfee/ *n.* **1. HANDWRITING** the art of handwriting (*technical*) **2.** = **calligraphy**

chi·ro·man·cy /kī́rə mànsee/ *n.* = **palmistry**

Chi·ron /kī́ ròn/ *n.* in Greek mythology, the centaur, known for his great wisdom, who was the tutor of Greek heroes such as Hercules, Achilles, and Jason

chi·ron·o·mid /kī rónnəmid/ *n.* a small nonbiting midge that gathers in large breeding swarms, especially near water. Family: Chironomidae. [Late 19thC. From modern Latin *Chironomidae*, from the genus name *Chironomus*, from Greek *kheironomos* "pantomime dancer."]

chi·rop·o·dy /ki róppədee/ *n. U.K.* = **podiatry** — **chi·rop·o·dist** *n.*

chi·ro·prac·tic /kī́rə práktik/ *n.* a medical system based on the theory that disease and disorders are caused by a misalignment of the bones, especially in the spine, that obstructs proper nerve functions [Late 19thC. Formed from CHIRO- and Greek *praktikos* "effective."] —**chi·ro·prac·tor** /kī́rə pràktər/ *n.*

chi·rop·ter·an /kī róptərən/, **chi·rop·ter** /kī róptər/ *n.* ZOOL a flying mammal, such as the bat, with forelimbs that have evolved as membranous wings (*technical*) [Mid-19thC. From modern Latin *Chiroptera*, from CHIRO- + Greek *pteron* "wing."]

chirp /churp/ *n.* **SHORT HIGH-PITCHED SOUND** a short high-pitched sound, especially as made by a bird ■ *v.* **(chirped, chirp·ing, chirps) 1.** *vi.* **MAKE A CHIRP** to make a short high-pitched sound **2.** *vti.* **SPEAK IN CHEERFUL MANNER** to speak, or say something, in a cheerful, lively, or pert voice [15thC. An imitation of the sound.]

chirp·y /chúrpee/ **(-i·er, -i·est)** *adj.* cheerful and lively (*informal*) —**chirp·i·ly** *adv.* —**chirp·i·ness** *n.*

chirr /chur/ *n.* **SHRILL INSECT SOUND** a shrill harsh trilled sound made by some insects, e.g., grasshoppers ■ *vi.* **(chirred, chir·ring, chirrs) MAKE A CHIRR** to make a harsh trilled sound [Early 17thC. An imitation of the sound.]

chir·rup /chúrrəp, cheèrəp/ *v.* **(-ruped, -rup·ing, -rups) 1.** *vi.* **TWITTER** to utter a series of chirps **2.** *vti.* **SPEAK IN HIGH CHEERFUL VOICE** to speak or say something in a high-pitched voice, and in a cheerful and lively fashion **3.** *vi.* **MAKE CLUCKING SOUND WITH LIPS** to make a clucking sound with the lips, e.g., when encouraging a horse to move faster ■ *n.* **CHIRP** a repeated series of chirping or clucking sounds [Late 16thC. Alteration of CHIRP.] —**chir·rup·y** *adj.*

Chisel

chis·el /chízz'l/ *n.* **TOOL WITH FLAT BEVELED BLADE** a tool for cutting and shaping wood or stone, consisting of a straight flat beveled blade with a sharp square-cut bottom edge inserted in a handle. The chisel is often held in one hand and struck with a hammer or mallet, but is also used freehand. ■ *v.* **(-eled, -el·ing, -els) 1.** *vti.* **CARVE SOMETHING WITH CHISEL** to carve, cut, or work wood or stone using a chisel **2.** *vti.* **CHEAT SOMEBODY** to cheat or swindle somebody (*informal*) **3.** *vt.* **OBTAIN BY CHEATING** to obtain something by cheating or deception (*informal*) [14thC. Via Old French from, ultimately, Latin *caes-*, stem of *caedere* "to cut" (source of English *scissors*).]

chis·eled /chízz'ld/ *adj.* clear-cut or sharply defined in shape or profile ○ *a finely chiseled face*

chis·el·er /chízzlər/ *n.* a cheat or swindler (*informal*)

Chis·holm /chízzəm/, **Shirley Anita** (*b.* 1924) U.S. politician. She was the first African American woman to serve in the U.S. House of Representatives (1969–83).

Chis·holm Trail *n.* an important trail formerly used to drive cattle to market, running from San Antonio, Texas to Abilene, Kansas [Mid-19thC. Named for Jesse *Chisholm*, a Cherokee Native American.]

Chi·şi·nău /keeshi nów/ city and capital of Moldova, situated on a tributary of the Dniester, 90 mi./145 km northwest of Odessa, Ukraine. Population: 753,500 (1991). Former name **Kishinev** (1940–91)

chi-square *n.* a statistical calculation used to test how well the distribution of a set of observed data matches a theoretical probability distribution. The calculated value is equal to the sum of the squares of the differences divided by the expected values.

chi-square dis·tri·bu·tion *n.* a probability function widely used in testing a statistical hypothesis, e.g., the likelihood that a given statistical distribution of results might be reached in an experiment

chit[1] /chit/ *n.* a note, bill, or any small slip of paper with writing on it, especially a statement of money owed for food and drink (*dated*) [Late 18thC. Shortening of *chitty*, via Hindi *ciṭṭhī*, from Sanskrit *citra* "spot, mark," referring to the writing.]

chit[2] /chit/ *n.* a child, girl, or young woman, especially one whose physical slightness seems to be at odds with an impertinent, forceful, or self-confident manner

chi·tal /cheét'l/ (*plural* **-tal** *or* **-tals**) *n.* = **axis deer** [Late 19thC. From Hindi *cittal*, from Sanskrit *citrala* "spotted."]

chit·chat /chít chàt/ *n.* SMALL TALK casual conversation or small talk, or a casual conversation with somebody (*informal*) ■ *vi.* (**-chat·ted, -chat·ting, -chats**) MAKE SMALL TALK to engage in casual conversation or small talk (*informal*) ○ *What are you chitchatting about now?* [Late 17thC. A playful elaboration of CHAT.]

chi·tin /kítin/ *n.* a tough semitransparent substance that forms part of the protective outer casing (**cuticle**) of some insects and other arthropods, and the cell walls of some fungi [Mid-19thC. From French *chitine*, from Greek *khitōn* "tunic, coat of mail."] — **chi·ti·noid** *adj.* —**chi·tin·ous** *adj.*

chit·lins /chíttlinz/, **chit·lings** *npl. Southern U.S.* = **chitterlings** [Mid-19thC. Contraction of CHITTERLINGS.]

chi·ton /kít'n, -tòn/ *n.* **1.** SMALL MARINE MOLLUSK a small primitive marine mollusk that lives on rocks and has an elongated body protected by a shell consisting of eight overlapping plates. Class: Polyplacophora. **2.** TUNIC OF ANCIENT GREECE AND ROME a loose knee-length woolen tunic worn by women and men in ancient Greece [Early 19thC. From Greek *khiton* "tunic, coat of mail."]

Chit·ta·gong /chíttə gòng/ chief port of Bangladesh and an important industrial city. It is situated on the southeastern coast of the country. Population: 1,364,000 (1991).

chit·ter /chíttər/ (**-tered, -ter·ing, -ters**) *vi.* to chirp or twitter [12thC. An imitation of the sound.]

chit·ter·lings /chíttlinz/ *npl.* the small intestines of pigs, especially when prepared as food [13thC. Origin unknown.]

chiv /chiv, shiv/, **chive, shiv** /shiv/ *n.* KNIFE a pocketknife, often a switchblade, or razor (*slang*) ■ *vt.* (**chivved, chiv·ving, chivs; chived, chiv·ving, chives; shivved, shiv·ving, shivs**) SLASH SOMEBODY WITH KNIFE to slash or stab somebody with a switchblade or razor (*slang*) [Late 17thC. Origin uncertain: perhaps from Romany, "blade."]

chi·val·ric /shi vállrik, shívvəlrik/ *adj.* relating to knights, knighthood, and the knightly code of honor

chiv·al·rous /shívvəlrəss/ *adj.* **1.** RELATING TO KNIGHTHOOD CODE relating to, or reflecting the values of, the medieval code of knighthood, especially courtesy, self-sacrifice, and a sense of fair play **2.** CONSIDERATE AND COURTEOUS considerate and courteous, especially toward women —**chiv·al·rous·ly** *adv.* — **chiv·al·rous·ness** *n.*

chiv·al·ry /shívvəlree/ (*plural* **-ries**) *n.* **1.** QUALITIES OF IDEAL KNIGHT the combination of qualities expected of the ideal medieval knight, especially courage, honor, loyalty, and consideration for others, especially women **2.** CHIVALROUS BEHAVIOR courteous and considerate behavior, especially toward women **3.** MEDIEVAL KNIGHTHOOD the medieval concept of knighthood, and the customs, practices, social system, and religious and personal ideals associated with knights and their way of life **4.** GROUP OF KNIGHTS knights, noblemen, or armed mounted soldiers, collectively or in a group (*archaic*) [13thC. Via Old French *chevalerie* from medieval Latin *caballerius*, from Latin *caballus* "horse" (source of English *cavalier*).]

chive /chīv/ *n.* a plant with long fine hollow leaves that has a strong onion flavor and purple ball-shaped flowers. Its leaves are used to season food. Latin name: *Allium schoenoprasum.* [14thC. From French dialect, variant of *cive*, from Latin *cepa* "onion" (source of English *chipolata*).]

chla·myd·es plural of **chlamys**

chla·myd·i·a /klə míddee ə/ *n.* **1.** MICROBIOL PATHOGENIC BACTERIUM a spherical bacterium that causes several eye and urogenital diseases in humans and other animals, and psittacosis in pet birds *Genus[Chlamydia]* **2.** MED SEXUALLY TRANSMITTED DISEASE a sexually transmitted disease, the most common in developed countries, caused by the bacterium *Chlamydia trachomatis.* Often producing no symptoms, it can cause infertility, chronic pain, or a tubal pregnancy if left untreated. [Mid-20thC. Via modern Latin from Greek *khlamyd-*, stem of *khlamus* "mantle, chlamys."]

chla·myd·i·al /klə míddee əl/ *adj.* used to describe infections that are caused by a bacterium of the genus *Chlamydia*, e.g., trachoma and sexually transmitted infections such as urethritis

chla·myd·o·spore /klə míddə spàwr/ *n.* an asexual thick-walled spore produced by some fungi. It is capable of remaining dormant for long periods and surviving adverse conditions. [Late 19thC. Coined from the Greek stem *khlamyd-* "mantle" + SPORE.]

chlam·ys /klámmiss, kláy-/ (*plural* **-ys·es** *or* **-y·des** /klámmi deez/) *n.* a short cloak gathered and fastened at the shoulder, worn by men in ancient Greece [Late 17thC. From Greek *khlamus* "mantle."]

chlo·as·ma /klō ázmə/ (*plural* **-ma·ta** /-mətə/) *n.* dark coloration on the skin of the face caused by hormonal changes related to pregnancy, liver disease, or the use of birth control pills. It is made worse by sunlight. [Mid-19thC. Formed from Greek *khloazein* "to become green."]

chlor- *prefix.* = **chloro-** (*used before vowels*)

chlo·ral /kláwrəl/ *n.* a colorless oily toxic liquid with a strong odor, used in making chloral hydrate and DDT. Formula: CCl_3CHO. [Mid-19thC. Coined from CHLOR- + -AL.]

chlo·ral hy·drate *n.* a colorless crystalline solid that is soluble in water and is used as a sedative and hypnotic. Formula: $C_2H_3Cl_3O_2$.

chlo·ra·mine /kláwrə meen/ *n.* an unstable colorless liquid with a pungent odor. It is used to make hydrazine. Formula: NH_2Cl.

chlo·ram·phen·i·col /klàw ram fénni kòl/ *n.* a powerful antibiotic derived from a soil bacterium, the use of which is limited by its tendency to cause the failure of blood cell production (**aplastic anemia**). Formula: $C_{11}H_{12}Cl_2N_2O_5$. [Mid-20thC. Coined from CHLOR- + AMIDE+ PHEN- + NITRO- + GLYCOL.]

chlo·rate /kláw ràyt/ *n.* any salt of chloric acid [Early 19thC. Formed from CHLORIC.]

chlor·dane /kláwr dàyn/, **chlor·dan** *n.* a thick, toxic, colorless to amber-colored liquid that can exist with several different molecular structures (**isomers**) and is used as an insecticide and a fumigant. Chlordane has been found to be so highly toxic to humans that it has been outlawed in some U.S. states. Formula: $C_{10}H_6Cl_8$. [Mid-20thC. Coined from CHLOR- + INDENE + -ANE.]

chlor·di·az·e·pox·ide /klàwrdī azzə pók sīd/ *n.* a yellow crystalline powder that is used as a tranquilizer and as a treatment for alcoholism. Formula: $C_{16}H_{14}ClN_3O$. [Mid-20thC. Coined from CHLOR- + DI- +AZO- + EPI- + OXIDE.]

chlo·rel·la /kləréllə/ *n.* a single-celled green alga that is often used in research. Genus: *Chlorella.* [Early 20thC. From modern Latin, literally "little green (thing)," from Greek *khlōros* "green."]

chlo·ren·chy·ma /klə réngkəmə/ *n.* plant tissue that contains chloroplasts, found mainly in leaves [Late 19thC. Coined from CHLOROPHYLL + -ENCHYMA.]

chlo·ric /kláwrik/ *adj.* containing chlorine, especially with a valence of 5 [Early 19thC. Formed from CHLORINE.]

chlo·ric ac·id *n.* a toxic unstable acid, known only in solution and as chlorate salts. Formula: $HClO_3 \cdot 7H_2O$.

chlo·ride /kláw rīd/ *n.* a compound containing chlorine and one other element [Early 19thC. Formed from CHLORINE.] —**chlo·rid·ic** /klə ríddik/ *adj.*

chlo·ride of lime *n.* a powder used as a bleach (*technical*)

chlo·ri·nate /kláwri nayt/ (**-nat·ed, -nat·ing, -nates**) *vt.* to combine or treat something with chlorine, especially in order to kill harmful organisms — **chlo·ri·nat·ed** *adj.* —**chlo·ri·na·tion** /klàwri náysh'n/ *n.* —**chlo·ri·na·tor** /kláwri nàytər/ *n.*

chlo·rine /kláw reen/ *n.* a gaseous, poisonous, corrosive, greenish-yellow chemical element of the halogen group that combines with nearly every other element. It is widely used to purify water and as a disinfectant. Symbol **Cl** [Early 19thC. Formed from Greek *khlōros* "green," from the color of the gas.]

chlo·rite[1] /kláw rīt/ *n.* a group of soft black or green aluminosilicate minerals found in metamorphic rocks. Formula: $(Mg,Fe,Al)_6(Si,Al)_4O_{10}(OH)_8$. [Late 18thC. Via Latin *chloritis* from Greek *khlōritis*, a green precious stone.]

chlo·rite[2] /kláw rīt/ *n.* any salt of chlorous acid [Mid-19thC. Formed from CHLORINE.]

chloro- *prefix.* **1.** green○ *chlorophyll* **2.** chlorine ○ *chlorobenzene* [From Greek *khlōros* "green"]

chlo·ro·ben·zene /klàwrō bén zeen/ *n.* a combination of chlorine and benzene that produces a colorless flammable liquid with an almond smell, used especially in the production of solvents and DDT. Formula: C_6H_5Cl.

chlo·ro·fluor·o·car·bon /klàw rō flŏŏrō kaárbən, klàw rō flawrō kaárbən/ *n.* full form of **CFC** [Mid-20thC. Coined from CHLORO- + FLUORO- + CARBON.]

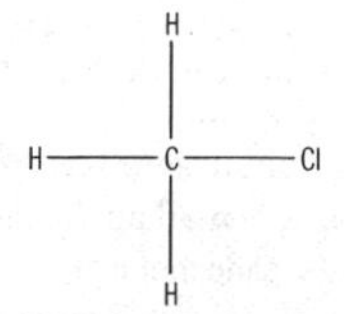

Chloroform

chlo·ro·form /kláwrə fàwrm/ *n.* LIQUID CAUSING UNCONSCIOUSNESS a colorless sweet-smelling toxic liquid that rapidly changes to a vapor and causes unconsciousness if inhaled, used as a solvent and cleaning agent. It was formerly used as an anesthetic for surgical operations and is still sometimes used as such in veterinary medicine. Formula: $CHCl_3$. ■ *vt.* RENDER UNCONSCIOUS WITH CHLOROFORM to make a person or animal breathe in chloroform in order to cause unconsciousness [Mid-19thC. Coined from CHLORO- + FORMIC.]

chlo·ro·me·thane *n.* = **methyl chloride**

Chlo·ro·my·ce·tin /klàwrō mī seét'n/ *tdmk.* a trademark for the antibiotic chloramphenicol

chlo·ro·phyll /kláwrəfil/, **chlo·ro·phyl** *n.* the green or purple pigment found in plants, algae, and some bacteria that is responsible for capturing the light energy needed for photosynthesis. In plants and algae, chlorophyll is contained within numerous minute membranous sacs (**chloroplasts**) within cells of the stems and leaves. [Early 19thC. From French *chlorophylle*, from Greek *khlōros* (see CHLORO-) + *phullon* "leaf."] —**chlo·ro·phyl·lose** /kláwrəfi lōss, klàwrə fí lōss/ *adj.*

chlo·ro·pic·rin /klàwrə píkrin/ *n.* a colorless toxic liquid that causes tears and vomiting and is used as a tear gas. It also has industrial uses as an insecticide, a disinfectant, and in dyes. Formula: CCl_3NO_2. [Mid-19thC. Coined from CHLORO- + PICRO- + -IN.]

chlo·ro·plast /kláwrə plàst/ *n.* a membranous sac (**plastid**) that contains chlorophyll and other pigments and is the place where photosynthesis occurs within the cells of plants and algae. Plant cells contain numerous chloroplasts, algal cells often have just one. Each consists of interconnected stacks of disk-shaped membranes in fluid, surrounded by a double membrane. [Late 19thC. Coined from CHLORO- + -PLAST.] —**chlo·ro·plas·tic** /kláwrə plástik/ *adj.*

chlo·ro·prene /kláwrə prèen/ *n.* a colorless liquid used in the manufacture of the synthetic rubber, neoprene. Formula: C_4H_5Cl. [Mid-20thC. Coined from CHLORO- + ISOPRENE.]

chlo·ro·quine /kláwrə kwìn, kláwrə kwèen/ *n.* a synthetic drug that is taken orally and is used to treat malaria and amebiasis. Formula: $C_{18}H_{26}ClN_3$. [Mid-20thC. Coined from CHLORO- + QUINOLINE, from which it is derived.]

chlo·ro·sis /klə rósiss/ *n.* **1. LOSS OF GREENNESS THROUGH CHLOROPHYLL DEFICIENCY** a yellowing or whitening of a plant's leaves and stems caused by a lack of the green pigment chlorophyll **2. IRON-DEFICIENCY ANEMIA** severe iron-deficiency anemia, formerly common in adolescent girls, that produces a greenish tint in the skin [Late 17thC. Coined from CHLORO- + -OSIS.] —**chlo·rot·ic** /klə róttik/ *adj.* —**chlo·rot·i·cal·ly** /-əlee/ *adv.*

chlo·ro·thi·a·zide /klàw rō thí ə zìd/ *n.* a water-soluble powder used in the treatment of high blood pressure, swelling, and heart failure to relieve fluid retention in the body

chlor·ous /kláwrəss/ *adj.* relating to or containing chlorine with a valence of 3 [Mid-19thC. Coined from CHLORINE + -OUS.]

chlor·prom·a·zine /klawr prómmə zèen, -prṓmə-/ *n.* a drug used as a sedative and tranquilizer in the treatment of psychiatric disorders such as schizophrenia [Mid-20thC. Coined from CHLOR- + PROMETHAZINE.]

chlor·prop·a·mide /klawr próppə mìd/ *n.* a drug that lowers blood sugar, used in the treatment of diabetes. Formula: $C_{10}H_{13}ClN_2O_3S$. [Mid-20thC. Coined from CHLOR- + PROPANE + AMIDE.]

chlor·tet·ra·cy·cline /klawr tèttrə síklin, -sí klèen/ *n.* an antibiotic drug, derived from a soil bacterium, that is used to treat a wide range of infections in humans and to stimulate growth in livestock. Formula: $C_{22}H_{23}ClN_2O_8$.

ChM *abbr.* Master of Surgery [Latin *Chirurgiae Magister*]

chm., **Chm.** *abbr.* **1.** chairman **2.** checkmate

choc·a·hol·ic *n.* = **chocoholic**

chock /chok/ *n.* **1. BLOCK TO STOP SOMETHING MOVING** a block of wood or metal used to prevent a wheel from turning, an object from moving, or to support something when it is raised off the ground **2.** SHIPPING **SHIP'S HORN-SHAPED FITMENT FOR SECURING CABLES** a heavy metal fitment attached to the deck of a ship that has two inward-curving horn-shaped projections around which a cable can be secured **3.** MOUNTAINEERING **METAL ANCHOR FOR CLIMBING** a metal device used to provide anchoring systems for climbing or caving ■ *vt.* **USE CHOCK FOR BRACE** to keep something from turning, moving, or falling by using a chock to block or brace it ○ *chock the plane's wheels* [14thC. Probably from an assumed Old Norman French variant of Old French *ço(u)che* "log," of unknown origin.]

chock-a-block *adj.* **1. PACKED FULL** so crammed with things or crowded with people as to make it virtually impossible to get anything or anybody else in or to move around (*informal*) **2.** NAUT **HAVING BLOCKS IN TIGHTEST POSITION** having the two blocks in a block and tackle tight up against each other [Mid-19thC. Alteration of an earlier nautical term *block and block*, "with pulleys drawn close together," influenced by CHOCK-FULL.]

chock-full *adj.* completely full, or containing an enormous number of things (*informal*) [14thC. *Chock* perhaps from CHOCK "wooden block," hence, originally, "stuffed with blocks of wood," or an alteration of CHEEK, hence, originally, "full up to the cheeks."]

choc·o·hol·ic /chòkə hóllik/, **choc·a·hol·ic** *n.* somebody who is extremely fond of or apparently addicted to chocolate, and who craves it or eats it in large quantities (*humorous*) [Late 20thC. Coined from CHOCOLATE + -AHOLIC.]

choc·o·late /chóklət/ *n.* **1.** FOOD **SMOOTH SWEET BROWN FOOD** a food or flavoring, typically a smooth sweet brown and sometimes brittle solid, made from roasted and ground cacao seeds usually sweetened and mixed with cocoa butter and dried milk. Chocolate is made into bars or candy, or used to flavor other foods, especially cakes, desserts, sauces, and cookies. (*often used before a noun*) ○ *a bar of chocolate* ○ *chocolate cake* **2.** FOOD **CANDY COVERED IN CHOCOLATE** a small piece of chocolate-coated candy with a hard or soft center **3.** BEVERAGES **CHOCOLATE DRINK** a drink, usually served hot or warm, made from sweetened powdered chocolate mixed with water or milk **4.** COLORS **BROWN COLOR** a deep warm brown color ■ *adj.* **BROWN-COLORED** of a deep warm brown color [Early 17thC. Directly or via French *chocolat* "drinking chocolate," from Spanish *chocolate*, from Nahuatl *chocolatl*, literally "bitter water."] —**choc·o·lat·ey** *adj.*

choc·o·late-box *adj.* depicting pretty scenes or pretty people in a stereotyped and usually sentimental or romanticized way ○ *chocolate-box portraits*

choc·o·late chip *n.* a small piece of chocolate, used especially in making cookies and desserts ○ *chocolate chip cookies*

choc·o·late tree *n.* = **cacao** *n.* 1

choc·o·la·tier /chókə làttee ər/ *n.* a maker or seller of chocolates

Choc·taw /chók tàw/ (*plural* **-taw** *or* **-taws**) *n.* **1.** PEOPLES **MEMBER OF NATIVE AMERICAN PEOPLE** a member of a Native American people who originally occupied lands in central and southern parts of Mississippi, and whose members now live mainly in Oklahoma and southern Mississippi. The Choctaw were one of the Five Civilized Nations who, under the Removal Act of 1830, were sent to live on reservations in Oklahoma. **2.** LANG **CHOCTAW LANGUAGE** the Muskogean language of the Choctaw people. Choctaw is spoken by about 10,000 people. [Early 18thC. From Choctaw *čahta*.] —**Choc·taw** *adj.*

choice /choyss/ *n.* **1. ACT OF CHOOSING SOMETHING OR SOMEBODY** a decision to choose one thing, person, or course of action in preference to others ○ *Think very carefully before you make a choice.* **2. POWER TO CHOOSE** the chance or ability to choose between different things ○ *They gave us no choice* **3. SELECTION OF THINGS** a variety of things, people, or possibilities from which to choose ○ *a wide choice of styles and colors* **4. CHOSEN OBJECT** a person, thing, or course of action chosen by somebody from among a range of possibilities ○ *Red would not have been my choice.* **5. BEST PART** the best or most desirable part ■ *adj.* (**choic·er, choic·est**) **1. HIGH-QUALITY** being of particularly good quality **2. RUDE OR EMPHATIC** carefully chosen for effectiveness and usually expressing displeasure or dislike in a sufficiently emphatic way (*used euphemistically*) ○ *a few choice words* [13thC. From Old French *chois*, from *choisir* "to choose," ultimately from a prehistoric Germanic word that is also the ancestor of English *choose*.] —**choice·ness** *n.* ◇ **of choice** chosen from among several as being the best or most suitable ○ *the newspaper of choice*

choir /kwīr/ *n.* **1. GROUP OF SINGERS** an organized group of singers who perform together, especially in church, typically combining smaller groups of singers who sing different parts at different pitches **2. AREA WHERE CHOIR SINGS** the part of a church where the choir performs **3. INSTRUMENT GROUP** a group of instruments of the same type **4.** = **choir organ** [13thC. Via Old French *quer*, from Latin *chorus* "choral dance" (source of English *chorus*), on which the English spelling was modeled, from Greek *khoros* "group of singers and dancers."]

choir·boy /kwír bòy/ *n.* a boy who sings in a church choir

choir·girl /kwír gùrl/ *n.* a girl who sings in a church choir

choir loft *n.* a raised gallery or part of the upper story in a church, where the choir performs during services

choir·mas·ter /kwír màstər/ *n.* somebody who instructs, trains, and conducts a choir

choir or·gan *n.* a manual or section of a large organ with sets of soft-toned pipes suitable for accompanying a choir. ◊ **great organ**

choir school *n.* a school where the members of a cathedral or church choir are educated and attend regular lessons as well as receiving special musical training

choke[1] /chōk/ *v.* (**choked, chok·ing, chokes**) **1.** *vi.* **STOP BREATHING THROUGH BLOCKAGE OF THROAT** to stop breathing, or breathe with great difficulty, because of a blockage or restriction of the throat **2.** *vt.* **PREVENT BREATHING BY CONSTRICTING THROAT** to prevent somebody from breathing by blocking or squeezing the throat **3.** *vt.* **BLOCK PASSAGE OR CHANNEL** to form an obstruction in a passage, channel, pipe, or roadway and prevent anything from passing along it **4.** *vt.* **PREVENT PLANTS FROM GROWING** to prevent plants from developing by growing over them and depriving them of light and air ○ *the bed was choked with weeds* **5.** *vti.* **BE TOO MOVED TO SPEAK** to be overcome with emotion and unable to speak, or make somebody feel so much emotion that he or she cannot speak (*informal*) **6.** *vi.* **LOSE NERVE AND FALTER** to lose nerve or confidence and falter in the middle of saying or doing something (*informal*) ○ *He gets ahead, two sets to one, and then he chokes!* **7.** *vi.* **REFUSE TO COOPERATE** to refuse to cooperate when presented with something unacceptable (*informal*) ○ *We choked on their last demand.* ■ *n.* **1. NOISE OF CHOKING** a sound or movement made by somebody choking, or indicative of somebody choking **2. FUEL MIXTURE REGULATOR FOR ENGINE** a device that controls the ratio of air to fuel in the mixture supplied to an internal-combustion engine ○ *pull the choke out* [Old English *ācēocian* from, ultimately, *cēoce* "cheek." The underlying idea is of cutting off the air supply by constricting the cheeks.] —**chok·ing** *adj.* —**chok·ing·ly** *adv.*

choke back *vt.* to stop the expression of an emotional response to something by a deliberate effort of self-control ○ *I couldn't choke back my tears any longer.*

choke off *vt.* to stop the flow, supply, or development of something, usually abruptly

choke[2] /chōk/ *n.* **1. INEDIBLE CENTRAL PART OF ARTICHOKE** the bristly inner inedible part of an artichoke **2. ARTICHOKE** an artichoke (*informal*) [Shortening]

choke·ber·ry /chṓk bèrree/ (*plural* **-ries**) *n.* **1.** (*plural* **-ries** *or* **-ry**) **N. AMERICAN SHRUB WITH SOUR FRUITS** a North American shrub of the rose family that bears small red or purplish sour fruits and small white or pink flowers. Genus: *Aronia.* **2. BITTER FRUIT OF CHOKEBERRY** the small bitter fruit of the chokeberry [Late 18thC. From its bitter fruit.]

choke·bore /chṓk bawr/ *n.* **1. TAPERING BORE** a shotgun bore that tapers toward the muzzle to prevent wide scattering of the shot **2. SHOTGUN WITH CHOKEBORE** a shotgun with a bore that tapers toward the muzzle

choke chain *n.* a chain serving as a collar and short leash that fits in a sliding loop around an animal's neck, so that when the animal pulls away the chain gets tighter. Choke chains are used in obedience training for dogs and to restrain powerful animals.

choke·cher·ry /chṓk chèrree/ (*plural* **-ries**) *n.* **1.** (*plural* **-ries** *or* **-ry**) **N AMERICAN WILD CHERRY** a North American wild cherry that produces long clusters of small white flowers, followed by dark red or black bitter fruit. Latin name: *Prunus virginiana.* **2. FRUIT OF CHOKECHERRY** the fruit of the chokecherry

choke coil *n.* a type of induction coil used to limit or suppress the flow of alternating current without stopping the flow of direct current

choke col·lar *n.* = **choke chain**

choked /chōkt/ *adj. U.K.* = **choked up** (*informal*)

choke·damp /chṓk dàmp/ *n.* MINING = **blackdamp**

choked up *adj.* overcome by emotion, usually unhappiness, disappointment, or resentment (*informal*)

choke·hold /chṓk hōld/ *n.* = **stranglehold**

choke·point /chṓk pòynt/ *n.* **1. AREA OF BLOCKAGE** a congested or narrow part where a blockage can occur **2.** NAVY **NARROW SHALLOW SEA CORRIDOR** a place at sea where geography and water depth combine to create a narrow shallow corridor for submarines and surface ships **3. STICKING POINT** a point or situation that is an obstacle to an agreement or results in an impasse ○ *amnesty being the choke point in the political settlement*

chok·er /chṓkər/ *n.* **1. NECK ORNAMENT** a short length of cloth or ribbon, or a short necklace, that fastens closely around the neck and is worn as an ornament **2. HIGH CLOSE-FITTING COLLAR** a high close-fitting collar, e.g., a clerical collar

cho·lan·gi·og·ra·phy /kō lànjee óggrəfee/ *n.* X-ray examination of the bile ducts to check for obstructions, carried out after the patient has swallowed a substance that shows up on an X-ray [Mid-20thC. Coined from CHOLE- + ANGIOGRAPHY.] —**cho-**

lan·gi·o·gram /kō lánjee ə gràm/ *n.* —**cho·lan·gi·o·graph·ic** /kō lànjee ə gráffik/ *adj.*

chole- *prefix.* bile, bile ducts, gall bladder ○ *cholelithiasis* [From Greek *kholē*. Ultimately from an Indo-European base meaning "yellow-colored, bile," which is also the ancestor of English *bile, gall,* and *yellow.*]

cho·le·cal·cif·er·ol /kōləkal siffə ròl, -ràwl/ *n.* = **vitamin D_3**

cho·le·cyst /kṓlə sìst/ *n.* the gallbladder (*technical*)

cho·le·cys·tec·to·my /kōlə-/ (*plural* **-mies**) *n.* a surgical operation to remove the gallbladder —**cho·le·cys·tec·to·mize** /kōlə sis téktə mīz/ *vt.*

cho·le·cys·ti·tis /kòlə si stī́ tiss/ *n.* inflammation of the gallbladder, usually caused by a bacterial infection or gallstones

cho·le·cys·to·du·o·de·nos·to·my /kōlə sistō doo odd'n óstəmee, kóllə-/ (*plural* **-mies**) *n.* a surgical procedure in which the gallbladder is connected directly to the first part of the small intestine (**duodenum**)

cho·le·cys·tog·ra·phy /kōlə sis tóggrəfee, kóllə-/ (*plural* **-phies**) *n.* X-ray examination of the gallbladder after the patient has swallowed a substance that shows up on an X-ray

cho·le·cys·to·ki·nin /kōlə sístə kī́nin/ *n.* a hormone secreted by cells at the top of the small intestine that stimulates the gallbladder, making it contract and release bile [Early 20thC. Coined from CHOLECYST + KININ.]

cho·le·li·thi·a·sis /kōlə li thī́ əsiss/ *n.* the formation or presence of gallstones in the gallbladder or bile ducts

chol·er /kóllər/ *n.* **1. BAD TEMPER** anger or bad temper (*archaic or literary*) **2. BODILY FLUID CAUSING BAD TEMPER** one of the four basic fluids (**humors**) of the body according to medieval medicine, thought to make somebody whose body contained too much of it prone to anger and irritability (*archaic*) [14thC. Via French *colère* from Latin *cholera* "bile" (see CHOLERA), believed to cause bad temper.]

chol·er·a /kóllərə/ *n.* an acute and often fatal intestinal disease that produces severe diarrhea, vomiting, dehydration, and gastric pain, and is usually caused by swallowing food or water contaminated with a bacterium *Vibrio cholerae* [14thC. Via Latin, "bile," originally "illness caused by bile," from Greek *kholera,* from *kholē* "bile." Revived in its modern sense in the 17thC.] —**chol·e·ra·ic** /kòllə ráy ik/ *adj.* —**chol·e·roid** /kóllə ròyd/ *adj.*

chol·er·ic /kóllərik, kə lérrik/ *adj.* liable to become angry or irritated, or showing anger or irritation (*literary*) [14thC. Directly and via French *cholérique* from Latin *cholericus* "bilious," from, ultimately, Greek *kholera* (see CHOLERA).] —**chol·er·i·cal·ly** *adv.*

cho·le·sta·sis /kōli stáyssiss, -stássiss/ *n.* a stoppage or slowing of the flow of bile —**cho·le·stat·ic** /kōli státtik/ *adj.*

cho·les·te·a·to·ma /kə lèstee ə tṓmə, kōləstee ə tṓmə/ *n.* a potentially dangerous condition of the middle ear in which a mass of cholesterol and skin scales forms, grows, and invades the local structures, including bone

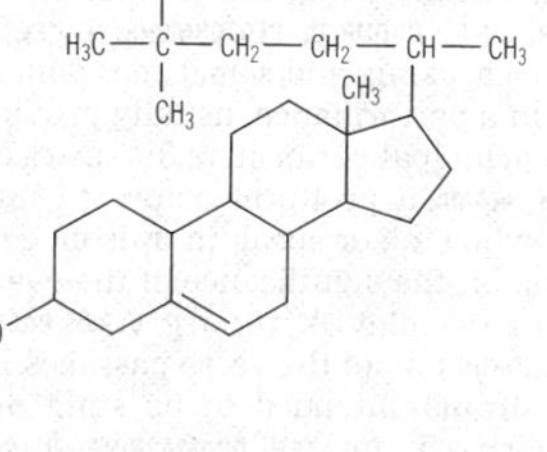

Cholesterol

cho·les·ter·ol /kə léstə ràwl/ *n.* a steroid alcohol (**sterol**) found in animal tissue, bile, blood, eggs, and fats, high levels of which in the blood are linked to atherosclerosis, heart disease, and gallstones. Cholesterol is important to the body as a constituent of cell membranes, and is involved in the formation of bile acid and some hormones. Formula: $C_{27}H_{45}OH$. [Late 19thC. Coined from CHOLE- + Greek *stereos* "stiff" + -OL.]

cho·le·styr·a·mine /kōli steérə meen, kō léstər á meen/ *n.* a synthetic resin used to lower cholesterol in the blood by binding it with bile acids [Mid-20thC. Coined from CHOLE- + STYRENE + -AMINE.]

cho·li /chṓlee/ (*plural* **-lis**) *n.* a short fitted top with short sleeves, worn underneath a sari [Early 20thC. From Hindi *colī.*]

cho·line /kṓ leen/ *n.* a soluble ammonia derivative (**amine**) that is found in animal and plant tissue and helps to prevent fat from being deposited in the liver. Choline is also involved in the formation of acetylcholine. Formula: $C_5H_{15}NO_2$. [Mid-19thC. Coined from CHOLE- + -INE.]

cho·lin·er·gic /kōlə núrjik/ *adj.* **1. ACTIVATED BY OR RELEASING ACETYLCHOLINE** used to describe nerve cells or fibers that are activated by acetylcholine or that release it **2. RESEMBLING ACETYLCHOLINE** used to describe drugs that resemble acetylcholine in the way they work or the effect they have [Mid-20thC. Coined from CHOLINE + Greek *ergon* "work."] —**cho·lin·er·gi·cal·ly** *adv.*

cho·lin·es·ter·ase /kōli néstə ràyss, -ràyz/ *n.* **1. ENZYME** an enzyme of the blood, brain, and heart that decomposes acetylcholine into acetic acid and choline, suppressing its stimulatory effect on nerves **2.** = **acetylcholinesterase** [Mid-20thC. Coined from CHOLINE + ESTERASE.]

chol·la /chóy ə/ (*plural* **-las** *or* **-la**) *n.* a cactus of the southwestern United States and Mexico that has cylindrical stem segments and yellow spines. Some cultivated types have vividly colored flowers. Genus: *Opuntia.* [Mid-19thC. From Mexican Spanish, from obsolete Spanish, "top of the head," perhaps from Old French *cholle* "round lump."]

Cho·lu·la /chə lóollə/ town in Puebla State, central Mexico, situated 8 mi./13 km west of the city of Puebla. Population: 77,923 (1990).

chomp /chomp/, **chump** /chump/ *vti.* (**chomped, chomp·ing, chomps; chumped, chump·ing, chumps**) **CHEW NOISILY** to take big bites of food and chew steadily, noisily, and with obvious satisfaction (*informal*) ■ *n.* (*informal*) **1. NOISY BITE** a big noisy bite into something **2. SOUND OF BITE** the sound made by noisy energetic biting or chewing [Mid-17thC. Variant of CHAMP, and imitative of the sound.]

Chom·sky /chómskee/, **Noam** (*b.* 1928) U.S. linguist. He is known for his transformational-generative grammar, which revolutionized linguistics, and for his political writings. Full name **Avram Noam Chomsky**

chon /chōn/ (*plural* **chon**) *n.* **1. KOREAN UNIT OF CURRENCY:** a subunit of currency of North and South Korea. See table at **currency 2. COIN OR BILL WORTH ONE CHON** a coin bill worth one chon [Mid-20thC. From Korean.]

chondr- *prefix.* = **chondro-**

chon·dral /kóndrəl/ *adj.* relating to or consisting of cartilage

chondri- *prefix.* = **chondro-**

chon·dri·fy /kóndrə fī/ (**-fied, -fy·ing, -fies**) *vti.* to change tissue into cartilage, or be changed into cartilage [Late 19thC. Formed from Greek *khondros* "cartilage."] —**chon·dri·fi·ca·tion** /kòndrəfi káysh'n/ *n.*

chon·drite /kón drīt/ *n.* a stony meteorite that contains spherical masses (**chondrules**) of mainly silicate minerals [Mid-19thC. Coined from Greek *khondros* "granule, cartilage" + -ITE.] —**chon·drit·ic** /drítik/ *adj.*

chondro- *prefix.* **1.** cartilage ○ *chondrocranium* **2.** granule ○ *chondrule* [From Greek *khondros*]

chon·dro·blast *n.* a cell that secretes chondrin for the formation of cartilage

chon·dro·cra·ni·um /kòn drō kráy nee əm/ (*plural* **-ums** *or* **-a** /-ə/) *n.* the part of an embryo's skull that consists of cartilage that later hardens into bone

chon·dro·ma /kon drṓmə/ (*plural* **-mas** *or* **-ma·ta** /-mətə/) *n.* a benign abnormal growth of cartilage

chon·drule /kón drool/ *n.* a small spherical mass of mineral matter from outer space, sometimes found in meteorites. Chondrules usually consist of olivine or pyroxene. [Late 19thC. Coined from CHONDRITE + -ULE.]

Chong /chong/, **Son** (1676–1759) Korean artist. He was the first Korean to paint in a non-Chinese style, and was noted for his landscapes.

Chong·qing /chŏong chíng/ city on the Yangtze River in southern Szechwan Province, south central China. It was China's capital from 1937 to 1946. Population: 2,980,000 (1991).

Chon·ju /jŏong jóo/, **Chŏn·ju** town and capital of North Chŏlla Province, South Korea, situated 120 mi./193 km south of Seoul. Population: 563,406 (1995).

choo-choo /chóo chòo/, **choo-choo train** *n.* a railroad train or locomotive (*babytalk*) [Early 20thC. Imitation of the sound of a steam train.]

choose /chooz/ (**chose** /chōz/, **cho·sen** /chṓz'n/, **choos·ing, choos·es**) *vti.* **1. DECIDE FROM AMONG RANGE OF OPTIONS** to decide which of a number of different things or people is best or most suitable **2. MAKE A DELIBERATE DECISION** to make a deliberate decision to do something [Old English *cēosan*. Ultimately from an Indo-European word that is also the ancestor of Latin *gustus* "taste" (source of English *gusto*).] —**choos·er** *n.*

choose up *vti.* to pick the players wanted on a team for a game

choos·y /chóozee/ (**-i·er, -i·est**), **choos·ey** (**-i·er, -i·est**) *adj.* very precise or discriminating in preferences (*informal*) —**choos·i·ness** *n.*

Cho O·yu /chṑ ō yóo/ mountain in the Himalaya range, one of the world's highest peaks. Height: 26,906 ft./8,201 m.

chop[1] /chop/ *v.* (**chopped, chop·ping, chops**) **1.** *vt.* **CUT UP SOMETHING WITH SHARP TOOL** to cut something into pieces with downward strokes of an ax, knife, or other sharp-bladed tool ○ *a dish of chopped liver* **2.** *vt.* **CUT OFF SOMETHING** to use a quick sharp blow or blows to sever or fell something ○ *chopped down the tree* **3.** *vi.* **MAKE CHOPPING MOVEMENTS** to make downward cutting movements with a tool or with the hand **4.** *vt.* **FORM BY CHOPPING** to make something such as a hole or path by chopping with an ax or other tool ○ *He chopped his way through the undergrowth.* **5.** *vt.* SPORTS **HIT BALL WITH SHARP DOWNWARD MOVEMENT** to hit a ball with a quick sharp downward movement of the racket or bat, often in order to give the ball backspin **6.** *vt.* **HIT SHARPLY DOWNWARD** to hit somebody or something with a sharp downward motion ■ *n.* **1.** FOOD **SLICE OF MEAT WITH BONE** a small piece of red meat cut from the ribs, loin, or shoulder, and usually with the bone still attached ○ *pork chops* **2. SHARP STROKE DOWNWARD** a sudden strong downward blow with the hand or a cutting tool ○ *a karate chop* **3.** *U.K.* **DISMISSAL** dismissal from a job (*informal*) ○ *was given the chop* **4. IRREGULAR WAVE MOTION** turbulent irregular motion in waves or water **5. DISTURBED SEA** a stretch of choppy water, especially on the sea [14thC. Variant of CHAP "to crack open."]

chop[2] /chop/ (**chopped, chop·ping, chops**) *vi.* to change direction or have a change of mind, especially suddenly or frequently [15thC. Variant of CHAP "jaw."]

chop[3] /chop/ *n.* a trademark, official stamp, or mark of quality, especially in the Far East

chop-chop *interj.* used to indicate, often in a bossy or arrogant way, that somebody should hurry or do something quickly or right away (*informal*) [Mid-19thC. Repetition of Pidgin English *chop,* an alteration of Cantonese Chinese *gap* "urgent."] —**chop-chop** *adv.*

chop·house /chóp hòwss/ (*plural* **chop·hous·es** /-hòwzəz/) *n.* a restaurant serving grilled meat, e.g., chops and steaks, as its specialty, especially formerly

Frédéric François Chopin

Chop·in /shō pán, -páN/, **Frédéric François** (1810–49) Polish composer and pianist. His piano compositions include mazurkas, études, preludes, nocturnes, waltzes, polonaises, sonatas, and two concertos.

Chop·in, Kate (1850–1904) U.S. novelist, short-story writer, and poet. She wrote *The Awakening* (1899), a pioneering novel of female sexual discovery.

cho·pine /chō pe͞en, chóppin/, **cho·pin** *n.* a type of high shoe with a very thick sole worn by European women in the 16th and 17th centuries [Late 16thC. Via Spanish *chapín* from Old French *chapin*.]

chop·log·ic /chóp lòjjik/ *n.* the presentation of an argument in a way that is either illogical or pedantic and over-complicated [Early 16thC. *Chop* in the obsolete sense "an exchange."]

chop·per /chóppər/ *n.* **1. HELICOPTER** a helicopter (*informal*) **2. BIKE WITH HIGH HANDLEBARS** a motorcycle or bicycle with a lowered seat, raised handlebars, and lengthened forks holding the front wheel **3. CLEAVER** a cutting tool with a handle and a sharp broad blade, used especially for chopping up meat or wood **4.** ELEC ENG **INTERRUPTING DEVICE** a device that regularly interrupts an electric current, a beam of light, or some other stream of radiation in order to produce a pulsing flow or beam ■ **chop·pers** *npl.* **TEETH** teeth, especially large or false ones (*slang*) ■ *vti.* **GO BY HELICOPTER** to transport something or somebody by helicopter, or travel by helicopter (*informal*)

chop·ping board *n. U.K.* = **cutting board**

chop·py /chóppee/ (**-pi·er, -pi·est**) *adj.* rough, with the surface of the water broken up into many small waves made by strong winds —**chop·pi·ly** *adv.* —**chop·pi·ness** *n.*

chops /chops/ *npl.* **1. JAWS** the jaws, or the skin covering the jaws (*informal*) **2.** MUSIC **MUSICAL TALENT** technique or virtuosity in playing an instrument, especially a wind instrument (*slang*)

chop shop *n.* a workshop or garage where stolen vehicles are disguised or broken up for spare parts (*slang*)

chop·sock·y /chóp sòkee/ *n.* the genre of movies in which martial arts, e.g., kung fu, feature prominently ○ *his latest chopsocky extravaganza* [Formed from CHOP + SOCK]

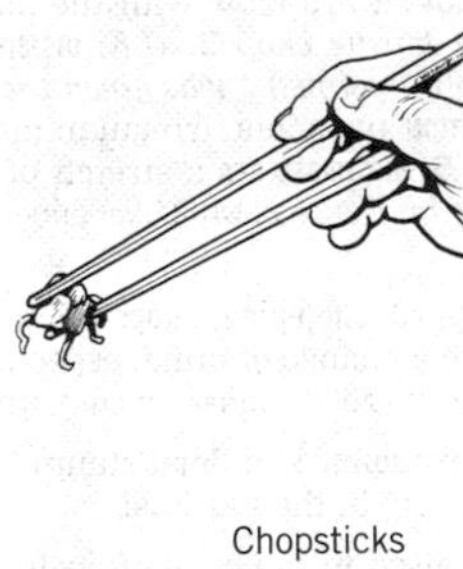

Chopsticks

chop·stick /chóp stìk/ *n.* either of a pair of narrow sticks that are held together in one hand and used when eating or preparing East Asian food [Late 17thC. *Chop* from Pidgin English, (see CHOP-CHOP). Translation of Chinese dialect *kuaizi*, literally "nimble ones."]

chop su·ey /chop so͞o ee/ *n.* a Chinese-style dish made typically of shredded meat and mixed vegetables. It is Chinese-American rather than Chinese in origin. [Late 19thC. From Cantonese Chinese *tsaâp suì* literally, "mixed bits."]

cho·ra·gus /kə ráygəss/ (*plural* **-gi** /-jī/ *or* **-gus·es**) *n.* the leader of the chorus in ancient Greek drama [Early 17thC. Via Latin from Greek *khoragos*, literally "to lead a chorus."] —**cho·rag·ic** /kaw rájjik/ *adj.*

cho·ral /káwrəl/ *adj.* **1. PERFORMED BY CHOIR** arranged for or performed by a chorus or choir ○ *choral singing* **2. RELATING TO CHORUS OR CHOIR** concerned with choral singing, choruses, or choirs ○ *a choral society* [Late 16thC. From medieval Latin *choralis*, from Latin *chorus* (see CHORUS).] —**cho·ral·ly** *adv.*

cho·rale /kə rál, kaw raál/ *n.* **1. GROUP OF SINGERS** a group of singers specializing in a particular style of music, especially church music **2. LUTHERAN HYMN TUNE** a hymn tune, especially a slow and stately one, originally intended for congregational singing in the Lutheran church **3. PIECE OF MUSIC BASED ON CHORALE** a piece of music, especially a choral work, based on a chorale tune or in a style reminiscent of traditional Lutheran church music [Mid-19thC. From German *Choral(gesang)*, a translation of Medieval Latin *(cantus) choralis* "choral song."]

cho·rale pre·lude *n.* an organ prelude based on a chorale tune, used to introduce congregational singing of the chorale on which it is based or performed as a separate piece

chord[1] /kawrd/ *n.* **NOTES STRUCK TOGETHER** two or more musical notes played or sung simultaneously ○ *an F minor chord* ■ *vt.* **SUPPLY CHORDS FOR SOMETHING** to play or produce chords to harmonize and embellish a melody [15thC. Shortening and alteration of ACCORD on the model of Latin *chorda*.]

WORD KEY: USAGE

chord or **cord**? In musical and mathematical contexts the spelling is ***chord***, and this form is also used in figurative meanings that have to do with feelings: *They struck the right chord.* In anatomical contexts (*spinal cord, umbilical cord, vocal cords*), **cord** is more usual. **Cord** has to be used when referring to a kind of thick string.

chord[2] /kawrd/ *n.* **1.** GEOM **LINE THROUGH ARC** a straight line connecting two points on an arc or circle **2.** BUILDING **HORIZONTAL CONNECTING PART** the horizontal part of a truss designed to absorb tension, e.g., in a roof **3.** AIR **AIRFOIL MEASURE** the shortest distance between the leading and trailing edges of an airfoil **4.** ANAT = **cord** [Mid-16thC. Alteration of CORD, on the model of Latin *chorda*.] ◇ **strike** *or* **touch a chord** to produce an emotional, especially a sympathetic, response in somebody, or jog somebody's memory

chord·al /káwrd'l/ *adj.* **1. RELATING TO CHORDS** consisting of chords, or played as a chord **2. BASED ON CHORDS** based principally on musical chords rather than linear melody

chor·date /káwr dàyt/ *n.* any animal that at some stage in its development has a main dorsal nerve cord, a skeletal rod (**notochord**), and gill slits. The chordates include all vertebrates and some primitive invertebrate marine animals. Phylum: Chordata. [Late 19thC. Formed from modern Latin *chordata*, from *chorda* "cord."] —**chor·date** *adj.*

chor·do·phone /káwrdə fōn/ *n.* any musical instrument that produces a sound through vibrating strings [Mid-20thC. Coined from CHORD + -PHONE.]

chord or·gan *n.* a small electronic organ with special keys to produce chords for accompanying a melody

chore /chawr/ *n.* **1. ROUTINE TASK** a task, especially an ordinary household task, that has to be done regularly (*often used in the plural*) **2. UNENJOYABLE TASK** something that is unpleasant, difficult, awkward, or boring to do [Mid-18thC. Alteration of CHAR.]

-chore *suffix.* a plant distributed by a particular means ○ *anemochore* [From Greek *khōrein* "to spread" (source also of English *anchorite*)]

cho·re·a /kaw reé ə/ *n.* jerky spasmodic movements of the limbs, trunk, and facial muscles, common to various diseases of the central nervous system [Late 17thC. Via Latin from Greek *khoreia* "dance." Probably a shortening of the Latin phrase *chorea sancti Viti* "St. Vitus's dance," a disease with this symptom.] —**cho·re·al** *adj.* —**cho·re·ic** *adj.*

cho·re·o·graph /káwree ə gràf/ *v.* **1.** *vti.* **PLAN OUT DANCE ROUTINE** to plan out the movements that dancers are to make to a piece of music **2.** *vt.* **ORGANIZE** to plan, coordinate, and supervise an event or activity ○ *His job is to choreograph royal weddings and other state occasions.* [Mid-20thC. Back-formation from CHOREOGRAPHY.] —**cho·re·og·ra·pher** /kàwree óggrəfər/ *n.*

cho·re·og·ra·phy /kàwree óggrəfee/ (*plural* **-phies**) *n.* **1. COMPOSING DANCES** the work or skill of planning dance movements to accompany music **2. DANCE MOVEMENTS FOR PIECE** the steps and movements planned for a ballet or dance routine, or a written record of them **3. PLANNED MOVEMENT** the carefully planned or executed organization of an event, or the maneuvering of people or things [Late 18thC. From French *choreographie*, literally "dance writing," from *choreo-* "dance" (modeled on Greek *khoreia*) + *-graphie* "writing."] —**cho·re·o·graph·ic** /kàwree ə gráffik/ *adj.* —**cho·re·o·graph·i·cal·ly** /-gráffikəlee/ *adv.*

cho·ri·amb /káwree àmb, káwree àm/ *n.* a poetic foot consisting of two short syllables between two long ones, or two unstressed syllables between two stressed ones [Early 17thC. Via late Latin *choriambus* from Greek *khoriambos*, literally "iamb of a chorus."] —**cho·ri·am·bic** /kàwree ámbik/ *adj.*

cho·ric /káwrik/ *adj.* performed by or written for a chorus, especially a chorus in classical Greek theater [Early 19thC. Via late Latin *choricus* from, ultimately, Greek *khoros*.]

cho·rine /káw reèn/ *n.* a chorus girl (*dated*) [Early 20thC. Coined from CHORUS + -INE.]

cho·ri·o·al·lan·to·is /kàwri ō ə lán tō iss/ *n.* a membrane surrounding the embryo and lying next to the shell in a bird's or reptile's egg. It is a fusion of the chorion and allantois membranes. In mammals, the chorioallantois of the egg forms a major part of the placenta. [Mid-20thC. Coined from CHORION + ALLANTOIS.] —**cho·ri·o·al·lan·to·ic** /kàwri ō allən tṓ ik/ *adj.*

cho·ri·on /káwri òn/ *n.* the outer membrane enclosing the embryo of mammals, reptiles, and birds. It has a dense concentration of blood vessels and aids in the formation of the placenta in mammals. ◊ **amnion** [Mid-16thC. From Greek *khorion*.] —**cho·ri·on·ic** /kàwree ónnik/ *adj.*

cho·ri·on·ic go·nad·o·tro·pin *n.* a hormone that stimulates the production of the estrogen and progesterone needed for the maintenance of pregnancy

cho·ri·on·ic vil·lus *n.* any of the tiny outgrowths from the outer membrane (**chorion**) surrounding an embryo that move into the womb wall to form the placenta (*often used in the plural*)

cho·ri·on·ic vil·lus sam·pling *n.* a prenatal test for birth defects carried out by examining cells from the tiny hairy outgrowths (**villi**) of the outer membrane (**chorion**) surrounding an embryo, which have the same DNA as the fetus

cho·ris·ter /káwristər/ *n.* a member of a chorus, choir, or other group of singers [14thC. Via an Anglo-Norman form of Old French *cuerist* from, ultimately, Latin *chorus* (see CHORUS). The spelling was changed in the 16thC on the model of CHOIR.]

cho·ri·zo /chə reé zō/ (*plural* **-zos**) *n.* a very spicy Mexican or Spanish pork sausage [Mid-19thC. From Spanish.]

C-ho·ri·zon, C ho·ri·zon *n.* the lowermost layer of soil immediately above bedrock

cho·rog·ra·phy /kə róggrəfee/ *n.* the preparation of maps in which specific areas or regions are delineated and often highlighted in some way, e.g., by color-coding [Mid-16thC. Directly or via French from Latin *chorographia*, from Greek *khōrographia*, literally "place writing."] —**cho·rog·ra·pher** *n.* —**cho·ro·graph·ic** /kàwrə gráffik/ *adj.* —**cho·ro·graph·i·cal·ly** /-alee/ *adv.*

cho·roid /káw ròyd/ *n.* **choroid, choroid coat MEMBRANE OF THE EYE** a brownish membrane between the retina and the white of the eye in vertebrates that contains blood vessels and large pigmented cells ■ *adj.* **LIKE THE CHORION** resembling the chorion in being vascular or membranous [Mid-17thC. From Greek *khoroeidēs*, from *khorion* "chorion."]

cho·roid plex·us *n.* a membrane with many small blood vessels in the fluid spaces of the brain that secrets cerebrospinal fluid

chor·tle /cháwrt'l/ *n.* **GLEEFUL LAUGH** a noisy gleeful laugh ■ *vi.* (**-tled, -tling, -tles**) **GIVE A CHORTLE** to laugh in a noisy gleeful way [Late 19thC. Blend of CHUCKLE and SNORT, originated by Lewis CARROLL in *Through the Looking-Glass* (1872).] —**chor·tler** *n.*

cho·rus /káwrəss/ *n.* **1.** MUSIC **REPEATED PART OF A SONG** a set of lines that are sung at least twice in the course of a song, usually being repeated after each verse **2.** THEATER, ARTS **GROUP OF PERFORMERS** a group of people who appear, sing, and sometimes dance together as a unit in a performance, usually providing backing for the principal performers **3.** THEATER **GROUP OF ACTORS IN GREEK DRAMA** a group of actors in ancient Greek drama who sing or speak in unison, generally commenting on the significance of the events that take place in the play **4.** THEATER **VERSE PASSAGE FOR GREEK DRAMA CHORUS** any of the verse passages in an ancient Greek drama intended to be sung or spoken by the chorus **5.** THEATER **DRAMA ROLE** a role in some Elizabethan and historical dramas for a solo actor, who speaks the introductory prologue, comments on the action, and delivers the epilogue **6.** MUSIC **MUSIC FOR GROUP** a musical composition written for a large group of singers, usually with different parts for the different voice types ○ *the Hallelujah Chorus* **7. MANY VOICES TOGETHER** the words spoken or feelings expressed by a group of people all giving voice at the same time ○ *a chorus of complaints* **8. GROUP**

SPEAKING OR MAKING NOISE TOGETHER a group of people or animals all speaking or making a noise together ■ *vt.* **(-rused, -rus·ing, -rus·es) SAY TOGETHER** to speak at the same time, saying the same thing or expressing the same feeling or opinion [Mid-16thC. Via Latin from Greek *khoros.*] ◇ **in chorus** all speaking or making a noise together

cho·rus boy *n.* a man or boy who sings and dances as one of the supporting group of performers in a stage or movie production

cho·rus girl *n.* a woman or girl who sings and dances as one of the supporting group of performers in a stage or movie production

cho·rus line *n.* the chorus of supporting singers and dancers in a musical or variety show

cho·rus·mas·ter /káwrəss màstər/ *n.* somebody who trains, rehearses, and directs a chorus

-chory *suffix.* = **-chore**

chose past tense of **choose**

cho·sen past participle of **choose** ■ *adj.* **SELECTED** picked out from or preferred to the rest ○ *one of the chosen few* ■ *npl.* RELIG = **elect**

cho·sen peo·ple *npl.* the Jews, who, according to the Bible and their own belief, were selected by God to play a unique role in world history

chou /shoo/ (*plural* **choux** /shoo/) *n.* **1.** = **choux pastry 2.** *U.K.* **FILLED SWEET PASTRY** a small pastry with a fruit or cream filling [Early 18thC. From French, "cabbage."]

chouette /shoo ét/ *n.* a variation of backgammon in which one player plays against two or more opponents in one game [Late 19thC. From French, literally "barn owl."]

chough /chuf/ *n.* a Eurasian bird of the crow family, roughly the size of a pigeon, that has glossy black plumage, red legs and feet, and a red or yellow bill. Genus: *Pyrrhocorax.* [12thC. Probably an imitation of its call.]

chouse /chowss/ *vt.* to herd livestock roughly (*regional*) [Early 20thC. Origin unknown.]

Chou·teau /shoo tṓ/, **René Auguste** (1749–1829) U.S. pioneer. He founded St. Louis, Missouri (1764), and was an important figure in the local fur trade.

choux pas·try *n.* a soft glossy egg-rich pastry that puffs up into a hollow case when baked. It is used in making filled pastries such as cream puffs and éclairs.

chow[1] /chow/ *n.* food (*slang*) [Late 18thC. Shortening of Chinese Pidgin English *chow-chow* "food, mixture," perhaps from Chinese *cha* "mixed."]

chow down *vi.* to eat food enthusiastically (*informal*)

chow[2] /chow/, **chow chow** *n.* a stocky thick-coated dog belonging to a breed originally from China, with a tail that curls over its back and a large dark purplish tongue [Late 19thC. From Pidgin English, possibly from Cantonese Chinese *gǒu* "dog."]

chow[3] /chow/ *n.* FOOD = **chow-chow**

chow chow *n.* ZOOL = **chow**[2]

chow-chow, **chow** *n.* **1. CHINESE MIXED VEGETABLE PICKLE** a Chinese mixed vegetable pickle in a yellow sauce, similar to piccalilli **2. TANGY SWEET MIXTURE IN SYRUP** a Chinese mixture of fruit and candied peel in syrup, with stem ginger

chow·der /chówdər/ *n.* a thick soup, especially one made with seafood or fish [Mid-18thC. Probably via French *chaudière* "stew pot," from, ultimately, Latin *caldarium* "hot bath," source of English *caldron*).]

chow·der·head /chówdər hèd/ *n.* a fool or idiot (*informal*) [Mid-19thC. Alteration of English dialect *jolterhead*, by association with CHOWDER.] —**chow·der·head·ed** *adj.*

chow·hound /chów hòwnd/ *n.* somebody who especially enjoys eating (*informal*)

chow line *n.* a line of people waiting for a meal (*informal*)

chow mein /chòw máyn/ *n.* a Chinese-style dish of soft fried noodles, usually cooked with chopped meat and vegetables [From Mandarin Chinese *chǎo miàn* "fried noodles"]

Chr *abbr.* BIBLE Chronicles

Chr. *abbr.* **1.** Christ **2.** Christian

chres·tom·a·thy /kre stómməthee/ (*plural* **-thies**) *n.* a collection of literary passages, especially one assembed for language study [Mid-19thC. Directly or via French *chrestomathie* from Greek *khrēstomatheia*, literally "useful learning."] —**chres·to·math·ic** /krèstə máthik/ *adj.*

Chré·ti·en /kràỳ tyáN/, **Jean** (*b.* 1934) Canadian politician. He became leader of the Liberal party and prime minister of Canada in 1990. Full name **Jean Joseph-Jacques Chrétien**

Chré·ti·en de Troyes /kràỳ tyaN də trwaá/ (*fl.* 1170) French poet. His epics were the first to incorporate Arthurian legends and the quest for the Holy Grail.

chrism /krízzəm/ *n.* **1. ANOINTING OIL** consecrated oil, or a consecrated mixture of balsam and oil, used for anointing people at some ceremonies in the Roman Catholic, Anglican, and Orthodox churches **2. ANOINTING WITH HOLY OIL** a ceremonial anointing with holy oil, especially at confirmation in the Eastern Orthodox churches [Pre-12thC. Via medieval Latin *crisma* from Greek *khrisma* "an anointing," from *khriein* "to anoint" (source of English *Christ* and *cream*).] —**chris·mal** /krízm'l/ *adj.*

chris·ma·tion /kriz máysh'n/ *n.* in the Eastern Orthodox tradition, the act of anointing somebody, or being anointed, with holy oil in a religious ceremony such as confirmation [Mid-16thC. From the medieval Latin stem *chrismation-*, from *crisma* (see CHRISM).]

chris·om /krízzəm/ *n.* a white robe or shawl worn by an infant for his or her baptism (*formal*) [13thC. Alteration of CHRISM, which was popularly pronounced with two syllables.]

chris·om child *n.* a baby that dies within a month of its baptism (*archaic*)

Christ /krīst/ *n.* **1.** CHR = **Jesus Christ 2.** RELIG **THE MESSIAH** according to the Bible, a savior who would come to deliver God's chosen people **3.** RELIG **PAINTING OF JESUS CHRIST** an artistic representation of Jesus Christ ■ *interj.* **SWEARWORD** used to express surprise, annoyance, exasperation, or alarm (*taboo*) [Pre-12thC. Via Latin *Christus* from Greek *Khristos*, literally "anointed," from *khriein* "to anoint" (source of English *chrism*), a translation of Hebrew *māšīăh* "Messiah."] —**Christ·hood** *n.* —**Christ·ly** *adj.*

Chris·ta·del·phi·an /krìstə délfee ən/ *n.* a member of a religious group founded by John Thomas in the United States around 1848. Christadelphians reject the doctrine of the Trinity as not in the Bible and believe in the dead being resurrected with the Second Coming of Christ. [Mid-19thC. Formed from late Greek *Khristadelphos*, literally "in brotherhood with Christ."] —**Chris·ta·del·phi·an** *adj.*

Christ·church city situated near the eastern coast of South Island, New Zealand, 8 mi./13 km northwest of Lyttelton. Population: 331,443 (1996).

chris·ten /kríss'n/ *vt.* **1. BAPTIZE AND NAME** to make somebody, especially a baby, a member of the Christian church in a ceremony that includes a form of baptism and, usually, the giving of a Christian name or names **2. GIVE NAME TO SOMETHING OR SOMEBODY** to give a name to something or somebody, with or without an accompanying ceremony ○ *christen a ship* **3. USE FOR FIRST TIME** to use or wear something for the first time (*informal*) ○ *Shall we christen our new coffee pot?* [Pre-12thC. Formed from Old English *crīsten* "Christian," from Latin *christianus.*] —**chris·ten·er** *n.*

Chris·ten·dom /kríss'ndəm/ *n.* **1. CHRISTIAN COUNTRIES** all the areas of the world where Christianity is accepted as the main religion **2. CHRISTIANS AS A GROUP** all Christian people considered as a group (*archaic or formal*) ◊ **Christianity** *n.* 3 [Old English *cristendom*, literally "condition of being Christian," from *crīsten*]

chris·ten·ing /kríssəning/ *n.* a ceremony in a Christian church in which somebody, especially a baby, is baptized and usually given a Christian name or names

Chris·tian /kríschən/ *n.* **BELIEVER IN JESUS CHRIST AS SAVIOR** somebody who believes that Jesus of Nazareth was sent to the world by God to save humanity, and who tries to follow his teachings and example ■ *adj.* **1.** CHR **FROM THE TEACHINGS OF JESUS CHRIST** based on or relating to a belief in Jesus of Nazareth as the son of God and Messiah, and acceptance of his teachings, contained in the Gospels **2. RELATING TO CHRISTIANITY** relating to Christianity, or belonging to or maintained by a Christian organization, especially a church ○ *Christian theology* ○ *a Christian school* **3. KIND AND UNSELFISH** showing qualities such as kindness, helpfulness, and concern for others (*dated*) [13thC. From Latin *Christianus*, from *Christus* (see CHRIST).] —**Chris·tian·ly** *adv.*

Chris·tian VIII (1786–1848) Danish ruler who was elected to the Norwegian throne in 1814 but ousted the same year. During his Danish reign (1839–48), his Schleswig-Holstein policy precipitated war with Prussia (1848).

Chris·tian E·ra *n.* the period of history dating from the year in which Jesus Christ is believed to have been born. Dates in the early Christian Era are often indicated by A.D., and dates before the Christian Era by B.C.

Chris·ti·an·i·ty /krìschee ánnətee, krìsstee/ *n.* **1. RELIGION THAT FOLLOWS JESUS CHRIST'S TEACHINGS** the religion based on the life, teachings, and example of Jesus Christ **2. HOLDING CHRISTIAN BELIEFS** the fact of holding Christian beliefs or being a Christian **3. CHRISTIANS AS A GROUP** all Christian people considered as a group. ◊ **Christendom**

Chris·tian·ize /kríschə nīz/ (**-ized, -iz·ing, -iz·es**) *vt.* **1. CHANGE BELIEFS TO CHRISTIAN ONES** to change the religious beliefs and practices of a person or group of people from another religion to Christianity **2. MAKE CHRISTIAN** to make somebody or something Christian by imbuing him, her, or it with Christian principles or a Christian spirit —**Chris·tian·i·za·tion** /krìschəni záysh'n/ *n.* —**Chris·tian·iz·er** /kríschə nīzər/ *n.*

Chris·tian name *n.* a given name, especially one given at christening

Chris·tian Sci·ence *n.* a religious group whose members believe that illness should be overcome or managed through religious faith and practice alone. It is based on the teachings and writings of Mary Baker Eddy.

Chris·tian Sci·en·tist *n.* a member of the Church of Christ, Scientist, and a believer in the principles of Christian Science

Chris·tian Scrip·tures *npl.* the New Testament of the Bible as opposed to the Old Testament (**Hebrew Scriptures**)

Chris·tian·sted /kríschən stèd/ town situated on the northeastern coast of St. Croix Island, U.S. Virgin Islands. Population: 2,555 (1990).

chris·tie /krístee/, **chris·ty** (*plural* **chris·ties**) *n.* in skiing, a type of turn used for stopping or rapidly changing direction, in which the skier twists sharply aside while keeping the skis parallel [Early 20thC. Shortening of *Christiania*, the former name of Norway's capital city, Oslo.]

Dame Agatha Christie

Chris·tie /krístee/, **Dame Agatha** (1891–1976) British novelist and playwright. She wrote over seventy detective novels featuring the sleuths Hercule Poirot and Miss Marple.

Chris·ti·na /kriss téénə/ (1626–89) Swedish monarch who, in 1644, negotiated the Peace of Westphalia, bringing to an end the Thirty Years' War.

Christ·mas /krísməss/ *n.* **1. Christmas CHRISTIAN FESTIVAL CELEBRATING BIRTH OF JESUS CHRIST** an annual Christian festival on December 25, celebrating the birth of Jesus Christ **2. SECULAR HOLIDAY ON DECEMBER 25** a secular holiday on December 25 when people traditionally exchange presents and greetings. It is a public holiday in many countries. **3. CHRISTMAS PERIOD** the period around December 25, or the church season extending from December 24 to January 6 **4. QUARTER DAY** in England, Wales, and Ireland, one of the four quarter days, falling on December 25 [Old English *Cristes mæsse*, literally "mass of Christ"]

Christ·mas cac·tus *n.* a branching Brazilian cactus that is cultivated as an ornamental plant for its red, pink, white, or purplish-red flowers that appear in winter. Latin name: *Schlumbergera truncata.*

Christ·mas car·ol *n.* a Christian song celebrating Christmas

Christ·mas Day *n.* = **Christmas** *n.* 1, **Christmas** *n.* 2

Christ·mas dis·ease *n.* a form of hemophilia caused by lack of a protein needed for blood clotting [Mid-20thC. Named for Stephen *Christmas,* a 20th-century Englishman who had the disease.]

Christ·mas Eve *n.* the day or evening of December 24

Christ·mas fern *n.* a North American evergreen fern with dense clusters of thin fronds. Latin name: *Polystichum acrostichoides.*

Christ·mas rose *n.* an evergreen flowering plant, native to Europe and Asia, that has drooping white flowers during the winter. Latin name: *Helleborus niger.*

Christ·mas stock·ing *n.* a stocking or large sock hung up on Christmas Eve by children, in the belief that it will be filled with presents by Santa Claus during the night

Christ·mas·sy *adj.* suggesting the Christmas period or suitable for Christmas ○ *The decorations look really Christmassy.*

Christ·mas·time /krísməss tīm/ *n.* = **Christmas** *n.* 3

Christ·mas tree *n.* an evergreen tree, especially a conifer or an artificial version of one, that is decorated with lights and ornaments at Christmas

Chris·to /krístō/ (*b.* 1935) Bulgarian-born U.S. artist. He is known for his modern conceptual art, in particular "wrapping" monuments and buildings. Full name **Christo Javacheff**

Chris·to·cen·tric /krìstə séntrik/ *adj.* **1. ASSUMING CHRISTIANITY** assuming, implying, or based on Christian values and beliefs, often where this is inappropriate **2. CENTERED ON JESUS CHRIST** concentrating or based strongly on Jesus Christ and his teachings

Chris·to·gram /krístə gràm/ *n.* = **Chi-Rho**

Chris·tol·o·gy /kri stólləjee/ *n.* the branch of theology concerned with the study of the nature, character, and actions of Jesus Christ —**Chris·to·log·i·cal** /krìstə lójjik'l/ *adj.* —**Chris·tol·o·gist** /kri stólləjist/ *n.*

Chris·tophe /krees tóff/, **Henri** (1767–1820) Haitian politician. He was president of Haiti from 1807 to 1811, when he became self-declared king (1811–20).

Chris·toph·er /krístəfər/, **St.** (*fl.* 3rd century) According to legend, he carried Jesus Christ as a child across a river. He is the patron saint of travelers.

Chris·toph·er, Warren (*b.* 1925) U.S. diplomat. He served as secretary of state under Presdent Bill Clinton (1993–97).

Christ's thorn, Christ thorn *n.* a thorny Asian shrub or tree, especially a jujube or a Jerusalem thorn, whose branches are popularly believed to have been used for Jesus Christ's crown of thorns

christy /krístee/ *n.* SKIING = **christie**

Chris·ty /krístee/, **Edwin Pearce** (1873–1952) U.S. entertainer. He is known for his minstrel troupe *The Christy Minstrels,* whose members were white singers performing in blackface (1840s-50s).

chrom- *prefix.* = **chromo-** (*used before vowels*)

chro·ma /krṓmə/ *n.* = **saturation** [Late 19thC. From Greek *khrōma* "color."]

chro·maf·fin /krṓməfin/ *adj.* used to describe cell components that can be easily and deeply stained with chromium salts, thereby indicating the presence of epinephrine or norepinephrine [Early 20thC. Coined from CHROMO- + Latin *affinis* "related."]

chromat- *prefix.* = **chromato-** (*used before vowels*)

chro·mate /krṓ màyt/ *n.* any salt or ester of chromic acid [Early 20thC. Formed from CHROMIC.]

chro·mat·ic /krō máttik/ *adj.* **1.** MUSIC **RELATING TO CHROMATIC SCALES** used to describe a musical scale that runs through all the semitones in an octave, e.g., using all the keys, black and white, on a keyboard **2.** MUSIC **HAVING FREQUENT ACCIDENTALS** used to describe music that is based on the chromatic scale or that makes frequent use of notes that are outside the key in which it is written **3. RELATING TO COLOR** relating to color and phenomena connected with it [15thC. Directly or via French *chromatique* from, ultimately, Greek *chrōmatikos,* from *khrōma* "color."] —**chro·mat·i·cal·ly** *adv.*

chro·mat·ic ab·er·ra·tion *n.* an optical aberration in a lens, caused by a defect and leading to different colored light being refracted differently

chro·mat·i·cism /krō mátti sìzzəm/ *n.* the use in music of the chromatic scale, or of many notes and harmonies that are foreign to the basic key

chro·ma·tic·i·ty /krṑmə tíssətee/ *n.* the color quality of light precisely and uniquely defined in terms of three factors (**chromaticity coordinates**)

chro·mat·ics /krō máttiks/ *n.* the science or study of color (*takes a singular verb*) —**chro·ma·tist** /krṓmətist/ *n.*

chro·mat·ic scale *n.* a scale whose octave consists of twelve notes in which every member is a semitone apart from the next

chro·ma·tid /krṓmətid/ *n.* either of the two strands into which a chromosome divides in the process of duplicating itself in cell division [Early 20thC. Formed from the Greek stem *khrōmat-,* from *khrōma* "color."]

chro·ma·tin /krṓmətin/ *n.* the substance that forms chromosomes and contains DNA, RNA, and various proteins [Late 19thC. Formed from the Greek stem *khrōmat-,* from *khrōma* "color."] —**chro·ma·tin·ic** /krṑmə tínnik/ *adj.*

chromato- *prefix.* **1.** color ○ *chromatography* **2.** chromatin ○ *chromatolysis* [From Greek *khrōmat-,* the stem of *khrōma* "color"]

chro·mat·o·gram /krō máttə gràm/ *n.* a pattern formed by substances that have been separated by chromatography

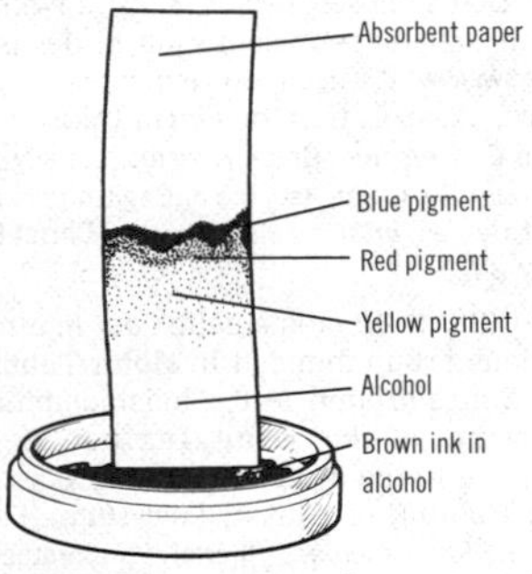

Chromatography

chro·ma·tog·ra·phy /krṑmə tóggrəfee/ *n.* a method of finding out which components a gaseous or liquid mixture contains that involves passing it through or over something that absorbs the different components at different rates —**chro·mat·o·graph** /krō máttə gràf/ *n.* —**chro·ma·tog·ra·pher** /krṑmə tóggrəfər/ *n.* —**chro·mat·o·graph·ic** /krō màttə gráffik/ *adj.* —**chro·mat·o·graph·i·cal·ly** /-əlee/ *adv.*

chro·ma·tol·y·sis /krṑmə tóllississ/ *n.* the breakdown of the substance that forms chromosomes (**chromatin**) within an injured cell nucleus [Late 19thC. Coined from CHROMATO- + -LYSIS.]

chro·mat·o·phore /krō máttə fàwr/ *n.* **1.** ZOOL **PIGMENT-CONTAINING CELL** a pigment-containing cell in many animals that, when it expands or contracts, causes a change in the animal's skin coloring. Octopus, squid, and some frogs and lizards contain these cells. **2.** BOT = **chromoplast** —**chro·mat·o·phor·ic** /krō màttə fáwrik/ *adj.*

chrome /krōm/ *n.* **1. CHROMIUM-PLATED METAL** shiny chromium-plated metal, e.g., that used formerly to trim cars **2. COMPOUND CONTAINING CHROMIUM** an alloy, dye, or pigment containing chromium **3.** CHEM = **chromium** ■ *vt.* (**chromed, chrom·ing, chromes**) **1. COAT WITH CHROMIUM** to electroplate a metal with chromium in order to make it shiny and protect it against corrosion **2. TREAT WITH CHROMIUM COMPOUND** to treat a substance with a chromium compound, usually when dyeing or tanning it [Early 19thC. Via French from Greek *khrōma* "color,"; because compounds containing it are often brightly colored.]

-chrome *suffix.* color, pigment ○ *phytocrome* [From Greek *khrōma* "color"]

chrome al·um *n.* a red-violet crystalline solid used as a fixing agent in dyeing, tanning, and photography. Formula: $CrK(SO_4)_2.12H_2O$.

chrome green *n.* a brilliant green pigment containing chrome yellow and iron blue, used to dye fabrics

chrome red *n.* a bright red-orange pigment containing lead chromate and lead oxide, used in paints and dyes

chrome tape *n.* magnetic recording tape that is coated with chromium dioxide

chrome yel·low *n.* a yellow pigment containing lead chromate and lead sulfate

chro·mic /krṓmik/ *adj.* relating to or containing chromium with a valence of 3

chro·mic ac·id *n.* an unstable oxidizing acid existing only in solution or in the form of a salt. Formula: H_2CrO_4.

chro·mite /krṓ mīt/ *n.* a brownish-black mineral ore consisting of an oxide of iron and chromium. It is the only commercial source of chromium. Formula: $FeCr_2O_4$.

chro·mi·um /krṓmee əm/ *n.* a bluish-white metallic element used in alloys and electroplating to increase hardness and resistance to corrosion. Its compounds are used as pigments, as catalysts, and in tanning. Symbol **Cr**

chro·mi·um di·ox·ide *n.* a black crystalline solid used to coat recording tape because of its magnetic properties. Formula: CrO_2.

chro·mo /krṓ mō/ (*plural* **-mos**) *n.* a chromolithograph [Mid-19thC. Shortening.]

chromo- *prefix.* **1.** color, pigment ○ *chromolithograph* ○ *chromogen* **2.** chromium ○ *chromite* [From Greek *khrōma* "color"]

chro·mo·dy·nam·ics /krṑ mō dī námmiks/ *n.* = **quantum chromodynamics**

chro·mo·gen /krṓməjən/ *n.* **1. POTENTIAL PIGMENT** any substance that is capable of being converted into a biological pigment or a dye, e.g., through oxidation **2. PIGMENT-PRODUCING MICROORGANISM** any microorganism that produces a pigment —**chro·mo·gen·ic** /krṑmə jénnik/ *adj.*

chro·mo·lith·o·graph /krṑmə líthə gràf/ *n.* a colored picture produced by making and superimposing multiple lithographs, each of which adds a different color —**chro·mo·li·thog·ra·pher** /krṑməli thóggrəfər/ *n.* —**chro·mo·lith·o·graph·ic** /krṑmə lithə gráffik/ *adj.* —**chro·mo·li·thog·ra·phy** /krṑməli thóggrəfee/ *n.*

chro·mo·mere /krṓmə meer/ *n.* a small, dense, bead-shaped granule of chromatin, found at intervals along a chromosome during cell division —**chro·mo·mer·ic** /krṑmə méerik, -mérrik/ *adj.*

chro·mo·ne·ma /krṑmə néemə/ (*plural* **-ma·ta** /-mətə/) *n.* the coiled central filament that forms the core of a chromosome strand (**chromatid**) [Early 20thC. Coined from CHROMO- + Greek *nēma* "thread."] —**chro·mo·ne·mal** *adj.*

chro·mo·phore /krṓmə fàwr/ *n.* a group of atoms in a molecule that produces color in dyes and other compounds through selective absorption of light, e.g., the azo group —**chro·mo·phor·ic** /krṑmə fáwrik/ *adj.*

chro·mo·plast /krṓmə plàst/ *n.* a membrane-surrounded structure (**plastid**) in a plant cell that contains pigment. Red, yellow, or orange chromoplasts contain carotenoid pigments, and green chromoplasts (**chloroplasts**) contain chlorophyll.

chro·mo·pro·tein /krṑmə prṓ teen/ *n.* any protein that contains a pigmented, nonprotein, metal-containing chemical group. Hemoglobins and carotenoids are chromoproteins.

chro·mo·some /krṓmə sōm/ *n.* a rod-shaped structure

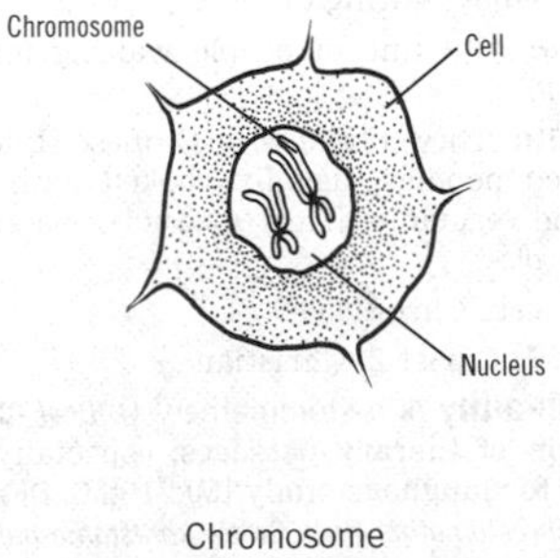

Chromosome

in a cell nucleus carrying the genes that determine sex and the characteristics an organism inherits from its parents. A normal human body cell contains 46 chromosomes arranged in 23 pairs. [Late 19thC. From German *Chromosom,* formed from Greek *khrōma* "color" + *sōma* "body,"; because chromosomes readily take up dye.] —**chro·mo·so·mal** /krṑmə sṓm'l/ *adj.*

chro·mo·some band *n.* one of the sections that chromosomes are made up of, visible as bands and used to identify chromosome types

chro·mo·some map *n.* a diagram that shows the positions of genes on a chromosome

chro·mo·some num·ber *n.* the number of chromosomes present in the cell nucleus of a species of plant or animal. A normal human body has a chromosome number of 46.

chro·mo·sphere /krṓmə sfeer/ *n.* **1.** LOWER REGION OF SUN'S ATMOSPHERE the lower region of the Sun's atmosphere, between the photosphere and the corona **2.** LOWER ATMOSPHERE OF STAR the lower region of the atmosphere of any star —**chro·mo·spher·ic** /krṑmə sférrik, krṑmə sfeérik/ *adj.*

chro·mous /krṓməss/ *adj.* relating to or containing chromium, especially chromium in its divalent state [Mid-19thC. Formed from CHROMIUM.]

chron. *abbr.* **1.** chronicle **2.** chronological **3.** chronology

Chron. *abbr.* BIBLE Chronicles

chron- *prefix.* = **chrono-** (*used before vowels*)

chron·ic /krónnik/ *adj.* **1.** MED LONG-LASTING used of an illness or medical condition that lasts over a long period and sometimes causes a long-term change in the body **2.** MED WITH LONG-TERM ILLNESS having a particular long-term illness or condition **3.** ALWAYS PRESENT always present or recurring **4.** HABITUAL repeatedly doing something or behaving compulsively ○ *a chronic liar* [15thC. Via French *chronique* from, ultimately, Greek *khronikos* "to do with time," from *khronos* "time."] —**chron·i·cal·ly** *adv.* —**chro·nic·i·ty** /krə níssətee/ *n.*

chronic fatigue syndrome *n.* an illness without a known cause that is characterized by long-term exhaustion, muscle weakness, depression, and sleep disturbances, possibly as a reaction to a viral infection in somebody already debilitated

chron·i·cle /krónnik'l/ *n.* **1.** HISTORICAL ACCOUNT an account of events presented in chronological order **2.** NARRATIVE a narrative or fictional account ■ *vt.* (**-cled, -cling, -cles**) MAKE RECORD OF to record an event or series of events in chronological order [14thC. Via Anglo-Norman *cronicle* from, ultimately, Greek *khronika* (plural) "annals," from *khronos* "time."] —**chron·i·cler** *n.*

chron·i·cle play *n.* a play based on historical events, especially one from the Elizabethan period

Chron·i·cles *n.* either of two books of the Bible that tell the story of the Israelites from the creation of Adam to the middle of the 6th century B.C. (*takes a singular verb*)

chrono- *prefix.* TIME time ○ *chronograph* [From Greek *khronos* "time"]

chron·o·bi·ol·o·gy /krṑnnə bī óllejee/ *n.* the study of recurring cycles of events in the natural world —**chron·o·bi·o·log·ic** /-bī́ ə lójjik/ *adj.* —**chron·o·bi·ol·o·gist** /-bī óllәjist/ *n.*

chron·o·gram /krónnə gràm, krṓnə-/ *n.* **1.** INSCRIPTION WITH HIDDEN DATE a phrase or inscription containing letters indicating a date. Roman numerals are often used in this way. **2.** CHRONOGRAPH RECORD a record produced by a chronograph —**chron·o·gram·mat·ic** /krṑnnə grə máttik, krṑnə-/ *adj.* —**chron·o·gram·mat·i·cal·ly** /-máttiklee/ *adv.*

chron·o·graph /krónnə graf, krṓnə-/ *n.* an instrument, e.g., a stopwatch, that records time with great accuracy —**chron·o·graph·ic** /krṑnnə gráffik, krṑnə-/ *adj.* —**chron·o·graph·i·cal·ly** /-gráffiklee/ *adv.*

chronol., **chron.** *abbr.* **1.** chronological **2.** chronology

chron·o·log·i·cal /krṑnnə lójjik'l, krṑnə-/ *adj.* **1.** IN ORDER OF TIME presented or arranged in the order in which events occur or occurred **2.** OF CHRONOLOGY relating to chronology —**chron·o·log·i·cal·ly** *adv.*

chron·o·log·i·cal age *n.* somebody's real age, as opposed to the age suggested by mental or physical development

chro·nol·o·gist /krə nóllәjist/ *n.* somebody who studies, or is an expert in applying, the methods used for determining the correct sequence of events

chro·nol·o·gy /krə nóllәjee/ (*plural* **-gies**) *n.* **1.** ORDER OF EVENTS the order in which events occur, or their arrangement according to this order **2.** LIST OF EVENTS a list or table of events arranged in order of occurrence **3.** STUDY OF ORDER IN TIME the study of, or the science of determining, the order in which things occur [Late 16thC. From modern Latin *chronologia,* formed from Greek *khronos* "time."]

chro·nom·e·ter /krə nómmətər/ *n.* any instrument designed to measure time accurately

chron·o·met·ric /krṑnnə méttrik, krṑnə-/, **chron·o·met·ri·cal** /krṑnnə méttrik'l, krṑnə-/ *adj.* relating to or designed for the accurate measurement of time —**chron·o·met·ri·cal·ly** *adv.*

chro·nom·e·try /krə nómmətree/ *n.* the study or science of the accurate measurement of time

chron·on /krṓ nòn/ *n.* a unit of time equal to the time that it would take for a photon to cross the diameter of an electron, taken as approximately 10^{-24} seconds [Coined from CHRONO- + -ON]

chron·o·scope /krṑnnə skṓp, krṑnə-/ *n.* an instrument that measures very small intervals of time —**chron·o·scop·ic** /krṑnnə skóppik, krṑnə-/ *adj.*

chrys·a·lid /krísselid/ *adj.* AT THE CHRYSALIS STAGE used to describe the stage between larva and adult in an insect and the protective covering formed at this time ■ *n.* (*plural* **chrys·a·lids** *or* **chry·sal·i·des**) = **chrysalis** [Late 18thC. From Latin *chrysa(l)lid-,* the stem of *chrysa(l)lis* (see CHRYSALIS).]

chrys·a·lis /kríssəliss/ *n.* **1.** INSECT BETWEEN LARVA AND ADULT an insect at the stage of changing from larva to adult, during which it is inactive and encased in a hard cocoon **2.** INSECT COCOON the hard cocoon that protects a butterfly, moth, or other pupa during its change from larva to adult **3.** THING DEVELOPING anything in an early or intermediate stage of development (*literary*) [Early 17thC. Via Latin *chrysal(l)is* from Greek *khrūsalis,* from *khrūsos* "gold," from the gold color or metallic sheen of the pupae of some species.]

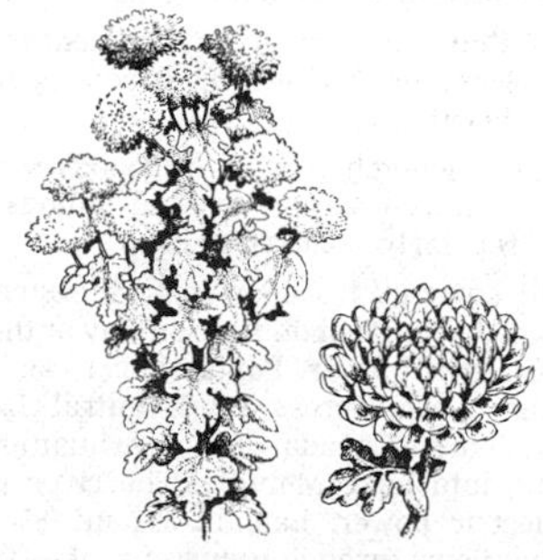

Chrysanthemum

chry·san·the·mum /kri sánthəməm, kri zánthəməm/ *n.* a plant with brightly colored globe-shaped flowers and small densely clustered petals. Genus: *Chrysanthemum.* [Mid-16thC. From Greek *khrūsanthemon,* literally "gold flower," from the color of the corn marigold, a member of the species, to which the name was originally applied.]

chrys·el·e·phan·tine /krìss ellə fán tìn, krìss ellə fán teén/ *adj.* used to describe classical Greek sculptures that are made of or overlaid with gold and ivory [Early 19thC. From Greek *khrūselephantinos,* from *khrūsos* "gold" + *elephas* "elephant, ivory."]

Chrys·ler /krī́sslər/, **Walter Percy** (1875–1940) U.S. automobile manufacturer. He introduced the Chrysler automobile (1924) and founded the Chrysler Corporation (1925).

chryso- *prefix.* gold, golden ○ *chrysophyte* [From Greek *khrusos* "gold," of Semitic origin]

chrys·o·ber·yl /kríssə bèrrəl/ *n.* a green, yellow, or brown mineral used as a gemstone [Mid-17thC. From Latin *chrysoberyllus,* from Greek *khrūsos* "gold" + *bērullos* "beryl."]

chrys·o·lite /kríssə lìt/ *n.* the mineral olivine (*no longer used technically*) [Middle English. Via Old French from, ultimately, Greek *khrūsolithos,* literally "gold stone."]

chrys·o·mel·id /krìssə méllid, krìssə meélid/ *n.* a small, brightly colored, leaf-eating beetle. Colorado potato beetles are chrysomelids. Family: Chrysomelidae. [Late 19thC. Via modern Latin *Chrysomelidae* (plural) from *Chrysomela,* from Greek *khrusomēlon* "quince" (literally "golden apple"), influenced by Greek *khrusomēlolonthion,* literally "little golden chafer."]

chrys·o·prase /kríssə pràyz/ *n.* a bright green variety of chalcedony, used as a gemstone [13thC. Via Old French from, ultimately, Greek *khrūsoprasos,* literally "golden leek." The word originally denoted a golden-green variety of beryl.]

Chry·sos·tom /kríssə stəm/, **John, St.** (349?–407) Syrian theologian and orator. He was Bishop of Constantinople and a Church Father of both the Roman and the Orthodox Christian traditions.

chrys·o·tile /kríssə tìl/ *n.* a green, gray, or white variety of the mineral serpentine. It is an important source of asbestos. [Mid-19thC. Coined from CHRYSO- + Greek *tilos* "fiber," from *tillein* "to pluck."]

chthon·ic /thónnik/, **chtho·ni·an** /thṓnee ən/ *adj.* relating to the underworld as described in Greek mythology [Late 19thC. Formed from Greek *khthōn* "earth."]

chub /chub/ (*plural* **chubs** *or* **chub**) *n.* a minnow with a stout rounded body belonging to a family that includes some North American sea and river fishes and the European carp. Family: Cyprinidae. [15thC. Origin unknown.]

chub·by /chúbbee/ (**-bi·er, -bi·est**) *adj.* pleasantly or charmingly plump, especially in the way that healthy babies and toddlers often are —**chub·bi·ly** *adv.* —**chub·bi·ness** *n.*

chuck[1] /chuk/ *vt.* (**chucked, chuck·ing, chucks**) **1.** THROW CARELESSLY to throw something, especially in a careless or casual way (*informal*) **2.** GET RID OF to get rid of something unwanted (*informal*) **3.** FORCE TO LEAVE to force somebody to leave a place, or take away somebody's membership of an organization (*informal*) **4.** GIVE UP to give something up, especially a job (*informal*) **5.** TICKLE AFFECTIONATELY UNDER CHIN to give somebody an affectionate pat or tickle under the chin ■ *n.* **1.** CARELESS THROW a throw, especially a careless or casual throw (*informal*) **2.** AFFECTIONATE TICKLE UNDER THE CHIN an affectionate pat or tickle under somebody's chin [Early 16thC. Perhaps from Old French *chuquer* "to knock, bump." Originally in the sense "to pat under the chin," hence "to use a similar small movement to throw something."]

chuck[2] /chuk/ *n.* **1.** TECH CLAMP ON LATHE OR DRILL a clamping device with three or four adjustable jaws, used to hold a piece of woodwork or metalwork in a lathe or a bit in a drill **2.** FOOD CUT OF BEEF a cut of beef that extends from the neck to the shoulder blade **3.** FOOD food (*regional*) [Late 17thC. A variant of CHOCK.]

chuck[3] /chuk/ *vi.* (**chucked, chuck·ing, chucks**) = **cluck** ■ *n.* = **cluck** (*archaic*) [14thC. An imitation of the sound.]

chuck-a-luck *n.* a game in which players bet on the possible combinations of three dice when thrown

chuck·hole /chúk hṑl/ *n. Midwest* a pothole [Mid-19thC. From CHUCK[1].]

chuck·le /chúk'l/ *vti.* (**-led, -ling, -les**) LAUGH QUIETLY to laugh quietly or to yourself ■ *n.* QUIET LAUGH a quiet or inward laugh [Late 16thC. Formed from CHUCK[3]. The word originally meant "to laugh heartily."] —**chuck·ler** *n.* —**chuck·ling·ly** *adv.*

chuck wag·on *n.* a vehicle carrying food and cooking supplies, originally a horse-drawn wagon for transients such as cowboys (*informal*) [*Chuck* of uncertain origin: perhaps from CHUCK[2]]

chuck·wal·la /chúk wàwlə/ (*plural* **-las** *or* **-la**) *n.* a large lizard with a dark body and a blunt yellow tail, found in the deserts of the southwestern United States and Mexico. Latin name: *Sauromalus obesus.* [Late 19thC. Via Mexican Spanish *chachuala* from Cahuilla *tcàxwal.*]

chuck-will's-wid·ow *n.* a large nightjar of the east central and southern United States with mottled brown markings and a call that sounds like its name. Latin name: *Caprimulgus carolinensis.* [Late 18thC. An imitation of its call.]

chu·fa /chóofə/ *n.* an African plant of the sedge family with an edible tuber that looks like a nut. Latin name: *Cyperus esculentus.* [Mid-19thC. From Spanish, literally "fluff, nonsense."]

chuffed /chuft/ *adj. U.K.* very pleased or satisfied (*informal*) [Mid-20thC. Formed from northern English dialect *chuff* "chubby, happy," of unknown origin.]

chug[1] /chug/ *vi.* (**chugged, chug·ging, chugs**) **1.** MAKE REPEATED THUDDING SOUND to make a repetitive thudding sound like that of a small engine **2.** MOVE WITH CHUGGING

SOUND to move along slowly with a chugging sound under the power of an engine **3.** CONTINUE IN STEADY FASHION to continue steadily doing the usual things (*informal*) ■ *n.* CHUGGING NOISE the chugging noise that an engine makes [Mid-19thC. An imitation of the sound.]

chug[2] /chug/ (**chugged, chug·ging, chugs**) *vt.* to drink something, especially beer, quickly and without pausing (*slang*)

Chugach Mountains /cho͞o gach-/ mountain range in southern Alaska, stretching 300 mi./480 km from St. Elias Mountains in the east to Cook Inlet in the west. The highest point is Mount Marcus Baker 13,176 ft./4,016 m.

chug·a·lug /chúggə lùg/ (**-lugged, -lug·ging, -lugs**) *vt.* = **chug** (*informal*) [Mid-20thC. An imitation of the sound of somebody swallowing.]

chu·kar /chúkər/ *n.* a grayish-brown South Asian partridge with red legs and bill, introduced into the western United States as a game bird. Latin name: *Alectoris chukar*. [Early 19thC. From Hindi *cakor*; probably ultimately an imitation of the sound it makes.]

Chuk·chi /cho͝okchee/ (*plural* **-chi** *or* **-chis**), **Chuk·chee** (*plural* **-chee** *or* **-chees**) *n.* **1.** PEOPLES MEMBER OF A SIBERIAN PEOPLE a member of a people who live in the far northeastern corner of Siberia. The Chukchi were the first to breed huskies as working dogs. **2.** LANG SIBERIAN LANGUAGE a language spoken in the Chukchi Peninsula of northeastern Siberia. Chukchi is spoken by about 12,000 people. [Early 18thC. From Russian.] —**Chuk·chi** *adj.*

Chuk·chi Sea part of the Arctic Ocean, situated north of the Bering Strait between Asia and North America

chuk·ka /chúkə/ *n.* **1. chuk·ka, chuk·ka boot** CLOTHES ANKLE-LENGTH BOOT a casual ankle-high lace-up boot, typically made of suede **2.** SPORTS = **chukker**

chuk·ker /chúkər/ (*plural* **-kers** *or* **-kas**) *n.* any of the six periods of continuous play in a polo match, each lasting approximately 7.5 minutes [Late 19thC. From Hindi *cak(k)ar* "circular course, turn," ultimately from an Indo-European word that is also the ancestor of English *cycle* and *wheel*.]

Chu·la·long·korn /cho͞olə láwng kàwrn/, **Rama V** (1853–1910) Siamese monarch who ruled from 1868 until 1910, and was noted for his modernization programs.

Chu·la Vis·ta /cho͞olə vístə/ city in southwest California, a southern suburb of San Diego, close to the U.S.-Mexico border. Population: 151,963 (1996).

chum[1] /chum/ *n.* **1.** FRIEND a close friend (*informal*) **2.** WAY OF ADDRESSING MAN used as a term of address for a man (*dated informal*) ■ *v.* (**chummed, chum·ming, chums**) **1.** *vi.* BE FRIENDS to be friends with somebody, or behave in a friendly way toward somebody **2.** *vi.* SHARE ROOM WITH SOMEBODY to share a room with somebody, e.g., in a school dormitory (*dated*) **3.** *vt. Scotland* GO WITH to accompany somebody somewhere (*regional*) [Late 17thC. Origin uncertain: probably short for *chamber-fellow*. Originally the slang word for a roommate at Oxford University.]

chum[2] /chum/ *n.* **1.** FISHBAIT an angler's bait, especially chopped fish, scattered on the water **2.** CHEAP TRINKETS inexpensive trinkets such as cufflinks and pins bearing, e.g., the U.S. Presidential seal (*slang*) ■ *vti.* (**chummed, chum·ming, chums**) USE FISH CHUM to fish using chum on the water [Mid-19thC. Origin unknown.]

chum[3] /chum/ (*plural* **chums** *or* **chum**) *n.* = **chum salmon** [Early 20thC. From Chinook Jargon *tzum (samun)*, literally "spotted (salmon)."]

Chu·mash /cho͞o màsh/ (*plural* **-mash** *or* **-mash·es**) *n.* a member of a Native American people who used to live in the coastal regions of southwestern California. A small population remains in the Santa Barbara area. —**Chu·mash** *adj.*

chum·my /chúmmee/ (**-mi·er, -mi·est**) *adj.* friendly or close (*informal*) —**chum·mi·ly** *adv.* —**chum·mi·ness** *n.*

chump[1] /chump/ *n.* somebody who is unwise or easily deceived (*informal*) [Early 18thC. Origin uncertain: perhaps a blend of CHUNK and LUMP or STUMP. The word originally denoted a thick piece of wood; the sense "fool" developed from this.]

chump[2] *vti., n.* = **chomp**

chump change *n.* a small amount of change or an insignificant amount of money (*slang*)

chum salm·on *n.* a salmon with wavy vertical green streaks and blotches, found in northern Pacific waters. Latin name: *Oncorhynchus keta*.

chunk[1] /chungk/ *n.* **1.** PIECE a thick squarish piece of something, e.g., bread, wood, or meat **2.** LARGE PORTION a large amount or part of something [Late 17thC. An alteration of CHUCK[2].]

chunk[2] /chungk/ *vi.* (**chun·ked, chunk·ing, chunks**), *n.* = **clunk** [Late 19thC. An imitation of the sound.]

chunk·y /chúngkee/ (**-i·er, -i·est**) *adj.* **1.** WITH LUMPS containing lumps or small pieces **2.** SQUARE AND SOLID solid and square-shaped ○ *a chunky table* **3.** SHORT AND BROAD short, broad, and sometimes overweight (*informal*) —**chunk·i·ly** *adv.* —**chunk·i·ness** *n.*

Chun·nel /chúnn'l/ *n.* a nickname for the Channel Tunnel (*informal*) [Early 20thC. Blend of CHANNEL and TUNNEL.]

chup·pah *n.* JUDAISM = **huppah**

church /church/ *n.* **1.** RELIGIOUS BUILDING a building for public worship, especially in the Christian religion **2.** RELIGIOUS SERVICES the religious services that take place in a church **3.** CLERGY the clergy as distinct from lay people **4. church, Church** RELIGIOUS AUTHORITY religious authority as opposed to the authority of the state **5. church, Church** RELIGION'S FOLLOWERS AS GROUP all the followers of a religion, especially the Christian religion, considered collectively **6. church, Church** BRANCH OF CHRISTIAN RELIGION any of several denominations of the Christian religion ■ *vt.* (**churched, church·ing, church·es**) GIVE CHURCH BLESSING TO to give somebody, especially a woman who has recently given birth, a blessing in church (*archaic*) (*often passive*) [Old English *cir(i)ce*, from a prehistoric Germanic word that is also the ancestor of German *Kirche*; ultimately from Greek *kuriakon doma* "house of the lord," from *kurios* "lord"] ◇ **right church, wrong pew** used to indicate that somebody is correct in a general way, but wrong in a particular way

Church /church/, **Frederick Edwin** (1826–1900) U.S. painter. A leader of the Hudson River school, he painted landscapes such as *Niagara Falls* (1857).

church fa·ther *n.* any of the pre-8th century Christian scholars who set down the doctrines and practices of Christianity

church·go·er /chúrch gōər/ *n.* somebody who is attending a church service or who attends church services regularly —**church·go·ing** *n., adj.*

Chur·chill /chúrchil/ **1.** seaport in northeastern Manitoba, Canada, situated on Hudson Bay at the mouth of the Churchill River. Population: 1,143 (1991). **2.** river that flows across south-central Labrador, Newfoundland, Canada, from Ashuanipi Lake, emptying into Lake Melville. The river provides hydroelectric power. Length: 532 mi./856 km. **3.** river that flows through numerous lakes from Lac la Loche in Saskatchewan through Manitoba, into Hudson Bay. Length: 1,000 mi./1,609 km.

Sir Winston Churchill

Chur·chill, Sir Winston (1874–1965) British statesman and writer. As Prime Minister (1940–45, 1951–55) he led Britain through World War II. He wrote *The Second World War* (1948–54) and won the Nobel Prize in literature (1953). Full name **Sir Winston Leonard Spencer Churchill**

Chur·chill Falls falls on the Churchill River, western Labrador, Newfoundland, Canada, situated 225 mi./362 km from Lake Melville. Height: 300 ft./90 m.

church key *n.* a metal tool with a sharp-pointed triangular head for opening cans at one end and a bottle opener at the other end

church·ly /chúrchlee/ *adj.* similar to, suitable for, or typical of a church —**church·li·ness** *n.*

church·man /chúrchmən/ (*plural* **-men**) *n.* **1.** CLERGYMAN a male member of the clergy **2.** CHURCH MEMBER a man who is a practicing member of a church —**church·man·ship** *n.*

church mode *n.* any of the eight scales used for church music in the Middle Ages, e.g., the Dorian, Phyrgian, or Lydian modes

Church of Christ, Sci·en·tist *n.* the official name of the Christian Science Church

Church of Eng·land *n.* the established church of England, ruled by a system of government by bishops and with the reigning monarch as its titular head

Church of Je·sus Christ of Lat·ter-Day Saints *n.* the official name of the Mormon Church

Church of Rome *n.* = **Roman Catholic Church**

Church of the Breth·ren *n.* a conservative Protestant church active mainly in the Midwest and Middle-Atlantic states

church school *n.* a private school affiliated with a church that provides children with a general education as well as religious instruction

Church Sla·von·ic *n.* = **Old Church Slavonic**

church·war·den /chúrch wàwrd'n/ *n.* **1.** LAYPERSON WITH CHURCH DUTIES a layperson who manages secular matters in an Anglican church **2.** PIPE WITH LONG STEM a long-stemmed clay tobacco pipe

church·wom·an /chúrch wo͝ommən/ (*plural* **-en** /-wìmmin/) *n.* **1.** CLERGYWOMAN a woman member of the clergy **2.** WOMAN MEMBER OF CHURCH a woman who is a practicing member of a church

church·y /chúrchee/ (**-i·er, -i·est**) *adj.* **1.** OVERLY RELIGIOUS overzealously or intolerantly religious **2.** LIKE A CHURCH resembling or suggesting a church

church·yard /chúrch yaàrd/ *n.* an area surrounding a church that is sometimes used as a graveyard

churl /churl/ *n.* **1.** BAD-MANNERED PERSON somebody who has no manners **2.** HIST = **ceorl** [Old English *ceorl* "man," specifically "freeman of the lowest rank" (as opposed to a nobleman), from a prehistoric Germanic word that is also the ancestor of German *Kerl* "fellow"]

churl·ish /chúrlish/ *adj.* **1.** CRASS characteristic of somebody who is ill-bred **2.** UNKIND AND GRUMPY surly, sullen, or miserly —**churl·ish·ly** *adv.* —**churl·ish·ness** *n.*

churn /churn/ *n.* BUTTER MAKER a container or device in which milk or cream is stirred vigorously to produce butter ■ *v.* (**churned, churn·ing, churns**) **1.** *vt.* STIR TO MAKE BUTTER to stir or beat milk or cream vigorously to make butter **2.** *vt.* MAKE BUTTER to make butter by beating milk or cream **3.** *vti.* SPLASH VIOLENTLY to move violently, or cause a liquid or soft solid to move violently **4.** *vi.* FEEL UNSETTLED to move unpleasantly, as if in a churn ○ *my stomach was churning* **5.** *vt.* STOCK EXCH TRADE FREQUENTLY FOR COMMISSION to buy and sell stocks and bonds on a frequent basis in order to earn brokerage commissions [Old English *cyrin*, of uncertain origin; perhaps from a prehistoric Germanic word that is also the ancestor of English *corn*, from the "grainy" appearance of stirred cream] —**churn·er** *n.*

churn out *vt.* to produce or issue something quickly or regularly and in large quantities

churr /chur/, **chirr** *vi.* (**churred, churr·ing, churrs; chirred, chirr·ing, chirrs**) MAKE BIRDS' AND INSECTS' VIBRATING NOISE to make the high-pitched vibrating sound typical of some birds, e.g., the nightjar, and some insects, e.g., the cicada ■ *n.* CHURRING SOUND a high-pitched vibrating sound [Mid-16thC. An imitation of the sound.]

chur·ro /cho͞or ō/ (*plural* **-ros**) *n.* a thick fritter made from a coil of dough [From Spanish, perhaps from dialect *xurro* "dirty, Valencian"]

chute[1] /shoot/ *n.* **1.** SLOPE TO DROP THINGS DOWN an inclined channel or passage that something can slide down **2.** LEISURE CHILDREN'S SLIDE a children's slide in a park or swimming pool **3.** SPORTS SNOW-COVERED SLOPE a snow- or ice-covered slope or channel for sports such as tobogganing or bobsledding **4.** AGRIC SLOPING PASSAGE FOR ANIMALS a narrow passageway through which animals are driven to be branded, sheared, loaded, dipped, or sprayed **5.** SPORTS SLOPE OR DROP ON WATERCOURSE a waterfall, rapids, or steep descent in a river or stream ■ *vt.* (**chuted, chut·ing, chutes**) DROP SOMETHING DOWN CHUTE to convey something, e.g., coal or dirty laundry, down a chute [Early 19thC. From French, literally "fall," ultimately from Latin *cadere* "to fall."]

chute[2] /shoot/ *n.* a parachute (*informal*) [Early 20thC. Shortening.] —**chut·ist** *n.*

chut·ney /chútnee/ (*plural* **-neys**) *n.* **1.** FOOD **SPICY RELISH** a sweet and spicy relish made from fruit, spices, sugar, and vinegar **2.** *Carib* MUSIC **RHYTHMIC CARIBBEAN SONG** a popular Caribbean form of song with a quick beat, much influenced by calypso in rhythm and choice of subjects [Early 19thC. From Hindi *caṭnī*.]

chutz·pah /ho͝otspə, kh-/, **hutz·pah, chutz·pa** *n.* (*informal*) **1. SELF-CONFIDENCE** boldness coupled with supreme self-confidence **2. RUDENESS** impudent rudeness or lack of respect [Late 19thC. Via Yiddish from Aramaic *ḥuṣpā*.]

Chu·vash /cho͞o va̋ash, choo va̋ash/ *n.* a language spoken west of the Urals in central Russia, belonging to the Turkic family of Altaic languages. Chuvash is spoken by about two million people. [Via Russian from Chuvash *čăvaš*] —**Chu·vash** *adj.*

chyle /kīl/ *n.* a milky fluid consisting of lymph and emulsified fat that forms in the small intestine during digestion [15thC. Via late Latin from Greek *khūlos* "animal or plant juice."] —**chy·la·ceous** /kī láyshəss/ *adj.* —**chy·lous** /kīləss/ *adj.*

chy·lo·mi·cron /kìlə mī krŏn/ *n.* a microscopic particle, containing fats, cholesterol, phospholipids and protein, formed in the small intestine and absorbed into the blood during digestion

chyme /kīm/ *n.* a thick fluid mass of partially digested food and gastric secretions passed from the stomach to the small intestine [Early 17thC. Via late Latin from Greek *khūmos* "animal or plant juice," ultimately "tube through which something flows," from an Indo-European word that is also the ancestor of English *funnel*.] —**chy·mous** *adj.*

chy·mo·pa·pa·in /kìmō pə páy in, -pə pī in/ *n.* an enzyme found in papaya juice that aids the breakdown of proteins and is used in medical procedures and as a meat tenderizer [Late 20thC. Formed from CHYME + PAPAIN.]

chy·mo·tryp·sin /kìmō trípsin/ *n.* a digestive enzyme produced in the pancreas —**chy·mo·tryp·tic** *adj.*

chy·mo·tryp·sin·o·gen /kìmō trip sínnəjən/ *n.* the inactive form of chymotrypsin that is converted into chymotrypsin by the enzyme trypsin

chy·pre /sheeprə/ *n.* perfume made from sandalwood [Late 19thC. From French, literally "Cyprus," perhaps where the perfume was originally made.]

ci *abbr.* MEASURE cubic inch

Ci[1] *abbr.* METEOROL cirrus

Ci[2] *symbol.* MEASURE, PHYS curie

CI *abbr.* **1.** INSUR certificate of insurance **2.** FREIGHT cost and insurance **3.** Cayman Islands

CIA *n.* a U.S. federal bureau responsible for intelligence and counterintelligence activities outside the United States. In conjunction with the FBI, it is also involved in domestic counterintelligence. Full form **Central Intelligence Agency**

CIAA *abbr.* Central Intercollegiate Athletic Association

cia·bat·ta /chə bátta/ (*plural* **-tas** *or* **-te**) *n.* a flat white Italian bread made with olive oil [Late 20thC. From Italian, literally "slipper," from the shape of the loaf.]

ciao /chow/ *interj.* used to say hello or goodbye (*informal*) [Early 20thC. From Italian dialect, literally "(I am your) slave."]

Ciar·di /chaárdee/, **John** (1916–86) U.S. poet and critic. In addition to poems and translations he wrote accessible critical works such as *How Does a Poem Mean?* (1950).

ci·bo·ri·um /si báwree əm/ (*plural* **-a** /si báwree ə/) *n.* **1. ALTAR CANOPY** a canopy that stands on four pillars over the altar in some Christian churches **2. HOLY WAFER BOX** a small container with a lid, used to hold the consecrated wafers for Holy Communion [Mid-16thC. Via medieval Latin from Greek *kibōrion*, denoting the cup-shaped seed vessel of a species of water lily.]

CIC *abbr.* Counterintelligence Corps

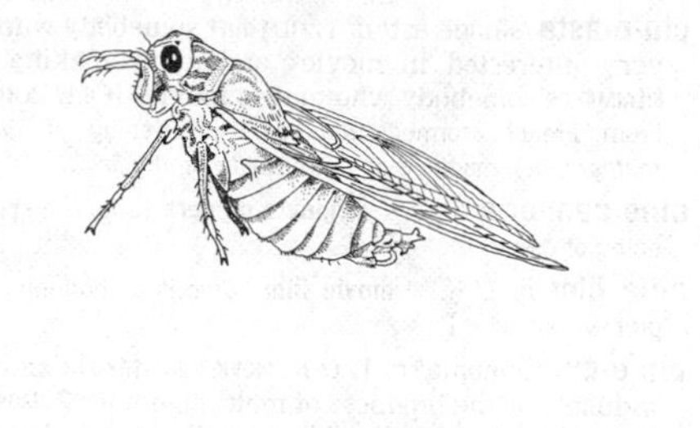

Cicada

ci·ca·da /si káydə, -kaádə/ (*plural* **-das** *or* **-dae** /-dee/) *n.* a large winged insect that lives in trees and tall grass, the male of which makes a shrill sound. Family: Cicadidae. [15thC. From Latin, of uncertain ultimate origin.]

ci·ca·da kill·er *n.* a large hunting wasp that feeds on adult cicadas. Latin name: *Sphecius speciosus.*

ci·ca·la /si kaálə/ (*plural* **-las** *or* **-le** /-lay/) *n.* = **cicada** [Late 18thC. Via Italian or directly from Latin, variant of *cicada*. The irregular plural comes from Italian.]

cic·a·trix /síkə triks/ (*plural* **-tri·ces**) *n.* **1.** MED **SCAR** a scar (*technical*) **2.** BOT **MARK OF LEAF ATTACHMENT** a scar left on a stem where a leaf used to be attached [Mid-17thC. From Latin, "scar."] —**cic·a·tri·cial** /sìkə trísh'l/ *adj.* —**ci·cat·ri·cose** /si káttri kōss/ *adj.*

cic·a·trize /síkə trīz/ (**-trized, -triz·ing, -triz·es**) *vti.* to heal, or cause a wound to heal, and form a scar (*technical*) [15thC. From French *cicatriser*, from *cicatrice* "scar."] —**cic·a·tri·za·tion** /sìkətri záysh'n/ *n.*

cic·e·ly /síssəlee/ *n.* = **sweet cicely**

cic·e·ro /síssərō/ *n.* a size of printed character slightly larger than the pica [From its first use (1458) for an edition of the works of CICERO]

Cic·e·ro /síssərō/ town in northeastern Illinois; a southwestern suburb of Chicago. Population: 70,915 (1996).

Cic·e·ro, Marcus Tullius (106–43 B.C.) Roman philosopher, writer, and statesman. He was Rome's greatest orator during a long political career. His letters and essays are known for their rich prose style. —**Cic·e·ro·ni·an** /sìssə rōnee ən/ *adj.*

cic·e·ro·ne /sìssə rōnee, chìchə-/ (*plural* **-nes** *or* **-ni** /-nee/) *n.* somebody who guides and informs tourists [Early 18thC. From Italian, named for CICERO, because of the guide's knowledge and eloquence.]

cich·lid /síklid/ *n.* a tropical freshwater fish with spiny fins, popular as an aquarium fish. Family: Cichlidae. [Late 19thC. From modern Latin *Cichlidae*, family name, from Greek *kikhlē*, denoting a kind of fish.]

Cid, El /èl síd/ (1040?–99) Spanish military leader. Legend obscures the true nature of "The Lord Champion" who fought both for and against Spain's Moorish rulers, and was virtual dictator of Valencia from 1094 to 1099. Born **Rodriguez Díaz de Vivar**

CID, C.I.D. *n.* the detective branch of the U.K. police force. Full form **Criminal Investigation Department**

-cide *suffix.* **1.** killer ○ *fungicide* **2.** killing ○ *tyrannicide* [Via Old French from Latin *-cida* "killer," and from Latin *-cidium* "killing," both from Latin *caedere* "to strike, kill" (source also of English *chisel, scissor, incise,* and *decide*)] —**-cidal** *suffix.*

ci·der /sídər/ *n.* **1. NONALCOHOLIC FRESH APPLE DRINK** a nonalcoholic drink made from freshly-pressed apples **2. FERMENTED APPLE JUICE** an alcoholic drink made from fermented apple juice [13thC. Via Old French *sidre* from, ultimately, Hebrew *šēkār* "alcoholic drink."]

ci·der vin·e·gar *n.* a light vinegar made from cider

ci-de·vant /si də vaáN/ *adj., adv.* used to indicate that what follows was somebody's former name, office, or title (*formal*) [Early 18thC. From French, literally "before this."]

c.i.f., C.I.F. *abbr.* **1.** cost, insurance, and freight. ◊ **C.F.I. 2.** central information file

c.i.f.c.i. *abbr.* cost, insurance, freight, commission, and interest (*used in quotes to indicate what is included in the price*)

cig /sig/ *n.* a cigarette (*informal*) [Late 19thC. Shortening.]

ci·gar /si gaár/ *n.* a cylindrical roll of tobacco leaves for smoking, with thin brown paper or a single tobacco leaf as an outer covering [Early 18thC. Directly or via French *cigare* from Spanish *cigarro*, probably from Mayan *sik'ar* "smoking."] ◇ **close but no cigar** the answer, response, or result is not good enough (*informal*)

cig·a·rette /síggə rèt/ *n.* **1. ROLL OF SHREDDED TOBACCO** a cylindrical roll of shredded tobacco leaves for smoking, with an outer covering of thin, usually white, paper **2. ROLL OF ANY LEAVES FOR SMOKING** a roll of shredded leaves of any kind for smoking, e.g., marijuana leaves or leaves of herbs [Mid-19thC. From French, literally "small cigar," from *cigare* (see CIGAR).]

Cig·a·rette /síggə rèt/ *tdmk.* a trademark for a long, sleek, high-performance, high-powered motorboat

cig·a·rette hold·er *n.* a hollow cylindrical device for holding a smoking cigarette. Some cigarette holders include filters.

cig·a·rette light·er *n.* = **lighter**

cig·a·rette pa·per *n.* a sheet of thin paper with gum on one edge, used with loose tobacco to roll cigarettes

cig·a·ril·lo /sìggə rílló/ (*plural* **-los**) *n.* a slender cigar about the same size as a cigarette [Mid-19thC. From Spanish *cigarillo*, literally "small cigar," from *cigarro* (see CIGAR).]

ci·gar-store In·di·an *n.* a wooden figure of a Native American man holding a bunch of cigars in his hands, formerly used as a sign indicating that a store sold tobacco products

cig·gy /síggee/ (*plural* **-gies**) *n.* a cigarette (*informal*)

ci·lan·tro /si laántrō, si lántrō/ *n.* the leaves of the coriander plant, used as a flavorful herb, especially in Latin American and Southwestern U.S. cooking [Early 20thC. Via Spanish from, ultimately, Latin *coriandrum* "coriander," source of English *coriander*.]

cil·i·a plural of **cilium**

cil·i·ar·y /síllee èrree/ *adj.* **1.** BIOL used to describe the short threads (**cilia**) projecting from some cells and the beating movement they make **2.** ANAT used to describe the tissue and muscle that surrounds the lens of the eye [Late 17thC. Formed from CILIUM.]

cil·i·ar·y bod·y *n.* the ring-shaped part at the front of eye that connects the pigmented layer (**choroid**) of the eyeball with the iris diaphragm. It also contains the ciliary muscle, which alters the curvature of the lens.

cil·i·ate /síllee àyt, síllee ət/ *n.* **ORGANISM PROPELLED BY THRASHING THREADS** a simple microscopic organism with projecting threads that thrash to help it to move along. Phylum: Ciliophora. ■ *adj.* = **ciliated** [Mid-18thC. Formed from CILIUM.]

cil·i·a·ted /síllee àytəd/, **cil·i·ate** *adj.* used to describe cells with projecting threads (**cilia**) or organisms with cells of this type —**cil·i·a·tion** /sìllee áysh'n/ *n.*

cil·ice /síllis/ *n.* **1.** TEXTILES = **haircloth 2.** CLOTHES **HAIRCLOTH GARMENT** a garment made of haircloth [Late 16thC. Via French from, ultimately, Greek *Kilikia*, Cilicia (an ancient district of Anatolia, now in southern Turkey), because the cloth was originally made of Cilician goats' hair.]

cil·i·um /síllee əm/ (*plural* **-a** /ə/) *n.* **1.** BIOL **MICROSCOPIC PROJECTION ON CELL** a tiny projecting thread, found with many others on a cell or microscopic organism, that beats rhythmically to aid the movement of a fluid past the cell or movement of the organism through liquid **2. EYELASH** an eyelash (*technical*) [Early 18thC. From Latin, literally "eyelash."]

Cim·ar·ron /símmə ròn/ river rising in northeastern New Mexico and flowing across Kansas and Oklahoma to the Arkansas River near Tulsa. Length: 600 mi./970 km.

cim·bal·om /símbələm, tsímb-/ *n.* a musical instrument similar to the hammered dulcimer. It is used especially in Hungarian folk and gypsy music. [Late 19thC. Via Hungarian from Italian *cimbalo* "dulcimer."]

Cim·bri /sím brī, kímbree/ *npl.* a Germanic people who lived in parts of Jutland and the Rhine valley during the second century B.C. They began to spread southwards, but were routed by the Romans in 101 B.C. [From Latin]

ci·met·i·dine /sī méttə deen/ *n.* a drug that limits the production of acid in the stomach and is used to treat peptic ulcers. Formula: $C_{10}H_{16}NS$. [Late 20thC. Coined from CYANO- + METHYL + -IDINE.]

ci·mex /sī mèks/ (*plural* **cim·i·ces** /sĭmi seez/) *n.* a bedbug or related insect that feeds on birds, humans, and other mammals. Genus: *Cimex.* [Late 16thC. From Latin, "bedbug."]

Cim·me·ri·an /sə meéree ən/ *adj.* DARK dark and gloomy (*literary*) ■ *n.* MYTHOL INHABITANT OF DARK LAND according to Greek mythology, a member of a people who lived in a land of perpetual darkness [Late 16thC. Formed from Latin *Cimmerius,* from Greek *Kimmerios.*]

CINC, C in C *abbr.* MIL Commander in Chief

cinch /sinch/ *n.* 1. SOMETHING EASILY DONE something that can be done or achieved with very little effort (*informal*) 2. SOMETHING CERTAIN something that is absolutely certain to happen (*informal*) 3. RIDING STRONG GIRTH a girth for a saddle, consisting of a thick strap secured by passing the end through two metal rings 4. FIRM GRIP a firm grip (*archaic*) ■ *vt.* (**cinched, cinch·ing, cinch·es**) 1. TIGHTEN to tighten something by constricting it 2. RIDING PUT CINCH ON HORSE to put a cinch on a horse 3. GRASP SOMETHING AROUND MIDDLE to grasp something around the middle, as a belt does (*informal*) 4. MAKE CERTAIN OF to make certain of something (*dated informal*) [Mid-19thC. From Spanish *cincha* "girth," ultimately from Latin *cingere* "to gird" (see CINCTURE).]

cinch belt *n.* a waist belt fashionable for women in the 1950s that was worn tight to make the waist appear smaller

cinch bug *n.* = **chinch bug** (*regional*)

cin·cho·na /sing kṓnə, sin chṓnə/ *n.* 1. TREE WITH BARK PRODUCING QUININE a South American evergreen tree or shrub whose bark is used to produce quinine and some other drugs. Genus: *Cinchona.* 2. **cin·cho·na, cin·cho·na bark** DRIED BARK OF THE CINCHONA the dried bark of a cinchona tree, used to produce quinine and some other drugs [Mid-18thC. From modern Latin, named for the Countess of *Chinchón* (1576–1641), vicereine of Peru, who was cured of a fever by the drug and who introduced it into Spain.] —**cin·chon·ic** /sing kónnik, sin chónnik/ *adj.*

cin·cho·nine /síngkə neèn, sínchə-/ *n.* a colorless crystalline solid obtained from the dried bark of the cinchona tree, which has been used in treating malaria. Formula: $C_{19}H_{22}N_{20}$.

cin·cho·nism /síngkə nìzzəm, sínchə-/ *n.* a condition resulting from the excessive use of quinine and other drugs derived from cinchona bark. The symptoms are headache, ringing in the ears, temporary deafness, and dizziness.

Cin·cin·na·ti /sìnsə náttee, -náttə/ city in southwestern Ohio on the Ohio-Kentucky border, on the Ohio River, southwest of Dayton. Population: 345,818 (1996).

Cin·co de May·o /seéngkō də máayō/ *n.* a celebration on May 5, among Mexican communities in Mexico and North America, of the Mexican defeat of French troops at the Battle of Puebla in 1862 [From Spanish, literally "5th of May"]

cinc·ture /síngkchər/ *n.* 1. BELT a girdle or belt, especially a cord or sash tied around a priest's, monk's, or nun's habit 2. ENCOMPASSING the act of encircling something, or something that encircles (*archaic*) [Late 16thC. Via Latin *cinctura* "girdle" from, ultimately, *cingere* "to gird," source of English *cinch, precinct,* and *succinct.*]

cin·der /síndər/ *n.* BURNED WOOD OR FUEL a small piece of charred wood or coal, especially one that continues to glow ■ **cin·ders** *npl.* 1. ASHES the ashes that remain after a fire has burned out 2. INDUST SLAG waste material produced by smelting 3. GEOL = **scoria** [Old English *sinder* "slag," from prehistoric Germanic. The modern spelling arose by association with French *cendre* "cinders, ash" (not related to the English word).] —**cin·der·y** *adj.*

cin·der block *n.* a light usually hollow block made from coal ashes mixed with cement that is used in building and construction work

Cin·der·el·la /sìndə réllə/ *n.* NEGLECTED PERSON OR THING somebody who or something that suffers undeserved neglect ■ *adj.* RAGS-TO-RICHES achieving sudden recognition or success, or relating to somebody who, or something that, achieves this [Mid-19thC. Named for the fairy-tale character *Cinderella,* who is neglected by her sisters but enabled by her fairy godmother to attend a ball and meet a prince.]

cine- *prefix.* CINEMA film, motion picture ○ *cinephile* [From CINEMA]

cin·e·aste /sínnee àst/ *n.* 1. FILM BUFF somebody who is very interested in movies and movie-making 2. FILMMAKER somebody who makes movies [Early 20thC. From French, formed from *ciné* (shortening of *cinématographe*), modeled on *enthusiaste* "enthusiast."]

cine cam·er·a *n. U.K.* = **movie camera** [*Cine* is a shortening of CINEMATOGRAPHIC]

cine film *n. U.K.* = **movie film** [*Cine* is a shortening of CINEMATOGRAPHIC]

cin·e·ma /sínnəmə/ *n.* 1. *U.K.* MOVIE INDUSTRY the movie industry or the business of making movies 2. MOVIES COLLECTIVELY movies considered collectively (*formal*) 3. *U.K.* MOVIE THEATER a movie theater [Early 20thC. From French *cinéma,* shortening of *cinématographe,* from Greek *kinēma* "movement."]

cin·e·ma·go·er /sínnəmə gṑ ər/ *n. U.K.* = **moviegoer**

cin·e·mat·ic /sìnnə máttik/ *adj.* 1. APPROPRIATE TO MOVIES typical of the style in which movies are made 2. OF MOVIES relating to movies or movie-making — **cin·e·mat·i·cal·ly** *adv.*

cin·e·ma·tog·ra·pher /sìnnəmə tóggrəfər/ *n.* somebody responsible for the lighting and camera work for a motion picture and the general look of the motion picture

cin·e·ma·tog·ra·phy /sìnnəmə tóggrəfee/ *n.* the art or technique of photographing and lighting motion pictures —**cin·e·mat·o·graph·ic** /sìnnə mattə gráffik/ *adj.* —**cin·e·mat·o·graph·i·cal·ly** /-gráffiklee/ *adv.*

ci·né·ma vé·ri·té /sìnnəmə verri táy, seenay maà verri táy/ *n.* a style of filmmaking characterized by a search for an authentic documentary feel. The term was first applied to a series of French documentary films in the 1960s. [Mid-20thC. From French, literally "cinema of truth."]

cin·e·phile /sínnə fìl/ *n.* somebody who is very interested in movies and moviemaking

cin·e·rar·i·a /sìnnə ráiree ə/ *n.* PLANT WITH DAISYLIKE FLOWERS a plant native to the Canary Islands, cultivated for its mass of blue, purple, or red flowers resembling daisies. Latin name: *Senecio hybridus.* ■ plural of **cinerarium** [Late 16thC. From modern Latin, formed from the Latin stem *ciner-* "ashes," from the fluffy gray leaves of the silver ragwort, the plant originally designated.]

cin·e·rar·i·um /sìnnə ráiree əm/ (*plural* **-a** /-ə/) *n.* a place where the ashes of a corpse are stored [Mid-18thC. From late Latin, formed from the Latin stem *ciner-* "ashes."]

cin·er·ar·y /sínnə rèrree/ *adj.* relating to ashes, especially human ashes [Mid-18thC. From Latin *cinerarius,* formed from the stem *ciner-* "ashes."]

ci·ne·re·ous /sə neéree əss/ *adj.* (*literary*) 1. LIKE OR OF ASHES resembling or consisting of ashes 2. ASH-GRAY of an ash-gray color like ashes ■ *n.* ASH-GRAY an ash-gray color (*literary*) [15thC. Formed from Latin *cinereus,* from the stem *ciner-* "ashes."]

cin·er·in /sínnərən/ *n.* an oily liquid compound extracted from pyrethrum and used in insecticides [Mid-20thC. Formed from the Latin stem *ciner-* "ashes."]

cin·gu·lum /síng gyələm/ (*plural* **-la** /-gyələ/) *n.* 1. ANAT BODY PART ENCIRCLING ANOTHER any part of the body that surrounds or encircles another part 2. BIOL STRIPE AROUND PLANT OR ANIMAL a band or stripe that encircles a plant or animal [Early 19thC. From Latin, literally "girdle," from *cingere* "to gird" (see CINCTURE).] — **cin·gu·late** /síng gyələt/ *adj.*

cin·na·bar /sínnə baàr/ *n.* 1. MINERALS MINERAL SOURCE OF MERCURY a reddish-brown mineral that is the principal source of mercury and is found near areas of volcanic activity 2. CHEM RED PIGMENT red mercuric sulfide used as a pigment 3. COLORS BRIGHT RED a bright red color tinged with orange ■ *adj.* OF A BRIGHT RED COLOR of a bright red color tinged with orange [Middle English. Via Latin from Greek *kinnabari,* ultimately from an oriental language.] —**cin·na·bar·ine** /sínnəbə reèn, sínnəbərin/ *adj.*

cin·na·bar moth *n.* a large European moth that has orange-red wings. It was introduced into the western United States in an attempt to control ragwort, the main food of its orange- and black-striped caterpillars. Latin name: *Hypocrita jacobaeae.*

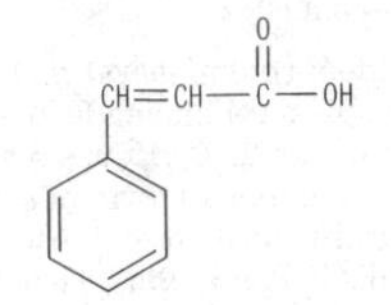

Cinnamic acid

cin·nam·ic ac·id /sə nàmmik-/ *n.* a white odorless acid that is insoluble in water, used in the perfume industry. Formula: $C_9H_8O_2$. [From its presence in cinnamon oil]

cin·na·mon /sínnəmən/ *n.* 1. FOOD SPICE OBTAINED FROM BARK the dried bark of any of several Asian trees, used to spice foods and drinks 2. TREES ASIAN TREE WITH CINNAMON BARK a small evergreen tree found in tropical regions of Asia whose dried bark is the source of cinnamon. Genus: *Cinnamomum.* 3. COLORS REDDISH-BROWN COLOR a warm reddish-brown color ■ *adj.* OF A REDDISH BROWN COLOR of a warm reddish-brown color [14thC. From French *cinnamome,* ultimately perhaps via Greek *kinnamon* from Malay.] —**cin·nam·ic** /sə námmik/ *adj.*

cin·na·mon bear *n.* a variety of the North American black bear that has reddish-brown fur

cin·na·mon stone *n.* = **essonite** [From its color]

cin·quain /sing káyn, síng kàyn/ *n.* a stanza of poetry that consists of five lines [Late 19thC. From French, literally "set of five," formed from *cinq* "five."]

cin·que·cen·to /chìngkwə chéntō/ *n.* the 16th century, especially with reference to Italian art and architecture [Mid-18thC. From Italian, literally "500," shortened from *milcinquecento* "1500," used to refer to the years 1500–99.]

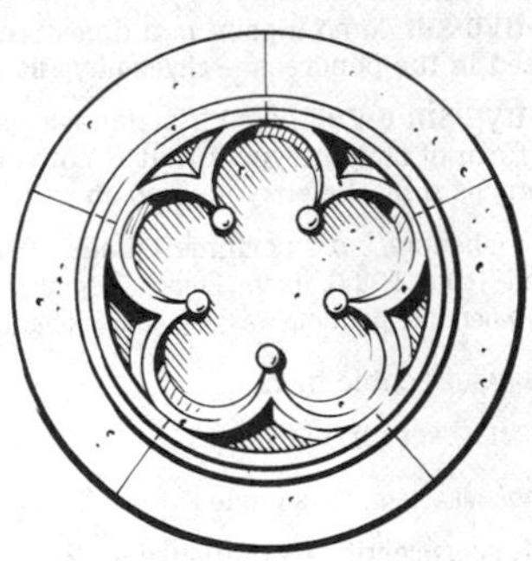

Cinquefoil

cinque·foil /síngk fòyl, sángk-/ (*plural* **-foils** *or* **-foil**) *n.* 1. PLANTS = **potentilla** 2. ARCHIT FIVE-ARC DESIGN an architectural design in the form of five arcs joined together [13thC. From Latin *quinquefolium,* literally "five leaves."]

CIO, C.I.O. *abbr.* Congress of Industrial Organizations

ciop·pi·no /chə peénō/ *n.* a thick seafood soup or stew with tomatoes, spices, and herbs [Mid-20thC. Perhaps from Italian dialect.]

Ci·pan·go /si páng gō/ *n.* in medieval mythology, an island off the eastern coast of Asia, perhaps modern-day Japan

ci·pher /sífər/, **cy·pher** *n.* 1. WRITTEN CODE a written code in which the letters of a text are substituted according to a system 2. CIPHER KEY the key to a cipher 3. TEXT IN CIPHER a text written in cipher 4. DESIGN DESIGN OF INTERLACING INITIALS a decorative design consisting of a set of interlaced initials 5. MUSIC FAULT IN ORGAN VALVE a fault in an organ valve that causes a pipe to sound continuously without the key having been pressed ■ *v.* 1. *vt.* WRITE IN CODE to write a text or message in cipher 2. *vi.* MUSIC SOUND OWING TO FAULT to sound continuously because of a faulty valve (*refers to an organ or organ pipe*) [14thC. Via Old French *cif(f)re* from, ultimately, Arabic *ṣifr* "zero," source of English *zero.*]

ci·pol·in /síppəlin/ *n.* a type of Italian marble with green and white streaks [Late 18thC. Directly or via

French from Italian *cipollino*, literally "small onion," from *cipolla* "onion," because the streaked structure resembles the layers of an onion.]

cir. *abbr.* **1.** circle **2.** circa **3.** circuit **4.** circulation **5.** circumference

cir·ca /súrkə/ *prep.* used before a date to indicate that it is approximate or estimated [Mid-19thC. From Latin, ultimately from *circus* "circle" (see CIRCUS).]

cir·ca·di·an /sər káydee ən/ *adj.* used to describe a pattern repeated approximately every 24 hours [Mid-20thC. Formed from Latin *circa* "about, in" + *dies* "day."]

Cir·cas·sian /sər kásh'n, -káshee ən/ *n.* a group of languages spoken in southern Russia, northern Georgia, and by many émigré communities in Turkey. It belongs to the Abkhaz-Adyghean branch of North Caucasian languages. Circassian is spoken by about 1,500,000 people and its dialects include Adyghe and Kabardian. [Mid-16thC. Formed from *Circassia*, Latinized form of Russian *Cherkes*.] —**Cir·cas·sian** *adj.*

Cir·ce /súrsee/ *n.* in Greek mythology, the daughter of Hecate and the Sun, who lured sailors to her island where she made love with them and then turned them into pigs [12thC. Via Latin from Greek *Kirkē*.] —**Cir·ce·an** /súrsee ən, sur sée ən/ *adj.*

cir·ci·nate /súrsə nàyt/ *adj.* used to describe leaves or fronds that are coiled with the tip in the center, as in most ferns [Early 19thC. From Latin *circinatus*, past participle of *circinare* "to make round," from *circinus* "pair of compasses," from *circus* "circle" (see CIRCUS).] —**cir·ci·nate·ly** *adv.*

Cir·ci·nus /súrsinəss/ *n.* a small inconspicuous constellation in the southern hemisphere near Centaurus [Early 19thC. From Latin *circinus* "pair of compasses."]

cir·cle /súrk'l/ *n.* **1.** GEOM **SHAPE OF PERFECT HOLLOW RING** a curved line surrounding a center point, every point of the line being an equal distance from the center point **2. AREA INSIDE CIRCLE** the area enclosed by a circle **3. CIRCLE-SHAPED THING** an area or object in the shape of a circle **4. CIRCLE-SHAPED PATTERN** an arrangement or pattern in the shape of a circle **5. GROUP OF PEOPLE** a group of people who share a common interest, profession, activity, or social background **6. CURVED ROUTE** a course or route that follows a curved path **7.** THEATER **RAISED THEATER SEATING** a section of tiered seating in a theater that is above ground level **8. CYCLE** a process or series of events that ends at the point at which it began, or that repeats itself continuously ■ *v.* (**-cled, -cling, -cles**) **1.** *vti.* **MOVE ALONG CURVING ROUTE** to move or move around something, following a curving route or path that ends where it began and usually repeats its cycle **2.** *vt.* **MAKE MARK AROUND** to draw a ring around something in order to mark it or draw attention to it **3.** *vt.* **SURROUND** to surround a place or an area with people [Pre-12thC. Via French from Latin *circulus*, literally "small circle," from *circus* "circle" (see CIRCUS).] —**cir·cler** *n.* ◇ **come full circle** to return to an earlier or first position or situation after leaving it ◇ **go** *or* **run around in circles** to be very busy without actually achieving anything

cir·cle graph *n.* = **pie chart**

cir·clet /súrklət/ *n.* **1. RINGLIKE DECORATION** a circular decoration, especially a decorative band worn on the head **2. SMALL CIRCLE** a small circle (*literary*)

cir·cuit /súrkit/ *n.* **1. CIRCULAR PATH** a route or path that follows a curved course and finishes at the point at which it began **2. AREA BOUNDED BY CIRCULAR PATH** an area that lies inside a circular route or path **3. SINGLE JOURNEY AROUND CIRCULAR PATH** a single complete journey around a circular route or path **4. REGULAR JOURNEY** a journey that somebody, e.g., a salesperson or circuit court judge, regularly makes around an area **5.** LAW **STOPS ON JOURNEY** the places visited by somebody on a regular circuit, especially those where a circuit court judge sits periodically **6. ROUND OF EVENTS** a series of events or places regularly attended or visited by the same group of people **7.** SPORTS **ONGOING SERIES OF COMPETITIONS** an ongoing series of competitions or tournaments regularly attended by the same group of people **8.** ELEC **ROUTE FOR ELECTRICITY** a route around which an electrical current can flow, beginning and ending at the same point **9.** ARTS **CHAIN OF ARTS LOCATIONS** a group of theaters, cinemas, or clubs, under the same management or showing the same performances or movies in rotation **10.** SPORTS **SET OF EXERCISES** a complete round of exercises in circuit training **11.** CHR **LOCAL GROUP OF METHODIST CHURCHES** a group of Methodist churches that form a local division of the Church's national administration ■ *vti.* (**-cuit·ed, -cuit·ing, -cuits**) **MOVE AROUND ALONG CIRCULAR PATH** to follow a circuit around something (*formal*) [14thC. Via French from Latin *circuitus*, from *circuire* "to go around," from *ire* "to go."]

cir·cuit board *n.* COMPUT = **printed circuit board**

cir·cuit break·er *n.* a device that can automatically stop the flow of electricity in a circuit if there is too much current to operate safely. Circuit breakers are easier to use than fuses because they just need to be reset instead of replaced.

cir·cuit court *n.* a court that moves from place to place within a particular judicial district

cir·cu·i·tous /sər kyóo itəss/ *adj.* lengthy because very indirect [Mid-17thC. From medieval Latin *circuitosus*, from Latin *circuire* (see CIRCUIT).] —**cir·cu·i·tous·ly** *adv.* —**cir·cu·i·tous·ness** *n.*

cir·cuit rid·er *n.* formerly, a clergyman who traveled from church to church preaching, especially in rural areas

cir·cuit·ry /súrkətree/ *n.* **1. CIRCUIT COMPONENTS** the components of an electric circuit **2. ELECTRICAL SYSTEM** the system of circuits in an electrical or electronic device **3. ELECTRIC CIRCUIT'S LAYOUT** the design or layout of an electric circuit

cir·cuit train·ing *n.* a form of sports training that involves performing different exercises in rotation

cir·cu·i·ty /sər kyóo itee/ (*plural* **-ties**) *n.* the indirect and lengthy nature of something, especially the way somebody speaks, argues, or reasons [Mid-16thC. From French *circuité*, ultimately from Latin *circuire* (see CIRCUIT).]

cir·cu·lar /súrkyələr/ *adj.* **1. LIKE A CIRCLE** shaped like, or resembling a circle **2. ENDING WHERE BEGINNING** following a curved route or path that ends at the point where it began **3.** LOGIC **NOT LOGICAL** used to describe an argument that does not move logically to a satisfactory conclusion because it assumes as true something that needs to be proved or demonstrated **4. CIRCUITOUS** indirect and complicated **5. WIDELY DISTRIBUTED** intended for distribution to a large number of people ■ *n.* **WIDELY DISTRIBUTED NOTICE** a letter, advertisement, or other notice distributed to a large number of people [14thC. Via Anglo-Norman from, ultimately, late Latin *circularis*, from Latin *circulus* (see CIRCLE).] —**cir·cu·lar·ly** *adv.*

cir·cu·lar breath·ing *n.* the technique of using the cheeks to force air out of the mouth while breathing in through the nose, used by woodwind and brass players to hold long notes

cir·cu·lar file *n.* a waste basket (*informal humorous*)

cir·cu·lar func·tion *n.* GEOM = **trigonometric function**

cir·cu·lar·i·ty /sùrkyə lérrətee/ *n.* **1. CIRCULAR SHAPE** the quality or fact of being circular in shape **2.** LOGIC **ILLOGICAL NATURE** the illogical nature of something such as an argument or piece of reasoning **3. COMPLEXITY AND INDIRECTNESS** the indirect and complicated nature of something such as a method or route [Late 16thC. From medieval Latin *circularitas*, from *circularis* (see CIRCULAR).]

cir·cu·lar·ize /súrkyələ rìz/ (**-ized, -iz·ing, -iz·es**) *vt.* **1. PUBLICIZE** to publicize something by distributing leaflets or notices widely **2. CANVASS OR POLL** to ask people for support or to survey public opinion by sending out questionnaires, letters, or leaflets —**cir·cu·lar·i·za·tion** /sùrkyələri záysh'n/ *n.*

cir·cu·lar meas·ure *n.* the measurement of an angle by relating it to the angle formed in the center of a circle by a sector, in units called radians

cir·cu·lar saw *n.* an electrically powered saw with a circular toothed blade that rotates at high speed

cir·cu·late /súrkyə làyt/ (**-lat·ed, -lat·ing, -lates**) *v.* **1.** *vi.* **MOVE AROUND CIRCULAR SYSTEM** to move freely through a circuit or to follow a circular route **2.** *vti.* **PASS AROUND** to distribute or pass something from person to person or from place to place, or be passed in this way **3.** *vi.* **FLOW** to move or flow freely in an enclosed space or defined area **4.** *vi.* **MINGLE** to move from person to person or group to group at a social gathering in order to talk with different people (*informal*) [15thC. From Latin *circulat-*, past participle stem of *circulare*, from *circulus*, literally "small circle."] —**cir·cu·lat·a·ble** *adj.* —**cir·cu·la·tor** *n.*

cir·cu·lat·ing dec·i·mal *n.* MATH = **repeating decimal**

cir·cu·lat·ing li·brar·y *n.* = **lending library, bookmobile**

cir·cu·lat·ing me·di·um *n.* anything used as money, e.g., a valuable commodity, paper money, or illegal drugs

cir·cu·la·tion /sùrkyə láysh'n/ *n.* **1.** PHYSIOL **MOVEMENT OF BLOOD AROUND BODY** the movement of blood through the body **2. FLOW** the free movement of something, e.g., air or water **3. DISTRIBUTION OR COMMUNICATION** the passing or communication of something, e.g., news, information, or money, from place to place or from person to person **4.** PUBL **NUMBER DISTRIBUTED OF PUBLICATION** the number of copies of a publication that are sold or distributed to readers in a given period **5.** FIN **USE AS MONEY** valid use as currency **6.** LIBRARIES **LIBRARY DEPARTMENT** the department of a lending library that oversees the lending and retrieval of books and other items

cir·cu·la·tor·y /súrkyələ tàwree/ *adj.* relating to the circulation of the blood

cir·cu·la·tor·y sys·tem *n.* the system consisting of the heart, blood vessels, and lymph vessels that pumps blood and lymph around the body

circum. *abbr.* circumference

circum- *prefix.* around ○ *circumlunar* [From Latin, formed from *circus* (see CIRCLE)]

cir·cum·am·bi·ent /sùrkəm ámbee ənt/ *adj.* surrounding (*literary*) —**cir·cum·am·bi·ent·ly** *adv.*

cir·cum·am·bu·late (**-lated, -lat·ing, -lates**) *v.* **1.** *vti.* **WALK AROUND** to walk around something, e.g., around the dead, a tomb, or a sacred site, as part of a ritual (*formal or humorous*) **2.** *vi.* **EVADE THE ISSUE** to avoid the point of a subject or discussion (*literary*) —**cir·cum·am·bu·la·tion** /sùrkəm ambyə láysh'n/ *n.*

cir·cum·cise /súrkəm sìz/ (**-cised, -cis·ing, -cis·es**) *vt.* **1. REMOVE MALE'S FORESKIN** to remove all or part of the foreskin from the penis, either for hygiene reasons or as part of a religious ritual **2. REMOVE FEMALE'S CLITORIS OR PREPUCE** to cut away the skin (**prepuce**) covering the clitoris, or remove the clitoris, usually as part of a religious ritual [13thC. Via Old French from Latin *circumcidere* "to cut around" (a literal translation of Greek *peritemnein*), from *caedere* "to cut."] —**cir·cum·cis·er** *n.*

cir·cum·ci·sion /sùrkəm sízh'n/ *n.* **1. REMOVAL OF MALE'S FORESKIN** the removal of all or part of the foreskin from the penis **2. REMOVAL OF CLITORIS OR ITS PREPUCE** the cutting away of the skin (**prepuce**) covering the clitoris, or the removal of the clitoris **3. RELIGIOUS CEREMONY WITH CIRCUMCISION** a religious ceremony during which a circumcision is performed, especially in Judaism or Islam

Cir·cum·ci·sion *n.* a Roman Catholic festival held on January 1 to commemorate the circumcision of Jesus

cir·cum·fer·ence /sər kúmfərəns, -kúmfrəns/ *n.* **1.** GEOM **DISTANCE AROUND CIRCLE** the distance around the edge of a circle **2. DISTANCE AROUND SOMETHING** the distance around the edge of an object or a place that is roughly circular **3. EDGE** the edge of a round object or area [14thC. From, ultimately, Latin *circumferentia*, from *circumferens*, the present participle of *circumferre*, literally "to carry around," from *ferre* "to carry."] —**cir·cum·fer·en·tial** /sər kùmfə rénsh'l/ *adj.* —**cir·cum·fer·en·tial·ly** /-rénshəlee/ *adv.*

cir·cum·flex /súrkəm flèks/, **cir·cum·flex ac·cent** *n.* a mark ^ placed above a letter to indicate a specific pronunciation or a contraction, usually different from that of the unaccented letter. Circumflexes may be written over vowels as in French, or over consonants as in Esperanto. [Late 16thC. From Latin *circumflexus*, the past participle of *circumflectere*, literally "to bend around," from *flectere* "to bend."]

cir·cum·flu·ent /sər kúmfloo ənt/, **cir·cum·flu·ous** /-əss/ *adj.* flowing all around a thing or place (*literary*)

cir·cum·fuse /súrkəm fyóoz/ (**-fused, -fus·ing, -fus·es**) *vt.* to surround or cover something, especially with liquid (*formal or literary*) —**cir·cum·fu·sion** /sùrkəm fyóozh'n/ *n.*

cir·cum·lo·cu·tion /sùrkəm lō kyóosh'n/ *n.* **1. INDIRECT WAY OF SAYING SOMETHING** the use of more words than necessary to express something, especially to avoid saying it directly **2. INDIRECT EXPRESSION** something said using more words than necessary, especially to avoid expressing it directly [15thC. Directly or via French from the Latin stem *circumlocution-*, literally "speaking around," from the stem *locution-* "speaking" (see

LOCUTION).] —**cir·cum·loc·u·to·ry** /sùrkəm lókyə tàwree/ *adj.*

cir·cum·lu·nar /sùrkəm lóonər/ *adj.* around or surrounding the moon

cir·cum·nav·i·gate /sùrkəm návvi gàyt/ (**-gat·ed, -gat·ing, -gates**) *vt.* to sail or fly around something, e.g., an island (*formal*) —**cir·cum·nav·i·ga·ble** *adj.* —**cir·cum·nav·i·ga·tion** *n.* —**cir·cum·nav·i·ga·tor** *n.*

cir·cum·po·lar /sùrkəm pṓlər/ *adj.* located or living near one or both poles of the earth or some other planet (*technical*)

cir·cum·po·lar star *n.* a star that is always visible above the horizon at a given latitude

cir·cum·scribe /súrkəm skrīb/ (**-scribed, -scrib·ing, -scribes**) *v.* **1.** *vt.* RESTRICT to limit the power of something or somebody to act independently (*formal*) (*often passive*) **2.** GEOM ENCLOSE WITHIN GEOMETRICAL SHAPE to draw one geometrical figure around another so that they touch at every corner (**vertex**) of the enclosed figure or at every side of the enclosing figure without cutting across each other [14thC. From Latin *circumscribere*, literally "to write around," from *scribere* "to write."] —**cir·cum·scrib·a·ble** /sùrkəm skrībəb'l/ *adj.* —**cir·cum·scrib·er** /súrkəm skrībər/ *n.*

cir·cum·scrip·tion /sùrkəm skrípshən/ *n.* **1.** RESTRICTION OF POWER the limiting of the power of something or somebody to act independently (*formal*) **2.** GEOM ENCLOSING OF SOMETHING WITHIN GEOMETRICAL SHAPE the act of drawing one geometrical figure around another so that they touch at every corner (**vertex**) of the enclosed figure or at every side of the enclosing figure without cutting across each other **3.** GEOM DRAWN SHAPE a shape drawn or enclosed by circumscription **4.** COINS INSCRIPTION ROUND CIRCULAR EDGE a circular inscription around the edge of a coin or medal —**cir·cum·scrip·tive** *adj.* —**cir·cum·scrip·tive·ly** *adv.*

cir·cum·so·lar /sùrkəm sṓlər/ *adj.* around or surrounding the sun

cir·cum·spect /súrkəm spèkt/ *adj.* showing unwillingness to act without first weighing the risks or consequences [15thC. From, ultimately, the Latin stem *circumspect-*, the past participle of *circumspicere*, literally "to look around," from *specere* "to look."] —**cir·cum·spec·tive** /-tiv/ *adj.* —**cir·cum·spect·ly** /súrkəm spèktlee/ *adv.*

WORD KEY: SYNONYMS

See Synonyms at ***cautious***.

cir·cum·stance /súrkəm stàns/ *n.* **1.** CONDITION AFFECTING SITUATION a condition that affects what happens or how somebody reacts in a particular situation (*usually used in the plural*) ○ *Under the circumstances, the team played well.* **2.** UNCONTROLLABLE CONDITIONS the conditions that affect somebody's life and that are beyond his or her control **3.** EVENT an event or occurrence (*formal*) **4.** WAY SOMETHING HAPPENS the way an event happens or develops ■ **cir·cum·stanc·es** *npl.* CONDITIONS the social, financial, material, or spiritual conditions that somebody lives in [12thC. Via French or directly from Latin *circumstantia*, from *circumstant-*, the present participle stem of *circumstare*, literally "to stand around," from *stare* "to stand."]

cir·cum·stanced /súrkəm stànst/ *adj.* living in a particular state or set of conditions (*formal*)

cir·cum·stan·tial /sùrkəm stánsh'l/ *adj.* **1.** LAW BASED ON INFERENCE containing or based on facts that allow a court to deduce that somebody is guilty without conclusive proof ○ *circumstantial evidence* **2.** SPECIAL related to particular circumstances **3.** FORMAL with a great deal of formality and ceremony **4.** DETAILED thorough and very detailed (*formal*) —**cir·cum·stan·ti·al·i·ty** /sùrkəm stanshee állətee/ *n.* —**cir·cum·stan·tial·ly** /-stánshəlee/ *adv.*

cir·cum·stan·ti·ate /sùrkəm stánshee àyt/ (**-at·ed, -at·ing, -ates**) *vt.* to provide evidence to support an argument or allegation (*formal*) —**cir·cum·stan·ti·a·tion** /sùrkəm stanshee áysh'n/ *n.*

cir·cum·stel·lar /sùrkəm stéllər/ *adj.* around or surrounding a star

cir·cum·ter·res·tri·al /sùrkəm tə réstree əl/ *adj.* around or surrounding the Earth

cir·cum·val·late /sùrkəm vá làyt/ (**-lat·ed, -lat·ing, -lates**) *vt.* to protect a town or camp by surrounding it with a rampart or a defensive wall (*archaic or formal*) [Mid-17thC. From Latin *circumvallare*, literally "to fortify with a rampart around," from, ultimately, *vallum* "rampart," from *vallus* "stake."] —**cir·cum·val·la·tion** /sùrkəm va láysh'n/ *n.*

cir·cum·vent /sùrkəm vént, súrkəm vènt/ (**-vent·ed, -vent·ing, -vents**) *vt.* **1.** GET AROUND RESTRICTION to find a way of avoiding restrictions imposed by a rule or law without actually breaking it ○ *an attempt to circumvent the ban* **2.** OUTWIT SOMEBODY to anticipate and counter somebody's plans [15thC. From Latin *circumvent-*, the present participle stem of *circumvenire*, literally "to come around," from *venire* "to come" (source of English *convene*).] —**cir·cum·vent·er** *n.* —**cir·cum·ven·tion** *n.* —**cir·cum·ven·tive** *adj.*

cir·cum·vo·lu·tion /sùrkəm və lóosh'n/ *n.* a turning or winding movement around a central axis (*formal*) [15thC. From Latin *circumvolut-*, the past participle stem of *circumvolvere*, literally "to turn around," from *volvere* "to turn."] —**cir·cum·vo·lu·to·ry** /sùrkəm vóllyə tàwree/ *adj.*

cir·cus /súrkəss/ *n.* **1.** TRAVELING SHOW a group of traveling entertainers, including clowns, acrobats and sometimes animal trainers and their animals **2.** SHOW a performance given by circus entertainers, or the place where they perform **3.** SELF-IMPORTANT EVENT a confused, noisy, or overwhelming event or situation, especially one that seems full of self-importance (*informal*) ○ *a media circus* **4.** ARCHIT ROMAN STADIUM an open stadium built by the ancient Romans to stage chariot races or fights between gladiators **5.** ROMAN SHOW a performance staged in a Roman stadium **6.** *U.K.* PLACE WHERE STREETS MEET a round or roundish open space where several streets meet ○ *Piccadilly Circus* [14thC. From Latin, literally "ring, circle" (source of English *circle* and *search*). Ultimately from an Indo-European word meaning "to bend," which is also the ancestor of English *curve*.] —**cir·cus·y** *adj.*

WORD KEY: ORIGIN

Circus is derived from the Latin word *circus*, meaning "ring" or "circle," which is also the source of English *circle, circuit, circulate,* and *search*.

cir·cus catch *n.* a catch in baseball or football involving a leap, a dive, or a roll (*informal*) [From baseball, presumably alluding to acrobats' feats at the circus]

Cir·cus Max·i·mus /-máksiməss/ *n.* a stadium in Rome used to stage chariot races and fights between gladiators [From Latin, literally "biggest racetrack"]

ci·ré /sə ráy/ *adj.* SHINY used to describe fabric with a shiny highly glazed finish ■ *n.* **1.** SHINY FINISH a very shiny highly glazed finish achieved by treating a fabric with wax or with a heat process **2.** SHINY FABRIC a fabric with a shiny finish [Early 20thC. From French, from the past participle of *cirer* "to wax," from *cire* "wax," from Latin *cera*.]

ci·re per·due /sèer pur dóo/ *n.* = **lost wax** (*technical*) [Late 19thC. From French, literally "lost wax."]

cirque /surk/ *n.* a semicircular hollow with steep walls formed by glacial erosion on mountains. It often forms the head of a valley. [Mid-19thC. From French, from Latin *circus* (see CIRCUS).]

cir·rate /séer àyt, séerət/ *adj.* **1.** BIOL WITH TENTACLES bearing structures resembling tentacles or tendrils (**cirri**) **2.** SHAPED LIKE TENTACLE like a tentacle or tendril in shape [Early 19thC. From the Latin stem *cirrat-* "curled," from *cirrus* "curl."]

cir·rho·sis /si rṓssiss/ *n.* a chronic progressive disease of the liver characterized by the replacement of healthy cells with scar tissue [Early 19thC. From modern Latin, formed from Greek *kirrhos* "orange-colored." From the presence of yellowish granules.] —**cir·rhot·ic** /si róttik/ *adj.*

cir·ri plural of **cirrus**

cir·ri·form /séerə fàwrm/ *adj.* shaped like a long slender tendril or tentacle [Early 19thC. Coined from Latin *cirrus* (see CIRRUS) + -FORM.]

cir·ri·ped /séerə pèd/, **cir·ri·pede** /séerə pèed/ *n.* a marine crustacean that lives fixed in one spot and draws food by means of slender hairs (**cirri**). Subclass: Cirripedia. [Mid-19thC. From modern Latin *Cirripedia*, literally "with curly legs," subclass name, from Latin *cirrus* "curl."]

cir·ro·cu·mu·lus /sèerō kyóomyələss/ (*plural* **-li** /-lī/) *n.* a high-altitude cloud formed of icy particles that occurs in lines of small rounded clouds. Cirrocumulus clouds often make a pattern resembling fish scales, called a mackerel sky, indicating unsettled weather.

cir·rose /séerōss/ *adj.* consisting of thin wisps, as formed by cirrus clouds

cir·ro·stra·tus /sèerō stráttəss, -stráytəss/ (*plural* **-ti** /-tī/) *n.* a cirrus cloud resembling a transparent white veil high in the sky. It indicates wet weather.

cir·rus /séerəss/ (*plural* **-ri** /-rī/) *n.* **1.** METEOROL HIGH-ALTITUDE WISPY CLOUD a thin wispy cloud, occurring as narrow bands of tiny ice particles, that forms at the highest and coldest point of the cloud region **2.** ZOOL SLENDER TENTACLE a slender tentacle with sensory or locomotive function, or a part resembling one [Early 18thC. From Latin, "curl, fringe."]

cis /siss/ *adj.* having two atoms or groups on the same side of a double bond between carbon atoms [Late 18thC. From Latin (see CIS-).]

CIS *abbr.* Commonwealth of Independent States

cis- *prefix.* GEOG on the near side of ○ *cisatlantic* [From Latin *cis*. Ultimately from an Indo-European base meaning "this," which is also the ancestor of English *here, hither,* and *he*.]

cis·al·pine /siss ál pīn/ *adj.* **1.** GEOG SOUTH OF ALPS situated south of the Alps **2.** CHR LIMITING PAPAL POWER relating to a movement in the Roman Catholic Church to limit papal power and encourage the independence of local churches [Mid-16thC. From Latin *cisalpinus* "on this side of the Alps" (as viewed from Rome), from *alpinus* "alpine."]

cis·at·lan·tic /sìss ət lántik/ *adj.* situated on the same side of the Atlantic Ocean as the writer or speaker

CISC *abbr.* complex instruction set computer

cis·co /sískō/ (*plural* **-coes** *or* **-cos**) *n.* a silvery freshwater whitefish, found in deep lakes in North America. Genus: *Coregonus*. [Mid-19thC. Back-formation from Canadian French *ciscoette*, alteration (influenced by *-ette* "small") of Ojibwa *bemidewiskawed*, literally "that which has oily skin."]

cis·lu·nar /siss lóonər/ *adj.* situated between the Earth and the Moon

cis·mon·tane /siss món tàyn/ *adj.* on the same side of the mountains as the writer or speaker

cis·pa·dane /sìspə dáyn/ *adj.* situated on the southern side of the River Po [Late 18thC. Formed from CIS- + Latin *Padus* "the Po."]

ciss·ing /sissing/ *n.* the appearance of marks such as bubbles or pits in paintwork. This is a result of the paint not adhering properly to the surface. [Late 20thC. Origin unknown.]

cis·sus /síssəss/ *n.* an evergreen woody climbing plant, grown for its green foliage. Genus: *Cissus*. [Late 20thC. Via modern Latin from Greek *kissos* "ivy," of uncertain origin; perhaps formed from *iskhein* "to hold."]

cist /sist/, **kist** /kist/ *n.* a wood or stone coffin , dating from the latter part of the Stone Age [Early 19thC. From Welsh, literally "chest," from *cist faen* "stone chest."]

Cis·ter·cian /si stúrshən/ *adj.* RELATING TO A RELIGIOUS GROUP relating to an austere contemplative Christian order of monks and nuns founded by reformist Benedictines in 1098 ■ *n.* MONK OR NUN a member of the Cistercian order of monks and nuns [15thC. Via French from Latin *Cistercium* "Cîteaux," near Dijon, France.]

cis·tern /sístərn/ *n.* **1.** CONSTR WATER TANK a tank for storing water, especially one connected to a toilet **2.** UNDERGROUND TANK an underground tank for storing rainwater **3.** ANAT = **cisterna** [13thC. Via French from Latin *cisterna*, from *cista* "chest," from Greek *kistē* (source of English *chest*).]

cis·ter·na /si stúrnə/ (*plural* **-nae** /-nee/) *n.* a pouch or cavity that contains a body fluid [Late 19thC. From, ultimately, Latin *cisterna* (see CISTERN).] —**cis·ter·nal** *adj.*

cis·tron /síssə tròn/ *n.* a section of DNA containing the genetic code for a short chain of amino acids (**polypeptide**), the smallest functional unit carrying genetic information [Mid-20thC. Coined from CIS- + TRANS- + -ON.] —**cis·tron·ic** /siss trónnik/ *adj.*

cis·tus /sístəss/ *n. U.K.* an evergreen shrub grown for its white, red, or yellow flowers. Genus: *Cistus*. ◊ **rockrose** [Mid-16thC. From, ultimately, Greek *kistos* "red-flowered shrub."]

cit. *abbr.* **1.** cited **2.** citizen

cit·a·del /síttəd'l, síttə dèl/ *n.* **1.** FORTRESS a fortress or strongly fortified building in or near a city, used as a place of refuge **2.** DEFENDER a strong defender of a particular way of life or principle [Mid-16thC. Via French or directly from Italian *cittadella*, literally "little city," from *cittade* "city," variant of *città*, from Latin *civitas* (see CITY).]

Cit·a·del *n.* a military academy in Marion Square, South Carolina, named for the building in which it was first housed, a 19th-century fortress

ci·ta·tion /sī táysh'n/ *n.* **1. OFFICIAL ACKNOWLEDGMENT OF MERIT** an official document or speech that praises somebody's actions, accomplishments, or character **2. EXTRACT FROM WORK** a quotation from an authoritative source, used, e.g., to support an idea or argument **3. ACT OF CITING SOMETHING** the act or process of citing something **4.** LAW **ORDER TO APPEAR IN COURT** a writ for somebody to appear in a court of law **5.** LAW **REFERENCE TO PREVIOUS DECISION** a reference to a previous decision by a court or legal authority, specifying precisely where it is documented **6.** LAW **USE OF PRECEDENT** the legal practice or process of referring to precedent —**ci·ta·tion·al** *adj.* —**ci·ta·to·ry** /sítə tàwree/ *adj.*

cite /sīt/ *vt.* (**cit·ed, cit·ing, cites**) **1. QUOTE SOMETHING OR SOMEBODY** to mention something or somebody as an example to support an argument or help explain what is being said (*formal*) **2.** LAW **NAME SOMEBODY** to name somebody officially in a court case **3.** LAW **ORDER TO APPEAR IN COURT** to order somebody officially to appear in court **4.** MIL **OFFICIALLY PRAISE SOMEBODY** to praise the actions of a member of the armed services in an official document (*often passive*) ■ *n.* **CITATION** a citation (*informal*) [15thC. From, ultimately, Latin *citare*, literally "to summon repeatedly," from *citus*, past participle of *ciere* "to summon" (source of English *excite*).]

WORD KEY: ORIGIN

Cite is derived from the Latin word *ciere*, meaning "to summon," which is also the source of English *excite*, *incite*, *recite*, and *solicit*.

cith·a·ra /síthərə, síthrə/, **kith·a·ra** /kíthərə, kíthrə/ *n.* a stringed musical instrument similar to a lyre, played in ancient Greece [Late 18thC. Via Latin from Greek *kithara* (source of English *guitar* and *zither*).]

cit·ied /síttid/ *adj.* having a city or cities

cit·i·fied /sítti fīd/ *adj.* oversophisticated, in a way often associated with those who live in cities by those who do not (*disapproving*)

cit·i·fy /sítti fī/ (**-fied, -fy·ing, -fies**) *vt.* (*disapproving*) **1. TURN PLACE INTO CITY** to develop an area and make it more urban **2. MAKE SOMEBODY TOO SOPHISTICATED** to make somebody adopt the customs, behavior, or dress of those who live in cities —**cit·i·fi·ca·tion** /sítti fi káysh'n/ *n.*

cit·i·zen /síttiz'n/ *n.* **1. LEGAL RESIDENT** somebody who has the right to live in a country because he or she was born there or because he or she has been legally accepted by that country **2. SOMEBODY WHO LIVES IN A CITY** somebody who lives in a city or town rather than in a rural area **3. CIVILIAN** a civilian, rather than a member of the armed forces, a police officer, or a public official [13thC. From Anglo-Norman *citezein*, from Old French *citeain*, from the Latin stem *civitat-* "city."] —**cit·i·zen·ly** *adj.*

WORD KEY: CULTURAL NOTE

Citizen Kane, a movie by U.S. director Orson Welles (1941). Repeatedly nominated as one of the greatest movies of all time, it is the story of the rise and the tormented private life of a fictional media baron, Charles Foster Kane (supposedly based on the life of the billionaire publisher William Randolph Hearst). The film's many stylistic innovations include the use of mock-newsreel footage and striking deep-focus photography. The term ***Citizen Kane*** is often used as a description of real people and situations, for example, in *a private life reminiscent of Citizen Kane*.

cit·i·zen·ry /síttiz'nree/ (*plural* **-ries**) *n.* the citizens of a place or area collectively

cit·i·zen's ar·rest *n.* an arrest made by an ordinary citizen rather than by a police officer

cit·i·zens band *n.* radio frequencies used by the general public to talk to one another over short distances

cit·i·zen·ship /síttiz'n shìp/ *n.* **1. LEGAL STATUS OF CITIZEN** the legal status of being a citizen of a country **2. SOCIAL CONDUCT** the duties and responsibilities that come with being a member of a community

Ci·tlal·té·petl /sèe tlaal táy pèt't'l/ volcanic peak in central Veracruz state, eastern Mexico, and the highest point in Mexico. Height: 18,700 ft./5,700 m.

ci·tole /síttōl/ *n.* MUSIC = **cittern** [14thC. From French, of uncertain origin; probably literally "little cithara," formed from Latin *cithara* "cithara" (see CITHARA).]

cit·ral /sítrəl/ *n.* a volatile pale yellow liquid with a pleasant odor found in lemon grass oil. Formula: $C_{10}H_{16}O$.

cit·rate /sít ràyt/ *n.* a salt or ester of citric acid

cit·ric /síttrik/ *adj.* relating to citrus fruit

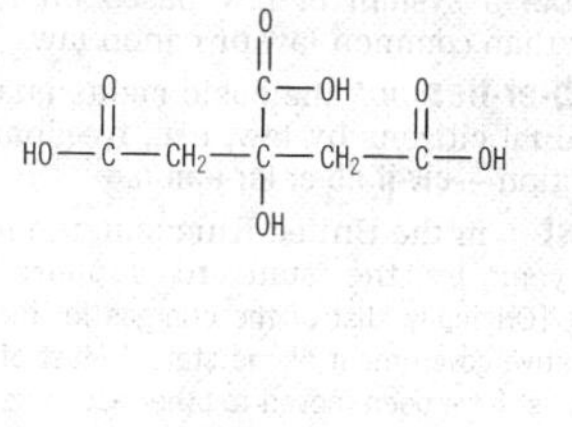

Citric acid

cit·ric ac·id *n.* a weak colorless acid present in citrus and other fruit. It is obtained commercially mainly from lemon, lime, or pineapple juice or from fermentation of sugars, and is used in flavorings.

cit·ric ac·id cy·cle *n.* = **Krebs cycle**

cit·ri·cul·ture /síttri kùlchər/ *n.* the cultivation of citrus fruits [Early 20thC. From CITRUS + CULTURE.] —**cit·ri·cul·tur·ist** *n.*

ci·trine *n.* /si trèen, sí trèen/ **1.** MINERALS **YELLOW QUARTZ** a brownish-yellow semiprecious variety of quartz **2.** COLORS **GREENISH-YELLOW COLOR** a greenish-yellow color, like that of a lemon ■ *adj.* /si trèen/ COLORS **GREENISH-YELLOW** of a greenish-yellow color, like that of a lemon [Late 16thC. From the color of the citron or lemon.]

cit·ron /síttrən/ *n.* **1.** TREES **THORNY CITRUS TREE** a small thorny evergreen citrus tree with edible fruit. Latin name: *Citrus medica.* **2.** FOOD **CITRUS FRUIT LIKE LARGE LEMON** the fruit of the citron tree, resembling a large lemon with a thick aromatic rind **3.** FOOD **CANDIED RIND** the candied rind of a fruit from a citron tree, used to decorate and flavor food **4.** PLANTS **WATERMELON** a small watermelon that has inedible white flesh and a hard rind. Latin name: *Citrullus lanatus* var. *citroides.* **5.** COLORS = **citrine** *n.* **2** [Early 16thC. From French, alteration (influenced by *limon* "lemon") of Latin *citrus* (see CITRUS).]

cit·ro·nel·la /sìttrə néllə/ *n.* **1. cit·ro·nel·la, cit·ro·nel·la grass** PLANTS **LEMON-SCENTED GRASS** a tropical Asian grass that has bluish green lemon-scented leaves and contains an aromatic oil. Latin name: *Cymbopogon nardus.* **2. cit·ro·nel·la, cit·ro·nel·la oil** CHEM **AROMATIC OIL** a pale yellow aromatic oil obtained from citronella and used in perfumes and as an insect repellent [Mid-19thC. Via modern Latin from French *citronnelle* "lemon oil," literally "little citron," from *citron* "citron," from Latin *citrus* (see CITRUS).]

cit·ro·nel·lal /sìttrə néllàl/ *n.* a colorless liquid, smelling like lemons, that is the main component of citronella oil. It is used in making perfumes and flavorings. Formula: $C_{10}H_{18}O$.

cit·ro·nel·lol /sìttrə né lawl, sìttrə né lòl/ *n.* an alcohol derived from citronellal. Formula: $C_{10}H_{20}O$.

cit·ron wood *n.* the wood of the citron tree or of the sanderac tree

cit·rul·line /síttrə lèen, síttrəlin/ *n.* an amino acid found in watermelon and also formed in the liver as part of the process of urea production. Formula: $C_6H_{13}N_3O_3$. [Mid-20thC. From medieval Latin *citrullus* "watermelon," literally "little citron tree," from Latin *citrus* (see CITRUS).]

cit·rus /síttrəss/ *n.* **1. FRUIT TREE WITH EDIBLE FRUIT** a spiny evergreen tree with edible fruit of a genus that includes the orange, lemon, lime, grapefruit, and pomelo. Though native to southern and southeastern Asia, citrus species are now grown throughout the world. Genus: *Citrus.* **2.** FOOD **FRUIT** the fruit of citrus trees collectively (*often used before a noun*) ○ *citrus flavor* [Early 19thC. From Latin, "citron tree, citrus tree," of uncertain origin.]

Cit·rus Heights /sìttrəss-/ city in Sacramento County, central California, situated northeast of Sacramento. Population: 107,439 (1990).

cit·tern /síttərn/ *n.* a medieval stringed instrument similar to a lute but with wire strings and a flat back [Mid-16thC. Origin uncertain: probably a blend of Latin *cithara* and *gittern*, both ultimately from Greek *kithara* "cithara."]

cit·y /síttee/ (*plural* **-ies**) *n.* **1. VERY LARGE TOWN** an extensive built-up area where large numbers of people live and work **2. PEOPLE IN A CITY** the inhabitants of a city collectively **3. EXTREME THING** a thing, place, or situation that is a good or extreme example of its type (*slang*) (*used in combination*) ○ *It was panic city outside.* **4. U.S. URBAN CENTER OF GOVERNMENT** an incorporated urban center in the United States that has self-government, boundaries, and legal rights established by state charter **5.** *Can* **CANADIAN URBAN AREA** a Canadian town or urban area that has been incorporated and given the title of city by the provincial government **6.** *U.K.* **LARGE BRITISH TOWN** a large town in Britain that has received the title of city from the Crown. It is usually the seat of a bishop, and so often has a cathedral. [12thC. Via Old French *cité* from Latin *civitas* "citizenship, community," from *civis* "citizen" (source of English *civil*).]

WORD KEY: SYNONYMS

city, conurbation, metropolis, town, municipality

CORE MEANING: an urban area where a large number of people live

city in the United States, a large municipal center governed under a charter granted by the state; in Canada, a large municipal unit incorporated by the provincial government, but now used generally for any large urban area; **conurbation** an urban region formed or enlarged by the merging of adjacent cities and towns through expansion or development; **metropolis** a large or important city, sometimes the capital of a country, state, or region, often used ironically to indicate a fairly small town; **town** a populated area smaller than a city and larger than a village; **municipality** a city, town, or area with some degree of self-government.

Cit·y /síttee/ *n.* = **City of London**

cit·y coun·cil *n.* a group of elected officials responsible for the government of a city or other municipality

cit·y desk *n.* a newspaper department that deals with local news

cit·y ed·i·tor *n.* the newspaper editor in charge of local news

cit·y hall *n.* **1. CITY ADMINISTRATORS** the administrators and elected officials who run a city **2. BUREAUCRACY** the bureaucracy that runs a city, especially when regarded as insensitive or inflexible **3. city hall, City Hall CITY COUNCIL BUILDING** the building where a city council has its main administrative offices

cit·y man·ag·er *n.* an administrator appointed by a municipal council to run its affairs

Cit·y of Lon·don the oldest part of London, England, and its business and financial heart. Its head of government is the Lord Mayor. Population: 4,142 (1991). Area: 1 sq. mi./2.6 sq. km.

cit·y room *n.* the department of a newspaper that deals with local news

cit·y·scape /sítti skàyp/ *n.* **1. VIEW OF CITY** a view of a city or town landscape **2.** PAINTING, PHOTOGRAPHY **PHOTOGRAPH OR PAINTING OF CITY** a photograph or painting of a view of part of a city or town

cit·y slick·er *n.* somebody who lives in a city and is extremely or excessively sophisticated (*informal disapproving*)

cit·y-state *n.* a independent state consisting of a sovereign city and its surrounding territory

cit·y·wide /sítti wīd/ *adj.* **INVOLVING AN ENTIRE CITY** involving the whole of a particular city ■ *adv.* **ALL OVER A CITY** so as to involve the whole of a particular city

Ci·u·dad Bo·lí·var /see ōō daad bə lèe vaar/ river port and capital of Bolívar State, eastern Venezuela, situated on the Orinoco River. Population: 258,112 (1992).

Ci·u·dad Juá·rez /-hwaa rèss, -waa-/ city in Chihuahua State, northern Mexico, across the Rio Grande from El Paso, Texas. Population: 797,679 (1990).

Ci·u·dad Vic·to·ri·a /-vik táwree ə/ town and capital of Tamaulipas state, central Mexico, situated 150 mi./241 km southeast of Monterrey

civ·et /sívvət/ *n.* **1. civ·et, civ·et cat** ZOOL **WILD ANIMAL LIKE CAT** a small carnivorous African or Asian mammal that looks like a cat. It secretes from its anal glands a greasy substance that smells like musk. Family: Viverridae. **2.** COSMETICS **SUBSTANCE USED IN PERFUME** a yellow or brown substance of the consistency of butter and smelling strongly of musk, secreted by the civet. It is used in the manufacture of perfume. **3. FUR** the fur of a civet [Mid-16thC. Via French *civette* from Italian *zivetto,* from medieval Latin *zibethum,* from Arabic *zabād* "civet perfume."]

civ·ic /sívvik/ *adj.* **1.** PUBLIC ADMIN **CONNECTED WITH CITY ADMINISTRATION** related to the government of a town or city ○ *civic reception* **2. RELATING TO COMMUNITY** connected with the duties and obligations of belonging to a community ○ *civic pride* [Mid-17thC. From, ultimately, Latin *civicus,* from *civis* "citizen" (see CITY).] —**civ·i·cal·ly** *adv.*

civ·ic cen·ter *n.* a municipal entertainment complex containing an indoor arena that can be used for sports, concerts, and trade shows

civ·ic-mind·ed *adj.* taking an active interest in the community needs and affairs of a town or city —**civ·ic-mind·ed·ness** *n.*

civ·ics /sívviks/ *n.* the study of the rights and duties of citizens (*takes a singular verb*)

civ·il /sívv'l/ *adj.* **1. RELATING TO CITIZENS** relating to what happens within the state or between different citizens or groups of citizens ○ *civil war* **2. NOT MILITARY** connected with ordinary citizens and organizations as opposed to the armed forces ○ *the civil authorities* **3. NOT RELIGIOUS** performed by a state official such as a registrar rather than a member of the clergy ○ *civil marriage* **4.** LAW **BETWEEN INDIVIDUALS** involving individual people or groups in legal action other than criminal proceedings ○ *a civil action* **5. POLITE** polite, but in a way that is cold and formal **6.** = **civic** *adj.* 2 [14thC. From, ultimately, Latin *civilis,* from *civis* "citizen" (see CITY).]

civil code *n.* the codified body of statutes in Quebec that derives from Roman and Napoleonic civil law

civ·il day *n.* = **calendar day** [*Civil* as in "legally recognized" (as opposed to "natural," "astronomical," etc.)]

civ·il de·fense *n.* **1. ORGANIZING OF CIVILIAN VOLUNTEERS** the organization and training of civilian volunteers to help the armed forces, police, and emergency services in the event of a war, a national emergency, or a natural disaster **2. VOLUNTEER GROUP** civilian volunteers who take part in civil defence

civ·il dis·o·be·di·ence *n.* the deliberate breaking of a law by ordinary citizens, carried out as nonviolent protest or passive resistance

civ·il en·gi·neer·ing *n.* the branch of engineering concerned with the planning, design, and construction of such things as roads, bridges, and dams —**civ·il en·gi·neer** *n.*

ci·vil·ian /si víllyən/ *n.* **NONSOLDIER** somebody who is an ordinary citizen rather than a member of the armed forces ■ *adj.* **RELATING TO CIVILIANS** relating to ordinary citizens as opposed to members of the armed forces [Early 14thC. From Old French *civilien* "of civil law," from *civil* "civil," from Latin *civilis* (see CIVIL). Originally referring to "civil law"; the modern sense dates from the early 19thC.]

ci·vil·ian·ize /si víllyə nīz/ (**-ized, -iz·ing, -iz·es**) *vt.* to change something from military to civilian use —**ci·vil·ian·i·za·tion** /si vìllyəni záysh'n/ *n.*

ci·vil·i·ty /si víllətee/ (*plural* **-ties**) *n.* **1. POLITENESS** the formal politeness that results from observing social conventions **2. POLITE ACT** something said or done in a formally polite way

civ·i·li·za·tion /sìvv'li záysh'n/ *n.* **1. HIGHLY DEVELOPED SOCIETY** a society that has a high level of culture and social organization **2. ADVANCED DEVELOPMENT OF SOCIETY** an advanced level of development in society that is marked by complex social and political organization, and material, scientific, and artistic progress **3. ADVANCED SOCIETY IN GENERAL** all the societies at an advanced level of development considered collectively **4. POPULATED AREAS** places where people live, rather than uninhabited areas **5. COMFORT** the level of material comfort that somebody is used to **6. CIVILIZING PROCESS** the process of creating a high level of culture and ending barbaric or primitive practices in a particular society or region

civ·i·lize /sívv'l īz/ (**-lized, -liz·ing, -liz·es**) *vt.* **1. TEACH ABOUT SOCIETY** to create a high level of culture and end barbaric or primitive practices in a society or region **2. MAKE MORE REFINED** to teach somebody to behave in a more socially and culturally acceptable way —**civ·i·liz·a·ble** *adj.* —**civ·i·liz·er** *n.*

civ·i·lized /sívv'l īzd/ *adj.* **1. CULTURALLY ADVANCED** having advanced cultural and social development **2. REFINED** refined in tastes

civ·il law *n.* **1. LAW OF CITIZENS' RIGHTS** the law of a state dealing with the rights of private citizens **2. ANCIENT ROMAN LAW** the law of ancient Rome, especially the part concerned with private citizens **3. LAW BASED ON ROMAN LAW** a system of law based on Roman law rather than common law or canon law

civ·il lib·er·ties *npl.* the basic rights guaranteed to individual citizens by law, e.g., freedom of speech and action —**civ·il lib·er·tar·i·an** *n.*

civ·il list *n.* in the United Kingdom, the money paid each year by the state to support the royal family [Originally "list of the charges for the civil or administrative government of the state." Most of the charges on that list have been moved to other accounts.]

civ·il·ly /sívv'lee/ *adv.* showing politeness in a cold formal way

civ·il rights *npl.* rights that all citizens of a society are supposed to have, e.g., the right to vote or to receive fair treatment from the law. These rights as conceived in U.S. law are set forth in the 13th and 14th Amendments to the U.S. Constitution and in some congressional acts.

civ·il ser·vant *n.* somebody who works in a state or federal government department

civ·il serv·ice *n.* all the government departments of a state and the people who work in them

civ·il war *n.* a war between opposing groups within a country

Civ·il War *n.* **1. 19C U.S. WAR** the civil war fought in the United States from 1861 to 1865 between the North and the slave-owning states of the South **2. 17C ENGLISH WAR** the civil war fought between the Royalist supporters of Charles I and the Parliamentarians led by Oliver Cromwell, between 1642 and 1648

civ·il year *n.* = **calendar year** [See CIVIL DAY]

civ·vies /sívviz/ *npl.* ordinary clothes as opposed to a military uniform (*informal*) [Late 19thC. Shortening and alteration of CIVILIAN, in the plural probably because it is modeled on CLOTHES.]

civ·vy /sívvee/ (*plural* **-vies**) *n.* MIL a civilian (*informal*) [Early 20thC. Shortening and alteration.]

C.J. *abbr.* **1.** *U.K.* Chief Justice **2.** Chief Judge

CJD *abbr.* Creutzfeldt-Jakob disease

ck. *abbr.* **1.** cask **2.** BANKING check

cl *abbr.* **1.** MEASURE centiliter **2.** class **3.** classification **4.** RELIG clergy **5.** FURNITURE closet **6.** CLOTHES cloth **7.** TRANSP carload

Cl *symbol.* chlorine

CL *abbr.* Sri Lanka (*international vehicle registration*)

clab·ber /klábbər/ *n.* sour milk that has curdled (*regional*) [Early 19thC. Shortening of *bonny-clabber,* from Irish *bainne clabair,* from *bainne* "milk" + *clabair,* of uncertain origin: probably "of the agitator of a churn."]

clack /klak/ *v.* **1.** *vti.* **MAKE NOISE** to cause or make a short hard loud noise, or cause something to make such a noise **2.** *vi.* **CHATTER** to chatter constantly or rapidly (*informal*) **3.** *vi.* = **cluck** ■ *n.* **SHARP NOISE** a short hard noise made by two things hitting each other [13thC. An imitation of the sound.]

clack·er /klákər/ *n.* a rattle or toy that makes a clacking noise

clack valve *n.* a valve with a hinged flap that swings open

Clac·to·ni·an /klak tṓnee ən/ *n.* a Lower Paleolithic culture of northwestern Europe that made stone chopping tools [Named for CLACTON-ON-SEA] —**Clac·to·ni·an** *adj.*

Clac·ton-on-Sea /klàktən on sée/ popular seaside resort on the North Sea coast of Essex, England. Population: 45,065 (1991).

clad¹ /klad/ *adj.* **1. DRESSED** wearing particular clothes ○ *clad in blue* **2. COVERED** covered in a particular thing (*literary*) (*often used in combination*) ○ *iron-clad* [13thC. From Old English *clā-ed,* the past participle of *clā-ian,* an earlier form of CLOTHE.]

clad² /klad/ (**clad, clad·ding, clads**) *vt.* **1.** BUILDING **COVER WITH CLADDING** to cover a wall or building with cladding **2.** TECH **COVER METAL WITH METAL** to cover or plate a metal with a layer of another metal, especially to make armor plating [Mid-16thC. Origin uncertain: probably from CLAD¹.]

clad- *prefix.* = **clado-**

Clad·dagh ring /klá dàk-/ *n.* an elaborate ring originally given in Ireland as a token of affection. The most common design is of two hands clasping a heart surmounted by a crown. [Late 20thC. From *Claddagh,* fishing village in Galway, Ireland, where the first Claddagh ring is said to have been made in the late 17thC.]

clad·ding /kládding/ *n.* **1.** BUILDING **OUTER LAYER ON BUILDING** a layer of stone, tiles, or wood added to the outside of a building to protect it or improve its insulation or appearance **2.** TECH **METAL COATING** a protective metal coating bonded onto another metal

clade /klayd/ *n.* a group of organisms, e.g., a species, that are considered to share a common ancestor [Mid-20thC. From Greek *klados* "branch."]

clad·ist /kláy dist/ *n.* a biologist who classifies organisms according to the principles of cladistics —**clad·ism** *n.*

cla·dis·tics /klə dístiks/ *n.* a system of biological classification that groups organisms on the basis of their observed shared characteristics in order to deduce the common ancestors (*takes a singular verb*) —**cla·dis·tic** *adj.* —**cla·dis·ti·cal·ly** *adv.*

clado- *prefix.* branch, shoot ○ *cladogram* [From Greek *klados.* Ultimately from an Indo-European base meaning "to strike, cut," which is also the ancestor of English *holt, hilt,* and *gladiator.*]

cla·doc·er·an /klə dóssərən/ *n.* **FRESHWATER CRUSTACEAN** a tiny freshwater crustacean. Water fleas are cladocerans. Order: Cladocera. ■ *adj.* **RELATING TO CLADOCERANS** belonging to or relating to the cladocerans [Early 20thC. Formed from modern Latin *Cladocera,* order name, from Greek *klados* "branch" + *keras* "horn."]

clad·ode /klá dōd/ *n.* BOT = **cladophyll** —**cla·do·di·al** /klə dṓdee əl/ *adj.*

clad·o·gen·e·sis /klàddō jénnəssiss, klày-/ *n.* evolutionary change regarded as taking place by the splitting of an ancestral species into two or more different descendant species —**clad·o·ge·net·ic** /klàddō jə néttik, klày-/ *adj.* —**clad·o·ge·net·i·cal·ly** /-jə néttikəlee, klày-/ *adv.*

clad·o·gram /kláydə gràm/ *n.* a tree-shaped evolutionary diagram in which the end of each branch represents one species. It shows evolutionary relationships and the points where species appear to have diverged from common ancestors.

clad·o·phyll /kláydəfil/ *n.* a flattened stem similar to a leaf

cla·fou·ti /klaà foo tée/ *n.* a fruit and batter pastry, typically made with cherries [Late 20thC. From French *clafoutis,* from dialect *clafir* "to stuff," originally "to attach with nails" (from Latin *clavo figere,* from *clavus* "nail" + *figere* "to attach") + French *foutre* "to stuff."]

claim /klaym/ *vt.* **1. MAINTAIN SOMETHING IS TRUE** to say, without proof or evidence, that something is true ○ *He claims we've already met.* **2. DEMAND SOMETHING AS ENTITLEMENT** to demand something officially that somebody has a right to or owns **3. END SOMEBODY'S LIFE** to cause the loss of somebody's life **4. WIN TITLE** to take a title, prize, or record **5. DEMAND ATTENTION** to force somebody to give attention ■ *n.* **1. SOMETHING THAT MAY BE TRUE** an assertion that something is true, unsupported by evidence or proof **2. BASIS FOR GETTING SOMETHING** the basis for demanding or getting something **3. DEMAND** a demand for something somebody has a right to or owns **4.** INSUR, SOC WELFARE **OFFICIAL REQUEST FOR MONEY** an official request for money or other benefits from the state or an organization **5. MONEY REQUESTED** the amount of money requested in a claim **6.** LAW **LEGAL RIGHT TO LAND** the legal right to own a piece of land and to mine it for minerals **7.** LAW **PIECE OF LAND** the piece of land to which somebody claims a legal right [14thC. From Old French *clamer* "to call," from Latin *clamare* (source of English *clamor*). Ultimately from an Indo-European word that is also the ancestor of English *éclair.*] —**claim·a·ble** *adj.* —**claim·er** *n.* ◇ **lay claim to something** to say that you have a right to something, or take what you think you have a right to

WORD KEY: ORIGIN

Claim is derived from the Latin word *clamare*, meaning "to call," which is also the source of English *acclaim*, *clamor*, *exclaim*, and *proclaim*.

claim·ant /kláymənt/ *n.* somebody who is claiming or receiving something, e.g., benefits or an inheritance

clair de lune /klàir də lo͞on/ *n.* **1.** CERAMICS **TYPE OF GLAZE** a pale blue or grayish-blue glaze used on porcelain **2.** COLORS **PALE BLUISH-GRAY** a pale bluish-gray color ■ *adj.* COLORS **OF A PALE BLUISH-GRAY** of a pale bluish-gray color [Late 19thC. From French, literally "light of the moon."]

claire-ob·scure /klàir əb skyo͞or/ *n.* = **chiaroscuro** [Early 18thC. From French *clair-obscur*, literally "light-dark," a translation of Italian *chiaroscuro*.]

clair·voy·ance /klair vóyənss/, **clair·voy·an·cy** /-ənsee/ *n.* the supposed ability to see things beyond the range of normal human vision [Mid-19thC. From French, from *clairvoyant* "clear-sighted," from *voyant*, the present participle of *voir* "to see."]

clair·voy·ant /klair vóyənt/ *n.* **PSYCHIC PERSON** somebody supposedly able to see things beyond the range of normal human vision ■ *adj.* **PSYCHIC** supposedly able to see things beyond the range of normal human vision [Mid-19thC. See CLAIRVOYANCE.] —**clair·voy·ant·ly** *adv.*

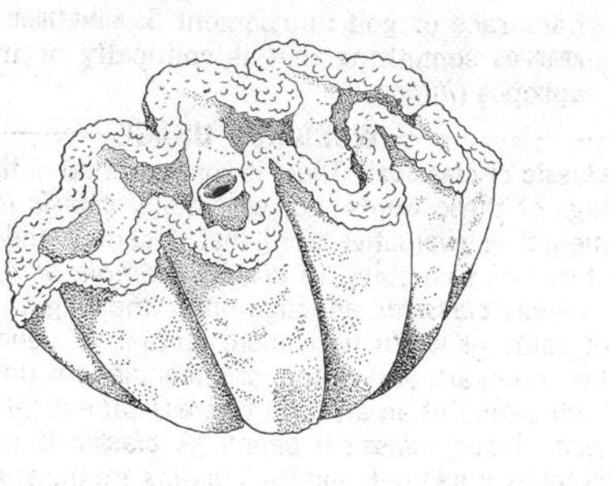

Clam

clam /klam/ *n.* **1.** **BURROWING SHELLFISH** a freshwater or marine mollusk that has a muscular foot with which it can burrow into sand. Many are edible and the largest is nearly 5 ft./1.5 m long. Class: Pelecypoda. **2.** FOOD **CLAM FLESH** the soft edible flesh of the clam **3.** **SECRETIVE PERSON** somebody who is shy or secretive, especially somebody who can keep a secret (*informal*) **4.** **DOLLAR** a dollar (*slang*) ■ *vi.* (**clammed, clam·ming, clams**) FOOD **COLLECT CLAMS** to gather clams [Early 16thC. From obsolete *clam-shell*, literally "clamp-shell," from Old English *clamm* "bond, grip"; ultimately from an Indo-European word meaning "to form into a ball."]

clam up *vi.* to become suddenly secretive or unwilling to talk (*informal*)

cla·mant /kláymənt/ *adj.* **1.** **LOUD** loud or noisy (*archaic*) **2.** **URGENT** demanding attention (*literary*) [Mid-17thC. From Latin *clamant-*, the present participle stem of *clamare* (see CLAIM).] —**cla·mant·ly** *adv.*

clam·bake /klám bàyk/ *n.* **1.** **SEAFOOD PICNIC** a picnic in which seafood such as clams and other foods are cooked and eaten **2.** **PARTY** a relaxed party or other gathering (*informal*)

clam·ber /klámbər/ *vi.* **CLIMB AWKWARDLY** to climb quickly but awkwardly, using hands and feet ■ *n.* **AWKWARD CLIMB** a climb that involves clambering [14thC. Origin uncertain: probably literally "to climb repeatedly," from *clamb*, former past tense of CLIMB.] —**clam·ber·er** *n.*

clam chow·der *n.* a thick soup made from clams and potatoes

clam·dig·gers *npl.* casual pants reaching to the middle of the wearer's calf [From the fact that they were originally worn for digging clams]

clam-flat *n.* a bank of mud left exposed by the tide where clams are plentiful (*regional*)

clam·mer /klámmər/ *n.* somebody who digs or dredges for clams

clam·my /klámmee/ (**-mi·er, -mi·est**) *adj.* **1.** **COLD AND DAMP** slightly damp and unpleasantly cold **2.** **HUMID** warm and damp [14thC. Origin uncertain: probably from *clam* "to smear," a back-formation from *clamde*, past tense of Old English *clæman*, from a prehistoric Germanic word meaning "clay."] —**clam·mi·ly** *adv.* —**clam·mi·ness** *n.*

clam·or /klámmər/ *vi.* **1.** **DEMAND NOISILY** to demand something noisily or desperately **2.** **SHOUT** to shout at the same time as other people, and make a lot of noise ■ *n.* **1.** **PERSISTENT DEMAND** a persistent demand for something, made in an excited or angry way **2.** **LOUD NOISE** a loud noise, especially one made by people shouting together [14thC. The verb came from the noun, from Old French *clamor*, from the Latin stem *clamor-*, from *clamare* (see CLAIM).] —**clam·or·er** *n.*

clam·or·ous /klámmərəss/ *adj.* **1.** **DEMANDING ATTENTION** demanding attention loudly and insistently **2.** **LOUD** loud and excited or angry **3.** **NOISY** making a loud noise —**clam·or·ous·ly** *adv.* —**clam·or·ous·ness** *n.*

clam·our *vi., n.* U.K. = **clamor**

clamp /klamp/ *n.* **1.** **HOLDING DEVICE** a mechanical device with movable jaws used to hold two things firmly together or one object firmly in position **2.** *U.K.* CARS = **boot** ■ *vt.* (**clamped, clamp·ing, clamps**) **1.** **FASTEN THINGS TOGETHER** to fasten two or more things firmly together using a clamp **2.** **HOLD FIRMLY** to hold something firmly and tightly in position **3.** *U.K.* CARS = **boot** [15thC. Origin uncertain: probably from assumed Middle Dutch or Middle Low German *klampe*.]

clamp down *vi.* to take firm action to control or limit something bad or somebody doing something bad ○ *Police have clamped down on illegal parking in the area.*

clamp·down /klámp dòwn/ *n.* firm official action taken to control or limit something bad or somebody doing something bad

clamp·er /klámpər/ *n.* a spiked metal frame fastened under a shoe to avoid slipping on ice or snow

clam·shell /klám shèl/ *n.* **1.** **SHELL** the shell of a clam **2.** **DREDGING BUCKET** a dredging bucket that has two hinged jaws (*informal*)

clam·worm /klám wùrm/ *n.* any segmented marine worm that burrows into sand or mud. They are dug up and used by fishermen as bait. Genus: *Nereis*. [*Clam*] from the fact that clams live buried in sand or mud]

clan /klan/ *n.* **1.** ETHNOL **GROUP OF FAMILIES** a group of families related through a common ancestor or marriage **2.** **LARGE FAMILY** a group of people who are all members of a particular family (*informal*) **3.** SOC SCI **RELATED SCOTTISH FAMILIES** a group of Scottish families with common ancestors and surname and a single chief **4.** **GROUP WITH SHARED AIM** a group of people who act together because they have the same interests or aims (*informal*) [15thC. From Gaelic *clann* "offspring," from Old Irish *cland*, from Latin *planta* "sprout."]

Clan·cy /klánsee/, **Tom** (*b.* 1947) U.S. writer. His thriller novels include *The Hunt for Red October* (1984). Full name **Thomas L. Clancy, Jr.**

clan·des·tine /klan déstin/ *adj.* secret or furtive, and usually illegal [Mid-16thC. From, ultimately, Latin *clandestinus*, from *clam* "secretly."] —**clan·des·tine·ly** *adv.* —**clan·des·tine·ness** *n.* —**clan·des·tin·i·ty** /klàndə stínnətee/ *n.*

clang /klang/ *vti.* **1.** **MAKE LOUD RINGING NOISE** to make the ringing sound of two metal objects hitting each other **2.** **MOVE MAKING CLANGING SOUND** to move or operate with a clanging sound ■ *n.* **LOUD RINGING NOISE** a ringing sound made by two metal objects hitting each other [Late 16thC. From Latin *clangere* "to emit a ringing sound." Ultimately from an Indo-European word meaning "to cry," an imitation of sounds made by people and animals.]

clang·er /klángər/ *n.* *U.K.* an unwise or embarrassing mistake (*informal*) ○ *drop a clanger*

clan·gor /kláng gər/ *n.* **1.** **CLANGING** a clang, or a repeated loud clanging **2.** **NOISE** a din or uproar —**clan·gor·ous** *adj.* —**clan·gor·ous·ly** *adv.*

clank /klangk/ *vti.* **1.** **MAKE METALLIC NOISE** to make the short loud sound of two heavy metal objects hitting each other **2.** **MOVE MAKING CLANKING SOUND** to move or operate with a clanking sound ■ *n.* **METALLIC NOISE** a short loud noise made by two heavy metal objects hitting each other [Mid-17thC. Origin uncertain: perhaps an imitation of the sound, with influence from CLANG and CLINK.] —**clank·ing·ly** *adv.* —**clank·y** *adj.*

clan·nish /klánnish/ *adj.* inclined to stick together as a group and exclude outsiders —**clan·nish·ly** *adv.* —**clan·nish·ness** *n.*

clans·man /klánz mən/ (*plural* **-men** /-mən/) *n.* a male member of a Scottish clan

clap[1] /klap/ *v.* (**clapped, clap·ping, claps**) **1.** *vti.* **APPLAUD** to hit the hands together repeatedly to express approval **2.** *vti.* **HIT HANDS TOGETHER** to hit the hands together quickly and loudly **3.** *vti.* **HIT HANDS IN RHYTHM** to hit the hands together repeatedly in time with a beat **4.** *vt.* **PUT QUICKLY** to move something to or against something quickly ■ *n.* **1.** **SUDDEN LOUD SOUND** the sound made by striking the palms together once, or any sudden loud sharp sound **2.** **EXPRESSION OF APPROVAL THROUGH APPLAUSE** an expression of approval by loud continuous clapping **3.** **CLAPPING RHYTHMICALLY** a session of rhythmic clapping [Old English *clæppan*, from a prehistoric Germanic word that was an imitation of the sound]

clap on *vt.* to put clothing or equipment on hastily (*dated*)

clap[2] /klap/ *n.* gonorrhea (*slang*) [Late 16thC. Origin uncertain: perhaps from French *clapoir* "bubo," from Old French *clapiore* "brothel."]

clap·board /kláp bàwrd, klábərd/ *n.* a long narrow wooden board that has one edge thicker than the other, used to clad building. Boards are nailed to a wooden frame and overlap to form a wall or roof. [Mid-17thC. Partial translation of earlier *clapholt*, from Low German *klappholt*, from *klappen* "to clap, split" + *holt* "wood."]

clapped-out *adj.* *U.K.* worn out and in very poor condition (*informal*) (*not hyphenated after a verb*)

clap·per /kláppər/ *n.* **1.** **PART MAKING BELL RING** a piece of metal inside a bell that strikes its side, making it ring **2.** **SOMEBODY WHO CLAPS** somebody who claps his or her hands ■ **clap·pers** *npl.* MUSIC **MUSICAL INSTRUMENT** a musical instrument consisting of two flat pieces of wood that are held between the thumb and forefinger and clapped together

Clapperboard

clap·per·board /kláppər bàwrd/ *n.* a pair of hinged boards filmed at the start of each take in a movie and clapped together to help to synchronize the soundtrack with the movie

clap·trap /kláp tràp/ *n.* pompous or important-sounding nonsense (*informal*) [Late 18thC. Originally, in the theater, a device or line to elicit applause; that is, a trap to catch a clap.]

claque /klak/ *n.* **1.** **PAID AUDIENCE** a group of people hired to applaud a performance **2.** **ENTOURAGE** a group of people around a rich or famous person whom they praise and support uncritically [Mid-19thC. From French, from *claquer* "to clap," an imitation of the sound.]

cla·queur /klákər/ *n.* somebody who goes around with a rich or famous person and gives him or her praise and uncritical support [Mid-19thC. From French, literally "clapper," from *claquer* (see CLAQUE).]

cla·ra·bel·la /klèrrə béllə/, **cla·ri·bel·la** *n.* an eight-foot flute stop on an organ [Mid-19thC. From Latin *clara bella*, literally "clear and beautiful."]

Clare /klair/ city in Clare County, central Michigan, situated 15 mi./24 km north of Mount Pleasant. Population: 3,021 (1990).

Clare·mont /klármont, kláir-/ city in southwestern California; an eastern suburb of Los Angeles. Population: 33,507 (1996).

clar·ence /klérrənss/ *n.* an enclosed four-wheeled carriage that seats four and has a glass front [Mid-19thC. Named for the Duke of *Clarence*, later William IV.]

Clar·en·don /klérrəndən/ *n.* a style of boldface roman type [Mid-19thC. Origin uncertain; probably named for the *Clarendon* Press in Oxford, England.]

clar·et /klérrət/ *n.* **1.** WINE **RED WINE** a red wine from the Bordeaux region of France **2.** COLORS **DEEP RED** a deep purplish-red color, like that of claret ■ *adj.* COLORS

OF A DEEP RED COLOR of a deep purplish-red color, like claret [Early 18thC. From Old French *(vin) claret* "light-colored (wine)," from Latin *vinum claratum* "clarified wine," *claratum* a form of *clarare* "to clarify," from *clarus* "clear."]

clar·et cup *n.* an iced summer drink made from claret, brandy, lemon, and sugar, sometimes with sherry or curaçao added

cla·ri·bel flute *n.* = **clarabella**

cla·ri·bel·la *n.* = **clarabella**

clar·i·fi·ca·tion /klèrrəfi káysh'n/ *n.* **1.** EXPLANATION a detailed explanation needed because something is unclear **2.** COOK PURIFYING OF FAT the process of making butter or fat become clear by heating it gently and removing impurities **3.** PURIFYING OF LIQUID the process of making a liquid clear and pure

clar·i·fi·er /klérrə fìr/ *n.* a device for removing impurities, e.g., from water

clar·i·fy /klérrə fì/ (**-fied, -fy·ing, -fies**) *v.* **1.** *vt.* MAKE SOMETHING CLEARER to make something clearer by explaining it in greater detail **2.** *vti.* COOK MAKE BUTTER CLEAR to make butter or fat clear, or become clear, by gently heating it to remove impurities **3.** *vti.* FOOD TECH MAKE A LIQUID CLEAR to make a liquid clear and pure, or become clear and pure, usually by filtering [14thC. Via Old French from late Latin *clarificare*, literally "to make clear," from Latin *clarus* "clear" (see CLARITY).]

clar·i·net /klérrə nét/ *n.* **1.** WOODWIND INSTRUMENT a musical instrument of the woodwind family, with a straight body and a single reed **2.** CLARINET PLAYER somebody who plays the clarinet, especially in an orchestra or group [Mid-18thC. From French *clarinette*, literally "little clarion," from *clarine* "clarion," from, ultimately, Latin *clarus* "clear" (see CLARITY).]

clar·i·net·tist /klèrrə néttist/, **clar·i·net·ist** *n.* somebody who plays the clarinet

clar·i·on /klérree ən/ *n.* **1.** ORGAN STOP a four-foot organ stop that sounds like a trumpet **2.** MEDIEVAL TRUMPET a medieval trumpet with a clear high-pitched tone [14thC. From the medieval Latin stem *clarion-*, from Latin *clarus* "clear" (see CLARITY).]

clar·i·on call *n.* an urgent or inspiring appeal to people to do something [From the use of the clarion as a signal in war]

clar·i·ty /klérrətee/ *n.* **1.** CLEARNESS OF EXPRESSION the quality of being clearly expressed **2.** CLEARNESS OF THOUGHT clearness in what somebody is thinking **3.** CLEARNESS OF REPRODUCTION the quality of being clear in sound or image **4.** TRANSPARENT QUALITY the quality of being clear, pure, or transparent ○ *wine of great clarity* [Early 17thC. From the Latin stem *claritat-*, from *clarus* "clear" (source of English *declare* and *chiaroscuro*).]

Clark /klaark/, **George Rogers** (1752–1818) U.S. soldier. He led troops against British forces in the American War of Independence (1775–83).

Clark, Mark Wayne (1896–1984) U.S. army general. He led the Allied armies in Italy (1943–45) and commanded UN forces in Korea (1952–53).

Clark, Tom Campbell (1899–1977) U.S. Supreme Court justice. He was appointed in 1949 by President Truman after serving as his attorney general (1945–49).

Clark, William (1770–1838) U.S. explorer. He was coleader of the Lewis and Clark Expedition that explored the Far West (1804–06).

Clark cell *n.* a standard battery cell with a mercury anode surrounded by a paste of mercury sulfate, and a zinc cathode immersed in saturated zinc sulfate solution [Late 19thC. Named for the English engineer Josiah Latimer *Clark* (1822–98), who invented it.]

Clarks·burg /klaárks bùrg/ city in northern West Virginia, on the West Fork River, northeast of Charleston. Population: 17,410 (1996).

Clarks·dale /klaárks dàyl/ city in northwestern Mississippi on the Sunflower River, southwest of Oxford. Population: 19,381 (1996).

Clarks·ville /klaárks vìl/ city in northwestern Tennessee, northwest of Nashville, where the Red and Cumberland rivers meet. Population: 94,879 (1996).

cla·ro /klaárō/ (*plural* **-ros**) *n.* a mild light-colored cigar [Late 19thC. Via Spanish, literally "clear, light," from Latin *clarus*.]

clar·sach /klaár sàkh, -səkh/ *n.* a small harp of ancient Scotland and Ireland [15thC. From Irish *cláirseach* and Gaelic *clársach*.]

clar·y /kláiree/ (*plural* **-ies**) *n.* a perennial plant of the mint family native to southern Europe. Some are cultivated for their violet, pink, or white flowers, or for an aromatic oil used in liquors and toiletries. Genus: *Salvia*. [14thC. Via obsolete French *clarie* from medieval Latin *sclarea*.]

clash /klash/ *v.* (**clashed, clash·ing, clash·es**) **1.** *vi.* FIGHT OR ARGUE to come into verbal or physical conflict with somebody **2.** *vi.* BE AT ODDS WITH SOMETHING to be incompatible ○ *The conclusions clash with the evidence.* **3.** *vti.* MAKE LOUD NOISE to make a loud harsh metallic noise, or hit things together to make such a noise **4.** *vi.* NOT HARMONIZE to look unpleasant or inharmonious when together ○ *The orange of the upholstery clashes with the pink of the paintwork.* ■ *n.* **1.** FIGHT OR ARGUMENT verbal or physical conflict with another person or group **2.** LOUD METALLIC SOUND a loud harsh metallic noise **3.** LACK OF HARMONY a jarring or unpleasant juxtaposition of incompatible colors **4.** CONFLICT CAUSED BY DIFFERENCE a difference of opinions or qualities that causes conflict ○ *a clash of personalities* [Early 16thC. An imitation of the sound.]

clasp /klasp/ *vt.* (**clasped, clasp·ing, clasps**) **1.** HOLD WITH HANDS OR ARMS to hold somebody or something tightly with the hands or arms ○ *She clasped the baby tightly to herself in the surging crowd.* ○ *I clasped the handrail as the boat lurched.* **2.** FASTEN to fasten or hold two things together with a device designed for this purpose ■ *n.* **1.** SMALL BUCKLE OR FASTENING a small fastening for holding things, e.g., bags or jewelry, closed or together **2.** TIGHT ARM OR HAND HOLD a firm tight hold with the arms, a hand, or a device for fastening or holding things together **3.** MIL IDENTIFYING ATTACHMENT ON MILITARY MEDAL a small metal bar on the ribbon of a medal that identifies the military action or service for which the honor was awarded [14thC. Origin unknown.]

clasp·er /kláspər/ *n.* **1.** GRASPING ORGAN OF INSECTS either of a pair of structures located in the anal region of particular male insects and crustaceans and used to grasp a female during copulation **2.** REPRODUCTIVE ORGAN ON FIN either of a pair of elongated reproductive organs on the pelvic fins of male sharks and rays

clasp knife *n.* a pocket knife with one or more blades and sometimes other devices that can be folded back into the handle

class /klass/ *n.* **1.** GROUP TAUGHT TOGETHER a group of students or pupils who are taught or study together **2.** PERIOD OF TEACHING a period when students meet to be taught a particular subject ○ *When's our next biology class?* **3.** SPECIFIC SUBJECT TAUGHT a specific course of instruction **4.** STUDENTS WHO GRADUATE TOGETHER the group of students who graduate from an institution in the same year **5.** GROUP WITHIN A SOCIETY a group of people within a society who share the same social and economic status **6.** STRUCTURE OF SOCIETY the structure of divisions in a society determined by the social or economic grouping of its members **7.** ELEGANCE IN STYLE elegance in appearance, behavior, or lifestyle (*informal*) ○ *a First Lady of real class* **8.** EXCELLENCE admirable skill or excellence in performance (*informal*) ○ *a player of real class* **9.** DIVISION ACCORDING TO QUALITY a categorization of services or goods according to quality ○ *This airline has several classes of seating.* **10.** *U.K.* UNIV UNIVERSITY HONORS DEGREE GRADE a grade assigned to university honors degrees in the U.K. **11.** GROUP OF SIMILAR ITEMS a group of things with at least one common characteristic **12.** BIOL SET OF RELATED ORGANISMS a major category in the taxonomic classification of related organisms, comprising a group of orders ○ *Elephants and dolphins both belong to the class Mammalia.* **13.** ETHNOL SOCIAL GROUP WITH SIMILAR OPPORTUNITIES a category of people who have a similar level of opportunity to obtain economic resources and prestige **14.** MATH, LOGIC = **set** ■ *vt.* (**classed, class·ing, clas·ses**) ASSIGN TO A GROUP to assign somebody or something to a particular category or group ○ *if you're classed as eligible to vote* [Mid-16thC. From Latin *classis* "political class."]

class. *abbr.* **1.** classic **2.** classical **3.** classification **4.** classified

class act *n.* a person or thing regarded as an example of excellence (*informal*)

class ac·tion *n.* an action brought by one or a number of litigants representing others sharing the same legal problem and seeking remedy or relief for all

class-con·scious *adj.* **1.** AWARE OF OWN SOCIAL CLASS aware of your position in a social class system in relation to members of other classes **2.** BELIEVING IN CLASS STRUGGLE used to describe a person or political party that believes in class struggle —**class-con·scious·ness** *n.*

clas·ses /klássəz/ plural of **classis**

clas·sic /klássik/ *adj.* **1.** TOP QUALITY generally considered to be of the highest quality or lasting value, especially in the arts **2.** DEFINITIVE authoritative and perfect as a standard of its kind ○ *a classic example of mixed metaphor English* **3.** EXHIBITING STYLISTIC RESTRAINT AND REFINEMENT simple, restrained, and refined in style ○ *The new sports car, with its classic lines, was the hit of the auto show.* **4.** ALWAYS FASHIONABLE always fashionable and elegant, usually because of simplicity and restraint in style ○ *the classic "little black dress"* **5.** GENERALLY ACCEPTED conforming to generally accepted principles or methods **6.** EXTREMELY AND USUALLY COMICALLY APROPOS apropos to an extreme degree, usually with a comical or ironic twist (*informal*) ■ *n.* **1.** WORK OF THE HIGHEST QUALITY something created or made, especially a work of art, music, or literature, that is generally considered to be of the highest quality and of enduring value ○ *the novel has become a 20th-century classic* **2.** SIMPLE ELEGANT GARMENT a piece of clothing of a simple and enduring style **3.** TOP QUALITY ARTIST OR WRITER a creator of works of art or literature that have enduring excellence ○ *As a children's book illustrator she's a classic.* **4.** MAJOR SPORTING EVENT a major sporting event, e.g., a horserace or golf tournament **5.** SOMETHING COMICALLY APROPOS something that is comically or ironically apropos (*informal*)

WORD KEY: USAGE

classic or **classical**? There is some overlap in the meanings of these words, but essentially ***classic*** is a judgmental or evaluative word that describes the value or status of something (*a classic example of Art Deco*), whereas ***classical***, although often implying a judgment of value or worth, is a more factual reference to the literature, art, and culture of the ancient world or to the high period of an art form (*a classical education, classical music, classical ballet*). A ***classic*** is something notable of its kind, and the *classics* are the study of the language and culture of ancient Greece and Rome.

clas·si·cal /klássik'l/ *adj.* **1.** RELATING TO ANCIENT GREECE OR ROME relating to or belonging to the ancient Greeks and Romans or their culture **2.** IN ANCIENT GREEK OR ROMAN STYLE in the style of ancient Greece or Rome, especially in architecture **3.** OF MUSIC CONSIDERED TO BE SERIOUS used to describe music that is considered serious or intellectual and is usually written in a traditional or formal style, as opposed to such genres as pop, rock, and folk music **4.** OF 18THC AND 19THC MUSIC used to describe the style of music composed in Europe in the 18th and 19th centuries **5.** STUDYING LATIN AND GREEK consisting of or involving the study of the ancient Greek and Latin languages and literature ○ *a classical education* **6.** KNOWLEDGEABLE ABOUT ANCIENT GREECE AND ROME highly knowledgeable about ancient Greek and Roman culture and art ○ *a classical scholar* **7.** ORTHODOX OR CONSERVATIVE considered as the traditional or authoritative form of something ○ *a classical Freudianism* **8.** = **classic** *adj.* **2**, **classic** *adj.* **3** **9.** PHYS EXCLUDING QUANTUM THEORY AND RELATIVITY not taking into account quantum theoretical or relativistic effects [Late 16thC. Formed from Latin *classicus* "of the first class" (source of English *classic*).] —**clas·si·cal·i·ty** /klàssi kállətee/ *n.* —**clas·si·cal·ness** /klássik'lnəss/ *n.*

WORD KEY: USAGE

See Usage note at ***classic***.

clas·si·cal con·di·tion·ing *n.* the teaching of a response to a new stimulus by pairing it repeatedly with a stimulus for which there is a biological reflex. The best-known example is Pavlov's experiment in which dogs heard a bell ring every time food appeared and eventually started salivating at the sound of the bell alone. ◊ **operant conditioning**

clas·si·cal·ism *n.* = **classicism**

clas·si·cal·ly /klássikəlee/ *adv.* **1.** SIMPLY STYLED in a simple and elegant style **2.** AS TRADITIONALLY ACCEPTED OR DONE in a manner that is traditionally accepted and belongs in the mainstream of the relevant art **3.** IN MANNER OF GRECO-ROMAN CULTURE in the manner or style of ancient Greece or Rome **4.** AS USUALLY OCCURS used to indicate what usually or typically happens ○ *Classically, cases like this are solved through painstaking investigation.* **5. AS TYPICAL EXAMPLE** as a classic example of something **6. IN CLASSIC WAY** in a classic or classical manner

clas·si·cism /klássi sìzzəm/, **clas·si·cal·ism** /klássik'l izzəm/ *n.* **1. RESTRAINED STYLE IN THE ARTS** a style of art and architecture based on Greek and Roman models or principles, characterized by regularity of form and restraint of expression **2. GREEK OR LATIN IDIOM** a Greek or Latin phrase or expression **3. STUDY OF GRECO-ROMAN CULTURE** the study or knowledge of ancient Greece and Rome

clas·si·cist /klássissist/ *n.* **1. SCHOLAR OF ANCIENT GREEK AND LATIN** somebody who studies ancient Greek and Latin **2. ADVOCATE OF ARTISTIC CLASSICISM** a supporter of classicism in the arts

clas·si·cize /klássi sīz/ (**-cized, -ciz·ing, -ciz·es**) *v.* **1.** *vt.* **MAKE SOMETHING CLASSIC OR CLASSICAL** to imbue something with classical traits, qualities, or characteristics ○ *classicized the design of the windows* **2.** *vi.* **BE STYLISTICALLY CLASSIC OR CLASSICAL** to be in a classic or classical style

clas·sics /klássiks/ *n.* **clas·sics, Clas·sics STUDY OF ANCIENT GREECE AND ROME** the academic study of the language, literature, and history of ancient Greece and Rome (*takes a singular verb*) ■ *npl.* **COLLECTION OF ANCIENT GRECO-ROMAN LITERATURE** a body of ancient Greek and Roman literature (*takes a plural verb*) [So called because Greek and Roman culture was considered to be of the highest quality]

clas·sics /klássiks/ *npl.* the languages of ancient Greece and Rome ○ *expanding the Classics curriculum*

clas·si·fi·a·ble /klássi fī əb'l/ *adj.* **1. ABLE TO BE CLASSED** being such that the one designated can be easily put into a particular category or classification ○ *classifiable insect specimens* ○ *remarks not easily classifiable as threats, yet disconcerting and ominous* **2. DESERVING TREATMENT AS SENSITIVE INFORMATION** being of such content and nature as to be deemed sensitive and therefore restricted for reasons of national security ○ *classifiable information, such as the number of aircraft in the region*

clas·si·fi·ca·tion /klàssifi káysh'n/ *n.* **1. ORGANIZATION INTO GROUPS** the allocation of items to groups according to type ○ *classification of members according to abilities and interests* **2. CATEGORY** a group or category within a system ○ *the classification "history" can be further subdivided.* **3.** BIOL **CATEGORIZATION OF LIVING THINGS** the categorization of organisms into defined groups on the basis of identified characteristics. The Linnean classification groups organisms into species, genera, families, and higher taxonomic groups on the basis of visible resemblances, while other systems may determine, e.g., the molecular relationships among the groups. **4.** BIOL **CATEGORY FOR LIVING THINGS** each of several categories into which biologists organize living things based on structural resemblance or evolutionary relationships ○ *genus and species classifications* **5. DESIGNATION AS SENSITIVE INFORMATION** the restriction of sensitive government or military information to authorized individuals [Late 18thC. From French, formed from *classe* "class," which came from Latin *classis* (see CLASS).] —**clas·si·fi·ca·tion·al** *adj.* —**clas·si·fi·ca·to·ry** /klássifikə tàwree, kla síffikə-/ *adj.*

clas·si·fi·ca·tion sched·ule *n.* the complete plan and content of a library's cataloging system

clas·si·fied /klássi fīd/ *adj.* **1. SECRET OR SENSITIVE** available only to authorized people for reasons of national security. The basic categories of classified information are confidential, secret, and top secret. **2. GROUPED BY TYPE** arranged in groups according to a classification system ■ **clas·si·fieds** *npl.* **GROUP OF ADVERTISEMENTS** classified advertisements printed together in a newspaper or magazine (*informal*)

clas·si·fied ad·ver·tise·ment, **clas·si·fied ad** *n.* a small advertisement positioned with others of similar content in a newspaper or magazine

clas·si·fi·er /klássi fīr/ *n.* **1. ASSIGNER TO CLASSIFICATIONS** somebody who assigns things to classes **2. OFFICIAL WHO DETERMINES WHAT IS SECRET** an official who decides if particular information is secret and thus available only to authorized people

clas·si·fy /klássi fī/ (**-fied, -fy·ing, -fies**) *vt.* **1. CATEGORIZE THINGS OR PEOPLE** to assign things or people to classes or groups **2. DECLARE INFORMATION SENSITIVE AND THUS RESTRICTED** to designate information as being available only to authorized people for reasons of security [Late 18thC. Back-formation from CLASSIFICATION.]

class in·ter·val *n.* any of the intervals into which adjacent discrete values of a variable are divided

clas·sis /klássiss/ (*plural* **-ses** /-seez/) *n.* **1. CHURCH GOVERNING BODY** in some Reformed churches, a governing body composed of elders and pastors **2. GROUP OF GOVERNED CHURCHES** a district or group of churches governed by a classis [Late 16thC. From Latin *classis* "political class."]

class·ism /klá sìzzəm/ *n.* discrimination or prejudice based on social or economic class —**class·ist** *adj., n.*

class·less /klássləss/ *adj.* **1. LACKING SOCIAL CLASSES** not having social or economic classes **2. NOT HAVING A SOCIAL CLASS** not belonging to or associated with a particular social or economic class —**class·less·ness** *n.*

class·mate /kláss màyt/ *n.* somebody who is or was in the same class as another at school

class·room /kláss ro͞om, -ro͝om/ *n.* a room, especially in a school or college, where classes are held

class strug·gle *n.* the Marxist principle of a continuous struggle for political and economic power between the ruling and working classes

class·y /klássee/ (**-i·er, -i·est**) *adj.* very stylish and elegant (*informal*) —**class·i·ly** *adv.* —**class·i·ness** *n.*

clast /klast/ *n.* a fragment of rock produced by the breaking down of larger rocks [Mid-20thC. Back-formation from CLASTIC.]

clas·tic /klástik/ *adj.* **1. ABLE TO BE TAKEN APART** able to be separated into parts or have parts removed to enable better study ○ *Clastic models are often used to teach anatomy.* **2.** GEOL **MADE FROM ROCK FRAGMENTS** used to describe rock that is composed of fragments of other rocks [Late 19thC. Via French *clastique* from Greek *klastos* "broken in pieces."]

clath·rate /kláth ràyt/ *n.* **CRYSTAL WITH EMBEDDED SUBSTANCE** a solid compound with a physical structure in which molecules of one substance are fully enclosed within the crystal structure of another ■ *adj.* **1. WITH CRYSTAL-EMBEDDED SUBSTANCE** having molecules of one substance enclosed fully within the crystal structure of another substance **2. LIKE A LATTICE** resembling a lattice in structure or appearance [Mid-19thC. From Latin *clathrare* "to fit with bars," from *clathri* "lattice," from Greek *klēthra* "bars."]

clat·ter /kláttər/ *v.* (**-tered, -ter·ing, -ters**) **1.** *vti.* **MAKE RATTLING NOISE** to make a loud rattling noise, or cause something to make a rattling noise ○ *a clattering old truck* **2.** *vi.* **CHATTER NOISILY** to chatter or prattle, especially noisily ■ *n.* **1. BANGING METALLIC SOUND** a loud metallic banging or rattling noise ○ *the clatter of pots and pans in the kitchen* **2. NOISY CHATTER** noisy chatter and prattling talk **3. LOUD COMMOTION** a noisy disturbance [Assumed Old English *clatrian*. Ultimately from an ancient Germanic word thought to be an imitation of the sound.] —**clat·ter·er** *n.* —**clat·ter·ing·ly** *adv.*

clau·di·ca·tion /klàwdi káysh'n/ *n.* **1. LIMPING** limping or lameness, especially as a result of reduced blood supply to the leg muscles **2.** = **intermittent claudication** [15thC. From the Latin stem *claudication-*, from *claudicare* "to limp," from *claudus* "lame."]

clause /klawz/ *n.* **1.** GRAM **GROUP OF WORDS** a group of words consisting of a subject and its predicate. A clause usually contains a verb and may or may not be a sentence in its own right. The sentence "she left before he arrived" contains two clauses, "she left" and "before he arrived." **2.** LAW **SECTION OF LEGAL DOCUMENT** a distinct section of a document, especially a legal document, that is usually separately numbered [13thC. Via French and assumed Latin *clausa* "close of a rhetorical period or legal argument" from, ultimately, *claudere* "to close" (source of English *close* and *cloister*).] —**claus·al** *adj.*

claus·tro·phobe /kláwstrə fōb/ *n.* = **claustrophobic** [Mid-20thC. Back-formation from CLAUSTROPHOBIA.]

claus·tro·pho·bi·a /klàwstrə fōbee ə/ *n.* an abnormal fear of being in a confined or enclosed space [Late 19thC. From modern Latin, coined from *claustrum* (see CLOISTER) + -PHOBIA.]

claus·tro·pho·bic /klàwstrə fōbik/ *adj.* **1. CONFINED OR CRAMPED** unpleasantly or uncomfortably confined ○ *The room is claustrophobic but painting the walls a light color might help.* **2. OF OR HAVING CLAUSTROPHOBIA** affected by claustrophobia ■ *n.* **SOMEBODY WHO FEARS ENCLOSED SPACES** somebody who is affected by claustrophobia —**claus·tro·pho·bi·cal·ly** *adv.*

cla·vate /kláy vàyt/ *adj.* with one end thicker than the other ○ *Some protozoa have clavate cilia.* [Early 19thC. From modern Latin *clavatus*, from Latin *clava* "club."] —**cla·vate·ly** *adv.*

clave /klaá vày/ *n.* either of a pair of hardwood sticks that are hit together to make a clicking sound [Early 20thC. Via American Spanish from Spanish, "keystone," from Latin *clavis* "key."]

clav·i·cem·ba·lo /klàvvi chémbəlō/ (*plural* **-los**) *n.* MUSIC = **harpsichord** [Mid-18thC. Via Italian from medieval Latin *clavicymbalum*, literally "key cymbal."]

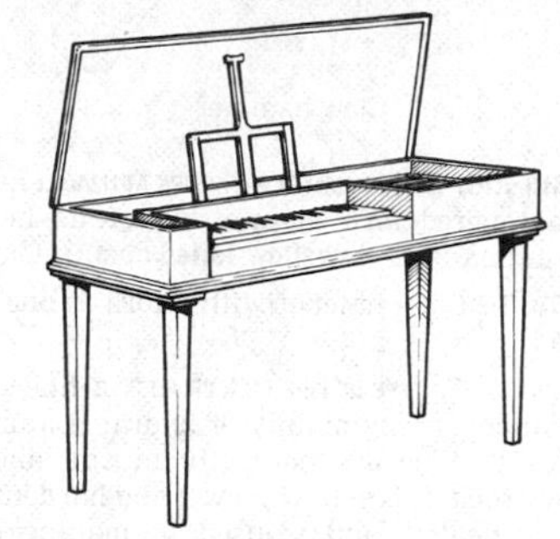

Clavichord

clav·i·chord /klávvi kàwrd/ *n.* a keyboard instrument of the 15th to 19th centuries, a precursor of the modern piano, in which small wedges strike horizontal strings to produce a soft sound [15thC. From medieval Latin *clavichordium*, formed from Latin *clavis* "key" + *chorda* "string."] —**clav·i·chord·ist** *n.*

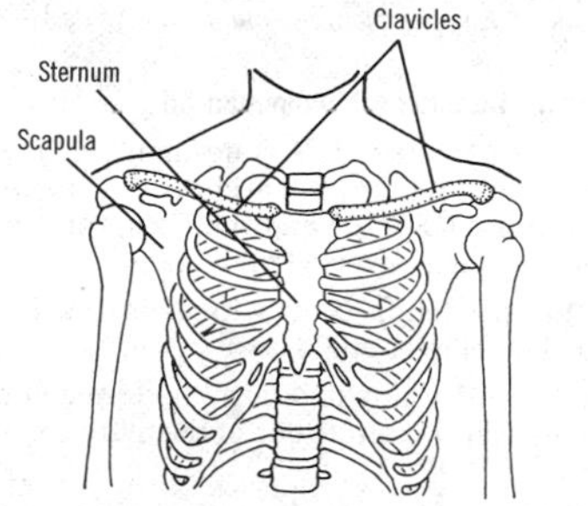

Clavicle

clav·i·cle /klávvik'l/ *n.* **1.** ANAT **BONE AT FRONT OF HUMAN SHOULDER** the long curved bone that connects the upper part of the breastbone with the shoulder blade at the top of each shoulder in humans **2.** ZOOL **BONE IN ANIMALS** a bone or structure with a function similar to that of the human clavicle in some other animals. It is reduced or absent in many mammals. [Early 17thC. From Latin *clavicula*, literally "small key," from *clavis* "key." From its shape.] —**cla·vic·u·lar** /klə víkyələr, kla-/ *adj.*

cla·vier /klə veér, klávvee ər/ *n.* **1. STRINGED KEYBOARD INSTRUMENT** any stringed keyboard musical instrument **2. MUSICAL KEYBOARD** the keyboard of a musical instrument [Early 18thC. Directly or via German *Klavier* from French, from medieval Latin *claviarius* "key-bearer," from Latin *clavis* "key."]

claw /klaw/ *n.* **1. ANIMAL'S SHARP NAIL** a pointed curved nail on the end of each toe in birds, some reptiles, and some mammals **2. PINCER** an appendage used for grasping in crabs and other invertebrates **3. APPENDAGE RESEMBLING CLAW** something resembling a claw in shape or function, e.g., a mechanical grabbing device ■ *v.* (**clawed, claw·ing, claws**) **1.** *vti.* **ATTACK WITH CLAWS** to scratch or dig at something or somebody with claws, fingernails, or something similar ○ *The dogs had clawed at the door* **2.** *vt.* **FORM SOMETHING BY SCRATCHING** to form something by digging or scratching with claws or something similar ○ *Using our bare hands we clawed a hole in the sand* [Old English *clawu*. Ultimately from a prehistoric Germanic word that is also the ancestor of German *Klaue* "claw."] —**claw·less** *adj.*

claw off *vi.* to avoid the dangers of a lee shore or other hazard by sailing as close to the wind as possible on alternate tacks

clawed /klawd/ *adj.* having claws or similar projections for scratching or grasping

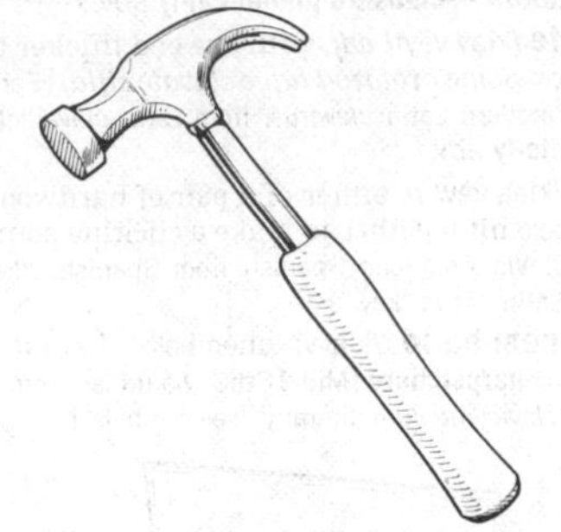

Claw hammer

claw ham·mer *n.* **1.** HAMMER WITH FORK AT HEAD a hammer with a tapered fork at one end of its head for removing nails **2.** = **swallow-tailed coat** (*informal*)

claw hatch·et *n.* a hatchet with a fork at one end of its head

clay /klay/ *n.* **1.** TYPE OF FINE SOIL OR ROCK a fine-grained material consisting mainly of hydrated aluminum silicates that occurs naturally in soil and sedimentary rock. It is soft when wet and hardens when dried or heated, and is used in making bricks, ceramics, and cement. **2.** MODELING SUBSTANCE a claylike substance used for modeling **3.** DIRT OR SOIL soil, especially heavy sticky wet soil **4.** HUMAN BODY AND ITS BASIC CONSTITUENTS the physical body of a human being, particularly the matter of which it is composed (*literary*) ○ *From clay we are made* **5.** = **clay court 6.** = **clay pigeon** *n.* 1 ■ *vt.* (**clayed, clay·ing, clays**) COVER WITH CLAY to cover something with clay [Old English *clæg*. Ultimately from an Indo-European word that is also the ancestor of English *clammy, climb,* and *glue*.] —**clay·ey** *adj.*

Clay /klay/, **Cassius** ➧ **Muhammad Ali**

Clay, Henry (1777–1852) U.S. statesman. He long served in Congress and was the architect of the Missouri Compromise (1820–21) and the Compromise of 1850 that temporarily averted civil war.

clay court *n.* a tennis court with a hard surface made of crushed clay or shale

clay min·er·al *n.* any of several hydrated aluminum silicates that constitute one of the main components of clay

clay·more /kláy màwr/ *n.* **1.** LARGE SWORD a large double-edged broadsword formerly used by Scottish Highlanders **2.** = **claymore mine** [Early 18thC. From Gaelic *claidheamh mor*, literally "great sword."]

clay·more mine *n.* a land mine in the shape of a convex disk that is placed above ground and detonates horizontally. It is designed to kill or maim approaching personnel.

clay·pan /kláy pàn/ *n.* hardpan that is composed mainly of clay

clay pig·eon *n.* **1.** MOVING TARGET FOR SHOOTING a clay disk hurled into the air from a machine and used as a target for shooting **2.** DEFENSELESS PERSON somebody who is vulnerable to attack (*slang*)

clay·stone /kláy stōn/ *n.* a compact fine-grained rock containing primarily clay particles

cld. *abbr.* STOCK EXCH called

clean /kleen/ *adj.* **1.** NOT DIRTY free from dirt or impurities ○ *clean hands* **2.** UNADULTERATED containing no foreign matter or pollutants ○ *a clean water supply* **3.** FREE OF DISEASE OR INFECTION not infected or diseased ○ *a clean wound* **4.** WASHED freshly laundered or washed after use ○ *fetch some clean shirts* **5.** taking pains over personal hygiene or grooming ○ *he is very clean in his habits* **6.** EMPTY containing nothing at all (*informal*) ○ *The apartment was stripped clean by the previous tenants* **7.** MORALLY UPRIGHT morally pure and upright **8.** HONESTLY FAIR just and fair ○ *a clean verdict* **9.** NOT RUDE not rude or obscene **10.** BLANK without anything on it, especially anything written ○ *a clean sheet of paper* **11.** WITH NO POLICE RECORD having or showing no record of convictions or penalties, e.g., for driving offenses ○ *Don's record is clean* **12.** FREE OF PROBLEMS without problems or difficulties ○ *The doctor gave me a clean bill of health.* **13.** SMOOTH-EDGED without rough or jagged edges ○ *a clean blow of the ax* **14.** STREAMLINED simple and flowing in design, without projections or additions ○ *the aircraft's clean silhouette* **15.** COMPLETE complete and unqualified ○ *made a clean break with the past* **16.** WITH NO FLAWS used to describe a gemstone that is free of flaws **17.** AGRIC FREE OF WEEDS cleared of weeds and unwanted undergrowth **18.** PRINTING NOT HEAVILY CORRECTED containing relatively few mistakes or corrections **19.** SPORTS PERFORMED PRECISELY precisely performed and in accordance with the best technique ○ *a clean jump* **20.** SPORTS WITH NO FOULS OR RULE-BREAKING played, fought, or won by strict compliance with the rules ○ *a clean victory for our team* **21.** NOT POLLUTING producing the least possible pollution ○ *a clean source of energy* **22.** MINIMALLY RADIOACTIVE producing the least possible radioactive fallout or contamination **23.** WITH NO CONCEALED ARMS not carrying concealed weapons (*slang*) ○ *A body search revealed that the suspect was clean.* **24.** WITH NO ILLEGAL DRUGS not containing or possessing illegal drugs (*slang*) **25.** UNADDICTED free from addiction to narcotic drugs or other substances (*slang*) **26.** INNOCENT not guilty of a particular crime (*slang*) **27.** JUDAISM RITUALLY UNDEFILED used to describe somebody who is ritually undefiled according to Jewish law **28.** JUDAISM ABLE TO BE LAWFULLY EATEN used to describe food that may be eaten according to Jewish law **29.** CHR PURE IN SPIRIT spiritually pure or purified ■ *v.* (**cleaned, clean·ing, cleans**) **1.** *vti.* RID SOMETHING OF DIRT to rid something of dirt or impurities **2.** *vt.* ERADICATE UNWANTED DIRT to remove or eradicate unwanted dirt, stains, or marks ○ *we spent the day cleaning out the spare room* **3.** *vi.* GET FREE OF DIRT to become free of dirt, chiefly because of a content or structure that easily repels it ○ *This acrylic rug cleans easily.* **4.** *vt.* RID OF CORRUPTION to free something of dishonest practices ○ *bent on cleaning the system of corruption.* **5.** *vt.* PREPARE DEAD ANIMAL FOR COOKING to prepare a dead animal for cooking by removing its entrails **6.** *vt.* REMOVE CONTENTS to use up the contents of something ○ *The children cleaned their plates and asked for more.* ■ *n.* SESSION OF CLEANING a spell of removing unwanted dirt or marks ■ *adv.* **1.** IN ORDER TO FREE OF DIRT so as to make something free from dirt **2.** IN ORDER TO RID OF EVIDENCE so as to rid something of incriminating evidence **3.** WITH NO OBSTRUCTION directly, especially without having any obstruction **4.** CLEANLY in a clean way ○ *Does this type of gas burn clean?* ○ *We wanted to play the game clean.* **5.** ENTIRELY completely or utterly (*informal*) ○ *I clean forgot to call.* [Old English *clǣne*. Ultimately from a prehistoric Germanic word meaning "clear, pure."] —**clean·a·bil·i·ty** /kleenə bíllətee/ *n.* —**clean·a·ble** /kleénəb'l/ *adj.* —**clean·ness** /kleén nəss/ *n.* ◇ **come clean** to confess or tell the truth about something (*informal*)

clean out *vt.* to use up or steal all of somebody's money or belongings (*informal*) ○ *Buying the new bike cleaned me out.*

clean up *v.* **1.** *vti.* MAKE CLEAN OR NEAT to make somebody or something clean or neat ○ *Can you just give me a minute to clean up in here?* **2.** *vt.* ERADICATE SOMETHING UNPLEASANT to rid a place of something unpleasant, e.g., pollution or crime **3.** *vi.* MAKE MONEY to acquire a large amount of money (*slang*) ○ *They really cleaned up on the stock market last year.* ◇ **clean up your act** to improve your behavior or the way you conduct your life (*slang*)

clean and jerk *n.* a movement in weightlifting in which the weight is lifted to shoulder height, held there briefly, and then quickly pushed above the head

clean-cut *adj.* **1.** NEAT-LOOKING neat in dress or appearance ○ *a clean-cut young officer in a spotless uniform* **2.** WITH SHARP OUTLINE distinctly outlined or designed **3.** = **clear-cut** *adj.* 1

clean·er /kleénər/ *n.* **1.** SOMEBODY EMPLOYED TO CLEAN INSIDE PLACES somebody whose job is to clean the interior of a building **2.** SOMETHING USED IN CLEANING a chemical or machine used for cleaning ■ **clean·ers** *npl.* SHOP PROVIDING DRYCLEANING SERVICE a shop where clothes and other items are taken to be drycleaned ○ *My best suit is at the cleaners.* ◇ **take somebody to the cleaners** to deprive somebody of his or her money or possessions by dishonest means (*slang*)

clean-limbed *adj.* having a well-proportioned and youthful-looking body

clean·li·ness /klénlinəss/ *n.* the degree to which somebody keeps clean or a place is kept clean ○ *a small hotel noted for its cleanliness*

clean·ly[1] /kleénlee/ *adv.* **1.** EASILY OR EFFICIENTLY with ease or efficiency ○ *a cleanly executed triple jump on the ice* **2.** WITHOUT JAGGED EDGES in a manner that does not leave rough edges ○ *the saw cut cleanly* **3.** FAIRLY in a fair manner **4.** IN CLEAN WAY in a way that is clean ○ *work cleanly in the kitchen, avoiding spills*

clean·ly[2] /klénnlee/ *adj.* habitually or fastidiously clean and neat (*archaic*)

clean room *n.* a room maintained with minimal contamination from dust or bacteria. Such rooms are used in the aerospace and electronics industries and in various kinds of scientific research.

cleanse /klenz/ (**cleansed, cleans·ing, cleans·es**) *vt.* **1.** MAKE THOROUGHLY CLEAN to remove dirt from somebody or something, especially by washing thoroughly **2.** MAKE FREE FROM UNPLEASANTNESS to free a place, person, or society from something wrong or unwelcome ○ *to cleanse the government of corrupt influences* **3.** MAKE FREE FROM SIN to free somebody or something from sin or guilt [Old English *clǣnsian*, from *clǣne* (see CLEAN)] —**cleans·ing** *n.*

cleans·er /klénzər/ *n.* **1.** CLEANING PRODUCT a substance for cleaning something thoroughly **2.** a cosmetic product for cleaning the face

clean-shav·en *adj.* with the facial hair shaved off

clean-up /kleén ùp/ *n.* **1.** THOROUGH CLEANING a thorough cleaning ○ *This garage needs a good cleanup.* **2.** ELIMINATION OF SOMETHING BAD an elimination of something unpleasant or unwanted **3.** LARGE GAIN a large and often illicit acquisition of assets (*slang*) **4.** BATTING POSITION IN BASEBALL in baseball, the fourth position in the batting order, usually held out for a known heavy hitter who can drive in runs

clear /kleer/ *adj.* **1.** FREE FROM WHAT DIMS free from anything that darkens or obscures ○ *a clear stream* **2.** TRANSPARENT able to be seen through ○ *clear glass* **3.** FREE FROM CLOUDS free from clouds, mist, or airborne particles ○ *a clear blue sky* **4.** PURE IN HUE pure in color or hue ○ *a clear red* **5.** PERFECT AND UNBLEMISHED free from any defect or impurity ○ *a clear complexion* **6.** EASILY HEARD OR SEEN easily heard or seen ○ *clear outlines* **7.** SOUNDING PLEASANT having a pleasant sound ○ *a clear singing voice* **8.** OUT-AND-OUT completely certain, allowing for no doubt ○ *clear evidence of collusion* **9.** UNAMBIGUOUS easy to understand and without ambiguity ○ *clear instructions* **10.** UNDERSTOOD PRECISELY understood without confusion or uncertainty ○ *Is it clear what you have to do when the bell rings?* **11.** EVIDENT so obvious as to need no further explanation or guidance ○ *After half an hour of trying it was clear that the engine would not work properly.* **12.** MENTALLY SHARP AND DISCERNING able to think without confusion ○ *You'll do better in the exam if you keep your mind clear.* **13.** WITHOUT GUILT free from feelings of guilt or blame ○ *a clear conscience* **14.** UNOBSTRUCTED free from obstructions or hindrances ○ *keep aisles clear* **15.** EMPTY empty, with all movable items removed **16.** NOT ATTACHED TO OR TOUCHING SOMETHING free of, or freed from, connection or contact ○ *they struggled to clear the wreckage* **17.** NET net of deductions or charges ○ *I earn a clear $500 a week.* **18.** NOT FINANCIALLY OBLIGATED not having any debt or financial obligation **19.** SHOWJUMPING UNPENALIZED without any penalties being incurred ○ *jumped a clear round* ■ *adv.* **1.** OUT OF THE WAY completely away from something ○ *Please stand clear of the doors until the vehicle has stopped.* **2.** ALL THE WAY totally or completely ○ *they moved clear across the country* ■ *v.* (**cleared, clear·ing, clears**) **1.** *vi.* DISSIPATE AND DISPERSE to undergo the process of dissolving or dispersing, thereby disappearing ○ *By noon the fog had finally cleared.* **2.** *vi.* NO LONGER BE FOGGY OR DULL to brighten and become free of adverse conditions ○ *There will be rain in the morning but the skies will clear by the early afternoon.* **3.** *vti.* MAKE OR BECOME TRANSPARENT to become or make something transparent or translucent ○ *The water cleared as the particles sank to the bottom.* **4.** *vt.* RID SOMETHING OF EXTRANEOUS MATTER to free something of impurities or unwanted matter ○ *clear a drain of blockages* **5.** *vt.* RID THROAT OF OBSTRUCTIONS to rid the throat of phlegm or other obstructions by coughing **6.** *vt.* CLARIFY THOUGHTS to remove confusion or misunderstanding from the mind ○ *I'd like a few minutes to clear my head before going into the meeting.* **7.** *vi.* RETURN TO SENSES to become or make the mind free from the dulling effects of alcohol, drugs, illness, or a blow to the head ○ *After my head had cleared I was able to stand up again.* **8.** *vt.* PROVE SOMEBODY INNOCENT to free somebody from suspicion or blame ○ *anxious to clear her name* **9.** *vt.* **REMOVE OBJECTS OR OBSTRUCTIONS FROM SOMETHING** to empty a space of objects or obstructions ○ *the room had been cleared* **10.** *vt.* **FORM SPACE FOR SOMEBODY OR SOMETHING** to form a route for somebody or something to pass by removing obstructions **11.** *vt.* **REMOVE PEOPLE FROM A PLACE** to empty a building or place of people, e.g., for security reasons ○ *police had to clear the area* **12.** *vt.* **DISENTANGLE** to straighten out something that is snarled or otherwise in disarray or disorder ○ *Hurry up and clear that anchor line!* **13.** *vt.* **MOVE PAST WITHOUT TOUCHING** to move past or over something and without touching it ○ *If we stay on this course we should clear the buoy.* **14.** *vti.* **ALLOW TO UNLOAD OR DEPART** to be allowed to unload or depart, or allow a vehicle or cargo to unload or passengers to depart, after customs and other formalities have been dealt with **15.** *vt.* **AUTHORIZE SOMEBODY TO DO OR GO** to authorize somebody to do something or go somewhere ○ *You are now cleared to enter the restricted area.* **16.** *vt.* **GIVE OR GET AUTHORIZATION** to give or obtain authorization for an action **17.** *vt.* **GAIN MONEY AS PROFIT** to earn or acquire something as profit (*informal*) ○ *We cleared $5000 on the deal.* **18.** *vt.* **PAY OFF DEBT** to settle a debt **19.** *vi.* BANKING **MOVE BETWEEN ACCOUNTS** to be authorized and credited to the account of the payee ○ *Checks take three days to clear.* **20.** *vti.* BANKING **SETTLE BANKING ACCOUNTS** to settle the accounts of a banking transaction through a clearinghouse **21.** *vt.* SPORTS **GET BALL OUT OF DEFENSE AREA** to get the ball or puck out of the defense area **22.** *vt.* COMPUT **DELETE DATA** to delete data from a computer display or storage device ■ *n.* **OPEN SPACE** an empty or open area or space ○ *The deer were standing in the clear.* [13thC. Via Old French *cler* from Latin *clarus* "clear, bright."] —**clear·a·ble** *adj.* —**clear·er** *n.* —**clear·ness** *n.* ◇ **in the clear** free from suspicion or blame

WORD KEY: ORIGIN

Clear is derived from the Latin word *clarus,* meaning "clear" or "bright," which is also the source of English *claret, clarify, clarion, clerestory,* and *declare.*

clear away *vt.* to remove objects and straighten up, e.g., by removing papers and other materials from a desk

clear off *vi. U.K.* to go away (*dated informal*) ○ *Clear off and don't come back!*

clear out *v.* **1.** *vi.* **LEAVE FAST** to leave a place quickly or urgently (*informal*) ○ *We cleared out as fast as we could.* **2.** *vt.* **REMOVE SOMETHING** to remove the contents of something, e.g., a room or closet, or to neaten something by removing some of its contents ○ *clearing out the attic*

clear up *v.* **1.** *vi.* **BECOME BRIGHTER** to become brighter, e.g., after rain **2.** *vti.* **GET OR MAKE BETTER** to alleviate or cure something, or be alleviated or cured **3.** *vti.* **PUT SOMETHING IN ORDER** to straighten something by removing or arranging disorganized contents ○ *Will you please clear up all this mess before you leave?* ■ **SOLVE MYSTERY OR EXPLAIN MISUNDERSTANDING** to solve a mystery or explain a misunderstanding ○ *Here is a big problem that has never been fully cleared up.*

clear·ance /kleérəns/ *n.* **1.** **REMOVING UNWANTED OBJECTS** the removal of obstructions or unwanted objects, e.g., dilapidated buildings or overgrown bushes, before building or cultivating **2.** **PERMISSION FOR SOMETHING TO HAPPEN** permission to do something or for something to take place ○ *several aircraft awaiting clearance to take off* **3.** **WIDTH OR HEIGHT OF OPENING** the width or height of an opening or passage ○ *Clearance on these freeway overpasses is limited, so big trucks must detour.* **4.** **CHEAP SALE OF MERCHANDISE** a sale of goods at reduced prices in order to clear stock **5.** BANKING **PASSAGE OF COMMERCIAL DOCUMENTS** the passage of commercial documents through a clearing house **6.** SPORTS **GETTING BALL OUT OF DEFENSE AREA** in games, the process of clearing the ball or puck from the defense area **7.** **REMOVAL OF PEOPLE FROM LAND** the forcible removal from an area of land of the people who have traditionally lived there **8.** = **security clearance** **9.** FORESTRY = **clearing**

clear-cut *adj.* **1.** **UNAMBIGUOUS** so definite as to leave no possibility of ambiguity **2.** **DISTINCTLY OUTLINED** with a distinct outline or form ○ *a clear-cut silhouette of a naval frigate on the horizon* ■ *vt.* (**clear-cut, clear-cut·ting, clear-cuts**) **REMOVE ALL TREES FROM AREA** to cut down and remove all of the trees from a forest or other land area ■ *n.* **LAND WITH ALL TREES REMOVED** land from which all the trees and undergrowth have been cut and removed

clear-eyed *adj.* **1.** **DISCERNINGLY PERCEPTIVE** able to discern things clearly **2.** **SHARP-EYED** having sharp sight **3.** **BRIGHT-EYED** having bright eyes

Clear·field /kleér feèld/ city in northern Utah, east of the Great Salt Lake and northwest of Salt Lake City. Population: 22,153 (1996).

clear-head·ed *adj.* able to think clearly and decisively, especially in difficult circumstances —**clear-head·ed·ly** *adv.* —**clear-head·ed·ness** *n.*

clear·ing /kleéring/ *n.* **1.** FORESTRY **OPEN SPACE IN FOREST** a space without trees in an area of land that is wooded or overgrown **2.** BANKING **MOVEMENT OF CHECKS BETWEEN ACCOUNTS** exchange between banks of checks, drafts, and notes, and the settlement of consequent differences

clear·ing bank *n. U.K.* any bank that uses a central clearinghouse for transferring credits and checks between itself and other banks

clear·ing·house *n.* **1.** BANKING **INSTITUTION COORDINATING FINANCIAL DEALINGS BETWEEN BANKS** an institution at which financial transactions between member banks are canceled against each other, leaving only balances to be paid **2.** **INSTITUTION COORDINATING INFORMATION INTERCHANGES** an agency that collects and distributes information

Clear Lake lake in northwestern California, the largest freshwater lake within the state, popular for leisure activities. Length: 25 mi./40 km.

clear·ly /kleérlee/ *adv.* **1.** **WITHOUT ANY PROBLEM IN HEARING** in a way that is easy to hear **2.** **WITHOUT ANY PROBLEM IN SEEING** in a way that is easy to see **3.** **WITHOUT ANY PROBLEM IN UNDERSTANDING** in a way that is easy to understand ○ *a clearly phrased piece of legislation* **4.** **LOGICALLY** in a logical and unconfused manner ○ *a clearly written legal brief* **5.** **OBVIOUSLY** used to acknowledge that a statement is undeniably true ○ *Clearly, we must take immediate action.*

clear-out *n. U.K.* a session of removing the contents of something, e.g., a room, or of straightening it by removing some of its contents ○ *We had a great clear-out at the weekend and now we've got room for the new table.*

clear-sight·ed *adj.* **1.** **HAVING GOOD PERCEPTION OR JUDGMENT** having or showing good perception or judgment **2.** **WITH KEEN VISION** having sharp vision —**clear-sight·ed·ly** *adv.* —**clear-sight·ed·ness** *n.*

clear·sto·ry *n.* ARCHIT = **clerestory**

Clear·wa·ter /kleér wàwtər/ city in western Florida on the Gulf of Mexico, directly west of Tampa. Population: 100,132 (1996).

clear·way /kleér wày/ *n. U.K.* a section of road where drivers may not normally stop

clear·wing /kleér wìng/ *n.* a moth with scaleless transparent wings that is active during the daytime. Family: Sesiidae.

cleat /kleet/ *n.* **1.** **HARD PIECE ATTACHED UNDER SHOE** a small piece of metal or hard plastic attached onto the sole of a shoe to improve its grip **2.** **DEVICE FOR TYING BOAT TO** a device with two projections pointing in opposite directions to which a rope can be tied to secure a boat **3.** **DEVICE ON BOOT FOR CLIMBING TREES** a device with a blade or set of sharp projections that is attached to a boot to assist in climbing trees or poles **4.** **WEDGE-SHAPED SUPPORT** wooden or other wedge attached to a structure in order to support it ■ **cleats** *npl.* **PAIR OF SPORTS SHOES** a pair of shoes with small projections on the soles used for playing sports on soft surfaces ■ *vt.* (**cleat·ed, cleat·ing, cleats**) **1.** **PROVIDE WITH CLEATS** to fix a cleat or cleats to something **2.** **SECURE ROPE TO CLEAT** to tie a rope to a cleat **3.** **SUPPORT WITH CLEAT** to support something using a cleat or cleats [14thC. Ultimately from a prehistoric Germanic word meaning "firm lump," which is also the ancestor of English *clot.*]

cleav·a·ble /kleévəb'l/ *adj.* able to be split or divided

cleav·age /kleévij/ *n.* **1.** **ACT OF SPLITTING** division or splitting **2.** **SPLIT IN SOMETHING** a split, division, or separation of something **3.** **CREASE VISIBLE BETWEEN BREASTS** the hollow visible between a woman's breasts when a low-cut garment is worn **4.** GEOL, MINERALS **ROCK OR MINERAL FRACTURE** the splitting of minerals or rocks along natural planes of weakness. The angle of cleavage is one of the features used to identify minerals. **5.** EMBRYOL **REPEATED DIVISION OF FERTILIZED EGG** the repeated division of a fertilized ovum (**zygote**) before formation of the early embryo (**blastula**). The zygote does not increase in size during this process because the cells become progressively smaller after each division. **6.** CHEM **SPLITTING OF A MOLECULE** the splitting of a molecule into simpler molecules through the breaking of a chemical bond

cleave[1] /kleev/ (**cleaved** *or* **cleft** *or* **clove** /klōv/, **cleaved** *or* **cleft** *or* **clo·ven** /klṓv'n/, **cleav·ing, cleaves**) *vti.* **1.** **SPLIT** to split, or make something split, especially along a plane of natural weakness **2.** **CUT A PATH THROUGH** to make a way through something (*literary*) ○ *We watched the bows of the tall ships cleave through the waves* **3.** **PENETRATE** to penetrate or pierce something deep or dense such as water or heavy undergrowth [Old English *clēofan.* Ultimately from an Indo-European word that is also the ancestor of Greek *gluphein* "to carve" (source of English *hieroglyphics*).]

cleave[2] /kleev/ (**cleaved** *or* **clove** /klōv/ *or* **clave** /klayv/, **cleaved, cleav·ing, cleaves**) *vi.* to cling closely, steadfastly, or faithfully to something or somebody (*literary*) ○ *Is it wrong to cleave to such fond memories?* [Old English *cleofian.* Ultimately from an Indo-European word that is also the ancestor of English *clay, climb,* and *glue.*]

cleav·er /kleévər/ *n.* a heavy knife with a broad blade, used by butchers

cleav·ers /kleévər/ *n.* an annual plant of Europe and Asia with slender sprawling stems, narrow leaves, and tiny white flowers. Its spiny round fruits cling to animals and clothing. Latin name: *Galium aparine.* (*takes a singular verb*) [Old English. From CLEAVE[2], because its bristles stick to whatever they come in contact with.]

Cle·burne /kleébərn/ city in northern Texas, south of Fort Worth and north of Waco. Population: 23,904 (1996).

cleek /kleek/ *n.* a hickory-shafted iron golf club similar to the modern number 2 iron (*dated*) [15thC. Originally a northern English dialect verb meaning "to clutch," of uncertain origin.]

clef /klef/ *n.* in written or printed music, a symbol placed at the beginning of each staff to indicate the pitch [Late 16thC. Via French from Latin *clavis* "key."]

cleft[1] /kleft/ *n.* **1.** **SMALL INDENTATION** a small indentation in a surface, e.g., skin or land **2.** **GAP OR SPLIT** a substantial gap or division separating two things (*formal*) ○ *the ever widening cleft between the liberals and the conservatives in their approaches to welfare reform* [Old English *geclyft.* Ultimately from an ancient Germanic word that is also the ancestor of English *cleave.*]

cleft[2] /kleft/ *vti.* past tense, past participle of **cleave** ■ *adj.* **SPLIT** having been separated into two or more sections by division

cleft pal·ate *n.* a congenital fissure along the midline of the roof of the mouth. It is caused by a failure of the two sides of the hard palate to meet and fuse during fetal development and is often associated with a cleft lip.

cleg /kleg/ *n. N England, Scotland* a horsefly of northern Europe and Asia. Genus: *Haemotopota.* [15thC. From Old Norse *kleggi.*]

cleis·tog·a·mous /klī stóggəməss/ *adj.* relating to or bearing small flowers that do not open, are self-pollinated in the bud, and appear in addition to brighter flowers on the same plant [Late 19thC. Coined from Greek *kleistos* "closed" (from *kleiein* "to close") + -GAMY.] —**cleis·tog·a·mous·ly** *adv.* —**cleis·tog·a·my** *n.*

clem·a·tis /klémmətiss, klə máttiss/ (*plural* **-tis·es** *or* **-tis**) *n.* a climbing plant, native chiefly to northern temperate regions, with fluffy seed heads. Some types have large flat colorful flowers, typically blue, purple, pink or white. Genus: *Clematis.* [Mid-16thC. Via Latin, "clematis, periwinkle," from Greek *klēmatis,* from *klēma* "vine branch."]

clem·en·cy /klémmənsee/ *n.* **1.** **SHOWING MERCY** an instance of showing mercy or leniency, or the tendency to do this **2.** **ACT OF MERCY** an act that bestows or shows mercy toward another person over whom somebody has ultimate power ○ *the governor's clemency toward the convicted murderer* **3.** **MILDNESS IN WEATHER** mildness or temperateness, especially in the weather ○ *the clemency of areas affected by the Gulf Stream*

Clem·ens /klémmənz/, **Samuel Langhorne** ➧ **Mark Twain**

clem·ent /klémmənt/ *adj.* **1.** **MILD WEATHERWISE** showing or experiencing no extremes in weather conditions **2.** **MERCIFUL** showing mercy or leniency [15thC. From the stem of Latin *clemens* "mild, gentle."] —**clem·ent·ly** *adv.*

Cle·men·te /klə méntee/, **Roberto** (1934–72) Puerto Rican-born U.S. baseball player. Playing for the Pittsburgh Pirates (1954–72), he won 12 Gold Gloves for fielding and was also an outstanding batter.

cle·men·tine /klémmən tīn, -teen/ *n.* an orange-colored citrus fruit, bred by crossing a tangerine with a Seville orange [Early 20thC. From French *clémentine*, of uncertain origin: perhaps named for Père *Clément*, a French missionary to Africa.]

Clem·son /klémss'n/ city in northwestern South Carolina, on the northeastern shore of Hartwell Lake, northwest of Anderson. Population: 12,174 (1996).

clench /klench/ *v.* (**clenched, clench·ing, clench·es**) **1.** *vt.* **HOLD TEETH OR FIST TIGHTLY TOGETHER** to close your teeth or fist tightly, e.g., when angry **2.** *vt.* **CLUTCH SOMETHING** to hold or grip something tightly ○ *He clenched the rope in his teeth* **3.** *vti.* to contract suddenly, often as a result of sudden tension or emotion (*refers to muscles*) ○ *his jaw clenched as he waited* ■ *n.* **1. TIGHT HOLD** a tight grasp or hold ○ *She held the steering wheel in a tight clench.* **2. DEVICE THAT GRIPS TIGHTLY** a mechanical device that holds or grips something firmly ■ *vt.* (**clenched, clench·ing, clench·es**), *n.* NAUT = **clinch** *v.* 4 [Old English *beclencan*. Ultimately from a prehistoric Germanic word meaning "to stick," which is also the ancestor of English *cling*.]

clenched /klencht/ *adj.* held tightly or firmly together ○ *clenched fists*

cle·o·me /kli ṓmee/ *n.* an aromatic plant native to warm regions, often cultivated for its clusters of white or purplish flowers. Genus: *Cleome.* [Early 19thC. Via modern Latin from Greek, where it denoted a different plant.]

Cle·o·pat·ra /kleé ə páttrə/ (69–30 B.C.) Egyptian monarch. A queen (51–30 B.C.) of legendary beauty, she and her lover Mark Antony were defeated by Octavian's forces at Actium (31 B.C.).

Cle·o·pat·ra's Nee·dle *n.* either of two Egyptian obelisks originally erected at Heliopolis about 1500 B.C. One was moved to the Thames Embankment, London, in 1878, the other to Central Park, New York, in 1880.

CLEP *abbr.* College Level Examination Program

clep·sy·dra /klépsədrə/ (*plural* **-dras** *or* **-drae** /-dree/) *n.* an ancient device used for measuring time by noting the amount of water or mercury that passes through a small aperture over a particular period [Mid-17thC. Via Latin from Greek *klepsudra*, from *kleptein* "to steal" + *hudor* "water."]

Clerestory

clere·sto·ry /kleér stàwree/ (*plural* **-ries**), **clear·sto·ry** (*plural* **-ries**) *n.* the upper part of the wall of a church nave that contains windows, or the upper part of a wall in other buildings that contains windows [*Clere* from an earlier spelling of CLEAR]

clere·sto·ry coach *n.* a railroad carriage or coach with a raised central section along its roof, containing small windows

cler·gy /klúrjee/ (*plural* **-gies**) *n.* the body of people ordained for religious service, especially in the Christian Church (*takes a singular or plural verb*) [13thC. Partly from Old French *clergie* (from *clerc* "cleric") and partly from *clergé* "body of clerks," both from, ultimately, ecclesiastical Latin *clericus* (see CLERK).]

cler·gy·man /klúrjimən/ (*plural* **-men** /-mən/) *n.* a man who is a member of the clergy

cler·gy·wom·an /klúrji wòommən/ (*plural* **-en** /-wìmmin/) *n.* a woman who is a member of the clergy

cler·ic /klérrik/ *n.* an ordained priest, minister, or rabbi [Early 17thC. From ecclesiastical Latin *clericus* (see CLERK).]

cler·i·cal /klérrik'l/ *adj.* **1. OF OFFICE WORK** relating or belonging to office work, especially of a routine administrative kind **2. OF THE CLERGY** relating or belonging to the clergy **3. PROMOTING CLERICALISM** advocating or supporting clericalism —**cler·i·cal·ly** *adv.*

cler·i·cal col·lar *n.* a stiff white collar, continuous at the front, worn by some members of the clergy

cler·i·cal·ism /klérrik'l ìzzəm/ *n.* **1. SUPPORT FOR CLERGY** a policy of supporting the power or views of the clergy **2. POWER OF CLERGY** the power or influence of the clergy —**cler·i·cal·ist** *n.*

cler·i·cals /klérrik'lz/ *npl.* the characteristic clothing worn by some members of the clergy

cler·i·hew /klérrə hyòo/ *n.* a humorous or satirical verse consisting of two rhyming couplets in lines of irregular meter about somebody who is named in the verse [Early 20thC. Named for the English writer Edmund *Clerihew* Bentley 1875–1956, who invented it.]

clerk /klurk/ *n.* **1. GENERAL OFFICE WORKER** a worker who performs general office duties, such as keeping records or sending out correspondence **2.** = **sales clerk 3. SERVICE DESK WORKER** somebody at a service desk who helps and advises other people **4. GOVERNMENT WORKER WHO KEEPS RECORDS** somebody who keeps official transcripts and other records of a legislative or other official body **5.** LAW **ADMINISTRATOR IN COURT OF LAW** somebody who administers the business of a court **6.** LAW **LAWYER WHO WORKS FOR JUDGE** a lawyer, typically one just recently graduated from law school, who is employed to perform research, prepare draft opinions, and perform other such tasks for a sitting judge **7.** *U.K.* LAW **COURT LEGAL ADVISER** somebody with legal qualifications who advises lay magistrates on points of law in court **8.** CHR **CLERIC** a member of the clergy (*formal*) **9. SCHOLAR** a scholar or learned person (*archaic*) ■ *vi.* (**clerked, clerk·ing, clerks**) **WORK AS CLERK** to work as a clerk [Pre-12thC. Via ecclesiastical Latin *clericus* "of the clergy" from Greek *klērikos*, from *klēros* "heritage." From the role of the clergy as scribes and record-keepers in the Middle Ages.] —**clerk·dom** *n.* —**clerk·ish** *adj.* —**clerk·ship** *n.*

clerk·ly /klúrklee/ *adj.* behaving or looking like a clerk ○ *a clerkly attention to detail in the midst of a crisis* —**clerk·li·ness** *n.*

cler·uch /klí ròok/ *n.* in ancient Athens, a citizen who received a land allotment in foreign territory and lived there without losing citizenship [Mid-19thC. From Greek *klērou̇khos*, literally "lot-holder."]

cler·uch·y /kleé ròokee, -rə-/ (*plural* **-ies**) *n.* an ancient Athenian colony in foreign territory that remained dependent on Athens and whose settlers retained Athenian citizenship —**cler·uch·ial** /kli ròokee əl/ *adj.*

cle·veite /kleé vīt/ *n.* a crystalline form of uraninite [Late 19thC. Named for the Swedish chemist Per T. *Cleve* (1840–1905).]

Cleve·land /kleévlənd/ **1.** city and port in northeastern Ohio on the southeastern shore of Lake Erie. Population: 498,246 (1996). **2.** city in southeastern Tennessee, northeast of Chattanooga and southwest of Athens. Population: 33,503 (1996).

Cleve·land, Grover (1837–1908) U.S. statesman and 22nd and 24th president of the United States. As president (1885–89, 1893–97) he opposed special interests and the political spoils system. Full name **Stephen Grover Cleveland**

Cleve·land Heights city in northeastern Ohio, an eastern suburb of Cleveland. Population: 54,293 (1996).

clev·er /klévvər/ *adj.* **1. INTELLIGENT** having sharp mental abilities **2. SHOWING INTELLIGENCE** demonstrating mental agility and creativity **3. GLIBLY FACILE** showing highly capable mental abilities in a showy or superficial way ○ *Don't give me one of your clever answers.* **4. DEXTEROUS** highly skilled in using the hands **5.** *New England* **EASILY MANAGED** used to describe an animal that is easily managed and controlled **6.** *New England* **EASYGOING BUT NOT BRIGHT** friendly, easygoing, and affable in manner and personality but not particularly smart **7.** *Southern U.S.* **HAVING PLEASANT DISPOSITION** having a pleasant disposition and personality **8.** *U.K.* **WELL** in a state of good health (*regional*) [13thC. Origin uncertain. The present-day meaning evolved from "deft" via "sprightly" and "agile."] —**clev·er·ly** *adv.* —**clev·er·ness** *n.*

clev·is /klévviss/ *n.* a U-shaped device with a hole at the end of each prong through which a pin or bolt can be pushed to secure another part in place [Late 16thC. Origin uncertain.]

clew /kloo/ *n.* **1. BALL OF THREAD OR YARN** a wound ball of thread or yarn **2.** SAILING **CORNER OF FORE-AND-AFT SAIL** the rear lower corner of a triangular or four-sided sail set along the length of a boat **3.** SAILING **CORNER OF SAIL SET ACROSS BOAT** either of the two lower corners of a sail set parallel to the width of a boat, e.g., a square sail or a spinnaker ■ **clews** *npl.* NAUT **HAMMOCK CORDS** the cords by which a hammock is suspended ■ *vt.* (**clewed, clew·ing, clews**) **ROLL YARN INTO BALL** to roll thread or yarn into a ball [Old English *cliwen*, probably related to *claw*]

clew up *vt.* to furl a square sail by pulling on lines attached to its lower corners

CLI *abbr.* cost-of-living index

cli·an·thus /klī ánthəss/ (*plural* **-thus·es** *or* **-thus**) *n.* a plant of Australia or New Zealand with drooping clusters of slender scarlet flowers. Genus: *Clianthus.* [Mid-19thC. From modern Latin, formed from Greek *kleos* "glory" + *anthus* "flower."]

cli·ché /kli sháy/ *n.* **1. OVERUSED EXPRESSION** a phrase or word that has lost its original effectiveness or power from overuse **2. OVERUSED IDEA** an overused activity or notion [Mid-19thC. From French, the past participle of *clicher* "to stereotype," imitative of the sound made when a mold is dropped into molten metal to produce a stereotype plate.]

cli·chéd /kli sháyd/ *adj.* full of clichés

click[1] /klik/ *n.* **1. SHORT SHARP SOUND** a short sharp sound, often metallic but not resonant **2.** COMPUT **PRESS OF COMPUTER MOUSE BUTTON** a single action of pressing and releasing a button on a computer mouse **3.** MECH ENG **MECHANICAL COMPONENT FOR LOCKING POSITION** a component of a mechanical device that holds a part in a locking position, or the movement of the part between adjacent positions **4.** PHON **SOUND PRODUCED BY SUCKING IN AIR** a consonant sound produced by sucking in air by movements of the tongue against the soft palate. It is part of the phonemic system of some African languages, e.g., Xhosa, but in English is used only for the sound represented by "tut-tut" and the sound used for encouraging horses. Technical name **suction stop** ■ *v.* (**clicked, click·ing, clicks**) **1.** *vti.* **MAKE OR CAUSE SHORT SHARP SOUND** to make a short sharp sound, or cause something to make a short sharp sound **2.** *vti.* COMPUT **PRESS COMPUTER MOUSE BUTTON** to press and release a button of a computer mouse ○ *Click on "yes."* **3.** *vi.* **BECOME CLEAR FAST** to be understood suddenly (*informal*) ○ *The whole thing clicked: they had decided not to hire me.* **4.** *vi.* **EASILY COMMUNICATE OR WORK TOGETHER** to communicate or work together easily and readily (*informal*) ○ *It's too bad that the two venture partners in the deal just never clicked.* **5.** *vi.* **BE A SUCCESS** to be successful or popular (*informal*) ○ *The new show clicked from the very first performance.* [Late 16thC. An imitation of the sound.]

click[2] /klik/ *n.* a kilometer (*slang*) ○ *about twenty clicks from here* [Mid-20thC. Origin uncertain: possibly an alteration of KILOMETER and TICK.]

click bee·tle *n.* a beetle that can right itself when inverted by springing into the air with a clicking sound. Family: Elateridae.

click·er /klíkər/ *n.* a person who or device that clicks

click·stream /klík streem/ *n.* the path of mouse clicks that a computer user adopts to navigate the World Wide Web. Some Web sites trace and record their visitors' clickstreams as part of their marketing research.

cli·ent /klī ənt/ *n.* **1. SOMEBODY USING PROFESSIONAL SERVICE** a person or organization taking advice from an attorney, accountant, or other professional person **2. CUSTOMER** a person or organization to whom goods or services are provided and sold **3. USER OF SOCIAL SERVICE AGENCY** somebody who uses the services of a social services agency **4. PERSON OR ENTITY HELPED BY ANOTHER** a person or entity dependent on the protection or patronage of another person or entity ○ *the former Soviet Union and its clients in the Middle East* **5.** COMPUT **COMPUTER PROGRAM THAT REQUESTS DATA** a computer program used to contact and obtain data from a program on another computer, often one linked on a network. A World Wide Web browser is a specific kind of client. [14thC. Via Latin *cliens* "client, dependent" from, ultimately, *cluere* "to listen, obey."] —**cli·en·tal** *adj.* —**cli·ent·less** *adj.*

cli·ent·age /klī́ əntij/ *n.* a social system in which free commoners receive the patronage of wealthy or influential aristocrats. It was common in ancient Rome and has become a feature of some modern societies.

cli·ent-cen·tered ther·a·py *n.* a form of psychotherapy in which the therapist seeks to elicit solutions to problems by gaining the trust of the patient through careful questioning. It was founded by Carl Rogers in the 1940s and is still used widely as a counselling method.

cli·en·tele /klī ən tél, klèe-/ *n.* the clients or customers of a professional organization or business, considered as a group ○ *The clientele of our family law firm consists mostly of big corporations.* [Mid-16thC. Directly, or later via French *clientèle*, from Latin *clientela*, from *cliens* (see CLIENT).]

cli·ent-serv·er, cli·ent/serv·er *adj.* designed for use on a computer network in which processing is divided between a client program running on a user's machine and a network server program. One server can provide data to, or perform storage-intensive processing tasks in conjunction with, one or more clients.

cli·ent state *n.* a country that depends on another for economic, political, or military support

cliff /klif/ *n.* a high steep rock or ice face, especially a rock face extending along a coastline [Old English *clif*. Ultimately from a prehistoric Germanic word that is also the ancestor of German *Klippe*.] —**cliff·y** *adj.*

cliff brake *n.* a fern that typically grows in relatively dry rocky areas or on cliffs and has compound, often leathery, leaves. Genus: *Pellaea*. ["Brake," back-formation from BRACKEN (taken to be a plural in Middle English)]

cliff dwell·er *n.* a member of any cliff-dwelling people, specifically of any of the Anasazi groups who constructed buildings on large ledges found in cliffs in the southwestern United States

Barnaby's

Cliff dwelling: Mesa Verde, Colorado

cliff dwell·ing *n.* a building or group of buildings lived in by cliff dwellers

cliff·hang·er /klíf hàngər/ *n.* **1.** ARTS, LITERAT **ENDING LEFT TEASINGLY UNRESOLVED** an unresolved ending in a serialized drama or book that leaves the audience or reader desperate to know what will happen in the next part **2.** ARTS **DRAMA SERIAL WITH SUSPENSEFUL ENDINGS** a drama serial that has episodes that often end in suspenseful unresolved endings **3. TENSE SITUATION** a situation full of tension or suspense because it is not clear what will happen next [From early serial films in which characters were left hanging off the edge of a cliff, their fate unresolved until the next episode] —**cliff·hang·ing** *adj.*

Cliff·side Park /klífsīd-/ borough in northeastern New Jersey, northeast of Jersey City and opposite New York City. Population: 20,917 (1996).

cliff swal·low *n.* a North American swallow with a dark throat patch. It builds its nest of mud on cliff faces or under eaves. Latin name: *Hyrundo pyrrhonota*.

Clif·ton /klíftən/ city in northeastern New Jersey, northwest of Newark and Jersey City, near the Passaic River. Population: 71,305 (1996).

Clif·ton Park town in eastern New York , northeast of Schenectady. Population: 32,689 (1996).

cli·mac·ter·ic /klī máktərik, klī mak térrik/ *n.* **1. PERIOD OF IMPORTANT CHANGE** a period in which critically important changes take place **2.** PHYSIOL = **menopause** **3.** PHYSIOL = **male menopause** **4.** BOT **RIPENING STAGE IN FRUITS** a stage in the ripening of some fruits, e.g., apples, when the rate of respiration increases ■ *adj.* **1. IMPORTANT** crucially important **2.** PHYSIOL, BOT **RELATING TO CLIMACTERIC** relating to a physiological or botanical climacteric [Mid-16thC. Via French from, ultimately, Greek *klimaktēr* "rung of a ladder," from *klimax* "ladder" (see CLIMAX).] —**cli·mac·ter·i·cal·ly** *adv.*

cli·mac·tic /klī máktik/ *adj.* **1. EXCITING** extremely exciting or decisive **2. RELATING TO A CLIMAX** forming or relating to a climax [Late 19thC. Formed from CLIMAX, probably under the influence of CLIMACTERIC.] —**cli·mac·ti·cal·ly** *adv.*

cli·mate /klī́mət/ *n.* **1.** METEOROL **TYPICAL WEATHER IN REGION** the average weather or the regular variations in weather in a region over a period of years **2. PLACE WITH PARTICULAR WEATHER** a place with a particular kind of weather ○ *I prefer a warm climate* **3. SITUATION** the situation or atmosphere that prevails at a particular time or place **4. INDOOR ENVIRONMENT** the prevailing conditions or environment in an indoor setting such as an office [14thC. Via late Latin from Greek *klimat-*, the stem of *klima* "slope, region of the earth."] —**cli·mat·ic** /klī máttik/ *adj.* —**cli·mat·i·cal·ly** *adv.*

cli·mat·ic zone *n.* an area of the earth's surface that possesses a distinct type of climate. There are eight major climatic zones, roughly demarcated by lines of latitude.

cli·ma·tol·o·gy /klī̀mə tólləjee/ *n.* the scientific study of climates —**cli·ma·to·log·ic** /klī̀mətə lójjik/ *adj.* —**cli·ma·to·log·i·cal** *adj.* —**cli·ma·to·log·i·cal·ly** *adv.* —**cli·ma·tol·o·gist** /klī̀mə tólləjist/ *n.*

cli·max /klī́ màks/ *n.* **1. KEY MOMENT** the most exciting or important moment or point **2.** PHYSIOL **ORGASM** a sexual orgasm **3.** LING **EVER-INTENSIFYING SEQUENCE OF PHRASES** a sequence of phrases or sentences, each more forceful or intense than the last, or the conclusion of such a sequence **4.** ECOL **FINAL STAGE IN ECOLOGICAL COMMUNITY'S DEVELOPMENT** a late or final stage in the development of an ecological community in which the composition of plants and animals is relatively stable and well matched to environmental conditions ■ *v.* (**-maxed, -max·ing, -max·es**) **1.** *vti.* **REACH THE KEY POINT** to reach the most important or exciting point in something such as an event or a story, or bring something to its most important or exciting point **2.** *vi.* PHYSIOL **HAVE AN ORGASM** to have a sexual orgasm [Mid-16thC. Via late Latin from Greek *klimax* "ladder, progression." Ultimately from an Indo-European base meaning "to lean," which is also the ancestor of English *lean, incline*, and *ladder*.]

climb /klīm/ *v.* (**climbs, climbed, climb·ing, climbs**) **1.** *vti.* **GO UP USING HANDS AND FEET** to move toward the top of something using the hands and feet ○ *climb a ladder* **2.** *vti.* **MOVE UPWARD** to move upward, or move toward the top of something, by any means, and typically through continual or gradual effort ○ *climb the stairs* **3.** *vi.* **MOVE WITH EFFORT** to maneuver the body somewhere with effort or difficulty ○ *I managed to climb out of bed.* **4.** *vi.* **RISE STEEPLY IN AMOUNT** to rise sharply in value or amount **5.** *vi.* CLIMBING **BE A MOUNTAINEER** to go up mountains or rocks on foot or using hands and feet as a sport **6.** *vti.* **MOVE HIGHER SOCIALLY** to move to a higher social or professional position **7.** *vti.* BOT **GROW CLINGINGLY UPWARD** to grow upward by using plants or objects as a support, e.g., by producing shoots or tendrils that cling to them ■ *n.* **1. ACT OF CLIMBING** the process of moving to the top of something ○ *It was a steep climb to the top.* **2.** CLIMBING **HILL OR MOUNTAIN** a route used to go up a hill, mountain, or rock, or the hill, mountain, or rock itself **3. RISE IN VALUE OR AMOUNT** a rise in the value or amount of something [Old English *climban*. Ultimately from a prehistoric Germanic verb meaning "to adhere," from assumed West Germanic *klimban*, a nasalized variant, that is, one introducing m or n, of an assumed word meaning "to adhere" (source of English *cleave* "to adhere" and *cleavers*).] —**climb·a·ble** *adj.*

climb into *vt.* to put on clothes, usually easy-to-wear ones (*informal*)

climb out of *vt.* to take off clothes, usually easy-to-wear ones (*informal*)

climb·er /klī́mər/ *n.* **1.** CLIMBING **SOMEBODY WHO CLIMBS MOUNTAINS** somebody who climbs rocks or mountains as a sport **2.** BOT **PLANT THAT CLINGS** a plant that attaches itself to other plants or objects such as posts and walls as it grows **3. SOMEBODY ADVANCING SOCIALLY** somebody who rises to a higher social or professional position, especially an unscrupulous person obsessed with advancement (*usually used in combination*)

climb·ing /klī́ming/ *n.* the sport of climbing mountains or rocks

climb·ing fern *n.* a fern, belonging to a large genus of tropical and warm-temperate fern, that climbs and grows as pairs of twining fronds. They are used to make baskets, fish traps, and mats. Genus: *Lygodium*.

climb·ing fish *n.* a tropical freshwater fish found in Asia that can breathe out of water and that uses its gill plates and lower fins to pull itself along the ground. Latin name: *Anabas testudineus*.

climb·ing frame *n. U.K.* = **jungle gym**

climb·ing iron *n.* a spike-covered metal frame that attaches to the sole of a boot to help somebody climb up ice or trees

climb·ing perch *n.* = **climbing fish**

climb·ing rat *n.* = **black rat**

climb·ing wall *n.* a wall with handholds and footholds, often located indoors, that is designed to provide practice at rock-climbing

clime /klīm/ *n.* a place with a particular type of climate (*literary*) (*often plural*) ○ *off to sunnier climes* [Late 16thC. Via Latin from Greek *klima* (see CLIMATE).]

-clinal *suffix.* sloping, slanting ○ *isoclinal* [Formed from Greek *klinein* "to lean" (see CLINE)]

cli·nan·dri·um /kli nándree əm/ (*plural* **-a** /kli nándree ə/) *n.* a hollow in the upper column of the flower of an orchid, containing the anther [Mid-19thC. From modern Latin, literally "stamen bed," coined from Greek *klinē* "couch" + the modern Latin stem *-andrium* "stamen."]

clinch /klinch/ *v.* (**clinched, clinch·ing, clinch·es**) **1.** *vt.* **RESOLVE SOMETHING DECISIVELY** to settle the outcome of something that was uncertain, e.g., a business deal or an argument, in a positive way **2.** *vt.* HOME MAINTENANCE, CONSTR **FLATTEN NAIL'S END** to bend or flatten the protruding end of a nail or rivet, or attach two or more things together using nails or rivets in this way **3.** *vi.* SPORTS **PUT ARMS AROUND OPPONENT** in boxing or wrestling, to put your arms around an opponent's body so as to pin the arms and prevent an exchange of blows **4.** *vt.* NAUT **FASTEN WITH A PARTICULAR KNOT** to fasten or secure something with a knot in a rope that is created by making a half hitch, the rope's end being fastened by seizing it ■ *n.* **1. PASSIONATE EMBRACE** a tight passionate embrace between lovers **2.** SPORTS **TACTIC OF PINNING OPPONENT'S ARMS** a tactic in boxing and wrestling designed to prevent an exchange of blows by putting your arms around an opponent's body, pinning the arms to the sides **3.** HOME MAINTENANCE, CONSTR **BENT END OF NAIL** a nail or rivet with its protruding end bent over, or a fastening made in this way **4.** NAUT **KNOT IN ROPE** a knot in a rope that is created by making a half hitch, the rope's end being fastened by seizing it [Mid-16thC. Origin uncertain: perhaps a blend of CLENCH and its dialectal (northern English and Scottish) variant *clink*.]

clinch·er /klínchər/ *n.* **1. DECIDING FACTOR** the factor that decides the outcome of something, e.g., an argument or a contest (*informal*) **2.** HOME MAINTENANCE, CONSTR **NAIL WITH END BENT** a nail or rivet that has its protruding end bent over **3.** HOME MAINTENANCE, CONSTR **TOOL FOR BENDING NAIL** a tool for bending the ends of a nail or rivet

cline /klīn/ *n.* **1. CONTINUUM** a continuum between two extremes **2. VARIATION IN CHARACTERISTICS OF A SPECIES** a gradual variation in the characteristics of a plant or animal species that occurs when it is distributed over an area with differing environmental or geographic conditions [Mid-20thC. From Greek *klinein* "to lean."] —**clin·al** *adj.* —**cli·nal·ly** *adv.*

WORD KEY: ORIGIN

The ultimate Indo-European source of ***cline*** is also the ancestor of English *client, clinic, decline, incline, ladder, lean*, and *recline*.

Cline /klīn/, **Patsy** (1932–63) U.S. singer. Her slick, sentimental country songs such as "Crazy" (1961) attracted huge popular audiences. She died in a plane crash at the peak of her career. Born **Virginia Patterson Hensley**

-cline *suffix.* slope ○ *syncline* [Back-formation from -CLINAL]

cling /kling/ *vi.* (**clung** /klung/, **cling·ing, clings**) **1. HOLD TIGHTLY** to hold onto somebody or something tightly with the hands or arms **2. STICK TO SOMETHING** to adhere to something by sticking to it or staying very close to it **3. RETAIN IDEAS OR CUSTOMS** to refuse to give up something, e.g., a belief or tradition, that you have grown fond of or used to **4. NEED SOMEBODY EMOTIONALLY** to have a strong emotional attachment to somebody **5. HOVER OVER AND SUFFUSE** to linger, usually in the air, resisting dispersion or dissipation ■ *n.* **1. STICKING QUALITY** the tendency of something to stick to surfaces **2.** BOT = **clingstone** [Old English *clingan* "to adhere." Ultimately from a prehistoric Germanic base that also produced English *clench.*] —**cling·ing·ly** *adv.*

cling·er /klíngər/ *n.* somebody who depends upon others for reassurance and a sense of security (*informal*)

cling·fish /klíng fish/ (*plural* **-fish** *or* **-fish·es**) *n.* a small fish whose pelvic fins have been modified into a sucking disk that it uses to attach itself to rocks or other objects. Family: Gobiesocidae.

cling·ing vine *n.* a woman who clings emotionally to a man, and who wants to be with or near him all or most of the time (*dated disapproving*)

Cling·mans Dome /klìngmənz-/ peak in the Great Smoky Mountains southeast of Knoxville. Height: 6,643 ft./2,025 m.

cling·stone /klíng stōn/ *n.* a fruit with flesh that sticks to the pit. Some varieties of peach, nectarine, and plum have fruit of this type.

cling·y /klíngee/ (**-i·er, -i·est**) *adj.* **1. EMOTIONALLY DEPENDENT** too dependent on the company or emotional support of other people **2. STICKING TO THE BODY** sticking closely to the body (*informal*) ○ *a clingy fabric* —**cling·i·ness** *n.*

clin·ic /klínnik/ *n.* **1.** MED **MEDICAL CENTER** a medical center for outpatients, which may be attached to a hospital or form part of it **2.** MED **SPECIALIZED MEDICAL CENTER** a medical center that specializes in a particular condition or area of medicine **3.** MED **GROUP MEDICAL PRACTICE** a suite of offices or an office where a number of doctors practice general medicine as a partnership **4.** *U.K.* MED **PRIVATE HOSPITAL** a hospital that charges patients directly for their treatment, rather than one providing state-funded treatment **5.** MED **MEDICINE TAUGHT AT THE BEDSIDE** a teaching session during which student doctors are allowed to examine patients in hospital wards, or the teaching of medicine by this method **6.** MED **SESSION ATTENDED BY PATIENTS** a session in a hospital that patients attend for specialized treatment or advice **7.** SPORTS **SESSION OF PRACTICAL SPORTS INSTRUCTION** a teaching session in which experts in specific sports give practical instruction and advice on improving technique and solving problems [Mid-19thC. Via French *clinique* from Greek *klinikē (tekhnē)* "(method of treating) the bedridden," from *klinikos* "of a bed," from *klinē* "bed," from *klinein* "to lean, lie down" (see CLINE).]

-clinic *suffix.* having a particular number of obliquely intersecting axes ○ *triclinic* [From Greek *klinein* "to lean" (see CLINE)]

clin·i·cal /klínnik'l/ *adj.* **1.** MED **BASED ON MEDICAL TREATMENT OR OBSERVATION** based on or involving medical treatment, practice, observation, or diagnosis **2. UNEMOTIONAL** practical and unemotional **3. SEVERE IN DECOR OR DESIGN** plain and severe in design, usually with the implication of lack of comfort —**clin·i·cal·ly** *adv.*

clin·i·cal e·col·o·gy *n.* MED the branch of medicine dealing with the supposed effects of the modern technological environment on human health, especially the relationship of allergies to the increase in chemicals in the environment

clin·i·cal psy·chol·o·gy *n.* a branch of psychology that deals with the diagnosis and treatment of psychological and behavioral problems —**clin·i·cal psy·chol·o·gist** *n.*

clin·i·cal ther·mom·e·ter *n.* a thermometer used for measuring the temperature of somebody's body, which continues to register the observed temperature until reset

cli·ni·cian /kli nish'n/ *n.* **1. MEDICAL PROFESSIONAL DOING PRACTICAL WORK** a medical professional who works directly with patients, as distinct from one working in research **2. DOCTOR WHO CONDUCTS CLINIC** a medical professional who conducts or teaches in a clinic

clink[1] /klingk/ *vti.* (**clinked, clink·ing, clinks**) **MAKE RINGING SOUND** to make or cause something to make the short high-pitched slightly ringing sound that metal or glass objects make when they knock against each other ■ *n.* **RINGING SOUND** the short high-pitched slightly ringing sound that metal or glass objects make when they knock against each other [14thC. Origin uncertain: possibly an imitation of the sound, or perhaps from Middle Dutch *klinken.*]

clink[2] /klingk/ *n.* a correctional institution, especially a prison (*dated slang*) [Early 16thC. From the *Clink,* a noted former prison in Southwark, a borough of London.]

clink·er[1] /klíngkər/ *n.* **1. BALL OF COAL RESIDUE** a hard mass of ash and partially fused coal that remains after coal is burned in a fire or furnace **2. HARD BRICK** a very hard brick, or an overhard brick that has been fired in a kiln for too long ■ *vi.* (**-ered, -er·ing, -ers**) **FORM LUMPY BURNED RESIDUE** to form hard lumps of partially fused coal and ash after burning [Mid-17thC. Alteration of obsolete *clincard,* from obsolete Dutch *klinckaerd* "brick," from *klinken* "to sound, ring"; from the sound made by a brick when struck.]

clink·er[2] /klíngkər/ *n.* (*informal*) **1. SOMETHING OF POOR QUALITY** a failure or something of very poor quality **2.** MUSIC **WRONG NOTE** a wrong note in a piece of music [Mid-20thC. Formed from CLINK.]

clink·er-built *adj.* used to describe a boat that has a hull made of overlapping planks [From *clinker* "clinched nail," from *clink* "to secure a nail," a variant of CLENCH]

clink·et·y-clank *n.* the dull short ringing sounds produced when something metallic hits a surface repeatedly [Early 20thC. From CLINK and CLANK, an imitation of the sound.]

clink·stone /klínk stōn/ *n.* = **phonolite** [Translation of German *Klingstein,* literally "ringing stone"; from its metallic resonance when struck]

clino- *prefix.* slope, slant ○ *clinometer* [Formed from Greek *klinein* "to lean, slope" (see CLINE)]

cli·nom·e·ter /klī nómmətər/ *n.* any instrument used in surveying or geology to measure the angle of a slope or incline —**cli·no·met·ric** /klīnə méttrik/ *adj.* —**cli·no·met·ri·cal** *adj.* —**cli·nom·e·try** /klī nómmətree/ *n.*

clin·o·py·rox·ene /klīnō pī rók seen/ *n.* a silicate mineral of the pyroxene group, containing calcium, iron, and magnesium and forming monoclinic crystals, e.g., augite

cli·no·stat /klīnə stàt/ *n.* a piece of laboratory equipment with a turntable that allows a plant placed on it to be exposed to a stimulus, e.g., light, equally on all sides

-clinous *suffix.* **1.** having stamens and pistils in a particular number of flowers ○ *diclinous* **2.** descending from a particular line ○ *matriclinous* [Origin uncertain: ultimately from Greek *klinein* "to lean, decline" (see CLINE)]

Clin·ton /klíntən/ **1.** city in Iowa, on the western bank of the Mississippi River, southeast of Cedar Rapids. Population: 28,323 (1996). **2.** city in central Mississippi, west of Jackson and east of Vicksburg. Population: 21,992 (1996).

Bill Clinton and Hillary Rodham Clinton

Clin·ton, Bill (*b.* 1946) U.S. statesman and 42nd president of the United States (1993–). Before his election to the White House he was Democratic Governor of Arkansas (1979–81, 1983–92). In 1999 he was impeached and acquitted by the senate for perjury and obstruction of justice. Full name **William Jefferson Clinton**

Clin·ton, De Witt (1769–1828) U.S. statesman. He was governor of New York State (1817–23), and ran for the U.S. presidency in 1812.

Clin·ton, George (1739–1812) U.S. statesman. He was governor of New York State (1777–95 and 1801–04) and the 4th U.S. vice president (1805–12).

Clin·ton, Hillary Rodham (*b.* 1947) U.S. lawyer and first lady. In 1994, her proposals for the first national health care program were blocked by Congress.

clin·to·ni·a /klin tōnee ə/ *n.* a broad-leafed perennial plant of the lily family with white, yellow, or purplish flowers and blue or purple berries. Genus: *Clintonia.* [Mid-19thC. From modern Latin, genus name, named for De Witt CLINTON.]

Cli·o /klī ō/ (*plural* **-os**) *n.* **1.** MYTHOL **GREEK MUSE** in Greek mythology, the muse of history **2. ADVERTISING AWARD** an annual award for excellence in television or radio advertising

cli·o·met·rics /klī ō méttriks/ *n.* the study of economic history using statistics, advanced methods of data processing, analysis of mathematical data, and economic modeling (*takes a singular verb*) [Mid-20thC. Coined from CLIO + -METRICS, modeled on such words as *econometrics.*] —**cli·o·met·ric** *adj.* —**cli·o·me·tri·cian** /klī ō me trísh'n/ *n.*

clip[1] /klip/ *v.* (**clipped, clipping, clips**) **1.** *vt.* **CUT OR TRIM SOMETHING** to cut or trim something, or cut it off, e.g., with scissors or shears **2.** *vt.* **CUT SOMETHING OUT** to remove something from something else by cutting **3.** *vt.* **SHORTEN TIME TAKEN FOR SOMETHING** to reduce the time taken to complete something, especially traveling time **4.** *vt.* **SIDESWIPE** to make physical contact with somebody or something else with a light glancing slapping blow (*informal*) **5.** *vt.* PHON **TRUNCATE SPEECH SOUND** to shorten a speech sound **6.** *vt.* LING **ABBREVIATE WORD** to shorten a word or other expression by abbreviating it or dropping a syllable **7.** *vt.* **CURTAIL** to reduce or diminish power or influence **8.** *vi.* **GO FAST** to move at a brisk pace (*informal*) **9.** *vt.* **SWINDLE SOMEBODY** to cheat or swindle somebody, especially by overcharging (*slang*) ■ *n.* **1.** CINEMA, TV **FILM OR TV EXTRACT** an extract, especially a short piece from movie or television footage **2.** PRESS **EXTRACT FROM PRINT MEDIA** a news story or other article cut out of a print publication and used, e.g., as a sample of work **3. GLANCING BLOW** a sideswiping blow **4. RATE OF MOTION** the speed at which somebody or something moves (*informal*) **5. SINGLE OCCASION** a single time or occasion (*informal*) **6. THING OR AMOUNT CUT** something cut or removed, especially the amount of wool cut from a flock of sheep at one shearing [13thC. Origin uncertain: probably from Old Norse *klippa* "to cut short," which may be an imitation of the sound.]

clip[2] /klip/ *n.* **1. GRIPPING DEVICE** any of numerous devices that grip or clasp loose things together or that hold things firmly (*often used in combination*) **2.** ACCESSORIES **PIECE OF JEWELRY** a piece of jewelry with a gripping device that attaches to clothing **3.** ARMS **BULLET HOLDER** a container for bullets, slotted directly into an automatic firearm **4.** FOOTBALL **ILLEGAL BLOCKING** the act or an instance of illegally blocking a player on an opposing team by hitting that player with the body from behind ■ *v.* (**clipped, clip·ping, clips**) **1.** *vti.* **HOLD SOMETHING WITH GRIPPING DEVICE** to hold loose things together, or attach one thing to another, using a clip, or be attached in this way **2.** *vt.* FOOTBALL **BLOCK PLAYER ILLEGALLY** to block an opposing player illegally by hitting that person from behind [Old English *clyppan* "to embrace, fasten," of prehistoric West Germanic origin. The noun evolved from the verb in the 15thC. Ultimately from an Indo-European word meaning "to form into a ball." See CLING.]

clip art *n.* prepackaged artwork, available on graphics or desktop publishing software, for use in documents produced on computer [So called because it originally came in the form of *clip sheets,* pages of drawings that graphic designers could cut out and paste into layouts]

clip·board /klíp bàwrd/ *n.* a small portable board with a clip attached at the top, used for securing papers and providing a hard writing surface for somebody on the move

clip-clop /klip klóp/ *n., interj.* **SOUND OF HOOVES** used to represent or imitate the rhythmic sound made by a walking horse's hooves as they strike hard ground ■ *vi.* (**clip-clopped, clip-clop·ping, clip-clops**) **GO CLIP-CLOP** to make the sound of hooves striking hard ground [Early 20thC. An imitation of the sound.]

clip joint *n.* a shop or club that habitually overcharges its customers (*slang*) [From CLIP[1] "to swindle"]

clip-on *adj.* ATTACHING BY GRIPPING used to describe something, especially an item of clothing, that is attached by means of a clip ■ *n.* ACCESSORY THAT ATTACHES WITH CLIP an accessory, e.g., an earring or a tie, that is attached with a clip

clipped /klipt/ *adj.* **1.** NEATLY TRIMMED trimmed or cut back neatly **2.** WITH EACH WORD SPOKEN CLEARLY spoken with each word pronounced separately and distinctly

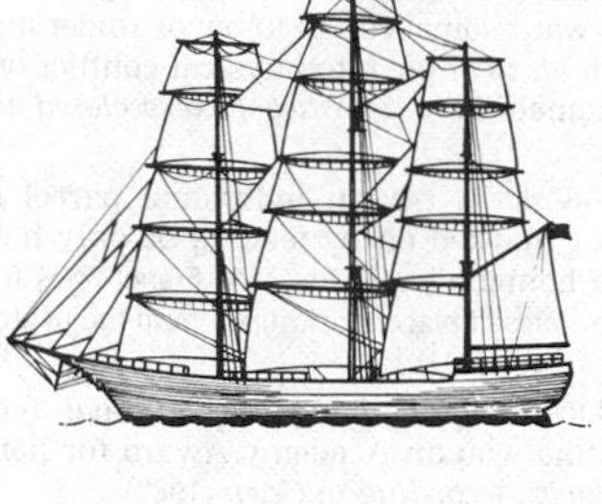

Clipper

clip·per /klíppər/ *n.* **1.** NAUT FAST SAILING SHIP a mid-19th-century tall ship with a sharp bow, designed for fast speeds **2.** METEOROL WEATHER FRONT a fast-moving weather front, usually one bringing cold air into a region **3.** SOMEBODY WHO USES CUTTING TOOL somebody who uses a cutting or shearing tool **4.** ELECTRON ENG = **limiter** ■ **clip·pers** *npl.* TOOL FOR CLIPPING SOMETHING a hand tool for cutting or clipping something. Clippers include the tool for trimming very short hair, that for trimming fingernails, and that for shearing sheep.

clip·ping /klípping/ *n.* **1.** NEWSPAPER ITEM CUT OUT an article cut out of a newspaper or magazine **2.** FOOTBALL = **clip** ■ **clip·pings** *npl.* TRIMMED-OFF HAIR OR GRASS pieces of grass or hair that have been cut or clipped off

clip·sheet /klíp shēet/ *n.* an item or items from a newspaper or magazine reprinted on one side of the paper only, used for distribution to interested parties

clique /kleek, klik/ *n.* a close group of friends or colleagues having similar interests and goals, and whom outsiders regard as excluding them [Early 18thC. From French, formed from *cliquer* "to click, clap," an imitation of the sound. The underlying meaning is apparently "a group of people who applaud one another."] —**cliqu·ey** *adj.* —**cliqu·ish** *adj.* —**cliqu·ish·ly** *adv.* **cliqu·ish·ness** *n.*

cli·tel·lum /klī téllәm/ (*plural* **-la** /-téllә/) *n.* a glandular section, similar in shape to a saddle, in the body wall of some worms, e.g., earthworms and leeches, that secretes a sticky substance during copulation. The substance is later used to form a sac in which the eggs are deposited. [Mid-19thC. Via modern Latin from Latin *clitellae* "packsaddle" (from its shape), literally "little litters."]

cli·tic /klíttik/ *adj.* used to describe a word that cannot be stressed and is pronounced as part of the word that follows or precedes it, e.g., in "ve" in "I've" [Mid-20thC. Back-formation from ENCLITIC and PROCLITIC.] —**cli·tic** *n.*

cli·tor·i·dec·to·my /klìttəri déktəmee/ (*plural* **-mies**) *n.* the cutting off of all or part of a woman's or girl's clitoris, practised in some societies as a social or cultural rite of passage

clit·o·ris /klíttəriss/ (*plural* **clit·o·ris·es** *or* **cli·tor·i·des** /kli táwri dēez/) *n.* a small highly sensitive erectile organ at the front junction of the labia minora in the vulva [Early 17thC. Via modern Latin from Greek *kleitoris*, literally "little hill."] —**clit·o·ral** *adj.*

Clive /klīv/, **Robert, Baron Clive of Plassey** (1725–74) British soldier and colonial administrator who was instrumental in establishing British rule in India. He served as governor of Bengal from 1765 to 1767 but became embroiled in scandal and committed suicide. Known as **Clive of India**

clk. *abbr.* clerk

clm. *abbr.* column

clo·a·ca /klō áykə/ (*plural* **-cae** /-sēe/) *n.* the terminal region of the gut in reptiles, amphibians, birds, and many fish as well as in some invertebrates. The intestinal, urinary, and genital canals open into it. [Late 16thC. From Latin, "sewer, canal." Ultimately from an Indo-European word meaning "to flush out," which is also the ancestor of English *cataclysm* and *clyster*).] —**clo·a·cal** *adj.*

cloak /klōk/ *n.* **1.** CLOTHES OUTER GARMENT a loose sleeveless outer garment that fastens at the neck **2.** ENSHROUDING OBJECT OR FORCE something that covers or conceals things (*literary*) ■ *vt.* (**cloaked, cloak·ing, cloaks**) ENSHROUD SOMETHING to cover or conceal something (*often passive*) [13thC. Via Old Northern French *cloke, cloque*, variants of Old French *cloche*, from medieval Latin *clocca* "bell, cape worn by travelers" (see CLOCK); from its bell-like shape.]

cloak-and-dag·ger *adj.* involving secrecy or intrigue, often as part of an espionage operation [Translation of French *de cape et d'épée* and Spanish *de capa y espada*, literally "of cape and sword," symbols of the rank of the chief characters in dramas of domestic intrigue]

cloak fern *n.* a fern of tropical and temperate America that is adapted to dry conditions and is often used as an ornamental plant. Genus: *Notholaena.*

cloak·room /klṓk ròom, klṓk rōōm/ *n.* **1.** = **coat check 2.** LEGISLATORS' LOUNGE a lounge for members of a legislature, near or connected to their chamber itself **3.** CLOSET FOR COATS a walk-in closet in a house, where coats and other outdoor items are stored **4.** *U.K.* = **restroom** (*informal*)

clob·ber /klóbbər/ (**-bered, -ber·ing, -bers**) *vt.* (*informal*) **1.** HIT SOMEBODY OR SOMETHING to hit somebody or something with great force **2.** UTTERLY DEFEAT SOMEBODY to defeat somebody heavily **3.** CRITICIZE SEVERELY to criticize something or somebody severely ○ *The proposal has been clobbered in the national media.* [Mid-20thC. Origin unknown.]

cloche /klōsh/ *n.* **1.** CLOTHES WOMAN'S HAT a woman's or girl's close-fitting hat with a very narrow brim, or no brim at all, especially popular in the 1920s and 1930s **2.** GARDENING PROTECTIVE COVER FOR PLANTS a small structure made of glass or clear plastic, placed over cold-sensitive garden plants in cold weather [Late 19thC. Via French, literally "bell," from medieval Latin *clocca* (see CLOCK); from the shape.]

clock[1] /klok/ *n.* **1.** TIME DEVICE DISPLAYING THE TIME a free-standing device that measures and records time, which it displays by a pointer on a dial or by a digital readout **2.** TECH MEASURING INSTRUMENT WITH DISPLAY a measuring instrument with a dial or a digital display, e.g., any of a vehicle's control gauges, especially the odometer **3.** BUSINESS = **time clock 4.** BOT SEED HEAD OF DANDELION the fluffy white seed head of a dandelion **5.** COMPUT ELECTRONIC CIRCUIT THAT SYNCHRONIZES COMPUTER PROCESSES an electronic circuit that generates pulses at a constant rate in order to synchronize the internal operations in a computer ■ *vt.* (**clocked, clock·ing, clocks**) **1.** RECORD SOMEBODY'S OR SOMETHING'S TIME to measure or record the time somebody or something takes, using a stopwatch or an electronic timing device **2.** PUNCH SOMEBODY to punch somebody (*slang*) [14thC. Via Middle Dutch and Middle Low German *klocke* from, ultimately, medieval Latin *clocca* "bell" (source of English *cloak*).] ◇ **against the clock** with limited time to finish something ◇ **around the clock, round the clock** day and night, without stopping ◇ **turn the clock(s) back, put the clock(s) back** to return to the conditions of an earlier time

clock in *vi.* to arrive for work, or record arrival for work by inserting a personalized card into a time clock

clock out *vi.* to leave work, or record departure from work by inserting a personalized card into a time clock

clock up *vt.* to reach a particular total

clock[2] /klok/ *n.* a design on the ankle or side of a stocking or sock [Mid-16thC. Origin uncertain: perhaps the pattern originally consisted of bell-shaped ornaments (see CLOCK[1]).]

clock golf *n.* a putting game in which the ball is played from each of several points on the edge of a circular lawn toward a single hole in the center

clock·mak·er /klók màykər/ *n.* somebody who makes and repairs clocks and watches for a living

clock ra·di·o *n.* an electronic device that incorporates a digital clock, an alarm clock, and a radio

clock speed *n.* the speed of a microprocessor's internal clock that controls how fast a computer can make calculations, usually measured in megahertz (MHz)

clock-watch·er *n.* somebody who is more interested in going home or to lunch on time than getting a job done —**clock-watch·ing** *n.*

clock·wise /klók wīz/ *adv., adj.* in the same direction that the hands of a clock move around a clockface

clock·work /klók wùrk/ *n.* **1.** MECHANICAL POWERING SYSTEM a mechanism consisting of cogs and a wound spring, used to drive a traditional clock or a moving toy **2.** UNVARYING REGULARITY precise unvarying regularity

clod /klod/ *n.* **1.** LUMP OF EARTH a large lump of earth or clay **2.** UNINTELLIGENT PERSON somebody who is unintelligent and stupid (*insult*) [14thC. Variant form of CLOT.] —**clod·dish** *adj.* —**clod·dish·ly** *adv.* —**clod·dish·ness** *n.* —**clod·dy** *adj.*

clod·hop·per /klód hòppər/ *n.* AWKWARD UNSOPHISTICATED PERSON somebody who is awkward and unsophisticated and behaves insensitively or clumsily (*insult*) ■ **clod·hop·pers** *npl.* CLOTHES BIG HEAVY SHOES OR BOOTS a pair of large heavy shoes or boots (*informal*) [Early 18thC. Originally "a plowman or other agricultural worker," from the idea of somebody who "hops" or walks over plowed land with clods of earth.]

clo·fi·brate /klō fī brayt, klō fí bràyt/ *n.* a drug used to reduce plasma levels of cholesterol, triglycerides, and uric acid. Formula: $C_{12}H_{15}ClO_3$. [Mid-20thC. Coined from *clofibric acid* (from, perhaps, CHLORO- + FIBR- + -ATE).]

clog /klog/ *v.* (**clogged, clog·ging, clogs**) **1.** *vti.* BLOCK GRADUALLY to block a tube or opening gradually with dirt or dust, or become gradually blocked with dirt or dust **2.** *vt.* TRANSP HINDER MOVEMENT IN SOMETHING to block something such as a road or tunnel, making movement difficult ■ *n.* **1.** CLOTHES HEAVY SHOE a heavy shoe traditionally made of wood, or a shoe with a heavy, traditionally wooden, sole **2.** OBSTRUCTION something that works against somebody as an obstacle or hindrance **3.** WEIGHT RESTRICTING ANIMAL'S MOVEMENT a wooden block fastened to an animal's leg to restrict its movement [14thC. Origin unknown. The original meaning of the word was "block, lump." The verb developed from the idea of impeding an animal with a wooden block.]

clog up *vti.* = **clog**

clog dance *n.* a dance performed by dancers wearing clogs, who tap or stamp in time to the music

clog·gy /klóggee/ *adj.* sticky, or lumpy in texture —**clog·gi·ness** *n.*

cloi·son·né /klòyz'n áy/ *adj.* DECORATED WITH PATTERN OF ENAMEL decorated with a pattern formed by pieces of enamel in various colors separated by strips of flattened wire ■ *n.* CLOISONNÉ WORK decorative work with a cloisonné pattern [Mid-19thC. From French, literally "partitioned," the past participle of *cloisonner*, from Old French *cloison* "partition," from, ultimately, Latin *claudere* (see CLOSE).]

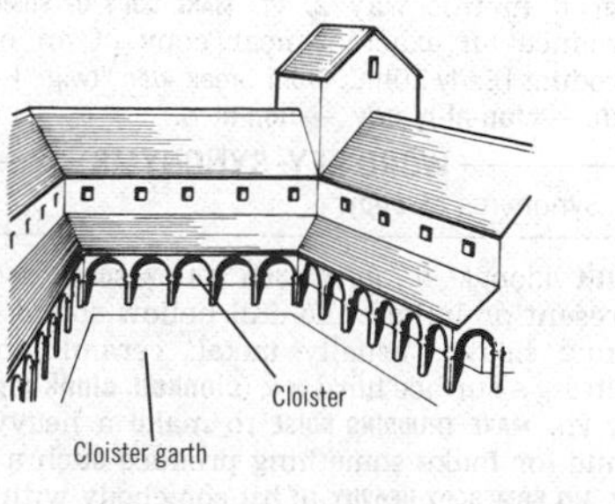

Cloister

clois·ter /klóystər/ *n.* **1.** RELIG MONASTERY OR CONVENT a place where people live a life of religious seclusion and contemplation, e.g., a monastery or convent **2.** RELIG PART OF MONASTERY WHERE MONKS LIVE an area within a monastery or convent where monks or nuns live. Some orders do not allow laypeople access to this area. **3.** RELIG LIFE OF RELIGIOUS SECLUSION the life of religious seclusion lived by a monk or nun ○ *He chose* *the cloister rather than the secular world.* **4.** **PLACE OF SECLUSION** a place where people can be private or secluded **5.** ARCHIT **COVERED WALKWAY AROUND COURTYARD** a continuous covered outdoor walkway built against buildings surrounding a central courtyard or quadrangle, especially in a monastery or college. The inner side of the walkway may be open or colonnaded. ■ *vr.* (**-tered, -ter·ing, -ters**) **FIND PRIVATE PLACE** to find a quiet private place where you can remain undisturbed [13thC. Via Old French *cloistre* from medieval Latin *claustrum*, from Latin, "bar, bolt," formed from *claudere* (see CLOSE). The underlying idea is of an enclosed place.]

clois·tered /klóystərd/ *adj.* **1.** **SECLUDED** secluded, or sheltered from the harsh realities of life ○ *had led a cloistered life* **2.** RELIG **IN A MONASTERY** living or occurring in a monastery or convent **3.** ARCHIT **WITH A CLOISTER** having a cloister for walking in

clois·tral /klóystrəl/ *adj.* **1.** RELIG **OF RELIGIOUS SECLUSION** relating to a life of religious seclusion **2.** **LEADING A SHELTERED LIFE** sheltered from the harsh realities of life

clom·i·phene /klómmə fèen, klṓmə-/ *n.* a synthetic drug used to induce ovulation and treat infertility. Formula: $C_{26}H_{28}ClNO$. [Mid-20thC. Coined from CHLORO- + AMINE + PHENYL.]

clomp *n., vti.* = **clump**[2]

Clone: First clone of an adult animal ("Dolly"), Roslin Institute, Edinburgh (1997)

clone /klōn/ *n.* **1.** GENETICS **GENETICALLY IDENTICAL ORGANISM** a plant, animal, or other organism that is genetically identical to its parent, having developed by vegetative reproduction, e.g. from a bulb or a cutting, or experimentally from a single cell **2.** GENETICS **GROUP OF GENETICALLY IDENTICAL PROGENY** a collection of organisms, cells, or molecular segments that are genetically identical direct descendants of a single parent by asexual reproduction, e.g., plant cuttings or grafts. Some plant varieties are clones. **3.** COMPUT **NEAR COPY OF HARDWARE OR SOFTWARE** a hardware device, e.g., a PC, or a piece of software that is a functional copy of another, popular, more expensive product developed by another manufacturer ■ *v.* (**cloned, clon·ing, clones**) **1.** *vti.* GENETICS **PRODUCE GENETICALLY IDENTICAL ORGANISMS** to produce an organism that is genetically identical to its parent, by vegetative reproduction or a laboratory technique, or be produced in this way **2.** *vt.* **MAKE COPY OF SOMETHING** to produce an exact or near copy of an object or product [Early 20thC. From Greek *klōn* "twig."] —**clon·al** *adj.* —**clon·al·ly** *adv.* —**clon·er** *n.*

WORD KEY: SYNONYMS

See Synonyms at ***copy***.

clonk /klongk/ *n., interj.* **DULL HOLLOW SOUND** used to represent or imitate the dull hollow sound of something heavy, usually metal, ceramic, or glass, hitting a surface hard ■ *v.* (**clonked, clonk·ing, clonks**) **1.** *vti.* **MAKE THUDDING NOISE** to make a heavy hollow thud, or make something produce such a noise **2.** *vt.* **HIT SOMEBODY HEAVILY** to hit somebody with a heavy blow, usually on a particular part of the body (*informal*) [Mid-19thC. An imitation of the sound.]

clo·nus /klṓnəss/ *n.* a series of rapid repetitive contractions and relaxations in a muscle during movement, which is characteristic of certain nervous disorders. Spontaneous clonus is a principal feature of grand-mal epilepsy seizures but is otherwise uncommon. [Early 19thC. Via Latin from Greek *klonos* "turmoil, agitation."] —**clo·nic** /klónnik, klṓnik/ *adj.* —**clo·nic·i·ty** /klō nìssətee, klo nìssətee/ *n.*

Cloo·ney /kloonee/, **George** (*b.* 1961) U.S. movie and television actor. He played Dr. Douglas Ross in the 1990s' television series *ER*.

clop /klop/ *n., interj.* **SOUND OF HOOVES** used to represent or imitate the sound that a walking horse's hooves make when they strike hard ground ■ *vi.* (**clopped, clop·ping, clops**) **MAKE SOUND OF HOOVES** to make the sound of a walking horse's hooves striking hard ground [Mid-19thC. An imitation of the sound.]

clo·que /klō káy/, **clo·qué** *n.* fabric with a raised woven or embossed pattern that gives it a quilted look [Early 20thC. Via French *cloqué*, literally "blistered," from dialectal *cloque* "blister," from medieval Latin *clocca* "bell."]

close[1] /klōss/ *adj.* (**clos·er, clos·est**) **1.** **NEAR** near in space or time ○ *The deadline was getting closer all the time.* **2.** **ABOUT TO HAPPEN** about to happen, or about to do something ○ *close to collapse* **3.** **KNOWING AND LIKING SOMEBODY** knowing somebody very well and liking him or her very much ○ *close friends* **4.** **CLOSELY RELATED** being a member of somebody's immediate family **5.** **INVOLVING REGULAR CONTACT** involving or having regular contact because of a shared interest in something **6.** **THOROUGH** involving great care and thoroughness ○ *give it close inspection.* **7.** **DECIDED BY A SMALL MARGIN** decided by, or likely to be decided by, a small margin ○ *a close contest* **8.** TEXTILES **ALLOWING LITTLE SPACE BETWEEN** so densely packed or woven as to allow only little spaces between **9.** **VERY SIMILAR** very similar to an original ○ *a close copy* **10.** **NEARLY CORRECT** nearly correct or exact ○ *You're not quite right, but you're pretty close.* **11.** **NEARLY A NUMBER OR QUANTITY** approximately the same as a particular number or quantity **12.** **SECRETIVELY SILENT** unwilling to talk about something or to reveal feelings **13.** **CUT VERY SHORT** cut so as to be very short **14.** **STINGY** unwilling to spend or give money **15.** **HARD TO GET** difficult to obtain **16.** **CLOSELY GUARDED** kept closely guarded **17.** **STUFFY** oppressively hot and airless **18.** SPORTS **DEFENSIVE, WITH SHORT PASSES** involving short passes only, so as to retain possession **19.** PHON **PRODUCED WITH TONGUE NEAR PALATE** used to describe a vowel sound that is produced with the tongue near the palate, e.g., the "ee" in "tee" ■ *adv.* (**clos·er, clos·est**) **1.** **NEAR TO SOMETHING** near in space or time **2.** **TIGHTLY** in a snug tight way [13thC. Via French *clos* from Latin *clausus*, the past participle of *claudere* "to close." The sense "near" developed from the idea of the closing off of the gap between two things if they are brought together.]

close[2] /klōz/ *v.* (**closed, clos·ing, clos·es**) **1.** *vti.* **COVER AN OPENING** to move or move something so that an opening or hole is covered or blocked **2.** *vti.* **COME OR BRING TOGETHER** to come together, or bring the edges or ends of something together, e.g., the eyelids **3.** *vti.* **SHUT DOWN BUSINESS FOR SHORT TIME** to stop working or operating, or shut a store or business, for a short period of time or overnight **4.** *vti.* = **close down** **5.** *vt.* = **close off** **6.** *vti.* **TERMINATE** to come to an end, or bring something to an end, e.g., an activity, period of time, or spoken or written text **7.** *vti.* **REDUCE THE DISTANCE** to reduce the distance between two people or things, especially in a race or chase **8.** *vt.* COMM **BRING DEAL TO CLOSURE** to complete a transaction successfully, e.g., a business deal or a house purchase **9.** *vi.* STOCK EXCH **HAVE AN END-OF-DAY VALUE** to have a particular value at the end of a day's trading on a stock exchange **10.** *vt.* COMPUT **DEACTIVATE AND STORE FILE OR PROGRAM** to perform the series of operations necessary to deactivate a file or program and store it for later use **11.** *vt.* ELEC ENG **COMPLETE AN ELECTRICAL CIRCUIT** to complete an electrical circuit ■ *n.* **1.** **END OF AN ACTIVITY** the end of an activity, period of time, or spoken or written text ○ *The meeting drew to a close.* **2.** MUSIC = **cadence** [13thC. From French *clos-*, the stem of *clore* "to close," from Latin *claudere* (see CLOSE[1]).] —**clos·a·ble** *adj.* —**clos·er** *n.*

WORD KEY: ORIGIN

Close is derived from the Latin word *claudere*, meaning "to close," which is also the source of English *clause, cloister, closet, conclude, include, preclude, recluse,* and *seclude*.

close down *vti.* to stop operating or trading permanently, or shut a factory, business, or school so that it stops operating permanently

close in *vi.* **1.** **APPROACH AND SURROUND SOMETHING** to move closer and eventually surround somebody or something **2.** **HAVE SHORTER DAYLIGHT PERIOD** to become progressively shorter, with fewer hours of daylight

close off *vt.* to prevent people from reaching a place or using a route by blocking access to it (*often passive*)

close out *vt.* **1.** **KEEP OUT WITH BARRIER** to keep something out by blocking or obstructing it **2.** COMM **SELL OFF** to get rid of old merchandise by selling it at reduced prices **3.** COMM **END BUSINESS OPERATIONS** to terminate business operations by selling the business to another party

close up *v.* **1.** *vti.* **LOCK BUILDING** to lock the doors of a building at the end of a working or trading session **2.** *vti.* **MOVE CLOSER TOGETHER** to move closer together, or make people or things move closer together **3.** *vti.* **BRING TOGETHER** to come together, or bring the ends or edges of something together **4.** *vi.* **HIDE EMOTIONS** to hide your true emotions deliberately because you do not want somebody to know or understand you

close with *vt.* to enter into physical conflict or a fight with somebody ○ *The two boxers closed with one another.*

close[3] /klōss/ *n.* LAW an individual parcel of land, whether marked off by fencing or only having invisible boundaries [13thC. Via French *clos* from Latin *clausum* "closed place, enclosure," from the neuter form of *clausus* (see CLOSE[1]).]

Close /klōss/, **Glenn** (*b.* 1947) U.S. stage and movie actor. She won an Academy Award for her role in *The World According to Garp* (1982).

close call *n.* a dangerous situation that could have resulted in death or injury, but from which somebody just manages to escape

close cor·po·ra·tion, closed cor·po·ra·tion *n.* a company, the stock of which is closely held by a limited number of shareholders, usually directors or managers, and not publicly traded

close-cropped *adj.* cut very short

closed /klōzd/ *adj.* **1.** **WHERE WORK HAS STOPPED** where work, operation, or trading has temporarily or permanently stopped **2.** **DENYING ACCESS** where access or passage is denied **3.** **NO LONGER TO BE DISCUSSED** about which there is to be no further discussion or investigation ○ *The subject is closed.* **4.** **RIGIDLY EXCLUDING OTHERS' IDEAS** rigidly rejecting ideas, beliefs, opinions, and influence from or by others ○ *He has a closed mind to all arguments.* **5.** **NOT ADMITTING OUTSIDERS** allowing no outsiders in, or tending not to meet with outsiders **6.** **CONFIDENTIAL AND PRIVATE** carried on or conducted in the strictest confidentiality or secrecy **7.** MATH **FULLY ENCLOSING AN AREA OR VOLUME** used to describe a curve, especially a circle, that fully encloses an area, or to describe a solid every surface of which is such a curve **8.** LING **HAVING LIMITED NUMBER OF MEMBERS** used to describe a word class that has a limited number of members, e.g., pronouns or conjunctions **9.** PHON **ENDING IN CONSONANT** used to describe a syllable that ends in a consonant

closed-cap·tioned *adj.* broadcast with captions, e.g., subtitles for the hard of hearing, that can be received on an adapted television set

closed cir·cuit *n.* an electrical circuit in which there is an uninterrupted endless path for current to flow when voltage is applied

closed-cir·cuit tel·e·vi·sion, closed-cir·cuit TV *n.* a television transmission system in which cameras transmit pictures by cable to connected monitors. Surveillance systems are based on this type of transmission.

closed cor·po·ra·tion *n.* = **close corporation**

closed cou·plet *n.* a pair of rhymed lines that form a complete sentence or unit of meaning

closed-door *adj.* restricted to members or those directly involved, and not open to the general public or the news media

closed-end fund *n.* an investment company with a fixed number of shares trading on the stock exchange

closed-end in·vest·ment com·pa·ny *n.* a corporation whose capitalization is fixed, and whose capital is invested in other companies, and whose own shares are traded by outside investors

closed in·ter·val *n.* a set consisting of all the numbers between two given numbers (**end points**), including the given numbers. All the whole numbers greater than or equal to 5 and less than or equal to 10 constitute a closed interval.

closed loop *n.* a system, usually computer-controlled, that adjusts itself to varying conditions by feeding output information back as input

closed-mind·ed, **close-mind·ed** *adj.* rigidly and obstinately averse to the consideration of new ideas or other people's arguments —**closed-mind·ed·ness** *n.*

close·down /klṓz dòwn/ *n.* a temporary or permanent stopping of work or operations

closed schol·ar·ship *n.* a scholarship for which only certain people may apply, e.g., students from a particular school or college

closed sea·son *n.* 1. PERIOD OF NO HUNTING the time of the year when it is illegal to hunt and kill certain animals, birds, or fish 2. PERIOD BETWEEN SEASONAL SPORTS COMPETITIONS the period between the end of one annual seasonal sports competition, e.g., a soccer season, and the start of the next one

closed set *n.* a set that includes the limits by which the set is defined, e.g., all the points within and on a circle

closed shop *n.* a place of work in which the employer has agreed to employ only members of a particular labor union. ◊ **open shop, union shop**

closed stance *n.* a stance, e.g., in baseball or golf, in which the front foot is closer to the line of play than the rear foot

close-fist·ed /klṑss-/ *adj.* reluctant to spend money (*informal*) —**close-fist·ed·ness** *n.*

close-fit·ting /klṑss-/ *adj.* fitting tightly on the body

close-grained /klṑss-/ *adj.* used to describe wood that has dense fibers and as a result a smooth texture

close har·mo·ny *n.* the arrangement of chord tones so that they are as close together as possible, used especially in music for vocal ensembles

close-hauled /klṑss-/ *adj.*, *adv.* with the sails set for sailing toward the direction from which the wind is blowing

close-in /klṑss-/ *adj.* 1. NEAR HUB OF ACTION being very near to a center of action or activity, e.g., the inlying suburbs of a metropolis 2. CLOSE-RANGE taking place at close range

close-knit /klṑss-/ *adj.* supportive and loyal to the other members of a community or group

close-lipped /klṑss-/ *adj.* unwilling to talk or to reveal anything

close·ly /klṓsslee/ *adv.* 1. CAREFULLY AND THOROUGHLY in a careful and thorough way ○ *listening closely* 2. IN A VERY SIMILAR WAY in a way that is very similar or strongly linked to something ○ *She closely resembles you.* 3. SO AS TO BE NEAR in a way that is near something in space or time ○ *We heard a bang, closely followed by another.* 4. SECRETLY in a secret or clandestine manner 5. INTIMATELY in an intimate manner ○ *worked closely with her*

close-mind·ed /klṑss-/ *adj.* = **closed-minded**

close·mouthed /klōz mówthd/ *adj.* unwilling to talk or to reveal anything

close·ness /klṓssnəss/ *n.* 1. NEARNESS the quality or state of being close to somebody or something in space, time, relationship, or intimacy 2. STUFFY AIRLESSNESS stuffy airlessness

close-or·der drill /klṑss-/ *n.* a formation or movement that is conducted with soldiers at close intervals

close·out /klṓz òwt/ *n.* a sale of all remaining merchandise, at very low prices

close punc·tu·a·tion *n.* punctuation in which a large number of commas, semicolons, and colons are used

close-run /klṑss-/ *adj.* having a very close result

close sea·son /klṑss-/ *n.* U.K. = **closed season**

close shave /klṑss-/ *n.* = **close call**

clos·et /klózzət/ *n.* 1. STORAGE PLACE a large cabinet or recessed area with a door, in which clothes or linens are stored 2. SMALL PRIVATE ROOM a small private room (*archaic*) 3. TOILET a water closet (*archaic*) ■ *adj.* 1. SECRET having beliefs or behavior that is not openly acknowledged but kept secret 2. IN THEORY ONLY regarded as something, or considering yourself as something, in theory or in your imagination but in not reality ○ *This game appeals to closet baseball managers.* ■ *vt.* (**-et·ed, -et·ing, -ets**) PUT SOMEBODY IN PRIVATE PLACE to put people in a small room where they can have privacy (*often passive*) [14thC. From Old French, literally "small enclosure," formed from *clos* "enclosure" (see CLOSE[3]).] —**clos·et·ful** *n.* ◇ **come out of the closet** to acknowledge openly something previously kept secret, especially the fact of being gay or lesbian

clos·et dra·ma *n.* a play or plays written to be read rather than performed

clos·et queen *n.* an offensive term for a gay man who does not reveal his sexual preference openly, or who actively conceals or denies it (*slang offensive*)

close-up /klṑss-/ *n.* 1. PHOTOGRAPHY, CINEMA, TV CLOSE-RANGE PHOTO OR SHOT a photograph, movie, or television shot taken from a position very close to the subject 2. DETAILED LOOK AT SOMETHING a detailed view or examination of something ■ *adj.* AT CLOSE RANGE seen from a position very near somebody or something else

clos·ing /klṓzing/ *adj.* FINAL forming or connected with the final part of an activity or period of time ■ *n.* 1. SOMETHING THAT CLOSES something that closes, e.g., a fastening on clothes 2. COMM, LAW TRANSFER OF PROPERTY OWNERSHIP a meeting among principals in a real estate transaction, during which legal papers related to the sale and purchase are signed and financial arrangements are made final and binding 3. LAW = **closing argument**

clos·ing ar·gu·ment, **clos·ing state·ment** *n.* an attorney's final summing up of a case before a judge or jury or both, during which he or she advocates the position of the state or of the individual client

clos·ing price *n.* the price of a share or bond on a stock exchange recorded at the official close of trading

clos·ing state·ment *n.* = **closing argument**

clos·ing time *n.* the time that an establishment such as a store, library, or bar closes and people have to leave

clos·trid·i·um /klo stríddee əm/ (*plural* **-ums** *or* **-a** /-dee ə/) *n.* a rod-shaped, usually motile, Gram-positive bacterium that can cause serious illnesses including botulism, tetanus, and gas gangrene. Genus: *Clostridium.* [Late 19thC. From modern Latin, genus name, literally "little spindle," coined from Greek *klōstēr* "spindle."] —**clos·trid·i·al** *adj.*

clo·sure /klṓzhər/ *n.* 1. PERMANENT END OF BUSINESS the permanent ending of a business or activity 2. BARRING OF ACCESS blocking the access to a place or blocking a route 3. SOMETHING THAT CLOSES AN OPENING a device for closing an opening, e.g., a zipper or a cap on a bottle, or the place where the opening closes 4. CLOSING SOMETHING an act or process of closing something, e.g., closing an opening or terminating an activity 5. POL = **cloture** 6. PSYCHOL SENSE OF FINALITY the sense of finality and coming to terms with an experience, felt or experienced over time 7. GEOL VERTICAL DISTANCE OF ROCK FORMATION the distance measured vertically between the top of a rock formation (**anticline**) and the lowest contour 8. POL = **cloture** 9. PHON CONTACT BETWEEN VOCAL ORGANS PRODUCING SOUND a contact made between vocal organs, e.g., the tongue and the soft palate, that produces a speech sound 10. MATH BEING A CLOSED SET IN MATHEMATICS the characteristic of a set in which the application of a given mathematical operation to any member of the set always results in another member of that set ■ *vt.* (**-sured, -sur·ing, -sures**) POL = **cloture**

clot /klot/ *n.* 1. STICKY LUMP a mass of thickened liquid, especially blood 2. ANY STICKY MASS a sticky mass of any substance, e.g., clay 3. CLUSTER a cluster of people or things ■ *vti.* (**clot·ted, clot·ting, clots**) THICKEN AND FORM LUMPS to thicken, or make a liquid thicken, and form lumps [Old English *clott.* Ultimately from an Indo-European word meaning "to form into a ball."] —**clot·tish** *adj.*

cloth /klawth/ *n.* 1. FABRIC fabric made by weaving, knitting, or felting thread or fibers 2. PIECE OF FABRIC a piece of fabric used for a particular purpose, e.g., a dishcloth (*often used in combination*) 3. CHR CLERGY the clergy, or the clothes worn by its members 4. SAILING SAIL a sail of a boat 5. THEATER PIECE OF FABRIC SCENERY a painted piece of fabric used as scenery [Old English *clāþ.* Ultimately from a prehistoric Germanic word (related to Danish *klæde* "cloth" and German *Kleid* "garment").]

cloth·bound /kláwth bòwnd/ *adj.* used to describe a book that has a cloth-covered hardback cover

cloth cap *n. U.K.* a man's unstiffened woolen cap with a visor, regarded as a symbol of the working class

clothe /klōth/ (**clothed** *or* **clad** *literary or archaic*, **cloth·ing, clothes**) *vt.* 1. DRESS SOMEBODY to put clothes on somebody (*often passive*) 2. PROVIDE CLOTHING FOR SOMEBODY to provide somebody with clothes 3. COVER SOMETHING to completely cover an area ○ *The hills were clothed in mist.* 4. COVER SOMETHING UP to obscure or conceal something as if wrapping something around it 5. ENDOW SOMEBODY OR SOMETHING to endow or invest somebody or something with some quality (*usually passive*) [Old English *clāþian*, from *clāþ* "cloth"(see CLOTH)]

clothes /klōthz, klōz/ *npl.* 1. THINGS WORN ON THE BODY garments that cover the body 2. WASHING all the garments, bed linen, and other articles that are washed when doing the laundry [Old English *clāþas*, the plural of *clāþ* "cloth" (see CLOTH)]

clothes·horse /klṓthz hàwrs, klṓz-/ *n.* 1. SOMEBODY WHO DRESSES FASHIONABLY somebody who insists on wearing the latest fashions or who wears conspicuously fashionable clothing (*informal*) 2. FRAME FOR CLOTHES a frame on which clothes are hung to dry indoors

clothes·line /klṓthz līn, klṓz-/ *n.* LINE FOR HANGING LAUNDRY a cord or wire on which clean laundry is hung to dry ■ *vt.* CATCH FOOTBALL PLAYER BY NECK in football, to knock down an opposing player by catching the player around the neck with an outstretched arm (*informal*)

clothes moth *n.* any of the small moths whose larvae feed on wool and fur. Family: Tineidae.

clothes peg *n. U.K.* = **clothespin**

clothes·pin /klṓthz pìn, klṓz pìn/ *n.* a small clip of plastic or wood, used to secure laundry to a clothesline

clothes press *n.* a piece of furniture for storing clothes, with hanging space and sometimes drawers or shelves

cloth·ier /klṓthyər/ *n.* somebody who sells clothes or cloth at retail [14thC. Alteration of obsolete *clother*, from CLOTH.]

cloth·ing /klṓthing/ *n.* 1. CLOTHES clothes collectively 2. COVERING a covering for something

Clo·tho /klṓ thō/ *n.* one of the three Fates of classical mythology. She holds the distaff and spins the thread of life. ◊ **Lachesis, Atropos** [From Greek *Klōthō*, literally "I spin"]

cloth of gold *n.* a luxury fabric of the Middle Ages woven from silk, or sometimes wool, intermixed with gold thread

clo·tri·ma·zole /klōtrímməzol/ *n.* an antifungal drug, used to treat yeast and fungal infections [Late 20thC]

clot·ted cream *n. U.K.* a thick cream made by removing the cream from the top of heated milk

clot·ting fac·tor *n.* any substance in the blood that is essential for blood to coagulate

clo·ture /klṓchər/ *n.* CLOSING OF DEBATE IN SENATE the process of closing a debate in the Senate by calling for a vote ■ *vt.* (**-tured, -tur·ing, -tures**) CLOSE DEBATE IN SENATE to close a debate in the Senate by calling for a vote [Late 19thC. From French *clôture*, literally "closing."]

cloud /klowd/ *n.* 1. MASS OF WATER IN SKY a visible mass of water or ice particles in the atmosphere from which rain and other forms of precipitation fall 2. MASS OF PARTICLES IN AIR a mass of particles in the air, e.g., dust or smoke ○ *a cloud of smoke* 3. FLYING MASS an airborne mass of insects or birds 4. DARKER PART a dark or dim area on something such as jewelry 5. SOMETHING WORRYING something that causes anxiety or fear ○ *Lack of financial independence was a cloud hanging over our future.* 6. GLOOMY CONDITION a condition of gloom or despondency ○ *a cloud of despair* ■ *v.* (**cloud·ed, cloud·ing, clouds**) 1. *vti.* BECOME CLOUDY to become covered with cloud or mist, or make something cloudy 2. *vt.* CONFUSE SOMETHING to make something more confusing ○ *cloud the issue* 3. *vt.* DETRACT FROM SOMETHING to make something appear less good ○ *It clouded their reputation.* 4. *vt.* IMPAIR SOMETHING to diminish a mental faculty 5. *vti.* LOOK TROUBLED to become or cause something to become troubled or gloomy ○ *His face clouded with disappointment.* 6. *vti.* BECOME OR MAKE SOMETHING OPAQUE to become or cause something to become opaque or murky ○ *The water was clouded with particles.* [Old English *clūd* "mass of rock, hill." The modern meaning (13thC) probably came from the supposed resemblance between cumulus clouds and lumps of rock.] ◇ **on cloud nine** extremely happy (*informal*) ◇ **under a cloud** in disgrace

cloud over, **cloud up** *vi.* 1. BECOME CLOUDY to become

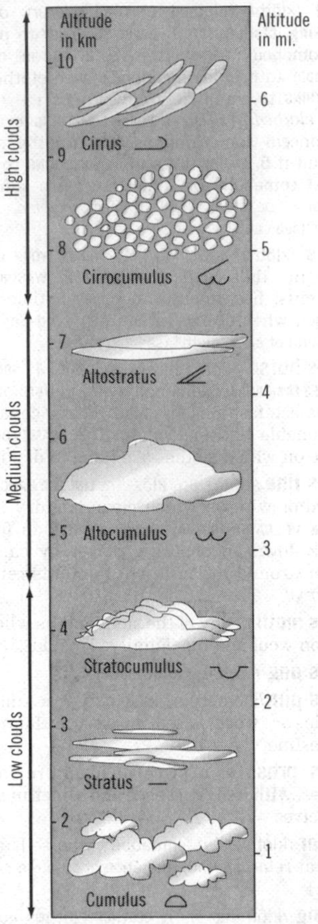

Cloud

covered with cloud or mist **2.** GROW TROUBLED to become troubled

cloud·ber·ry /klówd bèrree/ (*plural* **-ries**) *n.* a creeping perennial plant of the rose family found in Europe, North America, and Asia. It has white flowers and yellowish edible berries. Latin name: *Rubus chamaemorus.* [From CLOUD + BERRY, but the reason for the name is unknown]

cloud·burst /klówd bùrst/ *n.* a sudden heavy rain shower

cloud cham·ber *n.* a device in which the movement of high-energy particles is detected as they pass through a chamber of supersaturated vapor. Observable tracks are formed when droplets condense on the ionized molecules left by the high-energy particle.

cloud-cuck·oo-land *n.* an imaginary place in which problems do not exist [Translation of Greek *Nephelokokkygia*, an imaginary city in the air built by the birds in the comedy *Birds* by Aristophanes]

cloud·ed /klówdəd/ *adj.* **1.** TROUBLED appearing troubled **2.** OPAQUE opaque or murky

cloud·ed leop·ard *n.* a rare medium-sized cat that lives in forests from Nepal to Borneo and has short legs and a grayish to yellowish coat with darker irregular markings. It hunts by jumping from trees as well as by stalking. Latin name: *Neofelis nebulosa.*

cloud for·est *n.* a high-altitude tropical forest that is usually covered by cloud. Clinging plants (**epiphytes**), especially mosses and ferns, grow on the trees in profusion, encouraged by the moisture.

cloud·less /klówdləss/ *adj.* **1.** BRIGHT AND CLEAR bright and sunny without clouds ○ *a cloudless sky* **2.** WITHOUT PROBLEMS free of trouble —**cloud·less·ly** *adv.* —**cloud·less·ness** *n.*

cloud rack *n.* a group of clouds moving across the sky

cloud·scape /klówd skàyp/ *n.* a view or depiction of clouds

cloud seed·ing *n.* the technique or process of scattering substances such as silver iodide into clouds from an aircraft in order to precipitate rain

cloud·y /klówdee/ (**-i·er, -i·est**) *adj.* **1.** WITH CLOUDS covered with some clouds, usually a great deal **2.** OPAQUE opaque or murky ○ *a cloudy liquid* **3.** RESEMBLING CLOUDS having the appearance of clouds **4.** TROUBLED seeming troubled or gloomy **5.** NOT CLEAR obscure or difficult to understand —**cloud·i·ly** *adv.* —**cloud·i·ness** *n.*

clout /klowt/ *n.* **1.** POWER AND INFLUENCE the power to direct, shape, or otherwise influence things (*informal*) **2.** PUNCH a blow with the hand or fist **3.** ARCHERY TARGET in archery, a mark or target, epecially at a long distance ■ *vt.* (**clout·ed, clout·ing, clouts**) HIT SOMEBODY WITH HAND to hit somebody or something hard with the hand [Old English *clūt* "patch made of cloth, plate of metal." The reason behind the meaning "to hit," which dates from the 14thC, is unknown, and this group of senses may represent a different word.]

WORD KEY: REGIONAL NOTE

The use of ***clout*** to mean "influence," especially political influence originated in Chicago, and has spread throughout Illinois and the United States since the 1960s and the administration of Mayor Richard J. Daley.

clove[1] /klōv/ *n.* **1.** AROMATIC SPICE a strongly aromatic spice that is the dried flower bud of a tropical tree, used in both spicy and sweet dishes **2.** SPICE-YIELDING TROPICAL TREE an evergreen tree of the myrtle family, native to the Moluccas but grown in other tropical regions, with flower buds that are used dried as a spice. The buds, stalks, and leaves also yield aromatic oil of cloves. Latin name: *Syzgium aromaticum.* [12thC. From Old French *clou (de girofle)*, literally "nail (of the clove-tree)," from Latin *clavus* "nail" from the resemblance of a single clove-tree bud, with its stalk, to a nail.]

clove[2] *n.* one of the segments of a compound bulb ○ *a clove of garlic* [Old English *clufu*, from a prehistoric Germanic word that is also the ancestor of English *cleave* "to cut"]

clove[3] past tense of **cleave**

clove hitch *n.* a knot made of two half-hitches, used to attach a rope to a post or to another, thicker, rope [*Clove* is an old past participle of CLEAVE[1]]

clo·ven /klōv'n/ *v.* past participle of **cleave** ■ *adj.* SPLIT IN TWO split or divided into two parts (*archaic or literary*)

clo·ven hoof, cloven foot *n.* **1.** SPLIT HOOF OF ANIMAL the divided hoof of such animals as cattle, sheep, and pigs. Order: Artiodactyla. **2.** MARK OF DEVIL an indication of the presence of the Devil, traditionally represented in Christianity with a cloven hoof —**clo·ven-hoofed** *adj.*

clove oil *n.* = **oil of cloves**

clove pink *n.* = **carnation** [From CLOVE[1]; from the fact that the flower smells like the spice]

clo·ver /klōvər/ (*plural* **-ver** *or* **-vers**) *n.* **1.** PLANT WITH THREE-LOBED LEAVES a plant with three-lobed leaves and small rounded flower heads. Clover is often cultivated as a forage plant, for erosion control, and to provide nectar for bees. Genus: *Trifolium.* **2.** FORAGE PLANT any forage plant similar to clover. Genera: *Meliotus* and *Lespedeza* and *Medicago.* [Old English *clāfre*, ultimately from a prehistoric Germanic compound whose first part is also the ancestor of German *Klee* "clover"] ◇ **in clover** financially well off

clo·ver·leaf /klōvər leef/ (*plural* **clover·leaves** /-leevz/) *n.* **1.** THREE-LOBED LEAF the three-lobed leaf of a clover plant (*often used before a noun*) ○ *a cloverleaf motif* **2.** HIGHWAY INTERCHANGE an arrangement of highways resembling a four-leaf clover, with entrance and exit ramps enabling traffic to change direction rapidly without intersections

Clo·vis[1] /klōviss/ *adj.* used to describe a prehistoric North American culture characterized by leaf-shaped flint points that were used as parts of weapons to hunt game [Mid-20thC. Named for CLOVIS in New Mexico, where remains were first found.]

Clo·vis[2] /klōviss/ **1.** city in central California; an eastern suburb of Fresno. Population: 63,246 (1996). **2.** city in eastern New Mexico, near New Mexico's border with Texas, southeast of Santa Fe. Population: 34,663 (1996).

clown /klown/ *n.* **1.** ARTS COMIC CIRCUS PERFORMER a comic performer, usually in a circus, who does not speak and wears an outlandish costume and heavy makeup **2.** SOMEBODY FUNNY somebody who behaves comically **3.** PRANKSTER somebody who plays practical jokes **4.** ILL-MANNERED PERSON an ill-mannered or ineffectual person (*informal*) ■ *vi.* (**clowned, clown·ing, clowns**) **1.** BEHAVE COMICALLY to behave in a silly or funny way **2.** PLAY PRANKS to play practical jokes **3.** ARTS PERFORM AS CLOWN to perform as a circus clown [Mid-16thC. Origin uncertain. Originally "peasant."] —**clown·er·y** *n.*

clown a·nem·o·ne *n.* = **anemone fish**

clown fish *n.* = **anemone fish**

clown·ish /klównish/ *adj.* resembling or characteristic of a clown —**clown·ish·ly** *adv.* —**clown·ish·ness** *n.*

cloy /kloy/ (**cloyed, cloy·ing, cloys**) *vti.* to sicken somebody or become sickened with too much sweetness or sensation from something initially pleasing [Mid-16thC. Shortening of obsolete *accloy*, via French *encloer* "to drive in a nail" from medieval Latin *inclavare*, from, ultimately, Latin *clavus* "nail."] —**cloy·ing·ly** *adv.* —**cloy·ing·ness** *n.*

clo·za·pine /klōzə peen/ *n.* PHARM an antipsychotic drug used especially to alleviate symptoms of schizophrenia [Mid-20thC. Contraction of CHLORO- + BENZODIAZEPINE.]

cloze test /klōz-/ *n.* a test of comprehension and grammar in which a language student supplies appropriate missing words omitted from a text [*(Cloze)* shortening and alteration of CLOSURE]

CLU *abbr.* Chartered Life Underwriter

club /klub/ *n.* **1.** THICK STICK USED AS WEAPON a stout stick used as a weapon **2.** SPORTS STICK FOR HITTING BALL a stick or bat used in certain sports, especially golf, to hit a ball ○ *a golf club* **3.** ASSOCIATION FOR PARTICIPATING IN INTEREST an association of people with a common interest ○ *a gardening club* **4.** SPORTS ORGANIZATION FOR A SPORT an organization formed for the pursuit of a sport on an amateur or a professional basis ○ *a football club* **5.** PREMISES OF CLUB the premises where the activities of a club are pursued ○ *See you at the club tonight!* **6.** BUILDING PROVIDING FACILITIES TO MEMBERS a building that offers facilities and refreshments to members of the organization that owns or occupies it ○ *a gentlemen's club* **7.** COMM ORGANIZATION GIVING DISCOUNTS a plan or organization in which members receive price reductions in return for regular purchases ○ *a book club* **8.** SPORTS = **Indian club** **9.** NATIONS SHARING SOMETHING a group of nations or people who have a particular thing in common ○ *the nuclear club* **10.** = **nightclub** **11.** CARDS BLACK SYMBOL ON PLAYING CARD a black symbol shaped like a three-leaved clover on a playing card ■ *v.* (**clubbed, club·bing, clubs**) **1.** *vt.* HIT SOMEBODY WITH CLUB to hit a person or animal with a club ○ *The animal had been clubbed to death.* **2.** *vi.* FORM CLUB to join or form a club for social purposes or to pursue a common interest **3.** *vi.* NAUT DRIFT WITH ANCHOR LOWERED to drift with an anchor that drags to reduce the speed of the vessel [12thC. From Old Norse *klubba* "heavy stick," alteration of *klumpa*. With reference to cards, a translation of Spanish *basto* or Italian *baston*, from the stick on Spanish cards.] ◇ **join the club!** used to tell somebody that you are in the same position as he or she is

club together *vi.* **1.** CONTRIBUTE TO GROUP FUND to contribute money collectively for some purpose **2.** JOIN IN A GROUP to collaborate as a group

club·ba·ble /klúbbə b'l/, **club·a·ble** *adj.* sociable, and enjoying belonging to clubs —**club·ba·bil·i·ty** *n.*

clubbed /klubd/ *adj.* used to describe an appendage with a swelling at one end, like a club ○ *clubbed antennae*

club·ber /klúbbər/ *n.* **1.** MEMBER OF CLUB somebody who belongs to a club **2.** CLUB WIELDER somebody who uses a club

club·bing /klúbbing/ *n.* **1.** GOING TO NIGHTCLUBS the activity of going to nightclubs **2.** MED THICKENING OF FINGERS AND TOES a medical condition in which the tips of the fingers and toes become thickened, especially at the base of the nail. It may be associated with certain lung or heart diseases.

club·by /klúbee/ (**-bi·er, -bi·est**) *adj.* **1.** SOCIABLE enjoying the friendliness associated with clubs **2.** TYPICAL OF CLUB typical of a social club **3.** SNOBBISH socially exclusive and snobbish —**club·bi·ly** *adv.* —**club·bi·ness** *n.*

club chair *n.* a heavily upholstered chair with a low back and thick arms [From its use in gentlemen's clubs]

club class *n. U.K.* a class of travel on an aircraft between first class and economy class

club·face /klúb fàyss/ *n.* the surface of the head of a golf club with which the player strikes the ball

club·foot /klúb fo͝ot/ (*plural* **-feet**) *n.* **1. DEFORMITY OF FOOT** a congenital deformity of the foot, especially one in which the foot is twisted and turned inward **2. DEFORMED FOOT** a foot that is deformed by clubfoot —**club·foot·ed** *adj.*

club·hand *n.* **1. DEFORMITY OF HAND** a congenital deformity in which the hand is twisted and turned inward or outward **2. DEFORMED HAND** a hand deformed by clubhand —**club·handed** *adj.*

club·haul /klúb hàwl/ (**-hauled, -haul·ing, -hauls**) *vti.* to force a sailing vessel to change tack by dropping the lee-anchor and hauling in the anchor cable to swing the stern to windward

club·house /klúb hòws/ *n.* **1. BUILDING USED BY CLUB** the premises of a club, especially a sports club **2. LOCKER ROOM** a sports team's locker room

club·man /klúbmən/ (*plural* **-men** /-mən/) *n.* a man who belongs to one or more exclusive social clubs

club moss *n.* a nonflowering plant that typically has creeping stems with small overlapping leaves and reproduces by spores, often borne in club-shaped organs (**strobili**). Order: Lycopodiales.

club·room /klúb ro͞om, klúb ro͝om/ *n.* a room in which members of a club meet

club·root *n.* a disease affecting plants of the cabbage family, in which the roots become swollen and distorted. Latin name: *Plasmodiophora brassicae.*

clubs /klubs/ *n.* one of the four suits used in cards, with a black shape similar to a three-leaved clover as its symbol (*takes a singular or plural verb*)

club sand·wich *n.* a sandwich consisting of two layers of fillings between three slices of bread [Origin uncertain: perhaps from the variety of ingredients combined into one mass]

club so·da *n.* = **soda water** [Originally a proprietary name]

club steak *n.* = **Delmonico steak**

club·wom·an /klúb wo͝omən/ (*plural* **-en** /-wìmmin/) *n.* a woman who belongs to many clubs, especially social or civic organizations

cluck /kluk/ *interj.* **USED TO REPRESENT HEN'S CALL** used to imitate the short low clicking sound made by a hen ■ *v.* (**clucked, cluck·ing, clucks**) **1.** *vi.* **MAKE HEN'S SOUND** to make natural short low clicking sounds (*refers to hens*) **2.** *vti.* **EXPRESS SOMETHING WITH CLICKING SOUND** to show disapproval or concern by making short clicking sounds ■ *n.* **1. HEN'S CALL** a hen's short low clicking call **2. UNINTELLIGENT PERSON** a person who is considered mildly unintelligent (*informal*) [15thC. An imitation of the sound.]

clue /kloo/ *n.* **1. AID IN SOLVING MYSTERY** something that helps to solve a mystery or crime **2. AID IN SOLVING CROSSWORD** one of the numbered items of information used to solve a crossword puzzle **3. EXPLANATION FOR BEHAVIOR** an explanation or reason for something that is difficult to understand ■ *vt.* (**clued, clu·ing, clues**) **GIVE SOMEBODY INFORMATION** to supply somebody with useful information [Late 16thC. Alteration of CLEW. From the Greek myth of Theseus, who used a "clew" ("ball") of thread to escape from the Minotaur's labyrinth.] ◇ **not have a clue about something 1.** to know nothing about something (*informal*) **2.** to be very bad at something (*informal*)

clue in *vt.* to provide somebody with useful information ○ *She clued me in about office politics.*

clue·less /klo͞oləss/ *adj.* incompetent or ignorant (*informal*)

Cluj-Na·po·ca /klo͞ozh nə pṓkə/ industrial city and capital of Cluj County in Transylvania, northwestern Romania. Population: 326,017 (1994).

clum·ber span·iel /klúmbər/, **clum·ber** *n.* a thickset short-legged spaniel with a dense silky coat belonging to an English breed [Named for *Clumber* Park in Nottinghamshire, England]

clump[1] /klump/ *n.* **1. CLUSTER OF THINGS** a compact cluster or group of growing things ○ *a clump of moss* **2. MASS OF SIMILAR THINGS** an undifferentiated mass of something **3.** IMMUNOL **CLUSTER OF CELLS** a cluster of cells, e.g., bacteria or red blood cells, especially one formed during an immune response or when blood of incompatible blood groups is mixed ■ *v.* (**clumped, clump·ing, clumps**) **1.** *vti.* **COMBINE THINGS INTO MASS** to be gathered or gather things into a mass **2.** IMMUNOL **CAUSE MASSING OF CELLS** to cause cells, e.g., bacteria or red blood cells, to combine into a mass, especially as part of an immune response [13thC. Origin uncertain: probably from Low German *klump.*]

clump[2] /klump/, **clomp** *n.* **THUMPING SOUND** a heavy thumping sound ■ *vi.* (**clumped, clump·ing, clumps; clomped, clomp·ing, clomps**) **MOVE WITH CLUMP** to walk or move with a heavy thumping sound [Mid-17thC. An imitation of the sound.]

clump·y /klúmpee/ (**-i·er, -i·est**) *adj.* **1. LARGE AND UNGAINLY** large, heavy, and ungainly **2. CHARACTERIZED BY CLUMPS** composed of or growing in clumps —**clump·i·ly** *adv.* —**clump·i·ness** *n.*

clum·sy /klúmzee/ (**-si·er, -si·est**) *adj.* **1. MOVING AWKWARDLY** poorly coordinated physically **2. SAID OR DONE AWKWARDLY** said or done in an awkward or insensitive way ○ *a clumsy remark* [Late 16thC. Origin uncertain: perhaps formed from obsolete *clumse* "to be numb with cold," perhaps from Scandinavian.] —**clum·si·ly** *adv.* —**clum·si·ness** *n.*

clunk /klungk/ *n.* **1. DULL SOUND** a dull sound like that of a heavy piece of metal hitting something **2. BLOW OR SOUND IT MAKES** a blow, or the sound made by a blow (*informal*) **3. UNINTELLIGENT PERSON** somebody who is considered unintelligent or dull-witted (*informal*) ■ *vti.* (**clunked, clunk·ing, clunks**) **MAKE DULL SOUND** to make a dull heavy sound [Late 18thC. An imitation of the sound.]

clunk·er /klúngkər/ *n.* (*informal*) **1. DILAPIDATED MACHINE OR AUTOMOBILE** a dilapidated old motor vehicle or piece of machinery **2. SOMETHING WORTHLESS** something that is worthless, inferior, or unsuccessful

clunk·y /klúngkee/ (**-i·er, -i·est**) *adj.* awkwardly designed or made (*informal*)

Clu·ny lace /klo͞onee-/ *n.* a strong white lace made of silk, linen, or cotton [Late 19thC. Named for *Cluny*, a town in the Saône-et-Loire Department of France.]

clu·pe·id /klo͞opee id/ *n.* a soft-finned bony fish that has oily flesh, a narrow body, and a forked tail. Herrings, sardines, menhadens, and shad are clupeids. Family: Clupeidae. [Late 19thC. From modern Latin *Clupeidae*, family name, from, ultimately, Latin *clupea*, a small river fish.]

clus·ter /klústər/ *n.* **1. DENSE BUNCH** a small group of people or things that are closely packed together ○ *a cluster of diamonds* ○ *a little cluster of onlookers* **2.** ASTRON **STARS THAT APPEAR NEAR EACH OTHER** a group of galaxies or stars that are gravitationally interacting in space and appear to an observer on earth to be close together **3.** PHON **GROUP OF CONSONANTS** a group of consecutive consonants in the same syllable **4.** STATS **SUBSET IN STATISTICAL SAMPLE** a statistically significant subset within a population, used in sampling **5.** MUSIC **CHORD OF THREE OR MORE NOTES** a chord consisting of three or more notes spaced a semitone apart **6.** ARMY **DESIGN INDICATING MILITARY AWARDS** in the U.S. Army, a small metal design indicating that a medal has been awarded before to the same individual **7.** MIL **GROUP OF BOMBS** a group of bombs dropped together **8.** MIL **SET OF MINES** a basic unit of mines used in laying a minefield **9.** COMPUT **NETWORK OF SMALL COMPUTERS** a network of computers under the control of a larger, more powerful computer ■ *vti.* (**-tered, -ter·ing, -ters**) **FORM INTO CLUSTER** to gather something into or form a small group [Old English *clyster*, of uncertain origin: probably from the same prehistoric Germanic source as English *clot*] —**clus·tered** *adj.* —**clus·ter·y** *adj.*

clus·ter a·nal·y·sis *n.* a statistical technique that compares multiple characteristics of a population to determine whether individuals fall into different groups

clus·ter bomb *n.* a canister dropped from an aircraft to release a number of small bombs over a wide area

clus·ter con·trol·ler *n.* COMPUT a computer that sorts and files data transmitted by other smaller computers in a network

clus·ter head·ache *n.* a severe recurring headache associated with the release of histamine in the bloodstream, and marked by sudden sharp pain behind one eye or nostril

clutch[1] /kluch/ *v.* (**clutched, clutch·ing, clutch·es**) **1.** *vt.* **HOLD SOMETHING TIGHTLY** to grip something tightly **2.** *vi.* **MAKE GRABBING MOVEMENT** to try to grab hold of something **3.** *vi.* AUTOMOT **OPERATE CLUTCH** to engage the clutch of a motor vehicle ■ *n.* **1.** ENG **MECHANISM THAT CONNECTS SHAFTS** a device that enables two rotating shafts to be connected and disconnected smoothly, especially one in a motor vehicle that transmits power from the engine to the gearbox **2.** AUTOMOT **PEDAL ACTIVATING CLUTCH** the pedal that activates the clutch in a motor vehicle **3. CONTROLLING POWER** control and influence (*often used in the plural*) ○ *We were plainly in his clutches.* **4. CRUCIAL MOMENT** a crucial moment in a critical situation (*informal*) ○ *The clutch came in the seventh inning.* **5. GRIP ON SOMETHING** a tight grip on something ■ *adj.* **DEPENDABLE** dependable or accomplished at precisely the right moment [14thC. Variant of obsolete *clitch* "to bend, grasp," from Old English *clyccan* "to grasp," of uncertain origin.]

WORD KEY: SYNONYMS

See Synonyms at *catch*.

clutch[2] *n.* **1.** BIRDS **GROUP OF EGGS HATCHED TOGETHER** the number of eggs hatched by a bird or a pair of birds at one time **2.** BIRDS **GROUP OF CHICKENS HATCHED TOGETHER** all the chickens hatched together from one clutch of eggs **3. GROUP OF SIMILAR THINGS** a number of similar people or things (*informal*) [Early 18thC. Origin uncertain: probably a variant of dialectal *cletch*, from *cleck* "to hatch," from Old Norse *klekja.*]

clutch purse *n.* a purse that has no strap or handle and is carried under the arm or in the hand

clut·ter /klúttər/ *n.* **1. UNTIDY STUFF** an untidy collection of objects **2. DISORGANIZED MESS** a condition of disorderliness or overcrowding **3.** MIL **CONFUSING RADAR IMAGES** images on a radar screen that hinder observation ■ *vt.* (**-tered, -ter·ing, -ters**) **FILL SOMETHING WITH CLUTTER** to make a place untidy or overfilled with objects [Mid-16thC. Origin uncertain: probably a variant of obsolete *clotter*, literally "to clot repeatedly," from CLOT.]

Clydes·dale /klī́dz dàyl/ *n.* a strong heavy horse belonging to a breed originally developed in Scotland as draft animals [Late 18thC. Named for *Clydesdale*, the area of the river Clyde in Scotland where the horses originally were bred.]

clys·ter /klístər/ *n.* an enema (*archaic or literary*) [14thC. Directly or via French from Latin *clyster*, from Greek *klustēr* "syringe," from *kluzein* "to wash out" (source of English *cataclysm*).]

cm *symbol.* centimeter

Cm *symbol.* curium

c.m. *abbr.* **1.** PHYS center of mass **2.** court-martial

CMA, **C.M.A.** *abbr.* **1.** Canadian Medical Association **2.** certified medical assistant

CMC *abbr.* certified management consultant

Cmd. *abbr.* MIL Commander

cmdg. *abbr.* MIL commanding

Cmdr. *abbr.* MIL Commander

CMEA *abbr.* Council for Mutual Economic Assistance

cml. *abbr.* commercial

c'mon /kə món/ *contr.* come on (*nonstandard*)

CMOS /sée mòss/ *abbr.* COMPUT complementary metal oxide semi-conductor

CMSGT *abbr.* Chief Master Sergeant

CMV *abbr.* cytomegalovirus

cni·dar·i·an /ni dáiree ən/ *n.* **1.** MARINE BIOL **MARINE ANIMAL WITH TENTACLES** any marine invertebrate animal that has tentacles surrounding the mouth. Sea anemones, corals, and jellyfish are cnidarians. Phylum: Cnidaria. **2.** ZOOL = **coelenterate** [Early 20thC. From modern Latin *Cnidaria*, phylum name, from Greek *knidē* "nettle," from *knizein* "to cause to itch."] —**cni·dar·i·an** *adj.*

CNN *abbr.* Cable News Network

CNS *abbr.* central nervous system

CN Tower *n.* a tall tower in downtown Toronto,

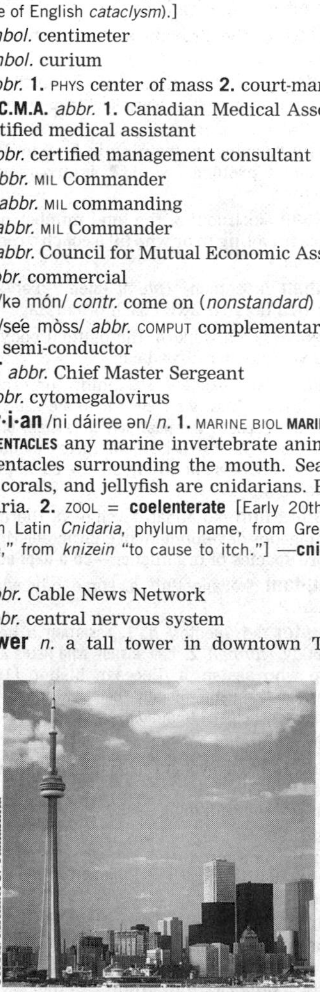
Corbis/Michael S. Yamashita

CN Tower, Toronto, Canada

Canada. It is more than 1800 ft./553 m high and was the world's tallest free-standing structure when it was built in 1976.

Co *symbol.* cobalt

CO[1] *abbr.* 1. Colombia (*international vehicle registration*) 2. Colorado

CO[2], **C.O.** *abbr.* 1. Commanding Officer 2. conscientious objector

Co. *abbr.* 1. Colorado 2. Company (*used in names of businesses*) 3. County (*used in place names*)

c.o.[1] *abbr.* 1. cash order 2. care of 3. ACCT carried over

c.o.[2] *prefix.* 1. together, jointly ○ *coauthor* 2. associate, alternate ○ *copilot* 3. to the same degree ○ *coeternal* 4. complement of an angle ○ *cotangent*

c/o *abbr.* 1. care of 2. ACCT carried over

CoA *abbr.* coenzyme A

coach /kōch/ *n.* 1. TRANSP **HORSE-DRAWN CARRIAGE** a large enclosed horse-drawn carriage 2. TRANSP **INEXPENSIVE TRAVEL CATEGORY** an inexpensive class of passenger accommodations on a bus, train, or aircraft 3. SPORTS **SOMEBODY WHO TRAINS SPORTS PLAYERS** somebody who trains sports players and athletes 4. RAIL **RAILROAD CAR** a railroad car 5. TRANSP **LONG-DISTANCE BUS** a bus designed for long-distance travel or sightseeing 6. CARS **CHEAP SMALL AUTOMOBILE** any inexpensive, usually two-doored automobile 7. ARTS **SOMEBODY WHO TRAINS PERFORMER** somebody who trains people in acting or singing 8. EDUC **TUTOR** somebody who instructs an individual in a specified subject ■ *v.* (**coached, coach·ing, coach·es**) 1. *vt.* SPORTS **TRAIN ATHLETE** to train somebody in a sport 2. *vt.* ARTS **TRAIN PERFORMER** to train somebody in acting or singing 3. *vt.* EDUC **TRAIN STUDENT** to give somebody private tuition in a particular subject or toward examinations 4. *vti.* **TRANSPORT PEOPLE IN COACH** to carry passengers in a horse-drawn coach, or travel by coach [Mid-16thC. Via French *coche* from German *Kutsche, Kotsche*, from Hungarian *kocsi (szekér)*, literally "(wagon) of Kocs," named for *Kocs*, a village in Hungary where carriages, carts, and suchlike were made.] —**coach·a·ble** *adj.*

coach bolt *n. U.K.* = **carriage bolt**

coach box *n.* the driver's seat on a horse-drawn carriage

coach dog *n.* a Dalmatian dog (*archaic*) [From the former practice of the dogs being kept to run in attendance on a carriage]

coach·ing /kṓching/ *n.* training in how to deal with emotional problems and interpersonal relationships

coach·load /kṓch lṑd/ *n.* the total number of people who are traveling in or who fill a coach ○ *coachloads of tourists*

coach·man /kṓchmən/ (*plural* **-men** /-mən/) *n.* the driver of a horse-drawn coach or carriage

coach·work /kṓch wùrk/ *n.* the painted bodywork of a road vehicle or railroad car

co·ac·tion /kō ákshən/ *n.* joint or reciprocal action [Early 17thC. Via French from the Latin stem *co-action-*, from *coact-*, the past participle stem of *coagere*, literally "to drive together," from *agere* "to drive."] —**co·ac·tive** *adj.* —**co·ac·tive·ly** *adv.* —**co·ac·tiv·i·ty** /kō ak tívvətee/ *n.*

co·ad·ap·ta·tion /kṑ addap táysh'n/ *n.* the mutually advantageous development of characteristics in two or more species of organisms —**co·a·dapt·ed** *adj.*

co·ad·ju·tant /kō ájjoot'nt/ *n.* somebody who helps another

co·ad·ju·tor /kō ájjootər/ *n.* 1. **ASSISTANT** a helper for somebody (*formal*) 2. CHR **BISHOP WHO HELPS ANOTHER** a bishop who assists a diocesan bishop [15thC. Via French from late Latin, literally "helper with," formed from Latin *adjutor* "helper," from *adjuvare* "to help."]

co·ag·u·la plural of **coagulum**

co·ag·u·lant /kō ággyələnt/ *n.* a substance that causes or assists coagulation of the blood, e.g., a natural clotting factor or a drug —**co·ag·u·lant** *adj.*

co·ag·u·lase /kō ággyə làyss, -làyz/ *n.* an enzyme, especially one produced by some bacteria, that causes coagulation of the blood [Early 20thC. Coined from COAGULATE + -ASE.]

co·ag·u·late /kō ággyə làyt/ *vti.* (**-lat·ed, -lat·ing, -lates**) 1. **MAKE OR BECOME SEMISOLID** to thicken, or cause liquid to thicken, into a soft semisolid mass 2. CHEM **GROUP TOGETHER IN LARGER MASS** to group together as a mass, or cause the particles in a colloid to group together, as, e.g., egg white does when heated ■ *n.* CHEM **COAGULATED MASS** a soft semisolid mass produced by coagulation of a colloid [15thC. From Latin *coagulat-*, the past participle stem of *coagulare* "to coagulate," from, ultimately, *coagere* "to drive together."] —**co·ag·u·la·bil·i·ty** /kō àggyələ bíllətee/ *n.* —**co·ag·u·la·ble** /-ággyələb'l/ *adj.* —**co·ag·u·la·tor** /-làytər/ *n.*

co·ag·u·la·tion /kō àggyə láysh'n/ *n.* 1. **BECOMING SEMISOLID** the thickening of a fluid into a soft semisolid mass 2. **CLOT** a clot or coagulum 3. CHEM **CHEMICAL FORMATION OF MASS** grouping together of the particles of a colloid to form a larger mass

co·ag·u·la·tion fac·tor *n.* = **clotting factor**

co·ag·u·lum /kō ággyələm/ (*plural* **-la** /-lə/) *n.* a clot or coagulated mass of something, especially blood [Mid-16thC. From Latin, formed from *coagere* (see COAGULATE).]

coal /kōl/ *n.* 1. **BLACK ROCK USED AS FUEL** a hard black or dark brown sedimentary rock formed by the decomposition of plant material, widely used as a fuel 2. **PIECE OF COAL** a piece of coal 3. **SMALL PIECE OF BURNABLE MATERIAL** any small piece of combustible material 4. = **charcoal** ■ *v.* (**coaled, coal·ing, coals**) 1. *vt.* **CONVERT SOMETHING INTO CHARCOAL** to burn something combustible and convert it into charcoal 2. *vti.* **PROVIDE OR TAKE ON COAL** to supply something with coal or take on coal [Old English *col.* Ultimately from an Indo-European word meaning "glowing ember." The modern meaning "black fossil fuel" dates from the 13thC.] —**coal·y** *adj.*

coal black *adj.* 1. **VERY BLACK** completely black 2. **VERY DARK** very dark black in color

coal·er /kṓlər/ *n.* a ship or train that transports coal

co·a·lesce /kṑ ə léss/ (**-lesced, -lesc·ing, -lesc·es**) *vti.* to merge or cause things to merge into a single body or group [Mid-16thC. From Latin *coalescere*, literally "to grow up together," from *alescere* "to grow up," from *alere* "to nourish" (source of English *adolescent* and *alumnus*).] —**co·a·les·cence** *n.* —**co·a·les·cent** *adj.*

coal·face /kṓl fàyss/ *n.* the newly exposed rock surface in a mine, from which coal is being cut

coal·field /kṓl feeld/ *n.* an area with coal deposits

coal·fish /kṓl fish/ (*plural* **coal·fish** *or* **coal·fish·es**) *n.* a black-backed or dark-colored edible fish, e.g., sablefish or pollack

coal gas *n.* 1. **METHANE AND HYDROGEN MIXTURE** a flammable mixture of gases obtained by distilling coal, consisting mainly of methane and hydrogen. It is sometimes used as a fuel. 2. **GAS BURNED OFF COAL** the gas produced when coal is burned

coal·i·fi·ca·tion /kṑləfi káysh'n/ *n.* the process in which coal is formed by the action of pressure and heat on buried plant material. The moisture content of the plants is progressively removed and the material remaining is solidified.

co·a·li·tion /kṑ ə lísh'n/ *n.* 1. **POLITICAL ALLIANCE** a temporary union between two or more groups, especially political parties 2. **MERGING INTO SINGLE ENTITY** the merging of things into one body or mass [Early 17thC. From the medieval Latin stem *coalition-*, from Latin *coalit-*, the past participle stem of *coalescere* "to grow together" (see COALESCE).] —**co·a·li·tion·ist** *n.*

coal meas·ures *npl.* a series of strata containing economically workable coal deposits, e.g., the upper Carboniferous rocks of northwestern Europe

coal·mine /kṓl mīn/ *n.* a mine where coal is dug from the ground —**coal·min·er** *n.*

coalmin·er's lung *n.* = **anthracosis** [From the fact that the disease frequently affects coalminers]

coal pit *n.* = **coal mine**

Coal·port /kṓl pàwrt/ *n.* a variety of white, strongly patterned bone china made in Coalport, near Shrewsbury, England, in the 19th century

Coal·sack /kṓl sak/ *n.* 1. **INTERSTELLAR CLOUD SEEN IN SOUTHERN HEMISPHERE** a dark cloud of interstellar dust (**nebula**) that is part of the Crux constellation and is visible in the southern hemisphere in front of the Milky Way 2. **INTERSTELLAR CLOUD SEEN IN NORTHERN HEMISPHERE** a dark interstellar cloud (**nebula**) visible in the northern hemisphere near the constellation Cygnus

coal scut·tle *n.* a metal container for holding and pouring coal for a domestic fire

coal tar *n.* a thick black liquid obtained as a by-product in the production of coke. It yields chemicals that are used in making dyes, drugs, and soap.

coam·ing /kṓming/ *n.* a raised edging around the cockpit or hatchway of a boat for keeping out water [Early 17thC. Origin unknown.]

co·an·chor /kō ángkər, kṓ àngkər/ *n.* **JOINT BROADCASTER OF NEWS** either of two broadcasters who jointly present a television program ■ *vti.* (**co·an·chored, co·an·chor·ing, co·an·chors**) **BE CO-ANCHOR** to be co-anchor of a television program, especially a news program

co·apt /kō ápt/ (**-apt·ed, -apt·ing, -apts**) *v.* to join or bring displaced parts close together in their correct alignment, e.g., the edges of a wound or broken bone [Late 16thC. From late Latin *coaptare*, literally "to fit together," from, ultimately, Latin *aptus* "fastened, suitable."] —**co·ap·ta·tion** /kō ap táysh'n/ *n.*

co·arc·tate /kō áark tàyt/ *adj.* 1. MED **CONSTRICTED** used to describe any vessel or canal in the body that has become constricted, narrowed, or pressed together 2. ZOOL **IN HARD SHELL** used to describe a pupa that is enclosed in a horny oval case ■ *vi.* (**-tat·ed, -tat·ing, -tates**) **CONSTRICT** to become narrow, constricted, or pressed together (*refers to blood vessels or other body passages*) [15thC. From Latin *coar(c)tatus*, the past participle of *coar(c)tare*, literally "to press close together," from *artare* "to press close," from *artus* "confined, narrow."] —**co·arc·ta·tion** /kṑ aark táysh'n/ *n.*

coarse /kawrs/ (**coars·er, coars·est**) *adj.* 1. **ROUGH** harsh or rough to the touch 2. **WITH THICK GRAINS OR STRANDS** consisting of large grains or thick strands 3. **INDELICATE OR TASTELESS** lacking taste or refinement 4. **VULGAR** vulgar or obscene 5. **UNREFINED** not refined ○ *coarse metal* 6. **INFERIOR** of inferior quality [14thC. Originally *corse, course*, meaning "ordinary" (used of cloth); of uncertain origin: perhaps from COURSE (as in "of course" or "matter of course").] —**coarse·ly** *adv.* —**coarse·ness** *n.*

coarse-grained *adj.* 1. **WITH ROUGH GRAIN** having a large or rough grain 2. **VULGAR** coarse or vulgar in speech or manner

coars·en /káwrs'n/ (**-ened, -en·ing, -ens**) *vti.* to become or make something coarse or coarser

coast /kōst/ *n.* 1. **LAND NEXT TO SEA** land beside the sea ○ *sailed along the coast* 2. **SLOPE FOR SLEDDING** a slope suitable for sledding 3. **SLEDDING DOWN SLOPE** the action of sliding down a slope on a sled 4. **FRONTIER** a frontier (*archaic*) ■ *v.* (**coast·ed, coast·ing, coasts**) 1. *vti.* **MOVE BY MOMENTUM** to move forward by momentum, without applying power or cause something to move in this way 2. *vi.* **SUCCEED EFFORTLESSLY** to progress with very little effort 3. *vti.* NAUT **TRAVEL ALONG SHORE** to sail along a shore [14thC. Via Old French *coste* from Latin *costa* "rib, side" (source of English *accost* and *cutlet*).]

Coast *n.* the North American coast bordering the Pacific Ocean

coast·al /kṓst'l/ *adj.* along, near, or relating to a coast —**coast·al·ly** *adv.*

coast·er /kṓstər/ *n.* 1. **MAT FOR GLASS** a mat placed under a glass in order to protect a surface 2. = **roller coaster** 3. **SOMETHING THAT COASTS** something that coasts of its own momentum 4. SHIPPING **SHIP TRADING ALONG COAST** a ship that sails along a coast to trade 5. **TRAY FOR PASSING BOTTLE** a small tray, sometimes on wheels, for passing a bottle or decanter round a table

coast·er brake *n.* a bicycle brake operated by back-pedaling

coast guard *n.* 1. **SERVICE DEALING WITH COASTAL MATTERS** an emergency service that rescues people in difficulties at sea and acts against smuggling 2. **MEMBER OF COAST GUARD** a member of the coast guard

Coast Guard *n.* a U.S. military service that enforces maritime laws, acts in marine emergencies, and maintains navigational aids, in wartime supplementing the navy

coast·land /kṓst lànd/ *n.* the land along a coast (*often used in the plural*)

coast·line /kṓst līn/ *n.* the outline of a coast as viewed from the sea or on a map

Coast Moun·tains Canadian range following the Pacific Coast from Vancouver into Yukon Territory. The highest peak is Mount Waddington, 13,104 ft./3,994 m. Length: 745 mi./1,200 km.

Coast Rang·es long narrow mountain ranges on the west coast of North America, along the Pacific coast from southern Alaska to northwestern Mexico. Highest peak: 19,551 ft./5,959 m.

Coast Sa·lish *npl.* a Salish-speaking indigenous people who inhabit the northwestern Pacific coast from southwestern British Columbia to southwestern Washington state

coast-to-coast *adj.* from one coast to another of a continent, or a nation that is an island ○ *The debate had coast-to-coast coverage on the news media.*

coast·wise /kṓst wīz/ *adv.* ALONG COAST along the coast ■ *adj.* FOLLOWING THE COAST following the direction of the coast

coat /kōt/ *n.* **1.** WARM OUTER GARMENT an item of clothing with long sleeves that is usually at least knee-length and is worn outdoors over other clothes **2.** *U.S., NZ* SUIT JACKET a jacket worn as part of a suit, with a skirt or trousers (*dated*) **3.** COVERING ON ANIMAL the fur, wool, or hair that covers an animal **4.** THIN COVERING any thin layer that covers something ■ *vt.* (**coat·ed, coat·ing, coats**) **1.** INDUST COVER SURFACE to cover a surface with a thin layer of something (*often passive*) **2.** PROVIDE SOMEBODY WITH COAT to provide somebody with a coat (*usually used in the passive*) [14thC. From Old French *cote,* from prehistoric Germanic.] —**coat·er** *n.*

coat check, coat·room *n.* a room in a public building, such as a theater, club, or restaurant, where customers can leave coats, umbrellas, and other belongings during their stay

coat·dress *n.* a tailored dress that is shaped like a coat and fastened in front from the neck to the hem, usually with buttons

coat·ed /kṓtəd/ *adj.* **1.** WITH OUTER LAYER covered with a layer of something **2.** PAPER PREPARED FOR WRITING OR PRINTING ON treated with a fine layer of a mineral to make paper suitable for writing or printing on **3.** TEXTILES TREATED AGAINST MOISTURE with a treated surface or plastic coating that resists moisture ○ *coated fabric*

coa·tee /kō tée/ *n.* a military cutaway coat with shortened coat-tails

Coates·ville /kṓts vìl/ city in southeastern Pennsylvania, west of Philadelphia and east of Lancaster. Population: 10,827 (1996).

coat hang·er *n.* a curved frame with a hook, used to drape and hang clothes

co·a·ti /kō àatee/ (*plural* **-tis** *or* **-ti**), **co·a·ti·mun·di** (*plural* **-dis** *or* **-di**) *n.* a South or Central American omnivorous mammal related to the raccoon, that has a narrow flexible snout and a striped tail. Genus: *Nasua.* [Early 17thC. Via Portuguese from Tupi *kua'ti.*]

coat·ing /kṓting/ *n.* **1.** THIN LAYER a thin layer that covers something ○ *a coating of dust* **2.** CLOTH FOR COATS cloth used in making coats

Coat of arms

coat of arms *n.* **1.** DESIGN ON SHIELD a design on a shield that signifies a particular family, university, or city **2.** GARMENT WITH COAT OF ARMS a garment that is decorated with a coat of arms [Translation of French *cote d'armes*]

coat of mail *n.* a protective garment of armor worn in medieval times, consisting of linked metal rings

coat·rack /kṓt ràk/ *n.* a stand or rack fitted with hooks, used for hanging clothes on

coat·room /kṓt ro͞om, kṓt ro͝om/ *n.* = **coat check**

coat stand *n. U.K.* = **coat tree**

coat·tail /kṓt tàyl/ *n.* the part below the waist at the back of a coat, especially one of the parts when it is divided into two (*usually used in the plural*) ◇ **on somebody's coattails** helped by somebody else rather than succeeding alone

coat tree *n.* a stand with hooks, used to hang coats on

co·au·thor /kō áwthər/ *n.* JOINT AUTHOR somebody who writes something jointly with one or more other authors ■ *vt.* (**-thored, -thor·ing, -thors**) WRITE SOMETHING JOINTLY to write something jointly with one or more other authors

coax /kōks/ (**coaxed, coax·ing, coax·es**) *v.* **1.** *vti.* PERSUADE GENTLY to persuade somebody gently to do something **2.** *vt.* OBTAIN SOMETHING BY GENTLE PERSUASION to get something from somebody by gentle persuasion **3.** *vt.* GENTLY MAKE SOMETHING WORK to manipulate something patiently until it moves or works ○ *I finally coaxed the sticky drawers open.* [Late 16thC. Alteration of *cokes,* from obsolete *cokes* "simpleton," of uncertain origin. "To persuade gently" developed via "to treat as a simpleton or pet" and "to fondle."] —**coax·ing·ly** /kṓksinglee/ *adv.*

co·ax ca·ble /kō aks-/ *n.* = **coaxial cable** [*Coax* shortening of COAXIAL]

co·ax·i·al /kō áksee əl/ *adj.* **1.** SHARING AXIS having a common axis **2.** ELEC OF COAXIAL CABLE belonging or relating to a coaxial cable —**co·ax·i·al·ly** *adv.*

co·ax·i·al ca·ble *n.* a cable consisting of an inner core and outer flexible braided tube, both of conductive material separated by an insulator, used to transmit high-frequency signals at high speeds

cob[1] /kob/ *n.* **1.** CORE OF CORN EAR the hard core to which individual kernels of corn are attached **2.** ZOOL MALE SWAN a male swan **3.** RIDING SHORT-LEGGED RIDING HORSE a sturdy short-legged riding horse [15thC. Partly ultimately from a prehistoric Germanic word meaning "round, lumpy object," and partly a variant of dialect *cop* "head, top."]

cob[2] /kob/ *n.* a crude often irregularly shaped gold or silver coin that circulated in Spanish colonies in the Americas between the 16th and 18th centuries [From Spanish *cabo de barra,* literally "end of bar" from the crudely cut silver or gold coin-sized planchets that were sliced from the cast bar]

co·bal·a·min /kə báwləmin/ *n.* = **vitamin** B_{12} [Mid-20thC. Blend of COBALT and VITAMIN.]

co·balt /kṓ bàwlt/ *n.* a tough brittle silvery-white metallic chemical element found in iron, nickel, and copper ores. It is used to color ceramics and in alloys. Symbol **Co** [Late 17thC. From German *Kobalt,* variant of *Kobold* "harmful goblin," from the belief of miners that the cobalt ore was harmful to neighboring silver ores.]

co·balt 60 *n.* a naturally radioactive isotope of cobalt that has a mass number of 60, spontaneously emits strong gamma radiation, and is used in radiotherapy and in industry

co·balt bloom *n.* = **erythrite** [Translation of German *Kobaltblüte*]

co·balt blue *adj.* of a deep blue color with a tinge of green —**co·balt blue** *n.*

co·balt bomb *n.* a device containing cobalt 60, used in radiotherapy

co·balt·ic /kō báwltik/ *adj.* relating to or containing cobalt, especially with a valence of 3

co·balt·ite /kō báwl tīt/ *n.* a rare silvery-white or grayish mineral consisting of cobalt sulfide and arsenide. It is used in ceramics.

co·balt·ous /kō báwltəss/ *adj.* relating to or containing cobalt, especially with a valence of 2

Cobb /kob/, **Irvin Shrewsbury** (1876–1944) U.S. humorist. He was known for his unpretentious Judge Priest stories.

Cobb, Ty (1886–1961) U.S. baseball player. Considered one of the game's most outstanding players of all time, he retired from the Detroit Tigers (1905–28) with a career batting average of .367. Full name **Tyrus Raymond Cobb.** Nickname **Georgia Peach**

cob·ble[1] /kóbb'l/ *n.* **1.** TRANSP = **cobblestone 2.** GEOL ROCK FRAGMENT a naturally rounded rock fragment between 64 and 256 mm in diameter ■ *vt.* (**cob·bled, cob·bling, cob·bles**) TRANSP PAVE ROAD WITH COBBLESTONES to pave a road with cobblestones [Early 17thC. Shortening of earlier *cobelstone,* from assumed *cobel* (perhaps literally "little lump," formed from COB[1] (+ STONE).]

cobble together *vt.* to assemble or make something roughly and quickly

cob·ble[2] /kóbb'l/ (**cob·bled, cob·bling, cob·bling, cob·bles**) *vt.* to make, repair, or patch footwear [15thC. Back-formation from COBBLER.]

cob·bled /kóbb'ld/ *adj.* paved with cobblestones

cob·bler[1] /kóbblər/ *n.* somebody who makes, repairs, or patches footwear [13thC. Origin unknown.]

cob·bler[2] /kóbblər/ *n.* **1.** DESSERT WITH CRUST a baked fruit dessert with a soft thick crust **2.** ICED ALCOHOLIC DRINK an iced drink made of wine, rum or whiskey, and sugar, often garnished with fruit and mint [Early 19thC. Origin uncertain: probably representing uses of COBBLER.]

cob·bler's wax *n.* a resin used to wax thread

cob·ble·stone /kóbb'l stōn/ *n.* a small rounded stone used for paving streets [15thC. See COBBLE[1].] —**cob·ble·stoned** *adj.*

co·bel·lig·er·ent /kō bə líjjərənt/ *n.* a country that or individual who is an ally in a fight or war

co·bi·a /kóbee ə/ (*plural* **co·bi·a** *or* **co·bi·as**) *n.* a large bony dark-striped fish found in tropical and subtropical seas that is related to the perch and sea bass. Latin name: *Rachycentron canadum.* [Mid-19thC. Origin unknown.]

CO·BOL /kṓ bawl/, **Co·bol** *n.* a high-level computer programming language, widely adopted for corporate business applications [Mid-20thC. Acronym formed from *common business-oriented language.*]

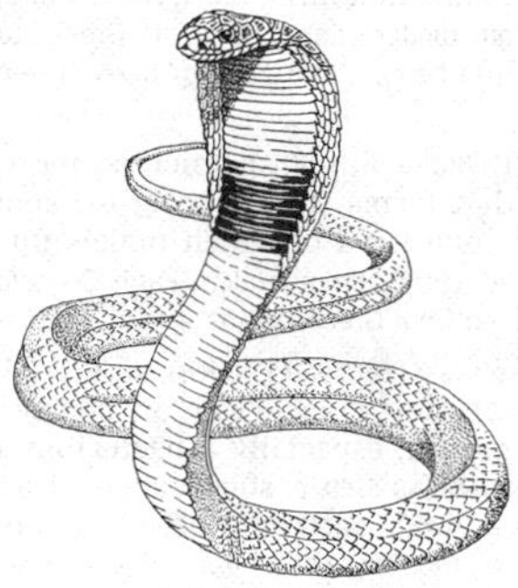

Cobra

co·bra /kṓbrə/ *n.* a venomous snake found in tropical Asia and Africa that, when excited, rears up and spreads the skin behind its head to form a hood. Genus: *Naja* and *Ophiophagus.* [Early 19thC. Shortening of *cobra de capello,* literally "snake with a hood"; *cobra* ultimately from Latin *cubra* "snake."]

co·burg /kṓ bùrg/ *n.* TEXTILES a thin fabric made of wool and cotton or silk, twilled on one surface and used as a dress fabric or lining cloth [Early 19thC. Named for Prince Albert of Saxe-*Coburg* (1819–61), consort of Queen Victoria of England.]

cob·web /kób wèb/ *n.* **1.** DUSTY SPIDER'S WEB a fine thread or web of fine threads spun by spiders, especially when covered with dust **2.** SOMETHING RESEMBLING COBWEB something that resembles a cobweb in being flimsy and insubstantial or in acting as a trap or snare ■ **cob·webs** *npl.* SLUGGISH MENTAL STATE mental sluggishness and tiredness ○ *I need to blow the cobwebs away.* [14thC. Cob from obsolete *coppe* "spider," ultimately from Old English *ātorcoppe,* probably literally "poison-head," from the idea that spiders are venomous.] —**cob·webbed** *adj.* —**cob·web·by** *adj.*

co·ca /kṓkə/ (*plural* **-ca**) *n.* **1.** PLANTS SHRUB YIELDING COCAINE a shrub, native to the Andes, that has yellow flowers and whose leaves yield cocaine and other alkaloids. Latin name: *Erythroxylum coca.* **2.** DRIED LEAVES OF COCA the dried leaves of coca, chewed as a stimulant or processed for cocaine and other alkaloids [Late 16thC. Via Spanish from Aymara *kuka* or Quechua *koka.*]

Co·ca-Co·la /kṑkə kṓlə/ *tdmk.* a trademark for a cola-flavored soft drink

co·caine /kō káyn, kṓ kàyn/ *n.* an addictive narcotic drug obtained from the leaves of the coca plant, taken illegally as a stimulant. It is now only used medicinally as a surface anesthetic. Formula: $C_{17}H_{21}NO_4$. [Mid-19thC. Coined from COCA + -INE.]

co·cain·ism /kō káy nìzzəm, kṓ kay-/ *n.* an addiction to or overuse of cocaine, resulting in physical or mental impairment (*dated*)

co·cain·ize /kō káy nīz, kṓ kay-/ (**-ized, -iz·ing, -iz·es**) *vt.* to anesthetize somebody using cocaine as a surface (**topical**) application in paste form in the nose. Cocaine is no longer used in this way, having been succeeded by synthetic analogues. —**co·cain·i·za·tion** /kō kàyni záysh'n, kō kayni záysh'n/ *n.*

co·car·cin·o·gen /kō kaárs'nəjèn, kō kaar sínnəjən/ *n.* a substance that does not cause cancer on its own but can increase the effect of carcinogenic factors or substances when acting together with them — **co·car·cin·o·gen·ic** /kō kaárs'nə jénnik, kō kaar sínnə jénnik/ *adj.*

coc·ci plural of **coccus**

coc·cid /kóksid/ *n.* any insect that folds its wings over its back when not flying. Scale insects and mealybugs are coccids. Family: Coccidae. [Late 19thC. Formed from modern Latin *Coccus*, genus name (see COCCUS).] —**coc·cid** *adj.*

coc·cid·i·a plural of **coccidium**

coc·cid·i·oi·do·my·co·sis /kok sìddə óydō mī kṓssiss/ *n.* a respiratory disease of humans and domestic animals in North America, marked by flu-like symptoms, that is caused by inhalation of spores from a fungus. Latin name: *Coccidioides immitis.*

coc·cid·i·o·sis /kok sìddi ṓsis/ *n.* a disease of domestic animals and birds, and occasionally humans, caused by coccidia in the intestines, and causing diarrhea

coc·cid·i·um /kok síddee əm/ (*plural* **-a** /-síddee ə/) *n.* a parasitic sporozoan that can cause disease in the gut of humans and animals. Order: Coccidia. [Mid-19thC. From modern Latin, from the Greek stem *kokkid-*, literally "little berry," from *kokkos* "berry."] —**coc·cid·i·al** *adj.*

coc·co·lith /kókə lìth/ *n.* a microscopic calcareous platelet that forms the covering for some marine plankton, one form of which makes up chalk deposits [Mid-19thC. From modern Latin *Coccolithus*, genus name, coined from Greek *kokkos* "grain" + *lithos* "stone."]

coc·cus /kókəss/ (*plural* **-ci** /kók sī, kó kī/) *n.* **1.** MICROBIOL **TYPE OF BACTERIUM** a spherical or nearly spherical microorganism, especially a bacterium **2.** BOT **PART OF FRUIT CONTAINING SEED** a subdivision of a fruit that contains a single seed and resembles a berry [Early 19thC. Via modern Latin from Greek *kokkos* "grain, berry."] —**coc·cal** *adj.* —**coc·coid** *adj.* —**coc·cous** *adj.*

-coccus *suffix.* a spherical microorganism ○ *pneumococcus* [From COCCUS]

coc·cyx /kók siks/ (*plural* **-cy·ges** /-sí jeez/ *or* **-cy·xes**) *n.* a small triangular bone at the base of the spinal column [Late 16thC. Via Latin from Greek *kokkux*, originally "cuckoo"; from its resemblance to a cuckoo's beak.] — **coc·cyg·e·al** /kok síjjee əl/ *adj.*

co·chan·nel /kō chánn'l, kō chànn'l/ *adj.* relating to a transmission occupying the same frequency band as another

Co·chin /kṓ chìn/ major port and town in Kerala State, southwestern India. Population: 564,000 (1991).

coch·i·neal /kòchə néel, kóchə néel/ *n.* a red dye obtained from the crushed dried bodies of female cochineal insects, used to color food and drinks and to dye fabrics [Late 16thC. Via French *cochenille* or Spanish *cochinilla* from Latin *coccinus* "scarlet," from, ultimately, Greek *kokkos* "berry," because the dried body of the insect was believed to be a berry.]

coch·i·neal in·sect *n.* a small red scale insect found in Mexico and the West Indies that feeds on cacti. The dye cochineal is derived from the crushed bodies of cochineal insects. Latin name: *Coccus cacti.*

Co·chise /kò chéess, -chéez/ (1815?–74) U.S. Native American leader. The chief of the Chiricahua Apache, he led fighting against European settlers in Arizona Territory (1862–71).

coch·le·a /kóklee ə, kṓklee ə/ (*plural* **-ae** /-ee, -ī/ *or* **-as**) *n.* a spiral structure in the inner ear that looks like a snail shell and contains over 10,000 tiny hair cells that move in response to sound waves. These movements stimulate nerve cells to send messages to the brain, which the brain interprets as sound. [Mid-16thC. Via Latin *coc(h)lea* "snail shell, screw" from Greek *kokhlias* "snail."] —**coch·le·ar** /kóklee ər, kṓklee ər/ *adj.*

coch·le·ar im·plant *n.* a device implanted under the skin that picks up sounds and converts them to impulses transmitted to electrodes placed in the cochlea, restoring some hearing to people with a hearing impairment

coch·le·ate /kóklee ət, kóklee àyt/ *adj.* shaped in a spiral like the shell of a snail

Coch·ran /kókrən/, **Jacqueline** (1910–80) U.S. aviator. She was the first woman pilot to break the sound barrier (1953).

cock[1] /kok/ *n.* **1. ADULT MALE CHICKEN** an adult male of a domestic fowl, normally only kept for breeding **2. MALE BIRD** the adult male of a bird **3.** *U.K.* **MALE ANIMAL** an adult male salmon, crab, or lobster **4. WEATHERVANE SHAPED LIKE ROOSTER** a weathervane shaped like a rooster **5.** ARMS **PART OF GUN** the hammer of a gun that, when released by the action of the trigger, makes the gun fire **6.** ARMS **RAISED POSITION OF HAMMER OF GUN** the raised position of the hammer of a gun when it is ready to fire **7. OFFENSIVE TERM** an offensive term for a man's penis (*slang taboo*) **8. STOPCOCK** a stopcock **9. TILTED POSITION** the tilt or angle in the position of somebody's head or hat, often suggesting that he or she is in a good mood ■ *vt.* (**cocked, cock·ing, cocks**) **1.** ARMS **PREPARE GUN FOR FIRING** to pull back the hammer of a gun so that it is ready to be fired when the trigger is pulled **2. TURN EARS OR EYES** to turn one or both ears or eyes in a particular direction to listen for or look out for somebody or something **3. TILT BACK OR ANGLE SOMETHING** to tilt or raise something, often as a way of expressing that you are full of confidence or in good humor **4. RAISE LIMB IN AIR** to lift or raise a part of the body **5. SET SOMETHING TO OPERATE** to set a device or mechanism so that it will release something, e.g., a camera shutter [Pre-12thC. Origin uncertain, probably from medieval Latin *coccus*, ultimately an imitation of a rooster's crow.]

cock[2] /kok/ (**cocked, cock·ing, cocks**) *n.* straw, hay, or grain piled in the shape of a cone (*dated*) [14thC. From Scandinavian.]

cock·ade /ko káyd/ *n.* a rosette, ribbon, or other ornament worn, usually on a hat, as an identifying badge or as part of a livery [Mid-17thC. From French *bonnet à la coquarde*, literally "bonnet worn proudly," from obsolete *coquard* "proud, saucy," from *coq* "cock."] — **cock·ad·ed** *adj.*

cock-a-doo·dle-doo *n., interj.* used as a description or imitation of the sound a rooster makes when it crows —**cock-a-doo·dle-doo** *vi.*

cock-a-hoop *adj.* **1. ELATED** extremely happy or excited about something **2. VERY PROUD OF SOMETHING** boastful about something that has been achieved [From *set the cock on the hoop* "to celebrate," of uncertain origin: perhaps referring to a wine-barrel tap, or a rooster eating *hoop* "grain"]

cock-a-leek·ie *n.* a Scottish soup made from a whole chicken and leeks and sometimes containing prunes

cock·a·ma·mie /kòkə máymee/, **cock·a·ma·my** *adj.* (*informal*) **1. TRIVIAL** having very little importance or meaning **2. RIDICULOUS** having little or nothing to do with reality ○ *cockamamie excuse* [Mid-20thC. Origin uncertain: probably an alteration of DECALCOMANIA.]

cock-and-bull sto·ry (*plural* **cock-and-bull sto·ries**), **cock-and-bull** *n.* a ridiculous and scarcely credible story that somebody tries to convince people is true, usually either to impress them or as an excuse for something [Origin uncertain: perhaps from the popularity of fables with animal characters. The theory involving stories exchanged by travelers near the Bull Inn and Cock Inn is folk etymology.]

cock·a·poo /kókə pòo/ (*plural* **-poos**) *n.* a dog that is a cross between a cocker spaniel and a small poodle [Late 20thC. Blend.]

cock·a·tiel /kòkə téel/, **cock·a·teel** *n.* a small gray Australian parrot with a white patch on its wing and a prominent crest that is yellow in males. Latin name: *Nymphicus hollandicus.* [Late 19thC. From Dutch *kaktielje*, of uncertain origin: probably a diminutive of *kaketoe* (see COCKATOO).]

cock·a·too /kókə tòo/ (*plural* **-toos**) *n.* a parrot with a prominent crest, found in Australia, New Guinea, the East Indies, and the Philippines. Many have white or light-colored plumage. Genera: *Cacatua* and *Callocephalon* and *Calyptorhynchus.* [Mid-17thC. Via Dutch *kaketoe* from Malay *kakatua*; influenced by COCK.]

cock·a·trice /kókətriss/ *n.* a mythological serpent that was supposed to have hatched from a cock's egg, and to be able to kill with its stare [14thC. Via Old French *cocatris* from medieval Latin *calcatrix* "tracker," from Latin *calcare* "to track," from *calx* "heel" (see CAULK).]

cock·boat /kók bṑt/ *n.* a small rowboat, especially one that belongs to a larger ship. Cockboats are often used to ferry stores and provisions between ship and shore. [15thC. *Cock* via Old French *coque* from, ultimately, Latin *codex* "block of wood" (source of English *code*).]

Cockatoo

cock·chaf·er /kók chàyfər/ *n.* INSECTS a large European beetle with larvae that destroy trees and other plants. Family: Scarabaeidae.

cock·crow /kók krō/ *n.* the time of day when the sun begins to show above the horizon (*archaic or literary*)

cocked hat *n.* a two- or three-cornered hat with a wide turned up brim, popular in the 18th century. A cocked hat was especially worn as part of a uniform or livery. ◇ **knock somebody** *or* **something into a cocked hat 1.** *U.K.* to be much better than somebody or something else (*informal*) **2.** to ruin or damage something utterly

cock·er[1] /kókər/ *n.* **1.** = **cocker spaniel 2. TRAINER OF GAMECOCKS** somebody who raises and trains roosters for fighting **3. SOMEBODY INVOLVED IN COCKFIGHTING** somebody who is involved in cockfighting either as a breeder or as a trainer of cocks, or as a regular spectator

cock·er[2] /kókər/ (**-ered, -er·ing, -ers**) *vt.* to treat somebody in an over-protective or indulgent way [15thC. Origin unknown.]

cock·er·el /kókərəl/ *n.* a young male chicken, usually one that is less than a year old [15thC. Literally "small rooster," formed from COCK.]

cock·er span·iel *n.* ZOOL a small dog with long floppy ears and a soft wavy coat, belonging to a breed of spaniels originally bred for flushing out game [So called because the breed was developed for rousing woodcock for shooting]

cock·eye /kók ī/ *n.* an eye that is turned inward or outward from the nose, making parallel vision impossible (*informal offensive*)

cock·eyed /kók īd/ *adj.* **1. FOOLISH** not sensible or properly thought out (*informal*) **2. NOT ALIGNED** positioned at an awkward or crooked angle **3. VERY DRUNK** so drunk that it is impossible to see straight (*informal*) ○ *Boy, did I get cockeyed last night!* **4. AFFECTED BY A SQUINT** having one eye that turns inward or outward from the nose (*informal offensive*)

cock feath·er *n.* the feather on an arrow positioned at right angles to the notch into which the bow string fits [*Cock* from COCK in the sense "to stick up"]

cock·fight /kók fìt/ *n.* an organized fight between two roosters, each of which is equipped with sharp metal spurs

cock·fight·ing /kók fìting/ *n.* the practice of setting two cocks to fight each other in front of spectators who often make bets on the outcome. The cocks are equipped with metal spurs designed to inflict the maximum harm on the opposing bird, and the sport is illegal in many countries.

cock·horse /kók hàwrs/ *n.* a rocking horse or a stick with an imitation horse's head on one end

cock·le[1] /kók'l/ *n.* **1. MOLLUSK WITH HEART-SHAPED SHELL** a small mollusk that has a rounded or heart-shaped ridged shell in two parts. Family: Cardiidae. **2.** = **cockleshell** *n.* 1 **3.** = **cockleshell** *n.* 2 **4. WRINKLE** a crease or pucker in a piece of material such as paper or cloth ■ *vti.* (**-led, -ling, -les**) **BECOME OR MAKE WRINKLED** to become wrinkled or puckered or make something such as a piece of material wrinkled or puckered [14thC. Via French *coquille* "shell" from, ultimately, Greek *kogkhē* "conch" (source of English *conch*).] ◇ **warm the cockles of somebody's heart** to give somebody a feeling of well-being or sentimental contentment

cock·le[2] /kók'l/ *n.* a weedy plant that belongs to the pink family, especially the corn cockle, which grows in cornfields [Pre-12thC. Origin uncertain: perhaps from assumed medieval Latin *cocculus*, literally "small berry," from Latin *coccus* (see COCOON).]

cock·le·boat /kók'l bōt/ *n.* NAUT = **cockboat** [Early 17thC. *Cockle* from COCKLE[1].]

cock·le·bur /kók'l bùr/ *n.* a coarse annual plant with prickly seed husks that attach easily to people's clothes or animals' fur. Genus: *Xanthium.* [Mid-19thC. *Cockle* from COCKLE[2].]

cock·le·shell /kók'l shèl/ *n.* **1.** SHELL OF COCKLE a shell of a marine cockle, or any similar mollusk **2.** NAUT SMALL BOAT a small, light shallow boat

cock·ney /kóknee/ (*plural* **-neys**) *n.* **1. cock·ney, Cock·ney** SOMEBODY FROM LONDON'S EAST END somebody born in London, traditionally within a two-mile radius of the bells of St. Mary-le-Bow church in London's East End. Cockneys are considered to be the "true" Londoners. **2. cock·ney, Cock·ney** LONDON DIALECT the accent or dialect of native Londoners from the East End [14thC. Middle English *coken* generative plural of *cok* (see COCK[1]) + obsolete *ey* "egg," from Old English _*æg.* Originally "small or misshapen egg" (supposedly laid by a rooster), "pampered child"; hence "town-dweller" (originally pejorative).] —**cock·ney·ism** *n.*

cock-of-the-rock (*plural* **cocks-of-the-rock**) *n.* a tropical South American bird, the males of which have bright orange or red plumage and crests that extend over the bill. Genus: *Rupicola.* [From the bird's practice of nesting on rocks]

cock·pit /kók pìt/ *n.* **1.** AEROSP PILOT'S PART OF AIRCRAFT the compartment in an aircraft or spacecraft where the pilot and other crew members sit **2.** MOTOR SPORTS AREA FOR DRIVER IN RACING CAR a space for the driver in a racing car **3.** SPORTS PLACE FOR COCKFIGHTING an enclosed place where cockfights are held **4.** NAUT ENCLOSURE FOR WHEEL OR TILLER an enclosure at the stern of a ship for the wheel or tiller **5.** MIL FREQUENT BATTLEGROUND a place where many battles have been fought [Late 16thC. Originally "pit for cockfighting," later "place for treating wounded below decks in warship" (from the association of blood and noise), later "well at yacht stern where helm is."]

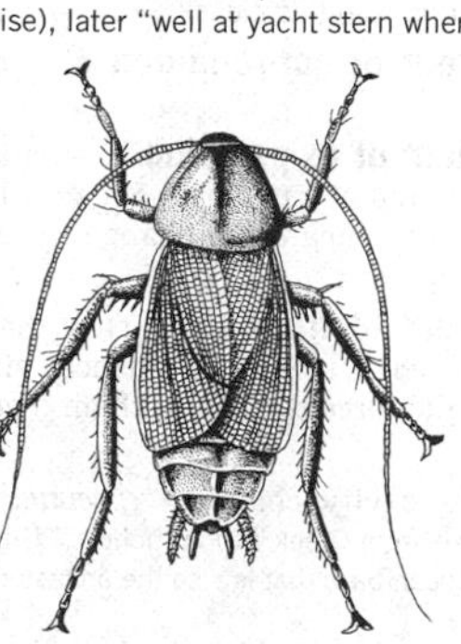

Cockroach

cock·roach /kók rōch/ *n.* a nocturnal insect with a flat oval body, long antennae, and chewing mouthparts, some species of which are household pests. Order: Blattodea. [Early 17thC. From Spanish *cucaracha*, changed by assimilation with COCK and ROACH.]

cocks·comb /kóks kōm/ *n.* **1.** CREST OF ROOSTER the red fleshy crest that grows on the top of a rooster's head **2.** PLANT WITH CREST OF RED FLOWERS a tropical plant with a broad crest or plume of orange or red flowers resembling a cockscomb, often grown as a houseplant. Latin name: *Celosia cristata.* **3.** = **coxcomb** *n.* 1

cock·shot /kók shòt/ *n.* = **cockshy** *n.*

cock·shy /kók shì/ (*plural* **-shies**) *n. U.K.* a throw at a cockshy (*dated*) [Early 19thC. So called because originally a cock was the target and prize; contestants had to catch the cock or break a pot containing the bird.]

cock·spur /kók spur/ *n.* a spur on the foot of some male birds

cock·suck·er /kók sùkər/ *n.* (*taboo offensive*) **1.** OFFENSIVE TERM a highly offensive term of abuse for a man **2.** OFFENSIVE TERM somebody who performs fellatio

cock·sure /kok shoor, kók shoor/ *adj.* **1.** CERTAIN ABOUT SOMETHING absolutely sure of being correct about something or succeeding in some effort **2.** OVERCONFIDENT arrogantly confident and self-assured [Early 16thC. From *cock* as a euphemism for "God." Originally "absolutely sure, safe"; later associated with the bird, regarded as swaggering in front of the hens.] —**cock·sure·ly** *adv.* —**cock·sure·ness** *n.*

cock·tail /kók tàyl/ *n.* **1.** MIXED BEVERAGE a drink that is made up of a mixture of different beverages, e.g., fruit juice or soda and usually alcohol, and served iced or chilled **2.** LIGHT SNACK a light appetizer before a main meal, consisting usually of seafood or fruit served with a sauce (*usually used in combination*) ○ *a shrimp cocktail* **3.** MIXTURE OF THINGS a mixture of different things or elements combined together ○ *a malicious cocktail of lies and gossip* **4.** MED COMBINATION TREATMENT a combination of two or more drugs or therapeutic agents given as a single treatment ■ **cock·tails** *npl.* GATHERING TO CONSUME ALCOHOLIC BEVERAGES a gathering where alcoholic beverages are consumed, sometimes with light snacks, often taking place early in the evening before another planned event ■ *adj.* SMALL extra small, designed to be eaten as a snack with the fingers or on a cocktail stick ○ *cocktail sausage* [Early 17thC. Originally "having a tail like a cock," later "horse with docked tail (that sticks up)" (used for carthorses), hence "non-thoroughbred racehorse," hence "mixture."]

cock·tail lounge *n.* a bar, sometimes a room in a hotel or restaurant, where cocktails and other drinks are served

cock·tail party *n.* a party where cocktails and light snacks are served, often taking place early in the evening before another social event

cock·tail stick *n.* a small pointed wooden or plastic stick on which olives or cherries are placed in cocktails, or small items of food, e.g., sausages or cubes of cheese, are served

cock·tail ta·ble *n.* = **coffee table**

cock-teas·er, cock-tease *n.* an offensive term used to describe somebody who makes sexual advances towards a man (*slang offensive*)

cock·y /kókee/ (**-i·er, -i·est**) *adj.* confident and sure of yourself to the point of being arrogant (*informal*) [Mid-16thC. From the image of a rooster strutting about, apparently showing off to his hens.] —**cock·i·ly** *adv.* —**cock·i·ness** *n.*

co·co /kṓkō/ (*plural* **-cos**) *n.* = **coconut** [Mid-16thC. From Spanish and Portuguese, literally "grinning face" (because of the appearance of the base of the shell).]

co·coa /kṓkō/ *n.* **1.** CHOCOLATE BASE an unsweetened brown powder made from roasted and ground cacao beans, used in making chocolate, in cooking, and as the base for a hot drink **2.** HOT DRINK MADE WITH COCOA POWDER a hot drink made with milk or water, cocoa powder, and sugar **3.** LIGHT TO MEDIUM BROWN COLOR a light to medium brown color [Early 18thC. Alteration of CACAO.]

Co·coa Beach /kōkō-/ city in eastern Florida, southeast of Orlando and just south of Cape Canaveral. Population: 12,635 (1996).

co·coa bean *n.* the bean-shaped seed of the cacao tree, used to make cocoa powder and chocolate

co·coa but·ter *n.* a thick oily solid obtained from cocoa beans and used in making chocolate, cosmetics, and suntan oils

co·coa-pay·ol *n. Carib* somebody of Spanish, usually Venezuelan, ancestry (*informal*) [Early 19thC. *Payol* from Spanish *español* "Spanish."]

co·co-de-mer /kōkō də máir/ (*plural* **co·cos-de-mer**) *n.* **1.** LARGE FAN PALM a fan palm, now found only in nature reserves in the Seychelles, that produces the largest seed in the world. Latin name: *Lodoicea maldivica.* **2.** COCO-DE-MER NUT the edible two-lobed fruit of the coco-de-mer palm [Early 19thC. From French, literally "coco from the sea" (because it was first known from nuts found floating in the sea).]

co·co·nut /kṓkə nùt/ (*plural* **-nut** *or* **-nuts**), **co·co** (*plural* **-cos**) *n.* **1.** HARD-SHELLED FRUIT CONTAINING SWEET JUICE the fruit of the coconut palm, consisting of a hard fibrous husk surrounding a single-seeded nut with firm white flesh and a hollow core containing sweet-tasting liquid (**coconut milk**). The flesh is eaten raw or is dried to make copra, and the husk fibers are used for matting and compost. **2.** WHITE FLESH OF COCONUT FRUIT the sweet white flesh of the coconut fruit, used widely in cooking and confectionery in the form of small dried flakes **3.** TREES = **coconut palm**

co·co·nut but·ter *n.* solidified coconut oil used in the manufacture of soap and candles

Coconut

co·co·nut crab *n.* a large hermit crab that lives on islands in the Pacific and Indian oceans. It burrows in the ground, can climb trees, and feeds on coconuts and other vegetation as well as carrion. Latin name: *Birgus latro.*

co·co·nut mat·ting *n.* coarse floor matting made from the fibres that grow on coconut shells

co·co·nut milk *n.* the sweet watery juice that is contained within a coconut and is used in drinks and cooking

co·co·nut oil *n.* a thick sweet-smelling oil extracted from the flesh of the coconut and used widely in food and cosmetics

co·co·nut palm *n.* a tall palm tree widely cultivated in tropical countries for its large fruit and from which beverages, oil, fiber, utensils, and thatch are produced. Latin name: *Cocos nucifera.*

co·coon /kə kóon/ *n.* **1.** ZOOL SHEATH FOR CATERPILLAR the silky covering with which a caterpillar or other insect larva encloses itself during its transition to an adult state **2.** ZOOL EGG COVERING a protective covering on the eggs of spiders, leeches, and other invertebrates **3.** ZOOL SHEATH FOR SPIDER'S PREY a sheath in which spiders wrap their prey **4.** TECH COVERING THAT PROTECTS SOMETHING FROM WATER a cover or protective spray used to seal machinery and make it waterproof, especially military equipment for storage or transport **5.** SOMETHING SIMILAR TO COCOON something that resembles a cocoon in the way that it provides protection or a sense of safety ■ *v.* (**-cooned, -coon·ing, -coons**) **1.** *vt.* WRAP SOMETHING OR SOMEBODY SAFELY to cover or envelop something or somebody for warmth or protection ○ *cocooned in a pile of bedclothes* **2.** *vt.* KEEP SAFE FROM SOMETHING to protect somebody from unpleasantness or danger **3.** *vi.* WITHDRAW INTO PRIVACY to withdraw into a state of personal privacy in order to escape stressful everyday life (*informal*) [Late 17thC. Via French *cocon* from, ultimately, Latin *coccus* "berry," from Greek *kokkos* (source of English *cochineal*).] —**co·cooned** *adj.*

co·co plum *n.* a tropical American and African tree, cultivated for its edible fruit that is usually eaten preserved and, in West Africa, for an oil obtained from its seeds. Latin name: *Chrysobalanus icaco.*

co·cos wood *n.* = **cocuswood** *n.* 2

co·cotte /kō kót, kə-/ *n.* **1.** PROSTITUTE a promiscuous woman or prostitute (*literary*) **2.** SMALL HEATPROOF DISH FOR COOKING FOOD a heatproof dish in which food can be cooked and served in small portions [Early 20thC. Via French *cocasse* from Latin *cucuma* "cooking pot."]

co·coun·sel·ing *n.* a form of counseling in which participants receive training as counselors and work alternately as counselor and client

Coc·teau /kok tṓ, kawk tṓ/, **Jean** (1889–1963) French

Jean Cocteau

writer and movie director. His works include the novel *Les enfants terribles* (1929) and the film *La belle et la bête* (1945).

co·cur·ric·u·lar /kō kə ríkyələr/ *adj.* something that is not part of the official curriculum but that complements it

co·cus·wood /kṓkəss wŏŏd/ (*plural* **-wood**) *n.* **1.** WEST INDIAN HARDWOOD TREE a West Indian tree that yields a hard wood. Latin name: *Brya ebenus.* **2.** WOOD OF COCUSWOOD TREE the hard wood of the cocuswood tree, which turns black with age and is used to make musical instruments, backs of brushes, and inlays [Mid-17thC. *Cocus* of unknown origin.]

Co·cy·tus /kō kítəss, -sítəss/ *n.* one of the tributaries of the river Styx that, in Greek mythology, flowed through the underworld [From Greek *Kōkutos,* literally "wailing"]

cod[1] /kod/ (*plural* **cod** *or* **cods**) *n.* a saltwater food fish that has three dorsal fins and slender feelers like whiskers (**barbels**) on its jaw and lives close to the seabed. Family: Gadidae. [14thC. Origin unknown.]

cod[2] /kod/ *n.* (*archaic*) **1.** BAG a bag **2.** SAC CONTAINING TESTES a sac of skin that contains the testes of male mammals [Old English *cod(d),* from a prehistoric Germanic word that is also the ancestor of English *cuttlefish*]

COD, C.O.D. *abbr.* **1.** cash on delivery **2.** collect on delivery

cod., Cod. *abbr.* codex

co·da /kṓdə/ *n.* **1.** FINAL SECTION OF MUSICAL PIECE in some pieces of music, a final section that adds dramatic energy to the work as a whole, usually through intensified rhythmic activity **2.** EXTRA TEXT an additional section at the end of a text, e.g., a literary work or speech, that is not necessary to its structure but gives additional information [Mid-18thC. Via Italian from Latin *cauda* "tail" (source of English *cue* and *queue*).]

cod·dle /kódd'l/ (**-dled, -dling, -dles**) *vt.* **1.** BE OVERPROTECTIVE OF SOMEBODY to treat somebody in an overprotective and indulgent way **2.** COOK EGG GENTLY to cook an egg in water just below the boiling point [Late 16thC. Origin uncertain: perhaps a variant of CAUDLE.] —**cod·dler** *n.*

code /kōd/ *n.* **1.** SYSTEM OF LETTERS, NUMBERS, OR SYMBOLS a system of letters, numbers, or symbols into which normal language is converted to allow information to be communicated secretly, briefly, or electronically **2.** INFORMATION SYSTEM OF LETTERS OR NUMBERS a system of letters or numbers that gives information about something, e.g., postal or telephone areas **3.** COMPUT COMPUTER INFORMATION a system of symbols, numbers, or signals that conveys information to a computer **4.** LAW, PUBLIC ADMIN RULES AND REGULATIONS a system of accepted laws and regulations that govern procedure or behavior in particular circumstances or within a particular profession **5.** WAY OF BEHAVING a set of unwritten rules concerning acceptable standards of behavior **6.** MED PATIENT WITH NO HEARTBEAT OR BREATHING a patient whose heart has stopped beating or who has stopped breathing (*slang*) ■ *v.* (**cod·ed, cod·ing, codes**) **1.** *vt.* PUT SOMETHING IN CODE to put a message or text into code **2.** GENETICS PROVIDE GENETIC INFORMATION to act as or provide the genetic information that enables a polypeptide, RNA molecule, or one of their constituent groups to be produced (*refers to codons or genes*) **3.** *vi.* MED UNDERGO HEART OR BREATHING STOPPAGE to go into a state in which the heart has stopped beating or the lungs have ceased to function (*slang*) **4.** *vt.* COMPUT WRITE COMPUTER PROGRAM to write a computer program that provides instructions to a computer [Late 16thC. From, ultimately, Latin *codex* "block of wood, block split into waxed tablets for writing on, book," hence "set of statutes."]

code blue, Code blue *n.* a medical emergency, e.g., in a hospital, when a patient's heart stops beating or lungs stop functioning

code·book /kṓd bŏŏk/ *n.* a book containing a key to a code or codes

co·deine /kṓ deen/ *n.* a white crystalline drug derived from opium, but milder in action, used as a painkiller and to relieve coughing [Mid-19thC. Coined from Greek *kōdeia* "poppy head" + -INE.]

code name *n.* a name used to disguise the identity or nature of somebody or something, e.g. a military operation —**code-name** *vt.*

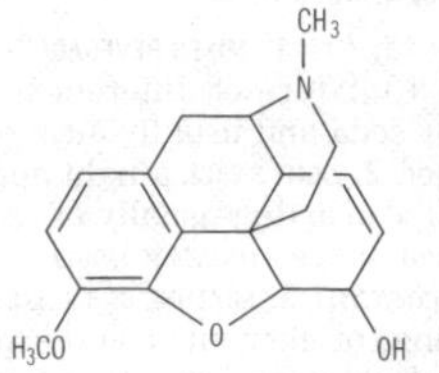

Codeine

Code Na·po·lé·on *n.* the codification of French laws drawn up under Napoleon between 1804 and 1810 and forming the basis of modern French civil law

code of con·duct *n.* a set of unwritten rules according to which people in a particular group, class, or situation are supposed to behave

code of prac·tice *n.* a set of rules according to which people of a particular profession are expected to behave

co·de·pen·den·cy /-ənsee/, **co·de·pen·dence** /kō di péndənss/ *n.* **1.** MUTUAL NEED the dependence of two people, groups, or organisms on each other, especially when this reinforces mutually harmful behavior patterns **2.** COUNSELLING RELATIONSHIP OF MUTUAL NEED a situation in which one person feels a need to be needed by another person, e.g., the partner of an alcoholic or a parent of a drug-addicted child —**co·de·pen·dent** *n., adj.*

cod·er /kṓdər/ *n.* **1.** CONVERTER OF SOMETHING INTO CODE somebody or something that converts texts, messages, or symbols into code **2.** DEVICE TRANSFORMING SIGNALS INTO CODE an electronic device that transforms signals into coded form

co·de·ter·mi·na·tion /kō di turmi náysh'n/ *n.* cooperation between management and employees in making decisions

code word *n.* **1.** SECRET WORD IDENTIFYING SOMEBODY OR SOMETHING a secret word or phrase that is used to identify a person, operation, or organization whose true identity is to be kept hidden, or is used as a password in a secret operation **2.** EUPHEMISM a word or phrase used to describe something in a euphemistic way ○ *corporate reengineering is often just a code word for layoffs*

co·dex /kṓ dèks/ (*plural* **-di·ces** /-seez/) *n.* a collection of ancient manuscript texts, especially of the Scriptures, in book form [Late 16thC. From Latin (see CODE).]

Co·dex Ju·ris Ca·non·i·ci /kō deks jooriss kə nónni sì/ *n.* the official code of canon law of the Roman Catholic Church since 1918, when it replaced the Corpus Juris Canonici. It was revised in 1983. [From ecclesiastical Latin, "Code of Canon Law"]

cod·fish /kód fish/ (*plural* **-fish** *or* **-fish·es**) *n.* = **cod**[1] *n.*

codg·er /kójjər/ *n.* a man, especially a man of advanced years who is seen as slightly eccentric or amusing (*informal*) [Mid-18thC. Origin uncertain: perhaps a variant of CADGER.]

co·di·ces plural of **codex**

cod·i·cil /kóddəssil/ *n.* **1.** EXTRA PART OF WILL an additional part of a will that either modifies it or revokes part of it **2.** APPENDIX TO TEXT an appendix or supplement to a text (*formal*) [15thC. From Latin *codicillus,* diminutive of *codex* (see CODE).] —**cod·i·cil·la·ry** /kòddə sílləree/ *adj.*

cod·i·col·o·gy /kòddə kólləjee/ *n.* the study of manuscripts [Mid 20thC. From French *codicologie,* literally "science of books," from Latin *codic-,* stem of *codex* (see CODE).] —**cod·i·co·log·i·cal** /kòddəkə lójjik'l/ *adj.*

cod·i·fi·ca·tion /kòddifi káysh'n/ *n.* the act of arranging laws, rules, or codes of behavior into organized systems, or any arrangement of these

cod·i·fy /kóddi fì/ (**-fied, -fy·ing, -fies**) *vt.* to arrange things, especially laws, rules, or principles, into an organized system or code —**cod·i·fi·er** *n.*

cod·ling /kóddling/ (*plural* **-lings** *or* **-ling**) *n.* a small or young codfish

cod·ling moth, cod·lin moth *n.* a small stout-bodied moth whose larvae feed on apples, pears, and other fruit. Latin name: *Laspeyresia pomonella.*

cod·liv·er oil *n.* an oil rich in vitamins A and D that is extracted from the liver of the codfish and is often used as a food supplement

co·dom·i·nant /kō dómminənt/ *adj.* **1.** GENETICS WITH EQUAL GENETIC EFFECT used to describe genes that each have equal effect in making the character they control appear in offspring. The genes for A and B blood groups are codominant and give rise to the AB blood group if they are both inherited. **2.** ECOL INFLUENCING WHICH SPECIES ARE PRESENT determining the kinds of species that exist in an ecological community —**co·dom·i·nance** *n.*

co·don /kṓ dòn/ *n.* a unit in messenger RNA consisting of a set of three consecutive nucleotides, which specifies a particular amino acid in protein synthesis [Mid-20thC. Coined from CODE + -ON.]

cod·piece /kód peess/ *n.* a decorative pouch attached to the crotch of breeches or hose worn by men in the 15th and 16th centuries [15thC. *Cod* from COD[2].]

co·driv·er *n.* somebody who does a share of the driving on a car trip or in a rally

co·ed, co-ed *n.* WOMAN AT TWO-GENDER COLLEGE a woman student who attends a college or university where men and women are educated together (*dated*) ■ *adj.* EDUCATING MEN AND WOMEN TOGETHER with both male and female students (*informal*) [Late 19thC. Shortening of COEDUCATIONAL.]

co·e·di·tion *n.* a book published by two or more publishers jointly

co·ed·u·ca·tion /kō éjjə káysh'n/ *n.* the education of both sexes together —**co·ed·u·ca·tion·al** *adj.* —**co·ed·u·ca·tion·al·ly** *adv.*

coef. *abbr.* coefficient

co·ef·fi·cient /kō ə físhənt/ *n.* **1.** MATH NUMERICAL PART OF ALGEBRAIC TERM the number placed before a letter that represents a variable in algebra, e.g., the "3" of "3x" in the equation "3x = 6" **2.** PHYS FIGURE MEASURING PROPERTY OF SUBSTANCE a constant that is a measure of a property of a substance [Mid-17thC. From modern Latin *coefficient-,* stem of *coefficiens* "combining to produce a result," from Latin *efficiens.*]

co·ef·fi·cient of cor·re·la·tion *n.* = **correlation coefficient**

co·ef·fi·cient of ex·pan·sion *n.* PHYS the change in length or area of a material per unit length or unit area that accompanies a change in temperature of one degree

co·ef·fi·cient of fric·tion *n.* PHYS the ratio of the force needed to make two surfaces slide over each other to the force that holds them together. Symbol μ

-coel *suffix.* cavity, chamber ○ *pseudocoel* [Via modern Latin *-coela* from Greek *koilos* "hollow." Ultimately from an Indo-European base that is also the ancestor of English *cave* and *concave.*]

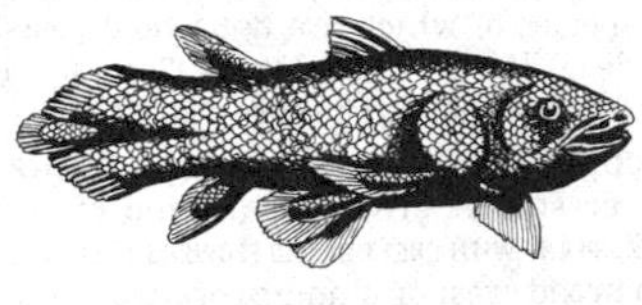

Coelacanth

coe·la·canth /seelə k'anth/ *n.* a fish found off the east coast of Africa that crawls on the sea bottom using its fins to move. Coelacanths, ancient forms of which are believed to be ancestors of the vertebrates, were considered to have been extinct for 70 million years until a living species was discovered in 1938. Latin name: *Latimeria chalumnae.* [Mid-19thC. From modern Latin *Coelacanthus,* genus name, from Greek *koilos* "hollow" + *akantha* "spine" (because the fins of the fish have hollow spines).] —**coe·la·can·thine** /seelə kán thìn, seelə kánthin/ *adj.* —**coe·la·can·thous** /-kánthəss/ *adj.*

-coele *suffix.* = **-coel**

coe·len·te·ra plural of **coelenteron**

coe·len·ter·ate /si léntə ràyt, -rət/ *n.* a marine invertebrate animal that has an internal body cavity (**coelenteron**), e.g., sea anemones, corals, jellyfish, or comb jellies. Phyla: *Cnidaria* and *Ctenophora.* Now called **cnidarian** [Late 19thC. From modern Latin *Coelenterata,* from Greek *koilos* "hollow" + *enteron* "intestine."] —**coe·len·ter·ic** /sèelən térrik/ *adj.*

coe·len·ter·on /si léntə ròn/ (*plural* **-te·ra** /-tərə/) *n.* the internal body cavity of a marine invertebrate animal (**coelenterate**)

coe·li·ac /séelee àk/ *adj.* = **celiac**

coe·lom /séeləm/ (*plural* **-loms** *or* **-lo·ma·ta** /-lṓmətə, -lómmətə/), **ce·lom** (*plural* **-loms** *or* **-lo·ma·ta** /-lṓmətə, -lómmətə/), **coe·lome** *n.* the cavity between the body wall and the gut of many animals, formed when the embryonic mesoderm is divided into two layers [Late 19thC. Via German *Koelom* from Greek *koilōma* "a hollow."] —**coe·lom·ic** /si lómmik, si lṓmik/ *adj.*

coe·lo·mate /séelə màyt/ *adj.* having a cavity between the body wall and the digestive tract —**coe·lo·mate** *n.*

coe·lo·stat /séelə stàt/ *n.* an instrument with a mirror that rotates parallel to the Earth's axis in order to reflect light from a celestial body onto a second mirror aimed at a fixed telescope [Late 19thC. Coined from Latin *caelum* "sky" + -STAT.]

co·emp·tion /kō émpshən/ *n.* the purchase of all available supplies of a particular commodity [14thC. From the Latin stem *coemption-*, literally "buying up," from, ultimately, *emere* "to take or buy" (source of English *exempt*).]

Co·en /koon/, **Jan Pieterszoon** (1587–1629) Dutch colonial administrator. He secured the East Indies for Holland and founded its capital in Batavia, present-day Jakarta (1618).

coen- *prefix.* = **coeno-** (*used before vowels*)

coeno- *prefix.* general, common ○ *coenocyte* [From Greek *koinos.* Ultimately from an Indo-European base meaning "together," which is also the ancestor of English *com-* and *contra-*.]

coen·o·bite /sénnə bīt/ *n.* = **cenobite** —**cen·o·bit·i·cal** /sènnə bíttik'l/ *adj.*

coe·no·cyte /sénnə sīt/ *n.* a cell, part, or organism that contains many nuclei not separated by cell walls, e.g., the threads (**hyphae**) of many fungi or the bodies of some algae —**coe·no·cyt·ic** /sènnə ssíttik/ *adj.*

coe·no·sarc /sénnə saàrk/ *n.* material linking the stems of individuals within a colony of polyps that contains a highly branched canal system with digestive and circulatory functions [Mid-19thC. Coined from COENO- + the Greek stem *sark-* "flesh."]

co·en·zyme /kō én zīm/ *n.* a nonprotein compound or molecule that combines with a protein (**apoenzyme**) to form an active enzyme

co·en·zyme A *n.* a complex compound derived from vitamin B_5 that acts together with specific enzymes in the metabolism of carbohydrates and fats

co·en·zyme Q *n.* = **ubiquinone**

co·e·qual /kō éekwəl/ *adj.* EQUAL TO SOMEBODY OR SOMETHING of the same size or belonging to the same rank or status ■ *n.* SOMEBODY OF SAME STATUS somebody who belongs to the same rank or status as another [14thC. From Latin *coaequalis* "of the same age," from *aequalis* (see EQUAL).] —**co·e·qual·i·ty** /kō i kwáwlətee/ *n.* —**co·e·qual·ly** /kō éekwəlee/ *adv.* —**co·equal·ness** /-éekwəlnəss/ *n.*

co·erce /kō úrss/ (**-erced, -erc·ing, -erc·es**) *vt.* to force somebody to do something that he or she does not want to do [15thC. From Latin *coercere,* literally "to shut in together," from *arcere* "to shut in" (source of English *arcane* and *exercise*).] —**co·erc·er** *n.* —**co·erc·i·ble** *adj.*

co·er·cion /kō úrsh'n/ *n.* **1.** FORCING SOMEBODY TO DO SOMETHING the use of force or threats to make people do things against their will **2.** FORCE USED TO COMPEL SOMEBODY force used to make somebody do something against his or her will —**co·er·cion·ar·y** /kō úrsh'n èrree/ *adj.* —**co·er·cion·ist** *n., adj.*

co·er·cive /kō úrssiv/ *adj.* using force, or having the power to use force, to make people do things against their will —**co·er·cive·ly** *adv.* —**co·er·cive·ness** *n.*

co·er·cive force *n.* the magnetic force necessary to demagnetize a substance

co·er·civ·i·ty /kō ur sívvətee/ *n.* = **coercive force**

co·es·sen·tial /kō i sénshəl/ *adj.* with the same essence or nature [Late 15thC. From ecclesiastical Latin *coessentialis* "of the same substance" (used as an attribute of the persons of the Trinity), from late Latin *essentialis* (see ESSENTIAL).] —**co·es·sen·ti·al·i·ty** /kō i senshee állətee/ *n.* —**co·es·sen·tial·ly** /kō i sénshəlee/ *adv.* —**co·es·sen·tial·ness** /-nəss/ *n.*

co·e·ta·ne·ous /kō i táynee əss/ *adj.* having the same age, duration, or period (*formal*) [Early 17thC. From Latin *coaetaneus,* literally "of the same age," from *aetas* "age."] —**co·e·ta·ne·ous·ly** *adv.* —**co·e·ta·ne·ous·ness** *n.*

co·e·ter·nal /kō i túrn'l/ *adj.* existing together throughout eternity (*formal*) [14thC. From ecclesiastical Latin *coaeturnus,* from Latin *aeternus* (see ETERNAL).] —**co·e·ter·nal·ly** *adv.*

co·e·ter·ni·ty /kō i túrnətee/ *n.* eternal existence with somebody or something else [Late 16thC. From late Latin *coaeternitas,* from Latin *aeternitas* (see ETERNITY).]

Coeur d'A·lene /kàwrd'l áyn/ city and resort in northeastern Idaho, on the northern shore of Coeur D'Alene Lake. Population: 31,076 (1996).

co·e·val /kō éevəl/ *adj.* having the same age, duration, or date of origin (*formal*) [Early 17thC. From late Latin *coaevus,* from Latin *aevum* "age," from Greek *aion* (source of English *eon* and *age*).] —**co·e·val·i·ty** /kō i vállitee/ *n.* —**co·e·val·ly** /kō éevəlee/ *adv.*

co·ev·o·lu·tion /kō evvə lo͞osh'n/ *n.* the joint development of two or more interdependent species, e.g., parasites and the animals they live on, such that they adapt to external changes together —**co·ev·o·lu·tion·ar·y** /kō evə lo͞osh'n èrree/ *adj.*

co·e·volve /kō i vólv/ (**-volved, -volv·ing, -volves**) *vi.* to evolve and adapt together, e.g., in the way that parasites and host organisms do (*refers to two different species*)

co·ex·ist /kō ig zíst/ (**-ist·ed, -ist·ing, -ists**) *vi.* **1.** BE IN EXISTENCE TOGETHER to exist together at the same time and in the same place **2.** LIVE TOGETHER PEACEFULLY to occupy the same place in a peaceful way —**co·ex·is·tence** *n.* —**co·ex·is·tent** *adj.*

co·ex·tend /kō ik sténd/ (**-tend·ed, -tend·ing, -tends**) *vti.* to extend or make things extend in or through the same space or length of time —**co·ex·ten·sion** /kō ik sténshən/ *n.*

co·ex·ten·sive /kō ik sténsiv/ *adj.* sharing the same limits, boundaries, or scope —**co·ex·ten·sive·ly** *adv.*

co·fac·tor /kō fáktər/ *n.* a substance, e.g., a coenzyme or metal ion, that acts with and is essential to the activity of an enzyme

C. of C. *abbr.* chamber of commerce

C. of E. *abbr.* Church of England

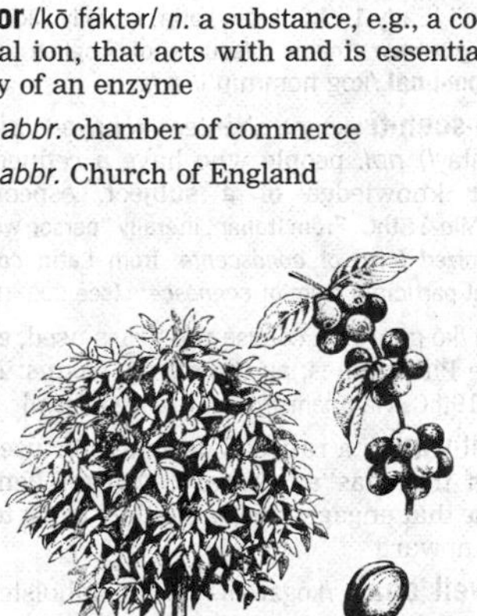

Coffee

cof·fee /kóffee/ *n.* **1.** STRONG CAFFEINE-RICH DRINK a drink made from ground or processed coffee beans that contains caffeine and has a mildly stimulating effect. Coffee may be drunk hot, often with cream or milk and sweetened with sugar, or iced. **2.** BEANS FOR MAKING COFFEE the beans used to make coffee. They are either roasted and ground, or made into powder or granules that dissolve in hot water. **3.** BUSH YIELDING COFFEE BEANS a bush cultivated as a source of the beans used in making coffee. Genus: *Coffea.* **4.** PALE BROWN COLOR a pale brown color, like that of milky coffee [Late 16thC. Via Turkish *kahve* from, ultimately, Arabic *ḳahwa.*]

cof·fee bag *n.* a small porous bag containing ground coffee powder that is steeped in boiling water to make coffee

cof·fee bean *n.* a seed of the coffee tree that is roasted and ground, or processed in other ways, to make coffee

cof·fee break *n.* a short break for coffee or other refreshment

cof·fee·cake /kóffi kàyk/ *n.* **1.** CAKE EATEN WITH COFFEE a sweet cake or roll, often containing nuts and raisins, that is eaten with coffee **2.** *U.K.* COFFEE-FLAVORED CAKE a cake flavored with coffee

cof·fee cup *n.* a cup intended for drinking coffee, generally with a saucer underneath

cof·fee grind·er *n.* an electric or hand-operated device for grinding roasted coffee beans

cof·fee·house (*plural* **-hous·es**) *n.* a place where coffee, and other refreshments are served

cof·fee klatch, **cof·fee klatsch** *n.* a small social gathering where people share coffee and casual conversation (*informal*) [Late 19thC. Anglicization of KAFFEEKLATSCH.]

cof·fee·mak·er /kóffi màykər/ *n.* an apparatus for brewing coffee, usually an electric device

cof·fee mill *n.* = **coffee grinder**

cof·fee·pot /kóffi pòt/ *n.* a pot with a spout and lid designed for brewing or serving coffee

cof·fee room *n.* a place provided in a business or academic department where coworkers or colleagues gather to relax while they drink coffee or other drinks

cof·fee roy·al (*plural* **cof·fee roy·als** *or* **cof·fee roy·al**) *n.* a cup of coffee to which a liqueur has been added, sometimes served topped with whipped cream

cof·fee shop *n.* **1.** INFORMAL RESTAURANT an informal restaurant serving anything from a snack to a full meal **2.** CAFÉ AND COFFEE-SELLER a place where coffee and snacks are served and coffee beans are sold

cof·fee ta·ble *n.* a low table, for use in a living room

cof·fee-ta·ble book *n.* a large, typically expensive book with lavish illustrations, usually used for display or casual perusal rather than reading

cof·fer /kóffər/ *n.* **1.** STRONGBOX a strong chest or box used for keeping valuables or money safe **2.** ARCHIT CEILING PANEL an ornamental sunken panel in a ceiling or dome **3.** CONSTR = **cofferdam** *n.* 1 ■ **cof·fers** *npl.* FUNDS a supply or store of money, often belonging to an organization ■ *vt.* (**-fered, -fer·ing, -fers**) **1.** STORE SOMETHING VALUABLE IN STRONGBOX to put money or valuables in a coffer **2.** DECORATE CEILING WITH COFFERS to decorate something, especially a ceiling, with coffers [13thC. Via French *coffre* from Latin *cophinus* (see COFFIN).]

cof·fer·dam /kóffər dàm/ *n.* **1.** CONSTR UNDERWATER CONSTRUCTION AREA a temporary watertight structure that is pumped dry to enclose an area underwater and allow construction work on a ship, bridge, or rig to be carried out **2.** BUFFER ON SHIP an empty space that acts as a protective barrier between two floors or bulkheads on a ship

cof·fin /kóffin/ *n.* **1.** BOX FOR CORPSE a long oblong container, usually made of wood, in which a dead body is placed for burial or cremation **2.** PRINTING TYPE OF PRINTING FRAME a frame that holds electrotype or stereotype printing plates ■ *vt.* (**-fined, -fin·ing, -fins**) PUT SOMETHING IN A COFFIN to place somebody or something in a coffin or in something resembling a coffin [14thC. From Old French *cof(f)in* "little basket or case," from Latin *cophinus* "basket," from Greek *kophinos.*]

cof·fin block *n.* = **coffin** *n.* 2

cof·fin bone *n.* the main bone in a horse's hoof

cof·fin cor·ner *n.* in football, a corner of the field within ten yards of the goal line of the defending team. Kickers try to kick the ball so that it will bounce out of bounds from this area, forcing the defending team to start their downs close to their own goal.

cof·fin nail *n.* a cigarette (*dated slang*)

C. of S. *abbr.* chief of staff

cog[1] /kog/ *n.* **1.** TOOTH ENGAGING WITH WHEEL FOR MOTION a projection on the edge of a gearwheel that engages with corresponding parts on another wheel to transfer motion from one wheel to the other **2.** = **cogwheel** [13thC. Origin uncertain: probably of Scandinavian origin.] —**cogged** *adj.*

cog /kog/[2] (**cogged, cog·ging, cogs**) *vti.* to cheat in a gambling game by loading the dice (*slang*) [Mid-16thC. Origin unknown.]

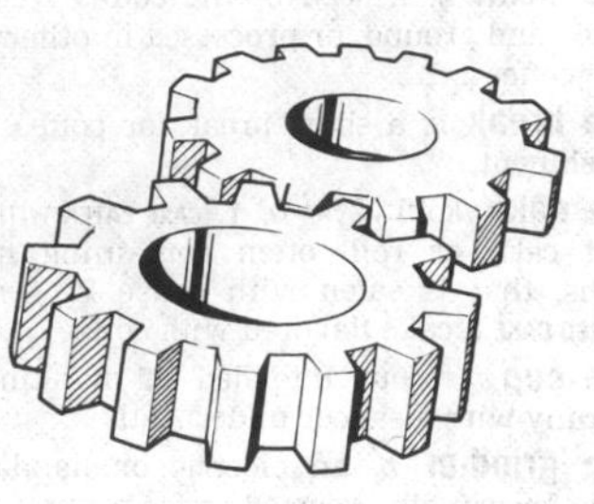
Cog

cog /kog/[3] *n.* **TIMBER BEAM JOINT** a piece that projects from the end of a timber beam and is designed to fit into an opening in another beam to form a joint ■ *vt.* **(cogged, cog·ging, cogs) JOIN TIMBER BEAMS** to join two timber beams with a cog [Early 19thC. Origin uncertain: probably a variant of *cock* "to pamper," shortening of COCKER[2].]

cog. *abbr.* GRAM cognate

co·gen·cy /kṓjənsee/ *n.* the power of an argument or piece of reasoning to convince somebody on an intellectual and rational level (*formal*)

co·gen·er·a·tion /kō jènnə ráysh'n/ *n.* the production of two types of energy, such as heat or electricity, from one source in such a way that both are usable rather than one being treated as waste energy —**co·gen·er·a·tor** /kō jénnə ràytər/ *n.*

co·gent /kṓjənt/ *adj.* forceful and convincing to the intellect and reason ○ *a cogent argument* [Mid-17thC. From Latin *cogent-*, present participle stem of *cogere* "to drive together," from *agere* "to drive" (source of English *agent*).] —**co·gent·ly** *adv.*

cog·i·tate /kójji tàyt/ **(-tat·ed, -tat·ing, -tates)** *vti.* to think deeply and carefully about something (*formal*) [Late 16thC. From, ultimately, Latin *cogitare*, literally "to disturb together," from *agitare* "to disturb" (see AGITATE).]

cog·i·ta·tion /kòjji táysh'n/ *n.* (*formal*) **1. DEEP THOUGHT** deep thought or consideration that somebody gives to a particular problem or subject **2. ACT OF DEEP THOUGHT** an act of thinking deeply about something

cog·i·ta·tive /kójji tàytiv/ *adj.* thinking deeply about or seriously considering something (*formal*) —**cog·i·ta·tive·ly** *adv.* —**cog·i·ta·tive·ness** *n.*

co·gnac /kṓn yàk/ *n.* a high-quality brandy distilled from white grapes in Cognac, western France

cog·nate /kóg nàyt/ *adj.* **1.** LING **DERIVED FROM SAME ROOT OR ORIGIN** having the same linguistic root or origin **2. WITH SAME ANCESTOR** related by blood or having an ancestor in common (*formal*) ■ *n.* **1.** LING **WORD WITH SAME ORIGIN AS ANOTHER** one of two or more words that have the same root or origin **2. SOMEBODY IN SAME FAMILY** somebody who is related by blood to somebody else or shares a common ancestor with somebody else [14thC. From Latin *cognatus*, literally "born together," from *gnatus*, past participle of *(g)nasci* "to be born" (source of English *native*).] —**cog·na·tion** /kog náysh'n/ *n.*

cog·nate ob·ject *n.* a noun that functions as the object of a verb that is from the same etymological root, as in "to dream a dream" or "to think a thought"

cog·ni·tion /kog nísh'n/ *n.* **1. ABILITY TO ACQUIRE KNOWLEDGE** the mental faculty or process of acquiring knowledge by the use of reasoning, intuition or perception **2. KNOWLEDGE ACQUIRED** knowledge that is acquired through processes such as reasoning, intuition or perception [15thC. From the Latin stem *cognition-*, from *cognoscere* "to get to know," from *(g)noscere* "to know" (see NOTION).] —**cog·ni·tion·al** *adj.*

cog·ni·tive /kógnitiv/ *adj.* **1. CONCERNED WITH ACQUISITION OF KNOWLEDGE** relating to the process of acquiring knowledge by the use of reasoning, intuition, or perception **2. RELATING TO THOUGHT** relating to thought processes [Late 16thC. From medieval Latin *cognitivus*, from Latin *cognoscere* (see COGNITION).] —**cog·ni·tive·ly** *adv.*

cog·ni·tive dis·so·nance *n.* a state of psychological conflict or anxiety resulting from a contradiction between a person's simultaneously held beliefs or attitudes

cog·ni·tive map *n.* a map of three-dimensional space maintained in the brain

cog·ni·tive psy·chol·o·gy *n.* the branch of psychology concerned with the study of mental states

cog·ni·tive sci·ence *n.* the scientific study of knowledge and how it is acquired, combining elements of philosophy, psychology, linguistics, anthropology, and artificial intelligence

cog·ni·tive ther·a·py *n.* a treatment of psychiatric disorders such as anxiety or depression that encourages patients to confront and challenge the distorted way of thinking that characterizes their disorder

cog·ni·tiv·ism /kógniti vìzzəm/ *n.* the theory that moral judgments are statements of fact and can therefore be classed as true or false

cog·ni·za·ble /kógnizəb'l, kog nízəb'l/ *adj.* **1. ABLE TO BE KNOWN** able to be known or perceived by the human mind (*formal*) **2.** LAW **WITHIN LAW COURT'S JURISDICTION** falling within the jurisdiction of a particular court of law and therefore able to be tried by that court —**cog·ni·za·bly** *adv.*

cog·ni·zance /kógnizəns/ *n.* **1. KNOWLEDGE** knowledge or awareness of something (*formal*) **2. SOMEBODY'S SCOPE OF KNOWLEDGE** the extent or range of what somebody can know and understand (*formal*) **3. COURT'S RIGHT TO DEAL WITH SOMETHING** the right of a court of law to deal with a particular matter **4. TAKING NOTICE OF A FACT** notice of a fact or facts taken by a court of law **5.** HERALDRY **DISTINGUISHING SIGN** a badge or other sign that is worn to distinguish the wearer [14thC. Via Old French *conis(s)aunce* from, ultimately, Latin *cognoscere* (see COGNITION).]

cog·ni·zant /kógnizənt/ *adj.* being fully aware or having knowledge of something (*formal*)

WORD KEY: SYNONYMS

See Synonyms at ***aware***.

cog·nize /kóg nìz/ **(-nized, -niz·ing, -niz·es)** *vt.* to become aware of or know something (*formal*) [Mid-17thC. Back-formation from COGNIZANCE, modeled on *recognizance, recognize*.] —**cog·niz·er** *n.*

cog·no·men /kog nṓmən/ (*plural* **-no·mens** *or* **-nom·i·na** /-nómmənə/) *n.* **1. NICKNAME** a nickname or name that describes somebody, e.g., "Billy the Kid" (*formal*) **2.** HIST **ROMAN SURNAME** a surname or family name, especially the third name given to a citizen of ancient Rome, e.g., "Cicero" in "Marcus Tullius Cicero" [Early 17thC. From Latin, literally "added name," from *(g)nomen* "name" (source of English *noun*).] —**cog·nom·i·nal** /kog nómmin'l/ *adj.*

cog·no·scen·ti /kògnə shéntee, kònnyə-/ (*singular* **-te** /-shéntay/) *npl.* people who have a refined and superior knowledge of a subject, especially the arts [Mid-18thC. From Italian, literally "person who knows," a Latinized form of *conoscente*, from Latin *cognoscent-*, present participle stem of *cognoscere* (see COGNITION).]

co·gon /kō gṓn/ *n.* a coarse tall grass used, especially in the Philippines, as thatching. Genus: *Imperata*. [Late 19thC. Via Spanish from Tagalog *kúgon*.]

cog rail·way *n.* a railroad designed for use on steep slopes that has a central cogwheel beneath the engine that engages with a toothed track to pull the train upward

Cogs·well chair /kógzwell-/ *n.* an upholstered armchair with an open part under the armrests and cabriole legs [*Cogswell* of uncertain origin: probably from the name *Cogswell*]

cog·wheel /kóg weel, kóg hweel/ *n.* a wheel with a series of projections around the rim that enable it to engage with projections on another wheel or rack to create traction and so produce motion

co·hab·it /kō hábbit/ **(-it·ed, -it·ing, -its)** *vi.* to live together, especially without being formally married (*formal*) [Mid-16thC. From Late Latin *cohabitare*, from *habitare* "to dwell," literally "to have usually" (see INHABIT).] —**co·hab·i·tant** *n.* —**co·hab·it·ee** /kō habbi tée/ *n.* —**co·hab·it·er** /kō hábbitər/ *n.*

co·hab·i·ta·tion /kō hàbbi táysh'n/ *n.* the state or practice of living with another person, especially without being formally married (*formal*) —**co·hab·i·ta·tion·al** *adj.*

Co·han /kṓ hàn/, **George M.** (1878–1942) U.S. actor, songwriter, and playwright. He wrote twenty plays and musicals and numerous songs such as *"I'm a Yankee Doodle Dandy"* (1904). Full name **George Michael Cohan**

co·hen /kṓ ən/ (*plural* **-hens** *or* **-han·im** /kṓ ənim/) *n.* in Judaism, a person recognized as a descendant of Aaron. The cohens were priests in the Temple in ancient Jerusalem, and a male identified as a cohen still retains certain obligations in Orthodox Judaism today.

Co·hen /kṓ ən/, **Leonard** (*b.* 1934) Canadian poet, novelist, singer, and songwriter. His albums include *The Songs of Leonard Cohen* (1967) and *I'm Your Man* (1988).

Co·hen, Morris Raphael (1880–1947) Russian-born U.S. philosopher. His philosophy was a combination of logic, pragmatism, and linguistic analysis.

co·here /kō héer/ **(-hered, -her·ing, -heres)** *vi.* **1. STICK TOGETHER** to stick or hold together in a mass that is not easily separated (*formal*) **2. BE LOGICALLY CONSISTENT** to be logically consistent so that all the separate parts fit together and add up to a harmonious or believable whole (*formal*) **3.** PHYS **BE HELD TOGETHER BY MOLECULAR FORCES** to be held together by the molecular forces of cohesion [Mid-16thC. From Latin *cohaerere*, from *haerere* "to stick" (source of English *adhere*).]

co·her·ence /kō héerəns/, **co·her·en·cy** /kō héerənsee/ *n.* **1. LOGICAL OR AESTHETIC CONSISTENCY** the quality of being logically or aesthetically consistent, with all separate parts fitting together to form a harmonious or credible whole **2.** PHYS = **cohesion** *n.* 2

co·her·ent /kō héerənt/ *adj.* **1. LOGICALLY OR AESTHETICALLY CONSISTENT** logically or aesthetically consistent and holding together as a harmonious or credible whole **2. SPEAKING LOGICALLY** able to speak clearly and logically ○ *He was so confused and dazed he was barely coherent.* **3. STICKING TOGETHER** being able to hold together to form an inseparable mass (*formal*) **4.** PHYS **DESCRIBING ELECTROMAGNETIC WAVES** used to describe electromagnetic waves that have the same wavelength and a fixed phase relationship. Coherent light is produced by lasers. **5. FORMING MEASUREMENTS FROM BASIC UNITS** forming a system of measurements, all units of which are multiples of several basic well-defined units —**co·her·ent·ly** *adv.*

co·he·sion /kō héezh'n/ *n.* **1. STICKING OR WORKING TOGETHER** the state or condition of joining or working together to form a united whole, or the tendency to do this **2.** PHYS **MOLECULAR ATTRACTION** the force of attraction by which the molecules of a solid or liquid tend to remain together [Mid-17thC. From Latin *cohaes-*, past participle stem of *cohaerere* (see COHERE).] —**co·he·sion·less** *adj.*

co·he·sive /kō héessiv/ *adj.* sticking, holding, or working together to form a united whole ○ *She had welded the team into a cohesive unit.* [Early 18thC. From Latin *cohaes-*, present participle stem of *cohaerere* (see COHERE).] —**co·he·sive·ly** *adv.* —**co·he·sive·ness** *n.*

co·ho /kṓhō/ (*plural* **-hos** *or* **-ho**) *n.* = **coho salmon**

co·hort /kṓ hàwrt/ *n.* **1. GROUP OF PEOPLE** a united group of people **2. SUPPORTER** a supporter, accomplice, or associate of a leader, especially one to whom special treatment and preference is given (*disapproving*) **3.** STATS **GROUP WITH STATISTICAL SIMILARITIES** a group of people sharing a common factor, e.g., the same age or the same income bracket, especially in a statistical survey **4.** HIST **UNIT OF ROMAN ARMY** an ancient Roman military unit that formed one tenth of a legion and that consisted of 300 to 600 men **5. SOLDIERS** a group of soldiers or warriors [15thC. From, ultimately, the Latin stem *cohort-*, literally "enclosure," thus "people within an enclosure," hence "company of infantry," variant of *cort-*.]

co·ho salm·on *n.* a small Pacific salmon with light-colored flesh. The coho salmon has been successfully introduced in the Great Lakes of North America and other inland waters. Latin name: *Oncorhynchus kisutch*. [Mid-19thC. Origin unknown.]

co·hosh /kṓ hòsh/ *n.* a North American plant such as black cohosh or blue cohosh. Latin name: *Cimicifuga racemosa* and *Caulophyllum thalictroides*. [Late 18thC. From Eastern Abenaki *kkwàhas*.]

co·hune /kō hóon/ *n.* a Central American palm with feathery leaves that produces a nut yielding an oil similar to coconut oil, often used in soaps and cosmetics. Latin name: *Orbignya cohune*. [Mid-18thC. From Miskito.]

coif /koyf/ *n.* **1. TYPE OF SKULLCAP FOR WOMEN** a close-fitting linen cap worn by women in the Middle Ages, and now worn by some nuns under their veils **2.** =

coiffure (*informal*) 3. LAWYER'S SKULLCAP a close-fitting white cap worn in the past by English sergeants-at-law (*archaic*) 4. LEATHER SKULLCAP a thick, close-fitting leather cap formerly worn under a hood of chain mail ■ *vt.* (**coifed, coif·ing, coifs**) 1. COVER HEAD WITH COIF to cover somebody's head with a coif or with something like a coif 2. ARRANGE HAIR to arrange or style somebody's hair (*formal*) [14thC. Via Old French *coife* "headdress" from late Latin *cofia* "helmet," ultimately from prehistoric Germanic.]

coif·feur /kwaa fúr/ (*plural* **-feurs** /-fúr/) *n.* a male hairdresser (*formal*) [Mid-19thC. From French, ultimately from Old French *coife* (see COIF).]

coif·feuse /kwaa fōōz/ (*plural* **-feus·es**) *n.* a woman hairdresser (*formal*) [Late 18thC. From French, feminine of COIFFEUR.]

coif·fure /kwaa fyŏŏr/ *n.* SOMEBODY'S HAIRSTYLE the way somebody wears his or her hair (*formal*) ■ *vt.* (**-fured, -fur·ing, -fures**) STYLE HAIR to style or arrange somebody's hair (*formal*) [Mid-17thC. From French, where it was formed from *coiffer* "to arrange the hair," ultimately from Old French *coife* (see COIF).] —**coif·fured** *adj.*

coign *n.* = **quoin**

coign of van·tage *n.* a good position from which to be able to observe somebody or something or to take action (*literary*) [*Coign* is a variant of COIN or QUOIN]

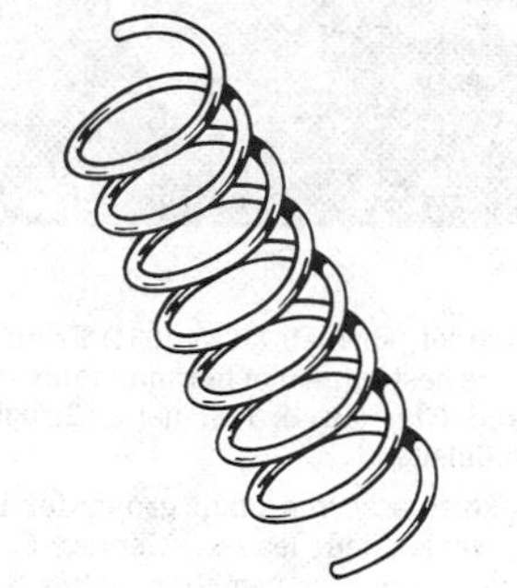

Coil

coil[1] /koyl/ *n.* 1. SERIES OF LOOPS a series of connected loops into which something has been wound or gathered 2. LOOP one of a series of loops into which something has been wound or gathered 3. SPIRAL something that curls or is curled into a spiral shape 4. PIPES ARRANGED IN ROWS OR SPIRAL a series of pipes arranged in rows or in a spiral, e.g., in a radiator or condenser 5. ELEC ENG WIRE SPIRAL FOR ELECTRIC CURRENT a spiral of wire through which an electric current is passed to create a magnetic field or to function as an inductor 6. ELEC ENG DEVICE SUPPLYING ELECTRICITY TO SPARK PLUGS a device that supplies a high voltage to the spark plugs in an internal-combustion engine 7. MED CONTRACEPTIVE DEVICE a coil-shaped device made of plastic or metal that is placed inside the womb to prevent a woman from becoming pregnant 8. ROLL OF STAMPS a roll of postage stamps dispensed by a vending machine ■ *v.* (**coiled, coil·ing, coils**) 1. *vti.* WIND SOMETHING INTO LOOPS to wind something into a series of connected loops or form a series of connected loops ○ *The rope had coiled itself around the propeller.* 2. *vi.* CURVE OR BEND to move in a curving, sinuous way [Early 16thC. Via Old French *coillir* "to gather" from Latin *colligere* (see COLLECT).] —**coil·er** *n.*

coil[2] /koyl/ *n.* a commotion or disturbance (*archaic*) [Late 16thC. Origin unknown.]

coil pot *n.* a pot formed from a structure of coils or ropes of clay laid one on top of the other in a spiral

coin /koyn/ *n.* 1. PIECE OF METAL MONEY a usually circular flat piece of metal stamped with its value as money 2. METAL MONEY money in the form of coins rather than bills or checks 3. PAPER OR METAL MONEY money in whatever form, as opposed to such things as checks 4. ALTERNATE BUT EQUIVALENT FORM OF EXPRESSION something considered acceptable as an alternative form of expression ○ *Honesty is her coin of choice.* ■ *vt.* (**coined, coin·ing, coins**) 1. MINT COINS to make a coin or coins 2. MAKE METAL INTO COINS to make a metal, e.g., gold or silver, into coins 3. CREATE EXPRESSION to invent or devise a word or phrase ■ *adj.* COIN-OPERATED requiring a coin or coins to be inserted to make it operate (*usually used in combination*) [14thC. From Old French *coin(g)*, literally "wedge, cornerstone," later "die (usually wedge-shaped) for stamping coins," from Latin *cuneus* "wedge."] —**coin·a·ble** *adj.* —**coin·er** *n.* ◇ **the other side of the coin** the contrasting or contrary aspect of something

coin·age /kóynij/ *n.* 1. COINS currency in the form of coins 2. CURRENCY a system or type of coins in use as currency ○ *decimal coinage* 3. MAKING OF METAL MONEY the act or process of minting coins 4. INVENTION OF NEW WORD OR PHRASE the invention of a new word or phrase 5. NEW WORD OR PHRASE a newly used word or phrase ○ *"Cyberspace" was a popular coinage of the 1980s.*

coin box *n.* a box into which coins are inserted to get something from a coin-operated machine

co·in·cide /kō in sīd/ (**-cid·ed, -cid·ing, -cides**) *vi.* 1. HAPPEN AT SAME TIME to happen at or around the same time 2. BE SAME IN POSITION OR FORM to occupy the same place or be exactly alike in position or form 3. AGREE to agree exactly [Early 18thC. From medieval Latin *coincidere*, literally "to fall upon together," from Latin *incidere* "fall upon," from *cadere* "to fall" (see CADENCE).]

co·in·ci·dence /kō ínsidəns/ *n.* 1. CHANCE HAPPENING something that happens by chance in a surprising or remarkable way 2. HAPPENING WITHOUT PLANNING the fact of happening by chance ○ *It was pure coincidence that we met.* 3. HAVING IDENTICAL FEATURES the fact or condition of happening at the same time or place or being identical (*formal*)

co·in·ci·dent /kō ínsidənt/ *adj.* (*formal*) 1. SHARING SAME PLACE OR TIME happening at the same time or occupying the same position in space 2. AGREEING EXACTLY being in exact agreement or matching — **co·in·ci·dent·ly** *adv.*

co·in·ci·den·tal /kō insi dént'l/ *adj.* 1. HAPPENING BY CHANCE happening by chance rather than intentionally 2. OCCURRING AT SAME TIME happening or existing at the same time —**co·in·ci·den·tal·ly** *adv.*

Coin·treau /kwaan trṓ/ *tdmk.* a trademark for a colorless orange-flavored liqueur

coir /kóyr/ *n.* a kind of coarse fiber that comes from the husk of the coconut and is used to make matting and rope [Late 16thC. From Malayalam *kayaru* "cord, coir."]

co·i·tion /kō ísh'n/ *n.* = **coitus** [Mid-16thC. From the Latin stem *coition-*, from *coire* (see COITUS).]

co·i·tus /kṓ itəss/ *n.* sexual intercourse (*formal or technical*) [Mid-19thC. From Latin, past participle of *coire*, literally "to go together," from *ire* "to go."] —**co·i·tal** *adj.* — **co·i·tal·ly** *adv.*

co·i·tus in·ter·rup·tus /kṓ itəss intə rúptəss/ *n.* during sexual intercourse, the deliberate withdrawal of the penis from the vagina before semen is ejaculated, used as a method of contraception [From modern Latin, "interrupted coitus"]

co·jones /kə hṓneez/ *npl.* (*slang*) 1. TESTICLES testicles 2. COURAGE courage or nerve [Mid-20thC. From Spanish, plural of *cojón* "testicle."]

coke[1] /kōk/ *n.* CARBON FUEL a solid residue consisting mainly of carbon, left after the volatile elements have been driven from bituminous coal or other petroleum material. Coke is used as a fuel and in steelmaking. ■ *vti.* (**coked, cok·ing, cokes**) CHANGE INTO COKE to change something, e.g., bituminous coal, into coke, or to become coke or like coke [Mid-17thC. Origin unknown.]

coke[2] /kōk/ *n.* cocaine used as an illicit drug (*slang*) [Early 20thC. Contraction.]

Coke /kōk/ *tdmk.* a trademark for a cola-flavored soft drink

coke·head /kōk hèd/ *n.* somebody who takes cocaine frequently or is addicted to it (*slang*)

col /kol/ *n.* 1. LOW POINT OF MOUNTAIN RIDGE a low point in a ridge of mountains, often forming a pass between two peaks 2. REGION OF LOW ATMOSPHERIC PRESSURE a pattern of atmospheric pressure distribution that develops between two anticyclones and two depressions arranged alternately, characterized by light variable winds and often thundery weather in summer or foggy conditions in winter [Mid-19thC. Via French from Latin *collum* "neck."]

Col *abbr.* BIBLE Colossians

COL *abbr.* 1. cost of living 2. computer-oriented language

col. *abbr.* 1. collect 2. college 3. colony 4. color 5. column

Col., **Col** *abbr.* 1. BIBLE Colossians 2. Columbia 3. Columbian 4. Colonel 5. **Col.**, **Colo.** Colorado

col-[1] *prefix.* = **colo-** (*used before vowels*)

col-[2] *prefix.* = **com-** (*used before l*)

co·la[1] /kṓlə/, **ko·la** *n.* 1. TYPE OF SODA a sweet carbonated drink that is flavored with cola nuts 2. **co·la, ko·la** TROPICAL TREE BEARING COLA NUTS a tropical evergreen tree cultivated for its reddish seeds (**cola nuts**). Genus: *Cola.* [Early 17thC. From Temni *k'ola* "cola nut."]

co·la[2] plural of **colon**

COLA *abbr.* cost-of-living adjustment

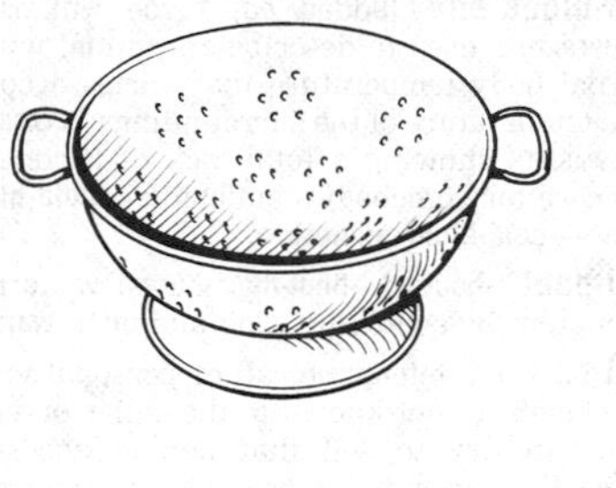

Colander

col·an·der /kúlləndə, kóllən-/ *n.* a bowl-shaped dish with holes in it, used for draining food that has been cooked in water or for washing vegetables or fruit [14thC. Origin uncertain: perhaps via Old Provençal *colador* from, ultimately, Latin *colare* "to strain," from *colum* "sieve" (source of English *percolate*).]

co·la nut, **ko·la nut** *n.* the small hard seed of the cola tree, which contains caffeine and theobromine and is used in carbonated drinks and medicines

co·lat·i·tude /kō láttə tōōd/ *n.* the difference between a latitude and 90°

Col·bert /kawl báir/, **Claudette** (1905–96) French-born U.S. movie actor. She acted in Hollywood movies and won an Academy Award for *It Happened One Night* (1934).

col·can·non /kol kánnən/ *n.* an Irish dish made of cabbage and potatoes boiled and mashed together and served with butter or cream [Late 18thC. Origin uncertain: perhaps from COLE, or Irish *cál ceannan*, literally "white-headed cabbage."]

Col·ches·ter /kṓlchəstər/ city in northwestern Vermont, east of Lake Champlain and northeast of Burlington. Population: 16,092 (1996).

col·chi·cine /kólchi sēen, kólk-/ *n.* a poisonous pale yellow extract obtained from autumn crocus plants, used in plant breeding to inhibit cell division and cause chromosome doubling, and in medicine to treat gout. Formula: $C_{22}H_{25}NO_6$.

cold /kōld/ *adj.* 1. AT LOW TEMPERATURE at or with a low, relatively low, uncomfortably low, or unusually low temperature ○ *The weather turned colder.* ○ *a cold drink* 2. MAKING PLACE SEEM COOLER giving a place a feeling of coolness rather than warmth ○ *blue is a cold color* 3. COOK COOKED HOT THEN COOLED cooked or prepared as a hot food and then cooled ○ *Serve the pie cold, with ice cream.* 4. TACITURN AND EMOTIONLESS showing no emotion, sympathy, or kindness 5. UNFRIENDLY AND UNCARING feeling or exhibiting no friendship or sense of caring 6. STRONG BUT CONTROLLED intense but expressed or shown in a controlled way ○ *cold fury* 7. SEXUALLY FRIGID giving or feeling no sexual response 8. HARD TO FOLLOW no longer recent or fresh and so difficult to track or follow ○ *The trail had gone cold.* 9. NOT NEAR OBJECT OF SEARCH not close to the correct answer or to something being searched for (*informal*) 10. DEAD dead, especially from a long time before 11. METALL PROCESSED AT LOW TEMPERATURE processed at a temperature below that at which recrystallization takes place ■ *n.* 1. MED VIRAL INFECTION OF NOSE AND THROAT a viral infection of the nose, throat, and bronchial tubes, characterized by coughing, sneezing, headaches, and nasal congestion 2. COLD WEATHER low-temperature weather or conditions ○ *The cold made me shiver.* 3. CONDITION CAUSED BY LOW TEMPERATURE the state of being subjected to low temperatures, or the condition caused by being subjected to low temperatures ■ *adv.* 1. EXTEMPORANEOUSLY without any preparation ○ *sang the part cold* 2. COMPLETELY completely and without any possibility of a change of mind ○ *turned the proposal down cold* [Old English *cald, ceald.* Ultimately from an

Indo-European word that is also the ancestor of English *chill* and *cool*. Perhaps originally a past participle meaning "cooled."] —**cold·ness** *n.* ◇ **left out in the cold** ignored or denied benefits that other people are getting ◇ **out cold** unconscious or in a deep sleep ◇ **blow hot and cold** to have wide extremes of attitude or mood ◇ **the cold light of day** conditions when things are seen for what they really are rather than being seen in an unrealistically favorable light ◇ **come** *or* **be brought in from the cold** to be allowed to take part in something after being previously excluded ◇ **leave somebody cold** to fail to impress or excite somebody

cold-blood·ed /-blúddəd/ *adj.* **1.** ZOOL **WITH VARYING BODY TEMPERATURE** used to describe an animal with an internal body temperature that varies according to the temperature of the surroundings **2. LACKING IN PITY OR WARMTH** showing a total lack of kindness, pity, or care for somebody's suffering —**cold·blood·ed·ly** *adv.* —**cold·blood·ed·ness** *n.*

cold·boot (**-boot·ed, -boot·ing, -boots**) *vt.* to restart a computer by switching it off and on. ◊ **warmboot**

cold call *n.* a telephone call or personal visit made to somebody not known to the caller or visitor, in order to try to sell that person goods or services [From the fact that the call is unsolicited and comes *cold*] —**cold-call** *vt.*

cold cash *n.* money that is immediately available

cold chis·el *n.* a tool consisting of a solid metal shaft with a sharply beveled point or edge that is struck with a hammer or mallet to break up or shape hard materials such as metal or stone [From the chisel's being so tempered as to be able to cut cold metal when struck with a hammer]

cold·cock /kṓld kòk/ (**-cocked, -cock·ing, -cocks**) *vt.* to knock somebody unconscious, usually by surprise (*slang*) [Early 20thC. Probably from the idea of knocking somebody cold with a blunt instrument such as a COCK "faucet, valve."]

cold com·fort *n.* something intended as encouraging or reassuring that does not help in practice

cold cream *n.* a thick cream used for cleaning and softening the skin, especially on the face

cold cuts *npl.* slices of cooked meat that are served cold

cold drink *n.* **1. CHILLED DRINK** a chilled drink of water, juice, or something similar **2.** *Southern U.S., S Africa* **SOFT DRINK** a nonalcoholic drink

cold duck *n.* a cocktail made with sparkling burgundy and champagne [Translation of German *kalte Ente*, by folk etymology from *kaltes Ende* "cold end," supposedly because leftover champagne and burgundy were poured by servers into a single bottle]

cold feet *npl.* a loss of nerve about something planned, causing a person not to go ahead as originally intended [From the fact that a soldier with cold or frozen feet is prevented from fighting]

cold fish *n.* somebody who shows no warmth or friendship

cold frame *n.* a box with glass or clear plastic sides and an opening roof, used in gardens for protecting seedlings and other plants from cold weather

cold front *n.* the boundary zone of an advancing cold-air mass as it replaces warmer air

cold fu·sion *n.* a hypothetical form of nuclear fusion held to take place at room temperature

cold-heart·ed *adj.* showing no sympathy or warmth to other people —**cold-heart·ed·ly** *adv.* —**cold-heart·ed·ness** *n.*

Col·ditz /kṓldits/ site of Colditz Castle, a German prisoner-of-war camp during World War II, from which many prisoners made daring escapes. It is situated about 30 mi./48 km southwest of Leipzig.

cold light *n.* light produced from a low-temperature source, e.g., phosphorescence, containing no infrared wavelengths and therefore having no heating effects

cold·ly /kṓldlee/ *adv.* without emotion, affection, friendliness, or sympathy

cold pack *n.* **1.** MED **SOMETHING COLD PRESSED ON BODY** a bag, cloth, or sheet that is soaked with water or filled with something cold and applied to the body to relieve pain or inflammation **2.** FOOD TECH **CANNING PROCESS** the packing and sterilization of uncooked food in jars or cans

cold-pressed *adj.* used to describe high-grade olive oil produced from the first pressing of the raw olives. The pressed olives are subsequently heated to extract further amounts of oil.

cold-rolled *adj.* used to describe metal that is rolled into sheets under pressure at room temperature in order to retain the crystalline structure of the metal and produce a smooth surface —**cold-rol·ling** *n.*

cold rub·ber *n.* a durable synthetic rubber made through polymerization at low temperature and used for retreading tires

cold shoul·der *n.* a refusal to behave in a friendly or pleasant way toward somebody ○ *He gave me the cold shoulder.* [From the former practice of giving only a cold shoulder of mutton to an unwelcome guest]

cold·shoul·der /kṓld shṓldər/ (**-dered, -der·ing, -ders**) *vt.* to ignore somebody or behave in an unfriendly way toward somebody

cold snap *n.* a sudden short period of very cold weather

cold sore *n.* a small painful blister on or near the lips, or sometimes the nose, caused by a virus *Herpes simplex* [From the fact that the sores often accompany colds]

cold stor·age *n.* chilled or refrigerated conditions in which perishable objects, especially food or furs, are kept to preserve them ◇ **in cold storage** ready to be put into action at some later date, but not being currently being acted on

cold store *n.* a refrigerated building or area for keeping goods, especially food or furs, in cold conditions to preserve them

cold sweat *n.* a very nervous, anxious, or frightened state, often with sweating and cold clammy skin

cold turk·ey *n.* **1. ABRUPT WITHDRAWAL OF ADDICTIVE DRUGS** a method of stopping drug addiction by not taking any further drugs and not having any other treatment to protect the addict from the withdrawal symptoms **2. WITHDRAWAL SYMPTOMS** the unpleasant symptoms, usually including nausea and shivering, that accompany a sudden withdrawal from an addictive drug ■ *adv.* **BLUNTLY AND UNDIPLOMATICALLY** so as to convey the meaning to somebody in a way that cannot be misunderstood (*slang*) [Origin uncertain; perhaps from the goose bumps, suggesting turkey flesh, experienced by addicts withdrawing from drugs]

cold type *n.* typesetting that is done without casting metal

cold war *n.* a relationship between two people or groups that is unfriendly or hostile but does not involve actual fighting or military combat. ◊ **hot war** [From the fact that the antagonism stops short of military conflict and so never heats up into an actual war]

Cold War *n.* the hostile yet nonviolent relations between the former Soviet Union and the United States, and their respective allies, from around 1946 to 1989

cold-wa·ter *adj.* with cold running water provided but no heating

cold wave *n.* **1.** METEOROL **COLD PERIOD** a sudden fall in temperature associated with the passage of air of continental polar origin **2.** HAIR **PERMANENT WAVE IN HAIR** a permanent wave in hair that is produced using chemicals, rather than heat (*dated*)

cold-weld (**cold-weld·ed, cold-weld·ing, cold-welds**) *vt.* to join two metal surfaces using pressure rather than heat —**cold-weld·ing** *n.*

cole /kōl/ *n.* = **kale** [Pre-12thC. From Latin *caulis* "stem, stalk, cabbage" (source of English *cauliflower* and *kohlrabi*).]

Cole /kōl/, **Thomas** (1801–48) British-born U.S. artist. He painted North American landscapes and is often considered the forerunner of the Hudson River School.

co·lec·to·my /kə léktəmee/ (*plural* **-mies**) *n.* an operation in which part or all of the colon is removed [Late 19thC. Coined from COLON + -ECTOMY.]

cole·man·ite /kṓlmə nīt/ *n.* a milky white or colorless crystalline mineral consisting of hydrous calcium borate. It is a source of borax. [Late 19thC. Named for William T. *Coleman* (1824–93), U.S. mine owner.]

co·le·op·ter·an /kòlee óptərən, kòll-/ *n.* an insect with modified forewings that function as tough covers for the membranous hind wings. Beetles, fireflies, and weevils are coleopterans. Order: Coleoptera. —**co·le·op·ter·ous** *adj.*

co·le·op·tile /kòlee ópt'l, kòll-/ *n.* BOT the first leaf in some grasses that forms a protective sheath around the stem tip (**plumule**) [Mid-19thC. Coined from Greek *koleos* "sheath" (see COLEUS) + *ptilon* "feather, down."]

co·le·o·rhi·za /kòli ō rízə, kòll-/ (*plural* **-zae** /-zee, kòll-/) *n.* BOT a protective sheath surrounding the young root of a germinating grass seed [Mid-19thC. Coined from Greek *koleos* "sheath" (see COLEUS) + *rhiza* "root."]

Col·e·ridge /kṓlərij/, **Samuel Taylor** (1772–1834) British poet. His collection *Lyrical Ballads* (1798), published with William Wordsworth, launched romanticism in English poetry.

cole·slaw /kṓl slàw/ *n.* a salad made with shredded raw cabbage and carrots in a mayonnaise dressing [Late 18thC. From Dutch *koolsla*, literally "cabbage salad," from *kool* "cabbage" + *sla* "salad."]

cole·tit /kṓl tìt/ *n.* = **coal tit**

AKG London

Colette

Co·lette /ko lét, kaw lét/ (1873–1954) French novelist. Among the best known of her many novels are *Chéri* (1926) and *Gigi* (1945). Full name **Sidonie Gabrielle Claudine Colette**

co·le·us /kṓlee əss/ *n.* a plant grown for its brightly colored variegated leaves. Genus: *Coleus.* [Mid-19thC. Via modern Latin from Greek *koleos* "sheath," from the way the plant's filaments are joined.]

cole·wort /kṓl wùrt, -wàwrt/ *n.* = **kale**

Col·fax /kṓl fàks/, **Schuyler** (1823–85) U.S. statesman and vice president of the United States. He was a Republican U.S. representative (1855–69), and Ulysses S. Grant's vice president (1869–73).

coli- *prefix.* = **colo-** (*used before vowels*)

col·ic /kóllik/ *n.* **1.** MED **PAIN IN ABDOMEN** a sudden attack of abdominal pain, often caused by spasm, inflammation, or obstruction **2.** MED **CRYING IN BABIES** excessive crying and irritability in infants from a variety of causes, especially stomach or intestinal discomfort **3.** VET **SERIOUS DIGESTIVE DISEASE IN HORSES** a serious disease of the digestive system in horses, sometimes leading to fatal intestinal blockage ■ *adj.* MED **OF INTERMITTENT ABDOMINAL PAIN** relating to spasmodic sharp pain in the abdomen [15thC. Via French from Latin *colicus*, from Greek *kolikos* "suffering in the large intestine," from *kolon* "large intestine" (source of English *colon*[2]), of unknown origin.]

col·ick·y /kóllikee/ *adj.* experiencing bouts of abdominal pain (**colic**)

co·li·form /kṓlə fàwrm, kól-/ *adj.* used to describe rod-shaped bacteria that are normally found in the colons of humans and animals and become a serious contaminant when found in the food or water supply. ◊ **E coli** [Early 20thC. Coined from modern Latin *coli*, species name, literally "of the large intestine" (a form of Latin *colon, colum* "large intestine") + -FORM.]

co·lin·e·ar /kō línnee ər/ *adj.* **1. ARRANGED IN LINEAR ORDER** with corresponding parts arranged in a regular linear order **2.** MATH = **collinear** [Early 20thC. Coined from CO- + LINEAR.] —**co·lin·e·ar·i·ty** /kōlinnee érrətee/ *n.*

col·i·se·um /kòllə sée əm/ *n.* a large building used as a theater or for sports events [Early 16thC. Via medieval Latin *coliseum*, literally "something colossal," from Latin *colosseus* "colossal," from *colossus* "colossus" (source of English *colossal*).]

co·lis·tin /kə lístin/ *n.* an antibiotic effective against a wide range of organisms and used to treat gastrointestinal infections. It is obtained from a soil bacterium. [Mid-20thC. From modern Latin *(Bacillus) colistinus*, scientific name for the bacterium that produces it, from *coli* (see COLIFORM).]

co·li·tis /kə lī́tiss/ *n.* inflammation of the colon, characterized by lower-bowel spasms and upper abdominal cramps [Mid-19thC. Coined from COLON[2] + -ITIS.] —**co·lit·ic** /kə líttik/ *adj.*

coll. *abbr.* **1.** COMM collateral **2.** colleague **3.** MAIL collect **4.** MAIL collection **5.** MAIL collector **6.** EDUC college **7.** EDUC collegiate **8.** LANG colloquial

coll- *prefix.* = **collo-** (*used before vowels*)

col·lab·o·rate /kə lábbə ràyt/ (**-rat·ed, -rat·ing, -rates**) *vi.* **1. WORK WITH OTHERS** to work with another person or group in order to achieve something **2.** MIL **WORK WITH ENEMY** to betray others by working with an enemy, especially an occupying force [Late 19thC. From late Latin *collaborat-*, the past participle stem of *collaborare*, literally "to work together," ultimately from Latin *labor* "toil" (see LABOR).]

col·lab·o·ra·tion /kə làbbə ráysh'n/ *n.* **1. A WORKING TOGETHER** the act of working together with one or more people in order to achieve something **2.** MIL **A WORKING WITH ENEMY** the betrayal of others by working with an enemy, especially an occupying force —**col·lab·o·ra·tion·ist** *n., adj.* —**col·lab·o·ra·tion·ism** *n.*

col·lab·o·ra·tive /kə lábbə ràytiv, -rətiv/ *adj.* achieved by working together or with others —**col·lab·o·ra·tive·ly** *adv.*

col·lab·o·ra·tor /kə lábbə ràytər/ *n.* **1. SOMEBODY WORKING WITH OTHERS** somebody working with one or more other people to achieve something **2.** MIL **SOMEBODY WORKING WITH ENEMY** somebody who betrays others by working with an enemy, especially an occupying force

col·lage /kə laázh/ *n.* **1.** CRAFT **PICTURE WITH PIECES STUCK ON SURFACE** a picture made by sticking cloth, pieces of paper, photographs, and other objects onto a surface **2.** CRAFT **ART OF MAKING COLLAGES** the art of making pictures by sticking cloth, pieces of paper, photographs, and other objects onto a surface **3. COMBINATION OF DIFFERENT THINGS** a combination of different things ■ *vti.* (**-laged, -lag·ing, -lages**) CRAFT **MAKE COLLAGE** to make a picture by sticking cloth, pieces of paper, photographs, and other objects onto a surface [Early 20thC. From French, from *coller* "to glue," from *colle* "glue," from, ultimately, Greek *kolla* (see COLLO-).] —**col·lag·ist** *n.*

col·la·gen /kóllәjәn/ *n.* a fibrous protein found in skin, bone, cartilage, tendon, and other connective tissue that yields gelatin when boiled in water [Mid-19thC. From French *collagène*, from Greek *kolla* "glue" (see COLLO-).] —**col·la·gen·ic** /kòllə jénnik/ *adj.* —**col·lag·e·nous** /kə lájjənəss/ *adj.*

col·lag·e·nase /kóllәjә nàyss, -nàyz/ *n.* any enzyme that assists in the breakdown of collagen and gelatin

col·lap·sar /kə láp saàr/ *n.* ASTRON = **black hole** [Late 20thC. Coined from COLLAPSE (verb), on the model of PULSAR and QUASAR.]

col·lapse /kə láps/ *v.* (**-lapsed, -laps·ing, -laps·es**) **1.** *vi.* **FALL DOWN** to fall down suddenly, generally as a result of damage, structural weakness, or lack of support ○ *A section of cliff had collapsed into the sea.* **2.** *vi.* **FAIL ABRUPTLY** to fail or come to an end suddenly ○ *Their partnership nearly collapsed under the strain.* **3.** *vi.* MED **FALL SUDDENLY** to fall or faint because of illness, exhaustion, or weakness ○ *He collapsed from overwork.* **4.** *vi.* **SUDDENLY SIT OR LIE DOWN** to sit or lie down suddenly and relax completely or give way to emotion ○ *I collapsed into an armchair.* **5.** *vi.* **BEND DOUBLE WITH EMOTION** to bend over double or otherwise contort the body, typically in the throes of emotion such as laughter or crying **6.** *vti.* **DEFLATE** to fold up or become flat from lack of pressure or loss of air, or to cause something such as a parachute to do this ○ *The left lung had collapsed.* **7.** *vti.* **FOLD SOMETHING TO MAKE SMALLER** to fold something up so that it is smaller or takes up less space, or to fold up in this way ■ *n.* **1. FAILURE OR END** a failure or sudden end to something ○ *The abrupt collapse of the campaign.* **2. A FALLING DOWN** the act of falling down suddenly, generally as a result of damage, structural weakness, or lack of support ○ *The roof was in danger of collapse.* **3. DECREASE IN VALUE** a sudden reduction or decrease in value ○ *the threatened collapse of the yen* **4.** MED **SUDDEN ILLNESS** a sudden onset of severe illness, resulting in hospitalization or bed rest ○ *in a state of nervous collapse* [Mid-18thC. Back-formation from *collapsed*, from Latin *collapsus*, the past participle of *collabi*, literally "to fall together," from *labi* "to fall."]

col·laps·i·ble /kə lápsəb'l/ *adj.* designed to fold up so as to take up less space —**col·laps·i·bil·i·ty** /kə làpsə bíllətee/ *n.*

col·lar /kóllər/ *n.* **1.** CLOTHES **GARMENT'S NECKBAND** the upright or turned-over neckband of a coat, jacket, dress, shirt, or blouse **2. BAND AROUND NECK OF AN ANIMAL** a stiff band of leather, plastic, strong fabric, or metal placed around the neck of an animal to identify it or attach it to a lead or leash **3. AREA RESEMBLING A COLLAR** an area round the neck of a bird or animal that has a color or marking different from the rest **4.** AGRIC **PART OF A HARNESS** the cushioned ring or other part of a harness that presses against a draft animal's shoulders **5.** MECH ENG **RING-SHAPED DEVICE OR PART** a ring-shaped device or part on a shaft that guides, seats, or restricts another mechanical part **6.** ACCESSORIES **NECKLACE** a close-fitting necklace or one that lies flat over the shoulders **7.** FOOD **MEAT FROM NECK** a cut of meat, especially bacon, taken from an animal's neck **8. POLICE ARREST** an arrest made by a police officer (*slang*) ■ *vt.* (**-lared, -lar·ing, -lars**) **1. FIND OR STOP SOMEBODY** to find or stop somebody you want to talk to (*informal*) **2. CATCH SOMEBODY** to catch somebody and hold him or her to prevent escape (*slang*) **3. MAKE A POLICE ARREST** to arrest a criminal suspect in your capacity as a police officer (*slang*) **4. PUT A COLLAR ON SOMETHING** to put a collar on something, e.g., an animal, a garment, or a machine part [14thC. Via Old French *colier* from Latin *collare*, from *collum* "neck." Ultimately from an Indo-European word meaning "to turn around," which is also the ancestor of English *cycle*, *wheel*, and *palindrome*.] —**col·lared** *adj.* —**col·lar·less** *adj.* ◇ **hot under the collar** angry, irritated, or generally agitated (*informal*)

col·lar·bone /kóllər bōn/ *n.* = **clavicle** *n.* 1

col·lard /kóllərd/ *n.* **KALE** a variety of kale with a crown of smooth edible leaves ■ **collards** *npl.* = **collard greens** [Mid-18thC. An alteration of *colewort*.]

col·lard greens *npl.* the leaves of the kale plant, cooked and eaten as a vegetable

col·lared pec·ca·ry *n.* = **peccary**

collat. *abbr.* collateral

col·late /kṓ làyt, kə láyt/ (**-lat·ed, -lat·ing, -lates**) *vt.* **1.** COMM **PUT PAGES IN ORDER** to assemble pages in the correct order **2. COMPARE INFORMATION** to bring together pieces of information and compare them in detail **3.** PRINTING **EXAMINE SHEETS OR PAGES** to examine sheets or pages so as to put them into the proper sequence prior to binding **4.** PRINTING **VERIFY PAGE SEQUENCING** to verify the correct sequencing and completeness of the pages in a book **5.** CHR **ADMIT CLERIC TO BENEFICE** to admit a member of the clergy to a benefice [Mid-16thC. From Latin *collat-*, used as the past participle stem of *conferre*, literally "to bring together," from *ferre* "to bring" (source of English *confer*).]

col·lat·er·al /kə láttərəl/ *n.* **1.** FIN **PROPERTY AS SECURITY AGAINST LOAN** property or goods used as security against a loan and forfeited if the loan is not repaid **2.** SOC SCI **DESCENDANT FROM DIFFERENT LINE** a relative descended from the same ancestor as another person but through a different set of parents, grandparents, and other forebears ■ *adj.* **1. PARALLEL** running side by side in parallel or corresponding in some way, e.g., in size **2.** SOC SCI **DESCENDED FROM SAME ANCESTOR** having the same ancestor but descended through a different set of parents, grandparents, and other forebears **3. ADDITIONAL** additional to and in support of something **4. ACCOMPANYING** accompanying or additional but secondary **5.** FIN **WITH PROPERTY AS SECURITY** obtained by putting up property or goods as security, to be forfeited if the loan cannot be paid [14thC. From medieval Latin *collateralis*, literally "side by side with," from Latin *lateralis* "on the side" (see LATERAL).] —**col·lat·er·al·i·ty** /kə làttə rállətee/ *n.* —**col·lat·er·al·ly** /kə láttərəlee/ *adv.*

col·lat·er·al dam·age *n.* unintended damage to civilian life or property during a military operation

col·lat·er·al·ize /kə láttərə lī̀z/ (**-ized, -iz·ing, -izes**) *vt.* **1. PLEDGE AS COLLATERAL** to pledge property or goods as security for getting a loan **2. SECURE LOAN** to secure a loan by use of property or goods as security

col·la·tion /kə láysh'n, kō láysh'n/ *n.* **1. COMPARISON OF INFORMATION** a detailed comparison between different items or forms of information **2.** PRINTING **ASSEMBLY OF PAGES IN ORDER** the assembling of pieces of paper in the right order, particularly the sections of a book prior to binding **3.** PRINTING **TECHNICAL DESCRIPTION OF BOOK** the technical description of a book, including its bibliographical details and information about its physical construction, or the act of compiling a description **4.** COOK **LIGHT MEAL** a light meal or refreshment ○ *a cold collation* **5.** CHR **APPOINTMENT OF CLERGY** the appointment of clergy to a benefice **6.** CHR **READING OF RELIGIOUS TEXT** the reading of a religious text to a gathering of monks [14thC. From medieval Latin and Latin *collation-* "a bringing together" from *collat-* (see COLLATE).]

col·la·tive /kə láytiv, kō láytiv/ *adj.* CHR used to describe an ecclesiastical benefice to which a member of the clergy is appointed [Early 17thC]

col·la·tor /kṓ làytər, kə láytər/ *n.* a person or machine that reads, compares, and sorts pages, e.g., of a book [Early 17thC. Directly or via French from medieval Latin *collator*, from Latin, "contributor," literally "one who brings together," from the stem *collat-* "brought together" (see COLLATE).]

col·league /kó leèg/ *n.* a person somebody works with, especially in a professional or skilled job [Early 16thC. Via French from Latin *collega*, literally "someone one commissions with," from *legare* "to commission, entrust," from *lex* "law" (source of English *privilege*).] —**col·league·ship** *n.*

col·lect[1] /kə lékt/ *v.* (**-lect·ed, -lect·ing, -lects**) **1.** *vt.* **BRING THINGS TOGETHER** to gather things and bring them together ○ *I collected up my belongings and left.* **2.** *vt.* **KEEP THINGS OF SAME TYPE** to obtain and keep objects of a similar type because of their interest, value, or beauty **3.** *vt.* **FETCH AND BRING SOMEBODY OR SOMETHING** to fetch people or objects and bring them somewhere ○ *They collected me from the airport.* **4.** *vt.* **TAKE MONEY OR PRIZE** to take the money or prize to which a person is entitled **5.** *vti.* **ASK FOR DONATIONS** to ask for money from people for a particular purpose **6.** *vti.* **ACCUMULATE SOMEWHERE** to gather and gradually accumulate in a place **7.** *vi.* **GRADUALLY ASSEMBLE** to come together gradually in a place and form a group or crowd of people ○ *By now an angry crowd had collected.* **8.** *vr.* **GET CONTROL OF YOURSELF** to gain or regain control of yourself and deliberately calm yourself or prepare yourself psychologically **9.** *vi.* **GET MONEY FROM SOMETHING** to obtain money that is due, e.g., from an insurance policy ■ *adv.* TELECOM **SO THAT CALL RECIPIENT PAYS** so as to be charged to the receiver of a call that is placed ■ *adj.* TELECOM **PAYABLE BY RECEIVER** charged by the caller to the receiver [Mid-16thC. Directly or via French from medieval Latin *collectare*, from Latin *collect-*, past participle stem of *colligere*, literally "to gather together," from *legere* "to gather, read" (source of English *lecture*).]

WORD KEY: SYNONYMS

collect, accumulate, gather, amass, assemble, stockpile, hoard

CORE MEANING: to bring dispersed things together in a group or mass

collect a general term, with the additional sense that the things brought together have been selected or arranged in an orderly way, especially as a hobby; **accumulate** to collect over a period of time; **gather** to collect or accumulate, with the suggestion of bringing together things from various locations; **amass** to accumulate, with the suggestion of a large amount; **assemble** to bring things together in an orderly way for a specific purpose; **stockpile** to collect and keep for future use, or permanently; **hoard** a term similar to "stockpile," often suggesting greed or secrecy.

col·lect[2] /kóllikt, kó lèkt/ *n.* a short formal prayer that can vary according to the day, said before the reading of the epistle in certain Christian church services [13thC. Via Old French from late Latin *collecta* "assembly," from Latin, a form of *collectus* "gathered together" (see COLLECT[1]).]

col·lect·a·ble *n.* = **collectible**

col·lec·ta·ne·a /kò lek táynee ə/ *npl.* a selection of pieces of writing by an author or by several authors [Mid-17thC. From Latin, literally "things collected," a form of *collectaneus* "collected," from *collectus* "gathered together" (see COLLECT[1]).]

col·lect·ed /kə léktəd/ *adj.* **1. CALM AND COMPOSED** calm and in control of yourself **2.** LITERAT **BROUGHT TOGETHER AS WHOLE** gathered together in one book or set of volumes as the whole of an author's work or work of a particular type **3.** EQU **CONTROLLED IN GAIT** moving with a controlled gait [Early 17thC. The underlying idea is of having pulled yourself together.] —**col·lect·ed·ly** *adv.* —**col·lect·ed·ness** *n.*

col·lect·i·ble /kə léktəb'l/, **col·lect·a·ble** *n.* COLLECTING **OBJECT VALUED BY COLLECTORS** an object of a type that is valued or sought after by collectors ■ *adj.* **POPULAR**

WITH COLLECTORS good for collecting or popular with collectors and much sought after

col·lec·tion /kə léksh'n/ *n.* **1.** GROUP OF THINGS OR PEOPLE a group of things or people together in one place **2.** SEVERAL DIFFERENT WORKS TOGETHER a number of different pieces of writing or music together in one book, CD, or record **3.** OBJECTS HELD BY COLLECTOR a set of objects collected for their interest, value, or beauty **4.** PAINTINGS OR OBJECTS IN MUSEUM all the paintings or objects of one kind held by an art gallery or museum **5.** TAKING OF DONATIONS the act of taking money due or given ○ *They took up a collection for him when he was in the hospital.* **6.** CHR TAKING OF MONEY IN CHRISTIAN CHURCH the act of accepting money from worshipers in a Christian church service, or the money so collected **7.** FASHION RANGE OF NEW CLOTHES a range of newly designed clothes for a particular season ○ *the spring collection* **8.** MAIL TAKING OF SOMETHING the taking of something on a regular basis, e.g., letters from mailboxes by the Postal Service, or garbage from buildings **9.** GATHERING TOGETHER the act of gathering things together (*formal*) [14thC. Via Old French from the Latin stem *collection-*, from the stem *collect-* "gathered together" (see COLLECT[1]).]

col·lec·tive /kə léktiv/ *adj.* **1.** SHARED BY ALL made or shared by everyone in a group **2.** COLLECTED TO FORM WHOLE collected together to form a whole or added up to form a total from different sources or groups **3.** APPLYING TO MANY applying to a number of individuals taken together ○ *staff training was the collective responsibility of the three personnel officers* **4.** BUSINESS, POL WORKER-RUN UNDER STATE SUPERVISION used to describe a business or other enterprise run by the people who work in it but under the jurisdiction of the state ■ *n.* **1.** BUSINESS, POL WORKER-RUN ENTERPRISE an enterprise, such as a farm or factory, that is run by its workers under state control **2.** BUSINESS, POL MEMBERS OF COLLECTIVE the members of a collective who work in and run the business **3.** GRAM = **collective noun** —**col·lec·tive·ly** *adv.* —**col·lec·tive·ness** *n.*

col·lec·tive a·gree·ment *n.* a contract of employment negotiated between a management and union

col·lec·tive bar·gain·ing *n.* negotiations between a management and union about pay and conditions of employment on behalf of all the workers in the union [Coined by Beatrice Webb of the Fabians]

col·lec·tive farm *n.* a farm that is state-supervised but operated by its laborers

col·lec·tive noun *n.* a noun that refers to a group of people or things considered as a single unit. "Committee" and "government" are collective nouns.

WORD KEY: USAGE

Collective nouns: Examples of collective nouns are *audience, clergy, committee, crowd, flock, government, jury,* and *orchestra*, all of which are singular in form but plural in the sense of being made up of a number of individuals or individual things. Such nouns take singular verbs when they are regarded as units: *The jury has handed down a unanimous verdict.* But they take plural verbs when emphasis is placed on the individuals making up the unit: *The jury have been arguing among themselves for 12 hours, and no verdict is expected.* Nouns that denote a class of objects, for example, *furniture* and *luggage*, are always singular: *My luggage is missing.* It is important to avoid inconsistency in your choice of verb and pronoun number when using collective nouns. For instance, this example contains inconsistencies: *The committee has [*singular*] decided to reject the proposal and will give their [*plural*] reasons in writing tomorrow.*

col·lec·tive se·cu·ri·ty *n.* the maintenance of peace and security through the united action of nations

col·lec·tive un·con·scious *n.* the inherited part of unconscious thought, memories, and instinct, which, according to Jungian principles, is common to members of a people and is observable through dreams and behavior

col·lec·tiv·ism /kə léktə vìzzəm/ *n.* the system of control and ownership of factories and farms and of the means of production and distribution of products by a nation's people [Mid-19thC. From COLLECTIVE, on the model of French *collectivisme.*] —**col·lec·tiv·ist** *n.* —**col·lec·tiv·is·tic** /kə lèktə vístik/ *adj.* —**col·lec·tiv·is·ti·cal·ly** /-vístiklee/ *adv.*

col·lec·tiv·i·ty /kò lek tívvətee/ (*plural* **-ties**) *n.* **1.** STATE OF BEING TOGETHER a state or situation in which people or things are together or work together to form a whole **2.** POL AGGREGATE a group regarded as an aggregate, especially a people [Mid-19thC]

col·lec·tiv·ize /kə léktə vìz/ (**-ized, -iz·ing, -iz·es**) *vt.* to run or organize something such as a farm according to principles of collective control — **col·lec·tiv·i·za·tion** /kə lèktəvi záysh'n/ *n.*

col·lec·tor /kə léktər/ *n.* **1.** SOMEBODY WHO COLLECTS OBJECTS somebody who collects objects of a particular type for their interest, value, or beauty ○ *a stamp collector* **2.** SOMEBODY WHO COLLECTS SOMETHING somebody whose job is to collect something, e.g., money owed, tickets, or garbage **3.** CONTAINER WHERE THINGS COLLECT something in which things are collected intentionally or where unwanted things collect **4.** ELECTRON ENG TRANSISTOR REGION the region of a transistor toward or through which charge carriers flow [14thC] —**col·lec·tor·ship** *n.*

col·lec·tor's i·tem *n.* an object that is sought after or valued highly by collectors

col·leen /kə leén, kólleen/ *n.* **1.** *Ireland* GIRL a girl, especially a young girl **2.** IRISH GIRL a girl living or born in Ireland or a girl of Irish descent [Early 19thC. From Irish *cailín*, literally "little girl," from *caile* "girl."]

col·lege /kóllij/ *n.* **1.** INSTITUTION OF HIGHER LEARNING an institution of higher learning that provides education to undergraduates and awards bachelor's and sometimes master's degrees **2.** UNIVERSITY SCHOOL OR DIVISION a school or a division of a university that usually has its own dean and other administrators and whose faculty teaches and confers degrees in specific academic fields **3.** FACULTY AND STUDENTS OF COLLEGE the faculty and students of a college **4.** *U.K.* PART OF BRITISH UNIVERSITY a division of some British universities, e.g., Oxford or Cambridge **5.** PROFESSIONAL BODY a group of people, usually of the same profession, who have agreed duties and rights **6.** COLLEGE BUILDING OR BUILDINGS the building or buildings of a college **7.** *U.K.* BRITISH SCHOOL used as part of the name of some British private schools **8.** CHR BODY OF CLERGY a group or body of clergy who live together [14thC. Directly or via Old French from Latin *collegium* "association, corporation," from *collega* "colleague" (see COLLEAGUE).]

Col·lege Board a service mark for administration of aptitude and achievement tests, used by some U.S. colleges and universities in their admittance and placement of prospective students

Col·lege of Arms *n.* a British institution that specializes in matters relating to heraldry, the granting of arms, and tracing genealogies

Col·lege of Car·di·nals *n.* the body of cardinals who elect popes, assist the pope in church governance, and manage the Holy See in the absence of a living or elected pope [Shortening of *Sacred College of Cardinals*, its official name]

Col·lege Park /kòllij/ city in western Maryland, and home to the University of Maryland. Population: 24,987 (1996).

Col·lege Sta·tion city in eastern Texas, southwest of Huntsville, that is home to Texas A&M University. Population: 58,757 (1996).

col·lege try *n.* an all-out effort to achieve something (*informal*) ○ *I'll give it the old college try.*

col·le·gi·al /kə leéjee əl, -leéjəl/ *adj.* **1.** POWER-SHARING with power shared equally between colleagues **2.** CHR OF POWER-SHARING BY BISHOPS relating to a situation or system in the Roman Catholic Church in which the bishops share equal power **3.** OF COLLEGE OR UNIVERSITY involving, typical of, or belonging to a college or university [14thC. Directly or via Old French from late Latin *collegialis*, from Latin *collegium* (see COLLEGE).] —**col·le·gi·al·i·ty** /kə leèjee állətee/ *n.* —**col·le·gi·al·ly** /kə leéjee əlee, -leéjəlee/ *adv.*

col·le·gian /kə leéjee ən/ *n.* a college undergraduate, graduate student, or recent graduate [15thC. From medieval Latin *collegianus*, from Latin *collegium* "association, corporation" (see COLLEGE).]

col·le·giate /kə leéjət, kə leéjee ət/ *adj.* **1.** OF COLLEGE involving, belonging to, appropriate to, or being a college, including its students and their pursuits **2.** WITH SEPARATE COLLEGES consisting of separate university colleges ■ *n. Can* = **collegiate institute** [15thC. From medieval Latin *collegiatus* "(member) of a college," from Latin *collegium* (see COLLEGE).] —**col·le·gi·ate·ly** *adv.*

col·le·giate church *n.* **1.** CHURCH WITH CANONS a Roman Catholic or Anglican church that has a chapter of canons but is not a cathedral **2.** GROUP OF CHURCHES a group or association of churches that have pastors in common

col·le·giate in·sti·tute *n.* in some Canadian provinces, a high school that offers a high level of courses and facilities

col leg·no /kō láy nō/ *adv.* to be played by tapping the strings of a stringed instrument with the back of the bow (*used as a musical direction*) [20thC. From Italian, literally "with the wood."]

col·lem·bo·lan /kə lémbələn/ *n.* INSECTS = **springtail** [Late 19thC. From modern Latin *Collembola*, order name, from Greek *kolla* "glue" + *embolon* "peg, stopper." From its ventral tube, which can secrete an adhesive substance.] —**collem·bo·lous** *adj.*

col·len·chy·ma /kə léngkimə/ *n.* a layer of supportive plant tissue that consists of elongated living cells that have walls unevenly thickened with cellulose and pectin [Mid-19thC. Coined from COLLO- + -ENCHYMA.] —**col·len·chym·a·tous** /kòllən kímmətəss/ *adj.*

Colles' frac·ture /kólliz-/ *n.* a fracture of the radius bone in which a piece broken off at the end is displaced toward the back of the wrist. The fracture is commonly caused by falling on the palm of the hand. [Late 19thC. Named for Abraham *Colles* (1773–1843), Irish surgeon.]

col·let /kóllət/ *n.* **1.** CONE-SHAPED MECHANICAL PIECE a slotted cone-shaped piece that encloses and grips a rod or shaft when inserted into the sleeve of a lathe or other machine **2.** SETTING FOR GEMSTONE a band or claw that holds a gemstone **3.** BAND ATTACHED TO SPRING IN WATCH a ring that holds the hairspring in a watch [16thC. From French *collet*, literally "little collar," from *col* "collar," from Latin *collum* "neck" (see COLLAR).]

col·le·te·ri·al gland *n.* a reproductive gland in female insects that secretes a sticky material that binds eggs together or to a surface [Late 19thC. *Colleterial* from modern Latin *colleterium*, from Greek *kollan* "to glue" (see COLLO-).]

col·lide /kə líd/ (**-lid·ed, -lid·ing, -lides**) *vi.* **1.** CRASH INTO SOMETHING to hit a person or object moving toward you or a person or object you are moving toward ○ *I collided with her in the corridor.* **2.** COME INTO CONFLICT WITH SOMEBODY to come into conflict with somebody else or another group [Early 17thC. From Latin *collidere* "to shatter," literally "to strike together," from *laedere* "to strike, injure" (source of English *elide* and *lesion*).]

col·lid·er /kə lídər/ *n.* a particle accelerator in which two oppositely moving particle beams are made to collide. This allows the particles to use more of their energy to create new particles than when they collide with a fixed target.

Collie

col·lie /kóllee/ *n.* ZOOL a dog with a long narrow muzzle, originally bred to herd sheep. There are short-haired (smooth) and long-haired (rough) collies. ◊ **Border collie** [Mid-17thC. Origin uncertain; perhaps formed from COAL, from its color.]

col·lier /kóllyər/ *n.* **1.** MINING COAL MINER a coal miner (*dated*) **2.** SHIPPING COAL-TRANSPORT VESSEL a ship designed to transport coal [13thC. Formed from COAL. Originally in the meaning of "charcoal burner."]

col·lier·y /kóllyəree/ (*plural* **-ies**) *n.* a coal mine and the buildings associated with it

col·lin·e·ar /kō línnee ər/, **co·lin·e·ar** *adj.* MATH lying on or passing through a single straight line [Mid-19thC. Coined from COL- + LINEAR.] —**col·lin·e·ar·i·ty** /kō linnee érrətee/ *n.*

col·lins /kóllinz/ (*plural* **-lins·es**) *n.* an iced drink made with spirits such as gin or vodka and fruit juice such as lemon or lime [Mid-19thC. Origin uncertain; possibly from the name of the bartender who originally dispensed it.]

Col·lins /kóllinz/, **Jackie** (*b.* 1939) British novelist. Her popular novels include *The Bitch* (1978).

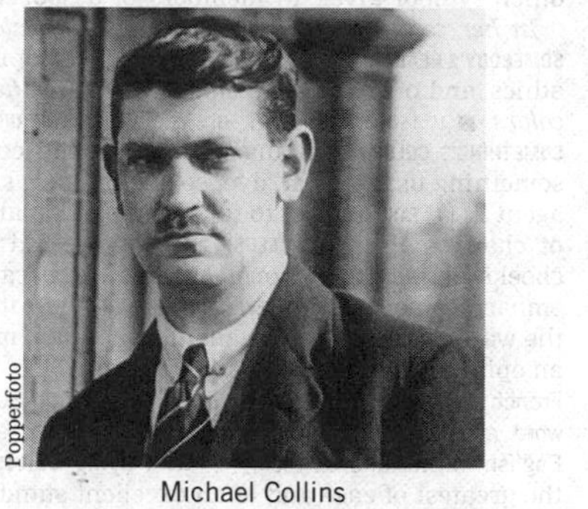

Michael Collins

Col·lins, Michael (1890–1922) Irish politician. A creator of the Irish Free State (1922), he was shot by Republicans who opposed the Anglo-Irish Treaty.

col·lin·si·a /kə línzee ə, -línsee ə/ *n.* a North American plant with blue, white, or purple flowers. Genus: *Collinsia.* [Early 19thC. Named for Zaccheus *Collins* (1764–1831), U.S. botanist.]

Col·lins·ville /kóllinz vìl/ city in southwestern Illinois, northeast of East St. Louis. Population: 23,057 (1996).

Col·lip /kóllip/, **James Bertram** (1892–1965) Canadian biochemist. He perfected a technique for producing pure insulin (1921) and researched other endocrine glands and hormones.

col·li·sion /kə lízh'n/ *n.* **1.** CRASH the action of two moving vehicles, ships, aircraft, or other objects hitting each other **2.** INSUR AUTOMOBILE INSURANCE COVERAGE automobile insurance that covers damages done to the insured's motor vehicle in the event that it collides with another vehicle or with some other object **3.** CONFLICT BETWEEN IDEAS a conflict between people or their ideas or beliefs **4.** PHYS EXCHANGE OF ENERGY BETWEEN PARTICLES an encounter between two or more particles that come together or close to each other, and exchange or transfer energy [15thC. From the late Latin stem *collision-*, from Latin *collis-*, the past participle stem of *collidere* "to smash together" (see COLLIDE).] —**col·li·sion·al** *adj.* —**col·li·sion·al·ly** *adv.*

col·li·sion course *n.* a path or course of action that inevitably leads to conflict ○ *The two of them were clearly headed on a collision course.*

col·li·sion zone *n.* an extensive linear feature marking the collision of two continental plates, characterized by young fold mountains and earthquakes

collo- *prefix.* glutinous, gelatinous ○ *collotype* [Via modern Latin from Greek *kolla* "glue" (source of English *collage* and *protocol*)]

col·lo·cate /kóllə kàyt/ *v.* (**-cat·ed, -cat·ing, -cates**) **1.** *vi.* LING OCCUR FREQUENTLY WITH ANOTHER WORD to occur frequently in conjunction with another word **2.** *vt.* PUT SOMETHING NEXT TO SOMETHING to arrange something so that it is next to or close to something else (*formal*) ■ *n.* LING WORD THAT OCCURS WITH ANOTHER a word that is frequently or typically used with another word [Early 16thC. From Latin *collocat-*, the past participle stem of *collocare*, literally "to place together," from *locare* "to place."]

col·lo·ca·tion /kòllə káysh'n/ *n.* **1.** LING CO-OCCURRENCE OF WORDS the association between two words that are typically or frequently used together **2.** CLOSENESS OF THINGS an arrangement in which things are placed next to each other or close together [Early 17thC] —**col·lo·ca·tion·al** *adj.*

col·lo·di·on /kə lṓdee ən/ *n.* a thick colorless solution of pyroxylin, ether, and alcohol. It is used in medicine to treat wounds and hold surgical dressings, and formerly in photography to make plates. [Mid-19thC. From Greek *kollōdēs* "gluelike," from *kolla* "glue" (see COLLO-).]

col·loid /kó lòyd/ *n.* **1.** CHEM SUSPENSION OF SMALL PARTICLES a suspension of small particles dispersed in another substance **2.** CHEM PARTICLES IN COLLOID the particles that are suspended in a colloid solution **3.** PHYSIOL SUBSTANCE IN THYROID GLAND a thick gelatinous substance that is produced in the thyroid gland and stores hormones ■ *adj.* CHEM OF COLLOID relating to or resembling a colloid [Mid-19thC. Coined from Greek *kolla* "glue" (see COLLO-) + -OID).] —**col·loid·al** /kə lóyd'l, ko lóyd'l/ *adj.*

col·lop /kólləp/ *n.* **1.** FOOD SLICE OF MEAT a slice of meat, especially fried bacon **2.** *U.S., Scotland* FAT FLESH a small roll of fat on the body **3.** PIECE a small piece of something [14thC. From Scandinavian.]

colloq. *abbr.* colloquial

col·lo·qui·a plural of **colloquium**

col·lo·qui·al /kə lṓkwee əl/ *adj.* **1.** INFORMAL appropriate to, used in, or characteristic of spoken language or of writing that is used to create the effect of conversation **2.** BY WAY OF CONVERSATION expressed by way of conversation (*archaic*) [Mid-18thC. Formed from Latin *colloquium* (see COLLOQUIUM).] —**col·lo·qui·al·i·ty** /kə lṑkwee álləteе/ *n.* —**col·lo·qui·al·ly** /kə lṓkwee əlee/ *adv.* —**col·lo·qui·al·ness** /kə lṓkwee əlnəss/ *n.*

col·lo·qui·al·ism /kə lṓkwee ə lìzzəm/ *n.* an informal word or phrase that is more common in conversation than in formal speech or writing

col·lo·qui·um /kə lṓkwee əm/ (*plural* **-ums** *or* **-a** /-lṓkwee ə/) *n.* **1.** UNIV ACADEMIC SEMINAR an academic conference or seminar in which a particular topic is discussed, often with guest speakers **2.** DISCUSSION MEETING an informal meeting to discuss something [Late 16thC. From Latin, "conversation," formed from *colloqui*, literally "to speak with," from *loqui* "to speak" (source of English *eloquent*).]

col·lo·quy /kólləkwee/ (*plural* **-quies**) *n.* **1.** DISCUSSION a formal conversation or discussion (*formal*) **2.** LITERAT WRITTEN DIALOGUE a literary or other written work in the form of a dialogue [15thC. Formed from Latin *colloquium* (see COLLOQUIUM).]

col·lo·type /kóllə tìp/ *n.* **1.** PRINTING PROCESS a process for making lithographic prints **2.** PRINT MADE BY COLLOTYPE a print that is made by use of the collotype process [Late 19thC. Coined from Greek *kolla* "glue" (see COLLO-) + -TYPE.]

col·lude /kə lo͞od/ (**-lud·ed, -lud·ing, -ludes**) *vi.* to cooperate with somebody secretly in order to do something illegal or undesirable [Early 16thC. From Latin *colludere*, literally "to play with," from *ludere* "to play," from *ludus* "game, play" (source of English *ludicrous*).] —**col·lud·er** *n.*

col·lu·sion /kə lo͞ozh'n/ *n.* secret cooperation between people in order to do something illegal or underhanded [14thC. Directly or via Old French from the Latin stem *collusion-*, from *collus-*, past participle stem of *colludere* (see COLLUDE).]

col·lu·sive /kə lo͞ossiv/ *adj.* secretly cooperating or involving secret cooperation in order to do something illegal or underhanded [Late 17thC. From Latin *collus-*, past participle stem of *colludere* (see COLLUDE).] —**col·lu·sive·ly** *adv.* —**col·lu·sive·ness** *n.*

col·lu·vi·um /kə lo͞ovee əm/ (*plural* **-a** /-ə/ *or* **-ums**) *n.* loose rock and soil at the base of a cliff or steep slope [Mid-20thC. From Latin, formed from *colluvies*, from *colluere*, literally "to wash thoroughly," from *lavere* "to wash" (source of English *lotion*).] —**col·lu·vi·al** /kə lo͞ovee əl/ *adj.*

col·ly·wob·bles /kólli wòbb'lz/ *npl.* (*informal*) **1.** STOMACH PAINS pains or cramps, or both, in the stomach or bowels (*takes a singular or plural verb*) **2.** *U.K.* NERVOUSNESS a feeling of nervousness about something [Early 19thC. Origin uncertain: probably formed from COLIC and WOBBLE, the underlying idea being of intestines wobbling.]

Colo. *abbr.* Colorado

colo-[1] *prefix.* relating to the colon [Via modern Latin from, ultimately, Greek *kolon* "large intestine" (see COLON[2])]

colo-[2] *prefix.* intestine ○ *colorectal* [From COLON]

col·o·bo·ma /kòllə bṓmə/ *n.* a structural defect in the retina, iris, or other tissue of the eye, usually present at birth [Mid-19thC. Via modern Latin from Greek *koloboma* "part removed in mutilation," from *kolobos* (see COLOBUS).] —**col·o·bo·ma·tous** *adj.*

col·o·bus /kólləbəss/ (*plural* **-bus·es** *or* **-bi** /-bì/), **col·o·bus mon·key** *n.* a large slender monkey native to Africa that has a long tail and long silky fur but lacks developed thumbs. Genus: *Colobus.* [Late 19thC. Via modern Latin from Greek *kolobos* "docked, maimed." Ultimately from an Indo-European word meaning "to cut," which is also the ancestor of English *calamity*.]

col·o·cynth /kólləsinth/ *n.* **1.** PLANTS VINE WITH BITTER FRUIT a European vine related to the pumpkin and squash that bears bitter yellow fruit about the size of a lemon but speckled with green. Latin name: *Citrulus colocynthis.* **2.** PLANTS, PHARM FRUIT OF COLOCYNTH the spongy bitter fruit of the colocynth that yields a powerful laxative or purgative [Mid-16thC. Via Latin from Greek *kolokunthis*, from *kolokunthē* "pumpkin, round gourd."]

co·logne /kə lṓn/ *n.* a scented liquid that is lighter than perfume [Early 19thC. Named for the city of *Cologne*, Germany, where it was first made.]

Co·logne /kə lṓn/ river port and largest city in the North Rhine-Westphalia state of Germany. Population: 958,600 (1992).

Colombia

Co·lom·bi·a /kə lúmbee ə, -lóm-/ republic in northwestern South America surrounded by the Caribbean Sea, Venezuela, Brazil, Peru, Ecuador, Panama, and the Pacific Ocean. Language: Spanish. Currency: peso. Capital: Bogotá. Population: 37,852,050 (1997). Area: 440,831 sq. mi./1,141,748 sq. km. Official name **Republic of Colombia** —**Co·lom·bi·an** *n., adj.*

Co·lom·bo /kə lúmbō/ commercial capital of Sri Lanka, situated on the west coast. It is also a port with a large artificially created harbor. Population: 615,000 (1990).

co·lon[1] /kṓlən/ *n.* **1.** LANG PUNCTUATION MARK the punctuation mark (:) used to divide distinct but related elements, e.g., clauses in which the second elaborates on the first, or to introduce a list, quotation, or speech **2.** MARK (:) USED IN PHONETICS a mark (:) after a vowel in a system of phonetic writing that shows that the vowel is lengthened **3.** (*plural* **cola**) LITERAT UNIT OF CLASSICAL POETRY in Greek or Roman verse, a rhythmic unit consisting of two to six metrical feet with one main accent [Mid-16thC. Via Latin from Greek *kōlon*, originally "limb," hence "unit of verse," hence "clause."]

co·lon[2] /kṓlən/ (*plural* **-lons** *or* **-la** /-lə/) *n.* the section of the large intestine that runs from the cecum to the rectum [14thC. Via Latin from Greek *kolon* "large intestine, food, meat," of unknown origin.]

co·lon[3] /kə lṓn/ (*plural* **-lons** *or* **-lo·nes** /kə lṓ nàyss/) *n.* **1.** see table at **currency 2.** COIN OR BILL WORTH ONE COLON a coin or bill worth one colon [Late 19thC. Named for Cristóbal *Colón*, Spanish name of Christopher Columbus.]

Co·lón /kə lṓn/ city and capital of Colón Province, central Panama, situated on Limón Bay at the entrance to the Panama Canal. Population: 54,654 (1990).

co·lon ba·cil·lus *n.* a bacterium found in the colon of humans and animals that becomes a serious contaminant when found in the food or water supply. Latin name: *Escherichia coli.*

colo·nel /kúrn'l/ *n.* **1.** MILITARY RANK IN UNITED STATES an officer whose rank in the U.S. Army, Marine Corps, or Air Force is between a brigadier general and a lieutenant colonel **2.** *U.K.* MILITARY RANK IN U.K. an officer whose rank in the British Army or Royal Marines is between a brigadier and a lieutenant colonel **3.** MILITARY RANK IN CANADA a high-ranking commissioned officer in the army or air force of Canada, ranking above lieutenant colonel and below brigadier general, equivalent in rank to a commander in the navy **4.** HONORARY TITLE an honorary title in an official state militia, given to respected citizens by the governor in some southern and central states. This practice is most closely associated with Kentucky, but also occurs in the states of Louisiana and Tennessee. [Mid-16thC. Via obsolete French *coronel* from Italian *colonnella,* literally "little column," from *colonna* "column," from Latin columna (see COLUMN).] —**colo·nel·ship** *n.*

colo·nel·cy /kúrn'lsee/ (*plural* **-cies**) *n.* the rank or commission of a colonel in the armed forces

co·lo·nes plural of **colon**[3]

co·lo·ni·a /kòlō neé ə/ *n.* a poor Hispanic-American community, especially along the border between the United States and Mexico [Late 20thC. From Spanish, literally "colony."]

co·lo·ni·al /kə lṓnee əl/ *adj.* **1.** RELATING TO COLONY possessing, ruling over, living in, or relating to a colony **2. co·lo·ni·al, Co·lo·ni·al** HIST RELATING TO BRITISH COLONIES IN AMERICA relating to the 13 original British colonies in North America before their independence in 1776 **3. co·lo·ni·al, Co·lo·ni·al** HIST OF THE BRITISH EMPIRE relating to the colonies of the former British Empire, or to the Empire as a whole **4.** ARCHIT, FURNITURE IN STYLE OF NORTH AMERICAN COLONIES dating from or in a style typical of British North America from the late 17th through the early 19th centuries **5.** ZOOL LIVING IN COLONIES used to describe animals that live in groups or colonies and are dependent on each other. Some, e.g., corals, are physically joined, while others, e.g., insects, show social organization and specialized functions. ■ *n.* **1.** SOMEBODY WHO LIVES IN COLONY somebody who lives in a colony but who is a national of the colonizing country **2.** SOMEBODY FROM A COLONY somebody whose native country is a colony **3.** ARCHIT COLONIAL-STYLE HOUSE a house built in the neoclassical style popular in the 17th and 18th centuries in the British colonies in America [Late 18thC. From COLONY, perhaps on the model of French *colonial.*] —**co·lo·ni·al·ly** *adv.* —**co·lo·ni·al·ness** *n.*

co·lo·ni·al·ism /kə lṓnee ə lìzzəm/ *n.* a policy in which a country rules other nations and develops trade for its own benefit —**co·lo·ni·al·ist** *n.* —**co·lo·ni·al·is·tic** /kə lṓnee ə lístik/ *adj.*

co·lo·ni·al·ize /kə lṓnee ə lìz/ (**-ized, -iz·ing, -iz·es**) *vt.* to enter a nation or other landmass and try to restructure it into a colony —**co·lo·ni·al·i·za·tion** /kə lṓnee ələ záysh'n/ *n.*

co·lon·ic /kō lónnik, kə-/ *adj.* MED, ANAT OF COLON relating to or situated in the colon ■ *n.* MED, ALTERN MED CLEANSING OF COLON a medical treatment in which fluids are injected through the anus into the colon to clean it out

col·o·nist /kóllənist/ *n.* **1.** SOMEBODY LIVING IN NEW COLONY somebody who goes to live in a new colony or is among the founders of a colony **2. col·o·nist, Col·o·nist** HIST EUROPEAN SETTLER OF NORTH AMERICA one of the early European settlers of North America before it became the United States **3.** BIOL ORGANISM MOVING INTO NEW ECOSYSTEM an organism, including a plant such as a weed, that moves into and establishes itself in a new ecosystem

co·lon·i·tis /kòlə nítiss/ *n.* = **colitis**

col·o·nize /kóllə nīz/ (**-nized, -niz·ing, -niz·es**) *v.* **1.** *vti.* ESTABLISH COLONY to establish a colony in another country or place **2.** *vt.* GO TO NEW LAND to go to and live in a colony or other civilized setting established in a foreign, hitherto sparsely inhabited or virtually unsettled land **3.** *vti.* BIOL BECOME ESTABLISHED IN NEW ECOSYSTEM to establish plants or animals, or become established, in a biological colony in a new ecosystem —**col·o·niz·a·ble** *adj.* —**col·o·ni·za·tion** *n.* —**col·o·ni·za·tion·ist** /kòllənə záysh'nist/ *n.* —**col·o·niz·er** /kóllə nīzər/ *n.*

col·on·nade /kòllə náyd, kóllə nàyd/ *n.* **1.** ARCHIT ROW OF SUPPORTING COLUMNS a row of columns, usually supporting a roof or arches **2.** GARDENING ROW OF TREES a row of evenly spaced trees [Early 18thC. From French, formed on the model of Italian *colonnato* from French *colonne* "column," from Latin *columna* (see COLUMN).] —**col·on·nad·ed** *adj.*

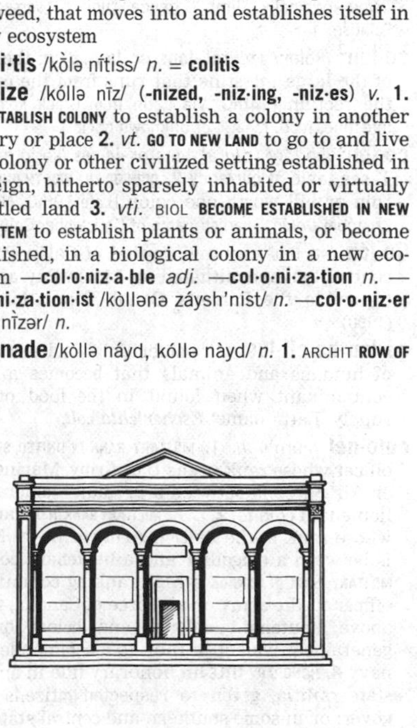

Colonnade

co·lon·o·scope /kə lónnə skōp/ *n.* a long flexible instrument (**endoscope**) used by a physician for viewing the interior of the colon, and often equipped with a device that can remove tissue for biopsy

co·lon·os·co·py /kòlə nóskəpee/ (*plural* **-pies**) *n.* a medical examination of the colon by a physician using a colonoscope [Coined from COLON[2] + -SCOPY] —**co·lon·o·scop·ic** /kòlənə skóppik/ *adj.*

col·o·ny /kólləne e/ (*plural* **-nies**) *n.* **1.** COUNTRY RULED BY ANOTHER a country or area that is ruled by another country **2.** HIST SETTLEMENT IN NORTH AMERICA one of the early settlements in North America that formed the 13 founding states of the United States after independence (*often used in the plural*) **3.** GROUP OF COLONISTS the group of people who have gone to live in a colony **4.** GROUP OF SIMILAR PEOPLE a group of people of the same nationality or ethnic group, doing the same work, or living in the same circumstances, who reside together or near one another ○ *a colony of artists* **5.** AREA WHERE GROUP LIVES the area, e.g., in a city, where a group of people of the same or similar ethnicity or interests or jobs lives **6.** BIOL GROUP OF ANIMALS OR PLANTS a group of animals, insects, or organisms of the same kind that are living together and dependent on each other, or a group of plants growing in the same place **7.** MICROBIOL MASS OF ORGANISMS a localized mass or growth of organisms, e.g., bacteria, in or on a nutrient medium [14thC. From Latin *colonia* "farm, settlement," from *colonus* "tiller, settler," from *colere* "to cultivate, dwell."]

col·o·phon /kóllə fòn/ *n.* **1.** PUBLISHER'S EMBLEM ON BOOK the symbol or emblem that is printed on a book and represents a publisher or publisher's imprint **2.** PUBLICATION DETAILS IN BOOKS the details of the title, printer, publisher, and publication date given at the end of a book. Colophons are commonly found in early printed books and in modern private press editions. [Early 17thC. Via late Latin from Greek *kolophōn* "summit, finishing touch."]

co·lo·phon·y /kóllə fōnee, kə lóffənee/ (*plural* **-ies**) *n.* = **rosin** [14thC. From Latin *colophonia,* from *Colophonia resina* "resin of Colophon," named for a city in the ancient kingdom of Lydia, in what is now Turkey.]

col·or /kúllər/ *n.* **1.** PROPERTY CAUSING VISUAL SENSATION the property of objects that depends on the light that they reflect and that is perceived as red, blue, green, or other shades **2.** PAINTING PIGMENT a pigment used in painting **3.** NOT BLACK OR WHITE a color such as red or green, as opposed to black, white, or gray **4.** SOMETHING THAT ADDS COLOR something such as paint, cosmetics, or dye that is used to add color to something **5.** NATURAL SHADE OF COMPLEXION the natural shade or color of somebody's skin as characteristic of race, especially of somebody who is not Caucasian ○ *a person of color* **6.** NONWHITE a skin color other than that normally described as white **7.** HEALTHY LOOK TO SKIN the normal look of a person's skin, especially in the face, when healthy **8.** EXTRA FACIAL REDNESS an extra redness in somebody's face, e.g., caused by embarrassment or exposure to cold wind **9.** VARIETY OF COLORS brightness and variety in the colors something such as a room or picture has **10.** INTEREST OR VIVIDNESS a quality in something that gives it interest or immediacy **11.** PAINTING USE OF COLOR IN PAINTING the use of color in painting, as distinct from line, form, or composition ○ *liked her handling of color* **12.** MUSIC SOUND QUALITY the quality of a particular sound **13.** LAW CLAIM OF LEGALITY a claim or appearance of legal right ○ *by color of law* **14.** PHYS HYPOTHETICAL QUANTUM CHARACTERISTIC a hypothetical property of quarks that takes three forms designated red, blue, and green **15.** PHYS HUE AND SATURATION the property or aspect of something that involves hue, lightness, and saturation or, in the case of light, hue, brightness, and saturation **16.** OPTICS ABILITY TO SEE COLORS the aspect of visual perception by which an observer recognizes colors **17.** PRINTING TYPE OF PRINTING INK the type and amount of inks used in a printing job ○ *a four-color brochure* **18.** MINING GOLD FOUND IN GRAVEL a particle of gold found in gravel or sand ■ **col·ors** *npl.* **1.** NATIONAL, STATE, OR MILITARY FLAG the flag of a nation, state, or military unit, or all of these combined, especially when on parade **2.** COLORS REPRESENTING TEAM OR GROUP the colors that are used to represent a team, school, or other group **3.** CLOTHING WORN IN SPORT the clothing worn by a jockey or an athlete that indicates the horse's owner or the team to which the athlete belongs **4.** HERALDRY HERALDIC COLOR the main heraldic colors (**tinctures**) of azure, vert, sable, gules, and purpure **5.** *U.K.* SPORTS TEAM MEMBERS' BADGE a badge or other symbol given to members of a sports team ○ *In her second year she got her rowing colors.* **6.** SOMEBODY'S REAL SELF somebody's real beliefs, opinions, ethics, and principles ○ *It showed her up in her true colors.* ■ *v.* (**-ored, -or·ing, -ors**) **1.** *vt.* CHANGE OR ADD TO SOMETHING'S COLOR to change or add to the color of something using paint, dye, cosmetics, or a similar agent **2.** *vi.* TAKE ON COLOR to take on a particular color or change color **3.** *vi.* BLUSH to get more red in the cheeks or face than normal, generally because of embarrassment **4.** *vt.* SKEW OPINION OR JUDGMENT to skew the way somebody thinks about something, making an opinion or judgment less objective [13thC. Via Old French from Latin *color.* Ultimately from an Indo-European word meaning "to cover," which is also the ancestor of English *holster* and *calypso.*] ◇ **with flying colors** with the greatest of ease and to an excellent standard ◇ **nail your colors to the mast** to make it obvious what your opinions or intentions are ○ *They've nailed their colors to the mast and announced that they will not sell their property for redevelopment.*

col·or·a·ble /kúllərəb'l/ *adj.* **1.** LOOKING REASONABLE BUT NOT SO appearing to be reasonable or true, but in fact being neither ○ *a colorable explanation* **2.** FEIGNING VALIDITY pretending to be true or valid [14thC. From Old French *colorable* "brightly colored," from *color* (see COLOR).] —**col·or·a·bil·i·ty** /kùllərə bíllətee/ *n.* —**col·or·a·ble·ness** /kúllərəb'lnəss/ *n.* —**col·or·a·bly** /kúllərəblee/ *adv.*

Colorado

Col·o·ra·do /kòllə ráddō, -raádō/ **1.** state in the western United States bordering on seven other states, including Utah to the west. Capital: Denver. Population: 3,892,644 (1997). Area: 104,100 sq. mi./269,618 sq. km. **2.** major North American river, rising in northern Colorado and flowing southwest through the Grand Canyon. Length: 1,450 mi./2,330 km. **3.** river in Texas, the longest entirely within the state. It rises in northwestern Texas and flows southeastward into the Gulf of Mexico. Length: 600 mi./965 km.

Col·o·ra·do bee·tle *n.* = **Colorado potato beetle**

Col·o·ra·do blue spruce *n.* = **blue spruce**

Col·o·ra·do Des·ert desert area of southeastern California west of the Colorado River. It includes the Salton Sea and the Imperial Valley.

Col·o·ra·do Pla·teau high, arid region covering parts of southeastern Utah, southwestern Colorado, northwestern New Mexico, and northern Arizona. Area: 50,000 sq. mi./130,000 sq. km.

Col·o·ra·do po·ta·to bee·tle *n.* a small black-and-yellow striped beetle that feeds on the leaves of potato plants and is a serious agricultural pest. Latin name: *Leptinotarsa decemlineata.* [From the fact that the beetle is native to the state of COLORADO]

Col·o·ra·do ru·by *n.* a type of red garnet crystal found in the state of Colorado

Col·o·ra·do Springs city in central Colorado, south of Denver and east of Pikes Peak. Population: 345,127 (1996).

Col·o·ra·do to·paz *n.* **1.** TOPAZ FOUND IN COLORADO a brownish-yellow topaz found in the state of Colorado **2.** BROWNISH-YELLOW QUARTZ a type of brownish-yellow quartz that resembles true Colorado topaz

col·or·ant /kúllərənt/ *n.* a dye, pigment, ink, or similar agent that is used to add or change color

col·or·a·tion /kùllə ráyshən/ *n.* **1.** COLOR APPEARANCE the appearance or pattern of color on an object **2.** COLORING OF AN ORGANISM the pattern of colors naturally occurring on an insect, bird, animal, or plant [Early 17thC]

col·or·a·tu·ra /kùllərə tóörə, kòllər-/ *n.* a passage or piece of vocal music characterized by florid and demanding ornamentation, usually consisting of a rapid succession of notes. Coloratura passages are frequent in 18th- and 19th-century arias. [Mid-18thC. From obsolete Italian, literally "coloring."]

col·or·a·tu·ra so·pran·o *n.* a soprano with a light versatile voice capable of performing coloratura roles

col·or bar *n.* = **color line**

col·or·blind *adj.* **1.** UNABLE TO DISTINGUISH BETWEEN CERTAIN COLORS partially or completely unable to see or to distinguish between certain colors because of a defect in vision **2.** NOT DISCRIMINATING not discriminating between people on the grounds of their ethnic group or the color of their skin [Mid-19thC. Coined by Sir David Brewster (1781–1868), the inventor of the kaleidoscope.] —**col·or·blind·ness** *n.*

col·or·breed /kúllər brēed/ (**-bred, -breed·ing, -breeds**) *vt.* to breed plants or animals selectively so that the offspring are of the desired color

col·or·cast /kúllər kàst/ (**col·or·cast** *or* **col·or·cast·ed, col·or·cast·ing, col·or·casts**) *n.* a television program broadcast in color [Mid-20thC. From COLOR + BROADCAST.] —**col·or·cast·er** *n.*

col·or-code (**col·or-cod·ed, col·or-cod·ing, col·or-codes**) *vt.* to classify different types of things by different colors

col·or con·trast *n.* the perceived difference in a color that occurs when it is surrounded by another color

col·o·rec·tal /kōlō rékt'l/ *adj.* relating to both the colon and rectum [Mid-20thC. Coined from COLO- + RECTAL.]

col·ored /kúllərd/ *adj.* **1.** HAVING COLOR having a particular color or colors (*often used in combination*) ○ *dark colored* ○ *honey colored* **2.** OFFENSIVE TERM an offensive term meaning belonging to an ethnic group whose members have dark-colored skin (*dated offensive*) **3. Col·ored, col·ored** *S Africa* OF MIXED ETHNIC ORIGIN belonging to a group of mixed ethnic origin (*dated*) ◊ **Cape Colored 4.** DISTORTED OR BIASED biased or sensationalized ○ *a highly colored account* ■ *n.* OFFENSIVE TERM an offensive term for somebody who belongs to an ethnic group that is predominantly dark-skinned (*dated offensive*)

col·or·fast /kúllər fàst/ *adj.* containing a dye that will not fade or wash out [Early 20thC. From FAST "firm."] —**col·or·fast·ness** *n.*

col·or fil·ter *n.* a filter made of colored glass or gelatin that absorbs light of a given color before it reaches the camera lens. It is used to achieve artistic effects or to compensate for weather conditions.

col·or·ful /kúllərfəl/ *adj.* **1.** WITH BRIGHT COLORS having bright or varied colors ○ *colorful costumes* **2.** INTERESTING interesting and exciting ○ *She has a colorful past.* **3.** NOT ORDINARY OR PREDICTABLE likely to behave in unusual and unexpected ways **4.** FULL OF SWEARWORDS characterized by coarse words or obscenities (*informal*) (*used euphemistically*) ○ *colorful language* —**col·or·ful·ly** *adv.* —**col·or·ful·ness** *n.*

col·or·if·ic /kùllə ríffik/ *adj.* producing or giving color to something

col·or·im·e·ter /kùllə rímmətər/ *n.* **1.** INSTRUMENT THAT MEASURES COLOR an instrument that determines the quality of colors by reference to a set of standard colors **2.** DEVICE USED TO FIND CONCENTRATIONS an instrument that determines the concentration of a solution of a colored substance by reference to standard solutions or standard color slides [Mid-19thC. Coined from Latin *color* (see COLOR) + -METER.] —**col·or·i·met·ric** /kùlləri méttrik/ *adj.* —**col·or·i·met·ri·cal·ly** /-méttrikəlee/ *adv.* —**col·or·im·e·try** /kùllə rímmətree/ *n.*

col·or·ing /kúlləring/ *n.* **1.** ACT OF GIVING COLOR the act of giving color to something **2.** COLORING SUBSTANCE a substance that gives color to something, e.g., a food dye **3.** TYPE OF COMPLEXION the shade of somebody's skin or hair color **4.** CHARACTERISTIC COLORS the characteristic colors of a bird's plumage or an animal's coat

col·or·ing book *n.* a book with drawings for a child to color

col·or·ist /kúllərist/ *n.* **1.** ARTIST KNOWN FOR USE OF COLORS a painter whose technique involves special use of color **2.** COLORER somebody whose work involves coloring things **3.** HAIR STYLIST a hair stylist who is professionally qualified to dye hair [Late 17thC. Formed from COLOR, on the model of Italian *colorista.*] —**col·or·is·tic** /kùllə rístik/ *adj.* —**col·or·is·ti·cal·ly** *adv.*

col·or·ize /kúllə rīz/ (**-ized, -iz·ing, -izes**) *vt.* to add color to a black and white movie, e.g., by using computer techniques

col·or·less /kúllərləss/ *adj.* **1.** WITHOUT COLOR lacking color **2.** CHARACTERLESS not interesting or exciting ○ *a colorless personality* **3.** PALE pale or lacking distinct color —**col·or·less·ly** *adv.* —**col·or·less·ness** *n.*

col·or line *n.* the legal, social, and traditional barriers that separate people of different ethnic groups

col·or phase *n.* **1.** SEASONAL VARIATION IN COLOR a seasonal variation in the colors of a bird's plumage or an animal's coat **2.** PERMANENT VARIATION IN COLOR a distinct and permanent color variation shown by a group of animals within a species

col·or·point short·hair *n.* a domestic cat belonging to a breed with a light-colored coat and darker markings on the face, ears, feet, and tail

col·or scheme *n.* a combination of colors used in interior decoration

col·or sub·car·ri·er *n.* the component of a television signal that transmits color information to the receiver

col·or·way *n.* one of range of possible colors available ○ *The shirt comes in three exciting colorways, taupe, red, and navy.*

col·or wheel *n.* the spectrum represented as a circular diagram that shows how colors are related to one another

co·los·sal /kə lóssəl/ *adj.* **1.** VERY LARGE unusually or impressively large **2.** VERY GREAT very great or impressive ○ *Our opponents made a colossal blunder.* ○ *a colossal increase in consumer spending* **3.** SCULPTURE TWICE LIFE SIZE used to describe sculptures that are twice life size —**co·los·sal·ly** *adv.*

col·os·se·um *n.* = **coliseum**

Colosseum, Rome, Italy

Colosseum /kòllə sée əm/ *n.* a large amphitheater in Rome, Italy, built in the 1st century A.D. for sports and entertainment

Co·los·sians /kə lósh'nz/ *n.* the twelfth book of the New Testament, a letter from St. Paul to the church in the Phrygian city of Colossae written between 55 and 63 A.D. See table at **Bible** [Early 16thC]

co·los·sus /kə lóssəss/ (*plural* **-si**) *n.* **1.** SCULPTURE HUGE STATUE a statue that is several times larger than life size **2.** SOMETHING ENORMOUSLY LARGE OR POWERFUL an enormously large or powerful person or thing ○ *a colossus among contemporary fashion designers* [14thC. Via Latin from Greek *kolossos*, of uncertain origin: possibly from a non-Indo-European Mediterranean language.]

co·los·to·my /kə lóstəmee/ (*plural* **-mies**) *n.* **1.** OPERATION CREATING AN ARTIFICIAL ANUS a surgical operation that creates an artificial anus through an opening made in the abdomen from the colon **2.** ARTIFICIAL ANUS an opening surgically created in the abdomen that functions as an anus [Late 19thC. Coined from COLO- + -STOMY.]

co·los·trum /kə lóstrəm/ *n.* a yellowish fluid rich in antibodies and minerals that a mother's breasts produce after giving birth and before the production of true milk. It provides newborns with immunity to infections. [Late 16thC. From Latin, of unknown origin.]

col·our *n., vti.* U.K. = **color**

col·our·point cat *n. U.K.* = **Himalayan cat**

col·our sup·ple·ment *n. U.K.* a magazine printed in color and forming a section of a newspaper

col·pi·tis /kol pítiss/ *n.* MED = **vaginitis** (*technical*)

colpo- *prefix.* vagina ○ *colposcope* [From Greek *kolpos* (source also of English *gulf*)]

col·po·scope /kóllpə skōp/ *n.* a magnifying and photographic instrument used to examine the vagina [Mid-20thC. From Greek *kolpos* "womb."] —**col·po·scop·ic** /kòlpə skóppik/ *adj.* —**col·pos·co·py** /kol póskəpee/ *n.*

colt /kōlt/ *n.* **1.** YOUNG MALE HORSE a young uncastrated male horse, usually under four years of age **2.** INEXPERIENCED YOUNG PERSON somebody who is young and inexperienced (*literary*) [Old English. Origin unknown.]

Colt /kōlt/ *tdmk.* a trademark for a brand of firearm

Colt /kōlt/, **Samuel** (1814–62) U.S. inventor. He patented a pistol with a revolving cylinder (1836) that was used in the Mexican War (1846–48).

col·ter *n.* = **coulter**

colt·ish /kṓltish/ *adj.* energetic and playful in nature [14thC. From the wild behavior of a colt.] —**colt·ish·ly** *adv.* —**colt·ish·ness** *n.*

Col·ton /kṓlt'n/ city in southern California, a southern suburb of San Bernardino. Population: 43,309 (1996).

Col·trane /kōl tràyn/, **John** (1926–67) U.S. saxophonist and composer. He was a leading proponent of free-form jazz in the 1960s. His compositions include *"Giant Steps."*

colts·foot /kṓlts fòot/ (*plural* **-foots** *or* **-foot**) *n.* a plant of the daisy family found in Europe, Asia, and North America, with yellow flower heads and large hoof-shaped leaves. The dried leaves and flowers are used in herbal medicine to treat coughs. Latin name: *Tussilago farfara.* [Mid-16thC. From the shape of the leaves.]

col·u·brid /kóllәbrid/ (*plural* **-brid** *or* **-brids**) *n.* a snake belonging to a family of mostly nonvenomous snakes. King snakes, garter snakes, and water snakes are colubrids. Family: Colubridae. [Late 19thC. From modern Latin *Colubridae*, family name, which was coined from Latin *colubrid-*, the stem of *coluber* "snake" (see COBRA).]

col·u·brine /kóllə brīn, -brin/ *adj.* **1.** LOOKING LIKE A SNAKE resembling a snake **2.** RELATING TO COLUBRIDS belonging or relating to the colubrid snakes [Early 16thC. From Latin *colubrinus*, from *coluber* "snake" (see COLUBRID).]

co·lu·go /kə lóo gō/ (*plural* **-gos** *or* **-go**) *n.* = **flying lemur** [Early 18thC. From Malay.]

col·um·bar·i·um /kòlləm báiree əm/ (*plural* **-a** /-ə/), **col·um·bar·y** /kólləm bèrree/ (*plural* **-ies**) *n.* **1.** PLACE FOR STORING FUNERAL URNS a chamber or wall in which urns containing the ashes of the dead are stored **2.** NICHE FOR FUNERAL URN one of the niches in a building used to store funeral ashes [Mid-18thC. From Latin, formed from *columba* "dove" (see COLUMBINE[1]).]

Co·lum·bi·a /kə lúmbee ə/ **1.** river that flows through southwestern Canada and the northwestern United States and empties into the Pacific Ocean below Portland, Oregon. Length: 1,240 mi./2,000 km. **2.** city in central Missouri, northwest of Jefferson City, that is home to the University of Missouri. Population: 76,756 (1996). **3.** city in central Tennessee, on the south bank of the Duck River, south of Nashville. Population: 32,043 (1996). **4.** capital of South Carolina, on the east bank of the Congaree River, northwest of Charleston. Population: 112,773 (1996).

Co·lum·bi·a Heights city in southeastern Minnesota, on the Mississippi River, a northern suburb of Minneapolis. Population: 18,368 (1996).

Co·lum·bi·an /kə lúmbee ən/ *adj.* relating to or typical of the United States, or its people or culture. ◊ **pre-Columbian**

Co·lum·bi·a Pla·teau region of the western United States, including parts of Washington, Oregon, and Idaho. Area: 200,000 sq. mi./520,000 sq. km.

col·um·bine[1] /kólləm bīn/ (*plural* **-bines** *or* **-bine**) *n.* a plant native to northern temperate zones that has five-petaled flowers with long spurs. Genus: *Aquilegia.* [14thC. Via Old French from medieval Latin *columbina (herba),* literally "dovelike (plant)," from Latin *columbinus* (see COLUMBINE[2]); from the resemblance of the flower to a cluster of pigeons.]

col·um·bine[2] *adj.* resembling or relating to doves [14thC. Via Old French from Latin *columbinus* "dovelike," which was formed from *columba* "dove, pigeon."]

co·lum·bite /kə lúm bīt/ *n.* a black, reddish-brown, or transparent mineral that is an ore of niobium and is made up of iron and manganese. Formula: $(Fe,Mn)(Nb,Ta)_2O_6$. [Early 19thC. Coined from COLUMBIUM + -ITE.]

co·lum·bi·um /kə lúmbee əm/ *n.* the element niobium (*no longer in technical use*) Symbol **Cb** [Early 19thC. Formed from modern Latin *Columbia* "America," named for Christopher *Columbus* (from the fact that the element was discovered in ore from Massachusetts).] —**co·lum·bic** *adj.* —**co·lum·bous** *adj.*

Co·lum·bus /kə lúmbəss/ **1.** capital of Ohio, and its largest city. It is home to Ohio State University. Population: 657,053 (1996). **2.** city in western Georgia, on the Chattahoochee River, east of Phoenix City, Alabama. Population: 182,828 (1996). **3.** city in Indiana, southwest of Indianapolis, where the Big Blue River and Flatrock Creek meet. Population: 32,963 (1996).

Co·lum·bus, Christopher (1451–1506) Italian explorer. He reached the West Indies in 1492, thereby opening the Americas to European trade and colonization.

Co·lum·bus Day *n.* a U.S. holiday, falling on October 12, that celebrates Christopher Columbus's first voyage to the Americas in 1492

col·u·mel·la /kòllə méllə/ (*plural* **-lae**) *n.* a tiny bone in the middle ear of all land vertebrates that transmits sound waves from the eardrum to the inner ear and corresponds to the stapes in mammals [Late 16thC. From Latin, literally "little column," formed from *columna* "column" (see COLUMN).] —**col·u·mel·lar** *adj.* —**col·u·mel·late** /-méllət, -mé làyt/ *adj.*

col·umn /kólləm/ *n.* **1. ROUND PILLAR** an upright support shaped like a long cylinder ○ *a Corinthian column* ○ *the white columns of Mount Vernon* **2. SOMETHING SHAPED LIKE A COLUMN** something compared to a column in form ○ *a column of smoke* **3. REGULAR ARTICLE** an item in a newspaper or magazine that is always written by the same person, or is always about the same subject **4. VERTICAL ARRANGEMENT OF NUMBERS** a vertical arrangement of figures or mathematical terms **5. SECTION OF PAGE** one of two or more vertical sections of printed material on a page **6. LINE OF PEOPLE OR THINGS** a long line of people or vehicles **7.** ANAT, BOT **PART SHAPED LIKE COLUMN** any long part of a plant or animal ○ *spinal column* [15thC. Directly or via Old French from Latin *columna* (source of English *colonel*), of uncertain origin; probably formed from *columen, culmen* "top, summit" (source of English *culminate*).] —**col·umned** *adj.*

col·um·ne·a /kə lúmnee ə/ (*plural* **-as** *or* **-a**) *n.* a tropical American bushy or trailing plant grown as a houseplant for its colorful tubular flowers. Genus: *Columnea.* [Mid to late 18thC. From modern Latin *columna,* the Latinized form of the name of Fabio *Colonna* (1567–1640), Italian writer on plants.]

col·umn inch *n.* an area on a page one column wide and one inch deep, used to measure the amount of type that would fill that space

col·um·nist /kólləmnist/ *n.* somebody who writes a regular column for a newspaper or magazine ○ *a gossip columnist*

col·ure /kə lóor/ *n.* either of two great circles on the celestial sphere that intersect at the celestial poles, one of which connects the equinoctial points on the ecliptic while the other connects the solstitial points [14thC. Via late Latin *coluri* from Greek *kolourai (grammai)* "truncated (lines)," from *kolouros,* from *kolos* "docked" + *oura* "tail."]

col·y /kólee/ (*plural* **-ies** *or* **-y**) *n.* a gregarious African bird that has soft hairy plumage, a crest on its head, and a very long tail. Family: Coliidae. [Mid-19thC. Via modern Latin *Colius,* genus name, from Greek *kolios* "green woodpecker," of uncertain origin; from the bird's pecking.]

com /kom/ *abbr.* company (*used in e-mail addresses*)

COM /kom/ *n.* a process of converting computer output directly to microfilm. Full form **computer output on microfilm**

com. *abbr.* **1.** comedy **2.** comic **3.** commerce **4.** commercial **5.** committee **6.** commune

Com. *abbr.* **1.** Commander **2.** Commodore **3.** Communist

com- *prefix.* together, with, jointly (*used before b, n, or p*) ○ *commix* [From Latin *com.* Ultimately from an Indo-European base meaning "together," which is also the ancestor of English *contra-* and *coeno-*.]

co·ma[1] /kṓmə/ *n.* a prolonged state of deep unconsciousness [Mid-17thC. Via modern Latin from Greek *kōma* "deep sleep," of uncertain origin: perhaps related to Greek *koiman* "to put to sleep" (source of English *cemetery*).]

co·ma[2] /kṓmə/ (*plural* **-mae** /-mee/) *n.* **1.** ASTRON **CLOUD AROUND HEAD OF COMET** a luminous cloud of gas and dust surrounding the head of a comet **2.** OPTICS **DISTORTION OF IMAGE** a lens defect that produces a blurred, comet-shaped image of a point, or the image produced [Early 17thC. Via Latin from Greek *komē* "hair of the head," of unknown origin.] —**co·mal** *adj.*

Co·ma Ber·e·ni·ces /kṓmə berrə nī́ seez/ *n.* a faint constellation in the sky of the northern hemisphere between Virgo and the Big Dipper

comal /kō maál/ *n. Southwest U.S.* a griddle

Co·man·che /kə mánchee/ (*plural* **-che** *or* **-ches**) *n.* **1. MEMBER OF NATIVE AMERICAN PEOPLE** a member of a Native American people who formerly led a nomadic life in areas of Kansas, Oklahoma, and Texas and who now live mainly in Oklahoma **2. COMANCHE LANGUAGE** the Shoshonean language of the Comanche people. Comanche is spoken by about 500 people. [Early 19thC. Via Spanish from Southern Paiute or another Numic language.] —**Co·man·che** *adj.*

Co·man·che·an /kə mánchee ən/ *n.* a part of the early Cretaceous period in North America, which lasted from 140 to 100 million years ago [Named for *Comanche,* a county in Texas where limestone rocks of this period were first found] —**Co·man·che·an** *adj.*

Co·ma·ne·ci /kòmmə néchee, -neéch/, **Nadia** (*b.* 1961) Romanian-born U.S. gymnast. At the age of 14 she was the youngest person to win an Olympic gold medal in gymnastics and the first to attain a perfect 10 mark (1976).

co·ma·tose /kṓmətōss/ *adj.* **1. IN A COMA** in a coma **2. UNABLE TO FUNCTION** in a very tired or drunken state (*informal*) ○ *After driving 14 hours in a snowstorm, I was comatose the entire next day.* [Late 17thC. Formed from Greek *kōmat-,* the stem of *kōma* "deep sleep" (see COMA[1]).] —**co·ma·tose·ly** *adv.*

co·mat·u·lid /kə máchəlid/ (*plural* **-lids** *or* **-lid**), **co·mat·u·la** /kə máchələ/ (*plural* **-lae** /-lee/ *or* **-la**) *n.* a marine invertebrate animal that is free-swimming when it reaches maturity. Feather stars are comatulids. Order: Comatulida. [Late 19thC. From modern Latin *Comatulidae,* family name, from late Latin *comatulus* "with neatly curled hair," from Latin *comatus* "having hair."]

comb /kōm/ *n.* **1. INSTRUMENT FOR ARRANGING HAIR** an instrument with a row of long thin teeth, used to arrange hair **2. FASTENING FOR HAIR** a piece of plastic or wood with long thin teeth, used to fasten back the hair **3.** TEXTILES **TOOL FOR CLEANING WOOL** a tool or part of a machine with long slender teeth, used for cleaning wool or other materials **4.** EQU = **currycomb 5.** ZOOL **CREST OF ROOSTER** the fleshy red growth on the head of a rooster or other bird **6.** ZOOL **HONEYCOMB** a honeycomb ■ *vt.* (**combed, comb·ing, combs**) **1. ARRANGE HAIR WITH COMB** to arrange hair or fur with a comb **2.** TEXTILES **CLEAN OR ARRANGE FIBERS** to clean or arrange the fibers of wool or other materials using a comb **3. SEARCH PLACE THOROUGHLY** to search an area thoroughly ○ *We combed the house for his keys.* [Old English *camb, comb.* Ultimately from an Indo-European word meaning "tooth, nail," which is also the ancestor of English *gem.*] ◇ **go over something with a fine-tooth(ed) comb, go through something with a fine-tooth(ed) comb** to study or search something extremely carefully

comb. *abbr.* **1.** combination **2.** combining **3.** combustion

com·bat *n.* /kóm bàt/ **1. FIGHTING** fighting between groups or individuals, especially between armies (*often used before a noun*) ○ *He had never seen combat.* ○ *combat troops* **2. FIGHT OR STRUGGLE** a struggle between opposing individuals or forces ○ *combat between good and evil* ■ *vt.* /kəm bát, kóm bàt/ (**-bat·ed** *or* **-bat·ted, -bat·ing** *or* **-bat·ting, -bats**) **1. TRY TO DESTROY SOMETHING DANGEROUS** to attempt to destroy or control something harmful ○ *measures to combat pollution* **2. RESIST SOMETHING** to resist somebody or something actively [Mid-16thC. Via French *combattre* "to fight" from assumed late Latin *combattere,* literally "to fight with," from, ultimately, Latin *battuere* "to beat" (see BATTER).] —**com·bat·a·ble** /kəm báttəb'l/ *adj.* —**com·bat·er** /-báttər/ *n.*

com·bat·ant /kəm bátt'nt/ *n.* **1. SOMEBODY TAKING PART IN WAR** a person or group taking part in a war **2. SOMEBODY INVOLVED IN ARGUMENT** somebody who is involved in a struggle or argument

Com·bat Arms *npl.* in the U.S. Army, the units that actually engage the enemy in combat, e.g., the infantry, armor, or field artillery

com·bat fa·tigue *n.* a psychological disorder resulting from the stress of being involved in a battle and characterized by acute anxiety, depression, and loss of motivation

com·bat·ive /kəm báttiv/ *adj.* eager to fight or argue —**com·bat·ive·ly** *adv.* —**com·bat·ive·ness** *n.*

comb·er /kṓmər/ *n.* **1.** TEXTILES **SOMEBODY OR SOMETHING THAT COMBS YARN** a person or machine that combs wool or other materials **2. BIG WAVE HITTING BEACH** a long high wave that crashes onto a beach

com·bi·na·tion /kòmbi náysh'n/ *n.* **1. MIXTURE** a mixture of different things or factors, or the act of mixing them ○ *We were saved by a combination of skill and good luck.* **2. COMBINED SET** two or more things or people that are combined to form a set ○ *The red shirt and navy vest make a striking color combination.* **3. NUMBERS THAT OPEN A LOCK** a series of numbers or letters needed to open a combination lock **4.** BOXING **SERIES OF PUNCHES** in boxing, two or more punches quickly delivered one after the other **5. ALLIANCE** an association between groups or individuals established in order to accomplish something **6.** MATH **ARRANGEMENT OF NUMBERS IN SUBSETS** an arrangement of the numbers or symbols in a mathematical set into smaller subsets without regard to the order in which those numbers or symbols appear **7.** MATH **SUBSET** a subset containing a specified number of the elements of a given set, selected without regard to the order in which they were chosen **8.** CHESS **SEQUENCE OF MOVES INVOLVING MULTIPLE PIECES** a series of tactical moves involving two or more chess pieces **9.** CHEM **FORMATION OF A COMPOUND** the union of substances in the formation of a chemical compound —**com·bi·na·tion·al** *adj.*

com·bi·na·tion lock *n.* a lock that operates by means of a set of wheels, each having a sequence of numbers from 0 to 9. It opens only when the wheels are aligned to give a specific sequence of numbers.

com·bi·na·tion tone *n.* MUSIC = **resultant tone**

com·bi·na·to·ri·al a·nal·y·sis *n.* a branch of mathematics dealing with combinations and permutations, especially those relating to probability and statistics

com·bine *v.* /kəm bī́n/ (**-bined, -bin·ing, -bines**) **1.** *vti.* **JOIN OR MIX TOGETHER** to join or mix together, or join or mix people or things together ○ *Combine the ingredients in a large mixing bowl.* ○ *All these factors combine to make for a truly successful product.* **2.** *vt.* **DO THINGS SIMULTANEOUSLY** to undertake two or more activities at the same time ○ *She has successfully combined a career as an attorney and a state senator.* **3.** *vti.* CHEM **UNITE CHEMICALLY** to join together or to make substances join together to form a chemical compound **4.** *vti.* AGRIC **HARVEST CROPS WITH MACHINE** to harvest crops using a combine harvester ■ *n.* /kóm bīn/ **1. ASSOCIATION** an illegal association of business organizations **2.** AGRIC = **combine harvester** [15thC. From late Latin *combinare,* literally "to put two things together," from Latin *bini* "two at a time," from *bi-* "twice" (see BI-).] —**com·bin·a·ble** *adj.* —**com·bi·na·tive** /kómbi nàytiv/ *adj.* —**com·bin·er** /kəm bī́nər/ *n.*

com·bined /kəm bī́nd/ *n.* SKIING a skiing event involving competition in downhill and slalom runs that are slightly less arduous than either run as a single event

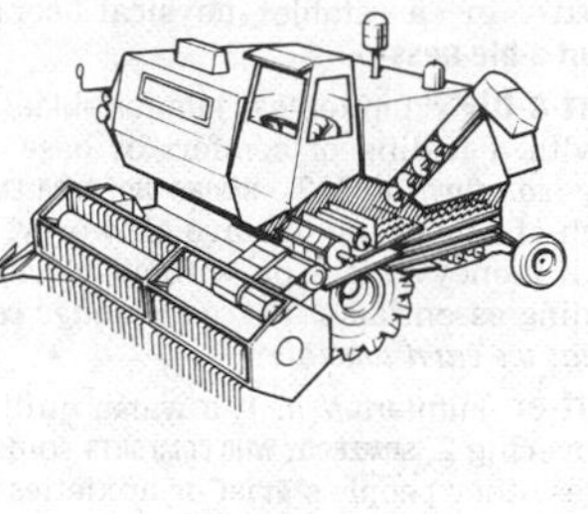

Combine harvester

com·bine har·vest·er *n.* a large farm machine that is used to harvest crops

comb·ings /kómingz/ *npl.* small loose pieces of hair, wool, or other fiber that are collected during combing

com·bo /kóm bō/ (*plural* **-bos**) *n.* **1. JAZZ GROUP** a small jazz or dance band **2. SOMEBODY OR SOMETHING JOINED** a combination of several people or elements (*informal*) ○ *a burger, fries, and shake combo* [Early 20thC. Formed from COMBINATION.]

com·bust /kəm búst/ (**-bust·ed, -bust·ing, -busts**) *vti.* to react vigorously with oxygen to produce heat and light, seen as a flame [15thC. Partly from obsolete *combust* "burned," from Latin *combustus* (see COMBUSTION); partly a back-formation from COMBUSTION.]

com·bus·ti·ble /kəm bústəb'l/ *adj.* **1. LIKELY TO CATCH FIRE** able or likely to catch fire and burn **2.** CHEM **REACTING WITH OXYGEN TO PRODUCE FLAME** able to react vigorously with oxygen to produce heat and light, seen as a flame —**com·bus·ti·bil·i·ty** /kəm bùstə bíllətee/ *n.* —**com·bus·ti·bly** /kəm bústiblee/ *adv.* —**com·bus·ti·ble** /kəm bústib'l/ *n.*

com·bus·tion /kəm búschən/ *n.* **1. IGNITION** the burning of fuel in an engine to provide power **2. CHEMICAL REACTION** a chemical process in which a substance reacts vigorously with oxygen to produce heat and light, seen as a flame **3. EXTREME AGITATION** a state of extreme discontent and agitation [15thC. From Latin *combustos*, the past participle of *comburere* "burn up," from, ultimately, *urere* "burn."] —**com·bus·tive** *adj.*

com·bus·tion cham·ber *n.* an enclosed space in which combustion takes place, e.g., in a jet engine or internal-combustion engine

com·bus·tor /kəm bústər/ *n.* a combustion system in a jet engine or gas turbine, consisting of the fuel injection system, the igniter, and the combustion chamber

comd. *abbr.* MIL command

comdg. *abbr.* MIL commanding

Comdr. *abbr.* Commander

Comdt. *abbr.* Commandant

come (**came, coming, comes**) CORE MEANING: a basic intransitive verb expressing movement toward a specified place or person. This verb often expresses the concept of movement coupled with the arrival at a place where an activity will take place. ○ *Come and sit by me.* ○ *Come to my house tomorrow.*

1. *vi.* **ORIGINATE FROM** to originate from a place or thing ○ *The meat came from Canadian herds.* **2.** *vi.* **ARRIVE OR HAPPEN** to happen or exist at a particular point or time ○ *I never thought this day would come.* **3.** *vi.* **RESULT FROM** to result from something ○ *We hoped some good would come of it.* **4.** *vi.* **BE PRODUCED** to be produced in a particular size, color, or style ○ *This model also comes in red.* **5.** *vi.* **REACH** to reach or extend to a particular point or place ○ *Her hair came down to her waist.* **6.** *v. vti.* **OCCUR IN THE MIND** to occur in the mind ○ *An afterthought came to me while I was shaving.* **7.** *vi.* **REACH A STATE** to reach or be brought into a particular state or situation ○ *It just came apart in my hands.* **8.** *vi.* **HAVE AN ORGASM** to reach sexual climax (*slang*) (*considered offensive by some speakers*) **9.** *vi.* **AMOUNT TO** to add up to a particular total ○ *That comes to $14.50.* **10.** *prep.* by a particular time in the future ○ *Come July there will be an extra fifty cases to deal with.* **11.** *n.* **SEMEN** a man's semen (*slang offensive*) ◇ **come again?** used to ask someone to repeat or explain something (*informal*) ◇ **come to pass** to happen (*archaic or literary*)

come about *vi.* to take place or occur

come across *v.* **1.** *vt.* **FIND SOMEBODY OR SOMETHING** to find something or meet somebody by chance ○ *I came across a reference to her in the newspaper.* **2.** *vi.* **BE COMMUNICATED** to be clearly communicated ○ *The point came across loud and clear: cutbacks are inevitable.* **3.** *vi.* **GIVE AN IMPRESSION** to give a particular impression ○ *She came across as very positive.*

come along *vi.* **1. APPEAR** to appear or arrive ○ *We'll deal with whatever comes along.* **2. PROGRESS** to progress or develop (*only used in continuous tenses, usually in questions or with an adverb*) ○ *How's the new recruit coming along?* **3. ACCOMPANY SOMEBODY ELSE** to go somewhere with somebody **4.** *U.K.* **HURRY UP** to move or act more quickly ○ *Come along or we'll be late for dinner.*

come apart *vi.* to tear or disintegrate ○ *The dress just came apart when I washed it.*

come around *vi.* **1. CHANGE YOUR OPINION** to change your opinion to that of somebody else ○ *They soon came around to our way of thinking.* **2. REGAIN CONSCIOUSNESS** to regain consciousness after being knocked out, e.g. ○ *He finally came around after being unconscious for nearly three hours.* **3. RECUR** to happen again at the expected time ○ *There's excitement in the air when the first football game comes around every year.* **4. VISIT** to visit somebody ○ *Why don't you all come around to my place and have some coffee?*

come at *vt.* **1. ATTACK SOMEBODY** to set upon and attack somebody ○ *He came at his opponent on a dark side street.* **2.** *U.K.* **ARRIVE AT SOMETHING** to reach or discover something with difficulty ○ *The only way to come at the facts is to ask pertinent questions.*

come away *vi.* *U.K.* to become detached from something ○ *The handle came away in my hand.*

come back *vi.* **1. BE POPULAR AGAIN** to become popular again ○ *Seventies fashions came back briefly during the mid-nineties.* **2. COME INTO SOMEBODY'S MIND** to appear or become clear again from somebody's memory ○ *I can't remember the address, but give me a moment and it'll come back to me.* **3. RETORT** to reply energetically or aggressively to somebody ○ *She came back at him immediately with a counterblast.*

come back to *vt.* **1. CONSIDER SOMETHING AGAIN** to reconsider or refer to something again (*informal*) ○ *I'll come back to that question in a moment.* **2. REPLY AFTER INTERVAL** to speak to somebody again about something at a later time ○ *Do you mind if I come back to you on that one?*

come before *vt.* be submitted for consideration or judgment before a group of people with authority ○ *The report is due to come before the committee.*

come between *vt.* **1. INTERFERE IN SOMEBODY'S RELATIONSHIP** to disrupt a relationship ○ *I won't let anything come between us.* **2. STOP SOMEBODY GETTING OR DOING SOMETHING** to prevent somebody from having or doing something ○ *He won't let anything come between him and his Saturday football.*

come by *vt.* to manage to acquire something ○ *Jobs are not so easy to come by nowadays.*

come down *vi.* **1. DECREASE** to decrease in value or amount ○ *Prices are coming down.* **2. REACH A DECISION** to make a decision or judgment ○ *The judge came down in favor of the plaintiff's motion.* **3. BE HANDED DOWN** to be passed down from one generation to another ○ *written records that have come down to us from that period* **4. RETURN TO NORMAL CONSCIOUSNESS** to return to a normal state of consciousness after being affected by drugs (*informal*) **5. HAPPEN** to be happening in the present (*slang*) ○ *Hey, dude! What's coming down?* ◇ **come down in the world** to have less money or power than previously ◇ **come down to earth** to come back to reality after a period of happiness or unrealistic hopes

come down on *vt.* to punish or criticize somebody severely

come down to *vt.* to mean or represent something fundamentally, when all nonessential detail has been disregarded

come down with *vt.* to catch a cold, the flu, or another minor illness

come for *vt.* to arrive at a place to pick somebody or something up

come forward *vi.* to present yourself and show that you are willing to undertake something

come from *v.* **1.** *vti.* **ORIGINATE OR ARISE** to have a particular place as your original home or a particular source of something ○ *She came from Ohio.* **2.** *vi.* **BE DESCENDED FROM** be descended from a particular line, family, or stock

come in *vi.* **1. FINISH IN A PARTICULAR POSITION** to finish a race in a particular position ○ *The American yacht came in fifth.* **2. ARRIVE** to arrive or be received and become available for use, sale, or communication ○ *The spring fashions will be coming in next month.* **3. BECOME FASHIONABLE** to become fashionable ○ *Long hair for men came in during the 1960s.* **4. PARTICIPATE** to become involved in something ○ *There are three other venture capitalists interested in coming in on the deal.* **5.** RADIO **BEGIN SPEAKING** to begin speaking during a discussion or in reply to a radio signal ○ *Senator, do you want to come in on that point? We've only 60 seconds left.* **6. PROVE** to turn out to have a particular level of usefulness ○ *That little knife came in very handy when we went camping.* **7.** TRANSP **APPROACH DESTINATION** to approach or arrive at a destination **8. BECOME HIGHER** to become higher, driving water up over the shore (*refers to the tide*) **9. SUBSTITUTE** to enter a game as a substitute for somebody else ○ *It looks like a new defensive lineman has just come in.*

come in for *vt.* to be the object of criticism or scrutiny ○ *The policy has come in for scathing attacks by the media.*

come into *vt.* to inherit money or property ○ *When her uncle died, she came into a great deal of money.*

come of *vt.* to be the result of something ○ *Did anything ever come of your lawsuit?*

come off *v.* **1.** *vt.* **COME LOOSE** to become detached or to be detachable from something ○ *The top comes off easily.* **2.** *vi.* **HAPPEN** to take place as planned or predicted (*informal*) ○ *Let's hope the trip comes off.* **3.** *vt.* **STOP TAKING MEDICINE** to stop taking a drug or a medicine ○ *When I came off the prescription painkillers, the doctor put me on aspirin.* **4.** *vt.* **BE DEDUCTED FROM SOMETHING** to be deducted from something

come on *v.* **1.** *vi.* **START TO OPERATE** to become available for use or to begin to function (*refers to a power source or machine*) ○ *The street lights come on at dusk.* **2.** *vi.* **HURRY** to hurry up (*usually used in the imperative*) ○ *Come on, I haven't got all day!* **3.** *vi.* **USED TO ENCOURAGE SOMEBODY** used to encourage somebody who is tired or unwilling (*usually used in the imperative*) ○ *Come on, you can do it if you try.* **4.** *vi.* **USED TO SHOW DISBELIEF** used to tell somebody to stop exaggerating or lying ○ *Come on! You don't expect me to believe that, do you?* **5.** *vi.* **TO TELL SOMEBODY TO STOP PRETENDING** used to tell somebody to drop a pretense or stop behaving in a superior way (*usually used in the imperative*) ○ *Come on! You know you can't afford that car.* **6.** *vt.* **APPEAR OR SPEAK ON BROADCAST MEDIUM** to appear or speak on television or radio ○ *I noticed her voice when she came on the phone.* **7.** *vi.* **BEGIN AT SCHEDULED TIME** to begin at a particular time (*refers to radio or television programs or a stage performer*) ○ *Her favorite show is coming on in an hour, and she never misses it.* **8.** *vi.* **DEVELOP GRADUALLY** to develop gradually ○ *It grew chilly as night came on.* **9.** *vi.* THEATER **ENTER DURING PLAY** to go onto the stage as part of the action ○ *The villain doesn't come on until Act 2.* **10.** *vi.* **ADVANCE** to move forward, especially in battle ○ *Our cannon fire tore huge holes in their ranks, but still they came on.*

come on to *vt.* to make sexual advances to somebody (*slang*)

come out *vi.* **1. REVEAL OR BE REVEALED** to reveal something or be revealed ○ *The facts only came out when journalists began to dig a little deeper.* **2.** PUBL **BE PUBLISHED** to be published ○ *Her new novel is coming out next month.* **3. DECLARE SOMETHING** to state something openly ○ *The majority came out in favor of raising the age limit.* **4. ACKNOWLEDGE SEXUALITY** to declare openly that one is gay or lesbian **5. REVEAL SOMETHING SECRET ABOUT YOURSELF** to reveal to other people something about yourself that you have kept secret **6. BECOME ACTIVE IN SAME-SEX RELATIONSHIPS** to become active in sexual relationships with others of the same sex for the first time ○ *I think she came out when she was 17, with her best friend.* **7. MAKE DEBUT IN SOCIETY** to make a first appearance in society **8. BE UTTERED** to be uttered involuntarily or with an unintended effect ○ *We had no intention of revealing the story; it came out by accident.* **9. BECOME VISIBLE IN SKY** to become visible in the sky ○ *The sun came out from behind a cloud.* **10. BE REMOVABLE** to disappear after cleaning ○ *Even the toughest stains come out with this new detergent.* **11.** *U.K.* **STRIKE** to begin a strike ○ *The train drivers came out in sympathy.*

come out in *vt.* *U.K.* to have something such as spots or a rash appear on the skin

come out of *vt.* **1. SURVIVE HAZARD OR ILLNESS** to survive a hazard or illness ○ *I'd say she came out of the ordeal* *in pretty good shape.* **2. BE DEDUCTED** to be deducted from an amount of money ○ *The new window will have to come out of your allowance.*

come out with *vt.* to say something surprising ○ *never know what children will come out with*

come over *vi. U.K.* to change an opinion or allegiance ○ *She says she'll come over if we guarantee her a seat on the board.*

come round *vi.* U.K. = **come around**

come through *v.* **1.** *vi.* **PERFORM WELL WHEN MOST NEEDED** to supply something desperately needed at a critical moment (*informal*) ○ *They could always count on him to come through for them in difficult times.* **2.** *vi.* **SURVIVE** to survive a dangerous or unpleasant experience **3.** *vi.* **BE RECEIVED** to be received or heard, usually through a telecommunications medium **4.** *vti.* **MOVE THROUGH A PLACE** to move between one place and another ○ *The porch was so crowded, we had to come through the kitchen.* ○ *Coming through! Coming through! These plates are hot!*

come to *v.* **1.** *vi.* **REGAIN CONSCIOUSNESS** to regain consciousness or wake up ○ *The patient came to in the recovery room.* **2.** *vt.* **TOTAL** to amount to a particular total **3.** *vi.* NAUT **SLOW DOWN OR STOP** to slow down or stop (*refers to a ship*)

come under *vt.* **1. UNDERGO SOMETHING** to be subjected to something ○ *She came under attack from members of her own party.* **2. BE CLASSIFIED** to be classified under a particular heading ○ *Hawthorne comes under American authors.*

come up *vi.* **1. EMERGE FROM WATER** to rise to the surface of water ○ *She'll have to come up for air in a minute.* **2. APPEAR ABOVE HORIZON** to appear above the horizon ○ *I enjoy watching the sun come up.* **3. BE MENTIONED** to be mentioned or discussed ○ *a topic that came up in conversation* **4. OCCUR UNEXPECTEDLY** to happen unexpectedly ○ *I won't be able to make lunch; something's come up at work.* **5. BE HAPPENING SOON** to be going to happen in the near future ○ *Coming up next, the news.* **6. APPEAR IN COURT** to be tried by a court of law ○ *Her case comes up next week.* **7. BE SELECTED AS WINNER** to win a prize in a game involving luck ○ *if my numbers come up*

come up against *vt.* to meet with something that has to be faced or dealt with ○ *He has come up against fierce criticism.*

come up for *vt.* to become due for something ○ *The case is coming up for review.*

come upon *vt.* to find something or meet somebody by chance

come up to *vt.* to be as good as somebody's expectations

come up with *vt.* to produce or discover something, in response to a need or challenge ○ *She's come up with a brilliant solution.*

come·back /kúm bàk/ *n.* **1. RETURN TO SUCCESS** a return to a successful position or activity ○ *Rumor has it that she's planning a comeback.* **2. SHARP REPLY** a sharp or witty reply ○ *He's always been one for the quick comeback.*

Come·con /kómmə kòn/, **COME·CON** *n.* an organization of the former U.S.S.R and satellite Communist countries aimed at encouraging economic development. It existed between 1949 and 1991. Full form **Council for Mutual Economic Assistance** [Mid-20thC]

co·me·di·an /kə meédee ən/ *n.* **1. COMIC ENTERTAINER** a humorous entertainer **2. COMIC ACTOR** an actor who plays comic roles **3. AMUSING PERSON** somebody who is or tries to be amusing (*often used ironically*) ○ *Some comedian put salt in the sugar bowl.*

co·me·di·enne /kə meédee én/ *n.* **1. FEMALE COMIC ENTERTAINER** a female entertainer who tells jokes **2. COMIC ACTRESS** a female actor who takes comic roles **3. AMUSING WOMAN** a woman who is, or tries to be amusing (*often used ironically*)

com·e·do /kómmə dō/ (*plural* **-do·nes** /-dṓ neéz/) *n.* MED a blackhead [Mid-19thC. From Latin, "glutton, worm that devours the body," formed from *comedere* "to devour" (see COMESTIBLE). From the shape of the contents when squeezed out.]

come·down /kúm dòwn/ *n.* a decline in status or position (*informal*)

com·e·dy /kómmədee/ (*plural* **-dies**) *n.* **1. FUNNY PLAY, MOVIE, OR BOOK** a play, movie, or book depicting amusing events **2. COMIC GENRE** comic works, especially plays, considered as a literary genre **3. COMIC ENTERTAINMENT** entertainment that is amusing **4. COMIC ELEMENT** the humorous elements of a situation or work of art [14thC. Via French *comédie* from, ultimately, Greek *kōmōidia*, from *kōmōidos* "comic actor, comic poet," from *kōmos* "revel" (see COMIC) + *aoidos* "singer," from *aeidein* "to sing."] —**co·me·dic** /kə meédik/ *adj.* —**co·med·i·cal·ly** /-meédikəlee/ *adv.*

come from a·way *n. Can* somebody who is a newcomer to the Atlantic region of Canada (*informal*)

come·ly /kúmmlee/ (**-li·er, -li·est**) *adj.* physically attractive (*archaic or literary*) (*refers to women*) [13thC. Origin uncertain: probably shortening of obsolete *becomely* "becoming, fitting," from BECOME "to be suitable to."] —**come·li·ness** *n.*

come-on *n.* **1. ENTICEMENT** something that arouses interest or desire, e.g., a free gift intended to encourage purchasers (*informal*) **2. COMMENT OR ACTION** a comment or action intended to indicate somebody's sexual interest in another person

com·er /kúmmər/ *n.* somebody or something that is likely to succeed (*informal*) ○ *In party power circles he's regarded as a real comer.*

co·mes·ti·ble /kə méstəb'l/ *n.* **FOOD** something edible, usually a cooked food (*formal*) ■ *adj.* **EDIBLE** fit for eating (*formal*) [15thC. Via French from medieval Latin *comestibilis*, from Latin *comestus*, past participle of *comedere*, literally "to eat completely," from *edere* "to eat" (see EDIBLE).]

Comet: Hale-Bopp comet, photographed over Bulgaria (1997)

com·et /kómmət/ *n.* a celestial body that is composed of a mass of ice and dust and has a long luminous tail produced by vaporization when its orbit passes close to the Sun [12thC. Directly or via Old French from Latin *(stella) cometa* "long-haired (star)," from Greek *(astēr) komētēs*, from, ultimately, *komē* "hair of the head."] —**com·et·ar·y** /kómmə tèrree/ *adj.* —**co·met·ic** /kə méttik/ *adj.*

come·up·pance /kum úppəns/ *n.* something unpleasant, regarded as a just punishment for somebody (*informal*) ○ *He got his comeuppance in the end.* [Mid-19thC. Formed from COME UP, probably in the sense "to be tried before a court."]

com·fit /kúmfit, -fit/ *n.* a candy consisting of a piece of fruit, a seed, or a nut in a sugar coating [14thC. Via Old French from Latin *confectum*, *confecta*, from *confectus* "prepared, made ready" (see CONFECT).]

com·fort /kúmfərt/ *n.* **1. STATE OF BEING COMFORTABLE** conditions in which somebody feels physically relaxed ○ *Enjoy the comfort of your own home.* **2. COMFORTABLE THING** something that makes you feel physically relaxed (*often used in the plural*) ○ *the comforts of home* **3. RELIEF FROM PAIN** relief from pain or anxiety ○ *They brought comfort to the wounded.* **4. SOMETHING PROVIDING RELIEF** somebody or something that provides relief from pain or anxiety ○ *The family has been such a comfort to me since my wife died.* ■ *vt.* (**-fort·ed, -fort·ing, -forts**) **1. CHEER SOMEBODY** to bring somebody relief from distress or anxiety ○ *The victim's parents were being comforted at home by relatives.* **2. MAKE SOMEBODY COMFORTABLE** to make somebody feel pleasantly relaxed ○ *She was comforted by the warmth.* [12thC. Via Old French *confort* from, ultimately, late Latin *confortare*, literally "to strengthen completely," from Latin *fortis* "strong" (see FORCE). Originally "to encourage, support."]

com·fort·a·ble /kúmftəb'l, -fərtəb'l/ *adj.* **1. RELAXED** feeling comfort or ease ○ *Sit down and make yourselves comfortable.* **2. MAKING SOMEBODY RELAXED** making somebody feel physically relaxed ○ *I changed into something more comfortable.* **3. NOT ANXIOUS** free from stress or anxiety ○ *I don't feel comfortable with that idea.* **4. WITH ADEQUATE INCOME** having enough income ○ *They're not what you'd call well-off, but they're certainly comfortable.* **5. ADEQUATE OR LARGE** large enough to prevent anxiety or risk ○ *The candidate won by a comfortable majority.* **6.** *U.K.* MED **STABLE PHYSICALLY** in a stable physical condition —**com·fort·a·ble·ness** *n.*

com·fort·a·bly /kúmftəblee, kúmfərtəblee/ *adv.* **1. AT EASE** with a feeling of comfort or ease ○ *Are you sitting comfortably?* **2. HAVING NO PROBLEMS** having enough of something to stave off worry, especially enough money to live on without worrying about providing essentials ○ *We can manage comfortably on what we earn together.*

com·fort·er /kúmfərtər/ *n.* **1.** a warm quilt used as a bed covering **2. SOMEBODY WHO COMFORTS** somebody who relieves other people's grief or anxieties

Com·fort·er *n.* the Holy Spirit [14thC. From Old French *confortere*, translation of Latin *consolator*, translation in turn of Greek *paraklētos* "advocate, intercessor" (see PARACLETE). The proper Latin translation would have been *advocatus*.]

com·fort food *n.* FOOD easily prepared unsophisticated food that is psychologically comforting, especially food that is high in carbohydrates (*informal*)

com·fort·ing /kúmfərting/ *adj.* relieving anxiety or pain —**com·fort·ing·ly** *adv.*

com·fort·less /kúmfərtləss/ *adj.* affording no comfort ○ *a sterile, comfortless room* —**com·fort·less·ly** *adv.* —**com·fort·less·ness** *n.*

com·fort lev·el, **com·fort zone** *n.* the set of physical or psychological circumstances in which somebody feels most at ease and free from physical discomfort or stress (*informal*) ○ *He said that the task was outside his workplace comfort zone.*

com·fort sta·tion *n.* a public toilet (*used euphemistically*)

com·frey /kúmfree/ (*plural* **-frey** *or* **-freys**) *n.* a plant native to Europe and Asia, with hairy leaves and stems and clusters of pink, white, or blue flowers. Herbalists used its grated roots in poultices to heal broken bones, or in linctuses for back pain and coughs. Genus: *Symphytum*. [13thC. Via Anglo-Norman and Old French from, ultimately, Latin *conferva*, from *confervere* "to heal," literally "to boil together," from *fervere* "to boil" (see FERVENT).]

com·fy /kúmfee/ (**-fi·er, -fi·est**) *adj.* comfortable (*informal*) [Early 19thC. Formed from a shortening of COMFORTABLE.]

com·ic /kómmik/ *adj.* **1. FUNNY** so amusing that it induces smiles or laughter **2.** THEATER **RELATING TO COMEDY** appearing in or characteristic of comedy ○ *a great comic routine* ■ *n.* **1.** THEATER **COMEDIAN** a comedian or comedienne **2.** PUBL = **comic book** ■ **com·ics** *npl.* **COMIC STRIP SECTION** the part of a newspaper that consists of comic strips [Late 16thC. Via Latin from Greek *kōmikos*, from *kōmos* "revel" (source of English *comedy*), of unknown origin.]

WORD KEY: USAGE

comic or **comical**? The two words are close in meaning, but ***comic*** generally denotes intention (*a comic act, a comic poet*) whereas ***comical*** denotes effect or result, whether intentional or not (*a comical performance; his attempts at skiing were comical*).

com·i·cal /kómmik'l/ *adj.* so amusing that it elicits smiles or laughter ○ *comical facial expressions* —**com·i·cal·i·ty** /kòmmi kállətee/ *n.* —**com·i·cal·ness** /kómik'lnəss/ *n.* —**com·i·cal·ly** /kómmiklee/ *adv.*

WORD KEY: USAGE

See Usage note at ***comic***.

com·ic book *n.* a magazine that consists almost entirely of stories told in a series of colored panels in which balloons over the characters' heads provide dialogue and the thoughts of the characters

com·ic o·pe·ra *n.* **1. OPERA WITH COMIC LIBRETTO** an opera with a humorous plot and a happy ending **2. MUSICAL GENRE** comic operas considered as a musical genre

com·ic strip *n.* a series of cartoons that tell a story or a joke

com·ing /kúmming/ *adj.* **1. HAPPENING SOON** about to happen or start ○ *In the coming election campaign you can expect a media barrage on TV.* **2. PROBABLY SUCCESSFUL** likely to be successful in the near future ○ *She's the coming power in this company.* ■ *n.* **ARRIVAL** the arrival of a person or an event

com·ing of age *n.* **1. REACHING ADULTHOOD** the reaching of the official age of adulthood and legal responsibility **2.** ADVANCED DEVELOPMENT the reaching of an advanced stage of development ○ *the coming of age of the computer*

com·ings and go·ings *npl.* busy activity in which people arrive and depart frequently

Com·in·tern /kómmintərn/ *n.* an international organization of Communist parties set up by Lenin in 1919 and abolished in 1943 [Early 20thC. From Russian *Komintern,* which was coined from *kommunisticheskii internatsional'nyi* "communist international."]

co·mi·ti·a /kō míshə/ (*plural* **-a**) *n.* a legislative assembly of citizens in ancient Rome [Early 17thC. From Latin, the plural of *comitium* "assembly," literally "going together," from *itus,* the past participle of *ire* "to go" (see ITINERARY).]

com·i·ty of nations *n.* the mutual recognition among nations of one another's laws, customs, and institutions

com·ix /kómmiks/ *npl.* comic books and comic strips for an adult audience, especially those containing nudity and obscenity [Late 20thC. Representation of the pronunciation of COMICS.]

coml. *abbr.* commercial

comm. *abbr.* **1.** commerce **2.** commercial **3.** commission **4.** committee **5.** commonwealth

com·ma /kómmə/ *n.* **1.** GRAM PUNCTUATION MARK a punctuation mark (,) that represents a slight pause in a sentence or is used to separate words and figures in a list **2.** MUSIC BRIEF PAUSE OR INTERVAL a short pause or interval in a piece of music **3.** ZOOL = **comma butterfly** [Late 16thC. Via Latin from Greek *komma* "piece cut off, short clause," from *koptein* "to cut." The original English meaning was "short clause."]

Com·mack /kō màk, kó-/ town in Suffolk County, New York, situated on central Long Island southeast of Huntington. Population: 36,124 (1990).

com·mand /kə mánd/ *n.* **1.** ORDER an order or instruction given by somebody in authority ○ *On the command to mount up, the crews scrambled into their tanks.* **2.** CONTROL control over somebody or something that is gained by personal power or authority ○ *She sized up the situation and took command.* **3.** THOROUGH KNOWLEDGE thorough knowledge of something, especially a language ○ *a fluent command of French* **4.** COMPUT OPERATING INSTRUCTION TO COMPUTER an instruction to a computer to carry out an operation **5.** AUTHORITY the authority to control and direct the actions of a group of people, especially a military unit ○ *A new officer arrived to take command of the regiment.* **6.** MILITARY CONTROL the ability to control an area militarily ○ *Our primary objective is to gain command of the high ground.* **7.** SOMETHING UNDER OFFICER'S JURISDICTION troops or a particular area that are controlled by an officer ○ *My new command consists of a mechanized unit.* **8.** GROUP OF OFFICERS IN CONTROL a group of officers who control part of an army ○ *the enemy command* **9.** MILITARY GROUP WITH SPECIFIC FUNCTION a unit or units, an organization, or an entire area under the control of one individual ■ *v.* (**-mand·ed, -mand·ing, -mands**) **1.** *vti.* ORDER SOMEBODY to give somebody an order or instruction ○ *I command you to let these men go.* **2.** *vti.* HAVE AUTHORITY OVER SOMETHING to control a military unit or a specific area ○ *an officer who commands a special operations battalion* **3.** *vt.* CONTROL OR DOMINATE AREA to control an area using military force ○ *a fort that commanded the single pass through steep mountains* **4.** *vt.* BE ABLE TO OBTAIN SOMETHING to deserve or be entitled to something ○ *With your qualifications you can command a high salary.* **5.** *vt.* LOOK OVER SOMETHING to be in a position that has a wide view over something ○ *The observation deck commands a breathtaking view of San Francisco Bay.* [13thC. Via Anglo-Norman and Old French from assumed late Latin *commandare,* literally "to enjoin strongly," from Latin *mandare* "to entrust, order" (see MANDATE).] —**com·mand·a·ble** *adj.*

com·mand and con·trol *n.* **1.** SYSTEM DIRECTING A MISSILE a system that directs the course of a missile **2.** COMMANDER'S EXERCISE OF AUTHORITY AND DIRECTION a military commander's exercise of authority and direction of operations

com·man·dant /kómmən dánt, kòmmən daánt/ *n.* an officer in command of a military establishment

Com·man·dant of the Ma·rine Corps *n.* the highest-ranking officer of the Marine Corps and its representative on the U.S. Joint Chiefs of Staff (*formal*)

com·mand car *n.* an armored vehicle that can travel over rough terrain

com·mand e·con·o·my *n.* an economy in which resources and business activity are controlled by the government

com·man·deer /kòmmən deér/ (**-deered, -deer·ing, -deers**) *vt.* **1.** SEIZE SOMETHING FOR MILITARY PURPOSES to take something from its owner for official or military purposes **2.** TAKE SOMETHING OVER to take or use something, sometimes using force (*disapproving*) **3.** FORCE SOMEBODY INTO MILITARY SERVICE to force somebody to serve in the armed forces [Early 19thC. Via Afrikaans *kommandeer* from Dutch *kommanderen* "to command," from French *commander* (see COMMAND).]

com·man·der /kə mándər/ *n.* **1.** MILITARY OFFICER an officer in command of a military unit **2.** NAVAL OR COAST GUARD RANK a naval or Coast Guard rank next below captain and above lieutenant commander, or an officer holding this rank **3.** a police officer in charge of a shift, a precinct, or a unit **4.** MEMBER WITH HIGH RANK a high-ranking member of some knightly and fraternal orders

com·man·der in chief (*plural* **com·mand·ers in chief**) *n.* an officer who has supreme command of military forces, in the United States the president

Com·mand·er in Chief *n.* used as an honorific title to denote the President of the United States, as commander of the nation's armed forces

com·mand·ing /kə mánding/ *adj.* **1.** IMPRESSIVE able to control or dominate ○ *a commanding presence* **2.** BEING HIGHER IN POSITION dominating a landscape or view **3.** DOMINATING demonstrating clear superiority ○ *a commanding lead* —**com·mand·ing·ly** *adv.*

com·mand·ing of·fi·cer *n.* an officer in command of a military unit or establishment

com·mand-line *adj.* COMPUT using letters or words instead of codes to instruct a computer to perform a task [From the fact that such instructions are entered all on a single line after a prompt character called the "command prompt"]

com·mand·ment /kə mándmənt/ *n.* a command from God, especially one of the Ten Commandments

com·mand mod·ule *n.* the part of a spacecraft that houses the controls and the crew's living quarters

com·man·do /kə mán dō/ (*plural* **-dos** *or* **-does**) *n.* **1.** SPECIALLY TRAINED SOLDIER a member of a military force specially trained to make dangerous raids **2.** UNIT a military unit made up of commandos **3.** BOER FIGHTING UNIT a force of Boer troops during the Boer War [Late 18thC. From Portuguese, "raiding party," literally "commanded (squad)," from *commandar* "to command."]

com·mand per·form·ance *n.* a performance of a play or film given by command of a ruler or state

com·mand post *n.* **1.** FIELD HEADQUARTERS a military headquarters for a command group and its officers during an operation **2.** TEMPORARY COMMUNICATIONS CENTER a temporary headquarters for a team of people involved in an operation

com·mand ser·geant ma·jor (*plural* **com·mand ser·geant ma·jors** *or* **com·mand ser·geants ma·jor**) *n.* a noncommissioned officer who ranks above a sergeant major

com·me·dia dell'arte /kə màydee ə də laártee/ *n.* an Italian form of popular comedy developed during the 16th and 17th centuries, characterized by the use of stock characters and familiar plots [Late 19thC. From Italian, literally "comedy of art."]

com·mem·o·rate /kə mémmə ràyt/ (**-rat·ed, -rat·ing, -rates**) *vt.* **1.** REMEMBER SOMETHING CEREMONIALLY to honor the memory of somebody or something in a ceremony ○ *a service held to commemorate the dead* **2.** BE MEMORIAL TO SOMETHING to serve as a memorial to something [Mid-17thC. From Latin *commemoratus,* the past participle of *commemorare* "to call to mind clearly," from *memorare* "to remind, speak of," from *memor* "mindful" (see MEMORY).] —**com·mem·o·ra·tor** *n.* —**com·mem·o·ra·to·ry** /-mémmərə tàwree/ *adj.*

com·mem·o·ra·tion /kə mèmmə ráysh'n/ *n.* **1.** CEREMONY HONORING SOMEBODY OR SOMETHING a ceremony or religious service to commemorate a person or an event **2.** ACT OF HONORING the act of honoring the memory of a person or an event —**com·mem·o·ra·tion·al** *adj.*

com·mem·o·ra·tive /kə mémmərətiv, -ràytiv/ *adj.* honoring the memory of a person or an event —**com·mem·o·ra·tive·ly** *adv.*

com·mence /kə méns/ (**-menced, -menc·ing, -menc·es**) *vti.* to begin happening or to begin something (*formal*) [14thC. Via Old French *com(m)encier* from assumed Vulgar Latin *cominitiare,* from Latin *initiare* "to begin" (see INITIATE).] —**com·menc·er** *n.*

com·mence·ment /kə ménsmənt/ *n.* **1.** THE BEGINNING OF SOMETHING the beginning of something (*formal*) ○ *the commencement of open hostilities* **2.** GRADUATION CEREMONY a ceremony during which degrees and diplomas are conferred at high schools, colleges, and universities, or the day on which this ceremony takes place

com·mend /kə ménd/ (**-mend·ed, -mend·ing, -mends**) *vt.* **1.** PRAISE SOMEBODY OR SOMETHING to praise somebody or something in a formal way ○ *She was commended for her bravery.* **2.** PROVE SOMETHING WORTHWHILE to prove something to possess worthwhile qualities ○ *The plan has much to commend it.* **3.** SURRENDER SOUL FOR SAFEKEEPING to entrust somebody, yourself, or your soul to somebody's safekeeping [14thC. From Latin *commendare,* literally "to entrust completely," from *mandare* "to entrust, commit" (see MANDATE).] —**com·mend·er** *n.*

com·mend·a·ble /kə méndəb'l/ *adj.* worthy of praise —**com·mend·a·ble·ness** *n.* —**com·mend·a·bly** *adv.*

com·men·da·tion /kòmmən dáysh'n/ *n.* **1.** ACT OF COMMENDING praise of somebody's abilities **2.** RECOGNITION OF ACCOMPLISHMENT an award or citation given to somebody in recognition of an outstanding achievement

com·men·da·to·ry /kə méndə tàwree/ *adj.* expressing praise

com·men·sal /kə méns'l/ *adj.* used to describe a relationship between organisms of two different species in which one derives food or other benefits from the association while the other remains unharmed and unaffected [Late 19thC. Directly or via French from medieval Latin *commensalis,* literally "at table together," from Latin *mensa* "table."] —**com·men·sal** *n.* —**com·men·sal·i·ty** /kò men sállətee/ *n.* —**com·men·sal·ly** /kə ménsəlee/ *adv.*

com·men·su·ra·ble /kə ménsərəb'l, -ménshər-/ *adj.* **1.** RELATED BY MEASUREMENT related by virtue of sharing the same system of measurement or by being measurable using the same units **2.** COMMENSURATE equal in terms of something else (*formal*) ○ *His salary is commensurable to his ability.* **3.** MATH DESCRIBING TWO QUANTITIES divisible by the same unit an even number of times [Mid-16thC. From late Latin *commensurabilis,* literally "completely measurable," from *mensurabilis* "measurable" (see MENSURABLE).] —**com·men·su·ra·bil·i·ty** /kə mènsərə bíllətee, -mènshərə-/ *n.* —**com·men·su·ra·bly** /kə ménsərəblee, -ménshər-/ *adv.*

com·men·su·rate /kə ménsərət, -ménshərət/ *adj.* **1.** EQUAL IN SIZE of the same size or extent **2.** IN PROPORTION properly or appropriately proportionate ○ *The rewards will be commensurate with the efforts made.* **3.** MEASURED USING SAME SYSTEM relating to, being, or measured in units belonging to the same system of measurement [Mid-17thC. From late Latin *commensuratus,* literally "measured with," from, ultimately, Latin *mensura* "measure" (source of English *measure*).] —**com·men·su·rate·ly** *adv.* —**com·men·su·rate·ness** *n.* —**com·men·su·ra·tion** /kə mensə ráysh'n, -menshə-/ *n.*

com·ment /kómmènt/ *n.* **1.** REMARK a remark that states a fact or expresses an opinion ○ *Comments are invited from all participants.* **2.** OBSERVATION an implied or indirect judgment ○ *The incident attracted a great deal of press comment.* **3.** EXPLANATORY NOTE a note that explains a passage in a text **4.** COMPUT NOTE EXPLAINING PROGRAM CODE a note embedded in a computer program that describes how the programming code that follows works ■ *v.* (**-ment·ed, -ment·ing, -ments**) **1.** *vti.* MAKE A COMMENT to state a fact or give an opinion **2.** *vt.* MENTION SOMETHING to make a reference to or discuss something [14thC. From, ultimately, Latin *commentum* "invention, fiction," from the past participle stem *comment-* of *comminisci* "to invent," literally "to think together."]

com·men·tar·y /kómmən tèrree/ *n.* (*plural* **-ies**) **1.** SERIES OF EXPLANATORY NOTES a series of notes explaining or interpreting a written text **2.** EXPLANATORY ESSAY an essay or book that explains a text **3.** CLARIFICATION OF A SITUATION an example illustrating a situation **4.** *U.K.* SPORTS = **play-by-play** ■ **com·men·tar·ies** *npl.* RECORD OF EVENTS a record of events, usually written by somebody who participated in them —**com·men·tar·i·al** /kòmmən térree əl/ *adj.*

com·men·tate /kómmən tàyt/ (**com·men·tat·ed, com·men·tat·ing, com·men·tates**) *vi.* **1. REPORT OR INTERPRET** to act as a commentator, either in radio or television broadcasting or on texts **2. EXPLAIN SOMETHING** to comment on something in a way that explains or interprets it [Mid-19thC. Back-formation from COMMENTATOR.]

com·men·ta·tor /kómmən tàytər/ *n.* somebody who reports on and analyzes events in the news for radio, television, or a newspaper [14thC. From Latin, formed from *commentari* "to comment," from *comminisci* (see COMMENT).]

com·merce /kómmərs/ *n.* **1. TRADE IN GOODS AND SERVICES** the large-scale buying and selling of goods and services **2. STUDY OF COMMERCE** the study of the principles and practices of commerce [Mid-16thC. From, ultimately, Latin *commercium,* literally "mutual trade."]

com·mer·cial /kə múrsh'l/ *adj.* **1. RELATING TO COMMERCE** relating to the buying and selling of goods or services **2. SUITABLE FOR TRADING** appropriate or sufficient for the purposes of trade **3. FOR INDUSTRIAL USE** produced in bulk for industrial use and often unrefined **4. DONE FOR PROFIT** done with the primary aim of making money **5. PAID FOR WITH ADVERTISING** supported by revenue from advertising ■ *n.* **ADVERTISEMENT ON RADIO OR TELEVISION** an advertisement broadcast on radio or television [Late 16thC. The noun first meant "commercial traveler," the current sense being a mid-20th-century development.] —**com·mer·ci·al·i·ty** /kə mùrshee állətee/ *n.*

com·mer·cial art *n.* graphic art produced for purposes such as advertising and packaging —**com·mer·cial art·ist** *n.*

com·mer·cial bank *n.* a bank whose primary business is providing financial services to companies

com·mer·cial break *n.* an interval during a radio or television program for the purpose of broadcasting advertisements

com·mer·cial col·lege *n.* a college that teaches primarily business-related subjects

com·mer·cial·ism /kə múrsh'l ìzzəm/ *n.* **1. COMMERCIAL PRINCIPLES** the principles and methods of commerce **2. ACTING FOR PROFIT** excessive emphasis on profit-making —**com·mer·cial·ist** *n.* —**com·mer·cial·is·tic** /-mùrsh'l ístik/ *adj.*

com·mer·cial·ize /kə múrsh'l ìz/ (**-ized, -iz·ing, -iz·es**) *vt.* **1. APPLY COMMERCIAL PRINCIPLES TO SOMETHING** to apply business principles to something or run it as a business **2. USE FOR PROFIT ONLY** to exploit something for financial gain —**com·mer·cial·i·za·tion** /kə mùrsh'li záysh'n/ *n.*

com·mer·cial·ly /kə múrsh'lee/ *adv.* in commercial terms or from a profit-making point of view

com·mer·cial pa·per *n.* very short-term debt obligations backed only by the good name of the company

com·mer·cial trav·e·ler *n.* a traveling company sales representative (*dated*)

com·messe /kómmess/ *n. Carib* in Trinidad, any kind of scandal, conflict, or illegal behavior (*informal*)

com·mie /kómmee/, **com·my** *n.* (*plural* **-mies**) **COMMUNIST** somebody who is a Communist (*informal disapproving*) ■ *adj.* **SUPPORTING COMMUNISM** holding or advocating Communist or left-wing views (*informal disapproving*) [Mid-20thC. Coined from COMMUNIST + -IE.]

com·mi·na·tion /kòmmi náysh'n/ *n.* (*formal*) **1. ACT OF DENOUNCING** a formal denunciation of somebody or something **2. THREAT OF PUNISHMENT** a warning of punishment or vengeance, especially punishment by God [15thC. From, ultimately, Latin *comminat-,* past participle stem of *comminari,* literally "to threaten with," from *minari* "to threaten" (see MENACE).] —**com·min·a·to·ry** /kə mínnə tàwree/ *adj.*

com·min·gle /kə míng'l/ (**-gled, -gling, -gles**) *vti.* to blend or mix two or more things, or become mixed or blended (*literary*)

com·mi·nute /kómmə nòot/ (**-nut·ed, -nut·ing, -nutes**) *v.* **1.** *vti.* MED **BREAK BONE INTO FRAGMENTS** to break, or cause a bone to break, into small parts **2.** *vt.* **PULVERIZE SOMETHING** to crush or grind something into a powder [Late 16thC. From, ultimately, Latin *comminuere,* literally "to lessen greatly," from *minuere* "to lessen."] —**com·mi·nut·ed** *adj.* —**com·mi·nu·tion** /kòmmə nòosh'n/ *n.*

com·mi·nut·ed frac·ture *n.* a fracture in which the bone is broken into fragments

com·mis·er·ate /kə mízzə ràyt/ (**-at·ed, -at·ing, -ates**) *vi.* to express sympathy or sorrow [Late 16thC. From, ultimately, Latin *commiserari,* literally "to lament with, be miserable with," from, ultimately, *miser* "miserable."] —**com·mis·er·a·tive** *adj.* —**com·mis·er·a·tive·ly** *adv.*

com·mis·er·a·tion /kə mìzzə ráysh'n/ *n.* **SYMPATHY** feelings of sympathy or compassion ■ **com·mis·er·a·tions** *npl.* **SYMPATHETIC WORDS** expressions of sympathy or sorrow

com·mis·sar /kómmi saar/ *n.* **1. FORMER SOVIET DEPARTMENT HEAD** in the former Soviet Union, the chief minister in a government department **2. COMMUNIST PARTY OFFICIAL** in the former Soviet Union, a Communist Party official, often attached to a military unit, responsible for providing political education [Early 20thC. From Russian *komissar,* from, ultimately, medieval Latin *commissarius* "officer in charge," from Latin *commiss-,* past participle stem of *committere* "to entrust" (see COMMIT).] —**com·mis·sar·i·al** /kòmmi sáiree əl/ *adj.*

com·mis·sar·i·at /kòmmi sáiree ət/ *n.* **1.** ARMY **ARMY SUPPLY DEPARTMENT** an army department responsible for organizing food and supplies **2.** ARMY **ARMY SUPPLIES** food and other supplies given to soldiers **3. FORMER SOVIET GOVERNMENT DEPARTMENT** a government department in the former Soviet Union. The term was used until 1946, after which it was called a ministry. [Late 16thC. From, ultimately, assumed medieval Latin *commissariatus,* from *commissarius* (see COMMISSAR).]

com·mis·sar·y /kómmi sèrree/ (*plural* **-ies**) *n.* **1. SUPERMARKET ON A MILITARY BASE** a store that sells groceries and household supplies, especially one located on a military base **2. REPRESENTATIVE** a deputy or representative **3.** FOOD **RESTAURANT** a cafeteria or restaurant, especially in a motion-picture or television studio [14thC. From medieval Latin *commissarius* (see COMMISSAR).]

com·mis·sion /kə mísh'n/ *n.* **1.** COMM **FEE PAID TO AGENT** a fee paid to an agent for providing a service, especially a percentage of the total amount earned by the agent **2. TASK** a job or task given to an individual or group, especially an order to produce a particular product or piece of work **3.** POL **GOVERNMENT GROUP** a government agency that has judicial or legislative powers **4. GROUP WITH TASK** a group of people authorized or directed to carry out a duty or task **5.** MIL **APPOINTMENT AS MILITARY OFFICER** an appointment to the rank of officer in the armed forces, or a document conferring such a rank **6. AUTHORITY TO ACT AS AGENT** the authority granted to an individual or organization to act as an agent for another **7. AUTHORITY OR INSTRUCTION** the authority to do something, or an instruction to do it (*formal*) **8. ACT OF COMMITTING SOMETHING** the committing of something, especially a crime or other offense ■ *vt.* (**-sioned, -sion·ing, -sions**) **1. ASSIGN** to assign a duty or task to somebody **2. ORDER SOMETHING SPECIAL** place an order for something that must be specially made or created ○ *have commissioned a new architectural firm to design the building* **3.** MIL **MAKE SOMEBODY OFFICER** to confer the rank of officer on somebody in the armed forces **4.** SHIPPING **EQUIP SHIP** to bring a ship into active service **5. START OPERATING** to bring a new project or facility such as a nuclear facility into operation [14thC. From, ultimately, Latin *commiss-* (see COMMISSAR).] —**com·mis·sion·al** *adj.* —**com·mis·sion·ar·y** *adj.* ◇ **on commission** with a percentage of the value of sales being full or partial payment for the work of selling ◇ **in commission 1.** in operational use or in working order **2.** in active service, especially as a ship ◇ **out of commission 1.** not in operational use or not in working order **2.** not in active service, especially as a ship

com·mis·sion·aire /kə mìshə náir/ *n.* **1.** *U.K.* **UNIFORMED WORKER** in the U.K., a uniformed attendant or usher at a hotel or theater **2. MEMBER OF CANADIAN VETERANS' ORGANIZATION** in Canada, a veteran of the armed forces who belongs to the Corps of Commissionaires, an organization whose uniformed members can be hired to watch or protect buildings and property [Mid-17thC. From, ultimately, medieval Latin *commissionarius,* from the Latin stem *commission-* "commission," from *commiss-* (see COMMISSAR).]

com·mis·sioned of·fi·cer *n.* a military officer who holds rank by appointment at or above the rank of second lieutenant or ensign

com·mis·sion·er /kə mísh'nər/ *n.* **1. COMMISSION MEMBER** a member of a commission **2. SOMEBODY WORKING FOR COMMISSION** somebody authorized by a commission to carry out prescribed duties or tasks **3. GOVERNMENT OFFICIAL** a government representative in an administrative area **4. DEPARTMENT HEAD** the head of a public service, such as the police or fire department, in a town or city **5.** SPORTS **SPORT EXECUTIVE** the administrative head of a sport —**com·mis·sion·er·ship** *n.*

com·mis·sion mer·chant *n.* an agent who buys and sells goods for others and is paid on a commission-only basis

com·mis·sion plan *n.* a system of local government in which an elected commission supervises the workings of a municipality's departments instead of the more common mayor or city council

com·mis·sure /kómmi shòor/ *n.* **1.** ANAT **PLACE WHERE CELLS OR ORGANS MEET** a line or point where two cells, organs, or body parts meet or connect **2.** ANAT **LINKING BAND OF NERVE TISSUE** a band of nerve tissue that connects opposite sides of the central nervous system, e.g., the tissue connecting the left and right sides of the brain **3.** BOT **PLACE WHERE PLANT PARTS JOIN** a junction or seam between two organs or parts, such as that between the carpels of a flower [15thC. From Latin *commissura* "juncture," from *commiss-* (see COMMISSAR).] —**com·mis·su·ral** /kə míshərəl/ *adj.*

com·mit /kə mít/ (**com·mit·ted, com·mit·ting, com·mits**) *v.* **1.** *vi.* **PROMISE DEVOTION** to pledge devotion or dedication to somebody or something ○ *he wasn't yet ready to commit to the relationship* **2.** *vt.* **PROMISE RESOURCES** to devote or pledge something, e.g., time or money, to an undertaking **3.** *vt.* **DO WRONG** to do something wrong or illegal ○ *commit a felony* **4.** *vt.* **ENTRUST TO** to entrust something or somebody to somebody else for protection **5.** *vt.* **RECORD FOR THE FUTURE** to consign or record something in order to preserve it **6.** *vt.* **ASSIGN FOR DESTRUCTION** to give something over for destruction or disposal **7.** *vt.* **INSTITUTIONALIZE** to legally confine somebody to an institution, e.g., to prison or a mental health facility **8.** *vt.* POL **REFER PROPOSED LAW FOR REVIEW** to refer a bill to a legislative committee for review [14thC. From Latin *committere,* literally "to put together," from *mittere* "to put, send" (source of English *missile*).] —**com·mit·ta·ble** *adj.* —**com·mit·ter** *n.*

com·mit·ment /kə mítmənt/ *n.* **1. RESPONSIBILITY** something that takes up time or energy, especially an obligation **2. LOYALTY** devotion or dedication, e.g., to a cause, person or relationship **3. PREVIOUSLY PLANNED ENGAGEMENT** a planned arrangement or activity that cannot be avoided **4. REFERRAL OF BILL FOR REVIEW** a referral of a bill to a legislative committee for review **5. INSTITUTIONALIZING SOMEBODY** an act of legally confining somebody to prison or a mental health facility **6. COURT ORDER** a written court order confining somebody to prison

com·mit·tal /kə mítt'l/ *n.* = **commitment** *n.* 5

com·mit·ted /kə míttəd/ *adj.* devoted to somebody or something such as a cause or relationship —**com·mit·ted·ly** *adv.*

com·mit·tee /kə míttee/ *n.* a group of people appointed or chosen to perform a function on behalf of a larger group [15thC. Originally "person to whom something is committed."]

com·mit·tee·man /kə míttimən/ (*plural* **-men** /kə míttimən/) *n.* a man who is a member of one or more committees

com·mit·tee of the whole (*plural* **com·mit·tees of the whole**) *n.* the entire membership of a legislative body gathering as a whole to consider a matter informally

com·mit·tee·wom·an /kə mítti wòomən/ (*plural* **-en** /-wìmmin/) *n.* a woman who is a member of one or more committees

com·mode /kə mód/ *n.* **1. CHAIR WITH CHAMBER POT** a chair or box-shaped piece of furniture holding a chamber pot covered by a lid **2. PORTABLE WASHSTAND** a movable washstand with a cupboard underneath containing a chamber pot or washbasin **3. DECORATED CABINET** a low cabinet or chest of drawers, usually elaborately decorated [Late 17thC. From French, originally "suitable," from Latin *commodus,* literally "conforming with due measure, quite fit," from *modus* "measure" (see MODE).]

com·mo·di·ous /kə módee əss/ *adj.* pleasantly spacious —**com·mo·di·ous·ly** *adv.* —**com·mo·di·ous·ness** *n.*

com·mod·i·ty /kə móddətee/ (*plural* **-ties**) *n.* **1.** FIN **TRADED ITEM** an item that is bought and sold, especially an unprocessed material **2. USEFUL THING** something that people value or find useful [15thC. From, ultimately, Latin *commodus* "useful" (see COMMODE).]

com·mod·i·ty art *n.* ARTS art that is marketable because its subject matter and style are tailored to appeal to a specific kind of buyer, and not purely an expression of the artist's ideas

com·mo·dore /kómmə dàwr/ *n.* **1.** NAVY **NAVAL OFFICER** an officer in the navy ranked above a captain and below a rear admiral **2.** SHIPPING **MERCHANT NAVY CAPTAIN** a senior captain in charge of a fleet of merchant ships **3.** SAILING **PRESIDENT OF YACHT CLUB** the head of a yacht or boat club [Late 17thC. Origin uncertain: probably an alteration of Dutch *komandeur* "commander," from French *commandeur*, ultimately from Old French *comander* "to command" (see COMMAND).]

com·mon /kómmən/ *adj.* **1.** **SHARED** belonging to or shared by two or more people or groups ○ *they shared a common goal* **2.** **OF OR FOR ALL** relating or belonging to the community as a whole ○ *the common good* **3.** **EVERYDAY** often occurring or frequently seen ○ *a common sight in cities* **4.** **WIDELY FOUND** used to describe a widely found species of plant or animal **5.** **NONSPECIALIST** used by ordinary people who have no specialist knowledge ○ *The common name for "Viscum album" is "mistletoe."* **6.** **GENERAL** done, used, or held by most people ○ *common practice* **7.** **ORDINARY** without special privilege, rank, or status ○ *the common man* **8.** **OF AN EXPECTED STANDARD** of the standard that most people expect ○ *common courtesy* **9.** **VULGAR** considered to be ill-bred or vulgar ○ *common behavior* **10.** MATH **WITH EQUAL MATHEMATICAL RELATIONSHIP** having an equal relationship to two or more mathematical entities **11.** POETRY **OF VARYING STRESS OR LENGTH** used to describe a syllable that, in a line of poetry, can be either long or short, or stressed or unstressed **12.** CHR **USEFUL FOR SEVERAL RELIGIOUS FESTIVALS** capable of being used as a service for any of a number of similar religious festivals ■ *n.* **1.** **PIECE OF PUBLIC LAND** an area of land available for anybody to use, e.g., as a public recreation area or as pasture for cattle **2.** LAW **RIGHT TO USE SOMEBODY'S LAND** the legal right to use somebody else's land or waters in a particular way, usually for grazing or fishing **3.** CHR **SERVICE FOR SEVERAL RELIGIOUS FESTIVALS** a religious service that can be used for any of a number of similar festivals **4.** FIN = **common stock** ■ *npl.* COMPUT **SHARED DATA STORE** data stored in the memory of one computer that is available to all computers linked to it by a network [13thC. From, ultimately, Latin *communis*, literally "duties together," from *munia* (plural) "duties." Ultimately from an Indo-European word meaning "exchange," which is also the ancestor of English *immune*.] —**com·mon·ness** /kaámən nəss/ *n.*

WORD KEY: USAGE

See Usage note at ***mutual***.

com·mon·age /kómmənij/ *n.* **1.** **RIGHT TO USE JOINTLY** the legal right to use something, especially a pasture, in common with other people, or the use that is made of it **2.** **PUBLIC OWNERSHIP OF LAND** the status of something, usually land, that is publicly owned and available **3.** **LAND FOR ALL TO USE** land that is publicly owned and available **4.** = **commonalty**

com·mon·al·i·ty /kòmmə nállətee/ (*plural* **-ties**) *n.* **1.** **POSSESSION OF COMMON ATTRIBUTES** the sharing of characteristics or qualities with other individuals **2.** **COMMON ATTRIBUTE** a shared characteristic or quality **3.** = **commonalty** [Late 16thC. Alteration of COMMONALTY.]

com·mon·al·ty /kómmən'ltee/ *n.* **1.** **COMMON PEOPLE** the ordinary people as distinct from the upper classes, especially when considered as a political class **2.** **GROUP** a group or society or its membership (*takes a singular or plural verb*) [13thC. Via Old French from medieval Latin *communalitas*, from Latin *communis* (see COMMON).]

com·mon bile duct *n.* the duct formed by the joining of the duct from the liver and and that from the gall bladder

com·mon blue *n.* a common European butterfly, the male of which is blue and the female usually brown with orange markings. Latin name: *Polyommatus icarus.*

com·mon car·ri·er *n.* **1.** **TRANSPORTATION COMPANY** an individual or company in the business of transporting goods or passengers **2.** **TELECOMMUNICATIONS COMPANY** a company that provides telecommunications services to the general public, e.g., a telephone company

com·mon chord *n.* a major or minor musical chord of three notes (**triad**) that contains a perfect fifth

com·mon cold *n.* = **cold** *n.* 1

com·mon de·nom·i·na·tor *n.* **1.** **NUMBER DIVISIBLE BY BOTTOM FRACTION PART** a whole number that can be divided exactly by the lower numbers (**denominators**) of two or more fractions. For example, 8 is a common denominator of $\frac{1}{4}$ and $\frac{1}{8}$. **2.** **SOMETHING IN COMMON** a shared belief or characteristic

com·mon dif·fer·ence *n.* the difference between successive terms in an arithmetic series. For example, 3 is the common difference in the series 2, 5, 8, 11.

com·mon di·vi·sor *n.* a number that two or more other numbers can be divided by exactly. For example, 4 is a common divisor of 8, 12, and 20.

com·mon·er /kómmənər/ *n.* an ordinary member of society who does not belong to the nobility

Com·mon E·ra *n.* the Christian Era, especially as used in reckoning dates. ◊ **Christian Era**

com·mon frac·tion *n.* = **simple fraction**

com·mon gen·der *n.* **1.** **GENDER OF NOUN FOR BOTH SEXES** in English, the gender of a noun that can refer to a person or animal of either sex, e.g., "leader" and "fox" **2.** **GENDER THAT EXCLUDES NEUTER** in some languages, the gender of those nouns that can be either masculine or feminine but not neuter

com·mon good *n.* the advantage or benefit of everyone

com·mon ground *n.* something mutually agreed upon especially as a basis for negotiation

com·mon knowl·edge *n.* something that is generally known

com·mon law *n.* the body of law developed as a result of custom and judicial decisions, as distinct from the law laid down by legislative assemblies. Common law forms the basis of all law that is applied in England and most of the United States. [A translation of Latin *jus commune*]

com·mon-law *adj.* **1.** LAW **WITHOUT OFFICIAL CEREMONY** used to describe a partner in a marriage that is recognized in some jurisdictions when both parties declare themselves married without an official ceremony **2.** **OF UNMARRIED COUPLE LIVING TOGETHER** used to describe a partner in a marriage so called because of the length of time the two unmarried people have lived together as husband and wife **3.** **OF COMMON LAW** based on or relating to common law

com·mon log·a·rithm *n.* a logarithm with ten as its base number

com·mon loon *n.* a large black-and-white diving bird found especially in North America. Latin name: *Gavia immer.*

com·mon·ly /kómmənlee/ *adv.* by most people or in most circumstances ○ *The measure was commonly held to be a success.*

com·mon mar·ket *n.* any economic association established, typically between nations, with the aim of removing or reducing trade barriers

Com·mon Mar·ket *n.* a term used in the1960s and 1970s to refer both to the European Community and the European Economic Community

com·mon meas·ure *n.* **1.** MUSIC = **common time** **2.** POETRY **4-LINE STANZA FORM FOR BALLADS** the stanza form used for ballads, with four iambic lines rhymed "abab" or "abac" **3.** MATH = **common divisor**

com·mon me·ter *n.* **1.** POETRY = **common measure** **2.** MUSIC **4-LINE VERSE FORM FOR HYMNS** the verse form used in many hymns, consisting of four-line verses that alternate lines of eight and six syllables

com·mon mul·ti·ple *n.* a number that can be divided exactly by two or more other numbers. For example, 12 is a common multiple of 2, 3, and 4.

com·mon noun *n.* a noun that refers to any of a class of people or things, e.g., "singer" and "place," as distinct from a proper noun, e.g., "Lennon" or "Washington." Common nouns can be preceded by words that modify their meaning, such as "some" and "any."

com·mon·place /kómmən plàyss/ *adj.* **1.** **EVERYDAY** encountered or happening often **2.** **DULL** uninteresting as a result of being unoriginal ■ *n.* **1.** **DULL REMARK** an unoriginal remark **2.** **SOMETHING ORDINARY** something that is encountered or seen often, or that happens often [Mid-16thC. Originally two words; a translation of Latin *locus communis*, a translation of Greek *koinos topos* "general theme."] —**com·mon·place·ness** *n.*

com·mon·place book *n.* a personal notebook used for copying down quotations and memorable passages from other books

com·mon pleas *n.* LAW = **court of common pleas** (*takes a singular verb*)

com·mon room *n.* **1.** **ROOM FOR THE RELAXATION OF RESIDENTS** a lounge available to everyone living in a residential community or institution **2.** EDUC **LOUNGE IN COLLEGE** a sitting room in a college or university where staff or students can relax

com·mons /kómmənz/ *npl.* **1.** **COLLEGE DINING HALL** a dining hall in a college or university (*takes a singular verb*) **2.** **com·mons, Com·mons** **MASSES** the common people as distinct from the ruling classes (*takes a singular or plural verb*)

Com·mons *npl.* (*takes a singular or plural verb*) **1.** **PARLIAMENTARY REPRESENTATIVES** the politicians who are elected to the lower house of the U.K. and Canadian parliament and represent all the people **2.** **LOWER PARLIAMENTARY HOUSE** the House of Commons in the parliaments of the United Kingdom and Canada

com·mon salt *n.* = **salt** *n.* 1

com·mon school *n.* a public elementary school

com·mon seal *n.* a gray seal with dark blotches on its skin that lives in northern Atlantic and Pacific waters. Latin name: *Phoca vitulina.*

com·mon sense *n.* sound practical judgment derived from experience rather than study

com·mon·sense /kòmmən sénss/ *adj.* based on common sense —**com·mon·sen·si·cal** *adj.* —**com·mon·sen·si·cal·ly** *adv.*

com·mon stock *n.* a stock that pays the holder a fluctuating dividend after the holders of preferred stock have been paid

com·mon time *n.* a musical meter with four quarter notes to the measure, commonly referred to as four-four time

com·mon touch *n.* the ability of a celebrity or somebody in public life to behave toward members of the general public in a naturally friendly, informal, and uncondescending way

com·mon·wealth /kómmən wèlth/ *n.* **1.** **NATION OR ITS PEOPLE** a nation or its people considered as a political entity **2.** **REPUBLIC** a nation or state in which the people govern **3.** **ASSOCIATION OF STATES** a group of states that have formed an association for the political and economic benefit of all members **4.** **PEOPLE WITH COMMON INTEREST** a group of people linked by something that they all have in common

Com·mon·wealth /kómmən wèlth/ *n.* **1.** **TERRITORY ASSOCIATED WITH UNITED STATES** a self-governing territory voluntarily associated with the United States. Puerto Rico and the Northern Mariana Islands are Commonwealths. **2.** **TITLE FOR SOME STATES** an official title used by the states of Kentucky, Massachusetts, Pennsylvania, and Virginia **3.** RELIG = **Commonwealth of Nations** **4.** POL **FEDERATED STATES OF AUSTRALIA** the official designation of the federated states of Australia, often used to refer to the federal government as opposed to the state governments **5.** HIST **REPUBLIC IN 17THC ENGLAND** the state and republican government in England from the death of Charles I in 1649 until the restoration of the monarchy in 1660

Com·mon·wealth Day *n.* a holiday observed in some countries of the Commonwealth of Nations, formerly on the anniversary of Queen Victoria's birth on May 24 but now on the second Monday in March. It was formerly known as Empire Day.

Com·mon·wealth of In·de·pen·dent States *n.* an association formed in 1991 by most of the republics of the former Soviet Union, with ceremonial headquarters in Minsk, Belarus

Com·mon·wealth of Na·tions *n.* an association consisting of Britain and sovereign states that were formerly British colonies or are ruled by Britain. The British monarch is acknowledged by member states as its head.

com·mon year *n.* an ordinary year of 365 days, as distinct from a leap year

com·mo·tion /kə mṓsh'n/ *n.* a scene of noisy confusion or activity [14thC. From the Latin stem *commotion-*, literally "intensive motion," from the stem *motion-* "motion" (see MOTION).] —**com·mo·tion·al** *adj.*

com·mu·nal /kə myo͝on'l/ *adj.* 1. SHARED used or owned by all members of a group or community 2. OF COMMUNITIES relating to communities or to living in communities 3. OF A COMMUNE belonging or relating to a commune 4. RELATING TO DIFFERENT SOCIAL GROUPS relating to or involving different groups within a society [Early 19thC. From, ultimately, late Latin *communalis,* from Latin *communis* (see COMMON).] —**com·mu·nal·ly** *adv.*

com·mu·nal·ism /kə myo͝on'l ìzzəm/ *n.* 1. COMMUNAL LIVING the principles and practices of communal living or ownership or support for a communal society 2. ALLEGIANCE TO AN ETHNIC GROUP a greater loyalty to an ethnic or religious group than to society in general —**com·mu·nal·ist** *n.* —**com·mu·nal·is·tic** /-ístik/ *adj.*

com·mu·nal·i·ty /kòmmyə nállətee/ *n.* 1. SHARING shared use or ownership 2. SPIRIT OF TOGETHERNESS the spirit of cooperation and solidarity that exists among members of a community or commune

com·mu·nal·ize /kə myo͝on'l ìz, kómmyən'l ìz/ (**-ized, -iz·ing, -iz·es**) *vt.* to put something into joint ownership among the members of a community

com·mu·nard /kómmyə naard/ *n.* somebody living in a commune

Com·mu·nard /kómmyə naard/ *n.* a member or supporter of the Paris Commune of 1871 [Late 19thC. From French, from *commune* "group of citizens, Commune," from medieval Latin *communia,* the neuter plural of Latin *communis* "common" (see COMMON).]

com·mune[1] /kóm yo͞on/ *n.* 1. COMMUNAL GROUP a mutually supportive community in which possessions and responsibilities are shared 2. PEOPLE LIVING IN COMMUNE a group of families or individuals living in a commune 3. SMALLEST ADMINISTRATIVE DISTRICT OF VARIOUS COUNTRIES the smallest administrative district of some countries, e.g., France, Italy, and Switzerland, governed by a mayor and a council [Late 17thC. Via French from medieval Latin *communia,* from Latin *communis* (see COMMON).]

com·mune[2] /kə myo͞on/ (**-muned, -mun·ing, -munes**) *vi.* to experience a deep emotional or spiritual relationship with something [14thC. From Old French *comuner* "to share," from *comun* "common," from Latin *communis* (see COMMON).]

com·mu·ni·ca·ble /kə myo͞onikəb'l/ *adj.* 1. READILY TRANSMITTABLE able to be passed from one person, animal, or organism to another ○ *a communicable disease* 2. EASILY EXPLAINED easily or simply communicated or capable of being communicated [14thC. From, ultimately, late Latin *communicabilis,* from Latin *communicare* (see COMMUNICATE).] —**com·mu·ni·ca·bil·i·ty** /kə myo͞onikə bíllətee/ *n.* —**com·mu·ni·ca·bly** /-myo͞onikkəblee/ *adv.*

com·mu·ni·cant /kə myo͞onikənt/ *n.* 1. CHR SOMEBODY WHO RECEIVES COMMUNION somebody who receives the Christian sacrament of Communion 2. SOMEBODY OR SOMETHING THAT INFORMS somebody or something such as a service that provides information [15thC. From the Latin present participle stem *communicant-* of *communicare* (see COMMUNICATE).]

com·mu·ni·cate /kə myo͞oni kàyt/ (**-cat·ed, -cat·ing, -cates**) *v.* 1. *vti.* EXCHANGE INFORMATION to give or exchange information, e.g., by speech or writing ○ *We communicate by e-mail.* 2. *vt.* CONVEY to transmit or reveal a feeling or thought by speech, writing, or gesture so that it is clearly understood 3. *vi.* UNDERSTAND ONE ANOTHER to share a good personal understanding 4. *vi.* HAVE COMMON ACCESS to be connected or provide access to each other 5. *vt.* MED TRANSMIT DISEASE to pass a disease or infection on to somebody 6. *vi.* CHR GIVE OR RECEIVE COMMUNION to give or receive the Christian sacrament of Communion [Early 16thC. From, ultimately, Latin *communicare* "to share," from *communis* (see COMMON).] —**com·mu·ni·ca·tor·y** /kə myo͞onikə tàwree/ *adj.*

com·mu·ni·ca·tion /kə myo͞oni káysh'n/ *n.* 1. EXCHANGE OF INFORMATION the exchange of information between individuals, e.g., by means of speaking, writing, or using a common system of signs or behavior 2. MESSAGE a spoken or written message 3. ACT OF COMMUNICATING the communicating of information 4. RAPPORT a sense of mutual understanding and sympathy 5. ACCESS a means of access or communication, e.g., a connecting door —**com·mu·ni·ca·tion·al** *adj.*

com·mu·ni·ca·tion cord *n. U.K.* = **emergency cord**

com·mu·ni·ca·tions /kəmyooni káysh'nz/ *n.* 1. SYSTEMS FOR COMMUNICATING the technology and systems used for sending and receiving messages, e.g., postal and telephone networks 2. EFFECTIVE VERBAL EXPRESSION the effective use of words to convey ideas or information (*takes a singular or plural verb*) 3. TRANSPORTATION OF TROOPS a system of routes and transportation for moving troops and supplies 4. STUDY OF HUMAN COMMUNICATION the study of the different means people use to communicate with each other, e.g., by gesture, speech, telecommunications, and writing (*takes a singular or plural verb*)

com·mu·ni·ca·tions sat·el·lite *n.* an artificial satellite used to relay data such as radio, telephone, and television signals around the world. Signals may be reflected, but more often they are strengthened using a solar-powered transponder. Satellites often follow a geostationary orbit, remaining in the same position relative to Earth.

com·mu·ni·ca·tions the·o·ry *n.* = **communication theory**

com·mu·ni·ca·tion the·o·ry, com·mu·ni·ca·tions the·o·ry *n.* the study of all forms of human communication, including branches of linguistics such as semantics, as well as telecommunications and other nonlinguistic forms

com·mu·ni·ca·tive /kə myo͞oni kàytiv/ *adj.* 1. TALKATIVE inclined or ready to talk 2. OF COMMUNICATION relating to communication or to systems for communication 3. STRESSING PRACTICAL COMMUNICATION in foreign language teaching, stressing the importance of language as a tool for communicating information and ideas —**com·mu·ni·ca·tive·ly** *adv.* —**com·mu·ni·ca·tive·ness** *n.*

com·mu·ni·ca·tor /kə myo͞oni kàytər/ *n.* 1. SOMEBODY COMMUNICATING somebody or something that communicates 2. SOMEBODY WHO CAN MAKE SOMETHING CLEAR somebody who has a particular ability to express things effectively ○ *She's a highly effective communicator.*

com·mun·ion /kə myo͞onyən/ *n.* 1. INTIMACY a feeling of emotional or spiritual closeness 2. CONNECTION an association or relationship 3. CHR RELIGIOUS GROUP WITH COMMON FAITH a religious group with its own set of beliefs and practices, especially a Christian denomination 4. CHR FELLOWSHIP BETWEEN RELIGIOUS GROUPS a sense of shared religious identity and fellowship, especially between members of different Christian denominations [14thC. From the Latin stem *communion-,* from *communis* (see COMMON).] —**com·mu·nion·al** *adj.* —**com·mu·nion·al·ly** *adv.*

Com·mu·nion /kə myo͞onyən/ *n.* 1. CHRISTIAN SACRAMENT a Christian sacrament that commemorates Jesus Christ's Last Supper, with the priest or minister consecrating bread and wine that is consumed by the congregation 2. PART OF THE COMMUNION SERVICE the celebration of the sacrament of Communion 3. CONSECRATED BREAD AND WINE the consecrated bread and wine received by worshippers at a Communion service

com·mu·ni·qué /kə myo͞oni káy, kə myo͞oni kày/ *n.* an official announcement, especially to the press or public [Mid-19thC. From French, from the past participle of *communiquer* "to communicate," from Latin *communicare* (see COMMUNICATE).]

com·mu·nism /kómmyə nìzzəm/ *n.* the political theory or system in which all property and wealth is owned in a classless society by all the members of a community. ◊ **Communism** [Mid-19thC. From French *communisme,* from *commun* "common," from Latin *communis* (see COMMON).]

Com·mu·nism /kómmyə nìzzəm/ *n.* 1. **Com·mu·nism, com·mu·nism** MARXIST-LENINIST SYSTEM the Marxist-Leninist version of a classless society in which capitalism is overthrown by a working-class revolution that gives ownership and control of wealth and property to the state 2. ONE-PARTY STATE any system of government in which a single, usually totalitarian, party holds power, and the state controls the economy

Com·mu·nism Peak mountain situated in central Tajikistan, and the highest peak in the country. Height: 24,590 ft./7,495 m. Also known as **Mount Communism**

com·mu·nist /kómmyənist/ *n.* 1. SUPPORTER OF COMMUNISM an advocate or supporter of any type of communism 2. SOMEBODY LEFT-WING somebody with left-wing views, especially somebody denounced as revolutionary or subversive 3. PRACTICER OF COMMUNAL LIVING somebody who practices communal living ■ *adj.* OF COMMUNISM relating to communism or its supporters [Mid-19thC. From French *communiste,* from *commun* "common," from Latin *communis* (see COMMON).] —**com·mu·nist·ic** /kòmmyə nístik/ *adj.*

Com·mu·nist /kómmyənist/ **com·mu·nist** *n.* a supporter of Communism or a member of an organization that supports or practices Communism —**Com·mu·nist** *adj.*

com·mu·ni·tar·i·an /kə myo͞oni táiree ən/ *n.* ADVOCATE OF COLLECTIVE WAY OF LIVING a member or supporter of a collectivist or cooperative community or system ■ *adj.* OF COMMUNITARIANS relating to communitarians or a collectivist or cooperative way of life [Mid-19thC. Coined from COMMUNITY + -ARIAN, modeled on words such as UNITARIAN.] —**com·mu·ni·tar·i·an·ism** *n.*

com·mu·ni·ty /kə myo͞onitee/ (*plural* **-ties**) *n.* 1. PEOPLE IN AREA a group of people who live in the same area, or the area in which they live ○ *a close-knit fishing community* 2. PEOPLE WITH COMMON BACKGROUND a group of people with a common background or with shared interests within society ○ *the financial community* 3. NATIONS WITH COMMON HISTORY a group of nations with a common history or common economic or political interests ○ *the international community* 4. SOCIETY the public or society in general ○ *a useful member of the community* 5. INTERACTING PLANTS AND ANIMALS all the plants and animals that live in the same area and interact with one another [14thC. Via Old French *communeté* from the Latin stem *communitat-,* from *communis* (see COMMON).]

com·mu·ni·ty an·ten·na tel·e·vi·sion *n.* = **cable television**

com·mu·ni·ty cen·ter *n.* a building used for a range of community activities

com·mu·ni·ty chest *n.* a fund raised by voluntary contributions for local charities and social welfare activities (*dated*)

com·mu·ni·ty col·lege *n.* in Canada or the United States, a nonresidential college usually supported by the government offering two-year or three-year courses and awarding diplomas or associate degrees

com·mu·ni·ty med·i·cine *n.* the branch of medicine devoted to the care of public health provision

com·mu·ni·ty po·lic·ing *n.* policing that seeks to integrate officers into the local community in order to reduce crime and foster good community relations

com·mu·ni·ty prop·er·ty *n.* property regarded by law as being jointly owned by husband and wife

com·mu·ni·ty re·la·tions *npl.* 1. RELATIONSHIPS BETWEEN GROUPS IN AREA the relationships between different cultural, ethnic, political, or religious groups who live in an area and may come into conflict 2. MEDIATION BETWEEN GROUPS mediation between different cultural, ethnic, political, or religious groups living in an area

com·mu·ni·ty ser·vice *n.* a penalty requiring that an offender convicted of a relatively minor crime do unpaid work that is beneficial to the community as an alternative to imprisonment

com·mu·nize /kómmyə nìz/ (**-nized, -niz·ing, -niz·es**) *vt.* 1. MAKE PUBLICLY OWNED to transfer something, e.g., land or property, from private to public ownership 2. RUN ON COMMUNIST PRINCIPLES to apply communist principles of organization to a government or people [Late 19thC. From Latin *communis* "common" (see COMMON) + -IZE.] —**com·mu·ni·za·tion** *n.*

com·mut·a·ble /kə myo͞otəb'l/ *adj.* 1. LAW CAPABLE OF BEING REDUCED capable of being shortened or made less severe ○ *a commutable sentence* 2. EXCHANGEABLE FOR MONEY able to be converted or exchanged, especially into or for money 3. TRANSP WITHIN COMMUTING DISTANCE close enough to make a daily journey to and from work practical —**com·mut·a·bil·i·ty** /kə myo͞otə bíllətee/ *n.*

com·mu·tate /kómmyə tàyt/ (**-tat·ed, -tat·ing, -tates**) *vt.* to convert alternating electric current to direct current or vice versa

com·mu·ta·tion /kòmmyə táysh'n/ *n.* 1. LAW REDUCTION IN SEVERITY OF LEGAL PENALTY the reduction of a prison sentence or other legal penalty to a less severe one 2. TRANSP the traveling undertaken by a commuter 3. ELEC CONVERSION OF ELECTRIC CURRENT the converting of an electric current from alternating to direct current or vice versa 4. CONVERSION any exchange or substitution, e.g., the substituting of one kind of payment for another (*formal*)

com·mu·ta·tion tick·et *n.* a passenger ticket valid for multiple trips over a given route during a limited period, sold for less than the total cost of tickets purchased separately for each trip

com·mu·ta·tive /kómmyə tàytiv/ *adj.* **1. OF SUBSTITUTION** involving or relating to exchanges or substitutions **2.** MATH **NOT DEPENDENT ON ORDER** giving the same result in mathematics or logic irrespective of the order in which two or more terms or quantities are placed. For example, addition and multiplication are commutative processes, while subtraction and division are not. —**com·mu·ta·tive·ly** *adv.* —**com·mu·ta·tiv·i·ty** /kə myòotə tívvətee/ *n.*

com·mu·ta·tor /kómmyə tàytər/ *n.* a device that maintains the direction of flow of electric current in a generator or reverses it in an electric motor

com·mute /kə myóot/ (**com·mut·ed, com·mut·ing, com·mutes**) *v.* **1.** *vi.* TRANSP **TRAVEL REGULARLY BETWEEN PLACES** to travel regularly from one place to another, especially between home and work **2.** *vt.* LAW **REDUCE SEVERITY OF PENALTY** to reduce a legal sentence to a less severe one **3.** *vti.* **REPLACE WITH SOMETHING ELSE** to be changed or substituted or to change or substitute one thing for another, e.g., one form of payment for another **4.** *vi.* **BE REPLACEMENT** to compensate or act as a substitute **5.** *vt.* ELEC = **commutate 6.** *vi.* MATH **GIVE SAME RESULT WITH DIFFERENT ORDER** to give the same mathematical result irrespective of the order in which two or more quantities are placed, e.g., as in addition but not subtraction [15thC. From Latin *commutare,* literally "to change altogether," from *mutare* "to change" (source of English *mutant*). First used of traveling in the 19thC.]

com·mut·er /kə myóotər/ *n.* **1. REGULAR TRAVELER FROM HOME TO WORK** somebody who travels regularly from one place to another, especially between home and work and usually between a suburb and a city **2. INTERCITY AIRLINE** an airline that provides short flights between major cities

com·my *n.* = **commie**

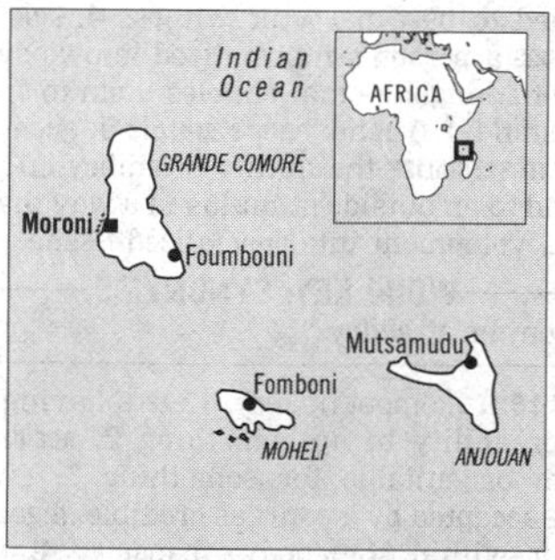

Comoros

Com·o·ros /kómmə rōz, kə máw rōz/ an independent state consisting of a group of islands in the Indian Ocean, 180 mi./290 km from Mozambique and 200 mi./320 km from Madagascar. Language: French, Arabic. Currency: Comorian Franc. Capital: Moroni. Population: 528,893 (1997). Area: 719 sq. mi./1,862 sq. km. Official name **Federal Islamic Republic of the Comoros**

comp[1] /komp/ *n.* **SOMETHING FREE** something supplied free of charge e.g., a complimentary theater ticket (*informal*) ■ *adj.* **FREE** complimentary or free of charge (*informal*) ■ *vt.* (**comped, comp·ing, comps**) **GIVE SOMEBODY A COMP** to supply somebody with something that is complimentary or free (*informal*) [Late 19thC. Shortening of COMPLIMENTARY.]

comp[2] /komp/ *n.* **JAZZ ACCOMPANIMENT** an accompaniment, especially a jazz accompaniment played on piano or guitar (*informal*) ■ *vti.* (**comped, comp·ing, comps**) **PLAY JAZZ ACCOMPANIMENT** to play a musical accompaniment, often improvised, especially in jazz (*informal*) [Mid-20thC. Shortening.]

comp[3] /komp/ *n.* compensation (*informal*) [Late 20thC. Shortening.]

comp. *abbr.* **1.** companion **2.** comparative **3.** compare **4.** compensation **5.** compilation **6.** compiled **7.** complete **8.** composer **9.** composite **10.** composition **11.** compound **12.** comprehensive **13.** comprising

com·pact[1] *adj.* /kəm pákt, kóm pàkt/ **1. PACKED TIGHTLY** closely clustered or packed together ○ *a compact bundle of papers* **2. SMALL AND EFFICIENTLY ARRANGED** small, with efficient use of available space **3. SHORT AND STURDY** short and stocky **4. CONCISE** brief and concise ■ *vti.* /kəm pákt/ (**-pact·ed, -pact·ed** *or* **-pact, -pact·ing, -pacts**) **PACK SOMETHING TIGHTLY** to become, or make something, more dense or firmly packed ■ *n.* /kóm pàkt/ **1.** COSMETICS **CASE FOR MAKEUP** a small flat case containing makeup, usually face powder, with a mirror inside the lid **2. SMALLISH CAR** a medium-sized car that is economical to run [14thC. From Latin *compactus,* the past participle of *compingere,* literally "to fasten together," from *pangere* "to fasten."] —**com·pact·i·ble** *adj.* —**com·pact·ly** *adv.* —**com·pact·ness** *n.*

com·pact[2] /kóm pàkt/ *n.* an agreement between two or more individuals or entities [Late 16thC. From Latin *compactum,* from the past participle of *compacisci,* literally "to make an agreement together," from *pacisci* "to make an agreement" (see PACT).]

com·pact disc, com·pact disk *n.* a hard plastic disk approximately $4\frac{3}{4}$ in./12 cm in diameter on which information, e.g., music or computer data, is digitally encoded in a format readable by laser beam

com·pact disc play·er, com·pact disk play·er *n.* a machine for playing compact disks

com·pact·er /kəm páktər/ *n.* = **compactor**

com·pac·tion /kəm pákshən/ *n.* **1. COMPRESSING** the pressing together of particles to make a denser mass, or the compressed state of the resulting mass **2.** GEOL **PROCESS OF ROCK FORMATION** a process in the formation of sedimentary rock in which pressure from overlying sediment forces water from unconsolidated sediment, reducing its volume and yielding solid rock

com·pac·tor /kəm páktər, kóm pàktər/, **com·pact·er** *n.* a machine used in the home to compress garbage into small bundles for easy disposal

com·pan·ion[1] /kəm pánnyən/ *n.* **1. SOMEBODY TO BE WITH** somebody who accompanies you, spends time with you, or is a friend **2. SOMEBODY WHOSE JOB IS ACCOMPANYING ANOTHER** somebody employed to live with another **3. MATCH FOR SOMETHING** an article that goes with another to make a pair **4.** PUBL **HANDBOOK** a guide or handbook on a particular subject **5.** ASTRON **FAINTER OF TWO STARS** the fainter of the stars that make up a double-star or multiple-star system ■ *vt.* (**-ioned, -ion·ing, -ions**) **ACCOMPANY SOMEBODY** to be a companion to somebody [13thC. From, ultimately, the late Latin stem *companion-,* literally "one who shares bread," from Latin *panis* "bread" (source of English *pantry*).] —**com·pan·ion·less** *adj.*

com·pan·ion[2] /kəm pánnyən/ *n.* a companionway, or a covering above a companionway [Mid-18thC. Alteration of obsolete Dutch *kompanje* "quarterdeck," from, ultimately, Italian *compagna* "(storeroom for) provisions," literally "(eaten) with bread," from, ultimately, Latin *panis* "bread" (see PANTRY).]

Com·pan·ion /kəm pánnyən/ *n.* **Com·pan·ion, com·pan·ion** a member of the lowest rank in a British order of knighthood

com·pan·ion·a·ble /kəm pánnyənəb'l/ *adj.* friendly, sociable, and good company ○ *They sat in a companionable silence.* —**com·pan·ion·a·bil·i·ty** /-pànnyənə bíllətee/ *n.* —**com·pan·ion·a·ble·ness** /kəm pánnyənəb'lnəss/ *n.* —**com·pan·ion·a·bly** /-əblee/ *adv.*

com·pan·ion·ate /kəm pánnyənət/ *adj.* **1. FITTING FOR A COMPANION** appropriate for a companion **2. WELL SUITED** right for each other

com·pan·ion·ate mar·riage *n.* SOCIOL marriage based on mutual affection and shared interests as opposed to purely economic or dynastic considerations

com·pan·ion cell *n.* a type of cell found in flowering plants that lies alongside a sap-conducting sieve-tube element, whose function it is thought to influence. Companion cells have a prominent nucleus and dense cytoplasm, and form fine cytoplasmic connections (**plasmodesmata**) with the adjacent sieve-tube element.

com·pan·ion piece *n.* a work, especially of music or literature, that is closely related to another, often by the same composer or author

com·pan·ion·ship /kəm pánnyən shìp/ *n.* **1. RELATIONSHIP OF FRIENDS** the company of friends and the relationship that exists between them **2. GROUP** an organized group of people

com·pan·ion·way /kəm pánnyən wày/ *n.* a stairway or ladder between decks on a boat or ship

com·pa·ny /kúmpənee/ *n.* (*plural* **-nies**) **1.** BUSINESS **BUSINESS** a business enterprise **2. BEING WITH SOMEBODY** being together with others ○ *He didn't feel at ease in company.* **3. GROUP** a gathering of people **4. COMPANIONS** the people that somebody associates with **5. PARTICULAR TYPE OF COMPANION** somebody seen as providing a particular type of companionship ○ *he can be very good company* **6. GUEST** a guest or visitor, especially for a meal or overnight stay ○ *We're having company this weekend.* **7.** BUSINESS **BUSINESS PARTNERS** the partners of a business enterprise whose names are not included in the firm's title **8.** THEATER **TROUPE** a group of performing artists, e.g., actors **9.** MIL **GROUP OF TROOPS** a unit of soldiers, usually consisting of two or more platoons **10.** NAVY **SHIP'S CREW** the crew and officers of a ship **11. FIREFIGHTERS** a unit of firefighters **12.** BUSINESS, HIST **TRADE GUILD** a medieval trade guild ■ *vi.* (**-nied, -ny·ing, -nies**) **JOIN** to associate with somebody (*archaic*) [13thC. From Anglo-Norman *compainie,* ultimately from the late Latin *companion-* (see COMPANION).]

com·pa·ny car *n.* a car owned or leased by a business for use by an employee, often as a fringe benefit of a job or position

com·pa·ny-grade of·fi·cer *n.* = **company officer**

com·pa·ny man *n.* an employee who puts loyalty to an employer before friendship or personal beliefs (*disapproving*)

com·pa·ny of·fi·cer *n.* a commissioned officer who holds the rank of captain or below

com·pa·ny town *n.* a town whose residents depend on a single business for employment, housing, and shops

com·pa·ny un·ion *n.* a labor union established within a company, not affiliated with any national union, and often dominated by the company's management rather than by its membership

compar. *abbr.* comparative

com·pa·ra·ble /kómpərəb'l/ *adj.* **1. CAPABLE OF BEING COMPARED** similar enough for a fair comparison to be made ○ *We ate a meal comparable to that of the finest restaurant.* **2. SIMILAR** as good as another or each other ○ *They both have comparable keyboarding skills.* —**com· pa·ra·bil·i·ty** /kòmpərə bíllətee/ *n.* —**com·pa·ra·ble·ness** /kómpərəb'lnəss/ *n.* —**com·pa·ra·bly** /kómpərəblee/ *adv.*

WORD KEY: USAGE

comparable to or **comparable with**? ***Comparable*** mimics the verb *compare* in being followed either by *to* or *with,* depending on whether a likening to or a contrasting with is intended: *The agency provides a service comparable to that of a good library. The hurricane was comparable with the ones that recently hit Florida and Louisiana.* See Usage note at ***compare.***

com·pa·ra·ble worth *n.* the belief that men and women should receive equal pay for jobs requiring comparable responsibility and skills

com·par·a·tist /kəm pérrətist/ *n.* somebody who uses a comparative method, e.g., in the study of linguistics [Mid-20thC. From French, formed from *comparatif* "comparative."]

com·par·a·tive /kəm pérrətiv/ *adj.* **1. INVOLVING COMPARISONS** based on or using comparisons of different elements or types in the investigation of something ○ *comparative linguistcs* **2. COMPARED TO OTHERS** considered relative to something known, mentioned, or expected ○ *He passed the test with comparative ease.* **3.** GRAM **IN A FORM EXPRESSING INCREASE** used to describe the form of an adjective or adverb that expresses an increase in quality, quantity, or degree e.g., "quicker" and "more importantly" ■ *n.* GRAM **COMPARATIVE FORM OF WORD** a comparative form of an adjective or adverb [15thC. Formed from Latin *comparat-,* the past participle stem of *comparare* (see COMPARE).] —**com·par·a·tive·ly** *adv.* —**com·par·a·tive·ness** *n.*

com·par·a·tive·ly /kəm pérrətivlee/ *adv.* in comparison to something else ○ *the costs were comparatively high*

com·pa·ra·tor /kəm pérrətər/ *n.* an instrument used to compare a measurable property of something, e.g., its color or shape, with a standard

com·pare /kəm páir/ *v.* (**-pared, -par·ing, -pares**) **1.** *vt.* **EXAMINE FOR SIMILARITIES** to examine two or more people or things in order to discover similarities and differences between them **2.** *vt.* **LIKEN** to consider or represent somebody or something as similar to another ○ *"Shall I compare thee to a summer's day?"* (William Shakespeare, *Sonnet*; 1564–1616) **3.** *vi.* **BE AS GOOD AS** to be equal or similar in quality or standing, especially to be as good as another ○ *As an athlete she can compare with the best in the sport.* **4.** *vi.* **CONTRAST** to have a patricular relationship with something or somebody else ○ *Its performance compares badly with that of rival engines.* **5.** *vi.* **MAKE COMPARISON** to make a comparison **6.** *vt.* GRAM **GIVE ALL ADJECTIVE'S OR ADVERB'S FORMS** to give the positive, comparative, and superlative forms of an adjective or adverb ■ *n.* **COMPARISON** comparison (*literary*) ○ *a painting beautiful beyond compare* [15thC. From, ultimately, Latin *comparare*, from *compar*, literally "equal with," from *par* "equal."] —**com·par·i·son** *n.*

WORD KEY: USAGE

Compare to or **compare with**? ***Compare to*** is used when things are being likened in general ways: *He compared her skin to ivory.* ***Compare with*** is used when the comparison is more specific and implies differences as well as similarities: *Tourists find our hotels good compared with those of European capitals.* When **compare** is used intransitively (i.e., without an object), *with* should always be used: *The new model compares well with others in the same price range.*

com·par·i·son-shop *vi.* to compare the prices and features of the same or similar items, especially in different stores, to find the best deal —**com·par·i·son shop·per** *n.*

com·part·ment /kəm paártmənt/ *n.* **1. PARTITIONED SPACE** one of the areas into which an enclosed space is divided **2. TRAIN CAR SECTION** a subdivision of a passenger train car, with a door and features such as two facing rows of seats or sleeping accommodation **3. SMALLER PART** a separate part of something larger ○ *He liked to divide his life into different compartments.* [Mid-16thC. Via French *compartiment* from, ultimately, late Latin *compartiri*, literally "to divide up," from Latin *partiri* "to divide," from *pars*.] —**com·part·ment·al** /kəm paárt mént'l/ *adj.* —**com·part·men·tal·ly** /-ee/ *adv.*

com·part·men·tal·ize /kəm paárt mént'l ɪz/ (**-ized, -iz·ing, -iz·es**) *vt.* to divide something into separate areas, categories, or compartments ○ *She had to compartmentalize her home life and work.* —**com·part·men·tal·i·za·tion** /kəm paárt ment'li záysh'n/ *n.*

com·pass /kúmpəss, kómpəss/ *n.* **1. DIRECTION FINDER** a device for finding directions, usually with a magnetized needle that automatically swings to magnetic north **2. PERSONAL DIRECTION** a sense of personal direction ○ *a leader who was devoid of moral compass* **3. SCOPE** the scope of something such as a subject or area ○ *beyond the compass of the inquiry* ■ *vt.* (**-passed, -pass·ing, -pass·es**) **1. UNDERSTAND SOMETHING** to understand something fully and completely (*formal*) ○ *far more than the average mind can compass* **2.** = **encompass 3. ACHIEVE SOMETHING** to achieve or attain something (*literary*) [14thC. Via French *compas* "scope, circle" and *compasser* "to measure" from assumed Vulgar Latin *compassare*, literally "to step off," from Latin *passus* "step" (see PACE).] —**com·pass·a·ble** *adj.*

com·pass card *n.* the circular diagram in a direction-finding compass over which the needle rotates. Also called **rose**[1] *n.* 10

com·pass·es /kúmpəssəz, kómp-/ *npl.* a device for drawing circles or measuring distances, e.g., on a map that consists of two rods, one pointed, the other often holding a pencil, joined by an adjustable hinge [Mid-16thC]

com·pas·sion /kəm pásh'n/ *n.* sympathy for the suffering of others, often including a desire to help [14thC. Via French from, ultimately, Latin *compass-*, the past participle stem of *compati* (see COMPATIBLE).] —**com·pas·sion·less** *adj.*

com·pas·sion·ate /kəm pásh'nət/ *adj.* showing feelings of sympathy for the suffering of others, often with a desire to help —**com·pas·sion·ate·ly** *adv.* —**com·pas·sion·ate·ness** *n.*

com·pas·sion·ate leave *n.* emergency leave in exceptional circumstances granted to somebody for personal reasons, e.g., the death of a close relative

com·pas·sion fa·tigue *n.* a loss or lessening of sympathy for the misfortune of others because too many demands have been made on your feelings

com·pass plant *n.* a plant found in prairie regions of the central United States, with yellow flowers similar to daisies and leaves that tend to point North and South. Latin name: *Silphium laciniatum.*

com·pass rose *n.* a circular diagram printed on a chart or map to show the direction of north and other main points of the compass [So called because its many-pointed design was thought to resemble a rose]

com·pass saw *n.* a handsaw with a tapering blade, used for cutting curved shapes

com·pat·i·ble /kəm páttəb'l/ *adj.* **1. HARMONIOUS** able to exist, live, or work together without conflict ○ *a highly compatible couple* **2. CONSISTENT** consistent or in keeping with something else ○ *an observation not compatible with the facts* **3.** COMPUT **ABLE TO BE USED WITH SOMETHING** able to be used together with or substituted for another piece of hardware or software ○ *The software isn't PC-compatible* **4.** BOT **ABLE TO CROSS-POLLINATE** used to describe plant varieties that are able to cross-pollinate successfully **5.** BOT **ABLE TO BE GRAFTED** used to describe plants that are able to be grafted onto each other successfully **6.** FUNGI **ABLE TO MATE** used to describe fungal strains that are able to mate successfully **7.** MED **ACCEPTABLE TO THE BODY** used to describe blood, organs, or tissue that can be transplanted or transfused into a person's body without being rejected [Mid-16thC. Via French from, ultimately, Latin *compati*, literally "to suffer together," from *pati* (see PATIENT).] —**com·pat·i·bil·i·ty** /kəm pàttə bíllətee/ *n.* —**com·pat·i·ble·ness** /kəm páttəb'lnəs/ *n.* —**com·pat·i·bly** /kəm páttəblee/ *adv.*

com·pa·tri·ot /kəm páytree ət/ *n.* **1. FELLOW CITIZEN OR SUBJECT** somebody from the same country as another **2.** a fellow worker or colleague [Late 16thC. Via French from late Latin *compatriota*, literally "fellow countryman," from *patriota* (see PATRIOT).]

compd. *abbr.* compound

com·peer /kóm peer, kəm péer/ *n.* (*formal*) **1. EQUAL** somebody who is the equal or peer of somebody else **2. COMPANION** a person who is a close companion or associate of somebody else [Via Old French *comper* from Latin *compar* "equal with" (see COMPARE)]

com·pel /kəm pél/ (**-pelled, -pel·ling, -pels**) *vt.* **1. FORCE SOMEBODY** to force somebody to do something ○ *I felt compelled to listen.* **2. FORCE SOMETHING TO HAPPEN** to make something happen by force [14thC. From Latin *compellere*, literally "to drive together," from *pellere* (see PULSE).] —**com·pel·la·ble** *adj.* —**com·pel·la·bly** *adv.* —**com·pel·ler** *n.*

com·pel·ling /kəm pélling/ *adj.* **1. HOLDING THE ATTENTION** attracting strong interest and attention ○ *a compelling account of a major scientific discovery* **2. MAKING SOMEBODY DO SOMETHING** tending to make somebody do something, make something happen, or be necessary ○ *I felt a compelling need to explain my actions.* —**com·pel·ling·ly** *adv.*

com·pend /kóm pènd/ *n.* = **compendium** *n.* 1 [Late 16thC. Anglicization of Latin *compendium* (see COMPENDIUM).]

com·pen·di·ous /kəm péndee əss/ *adj.* containing a wide range of information in a concise form —**com·pen·di·ous·ly** *adv.* —**com·pen·di·ous·ness** *n.*

com·pen·di·um /kəm péndee əm/ (*plural* **-ums** *or* **-a** /-ə/) *n.* **1. SHORT ACCOUNT** a comprehensive but brief account of a subject, especially in book form **2. LIST OF ITEMS** a list or compilation of various items ○ *Her letter was a compendium of complaints.* [Late 16thC. From Latin, formed from *compendere*, literally "to weigh together," from *pendere* (see PENSIVE).]

com·pen·sa·ble /kəm pénssəb'l/ *adj.* qualifying for compensation —**com·pen·sa·bil·i·ty** /kəm pènsə bíllətee/ *n.*

com·pen·sate /kómpən sàyt/ (**-sat·ed, -sat·ing, -sates**) *v.* **1.** *vt.* **PAY SOMEBODY FOR LOSS** to pay somebody for work done or for something lost ○ *adequately compensated for their efforts* **2.** *vti.* **COUNTERBALANCE** to counterbalance a force or quality **3.** *vi.* **MAKE AMENDS** to make amends or make up for something ○ *Nothing can compensate for the loss of a child.* **4.** *vi.* PSYCHOL **STRESS SOMETHING TO MAKE UP DEFICIENCY** to stress the development of one aspect of your personality to make up for deficiency in another. ◊ **overcompensate** [Mid-17thC. From Latin *compensat-*, the past participle stem of *compensare*, literally "to weigh together," from *pensare* (see PENSIVE).] —**com·pen·sa·tive** /kómpən sàytiv, kəm pénsətiv/ *adj.* —**com·pen·sa·tor** /kómpən sàytər/ *n.*

com·pen·sa·tion /kòmpən sáysh'n/ *n.* **1. MONEY PAID TO REPAIR A LOSS** an amount of money or something else given to pay for loss, damage, or work done ○ *claimed compensation for loss of earnings* **2. PAYMENT OF MONEY TO COVER LOSS** the giving of something to somebody to pay for work done, loss, or damage **3. AMENDS** something that makes amends or makes up for something else ○ *one of the compensations of living abroad* **4.** PSYCHOL **STRESSING A QUALITY** the stressing of one aspect of the personality to make up for deficiency in another —**com·pen·sa·tion·al** *adj.*

com·pen·sa·to·ry /kəm pénsə tàwree/ *adj.* serving to offset the negative effects or results of something else

com·pen·sa·to·ry dam·ag·es *npl.* damages that are awarded in order to compensate a plaintiff for personal injury or injury to property caused by the defendant's wrongful act

com·pen·sa·to·ry growth *n.* the growth in size of one part or organ of the body to make up for the failure or loss of another

com·pere /kóm pàir/ *n. U.K.* **HOST** a host of an entertainment show, especially on television ■ *vti.* (**-pered, -per·ing, -peres**) *U.K.* **ACT AS COMPERE** to act as a compere [Mid-18thC. Via French *compère*, literally "godfather," from medieval Latin *compater*, from Latin *pater* "father."]

com·pete /kəm péet/ (**-pet·ed, -pet·ing, -petes**) *vi.* **1. TRY TO WIN** to do something with the goal of outperforming others or of winning something **2. PUT UP REASONABLE CONTEST** to be able to put up a contest against somebody or something else and have a chance of winning ○ *This product just can't compete.* [Early 17thC. From late Latin *competere*, literally "to strive together," from Latin *petere* (see PETITION).]

com·pe·tence /kómpət'ns/, **com·pe·ten·cy** /kómpətən see/ *n.* **1. ABILITY** the ability to do something well or to a required standard ○ *I don't doubt his competence for a moment.* **2. SUFFICIENT INCOME** an income that is enough to live on (*formal*) **3.** LAW **BEING LEGALLY QUALIFIED** the condition of being accepted by a court as legally qualified to be a party or witness **4.** LING **LANGUAGE KNOWLEDGE** a person's internalized knowledge of the rules of a language that enables them to speak and understand it. ◊ **performance, parole 5.** EMBRYOL **ABILITY OF CELL TO SPECIALIZE** the ability of embryonic cells to respond to an outside stimulus in a way that affects their development into specialized tissue

WORD KEY: SYNONYMS

See Synonyms at ***ability.***

com·pe·tent /kómpət'nt/ *adj.* **1. ABLE** having enough skill or ability to do something **2. ADEQUATE** good enough or suitable for something **3.** LAW **LEGALLY CAPABLE** accepted by a court as credible, legally qualified, or within somebody's capacity **4.** MED, BIOL **FUNCTIONING NORMALLY** able to carry out its normal functions effectively ○ *a competent cervix* [14thC. Via French from Latin *competent-*, the present participle stem of *competere* (see COMPETE). The underlying sense is "adequate for the purpose."] —**com·pe·tent·ly** *adv.*

com·pe·ti·tion /kòmpə tísh'n/ *n.* **1. TRYING TO BEAT OTHERS** the activity of doing something with the goal of outperforming others or winning something ○ *several firms are in competition for the contract* **2. CONTEST** an activity in which people try to do something better than others or win something **3. OPPOSITION** those against whom one is competing, or the level of opposition they give ○ *keep one step ahead of the competition* **4.** ECOL **STRUGGLE FOR RESOURCES** the struggle between organisms of the same or different species for limited resources such as food or light [Early 17thC. From the late Latin stem *competition-*, from Latin *competit-*, the past participle stem of *competere* (see COMPETE).]

com·pet·i·tive /kəm péttitiv/ *adj.* **1. INVOLVING BEATING OTHERS** involving or decided by trying to do something better than others or win something ○ *a highly competitive sport* **2. WANTING TO BEAT OTHERS** inclined toward wanting to do something better than others **3. ATTRACTIVE** more attractive than others because of being good value or worth more ○ *competitive prices* —**com·pet·i·tive·ness** *n.*

com·pet·i·tive ex·clu·sion *n.* ECOL the concept that two or more species with identical requirements cannot coexist on the same limited resources because one will compete more successfully than the other

com·pet·i·tive·ly /kəm péttitivlee/ *adv.* **1. SO AS TO BEAT OTHERS** in a way that involves trying to do something better than others or win something ○ *You will have to play competitively to win.* **2. ATTRACTIVELY** in an attractive way because of being good value or worth more than something else ○ *competitively priced*

com·pet·i·tor /kəm péttitər/ *n.* **1. PARTICIPANT IN COMPETITION** a person, animal, or group taking part in a competition **2. MARKETPLACE OPPONENT** an opponent that somebody is competing against in a commercial market [Early 16thC. From Latin, formed from *competere* (see COMPETE).]

com·pi·la·tion /kòmpə láysh'n/ *n.* **1. GATHERING** the activity of gathering things together from various places **2. SOMETHING CREATED BY GATHERING** something created by gathering things together from various places ○ *a compilation of new poems*

com·pile /kəm pīl/ (**-piled, -pil·ing, -piles**) *vt.* **1. PUT THINGS TOGETHER** to gather things together from various places to form a whole **2. CREATE SOMETHING BY GATHERING THINGS** to create something by gathering things together **3.** COMPUT **TRANSLATE COMPUTER LANGUAGE** to convert a computer program written in a high-level language into an intermediate language (**machine language**) using a special program (**compiler**) [14thC. From French *compiler*, of uncertain origin: probably from Latin *compilare* "to plunder, plagiarize," literally "to heap together," from *pila* (see PILE[1]).]

com·pil·er /kəm pīlər/ *n.* **1. GATHERER** a person or group that gathers things together, especially to create a whole **2.** COMPUT **PROGRAM** a computer program that converts another program from a high-level language into an intermediate language (**machine language**)

com·pla·cent /kəm pláyss'nt/ *adj.* **1. SATISFIED** self-satisfied, usually in an unreflective way and without being aware of possible dangers **2. EAGER TO PLEASE** eager to please [Mid-17thC. From Latin *complacent-*, the present participle stem of *complacere*, literally "to please very much," from *placere* (see PLACID). The word's original sense was "pleasing."] —**com·pla·cen·cy** *n.* —**com·pla·cent·ly** *adv.*

com·plain /kəm pláyn/ (**-plained, -plain·ing, -plains**) *vi.* **1. EXPRESS UNHAPPINESS ABOUT SOMETHING** to express unhappiness about something **2. DESCRIBE SYMPTOMS OF SOMETHING** to say that you are experiencing something, especially pain or an illness ○ *complaining of chest pains* **3. ACCUSE** to accuse somebody of doing something illegal or undesirable, or make a protest about something ○ *The neighbors complained to the police about the noise.* [14thC. Via French *complaign-*, the stem of *complaindre*, from assumed Vulgar Latin *complangere*, from Latin *plangere* (see PLAINT).]

WORD KEY: SYNONYMS

complain, object, protest, grumble, grouse, carp, gripe, whine, nag

CORE MEANING: to indicate dissatisfaction with something

complain a general and neutral term; **object** to indicate dissatisfaction with and opposition to something; **protest** a more forceful term for *object*; **grumble** a term suggesting a moderate degree of dissatisfaction, and suggesting that the complaint is repeated or continual; **grouse** to complain regularly and continually, often in a way that is not constructive; **carp** to complain continually, especially about unimportant things; **gripe** an informal term for *complain*; **whine** to complain in an unreasonable, repeated, or irritating way; **nag** to find fault with somebody regularly and repeatedly.

com·plain·ant /kəm pláynənt/ *n.* a person or organization that takes legal action against another

com·plain·er /kəm pláynər/ *n.* somebody who is unhappy about something and expresses this, especially habitually

com·plaint /kəm pláynt/ *n.* **1. STATEMENT OF UNHAPPINESS** a statement expressing dissatisfaction with something ○ *If you have any complaints, talk to the manager.* **2. SOMETHING MAKING SOMEBODY UNHAPPY** something that makes somebody unhappy or dissatisfied **3. EXPRESSING OF DISSATISFACTION** the act of expressing dissatisfaction with something ○ *has cause for complaint* **4. AILMENT** a physical disorder, usually something minor **5.** LAW **STATEMENT** a statement setting out the reasons for a legal action **6.** LAW **FORMAL CHARGE** a formal charge that somebody has committed a crime ○ *swore out a complaint against him* [14thC. From French *complainte*, the feminine past participle of *complaindre* (see COMPLAIN).]

com·plai·sant /kəm pláyss'nt, -pláyz'nt/ *adj.* showing a willingness to please others by carrying out, or allowing them to carry out, their wishes [Mid-17thC. Via French, the present participle of *complaire* "to agree in order to please," from Latin *complacere* (see COMPLACENT).] —**com·plai·sance** *n.* —**com·plai·sant·ly** *adv.*

com·pleat /kəm pléet/ *adj.* having or exhibiting full knowledge of a particular field or skill (*literary*) [14thC. Variant of COMPLETE.]

com·plect·ed /kəm pléktəd/ *adj.* having a particular kind of complexion (*informal*) (*usually used in combination*) [Early 19thC. Back-formation from COMPLEXION.]

com·ple·ment /kómpləmənt/ *n.* **1. COMPLETING PART** something that completes or perfects something else **2. ONE OF TWO** either of two things that form a unit **3. FULL QUANTITY** a quantity of things or people that is considered complete ○ *the full complement of warships and replenishing vessels* **4.** LING **SENTENCE PART** the predicate part of a sentence that refers to the subject, not counting the verb **5.** MATH, LOGIC **ITEMS EXCLUDED FROM A SUBSET** the elements of a set that are not included in a particular subset of that set **6.** GEOM = **complementary angle 7.** IMMUNOL **GROUP OF BLOOD PROTEINS** a set of proteins in the bloodstream that, together with antibodies, recognize and attack foreign cells such as bacteria **8.** MUSIC **NOTE INTERVAL** an interval that, when added to a given interval, equals an octave ■ *vt.* (**-ment·ed, -ment·ing, -ments**) **COMPLETE SOMETHING** to complete, perfect, or accompany something else pleasingly ○ *a light dessert that complements a rich meal* [14thC. From Latin *complementum*, literally "something that fills up" from *complere* (see COMPLETE).] —**com·ple·men·tal** /kòmplə mént'l/ *adj.* —**com·ple·men·tal·ly** /-méntˈlee/ *adv.*

WORD KEY: USAGE

complement or **compliment**? The two words are close in spelling but their meanings are quite different. A ***complement*** is something added to enhance a thing and make it complete, whereas a ***compliment*** is an expression of praise. *A fine wine is the perfect complement to good cooking. The cook received many compliments from the guests that evening.* Both words are also used as verbs, and both have adjectival forms: ***complementary*** and ***complimentary***. ***Complimentary*** has the special meaning "given free of charge"; and so a ***complimentary*** copy of a book is one given without charge, whereas a ***complementary*** copy is one that completes a set of books.

com·ple·men·tar·i·ty /kòmplə men térratee/ (*plural* **-ties**) *n.* **1. RELATION OF PARTS** the condition of things that complement one another **2.** PHYS **PRINCIPLE GOVERNING EXPLANATION OF ATOMIC SYSTEMS** the concept that two different models may be necessary to describe an atomic or subatomic system, e.g., electrons may be regarded as particles or waves in different circumstances

com·ple·men·ta·ry /kòmplə méntəree, -méntree/ *adj.* **1. COMPLETING** completing something else **2. MAKING A WHOLE** making a pair or whole ○ *At this camp, we regard indoor and outdoor activities as complementary.* **3.** GENETICS **INTERDEPENDENT** used to describe genes that are interdependent and produce their effect only when present together **4.** MATH **NOT IN SUBSET** used to describe the elements of a mathematical set that are not included in a particular subset of that set **5.** GEOM = **complementary angle 6.** MED **RELATING TO COMPLEMENTARY MEDICINE** used in or using complementary medicine —**com·ple·men·ta·ri·ly** *adv.* —**com·ple·men·ta·ri·ness** *n.*

WORD KEY: USAGE

See Usage note at ***complement***.

com·ple·men·ta·ry an·gle *n.* GEOM either of two angles that together make up a right angle

com·ple·men·ta·ry col·or *n.* PHYS a color or colored light that, when combined with another, produces white or gray

com·ple·men·ta·ry gene *n.* a gene that produces an observable effect in an organism only in conjunction with another gene

com·ple·men·ta·ry med·i·cine *n.* a range of therapies based on the holistic treatment of physical disorders, generally addressing the causes of diseases rather than their symptoms and also taking steps in the prevention of disease. The term embraces therapies such as acupuncture, herbalism, and homeopathy. ◊ **alternative medicine**

com·ple·ment fix·a·tion *n.* the process in which a group of blood proteins (**complement**) is bound to a specific combined antibody-antigen pair as part of the immune reaction to foreign cells

com·ple·men·tiz·er /kómpləmən tīzər/ *n.* a word introducing a clause that acts as a complement ○ *"For" in "for Sam to be late is unusual" is a complementizer.*

com·plete /kəm pléet/ *adj.* **1. WHOLE** having every necessary part or everything that is wanted ○ *a complete set of Dickens* **2. FINISHED** having reached the normal or expected end ○ *The washer stops when the last spin cycle is complete.* **3. ABSOLUTE** being the greatest degree of something ○ *a complete waste of time* **4. ACCOMPLISHED** having all the necessary qualities or abilities for a particular role ○ *She is the complete diplomat.* **5.** FOOTBALL **SUCCESSFULLY CAUGHT** used to describe a forward pass in football that has been successfully caught **6.** BOT **HAVING ALL PRINCIPAL FLOWER PARTS** used to describe flowers that have all the principal flower parts, that is, carpels, petals, sepals, and stamens. ◊ **incomplete** ■ *v.* (**-plet·ed, -plet·ing, -pletes**) **1.** *vt.* **MAKE SOMETHING WHOLE** to make something whole by including every necessary part or everything that is wanted ○ *one more goblet to complete the set* **2.** *vt.* **FINISH SOMETHING** to finish something or bring something to an end ○ *You have 20 minutes to complete the quiz.* **3.** *vt.* **ACCOMPLISH SOMETHING** to carry out or accomplish something ○ *The terms of the sale have been completed.* **4.** *vti.* FOOTBALL to throw a successful forward pass ○ *The starting quarterback completed six passes in a row, gaining a total of 45 yards.* [14thC. Directly or via French from Latin *completus*, the past participle of *complere*, literally "to fill up," from *plere* "to fill" (source also of English *supply*).] —**com·plete·ly** *adv.* —**com·plete·ness** *n.* —**com·ple·tive** *adj.* ◇ **complete with** including a particular thing as a feature

WORD KEY: ORIGIN

Complete comes from the Latin word *plere*, meaning "to fill," which is also the source of English *accomplish, complement, compliment, comply, deplete, expletive, implement, replete, supplement*, and *supply*.

com·plete blood count *n.* a diagnostic test used to identify the levels of all blood-cell types in a quantity of blood

com·plete·ly /kəm pléetlee/ *adv.* used to emphasize the extent of something ○ *completely wrong* ○ *I completely forgot about it*

com·plete met·a·mor·pho·sis *n.* metamorphosis that involves the four stages of egg, larva, pupa, and adult in insects such as butterflies, beetles, flies, and bees

com·plet·er /kəm pléetər/ *n.* an item that serves to make a larger item, especially a set, whole ○ *an eight-piece completer set of china*

com·ple·tion /kəm pléesh'n/ *n.* **1. FINISHING** the finishing of something or making something whole **2. STATE OF BEING FINISHED** the state of being finished or brought to an end ○ *the building is nearing completion* **3.** *U.K.* LAW **FINAL STAGE OF SALE** the final stage of the sale of real estate, when ownership changes hands **4.** FOOTBALL **CAUGHT PASS** a forward pass that has been successfully caught

com·plex *adj.* /kəm pléks, kóm plèks/ **1. COMPLICATED** difficult to analyze, understand, or solve **2. HAVING MANY PARTS** made up of many interrelated parts ■ *n.* /kóm plèks/ **1. INTERCONNECTED WHOLE** a whole composed of various interrelated parts ○ *a building complex* **2. INFLUENCE ON BEHAVIOR** a set of related feelings, ideas, or impulses that may be repressed but that continues to influence thoughts and behavior ○ *a guilt complex* **3. EXAGGERATED FEELINGS** an exaggerated or obsessive set of feelings about something (*informal*) ○ *He has a complex about eating in restaurants.* **4.** CHEM **COMPOUND OF NONMETAL AND METAL ATOMS** a compound in which nonmetal molecules or ions form weak bonds (**coordinate bonds**) with a central metal atom [Mid-17thC. Directly and via French from Latin *complexus*, the past participle of *complecti*, literally "to weave together," from *plectere* "to plait"(see PLEXUS).] —**com·plex·ly** *adv.* —**com·plex·ness** *n.*

com·plex con·ju·gate *n.* MATH a complex number in a pair that have the same real components but opposite imaginary components. The complex conjugate of a + ib is a – ib.

com·plex frac·tion *n.* MATH a fraction with a mixed number or fraction in its numerator or denominator, or in both

com·plex·ion /kəm plékshən/ *n.* **1.** SKIN TYPE the quality and color of the skin, especially of the face **2.** CHARACTER the character of something or the way it appears ○ *This development puts an entirely new complexion on the matter.* [14thC. Via French, "bodily constitution," from, ultimately, Latin *complecti* "to entwine" (see COMPLEX). The original underlying sense was the "combination" of a person's bodily humors.] —**com·plex·ion·al** *adj.*

com·plex·ioned /kəm plékshənd/ *adj.* having a particular type of skin, especially on the face (*usually used in combination*) ○ *fair-complexioned*

com·plex·i·ty /kəm pléksitee/ (*plural* **-ties**) *n.* **1.** COMPLICATED NATURE the condition of being difficult to understand, or being made up of many interrelated things ○ *the increasing complexity of computing systems* **2.** COMPLICATED THING any one of the interrelated problems or difficulties involved in a complicated matter (*often used in the plural*)

com·plex num·ber *n.* a number in the form *a* + i*b*, where i = $\sqrt{-1}$, that may be either real or imaginary

com·plex plane *n.* MATH a plane whose coordinates are expressed as single complex numbers

com·plex sen·tence *n.* a sentence containing one or more subordinate clauses

com·pli·ance /kəm plī́ əns/, **com·pli·an·cy** /-ənsee/ *n.* **1.** CONFORMITY the state or act of conforming with or agreeing to do something ○ *in compliance with the court order* **2.** READINESS TO COMPLY readiness to conform or agree to do something

com·pli·an·cy /kəm plī́ ənsee/ *n.* = **compliance**

com·pli·ant /kəm plī́ ənt/ *adj.* **1.** READY TO CONFORM ready to conform or agree to do something **2.** CONFORMING TO REQUIREMENTS made or done according to requirements or instructions (*often used in combination*) ○ *compliant with the general statutes* ○ *Y2K-compliant* —**com·pli·ant·ly** *adv.*

com·pli·ca·cy /kómplikəssee/ (*plural* **-cies**) *n.* a complicated matter or situation (*formal*)

com·pli·cate /kómpli kàyt/ *vt.* (**-cat·ed, -cat·ing, -cates**) MAKE SOMETHING MORE COMPLEX to make something complex or difficult ○ *Further delay will only complicate matters.* ○ *a complicating factor* ■ *adj.* **1.** FOLDED used to describe things that are folded lengthwise, e.g., leaves or insect wings **2.** = **complicated** [Early 17thC. From Latin *complicat-*, the past participle stem of *complicare*, literally "to fold together," from *plicare* (see PLY[2]).]

com·pli·cat·ed /kómpli kàytəd/, **com·pli·cate** *adj.* **1.** HAVING MANY INTERRELATED PARTS composed of many interrelated parts and so difficult to understand or deal with ○ *a complicated diagram* **2.** DIFFICULT difficult to deal with because of the need to take different relationships or points of view into consideration ○ *Life is complicated enough as it is.* —**com·pli·cat·ed·ly** *adv.* —**com·pli·cat·ed·ness** *n.*

com·pli·ca·tion /kòmpli káysh'n/ *n.* **1.** DIFFICULT STATE a difficult or confused state caused by many interrelated factors **2.** DIFFICULTY something that makes something else more difficult or complex ○ *Far from being helpful, this is just a further complication.* **3.** PLOT DEVICE an event or character whose introduction into a story causes difficulty **4.** MEDICAL PROBLEM a disease or problem that arises in addition to the initial condition or during a surgical operation **5.** INTRODUCTION OF DIFFICULTY the act of making something complex or difficult

com·plice /kómpliss/ *n.* somebody who helps another, especially in doing something illegal (*archaic*) [15thC. Via French from late Latin *complic-*, the stem of *complex* "close associate," from *plicare* (see PLY[2]). The underlying meaning is "somebody who is bound together with you."]

com·plic·it /kəm plíssit/ *adj.* involved in something illegal or wrong ○ *It was clear that some of the staff were complicit in the attempt to cover up the scandal.* [Late 20thC. Back-formation from COMPLICITY.]

com·plic·i·ty /kəm plíssitee/ *n.* involvement with another in doing something illegal or wrong [Mid-17thC. Formed from COMPLICE.]

com·pli·ment /kómpləmənt/ *n.* **1.** STATEMENT OF PRAISE something said to express praise and approval **2.** ACT OR GESTURE something done to show respect and honor **3. com·pli·ments** RESPECT expressions of respect and good wishes ○ *My compliments to the chef.* ■ *vt.* (**-ment·ed, -ment·ing, -ments**) **1.** SAY SOMETHING NICE TO SOMEBODY to say something that expresses praise and approval to somebody **2.** GIVE SOMETHING TO SOMEBODY to give somebody a gift as a sign of respect or affection **3.** CONGRATULATE SOMEBODY to congratulate somebody [Mid-17thC. Via French from, ultimately, Latin *complere* (see COMPLETE). The underlying sense is "to fulfill the demands of courtesy."] ◇ **return the compliment** to respond to a gesture somebody has made toward you with a similar gesture

WORD KEY: USAGE

See Usage note at ***complement***.

com·pli·men·ta·ry /kòmplə méntəree, -méntree/ *adj.* **1.** ADMIRING expressing praise or approval ○ *a complimentary glance* **2.** FREE given free as a courtesy or favor ○ *complimentary seats* —**com·pli·men·ta·ri·ly** *adv.*

WORD KEY: USAGE

See Usage note at ***complement***.

com·pli·men·ta·ry close *n.* the part of a letter, e-mail, or similar communication immediately before the signature, expressing the sender's sentiments, e.g., "Sincerely yours"

com·pline /kómplin, kómp lìn/, **com·plin** /kómplin/ *n.* the last of the seven separate hours (**canonical hours**) that are set aside for prayer each day in the Roman Catholic Church [12thC. An alteration (probably influenced by "matins") of Old French *complie*, from medieval Latin *(hora) completa* "final (hour)," from Latin *completus* (see COMPLETE).]

com·ply /kəm plī́/ (**-plied, -ply·ing, -plies**) *vi.* to obey or conform to something, e.g., a rule, law, wish, or regulation [Late 16thC. Via obsolete French *complire* from Latin *complere* (see COMPLETE). The underlying sense is "to carry out completely, fulfill."] —**com·pli·er** *n.*

com·po /kómpō/ *n.* a material mixed from various ingredients, especially a mix of cement mortar (*slang*) [Early 19thC. Shortening of COMPOSITION.]

com·po·nent /kəm pṓnənt/ *n.* **1.** PART a part of something, usually of something bigger ○ *a manufacturer of vehicle components* ○ *one of several major components of our research* **2.** ELEC ELECTRIC PART a device, e.g., a resistor or transistor, that is part of an electronic circuit **3.** MATH VECTOR any one of a set of vectors whose combination (**resultant**) is another vector **4.** CHEM CONSTITUENT SUBSTANCE any one of the substances necessary to describe each phase of a chemical system ■ *adj.* FORMING PART forming part of a whole [Mid-16thC. From Latin *component-*, the present participle stem of *componere*, literally "to put together," from *ponere* (see POST).] —**com·po·nen·tial** /kòmpə nénsh'l/ *adj.*

com·port /kəm páwrt/ (**-port·ed, -port·ing, -ports**) *v.* (*formal*) **1.** *vr.* BEHAVE to behave in a particular way **2.** *vi.* BE CONSISTENT to agree or be consistent with something ○ *This does not comport with the established facts.* [14thC. From Latin *comportare*, literally "to bring together," from *portare* (see PORT[5]). The underlying meaning is "to collect yourself."]

com·port·ment /kəm pórtmənt/ *n.* the way in which somebody behaves (*formal*)

com·pose /kəm pṓz/ (**-posed, -pos·ing, -pos·es**) *v.* **1.** *vt.* BE THE PARTS OF SOMETHING to make something by combining together ○ *fertilizer composed of organic compounds* **2.** *vt.* PUT ELEMENTS TOGETHER to put things together to form a whole ○ *compose a light lunch, using cold cuts and salads* **3.** *vt.* ARRANGE ITEMS to arrange things in order to achieve an effect ○ *compose objects for a still life in oils* **4.** *vti.* CREATE to create something, especially a piece of music or writing ○ *She is trying to compose a rather difficult letter to her client.* **5.** *vt.* CALM to make somebody become calm ○ *please compose yourself* **6.** *vt.* RECONCILE ARGUMENT to settle a quarrel or dispute (*archaic*) **7.** *vti.* SET TYPE to set type in preparation for printing [14thC. From French *composer*, an alteration (influenced by *poser* "to place") of Latin *componere* (see COMPONENT).]

WORD KEY: USAGE

See Usage note at ***comprise***.

com·posed /kəm pṓzd/ *adj.* not agitated or distracted —**com·pos·ed·ly** /-pṓzədlee/ *adv.* —**com·pos·ed·ness** /-ədnəss/ *n.*

WORD KEY: SYNONYMS

See Synonyms at ***calm***.

com·pos·er /kəm pṓzər/ *n.* somebody who composes, especially a writer of music

com·pos·ite /kəm pózzit/ *adj.* **1.** COMPOUND made up of different parts **2.** BOT BELONGING TO DAISY FAMILY used to describe any plant belonging to a large family that has flower heads resembling a single flower but composed of many smaller flowers. Dandelions and daisies are composite plants. Family: Compositae. ■ *n.* **1.** SOMETHING MADE OF PARTS something made from different parts ○ *The new law is a composite of previous suggested legislation.* **2.** CRIMINOL IMAGE OF SUSPECT an image of a suspect's face that is created by a police artist or photographer, based on input from witnesses (*informal*) **3.** BOT PLANT OF DAISY FAMILY a composite plant **4.** BUILDING BUILDING MATERIAL any building material made up of different ingredients [14thC. Directly or via French from Latin *compositus*, the past participle of *componere* (see COMPONENT).] —**com·pos·ite·ly** *adv.* —**com·pos·ite·ness** *n.*

Com·pos·ite *adj.* belonging to a Classical order of architecture that combines elements of the Ionic and Corinthian orders [Mid-16thC]

com·pos·ite con·struc·tion *n.* a building technique that combines the use of steel and concrete to make supporting columns, resulting in stronger, lighter, and less costly supports

com·pos·ite pho·to·graph *n.* an image or scene made up of two or more original images placed side by side, overlapped, or superimposed

com·pos·ite school *n.* in some Canadian provinces, a secondary school in which academic, business, and vocational programs are offered

com·po·si·tion /kòmpə zísh'n/ *n.* **1.** CONSTITUENTS the way in which something is made, especially in terms of its different parts **2.** ARRANGEMENT the way in which the parts of something are arranged, especially the elements in a visual image ○ *the artist's masterly composition of a group portrait* **3.** PUTTING TOGETHER the act or process of combining things to form a whole, or of creating something such as a piece of music or writing **4.** ARTS ARTISTIC CREATION something created as a work of art, especially a piece of music **5.** PIECE OF WRITING a short piece of writing, especially a school exercise **6.** PRODUCT a thing created by combining separate parts **7.** LAW SETTLEMENT a settlement whereby creditors agree to accept partial payment of debts by a bankrupt party, typically in return for a consideration such as immediate payment of a lesser amount **8.** LING WORD FORMATION the formation of compound words from separate words **9.** PRINTING TYPESETTING the setting of type in preparation for printing [14thC. Via French from, ultimately, Latin *composit-*, the past participle stem of *componere* (see COMPONENT).] —**com·po·si·tion·al** *adj.* —**com·po·si·tion·al·ly** *adv.*

com·pos·i·tor /kəm pózzitər/ *n.* somebody who sets text in type [Mid-16thC. From Latin, "compiler," formed from *composit-*, the past participle stem of *componere* (see COMPONENT).]

com·pos men·tis *adj.* sane or of sound mind [From Latin, literally "in control of one's mind"]

com·post /kóm pōst/ *n.* **1.** DECAYED PLANT MATTER a mixture of decayed plants and other organic matter used by gardeners for enriching soil **2.** COMPOUND a compound or composition of several elements ■ *v.* (**-post·ed, -post·ing, -posts**) **1.** *vti.* DECAY to convert organic matter to compost, or to be converted to compost **2.** *vt.* TREAT SOIL to treat soil or an area of ground by adding compost [14thC. Via Old French *composte* "mixture" (source of English *compote*) from Latin *composita*, from *composit-*, the past participle stem of *componere* (see COMPONENT).] —**com·post·a·ble** *adj.*

com·post·er /kóm pōstər/ *n.* a device, often shaped like a box or barrel, used to collect organic materials to be used later in composting

com·po·sure /kəm pṓzhər/ *n.* calm and steady control over the emotions

com·pote /kóm pōt/ *n.* **1.** STEWED FRUIT fruit cooked in sugar or syrup, served as a hot or cold dessert **2.** DISH a glass dish with a long stem, used for serving fruit, nuts, or candy [Late 17thC. Via French, literally "mixture," from Old French *composte* (see COMPOST).]

com·pound[1] *n.* /kóm pòwnd/ **1.** MIXTURE something made by the combination of two or more different things **2.** GRAM WORD MADE UP OF OTHER WORDS a word that is formed from two or more identifiable words, e.g., "blackbird," "cookbook," or "bullheaded," or, in some analyses, "mother-in-law" or "fire drill" ■ *adj.* /kóm pòwnd, kom pównd, kəm-/ **1.** HAVING PARTS made by the combination of two or more different things **2.** GRAM MADE FROM TWO OR MORE WORDS used to describe a word that is made up of two or more words or word parts **3.** BOT DIVIDED INTO PARTS used to describe a leaf that is divided into two or more parts (**leaflets**) attached to a single stalk. ◊ **simple** ■ *v.* /kom pównd, kəm pównd/ (**-pound·ed, -pound·ing, -pounds**) **1.** *vti.* ADD TOGETHER to add together, or add one thing to another or others, to form a whole ○ *hatred that was compounded with fear and revulsion* **2.** *vt.* MAKE SOMETHING BY COMBINING PARTS to make something by the adding together of different parts ○ *a medication compounded from several constituent elements* **3.** *vt.* INTENSIFY SOMETHING to make something more extreme or intense by adding something to it ○ *Further financial reverses compounded his despair.* **4.** *vt.* LAW TAKE BRIBE TO IGNORE CRIME to accept a bribe in return for not prosecuting or informing about a crime **5.** *vti.* SETTLE DEBT to settle a debt by paying a lesser amount owed, typically right away in a lump sum **6.** *vt.* FIN ADD INTEREST to calculate or pay interest based on both the principal and the interest that has previously accrued on it ○ *6% interest, compounded monthly* [14thC. Originally the past participle of earlier *compoune* "to put together," via Old French *compoun-*, the stem of *compondre*, from Latin *componere* (see COMPOSE).] —**com·pound·a·ble** /kəm pówndəb'l/ *adj.* —**com·pound·er** /kəm pówndər/ *n.*

com·pound[2] /kóm pownd/ *n.* an enclosed group of buildings for the segregation or restraint of a particular group of people [Late 17thC. Alteration of Malay *kampong* "enclosure, village."]

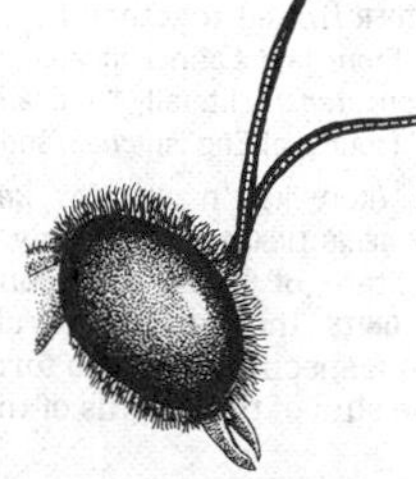

Compound eye

com·pound eye *n.* the eye that most insects and some crustaceans have, made up of several separate light-sensitive parts

com·pound fault *n.* GEOL a series of faults that lie closely together, following the same general direction

com·pound frac·tion *n.* MATH = **complex fraction**

com·pound frac·ture *n.* a bone fracture in which a broken bone pierces the skin or comes into contact with an open wound

com·pound in·ter·est *n.* interest that is calculated on the combined total of the original sum borrowed (**principal**) and the interest it has already accrued

com·pound me·ter *n.* MUSIC a meter in which the beats of the measure are grouped in threes

com·pound mi·cro·scope *n.* a microscope consisting of two lenses or lens systems and an eyepiece, mounted in a tube

com·pound sen·tence *n.* a sentence containing two or more clauses that can stand independently. The clauses are often linked by a conjunction that is sometimes preceded by a comma, as in "We waited for over an hour, but she didn't show up."

com·pound time *n. U.K.* MUSIC = **compound meter**

com·pre·hend /kòmprə hénd/ (**-hend·ed, -hend·ing, -hends**) *v.* **1.** *vti.* UNDERSTAND to grasp the meaning or nature of something ○ *It was hard to comprehend the sheer scale of the problem.* **2.** *vt.* INCLUDE SOMETHING to include something as a part of something else (*formal*) [14thC. From Latin *comprehendere*, literally "to grasp fully," from *prehendere* "to seize."] —**com·pre·hend·i·ble** *adj.*

com·pre·hen·si·ble /kòmprə hénsəb'l/ *adj.* capable of being understood or grasped [15thC. Directly or via French from Latin *comprehensibilis*, from *comprehens-*, the past participle stem of *comprehendere* (see COMPREHEND).] —**com·pre·hen·si·bil·i·ty** /kòmprə hensə bíllətee/ *n.* —**com·pre·hen·si·ble·ness** /kòmprə hénsəb'lnəss/ *n.* —**com·pre·hen·si·bly** /-hensəblee/ *adv.*

com·pre·hen·sion /kòprə hénsh'n/ *n.* **1.** UNDERSTANDING the grasping of the meaning of something **2.** INTELLECTUAL ABILITY the ability to grasp the meaning of something ○ *It's beyond my comprehension.* **3.** EDUC SET OF QUESTIONS ON TEXT an exercise consisting of a set of questions on a short text, designed to test students' understanding of it [15thC. Directly or via French from the Latin stem *comprehension-*, from *comprehens-*, the past participle stem of *comprehendere* (see COMPREHEND).]

com·pre·hen·sive /kòmprə hénsiv/ *adj.* **1.** INCLUSIVE covering many things or a wide area ○ *a comprehensive survey of public opinion* **2.** INCLUDING ALL including everything, so as to be complete ○ *comprehensive knowledge of the subject* **3.** COVERING MANY EVENTUALITIES used to describe insurance policies that provide coverage or benefit in most areas **4.** ABLE TO UNDERSTAND able to understand, or using the power of understanding (*archaic*) ○ *an unusually comprehensive mind* ■ *n.* **comprehensive, comprehensive examination** EDUC EXAMINATION a final graduate or undergraduate examination in a major field of study (*often used in the plural*) [17thC. Directly or via French from Latin *comprehensivus*, from *comprehens-*, the past participle stem of *comprehendere* (see COMPREHEND).] —**com·pre·hen·sive·ly** *adv.* —**com·pre·hen·sive·ness** *n.*

com·press *v.* /kəm préss/ (**-pressed, -press·ing, -press·es**) **1.** *vti.* SHRINK to make something smaller by applying pressure or by some analogous process **2.** *vt.* PRESS THINGS TOGETHER to press things, e.g., the lips, together **3.** *vt.* COMPUT MAKE FILES SHORTER to reduce the size of computer files or transmissions by means of algorithms ■ *n.* /kóm prèss/ **1.** MED TREATMENT PAD a cloth pad, often moistened or medicated, pressed firmly against a part of the body as a treatment, e.g., to stop bleeding **2.** MACHINE a machine for compressing material, especially cotton that is being packed [14thC. Via Old French from late Latin *compressare*, literally "to keep pressing together," from Latin *comprimere*, from *premere* (see PRESS).] —**com·press·i·ble** *adj.* —**com·press·i·bil·i·ty** /kəm prèssə bíllətee/ *n.* —**com·press·i·ble·ness** /-préssəb'lnəss/ *n.* —**com·press·i·bly** /-préssəblee/ *adv.*

com·pressed /kəm prést/ *adj.* squeezed or condensed and made smaller or shorter

com·pressed air *n.* air that is kept in a container under pressure, often used to power machines

com·pres·sion /kəm présh'n/ *n.* **1.** REDUCTION IN SIZE the reduction of the volume or mass of something by applying pressure, or the state of having been treated in this way **2.** PHASE IN ENGINE a phase in the working of an internal-combustion engine in which a combination of fuel and air is compressed in a cylinder before being ignited [14thC. Via French from, ultimately, Latin *compress-*, the past participle stem of *comprimere* (see COMPRESS).] —**com·pres·sion·al** *adj.*

com·pres·sion ra·tio *n.* the ratio between the largest and smallest possible volumes in the cylinder of an internal-combustion engine that contains a combination of fuel and air being compressed

com·pres·sion wave *n.* a longitudinal wave created in a fluid by a compressing force, e.g., a sound wave in air

com·pres·sive /kəm préssiv/ *adj.* having the power or tendency to compress [14thC. Via French from, ultimately, Latin *compress-*, the past participle stem of *comprimere* (see COMPRESS).] —**com·pres·sive·ly** *adv.*

com·pres·sor /kəm préssər/ *n.* **1.** MACHINE THAT COMPRESSES GAS a machine that compresses gas so that the power produced when the gas is released can be used to power another machine, e.g., a pneumatic drill **2.** ANAT MUSCLE a muscle that compresses or flattens a part of the body

com·pri·mar·i·o /kòmpri máiriee ō, kòmpri maáree ō/ *n.* a secondary role in an opera or ballet, or somebody who performs such a role [From Italian, literally "co-primary"]

com·prise /kəm príz/ (**-prised, -pris·ing, -pris·es**) *vt.* **1.** INCLUDE SOMETHING to incorporate or contain something **2.** CONSIST OF SOMETHING to be made up of something **3.** CONSTITUTE SOMETHING to make up the whole of something [15thC. Formed from French *compris*, the past participle of *comprendre* "to include," from Latin *comprehendere* (see COMPREHEND).] —**com·pris·a·ble** *adj.*

WORD KEY: USAGE

comprise, include, compose, consist of or **constitute**? ***Comprise*** and ***consist of*** are concerned with a whole having a number of parts. They are used in the active voice, with the whole as their subject and the parts as their object: *the house comprises three bedrooms, a bathroom, a kitchen, and a living room; the meal consisted of several small dishes that everybody dipped into and shared.* If some rather than all the parts are mentioned, ***include*** may be used instead: *the house includes a kitchen and a living room on the first floor.* ***Compose*** and ***constitute*** are concerned with parts making up a whole. ***Compose*** is normally used in the passive and ***constitute*** in the active: *The team is composed of several experts in the field. The following commodities constitute the average household diet.*

com·pro·mise /kómprə mìz/ *n.* **1.** AGREEMENT a settlement of a dispute in which two or more sides agree to accept less than they originally wanted ○ *After hours of negotiations a compromise was reached.* **2.** SOMETHING ACCEPTED RATHER THAN WANTED something that somebody accepts because what was wanted is unattainable **3.** POTENTIAL DANGER OR DISGRACE exposure to danger or disgrace ■ *v.* (**-mised, -mis·ing, -mis·es**) **1.** *vi.* AGREE BY CONCEDING to settle a dispute by agreeing to accept less than what was originally wanted **2.** *vt.* LESSEN VALUE OF SOMETHING to undermine or devalue something or somebody by making concessions ○ *Don't compromise your integrity by telling half-truths.* **3.** *vt.* EXPOSE TO DANGER to expose somebody or something to danger or risk ○ *This scandal could compromise his chances for reelection .* ○ *drugs that can compromise the immune system* [15thC. Via French *compromis* from Latin *compromissum* "mutual agreement," from the past participle of *compromittere*, literally "to make mutual promises," from *promittere* (see PROMISE).] —**com·pro·mis·er** *n.*

com·pro·mis·ing /kómprə mìzing/ *adj.* liable to expose somebody to disgrace or humiliation —**com·pro·mis·ing·ly** *adv.*

compt. *abbr.* compartment

Comp·ton /kómptən/ city in southwestern California, a southern suburb of Los Angeles situated northeast of Torrance. Population: 91,700 (1996).

Comp·ton, Arthur Holly (1892–1962) U.S. physicist. He discovered the Compton effect (1922), for which he received the 1927 Nobel Prize in Physics.

Comp·ton ef·fect *n.* the decrease in energy and increase in wavelength experienced by a photon after colliding or interacting with an electron [Early 20thC. Named for A. H. COMPTON.]

comp·trol·ler /kən trólər/ *n.* FIN = **controller** *n.* 2 [15thC. Variant of CONTROLLER, by association with *compt*, an older spelling of *count*.] —**comp·trol·ler·ship** *n.*

com·pul·sion /kəm púlshən/ *n.* **1.** FORCE a force that makes somebody do something **2.** COMPELLING an act of compelling or the state of being compelled ○ *You are under no compulsion to leave.* **3.** PSYCHOL PSYCHOLOGICAL FORCE a psychological and usually irrational force that makes somebody do something, often unwillingly ○ *felt an irresistible compulsion* [14thC. Via French from, ultimately, Latin *compuls-*, the past participle stem of *compellere* (see COMPEL).]

com·pul·sive /kəm púlsiv/ *adj.* **1.** DRIVEN driven by an irresistible inner force to do something ○ *a compulsive liar* **2.** POWERFULLY INTERESTING exerting a powerful attraction or interest ■ *n.* SOMEBODY UNDER PSYCHOLOGICAL COMPULSION somebody whose actions are driven by a usually irrational psychological force —**com·pul·sive·ly** *adv.* —**com·pul·sive·ness** *n.* —**com·pul·siv·i·ty** /kòm pul sívvətee/ *n.*

com·pul·so·ry /kəm púlsəree/ *adj.* **1.** NECESSARY required by law or an authority ○ *attendance at the lecture is compulsory* **2.** FORCED caused by force, or using force to make somebody do something ■ *n.* (*plural* **-ries**) REQUIRED ROUTINE an exercise or routine that participants in a sport such as gymnastics or figure skating must perform as part of a competition (*often used in the plural*) [Early 16thC. From medieval Latin *compulsorius*, from Latin *compuls-*, the past participle stem of *compellere* (see COMPEL).] —**com·pul·so·ri·ly** *adv.* —**com·pul·so·ri·ness** *n.*

com·punc·tion /kəm púngkshən/ *n.* feelings of shame and regret about doing something wrong [14thC. Via French *componction* from, ultimately, Latin *compunct-*, the past participle stem of *compungere*, literally "to sting strongly," from *pungere* (see PUNGENT).] —**com·punc·tious** *adj.* —**com·punc·tious·ly** *adv.*

com·put·a·ble /kómpyətəb'l/ *adj.* capable of being worked out by calculation, especially using a computer —**com·put·a·bil·i·ty** /kòmpyətə bíllətee/ *n.*

com·pu·ta·tion /kòmpyə táysh'n/ *n.* **1.** USE OF COMPUTER the use of a computer, especially for calculation, or something calculated using a computer **2.** CALCULATION the calculating of something, or the result of a calculation —**com·pu·ta·tion·al** *adj.*

com·pu·ta·tion·al /kòmpyətáyshənəl/ *adj.* relating to or involving the use of computers ○ *computational linguistics* —**com·pu·ta·tion·al·ly** *adv.*

com·pute /kəm pyóot/ (**-put·ed, -put·ing, -putes**) *v.* **1.** *vt.* CALCULATE SOMETHING to calculate an answer or result, especially using a computer **2.** *vi.* USE COMPUTER OR CALCULATOR to use a computer or calculator **3.** *vi.* YIELD RESULT to yield a result, especially a correct result, from calculation ○ *These numbers just don't compute.* [Early 17thC. From Latin *computare*, literally "to reckon together" source of COUNT[1].]

com·put·ed to·mog·ra·phy *n.* MED a technique for producing images of cross-sections of the body. A computer processes data from X-rays penetrating the body from many directions and projects the results on a screen. This is the technology used when conducting a CT scan.

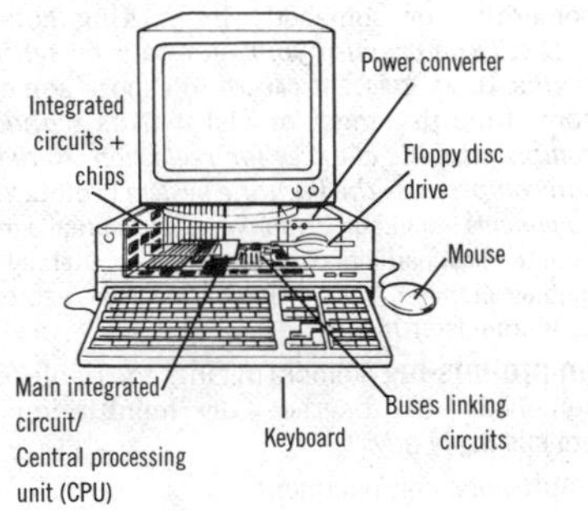

Computer

com·put·er /kəm pyóotər/ *n.* **1.** ELECTRONIC DATA PROCESSOR AND STORER an electronic device that accepts, processes, stores, and outputs data at high speeds according to programmed instructions **2.** SOMEBODY WHO COMPUTES a person who calculates numbers or amounts using a machine —**com·put·er·less** *adj.*

com·put·er con·fer·enc·ing *n.* the use of computers to allow people at distant sites to exchange text and graphic messages as they would at a meeting

com·put·er crime *n.* illegal activities carried out on or by means of a computer. Computer crime includes criminal tresspass into another's computer system, theft of computerized data, and the use of an on-line system to commit or aid in the commission of fraud.

com·put·er dat·ing *n.* the business or practice of putting people's personal information and preferences into a computer that then matches apparently compatible couples

com·put·er·ese /kəm pyòotə réez, -réess/ *n.* the technical language used by people involved with computers (*humorous*)

com·put·er game *n.* a game in the form of computer software, run on a personal computer or games machine and played by one or more people using a keyboard, mouse, control pad, or joystick. Computer games usually combine sound and graphics and range from traditional games such as chess to fast-moving action games or complex puzzles.

com·put·er graph·ics *n.* GENERATION OF PICTURES ON COMPUTER the use of a computer and specialized software to produce and manipulate pictorial images for purposes of animation, business presentations, and scientific research. The graphic images may be stored as mathematical representations called "vector graphics," which may be sized and scaled as desired, or as "bit-mapped graphics," which are patterns on the screen (**pixels**). (*takes a singular verb*) ■ *npl.* COMPUTER-GENERATED IMAGES the images produced by computer graphics

com·put·er·ize /kəm pyóotə rìz/ (**-ized, -iz·ing, -iz·es**) *vt.* **1.** CONVERT TO COMPUTER-BASED SYSTEM to install or start using a computer system to organize, control, or automate something, such as a mechanical process or calculations **2.** PUT DETAILS OF SOMETHING ON COMPUTER to store information in a computer system or process it by computer —**com·put·er·iz·a·ble** *adj.* —**com·put·er·i·za·tion** /kəm pyòotəri záysh'n/ *n.*

com·put·er·ized /kəm pyóotə rìzd/ *adj.* **1.** RUN BY COMPUTER operated, organized, controlled, or performed by computer **2.** KEPT ON COMPUTER processed by or stored in a computer or computer system

com·put·er·ized ax·i·al to·mog·ra·phy *n.* = **computed tomography**

com·put·er·ized to·mog·ra·phy *n.* = **computed tomography**

com·put·er lan·guage *n.* = **programming language**

com·put·er lit·er·a·cy *n.* the ability to use computers competently and to understand computer terminology

com·put·er lit·er·ate *adj.* having a good understanding and experience of working with a computer or computer system

com·put·er·phobe /kəm pyóotər fòb/ *n.* somebody who dislikes, avoids, or worries about using computers (*informal*) —**com·put·er·pho·bi·a** /kəm pyòotər fóbee ə/ *n.* —**com·put·er·pho·bic** *adj.*

com·put·er sci·ence *n.* the study of the mathematics and technology of computers and their applications

com·put·er vi·rus *n.* = **virus** *n.* **3**

com·put·ing /kəm pyóoting/ *n.* the use of computers or computing systems

Comr. *abbr.* Commissioner

com·rade /kóm ràd, -rad/ *n.* **1.** FRIEND OR COMPANION somebody who is either a close friend or a companion, often resulting from shared experiences **2. com·rade, Com·rade** FELLOW SOLDIER, MEMBER, OR COWORKER a fellow member of a group, especially a fellow soldier or a fellow supporter of a Communist or Socialist party [Mid-16thC. Via French *camerade* from Spanish *camarada* "barracks mate," from *camara* "room," from Latin *camera* (see CAMERA).] —**com·rade·ly** *adj.* —**com·rade·ship** *n.*

com·rade-in-arms (*plural* **com·rades-in-arms**) *n.* somebody who is fighting on the same side in a war, battle, or other armed struggle (*formal*)

Com·stock·er·y /kóm stòkəree, kúm stòkəree/ *n.* the removal of, or strong opposition to, anything that could be seen as immoral or obscene in literary, artistic, or broadcast material [Early 20thC. Named for the U.S. moral crusader Anthony *Comstock* 1844–1915, who founded the New York Society for the Suppression of Vice.]

Comte /koNt/, **Auguste** (1798–1857) French philosopher. He was a pioneer of "positivism" who, through his theories of social evolution, both named and established the science of sociology. Full name **Isidore Auguste Marie François Xavier Comte** —**Com·ti·an** *n., adj.* —**Com·tism** *n.*

Co·mus /kómәss/ *n.* the Roman god of revelry

con[1] /kon/ *vt.* (**conned, con·ning, cons**) **1.** TRICK SOMEBODY to cheat somebody, usually out of money or property, by first convincing the victim of something that is untrue **2.** LIE to tell somebody something untrue or misleading **3.** PERSUADE SOMEBODY to get somebody to agree to something (*informal*) ○ *See if you can con him into a game of basketball!* ■ *n.* DISHONEST TRICK a trick or dishonest business ploy that takes advantage of somebody's trust, such as telling lies in order to get money or property unfairly [Late 19thC. Shortening of CONFIDENCE TRICK.]

con[2] /kon/ *n.* **1.** REASON NOT TO DO SOMETHING an argument against doing something, or evidence or an opinion stating that something should not be done ○ *the pros and cons* **2.** PERSON NOT IN FAVOR somebody who opposes or votes against something [Late 16thC. Shortening of Latin *contra* "against."]

con[3] /kon/ *n.* a convict (*slang*) [Late 19thC. Shortening.]

con[4] /kon/ (**conned, con·ning, cons**) *vt.* (*archaic*) **1.** EXAMINE SOMETHING to study something with great care and attention **2.** LEARN OR MEMORIZE to learn or memorize something [Partly from Old English *cunnan* "to know how" (source of English *can*); partly from Old English *cunnian* "to explore." Both ultimately from an Indo-European word that also produced English *know.*]

con[5] /kon/, **conn** *vt.* (**conned, con·ning, cons; conned, con·ning, conns**) DIRECT STEERING OF SHIP to control or direct the steering of a ship ■ *n.* DIRECTING OF SHIP'S STEERING control of the steering of a ship, or the controls so used [Early 17thC. Shortened from French *conduire*, from Latin *conducere* "conduct."]

con[6] /kon/ *prep.* used to mean "with" in a musical direction [From Italian, "with"]

con. *abbr.* **1.** MUSIC concerto **2.** LAW conclusion **3.** connection **4.** consolidated **5.** continued **6.** contra

Con. *abbr.* **1.** Consul **2.** Conservative

con- *prefix.* = **com-** (*used before sounds other than b, l, m, or p.*)

Con·a·kry /kónnə kree, kònnə krée/ capital, largest city, and chief Atlantic port of Guinea, in western Africa. Population: 705,280 (1983).

con a·mo·re /kòn ə máwree, kàwn aa máw ràyl/ *adv.* with tender feeling (*used as a musical direction*) [From Italian, literally "with love"]

Co·nant /kónənt/, **James Bryant** (1893–1978) U.S. educator and chemist. He campaigned for national educational reform and was president of Harvard University (1933–53).

co·na·tion /kō náysh'n/ *n.* in psychology, a mental process involving the will, such as impulse, desire, or resolve [Mid-19thC. From the Latin stem *conation-*, from *conat-*, the past participle stem of *conari* "to try."] —**co·na·tion·al** *adj.* —**co·na·tive** /kónətiv, kónn-/ *adj.*

con bri·o /kon brée ō, kōn-/ *adv.* with spirit or vigor (*used as a musical direction*) [From Italian, literally "with vigor"]

conc. *abbr.* **1.** concentrated **2.** concentration **3.** concerning **4.** concerto **5.** concrete

con·cat·e·nate *vt.* /kon kátt'n àyt, kən-/ (**-nat·ed, -nat·ing, -nates**) **1.** BRING TOGETHER to connect separate units or items into a linked system **2.** COMPUT LINK UNITS TOGETHER to link two or more information units, such as character strings or files, so that they form a single unit ■ *adj.* /kon kátt'nət, -kátt'n àyt, kən-/ COMPUT LINKED TOGETHER linked together in a sequence or chain [15thC. From late Latin *concatenat-*, the past participle stem of *concatenare*, literally "to chain together," from *catena* "chain" (source of English *chain* and *catenary*).]

con·cat·e·na·tion /kon kàtt'n áysh'n, kən-/ *n.* **1.** PROCESS OR STATE OF BEING LINKED the linking of things together or the state of being interconnected **2.** COMPUT LINKING OF UNITS the linking of characters, strings, or files in a specified order to form a single entity equal to the sum of the lengths of the original entities

con·cave /kon káyv, kón kayv/ (**-caved, -cav·ing, -caves**) *adj.* **1.** CURVED INWARD curved inward like the inner surface of a bowl or sphere **2.** MATH CONTAINING AN ANGLE GREATER THAN 180° used to describe a polygon with an interior angle greater than 180° [From Latin *concavus*, literally "hollowed out," from *cavus* (see CAVE)] —**con·cave·ly** *adv.* —**con·cave·ness** *n.*

con·cav·i·ty /kon kávvətee/ (*plural* **con·cav·i·ties**) *n.* **1.** STATE OF BEING CONCAVE the state of being concave **2.** CONCAVE PART OR SURFACE a concave part or surface

con·cav·o-con·cave /kon kàyvō kon káyv/ *adj.* OPTICS used to describe a lens that is concave on both surfaces

con·cav·o-con·vex /kon kàyvō-/ *adj.* OPTICS used to describe a lens that is concave on one surface and convex on the other

con·ceal /kən séel/ (**-cealed, -ceal·ing, -ceals**) *vt.* **1.** HIDE PERSON OR THING to put or keep something or somebody out of sight or prevent the person or thing from being found ○ *he was found carrying a concealed weapon on him* **2.** HIDE FACT OR FEELING to keep something secret or prevent it from being known [13thC. Via Old French *conceler* from Latin *concelare* "to hide well," from *celare* "to hide."] —**con·ceal·a·ble** *adj.* —**con·ceal·er** *n.*

con·ceal·er /kən séelər/ *n.* **1.** MAKEUP FOR HIDING BLEMISHES flesh-colored makeup that can be applied to the skin to hide blemishes **2.** SOMEBODY OR SOMETHING THAT CONCEALS somebody or something that conceals

con·ceal·ment /kən séelmənt/ *n.* **1.** HIDING SOMETHING OR SECRECY secrecy, or the act of hiding somebody or something **2.** MIL MILITARY COVER the protection of troops from observation in combat, or something that provides such protection

con·cede /kən se͞ed/ (-ced·ed, -ced·ing, -cedes) *v.* **1.** *vt.* RELUCTANTLY ACCEPT SOMETHING TO BE TRUE to admit or acknowledge something, often grudgingly or with reluctance **2.** *vt.* RELIG GRANT RIGHTS TO to allow or yield something such as a right or privilege to another person or country **3.** *vti.* POL ADMIT FAILURE BEFORE END to accept and acknowledge defeat in a contest, debate, election, or fight, often without waiting for the final result **4.** *vt.* *U.K.* SPORTS GIVE SOMETHING AWAY to allow your opponent or opposing team to gain something valuable, usually a goal or points [15thC. Via French from Latin *concedere*, literally "to yield completely," from *cedere* (see CEDE).] —**con·ced·er** *n.*

con·ceit /kən se͞et/ *n.* **1.** TOO MUCH PRIDE IN YOURSELF a high opinion of your own qualities or abilities, especially one that is not justified **2.** LITERAT EXAGGERATED COMPARISON IN LITERATURE an imaginative poetic image, or writing that contains such an image, especially a comparison that is extreme or far-fetched **3.** WHIMSICAL OBJECT an object created from the imagination **4.** IMAGINATIVE IDEA an idea, opinion, or theme, especially one that is fanciful or unusual in some way **5.** WITTY EXPRESSION a witty, inventive, or amusing expression (*archaic*) ■ *vt.* (-ceited) **1.** APPREHEND MENTALLY to think of, to consider, to imagine, or to understand something (*archaic*) **2.** *N England* LIKE SOMETHING to like or tolerate something [14thC. Formed from CONCEIVE, on the model of "deceit." The underlying sense is "something conceived in the mind."]

con·ceit·ed /kən se͞etəd/ *adj.* **1.** TOO PROUD having or showing an excessively high opinion of your own qualities or abilities **2.** CREATIVELY WITTY imaginative, fanciful, witty, or ingenious (*archaic*) —**con·ceit·ed·ly** *adv.*

con·ceit·ed·ness /kən se͞etədnəss/ *n.* = **conceit** *n.* 1

con·ceiv·a·ble /kən se͞evəb'l/ *adj.* possible to imagine, understand, or believe ○ *we tried every means conceivable to contact her* —**con·ceiv·a·bil·i·ty** /kən se͞evə bíllətee/ *n.* —**con·ceiv·a·ble·ness** /kən se͞evəb'lnəss/ *n.*

con·ceiv·a·bly /kən se͞evəblee/ *adv.* possibly, even if only a remote possibility ○ *you could just conceivably be wrong*

con·ceive /kən se͞ev/ (-ceived, -ceiv·ing, -ceives) *v.* **1.** *vti.* THINK OF OR IMAGINE SOMETHING to form an idea or concept of something in your mind **2.** *vt.* INVENT, DEVISE, OR ORIGINATE SOMETHING to think up something that could be put into action such as a plan or an invention ○ *Conceived and written by John Sander* **3.** START TO EXPERIENCE to produce something from the mind such as an emotion **4.** *vti.* BECOME PREGNANT to become pregnant with a child or with young **5.** *vt.* UNDERSTAND to understand something [13thC. Via Old French *conceiv-*, the stem of *concevoir*, from Latin *concipere*, literally "to take in," from *capere* (see CAPTURE).] —**con·ceiv·er** *n.*

con·cel·e·brant /kən sélləbrənt/ *n.* a priest who celebrates the Christian Mass or Holy Communion together with one or more other priests

con·cel·e·brate /kən séllə bràyt/ (-brat·ed, -brat·ing, -brates) *vti.* to celebrate the Christian Mass or Holy Communion jointly with one or more other priests [Late 16thC. From Latin *concelebrat-*, the past participle stem of *concelebrare*, literally "to celebrate together," from *celebrare* (see CELEBRATE).] —**con·cel·e·bra·tion** /kən sèllə bráysh'n/ *n.*

con·cen·ter /kən séntər, kon-/ (-tered, -ter·ing, -ters) *vti.* MATH to direct things to a common center or to converge at a common center [Late 16thC. From French *concentrer*, from *con-* "together" and *centre* "center."]

con·cen·trate /kóns'n tràyt/ *v.* (-trat·ed, -trat·ing, -trates) **1.** *vti.* SILENTLY AND INTENSELY THINK ABOUT SOMETHING to focus all of your thoughts or mental activity on one subject or activity, usually in silence ○ *I found myself unable to concentrate on my work* **2.** *vti.* DEVOTE EFFORTS TO ONE THING to direct attention, time, and resources to one particular area or activity, usually over a period of time **3.** *vti.* CLUSTER TOGETHER to bring things to a common center or close together in the same area, or to come together in the same place **4.** *vt.* MAKE PURER to make a substance purer by the removal of another substance, especially by removing a liquid **5.** *vti.* COOK MAKE THICKER OR STRONGER to remove water from a substance, usually a liquid, leaving a smaller quantity that is thicker in consistency and stronger in flavor **6.** *vti.* BIOL ACCUMULATE IN TISSUE to accumulate or be stored, or to cause to accumulate or be stored, in biological tissue over a period of time **7.** *vt.* MINERALS PURIFY ORE to remove rock and other material from ore to purify it ■ *n.* **1.** PURE SUBSTANCE a substance made purer by the removal of another, especially a liquid **2.** FOOD THICK FOOD SUBSTANCE a food substance, especially a liquid, made thicker or stronger in flavor by the removal of liquid [Mid-17thC. Formed from CONCENTER.] —**con·cen·tra·tive** *adj.* —**con·cen·tra·tive·ly** *adv.*

con·cen·trat·ed /kóns'n tràytəd/ *adj.* **1.** CHEM, FOOD STRONG used to describe a substance, especially a liquid, made thicker or stronger by the removal of water **2.** FOCUSED involving or characterized by the focusing or intensifying of an activity or process —**con·cen·trat·edly** *adv.*

con·cen·tra·tion /kòns'n tráysh'n/ *n.* **1.** FOCUS OF MIND OR RESOURCES the direction of all thought or effort toward one particular task, idea, or subject **2.** CLUSTER OR NUMBER a large number of things or amount of something collected together in one area ○ *the concentration of computing talent in one part of the country* **3.** CHEM STRENGTH OF SOLUTION the amount of a substance dissolved in another. Symbol *c* **4.** CHEM, COOK MAKING A LIQUID THICKER OR STRONGER the removal of water from something, usually a liquid, to make it thicker or stronger **5.** EDUC FOCUS OF MAJOR IN COLLEGE the main area of study within a student's major in college

con·cen·tra·tion camp *n.* **1.** HIST NAZI CAMP FOR EXTERMINATING PRISONERS one of the prison camps used under the rule of Hitler in Nazi Germany **2.** PRISON CAMP FOR CIVILIANS IN WAR a prison camp used for the incarceration of political prisoners or civilians [Originally used in the Boer War to denote camps into which civilians were "concentrated" so that they did not hinder military operations]

con·cen·tra·tor /kóns'n tràytər/ *n.* **1.** COMPUT TELECOMMUNICATIONS DEVICE a telecommunications device that combines outgoing messages into one message, or extracts individual messages from one transmission into which they have been combined **2.** MINERALS FACTORY THAT PROCESSES MINERAL ORE an industrial plant that produces purified or concentrated mineral ore **3.** ENERGY MIRROR SYSTEM FOR PRODUCING SOLAR ENERGY a set of mirrors used to concentrate sunlight in the collection of energy from the sun

con·cen·tric /kən séntrik, kon-/ *adj.* **1.** WITH COMMON MIDDLE POINT used to describe circles and spheres of different sizes with the same middle point **2.** WITH COMMON AXIS with a common axis, as when rotating elements are mounted on shafts that have a common center line [14thC. From Medieval Latin *concentricus*, literally "having the same center," formed from Latin *centrum* (see CENTER).] —**con·cen·tri·cal·ly** *adv.* —**con·cen·tric·i·ty** /kòns'n trísseetee/ *n.*

Con·cep·ción /kàwn sep syáwn, kən sèpsi ṓn/ city and capital of Bío-Bío Region, central Chile, situated on the Bío-Bío River, 260 mi./418 km southwest of Santiago. Population: 326,784 (1992).

con·cept /kón sèpt/ *n.* **1.** SOMETHING THOUGHT OR IMAGINED something that somebody has thought up, or that somebody might be able to imagine **2.** BROAD PRINCIPLE AFFECTING PERCEPTION AND BEHAVIOR a broad abstract idea or a guiding general principle, such as one that determines how a person or culture behaves, or how nature, reality, or events are perceived ○ *the concept of time* **3.** UNDERSTANDING OR GRASP the most basic understanding of something **4.** WAY OF DOING OR PERCEIVING SOMETHING a method, plan, or type of product or design [Mid-16thC. From late Latin *conceptus*, from the past participle of Latin *concipere* (see CONCEIVE).]

con·cept art *n.* = **conceptual art**

con·cep·tion /kən sépshən/ *n.* **1.** BIOL CONCEIVING OF YOUNG the fertilization of an egg by a sperm at the beginning of pregnancy **2.** = **concept** *n.* 1 **3.** BROAD UNDERSTANDING a general understanding of something **4.** FORMULATION OF IDEA the process of arriving at an abstract idea or belief or the moment at which such an idea starts to take shape or emerge **5.** ORIGIN OR BEGINNINGS the beginnings or origin of something **6.** SOMETHING CONCEIVED IN THE MIND a result of thought, such as an idea, invention, or plan **7.** BIOL EMBRYO OR FETUS an embryo or fetus (*technical*) [14thC. Via French from, ultimately, Latin *concipere* (see CONCEIVE).] —**con·cep·tion·al** *adj.* —**con·cep·tive** *adj.* —**con·cep·tive·ly** *adv.*

con·cep·tu·al /kən sépchoo əl/ *adj.* coming from or belonging to the concepts, ideas, or principles something is based on —**con·cep·tu·al·ly** *adv.*

con·cep·tu·al art, con·cept art *n.* art designed to present an idea rather than to be appreciated for its creative skill or beauty, and that often makes use of unconventional media instead of painting or sculpture

con·cep·tu·al art·ist *n.* an artist specializing in conceptual art

con·cep·tu·al·ism /kən sépchoo ə lìzzəm/ *n.* **1.** PHILOS THEORY THAT MENTAL CONCEPTS DETERMINE REALITY the philosophical theory that the existence of something is dependent on our having a mental concept of it **2.** ARTS THEORY OF ART FOCUSING ON IDEAS a school of art concerned primarily with the ideas that lie behind a work of art rather than the artwork itself —**con·cep·tu·al·is·tic** /-sèpchoo ə lístik/ *adj.* —**con·cep·tu·al·is·ti·cal·ly** /-əlee/ *adv.*

con·cep·tu·al·ist /kən sépchoo əlist/ *n.* **1.** PHILOS BELIEVER IN CONCEPTUALISM a person who believes in conceptualism **2.** ARTS = **conceptual artist**

con·cep·tu·al·ize /kən sépchoo ə lìz/ (-ized, -iz·ing, -iz·es) *vti.* **1.** INTERPRET OBSERVATIONS WITH A CONCEPT to arrive at a concept or generalization as a result of things seen, experienced, or believed **2.** IMAGINE picture, imagine, or perceive something —**con·cep·tu·al·i·za·tion** /kən sèpchoo əli záysh'n/ *n.* —**con·cep·tu·al·iz·er** *n.*

con·cep·tus /kən séptəss/ (*plural* -tus·es) *n.* an embryo or fetus along with all the tissues that surround it throughout pregnancy, including the placenta, amniotic sac and fluid, and the umbilical cord [Mid-18thC. From Latin, literally "something conceived," from the past participle of *concipere* (see CONCEIVE).]

con·cern /kən súrn/ *n.* **1.** WORRY OR SOMETHING CAUSING IT a reason to worry, or something that causes worry ○ *His condition is giving rise to concern* **2.** CARING FEELINGS emotions such as worry, compassion, sympathy, or regard for somebody or something **3.** AFFAIR THAT SHOULD INVOLVE SOMEBODY a matter that affects somebody, or that somebody has the right to be involved with ○ *it's no concern of yours* **4.** BUSINESS a commercial enterprise **5.** OBJECT a gadget or trivial object (*dated*) ■ *vt.* (-cerned, -cern·ing, -cerns) **1.** MAKE SOMEBODY WORRIED to give somebody an uneasy or anxious feeling **2.** BE INTERESTING OR IMPORTANT TO SOMEBODY to have a direct effect on, or be a matter of significance to, somebody or something **3.** INVOLVE SOMEBODY OR GET INVOLVED to require somebody to be involved with something, or to get involved with or interested in something **4.** BE ON THE SUBJECT OF to be about a particular topic [Late 14thC. Via French from late Latin *concernere*, literally "to sift together," from Latin *cernere* (see CERTAIN). The meaning evolved from "to sort out" through "decide" to "relate to."]

con·cerned /kən súrnd/ *adj.* **1.** ANXIOUS OR WORRIED worried or apprehensive, particularly about something such as a situation that is developing or that has newly arisen **2.** INTERESTED caring and interested in general, or giving care and attention to a particular thing or area **3.** INVOLVED having an active role in something, or anything to do with something ○ *a message was conveyed to the families concerned*

con·cern·ing /kən súrning/ *prep.* to do with or involving something or somebody

con·cert *n.* /kón sùrt, kónsərt/ **1.** MUSIC PUBLIC MUSICAL PERFORMANCE an event where an individual musician or a group of musicians, such as a choir or an orchestra, performs in front of an audience **2.** AGREEMENT harmony or accord, e.g., in purpose or action **3.** UNIFIED PAIR OR GROUP a combination of people or things in agreement or harmony, especially one resulting from a consensus of opinions and ideas ■ *v.* /kən súrt/ (-cert·ed, -cert·ing, -certs) **1.** *vti.* ACT IN AGREEMENT OR UNITY to do or plan something in cooperation or in harmony with another person or group **2.** *vt.* REACH A CONSENSUS to settle or adjust something, such as a contract or disagreement, by discussion and mutual consent [Late 16thC. Via French from Italian *concerto* "harmony, agreement" (see CONCERTO).] ◇ **in concert 1.** MUSIC playing music or singing at a live concert **2.** working or acting together, especially in a united or harmonious way

con·cer·tan·te /kònsər taántee, kònchər taántee, -tày/ *adj.* **1.** RELATING TO BAROQUE CONCERTO relating to or resembling a concerto, especially one in the Baroque style **2.** WITH SOLO PASSAGES relating to a symphonic work that highlights individual instruments within the orchestra [Early 18thC. From Italian, the present participle of *concertare* "to be in harmony," from *concerto* (see CONCERTO).]

con·cert·ed /kən súrtəd/ *adj.* **1. ACHIEVED OR PERFORMED TOGETHER** planned or carried out by two or more people working together or with the same goal **2.** MUSIC **ARRANGED FOR ORCHESTRA OR CHAMBER ENSEMBLE** written for several soloists to perform together in an ensemble, or within the context of a larger-scale work —**con·cert·ed·ly** *adv.* —**con·cert·ed·ness** *n.*

con·cert·go·er /kónsərt gō ər/ *n.* somebody who is or will be attending a concert, or who often goes to concerts —**con·cert·go·ing** *adj.*

con·cert grand *n.* the largest size of grand piano, between 9 ft./2.74 m and 12 ft./3.66 m long, designed for use in a concert hall

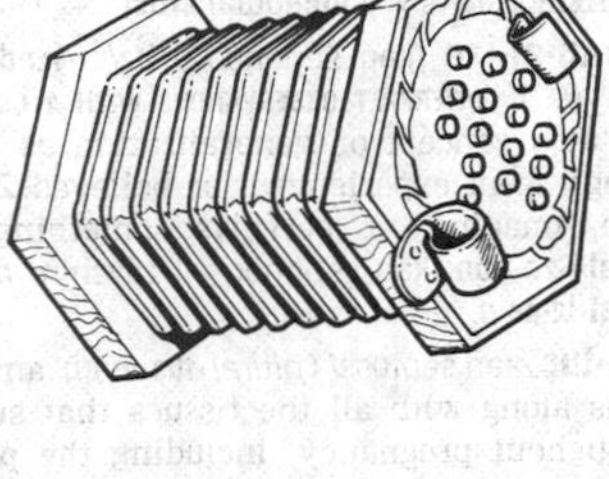

Concertina

con·cer·ti·na /kònsər teénə/ (**-naed, -na·ing, -nas**) *n.* a small octagonal accordion with button keys [Mid-19thC. Formed from CONCERT + the Italian suffix *-ina.*] —**con·cer·tin·ist** *n.*

con·cer·ti·no /kòn chər teénō/ (*plural* **-nos** *or* **-ni** /-nee/) *n.* **1. SOLOIST GROUP** the solo instrumental group in a piece of music played by a small group of soloists and a larger ensemble (**concerto grosso**) **2. SMALL-SCALE CONCERTO** a small-scale concerto for a single solo instrument [Late 18thC. From Italian, literally "little concerto," from *concerto* "CONCERTO."]

con·cer·tize /kónsər tìz/ (**-tized, -tiz·ing, -tiz·es**) *vi.* MUSIC to perform in concerts (*refers to a soloist or conductor*)

con·cert·mas·ter /kónsərt màstər/ *n.* MUSIC the leader of the first violin section of an orchestra, usually next in rank below the conductor [Late 19thC. Translation of German *Konzertmeister.*]

con·cert·mis·tress /kónsərt mìstrəss/ *n.* a woman who is the leader of the first violin section of an orchestra, usually next in rank below the conductor

con·cer·to /kən cháirtō/ (*plural* **-tos** *or* **-ti** /-cháirtee/) *n.* **1. MUSICAL COMPOSITION FOR SOLOIST AND ORCHESTRA** an instrumental work for orchestra that highlights a soloist or group of soloists **2. ORGAN-ACCOMPANIED VOICES** in music before 1650, a work for voices with organ or continuo [Early 18thC. From Italian, of uncertain immediate origin: possibly from Latin *concertus*, the past participle of *concernere* (see CONCERN).]

con·cer·to gros·so /kən chàirtō grṓssō/ (*plural* **con·cer·ti gros·si** /-chàirti grṓssee/ *or* **con·cer·to gros·sos**) *n.* a genre of orchestral composition, popular in the 17th century, that contrasts a small group of soloists (**concertino**) with a larger ensemble (**ripieno**) [From Italian, literally "big concerto"]

con·cert o·ver·ture *n.* a short orchestral composition similar to an opera overture but intended for concert performance on its own

con·cert pitch *n.* **1.** MUSIC **STANDARD PITCH TO WHICH INSTRUMENTS TUNED** the internationally agreed standard pitch to which orchestral instruments are tuned, typically using the A above middle C as a reference. In an instrument tuned to concert pitch, the A above middle C is at a pitch of 440 hertz per second. **2.** MUSIC **PITCH OF NOTE IN TRANSPOSED MUSIC** the sounding pitch of a note played by an instrument when transposing a piece of written music to a different key, as opposed to the written pitch **3. READINESS** a state of readiness for action

con·cert·stück /kən súrt shtŏŏk/ *n.* a short character piece, usually for piano [From German *Konzertstück*, literally "concert piece"]

con·ces·sion /kən sésh'n/ *n.* **1. RELUCTANT YIELDING** an act or an example of conceding, yielding, or compromising in some way, often grudgingly or unwillingly **2. SPECIAL PRIVILEGE** something such as a particular privilege, right, or kindness, that is allowed or granted to a individual or group, usually in view of special circumstances **3. SOMETHING UNWILLINGLY ADMITTED** something acknowledged or admitted, even if unwillingly or grudgingly **4.** COMM **SMALL BUSINESS OUTLET INSIDE ANOTHER ESTABLISHMENT** a branch of a business set up and operating in a place belonging to another commercial enterprise, or a business agreement that grants the right to do this **5. RIGHT TO USE LAND** an official license granted by a landowner or government that allows work such as drilling for oil to be carried out in a specified area of land **6.** *U.K.* **CHEAP TICKET** a special reduced price at which tickets for travel or entertainment are sold to some groups of people, such as senior citizens, students, or the unemployed **7.** *Can* **LAND SUBDIVISION** a subdivision of land in a township survey, mainly in Ontario and Quebec, that was formerly one of the rows of 32 200-acre lots into which each new township was divided **8.** *Can* = **concession road** [Early 17thC. Directly or via French from, ultimately, Latin *concess-*, the past participle stem of *concedere* (see CONCEDE).] —**con·ces·si·ble** /kən séssəb'l/ *adj.* —**con·ces·sion·al** *adj.*

con·ces·sion·aire /kən sèsh'n áir/, **con·ces·sion·er** /kən sésh'nər/ *n.* somebody who has been given land by a government concession or who has a concession to operate a business or sell a product in a specific place (*formal*) [Mid-19thC. From French, formed from *concession* (see CONCESSION).]

con·ces·sion·ar·y /kən sésh'n èrree/ *adj.* created or executed as a compromise or goodwill gesture, especially within a negotiating process

con·ces·sion·er *n.* = **concessionaire**

con·ces·sion road, **con·ces·sion line** *n.* *Can* in Canada, particularly Quebec and Ontario, a rural road running along the line of the survey of Canada that divided farmland into lots called concessions

con·ces·sive /kən séssiv/ *adj.* **1.** GRAM **SHOWING WILLINGNESS TO CONCEDE SOMETHING** relating to a word or part of a sentence that expresses concession, e.g., the word "although" **2. WITH CONCESSION** relating to or containing a concession [Early 18thC. From late Latin *concessivus*, from Latin *concess-*, the past participle stem of *concedere* (see CONCEDE).] —**con·ces·sive·ly** *adv.*

conch /kongk, konch/ (*plural* **conch·es** *or* **conchs**) *n.* **1. TROPICAL SEA ANIMAL WITH SHELL** a tropical marine mollusk with a large, often brightly colored, spiral shell **2. LARGE SPIRAL SHELL** the large spiral shell of a conch, often used as a horn or trumpet, as an ornament, or to make jewelry **3.** ANAT = **concha** *n.* 1 [14thC. Via Latin *concha* from Greek *konkhē* "shell, shellfish" (source of English *cockle*).]

conch- *prefix.* = **concho-** (*used before vowels*)

con·cha /kóngkə/ (*plural* **-chae** /-kee/) *n.* **1.** ANAT **SHELL-SHAPED PART OF BODY** a part of the body shaped like a conch shell, such as the external ear or the central cavity of the ear **2.** ARCHIT **APSE OR PART OF IT** an apse, or the plain partial dome of one [Late 16thC. From Latin, "shell" (see CONCH).] —**con·chal** /kóngk'l/ *adj.*

conchi- *prefix.* = **concho-**

con·chi·glie /kən keélee/ *n.* FOOD pasta formed into small shell shapes [Via Italian, literally "little shells," from, ultimately, Latin *concha* "shell" (see CONCH)]

con·chi·o·lin /kong kī́ əlin, kon kī́-/ *n.* BIOCHEM a fibrous protein that makes up the inner part of the shell of a mollusk [Late 19thC. Formed from modern Latin *conchiola*, literally "little shell," from Latin *concha* (see CONCH).]

concho- *prefix.* shell ○ *conchology* [From Latin *concha* "shell" (see CONCH)]

con·chol·o·gy /kong kóllǝjee/ *n.* a branch of zoology dealing with the study of sea shells and the animals that inhabit them —**con·cho·log·i·cal** /kòngkə lójjik'l/ *adj.* —**con·chol·o·gist** /kong kólləjist/ *n.*

con·cierge /kōn syáirzh/ (*plural* **-cierges**) *n.* **1. CHIEF ASSISTANT IN HOTEL** a person employed at a hotel or apartment building to help the guests or residents, e.g., by dealing with luggage, making travel arrangements, or delivering messages **2. CARETAKER OF APARTMENT BUILDING** especially in France, somebody whose job is to staff or watch the entrance to a large residential building, and who usually also lives on the premises (*dated*) [Mid-16thC. Via French from, ultimately, Latin *conservus* "fellow slave," from *servus* "slave" (source also of English *serve, serf,* and *sergeant*).]

con·cil·i·ar /kən síllee ər/ *adj.* belonging to, issued by, or relating to a council [Late 17thC. Formed from Latin *concilium* (see COUNCIL).] —**con·cil·i·ar·ly** *adv.*

con·cil·i·ate /kən síllee àyt/ (**-at·ed, -at·ing, -ates**) *vti.* **1. BRING DISPUTING SIDES TOGETHER** to work with opposing parties with the goal of bringing them to an agreement or reconciliation **2. GET SOMEBODY'S SUPPORT OR FRIENDSHIP BACK** to bring a disagreement with somebody to an end, or to overcome somebody's anger, suspicion, or hostility **3. BE CHARMING TO GAIN SOMETHING** to gain something, especially somebody's friendship, goodwill, or respect, by behaving pleasantly [Mid-16thC. From Latin *conciliat-*, the past participle stem of *conciliare*, from *concilium* (see COUNCIL).] —**con·cil·i·a·ble** *adj.* —**con·cil·i·a·tive** *adj.*

con·cil·i·a·tion /kən sìllee áysh'n/ *n.* action taken to reach agreement or restore trust, friendship, or goodwill that has been lost, especially as a deliberate process used in a dispute

con·cil·i·a·tor /kən síllee àytər/ *n.* somebody who works to overcome disagreement between other parties, or who tries to overcome somebody's anger or distrust with friendly actions and discussion

con·cil·i·a·to·ry /kən síllee ə tàwree/ *adj.* done or said to appease somebody, to bring about agreement, or to restore trust or goodwill —**con·cil·i·a·to·ri·ly** *adv.* —**con·cil·i·a·to·ri·ness** *n.*

con·cin·ni·ty /kən sínnətee/ (*plural* **-ties**) *n.* **1.** LITERAT **PLEASING STYLISTIC ARTISTIC HARMONY** a balanced, graceful, and polished quality, particularly in a literary work **2. GENERALLY HARMONIOUS STRUCTURE** a harmonious structuring of all parts of something in terms of the whole [Mid-16thC. Formed from Latin *concinnitas*, from *concinnus* "skillfully put together."] —**con·cin·nous** *adj.*

con·cise /kən sī́ss/ *adj.* using as few words as possible to give the necessary information, or compressed in order to be brief [Late 16thC. Directly or via French from Latin *concisus*, the past participle of *concidere*, literally "to cut down," from *caedere* (see CAESURA).] —**con·cise·ly** *adv.* —**con·cise·ness** *n.* —**con·ci·sion** *n.*

con·clave /kón klàyv, kóng klàyv/ *n.* **1. SECRET MEETING** a private gathering of a select group of people, where discussions are kept secret **2.** CHR **MEETING TO SELECT ROMAN CATHOLIC POPE** the secret meeting at which Roman Catholic cardinals elect a new pope **3.** CHR **ROOMS WHERE POPE IS ELECTED** the private rooms in which the college of Roman Catholic cardinals meets to elect a new pope [14thC. Via French from Latin "locked room," formed from *clavis* "key" (see CLEF).] —**con·clav·ist** *n.*

con·clude /kən klóod/ (**-clud·ed, -clud·ing, -cludes**) *v.* **1.** *vt.* **COME TO A CONCLUSION** to form an opinion or make a logical judgment about something after considering everything known about it **2.** *vti.* **FINISH** to come to an end or bring something to an end **3.** *vt.* **SETTLE SOMETHING** to make a formal agreement complete and fixed, especially after detailed or prolonged discussions or arrangements **4.** *vti.* **DIVIDE** to reach a decision about something (*dated*) [13thC. From Latin *concludere*, literally "to close completely," from *claudere* (see CLOSE).] —**con·clud·er** *n.*

WORD KEY: SYNONYMS

See Synonyms at ***deduce***.

con·clu·sion /kən klóozh'n/ *n.* **1. DECISION BASED ON FACTS** a decision made or an opinion formed after considering the relevant facts or evidence **2. FINAL PART OF SOMETHING** an ending or the part that brings something to a close (*formal*) **3. FINAL SETTLEMENT OF SOMETHING** the completion of a formal agreement or deal, especially after long or detailed discussions and arrangements **4.** LAW **CLOSING ARGUMENT IN TRIAL** the summation or closing argument at the end of case being tried **5.** LOGIC **PART OF ARGUMENT DEDUCED FROM EVIDENCE** the portion of an argument for which evidence is presented [14thC. Via French from, ultimately, Latin *conclus-*, the past participle stem of *concludere* (see CONCLUDE).]

con·clu·sive /kən klóossiv/ *adj.* being such that what is specified proves a matter beyond all doubt [Late 16thC. From late Latin *conclusivus*, from Latin *conclus-*, the past participle stem of *concludere* (see CONCLUDE).] —**con·clu·sive·ly** *adv.* —**con·clu·sive·ness** *n.*

con·clu·so·ry /kən klo͞ossəree/ *adj.* LAW convincing, but not to the extent that it cannot be contradicted

con·coct /kən kókt/ (**-coct·ed, -coct·ing, -cocts**) *vt.* **1.** MIX INGREDIENTS TO MAKE SOMETHING NEW to create something by mixing or combining various ingredients in a new way, especially in cooking **2.** MAKE SOMETHING UP to think up a story or plan, especially something ingenious or imaginative [Mid-16thC. From Latin *concoct-*, the past participle stem of *concoquere*, literally "to cook together," from *coquere* (see COOK).] —**con·coc·ter** *n.* —**con·coc·tive** *adj.*

con·coc·tion /kən kókshən/ *n.* **1.** NEW AND UNUSUAL MIXTURE something that has been concocted, especially a drink or dish created by mixing together ingredients **2.** CONCOCTING A MIXTURE the act or process of mixing or combining ingredients to create something new and unusual **3.** LIE OR TRICK something such as a story or plan devised to be deceitful

con·com·i·tance /kən kómmitəns/ *n.* **1.** EXISTENCE OR OCCURRENCE TOGETHER the existence or occurrence of something at the same time as, or in connection with, something else **2.** SOMETHING CONNECTED WITH SOMETHING ELSE something that exists at the same time, or in connection with, something else **3.** CHR CHRISTIAN BELIEF REGARDING EUCHARIST the Christian doctrine that the body and blood of Jesus Christ are embodied in the elements of the Eucharist

con·com·i·tant /kən kómmətənt/ *adj.* HAPPENING AT THE SAME TIME happening or existing along with or at the same time as something else ○ *parenthood and all its concomitant responsibilities* ■ *n.* SOMETHING THAT ACCOMPANIES SOMETHING ELSE something that happens or exists along with or at the same time as something else [Early 17thC. From late Latin *concomitant-*, the present participle stem of *concomitari* "to accompany," from *comit-*, the stem of *comes* "companion," source of English *count*[2].] —**con·com·i·tant·ly** *adv.*

con·cord /kón kàwrd, kóng kàwrd/ *n.* **1.** PEACEFUL COEXISTENCE agreement, friendly relations, or peace **2.** PEACE TREATY a peace treaty **3.** MUSIC PLEASING COMBINATION OF SOUNDS a pleasing sound made when two or more notes are played together **4.** GRAM = **agreement** [13thC. Via Old French from, ultimately, Latin *concord-*, the stem of *concors*, literally "of one heart," from *cor* "heart" (see CORDIAL).]

Con·cord /kóng kàwrd/ **1.** city in western California, a northern suburb of the Oakland-San Francisco area, northeast of Berkeley. Population: 114,850 (1996). **2.** town in northeastern Massachusetts, west of Boston, on the Concord River. Population: 17,792 (1996). **3.** capital of New Hampshire, in the south of the state, on the Merrimack River. Population: 37,021 (1996). **4.** city in southwestern North Carolina, northeast of Charlotte. It was a gold-mining town in the 18th century. Population: 32,944 (1996).

con·cor·dance /kən káwrd'ns/ *n.* **1.** SIMILARITY OR AGREEMENT similarity or agreement between two or more things **2.** LITERAT INDEX OF WORDS USED BY AUTHOR an index of words, e.g., of all the words contained in a single work, or in the combined works of an author, or in any body or bank of text, arranged in alphabetical order. A concordance often gives information about the meaning and context of a listed word. [14thC. Via French from medieval Latin *concordantia*, from Latin *concordant-*, the stem of *concordare* (see CONCORDANT).]

con·cor·dant /kən káwrd'nt/ *adj.* showing harmony, unity, or agreement [15thC. Via French from Latin *concordant-*, the present participle stem of *concordare*, literally "to bring into harmony," from *concord-*, the stem of *concors* (see CONCORD).] —**con·cor·dant·ly** *adv.*

con·cor·dat /kən káwr dàt/ *n.* an official agreement, especially a formal contract between the Pope and a national government concerning the religious affairs of a country [Early 17thC. Via French from Latin *concordatum*, the past participle of *concordare* (see CONCORDANT).]

Con·corde /kóng kàwrd/ *tdmk.* a trademark for a supersonic commercial passenger aircraft developed jointly by the British and French governments

Con·cord grape *n.* a blue-black sweet grape with a distinctive foxy aroma, produced by a variety of the native North American grapevine. It is used for sparkling and dessert wines, jellies, and grape juice. Latin name: *Vitis labrusca.* [Mid-19thC. Named for the town of *Concord*, Massachusetts, where it was developed.]

con·cours /kóN koor/, **con·cours d'é·lé·gance** /-daylay gáNss/ *n.* a meeting at which classic or vintage automobiles are exhibited and prizes awarded

con·course /kón kàwrs, kóng kàwrs/ *n.* **1.** LARGE OPEN SPACE a large space where people can gather in a public place or building, e.g., at an airport or train station **2.** CROWD a large number of people who have gathered for a special event **3.** GATHERING TOGETHER coming or moving together, or an example of this [14thC. Via French from Latin *concursus* "assembly," from *concurs-*, the past participle stem of *concurrere* (see CONCUR).]

con·cres·cence /kən kréss'ns/ *n.* **1.** BIOL GROWING TOGETHER OF PARTS the growing or coming together of body parts or organs, especially in the normal early formation of an embryo **2.** MED = **concretion** [Early 17thC. Formed from Latin *concrescent-*, the present participle stem of *concrescere* (see CONCRETE).] —**con·cres·cent** *adj.*

con·crete *n.* /kón kreet, kon kreet, kóng-, kong-/ **1.** CONSTR HARD CONSTRUCTION MATERIAL a mixture of cement, sand, gravel, and water in specific proportions that hardens to a strong stony consistency over varying lengths of time **2.** PHYS MASS FORMED WHEN PARTICLES COALESCE a mass formed when particles coalesce ■ *adj.* /kon kreet, kong-/ **1.** SOLID AND REAL, NOT IMAGINARY able to be seen or touched because it exists in reality, not just as an idea **2.** DEFINITE certain and specific rather than vague or general ○ *concrete proposals for reform* **3.** PHYS SOLIDIFIED made solid by coalescence ■ *vt.* /kón kreet, kon kreet, kóng-, kong-/ (**-cret·ed, -cret·ing, -cretes**) COVER WITH CONCRETE to cover an area with concrete [14thC. Via French from Latin *concretus*, the past participle of *concrescere*, literally "to grow together," from *crescere* (see CRESCENT).] —**con·crete·ly** *adv.* —**con·crete·ness** *n.*

con·crete jun·gle *n.* an urban area completely covered with walkways, roads, and buildings, and perceived as a hostile environment

con·crete mu·sic *n.* electronic music assembled from recordings of live sounds, usually including natural and mechanical sources, manipulated for effect [Translation of French *musique concrète*, literally "real music," so called because it is created from real-life sounds]

con·crete noun *n.* a noun that refers to a physical, and usually visible or touchable, object or substance, e.g., "clock" or "elephant"

con·crete po·et·ry *n.* verse that uses physical arrangement of the words on the page to add to its meaning and effect

con·cre·tion /kən kreesh'n/ *n.* **1.** FORMATION OF WHOLE FROM PARTS the act or process of separate parts or particles coming together into a solid mass **2.** SOLID FORMED BY UNIFICATION OF PARTS a hard solid mass formed by parts uniting into a whole **3.** GEOL ROUNDED MASS a rounded mass of compact concentric layers within a sediment, built up around a nucleus such as a fossil **4.** MED INORGANIC MASS IN BODY a mass of inorganic material in a body organ or tissue, usually caused by disease [Mid-16thC. Via French from, ultimately, Latin *concret-*, the past participle stem of *concrescere* (see CONCRETE).] —**con·cre·tion·ar·y** *adj.*

con·cret·ism /kon kreet ìzzəm/ *n.* the creation of physical things to represent abstract ideas, especially by the use of concrete poetry —**con·cret·ist** *n.*

con·cre·tize /kóngkrə tìz/ (**-tized, -tiz·ing, -tiz·es**) *vt.* to make something solid, real, or specific —**con·cre·ti·za·tion** /kòngkrəti záysh'n/ *n.*

con·cu·bi·nage /kon kyo͞obinij, kən-/ *n.* the state of being or keeping a concubine

con·cu·bine /kóngkyə bìn, kónkyə-/ *n.* **1.** HIST OFFICIAL MISTRESS IN SOME CULTURES a woman who is the lover of a wealthy married man but with the social status of a subordinate form of wife, often kept in a separate home. The term usually refers to such a woman in imperial China. **2.** MAN'S FEMALE LIVE-IN LOVER a woman who lives with a man and has a sexual relationship with him but is not married to him [13thC. Via Old French from Latin *concubina*, literally "bedmate," from *cubare* "to lie down" (see CUBICLE).] —**con·cu·bi·na·ry** /kon kyo͞obi nèrree/ *adj.*

con·cu·pis·cence /kon kyo͞opiss'nss/ *n.* powerful feelings of physical desire (*literary*) [14thC. Via French from, ultimately, late Latin *concupiscentia*, from Latin *concupiscere*, literally "to start longing for," from *cupere* (see COVET).] —**con·cu·pis·cent** *adj.*

con·cur /kən kúr/ (**con·curred, con·cur·ring, con·curs**) *v.* **1.** *vti.* AGREE to have the same opinion or reach agreement on a specified point **2.** *vi.* COINCIDE to happen at the same time [14thC. From Latin *concurrere*, literally "to run together," from *currere* (see CURRENT).] —**con·cur·ring·ly** *adv.*

WORD KEY: SYNONYMS

See Synonyms at ***agree***.

con·cur·rent /kən kúrənt/ *adj.* **1.** HAPPENING TOGETHER taking place or existing at the same time, or running parallel **2.** GEOM = **convergent** [14thC. From Latin *concurrent-*, the present participle stem of *concurrere* (see CONCUR).] —**con·cur·rent·ly** *adv.* —**con·cur·rence** *n.*

con·cuss /kən kúss/ (**-cussed, -cuss·ing, -cuss·es**) *vt.* to cause concussion, usually by a blow to the head or a jarring fall or jolt [Late 16thC. From Latin *concuss-*, the past participle stem of *concutere*, literally "to strike together," from *quatere* "to strike" (source of English *discuss*, *percussion*, and *rescue*).]

con·cus·sion /kən kúsh'n/ *n.* **1.** MED MILD TO MODERATE BRAIN INJURY an injury to the brain, often resulting from a blow to the head, that can cause temporary disorientation, memory loss, or unconsciousness **2.** MED INJURY TO A BODILY ORGAN an injury to an organ of the body, usually caused by a violent blow or shaking **3.** SUDDEN JOLT OR SHOCK any sudden violent jolting or shaking —**con·cus·sive** /-kússiv/ *adj.*

con·demn /kən dém/ (**-demned, -demn·ing, -demns**) *vt.* **1.** GIVE SOMEBODY A LEGAL SENTENCE to make a judicial pronouncement stating what punishment has been imposed on a person found guilty of a crime, especially in the case of a heavy penalty or a death sentence **2.** CONSIDER SOMEBODY GUILTY to judge that a person or thing is to blame for something **3.** PRONOUNCE SOMETHING OR SOMEBODY AS BAD to state that something or somebody is in some way wrong or unacceptable **4.** MAKE SOMEBODY EXPERIENCE SOMETHING to force or oblige somebody to experience something very unpleasant, especially something permanent or long-lasting **5.** BAN USE OR CONSUMPTION OF SOMETHING to issue an official order saying that something such as a building is unfit to be used **6.** PROVE GUILTY to serve as proof of guilt **7.** LAW APPROPRIATE PROPERTY to take property under eminent domain for public use [14thC. Via French *condemner* from Latin *condemnare*, literally "to pass final sentence," from Latin *damnare* "to sentence" (see DAMN).] —**con·dem·na·ble** *adj.* —**con·dem·na·tion** /kòn dem náysh'n, -dəm-/ *n.* —**con·dem·na·to·ry** /kən démnə tàwree/ *adj.*

WORD KEY: SYNONYMS

See Synonyms at ***criticize***.

con·demned cell *n. U.K.* = **death row cell**

con·den·sate /kóndən sàyt, kən dén sàyt/ *n.* a substance resulting from condensation, especially a liquid from a vapor

con·den·sa·tion /kòn den sáysh'n, kòndən sáysh'n/ *n.* **1.** FILM OF WATER DROPLETS tiny drops of water that form on a cold surface such as a window when warmer air comes into contact with it **2.** MAKING SOMETHING SHORTER the state of being compressed or made briefer, or the act or result of summarizing or compressing something **3.** PHYS CONVERSION OF GAS TO LIQUID the process by which a vapor loses heat and changes into a liquid **4.** CHEM FORMATION OF DENSER MOLECULES the bonding of molecules of a substance to form a larger denser molecule, usually with the release of simpler substances, such as water —**con·den·sa·tion·al** *adj.*

con·den·sa·tion trail *n.* AIR = **vapor trail**

con·dense /kən déns/ (**-densed, -dens·ing, -dens·es**) *v.* **1.** *vti.* PHYS CHANGE FROM GAS TO LIQUID to lose heat and change from a vapor into a liquid, or to make a vapor change to a liquid **2.** *vt.* MAKE SOMETHING SHORTER to reduce the length of a text by removing unnecessary words or passages or by expressing the content more concisely **3.** *vti.* COOK THICKEN BY REMOVING WATER to make something, especially a food, denser by removing water, or to become denser in this way **4.** *vti.* CHEM FORM DENSER MOLECULES to bond together to form a larger denser molecule, or to make molecules undergo this process [15thC. Via French from Latin *condensare* "to thicken," from *condensus* "very dense," from Latin *densus* (see DENSE).] —**con·dens·a·bil·i·ty** /kən dènsə bíllətee/ *n.* —**con·dens·a·ble** *adj.*

con·densed milk *n.* milk thickened by evaporating most of the water content and then sweetened. ◊ **evaporated milk**

con·dens·er /kən dénsər/ *n.* **1.** PHYS **CONVERTER OF GAS TO LIQUID** a device that converts a gas to a liquid to obtain either the substance or the released heat **2.** OPTICS **LENS OR MIRROR FOR CONCENTRATING LIGHT** a lens or mirror used to concentrate light onto, e.g., a transparency or specimen **3.** ELEC = **capacitor**

con·de·scend /kòndə sénd/ (**-scend·ed, -scend·ing, -scends**) *vi.* **1. ACT IN A SUPERIOR WAY** to behave toward other people as though they are less important or less intelligent than you are **2. MAKE CONCESSIONS FOR OTHERS** to do something that you would normally consider yourself too important or dignified to do [14thC. Via French *condescendre* from ecclesiastical Latin *condescendere* "to lower oneself," from Latin *descendere* (see DESCEND).] —**con·de·scend·er** *n.*

con·de·scend·ing /kòndə sénding/ *adj.* behaving toward other people in a way that shows you consider yourself socially or intellectually superior to them, especially when explaining or giving something —**con·de·scend·ing·ly** *adv.*

con·de·scen·sion /kòndə sénshən/ *n.* behavior or an example of behavior that implies that somebody is graciously lowering himself or herself to the level of people less important or intelligent

con·dign /kən dīn/ *adj.* well deserved and completely appropriate (*formal*) [14thC. Via French from Latin *condignus*, literally "wholly worthy," from *dignus* (see DIGNITY).] —**con·dign·ly** *adv.*

con·di·ment /kóndimənt/ *n.* salt, pepper, mustard, relish, or a similar substance added to food to improve or adjust its flavor. Condiments are usually served at the table and added according to individual taste. [15thC. Via French from Latin *condimentum*, from *condire* "to preserve, pickle."]

con·di·tion /kən dísh'n/ *n.* **1. STATE OF REPAIR** the particular state of repair or ability to function of an object or piece of equipment ○ *The meter is still in good condition.* **2. STATE OF HEALTH** a state of physical fitness or general health ○ *out of condition* **3. DISRDER** a physical disorder **4. WAY OF BEING** a general state or mode of existence, especially one characterized by hardship or suffering **5. STATUS** position, rank, or social status (*formal*) **6. SOMETHING STATED AS NECESSARY FOR AGREEMENT** something that is necessary for something else to happen, e.g., to bring a situation about or make a contract valid ■ **conditions** *npl.* **FACTORS AFFECTING PEOPLE** the factors or circumstances that affect the situation somebody is living or working in ○ *poor working conditions* ■ *vt.* (**-tioned, -tion·ing, -tions**) **1.** PSYCHOL **TRAIN SOMEBODY** to make people or animals act or react in a certain way by gradually getting them used to a certain pattern of events **2. MAKE STRONG, HEALTHY, OR READY** to give somebody or something a treatment to improve general health, soundness, readiness for use, appearance, or performance **3.** HAIR **IMPROVE HAIR'S CONDITION** to put conditioner or a similar substance on the hair in order to improve its appearance and texture **4. SPECIFY A REQUIREMENT OR PREREQUISITE** to state a requirement that must be fulfilled, or to make something dependent on a requirement, especially in a legal contract (*formal*) **5. ADAPT TO SOMETHING** to become accustomed to specific conditions or activities, or to make yourself adapt to these **6. COOL** to make air cooler ○ *Heat pumps condition the air on the first floor.* [13thC. Via Old French from the Latin stem *condition-* "agreement, stipulation," from *condicere*, literally "to talk together," from *dicere* (see DICTATE).] —**con·di·tion·a·ble** *adj.*

con·di·tion·al /kən díshən'l, -díshnəl/ *adj.* **1. DEPENDENT ON SOMETHING ELSE BEING DONE** used to describe something that will be done or will happen only if and when another thing is done or happens **2.** GRAM **STATING A CONDITION OR LIMITATION** used to describe a clause, conjunction, verb form, or sentence that expresses a condition or limitation **3.** MATH **TRUE ONLY FOR CERTAIN MATHEMATICAL VALUES** true only for certain values of one or more variables in a mathematical equation **4.** MATH **DESCRIBING SERIES OF NUMBERS** used to describe a convergent series of numbers that becomes a divergent series when its terms are converted to their absolute values ■ *n.* GRAM **CONDITIONAL CLAUSE, CONJUNCTION, OR VERB FORM** a conditional clause, conjunction, verb form, or sentence —**con·di·tion·a·ble** *adj.* —**con·di·tion·al·i·ty** /kən dìsh'n állətee/ *n.*

con·di·tion·al·i·za·tion /kən dìshən'li záysh'n, -dìshnəli-/ *n.* the process of turning a statement into a conditional statement, e.g., changing "It will rain" into "If it is cloudy, then it will rain"

con·di·tion·al·ly /kən díshənəlee, -díshnəlee/ *adv.* with the proviso that all valid conditions be met

con·di·tion·al prob·a·bil·i·ty *n.* the probability that one event will occur, given that another event has occurred or is certain to occur

con·di·tioned /kən dísh'nd/ *adj.* **1. AT SPECIFIED PERFORMANCE OR QUALITY LEVEL** having reached or been brought to a specified or high level of fitness, quality, or performance **2.** PSYCHOL **INVOLUNTARILY PRODUCED AS LEARNED RESPONSE** brought on unconsciously by a stimulus that triggers a reaction because of a learned association with something else

con·di·tioned re·sponse, **con·di·tioned re·flex** *n.* PSYCHOL a response to a new second stimulus as a result of association with a prior stimulus. The classic example is Pavlov's experiment in which dogs began to salivate at the sound of a bell, having previously been fed when the bell was rung.

con·di·tioned stim·u·lus *n.* in classical psychological conditioning, an otherwise ineffective stimulus that, when paired with an unconditioned stimulus, is able to evoke a conditioned response

con·di·tion·er /kən dísh'nər/ *n.* **1.** HAIR **PRODUCT FOR IMPROVING HAIR TEXTURE** a liquid or cream applied to hair, either after or with shampoo and usually while the hair is still wet, to make it more manageable or healthier **2. SOMETHING THAT CONDITIONS** a substance that makes something, e.g., bread dough or soil, easier to manage

con·di·tion·ing /kən dísh'ning/ *n.* PSYCHOL a method of controlling or influencing the way people or animals behave or think by using a gradual training process

con·do /kón dō/ (*plural* **-dos**) *n.* a condominium (*informal*) [Mid-20thC. Shortening.]

con·dole /kən dṓl/ (**-doled, -dol·ing, -doles**) *vi.* to express sympathy to somebody who is experiencing grief, loss, or pain, especially over a death (*formal*) [Late 16thC. From Christian Latin *condolere*, literally "to grieve together," from *dolere* "to suffer" (source of English *doleful* and *indolent*).] —**con·do·la·to·ry** *adj.* —**con·dol·er** *n.* —**con·dol·ing·ly** *adv.*

WORD KEY: USAGE

condole or **console**? These words are easy to confuse because they are both connected with reassuring people in distress. The more common word is ***console***, which takes an object and means "to comfort." *He tried to console his father when his mother died.* ***Condole*** means "to express sympathy," and does not take an object but uses *with* instead. *He condoled with his father over the death of his mother.*

con·do·lence /kən dṓləns/ *n.* an expression of sorrow and sympathy, usually to somebody who is grieving over a death (*often used in the plural*) —**con·do·lent** *adj.* —**con·do·lent·ly** *adv.*

con do·lo·re /kòn də láwree, kàwn də láw rày/ *adv.* in a sad or sorrowful way (*used as a musical direction*) [From Italian, literally "with sorrow"] —**con do·lo·re** *adj.*

con·dom /kóndəm, kúndəm/ *n.* a close-fitting rubber covering worn by a man over the penis during sexual intercourse to prevent pregnancy or the spread of sexually transmitted disease. ◊ **female condom** [Early 18thC. Origin unknown.]

con·do·min·i·um /kòndə mínnee əm/ *n.* **1.** ARCHIT **INDIVIDUALLY OWNED APARTMENT** an individually owned unit of real estate, especially an apartment or townhouse, in a building or on land that is owned in common by the owners of the units **2.** ARCHIT **BUILDING CONTAINING CONDOMINIUMS** a building or complex containing condominium apartments or townhouses **3.** POL **STATE RULED BY FOREIGN COUNTRIES** a country governed by two or more different countries with joint responsibility **4.** POL **JOINT GOVERNMENT OF TERRITORY** the system under which a country or state is ruled by two or more other nations [Early 18thC. From modern Latin, literally "joint right of ownership," from Latin *dominium* "property" (see DOMINION).] —**con·do·min·i·al** *adj.*

con·done /kən dṓn/ (**-doned, -don·ing, -dones**) *vt.* to regard something that is considered immoral or wrong in a tolerant way, without criticizing it or feeling strongly about it [Mid-19thC. From Latin *condonare*, literally "to give up," from *donare* (see DONATE). The underlying meaning is "to give up your objections."] —**con·don·a·ble** *adj.* —**con·do·na·tion** /kòndə náysh'n, -dō-/ *n.* —**con·don·er** *n.*

Condor

con·dor /kón dàwr, kóndər/ *n.* a large vulture of the Andes that has dull black plumage with white around the neck. Latin name: *Vultur gryphus.* [Early 17thC. Via Spanish *cóndor* from Quechua *kuntur.*]

con·dot·tie·re /kon dòttee érree, kóndə tyé rày/ (*plural* **-ri** /-ree/) *n.* **1. CAPTAIN OF MERCENARY SOLDIERS DURING RENAISSANCE** a man who led a group of hired soldiers, or one of the hired soldiers in such a group, especially during the period of the Italian Renaissance, between the 13th and 16th centuries **2. MERCENARY** a hired soldier [Late 18thC. From Italian, literally "contractor."]

con·duce /kən dóoss/ (**-duced, -duc·ing, -duc·es**) *vi.* to help, contribute, or lead to bringing about an action or event (*formal*) [14thC. From Latin *conducere*, literally "to bring together," from *ducere* (see DUCT).] —**con·duc·er** *n.* —**con·duc·i·ble** *adj.* —**con·duc·ing·ly** *adv.*

con·du·cive /kən dóossiv/ *adj.* tending to encourage or bring about a good or intended result

con·duct *v.* /kən dúkt/ (**con·duct·ed, con·duct·ing, con·ducts**) **1.** *vti.* **LEAD INSTRUMENTAL OR VOCAL GROUP** to lead a group of musicians or a musical performance by signaling the beat with a baton or hand gestures, giving cues, and offering suggestions for interpretation or expression **2.** PHYS, ELEC **TRANSMIT ENERGY** to transmit energy, e.g., heat, light, sound, or electricity **3.** *vt.* **GUIDE SOMEBODY ALONG** to lead a person or group of people by going along with them **4.** *vt.* **DO OR RUN SOMETHING** to carry out, manage, or control something **5.** *vr.* **BEHAVE** to behave in a specified way ○ *He conducted himself with great dignity.* ■ *n.* /kón dùkt/ **1. BEHAVIOR** the way a person behaves, especially in public **2. HOW SOMEBODY DOES OR HANDLES SOMETHING** the management or execution of matters such as work or official affairs **3. LEADER OR GUIDE** somebody who leads, guides, or escorts another or others (*archaic*) [15thC. Directly and via *conduit* from Latin *conduct-*, the past participle stem of *conducere* (see CONDUCE).] —**con·duct·i·bil·i·ty** /kən dùktə bíllətee/ *n.* —**con·duct·i·ble** /kən dúktəb'l/ *adj.*

WORD KEY: SYNONYMS

See Synonyms at ***guide***.

con·duc·tance /kən dúktəns/ *n.* a measure of the ability of an object to transmit electricity. ◊ **conductivity** *n.* 1. Symbol *G*

con·duc·tion /kən dúkshən/ *n.* **1.** PHYS **TRANSMISSION OF ENERGY** the passage of energy through something, particularly heat or electricity **2. TRANSMISSION THROUGH A NERVE FIBER** the transmission of biochemical or electrical energy through a nerve fiber **3. CONVEYANCE THROUGH PASSAGE** the passage of something through or along something, e.g., water through a pipe

con·duc·tive /kən dúktiv/ *adj.* **1.** PHYS **CONDUCTING ENERGY** transmitting or able to transmit energy, particularly heat or electricity **2.** BIOL **TRANSMITTING NERVE IMPULSE** used to describe a cell that allows a physiological disturbance, e.g., a nerve impulse, to pass through it

con·duc·tiv·i·ty /kòn duk tívvətee/ *n.* **1.** ELEC **ABILITY TO TRANSMIT ELECTRICITY** a mathematical relationship between the dimensions of an object and its ability to transmit electricity. ◊ **conductance.** Symbol σ **2.** BIOL **TRANSMISSION OF NERVE IMPULSES** the ability of tissue to transmit nerve impulses

con·duc·tor /kən dúktər/ *n.* **1.** TRANSP **SOMEBODY WHO COLLECTS FARES ON BUS** somebody who takes tickets or money for the fare on a bus or streetcar **2.** TRANSP **RAILROAD EMPLOYEE IN CHARGE OF PASSENGERS** a railroad employee who is in charge of a train and whose job is to check tickets, announce stops, and attend to passengers' needs and safety **3.** MUSIC **DIRECTOR OF ORCHESTRA OR CHOIR** somebody in charge of an orchestra or choir who marks time and signals musicians or singers when and how to play or sing **4.** PHYS **SOMETHING THAT CONVEYS HEAT OR ELECTRICITY** a substance, body, or medium that allows heat, electricity, light, or sound to pass along it or through it. Metals are good conductors of heat because of the high concentration of free electrons they contain. **5.** ENG = **lightning rod** —**con·duc·to·ri·al** /kòn duk táwree əl/ *adj.* —**con·duc·tor·ship** /kən dúktər shìp/ *n.*

con·duit /kón doò it, kóndwit/ *n.* **1.** UTIL **CHANNEL FOR LIQUID** a pipe or channel that carries liquid to or from a place **2.** CONSTR **PROTECTIVE COVER FOR CABLE** a pipe or tube that covers and protects electrical cables **3.** **CONVEYER OF INFORMATION** somebody or something that conveys information, especially if in secret [14thC. Via French *conduit* from, ultimately, Latin *conduct-*, stem of *conducere*, literally "to lead with" (source of English *conduct*).]

con·dyle /kón dìl, kónd'l/ *n.* a rounded part at the end of a bone that forms a moving joint with a cup-shaped cavity in another bone. The ball part of a ball-and-socket joint, such as the hip or shoulder joint, is a condyle. [Mid-17thC. Via French from, ultimately, Greek *kondulos* "knuckle."] —**con·dy·lar** /kónd'lər/ *adj.*

con·dy·loid /kónd'l òyd/ *adj.* rounded like the protruding surface at the end of a bone

con·dy·lo·ma /kònd'l ṓmə/ (*plural* **-mas** *or* **-ma·ta** /-mətə/) *n.* a growth resembling a wart on the skin or a mucous membrane, usually of the genitals or anus [14thC. Via Latin from Greek *kondulōma* "callous knob or lump," from *kondulos* "knuckle."]

cone /kōn/ *n.* **1.** **POINTED OBJECT WITH ROUND BASE** any object or shape that has a circular base and tapers to a point at the top, or has a circular top and tapers to a point at the bottom **2.** GEOM **POINTED FIGURE WITH CURVED FLAT BASE** a three-dimensional geometric figure formed by straight lines through a fixed point (**vertex**) to the points of a fixed curve (**directrix**). A circular cone has a directrix that is a circle. **3.** FOOD **CONE-SHAPED WAFER FOR ICE CREAM** a cone-shaped or cup-shaped wafer used for serving ice cream, or such a wafer with ice cream in it **4.** TRANSP **PLASTIC CONE-SHAPED ROAD MARKER** a plastic cone-shaped object used as a temporary road marker or barrier, e.g., to close off part or all of a road during repairs or after an accident **5.** BOT **SEED-BEARING STRUCTURE OF PINES AND FIRS** a tightly packed cluster of scales that bears the reproductive organs of coniferous plants such as pines and firs. Male cones produce pollen, and female cones bear seeds. Technical name **strobilus** **6.** BOT **REPRODUCTIVE PART OF NONFLOWERING PLANTS** a club-shaped, umbrella-shaped, or poker-shaped cluster of fertile leaves that bears the spore-producing organs of a clubmoss or horsetail **7.** ANAT **LIGHT RECEPTOR CELL IN EYE** a cone-shaped cell sensitive to light and color in the retina of the eye of a human being or any other vertebrate animal. There are three different types of cone cells, responding to blue, green, or red light. **8.** MARINE BIOL **SEA SNAIL WITH CONE-SHAPED SHELL** a sea snail found in the South Pacific and Indian oceans that has a cone-shaped, vividly marked shell and a poisonous, sometimes fatal, sting. Family: Conidae. **9.** GEOG **VOLCANO** a cone-shaped mountain, especially a volcano ■ *vt.* (**coned, con·ing, cones**) **MAKE SOMETHING INTO CONE SHAPE** to shape something into the form of a cone [15thC. Via French from, ultimately, Greek *kōnos* "pine cone, cone."]

cone·flow·er /kṓn flòwr/ *n.* a plant, originally from North America, with variously colored flowers that have a brown or black cone-shaped center. Genera: *Echinacea* and *Rudbeckia* and *Ratibida*.

cone·nose /kṓn nṑz/, **cone-nosed bug** *n.* a blood-sucking insect found in Mexico and the southern and western United States that feeds on other insects, inflicts painful bites on humans, and transmits diseases. Family: Reduviidae.

cone shell *n.* = **cone** *n.* 8

con es·pres·si·o·ne /kòn ə spressi ṓ nàу, káwn-/ *adv.* with feeling and expression (*used as a musical direction*) [From Italian, literally "with expression"]

Con·es·to·ga wag·on /kònnə stṓgə-/ *n.* a heavy covered wagon used by U.S. pioneers in the 19th century to travel west [Early 18thC. Named for *Conestoga*, Pennsylvania, where it was first made.]

co·ney /kṓnee/ (*plural* **-neys**), **co·ny** (*plural* **-nies**) *n.* **1.** ZOOL **EUROPEAN RABBIT** a rabbit, especially the common domesticated European rabbit **2.** INDUST **RABBIT FUR** rabbit fur used for coats and other articles of clothing **3.** ZOOL = **hyrax 4.** ZOOL = **pika 5.** *Southeast U.S., Carib* ZOOL **CARIBBEAN FISH** a fish with varying color phases that lives along reefs of the Caribbean Sea [14thC. Via Anglo-Norman from, ultimately, Latin *cuniculus* "rabbit, burrow," of uncertain origin: perhaps from *cunus* "female pudenda."]

Co·ney Is·land formerly a resort, now an amusement area in southern Brooklyn, New York City, New York. It was an island, but has become part of Long Island since the silting up of Coney Island Creek.

conf, **conf.** *abbr.* **1.** confer **2. conf.** conference **3. conf.** LAW confessor **4. conf.** confidential

con·fab /kón fàb/ *n.* (*informal*) **1.** **TALK** a chat or casual discussion **2.** **GATHERING OF PEOPLE** a gathering of people for discussion or decision-making ■ *vi.* (**-fabbed, -fab·bing, -fabs**) **TALK ABOUT SOMETHING** to have a chat or discussion about something (*informal*) [Early 18thC. Shortening of CONFABULATION.]

con·fab·u·late /kən fábbyə làyt/ (**-lat·ed, -lat·ing, -lates**) *vi.* **1.** **CONFER ABOUT SOMETHING** to discuss or have a chat about something (*formal*) **2.** PSYCHOL **CREATE MEMORY OF SUPPOSED PAST EVENTS** to give fictitious accounts of past events, believing they are true, in order to cover a gap in the memory caused by a medical condition such as dementia or Korsakoff's syndrome [Early 17thC. From Latin *confabulat-*, stem of *confabulari*, literally "to talk together," from, ultimately, *fabula* "story" (see FABLE).] —**con·fab·u·la·tion** /kən fàbbyə láysh'n/ *n.* —**con·fab·u·la·tor** /-fábbyə làytər/ *n.* —**con·fab·u·la·to·ry** /-lə tàwree/ *adj.*

con·fect /kən fékt/ *vt.* (**-fect·ed, -fect·ing, -fects**) **1.** COOK **MAKE CANDY OR PRESERVES** to make candy by combining ingredients such as sugar, fruit, and nuts, or make preserves (*formal*) **2.** **MAKE** to create something by combining different materials or items ○ *Using scrap lumber, they succeeded in confecting a house of sorts.* ■ *n.* **SWEET CONFECTION** something, e.g., candy, that is a sweet confection (*formal*) [14thC. From Latin *confect-*, stem of *conficere*, literally "to put or make together," from *facere* "to make."]

con·fec·tion /kən fékshən/ *n.* **1.** FOOD **SOMETHING SWEET** a sweet food made by combining ingredients such as fruit, nuts, and sugar **2.** **COMBINATION** a combining of elements or materials or its result ○ *a confection of lies and half-truths* **3.** **ELABORATE CREATION** an often elaborate piece of craftsmanship and skill, e.g., an ornate piece of women's clothing ○ *Her gown was a marvelous confection of lace and tulle.* **4.** PHARM **SWEET MEDICINE** a medicine that has been sweetened with honey or sugar (*archaic*)

con·fec·tion·ar·y /kən fékshən èrree/ *n.* (*plural* **-ies**) FOOD = **confectionery** *n.* 1, **confectionery** *n.* 3 ■ *adj.* **RELATING TO CONFECTIONERY** relating to confectionery and confectioners (*formal*)

con·fec·tion·er /kən fékshənər/ *n.* somebody who makes or sells candies

con·fec·tion·ers' sug·ar *n.* finely powdered sugar with cornstarch added, used for making cake icing or for dusting pastries and some types of bread

con·fec·tion·er·y /kən fékshə nèrree/ (*plural* **-ies**) *n.* **1.** FOOD **CONFECTIONS** candies, considered collectively **2.** COOK **CANDY-MAKING** the skill, technique, or practice of making candy **3.** COMM **CONFECTIONER'S STORE** a store where candy is sold

confed., **Confed.** *abbr.* POL **1.** confederation **2.** confederate *or* Confederate

con·fed·er·a·cy /kən féddərəssee/ *n.* **1.** **POLITICAL UNION** an alliance of people, states, or parties for some common purpose, or the people, states, or parties in an alliance **2.** **GROUP DOING SOMETHING UNLAWFUL TOGETHER** a group of people who have joined together to do something unlawful

Con·fed·er·a·cy *n.* = **Confederate States of America**

con·fed·er·al /kən féddərəl/ *adj.* **1.** **OF A CONFEDERATION** relating to a confederation **2.** **CONCERNING TWO OR MORE NATIONS** relating to the activities of two or more nations —**con·fed·er·al·ist** *n.*

con·fed·er·ate *n.* /kən féddərət/ **1.** **ALLY** one of two or more people, groups, or nations that have formed an alliance for some common purpose **2.** **ACCOMPLICE** somebody who is part of a plot or conspiracy ■ *adj.* /kən féddərət/ **ASSOCIATED** joined in common purpose ■ *vti.* /kən féddə ràyt/ (**-at·ed, -at·ing, -ates**) **UNITE PEOPLE OR THINGS** to form people, groups, or nations into a confederacy, or become part of a confederacy [14thC. From late Latin *confoederat-*, the past participle stem of *confoederare*, literally "to league together," from, ultimately, the stem *foeder-* "league" (see FEDERAL).] —**con·fed·er·a·tive** /kən féddə ràytiv/ *adj.*

Con·fed·er·ate /kən féddərət/ *n.* **SUPPORTER OF CONFEDERATE STATES OF AMERICA** a supporter or soldier of the Confederate States of America during the Civil War ■ *adj.* **RELATING TO CONFEDERATE STATES OF AMERICA** relating to the Confederate States of America during the Civil War

Con·fed·er·ate Me·mo·ri·al Day *n.* a holiday remembering Civil War dead and observed by descendants of Confederate soldiers. It is celebrated on various days in the spring in most former Confederate states. Though still an official holiday in several states, it is often only observed by memorial organizations.

Con·fed·er·ate States of A·mer·i·ca *n.* the confederation of the 11 southern states that seceded from the United States in 1861, an act that started the Civil War. Alabama, Arkansas, Florida, Georgia, Louisiana, Mississippi, North Carolina, South Carolina, Tennessee, Texas, and Virginia were the states that seceded.

con·fed·er·a·tion /kən fèddə ráysh'n/ *n.* **1.** **GROUP OF LOOSELY ALLIED STATES** a group of states that are allied together to form a political unit in which they keep most of their independence but act together for certain purposes such as defense **2.** **BODY REPRESENTING INDEPENDENT ORGANIZATIONS** a body comprising representatives of independent organizations that wish to cooperate for some common beneficial purpose **3.** *Can* **FEDERATION** a federation **4.** **CONFEDERATING** the formation of or state of being a confederation —**con·fed·er·a·tion·ism** /kən fèddə ráysh'n ìzzəm/ *n.* —**con·fed·er·a·tion·ist** *n.*

Con·fed·er·a·tion *n.* **1.** **ORIGINAL UNITED STATES** the union of the original 13 states of the United States under the Articles of Confederation from 1781 to 1789 **2.** **CANADA IN 1867** the original union of Ontario, Quebec, New Brunswick, and Nova Scotia in 1867 into the federation of Canada, afterwards joined by the six other provinces

con·fer /kən fúr/ (**-ferred, -fer·ring, -fers**) *v.* **1.** *vi.* **DISCUSS SOMETHING WITH SOMEBODY** to talk with somebody in order to compare opinions or make a decision **2.** *vt.* **GIVE HONOR OR TITLE TO SOMEBODY** to give something such as a title, honor, or favor to somebody (*formal*) ○ *The university conferred an honorary Doctor of Arts degree on the president.* **3.** *vt.* **GIVE SOMEBODY OR SOMETHING SOME CHARACTERISTIC** to give somebody or something a certain status or characteristic ○ *His demeanor conferred a sense of dignity on the whole affair.* [15thC. From Latin *conferre*, literally "to bring together," from *ferre* "to bring."] —**con·fer·ment** *n.* —**con·fer·ra·ble** *adj.* —**con·fer·ral** *n.* —**con·fer·rer** *n.*

con·fer·ee /kònfə rée/, **con·fer·ree** *n.* **1.** **PARTICIPANT AT CONFERENCE** somebody who takes part in a conference **2.** **SOMEBODY HONORED** somebody who is given a title, honor, or favor

con·fer·ence /kónfərəns/ *n.* **1.** **MEETING FOR LECTURES AND DISCUSSION** a meeting, sometimes lasting for several days, in which people with a common interest participate in discussions or listen to lectures to obtain information **2.** **MEETING FOR SERIOUS DISCUSSION** a meeting to discuss serious matters, e.g., policy or business **3.** **MEETING OF REPRESENTATIVES OF ORGANIZATION** a usually annual gathering of local representatives of an organization, such as a political party, trade union, or church, where policy matters and other issues are discussed or decided ○ *the Democratic Party Conference* **4.** POL **MEETING OF TWO LEGISLATIVE COMMITTEES** a meeting of select members or committees from two legislative bodies, for the purpose of settling differences in bills they have passed **5.** CHR **AREA ORGANIZATION OF CHURCHES** in some Protestant churches, a regional or national body to which a number of local churches belong ○ *the Friends General Conference* **6.** SPORTS **SPORTS LEAGUE** an association or league of athletic teams that compete with each other **7.** **CON-**

FERRING OF SOMETHING the conferring of something such as a degree or honor on somebody (*archaic*)

con·fer·ence call *n.* a conversation involving three or more people linked together by telephone

con·fer·enc·ing /kónfərənssing/ *n.* the holding of a conference, meeting, or discussion in which the participants are linked by telephone (**audioconferencing**), by telephone and video equipment (**videoconferencing**), or by computer (**computer conferencing**)

con·fer·ree *n.* = **conferee**

con·fess /kən féss/ (**-fessed, -fess·ing, -fess·es**) *v.* **1.** *vti.* ADMIT HAVING DONE SOMETHING WRONG to admit openly a wrongdoing, crime, or error ○ *She confessed to having taken the watch.* ○ *I eventually confessed that I had made the call that night.* **2.** *vt.* ACKNOWLEDGE TO BE TRUE to admit the truth of something, e.g., something that might reflect badly or be embarrassing ○ *I confess I didn't really want to come here tonight.* ○ *I confess myself unworthy of the honor you are bestowing on me.* **3.** *vti.* CHR ADMIT SINS to reveal sins to a priest or to God and ask for forgiveness ○ *It had been some months since I had confessed.* **4.** *vt.* CHR HEAR SOMEBODY'S CONFESSION to listen to somebody's confession of sins ○ *A priest visited her to declare confess her every day.* **5.** *vt.* ACKNOWLEDGE FAITH IN to declare faith or belief in something or somebody (*archaic*) ○ *On that day everyone will confess him Lord and God.* [14thC. Via French *confesser* from Latin *confess-*, past participle stem of *confiteri* "to acknowledge," literally "to declare utterly," from *fateri* "to declare."] —**con·fess·a·ble** *adj.*

con·fessed /kən fést/ *adj.* openly admitted ○ *a confessed admirer of your films*

con·fess·ed·ly /kən féssədlee/ *adv.* used to indicate that something is admitted to be the case

con·fes·sion /kən fésh'n/ *n.* **1.** ADMISSION OF WRONGDOING an admission of having done something wrong or embarrassing **2.** LAW ADMISSION OF GUILT a voluntary written or verbal statement admitting the commission of a crime **3.** OPEN ACKNOWLEDGMENT OF FEELINGS a profession of emotions or beliefs such as love, loyalty, or faith **4.** CHR DECLARATION OF SINS a formal declaration of sins confidentially to a priest or to God **5.** SOMETHING ADMITTED something that is confessed or disclosed **6.** RELIG DECLARATION OF BELIEFS OR DOCTRINES a declaration of the beliefs or doctrines of a religious body **7.** CHR RELIGIOUS GROUP SHARING BELIEFS a religious group that has a specific set of beliefs and practices

con·fes·sion·al /kən féshən'l, -féshnəl/ *adj.* **1.** RESEMBLING CONFESSION suited to, typical of, or resembling an act of confession **2.** BEING OF AN INTIMATE NATURE relating to or being something intimately autobiographical in nature or content ■ *n.* CHR PLACE FOR CONFESSION IN CHURCH a small wooden stall in a Roman Catholic church with a partition behind which a priest sits to hear confession

con·fes·sor /kən féssər/ *n.* **1.** CHR PRIEST a priest who hears confessions and sometimes acts as a spiritual adviser **2.** CHR CHRISTIAN NOT DETERRED BY PERSECUTION somebody who demonstrates Christian faith by living a holy life, especially in the face of persecution but without being a martyr (*archaic*) **3.** SOMEBODY WHO CONFESSES somebody who makes a confession

con·fet·ti /kən féttee/ *n.* COLORED PAPER PIECES FOR THROWING small pieces of colored paper or dried flowers thrown over people at festive occasions, e.g., the bride and groom at a wedding ■ *adj.* RESEMBLING CONFETTI similar to confetti in shape or color [Early 19thC. From Italian, plural of *confetto* "small sweet thrown at carnivals," from, ultimately, Latin *conficere* (see CONFECT).]

con·fi·dant /kónfi dànt, kònfi daánt/ *n.* a trusted person with whom personal matters and problems are discussed [Mid-17thC. Alteration of CONFIDENT.]

con·fi·dante /kónfi dànt, kònfi daánt/ *n.* a trusted woman with whom personal matters and problems are discussed [Mid-17thC. Alteration of CONFIDENT.]

con·fide /kən fíd/ (**-fid·ed, -fid·ing, -fides**) *v.* **1.** *vti.* TELL SOMETHING SECRET TO SOMEBODY to tell somebody something that is to remain secret or private ○ *He later confided to me that he had not wanted the position at all.* **2.** *vt.* GIVE SOMETHING OVER TO SOMEBODY'S CARE to entrust somebody with something such as a valuable object or an important task (*archaic*) ○ *He had been confided with the task of taking the message to the king.* **3.** *vi.* TRUST IN SOMEBODY to have trust or confidence in somebody (*archaic*) [15thC. From Latin *confidere* "to put your trust in," from *fidere* "to trust," from *fides* "trust" (source of English *faith*).] —**con·fid·er** *n.*

con·fi·dence /kónfidənss/ *n.* **1.** BELIEF IN OWN ABILITIES a belief or self-assurance in your ability to succeed **2.** FAITH IN SOMEBODY TO DO RIGHT belief or assurance in somebody or something or the ability of somebody or something to act in a proper, trustworthy, or reliable manner **3.** SECRET something told to somebody that is to be kept private **4.** TRUSTING RELATIONSHIP a relationship based on trust and intimacy ○ *He took me into his confidence.*

con·fi·dence game *n.* a fraud in which somebody obtains something of value by first gaining the trust of the victim, then betraying that person

con·fi·dence in·ter·val *n.* a range of statistical values within which a result is expected to fall with a specific probability

con·fi·dence lim·it *n.* the highest and lowest values of a confidence interval

con·fi·dence trick *n.* U.K. = **confidence game** —**con·fi·dence trick·ster** *n.*

con·fi·dent /kónfidənt/ *adj.* **1.** SELF-ASSURED certain of having the ability, judgment, and resources needed to succeed **2.** CONVINCED sure about the nature or facts of something ○ *We are confident that the market for our products is expanding.* **3.** EXCESSIVELY FORWARD bold and presumptuous in manner [Late 16thC. Via French from *confidere* (see CONFIDE).] —**con·fi·dent·ly** *adv.*

con·fi·den·tial /kònfi dénsh'l/ *adj.* **1.** PRIVATE AND SECRET carried out or revealed in the expectation that anything done or revealed will be kept private **2.** FOR A SELECT GROUP not available to the public, e.g., because it is commercially or industrially sensitive or concerns matters of national security **3.** DEALING WITH PRIVATE AFFAIRS entrusted with somebody's personal or private matters **4.** SUGGESTING A CLOSE RELATIONSHIP suggesting familiarity or intimacy that may not exist ○ *a confidential whisper* —**con·fi·den·ti·al·i·ty** /-denshee álləteе/ *n.* —**con·fi·den·tial·ly** /-dénsh'lee/ *adv.*

con·fi·den·tial com·mu·ni·ca·tion *n.* privileged communication with somebody such as a doctor, priest, lawyer, or spouse that a court cannot legally order to be disclosed

con·fid·ing /kən fíding/ *adj.* willing to trust others with the knowledge of private or personal matters —**con·fid·ing·ly** *adv.*

con·fig·u·ra·tion /kən fìggyə ráysh'n/ *n.* **1.** ARRANGEMENT OF PARTS the way the parts or elements of something are arranged and fit together ○ *I don't quite grasp the configuration of this engine.* **2.** SHAPE OR OUTLINE the shape or outline of something, determined by the way its parts or elements are arranged ○ *Geese fly in a V-shaped configuration.* **3.** CHEM, PHYS ARRANGEMENT OF ATOMS IN MOLECULE the fixed stable spatial arrangement of atoms within a molecule **4.** PSYCHOL = **gestalt 5.** COMPUT COMPUTER SYSTEM'S SETUP the manner in which the software and internal and external hardware components of a computer system are arranged and interconnected, so that the system functions correctly —**con·fig·u·ra·tive** /kən fíggyə ràytiv/ *adj.* —**con·fig·u·ra·tion·al** /kən fìggyə ráyshən'l, kən fìggyə ráyshnəl/ *adj.* —**con·fig·u·ra·tion·al·ly** *adv.*

con·fig·ure /kən fíggyər/ (**-ured, -ur·ing, -ures**) *vt.* to set up, design, or arrange the parts of something for a specific purpose [14thC. From Latin *configurare* "to fashion after a pattern," literally "to form together," from *figura* "shape" (source of English *figure*).]

con·fine *vt.* /kən fín/ (**-fined, -fin·ing, -fines**) **1.** KEEP SOMEBODY OR SOMETHING WITHIN LIMITS to keep within certain limits or boundaries ○ *Please confine your comments to the matters at hand.* **2.** KEEP IN SOME PLACE to keep somebody or something from leaving an enclosed or limited space such as a prison, room, or bed ■ *n.* /kón fìn/ **1.** LIMITATION restriction within limits (*archaic literary*) **2.** PRISON a place of confinement (*archaic*) ■ **confines** *npl.* BOUNDARIES OR SCOPE the boundaries, limits, or scope that restricts somebody or something ○ *Their goals were defined by the confines of the project requirements.* [15thC. From French *confiner*, from *confins* (plural) "boundaries," from, ultimately, Latin *confinis* "ending with," from *finis* "end" (see FINAL).] —**con·fin·a·ble** *adj.* —**con·fin·er** *n.*

con·fined /kən fínd/ *adj.* **1.** LIMITED restricted in scope or application ○ *a problem that is not confined to the inner cities* **2.** CONSTRICTED small, cramped, and completely enclosed **3.** MED IN PROCESS OF GIVING BIRTH giving birth, or about to give birth, to a child (*dated*) —**con·fined·ness** /-fínədnəss/ *n.*

con·fine·ment /kən fínmənt/ *n.* **1.** MED PROCESS OR TIME OF GIVING BIRTH the period of time or the process of giving birth, beginning when a woman goes into labor and ending when a child is born (*dated*) **2.** RESTRAINT restriction or limitation within the boundaries or scope of something

con·firm /kən fúrm/ (**-firmed, -firm·ing, -firms**) *v.* **1.** *vt.* PROVE TO BE TRUE to verify the truth or validity of something thought to be true or valid **2.** *vti.* MAKE SOMETHING DEFINITE to make certain that a tentative arrangement or one made earlier is firm ○ *call to confirm the reservation* **3.** *vt.* LEGALLY APPROVE to ratify or make something valid with a formal or legal act ○ *confirmed his appointment to the post with a unanimous vote* **4.** *vt.* JUD-CHR ADMIT INTO RELIGIOUS BODY in Judaism and Christianity, to admit somebody into full membership of a religious body or community **5.** *vt.* STRENGTHEN to make something stronger (*formal*) [13thC. Via Old French *confermer* from Latin *confirmare*, literally "to strengthen together," from *firmare* "to strengthen."] —**con·firm·a·bil·i·ty** /kən fùrmə bílləteе/ *n.* —**con·firm·a·ble** /-fúrməb'l/ *adj.* —**con·firm·a·to·ry** /-fúrmə tàwree/ *adj.* —**con·firm·er** *n.*

con·fir·mand /kən fúrmənd/ *n.* somebody who is being confirmed in a religious ceremony (*formal*) [Mid-18thC. From Latin *confirmandus* "fit to be confirmed," from *confirmare* (see CONFIRM).]

con·fir·ma·tion /kònfər máysh'n/ *n.* **1.** CONFIRMING SOMETHING verification that something has been or will be done **2.** SOMETHING THAT CONFIRMS SOMETHING ELSE something that supports, validates, or verifies something ○ *a confirmation of my worst fears* **3.** CHR ACCEPTANCE INTO CHURCH a religious ceremony that marks somebody's formal acceptance into a Christian church **4.** JUDAISM CEREMONY MARKING BEGINNING OF RESPONSIBLE ADULTHOOD in Reform Judaism, a ceremony that marks the completion of somebody's religious training and entry into full adult membership of the community —**con·fir·ma·tion·al** *adj.*

con·firmed /kən fúrmd/ *adj.* **1.** SETTLED AND UNLIKELY TO CHANGE firmly settled in a particular habit and unlikely to change **2.** ESTABLISHED AS TRUE having been found or shown to be true or definite ○ *confirmed cases of infection* **3.** CHR MADE MEMBER OF CHURCH received into a Christian church as a full member

con·firm·ed·ly /kənfúrmədlee/ *adv.* to an extent or in a way that is unlikely to change

con·fis·ca·ble /kən fískəb'l/ *adj.* at risk of being confiscated (*formal*) ○ *confiscable goods*

con·fis·cate *vt.* /kónfi skàyt/ (**-cat·ed, -cat·ing, -cates**) **1.** TAKE AWAY FROM SOMEBODY to take somebody's property with authority, or appropriate it for personal use as if with authority ○ *I'll confiscate that ruler if you don't stop playing with it.* **2.** TAKE PROPERTY AS LEGAL PENALTY to seize property legally forfeited to the public treasury as a penalty ○ *The goods were confiscated by customs.* ■ *adj.* /kónfi skàyt, kónfiskət/ (*formal*) **1.** TAKEN BY AUTHORITY taken legally or forfeited **2.** HAVING FORFEITED PROPERTY having had property taken away legally or by forfeiture [Mid-16thC. From Latin *confiscare* "to appropriate for the public treasury," from *fiscus* (see FISCAL).] —**con·fis·cat·a·ble** *adj.* —**con·fis·ca·tor** *n.* —**con·fis·ca·to·ry** /kən fískə tàwree/ *adj.*

con·fit /kon fée, kōn-/ *n.* meat cooked and preserved in its own fat, e.g., goose, duck, or pork [Mid-20thC. From French, originally the past participle of Old French *confire* "to prepare," from Latin *conficere* "to put together" (see CONFECT).]

Con·fi·te·or /kən féetee ər, -àwr/ *n.* a Roman Catholic prayer of confession and plea for forgiveness [13thC. From Latin, "I confess," from the opening words *Confiteor Deo Omnipotenti...* "I confess to Almighty God...."]

con·fi·ture /kónfi chòor/ *n.* fruit jam or preserve [Mid-16thC. From French, where it was formed from *confit* (see CONFIT).]

con·fla·grant /kən fláygrənt/ *adj.* burning intensely (*literary*) [Mid-17thC. From Latin *conflagrant-*, present participle stem of *conflagrare* (see CONFLAGRATION).]

con·fla·gra·tion /kònflə gráysh'n/ *n.* a large fire that causes a great deal of damage [15thC. From the Latin stem *conflagration-*, ultimately from *conflagrare* "to burn up," from *flagrare* "to blaze" (source of English *flagrant*).]

con·flate /kən fláyt/ (**-flat·ed, -flat·ing, -flates**) *v.* (*formal*) **1.** *vti.* COMBINE THINGS to join or merge two or more things into a unified whole **2.** *vt.* MIX THINGS to fuse or bring things together ○ *I'm afraid you've mistakenly conflated two separate sets of facts.* [15thC. From Latin *conflat-*, past participle stem of *conflare* "to melt together," from *flare* "to blow" (source of English *flavor* and *soufflé*).] —**con·fla·tion** /kən fláysh'n/ *n.*

con·flict *n.* /kón flìkt/ **1.** MIL **WAR** a continued struggle or battle, especially open warfare between opposing forces ○ *news that the conflict had reached the outskirts of the capital* **2. DIFFERENCE** a disagreement or clash between ideas, principles, or people ○ *The two sides came into conflict over the proposed contract.* **3.** PSYCHOL **MENTAL STRUGGLE** a psychological state resulting from the often unconscious opposition between simultaneous but incompatible desires, needs, drives, or impulses **4.** LITERAT **PLOT TENSION** opposition between or among characters or forces in a literary work that shapes or motivates the action of a plot ■ *vi.* /kən flíkt/ (**-flict·ed, -flict·ing, -flicts**) **DIFFER** to be incompatible, in opposition, or in disagreement ○ *The latest findings conflict with those of the original report.* [15thC. From Latin *conflictus*, past participle of *confligere* "to strike together, fight," from *fligere*, to strike (source of English *profligate* and *inflict*).] —**con·flic·tion** /kən flíkshən/ *n.* —**con·flic·tive** /kən flíktiv/ *adj.* —**con·flic·to·ry** /-flíktəree/ *adj.* —**con·flic·tu·al** /kən flíkchoo əl/ *adj.*

con·flict·ed /kən flíktəd/ *adj.* confused or ambivalent because of conflicting desires, possibilities, or impulses (*informal*) ○ *I haven't known him when he wasn't conflicted about one thing or another.*

con·flict·ing /kən flíkting/ *adj.* **1. DIFFERENT AND INCOMPATIBLE** inconsistent or contradictory and unable to be reconciled ○ *We've been receiving conflicting reports about the whereabouts of the kidnappers.* **2. REQUIRING DIFFERENT AND INCOMPATIBLE ACTIONS** not able to be followed or acted on, because each requires different and incompatible actions ○ *In the confusion, the men were ordered to do conflicting and impossible things.* —**con·flict·ing·ly** *adv.*

con·flict of in·ter·est *n.* a conflict between the public and private interests of somebody in an official position or conflicts between a number of public positions

con·flu·ence /kón floo ənss/ *n.* **1.** GEOG **MEETING OF STREAMS** a flowing together of two or more streams, a point at which streams combine, or a stream formed by their combining **2. MEETING OF TWO OR MORE THINGS** a meeting or gathering together of two or more things, or the place where two or more things meet or join

con·flu·ent /kón floo ənt/ *adj.* **1.** GEOG **MERGING INTO ONE** used to describe streams that blend or flow into one **2.** MED **MERGING TOGETHER** used to describe skin eruptions that merge or spread into one another ■ *n.* GEOG **STREAM** one of two or more streams that flow together [15thC. From Latin *confluent-*, present participle stem of *confluere* "to flow together," from *fluere* "to flow" (see FLUID).]

con·flux /kón flùks/ *n.* = **confluence** *n.* 1 (*formal*) [Early 17thC. From Latin *confluxus* "flowed together," from *confluere* (see CONFLUENT).]

con·fo·cal /kon fṓk'l/ *adj.* having the same focus or foci [Mid-19thC. Coined from Latin *con-* "with" + FOCAL.] —**con·fo·cal·ly** *adv.*

con·form /kən fáwrm/ (**-formed, -form·ing, -forms**) *v.* **1.** *vi.* **BEHAVE ACCEPTABLY** to behave or think in a socially acceptable or expected way ○ *the constant pressure to conform* **2.** *vi.* **FOLLOW A STANDARD** to comply with a fixed standard, regulation, or requirement ○ *a transformer that doesn't conform to U.K. standards* **3.** *vti.* **BE OR MAKE SIMILAR** to be the same as or very similar to something or somebody, or make something similar ○ *The Assyrian account of the great flood conforms closely with the biblical account.* [14thC. Via French *conformer* from Latin *conformare* "to shape after," from *forma* "shape" (source of English *form*).] —**con·form·er** *n.*

con·form·a·ble /kən fáwrməb'l/ *adj.* **1. IN AGREEMENT** consistent with something ○ *This gradual increase in the number of species in a group is conformable with the theory.* **2. SIMILAR** similar in form or shape ○ *I think this software is conformable with what you already have on your system.* **3. COMPLIANT** eager to obey or comply with the wishes of others ○ *I've always found him a conformable sort of person.* **4.** GEOL **LYING ABOVE LAYER DEPOSITED IMMEDIATELY BEFORE** used to describe a layer of rock that lies on the stratum that was deposited immediately before it, so there is no break in stratigraphic sequence or intervening erosion —**con·form·a·bil·i·ty** /kən fàwrmə bíllətee/ *n.* —**con·form·a·ble·ness** *n.* —**con·form·a·bly** *adv.*

con·for·mal /kən fáwrm'l/ *adj.* **1.** MATH **MAINTAINING THE SAME ANGLES** used to describe a mathematical transformation that leaves the angles between intersecting curves unchanged **2.** MAPS **WITH ACCURATE SHAPE AND SCALE** used to describe a map that shows the correct shape and scale of a small area [Late 19thC. Formed from German *conform*, literally "of the same shape," ultimately from Latin *forma* "shape" (see FORM).]

con·for·mance /kən fáwrmənss/ *n.* the act of conforming or bringing about accord or compliance

con·for·ma·tion /kòn fawr máysh'n/ *n.* **1. SOMETHING'S STRUCTURE** the shape, outline, or form of something, determined by the way in which its parts are arranged ○ *He attempted to discover whether different conformations of bodily organs caused alterations to the state of the mind.* **2. SYMMETRY** the symmetrical arrangement of parts or elements of something ○ *That sculpture shows excellent conformation.* **3.** CHEM **MOLECULAR ARRANGEMENT** any of the arrangements of a molecule that result from atoms being rotated about a single bond **4. CREATION OF CONFORMITY** a bringing of one thing into accord with another —**con·for·ma·tion·al** *adj.* —**con·for·ma·tion·al·ly** *adv.*

con·form·ist /kən fáwrmist/ *n.* **SOMEBODY WHO FOLLOWS CUSTOMS AND RULES** somebody who behaves or thinks in a socially acceptable or expected way ■ *adj.* **SOCIALLY ACCEPTABLE** characterized by adherence to accepted norms of behavior or thought —**con·form·ism** *n.*

con·form·i·ty /kən fáwrmətee/ *n.* **1. DOING AND THINKING AS OTHERS** behaving or thinking in a socially acceptable or expected way ○ *a certain lack of conformity in his attitudes* **2. FOLLOWING A STANDARD** compliance with a fixed standard, regulation, or requirement **3. AGREEMENT IN FORM** agreement, correspondence, or similarity in structure, manner, or character

con·found /kən fównd/ (**-found·ed, -found·ing, -founds**) *vt.* **1. BEWILDER** to puzzle or confuse somebody **2. MAKE SITUATION WORSE** to cause a confused situation to become even more confused ○ *Shouting at her like that only confounded the problem.* **3. GET THINGS MIXED UP** to fail to distinguish between two or more things ○ *He often confounds fact and opinion.* **4. REFUTE** to prove somebody or something to be wrong **5. EXPRESSING ANGER** a word used to express anger at something or somebody ○ *Confound his insolence!* **6. PUT TO SHAME** to cause somebody to feel ashamed or embarrassed ○ *Her presentation confounded everyone who had criticized her.* **7. FRUSTRATE SOMEBODY OR SOMETHING** to prevent somebody or something from succeeding ○ *The lack of progress confounded him and he left in disgust.* **8. BRING TO RUIN** to ruin or destroy somebody or something (*archaic*) [13thC. Via Anglo-Norman *conf(o)undre* from, ultimately, Latin *confundere*, literally "to pour together," hence "to mix up," from *fundere*, "to melt, pour" (see FOUND).] —**con·found·er** *n.* —**con·found·ing·ly** *adv.*

con·found·ed /kən fówndəd/ *adj.* **1. EXPRESSING ANNOYANCE** used to express annoyance or irritation (*dated informal*) **2. BEWILDERED** puzzled or confused by something ○ *"I don't know what's happened," he sputtered, completely confounded.* —**con·found·ed·ly** *adv.* —**con·found·ed·ness** *n.*

con·fra·ter·ni·ty /kònfrə túrnətee/ (*plural* **-ties**) *n.* a group of people united in a common profession or for some purpose, often a group of Christians who have joined together to perform charitable acts [15thC. Via French *confraternité* from, ultimately, Latin *confrater*, literally "brother with," hence "colleague."]

con·frère /kón fràir/ *n.* a fellow member of a professional, charitable, or other group (*formal*) [15thC. Via French from, ultimately, Latin *confrater* (see CONFRATERNITY).]

con·front /kən frúnt/ (**-front·ed, -front·ing, -fronts**) *vt.* **1. CHALLENGE FACE TO FACE** to come face to face with somebody, especially in a challenge, and usually with hostility, criticism, or defiance **2. MAKE AWARE OF SOMETHING** to bring somebody face to face with something such as contradictory facts or evidence **3. ENCOUNTER DIFFICULTY** to meet something face to face, especially an obstacle that must be overcome ○ *This is just one of the difficulties students confront these days.* **4. BE MET BY DIFFICULTY** to be met face to face by something that must be overcome ○ *The hardships that would confront the settlers were blissfully unknown when they started out.* [Mid-16thC. Via French *confronter* from medieval Latin *confrontare*, from Latin *front-*, stem of *frons* "forehead, face, front."] —**con·front·er** *n.*

con·fron·ta·tion /kònfrən táysh'n/ *n.* **1. ENCOUNTER** a face-to-face meeting or encounter with somebody or something **2.** RELIG **HOSTILITY WITHOUT WARFARE** hostility between nations often involving armed forces, yet stopping short of actual warfare **3. CONFLICT BETWEEN IDEAS OR PEOPLE** conflict between ideas, beliefs, or opinions, or between the people who hold them ○ *This country is headed for a confrontation over natural resources and whether exploiting them is a right or a privilege.* **4. COMPARISON OR OPPOSITION** a comparison or contrast between elements that have been brought together into a whole ○ *Her sculpture is a superb confrontation of traditional and modern elements.* —**con·fron·ta·tion·al** *adj.* —**con·fron·ta·tion·ist** *n., adj.*

Con·fu·cian /kən fyóosh'n/ *adj.* **RELATING TO CONFUCIUS'S TEACHINGS** relating to the teachings of Confucius or his followers, emphasizing self-control, adherence to a social hierarchy, and social and political order ■ *n.* **FOLLOWER OF CONFUCIUS'S TEACHINGS** somebody who follows the teachings of Confucius —**Con·fu·cian·ism** *n.* —**Con·fu·cian·ist** *n.*

Con·fu·cius /kən fyóoshəss/ (551?–479? B.C.) Chinese philosopher, administrator, and moralist. His social and moral teachings, collected in the *Analects*, tried to replace former religious observances.

con fuo·co /kòn foo ṓkō, kŏn foo ṓkō/ *adv.* to be played with energy, passion, and fire (*used as a musical direction*) [From Italian, literally "with fire"] —**con fuo·co** *adj.*

con·fuse /kən fyóoz/ (**-fused, -fus·ing, -fus·es**) *vt.* **1. MAKE UNABLE TO THINK INTELLIGENTLY** to make somebody unable to think or reason clearly or act sensibly **2. MAKE HARD TO UNDERSTAND** to make something hard or harder to understand **3. GET THINGS MIXED UP** to mistake one person or thing for another **4. EMBARRASS** to make somebody feel embarrassed or ill at ease **5. UPSET THE ORDER OF** to cause disorder in something or somebody ○ *The dense fog utterly confused traffic on the highway.* [14thC. Via French *confus* "perplexed" from Latin *confusus* "mixed up," from *confundere* "to mix together" (see CONFOUND).] —**con·fus·a·bil·i·ty** /kən fyóozə bíllətee/ *n.* —**con·fus·a·ble** *adj.*

con·fused /kən fyóozd/ *adj.* **1. UNABLE TO THINK INTELLIGENTLY** unable to think or reason clearly or to act sensibly **2. DISORDERED** in no logical or sensible order **3. EMBARRASSED** embarrassed and not knowing what to say or how to act **4. NOT DIFFERENTIATED** mistaken for each other **5. DISORIENTED** having impaired psychological capacity to the extent of being forgetful and no longer able to carry out simple everyday tasks —**con·fus·ed·ly** /-fyóozədlee/ *adv.* —**con·fus·ed·ness** *n.*

con·fus·ing /kən fyóozing/ *adj.* unclear and difficult to understand —**con·fus·ing·ly** *adv.*

con·fu·sion /kən fyóozh'n/ *n.* **1. BEWILDERMENT** the act of confusing somebody or something, or the state of being confused or perplexed **2. LACK OF CLARITY** misunderstanding of a situation or the facts **3. MISTAKING ONE FOR ANOTHER** a failure to distinguish between people or things **4. DISORDER** a chaotic or disordered state **5. EMBARRASSMENT** self-consiousness or embarrassment **6. DISORIENTED STATE OF MIND** a psychological state in which somebody is disoriented and unable to think clearly —**con·fu·sion·al** *adj.*

con·fu·ta·tion /kònfyə táysh'n/ *n.* (*formal*) **1. PROVING SOMETHING WRONG** proving that somebody is wrong or that something is false, invalid, or faulty ○ *The lawyer's confutation of the witness's testimony was decisive.* **2. SOMETHING THAT REFUTES SOMETHING ELSE** a fact, observation, or piece of evidence proving that somebody is wrong or that something is false, invalid, or faulty (*often used in the plural*) —**con·fu·ta·tive** /kən fyóotətiv/ *adj.*

con·fute /kən fyóot/ (**-fut·ed, -fut·ing, -futes**) *vt.* to prove conclusively that somebody is wrong or that something is false, invalid, or faulty (*formal*) [Early 16thC. From Latin *confutare* "to restrain, answer conclusively."] —**con·fut·a·ble** *adj.* —**con·fut·er** *n.*

cong. *abbr.* **1.** POL congress **2.** POL congressional **3.** RELIG congregational **4.** MEASURE, PHARM congius

Cong. *abbr.* **1.** POL Congress **2.** POL Congressional **3.** RELIG Congregational

con·ga /kóng gə/ *n.* **1. DANCE DONE IN A LINE** a Latin American dance in which people form a line and, holding the waist of the person ahead, move three steps forward rhythmically, then kick out a leg **2.** MUSIC FOR CONGA a piece of music to which people dance the conga **3.** = conga drum ■ *vi.* (**-gaed, -ga·ing, -gas**) DANCE to dance the conga [Mid-20thC. Via American Spanish *(danza) Conga* "dance from the Congo" from Spanish *Congo.*]

con·ga drum *n.* a tall tapering drum, played with both hands and used in Latin American and African music

con game *n.* a confidence game (*informal*)

con·gé /kón jày, kawN zháy/ (*plural* **-gés**), **con·gee** /kónjee, kən jée/ *n.* **1.** PERMISSION formal permission for somebody to leave (*formal*) **2.** DISMISSAL a dismissal, especially an abrupt one (*formal*) **3.** LEAVE-TAKING a departure (*formal*) **4.** BOW a formal bow (*formal*) **5.** ARCHIT CONCAVE MOLDING an architectural molding that is concave in shape [14thC. Via French *congié* from, ultimately, Latin *commeare* "to come and go."]

con·geal /kən jéel/ (**-gealed, -geal·ing, -geals**) *vti.* **1.** BECOME OR MAKE LIQUID THICK to become thick and solid or cause a liquid to thicken and solidify **2.** BECOME OR MAKE FIRM to become, or cause to become, firm and strong ○ *Let's act before opposition to our plan congeals.* [14thC. Via French *congeler* from Latin *congelare*, literally "to freeze together," from *gelu* "frost" (see GEL).] —**con·geal·er** *n.* —**con·geal·ment** *n.*

con·gealed sal·ad *n. Southern U.S.* a dish made of flavored gelatin and chopped fruit or vegetables and sometimes nuts, cottage cheese, or marshmallows that is set in a mold and served cold

con·gee *n.* = congé

con·ge·la·tion /kònjə láysh'n/ *n.* **1.** SOLIDIFYING OR SOLIDIFIED STATE the process of turning from a liquid into a solid, or the state of being solid as a result of congealing (*formal*) **2.** CONGEALED LIQUID a liquid that has solidified [15thC. Directly or via French from the Latin stem *congelation-*, from *congelare* (see CONGEAL).]

con·ge·ner /kónjənər, kən jéenər/ *n.* somebody or something that belongs to the same class, group, or type, e.g., an animal or plant of the same genus as another animal or plant, or two elements belonging to the same group [Mid-18thC. Formed from Latin *congenus* "of the same race," from *genus* "race" (see GENUS).]

con·ge·ner·ic /kònjə nérrik/ *adj.* used to describe organisms belonging to the same class, group, or type —**con·gen·er·ous** /kən jénnərəss, kon-/ *adj.*

con·gen·ial /kən jéenyəl, kən jéenee əl/ *adj.* **1.** AGREEABLE pleasant and suitable to somebody's character or taste or to a situation ○ *a very congenial atmosphere* **2.** KINDRED OR SIMILAR compatible in tastes, interests, attitudes, or backgrounds **3.** FRIENDLY having an outgoing pleasant character ○ *Her congenial nature makes her well-loved in the town.* [Early 17thC. Formed from Latin *con-* + GENIAL.] —**con·ge·ni·al·i·ty** /kən jèenee állətee/ *n.* —**con·gen·ial·ly** /-jéenyəlee, -jéenee əlee/ *adv.* —**con·gen·ial·ness** *n.*

con·gen·ic /kən jénnik/ *adj.* used to describe animal cells that are genetically identical except for the arrangement of genes in a single restricted chromosome region (**locus**)

con·gen·i·tal /kən jénnit'l/ *adj.* **1.** MED EXISTING AT BIRTH used to describe an abnormal condition present at birth **2.** INGRAINED IN SOMEBODY'S CHARACTER firmly established as part of somebody's character or beliefs [Late 18thC. Formed from Latin *congenitus*, literally "born with," from *genitus* "born" (see GENITAL).] —**con·gen·i·tal·ly** *adv.* —**con·gen·i·tal·ness** *n.*

con·gen·i·tal a·nom·a·ly *n.* a birth defect (*technical*)

con·ger eel /kóng gər-/, **con·ger** *n.* a large scaleless eel found in temperate and tropical coastal waters of the Atlantic Ocean. Latin name: *Conger oceanicus.* [14thC. Via French *congre* from, ultimately, Greek *gongros*.]

con·ge·ries /kən jéer eez, kónjə reez/ (*plural* **-ries**) *n.* a collection or assortment of things (*takes a singular verb*) [Mid-16thC. From Latin, "heap, pile," from *congerere* (see CONGEST).]

con·gest /kən jést/ (**-gest·ed, -gest·ing, -gests**) *vti.* **1.** BLOCK OR BECOME BLOCKED to overcrowd a street or area, or become overcrowded so that movement is slow or difficult **2.** MED HAVE TOO MUCH FLUID to accumulate an abnormal amount of blood or fluid in an organ or body part, as a result of disease or infection [15thC. From Latin *congest-*, past participle stem of *congerere* "to collect, heap up," literally "to carry together," from *gerere* "to carry" (see GESTURE).] —**con·gest·i·ble** *adj.* —**con·ges·tive** *adj.*

con·gest·ed /kən jéstəd/ *adj.* **1.** PACKED WITH TRAFFIC OR PEOPLE overcrowded with traffic or people, making movement slow and difficult **2.** MED CONTAINING TOO MUCH FLUID having an abnormal amount of blood or other fluid in a vessel or organ, as a result of disease or infection

con·ges·tion /kən jéschən/ *n.* **1.** EXCESSIVE TRAFFIC OR PEOPLE a state of overcrowding in a street or other area, making movement slow or difficult **2.** MED ABNORMAL ACCUMULATION OF FLUID the condition of having an abnormal amount of blood or fluid accumulate in an organ or body part, as a result of disease or infection **3.** COMPUT HAVING TOO MUCH INFORMATION TO TRANSFER in computing, a situation that arises when the amount of information to be transferred is greater than the data communication path can carry

con·ges·tive heart fail·ure *n.* a form of heart failure in which the heart is unable to pump away the blood returning to it fast enough, causing congestion in the veins

con·gi·us /kónjee əss/ (*plural* **-i** /-ī/) *n.* **1.** PHARM LIQUID MEASURE EQUAL TO ONE GALLON in pharmacy, a unit of measure for liquids equal to one gallon, which is 4.546 liters in the United Kingdom or 3.7854 liters in the United States **2.** HIST ROMAN MEASURE a unit of measure used by the ancient Romans equal to approximately 0.84 U.S. gallons/3.3 liters [14thC. From Latin, measure of one eighth of an amphora.]

con·glo·bate /kən glṓ bàyt, kóng glṑ bayt/ *vti.* (**-bat·ed, -bat·ing, -bates**) MAKE OR BECOME BALL-SHAPED to form or be formed into a globe or ball (*formal*) ■ *adj.* BALL-SHAPED shaped like a ball (*archaic*) [Mid-17thC. From Latin *conglobat-*, past participle stem of *conglobare* "to make into a ball," from *globus* "ball" (source of English *globe*).] —**con·glo·ba·tion** /kòng glō báysh'n/ *n.*

con·globe /kon glṓb/ (**-globed, -glob·ing, -globes**) *vti.* = **conglobate** *v.* (*formal*)

con·glom·er·ate *n.* /kən glómmərət/ **1.** BUSINESS BUSINESS ORGANIZATION INVOLVED IN MANY AREAS a large business organization that consists of a number of companies that deal with a variety of different business, manufacturing, or commercial activities **2.** SOMETHING MADE BY COMBINING THINGS something formed by gathering together a number of dissimilar materials or elements **3.** GEOL ROCK COMPRISING PIECES OF OTHER ROCKS coarse-grained sedimentary rock containing fragments of other rock larger than 0.08 in./2 mm in diameter, held together with another material such as clay ■ *adj.* /kən glómmərət/ FORMED BY COMBINING DIFFERENT THINGS consisting of a mass or accumulation of dissimilar materials or elements ■ *vti.* /kən glómmə ràyt/ (**-at·ed, -at·ing, -ates**) BRING THINGS TOGETHER TO FORM MASS to gather together materials or elements, or to be gathered together into a mass [Late 16thC. From Latin *conglomeratus* "wound into a ball," from *glomer-*, stem of *glomus* "ball."] —**con·glom·er·at·ic** /kən glòmmə ráttik/ *adj.* —**con·glom·er·it·ic** /-ríttik/ *adj.* —**con·glom·er·a·tor** /kən glómmə ràytər/ *n.*

con·glom·er·at·ed /kən glómmə ràytəd/ *adj.* made up of and controlling many parts of an industry ○ *a conglomerated corporation*

con·glom·er·a·tion /kən glòmmə ráysh'n/ *n.* **1.** MASS OF DIFFERENT THINGS an accumulation or mass of dissimilar materials or elements **2.** FORMATION OF A MASS the gathering together of different materials or elements, or the state of being gathered together into a mass —**con·glom·er·a·tive** /kən glómmərətiv, -ràytiv/ *adj.*

con·glu·ti·nate /kən glóot'n àyt, kon-/ (**-nat·ed, -nat·ing, -nates**) *vti.* to become stuck together, or cause two or more things to become stuck together (*formal*) [15thC. From Latin *conglutinat-*, past participle stem of *conglutinare* "to glue together," from *gluten* "glue" (source of English *glue*).] —**con·glu·ti·na·tive** *adj.*

Con·go /kóng gō/ Africa's second longest river, which provides a major transportation network. It rises in the north of the Democratic Republic of Congo and empties into the Atlantic Ocean. Length: 2,710 mi./4,374 km. Former name **Zaire River**

Con·go, Dem·o·crat·ic Re·pub·lic of large equatorial country of Central Africa with a coastline on the Atlantic Ocean. Language: French. Currency: new zaire. Capital: Kinshasa. Population: 447,589,551 (1997). Area: 905,365 sq. mi./2,344,885 sq. km. Official name **Democratic Republic of the Congo**. Former name **Congo Free State** (1880s-1908). Former name **Belgian Congo** (1908–60). Former name **Zaire**

Democratic Republic of Congo

(1971–97) —**Con·go·lese** /kòng gə léez, -léess/ *adj.*, *n.*

Con·go, Re·pub·lic of republic in West Africa, on the coast of the Atlantic Ocean. Language: French. Currency: CFA franc. Capital: Brazzaville. Population: 2,599,713 (1997). Area: 132,000 sq. mi./342,000 sq. km. Former name **People's Republic of the Congo** —**Con·go·lese** *adj.*, *n.*

Republic of Congo

con·go dye *n.* any of a number of dyes containing nitrogen, usually derived from benzidine [*Congo* from the perception that it is associated either with the region of the Congo, or with African Americans from this region]

Con·go eel *n.* an amphibian of the southeastern United States that has a long body with gill slits and two pairs of rudimentary limbs that enable it to travel on land. Latin name: *Amphiuma means.* [As CONGO DYE]

Con·go Free State former name for **Congo [Democratic Republic of]**

Con·go red *n.* a dye that is red in alkaline solutions and blue in acid solutions. It is used as a chemical indicator, a biological stain, and a dye for cotton and wool. [As CONGO DYE]

Con·go snake *n.* = **Congo eel**

con·gou /kóng gō, kóng gȯȯ/ *n.* a fine grade of Chinese black tea, made from the largest leaf gathered from the tip of a shoot on a tea plant [Early 18thC. Shortening of Cantonese Chinese *kungfúch'a* and Mandarin *gōngfu chá* "tea made for refined tastes," literally "effort tea."]

con·grats /kən gráts/ *npl.*, *interj.* an expression of congratulations (*informal*) [Early 20thC. Shortening.]

con·grat·u·late /kən gráchə làyt/ (**-lat·ed, -lat·ing, -lates**) *v.* **1.** *vt.* EXPRESS PLEASURE AT SOMEBODY'S GOOD FORTUNE to express pleasure or approval to somebody for an achievement or good fortune or on a special occasion **2.** *vr.* FEEL PLEASED WITH SOMETHING to feel self-satisfied in having success or good fortune ○ *I was congratulating myself on my driving skills, when I skidded into a snow bank.* [Mid-16thC. From Latin *congratulat-*, past participle stem of *congratulari* "to rejoice with," from *gratus* "pleasing, thankful" (source of English *grateful*).] —**con·grat·u·la·tor** /-làytər/ *n.* —**con·grat·u·la·to·ry** /-lə tàwree/ *adj.*

con·grat·u·la·tion /-gràchə láysh'n/ *n.* ACT OF CONGRATULATING SOMEBODY the expressing of pleasure to somebody for an achievement or good fortune or on a special occasion ○ *The bride's father made a short speech of congratulation to the newly married couple.* ■ *npl.*, *interj.* **con·grat·u·la·tions** EXPRESSION OF JOY FOR SOMEBODY'S ACHIEVEMENT an expression of pleasure or acknowledgment of somebody's success or good fortune or on a special occasion

con·gre·gant /kóng grəgənt/ *n.* a member of a religious congregation [Late 19thC. From Latin *congregant-*, present participle stem of *congregare* (see CONGREGATE).]

con·gre·gate *vti.* /kóng grə gàyt/ (**-gat·ed, -gat·ing, -gates**) **ASSEMBLE PEOPLE OR ANIMALS** to come together in a group, or gather people or animals together in a group ■ *adj.* /kóng grəgət/ (*formal*) **1. HAVING COME TOGETHER** gathered or assembled in a group **2. RELATING TO A GATHERING** relating to an assembled group [15thC. From Latin *congregat-*, past participle stem of *congregare* "to collect together," from *greg-*, stem of *grex* "flock" (source of English *egregious*).] —**con·gre·ga·tive** *adj.* —**con·gre·ga·tor** *n.*

con·gre·ga·tion /kòng grə gáysh'n/ *n.* **1.** RELIG **GROUP OF WORSHIPERS** a group of people who have gathered together for a religious service **2.** RELIG **MEMBERS OF SAME CHURCH** the members of a particular church **3.** CHR **ROMAN CATHOLIC RELIGIOUS BODY** a Roman Catholic religious body whose members follow a common rule of life and are bound by simple vows (*formal*) **4.** CHR **DIVISION OF ROMAN CATHOLIC CENTRAL ADMINISTRATION** a section of the central administrative organization (**Curia**) of the Roman Catholic Church **5.** CHR **COMMITTEE OF ROMAN CATHOLIC BISHOPS** a committee of Roman Catholic bishops responsible for handling the business of a general council (*formal*) **6. GATHERING** a group of people or things gathered together ○ *A congregation of reporters waited outside the courthouse.* **7. COMING TOGETHER** the act of gathering together or assembling (*formal*) ○ *Congregation in the halls is not allowed.*

con·gre·ga·tion·al /kòng grə gáyshən'l, -gáyshnəl/ *adj.* relating to a congregation

Con·gre·ga·tion·al *adj.* relating to Congregationalism or its followers

Con·gre·ga·tion·al Church *n.* a Protestant denomination in which each church is self-governing

con·gre·ga·tion·al·ism /kòng grə gáyshən'l ìzzəm, -gáyshnə-/ *n.* a system of church organization in which each church is self-governing —**con·gre·ga·tion·al·ist** *n., adj.*

Con·gre·ga·tion·al·ism *n.* a Protestant denomination with a system of government in which each local church governs itself —**Con·gre·ga·tion·al·ist** *n., adj.*

con·gress /kóng grəss/ *n.* **1. CONFERENCE OR MEETING OF REPRESENTATIVES** a conference or formal meeting of delegates or representatives, such as the representatives of a group of nations, to discuss matters of interest or concern **2. ORGANIZED GROUP** a society or organization of people with common interests and concerns **3. GATHERING FOR A MEETING** the act of meeting, especially a single occurrence for a special purpose (*dated formal*) **4. SEXUAL INTERCOURSE** sexual intercourse (*dated formal*) [15thC. From Latin *congressus*, past participle of *congredi* "to go together," from *gradi* "to proceed, step" (source of English *aggressive*).]

Con·gress *n.* **1. U.S. LEGISLATURE** the national legislative body of the United States, consisting of the House of Representatives and the Senate **2. SESSION OF CONGRESS OR ITS MEMBERS** a two-year term of Congress, or the members of Congress during such a term ○ *the 22nd Congress* **3. GOVERNING AND LAW-MAKING BODY** the governing and law-making body in some countries ○ *the National People's Congress* **4. NAME OF CERTAIN POLITICAL PARTIES** shortened name of a number of political parties whose name includes the word "Congress," e.g., the African National Congress or the Indian Congress Party

con·gres·sion·al /kən gréshən'l, -gréshnəl/ *adj.* relating to a congress —**con·gres·sion·al·ist** *n.* —**con·gres·sion·al·ly** *adv.*

Con·gres·sion·al *adj.* relating to the U.S. Congress or its members

con·gres·sion·al dis·trict *n.* a district within a U.S. state that is entitled to elect one representative to the House of Representatives

Con·gres·sion·al Med·al of Hon·or *n.* the highest military decoration in the United States, awarded by Congress for outstanding bravery in action

Con·gres·sion·al Rec·ord *n.* a government journal in the United States that records and publishes the proceedings of Congress

con·gress·man /kóng grəssmən/ (*plural* **-men** /-mən/) *n.* a man who is a member of the U.S. Congress, especially of the House of Representatives

Con·gress of In·dus·tri·al Or·ga·ni·za·tions *n.* a federation of industrial trade unions formed in the United States in 1935 and merged with the American Federation of Labor in 1955 to form the AFL-CIO

Con·gress of Vi·en·na *n.* a congress held in Vienna between 1814 and 1815 to deal with the territorial and jurisdictional problems remaining after the defeat of Napoleon in the Napoleonic Wars

con·gress·per·son /kóng grəss pùrs'n/ (*plural* **-peo·ple** /-pèep'l/) *n.* a member of the U.S. Congress, especially of the House of Representatives

con·gress·wom·an /kóng grəss wòommən/ (*plural* **-en** /-wìmmin/) *n.* a woman who is a member of the U.S. Congress, especially of the House of Representatives

con·gru·ence /kóng groo əns, kən gróo əns/ *n.* **1. AGREEMENT** a coinciding, agreeing, or being in harmony **2.** MATH **STATEMENT ABOUT NUMBERS OR GEOMETRICAL SHAPES** a statement that two quantities or geometrical structures are congruent

con·gru·ent /kóng groo ənt, kən gróo-/ *adj.* **1. IN AGREEMENT** corresponding to or consistent with each other or something else (*formal*) ○ *We receive congruent sensations from the world around us.* **2.** GEOM **WITH THE SAME SHAPE** with identical geometric shapes **3.** MATH **DIFFERING BY EXACTLY DIVISIBLE AMOUNT** used to describe two numbers whose difference is exactly divisible by a third number (**modulus**) [15thC. From Latin *congruent-*, present participle stem of *congruere* "to meet together, agree," from *ruere* "to fall."] —**con·gru·ent·ly** *adv.*

con·gru·i·ty /kən gróo ətee/ *n.* (*formal*) **1. AGREEMENT OR CONSISTENCY** the state or fact of agreeing or being consistent with each other or with something else **2. APPROPRIATENESS** the quality or fact of being suitable or appropriate for something **3. SOMETHING AGREED UPON** a point on which there is agreement

con·gru·ous /kóng groo əss/ *adj.* **1. APPROPRIATE** appropriate to or suitable for a particular thing or situation (*formal*) **2. CORRESPONDING OR CONSISTENT** corresponding to or consistent with each other or something else [Late 16thC. Formed from Latin *congruus* "agreeing, suitable," from *congruere* (see CONGRUENT).] —**con·gru·ous·ly** *adv.* —**con·gru·ous·ness** *n.*

con·ic /kónnik/ *adj.* = **conical** ■ *n.* = **conic section** [Late 16thC. Via modern Latin *conicus* from Greek *kōnikos*, from *kōnos* (see CONE).]

con·i·cal /kónnik'l/ *adj.* **1. CONE-SHAPED** shaped like a cone **2.** GEOM **OF A CONE** relating to or having the form of a geometrical cone

con·ic pro·jec·tion *n.* a method of making a map by projecting the globe onto a surrounding cone whose point is above one of the poles and then flattening the cone, or a map so made. On a conic projection, the parallels of latitude appear as concentric circles, and the lines of longitude radiate from the center as equal radii.

con·ics /kónniks/ *n.* the branch of geometry involving the study of conic sections

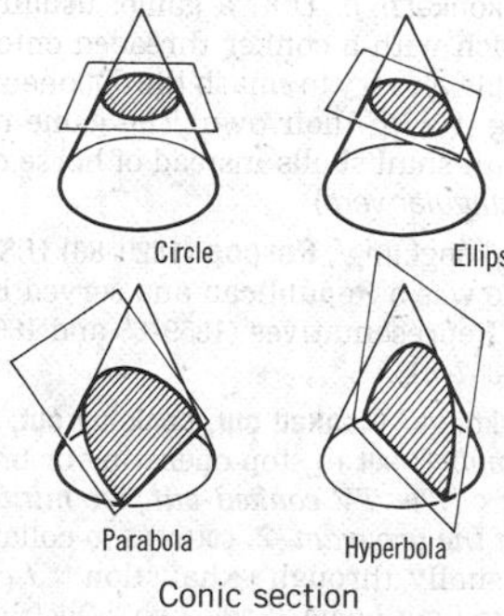

Conic section

con·ic sec·tion *n.* a curve produced by the intersection of a plane with a circular cone, e.g., a circle, ellipse, hyperbola, or parabola

co·nid·i·a plural of **conidium**

co·nid·i·o·phore /kə níddee ə fàwr/ *n.* a simple or branched part (**hypha**) of a fungus that produces spores asexually [Late 19thC. Coined from CONIDIUM + -PHORE.] —**co·nid·i·oph·or·ous** /kə nìddee óffərəss/ *adj.*

co·nid·i·um /kə níddee əm/ (*plural* **-a** /-ə/) *n.* an asexually produced spore of certain types of fungi [Late 19thC. From modern Latin, from Greek *konis* "dust."] —**co·nid·i·al** *adj.*

co·ni·fer /kónnəfər/ *n.* any tree that has thin leaves (**needles**) and produces cones. Many types are evergreen. Pines, firs, junipers, larches, spruces, and yews are conifers. Order: Coniferales. [Mid-19thC. From Latin, literally "cone-bearing," from Greek *kōnos* "cone."] —**co·nif·er·ous** /kə níffərəss/ *adj.*

co·ni·ine /kṓnee èen/ *n.* a colorless substance with poisonous properties found in poison hemlock. Formula: $C_8H_{17}N$. [Mid-19thC. Coined from *conium* "hemlock" from Latin+ -ine.]

conj. *abbr.* **1.** GRAM conjugation **2. conj.** ASTRON, GRAM conjunction **3. conj.** GRAM conjunctive

con·jec·tur·al /kən jékchərəl/ *adj.* **1. BASED ON GUESSWORK** based on or involving conjecture **2. INCLINED TO SPECULATE** inclined to make guesses or speculations —**con·jec·tur·al·ly** *adv.*

con·jec·ture /kən jékchər/ *n.* **1. GUESSWORK** the formation of judgments or opinions on the basis of incomplete or inconclusive information **2. SOMETHING BASED ON GUESSWORK** a conclusion, judgment, or statement based on incomplete or inconclusive information ■ *vti.* (**-tured, -tur·ing, -tures**) **GUESS** to form an opinion or judgment based on incomplete or inconclusive information [14thC. Directly or via French from Latin *conjectura*, from, ultimately, *conjicere*, literally "to throw together," from *jacere* "to throw."] —**con·jec·tur·a·ble** *adj.* —**con·jec·tur·a·bly** *adv.* —**con·jec·tur·er** *n.*

con·join /kən jóyn/ (**-joined, -join·ing, -joins**) *vti.* to join two or more things together, or become joined together (*formal*) [14thC. Via French *conjoindre* from Latin *conjungere*, literally "to join together," from *jungere* "to join" (see JOIN).] —**con·join·er** *n.*

con·joint /kən jóynt/ *adj.* **1. BY TWO COMBINED THINGS** done by, involving, or relating to two or more combined entities ○ *a conjoint project* **2. LINKED** joined together or combined —**con·joint·ly** *adv.*

con·ju·gal /kónjəg'l/ *adj.* relating to marriage or to husbands and wives [Early 16thC. From Latin *conjugalis*, from *conjugare* (see CONJUGATE).] —**con·ju·gal·i·ty** /kònjə gállətee/ *n.* —**con·ju·gal·ly** /kónjəgəlee/ *adv.*

con·ju·gal rights *npl.* the rights that husbands or wives are entitled to in a marriage, especially the right to have sexual relations with their spouse

con·ju·gal vis·it *n.* a visit to a jail by the husband or wife of a prisoner, during which the couple is allowed some privacy, e.g., to allow them to have sexual relations

con·ju·gant /kónjəgənt/ *n.* either of a pair of organisms, cells, or gametes in the process of reproducing [Early 20thC. From Latin *conjugant-*, present participle stem of *conjugare* (see CONJUGATE).]

con·ju·gate *v.* /kónjə gàyt/ (**-gat·ed, -gat·ing, -gates**) **1.** *vti.* GRAM **STATE DIFFERENT GRAMMATICAL FORMS OF VERB** to state systematically the different forms a verb has according to tense, mood, person, and number **2.** *vi.* GRAM **HAVE DIFFERENT GRAMMATICAL FORMS** to have different grammatical forms according to tense, mood, number, and person (*refers to verbs*) **3.** *vt.* CHEM **JOIN SUBSTANCES** to join two substances together in such a way that they can easily be separated again, especially in chemical reactions **4.** *vi.* BIOL **REPRODUCE** to reproduce by physically joining in order to transfer genetic information (*refers to organisms that normally reproduce by division*) ■ *adj.* /kónjəgət, -gàyt/ **1. PAIRED** joined together in pairs (*formal*) **2.** MATH **ADDING UP TO 360 DEGREES** used to describe a pair of angles that together add up to 360 degrees **3.** CHEM **DIFFERING BY ONE PROTON** used to describe substances that have such similar molecular structures that one becomes the other through the gain or loss of a proton **4.** CHEM **EXISTING TOGETHER IN STATE OF EQUILIBRIUM** used to describe a state of chemical equilibrium in which two liquids coexist in separate forms, one being the solute and the other the solvent ■ *n.* /kónjəgət, -gàyt/ **1.** GRAM **VERB FORM** one of the different forms of a verb according to tense, mood, person, or number **2. RESULT OF JOINING TWO THINGS** a product of joining or union **3.** MATH = **conjugate complex number** [15thC. From Latin *conjugatus*, past participle of *conjugare*, literally "to yoke together," hence "to marry." The grammatical sense comes from the idea of a set of verbs belonging together.] —**con·jug·a·ble** /kónjəgəb'l/ *adj.* —**con·ju·gate·ly** /-gətlee, -gàytlee/ *adv.* —**con·ju·gate·ness** *n.* —**con·ju·ga·tive** *adj.* —**con·ju·ga·tor** *n.*

con·ju·gate com·plex num·ber *n.* either of a pair of complex numbers that are symmetrically located on either side of an x-axis, differing only in the sign of the imaginary component

con·ju·gat·ed /kónjə gàytəd/ *adj.* **1. CONTAINING ALTERNATING CHEMICAL BONDS** containing two or more double or triple bonds in alternation with single bonds **2. SEPARATED BY SINGLE CHEMICAL BOND** used to describe a double chemical bond separated by a single bond

con·ju·gat·ed pro·tein *n.* a compound containing a series of amino acids that form a simple protein attached to a nonprotein, e.g., a carbohydrate or lipid group

con·ju·ga·tion /kònjə gáysh'n/ *n.* **1.** GRAM **INFLECTION OF VERB** the different patterns of inflection of a given verb **2.** GRAM **GROUP OF VERBS WITH SAME INFLECTIONS** a group of verbs that use the same patterns of inflection **3.** GRAM **SET OF VERB INFLECTIONS** the complete set of inflections for a given verb **4. ACT OF JOINING TOGETHER** the act of joining together or uniting, or the state of being joined together **5.** BIOL **REPRODUCTION IN SIMPLE ORGANISMS** the simplest form of reproduction, in which two single-celled organisms, e.g., bacteria or protozoans, link together, exchange genetic information, and then separate **6.** BIOL **FUSION OF NUCLEI** the fusion of the nuclei of a male and a female gamete in algae and fungi **7.** GENETICS **PAIRING OF CHROMOSOMES** the distribution of pairs of chromosomes into the four nuclei produced by the division of a parent nucleus **8.** CHEM **ALTERNATION OF NUMBER OF BONDS** the occurrence of two or more double or triple bonds in alternation with single bonds in a molecule —**con·ju·ga·tion·al** *adj.* —**con·ju·ga·tion·al·ly** *adv.*

con·junct *adj.* /kən júngkt, kón jùngkt/ **1. ATTACHED OR JOINED** attached or joined very close to something **2.** LING **ADJACENT TO CONSONANT** used to describe consonants that are next to each other within a word without a vowel or vowels between **3.** MUSIC **CONSISTING OF SINGLE STEPS IN SCALE** relating to or consisting of adjacent notes in a musical scale ■ *n.* /kón jùngkt/ LOGIC **EITHER PROPOSITION IN CONJUNCTION** either of the two propositions or formulas in a conjunction in logic [15thC. From Latin *conjunctus*, the past participle of *conjungere* (see CONJOIN).] —**con·junct·ly** /kən júngktlee/ *adv.*

con·junc·tion /kən júngkshən/ *n.* **1. COMBINING OF SEVERAL THINGS** the joining together or combining of two or more things **2. SIMULTANEOUS OCCURRENCE** a simultaneous occurrence of events or circumstances **3.** GRAM **CONNECTING WORD** a word that is used to link sentences, clauses, phrases, or words, e.g., "and," "but," or "if" **4.** ASTRON **ALIGNMENT WITH SUN** the position of a planet or the Moon when aligned with the Sun, as seen from Earth **5.** ASTRON **CLOSE PROXIMITY OF PLANETS** the appearance of two planets very close to each other or in the same place on the celestial sphere **6.** ASTROL **ASPECT OF 0° BETWEEN PLANETS** in astrology, an aspect of 0° between two planets **7.** LOGIC **TYPE OF COMPOUND STATEMENT** a proposition in logic of the form "A and B" that is true only if both A and B are true [14thC. From the Latin stem *conjunction-*, from *conjunct-*, the past participle stem of *conjungere* (see CONJOIN).] —**con·junc·tion·al** *adj.* —**con·junc·tion·al·ly** *adv.* ◇ **in conjunction with** together with or combined with something

con·junc·ti·va /kòn jungk tívə/ (*plural* **-vas** *or* **-vae** /-vee/) *n.* a delicate mucous membrane that covers the internal part of the eyelid and is attached to the cornea [14thC. From medieval Latin *(tunica) conjunctiva* "connective (membrane)," from Latin *conjunct-*, the past participle stem of *conjungere* (see CONJOIN).] —**con·junc·ti·val** *adj.*

con·junc·tive /kən júngktiv/ *adj.* **1. CONNECTIVE** serving to join things together **2. COMBINED** joined together or combined with something else **3.** GRAM **OF GRAMMATICAL CONJUNCTIONS** relating to conjunctions or their grammatical function, or consisting of conjunctions ■ *n.* GRAM **CONJUNCTION** a conjunction (*archaic*) [15thC. From late Latin *conjunctivus*, from Latin *conjunct-*, the past participle stem of *conjungere* (see CONJOIN).] —**con·junc·tive·ly** *adv.*

con·junc·tive ad·verb *n.* an adverb or adverbial phrase that is used to connect parts or clauses of a sentence

con·junc·tive eye move·ment *n.* a simultaneous movement of both eyes in the same direction

con·junc·ti·vi·tis /kən jùngkti vítiss/ *n.* inflammation of the conjunctiva caused by infection, injury, or allergy

con·ju·ra·tion /kònjə ráysh'n/ *n.* **1. MAGIC SPELL** a word or phrase that a magician says when casting a spell (*literary*) **2. INVOCATION OF SUPERNATURAL FORCE** a summoning or invoking, usually of a supernatural force, by pronouncing a sacred name (*literary*) **3. MAGIC TRICK** a magic or supernatural occurrence achieved by pronouncing a spell or chanting **4. PERFORMANCE OF TRICKS** the performance of illusions or tricks (*archaic*) **5. BEGGING** pleading or begging (*archaic*)

con·jure /kónjər/ (**-jured, -jur·ing, -jures**) *v.* **1.** *vi.* **PERFORM MAGIC TRICKS** to perform illusions and magic tricks that require agile hand movements, usually for entertainment **2.** *vti.* **INVOKE SUPERNATURAL FORCES** to call upon or order a supernatural force or being by reciting a spell ○ *He was struck dumb by the very demons he was conjuring.* **3.** *vt.* **INFLUENCE WITH SPELL** to change or influence something by reciting a spell or invocation **4.** *vt.* **COMMAND SOLEMNLY** to command somebody solemnly to do something (*archaic*) **5.** *vt.* **IMPLORE** to implore somebody to do something (*archaic*) ○ *I conjure you to show me mercy.* [13thC. Via Old French from, ultimately, Latin *conjurare* "to bind with an oath," literally "to swear together," from *jurare* (see JURY).]

conjure up *vt.* **1. EVOKE** to create something in the mind ○ *This music conjures up images of rural scenes.* **2. PRODUCE AS IF BY MAGIC** to produce or create something difficult or unexpected as if by magic ○ *She conjured up a delicious meal from the most basic ingredients.* **3. SUMMON SUPERNATURAL BEING** to call upon a supernatural force or being by reciting a spell or chanting magic words

con·jur·er /kónjərər/, **con·jur·or** *n.* **1. ENTERTAINER WHO PERFORMS TRICKS** somebody who performs tricks involving manual agility and the illusion of magic, as an entertainment **2. SORCERER** somebody who is believed to practice magic or conjure supernatural forces or beings

conk[1] /kongk/ *n.* **BLOW TO THE HEAD** a blow, especially on the head (*slang*) ■ *vt.* (**conked, conk·ing, conks**) **HIT ON HEAD** to hit somebody, especially on the head (*slang*) [Early 19thC. Origin uncertain: possibly an alteration of CONCH.]

conk[2] /kongk/ *n.* the hard fruiting body, shaped like a shelf, of certain fungi that grow on trees or decaying wood [Mid-19thC. Origin uncertain: possibly an alteration of CONCH.]

conk[3] /kongk/ *n.* **STRAIGHT HAIRSTYLE** a hairstyle in which very curly hair is straightened by applying a chemical treatment ■ *vt.* (**conked, conk·ing, conks**) **STRAIGHTEN HAIR** to straighten very curly hair by applying a chemical treatment [Mid-20thC. Origin uncertain: possibly a shortening of *congolene*, a substance for straightening hair.]

conk·er /kónkər/ *n. U.K.* a horse chestnut, without its spiny outer casing, used in the game of conkers [Mid-19thC. Origin uncertain: apparently a blend of CONCH, CONK, and CONQUER.]

conk·ers /kónkərz/ *n. U.K.* a game, usually for two people, each with a conker threaded onto a string, in which players try to smash the opponent's conker by hitting it with their own. The game used to be played with snail shells instead of horse chestnuts. (*takes a singular verb*)

Conk·ling /kóngkling/, **Roscoe** (1829–88) U.S. political leader. He was a Republican and served in the U.S. House of Representatives (1859–63 and 1865–67) and Senate (1867–81).

conk out /kongk/ (**conked out, conk·ing out, conks out**) *vi.* (*informal*) **1. FAIL** to stop operating or break down suddenly ○ *The TV conked out five minutes before the end of the program.* **2. COLLAPSE** to collapse or fall asleep, usually through exhaustion ○ *I conked out the minute I got home.* [Early 20thC. Origin unknown.]

con man (*plural* **con men**) *n.* somebody who uses deception and persuasive speech to get people to part with their money (*informal*) [*Con* shortening of CONFIDENCE, shortening of CONFIDENCE MAN]

con mo·to /kon mṓtō/ *adv.* to be performed in a lively or brisk way (*used as a musical direction*) [Early 19thC. From Italian, literally "with movement."]

conn *vt., n.* = **con**

con·nate /kó nàyt, kə náyt/ *adj.* **1.** BOT **UNITED BY GROWTH** used to describe parts that have grown closely joined to a single structure in a plant or animal **2.** GEOL **FORMED SIMULTANEOUSLY WITH SURROUNDING ROCK** used to describe water, usually very saline, that has been trapped in sedimentary rock since the original deposits were laid down [Mid-17thC. From late Latin *connatus*, the past participle of *connasci*, literally "to be born with," from Latin *nasci* (see NATIVE).] —**con·nate·ly** *adv.* —**con·nate·ness** *n.*

con·nect /kə nékt/ (**-nect·ed, -nect·ing, -nects**) *v.* **1.** *vti.* **LINK TWO THINGS** to link or join two or more parts, things, or people ○ *All you have to do is connect these two wires, and it should work.* ○ *A flagstone walk connected the main house with the toolshed.* **2.** *vt.* **ASSOCIATE WITH SOMETHING ELSE** to make a psychological or emotional association between people, things, or events ○ *She always connected that house with family celebrations.* ○ *There was no evidence to connect them to the robbery.* **3.** *vt.* TELECOM **ESTABLISH TELECOMMUNICATION** to set up a communication link between people, organizations, or places ○ *All my friends are connected to the Internet.* **4.** *vt.* PUBL **LINK UP TO UTILITY** to link people or equipment to a source of electricity, water, or gas ○ *Have they connected your cable yet?* ○ *After we paid the fee, they finally connected our gas line.* **5.** *vi.* TRANSP **ALLOW TIME FOR PASSENGERS TO TRANSFER** to arrive shortly before another vehicle or vessel departs, or shortly after another arrives, so as to allow passengers to change from one to the other ○ *The local train connects with the express twice a day.* **6.** *vi.* TRANSP **MAKE TRANSPORTATION CONNECTION** to change from one vehicle or vessel to another ○ *those wishing to connect with the overseas flight* **7.** *vi.* **HIT SOMETHING FIRMLY** to strike, punch, or kick firmly, with good contact between the striking surface and the object struck (*informal*) ○ *The punch connected, and he sank to the ground.* **8.** *vi.* **GET ALONG WELL WITH SOMEBODY** to have a good rapport with somebody ○ *The interview was a disaster – we never really connected.* [15thC. From Latin *connectere*, literally "to tie together," from *nectere* (see NEXUS).] —**con·nect·i·ble** *adj.*

connect up *vti.* = **connect**

con·nect·ed /kə néktəd/ *adj.* **1. JOINED TOGETHER** joined or linked firmly together **2. WITH BENEFICIAL SOCIAL CONNECTIONS** with useful business or social connections (*often used in combination*) **3.** *U.K.* **WITH WEALTHY RELATIVES** with upper-class or wealthy relatives (*often used in combination*) ○ *Her husband is well connected.* **4. LOGICAL AND INTELLIGIBLE** ordered in a logical and intelligible way **5.** MATH **DESCRIBING MATHEMATICAL RELATION** used to describe a mathematical relation for which either the relation or its converse is true for any two members in a set —**con·nect·ed·ly** *adv.* —**con·nect·ed·ness** *n.*

con·nect·er *n.* = **connector**

Connecticut

Con·nect·i·cut /kə néttikət/ **1.** southernmost state in New England. It is bordered on the north by Massachusetts, on the east by Rhode Island, on the south by the Long Island Sound, and on the west by New York State. Population: 3,287,116 (1990). Area: 5,544 sq. mi./14,359 sq. km. **2.** longest river of New England, flowing southward from Massachusetts to enter Long Island Sound. Length: 407 mi./655 km.

con·nect·ing rod *n.* a rod that transmits motion, especially the rod that connects the crankshaft to the piston in an internal combustion engine

con·nec·tion /kə nékshən/ *n.* **1. LINKING THINGS TOGETHER** the linking or joining of two or more parts, things, or people **2. PHYSICAL LINK** something that links two or more things ○ *check for a loose connection* **3. LOGICAL LINK** a linking association between people, things, or events **4. TRANSPORTATION LINK** an opportunity for passengers to use any of a variety of transportation options, or to change from one form of transportation to another ○ *If we don't hurry, we'll miss our connection in Boston.* **5.** VEHICLE SCHEDULED TO PERMIT TRANSFER a particular bus, train, ferry, or plane that is scheduled to arrive at such a time as to allow passengers to transfer onto it from another scheduled form of transport ○ *Your connection will arrive on platform ten at 9:15.* **6.** COMMUNICATION LINK a communication link, especially between telephones **7.** CONTEXT the relationship of something with its context ○ *In this connection, we need to tighten up all the safety procedures.* **8.** INFLUENTIAL CONTACT a friend, relative, or associate who either has or has access to influence or power (*often used in the plural*) ○ *She used her connections to finagle an interview with the lead singer.* **9.** RELATION somebody who is related to another person, usually distantly or by marriage (*often used in the plural*) **10.** SUPPLIER OF ILLEGAL SUBSTANCES a supplier of illegal substances, usually drugs (*slang*) [14thC. From the Latin stem *connexion-*, from *connex-*, the past participle stem of *connectere* (see CONNECT). The spelling was influenced by CONNECT.] —**con·nec·tion·al** *adj.*

con·nec·tion·ism /kə néksh'ə nìzzəm/ *n.* the theory that thoughts and behavior are based on patterns of stimulus and response that have either been inherited or learned

con·nec·tive /kə néktiv/ *adj.* LINKING linking or joining two or more parts, things, or people ■ *n.* **1.** LINK something that links or joins two or more parts, things, or people **2.** LING LINKING WORD a word that links sentences, phrases, clauses, or words **3.** BOT STAMEN TISSUE the tissue that joins the two lobes of an anther in the stamen of a plant —**con·nec·tive·ly** *adv.*

con·nec·tive tis·sue *n.* animal tissue that supports, connects, and surrounds organs and other body parts. It may consist mainly of collagen, elastic and reticular fibers, fatty tissue, cartilage, or bone.

con·nec·tiv·i·ty /kò nek tívvətee/ *n.* the ability to connect with something, especially to communicate with another machine, e.g., a computer or computer system

con·nect·or /kə néktər/, **con·nect·er** *n.* something that connects things, especially two pieces of equipment, or components of a single device or structure

con·nect-the-dots *adj.* (*slang*) **1.** BUSINESS SKILLFULLY ASSEMBLED gathering information or facts from different sources to make a coherent whole ○ *The article was a model of connect-the-dots journalism.* **2.** EASY TO DO straightforward or obvious ○ *It's a connect-the-dots problem, easily solvable.* [From the method of producing a picture by connecting printed dots in order to form its outline]

con·nect time *n.* the period of time a user is logged on to a remote computer, e.g., when browsing the Internet

Con·nel·ly /kónnəlee/, **Marc** (1890–1980) U.S. playwright, screenwriter, director, and actor. His works include the Pulitzer Prize-winning play *The Green Pastures* (1930). Full name **Marcus Cook Connelly**

Con·ne·ry /kónnəree/, **Sean** (*b.* 1930) Scottish movie actor. He played the starring role in several James Bond movies and won an Academy Award for best supporting actor for *The Untouchables* (1987). Full name **Thomas Sean Connery**

con·nex·ion *n. U.K.* = **connection**

con·ning tow·er *n.* **1.** SUBMARINE CONTROL DECK a structure on the top of a submarine that is used as the navigation bridge and main point of entrance **2.** ARMORED PILOTHOUSE the armored pilothouse in the shape of a low dome found on the deck of a warship [Formed from CONN]

con·nip·tion /kə nípshən/ *n.* a hysterical fit caused by extreme excitement or anger (*informal*) (*often used in the plural*) [Mid-19thC. Origin unknown.]

con·niv·ance /kə nívəns/, **con·niv·ence** *n.* **1.** SECRET PLOTTING secret joint conspiracy or plotting **2.** TACIT ENCOURAGEMENT OF WRONGDOING unspoken encouragement of, or consent to, somebody else's wrongdoing

con·nive /kə nív/ (**-nived, -niv·ing, -nives**) *vi.* **1.** PLOT to plan secretly to do something, usually something wrong or illegal **2.** GIVE TACIT CONSENT TO SOMETHING WRONG to pretend not to know about or do nothing to stop a wrongful or illegal act, thus showing encouragement of or consent to the act ○ *He connived at his brother's shoplifting with the understanding that he would share the loot.* [Early 17thC. Via French from Latin *connivere* "to close your eyes," (related to *nictare* "to wink," the source of English *nictitate*).] —**con·niv·er** *n.* —**con·niv·er·y** *n.*

con·niv·ence *n.* = **connivance**

con·ni·vent /kə nívənt/ *adj.* used to describe insect wings and flower petals or stamens that converge and touch but remain separate and not fused

con·niv·ing /kə níving/ *adj.* devious and scheming —**con·niv·ing·ly** *adv.*

con·nois·seur /kònnə súr/ *n.* somebody who has specialist knowledge of or training in a particular field of the fine or domestic arts, or whose taste in such a field is considered to be discriminating [Early 18thC. From French, formed from *connoistre* "to know," from Latin *cognoscere* (see COGNITION).] —**con·nois·seur·ship** *n.*

Con·nol·ly /kónn'lee/, **Maureen** (1934–69) U.S. tennis player. She was the first woman to win all four grand slam tournaments in one year (1953). Full name **Maureen Catherine Connolly**. Known as **Little Mo**

Con·nors /kónnərs/, **Jimmy** (*b.* 1952) U.S. tennis player. He won 109 professional singles titles, including eight grand slam tournaments, during the 1970s and 1980s. Full name **James Scott Connors**. Known as **Jimbo**

con·no·ta·tion /kònnə táysh'n/ *n.* **1.** IMPLIED ADDITIONAL MEANING an additional sense or senses associated with or suggested by a word or phrase. Connotations are sometimes, but not always, fixed, and are often subjective. ○ *Patriotism has different connotations for different people.* **2.** SUGGESTING MEANING FOR WORD the implying or suggesting of an additional meaning for a word or phrase apart from the explicit meaning **3.** DEFINING CHARACTERISTIC in logic, the characteristic or set of characteristics that makes up the meaning of a term and thus defines the objects to which a term can be applied —**con·no·ta·tive** /kónnə tàytiv/ *adj.* —**con·no·ta·tive·ly** *adv.*

con·note /kə nṓt/ (**-not·ed, -not·ing, -notes**) *vt.* **1.** HAVE AS ADDITIONAL IMPLIED MEANING to imply or suggest something in addition to the main or literal meaning ○ *The word "hearth" often connotes coziness and warmth.* **2.** IMPLY SOMETHING ELSE to mean that something else is necessarily either a condition or a consequence ○ *His reluctance to act connotes cowardice.* [Mid-17thC. From medieval Latin *connotare*, literally "to mark along with," from Latin *notare* "to mark," from *nota* "sign" (source of English *note* and *annotate*).]

con·nu·bi·al /kə nóobee əl/ *adj.* dealing with or relating to marriage (*formal*) [Mid-17thC. From Latin *connubialis* "concerning marriage," from *connubium* "marriage," from *nubere* "to marry" (source of English *nubile* and *nuptial*).] —**con·nu·bi·al·ly** *adv.*

co·no·dont /kṓnə dònt, kónnə-/ *n.* a very small tooth-shaped fossil thought to be the remains of a marine organism. Conodonts are commonly found in marine limestone beds from the Paleozoic era and are used by geologists to date rock layers. [Mid-19thC. Coined from Greek *kōnos* "cone" + -DONT.]

con·quer /kóngkər/ (**-quered, -quer·ing, -quers**) *v.* **1.** *vt.* SEIZE AREA BY MILITARY FORCE to take control of a place by force of arms **2.** *vt.* DEFEAT PEOPLE IN WAR to win a victory over a people in war **3.** *vt.* MASTER SOMETHING DIFFICULT to overcome or gain control of something that is difficult to overcome ○ *the first woman to conquer Everest* ○ *conquered inflation by controlling public expenditure* **4.** *vt.* WIN SOMEBODY'S ADMIRATION to win somebody's love, affection, or admiration, often through strength of character or seduction, and sometimes somewhat against the person's will ○ *By the end of the last song, she had conquered their hearts.* **5.** *vi.* WIN to be victorious [13thC. Via Old French *conquerre* from assumed Vulgar Latin *conquaerere*, literally "to seek diligently," from *quaerere* (see QUERY).] —**con·quer·a·ble** *adj.*

WORD KEY: SYNONYMS

See Synonyms at ***defeat***.

con·quer·or /kóngkərər/ *n.* **1.** VICTOR OVER ENEMY somebody who has enjoyed great success in war and has defeated an enemy or enemies **2.** VICTOR IN CONTEST somebody who has beaten an opponent in a contest

con·quest /kón kwèst, kóng kwèst/ *n.* **1.** SUBJUGATION OF ENEMY AFTER FIGHTING taking control of a place or people by force of arms **2.** SOMETHING ACQUIRED BY CONQUERING something that has been acquired through force of arms, e.g., land, people, or goods **3.** ADMIRER GAINED BY PERSISTENT ATTENTION somebody whose love, affection, or admiration has been won, often through strength of character or seduction, and sometimes somewhat against the person's will ○ *boasting about his conquests* [13thC. Via Old French from assumed Vulgar Latin *conquaesita*, the feminine past participle of *conquaerere* (see CONQUER).]

con·qui·an /kóngkee ən/ *n.* CARDS = **cooncan**

con·quis·ta·dor /kon keéstə dàwr, kəng-, -kweéstə-/ (*plural* **-dors** *or* **-dor·es** /-dáw ràyz/) *n.* a Spanish conqueror or adventurer, especially one of those who conquered Mexico, Peru, and Central America in the16th century [Mid-19thC. Via Spanish from, ultimately, Latin *conquirere* "to conquer."]

AKG London

Joseph Conrad

Con·rad /kón ràd/, **Joseph** (1857–1924) Polish-born British writer. His novels and stories include *Nostromo* (1904), *Lord Jim* (1900), and *Heart of Darkness* (1902).

Con·roe /kón rō/ city in eastern Texas, northwest of Houston. Population: 33,748 (1996).

cons. *abbr.* **1.** consigned **2.** consignment **3.** consecrated **4.** consonant **5. cons., cons** constitution **6.** constitutional **7.** construction

Cons. *abbr.* **1. Cons, Cons.** Constitution **2.** Constable **3.** Consul

con·san·guin·e·ous /kòn san gwínnee əss, -sang-/, **con·san·guine** /kon sángwin/ *adj.* descended from the same family or ancestors [Early 17thC. Formed from Latin *consanguineus*, literally "of the same blood," from *sanguineus* (see SANGUINE).] —**con·san·guin·e·ous·ly** *adv.*

con·san·guin·i·ty /kòn san gwínnətee/ *n.* **1.** RELATIONSHIP BY BLOOD relationship by descent from the same ancestor, rather than by marriage or affinity **2.** CLOSE CONNECTION a close relationship or connection

con·science /kónshəns/ *n.* **1.** SENSE OF RIGHT AND WRONG the internal sense of what is right and wrong that governs somebody's thoughts and actions, urging him or her to do right rather than wrong ○ *Let your conscience be your guide.* **2.** OBEDIENCE TO CONSCIENCE behavior in compliance with what your internal sense of right and wrong tells you is right ○ *a person of strict conscience* **3.** SHARED MORAL VIEWPOINT a shared concern for moral issues ○ *a social conscience* **4.** PSYCHOANAL PART OF SUPEREGO the part of the superego that passes judgment on thought and behavior to the ego for further consideration [13thC. Via Old French from Latin *conscientia* "consciousness," from *conscire* "to be conscious," literally "to know thoroughly," from *scire* (see SCIENCE).] —**con·science·less** *adj.* ◇ **in (all) (good) conscience 1.** while being fair and reasonable **2.** used to emphasize that what you are saying is truly the case ◇ **on somebody's conscience** causing somebody to feel guilty or anxious about something

con·science clause *n.* a clause in an act, law, or contract that exempts those who have moral or religious objections to complying

con·science mon·ey *n.* money paid voluntarily in compensation for a previous act of wrongdoing by which somebody has been harmed

con·science-strick·en, **con·science-smit·ten** *adj.* feeling guilty or anxious about having done something wrong

con·sci·en·tious /kònshee énshəss/ *adj.* **1.** PAINSTAKING thorough and diligent in performing a task **2.** IN ACCORDANCE WITH SOMEBODY'S CONSCIENCE governed by or done according to somebody's sense of right and wrong ○ *a conscientious decision to dedicate an hour a week to volunteer work* [Early 17thC. Via French *consciencieux* from, ultimately, Latin *conscientia* (see CONSCIENCE).] —**con·sci·en·tious·ly** *adv.* —**con·sci·en·tious·ness** *n.*

WORD KEY: SYNONYMS

See Synonyms at *careful*.

con·sci·en·tious ob·jec·tor *n.* somebody who, for moral or religious reasons, believes it is wrong to wage war and therefore refuses to join or serve in any branch of the armed services

con·scio·na·ble /kónshənəb'l/ *adj.* acceptable according to somebody's conscience (*archaic*) [Mid-16thC. Formed from *conscions*, a variant of CONSCIENCE.] —**con·scio·na·ble·ness** *n.* —**con·scio·na·bly** *adv.*

con·scious /kónshəss/ *adj.* **1. AWAKE** awake and responsive to stimuli ○ *He's been seriously injured but he's still conscious.* **2. KEENLY AWARE OF SOMETHING** aware of something, and attaching importance to it ○ *I'm conscious of all you've done for us.* **3. CONSIDERED AND DELIBERATE** considered and deliberate, or done with critical awareness ○ *a conscious effort not to lose her temper* **4. AWARE AND WELL-INFORMED** aware of issues relating to a particular topic of serious significance (*often used in combination with adverbs*) ○ *environmentally conscious* **5. CONCERNED WITH SOMETHING** aware of and interested in a specified topic (*used hyphenated in combination with nouns*) ○ *fashion-conscious* **6.** PSYCHOL **FUNCTIONING WITH INDIVIDUAL'S KNOWLEDGE** concerned with or relating to a part of the mind that is capable of thinking, choosing, or perceiving ■ *n.* PSYCHOL **AREA OF MIND AWARE OF SURROUNDINGS** the part of the human mind that is aware of the feelings, thoughts, and surroundings [Late 16thC. From Latin *conscius* "knowing," from *scire* (see SCIENCE).] —**con·scious·ly** *adv.*

WORD KEY: SYNONYMS

See Synonyms at *aware*.

con·scious·ness /kónshəssnəss/ *n.* **1. BEING AWAKE AND AWARE OF SURROUNDINGS** the state of being awake and aware of what is going on around you **2. SOMEBODY'S MIND** somebody's mind and thoughts ○ *In time, this experience will fade from your consciousness.* **3. SHARED FEELINGS AND BELIEFS** the set of opinions, feelings, and beliefs of a group **4. BEING AWARE OF SPECIFIC ISSUES** awareness of or sensitivity to issues in a particular field **5. AWARENESS OF THOUGHTS AND FEELINGS** the part of the human mind that is aware of the feelings, thoughts, and surroundings

con·scious·ness-rais·ing *n.* **1. IMPROVING GROUP UNDERSTANDING OF ISSUE** the aim of increasing people's awareness of a moral or social issue with a view to encouraging them to take action **2. INCREASING SELF-AWARENESS** increasing self-awareness, usually through group therapy —**con·scious·ness-rais·er** *n.*

con·script *vt.* /kən skrípt/ (**-script·ed, -script·ing, -scripts**) **COMPEL TO DO MILITARY SERVICE** to enroll somebody compulsorily in the armed forces or for military service ■ *n.* /kón skrìpt/ **MILITARY RECRUIT** somebody who has been enrolled compulsorily for service, usually in the armed forces [15thC. From Latin *conscript-*, the past participle stem of *conscribere* "to enroll," literally "to write down," from *scribere* (see SCRIBE).]

con·scrip·tion /kən skrípshən/ *n.* **1. COMPULSORY ENROLLMENT FOR NATIONAL SERVICE** obligatory enrollment of citizens for a period of service, usually in the armed forces **2. COMPULSORY WARTIME LEVY OF MONEY** a compulsory monetary contribution levied by a government in wartime (*archaic*)

con·se·crate /kónsə kràyt/ (**-crat·ed, -crat·ing, -crates**) *vt.* **1. DECLARE PLACE HOLY** to declare or set apart a building, area of ground, or specific spot as holy or sacred ○ *The cathedral was consecrated in the 12th century.* **2. DEDICATE TO SPECIFIC PURPOSE** to dedicate something or somebody to a specific purpose **3. BLESS COMMUNION BREAD AND WINE** to sanctify the bread and wine for use in the Eucharist or Communion service, as symbols of the body and blood of Jesus Christ **4. ORDAIN AS BISHOP** to ordain a priest as a bishop **5. MAKE CUSTOM REVERED** to cause a custom to be revered [14thC. From Latin *consecrat-*, the past participle stem of *consecrare*, literally "to make sacred," from *sacer* (see SACRED).] —**con·se·cra·tive** *adj.* —**con·se·cra·tor** *n.* —**con·se·cra·to·ry** /kónsəkrə tàwree/ *adj.*

con·se·cra·tion /kónsə kráysh'n/ *n.* **1. CONSECRATING CEREMONY** the ceremony in which somebody or something is consecrated **2. Con·se·cra·tion SANCTIFICATION OF COMMUNION BREAD AND WINE** the process or ceremony of sanctifying the bread and wine during Communion, as symbols of the body and blood of Jesus Christ

con·sec·u·tive /kən sékyətiv/ *adj.* **1. SUCCESSIVE** following one after another without interruption or break ○ *He hasn't shown up for work for three consecutive days.* **2. FOLLOWING LOGICAL SEQUENCE** following a logical or chronological sequence [Early 17thC. Via French from, ultimately, Latin *consecut-*, the past participle stem of *consequi* (see CONSEQUENT).] —**con·sec·u·tive·ly** *adv.* —**con·sec·u·tive·ness** *n.*

con·sen·su·al /kən sénshoo əl/ *adj.* **1. BY MUTUAL CONSENT** involving the agreement of all involved **2.** LAW **REQUIRING CONSENT ONLY** requiring only the consent of the parties involved to make it binding **3.** PHYSIOL **RESPONDING INVOLUNTARILY TO INDIRECT STIMULUS** used to describe an involuntary response to a voluntary movement from another body part, e.g., the pupil of one eye constricting when the other eye is exposed to light [Mid-18thC. Formed from Latin *consens-*, the past participle stem of *consentire* (see CONSENT).] —**con·sen·su·al·ly** *adv.*

con·sen·sus /kən sénsəss/ *n.* **1. BROAD UNANIMITY** general or widespread agreement among all the members of a group ○ *The consensus of opinion among journalists was that the vote could make or break this administration.* **2. VIEW OF SOCIETY IN EQUILIBRIUM** a concept of society in which the absence of conflict is seen as the equilibrium state of society [Mid-17thC. From Latin, from the past participle of *consentire* (see CONSENT).]

WORD KEY: USAGE

Tautology trap: Since ***consensus*** already means "a view or opinion that is generally shared," expressions such as *general consensus* and *consensus of opinion* are, strictly speaking, tautologies (i.e., they say the same thing twice), in which "general" and "of opinion" are redundant. However, occasionally a modifier such as "of opinion" can be justified, as in *There was a consensus of feeling, but no consensus of opinion.* It is always best to begin by considering whether or not the word without modifiers expresses what you mean.

WORD KEY: USAGE

The word ***consensus*** is often misspelled *concensus*, probably from the erroneous influence of the word *census*.

con·sent /kən sént/ *vi.* (**-sent·ed, -sent·ing, -sents**) **1. GIVE PERMISSION FOR SOMETHING** to give permission or approval for something to happen ○ *As soon as they met Robert, her parents consented to the marriage.* ○ *I will never consent to do that.* **2. AGREE ABOUT SOMETHING** to be of the same opinion (*archaic*) ■ *n.* **1. PERMISSION FOR SOMETHING** acceptance of or agreement to something proposed or desired by another **2. CONSENSUS** agreement on an opinion or course of action ○ *It was by common consent the best.* [13thC. Via Old French from Latin *consentire*, literally "to feel with," from *sentire* (see SENTIENT). The underlying meaning is "to feel the same."] —**con·sent·er** *n.*

WORD KEY: SYNONYMS

See Synonyms at *agree*.

con·sent de·cree *n.* a judicial decree expressing voluntary agreement between parties to a dispute

con·sent·ing a·dult *n.* somebody who is no longer a minor, or is above the legal permitted age for any specific activity, who is willing to participate in that activity, especially sexual activities

con·se·quence /kónsəkwənss/ *n.* **1. RESULT** something that follows as a result ○ *This is a direct consequence of your negligence.* **2. RELATION BETWEEN RESULT AND CAUSE** the relation between a result and its cause **3. IMPORTANCE** importance or significance (*formal*) (*often used in negative statements*) ○ *Your opinion is of no consequence whatsoever to me.* **4. LOGICAL CONCLUSION** a conclusion reached through valid deductive reasoning ■ **con·se·quen·ces** *npl.* **NEGATIVE RESULTS** the unpleasant or difficult results of a previous action [14thC. Via French from Latin *consequentia*, from *consequi* (see CONSEQUENT).] ◇ **in consequence** as a result of something (*formal*)

con·se·quent /kónsəkwənt/ *adj.* **1. FOLLOWING AS RESULT** following as a result or effect ○ *weeks of rain and the consequent flooding* **2.** LOGIC **AS LOGICAL CONCLUSION** following as a logical conclusion ■ *n.* **1.** LOGIC **RESULT OF SOMETHING** something that follows as a result **2.** LOGIC **SECOND HALF OF CONDITIONAL SENTENCE** the part of a conditional sentence that expresses the result and is the q clause in a proposition of the form "if p then q" **3.** MATH **SECOND TERM OF RATIO** the second term in a mathematical ratio [15thC. Via Old French from Latin *consequent-*, the present participle stem of *consequi*, literally "to follow along with," from *sequi* (see SEQUENCE.]

con·se·quen·tial /kònsə kwénsh'l/ *adj.* **1.** INSUR **ARISING AS INDIRECT COST** used to describe costs, loss, or damage beyond the market value of the object lost or damaged, including other indirect costs arising **2. IMPORTANT** of considerable importance, significance, or value ○ *a consequential figure on the classical music circuit* **3. TOO SELF-IMPORTANT** having an exaggerated opinion of your own importance —**con·se·quen·ti·al·i·ty** /kònsə kwenshee állətee/ *n.* —**con·se·quen·tial·ly** /kònsə kwénshəlee/ *adv.* —**con·se·quen·tial·ness** *n.*

con·se·quen·tial·ism /kònsə kwénshə lìzzəm/ *n.* the tenet by which an action is considered right or wrong depending on whether its outcome is good or bad

con·se·quent·ly /kónsəkwəntlee/ *adv.* as a result or in view of this (*formal*) ○ *The joke backfired and the relationship consequently deteriorated.*

con·ser·van·cy /kən súrvənsee/ (*plural* **-cies**) *n.* an area designated for the protection both of the land and of its wildlife and their habitat

con·ser·va·tion /kònsər váysh'n/ *n.* **1. PROTECTION OF VALUED RESOURCES** the preservation, management, and care of natural and cultural resources **2. PROTECTION FROM CHANGE** the keeping or protecting of something from change, loss, or damage —**con·ser·va·tion·al** *adj.*

con·ser·va·tion·ist /kònsər váysh'nist/ *n.* somebody who campaigns for, supports, or works toward the preservation, management, and care of the environment, especially of natural resources in the countryside

con·ser·va·tion of charge *n.* the principle that the total electric charge of an isolated system remains constant no matter what internal changes take place

con·ser·va·tion of en·er·gy *n.* the principle that the amount of energy in an isolated system remains the same, even though the form of energy may change

con·ser·va·tion of mass, **con·ser·va·tion of mat·ter** *n.* the principle that the total mass of an isolated system remains constant, no matter what physical or chemical changes take place

con·ser·va·tion of mo·men·tum *n.* the principle that the total linear or angular momentum of an isolated system remains the same

con·ser·va·tism /kən súrvə tìzzəm/ *n.* **1. RELUCTANCE TO ACCEPT CHANGE** unwillingness or slowness to accept change or new ideas **2. RIGHT-WING POLITICAL VIEWPOINT** a right-of-center political philosophy based on a tendency to support gradual rather than abrupt change and to preserve the status quo **3. DESIRE TO PRESERVE CURRENT SOCIETAL STRUCTURE** an ideology that views the existing form of society as worthy of preservation

Con·ser·va·tism *n.* the principles and practice of Conservative politicians or supporters, e.g., in the United Kingdom or Canada

con·ser·va·tive /kən súrvətiv/ *adj.* **1. RELUCTANT TO ACCEPT CHANGE** in favor of preserving the status quo and traditional values and customs, and against abrupt change **2. OF CONSERVATISM** associated with, characteristic of, or displaying conservatism **3. CAUTIOUS AND ON THE LOW SIDE** cautiously moderate and therefore often less than the final outcome ○ *Several hundred dollars is probably a very conservative estimate.* **4. CONVENTIONAL IN APPEARANCE** conventional or restrained in style and avoiding showiness ○ *a conservative suit* **5. USING MINIMUM MEDICAL INTERVENTION** designed to help relieve symptoms or preserve health with a minimum of medical intervention ■ *n.* **1. TRADITIONALIST PERSON** somebody who is reluctant to consider new ideas or accept change **2. SUPPORTER OF CONSERVATISM** somebody who supports the doctrine or beliefs of conservatism —**con·ser·va·tive·ly** *adv.* —**con·ser·va·tive·ness** *n.*

Con·ser·va·tive *adj.* **1. OF CONSERVATIVE PARTY** supporting, belonging to, or associated with a Conservative Party, e.g., in the United Kingdom or Canada **2. OF CONSERVATIVE JUDAISM** relating to, associated with, or characteristic of Conservative Judaism ■ *n.* **SUPPORTER OF CONSERVATIVE PARTY** somebody who is a member of or supports a Conservative Party, e.g., in the United Kingdom or Canada

Con·ser·va·tive Ju·da·ism *n.* a form of Judaism that accepts most of the principles and practices of traditional Judaism but supports the modification and relaxing of certain laws. The movement arose around the turn of the 20th century as a reaction against the more liberal Reform Judaism.

Con·ser·va·tive Par·ty *n.* **1.** MAIN U.K. RIGHT-WING POLITICAL PARTY in the United Kingdom, the principal right-of-center political party. It supports low personal taxation, home ownership, and the maintenance of the present form of government. It was founded in the early 1830s as a successor to the Tory Party. **2.** CANADIAN RIGHT-WING POLITICAL PARTY in Canada, the Progressive Conservative Party, which originally derived its political principles from British Toryism. It added Progressive to its name in 1942. **3.** POLITICAL PARTY OPPOSED TO CHANGE in countries other than the United Kingdom and Canada, a political party that is opposed to change (*takes a singular or plural verb*)

con·ser·va·tize /kən súrvə tīz/ (**-tized, -tiz·ing, -tiz·es**) *vti.* to become, or make an organization or person become, conservative or increasingly conservative

con·ser·va·toire /kən sùrvə twaár/ *n.* = **conservatory** *n.* 2 [Late 18thC. Via French from Italian *conservatorio*, originally a home for orphans that provided an education in music, from late Latin *conservatorium* (see CONSERVATORY).]

con·ser·va·tor /kən súrvətər/ *n.* **1.** RESTORER OF WORKS OF ART somebody who is responsible for looking after or restoring exhibits in a museum or collection, or other works of art **2.** PROTECTOR OF INTERESTS OF INCOMPETENT PERSON a person or institution responsible for protecting the interests of an incompetent —**con·ser·va·to·ri·al** /kən sùrvə táwree əl/ *adj.* —**con·ser·va·tor·ship** /kən súrvətər shìp/ *n.*

con·ser·va·to·ry /kən súrvə tàwree/ (*plural* **-ries**) *n.* **1.** GREENHOUSE a room with glass walls and roof where plants are grown or displayed, often built onto the side of a house **2.** ADVANCED MUSIC OR DRAMA SCHOOL an institution or school where students are taught one of the arts, most commonly music or drama, to a professional standard [Mid-16thC. From late Latin *conservatorium*, from Latin *conservare* (see CONSERVE).]

con·serve *vt.* /kən súrv/ (**-served, -serv·ing, -serves**) **1.** PROTECT FROM HARM OR DECAY to keep something, especially an important environmental or cultural resource, from harm, loss, change, or decay ○ *the importance of conserving our national heritage* **2.** USE SPARINGLY to use something sparingly so as not to exhaust supplies ○ *some drastic measures to conserve water* **3.** PRESERVE FOOD IN SUGAR to preserve food, especially fruit, in sugar **4.** KEEP MATTER OR ENERGY CONSTANT to keep something constant through physical changes or chemical reactions ■ *n.* /kaán sùrv, kən/ FRUIT IN SYRUP a food consisting of fruit in a thick sugar syrup, like jam but less firmly set and usually containing larger pieces of fruit [14thC. Via French from Latin *conservare*, literally "to preserve well," from *servare* (see SERVE).] —**con·serv·a·ble** *adj.* —**con·serv·er** *n.*

con·sid·er /kən síddər/ (**-ered, -er·ing, -ers**) *v.* **1.** *vti.* THINK CAREFULLY to think carefully about something ○ *You should consider your next move carefully.* ○ *time to consider whether this is what you really want* **2.** *vt.* JUDGE to have something as an opinion or point of view ○ *He considers himself lucky to be alive.* ○ *I consider it unlikely that they'll accept your proposal.* **3.** *vt.* RESPECT to show respect for or be thoughtful of somebody's feelings or position ○ *They never seem to consider the feelings of others.* **4.** *vt.* WEIGH POSSIBILITIES BEFORE DECIDING to weigh the pros and cons of the situation before making a decision on a course of action ○ *I'm considering my options.* ○ *They're considering buying a new house.* **5.** *vt.* EXAMINE to examine a problem and discuss it in detail ○ *On this week's show, we're going to consider the following question.* **6.** *vt.* TAKE INTO ACCOUNT to take something into account, often in a sympathetic way ○ *We've done very well, all things considered.* **7.** *vt.* LOOK CAREFULLY AT to look at something carefully and with concentration (*formal*) [14thC. Via French *considérer* from Latin *considerare*, of uncertain origin: probably formed from *sidus* "star," the underlying idea being one of examining the stars carefully to divine the future.] —**con·sid·er·er** *n.*

con·sid·er·a·ble /kən síddərəb'l/ *adj.* **1.** LARGE large enough to be important ○ *needs a considerable income to afford this apartment* **2.** MUCH with a far from negligible amount of something ○ *a woman of considerable influence* **3.** SIGNIFICANT worthy of consideration or respect ○ *a considerable figure in the art world* ■ *n.* GREAT AMOUNT a great deal or amount (*informal*)

con·sid·er·a·bly /kən síddərəblee/ *adv.* to a significant degree ○ *He's considerably older than I am.*

con·sid·er·ate /kən síddərət/ *adj.* mindful of the needs, wishes, and feelings of others —**con·sid·er·ate·ly** *adv.* —**con·sid·er·ate·ness** *n.*

con·sid·er·a·tion /kən sìddə ráysh'n/ *n.* **1.** CAREFUL THOUGHT careful thought or deliberation (*formal*) ○ *Your application will be given the fullest consideration.* **2.** RESPECT thoughtful concern for or sensitivity toward the feelings of others **3.** RELEVANT FACTOR IN ASSESSING SOMETHING something to be taken into account when weighing up the pros and cons before making a decision ○ *Value for money is one of the most important considerations for our customers.* **4.** DETAILED EXAMINATION detailed discussion or scrutiny ○ *The issue for consideration on today's show is cosmetic surgery.* **5.** OPINION a carefully thought-out opinion ○ *It is my consideration that you are not suitable for this position.* **6.** PAYMENT a payment or fee in return for a service (*formal*) **7.** HIGH REGARD high regard or esteem (*formal*) ○ *She has always been held in great consideration by this congregation.* **8.** SOMETHING MAKING CONTRACT BINDING something done by one of the parties as part of a contractual arrangement that makes it binding, e.g., the payment of the price in a sales agreement ◇ **take something into consideration** to take account of special circumstances, often in a sympathetic way ◇ **of little consideration, of no consideration** not important or significant (*formal*) ◇ **in consideration of** **1.** because of (*formal*) **2.** as payment for (*formal*)

con·sid·ered /kən síddərd/ *adj.* **1.** THOUGHT OUT carefully thought out ○ *my considered opinion* **2.** REGARDED regarded in a particular way (*formal*) (*usually used in combination*) ○ *highly considered*

con·sid·er·ing /kən síddəring/ *prep., conj.* TAKING INTO ACCOUNT taking something into account ○ *It's a tremendous bargain, considering the price and how much we need one.* ■ *adv.* ALL IN ALL taking everything into account, often in a sympathetic way (*spoken*) (*usually used at the end of a phrase or sentence*) ○ *We've done a really good job, considering.*

con·si·glie·re /kòn seel yérrə/ (*plural* **-sig·lie·ri** /-yérree/) *n.* somebody who advises the leader of a crime syndicate [Early 17thC. Via Italian from, ultimately, Latin *consilium* (see COUNSEL).]

con·sign /kən sín/ (**-signed, -sign·ing, -signs**) *vt.* **1.** ENTRUST to hand somebody or something over to the care of another ○ *The children were consigned to the care of the nanny.* **2.** GET RID OF to dispose of something or somebody, usually for a very long time if not permanently, and often to somewhere unpleasant or difficult ○ *Before fleeing, they consigned the documents to the flames.* **3.** DELIVER to address, deliver, or hand over for later delivery something for sale, safekeeping, or disposal [15thC. Via French from Latin *consignare* "to certify with a seal," from *signum* (see SIGN).] —**con·sign·a·ble** *adj.*

con·sign·ee /kòn sī née/ *n.* the person, people, or organization to whom something is delivered or addressed (*formal*)

con·sign·er *n.* = **consignor**

con·sign·ment /kən sínmənt/ *n.* **1.** DELIVERY a quantity or package of goods delivered or to be delivered **2.** DISPOSAL TO SOMEWHERE DISAGREEABLE the disposing of somebody or something, or being disposed, to an unpleasant or difficult place or task, usually for a very long time if not forever **3.** ENTRUSTING OF SOMEBODY TO ANOTHER'S CARE the handing over of somebody or something to the care of another ◇ **on consignment** on the understanding that payment will be made only when the goods have been sold and that any remaining unsold articles can be returned

con·sign·ment store *n.* a retail outlet that stocks and sells goods on a sale-or-return basis, or as an agent selling on behalf of others and receiving a percentage

con·sign·or /kən sínər/, **con·sign·er** *n.* a person who or organization that delivers goods

con·sist /kən síst/ (**-sist·ed, -sist·ing, -sists**) *vi.* **1.** BE MADE UP OF SOMETHING to be made up of diverse elements ○ *This dressing consists of oil, lemon juice, and mustard.* **2.** BE BASED ON SOMETHING to be based on or defined by something ○ *Her talent consists in her superb musicianship.* [Early 16thC. From Latin *consistere* "to be made of," literally "to stand together," from *sistere* "to make stand," from *stare* "to stand" (see STATION).]

WORD KEY: USAGE

See Usage note at ***comprise***.

con·sis·ten·cy /kən sístənsee/ (*plural* **-cies**), **con·sis·tence** /kən sístəns/ *n.* **1.** CONSTANCY the ability to maintain a particular standard or repeat a particular task with minimal variation ○ *Consistency is important in performing this job.* ○ *"A foolish consistency is the hobgoblin of small minds."* (Ralph Waldo Emerson *Self-Reliance*; 1841) **2.** COHERENCE reasonable or logical harmony between parts ○ *The plot lacked consistency.* **3.** LEVEL OF THICKNESS OR SMOOTHNESS level of thickness or smoothness of a mixture ○ *Blend the mixture until it reaches the consistency of thick cream.*

con·sis·tent /kən sístənt/ *adj.* **1.** COHERENT reasonably or logically harmonious ○ *The evidence is consistent with the defendant's statement.* ○ *Their accounts of the incident just aren't consistent.* **2.** RELIABLE able to maintain a particular standard or repeat a particular task with minimal variation ○ *He's one of the most consistent hitters in the league.* **3.** WITH COMMON SOLUTIONS with a set of solutions in common, especially for two or more equations or inequalities **4.** FREE OF CONTRADICTION containing no provable contradiction [Late 16thC. From Latin *consistent-*, the present participle stem of *consistere* (see CONSIST).] —**con·sis·tent·ly** *adv.*

con·sis·to·ry /kən sístəree/ (*plural* **-ries**) *n.* **1.** RELIG ASSEMBLY OF CARDINALS AND POPE in the Roman Catholic Church, an assembly of cardinals convoked and led by the Pope **2.** *U.K.* RELIG ANGLICAN DIOCESAN COURT in the Anglican Church, the court of any diocese except Canterbury **3.** RELIG CONGREGATIONAL GOVERNING BODY in certain Reformed churches, the governing body of a congregation **4.** RELIG REGULATORY COURT IN LUTHERAN CHURCHES in Lutheran state churches, a court appointed to regulate ecclesiastical affairs **5.** HIST HISTORICAL COUNCIL OR ASSEMBLY a council or assembly, e.g., in the Roman Empire [13thC. Via Anglo-Norman from late Latin *consistorium* "place of assembly," from Latin *consistere* "to stand together" (see CONSIST).] —**con·sis·to·ri·al** /kònsi stáwree əl/ *adj.*

con·so·ci·ate *vti.* /kən sṓshee àyt/ (**-at·ed, -at·ing, -ates**) JOIN OR WELCOME ASSOCIATION to enter or welcome somebody into a friendly association (*formal*) ■ *adj.* /kən sṓshee ət/ ASSOCIATED associated or united (*formal*) ■ *n.* /kən sṓshee ət/ PARTNER an associate or partner (*formal*) [15thC. From Latin *consociat-*, the past participle stem of *consociare* "to associate," from *socius* "companion" (see SOCIAL).]

con·so·ci·a·tion /kən sṓshee áysh'n/ *n.* **1.** FRIENDLY ASSOCIATION a friendly association or alliance (*formal*) **2.** ECOL ECOLOGICAL COMMUNITY WITH ONE MAIN SPECIES an ecological community that has one dominant species, e.g., a wood consisting predominantly of beech trees **3.** POL POLITICAL COALITION a grouping of political parties or pressure groups within a region or country that work together to share power **4.** CHR ASSOCIATION OF REFORMED CHURCHES an association of churches or religious societies, especially Congregational churches in New England and Presbyterian churches —**con·so·ci·a·tion·al** *adj.*

con·so·la·tion /kònsə láysh'n/ *n.* **1.** SOURCE OF COMFORT a source of comfort to somebody who is upset or disappointed ○ *The fortune she left was little consolation for him.* **2.** COMFORT TO SOMEBODY IN DISTRESS comfort to somebody who is distressed or disappointed ○ *Most of those at the funeral murmured some words of consolation as they left.* **3.** GAME FOR EARLIER LOSERS a game or contest held for people or teams who have lost earlier in a tournament

con·so·la·tion prize *n.* a prize given to comfort the loser or losers in a game or competition

con·sole[1] /kən sṓl/ (**-soled, -sol·ing, -soles**) *vt.* to be or provide a source of comfort to somebody who is distressed or disappointed [Mid-17thC. Via French from Latin *consolare*, from *solari* "to soothe" (see SOLACE).] —**con·sol·a·ble** *adj.* —**con·so·la·to·ry** *adj.* —**con·sol·er** *n.* —**con·sol·ing·ly** *adv.*

WORD KEY: USAGE

See Usage note at ***condole***.

con·sole[2] /kón sòl/ *n.* **1.** CABINET FOR TELEVISION OR HI-FI a free-standing cabinet, especially one used to house a television or hi-fi system **2.** CONTROL PANEL a desk, table, display, or keyboard onto which the controls of an electronic system or some other machine are fixed **3.** STORAGE COMPARTMENT IN AUTOMOBILE a small storage compartment in an automobile, fixed between individual seats **4.** ORGAN CONTROLS the part of an organ that houses the keyboards or manuals, pedals, and stops **5.** ORNAMENTAL BRACKET an ornamental bracket, often in the shape of a scroll, used for decoration and for supporting wall fixtures **6.** = **console table** [Mid-17thC. From French, of uncertain origin: perhaps a shortening of *consolider* "to consolidate."]

con·sole ta·ble *n.* a small table with curved legs designed to stand against a wall

con·sol·i·date /kən sólli dàyt/ (**-dat·ed, -dat·ing, -dates**) *vti.* **1.** UNITE BUSINESS ACTIVITIES to bring businesses or business activities together, or come together, into a single unit **2.** STRENGTHEN YOUR POSITION to increase the strength, stability, or depth of your success or position ○ *This excellent performance has enabled her to consolidate her lead.* **3.** COMBINE INTO SINGLE MASS to combine separate items or scattered material into a single mass [Early 16thC. From Latin *consolidat-*, the past participle stem of *consolidare*, literally "to make solid," from *solidus* (see SOLID).] —**con·sol·i·da·tor** *n.*

con·sol·i·dat·ed school *n.* a public school for students from several neighboring, often rural, districts

con·sol·i·da·tion /kən sòlli dáysh'n/ *n.* **1.** COMBINING OF BUSINESS ACTIVITIES the bringing together of two or more businesses or business activities into a single unit **2.** STRENGTHENING increasing of the strength, stability, or depth of a person's or group's success ○ *The final six weeks saw a consolidation of their position at the top of the league.* **3.** COMBINATION INTO SINGLE MASS the combination of separate items or scattered material into a single mass **4.** GEOL COMPACTION INTO ROCK any process by which a loose deposit is compacted into hard rock **5.** PSYCHOL PSYCHOLOGICAL PROCESS THAT RETAINS MEMORY the process in the brain that enables somebody to have a lasting memory of a particular event

con·som·mé /kònsə máy/ *n.* a thin clear soup made from meat or chicken stock. It can be eaten hot, or cold in jellied form. [Early 19thC. From French, from the past participle of *consommer* "to use up," from Latin *consummare* (see CONSUMMATE).]

con·so·nance/kónsənəns/, **con·so·nan·cy** /kónsənən see/ (*plural* **-cies**) *n.* **1.** AGREEMENT agreement or harmony (*formal*) **2.** SIMILARITY BETWEEN CONSONANTS a close similarity between consonants or groups of consonants, especially at the ends of words, e.g., between "strong" and "ring" **3.** PLEASANT COMBINATION OF MUSICAL NOTES a combination of notes that sounds pleasing when played simultaneously

con·so·nant /kónsənənt/ *n.* SPEECH SOUND OTHER THAN VOWEL a speech sound produced by partly or totally blocking the path of air through the mouth, or the corresponding letter of the alphabet ■ *adj.* **1.** IN AGREEMENT WITH SOMETHING in agreement or harmony with something (*formal*) ○ *I was delighted to learn that their views were consonant with my own.* **2.** PLEASING IN HARMONY containing chords or harmonies that are pleasing to hear **3.** HAVING SIMILAR SOUNDS having similar sounds or showing consonance [14thC. Via French from Latin *consonant-*, the stem of *consonans*, literally "sounding together," from *sonare* (see SONANT).] —**con·so·nant·ly** *adv.*

con·so·nan·tal /kònsə nánt'l/ *adj.* **1.** OF CONSONANT consisting of, relating to, or functioning like a consonant **2.** CONTAINING CONSONANTS containing consonants or nothing but consonants —**con·so·nan·tal·ly** *adv.*

con sor·di·no /kòn sawr deénō/ *adv.* to be played with a mute or the mute pedal (*used as a musical direction*) [Early 19thC. From Italian, literally "with a mute."]

con·sort *vi.* /kən sáwrt/ (**-sort·ed, -sort·ing, -sorts**) ASSOCIATE WITH UNDESIRABLES to associate with or spend time in the company of undesirable people (*formal*) ○ *consorting with known criminals* ■ *n.* /kón sàwrt/ **1. con·sort, Con·sort** SPOUSE OF REIGNING MONARCH the husband or wife of a reigning monarch **2.** PARTNER a partner or companion (*formal*) **3.** SHIP THAT ESCORTS ANOTHER a ship that accompanies or escorts another on a journey **4.** CHAMBER GROUP SPECIALIZING IN EARLY MUSIC a small group of musical instruments, often of the baroque or other early period, or a group of players of such instruments [15thC. Via French from Latin *consort-*, the stem of *consors*, literally "having the same fate," from *sors* "fortune" (see SORT).] ◇ **in consort with** in association or together with others (*archaic or formal*)

con·sor·ti·um /kən sáwrtee əm, -sáwrshəm, -sáwrshee əm/ (*plural* **-a** /-tee ə, -shə, -shee ə/) *n.* **1.** COMBINATION OF ORGANIZATIONS FOR COMMON PURPOSE an association or grouping of institutions, businesses, or financial organizations, usually set up for a common purpose that would be beyond the capabilities of a single member of the group **2.** RIGHT TO MARITAL COMPANY AND AFFECTION the right of husbands or wives to the company, affection, and help of their spouses (*archaic*) [Early 19thC. From Latin, "fellowship," from *consors* "fellow" (see CONSORT).] —**con·sor·ti·al** *adj.*

con·spe·cif·ic /kònspə síffik/ *adj.* OF SAME SPECIES of the same species as another organism ■ *n.* ORGANISM OF SAME SPECIES an organism of the same species as another

con·spec·tus /kən spéktəss/ *n.* **1.** MENTAL OVERVIEW OF SOMETHING a general mental survey or overview of something **2.** SYNOPSIS OF SOMETHING an overview of something in outline or synopsis (*technical*) [Mid-19thC. From Latin, formed from *conspect-*, the past participle stem of *conspicere* (see CONSPICUOUS).]

con·spic·u·ous /kən spíkyoo əss/ *adj.* **1.** EASILY VISIBLE easily or clearly visible ○ *The building's most conspicuous feature is its dome-shaped roof.* **2.** ATTRACTING ATTENTION attracting attention through being unusual or remarkable ○ *He felt uncomfortably conspicuous, since he was the only man in evening dress.* [Mid-16thC. Formed from Latin *conspicuus*, from *conspicere*, literally "to observe carefully," from the verb *specere* (see SPECTACLE).] —**con·spic·u·ous·ly** *adv.* —**con·spic·u·ous·ness** *n.*

con·spic·u·ous con·sump·tion *n.* spending large quantities of money, often extravagantly, to impress others [The term was introduced by Thorstein Veblen in his *Theory of the Leisure Class*, 1899]

con·spir·a·cist /kən spírrəssist/ *n.* somebody who believes in a conspiracy theory about some event

con·spir·a·cy /kən spírrəssee/ (*plural* **-cies**) *n.* **1.** PLAN TO COMMIT ILLEGAL ACT TOGETHER a plan or agreement between two or more people to commit an illegal or subversive action **2.** AGREEMENT AMONG CONSPIRATORS the making of an agreement or plot to commit an illegal or subversive action **3.** GROUP OF CONSPIRATORS a group of conspirators [14thC. Via Anglo-Norman *conspiracie* from, ultimately, Latin *conspirat-*, the past participle stem of *conspirare* (see CONSPIRE).]

con·spir·a·cy of si·lence *n.* an agreement among a group of people to say nothing in public about something of public interest or importance, in order to protect or promote selfish interests

con·spir·a·cy the·o·ry *n.* a belief that a particular event is the result of a secret plot rather than the actions of an individual or chance —**con·spir·a·cy the·o·rist** *n.*

con·spir·a·tor /kən spírrətər/ *n.* a member of a group of people planning or agreeing to commit an illegal or subversive act

con·spir·a·to·ri·al /kən spìrrə táwree əl/ *adj.* indicating or betraying knowledge of or involvement in a secret plot —**con·spir·a·to·ri·al·ly** *adv.*

con·spire /kən spír/ (**-spired, -spir·ing, -spires**) *vi.* **1.** PLAN SECRETLY TO ACT ILLEGALLY to plan or agree in secret with others to commit an illegal or subversive act ○ *In court, the three defendants admitted to conspiring against the government.* **2.** JOINTLY CAUSE TROUBLE to combine so as to cause harm, inconvenience, or difficulty ○ *Rain and tears conspired to smudge her carefully applied mascara.* [14thC. Via French from Latin *conspirare* "to agree," literally "to breathe or whisper together," from *spirare* (see SPIRIT).] —**con·spir·ing·ly** /kən spíringlee/ *adv.*

con·spi·ri·o·lo·gist /kən spìrri óllәjist/ (*plural* **-gists**) *n.* POL somebody who engages in conspiracy theories

con spi·ri·to /kòn spírritō/ *adv.* to be performed in a lively or spirited way (*used as a musical direction*) [Late 19thC. From Italian, literally "with spirit."]

const. *abbr.* **1.** constant **2. const., const** constitution **3.** constitutional

Const. *abbr.* **1. Const, Const.** Constitution **2. Const, Const., const, const.** Constable

con·sta·ble /kónstəb'l, kúnstəb'l/ *n.* **1.** LAW OFFICER BELOW SHERIFF a low-ranking law officer in some towns or townships **2.** LAW BRITISH POLICE OFFICER in Great Britain, a police officer of the lowest rank **3.** CASTLE WARDEN the warden of a royal castle or fortress **4.** ROYAL HOUSEHOLD OFFICIAL IN MIDDLE AGES the chief administrative and military officer in a royal household, especially in medieval France and England [12thC. From Old French *conestable*, from late Latin *comes stabilis*, literally "count of the stable," later "chief household officer of the Frankish kings."] —**con·sta·ble·ship** *n.*

con·stab·u·lar·y /kən stábbyə lèrree/ (*plural* **-ies**) *n.* **1.** FORCE OF CONSTABLES an organized force of constables operating in a city or district **2.** MIL MILITARY STYLE POLICE FORCE an armed police force that has been organized according to a military model but is separate from the army **3.** LAW BRITISH POLICE FORCE in Great Britain, a police force for a city or a district —**con·stab·u·lar** *adj.*

con·stan·cy /kón stənsee/ *n.* **1.** LOYALTY the quality of remaining faithful to a person, belief, or decision, especially in the face of difficulties ○ *The church would never have been finished if not for the constancy of a few citizens over the past six years.* **2.** UNCHANGING QUALITY the quality or fact of remaining the same despite change or variation in other things

con·stant /kón stənt/ *adj.* **1.** EVER PRESENT always present or available ○ *constant whining* **2.** HAPPENING OR DONE REPEATEDLY occurring or made again and again ○ *constant visits to the doctor* **3.** NOT CHANGING OR VARYING remaining the same and not varying with change in other things ○ *kept at a constant pressure* **4.** FAITHFUL faithful and loyal, especially to a husband, wife, or loved one ■ *n.* **1.** SOMETHING UNCHANGING an object, quality, or fact that is invariable ○ *This preoccupation has become a constant in our daily lives.* **2.** MATH QUANTITY WITH FIXED VALUE a quantity that retains a fixed value in any circumstances or throughout a particular set of calculations. Pi, the ratio of the circumference to the radius of any circle, is a constant. **3.** PHYS UNVARYING PROPERTY a property, condition, or quantity that is assumed not to vary for the purposes of a theory or experiment, e.g., the speed of light [14thC. Via French from Latin *constant-*, present participle stem of *constare* "to stand together," from *stare* "to stand" (see STAGE).]

con·stan·tan /kónstən tàn/ *n.* an alloy of copper and nickel whose electrical resistance is unaffected by changes in temperature. It is used mainly in resistors and thermocouples. [Early 20thC. Formed from CONSTANT.]

con·stant dol·lars *npl.* FIN dollars valued not at the current rate but at the rate that applied on a particular date in the past

Con·stan·tine II /kónstən teen, -tìn/, **King of the Hellenes** (*b.* 1940). Succeeding in 1964, he was exiled in 1967 by a military junta and deposed in 1973. A referendum abolished the Greek monarchy in 1974.

Con·stan·tine (the Great), Emperor of Rome (274–337). He converted to Christianity in 312 and made it a state religion in 324. He moved his capital to Byzantium, renamed Constantinople in 330. Real name **Flavius Valerius Aurelius Constantinus**

Con·stan·ti·no·ple /kòn stant'n ṓp'l/ former name for **Istanbul**

con·stant·ly /kón stəntlee/ *adv.* always and without interruption, or again and again without end ○ *She's been on my mind constantly since I heard the news.*

con·sta·tive /kónstətiv/ *adj.* **1.** PHILOS OF TRUE OR FALSE STATEMENT relating to a statement, question, or command that can be considered true or false **2.** GRAM OF PAST VERB FORMS relating to verb forms indicating that something has been completed in the past [Early 20thC. Formed from Latin *constat-*, past participle stem of *constare* (see CONSTANT).]

con·stel·late /kónstə lày t/ (**-lat·ed, -lat·ing, -lates**) *vti.* to form clusters, in or as if in constellations (*formal*) [Late 16thC. From late Latin *constellatus*, literally "stars together," from, ultimately, Latin *stella* "star."]

con·stel·la·tion /kònstə láysh'n/ *n.* **1.** ASTRON GROUP OF STARS FORMING SHAPE a group of stars visible from Earth that forms a distinctive pattern and has a name linked to its shape, often derived from Greek mythology. There are 88 constellations and the groupings are historical rather than scientific. **2.** ASTRON **AREA OF SKY CONTAINING CONSTELLATION** the area of the sky within and around a constellation **3. GATHERING OF CELEBRITIES** a gathering of famous or important people ○ *a glittering constellation of Hollywood stars* **4. GROUP OF RELATED THINGS** a group of things or circumstances felt to be related to each other in some way ○ *Problems tend to occur not singly, but in constellations.* **5.** ZODIAC **ASTROLOGICAL ARRANGEMENT OF PLANETS** the arrangement of the planets in the zodiac at a particular time, believed by astrologers to influence human character or events on earth —**con·stel·la·tion·al** *adj.* —**con·stel·la·to·ry** /kən stéllə tàwree/ *adj.*

con·ster·nate /kónstər nàyt/ (**-nat·ed, -nat·ing, -nates**) *vt.* to fill somebody with alarm, confusion, or dismay (*formal*) [Mid-17thC. From Latin *consternat-*, past participle stem of *consternare*, literally "to make prostrate with fear," from *sternare* "to lay low."]

con·ster·na·tion /kònstər náysh'n/ *n.* a feeling of bewilderment and dismay, often caused by something unexpected ○ *The news caused worldwide consternation and a panic on the stock exchange.*

con·sti·pate /kónsti pàyt/ (**-pat·ed, -pat·ing, -pates**) *vt.* to cause somebody or something to become constipated [Mid-16thC. From Latin *constipat-*, past participle stem of *constipare* "to cram together," from *stipare* "to press."]

con·sti·pat·ed /kónsti pàytəd/ *adj.* **1. HAVING DIFFICULTY WITH DEFECATION** having difficulty in eliminating solid waste from the body with feces being hard and dry **2. BLOCKED OR OBSTRUCTED** unable to flow or produce at the normal rate because of blockage or obstruction

con·sti·pa·tion /kònsti páysh'n/ *n.* **1. DIFFICULTY IN DEFECATION** a condition in which a person or animal has difficulty in eliminating solid waste from the body and the feces are hard and dry **2. BLOCKAGE OR OBSTRUCTION** a state in which the normal flow of something is blocked or obstructed

con·stit·u·en·cy /kən stíchoo ənsee/ (*plural* **-cies**) *n.* **1.** POL **ELECTORAL DISTRICT** one of the areas into which a country is divided for election purposes, from which a representative is elected to serve in a legislative body ○ *Members of Congress returned to their constituencies this week.* **2.** POL **VOTERS IN A CONSTITUENCY** the voters or residents in a particular electoral district **3. GROUP WITH COMMON OUTLOOK** a group of people thought to have common aims or views, and therefore sometimes appealed to for support ○ *people outside his usual constituency of young married couples* **4. CUSTOMERS CONSIDERED AS A GROUP** a group of people served by an organization, especially a business ○ *enlarging its constituency via a website*

con·stit·u·ent /kən stíchoo ənt/ *n.* **1.** POL **RESIDENT OF CONSTITUENCY** a person living in an electoral district, especially one having the right to vote **2. INGREDIENT** one of the materials or elements that make up something ○ *one of the constituents of cement* **3.** GRAM **WORD, PHRASE, OR CLAUSE** a word, phrase, or clause in a larger construction such as a sentence. ◊ **immediate constituent, ultimate constituent** **4.** LAW **CLIENT** somebody who appoints another person to act on his or her behalf (*formal*) ■ *adj.* **1. FORMING A PART** forming a part of something (*formal*) ○ *a constituent part of sth* **2.** POL **WITH POWER TO DRAW UP CONSTITUTION** having the power to draw up or alter a constitution [15thC. Directly or via French *constituant*, from Latin *constituent-*, present participle stem of *constituere* (see CONSTITUTE).] —**con·stit·u·ent·ly** *adv.*

con·sti·tute /kónsti tòot/ (**-tut·ed, -tut·ing, -tutes**) *vt.* **1. BE** to be, amount to, or have the status of a particular thing ○ *This letter does not constitute an offer of employment.* **2. BE INGREDIENT OF** to make up the whole or a stated part of something ○ *a panel constituted of four individuals* **3. FORMALLY ESTABLISH** to create and establish something formally, especially an official body (*formal*) ○ *constitute an assembly* **4. FORMALLY APPOINT** to appoint somebody formally to a position (*formal*) [15thC. From Latin *constitut-*, past participle stem of *constituere* "to establish, appoint," from *statuere* "to set up."] —**con·sti·tut·er** *n.*

WORD KEY: USAGE

See Usage note at ***comprise***.

con·sti·tu·tion /kònstə tóosh'n/ *n.* **1.** POL **STATEMENT OF FUNDAMENTAL LAWS** a written statement outlining the basic laws or principles by which a country or organization is governed **2.** POL **DOCUMENT CONTAINING FUNDAMENTAL LAWS** the document or statute setting out the fundamental laws or bylaws of a country or organization **3. SOMEBODY'S HEALTH** somebody's general condition of health, especially the body's ability to remain healthy and withstand disease or hardship **4. COMPOSITION OF SOMETHING** the parts or members of something, or the way in which they combine to form it ○ *challenge the constitution of the jury* **5. ACT OR PROCESS OF ESTABLISHING SOMETHING** the formal creation or establishment of something

Con·sti·tu·tion *n.* POL the Constitution of the United States, containing seven articles and 26 amendments, that has been in effect since its adoption in 1789

Con·sti·tu·tion Act *n.* the constitution of Canada, embodied in 1982 and including the Canadian Charter of Rights and Freedoms as well as provisions of the British North America Act

con·sti·tu·tion·al /kònstə tóoshən'l, kònstə tóoshnəl/ *adj.* **1.** POL **IN ACCORDANCE WITH A CONSTITUTION** authorized by a constitution, especially the Constitution of the United States ○ *The Supreme Court has to decide whether such punishments are constitutional.* **2.** POL **INVOLVING CONSTITUTION** involving the constitution of a country or an organization **3.** POL **GOVERNED BY CONSTITUTION** governed or regulated by a constitution **4. RELATING TO BODY AND HEALTH** being part of, or a consequence of, a person's physical and sometimes psychological makeup **5. HEALTH-GIVING** beneficial to a person's health (*dated*) **6. RELATING TO SOMETHING'S STRUCTURE AND MAKEUP** used to describe or relate to the way something is composed ○ *a constitutional analysis of the substance* ■ *n.* **WALK** a short walk, taken regularly for health reasons

con·sti·tu·tion·al·ism /kònstə tóoshən'l ìzzəm, -tóoshnə lìzzəm/ *n.* **1. GOVERNMENT BY CONSTITUTION** the principles or practice of government regulated by a constitution, especially a written one **2. BELIEF IN IDEA OF CONSTITUTION** belief in constitutional government —**con·sti·tu·tion·al·ist** *n., adj.*

con·sti·tu·tion·al·i·ty /kònstə toosh'n állətee/ *n.* validity or permissibility in terms of the provisions or principles of a constitution, especially the Constitution of the United States

con·sti·tu·tion·al·ize /kònstə tóoshən'l ìz, -tóoshnə lìz/ (**-ized, -iz·ing, -iz·es**) *vt.* **1. INCORPORATE INTO CONSTITUTION** to incorporate a piece of legislation into a constitution, or to authorize a practice through a constitution **2. SUBJECT TO CONSTITUTION** to make a form of government, a country, or an organization subject to a constitution —**con·sti·tu·tion·al·i·za·tion** /kònstətooshən'lə záysh'n, kònstətooshnələ záysh'n/ *n.*

con·sti·tu·tion·al·ly /kònstə tóoshən'lee, -tóoshnəlee/ *adv.* POL in accordance with a political constitution

con·sti·tu·tion·al mon·ar·chy (*plural* **con·sti·tu·tion·al mon·ar·chies**) *n.* **1. POLITICAL SYSTEM** a political system in which the head of state is a king or queen ruling to the extent allowed by a constitution **2. ROYAL-RULED COUNTRY** a country with a constitutional monarchy —**con·sti·tu·tion·al mon·arch** *n.*

Con·sti·tu·tion State *n.* the state of Connecticut (*informal*)

con·sti·tu·tive /kónstə tòotiv/ *adj.* **1. FORMING A PART** forming a part of something **2. ESSENTIAL** essential to the particular nature or character of something **3.** BIOCHEM **FORMED CONTINUOUSLY** used to describe enzymes that are formed continuously and at a constant rate within the body regardless of the physiological demands of the cell **4.** POL **HAVING POWER TO ESTABLISH INSTITUTION** having the power to create or establish a system of government, legislative body, or other institution, or to appoint members of official bodies —**con·sti·tu·tive·ly** *adv.*

constr. *abbr.* construction

con·strain /kən stráyn/ (**-strained, -strain·ing, -strains**) *vt.* **1. FORCE TO ACT** to force somebody to do something, especially through pressure of circumstances or a sense of obligation ○ *Many companies have been constrained to lay off workers.* **2. LIMIT** to limit or restrict somebody or something, especially to prevent the free expression of something ○ *We felt constrained by the presence of the others.* **3. RESTRAIN** to hold somebody or something back from an action [14thC. Via Old French *constraindre* from Latin *constringere* "to bind tightly together," from *stringere* "draw tight."] —**con·strain·a·ble** *adj.* —**con·strain·er** *n.*

con·strained /kən stráynd/ *adj.* lacking naturalness or spontaneity because of self-consciousness, reserve, or inhibiting circumstances —**con·strain·ed·ly** /kən stráynədlee/ *adv.*

con·straint /kən stráynt/ *n.* **1. LIMITING FACTOR** something that limits the freedom to act spontaneously ○ *Even in a free society individual liberty must be subject to certain constraints.* **2. LACK OF SPONTANEITY** a lack of warmth and spontaneity in somebody's manner, or in the atmosphere on a particular occasion **3. STATE OF RESTRICTION** a state in which freedom of action is severely restricted **4. FORCE OR COMPULSION** physical, moral, or other force that compels somebody to do something or that limits somebody's freedom of action ○ *Constraint was needed to get the parties to agree to negotiate.* [14thC. From French *costreinte*, feminine past participle of *constraindre* (see CONSTRAIN).]

con·strict /kən stríkt/ (**-strict·ed, -strict·ing, -stricts**) *v.* **1.** *vti.* **NARROW** to make something, especially a blood vessel, narrower, or to become narrower **2.** *vt.* **LIMIT OR RESTRICT** to limit the movement of a person or part of the body in an uncomfortable way **3.** *vt.* **RESTRICT FLOW** to stop or slow down the flow of something, e.g., air, liquid, or blood **4.** *vt.* **SQUEEZE** to squeeze something with great force ○ *"For a moment I felt my chest constricted as with a band of iron."* (George van Schaick, *A Top-Floor Idyl*; 1917) **5.** *vt.* **SUFFOCATE PREY BY SQUEEZING** to squeeze prey animals until they suffocate, as many snakes do [Mid-18thC. From Latin *constrict-*, past participle stem of *constringere* (see CONSTRAIN).] —**con·stric·tive** *adj.* —**con·stric·tive·ly** *adv.* —**con·stric·tive·ness** *n.*

con·stric·tion /kən stríkshən/ *n.* **1. BECOMING CONSTRICTED** the process of becoming narrower, or of making something narrower, e.g., blood vessels **2. COMPRESSION BY SQUEEZING** the process of squeezing or compressing something, e.g., the prey of a snake **3. NARROW PLACE** a narrow place or part ○ *A constriction in the tube prevents the mercury from returning to the bulb.* **4. FEELING OF TIGHTNESS** a feeling of tightness or pressure, especially in the chest or throat **5. RESTRICTION** something that severely restricts a person's freedom of movement, action, or expression **6. CONSTRICTING THING** something that constricts somebody or something

con·stric·tor /kən stríktər/ *n.* **1.** ZOOL **SNAKE THAT SQUEEZES PREY TO DEATH** a large nonvenomous snake, such as an anaconda, boa, or python, that coils itself around its prey and crushes it to death **2.** ANAT **MUSCLE** a muscle that tightens to make a part of the body narrower **3. SOMETHING THAT CONSTRICTS** something that constricts

con·stringe /kən strínj/ (**-stringed, -string·ing, -string·es**) *vt.* to cause something to contract or grow narrower (*archaic*) [Late 16thC. From Latin *constringere* (see CONSTRAIN).] —**con·strin·gen·cy** *n.* —**con·strin·gent** *adj.*

con·struct *vt.* /kən strúkt/ (**-struct·ed, -struct·ing, -structs**) **1. BUILD** to build or assemble something by putting together separate parts in an ordered way **2. CREATE IN THE MIND** to create something, such as a theory, as a result of systematic thought **3.** GEOM **DRAW ACCURATELY** to draw something accurately using given measurements ■ *n.* /kón strùkt/ **CONSTRUCTED THING OR CONCEPT** something that has been systematically put together, usually in the mind, especially a complex theory or concept [15thC. From Latin *construct-*, past participle stem of *construere*, literally "to pile together," from *struere* "to pile, build."] —**con·struct·i·ble** *adj.* —**con·struc·tor** *n.*

WORD KEY: SYNONYMS

See Synonyms at ***build***.

con·struc·tion /kən strúkshən/ *n.* **1.** BUILDING **ACT OR PROCESS OF CONSTRUCTING** the building of something, especially a large structure such as a house, road, or bridge **2.** BUILDING **BUILT STRUCTURE** a structure or thing that has been built **3. WORKMANSHIP AND MATERIALS** the way in which something has been built, especially with regard to the type and quality of the structure, materials, and workmanship **4.** BUILDING **BUILDING INDUSTRY** the building industry regarded as a whole **5. CREATION OF SOMETHING** the creation of something such as a system or concept from a number of different elements **6.** GRAM **COMBINATION OF WORDS** a group of words governed by particular grammatical rules **7.** GEOM **GEOMETRIC SHAPE** a geometric figure drawn accurately in accordance with given measurements **8.** ARTS

WORK OF ART a visual work of art that is put together from a variety of different materials, abstract in design, and usually three-dimensional —**con·struc·tion·al** *adj.* —**con·struc·tion·al·ly** *adv.*

con·struc·tion·ist /kən strúkshənist/ *n.* LAW somebody who construes the meaning of a legal text or document in a particular way

con·struc·tion pa·per *n.* ARTS thick paper produced in a variety of colors and used especially for school artwork

con·struc·tive /kən strúktiv/ *adj.* **1.** USEFUL carefully considered and meant to be helpful ○ *constructive criticism* **2.** LAW BASED ON INFERENCE based on what somebody infers from other statements or circumstances **3.** BUILDING STRUCTURAL involved in construction, especially forming part of the basic structure of a building —**con·struc·tive·ly** *adv.* —**con·struc·tive·ness** *n.*

con·struc·tive mar·gin *n.* a boundary between two tectonic plates at which new crust is formed, e.g., the mid-ocean ridges

con·struc·tiv·ism /kən strúkti vìzzəm/ *n.* ARTS a modern art movement originating in Moscow in the 1920s that produced large nonrepresentational structures made of industrial materials such as plastic, glass, and sheet metal. Its leading figures were Naum Gabo and Antoine Pevsner. [Early 20thC. Formed from CONSTRUCTIVE, modeled on Russian *konstruktivism*.] —**con·struc·tiv·ist** *n.*

con·strue /kən stróo/ (**-strued, -stru·ing, -strues**) *v.* **1.** *vt.* INTERPRET to interpret or understand the meaning of a word, gesture, or action in a particular way ○ *His silence could be construed as an admission of guilt.* **2.** *vti.* GRAM ANALYZE SYNTAX to analyze the grammar of a piece of text, such as text that is to be translated **3.** *vt.* GRAM USE WORD IN PARTICULAR WAY to use a word in a grammatical structure, e.g., by making it singular or plural ○ *"Folk" is construed as plural, except when it means "folk music."* **4.** *vti.* EDUC TRANSLATE ALOUD to translate something aloud, often word for word and especially from Latin or Greek (*dated*) [14thC. From Latin *construere* (see CONSTRUCT), used in late Latin to mean "to parse."] —**con·stru·a·ble** *adj.* —**con·stru·a·bil·i·ty** /kən stròo ə bíllətee/ *n.* —**con·stru·er** /kən stróo ər/ *n.*

con·sub·stan·tial /kòn səb stánsh'l/ *adj.* CHR having the same substance as something else, e.g., another member of the Holy Trinity [14thC. From ecclesiastical Latin *consubstantialis*, literally "substance together," from Latin *substantia* "substance."] —**con·sub·stan·ti·al·i·ty** /kònsəb stanshee állətee/ *n.*

con·sub·stan·ti·ate /kònsəb stánshee àyt/ (**-at·ed, -at·ing, -ates**) *vti.* CHR to become united, or to unite two things, in one single substance, as the body and blood of Jesus Christ are believed to become one with bread and wine in the Christian doctrine of transubstantiation [Late 16thC. From late Latin *consubstantiatus* "united in one substance," from *substantiat-*, past participle stem of *substantiare* (see SUBSTANTIATE).]

con·sub·stan·ti·a·tion /kònsəb stanshee áysh'n/ *n.* **1.** CHRISTIAN EUCHARISTIC DOCTRINE the Christian belief that the body and blood of Jesus Christ coexist in the bread and wine consecrated at Holy Communion with the natural elements of which bread and wine are made. ◊ **transubstantiation 2.** PROCESS IN CHRISTIAN COMMUNION SERVICE the process by which the body and blood of Jesus Christ are believed by some Christians to become present in the bread and wine consecrated at Holy Communion

con·sue·tude /kónswi tòod/ *n.* established custom or usage (*archaic*) [14thC. Directly or via French from Latin *consuetudo*, literally "complete accustomedness," from, ultimately, *suescere* "to become accustomed."]

con·sul /kóns'l/ *n.* **1.** POL GOVERNMENT OFFICIAL WORKING ABROAD a government official living in a foreign city to promote the commerce of the official's own state and protect its citizens **2.** HIST ANCIENT ROMAN MAGISTRATE one of the two chief magistrates who were elected annually to govern ancient Rome **3.** HIST FORMER FRENCH OFFICIAL one of the three chief magistrates of the first French Republic between1799 and 1804 [14thC. From Latin, from or related to consultive "to seek advice."] —**con·sul·ship** *n.*

con·su·lar /kónsələr/ *adj.* having the position or rank of a consul, carried out by a consul, or belonging to a consul or consulate

con·su·late /kónsələt/ *n.* **1.** RELIG CONSUL'S OFFICE a consul's office or official residence **2.** SCOPE OF CONSUL'S RESPONSIBILITIES the political office or period of office of a consul, or the jurisdiction of a consul **3.** HIST ANCIENT ROMAN GOVERNMENT the ancient Roman government administered by consuls

Con·su·late /kónsələt/ *n.* HIST **1.** FORMER FRENCH GOVERNMENT the government, consisting of three consuls, that ruled France from 1799 to 1804 **2.** PERIOD IN FRENCH HISTORY the period from 1799 to 1804 during which France was ruled by three consuls

con·su·late gen·er·al (*plural* **con·su·late gen·er·als** *or* **con·su·lates gen·er·al**) *n.* the building where a consul general lives or works

con·sul gen·er·al (*plural* **con·sul gen·er·als** *or* **con·suls gen·er·al**) *n.* a consul of the highest rank, usually based in a major foreign city that is important for trade

con·sult /kən súlt/ *v.* (**-sult·ed, -sult·ing, -sults**) **1.** *vti.* ASK FOR SPECIALIST ADVICE to ask for specialist advice or information, especially from a professional ○ *If symptoms persist, consult a doctor.* **2.** *vti.* DISCUSS to ask for somebody's opinion or permission before taking action ○ *You'd be wise to consult the boss before you make any major changes.* **3.** *vt.* REFER TO FOR INFORMATION to look at something, such as a reference book, in order to get information **4.** *vi.* GIVE PROFESSIONAL ADVICE to provide specialist advice for a fee ○ *After 15 years in computer programming, I now consult from home.* ■ *n.* CONSULTATION a consultation or discussion about something (*informal*) [Early 16thC. Via French *consulter*, from Latin *consultare* "to confer," from *consulere* "to seek advice."] —**con·sult·a·ble** *adj.* —**con·sult·er** *n.*

con·sul·tan·cy /kən súltənsee/ (*plural* **-cies**) *n.* **1.** WORK OF BEING A CONSULTANT the work or business of offering expert advice or services in a particular field ○ *We charge $50 per hour for consultancy.* **2.** COMPANY PROVIDING SPECIALIST ADVICE a business or professional practice that provides expert advice in a particular field **3.** CONSULTANT'S POSITION a position as a consultant

con·sult·ant /kən súltənt/ *n.* **1.** PROFESSIONAL ADVISER an expert who charges a fee for providing advice or services in a particular field **2.** *U.K.* MED SENIOR DOCTOR a senior doctor who is fully qualified in a particular branch of medicine —**con·sult·ant·ship** *n.*

con·sul·ta·tion /kòns'l táysh'n/ *n.* **1.** EXCHANGE OF OPINIONS a discussion, especially in order to ascertain opinions or reach an agreement ○ *After a quick consultation with his wife, he signed the paper.* **2.** MEETING a meeting with an expert in a particular field to obtain advice ○ *an appointment for a consultation with the heart surgeon* **3.** DISCUSSION FOR ADVICE the process of discussing something either with experts or with other participants and asking for their opinions or advice ○ *Insufficient time was allowed for consultation before the project began.* **4.** REFERENCE TO SOMETHING the act of referring to a book or person for information or advice ○ *Consultation of the manual confirmed the problem was the gearbox.* **5.** = **consultancy** *n.* 1

con·sul·ta·tive /kən súltətiv/ *adj.* available for consultation or involved in consultation —**con·sul·ta·tive·ly** *adv.*

con·sult·ing /kən súlting/ *adj.* **1.** PROVIDING SPECIALIST ADVICE providing specialist advice to other people who work in the same field **2.** OF CONSULTANTS OR CONSULTATION relating to a consultant or consultation ○ *a consulting fee* ■ *n.* BUSINESS OF CONSULTATION the business of being a consultant

con·sul·tor /kən súltər/ *n.* somebody, usually a priest, who advises a Roman Catholic bishop or the Curia

con·sum·a·ble /kən sóoməb'l/ *adj.* ABLE TO BE CONSUMED able or intended to be used up or discarded after use rather than saved ■ **con·sum·a·bles** *npl.* CONSUMABLE GOODS goods that have to be bought regularly because they wear out or are used up, such as food and clothing

con·sume /kən sóom/ (**-sumed, -sum·ing, -sumes**) *v.* **1.** *vt.* EAT OR DRINK to eat or drink something, especially in large amounts **2.** *vt.* USE UP to use something in such a way that it cannot be reused or recovered afterwards ○ *The newer models consume less gasoline.* **3.** *vt.* ENGROSS OR OVERCOME to fill somebody's mind or attention fully (*usually passive*) ○ *consumed by a desire for new experiences* **4.** *vt.* DESTROY COMPLETELY to destroy something or somebody completely, especially by fire or disease **5.** *vti.* BUY FROM OTHERS to buy goods or services produced by other people [14thC. Directly or via French *consumer* from Latin *consumere* "to take up completely, devour," from *sumere* "to take."]

con·sum·er /kən sóomər/ *n.* **1.** BUYER somebody who buys goods or services **2.** SOMEBODY OR SOMETHING THAT CONSUMES SOMETHING somebody or something that consumes something, by eating it, drinking it, or using it up ○ *The country is one of the largest consumers of paper products.* **3.** ECOL ORGANISM THAT FEEDS ON OTHERS in an ecological community or food chain, an organism that feeds on other organisms, or on material derived from them. Consumers include herbivorous and carnivorous animals, which feed on plants and other animals respectively, and also organisms such as worms, fungi, and bacteria, which feed on nonliving organic material. —**con·sum·er·ship** *n.*

con·sum·er cred·it *n.* money lent by financial institutions to enable members of the public to buy consumer goods or services. Buying items with monthly payments, credit cards, and charge accounts are all forms of consumer credit.

con·sum·er du·ra·bles *npl.* items such as computers or washing machines, that last a relatively long time and are purchased infrequently

con·sum·er goods *npl.* goods that are bought by consumers and are not used to produce other goods

con·sum·er·ism /kən sóomə rìzzəm/ *n.* **1.** PROTECTION OF CONSUMERS' RIGHTS the protection of the rights and interests of consumers, especially with regard to price, quality, and safety **2.** MATERIALISTIC ATTITUDE an attitude that values the acquisition of material goods (*disapproving*) **3.** ECON BELIEF IN BENEFITS OF CONSUMPTION the belief that the buying and selling of large quantities of consumer goods is beneficial to an economy or a sign of economic strength —**con·sum·er·ist** *n., adj.*

con·sum·er price in·dex *n.* a government-issued index of the retail prices of basic household goods and services

con·sum·er so·ci·e·ty *n.* a society in which the consumption of mass-produced goods is encouraged through mass communication

con·sum·ing /kən sóoming/ *adj.* so intense as to take up all of somebody's attention, time, and energy ○ *a consuming interest in horses* —**con·sum·ing·ly** *adv.*

con·sum·mate *v.* /kónsə màyt/ (**-mat·ed, -mat·ing, -mates**) **1.** *vt.* COMPLETE MARRIAGE to make a marriage legally complete and fully valid by having sexual intercourse **2.** *vt.* FULFILL RELATIONSHIP THROUGH SEX to bring a relationship to completion or to gratify desire, especially by having sexual intercourse (*often passive*) **3.** *vti.* CONCLUDE to bring something such as a business deal to a conclusion, or to be brought to a conclusion (*formal*) ○ *Leaving her business partner to consummate the deal, she boarded a flight for New York.* **4.** *vt.* ACHIEVE to achieve or fulfill something, especially something long sought (*formal*) (*often passive*) ○ *Twelve years of effort and struggle were consummated when the foundation stone for the new theater was laid.* **5.** *vti.* BRING TO PERFECTION to develop a skill to the point of perfection, or to be brought to the point of perfection (*literary*) ■ *adj.* /kónsəmət, kən súmmət/ **1.** SUPREME OR PERFECT excellent, skillful, or accomplished ○ *with consummate ease* **2.** UTTER OR TOTAL possessing or showing a bad quality to an extreme degree ○ *consummate arrogance* [15thC. From Latin *consummat-*, past participle stem of *consummare* "to accomplish, to finish," from *summa* "the highest thing."] —**con·sum·mate·ly** *adv.* —**con·sum·ma·tive** /kónsə màytiv/ *adj.* —**con·sum·ma·tor** /-màytər/ *n.* —**con·sum·ma·to·ry** /kən súmmə tàwree/ *adj.*

con·sum·ma·tion /kòn sə máysh'n/ *n.* **1.** PERFECT ENDING the bringing of something to a satisfying conclusion, or the final satisfying completion or achievement of something ○ *The publication of her book was a consummation of her whole life's work.* **2.** LEGAL COMPLETION OF MARRIAGE BY SEX the legal completion of a marriage by an act of sexual intercourse between the spouses **3.** COMPLETION OF DEAL the completion of something, such as a business deal

con·sump·tion /kən súmpshən/ *n.* **1.** ACT OF EATING OR DRINKING the eating or drinking of something, or the amount that a person eats or drinks ○ *unfit for human consumption* **2.** ACT OF USING SOMETHING UP the use of natural resources or fuels or the amount of resources or fuels used ○ *consumption of fossil fuels*

3. CONSUMER EXPENDITURE the purchase and use of goods and services by consumers, or the quantity of goods and services purchased **4.** WASTING DISEASE any condition that causes progressive wasting of the tissues, especially tuberculosis of the lungs (*dated*) [14thC. Via French *consomption* from the Latin stem *consumption-*, from *consumere* (see CONSUME).]

con·sump·tive /kən súmptiv/ *adj.* **1.** AFFECTED BY TUBERCULOSIS affected by a wasting disease, especially tuberculosis of the lungs, or connected with such a disease (*dated*) **2.** ENGAGED IN OR CAUSING CONSUMPTION engaged in, causing, or encouraging the consumption of food, materials, or goods, especially in a wasteful or destructive way ■ *n.* SOMEBODY WITH TUBERCULOSIS somebody affected by a wasting disease, particularly tuberculosis of the lungs (*dated*) ○ *a chronic consumptive* [Mid-17thC. From medieval Latin *consumptivus*, from Latin *consumere* (see CONSUME).] —**con·sump·tive·ly** *adv.* —**con·sump·tive·ness** *n.*

cont. *abbr.* **1.** containing **2.** PUBL contents **3.** GEOG continent **4.** GEOG continental **5.** continued **6.** MED, GRAM contraction **7.** GRAM continuous **8.** control

con·tact /kón tàkt/ *n.* **1.** STATE OF COMMUNICATION a state or relationship in which communication happens or is possible ○ *Our only means of contact with the base was a small radio receiver.* **2.** ACT OF COMMUNICATING an act of communicating with somebody ○ *All my contacts with him to date have been about business.* **3.** PHYSICAL CONNECTION a situation or state in which two or more things or people actually touch or strike against one another ○ *White phosphorus ignites on contact with the air.* **4.** INTERACTION a state in which somebody has access to, and can be affected or influenced by, people, situations, ideas, or information ○ *You'll come into contact with a number of people.* **5.** SOMEBODY WHO CAN HELP somebody who may be useful either professionally or socially by providing a connection to a professional field or social circle **6.** MED INFECTIOUS PERSON somebody associated with and seen as a possible carrier of an infectious disease **7.** ELEC DEVICE MAKING ELECTRICAL CONNECTION a movable part, such as a component of a switch, that can be made to touch another conductive part in order to enable an electrical current to pass **8.** ELEC ELECTRICAL CONNECTION a connection between, or the connection of, two or more electrical conductors so that current flows between them ■ **con·tacts** *npl.* CONTACT LENSES a set of contact lenses (*informal*) ■ *v.* (**-tact·ed, -tact·ing, -tacts**) **1.** *vt.* REACH IN ORDER TO COMMUNICATE to send a message to somebody, or reach somebody, e.g., by telephone or letter, in order to communicate ○ *You can contact me at this number.* **2.** *vti.* TOUCH to touch or strike against something ■ *adj.* **1.** USED FOR COMMUNICATING WITH SOMEBODY used as a means to contact somebody ○ *a contact address* **2.** WORKING BY TOUCHING working or happening by touching or being touched by something or somebody **3.** CAUSED BY TOUCH caused by touching something that irritates ○ *contact dermatitis* [Early 17thC. From Latin *contactus*, past participle of *contingere*, literally "to touch with," from *tangere* "to touch."] —**con·tac·tu·al** /kən tákchoo əl/ *adj.* —**con·tac·tu·al·ly** /-tákchoo əlee/ *adv.*

con·tact·a·ble /kən táktəb'l/ *adj.* able to be contacted by somebody wishing to send a message or communicate

con·tact bi·na·ry *n.* ASTRON a binary star system in which one of the components is transferring matter to its companion star

con·tact flight, **con·tact fly·ing** *n.* navigation of an aircraft by observing landmarks and other visible guides without the use of navigational aids

con·tact group *n.* a group of people who are neutral in a dispute and meet both sides to try to resolve disagreements through discussion

con·tact in·hi·bi·tion *n.* the normal cessation of cell division and growth caused by physical contact with other cells. This normal end to cell division does not function when cancer is present, resulting in uncontrolled reproduction of cells.

con·tact lan·guage *n.* a simplified language variety retaining features of other languages contributing to it, used as a means of communication in regions where the majority of speakers share no common language

con·tact lens *n.* a small plastic or glass lens placed directly onto the front of the eye to correct defective vision or make the iris appear a different color

con·tac·tor /kón tàktər/ *n.* a switch that controls the flow of electric current by repeatedly opening and closing a circuit

con·tact print *n.* a photographic print made by placing a negative directly on top of photosensitive paper and exposing it to light. This is usually done to check the images on a roll of film before making enlargements from individual negatives.

con·tact sport *n.* a sport such as boxing or hockey in which physical contact between players is an integral part of the game

con·ta·gion /kən táyjən/ *n.* **1.** SPREAD OF DISEASE BY PHYSICAL CONTACT the transmission of disease, especially by physical contact between persons or contact with infected objects such as bedding or clothing **2.** DISEASE SPREAD BY PHYSICAL CONTACT an illness that spreads from one person to another, especially by physical contact between persons or contact with infected objects **3.** HARMFUL INFLUENCE a harmful or corrupting influence with a tendency to spread **4.** SPREAD OF FEELING the spreading of an attitude or emotion from person to person among a number of people (*literary*) ○ *the contagion of happiness* [14thC. From the Latin stem *contagion-*, from *contingere* (see CONTACT).]

con·ta·gious /kən táyjəss/ *adj.* **1.** ABLE TO BE PASSED BY CONTACT transmitted from one person to another either by direct contact, such as touching an infected person, or indirect contact **2.** CAPABLE OF TRANSMITTING DISEASE affected by or carrying a disease that can be transmitted by direct or indirect contact **3.** LIKELY TO AFFECT OTHERS quickly spread from one person to another ○ *Laughter is contagious.* [14thC. From late Latin *contagiosus*, from Latin *contingere* (see CONTACT).] —**con·ta·gious·ly** *adv.* —**con·ta·gious·ness** *n.*

con·ta·gious a·bor·tion *n.* VET a contagious or infectious disease of farm animals, e.g., brucellosis, that is characterized by abortion

con·tain /kən táyn/ (**-tained, -tain·ing, -tains**) *vt.* **1.** HAVE WITHIN to have something inside, or to hold something **2.** BE CAPABLE OF HOLDING PARTICULAR AMOUNT to be capable of holding something within, especially a particular amount **3.** INCLUDE OR CONSIST OF to include something as part of its contents or makeup **4.** CONTROL EMOTION to keep an emotion under control ○ *I couldn't contain myself any longer.* **5.** HOLD BACK OR RESTRICT to restrict the movement, spread, or influence of a strong enemy, force, disease, or idea **6.** MATH BE DIVISIBLE BY to be divisible by a number, leaving no remainder **7.** GEOM FORM SIDES OF ANGLE to form the boundaries that define an angle [13thC. Via French *contenir* from Latin *continere* "to hold together," from *tenere* "to hold."] —**con·tain·a·ble** *adj.*

con·tain·er /kən táynər/ *n.* **1.** OBJECT USED TO HOLD SOMETHING an object such as a box, jar, or bottle that is used to hold something, especially when it is being stored or transported **2.** FREIGHT BOX FOR CARGO a large box of a standard size into which goods are packed so that they can be transported securely and efficiently from departure point to destination by road, ship, or rail, without having to be repacked in any way

con·tain·er·board /kən táynər bàwrd/ *n.* heavy corrugated or solid cardboard used to make containers

con·tain·er·ize /kən táynə rìz/ (**-ized, -iz·ing, -iz·es**) *vt.* **1.** MOVE CARGO IN LARGE CONTAINERS to pack something in freight containers for transportation by sea, road, or rail, especially commercially **2.** MODERNIZE TO ACCEPT CONTAINERS to convert a port, transport system, or industry so that it can use or handle standard-sized cargo containers —**con·tain·er·i·za·tion** /kən tàynəri záysh'n/ *n.*

con·tain·er·port /kən táynər pàwrt/ *n.* a port capable of handling containerized cargo

con·tain·er ship *n.* a ship specially designed to carry cargo that is packed in freight containers

con·tain·ment /kən táynmənt/ *n.* **1.** ATTEMPT TO STOP SPREAD OF SOMETHING action taken to restrict the spread of something hostile such as an enemy, or something undesirable such as a disease **2.** NUCLEAR PHYS CONTROL MEASURE IN NUCLEAR REACTIONS the use of magnetic fields to prevent the reacting particles from touching the containing vessel's walls in a reactor **3.** ACT OR PROCESS OF CONTAINING SOMETHING the act or process of being contained or of containing something

con·tam·i·nant /kən támminənt/ *n.* a substance, such as a toxin in food, that contaminates something else

con·tam·i·nate /kən támmi nàyt/ (**-nat·ed, -nat·ing, -nates**) *vt.* **1.** MAKE DIRTY OR IMPURE to make something impure, unclean, or polluted, especially by mixing harmful impurities into it or by putting it in contact with something harmful **2.** NUCLEAR PHYS MAKE RADIOACTIVE to make something radioactive by mixing it or putting it in contact with a radioactive substance [15thC. From, ultimately, Latin *contaminare*, from *contamen* "contact, pollution," literally "touching with," from *tangere* "to touch."] —**con·tam·i·na·ble** *adj.* —**con·tam·i·na·tive** *adj.* —**con·tam·i·na·tor** *n.*

con·tam·i·na·tion /kən tàmmi náysh'n/ *n.* **1.** ACT OF CONTAMINATING SOMETHING the act or process of contaminating something or becoming contaminated, or the unclean or impure state that results from this **2.** SOMETHING THAT CONTAMINATES something that physically contaminates a substance or that corrupts a person morally ○ *The investigators found considerable contamination in the rivers.* **3.** LING ALTERATION OF WORD OR PHRASE the process by which a word or phrase changes as a result of mistaken association with another word or phrase

con·tan·go /kən táng gō/ *n.* (*plural* **-gos**) **1.** FIN BASIC PRICING SYSTEM IN FUTURES TRADING in futures and options trading, a system of pricing whereby longer-term contracts are priced higher than near-term contracts. The higher price on the longer-term contracts is a result of the cost of carrying those commodities for future delivery. **2.** *U.K.* POSTPONEMENT OF STOCK DELIVERY formerly on the London Stock Exchange, the postponement of the delivery of stock to a broker and payment for it, from one account day to the next **3.** *U.K.* INTEREST PAYABLE ON CONTANGO interest payable by a broker when the delivery of and payment for stock is postponed ■ *vt.* *U.K.* ARRANGE A CONTANGO to arrange for delivery and payment to be postponed when transferring stock in a stock exchange [Mid-19thC. Origin uncertain: perhaps an alteration of CONTINUE, or of Latin *contingo*, first person singular present tense of *contingere* (see CONTACT).]

contd. *abbr.* continued

conte /kawNt/ *n.* **1.** SHORT STORY a short story (*literary*) **2.** LITERAT MEDIEVAL NARRATIVE a narrative tale from the Middle Ages [Late 19thC. From French, where it was formed from Old French *counter* (see COUNT[1]).]

con·temn /kən tém/ (**-temned, -temn·ing, -temns**) *vt.* to view or treat somebody with contempt (*literary*) [15thC. Directly or via Old French *contemner* from Latin *contemnere* (see CONTEMPT).] —**con·temn·er** *n.* —**con·tem·ni·ble** *adj.* —**con·tem·ni·bly** *adv.*

contemp. *abbr.* contemporary

con·tem·plate /kón təm plàyt/ (**-plat·ed, -plat·ing, -plates**) *v.* **1.** *vt.* LOOK AT THOUGHTFULLY to look at something thoughtfully and steadily **2.** *vt.* CONSIDER to think about something seriously and at length, especially in order to understand it more fully ○ *I sat there, contemplating what she'd said.* **3.** *vt.* HAVE AS POSSIBLE INTENTION to think about something as a possible course of action ○ *contemplating moving house* **4.** *vi.* THINK ABOUT SPIRITUAL MATTERS to think calmly and at length, especially as a religious or spiritual exercise [Late 16thC. From Latin *contemplat-*, past participle stem of *contemplari* "to observe carefully," from *templum* "space for observing omens."] —**con·tem·pla·tor** *n.*

con·tem·pla·tion /kòntəm pláysh'n/ *n.* **1.** THOUGHT ABOUT SOMETHING long and attentive consideration or observation of something **2.** DEEP SPIRITUAL THOUGHT OR MEDITATION concentration of the mind on spiritual matters such as achieving closer unity with God

con·tem·pla·tive /kən témplətiv/ *adj.* MEDITATIVE calm and thoughtful, or inclined to be this way ■ *n.* SOMEBODY WHO PRACTICES CONTEMPLATION somebody who practices contemplation as a spiritual exercise, especially a member of a Christian monastic order —**con·tem·pla·tive·ly** *adv.* —**con·tem·pla·tive·ness** *n.*

con·tem·po·ra·ne·ous /kən tèmpə ráynee əss/ *adj.* existing, occurring, or beginning at the same time or during the same period of time as something else [Mid-17thC. Formed from Latin *contemporaneus*, literally "time together," from *tempor-* (see CONTEMPORARY).] —**con·tem·po·ra·ne·i·ty** /kən tèmpərə nee itee, kən tèmpərə náy itee/ *n.* —**con·tem·po·ra·ne·ous·ly** /kən tèmpə ráynee əsslee/ *adv.* —**con·tem·po·ra·ne·ous·ness** /-nəss/ *n.*

con·tem·po·rar·y /kən témpə ràiree/ *adj.* **1.** OF THE SAME TIME existing or occurring at, or dating from, the same period of time as something or somebody else **2.** EXISTING in existence now **3.** MODERN IN STYLE distinctively modern in style ○ *a variety of favorite contemporary styles* **4.** OF THE SAME AGE of the same, or approximately the same, age as somebody else ○ *She and I are more or less contemporary.* ■ *n.* (*plural* **-ies**) **1. SOMEBODY OR SOMETHING OF SAME TIME** somebody who lived or something that existed during the same general span of time as somebody or something else ○ *This 18th-century table is a contemporary of the Shaker furniture in the other room.* **2. SOMEBODY OF SAME AGE** somebody who is approximately the same age as somebody else ○ *It was nice to spend time with my Dad's contemporaries.* **3. MODERN PERSON OR THING** somebody or something in existence at the present time **4.** *U.K.* PRESS, PUBL **RIVAL NEWSPAPER OR MAGAZINE** a newspaper or magazine that is regarded as a rival or competition by another paper or periodical [Mid-17thC. From medieval Latin *contemporarius*, from Latin *tempor-*, stem of *tempus* "time" (source of English *tempo*, *temporary*, and *tense*).] —**con·tem·po·rar·i·ly** *adv.* —**con·tem·po·rar·i·ness** *n.*

con·tem·po·rize /kən tém pərīz/ (**-rized, -riz·ing, -riz·es**) *vt.* **1. MAKE MODERN** to make something modern or fashionable **2. DATE THINGS FROM SAME PERIOD** to place somebody or something in the same period as somebody or something else [Mid-17thC. Formed from late Latin *contemporare* "to make contemporary," from Latin *tempor-* (see CONTEMPORARY).] —**con·tem·po·ri·za·tion** /kən tèmpəri záysh'n/ *n.*

con·tempt /kən témpt/ *n.* **1. ATTITUDE OF UTTER DISGUST OR HATRED** a powerful feeling of dislike toward somebody or something considered to be worthless, inferior, or undeserving of respect **2.** LAW = **contempt of court** [14thC. From Latin *contemptus* "scorn," from *contemnere* "to despise utterly," from *temnere* "to scorn."]

con·tempt·i·ble /kən témptəb'l/ *adj.* deserving to be treated with contempt —**con·tempt·i·bil·i·ty** /kən tèmptə bíllətee/ *n.* —**con·tempt·i·ble·ness** /kən témptəb'lnəss/ *n.* —**con·tempt·i·bly** /-témtəblee/ *adv.*

con·tempt of court *n.* the crime of deliberately failing to obey or respect the authority of a court of law or legislative body

con·temp·tu·ous /kən témpchoo əss/ *adj.* feeling, expressing, or demonstrating a strong dislike or utter lack of respect for somebody or something [Early 16thC. From medieval Latin *contemptuosus*, from Latin *contemnere* (see CONTEMPT).] —**con·temp·tu·ous·ly** *adv.* —**con·temp·tu·ous·ness** *n.*

con·tend /kən ténd/ (**-tend·ed, -tend·ing, -tends**) *v.* **1.** *vi.* **STATE SOMETHING** to argue or claim that something is true **2.** *vti.* **COMPETE** to compete for something, especially a prize or trophy ○ *the teams contending for the cup* **3.** *vi.* **STRUGGLE OR DEAL WITH SOMETHING** to fight with, struggle against, or deal with somebody or something ○ *Their lawyers have a number of awkward issues to contend with.* **4.** *vi.* **DEBATE WITH SOMEBODY** to debate or dispute with somebody (*literary*) [15thC. Directly or via French *contendre* from Latin *contendere* "to strive together," from *tendere* "to strive, stretch."]

con·tend·er /kən téndər/ *n.* **1. COMPETITOR** a competitor, especially somebody who has a good chance of winning **2. ANY COMPETITOR** any competitor in a contest for a prize or title

WORD KEY: SYNONYMS

See Synonyms at ***candidate***.

con·tent[1] /kón tènt/ *n.* **1. AMOUNT OF SOMETHING IN SOMETHING ELSE** the amount of something contained in something else **2. SUBJECT MATTER** the various issues, topics, or questions dealt with in speech, discussion, or a piece of writing **3.** LITERAT **MEANING OR MESSAGE** the meaning or message contained in a creative work as distinct from its appearance, form, or style **4.** COMPUT **INFORMATION AVAILABLE ELECTRONICALLY** information made available by an electronic medium or product **5. INTELLECTUALLY INTERESTING MATERIAL** material or ideas that are considered to be interesting, challenging, or worthwhile **6. CAPACITY** the capacity of a container ■ **con·tents** *npl.* **1. SOMETHING CONTAINED** everything that is inside a particular container ○ *picked up the file and emptied its contents onto the desk* **2. SUBJECT OF TEXT** the subject matter of a publication **3. LIST OF SUBJECT OR CHAPTER HEADINGS** a list at the front of a publication that gives the title and number of the first page of each new chapter, article, or part [15thC. From medieval Latin *contentum* "something contained," a form of Latin *contentus*, past participle of *continere* (see CONTAIN).]

con·tent[2] /kən tént/ *adj.* **1. QUIETLY SATISFIED AND HAPPY** reasonably happy and satisfied with the way things are **2. READY TO ACCEPT SOMETHING** willing to accept or comply with a situation or course of action ■ *v.* (**-tent·ed, -tent·ing, -tents**) **1.** *vt.* **CAUSE TO FEEL CONTENT** to make somebody feel happy or satisfied with something **2.** *vr.* **ACCEPT OR MAKE DO WITH SOMETHING** to accept or make do with something, rather than taking further action or making more demands ○ *He contented himself with a few cutting remarks about lack of discipline and did not take the matter further.* ■ *n.* = **contentment** *n.* 1 [15thC. Via French from Latin *contentus*, past participle of *continere* (see CONTAIN). The underlying sense is of having your desires limited to what you have.] —**con·tent·ly** *adv.*

con·tent·ed /kən téntəd/ *adj.* peacefully happy and satisfied with the way things are, or with what you have done or achieved —**con·tent·ed·ly** *adv.* —**con·tent·ed·ness** *n.*

con·ten·tion /kən ténshən/ *n.* **1. ASSERTION IN AN ARGUMENT** an opinion or claim stated in the course of an argument ○ *It is my contention that the plan was bound to fail.* **2. DISAGREEMENT** angry disagreement between people ○ *a lot of contention over the quality of the goods* **3. RIVALRY** competition between rivals or opponents ○ *fierce contention for the title* [14thC. Directly or via French from the Latin stem *contention-*, from *contendere* (see CONTEND).]

con·ten·tious /kən ténshəss/ *adj.* **1. CREATING DISAGREEMENT** causing or likely to cause disagreement and disputes between people with differing views ○ *It should have been possible to word the statement in a less contentious way.* **2. ARGUMENTATIVE** frequently engaging in and seeming to enjoy arguments and disputes **3.** LAW **SUBJECT TO LITIGATION** contested by another interested party ○ *a contentious will* [15thC. Via French *contentieux* from Latin *contentiosus*, from *contendere* (see CONTEND).] —**con·ten·tious·ly** *adv.* —**con·ten·tious·ness** *n.*

con·tent·ment /kən téntmənt/ *n.* **1. SATISFACTION** a feeling of calm satisfaction **2. SOMETHING THAT MAKES SOMEBODY CONTENTED** a circumstance, or a feature or characteristic of something, that gives rise to satisfaction (*formal or literary*)

con·tent word *n.* LING a word that refers to a real world object and primarily conveys meaning. ◊ **function word**

con·ter·mi·nous /kən túrminəss/, **co·ter·mi·nous** /kō-/ *adj.* **1. INSIDE SAME BOUNDARY** enclosed inside a common boundary **2. ADJACENT** next to and sharing a common boundary with something **3. MEETING IN TIME OR PLACE** meeting end to end, so that where or when one finishes the next begins **4. OF EQUAL EXTENT OR SCOPE** equal in length or extent, either in space or time, or having the same range of meaning as another term (*formal*) [Mid-17thC. From Latin *conterminus*, literally "boundary with," from *terminus* "boundary."] —**con·ter·mi·nous·ly** *adv.* —**con·ter·mi·nous·ness** *n.*

con·tes·sa /kən téssə, kon-/ *n.* an Italian countess [Early 19thC. Via Italian from medieval Latin *comitissa*, feminine of *comes* (see COUNT[2]).]

con·test *n.* /kón tèst/ **1. COMPETITION TO FIND THE BEST** an organized competition for a prize or title, especially one in which the entrants appear or demonstrate their skills individually and the winner is chosen by a group of judges **2. STRUGGLE FOR CONTROL** a struggle between rival or opposing individuals, organizations, or forces for victory or control ■ *vt.* /kən tést/ (**-test·ed, -test·ing, -tests**) **1. CHALLENGE** to challenge or question something **2. TAKE PART IN CONTEST** to take part in a contest or competition [Late 16thC. Directly or via French from Latin *contestari* "to begin a lawsuit by calling witnesses together," from *testari* "to be a witness."] —**con·test·a·ble** /kən téstəb'l/ *adj.* —**con·test·a·bly** /-téstəblee/ *adv.* —**con·test·er** /-téstər/ *n.*

con·tes·tant /kən téstənt/ *n.* **1. SOMEBODY COMPETING IN CONTEST** somebody who takes part in a competition **2.** LAW **FORMAL CHALLENGER** somebody who enters a formal challenge to something such as a will, verdict, or decision

WORD KEY: SYNONYMS

See Synonyms at ***candidate***.

con·text /kón tèkst/ *n.* **1. TEXT SURROUNDING A WORD OR PASSAGE** the words, phrases, or passages that come before and after a particular word or passage in a speech or piece of writing and help to explain its full meaning **2. SURROUNDING CONDITIONS** the circumstances or events that form the environment within which something exists or takes place [15thC. From Latin *contextus* "cohering, connected," from *contexere* "to weave together," from *texere* "to weave."]

con·tex·tu·al /kən tékschoo əl/ *adj.* forming, relating to, or contained in the context of a word or event —**con·tex·tu·al·ly** *adv.*

con·tex·tu·al·ize /kən tékschoo ə līz/ (**-ized, -iz·ing, -iz·es**) *vt.* to place a word, phrase, or idea within a suitable context —**con·tex·tu·al·i·za·tion** /kən tèkschoo əli záysh'n/ *n.*

con·tex·ture /kən tékschər/ *n.* **1. WEAVING TOGETHER** the process of weaving together separate strands, e.g., of an argument, to form a complex but coherent whole **2. INTERWOVEN STRUCTURE** a structure resulting from the complex interweaving of separate strands or parts [Early 17thC. From French, literally "weaving together," from, ultimately, Latin *textura* "weaving."] —**con·tex·tur·al** *adj.*

Con·ti /kóntee/, **Tom** (*b.* 1942) Scottish-born British stage and movie actor. He is a versatile character actor whose success dates from his Tony award for the Broadway production of *Whose Life Is It Anyway?* (1974).

con·ti·gu·i·ty /kòntə gyoō ətee/ (*plural* **-ties**) *n.* (*formal*) **1. CLOSENESS OR CONTACT** closeness in space or time to something, or actual contact with it along one side **2. SOMETHING CONTINUOUS** a continuous line, mass, or series ○ *a contiguity of roofs*

con·tig·u·ous /kən tíggyoo əss/ *adj.* (*formal*) **1. ADJOINING** sharing a boundary or touching each other physically **2. NEIGHBORING** situated next to something else or to each other **3. CONTINUOUS** connected together so as to form an unbroken sequence in time or an uninterrupted expanse in space [Early 16thC. Formed from Latin *contiguus* "touching together," from *contingere* (see CONTACT).] —**con·tig·u·ous·ly** *adv.* —**con·tig·u·ous·ness** *n.*

con·ti·nence /kóntinəns/ *n.* **1. CONTROL OVER URINATION AND BOWELS** the ability to prevent involuntary urination and bowel movements **2. SELF-RESTRAINT** control over physical, especially sexual, impulses leading to self-restraint, moderation, or abstinence [14thC. Directly or via French from Latin *continentia*, from *continere* (see CONTAIN).]

con·ti·nent[1] /kóntinənt/ *n.* **1. LAND MASS** any one of the seven large continuous land masses that constitute most of the dry land on the surface of the earth. They are Africa, Antarctica, Asia, Australia, Europe, North America, and South America. **2.** GEOG **LAND ABOVE SEA LEVEL** the part of the earth's crust that rises above the oceans [Mid-16thC. From Latin *terra continens* "continuous land," from the present participle of *continere* (see CONTAIN).]

con·ti·nent[2] /kóntinənt/ *adj.* **1. ABLE TO CONTROL URINATION AND BOWELS** able to exercise control over urination and bowel movements **2. MODERATE OR CELIBATE** restrained, especially abstaining from sexual activity [14thC. From Latin *continent-*, present participle stem of *continere* (see CONTAIN).]

Con·ti·nent *n.* the mainland of Europe, not including the British Isles

con·ti·nen·tal /kònti nént'l/ *adj.* **1. RELATING TO EARTH'S CONTINENTS** relating to, typical of, or belonging to the continents of the earth **2.** FOOD **OF CLASSIC EUROPEAN CUISINE** relating to the traditional food and dishes of western European countries, especially France ■ *n.* **1. WHIT** something small and worthless ○ *I wouldn't give a dime for that cheap merchandise, and I don't care a continental what the manufacturer thinks.* **2.** HIST **BANKNOTE** a banknote that was issued by the Continental Congress during the American Revolution —**con·ti·nen·tal·ism** *n.* —**con·ti·nen·tal·ist** *n.* —**con·ti·nen·tal·ly** *adv.*

Con·ti·nen·tal *adj.* **1. Con·ti·nen·tal, con·ti·nen·tal OF MAINLAND EUROPE** from or relating to mainland Europe **2.** HIST **OF THE ORIGINAL 13 AMERICAN COLONIES** from or relating to the 13 colonies that later became the United States. ◊ **Continental Congress** ■ *n.* **1. Con·ti·nen·tal, con·ti·nen·tal MAINLAND EUROPEAN** somebody from mainland Europe (*informal*) **2.** HIST **AMERICAN SOLDIER DURING REVOLUTION** a soldier in the American army during the Revolution

con·ti·nen·tal break·fast *n.* a light breakfast usually consisting of fruit juice, a roll, croissant, or pastry with jam and butter, and coffee or tea [continental from the fact that this kind of breakfast is common on the Continent]

Con·ti·nen·tal Con·gress *n.* HIST the congress of delegates from the American colonies held before, during, and after the American Revolution. It issued the Declaration of Independence (1776) and drafted the Articles of Confederation (1777).

con·ti·nen·tal crust *n.* GEOG the part of the outer shell of the solid earth that constitutes the continents and the rocks beneath them as deep as the mantle. It is approximately 22 mi./35 km thick in most areas and is composed of sedimentary rocks near the surface and metamorphic rocks at a lower depth.

con·ti·nen·tal di·vide *n.* GEOG a massive area of high ground in the interior of a continent, from either side of which a continent's river systems flow in different directions

Con·ti·nen·tal Di·vide *n.* the series of mountain ridges running from Alaska to Mexico and including the Rocky Mountains that forms the main watershed of North America

con·ti·nen·tal drift *n.* a theory that explains the formation, alteration, and extremely slow movement of the continents across the earth's crust. The continents are thought to have been formed from one large landmass that split, drifted apart, and in places collided again. ◊ **plate tectonics**

con·ti·nen·tal shelf *n.* the gently sloping undersea area surrounding a continent at depths of up to 656 ft./200 m, at the edge of which the continental slope drops steeply to the ocean floor

con·ti·nen·tal slope *n.* the steep slope from the continental shelf down to the ocean floor

con·ti·nen·tal U·nit·ed States *n.* the United States excluding its island possessions and the state of Hawaii

con·tin·gence /kən tínjəns/ *n.* **1.** CONTACT physical contact between objects **2.** = **contingency** *n.* 1

con·tin·gen·cy /kən tínjənsee/ (*plural* **-cies**) *n.* **1.** SOMETHING THAT MAY HAPPEN an event that may occur in the future, especially a problem, emergency, or expense that might arise unexpectedly, needs to be dealt with, and therefore must be prepared for **2.** SOMETHING INCIDENTAL OR DEPENDENT something that occurs or exists only as a result of something else or that depends on something else **3.** DEPENDENCE UPON CHANCE dependence upon chance or factors and circumstances that are presently unknown **4.** GRAM CHANGE IN MEANING PRODUCED BY CLAUSE in systemic grammar, a change in the meaning of the main clause brought about by the addition of a dependent clause introduced by "if," "when," "though," or "since"

con·tin·gen·cy fee *n.* a payment for professional services, such as those of a lawyer, that is made only if the client receives a satisfactory result

con·tin·gen·cy force *n.* MIL = **rapid-deployment force**

con·tin·gen·cy plan *n.* a plan designed to deal with a particular problem, emergency, or state of affairs if it should occur

con·tin·gent /kən tínjənt/ *adj.* **1.** DEPENDENT ON WHAT MAY HAPPEN dependent on or resulting from a future and as yet unknown event or circumstance ○ *Payment is contingent upon winning the case.* **2.** POSSIBLE BUT NOT CERTAIN possible, but not certain to happen ○ *"... all the advantages of a long slow ramble with Elfride, without the contingent possibility of the enjoyment being spoilt by her becoming weary."* (Thomas Hardy, *A Pair of Blue Eyes*; 1889) **3.** CHANCE happening by chance **4.** LOGIC TRUE ONLY UNDER CERTAIN CONDITIONS true only under certain conditions or under existing conditions, and therefore not universally true or valid ■ *n.* **1.** GROUP OF PEOPLE a group of people representing a particular organization or belief, or from a particular region or country, and forming part of a larger group **2.** MIL GROUP OF MILITARY PERSONNEL a group, particularly of soldiers, forming part of a larger force **3.** = **contingency** *n.* 1 [14thC. From Latin *contingent-*, present participle stem of *contingere* "to happen, have contact with." The underlying idea is of being affected by things happening.] —**con·tin·gent·ly** *adv.*

con·tin·gent fee *n.* = **contingency fee**

con·tin·gent work·er *n.* a temporary employee, often employed for a specific task

con·tin·u·al /kən tínnyoo əl/ *adj.* **1.** RECURRING VERY FREQUENTLY happening again and again, especially regularly **2.** UNINTERRUPTED continuing without interruption or ending [14thC. From French *continuel*, from *continuer* (see CONTINUE).] —**con·tin·u·al·ness** *n.*

WORD KEY: USAGE

continual or **continuous**? Something ***continual*** stops from time to time but continues intermittently over a long period, whereas something ***continuous*** goes on without a break. So a ***continual*** noise is one that is constantly repeated, like a dog's barking, and a ***continuous*** noise is one that continues unbroken, like the roar of a waterfall. The same distinction applies to the adverbs *continually* and *continuously*: *The speaker was continually interrupted by hecklers. She drove continuously for ten hours.*

con·tin·u·al·ly /kən tínnyoo əlee/ *adv.* **1.** REGULARLY OR FREQUENTLY with great frequency or regularity **2.** WITHOUT INTERRUPTION all the time, without stopping or without interruption ○ *hard to think with the kids continually screaming*

WORD KEY: USAGE

See Usage note at ***continual***.

con·tin·u·ance /kən tínnyoo əns/ *n.* **1.** CONTINUATION OF SOMETHING the fact or quality of continuing to be in a particular situation, to exist, or to occur beyond the present time into the future **2.** LENGTH OF TIME SOMETHING LASTS the period of time that something lasts or continues **3.** LAW ADJOURNMENT a postponement of legal proceedings until a later date

con·tin·u·ant /kən tínnyoo ənt/ *n.* a speech sound, such as "l," "f," or "s," made with the vocal passage partly open for breath to pass through, thus enabling the sound to be prolonged at will. ◊ **stop**

con·tin·u·a·tion /kən tìnnyoo áysh'n/ *n.* **1.** PROCESS OF CONTINUING the process of continuing something without interruption **2.** ADDITION OR EXTENSION an additional part that extends something that already exists or has already begun **3.** STARTING AGAIN AFTER INTERRUPTION the renewal of an action, event, or process after it has been interrupted

con·tin·u·a·tive /kən tínnyoo ətiv, -àytiv/ *adj.* **1.** AIDING CONTINUITY causing or helping something to continue (*formal*) **2.** GRAM EXPRESSING CONTINUATION expressing the continuation of an action ■ *n.* GRAM WORD EXPRESSING CONTINUATION a continuative clause, phrase, or word —**con·tin·u·a·tive·ly** *adv.*

con·tin·u·a·tor /kən tínnyoo àytər/ *n.* somebody who continues something, especially work started by another person

con·tin·ue /kən tínnyoo/ (**-ued, -u·ing, -ues**) *v.* **1.** *vti.* KEEP GOING to last, or to make something last, beyond the present **2.** *vti.* LAST to last or to make something last throughout a particular period of time **3.** *vti.* NOT STOP to keep up an activity or state already begun **4.** *vti.* START SOMETHING AGAIN to start, or to start doing something again after an interruption or pause **5.** *vti.* UTTER OR BEGIN SPEAKING AGAIN to begin speaking again, or to say something, after an interruption or pause **6.** *vti.* MAKE SOMETHING LONGER to extend, or to extend something, beyond a particular point or beyond its original length **7.** *vi.* MOVE FURTHER to move or travel further in a particular direction **8.** *vt. U.S., Scotland* LAW POSTPONE CASE to postpone legal proceedings [14thC. Via French *continuer* from Latin *continuare* "to make or be continuous," from, ultimately, *continere* (see CONTAIN).] —**con·tin·u·a·ble** *adj.* —**con·tin·u·er** *n.*

con·tin·ued /kən tínnyood/ *adj.* **1.** UNINTERRUPTED uninterrupted or unchanged from its beginning up to the present time **2.** BEGUN AGAIN begun again after a break or interruption

con·tin·ued frac·tion *n.* a fraction with a whole number as numerator, a number plus a fraction as denominator, which in turn has a number plus a fraction as its denominator. If there is a finite number of terms, it is said to be terminating, otherwise it is nonterminating.

con·tin·u·ing /kən tínnyoo ing/ *adj.* having existed for some time, currently in existence, and likely to remain so in the future —**con·tin·u·ing·ly** *adv.*

con·tin·u·ing ed·u·ca·tion *n.* **1.** LIFELONG ADULT EDUCATION adult education, usually in the form of short or part-time courses, continuing throughout an individual's life **2.** SPECIALIST COURSES TO UPDATE PROFESSIONALS regular courses or training designed to bring professionals up to date with the latest developments in their particular field

con·ti·nu·i·ty /kònti nóo ətee/ (*plural* **-ties**) *n.* **1.** UNCHANGING QUALITY the fact of staying the same, of being consistent throughout, or of not stopping or being interrupted ○ *measures to ensure continuity of care* **2.** CONSISTENT WHOLE something that remains consistent or uninterrupted throughout ○ *This program has benefited from two important continuities, in staffing and leadership.* **3.** CINEMA, BROADCAST CONSISTENCY BETWEEN FILM OR BROADCAST PARTS consistency in the details from one part of a film or broadcast to another ○ *discrepancies in continuity* **4.** CINEMA, BROADCAST SEAMLESSNESS OF NARRATIVE smoothness in the narrative flow in a film or broadcast **5.** CINEMA DETAILED SCRIPT a comprehensive script that includes full details of the contents of each shot or scene, including such items as camera positions and settings and costume features **6.** BROADCAST SPOKEN LINK IN BROADCASTING things said by a television or radio announcer to fill the time between the end of one program and the beginning of the next, or between parts of programs

con·tin·u·o /kən tínnyoo ō/ (*plural* **-os**) *n.* an instrumental bass accompaniment, usually played on a keyboard, with numbers written beneath the notes so that musicians can improvise and provide harmony [Early 18thC. From Italian, literally "continuous," from Latin *continuus* (see CONTINUOUS).]

con·tin·u·ous /kən tínnyoo əss/ *adj.* **1.** UNCHANGED OR UNINTERRUPTED continuing without changing, stopping, or being interrupted in space or time ○ *three days of continuous rain* **2.** UNBROKEN having no gaps, holes, or breaks ○ *a continuous line* **3.** GRAM = **progressive 4.** MATH RELATING TO DIFFERENCE OF FUNCTION VALUES relating to a line or curve along which the difference between function values at any two points within a given interval will approach zero if the interval is decreased sufficiently **5.** RELATING TO UNINTERRUPTED CHEMICAL MANUFACTURING relating to chemical manufacturing in which material is processed in an uninterrupted stream. Continuous processes are usually advantageous for large-scale chemical production. [Mid-17thC. Formed from Latin *continuus* "uninterrupted," from *continere* (see CONTAIN).] —**con·tin·u·ous·ness** *n.*

WORD KEY: USAGE

See Usage note at ***continual***.

con·tin·u·ous cre·a·tion the·o·ry *n.* ASTRON = **steady-state theory**

con·tin·u·ous·ly /kən tínnyoo əsslee/ *adv.* **1.** WITHOUT INTERRUPTION without any break or interruption ○ *It had rained continuously for three days.* See Usage note at **continual 2.** RECURRENTLY frequently or regularly

con·tin·u·ous spec·trum *n.* a sequence of frequencies that is without breaks over a relatively wide range of wavelengths

con·tin·u·ous wave *n.* an electromagnetic wave generated as an unbroken train of constant frequency and amplitude, rather than in pulses

con·tin·u·um /kən tínnyoo əm/ (*plural* **-a** /-nyoo ə/ *or* **-ums**) *n.* **1.** CONTINUOUS SEAMLESS SERIES a link between two things, or a continuous series of things, that blend into each other so gradually and seamlessly that it is impossible to say where one becomes the next ○ *A rainbow forms a continuum of color.* **2.** MATH SET OF NUMBERS a set of real numbers between any two of which a third can always be found, and in which there are no gaps [Mid-17thC. From Latin, a form of *continuus* (see CONTINUOUS).]

con·tort /kən táwrt/ (**-tort·ed, -tort·ing, -torts**) *v.* **1.** *vti.* TWIST OUT OF NATURAL SHAPE to become so twisted as to take on an unnatural or grotesque shape or to twist something, especially a part of the body, in this way ○ *Fear had contorted their faces.* **2.** *vt.* MAKE UNRECOGNIZABLE to change something so greatly that it becomes unrecognizable ○ *to contort the truth* [15thC. From Latin *contort-*, past participle stem of *contorquere* "to twist violently," from *torquere* "to twist."] —**con·tor·tive** *adj.*

con·tort·ed /kən táwrtəd/ *adj.* **1.** VERY TWISTED greatly or violently twisted out of shape **2.** OVERLAPPING used to describe plant parts such as sepals or leaves whose margins overlap in the bud like playing cards in a hand, so that they appear to be twisted —**con·tort·ed·ly** *adv.* —**con·tort·ed·ness** *n.*

con·tor·tion /kən táwrsh'n/ *n.* **1.** TWISTED SHAPE OR POSITION a twisting of something, especially a part of the body, out of its natural shape **2.** COMPLEX MANEUVER a bewilderingly complex maneuvering or manipulation of something ○ *verbal contortions*

con·tor·tion·ist /kən táwrshənist/ *n.* **1. SOMEBODY WHO PERFORMS BENDING FEATS** somebody who bends his or her body into unnatural shapes, especially as entertainment ○ *You'd have to be a contortionist to get into those jeans.* **2. SKILLFUL MANIPULATOR OR MANEUVERER** somebody who twists or distorts things, e.g., things people say, or who wriggles out of things, e.g., difficult situations ○ *a debater skilled as a logical contortionist* —**con·tor·tion·is·tic** /kən tàwrshə nístik/ *adj.*

con·tour /kòn to͝or/ *n.* **1. OUTLINE** an outline, especially of something curved or irregular (*often used in the plural*) ○ *The contours of the hills were characteristically rounded.* **2. GENERAL NATURE** the general character or nature of something ○ *scenes that establish the contour of the play* **3.** = **contour line** ■ *adj.* **1. SHAPED OR FITTED** shaped to fit something, especially the shape of somebody's body ○ *contour furniture* **2. FOLLOWING LAND'S SHAPE** following the lay of the land, rather than cutting through or across it ○ *contour farming* ■ *vt.* (**-toured, -tour·ing, -tours**) **1. SHAPE TO FIT** to shape one thing so that it fits the outlines of another ○ *furniture that is contoured to the human body* **2. PUT CONTOUR LINES ON** to mark contour lines on something such as a map **3. CAUSE TO FIT LAND'S SHAPE** to build or operate something so that it follows the natural shape of the land ○ *roads that are sensitively contoured* [Mid-17thC. Via French from, ultimately, Italian *contornare* "to draw in outline," literally "to turn with," from Latin *tornare* "to turn (in a lathe)" (see TURN).]

con·tour feath·er *n.* a medium-sized feather of a bird, excluding those on the wings and tail, that makes up its external covering and determines its shape

con·tour in·ter·val *n.* the interval between contour lines on a map, or the altitude the interval represents ○ *at contour intervals of 50 to 100 feet*

con·tour line *n.* a line on a map connecting points on a land surface that are the same elevation above sea level ○ *On this map, contour lines show you where the mountains are.*

con·tour map *n.* a map that uses contour lines to show the shapes and elevations of land surfaces

contr. *abbr.* **1.** GRAM contraction **2.** MUSIC contralto **3.** control

contra /kóntrə/ *n.* a member of the United States-backed counterrevolutionary force whose aim was to bring down the Nicaraguan government in the 1980s [From Spanish *contrarevolucionario* "counter-revolutionary"]

contra- *prefix.* **1.** against, opposite, contrasting ○ *contraindicate* **2.** lower in pitch ○ *contrabass* [From Latin *contra* "against." Ultimately from an Indo-European base meaning "together," which is also the ancestor of English *com-*.]

con·tra·band /kóntrə bànd/ *n.* **1. ILLEGAL IMPORTS AND EXPORTS** goods that are illegally imported or exported, e.g., goods that evade duty or are prohibited by law from being taken into or out of a country ○ *dealers in contraband* **2. ILLEGAL TRADE** illegal trade, especially the illegal importing or exporting of goods **3. SUPPLIES FORBIDDEN TO WARRING SIDES** goods that a neutral country must not supply to either side in a war **4. SLAVE IN UNION TERRITORY** a slave who escaped to, or was taken behind, Union lines during the Civil War ■ *adj.* **1. ILLEGALLY TRADED** bought or sold, especially imported or exported, illegally ○ *truckloads of contraband cigarettes* **2. FORBIDDEN FROM BEING IMPORTED OR EXPORTED** forbidden by law from being traded, especially as an import or export [Late 16thC. Via Spanish *contrabanda* from Italian *contrabbando*, literally "against proclamation," from *bando* "proclamation," ultimately from prehistoric Germanic.] —**con·tra·band·age** *n.* —**con·tra·band·ist** *n.*

con·tra·bass /kóntrə bàyss/ *n.* **1. DOUBLE BASS** a double bass **2. INSTRUMENT PITCHED LOWEST OF ITS FAMILY** an instrument pitched an octave below the usual range for that family of instruments **3. CONTRABASSIST** an instrumentalist in an orchestra or band who plays the contrabass ■ *adj.* **PITCHED AN OCTAVE BELOW** pitched an octave below the usual range of that instrument ○ *contrabass clarinet* [Early 19thC. From Italian *contrabbasso*, from *basso* "bass."] —**con·tra·bass·ist** /kòntrə báyssist/ *n.*

con·tra·bas·soon /kòntrə bə so͞on/ *n.* **1. LARGEST INSTRUMENT OF OBOE FAMILY** a U-shaped woodwind instrument that is the largest in the oboe family and has a pitch an octave below the bassoon **2. CONTRABASSOONIST** an instrumentalist in an orchestra or chamber group who plays the contrabassoon —**con·tra·bas·soon·ist** *n.*

con·tra·cep·tion /kòntrə sépshən/ *n.* a way of avoiding pregnancy, using either artificial methods such as condoms and birth-control pills or natural methods such as avoiding sex during the woman's known fertile periods [Late 19thC. Coined from CONTRA- + CONCEPTION.]

con·tra·cep·tive /kòntrə séptiv/ *n.* **DEVICE PREVENTING FERTILIZATION** a device used to prevent fertilization of an egg, e.g., a condom worn by a man during intercourse or a pill taken regularly by a woman ■ *adj.* **PREVENTING INSEMINATION** designed to prevent sperm from fertilizing an egg ○ *various contraceptive methods and devices*

con·tract *n.* /kón tràkt/ **1. FORMAL AGREEMENT** a formal or legally binding agreement, such as one for the sale of something, or one setting out terms of employment ○ *Such actions would be in breach of contract.* **2. DOCUMENT RECORDING AGREEMENT** a document that records a formal or legally binding agreement ○ *sign a contract* **3. AGREEMENT TO MARRY** a formal agreement to marry (*dated*) **4. PAID ASSASSIN'S ASSIGNMENT** a hiring of an assassin to kill somebody (*informal*) **5. AGREEMENT BETWEEN CLIENT AND THERAPIST** a verbal or written agreement drawn up between a client and therapist in a first session describing the conditions for future counseling or therapy sessions. It may include agreements on the number, duration, and cost of sessions, and procedures for nonattendance and confidentiality. **6.** BRIDGE **HIGHEST BRIDGE BID IN ONE HAND** a winning bid in a single hand of bridge, in which partners agree regarding the number of tricks they can take **7.** BRIDGE **NUMBER AND SUIT OF CONTRACT** the number and suit of the tricks agreed on by the highest bidders **8.** BRIDGE = **contract bridge 9. con·tracts** LAW **BRANCH OF LAW** the branch or category of law and legal education that deals with contracts ○ *She made a career in contracts.* ■ *v.* /kən trákt, kón tràkt/ (**-tract·ed, -tract·ing, -tracts**) **1.** *vti.* **SHRINK OR LESSEN** to shrink or become smaller, or make something shrink or become smaller ○ *metals expanding and contracting as temperatures change* **2.** *vti.* **TIGHTEN OR DRAW TOGETHER** to become tighter or draw together, or make something tighter or draw something together ○ *see the muscles contracting under the skin* **3.** *vi.* **FORMALLY OR LEGALLY AGREE** to make a formal or legally binding agreement to do something, especially work (*often passive*) ○ *I'm not contracted to work on Sundays.* **4.** *vt.* **GET ILLNESS** to catch or develop an illness or disease **5.** *vt.* **SHORTEN WORD OR PHRASE** to shorten a word by leaving out letters or syllables, or a phrase by leaving out words **6.** *vt.* **ARRANGE MARRIAGE** to arrange a marriage formally (*dated*) [14thC. Directly or via French from Latin *contractus*, past participle of *contrahere* "to draw together," from *trahere* "to draw" (see TRACTOR).] —**con·tract·i·bil·i·ty** /kən tràktə bíllətee/ *n.* —**con·tract·i·ble** /kən tráktəb'l/ *adj.* —**con·tract·i·ble·ness** *n.* —**con·tract·i·bly** *adv.*

contract out *v.* **1.** *vt.* **GIVE WORK TO OUTSIDERS** to offer work to outside companies or individuals **2.** *vi.* *U.K.* **WITHDRAW FORMALLY** to withdraw from something by making a formal or legally binding declaration ○ *employees contracting out of the state pension scheme*

con·tract bridge *n.* the most common variety of bridge, in which points are awarded only for tricks bid as well as won

con·trac·tile /kən trákt'l/ *adj.* able or tending to shrink, tighten, or become narrower —**con·trac·til·i·ty** /kòn trak tíllətee/ *n.*

con·trac·tile vac·u·ole *n.* BIOL a membrane-surrounded cavity within a cell that regulates the water content of the cell by absorbing water and then contracting to expel it

con·trac·tion /kən trákshən/ *n.* **1. REDUCTION IN SIZE** a shrinking or reducing ○ *alternate expansion and contraction* **2. CONTRACTING OF BODY PART** a tightening or narrowing of a muscle, organ, or other body part **3. TIGHTENING OF WOMB MUSCLES EFFECTING CHILDBIRTH** a tightening of the muscles of the womb that occurs at increasingly frequent intervals immediately before childbirth and eventually pushes the baby out of the womb **4. SHORTENED WORD** a shortened form or shortening of a word or phrase, e.g., "he'll" for "he will," or "Dr." for "Doctor." In English the omitted letter or letters are usually marked with an apostrophe or a period, depending on the type of contraction. —**con·trac·tion·al** *adj.* —**con·trac·tion·ar·y** *adj.* —**con·trac·tive** /-tráktiv/ *adj.*

con·trac·tor /kón tràktər/ *n.* **1. COMPANY OR PERSON UNDER CONTRACT** a company or individual with a formal contract to do a specific job, supplying labor and materials and providing and overseeing staff if needed ○ *a building contractor* ○ *The contractors are handling the electrical wiring.* **2. THING THAT CONTRACTS** something that contracts, e.g., a muscle **3. SOMEBODY WHO MAKES A CONTRACT** one of the parties to a contract

con·trac·tu·al /kən trákchoo əl/ *adj.* contained in, arising from, or in the form of a formal or legally binding agreement ○ *fulfilling your contractual obligations* —**con·trac·tu·al·ly** *adv.*

con·trac·ture /kən trákchər/ *n.* a permanent abnormal tightening or shortening of a body part, such as a muscle, a tendon, or the skin, often resulting in deformity

con·tra·dance, **con·tra·danse** *n.* = **contredanse**

con·tra·dict /kòntrə díkt/ (**-dict·ed, -dict·ing, -dicts**) *vt.* **1. DISAGREE WITH** to argue against the truth or correctness of somebody's statement or claim **2. SHOW TO BE WRONG** to show that something is not true, or show that the opposite is true ○ *The results contradicted all previously held theories.* [Late 16thC. From Latin *contradict-*, past participle stem of *contradicere* "to speak against," from *dicere* "to speak" (source of English *dictate* and *diction*).] —**con·tra·dict·a·ble** *adj.* —**con·tra·dict·er** *n.* —**con·tra·dic·tive** *adj.* —**con·tra·dic·tive·ly** *adv.* —**con·tra·dic·tive·ness** *n.*

WORD KEY: SYNONYMS

See Synonyms at ***disagree***.

con·tra·dic·tion /kòntrə díksh'n/ *n.* **1. SOMETHING ILLOGICAL** something that contains parts or elements that are illogical or inconsistent with each other ○ *a contradiction in terms* **2. OPPOSING STATEMENT** a statement or the making of a statement that opposes or disagrees with somebody or something ○ *I can say without fear of contradiction that she is our best worker.*

con·tra·dic·to·ry /kòntrə díktəree/ *adj.* **1. INCONSISTENT** inconsistent either within itself or in relation to one or more others **2. OPPOSING** holding or consisting of an opposite view in relation to something **3. ARGUMENTATIVE** fond of or given to taking opposite views —**con·tra·dic·to·ri·ly** *adv.* —**con·tra·dic·to·ri·ness** *n.*

con·tra·dis·tinc·tion /kòntrə di stínkshən/ *n.* differentiation between two things by identifying their contrasting qualities —**con·tra·dis·tinc·tive** *adj.* —**con·tra·dis·tinc·tive·ly** *adv.*

con·trail /kón tràyl/ *n.* = **vapor trail** [Mid-20thC. Contraction of condensation trail.]

con·tra·in·di·cate /kòntrə índi kàyt/ (**-cat·ed, -cat·ing, -cates**) *vt.* to state something to be inadvisable while taking certain medication because of a likely adverse reaction ○ *Taking aspirin with this drug is contraindicated.* —**con·tra·in·di·cant** *n.* —**con·tra·in·di·ca·tion** /kòntrə indi káysh'n/ *n.* —**con·tra·in·dic·a·tive** /kòntrə in díkətiv/ *adj.*

con·tra·lat·er·al /kòntrə láttərəl/ *adj.* used to describe a body part on the opposite side of the body or that acts in conjunction with such a part

con·tral·to /kən tráltō/ (*plural* **-tos**) *n.* **1. LOWEST FEMALE VOCAL RANGE** the lowest vocal range for women's voices, below soprano and mezzo-soprano **2. SOMEBODY WITH CONTRALTO SINGING VOICE** a singer, usually a woman, with a contralto voice **3. PART FOR CONTRALTO** a singing part for a contralto **4. LOW SPEAKING VOICE** a naturally low speaking voice in a woman ○ *warm contralto tones* [Mid-18thC. From Italian, literally "below alto."]

con·tra·po·si·tion /kòntrəpə zísh'n/ *n.* **1. POSITION OPPOSITE** a position opposite to or against something ○ *took up a stand in contraposition to government policy* **2.** LOGIC **ANTITHESIS** the relation of a proposition to its contrapositive [Mid-16thC. From the late Latin stem *contraposition-*, from Latin *contraponere* "to place opposite," from *ponere* "to place" (see POSE).]

con·tra·pos·i·tive /kòntrə pózzətiv/ *n.* LOGIC a conditional proposition that negates another conditional proposition and also reverses its clauses. The proposition "if not q then not p" is the contrapositive of the proposition "if p then q."

con·trap·pos·to /kòntrə pó stō/ (*plural* **-tos**) *n.* a relaxed asymmetrical pose of the human body in art, especially sculpture, in which the shoulders and hips are turned in different planes [Early 20thC. From Italian, past participle of *contrapporre*, from Latin *contraponere* (see CONTRAPOSITION).]

con·trap·tion /kən trápshən/ *n.* a device or machine, especially one that appears strange or improvised ○ *They'd rigged up a contraption for opening the door.* [Early 19thC. Origin uncertain: perhaps a blend of CONTRIVE and TRAP.]

con·tra·pun·tal /kòntrə púntəl/ *adj.* used to describe polyphonic music with very active and strongly differentiated parts [Mid-19thC. From Italian *contrapunto* "counterpoint," from *punto* "point, note," from Latin *punctum* (see POINT).] —**con·tra·pun·tal·ly** *adv.*

con·tra·pun·tist /kòntrə púntist/ *n.* MUSIC somebody who writes counterpoint or who composes in a contrapuntal style [Late 18thC. From Italian *contrapuntista*, from *contrapunto* "counterpoint."]

con·trar·i·an /kən tráiree ən/ *n.* **1.** SOMEBODY DISPOSED TO TAKING OPPOSITE POSITION somebody who is prone to opposing policies, opinions, or accepted wisdom ○ *a thoroughgoing contrarian, accepting nothing anyone says* **2.** FIN MAVERICK INVESTOR an investor who goes against current market trends, e.g., by buying stocks that most other investors are selling

con·tra·ri·e·ty /kòntrə rí ətee/ (*plural* **-ties**) *n.* **1.** OPPOSITENESS the state or quality of opposing or being contrary **2.** POINT OF DIFFERENCE a point of difference or inconsistency

con·trar·i·ous /kən tráiree əss/ *adj.* **1.** UNCOOPERATIVE willfully disobedient or uncooperative **2.** OBSTRUCTIVE obstructing or hindering progress ○ *beset by contrarious circumstances* —**con·trar·i·ous·ly** *adv.* —**con·trar·i·ous·ness** *n.*

con·trar·i·wise /kón trerri wìz, kən trérri wìz/ *adv.* **1.** IN THE OPPOSITE WAY in the opposite way or direction or on the opposite side **2.** ON THE OTHER HAND used to introduce a statement in direct opposition to what has already been said **3.** UNHELPFULLY in a way that obstructs or hinders progress ○ *Unfortunately, things turned out contrariwise, and we had to give up the idea.*

con·trar·y /kón trèrree/ *adj.* **1.** CONFLICTING not at all in agreement with something ○ *Such arrangements were contrary to his moral code.* **2.** OPPOSITE opposite in direction **3.** OBSTRUCTING OR HINDERING PROGRESS making forward motion extremely hard ○ *slowed by contrary winds* **4.** DELIBERATELY DISOBEDIENT willfully disobedient or uncooperative ○ *a contrary child* **5.** LOGIC UNABLE TO BE TRUE AT ONCE used to describe a pair of propositions that cannot both be true, though they may both be false ■ *n.* THE OPPOSITE the opposite of something ○ *Actually, the contrary is true.* [13thC. Via Anglo-Norman *contrarie* from Latin *contrarius*, from *contra* "against."] —**con·trar·i·ly** /kón trèrrilee/ *adv.* —**con·trar·i·ness** /kón trèrrinəss/ *n.* ◇ **contrary to** differently from ◇ **on** *or* **to the contrary** quite the reverse is true

con·trast *n.* /kón tràst/ **1.** MARKED DIFFERENCE a difference, or something that is different, compared with something else ○ *in stark contrast to the luxury they formerly enjoyed* **2.** JUXTAPOSITION OF DIFFERENT THINGS an effect created by placing or arranging very different things, e.g., colors, shades, or textures, next to each other **3.** DEGREE OF LIGHTNESS AND DARKNESS the difference or the use of differences between the lightest and the darkest parts of something, e.g., to create a special effect in a painting, photograph, or television image ■ *vti.* /kən trást, kón tràst/ (**-trast·ed, -trast·ing, -trasts**) BE OR SHOW TO BE DIFFERENT to compare different things or arrange them in a way that highlights their differences, or to be markedly different when compared with something ○ *These poems have a mature voice when contrasted with her earlier work.* [15thC. Via French from Italian *contrastare* "to stand against," from Latin *stare* "to stand" (source of English *statue*).] —**con·trast·a·ble** /kən trástəb'l/ *adj.* —**con·trast·a·bly** /-blee/ *adv.* —**con·trast·ing** /kən trásting/ *adj.* —**con·trast·ing·ly** /kən trástinglee/ *adv.*

con·trast·ive /kən trástiv/ *adj.* forming a contrast, or using contrasting colors, tones, or textures —**con·trast·ive·ly** *adv.* —**con·trast·ive·ness** *n.*

con·trast me·di·um *n.* a substance opaque to X-rays that is used to fill a body cavity, making the outline of the body part easier to see on an X-ray photograph. Barium is frequently used as a contrast medium.

con·trast·y /kón tràstee/ *adj.* showing sharp contrast between the lightest and darkest areas in a photograph or television or motion picture image

con·tra·vene /kòntrə veén/ (**-vened, -ven·ing, -venes**) *vt.* **1.** VIOLATE RULE OR LAW to break a rule or law ○ *outdated equipment that contravenes the safety regulations* **2.** CONTRADICT SOMETHING to disagree with or oppose a statement or decision ○ *There was no question of contravening the committee's findings.* [Mid-16thC. From late Latin *contravenire*, literally "to come against," from Latin *venire* "to come."] —**con·tra·ven·er** *n.* —**con·tra·ven·tion** /kòntrə vénshən/ *n.*

con·tre·coup /kóntrə ko͞o/ *n.* an injury to one side of an organ, especially the brain, as a result of a blow that causes it to swing inside the retaining cavity [Mid-18thC. From French, literally "a blow opposite," from *coup* (see COUP).]

con·tre·danse /kóntrə dàns, -daáns/, **con·tra·dance, con·tra·danse** *n.* **1.** KIND OF FOLK DANCE a folk dance for pairs of dancers who face each other in groups of two pairs **2.** MUSIC FOR CONTREDANSE music that is written for or in the rhythm of contredanse [Early 19thC. From French, by folk etymology (by association with *contre* "against") from English *country dance*.]

con·tre·temps /kóntrə taáN, káwntrə taáN/ *n.* an unfortunate occurrence, especially an awkward or embarrassing one [Late 17thC. From French, literally "against the time."]

contrib. *abbr.* **1.** contribution **2.** contributor

con·trib·ute /kən tríbbyoot/ (**-ut·ed, -ut·ing, -utes**) *v.* **1.** *vti.* GIVE MONEY FOR SPECIFIC PURPOSE to give money to something, such as a fund or charity, for a specific purpose, especially along with others ○ *Some organizations contribute thousands to political parties.* **2.** *vti.* DO OR GIVE SOMETHING WITH OTHERS to do or give something, especially along with others, that helps to achieve a specific purpose or goal ○ *I felt I had nothing to contribute to the discussion.* **3.** *vi.* BE PARTIAL CAUSE OF SOMETHING to be one of the factors that causes something ○ *a heart condition that contributed to his early death* **4.** *vti.* PROVIDE WORKS FOR PUBLICATION to supply material for a publication or broadcast [Mid-16thC. From Latin *contribut-*, past participle stem of *contribuere* "to bring in together," from *tribuere* "to grant" (source of English *tribute*).] —**con·trib·u·tive** *adj.* —**con·trib·u·tive·ly** *adv.* —**con·trib·u·tive·ness** *n.* —**con·trib·u·tor** *n.*

con·tri·bu·tion /kòntri byo͞osh'n/ *n.* **1.** SOMETHING GIVEN something given, such as money or time, especially to a common fund or for a specific purpose ○ *My grandparents sent money as a contribution to my college education.* **2.** MATERIAL SUPPLIED FOR PUBLICATION OR BROADCAST a piece of material that forms part of a publication or broadcast **3.** REGULAR PAYMENT a regular fixed amount paid, e.g., to a retirement fund, often deducted from somebody's wages

con·trib·u·to·ry /kən tríbbyə tàwree/ *adj.* **1.** HELPING SOMETHING HAPPEN partly responsible for something ○ *Poor diet is often a contributory factor.* **2.** GIVEN ALONG WITH OTHERS given with others to a common fund or project **3.** REQUIRING EMPLOYEE TO PAY IN PART requiring that premiums be paid by the employee as well as by the employer, usually referring to health insurance or retirement plans ■ *n.* (*plural* **-ries**) GIVER OF MONEY OR TIME somebody who donates money or effort

con·trib·u·to·ry neg·li·gence *n.* a victim's share in the responsibility for an accident, when care to prevent it could have been taken by the victim as well as the other party

con·trite /kən trít/ *adj.* **1.** VERY SORRY genuinely and deeply sorry about something ○ *She was suitably contrite.* **2.** ARISING FROM SENSE OF GUILT done or said out of a sense of guilt or remorse ○ *full of contrite promises* **3.** ASHAMED OF OWN SIN deeply ashamed of past sins and determined not to sin in the future [13thC. Via French *contrit* from Latin *contritus*, past participle of *contrerere* "to rub together," from *terere* "to rub or grind" (source of English *trite*).] —**con·trite·ly** *adv.* —**con·trite·ness** *n.*

con·tri·tion /kən tríshən/ *n.* **1.** REPENTANCE deep and genuine feelings of guilt and remorse **2.** SHAME OVER PAST SINS a deep sense of shame over past sins and a firm resolve not to sin in the future ○ *acts of contrition*

con·tri·vance /kən trívənss/ *n.* **1.** GADGET a cleverly made device or machine, especially one that is unusual ○ *a clumsy-looking contrivance for keeping your back straight* **2.** CREATIVE SOLUTION something clever done to accomplish something ○ *a contrivance to fool the enemy* **3.** DEVIOUS PLOT a plan intended to deceive **4.** SCHEMING the making of cunning or deceitful plans

con·trive /kən trív/ (**-trived, -triv·ing, -trives**) *v.* **1.** *vti.* DO SOMETHING CREATIVELY to accomplish something by being clever and creative ○ *She contrived a meeting between the warring factions.* **2.** *vt.* MAKE SOMETHING INGENIOUS to make or invent something clever, especially from whatever materials are available ○ *A tree house had been contrived from bits of scrap.* **3.** *vt.* DO CLEVERLY to accomplish something with cleverness and skill ○ *She somehow contrived to be both an effective and a well-liked teacher.* **4.** *vti.* PLOT to formulate clever or deceitful schemes ○ *The gang contrived a way to hack into the main computer system.* [13thC. Via Old French *contro(u)ver* "to invent" from medieval Latin *contropare* "to compare," from Latin *tropus* "turn, manner," from Greek *tropos* (source of English *trope*).] —**con·triv·a·ble** *adj.* —**con·triv·er** *n.*

con·trived /kən trívd/ *adj.* **1.** NOT SPONTANEOUS intended to appear spontaneous or genuine but really planned or affected ○ *Her apology was very contrived.* **2.** UNLIKE REALITY unrealistic and unconvincing ○ *a movie with a contrived ending* —**con·triv·ed·ly** /kən trívədlee/ *adv.*

con·trol /kən trṓl/ *vt.* (**-trolled, -trol·ling, -trols**) **1.** OPERATE MACHINE to work or operate something such as a vehicle or machine ○ *Computers control many of the safety features on board.* **2.** RESTRAIN OR LIMIT to limit or restrict the occurrence or expression of somebody or something, especially to keep it from appearing, increasing, or spreading ○ *The last administration set out to control inflation.* **3.** MANAGE to exercise power or authority over something such as a business or nation ○ *The company is controlled largely by foreign interests.* **4.** OVERSEE FINANCIAL AFFAIRS to regulate the financial affairs of a business or other large organization **5.** VERIFY ACCOUNTS to examine financial accounts and verify them as correct ■ *n.* **1.** ABILITY TO RUN SOMETHING ability or authority to manage or direct something ○ *circumstances beyond our control* **2.** OPERATING SWITCH a mechanical or electronic device used to operate a vehicle or machine ○ *a pilot at the controls of a plane* **3.** SKILL skill in using something or in performing (*often used in combination*) ○ *players with excellent ball control* **4.** LIMITS AND RESTRICTIONS the limiting or restricting of something, or the methods used in restricting something ○ *an era of price and wage controls* **5.** PLACE OF INSPECTION OR DIRECTION a place where something is checked or inspected, or from which something is directed (*usually used in combination*) ○ *passengers filing through passport control* **6.** COMPARATIVE STANDARD IN EXPERIMENT a subject taking part in an experiment or survey who is not involved in the procedures affecting the rest of the experiment, thus acting as the standard against which the results are compared ○ *We have sixteen mice, of which the eight controls have been matched for age, weight, and species.* **7.** SUPERVISING PERSON OR GROUP somebody or a group that supervises or monitors operations or operatives ○ *Their intelligence agents report to control twice a week* **8.** COMPUT SPECIAL COMPUTER KEY a computer key pressed in conjunction with others to perform any of a set of functions **9.** SPIRIT THAT GUIDES SÉANCE a spirit that is believed to help a medium gain access to other spirits being called up in a séance **10.** BASEBALL PITCHER'S PRECISION the ability of a pitcher to place a pitch precisely, especially in the strike zone ○ *The pitcher had great control in the top of the seventh.* [15thC. Via Anglo-Norman *contreroller* from medieval Latin *contrarotulare* "to check against a duplicate register" (the original sense in English), from *rotulus* "roll" (see ROLL).] —**con·trol·la·bil·i·ty** /kən trṑlə bíllətee/ *n.* —**con·trol·la·ble** /kən trṓləb'l/ *adj.* —**con·trol·la·bly** /-blee/ *adv.*

con·trol freak *n.* somebody who feels an excessive need to exert control over people and over his or her own life (*slang*)

con·trol gene *n.* one of the group of genes that regulates the development and specialization of cells

con·trol grid *n.* = **grid** *n.* 5

con·trol group *n.* in an experiment, the group of test subjects left untreated or unexposed to some procedure and then compared with treated subjects in order to validate the results of the test

con·trolled /kən trṓld/ *adj.* **1.** DONE WITH SKILL AND DISCIPLINE showing the skill, judgment, and discipline needed in order to achieve a desired result, without doing too little or too much ○ *His controlled performance as Lear was masterful.* **2.** CAREFULLY REGULATED carefully measured and regulated, especially in relation to medical treatments or scientific experiments ○ *They tested the effectiveness of controlled doses of the drug.* **3.** KEPT UNDER CONTROL kept in check and not expressed fully or at all ○ *She spoke with scarcely controlled fury.*

con·trolled sub·stance *n.* a substance subject to statutory control, especially a drug that can be obtained legally only with a doctor's prescription

con·trolled us·er *n.* somebody who maintains a normal lifestyle while being addicted to drugs

con·trol·ler /kən trṓlər/ *n.* **1.** SOMEBODY WHO CONTROLS OR ORGANIZES SOMETHING somebody in a managing, supervising, or monitoring position **2. con·trol·ler, comp·trol·ler** FIN FINANCIAL SUPERVISOR somebody whose job is to oversee financial matters in a business or government department **3.** CONTROLLING DEVICE a device or mechanism that controls something, such as part of an operation —**con·trol·ler·ship** *n.*

con·trol·ling in·ter·est *n.* ownership of enough of a company's stock to allow the holder to control the business

con·trol rod *n.* a rod or cylinder made of or containing neutron-absorbing material such as graphite, used to control the rate of fission in a nuclear reactor

con·trol sur·face *n.* a movable surface, such as a rudder or elevator, that controls the direction of an aircraft, rocket, or missile

con·trol tow·er *n.* a high building at an airport, from which air-traffic controllers organize the movements of incoming and outgoing aircraft by radioing their pilots

con·tro·ver·sial /kòntrə vúrsh'l/ *adj.* **1.** CAUSING ARGUMENT provoking strong disagreement or disapproval, e.g., in public debate ○ *The CEO heading up the company is a controversial figure.* **2.** ARGUMENTATIVE enjoying or habitually engaging in controversy ○ *a controversial writer* —**con·tro·ver·sial·ism** *n.* —**con·tro·ver·sial·ist** *n.* —**con·tro·ver·si·al·i·ty** /kòntrə vurshee állətee/ *n.* —**con·tro·ver·sial·ly** /kòntrə vérsh'lee/ *adv.*

con·tro·ver·sy /kóntrə vùrsee/ (*plural* **-sies**) *n.* disagreement on a contentious topic, strongly felt or expressed by all those concerned [14thC. From Latin *controversia*, from *controversus* "disputed," literally "turned against," from *vertere* "to turn" (source of English *versus*).]

con·tro·vert /kóntrə vùrt/ (**-vert·ed, -vert·ing, -verts**) *vt.* to argue strongly against something (*formal*) [Mid-16thC. From Latin *contro-* "against" + *vertere* "to turn" (see CONTROVERSY).] —**con·tro·vert·er** *n.* —**con·tro·vert·i·ble** /kòntrə vúrtəb'l/ *adj.* —**con·tro·vert·i·bly** /-blee/ *adv.*

con·tu·ma·cious /kòn too máyshəss/ *adj.* **1.** VERY RESISTANT TO AUTHORITY flagrantly insubordinate or rebellious **2.** LAW DISOBEYING COURT OF LAW persistently refusing to appear in court or to obey a court order without good reason —**con·tu·ma·cious·ly** *adv.* —**con·tu·ma·cious·ness** *n.*

con·tu·ma·cy /kən tóomәssee/ *n.* **1.** DEFIANCE OF AUTHORITY flagrant disobedience or rebelliousness **2.** LAW REFUSAL TO SUBMIT TO COURT'S AUTHORITY persistent refusal to appear in court or to obey a court order without good reason [13thC. From Latin *contumacia*, from *contumac-*, stem of *contumax* "insolent."]

con·tu·me·li·ous /kòntə méelee əss/ *adj.* having or showing an insulting, scornful, or contemptuous attitude (*archaic or literary*) —**con·tu·me·li·ous·ly** *adv.* —**con·tu·me·li·ous·ness** *n.*

con·tume·ly /kən tóoməlee, kón toomәlee, kóntəmlee/ (*plural* **-lies**) *n.* (*archaic or literary*) **1.** CONTEMPT insulting, scornful, or contemptuous language or treatment **2.** DERISIVE REMARK an openly insulting, scornful, or contemptuous remark [14thC. Via Old French *contumelie* from Latin *contumelia*.]

con·tuse /kən tóoz/ (**-tused, -tus·ing, -tus·es**) *vt.* to bruise a body part (*technical*) [14thC. From Latin *contus-*, past participle stem of *contundere* "to beat small, bruise," from *tundere* "to beat."]

con·tu·sion /kən tóozh'n/ *n.* an injury to the body in which skin and bone are not broken, but damage is done to tissues under the skin, causing a bruise or bruises (*technical*)

co·nun·drum /kə núndrəm/ *n.* **1.** WORD PUZZLE a riddle, especially one with an answer in the form of a play on words **2.** SOMETHING CONFUSING something puzzling, confusing, or mysterious [Early 17thC. Origin unknown.]

con·ur·ba·tion /kònnər báysh'n/ *n.* a large urban area created when neighboring towns spread into and merge with each other [Early 20thC. Coined from CON- + the Latin stem *urb-* "city" (see URBAN) + -ATION.]

WORD KEY: SYNONYMS

See Synonyms at ***city***.

conv. *abbr.* **1.** conversation **2.** convertible **3.** convocation

Conv. *abbr.* Conventual

con·va·lesce /kònvə léss/ (**-lesced, -lesc·ing, -lesc·es**) *vi.* to spend time recovering from an illness or medical treatment, especially by resting [15thC. From Latin *convalescere*, from *valescere* "to grow strong," from *valere* "to be strong" (source of English *valid*).]

con·va·les·cence /kònvə léss'ns/ *n.* gradual return to good health after an illness or medical treatment, or the period spent recovering

con·va·les·cent /kònvə léssənt/ *n.* somebody who is recovering after a period of illness or medical treatment such as surgery —**con·val·es·cent** *adj.*

con·vec·tion /kən vékshən/ *n.* **1.** CIRCULATORY MOTION IN LIQUID OR GAS circulatory movement in a liquid or gas, resulting from regions of different temperatures and different densities rising and falling in response to gravity **2.** METEOROL HEAT TRANSFER LEADING TO CLOUD FORMATION heat transfer within the atmosphere involving the upward movement of huge volumes of warm air, leading to subsequent condensation and cloud formation [Mid-19thC. From the late Latin stem *convection-*, from Latin *convehere* "to bring together," from *vehere* "to carry" (source of English *vehicle*).] —**con·vec·tion·al** *adj.* —**con·vec·tive** *adj.* —**con·vec·tive·ly** *adv.*

con·vec·tion heat·er *n.* = **convector**

con·vec·tion ov·en *n.* an oven with a fan that circulates heat throughout the oven, so that food on all levels cooks uniformly

con·vec·tor /kən véktər/ *n.* a heater that depends on convection of air to transfer heat from the heating element [Early 20thC. Formed from CONVECTION.]

con·ve·nance /kónvə naàns, kónvənəns/ *n.* suitable or acceptable behavior (*literary*) [15thC. From French, where it was formed from *convenir* "to be suitable, to agree," from Latin *convenire* (see CONVENE).]

con·vene /kən véen/ (**-vened, -ven·ing, -venes**) *v.* **1.** *vti.* GATHER FOR A MEETING to come together for or arrange a formal meeting ○ *A meeting of the working group has been convened for tomorrow.* **2.** *vt.* LAW CALL BEFORE COURT to order somebody to appear before a court, tribunal, or other decision-making body [15thC. From Latin *convenire* "to come together, to agree or suit," from *venire* "to come."] —**con·ven·a·ble** *adj.* —**con·ven·er** *n.*

con·ven·ience /kən véenyəns/ *n.* **1.** QUALITY OF BEING CONVENIENT the quality of being easy, useful, or of increasing comfort ○ *have the convenience of working at home* **2.** SOMEBODY'S PERSONAL COMFORT personal comfort, or circumstances that promote somebody's personal comfort ○ *All rooms have cooking facilities, for our guests' convenience.* **3.** SOMETHING PROVIDING EASE OR COMFORT something that makes life easier or more comfortable, especially a labor-saving device ○ *apartments supplied with every modern convenience* **4.** *U.K.* LAVATORY a lavatory, especially in a public place

con·ven·ience food *n.* packaged food that can be prepared quickly and easily, e.g., in a microwave or by adding boiling water

con·ven·ience store *n.* a small store near a residential area that stocks food and general goods and is open all or most of the day and night

con·ven·ient /kən véenyənt/ *adj.* useful or suitable, because it makes things easier, is close by, or does not involve much effort or trouble ○ *Choose a time convenient for you.* [14thC. From Latin *convenient-*, present participle stem of *convenire* (see CONVENE).] —**con·ven·ient·ly** *adv.*

con·vent /kónvənt, kón vènt/ *n.* **1.** RELIGIOUS COMMUNITY a community of women who live a life devoted largely to religious worship **2.** RELIGIOUS COMMUNITY'S BUILDING the building occupied by a community of religious women [13thC. Via Anglo-Norman *covent* from Latin *conventus* "assembly, company," from *convenire* (see CONVENE). Originally covent, now only in place names such as Covent Garden, London.]

con·ven·ti·cle /kən véntik'l/ *n.* an unlawful or secret religious gathering or the building where it is held (*formal*) [14thC. From Latin *conventiculum*, literally "small assembly," ultimately from *convenire* (see CONVENE).] —**con·ven·ti·cler** *n.*

con·ven·tion /kən vénshən/ *n.* **1.** GATHERING a gathering of people who have a common interest or profession ○ *He's attending an optometrists' convention in Iowa.* **2.** PEOPLE ATTENDING FORMAL MEETING the people present at a convention **3.** MEETING TO SELECT CANDIDATES a meeting of delegates of a political party for the purpose of selecting candidates, or the delegates attending such a meeting ○ *the Democratic and Republican conventions* ○ *The convention roared as the president stepped to the podium.* **4.** FORMAL AGREEMENT an agreement between groups, especially an international agreement slightly less formal than a treaty ○ *under the terms of the Geneva Convention* **5.** USUAL WAY OF DOING THINGS the customary way in which things are done within a group ○ *designs that flout convention* **6.** FAMILIAR DEVICE a standard technique or well-used device, especially in the arts ○ *Her style does not follow the usual literary conventions.* **7.** BRIDGE CODED BID a bid in bridge intended for a partner to understand differently than its face value, because of a prearranged bidding system [15thC. Via French from the Latin stem *convention-*, from, ultimately, *convenire* (see CONVENE).]

con·ven·tion·al /kən vénshən'l/ *adj.* **1.** SOCIALLY ACCEPTED conforming to socially accepted customs of behavior or style, especially in a way that lacks imagination ○ *They didn't want a conventional wedding.* **2.** USUAL OR ESTABLISHED using well-established methods or styles ○ *conventional cooking in a stove rather than a microwave* **3.** RELATING TO A GATHERING relating to a large gathering of people with a common interest or purpose **4.** ARMS ENGAGED IN WITHOUT NUCLEAR ENERGY not involving the use of nuclear weapons or energy **5.** LAW BASED ON CONSENT based or dependent on the consent of the various parties —**con·ven·tion·al·ism** *n.* —**con·ven·tion·al·ist** *n.* —**con·ven·tion·al·ly** *adv.*

con·ven·tion·al·i·ty /kən vènshə nállətee/ (*plural* **-ties**) *n.* **1.** ADHERENCE TO SOCIAL CONVENTIONS adherence to social conventions in behavior, tastes, or methods **2.** SOMETHING CONVENTIONAL a socially accepted way of behaving or of doing something ○ *the conventionalities of a formal occasion*

con·ven·tion·al·ize /kən vénshənə lìz/ (**-ized, -iz·ing, -iz·es**) *vt.* to make conventional, especially in style or taste ○ *His flights of fancy had become conventionalized as the Gothic style.* —**con·ven·tion·al·i·za·tion** /kən vènsh'nəli záysh'n/ *n.*

con·ven·tion·al wis·dom *n.* a generally held view, notion, or opinion ○ *Conventional wisdom dictates that such skills merit high rewards.*

con·ven·tion·eer /kən vènshə néer/ *n.* somebody who attends and participates in a convention

con·ven·tu·al /kən vénchoo əl/ *adj.* RELATING TO A CONVENT relating to or resembling a convent in quietness, simplicity, or discipline ○ *living a quiet conventual life* ■ *n.* SOMEBODY LIVING IN CONVENT a woman who lives in a convent —**con·ven·tu·al·ly** *adv.*

Con·ven·tu·al *n.* a member of a branch of a Franciscan order of friars who live a less austere life than in other branches

con·verge /kən vúrj/ (**-verged, -verg·ing, -verg·es**) *vi.* **1.** MEET to reach the same point coming from different directions ○ *the place where the roads converge* **2.** BECOME THE SAME to become gradually less different and eventually the same ○ *rapidly converging political parties* **3.** ARRIVE AT SAME DESTINATION to gather or meet at the same destination ○ *Delegates from all over the world are converging on the city of New York.* **4.** MATH APPROACH FINITE LIMIT to approach a finite limit as the number of terms in an infinite series increases **5.** BIOL DEVELOP SIMILAR CHARACTERISTICS to independently develop superficially similar characteristics in response to a set of environmental conditions, e.g., the development of wings in birds and insects [Late 17thC. From late Latin *convergere* "to lean together," from Latin *vergere* "to bend or turn" (source of English *verge*).]

con·ver·gence /kən vúrjəns/ *n.* **1. con·ver·gence, con·ver·gen·cy** COMING TOGETHER a coming together from different directions, especially a uniting or merging of groups or tendencies that were originally opposed or very different **2. con·ver·gence, con·ver·gen·cy** MATH **SERIES WITH CONSTANT OR INCREASING DIFFERENCES** the characteristic of a series or sequence of numbers in which the difference between each term and the following term remains constant or increases. ◊ **divergence 3.** BIOL **SIMILAR EVOLUTIONARY DEVELOPMENT** the tendency of different species to develop similar characteristics in response to a set of environmental conditions. ◊ **divergence 4.** METEOROL **MEETING OF AIR MASSES** the meeting of different air masses, often resulting in vertical air currents **5.** OPHTHALMOL **TURNING THE EYES INWARD** the turning inward of both eyes in order to look at something nearer than the previous object viewed —**con·ver·gent** *adj.*

con·ver·gent ev·o·lu·tion *n.* BIOL = **convergence** *n.* **3**

con·ver·gent mar·gin *n.* a boundary between two tectonic plates that are moving together, one dipping under the other

con·ver·sance /kən vúrsəns/, **con·ver·san·cy** /-ee/ *n.* knowledge of or familiarity with something

con·ver·sant /kən vúrsənt/ *adj.* knowing about something, or familiar with it, from experience or study ○ *not conversant with local customs* [14thC. From French, present participle of *converser,* from Latin *conversare* "to live or associate with" (see CONVERSE).] —**con·ver·sant·ly** *adv.*

con·ver·sa·tion /kònvər sáysh'n/ *n.* **1. CASUAL TALK** an informal talk with somebody, especially about opinions, ideas, feelings, or everyday matters ○ *a telephone conversation* **2. TALKING** the activity of talking to somebody informally ○ *in conversation with one of the cleaners* **3. INFORMAL TALK ABOUT ISSUE** an informal talk about something involving representatives from various interested groups **4.** COMPUT **REAL-TIME INTERACTION WITH COMPUTER** an interaction with a computer carried on in real time **5. NONVERBAL EXCHANGE** a nonverbal exchange that is perceived to have the qualities of conversation ○ *Critics spoke of the conversation between the new building and its neighbors.* **6.** = **criminal conversation** [14thC. Via French from the Latin stem *conversation-,* from *conversari* (see CONVERSE[1]).]

con·ver·sa·tion·al /kònvər sáyshən'l, kònvər sáyshnəl/ *adj.* **1. CONNECTED WITH CONVERSATION** relating to informal talking, especially to the ability to say interesting things ○ *got stuck with a seatmate who was a conversational dud* **2. INFORMAL IN LANGUAGE** informal in language and style, and usually dealing with simple subjects ○ *She writes in an easy conversational style.* **3. APPROPRIATE FOR INFORMAL TALK** suitable in style and vocabulary for informal talk on simple subjects, usually applied to skill in a foreign language ○ *conversational German* —**con·ver·sa·tion·al·ly** *adv.*

con·ver·sa·tion·al·ist /kònvər sáysh'nəlist/, **con·ver·sa·tion·ist** /-sáysh'nist/ *n.* somebody who enjoys talking to people or has the ability to converse in an interesting engaging manner ○ *Her husband's not much of a conversationalist.*

con·ver·sa·tion piece *n.* **1. OBJECT USED AS CONVERSATION TOPIC** something that attracts people's interest and leads to conversation ○ *I don't think much of the sculpture in their front yard, but I guess it makes a good conversation piece.* **2. GROUP PORTRAIT** a portrait painting of a group of stylish people in a domestic or landscape setting

con·ver·sa·zi·o·ne /kònvər saatsi ṓnee/ (*plural* **-ni** /-ṓnee/ *or* **-nes**) *n.* a social gathering to hear a talk on or discuss a topic related to the arts (*formal*) [Mid-18thC. From Italian, literally "conversation," ultimately from Latin *conversare* (see CONVERSE[1]).]

con·verse[1] *vi.* /kən vúrs/ (**-versed, -vers·ing, -vers·es**) **1. TALK** to have a conversation ○ *a place where they can converse uninterrupted* **2.** COMPUT **INTERACT WITH COMPUTER** to interact with a computer as if engaged in a dialog **3. INTERACT SOCIALLY WITH SOMEBODY** to be in somebody's company or associate with him or her socially (*archaic*) **4. ENGAGE IN SEXUAL INTERCOURSE** to have sexual intercourse with somebody (*archaic*) ■ *n.* /kón vùrs/ **1. CONVERSATION** conversation with somebody ○ *They were deep in converse with one another.* **2. SOCIAL ASSOCIATION** being with somebody socially (*archaic*) ○ *Their converse was always cordial.* **3. SEXUAL RELATIONS** sexual relations (*archaic*) [14thC. Via French *converser* from Latin *conversare* "to live or associate with," from *versari* "to occupy yourself," ultimately from *vertere* "to turn."] —**con·vers·er** *n.*

con·verse[2] /kón vùrs, kən vúrs/ *n.* **1. POLAR OPPOSITE** the opposite of something ○ *Actually, the converse is true.* **2.** LOGIC **REVERSED CATEGORICAL SENTENCE** a categorical sentence in which the subject and predicate have been reversed, e.g., "all dogs are collies" from "all collies are dogs" ■ *adj.* **OPPOSITE** opposite or reverse [14thC. From Latin *conversus,* past participle of *convertere* (see CONVERT).] —**con·verse·ly** *adv.*

con·ver·sion /kən vúrzh'n/ *n.* **1. ALTERATION** a change in the nature, form, or function of something ○ *a conversion of waste land into a sports field* **2. SOMETHING ALTERED** something that has been changed in nature, form, or function, especially a building or room ○ *These apartments are conversions.* **3. CHANGE OF MEASURING SYSTEM** a change from one measuring or calculating system to another, or a calculation done to bring about the change ○ *the conversion from miles to kilometers* **4. CHANGING OF SOMEBODY'S BELIEFS** an adoption of new opinions or beliefs, especially in religion ○ *his conversion to Islam* **5.** FOOTBALL an act of converting following a touchdown or a down. A conversion by kick earns one point, but a conversion by run or pass into the end zone earns two. **6.** RUGBY, FOOTBALL **KICK FOLLOWING TOUCHDOWN** a kicking of the ball over the crossbar following a touchdown, and the score made with a successful kick **7.** LOGIC **REVERSING TERMS IN CATEGORICAL SENTENCE** the reversing of the subject and predicate in a categorical sentence, forming a new sentence, e.g., "all dogs are collies" from "all collies are dogs" **8.** LAW **UNLAWFUL HOLDING OF ANOTHER'S PROPERTY** unlawful treating of somebody else's property as your own **9.** LAW **CHANGING OF PROPERTY CLASSIFICATION** the changing of one type of property to another, e.g., from real to personal property [14thC. Via French from the Latin stem *conversion-,* from *convers-,* past participle stem of *convertere* (see CONVERT).] —**con·ver·sion·al** *adj.* —**con·ver·sion·ar·y** *adj.*

con·ver·sion dis·or·der *n.* a neurosis marked by the appearance of physical symptoms, such as partial paralysis, without physical cause but in the presence of psychological conflict

con·vert *v.* /kən vúrt/ (**-vert·ed, -vert·ing, -verts**) **1.** *vti.* **CHANGE SOMETHING'S CHARACTER** to change the nature or form of something, or to be changed in nature or form ○ *a process for converting waste into usable fuel* **2.** *vti.* **CHANGE THING'S FUNCTION** to change the function or use of something or be able to change in function or use ○ *sofas that convert into beds* **3.** *vt.* **CHANGE MEASURING OR CALCULATING UNITS** to change units of one measuring or calculating system into units of another ○ *the formula for converting liters into gallons* **4.** *vti.* **CHANGE SOMEBODY'S BELIEFS** to adopt new opinions or beliefs or to change the opinions or beliefs of another, especially religious beliefs ○ *His wife converted to Judaism.* **5.** *vi.* FOOTBALL **SCORE AFTER TOUCHDOWN** to score following a touchdown by kicking the ball between the goal posts, which earns one point, or running or passing the ball into the end zone, which earns two **6.** *vt.* LOGIC **REVERSE TERMS IN CATEGORICAL SENTENCE** reverse the subject and predicate in a categorical sentence, forming a new sentence, e.g., "all dogs are collies" from "all collies are dogs" **7.** *vt.* LAW **UNLAWFULLY HOLD ANOTHER'S PROPERTY** to unlawfully treat somebody else's property as your own **8.** *vt.* LAW **CHANGE CLASSIFICATION OF PROPERTY** to change the classification of property, e.g., from real to personal property, in the course of certain transactions ■ *n.* /kón vùrt/ **SOMEBODY WITH CHANGED BELIEFS** somebody who has changed from one way of perceiving or understanding something, such as a belief system, to another ○ *a convert to Christianity* ○ *a convert to health food* [13thC. Via Old French *convertir* from, ultimately, Latin *convertere* "to turn around or transform," from *vertere* "to turn" (source of English *verse*).] ◇ **preach to the converted** to advocate a viewpoint to people who already have it

WORD KEY: SYNONYMS

See Synonyms at ***change***.

con·vert·a·plane *n.* = **convertiplane**

con·vert·er /kən vúrtər/, **con·ver·tor** *n.* **1.** TECH **DEVICE THAT CONVERTS** a device that converts something, e.g., an electrical device that converts alternating current into direct current **2.** PHYS **FREQUENCY CHANGER** an electronic component for changing one frequency to another **3.** METALL **FURNACE** a furnace for refining molten metal **4.** COMPUT **DATA CODE CHANGER** a device for changing data from one form to another, e.g., from analog to digital **5.** PHYS = **converter reactor**

con·vert·er re·ac·tor *n.* a type of nuclear reactor that converts one nuclear fuel into another, especially fertile into fissile material

con·vert·i·ble /kən vúrtəb'l/ *adj.* **1. CAPABLE OF BEING CONVERTED** capable of being changed from one form, function, or use to another **2.** FIN **EXCHANGEABLE FOR GOLD OR ANOTHER CURRENCY** able to be legally exchanged for gold or for another currency **3.** FIN **EXCHANGEABLE FOR STOCK** exchangeable for other assets, especially a fixed number of shares in ordinary stock ■ *n.* **1. CAR WITH REMOVABLE ROOF** a car with a roof that can be folded back or taken off ○ *a flashy red convertible* **2.** FIN = **convertible security 3. SOMETHING CONVERTIBLE** something that can be converted to another use, e.g., a sofa that folds out into a bed ○ *Both the sofa and the love seat are convertibles.* —**con·vert·i·bil·i·ty** /kən vùrtə bíllətee/ *n.* —**con·vert·i·ble·ness** /kən vúrtəb'lnəss/ *n.* —**con·vert·i·bly** *adv.*

con·vert·i·ble se·cu·ri·ty (*plural* **con·vert·i·ble se·cu·ri·ties**) *n.* FIN a security that may be exchanged for other assets, especially a fixed number of shares in ordinary stock

con·vert·i·plane /kən vúrtə plàyn/, **con·vert·a·plane** *n.* an airplane that takes off and lands vertically by altering the direction of its engines' thrust, reconverting to normal horizontal thrust for forward flight [Mid-20thC. Blend of CONVERTIBLE and AIRPLANE.]

con·ver·tor *n.* = **converter**

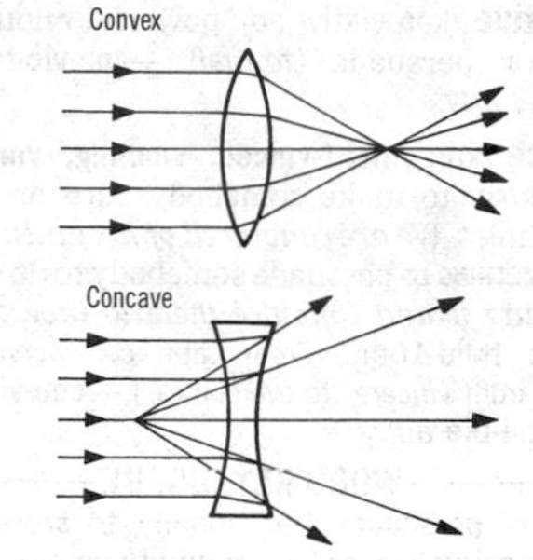

Convex: Convex and concave lenses

con·vex *adj.* /kón vèks/ **1. OUTWARDLY CURVING** with a surface that curves outward rather than inward **2.** OPTICS **SHAPED LIKE A SPHERE'S EXTERIOR** shaped like the exterior of a sphere, paraboloid, ellipsoid, or any other outwardly curved surface ○ *a convex lens* **3.** MATH **CONTAINING NO ANGLE ABOVE 180°** used to describe a polygon with no interior angle greater than 180° ■ *vti.* /kón vèks, kən véks/ (**-vexed, -vex·ing, -vexes**) **CURVE OUTWARD** to curve outward, or make something curve outward [Late 16thC. From Latin *convexus* "vaulted, arched."] —**con·vex·ly** /kon vékslee/ *adv.*

con·vex·i·ty /kon véksətee/ (*plural* **-ties**) *n.* **1. CURVING OUTWARD** outwardly curving quality **2. SOMETHING THAT CURVES OUTWARD** an outwardly curving surface or part

con·vex·o-con·cave /kon vèksō-/ *adj.* used to describe a lens that is convex on one side and concave on the other

con·vex·o-con·vex *adj.* used to describe a lens that is convex on both sides

con·vey /kən váy/ (**-veyed, -vey·ing, -veys**) *vt.* **1. TAKE SOMEWHERE** to take somebody or something somewhere (*formal*) **2. COMMUNICATE** to communicate something and make it known ○ *a look that conveyed all the tenderness he felt for her* **3. MEAN** have something as a meaning or connotation ○ *"Majesty" conveys grandeur.* **4. TRANSFER THROUGH CARRIER** to transfer or transmit something along a wire, pipe, tube, or other carrier **5.** LAW **TRANSFER OWNERSHIP** to transfer ownership of something ○ *The title to the property was conveyed last June.* [14thC. Via Old French *conveier* (source of English *convoy*) from medieval Latin *conviare,* literally "to go together on the road," from Latin *via* "road."] —**con·vey·a·ble** *adj.*

con·vey·ance /kən váyəns/ *n.* **1. MOVING SOMETHING** the conveying of something, especially the transportation or transmission of something from one place to another ○ *the conveyance of information from the mainland to the islands* **2. VEHICLE** a vehicle or other means of transportation (*formal*) ○ *public conveyances* **3.** LAW **TRANSFER OF OWNERSHIP** a document that legally transfers ownership or the transfer itself —**con·vey·anc·er** *n.* —**con·vey·anc·ing** *n.*

con·vey·er *n.* **1. CONVEYING DEVICE** a device that transports or transmits something, especially a conveyor belt **2. MEANS OF TRANSMITTING** somebody or something that transmits something, especially news ○ *conveyor of good tidings*

con·vey·or belt *n.* a device that consists typically of a continuous wide flat rubber loop moved by electrically operated rollers, used to move objects from one place to another nearby

con·vict *v.* /kən víkt/ (**-vict·ed, -vict·ing, -victs**) **1.** *vt.* **RULE THAT SOMEBODY IS GUILTY** to declare somebody guilty of a crime in a court of law (*often passive*) ○ *had been previously convicted of fraud* **2.** *vi.* **ARRIVE AT GUILTY VERDICT** to reach a verdict of guilty ○ *juries who will convict on the slimmest evidence* **3.** *vt.* **SHOW TO BE AT FAULT** to show that somebody is in the wrong in some respect ○ *actions that convicted her of selfishness* ■ *n.* /kón vìkt/ **SOMEBODY IN PRISON** somebody serving a prison sentence ○ *an escaped convict* [14thC. From Latin *convict-*, past participle stem of *convincere* (see CONVINCE).] —**con·vict·a·ble** /kən víktəb'l/ *adj.*

con·vic·tion /kən víksh'n/ *n.* **1. FIRMLY HELD BELIEF** a belief or opinion that is held firmly ○ *my conviction that they are lying* **2. FIRMNESS OF BELIEF** firmness of belief or opinion ○ *said with complete conviction* **3. GUILTY VERDICT** the finding or an instance of finding somebody guilty or of being found guilty of a crime ○ *The accused has no previous convictions.* —**con·vic·tion·al** *adj.*

con·vic·tive /kən víktiv/ *adj.* powerful enough to convince or persuade (*formal*) —**con·vic·tive·ly** /kən víktivlee/ *adv.*

con·vince /kən víns/ (**-vinced, -vinc·ing, -vinc·es**) *vt.* **1. MAKE CERTAIN** to make somebody sure or certain of something ○ *We are convinced of his guilt.* **2. PERSUADE TO DO SOMETHING** to persuade somebody to do something ○ *Nothing would convince them to invest in such a scheme.* [Mid-16thC. From Latin *convincere* "to prove wrong," from *vincere* "to overcome."] —**con·vinc·er** *n.* —**con·vinc·i·ble** *adj.*

WORD KEY: USAGE

convince or **persuade**? Traditionally, to ***convince*** somebody is to bring him or her around to an opinion, and to ***persuade*** somebody is to induce him or her to act: *She convinced him that he had talent, and persuaded him to study music.* Because of this distinction, some object to the use of an infinitive after ***convince,*** pointing out that *She convinced him to ...* will tend to involve action. All the same, somebody who is ***persuaded*** to act has probably also been ***convinced*** of the merit of doing so. In many contexts the two words are completely interchangeable, and in others are nearly so.

con·vinc·ing /kən vínsing/ *adj.* **1. PERSUASIVE** persuading somebody to believe something is true or real ○ *The special effects were very convincing.* **2. ABLE TO PERSUADE PEOPLE** skilled at making people believe something ○ *a convincing impostor* **3. BEYOND DOUBT** impressively clear or definite ○ *a convincing victory* —**con·vinc·ing·ly** *adv.* —**con·vinc·ing·ness** *n.*

con·viv·i·al /kən vívvee əl/ *adj.* **1. PLEASANT** enjoyable because of its friendliness ○ *spent many a convivial evening at the club* **2. SOCIABLE** enjoying the company of others ○ *He was famously convivial.* [Mid-17thC. From Latin *convivialis*, from *convivium* "feast," from *vivere* "to live" (source of English *vivid*).] —**con·viv·i·al·ist** *n.* —**con·viv·i·al·i·ty** /kən vìvvee álləteе/ *n.* —**con·viv·i·al·ly** /kən vívvee əlee/ *adv.*

con·vo·ca·tion /kònvə káysh'n/ *n.* **1. FORMAL ASSEMBLY** a large formal assembly, e.g., of a college or university community, or the senior members of a church **2. CALLING A MEETING** the arranging or calling of a formal meeting [14thC. From the Latin stem *convocation-*, from *convocare* (see CONVOKE).] —**con·vo·ca·tor** /kónvə kàytər/ *n.*

con·voke /kən vṓk/ (**-voked, -vok·ing, -vokes**) *vt.* to call a formal meeting or call people together for such a meeting [Late 16thC. From Latin *convocare* "to call together," from *vocare* "to call" (source of English *vocation*).] —**con·voc·a·tive** /-vókətiv/ *adj.* —**con·vok·er** /kən vṓkər/ *n.*

con·vo·lute /kónvə lòot/ *vti.* (**-lut·ed, -lut·ing, -lutes**) **TWIST** to twist or coil something in folds ○ *The snake's coils were tightly convoluted.* ■ *adj.* BOT **TIGHTLY TWISTED** used to describe petals or leaves that are rolled from the sides so that one side is wrapped around the other [Late 17thC. From Latin *convolut-*, past participle stem of *convolvere* "to twist or coil around," from *volvere* "to roll."] —**con·vo·lute·ly** *adv.*

con·vo·lut·ed /kónvə lòotəd/ *adj.* **1. EXTREMELY INTRICATE** too complex or intricate to understand easily ○ *convoluted sentences* **2. VERY TWISTED** having many twists, coils, or whorls ○ *the brain's convoluted surface* —**con·vo·lut·ed·ly** *adv.* —**con·vo·lut·ed·ness** *n.*

con·vo·lu·tion /kònvə lóosh'n/ *n.* **1. TWISTED SHAPE** a curve, coil, or twist **2. TWISTED RIDGE ON BRAIN SURFACE** any of the ridges on the brain's surface **3. INTRICACY** a complexity or intricacy, especially one of many ○ *The plot had so many convolutions it was difficult to follow.* —**con·vo·lu·tion·al** *adj.* —**con·vo·lu·tion·ar·y** *adj.*

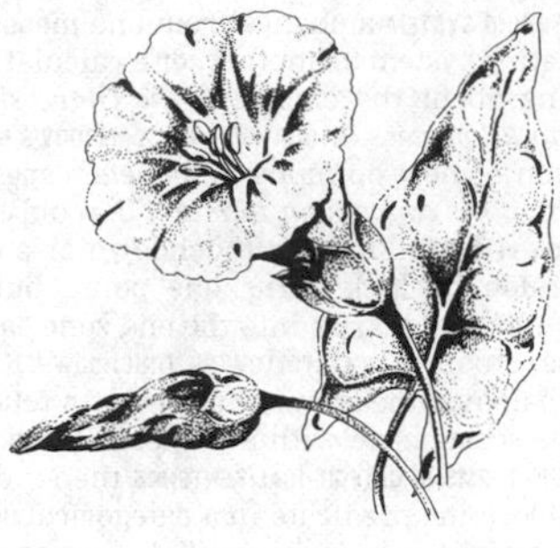

Convolvulus

con·vol·vu·lus /kən vólvyələss/ (*plural* **-lus·es** *or* **-li**) *n.* a plant of the morning-glory family with trumpet-shaped flowers. Most types are twining plants and some are cultivated. Genus: *Convolvulus.* [Mid-16thC. From Latin, where it was formed from *convolvere* (see CONVOLUTE).]

con·voy /kón vòy/ *n.* **1. VEHICLES OR SHIPS TRAVELING TOGETHER** a group of vehicles or ships traveling together, often with an escort for protection ○ *convoys of trucks on the highway* ○ *traveling in convoy* **2. VEHICLES' OR SHIPS' ESCORT** a protective escort for a group of vehicles or ships ■ *vt.* (**-voyed, -voy·ing, -voys**) **ESCORT VEHICLES OR SHIPS** to travel as an escort to protect a group of vehicles or ships [14thC. Via French *convoi* from Old French *conveier* (see CONVEY).]

con·vul·sant /kən vúlsənt/ *adj.* **CAUSING CONVULSIONS** causing convulsions ■ *n.* **DRUG CAUSING CONVULSIONS** a drug that causes convulsions

con·vulse /kən vúls/ (**-vulsed, -vuls·ing, -vuls·es**) *v.* **1.** *vti.* **SHAKE UNCONTROLLABLY** to jerk or shake violently and uncontrollably, or to make a muscle or body part go into a repetitive spasm **2.** *vt.* **CAUSE TO SHAKE** to make somebody shake with laughter or a strong emotion (*often passive*) ○ *convulsed with panic* **3.** *vt.* **DISRUPT** to cause extreme disruption or disturbance in something ○ *Problems in the Far Eastern economies convulsed the New York markets.* [Mid-17thC. From Latin *convuls-*, past participle stem of *convellere* "to wrench or pull violently," from *vellere* "to pluck or pull" (source of English *svelte*).]

con·vul·sion /kən vúlshən/ *n.* (*often used in the plural*) **1. UNCONTROLLABLE SHAKING** a violent shaking of the body or limbs caused by uncontrollable muscle contractions, which can be a symptom of brain disorders and other conditions **2. DISTURBANCE** an extreme disruption or disturbance (*literary*) ■ **con·vul·sions** *npl.* **LAUGHTER** fits of laughter —**con·vul·sion·ar·y** *adj.*

con·vul·sive /kən vúlsiv/ *adj.* **1. JERKY** sudden, jerky, or uncontrollable **2. HAVING OR PRODUCING CONVULSIONS** undergoing or producing uncontrollable jerking of the body or limbs —**con·vul·sive·ly** *adv.* —**con·vul·sive·ness** *n.*

Con·way /kón wày/ city in central Arkansas, north of Little Rock and directly east of the Arkansas River. Population: 35,827 (1996).

coo /koo/ *v.* (**cooed, coo·ing, coos**) **1.** *vi.* **MAKE SOUND OF PIGEON** to make the soft warbling sound that is characteristic of pigeons **2.** *vti.* **SPEAK VERY TENDERLY** to speak or say something with affected or exaggerated admiration ○ *young lovers cooing to each other* ■ *n.* (*plural* **coos**) **BIRD'S SOUND** the soft warbling sound that pigeons make [Mid-17thC. An imitation of the sound.]

co-oc·cur (**co-oc·curred, co-oc·cur·ring, co-oc·curs**) *vi.* **1. HAPPEN TOGETHER** to happen at the same time and place **2.** LING **SHARE SAME LINGUISTIC CONTEXT** to appear together in the same contexts (*refers to linguistic elements, for example, sound*) —**co-oc·cur·rence** *n.*

cook /kòok/ *v.* (**cooked, cook·ing, cooks**) **1.** *vti.* **PREPARE FOOD** to prepare food for a meal **2.** *vti.* **MAKE OR BECOME HOT** to make food safe and appetizing by heating it, or to become ready to eat by heating ○ *The onions have been cooking for a while.* ○ *Cook the beef until it is tender.* **3.** *vi.* **BE UNCOMFORTABLE IN HEAT** to feel extreme discomfort in hot conditions (*informal*) ○ *cooking in an overcrowded bus* **4.** *vt.* **CHANGE IN ORDER TO DECEIVE** to alter or tamper with information or evidence fraudulently (*informal*) ○ *accountants who had cooked the books* **5.** *vi.* **HAPPEN** to be happening or developing (*informal*) ○ *I had the feeling that something was cooking.* **6.** *vi.* **WORK WELL** to be working or performing superbly (*slang*) ○ *It only took a couple of songs before the band was really cooking.* **7.** *vt.* **HEAT ILLEGAL DRUG** to heat an illegal drug, e.g., heroin (*slang*) **8.** *vt.* **SHOW TO BE WRONG** to show that a presented problem is wrong, especially because it has more than one solution ■ *n.* **1. SOMEBODY WHO PREPARES FOOD** somebody who prepares food, or whose job is preparing food **2. PROOF THAT A PROBLEM IS WRONG** something that shows that a presented problem is wrong, especially because it has more than one solution [Pre-12thC. Via assumed Vulgar Latin *cocus* "a cook" from Latin *coquus*, from *coquere* "to cook" (source of English *kitchen, concoct,* and *biscuit*).] —**cook·a·ble** *adj.* —**cook·er** *n.*

cook up *vt.* **1. PREPARE MEAL QUICKLY** to prepare or improvise a meal quickly **2. INVENT** to invent something untrue or dishonest such as an excuse (*informal*) **3.** = **cook** *v.* 7 (*slang*)

Cook /kòok/, **James, Captain** (1728–79) British explorer and cartographer. During three great voyages (1768–71, 1772–75, 1776–79) he charted New Zealand and Australia and explored the Antarctic and the northwestern coast of North America.

Cook, Mount peak of the St. Elias Range in southwestern Yukon Territory. Height: 13,760 ft./4,194 m.

cook·book /kòok bòok/ *n.* a book containing recipes for preparing food or, more generally, detailed directions for a process of any kind

Cooke /kòok/, **Jay** (1821–1905) U.S. banker. He helped to finance the federal government during the Civil War. His failed attempt to finance the building of the Northern Pacific Railroad caused the financial panic of 1873.

cook·er /kóokər/ *n.* *U.K.* = **stove**

cook·er·y /kóokəree/ (*plural* **-ies**) *n.* **1. PREPARATION OF FOOD** the skill or activity of preparing food **2. STYLE OF PREPARING FOOD** a type or style of cooking, such as a national variety or one that meets specific dietary requirements **3. PLACE FOR COOKING** a place where food is prepared and cooked

Cooke·ville /kòok vìl/ city in north central Tennessee, southeast of Nashville and north of Chattanooga. Population: 25,224 (1996).

cook·ie /kóokee/, **cook·y** (*plural* **-ies**) *n.* **1. SMALL FLAT SWEET CAKE** a small flat crisp baked cake, especially one made from sweetened dough ○ *a box of cookies* **2. TYPE OF PERSON** somebody who has a particular characteristic (*informal*) ○ *She's one smart cookie.* **3.** COMPUT **COMPUTER FILE CONTAINING USER INFORMATION** on the Internet or in a computer network, a file containing information about a user that is sent to the central computer each time a request is made. The server uses this information to customize data sent back to the user and to log the user's requests. [Early 18thC. From Dutch *koekje*, literally "little cake," from *koek* "cake."] ◇ **toss your cookies** to vomit (*slang humorous*) ◇ **that's the way the cookie crumbles** that is the way things tend to happen (*informal*)

cook·ie cut·ter *n.* a shaped template with a sharp edge, used for pressing into a sheet of dough to make cookie shapes

cook·ie-cut·ter *adj.* seemingly mass-produced without distinctive features ○ *cookie-cutter houses*

cook·ie sheet *n.* = **baking sheet**

cook·ing /kóoking/ *n.* **1. PREPARATION OF FOOD** the skill or practice of preparing food **2. PREPARED FOOD** food that has been prepared for eating ○ *She doesn't like my cooking.* ■ *adj.* **USED IN COOKING** intended for use in cooking rather than for consumption on its own ○ *a bottle of cooking sherry*

cook-off *n.* a final round of a cooking competition, in which only the top contestants compete

cook·out /kòok òwt/ *n.* a party at which food is cooked and eaten outdoors

Cook's tour *n.* a quick tour or survey, with attention only to the main features (*informal*) ○ *The book doesn't try to give anything more than a Cook's tour of European history.* [Named for the English travel agent Thomas Cook (1808–92)]

cook·stove /ko͝ok stòv/ *n.* **1. STOVE FOR COOKING** a stove used for cooking, as distinct from one designed to heat a room **2.** CAMPING **STOVE USED WHEN CAMPING** a portable stove used for cooking on camping trips

cook·top /ko͝ok tòp/ *n.* a flat cooking area on a stove that includes heating units and a surface that can be used for food preparation

cook-up *n.* a Caribbean dish of mixed meats, seafood, and rice

cook·ware /ko͝ok wàir/ *n.* utensils, e.g., pots, pans, and dishes, used in cooking

cook·y /ko͝okee/ *n.* **1.** = **cookie 2. COOK** a cook (*informal*)

cool /kool/ *adj.* **1. COLDISH** somewhat cold, usually pleasantly so **2. STAYING CALM** staying calm or not showing emotions, especially nervousness or fear **3. FASHIONABLE** fashionable and sophisticated ○ *looking cool* **4. UNFRIENDLY** unfriendly or unenthusiastic ○ *They gave us a somewhat cool reception.* **5.** MUSIC **HAVING RELAXED RHYTHM** used to describe a style of jazz, popular in the mid-20th century, characterized by a relaxed rhythm **6. EMPHASIZING SUM OF MONEY** used to emphasize how large a sum of money is (*informal*) ○ *a cool $3.2 million* **7. EXCELLENT** very good (*slang*) ○ *a cool idea* **8. OK** acceptable, untroubling (*slang*) ○ *That's cool, no problem.* **9. SEEMING COLD** giving an impression of coldness ○ *a cool mint green* **10. KEEPING TEMPERATURE LOW** made of fabric that keeps the body at a pleasant temperature in hot conditions ■ *vti.* **(cooled, cooling, cools) 1. MAKE OR BECOME LESS WARM** to become or cause somebody or something to become less warm ○ *Wait until the mixture cools* **2. MAKE OR BECOME LESS INTENSE** to make somebody or something less intense, or to become less intense ○ *anything that might cool his anger* ■ *n.* **1. CALMNESS** the ability to remain calm in difficult circumstances (*informal*) **2. STYLISHNESS** stylishness that is attractive without being ostentatious (*informal*) **3. SLIGHT CHILL** moderate coldness, especially in relation to greater heat or coldness ○ *the cool of the evening* ■ *adv.* **CALMLY** in a calm self-controlled way (*informal*) ○ *Just act cool.* ■ *interj.* **EXPRESSING PLEASURE** used to express delight or excitement at a prospect or event (*informal*) ○ *You're coming too? Cool!* [Old English *cōl*. Ultimately from an Indo-European word denoting "cold" that is also the ancestor of English *chill, congeal,* and *glacier.*] —**cool·ing·ly** *adv.* —**cool·ness** *n.* ◇ **cool it** used to tell somebody to calm down (*slang*) ◇ **keep your cool** to remain calm ◇ **lose your cool** to become angry and excitable

cool down *vti.* **1. MAKE OR BECOME LESS WARM** to make somebody or something less warm, or to become less warm ○ *Wait till the engine cools down before you lift the hood.* **2. MAKE OR BECOME CALM** to make somebody or something calm or calmer after strong feeling or excitement, or become calm or calmer ○ *Only when studio officials had cooled the two men down was the show able to continue.*

cool off *v.* **1.** *vi.* **BECOME COOL AGAIN** to become comfortably cool again ○ *I went for a swim to cool off.* **2.** *vti.* **REGAIN CALMNESS** to become calm or unemotional again after being angry or passionate (*informal*) ○ *After a few months, their relationship cooled off.*

cool out *vi. Carib* to relax (*informal*)

cool·ant /ko͞olənt/ *n.* a substance, usually a liquid, used to prevent overheating in an engine or other mechanism

cool bag, cool box *n. U.K.* = **cooler**

cool·er /ko͞olər/ *n.* **1. INSULATED FOOD CONTAINER** a portable insulated container used to keep food cool outdoors **2. LONG DRINK** a long refreshing drink, especially an iced mixture of wine, fruit juice, and soda water. **3. PRISON** a prison or prison cell (*dated slang*) **4. COOL PLACE OR CONTAINER** a compartment or container in which something is cooled or kept cool

Cool·gar·die /kool gaárdee/ gold-mining town in southern Western Australia. It was once the third largest town in the state. Population: 1,258 (1996).

cool-head·ed *adj.* staying calm in tense situations

Coolidge /ko͞olij/, **Calvin** (1872–1933) U.S. statesman and 30th President of the United States. A probusiness Republican, he presided over a period of prosperity, but his presidency (1923–29) ended with the Wall Street Crash. Full name **John Calvin Coolidge**

coo·lie /ko͞olee/ *n.* (*offensive*) **1. OFFENSIVE TERM** an offensive term in India, China, and other parts of Asia for a local man hired cheaply to do laboring or portering work **2. OFFENSIVE TERM** an offensive term for somebody brought to the United States from China during the 19th century to construct railroads **3. POORLY TREATED WORKER** an employee who is treated as merely one of many unworthy of concern [Mid-17thC. From Hindi *kūlī*, of uncertain origin: possibly a blend of Telugu *kūli* "hire" and Urdu *kulī* "slave," or from *Kulī*, a Gujarati people.]

cool·ing-off pe·ri·od /ko͞oling-/ *n.* **1. BREAK IN DISPUTE** an agreed pause in a dispute to allow tempers to cool and peaceful solutions to be examined **2. TIME TO RECONSIDER** a period of reflection allowed before making a legally binding commitment

cool·ing tow·er *n.* a tall chimney in which the steam produced by an industrial process is condensed

cool jazz *n.* a kind of jazz with a lighter tone and more relaxed character, popular in the 1940s and 1950s, especially on the West Coast of the United States

cool·ly /ko͞olee/ *adv.* **1. CALMLY** in a calm or relaxed way ○ *She coolly marched up to the desk and demanded to see the manager.* **2. IN COLD MANNER** without friendliness or enthusiasm ○ *He greeted her coolly.*

coolth /koolth/ *n.* **1. COOLNESS** pleasant coolness or coldness relative to greater heat or cold (*informal or humorous*) **2. HIPNESS** the quality of being very self-confident and informed about current trends (*slang*) ○ *Don't you admire her coolth?* [Mid-16thC. Formed from COOL, on the model of WARMTH.]

coon[1] /koon/ *n.* a raccoon (*informal*) [Mid-18thC. Shortening of RACCOON.] ◇ **in a coon's age** in a long time (*informal*)

coon[2] /koon/ *n.* a highly offensive term for a Black person (*offensive taboo*) [Mid-19thC. Shortening of Portuguese *barracoos* "buildings specially constructed to hold slaves for sale."]

coon·can /ko͞on kàn/ *n.* a card game from Mexico that is similar to rummy and played with one or two packs [Late 19thC. By folk etymology from American Spanish *conquián*, from Spanish *con quién?* "with whom?".]

coon·hound /ko͞on hòwnd/ *n.* a smooth-haired dog trained to hunt raccoons

Coon Rap·ids /koon-/ city in southeastern Minnesota, on the Mississippi River, a northwestern suburb of Minneapolis. Population: 62,790 (1996).

coon·skin /ko͞on skìn/ *n.* the skin of a raccoon, or clothing made from it

coon·tie /ko͞ontee/ (*plural* **-ties** *or* **-tie**) *n.* **1. TROPICAL EVERGREEN PLANT** an evergreen plant found in southern Florida and Mexico that resembles a palm and has compound leaves, cones, and thick underground stems that yield an edible starch similar to arrowroot. Genus: *Zamia.* **2. STARCHY FOOD** the edible starch, similar to arrowroot, obtained from the underground stem of the coontie plant [Late 18thC. From Seminole *kunti.*]

coop /koop/ *n.* **1. ENCLOSURE FOR POULTRY** an enclosure or hut in which poultry is kept **2. FISHING BASKET** a wicker basket used for catching fish **3. PRISON** a prison or prison cell (*dated slang*) [13thC. Origin uncertain: possibly via Middle Dutch *kūpe* "basket, tub" from, ultimately, Latin *cupa* "cask." The earliest meaning in English was "basket."] ◇ **fly the coop** to escape or leave a place (*informal*)

coop up *vt.* to keep somebody in a confined space

co-op /kṓ òp, -óp/, **coop** *n.* (*informal*) **1. COOPERATIVE** a cooperative organization or venture, especially an apartment building or a marketing enterprise **2. PROGRAM OF STUDY** a program of study that allows students to combine liberal-arts and technical courses by using the resources of two different colleges or universities [Mid-19thC. Shortening.]

coop·er /ko͞opər/ *n.* **BARREL-MAKER** somebody skilled in making and repairing wooden barrels ■ *vti.* **(-ered, -er·ing, -ers) MAKE BARRELS** to make or repair wooden barrels [15thC. From Middle Dutch *kūper*, from *kūpe* "cask" (see COOP).]

Coo·per /ko͞opər/, **Gary** (1901–61) U.S. movie actor. He starred in Westerns, winning Academy Awards for *Sergeant York* (1941) and *High Noon* (1952).

Coo·per, James Fenimore (1789–1851) U.S. writer. Among his Leather-Stocking Tales about frontier life is the novel *The Last of the Mohicans* (1826).

Coo·per, Peter (1791–1883) U.S. industrialist and philanthropist. He manufactured the first U.S. steam locomotive (1830) and promoted public education.

coop·er·age /ko͞opərij/ *n.* **1. COOPER'S CRAFT** the craft of making and repairing wooden barrels **2. COOPER'S WORKPLACE** a place where wooden barrels are made and repaired **3. COOPER'S FEE** the fee charged by a cooper for making or repairing barrels

co·op·er·ate /kō óppə ràyt/ **(-at·ed, -at·ing, -ates), co-op·er·ate (co-op·er·at·ed, co-op·er·at·ing, co-op·er·ates)** *v.* **1.** *vi.* **WORK TOGETHER** to work or act together to achieve a common aim **2. COMPLY** to do what is asked or required ○ *to cooperate with police investigations* [Late 16thC. From ecclesiastical Latin *cooperat-*, past participle stem of *cooperari*, literally "to work together," from Latin *operari* "to work."] —**co·op·er·a·tor** *n.*

co·op·er·a·tion /kō òppə ráysh'n/, **co-op·er·a·tion** *n.* **1. WORKING TOGETHER** the act of working together to achieve a common aim **2. COMPLIANCE** doing what is asked or required —**co·op·er·a·tion·ist** *n.*

co·op·er·a·tive /kō óppərətiv/, **co-op·er·a·tive** *adj.* **1. WILLING TO HELP** doing, or willing to do, what is asked or required ○ *She's a good worker and very cooperative.* **2. WORKING TOGETHER** working or acting together with others, or done by people working or acting together ○ *a cooperative effort* **3. OF JOINTLY OWNED APARTMENT BUILDING** relating to a building with apartments owned by a corporation of tenants in which shares of expenses are calculated on the basis of the value of the tenant's apartment **4. OPERATED COLLECTIVELY** owned jointly by all its members or workers, who share all profits equally ○ *a cooperative farm* ■ *n.* **1. JOINTLY OWNED APARTMENT BUILDING** an apartment building that is jointly owned by the residents, or an apartment in such a building **2. BUSINESS OWNED BY WORKERS** a business that is jointly owned by the people who run it, with all profits shared equally ○ *the workers' cooperative* —**co·op·er·a·tive·ly** *adv.* —**co·op·er·a·tive·ness** *n.*

Coo·per's hawk *n.* a small bluish-gray short-winged North American hawk with a barred rust-colored breast and long tail. Latin name: *Accipiter cooperii.* [Early 19thC. Named for the U.S. naturalist William Cooper (1798–1864).]

Coo·pers·town /ko͞opərz tòwn/ village in central New York on Otsego Lake, home to the Baseball Hall of Fame. Population: 2,033 (1996).

co-opt /kō ópt/ **(co-opt·ed, co-opt·ing, co-opts)** *vt.* **1. ADOPT OR APPROPRIATE** to adopt or appropriate something, e.g., a political issue or idea, as your own **2. TAKE INTO LARGER GROUP** to absorb an opponent or opposing group into a larger group or society by making promises and concessions **3. APPOINT BY AGREEMENT** to appoint somebody to a body by agreement with the other members [Mid-17thC. From Latin *cooptare*, literally "to choose mutually," from *optare* "to choose" (source of English *opt* and *adopt*).] —**co-op·ta·tion** *n.* —**co-op·tion** *n.* —**co-op·ta·tive** *adj.* —**co-op·tive** *adj.*

co·or·di·nate, co-or·di·nate *v.* /kō áwrdə nàyt/ **(-nat·ed, -nat·ing, -nates) 1.** *vt.* **ORGANIZE SOMETHING COMPLEX** to organize a complex enterprise in which numerous people are involved and bring their contributions together to form a unified whole ○ *responsible for coordinating the campaign* **2.** *vti.* **MAKE PARTS MOVE TOGETHER** to make moving parts, e.g., parts of the body, work together in sequence or in time with one another, or to work together in this way ○ *hand and eye coordinating perfectly for the overhead shot* **3.** *vt.* **PUT TOGETHER** to place or class things together ○ *Before we can proceed, all of our files have to be coordinated.* **4.** *vi.* **WORK TOGETHER** to work together as a unit ○ *members of the team coordinating brilliantly* **5.** *vti.* **GO WELL TOGETHER** to make a pleasing combination or match ○ *outfit and accessories that coordinate stylishly* ■ *n.* /kō áwrdənət/ **1.** GEOM **NUMBER SPECIFYING POSITION** each of a set of numbers that together describe the exact position of something such as a place on a map with reference to a set of axes ○ *Did you receive the coordinates for your target?* **2. SOMEBODY OR SOMETHING EQUAL** somebody or something that is equal in rank or importance **3.** CHEM, PHYS **VARIABLE** a variable used with others to describe the state of a physical or chemical system ■ **co·or·di·nates** *npl.* **MATCHING CLOTHES** clothes that are designed to be worn together ■ *adj.* /kō áwrdənət/ **1. EQUAL** equal in rank or importance **2.** GRAM **HAVING SAME GRAMMATICAL FUNCTION** having the same grammatical function in a syntactic structure ○ *Both "got up"* *and "ate" are coordinate verbs in the sentence "I got up and ate breakfast."* **3.** CHEM, PHYS **INVOLVING SET OF VARIABLES** involving the use of coordinates [Mid-17thC. Coined from co- + Latin *ordinare* "to set in order," on the model of SUBORDINATE.] —**co·or·di·nat·ed** *adj.* —**co·or·di·nate·ly** *adv.* —**co·or·di·nate·ness** *n.* —**co·or·di·na·tive** *adj.*

co·or·di·nate bond *n.* a chemical bond between two atoms created by the sharing of a pair of electrons, both supplied by one atom. A coordinate bond is a type of covalent bond.

co·or·di·nate clause *n.* any of two or more clauses in a sentence that have the same grammatical function or status, usually joined by a coordinating conjunction such as "and" or "but." ◊ **subordinate clause, main clause**

co·or·di·nate ge·om·e·try *n.* = **analytic geometry**

co·or·di·nat·ing con·junc·tion *n.* a word such as "and" or "but" that joins two words or clauses with the same grammatical function or status

co·or·di·na·tion /kō àwrdə náysh'n/, **co·or·di·na·tion** *n.* **1. MOVEMENT OF PARTS TOGETHER** the skillful and balanced movement of different parts, especially parts of the body, at the same time **2. COMING OR WORKING TOGETHER** the combining of diverse parts or groups to make a unit, or the way these parts work together

co·or·di·na·tion com·plex, co·or·di·na·tion com·pound *n.* a chemical compound containing one or more ions, atoms, or molecules bound by coordinate bonds to a central metallic atom

co·or·di·na·tion num·ber *n.* the number of ions, atoms, or molecules attached by coordinate bonds to the metallic atom in a complex

co·or·di·na·tor /kō áwrdə nàytər/, **co·or·di·na·tor** *n.* **1. SOMEBODY BRINGING TOGETHER DIFFERENT ELEMENTS** somebody responsible for organizing diverse parts of an enterprise or groups into a coherent or efficient whole **2.** = **coordinating conjunction**

Coo·sa /kóossə/ river in the southern United States, formed in northern Georgia by the confluence of the Etowah and Oostanaula rivers. Length: 286 mi./460 km.

Coos Bay /kooss-/ city in southwestern Oregon, on an inlet of Coos Bay on the Pacific Ocean. Population: 15,448 (1996).

Coot

coot /koot/ (*plural* **coots** *or* **coot**) *n.* **1. WATER BIRD** an aquatic bird of Europe, Asia, and North America that has long toes, dark plumage, and a white bill and forehead. Genus: *Fulica.* **2. UNCONVENTIONAL PERSON** an odd, eccentric, or unreasonably stubborn person (*informal insult*) [13thC. Origin uncertain: possibly from Middle Dutch *coet.*]

coot·er /kóotər/ *n.* a large freshwater turtle of the eastern United States. Genus: *Chrysemys.* [Early 19thC. From Gullah.]

coo·tie /kóotee/ *n. U.S., NZ* a louse of the kind that infests people (*informal*) [Early 20thC. Origin uncertain: probably from Malay *kutu.*]

cop[1] /kop/ *n.* **POLICE OFFICER** a police officer (*slang*) ■ *vt.* (**copped, cop·ping, cops**) **1. GRAB** to seize or grab something (*informal*) **2. STEAL** to steal something (*informal*) ○ *Those kids copped candy bars from the store.* **3.** DRUGS **OBTAIN DRUGS** to obtain illegal drugs (*slang*) [Early 18thC. "Police officer": related to COPPER², literally "grabber." Verb senses from a variant of *cap* "to catch," which came via French *caper* from Latin *capere* "to seize, take."] ◇ **cop a plea** to negotiate with a prosecutor in order to avoid prosecution for a serious crime by agreeing to plead guilty to a lesser crime (*slang*)

cop out *vi.* to withdraw from an activity because of lack of nerve or inclination (*slang*)

cop[2] /kop/ *n.* a cone-shaped roll of thread on a spindle [Old English *coppe* "summit," of unknown origin]

cop. *abbr.* copyright

Co·pa·ca·ba·na /kōpə kə bánnə/ beach resort and residential area in southern Rio de Janeiro, Brazil

co·pa·cet·ic /kòpə séttik/, **co·pa·set·ic** *adj.* excellent or very good (*slang*) [Early 20thC. Origin unknown.]

co·pal /kṓp'l, kṓ pàl/ *n.* a hard resin from various tropical trees, used to make varnish [Late 16thC. Via Spanish from Nahuatl *copalli.*]

Co·pán /kō paán/ ancient city of the Mayan people, in northwestern Honduras. It is an important archaeological site.

co·par·ent·ing *n.* **1. SHARED RESPONSIBILITY FOR CHILDREN** the care and raising of children by two people who have divorced or separated **2. RAISING CHILDREN TOGETHER** shared responsibilty for raising children between two people who are not legally married, especially a same-sex couple —**co·par·ent** *n.*

co·part·ner /kō paártnər/ *n.* a close partner or associate, especially one who has an equal stake in a company —**co·part·ner·ship** *n.*

co·pa·set·ic *adj.* = **copacetic**

co·pay·ment *n.* an arrangement by which two or more parties make complementary payments on a loan or other financial obligation, or a payment made in this way, especially a patient's payment for a medical expense partially covered by insurance

cope[1] /kōp/ (**coped, cop·ing, copes**) *vi.* to deal successfully with a difficult problem or situation [14thC. Via French *couper* "to strike, cut" from, ultimately, Greek *kolaphos* "a blow." The underlying meaning is "to come to blows or contend with."] —**cop·er** *n.*

cope[2] /kōp/ *n.* a long sleeveless ceremonial cape worn by priests in some Christian Churches [13thC. Via medieval Latin *capa* "cloak, hood" from late Latin *cappa* (source of English *cape* and *chaperone*).] —**coped** *adj.*

cope[3] /kōp/ *n.* = **coping** ■ *vt.* (**coped, cop·ing, copes**) **PROVIDE WALL WITH COPING** to lay a protective top course of brick or stone (**coping**) on a wall [16thC. From COPE².)]

co·peck *n.* = **kopeck**

Co·pen·ha·gen /kṓpən hàygən, kṓpən haágən/ capital and largest city of Denmark, situated on the eastern coast of Sjælland Island and the northern coast of Amager Island. Population: 1,339,395 (1994). Danish **København**

Co·pen·ha·gen blue *adj.* of a grayish-blue color —**Co·pen·ha·gen blue** *n.*

co·pe·pod /kṓpə pòd/ (*plural* **-pods** *or* **-pod**) *n.* a tiny marine or freshwater crustacean that lives among plankton and is an important food source for many fish. Subclass: Copepoda. [Late 19thC. From modern Latin *Copepoda*, subclass name, from Greek *kōpē* "oar" + -POD, because of its paddle-shaped feet.]

Co·per·ni·can /kə púrnikən/ *adj.* **1. OF COPERNICUS** relating to Copernicus, especially to his theory that the Earth and other planets revolve around the sun **2. FAR-REACHING** profoundly important or far-reaching (*literary*) ○ *a Copernican change in attitudes*

Co·per·ni·can sys·tem *n.* the theory of Copernicus regarding the mechanics of the solar system, published in 1543, in which he argued that the Earth and other planets revolve around the Sun. This theory challenged the Ptolemaic system of astronomy that had prevailed since the second century.

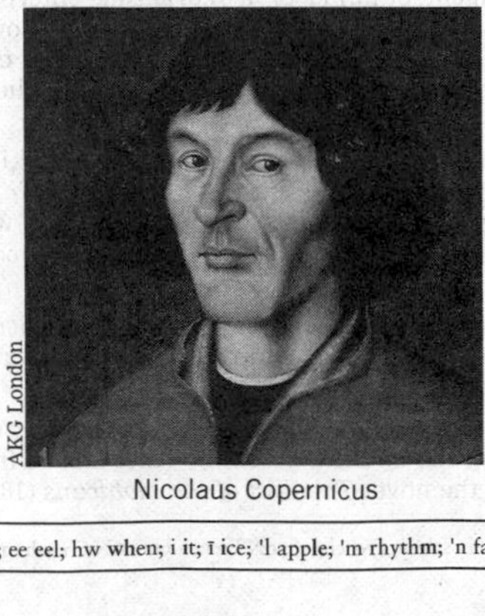

Nicolaus Copernicus

Co·per·ni·cus /kō púrnikəss, kə-/, **Nicolaus** (1473–1543) Polish astronomer. His major work, *De Revolutionibus Orbium Coelestium* (1543), postulated that the Earth orbited the Sun and laid the foundations of modern astronomy. Born **Mikołaj Kopernik**

cope·stone /kṓp stṑn/ *n.* one of the stones that form the top edge of a wall [Mid-16thC. Formed from COPE³.]

cop·i·er /kóppee ər/ *n.* **1. DEVICE FOR MAKING COPIES** a device, especially a photocopier, that makes copies of documents **2. SOMEBODY WHO MAKES COPIES** somebody who makes copies of things, especially handwritten copies of manuscripts in former times

co·pi·lot /kṓ pìlət/ *n.* a second pilot in an aircraft, who shares the flying but is not in command

cop·ing /kṓping/ *n.* the top, often sloping, course of brick or stone on top of a wall that forms a protective cap against the weather [Mid-16thC. Formed from COPE³.]

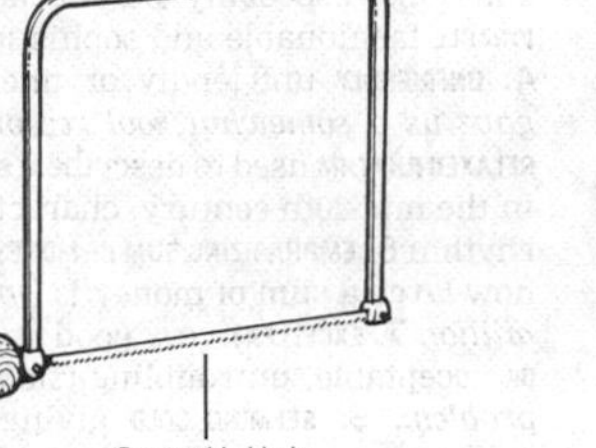

Coping saw

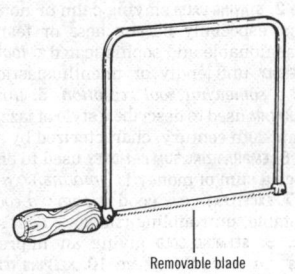

cop·ing saw *n.* a saw with a thin flexible blade held tight in a U-shaped frame that is used for cutting curves in wood

co·pi·ous /kṓpee əss/ *adj.* **1. ABUNDANT** produced or existing in large quantities **2. USING WORDY STYLE** using many words in writing or speech (*archaic*) [14thC. Directly or via French from Latin *copiosus*, from *copia* "abundance" (source of English *cornucopia* and *copy*).] —**co·pi·ous·ly** *adv.* —**co·pi·ous·ness** *n.*

co·pi·ta /kō peétə/ *n.* a traditional Spanish tulip-shaped sherry glass, or a drink of sherry served in one [Mid-19thC. From Spanish, literally "little cup."]

co·pla·nar /kō pláynər/ *adj.* lying in the same plane —**co·pla·nar·i·ty** /kō plày nérrətee/ *n.*

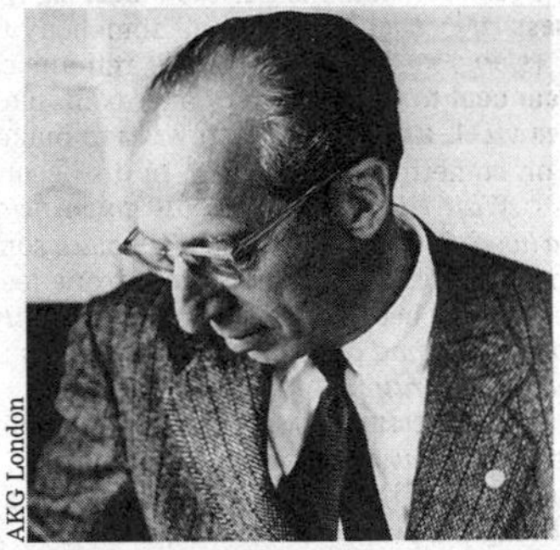

Aaron Copland

Cop·land /kṓplənd/, **Aaron** (1900–90) U.S. composer whose music was often based on folk themes. He won the Pulitzer Prize in music for *Appalachian Spring* (1944).

Cop·ley /kópplee/, **John Singleton** (1738–1815) American portrait painter. The foremost artist of colonial America, he painted many portraits of political figures.

co·pol·y·mer /kō póllimər/ *n.* a substance with a high molecular weight that results from chemically combining two or more monomers —**co·pol·y·mer·ic** /kō pòlli mérrik/ *adj.*

co·pol·y·mer·ize /kō pə límmə rīz, -póllimə-/ (**-ized, -iz·ing, -iz·es**) *vt.* to unite two or more monomers chemically to form a copolymer —**co·pol·y·mer·i·za·tion** /kō pə limmərə záysh'n, kō pòllimərə-/ *n.*

cop-out *n.* (*slang*) **1. EVASION OF RESPONSIBILITY** a feeble avoidance of a responsibility or commitment **2. EXCUSE FOR NOT TAKING ACTION** a feebly transparent excuse or explanation for refusing to face up to something **3. SOMEBODY WHO BACKS OUT OF SOMETHING** somebody who refuses to follow through on or fulfill a commitment ○ *What a bunch of cop-outs!*

cop·per[1] /kóppər/ *n.* **1. REDDISH-BROWN METAL** a reddish-brown metallic chemical element that bends easily and is a good conductor of electricity and heat. Symbol **Cu 2. REDDISH-BROWN COLOR** a reddish-brown color, like that of polished copper **3. SMALL COIN** a low-value coin made of copper or brass (*informal*) ○ *a pocketful of coppers* **4.** ZOOL **REDDISH-BROWN BUTTERFLY** a small reddish-brown butterfly. Genera: *Lycaena* and *Heodes.* ■ *adj.* **OF REDDISH-BROWN COLOR** of a reddish-brown color, like that of polished copper ■ *vt.* **(-pered, -per·ing, -pers) COVER WITH COPPER** to cover or coat something with copper (*often passive*) [Pre-12thC. Via late Latin *cuprum* from, ultimately, Greek *Kupros* "Cyprus," an important ancient source of copper.] —**cop·per·y** *adj.*

cop·per[2] /kóppər/ *n.* a police officer (*slang insult*) [Mid-19thC. Formed from COP[1].]

cop·per·as /kóppərəss/ *n.* = **ferrous sulfate** [15thC. Via French from medieval Latin *cuperosa*, of uncertain origin: probably an alteration of assumed *aqua cuprosa* "copper water," from late Latin *cuprum* (see COPPER).]

Cop·per·as Cove city in central Texas, north of Austin. It is home to the U.S. Army base at Fort Hood. Population: 30,311 (1996).

cop·per-bot·tomed *adj.* **1. HAVING COPPER BOTTOM** having a copper coating on the base **2. SOUND** certain or reliable, especially financially

Cop·per·field /kóppər fèeld/, **David** (*b.* 1956) stage magician. He has reached a large audience through his lavish televised magic shows.

cop·per·head /kóppər hèd/ (*plural* **-heads** *or* **-head**) *n.* **1. REDDISH-BROWN SNAKE** a reddish-brown poisonous snake of the viper family found in the eastern and central United States. Latin name: *Agkistrodon contortrix.* **2.** HIST **SUPPORTER OF SOUTH DURING CIVIL WAR** somebody living north of the Mason-Dixon line who sympathized with the South during the Civil War (*informal*) [Late 18thC]

Cop·per·mine /kóppər mīn/ river in northern Canada, flowing north from the Northwest Territories, through Nunavut, and into the Arctic Ocean. Length: 525 mi./845 km.

cop·per·plate /kóppər plàyt/ *n.* **1. PRINTING PLATE** a polished copper printing plate with a design etched or engraved on it **2. PRINT** a print made from a copperplate **3. NEAT HANDWRITING** neat handwriting, especially in the style of copybooks produced from copper plates

cop·per py·rites *n.* = **chalcopyrite**

cop·per·smith /kóppər smìth/ *n.* **1. SOMEBODY WHO MAKES COPPER ARTICLES** somebody who makes or repairs articles of copper **2. ASIAN BIRD WITH METALLIC CALL** a small greenish bird of Southeast Asia belonging to the barbet family that has a distinctive metallic call. Latin name: *Megalaima haemacephala.*

cop·per sul·fate *n.* a poisonous blue compound containing copper and sulfur that is used in dyeing and as a fungicide. Formula: $CuSO_4$.

cop·per·ware /kóppər wàir/ *n.* objects made of copper, especially cooking pots and pans

cop·pice /kóppiss/ *n.* **GROVE OF SMALL TREES** an area of densely growing small trees, especially one in which the trees are regularly cut back to encourage more growth ■ *vt.* **(-piced, -pic·ing, -pic·es) PRUNE TREES** to cut back trees periodically to encourage young growth [Mid-14thC. From Old French *copeïz*, from *coper* "to cut" (see COPE[1]).]

Express Newspapers

Francis Ford Coppola

Cop·po·la /kóppələ/, **Francis Ford** (*b.* 1939) U.S. movie director. He directed the *Godfather* trilogy (1972, 1974, 1990).

co·pra /kóprə, kóp-/ *n.* the dried flesh of the coconut from which coconut oil is obtained [Late 16thC. Via Portuguese from Malayalam *koppara*.]

copro- *prefix.* dung, excrement ○ *coprophilous* [From Greek *kopros* "dung"]

co·pro·ces·sor /kō pró sèssər/ *n.* a second processor in a computer, designed to improve performance time by handling specialized tasks

cop·ro·la·li·a /kòpprə láylee ə/ *n.* the uncontrolled use of violent and obscene language, especially as a result of an illness such as Tourette's syndrome

cop·ro·lite /kóppro līt/ *n.* fossilized dung from which information about eating patterns in prehistoric times can be discovered —**cop·ro·lit·ic** /kòpprə líttik/ *adj.*

cop·rol·o·gy /kə prólləjee/ *n.* an obsession with defecation especially as expressed in art and literature

cop·roph·a·gy /kə próffəjee/ *n.* the eating of dung by certain species of insects or animals —**cop·roph·a·gous** /kə próffəgəss/ *adj.*

cop·ro·phil·i·a /kòpprə fíllee ə/ *n.* an obsessive and often sexual interest in feces and defecation —**cop·ro·phil·i·ac** *n.* —**cop·ro·phil·ic** *adj.*

cop·roph·i·lous /kə próffiləss/ *adj.* used to describe organisms such as some insects or fungi that live on or in dung

copse /kops/ *n.* = **coppice** [Late 16thC. Alteration of COPPICE.]

Copt /kopt/ *n.* **1. MEMBER OF COPTIC CHURCH** a member of the Coptic Church **2. NON-ARAB EGYPTIAN** an Egyptian of non-Arab descent [Early 17thC. Via French or modern Latin from Arabic *al-ḳibṭ* "the Copts," from Coptic *Gyptios* "Egyptian," from Greek *Aiguptios*.]

Copt. *abbr.* Coptic

cop·ter /kóptər/ *n.* a helicopter (*informal*) [Mid-20thC. Shortening.]

Cop·tic /kóptɪk/ *n.* **FORMER EGYPTIAN LANGUAGE** a language formerly spoken in Egypt, a later form of ancient Egyptian and one of the Afro-Asiatic languages. Coptic survives as the liturgical language of Egyptian Monophysite Christians. ■ *adj.* **OF THE COPTS** relating or belonging to the Copts, Coptic, or Egyptian Monophysite Christian Church

Cop·tic Church *n.* the Egyptian Christian Church, established in the 6th century and adhering to the doctrine of the Monophysites

cop·u·la /kóppyələ/ (*plural* **-las** *or* **-lae** /-lèe/) *n.* **1.** GRAM **LINKING VERB** a verb such as "be" or "seem" that links the subject of a sentence with an adjective or noun phrase (**complement**) relating to it (*technical*) **2.** LOGIC **LINK BETWEEN SUBJECT AND PREDICATE** a form of the verb "to be" linking the subject and the predicate in certain propositions, such as "are" in "Some dogs are poodles" (*technical*) **3. LINK BETWEEN TWO THINGS** anything that provides a link between two things (*formal*) [Early 17thC. From Latin, "link" (source of English *couple*). Ultimately from an Indo-European word meaning "to reach" that is also the ancestor of English *apt, apex*, and *attitude*.] —**cop·u·lar** *adj.*

cop·u·late /kóppyə làyt/ **(-lat·ed, -lat·ing, -lates)** *vi.* to have sexual intercourse (*formal*) [Early 17thC. From Latin *copulat-*, past participle stem of *copulare* "to join together," from *copula* (see COPULA).] —**cop·u·la·tion** /kòppyə láysh'n/ *n.* —**cop·u·la·to·ry** /kóppyələ tàwree/ *adj.*

cop·u·la·tive /kóppyə làytiv, -lə-/ *adj.* **1. LINKING** linking or joining (*formal*) **2.** GRAM **RELATING TO LINKING VERB** relating to a verb that links the subject with its complement, or to the function of such a verb —**cop·u·la·tive·ly** *adv.*

cop·y /kóppee/ *n.* (*plural* **-ies**) **1. REPRODUCTION** something that is made exactly like something else in appearance or function **2. ONE OF MANY** any of many identical specimens of something that is produced in large numbers, especially something printed or published **3. WRITTEN TEXT** the written text to be published in a book, newspaper, or magazine, as distinct from visual material or graphics ■ *v.* **(-ied, -y·ing, -ies) 1.** *vt.* **MAKE IDENTICAL VERSION** to make another example or specimen that is exactly the same as something **2.** *vt.* **DO SAME AS** to do exactly what somebody else does **3.** *vti.* **CHEAT BY DOING SAME** to reproduce the work of another fraudulently **4.** *vt.* **SEND COPY TO SOMEBODY** to send a copy to somebody, especially a copy of a letter or other document ○ *All heads of departments should have been copied.* [14thC. Via French from, ultimately, Latin *copia* "abundance, power, right" (see COPIOUS), in phrases meaning "the right to transcribe."] —**cop·y·a·ble** *adj.*

WORD KEY: SYNONYMS

copy, reproduce, duplicate, clone, replicate, recreate

CORE MEANING: to make something that resembles something else to a greater or lesser degree

copy the most general term; **reproduce** to make a copy that is careful and exact; **duplicate** to copy something two or more times; **clone** to produce a copy that is very nearly identical to the original, particularly a piece of equipment or an organism; **replicate** to copy something repeatedly and exactly; **recreate** to make something that appears to be the same as something that no longer exists, or that exists in a different place.

copy down *vt.* to make a written copy of something ○ *Journalists copied down his every word.*

cop·y·book /kóppi bòok/ *n.* **BOOK OF HANDWRITING SPECIMENS** a book containing models of handwriting for young students to copy ■ *adj.* **UNORIGINAL** following guidelines slavishly and showing no originality

cop·y boy /kóppi boy/, **cop·y·boy** *n.* somebody, usually a young man, who runs errands in a newspaper office

cop·y·cat /kóppi kàt/ *n.* **SOMEBODY WHO IMITATES OTHERS** somebody, especially a child, who slavishly imitates another (*informal*) ■ *adj.* **DONE IN IMITATION** done in close imitation of somebody or something else (*informal*)

cop·y desk *n.* a desk at which written material is edited for publication

copy·ed·it **(-it·ed, -it·ing)** *vti.* to read written material and correct it for publication

cop·y ed·i·tor /kóppee èddətər/, **copy·ed·i·tor** *n.* somebody who reads written material and corrects it for publication [Late 19thC]

copy·graph /kóppi gràf/ *n.* = **hectograph**

cop·y·hold·er /kóppi hòldər/ *n.* **1. DOCUMENT STAND** a stand that holds documents upright while they are being read or keyed **2. ASSISTANT TO PROOFREADER** somebody who reads written material aloud to a proofreader

cop·y·ist /kóppee ist/ *n.* **1. SOMEBODY WHO MAKES WRITTEN COPIES** somebody whose job is making copies of handwritten documents or music **2. UNIMAGINATIVE IMITATOR** somebody who merely imitates others

cop·y pro·tec·tion *n.* a means of preventing unauthorized duplication of computer software —**cop·y·pro·tect·ed** *adj.*

cop·y·read·er /kóppi rèedər/ *n.* somebody who reads and edits newspaper articles to prepare them for publication

cop·y·right /kóppi rīt/ *n.* **CREATIVE ARTIST'S CONTROL OF ORIGINAL WORK** the legal right of creative artists or publishers to control the use and reproduction of their original works ■ *adj.* **PROTECTED BY COPYRIGHT** controlled or restricted by a copyright ■ *vt.* **(-right·ed, -right·ing, -rights) GET COPYRIGHT OF** to secure the copyright on a creative work —**cop·y·right·a·ble** *adj.* —**cop·y·right·er** *n.*

cop·y·right de·pos·it li·brar·y *n.* any of a small number of libraries that receives a free copy of every book published in the United States

cop·y·writ·er /kóppi rītər/ *n.* somebody who writes the texts for advertisements and other publicity material —**cop·y·writ·ing** *n.*

coq au vin /kòk ō váN, -ván/ (*plural* **coqs au vin** /kòk-/ *or* **coq au vins**) *n.* a French dish of chicken cooked in red wine with other ingredients [From French, literally "cock in wine"]

co·quet /kō két/ *vi.* **(-quet·ted, -quet·ting, -quets)** (*literary*) **1. FLIRT** to act coyly and flirtatiously **2. ACT FRIVOLOUSLY** to act casually or frivolously ■ *n.* **MAN WHO FLIRTS** a flirtatious man (*literary*) [Late 17thC. From French, literally "little cock," from *coq* "cock" (see COCKADE).]

co·quet·ry /kṓkətree/ (*plural* **-ries**) *n.* flirtatious behavior (*literary*)

co·quette /kō két/ *n.* a flirtatious woman (*literary*) [Mid-17thC. From French, the feminine form of *coquet* "COQUET."] —**co·quet·tish** *adj.* —**co·quet·tish·ly** *adv.* —**co·quet·tish·ness** *n.*

co·quil·la nut /kə kíllə-, kō kéeyə-/ *n.* the nut of a Brazilian palm tree, with a thick hard shell used for carving [Coquilla of uncertain origin: possibly an alteration of Portuguese *coquilho*, literally "little coconut," from *côco* "coconut" (see COCO)]

co·quille /kō kéel/ *n.* **1. SEAFOOD DISH** a dish of seafood baked and served in a scallop shell or a scallop-shaped dish **2. SHELL OR SHELL-SHAPED DISH** a scallop shell or a scallop-shaped dish **3.** FENCING **GUARD ON FOIL** a bell-shaped guard on a fencing foil [From French, "cockle shell" (see COCKLE)]

co·qui·na /kō kéenə/ *n.* **1. SOFT LIMESTONE** a soft limestone formed largely from crushed shells and coral, used as a building material in the West Indies and the southeastern United States **2. SEA CLAM** a small clam common in the seas around the eastern and southern United States. Genus: *Donax.* [Mid-19thC. From Spanish, "cockle shell," of uncertain origin: probably via *concha* "mollusk shell" from Latin, "mussel."]

co·qui·to /kō kéetō/ (*plural* **-tos** *or* **-to**) *n.* a Chilean palm tree with edible nuts and a sweet sap that is used to make wine. Latin name: *Jubaea chilensis.* [Mid-19thC. Via Spanish, literally "little coco shell," from, ultimately, Portuguese *côco* "coconut" (see COCO).]

cor. *abbr.* **1.** corner **2.** cornet **3.** correction **4.** correspondence **5.** PRESS correspondent

Cor. *abbr.* BIBLE Corinthians

cor·a·cle /káwrəkəl/ *n.* a small round boat made from animal skins stretched over a wicker frame [Mid-16thC. Via Welsh *corwgl* from Middle Irish *curach* "currach" (see CURRACH).]

cor·a·coid /káwrə kòyd/ *n.* a bony projection on the shoulder blade in most mammals [Mid-18thC. Via modern Latin from Greek *korakoeidēs* "crowlike" (from its resemblance to a crow's beak), from *korax* "raven, crow."]

Coral

cor·al /káwrəl/ *n.* **1. MARINE ORGANISM** a marine organism that lives in colonies and has an external skeleton. Class: Anthozoa. **2. HARD MARINE DEPOSIT** a hard deposit consisting of coral skeletons, often forming marine reefs **3. SOMETHING MADE OF CORAL** a piece of coral or an article made from it **4. DEEP REDDISH-ORANGE COLOR** a deep reddish-orange color **5. LOBSTER'S OR CRAB'S EGGS** the unfertilized eggs of a crab or lobster that turn pinkish-orange when cooked ■ *adj.* **DEEP REDDISH-ORANGE** of a deep reddish-orange color [14thC. Via Old French from, ultimately, Greek *korallion.*]

cor·al bean *n.* = **coral tree**

cor·al-bells *n.* a perennial plant that produces clusters of tiny pinkish-orange bell-shaped flowers. Latin name: *Heuchera sanguinea.* (*takes a singular or plural verb*)

cor·al·ber·ry /káwrəl bèrree/ (*plural* **-ries** *or* **-ry**) *n.* **1. PLANT WITH RED BERRIES** a North American shrub of the honeysuckle family that produces dark red berries. Latin name: *Symphoricarpos orbiculatus.* **2. EASTERN ASIAN SHRUB** an evergreen shrub of eastern Asia. Genus: *Ardisia.*

Cor·al Ga·bles /káwrəl-/ city on Biscayne Bay in Florida, west of Miami, that is home to the University of Miami. Population: 39,916 (1996).

cor·al·line /káwrə lìn, -lin/ *adj.* **1. OF OR LIKE CORAL** relating to or resembling coral **2. PINKISH-RED OR PINKISH-ORANGE** of the pinkish-red or pinkish-orange color of coral ■ *n.* **1. CALCIUM-COVERED RED ALGA** a red alga whose fronds are covered or impregnated with calcium deposits. Genus: *Corallina.* **2. ORGANISM THAT RESEMBLES CORAL** a sponge or other organism that resembles coral

cor·al·loid /káwrə lòyd/ *adj.* relating to or resembling coral

cor·al reef *n.* a marine reef composed of the skeletons of living coral, together with minerals and organic matter

cor·al·root /káwrəl ròot/ (*plural* **-roots** *or* **-root**) *n.* a leafless orchid with small insignificant flowers that feeds through roots that resemble coral. Genus: *Corallorhiza.*

Cor·al Sea sea in the southwestern Pacific Ocean bounded by Australia, New Guinea, the Solomon Islands, and Vanuatu

cor·al snake *n.* **1. POISONOUS SNAKE OF N AND S AMERICA** a poisonous snake of North and South America that is strikingly marked with red, black, and yellow or white bands. Coral snakes are mostly nocturnal and feed on other snakes and lizards. Genera: *Micrurus* and *Micruroides.* **2. AUSTRALIAN POISONOUS SNAKE** a poisonous snake of eastern Australia that is red with yellow and black bands. Latin name: *Brachyurophis australis.*

Cor·al Springs city in southeastern Florida, northwest of Fort Lauderdale and southwest of Boca Raton. Population: 105,275 (1996).

cor·al tree *n.* a thorny shrub or small tree of tropical and subtropical regions with large red or orange flowers that are pollinated by birds and brightly colored seeds that grow in long pods. Genus: *Erythrina.*

cor·am pop·u·lo /k'awram póppyəlō/ *adv.* where other people can see what is being done (*literary*) [From Latin, literally "before the people"]

cor an·glais /kàwr awng gláy/ (*plural* **cor an·glais** *or* **cors an·glais** /kàwr awng gláy/) *n.* = **English horn** [From French, literally "English horn"]

co·ran·to /kə rántō, -raà-/ (*plural* **-tos**) *n.* = **courante** [Mid-16thC. Alteration of French *courante* (see COURANTE), influenced by Italian *corranta* (also from French).]

cor·ban /káwr bàn, -baàn, kawr bán, -baán/ *n.* **1. HEBREW OFFERING TO GOD** an offering to God made by the ancient Hebrew people **2. TEMPLE TREASURY** the treasury of the Temple of Jerusalem, or an offering made to it [14thC. Via Greek from Hebrew *qorbān* "offering," from *qārab* "to approach."]

cor·beil /káwrb'l/, **cor·beille** *n.* a stone carving of a basket of fruit or flowers as a feature on a building [Mid-18thC. Via French from late Latin *corbicula*, literally "small basket," from Latin *corbis* "basket."]

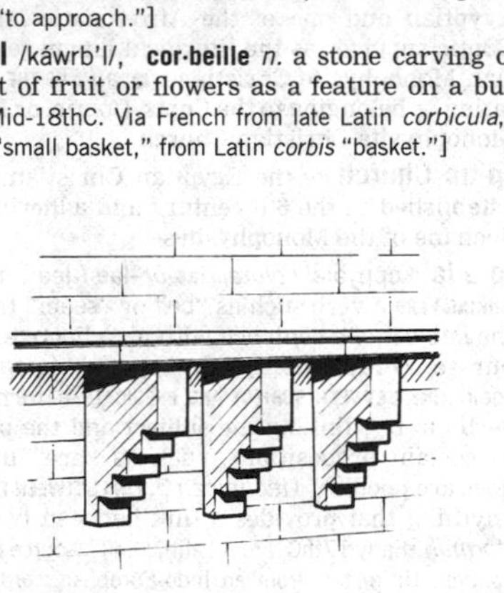
Corbel

cor·bel /káwrb'l, -bèl/ *n.* **SUPPORTING STONE BRACKET** a bracket of brick or stone that juts out of a wall to support a structure above it ■ *vt.* **(-beled, -bel·ing, -bels) 1. LAY MASONRY UNITS TO FORM PROJECTION** to lay stones or bricks in layers so that each juts out above the one below to form a supporting bracket **2. SUPPORT WITH CORBELS** to support a cornice or other structure on corbels [14thC. From Old French, literally "little raven," from *corp* "raven," from Latin *corvus* (see CORVINE); from its original beaklike profile from being cut slantwise.]

cor·bel·ing /káwrbəling, -bèlling/ *n.* a structural system using corbels as supports

Cor·bett /káwrbət/, **James John** (1866–1933) U.S. boxer. He was the world heavyweight boxing champion from 1892 to 1897. Known as **Gentleman Jim**

cor·bie /káwrbee/ (*plural* **-bies** *or* **-bie**) *n. Scotland* a crow, especially a raven [15thC. Via Old French *corbin* from late Latin *corvinus* "ravenlike" (see CORVINE).]

cor·bie ga·ble *n.* a gable with top edges shaped like a series of steps [Corbie from CORBIE-STEP]

cor·bie-step /káwrbi stèp/, **cor·bie·step** *n.* each of a series of decorative steps going up the side of a gable [*Corbie* from the idea that only crows can reach them]

cor·bi·na /kawr béenə/ (*plural* **-nas** *or* **-na**), **cor·vi·na** /kawr véenə/ (*plural* **-nas** *or* **-na**) *n.* a Pacific food and game fish that is popular with anglers along the coast of California. Latin name: *Menticirrhus undulatus.* [Early 20thC. Via American Spanish from Spanish *corvino* "ravenlike" (because of its color), from Latin *corvinus* (see CORVINE).]

cord /kawrd/ *n.* **1. STRING OR ROPE** thick strong string or thin rope ○ *cords of Venetian blinds* **2. ELECTRICAL CABLE** flexible insulated electric cable **3. BODY PART RESEMBLING ROPE** a part of the body resembling cord, e.g., the spinal cord or the umbilical cord **4. FASTENING OR BELT** a length of cord used as a fastening or belt **5. RIBBED FABRIC** any fabric that has a ribbed surface, especially corduroy **6. UNIT OF VOLUME** a unit of volume for measuring cut wood, equal to 128 cu. ft./3.62 cu. m ■ **cords** *npl.* **PANTS** corduroy pants (*informal*) ○ *a pair of cords* ■ *vt.* **(cord·ed, cord·ing, cords) 1. TIE WITH CORD** to fasten or tie something with cord or rope ○ *Are the packages corded and ready to ship?* **2. STACK WOOD IN CORDS** to stack wood in units with a volume of one cord [13thC. Via Old French and Latin from Greek *khordē* "string." Ultimately from an Indo-European word meaning "gut, entrail" that is also the ancestor of English *yarn, chord,* and *hernia.*] —**cord·er** *n.*

WORD KEY: USAGE

See Usage note at ***chord.***

cord·age /káwrdij/ *n.* **1. AMOUNT OF WOOD** the amount of wood in a stack, measured in cords **2. CORDS AS GROUP** ropes or cords collectively, especially the lines and rigging of a ship

cor·date /káwr dàyt/ *adj.* BOT used to describe a leaf that is heart-shaped [Mid-18thC. Via modern Latin *cordatus* from the Latin stem *cord-* (see CORDIAL).] —**cor·date·ly** *adv.*

cord·ed /káwrdəd/ *adj.* **1. RIBBED** used to describe a fabric with a ribbed surface **2. TIED UP** securely tied up with string or rope **3. WITH TIGHT MUSCLES** having tensed or well-developed muscles visible as ridges or ripples

cord grass *n.* a coarse grass found on coastal salt marshes or mudflats. Genus: *Spartina.*

cor·dial /káwrjəl/ *adj.* **1. WARM** friendly and affectionate **2. DEEPLY FELT** sincere or profound ○ *cordial greeting* (*literary*) **3. REFRESHING** stimulating or invigorating (*literary*) ■ *n.* **1. LIQUEUR** an alcoholic drink usually served at the end of a meal **2. TONIC** a stimulating or medicinal drink [14thC. Via medieval Latin *cordialis* "of the heart" from the Latin stem *cord-* from *cor* "heart" (source of English *courage* and *accord*).] —**cor·dial·ly** *adv.* —**cor·dial·ness** *n.*

cor·di·al·i·ty /kàwrjee állətee/ *n.* friendliness and affection ○ *We were surprised by the cordiality of their response.*

cor·di·er·ite /káwrdee ə rìt/ *n.* a purplish-blue or gray mineral that is a silicate of magnesium, aluminum, and iron and is found in metamorphic rock [Early 19thC. Named for the French geologist, Pierre L. *Cordier* (1777–1861) who discovered it.]

cor·dil·le·ra /kàwrd'l yáirə/ (*plural* **-ras**) *n.* a system of mountain ranges consisting of approximately parallel ridges [Early 18thC. From Spanish, from *cordilla*, literally "small cord," from *cuerda* "cord," from Latin *chorda* (see CORD).]

cord·ite /káwr dìt/ *n.* a smokeless explosive, usually made of gunpowder and nitroglycerin [Late 19thC. Formed from CORD, because of its stringy appearance.]

cord·less /káwrdləss/ *adj.* powered by an internal battery and not needing to be continuously attached by a cable to an external electricity supply

cord·less tel·e·phone *n.* a telephone, powered by a recharging battery, with a portable handset that can be removed from its base unit and has a short-range radio link to it

cór·do·ba /káwrdəbə/ *n.* **1.** see table at **currency 2. COIN WORTH ONE CÓRDOBA** a coin worth one córdoba [Early 20thC. Named for the Spanish explorer, Francisco Fernández de *Córdoba* (1475–1526).]

Cór·do·ba /káwrdəbə/ **1.** city and capital of Córdoba Province in central Argentina. It is the site of the National University of Córdoba, founded in 1613. Population: 1,148,305 (1991). English **Cordova 2.** city in Andalusía, southern Spain. It is the capital of Córdoba Province. Population: 300,229 (1991).

English **Cordova** 3. resort and trading city in east central Mexico. Population: 137,641 (1990).

cor·don /káwrd'n, -dòn/ *n.* 1. PEOPLE OR VEHICLES ENCIRCLING AREA a chain of police officers or soldiers, or their vehicles, surrounding an area to control access to it 2. RIBBON a piece of ribbon worn for decoration or as a sign of rank or a mark of honor 3. GARDENING FRUIT TREE WITH NO SIDE BRANCHES a fruit tree grown as a main stem with spurs, but with its side branches removed 4. ARCHIT = **stringcourse** [Late 16thC. From Old French, literally "small cord," from *corde* (see CORD).]

cordon off (cordoned off, cordoning off, cordons off) *vt.* to surround an area with a line of police officers, soldiers, or their vehicles, to control access to it

cor·don bleu /kàwr dawn blóo, -dawN-/ *adj.* 1. OF HIGHEST CLASS used to describe a cook or cooking of the highest class 2. WITH CHEESE AND HAM used to describe a way of preparing meat, especially veal, by rolling a thin slice around cheese and ham and then coating in breadcrumbs ■ *n.* (*plural* **cor·don bleus**) 1. MASTER CHEF a cook of the very highest class, especially a master chef 2. HIST KNIGHT'S RIBBON a blue ribbon worn by knights of the highest order in Bourbon France [Early 18thC. From French, literally "blue ribbon."]

cor·don sa·ni·taire /kàwr dawN saani táir/ *n.* 1. DISEASE-CONTROLLING BARRIER a barrier erected to control the spread of a disease by restricting movement to and from the infected area 2. AREA SEPARATING WARRING NATIONS a neutral state, or a string of neutral states, lying between two states that are hostile to each other [Mid-19thC. From French, literally "sanitary line."]

Cor·do·va /kawr dővə/ city in southeastern Alaska, on the north shore of Prince William Sound, southeast of Anchorage. Population: 2,256 (1996).

cor·do·van /káwrdəvən/ *n.* a fine soft leather originally made from goatskin and now usually made from horsehide [Late 16thC. From Spanish *cordován*, named after the Spanish city of CORDOBA where it was made.]

cor·du·roy /káwrdə ròy/ *n.* RIBBED COTTON FABRIC a heavy cotton fabric with a ribbed nap running lengthwise ■ **cor·du·roys** *npl.* PANTS pants made of corduroy [Late 18thC. Origin uncertain: probably coined from CORD + *duroy*, a kind of coarse woollen fabric.]

cor·du·roy road *n.* a road made of logs across muddy or swampy ground [*Corduroy* from the resemblance of its surface to corduroy fabric]

cord·wain /káwrd wàyn/ *n.* = **cordovan** (*archaic*) [14thC. Via Old French *cordewan* from Spanish *cordován* (see CORDOVAN).]

cord·wain·er /káwrd wàynər/ *n.* somebody who makes shoes and other articles from fine soft leather (**cordovan**) (*archaic*) —**cord·wain·er·y** *n.*

cord·wood /káwrd wòod/ *n.* wood in stacks with a volume of one cord, or cut into lengths of 4 ft./1.2 m for stacking in cords

core /kawr/ *n.* 1. CENTRAL PART OF FRUIT the fibrous central part of some kinds of fruit, containing the seeds 2. ESSENTIAL PART the central or most important part of something 3. GEOL CENTER OF EARTH the central part of the Earth, or the corresponding part of another celestial body. The Earth's core is molten in parts and is composed of an alloy of iron and nickel. 4. COMPUT COMPUTER MEMORY the main memory of a computer, which was composed of arrays of ring-shaped magnets, before the introduction of semiconductor memories 5. COMPUT PIECE OF COMPUTER MEMORY a ring-shaped piece of magnetic material formerly used to store digital data in a computer, each core representing one binary digit (**bit**) 6. GEOL SAMPLE OBTAINED BY DRILLING a tubular segment of rock, ice, or other material obtained as a study sample by drilling 7. PHYS CENTRAL PART OF NUCLEAR REACTOR the central part of a nuclear reactor in which fission takes place 8. ELEC IRON IN TRANSFORMER a block of iron in a coil or transformer, used to intensify and direct the magnetic field produced by a current in surrounding coils 9. STONE USED TO MAKE TOOLS a block of stone from which tools or flakes are chipped ■ *adj.* ESSENTIAL of central or fundamental importance ■ *vt.* (**cored, cor·ing, cores**) TAKE CORE OUT OF to remove the core from a piece of fruit [13thC. Origin unknown.]

CORE /kawr/ *abbr.* Congress of Racial Equality

core cit·y *n.* = **inner city**

core com·pe·ten·cy *n.* an area of expertise that is fundamental to a particular job or function

core cur·ric·u·lum *n.* the subjects that all students are required to study at school

core dump *n.* 1. TRANSFER OF DATA a transfer of data stored in the core memory of a computer, usually to external storage 2. LONG-WINDED ANSWER a long-winded response to a simple question (*informal humorous*)

co·ref·er·en·tial /kō reffə rénshəl/ *adj.* referring to the same person or thing ○ *In the sentence "Mary lost her purse," "Mary" and "her" are coreferential.*

co·re·lig·ion·ist /kō ri líjjənist/ *n.* somebody who practices the same religion as another person

core mem·o·ry *n.* = **core** *n.* 4 (*technical*)

co·req /kōrék/ *n.* a corequisite (*informal*)

co·req·ui·site /kō rékwizit/ *n.* a course of study that must be taken along with another [Mid-20thC. Modeled on *prerequisite*.]

cor·er /káwrər/ *n.* a utensil with a near-cylindrical blade used for removing the cores of apples and other fruit

co·re·spon·dent /kō ri spóndənt/, **co·re·spon·dent** *n.* somebody named in a divorce suit as the alleged adulterous sexual partner of the respondent —**co·re·spon·den·cy** *n.*

core sub·ject *n.* any of a number of subjects that all students are required to study at school

core time *n.* the part of the working day during which workers on flextime must be present at work

corf /kawrf/ (*plural* **corves** /kawrvz/) *n.* MINING a wagon used inside a mine for transporting mined coal or ore [15thC. Via Middle Dutch or Middle Low German *korf* "basket" from Latin *corbis*. Its earliest meaning in English was "basket."]

Cor·fam /káwr fàm/ *tdmk.* a trademark for a synthetic water-resistant substitute for leather, used in the making of shoes

Cor·fu /kawr fóo, káwr fòo/ most northerly island in the Ionian Islands, west of Greece. It is a major tourist center. Population: 107,592 (1991). Area: 247 sq. mi./641 sq. km. Greek **Kérkira**

cor·gi /káwrgee/ (*plural* **-gis**) *n.* a small dog with short legs and smooth hair. There are two breeds of corgi, the Cardigan Welsh corgi and the Pembroke Welsh corgi. [Early 20thC. From Welsh, formed from *cor* "dwarf" + *ci* "dog."]

cor·i·a·ceous /kàwree áyshəss/ *adj.* like leather in texture or appearance [Late 17thC. From late Latin *coriaceus*, from Latin *corium* "leather."]

co·ri·an·der /kàwree ándər/ *n.* 1. AROMATIC PLANT an annual plant native to Asia and the Mediterranean, grown for its aromatic leaves and seeds that are used as a flavoring in cooking. Latin name: *Coriandrum sativum.* 2. FOOD FLAVORING the leaves or seeds of the coriander plant, or a powder made from the crushed seeds, used to season food [13thC. Via Old French from, ultimately, Greek *koriandron*.]

Cor·inth /káwrinth/ 1. ancient Greek city and modern town 3 mi./5 km to the northeast. The ruins of the ancient city are about 50 mi./80 km west of Athens. Population: 29,600 (1995). 2. city in the northeastern corner of Mississippi, the site of a famous Civil War battle. Population: 12,264 (1996).

Co·rin·thi·an /kə rínthee ən/ *adj.* 1. OF CORINTH relating to or typical of the ancient or modern Greek city of Corinth 2. ARCHIT SLENDER AND ORNATE AT TOP used to describe a slender column with an ornate capital 3. DEBAUCHED debauched or ostentatiously luxurious (*literary*) ■ *n.* 1. SOMEBODY FROM CORINTH somebody from the city of Corinth 2. WEALTHY SPORTSPERSON a wealthy amateur sportsperson, especially somebody fond of yachting (*humorous*) 3. MAN ABOUT TOWN a man who enjoys good living

Co·rin·thi·an or·der *n.* an ancient Greek order of architecture characterized by a slender column with an ornate capital [Corinthian from the origin of the order in CORINTH, Greece]

Co·rin·thi·ans /kə rínthee ənz/ *n.* either of two books in the New Testament, originally written as letters by St. Paul to the church at Corinth. See table at **Bible**

Co·ri·o·la·nus /kàwree ə láynəss, kə rī ə lánnəss/ *n.* in Roman legend the defeater of the Volsci in the 5th century B.C. He later joined his former enemies, and was dissuaded from leading a Volscian attack on Rome by the pleas of his wife and mother.

Co·ri·o·lis ef·fect /kawri ṓlis-/ *n.* the observed deflection of something such as a missile in flight relative to the Earth's surface, caused by the Earth's rotation beneath the object. The deflection is to the right in the northern hemisphere and to the left in the southern hemisphere. [Named for the French mathematician Gaspard de *Coriolis* 1792–1843]

Co·ri·o·lis force *n.* an apparent but nonexistent force used to describe the effect of the Earth's rotation on the motion of moving objects

co·ri·um /káwree əm/ (*plural* **-a** /-ree ə/) *n.* 1. MED = **dermis** 2. INSECTS PART OF INSECT'S WING the leathery middle part of the forewing of some insects [Early 19thC. From Latin, "hide, leather" (source of English *excoriate*).]

co·ri·val *n.* = **corrival**

cork /kawrk/ *n.* 1. INDUST OUTER BARK OF CORK OAK the light, flexible, outer bark of the cork oak tree commonly used to make bottle stoppers and as an insulator 2. BOTTLE STOPPER a usually cylindrical piece of cork or other material used as a bottle stopper 3. ANGLING FLOAT USED IN FISHING a small float used in fishing to maintain a hook or net suspended in the water 4. BOT LAYER OF PLANT TISSUE dead tissue that forms a protective outer layer on plants and is part of the bark in woody plants ■ *vt.* (**corked, cork·ing, corks**) 1. SEAL CONTAINER WITH CORK to stop or seal something, especially a bottle, with a cork 2. RESTRAIN FEELINGS to restrain feelings, especially strong negative ones such as anger or grief 3. BLACKEN FACE AND HANDS to blacken something, especially somebody's face and hands, with charred cork [13thC. Origin uncertain: probably via Middle Dutch from, ultimately, Arabic dialect *kurk* "cork-soled sandal," which may have been borrowed from Latin *quercus* "oak tree."] ◇ **blow** *or* **pop your cork** to lose your temper (*informal*)

Cork /kawrk/ county town of County Cork, southern Ireland. It is a port on the Lee River and the second largest city in the Republic of Ireland. Population: 127,024 (1991).

cork·age /káwrkij/ *n.* a fee charged at some restaurants for serving wine and other alcoholic drinks that guests bring in from elsewhere

cork·board /káwrk bàwrd/ *n.* 1. THIN SHEET OF COMPRESSED CORK GRANULES a thin sheet made from compressed cork granules, typically used as a floor covering and as wall insulation before plastic was available 2. BULLETIN BOARD a bulletin board made with compressed cork granules

cork cam·bi·um *n.* a zone of actively dividing tissue near the outer surface of a woody plant that produces cork

corked /kawrkt/ *adj.* 1. SEALED sealed or stopped with a cork or other object 2. WINE TAINTED BY CORK given an unpleasant flavor by substances from a tainted cork ○ *Waiter, this wine's corked!* 3. BLACKENED blackened with burnt cork

cork·er /káwrkər/ *n.* 1. PARTICULARLY STRIKING PERSON OR THING somebody or something particularly striking or special (*dated slang*) ○ *It was a corker of a day.* 2. PERSON OR MACHINE THAT FITS CORKS a person or machine that fits corks, especially into bottles

cork·ing /káwrking/ *adj.* excellent or splendid (*dated slang*)

cork oak (*plural* **cork oaks** *or* **cork oak**) *n.* a Mediterranean evergreen oak tree whose thick bark is a source of cork. Latin name: *Quercus suber.*

cork·screw /káwrk skròo/ *n.* DEVICE FOR REMOVING CORKS FROM BOTTLES a device for taking corks out of bottles, usually a pointed spiral of metal attached to a handle or simple lever ■ *v.* (**-screwed, -screw·ing, -screws**) 1. *vi.* MOVE IN SPIRAL PATH to move in a spiral path ○ *watched anxiously as the plane corkscrewed toward the ground* 2. *vt.* WIND IN SPIRAL to wind or twist something in a spiral ■ *adj.* SPIRAL-SHAPED shaped like a spiral ○ *corkscrew curls*

cork tree *n.* = **cork oak**

cork·wood /káwrk wòod/ (*plural* **-woods** *or* **-wood**) *n.* 1. TREES TREE WITH LIGHTWEIGHT WOOD a deciduous shrub or small tree that grows in wetlands of the southeastern United States and has light porous wood. Latin name: *Leitneria floridana.* 2. INDUST LIGHTWEIGHT WOOD the light, porous wood of the corkwood or any similar wood, such as balsa

cork·y /káwrkee/ (**-i·er, -i·est**) *adj.* 1. OF OR LIKE CORK made from or resembling cork 2. TASTING OR SMELLING OF CORK having the taste or smell of cork —**cork·i·ness** *n.*

corm /kawrm/ *n.* a short swollen underground stem base in some plants, e.g., crocus and gladiolus, that stores food over the winter and produces new foliage in the spring. New corms often form on top of old ones and are used as a means of propagating new plants. [Mid-19thC. Via modern Latin *cormus* from Greek *kormos* "lopped-off tree trunk."] —**cor·mous** *adj.*

Cormorant

cor·mo·rant /káwrmərənt/ *n.* **1. LARGE MARINE BIRD** a large marine diving bird with webbed feet, a hooked bill, and a long neck that can expand to swallow fish. Family: Phalacrocoracidae. **2. SOMEBODY GREEDY** somebody greedy or rapacious (*informal*) [13thC. Alteration of Old French *cormaran*, literally "sea raven," from *corp* "raven" (source of English *corbel*) + *marenc* "of the sea" (from Latin *marinus*, source of English *marine*).]

corn[1] /kawrn/ *n.* **1. TALL CEREAL CROP** a tall annual cereal crop that yields densely packed ears of grains attached to a central core. Native to Central and South America, it has been cultivated as a food crop since ancient times. The grains are a staple food for both humans and livestock in many countries, and the entire plant is sometimes used for silage. Latin name: *Zea mays.* **2. GRAINS OF CORN PLANT** the grain of the corn plant, used as a vegetable, ground for flour, to produce oil, or for livestock feed **3.** *U.K., Ireland* **CEREAL CROP** any cereal crop, especially wheat, barley, or oats **4.** METEOROL, SKIING = **corn snow 5.** BEVERAGES = **corn whiskey 6. CORNY ITEM OR MATERIAL** something trite or overly sentimental (*informal*) ■ *vt.* FOOD TECH **PRESERVE FOOD WITH SALT OR BRINE** to preserve food using grains of salt or brine [Old English. Ultimately from an Indo-European word meaning "grain" that is also the ancestor of English *grain, kernel, granite,* and *grenade.*]

corn[2] /kawrn/ *n.* MED a hardened or thickened, often painful, area of skin, usually on a toe, caused by friction or pressure [Late 14thC. Via French, from Latin *cornu* "horn." Ultimately from an Indo-European base that is also the ancestor of English *horn, cranium, reindeer,* and *carrot.*]

corn·ball /káwrn bàwl/ *n.* **SOMEBODY VERY SENTIMENTAL** somebody who is very sentimental or unsophisticated ■ *adj.* **VERY SENTIMENTAL** trite or overly sentimental ○ *a cornball movie* [Mid-20thC. Originally used for a ball of popcorn and molasses or syrup, often sold at carnivals and circuses. The underlying meaning is "something popular with unsophisticated rural audiences."]

Corn Belt *n.* the area of the Great Plains and the Midwest where corn and soybeans are the principal crops

corn bor·er *n.* ZOOL a moth whose larvae bore into corn. Family: Pyralidae.

corn·braid /káwrn bràyd/ *vt., n.* = **cornrow**

corn cake /káwrn kàyk/, **corn·cake** *n. Southern U.S.* = **johnnycake**

corn chip *n.* a crisp thin piece of fried cornmeal batter, eaten as a savory snack food

corn·cob /káwrn kòb/ *n.* the hard core of an ear of corn, on which the kernels grow

corn·cob pipe, corn·cob *n.* a pipe with a bowl made from part of a dried corncob

corn·cock·le /káwrn kòk'l/ (*plural* **-les** *or* **-le**), **corn cock·le** *n.* an annual Mediterranean plant of the pink family with reddish-purple flowers and poisonous seeds, once common as a weed in grainfields. Latin name: *Agrostemma githago.* [Early 18thC. From *corn*[1] + *cockle* "corncockle," from Old English *coccul.*]

corn·crake /káwrn kràyk/ *n.* a speckled bird with a harsh call, a short bill, and reddish wings that lives in fields and meadows in Europe and Asia. Latin name: *Crex crex.*

corn·crib /káwrn krìb/ *n.* a ventilated building used for the storage and drying of corn

corn·dodg·er /káwrn dòjjər/ *n. Southern U.S.* a ball of cornmeal batter that is deep-fried, baked, or boiled

corn dog *n.* a hot dog on a stick, coated in cornmeal batter and deep-fried. It is typically sold at fairs and carnivals.

corn·dog·ging /káwrn dògging/ *n.* a surfing initiation ritual in which a surfer is rolled in sand after surfing by his or her fellow surfers (*slang*)

cor·ne·a /káwrnee ə/ (*plural* **-as** *or* **-ae** /-'ee/) *n.* the transparent convex membrane that covers the pupil and iris of the eye [14thC. From medieval Latin *cornea tela* "horny tissue," because of its fibrous consistency, from, ultimately, Latin *cornu* "horn" (source of English *corn*[2]).] —**cor·ne·al** *adj.*

corn ear·worm *n.* a large striped American moth larva that feeds destructively on corn, tomatoes, cotton bolls, and many other plants. Latin name: *Helicoverpa zea.*

corned /kawrnd/ *adj.* cooked and then preserved in salt or brine ○ *corned mutton* [Early 17thC. From corn "to preserve with grains of salt," from CORN[1].]

corned beef *n.* beef that has been cooked, preserved in salt or brine, and often canned

cor·nel /káwrn'l/ (*plural* **-nels** *or* **-nel**) *n.* **1.** any plant related to dogwood. Genus: *Cornus.* **2.** = **cornelian cherry** [Mid-16thC. Via French *corneille* or German *Kornelbaum* from, ultimately, Latin *cornus.*]

cor·nel·ian /kawr neélyən/ *n.* = **carnelian**

cor·nel·ian cher·ry *n.* a small deciduous tree that is native to southern Europe but is widely cultivated for its clusters of bright yellow flowers, which it bears in early spring, and its small red fruits. The fruits are edible but sour, and were formerly used in jellies and preserves. Latin name: *Cornus mas.*

Cor·nell /kawr nél/, **Joseph** (1903–72) U.S. sculptor. He is best known for his assemblages of often surreal objects enclosed in small glass-fronted wooden boxes.

Cor·nell, Katharine (1898–1974) U.S. stage actor who achieved international recognition from the 1920s until 1960.

cor·ner /káwrnər/ *n.* **1. MEETING OF LINES OR SURFACES** the angle formed where two or more lines or surfaces meet ○ *a corner of the room* **2. AREA ENCLOSED BY CONVERGING LINES** the area enclosed where two lines or surfaces meet **3. PROJECTING PART OF SOMETHING** a projecting angular part of something **4. PLACE WHERE TWO ROADS MEET** the place where two roads or streets meet **5. DIFFICULT SITUATION** a difficult or embarrassing position, especially one from which there is no easy way of escape ○ *got himself into a corner about his previous statements* **6. QUIET PLACE** a secluded, peaceful, or secret place **7. REMOTE PLACE** any area or place, especially one that is remote **8. OBJECT FITTED OVER CORNER** an object made to fit over a corner of something, especially to protect it ○ *a diary with metal corners* **9.** COMM **CONTROL OF A MARKET** a monopoly of a particular commodity acquired in order to control its market price **10.** BASEBALL **PART OF BASEBALL STRIKE ZONE** in baseball, a location on either edge of home plate, forming part of the strike zone **11.** SPORTS **PART OF PLAYING FIELD OR SURFACE** in various sports, part of the playing field or surface where two boundaries meet **12.** SOCCER, HOCKEY **KICK OR SHOT FROM CORNER** in some games, a free kick or shot from a corner of the field given to the attacking team when a defending player knocks the ball over the goal line **13.** BOXING, WRESTLING **PART OF RING** in boxing and wrestling, any of the four parts of a ring where the ropes are attached to the posts, especially the two where the competitors rest between rounds ■ *adj.* **1. LOCATED ON CORNER** situated on a street corner ○ *a corner store* **2. INTENDED FOR CORNER** intended to be put in a corner ○ *a corner cabinet* **3. IN CORNER OF SOMETHING** at or in a corner of something ○ *sat at a corner table* ■ *v.* (**-nered, -ner·ing, -ners**) **1.** *vt.* **FORCE INTO DIFFICULT POSITION** to force a person or an animal into a position from which escape is difficult **2.** *vt.* **PUT IN CORNER** to place somebody or something in a corner **3.** *vt.* **PROVIDE WITH CORNERS** to give corners to something **4.** *vt.* COMM **ACQUIRE MONOPOLY OF** to acquire a monopoly of a particular commodity and so be able to control its market price **5.** *vi.* **TURN CORNER** to turn a corner (*refers to vehicles or their drivers*) **6.** *vti.* SOCCER, HOCKEY **TAKE CORNER KICK** in some games, to take a free kick or hit from a corner of the field on an opponents' goal line [13thC. Via Anglo-Norman from, ultimately, Latin *cornua* "horns, points," the plural of *cornu* "horn, point" (source of English *corn*[2]).] ◇ **cut corners** to do something in a quicker, cheaper, or less careful way than is desirable or wise ◇ **in somebody's corner** providing somebody with support ○ *You can't lose with him in your corner.* ◇ **turn the corner** to get past the worst part of a difficult or dangerous situation

cor·ner·back /káwrnər bàk/ *n.* in football, either of two defensive halfbacks placed behind the linebackers and near the sidelines

Cor·ner Brook /káwrnər-/ city on the western coast of the province of Newfoundland, Canada, on the Humber River. Population: 21,893 (1996).

cor·nered /káwrnərd/ *adj.* **1. IN DIFFICULT POSITION** in a difficult or embarrassing position, especially when there is no easy way of escape **2. WITH PARTICULAR CORNERS** with a particular number or type of corners (*usually used in combination*) **3. WITH NUMBER OF CONTENDERS** with a specified number of contenders ○ *a three-cornered struggle for the championship*

cor·ner·man /káwrnərmən/ (*plural* **-men** /-mən/) *n.* **1. PLAYER IN CORNERS** in various sports, a team member assigned to play, or adept at playing, in the corners, such as a basketball forward or a football cornerback **2.** BOXING **BOXER'S ASSISTANT** a supporter in a boxer's corner who gives advice, refreshment, and encouragement between rounds **3. POLITICAL AIDE** somebody who provides support and advice, especially to a political candidate (*slang*)

cor·ner·stone /káwrnər stōn/ *n.* **1. FUNDAMENTALLY IMPORTANT PERSON OR THING** somebody or something that is fundamentally important to something **2.** BUILDING **STONE AT CORNER OF TWO WALLS** a stone joining two walls where they meet at a corner **3.** BUILDING **FIRST STONE OF NEW BUILDING** the first stone laid at a corner where two walls begin and form the first part of a new building [13thC. Modeled on Latin *lapis angularis.*]

cor·ner·wise /káwrnər wìz/, **cor·ner·ways** /káwrnər wàyz/ *adv., adj.* diagonal or diagonally, or with a corner at the front

cor·net /kawr nèt/ *n.* **1.** MUSIC **BRASS INSTRUMENT LIKE TRUMPET** a three-valved brass instrument shaped like a compressed trumpet. Its tubing is more conical than a trumpet and it has a softer warmer sound. **2.** MUSIC = **cornetist 3.** FOOD **PAPER CONE FOR HOLDING CANDY** a piece of paper folded into a cone shape and used to hold small edible things, especially candy **4.** CLOTHES **WOMAN'S HEADDRESS** a headdress of starched cloth worn by women from the 12th to the 15th centuries **5.** CLOTHES, CHR **NUN'S HEADDRESS** a large white headdress worn by some Christian nuns [14thC. From French, literally "small horn," from *corne* "horn," from, ultimately, Latin *cornu* "horn" (source of English *corn*[2]).]

cor·net·fish /kawr nét fish/ (*plural* **-fish** *or* **-fishes**) *n.* a tropical or subtropical sea fish that has a long tubular snout ending in a small mouth and a forked tail with a long trailing extension from its center. Family: Fistularidae.

cor·net·ist /kawr néttist/, **cor·net·tist** *n.* somebody who plays a cornet

cor·nett /kawr nét/ *n.* Renaissance and Baroque wooden horn with six keys and a cup mouthpiece [Late 19thC. Variant of CORNET, modeled on Italian *cornetto*, literally "small horn."]

corn-fed *adj.* **1. FED ON CORN** fed or fattened on corn **2. RUSTIC** robust but unsophisticated (*informal*)

corn·field /káwrn feèld/ *n.* a field in which corn is growing

corn·flakes /káwrn flàyks/, **corn flakes** *npl.* a breakfast cereal consisting of small pieces of toasted corn, usually eaten with cold milk

corn·flour /káwrn flòwr/ *n. U.K.* = **cornstarch**

corn·flow·er /káwrn flòwr/ *n.* an annual plant found in Europe and Asia and naturalized in North America, with blue, pink, white, or purple flowers when cultivated. Latin name: *Centaurea cyanus.*

corn·flow·er blue *n.* a deep brilliant blue color with a tinge of purple

corn·husk /káwrn hùsk/ *n.* the leafy outer covering of an ear of corn

corn·husk·er /káwrn hùskər/ *n.* **1. REMOVER OF CORNHUSKS** somebody or something that removes the husks from corn **2. corn·husk·er, Corn·husk·er** SOMEBODY FROM NEBRASKA somebody who comes from or lives in Nebraska

Corn·husk·er State *n.* the state of Nebraska (*informal*)

corn·husk·ing /káwrn hùsking/ *n.* **1.** SOCIAL EVENT a social event in which participants husk corn and later eat, dance, and sing **2.** REMOVAL OF CORNHUSKS the removal of the husks from ears of corn

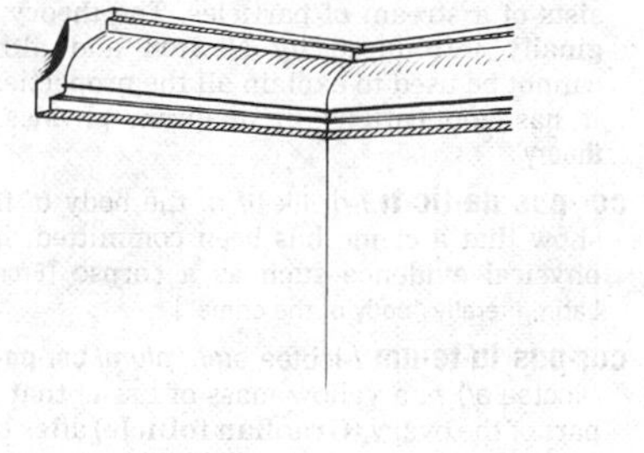

Cornice

cor·nice /káwrniss/ *n.* **1.** ARCHIT **PROJECTING MOLDING ALONG WALL** a projecting horizontal molding along the top of a wall or building **2.** ARCHIT **DECORATIVE PLASTER MOLDING** a decorative plaster molding around a room where the walls and ceiling meet **3.** ARCHIT **PART OF CLASSICAL BUILDING** the top projecting section of the part of a classical building that is supported by the columns (**entablature**) **4.** MOUNTAINEERING **OVERHANG OF SNOW** an overhanging mass of snow or ice formed by wind action ■ *vt.* (**-niced, -nic·ing, -nic·es**) ARCHIT **DECORATE WALL WITH CORNICE** to decorate or finish a wall or building with a cornice [Mid-16thC. From French and Italian, of uncertain origin: perhaps from the Latin stem *cornic-* "crow" (because it resembles a crow's beak), influenced by Greek *korōnis* "copestone."]

cor·niche /káwrnish, kawr néesh/ *n.* a coast road, especially one cut into a cliff [Mid-19thC. From French, a variant of *cornice* "CORNICE."]

cor·nic·u·late /kawr níkyələt/ *adj.* **1.** HAVING HORNS having horns or projections like horns **2.** OF HORNS relating to or resembling a horn [Mid-17thC. Formed from Latin *cornicula*, literally "little horn," from *cornu* "horn" (see CORN[2]).]

cor·ni·fi·ca·tion /kàwrnəfi káysh'n/ *n.* the conversion of skin cells into keratin or other horny material, such as nails or scales [Mid-19thC. Coined from Latin *cornu* "horn" (see CORN[2] + -FICATION).]

Corn·ing /káwrning/ city in southern New York, northwest of Elmira, on the Cohocton River. Population: 11,356 (1996).

Cor·nish /káwrnish/ *adj.* OF CORNWALL relating to or typical of Cornwall in southwestern England or its people, language, or culture ■ *npl.* PEOPLES PEOPLE OF CORNWALL the people of Cornwall in southwestern England ■ *n.* (*plural* **-nish**) LANG, HIST **EXTINCT CELTIC LANGUAGE** a Celtic language spoken in Cornwall until the late 18th century. Breton is the living language most closely related to Cornish.

Corn Laws *npl.* HIST a group of laws introduced in Great Britain in 1804 and repealed in 1846 that were designed to restrict the importation of foreign grain by imposing duty on it. This caused bread prices to rise and led to riots.

corn lil·y *n.* a southern African plant of the iris family, widely grown for its ornamental flowers of various colors that resemble lilies. Genus: *Ixia.*

corn·meal /káwrn mèel/, **corn meal** *n.* flour made from corn

corn oil *n.* oil extracted from corn, used in cooking, in margarine, as salad oil, and in some soaps

corn on the cob *n.* an ear of corn that is cooked and served whole

Corn·plant·er /káwrn plàntər/ (1735?–1836) Native American leader who made treaties with settlers, and was rejected by his people. Born **Galant-waka**

corn·pone /káwrn pōn/, **corn pone** *n.* *Southern U.S.* CORNMEAL BREAD bread made with cornmeal but often without eggs or milk, shaped into ovals, then fried or baked ■ *adj.* TYPICAL OF COUNTRY LIFE typical of country life and people in being simple, unpretentious, and homely (*informal*)

corn pop·py *n.* a common wild plant of Europe and Asia that has large scarlet flowers and often grows in cultivated fields. Latin name: *Papaver rhoeas.*

corn·row /káwrn rō/ *n.* BRAIDED ROW OF HAIR any of a group of narrow parallel braids of hair lying flat against the scalp ■ *vt.* (**-rowed, -row·ing, -rows**) FIX HAIR INTO CORNROWS to style hair in cornrows [Late 20thC. Because the braids resemble rows of corn.]

corn sal·ad *n.* a plant of the valerian family that often grows in grain fields and has edible leaves. Latin name: *Valerianella locusta.*

corn silk *n.* the tuft of silky styles and stigmas growing at the tip of a corn ear. It is used in herbal medicine as a diuretic.

corn smut *n.* a fungal disease of corn that produces dark swellings on the grain

corn snow *n.* fallen snow that has a grainy surface because it has thawed and refrozen

corn·starch /káwrn staarch/ *n.* fine-grained, starchy flour made from corn, especially used as a thickener in cooking

corn sug·ar *n.* a type of sugar (**dextrose**) extracted from cornstarch

corn syr·up *n.* syrup made from cornstarch, used as a sweetener in many foods

cor·nu /káwr nōō/ (*plural* **-nu·a** /-noo ə/) *n.* a part that resembles a horn or has a horn-shaped pattern [Late 17thC. From Latin, "horn" (see English CORN[2]).] —**cor·nu·al** *adj.*

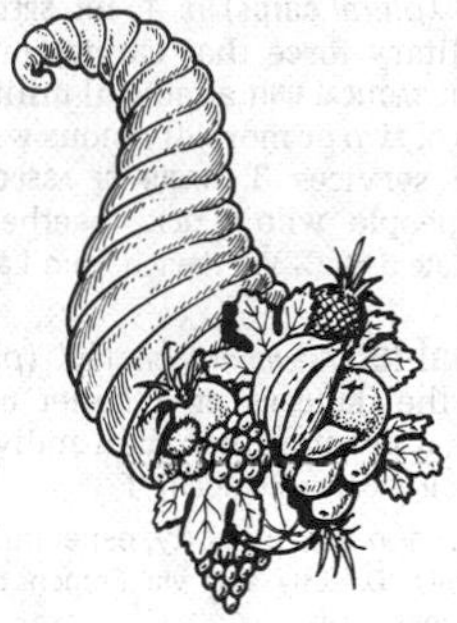

Cornucopia

cor·nu·co·pi·a /kàwrnə kṓpee ə/ *n.* **1.** ABUNDANCE a great abundance of something **2.** ARTS **GOAT'S HORN OVERFLOWING WITH PRODUCE** a painting or other representation of a goat's horn overflowing with fruits, flowers, and vegetables, used to symbolize plenty or prosperity **3.** HORN-SHAPED CONTAINER an ornament or container shaped like a goat's horn **4.** MYTHOL **HORN OF GOAT THAT SUCKLED ZEUS** in Greek mythology, the horn of the goat that suckled Zeus [Early 16thC. Via late Latin from Latin *cornu copiæ*, literally "horn of plenty."] —**cor·nu·co·pi·an** *adj.*

cor·nute /kawr nṓōt/, **cor·nut·ed** /-nṓōtəd/ *adj.* resembling a horn, or having horns or horny parts [Early 17thC. From Latin *cornutus* "horned," from *cornu* "horn" (see English CORN[2]).]

Corn·wall /káwrn wàwl, -wəl/ **1.** southwesternmost county of England, bordered on three sides by the sea. It used to be a major tin-mining area. Population: 482,700 (1995). **2.** city on the St. Lawrence River in southeastern Ontario, Canada, 68 mi./110 km southwest of Montreal. Population: 47,403 (1996).

Corn·wal·lis /kawrn wáwliss/, **Charles, 1st Marquis and 2nd Earl Cornwallis** (1738–1805) British general and statesman. He commanded forces in North Carolina during the American Revolution and was defeated at Yorktown.

corn whis·key *n.* whiskey distilled from mash made mostly of corn

corn·y /káwrnee/ (**-i·er, -i·est**) *adj.* unsophisticated and trite ○ *a corny love scene* [Late 16thC. Formed from CORN[1].] —**corn·i·ly** *adv.* —**corn·i·ness** *n.*

corol., **coroll.** *abbr.* corollary

co·rol·la /kə róllə, -rṓlə/ *n.* the petals of a flower collectively, forming a ring around the reproductive organs and surrounded by an outer ring of sepals [Mid-18thC. From Latin, "garland," literally "little crown," from *corona* "crown, wreath" (source of *crown*).]

cor·ol·lar·y /káwrə lèrree/ *n.* (*plural* **-ies**) **1.** NATURAL CONSEQUENCE something that is a natural consequence of or accompaniment to something else **2.** LOGIC STATEMENT EASILY PROVED FROM ANOTHER a proposition that follows, with little or no further reasoning, from the proof of another **3.** LOGIC **OBVIOUS DEDUCTION** something that is very obviously or easily deduced from something already proven **4.** SOMETHING ADDED something added to something else, e.g. something appended to a document ■ *adj.* FOLLOWING following as a consequence or result [14thC. From Latin *corollarium* "money paid for a garland, gratuity, deduction," from *corolla* (see COROLLA).]

cor·o·man·del /kàwrə mánd'l/ *n.* = **calamander** [Mid-19thC. Named for the *Coromandel* Coast, where it is found.]

Cor·o·man·del Coast /kàwrə mánd'l-/ southern part of the eastern Indian coastline in the states of Tamil Nadu and Andhra Pradesh, on the Bay of Bengal

co·ro·na /kə rṓnə/ (*plural* **-nas** *or* **-nae** /-nee/) *n.* **1.** ASTRON **RING OF LIGHT AROUND MOON** a ring of light visible around a luminous body, especially the Moon, typically as a result of optical effects caused by thin cloud, water droplets or ice in the Earth's atmosphere **2.** ASTRON **OUTERMOST PART OF SUN'S ATMOSPHERE** the outermost part of the Sun's atmosphere **3.** BOT **LIP OF FLOWER TRUMPET** the prominent, sometimes frilly lip of the petal tube or trumpet corolla of some flowers such as daffodils and narcissi **4.** ANAT **TOP OF BODY PART** the top of a part of the body such as the crown of the head or a tooth **5.** PHYS = **corona discharge 6.** ARCHIT **PART OF CORNICE** the flat vertical surface of a cornice just above the bottom surface (**soffit**) **7.** LONG CIGAR a long cigar with a blunt rounded mouth end **8.** CIRCULAR CHANDELIER a circular hanging chandelier, especially in a church [Mid-16thC. From Latin *wreath crown* (see CROWN).]

Co·ro·na /kə rṓnə/ city in southern California, southwest of Riverside. Population: 100,208 (1996).

Co·ro·na Aus·tra·lis /-aw stráyliss, -strálliss/ *n.* a constellation in the southern hemisphere near Sagittarius

Co·ro·na Bo·re·al·is /-báwree áyliss, -álliss/ *n.* a constellation in the northern hemisphere between Hercules and Boötes

co·ro·na dis·charge *n.* a luminous discharge from the surface of an object that is highly charged electrically, caused by ionization of the surrounding gas

Cor·o·na·do /kàwrə naadō/ city in southwestern California, across the bay from San Diego. Population: 25,701 (1996).

Co·ro·na·do, Francisco Vásquez de (1510–54) Spanish explorer. He led the first European expeditions to what is now the southwestern United States.

co·ro·na·graph /kə rṓnə gràf/, **co·ro·no·graph** *n.* a telescope that masks the bright disk of the Sun so that the Sun's corona can be studied

cor·o·nal /káwrən'l, kə rṓn'l/ *adj.* **1.** OF TOP OF BODY PART relating to the top of a body part (**corona**) **2.** RELATING TO JOINT OF SKULL BONES relating to the top of the skull where the bony plates join **3.** OF IMAGINARY PLANE DIVIDING BODY relating to, involving, or in the direction of an imaginary plane dividing the body into front and back parts [Mid-16thC. Via French from, ultimately, Latin *corona* "crown" (source also of English *crown*).]

cor·o·nal su·ture *n.* a junction extending side-to-side across the crown of the skull between the two parietal bones and the frontal bone

cor·o·nar·y /káwrə nèrree/ *n.* (*plural* **-ies**) **1.** = **coronary thrombosis 2.** HEART ATTACK a heart attack (*informal*) ■ *adj.* **1.** SUPPLYING OR DRAINING BLOOD FROM HEART used to describe the arteries that supply blood to the muscle tissue of the heart, or the veins that take blood away from it **2.** INVOLVING THE CORONARY ARTERIES AND VEINS relating to disease of the coronary arteries and veins, and conditions associated with it ○ *coronary care* [Early 17thC. From Latin *coronarius* "crownlike," from *corona* "crown" (source of English *crown*). The underlying idea is something that encircles, like the arteries of the heart.]

cor·o·nar·y ar·ter·y *n.* an artery supplying blood to the muscles of the heart, one of a pair arising from the aorta. The left artery divides into two almost immediately, giving rise to the common assumption that there are three coronary arteries.

cor·o·nar·y by·pass *n.* an operation in which a new blood vessel is grafted onto the heart to replace a blocked coronary artery

cor·o·nar·y throm·bo·sis *n.* the blocking of a coronary artery by a blood clot, which obstructs the blood supply to the heart muscle, resulting in death of the muscle and, often, a heart attack

cor·o·nar·y vein *n.* any of the veins that drain blood from the muscles and other tissues of the heart

cor·o·na·tion /kàwrə náysh'n/ *n.* the ceremony or act of crowning a monarch [14thC. Via Old French from the medieval Latin stem *coronation-*, from, ultimately, Latin *corona* "crown" (source also of English *crown*).]

cor·o·ner /káwrənər/ *n.* a public official formerly responsible for investigating deaths that appear not to have natural causes. They are now largely replaced by medical examiners. [13thC. From Anglo-Norman *coruner* "officer of the crown," from *coroune* "crown" (source also of English *crown*).] —**cor·o·ner·ship** *n.*

cor·o·net /kàwrə nét, káwrə nèt/ *n.* **1. SMALL CROWN** a small crown, especially one worn by a prince or a peer rather than a reigning monarch **2. WOMAN'S HEAD DECORATION** a circular ornamental band worn by women on the head **3.** VET **TOP OF HORSE'S HOOF** the upper part of a horse's hoof, where the horn of the hoof meets the skin of the pastern [14thC. From French, literally "little crown," from *corone* (see CROWN).]

co·ro·no·graph *n.* = **coronagraph**

co·ro·tate /kō rṓ tàyt/ (**-tat·ed, -tat·ing, -tates**) *vi.* to turn in conjunction with another turning object —**co·ro·ta·tion** /kṓ rō táysh'n/ *n.* —**co·ro·ta·tion·al** *adj.*

corp. *abbr.* corporation

Corp. *abbr.* MIL Corporal

cor·po·ra plural of **corpus**

cor·po·ral[1] /káwrpərəl, -prəl/ *adj.* relating or belonging to the body ○ *corporal punishment* [14thC. Via French from Latin *corporalis*, "bodily," from *corpus* (see CORPUS).] —**cor·po·ral·ly** *adv.*

WORD KEY: USAGE

corporal or **corporeal**? ***Corporal*** means "relating to the human body" and is mainly used in the expression *corporal punishment*, in reference to physical abuse. ***Corporeal*** means "bodily or physical as distinct from spiritual": *The gods of antiquity were not just spirits but enjoyed a corporeal existence.*

cor·po·ral[2] /káwrpərəl, -prəl/ *n.* a noncommissioned officer in various armed forces, ranking immediately below sergeant, or, in Canada, a master corporal [Mid-16thC. Via French from, ultimately, Italian *caporale*, literally "of the head," from *capo* (see CAPO). The underlying meaning is "head of a company of troops."] —**cor·po·ral·cy** *n.* —**cor·po·ral·ship** *n.*

cor·po·ral[3] /káwrpərəl, káwrprəl/ *n.* a white, usually linen, cloth on which the consecrated bread and wine are placed in the Christian sacrament of Eucharist [14thC. Directly or via French from medieval Latin *(pallium) corporale*, literally "(cloth) for the body."]

cor·po·ral·i·ty /kàwrpə rállətee/ *n.* the state of being in physical or bodily form rather than spiritual form

cor·po·ral pun·ish·ment *n.* the striking of a person's body as punishment

cor·po·rate /káwrpərət, -prət/ *adj.* **1. INVOLVING A CORPORATION** relating or belonging to a corporation **2. OF CORPORATE EMPLOYEES** designed for, suitable for, or typical of people who work for large corporations ○ *corporate fashions* **3. INCORPORATED** legally united to form a body that can act as a unit **4. OF GROUP AS A WHOLE** relating to or involving a group as a whole (*formal*) [16thC. From Latin *corporatus*, the past participle of *corporare* "to form a body," from *corpus* "body" (see CORPUS).] —**cor·po·rate·ly** *adv.*

cor·po·rate raid·er *n.* a company or person who attempts to take control of a business by acquiring a substantial number of its shares or by manipulating proxies

cor·po·rate wel·fare *n.* laws and government subsidies that are seen to favor corporations unfairly at the expense of ordinary taxpayers

cor·po·ra·tion /kàwrpə ráysh'n/ *n.* **1. GROUP REGARDED AS INDIVIDUAL BY LAW** a company recognized by law as a single body with its own powers and liabilities, separate from those of the individual members. Corporations perform many of the functions of private business, governments, educational bodies, and the professions. **2. LOCAL GOVERNING AUTHORITY** the governing authority of an incorporated municipality, e.g., a city or town **3. GROUP ACTING AS SINGLE ENTITY** a group of people acting as a single entity [15thC. From late Latin *corporation-*, from *corporatus* (see CORPORATE).]

cor·po·rat·ism /káwrpərə tìzzəm, káwrprə-/, **cor·po·ra·tiv·ism** /káwpərətiv ìzzəm, káwprətiv-/ *n.* a system of running a state using the power of organizations like businesses and trade unions that act, or purport to act, for large numbers of individuals —**cor·po·ra·tist** *adj.*, *n.*

cor·po·ra·tor /káwrpə ràytər/ *n.* a member of a corporation, especially a founding member (*archaic*) [Late 18thC. Back-formation from CORPORATION.]

cor·po·re·al /kawr páwree əl/ *adj.* **1. CONCERNING THE PHYSICAL BODY** relating to or involving the physical body rather than the mind or spirit **2. MATERIAL** material or physical rather than spiritual [Early 17thC. From late Latin *corporealis*, from, ultimately, Latin *corpus* (see CORPUS).] —**cor·po·re·al·i·ty** /kawr pàwree állətee/ *n.* —**cor·po·re·al·ly** /kàwr páwree əlee/ *adv.*

WORD KEY: USAGE

See Usage note at ***corporal***.

cor·po·re·i·ty /kàwrpə reé ətee/ *n.* the state of existing as something material or physical [Early 17thC. From French *corporéite*, from, ultimately, Latin *corpus* (see CORPUS).]

cor·po·sant /káwrpə sànt, -pəss'nt/ *n.* St. Elmo's fire. (*archaic*) [Mid-16thC. From Old Spanish or Italian *corpo santo*, literally "holy body."]

corps /kawr/ (*plural* **corps**) *n.* **1.** MIL **SPECIALIZED MILITARY FORCE** a military force that carries out specialized duties **2.** MIL **TACTICAL UNIT** a tactical military unit that is made up of two or more divisions with additional supporting services **3. GROUP OF ASSOCIATED PEOPLE** a group of people who work together or are associated [Late 16thC. Via French from Latin *corpus* (see CORPUS).]

corps de bal·let /kàwr də ba láy/ (*plural* **corps de bal·let**) *n.* the dancers of a ballet company who perform as a group rather than individually [From French, literally "dance company"]

corpse /kawrps/ *n.* a dead body, especially of a human being [14thC. Directly and via French *cors* from Latin *corpus* (see CORPUS).]

corps·man /káwr mən, káwrz-/ (*plural* **-men** /káwr men, káwrz-/) *n.* in the U.S. armed forces, an enlisted person with training in giving first aid and basic medical treatment

cor·pu·lence /káwrpyələns/, **cor·pu·lenc·y** /-ee/ *n.* obesity (*formal or literary*)

cor·pu·lent /káwrpyələnt/ *adj.* obese (*formal or literary*) [15thC. From Latin *corpulentus*, literally "abundant in body," from *corpus* (see CORPUS).] —**cor·pu·lent·ly** *adv.*

cor pul·mo·na·le /kawr pŏŏlmə náll ee, -pùlmə-, -pŏŏlmə naálee, -pùlmə-/ *n.* a disease in which the right ventricle of the heart becomes enlarged and fails, caused by disease of the lungs or pulmonary blood vessels [From modern Latin, literally "pulmonary heart"]

cor·pus /káwrpəss/ (*plural* **-po·ra** /-pərə/) *n.* **1. BODY OF WRITINGS** a body of writings by a particular person, on a particular subject, or of a particular type ○ *one of the most popular works in the Shakespearean corpus* **2. MAIN PART** the main part of something **3.** ANAT **PART OF ORGAN** the main portion of something, such as an organ or other body part, or a mass of tissue with a distinct function ○ *the corpus of the uterus* **4.** FIN **CAPITAL** the capital or principal of a sum of money **5.** LING **COLLECTION OF LANGUAGE USE** a large collection of written, and sometimes spoken, examples of the usage of a language, used for linguistic analysis [Early 18thC. From Latin, "body." Ultimately from an Indo-European word that is also the ancestor of English *corpse, corset, corsage*, and possibly *midriff*.]

cor·pus cal·lo·sum /-kə lṓssəm/ (*plural* **cor·po·ra cal·lo·sa** /-kə lṓssə/) *n.* the thick band of nerve fibers that connects the two hemispheres of the brain in higher mammals and allows the hemispheres to communicate [From modern Latin, literally "callous body"]

Cor·pus Chris·ti[1] /-krístee/ *n.* a mainly Roman Catholic festival in honor of the sacrament of the Eucharist, observed on the Thursday that follows Trinity Sunday [From medieval Latin, literally "body of Christ"]

Cor·pus Chris·ti[2] /-krístee/ city and port in southeastern Texas, on the south shore of Corpus Christi Bay. Population: 280,260 (1996).

cor·pus·cle /káwrpəss'l, -pùss'l/ *n.* **1.** ANAT **UNATTACHED CELL** any small independent body, especially a cell in the blood or lymph **2.** PHYS **PARTICLE** a discrete particle, especially a photon **3. SMALL PARTICLE** a very small particle of anything [Mid-17thC. From Latin *corpusculum*, literally "small body," from *corpus* (see CORPUS).] —**cor·pus·cu·lar** /kawr púskyələr/ *adj.*

cor·pus·cu·lar the·o·ry *n.* the theory that light consists of a stream of particles. The theory was originally introduced by Newton and although it cannot be used to explain all the properties of light it has applications in quantum physics. ◊ **wave theory**

cor·pus de·lic·ti /-di lík tī/ *n.* the body of facts that show that a crime has been committed, including physical evidence such as a corpse [From modern Latin, literally "body of the crime"]

cor·pus lu·te·um /-lṓotee əm/ (*plural* **cor·po·ra lu·te·a** /-lṓotee ə/) *n.* a yellow mass of tissue that forms in part of the ovary (**Graafian follicle**) after ovulation in mammals and secretes the hormone progesterone. If no pregnancy is established, the corpus luteum degenerates, whereas it continues to secrete the hormone if pregnancy occurs. [From modern Latin, literally "yellow body"]

cor·pus stri·a·tum /-strī áytəm/ (*plural* **cor·po·ra stri·a·ta** /-strī áytə/) *n.* a mass of striped gray and white nervous tissue, one of which occurs in each hemisphere of the brain [From modern Latin, literally "striated body"]

corr. *abbr.* **1.** correction **2.** correct **3.** corrected **4.** correspondence **5.** correspondent

cor·ral /kə rál/ *n.* **1.** AGRIC **PLACE FOR KEEPING LIVESTOCK** a fenced area in which livestock or horses are kept **2.** HIST **CIRCLE OF WAGONS** a temporary defensive enclosure formed by wagons arranged in a circle ■ *vt.* (**-ralled, -ral·ling, -rals**) **1.** AGRIC **DRIVE ANIMALS INTO CORRAL** to gather animals together and drive them into a corral **2.** HIST **PUT WAGONS IN CIRCLE** to form wagons into a corral **3. GATHER AND CONTROL** to gather together and take control of people or things ○ *hopes to corral sufficient funding for the project* [Late 16thC. From Spanish, of uncertain origin: perhaps from Khoisan, or perhaps from, ultimately, Latin *currus* "vehicle" (source of English *car*).]

cor·ra·sion /kə ráyzh'n/ *n.* the mechanical erosion of a surface by fragments of rock carried by water, wind, or ice [Late 19thC. From Latin *corras-*, the past participle stem of *corradere* "to scrape together," from *radere* "to scrape" (source of English *raze*).] —**cor·ra·sive** /kə ráyssiv, -ziv/ *adj.*

cor·rect /kə rékt/ *vt.* (**-rect·ed, -rect·ing, -rects**) **1. REMOVE ERRORS FROM** to take the errors out of something **2. POINT OUT ERRORS IN** to point out or mark the errors in something **3. RECTIFY DEFECT** to rectify a defect in something or counteract something wrong or undesirable ○ *wears glasses to correct his astigmatism* **4. MODIFY** to modify something, e.g., behavior, to make it acceptable or bring it up to a particular standard **5. PUNISH TO GAIN IMPROVEMENT** to punish or scold somebody, especially a child, to bring about improvement or reform (*dated*) ■ *adj.* **1. ACCURATE** accurate or without errors ○ *the correct time* **2. ACCEPTABLE** acceptable or meeting a particular standard ○ *correct dress* [14thC. From Latin *correct-*, the past participle stem of *corrigere*, literally "to rule completely," from *regere* "to rule" (source of English *regent*).] —**cor·rect·a·ble** *adj.* —**cor·rect·ly** *adv.* —**cor·rect·ness** *n.* —**cor·rec·tor** *n.*

cor·rec·tion /kə rékshən/ *n.* **1. ALTERATION THAT IMPROVES** an alteration that removes an error **2. WRITTEN COMMENT ON ERROR** something written beside an error in a text to point out what should be there instead **3. REMOVING OF ERRORS** the removing of errors from something or the indicating of errors in something **4. MODIFICATION TO CALCULATION** an adjustment made to a calculation or measurement to compensate for an observed deviation from ideal conditions **5. PUNISHMENT MEANT TO IMPROVE** punishment, especially when meant to improve or reform the person punished (*dated*) **6.** FIN **FALL IN PRICES** a fall in prices or activity in a stock market following a rise or busy period ■ **cor·rec·tions** *npl.* LAW **TREATMENT OF OFFENDERS** the system of dealing with criminals by imprisonment, rehabilitation, parole, and probation

cor·rec·tion·al /kə rékshən'l/ *adj.* **1.** OF CORRECTION about, involving, or intended as correction **2.** OF CORRECTIONS of or involved in the system of dealing with criminals by imprisonment, rehabilitation, parole, and probation

cor·rec·tion·al fa·cil·i·ty *n.* a prison or other institution where criminals are held and treated

cor·rec·ti·tude /kə réktə to͞od/ *n.* the fact of being correct, especially in behavior and manners (*formal*) [Late 19thC. Blend of CORRECT and RECTITUDE.]

cor·rec·tive /kə réktiv/ *adj.* CORRECTING acting to correct or intended to correct something ○ *corrective action* ■ *n.* SOMETHING INTENDED TO CORRECT something that corrects or is meant to correct something —**cor·rec·tive·ly** *adv.*

cor·rec·tive shoe *n.* a specially fitted shoe that compensates for physical deformity in the foot

Cor·reg·i·dor /kə réggi dàwr/ island at the entrance to Manila Bay in the Philippines. Area: 2 sq. mi./5 sq. km.

correl. *abbr.* correlative

cor·re·late *v.* /kàwrə làyt/ (**-lat·ed, -lat·ing, -lates**) **1.** *vti.* HAVE OR SHOW MUTUAL RELATIONSHIP to have a mutual or complementary relationship, or show two or more things, e.g., a cause and an effect, to have a mutual or complementary relationship ○ *How do these results correlate with your findings?* **2.** *vt.* GATHER AND COMPARE THINGS to gather together and compare related things, e.g., results or reports ○ *Her job is to correlate the statistics from a range of sources and prepare a report.* ■ *adj.* /kàwrə lət, -làyt/ HAVING SHARED PROPERTIES having mutual or complementary properties ■ *n.* /kàwrə lət, -làyt/ **1.** COMPLEMENTARY THING something that shares mutual or complementary properties with something else **2.** STATS VARIABLE RELATED TO ANOTHER VARIABLE either of two variables that are related with the result that a variation in one is accompanied by a linear variation of the other [Mid-18thC. Back-formation from CORRELATION.] —**cor·re·lat·a·ble** *adj.* —**cor·re·la·tor** *n.*

cor·re·la·tion /kàwrə láysh'n/ *n.* **1.** MUTUAL OR COMPLEMENTARY RELATIONSHIP a relationship in which two or more things are mutual or complementary, or one is caused by another ○ *the close correlation between the two factors* **2.** ACT OF CORRELATING the act of correlating, or the state of being correlated **3.** STATS RELATEDNESS OF VARIABLES the degree to which two or more variables are related and change together [Mid-16thC. From the medieval Latin stem *correlation-*, literally "mutual relationship," from Latin *relation-*, (see RELATION).] —**cor·re·la·tion·al** *adj.*

cor·re·la·tion co·ef·fi·cient *n.* a number or function indicating the degree of correlation between two variables. It ranges between 1 for high positive correlation to –1 for high negative correlation, with 0 indicating a purely random relationship.

cor·rel·a·tive /kə réllətiv/ *adj.* **1.** BEING CORRELATES in a mutual or complementary relationship **2.** GRAM TOGETHER BUT NOT ADJACENT often used together but not usually adjacent, as are the conjunctions "either" and "or" ■ *n.* **1.** = **correlate** *n.* 1 **2.** GRAM CORRELATIVE WORD a word, especially a conjunction, that is often used together with but not usually adjacent to another —**cor·rel·a·tive·ly** *adv.* —**cor·rel·a·tive·ness** *n.* —**cor·rel·a·tiv·i·ty** /kə rèllə tívvətee/ *n.*

cor·re·spond /kàwrə spónd/ (**-spond·ed, -spond·ing, -sponds**) *vi.* **1.** CONFORM OR BE CONSISTENT to conform, be consistent, or be in agreement with something else **2.** BE SIMILAR to be similar or equivalent **3.** WRITE TO ONE ANOTHER to communicate with somebody by exchanging written messages [Early 16thC. Via French from medieval Latin *correspondere*, literally "to respond to each other," from Latin *respondere* (see RESPOND).]

cor·re·spon·dence /kàwrə spóndəns/ *n.* **1.** WRITTEN COMMUNICATION communication by means of exchanged written messages, e.g., letters or e-mail **2.** WRITTEN MESSAGES written messages, especially letters **3.** CONFORMITY conformity, consistency, or agreement between two or more things **4.** SIMILARITY similarity or equivalence between two or more things

cor·re·spon·dence course *n.* an educational course in which the teaching organization sends lessons and tests to students by mail and students return completed work in the same way

cor·re·spon·dence school *n.* an educational organization that carries out teaching by mail

cor·re·spon·dent /kàwrə spóndənt/ *n.* **1.** SOMEBODY COMMUNICATING BY WRITING somebody who communicates in writing or electronically ○ *Most of my correspondents have e-mail now.* **2.** PRESS SOMEBODY PROVIDING SPECIAL REPORTS somebody employed by a news organization, especially a newspaper or broadcasting company, to provide reports from a particular place or on a particular subject ○ *our Paris correspondent* **3.** BUSINESS BUSINESS DEALING WITH A DISTANT BUSINESS a person or company that regularly does business with another, especially one that is distant **4.** SOMETHING THAT CORRESPONDS something that conforms or agrees with, or is similar to, something else (*formal*) ■ *adj.* = **corresponding**

cor·re·spond·ing /kàwrə spónding/ *adj.* **1.** CONSISTENT consistent, conforming, or in agreement with something else ○ *Line up the prongs on one half with the corresponding sockets on the other.* **2.** ANALOGOUS similar or equivalent to something else in one or more important respects ○ *the corresponding word in her own language* **3.** WORKING FROM A DISTANCE interacting or contributing from a distance, e.g., by mail ○ *a corresponding member based in China* **4.** DEALING WITH CORRESPONDENCE handling correspondence, or assigned to handle correspondence

cor·re·spond·ing an·gles *npl.* the angles formed on the same side of two lines and a third line (**transversal**) that intersects them, each of the four angles at each intersection corresponding to the four angles at the other

cor·re·spond·ing·ly /kàwrə spóndinglee/ *adv.* in a way that is consistent, equivalent, or similar ○ *A large company has correspondingly large problems.*

cor·ri·da /kaw reédə/ *n.* a program of bullfights [Late 19thC. From Spanish, literally "running" (of bulls), from, ultimately, Latin *currere* "to run" (source also of English *current*).]

cor·ri·dor /kàwridər/ *n.* **1.** ARCHIT PASSAGE INSIDE BUILDING a passage between parts of a building, often with a series of rooms opening onto it **2.** RAIL, SHIPPING PASSAGEWAY IN RAILROAD CAR OR SHIP a passageway in a railroad car or ship giving access to cabins or compartments **3.** GEOG STRIP OF LAND a narrow strip of land belonging to one country and projecting through another, e.g., to give a landlocked country access to a port **4.** GEOG POPULATED STRIP BETWEEN URBAN AREAS a densely populated strip of land connecting two or more urban areas ○ *the northeastern corridor* **5.** AIR REGION OF AIRSPACE FOR AIR TRAFFIC a particular region of airspace designated for use by air traffic **6.** AEROSP SPACECRAFT FLIGHT PATH a predetermined flight path that a spacecraft follows upon reentry into the earth's atmosphere [Late 16thC. Via French and Italian from, ultimately, Latin *currere* "to run" (source also of English *current*). The underlying meaning is "a place to run."]

Cor·rie·dale /kàwri dàyl/ (*plural* **-dales** *or* **-dale**) *n.* a sheep belonging to a breed without horns developed in New Zealand and kept for both wool and meat [Early 20thC. Named for *Corriedale*, an estate in northern Otago, New Zealand.]

cor·ri·gen·da /kàwri jéndə/ *n.* = **errata** (*takes a singular or plural verb*)

cor·ri·gen·dum /kàwri jéndəm/ (*plural* **-da**) *n.* an error to be corrected [Early 19thC. From Latin, literally "thing to be corrected."]

cor·ri·val /kō rī́v'l, kō rī́v'l/, **co·ri·val** *n.* a rival (*archaic*) [Late 16thC. Directly and via French from Latin *corrivalis*, literally "completely rivaling," from *rivalis* "rivaling" (see RIVAL).] —**cor·ri·val·ry** *n.*

cor·rob·o·rate /kə róbbə ràyt/ (**-rat·ed, -rat·ing, -rates**) *vt.* to give or represent evidence of the truth of something ○ *The photographs corroborate the verbal account.* [Mid-16thC. From Latin *corroborat-*, the past participle stem of *corroborare*, literally "to strengthen together," from *roborare* "to strengthen."] —**cor·rob·o·ra·tive** *adj.* —**cor·rob·o·ra·tive·ly** *adv.* —**cor·rob·o·ra·to·ry** /-rə tàwree/ *adj.* —**cor·rob·o·ra·tor** /-ràytər/ *n.*

cor·rob·o·ra·tion /kə ròbbə ráysh'n/ *n.* **1.** CONFIRMATION something that supports or confirms something else **2.** ACT OF CONFIRMING the supporting or confirming of something else

cor·rob·o·ree /kə róbbəree, -reé/ *n. Aus* **1.** ABORIGINAL GATHERING a gathering of an Aboriginal people **2.** NOISY GATHERING any noisy gathering of people, especially a party (*informal*) [Late 18thC. From Dharuk (an Australian Aboriginal language) *garaabara*.]

cor·rode /kə rṓd/ (**-rod·ed, -rod·ing, -rodes**) *v.* **1.** *vti.* CHEM DESTROY PROGRESSIVELY BY CHEMICAL ACTION to destroy something progressively, or be destroyed progressively, by chemical action **2.** *vt.* UNDERMINE to undermine or destroy something gradually ○ *His continual scorn had corroded her pride.* [14thC. From Latin *corrodere*, literally "to gnaw away," from *rodere* "to gnaw" (source of English *rodent*).] —**cor·ro·dant** *n.* —**cor·rod·er** *n.* —**cor·ro·di·bil·i·ty** /kə rṑdə bíllətee/ *n.* —**cor·rod·i·ble** /kə rṓdəb'l/ *adj.* —**cor·ro·si·ble** /kə rṓssəb'l/ *adj.*

cor·ro·sion /kə rṓzh'n/ *n.* **1.** CHEM DESTRUCTION BY CHEMICAL ACTION a process in which something, especially a metal, is destroyed progressively by chemical action, as iron is when it rusts **2.** MATERIAL PRODUCED BY CORROSION material produced by corrosion, e.g., rust **3.** GRADUAL DESTRUCTION the gradual destruction or undermining of something ○ *the steady corrosion of civil rights* **4.** RESULT OF CORROSION the condition produced by corrosion [14thC. Via French and late Latin from, ultimately, Latin *corros-*, the past participle stem of *corrodere* (see CORRODE).]

cor·ro·sive /kə rṓssiv/ *adj.* **1.** CHEM PROGRESSIVELY DESTRUCTIVE able to destroy something progressively by chemical action **2.** DESTROYING GRADUALLY destroying something gradually **3.** VERY SARCASTIC very strongly sarcastic or bitter ○ *a corrosive review* ■ *n.* CHEM DESTRUCTIVE SUBSTANCE a substance that is able to destroy something progressively by chemical action, e.g., an acid [14thC. Via French, ultimately from Latin *corros-*, the past participle stem of *corrodere* (see CORRODE).] —**cor·ro·sive·ly** *adv.* —**cor·ro·sive·ness** *n.*

cor·ro·sive sub·li·mate *n.* = **mercuric chloride**

cor·ru·gate /kàwrə gàyt/ *vti.* (**-gat·ed, -gat·ing, -gates**) FOLD INTO RIDGES AND TROUGHS to become folded into parallel ridges and troughs, or fold something, e.g., a sheet of cardboard, into parallel ridges and troughs ■ *adj.* = **corrugated** [Early 17thC. From Latin *corrugat-*, the past participle stem of *corrugare*, literally "to wrinkle completely," from *rugare* "to wrinkle."]

cor·ru·gat·ed /kàwrə gàytəd/ *adj.* **1.** WITH RIDGES AND TROUGHS folded into parallel ridges and troughs **2.** MADE FROM SOMETHING CORRUGATED made from a corrugated material ○ *a shed with a corrugated roof*

cor·ru·ga·tion /kàwrə gáysh'n/ *n.* **1.** FOLD IN CORRUGATED SURFACE any of the folds in a corrugated surface **2.** PARALLEL RIDGES AND TROUGHS parallel ridges and troughs formed by folding

cor·ru·ga·tor /kàwrə gàytər/ *n.* a muscle that wrinkles the skin when it contracts

cor·rupt /kə rúpt/ *adj.* **1.** IMMORAL OR DISHONEST immoral or dishonest, especially as shown by the exploitation of a position of power or trust for personal gain **2.** DEPRAVED extremely immoral or depraved **3.** COMPUT CONTAINING ERRORS unusable because of the presence of errors that have been introduced unintentionally ○ *a corrupt file* **4.** CONTAINING COPYING ERRORS containing undesirable changes in meaning or errors made in copying ○ *a corrupt transcription of the manuscript* **5.** CONTAMINATED contaminated or tainted by something else (*archaic*) ○ *a corrupt fountain* **6.** ROTTEN putrid or decomposing (*archaic*) ○ *corrupt flesh* ■ *v.* (**-rupt·ed, -rupt·ing, -rupts**) **1.** *vti.* MAKE OR BECOME DISHONEST to become dishonest, or destroy or compromise somebody's morality or honesty **2.** *vti.* MAKE OR BECOME DEPRAVED to become or cause somebody to become immoral or depraved **3.** *vt.* COMPUT INTRODUCE ERRORS INTO DATA to introduce unintentional errors into data or a program, making it unusable or unreliable **4.** *vt.* SPOIL TEXT WITH COPYING ERRORS to make undesirable changes in meaning or errors in a text during copying **5.** *vt.* CONTAMINATE to contaminate or taint something or somebody (*archaic*) **6.** *vt.* CAUSE TO ROT to make something rot or become putrid (*archaic*) [14thC. From Latin *corruptus*, the past participle of *corrumpere*, literally "to break completely," from *rumpere* "to break" (source of English *rupture*).] —**cor·rup·ter** *n.* —**cor·rupt·ly** *adv.* —**cor·rupt·ness** *n.*

cor·rupt·i·ble /kə rúptəb'l/ *adj.* capable of or susceptible to being corrupted —**cor·rupt·i·bil·i·ty** /kə rùptə bíllətee/ *n.* —**cor·rupt·i·ble·ness** /kə rúptəb'lnəss/ *n.* —**cor·rupt·i·bly** /-blee/ *adv.*

cor·rup·tion /kə rúpsh'n/ *n.* **1.** DISHONESTY FOR PERSONAL GAIN dishonest exploitation of power for personal gain **2.** DEPRAVITY extreme immorality or depravity **3.** LING WORD OR PHRASE ALTERED FROM ORIGINAL a word or phrase that has been altered from its original form **4.** UNDESIRABLE CHANGE an undesirable change in meaning or error introduced into a text during copying **5.** CORRUPTING OF SOMETHING the corrupting of something or somebody, or the state of being corrupt **6.** ROTTING rotting or putrefaction, or the state of being rotten or putrid (*archaic*)

cor·rup·tion·ist /kə rúpsh'nist/ *n.* somebody who takes part in corruption or defends it, especially in politics

cor·rup·tive /kə rúptiv/ *adj.* having a bad effect on somebody's character or behavior —**cor·rup·tive·ly** *adv.*

cor·sac /káwr sàk/ *n.* a small yellowish or reddish brown fox from Central Asia. Latin name: *Vulpes corsac.* [Mid-19thC. Via Russian *korsak* from Turkic *karsak.*]

cor·sage /kawr sáazh/ *n.* **1.** FLOWERS ON DRESS a small bouquet worn on the bodice of a dress or the lapel of a jacket **2.** BODICE the bodice of a dress (*archaic*) [Early 19thC. From French, formed from Old French *cors* "body."]

cor·sair /káwr sàir/ *n.* **1.** PIRATE a pirate, especially one based on the northern African coast between the 16th and 19th centuries **2.** OFFICIAL PIRATE SHIP a privately owned ship commissioned by a government to attack foreign ships, especially one based on the coast of northern Africa **3.** OWNER OF PIRATE SHIP the owner of a ship commissioned by a government to attack ships of other countries [Mid-16thC. Via French from medieval Latin *cursarius,* from Latin *cursus,*"hostile incursion, plunder" from the past participle of *currere* "to run" (see COURSE).]

cor·se·let /káwrsslət/ *n.* **1. corse·let, corse·lette** FOUNDATION GARMENT a garment combining a corset and a bra **2. corse·let, cors·let** ARMS BREASTPLATE armor covering the upper body [15thC. From French, formed from Old French *cors* "body."]

cor·set /káwrssət/ *n.* **1.** STIFF GARMENT a stiffened garment worn by women to shape the waist and breasts **2.** STIFF UNDERGARMENT a stiff undergarment with laces to fasten it tightly, worn in former times to shape and support the body **3.** MED INJURY SUPPORT a garment like a corset worn by men or women for support when injured [13thC. From French, formed from Old French *cors* "body."] —**cor·set·ed** *adj.*

cor·set·i·ère /kàwrssə tyáir/ *n.* somebody who makes or fits corsets [Mid-19thC. From French, formed from *corset* "CORSET."]

cor·set·ry /káwrssətree/ *n.* corsets in general

Cor·si·ca /káwrssikə/ mountainous island in the Mediterranean Sea, an administrative region of France. Population: 249,237 (1990). Area: 3,351 sq. mi./8,680 sq. km. —**Cor·si·can** *adj., n.*

Cor·si·ca·na /kàwrssi kánnə/ city in Texas, south of Dallas, noted as a center for oil products since 1896. Population: 23,320 (1996).

Cor·tá·zar /káwrtə zaar/, **Julio** (1914–84) Belgian-born Argentine writer, who is known for his surrealist works, including the novel *Hopscotch* (1963).

cor·tege /kawr tézh/, **cor·tège** *n.* **1.** PROCESSION a procession, especially a funeral procession **2.** ATTENDANTS a retinue of servants or attendants [Mid-17thC. Via French from Italian *corteggio,* from *corteggiare* "to attend court," from *corte* "court," from Latin *cohors* (see COHORT).]

Cor·tés /kawr téz/, **Hernán** (1485–1547) Spanish explorer. He conquered Mexico in 1521 for Spain, and served as its governor (1523–28).

cor·tex /káwr tèks/ (*plural* **-ti·ces** /-ti seez/ *or* **-tex·es**) *n.* **1.** ANAT OUTER LAYER OF BODY PART the outer layer of a solid organ or part of the body, e.g., the outer covering of the kidney or brain (**cerebral cortex**) **2.** BOT TISSUE LAYER the tissue in plant stems and roots between the outer layer (**epidermis**) and the central core (**stele**) [Mid-17thC. From Latin, literally "bark." Ultimately from an Indo-European base meaning "to cut," which is also the ancestor of English *shear, shirt, carnage,* and *corm.*] —**cor·ti·cal** /káwrtik'l/ *adj.*

cortic- *prefix.* = **cortico-** (*used before vowels*)

cortico-[2] *prefix.* cortex, cortical ○ *corticospinal* [From Latin *cortic-,* the stem of *cortex* (see CORTEX)]

cor·ti·coid /káwrti kòyd/ *n.* a drug that acts in a similar way to the hormone produced by the outer layer of the adrenal gland

cor·ti·co·spi·nal /kàwrtikō spín'l/ *adj.* relating to or connecting the outer covering of the brain (**cerebral cortex**) and the spinal cord

cor·ti·co·ste·roid /kàwrtikō sté ròyd, -steer-/ *n.* **1.** MED NATURAL STEROID a steroid hormone produced by the adrenal gland and involved in metabolism and immune response **2.** PHARM SYNTHETIC STEROID a synthetic drug similar or identical to a natural corticosteroid, used to reduce inflammation, control allergic disorders, and prevent graft rejection

cor·ti·co·tro·pin /kàwrtikō trṓpin/, **cor·ti·co·tro·phin** /-fin/ *n.* = **ACTH** [Mid-20thC. Contraction of *adrenocorticotrophic hormone.*]

cor·ti·sol /káwrti sàwl, -zàwl, -sòl, -zòl/ *n.* = **hydrocortisone** [Mid-20thC. Coined from CORTISONE + -OL.]

cor·ti·sone /káwrti zṑn/ *n.* a hormone secreted by the adrenal gland and used to treat rheumatoid arthritis and allergies [Mid-20thC. Contraction of *corticosterone,* a type of CORTICOSTEROID.]

Cort·land /káwrtlənd/ city in New York, on the Tioughnioga River, northwest of Binghamton. Population: 18,733 (1996).

co·run·dum /kə rúndəm/ *n.* a hard mineral of aluminum oxide, with crystals in a range of colors and used as an abrasive or a gemstone. The best-known varieties are ruby and sapphire. [Early 18thC. From Tamil *kuruntam.*]

co·rus·cant /kə rúskənt/ *adj.* sparkling or glittering (*literary*)

cor·us·cate /káwrə skàyt/ (**-cat·ed, -cat·ing, -cates**) *vi.* (*literary*) **1.** GLITTER to give off flashes of bright light **2.** BE BRILLIANT to show brilliance or virtuosity ○ *a journalist renowned for her coruscating wit* [Early 18thC. From Latin *coruscat-,* the past participle stem of *coruscare* "to glitter."] —**cor·us·cat·ing** *adj.* —**cor·us·ca·tion** /kàwrə skáysh'n/ *n.*

Cor·val·lis /kawr válliss/ city in western Oregon, southwest of Salem, on the Willamette River. Population: 47,518 (1996).

cor·vée /kawr váy, káwr vày/ *n.* **1.** FEUDAL SERVICE a day of unpaid labor required of a serf for a manorial lord **2.** SERVICE FOR GOVERNMENT a period of labor sometimes required by the state in lieu of taxes [14thC. Via French from, ultimately, Latin *corrogata,* the past participle of *corrogare,* literally "to summon together," from *rogare* "to ask, beg."]

corves plural of **corf**

cor·vette /kawr vét/ *n.* **1.** NAVAL ESCORT SHIP an armed naval escort vessel, smaller than a destroyer **2.** SMALL WARSHIP in former times, a small wooden warship with one tier of guns [Mid-17thC. Via French from, ultimately, Dutch *korf* "small ship," literally "basket," from Latin *corbis* (source also of English *corf*).]

cor·vid /káwrvid/ *n.* a bird of the family that includes crows, jays, and magpies. Family: Corvidae. [Mid-20thC. From modern Latin *Corvidae,* family name, from Latin *corvus* (see CORVINE).]

cor·vi·na *n.* = **corbina**

cor·vine /káwr vīn/ *adj.* belonging to the crow family, or characteristic of birds of the crow family such as crows and ravens (*formal or literary*) [Mid-17thC. From Latin *corvinus,* from *corvus* "raven." Ultimately from an Indo-European word that is also the ancestor of English *screech, shrike, raven,* and *rook.*]

Cor·vus /káwrvəss/ *n.* a small constellation situated in southern skies between Virgo and Hydra

Cor·y·bant /káwri bànt/ (*plural* **-bants** *or* **-ban·tes** /-bán teez/) *n.* **1.** RELIG PRIEST OF CYBELE in ancient Phrygia, a priest of the goddess Cybele who performed wild ecstatic dances **2.** MYTHOL ATTENDANT OF GODDESS CYBELE in ancient mythology, any of the goddess Cybele's attendants [15thC. From Latin *Corybant-,* the stem of *Corybas,* from Greek *Korubas.*] —**Cor·y·ban·tic** /kàwri bántik/ *adj.*

cor·ymb /káw rìmb, -rim/ *n.* a flat flower head (**inflorescence**) consisting of flowers whose stalks grow from different points on the flower stem but reach approximately the same height [Early 18thC. Via French from, ultimately, Greek *korumbos* "summit." Ultimately from an Indo-European base meaning "head, horn."] —**cor·ymbed** *adj.* —**cor·ym·bose** /káwrim bōss/ *adj.* —**co·rym·bous** /kaw rimbəss/ *adj.*

cor·y·phée /kàwri fáy/ *n.* a leading dancer in a ballet company who usually performs with a small group of other dancers [Early 19thC. Via French from, ultimately, Greek *koruphaios* "chorus leader," from *koruphe* "head top."]

co·ry·za /kə rī́zə/ *n.* **1.** MED NASAL CONGESTION severe nasal congestion **2.** MED COLD a common cold (*technical*) **3.** VET BIRD DISEASE a respiratory disease of chickens and turkeys, caused by bacteria [Early 16thC. Via Latin from Greek *koruza* "nasal mucus, catarrh," of unknown origin.] —**co·ry·zal** *adj.*

cos[1] /koss/ (*plural* **cos·es** *or* **cos**) *n. U.K.* = **romaine** [Late 17thC. Named for the island of *Cos* in Greece, from which it was introduced.]

cos[2] /kōz/ *abbr.* cosine

'cos /kəz, kawz/ *conj.* because (*informal*) [Early 19thC. Shortening and alteration of BECAUSE.]

COS *abbr.* **1.** cash on shipment **2.** chief of staff

c.o.s. *abbr.* cash on shipment

Co·sa Nos·tra /kṓssə nṓstrə/ *n.* a criminal organization in the United States, linked with the Mafia of Sicily [Mid-20thC. From Italian, literally "our concern."]

Cos·by /kózbee/, **Bill** (*b.* 1937) U.S. comedian, actor, producer, and writer best known for his work in television, in particular his role in *The Cosby Show* (1984–92). Full name **William Henry Cosby, Jr.**

co·sec /kṓ sèk/ *abbr.* cosecant

co·se·cant /kō séekənt/ *n.* for a given angle in a right triangle, a trigonometric function equal to the length of the hypotenuse divided by that of the side opposite the angle

co·seis·mal /kō sī́zməl/ *n.* a line on a map that connects places where the effects of an earthquake were felt at the same time

cosh /kosh/ *n. U.K.* BLUNT WEAPON a blunt weapon that resembles a blackjack, usually made of rubber or metal ■ *vt.* (**coshed, cosh·ing, cosh·es**) *U.K.* HIT WITH A COSH to attack somebody using a cosh [Mid-19thC. Origin uncertain: possibly from Romany *kosh* "stick."]

co·sig·na·to·ry /kō sígnə tàwree/ (*plural* **-ries**) *n.* a person, government, or organization that signs a document or treaty jointly with others

co·sine /kṓ sīn/ *n.* for a given angle in a right triangle, a trigonometric function equal to the length of the side adjacent to the angle divided by the hypotenuse

cos·me·ceut·i·cal /kòzmə sóotək'l/ *n.* a product that falls between the categories designated as pharmaceuticals and cosmetics, especially in terms of marketing

cos·met·ic /koz méttik/ *n.* (*often used in the plural*) **1.** BEAUTIFYING SUBSTANCE a preparation, e.g., lipstick, that is applied to the face or the body to make it more attractive **2.** SUPERFICIALLY ATTRACTIVE ASPECT something added or done to something else to cover up defects ■ *adj.* **1.** BEAUTIFYING intended to improve somebody's physical appearance ○ *cosmetic surgery* **2.** ONLY FOR APPEARANCES done to make something seem better but having no real value ○ *The changes to the code of conduct were purely cosmetic, since attitudes remained fundamentally the same.* **3.** DECORATIVE designed or added for decorative purposes rather than for any real function [Early 17thC. Via French *cosmétique* from Greek *kosmētikos* "skilled in ornamenting," from *kosmein* "to arrange," from *kosmos* (see COSMOS[1]).] —**cos·met·i·cal·ly** *adv.*

cos·me·ti·cian /kòzmə tísh'n/ *n.* somebody who makes or sells cosmetics, or who applies them professionally

cos·me·tol·o·gist /kòzmə tólləjist/ *n.* an expert in cosmetics and their use

cos·me·tol·o·gy /kòzmə tólləjee/ *n.* the study of cosmetics or the art or profession of using them [Mid-19thC. From French *cosmétologie,* from *cosmétique.*]

cos·mic /kózmik/ *adj.* **1.** OF WHOLE UNIVERSE relating to the whole universe **2.** ASTRON OF UNIVERSE APART FROM EARTH used to describe outer space or a part of the universe other than the Earth **3.** GREAT very great in size or significance ■ *interj.* EXPRESSING AMAZEMENT used to express amazement or wonder [Mid-17thC. From Greek *kosmikos,* from *kosmos* (see COSMOS[1]).] —**cos·mi·cal·ly** *adv.*

cos·mic dust *n.* small particles of solid matter found in outer space, often collected in clouds

cos·mic ray *n.* a stream of high-energy radiation that reaches the earth from outer space

cos·mic string *n.* an extremely long and thin astronomical object theorized to be a space-time defect formed when the universe began

cosmo- *prefix.* the universe, space ○ *cosmochemistry* [From Greek *kosmos* "order, the world" (source of English *microcosm*)]

cos·mog·o·ny /koz móggənee/ (*plural* **-nies**) *n.* **1. STUDY OF UNIVERSE'S ORIGIN** the study of the origin of the universe or a part of it **2. THEORY OF UNIVERSE'S ORIGIN** a theory that explains the origin of the universe [Late 17thC. From Greek *kosmogonia* "creation of the world," from *kosmos* "COSMOS[1]."] —**cos·mo·gon·ic** /kòzmə gónnik/ *adj.* —**cos·mo·gon·i·cal** *adj.* —**cos·mo·gon·i·cal·ly** *adv.* —**cos·mog·o·nist** /koz móggənist/ *n.*

cos·mog·ra·phy /koz móggrəfee/ (*plural* **-phies**) *n.* the study and description or mapping of the entire world or the universe [14thC. Via late Latin from Greek *kosmographia,* from *kosmos* "COSMOS[1]."] —**cos·mog·ra·pher** *n.* —**cos·mo·graph·ic** /kòzmə gráffik/ *adj.* —**cos·mo·graph·i·cal** *adj.* —**cos·mo·graph·i·cal·ly** *adv.*

cos·mo·log·i·cal ar·gu·ment *n.* a logical argument that tries to prove the existence of God from empirical information about the universe

cos·mo·log·i·cal prin·ci·ple *n.* the principle that the universe would look the same to observers at any point in it as it does to us

cos·mol·o·gy /koz móllәjee/ (*plural* **-gies**) *n.* **1.** PHILOS **STUDY OF UNIVERSE** the philosophical study and explanation of the nature of the universe **2.** COSMOL **SCIENTIFIC STUDY OF UNIVERSE** the scientific study of the origin and structure of the universe [Mid-17thC. From modern Latin *cosmologia,* from, ultimately, Greek *kosmos* "COSMOS[1]."] —**cos·mo·log·ic** /kòzmə lójjik/ *adj.* —**cos·mo·log·i·cal** *adj.* —**cos·mo·log·i·cal·ly** *adv.* —**cos·mol·o·gist** /koz móllәjist/ *n.*

cos·mo·naut /kózmə nàwt/ *n.* an astronaut in the space programs of Russia and the former Soviet Union [Mid-20thC. From Russian *kosmonavt,* coined from Greek *kosmos* "COSMOS" + *nautēs* "sailor," on the model of *aeronavt* "aeronaut."]

cos·mop·o·lis /koz móppəliss/ *n.* a large city where people from many different countries and cultures live [Mid-19thC. Coined from COSMOS-, on the model of METROPOLIS.]

cos·mo·pol·i·tan /kòzmə póllit'n/ *adj.* **1. WITH FEATURES OF DIFFERENT COUNTRIES** composed of or containing people from different countries **2. WELL-TRAVELED** familiar with many different countries and cultures **3. UNPREJUDICED** free from national prejudices **4. KNOWLEDGEABLE AND REFINED** showing a breadth of knowledge and refinement from having traveled widely **5.** ECOL **OCCURRING WORLDWIDE** growing or occurring in many different parts of the world ■ *n.* **WELL-TRAVELED PERSON** somebody who has traveled to many different countries around the world [Mid-17thC. Formed from COSMOPOLITE.] —**cos·mo·pol·i·tan·ism** *n.*

cos·mop·o·lite /koz móppə lìt/ *n.* = **cosmopolitan** [Early 17thC. Via French from Greek *kosmopolitēs,* literally "citizen of the world."] —**cos·mop·o·lit·ism** *n.*

cos·mos[1] /kóz mòss, -məss/ *n.* **1.** PHILOS, COSMOL **WHOLE UNIVERSE** the universe thought of as an ordered and integrated whole **2. ORDERED SYSTEM** an ordered system or harmonious whole [13thC. From Greek *kosmos* "order, universe, ornament" (source also of English *microcosm*).]

cos·mos[2] /kóz mòss, -məss/ (*plural* **-mos·es** *or* **-mos**) *n.* a tropical American plant with flowers of various colors that resemble large daisies. Genus: *Cosmos.* [Early 19thC. Via modern Latin from Greek *kosmos* "ornament" (source of English COSMOS[1]). So called because of its elegant foliage.]

co·spon·sor /kō spónsər/ *n.* **JOINT SPONSOR** a sponsor who supports a person, organization, or project jointly with others ■ *vt.* (**-sor·ed, -sor·ing, -sors**) **SPONSOR JOINTLY** to sponsor something jointly with one or more other people or organizations —**co·spon·sor·ship** *n.*

Cos·sack /kó sàk/ *n.* **1.** HIST **RUSSIAN PEASANT** a peasant of Polish or Russian descent living in southeastern Russia, Ukraine, or Siberia. Cossacks were noted for their skill in horsemanship. **2.** MIL **COSSACK SOLDIER** a member of a Russian army unit whose soldiers are Cossacks [Late 16thC. Via Russian *kazak* (source of English *Kazakh*) from Turkic, literally "nomad, adventurer." The spelling was influenced by French *Cosaque.*]

cos·set /kóssət/ (**-set·ed, -set·ing, -sets**) *vt.* to give somebody or something excessive care and protection [Mid-16thC. Origin uncertain: perhaps via Anglo-Norman *coscet* "lamb reared by hand" from Old English *cotsǣta,* literally "cottage-dweller."]

cost /kawst/ *v.* (**cost, cost·ing, costs**) **1.** *vt.* **BE PRICED AT** to require the payment of a particular sum **2.** *vti.* **BE EXPENSIVE** to require payment of a large sum of money (*informal*) **3.** *vt.* **CAUSE LOSS OF** to cause somebody or something to lose, sacrifice, or suffer something **4.** (*past and past participle* **cost·ed**) *vt.* **CALCULATE MONEY REQUIRED** to calculate the price or expense of something ■ *n.* **1. AMOUNT PAID FOR SOMETHING** the amount of money required to be paid for something **2. MONEY SPENT DOING SOMETHING** the amount of money spent in producing or doing something **3. LOSS OR EFFORT** the loss, sacrifice, suffering, or effort involved in doing something **4.** = **cost price** ■ **costs** *npl.* LAW **LEGAL EXPENSES** the amount of money that is spent pursuing a legal action, especially those expenses that the losing party is required to pay [14thC. Via Old French from, ultimately, Latin *constare* "to be fixed."] —**cost·less** *adj.* —**cost·less·ly** *adv.* —**cost·less·ness** *n.*

cos·ta /kóstə/ (*plural* **-tae** /-tee/) *n.* **1.** ANAT **RIB** a rib (*technical*) **2.** BIOL **PART LIKE RIB** a part of something, e.g., a leaf or a wing, that resembles a rib [Mid-19thC. From Latin, "rib" (source also of English *accost, coast* and *cutlet*).] —**cos·tal** *adj.*

cost ac·count·ant *n.* an accountant who calculates and provides detailed information on the cost of producing something or carrying out some operation in a business, and compares actual costs with expected costs

cost ac·count·ing *n.* accounting that is concerned with providing detailed information on the cost of producing something or carrying out an operation in a business

cos·tae plural of **costa**

Cos·ta Me·sa /-máyssə/ city in southwestern California, south of Long Beach, on the shores of the Pacific Ocean. Population: 100,938 (1996).

co·star /kṓ staar/, **co-star** *n.* **JOINT STAR** somebody who stars jointly with another person or other people in a production ■ *v.* (**-starred, -star·ring, -stars**) **1.** *vi.* **STAR JOINTLY WITH OTHERS** to star jointly with another actor or actors in a production **2.** *vt.* **FEATURE AS JOINT STAR** to include or feature somebody as a costar

cos·tard /kóstərd/ *n.* a large English cooking apple [13thC. From Anglo-Norman, formed from *coste* "rib," from Latin *costa* (see COSTA). So called because of its prominent ridges.]

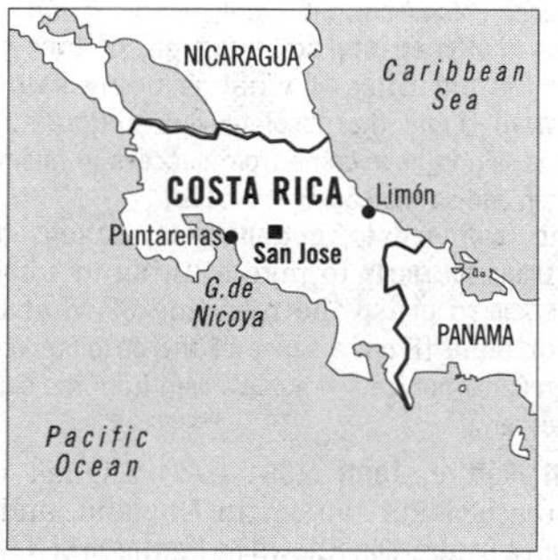

Costa Rica

Cos·ta Ri·ca /kòstə réekə, kòstə-/ republic in southern Central America between the Caribbean Sea and the Pacific Ocean. Language: Spanish. Currency: colón. Capital: San José. Population: 3,534,174 (1997). Area: 19,714 sq. mi./51,060 sq. km. Official name **Republic of Costa Rica** —**Cos·ta Ri·can** *n., adj.*

cos·tate /káw stàyt/ *adj.* BOT used to describe a leaf that has ridges or is ribbed [Early 19thC. From Latin *costatus,* formed from *costa* (see COSTA).]

cost-ef·fec·tive *adj.* economically worthwhile in terms of what is achieved for the amount of money spent —**cost-ef·fec·tive·ly** *adv.* —**cost-ef·fect·ive·ness** *n.*

cost·ing /káwsting/ *n.* the cost that has been calculated for undertaking a project (*often used in the plural*)

cos·tive /kóstiv/ *adj.* **1.** MED **CONSTIPATED** constipated, or causing constipation (*technical*) **2. HESITANT** slow to act or speak [14thC. Via Old French from Latin *constipatus,* the past participle of *constipare* (see CONSTIPATE).] —**cos·tive·ly** *adv.* —**cos·tive·ness** *n.*

cost·ly /káwstlee/ (**-li·er, -li·est**) *adj.* **1. EXPENSIVE** costing a lot of money to buy **2. LUXURIOUS** using expensive and luxurious materials **3. INVOLVING TIME OR EFFORT** involving a great deal of effort, time, or sacrifice **4. DAMAGING** causing great loss, damage, or suffering —**cost·li·ness** *n.*

Cost·ner /kóstnər/, **Kevin** (*b.* 1955) U.S. movie actor and director. He won seven Academy Awards for *Dances With Wolves* (1990), a movie about the Sioux.

cost of liv·ing *n.* the amount of money spent on food, clothing, accommodation, and other basic necessities (*hyphenated when used before a noun*)

cost-of-liv·ing ad·just·ment *n.* an increase in wages or salary to compensate for an increase in the cost of living

cost-of-liv·ing in·dex *n.* = **consumer price index**

cost-plus *n.* a pricing system that calculates the price of a product by adding a specified percentage as profit to the production cost

cost price *n.* the price that somebody selling something paid for it

cos·tume /kós toom/ *n.* **1. SPECIAL CLOTHES** clothes worn to make somebody look like somebody or something else, e.g., when performing in a play **2. CLOTHES OF PERIOD OR GROUP** the clothes worn during a specific period of time or in a specific location **3. CLOTHES FOR CERTAIN ACTIVITY** the clothing appropriate for a particular activity, e.g., swimming ■ *vt.* (**-tumed, -tum·ing, -tumes**) **1. DRESS IN A COSTUME** to provide somebody with a costume **2. PROVIDE COSTUMES** to provide costumes for a production [Early 18thC. Via French from Italian *costume,* literally "custom, fashion," from Latin *consuetudo* (see CUSTOM).]

cos·tume jew·el·ry *n.* jewelry that is decorative but cheap

cos·tum·i·er /ko stóomee ər, kàwss toom yáy/, **cos·tum·er** /kós toomər, ko stóomər/ *n.* somebody who makes or supplies costumes for a play, show, or festivity [Mid-19thC. From French, from *costumer* "to provide with a costume."]

co-sur·vi·vor *n.* PSYCHOL a close relative or friend of somebody who has experienced a traumatizing event, e.g., a rape victim, AIDS patient, or victim of a disaster

co·sy *adj., n.* U.K. = **cozy**

cot[1] /kot/ *n.* **1. COLLAPSIBLE LIGHTWEIGHT BED** a narrow collapsible bed for occasional or camping use, usually consisting of a lightweight metal or wood frame and a canvas surface or thin mattress **2.** *U.K.* = **crib** [Mid-17thC. From Hindi *khāṭ,* a framework strung with rope and used as a bed or seat, via Sanskrit *khaṭvā* from Tamil *kaṭṭu* "to tie."]

cot[2] /kot/ *n.* **1. COTTAGE** a small cottage (*archaic or literary*) **2.** MED **COVER FOR SORE FINGER** a cover for an injured finger, shaped like the finger of a glove [Old English, from prehistoric Germanic (see COTE)]

cot[3] /kot/ *abbr.* cotangent

cot[4] *n.* = **cote**

co·tan /kṓ tàn/ *abbr.* cotangent

co·tan·gent /kō tánjənt/ *n.* for a given angle in a right triangle, a trigonometric function equal to the length of the side adjacent to the angle divided by that of the side opposite —**co·tan·gen·tial** /kō tan jénshəl/ *adj.*

cot death *n. U.K.* = **crib death**

cote /kōt/, **cot** /kot/ *n.* a small shelter, especially one for birds or animals (*usually used in combination*) [Old English. Ultimately from a prehistoric Germanic word that is also the ancestor of English *cot[2]*.]

cot·eau /kə tṓ/ (*plural* **-eaus**) *n. Midwest, Can* in western North America, a hilly upland or divide between valleys [Mid-19thC. From French, "hillside, slope."]

Côte d'I·voire /kòt di vwaár/ republic in western

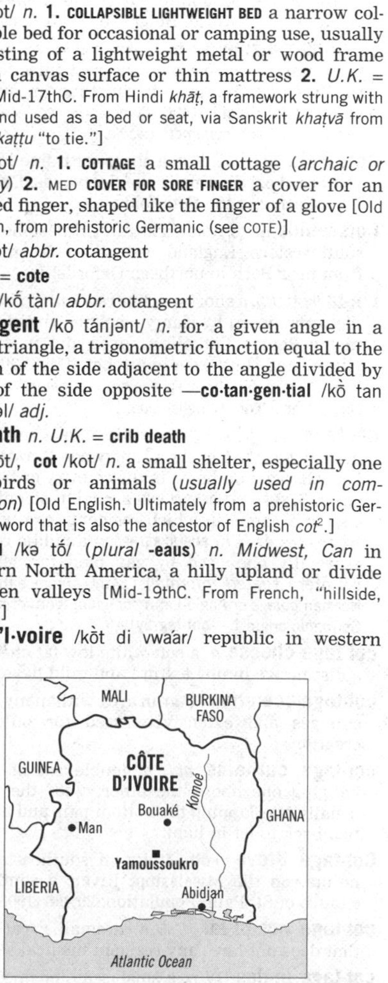

Côte d'Ivoire

Africa, situated north of the Gulf of Guinea and east of Liberia. Language: French. Currency: CFA franc. Capital: official, Yamoussoukro; seat of government, Abidjan. Population: 15,074,684 (1997). Area: 124,503 sq. mi./322,462 sq. km. Official name **Republic of Côte d'Ivoire**

co·ter·ie /kṓtəree, kōtə reé/ *n.* a small exclusive group of people who share the same interests [Early 18thC. Via French from, ultimately, Middle Low German *kote* "cottage." In Old French, the word meant "tenants."]

co·ter·mi·nous *adj.* = **conterminous**

Côtes du Rhône /kōt də rṓn/ *n.* a red or white wine produced in the Rhône valley, France

coth /kawth/ *abbr.* hyperbolic cotangent [Late 19thC. From COT^3 + *h* for HYPERBOLIC.]

co·tid·al /kō tíd'l/ *adj.* used to describe a line that joins together locations on a coastal map where tides occur simultaneously

co·til·lion /kə tíllyən, kō-/, **co·til·lon** /kə-, kō-/ *n.* **1.** FRENCH DANCE a complicated French dance popular in the 18th century **2.** BALL a formal ball **3.** DANCE LIKE QUADRILLE a dance similar to a quadrille **4.** MUSIC MUSIC the music for a cotillion [Early 18thC. From French *cotillon*, literally "petticoat," from *cotte* (see COAT).]

co·tin·ga /kō tíng gə, kə-/ *n.* a brightly colored bird of Central and South America. Family: Cotingidae. [Late 18thC. Via French from Tupi *cutinga*.]

co·ton à broder /kaw tōn aa brō dáir/ *n.* fine flat cotton thread with a slight sheen, used for embroidery [From French, literally "cotton for embroidery"]

co·to·ne·as·ter /kə tṓnee àstər/ *n.* a shrub of European or Asian origin with small white or pink flowers and black or red berries. Genus: *Cotoneaster*. [Mid-18thC. From modern Latin, genus name, from Latin *cotoneum* (see QUINCE).]

co·ton perlé /kaw tōn pur láy/ *n.* shiny twisted two-ply thread available in various thicknesses, used for embroidery [From French, literally "pearly cotton"]

Co·to·pa·xi /kòtə páksee/ volcano in central Ecuador, in the Andes Mountains. It is the highest active volcano in the world. Height: 19,347 ft./5,897 m.

co·tri·mox·a·zole /kō trī móksi zōl/ *n.* an antibiotic used mainly to treat urinary tract infections, that consists of a mixture of trimethoprim and sulfamethoxazole [Late 20thC. Coined from CO- + a blend of *trimethoprim* and *sulfamethoxazole*.]

Cots·wold /kóts wòld/ *n.* a sheep with fine long wool of a breed originating in the Cotswolds, England. ■ *adj.* relating to the Cotswolds

Cots·wolds /kóts wōldz/ range of limestone hills in southwestern England, extending 50 mi./80 km from near Bath to northern Oxfordshire

cot·ta /kóttə/ *n.* a short surplice reaching to just above the waist, worn by clergy, acolytes and choristers, in the Roman Catholic Church and in some Anglican and Lutheran churches [Mid-19thC. From Italian, ultimately from an ancient Germanic word that is also the ancestor of English *coat*.]

cot·tage /kóttij/ *n.* **1.** SMALL RURAL HOUSE a small house, usually situated in the countryside **2.** VACATION HOME a small vacation home in the country or beside the ocean **3.** SMALL RESIDENTIAL UNIT a small residential unit, e.g., at a camp, in which residents can be housed in groups **4.** *U.K.* PUBLIC BATHROOM a public restroom, especially one used by gay men for sexual encounters (*dated informal*) [14thC. From either Anglo-Norman *cotage* or Anglo-Latin *cotagium*, both of prehistoric Germanic origin.] —**cot·tag·ey** *adj.*

cot·tage cheese *n.* a soft white low-fat cheese with a distinctive lumpy texture and mild flavor

cot·tage coun·try *n. Can* an area with many summer cottages and extensively used for outdoor recreation

cot·tage cur·tains *npl.* a double set of curtains hanging one above the other, with the top pair usually overlapping the bottom pair and able to be tied back to let in light

Cot·tage Grove /kòttij-/ city in southeastern Minnesota, on the Mississippi River; a southeastern suburb of St. Paul. Population: 29,486 (1996).

cot·tage hos·pi·tal *n. U.K.* a small rural hospital that does not have any resident medical staff

cot·tage in·dus·try *n.* a small-scale business where people mostly work at home

cot·tage pud·ding *n.* a plain cake with a sweet sauce over it

cot·tag·er /kóttijər/ *n.* **1.** SOMEBODY WHO VACATIONS IN A COTTAGE somebody who vacations in a cottage **2.** *Can* LEISURE SUMMER RESIDENT a summer resident in a resort **3.** *U.K.* SOMEBODY WHO ENGAGES IN COTTAGING somebody who has gay sex or looks for gay partners in public restrooms (*slang*)

cot·tag·ing /kóttijing/ *n. U.K.* gay sex or looking for gay partners in public restrooms, a practice that was especially prevalent in the years when gay sex was a criminal offense (*slang*)

cot·tar /kóttər/, **cot·ter** *n.* **1.** FARM WORKER OCCUPYING COTTAGE formerly in Scotland, a farm worker who was allowed to occupy a cottage in return for labor **2.** = **cottier** [Mid-16thC. Origin uncertain: perhaps from medieval Latin *cotarius* (from Old English *cotsæta*, literally "cottage-dweller"), or formed from COT^2 + a Scots variant of -ER.]

cot·ter[1] /kóttər/ *n.* **1.** WEDGE OR BOLT KEEPING THINGS TOGETHER a wedge, key, or bolt used to keep two parts of something, e.g., machinery, together **2.** = **cotter pin** [14thC. Origin unknown.] —**cot·tered** *adj.* —**cot·ter·less** *adj.*

cot·ter[2] *n.* = **cottar**

cot·ter pin *n.* a split pin inserted through a hole in a machine part and then bent so it holds the part in place

cot·ti·er /kóttee ər/ *n.* formerly in Ireland, a tenant who farmed land he had acquired as the highest bidder [14thC. From Old French *cotier*. Ultimately of prehistoric Germanic origin.]

cot·ton /kótt'n/ *n.* **1.** PLANTS BUSH PRODUCING DOWNY FIBER a tropical or subtropical bush producing soft white downy fibers and oil-rich seeds. Genus: *Gossypium*. **2.** INDUST SOFT FIBER the soft white downy fiber that grows in the seed pods of the cotton plant, used for making textiles **3.** TEXTILES FABRIC MADE FROM COTTON fabric woven or knitted from spun cotton fiber **4.** SEW YARN OR THREAD yarn or thread made from cotton fiber, or a synthetic substitute **5.** SOMETHING MADE OF COTTON something made of cotton fabric (*often used in the plural*) **6.** INDUST SUBSTANCE RESEMBLING COTTON a substance that resembles cotton fiber but is produced by another plant, e.g., the cottonwood [14thC. Via French *coton* from, ultimately, Arabic *kuṭun*.]

cotton on (**cottoned on, cottoning on, cottons on**) *vi.* to grasp the meaning of what is being said or done (*informal*) [From the obsolete verb *cotton* "to prosper," which is said to have come from success in raising the nap of cotton and so increasing its value]

cotton to (**cottoned to, cottoning to, cottons to**) *vt.* **1.** START LIKING SOMEBODY to take a liking to somebody **2.** UNDERSTAND to grasp the meaning of what has been said or done [From a sense of the obsolete verb COTTON "to agree, harmonize," which evolved from the earlier sense "to prosper"]

Cot·ton /kótt'n/, **John** (1584–1652) English minister. He preached Puritanism in England, and then in America from 1633. Known as **Patriarch of New England**

Cot·ton Belt *n.* an extensive agricultural area in the southeast United States where cotton is the main crop

cot·ton can·dy *n.* a very sweet, usually pink, candy consisting of a mass of fluffy threads of spun sugar, often sold wrapped around a paper tube

cot·ton grass *n.* a reed-like marsh plant of northern temperate areas that has white tufted cottony flower heads. Genus: *Eriophorum*.

cot·ton moth *n.* a migratory owlet moth found in North America, especially as a pest in cotton fields. Latin name: *Alabama argillacea*.

cot·ton·mouth /kótt'n mòwth/ (*plural* **-mouths** /-thz, -ths/) *n.* = **water moccasin** [Mid-19thC. From the whitish color inside its mouth.]

cot·ton-pick·ing *adj.* used to indicate disapproval or annoyance, or simply for emphasis (*informal*) [From the fact that cotton-picking was done by only the poorest laborers]

cot·ton sedge *n. Can* = **cotton grass**

cot·ton·seed /kótt'n seèd/ *n.* the seed of the cotton plant, used to give oil and make meal

cot·ton·seed cake *n.* a hard cake produced as a residue after the extraction of oil from cottonseeds and used as a feed for livestock. It is usually ground for feeding.

cot·ton stain·er *n.* an insect that pierces cotton seed pods (**bolls**) and stains the fibers. Genus: *Dysdercus*.

Cot·ton State *n.* the state of Alabama (*informal*)

cot·ton swab *n.* a short stick with a small amount of absorbent cotton wound tightly onto one or both ends, used, e.g., to clean ears or apply makeup

cot·ton·tail /kótt'n tàyl/ *n.* a small North American rabbit with brown or gray fur and a tail with a white cottony underside. Genus: *Sylvilagus*.

cot·ton waste *n.* waste cotton yarn used as a cleaning material

cot·ton·wood /kótt'n wòod/ (*plural* **-woods** *or* **-wood**) *n.* a North American poplar tree that has seeds with cottony tufts. Latin name: *Populus deltoides*.

cot·ton wool *n.* **1.** *U.K.* = **absorbent cotton** (*hyphenated when used before a noun*) **2.** UNPROCESSED COTTON raw unprocessed cotton

cot·ton·y /kótt'nee/ *adj.* looking or feeling like cotton

cot·ton·y-cush·ion scale *n.* a small sap-sucking insect, native to Australia, that damages citrus crops in California and elsewhere. Latin name: *Icerya purchasi*.

-cotyl *suffix.* cotyledon ○ *hypocotyl* [From COTYLEDON]

cot·y·le·don /kòtt'l eéd'n/ *n.* **1.** FIRST LEAF the first leaf, or one of the first pair of leaves, produced by the seed of a flowering plant. They may serve as food stores, remaining in the seed at germination, or produce food by photosynthesis. **2.** TUFT ON MAMMALIAN PLACENTA a tuft of projections (**villi**) on the placenta of a mammal [Mid-16thC. Via Latin, literally "navelwort," from Greek *kotulēdōn* "cup-shaped cavity," from *kotulē* "cup, socket."] —**cot·y·le·don·al** *adj.* —**cot·y·le·don·ar·y** *adj.* —**cot·y·le·don·ous** *adj.*

cot·y·lo·saur /kótt'lə sàwr/ *n.* an extinct reptile with a heavy body and short legs. The cotylosaurs were probably the first land vertebrates. Order: Cotylosauria. [Early 20thC. Coined from Greek *kotulē* "cup, socket" + *sauros* "lizard." So called from its vertebrae, which are concave at both ends.]

cou·cal /kōo kàl, -k'l/ *n.* a tropical bird of the cuckoo family with a large hooked beak and long broad tail, found in Africa, southern Asia, and Australasia. Genus: *Centropus*. [Early 19thC. From French, said to be a blend of *coucou* "cuckoo" and *alouette* "lark."]

couch[1] /kowch/ *n.* **1.** LONG SEAT a piece of upholstered furniture on which two or more people can sit side by side. It usually has a back and arms. **2.** DOCTOR'S LONG SEAT a long seat with a headrest that a patient lies on, e.g., during a medical examination **3.** MALTING FRAME a frame on which barley grain is spread during malting **4.** PAINTING FIRST COAT OF PAINT a layer of paint or varnish applied to a canvas as a first coat ■ *v.* (**couched, couch·ing, couch·es**) **1.** *vt.* PHRASE IN CERTAIN WAY to express something using a particular style or choice of words **2.** *vt.* SPREAD FOR MALTING to spread barley on a frame for malting **3.** *vti.* LIE OR LAY DOWN to lie down, or lay somebody or something down (*archaic or literary*) (*often passive*) **4.** *vi.* LIE IN AMBUSH to lie in ambush (*archaic or literary*) **5.** *vt.* ARMS LOWER LANCE to lower a lance into position for an attack **6.** *vt.* SURG REMOVE CATARACT to remove a cataract by pushing down the lens of the eye **7.** *vt.* SEW EMBROIDER BY HOLDING DOWN THREADS to embroider a pattern by holding down threads by means of other threads passed through the material [14thC. The noun is via French *couche*, the verb directly from *coucher* "to lie or set down," from Latin *collocare*, literally "to place together."] —**couch·er** *n.*

couch[2] *n.* = **couch grass** [Late 16thC. Variant of QUITCH.]

couch·ant /kówchənt/ *adj.* used in heraldry to describe an animal lying down with its head raised [15thC. From French, the present participle of *coucher* (see COUCH[1]).]

cou·chette /koo shét/ *n.* **1.** SEAT CONVERTIBLE TO BED a seat in a compartment on a continental European train that can be converted into a sleeping berth **2.** COMPARTMENT WITH COUCHETTES a compartment of a train containing couchettes [Early 20thC. From French, literally "small bed," from *couche* (see COUCH[1]).]

couch grass *n.* a type of grass with rapidly spreading underground roots, that is a troublesome weed in gardens. Latin name: *Agropyron repens*.

couch po·ta·to *n.* an inactive person who spends too much time sitting watching television (*disapproving informal*) [A pun on the idea that somebody who watches the "boob tube" is a "tuber"; also with reference to snacking on potato chips]

cou·dé /koo dáy/, **cou·dé tel·e·scope** *n.* an astronomical telescope that reflects light from a main mirror onto a detector to one side [Late 19thC. From French, the past participle of *couder* "to bend at right angles," from *coude* "elbow," from Latin *cubitum* "elbow, forearm, cubit."]

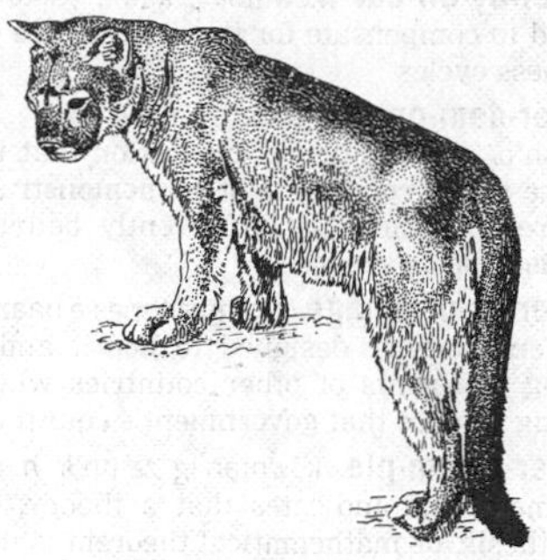
Cougar

cou·gar /kóogər, -aar/ (*plural* **-gars** *or* **-gar**) *n.* = **mountain lion** [Late 18thC. Via French *couguar* from, ultimately, Guarani *cuguaçuarana.*]

cough /kawf/ *v.* (**coughed, cough·ing, coughs**) **1.** *vi.* EXPEL AIR FROM LUNGS NOISILY to release air through the windpipe and mouth sharply and noisily **2.** *vt.* EXPEL BY COUGHING to expel something from the lungs or windpipe by coughing **3.** *vi.* MAKE COUGHING NOISE to make a noise that is similar to the sound of somebody coughing ■ *n.* **1.** ACT OR SOUND OF COUGHING a sudden noisy release of air through the windpipe and mouth, often expelling an obstruction **2.** MED ILLNESS CAUSING COUGHING an illness causing coughing because of an infection in the lungs [14thC. Ultimately from a prehistoric Germanic word that imitated the sound.] —**cough·er** *n.*

cough up *vti.* to give something such as money or information reluctantly (*informal*)

cough drop *n.* a medicated candy for soothing a cough or sore throat

cough syrup *n.* a medicated, often sweet-tasting, syrup that is taken to soothe or suppress a cough

could /kŏŏd/ CORE MEANING: a modal verb used to form the past tense of "can" ○ *My mother did the best she could for my brother and me, often against very stiff odds.* ○ *She could perform illusions and she was a trapeze artist.* ○ *His feet had swollen so he could hardly walk.* ○ *We were so tired we couldn't stay awake.*

vi. **1.** EXPRESSING POSSIBILITY used to express that something is possibly true or happening in the future ○ *She thinks that medical technology could be the field for her.* **2.** EXPRESSING REQUEST used when making polite requests ○ *Could you close the window please?* **3.** INDICATING A POSSIBLE PAST SITUATION used to indicate a possible situation in the past that did not happen ○ *We could have gone.* **4.** EXPRESSING POLITE OFFER used to make polite offers and suggestions **5.** FOR EMPHASIS used in questions to emphasize strong feelings about something ○ *How could you do that?* [Old English *cūþe*, past tense of *cunnan* "to know" (see CAN[2]; altered on the model of SHOULD and WOULD]

could·n't /kŏŏdd'nt/ *contr.* could not

could've /kŏŏddəv/ *contr.* could have

cou·lee /kóolee/ *n.* **1.** GEOL LAVA FLOW a thick short flow of viscous molten lava **2.** *Northwestern U.S., Can* GEOG DEEP GULLY DRY IN SUMMER a deep gully formed by rain or melting snow and usually dry in the summer **3.** *Southern U.S.* GEOG SMALL STREAM a small stream, canal, or bayou **4.** *Southern U.S.* GEOG STREAMBED a streambed, sometimes dry **5.** *Midwest* GEOG SHALLOW VALLEY a broad shallow valley [Early 19thC. From French, literally "flow," from the feminine past participle of *couler* "to flow," from Latin *colare* "to strain" (see COLANDER).]

cou·lis /kóolee/ (*plural* **-lis** /-lee/) *n.* a thin puree of fruit or vegetables used as a garnish [Late 20thC. Via French from Old French *coleïs*, literally "flowing."]

cou·lisse /koo léess/ *n.* in the theater, a piece of side scenery on a stage or the space between two of these pieces (*often used in the plural*) [Early 19thC. From French, from *(porte) coulisse* "sliding (door)," from Old French (see PORTCULLIS).]

cou·loir /kool waár/ *n.* a broad mountain gully, especially one prone to avalanches [Early 19thC. From French, literally "channel," from *couler* "to flow" (see COULEE).]

cou·lomb /kŏŏ lòm/ *n.* an SI unit of electric charge equal to the amount of electricity transferred by a current of one ampere in one second. Symbol **C** [Late 19thC. Named for the French physicist Charles Augustin de *Coulomb* (1736–1806), because of his work in electrostatics.]

Cou·lomb's law *n.* a law of electricity stating that the force of attraction or repulsion between two electric charges is proportional to their product and inversely proportional to the square of the distance between them [Mid-19thC. Named after the physicist who formulated it (see COULOMB).]

cou·lom·e·try /koo lómmətree/ *n.* a means of analyzing the results of a process of electrolysis by measuring the amount of electricity used in the process to determine the amount of the substance produced [Mid-20thC. Coined from COULOMB + -METRY.] —**cou·lo·met·ric** /kòolə méttrik/ *adj.* —**cou·lo·met·ri·cal·ly** /-méttrikəlee/ *adv.*

coul·ter /kóltər/, **col·ter** *n.* a vertical blade attached to a plow that cuts into the soil in front of a plowshare [Pre-12thC. From Latin *culter* "knife, plowshare" (source of English *cutlass* and *cutlery*). Ultimately from an Indo-European word meaning "to cut," which also produced English *shell, scale,* and *skill.*]

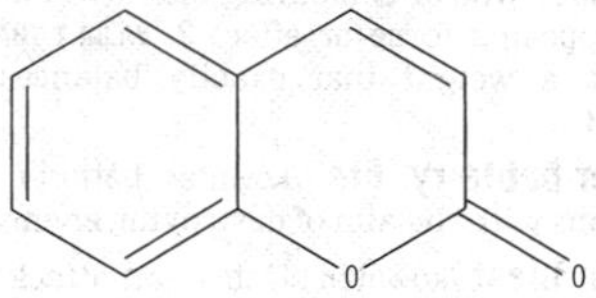

Coumarin

cou·ma·rin /kóomərin/ *n.* a fragrant compound found naturally in plants or made synthetically, used in perfumes and in medicine. Formula: $C_9H_6O_2$. [Mid-19thC. Via French from, ultimately, Tupi *cumarú* "tonka bean tree," one of the plants from which coumarin is obtained.] —**cou·ma·ric** *adj.*

coun·cil /kówns'l/ *n.* **1.** PUBLIC ADMIN PEOPLE RUNNING LOCAL AFFAIRS a group of people elected to govern a local district **2.** COMMITTEE an appointed or elected body of people with an administrative, advisory, or representative function **3.** CHR CHURCH ASSEMBLY an assembly of church representatives who meet to decide matters of discipline and doctrine **4.** COUNCIL MEETING a meeting of a council **5.** MEETING FOR DISCUSSION a meeting to discuss or decide something [Pre-12thC. Via Anglo-Norman *cuncile* from Latin *concilium*, literally "calling together." Ultimately from an Indo-European word meaning "to call," which also produced English *low, claim,* and *calendar.*]

WORD KEY: USAGE

council or **counsel**? ***Council*** is a noun only, meaning an assembly or a body of persons or their deliberations. ***Counsel*** is both a noun and a verb, and has to do with advice, particularly of a professional nature, and the giving of it. The noun ***counsel*** most often means a lawyer or lawyers dealing with a legal case, whereas a ***counselor*** gives some other kind of professional advice. The verb describes the activity of such advisers: *The company psychologist counsels employees having stress problems. International financial analysts counseled caution.*

Coun·cil Bluffs /kówns'l blúffs/ city in southwestern Iowa, on the Missouri River, directly east of Omaha, Nebraska. Population: 55,569 (1996).

coun·cil·lor *n.* = **councilor**

coun·cil·man /kówns'lmən/ (*plural* **-men** /-mən/) *n.* a man who is a member of a council, especially of a local government

coun·cil-man·ag·er plan *n.* a type of city government in the United States where an elected city council hires a professional administrator to run the public services and other operations of the city

Coun·cil of Eu·rope *n.* an organization of European states founded in 1949 to further political unity

Coun·cil of Trent *n.* a Roman Catholic Church council held in Trento, Italy, from 1545 to 1563 to respond to the threat from Protestantism. The council reaffirmed and defined Roman Catholic beliefs and laid the foundation for the Counter-Reformation.

coun·cil·or /kównsələr/, **coun·cil·lor** *n.* **1.** MEMBER OF LOCAL GOVERNMENT COUNCIL a member of a council elected to govern a local district **2.** MEMBER OF ADVISORY COUNCIL an elected or appointed member of an advisory council [14thC. Alteration of COUNSELLOR by association with COUNCIL.] —**coun·cil·or·ship** *n.*

coun·cil·wom·an /kówns'l wŏŏmmən/ (*plural* **-en** /-wìmmən/) *n.* a woman member of a council, especially of a local government

coun·sel /kówns'l/ *n.* **1.** COURT LAWYER a lawyer or group of lawyers who conduct cases in court or give legal advice **2.** SOMEBODY WHO GIVES ADVICE somebody whose advice is sought, or who acts as an official advisor (*takes singular or plural verb*) **3.** ADVICE advice sought from or given by somebody, especially somebody who is wise or knowledgeable (*formal or literary*) (*often used in the plural*) **4.** CONSULTATION consultation with others (*archaic or literary*) ■ *vt.* (**-seled, -sel·ing, -sels**) **1.** ADVISE TO DO SOMETHING to advise somebody on a particular course of action (*formal or literary*) **2.** ADVISE ON PERSONAL PROBLEMS to give somebody advice and support on personal or psychological matters, usually in a professional context [12thC. Via Old French *conseil* from, ultimately, Latin *consilium* "consultation, deliberating body," from *consulere* "to seek advice."] ◇ **keep your own counsel** to keep your thoughts and intentions secret

WORD KEY: USAGE

Counsel, meaning a lawyer, is often mispronounced "consul," the latter word meaning a foreign service officer attached to and running a consulate. See also Usage note at ***council.***

coun·se·lee /kòwnsə leé/ *n.* somebody who is receiving counseling

coun·sel·ing /kówns'ling/, **coun·sel·ling** *n.* **1.** HELP WITH PERSONAL PROBLEMS help with personal or psychological matters usually given by a professional **2.** MEETINGS WITH COUNSELOR meetings with a counselor to receive help with personal or psychological problems

coun·sel·or /kówns'lər/, **coun·sel·lor** *n.* **1.** SOMEBODY WHO GIVES ADVICE somebody, e.g., a friend, who gives advice **2.** SOC WELFARE ADVISER ON PERSONAL PROBLEMS somebody, usually a professional, who helps others with personal, social, or psychological problems **3.** EDUC, MED ADVISER ON SPECIAL SUBJECT a professional who gives advice on such matters as careers, education, or health **4. coun·sel·or, coun·sel·lor, coun·sel·or-at-law** (*plural* **coun·sel·ors-at-law**), **coun·sel·lor-at-law** (*plural* **coun·sel·lors-at-law**) LAW ATTORNEY an attorney, especially one who acts for a client in a trial **5.** PUBLIC ADMIN HIGH-RANKING DIPLOMAT a diplomat ranking below an ambassador or minister **6.** LEISURE CHILDREN'S SUPERVISOR somebody who supervises young people at a summer camp [12thC. Partly from French *conseiller* (from Latin *consiliarius*), and partly from French *conseilleur* (from Latin *consiliator*), both ultimately from Latin *consilium* (see COUNSEL).] —**coun·se·lor·ship** *n.*

count[1] /kownt/ *v.* (**count·ed, count·ing, counts**) **1.** *vti.* SAY NUMBERS to say numbers in order, usually starting at one **2.** *vti.* ADD UP to add things up to see how many there are or to find the value of an amount of money **3.** *vt.* INCLUDE to include somebody or something in a calculation **4.** *vti.* CONSIDER OR BE CONSIDERED to consider somebody or something, or be considered, in a particular way or as a particular thing **5.** *vi.* BE OF IMPORTANCE to be of importance or value **6.** *vi.* HAVE A VALUE to have a specific value **7.** *vti.* MUSIC, DANCE KEEP TIME to keep time by counting beats ■ *n.* **1.** SAYING OF NUMBERS an act of saying numbers in order **2.** FINDING OF TOTAL an addition of people or things to find a total **3.** TOTAL a total that is reached by adding up **4.** ONE OF MANY POINTS any one of a number of points, e.g., in a discussion **5.** LAW CHARGE AGAINST SOMEBODY a charge against somebody who is on trial **6.** BASEBALL BALLS AND STRIKES ON BASEBALL BATTER in baseball, the number of balls and strikes that a batter has accumulated during a turn at bat **7.** BOXING BOXING REFEREE'S COUNT a count to ten by the referee in a boxing match during which a boxer who has been knocked down must stand up or lose the match **8.**

WRESTLING **WRESTLING REFEREE'S COUNT** a count to three by the referee at a wrestling match during which a wrestler being held on the floor must break the hold or lose the point [14thC. The noun is via old French *conte*; the verb directly from Old French *conter* "to reckon," from Latin *computare*, literally "to reckon together."] ◇ **keep count** to count and remember the number of people or things counted ◇ **lose count** to fail to count accurately or remember the number of people or things counted ◇ **out** *or* **down for the count 1.** unconscious or deeply asleep and unlikely to wake again for some time (*informal*) **2.** BOXING unable to stand up, after being knocked down, within the ten-second count given by the referee, and therefore losing the match

count down *vi.* to count backward from a number to zero, or from a given time to something such as the launch of a rocket

count in *vt.* to include somebody in a plan

count on *vt.* **1. RELY ON** to rely on somebody to do something **2. BE SURE OF** to be sure that something will happen

count out *vt.* **1. COUNT ONE BY ONE** to count something, e.g., money, one item at a time **2. NOT INCLUDE** to exclude somebody from a plan **3.** BOXING **DECLARE BOXER DEFEATED BY COUNTING TEN** to disqualify a boxer who has been knocked down and fails to get up within ten seconds

count toward, count to·wards *vt.* to be included as part of something

count upon *vt.* = **count on**

count[2] /kownt/ *n.* a nobleman in certain European countries, with a rank equal to that of a British earl [14thC. Via old French *conte* from Latin *comit-*, the stem of *comes* "companion," later "member of the imperial court," literally "somebody who goes with."]

count·a·ble /kówntəb'l/ *adj.* **1. THAT CAN BE COUNTED** able to be counted **2.** GRAM **ABLE TO FORM A PLURAL** used to describe a noun that can be used with "a" or "an" and with a plural verb, usually in a distinct plural form —**count·a·bil·i·ty** /kòwntə bíllətee/ *n.* —**count·a·bly** /kówntəblee/ *adv.*

count·down /kównt dòwn/ *n.* **1. BACKWARD COUNT** a count in descending order before an event such as a rocket launch **2. ACTIVITIES BEFORE AN EVENT** the activities carried on during the period of time before something such as a rocket launch **3. PREPARATORY PERIOD** the period immediately preceding an important event

coun·te·nance /kówntənəns/ *n.* **1. FACE OR EXPRESSION** somebody's face, or the expression on it **2. COMPOSURE** composure or self-control ■ *vt.* (**-nanced, -nanc·ing, -nanc·es**) **TOLERATE OR APPROVE** to tolerate, accept, or give approval to something (*formal*) [13thC. From old French *contenance* "demeanor," literally "contents," from *contenir* (see CONTAIN).] —**coun·te·nanc·er** *n.*

count·er[1] /kówntər/ *n.* **1. FLAT SURFACE** a flat surface on which food or drink is served, merchandise is displayed, or business is transacted **2. FLAT SURFACE IN KITCHEN** a flat surface in a kitchen on which food can be prepared or dishes laid out **3.** LEISURE **SMALL MARKER** a small object, often a flat disk, used in games to mark a player's position or to keep score **4. IMITATION COIN** an object, usually a flat disk, used as a substitute for a coin [14thC. Via Anglo-Norman *counteor* from medieval Latin *computatorium*, literally "place for counting," from Latin *computare* (see COUNT[1]).] ◇ **under the counter** secretly and unofficially, usually because there is something illegal about what is being done

count·er[2] /kówntər/ *vti.* (**coun·tered, coun·ter·ing, coun·ters**) **1. CONTRADICT OR OPPOSE** to say something that contradicts or opposes what somebody has said **2. DO SOMETHING IN OPPOSITION** to do something in opposition to what somebody is doing, to make it less effective **3.** BOXING **PUNCH OPPONENT IN RETURN** to defend yourself against a punch from an opponent and deliver a punch in return ■ *adv.* **1. OPPOSITE** in the opposite direction **2. CONTRARILY** in a contrary manner ■ *adj.* **CONTRADICTING** contradicting or opposing something ○ *a counter blow* ■ *n.* **1. RESPONSE** a response made in retaliation to something that has been said **2. OPPOSITE** something that is the opposite of something else or that is done in opposition to something else **3.** BOXING **RETURN PUNCH** a punch that counters a punch aimed by an opponent **4.** FENCING **PARRY** in fencing, a parry in which the foils make a circular movement **5.** NAUT **END OF SHIP'S STERN** the part of the stern of a ship or boat that juts out above the waterline **6.** PRINTING **HOLLOW PART OF TYPEFACE** a hollow part of a piece of type, such as the inner parts of the letters "p" and "d" **7.** CLOTHES **LEATHER AROUND HEEL OF SHOE** a piece of leather around the heel of a shoe or boot **8.** FOOTBALL **MOVE AWAY FROM ATTACKING LINEMEN** a move in which the player carrying the ball runs to the side of the field away from the attacking linemen [14thC. From COUNTER-. The underlying meaning is "to go against."]

count·er[3] /kówntər/ *n.* **1. DEVICE THAT COUNTS** a device that counts automatically **2. SOMEBODY WHO COUNTS** somebody whose job is to count something, e.g., votes

counter- *prefix.* **1.** contrary, opposing ○ *counterattack* **2.** complementary, corresponding ○ *counterpart* [Via Anglo-Norman *countre-* from, ultimately, Latin *contra* (see CONTRA-)]

coun·ter·act /kòwntər ákt/ (**-act·ed, -act·ing, -acts**) *vt.* to prevent something having an effect, or lessen its effect —**coun·ter·ac·tion** *n.* —**coun·ter·ac·tive** *adj.* —**coun·ter·ac·tive·ly** *adv.*

coun·ter·ar·gu·ment /kówntər aargyəmənt/ *n.* a fact or opinion that challenges the reasoning behind somebody's proposal and shows that there are grounds for taking an opposite view

coun·ter·at·tack /kówntər ə tàk/ *n.* **RESPONSE TO ATTACK** an attack made in response to an attack by an enemy or opponent ■ *vti.* (**-tacked, -tack·ing, -tacks**) **LAUNCH COUNTERATTACK** to launch a counterattack against an enemy or opponent

coun·ter·bal·ance /kówntər bàlləns/ *vt.* (**-anced, -anc·ing, -anc·es**) **1. HAVE EQUAL AND OPPOSING EFFECT ON** to be or have an equal and opposing force or effect on something **2. BALANCE WITH EQUAL WEIGHT** to make something balance by putting equal weight on the opposite side ■ *n.* **1. COUNTERBALANCING PERSON OR THING** somebody who or something that is or has an equal and opposing force or effect **2. WEIGHT THAT BALANCES ANOTHER** a weight that exactly balances another weight

coun·ter·bat·te·ry fire /kówntər bàttəri-/ *n.* firing weapons with the aim of destroying enemy artillery

coun·ter·blast /kówntər blàst/ *n.* an attack on somebody in speech or writing, made in response to an attack by that person

coun·ter·change /kówntər chàynj/ (**-changed, -chang·ing, -chang·es**) *v.* **1.** *vti.* **INTERCHANGE** to interchange the parts or positions of two things **2.** *vt.* **CHECKER** to checker or dapple something with colors

coun·ter·charge /kówntər chaarj/ *n.* **1. ACCUSATION AGAINST ACCUSER** a charge or accusation made against the person or group who has accused another of something **2.** MIL **CHARGE COUNTERING ENEMY'S CHARGE** a military charge made to counter an enemy's charge ■ *vt.* (**-charged, -charg·ing, -charg·es**) **CHARGE ACCUSER WITH SOMETHING** to bring a charge against an accuser

coun·ter·check /kówntər chèk/ *n.* **1. SECOND CHECK** a check made to ensure that a previous check was correct **2. RESTRAINT ON SOMETHING** something that acts to block or restrain something else ■ *v.* (**-checked, -check·ing, -checks**) **1.** *vti.* **CHECK AGAIN** to carry out a second check on something, in order to ensure that the first was accurate **2.** *vt.* **RESTRAIN** to act in order to block the force or action of something

coun·ter·claim *n.* /kówntər klàym/ **CLAIM ENTERED BY DEFENDANT** a claim entered by the defendant in a court of civil law, as a response to the original claim that was entered against the defendant by the plaintiff ■ *vti.* /kòwntər kláym/ (**-claimed, -claim·ing, -claims**) **RESPOND TO ONE CLAIM WITH ANOTHER** to make a claim in response to, or as a defense against, an earlier claim —**coun·ter·claim·ant** /kòwntər kláymənt/ *n.*

coun·ter·clock·wise /kòwntər klók wìz/ *adv.* **IN THE DIRECTION OPPOSITE TO CLOCKWISE** in the direction opposite to the one that the hands of a clock move ■ *adj.* **MOVING OPPOSITE TO CLOCKWISE** moving in the direction opposite to the one that the hands of a clock move

coun·ter·con·di·tion·ing /kòwntər kən dísh'ning/ *n.* a process of psychological conditioning that attempts to replace somebody's undesired habitual response to a particular situation with a desired learned response

coun·ter·coup /kówntər koo/ *n.* a coup made against a group that has seized political power in an earlier coup

coun·ter·cul·ture /kówntər kùlchər/ *n.* a culture that has ideas and ways of behaving that are consciously and deliberately very different from the cultural values of the larger society that it is part of —**coun·ter·cul·tur·al** *adj.* —**coun·ter·cul·tur·ist** *n.*

coun·ter·cur·rent /kówntər kùrrənt/ *n.* **CURRENT FLOWING OPPOSITE WAY** a current that flows in the opposite direction of another current ■ *adj.* **1. FLOWING IN OPPOSITE DIRECTION** flowing in the opposite direction of another current **2. USING OPPOSING CURRENTS** involving the flow of two currents in opposite directions —**coun·ter·cur·rent·ly** *adv.*

coun·ter·cy·cli·cal /kòwntər síklik'l, -sík-/ *adj.* designed to compensate for the undesirable effects of business cycles

coun·ter·dem·on·stra·tion /kòwntər demmən stráysh'n/ *n.* a public demonstration that is held to oppose the purpose of another demonstration that was recently held or is currently being held —**coun·ter·dem·on·stra·tor** *n.*

coun·ter·es·pi·o·nage /kòwntər éspee ə naazh/ *n.* government activity designed to detect and prevent spying by agents of other countries who are operating against that government's country

coun·ter·ex·am·ple /kówntər ig zàmp'l/ *n.* a fact or argument that indicates that a theory, scientific hypothesis, or mathematical theorem is not true

coun·ter·fac·tu·al /kòwntər fákchoo əl/ *adj.* not reflecting or taking into account the facts

coun·ter·feit /kówntər fèet/ *adj.* **1. FORGED** made as a copy of something, especially money, in order to defraud or deceive people **2. FALSE** pretended in order to deceive somebody ○ *counterfeit geniality* ■ *vti.* (**-feit·ed, -feit·ing, -feits**) **1. FORGE** to make realistic copies of something, especially money, in order to defraud or deceive people **2. PRETEND** to pretend to have an emotion in order to deceive somebody ■ *n.* **FORGERY** a copy of something, especially money, made in order to defraud or deceive people [14thC. From Anglo-Norman *countrefet*, the past participle of *countrefaire* "to counterfeit," from medieval Latin *contrafacere*, from Latin *contra-* "against"+ *facere* "to make" (see FACT).] —**coun·ter·feit·er** *n.*

coun·ter·foil /kówntər fòyl/ *n.* the part of a check, ticket, or other paper used in a financial transaction that is detached and kept by the issuer as a record

coun·ter·fort /kówntər fàwrt/ *n.* a type of buttress that sticks out at right angles from a wall [Late 16thC. From French *contrefort*, from Old French *contreforcier* "buttress."]

coun·ter·glow /kówntər glō/ *n.* = **gegenschein** [Mid-19thC. Translation of German *Gegenschein*.]

coun·ter·heg·e·mon·ic /kòwntər hejjə mónnik/ *adj.* contrary to the prevailing fashion, especially in intellectual matters [Late 20thC. Formed from COUNTER- + HEGEMONY.]

coun·ter·in·sur·gen·cy /kòwntər in súrjənsee/ *n.* military and political activities undertaken by a government to defeat a rebellion or guerrilla movement —**coun·ter·in·sur·gent** *n.*

coun·ter·in·tel·li·gence /kòwntər in téllijəns/ *n.* government and military activities designed to gather information about enemy spies, thwart their activities, and supply them with false information

coun·ter·in·tu·i·tive /kòwntər in too itiv/ *adj.* not in accordance with what would naturally be assumed or expected ○ *I know it's counterintuitive, but the highest grade in this system is D and the lowest is A.* —**coun·ter·in·tu·i·tive·ly** *adv.*

coun·ter·ir·ri·tant /kòwntər írrit'nt/ *n.* **1. WORRY THAT DIVERTS ATTENTION FROM ANOTHER** a worry or annoyance that distracts somebody from attending to another worry or annoyance **2. SKIN IRRITANT SUPPOSED TO REDUCE INFLAMMATION** a substance applied to the skin in the belief that the irritation produced will reduce the inflammation of underlying tissue —**coun·ter·ir·ri·ta·tion** /kòwntər írri táysh'n/ *n.*

coun·ter·man /kówntər màn, kówntərmən/ (*plural* **-men** /-mèn, -mən/) *n.* a man who serves food at a counter, e.g., in a diner, delicatessen, or luncheonette

coun·ter·mand /kówntər mànd, kòwntər mánd/ *vt.* (**-mand·ed, -mand·ing, -mands**) **1. CANCEL A COMMAND** to give an order or instruction that a previous order or instruction should not be followed **2. RECALL** to recall somebody or something sent somewhere by a previous order ■ *n.* **ORDER CANCELING ANOTHER** an order canceling a previous order [15thC. From old French *contremander*, from, ultimately, Latin *mandare* "to command" (see MANDATE).]

coun·ter·march /kówntər maarch/ *n.* **1. RETURN MARCH** a march, especially one undertaken by soldiers, back from a position following the same route as that taken on the outward march **2.** CHANGE IN MARCHING DIRECTION a marching maneuver in which soldiers change the direction they are marching in while retaining their positions within a formation **3.** COMPLETE CHANGE OF APPROACH a complete change in somebody's behavior or way of doing things ■ *v.* **(-marched, -march·ing, -march·es) 1.** *vti.* MARCH BACK to return from a position by marching back along the same route, or to make soldiers do this **2.** *vi.* CHANGE DIRECTION OF MARCHING to change the direction of a formation of marching soldiers without altering the positions of the individual soldiers

coun·ter·mea·sure /kówntər mèzhər/ *n.* something that is done in reaction to and as defense against a hostile action by somebody else, or is done in order to deal with a threatening situation

coun·ter·mine /kówntər mīn/ *v.* **(-mined, -min·ing, -mines) 1.** *vti.* EXPLODE ENEMY'S MINES IN AN AREA to place explosive mines in an area in order to explode mines placed there by an enemy **2.** *vti.* DIG TUNNELS AGAINST ENEMY'S TUNNELS to dig underground tunnels in order to intercept or destroy tunnels dug by an enemy **3.** *vt.* SECRETLY FOIL PLOT to take secret action against somebody's plans ■ *n.* **1.** TUNNEL DUG AGAINST ENEMY'S TUNNELS a tunnel dug to intercept or destroy tunnels dug by an enemy **2.** SECRET ACTION TO FOIL PLOT a secret action designed to undermine or destroy a plot or scheme

coun·ter·move /kówntər mo͞ov/ *n.* RESPONSE a move made in response to an opponent's move, e.g., in a game ■ *vi.* **(-moved, -mov·ing, -moves)** RESPOND to act in response to an opponent's action, e.g., in a game —**coun·ter·move·ment** *n.*

coun·ter·of·fen·sive /kòwntər ə fénsiv/ *n.* a major attack or series of attacks made by a military force in response to the attacks made by an enemy

coun·ter·of·fer /kówntər òffər/ *n.* a revised offer from somebody who rejects another person's offer as unsatisfactory, made in part to continue their negotiations toward a purchase or agreement

coun·ter·pane /kówntər pàyn/ *n.* a cover for a bed and its bedding (*dated*) [15thC. Alteration, under the influence of pane "panel," of earlier *counterpoint*, via Old French from, ultimately, medieval Latin *culcita puncta*, literally "stitched quilt."]

coun·ter·part /kówntər paart/ *n.* **1.** SOMEBODY OR SOMETHING CORRESPONDING TO ANOTHER somebody who or something that has very similar characteristics to another person or thing, or plays a very similar part in a different system or organization **2.** MATCHING PART OR THING either of two parts that fit together, or either of two things that complement each other ○ *I identified bolt A but could not find its counterpart, socket B.* **3.** ARTS ACTOR PLAYING OPPOSITE ANOTHER somebody who plays opposite another person in a play or film **4.** LAW COPY OF LEGAL DOCUMENT a copy of a lease, contract, or other legal document that is held by one party to a transaction and that duplicates the copy held by the other party

coun·ter·per·son /kówntər pùrs'n/ *n.* somebody who serves food at a counter, e.g., in a diner, delicatessen, or luncheonette

coun·ter·plan /kówntər plàn/ *n.* **1.** OPPOSING PLAN a plan made to defeat or respond to another plan **2.** ALTERNATIVE PLAN a plan prepared as an alternative or substitute for the primary plan

coun·ter·plea /kówntər plee/ *n.* a plea made by the plaintiff in a court of law in response to the plea made by the defendant

coun·ter·plot /kówntər plòt/ *n.* PLOT MADE AGAINST PLOT a plot made in order to defeat an enemy's or opponent's plot ■ *vi.* **(-plot·ted, -plot·ting, -plots)** MAKE COUNTERPLOT to make a plot designed to defeat an enemy's or opponent's plot

coun·ter·point /kówntər pòynt/ *n.* **1.** SOUNDING TOGETHER OF MELODIES the sounding together of two or more melodic lines in a piece of music, each of which displays an individual and differentiated melodic contour and rhythmic profile **2.** MELODY COMBINED WITH ANOTHER in a piece of music, a melodic line or part that is sung or played at the same time as another **3.** CONTRASTING ELEMENT a theme or element in a work of art that forms a contrast with another ■ *vt.* **(-point·ed, -point·ing, -points) 1.** CONTRAST WITH to make an effective contrast with something, especially in a work of art ○ *Richard's social ease counterpoints his sister's awkwardness.* **2.** ARRANGE MUSIC IN COUNTERPOINT to add one or more melodic lines in counterpoint in a piece of music [15thC. Via French from, ultimately, medieval Latin *(cantus) contrapunctus*, literally "(song) with notes marked opposite (the melody)."]

coun·ter·poise /kówntər pòyz/ *n.* **1.** COUNTERACTING WEIGHT a weight that balances another weight **2.** COMPENSATING FACTOR something that has the effect of diminishing or compensating for the effect of something else ○ *The government had covertly encouraged the fascists as a counterpoise to the reformers.* **3.** BALANCED STATE a state of balance ■ *vt.* **(-poised, -pois·ing, -pois·es) 1.** OPPOSE AND BALANCE SOMETHING to counteract or compensate for something by providing an equal force, influence, or weight **2.** MAKE BALANCED to bring something into a state of balance [15thC. Alteration, under the influence of *poise* "balance," of French *contrepeis*, literally "counterweight."]

coun·ter·pro·duc·tive /kòwntər prə dúktiv/ *adj.* producing problems or difficulties instead of helping to achieve a goal ○ *A direct challenge to her authority is likely to be very counterproductive.* —**coun·ter·pro·duc·tive·ly** *adv.*

coun·ter·pro·pos·al /kówntər prə pṓz'l/ *n.* a suggestion made in response to, and with the hope of modifying or replacing, another suggestion in a negotiation

coun·ter·punch /kówntər pùnch/ *n.* COUNTERATTACKING PUNCH a punch made by a boxer in response to an opponent's punch ■ *vi.* **(-punched, -punch·ing, -punch·es)** BOX BACK to punch in response to an opposing boxer's punches —**coun·ter·punch·er** *n.*

coun·ter·ref·or·ma·tion /kòwntər reffər máysh'n/ *n.* a reform or reform movement that seeks to reverse the effects of earlier reforms

Coun·ter Ref·or·ma·tion, **Coun·ter-Ref·or·ma·tion** *n.* the movement of reform and regeneration instituted by the Roman Catholic Church in 1545 to counter the increasing strength of Protestantism in Europe as a result of the Reformation

coun·ter·rev·o·lu·tion /kòwntər revvə lo͞osh'n/ *n.* **1.** REVOLUTION OPPOSING PREVIOUS REVOLUTION a revolution with the aim of undoing the effects of a previous revolution and overthrowing the government or social system that it produced **2.** ACTIVITY AGAINST RESULTS OF REVOLUTION subversive activity aimed at undoing the results of a revolution and overthrowing the government or social system that it produced —**coun·ter·rev·o·lu·tion·ist** *n.*

coun·ter·rev·o·lu·tion·ar·y *n.* (*plural* **-ies**) **1.** SOMEBODY FIGHTING REVOLUTIONARY GOVERNMENT somebody, especially a member of a military force, who seeks to overthrow a national government or social system established by a revolution **2.** SOMEBODY OPPOSED TO REVOLUTION somebody who is opposed to revolution as a means of political and social change ■ *adj.* OPPOSED TO REVOLUTION opposed to a specific revolution or to revolution as a means of political and social change

coun·ter·sank past tense of **countersink**

coun·ter·scarp /kówntər skaarp/ *n.* the slope or bank on the outer side of the ditch outside a fort [Late 16thC. Via French *contrescarpe* from Italian *controscarpa*, from *scarpa* (see SCARP).]

coun·ter·shad·ing /kówntər shàyding/ *n.* a pattern of coloring on an animal's skin or coat where the upper parts are darker than the lower, counteracting the effects of sun and shade and camouflaging the animal

coun·ter·shaft /kówntər shàft/ *n.* an intermediate shaft that transmits power from the main shaft to a working part but rotates in the opposite direction, especially in a belt drive or gear drive

coun·ter·sign /kówntər sīn/ *vt.* **(-signed, -sign·ing, -signs)** SIGN DOCUMENT ALREADY SIGNED to sign a document that somebody else has signed, e.g., as a witness to the signature or to confirm an authorization ■ *n.* **1.** MIL SECRET PASSWORD an agreed and secret sign, word, or signal given as a password to a military sentry in order to pass **2.** = **countersignature**

coun·ter·sig·na·ture /kòwntər sígnəchər, -cho͝or/ *n.* a signature added to a document that has already been signed, e.g., to witness the first signature or to confirm an authorization

coun·ter·sink /kówntər sìngk/ *vt.* **(-sunk /-sùngk/, -sunk, -sink·ing, -sinks) 1.** MAKE SCREW HEADS LEVEL WITH SURFACE to place screws, bolts, or nails in wood or another material so that their heads are level with or below the surface of the material **2.** MAKE HOLE TO INCLUDE SCREW HEAD to widen the top of the hole for a screw or bolt so that the head will fit into the hole and be flush with or below the surface ■ *n.* **1.** HOLE THAT ACCEPTS SCREW HEAD a hole for a screw or bolt that is wider at the top so that the head will fit into the hole and be flush with or below the surface **2.** COUNTERSINKING TOOL a special drill bit or other tool for countersinking holes for screws or bolts

coun·ter·spy /kówntər spī/ (*plural* **-spies**) *n.* a spy who spies on and seeks to thwart enemy spies

coun·ter·stain /kówntər stàyn/ *n.* ADDITIONAL STAIN FOR MICROSCOPE SPECIMEN an additional stain applied to a specimen to be examined under a microscope, in order to bring out features not revealed by the primary stain ■ *vt.* **(-stained, -stain·ing, -stains)** ADD COUNTERSTAIN to use a counterstain on a microscope specimen

coun·ter·sub·ject /kówntər sùbjəkt/ *n.* a second theme or melodic line that contrasts with the main one in a fugue or other piece of music employing counterpoint

coun·ter·sue /kówntər so͞o/ **(-sued, -su·ing, -sues)** *vti.* to bring a lawsuit against somebody who is suing you

coun·ter·sunk past tense, past participle of **countersink**

coun·ter·ten·or /kówntər tènnər/ *n.* **1.** HIGH MALE SINGING VOICE an adult male singing voice that is higher than tenor and covers the alto range, produced by singing in falsetto **2.** MAN WITH HIGH SINGING VOICE a man whose singing voice is a countertenor [14thC. Via French *contrateneur* from obsolete Italian *contratenore*, literally "against the tenor."]

coun·ter·ter·ror /kówntər tèrrər/ *adj.* intended or used to combat terrorism

coun·ter·ter·ror·ism /kòwntər terrə rìzzəm/ *n.* military or political activities intended to combat or prevent terrorism —**coun·ter·ter·ror·ist** *adj.*, *n.*

coun·ter·top /kówntər tòp/ *n.* the surface of a counter, especially a kitchen counter, or of the top of a display or storage case in a store

coun·ter·trade /kówntər tràyd/ *n.* a system of international trade in which countries exchange goods or services, rather than paying for imports with currency —**coun·ter·trad·er** *n.*

coun·ter·trans·fer·ence /kòwntər trans fúrrəns, -trànsfərəns/ *n.* a process that sometimes occurs in psychoanalytic therapy where repressed emotions in the therapist are awakened by identification with the experiences and feelings of the patient

coun·ter·type /kówntər tīp/ *n.* **1.** OPPOSITE TYPE a type that is the complete opposite of another type **2.** CORRESPONDING TYPE a type that corresponds with or is equivalent to another type

coun·ter·vail /kòwntər váyl, kówntər vàyl/ **(-vailed, -vail·ing, -vails)** *v.* **1.** *vti.* EXERT COUNTERACTING EFFECT to exert a counteracting power or influence against something, especially against a harmful force, idea, or influence **2.** *vt.* OFFSET to offset or compensate for something [14thC. From Anglo-Norman *contrevaloir*, literally "to be worth against."]

coun·ter·weigh /kòwntər wáy/ **(-weighed, -weigh·ing, -weighs)** *vt.* to counterbalance something, or use something to counterbalance something

coun·ter·weight /kówntər wàyt/ *n.* **1.** COUNTERBALANCING WEIGHT a weight that balances another weight **2.** SOMETHING WITH COMPENSATORY EFFECT something that counteracts or compensates for something else, e.g., a force, idea, or influence —**coun·ter·weight·ed** *adj.*

coun·ter·wom·an /kówntər wo͝omən/ (*plural* **-en** /-wìmmin/) *n.* a woman who serves food at a counter, e.g., in a diner, delicatessen, or luncheonette

coun·ter·work /kówntər wùrk/ *n.* **1.** WORK COUNTERACTING OTHER WORK work or action undertaken to counteract other work or another action **2.** MIL FORTIFICATIONS fortifications against an attack

count·ess /kówntəss/ *n.* **1.** WIFE OF COUNT OR EARL a woman who is married to a count or an earl, or who is the widow of a count or an earl **2.** FEMALE EQUIVALENT OF COUNT OR EARL a woman who holds the rank of count or earl in her own right [12thC. Via Old French *contesse* from medieval Latin *comitissa*, the feminine form of *comes* (see COUNT[2]).]

count·ing·house /kównting hòwss/ (*plural* **-houses** /-hòwzəz/) *n.* the place where the financial work of a business is done or where its accounts are kept (*archaic*)

count·less /kówntləss/ *adj.* many more than it is possible or convenient to count ○ *I've told him countless times to be more careful.* —**count·less·ly** *adv.*

count noun *n.* a noun that refers to one thing rather than a mass of something and that can be used with "a" or "an," with a number, and in the plural. Examples of English count nouns are "cat," "sheep," and "child."

count pa·la·tine (*plural* **counts pa·la·tine**) *n.* **1.** LOCAL RULER IN HOLY ROMAN EMPIRE a count who ruled over his own domain (**county palatine**) in the Holy Roman Empire, or an official who ruled an area of the empire as the emperor's representative **2.** SOMEBODY WITH JUDICIAL POWER OVER COUNTY in former times, an earl or other nobleman in England or Ireland who held the highest judicial authority and other supreme powers within his own domain (**county palatine**) **3.** ROMAN PALACE OFFICIAL a palace official with judicial authority in the late Roman Empire

coun·tri·fied /kúntri fīd/, **coun·try·fied** *adj.* **1.** WITH A COUNTRY AIR having a style or quality appropriate to the country ○ *a pretty, countrified row of houses* **2.** UNSOPHISTICATED not fashionable or sophisticated and of a style or quality that is typical of rural areas

coun·try /kúntree/ *n.* (*plural* **-tries**) **1.** SEPARATE NATION a nation or state that is politically independent, or a land that was formerly independent and remains separate in some respects **2.** HOMELAND the nation or state where somebody was born or is a citizen **3.** GEOGRAPHICALLY DISTINCT AREA a large area of land regarded as distinct from other areas, e.g., because of its natural boundaries or because it is inhabited by a particular people ○ *The country was settled by Europeans in the 16th century.* **4.** FARMED AND UNDEVELOPED AREA an area that is farmed or remains in a relatively undeveloped state, as distinct from cities, towns, and other built-up areas ○ *a house in the country* **5.** REGION WITH SPECIAL CHARACTER a region that is distinguished by particular characteristics or is associated with a particular activity, person, or group of people ○ *This was rebel country and there were checkpoints along the road.* **6.** NATION'S PEOPLE the people of a nation or state, especially when affected as a group by political or other events ○ *a scandal that rocked the country* **7.** = **country music** ■ *adj.* **1.** TYPICAL OF RURAL AREAS typical of rural areas or the people living there **2.** OF COUNTRY MUSIC typical of, similar to, or performing country music [13thC. Via Old French *cuntrée* from assumed Vulgar Latin *(terra) contrata*, literally "(land) lying opposite," from Latin *contra* "against."] —**coun·try·ish** *adj.*

coun·try and west·ern *n.* = **country music** (*hyphenated when used before a noun*)

coun·try bump·kin *n.* = **bumpkin**

coun·try club *n.* a club for social and leisure activities that has facilities for golf, tennis, or other outdoor sports, usually located in the suburbs or the country

coun·try cous·in *n.* somebody from a rural area whose unsophisticated reactions to city life are amusing (*dated*)

coun·try-dance *n.* a folk dance in which several couples form a square, a circle, or two lines, and perform a set of movements —**coun·try-danc·ing** *n.*

coun·try·fied *adj.* = **countrified**

coun·try gen·tle·man *n.* a man who owns an estate in the country

coun·try house *n.* a house in the country, usually a large residence or a second home

coun·try·man /kúntrimən/ (*plural* **-men** /-mən/) *n.* **1.** SOMEBODY FROM SAME NATION somebody who was born in or has become a citizen of the same nation as somebody else **2.** SOMEBODY FROM PARTICULAR NATION somebody who is from or is a citizen of a particular nation **3.** SOMEBODY FROM THE COUNTRY somebody who lives in the country, especially somebody brought up there and familiar with rural life and pursuits

coun·try mar·riage *n. Can* formerly in Canada, a common-law marriage between a fur trader of European origin and an Aboriginal or Métis woman

coun·try mile *n.* a long distance (*regional informal*)

coun·try mu·sic *n.* a type of popular music, based on the traditional music of the rural South and the cowboy music of the West, whose songs express strong personal emotions. Country musicians typically play such instruments as the guitar and fiddle. —**coun·try mu·si·cian** *n.*

coun·try rock *n.* **1.** MUSIC COUNTRY-INFLUENCED ROCK MUSIC a type of rock music that is strongly influenced by country music **2.** GEOL ROCK SURROUNDING OTHER ROCK rock that has been intruded by magma or that surrounds veins of mineral ore

coun·try·seat *n.* an estate or a large house in the country that is the hereditary property of a particular family

coun·try·side /kúntri sīd/ *n.* **1.** RURAL LAND an area of land that is farmed or in a relatively undeveloped state ○ *a village set in the wooded countryside* **2.** INHABITANTS OF RURAL AREA the people who live in a rural area ○ *The entire countryside was up in arms against the proposed development.*

coun·try·wide /kúntri wīd/ *adj., adv.* throughout an entire nation ○ *a countrywide organization for professional women* ○ *rates that were increased countrywide*

coun·try·wom·an /kúntri wŏŏmmən/ (*plural* **-en** /-wìmmin/) *n.* **1.** WOMAN FROM SAME NATION a woman who was born in or is a citizen of the same nation as somebody else **2.** WOMAN FROM PARTICULAR NATION a woman who was born in or is a citizen of a particular nation **3.** WOMAN FROM THE COUNTRY a woman who lives in the country, especially one brought up there and familiar with rural life and pursuits

coun·ty /kówntee/ (*plural* **-ties**) *n.* **1.** LOCAL GOVERNMENT AREA a unit of local government and one of the administrative subdivisions that the states of the United States and, excepting major cities, all of England and Wales are divided into **2.** PEOPLE OF A COUNTY the people who live in a county **3.** COUNT'S OR EARL'S DOMAIN the lands controlled by a count or an earl (*archaic*) [13thC. Via Anglo-Norman *counté* from, ultimately, Latin *comitatus*, literally "group of companions," from *comes* (see COUNT²).]

coun·ty a·gent *n.* a government employee who provides advice to the residents of a rural county on subjects such as agriculture and home economics

coun·ty clerk *n.* a local government official who keeps records and maintains documents for a county and its residents

coun·ty coun·cil *n.* a local government body administering a county in the United Kingdom and some parts of the United States

coun·ty court *n.* a local court of a state having jurisdiction in civil and criminal matters in one or more counties

coun·ty pa·la·tine (*plural* **coun·ties pa·la·tine**) *n.* **1.** COUNT PALATINE'S DOMAIN the lands governed by a nobleman or imperial official with the rank of count palatine in the Holy Roman Empire **2.** EARL'S OR COUNT'S DOMAIN in England and Ireland in former times, the lands administered by an earl or other nobleman who exercised judicial authority [See COUNT PALATINE]

coun·ty seat *n.* a town that is the seat of local government for a county

coun·ty town *n. U.K.* = **county seat**

coun·ty·wide /kówntee wīd/ *adj., adv.* throughout an entire county

coup /koo/ *n.* **1.** SEIZURE OF POLITICAL POWER the sudden overthrow of a government and seizure of political power, especially in a violent way and by the military **2.** SUCCESSFUL ACTION a success that is unexpected and achieved with exceptional skill ○ *Getting the author to come and speak was quite a coup.* **3.** FEAT OF BRAVERY among some Native American peoples, a feat of bravery during battle, especially touching an enemy warrior without harming him [Late 18thC. Via French, "blow," from, ultimately, Greek *kolophos* "blow with the fist."]

coup de fou·dre /kŏŏ də fóodrə/ (*plural* **coups de fou·dre** /kŏŏ də foodrə/) *n.* a sudden overwhelming feeling of love for somebody [From French, literally "stroke of lightning"]

coup de grâce /kŏŏ də graáss/ (*plural* **coups de grâce** /kŏŏ-/) *n.* **1.** DEATH BLOW a final stroke or shot that kills a person or animal, especially one intended to end suffering **2.** ACT THAT ASSURES VICTORY the final action that assures victory or success, especially in a sporting event [From French, literally "stroke of mercy"]

WORD KEY: USAGE

Pronunciation trap: When foreign words and expressions enter our language, how much adaptation does their pronunciation undergo? At first a borrowed word is generally recognized as foreign, and is pronounced much as it would be in its original language. As time goes on, pronunciation and even spelling are likely to be modified so as to be more typical of English, until the word's foreign origins are invisible except to etymologists. *Discotheque, laissez-faire, mayonnaise,* and *uncle*, for example, are at various points along this continuum of assimilation. Curiously, ***coup de grâce*** is often mistakenly pronounced *kŏŏ də graá*, as people, perhaps having heard, for example, *bourgeois, esprit de corps,* and *foie gras* pronounced without their final consonants, imagine the expression should be pronounced in French. But the correct French pronunciation is more like the correct English pronunciation: *kŏŏ də graáss.*

coup de main /kŏŏ də máyn/ (*plural* **coups de main** /kŏŏ də máyn/) *n.* a sudden, fierce, and successful surprise attack against an enemy [From French, literally "blow of the hand"]

coup d'é·tat /kŏŏ day taá/ (*plural* **coups d'é·tat** *or* **coup d'é·tats** /kŏŏ day taá/) *n.* = **coup** *n.* 1 [From French, literally "stroke of state"]

coup de thé·â·tre /kŏŏ də tay aátrə/ (*plural* **coups de thé·â·tre** /kŏŏ də tay aátrə/) *n.* **1.** SURPRISING TURN OF EVENTS something that occurs in a very dramatic way, especially a sensational and unexpected turn of events **2.** THEATER EFFECTIVE PIECE OF THEATER a strongly dramatic moment in a play or other theatrical production, produced by an exceptional piece of writing, performance, or staging **3.** THEATER SUCCESSFUL PLAY a play or other theatrical performance that is very successful [From French, literally "stroke of theatre"]

coup d'oeil /kŏŏ dŏyə/ (*plural* **coups d'oeil** /kŏŏ-/) *n.* a quick look at something, especially one that provides an overall general impression (*literary*) [From French, literally "stroke of the eye"]

coupe[1] /koop/ *n.* **1.** ICE CREAM WITH FRUIT a dessert of ice cream and fruit **2.** GLASS DISH a small shallow glass bowl, often with a stem, for fruit and ice cream [Late 19thC. Via French, literally "goblet," from medieval Latin *cuppa* (see CUP).]

coupe[2] /koop/ *n.* a car with two doors and a hard, fixed roof that seats two people or has a small rear seat [Early 20thC. Variant of COUPÉ.]

cou·pé /koo páy, koop/ *n.* **1.** CARS = **coupe**[2] **2.** TRANSP TWO-SEATER CARRIAGE a closed four-wheeled carriage that has two inside seats for passengers and a driver's seat outside in the front [Mid-19thC. From French *(carrosse) coupé*, literally "cut-down (carriage)" (because it was smaller than earlier models), the past participle of *couper* "to cut" (see COPE).]

cou·ple /kúpp'l/ *n.* **1.** TWO SIMILAR THINGS two things of the same kind that are together or are considered as a pair ○ *found a couple of mugs in the cupboard* **2.** SEVERAL a few things of the same kind (*spoken*) ○ *There are a couple of things I'm not sure about.* **3.** TWO PEOPLE SHARING LIVES two people who are married, are living together, or have an intimate relationship **4.** TWO PEOPLE DOING SOMETHING TOGETHER two people, especially a man and a woman, who are sitting, walking, dancing, or working together ○ *There were only a few couples on the dance floor.* **5.** SOMETHING THAT JOINS something that links or joins two similar things **6.** ENG SYSTEM OF OPPOSING FORCES a system of two equal forces that are parallel and in opposite directions **7.** HUNT PAIR OF DOGS a pair of hunting dogs attached to each other by a leash, or the double collar and leash on which they are held **8.** PHYS ELECTRICAL CONTACT a connection of two dissimilar metals that develops an electric current in the presence of an electrical conductor (**electrolyte**) ■ *v.* (**-pled, -pling, -ples**) **1.** *vt.* ASSOCIATE TWO THINGS to associate or combine something or somebody with another ○ *High prices coupled with poor living conditions made their lives difficult.* **2.** *vt.* JOIN TWO THINGS to join or link two things or people ○ *to couple freight cars* **3.** *vi.* HAVE SEXUAL INTERCOURSE to have sexual intercourse (*formal*) ■ *adj.* A FEW two or a few [13thC. Via Old French from Latin *copula* (see COPULA).]

WORD KEY: USAGE

Singular or plural? When ***couple*** refers to two married people or partners, it may be treated as either singular or plural: *The couple wants to be married before the end of the year* but *The couple have not reconciled, and continue to live apart.* If there is a pronoun referring to the word, it is almost always plural (*their*), and then any verb should be plural as well: *The couple have repeatedly asked that their privacy be respected.* In other uses, the word is often followed by *of* and a plural noun, in which case it is treated as plural: *A couple of books were on the table.* In informal uses the idea of "two" may be very approximate. If somebody says, e.g., *A couple of us are going out for coffee,* no one should be surprised if three people go.

cou·pler /kúpplər/ *n.* **1.** RAIL **CONNECTOR FOR RAILROAD CARS** a device on a railroad car that enables the cars to be connected to form a train **2.** ENG = **coupling** *n.* 4 **3. MEANS OF COUPLING THINGS** something or somebody that joins or combines two things together **4.** MUSIC **DEVICE CONNECTING KEYBOARDS** a mechanical or electronic device that connects two keyboards on an organ or harpsichord so that all the keys can be played from one keyboard

cou·plet /kúpplət/ *n.* two lines of verse that form a unit alone or as part of a poem, especially two that rhyme and have the same meter [Late 16thC. From French, literally "little couple," from *couple* "COUPLE."]

cou·pling /kúppling/ *n.* **1. SOMETHING THAT JOINS TWO THINGS** something that joins two things, especially a device for connecting two pieces of pipe, hose, or tube **2. JOINING TWO THINGS TOGETHER** a joining together or linking of two persons or things ○ *a disastrous coupling of two very unlike singers* **3. ACT OF SEXUAL INTERCOURSE** an act of sexual intercourse **4.** MECH ENG **LINK THAT TRANSFERS POWER** a part of a mechanical system by which power is transmitted from one rotating part to another part **5.** RAIL = **coupler 6.** ZOOL **TRUNK OF ANIMAL'S BODY** the part of the body of a four-legged animal between the forequarters and hindquarters **7.** ELECTRON ENG **CONNECTION OF ELECTRICAL CIRCUITS** a means of connecting two electrical circuits so that power can be passed between them, or the process of connecting electrical circuits in this way

cou·pon /kóo pòn, kyóo-/ *n.* **1. VOUCHER REDEEMED BY STORE OR COMPANY** a voucher that entitles somebody to a discount, refund, or gift, typically issued as a sales promotion **2. ORDER FORM** a printed form, e.g., in an advertisement, that may be filled in and returned to order a product or request information **3. FORM FOR PAYMENT BY INSTALLMENTS** a form or card showing the payment due on a certain date for something that is paid for on an installment plan. The card is returned with the payment. **4.** FIN **CERTIFICATE OF INTEREST ON BOND** a detachable part of a bond that indicates a date and the amount of interest paid on that date. It must be presented to receive payment of the interest. **5. TICKET IN RATIONING SYSTEM** a ticket issued under a rationing system that entitles somebody to a certain amount of a rationed item and that must be handed in to buy or receive that item [Early 19thC. From French, literally "piece cut off," from *couper* (see COPE).]

cou·pon·ing /kóo pònning, kyóo-/ *n.* the use of coupons as a means of promoting a product's sales or of saving money on purchases

cour·age /kúrrij/ *n.* the ability to face danger, difficulty, uncertainty, or pain without being overcome by fear or being deflected from a chosen course of action ○ *He showed great courage throughout this difficult time.* [13thC. From Old French *corage,* from, ultimately, Latin *cor* "heart" (the source also of English *cordial* and *discord*).]

WORD KEY: SYNONYMS

courage, bravery, fearlessness, nerve, guts, pluck, mettle

CORE MEANING: personal resoluteness in the face of danger or difficulties

courage the most general term, indicating fearlessness and determination, whether physical, mental, or moral, against a wide range of difficulties or dangers; **bravery** a slightly narrower term, emphasizing a lack of physical fear; **fearlessness** a term similar to *bravery,* but less commonly used; **nerve** coolness and steadiness, sometimes with the suggestion of calculated risk-taking; **guts** a widely used slang term suggesting boldness or fortitude when faced with a difficult or potentially dangerous situation; **pluck** a dated somewhat formal term similar to *guts,* suggesting resolution and a willingness to continue struggling against the odds; **mettle** a somewhat literary term similar to "pluck," suggesting a spirited determination.

WORD KEY: CULTURAL NOTE

The Red Badge of Courage, a novel by Stephen Crane (1895). Set during the Civil War, it tells the story of an idealistic soldier, Henry Fleming, who panics in battle and temporarily deserts. During a scuffle with another deserter, he receives a minor wound. Returning to battle bearing this "badge of courage," he performs with heroism but is wracked by guilt.

cou·ra·geous /kə ráyjəss/ *adj.* acting with or showing courage —**cou·ra·geous·ly** *adv.* —**cou·ra·geous·ness** *n.*

cou·rante /koo raánt/ *n.* **1.** MUSIC **PIECE OF FAST MUSIC** a musical composition in quick time with three beats to the measure, frequently a part of a baroque suite **2.** DANCE **QUICK DANCE** a dance of French and Italian origin with short quick steps, performed to music in quick time with three beats to the measure [Late 16thC. From French, literally "running."]

cou·reur de bois /kòo rör də bwaá/ (*plural* **cou·reurs de bois** /kòo rör-/) *n.* somebody of French or French and Native American descent who trapped and traded furs in the 18th and 19th centuries in the north and northwest of what is now Canada [Early 18thC. From French, literally "woods runner."]

cour·gette /koor zhét/ *n.* *U.K.* = **zucchini** [Mid-20thC. From French, literally "small gourd," via Old French *cohourde* from Latin *cucurbita* (source of English *gourd* and *zucchini*).]

cou·ri·er /kóoree ər, kúrri-/ *n.* **1. OFFICIAL MESSENGER** a diplomat, soldier, or other person with the responsibility of carrying and delivering official documents **2. SECRET MESSENGER** somebody who carries and delivers something secretly, e.g., illegal drugs, smuggled goods, or information gained through espionage **3.** *U.K.* **SOMEBODY PROVIDING DELIVERY SERVICE** a person or company that delivers documents or small and valuable packages by hand **4.** *U.K.* **TRAVELERS' GUIDE** a paid guide and helper who accompanies a group of travelers and makes arrangements for them, especially somebody employed by a travel agency to do this ■ *vt.* (**-ered, -er·ing, -ers**) *U.K.* **SEND BY COURIER** to send a document or package by a commercial courier service [14thC. From French, literally "runner," from, ultimately, Latin *currere* "to run" (see CURRENT).]

cour·lan /kóorlən, koor laán/ *n.* BIRDS = **limpkin** [Late 19thC. From French, of uncertain origin: probably ultimately from Galibi *kurliri.*]

course /kawrs/ *n.* **1. SEQUENCE OF EVENTS** the progression or development of a sequence of events, especially a development that is normal or expected ○ *events that changed the course of history* **2. PERIOD OF TIME** the progression or development of a period of time ○ *in the course of the afternoon* **3. DIRECTION TRAVELED** the direction or route along which something travels **4. ACTION CHOSEN** an action or series of actions that somebody decides to take ○ *The simplest course would be to say nothing.* **5.** EDUC **CLASS TAUGHT AT EDUCATIONAL INSTITUTION** a session or series of sessions that students attend to learn a subject, often as part of a school curriculum that leads to a degree or certificate **6.** EDUC **PROGRAM OF STUDY** a program of study or training, especially one that leads to a degree or certificate from an educational institution **7. PART OF MEAL** one of two or more different dishes or types of food that are served in sequence during a meal **8. PATH OF RIVER** the route followed by a river or stream or by something very long such as a road or boundary **9. ONWARD MOVEMENT** swift onward movement ○ *Nothing could interrupt his headlong course.* **10.** MED **ESTABLISHED SEQUENCE OF TREATMENT** a sequence of treatment, exercise, or medication that is followed over a period of time **11.** SPORTS **PLACE FOR RACE OR SPORT** an area where a race is run or where a sport in which players progress over the area is played **12.** BUILDING **LAYER OF BRICKS** one of the layers of bricks that make up a wall **13.** SAILING **LOWEST SAIL ON SHIP** the lowest sail or row of sails on a square-rigged ship **14.** SPORTS **GREYHOUND CHASE** a chase or race by dogs such as greyhounds ■ *v.* (**coursed, cours·ing, cours·es**) **1.** *vi.* **RUN FAST** to flow or run swiftly **2.** *vi.* **TRAVEL** to travel or range over an area (*literary*) **3.** *vti.* HUNT **HUNT ANIMALS WITH GREYHOUNDS** to hunt animals, especially hares, with greyhounds or other dogs that hunt by sight **4.** *vt.* HUNT **USE GREYHOUNDS FOR HUNTING** to use greyhounds or other dogs that hunt by sight [13thC. Via French *cours* from Latin *cursus,* the past participle of *currere* (see CURRENT).] ◇ **be par for the course** to be what would be expected ◇ **in due course** after the lapse of an appropriate period of time ◇ **of course 1.** without any question or doubt **2.** used to show that the speaker has just understood something **3.** used to point out a possibility that somebody may not have considered

cours·er[1] /káwrsər/ *n.* **1. DOG THAT HUNTS BY SIGHT** a dog that is trained to hunt its quarry by sight instead of by scent **2. HUNTER WITH COURSERS** somebody who hunts with coursers [Early 17thC. Formed from COURSE.]

cours·er[2] /káwrsər/ *n.* a strong swift horse (*literary*) [13thC. From Old French *corsier,* from, ultimately, Latin *cursus* "course" (see COURSE).]

cours·er[3] /káwrsər/ *n.* a bird related to the plovers that lives in arid regions of Africa and Asia and is a swift runner. Subfamily: Cursoriinae. [Mid-18thC. Anglicization of modern Latin *Cursorius,* genus name, from Latin *cursor* "runner" (see CURSOR).]

course·ware /káwrs wàir/ *n.* computer software designed for educational use [Late 20thC. Formed from COURSE + SOFTWARE.]

course·work /káwrs wùrk/ *n.* work that is assigned to students as part of an educational course and counts toward the grade given for the course

cours·ing /káwrsing/ *n.* the sport of hunting with dogs such as greyhounds that follow their quarry using sight instead of scent

court[1] /kawrt/ *n.* **1. MEETING WHERE LEGAL JUDGMENTS ARE MADE** a session of an official body that has authority to try criminals, resolve disputes, or make other legal decisions **2. JUDGE** the constituted authority presiding over a court of law **3. COURTROOM OR COURTHOUSE** a place where a court of law is held **4. OPEN SPACE WITHIN WALLS** an open space surrounded by buildings and walls, or a roofless area within a building **5. AREA FOR BALL GAME** an area marked out for playing a sport such as tennis or basketball, or a walled area where squash or a similar sport is played **6. MONARCH'S ATTENDANTS** the ministers, courtiers, and officials of the royal household who attend a king or queen **7. MEETING OF MONARCH AND ATTENDANTS** an occasion when a king or queen and the ministers, courtiers, and officials of the royal household are assembled **8. PLACE WHERE MONARCH LIVES** the place where a king or queen and the court are usually in residence **9. IMPORTANT PERSON'S FOLLOWERS** a group of people who devote their time to the service and flattery of a noble, rich, or important person **10. SHORT STREET** a short street of houses that is closed at one end **11. GROUP OF HOUSES** a group of houses built around an open space **12. LARGE APARTMENT BUILDING** a large building containing many apartments or offices **13. LARGE HOUSE** a large and imposing house and the land surrounding it (*often used in place names*) **14. GOVERNING BODY** the governing body or council of an organization such as a corporation or academic institution [13thC. From Anglo-Norman *curt,* ultimately from Latin *cohort-,* the stem of *cohors* "enclosed space, retinue."] ◇ **be laughed out of court** to be ridiculed so severely that what you have to say is not considered seriously ◇ **pay court to somebody 1.** to try to win influence with somebody or to win somebody's approval or favor through flattery or attentiveness **2.** to try to win somebody's love (*dated*) ◇ **rule something out of court** to refuse absolutely to allow something to take place

court[2] /kawrt/ (**court·ed, court·ing, courts**) *v.* **1.** *vt.* **BE ATTENTIVE TO** to try to win influence with somebody or to win somebody's approval or favor through flattery or attentiveness **2.** *vt.* **TRY TO GAIN** to try to gain something, e.g., somebody's attention or admiration, by behaving in ways that are intended to attract or encourage it **3.** *vt.* **RISK EXPERIENCING SOMETHING BAD** to behave in a way that increases the likelihood of failure, injury, or other trouble **4.** *vti.* **TRY TO WIN SOMEBODY'S LOVE** to try to win somebody's love (*dated*) **5.** *vti.* ZOOL **TRY TO ATTRACT MATE** to engage in behavior that is designed to attract another animal or bird as a mate **6.** *vi.* **BE SWEETHEARTS** to spend time together in a romantic relationship as a prelude to getting married (*dated*) ○ *We used to come here when we were courting.* [Early 16thC. From Old Italian *corteare,* which came from Latin *cohors* (see COURT[1]).]

court bouil·lon /koor bóol yòn, kawr bóol yón/ *n.* a liquid used for poaching fish, made with water flavored with vegetables, herbs, and wine or vinegar. The liquid is discarded after the fish is poached. [From French, literally "short broth"]

court card *n. U.K.* = **face card**

cour·te·ous /kúrtee əss/ *adj.* polite in a way that shows consideration of others or good manners [13thC. From Old French *corteis* "courtly," from *cort* "court" (see COURT[1]).] —**cour·te·ous·ly** *adv.* —**cour·te·ous·ness** *n.*

cour·te·san /káwrtəzən/ *n.* a prostitute or mistress, especially one associated with a rich, powerful, or upper-class man who provides her with luxuries and status [Mid-16thC. Via French *courtisane* from a dialect form of Italian *cortigiana* "female courtier," from *corte* "court," from the Latin stem *cohort-* (see COHORT).]

cour·te·sy /kúrtəssee/ *n.* (*plural* **-sies**) **1.** POLITE OR CONSIDERATE BEHAVIOR politeness that shows consideration for other people or good manners ○ *He didn't even have the courtesy to offer me a seat.* **2.** POLITE OR CONSIDERATE ACTION something done out of politeness or consideration for another person ○ *We should certainly go, if only as a courtesy to Helen.* ■ *adj.* **1.** FOR SAKE OF POLITENESS given or done as a courtesy ○ *a courtesy call* **2.** PROVIDED FREE provided free of charge ○ *Your courtesy limousine will take you to the airport.* [13thC. From Old French *curtesie* (source also of English *curtsy*), from *corteis* "courtly" (see COURTEOUS).]

cour·te·sy card *n.* a card given to customers of a supermarket or other business that entitles them to special benefits or privileges

cour·te·sy light *n.* a light inside the passenger compartment of a vehicle that turns on automatically when the door is opened

cour·te·sy ti·tle *n.* a personal title that is used to address somebody out of politeness or as a social convention even though the person is not professionally or socially entitled to it

court·house /káwrt hòwss/ *n.* **1.** BUILDING FOR LAW COURT a building where a court of law is held **2.** COUNTY GOVERNMENT BUILDING a building where the offices of a county government are located

court·i·er /káwrtyər/ *n.* **1.** SOMEBODY AT ROYAL COURT somebody who spends time at a royal court or attends a king or queen **2.** FLATTERER OF IMPORTANT PERSON somebody who is insincerely polite or flattering to a more important person [13thC. Alteration of Anglo-Norman *courteour*, from Old French *courtoyer* "to be at court," from *cort* "court" (see COURT).]

court·ly /káwrtlee/ (**-li·er, -li·est**) *adj.* **1.** WITH REFINED MANNERS showing great delicacy and refinement in behavior **2.** INSINCERELY POLITE insincerely polite or deferential in order to win somebody's favor **3.** OF THE HIGHEST QUALITY rich or fine and suitable for a royal court —**court·li·ness** *n.*

court·ly love *n.* a medieval code of behavior that idealized the love of a knight for a usually married noblewoman and prescribed how they should act toward each other

court-mar·tial *n.* (*plural* **courts-mar·tial** *or* **court-mar·tials**) **1.** MILITARY COURT a military court that tries members of the military and others for offenses under military law **2.** MILITARY TRIAL a trial by court-martial ■ *vt.* (**court-mar·tialed, court-mar·tial·ing, court-mar·tials**) TRY BY MILITARY COURT to try somebody by a military court for an offense under military law

court of ap·peals *n.* a court that has authority to hear appeals of the judgments of lower courts

Court of Ap·peals *n.* the supreme court of the state of New York

court of chan·cer·y *n.* a court of equity, ruling on matters not covered by common law

court of claims *n.* a federal court in the United States that has jurisdiction over claims brought against the government

court of com·mon pleas *n.* a court that has general jurisdiction in some states

court of do·mes·tic re·la·tions *n.* = **family court**

court of hon·or *n.* a military court that investigates questions involving personal honor

court of in·quir·y *n.* a military tribunal that investigates a matter of concern, especially in order to determine whether official charges should be brought

court of law *n.* a court that hears legal cases and issues rulings based on legal statutes or common law

court of rec·ord *n.* a court that has its proceedings placed on an official permanent record and has the power to give penalties for contempt of court

Court of Saint James's *n.* the court of the monarch of the United Kingdom, to which ambassadors are accredited (*technical*)

court or·der *n.* an official order issued by the judge of a court, requiring or forbidding somebody to do something

court plas·ter *n.* cloth treated on one side with isinglass or another adhesive substance, formerly used to bandage small cuts, hide skin blemishes, and simulate beauty marks [So called because of its use by ladies at court]

court re·cord·er *n. U.K.* = **court reporter**

court re·port·er *n.* a stenographer who records the proceedings of a law court and prepares a verbatim report of them

court·room /káwrt ro͝om, -ro͞om/ *n.* a room used for holding a session of a court of law

court·ship /káwrt shìp/ *n.* **1.** TRYING TO GAIN SOMEBODY'S LOVE the act of paying attention to somebody with a view to developing a more intimate relationship **2.** PRELUDE TO MARRIAGE the period of a romantic relationship before marriage **3.** INGRATIATING BEHAVIOR friendly and often ingratiating attention for the purpose of winning a favor or establishing an alliance or other relationship **4.** ZOOL MATING BEHAVIOR behavior designed to attract another animal or bird as a mate, or the time during which an animal or bird engages in this

court shoe *n. U.K.* = **pump**[2] *n.* 1

court·side /káwrt sìd/ *adj., adv.* at the side of an athletic court where a match or game such as tennis or basketball is being played

court ten·nis *n.* the original form of tennis, played on an indoor court whose sides have walls off which the ball may be played

court-watch *vt.* to follow a trial closely by sitting in a courtroom throughout the proceedings, e.g., to demonstrate support for somebody involved in the trial

court·yard /káwrt yaàrd/ *n.* an area of ground that is surrounded by buildings, lies inside a large building, or is adjacent to a building and enclosed by walls

cous·cous /ko͞oss ko͞oss/ *n.* **1.** SAVORY FOOD MADE OF SEMOLINA a food made from semolina and resembling tiny grains. It is cooked by steaming or briefly soaking in boiling water, and is served in the same way as rice. **2.** DISH OF STEW AND COUSCOUS a North African dish consisting of a spicy stew of meat and vegetables served with couscous [Late 16thC. Via French from Arabic *kuskus*, from *kaskasa* "to pulverize."]

cous·in /kúzz'n/ *n.* **1.** UNCLE'S OR AUNT'S CHILD a child of somebody's uncle or aunt **2.** DISTANT RELATIVE somebody to whom somebody is related through the brother or sister of a grandparent, great-grandparent, or even older ancestor **3.** SOMEBODY WITH MUCH IN COMMON somebody with whom somebody feels connected because of similar ancestry or ethnic background, or interests ○ *our Canadian cousins* **4.** TERM OF ADDRESS BETWEEN SOVEREIGNS used by European sovereigns as a term of address for another sovereign or a member of a royal family [13thC. Via Old French from Latin *consobrinus* "mother's sister's child," from *sobrinus* "maternal cousin."] —**cous·in·hood** *n.* —**cous·in·ly** *adj.*

cous·in-ger·man (*plural* **cousins-ger·man**) *n.* = **cousin** *n.* 1 [14thC. from French *cousin germain*; *germain* from, Latin *germanus* "having the same parents" (see GERMANE).]

Cou·sy /kówzee/, **Bob** (*b.* 1928) U.S. basketball player. He led the Boston Celtics to six championships between 1950 and 1963. Full name **Robert Cousy**

couth /kooth/ *adj.* VERY SOPHISTICATED showing very good manners or great social sophistication (*humorous*) ■ *n.* SOCIAL SOPHISTICATION very good manners or great social sophistication (*humorous*) [Late 19thC. Back-formation from UNCOUTH. In Scots it survives from Old English *cūþ* (see UNCOUTH).]

cou·ture /koo to͝or/ *n.* **1.** FASHION DESIGN the design and production of fashionable high-quality custom-made clothes **2.** HIGH-FASHION CLOTHING high-quality clothing made to order by a fashion designer [Early 20thC. Via French from late Latin *consutura*, literally "sewing together," from Latin *suere* "to sew" (see SUTURE).]

cou·tu·rier /koo to͝oree ər, koo to͝oree àyl/ *n.* a designer of fashionable high-quality custom-made clothes [Late 19thC. From French, "dressmaker," formed from *couture* "COUTURE."]

cou·tu·rière /koo to͝oree ər, -èr/ *n.* a woman who is a designer of fashionable high-quality custom-made clothes [Early 19thC. From French, the feminine form of *couturier* "COUTURIER."]

cou·tur·i·fy /koo to͝orə fì/ (**-fied, -fy·ing, -fies**) *vt.* to make a garment more stylish or fancier by using fine fabrics, unusual colors, handwork, and other elements of designer clothing (*informal*) [Late 20thC. Formed from COUTURE.]

cou·vade /koo vaàd/ *n.* the mimicking of childbirth by the father while it is taking place, a custom in some Native South American societies [Mid-19thC. From French, literally "hatching," from *couver* "to hatch," from Latin *cubare* "to lie down" (see CUBICLE).]

co·va·lence /kō váyləns/ *n.* chemical valence involving the sharing of electrons

co·va·len·cy /kō váylənsee/ *n. U.K.* = **covalence**

co·va·lent /kō váylənt/ *adj.* used to describe a chemical bond in which the attractive force between atoms is created by the sharing of electrons —**co·va·lent·ly** *adv.*

co·va·lent bond *n.* a chemical bond between two atoms created by the sharing of a pair of electrons

co·var·i·ance /kō váiree əns/ *n.* a statistical measure of the tendency of two variables to change in conjunction with each other. It is equal to the product of their standard deviations and correlation coefficients.

co·var·i·ant /kō váiree ənt/ *adj.* exhibiting a tendency to change in conjunction with another statistical variable

Co·var·ru·bi·as /kōvə ro͞obee əss/, **Miguel** (1904–57) Mexican artist, author and ethnologist. He was known for his book and magazine illustrations, and his ethnographic studies of Native Americans.

cove /kōv/ *n.* **1.** BAY IN SHORELINE a small bay on the shore of the sea or a lake, especially one that is enclosed by high cliffs **2.** NOOK IN CLIFF a small semicircular recessed valley in the side of a hill or cliff **3.** CURVE AT TOP OF WALL an inwardly curved surface at the point where a wall meets a ceiling **4.** CURVED MOLDING a molding that curves inward ■ *vti.* (**coved, cov·ing, coves**) MAKE WITH OR HAVE INWARD CURVE to have a cove, or design or build a wall with a cove [Old English *cofa* "bedchamber, alcove." Ultimately from a prehistoric Germanic word meaning "hollow place providing shelter," which is also the ancestor of English *cubby*.]

co·vel·lite /kō vé lìt, kōvə-/ *n.* a purple mineral consisting of thin sheets of copper sulfide [Mid-19thC. Named for the Italian mineralogist Nicolò *Covelli* (1790–1829).]

cov·en /kúvv'n, kōv'n/ *n.* a meeting or group of witches, usually 13 in number [Mid-17thC. From Anglo-Norman "assembly" (see CONVENT) from, ultimately, Latin *convenire* (see CONVENE).]

cov·e·nant /kúvvənənt/ *n.* **1.** SOLEMN AGREEMENT a solemn agreement that is binding on all parties **2.** LAW LEGALLY BINDING AGREEMENT a formal and legally binding agreement or contract such as a lease, or one of the clauses in an agreement of this kind. A covenant is often used to require an owner or user of a parcel of land to do or refrain from doing something. **3.** LAW LAWSUIT FOR BREACH OF AGREEMENT a lawsuit for damages that is brought because of the breaking of a legal covenant **4.** BIBLE MUTUAL PROMISES OF GOD AND ISRAELITES the promises that were made in the Bible between God and the Israelites, who agreed to worship no other gods ■ *vti.* (**-nant·ed, -nant·ing, -nants**) AGREE IN COVENANT to promise something in a covenant [13thC. From Old French, the present participle of *convenir* "to agree" (see CONVENE).] —**cov·e·nant·al** /kùvvə nánt'l/ *adj.* —**cov·e·nant·al·ly** *adv.*

Cov·e·nant *n.* any of several agreements in the 17th century by which Scottish Presbyterians united to defend their church

cov·e·nan·tee /kùvvənən teé/ *n.* somebody to whom something is promised in a covenant

cov·e·nan·ter /kúvvənəntər/, **cov·e·nan·tor** *n.* somebody who joins in a covenant or undertakes an obligation in a covenant

Cov·e·nant·er *n.* somebody who joined in a Covenant

during the 17th century to defend the Scottish Presbyterian church

Cov·en·try /kóvvəntree, kúvvən-/ **1.** historic cathedral city in Warwickshire, England, and the home of Warwick University. It has also been a car manufacturing center. Population: 303,600 (1995). **2.** town in western Rhode Island, on the northern bank of the Pawtuxet River. Population: 32,221 (1996).

co-ven·ture, coven·ture *vti.* **UNDERTAKE AS JOINT VENTURE** to undertake a business venture in partnership with another individual or company ■ *n.* **BUSINESS PARTNERSHIP** a business agreement, deal, partnership involving two or more companies

cov·er /kúvvər/ *v.* (**cov·ered, cov·er·ing, covers**) **1.** *vt.* **PUT SOMETHING OVER** to put something over the whole of or the upper surface of something, e.g., in order to hide, protect, or decorate it **2.** *vt.* **BE ALL OVER** to lie across or in a layer over the whole of or the upper surface of something ○ *rocks covered with seaweed* **3.** *vt.* **KEEP WARM** to put something such as a blanket over or around somebody for warmth ○ *She covered him with the quilt.* **4.** *vt.* **BE WRAPPED AROUND** to be lying over or wrapped around somebody to provide warmth ○ *He was covered only by a thin blanket.* **5.** *vt.* **PUT CLOTHING ON** to put a piece of clothing on part of your own or somebody else's body ○ *Keep your head covered if you are going out.* **6.** *vt.* **BE WORN ON** to be worn on part of the body **7.** *vt.* **PUT LID ON** to put a lid or protective covering over something **8.** *vt.* **TALK OR WRITE ABOUT** to deal with a subject in a discussion, speech, book, or article ○ *His talk covered several aspects of company law.* **9.** *vt.* **PROVIDE NEWS OF** to be responsible for reporting, videotaping, or photographing an event or a particular class of events for a newspaper or a broadcasting company ○ *We cover everything that has a financial angle.* **10.** *vt.* **INCLUDE PARTICULAR INSTANCE** to take something into account and provide an adequate treatment of it ○ *Unfortunately, the law does not cover cases of this sort.* **11.** *vt.* **EXTEND OVER** to include the whole of a particular area, either physically or as a field of operations or responsibility ○ *an office complex covering three blocks* ○ *a police operation that covered the whole city* **12.** *vt.* **TRAVEL CERTAIN DISTANCE** to travel a particular distance **13.** *vt.* **HIDE STATE OF** to conceal a feeling, action, or situation by presenting a different appearance or directing attention elsewhere ○ *I managed to cover my mistake by changing the subject.* **14.** *vt.* INSUR **INSURE** to provide insurance protection to somebody **15.** *vt.* INSUR **INSURE AGAINST** to provide insurance protection against a type of hazard or risk **16.** *vt.* **PAY FOR** to be sufficient to pay for something **17.** *vt.* **PROTECT FROM ATTACK** to protect somebody, a part of an army, or a piece in chess or another game from attack by occupying a position nearby from which a counterattack can be made **18.** *vt.* **AIM GUN AT** to have a person or place in the aim or range of a gun, especially in order to provide protection against a possible attack **19.** *vt.* **PATROL** to maintain a watch on or a patrol of something, e.g., to track somebody's movements ○ *One police officer covered the rear exit while the others knocked at the front door.* **20.** *vt.* **INFUSE WITH A QUALITY** to bring an overwhelming amount of some quality upon yourself or somebody else (*often passive*) **21.** *vi.* **DO SOMEBODY'S JOB** to do the work of somebody who is absent for a time **22.** *vi.* **TELL LIES FOR SOMEBODY** to keep people from learning something about somebody that is not as it should be ○ *to cover for him by lying* **23.** *vt.* ZOOL **COPULATE WIH FEMALE** to copulate with a female animal, especially a mare **24.** *vt.* CARDS **PLAY HIGHER CARD** to play a card that has a higher value than one already played by another person **25.** *vti.* FIN **BUY REPLACEMENT STOCK** to buy shares of stock or commodities to replace others that were borrowed from a broker and sold with the expectation that the price would fall **26.** *vt.* GAMBLING **MATCH ANOTHER'S BET** to match the amount of money bet by another gambler **27.** *vt.* MUSIC **RECORD NEW VERSION OF SONG** to record a new version of a song that was first sung or made popular by another performer **28.** *vt.* SPORTS **DEFEND AREA AGAINST OPPONENT** to play defense against an opponent or in a particular position or area on a sports field **29.** *vt.* BIRDS **SIT ON EGGS** to sit on eggs in a nest to hatch them ■ *n.* **1. SOMETHING THAT COVERS SOMETHING** something that hides, protects, or covers something, or is used to cover something **2. LID** something that covers the top of a container, e.g., a lid **3. BINDING OF BOOK OR MAGAZINE** the protective binding, thick paper, or boards at the front and back of a book or magazine **4. CLOTH THAT COVERS FURNITURE** a cloth or plastic covering for a piece of furniture or bedding **5. SHELTER FROM WEATHER** something that provides shelter from the weather **6. HIDING PLACE** something that provides concealment or protection, especially undergrowth where animals can hide or a shelter from attack **7. VEGETATION** the plants that cover an area of land **8. DEFENSE AGAINST ATTACK** protection provided, especially to an attacking force, by other forces located nearby or in the air ○ *air cover* **9. PROTECTIVE PRETENSE** a false identity or a pretext that provides protection for somebody such as a spy or a detective **10. SUBSTITUTES FOR WORKERS** people who are available to do other people's jobs when they are absent ○ *We no longer have enough staff to provide cover in emergencies.* **11. PLACE SET AT A TABLE** a place set at a table, especially in a restaurant **12.** = **cover charge 13.** *U.K.* = **coverage 14.** MUSIC **NEW RECORDING OF WELL-KNOWN SONG** a recording by a performer of a song that was first sung or popularized by another performer **15.** MUSIC **UNDERSTUDY** an understudy for a musical role **16.** *U.K.* FIN **ENOUGH MONEY** sufficient funds or guaranteed income to meet a liability or cover a planned expenditure **17.** STAMPS **ENVELOPE** a postmarked envelope ■ **covers** *npl.* **1. COVERINGS ON BED** the sheets, blankets, and other coverings on a bed **2.** *U.K.* SPORTS = **groundcloth** (*usually plural*) **3.** CRICKET **OFF-SIDE FIELD** the area of a cricket field in front of the batsman on the off side that is between cover point and extra cover [13thC. Via Old French *covrir* from Latin *cooperire*, literally "to cover completely," from *operire* "to cover."] —**cov·er·a·ble** *adj.* —**cov·er·er** *n.* —**cov·er·less** *adj.* ◇ **blow somebody's cover** to expose a disguise, lie, or pretense that somebody was using to conceal something ◇ **under cover of something** hidden or protected by something ◇ **under separate cover** in another envelope or package

cover up *v.* **1.** *vti.* **COVER SOMETHING COMPLETELY** to cover somebody or something completely **2.** *vti.* **CONCEAL SOMETHING BAD** to try to conceal that something illegal, immoral, or undesirable has happened or how or why it happened **3.** *vi.* BOXING **PROTECT HEAD AND UPPER BODY** to hide the head and upper body behind the arms as protection against another boxer's blows

cov·er·age /kúvvərij/ *n.* **1. MEDIA ATTENTION** the attention given to an event or topic by newspapers, radio, and television in their reporting **2.** INSUR **INSURANCE PROTECTION** the amount or type of protection provided by an insurance policy **3. MEDIA AUDIENCE** the percentage of all the people in a given area who are reached by a newspaper or radio or television station **4. DEGREE OF COVERING** the degree to which something is covered by something else ○ *the coverage of the ground by the snow* **5.** FIN **AVAILABLE FUNDS** the amount of funds available to cover financial liabilities or commitments

cov·er·alls /kúvvə ràwlz/ *npl.* a one-piece outer garment that covers and protects the clothes

cov·er boy *n.* a young man, especially a handsome model, whose picture is on a magazine cover

cov·er charge *n.* a fixed charge that is added per head to the cost of drinks and food in a nightclub or restaurant, e.g., for bread or entertainment

cov·er crop *n.* a crop planted between main crops to prevent erosion or to plow in to enrich the soil

cov·ered-dish /kúvvərd-/, **cov·er-dish** /kúvvər dìsh/ *adj.* used to describe a community meal of hot dishes (*regional*) ○ *a covered-dish supper*

WORD KEY: REGIONAL NOTE

Covered-dish meal is widespread, from New York State westward across the North and South. It is absent from the Rocky Mountain and Pacific Coast states.

cov·ered wag·on *n.* a large wagon with a canvas roof stretched over arched supports, used by pioneers crossing the plains of North America

cov·er girl *n.* a young woman, usually a glamorous model, whose picture is on the cover of a magazine

cov·er glass *n.* a piece of thin glass used to cover a specimen on a microscope slide

cov·er·ing /kúvvəring/ *n.* something that protects, hides, or covers something

cov·er·ing fire *n.* weapon fire used to protect friendly troops from direct fire from the enemy's weapons

cov·er·ing let·ter *n.* = **cover letter**

cov·er·let /kúvvərlət/ *n.* a usually decorative cover for a bed, placed over the other covers when the bed is not being used [13thC. From Old French *couvre lit* "bed cover."]

cov·er let·ter *n.* a letter sent with another document or package, providing necessary or additional information

cov·er page, cov·er sheet *n.* a form sent along with a fax that gives information about the sender, e.g., the name, address, telephone number, and fax number

cov·er slip *n.* = **cover glass**

cov·er sto·ry *n.* **1. MAIN FEATURE IN MAGAZINE** a magazine feature that is illustrated on the front cover and is the most important article in the issue **2. FALSE STORY** a story made up to deceive somebody, e.g., to provide a false identity for an undercover investigator

cov·ert /kúvvərt, kṓ-, kō vúrt/ *adj.* **SECRET** not intended to be known, seen, or found out ■ *n.* **1. UNDERGROWTH PROVIDING COVER** a thicket or undergrowth in which game can shelter or hide **2. SHELTER** a shelter or hiding place **3. SMALL FEATHER** a small feather around the base of a quill on the wing or tail of a bird **4.** TECH **FLOCK OF COOTS** a flock of coots [13thC. From Old French, "covered," from the past participle of *covrir* "to cover" (see COVER).] —**cov·ert·ly** *adv.* —**cov·ert·ness** *n.*

cov·er·ture /kúvvər chŏŏr, -ər/ *n.* **1. SHELTER** a shelter or covering **2.** LAW **CONDITION OF BEING MARRIED WOMAN** the condition of being a married woman considered to be under the protection and guidance of a husband [13thC. From Old French, formed from *covrir* (see COVER).]

cov·er-up *n.* **1. CONCEALMENT OF SOMETHING UNFAVORABLE** a concealment of something illegal, immoral, or undesirable **2. OUTER GARMENT** a loose item of clothing worn over another garment, e.g., a wrap over an evening dress or a T-shirt over a bathing suit

cov·er ver·sion *n.* = **cover** *n.* 14

cov·et /kúvvət/ (**-et·ed, -et·ing, -ets**) *v.* **1.** *vti.* **WANT SOMEBODY ELSE'S PROPERTY** to have a strong desire to possess something that belongs to somebody else **2.** *vt.* **YEARN TO HAVE** to want to have something very much [13thC. From Old French *coveitier*, from, ultimately, Latin *cupiditas* "cupidity."] —**cov·et·a·ble** *adj.* —**cov·et·er** *n.* —**cov·et·ing·ly** *adv.*

cov·et·ous /kúvvətəss/ *adj.* **1. WANTING SOMEBODY ELSE'S PROPERTY** having a strong desire to possess something that belongs to somebody else **2. YEARNING FOR SOMETHING** wanting to have something very much —**cov·et·ous·ly** *adv.* —**cov·et·ous·ness** *n.*

cov·ey /kúvvee/ (*plural* **-eys**) *n.* **1. GROUP OF GAME BIRDS** a small group of game birds such as partridge, grouse, or quail **2. GROUP OF PEOPLE OR THINGS** a small group of people or things [14thC. From French *covée* "brood," from, ultimately, Latin *cubare* "to lie down" (source of English *cubicle*).]

Co·vi·na /kō veénə/ city in southwestern California, an eastern suburb of Los Angeles. Population: 44,290 (1996).

cov·ing /kṓving/ *n.* = **cove** *n.* 3

Cov·ing·ton /kúvvingtən/ city in the northern part of Kentucky, directly north of Lexington, across the Kentucky-Ohio border from Cincinnati, Ohio. Population: 40,971 (1996).

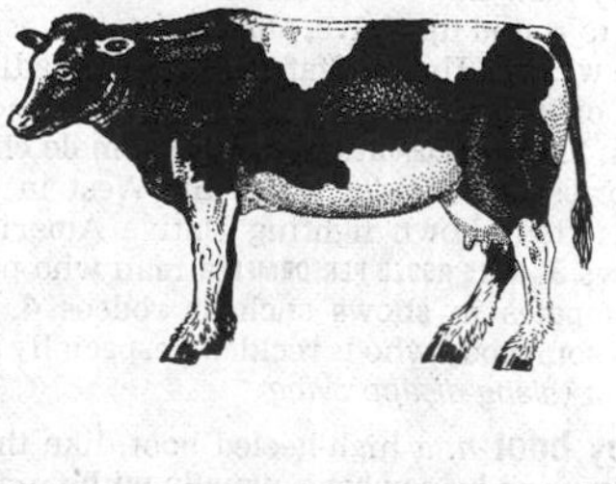

Cow

cow¹ /kow/ *n.* **1. LARGE FEMALE MAMMAL KEPT FOR MILK** an adult female grass-eating quadruped, raised as a farm animal for the milk it produces or for breeding. Genus: *Bos.* **2. MALE OR FEMALE OF DOMESTIC CATTLE** a male or female, whether adult or not, belonging to any breed of domestic cattle **3. LARGE FEMALE MAMMAL** an adult female of a large mammal species other than cattle, e.g., the whale, elephant, seal, or moose [Old English *cū*. Ultimately from an Indo-European word that is also the ancestor of English *beef, bovine* and *bugle*.] ◇ **have a cow** to become suddenly and greatly excited or angry (*slang*) ◇ **till** *or* **until the cows come home** until an extremely long time has elapsed

cow[2] /kow/ **(cowed, cow·ing, cows)** *vt.* to frighten somebody into submission or obedience [Late 16thC. Probably from Old Norse *kúga* "to tyrannize over, oppress."]

cow·ard /kówərd/ *n.* somebody who is too easily or too greatly frightened [13thC. From Old French *cuard*, from Latin *cauda* "tail," the underlying idea probably being the same as in "to turn tail" or "run away with your tail between your legs."]

Cow·ard /kówərd/, **Sir Noel** (1899–1973) British dramatist, actor, and songwriter. He was the author of *The Vortex* (1924), *Private Lives* (1930), *Blithe Spirit* (1941), and *Brief Encounter* (1946).

cow·ard·ice /kówərdis/ *n.* a lack of courage, or behavior that shows such a lack

cow·ard·ly /kówərdlee/ *adj.* **1. NOT BRAVE** caused by a lack of courage, or lacking courage **2. CRUEL AND SPINELESS** showing meanness or cruelty to those who are weaker and fear of those who are equal or stronger —**cow·ard·li·ness** *n.* —**cow·ard·ly** *adv.*

WORD KEY: SYNONYMS

cowardly, faint-hearted, spineless, gutless, pusillanimous, craven, yellow, chicken

CORE MEANING: lacking in courage

cowardly the most general and widely used term, applied to people and their actions; **faint-hearted** a less strong term than *cowardly*, suggesting timidity and lack of resolve; **spineless** a disapproving term suggesting contemptible weakness of character; **gutless** a slang term for *spineless*; **pusillanimous** a formal term suggesting an extreme and contemptible degree of cowardice; **craven** a formal or literary term suggesting an extreme and contemptible degree of cowardice and weakness of will; **yellow** an insulting slang term suggesting extreme cowardice and implying utter contempt; **chicken** an informal term, often used by children and young people of peers who refuse to take part in something daring.

cow·bane /ków bàyn/ (*plural* **-bane**) *n.* **1. POISONOUS N AMERICAN PLANT** a poisonous North American marsh plant of the carrot family. Latin name: *Oxypalis rigidior*. **2. POISONOUS EURASIAN PLANT** a poisonous Eurasian marsh plant of the carrot family, e.g., the water hemlock. Genus: *Cicuta*.

cow·bell /ków bèl/ *n.* **1. BELL ON COW'S NECK** a bell that is fastened to a collar around a cow's neck and clangs as the cow moves, making the animal easier to find **2. PERCUSSION INSTRUMENT** a bell without a clapper, played as a percussion instrument by being struck with a drumstick

cow·ber·ry /ków bèrree/ *n.* **1.** (*plural* **-ries** *or* **-ry**) **CREEPING SHRUB** a creeping flowering shrub that grows in northern temperate areas and produces edible berries. Latin name: *Vaccinium vitis-idaea*. **2.** (*plural* **-ries**) **EDIBLE BERRY** the edible berry of the cowberry plant

cow·bird /ków bùrd/ *n.* a North American blackbird belonging to either of two species that lay their eggs in the nests of other birds and often feed alongside grazing cattle. Genus: *Molothrus*.

cow·boy /ków bòy/ *n.* **1. MAN WHO TENDS CATTLE** a man hired to round up, drive, and tend cattle, especially in the western United States. Cowboys traditionally work on horseback, but now also use motor vehicles. **2. MALE CHARACTER IN WESTERNS** a male character in stories and movies about the West in the late 1800s, often shown fighting Native Americans or outlaws **3. MALE RODEO PERFORMER** a man who performs or competes in shows such as rodeos **4. RECKLESS PERSON** somebody who is reckless, especially a driver or pilot (*slang disapproving*)

cow·boy boot *n.* a high-heeled boot, like those originally worn by cowboys, usually with pointed toes and ornamental stitching

cow·boy hat *n.* a hat, usually felt, with a high crown and a wide brim, originally worn by cowboys, now widely worn in the Southwest and Midwest

cow·boys and In·di·ans *n.* a children's game involving two sides, pretending to be cowboys and Native Americans fighting against each other (*takes a singular verb*)

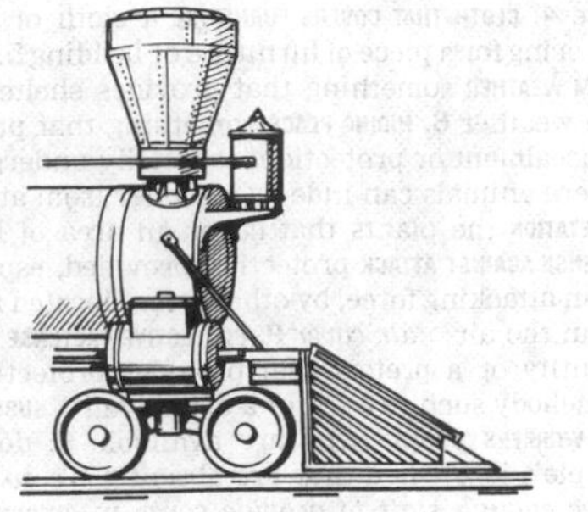

Cowcatcher

cow·catch·er /ków kàchər/ *n.* an angled metal frame formerly fixed to the front of a steam locomotive to clear animals and other obstructions from the track

cow col·lege *n.* **1. AGRICULTURAL COLLEGE** an agricultural college or university (*informal*) **2. SMALL RURAL COLLEGE** a small college or university in a rural area, regarded as unsophisticated (*informal insult*)

cow·er /kówər/ **(-ered, -er·ing, -ers)** *vi.* to cringe or move backward defensively in fear [13thC. From Middle Low German *kūren* "to lie in wait," of unknown origin.]

cow·fish /ków fìsh/ (*plural* **-fish** *or* **-fish·es**) *n.* **1. FISH WITH SPINES ABOVE EYES** a small brightly colored warm-water marine fish with spines that resemble horns above the eyes. Family: Ostraciidae. **2. DOLPHIN, PORPOISE, OR MANATEE** an aquatic mammal, e.g., certain species of dolphin or porpoise, or a manatee

cow·girl /ków gùrl/ *n.* **1. WOMAN WHO TENDS CATTLE** a woman hired to round up, drive, and tend cattle, especially in the western United States **2. WOMAN CHARACTER IN WESTERNS** a woman character in stories and movies about the West in the late 1800s, usually accompanying or assisting a cowboy in his exploits **3. FEMALE RODEO PERFORMER** a woman who performs or competes in shows such as rodeos

cow·hand /ków hànd/ *n.* somebody hired to tend cattle

cow·herb /ków ùrb, -hùrb/ *n.* an annual European plant with clusters of pink flowers that has become a weed in North America. Latin name: *Vaccaria pyramidata*.

cow·herd /ków hùrd/ *n.* somebody who tends cattle, usually on foot (*archaic or literary*)

cow·hide /ków hìd/ *n.* **1. SKIN OF COW** the skin of a cow or bull, especially removed and processed **2. LEATHER** leather made from a cowhide **3. LEATHER WHIP** a whip made of braided leather or rawhide ■ *vt.* **(-hid·ed, -hid·ing, -hides) WHIP SOMEBODY** to beat somebody with a whip made of braided leather or rawhide

cow horse *n.* = **cow pony**

Cowichan sweater /kówichən-/ *n.* *Can* a heavy homespun sweater, originally black and white and knitted with symbolic designs by Aboriginal peoples of the Pacific Northwest coast [*Cowichan* from the name of an Aboriginal people of Canada]

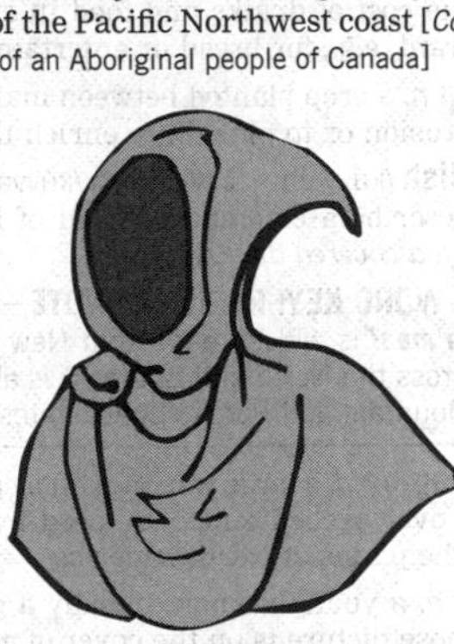

Cowl

cowl /kowl/ *n.* **1. MONK'S HOOD** the hood on a monk's cloak or a monk's hooded cloak **2.** = **cowl neck 3. HOOD FOR CHIMNEY** a hood-shaped, sometimes revolving, cover fitted to a chimney or vent to improve ventilation and prevent downdrafts **4. PART OF VEHICLE BODY** the part of the body of an automobile to which the windshield, hood, and dashboard are attached **5.** ENG = **cowling** [Pre-12thC. Via prehistoric Germanic from, ultimately, Latin *cucullus* "hood."]

cow·lick /ków lìk/ *n.* a tuft of hair growing in a different direction from the rest of the hair on somebody's head and usually sticking up [From its resemblance to a ridge of hair on a cow's hide where hair growing in different directions meets, thought to be caused by the animal licking itself]

cowl·ing /kówling/ *n.* a streamlined removable metal covering for an aircraft engine, fuselage, or nacelle

cowl neck /kówl nèk/ *n.* a collar on a woman's garment, e.g., a sweater, that drapes in large folds around the neck (*hyphenated when used before a noun*)

cow·man /kówmən, -màn/ (*plural* **-men** /-, -mèn/) *n.* **1. CATTLE OWNER** a man who owns cattle or a cattle ranch **2.** = **cowherd**

co·work·er /kṓ wùrkər/ *n.* somebody who works along with one or more other people

cow pars·nip *n.* a tall perennial plant that grows in northern temperate regions and has a thick stem and flattened clusters of tiny white and purple flowers. Genus: *Heracleum*.

cow·pat /ków pàt/ *n.* a circular flat mass of dung excreted by a cow

cow·pea /ków pèe/ *n.* = **black-eyed pea**

Cow·per's gland /kówpərz-, kŏŏp-/ *n.* either of two small glands, just below the prostate, that secrete into the urethra a lubricant fluid that is released just prior to ejaculation of semen. ◊ **Bartholin's gland** [Mid-18thC. Named for the English anatomist William *Cowper* (1666–1709), who first described it.]

cow·pie /ków pì/ *n.* a cowpat (*slang*)

cow·poke /ków pōk/ *n.* a cowboy or cowgirl (*informal*)

cow pon·y *n.* a horse trained for use in cattle herding

cow·pox /ków pòks/ *n.* a mild viral skin disease in cattle, usually affecting the udder with a pustular rash. Cowpox virus was once used to inoculate humans against smallpox. Technical name **vaccinia**

cow·punch·er /ków pùnchər/ *n.* a cowboy or cowgirl (*informal*)

cow·rie /kówree/, **cow·ry** (*plural* **-ries**) *n.* **1. BRIGHTLY COLORED MOLLUSK** a tropical marine mollusk that has a glossy brightly colored shell with a long central toothed opening. Family: Cypraeidae. **2. SHELL USED AS MONEY** the shell of the cowrie, formerly used as money in parts of Africa and Asia [Mid-17thC. From Hindi *kaurī*.]

co·write /kō rìt/ **(-writ·ten** /kō rítt'n/, **-wrote** /kō rṓt/, **-writ·ing, -writes)** *vt.* to write something, e.g., a screenplay or report, jointly with somebody —**co·writ·er** *n.*

cow·ry *n.* = **cowrie**

cow shark *n.* a large flabby bottom-dwelling shark that has a weak jaw and small teeth and lives in warm and temperate seas. Family: Hexanchidae.

cow·shed /ków shèd/ *n.* a building in which cattle are housed

cow·slip /ków slìp/ *n.* **1. PRIMROSE** a common primrose with long-stemmed fragrant yellow flowers that grows in grassy areas in temperate regions of Europe, Africa, and Asia. Latin name: *Primula veris*. **2.** = **marsh marigold** [Old English *cūslyppe* "cow dung," probably from a belief that it grew where a cowpat had fallen]

cow town *n.* **1. CATTLE-MARKETING CENTER** a city or town that is a main market center or shipping point for cattle **2. SMALL RURAL TOWN** a small town in a cattle-breeding area

cox /koks/ *n.* = **coxswain** *n.* 1 ■ *vti.* **(coxed, cox·ing, cox·es)** = **coxswain** *v.* [Late 19thC. Shortening of COXSWAIN.] —**cox·less** *adj.*

Cox /koks/, **David** (1783–1859) British artist. He is known for his watercolors of landscapes in northern Wales, characterized by broad washes and atmopheric effects.

Cox, James Middleton (1870–1957) U.S. statesman. He was governor of Ohio (1913–15 and 1917–21), and ran for the U.S. presidency in 1920.

cox·a /kóksə/ (*plural* **-ae** /-èe/) *n.* **1.** ANAT **HIP** the hipbone or hip joint (*technical*) **2.** ZOOL **PART OF INSECT LEG** the base segment of the leg in most insects and other arthropods [Early 19thC. From Latin, "hip."] —**cox·al** *adj.*

cox·al·gi·a /kok sáljə/ *n.* pain in the hip, or a disease of the hip —**cox·al·gic** *adj.*

cox·comb /kóks kōm/ *n.* (*archaic*) **1. CONCEITED MAN** a conceited man with an excessive interest in clothes and fashion **2. JESTER'S CAP** the cap worn by a medieval jester, shaped like a rooster's crest [Mid-16thC. Alteration of COCKSCOMB.]

cox·comb·ry /kók skōmree, kókskəmree/ (*plural* **-ries**) *n.* foolishly excessive conceit or concern about clothes and fashion, or an instance of this (*archaic*)

cox·sack·ie vi·rus /kŏok saáki-, kok sáki-/, **Cox·sack·ie vi·rus** *n.* an enterovirus belonging to a group that occurs in the human intestinal tract and causes diseases such as viral meningitis and a condition similar to poliomyelitis [Mid-20thC. Named for *Coxsackie* in New York State, where the first cases were identified.]

cox·swain /kóks'n, -swàyn/, **cock·swain** *n.* **1.** ROWING **SOMEBODY IN CHARGE OF ROWING BOAT** the member of a rowing crew who faces forward, steers the boat, and directs the speed and rhythm of the rowers **2. SOMEBODY IN CHARGE OF SHIP'S BOAT** somebody who is in charge of a ship's boat and its crew, and who usually steers it ■ *vti.* (**-swained, -swain·ing, -swains**) **BE COXSWAIN** to be the coxswain of a boat [14thC. From COCK "ship's boat" + SWAIN.]

coy /koy/ *adj.* **1. PRETENDING TO BE SHY** pretending, in a teasing or provocative way, to be reserved or modest **2. SHY** shy or reserved in social situations **3. EVASIVE** annoyingly reluctant to make a commitment or to divulge something [14thC. Via French *coi* "quiet" from, ultimately, Latin *quietus* (source of English *quiet*).] —**coy·ish** *adj.* —**coy·ly** *adv.* —**coy·ness** *n.*

coy·dog /kóy dòg/ *n.* the supposed offspring of a coyote and feral dog, despite a lack of evidence that they interbreed in the wild [Mid-20thC. Blend of COYOTE and DOG.]

coy·o·te /kī ótee, kí ōt/ (*plural* **-tes** *or* **-te**) *n.* **1. N AMERICAN CANINE MAMMAL** a carnivorous North American canine mammal, similar to but smaller than the wolf. Coyotes are known for their howling and yapping at night and are considered pests in crowded residential and farming areas. Latin name: *Canis latrans.* **2. SMUGGLER OF ILLEGAL ALIENS** somebody who brings illegal immigrants into the United States (*slang*) [Mid-18thC. Via Mexican Spanish from Nahuatl *coyotl*.]

coy·o·til·lo /kòyə tíllō, -teéyō, kīə tíllō, -teéyō/ (*plural* **-los**) *n.* a thorny shrub that grows in Mexico and the southwestern United States, with small green flowers and poisonous black berries. Latin name: *Karwinskia humboldtiana.* [Late 19thC. From Mexican Spanish, literally "little coyote."]

Coypu

coy·pu /kóy pōō/ (*plural* **-pus** *or* **-pu**) *n.* a large semiaquatic rodent with webbed feet and a long tail, native to South America. It is reared in captivity for its fur. [Late 18thC. From Araucanian.]

coz /kuz/ *n.* a cousin (*informal*) [Mid-16thC. Shortening.]

coz·en /kúzz'n/ (**-ened, -en·ing, -ens**) *vti.* to deceive, cheat, or defraud somebody (*archaic*) [Late 16thC. Perhaps from obsolete Italian *cozzonare* "to cheat" or Old French *coçoner* "to act as a middle man," both from, ultimately, Latin *coctio* "dealer."] —**coz·en·er** *n.*

coz·en·age /kúzz'nij/ *n.* a getting of something, or persuading of somebody to do something, by trickery or wheedling persuasion

co·zy up *v.* **1.** *vi.* **CUDDLE UP** to sit or lie as close as possible to somebody for warmth or affection **2. INGRATIATE YOURSELF** to try to ingratiate yourself, or become friendly or intimate, with somebody

cp *abbr.* candlepower

cP *abbr.* centipoise

CP *abbr.* **1.** Canadian Press **2.** chemically pure **3.** command post **4.** Communist Party

cp. *abbr.* **1.** compare **2.** coupon

C.P. *abbr.* **1.** command post **2.** Cape Province

CPA *abbr.* **1. CPA, C.P.A.** ACCT certified public accountant **2.** COMPUT critical path analysis

CPB, C.P.B. *abbr.* Corporation for Public Broadcasting

cpd. *abbr.* compound

CPFF *abbr.* cost plus fixed fee

cpi *abbr.* characters per inch

CPI *abbr.* consumer price index

Cpl. *abbr.* Corporal

cpm, CPM *abbr.* **1.** cost per thousand **2.** cycles per minute

CPO *abbr.* Chief Petty Officer

CPOM *abbr.* Master Chief Petty Officer

CPOS *abbr.* Senior Chief Petty Officer

CPR *abbr.* **1.** cardiopulmonary resuscitation **2.** Canadian Pacific Railway

cps *abbr.* **1.** COMPUT characters per second **2.** PHYS cycles per second

CPS, C.P.S. *abbr.* certified professional secretary

CPSC *abbr.* Consumer Product Safety Commission

CPSU *abbr.* Communist Party of the Soviet Union

Cpt., CPT *abbr.* Captain

CPU *abbr.* central processing unit

CQ[1] *n.* the code letters transmitted at the start of a radio message indicating that the message is meant for all receivers and requesting a response

CQ[2] *abbr.* **1.** call to quarters **2.** charge of quarters

Cr *symbol.* chromium

CR *abbr.* PSYCHOL **1.** conditioned reflex **2.** conditioned response

cr. *abbr.* **1.** credit **2.** creditor **3.** creek **4.** crown

C.R. *abbr.* Costa Rica

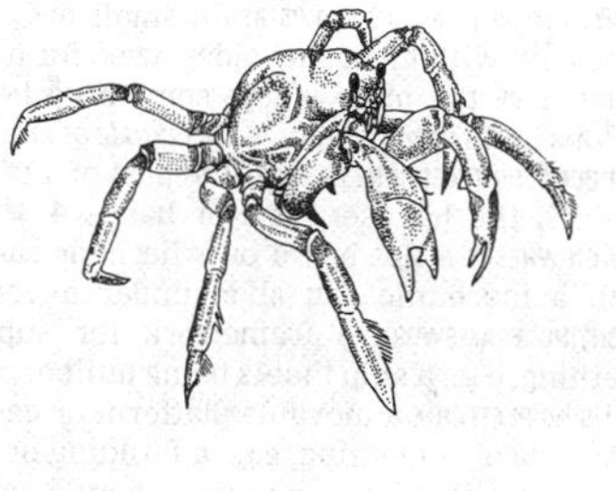

Crab

crab[1] /krab/ *n.* **1. FLAT CRUSTACEAN** a crustacean with a broad flat shell, antennae, a small abdomen, and five pairs of legs, the front pair of which are in the form of grasping pincers. Suborder: Brachyura. **2. CRUSTACEAN RESEMBLING CRAB** an animal similar or related to the true crab, e.g., the hermit crab, horseshoe crab, and king crab **3. FLESH OF CRAB** the flesh of a crab when used as food **4. PARASITIC LOUSE IN PUBIC HAIR** a parasitic louse resembling a tiny crab that infests the pubic hair of humans, causing inflammation and itching of the skin. Latin name: *Phthirius pubis.* **5.** MECH ENG **CRANE** a machine similar to a crane designed to lift and move heavy weights **6.** AIR **FLYING MANEUVER** a flying maneuver in which an aircraft is steered into a crosswind slightly to compensate for drifting off course ■ **crabs** *npl.* **LICE INFESTATION** an infestation of crab lice (*informal*) ■ *v.* (**crabbed, crab·bing, crabs**) **1.** *vti.* **SCURRY SIDEWAYS** to move sideways as a crab does, or to cause something to move in this way **2.** *vi.* **CATCH CRABS** to go fishing or hunting for crabs **3.** *vti.* AIR **FLY INTO CROSSWIND** to fly an aircraft slightly into a crosswind to compensate for drifting off course **4.** *vi.* NAUT **SAIL WITH SIDEWAYS DRIFT** to sail forward with a slight sideways drift caused by a current [Old English *crabba*. Ultimately from an Indo-European word meaning "scratch," which also produced English *carve* and *graffito*.] ◇ **catch a crab** in rowing, to make a faulty stroke by failing to make contact with the water or plunging the oar blade in too deeply

crab[2] /krab/ *n.* = **crab apple** [15thC. Origin uncertain: possibly an alteration by folk etymology (because a bad-tempered crab was likened to a sour apple) of dialect *scrab*, from a Scandinavian language.]

crab[3] /krab/ *n.* **SOMEBODY BAD TEMPERED** somebody who is bad tempered or disagreeable by nature (*informal insult*) ■ *v.* (**crabbed, crab·bing, crabs**) **1.** *vi.* **CRITICIZE** to criticize or grumble about somebody or something (*informal*) **2.** *vt.* **SPOIL** to ruin or spoil something through interference (*informal*) **3.** *vt.* **MAKE BAD TEMPERED** to make somebody bad tempered or bitter [Late 16thC. Probably a back-formation from CRABBED.]

Crab *n.* ZODIAC = **Cancer**

crab ap·ple *n.* **1. SMALL SOUR APPLE** the small sour fruit of a type of apple tree. Crab apples are too sour to eat but are used in jellies. **2. APPLE TREE** an apple tree with white, pink, or red flowers that produces small sour fruit. Genus: *Malus.*

crab·bed /krábbəd/ *adj.* **1. GROUCHY** bad tempered, irritable, or disagreeable by nature **2. HARD TO READ** hard to read, because the words and letters are compressed **3. COMPLICATED** complicated and hard to follow (*dated*) ○ *crabbed logic* [13thC. Formed from CRAB[1] because the way crabs threaten with their claws and their sideways walk suggest bad temper; reinforced by the idea of "sourness" found in CRAB[2].] —**crab·bed·ly** *adv.* —**crab·bed·ness** *n.*

crab·ber /krábbər/ *n.* **1. CATCHER OF CRABS** somebody who fishes for crabs **2. CRAB BOAT** a boat used in fishing for crabs

crab·bing /krábbing/ *n.* fishing or hunting for crabs

crab·by /krábbee/ (**-bi·er, -bi·est**) *adj.* bad tempered or irritable in character [Mid-16thC. Formed from both CRAB[1] and CRAB[2].] —**crab·bi·ly** *adv.* —**crab·bi·ness** *n.*

crab cac·tus *n.* = **Christmas cactus**

crab·grass (*plural* **-grass·es** *or* **-grass**) *n.* a coarse grass that grows in warm regions, has creeping stems that root freely, and is considered a weed in lawns and gardens. Genus: *Digitaria.*

crab louse *n.* = **crab**[1] *n.* 4

crab·meat /kráb meèt/ *n.* the flesh of a crab when used as food

Crab Neb·u·la *n.* the gaseous remains of an exploded star in the constellation Taurus, about 5,000 light years from the Earth

crab's eye *n.* = **rosary pea**

crab stick *n.* a stick-shaped piece of processed fish that has been flavored and colored to resemble crabmeat

crab·stick /kráb stìk/ *n.* **1. STICK OF CRAB APPLE WOOD** a stick or club made from the wood of a crab apple **2. GROUCH** somebody bad tempered or irritable (*informal*)

crab·wise /kráb wīz/ *adv., adj.* **1. SIDEWAYS** sideways, as crabs usually move **2. BY INDIRECT MEANS** in roundabout and cautious way

crack /krak/ *v.* (**cracked, crack·ing, cracks**) **1.** *vti.* **BREAK WITHOUT COMING FULLY APART** to break, or make something break, in such a way that a fine split or splits appear but the split sections do not come apart **2.** *vti.* **BREAK INTO PIECES** to break into pieces, or to break something into pieces **3.** *vti.* **BREAK WITH SHARP NOISE** to break, or make something break, with a sudden sharp noise **4.** *vti.* **MAKE SHARP NOISE** to make a loud sharp sound, or to cause something, e.g., a whip or a rifle, to make such a sound **5.** *vt.* **HIT HARD** to hit something with a powerful impact **6.** *vti.* **BREAK OPEN UNDER PRESSURE** to break open because of pressure, or to make something, e.g., a nut, break or open by pressure **7.** *vti.* **FAIL OR MAKE SOMETHING FAIL** to fail, give way, or break down, or to make somebody or something do so **8.** *vti.* **BREAK DOWN PSYCHOLOGICALLY** to break down psychologically, or to cause somebody to break down psychologically, e.g., under stress or torture **9.** *vi.* **BECOME HOARSE OR CHANGE IN PITCH** to become slightly hoarse or suffer from uncontrollable changes in pitch, especially because of emotion or stress (*refers to the voice*) **10.** *vt.* **TELL JOKE** to tell something, especially a joke (*informal*) **11.** *vt.* **DECODE OR SOLVE** to decipher or solve something, e.g., a code, puzzle, or problem **12.** *vt.* **BREAK INTO** to force a way into something, especially a safe (*informal*) **13.** *vt.* **OPEN SOMETHING TO USE** to open something, e.g., a bottle or book, in order to consume or use its contents (*informal*) 14. *vt.* INDUST **BREAK DOWN INTO SMALLER MOLECULES** to break down something, especially the heavier hydrocarbons in petroleum, into smaller molecules by using heat or catalysis ■ *n.* 1. **THIN BREAK** a break or flaw in something, e.g., a mirror, that is visible as a fine line 2. **LONG NARROW OPENING** a relatively long and narrow break, hole, or opening in something 3. **SHARP NOISE** a sudden loud sharp noise 4. **WEAKNESS** a flaw, defect, or weak spot 5. **BLOW** a hard blow from somebody or something (*informal*) 6. **SARCASTIC COMMENT** a sarcastic, funny, or rude remark, especially at somebody's expense (*informal*) 7. **ATTEMPT** an attempt at something (*informal*) 8. **UNEVEN VOICE TONE** a hoarseness or uncontrollable change in pitch in somebody's voice 9. **EXACT MOMENT** the exact moment when something happens or begins ○ *at the crack of dawn* 10. **crack PURIFIED FORM OF COCAINE** a purified and extremely addictive form of cocaine (*slang*) ■ *adj.* **EXCELLENT** excellent, expert, or trained to a high degree of efficiency [Old English *cracian*, from the same prehistoric Germanic ancestor as Dutch *kräken* and German *krachen*. The original idea was of making a loud noise, the idea of breaking coming from this.] ◇ **be not all he's** *or* **she's** *or* **it's cracked up to be** to be not as good as promised or reputed ◇ **fall between** *or* **through the cracks** to be overlooked or forgotten

crack down *vi.* to take strong and decisive action against something undesirable or illegal or against somebody involved in such activity (*informal*)

crack up *v.* 1. *vi.* **HAVE BREAKDOWN** to experience a psychological or, sometimes, physical breakdown, usually because of stress (*informal*) 2. *vi.* **BREAK INTO PIECES** to crack and break into pieces 3. *vti.* **LAUGH UNCONTROLLABLY** to laugh, or cause somebody to laugh, uncontrollably (*informal*) 4. *vti.* **CRASH** to crash a car, boat, or aircraft (*informal*)

crack·brained /krák brāynd/ *adj.* extremely irrational or eccentric

crack co·caine *n.* = **crack** *n.* 10

crack·down /krák dòwn/ *n.* a strong and decisive measure taken against something undesirable or illegal, or against somebody involved in such activity

cracked /krakt/ *adj.* 1. **HAVING CRACKS** marked with a crack or cracks 2. **IRRATIONAL** extremely irrational (*informal*) 3. **COARSELY CRUSHED** broken or crushed into coarse pieces ○ *cracked wheat* 4. **HOARSE** sounding rough or hoarse vocally, often because of emotion or stress

cracked wheat *n.* whole grains of wheat that have been chopped into little pieces

crack·er /krákər/ *n.* 1. **FLAT CRISP WAFER** a thin crisp, usually unsweetened, and sometimes salted flatbread, often eaten with cheese 2. = **firecracker** 3. **SOMEBODY OR SOMETHING THAT CRACKS** somebody who or something that cracks something 4. **POOR WHITE RURAL SOUTHERNER** a poor white person living in a rural area, especially in the South (*offensive*) 5. **SOMEBODY FROM GEORGIA OR FLORIDA** somebody who comes from or lives in the states of Georgia or Florida (*informal humorous*) 6. INDUST **DEVICE FOR CRACKING PETROLEUM COMPOUNDS** a device in which petroleum oils and tars are broken down to yield more valuable light fuels 7. COMPUT **SOMEBODY WHO ACCESSES COMPUTER SYSTEM ILLICITLY** somebody who gains unauthorized access to a computer system, especially to acquire or interfere with data 8. *U.K.* **CARDBOARD TUBE HOLDING PARTY FAVOR** a cardboard tube, containing a party favor, that is wrapped in colored paper and opens with an explosive noise when both its ends are pulled

crack·er-bar·rel *adj.* expressing unsophisticated but practical sense or wisdom, such as is regarded as typical of a rural community [The image comes from the village store being a social center, where people might sit on cracker barrels and discuss the world]

Crack·er Jack *tdmk.* a trademark for a snack food consisting of candy-coated popcorn and peanuts

crack·head /krák hèd/ *n.* somebody who is addicted to crack cocaine (*slang*)

crack house *n.* a house or apartment where crack cocaine is sold to addicts and where, sometimes, it is also made (*slang*)

crack·ing /kráking/ *adv.* **VERY** extremely (*informal*) ■ *n.* **BREAKING DOWN INTO SMALLER MOLECULES** the breaking down of something, especially the heavier hydrocarbons in petroleum, into smaller molecules using heat or catalysis

crack·le /krák'l/ *v.* (**-led, -ling, -les**) 1. *vti.* **MAKE RAPID SNAPPING NOISE** to make, or cause something to make, repeated short sharp snapping or popping noises, such as dry wood makes when burning 2. *vi.* **SCINTILLATE** to be lively, energetic, or scintillating ○ *The play crackles with wit.* 3. *vt.* **DECORATE WITH CRACKS** to decorate a piece of pottery or porcelain with a network of fine cracks in the surface of its glaze ■ *n.* 1. **REPEATED SNAPPING NOISES** a series of repeated short sharp snapping or popping noises 2. **FINE DECORATIVE CRACKS** a network of fine cracks created as decoration in the surface of the glaze of pottery or porcelain 3. **crack·le, crack·le·ware PORCELAIN DECORATED WITH FINE CRACKS** pottery or porcelain decorated with a network of fine cracks in the surface of its glaze

crack·ling /krákling/ *n.* **SNAPPING OR POPPING NOISES** a series of repeated short sharp snapping or popping noises ■ **crack·lings** *npl.* FOOD **CRISP PIECES OF FATTY MEAT** the crisp pieces left after the fat has been rendered from fatty pieces of meat or skin, especially of pork

crack·ly /kráklee/ (**-li·er, -li·est**) *adj.* 1. **BRITTLE** brittle or crisp 2. **MAKING SNAPPING NOISES** making or consisting of a series of repeated short sharp snapping or popping noises

crack·nel /kráknəl/ *n.* **BRITTLE BISCUIT** a hard light brittle biscuit ■ **crack·nels** *npl.* **CRACKLINGS** cracklings [14thC. Via Old French *craquelin* from Middle Dutch *krākeline*, a type of small cake, from *krāken* "to crack."]

crack·pot /krák pòt/ *n.* **SOMEBODY UNCONVENTIONAL** somebody who has unconventional or wild ideas (*informal insult*) ■ *adj.* **UNREALISTIC** extremely eccentric or unrealistic (*informal*) ○ *another of his crackpot money-making schemes*

crack-up *n.* (*informal*) 1. **BREAKDOWN** a psychological or sometimes a physical breakdown 2. **CRASH** a motor vehicle or aircraft crash

Cra·cow /kráa kòw, krá k-/ university city on the Vistula River in southern Poland. Its medieval architecture attracts many tourists, but it is also an important industrial center. Population: 745,400 (1995).

-cracy *suffix.* rule, government, power ○ *technocracy* [Via French *-cratie* from, ultimately, Greek *kratos* "power, strength." Ultimately from an Indo-European word meaning "hard," which is also the ancestor of English *hard* and *hardy*.]

cra·dle /kráyd'l/ *n.* 1. **BABY'S BED** a small bed, usually on rockers, with enclosing sides, used for a baby 2. **STARTING PLACE** the place where something begins or develops in its early stages ○ *the cradle of civilization* 3. **SUPPORT FOR TELEPHONE HANDSET** the part of a telephone on which the handset rests or hangs 4. **MECHANIC'S BOARD ON WHEELS** a flat board on wheels or casters on which a mechanic can slide under a vehicle 5. **SUPPORTING FRAMEWORK** a framework for supporting something, e.g., a ship that is being built or repaired 6. **HANGING PLATFORM** a movable platform or cage hung on the side of something, e.g., a building or ship, to hold somebody who is working there 7. **PROTECTIVE FRAME SUPPORTING SHEET OR BLANKET** a frame placed beneath a top sheet or blanket covering a patient to keep it from touching a sensitive part of the body, e.g., after injury or an operation 8. **PANNING DEVICE** a rocking device like a box used in panning for gold ■ *vt.* (**-dled, -dling, -dles**) 1. **HOLD CAREFULLY** to hold or support somebody or something tenderly, carefully, or protectively, especially in a hollow formed with the arms or hands 2. **PUT INTO CRADLE** to put somebody or something into a cradle or something like a cradle 3. **SUPPORT IN FRAMEWORK** to support something in a framework, e.g., a ship that is being built or repaired 4. **NURTURE** to look after a young child, or support something in the early stages of its development 5. **WASH SOIL** to wash gold-bearing soil in a cradle [Old English *cradol*, of uncertain origin: possibly from a prehistoric Germanic word that is also the ancestor of German *Kratte* "basket"] —**cra·dler** *n.* ◇ **rob the cradle** to be romantically or sexually involved with somebody who is much younger (*informal*)

cra·dle·board /kráyd'l bawrd/ *n.* a wooden frame supporting a cloth enclosure for a baby, traditionally worn on the back by some Native Americans in order to carry a baby while working or traveling. Cradleboards are often highly decorated with beadwork.

cra·dle cap *n.* a skin condition that commonly affects the scalp of young babies, causing thick scaling and flaking

cra·dle·song /kráyd'l sòng/ *n.* = **lullaby**

craft /kraft/ *n.* 1. **MAKING THINGS BY HAND** a profession or activity such as weaving, pottery, or wood carving, involving the skillful making of decorative or practical objects by hand (*often used in combination*) 2. **OBJECT PRODUCED BY SKILLFUL HANDWORK** something such as a piece of pottery or carving produced skillfully by hand, especially in a traditional manner 3. **SKILL** skill in making or doing things, especially by hand 4. **SKILLED PROFESSION OR ACTIVITY** a profession or activity that requires skill and training, or experience, or specialized knowledge (*often used in combination*) 5. **GUILD** the people engaged in a skilled trade or profession, considered as a group (*dated*) 6. **DEVIOUSNESS** skill in trickery or deceiving others 7. (*plural* **craft**) **VESSEL** a vessel used for traveling, e.g., a boat, ship, airplane, or space vehicle (*often used in combination*) ■ *vt.* (**craft·ed, craft·ing, crafts**) 1. **MAKE WITH SKILL** to produce or create something with skill and care 2. **MAKE SOMETHING BY HAND** to make something skillfully by hand [Old English *cræft* of prehistoric Germanic origin. Originally "strength, power"; this sense died out in the 16thC.] —**craft·er** *n.*

WORD KEY: SYNONYMS

See Synonyms at ***boat***.

craft beer *n.* a beer that is brewed on a small scale and only distributed locally

craft-brewed *adj.* made by a small-scale brewery in small quantities

crafts·man /kráftsmən/ (*plural* **-men** /-mən/) *n.* 1. **SOMEBODY WHO MAKES THINGS BY HAND** somebody who makes decorative or practical objects skillfully by hand 2. **SKILLFUL PERSON** somebody who does something with great skill and expertise —**crafts·man·like** *adj.* —**crafts·man·ly** *adj.* —**crafts·man·ship** *n.*

crafts·per·son /kráfts pùrs'n/ (*plural* **-peo·ple** /-peep'l/ *or* **-per·sons**) *n.* somebody who makes decorative or practical objects skillfully by hand

crafts·wom·an /kráfts wŏŏmmən/ (*plural* **-en** /-wìmmin/) *n.* a woman who makes decorative or practical objects skillfully by hand

craft un·ion *n.* a labor union for people who work at a particular skilled trade, as distinct from an organization for everyone employed in a particular industry

craft·y /kráftee/ (**-i·er, -i·est**) *adj.* using cunning or trickery to deceive other people —**craft·i·ly** *adv.* —**craft·i·ness** *n.*

crag /krag/ *n.* a steep rough mass of rock forming part of a cliff or mountain peak [14thC. From a Celtic word, probably either Welsh *craig* or Gaelic *creagh*.] —**crag·ged** *adj.*

crag·gy /krággee/ (**-gi·er, -gi·est**) *adj.* 1. **ROCKY AND STEEP** steep and rocky, and forming part of a cliff or mountain peak 2. **RUGGED** rugged-looking with strong prominent masculine features —**crag·gi·ly** *adv.* —**crag·gi·ness** *n.*

Craig /krayg/, **Sir James Henry** (1748–1812) British-born Canadian statesman and soldier. He served as Governor-General of Canada (1807–11).

crake /krayk/ *n.* a short-billed long-legged Eurasian marsh bird of the rail family, e.g., the corncrake or spotted crake [14thC. From Old Norse *kráka*, *krákr* used of several birds, including the raven; probably an imitation of their sound.]

cram /kram/ *v.* (**crammed, cram·ming, crams**) 1. *vt.* **FORCE INTO SOMETHING** to force people or objects into a space or container that is too small to hold them comfortably 2. *vti.* **EAT GREEDILY** to eat food hastily and greedily 3. *vt.* **FORCE TO EAT** to encourage or force a person or animal to eat more than is necessary 4. *vti.* **STUDY INTENSIVELY** to study a subject intensively for an imminent exam (*informal*) ■ *n.* 1. **TIGHTLY PACKED STATE** a situation in which a group of people or things is crushed, crowded, or tightly packed together 2. **PERIOD OF INTENSIVE STUDY** a period of intensive study, especially for an imminent exam (*informal*) [Old English *(ge)crammian*, from a prehistoric Germanic base that also produced English *grapnel* and *crampon*] —**cram·mer** *n.*

Cram /kram/, **Ralph Adams** (1863–1942) U.S. architect. He was a leading exponent of the Gothic revival, particularly in U.S. university buildings.

cram·bo /krámbō/ (*plural* **-boes** *or* **-bos**) *n.* a game in which one player gives a word or a line of verse for which the other players must find a rhyming word or line (*dated*) [Mid-17thC. Alteration of obsolete *crambe* "cabbage, distasteful repetition," via Latin from Greek *krambē* "cabbage" (usually referring to Latin *crambe repetita* "something unpleasant to have repeated," literally "warmed-up cabbage").]

cramp[1] /kramp/ *n.* **1.** PAINFUL MUSCLE CONTRACTION a sudden painful involuntary contraction of a muscle **2.** MUSCLE PARALYSIS the temporary paralysis of a muscle or muscle group caused by repetitive use or overexertion ○ *writer's cramp* ■ **cramps** *npl.* ABDOMINAL PAIN severe pain in the abdomen or adjoining areas, usually of gastrointestinal or uterine origin ■ *vi.* **(cramped, cramp·ing, cramps)** BE AFFECTED WITH CRAMP to experience a cramp [14thC. Via Old French *crampe* from Middle Dutch *krampe.*]

cramp[2] /kramp/ *vt.* **(cramped, cramp·ing, cramps) 1.** CONFINE to confine or enclose somebody or something in a small space (*usually passive*) **2.** HAMPER to hamper or obstruct somebody or something **3.** HOLD TOGETHER to fasten, hold, or press something together with an adjustable clamp **4.** TURN SHARPLY to make the wheels of a vehicle turn sharply ■ *n.* **1.** RESTRICTION something that confines, restricts, or restrains, e.g., a set of shackles **2.** CONFINED PLACE a confined or restricted position or place **3.** DEVICE FOR HOLDING THINGS TOGETHER an adjustable clamp for temporarily holding or pressing objects together **4.** BAR WITH BENT ENDS a metal bar with ends bent at right angles, used in building to hold objects together, e.g., bricks or timbers [14thC. From Middle Dutch *krampe.* Ultimately from a prehistoric Germanic word meaning "bending, compression," which also produced English *cramp*[1], *crimp*, and *cripple*.] ◇ **cramp somebody's style** to restrict or hinder somebody from doing something freely (*informal*)

cramped /krampt/ *adj.* **1.** LACKING SPACE inconveniently or uncomfortably small and confining **2.** PACKED IN packed into too small a space for comfort **3.** HARD TO READ written or printed in small characters that are close together and hard to read

cramp·fish /krámp fìsh/ (*plural* **-fish** *or* **-fish·es**) *n.* = **electric ray**

cramp i·ron *n.* = **cramp**[2] *n.* 4

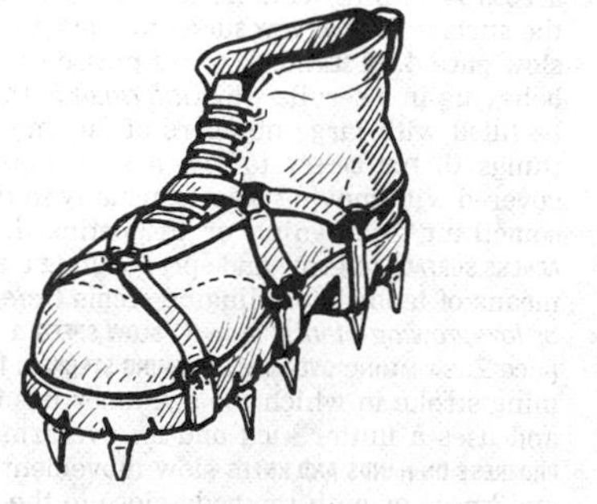

Crampon

cram·pon /krám pòn/ *n.* **1.** SPIKES ON CLIMBING BOOT a set of metal spikes fastened to the sole of a boot or shoe to provide better traction on ice or snow (*usually used in the plural*) **2.** GRAPPLING IRON a grappling iron (*archaic*) (*often used in the plural*) [13thC. Via Old French from Frankish.]

Cra·nach /kraá naakh/, **Lucas, the Elder** (1472–1553) German painter and engraver. Despite his stylized sensuous nudes, he was a friend of Martin Luther, whose portrait he painted. He was also a propagandist for the Reformation. Real name **Lucas Müller**

cran·ber·ry /krán bèrree/ (*plural* **-ries**) *n.* **1.** RED BERRY a sour red or reddish berry, used especially to make a sauce to accompany roast turkey **2.** PLANT PRODUCING RED BERRIES a low-growing evergreen plant of the heath family that yields cranberries. Genus: *Vaccinium.* [Mid-17thC. From German *Kranbeere*, literally "crane berry," because the stamens are said to look like a crane's beak.]

cran·ber·ry bush, **cran·ber·ry tree** *n.* a North American shrub that produces acid red fruit. Latin name: *Viburnum trilobum.*

Cran·brook /krán broòk/ city in southeastern British Columbia, Canada, some 30 mi./60 km north of the U.S. border. Population: 18,131 (1996).

Crane

crane /krayn/ *n.* **1.** LIFTING MACHINE a large machine used to lift and move heavy objects by means of a hook attached to cables suspended from a supporting, usually movable, beam **2.** MOVING SUPPORT FOR CAMERA a moving platform with a long support for a motion-picture or television camera **3.** MOVABLE SUPPORT WITH LONG ARM a device with a long arm for supporting something, e.g., one for swinging and holding a pot or kettle over a fire **4.** BIRDS LONG-LEGGED BIRD a large long-necked long-legged short-tailed bird that lives on plains and in marshes. Family: Gruidae. **5.** BIRDS BIRD LIKE CRANE any bird, e.g., a heron or stork, that looks like a true crane ■ *v.* **(craned, cran·ing, cranes) 1.** *vti.* STRETCH NECK TO SEE to stretch the neck in order to get a better view of something **2.** *vt.* MOVE BY CRANE to lift or move something using a crane [Old English *cran.* Ultimately from an Indo-European word that was probably an imitation of the sound of the bird, and which also produced English *geranium.*]

Crane /krayn/, **Hart** (1899–1932) U.S. poet. His work celebrated modern civilization in poems such as *The Bridge* (1930). Full name **Harold Hart Crane**

Crane, Stephen (1871–1900) U.S. writer. He is known for his novel *The Red Badge of Courage* (1895) and other fiction and poetry.

crane fly *n.* a large two-winged fly with a long thin body and long legs. Family: Tipulidae.

cranes·bill /kráynz bìl/ *n.* = **geranium** *n.* 2

crani- *prefix.* = **cranio-**

cra·ni·a plural of **cranium**

cra·ni·al /kráynee əl/ *adj.* relating to, involving, or in the skull, especially the part covering the brain

cra·ni·al in·dex *n.* = **cephalic index**

cra·ni·al nerve *n.* one of a pair of nerves that originate in the brainstem and pass out of the skull to the surface of the body. There are 12 pairs of cranial nerves in mammals, birds, and reptiles, and usually 10 in fish and amphibians.

cra·ni·ate /kráynee ət, -àyt/ *adj.* having a skull or cranium

cranio- *prefix.* cranium, skull ○ *craniofacial* [From CRANIUM]

cra·ni·o·fa·cial /kràyni ō fáysh'l/ *adj.* relating to or involving both the cranium and the face

cra·ni·ol·o·gy /kràynee óllәjee/ *n.* the scientific study of the shapes, sizes, and other characteristics of human skulls —**cra·ni·o·log·i·cal** /-ə lójjik'l/ *adj.* —**cra·ni·o·log·i·cal·ly** *adv.* —**cra·ni·ol·o·gist** /-ólləjist/ *n.*

cra·ni·om·e·ter /kràynee ómmətər/ *n.* an instrument used to take measurements of the skull

cra·ni·om·e·try /kràynee ómmətree/ *n.* the scientific measurement of skulls —**cra·ni·o·met·ric** /kràynee ə méttrik/ *adj.* —**cra·ni·o·met·ri·cal** *adj.* —**cra·ni·o·met·ri·cal·ly** *adv.* —**cra·ni·om·e·trist** /-ómmətrist/ *n.*

cra·ni·o·sac·ral /kràyni ō sákrəl, -sáy-/ *adj.* = **parasympathetic**

cra·ni·o·sac·ral ther·a·py *n.* gentle manipulation of the bones of the face, skull, and spine, intended to relieve conditions including migraine, sinusitis, and musculoskeletal problems

cra·ni·ot·o·my /kràynee óttəmee/ (*plural* **-mies**) *n.* cutting open the skull to expose the brain, especially for brain surgery

cra·ni·um /kráynee əm/ (*plural* **-ums** *or* **-a** /-nee ə/) *n.* the skull of a vertebrate, especially the part that covers the brain [15thC. Via medieval Latin from Greek *kranion.*]

crank[1] /krangk/ *n.* **1.** MECHANICAL DEVICE FOR TRANSMITTING MOTION a device consisting of an arm or handle that is connected to a shaft at right angles, enabling the transmission of motion to or from the shaft. A crank may be used for changing rotary motion to reciprocating motion or vice versa. **2.** SOMEBODY ECCENTRIC somebody who has unusual or eccentric ideas and opinions, especially ones that are strongly held (*informal*) **3.** GROUCH somebody who is disagreeable and bad tempered (*informal*) ■ *v.* **(cranked, crank·ing, cranks) 1.** *vti.* USE CRANK TO DO SOMETHING to start, move, or operate something by turning a crank **2.** *vt.* FORM INTO CRANK SHAPE to form something into the shape of a crank ■ *adj.* **1.** ECCENTRIC typical of or done by somebody who has unusual or eccentric, often strongly held, ideas and opinions (*disapproving*) **2.** FROM SOMEBODY MALICIOUS typical of or done by somebody who is malicious or playing a prank [Old English *cranc*, from a prehistoric Germanic word meaning "bent, crooked"]

crank out *vt.* to produce something, especially quickly, mechanically, regularly, and in large quantities (*informal*)

crank up *v.* **1.** *vti.* START WITH CRANK to start something, especially an engine, with a crank **2.** *vt.* INCREASE to increase the force, volume, or intensity of something (*informal*) **3.** *vt.* START to get something started (*informal*) **4.** *vi.* TAKE DRUGS to take or inject an illegal drug (*slang*)

crank[2] /krangk/ *adj.* unsteady on the water and likely to capsize [Early 17thC. Origin uncertain: possibly from CRANK[1].]

crank·case /krángk kàys/ *n.* the metal casing that encloses the crankshaft in some engines, especially internal-combustion engines

crank·pin /krángk pìn/ *n.* a short cylindrical bearing piece in the arm of a crank, attached to a connecting rod

crank·shaft /krángk shàft/ *n.* a shaft driving or driven by a crank, e.g., one attached to a connecting rod in an internal-combustion engine

crank·y[1] /krángkee/ (**-i·er, -i·est**) *adj.* **1.** GROUCHY disagreeable and easily irritated (*informal*) **2.** WORKING UNPREDICTABLY not working well and likely to break down or operate unreliably **3.** ECCENTRIC eccentric or obsessive (*informal*) **4.** CROOKED characterized by turns and twists —**crank·i·ly** *adv.* —**crank·i·ness** *n.*

cranky[2] /krángkee/ (**crank·i·er, crank·i·est**) *adj.* SAILING = **crank**[2] *adj.*

cran·nog /kránnəg/ *n.* an ancient Celtic settlement in Scotland or Ireland, usually fortified, built on a natural or constructed island in a lake or swamp [Early 17thC. From Irish *crannóg* or Gaelic *crannag* "timber structure," formed from *crann* "tree, beam."]

cran·ny /kránnee/ (*plural* **-nies**) *n.* a small narrow crack, hole, or opening in a wall or rock [15thC. From French *crané* "notched," from, ultimately, popular Latin *crena* "small notch" (source of English *crenate*).] —**cran·nied** *adj.*

Cran·ston /kránstən/ city in eastern Rhode Island; a southwestern suburb of Providence. Population: 74,324 (1996).

crap /krap/ *n.* (*slang offensive*) **1.** NONSENSE nonsense, or something worthless or annoying **2.** EXCREMENT solid waste matter passed out of the body through the anus **3.** DEFECATION an act of passing solid waste matter out of the body through the anus ■ *adj.* WORTHLESS OR USELESS worthless, useless, or lacking in ability (*slang offensive*) ■ *vti.* **(crapped, crap·ping, craps)** DEFECATE to pass solid waste matter out of the body through the anus (*slang offensive*) [Late 19thC. From Middle English *crap* "chaff," of uncertain origin: perhaps from Dutch *krappe* "something separated"; or via French *crape* "siftings" from medieval Latin *crappa* "chaff."]

crap /krap/ *n.* (*takes a singular or plural verb*) **1.** DICE GAME a U.S. gambling game played with two dice **2.** LOSING THROW a losing throw of the dice in the game of craps [Early 18thC. Origin uncertain: probably from French, variant of *crabs* "score of two ones at dice," from English, plural of CRAB[1], the black dots perhaps being likened to a crab's eyes.]

crap out *vi.* (*slang*) **1.** MAKE LOSING THROW to make a losing throw in the game of craps **2.** AVOID DOING SOMETHING to avoid or discontinue an activity, especially out of fear **3.** RENEGE to fail to fulfill a promise

crape /krayp/ *n.* **1.** = **crepe 2.** BLACK BAND INDICATING MOURNING a band of crepe worn as a sign of mourning around the arm or, in the past, around a hat [Early 16thC. From French *crêpe* (see CRĘPE).]

crape myr·tle *n.* a deciduous Asian shrub or tree, cultivated for its white, pink, or red flowers. Latin name: *Lagerstroemia indica.*

crap·per /kráppər/ *n.* a toilet (*slang offensive*)

crap·pie /kráppee/ (*plural* **-pies** *or* **-pie**) *n.* a freshwater sunfish, with equal-sized anal and dorsal fins, found in lakes and ponds in North America. Genus: *Pomoxis.* [Mid-19thC. Origin unknown.]

crap·py /kráppee/ (**-pi·er, -pi·est**) *adj.* worthless, useless, of poor quality, or badly made or done (*slang*)

crap·shoot /kráp shoo͝t/ *n.* **1.** GAMBLING **CRAPS GAME** a game of craps **2. MATTER OF CHANCE** something that is risky or a matter of chance, the outcome of which cannot be predicted (*informal*)

crap·shoot·er /kráp shoo͞tər/ *n.* somebody who plays craps

crap·u·lence /kráppyələns/ *n.* **1. OVERINDULGENCE** overindulgence, especially in alcoholic drink **2. SICKNESS** sickness caused by overindulgence in good food and, especially, alcoholic drink (*dated*) —**crap·u·lent** *adj.*

crap·u·lous /kráppyələss/ *adj.* (*dated*) **1. REGULARLY OVERINDULGING** regularly overindulging in good food and, especially, alcoholic drink **2. SICK FROM OVERINDULGENCE** suffering from the effects of overindulgence in good food and, especially, alcoholic drink [Mid-17thC. From late Latin *crapulentus* "very drunk," from, ultimately, Greek *kraipalē* "drunken headache, hangover."] —**crap·u·lous·ly** *adv.* —**crap·u·lous·ness** *n.*

cra·que·lure /kra kloo͝r/ *n.* a network of small cracks that sometimes appear on the surface of an oil painting as it ages [Early 20thC. From French.]

crash[1] /krash/ *n.* **1. VEHICLE COLLISION** a collision involving a moving vehicle or aircraft **2. LOUD NOISE** a loud noise such as that made by thunder or by something breaking violently into pieces **3. COMPUTER BREAKDOWN** a sudden complete failure of a computer system, device, or program, usually with an accompanying loss of data ○ *a system crash* **4. FINANCIAL COLLAPSE** the financial collapse or failure of something such as a stock market, involving a massive drop in stock prices, or the collapse of a commercial business ■ *v.* (**crashed, crash·ing, crash·es**) **1.** *vti.* **COLLIDE VIOLENTLY** to strike against something with great force, causing damage or destruction, or to cause something, e.g., a car, to strike against something in this way **2.** *vti.* **MAKE LOUD NOISE** to make a loud noise, or to cause something to make such a noise **3.** *vti.* **BREAK IN PIECES NOISILY** to break into pieces violently and noisily, or break an object in this way **4.** *vti.* **MOVE NOISILY** to move, or cause something to move, noisily, destructively, or violently **5.** *vti.* **HAVE OR CAUSE COMPLETE COMPUTER FAILURE** to experience a sudden complete failure, or cause a computer system to have a sudden complete failure **6.** *vi.* **COLLAPSE FINANCIALLY** to suffer financial collapse or failure **7.** *vi.* **DROP SHARPLY** to decrease in value rapidly and steeply **8.** *vti.* **ATTEND UNINVITED** to attend an event, such as a party, without an invitation (*informal*) **9.** *vi.* **SLEEP** to sleep, especially somewhere other than usual when exhausted, or stay temporarily somewhere other than home (*informal*) **10.** *vi.* **BECOME DEPRESSED** to become depressed as the effects of a drug-induced high wear off (*slang*) ■ *adj.* **RAPID AND INTENSIVE** done intensively over a short period of time in order to achieve the desired results quickly [14thC. Origin uncertain: possibly an imitation of the sound of a crash, perhaps influenced by DASH and CRAZE.] —**crash·er** *n.* ◇ **crash and burn 1.** to fail utterly (*slang*) **2.** to fall asleep or collapse from exhaustion (*slang*)

crash[2] /krash/ *n.* a coarse linen or cotton cloth used for towels and curtains and in the bindings of books [Early 19thC. From Russian *krashenina* "dyed coarse linen."]

crash dive *n.* a steep rapid dive from the surface of a body of water by a submarine

crash-dive (**crash-dived** *or* **crash-dove, crash-div·ing, crash-dives**) *vti.* **1. DESCEND AND CRASH** to dive steeply through the air and crash, or cause an aircraft to do this **2. MAKE RAPID DIVE IN WATER** to make a steep rapid descent from the surface of a body of water, or cause a submarine to do this

crash hel·met *n.* a hard padded helmet worn by motorcyclists, racing drivers, and others to protect the head in case of an accident

crash·ing /kráshing/ *adj.* complete and utter (*informal*) ○ *a crashing bore*

crash land·ing *n.* an emergency landing by an aircraft, usually causing damage to the aircraft —**crash-land** *vti.*

crash pad *n.* **1. PROTECTIVE PADDING IN VEHICLE** padding inside a vehicle to protect the occupants in a crash **2. PLACE TO SLEEP** a place, other than home, where somebody sleeps or stays temporarily (*dated slang*)

crash-test (**crash-test·ed, crash-test·ing, crash-tests**) *vt.* **1. TEST TO BREAKING POINT** to establish the safety and reliability of something by subjecting it to tests, e.g., using heat, pressure, or strain, until it reaches its breaking point **2. TEST VEHICLE IN CRASH** to test a vehicle by deliberately crashing it into a wall to learn how it and its occupants will be affected in an accident

crash·wor·thy /krásh wùrthee/ *adj.* able to withstand a crash —**crash·wor·thi·ness** *n.*

crass /krass/ *adj.* **1. THOUGHTLESS AND VULGAR** so thoughtless, vulgar, and insensitive as to lack all refinement or delicacy **2. UTTER** extreme or flagrant ○ *crass stupidity* [15thC. From Latin *crassus* "thick, solid, fat" (source of English *grease* and *cresset*).] —**crass·i·tude** *n.* —**crass·ly** *adv.* —**crass·ness** *n.*

-crat *suffix.* somebody who supports or is a member of a particular kind of government ○ *technocrat* [Via French *-crate* from, ultimately, Greek *kratos* (see -CRACY)]

crate /krayt/ *n.* **1. BOX** a large open sturdy box used to carry or store objects or built to fit and protect something during shipping **2. OLD VEHICLE** an old rickety airplane or automobile (*dated informal*) ■ *vti.* (**crat·ed, crat·ing, crates**) **PUT IN CRATE** to put or pack something in a crate [14thC. Origin uncertain: perhaps from Latin *cratis* "wickerwork" or Dutch *krat* "tailboard of a wagon." Originally "hurdle, grillwork."]

cra·ter /kráytər/ *n.* **1. VOLCANO SUMMIT** a circular funnel-shaped depression produced by volcanic eruption **2. METEORITE IMPACT AREA** a bowl-shaped hole on the surface of the Moon or a planet caused by the impact of a meteorite **3. EXPLOSION HOLE** a large hole in the ground or a surface caused by an explosion **4.** *U.K.* = **krater** ■ *vti.* (**-tered, -ter·ing, -ters**) **FORM CRATERS** to form craters or make craters form in something [Early 17thC. Via Latin from Greek *kratēr* "(mixing) bowl."] —**cra·ter·like** *adj.*

Cra·ter *n.* a small constellation in the southern hemisphere near Hydra and Virgo

Cra·ter Lake Na·tion·al Park /kràytər-/ park in southern Oregon. Established in 1902, the park includes the circular Crater Lake, situated in the crater of an extinct volcano and the deepest U.S. lake. Area: 183,224 acres/74,148 hectares.

C ra·tion *n.* a canned field ration formerly issued to U.S. soldiers [*C* from *canned*]

cra·ton /kráy tòn/ *n.* the extensive interior of a large block of the earth's crust that has been relatively stable for many millions of years [Mid-20thC. Origin uncertain: either an alteration of *kratogen*, from Greek *kratos* "strength" + -GEN ; or from German *Kraton*, alteration of Greek *kratos.*] —**cra·tonic** /kray tónnik/ *adj.*

cra·vat /krə vát/ *n.* a scarf or band of fabric worn around a man's neck and tied in front. In the United States a cravat may be worn on formal occasions instead of a bow tie. [Mid-17thC. From French *cravate*, from *Cravate* "Croatian," from German *Krabat(e)*, from Serbo-Croat *Hrvāt* "a Croat." From the linen scarfs worn by Croatian mercenaries in French service.]

crave /krayv/ (**craved, crav·ing, craves**) *v.* **1.** *vti.* **DESIRE** to have a strong desire for something **2.** *vt.* **BEG FOR** to beg or implore something from somebody (*archaic*) [Old English *crafian* "to demand," from a prehistoric Germanic word perhaps meaning "to force," which may also be the ancestor of English *craft*] —**crav·er** *n.* —**crav·ing·ly** *adv.*

cra·ven /kráyvən/ *adj.* so lacking in courage as to be worthy of contempt (*literary*) [12thC. Origin uncertain: perhaps via Anglo-Norman from Old French *cravanté* "defeated," past participle of *cravanter* "to crush," from Latin *crepant-*, the present participle stem of *crepare* "to break."] —**cra·ven·ly** *adv.* —**cra·ven·ness** *n.*

WORD KEY: SYNONYMS

See Synonyms at ***cowardly.***

crav·ing /kráyving/ *n.* a strong desire for something

craw /kraw/ *n.* **1.** = **crop** *n.* 7, **crop** *n.* 8 **2. STOMACH** the stomach of an animal (*informal*) **3.** *Ireland* **THROAT** the throat or gullet [14thC. From or related to Middle Low German *krage* or Middle Dutch *crāghe* "neck, throat."] ◇ **stick in your craw** to go against your sense of what is right, making you feel anger or resentment (*informal*)

craw·dad /kráw dàd/ *n.* *Southern U.S.* a crayfish [Early 20thC. Origin uncertain: probably an alteration of CRAWFISH.]

craw·fish /kráw fìsh/ (*plural* **-fish** *or* **-fish·es**) *n.* = **crayfish** [Early 17thC. Variant of CRAYFISH.]

Joan Crawford

Craw·ford /kráwfərd/, **Joan** (1908–77) U.S. actor. She starred in over 70 movies, including the Academy Award-winning *Mildred Pierce* (1945). Real name **Lucille Le Sueur**

Craw·fords·ville /kráwfərdz vìl/ city in western Indiana, northwest of Indianapolis. Population: 14,219 (1996).

crawl /krawl/ *vi.* (**crawled, crawl·ing, crawls**) **1. MOVE CLOSE TO GROUND** to move slowly along on hands and knees or with the body close to the ground or a surface **2. MOVE SLOWLY CLOSE TO SURFACE** to move slowly across something with the body close to or touching the surface **3. MOVE VERY SLOWLY** to move forward at a slow pace **4. BE SERVILE** to try to please somebody by behaving in a servile way (*informal*) **5. BE OVERRUN** to be filled with large numbers of moving people or things **6. FEEL CREEPY** to feel a sensation of being covered with moving insects, usually in reaction to something frightening or disgusting **7.** BOT **GROW ACROSS SURFACE** to grow and spread along a surface by means of tendrils or clinging stems (*refers to vines or low-growing plants*) ■ *n.* **1. SLOW SPEED** a very slow pace **2.** SWIMMING **OVERARM SWIMMING STROKE** a fast swimming stroke in which the swimmer lies face down and uses a flutter kick and an overarm stroke **3. PROGRESS ON HANDS AND KNEES** slow movement on hands and knees or with the body close to the ground **4.** CINEMA, TV **MOVING WORDS ON TELEVISION OR FILM** words or figures that are scrolled across a television or motion picture screen to convey information, e.g., programming credits or news bulletins [14thC. Origin uncertain: probably from Old Norse *krafla* "to paw with the hands."] —**crawl·ing·ly** *adv.*

crawl·er /kráwlər/ *n.* **1. SOMETHING THAT CRAWLS** an insect or other animal that crawls **2. VEHICLE WITH TRACKS** a vehicle that has continuous tracks of linked plates instead of wheels

crawl space *n.* a low unfinished space under a floor or above a ceiling in a building that gives access to plumbing, wiring, and ductwork [From having to crawl through it because of its restricted height]

crawl·y /kráwlee/ (**-i·er, -i·est**) *adj.* causing a shuddery disgust or unease

cray·fish /kráy fìsh/ (*plural* **-fish** *or* **-fish·es**) *n.* **1. ANIMAL RESEMBLING LOBSTER** a freshwater crustacean with large claws like those of a lobster. It is prized for its tail meat. Superfamily: Astacoidea. **2.** = **spiny lobster** [14thC. By folk etymology (influenced by FISH) from French *crevice* "crayfish," from, ultimately, an Indo-European word meaning "to scratch," which is also the ancestor of English *crawl.*]

cray·on /kráy òn/ *n.* **1. COLORED DRAWING STICK** a stick of colored wax, chalk, or charcoal, sometimes enclosed in wood like a pencil, used for drawing and coloring **2. DRAWING** a drawing made using crayons ■ *vti.*

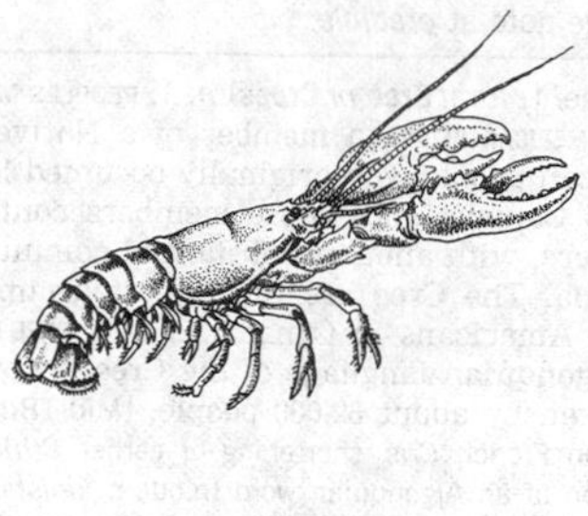

Crayfish

(-oned, -on·ing, -ons) **USE CRAYONS** to draw or color something with crayons [Mid-17thC. From French, "pencil," from *craie* "chalk," from Latin *creta* "chalk, clay" (source of English *cretaceous*).] —**cray·on·ist** *n.*

craze /krayz/ *n.* **1. FAD** a fashion that is extremely popular for a short time **2.** CERAMICS **FINE CRACK** a fine crack in the glaze of pottery. It happens when the glaze cools and contracts at a different temperature from the clay. ■ *vti.* **(crazed, craz·ing, craz·es) 1. MAKE OR BECOME UNBALANCED** to become or make somebody become psychologically unbalanced or unstable **2. PRODUCE CRACKS IN** to produce fine cracks in the glaze of pottery, or to become covered with such cracks [14thC. Origin uncertain: probably from assumed Old Norse *krasa* "to shatter," perhaps an imitation of the sound.]

crazed /krayzd/ *adj.* **1. PSYCHOLOGICALLY UNBALANCED** driven wild or uncontrollable, or showing signs of psychological disturbance **2.** CERAMICS **WITH SURFACE CRACKS** with fine cracks on the surface

craz·ing /kráyzing/ *n.* fine cracks in the glaze of a piece of pottery, produced when the glaze cools and contracts at a different temperature from the clay. When the effect is deliberate, it is often called crackle.

cra·zy /kráyzee/ *adj.* **(-zi·er, -zi·est) 1. UNBALANCED** affected by psychological disturbance or instability, or produced by an unbalanced mind **2. RIDICULOUS** not showing good sense or practicality (*informal*) **3. EXCESSIVELY FOND** excessively fond of somebody or something (*informal*) ■ *n.* (*plural* **-zies**) **UNBALANCED PERSON** somebody whose behavior shows signs of psychological disturbance or instability (*informal*) —**cra·zi·ly** *adv.* —**cra·zi·ness** *n.*

cra·zy bone *n.* = **funny bone** (*informal*)

Cra·zy Horse (1849?–77) Native American leader. As leader of the Oglala Sioux, he opposed and fought against European settlement. Original name **Ta-shunca Witco**

cra·zy quilt *n.* **1. QUILT OF IRREGULAR PATCHWORK** a quilt made of irregularly shaped and patterned pieces of cloth sewn together **2. HODGEPODGE** a confusing mix of things that do not belong or fit together ○ *a crazy quilt of confusing ideas and contradictory suggestions*

cra·zy·weed /kráyzi weed/ (*plural* **-weed** *or* **-weeds**) *n.* = **locoweed**

creak /kreek/ *vi.* **(creaked, creak·ing, creaks) 1. SQUEAK** to make a prolonged squeaking noise **2. MOVE WITH SQUEAKING** to move along while making prolonged squeaking noises ■ *n.* **PROLONGED SQUEAK** a prolonged squeaking noise [14thC. An imitation of the sound.] —**creak·ing·ly** *adv.*

creak·y /kreekee/ **(-i·er, -i·est)** *adj.* **1. CREAKING** making a prolonged squeaking noise **2. STIFF** not able to move easily, especially as a result of aging (*informal*) **3. OLD OR OLD-FASHIONED** showing signs of having deteriorated over time or of being old-fashioned (*informal*) —**creak·i·ly** *adv.* —**creak·i·ness** *n.*

cream /kreem/ *n.* **1. FATTY PART OF MILK** a high-fat liquid product separated from milk and used in cooking and as an accompaniment to desserts **2. CREAMY LOTION** a cosmetic or medicinal preparation that has a thick smooth consistency like cream **3.** FOOD **CREAMY FOOD** a food that contains cream or has a consistency like cream **4. BEST PART** the best part of something **5.** COLORS **WHITE TINGED WITH YELLOW** a white color with a faint yellowish tinge **6.** FOOD **SOFT-CENTERED CHOCOLATE** a chocolate with a soft smooth filling ■ *adj.* **WHITE WITH SOME YELLOW** white with a tinge of yellow ■ *v.* **(creamed, cream·ing, creams) 1.** *vt.* **MAKE CREAMY** to mix ingredients together to soften and combine them **2.** *vt.* **PREPARE WITH CREAM** to add cream to something while cooking it or on serving it **3.** *vti.* **FORM FOAM ON TOP** to form, or cause something to form a frothy layer resembling cream on the surface **4.** *vt.* to remove the cream from milk **5.** *vti.* **FORM CREAM** to form cream, or leave milk to form cream **6.** *vt.* **DEFEAT THOROUGHLY** to defeat somebody thoroughly (*informal*) ○ *We creamed them!* **7.** *vt.* **WRECK BY SMASHING** to wreck or damage something by smashing it into a hard object (*informal*) ○ *She creamed her car against the stone wall.* **8.** *vti.* **EJACULATE ON SOMETHING** to have an orgasm and ejaculate on something (*slang taboo*) [14thC. From French *creme*, blend of late Latin *cramum* (of uncertain origin: perhaps from Gaulish) and ecclesiastical Latin *chrisma* "ointment" (from Greek *khrisma*).]

cream off *vt.* **1. REMOVE AS BEING THE BEST** to take away the best part of something **2. TAKE ILLICITLY** to take and use something for an illicit or unintended purpose (*informal*)

cream cheese *n.* a soft white unmatured cheese with a high fat content

cream·cups /kreem kùps/ *npl.* an annual plant of the poppy family that has small pale yellow or cream-colored flowers. It is native to the southwestern United States and Mexico. Latin name: *Platystemon californicus.*

cream·er /kreemər/ *n.* **1. SMALL PITCHER** a small pitcher for serving cream **2. CREAM SUBSTITUTE** a cream substitute, used especially in coffee or tea

cream·er·y /kreeməree/ (*plural* **-ies**) *n.* **1. PLACE PRODUCING DAIRY PRODUCTS** a place where milk is processed and dairy products are produced **2. BUSINESS SELLING DAIRY PRODUCTS** a business that sells dairy products [Mid-19thC. Formed from CREAM on the model of French *crémerie*.]

cream of tar·tar *n.* potassium bitartrate, used as a leavening agent in cooking, usually in baking powder

cream puff *n.* **1. CREAM-FILLED PASTRY** a sweet pastry made of a flaky shell filled with whipped cream and dusted with powdered sugar **2. EFFEMINATE MAN** a weak effeminate man (*slang offensive*) **3. GOOD CAR** a used car in very good condition (*slang*)

cream sher·ry *n.* a type of smooth sweet sherry

cream so·da *n.* a carbonated soft drink flavored with vanilla

creamware /kreem wàir/ *n.* glazed earthenware of a deep creamy color, first produced in Britain about 1720

cream·y /kreemee/ **(-i·er, -i·est)** *adj.* **1. LIKE CREAM** with a texture, color, taste, or consistency like cream **2. CONTAINING CREAM** containing a large amount of cream —**cream·i·ly** *adv.* —**cream·i·ness** *n.*

crease /kreess/ *n.* **1. FOLD PUT IN FABRIC** a straight line formed in clothing or fabric by pressing **2. UNWANTED FABRIC FOLD** an unwanted line in clothing or fabric that has been crushed or folded **3. SKIN WRINKLE** a line or wrinkle on the skin **4.** HOCKEY **GOAL AREA** the rectangular area in front of an ice hockey goal **5.** LACROSSE **GOAL AREA** the semicircular area surrounding a lacrosse goal ■ *v.* **(creased, creas·ing, creas·es) 1.** *vti.* **MAKE OR ACQUIRE CREASES** to form lines, folds, or wrinkles in something, or to become lined, folded, or wrinkled **2.** *vt.* **GRAZE** to graze the skin and inflict a superficial wound [Late 16thC. Origin uncertain: probably an alteration of *creaste* "furrow, ridge," perhaps a variant of CREST, the ridges in creased cloth being likened to crests.] —**creas·er** *n.* —**creas·y** *adj.*

cre·ate /kree áyt/ **(-at·ed, -at·ing, -ates)** *v.* **1.** *vt.* **MAKE** to bring somebody or something into existence **2.** *vt.* **GIVE RISE TO** to produce something as a result, or make something happen **3.** *vti.* **PRODUCE ART OR INVENT** to use imagination to invent things or produce works of art **4.** *vt.* **APPOINT** to give somebody a new title, role, or office **5.** *vt.* ARTS **PERFORM FOR FIRST TIME** to be the first person to perform a particular role in a production [14thC. From Latin *creat-*, the past participle stem of *creare* "to bring forth, produce" (source of English *creature*), of uncertain origin: perhaps formed from *crescere* "to grow."]

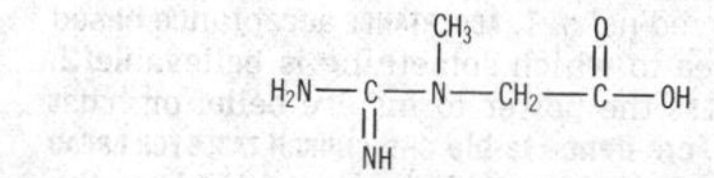

Creatine

cre·a·tine /kree ə teen, -t'n/, **cre·a·tin** /-tin/ *n.* an amino acid formed during metabolism and used as an energy-storage molecule in vertebrate muscle tissue, usually as phosphocreatine. Formula: $C_4H_9O_2N_3$. [Mid-19thC. Coined from assumed Greek *kreat-* the stem of assumed *kreas* "flesh" (source of English *pancreas*) + -INE.]

cre·a·tine ki·nase *n.* an enzyme that aids the breakdown of phosphocreatine into creatine and phosphoric acid, with a release of energy

cre·a·tine phos·phate *n.* = **phosphocreatine**

cre·at·i·nine /kree àtt'n een/ *n.* a derivative of creatine found in muscle, blood, and urine. Formula: $C_4H_7ON_3$. [Mid-19thC. Coined from CREATINE + -INE.]

cre·a·tion /kree áysh'n/ *n.* **1. MAKING SOMETHING** the bringing of something into existence **2. EARTH AND ITS INHABITANTS** the world and everything on it **3. SOMETHING CREATED BY SOMEBODY** a product of human imagination or invention **4. ELABORATE GARMENT** an elaborate or striking article of clothing —**cre·a·tion·al** *adj.*

Cre·a·tion *n.* **1. GOD'S MAKING OF UNIVERSE** the act of God that, according to the Bible, brought the universe and all living beings into existence **2. UNIVERSE** the universe as created by God, according to the Bible

cre·a·tion·ism /kree áysh'n ìzzəm/ *n.* the belief that the Bible's account of the Creation is literally true —**cre·a·tion·ist** *adj.*, *n.*

cre·a·tion sci·ence *n.* the attempt to provide scientific proof for the account of God's creation of the world that is described in the Bible

cre·a·tive /kree áytiv/ *adj.* **1. ABLE TO CREATE** able to create things **2. NEW AND ORIGINAL** using or showing use of the imagination to create new ideas or things ○ *a creative approach to the problem of lack of space* **3. RESOURCEFUL** making imaginative use of the limited resources available **4.** FIN **INTENTIONALLY DECEPTIVE ABOUT FINANCIAL INFORMATION** employing deceptive methods to distort financial records (*ironic*) ○ *creative accounting* ○ *creative bookkeeping* ■ *n.* **IDEAS PERSON** somebody who is responsible for coming up with new ideas and concepts for sales campaigns (*informal*) ○ *ad agency creatives hard at work on a TV infomercial series* —**cre·a·tive·ly** *adv.* —**cre·a·tive·ness** *n.*

cre·a·tive writ·ing *n.* the writing of fiction, poetry, or drama, often as an exercise, or the work written

cre·a·tiv·i·ty /kree ay tívvitee/ *n.* **1. BEING CREATIVE** the quality of being creative **2. IMAGINATIVE ABILITY** the ability to use the imagination to develop new and original ideas or things, especially in an artistic context

cre·a·tor /kree áytər/ *n.* somebody who brings something into existence —**cre·a·tor·ship** *n.*

Cre·a·tor *n.* God regarded as creator of the universe

crea·ture /kreechər/ *n.* **1. LIVING BEING** any living person or animal **2. UNPLEASANT LIVING BEING** an unpleasant or frightening living thing **3. CREATED THING** somebody or something that has been created ○ *a creature of your imagination* **4. TYPE OF PERSON** somebody of a particular type ○ *He's a harmless creature.* **5. SUBSERVIENT PERSON** somebody who is under the influence of somebody or something else [13thC. Directly or via French from late Latin *creatura*, from Latin *creat-* (see CREATE).] —**crea·tur·al** *adj.* —**crea·ture·hood** *n.*

crea·ture com·forts *npl.* things considered necessary for a comfortable life

crèche /kresh, kraysh/ *n.* **1. NATIVITY SCENE** a three-dimensional representation of the scene at the birth of Jesus **2. FOUNDLING HOSPITAL** a hospital for abandoned children **3.** *U.K.* **CHILDCARE FACILITY** a place where small children are looked after while their parents or guardians are working or doing something else [Late 18thC. Via French, "crib," from assumed Vulgar Latin *creppia*, from a prehistoric Germanic word that is also the ancestor of English *crib*.]

cre·dence /kreed'ns/ *n.* **1.** ACCEPTANCE acceptance based on the degree to which something is believable **2.** TRUSTWORTHINESS the power to inspire belief or trust **3. cre·dence, cre·dence ta·ble** CHR CHURCH TABLE FOR BREAD AND WINE a small shelf or table in a church where the bread, wine, and vessels used for the Eucharist are kept [14thC. Directly or via French from medieval Latin *credentia* "belief," from Latin *credent-*, the present participle stem of *credere* "to believe."]

cre·den·tial /krə dénshəl/ *n.* **1.** PROOF OF ABILITY OR TRUSTWORTHINESS a certificate, letter, or experience that qualifies somebody to do something **2.** AUTHENTICATION anything that provides authentication for a claim ■ **credentials** *npl.* OFFICIAL IDENTIFICATION a letter, badge, or other official identification that confirms somebody's position or status ■ *vt.* **(-tialed, -tial·ing, -tials)** GIVE CREDENTIALS to provide with official credentials [15thC. From medieval Latin *credentialis* "entitling confidence," from *credentia* belief (see CREDENCE).]

cre·den·tial·ism /krə dénsh'l ìzzəm/ *n.* an overemphasis on educational credentials when assessing somebody's qualifications, e.g., for a job

cre·den·za /krə dénzə/ *n.* **1.** BUFFET a buffet or sideboard, usually without legs **2.** LOW OFFICE CABINET a low piece of office furniture that has enclosed shelf space [Late 19thC. Via Italian from medieval Latin *credentia* "side table" (see CREDENCE).]

cred·i·bil·i·ty /krèddə bíllətee/ *n.* **1.** BELIEVABILITY the ability to inspire belief or trust **2.** WILLINGNESS TO BELIEVE a willingness to accept something as true

cred·i·bil·i·ty gap *n.* **1.** DISTRUST OF OFFICIAL STATEMENTS a situation in which the public distrusts the accuracy of official statements **2.** LACK OF TRUST any situation in which a lack of trust exists between two groups **3.** DISCREPANCY BETWEEN CLAIM AND TRUTH an apparent difference between what is claimed to be true and what is in fact true

cred·i·ble /kréddəb'l/ *adj.* **1.** BELIEVABLE easy to believe **2.** TRUSTWORTHY inspiring trust and confidence **3.** MIL MILITARILY EFFECTIVE of sufficient strength to function effectively as a military force [14thC. From Latin *credibilis*, from *credere* "to believe" (source of English *creed*, and *miscreant*).] —**cred·i·bly** *adv.* —**cred·i·ble·ness** *n.*

WORD KEY: USAGE

credible, creditable, or **credulous?** These three adjectives, and the corresponding nouns *credibility, credit,* and *credulity*, are sometimes confused. Something or somebody is ***credible*** when it (or he or she) can be easily or readily believed. Somebody is ***credulous*** when he or she is all too ready to believe. *My story may sound barely credible but I assure you it's true. Only the most credulous person would believe such a story.* ***Credible*** has the special newer meaning "inspiring confidence": *The government needs to develop a credible monetary policy.* ***Creditable*** is connected with the word *credit* and means "bringing credit": *An excellent squash player, she plays a creditable game of tennis as well.*

cred·it /kréddit/ *n.* **1.** RECOGNITION praise or recognition for something done or achieved **2.** SOURCE OF PRIDE somebody or something that is a source of pride or honor **3.** GOOD REPUTATION somebody's good reputation among or influence with other people ○ *She has a lot of credit with this commmunity.* **4.** COMM PAY-LATER SYSTEM an arrangement by which a buyer can take possession of something now and pay for it later or over time ○ *offer credit* ○ *buy on credit* **5.** COMM TIME TO PAY the time allowed for payment of something by credit **6.** FIN FINANCIAL STATUS somebody's financial status or reputation **7.** COMM SPENDING ENTITLEMENT AT STORE money that a customer is owed by a store and is entitled to spend there **8.** COMM BALANCE IN ACCOUNT the amount of money in an account after debts have been charged against it **9.** FIN MONEY PAID INTO ACCOUNT an amount of money paid into an account **10.** FIN AMOUNT BANK WILL LEND the amount of money that a financial institution is prepared to lend somebody **11.** ACKNOWLEDGMENT OF SOMEBODY'S ROLE a mention of the role that somebody played in an endeavor, especially an artistic one **12.** ACCT DEDUCTION OF PAYMENT FROM OWED AMOUNT the deduction from a business account of an amount owed paid from the amount **13.** ACCT ACCOUNT PAYMENTS COLUMN the right-hand side of an account record, where payments to the account are recorded **14.** ACCT PAYMENT RECORDED a payment recorded against an amount owed **15.** EDUC COURSE UNIT a unit of study, often equivalent to an hour of class time, in a course of higher education **16.** EDUC RECOGNITION OF COURSE COMPLETION official recognition that a student has satisfactorily completed a course of study ○ *get credit for a course* ■ **cred·its** *npl.* CINEMA, TV LIST OF ACKNOWLEDGMENTS a listing of the people involved in a film or television production, together with their roles or jobs ■ *vt.* **(-it·ed, -it·ing, -its) 1.** BELIEVE to accept that something is true **2.** RECOGNIZE to recognize somebody as the person responsible for an achievement **3.** ATTRIBUTE to ascribe something such as a personal quality to somebody **4.** FIN ADD TO BANK ACCOUNT to add an amount of money to somebody's account **5.** ACCT RECORD PAYMENT OF to record an amount of money as a payment in an accounting record **6.** ACCT RECORD PAYMENT TO to enter a credit in the record of somebody's account **7.** EDUC MAKE EDUCATIONAL AWARD TO to award a credit to a student for successful completion of a course of study [Mid-16thC. From French, ultimately from Latin *creditum* "loan," from the past participle of *credere* "to entrust, believe." The underlying idea is of something entrusted.] —**cred·it·al** *adj.* ◇ **to somebody's credit** commendable of somebody

WORD KEY: ORIGIN

Credit is derived from Latin *credere*, meaning "to believe," which is also the source of English *credible, creed, grant,* and *miscreant*.

cred·it·a·ble /krédditəb'l/ *adj.* bringing credit or worthy of praise —**cred·it·a·bil·i·ty** /krèdditə bíllətee/ *n.* —**cred·it·a·ble·ness** /krédditəb'lnəss/ *n.* —**cred·it·a·bly** *adv.*

WORD KEY: USAGE

See Usage note at ***credible***.

cred·it ac·count *n.* *U.K.* = **charge account**

cred·it bu·reau *n.* a business that provides information concerning somebody's creditworthiness to companies or banks

cred·it card *n.* a card issued by a bank or business that allows somebody to purchase goods and services and pay for them later, often with interest

cred·it hour *n.* a credit at a school or college that represents one hour of classroom study per week over the period of time that the course is taught

cred·it line *n.* **1.** FIN AVAILABLE CREDIT the maximum amount of credit that a lending institution or a credit card company will extend to a client **2.** WRITTEN RECOGNITION a printed acknowledgment of the author or source of something that was included in a publication

cred·i·tor /kréddìtər/ *n.* a person or organization owed money by another

cred·it rat·ing *n.* an estimate of somebody's ability to repay money given on credit

cred·it-ref·er·ence a·gen·cy *n.* U.K. = **credit bureau**

cred·it squeeze *n.* a reduction in the availability of credit or an increase in the interest charged for credit

cred·it un·ion *n.* a cooperative savings association that makes loans to its members at reduced interest rates

cred·it·wor·thy /kréddit wùrthee/ *adj.* considered to be financially reliable enough to be given credit or lent money —**cred·it·wor·thi·ness** *n.*

cre·do /kreé dō/ (*plural* **-dos**) *n.* a statement of principles or beliefs, especially one that is professed formally [12thC. From Latin, literally "I believe" (first words of the Apostles' and Nicene creeds), a form of *credere* (see CREDIBLE).]

Cre·do (*plural* **-dos**) *n.* **1.** STATEMENT OF CHRISTIAN BELIEFS the Apostles' Creed or Nicene Creed, both of which are ancient statements of the basic doctrines of Christianity **2.** MUSICAL SETTING OF THE CREDO a musical setting, especially in a Mass, of the Credo

cre·du·li·ty /krə dóolətee/ *n.* the tendency to believe something too readily

cred·u·lous /kréjjələss/ *adj.* **1.** GULLIBLE too easily convinced that something is true **2.** DUE TO READINESS TO BELIEVE resulting from a tendency to believe things too readily [Late 16thC. Formed from Latin *credulus*, from *credere* (see CREDIBLE).] —**cred·u·lous·ly** *adv.* —**cred·u·lous·ness** *n.*

WORD KEY: USAGE

See Usage note at ***credible***.

Cree /kree/ (*plural* **Cree** *or* **Crees**) *n.* **1.** PEOPLES MEMBER OF NATIVE AMERICAN PEOPLE a member of a Native North American people who originally occupied lands in central Canada, and whose members continue to live there, with another substantial community in Montana. The Cree are the largest group of the Native Americans in Canada. **2.** LANG CREE LANGUAGE the Algonquian language of the Cree people. Cree is spoken by about 62,000 people. [Mid-18thC. From Canadian French *Cris*, shortening of earlier *C(h)ristinaux*, alteration of an Algonquian word (modern *kinistiono*).] —**Cree** *adj.*

creed /kreed/ *n.* **1.** STATEMENT OF BELIEFS a formal summary of the principles of the Christian faith **2.** RELIGION a set of religious beliefs **3.** SET OF PRINCIPLES any set of beliefs or principles [Pre-12thC. From Latin *credo* (see CREDO).]

creek /kreek/ *n.* **1.** STREAM a stream, especially one that flows into a river **2.** *U.K.* NARROW TIDAL INLET a narrow tidal inlet or bay on a sea coast, especially in a saltmarsh [15thC. Directly or via French *crique* from Old Norse *kriki* "nook, corner." Perhaps also partly from Middle Dutch *krēke*.] ◇ **up the creek (without a paddle)** in a difficult situation, or in trouble (*informal*)

Creek (*plural* **Creek** *or* **Creeks**) *n.* **1.** PEOPLES MEMBER OF NATIVE AMERICAN PEOPLE a member of a Native American people who originally occupied lands in Alabama, Georgia, and Florida, and whose members now live mainly in central Oklahoma and southern Alabama. The Creek were one of the Five Civilized Nations who, under the Removal Act of 1830, were sent to live on reservations in Oklahoma. **2.** LANG CREEK LANGUAGE the Muskogean language of the Creek people. Creek is spoken by about 50,000 people. [Early 18thC. From CREEK; from the large number of creeks in their country.] —**Creek** *adj.*

creel /kreel/ *n.* **1.** WICKER BASKET FOR FISH a wicker basket used by anglers for holding fish **2.** WICKER FISH TRAP a wicker trap for catching fish or lobsters **3.** BOBBIN HOLDER a framework in a spinning machine that holds the bobbins [14thC. Origin uncertain: perhaps via assumed Old French *creille* "grill" from Latin *craticula* "fine wickerwork," from *cratis* "wickerwork" (source of English *griddle*).]

creep /kreep/ *vi.* **(crept** /krept/ *or* **creeped, creep·ing, creeps) 1.** MOVE QUIETLY to move along silently and stealthily **2.** MOVE NEAR THE GROUND to move along with the body close to the ground **3.** PROCEED SLOWLY to move along very slowly **4.** GRADUALLY DEVELOP to appear, approach, or develop gradually **5.** SHIVER WITH DISGUST to tingle uncomfortably as if covered with crawling insects, especially from fear or disgust **6.** BOT SPREAD OVER A SURFACE to grow along a surface by sending out tendrils, suckers, or roots **7.** BE DISPLACED SLIGHTLY to move slightly from the original or proper position **8.** INDUST DEFORM FROM HEAT OR STRESS to become deformed over a period of time due to stress or heat ■ *n.* **1.** CREEPING MOVEMENT a slow or stealthy pace or movement **2.** SOMEBODY REPELLENT somebody obnoxious or disliked (*informal*) **3.** SLIGHT DISPLACEMENT the slight movement of something **4.** GEOL MOVEMENT OF ROCK a gradual movement of rock and debris down a slope **5.** GEOL DEFORMATION OF ROCKS UNDER STRESS a slow deformation of rocks and minerals in response to prolonged stress **6.** METALL DEFORMATION OF METAL UNDER STRESS a gradual deformation of a hard material, especially metal, as a result of heat or stress ■ **creeps** *npl.* UNEASY FEELING an uneasy or unnerving feeling usually caused by fear or disgust (*informal*) [Old English *crēopan*, from a prehistoric Germanic word that may also be the ancestor of English *cripple*. The underlying idea would be of moving with back bent.]

creep out *vt.* to make somebody feel fear, disgust, or another emotion that produces extreme uneasiness (*slang*) ○ *It creeps me out to watch a horror film.*

creep up on *vt.* **1.** MAKE QUIET APPROACH TO to approach somebody or something stealthily **2.** GRADUALLY DAWN ON to enter somebody's consciousness or feelings gradually

creep·back /kreép bàk/ *n.* the tendency for employers to recruit new employees surreptitiously after excessive or heavy layoffs

creep·er /kreépər/ *n.* **1.** BOT CLINGING PLANT any plant that grows by means of tendrils, suckers, or roots that anchor it to a surface **2.** SOMEBODY OR SOMETHING THAT CREEPS a person or animal that moves by creeping

3. BIRDS **SMALL CLIMBING BIRD** a small climbing bird found in the woods of North America, Europe, Asia, and Africa with a slender curved beak and short legs. Family: Certhiidae. 4. CLOTHES **INFANT'S ONE-PIECE GARMENT** an infant's one-piece garment that has short or no pantlegs and can be unsnapped at the crotch 5. CARS = **cradle** *n.* 4 6. INSUR **UNDERWATER GRAPPLING DEVICE** a device with hooks that is used to drag for submerged objects in deep water 7. *Northeast U.S.* **SHOE SPIKES** a spiked or toothed device that is attached to the sole of a boot to provide traction on ice

creep·ing /kréeping/ *adj.* 1. **SLOWLY DEVELOPING** developing or advancing gradually over a period of time 2. BOT **GROWING BY CLINGING** growing and spreading by sending out tendrils, suckers, or roots

creep·ing Char·lie (*plural* **creep·ing Char·lies** *or* **creep·ing Char·lie**) *n.* = **moneywort**

creep·ing e·rup·tion *n.* a skin disease caused by hookworm or roundworm larvae, producing itching and eruptions in the form of spreading red lines on the skin

creep·ing Jen·nie, **creep·ing Jen·ny** *n.* = **moneywort**

creep·ing this·tle *n.* *U.K.* = **Canada thistle**

creep·y /kréepee/ (**-i·er, -i·est**) *adj.* (*informal*) 1. **UNNERVING THROUGH FEAR** unsettling because it causes fear, disgust, or uneasiness 2. **REPELLENT** repellent because of annoying, unpleasant, or disturbing qualities —**creep·i·ly** *adv.* —**creep·i·ness** *n.*

creep·y-crawl·y (*plural* **creep·y-crawlies**) *n.* a crawling insect or small animal (*informal*)

cre·mains /kri máynz/ *npl.* the ashes that remain after a body has been cremated [Mid-20thC. Blend of CREMATED and REMAINS.]

cre·mate /krée màyt/ (**-mat·ed, -mat·ing, -mates**) *vt.* to burn a dead body until nothing remains but ashes [Late 19thC. Either formed from Latin past participle stem *cremat-* (see CREMATION), or a back-formation from CREMATION.] —**cre·ma·tor** *n.*

cre·ma·tion /kri máysh'n/ *n.* 1. **INCINERATION OF DEAD BODY** the burning of a dead body until only ashes are left 2. **FUNERAL** a funeral ceremony during which the body is cremated [Early 17thC. From the Latin stem *cremation-*, from *cremat-*, the past participle stem of *cremare* "to burn."]

cre·ma·to·ri·um /krèemə táwree əm/ (*plural* **-ums** *or* **-a** /-ə/) *n.* a building or furnace where bodies are incinerated [Late 19thC. From modern Latin, where it was formed from Latin *cremat-* (see CREMATION).]

cre·ma·to·ry /kréemə tàwree, krémmə-/ *n.* (*plural* **-ries**) = **crematorium** ■ *adj.* **RELATING TO CREMATION** relating to or used for cremation

Cré·maz·ie /kráy maa zée/, **Octave** (1827–79) French-Canadian poet. He became Canada's official poet after writing his *"Chant du vieux soldat canadien"* (1855).

crème brû·lée /krèm broo láy/ (*plural* **crème brû·lées** /krèm broo láyz/ *or* **crèmes brû·lées** /krèm broo láy/) *n.* a rich baked custard with caramelized sugar on top. It is served chilled. [From French, literally "burnt cream"]

crème car·a·mel /krèm kaarə mél, -kerr-/ (*plural* **crème car·a·mels** /krèm kaarə mélz, -kerr-/ *or* **crèmes car·a·mel** /krèm-, krèmz-/) *n.* a custard cooked in a mold coated with caramelized sugar, which forms a sauce. It is chilled and removed from the mold before serving. [From French, literally "caramel cream"]

crème de ca·cao /krèm də kṓkō, -kaa kaa ṓ/ (*plural* **crème de ca·caos** /krèm də kṓkōz, -kaa kaa ṓz/ *or* **crèmes de ca·cao** /krèm də kṓkō, -kaa kaa ṓ/) *n.* a sweet chocolate-flavored liqueur [From French, literally "cream of cacao"]

crème de la crème /kèm də laa krém/ *n.* the very best of a group of people or things [From French, literally "cream of the cream"]

crème de menthe /krèm də ménth, -maáNt/ (*plural* **crème de menthes** *or* **crèmes de menthe** /krèm də ménth, -maáNt/) *n.* a sweet mint-flavored liqueur [From French, literally "cream of mint"]

crème fraîche /krèm frésh/ *n.* thickened French sour cream, used in cooking or served with other foods [From French, literally "fresh cream"]

cre·nate /kréé nàyt/, **cre·nat·ed** /-təd/ *adj.* with a scalloped edge or a surface with rounded projections [Late 18thC. From modern Latin *crenatus*, from Latin *crena* "small notch" (source of English *cranny*), of unknown origin.] —**cre·nate·ly** *adv.*

cre·na·tion /kri náysh'n/ *n.* 1. **ROUNDED PROTRUSION** a rounded protrusion from the edge or surface of something 2. **SCALLOPED EDGE OR SURFACE** a scalloped edge or a surface with rounded projections 3. MED **SHRINKAGE OF RED BLOOD CELLS** a medical condition in which the red blood cells shrink and develop multiple indentations and protrusions

cren·a·ture /krénnəchər, kréenəchər/ *n.* = **crenation** *n.* 1, **crenation** *n.* 2 (*technical*)

cren·el /krénn'l/, **cren·elle** /krə nél/ *n.* 1. **OPENING IN BATTLEMENT** any of the rectangular openings in the top of a castle wall or parapet 2. **ROUNDED PROTRUSION** a rounded protrusion from the edge or surface of something [15thC. From Old French, literally "small notch," from Latin *crena* (see CRENATE).]

cren·e·late /krénn'l àyt/ (**-lat·ed, -lat·ing, -lates**), **cren·el·late** (**-lat·ed, -lat·ing, -lates**) *vt.* 1. **BUILD WITH BATTLEMENTS** to provide a structure with battlements or decorative features resembling battlements 2. **MAKE WITH SQUARE INDENTIONS** to make something with square indentations like the openings (**crenels**) of a battlement [Early 19thC. Formed from French *créneler*, from Old French *crenel* (see CRENEL).] —**cren·e·lat·ed** *adj.* —**cren·e·la·tion** /krènn'l áysh'n/ *n.*

cren·elle *n.* = **crenel**

cren·shaw /krén shàw/ *n.* a variety of melon that has a green rind and sweet salmon-pink flesh. It is closely related to the casaba, honeydew, and winter melons. [Late 20thC. Origin unknown.]

cren·u·late /krénnyələt, -làyt/, **cren·u·lat·ed** /-làytəd/ *adj.* with a finely scalloped or notched wavy edge [Late 18thC. From modern Latin *crenulatus*, from *crenula*, literally "small notch," from Latin *crena* (see CRENATE).]

cren·u·la·tion /krènnyə láysh'n/ *n.* 1. **TINY NOTCH** a very small notch or indentation 2. **FINELY NOTCHED EDGING** very fine notching or indentation along an edge

cre·o·dont /kréé ə dònt/ (*plural* **-donts** *or* **-don·ta**) *n.* an extinct carnivorous mammal that lived during the Tertiary period. Suborder: Creodonta. [Late 19thC. From modern Latin *Creodonta*, literally "flesh-toothed ones," from Greek *kreas* "flesh" (source of English *pancreas*)+ *rodont-*, from *odous* "tooth."]

cre·ole /kréé ōl/ *n.* 1. LING **LANGUAGE OF MIXED ORIGIN** a language that has evolved from the mixture of two or more languages and has become the first language of a group 2. PEOPLES **AFRICAN DESCENDANT BORN IN AMERICAS** somebody of African or mixed African descent born in the Americas ■ *adj.* COOK **COOKED NEW ORLEANS STYLE** cooked in a spicy flavorful way typical of the French Creoles of New Orleans. Tomatoes, hot peppers, onions, and rice are characteristic ingredients. [Late 19thC. From CREOLE.]

Cre·ole /kréé ōl/ *n.* 1. **SOMEBODY OF FRENCH ANCESTRY** an inhabitant of the southern United States, especially southern Louisiana, who is descended from the early French settlers 2. **LANGUAGE OF LOUISIANA** the creolized French language spoken by the Creoles of New Orleans and southern Louisiana 3. **LANGUAGE OF CARIBBEAN ISLANDS** a group of creolized languages, based on English and French, spoken on many of the islands of the Caribbean 4. **HAITIAN LANGUAGE** the creolized language spoken in Haiti 5. **WEST INDIAN OF EUROPEAN ANCESTRY** somebody who was born in or is a citizen of a West Indian or Latin American country, and who is of European, especially Spanish, descent 6. **CREOLE SPEAKER** somebody of both European and African ancestry who speaks a form of Creole [Mid-18thC. From French, from Spanish *criollo* "native," from Portuguese *crioulo*, from *criar* "to bring up," from Latin *creare* (see CREATE).] —**Cre·ole** *adj.*

cre·olize /kréé ə līz/ (**-olized, -oliz·ing, -olizes**) *vt.* to form a new mixed language from two or more other languages —**cre·oliza·tion** /krèe əli záysh'n/ *n.*

cre·o·lized /kréé ə līzd/ *adj.* combining elements of two or more separate languages to form the new mixed language of a group of people

Cre·on /kréé òn/ *n.* in Greek mythology, the brother of Jocasta and the successor of Oedipus as king of Thebes. He was also the uncle of Antigone and issued an edict forbidding the burial of the body of her brother Polynices, which she defied.

cre·o·sol /kréé ə sòl/ *n.* a pale yellow or colorless oily liquid that is a component of creosote. Formula: $C_8H_{10}O_2$. [Mid-19thC. Coined from CREOSOTE + -OL.]

cre·o·sote /kréé ə sōt/ *n.* 1. **WOOD PRESERVATIVE** a thick yellowish to brown oily substance derived from coal tar, used as a wood preservative 2. **ANTISEPTIC** a yellow to colorless oily substance derived from wood tar, used as an antiseptic 3. **CHIMNEY TAR** a dark brown to black tar deposited inside a chimney flue when wood, especially pine or other resinous wood, is burned. The flammable tar is a fire hazard. ■ *vt.* (**-sot·ed, -sot·ing, -sotes**) **APPLY CREOSOTE TO** to apply creosote to wood as a preservative [Mid-19thC. From German *Kreosote*, literally "flesh-saving," from Greek *kreas* "flesh" (source of English *pancreas*) + *sōtēr* "preserver"; from its antiseptic properties.]

cre·o·sote bush *n.* a resinous evergreen shrub that is native to the deserts of the southwestern United States and Mexico and has leaves that smell like creosote. Latin name: *Larrea tridentata.*

crepe /krayp/; (*"pancake"*) /krayp, krep/, **crêpe** *n.* 1. **crepe** TEXTILES **LIGHT CRINKLED FABRIC** a light fine fabric with a crinkled surface 2. COOK **THIN PANCAKE** a thin pancake usually served rolled up or folded with a filling 3. = **crape** *n.* 2 4. = **crepe paper** 5. = **crepe rubber** [Late 18thC. From French, from Old French *crespe* "curled," from Latin *crispus* (the source also of English *crisp*).] —**crep·y** /kráypee/ *adj.*

crepe de Chine /kraáyp də shéen/ (*plural* **crepes de Chine** *or* **crepe de Chines** /kraáyp də shéenz/), **crêpe de Chine** (*plural* **crêpes de Chine** *or* **crêpe de Chines** /kraáyp də shéenz/) *n.* a light smooth silk fabric, used to make delicate articles of clothing [From French, literally "crepe of China"]

crepe myr·tle *n.* = **crape myrtle**

crepe pa·per, **crêpe pa·per** *n.* a thin, slightly stretchy, crinkled colored paper, used for wrapping presents or making decorations (*hyphenated when used before a noun*)

crep·e·rie /kráypəree, krép-/, **crêp·e·rie** *n.* a restaurant that specializes in thin pancakes (**crepes**) with fillings [From French *crêperie* from *crêpe* (see CREPE)]

crepe rub·ber, **crêpe rub·ber** *n.* rubber in the form of thin crinkled sheets, used especially for the soles of shoes

crêpe suz·ette /kràyp soo zét/ (*plural* **crêpes suz·ette** *or* **crêpe suz·ettes** /kràyp soo zéts/) *n.* a pancake prepared with orange sauce and flambéed with an orange-flavored liqueur or brandy [From French, said to be named after the French actress *Suzanne* Reichenberg (1853–1924)]

crep·i·tate /kréppi tàyt/ (**-tat·ed, -tat·ing, -tates**) *v.* 1. *vi.* **CRACKLE** to make a crackling or grating sound (*formal or literary*) 2. MED **CRACKLE OR GRATE** to make the crackling or grating sound of crepitus [Early 17thC. From Latin *crepitat-*, the past participle stem of *crepitare* "to crackle," from *crepare* "to rattle" (source of English *crevice*) an imitation of the sound.] —**crep·i·tant** *adj.* —**crep·i·ta·tion** /krèppi táysh'n/ *n.*

crep·i·tus /kréppitəss/ *n.* MED 1. **GRATING SOUND OF BROKEN BONE** the grating sound heard when the broken ends of a bone rub together 2. **CRACKLING CHEST NOISE** a crackling sound heard in the chest of somebody who has a lung disease, e.g., pneumonia [Early 19thC. From Latin, "rattling," from *crepare* (see CREPITATE).]

crept past tense, past participle of **creep**

cre·pus·cu·lar /krə púskyələr/ *adj.* 1. **LIKE TWILIGHT** relating to or resembling the fading light of dusk (*literary*) 2. ZOOL **ACTIVE IN LOW LIGHT** used to describe fish and land mammals that are active at dusk and dawn, when the light level is low [Mid-17thC. Formed from Latin *crepusculum* "twilight."]

Cre·rar /kréé raàr/, **Henry Duncan Graham** (1888–1965) Canadian soldier. He headed the Canadian army in Europe (1944–45) during World War II.

cresc. *abbr.* crescendo

cres·cen·do /krə shén dō/ *n.* (*plural* **-dos** *or* **-does** *or* **-di** /-dee/) 1. MUSIC **INCREASING LOUDNESS** a gradual increase in the volume of a passage of music 2. MUSIC **MUSIC PLAYED INCREASINGLY LOUD** a passage of music in which there is a gradual increase in volume 3. **INTENSIFICATION** an increase in volume or intensity similar to a crescendo in music 4. **CLIMAX** the climax of an increase in volume or intensity ■ *adj.* **INTENSIFYING** gradually increasing in volume or intensity ■ *adv.* MUSIC **WITH GREATER VOLUME** with increasing loudness ■ *vi.* (**-doed, -do·ing, -does**) **BECOME LOUDER OR STRONGER** to increase in volume or intensity [Late 18thC. From Italian, the present participle of *crescere* "to increase," from Latin *crescere* (see CRESCENT).]

WORD KEY: USAGE

A *crescendo* is properly a process and not the end of a process. This is usually well understood in musical contexts, because the word is a technical term. In figurative uses, though, it tends to be used as an alternative for *climax*, which is indeed the end point or culmination of a process. A noise or feeling can increase *to* a climax but it does so *in a* ***crescendo***. Correct: *The bird's calls rose in a crescendo and then subsided again.* Avoid: *The abusive calls reached a crescendo the following week.*

cres·cent /kréss'nt/ *n.* **1. ARC SHAPE** a curved shape like that of the moon when it is less than half illuminated **2. ARC-SHAPED THING** something shaped like a crescent **3. cres·cent, Cres·cent** ISLAM **ISLAMIC SYMBOL** the emblem of Islam or Turkey, shaped like a crescent moon **4. cres·cent, Cres·cent** ISLAM **ISLAMIC OR TURKISH POWER** Islamic or Turkish power **5. cres·cent, Cres·cent** TRANSP **ARC-SHAPED STREET** a curved street, especially one that opens onto the same street at each end **6.** HERALDRY **SYMBOL FOR SECOND SON** a crescent moon, used in heraldry to signify a second son ■ *adj.* **1. ARC-SHAPED** shaped like a crescent **2. GROWING** gradually increasing in size (*literary*) [14thC. Via Anglo-Norman *cressaunt* from, ultimately, Latin *crescent-*, the present participle stem of *crescere* "to grow."] —**cres·cen·tic** /krə séntik/ *adj.*

WORD KEY: ORIGIN

As well as being the source of ***crescent***, the Latin word *crescere*, meaning "to grow," is also the source of English *accretion, concrete, create, crescendo, crew, croissant, increase,* and *recruit.*

cre·sol /krée sòl/ *n.* a colorless compound derived from wood or coal tar, used as an antiseptic and disinfectant. Formula: C_7H_8O. [Mid-19thC. Alteration of CREOSOL.]

cress /kress/ (*plural* **cress** *or* **cress·es**) *n.* a plant of the mustard family with small pungently flavored leaves that are used in salads or as a garnish [Old English *cressa*, from prehistoric Germanic]

cres·set /kréssət/ *n.* a metal cup or basket mounted on a pole and filled with oil or pitch that was burned to give light [14thC. From Old French *cresset*, from *craisse*, variant of *graisse* "oil, grease," from, ultimately, Latin *crassus* "solid, fat" (source of English *crass*).]

Cres·si·da /kréssidə/ *n.* in medieval retellings of the Trojan War, a Trojan woman captured by the Greeks who is unfaithful to her Trojan lover, Troilus, by giving herself to the Greek Diomedes

crest /krest/ *n.* **1. TOP OF CURVE OR SLOPE** the top part of something that slopes or rises upward, e.g., a wave or a hill **2. CULMINATION** the highest stage or culminating point in an activity or achievement **3.** ZOOL **TUFT ON ANIMAL'S HEAD** a tuft or other growth on the top of the head of a bird or other animal **4. SOMETHING RESEMBLING CREST** something resembling the crest of a bird or other animal **5.** ARMS **HELMET ORNAMENT** a plume or other decoration on top of a helmet **6.** ZOOL **NECK RIDGE** a ridge along the neck of a horse, lion, or other animal, from which hair grows **7.** HERALDRY **SYMBOL OF FAMILY OR OFFICE** a small animal, bird, or other heraldic symbol of a family or office, placed above the shield in a coat of arms or used alone on a helmet **8.** HERALDRY = **coat of arms** ■ *v.* (**crest·ed, crest·ing, crests**) **1.** *vi.* **RISE** to reach or rise to a crest **2.** *vt.* **REACH TOP OF** to reach the top of something **3.** *vt.* **TOP SOMETHING** to be at the top of something [14thC. Via French *creste* from Latin *crista* "tuft, plume."]

crest·ed /kréstəd/ *adj.* **1.** CLOTHES **WITH FUR OR FEATHER CREST** used to describe an item of headgear that has a knot or row of hairs or feathers on its top **2.** ZOOL **TUFTED** used to describe a bird or other animal with a tuft or other growth on its head

crest·ed hon·ey·creep·er *n.* an endangered Hawaiian honeycreeper found only on Haleakala Mountain on the island of Maui. Latin name: *Palmeria dolei.*

crest·ed wheat·grass *n.* a perennial grass native to Europe and Asia, grown as forage, hay, and erosion control in North America. Genus: *Agropyron.*

crest·fall·en /krést fàwlən/ *adj.* disappointed or humiliated, especially after being enthusiastic or confident [From the drooping of a somebody's head when disappointed] —**crest·fall·en·ly** *adv.* —**crest·fall·en·ness** *n.*

crest·ing /krésting/ *n.* **1.** ARCHIT **DECORATIVE ROOF RIDGE** an ornamental ridge on a roof **2.** FURNITURE **FURNITURE ORNAMENT** an ornamental carving or rail on the top of a piece of furniture

cre·syl·ic /krə síllik/ *adj.* relating to or containing creosol or creosote

cre·syl·ic ac·id *n.* = **cresol**

cre·ta·ceous /krə táyshəss/ *adj.* resembling or consisting of chalk (*technical*) [Late-17thC. Formed from Latin *cretaceus* "chalklike, chalky," from *creta* "chalk" (source of English *crayon*).] —**cre·ta·ceous·ly** *adv.*

Cre·ta·ceous *adj.* belonging to or dating from the end of the Mesozoic era, 144 to 65 million years ago

Cre·tan /kréet'n/ *n.* **SOMEBODY FROM CRETE** somebody who was born or raised in Crete ■ *adj.* **RELATING TO CRETE** relating to or typical of Crete, or its people or culture

Crete /kreet/ the largest Greek island in the southern Aegean Sea. The chief town is Iráklion. Population: 540,054 (1991). Area: 3,218 sq. mi./8,335 sq. km. Greek **Kríti**

cre·tic /kréetik/ *n.* POETRY = **amphimacer** [Late 16thC. Via Latin *creticus*, literally "Cretan," from Greek *krētikos*, from *Krētē* "Crete."]

cre·tin /kréet'n/ *n.* **1. OFFENSIVE TERM** an offensive term that deliberately insults somebody's supposed intellectual capacity (*offensive*) **2.** MED **SOMEBODY WITH THYROID HORMONE DEFICIENCY** somebody affected by congenital myxedema (*dated*) [Late 18thC. Via French from Swiss French *creitin* "Christian mentally challenged," from Latin *Christianus* "Christian," from *Christus* "Christ."] —**cre·tin·ism** *n.* —**cre·tin·oid** *adj.* —**cre·tin·ous** *adj.*

cre·tonne /krée tòn, krə tón/ *n.* a heavy fabric made from cotton, linen, or rayon and usually printed with a colorful design, used for upholstery [Late 19thC. From French, from *Creton*, name of a village in Normandy, France, where it was first made.]

cre·tons /krə tóN/ *npl. Can* in Quebec, a dish of spiced shredded pork cooked with onions in lard [From Canadian French, of uncertain origin: probably from Middle Dutch *kerte* "cut"]

Creutz·feldt-Ja·kob dis·ease /kròyts felt yaá kawb-/ *n.* a rare fatal brain disease, a form of spongiform encephalopathy, that develops slowly, causing dementia and loss of muscle control. An abnormal protein (**prion**) is the suspected cause. A new variant of the disease, that develops rapidly and affects younger people, appeared in the late 1980s. [Late 20thC. Named for the German neurologists H. G. *Creutzfeldt* (1885–1964) and A. M. *Jakob* (1884–1931).]

cre·val·le /krə vállee, -vállə/ (*plural* **-le** *or* **-les**) *n.* a spiny-finned marine fish related to the pompano. Family: Carangidae. [Late 19thC. Alteration of CAVALLA.]

cre·vasse /krə váss/ *n.* **1. DEEP CRACK** a deep crack, e.g., in the ice of a glacier **2. LEVEE CRACK** a crack in a levee or dike ■ *vti.* (**-vassed, -vass·ing, -vass·es**) **FORM CREVASSES** to develop or make something develop crevasses [Early 19thC. From French, from Old French *crevace* (see CREVICE).]

crev·ice /krévviss/ *n.* a narrow crack or opening, especially in rock [14thC. From Old French *crevace* "a burst, split," from *crever* "to burst," from Latin *crepare* "to rattle" (source of English *decrepit*), an imitation of the sound.] —**crev·iced** *adj.*

crew[1] /kroo/ *n.* **1. ONBOARD STAFF** the people who work on a boat, ship, aircraft, or spacecraft **2. PEOPLE WORKING TOGETHER** a group of people who work together on a project or task **3. SHIP'S STAFF EXCLUDING OFFICERS** the members of a ship's crew who are not officers **4. SPECIALIZED STAFF ON CRAFT** a smaller group within the crew of a ship, aircraft, or spacecraft who are assigned a specific task **5. GROUP OF FRIENDS** a group of people who spend a lot of time together or are somehow associated with each other (*informal*) **6. ROWERS** the rowers and coxswain of a racing shell **7. ROWING** the sport of rowing racing shells ■ *v.* (**crewed, crew·ing, crews**) **1.** *vi.* **BE ON CREW** to be a member of a crew **2.** *vt.* **BE ON CREW OF** to serve as a member of the crew of a boat, ship, aircraft, or spacecraft (*often passive*) [15thC. From French *creüe* "increase, recruit," from the past participle of *croistre* "to grow," from Latin *crescere* (see CRESCENT). Originally "company of soldiers."]

crew[2] *U.K.* past tense of **crow**

crew chief *n.* **1.** AIR FORCE **MILITARY AIRCRAFT MAINTENANCE CHIEF** a noncommissioned officer in the air force who is in charge of the maintenance and ground handling of an aircraft **2.** MOTOR SPORTS **HEAD OF PIT CREW** the head of the maintenance crew that fuels and repairs an automobile or other motor vehicle during a race

crew cut *n.* a haircut, usually worn by men and boys, with the hair cut close to the head [Thought to be from its original adoption by boat crews at the U.S. universities of Harvard and Yale in the mid-20thC]

crewed /krood/ *adj.* operated by onboard personnel ○ *A crewed minisub explored the ocean floor.* ○ *"A crewed mission to Mars currently lies on the very edge of our technological ability and the realization of this ambition … would undoubtedly stand as a testament to the possibilities which technology presents to our civilization" (NASA) website; 1999)*

crew·el /kroó əl/ *n.* **1. WOOL EMBROIDERY YARN** a loosely twisted woolen yarn used in embroidery **2.** = **crewelwork** [15thC. Origin unknown.] —**crew·el·ist** *n.*

crew·el·work /kroó əl wùrk/ *n.* embroidery work done with crewel yarn

crew·mate /kroó màyt/ *n.* a fellow member of a crew, especially on board a boat or spacecraft

crew neck *n.* **1. ROUND NECKLINE** a close-fitting round neckline on a sweater, sweatshirt, or other garment **2. CREW-NECK SWEATER** a sweater with a close-fitting round neck [From the sweaters with such a neckline worn by boat crews] —**crew-neck** *adj.*

crew sock *n.* a thick short sock that is ribbed above the ankle

crib /krib/ *n.* **1. BABY'S BED** a bed for a baby or small child that has high usually vertically barred sides to keep the child from falling out **2.** AGRIC **GRAIN STORE** a small building with slatted sides used for storing grain, especially corn **3.** AGRIC **ANIMAL'S STALL** a stall for cattle or horses **4. PLAGIARISM** a theft of something from an intellectual or artistic work **5.** AGRIC **HAY RACK** a trough or box for hay or other fodder from which livestock can feed **6.** EDUC **CRIB SHEET** a crib sheet (*informal*) **7. PETTY THEFT** a theft of something of insignificant value **8. SOMEBODY'S HOME** somebody's home, especially an urban apartment (*slang*) **9. PROSTITUTE'S ROOM** a run-down house or room used by a prostitute **10. BASKET** a wicker basket **11.** CARDS **DEALER'S CARDS** the cards used by the dealer in cribbage, consisting of cards discarded by the other players **12.** CARDS **CRIBBAGE** cribbage (*informal*) ■ *v.* (**cribbed, crib·bing, cribs**) **1.** *vti.* **PLAGIARIZE** to steal somebody's ideas or work **2.** *vi.* EDUC **USE CRIB SHEET** to use a crib sheet in an examination (*informal*) **3.** *vt.* **PUT IN CRIB** to put somebody or something in a crib **4.** *vt.* **PROVIDE CRIB FOR** to construct or provide a crib for something [Old English *crib(b)* "manger, trough for fodder," from a prehistoric Germanic word that is also the ancestor of English *crèche*. *Plagiarize* came via thieves' slang "pilfer from basket."] —**crib·ber** *n.*

crib·bage /kríbbij/ *n.* a card game for two to four players in which the score is kept by moving pegs along rows of holes in a small board [Mid-17thC. Origin uncertain: probably from CRIB + -AGE.]

crib·bage board *n.* a board with holes in which pegs are placed for scoring in cribbage

crib·bing /kríbbing/ *n.* **1.** EDUC **CHEATING ON EXAMINATION** using a crib sheet to cheat on an examination (*informal*) **2.** CONSTR **BEAMS FOR MINESHAFT** the timbers used for a framework, e.g., of a mineshaft or foundation **3.** VET = **crib-biting**

crib-bit·ing *n.* a behavioral abnormality in horses in which animals kept in stables chew their stalls and salivate excessively. The disorder is partly an inherited condition and partly an expression of boredom. —**crib-bit·er** *n.*

crib death *n.* the sudden and unexplained death of a small baby while sleeping

crib·ri·form /kríbbrə fàwrm/ *adj.* with small holes like a sieve (*technical*) [Mid-18thC. Coined from Latin *cribrum* "sieve" + -FORM.]

crib sheet *n.* a list of answers or translation of a foreign text used for cheating in examinations or classwork

cri·ce·tid /krī séetid, -séttid/ (*plural* **-tids** *or* **-tid**) *n.* a small rodent of the family that includes the hamster, gerbil, muskrat, and vole. Family: Cricetidae. [Mid-20thC. From modern Latin *Cricetidae*, from *Cricetus* (genus name of hamsters), from medieval Latin *cricetus* "hamster," from or related to Old Czech *křeček*.] —**cri·ce·tid** *adj.*

Crich·ton /krī́t'n/, **Michael** (*b.* 1942) U.S. writer. He is known for his science-fiction thrillers including *Jurassic Park* (1990), which was made into a movie in 1993.

crick[1] /krik/ *n.* PAINFUL STIFFNESS a painful stiffness or muscle spasm in the neck or back ■ *vt.* **(cricked, crick·ing, cricks)** CAUSE CRICK IN to cause a painful stiffness or muscle spasm in the neck or back [15thC. Origin unknown.]

crick[2] /krik/ *n.* a creek (*regional*) [Variant]

crick·et[1] /kríkət/ *n.* **1.** LEAPING CHIRPING INSECT a leaping insect that has biting mouthparts, long legs, and antennae. The male produces a chirping sound by rubbing its forewings together. Family: Gryllidae. **2.** SMALL TOY THAT CLICKS a small metal toy or noise-maker that produces a sharp clicking sound when it is pressed [14thC. From French *criquet* "grasshopper, locust," from Old French *criquer* "to click," an imitation of the sound.]

Cricket: A batsman is bowled

crick·et[2] /kríkət/ *n.* BAT-AND-BALL GAME an outdoor sport played in England and Commonwealth countries by two teams of 11 players using a flat bat, a small hard ball, and wickets. A player scores by batting the ball and running, while the defenders can get a player out by bowling and hitting the wicket, catching a hit ball, or running the player out. ■ *vi.* to play cricket [Late 16thC. Origin uncertain: perhaps from Old French *criquet* "stick (used in a bowling game)," or Flemish *krick* "stick" or *krickstoel* "low stool" (resembling early wickets).]

crick·et[3] /kríkət/ *n.* a wooden footstool [Mid-17thC. Origin unknown.]

crick·et·er /kríkətər/ *n.* somebody who plays cricket

cri·coid /krī́ kòyd/ *adj.* relating to or in the region of the lowermost cartilage of the larynx [Mid-18thC. Via modern Latin *cricoides* "ring-shaped" from Greek *krikoeidēs*, from *krikos* "ring."]

cri·coid car·ti·lage *n.* the lowermost cartilage of the voice box (**larynx**), which has a shape like a signet ring

cri de coeur /krée də kúr/ (*plural* **cris de coeur** /krée-/) *n.* a heartfelt, usually anguished appeal [From French, literally "cry from the heart"]

cri·er /krī́r/ *n.* **1.** SOMEBODY OR SOMETHING THAT CRIES a person or animal that cries **2.** = **town crier 3.** LAW COURT ANNOUNCER an official who makes public announcements of the orders of a court of law **4.** VENDOR SHOUTING WARES a vendor who makes public announcements about the goods he or she has for sale

crim. *abbr.* criminal

crim. con. /crím còn/ *abbr.* LAW criminal conversation

crime /krīm/ *n.* **1.** ILLEGAL ACT an action prohibited by law, or a failure to act as required by law **2.** ILLEGAL ACTIVITY activity that involves breaking the law **3.** IMMORAL ACT any act considered morally wrong **4.** UNDESIRABLE ACT a shameful, unwise, or regrettable act (*informal*) ○ *It's a crime the way some people mistreat their pets.* [13thC. Via French from Latin *crimen* (stem *crimin-*) "judgment," from *cernere* "to decide" (source of English *certain* and *decree*).] —**crime·less** *adj.*

WORD KEY: CULTURAL NOTE

Crime and Punishment, a novel by Russian writer Fyodor Dostoevsky (1866). Set in St. Petersburg, it describes how a young student, Raskolnikov, plans and carries out the murder of a woman pawnbroker, ostensibly for money but in reality to prove that certain individuals are above the law. Ultimately, however, his conscience forces him to confess his crime.

Cri·me·a /krī mée ə/ peninsula in southeastern Ukraine between the Black Sea and the Sea of Azov. Area: 10,036 sq. mi./25,993 sq. km. —**Cri·me·an** *n., adj.*

crime a·gainst hu·man·i·ty *n.* a cruel and immoral act, e.g., torture, murder, or expulsion, committed against a large number of people

crime of pas·sion *n.* a crime that is motivated by an extreme emotion, especially sexual jealousy

crime wave *n.* a period during which more crimes than usual are committed

crim·i·nal /krímmin'l/ *n.* SOMEBODY ACTING ILLEGALLY somebody who has committed a crime ■ *adj.* **1.** PUNISHABLE AS CRIME punishable as a crime under the law **2.** PROSECUTING CRIMINALS involved in or relating to the prosecution and punishment of people accused of committing crimes **3.** RELATING TO CRIMINALS relating to or typical of criminals **4.** MORALLY WRONG morally wrong whether illegal or not **5.** UNWISE OR REGRETTABLE not showing good sense or fairness (*informal*) [15thC. Directly or via French *criminel* from late Latin *criminalis* "of crime," from the Latin stem *crimin-* (see CRIME).] —**crim·i·nal·ly** *adv.*

WORD KEY: SYNONYMS

See Synonyms at ***bad***.

crim·i·nal con·ver·sa·tion *n.* adultery considered as a legal breach of the marriage contract (*technical*)

crim·i·nal·i·ty /krìmmi nállətee/ *n.* **1.** CRIMINAL QUALITY a criminal character or quality **2.** TENDENCY TO LAW-BREAKING a tendency to commit crimes **3.** CRIME a criminal act or practice (*often used in the plural*)

crim·i·nal·ize /krímmin'l īz/ (**-ized, -iz·ing, -iz·es**) *vt.* **1.** MAKE ILLEGAL to make an action punishable as a crime under the law **2.** MAKE INTO CRIMINAL to make somebody become or treat somebody as a criminal —**crim·i·nal·i·za·tion** /krìmmin'li záysh'n/ *n.*

criminol. *abbr.* criminology

crim·i·nol·o·gy /krìmmi nólləjee/ *n.* the sociological study of crime, criminals, and the punishment of criminals —**crim·i·no·log·i·cal** /krìmminə lójjik'l/ *adj.* —**crim·i·no·log·i·cal·ly** *adv.* —**crim·i·nol·o·gist** *n.*

crimp /krimp/ *vt.* (**crimped, crimp·ing, crimps**) **1.** FOLD OR PRESS TOGETHER to fold or press the ends or edges of something together **2.** INTERFERE WITH to hinder, obstruct, or otherwise interfere with something such as a plan or process ○ *A slowdown in sales crimped the company's cash flow.* **3.** PLEAT to press or gather something into small folds, e.g., a piece of fabric **4.** HAIR CURL to make somebody's hair wavy with a curling iron **5.** COOK PINCH DECORATIVELY to pinch or press together the edges of pastry to form a seal or for decoration **6.** MANUF MOLD to mold or form leather into a shape **7.** METALL JOIN INTO SEAM to bend or fold the edges of sheet metal to form a seam for a tube or between two pieces ■ *n.* **1.** CRIMPING ACTION a pinching, folding, or other action that crimps something **2.** HINDRANCE somebody who or something that hinders, obstructs, or otherwise interferes with somebody or something else **3.** HAIR TIGHT HAIR WAVE a tight artificial wave in somebody's hair, usually made with a curling iron **4.** PINCHED EDGE a fold or crease made by pinching together two edges, e.g., of fabric or pastry **5.** CREASE FORMED BY BENDING a fold or crease formed by bending something, e.g., sheet metal **6.** CURL OF WOOL FIBERS the curl or wave of wool fibers [Late 17thC. Origin uncertain: probably via Dutch or Low German *krimpen* "to shrink, crimp" from a prehistoric Germanic word that is also the ancestor of English *cram.*] —**crimp·er** *n.*

crimp·y /krímpee/ (**-i·er, -i·est**) *adj.* with many small waves, folds, or wrinkles —**crimp·i·ness** *n.*

crim·son /krímz'n/ *adj.* OF DEEP RICH RED COLOR of a deep rich red color with a tinge of purple ○ *crimson lips* ■ *n.* DEEP RICH RED COLOR a deep rich red color tinged with purple ■ *v.* (**-soned, -son·ing, -sons**) **1.** *vti.* MAKE OR BECOME CRIMSON to become a vivid or deep red color, or make something become this color **2.** *vi.* BLUSH to blush, with embarrassment, shyness, or shame [15thC. Via Old Spanish *cremesín* from Arabic *ḳirmizī* "red color," from *ḳirmiz* "kermes insect."]

cringe /krinj/ *vi.* (**cringed, cring·ing, cring·es**) **1.** CROUCH OR MOVE BACK SUDDENLY to pull the head and body quickly away from something or somebody in a frightened or servile way **2.** BE EMBARRASSED OR UNCOMFORTABLE to react to something with embarrassment or discomfort, often showing this by physically flinching (*informal*) ○ *We always cringe at his jokes.* **3.** ACT HUMBLY to behave in a very humble or servile way (*disapproving*) ■ *n.* COWERING MOVEMENT a quick pulling away of the head and body from something or somebody in a frightened or servile way [13thC. Origin uncertain: probably from Old English *crincan* "to yield." Ultimately from a prehistoric Germanic word meaning "to bend, curl," which is also the ancestor of English *crank.*] —**cring·er** *n.*

crin·gle /kríng g'l/ *n.* a piece of rope with a metal ring (**grommet**) in it, fitted into the main rope (**boltrope**) around the edge of a sail [Early 17thC. From Low German *kringel*, literally "small ring." Ultimately from a prehistoric Germanic base meaning "to bend," which is also the ancestor of English *crinkle* and *cringe.*]

crin·kle /kríngk'l/ *vti.* **1.** CREASE OR WRINKLE ALL OVER to become, or make something become, finely folded, wrinkled, or wavy, e.g., by crushing or pressing it **2.** MAKE SOFT CRACKLING SOUND to make little crunching or rustling noises, like the sound of paper being crushed, or cause something to make these noises ■ *n.* TINY FOLD OR WAVE a little fold or wave, especially in paper or cloth [14thC. Origin uncertain: perhaps formed from Old English *crincan* (see CRINGE).] —**crin·kly** *adv.*

crin·kle·root /kríngk'l ròot/ (*plural* **-root** *or* **-roots**) *n.* a woodland plant of eastern North America that has pungent fleshy roots and clusters of pink and white flowers. Genus: *Dentaria.*

cri·noid /krī́ nòyd/ *n.* a type of primitive marine invertebrate animal (**echinoderm**) with a cup-shaped body and five feathery radiating arms. These animals are related to the starfish and the sea urchin. Class: Crinoidea. [Mid-19thC. From Greek *krinoeidēs* "lilylike," from *krinon* "lily."] —**cri·noid** *adj.*

crin·o·line /krínnəlin/ *n.* **1.** FABRIC FOR STIFFENING THINGS a stiff fabric made of horsehair and cotton or linen, used in the past for linings and petticoats **2.** STIFF PETTICOAT a petticoat of crinoline fabric or net, worn to expand a skirt **3.** HOOPED SKIRT a skirt or petticoat containing wire hoops, worn to expand the skirt [Mid-19thC. Via French from Italian *crinolino*, from *crino* "horsehair" + *lino* "flax."] —**crin·o·lined** *adj.*

cri·num /krī́nəm/ (*plural* **-num** *or* **-nums**) *n.* a tropical plant that grows from a bulb and has long thin leaves and clusters of flowers in various colors. Genus: *Crinum.* [Via modern Latin, genus name, from Greek *krinon* "lily," of unknown origin]

cri·ol·lo /kri ṓlō/ *n.* (*plural* **-los**) **1.** LATIN AMERICAN OF EUROPEAN DESCENT somebody who was born in or is a citizen of a Latin American country, and who is of European, especially Spanish, descent **2.** ANIMAL OF LATIN AMERICAN BREED any Latin American breed of domestic animal ■ *adj.* **1.** OF LATIN AMERICANS OF EUROPEAN DESCENT relating to or typical of Latin American people of European, especially Spanish, descent, or their language, or their culture **2.** BEING LATIN AMERICAN ANIMAL belonging to a Latin American breed of domestic animal ○ *a criollo pony* [Late 19thC. From Spanish (see CREOLE).] —**cri·ol·lo** *adj.*

cri·o·sphinx /krée ə sfìnks/ (*plural* **-sphinx·es** *or* **-sphing·es** /-sfínjeez/) *n.* in ancient Egyptian mythology and art, a figure that is like a sphinx in having a lion's body but has the head of a ram rather than a human head [Mid-19thC. Coined from Greek *krios* "ram" + SPHINX.]

cripes /krīps/ *interj.* used to express surprise or concern (*slang*) ○ *Cripes! That does it!* [Early 20thC. Alteration of CHRIST.]

crip·ple /krípp'l/ *n.* **1.** PHYSICALLY CHALLENGED PERSON somebody whose use of a limb or limbs is impaired (*offensive*) **2.** INCAPABLE PERSON somebody who is deficient in a particular area (*informal*) ○ *an emotional cripple* **3.** SOMETHING DAMAGED something that does not work correctly (*informal*) ■ *vt.* (**-pled, -pling, -ples**) **1.** MAKE SOMEBODY PHYSICALLY CHALLENGED to hurt or damage somebody seriously and often permanently, especially impairing the ability to move ○ *crippled by arthritis* **2.** DAMAGE SERIOUSLY to cause major problems to something, e.g., a machine or a business, so that it cannot operate properly ○ *a business crippled by debts and bad publicity* [Old English *crypel.* Ultimately from a prehistoric Germanic word denoting "bent," which was also the ancestor of English *creep.*] —**crip·pled** *adj.* —**crip·pling** *adj.* —**crip·pling·ly** *adv.*

Crip·ple Creek /krìpp'l-/ city in Colorado, United States, and seat of Teller County. It was a major gold-mining center (1891–1920). Population: 584 (1990).

cri·sis /krísiss/ (*plural* **-ses** /-seez/) *n.* **1. DANGEROUS OR WORRYING TIME** a situation or period in which things are very uncertain, difficult, or painful, especially a time when action must be taken to avoid complete disaster or breakdown **2. CRITICAL MOMENT** a time when something very important for the future happens or is decided **3.** MED **TURNING POINT IN DISEASE** a point in the course of a disease when the patient suddenly begins to get worse or better [15thC. Via Latin from Greek *krisis* "decisive moment," from *krinein* "to decide" (source of English *critic* and *criterion*).]

cri·sis cen·ter *n.* an office or meeting place where people can go in a time of great personal difficulty or distress for advice and support, often from volunteer staff

cri·sis man·age·ment *n.* the business or process of working through a crisis to solve or cope with problems as they arise

crisp /krisp/ *adj.* **1. HARD BUT EASILY BROKEN** dry and firm, and of a texture that breaks easily ○ *cereal that stays crisp in milk* **2. FRESH AND CRUNCHY** fresh and firm enough to snap when bitten into ○ *nice crisp lettuce* **3. SMOOTH, FIRM, AND CLEAN** with a stiff, uncreased, or unspoiled surface ○ *a crisp white tablecloth* **4. DISTINCT** distinct and clear, without ambiguity or distortion ○ *She was pleased with the crisp image of the print.* **5. SHARP AND CONCISE** sharp and concise, often to the point of brusqueness ○ *crisp responses* **6. INVIGORATING** invigorating and fresh ○ *It was a beautiful crisp December morning.* **7. QUICK AND PRECISE** performed in a quick and precise way ○ *some crisp passing* ■ *n.* **1. DESSERT WITH CRUNCHY TOPPING** a dish of prepared fruit covered with a mixture of flour, sugar, and fat baked until the top is crunchy **2.** *U.K.* = **potato chip** ○ *cheese and onion crisps* ■ *vti.* **(crisped, crisp·ing, crisps) MAKE OR BECOME CRISP** to become or make something crisp or crisper, usually in the oven [Mid-16thC. Originally in the sense "curly," from Latin *crispus* (the source also of English *crêpe*).] —**crisp·ly** *adv.* —**crisp·ness** *n.* ◇ **to a crisp** until it has become hard and crunchy, usually when it should not be (*informal*) ○ *toast burned to a crisp*

cris·pate /kriss páyt/ *adj.* used to describe leaves that have curled or wavy edges [Mid-19thC. From Latin *crispatus*, the past participle of *crispare* "to curl," from *crispus* "curled."]

cris·pa·tion /kriss páysh'n/ *n.* **1. ACT OF CURLING** the act of curling or the condition of being curled (*formal*) **2. MUSCLE CONTRACTION** a minor convulsive muscle contraction that produces a creeping feeling in the skin [Early 17thC. Formed from Latin *crispat-*, the past participle stem of *crispare* (see CRISPATE).]

crisp·bread /krísp brèd/ *n.* a flat, crisp, usually rectangular cracker made from rye, wheat, corn, or other grain

crisp·en /kríspən/ (**-ened, -en·ing, -ens**) *vti.* to become or make something crisp or crisper

crisp·er /kríspər/ *n.* a covered compartment in a refrigerator, where fruits and vegetables are placed to keep them fresh and crisp

crisp·y /kríspee/ (**-i·er, -i·est**) *adj.* with a pleasantly light, crunchy texture ○ *Do you like your bacon crispy?* —**crisp·i·ness** *n.*

cris·sa plural of **crissum**

Crisscross

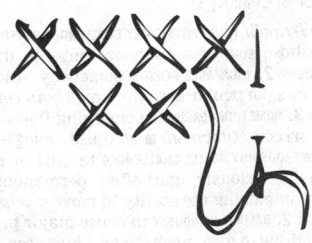

criss·cross /kríss kròss/ *n.* **CROSS OR LATTICE ARRANGEMENT** a pattern of lines that cross each other ■ *adj.* **WITH CROSSED VERTICAL AND HORIZONTAL LINES** running in different directions across each other, or made up of lines like this ■ *adv.* **BACK AND FORTH** in a way that makes a crisscross pattern of crossing lines ■ *v.* **(-crossed, -cross·ing, -cross·es) 1.** *vti.* **MAKE PATTERN OF CROSSED LINES** to create a crisscross pattern on something **2.** *vt.* **GO TO AND FRO ACROSS SOMETHING** to travel or move backward and forward or in all different directions over something [Early 17thC. Alteration of *cristcross* "sign of cross."]

cris·sum /kríssəm/ (*plural* **-sa** /-sə/) *n.* the feathers beneath the tail of a bird [Late 19thC. From modern Latin, formed from Latin *crissare* "to wiggle the hips."] —**cris·sal** *adj.*

cris·ta /krístə/ (*plural* **-tae** /-tee/) *n.* **1.** ANAT **CREST** a crest or ridge, e.g., the border of a bone **2.** CELL BIOL **FOLD** a fold in the inner membrane of a mitochondrion, providing a large surface area over which the enzymes responsible for energy metabolism are located [Mid-19thC. From Latin, "tuft of hair, ridge" (source of English *crest*).] —**cris·tate** *adj.*

cris·to·ba·lite /kri stṓbə lìt/ *n.* a white mineral form of silica that occurs in volcanic rocks. Formula: SiO_2. [Late 19thC. Named for the hill of San Cristóbal, near the town of Pachuca de Soto in Mexico.]

crit. *abbr.* 1. critic 2. critical 3. criticism

cri·te·ri·on /krī teéree ən/ (*plural* **-a** /-teéree ə/ *or* **-ons**) *n.* an accepted standard used in making decisions or judgments about something (*often used in the plural*) [Early 17thC. From Greek *kritērion*, from *kritēs* "judge" (see CRITIC).] —**cri·te·ri·al** *adj.*

WORD KEY: USAGE

criterion or **criteria**? *Criterion* is singular, and *criteria* is plural; it is incorrect to use *criteria* as a singular noun (with *criterias* as a bogus plural), although this is commonly seen and heard in the print and electronic media, and in some law contexts as well: *In two cases ... the courts expressly adopted that criteria* (P. P. Craig, *Administrative Law*). To form a correct singular noun, the phrase *set of criteria* is often used.

crit·ic /kríttik/ *n.* **1. SOMEBODY JUDGING SOMETHING** somebody who makes a judgment about or an appraisal of something or somebody and gives comments ○ *an eminent critic of postwar government* **2. WRITER OF REVIEWS** somebody, especially a journalist, who writes or broadcasts opinions on the quality of things such as drama productions, art exhibitions, and literary works ○ *the newspaper's TV critic* **3. SOMEBODY WHO FINDS FAULT** somebody who does not like something or somebody, or who finds fault with something or somebody [Mid-16thC. Via Latin from Greek *kritikos* "discerning," from *kritēs* "judge," from *krinein* (see CRISIS).]

crit·i·cal /kríttik'l/ *adj.* **1. NOT APPROVING** tending to find fault with a particular person or thing, or with people and things in general **2. GIVING COMMENTS OR JUDGMENTS** containing or involving comments and opinions that analyze or judge something, especially in a detailed way ○ *a critical analysis of modern economic theory* **3. CRUCIAL** extremely important because of being a time or happening at a time of special difficulty, trouble, or danger, when matters could quickly get either worse or better ○ *The decision was a critical one for the country.* **4. ESSENTIAL** absolutely necessary for the success of something ○ *The army's immediate response is critical to our campaign.* **5. LIFE-THREATENING** life-threatening as a medical condition, or in danger from such a condition ○ *a patient in critical condition* **6. UNDERGOING CHANGE** relating to a property of a system that is undergoing a sudden change ○ *critical temperature* **7. SUSTAINING NUCLEAR CHAIN REACTION** designed to or having the mass to sustain a nuclear chain reaction —**crit·i·cal·ly** *adv.* —**crit·i·cal·ness** *n.*

crit·i·cal an·gle *n.* **1. ANGLE PRODUCING COMPLETE REFLECTION** the angle between a ray of light and a surface at which the ray will be completely reflected by the surface **2.** = **stalling angle**

crit·i·cal·i·ty /krìtti kállətee/ *n.* **1. CRUCIALNESS** the condition of being crucial, decisive, or extremely serious **2. STAGE OF NUCLEAR REACTION** the point in an intensifying nuclear reaction at which it becomes self-sustaining

crit·i·cal mass *n.* **1. AMOUNT OF FISSIONABLE MATERIAL** the smallest amount of fissionable material needed to maintain a nuclear chain reaction **2. POINT OF CHANGE** a point or situation at which change occurs ○ *Support for the measure has reached critical mass.*

crit·i·cal point *n.* **1. POINT OF EQUILIBRIUM BETWEEN TWO STATES** a point at which two or more phases of a substance, e.g., liquid and gas, are identical or in equilibrium **2. ZERO POINT ON GRAPH** a point on a graph at which the tangent to a curve is parallel to either the horizontal or vertical axis

crit·i·cal re·gion *n.* the possible results of a statistical test that are outside the range of acceptable probabilities and, if observed, would lead to their rejection

crit·i·cal state *n.* = **critical point** *n.* 1

crit·i·cal think·ing *n.* disciplined intellectual criticism that combines research, knowledge of historical context, and balanced judgment

crit·i·cism /krítti sìzzəm/ *n.* **1. ACT OF CRITICIZING** a spoken or written opinion or judgment of what is wrong or bad about somebody or something **2. DISAPPROVAL** spoken or written opinions that point out one or more faults of somebody or something **3. ASSESSMENT OF CREATIVE WORK** considered judgment of or discussion about the qualities of something, especially a creative work **4.** = **critique** *n.* 1

crit·i·cize /krítti sìz/ (**-cized, -ciz·ing, -ciz·es**) *vti.* **1. COMPLAIN ABOUT SOMETHING WRONG** to comment on or point out the faults of people or things, or find something wrong or bad about them **2. GIVE CONSIDERED OPINION ON SOMETHING** to make a considered assessment of the qualities of something, especially a creative work —**crit·i·ciz·a·ble** /krítti sìzəb'l, kritti sízəb'l/ *adj.* —**crit·i·ciz·er** /-sìzər/ *n.*

WORD KEY: SYNONYMS

criticize, censure, castigate, blast, condemn, find fault with, pick holes in, nitpick

CORE MEANING: to express disapproval or dissatisfaction with somebody or something

criticize the most wide-ranging term; **censure** to make a formal, often public or official statement of disapproval; **castigate** to criticize severely, often with a suggestion of reprimanding; **blast** an informal term for "castigate"; **condemn** to give an unfavorable, absolute, and final judgment; **find fault with** to enumerate specific grounds for dissatisfaction; **pick holes in** to point out flaws in something, particularly an argument; **nitpick** to engage in petty fault-finding.

cri·tique /kri teék/ *n.* **1. REVIEW OF SOMEBODY'S WORK** a written or broadcast assessment of something, usually a creative work, with comments on its good and bad qualities **2.** = **criticism** *n.* 3 ■ *vt.* **(-tiqued, -tiqu·ing, -tiques) GIVE REVIEW OF** to discuss or comment on something, e.g., an artist's work or a political policy, giving an assessment of its good and bad features [Mid-17thC. Via French from Greek *kritikē* (*tekhnē*), literally "art of criticism," from *kritikos* (see CRITIC).]

crit·ter /kríttər/ *n.* a living thing, often a child or an animal (*informal humorous*) ○ *That dog was a mean old critter.* [Early 19thC. Alteration of CREATURE.]

croak /krōk/ *n.* **CRY OF ANIMAL OR BIRD** a rough, usually low-pitched, vibrating sound, especially made by a frog or a crow, or the rough-sounding voice of somebody with a dry or sore throat ■ *v.* **(croaked, croak·ing, croaks) 1.** *vi.* **GIVE HARSH GRATING CALL** to make a rough, usually low-pitched, vibrating call **2.** *vti.* **SPEAK HOARSELY** to speak or say something in a rough low uneven voice **3.** *vi.* **GRUMBLE** to grumble or mutter gloomily (*informal*) **4.** *vti.* **DIE OR KILL** to die, or to kill somebody (*slang*) [Mid-16thC. Origin uncertain: probably an imitation of the sound.] —**croak·i·ly** *adv.* —**croak·y** *adj.*

croak·er /krṓkər/ *n.* **1. FISH THAT MAKES CROAKING SOUND** a fish that makes croaking or grunting noises. Family: Sciaenidae. **2. CROAKING ANIMAL** a bird or other animal that croaks when it calls **3. DOCTOR** a doctor (*slang*)

Cro·at /krṓ àat, krṓ àt/ *n.* **1.** PEOPLES **SOMEBODY FROM CROATIA** somebody who was born or raised in Croatia, or who has Croatian citizenship **2.** LANG = **Croatian** *n.* 1 [Mid-17thC. Via modern Latin *Croata* from Serbo-Croatian *Hrvāt* (source of English *cravat*).] —**Croat** *adj.*

Cro·a·tia /krō áyshə, -shee ə/ formerly one of the six republics that made up the former Federal People's Republic of Yugoslavia, Croatia declared itself an independent republic in 1991. Language: Croatian. Currency: kuna. Capital: Zagreb. Population: 4,664,710 (1997). Area: 21,819 sq. mi./56,510 sq. km. Official name **Republic of Croatia**

Croatia

Cro·a·tian /krō áysh'n/ *adj.* **OF CROATIA** relating to or typical of Croatia, its people, culture, or language ■ *n.* **1.** LANG **OFFICIAL LANGUAGE OF CROATIA** the official language of Croatia, a variety of Serbo-Croat written in the Latin alphabet. Croatian is spoken by about five million people. **2.** PEOPLES = **Croat** *n.* 1

croc /kraak/ *n.* a crocodile (*informal*) ○ *Any crocs in this river?* [Late 19thC. Shortening.]

cro·ce·in /krṓssee in/ *n.* a red or orange acid azo dye [20thC. Formed from Latin *croceus* "saffron-colored," from *crocus* (see CROCUS).]

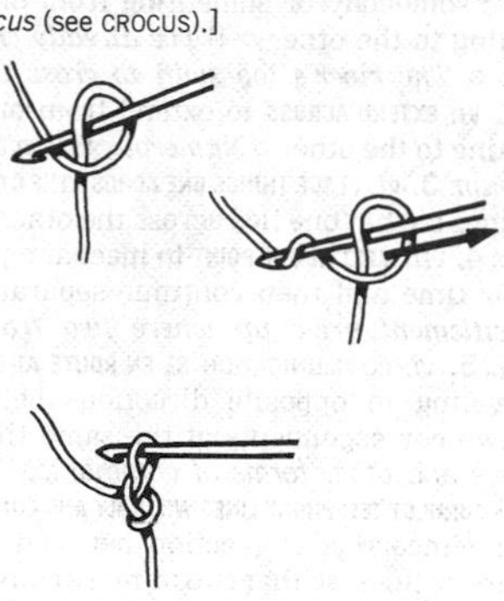

Crochet: Hooked needle is used to catch thread (top), which is twisted and pulled to create loop (center and bottom)

cro·chet /krō sháy/ *n.* **TYPE OF KNITTING USING HOOK** a form of needlework used to make clothes or decorative items from wool or thick stiff thread, by looping it through itself with a special hooked needle (**crochet hook**) ■ *vti.* (**-cheted, -cheted** /-sháyd/, **-chet·ing** /-sháy ing/, **-chets** /-sháyz/) **USE CROCHET TO MAKE SOMETHING** to make things, or a particular item, with crochet work [Mid-19thC. From French *crochet*, literally "little hook," from *croche* "hook," of Germanic origin.] —**cro·chet·er** /krō sháy ər/ *n.*

cro·ci plural of **crocus**

cro·cid·o·lite /krō síddə lìt/ *n.* a fibrous purplish blue form of the mineral riebeckite. It is a type of asbestos. [Mid-19thC. Coined from Greek *krokid-*, the stem of *krokis* "nap of woolen cloth" + -LITE.]

crock[1] /krok/ *n.* **1. CLAY POT** a pot made of clay **2. POTTERY FRAGMENT** a fragment of clay pottery **3. LIE** something, especially a story, that is ridiculous or untrue (*slang disapproving*) ○ *His story about working until midnight is just a crock!* [Old English *crocc*, of prehistoric Germanic origin]

crock[2] /krok/ *n.* **WORN-OUT THING** a worn-out person, vehicle, or machine (*informal insult*) ■ *vt.* (**crocked, crock·ing, crocks**) **DISABLE SOMETHING OR SOMEBODY** to disable or weaken somebody or something (*slang*) [15thC. Origin unknown.]

crock[3] /krok/ *n.* dirt or soot (*regional*) [Mid-17thC. Origin unknown.]

crocked /krokt/ *adj.* drunk (*slang*) [Early 20thC. Origin uncertain: possibly from CROCK[2].]

crock·er·y /krókəree/ *n.* plates, cups, saucers, and other household items made of earthenware [Early 18thC. Formed from earlier *crocker* "potter," from CROCK[1].]

crock·et /krókət/ *n.* any of various leaf shapes carved as decorations in Gothic architecture, often projecting along the angles on a spire or gable [Late 17thC. From Old French dialect *croquet* "shepherd's crook," a variant of Old French *crochet* (see CROCHET).]

Crock·ett /krókət/, **Davy** (1786–1836) U.S. frontiersman. He fought against the Creek Native Americans, and joined Congress in 1827. Full name **David Crockett**

Crock-Pot *tdmk.* a trademark for an electric pot used for slow cooking

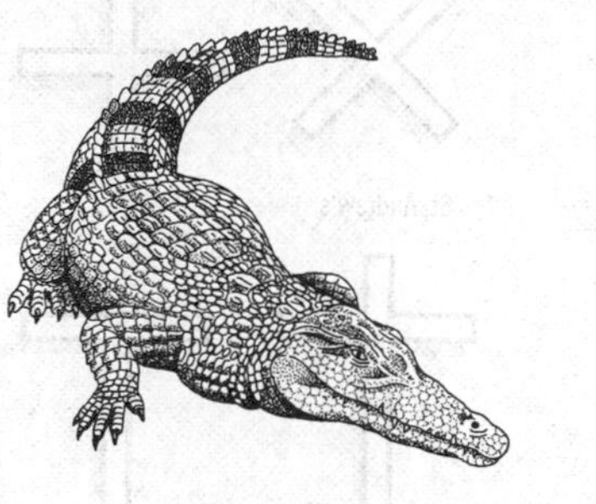

Crocodile

croc·o·dile /krókə dìl/ (*plural* **-diles** *or* **-dile**) *n.* **1. LARGE REPTILE WITH STRONG JAWS** a large tropical or subtropical carnivorous reptile that lives near water. It has a long, thick-skinned, body and a broad head with strong jaws. Crocodiles have longer and more tapering snouts than alligators. Family: Crocodylidae. **2.** = **crocodilian 3. LEATHER FROM CROCODILE SKIN** leather made from the skin of a crocodile ○ *crocodile shoes* [13thC. Via Old French *cocodril* from, ultimately, Greek *krokodilos*, a kind of small lizard.]

croc·o·dile bird *n.* a long-legged black-and-white African bird that lives near the sandy banks of rivers and lakes and feeds on insects parasitic to the crocodile. Latin name: *Pluvianus aegyptius.*

croc·o·dile clip *n. U.K.* = **alligator clip**

croc·o·dile tears *npl.* false tears or an insincere show of grief [Because crocodiles were once believed to have made sounds like weeping to attract prey, and to shed hypocritical tears over their victims]

croc·o·dil·i·an /krókə díllee ən/ *n.* any large predatory reptile belonging to a group that includes the alligator, caiman, crocodile, gavial, and related extinct animals. Order: Crocodylia. —**croc·o·dil·i·an** *adj.*

croc·o·ite /krókō ìt/, **cro·coi·site** /krō kṓ i sìt/ *n.* a rare orange or red mineral consisting of lead chromate. Formula: $PbCrO_4$. [Mid-19thC. Alteration of French *crocoise*, from Greek *krokoeis* "saffron-colored," from *krokos* "saffron."]

cro·cus /krṓkəss/ (*plural* **-cus·es** *or* **-ci** /-sì, -kee/) *n.* **1. SPRING FLOWER** a small perennial plant that grows from a corm and has white, purple, or yellow flowers in early spring. Genus: *Crocus.* **2. FLOWER SIMILAR TO CROCUS** any plant that has a flower like a true crocus, e.g., the autumn crocus **3. METAL POLISH** powdered ferric oxide, used to polish metal [14thC. Via French and Latin from Greek *krokos* "saffron, crocus."]

cro·cus sack, cro·cus bag *n. Southern U.S.* a gunnysack [Origin uncertain: possibly from CROCUS, because such sacks were used to carry saffron]

WORD KEY: REGIONAL NOTE

Crocus sack is a Virginian Piedmont term that spreads south below the South Midland territory, where *tow sack* prevails. In Southern regions, where /r/ is pronounced and not vocalized after a vowel, the spelling form *croker sack* recurs. As vocalization recedes, the latter has become far more common than the original form.

Croe·sus /kréessəss/ *n.* a name used for a very wealthy man [From CROESUS.]

Croe·sus /kréessəss/, **King of Lydia** (*fl.* 6th century B.C.) Lydian monarch who was proverbially wealthy ruler whose reign from about 560 to 546 B.C. ended in defeat and probable capture by Cyrus the Great.

croft /kroft/ *n.* a small plot of land, often with a house on it, that the owner or occupier farms, especially in Scotland [Old English. Of unknown origin.]

croft·er /króftər/ *n.* somebody who owns or rents and farms a small plot of land, often living in a house on it, especially in Scotland

Crohn's dis·ease /krṓnz-/ *n.* a chronic inflammatory disease, usually of the lower intestinal tract, marked by scarring and thickening of the intestinal wall and obstruction [Mid-20thC. Named for the U.S. pathologist B. B. *Crohn* (1884–1983), who identified it.]

crois·sant /krwaa saánt, -saán, -saáN/ *n.* a piece of baked dough or pastry shaped into a crescent, usually moist, flaky, and very rich in fat, originally made in France [Late 19thC. From French, literally "crescent."]

Croix de Guerre /krwaà də gúr/ (*plural* **Croix de Guerre**) *n.* a French military medal awarded for bravery in war [Early 20thC. From French, literally "war cross."]

cro·ker sack /krṓkər-/ *n. Southern U.S.* a gunnysack [Alteration of CROCUS SACK]

Cro-Mag·non /krō mágnən, -mánnyən/ *n.* the earliest known type of modern human being found in Europe and dating from between about 50,000 and 30,000 years ago [Mid-19thC. From the name of the *Cro-Magnon* hill in the Dordogne, France, where Cro-Magnon skeletons were first discovered.]

crom·lech /króm lèk/ *n.* **1. STONE CIRCLE** a group of prehistoric standing stones arranged in a circle **2. BURIAL CHAMBER** an ancient stone burial chamber [Late 17thC. From Welsh, formed from *crwm* "arched" and *llech* "flat stone."]

Crom·well /króm wèl, krómwəl/, **Oliver** (1599–1658) English soldier and statesman. He led the Parliamentarians to victory in the English Civil War (1642–48) and, after the execution of Charles I, ruled as Lord Protector of England (1653–58).

crone /krōn/ *n.* an offensive term that deliberately insults a woman's age, appearance, and temperament (*offensive*) [14thC. Via Old Northern French *carogne* "withered old woman," literally "carrion," from assumed Vulgar Latin *caronia*, from Latin *caro* "flesh."]

Cro·nus /krṓnəss/ *n.* in Greek mythology, one of the Titans who ruled the world until his son Zeus dethroned him. Roman equivalent **Saturn**

cro·ny /krṓnee/ (*plural* **-nies**) *n.* a close friend, especially one of long standing [Mid-17thC. From Greek *khronios* "long-lasting," from *khronos* "time" (source of English *chronic*). The word was originally Cambridge University slang.]

cro·ny·ism /krṓnìizzəm/ *n.* special treatment and preference given to friends or colleagues, especially the giving of political posts to people because of friendship rather than their ability (*informal disapproving*)

Cro·nyn /krṓnin/, **Hume** (*b.* 1911) Canadian-born U.S. stage and screen actor who starred in many movies, including *Cocoon* (1985). In 1994 Cronyn and his wife, Jessica Tandy, were awarded the first Tony award for lifetime theatrical achievement.

crook /krŏŏk/ *n.* **1. HOOK-SHAPED DEVICE** a curved or hooked tool, instrument, or part in a mechanism **2.** AGRIC **SHEPHERD'S HOOKED STICK** a long stick with a curved end used by a shepherd to catch or guide a sheep **3.** CHR = **crosier 4. BEND IN SOMETHING** a bent or curved part of something, e.g., the curve made by somebody's arm when the elbow is bent **5. DISHONEST PERSON** somebody who steals, cheats, or is involved in criminal activities (*informal disapproving insult*) ■ *vti.* (**crook·ed, crook·ing, crooks**) **BEND SOMETHING** to curve, or make something, e.g., a finger, take on a hooked or curved shape [12thC. From Old Norse *krókr* "hook."]

crook·ed /krŏŏkəd/ *adj.* **1. WITH BENT SHAPE** sharply curved, bent, or twisted, often in more than one place **2. AT ANGLE** not aligned properly, or at an angle ○ *That picture is crooked.* **3. NOT LEGAL** illegal or dishonest (*informal*) —**crook·ed·ly** *adv.* —**crook·ed·ness** *n.*

crook·er·y /krŏŏkəree/ *n.* illegal or dishonest activities

crook·neck /krŏŏk nèk/, **crook·neck squash, crook-necked squash** /krŏŏk nèkt-/ *n.* a yellow summer squash that has a long curved neck

croon /kroon/ *vti.* (**crooned, croon·ing, croons**) **1. SING OR MURMUR GENTLY** to sing or murmur something in a soft, low voice, especially to yourself or to a sleepy child **2. SING SENTIMENTALLY** to perform a song or songs in a smooth sentimental style ■ *n.* **GENTLE SINGING** a singing in a soft low way, or something sung in this way [15thC. From Middle Dutch *krōnen* "to lament" (perhaps ultimately an imitation of the sound).]

croon·er /kroonər/ *n.* a singer who favors slow songs, especially ballads, and whose style is generally sentimental

crop /krop/ *n.* **1.** AGRIC, BOT **PLANT GROWN FOR USE** any group of plants grown by people for food or other use, especially on a large scale in farming or horticulture **2.** AGRIC **AMOUNT PRODUCED** the amount harvested from a plant or area of land, during one particular period of time ○ *a good crop of tomatoes* **3.** AGRIC **ANIMALS REARED FOR PRODUCE** a group of animals reared in farming, or something produced from them ○ *a poor crop of lambs* **4. GROUP OF PEOPLE OR THINGS** a number of things occurring, or people doing or being something, at the same time ○ *last year's crop of students* **5.** EQU **WHIP HANDLE** the handle of a whip **6.** HAIR **SHORT HAIRSTYLE** a short hairstyle, usually for a woman **7.** BIRDS **POUCH IN GULLET OF BIRDS** a pouch in the gullet of many birds in which they store or partially digest food before regurgitating it to feed their young **8.** ZOOL **POUCH IN DIGESTIVE SYSTEM** a pouch in the digestive tract of an insect or earthworm ■ *v.* **(cropped, crop·ping, crops) 1.** *vti.* AGRIC **GRAZE** to eat the top parts of growing plants, especially grass **2.** *vt.* **CUT SOMETHING SHORT** to cut something short, e.g., hair or a lawn **3.** *vti.* AGRIC **GATHER PRODUCE** to cut or gather the produce of plants or of a cultivated area ○ *crop a field* **4.** *vti.* AGRIC **PRODUCE CROP** to produce a crop, or make an area of land produce a crop ○ *The tomatoes cropped well this summer.* **5.** *vt.* PHOTOGRAPHY **CUT PART OF PHOTO** to cut off or conceal unwanted parts of an image, especially a photograph [Old English *cropp* "ear of grain." Ultimately from a prehistoric Germanic word meaning "round mass," which is also the ancestor of English *croup* and *group*.]

crop out *vi.* = **outcrop**

crop up *vi.* to appear or arrive, especially unexpectedly or from time to time (*informal*) ○ *Her name keeps cropping up in conversation.*

crop cir·cle *n.* an area in a field of crops where the plants have been mysteriously flattened, usually overnight, into the shape of a circle or a more complex pattern

crop-dust·er, crop dust·er *n.* **1. CROP-SPRAYING AIRCRAFT** an aircraft used to spray powdered fungicide or insecticide onto crops from the air **2. FLIER OF CROP-SPRAYING AIRCRAFT** somebody who flies a crop-spraying aircraft

crop-dust·ing *n.* the spraying of powdered fungicide or insecticide onto crops from the air

crop·per /kröppər/ *n.* **1.** = **sharecropper 2. SOMEBODY OR SOMETHING THAT CROPS** a person, animal, or machine that crops **3. PLANT GIVING YIELD** a plant described in terms of its ability to yield produce ◇ **come a cropper 1.** to fail completely (*informal*) **2.** to experience a hurtful or embarrassing fall (*informal*)

crop ro·ta·tion *n.* a system of farming in which a piece of land is planted with different crops in succession, in order to improve soil fertility and control crop pests and diseases

cro·quet /krō káy/ *n.* **1. LAWN GAME WITH BALLS AND MALLETS** an outdoor game, usually played on a lawn, in which the players use long-handled wooden mallets to hit large wooden balls through a series of hoops (**wickets**) **2. STROKE IN CROQUET** a stroke played in the game of croquet whereby a player knocks away an opponent's ball by hitting his or her own ball when the two are touching ■ *vti.* **(-queted, -quet·ing, -quets) KNOCK SOMEBODY'S CROQUET BALL AWAY** to knock away an opponent's ball in the game of croquet by hitting your own ball when the two are touching [Mid-19thC. Origin uncertain: possibly from French dialect *croquet* "shepherd's crook," a variant of French *crochet* (see CROCHET).]

cro·quette /krō két/ *n.* a little flat cake or ball of a savory mixture, e.g., containing potato, meat, or fish, coated in egg and breadcrumbs, and fried [Early 18thC. From French, formed from *croquer* "to crunch," ultimately an imitation of the sound.]

cro·quis /krō kée/ (*plural* **-quis**) *n.* a rough sketch or draft of something (*technical*) [Early 19thC. From French, formed from *croquer* "to sketch."]

crore /krawr/ (*plural* **crores** *or* **crore**) *n. S Asia* ten million, especially ten million rupees or the equivalent, one million pounds, in sterling [Early 17thC. Via Hindi *kror* from Sanskrit *koṭiḥ*.]

Cros·by /krózbee/, **Bing** (1904?–77) U.S. singer and actor. Famous for songs such as "White Christmas" (1942), he also starred in many movies, including *High Society* (1956). Real name **Harry Lillis Crosby**

cro·sier /krṓzhər/, **cro·zier** *n.* **1.** CHR **ROD CARRIED BY BISHOP** a staff with a hooked end like a shepherd's crook, carried by Christian bishops, archbishops, or abbots, symbolizing their roles of caring for their congregations as shepherds tend flocks **2.** BOT **CURLED PLANT PART** a part of a plant that has a curled end, e.g., the frond of a fern [13thC. Via Old French *crosier* "crook bearer" from *croce* "crook" (also influenced by *crois* "cross"). Ultimately of Germanic origin.]

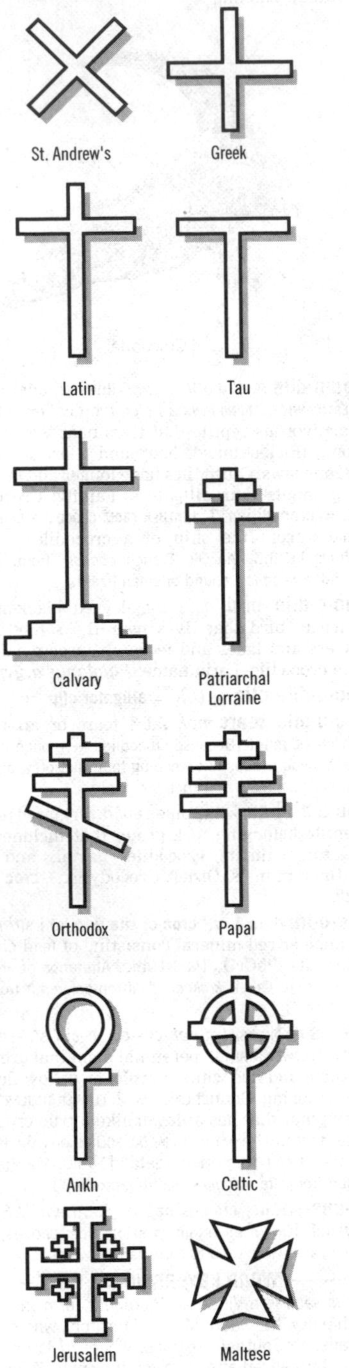

Cross

cross /kross/ *n.* **1. TWO INTERSECTING LINES** a sign or mark (X) made of two straight lines that bisect each other, used to mark or cancel something, or, in the past, as a signature by people who could not write **2. CHRISTIAN SYMBOL** a long vertical bar intersected at right angles, usually about two-thirds up, by a shorter horizontal bar, used as a symbol of Christianity, or of the crucifixion. The shape refers to the cross on which Jesus Christ was crucified. **3. Cross, cross WOODEN STRUCTURE JESUS CHRIST DIED ON** the specific wooden cross on which Jesus Christ was crucified **4. CROSS-SHAPED MEDAL OR INSIGNIA** a medal or emblem shaped like a cross **5. WOODEN EXECUTION POST WITH CROSSBAR** an upright wooden post with a shorter post fixed across it at right angles toward the top, on which, in the past, people were nailed or hanged in public executions **6. STONE MONUMENT** an upright stone or structure in the shape of a cross or holding a cross, erected to commemorate somebody or something (*often used in placenames*) **7. SOMETHING TO BE BORNE** a difficulty in somebody's personal life that is particularly testing, troubling, or painful ○ *What's happened to him is a shame, but we all have a cross to bear.* **8. MIXTURE** a thing or person that results from blending two different kinds together, or that combines the qualities of two different kinds ○ *a cross between a mystery and a historical novel* **9.** GENETICS **PRODUCTION OF HYBRID** the process of producing a crossbreed or hybrid from genetically different individuals **10.** GENETICS **HYBRID INDIVIDUAL** an animal or plant produced by breeding two genetically different individuals together **11.** BOXING **SIDEWAYS BLOW IN BOXING** a punch thrown at an opponent from the side, in response to and evading the opponent's jab or lead **12.** SOCCER **PASSING OF BALL ACROSS FIELD** in soccer, a kicked pass that sends the ball across the field, usually in the air **13.** SPORTS **PASS ACROSS GOAL** a pass that sends the ball across the field, e.g., in field hockey **14.** CONSTR **PIPE CONNECTION** a cross-shaped joint used to connect four pipes **15. ACT OF OPPOSITION** an act of opposition to somebody's plan or procedure **16.** LAW **CROSS-EXAMINATION** cross-examination ○ *On cross, the witness admitted he had lied.* **17. SOMETHING DISHONEST** something dishonest or fraudulent, especially a sports contest in which the outcome has been dishonestly decided before it begins (*slang*) ■ *v.* **(crossed, cross·ing, cross·es) 1.** *vti.* **GO ACROSS** to move or move somebody or something from one side of something to the other ○ *We've already crossed the border.* ○ *The river's too swift to cross the horses here.* **2.** *vi.* **EXTEND ACROSS** to extend from one side of something to the other ○ *Numerous fallen trees cross the stream.* **3.** *vt.* **PLACE THINGS ONE ACROSS THE OTHER** to put two things so that one lies across the other ○ *crossed her legs* **4.** *vti.* **MEET AT ONE POINT** to meet at a particular place or time and then continue separately again ○ *A settlement grew up where two trade routes crossed.* **5.** *vi.* COMMUNICATION **BE EN ROUTE AT ONE TIME** to be traveling in opposite directions between the same two correspondents at the same time (*refers to letters and other forms of communication*) **6.** *vti.* TELECOM **CONNECT TELEPHONE LINES WRONGLY AND CONFUSINGLY** to make an incorrect connection between telephone numbers or lines, so that two or more conversations intermingle with each other, or to be connected in this way (*often passive*) **7.** *vt.* GENETICS **INTERBREED PLANTS OR ANIMALS** to make plants or animals, especially those that are genetically different, interbreed or hybridize **8.** *vt.* CHR **MAKE CHRISTIAN BLESSING GESTURE WITH HAND** to draw the shape of a Christian cross in the air over somebody or something as a symbol of God's blessing **9.** *vti.* SPORTS **PASS BALL ACROSS FIELD** in soccer and some other games, to make a pass that sends the ball across, rather than up or down, the field **10.** *vt.* **THWART SOMEBODY** to do something that goes against somebody's wishes, or that annoys or frustrates somebody (*formal*) ○ *I wouldn't cross her; she gets mean when she's angry.* **11.** *vt.* **WRITE LINE ACROSS LETTER T** to draw a horizontal line across the vertical line of a letter t, to complete the letter ■ *adj.* **ANGRY** angry and upset ○ *exchanged a few cross words* [Pre-12thC. Via Old Norse *kross* and Old Irish *cros* from Latin *crux* (source of English *crucify, crucible, cruise,* and *crusade*). Perhaps ultimately of Phoenician origin.] —**cross·er** *n.* —**cross·ly** *adv.* —**cross·ness** *n.*

cross off *vt.* to remove something, especially a name or item written on a list, by drawing a line through it

cross out *vt.* to cancel something, especially a word or item that is wrong or not wanted, by drawing a line through it

cross- *prefix.* **1.** crossing ○ *crossover* **2.** opposing, opposite ○ *crosscurrent* **3.** reciprocal, mutual ○ *crosslink* [From CROSS]

cross·a·ble /kráwssəb'l/ *adj.* possible, easy, or safe to pass across from one side to the other — **cross·a·bil·i·ty** /kròssə bíllətee/ *n.*

cross ac·tion *n.* LAW a legal proceeding brought by a person who has been sued against the person who brought the original action, or against a fellow defendant

cross·bar /kráwss baar/ *n.* **1. LEVEL POLE** a bar that runs horizontally between two vertical posts, e.g., between goalposts or the uprights of a jump **2. LEVEL BAR IN BICYCLE FRAME** a horizontal metal bar that runs from below the handlebars to below the saddle, traditionally in a man's or boy's bicycle **3. TRANSVERSE STRIPE** a transverse bar, stripe, or band

cross·beam /kráwss be̅em/ *n.* a beam that passes between two supports in the structure of a building

cross·bear·er /kráwss bàirər/, **cross-bear·er** *n.* somebody who carries a cross in front of a bishop or archbishop in a ceremonial procession

cross-bed·ding *n.* layering of geological strata in which deposits were laid down at an angle with respect to those above and below, commonly seen in sandstone deposited as dunes —**cross-bed·ded** *adj.*

cross·bill /kráwss bìl/ (*plural* **-bills** *or* **-bill**) *n.* a large finch that lives in coniferous forests and has a beak with crossed tips that it uses to extract seeds from conifer cones. Genus: *Loxia.*

cross·bones /kráwss bōnz/ *npl.* a representation of two human thighbones crossing each other in the middle, traditionally placed beneath a skull as a symbol of death. The image of crossbones lying below a skull was traditionally used by pirates on their flag (**Jolly Roger**) and in modern times to show that something is poisonous. ◊ **skull and crossbones**

cross·bow /kráwss bō/ *n.* a medieval weapon, or its modern sports successor, consisting of a bow attached crosswise to a stock with a cranking mechanism and a trigger. A crossbow fires short, heavy arrows called bolts or quarrels. —**cross·bow·man** *n.*

cross·bred /kráwss bred/ *adj.* HYBRID produced by hybridization of genetically different individuals ■ *n.* = **crossbreed**

cross·breed /kráwss bre̅ed/ *vti.* (**-bred, -bred** /-brèd/, **-breed·ing, -breeds**) BREED FROM GENETICALLY DIFFERENT INDIVIDUALS to breed new strains of plants or animals from genetically different individuals ■ *n.* PRODUCT OF CROSSBREEDING an animal or plant produced by crossbreeding

cross·check /kráwss chèk/ (**-checked, -check·ing, -checks**), **cross-check** *vt.* **1.** VERIFY SOMETHING IN ANOTHER WAY to make sure that something such as a fact or figure is correct by looking it up in other sources or asking another person **2.** OBSTRUCT OPPONENT USING STICK in field hockey, ice hockey, and lacrosse, to obstruct an opposing player by using both hands to thrust a playing stick across his or her body —**cross·check** *n.*

cross-claim *n.* a claim made against another party on the same side of a lawsuit, e.g., a fellow defendant

cross-coun·try *adj.* NOT ON ROAD OR TRACK done over fields or hills, or through woods, not on roads or a specially prepared area ○ *a cross-country run* ■ *n.* RACING OVER FIELDS running, sporting activity, or a race or event, done cross-country ■ *adj.* **1.** ACROSS A COUNTRY from one side of a country to another, or throughout a country ○ *The band embarked on a cross-country tour.* **2.** OPERATING OFF ROADS designed or able to operate without roads ○ *a cross-country vehicle*

cross-coun·try ski·ing *n.* skiing on long narrow skis across open countryside on fairly level ground

cross·court /kráwss kàwrt/ *adj.* hit or thrown from one side of a playing court toward the other, especially in tennis or basketball

cross cous·in, cross-cous·in *n.* a cousin who is related to somebody through a brother and sister, being either a father's sister's child or a mother's brother's child. ◊ **parallel cousin**

cross-cul·tur·al *adj.* relating to or comparing two or more different cultures —**cross-cul·tur·al·ly** *adv.*

cross·cur·rent /kráwss kùrrənt/ *n.* **1.** CONTRARY FLOW a current that flows across another current, mainly in water but also in air **2.** OPPOSITE TENDENCY a movement or trend that conflicts with the general one, especially a trend in people's ideas or opinions

cross·cut /kráwss kùt/ *adj.* **1.** CUT AT ANGLE used to describe something such as wood, meat, or fabric that is cut across its main grain **2.** FOR CUTTING ACROSS made or used for cutting across the grain of wood ■ *v.* (**-cut, -cut·ting, -cuts**) **1.** *vt.* CUT WITH CROSSCUT SAW to cut across the grain of wood using a crosscut saw **2.** *vti.* CINEMA MOVE FROM ONE SHOT TO ANOTHER to alternate repeatedly brief scenes from one filmed sequence with scenes from another to give the impression that the events they show are happening at the same time ■ *n.* **1.** CUT ACROSS a cut made across something, e.g., a long piece of timber **2.** TUNNEL ACROSS VEIN OF ORE a tunnel in a mine that cuts across a vein of ore **3.** CINEMA EXAMPLE OF FILM TECHNIQUE an example of the film technique in which short segments of two or more scenes are alternated **4.** SHORTCUT a shorter and more direct route to place

cross·cut saw *n.* a saw used for cutting wood across the grain

cross·cut·ting /kráwss kùtting/ *n.* CINEMA repeated alternation between brief film sequences to give the impression that the events they show are happening at the same time

cross-dress (**cross-dressed, cross-dress·ing, cross-dress·es**) *vi.* to wear clothes usually worn by somebody of the opposite sex —**cross-dress·er** *n.* —**cross-dress·ing** *n.*

crosse /krawss, kross/ *n.* a wooden stick used in the game of lacrosse, curved at the top into a triangular frame that supports a tough leatherwork net [Mid-19thC. From French, "bishop's crook." See CROSIER.]

cross-ex·am·ine (**cross-ex·am·ined, cross-ex·am·in·ing, cross-ex·am·ines**) *vt.* **1.** QUESTION OPPOSING WITNESS to question a witness for the opposing side in a hearing or trial **2.** QUESTION SOMEBODY RELENTLESSLY to ask somebody a lot of detailed questions in a persistent or aggressive way (*informal*) —**cross-ex·am·in·er** *n.* —**cross-ex·am·i·na·tion** *n.*

cross-eyed *adj.* having one or both eyes turned in toward the nose (*offensive*)

cross-fade (**cross-fad·ed, cross-fad·ing, cross-fades**) *vti.* to gradually introduce a new sound or picture while causing another one to disappear

cross-fer·til·i·za·tion *n.* **1.** FERTILIZATION BY FUSION the fertilization of a female sex cell (**gamete**) of one individual by a male sex cell from a different individual, usually of the same species. ◊ **self-fertilization 2.** = **cross-pollination 3.** EXCHANGE OF IDEAS the exchange of ideas between two groups, especially cultures, that produces benefits for both —**cross-fer·tile** *adj.* —**cross-fer·til·ize** *vti.*

cross·fire /kráwss fìr/ *n.* **1.** GUNFIRE FROM DIFFERENT DIRECTIONS shots that come from more than one place, in such a way that the lines of fire converge **2.** FIERCE CLASH OF OPINIONS heated or lively conversation, with different and opposing views and ideas being put forward, or an example of this

cross-grained *adj.* **1.** WITH GRAIN RUNNING CROSSWISE with an irregular grain or a grain that runs across the length **2.** BAD-TEMPERED AND DIFFICULT difficult to deal with because of stubbornness, contrariness, or bad temper (*informal*)

cross hairs, cross·hairs /kráwss hàirz/ *npl.* a pair of fine lines or wires that cross at right angles inside a lens or sight, used, e.g., in focusing an optical instrument or in aiming a rifle

cross·hatch /kráwss hàtch/ (**-hatched, -hatch·ing, -hatch·es**) *vti.* to draw parallel or intersecting lines across part of a drawing or diagram, usually diagonally, especially to give the effect of shadow or different texture —**cross·hatch·ing** *n.*

cross·head /kráwss hèd/ *n.* a sliding metal block securing one end of a piston rod to a connecting rod

cross-in·dex (**cross-in·dexed, cross-in·dex·ing, cross-in·dex·es**) *v.* **1.** *vt.* CROSS-REFER ITEM IN INDEX to give a particular item one or more additional entries in an index, under different headings, as cross-references to it **2.** *vti.* GIVE CROSS-REFERENCES to supply cross-references in something

cross·ing /kráwssing/ *n.* **1.** POINT WHERE SOMEBODY CAN CROSS SOMETHING a place that has been specially constructed, chosen, or marked out as somewhere where something, e.g., a road or a border, may be crossed **2.** POINT WHERE ROUTES CROSS a place where a railway line and a road, two railway lines, roads, paths, or similar lines go across each other **3.** JOURNEY ACROSS WATER a journey across a body of water **4.** CENTRAL AREA OF CROSS-SHAPED CHURCH the place in a cross-shaped church where the nave and the transept meet

cross·ing o·ver, cross·ing-o·ver *n.* GENETICS the interchange of segments between homologous chromosomes during cell division (**meiosis**), resulting in new combinations of gene types (**alleles**) and therefore variability in inherited characteristics. ◊ **recombination**

cross·jack /kráwss jàk/ *n.* a sail on the mizzenmast of a ship

cross-leg·ged *adj.* WITH KNEES APART AND ANKLES CROSSED in a sitting position with the legs bent so that the knees are apart and the ankles are crossed in front ■ *adv.* WITH ONE LEG OVER OTHER with one leg lying over the other ○ *sitting cross-legged*

cross·let /kráwsslət/ *n.* on coats of arms, a cross that has a smaller cross at the end of each of its arms [15thC. Modeled on Anglo-Norman *croiselet*, literally "small cross."]

cross-link *n.* **cross-link, cross-link·age** CONNECTING LINK IN MOLECULE a transverse connecting element, such as an atom, chemical group, or covalent bond, between parallel chains of a complex organic molecule, especially a polymer or protein ■ *vt.* (**cross-linked, cross-link·ing, cross-links**) JOIN SOMETHING BY CROSS-LINK to join polymer chains by a cross-link

cross match·ing *n.* the process of testing for the compatibility of a donor's and recipient's tissues before blood transfusion or tissue transplantation —**cross-match** *vt.*

cross-mul·ti·ply (**cross-mul·ti·plied, cross-mul·ti·ply·ing, cross-mul·ti·plies**) *vi.* to multiply each numerator of two fractions by the denominator of the other —**cross-mul·ti·pli·ca·tion** *n.*

cross of Lor·raine *n.* a cross with two horizontal bars, a short bar near the top and a longer one near the bottom [Mid-19thC. Named for the former French province of *Lorraine*.]

Cross of Val·our *n.* the highest Canadian decoration for courage

cros·sop·te·ryg·i·an /kro sòptə ríjjən/ (*plural* **-ans** *or* **-an**) *n.* a bony fish with paired fleshy pectoral fins like limbs that is thought to be ancestral to amphibians and other land vertebrates. All except the coelacanth are extinct. Subclass: Crossopterygii. [Mid-19thC. From modern Latin *Crossopterygii*, subclass name, from Greek *krossoi* "fringe" and *pterux* "wing, fin."] —**cros·sop·te·ryg·i·an** *adj.*

cross·o·ver /kráwss ōvər/ *n.* **1.** CROSSING OR TRANSFER POINT a place for crossing from one side of something to the other, or from one line, system, or vehicle to another **2.** GENETICS = **crossing over 3.** GENETICS RESULT OF GENETIC CROSSING OVER a characteristic that is a result of genetic crossing over **4.** SOMEBODY VOTING AGAINST OWN PARTY a supporter of one political party who votes for a candidate of another party, especially in a primary election **5.** WIDENING OF POPULARITY the process by which an artistic work becomes popular outside the category in which it originated **6.** SOMETHING NOW POPULAR WITH DIFFERENT AUDIENCE an artist, musician, artistic creation, or piece of music that has become popular outside one original category —**cross·o·ver** *adj.*

cross·patch /kráwss pàch/ *n.* a bad-tempered, touchy person (*dated informal*) [Late 17thC. Formed from CROSS in the sense "annoyed" + PATCH, with the early meaning "fool."]

cross·piece /kráwss pe̅ess/ *n.* a piece that crosses a structure or implement from one side to the other, e.g., a beam in a building or part of the handle of a tool

cross-pol·li·na·tion *n.* the transfer of pollen from an anther of one flower to the stigma of another —**cross-pol·li·nate** *vti.*

cross prod·uct *n.* = **vector product**

cross-pur·pose *n.* a conflicting or contrary purpose ◇ **at cross-purposes** not understanding each other, usually through not realizing that the other person means or intends something different

cross-ques·tion *n.* a lawyer's question to a witness being cross-examined in a court case —**cross-ques·tion·ing** *n.* —**cross-ques·tion** *vt.*

cross-re·ac·tion *n.* the immunological reaction of one antigen with the antibodies developed against another similar antigen —**cross-re·act** *vi.* —**cross-re·ac·tive** *adj.* —**cross-re·ac·tiv·i·ty** *n.*

cross-re·fer (**cross-re·ferred, cross-re·fer·ring, cross-re·fers**) *vti.* to give a note that tells a reader of a book, index, or card catalog to look in another specified part of the same work or under another heading

cross-ref·er·ence *n.* DIRECTION TO READER TO LOOK ELSEWHERE a note, especially one printed in a book, index, or card catalog, that tells a reader to look in another specified place for information ■ *v.* (**cross-ref·er·enced, cross-ref·er·enc·ing, cross-ref·er·en·ces**) **1.** *vt.* PUT NOTES INTO TEXT to provide a text, index, or card catalogue with cross-references **2.** *vti.* = **cross-refer**

cross-re·sis·tance *n.* resistance developed by an organism to the effects of a toxin as a result of being exposed to a similar toxin

cross·road /kráwss rōd/ *n.* a road that runs across another one or that links two main roads

cross·roads /kráwss rōdz/ *npl.* (*takes a singular verb*) **1. INTERSECTION** a place where two or more roads meet or cross each other, especially in a rural or quiet area **2. RURAL COMMUNITY** a small town or community located at a crossroads **3. MEETING PLACE** a central meeting place that has a lot of activity **4. DECISIVE MOMENT** a time when an important decision must be made

cross·ruff /kráwss rùf/ *n.* **PLAN BETWEEN PARTNERS AT CARDS** a tactic used in the games of whist and bridge, in which two partners alternately trump each other's first card (**lead**) in each round ■ *vti.* (**-ruffed, -ruff·ing, -ruffs**) **TAKE TURNS TO TRUMP PARTNER** to play a crossruff, or to trump the card led by your partner or from the dummy in a crossruff [Late 16thC. Formed from CROSS + RUFF[2] "to trump."]

cross sec·tion, **cross-sec·tion** *n.* **1. PLANE CUTTING THROUGH AN OBJECT** a plane surface formed by cutting through an object at right angles to an axis, especially the longest axis **2. SOMETHING CUT IN CROSS SECTION** a piece cut as part of a cross section, or an image of such a piece ○ *draw a cross-section of a cone* **3. REPRESENTATIVE SAMPLE** a sample of something that represents all or most of the different elements that the whole contains **4. PROBABILITY OF PARTICLE INTERACTION** a measure of the probability of any specific interaction such as fission or ionization occuring between two elementary particles —**cross-sec·tion·al** *adj.*

cross-stitch *n.* **1. EMBROIDERY STITCH** a stitch made up of two diagonal stitches crossing each other **2. EMBROIDERY IN CROSS-SHAPED STITCHES** pictures, designs, or items of needlework sewn using cross-stitches ■ *vti.* (**cross-stitched, cross-stitch·ing, cross-stitch·es**) **SEW USING CROSS-STITCH** to do embroidery using cross-stitches, or to make something in cross-stitch

cross·talk /kráwss tàwk/ *n.* **1. UNWANTED SIGNALS** unwanted sounds or other signals picked up by one channel of an electronic communications system from another channel, e.g., between telephones or loudspeakers **2. SIDE CONVERSATION** talking that is not part of the main conversation and may distract from it

cross·tie /kráwss tī/ *n.* **1. CROSSWISE SUPPORT** a transverse supporting part of a structure, e.g., a beam or rod **2. RAILROAD TIE** a wooden beam that secures the rails on a railroad track

cross-tol·er·ance *n.* = **cross-resistance**

cross·town /kráwss tòwn/, **cross·town** *adj.* traveling or extending across a city or town —**cross·town** *adv.*

cross-train (**cross-trained, cross-training, cross-trains**) *vi.* SPORTS to train for more than one competitive sport at a time

cross-train·er /kráwss tràynər/ *n.* SPORTS **1. SOMEBODY TRAINING FOR DIFFERENT SPORTS** an athlete who trains for more than one competitive sport simultaneously **2. SNEAKER** a sneaker designed for more than one sporting activity

cross train·ing *n.* SPORTS fitness training in different sports, e.g., running and weightlifting, usually undertaken to enhance performance in one of the sports

cross-train·ing *adj.* SPORTS designed to be used for more than one kinds of sporting activity ○ *a cross-train·ing bike*

cross·tree /kráwss trēe/ *n.* either of a pair of horizontal pieces of wood or metal at the top of a ship's mast to which ropes are fixed to support the mast

cross vault, **cross vault·ing** *n.* a ceiling created by the crossing of two or more simple arched vaults (**barrel vaults**)

cross·walk /kráwss wàwk/ *n.* a place marked on a street where pedestrians can cross the street safely

cross·way /kráwss wày/ *n.* = **crossroad**

cross·ways /kráwss wàyz/ *adv.* **1.** = **crosswise 2. DIAGONALLY** from one side or corner to another, in a slanting line

cross·wind /kráwss wìnd/ *n.* a wind that blows across a particular route, flight path, or direction of travel

cross·wise /kráwss wīz/ *adv.* **SIDEWAYS ACROSS SOMETHING** in such a way as to cross something or be positioned across it ■ *adj.* **TRANSVERSE** crossing or lying across something else

cross·word /kráwss wùrd/, **cross·word puz·zle** *n.* a puzzle in which numbered clues are solved and words that form the answers entered horizontally or vertically into a correspondingly numbered grid of squares. Crossword puzzles are often printed in newspapers and magazines, usually with black squares in the grid among the blank squares.

crotch /kroch/ *n.* **1. PLACE WHERE LEGS JOIN BODY** the part of the human body where the legs join the trunk **2. PART OF GARMENT COVERING GENITALS** the area of a pair of pants or underpants that covers somebody's genitals **3. PLACE WHERE TREE DIVIDES** a part of a tree where it forks into two branches **4. FORKED STICK** a pole or stick with a forked end, or the fork itself. ◊ **crutch** [Mid-16thC. Probably a variant of CRUTCH, but influenced by Old North French *croche* "crook," ultimately of Germanic origin. (See CROZIER).] —**crotched** *adj.*

crotch·et /króchət/ *n.* **1. WHIM** a whim, or a perverse idea or opinion (*dated*) **2.** *U.K.* = **quarter note** [14thC. From Old French *crochet*, literally "small hook" (see CROCHET).]

crotch·et·y /króchətee/ *adj.* irritable and difficult to please (*informal*) —**crotch·et·i·ness** *n.*

cro·ton /krṓt'n/ (*plural* **-ton** *or* **-tons**) *n.* **1. TROPICAL PLANT** a tropical plant belonging to the spurge family. Most are shrubs or trees, and some are noted for their medicinal properties . Genus: *Croton*. **2. TROPICAL EVERGREEN PLANT** a tropical evergreen plant, grown for its leathery, variegated foliage. Latin name: *Codiaeum variegatum*. [Mid-18thC. Via modern Latin, genus name, from Greek *krotōn* "sheep-tick," because of the shape of the plant's seeds.]

Cro·ton bug /krṓt'n-/ *n.* = **German cockroach** [Mid-19thC. Named for the *Croton* River in southeastern New York, which formerly supplied water for New York City.]

cro·ton·ic ac·id /krō tònnik-/ *n.* a colorless, crystalline, organic acid used in organic synthesis and the manufacture of drugs and resins. Formula: $C_4H_6O_2$. [Formed from CROTON]

cro·ton oil *n.* a yellowish brown oil used in the past as a purgative and counterirritant, extracted from the seeds of a croton plant

crouch /krowch/ *v.* (**crouched, crouch·ing, crouch·es**) **1.** *vi.* **BEND DOWN LOW** to squat down on the balls of the feet with knees bent and body hunched over ○ *I had to crouch to get under the table.* **2.** *vi.* **BEND IN PREPARATION TO POUNCE** to stay down close to the ground with legs bent, waiting to spring or run forward (*refers to animals*) ○ *The mountain lion crouched in readiness to pounce.* **3.** *vti.* **CRINGE** to bow the head or bend the body down in a humble or frightened way (*dated*) ■ *n.* **SQUATTING POSITION** the position of a human squatting with back and knees bent, or the position of an animal with the body pressed low to the ground in readiness to spring [14thC. Origin uncertain: probably from a variant of Old French *crochir* "to be crooked," from *croche* "hook" (see CROCHET).]

croup[1] /kroop/ *n.* an inflammatory condition of the larynx and trachea, especially in young children, marked by a cough, hoarseness, and difficult breathing [Mid-18thC. From *croup* "to croak," probably an imitation of the sound.] —**croup·ous** *adj.* —**croup·y** *adj.*

croup[2] /kroop/, **croupe** *n.* the hindquarters of a four-legged animal, especially a horse. ◊ **crupper** [13thC. From Old French *croupe* (source also of English *crupper*).]

crou·pi·er /kroopee ày, -ər/ *n.* somebody in charge of a gaming table who collects and pays out the players' money and chips, and deals the cards or spins the roulette wheel [Mid-18thC. From French, literally "person who rides behind." The modern English meaning developed from "adviser standing behind a gambler."]

crous·tade /kroo staád/ *n.* an edible casing, usually of fried bread or pastry, for holding a savory filling e.g., fish, poultry, meat, or vegetables [Mid-19thC. Via French from, ultimately, Latin *crusta* (see CRUST).]

crou·ton /kroo tòn/ *n.* a small piece, usually a cube, of fried bread used as a garnish for soups, salads, and other dishes (*usually used in the plural*) [Early 19thC. From French, literally "little crust," from *croûte* (see CRUST).]

crow /krō/ *n.* **1. LARGE BLACK BIRD** a large bird with shiny black feathers and a raucous cry, belonging to a family whose members are found in most parts of the world. Rooks and ravens are crows. Genus: *Corvus*. **2.** = **crowbar 3. OFFENSIVE TERM** an offensive term for a woman that deliberately insults the pitch of her voice (*slang offensive*) **4. ROOSTER'S LOUD CRY** a long shrill call made by a bird, especially a rooster ■ *vi.* (**crowed** *or* **crew, crowed, crow·ing, crows**) **1. CRY LIKE ROOSTER** to give the loud shrill cry of a rooster **2. CRY OUT HAPPILY** to cry out with pleasure in the way that babies do **3. BRAG ABOUT SOMETHING** to boast about personal success or celebrate about something another person has failed to do in a noisy and exuberant way [The noun is from Old English *crāwe*; the verb from Old English *crāwan*. Ultimately from a prehistoric Germanic word that was also the ancestor of English *crack* and *croon*.] ◇ **eat crow** to be forced to admit that you have been wrong or have been humiliatingly defeated (*informal*) ◇ **as the crow flies** in a straight line

Crow /krō/ (*plural* **Crow** *or* **Crows**) *n.* **1. MEMBER OF NATIVE AMERICAN PEOPLE** a member of a Native North American people who used to live on the plains of North Dakota but who now inhabit areas of southern Montana and Wyoming **2. CROW LANGUAGE** the Siouan language of the Crow people. Crow is spoken by about five thousand people. [Early 19thC. Translation of French *(gens de) corbeaux*, literally "raven people," which in turn was a translation of the Native American name.] —**Crow** *adj.*

crow·bar /krṓ baàr/ (**-barred, -bar·ring, -bars**) *n.* an iron or steel bar with one flattened, often bent or forked end that is used to lever things up or off [Mid-18thC. So called because the flattened end resembles a crow's foot.] —**crow·bar** *vt.*

crow·ber·ry /krṓ bèrree/ (*plural* **-ries**) *n.* **1. EVERGREEN SHRUB** a low-growing evergreen shrub found in colder regions that has tiny pink or purple flowers and small black berries. Latin name: *Empetrum nigrum*. **2. BERRY OF CROWBERRY SHRUB** the flavorless edible berry of the crowberry shrub [Late 16thC. Probably a translation of German *Krähenbeere*.]

crowd[1] /krowd/ *n.* **1. PEOPLE GATHERED TOGETHER** a large group of people gathered in one place **2. SET OF PEOPLE** a group of people with something in common **3. AUDIENCE OR SPECTATORS** a group of people attending the same public event or entertainment **4. THE MASSES** the mass or majority of people **5. LARGE GROUP OF THINGS** a large number of things put or found together ■ *v.* (**crowd·ed, crowd·ing, crowds**) **1.** *vi.* **THRONG TOGETHER** to assemble or move in large numbers **2.** *vt.* **FILL OR PACK SOMETHING** to fill or cover something or a place in large numbers or to capacity **3.** *vti.* **PRESS NEAR SOMEBODY** to stand or move uncomfortably close to somebody **4.** *vti.* **HERD OR CRAM** to urge, herd, or force a closely packed group of people, animals, or things into a place **5.** *vti.* **ADVANCE BY SHOVING** to move forward by pushing and shoving, or shove past somebody **6.** *vt.* **PRESSURE SOMEBODY** to put pressure on somebody to do something, or make somebody feel forced into something [Old English *crūdan* "to press." The underlying sense is "pressing against something or into a space."] —**crowd·ed** *adj.* —**crowd·ed·ness** *n.* —**crowd·er** *n.*

crowd out *vt.* to exclude or push out somebody or something by force of numbers

crowd[2] /krowd/ *n.* MUSIC an ancient Celtic stringed instrument that was bowed or plucked [14thC. From Welsh *crwth*.]

crowd pleas·er *n.* a person, object, event, or occasion that has great popular appeal —**crowd-pleas·ing** *adj.*

crow·foot /krṓ fòot/ *n.* **1.** PLANTS **PLANT WITH LEAVES LIKE CROW'S FOOT** a plant related to the buttercup that has small yellow or white flowers and divided leaves resembling the feet of a crow. Some species grow in water. Genus: *Ranunculus*. **2.** PLANTS **PLANT RESEMBLING CROWFOOT** any of various plants that have leaves resembling a bird's foot **3.** (*plural* **-feet**) NAUT **ROPES SUPPORTING AWNING** a set of ropes to support an awning

crown /krown/ *n.* **1.** ACCESSORIES **HEADDRESS SYMBOLIZING ROYALTY** an ornate headdress worn as a symbol of sovereignty, often made of gold and set with gems **2. SYMBOL OF ACHIEVEMENT** a wreath or circlet worn on the head as a symbol of victory, success, or high achievement **3.** POL **MONARCH** the reigning monarch of a country **4. Crown, crown** POL **MONARCH'S POWER** the power or authority vested in a monarch **5. EMBLEM RESEMBLING CROWN** an emblem or ornament resembling or representing a crown **6. TOP-RANKING TITLE** a title or distinction that signifies victory or supreme achievement **7. PINNACLE** the highest point of quality, achievement, or fame **8. UPPERMOST PART** the top part of something, especially a hill **9.** ANAT **TOP OF HEAD** the top part of the head **10.** BOT **UPPER PART OF PLANT** the upper part of a tree or shrub, consisting of the foliage and branches **11.** ACCESSORIES **TOP OF HAT** the top part of a hat **12.** BOT **ROOTS AND LOWER STEM OF PLANT** the roots and lower stem of a plant, or a plant consisting only of these parts, used especially for propagation **13.** DENT **VISIBLE PART OF TOOTH** the visible part of a tooth, covered by enamel **14.** DENT **ARTIFICIAL TOOTH** an artificial replacement for the visible part of a tooth that has decayed or been damaged **15.** BOT = **corona 16.** BIRDS **BIRD'S CREST** the crest of a bird **17. TOP OF GEMSTONE** the upper part of a cut gemstone **18.** HIST, MONEY **BRITISH COIN** a former British coin worth five shillings, equivalent to 25 pence, now issued only to commemorate special events **19.** MONEY **EUROPEAN COIN** any of several European coins, such as the Norwegian and Danish krone or the Swedish krona, whose name is translated as "crown" **20.** ACCESSORIES **WINDING KNOB ON WATCH** a ridged winding knob on a watch **21.** NAUT **JUNCTION OF ANCHOR ARMS AND SHANK** the junction where the arms of an anchor join the shank **22.** PAPER **SIZE OF PAPER** a size of paper equal to 15 by 20 in./38 by 51 cm ■ *v.* **(crowned, crown·ing, crowns) 1.** *vt.* POL **CONFER ROYAL STATUS** to make somebody royal or place a crown on somebody's head to symbolize this **2.** *vt.* **REWARD SOMEBODY WITH CROWN** to place a crown on somebody's head, especially in recognition of a victory, success, or achievement **3.** *vt.* **RANK HIGHEST** to confer the top rank on somebody **4.** *vt.* **BE SUMMIT OF SOMETHING** to be or form the top of something **5.** *vt.* **PUT FINISHING TOUCH TO SOMETHING** to complete or be the consummation or confirmation of something **6.** *vt.* DENT **FIT CROWN TO TOOTH** to fit an artificial crown to a damaged or decayed tooth **7.** *vt.* BOARD GAMES **MAKE CHECKER A KING** to promote an ordinary checkers piece to the status of king **8.** *vt.* **TOP SOMETHING WITH SOMETHING ELSE** to put something on or at the top of something else **9.** *vt.* **HIT SOMEBODY ON HEAD** to hit somebody over the head (*informal*) **10.** *vi.* **SHOW BABY'S HEAD DURING LABOR** to progress during the birth of a baby to the point where part of the baby's head is showing at the vaginal opening (*informal*) [12thC. Via Anglo-Norman *corune* or Old French *corone* from Latin *corona* "wreath, garland" (source of English *corona*), from Greek *korōnē* "something curved" from *koronis* "curved."]

Crown at·tor·ney *n.* a lawyer who undertakes criminal prosecutions in Canada on behalf of a federal, provincial, or territorial government

crown col·o·ny *n.* a British colony in which the Crown has a whole or partial governing power

crown cor·po·ra·tion *n.* in Canada, a commerical company owned by a government but independently managed

Crown Der·by *n.* a soft-paste porcelain manufactured in the city of Derby, England, from 1784–1848 and usually marked with the letter "D" surmounted by a crown

crowned head *n.* a reigning monarch

crown gall *n.* a disease of fruit and roses that results in swellings on the roots or stems and is caused by a bacterium *Agrobacterium tumefaciens*

crown glass *n.* **1. OLD WINDOW GLASS** a traditional window glass made by spinning a bubble of molten glass on the end of a rod until it forms a flat disk **2. GLASS FOR LENSES** high-quality glass with a low index of refraction used for making lenses

crown·ing /krówning/ *n.* **1.** POL **INVESTITURE OF MONARCH** the process or ceremony of making somebody a monarch **2.** MED **STAGE IN LABOR** the stage in giving birth at which an infant's head passes through the vaginal opening ■ *adj.* **1. ULTIMATE IN ACHIEVEMENT** representing supreme achievement or the ultimate moment in something **2. FORMING SUMMIT** forming a crown or summit

crown jew·el *n.* the most valuable part of something, or the most prized asset

crown jew·els *npl.* the jewelry and regalia that a monarch wears on state occasions

crown land *n. Can* public land, especially forests, that is owned and regulated by a federal or provincial government

crown lens *n.* a lens made of crown glass, especially the converging component of an achromatic lens

crown-of-thorns (*plural* **crown-of-thorns**) *n.* **1.** ZOOL **SPINY STARFISH** a spiny Pacific starfish that feeds on live coral. Latin name: *Acanthaster planci.* **2.** PLANTS **SHRUB WITH SCARLET BRACTS** a Madagascan shrub, grown as a house plant or as a hedge in tropical areas, whose flowers have scarlet bracts. Latin name: *Euphorbia milii.* **3. HEAVY BURDEN** a painful or onerous burden [From the biblical accounts of the wreath of thorns placed on the head of Jesus Christ]

crown prince *n.* the principal male heir in a monarchy

crown prin·cess *n.* the principal female heir in a monarchy, or the wife of the male heir

Crown pros·e·cu·tor *n.* = **Crown attorney**

crown roast *n.* a cut of meat consisting of two rib sections sewn together to form a circle

crown saw *n.* a cylindrical saw with a row of teeth along one edge, designed for cutting round holes

crown vetch *n.* a European leguminous plant with small pink or white flowers that is cultivated for garden borders and erosion control. Latin name: *Coronilla varia.*

crow's feet *npl.* a network of wrinkles radiating from the outer corner of the human eye [Because they resemble the footprints of crows]

crow's-foot (*plural* **crow's-feet**) *n.* **1.** SEW **THREE-POINT STITCH** a sewing stitch with three points, used especially for finishing off a seam **2.** AIR **SET OF ROPES** a set of short ropes, used in airships and ballooning, that redistributes the pull of a single rope **3.** MIL = **caltrop** [From the shape]

crow's-nest *n.* **1.** NAUT **SHIP'S LOOKOUT POINT** a lookout point consisting of a railed platform at the top of a ship's mast or superstructure **2.** ARCHIT **LOOKOUT POINT ON LAND** a high enclosed lookout point on land

croze /krōz/ *n.* **1. GROOVE ON BARREL** a groove at the top of a barrel or cask into which the head is fitted **2. TOOL TO CUT CROZE** a cooper's tool used to cut grooves at the top of barrels and casks [Early 17thC. From French *creux* "hollow, groove," probably ultimately of Celtic origin.]

cro·zier *n.* = **crosier**

CRT[1] *abbr.* cathode-ray tube

CRT[2] (*plural* **CRTs**) *n.* a computer monitor containing a cathode-ray tube

cru /kroo/ *n.* **1. FRENCH VINEYARD** a vineyard or wine-growing area in France that meets specified standards of quality. The French government sometimes classifies a cru either as a "grand cru" or a "premier cru." **2. OFFICIAL CLASS OF FRENCH WINE** an official grade of French wine such as grand or premier cru [Early 19thC. Formed from French *crû*, past participle of *croître* "to grow," from, ultimately, Latin *crescere* (source of English *accretion* and *crescent*).]

cru·cial /kroósh'l/ *adj.* **1. VITAL TO SOLUTION** vital to the outcome of something **2. IMPORTANT** very important or significant (*informal*) [Early 18thC. Via French, from Latin *cruc-*, the stem of *crux* "cross" (source of English *crux*).] —**cru·cial·ly** *adv.*

WORD KEY: USAGE

Meaning trap: ***Crucial*** has been trivialized to the point that it often means nothing more than "important." This is especially true in media reports in which a hard-hitting word is often more attractive to the reporter: *If proportional representation is adopted, it is crucial to choose the best method.* ***Crucial*** would better be reserved for something decisive: *Her tie-breaking vote was crucial* and *Her vote was nearly crucial* are correct; *Her tie-breaking vote was very crucial* and *Her vote was somewhat crucial* are not, because the meanings of ***crucial*** are "of the greatest significance" and "most vital," thus admitting no comparatives or superlatives.

cru·cian /kroósh'n/ (*plural* **-cians** *or* **-cian**), **cru·cian carp** *n.* a carp that lives in Europe and Asia and has a dark-green back, golden-yellow sides, and reddish fins. Latin name: *Carassius carassius.* [Mid-18thC. Via an alteration of Low German *karu(s)se, karutze* from, ultimately, Latin *coracinus*, denoting a black fish of the Nile River, from Greek *korax* "raven."]

cru·ci·ate /kroóshee àyt/ *adj.* **1.** = **cruciform 2.** INSECTS **FORMING CROSS SHAPE** used to describe insect wings that form a cross shape when at rest [Late 17thC. From medieval Latin *cruciata*, from Latin *crux* "cross."]

cru·ci·ble /kroóssəb'l/ *n.* **1.** METALL **CONTAINER FOR MELTING SOMETHING** a heat-resistant container in which ores or metals are melted **2.** METALL **BOTTOM OF FURNACE** the hollow part at the bottom of a furnace where molten metal collects **3. ORDEAL** a severe trial or ordeal **4. TESTING CIRCUMSTANCES** a place or set of circumstances where people or things are subjected to forces that test them and often make them change [15thC. From medieval Latin *crucibulum* "nightlight, crucible" of uncertain origin: perhaps from Latin *crux* "cross" or from Old French *croisel* "cresset."]

WORD KEY: CULTURAL NOTE

The Crucible, a play by Arthur Miller (1953). Intended as a metaphor for the "un-American" McCarthy hearings of the 1950s, is set in Salem, Massachusetts, in 1692 and describes how the social fabric of a small town is ripped apart when a group of young girls starts to denounce townsfolk as witch-hunters. It was made into a movie by Nicholas Hytner in 1996.

cru·ci·ble steel *n.* a high-grade steel made by mixing steel and additives in a furnace

cru·ci·fer /kroóssəfər/ *n.* **1.** PLANTS **PLANT WITH FOUR-PETALED FLOWERS** a plant that has flowers with four petals in the shape of a cross and long narrow seed pods. Crucifers include cabbages, turnips, broccoli, and wallflowers. Family: Cruciferae. **2.** CHR **SOMEBODY CARRYING CROSS** somebody who carries a cross, especially in a religious ceremony [Mid-16thC. From ecclesiastical Latin, from Latin *cruc-* (the stem of *crux* "cross") + *-fer* "bearer."]

cru·cif·er·ous /kroo sífferəss/ *adj.* used to describe a plant that is a crucifer [Mid-17thC. Formed from Christian Latin *crucifer.*]

cru·ci·fix /kroóssə fiks/ *n.* a model or image of Jesus Christ on the Cross [12thC. Via French from Ecclesiastical Latin *crucifixus*, from Latin *cruci fixus* "fixed to a cross."]

cru·ci·fix·ion /kroóssə fíksh'n/ *n.* **1. EXECUTION BY HANGING ON CROSS** a form of execution used in ancient times that involved binding or nailing somebody to an upright cross until death **2. EXECUTION** an execution involving crucifixion **3. ORDEAL** a painful ordeal or victimization [15thC. From the ecclesiastical Latin stem *crucifixion-*, which was formed from *crucifigere* (see CRUCIFY).]

Cru·ci·fix·ion *n.* **1. AGONY AND DEATH OF JESUS CHRIST** the agony and death of Jesus Christ on the Cross at Calvary **2. DEPICTION OF THE CRUCIFIXION** a depiction of Jesus Christ on the Cross

cru·ci·form /kroóssi fàwrm/ *adj.* shaped like a cross [Mid-17thC. Coined from Latin *cruc-*, the stem of *crux* "cross" + -FORM.] —**cru·ci·form·ly** *adv.*

cru·ci·fy /kroóssi fī/ (**-fied, -fy·ing, -fies**) *v.* **1.** *vt.* **EXECUTE BY CRUCIFIXION** to execute somebody by crucifixion **2.** *vt.* **TREAT SOMEBODY CRUELLY** to defeat, torment, or victimize somebody in a thorough or cruel way **3.** *vr.* **SEVERELY DISCIPLINE YOUR BODY** to severely punish your body as a form of self-discipline [14thC. Via French *crucifier* from, ultimately, Ecclesiastical Latin *crucifigere*, from Latin *cruci figere* "to fix to a cross."] —**cru·ci·fi·er** *n.*

crud /krud/ *n.* **1. FILTH** a messy, dirty, or sticky substance (*slang*) **2.** MANUF **WASTE PRODUCT** an unwanted by-product, especially in the nuclear industry **3. SOMEBODY OR SOMETHING CONTEMPTIBLE** somebody or something that is disgusting or worthless (*informal*) **4.** SKIING **SLUSHY SNOW** slushy snow that is unfit for good skiing (*informal*) **5. NONSENSE** absolute nonsense (*informal*) [14thC. An earlier form of CURD, surviving in this sense in dialect; current senses date from the 20thC.] —**crud·dy** *adj.*

crude /krood/ *adj.* (**crud·er, crud·est**) **1. IN RAW STATE** in an unprocessed state or condition ○ *crude ore* **2. APPROXIMATE** not precisely accurate ○ *a crude estimate* **3.** roughly or unskillfully made or conceived ○ *a crude model of a ship* **4. UNCORRECTED OR UNEMBELLISHED** used to describe numerical results or collected data that have not been organized, analyzed, adjusted, or altered in any way ○ *crude data* ○ *crude facts* **5. VULGAR** vulgar or obscene ○ *a crude gesture* ■ *n.* = **crude oil** [14thC. From Latin *crudus* "raw, rough, cruel."] —**crude·ly** *adv.* —**crude·ness** *n.* —**cru·di·ty** *n.*

crude oil *n.* petroleum that has not yet been refined

cru·di·tés /kroódi táy/ *npl.* small pieces of raw vegetables such as carrots and cucumber eaten as an appetizer or snack, often served with a dip [Mid-20thC. From French, plural of *crudité* from Latin *cruditas*, from *crudus* "raw, rough, cruel."]

cru·el /kroó əl/ *adj.* **1. MERCILESS** deliberately and remorselessly causing pain or anguish, or insensitive to the pain and anguish of others **2. BRINGING ABOUT PAIN** bringing about pain and distress, or painful to bear [12thC. Via French from Latin *crudelis.* Ultimately, from an Indo-European word that also produced English *raw* and Latin *crudus* (source of English *crude*).] —**cru·el·ly** *adv.* —**cru·el·ness** *n.*

cru·el·ty /kro͞o əltee/ (*plural* **-ties**) *n.* **1. DELIBERATELY CRUEL ACT** an act that deliberately causes pain and distress **2. STATE OF BEING CRUEL** the quality or condition of being cruel **3.** LAW **PSYCHOLOGICAL OR PHYSICAL PAIN** the infliction of pain, distress, or anguish, especially when it is long-term and considered extreme enough to be grounds for divorce [13thC. Via Old French *crualté* from, ultimately, Latin *crudelitas*, from *crudelis* (see CRUEL).]

cru·et /kro͞o ət/ *n.* **1.** HOUSEHOLD **CONDIMENT CONTAINER** a small container for holding salt, pepper, oil, or vinegar **2.** HOUSEHOLD **CONDIMENT SET** a set of matching cruets on a stand **3.** CHR **SMALL BOTTLE USED IN EUCHARIST** either of two containers that hold the water and wine used in the Eucharist [13thC. From Anglo-Norman, literally "little flask," formed from Old French *crue* "flask." Ultimately from a prehistoric Germanic word that is also the ancestor of English *crock* "earthenware pot."]

cruise /krooz/ *v.* (**cruised, cruis·ing, cruis·es**) **1.** *vti.* LEISURE, NAUT **TRAVEL BY SEA** to travel by ship over a sea or other large body of water on a pleasure trip, usually calling at several places **2.** *vi.* **TRAVEL AT EASY RATE** to travel at a steady efficient rate, below top speed **3.** *vi.* **TRAVEL WHILE LOOKING FOR SOMETHING** to travel at a slow steady rate while searching or watching for something ○ *The police cruised the streets, looking for the suspect.* **4.** *vti.* **SEEK SEXUAL PARTNER** to go out looking for a sexual partner, or frequent a public place in search of a sexual partner (*slang*) **5.** *vi.* **PROCEED CASUALLY** to proceed in a leisurely casual way or with no particular destination **6.** *vi.* NAVY **PATROL SEA** to patrol an area of sea on the lookout for enemy vessels **7.** *vti.* FORESTRY **DETERMINE TIMBER YIELD** to inspect a forest to determine its potential yield of timber ■ *n.* LEISURE, NAUT **PLEASURE TRIP BY SEA** a journey by ship for pleasure [Mid-17thC. From Dutch *kruisen* "to cross," from *kruis* "cross" from, ultimately, Latin *crux* (source of English "cross").]

Cruise /krooz/, **Tom** (*b.* 1962) U.S. actor and star of many Hollywood movies, including *Jerry Maguire* (1996). Real name **Thomas Cruise Mapother IV**

cruise con·trol *n.* an electronic device in a motor vehicle that allows a selected speed to be maintained consistently

cruise mis·sile *n.* a long-range jet-propelled guided missile that flies low

cruis·er /kro͞ozər/ *n.* **1.** NAVY **SMALL WARSHIP** a fast and easily maneuverable warship that is smaller and less heavily armored than a battleship **2. SOMETHING OR SOMEBODY THAT CRUISES** a vehicle that cruises, e.g., a ship, aircraft, or motor vehicle, or a person that cruises (*slang*) **3. SOMEBODY SEEKING SEXUAL PARTNER** somebody who goes out looking for a sexual partner in a public place (*slang*) **4.** NAUT = **cabin cruiser 5. POLICE CAR** a police car, especially one used to patrol an area ■ *U.K.* BOXING = **cruiserweight** [Late 17thC. From Dutch *kruiser*, from *kruisen* (see CRUISE).]

cruis·er·weight /kro͞ozər wàyt/ *n. U.K.* a boxer between a light heavyweight and a heavyweight,with a maximum weight of 190 lb./86 kg

cruise·wear /kro͞oz wair/ *n.* light casual clothing appropriate for pleasure cruises or hot weather while on vacation

cruis·ing ra·di·us *n.* the maximum distance that a vessel or aircraft can travel without needing to refuel

crul·ler /krúllər/, **krul·ler** *n.* **1. CAKE LIKE DOUGHNUT** a small ring-shaped deep-fried cake **2. TWISTED UNRAISED DOUGHNUT** a type of unraised doughnut, usually twisted in shape [Early 19thC. From Dutch *kruller*, from *krullen* "to curl."]

WORD KEY: REGIONAL NOTE

In the sense of a small ring-shaped or twisted sweet cake, fried in deep fat, ***cruller*** belongs primarily to New England and the Middle Atlantic and North Central states, with a high incidence also in California. The sense "unraised doughnut" is found most frequently in New England and Pennsylvania.

crumb /krum/ *n.* **1. SMALL FRAGMENT OF BAKED FOOD** a very small fragment of bread, cake, cookie, or similar food **2. SMALL AMOUNT** any tiny amount of something **3.** COOK **INNER PART OF LOAF** the soft middle part of a loaf of bread **4. CONTEMPTIBLE PERSON** somebody who is unworthy of respect (*dated slang*) ■ *v.* (**crumbed, crumb·ing, crumbs**) **1.** *vt.* COOK **PUT CRUMBS ON OR IN FOOD** to coat or thicken food with crumbs, especially breadcrumbs **2.** *vti.* COOK **CRUMBLE** to break bread, cake, or cookies into small bits **3.** *vt.* **CLEAN CRUMBS FROM SOMETHING** to clear away crumbs from something [Old English *cruma*, of prehistoric Germanic origin. The final "b" was added in the 16thC.]

crum·ble /krúmb'l/ *v.* (**-bled, -bling, -bles**) **1.** *vti.* **REDUCE TO TINY BITS** to break or make something break into tiny bits **2.** *vi.* **DISINTEGRATE** to disintegrate or fall apart ■ *n. U.K.* = **crisp** [15thC. Probably ultimately from Old English *gecrymmian* "to break into crumbs," which was formed from *cruma* (see CRUMB).]

crum·bly /krúmblee/ (**-bli·er, -bli·est**) *adj.* **1. EASILY CRUMBLED** tending to crumble readily **2. WITH MANY CRUMBS** containing or covered with many crumbs — **crum·bli·ness** /krúmblinəss/ *n.*

crumb·y /krúmmee/ (**-i·er, -i·est**) *adj.* **1. FULL OF CRUMBS** full of or covered with crumbs **2. SOFT-TEXTURED** soft and spongy in texture, like the inside of a loaf of bread **3.** = **crummy**

crum·horn /krúm hàwrn/, **krumm·horn** *n.* a double-reed medieval woodwind instrument with an upward curving tube [Late 17thC. From German, literally "crooked horn."]

crum·my /krúmmee/ (**-mi·er, -mi·est**), **crumb·y** (**-i·er, -i·est**) *adj.* (*informal*) **1. OF LITTLE VALUE** inferior and of little worth **2. MISERABLE** miserable or unwell [Mid-19thC. Variant of CRUMBY.]

crump /krump/ *n.* **SOUND OF BURSTING BOMB** the thudding sound of an exploding shell or bomb ■ *vi.* (**crumped, crump·ing, crumps**) **1. MAKE THUDDING NOISE** to make a thudding noise like the sound of an exploding shell or bomb **2. MAKE CRUNCHING NOISE** to make a crunching noise like the sound of footsteps in crisp snow [Mid-17thC. An imitation of the sound.]

crum·pet /krúmpət/ *n.* a griddle cake with a slightly elastic texture and small holes that is made from a batter risen with yeast. Crumpets are usually eaten toasted with butter. [Late 17thC. Origin uncertain: perhaps from the earlier phrase *crompid cake*, literally "curled-up cake"; *crompid* "crooked."]

crum·ple /krúmp'l/ *v.* (**-pled, -pling, -ples**) **1.** *vti.* **CREASE AND WRINKLE** to become or make something become full of irregular creases and wrinkles **2.** *vti.* **COLLAPSE** to collapse, or make something collapse **3.** *vi.* **LOOK UPSET OR DISAPPOINTED** to lose the appearance of equanimity and control, especially when upset or disappointed and close to tears ■ *n.* **WRINKLE** a crease or wrinkle in something [14thC. Formed from Old English *crump* "to curl up."] —**crum·ply** *adj.*

crunch /krunch/ *v.* (**crunched, crunch·ing, crunch·es**) **1.** *vt.* **MUNCH NOISILY** to crush crisp foods audibly with the teeth **2.** *vti.* **SCRUNCH** to make or cause something to make a noisy scrunching sound ○ *the crunch of footsteps on gravel* **3.** *vt.* COMPUT **RAPIDLY PROCESS DATA** to process data or numbers at high speed (*informal*) ■ *n.* **1. SCRUNCHING NOISE** a loud short sound made when something is crushed **2. DECISIVE MOMENT** a critical time or situation, especially one when a decision or action must be taken ○ *when it comes to the crunch* **3. CRISIS** an emergency or crisis, especially fiscal ■ *adj.* **NEEDING DECISIVE ACTION** requiring a decision or action [Early 19thC. A variant of earlier *cranch* (an imitation of the sound), by association with MUNCH and CRUSH.] —**crunch·a·ble** *adj.* —**crunch·er** *n.*

crunch·y /krúnchee/ (**-i·er, -i·est**) *adj.* crisp and making a crunching sound when eaten or walked upon — **crunch·i·ly** *adv.* —**crunch·i·ness** *n.*

crup·per /krúppər/ *n.* **1.** RIDING **STRAP HOLDING ON SADDLE** a strap that passes under the tail of a horse and is attached to a saddle or harness to prevent it from sliding forward **2.** ZOOL **HORSE'S HINDQUARTERS** the hindquarters of a horse. ◊ **croup** [14thC. From Anglo-Norman *cropere* or Old French *cropiere*. Ultimately, from a prehistoric Germanic word that is also the ancestor of English *crop* and *croup* "rump."]

cru·ra plural of **crus**

cru·ral /kro͝orral/ *adj.* belonging or relating to the leg, or an elongated part resembling a leg [Late 16thC. Directly or via French from Latin *cruralis*, from *crus* "leg."]

crus /krooss, kruss/ (*plural* **cru·ra** /kro͝orə/) *n.* **1. SECTION OF LEG** the leg between the knee and ankle **2. ELONGATED BODY PART** a body part shaped like a leg or pair of legs [Late 16thC. From Latin, literally "leg."]

cru·sade /kroo sáyd/ *n.* **1. cru·sade, Cru·sade** HIST, CHR **RELIGIOUS WAR** any of several military expeditions made by European Christians in the 11th to 13th centuries to retake areas captured by Muslim forces **2.** RELIG **RELIGIOUSLY MOTIVATED EFFORT** a war or campaign that is religiously motivated, e.g., one with papal sanction **3. CONCERTED EFFORT** a vigorous concerted action to promote or eliminate something ■ *vi.* (**-sad·ed, -sad·ing, -sades**) **1. CAMPAIGN** to make a vigorous or concerted effort to promote or eliminate something **2.** HIST, RELIG **FIGHT TO RETAKE HOLY LAND** to go on a religious crusade, especially one to retake the Holy Land in the 11th to 13th centuries [15thC. Ultimately, from Latin *crux* "cross." Originally via Medieval Latin *cruciata*, later via French *croisade* or Spanish *cruzada*.]

cru·sad·er /kroo sáydər/ *n.* **1. cru·sad·er, Cru·sad·er SOLDIER IN CRUSADES** a soldier who took part in any of the crusades **2. CAMPAIGNER** somebody who campaigns vigorously for or against something

cru·sa·do /kroo zaa dō, kroo saa dō, kroo sáy dō/ (*plural* **-does** *or* **-dos**) *n.* a gold or silver coin with a cross imprinted on it that was a unit of currency in Portugal between the 15th and 20th centuries [Mid-16thC. From Portuguese *cruzado* (see CRUZADO).]

cruse /krooz/ *n.* a small earthenware container used to hold liquids (*archaic*) [Old English *crūse*, of prehistoric Germanic origin]

crush /krush/ *v.* (**crushed, crush·ing, crush·es**) **1.** *vti.* **COMPRESS SOMETHING** to compress somebody or something, or become compressed, causing injury, damage, or distortion **2.** *vti.* **CREASE SOMETHING** to compress a fabric or item of clothing, or to become compressed, causing creasing or crumpling **3.** *vti.* **GRIND SOMETHING** to grind something, or become ground, into bits **4.** *vt.* **QUELL PROTEST** to put down a protest or movement using force **5.** *vt.* **OVERWHELM SOMEBODY OR SOMETHING** to defeat, subdue, or suppress somebody or something overwhelmingly **6.** *vt.* **MASH FRUIT** to reduce fruit or vegetables to juice and pulp by pressing **7.** *vt.* **SQUASH SOMEBODY** to exert physical pressure on somebody by hugging, pressing, or pushing **8.** *vt.* **HUMILIATE SOMEBODY** to humiliate somebody by the force of a remark, criticism, or argument **9.** *vi.* **CROWD TOGETHER** to move in a mass or crowd ■ *n.* **1. CROWD** a crowd or mass, especially of people **2. CROWDING** a crowded situation or mass especially of people, or an action that results in this **3.** FOOD **FRUIT DRINK** a drink containing the juice from crushed fruit **4. TEMPORARY ROMANTIC ATTRACTION** a temporary romantic infatuation (*informal*) ○ *a teenage crush* **5. OBJECT OF SOMEBODY'S CRUSH** the person who is the object of somebody's romantic infatuation (*informal*) [14thC. From Anglo-Norman *crussier* or Old French *croissir*, of uncertain origin: perhaps from the prehistoric Germanic language.] —**crush·a·ble** *adj.* — **crush·er** *n.* —**crush·ing** *adj.* —**crush·ing·ly** *adv.*

crushed /krusht/ *adj.* used to describe a fabric or material that has been manufactured or treated to create permanent creases in it ○ *crushed velvet*

crush·proof /krúsh pro͞of/ *adj.* made to resist being crushed, creased, or wrinkled

crust /krust/ *n.* **1.** FOOD **OUTER PART OF BREAD** the thin, usually hard or crisp, outer part of a loaf or slice of bread **2.** FOOD **PIECE OF BREAD** a piece of bread that is mostly crust or is stale and dry **3.** FOOD **PASTRY FOR PIE** the pastry that wholly or partly encases a pie or tart **4. HARD UPPER LAYER** a crisp, hard, or thick outer layer or coating that develops on something **5.** GEOL **SOLID OUTER LAYER OF EARTH** the thin outermost layer of the Earth, approximately one percent of the Earth's volume, that varies in thickness and has a different composition than the interior. Other terrestial planets are believed to have crusts. **6.** MED **SCAB** a dry hardened outer layer of blood, pus, or other bodily secretion that forms over a cut or sore **7.** WINE **LAYER OF POTASSIUM TARTRATE** a thin layer of potassium tartrate that forms on the inside of some wine and port bottles as the contents mature **8.** BIOL **BODY COVERING** the hard outermost body covering in some living organisms such as lichens and crustaceans **9. IMPUDENCE** impudent or impertinent attitude or behavior (*dated informal*) ■ *vti.* (**crust·ed, crust·ing, crusts**) **1. FORM CRUST** to form into or develop a crust **2. MAKE OR BECOME ENCRUSTED** to cover something or become covered with a crust [14thC. Via Old French *crouste* (source of English *crouton* and *custard*) from Latin *crusta* "rind, shell, incrustation" (source of English *crustacean* and *encrust*).]

crus·ta·cean /kru stáysh'n/ *n.* an arthropod with several pairs of jointed legs, a hard protective outer shell, two pairs of antennae, and eyes at the ends of stalks. Lobsters, crabs, shrimps, crayfish, water-fleas, barnacles, and woodlice are crustaceans. Subphylum: Crustacea. [Mid-19thC. Formed from Modern Latin *Crustacea*, neuter plural of *crustaceus* "having a shell," from Latin *crusta* (see CRUST).] —**crus·ta·cean** *adj.* —**crus·ta·ceous** *adj.*

crust·al /krúst'l/ *adj.* used to describe the crust of the Earth or another celestial body [Mid-19thC. From Latin *crusta* (see CRUST).]

crus·tose /krús tōss/ *adj.* used to describe lichens or algae that resemble a crust on the surface they adhere to [Late 19thC. From Latin *crustosus*, from *crusta* (see CRUST).]

crust·y /krústee/ (**-i·er, -i·est**) *adj.* **1. WITH CRUST** with a crisp crust ○ *crusty bread* **2. CURT** gruff, curt, and candid in speech —**crust·i·ly** *adv.* —**crust·i·ness** *n.*

crutch /kruch/ *n.* **1.** MED **WALKING AID** a staff with a handgrip and a rest for the forearm or armpit, used to help somebody who is lame or injured to walk **2. SOMETHING PROVIDING HELP OR SUPPORT** something that sustains or supports somebody or something liable to collapse, fail, or falter **3.** ANAT = **crotch 4.** NAUT **FORKED SUPPORT** a forked supporting piece for a boom, oar, or spar **5.** RIDING **LEGREST ON SIDESADDLE** a forked leg support on a sidesaddle ■ *vt.* (**crutched, crutch·ing, crutch·es**) **SUPPORT WITH CRUTCH** to support something with a crutch or similar object [Old English *cryc(c)*. Ultimately, from a prehistoric Germanic word that is also the ancestor of English *crook, crochet, crotch,* and *encroach*).]

crux /kruks/ (*plural* **crux·es** *or* **cru·ces** /kroo seez/) *n.* **1. CRUCIAL POINT** an essential or deciding point or element in something, e.g., in an argument **2. PUZZLING PROBLEM** an extremely difficult or puzzling problem **3.** MOUNTAINEERING **ARDUOUS PART OF CLIMB** the most demanding part of a climb [Mid-17thC. From Latin, literally "cross" (source of English *cross*).]

Crux *n.* the Southern Cross (*formal*)

Manuel Zambrana/Corbis

Celia Cruz

Cruz /krooz/, **Celia** (*b.* 1924) Cuban-born U.S. vocalist. She is one of the leading singers of the popular Latin dance music called salsa.

cru·za·do /kroo zaa dō/ (*plural* **-does** *or* **-dos**) *n.* **1. FORMER BRAZILIAN UNIT OF CURRENCY** a unit of currency used in Brazil between 1986 and 1990, equivalent to 100 centavos **2. COIN OR BILL WORTH ONE CRUZADO** a coin or bill worth one cruzado **3.** = **crusado** [Mid-16thC. From Portuguese, literally "marked with a cross," from the past participle of *cruzar* "to mark with a cross," from, ultimately, Latin *crux* "cross."]

Cru·zan /kroo zán, kroo zàn/ *n.* somebody who was born or lives in St. Croix in the U.S. Virgin Islands. [Mid-20thC. From assumed American Spanish *cruzano*, from Spanish *Santa Cruz* "St. Croix."]

cru·zei·ro /kroo záy rō, -záir ō/ (*plural* **-ros**) *n.* **1. FORMER BRAZILIAN UNIT OF CURRENCY** a unit of currency formerly used in Brazil. **2. COIN WORTH ONE CRUZEIRO** a coin worth one cruzeiro [Early 20thC. From Portuguese, literally "large cross," (from the figure on the coin) from, ultimately, Latin *crux* "cross."]

cry /krī/ *v.* (**cried, cry·ing, cries**) **1.** *vti.* **SHED TEARS** to shed tears as the result of a strongly felt emotion **2.** *vti.* **SHOUT** to call or shout out loudly **3.** *vi.* ZOOL **MAKE DISTINCTIVE SOUND** to make a natural high-pitched call (*refers to a bird or animal*) **4.** *vt.* **ANNOUNCE FOR SALE** to proclaim something publicly as being for sale (*archaic*) **5.** *vt.* **GIVE SOMETHING AS REASON** to plead or profess something as a reason or explanation ■ *n.* (*plural* **cries**) **1. INARTICULATE SOUND** a loud inarticulate expression of rage, pain, or surprise **2.** ZOOL **CALL OF BIRD OR ANIMAL** the natural high-pitched call of a bird or animal **3. PERIOD OF WEEPING** an act or period of shedding tears **4. PUBLIC DEMAND** a public demand, especially an urgent one **5.** HUNT **BAYING OF HOUNDS** the sound of hounds baying as they chase their quarry **6.** HUNT **HOUNDS** a pack of hounds **7. PROCLAMATION** an announcement or advertisement called out in public (*archaic*) **8. UNIFYING CALL** a call to rally or unite [13thC. Via French *crier* from Latin *quiritare* "to raise a public outcry," literally "to call for the help of the Roman citizens," which was formed from *Quirites* "Roman citizens."] ◇ **in full cry** in enthusiastic pursuit of something

cry down *vt.* to say disparaging or belittling things about somebody or something

cry off *vi.* to withdraw from something you had previously agreed to do (*informal*)

cry out *v.* **1.** *vti.* **SHOUT LOUDLY** to exclaim loudly because of pain, shock, or fear **2.** *vi.* **BE IN NEED** to be in obvious and urgent need ◇ **for crying out loud!** used to express annoyance, impatience, frustration, or surprise (*informal*)

cry up *vt.* to praise somebody or something highly

cry·ba·by /krī bàybee/ (*plural* **-bies**) *n.* somebody, especially a child, who cries or complains a lot

cry·ing /krī ing/ *adj.* desperate or deplorable and demanding a remedy ○ *a crying shame*

cryo- *prefix.* freezing, cold ○ *cryosurgery* [From Greek *kruos* "icy cold." Ultimately from an Indo-European base meaning "to freeze over," which is also the ancestor of English *crust* and *crystal*.]

cry·o·bank /krī ə bànk/ *n.* a place where biological material such as semen and body tissues can be stored at extremely low temperatures

cry·o·bi·ol·o·gy /krì ə bī óllәjee/ *n.* the branch of biology that studies how extremely low temperatures affect organisms —**cry·o·bi·o·log·i·cal** /-bīə lójjik'l/ *adj.* —**cry·o·bi·o·log·i·cal·ly** /-əlee/ *adv.* —**cry·o·bi·ol·o·gist** /-bī óllәjist/ *n.*

cry·o·gen /krī ə jèn/ *n.* a substance, e.g., liquid nitrogen, used in producing extremely low temperatures

cry·o·gen·ic /krì ə jénnik/ *adj.* having or relating to extremely low temperatures —**cry·o·gen·i·cal·ly** *adv.*

cry·o·gen·ics /krì ə jénniks/ *n.* a branch of physics that studies the causes and effects of extremely low temperatures (*takes a singular verb*)

cry·o·lite /krī ə līt/ *n.* an uncommon white mineral that consists of a fluoride of sodium and aluminum. It is used in the production of aluminum. Formula: Na_3AlF_6. [Early 19thC. Coined from CRYO- "cold" (because it was first found in Greenland) + -LITE.]

cry·om·e·ter /krī ómmətər/ *n.* a thermometer that measures extremely low temperatures

cry·om·e·try /krī ómmətree/ *n.* the measurement or recording of extremely low temperatures, especially using a cryometer

cry·on·ics /krī ónniks/ *n.* **FREEZING OF CORPSE** the study or practice of keeping a newly dead body at an extremely low temperature in the hope of restoring it to life later with the help of future medical advances (*takes a singular verb*) ■ *npl.* **CRYOGENIC TECHNIQUES** the collective techniques involved in cryogenics (*takes a plural verb*) [Mid-20thC. Contraction of CRYOGENICS.] —**cry·on·ic** *adj.*

cry·o·phil·ic /krì ə fíllik/ *adj.* capable of living at low temperatures

cry·o·phyte /krī ə fīt/ *n.* an organism that can live or grow on snow or ice. Most cryophytes are algae.

cry·o·pre·cip·i·tate /krì ō pri síppə tàyt, -tət/ *n.* a substance that is precipitated at low temperatures, especially a precipitate of blood containing a blood-clotting factor

cry·o·pres·er·va·tion /krì ō prezzər váysh'n/ *n.* the process of storing semen, ova, corneas, embryos, or body tissue at extremely low temperatures for future use —**cry·o·pre·serve** /krì ō pri zúrv/ *vt.*

cry·o·probe /krī ə prōb/ *n.* an instrument used in cryosurgery for cooling body tissue to low temperatures

cry·o·pro·tec·tant /krì ō prə téktənt/ *n.* a substance, e.g., glycerol, used to protect stored living tissue from the effects of freezing

cry·o·scope /krī ə skōp/ *n.* an instrument used for determining the point at which a liquid freezes

cry·os·co·py /krī óskəpee/ *n.* the study or practice of determining the freezing point of liquids —**cry·o·scop·ic** /krì ə skóppik/ *adj.*

cry·o·stat /krīə stàt/ *n.* a regulating device for maintaining a constant low temperature

cry·o·sur·ger·y /krì ō súrjəree/ *n.* surgery in which low temperatures are applied, e.g., to destroy diseased tissue, or to seal down detached retinas —**cry·o·sur·geon** *n.* —**cry·o·sur·gi·cal** *adj.*

cry·o·ther·a·py /krì ō thérrəpee/ (*plural* **-pies**) *n.* medical treatment that involves cooling the body, especially by applying ice packs

crypt /kript/ *n.* **1.** ARCHIT **UNDERGROUND CHAMBER** an underground room or vault, often below a church, used as a burial chamber or chapel, or for storing religious artifacts **2.** ANAT **SMALL BODY CAVITY** a small recess, tubular gland, or follicle in the body [Late 18thC. Via Latin *crypta* from Greek *kruptē* "vault," feminine of *kruptos* "hidden."]

crypt- *prefix.* = **crypto-**

crypt·a·nal·y·sis /krìptə nálləssiss/ *n.* **1. CODE-BREAKING** the process or science of deciphering coded texts or messages **2. TECHNIQUES TO DECODE MESSAGES** the techniques and methods used in deciphering coded texts and messages, or the study of such methods —**crypt·an·a·lyst** /krip tánn'list/ *n.* —**crypt·an·a·lyt·ic** /krìp tannə líttik/ *adj.* —**crypt·an·a·lyt·i·cal** /-líttik'l/ *adj.*

crypt·an·a·lyze /krip tánnə līz/ (**-lyzed, -lyz·ing, -lyzes**) *vt.* to decipher coded texts or messages

cryp·tic /kríptik/ *adj.* **1. AMBIGUOUS OR OBSCURE** deliberately mysterious and seeming to have a hidden meaning **2. SECRET** secret or hidden in some way **3.** LEISURE **INDICATING SOLUTION INDIRECTLY** with an indirect solution or clue, e.g., crosswords, puzzles, or anagrams **4. USING CODES** using or relating to codes and similar techniques **5.** ZOOL **PROTECTIVE** used to describe body markings and color that camouflage an animal [Early 17thC. Via late Latin *crypticus* from Greek *kruptikos*, from *kruptē* (see CRYPT).] —**cryp·ti·cal·ly** *adv.* —**cryp·tic·ness** *n.*

crypto- *prefix.* secret, hidden ○ *cryptogram* [From Greek *kruptos*, from *kruptein* "to hide"]

cryp·to·clas·tic /krìptə klástik/ *adj.* used to describe rock composed of microscopic mineral fragments

cryp·to·coc·co·sis /krìp tō ko kōssiss/ *n.* an infectious disease that affects parts of the body, especially the brain and central nervous system, with lesions or abscesses caused by the fungus *Cryptococcus neoformans* [Mid-20thC. Coined from modern Latin *Cryptococcus* + -OSIS.]

cryp·to·coc·cus /krìptə kókəss/ (*plural* **-cocci** /-kók sī, -kó kī/) *n.* a budding fungus that resembles a yeast, some types of which cause illnesses, e.g., cryptococcosis. Genus: *Cryptococcus.* [Early 20thC. From modern Latin, literally "hidden coccus."]

cryp·to·crys·tal·line /krìp tō krístə līn, -lin/ *adj.* used to describe rocks that are composed of crystals too small to be seen with a petrological microscope

cryp·to·gam /kríptə gàm/ *n.* a plant that reproduces by means of spores instead of seeds. Ferns, moss, algae, and fungi are cryptogams. (*dated*) [Late 18thC. Via French *cryptogame* from, ultimately, modern Latin *cryptogamus*, literally "hidden marriage" (because the means of reproduction is not apparent).] —**cryp·to·gam·ic** /krìptə gámmik/ *adj.* —**cryp·tog·a·mous** /krip tóggəməss/ *adj.*

cryp·to·gen·ic /krìptə jénnik/ *adj.* = **idiopathic**

cryp·to·gram /kríptə gràm/ *n.* **1. CODED MESSAGE** a text or message that is in code or cipher **2. SECRET SYMBOL** a symbol with a secret meaning or significance

cryp·to·graph /kríptə gràf/ *n.* **1.** = **cryptogram 2. ENCODING OR DECODING MACHINE** a machine for writing or deciphering encoded messages

cryp·tog·ra·pher /krip tóggrəfər/, **cryp·tog·ra·phist** /krip tóggrəfist/ *n.* somebody who writes, transcribes, or decodes cryptograms, or studies such methods

cryp·tog·ra·phy /krip tóggrəfee/ *n.* **1. STUDY OF ENCODING** the study or analysis of codes and coding methods **2. SECRET WRITING** writing that is coded or secret —**cryp·to·graph·ic** /krìptə gráffik/ *adj.* —**cryp·to·graph·i·cal** /-gráffik'l/ *adj.* —**cryp·to·graph·i·cal·ly** /-gráffikəlee/ *adv.*

cryp·tol·o·gy /krip tólləjee/ *n.* **1.** = **cryptography** *n.* **1 2.** = **cryptanalysis** —**cryp·to·log·ic** /krìptə lójjik/ *adj.* —**cryp·to·log·i·cal** /-lójjik'l/ *adj.* —**cryp·tol·o·gist** /krip tólləjist/ *n.*

cryp·to·me·ri·a /krìptə meeree ə/ *n.* a tall coniferous tree native to China and Japan that has curved needle-shaped leaves arranged in spirals. Latin name: *Cryptomeria japonica.* [Mid-19thC. From modern

Latin, literally "hidden part," because its seeds are hidden by scales.]

crypt·or·chid /krip táwrkid/ *n.* a male human or animal with one or both testicles that have failed to descend into the scrotum [Late 19thC. From CRYPTORCHISM.]

crypt·or·chism /krip táwr kìzzəm/, **crypt·or·chi·dism** /krip táwrki dìzzəm/ *n.* a developmental condition affecting humans or animals in which one or both testicles fail to descend into the scrotum [Late 19thC. Coined from CRYPTO- + Latin *orchis* "testicle" (from Greek *orkhis*) + -ISM.]

cryp·to·spo·rid·i·o·sis /krìp tō spawridee óssiss/ *n.* an infectious condition of humans and domestic animals, characterized by fever, diarrhea, and stomach cramps. It is spread by a protozoan of the genus *Cryptosporidium.* [Formed from CRYPTOSPORIDIUM]

cryp·to·spor·i·di·um /krìp tō spə ríddee əm/ (*plural* **-a** /-ríddee ə/) *n.* MICROBIOL a water-borne protozoan parasite that contaminates drinking water supplies, causing intestinal infections in human beings and domestic animals [Late 20thC. From Modern Latin, genus name, from Greek *kruptos* (see CRYPTO-) + *sporidium*, literally "little spore," from *spora* (see SPORE).]

cryp·to·zo·ic /krìptə zṓ ik/ *adj.* used to describe invertebrates that live in dark or concealed places, such as under stones or in caves or holes

Cryp·to·zo·ic *adj.* **OCCURRING BEFORE COMPLEX ORGANISMS** belonging to a geological time in which only a few very primitive organisms existed ■ *n.* **GEOLOGICAL ERA** the Cryptozoic era of geological time

cryp·to·zo·ite /krìptə zṓ ìt/ *n.* a malarial parasite at the stage in its life cycle when it is present in the host's body tissue but before it invades the red blood cells [Coined from CRYPTO-+ Greek *zōion* "animal" + -ITE]

cryp·to·zo·ol·o·gy /krìp tō zō óllәjee/ *n.* the study of legendary creatures like the Loch Ness monster or the Yeti —**cryp·to·zo·o·log·i·cal** /krìp tō zō ə lójjik'l/ *adj.* —**cryp·to·zo·ol·o·gist** /-óllәjist/ *n.*

cryst. *abbr.* **1.** crystalline **2.** crystallography

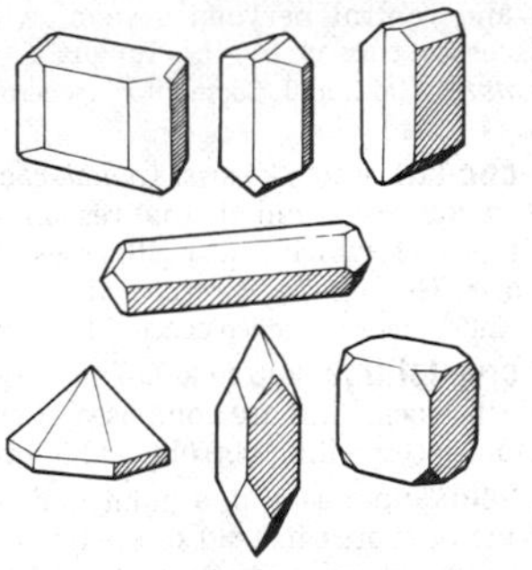

Crystal

crys·tal /kríst'l/ *n.* **1.** CHEM **SOLID WITH REPETITIVE INTERNAL STRUCTURE** a solid containing an internal pattern of atoms, molecules, or ions that is regular, repeated, and geometrically arranged **2.** MINERALS **PIECE OF CRYSTAL** a piece of a mineral in crystal form **3.** MINERALS **QUARTZ** a clear colorless mineral, especially quartz **4.** ELECTRON ENG **ELECTRONIC COMPONENT** a crystalline substance that has semiconducting or piezoelectric properties and is used as an electronic component, or the electrical device using it **5. SOMETHING LIKE CRYSTAL** something that has the form of a crystal, e.g., a frozen snowflake or a grain of salt **6.** CRAFT **HEAVY GLASS** a heavy transparent sparkling glass **7.** HOUSEHOLD **CRYSTAL GLASS OBJECTS** things made from crystal **8. GLASS OVER WATCH FACE** a transparent glass or plastic cover for the face of a clock or watch ■ *adj.* **VERY CLEAR** clear and sparkling [Pre-12thC. Via French *cristal* and Latin *crystallum* from Greek *krustallos* "ice" (the original sense in English). Ultimately, from an Indo-European word meaning "to freeze over" which is also the ancestor of English *crust* and cryo-.]

Crys·tal /kríst'l/ city in southeastern Minnesota, near the Mississippi River; a northwestern suburb of Minneapolis. Population: 23,292 (1996).

crys·tal ball *n.* **1. FORTUNE TELLER'S GLOBE** a clear solid sphere of glass or rock crystal that is used by a fortune teller to predict the future **2. MEANS TO PREDICT FUTURE** any means used to predict future events

crys·tal clear *adj.* **1. VERY CLEAN** clean and sparkling **2. OBVIOUS OR UNDERSTOOD** clear or obvious to the understanding

crys·tal gaz·ing *n.* predicting the future by any questionable means, most commonly by staring into a crystal ball in the belief that images of future events will appear —**crys·tal gaz·er** *n.*

crys·tal heal·ing *n.* use of pieces of crystal that are supposed to promote health and increase well-being

crys·tal·ize *vti.* = **crystallize**

crystall. *abbr.* crystallography

crystall- *prefix.* = **crystallo-** (*used before vowels*)

Crys·tal Lake city in northeastern Illinois, east of Rockford and northwest of Chicago. Population: 32,180 (1996).

crys·tal lat·tice *n.* the regular array of points in space that are occupied by the atoms, ions, or molecules that make up a crystal

crys·tal·lif·er·ous /krìstə líffərəss/, **crys·tal·lig·er·ous** /krìstə líjjərəss/ *adj.* forming or containing crystals

crys·tal·line /krístə lìn, krístəlin/ *adj.* **1. LIKE OR BEING CRYSTALS** relating to, made of, containing, or resembling crystals **2. VERY CLEAR** clear and sparkling **3. WITH A DEFINITE SHAPE** clear and definite in shape —**crys·tal·lin·i·ty** /krìstə línnitee/ *n.*

crys·tal·line lens *n.* the transparent lens behind the iris in the eyes of vertebrates

crys·tal·lite /krístə lìt/ *n.* a tiny rudimentary crystal, e.g., those found in some igneous rocks —**crys·tal·lit·ic** /krìstə líttik/ *adj.*

crys·tal·lize /krístə lìz/ (**-lized, -liz·ing, -liz·es**), **crys·tal·ize** (**-ized, -iz·ing, -iz·es**) *vti.* **1. MAKE OR BECOME WELL DEFINED** to become or make an idea or feeling become fixed or definite **2. FORM CRYSTALS** to form or make something form crystals **3.** COOK **COAT WITH SUGAR CRYSTALS** to coat or impregnate something, or become coated or impregnated, with crystals, especially sugar crystals —**crys·tal·liz·a·bil·i·ty** /krìstə lìzə bíllətee/ *n.* —**crys·tal·liz·a·ble** /krístə lìzəb'l/ *adj.* —**crys·tal·li·za·tion** /krìstəli záysh'n/ *n.* —**crys·tal·liz·er** /krístə lìzər/ *n.*

crystallo- *prefix.* crystal, crystalline ○ *crystallography* [From Greek *krustallos* (see CRYSTAL)]

crys·tal·log·ra·phy /krìstə lóggrəfee/ *n.* a branch of science dealing with the formation and properties of crystals —**crys·tal·log·ra·pher** *n.* —**crys·tal·lo·graph·ic** /krìstələ gráffik/ *adj.* —**crys·tal·lo·graph·i·cal·ly** /-gráffikəlee/ *adv.*

crys·tal·loid /krístə lòyd/ *n.* **1. SUBSTANCE FORMING CRYSTALS** a substance that can form crystals and in solution can pass through a semipermeable membrane **2.** BOT **PROTEIN IN PLANT CELL** a mass of protein resembling a crystal that commonly occurs in seeds and other storage organs ■ *adj.* **LIKE CRYSTAL** with the structure, properties, or appearance of a crystal —**crys·tal·loi·dal** *adj.*

crys·tal pleat *n.* one of a series of permanently pressed pleats of varying widths, often in a sheer fabric

crys·tal set *n.* an early form of radio receiver that used a quartz crystal as a detector

Cs *symbol.* cesium

CS *abbr.* **1.** FIN capital stock **2.** CIV ENG chartered surveyor **3.** chief of staff **4.** CHR Christian Science **5.** CHR Christian Scientist

cs. *abbr.* **1.** case **2.** census

C.S.A. *abbr.* Confederate States of America

csc *abbr.* cosecant

C-sec·tion *n.* = **cesarean section**

CSF *abbr.* cerebrospinal fluid

C-span *n.* a cable TV channel that focuses chiefly on public affairs such as Congressional hearings and cultural and social issues

CST *abbr.* **1.** Central Standard Time **2.** convulsive shock treatment

C.S.T. *abbr.* Central Standard Time

c-store, **C-store** *n.* a convenience store (*informal*)

CT *abbr.* **1.** TIME Central Time **2.** MED computerized tomography **3.** Connecticut

ct. *abbr.* **1.** carat **2.** cent **3.** certificate

Ct. *abbr.* **1.** Connecticut **2.** Count (*used in titles*)

C.T. *abbr.* Central Time

CTD *abbr.* MED cumulative trauma disorder

cte·nid·i·um /tə níddee əm/ (*plural* **-a** /-ə/) *n.* a gill found in mollusks that has a central axis with a fringe of filaments on either side. It is used in gas exchange and filter feeding. [Late 19thC. Via modern Latin from Greek *ktenidion*, literally "little comb," from *kteis* "comb."]

cten·oid /té nòyd, teé-/ *adj.* used to describe fish scales that have tiny projections like the teeth of combs, or fish that have such scales [Mid-19thC. Coined from Greek *kten-*, the stem of *kteis* "comb" +-OID.]

cten·o·phore /ténnə fàwr/ *n.* a marine invertebrate resembling a jellyfish but with eight rows of undulating filaments used for swimming. Sea gooseberries and sea walnuts are ctenophores. Phylum: Ctenophora. [Late 19thC. Formed from modern Latin *ctenophorus*, from the Greek stem *kten-* (see CTENOID).] —**cte·noph·o·ran** /tə nóffərən/ *adj., n.*

ctf. *abbr.* certificate

ctg., **ctge.** *abbr.* cartage

ctn *abbr.* cotangent

ctn. *abbr.* carton

ctr. *abbr.* **1.** center **2.** counter

Ctrl. *abbr.* COMPUT control

cts. *abbr.* cents

CT scan *n.* = **CAT scan**

CT scan·ner *n.* = **CAT scanner**

CTV *abbr.* Canadian Television Network Limited

Cu *symbol.* copper

cu. *abbr.* cubic

cua·dril·la /kwaa dreéyə/ *n.* a group of three banderilleros and two picadors who assist a matador in the bullring [Mid-19thC. From Spanish, literally "little square" (from a formation used), from *cuadra* "square," from, ultimately, the Latin stem *quadr-* (source of English *quadrille*).]

cub /kub/ *n.* **1.** ZOOL **YOUNG OF CARNIVOROUS MAMMAL** an offspring of some carnivorous mammals, e.g., a bear, lion, or tiger **2. NOVICE** an inexperienced person or apprentice (*dated*) **3. YOUNG PERSON** an inexperienced young person, often lacking in manners (*dated*) ■ *vi.* (**cubbed, cub·bing, cubs**) **PRODUCE YOUNG** to give birth to an animal cub [Mid-16thC. Origin unknown.] —**cub·bish** *adj.* —**cub·bish·ly** *adv.*

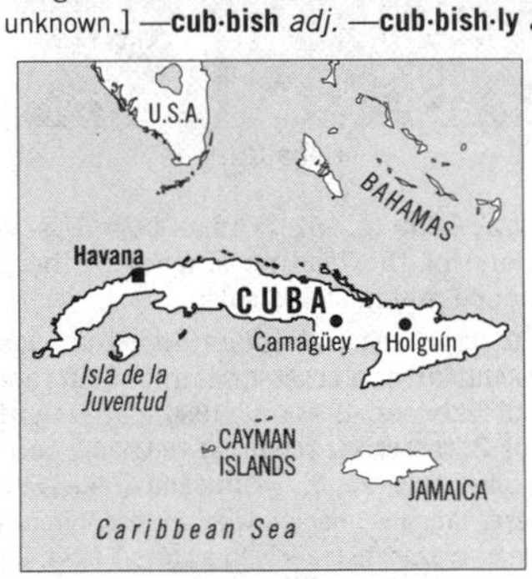

Cuba

Cu·ba /kyoóbə/ independent republic in the Caribbean Sea comprising two main islands and over 1,000 islets. Language: Spanish. Currency: peso. Capital: Havana. Population: 10,999,139 (1997). Area: 44,218 sq. mi./114,525 sq. km. Full name **Republic of Cuba**

cub·age /kyoóbij/ *n.* = **cubature** *n.* 2

Cu·ba li·bre /kyoòbə leébrə/ *n.* a drink made by mixing rum, cola, ice, and lime juice [From American Spanish, literally "free Cuba," used as a toast during the Cuban War of Independence, 1895–98]

Cu·ban /kyoóbən/ *n.* **1. SOMEBODY FROM CUBA** somebody who was born or raised in Cuba, or who is a citizen of Cuba **2. CIGAR** a Cuban cigar ■ *adj.* **RELATING TO CUBA** relating to or typical of the Republic of Cuba, or its people or culture

Cu·ban heel *n.* a straight broad heel of medium height for a shoe

Cu·ban sand·wich *n. Southern U.S.* a long narrow sandwich of Cuban origin, filled with ham, pork, cheese, and pickles, and often grilled

cu·ba·ture /kyoóbə choòr, -chər/ *n.* **1. DETERMINATION OF VOLUME OF SOLID** the process of working out the cubic content or volume of a solid **2.** CUBIC CONTENT the cubic content or volume of a solid [Late 17thC. Formed from CUBE, modeled on *quadrature*.]

cub·by·hole /kúbbi hòl/, **cub·by** (*plural* **-bies**) *n.* **1.** SMALL AREA a small space or room **2.** STORAGE COMPARTMENT a small storage compartment

cube[1] /kyo͞ob/ *n.* **1.** GEOM SOLID FIGURE OF SIX EQUAL SIDES a solid figure of six equal square plane faces, each set at right angles to the four sides adjacent to it **2.** CUBE-SHAPED OBJECT any solid shaped like a cube **3.** MATH PRODUCT OF THREE EQUAL NUMBERS the product of three equal numbers or quantities multiplied together, usually written in mathematical notation as a raised 3, e.g., 4^3 means 4 × 4 × 4 **4.** MEASURE, MECH ENG CUBIC INCHES cubic inches, especially of an internal-combustion engine (*informal*) ■ *vt.* **(cubed, cub·ing, cubes) 1.** MATH MULTIPLY ITEM BY ITSELF TWICE to multiply a number or quantity by itself twice, e.g., 6 cubed is 6 multiplied by 6 and then multiplied by 6 again **2.** COOK DICE to cut or shape food into cubes **3.** MATH WORK OUT CUBIC CONTENT to calculate the cubic content of something **4.** COOK TENDERIZE MEAT to score meat with a pattern of squares in order to make it more tender [Mid-16thC. Directly or via French from Latin *cubus*, from Greek *kubos* "cube" (and also "pelvis" because of its shape).] —**cub·er** *n.*

cu·be[2] /kyo͞o bày, kyoo báy/, **cu·bé** *n.* PLANTS a tropical American leguminous woody plant that is cultivated as a source of rotenone. Genus: *Lonchocarpus*. [Early 20thC. From American Spanish.]

cu·beb /kyo͞o bèb/ *n.* **1.** ASIAN CLIMBING PLANT a climbing plant of Southeast Asia that has heart-shaped leaves, spikes of small flowers, and brownish berries. Latin name: *Piper cubeba*. **2.** BERRY OF CUBEB PLANT a small unripe spicy berry of the cubeb plant, used in the past to treat respiratory and urinary disorders [13thC. Via French *cubèbe* from, ultimately, Arabic *kubāba*.]

cube root *n.* a number or quantity that, when multiplied by itself twice, equals a given number or quantity

cube steak *n.* a thin slice of beef that has been scored with squares to make it more tender

cube van *n. Can* a small truck with a cube-shaped storage compartment at the rear

cu·bic /kyo͞obik/ *adj.* **cu·bic, cu·bi·cal 1.** WITH THREE DIMENSIONS with three measurable dimensions **2.** EQUAL TO LINEAR MEASURE CUBED used to describe a unit of volume or capacity that is equal to the given unit of linear measurement raised to the power of three **3.** CUBE-SHAPED shaped like a cube **4.** MATH RELATING TO OR CONTAINING CUBED VARIABLE used to describe a mathematical expression or equation in which at least one variable is cubed but no variable is to be multiplied by itself more than two times ○ *a cubic equation* **5.** CRYSTALS WITH THREE EQUAL AXES used to describe a crystal that has three equal perpendicular axes ■ *n.* MATH MATHEMATICAL EQUATION a cubic expression, equation, or curve —**cu·bi·cal·ly** *adv.*

cu·bi·cle /kyo͞obik'l/ *n.* **1.** PARTITIONED WORK AREA IN A ROOM a work area that is partly separated from the rest of a room in an office or library **2.** PARTITIONED AREA OF ROOM a small partitioned area for private use in a larger, more public room, e.g., a changing room or dormitory [15thC. From Latin *cubiculum* "bedroom" (the original sense in English), from *cubare* "to lie down."]

cu·bic meas·ure *n.* a unit or system for measuring volume or capacity

cu·bic zir·co·ni·a *n.* a synthetic gemstone used as a substitute for diamonds in costume jewelry. It is formed by heating zirconia together with a stabilizing metallic oxide. Formula: ZrO_2.

cu·bi·form /kyo͞obi fàwrm/ *adj.* shaped like a cube

cub·ism /kyo͞o bìzzəm/, **Cu·bism** *n.* an artistic style, chiefly in painting and sculpture, that developed in the early 20th century and emphasized the representation of natural forms as geometric shapes seen from several angles [Early 20thC. From French *cubisme*, from *cube* (see CUBE).] —**cub·ist** *n.* —**cu·bis·tic** /kyoo bístik/ *adj.* —**cu·bis·ti·cal·ly** /-bístikəlee/ *adv.*

cu·bit /kyo͞obit/ *n.* an ancient unit of length, equal to the distance from the elbow to the tip of the middle finger, approximately 17–22 in./43–56 cm [14thC. From Latin *cubitum* "elbow, forearm, cubit."]

cu·bit·al /kyo͞obit'l/ *adj.* relating to the elbow, ulnar bone, or forearm [15thC. From Latin *cubitalis*, from *cubitum* "elbow, forearm, cubit."]

cu·boid /kyo͞o bòyd/ *n.* **1.** GEOM SOLID FIGURE OF SIX RECTANGULAR PLANES a solid figure of six rectangular plane faces, each set at right angles to the four sides adjacent to it **2.** ANAT BONE IN FOOT the outermost tarsal bone of the foot in vertebrates ■ *adj.* GEOM CUBE-SHAPED shaped like a cube —**cu·boi·dal** /kyoo bóyd'l/ *adj.*

cub re·port·er *n.* a young inexperienced newspaper reporter

cu·chi·fri·to /ko͝ochi frēētō/ (*plural* **-tos**) *n. Southwestern U.S.* a small deep-fried cube of pork [From American Spanish, from *cuchí* "pig" (alteration of Spanish *cochino* "little pig") + Spanish *frito*, past participle of *freir* "to fry," from Latin *frigere*]

cuck·ing stool /kúking-/ *n.* a punishment used in medieval times in which somebody was tied to a stool and pelted with rotting food [14thC. *Cucking* "defecating" (from obsolete *cuck* "to defecate," of Scandinavian origin), because a commode was sometimes used for this purpose.]

cuck·old /kúkəld/ *n.* MAN WHOSE WIFE IS UNFAITHFUL a husband whose wife has been unfaithful to him (*archaic*) ■ *vt.* **(-old·ed, -old·ing, -olds)** MAKE CUCKOLD OF SOMEBODY to make a cuckold of a husband (*archaic*) [Pre-12thC. From Old Northern French, a variant of Old French *cucuault*, from *cucu* "cuckoo," perhaps from the analogy that other birds' nests are invaded by cuckoos.] —**cuck·old·ry** *n.*

Cuckoo

cuck·oo /ko͞o ko͞o, ko͞o-/ *n.* (*plural* **-oos**) **1.** BIRDS BIRD LAYING IN OTHERS' NESTS a European songbird that lays its eggs in the nests of other birds who bring the nestlings up as their own. Latin name: *Cuculus canorus*. **2.** BIRDS RELATED BIRD a bird related to the European cuckoo **3.** BIRDS CUCKOO'S CALL the characteristic two-note call of the European cuckoo **4.** ECCENTRIC PERSON somebody who is very eccentric, strange, or extremely unconventional (*informal*) ■ *adj.* STRANGE very eccentric, strange, or extremely unconventional (*informal*) ■ *vi.* **(-ooed, -oo·ing, -oos)** GIVE THE CALL OF THE CUCKOO to make the characteristic two-note call of the cuckoo [13thC. From Old French *cucu*, an imitation of its call.]

WORD KEY: CULTURAL NOTE

One Flew Over the Cuckoo's Nest, a movie by U.S. director Milos Forman (1975). Based on Ken Kesey's 1962 novel, it describes how mischievous convict Randle McMurphy inspires his fellow inmates at a mental health facility to rebel against their disciplinarian nurse, Ratched. The movie can be seen as a metaphor for the conflict between individuality and creativity and society's pressure to conform.

cuck·oo clock *n.* a clock that indicates the hour with sounds like a cuckoo's call, usually accompanied by the appearance of a mechanical bird from behind a door

cuck·oo·flow·er /ko͞o ko͞o flòwr, ko͞o-/ *n.* **1.** PLANT WITH LIGHT PURPLE FLOWERS a plant often found in moist meadows, with light purple or occasionally white flowers and yellow anthers in April to June. Latin name: *Cardamine pratensis*. **2.** = **ragged robin** [Late 16thC. Because the plant is in flower at about the time of year when the bird is first heard.]

cuck·oo·pint /ko͞o koo pìnt, ko͞o ko͞o pìnt/ *n.* a perennial European plant, with leaves shaped like arrowheads and flowering stems consisting of a yellowish green cone around a reddish purple spike that later carries poisonous scarlet berries. Latin name: *Arum maculatum*. [15thC. Shortening of earlier *cuckoo pintle*, literally "cuckoo penis," from the shape of the spadix.]

cuck·oo spit *n.* **1.** FROTHY INSECT SECRETION ON PLANTS a white frothy secretion found on the stems and leaves of plants, produced by the larva of insects like the spittlebug **2.** SPITTLEBUG an insect that produces cuckoo spit [Because it was believed to have been spat out by cuckoos]

cu·cum·ber /kyo͞o kùmbər/ *n.* **1.** PLANTS PLANT WITH LONG GREEN FRUIT a climbing or trailing annual plant of the gourd family that is grown for its edible long green fruit. Latin name: *Cucumis sativus*. ◊ **squirting cucumber 2.** FOOD FRUIT OF CUCUMBER PLANT the long fruit of the cucumber plant that has dark green peel and crisp white watery flesh and is usually eaten raw in salads and sandwiches or pickled [14thC. From Latin *cucumer-*, the stem of *cucumis*, by association with Old French *cocombre*.] ◇ **cool as a cucumber** calm and composed, especially under pressure

cu·cum·ber tree *n.* a small tree that grows mainly in central and eastern North America, has greenish-yellow flowers, and produces cucumber-shaped fruit. Genus: *Magnolia*.

cu·cur·bit /kyoo kúrbit/ *n.* a tropical or subtropical climbing or trailing plant of the gourd family with large, fleshy, tough- or hard-skinned fruits, many of which are edible, e.g., cucumber, watermelon, or squash. Family: Cucurbitaceae. [14thC. Via French *curcurbite* from Latin *cucurbita* "gourd."]

Cú·cu·ta /ko͞okə tàa/ city in northeastern Colombia, capital of Norte de Santander Department near the Venezuelan frontier. Population: 459,887 (1993).

cud /kud/ *n.* **1.** ZOOL FOOD CHEWED TWICE partly digested food that cows and other ruminants return to the mouth, after it has passed into the first stomach, to chew again as an aid to digestion **2.** SOMETHING CONTINUOUSLY CHEWED something that is chewed repeatedly, such as tobacco (*informal*) [Old English *cudu*. Ultimately from an Indo-European word that probably also produced the first syllable of English *bitumen* (the underlying idea being "sticky substance").]

cud·bear /kúd bàir/ *n.* a violet dye extracted from some lichens [Mid-18thC. Alteration of *Cuthbert*, named for an 18th-century Scottish chemist *Cuthbert* Gordon, who patented it.]

cud·dle /kúdd'l/ *v.* **(-dled, -dling, -dles) 1.** *vti.* TENDERLY HUG OR NESTLE to nestle together or hold somebody or something close for affection, warmth, or comfort **2.** *vi.* ASSUME COMFORTABLE POSITION to get into a warm comfortable position ■ *n.* TENDER HUG a prolonged hug or embrace given to comfort or show affection [Early 16thC. Origin uncertain: perhaps formed from earlier *couth* (see UNCOUTH), in the sense "familiar, comfortable, cozy."] —**cud·dler** *n.* —**cud·dle·some** *adj.*

cud·dly /kúddlee/ **(-dlier, -dli·est)** *adj.* pleasant to hold because of being soft, warm, or endearingly attractive

cud·dy /kúddee/ (*plural* **-dies**) *n.* **1.** NAUT SMALL CABIN ON BOAT a small cabin or galley on a boat **2.** SMALL ROOM a small room or closet [Mid-17thC. Origin uncertain: probably via early modern Dutch *kajute* from French *cahute* "shanty," of unknown origin.]

cudg·el /kújjəl/ *n.* SHORT HEAVY CLUB a heavy stick used as a weapon ■ *vt.* **(-eled, -el·ing, -els)** BEAT WITH CUDGEL to beat somebody with a cudgel [Old English *cycgel*, of unknown origin] ◇ **take up the cudgels** to defend or support somebody or something actively and energetically

cud·weed /kúd wēēd/ (*plural* **-weeds** *or* **-weed**) *n.* a plant of the daisy family that has woolly leaves and clusters of white or yellow flowers and is found in temperate regions worldwide. Genera: *Gnaphalium* and *Filago*.

cue[1] /kyoo/ *n.* **1.** SIGNAL TO SPEAK OR ACT something said or done that provides the signal for somebody, especially an actor or performer, to say or do something **2.** PROMPT OR REMINDER something that prompts or reminds somebody to do something ○ *I took my cue from my brother and said nothing.* **3.** PSYCHOL RESPONSE-PRODUCING STIMULUS a stimulus or pattern of stimuli, often not consciously perceived, that results in a specific learned behavioral response **4.** SOMEBODY'S ROLE a part or function assigned to or expected of a person (*archaic*) ■ *vt.* **(cued, cu·ing, cues)** GIVE SIGNAL OR PROMPT TO to give somebody, especially an actor or performer, a signal to say or do something [Mid-16thC. Origin uncertain: perhaps standing for *qu*, an abbreviation of Latin *quando* "when," written on actors' scripts to remind them to come in.]

cue in *vt.* **1.** GIVE SIGNAL TO to signal that it is now time for somebody, especially a performer, to say or do something ○ *The conductor will cue you in.* **2. INSTRUCT OR REMIND** to give somebody information, instructions, or a reminder **3. INSERT INTO PERFORMANCE** to insert something, such as a speech or song, into a performance

cue² /kyoo/ *n.* **1.** CUE GAMES **STICK USED TO HIT BALL** a long tapering stick used to strike the cue ball in games such as billiards or pool (*often used before a noun*) **2.** GAME **LONG STICK USED IN SHUFFLEBOARD** a long stick with a semicircular piece attached at the end, used to push shuffleboard disks **3.** = **queue** *n.* 4 ■ *vt.* **(cued, cu·ing, cues) 1.** CUE GAMES **STRIKE WITH CUE** to strike a cue ball with a cue in such games as pool and billiards **2. TIE IN BRAID** to tie the hair at the back of the head in a braid [Mid-18thC. Variant of QUEUE.]

cue³ /kyoo/ *n.* the letter q [Mid-18thC. Representing the pronunciation of *q*.]

cue ball *n.* the white ball struck with the cue in games such as billiards or pool, which strikes the object ball in turn

cue bid *n.* BRIDGE in bridge, a bid made to show a partner that the bidder has either an ace or no cards in a particular suit

cue card *n.* in broadcasting, a large card containing the words that somebody is to say, held up out of sight of the viewing audience

cued speech *n.* a series of hand movements used to differentiate ambiguous mouth positions as an aid in lip reading

Cuen·ca /kwéng kaa, -kə/ city in a valley of the Andes Mountains in southern Ecuador. It is the capital of Azuay Province. Population: 194,981 (1990).

Cuer·na·va·ca /kwàirnə vaakə/ resort city and capital of Morelos State, south central Mexico. Population: 279,187 (1990).

cues·ta /kwéstə/ *n.* a ridge with a steep face on one side and a gentle slope on the other, especially in the southwestern United States [Early 19thC. Via Spanish, literally "slope," from Latin *costa* "rib, side" (source of English *coast* and *accost*).]

cuff¹ /kuf/ *n.* **1. END OF SLEEVE NEAREST WRIST** the part of a sleeve that covers the wrist, either turned back or with a band of fabric attached **2.** *U.S., Can, Aus* **FOLD AT BOTTOM OF TROUSER** a turned-up fold at the bottom of a pant leg **3. PART OF GLOVE COVERING LOWER ARM** the part of a glove or gauntlet that extends up the arm beyond the wrist **4.** MED **BAND USED IN MEASURING BLOOD PRESSURE** an inflatable band fastened around a patient's arm when measuring blood pressure **5. HANDCUFF** a handcuff (*slang*) **6. BAND ON SOCK** a ribbed or elasticized band at the top of a sock that serves to hold it up ■ *vt.* **(cuffed, cuff·ing, cuffs) 1.** *U.S., Can, Aus* **PUT CUFF ON PANTS** to give pants a cuff **2. PUT HANDCUFFS ON** to put handcuffs on somebody (*slang*) [14thC. Origin unknown.] —**cuff·less** *adj.*

cuff² *vt.* **(cuffed, cuff·ing, cuffs) HIT WITH OPEN HAND** to hit somebody lightly with an open hand ■ *n.* **OPEN-HANDED BLOW** a blow with an open hand [Mid-16thC. Probably an imitation of the sound of hitting.]

cuff link *n.* each one of a pair of ornamental fasteners for shirt cuffs used as an alternative to buttons (*often used in the plural*)

cui bo·no /kwi bṓnō/ *n.* **1. LEGAL PRINCIPLE** the legal principle that somebody who would gain something from a particular action or event is probably responsible for it **2. USEFULNESS AS MEASURE OF VALUE** the usefulness of something used to measure its value [Early 17thC. From Latin, literally "to whom is the benefit."]

cui·rass /kwi ráss/ *n.* **1. ARMOR FOR UPPER BODY** a piece of body armor made of metal or leather, covering the chest and sometimes the back **2. PROTECTION** a protective covering, or any means of protection **3.** ZOOL **ANIMAL'S HARD PROTECTIVE COVERING** a protective outer covering on some animals, e.g., scales or a shell [15thC. Via Old French *cuirace* from, ultimately, Latin *coriaceus* "made of leather," from *corium* "leather."]

cui·ras·sier /kweerə seer, kyoorə-/ *n.* a mounted soldier wearing a cuirass, especially in 16th-century Europe [Mid-16thC. From French, from *cuirasse*, from Old French *cuirace* (see CUIRASS).]

cuish *n.* = **cuisse**

cui·sine /kwi zeen/ *n.* **1. COOKING STYLE** a specified style of cooking, especially one that is notable for high quality. ◊ **haute cuisine 2. RANGE OF FOOD** the range of food prepared by a particular restaurant, country, or individual [Late 18thC. Via French, literally "kitchen," from Latin *coquina*, from *coquere* "to cook" (source of English *concoct*, *decoct*, and *precocious*).]

cui·sine min·ceur /-maN súr/ *n.* a low-calorie form of cooking originating in France [From French, literally "slimness cooking"]

cuisse /kwiss/, **cuish** /kwish/ *n.* a piece of armor formerly worn in battle to protect the thigh [13thC. Via Old French *cuiss(i)eus*, plural of *cuissel*, from late Latin *coxale*, from Latin *coxa* "hip" (source of English *cushion*).]

cuke /kyook/ *n.* a cucumber (*informal*) [Early 20thC. Shortening.]

Cul·bert·son /kúlbərtsən/, **Ely** (1891–1955) Romanian-born U.S. bridge player. He invented a contract-bridge bidding system, and wrote widely about the game.

cul-de-sac /kùl də sák/ (*plural* **culs-de-sac** *or* **cul-de-sacs**) *n.* **1. STREET CLOSED AT ONE END** a road with no exit at one end, often in a residential area **2. IMPASSE** a situation in which further progress is impossible **3.** ANAT **BODY CAVITY RESEMBLING POUCH** a body cavity or tubular structure open at one end only [From French, literally "bottom of a sack"]

cu·let /kyoolət/ *n.* the flat face at the back or base of a faceted gemstone [Late 17thC. From French, literally "little base," from *cul* (see CULOTTES).]

Cu·lia·can /koolyə kaan/ city in western Mexico, the capital of Sinaloa State. Population: 601,123 (1990).

cu·li·cid /kyooləsid, kyoo líssid/ *n.* an insect of the mosquito family. Family: Culicidae. [Early 20thC. From Latin *culic-*, the stem of *culex* "gnat."]

cu·li·nar·y /kúllə nèrree, kyoo-/ *adj.* relating to food or cooking [Mid-17thC. From Latin *culinarius*, from *culina* "kitchen" (source of English *kiln*).] —**cu·li·nar·i·ly** *adv.*

cull /kul/ *vt.* **(culled, cull·ing, culls) 1. REMOVE AS WORTHLESS** to remove an inferior thing or person from a larger group **2. SELECT** to select or gather things or people, especially those that are good examples of their kind ○ *The following cases are culled from the police reports.* **3.** VET **REMOVE FROM HERD** to remove an animal, especially a sick or weak one, from a herd or flock ■ *n.* **1.** VET **REDUCTION OF ANIMAL NUMBERS** a reduction of the numbers of an animal population achieved by killing some of its members **2. SOMETHING WITHOUT VALUE** something regarded as worthless, especially an unwanted or inferior animal removed from a herd [12thC. Via Old French *coillier* from Latin *colligere* "to gather together," from *legere* "to gather" (source of English *select*).]

Cul·len /kúllən/, **Countee** (1903–46) U.S. poet. An essentially lyric poet influenced by the work of the English poet John Keats, Cullen was a leading figure of the Harlem Renaissance.

cul·let /kúllət/ *n.* broken or waste glass returned for recycling [Early 19thC. Variant of COLLET in the obsolete sense "glass left on the end of a blowing iron when the finished article has been removed."]

cul·ly /kúllee/ *n.* (*plural* **-lies**) **GULLIBLE PERSON** somebody who is easily tricked (*archaic*) ■ *vt.* **(-lied, -ly·ing, -lies) DECEIVE** to cheat or deceive somebody (*archaic*) [Mid-17thC. Origin uncertain: perhaps a contraction of CULLION.]

culm¹ /kulm/ *n.* **1. COAL MINE WASTE** waste from a coal mine **2. SHALE CONTAINING MUCH COAL** shale that contains a lot of coal **3. INFERIOR ANTHRACITE** anthracite coal of poor quality [14thC. Origin uncertain: probably ultimately from Old English *col* (see COAL).]

culm² /kulm/ *n.* the jointed hollow stem of a grass or similar plant [Mid-17thC. From Latin *culmus*.]

cul·mi·nant /kúlmənənt/ *adj.* **1.** ASTRON **AT HIGHEST POINT** used to describe a planet or other celestial body that is at its highest altitude **2. CULMINATING** reaching its climax or point of highest development [Early 17thC. From late Latin *culminant-*, the present participle stem of *culminare* (see CULMINATE).]

cul·mi·nate /kúlmiə nàyt/ **(-nat·ed, -nat·ing, -nates)** *v.* **1.** *vti.* **COME OR BRING TO HIGHEST POINT** to reach a climax or point of highest development, or to bring something to this point ○ *a general feeling of dissatisfaction that culminated in his resignation* **2.** *vti.* **FINISH SPECTACULARLY** to come or bring something to a climax ○ *The festivities culminated in a procession through the town.* **3.** *vi.* **HAVE SOMETHING AT ITS HIGHEST END** to have something at its apex ○ *The tower culminates in a point.* **4.** *vi.* ASTRON **REACH HIGHEST OR LOWEST POINT** to reach the highest or, less commonly, the lowest point in the sky relative to an observer's horizon (*refers to celestial bodies*) [Mid-17thC. From late Latin *culminat-*, the past participle stem of *culminare* "to exalt or extol," from *culmen* "summit."]

cul·mi·na·tion /kùlmə náysh'n/ *n.* **1. HIGHEST POINT** the highest, most important, or final point of an activity **2. ACT OF CULMINATING** the arrival at, or the bringing of something to, a climax **3.** ASTRON **HIGHEST OR LOWEST ALTITUDE** the highest or, less commonly, the lowest point that a celestial body reaches relative to an observer's horizon

cu·lottes /koo lóts, koo lòts/ *npl.* a pair of women's knee-length shorts, cut to resemble a skirt [Mid-19thC. From French, literally "small bottom," later "knee breeches" (the original sense in English), from *cul* "bottom, rump" (source of English *tutu*), from Latin *culus*.]

cul·pa·ble /kúlpəb'l/ *adj.* deserving blame or punishment for a wrong [13thC. Via French *coupable* from Latin *culpabilis*, from *culpare* "to blame," from *culpa* "fault, blame."] —**cul·pa·bil·i·ty** /kùlpə bíllətee/ *n.* —**cul·pa·bly** /-blee/ *adv.*

cul·prit /kúlprit/ *n.* **1. WRONGDOER** somebody who is responsible for or guilty of an offense or misdeed **2.** CRIMINAL LAW **ACCUSED PERSON** somebody charged with a crime and awaiting trial, especially somebody who has pleaded not guilty **3. ORIGIN OF PROBLEM** a cause of a problem (*informal*) ○ *A faulty connection proved to be the culprit.* [Late 17thC. Origin uncertain: perhaps from an earlier abbreviation *cul. prist* (mistakenly taken as a form of address), from Anglo-Norman *Culpable; prest d'averer*, literally "You are guilty; we are ready to prove it."]

cult /kult/ *n.* **1. RELIGION** a system of religious or spiritual beliefs, especially an informal and transient belief system regarded by others as misguided or unorthodox **2. RELIGIOUS GROUP** a group of people who share religious or spiritual beliefs **3. IDOLIZATION OF SOMEBODY OR SOMETHING** extreme or excessive admiration for a person, philosophy of life, or activity (*often used before a noun*) ○ *a cult following* **4. OBJECT OF IDOLIZATION** a person, philosophy, or activity regarded with extreme or excessive admiration **5. FAD** something popular or fashionable among a devoted group of enthusiasts (*often used before a noun*) ○ *cult status* **6.** ETHNOL **SYSTEM OF SUPERNATURAL BELIEFS** a body of organized practices and beliefs supposed to involve interaction with and control over supernatural powers **7. ELITE GROUP** a self-identified group of people who share a narrowly defined interest or perspective [Early 17thC. Directly or via French from Latin *cultus* "worship" (the original sense in English), from *colere* (see CULTURE).] —**cul·tic** *adj.* —**cult·ish** *adj.* —**cult·ish·ly** *adv.* —**cult·ish·ness** *n.* —**cult·ism** *n.* —**cult·ist** *n.*

cul·ti plural of **cultus**

cul·ti·va·ble /kúltəvəb'l/, **cul·ti·vat·a·ble** /-vàytə-/ *adj.* used to describe land that is capable of being cultivated —**cul·ti·va·bil·i·ty** /kùltivə bíllətee/ *n.*

cul·ti·var /kúltə vaar/ *n.* a variety of a cultivated plant that is developed by breeding and has a designated name [Early 20thC. Blend of CULTIVATE and VARIETY.]

cul·ti·vat·a·ble *adj.* = **cultivable**

cul·ti·vate /kúltə vàyt/ **(-vat·ed, -vat·ing, -vates)** *vt.* **1. PREPARE LAND FOR CROPS** to work land or prepare soil for growing crops **2. GROW PLANTS** to grow a plant or crop **3. LOOSEN SOIL** to break up soil with a tool or machine, especially before sowing or planting **4. NURTURE** to improve or develop something, usually by study or education ○ *cultivating her interest in science* **5. DEVELOP, OFTEN SELFISHLY** to develop an acquaintance or intimacy with somebody, often for personal advantage **6. MAKE CULTURED** to civilize or educate a person or group [Mid-17thC. From medieval Latin *cultivat-*, the past participle stem of *cultivare*, from *cultivus* "cultured," from Latin *cult-* (see CULTURE).]

cul·ti·vat·ed /kúltə vàytəd/ *adj.* **1. KNOWLEDGEABLE** well-educated, knowledgeable, and well-mannered **2. FOR CROPS** prepared or used for growing crops **3. PRODUCED BY HORTICULTURAL OR AGRICULTURAL METHODS** developed or improved by horticultural or agricultural techniques

cul·ti·va·tion /kùltə váysh'n/ *n.* **1. PREPARATION OF LAND OR GROWING CROPS** planting, growing, and harvesting crops or plants, or preparing land for this purpose **2. IMPROVEMENT** improvement or development, especially through study or education **3. SOPHISTICATION** educated taste or sophistication [Via French, from *cultiver* "to cultivate," from, ultimately, Latin *cult-* (see CULTURE)]

cul·ti·va·tor /kúltə vàytər/ *n.* any gardening or farm tool or machine for breaking up soil [Mid-19thC. From CULTIVATE, modeled on French *cultivateur.*]

cul·tur·al /kúlchərəl/ *adj.* **1. OF SPECIFIC CULTURE** relating to a particular culture or civilization **2. OF THE ARTS** relating to the arts and intellectual activity —**cul·tur·al·ly** *adv.*

cul·tur·al an·thro·pol·o·gy *n.* the scientific study of human culture or the culture of specific societies, including social structure, language, religion, art, and technology —**cul·tur·al an·thro·pol·o·gist** *n.*

cul·tur·al lag, **cul·ture lag** *n.* SOCIOL a slower rate of change in one part of a culture or one society compared with another

cul·tur·al ma·te·ri·al·ism *n.* the anthropological theory that environment, resources, technology, and other material things are the major influences on cultural change

cul·tur·al rel·a·tiv·ism *n.* the principle that we should not judge the behavior of others using the standards of our own culture, and that each culture must be analyzed on its own terms

Cul·tur·al Rev·o·lu·tion *n.* a political and cultural reform movement in China from 1965 to 1968 that was intended to revolutionize political opinion and behavior and was characterized by social upheaval. The Red Guard played a prominent role in the movement, which was aimed at restoring principles associated with Mao Zedong.

cul·tu·ra·ti /kùlchə ráatee/ *npl.* people who have a passion for the arts (*informal*) [Mid-20thC. From CULTURE, modeled on *literati.*]

cul·ture /kúlchər/ *n.* **1. THE ARTS COLLECTIVELY** art, music, literature, and related intellectual activities ○ *Culture is necessary for a healthy society.* **2. KNOWLEDGE AND SOPHISTICATION** enlightenment and sophistication acquired through education and exposure to the arts ○ *They are people of culture.* **3. SHARED BELIEFS AND VALUES OF A GROUP** the beliefs, customs, practices, and social behavior of a particular nation or people ○ *Southeast Asian culture* **4. PEOPLE WITH SHARED BELIEFS AND PRACTICES** a group of people whose shared beliefs and practices identify the particular place, class, or time to which they belong **5. SHARED ATTITUDES** a particular set of attitudes that characterizes a group of people ○ *The company tries hard to avoid a blame culture.* **6. GROWING BIOLOGICAL MATERIAL IN SPECIAL CONDITIONS** the growing of biological material, especially plants, microorganisms, or animal tissue, in a nutrient substance in specially controlled conditions for scientific, medical, or commercial purposes **7.** BIOL **BIOLOGICAL MATERIAL GROWN IN SPECIAL CONDITIONS** biological material, especially plants, microorganisms, or animal tissue, grown in a nutrient substance (**culture medium**) in specially controlled conditions for scientific, medical, or commercial purposes **8. TILLAGE** the cultivation of the land or soil in preparation for growing crops or plants **9. IMPROVEMENT** the development of a skill or expertise through training or education ○ *physical culture* ■ *vt.* (**-tured, -tur·ing, -tures**) **1. GROW IN SPECIAL CONDITIONS** to grow biological material, especially plants, microorganisms, or animal tissue, in a nutrient substance in specially controlled conditions, for scientific, medical, or commercial purposes **2.** AGRIC **CULTIVATE** to cultivate plants or crops [13thC. Via French from Latin *cultura* "tillage," from *cult*, the past participle stem of *colere* "to inhabit, cultivate, worship." Originally in English "piece of tilled land."]

cul·tured /kúlchərd/ *adj.* **1. EDUCATED AND SOPHISTICATED** generally educated and informed about the arts and related intellectual activity **2.** BIOL **GROWN IN NUTRIENT SUBSTANCE** grown in a nutrient substance in a laboratory **3. ARTIFICIALLY PRODUCED** created artificially rather than by natural or organic processes

cul·tured pearl *n.* a pearl created artificially by introducing a foreign body into an oyster or clam shell to attract layers of mother-of-pearl around it

cul·ture lag *n.* SOCIOL = **cultural lag**

cul·ture shock *n.* the feelings of confusion and anxiety experienced when an individual or a group suddenly finds itself in an unfamiliar cultural environment

cul·ture vul·ture *n.* somebody who has a strong or obsessive interest in the arts (*informal*)

cul·tus /kúltəss/ (*plural* **-tus·es** *or* **-ti** /-tī/) *n.* a religious group (*formal*) [Early 17thC. From Latin *cultus,* "worship" (source of English *cult*), from *cult-* (see CULTURE).]

Cul·ver Cit·y /kùlvər-/ city in southwestern California, southwest of Los Angeles. It is a center for many film studios. Population: 39,292 (1996).

cul·ver·in /kúlvərən/ *n.* **1. HEAVY CANNON** a type of long-range cannon used in the 15th to 17th centuries **2. MEDIEVAL MUSKET** a type of musket used in the 15th and 16th centuries [15thC. From French *coulevrine,* from *couleuvre* "snake," from, ultimately, Latin *colubra.*]

cul·vert /kúlvərt/ *n.* **1. UNDERGROUND DUCT** a covered channel that carries water or cabling underground **2. STRUCTURE COVERING DRAINAGE CHANNEL** an arch, bridge, or part of a road that covers a culvert [Late 18thC. Origin unknown.]

cum /kum/ *prep.* together with, along with, in combination with, or functioning as (*informal*) ○ *He lives and works in an apartment cum office.* [Late 19thC. From Latin, "with."]

cum. *abbr.* cumulative

cum·ber /kúmbər/ *vt.* (*archaic or literary*) **1. HAMPER** to hamper or hinder **2. BURDEN** to burden or encumber [14thC. Origin uncertain: probably a shortening of ENCUMBER.]

Cum·ber·land /kúmbərlənd/ **1.** river in southern Kentucky and northern Tennessee, formed in southeastern Kentucky and emptying into the Ohio River. Length: 720 mi./1,160 km. **2.** city in the northwestern corner of Maryland, on the Potomac River, west of Hagerstown. Population: 22,341 (1996). **3.** town in northeastern Rhode Island, on Blackstone River, a northern suburb of Providence. Population: 29,274 (1996).

Cum·ber·land Falls *n.* waterfalls in the state of Kentucky, United States. They are situated in Cumberland Falls State Resort Park. Height: 68 ft./21 m.

Cum·ber·land Gap *n.* pass through the Cumberland Mountains near the point at which Tennessee, Virginia, and Kentucky meet. Height: 1,650 ft./503 m.

cum·ber·some /kúmbərsəm/ *adj.* **1. HEAVY OR BULKY** awkward to carry or handle because of weight, size, or shape **2. COMPLICATED OR PROBLEMATIC** difficult to use or deal with because of length or complexity —**cum·ber·some·ly** *adv.* —**cum·ber·some·ness** *n.*

cum·brous /kúmbrəss/ *adj.* large and unwieldy (*archaic or literary*) ○ *"this cumbrous and creaking structure"* (Thomas Hardy, *Tess of the d'Urbervilles*; 1891) —**cum·brous·ly** *adv.* —**cum·brous·ness** *n.*

cum·in /kúmmin/ *n.* **1. PLANT WITH AROMATIC SEEDS** a Mediterranean plant of the carrot family with small white or pink flowers, often grown for its aromatic seeds. Latin name: *Cuminum cyminum.* **2. SEEDS USED COOKING** the aromatic seeds of the cumin plant, used whole or ground as a spice [Pre-12thC. Via Latin *cuminum* from Greek *kuminon,* of Semitic origin.]

cum lau·de /kum lów dày, -dee/ *adv., adj.* with the lowest of the three grades of academic distinction awarded above the average graduate [From Latin, literally "with praise"]

cum·mer·bund /kúmmər bùnd/ *n.* a brightly colored pleated sash worn around the waist by men as part of formal dress [Early 17thC. From Urdu *kamar-band,* literally "loin-band, waistband."]

cum·mings, e. e. (1894–1962) U.S. poet. He is known for his experimental poetry, which was written only in lower case. Full name **Edward Estlin Cummings**

cum·quat *n.* = **kumquat**

cum·shaw /kúm shàw/ *n.* a tip or gift, originally one given to Chinese beggars (*dated*) [Early 19thC. From Chinese dialect *gǎmsiā,* an expression of thanks used by beggars.]

cu·mu·late *v.* /kyóomyə làyt/ (**-lat·ed, -lat·ing, -lates**) **1.** *vti.* = **accumulate** *v.* 1 **2.** *vt.* **MERGE** to combine two or more items into one ■ *adj.* /-lət, -làyt/ **HEAPED OR AMASSED** heaped up in a pile or mass [Mid-16thC. From Latin *cumulat-,* the past participle stem of *cumulare* "to gather in a heap" (the original sense in English), from *cumulus* "a heap."] —**cu·mu·la·tion** /kyóomyə láysh'n/ *n.*

cu·mu·la·tive /kyóomyə làytiv, -lət-/ *adj.* **1. GRADUALLY BUILDING UP** becoming successively larger, stronger, or more effective ○ *Many drugs have a cumulative effect on the body.* **2. CREATED BY GRADUAL ADDITIONS** resulting from successive additions **3.** FIN **ADDED TO NEXT PAYMENT** used to describe an interest or dividend payment that is added to the next payment rather than being paid out when it falls due **4.** STOCK EXCH **ENTITLING SHAREHOLDER TO CLAIM DIVIDEND ARREARS** used to describe preferred stocks whose holder has the right to claim dividend arrears before dividends are distributed to holders of common stock **5.** LAW **MORE SEVERE FOR REPEAT OFFENDER** used to describe a more severe punishment imposed on somebody who has previously committed the same crime **6.** LAW **CONSECUTIVE** following consecutively on from another sentence or term of imprisonment **7.** STATS **INCLUDING ALL GIVEN VALUES OF VARIABLE** relating to the sum of the number of times a variable has a particular value totalled over all the values of the variable that are less than a given value **8.** STATS **INCREASING WITH SUCCESSIVE MEASUREMENTS** used to describe an error that increases as more measurements are taken —**cu·mu·la·tive·ly** *adv.* —**cu·mu·la·tive·ness** *n.*

cu·mu·la·tive dis·tri·bu·tion func·tion *n.* a procedure that assigns to each possible value of a random variable the probability that this value will be found. If each value is equally likely to be found, the distribution is said to be uniform.

cu·mu·la·tive trau·ma dis·or·der *n.* MED = **repetitive strain injury**

cu·mu·li plural of **cumulus**

cu·mu·lo·nim·bus /kyóomyə lō nímbəss/ (*plural* **-bi** /-bī/ *or* **-bus·es**) *n.* a tall dark cumulus cloud in the shape of an anvil, often bringing thunderstorms

cu·mu·lous /kyóomyələss/ *adj.* having a piled up shape similar to a cumulus cloud

cu·mu·lus /kyóomyələss/ (*plural* **-li** /-lī/) *n.* **1. LARGE FLUFFY CLOUD** a large white or gray cloud with a flat base and a rounded fluffy top, or a mass of such clouds, developing as a result of rising hot air currents **2. HEAP** a mass or heap [Mid-17thC. From Latin, literally "heap, pile" (the original sense in English).]

cunc·ta·tion /kungk táysh'n/ *n.* hesitation or procrastination in the performance of something (*formal*) [Late 16thC. From the Latin stem *cunctation-,* from *cunctare* "to delay."] —**cunc·ta·tive** /kúngktətiv/ *adj.* —**cunc·ta·tor** /-tàytər/ *n.*

cu·ne·al /kyóonee əl/ *adj.* having the shape of a wedge [Late 16thC. Directly or via modern Latin, from medieval Latin *cunealis,* from Latin *cuneus* "wedge." Probably obsolete by the 18thC and revived in the 19th.]

cu·ne·ate /kyóonee àyt, -ət/ *adj.* BOT used to describe a leaf that is more or less triangular with the narrowest point of the triangle forming the tip [Early 19thC. Formed from Latin *cuneus* "wedge."] —**cu·ne·ate·ly** *adv.*

Cuneiform: Sumerian clay tablet (18th century B.C.)

cu·ne·i·form /kyóoni fàwrm, kyoo née ə-/ *adj.* **1. WEDGE-SHAPED** with the narrowly triangular shape of a wedge **2. USED IN ANCIENT WRITING SYSTEM** relating or belonging to any of several writing systems of the ancient Near East, e.g., Sumerian or Linear B, in which wedge-shaped impressions were made in soft clay **3. USED FOR CUNEIFORM WRITING** used to describe the clay tablets on which cuneiform script was written **4.** ANAT **OF ANKLE** used to describe any of three wedge-shaped bones of the ankle ■ *n.* **1. CUNEIFORM SCRIPT** writing that uses small wedge-shaped characters **2.** ANAT **WEDGE-SHAPED ANKLE BONE** any of the three cuneiform bones of the ankle (*informal*) [Late 17thC. From French *cunéiforme* or modern Latin *cuneiformis,* from Latin *cuneus* "wedge."]

cun·ner /kúnnər/ (*plural* **-ner** *or* **-ners**) *n.* a small fish of the wrasse family, found in the north Atlantic Ocean. Latin name: *Tautogolabrus adspersus.* [Early 17thC. Origin unknown.]

cun·ni·lin·gus /kùnni língəss/ *n.* sexual stimulation of a woman's genitals using the tongue and lips [Late 19thC. From Latin, literally "vulva-licker."]

cun·ning /kúnning/ *adj.* **1. CRAFTY AND DECEITFUL** clever or artful in a way that is intended to deceive **2. CLEVERLY THOUGHT OUT** showing skill, shrewdness, and ingenuity in planning or doing something **3. CUTE** attractive in a pleasant delicate way (*informal*) ■ *n.* **1. CRAFTINESS AND DECEITFULNESS** the ability to deceive in a clever subtle way **2. SKILLFUL PERFORMANCE** skillful ingenuity or grace in doing something [13thC. Probably ultimately from Old Norse *kunna* "to know." Originally in the sense "learned, knowledgeable."] —**cun·ning·ly** *adv.* —**cun·ning·ness** *n.*

Charles E. Rothin/Corbis
Merce Cunningham

Cun·ning·ham /kúnning hàm/, **Merce** (*b.* 1919) U.S. dancer and choreographer. He invented the "choreography by chance" technique and has played an important role in the development of avant-garde dance.

cunt /kunt/ *n.* (*taboo offensive*) **1. OFFENSIVE TERM** a highly offensive term for a woman's genitals **2. OFFENSIVE TERM** a highly offensive term for a woman **3. OFFENSIVE TERM** a highly offensive term for somebody who is viewed with great dislike or contempt, especially a man **4. OFFENSIVE TERM** a highly offensive term for sexual intercourse with a woman [13thC. Ultimately of prehistoric Germanic origin. First recorded in *Gropecuntlane*, a street in Oxford, England, where prostitutes worked; there were similar names in London, Norwich, and York.]

cup /kup/ *n.* **1. DRINKING CONTAINER** a small container, usually with a handle, used to hold liquids for drinking **2. CONTENTS OF CUP** the contents of a cup ○ *Will you have another cup?* **3.** *U.S., Can, Aus* COOK **MEASURE IN COOKING** a unit of capacity used in recipes, equivalent to 8 fluid ounces/237 ml **4. WINNER'S PRIZE IN SPORTS** an ornamental trophy, typically a large two-handled silver goblet, awarded as a prize in a competition **5. SPORTS COMPETITION** a sporting competition in which the winner's prize is a large ornamental goblet **6. BOWL-SHAPED OBJECT** something that has an open hollow rounded shape **7. PART OF BRA** either of the shaped sections of a bra that support and cover the breasts **8. ATHLETIC SUPPORT** an athletic support reinforced with plastic or metal, worn to protect the male genitals during team sports **9. BOWL-SHAPED PLANT OR BODY PART** an open hollow rounded part or structure in a plant or in the body **10. PARTY PUNCH** a mixed drink with a particular ingredient as its base, usually served from a large bowl at parties ○ *a champagne cup* **11. DISH SERVED IN CUP-SHAPED CONTAINER** a dessert or appetizer served in a small bowl or glass dish **12. COMMUNION CHALICE OR WINE** in Christian services, the vessel from which the consecrated wine is drunk during Holy Communion, or the wine itself **13.** GOLF **GOLF HOLE** the hole on a green that is the target in golf, or the metal lining of such a hole **14. SOMEBODY'S LOT IN LIFE** what a person is destined to receive, suffer, or enjoy in life (*literary*) ■ *vt.* **(cupped, cup·ping, cups) 1. FORM INTO CUP SHAPE** to form one or both of the hands into an open hollow rounded shape, usually to hold or receive something, e.g., water **2. HOLD IN HANDS** to hold something in cupped hands **3. DRAW TO SURFACE OF SKIN** formerly, to use a cupping glass to increase the blood supply to an area of the skin [Pre-12thC. From late Latin *cuppa*, probably from Latin *cupa* "tub" (source of English *coop* and *cupola*).] ◇ **in your cups** drunk (*archaic*)

cup-and-sau·cer plant *n.* a Mexican climbing plant with large brightly colored flowers. Latin name: *Cobaea scandens.*

cup·bear·er /kúp bairər/ *n.* a servant who pours wine, especially one employed in a royal household (*formal*)

cup·board /kúbbərd/ *n.* a piece of furniture, either built-in or freestanding, or a small room used for storing food and other kitchen necessities [14thC. Originally used for a table or sideboard on which cups and other crockery were displayed.]

cup·cake /kúp kàyk/ *n.* a small individual iced cake, baked in a paper or foil cup or in a cup-shaped mold

cu·pel /kyoo pél, kyóop'l/ *n.* **CONTAINER FOR SEPARATING PRECIOUS METALS** a small container in which precious metals are refined, especially in which gold and silver are separated from base metals during assaying ■ *vt.* **(-peled, -pel·ing, -pels) REFINE IN A CUPEL** to separate gold or silver from a base metal using a cupel [Early 17thC. From French *coupelle*, literally "little cup," from *coupe* "cup," from late Latin *cuppa* (see CUP).] —**cu·pel·ler** *n.*

cu·pel·la·tion /kyòopə láysh'n/ *n.* the recovery of precious metals in a cupel by exposure to a blast of hot air that oxidizes the unwanted base metals, such as lead, which are partly absorbed

Cu·per·ti·no /kòopər teénō/ city in western California, a western suburb of San Jose. Population: 42,831 (1996).

cup·ful /kúp fòol/ *n.* **1. AMOUNT HELD BY CUP** the amount held by a cup ○ *There's only about a cupful of water left.* **2.** *U.S., Can, Aus* = **cup** *n.* 3

cup fun·gus *n.* a cup-shaped and often bright red, orange, or yellow fungus with a spore-bearing often stalkless structure. Subdivision: *Ascomycotina.*

cu·pid /kyóopid/ *n.* a representation of the god Cupid as a symbol of love in painting or sculpture

Cu·pid *n.* the Roman god of love, the son of Venus, usually represented as a young boy with wings and a bow and arrow. Greek equivalent **Eros** [14thC. From Latin *Cupido*, literally "desire," from *cupere* "to desire."]

cu·pid·i·ty /kyoo píddətee/ *n.* greed, especially for money or possessions (*formal*) [15thC. Directly or via French from Latin *cupiditas* (source also of English *covet*), from *cupere* "to desire."]

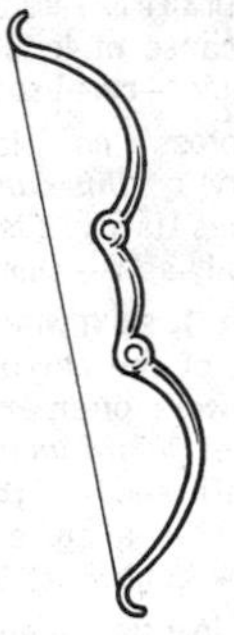
Cupid's bow

Cu·pid's bow *n.* **1. DOUBLE CURVE** a double curve, especially the curves of the upper lip **2.** ARCHERY **DOUBLE-CURVED BOW** a bow with two curves used in archery [From the shape of the bow used by Cupid]

cup of tea *n.* **1. PREFERRED THING** what somebody likes or prefers ○ *This is more my cup of tea.* **2. SOMETHING TO DEAL WITH** something to be dealt with

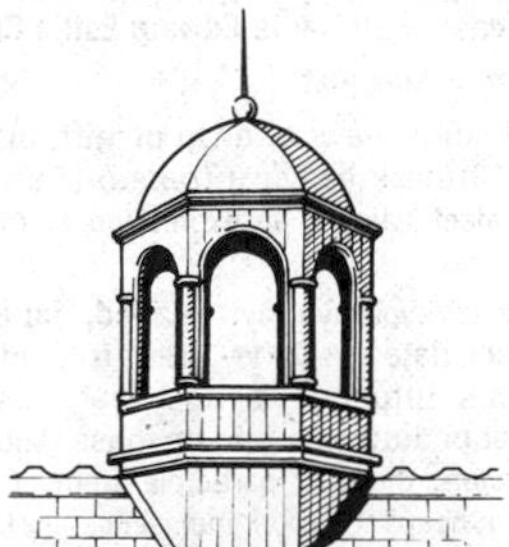
Cupola

cu·po·la /kyóopələ/ *n.* **1.** ARCHIT **DOME-SHAPED ROOF** a roof or ceiling in the form of a dome **2.** ARCHIT **DOME ON ROOF** a small dome on a roof, sometimes made of glass and providing natural light inside **3.** MIL **GUN TURRET** a domed structure protecting a gun, e.g., on a warship **4. SMALL OBSERVATION DOME** a glass observation dome on the roof of an armored vehicle or railroad caboose **5. BLAST FURNACE** a cylindrical blast furnace used in foundries for remelting iron or other metals [Mid-16thC. Via Italian from late Latin *cupula* "little cask, vault," from *cupa* "cask."]

cup·ping /kúpping/ *n.* MED a historical medical practice in which a cupping glass was used to increase the blood supply to an area of the skin

cup·ping glass *n.* MED a glass container in which a partial vacuum is created by heat or suction that is applied to the skin to increase the blood supply in the tissues below

cup·py /kúppee/ (**-pi·er, -pi·est**) *adj.* **1. CUP-SHAPED** with the shape of a cup **2. FULL OF SHALLOW DEPRESSIONS** with many small shallow hollows in the surface

cupr- *prefix.* = **cupro-** (*used before vowels*)

cu·pre·ous /kóopree əss/ *adj.* **1. COPPERY** consisting of or containing copper **2. OF REDDISH BROWN COLOR** having a reddish-brown color, like that of polished copper [Mid-17thC. Formed from late Latin *cupreus*, from *cuprum* "copper."]

cupri- *prefix.* = **cupro-**

cu·pric /kóoprik/ *adj.* containing copper with a valence of two. ◊ **cuprous** [Late 18thC. Formed from Late Latin *cuprum* "copper."]

cu·prif·er·ous /koo príffərəss/ *adj.* having copper as a constituent [Late 18thC. Coined from late Latin *cuprum* "copper" + -IFEROUS.]

cu·prite /kòo prìt/ *n.* a reddish-brown or black mineral consisting of copper oxide. It is an ore of copper. [Mid-19thC. Formed from Late Latin *cuprum* "copper."]

cupro- *prefix.* copper ○ *cupronickel* [From late Latin *cuprum* (see COPPER)]

cu·pro·nick·el /kòo prō ník'l/ *n.* a corrosion-resistant alloy of copper containing up to 40 percent nickel

cu·prous /kóoprəss/ *adj.* containing copper with a valence of 1. ◊ **cupric** [Mid-17thC. Formed from late Latin *cuprum* "copper."]

cu·pu·late /kyóopyə làyt, -lət/, **cu·pu·lar** /-lər/ *adj.* **1. SMALL AND CUP-SHAPED** shaped like a small cup or dome **2. HAVING CUPULES** having a cupule or cupules

cu·pule /kyóo pyòol/ *n.* a cup-shaped body part or plant part, such as that enclosing the base of an acorn [15thC. From late Latin *cupula* "little cask, vault," from *cupa* "cask."]

Cu·que·nan Wa·ter·fall /kòo kay nan-/ waterfall in Venezuela, one of the highest in the world. Height: 2,000 ft./610 m.

cur /kur/ *n.* **1. MONGREL DOG** a mixed-breed dog, especially an ill-natured or worthless one **2. CONTEMPTIBLE PERSON** a mean, cowardly, or otherwise unpleasant person (*dated insult*) [12thC. Originally in *cur-dog*; perhaps ultimately from Old Norse *kurr* "grumbling."]

cur. *abbr.* current

cur·a·ble /kyóorəb'l/ *adj.* **1. ABLE TO BE TREATED MEDICALLY** capable of being treated by medical procedures **2. ABLE TO BE HEALED** capable of being healed by medical procedures —**cur·a·bil·i·ty** /kyòorə bíllətee/ *n.* —**cur·a·bly** /-blee/ *adv.*

cu·ra·çao /kòorə sów, -sṓ/ *n.* an orange-flavored liqueur that originated on the Caribbean island of Curaçao

Cu·ra·çao /kóorə sòw, -sṑ, kyóorə-, -sṓ/ island in the Netherlands Antilles, in the Caribbean Sea, and the largest of the island group. Area: 171 sq. mi./444 sq. km.

cu·ra·cy /kyóorəssee/ (*plural* **-cies**) *n.* the position or term of office of a curate

cu·ra·re /kyoo ráaree/, **cu·ra·ri** *n.* **1. PLANT RESIN CAUSING PARALYSIS** a dark resin obtained from certain South American plants, used by indigenous hunters to poison their arrows and in medicine as a muscle relaxant **2. SOURCE OF CURARE** a tropical South American vine from which curare is obtained. Genera: *Strychnos* and *Chondodendron.* [Late 18thC. Via Spanish and Portuguese from Carib *kurari.*]

cu·ra·rize /kyóorə rìz/ (**-rized, -riz·ing, -riz·es**) *vt.* to treat somebody with curare —**cu·ra·ri·za·tion** /kyòorəri záysh'n/ *n.*

cu·ras·sow /kyóorə sṑ/ *n.* a large crested game bird of South and Central America with a long tail and a brightly colored bill. Genus: *Crax*. [Late 17thC. Alteration of CURAÇAO.]

cu·rate[1] /kyŏŏrət/ *n.* **1. PRIEST'S ASSISTANT** a member of the clergy who assists a vicar, rector, or priest **2. SOMEBODY RESPONSIBLE FOR PARISH** a member of the clergy in charge of a parish [14thC. From medieval Latin *curatus* "somebody who cares for a parish," from Latin *cura* "care" (source of English *cure*).]

cu·rate[2] /kyŏŏr àyt/ (**-rat·ed, -rat·ing, -rates**) *vti.* to be the curator of a museum, gallery, or other collection [Early 18thC. Back-formation from CURATOR.]

cu·ra·tive /kyŏŏrətiv/ *adj.* **CAPABLE OF CURING** able to restore health ■ *n.* **MEDICINE OR MEDICAL TREATMENT** a substance or treatment that can restore health —**cu·ra·tive·ly** *adv.* —**cu·ra·tive·ness** *n.*

cu·ra·tor /kyə ráytər, kyŏŏ ràytər/ *n.* the administrative head of a museum, gallery, or other collection [14thC. From Latin, from *curare* "to care for" (see CURE).] —**cu·ra·to·ri·al** /kyŏŏrə táwree əl/ *adj.* —**cu·ra·tor·ship** /kyə ráytər shìp, kyŏŏ raytər-/ *n.*

curb /kurb/ *n.* **1. EDGE OF SIDEWALK** a line of concrete or stones forming the edge of the sidewalk and part of the gutter at the side of a road **2. EDGING FOR LAWN** a line of stones that forms the edge of an area of lawn **3. IMPOSED LIMITATION** something that controls or limits something else **4. RAISED PART THAT SURROUNDS SOMETHING** an enclosing frame or raised margin, e.g., around a skylight or a well **5. HORSE'S BIT AND ATTACHED CHAIN** a horse's bit with a chain or strap attached, passed under the horse's jaw (*often used before a noun*) ○ *a curb chain* ■ *vt.* (**curbed, curb·ing, curbs**) **1. RESTRAIN** to restrain, control, or limit something **2. PROVIDE WITH CURB** to provide with a curb **3. LEAD DOG OFF SIDEWALK TO DEFECATE** to lead a dog off the sidewalk onto the curb or into the gutter to let it defecate [15thC. Probably a variant of earlier *courb* "to curve" (the underlying sense in English), which came via French *courber*, from Latin *curvare*. Originally, "horse's bit" (that bends the horse's neck).]

curb bit *n.* a horse's bit attached to a chain or strap

curb cut *n.* a small ramp built on a curb to make it easier for people in wheelchairs or people pushing strollers to move between the street and sidewalk

curb·ing /kúrbing/ *n.* **1. MATERIAL FOR CURBS** the material used to make a curb **2. CURBS LINING STREET** the whole length of curb along a street, or all the curbs of a street

curb roof *n.* a roof that has two or more different angles of slope on each side, e.g., a mansard or gambrel roof

curb ser·vice *n.* service to customers who remain in their vehicles, especially at fast food outlets

curb·side /kúrb sìd/ *n.* **1. SIDE BORDERED BY CURB** the edge of a street or a sidewalk bordered by a curb **2. SIDEWALK** a sidewalk

curb·side ser·vice *n.* = **curb service**

curb·stone /kúrb stòn/ *n.* any of the stones or pieces of concrete that form a curb

cur·cu·li·o /kur kyŏŏlee ò/ (*plural* **-os**) *n.* a weevil that damages fruit trees, vegetables, and other plants. Genus: *Conotrachelus*. [Mid-18thC. From Latin, literally "corn weevil."]

cur·cu·ma /kúrkyəmə/ *n.* a tropical plant from which turmeric and zedoary are obtained. Genus: *Curcuma*. [15thC. Via medieval Latin from Arabic *kurkum* "turmeric," from Sanskrit *kuṅkuma* "saffron." The change of meaning from "saffron" to "turmeric" presumably occurred because of the yellow coloring of both.]

curd /kurd/ *n.* **1. SOLID PART OF SOUR MILK** the solid substance formed when milk coagulates, used to make cheese **2. SUBSTANCE RESEMBLING MILK CURD** a food substance with a consistency similar to milk curd ■ *vti.* (**curd·ed, curd·ing, curds**) **CURDLE** to turn something into curd, or to become curd [14thC. Origin uncertain: perhaps from Celtic.] —**curd·y** *adj.*

curd cheese *n. U.K.* a mild soft cheese made from skim milk curds

cur·dle /kúrd'l/ (**-dled, -dling, -dles**) *vti.* **1. COAGULATE OR MAKE SOMETHING COAGULATE** to separate, or cause a liquid such as milk, to separate into curds and whey, e.g., by permitting or encouraging bacterial action **2. GO BAD OR SPOIL SOMETHING** to go bad or wrong, or to spoil something (*informal*) [Late 16thC. Formed from CURD. Literally "to keep on making into curd."]

cur dog *n. Southern U.S.* a mixed-breed worthless dog

WORD KEY: REGIONAL NOTE

Cur dog is common throughout the South, except in Louisiana, where the intrepid stock (usually hog) tender, the *Catahoula cur*, is the official state dog.

cure /kyoor/ *v.* (**cured, cur·ing, cures**) **1.** *vti.* **HEAL** to restore a sick person or animal to health ○ *Six months later she was completely cured.* **2.** *vt.* **TREAT SUCCESSFULLY** to bring about recovery from an illness, disorder, or injury ○ *Diseases like this are not easily cured.* **3.** *vt.* **SOLVE PROBLEM** to solve a problem ○ *curing unemployment* **4.** *vti.* **PRESERVE FOOD** to preserve food, especially meat or fish, usually by smoking, drying, or salting it, or to be preserved by one of these methods **5.** *vt.* **PRESERVE BY DRYING** to preserve a substance, especially leather or tobacco, by drying it **6.** *vt.* **FINISH WITH CHEMICAL PROCESS** to finish a material by applying chemicals **7.** *vt.* **MAKE RUBBER STRONGER** to strengthen rubber with additives in the presence of heat and pressure **8.** *vti.* **HARDEN** to make a material, especially concrete or cement, harden ■ *n.* **1. SOMETHING THAT RESTORES HEALTH** a medication or treatment that brings about a full recovery from an illness or injury ○ *working to find a cure for the disease* **2. RECOVERY** restoration or return to health ○ *I managed to achieve a complete cure.* **3. PROBLEM'S SOLUTION** something that resolves a problem **4. FOOD PRESERVATION PROCESS** the preservation of meat or fish, especially by smoking, drying, or salting **5. SPIRITUAL CARE** the spiritual and pastoral responsibility of the clergy for laypeople [13thC. Via Old French from Latin *curare* "to care for," or its source *cura* "care, concern" (the original sense in English). Current senses evolved via the obsolete sense "medical care."] —**cur·er** *n.*

WORD KEY: ORIGIN

Cure is derived from the Latin word *cura*, meaning "care" or "concern," which is also the source of English *curate*, *curious*, *scour*, *secure*, and *sinecure*.

cu·ré /kyoo ráy, kyə-/ *n.* a parish priest [Mid-17thC. Via French from medieval Latin *curatus* (see CURATE[1]).]

cure-all *n.* a treatment or remedy that is believed to be able to cure every ailment or problem

cu·ret *n.*, *vt.* = **curette**

cu·ret·tage /kyŏŏrə taázh/, **cu·rette·ment** /kyoo rétmənt/ *n.* a surgical procedure that involves scraping the inside surface of a body cavity with an instrument shaped like a spoon (**curette**) to remove abnormal growths or other tissue [Late 19thC. From French, from *curette* (see CURETTE).]

cu·rette /kyoo rét/, **cu·ret** *n.* **SURGICAL INSTRUMENT FOR SCRAPING** a spoon-shaped surgical instrument used to remove tissue from the inner surface of a body cavity ■ *vt.* (**-ret·ted, -ret·ting, -rettes; -ret·ted, -ret·ting, -rets**) **REMOVE TISSUE BY SCRAPING** to scrape tissue from the inner surface of a body cavity using a curette [Mid-18thC. From French, from *curer* "to clean out," from Latin *curare* "to care for."]

cu·rette·ment /kyoo rétmənt/ *n.* = **curettage**

cur·few /kúr fyoo/ *n.* **1. RESTRICTION ON PEOPLE'S MOVEMENTS** an official restriction on people's movements, requiring them to remain indoors after a specified time at night **2. TIME OR SIGNAL FOR CURFEW** the time at which a curfew takes effect, or the signal given at this time **3. LENGTH OF CURFEW** the duration of a curfew **4. MEDIEVAL REMINDER TO EXTINGUISH LIGHTS** in the Middle Ages, the ringing of a bell in the evening as a reminder to put out fires and lights ○ *"The curfew tolls the knell of parting day"* (Thomas Gray, *Elegy written in a Country Churchyard*; 1751) [13thC. From Anglo-Norman *coeverfu* or Old French *cuevrefeu*, literally "cover fire."]

cu·ri·a /kyŏŏree ə/ (*plural* **-ae** /-ee/) *n.* **1. PAPAL COURT** the administrative body at the Vatican, by which the Pope governs the Roman Catholic Church **2. SUBDIVISION OF ANCIENT ROMAN TRIBE** in ancient Rome, a subdivision of each tribe, or the place where it met **3. ANCIENT ROMAN SENATE** the senate or senate house in an ancient Roman city **4. MEDIEVAL COURT** a medieval monarch's court of justice [Early 17thC. From Latin, literally "council," perhaps formed from *co-* "together" + *vir* "man" (source of English *virile*).] —**cu·ri·al** *adj.*

cu·rie /kyŏŏree, kyoor ée/ *n.* a unit of radioactivity equal to 3.7 times 10^{10} disintegrations per second [Early 20thC. Named for the French physicists Pierre *Curie* (1859–1906) and Marie CURIE, who studied radioactivity.]

Marie Curie

Cu·rie /kyŏŏree/, **Marie** (1867–1934) Polish-born French chemist and physicist. She pioneered research into radioactivity and was awarded the Nobel Prize in 1903 and 1911. She died of leukemia. Her husband Pierre Curie collaborated with her and was jointly awarded the 1903 Nobel Prize. Born **Marja Sklodowska**

Cu·rie point, **Cu·rie tem·per·a·ture** *n.* the temperature at which in some substances, such as iron, there is a change in the magnetic characteristics, from ferromagnetic to paramagnetic behavior [Named for Pierre *Curie* (see CURIE), who discovered the laws that relate some magnetic properties to changes in temperature]

Cu·rie's law *n.* the law of physics stating that there is an inverse proportionality between the effect of a magnetic field on a paramagnetic material and its absolute temperature [Named for Pierre *Curie* (see CURIE), who formulated it]

Cu·rie-Weiss law /-vìss-/ *n.* a variation of Curie's law in which the temperature term is reduced by an amount equal to the Curie point [Named for Pierre *Curie* (see CURIE) and the French physicist Pierre Ernest *Weiss* (1865–1940), who constructed a mathematical description of phenomena such as the Curie point]

cu·ri·o /kyŏŏree ò/ (*plural* **-os**) *n.* an object that is valued and often collected for its interest or rarity [Mid-19thC. Shortening of CURIOSITY.]

cu·ri·o·sa /kyŏŏree óssə, -ózə/ *npl.* (*takes a plural verb*) **1. WRITINGS ON UNUSUAL SUBJECTS** books or other texts dealing with unusual topics, especially erotica **2. UNUSUAL OBJECTS** interesting and unusual objects [Late 19thC. From Latin, neuter plural of *curiosus* (see CURIOUS).]

cu·ri·os·i·ty /kyŏŏree óssətee/ (*plural* **-ties**) *n.* **1. DESIRE TO KNOW SOMETHING** eagerness to know about something or to get information **2. TENDENCY TO PRY** an excessive interest in other people's affairs **3. SOMEBODY OR SOMETHING THOUGHT STRANGE** an interesting and unusual object, person, or phenomenon [14thC. Via French *curiosité* from Latin *curiositas*, from *curiosus* (see CURIOUS).]

cu·ri·ous /kyŏŏree əss/ *adj.* **1. EAGER TO KNOW SOMETHING** eager to know about something or to get information ○ *I'm curious to know how they found out about the party.* **2. TOO INQUISITIVE** excessively eager to find out about other people's affairs **3. ODD** strange, unexpected, or hard to explain ○ *several curious events* **4. VERY INTRICATE** intricate or detailed (*archaic or literary*) [14thC. Via Old French *curios* from Latin *curiosus* "careful, assiduous, inquisitive," from *cura* "care, concern, solicitude" (source of English *cure*).] —**cu·ri·ous·ly** *adv.* —**cu·ri·ous·ness** *n.*

Cu·ri·ti·ba /kŏŏri teébə/ city in southern Brazil. It is the capital of Paraná State. Population: 1,290,142 (1991). Former name **Curytiba**

cu·ri·um /kyŏŏree əm/ *n.* a silvery-white metallic radioactive chemical element produced artificially from plutonium. Symbol **Cm** [Mid-20thC. Named for Pierre and Marie *Curie* (see CURIE), because of their research into radioactivity.]

curl /kurl/ *v.* (**curled, curl·ing, curls**) **1.** *vti.* **MAKE HAIR CURLY** to make naturally straight hair curly, usually by twisting it around something while it is damp, or to grow in ringlets naturally **2.** *vti.* **MAKE OR BECOME CURVED OR COILED** to bend, twist, or wind something into a curved or spiral shape, or to become curved or coiled ○ *He curled the silver ribbon into spirals.* ○ *The paper had begun to curl at the edges.* **3.** *vi.* **MOVE IN A SPIRAL MOTION** to move in a curve or spiral ○ *Smoke curled into the sky.* **4.** *vi.* **PARTICIPATE IN CURLING** to play the game of curling ■ *n.* **1. CURVED OR COILED HAIRS** a lock of hair curved into a round or spiral shape (*often used in the plural*) **2. TENDENCY TO CURL** the tendency of hair to grow or stay in ringlets ○ *My* *hair doesn't have much curl.* **3. CURVED OR COILED THING** something with a curved or coiled shape, e.g., a wood shaving or the crest of a breaking wave **4. CURLING OF SOMETHING** the forming of something into a curved or round shape **5.** GYM **WEIGHTLIFTING MANEUVER** a weightlifting move in which a barbell is held at thigh height with the underarms facing outward, then raised to the chest, and lowered without moving the shoulders, upper arms, or legs **6. MARKING ON WOOD** a curved or spiral marking in wood grain [14thC. From Middle Dutch *krul* "curly," of prehistoric Germanic origin.]

curl up *v.* **1.** *vi.* **CURVE BODY AND DRAW UP LEGS** to sit or lie with the body curved and the legs tucked up, usually in order to relax ○ *curl up into bed with a good novel* **2.** *vti.* **MAKE OR BECOME CURVED OR COILED** to become curved or coiled, or to bend, twist, or wind something into a curved or spiral shape ○ *The paper curled up in the fire before it burst into flames.* **3.** *vi.* **FEEL EXTREMELY EMBARRASSED** to be overcome with embarrassment, revulsion, or some other strong feeling (*informal*) ○ *When I realized my mistake I just wanted to curl up and disappear.*

curl·er /kúrlər/ *n.* **1. DEVICE FOR CURLING HAIR** a roller or other device used to curl hair **2. SOMEBODY PLAYING CURLING** somebody who takes part in the game of curling

Curlew

cur·lew /kúr lōō/ *n.* a large shore bird with brownish plumage, long legs, and a long slender bill that curves downward. Genus: *Numenius.* [14thC. From Old French *courlieu*, a variant, probably influenced by *courliu* "courier, messenger," of *courlis*, an imitation of the bird's cry.]

curl·i·cue /kúrli kyōō/ *n.* a curly ornamental twist, especially in calligraphy or design [Mid-19thC. From CURLY + CUE[2] (in the obsolete sense "pigtail").] —**curl·i·cued** *adj.*

curl·ing /kúrling/ *n.* a team game played on an ice rink, in which a heavy polished stone with a handle is slid toward a circular target (**tee**) [Early 17thC. From the curving path of the stone as it reaches the target.]

curl·ing i·ron *n.* a device consisting of a heated rod around which the hair is twisted to form a curl

curl·ing stone *n.* a heavy polished stone with a handle used in the game of curling

curl·ing tongs *npl. U.K.* = **curling iron**

curl·pa·per /kúrl pàypər/ *n.* a small piece of paper rolled around a lock of hair, which is then twisted and left to set into a curl

curl·y /kúrlee/ (**-i·er, -i·est**) *adj.* **1. WITH CURLS** arranged in curls, or curling naturally **2. CURVED OR COILED** bent or twisted into a wavy, curved, or spiral shape ○ *The paper has gone all curly.* **3. WITH CURVES IN GRAIN** used to describe wood that has irregular curved or wavy markings in the grain —**curl·i·ness** *n.*

curl·y-coat·ed re·triev·er *n.* a dog with a short curly black or brown coat, belonging to a breed used for hunting

curl·y top *n.* a viral disease of beets, tomatoes, beans, and other plants that makes the leaves curl

cur·mudg·eon /kur mújjən/ *n.* a bad-tempered, disagreeable, or stubborn person (*disapproving*) [Late 16thC. Origin uncertain: perhaps thought to suggest the sound of grumbling.] —**cur·mudg·eon·ly** *adj.* —**cur·mud·geon·ry** *n.*

cur·rach /kúrrə/, **cur·ragh** *n. Ireland, Scotland* a boat like a coracle, formerly used on Scottish and Irish lakes and rivers [15thC. From Irish and Gaelic *curach* "small boat." Ultimately from a Celtic word which is also the ancestor of English *coracle.*]

cur·rant /kúrrənt/ *n.* **1. SMALL DRIED GRAPE** a small dark dried seedless grape originally from the Mediterranean, used in cooking **2. SMALL FRUIT-BEARING SHRUB** a small deciduous shrub cultivated in temperate regions that bears a small round edible fruit, especially the redcurrant or black currant. Genus: *Ribes.* **3. FRUIT OF CURRANT BUSH** the small round juicy fruit of a currant bush, especially a redcurrant or black currant [Early 16thC. Shortening of Anglo-Norman *raisins de Corauntz*, a variant of Old French *raisins de Corinthe*, literally "grapes from Corinth," where they originated.]

cur·ren·cy /kúrrənsee/ (*plural* **-cies**) *n.* **1. MONEY** a system of money, or the bills and coins themselves, used in a particular country **2. ACCEPTANCE OF IDEA OR TERM** widespread acceptance or use of an idea, theory, word, or phrase **3. CIRCULATION** the transmitting of something, especially money, from person to person **4. TIME WHEN SOMETHING IS CURRENT** the period of time during which something is current [Mid-17thC. Formed from CURRENT. In the financial sense, from the idea of being currently in circulation.]

cur·ren·cy-sta·bi·li·za·tion fund *n.* FIN a fund set aside for use in stabilizing the foreign exchange rate for a national currency in international markets

cur·rent /kúrrənt, kúr ənt/ *adj.* **1. EXISTING NOW** happening, existing, or in force at the present ○ *In my current job, I am in charge of 25 people.* **2. VALID** accepted as legally valid **3. PRESENTLY ACCEPTED** widely known, accepted, or believed ○ *The theory is no longer current.* **4.** FIN **UP-TO-DATE WITH PAYMENTS** having made all the payments required for the present time ■ *n.* **1. FLOW OF WATER OR AIR** the steady flow of water or air in a particular direction **2. STREAM** a mass of water or air flowing steadily in a particular direction **3. FLOW OF ELECTRIC CHARGE** the flow of electricity through a cable, wire, or other conductor **4. RATE OF FLOW OF ELECTRICITY** the rate of flow of an electric charge through a conductor **5. TENDENCY** a trend or tendency ○ *going against the current and moving upstate* [13thC. From Old French *corant*, the present participle of *courre* "to run," from Latin *currere*. The original and underlying sense is "running, flowing."] —**cur·rent·ness** *n.*

WORD KEY: ORIGIN

Current is derived from the Latin word *currere*, meaning "to run," which is also the source of English *corridor, courier, course, occur,* and *succor.*

cur·rent ac·count *n. U.K.* BANKING = **checking account**

cur·rent af·fairs *npl.* = **current events** (*often used before a noun*)

cur·rent as·sets *npl.* available cash and other assets that could be converted to cash within a year

cur·rent-cost ac·count·ing *n.* a method of accounting that assesses the value of assets as the cost of replacing them rather than as their original cost

cur·rent den·si·ty *n.* the ratio of the amount of current flowing through a conductor to the cross-sectional area of the conductor. Symbol *j, J*

cur·rent ef·fi·cien·cy *n.* in an electrolytic process, the mass of the substance liberated by a given current divided by the theoretical mass, as predicted by Faraday's law

cur·rent e·vents *npl.* important political and social events or issues of the present time (*often used before a noun*)

cur·rent li·a·bil·i·ties *npl.* business liabilities that are due to be cleared before the end of the financial year

cur·rent·ly /kúrrəntlee/ *adv.* at the present time ○ *They are currently living abroad.*

cur·rent ra·tio *n.* the ratio of current assets to current liabilities

cur·ri·cle /kúrrik'l/ *n.* a light two-wheeled open carriage drawn by a pair of horses side by side [Mid-18thC. From Latin *curriculum* , in the sense "racing chariot."]

cur·ric·u·lum /kə ríkyələm/ (*plural* **-la** /-lə/ *or* **-lums**) *n.* the subjects taught at an educational institution, or the elements taught in a particular subject [Early 19thC. From Latin, literally "running, course," from *currere* "to run" (source of English *current*).] —**cur·ric·u·lar** *adj.*

cur·ric·u·lum vi·tae /-vee tī, -vítee/ (*plural* **cur·ric·u·la vi·tae** /kə rìkyələ vee tī, -vítee/) *n.* a summary of a person's educational qualifications, skills, publications, and professional activities, prepared when applying for an academic position [Early 20thC. From Latin, literally "course of life."]

cur·ri·er /kúrree ər/ *n.* somebody who dresses and finishes leather after it has been tanned [14thC. Via Old French *corier* from Latin *coriarius*, from *corium* "leather."]

Cur·ri·er /kúrr iər/, **Nathaniel** (1813–88) U.S. lithographer. He formed half of Currier and Ives, noted for their colored prints of Victorian American life.

cur·rish /kúrrish/ *adj.* having a very hostile or disagreeable disposition [15thC. Formed from CUR.] —**cur·rish·ly** *adv.* —**cur·rish·ness** *n.*

cur·ry[1] /kúrree/ *n.* (*plural* **-ries**) (*often used before a noun*) **1. HIGHLY SPICED DISH** a dish containing meat, fish, or vegetables in a highly spiced sauce ○ *chicken curry* **2. SEASONING FOR CURRY** a mixture of spices in any of various forms, such as sauce, paste, or powder, used to prepare curry ○ *curry paste* ■ *vt.* (**-ried, -ry·ing, -ries**) **COOK IN HIGHLY SPICED SAUCE** to cook meat, fish, or vegetables in a highly spiced sauce [Late 16thC. From Tamil *kari* "sauce."]

cur·ry[2] /kúrree/ (**-ried, -ry·ing, -ries**) *vt.* **1. GROOM** to groom a horse **2. PUT THROUGH FINISHING PROCESS** to make leather flexible and waterproof as the final stage in its processing [13thC. Via Old French *correier*, "to arrange, prepare" from an assumed Vulgar Latin verb formed from Latin *con* "with" and a prehistoric Germanic base that is also the ancestor of English *ready.*]

Cur·ry /kúrree/, **John Steuart** (1897–1946) U.S. artist. He is known for his easel paintings and murals. Some of his murals adorn federal buildings in Washington, D.C.

cur·ry·comb /kúrri kōm/ *n.* **COMB USED TO GROOM HORSES** a comb with metal or rubber teeth, used to groom horses ■ *vt.* (**-combed, -comb·ing, -combs**) **GROOM WITH CURRYCOMB** to groom a horse with a currycomb [Late 16thC. From CURRY[2] + COMB.]

cur·ry pow·der *n.* a mixture of finely ground spices, usually turmeric, cumin, coriander, chili, and ginger, used to make curry

curse /kurs/ *n.* **1. SWEARWORD** a swearword, obscenity, or blasphemous oath **2. EVIL PRAYER** a malevolent appeal to a supernatural being for harm to come to somebody or something, or the harm that is thought to result from this **3. SOURCE OF HARM** a cause of unhappiness or harm ○ *the curse of poverty* **4. MENSTRUATION** menstruation or a menstrual period (*dated slang*) **5. RELIGIOUS BAN** an ecclesiastical pronouncement of censure or excommunication ■ *interj.* **curs·es USED AS OATH** used to express irritation or annoyance ■ *v.* (**cursed** *or* **curst, curs·ing, curs·es**) **1.** *vi.* **SWEAR** to utter swearwords or obscenities **2.** *vt.* **SWEAR AT** to swear at somebody **3.** *vt.* **WISH EVIL ON** to appeal malevolently to a supernatural being for harm to come to somebody or something **4.** *vt.* **CAUSE SUFFERING TO** to inflict something unpleasant on somebody ○ *cursed with a succession of mediocre assistants* [Old English *curs*, of unknown origin] —**curs·er** *n.*

curs·ed /kúrsəd, kurst/ *adj.* **1. HAVING BEEN WISHED EVIL** afflicted with harm thought to result from a curse **2. WICKED OR HATEFUL** evil to the point of being despicable **3. ANNOYING OR FRUSTRATING** stubborn to the point of causing irritation or annoyance (*informal*) —**curs·ed·ly** /kúrsədlee/ *adv.* —**curs·ed·ness** /-nəss/ *n.*

cur·sive /kúrsiv/ *adj.* **WRITTEN IN FLOWING STYLE** written in a flowing style with the letters joined together ■ *n.* **1. FLOWING SCRIPT** cursive writing **2. MANUSCRIPT WRITTEN IN FLOWING STYLE** a piece of cursive handwriting, especially an ancient manuscript **3.** PRINTING **TYPEFACE** a cursive typeface [Late 18thC. From medieval Latin *cursivus*, from Latin *currere* "to run."] —**cur·sive·ly** *adv.* —**cur·sive·ness** *n.*

cur·sor /kúrsər/ *n.* COMPUT **MARKER ON COMPUTER SCREEN** a moving marker on a computer screen, e.g., a flashing horizontal or vertical bar, that marks the point at which keyed characters will appear, be deleted, or be corrected ■ *vi.* COMPUT **MOVE CURSOR** to move the cursor in a particular direction on the screen of a computer ○ *As we cursor down, the hierarchy changes.* [14thC. From Latin (see CURSORY). Originally, "runner, messenger"; later used to denote part of a scientific instrument which slides backward and forward, specifically the slide of a sliderule.]

cur·so·ri·al /kur sáwree əl/ *adj.* ZOOL having a body or body parts that are particularly well-adapted for

CURRENCY: UNITS AND SUBUNITS

Country	Unit	Subunit
Afghanistan	afghani	100 puls
Albania	lek	100 qindars
Algeria	dinar	100 centimes
Andorra	peseta franc	100 centimos 100 centimes
Angola	readjusted kwanza	100 lwei
Antigua and Barbuda	dollar	
Argentina	peso argentino	
Armenia	dram	100 humma
Australia	dollar	100 cents
Austria*	schilling	100 groschen
Azerbaijan	manat	100 gyapiks
The Bahamas	dollar	100 cents
Bahrain	dinar	1000 fils
Bangladesh	taka	100 paisas
Barbados	dollar	100 cents
Belarus	ruble	
Belgium*	franc	100 centimes
Belize	dollar	100 cents
Benin	franc	
Bhutan	ngultrum	100 chetrums
Bolivia	boliviano	100 centavos
Bosnia-Herzegovina	dinar	
Botswana	pula	100 thebe
Brazil	real	100 centavos
Brunei	dollar/ringgit	100 cents
Bulgaria	lev	100 stotinki
Burkina Faso	franc	
Burundi	franc	100 centimes
Cambodia	riel	100 sen
Cameroon	franc	
Canada	dollar	100 cents
Cape Verde	escudo	100 centavos
Central African Republic	franc	
Chad	franc	
Chile	peso	100 centavos
China	yuan	10 jiao
Hong Kong	dollar	100 cents
Macao	pataca	100 avos
Colombia	peso	100 centavos
Comoros	franc	100 centimes
Democratic Republic of Congo	new zaire	100 makuta
Republic of Congo	franc	
Costa Rica	colón	100 centimos
Côte d'Ivoire	franc	
Croatia	kuna	100 lipa
Cuba	peso	100 centavos
Cyprus	pound/lira	
Czech Republic	koruna	100 haler
Denmark	krone	100 øre
Djibouti	franc	100 centimes
Dominica	dollar	
Dominican Republic	peso	100 centavos
Ecuador	sucre	100 centavos
Egypt	pound	100 piastres
El Salvador	colon	100 centavos
Equatorial Guinea	franc	
Eritrea	nakfa	100 cents
Estonia	kroon	100 sents
Ethiopia	birr	100 cents
Fiji	dollar	100 cents
Finland*	markka	100 pennis
France*	franc	100 centimes
Gabon	franc	
The Gambia	dalasi	100 bututs
Georgia	lari	
Germany*	mark	100 pfennig
Ghana	new cedi	100 pesewas
Greece	drachma	100 lepta
Grenada	dollar	
Guatemala	quetzal	100 centavos
Guinea	franc	100 centimes
Guinea-Bissau	franc	
Guyana	dollar	100 cents
Haiti	gourde	100 centimes
Honduras	lempira	100 centavos
Hungary	forint	100 fillér
Iceland	króna	100 aurar
India	rupee	100 paisa
Indonesia	rupiah	100 sen
Iran	rial	
Iraq	dinar	1000 fils
Ireland*	punt	100 pence
Israel	shekel	100 agorot
Italy*	lira	100 centesimi
Jamaica	dollar	100 cents
Japan	yen	100 sen
Jordan	dinar	1000 fils
Kazakhstan	tenge	
Kenya	shilling	100 cents
Kiribati	dollar	100 cents
Kuwait	dinar	1000 fils
Kyrgyzstan	som	100 tyiyn
Laos	new kip	
Latvia	lat	100 santims
Lebanon	pound	100 piastres
Lesotho	loti	100 lisente
Liberia	dollar	100 cents
Libya	dinar	1000 dirhams
Liechtenstein	franc	100 centimes
Lithuania	litas	100 centas
Luxembourg*	franc	100 centimes
Macedonia	denar	100 deni
Madagascar	franc	
Malawi	kwacha	100 tambala
Malaysia	ringgit	100 sen
Maldives	rufiyaa	100 laari
Mali	franc	
Malta	lira	100 cents
Marshall Islands	dollar	100 cents
Mauritania	ouguiya	5 khoums
Mauritius	rupee	100 cents
Mexico	peso	100 centavos
Micronesia	dollar	100 cents
Moldova	leu	
Monaco	franc	100 centimes
Mongolia	tugrik	100 mongo
Morocco	dirham	100 centimes
Mozambique	metical	100 centavos
Myanmar	kyat	100 pyas
Namibia	dollar	100 cents
Nauru	dollar	100 cents
Nepal	rupee	100 paisas
Netherlands*	guilder	100 cents
New Zealand	dollar	100 cents
Nicaragua	córdoba	100 centavos
Niger	franc	
Nigeria	naira	100 kobo
North Korea	won	100 chon
Norway	krone	100 øre
Oman	riyal	1000 baiza
Pakistan	rupee	100 paisas
Palau	dollar	100 cents
Panama	balboa	100 centesimos
Papua New Guinea	kina	100 toea
Paraguay	guarani	100 centimos
Peru	nuevo sol	100 centimos
Philippines	peso	100 centavos
Poland	zloty	100 groszy
Portugal*	escudo	100 centavos
Qatar	riyal	100 dirhams
Romania	leu	100 bani
Russia	ruble	100 kopeks
Rwanda	franc	100 centimes
St Kitts and Nevis	dollar	
St Lucia	dollar	
San Marino	lira	
St Vincent and the Grenadines	dollar	
Samoa	tala	100 sene
Sao Tome and Principe	dobra	100 centimos
Saudi Arabia	riyal	100 halalah
Senegal	franc	
Seychelles	rupee	100 cents
Sierra Leone	leone	100 cents
Singapore	dollar	100 cents
Slovakia	koruna	100 haliers
Slovenia	tolar	100 stotinas
Solomon Islands	dollar	100 cents
Somalia	shilling	100 cents
South Africa	rand	100 cents
South Korea	won	100 chon
Spain*	peseta	100 centimos
Sri Lanka	rupee	100 cents
Sudan	pound	100 piastres
Suriname	guilder	100 cents
Swaziland	lilangeni	100 cents
Sweden	krona	100 öre
Switzerland	franc	100 centimes
Syria	pound	100 piastres
Taiwan	dollar	100 cents
Tajikistan	ruble	100 tanga
Tanzania	shilling	100 cents
Thailand	baht	100 satang
Togo	franc	
Tonga	pa'anga	100 seniti
Trinidad and Tobago	dollar	100 cents
Tunisia	dinar	1000 millimes
Turkey	lira	100 kurus
Turkmenistan	manat	100 tenesi
Tuvalu	dollar	100 cents
Uganda	shilling	100 cents
Ukraine	hryvnia	
United Arab Emirates	dirham	100 fils
United Kingdom	pound	100 pence
United States	dollar	100 cents
Uruguay	peso	100 centesimos
Uzbekistan	soum	
Vanuatu	vatu	
Vatican City	lira	
Venezuela	bolivar	100 centimos
Vietnam	new dong	100 xu
Yemen	riyal	100 fils
Yugoslavia	new dinar	100 para
Zambia	kwacha	100 ngwee
Zimbabwe	dollar	100 cents

* Indicates member states of the European Union in which the Euro was introduced in 1999

running [Mid-19thC. Formed from Latin *cursor* (see CURSORY).]

cur·so·ry /kúrsəree/ *adj.* done in a quick or superficial way [Early 17thC. From Latin *cursorius*, from *cursor* "runner," from *currere* "to run." The underlying sense is "running rapidly over something."] —**cur·so·ri·ly** *adv.* —**cur·so·ri·ness** *n.*

curt /kurt/ *adj.* **1.** RUDELY BRIEF rude or abrupt **2.** TERSE using few words [14thC. From Latin *curtus* "cut short."] —**curt·ly** *adv.* —**curt·ness** *n.*

cur·tail /kur táyl/ (**-tailed, -tail·ing, -tails**) *vt.* to reduce the length or duration of something [15thC. By folk etymology from CURTAL, by association with TAIL and probably also with French *tailler* "to cut."] —**cur·tail·ment** *n.*

cur·tail step *n.* a wider lowest step on some flights of stairs, often rounded at one or both ends

cur·tain /kúrt'n/ *n.* **1.** CLOTH HUNG TO COVER SOMETHING a piece of cloth hung at a window, in a doorway, or around a bed, usually for privacy or to exclude light or drafts **2.** CLOTH AT FRONT OF STAGE in a theater, a hanging cloth that is raised and lowered at the front of the stage **3.** BEGINNING OR END OF SHOW the beginning or end of a performance, act, or scene, as marked by the raising or lowering of the curtain **4.** BARRIER OR SCREEN something that acts as a barrier or screen to divide, protect, or conceal something **5.** SOMETHING RESEMBLING CURTAIN something that resembles a curtain in appearance ○ *a curtain of water* **6.** ARCHIT WALL CONNECTING OTHER STRUCTURES a length of wall, especially one that connects two towers or gates ■ *vt.* (**-tained, -tain·ing, -tains**) **1.** COVER OR DIVIDE WITH CURTAIN to surround, separate, or conceal something with a curtain **2.** FIT WITH CURTAINS to provide something, especially a window, with curtains [13thC. Via Old French from Latin *cortina* "caldron," mistakenly rendering Greek *aulaia* "curtain," perhaps from association of *aulaia* (formed from *aulē* "court") with Latin *cohort-* "court."] ◇ **curtain raiser** any preliminary event

cur·tain call *n.* an appearance by actors, dancers, or singers at the front of the stage to receive the audience's applause at the end of a performance

cur·tain lec·ture *n.* a private reprimand given to a man by his wife (*archaic*) [From its originally being delivered within the privacy of drawn bed curtains]

cur·tain rais·er *n.* **1.** PRELIMINARY PERFORMANCE a short performance put on immediately before the main performance **2.** PRELIMINARY EVENT a smaller or less important event that takes place before a bigger or more important one

cur·tain speech *n.* **1.** TALK AFTER PLAY a speech addressed to the audience by somebody in front of the curtain after a play has ended **2.** LAST SPEECH the speech before the final curtain of an act or play

cur·tain time *n.* the time when a play starts or is set to start

cur·tain wall *n.* **1.** NONBEARING WALL an external wall that does not bear any of the load of the building it is attached to **2.** LOW CASTLE WALL a low wall outside a castle built for defense

cur·tal /kúrt'l/ *n.* an animal whose tail has been docked (*archaic*) [Early 16thC. From obsolete French *courtault*, from *court* "short" + the pejorative suffix *-ault*.]

cur·ti·lage /kúrt'lij/ *n.* an enclosed area occupied by a dwelling, grounds, and outbuildings [14thC. From Old French *co(u)rtillage*, from *co(u)rtil* "kitchen garden," literally "small court," from *cort*.]

Cur·tis /kúrtiss/, **Charles Brent** (1860–1936) U.S. politician. He was a Republican senator who served as vice president under President Hoover (1929–33).

Cur·tis, Cyrus H. K. (1850–1933) U.S. publisher. He built the *Saturday Evening Post* into the most successful U.S. magazine. Full name **Cyrus Hermann Kotzschmar Curtis**

Cur·tiss /kúrtiss/, **Glenn Hammond** (1878–1930) U.S. aviator. He made the first domestic public airflight (1908) and invented the first successful seaplane (1911).

Cur·tiz /kúrtiss/, **Michael** (1888–1962) Hungarian-born U.S. film director. He won an Oscar for *Casablanca* (1943) and directed over 125 Hollywood films.

curt·sy /kúrtsee/, **curt·sey** *vi.* (**-sied** *or* **-seyed, -sy·ing** *or* **-sey·ing, -sies** *or* **-seys**) BEND KNEES IN RESPECT to bend the knees, with one foot behind the other, as a gesture of respect. Women curtsy in formal situations where men bow, e.g., when acknowledging the applause of an audience after performing on stage, or when meeting royalty. ■ *n.* (*plural* **-sies**; *plural* **-seys**) WOMAN'S RESPECTFUL MOVEMENT a movement made by a woman as a sign of respect for somebody in which she bends her knees with one foot behind the other [Early 16thC. A variant of COURTESY.]

cu·rule /kyóo rōol, kyóo rōol/ *adj.* in ancient Rome, having the status to sit on an official chair (**curule chair**) and the privileges associated with this status [Mid-16thC. From Latin *curulis*, from *currus* "chariot," from *currere* "to run" (see CURRENT); from the conveying of the chief Roman magistrate in a chariot.]

cu·rule chair *n.* a folding chair with heavy legs and no back, used by high officials of ancient Rome

cur·va·ceous /kur váyshəss/ *adj.* having an attractive body with rounded hips and breasts [Mid-20thC. The suffix -ACEOUS is mainly botanical, here used humorously.] —**cur·va·ceous·ly** *adv.* —**cur·va·ceous·ness** *n.*

cur·va·ture /kúrvə chòor, -chər/ *n.* **1.** BEING CURVED the quality of being curved **2.** DEGREE OF CURVE the degree of curving in a line or surface ○ *the slight curvature of the land* **3.** GEOM RECIPROCAL OF RADIUS the reciprocal of the radius of the circle that best matches a curve at a given point [15thC. From Latin *curvatura* "bending," from *curvus* (see CURVE).]

curve /kurv/ *n.* **1.** ROUNDED LINE a line that bends smoothly and regularly from being straight or flat, like part of a circle or sphere **2.** SOMETHING SHAPED IN A CURVE something with a smooth round shape, such as a bend in a road **3.** STATS PLOTTED LINE a line plotted on a graph from statistical data **4.** EDUC STATISTICAL METHOD OF GRADING a method of distributing students' grades by plotting each individual's score on a graph and then dividing this line into grades **5.** MATH LINE REPRESENTING EQUATION a line whose points are defined by an equation and whose coordinates are functions of an independent variable **6.** BASEBALL = **curve ball** ■ *v.* (**curved, curv·ing, curves**) **1.** *vi.* MOVE IN CURVE to move or bend in a curve **2.** *vt.* CAUSE TO CURVE to make something move or bend in a curve **3.** *vt.* BASEBALL THROW A CURVE BALL to pitch somebody a curve ball **4.** *vt.* GRADE STUDENTS RELATIVELY TO ONE ANOTHER to grade students' work by plotting scores on a graph and then assigning individual grades according to a standard distribution [15thC. From Latin *curvus* "curved, crooked." English adopted the word as an adjective, and it was not used as a noun until the late 17thC.] ◇ **ahead of the curve** forward-thinking and ahead of a trend or trends ◇ **behind the curve** reactive, or slow to react, to a trend or trends ◇ **pitch** *or* **throw somebody a curve** to surprise somebody, usually with an unexpected and unwelcome question or response (*informal*)

curve ball *n.* in baseball, a ball that when pitched drifts to the left if thrown by a right-handed pitcher and to the right if thrown by a left-handed pitcher

curved /kurvd/ *adj.* with a rounded or bending shape

cur·vet /kur vét/ *n.* HORSE'S LEAP a leap by a horse in dressage in which its hind legs are raised just before the forelegs touch the ground ■ *vi.* (**-vet·ed** *or* **-vet·ted, -vet·ing** *or* **-vet·ting, -vets**) PERFORM CURVET to execute a curvet in dressage [Late 16thC. From Italian *corvetta*, literally "small curve," from *corve*, from, ultimately, Latin *curvus* "curved."]

cur·vi·lin·e·ar /kùrvə línnee ər/, **cur·vi·lin·e·al** /-əl/ *adj.* **1.** CURVED being a curve or having a curved part or parts ○ *a curvilinear polygon* **2.** MOVING IN CURVE moving along a curved path or line ○ *The ball followed a curvilinear trajectory.* [Early 18thC. Modeled on RECTILINEAR.] —**cur·vi·lin·e·ar·i·ty** /kùrvə linnee érrətee/ *n.* —**cur·vi·lin·e·ar·ly** *adv.*

curv·y /kúrvee/ (**-i·er, -i·est**) *adj.* **1.** ROUNDED with a rounded shape **2.** WINDING having many curves or bends

cus·cus /kús kùss/ *n.* a tree-dwelling nocturnal mammal inhabiting rainforests in northeastern Australia and New Guinea. Cuscuses have round heads, large eyes, large curved claws, and thick fur, and can grip with their tails. Genus: *Phalanger.* [Mid-17thC. Via French *couscous* or modern Latin *cuscus* from Dutch *koeskoes*, ultimately from a native word in New Guinea.]

cu·sec /kyóo sèk/ *n.* a unit of flow equal to one cubic foot per second [Early 20thC. Shortening of *cubic foot per second.*]

C·U·See·Me *n.* a computer program, developed at Cornell University, in Ithaca, New York, that enables users to engage in real-time video conferencing over the Internet

Cush /kōosh/, **Kush** *n.* **1.** BIBLE CANAAN'S BROTHER in the Bible, the oldest son of Ham and brother of Canaan (Genesis 10:6) **2.** ANCIENT AFRICAN REGION a region of northeastern Africa thought to be where the descendants of Cush settled. It is roughly equivalent to modern Ethiopia, part of northern Sudan, and southern Egypt.

Cush·ing /kúshing/, **Harvey** (1869–1939) U.S. neurosurgeon. He was a Harvard professor (1912–33) and in 1925 won the Pulitzer Prize for his *The Life of Sir William Osler*.

Cush·ing's dis·ease *n.* a form of Cushing's syndrome caused by excessive production of the hormone ACTH by the pituitary gland [Mid-20thC. Named for Harvey CUSHING, who described the condition.]

Cush·ing's syn·drome *n.* a condition caused by excessive production of corticosteroids by the adrenal cortex or pituitary gland and marked by obesity, muscular weakness, hypertension, striated skin, and fatigue [Mid-20thC. Named for Harvey Williams CUSHING, who described the syndrome.]

cush·ion /kōosh'n/ *n.* **1.** SOFT FILLED BAG FOR SITTING ON a fabric case filled with soft material, used to sit or lean on **2.** SOFT PROTECTIVE PAD a pad that is used for support, to rest against, to protect against damage, or as a shock absorber **3.** SOMETHING SOFT AND YIELDING something that gives slightly when pressed ○ *a cushion of moss at the foot of the tree* **4.** SOMETHING HELPFUL something that limits the effect of an unpleasant situation ○ *An unexpected inheritance provided a cushion when her savings ran out.* **5.** CUE GAMES BILLIARD TABLE RIM the raised rim around the top of a billiard table that borders its playing surface **6.** SEW LACEMAKING ACCESSORY a pillow used to support the tools used in lacemaking ■ *vt.* (**-ioned, -ion·ing, -ions**) **1.** PROTECT AGAINST IMPACT to protect somebody or something against the effects of physical impact ○ *A pile of sand cushioned his fall.* **2.** REDUCE UNPLEASANT EFFECT OF to lessen the effect of an unpleasant situation ○ *a generous payout to cushion the blow of early retirement* **3.** SUPPORT OR PLACE ON CUSHION to support or rest something on a cushion or other soft object **4.** PAD to pad something with cushions or some other soft spongy material [14thC. Via French *coussin* from, ultimately, assumed Vulgar Latin *coxinum*, literally "(support for the) hip," from Latin *coxa* "hip."] —**cush·ion·y** *adj.*

Cush·it·ic /kōo shíttik/ *n.* a branch of the Afro-Asiatic family of languages including about 30 languages spoken in areas of Ethiopia, Somalia, and Kenya [Early 20thC. Formed from CUSH.] —**Cush·it·ic** *adj.*

Cush·man /kúshmən/, **Charlotte** (1816–76) U.S. stage actor, known for her tragic roles such as Lady Macbeth. Full name **Charlotte Saunders Cushman**

cush·y /kōoshee/ (**-i·er, -i·est**) *adj.* (*informal*) **1.** WELL-PAID AND EASY providing a good salary, many perks, and little or no hard work ○ *a cushy job* **2.** LUXURIOUS luxuriously styled and crafted ○ *cushy sedans for executive types* [Early 20thC. Formed from Hindi *khūsh* "pleasant."] —**cush·i·ly** *adv.* —**cush·i·ness** *n.*

cusk /kusk/ (*plural* **cusk** *or* **cusks**) *n.* **1.** FOOD FISH OF COD FAMILY a large North Atlantic food fish of the cod family. Latin name: *Brosme brosme.* **2.** = **burbot** [Early 17thC. Origin unknown.]

cusp /kusp/ *n.* **1.** POINTED END a point or pointed end of something **2.** DENT RIDGE ON MOLAR TOOTH a ridge on the grinding surface of a molar tooth that helps in grinding and chewing food **3.** ANAT FLAP OF VALVE a triangular fold or flap of a valve in the heart or in lymph vessels that allows the flow of blood or lymph in one direction only **4.** GEOM POINT OF INTERSECTION a point where two arcs or branches of a curve intersect and the two tangents to the curve coincide **5.** ZODIAC BORDER BETWEEN ZODIAC SIGNS the border between two astrological star signs **6.** ARCHIT POINTED PROJECTION IN GOTHIC ARCHITECTURE a pointed projection formed by the intersection of two arcs, used especially in Gothic architecture **7.** ASTRON POINTED END OF CRESCENT MOON either of the pointed ends of a crescent moon, or of any celestial body appearing with the same curved shape [Late 16thC. From Latin *cuspis* "point, spear, pointed end of anything," of unknown origin.] —**cusped** *adj.*

cus·pid /kúspid/ *n.* DENT = **canine** [Mid-18thC. From Latin *cuspid-*, the stem of *cuspis* (see CUSP).]

cus·pi·date /kúspi dàyt/ *adj.* **1.** ANAT **WITH CUSP** ending in or having a cusp or cusps **2.** BOT **POINTED** used to describe a leaf that ends in a sharp point [Late 17thC. From Latin *cuspidatus*, the past participle of *cuspidare* "to make pointed," from *cuspid*, the stem of *cuspis* "point" (source of English *cusp* and *bicuspid*).]

cus·pi·dor /kúspi dàwr/ *n.* = **spittoon** [Mid-18thC. From Portuguese, formed from *cuspir* "to spit," from Latin *conspuere*, from *spuere* "to spit."]

cuss /kuss/ *vti.* (**cussed, cuss·ing, cuss·es**) **USE BAD LANGUAGE** to use vulgar and offensive language (*informal*) ■ *n.* (*informal*) **1. SOMEBODY ANNOYING** a person or animal with a particular, usually irritating trait **2. VULGAR OATH** an instance of vulgar or offensive language [Late 18thC. Colloquial variant of CURSE.]

cuss out *vt.* to rebuke somebody using angry, foul langauge (*informal*)

cuss·ed /kússəd/ *adj.* (*informal*) **1. ANNOYING** causing annoyance and anger, especially by being uncooperative **2. CURSED** cursed [Mid-19thC. Variant of CURSED.] —**cuss·ed·ly** *adv.* —**cuss·ed·ness** *n.*

cuss·word /kúss wùrd/ *n.* a swearword (*informal*)

cus·tard /kústərd/ *n.* a cooked mixture of sugar, eggs, and milk [15thC. Originally "open pie of meat or fruit," from Anglo-Norman *crustade*, from Old French *crouste* "crust" (source of English *crust*).] —**cus·tard·y** *adj.*

WORD KEY: ORIGIN

A ***custard*** was originally an open pie of meat or fruit, and the reference in the name is to the pie's pastry shell. The filling included stock or milk, often thickened with eggs. By around 1600 the term indicated a dish in its own right made of eggs beaten into milk and cooked.

cus·tard ap·ple *n.* **1.** FOOD **HEART-SHAPED GREEN FRUIT** a large heart-shaped fruit with large black seeds and soft whitish flesh inside a green skin **2.** TREES **WEST INDIAN TREE** a small West Indian tree that bears custard apples. Latin name: *Annona reticulata.* **3.** TREES **FRUIT TREE RELATED TO CUSTARD APPLE** a fruit-bearing tree related to the custard apple tree, such as the papaw, cherimoya, and sweetsop

cus·tard pie *n.* a pie filled with custard, whipped cream, or a substance resembling either of these, that is traditionally thrown at people in slapstick comedy routines

Cus·ter /kústər/, **George Armstrong** (1839–76) U.S. military leader. He was killed fighting against Native Americans at the Battle of the Little Bighorn (1876).

cus·to·di·al /kus tṓdee əl/ *adj.* **1. RELATING TO LEGAL CUSTODY** relating to the legal custody of, and responsibility for, a child ○ *a custodial parent* **2. JANITORIAL** connected with the work of a custodian or janitor **3. INVOLVING DETENTION** involving or consisting of detention in a prison ○ *a custodial sentence*

cus·to·di·al care *n.* assistance, usually on a long-term basis, with the tasks of daily living, provided to people who are unable to look after themselves

cus·to·di·an /kus tṓdee ən/ *n.* **1.** LAW **SOMEBODY RESPONSIBLE FOR SOMETHING VALUABLE** somebody responsible for holding or looking after valuable property on behalf of a company or another person **2. JANITOR** somebody responsible for general maintenance and cleaning, especially of a school or other building **3. UPHOLDER OF SOMETHING VALUABLE** somebody who wants to protect and uphold something seen as valuable and endangered, e.g., traditions or moral values [Late 18thC. Formed from *custody*, on the model of GUARDIAN.] —**cus·to·di·an·ship** *n.*

cus·to·dy /kústədee/ *n.* **1.** LAW **RIGHTS OVER CHILD** the legal right and responsibility for raising a child and personally supervising the child's upbringing, especially the right to keep the child in your home **2.** CRIMINOL **DETENTION** the state of being detained by the police or other authorities ○ *arrested and in custody* **3. PROTECTION** the state of being held under the protection of somebody or something or being in somebody's care [15thC. From Latin *custodia* "guarding, keeping," from *custos* "guardian," of unknown origin.]

cus·tom /kústəm/ *n.* **1. TRADITION** something that people always do or always do in a particular way by tradition **2. HABIT** the way somebody normally or routinely behaves in a situation **3. TRADITION LIKE LAW** a traditional practice that is so long-established and universal that it has acquired the force of law ○ *custom and practice* **4.** = **patronage 5.** HIST **FEUDAL RENT** a tribute, rent, or other obligation paid by a feudal vassal to a lord ■ *adj.* **1. MADE TO ORDER** made or built to order **2. MAKING GOODS TO ORDER** making or selling custom-made goods ○ *a custom tailor* **3. CHANGED TO SUIT BETTER** altered in order to fit somebody's requirements better [12thC. Via Old French *costume* "habitual practice" (source of English *costume*) from the Latin stem *consuetudin-*, from *consuescere*, literally "to accustom completely," from *suescere* "to become accustomed."]

cus·tom·a·ble /kústəməb'l/ *adj.* liable to import or export duties

cus·tom·ar·y /kústə mèrree/ *adj.* **1. USUAL** conforming to what is usual or normal **2. TYPICAL** usual for somebody or typical of somebody's normal behavior ○ *his customary good humor* **3.** LAW **BY CUSTOM** based on tradition and custom rather than written law —**cus·tom·ar·i·ly** /kùstə mérrilee/ *adv.* —**cus·tom·ar·i·ness** /-mérrinəss/ *n.*

cus·tom-built *adj.* designed and built to meet the requirements of a particular customer —**cus·tom-build** *vt.*

cus·tom·er /kústəmər/ *n.* **1. BUYER** a person or company who buys goods or services **2. TYPE OF PERSON** a person who interacts with others in a characteristic way (*informal*) ○ *a tough customer* [15thC. From the idea of "customary business practice."]

cus·tom·er serv·ice *n.* a department of a business that deals with complaints from or disputes with customers, or that handles routine inquiries from callers ○ *a toll-free customer-service line*

cus·tom·house /kústəm hòwss/, **cus·toms·house** *n.* an office at a port where customs are collected and where ships are given permission to enter or leave

cus·tom·ize /kústə mìz/ (**-ized, -iz·ing, -iz·es**) *vt.* to alter something in order to make it fit somebody's requirements better ○ *She has customized the software to suit our needs.* —**cus·tom·i·za·tion** /kùstəmi záysh'n/ *n.* —**cus·tom·iz·er** *n.*

cus·tom-made *adj.* designed and made to meet the requirements of a particular customer ○ *custom-made shoes*

cus·toms /kústəmz/ *n.* (*takes a singular or plural verb*) **1. cus·toms, Cus·toms PLACE WHERE DUTIABLE GOODS ARE EXAMINED** the place where goods and baggage are examined on entering a country to see what duty is payable on them and to check for smuggled goods ○ *pass through customs* **2. cus·toms, Cus·toms GOVERNMENT AGENCY** the government department responsible for collecting taxes on imports and for prevention of illegal imports **3. DUTIES ON GOODS** taxes payable on imports and exports [14thC. From the term used for the "customary tax" levied by a lord or local authority on goods bound for market.]

cus·toms·house *n.* = **customhouse**

cus·toms un·ion *n.* an association of countries that enjoy free trade among themselves and agree on tariffs for nonmembers

cus·tom·tai·lor (**cus·tom·tai·lored, cus·tom·tai·lor·ing, cus·tom·tai·lors**) *vt.* to plan, build, or change something in order to meet particular requirements

cut /kut/ *v.* (**cut, cut·ting, cuts**) **1.** *vti.* **DIVIDE SOMETHING WITH SHARP TOOL** to divide something into pieces using a knife, scissors, or a similar sharp-edged tool **2.** *vt.* **SEVER USING SHARP TOOL** to sever something or separate a part of something using a sharp-edged tool such as a knife, scissors, or a saw ○ *cut a slice of bread* **3.** *vti.* **MAKE HOLE IN SOMETHING** to pierce something or make a hole in something using a sharp instrument **4.** *vi.* **BE SHARP** to be sharp enough to slice or pierce things easily ○ *These scissors won't cut.* **5.** *vi.* **YIELD TO BLADE** to be easily sliced or pierced by a sharp tool such as a knife ○ *The cheese cuts well and doesn't crumble.* **6.** *vt.* MED **INJURE WITH SHARP EDGE** to injure yourself or somebody with something sharp, usually enough to draw blood **7.** *vt.* **SHORTEN WITH SHARP TOOL** to make something shorter by removing some of it with a sharp tool such as scissors ○ *I'm having my hair cut this afternoon.* **8.** *vt.* FASHION **FASHION A GARMENT** to shape fabric in a particular way in order to fashion a garment ○ *a skirt cut on the bias* **9.** *vi.* **TAKE OR BE A SHORTCUT** to cross, travel, or make a line through or across an area, especially in order to save time ○ *This path cuts through the woods.* **10.** *vt.* **REDUCE A QUANTITY** to reduce an amount, e.g., of money or time, or remove an amount from something ○ *The budget cannot be cut any further without reducing services.* **11.** *vt.* **SHORTEN BY EDITING** to make a film, text, play, broadcast, or speech shorter by removing parts of it, or remove a part to make it shorter **12.** *vti.* COMPUT **DELETE DATA** to delete data from one place, usually with the intention of inserting it in another **13.** *vti.* CINEMA, BROADCAST **EDIT MOVIE OR VIDEO** to edit a movie or other work intended for performance or broadcast **14.** *vi.* CINEMA **STOP FILMING** to stop filming a particular scene (*usually used as a command*) **15.** *vi.* CINEMA **CHANGE SCENE** to switch suddenly from one scene to another when filming or showing a film **16.** *vt.* **STOP PROVIDING** to stop providing a service or supply of something ○ *cut the food supply to the refugee camps* **17.** *vt.* **SWITCH OFF** to stop something from operating ○ *cut the engine* **18.** *vti.* CARDS **DIVIDE DECK OF CARDS** to divide a deck of cards in two, usually after shuffling them **19.** *vt.* RECORDING **MAKE A RECORDING** to make a recording of a song or group of songs ○ *The band cut 12 new tracks for the album.* **20.** *vt.* **NOT ATTEND** to not go to a place you are supposed to be, such as school (*informal*) ○ *expelled for cutting classes* **21.** *vt.* **DILUTE** to add a substance to another, especially to a drug or an alcoholic drink, usually in order to make it weaker or cheaper **22.** *vti.* **REMOVE GRIME** to dissolve or clean something such as dirt or grease from something else **23.** *vti.* **INTERSECT** to cross something or cross each other at a particular point ○ *The road cuts the river in three places.* **24.** *vi.* **CHANGE DIRECTION SHARPLY** to make a sharp change in direction ○ *You need to cut to the right here.* **25.** *vt.* DENT **GROW TEETH THROUGH GUMS** to produce a tooth through the surface of the gums ○ *The baby's cutting a tooth.* **26.** *vt.* **NEGOTIATE SOMETHING** to negotiate an agreement **27.** *vt.* **SNUB** to pay no attention to somebody publicly or obviously, or stop a social relationship with somebody **28.** *vti.* **UPSET SOMEBODY** to hurt somebody's feelings ○ *a cruel remark that cut me to the quick* **29.** *vt.* **STOP DOING** to stop doing something that is annoying somebody ○ *Cut that racket!* **30.** *vt.* RACKET GAMES **HIT A BALL SO IT SPINS** to hit a ball in such a way that it spins as it flies through the air ■ *n.* **1. WOUND IN SKIN** an injury made when something sharp pierces the skin **2. INCISION** an incision made in something with a knife or other sharp-edged tool **3. REDUCTION** a reduction in the amount of something ○ *cuts in taxes and interest rates* **4.** HAIR **HAIRCUT** a haircut or hairstyle **5.** FASHION **GARMENT STYLE** the way of cutting a garment from fabric that determines its shape and fit **6. PRUNING OF TEXT** a removal of a section of a movie, text, play, broadcast, or speech in order to make it shorter or improve it, or a section removed ○ *The editor advised me to make some cuts in the final chapter.* **7.** CINEMA **VERSION** a particular edited version of a movie ○ *the director's cut of "Blade Runner"* **8. SHARE** somebody's share from an amount of money or something else to be divided (*informal*) **9. STOPPING OF SUPPLY** a stopping of the supply of something such as electricity ○ *power cuts* **10.** EDUC **NONATTENDANCE** an unauthorized absence from a class ○ *expelled for too many cuts* **11.** FOOD **PARTICULAR SEGMENT OF MEAT** a piece of meat cut in a standard way, ready to be cooked ○ *The chef only buys the more expensive cuts.* **12. ALLEY** a narrow alley or passageway (*archaic*) **13.** AGRIC **HARVEST** a harvest or set of harvests of a crop ○ *this year's cut of oats* **14.** RECORDING **SINGLE RECORDING** a track on a musical recording **15.** RACKET GAMES **SPIN ON A BALL** the spin given to a struck ball **16.** BASEBALL **SWING OF BASEBALL BAT** a swing of a baseball bat **17.** PRINTING **PRINTING DEVICE** a block for printing that has a design engraved, incised, or cut in relief on it (*often used in combination*) **18. HURTFUL WORDS** words or action intended to insult or hurt **19. SNUB** a snub (*archaic*) **20. ITEMS FOR DRAWING LOTS** one of several pieces of paper or straws used to draw lots **21.** CARDS **DIVIDING OF DECK OF CARDS** the action of dividing a deck of cards in two ■ *adj.* **1.** MED **INJURED WITH SOMETHING SHARP** injured or damaged by something sharp, usually enough to draw blood ○ *nursing a cut finger* **2. SEPARATED WITH KNIFE** separated or severed using a knife, scissors, or similar sharp tool **3.** BOT **DIVIDED** used to describe a leaf that is divided into segments [13thC. From assumed Old English *cytan.*] ◇ **a cut above** somebody or something superior to somebody or something ◇ **cut a fine** *or* **sorry figure** to look impressive *or* unimpressive ◇ **cut and run** to leave a place quickly to avoid being caught or detained ◇ **cut both ways** to have both advantages and disadvantages ◇ **cut it close** to allow barely enough of something, often time, for what has to be done ◇ **cut loose** *U.S., Aus* to behave in an unrestrained and relatively uncontrolled way (*informal*) ◇ **cut somebody dead** to ignore somebody deliberately and completely ◇ **not cut it, not be able to cut it** to fall short of requirements or be unable to cope with a situation (*informal*) ○ *His usual excuses just don't cut it with me.*

cut across *vt.* to affect a widely differing group of people or things equally

cut back *v.* **1.** *vti.* **REDUCE SOMETHING** to reduce the amount of something ○ *cut back on spending* **2.** *vt.* GARDENING **REMOVE TOP OF PLANT** to cut the tops or all of the stems or branches off a plant in order to remove dead growth or produce bushier growth ○ *cut back the roses*

cut down *v.* **1.** *vti.* **REDUCE SOMETHING** to consume, use, or do less of something, especially because it is considered harmful ○ *The doctor says I have to cut down on fried foods.* **2.** *vt.* **FELL OR CLEAR AWAY PLANTS** to cut through the trunk or stem of a plant so that it can be harvested or removed **3.** *vt.* **KILL** to kill somebody, especially suddenly or unexpectedly (*informal; usually passive*) **4.** *vt.* CLOTHES **MAKE CLOTHING SMALLER** to alter a piece of clothing so that it will fit somebody smaller **5.** *vt.* CARS **REMODEL BY REMOVING EXTRAS** to remodel a car by removing unnecessary extras, especially to make it more suitable for racing

cut in *v.* **1.** *vti.* **INTERRUPT** to interrupt when somebody is speaking **2.** *vti.* **JOIN MIDDLE OF LINE** to enter a line of people by pushing in front of others who have been waiting **3.** *vi.* TRANSP **JOIN TRAFFIC DANGEROUSLY** to join a lane of traffic too close in front of another car so that it has to brake sharply **4.** *vi.* TECH **START TO OPERATE** to start working as part of a machine or electrical device **5.** *vi.* DANCE **PARTNER SOMEBODY ALREADY DANCING** to interrupt a couple who are dancing and take one of them as your own partner **6.** *vt.* COOK **MIX FAT WITH FLOUR** to mix shortening into flour using a metal blade in order to ensure that it is evenly distributed **7.** *vt.* **ALLOW TO SHARE** to allow somebody to have a share in something, especially money (*informal*) ○ *cut us in on the profits*

cut off *v.* **1.** *vt.* **REMOVE PART OF SOMETHING** to remove something that is part of something else by cutting it **2.** *vt.* **STOP SUPPLY** to stop supplying something ○ *cut off the electricity* **3.** *vt.* **ISOLATE** to separate a person, place, or group from normal communication or contact ○ *a town cut off by the blizzard* **4.** *vt.* UTIL **DISCONNECT TELEPHONE CONNECTION** to disconnect people who are talking on the telephone **5.** *vt.* **STOP SOMEBODY TALKING** to interrupt what somebody is saying and stop him or her from talking ○ *cut him off in mid-sentence* **6.** *vt.* **DISINHERIT** to exclude somebody from an inheritance ○ *They cut their son off without a penny.* **7.** *vt.* **BRING TO ABRUPT END** to bring something to an abrupt end or somebody to an early death (*often passive*) ○ *She was cut off in her prime.* **8.** *vi.* **CEASE ABRUPTLY** to come to an abrupt end ○ *The machine cut off suddenly.*

cut out *v.* **1.** *vt.* **REMOVE BY CUTTING** to remove part of something using a cutting tool **2.** *vt.* **CUT SHAPE** to cut a shaped piece from a larger part or whole **3.** *vt.* **REMOVE PART FROM TEXT** to remove part of a text or broadcast **4.** *vt.* **STOP DOING** to stop consuming, using, or doing something, especially because it is considered harmful ○ *I've cut out all dairy products.* **5.** *vt.* **EXCLUDE** to exclude or eliminate somebody from a group or activity ○ *cut them out of future negotiations* **6.** *vt.* **OMIT** to exclude, eliminate, or omit something ○ *I followed the recipe but cut out the walnuts.* **7.** *vt.* **DISINHERIT** to change a will so that somebody will no longer inherit **8.** *vi.* **STOP WORKING** to stop functioning suddenly, especially to stop providing power ○ *The engine cut out.* **9.** *vt.* **STOP SOMETHING ANNOYING** to stop doing something that is annoying somebody (*informal*) (*often used as a command*) ○ *Cut out the wisecracks.* **10.** *vi.* **LEAVE QUICKLY** to leave a location or place hastily (*slang*) ○ *Let's cut out of here.* **11.** *vt.* AGRIC **SEPARATE ANIMAL FROM HERD** to separate an animal or animals, particularly cows, from a herd **12.** *vt. Southern U.S.* **TURN OFF** to turn off a light or electrical appliance ○ *cut the lights out* ■ *adj.* **NATURALLY SUITED** naturally suited for a particular activity or profession ○ *I wasn't cut out to be a driving instructor.*

cut over *vt.* COMPUT to transfer existing data, functions, or users of a system to new facilities or equipment in a synchronized manner, to ensure continuity and minimize disruption

cut through *vt.* to deal with an obstacle in a way that reduces or eliminates it ○ *Can't we cut through the formalities?*

cut up *v.* **1.** *vt.* **CUT IN PIECES** to cut something into pieces **2.** *vi.* **MISBEHAVE** to behave in a humorous and disruptive way (*slang*) ○ *cutting up in class* **3.** *vt.* MED **INJURE** to injure somebody, especially enough to draw blood ○ *He was badly cut up after the fight and had to be taken to the hospital.* **4.** *vt.* **CRITICIZE** to criticize somebody severely (*dated informal*) ■ *adj.* **UPSET** upset and distressed (*informal*) ○ *He was all cut up over his mother's death.*

cut-and-cov·er *adj.* used to describe a method of constructing a tunnel by digging a trench down from ground level and then roofing it

cut-and-dried *adj.* **1.** **DECIDED AND FIXED** clear, settled, and not needing changes or further work **2.** **PREDICTABLE** obvious or conforming to what is expected ○ *a cut-and-dried press conference* [From the earlier sense "prepared in advance, not spontaneous," from the idea of dried rather than fresh herbs offered for sale]

cut-and-paste *n.* COMPUT a facility of computers allowing data to be deleted in one place and inserted in another ○ *Use cut-and-paste to move that paragraph into the new document.*

cut-and-try *adj.* by trial and error, using experimental procedures ○ *a cut-and-try approach*

cu·ta·ne·ous /kyoo táynee əss/ *adj.* relating to the skin [Late 16thC. Formed from modern Latin *cutaneus*, from Latin *cutis* "skin."] —**cu·ta·ne·ous·ly** *adv.*

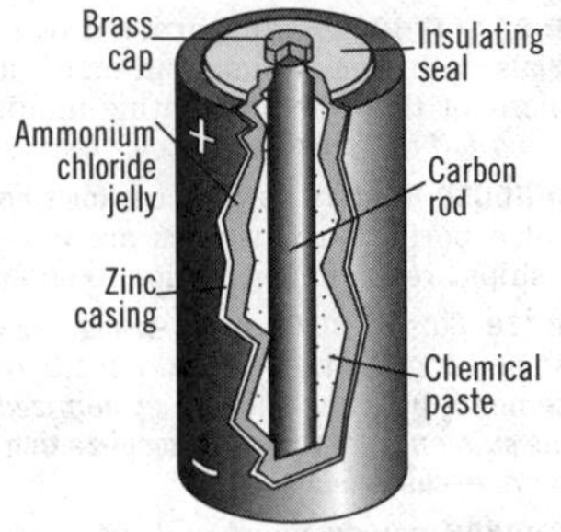

Cutaway: Cutaway view of a battery

cut·a·way /kúttə wày/ *n.* **1.** **MODEL WITH INSIDE VIEW** a drawing or model of something with part of its outside removed to give a view of the inside **2.** CLOTHES **MEN'S FORMAL COAT WITH TAILS** a formal coat for men, cut short at the front and with two long tails at the back **3.** CINEMA, VIDEO **SECONDARY SHOT WITH CAMERA** a cut to a camera shot of an action separate from the main action ■ *adj.* **1.** **GIVING INSIDE VIEW** constructed or represented so as to give a view of the inside **2.** CLOTHES **CUT DIAGONALLY** with the front cut diagonally away from the center, e.g., in the part of a tailcoat below the waist

cut·back /kút bàk/ *n.* a reduction in the amount of something ○ *cutbacks in public spending*

cutch /kuch/ *n.* = **catechu** [Mid-18thC. From Malay *kachu* "astringent vegetable extract" (source of English *catechu*), ultimately of Dravidian origin.]

cute /kyoot/ (**cut·er, cut·est**) *adj.* **1.** **ATTRACTIVE IN CHILDLIKE WAY** endearingly attractive in the way that some children and young animals are **2.** **PHYSICALLY ATTRACTIVE** young and physically attractive **3.** **PLEASING** smaller than the usual size but nicely arranged or appointed ○ *an apartment with a cute little kitchen* **4.** **SHREWD** sharply intelligent, shrewd, or wily (*dated*) [Early 18thC. Colloquial shortening of ACUTE.] —**cute·ly** *adv.* —**cute·ness** *n.* ◇ **get cute (with somebody)** to show insolence to somebody

cu·tes plural of **cutis**

cute·sy /kyóotsee/ (**-si·er, -si·est**) *adj.* too obviously attempting to be charming —**cute·si·ness** *n.*

cut·ey *n.* = **cutie**

cut glass *n.* glass with a decorative pattern cut into its surface (*hyphenated before a noun*)

cut·grass /kút gràss/ *n.* a marsh grass with rough or sharp edges along the leaf margin. Genus: *Leersia.*

cu·ti·cle /kyóotik'l/ *n.* **1.** ANAT **SKIN AT BASE OF NAILS** an edge of hard skin at the base of a fingernail or toenail **2.** ANAT = **epidermis** **3.** ANAT **DEAD EPIDERMIS** dead or hardened epidermis **4.** BOT **PROTECTIVE PLANT LAYER** the thin outermost noncellular layer covering the aboveground parts of plants and helping to prevent water loss **5.** ZOOL **HARD COVERING OF INVERTEBRATES** a hardened noncellular layer secreted by and covering the epidermis in many invertebrates [15thC. From Latin *cuticula*, literally "little skin," from *cutis* "skin."] —**cu·tic·u·lar** /kyoo tíkyələr/ *adj.*

cut·ie /kyóotee/, **cut·ey** (*plural* **-eys**) *n.* a cute person or animal (*informal*)

cu·tin /kyóot'n/ *n.* a waterproof mixture of waxy material containing derivatives of fatty acids, soaps, and other resinous substances that forms the protective layer (**cuticle**) of the aboveground parts of a plant [Mid-19thC. Coined from CUTIS + -IN.]

cut-in *n.* a camera shot that focuses in on a smaller portion of a scene already established

cu·tin·ize /kyóot'n ìz/ (**-ized, -iz·ing, -iz·es**) *vti.* to deposit cutin in the cell walls of aboveground plant parts —**cu·tin·i·za·tion** /kyóot'ni záysh'n/ *n.*

cu·tis /kyóotiss/ (*plural* **-tes** /-teez/) *n.* = **dermis** [Early 17thC. From Latin, "skin."]

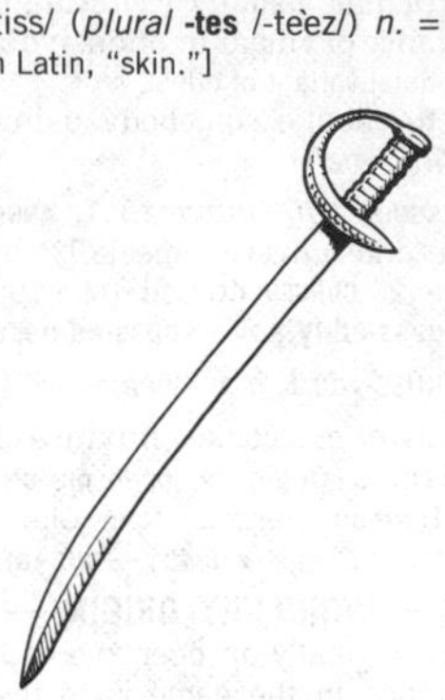

Cutlass

cut·lass /kúttləss/ *n.* **1.** **SHORT NAVAL SWORD** a short thrusting sword with a flat and slightly curved blade used in the past, especially by sailors **2.** *Carib* **MACHETE** a machete [Late 16thC. Via French *cutelas* "large knife," from, ultimately, Latin *cultellus*, literally "small knife," from *culter* "knife, ploughshare" (see COULTER).]

cut·lass fish *n.* a sea fish with a long slender body and long sharp teeth. Genus: *Trichiurus.*

cut·ler /kúttlər/ *n.* somebody whose job is to make, repair, or sell knives and other bladed tools (*archaic*) [14thC. From French *coutelier*, from *coutel* (see CUTLASS).]

cut·ler·y /kúttləree/ *n.* **1.** = **flatware** **2.** **TOOLS WITH BLADES** knives and other instruments with a blade **3.** **JOB OF CUTLER** the job of making knives and other bladed instruments (*dated*) [14thC. From French *coutellerie*, from *coutel* (see CUTLASS).]

cut·let /kúttlət/ *n.* **1.** **FLAT, BONELESS PIECE OF MEAT** a flat, boneless piece of meat that will serve one person **2.** **CHOPPED FRIED FOOD** a mixture of chopped meat, fish, nuts, vegetables, or other foods, made into a flat round shape, covered with breadcrumbs, and fried [Early 18thC. From French *côtelette*, literally "little rib," from, ultimately, Latin *costa* "rib" (source of English *coast*). The modern spelling reflects the idea of a "small cut" (of meat).]

cut·line /kút lìn/ *n.* a caption to an illustration

cut·off /kút àwf/ *n.* **1.** **LIMIT** a limit or date, beyond which something is stopped **2.** **END OF SUPPLY** an end to the supply of something ○ *a cutoff in oil imports* **3.** ENG **VALVE** a valve that controls the flow of fluid or gas through a pipe **4.** **SHORTCUT** a shorter route or bypass **5.** BASEBALL **RELAYED THROW** in baseball, a throw from the outfield to home plate or a base in two stages, using an infielder as an intermediary **6.** MUSIC **BREAK IN MUSIC** the end of a note, passage, or piece of music, especially when indicated by a sign from the conductor **7.** MUSIC **SIGNAL FROM MUSIC CONDUCTOR** a sign given by a conductor to indicate a cutoff in the music **8.** ELECTRON ENG **ELECTRICAL THRESHOLD** the value of voltage, frequency, or other variable that represents a minimum or maximum for effective operation **9.** GEOG **NEW RIVER CHANNEL** a short channel cut by a river across a bend in the river, forming an oxbow lake ■ **cut·offs** *npl.* CLOTHES **SHORTS MADE FROM PANTS** shorts made by cutting off the legs of a pair of pants, especially jeans

cut·off man *n.* in baseball, an infielder who catches a throw from an outfielder and relays it to home plate or a base

cut·out /kút òwt/ *n.* **1.** **SHAPE OF SOMEBODY OR SOMETHING** a two-dimensional shape of somebody or something usually made from stiff cardboard **2.** **SOMETHING CUT OUT** something that has been cut out from something else **3.** ELEC **SAFETY DEVICE FOR ELECTRIC CIRCUIT** a device that switches off an electric circuit or supply, e.g., to a machine, as a safety measure **4.** SPIES' GO-BETWEEN somebody trusted to pass messages between espionage agents (*informal*) **5.** RECORDING OUTDATED AUDIO RECORDING a recording sold at a discount because it is out-of-date and supply exceeds demand

cut·o·ver /kút ȍvər/ *n.* COMPUT SYSTEM TRANSFER the synchronized transfer of data, functions, or users to new facilities or equipment in order to ensure continuity and minimize disruption ■ *adj.* FORESTRY WITH TREES CUT used to describe forest land with the trees cut down for selling as timber

cut·purse /kút pùrs/ *n.* a pickpocket (*archaic*)

cut-rate *adj.* on sale or selling for less than the standard price, and often regarded as shoddy

CUTS *abbr.* Computer Users' Tape System

cut·ta·ble /kúttəb'l/ *adj.* capable of being shortened or divided by cutting

cut·ter /kúttər/ *n.* **1.** SHARP TOOL a tool used to cut through something (*often used in the plural*) ○ *wire cutters* **2.** SOMEBODY WHO CUTS SOMETHING somebody whose work involves cutting things, e.g., fabrics to be made into clothing **3.** SOMEBODY WHO REDUCES SOMETHING somebody who makes something shorter or reduces something in amount **4.** NAVY SMALL ARMED PATROL BOAT a small lightly armed patrol boat used by the Coast Guard or customs department **5.** SAILING SINGLE-MASTED SAILBOAT a single-masted sailing vessel on which the mast is positioned further aft than on a sloop **6.** NAUT BOAT FOR TRANSPORTING PASSENGERS a ship's boat, powered by a motor or by oars that is used for transporting passengers and light cargo **7.** TRANSP SMALL SLEIGH a small sleigh pulled by one horse, used in the past

cut·throat /kút thrȍt/ *adj.* **1.** WITH NO HOLDS BARRED aggressive and merciless in striving for supremacy **2.** MURDEROUS capable of murder or characteristic of a murderer (*archaic*) **3.** FOR 3 PLAYERS used to describe games for three players that are adapted from games for four partnered players ○ *cutthroat bridge* ■ *n.* **1.** DANGEROUS PERSON a murderer or a very aggressive dangerous person **2.** (*plural* **-throat** *or* **-throats**) ZOOL = **cutthroat trout**

cut·throat ra·zor *n. U.K.* = **straight razor**

cut·throat trout *n.* a trout of western North America that resembles the rainbow trout but has reddish-orange markings on either side of the throat. Latin name: *Salmo clarkii.*

cut time *n.* a meter in which two half notes receive the beat each bar, notated in the time signature by a "C" with a slash through it

cut·ting /kútting/ *n.* **1.** PART OF PLANT FOR PROPAGATION a piece taken from a stem, leaf, or root that will grow into a new whole plant **2.** *U.K.* = **clipping** *n.* 1 **3.** EDITING PROCESS the process of editing a text, film, or recording **4.** CINEMA CHANGING OF SHOTS IN FILM the technique of changing from one shot to another in the editing of a film ■ *adj.* **1.** ABRASIVE AND HURTFUL sharply expressed and likely to upset somebody's feelings ○ *a cutting remark* **2.** VERY COLD piercingly cold ○ *a cutting wind* —**cut·ting·ly** *adv.*

cut·ting board *n.* a piece of flat wood or rigid plastic used to protect a countertop or table while cutting food

cut·ting edge *n.* the most advanced and modern stage of something (*hyphenated when used before a noun*)

cut·ting horse *n.* a horse trained to separate cows, calves, or steers from a herd on the commands of its rider

cut·ting room *n.* a room where motion picture film is edited, normally by hand and by being physically cut

cut·tle·bone /kútt'l bȍn/ *n.* the white internal shell of a cuttlefish, used whole as a mineral supplement for caged birds and in powdered form for polishing [Late 16thC. *Cuttle* from Old English *cudele* "cuttlefish" (see CUTTLEFISH).]

cut·tle·fish /kútt'l fish/ (*plural* **-fish** *or* **-fish·es**) *n.* a marine mollusk that lives on the ocean floor and has ten arms, a flattened body, and an internal shell. Cuttlefish eject a dark inky fluid as a defense mechanism. Genus: *Sepia.* [Late 16thC. *Cuttle* from Old English *cudele*; related to *cod(d)* "bag" (see CODPIECE); so called because of the animal's shape.]

cut·up /kút ùp/ *n.* somebody known for telling jokes, showing off, and doing pranks (*informal*)

Cuttlefish

cut·wa·ter /kút wòttər/ *n.* **1.** NAUT FRONT OF SHIP'S PROW the foremost part of a ship's prow **2.** CIV ENG BUFFER PART OF BRIDGE SUPPORT a pointed or wedge-shaped upstream face of a bridge pier at water level, designed to minimize the effects of moving water, ice floes, and debris

cut·work /kút wùrk/ *n.* a form of openwork embroidery in which each part of the design is outlined in buttonhole stitch, then some parts of the fabric within the outlines are cut away

cut·worm /kút wùrm/ *n.* a nocturnal moth caterpillar that feeds on and eats through the base of young plant stems. Family: Noctuidae.

cu·vée /koo váy/ *n.* a single batch of wine [Mid-19thC. From French, "vatful," from *cuve* "cask, vat," from Latin *cupa* (source of English *coop*).]

cu·vette /koo vét/ *n.* a transparent tubular laboratory vessel or dish for holding a liquid [Late 17thC. From French, literally "small cask," from *cuve* (see CUVÉE).]

Cuy·a·ho·ga /kī ə hṓgə, -hó-/ river in northeastern Ohio, flowing southwest and then sharply north into Lake Erie. Length: 100 mi./160 km.

Cuy·a·ho·ga Falls city in northeastern Ohio, on the northern shore of the Cuyahoga River, northeast of Akron. Population: 49,278 (1996).

Cuz·co /ko͞oss kȍ/ city in southern Peru, and capital of Cuzco Department. It was the capital of the Inca empire until 1533. Population: 255,568 (1993).

CV *abbr.* **1.** cardiovascular **2. CV, cv** curriculum vitae **3.** MIL Cross of Valour

cv. *abbr.* BOT cultivar

C.V. *abbr.* Cape Verde

CVA *abbr.* **1.** cerebrovascular accident **2.** Columbia Valley Authority

CVS *abbr.* chorionic villus sampling

cw *abbr.* continuous wave

CW *abbr.* **1.** continuous wave **2.** chemical warfare **3.** chemical weapons

cw. *abbr.* clockwise

cwm /koom/ *n. U.K.* = **cirque** [Mid-19thC. From Welsh, "valley."]

CWO *abbr.* MIL Chief Warrant Officer

c.w.o. *abbr.* cash with order

cwt., **cwt** *abbr.* hundredweight [Early 16thC. *C* is the roman numeral that denotes one hundred.]

CY *abbr.* calendar year

-cy *suffix.* **1.** condition, quality ○ *buoyancy* **2.** action ○ *advocacy* **3.** rank, office ○ *baronetcy* [Via Old French *-cie, -tie* from Latin *-cia, -tia* and Greek *-k(e)ia, -t(e)ia*]

cy·an /sī ən, sī àn/ *n.* a deep greenish-blue color that, together with yellow and magenta, is one of the three primary colors used in printing and photographic processing [Late 19thC. From Greek *kuan(e)os* "dark blue," of unknown origin.] —**cy·an** *adj.*

cyan- *prefix.* = **cyano-** (*used before vowels*)

cy·an·am·ide /sī ánnə mīd/, **cy·an·am·id** /-mid/ *n.* **1.** CAUSTIC COMPOUND a white crystalline caustic compound. Formula: CH_2N_2. **2.** = **calcium cyanamide**

cy·a·nate /sī ə nàyt, -nət/ *n.* a salt or ester of cyanic acid

cy·an·ic /sī ánnik/ *adj.* COLORS of a greenish-blue color

cy·an·ic ac·id *n.* a weak colorless unstable acid. Formula: HOCN.

cy·a·nide /sī ə nīd/ *n.* **1.** POISONOUS SALT a poisonous salt of hydrocyanic acid that contains the radical CN **2.** = **potassium cyanide 3.** = **sodium cyanide** ■ *vt.* (**-nid·ed, -nid·ing, -nides**) **1.** METALL HARDEN METAL WITH CYANIDE to treat something, e.g., a metal surface, with cyanide to increase its hardness **2.** MINING TREAT ORE WITH SODIUM CYANIDE to treat ore with a weak solution of sodium cyanide to remove gold or silver [Early 19thC. Coined from CYANOGEN + -IDE.] —**cy·a·nid·a·tion** /sīənə dáysh'n/ *n.*

cy·a·nide proc·ess *n.* MINING a process for extracting gold or silver from ore by treating the ore with a weak solution of sodium cyanide and recovering the metal particles from the resulting solution

cy·a·nine /sī ə neen, -nin/ *n.* a chemical belonging to a group of blue dyes used to improve the sensitivity of photographic film to green, yellow, red, and infrared light

cy·a·nite /sī ə nīt/ *n.* = **kyanite**

cyano- *prefix.* **1.** blue ○ *cyanosis* **2.** cyanogen ○ *cyanic* **3.** cyanide ○ *cyanogen* [From Greek *kuanos* "dark blue"]

cy·a·no·ac·ry·late /sī ə nō ákrə làyt, -ákrələt/ *n.* a liquid acrylate monomer belonging to a group with adhesive properties, used in industry and medicine

cy·a·no·bac·te·ri·a /sī ənō bak téeree ə/ *npl.* bacteria belonging to a large group that have a photosynthetic pigment, carry out photosynthesis, and were classified in the past as blue-green algae. Family: Cyanophyta.

cy·a·no·co·bal·a·min /sī ə nō kō bálləmin/ *n.* = **vitamin** B_{12}

cy·an·o·gen /sī ánnəjən, -jèn/ *n.* **1.** POISONOUS GAS a flammable colorless poisonous gas used in organic synthesis. Formula: C_2N_2. **2.** CHEMICAL RADICAL a univalent radical found in cyanide compounds. Formula: CN. [Early 19thC. From French *cyanogène*, from, ultimately, Greek *kuan(e)os* "dark blue"; from its being a constituent of Prussian blue.]

cy·a·no·gen·e·sis /sī ə nō jénnəssiss/ *n.* the natural generation and release of hydrogen cyanide that occurs in some plants —**cy·a·no·gen·ic** *adj.* —**cy·a·no·ge·net·ic** /-jə néttik/ *adj.*

cy·a·no·hy·drin /sī ə nō hīdrin/ *n.* an organic compound containing both cyano and hydroxyl groups, usually linked to the same carbon atom

cy·a·no·sis /sī ə nṓssiss/ *n.* a condition in which the skin and mucous membranes take on a bluish color because there is not enough oxygen in the blood [Mid-19thC. Via modern Latin from Greek *kuanōsis* "blueness," from *kuan(e)os* "dark blue."] —**cy·a·not·ic** /sī ə nóttik/ *adj.*

cy·an·o·type /sī ánnə tīp/ *n.* = **blueprint**

Cyb·e·le /síbbəlee/ *n.* the Phrygian goddess of nature. She was worshiped by the Romans as the Great Mother of the Gods.

cyber- *prefix.* computers and information systems ○ *cyberphobia* [From CYBERNETICS and CYBERSPACE]

cy·ber·ca·fé /sībər ka fày, -kə fày/ *n.* **1.** COFFEE HOUSE OFFERING INTERNET ACCESS a coffee house that provides patrons with computer terminals for browsing the Internet for a fee **2.** VIRTUAL MEETING PLACE a virtual gathering place on the Internet where people communicate using a chat program or by posting messages on a BBS

cy·ber·nate /sībər nàyt/ (**-nat·ed, -nat·ing, -nates**) *vt.* to control a manufacturing process with a servomechanism or computer [Mid-20thC. Coined from CYBERNETICS.] —**cy·ber·nat·ed** *adj.* —**cy·ber·na·tion** /sībər náysh'n/ *n.*

cy·ber·ne·ti·cian /sībərnə tísh'n/, **cy·ber·net·i·cist** /sībər néttissist/ *n.* a specialist in cybernetics

cy·ber·net·ics /sībər néttiks/ *n.* (*takes a singular verb*) **1.** STUDY OF AUTOMATIC CONTROL SYSTEMS the science or study of communication in organisms, organic processes, and mechanical or electronic systems **2.** REPLICATION OF NATURAL SYSTEMS the replication or imitation of biological control systems with the use of technology [Mid-20thC. Formed from Greek *kubernētēs* "steersman, governor," from *kubernan* "to steer" (source of English *govern*). Coined by the U.S. mathematician Norbert Wiener (1894–1964).] —**cy·ber·net·ic** *adj.* —**cy·ber·net·i·cal** *adj.* —**cy·ber·net·i·cal·ly** *adv.*

cy·ber·pho·bi·a /sībər fṓbee ə/ *n.* a pathological fear of computers and information technology

cy·ber·punk /sībər pùnk/ *n.* a type of science fiction featuring characters living in a darkly frightening, futuristic world dominated by computer technology

cy·ber·space /sîbər spàyss/ *n.* **1.** **IMAGINED PLACE WHERE ELECTRONIC DATA GOES** the notional realm in which electronic information exists or is exchanged ○ *an e-mail message lost in cyberspace* **2.** **VIRTUAL REALITY** the imagined world of virtual reality

cy·ber·surf·er /sîbər sùrfər/ *n.* COMPUT somebody who spends a lot of time surfing the Internet (*slang*)

cy·borg /sî bàwrg/ *n.* a fictional being that is part human, part robot [Mid-20thC. Coined from CYBERNETICS + ORGANISM.]

cy·cad /sîkəd, -kàd/ *n.* a tropical tree that has a thick trunk, sharp pointed leaves like palm leaves, and cones. Order: Cycadales. [Mid-19thC. Via modern Latin *Cycad-*, the stem of *Cycas*, genus name, from Greek *kukas*, a miswriting of *koikas*, a plural form of *koix*, a type of palm tree.]

cycl- *prefix.* = **cyclo-**

cy·cla·mate /sîklə màyt/ *n.* a salt or ester of cyclamic acid, especially sodium cyclamate, a compound approved for use in some countries as an artificial sweetener [Mid-20thC. Contraction of *cyclohexylsulfamate*, its chemical name.]

cy·cla·men /síkləmən/ *n.* a small plant with heart-shaped leaves that grows wild under trees in parts of Europe, and is also cultivated in gardens for its white or pink flowers. Bigger, large-flowered types are cultivated as houseplants. Genus: *Cyclamen.* [Mid-16thC. Via Latin *cyclaminos* from Greek *kuklaminos*, which was probably formed from *kuklos* "circle," with reference to the flower's bulbous root.]

cy·cla·mic ac·id /sìkləmik-, sî-/ *n.* a synthetic crystalline acid used to produce cyclamates and as a food additive. Formula: $C_6H_{13}NO_3S$. [Contraction of *cyclohexylsulfamic acid*]

cy·clase /sî klàyss, -klàyz/ *n.* an enzyme that aids the formation of hydrocarbon rings (**cyclization**) in a compound

cy·cle /sîk'l/ *n.* **1.** **REPEATED SEQUENCE OF EVENTS** a sequence of events that is repeated again and again, especially a causal sequence **2.** **TIME BETWEEN REPEATED EVENTS** a period of time between repetitions of an event or phenomenon that occurs regularly ○ *a seven-year economic cycle* **3.** TECH **COMPLETE PROCESS** a complete process or sequence of processes in a machine or electronic device, or the time that this takes **4.** TIME **LONG TIME** a very long period of time **5.** ARTS **LINKED ARTWORKS** a series of linked songs, poems, stories, plays, or operas that deal with the same story, events, or characters ○ *Wagner's Ring cycle* **6.** PHYS **ONE COMPLETE OSCILLATION** one complete continuous change in the magnitude of an oscillating quantity or system that brings the system back to its original energy state ○ *running at 100 cycles per second* **7.** ASTRON **ORBIT** one complete orbit of a celestial body **8.** COMPUT **SET OF OPERATIONS** a set of instructions completed as a unit by a computer, or the time that completion takes **9.** CYCLING **BICYCLE** a bicycle or tricycle **10.** MOTORCYCLES = **motorcycle** ■ *v.* (**-cled, -cling, -cles**) **1.** *vti.* **GO THROUGH CYCLE** to put something through or go through a sequence of events ○ *programmed to cycle every hour* **2.** *vi.* **RIDE BICYCLE** to ride a bicycle or tricycle [14thC. Directly or via French from Latin *cyclus*, from Greek *kuklos* "circle" (source also of English *cyclone* and *encyclopedia*).]

cy·cle path *n.* = **bikeway**

cy·clic /sîklik, sík-/, **cy·cli·cal** /sîklik'l, sík-/ *adj.* **1.** **IN CYCLES** occurring or repeated in cycles **2.** CHEM **ARRANGED IN RING** used to describe organic compounds that are composed of a closed ring of atoms **3.** MUSIC **WITH RECURRENT THEME** containing a recurrent theme or motif —**cy·cli·cal·i·ty** /sîkli kállətee, sìkli-/ *n.* —**cy·cli·cal·ly** *adv.* —**cy·cli·cit·y** /sî klíssətee, -klíssətee/ *n.*

cy·clic AMP *n.* a cyclic form of adenosine monophosphate that is a constituent of plant and animal cells and is responsible for activating enzymes and enhancing hormonal processes within the cell

cy·clic GMP *n.* a cyclic form of guanosine that is a constituent of plant and animal cells and is responsible for aspects of cell division and growth

cy·clist /sîklist/ *n.* somebody who rides a bicycle, motorcycle, or other such vehicle

cy·cli·za·tion /sìklə záysh'n, sìklə-/ *n.* the formation of one or more hydrocarbon rings in an organic compound

cyclo- *prefix.* **1.** circle, cycle ○ *cyclometer* **2.** cyclic compound ○ *cyclopropane* [From Greek *kuklos* (see CYCLE)]

cy·clo·ad·di·tion /sî klō ə dísh'n/ *n.* the creation of a ring structure in an organic chemical compound by chemical action

cy·clo·al·i·phat·ic /sî klō allə fáttik/ *adj.* = **alicyclic**

cy·clo·gen·e·sis /sî klō jénnəssiss/ *n.* the formation and development of a cyclone [Mid-20thC. Coined from CYCLONE + -GENESIS.]

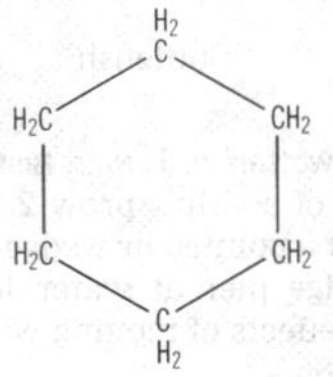

Cyclohexane

cy·clo·hex·ane /sî klō hék sàyn/ *n.* a pungent flammable colorless liquid hydrocarbon derived from benzene and used as a paint thinner and solvent, and in organic synthesis. Formula: C_6H_{12}.

cy·clo·hex·a·none /sî klō héksə nōn/ *n.* a colorless liquid ketone used as a solvent and in organic synthesis. Formula: $C_6H_{10}O$. [Early 20thC]

cy·clo·hex·i·mide /sî klō héksə mīd/ *n.* a colorless crystalline compound derived from a bacterium and used as a fungicide in agriculture. Formula: $C_{15}H_{23}NO_4$.

cy·cloid /sî klòyd/ *adj.* **1.** **LIKE CIRCLE** resembling a circle **2.** ZOOL **CIRCULAR** used to describe fish scales that are circular and thin with smooth edges **3.** PSYCHOL **MOODY** changing between states of depression and elation (*technical*) ■ *n.* **1.** GEOM **GEOMETRIC CURVE** a geometric curve formed by a point on the circumference of a circle that rolls along a straight line **2.** ZOOL **FISH WITH CYCLOID SCALES** a fish with scales that are circular and thin with smooth edges —**cy·cloi·dal** *adj.* —**cy·cloi·dal·ly** *adv.*

cy·clom·e·ter /sî klómmətər/ *n.* an instrument that counts the number of a times a wheel rotates and uses this to show the distance that a vehicle has traveled —**cy·clo·met·ric** /sìklə méttrik/ *adj.* —**cy·clom·e·try** *n.*

cy·clone /sî klōn/ *n.* **1.** METEOROL **LARGE-SCALE STORM SYSTEM** a large-scale storm system with heavy rain and winds that rotate counterclockwise in the Northern Hemisphere and clockwise in the Southern Hemisphere around and toward a low pressure center. ◊ **anticyclone** **2.** METEOROL **VIOLENT STORM** a violent rotating windstorm or tornado **3.** TECH **ROTATING DEVICE** a device that rotates rapidly, using centrifugal force to separate materials, e.g., particles from a gas [Mid-19thC. From Greek *kuklōma* "wheel, serpentine coil," from *kuklos* "circle" (see CYCLE).] —**cy·clon·ic** /sî klónnik/ *adj.* —**cy·clon·i·cal** *adj.* —**cy·clon·i·cal·ly** *adv.*

cy·clone cel·lar *n.* = **storm cellar**

cy·clo·pae·di·a *n.* = **cyclopedia**

cy·clo·pe·an /sìklə peé ən, sî klōpee ən/ *adj.* **1.** MYTHOL **LIKE THE CYCLOPS** relating to or resembling the Cyclops **2.** ARCHIT **MADE OF BIG STONES** constructed of massive irregular stone blocks **3.** OPTICS **DESCRIBING VISION** used to describe the phenomenon of apparent unity in binocular vision

cy·clo·pe·di·a /sìklə peédee ə/, **cy·clo·pae·di·a** *n.* = **encyclopedia** [Early 18thC. Shortening.] —**cy·clo·pe·dic** *adj.* —**cy·clo·pe·dist** *n.*

cy·clo·pen·tane /sî klō pén tàyn/ *n.* a colorless, flammable, pungent, liquid cycloalkane used as a paint remover, fuel, and solvent. Formula: C_5H_{10}.

cy·clo·pes /sî klō peez/ plural of **cyclops**

Cy·clo·pes plural of **Cyclops**

cy·clo·phos·pha·mide /sî klō fósfə mīd/ *n.* a toxic drug used to suppress the body's immune system in the treatment of leukemia, lymphoma, Hodgkin's disease, and tumors

cy·clo·ple·gia /sî klō pleéjə, -klə-/ *n.* paralysis of the eye muscles that adjust the size of the lens and are used for focusing —**cy·clo·ple·gic** *adj.*

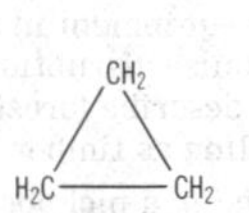

Cyclopropane

cy·clo·pro·pane /sî klō prō pàyn/ *n.* a flammable hydrocarbon gas used in medicine as a general anesthetic and in organic synthesis. Formula: C_3H_6.

cy·clops /sî klòps/ (*plural* **-clop·es** /-klō peéz/ *or* **-clops**) *n.* ZOOL an aquatic crustacean (**copepod**) with a single eye. Genus: *Cyclops.* [Mid-19thC. From modern Latin, genus name, from Latin (see CYCLOPS); from its characteristically centrally placed eye.]

Cy·clops (*plural* **-clo·pes** *or* **-clops** *or* **-clops·es**) *n.* MYTHOL one of a race of giants in Greek mythology who had only one eye in the middle of the forehead [Early 16thC. Via Latin from Greek *Kuklōps*, literally "round-eyed," from *kuklos* "circle" + *ōps* "eye."]

cy·clo·ram·a /sìklə rámmə/ *n.* **1.** PAINTING **CIRCULAR MURAL** a picture painted all the way around the wall of a circular room **2.** THEATER **STAGE BACKDROP** a large concave curtain or wall behind a stage [Mid-19thC. Coined from CYCLO- on the model of PANORAMA.] —**cy·clo·ram·ic** *adj.*

cy·clo·sis /sî klóssiss/ *n.* the rotary flow of protoplasm within some cells and protozoans [Mid-19thC. From Greek *kuklōsis* "encirclement."]

cy·clo·spor·ine /sî klō spáw reén, sî klō spáwrin/, **cy·clo·spor·in** /-rin/ *n.* a drug obtained from a soil fungus and used to suppress the body's immune system in order to prevent tissue rejection in transplant surgery [Late 20thC. Coined from CYCLO- + *polysporum*, name of the fungus that produces the drug + -INE[2].]

cy·clo·stome /sîklə stōm/ *n.* ZOOL a jawless fish with a circular sucking mouth and without true teeth. Lampreys and hagfish are cyclostomes. Class: Cyclostomata. [Mid-19thC. Coined from CYCLO- + Greek *stoma* "mouth."] —**cy·clos·to·mate** /sî klóstəmət, sî klō stō màyt/ *adj.* —**cy·clo·stom·a·tous** /sìklə stómmətəss, -stōmətəss/ *adj.*

cy·clo·thy·mi·a /sìklə thīmee ə/ *n.* a psychiatric disorder in which the patient has frequent, relatively mild mood swings between elation and depression [Early 20thC. Coined from CYCLO- + Greek *thumos* "mind, temper."] —**cy·clo·thy·mic** *adj.*

cy·clo·tron /sîklə tròn/ *n.* a circular particle accelerator in which charged particles are confined by a vertical magnetic field and accelerated by an alternating high-frequency applied voltage, in order to study the way they interact [Mid-20thC. Coined from CYCLO- + -TRON.]

cyg·net /sígnət/ *n.* a young or baby swan [15thC. Literally "little swan," formed from Old French *cigne* "swan" from, ultimately, Greek *kuknos*.]

Cyg·nus /sígnəss/ *n.* a constellation in the northern Hemisphere between Lyra and Pegasus and containing the star Deneb

cyl. *abbr.* **1.** cylinder **2.** cylindrical

cyl·in·der /síllindər/ *n.* **1.** **TUBE SHAPE** a shape with straight sides and circular ends of equal size **2.** ENG **CHAMBER FOR PISTON** a chamber in an internal combustion engine or a pump within which a piston moves back and forth **3.** ARMS **ROTATING PART OF REVOLVER** the rotating part of a revolver, containing chambers into which cartridges are loaded **4.** **LONG THIN CONTAINER** a long thin sealed container, such as one in which gas is kept under pressure **5.** GEOM **GEOMETRIC SOLID** a solid bounded by two equal parallel circles and a curved surface formed by moving a straight line so that its ends lie on the circles **6.** GEOM **GEOMETRIC SURFACE** a surface formed by a straight line moving in a circle around and parallel to a fixed straight line, forming a hollow tube shape **7.** **TUBE-SHAPED OBJECT** any object with straight sides and circular ends of equal size **8.** PRINTING **ROTATING PART OF PRINTING PRESS** any one of the revolving drums of a printing press that produce or receive the impression **9.** ARCHEOL **ANCIENT CYLINDRICAL CLAY OBJECT** a hollow barrel-shaped object of baked clay covered in cuneiform script **10.** HIST = **cylinder seal** [Late 16thC. Via Latin *cylindrus* from Greek *kulindros* "roller," from *kulindein* "to roll."] —**cyl·in·dered** *adj.*

cyl·in·der block *n.* = **engine block**

cyl·in·der head *n.* the closed detachable end of a cylinder in an internal-combustion engine

cyl·in·der press *n.* a printing press in which a flat bed holding the type matter moves under a revolving cylinder carrying the paper

cyl·in·der seal *n.* an engraved cylindrical clay or stone object used in ancient times, especially in Mesopotamia, as a seal that was rolled in wet clay to leave an impression

cy·lin·dri·cal /sə líndrik'l/, **cy·lin·dric** /sə líndrik/ *adj.* with straight sides, circular ends of equal size, and constant circular cross section —**cy·lin·dri·cal·i·ty** /sə lìndri kállətee/ *n.* —**cy·lin·dri·cal·ly** /sə líndrikəlee/ *adv.*

cyl·in·droid /sə lín dròyd/ *n.* GEOM a solid with straight sides and an elliptical cross section [Mid-17thC. Coined from CYLINDER + -OID.] —**cyl·in·droid** *adj.*

cy·ma /sī́mə/ (*plural* **-mae** *or* **-mas**) *n.* ARCHIT a projecting molding with an S-shaped profile [Mid-16thC. Via modern Latin from Greek *kuma* "billow, wave, wavy molding" from *kuein*, "to become pregnant."]

cy·mar /sə máar/, **ci·mar, si·mar** *n.* a loose jacket or robe for women that originated in the Renaissance and was popular in the 17th and 18th centuries [Mid-17thC. Via French from Italian *cimarra* "long robe."]

cy·ma·ti·um /sī máyshəm/ (*plural* **-a** /-ə/) *n.* ARCHIT **1.** = **cyma** *n.* **2.** **TOP CORNICE MOLDING** the top molding of a classical cornice [Mid-16thC. Via Latin, "ogee," from Greek *kumation*, literally "little cyma," from *kuma* (see CYMA).]

cym·bal /símb'l/ *n.* a circular brass percussion instrument played with a stick or by striking two of them together [Pre-12thC. Directly or via Old French *cymbale* from Latin *cymbalum*, from Greek *kumbalon*, from *kumbē* "bowl, drinking cup."] —**cym·bal·eer** /sìmbə léer/ *n.* —**cym·bal·er** /símb'lər/ *n.* —**cym·bal·ist** /-ist/ *n.*

cym·bid·i·um /sim bíddee əm/ (*plural* **-a** /-dee ə/ *or* **-ums**) *n.* an orchid native to tropical Asia and Australia whose brightly colored flowers have a boat-shaped lower petal. Genus: *Cymbidium*. [Early 19thC. From modern Latin, genus name, formed from Greek *kumbē* "cup"; because of a depression resembling a cup in the flower lip.]

cyme /sīm/ *n.* a flower cluster in which each flower stem ends in a single flower and other flower stems form below and to the side [Early 18thC. Via French, "summit, top," from Latin *cyma* (see CYMA).] —**cy·mif·er·ous** /sī mífərəss/ *adj.*

cy·mene /sī́ meen/ *n.* a colorless liquid benzene derivative, existing in three isomers, used as a solvent and in making resins. Formula: $(CH_3)_2CHC_6H_4CH_3$. [Mid-19thC. Coined from Greek *kummon* "cumin" + -ENE.]

cy·mo·gene /sī́mə jeen/ *n.* a flammable gaseous mix of petroleum derivatives consisting mainly of butane and used to produce low temperatures [Mid-19thC. Coined from CYMENE + GENE.]

cy·mo·graph /sī́mə gràf/ *n.* ARCHIT an instrument used to trace the outline of an architectural molding [Mid-19thC. Coined from CYMA + -GRAPH.] —**cy·mo·graph·ic** /sīmə gráffik/ *adj.*

cy·moid /sī́ mòyd/ *adj.* **1.** BOT **LIKE CYME** resembling a cyme **2.** ARCHIT **LIKE CYMA** resembling a cyma

cy·mo·phane /sī́mə fàyn/ *n.* chrysoberyl, especially an opalescent variety used as a gemstone [Early 19thC. From Greek *kuma* (see CYMA) + *-phanēs*, "showing, shining."]

cy·mose /sī́ mōss/, **cy·mous** /sī́məss/ *adj.* relating to, like, or being a cyme —**cy·mose·ly** *adv.*

Cym·ric /kúmmrik/ *n.* **WELSH LANGUAGE** the Welsh language (*dated*) ■ *adj.* **OF WALES** relating to or typical of Wales, or its people or culture [Mid-19thC. Formed from Welsh *Cymry* "the Welsh," from *Cymru* "Wales."]

Cym·ry /kúmree/ *npl.* **1.** **BRYTHONIC CELTS** members of the Brythonic branch of the Celtic peoples, which now comprises the Welsh, Cornish, and Breton peoples **2.** **WELSH PEOPLE** people who are born in or are citizens of Wales [Mid-19thC. See CYMRIC.]

cyn·ic /sínnik/ *n.* **1.** **BELIEVER THAT PEOPLE ARE INSINCERE** somebody who believes that human actions are insincere and motivated by self-interest **2.** **SOMEBODY SARCASTIC** somebody sneering and sarcastic ■ *adj.* = **cynical** [Late 16thC. From CYNIC.]

Cyn·ic /sínnik/ *n.* **ANCIENT GREEK PHILOSOPHER** a member of a group of ancient Greek philosophers who believed that virtue is the only good and that the only means of achieving it is self-control. The sect was founded by Antisthenes in the 4th century B.C. ■ *adj.* **RELATING TO CYNICS** belonging to, characteristic of, or relating to the Cynics [Mid-16thC. Via Latin from Greek *Kunikos*.]

cyn·i·cal /sínnik'l/, **cyn·ic** /sínnik/ *adj.* **1.** **DISTRUSTFUL OF HUMAN NATURE** doubting or contemptuous of human nature or of the motives, goodness, or sincerity of others ○ *Many people have developed a cynical distrust of politicians.* **2.** **SARCASTIC** mocking, scornful, or sneering ○ *cynical remarks to cover up disappointment* —**cyn·i·cal·ly** *adv.* —**cyn·i·cal·ness** *n.*

cyn·i·cism /sínni sìzzəm/ *n.* **1.** **CYNICAL QUALITY OR DISPOSITION** cynical attitude, beliefs, character, or quality **2.** **CYNICAL REMARK** a cynical action, comment, or idea

Cyn·i·cism *n.* the beliefs or philosophy of the ancient Greek Cynics

cyn·i·pid /sínnəpid/ *n.* a gall wasp (*technical*)

cy·no·sure /sī́nə shòor/ *n.* **1.** **CENTER OF ATTENTION** somebody or something that is the center of admiration, attention, or attraction **2.** **GUIDE** somebody or something acting as a guide or used for direction ○ *Guidebooks are the cynosure of the inexperienced traveler.* [Late 16thC. Via Latin *Cynosura* "the constellation Ursa Minor, containing the Pole Star" (hence "guiding star," hence "center of attention") from Greek *kunosoura*, literally "dog's tail."] —**cy·no·sur·al** *adj.*

Cyn·thi·a /sínthee ə/ *n.* **1.** **MOON** the Moon personified as a goddess (*literary*) **2.** = **Diana** [Late 16thC. Because the goddess Diana was said to have been born on Mount *Cynthus* in Delos.]

CYO *abbr.* Catholic Youth Organization

cy·pher /sī́fər/ *n.* = **cipher**

cy·pher·punk /sī́fər pùngk/ *n.* an experienced computer user who is adept at breaking codes and entering secure computer systems [Late 20thC. Coined from CYPHER + PUNK on the model of CYBERPUNK.]

cy pres /si práy/ *adv.* LAW as nearly as possible to the will or intention of a person whose wishes cannot be executed literally [Via Anglo-Norman from French *si près* "as near as"]

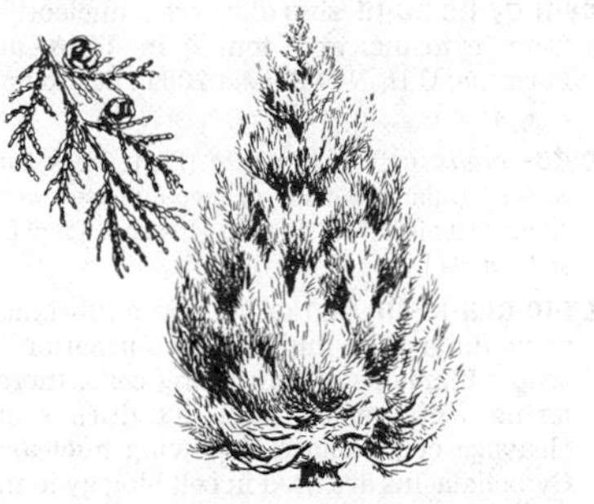

Cypress

cy·press[1] /sī́prəss/ *n.* **1.** **CONIFER** a coniferous evergreen tree, native to Eurasia and North America, that has hard wood and dark green leaves resembling scales. Genus: *Cupressus*. **2.** **TREE OR SHRUB RESEMBLING CYPRESS** a coniferous tree or shrub that is similar or related to the cypress, e.g., the bald or swamp cypress **3.** **WOOD** the hard wood of a cypress tree **4.** **CYPRESS BRANCHES AS SYMBOL OF MOURNING** the branches of a cypress tree used as a symbol of mourning [12thC. Via Old French *cipres* and late Latin *cypressus* from Greek *kuparisoss*.]

cy·press[2] /sī́prəss/, **cy·prus** *n.* a fine silk or cotton fabric, usually black, used for mourning clothes [15thC. Via Anglo-Norman *cipres* from Old French *Cipre* "Cyprus," because the fabric was originally brought from Cyprus.]

Cy·press /sī prəss/ city in southwestern California, a southeastern suburb of Los Angeles. Population: 47,032 (1996).

cy·press vine *n.* a tropical American climbing plant related to morning glory that has leaves divided into many thin segments and scarlet, orange, or white tubular flowers. Latin name: *Ipomoea quamoclit*.

Cyp·ri·an /síppree ən/, **St.** (200?–258) African-born Roman lawyer, bishop, and martyr. He was a Carthaginian bishop whose works, including *De Unitate Catholicae Ecclesiae* (251), influenced St. Augustine. Full name **Thascius Caecilius Cyprianus**

cyp·ri·nid /síppranid, sə prínnid/ (*plural* **-nid** *or* **-nids**) *n.* a freshwater fish of the family that includes the carps and minnows, typically with rounded scales, soft fins, and toothless jaws. Family: Cyprinidae. [Late 19thC. Formed from Latin *cyprinus* "carp," from ultimately, Greek *kuprinos*.] —**cyp·ri·nid** *adj.*

cy·prin·o·dont /sə prínnə dònt, -prī́nə-/ *n.* a small freshwater fish of North America, Eurasia, and Africa with soft fins and a toothed jaw. Killifishes and guppies are cyprinodonts. Family: Cyprinodontidae. [Mid-19thC. Coined from CYPRINOID + -ODONT.] —**cy·prin·o·dont** *adj.*

cyp·ri·noid /síppra nòyd/ *n.* any fish belonging to a large group that includes the carp [Mid-19thC. Formed from Latin *cyprinus* "carp," from ultimately, Greek *kuprinos*.] —**cyp·ri·noid** *adj.*

Cyp·ri·ot /síppree ət/, **Cyp·ri·ote** *n.* **SOMEBODY FROM CYPRUS** somebody who was born or raised in Cyprus or who has Cypriot citizenship ■ *adj.* **1.** **OF CYPRUS** relating to or typical of Cyprus, or its peoples or cultures **2.** **OF THE LANGUAGES OF CYPRUS** belonging or relating to the dialects of Greek and Turkish that are spoken on Cyprus [Late 16thC. From Greek *Kupriōtēs*, from *Kupros* "Cyprus."]

cy·pro·hep·ta·dine /sīprō héptə deen/ *n.* an antihistamine drug used especially to treat asthma, allergies, and skin disorders [Late 20thC. Coined from CYCLIC + PROPYL + HEPTA + PIPERIDINE.]

cy·prus *n.* = **cypress**[2]

Cyprus

Cy·prus /sī́ prəss/ island republic in the Mediterranean Sea. Since 1974, it has been partitioned between the Greek Cypriot south and the officially unrecognized Turkish Republic of Northern Cyprus. Language: Greek, Turkish. Currency: Cyprus pound. Capital: Nicosia. Population: 752,808 (1997). Area: 3,572 sq. mi./9,251 sq. km. Official name **Republic of Cyprus**

cyp·se·la /sípsələ/ (*plural* **-lae** /-lee/) *n.* a small hard one-seeded fruit with an attached calyx that does not split during seed dispersal. Plants with cypselae include daisies and dandelions. Family: Compositae. [Late 19thC. Via modern Latin from Greek *kupselē* "hollow vessel, chest."]

Cyr·e·na·ic /sìrrə náy ik/ *adj.* **1.** **OF CYRENE** relating to or typical of the ancient Greek city of Cyrene in North Africa, or its people or culture **2.** **OF CYRENAICA** relating to or typical of the ancient Cyrenaica, or its people or culture **3.** PHILOS **OF THE PHILOSOPHY OF PLEASURE** relating to or advocating the doctrines of the school of philosophy founded in the 4th century B.C. by Aristippus of Cyrene, who believed pleasure is the sole or supreme good ■ *n.* **1.** **SOMEBODY FROM CYRENE** somebody who was born in or was a citizen of ancient Cyrene **2.** PHILOS **BELIEVER IN CYRENAIC PHILOSOPHY** an adherent of the Cyrenaic school of philosophy **3.** PHILOS **HEDONIST** somebody who believes that pleasure is the sole good in life [Late 16thC. Via Latin *Cyrenaicus* from Greek *Kurēnaikos*, from *Kurēnē*, "Cyrene."] —**Cyr·e·na·i·cism** /sìrrə náy i sìzzəm/ *n.*

Cy·re·na·ica /sìrrə náy ikə, sīrə-/ historic region settled by the ancient Greeks that occupied the eastern half of Libya

Cy·re·ne /sī reénee/ ancient Greek town in Libya and the original capital of Cyrenaica, founded in about 630 B.C. The ruins are situated about 140 mi./225 km from Benghazi in northeastern Libya.

Cyr·il /sírrəl/, **St.** (827–869) Greek missionary. With his brother Methodius he brought Christianity to the Slavs of southeastern Europe, and is said to have devised the Cyrillic alphabet. Born **Constantine**

Cy·ril·lic /sə ríllik/ *adj.* **OF ALPHABET USED IN SLAVIC LANGUAGES** relating or belonging to the old alphabet derived from Greek script and attributed to St. Cyril, or a modified form used in modern Slavic languages such as Bulgarian and Russian. The Cyrillic alphabet is also used in the non-Slavic languages of some republics of the former Soviet Union. ■ *n.* **SLAVIC ALPHABET** the Cyrillic alphabet [Early 19thC. Named after ST. CYRIL.]

cyst /sist/ *n.* **1. ABNORMAL SPHERICAL SWELLING** a closed, usually spherical, membranous sac that develops abnormally in human or other animal tissue and contains fluid or semisolid material. Some types of cysts form when glands are blocked, and most cysts are benign. **2.** ANAT **HOLLOW ORGAN OR CAVITY** a thin-walled bladder, sac, or vesicle in an animal **3.** BOT, FUNGI **RESTING SPORE** a spore that is not undergoing cell division, in some algae and fungi **4.** ZOOL **PROTECTIVE SAC ENCLOSING ORGANISM** a sac or capsule that encloses and protects some organisms in a dormant or larval stage **5.** ZOOL **PROTECTIVE COVERING AROUND PARASITE** a protective covering around a parasite, produced by a host or by the parasite itself **6.** BOT **AIR-FILLED CAVITY IN SEAWEEDS** a small air-filled cavity resembling a bladder that occurs in some seaweeds, e.g., the bladderwrack [Early 18thC. Via late Latin *cystis* from Greek *kustis* "bladder, cyst."]

cyst- *prefix.* = **cysto-** (*used before vowels*)

cys·tec·to·my /siss téktəmee/ (*plural* **-mies**) *n.* **1. OPERATION TO REMOVE CYST** surgical removal of a cyst **2. OPERATION TO REMOVE BLADDER** surgical removal of the urinary bladder

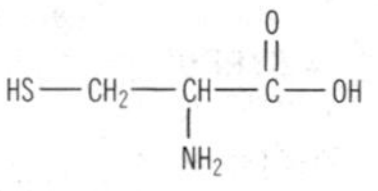

Cysteine

cys·te·ine /sís teèn, sístee eèn/ *n.* a crystalline sulfur-containing amino acid that is converted to cystine during metabolism. [Late 19thC. Coined from CYSTINE + *-eine*, a variant of - EIN.]

cys·tic /sístik/ *adj.* **1. RELATING TO CYST** used to describe a cyst or material that forms, contains, or is enclosed in a cyst **2. CONTAINING CYST** consisting of or containing a cyst or cysts **3. WITHIN CYST** enclosed within a cyst **4. RELATING TO BLADDER** relating to a bladder, especially the urinary bladder

cys·tic duct *n.* the duct of the gall bladder that joins the bile duct from the liver to form the common bile duct

cys·ti·cer·cus /sìstə súrkəss/ (*plural* **-ci** /-sī/) *n.* the larva of some tapeworms that consists of a folded inverted head encapsulated in a fluid-filled sac. It is found in the body tissues of infested people and animals. [Mid-19thC. From modern Latin *cysticercus*, from Greek *kustis* "bladder" (see CYST) + *kerkos* "tail."]

cys·tic fi·bro·sis /-fī brṓssiss/ *n.* a hereditary disease starting in infancy that affects various glands and results in secretion of thick mucus that blocks internal passages, including those of the lungs, causing respiratory infections. The pancreas is also affected, resulting in a deficiency of digestive enzymes and impaired nutrition.

cys·tine /sí steèn, sístin/ *n.* a crystalline amino acid found in many proteins, especially keratin. Formula: $C_6H_{12}N_2O_4S_2$. [Mid-19thC. Coined from Greek *kustis*, "bladder"+-IN.]

cys·tin·u·ri·a /sìstə nyoóree ə/ *n.* the excessive excretion of cystine in the urine and the formation of cystine stones in the kidney, characteristic of an inherited disorder of the metabolism

cys·ti·tis /sis títiss/ *n.* inflammation of the urinary bladder, often caused by infection

cysto- *prefix.* hollow structure, sac, cyst ○ *cystocarp* [Via modern Latin *cystis* "bladder" from Greek *kustis* (see CYST)]

cys·to·carp /sístə kaàrp/ *n.* the reproductive body of red algae produced after fertilization and consisting of a mass of asexual spores borne on filaments

cys·to·cele /sístə seèl/ *n.* a hernia of the urinary bladder that protrudes through the vaginal wall

cys·tog·ra·phy /sis tóggrəfee/ *n.* X-ray examination of the urinary bladder after the introduction of a liquid that is partially opaque to X-rays

cys·toid /sís tòyd/ *adj.* **LIKE A CYST** resembling a cyst ■ *n.* **STRUCTURE RESEMBLING CYST** a structure or mass of tissue that resembles a cyst but lacks an enclosing capsule

cys·to·lith /sístə lìth/ *n.* **1.** BOT **MINERAL DEPOSIT IN PLANT CELLS** a hard mineral deposit, usually of calcium carbonate, that occurs in the epidermal cells of some plants, e.g., figs or stinging nettles **2.** MED **BLADDER STONE** a stone that occurs in the bladder

cys·to·scope /sístə skṑp/ *n.* a narrow tubular instrument that is passed through the urethra to examine the interior of the urethra and the urinary bladder —**cys·to·scop·ic** /sìstə skóppik/ *adj.* —**cys·tos·co·py** /sis tóskəpee/ *n.*

cys·tos·to·my /sis tóttəmee/ (*plural* **-mies**) *n.* the surgical construction of an opening into the urinary bladder to permit the removal of stones

cyt- *prefix.* = **cyto-** (*used before vowels*)

cy·tas·ter /sī tástər/ *n.* = **aster** *n.* **2** [Late 19thC. Coined from CYTO- + ASTER.]

-cyte *suffix.* cell ○ *phagocyte* [Via modern Latin *-cyta* from Greek *kutos* "hollow vessel"]

Cyth·e·re·a /sə theèree ə/ *n.* = **Aphrodite**

Cyth·e·re·an /sə theèree ən/ *adj.* **1. OF VENUS** relating to the planet Venus **2. OF CYTHEREA** relating to Cytherea

cy·ti·dine /sítti deèn/ *n.* a compound (**nucleoside**) formed from cytosine and ribose. Formula: $C_9H_{13}N_3O_5$. [Early 20thC. Coined from CYTO- + -IDINE.]

cy·ti·dy·lic ac·id /sìttə díllik-/ *n.* a nucleotide derived from cytosine and found in DNA and RNA. Formula: $C_9H_{14}N_3O_8P$. [Mid-20thC. Coined from CYTIDINE + -YL + -IC.]

cyto- *prefix.* cell ○ *cytotoxin* [From Greek *kutos* "hollow vessel." Ultimately from an Indo-European word meaning "thing that hides," which is also the ancestor of English *hide* and *cuticle*.]

cy·to·cha·la·sin /sìtō kə láyzin/ *n.* a substance derived from fungi that inhibits the formation of microscopic filaments within living cells, thereby interfering with various cell activities such as the cleavage of cytoplasm following nuclear division. Cytochalasins are used in cell biology to investigate various phenomena, such as cytoplasmic movement and cell motility. [Mid-20thC. Coined from CYTO- + Greek *khalasis* "dislocation."]

cy·to·chem·is·try /sìtō kémmistree/ *n.* a branch of biochemistry dealing with the chemistry of the cells of organisms —**cy·to·chem·i·cal** *adj.* —**cy·to·chem·i·cal·ly** *adv.*

cy·to·chrome /sítə krṑm/ *n.* a compound containing protein and iron that plays a role in cell respiration

cy·to·chrome ox·i·dase *n.* an enzyme containing iron and porphyrin that is important in cell respiration

cy·to·gen·e·sis /sìtō jénnəssiss/ *n.* the origin, development, and variation of cells

cy·to·ge·net·ics /sìtō jə néttiks/ *n.* the study of the relationship between inheritance and the structure and function of cell components (*takes a singular verb*) —**cy·to·ge·net·ic** *adj.* —**cy·to·ge·net·i·cal·ly** *adv.* —**cy·to·ge·net·i·cist** *n.*

cy·tog·e·ny /sī tójjənee/ *n.* = **cytogenesis**

cy·to·kine /sítə kìn/ *n.* a protein secreted by cells of the lymph system that affects the activity of other cells and is important in controlling inflammatory responses. Interleukins and interferons are cytokines. [Mid-20thC. Coined from CYTO- + kinein "to move."]

cy·to·ki·ne·sis /sìtō ki neéssiss, sìtō kī neéssiss/ *n.* division of the cytoplasm of a cell during mitosis or meiosis —**cy·to·ki·net·ic** /sìtō ki néttik/ *adj.*

cy·to·ki·nin /sítə kínin/ *n.* a plant hormone that regulates cell division and growth. Kinetin and zeatin are cytokinins.

cy·tol·o·gy /sī tóllәjee/ *n.* **1. STUDY OF CELLS** a branch of biology dealing with the study of cells, especially their structures and functions **2.** MED **EXAMINATION OF CELLS** the examination of cells obtained from body tissue or fluids, especially to establish if they are cancerous —**cy·to·log·ic** /sìtə lójjik/ *adj.* —**cy·to·log·i·cal** /-lójjik'l/ *adj.* —**cy·to·log·i·cal·ly** /-əlee/ *adv.* —**cy·tol·o·gist** /sī tólləjist/ *n.*

cy·tol·y·sin /sī tólləsin, sìtə lís'n, -lís'n/ *n.* a substance that can destroy or dissolve cells [Early 20thC. Coined from CYTOLYSIS + -IN.]

cy·tol·y·sis /sī tólləssiss/ *n.* the destruction or dissolution of cells, e.g., by the immune system —**cy·to·lyt·ic** /sìtə líttik/ *adj.*

cy·to·me·gal·ic /sìtō mə gállik/ *adj.* characterized by, producing, or relating to enlarged cells [Mid-20thC. Coined from CYTO- + MEGALO- + -IC.]

cy·to·me·gal·ic in·clu·sion dis·ease *n.* a serious disease of newborn babies affecting the brain, liver, kidneys, and lungs. It is caused by cytomegalovirus infection of pregnant mothers and leads to enlargement of the affected cells.

cy·to·meg·a·lo·vi·rus /sìtō méggəlō vírəss/ *n.* a virus that causes enlargement of epithelial cells, usually resulting in mild infections. It causes more serious disorders in AIDS patients and in newborn babies. [Mid-20thC. Coined from CYTO- + MEGALO- + VIRUS.]

cy·to·path·o·gen·ic /sìtō pathə jénnik/, **cy·to·path·ic** /sìtō páthik/ *adj.* relating to or causing damage or disease to cells [Mid-20thC. Coined from CYTO- + PATHOGENIC.] —**cy·to·path·o·gen·i·ci·ty** /sìtō pathə jə níssətee/ *n.*

cy·to·path·ol·o·gy /sìtō pə thóllәjee/ (*plural* **-gies**) *n.* **1. PATHOLOGY OF CELL DISEASE** a branch of pathology dealing with cell disease and damage **2. FEATURES OF DISEASED CELL** the set of features or conditions associated with a diseased cell or cells

cy·top·a·thy /sī tóppəthee/ *n.* deterioration or disease in a living cell

cy·to·phar·ynx /sìtō férringks/ (*plural* **-pha·ryn·ges** /-fə rin jeèz/ *or* **-phar·ynx·es**) *n.* a tube in some protozoans, extending from the cytoplasm into the endoplasm

cy·to·pho·tom·e·ter /sìtō fō tómmətər/ *n.* an instrument that utilizes the variations in light intensity produced by stained cell cytoplasm to identify and locate chemical compounds within cells —**cy·to· pho·to·met·ric** /sìtō fōtə méttrik/ *adj.* —**cy·to·pho·to·met·ri·cal·ly** /-əlee/ *adv.* —**cy·to·pho·tom·e·try** /sìtō fə tómmətree/ *n.*

cy·to·plasm /sìtō plàzzəm/ *n.* the complex of chemical compounds and structures within a plant or animal cell excluding the nucleus. Cytoplasm contains the cytosol, organelles, vesicles, and cytoskeleton. —**cy·to·plas·mic** /sìtə plázmik/ *adj.* —**cy·to·plas·mi·cal·ly** /-plázmikəlee/ *adv.*

cy·to·plas·mic in·her·i·tance *n.* the inheritance of genes from the female parent that are not in the nucleus but in organelles such as mitochondria that are found in the cytoplasm. This type of inheritance is not controlled by Mendel's laws.

cy·to·plast /sítō plàst/ *n.* a plant or animal cell that has had the nucleus removed —**cy·to·plas·tic** /sìtə plástik/ *adj.*

cy·to·sine /sítə seèn, -ssin/ *n.* a component of nucleic acids that pairs with guanine to carry hereditary information in DNA and RNA in cells. Chemically, it is a pyrimidine base. Formula: $C_4H_5N_3O$. Symbol **C** [Late 19thC. Coined from CYTO- + -OSE[1] + -INE[2].]

cy·to·skel·e·ton /sìtō skéllət'n/ *n.* the internal network of protein filaments and microtubules in an animal or plant cell that controls the cell's shape and movement —**cy·to·skel·e·tal** *adj.*

cy·to·sol /sítə sòl, sítə sàwl/ *n.* the fluid component of a cell's cytoplasm excluding organelles and other structures —**cy·to·sol·ic** /sìtə sóllik/ *adj.*

cy·to·some /sítə sòm/ *n.* the cytoplasm in a cell, excluding the nucleus

cy·to·sta·tic /sítə státtik/ *adj.* STOPPING CELL GROWTH suppressing cell growth and multiplication ■ *n.* CYTOSTATIC AGENT a cytostatic agent —**cy·to·sta·tic·al·ly** *adv.*

cy·to·tax·is /sìtō táksiss/ *n.* the movement of cells or cell masses in relation to one another

cy·to·tax·on·o·my /sìtō tak sónnəmee/ *n.* the classification of organisms according to cell structure, especially the number, structure, and shape of chromosomes —**cy·to·tax·o·nom·ic** /-taksə nómmik/ *adj.* —**cy·to·tax·o·nom·i·cal·ly** /-əlee/ *adv.* —**cy·to·tax·on·o·mist** /-tak sónnəmist/ *n.*

cy·to·tech·nol·o·gist /sìtō tek nólləjist/ *n.* somebody trained to prepare cell samples and identify abnormalities —**cy·to·tech·nol·o·gy** *n.*

cy·to·tox·ic /sìtō tóksik/ *adj.* **1.** PREVENTING CELL DIVISION used to describe a drug that prevents cell division, often used in cancer treatment **2.** BIOL KILLING CELLS used to describe a type of cell in the immune system that destroys other cells —**cy·to·tox·ic·i·ty** /sìtō tok síssətee/ *n.*

cy·to·tox·ic T cell *n.* a killer cell (*technical*)

cy·to·tox·in /sìtō tóksin/ *n.* a substance, e.g., an antibody, that has a toxic effect on living cells

cy·to·trop·ic /sìtō tróppik/ *adj.* used to describe motile cells that are mutually attracted to each other

cy·to·trop·ism /sī tóttrə pìzzəm/ *n.* the movement or turning of cells or cell masses toward or away from one another

CZ, C.Z. *abbr.* Canal Zone

czar /zaar, tsaar/ *n.* **1.** HIST = **tsar 2.** PERSON WITH ABSOLUTE POWER a person with great authority, power, and control ○ *a drug czar* **3.** TYRANT a despotic and autocratic leader [Mid-16thC. Via Russian *tsar'* from Old Slavic *cěsarĭ*, ultimately (perhaps via Germanic) from Latin *Caesar* (source of English *Kaiser* and *caesarean*).] —**czar·dom** *n.* —**czar·ism** *n.* —**czar·ist** *adj., n.*

czar·das /chaar daash/, **csar·das** *n.* **1.** HUNGARIAN DANCE a Hungarian dance composed of a slow section followed by a faster one **2.** HUNGARIAN DANCE MUSIC a piece of music composed for a czardas [Mid-19thC. From Hungarian *csárdás*, from *csárda* "inn."]

czar·e·vitch *n.* = **tsarevitch**

cza·rev·na *n.* = **tsarevna**

cza·ri·na *n.* = **tsarina**

cza·rit·za *n.* = **tsaritsa**

Czech /chek/ *n.* **1.** SOMEBODY FROM CZECH REPUBLIC somebody who was born or raised in, or is a citizen of the Czech Republic **2.** SOMEBODY FROM CZECHOSLOVAKIA somebody who was born or raised in, or who was a citizen of the former Czechoslovakia **3.** OFFICIAL LANGUAGE OF CZECH REPUBLIC the official language of the Czech Republic, belonging to the West Slavic group of Indo-European languages. About 10 million people speak Czech. [Early 19thC. Via Polish from Czech *Čech*.] —**Czech** *adj.*

Czech·o·slo·va·ki·a /chèkəsslə vaakee ə, chèkō slō-/ former country in eastern Europe that was divided into the Czech Republic and the Slovak Republic, or Slovakia, on January 1, 1993

Czech·o·slo·vak·i·an /chèkəslə vaakee ən, chèkō slō vaakee ən/ *n.* **1.** = **Czech** *n.* 2 **2.** LANGUAGE OF CZECHOSLOVAKIA either Czech or Slovak, the languages of the former Czechoslovakia ■ *adj.* OF CZECHOSLOVAKIA relating to or typical of the former Czechoslovakia, or its people or culture [Early 20thC]

Czech Republic

Czech Re·pub·lic republic created in 1993 when the former Czechoslovakia was divided into the Czech Republic and the Slovak Republic, or Slovakia. Language: Czech. Currency: Czech koruna. Capital: Prague. Population: 10,298,324 (1997). Area: 30,450 sq. mi./78,864 sq. km.

Dd

d[1] /dee/ (*plural* **d's**), **D** (*plural* **D's** *or* **Ds**) *n.* **1.** LING **4TH LETTER OF ENGLISH ALPHABET** the fourth letter of the English alphabet **2.** MUSIC **2ND NOTE OF SCALE IN C** the second note of a scale in C major **3.** MUSIC **SOMETHING THAT PRODUCES A D** a string, key, or pipe tuned to produce the note D **4.** MUSIC **SCALE BEGINNING ON D** a scale or key that starts on the note D **5.** MUSIC **WRITTEN SYMBOL OF D** a graphic representation of the tone of D **6.** LING **PRINTED OR WRITTEN D OR D** a representation of the letter D or d in written or printed form **7.** PHON **SOUND REPRESENTED BY D OR D** a speech sound represented by the letter D or d **8. 4TH ITEM** the fourth item in a series **9. SOMETHING D-SHAPED** something shaped like a letter D **10.** EDUC **GRADE INDICATING POOR QUALITY** a grade or mark indicating that a student's work is of poor quality **11.** SPORTS **SEMICIRCLE AROUND FIELD HOCKEY GOAL** in field hockey, the semicircle surrounding the goal from which an attacker may try to score

d[2] *symbol.* **1.** deci- **2.** PHYS density **3.** PHYS deuteron **4.** PHYS down (*used of quark flavors*) **5.** the fourth vertical row of squares from the left on a chessboard

'd /d, əd/ *contr.* **1. DID** did ○ *Where'd she get that hat?* **2. HAD** had ○ *We'd already finished supper.* **3. SHOULD OR WOULD** should or would ○ *I'd like to stop at the store.*

D[1], **d** *n.* the Roman numeral for 500

D[2] *symbol.* **1.** PHYS dispersion **2.** drag **3.** MATH the first derivative of a function **4.** deuterium

D[3] *abbr.* **1.** Democrat **2.** democratic **3.** diameter **4.** drive (*used on gearshifts of automatic transmissions*)

d. *abbr.* **1.** ZOOL dam **2.** date **3.** daughter **4.** day **5.** degree **6.** departs **7.** depth **8.** deputy **9.** diameter **10.** died **11.** dollar **12.** drachma

D. *abbr.* **1.** December **2.** Department **3.** deputy **4.** Deus **5. D., d.** dinar **6.** OPTICS diopter **7.** Director **8.** JUD-CHR Dominus **9.** Don **10.** Duchess **11.** Duke

da *symbol.* deca-

DA[1] *abbr.* **1.** COMM deed of arrangement **2.** ARMS delayed action **3.** Department of Agriculture **4.** deposit account **5. DA, D.A.** district attorney **6.** don't answer (*used in telegraphy*)

DA[2] *n.* a man's hairstyle popular in the 1950s in which the hair is slicked back and drawn into a point at the back of the neck to look like a duck's tail (*informal*) Full form **duck's ass**

Da. *abbr.* Danish

D/A *abbr.* **1.** COMM days after acceptance **2.** COMM delivery on acceptance **3.** FIN deposit account **4.** COMPUT digital-to-analog **5.** COMM documents against acceptance

daal *n.* FOOD = **dahl**

dab[1] /dab/ *vti.* (**dabbed, dab·bing, dabs**) **1. TAP GENTLY** to pat or touch something lightly or gently ○ *She dabbed the tears from her eyes.* **2. APPLY GENTLY** to apply a substance using a quick light tapping action ○ *The nurse dabbed some ointment on the cut.* ■ *n.* **1. SMALL QUANTITY** a small quantity, especially of a moist or soft substance ○ *a dab of butter* **2. GENTLE TAP** a light or gentle tap, e.g., with the hand or a soft material [13thC. Thought to suggest the action. The modern meaning, "to pat gently," evolved from "to strike a blow with a weapon" through "to strike lightly."]

dab[2] /dab/ (*plural* **dabs** *or* **dab**) *n.* a small brown European flatfish eaten as food. Latin name: *Limanda limanda.* [15thC. Origin unknown.]

dab·ber /dábbər/ *n.* a pad used by engravers and printers to apply ink or color

dab·ble /dább'l/ (**-bled, -bling, -bles**) *v.* **1.** *vi.* **BECOME INVOLVED SUPERFICIALLY** to have a casual or superficial interest in something ○ *He dabbled in local politics for a few years.* **2.** *vi.* **SPLASH** to paddle, play, or splash in water **3.** *vt.* **DIP** to wet something by dipping it in a liquid ○ *We sat by the pool, dabbling our feet in the water.* **4.** *vt.* **SPLASH WITH LIQUID** to daub, splash, or spatter somebody or something with a liquid **5.** *vi.* ZOOL **MOVE UNDER WATER FOR FOOD** to move the bill to the bottom of shallow water in order to reach food (*refers to ducks*) [Mid-16thC. Origin uncertain: probably from Dutch *dabbelen,* literally "to keep tapping," from *dabben* "to tap."]

dab·bler /dábblər/ *n.* somebody whose involvement with something is superficial rather than serious

dab·chick /dáb chìk/ *n.* a small bird of the grebe family. Family: Podicipedidae.

dab·oia /də bóyə/ *n.* a colorful adder of Southeast Asia. Latin name: *Vipera russelii.* [Late 19thC. From Hindi *daboyā,* literally "lurker," from *dabnā* "to lurk."]

da ca·po /daa kaápō/ *adv.* MUSIC **REPEAT FROM BEGINNING** to be played or sung again from the beginning of the passage or piece (*used as a musical direction*) ◊ **dal segno** [Early 18thC. From Italian, literally "from the head."] —**da ca·po** *adj.*

Dac·ca = **Dhaka**

dace /dayss/ (*plural* **dace** *or* **dac·es**) *n.* **1. N AMERICAN FRESHWATER FISH** a small freshwater fish of North America. Family: Cyprinidae. **2. SMALL EUROPEAN FISH** a small European freshwater fish with a slim olive-green body. Latin name: *Leuciscus leuciscus.* [15thC. From Old French *dars,* "dace, dart." Because of its darting motion in the water.]

da·cha /daáchə/ *n.* a cottage or house in the suburbs or countryside in Russia [Mid-19thC. From Russian, literally "grant of land."]

Da·chau /daá kòw, -khòw/ site of a World War II Nazi concentration camp (1939–45) in Bavaria, about 10 mi./16 km northwest of Munich, southwestern Germany. It is now a memorial to those who died there.

Dachshund

dachs·hund /daáks hoǒnd, daáksənt/ *n.* a small dog of a breed that has a long body, short legs, and drooping ears [Late 19thC. From German, literally "badger dog." Because the breed was originally developed to hunt badgers.]

da·coit /də kóyt/, **da·koit** *n.* a member of a gang of armed robbers in India and Myanmar (Burma), especially in the past [Late 18thC. From Hindi *dakait,* from *dākā,* "gang robbery."]

da·coit·y /də kóytee/ (*plural* **-ies**), **da·koit·y** (*plural* **-ies**) *n.* robbery by a gang of armed robbers in India or Myanmar (Burma), especially in the past [Early 19thC. From Hindi *dakaitī.*]

Da·cron /dáy kròn/ *tdmk.* a trademark for a synthetic polyester fabric or fiber

dac·tyl /dákt'l/ *n.* **1. dac·tyl, dac·tyl·ic METRICAL FOOT OF THREE SYLLABLES** a metrical foot consisting of one long syllable followed by two short syllables in classical verse, or one stressed syllable followed by two unstressed syllables in modern verse **2.** ZOOL **FINGER OR TOE** a finger, toe, or related body part [14thC. Via Latin *dactylus* from Greek *daktulos,* "finger." *Metrical foot* from the length of the three joints in a finger.]

dactyl- *prefix.* = **dactylo-** (*used before vowels*)

-dactyl *suffix.* having fingers or toes of a particular kind or number ○ *polydactyl* [From Greek *daktulos* "finger"] —**-dactylous** *suffix.*

dac·tyl·ic /dak tíllik/ *adj.* **OF OR CONTAINING DACTYLS** relating to a dactyl or containing dactyls ■ *n.* = **dactyl** *n.* 1 —**dac·tyl·i·cal·ly** *adv.*

dac·tyl·ic hex·am·e·ter *n.* a line of verse consisting of six feet, the fifth of which is a dactyl, the first four dactyls or spondees, and the sixth a spondee or trochee. It is the meter of Greek and Roman epic and some other poetry.

dactylo- *prefix.* finger, toe ○ *dactylology* [From Greek *daktulos* "finger" (see -DACTYL)]

dac·ty·log·ra·phy /dàktə lóggrəfee/ *n.* the scientific examination of fingerprints for identification purposes [Coined from Greek *daktulos* "finger" + -OGRAPHY] —**dac·ty·lo·graph·ic** /dàktəlō gráffik, dak tìllə-/ *adj.*

dac·ty·lol·o·gy /dàktə lólləjee/ *n.* communication using signs made with the hands, often used by hearing-impaired people [Coined from Greek *daktulos* "finger" + -O- + -LOGY]

dad /dad/ *n.* used especially by a child or as a term of address, to refer to a father (*informal*) [Mid-16thC. Origin uncertain: perhaps an imitation of young children's speech.]

Da·da /daá daà/, **da·da, Da·da·ism** /-ìzzəm/, **da·da·ism** *n.* a European artistic and literary movement of the early 20th century founded on a rejection of traditional artistic and cultural values. Its work was characterized by anarchy, irrationality, and irreverence. [Early 20thC. From French, literally "hobby-horse." Said to have been chosen because of its meaningless sound and childish connotations.] —**Da·da·ist** *n., adj.*

dad-blamed *adj.* used to express surprise or mild annoyance (*informal*) [A euphemistic alteration of GOD-DAMNED]

dad·dy /dáddee/ (*plural* **-dies**) *n.* **1. FATHER** used especially by a young child or as a term of address, to refer to a father (*informal*) **2.** *U.S., Can, Aus* **SUPREME EXAMPLE** the earliest or finest example of something (*informal*) ○ *He was a fine trumpet player, the daddy of them all.* **3.** = **sugar daddy** (*slang*) [Early 16thC. Formed from DAD.]

dad·dy long·legs (*plural* **dad·dy long·legs**) *n.* **1. LONG-LEGGED ARACHNID** a long-legged arachnid with an oval body. Order: Opiliones. **2.** = **crane fly**

dad·dy track *n.* a career route taken by a man reducing his chances of career advancement by working flextime or fewer hours in order to look after a child or children (*informal*) ◊ **mommy track**

da·do /dáy dō/ *n.* (*plural* **-does** *or* **-dos**) **1.** ARCHIT = **die**[2] *n.* 5 **2.** BUILDING **LOWER PART OF INTERIOR WALL** the lower part of an interior wall, decorated or faced in a different manner from the upper part, usually with panels, paint, or wallpaper **3. RECTANGULAR GROOVE IN BOARD** a rectangular groove cut into a board so that a matching piece can be fitted into it to form a joint ■ *vt.* (**-doed, -do·ing, -does**) **1.** ARCHIT **PROVIDE WITH DADO** to fit a wall with a dado **2. CUT DADO IN SOMETHING** to cut a rectangular groove in something so that a matching piece can be fitted into it to form a joint **3. INSERT INTO DADO** to insert something into a rectangular groove to form a joint [Mid-17thC. From Italian, literally "die, cube."]

dae·dal /déed'l/, **de·dal** *adj.* (*literary*) **1. INTRICATE** complex or intricate **2. INGENIOUS** skillful or ingenious **3. DECORATED WITH MANY THINGS** adorned or decorated with many things, especially natural wonders ■ *n.* **INGENIOUS INVENTOR** an expert or ingenious inventor [Late 16thC. Via Latin *dædalus* from Greek *daidalos*, "skillful"; as noun, *Daidalos* "Daedalus," literally "skillful worker."]

Dae·da·lus /déddələss/ *n.* in Greek mythology, a craftsman and inventor who built a labyrinth on the island of Crete to house a half-bull, half-man monster (**Minotaur**). He made wings so that he could escape from Crete with his son (**Icarus**), but his son perished during the flight. —**Dae·da·li·an** /di dáylee ən/ *adj.*

dae·mon /déemən/, **dai·mon** /dī mōn/ *n.* **1.** MYTHOL **DEMIGOD** mythological being that is part-god and part-human **2.** MYTHOL **GUARDIAN SPIRIT** a guardian spirit **3. DEMON** a demon (*archaic*) [Variant of DEMON] —**dae·mon·ic** /di mónnik/ *adj.*

daff /daf/ *n.* a daffodil (*informal*) [Early 20thC. Shortening.]

Daffodil

daf·fo·dil /dáffə dìl/ *n.* **1. SPRINGTIME PLANT WITH TRUMPET-SHAPED FLOWERS** a European plant that has yellow trumpet-shaped flowers and long slender leaves growing from a bulb. Latin name: *Narcissus pseudonarcissus.* **2. BRIGHT YELLOW COLOR** a brilliant yellow color, like that of a daffodil ■ *adj.* **BRIGHT YELLOW** of a brilliant yellow color, like a daffodil [Mid-16thC. From medieval Latin *affodilus*, "asphodel." The modern spelling may have been influenced by Dutch *de affodil*, "the daffodil."]

daf·fy /dáffee/ (**-fi·er, -fi·est**) *adj.* silly in an amusing or harmless way (*informal*) [Late 19thC. Blend of DAFT and -Y.] —**daf·fil·y** *adv.* —**daf·fi·ness** *n.*

daft /daft/ *adj.* *U.K.* psychiatrically disordered (*informal*) [Old English *gedæfte*, "fitting," from a prehistoric Germanic word meaning "fit, suitable." The modern meaning, "silly," evolved from "suitable" via "compliant, gentle."] —**daft·ly** *adv.* —**daft·ness** *n.*

dag[1] /dag/ *n.* **1.** = **daglock** *n.* **2. DECORATIVE EDGING** a decorative edging on garments, used especially in medieval times ■ *vti.* (**dagged, dag·ging, dags**) **REMOVE SOILED WOOL FROM SHEEP** to cut off dung-coated wool from a sheep's coat [Early 17thC. Shortening of DAGLOCK.]

dag[2] *symbol.* decagram [Shortening and alteration]

Da·gan /daagən/ *n.* the god of the Earth in Babylonian mythology

Da·ges·tan·ian /daagə staánee ən/ *n.* **1.** LANG **CAUCASIAN LANGUAGE GROUP** a group of North Caucasian languages spoken in Dagestan, an autonomous republic in southwestern Russia. The main member of the group is Avar. No more than a few thousand people speak a Dagestanian language. **2.** PEOPLES **SOMEBODY FROM DAGESTAN** somebody who was born or raised in Dagestan, or who is a citizen of Dagestan [Formed from *Dagestan* in southwestern Russia] —**Da·ges·tan·ian** *adj.*

dag·ger /dággər/ *n.* **1. SHORT POINTED KNIFE** a short pointed knife used as a weapon **2. IRRITATION** something that torments or wounds somebody ○ *Such cutting words were a dagger to my heart.* **3. SIGN USED AS REFERENCE MARK** a sign (†) that is used as a reference mark, especially to a footnote ■ *vt.* (**-gered, -ger·ing, -gers**) **1. MARK SOMETHING WITH REFERENCE SIGN** to mark something with a dagger sign **2. STAB** to stab somebody or something with a dagger (*archaic*) [14thC. Origin uncertain: perhaps formed from obsolete *dag* "to stab"; or ultimately from Old Provençal or Old Italian *daga*, literally "Dacian knife," ultimately from Latin *Dacia* (see DACIAN).] ◇ **look daggers at somebody** to look at somebody in an angry or hostile way

dag·lock /dág lòk/ *n.* a lock of dung-coated wool on a sheep's hindquarters [Early 17thC. From earlier *dag*, "hanging part of something" + LOCK, "piece of hair."]

da·go /dáy gō/ (*plural* **-gos** *or* **-goes**), **Da·go** (*plural* **-gos** *or* **-goes**) *n.* a highly offensive term that refers to somebody of Italian, Spanish, or Portuguese birth or descent (*taboo insult*) [Mid-19thC. Variant of the name *Diego.*]

da·go·ba /daágəbə/ *n.* a dome-shaped shrine that contains Buddhist relics [Early 19thC. Via Sinhalese *dāgaba* from Pali *dhātu-gabbha*, "receptacle for relics."]

Da·gon /dáy gòn/ *n.* the chief god in Philistine mythology, often depicted as half man and half fish

Da·guerre /də gáir, daa-/, **Louis Jacques** (1789–1851) French painter and inventor. Originally a scene painter, he became a pioneer photographer who, working initially with French physicist Joseph Niepce (1829), perfected the daguerreotype process (1837). Full name **Louis Jacques Mandé Daguerre**

da·guerre·o·type /də gérrə tìp/ *n.* **1. EARLY PHOTOGRAPHIC PROCESS** an early photographic process in which an image was produced on a light-sensitive silver or silver-coated plate and developed in mercury vapor **2. EARLY PHOTOGRAPH** a photograph produced by the daguerreotype process ■ *vt.* (**-typed, -typ·ing, -types**) **TAKE PHOTOGRAPH OF** to make a daguerreotype of something or somebody [Mid-19thC. From French, named for Louis-Jacques Mandé *Daguerre.*] —**da·guerre·o·typ·er** *n.* —**da·guerre·o·typ·ist** *n.* —**da·guerre·o·typ·y** /də gérrə tìpee/ *n.*

Dag·wood sand·wich /dág wòod-/, **Dag·wood** *n.* a thick sandwich filled with a variety of meats and cheeses together with different dressings and seasonings [Late 20thC. Named for *Dagwood* Bumstead, a comic-strip character noted for his fondness for such sandwiches.]

dah /daa/ *n.* COMMUNICATION the spoken representation of a dash in Morse code and other telegraphic codes [Mid-20thC. An imitation of the sound made by a Morse code transmitter.]

dahl /daal/, **daal, dal** *n.* a thick Indian stew made from pulses, onions, and spices

Dahl /daal/, **Roald** (1916–90) British writer. He is best known for his many children's books, including *James and the Giant Peach* (1961) and *Charlie and the Chocolate Factory* (1964). His books for adults include *Kiss, Kiss* (1960).

Dahlia

dahl·ia /daályə, dál-/ *n.* a tall perennial plant native to Central America and Mexico that has large brightly colored flowers and tuberous roots. Many different varieties of dahlias are cultivated as garden plants. Genus: *Dahlia.* [Early 19thC. Named for Andreas *Dahl* (1751–89), a Swedish botanist who discovered this genus of plants in Mexico in 1788.]

Da·ho·mey /də hómee, -may/ former name for **Benin**

da·hoon /də hóon/ *n.* a small evergreen tree of the holly family that is native to the southern United States and has flat leathery, dark green leaves and orange, red, or yellow fruits. Latin name: *Ilex cassine.*

dai·kon /dī kòn, dīkən/ *n.* a long sweet white radish used in Asian cuisines. Latin name: *Raphanus sativus longipinnatus.* [Late 19thC. From Japanese, literally "big root."]

Dáil Eire·ann /dòyl áirən/, **Dáil** *n.* the lower house of the parliament of the Republic of Ireland [Early 20thC. From Irish, literally "Irish Assembly."]

dai·ly /dáylee/ *adj.* **1. DONE EVERY DAY** done or occurring every day **2. FOR EACH DAY** for each day or for a period of a day **3. LASTING A DAY** for the duration of or during a day ■ *adv.* **EVERY DAY** on each day ■ *n.* (*plural* **-lies**) **NEWSPAPER PUBLISHED EVERY DAY** a newspaper published every day, or every day except Sunday (*often used in the plural*) ■ **dai·lies** *npl.* CINEMA **DAY'S SHOOTING OF MOVIE SCENES** unedited prints of a day's shooting of scenes from a movie prepared each day for the director to view the following day [15thC. Formed from DAY.]

dai·ly dou·ble *n.* **1. BET ON TWO RACES** a bet, e.g., in horseracing, won by correctly choosing the winners of two specified races taking place on the same day **2. TWO RACES** the two races specified for a daily double bet

dai·ly doz·en *n.* a set of physical exercises to be done each day

dai·mi·o *n.* = **daimyo**

Daim·ler /dīmlər/, **Gottlieb** (1834–1900) German engineer and inventor. His high-speed gasoline-burning internal-combustion engine powered the first motorcycle and one of the earliest successful automobiles (1887).

dai·mon *n.* = **daemon**

dai·my·o /dīmyō/ (*plural* **-o** *or* **-os**), **dai·mi·o** (*plural* **-o** *or* **-os**) *n.* a great Japanese feudal lord who was a vassal of the emperor [Early 18thC. From Japanese, literally "great name."]

Dain·tree Riv·er Na·tion·al Park /dáyn tree-/ national park in northeastern Queensland, Australia, that forms part of the Wet Tropics of Queensland World Heritage Area. Area: 2,734 sq. mi./7,000 sq. km.

dain·ty /dáyntee/ *adj.* (**-ti·er, -ti·est**) **1. PRETTY** delicate and pretty ○ *dainty slippers* **2. TASTY** choice, delicious, or tasty ○ *a dainty morsel* **3. REFINED IN TASTE** having refined taste or manners **4. OVERLY NICE** excessively fastidious or particular ■ *n.* (*plural* **-ties**) **DELICACY** something delicious, especially a small piece of food [13thC. Via Anglo-Norman *dainte* and Old French *daintie* from Latin *dignitas* (see DIGNITY). "Delicate" evolved from "esteem" through "pleasure" and "luxury" to "delightful."] —**dain·ti·ly** *adv.* —**dain·ti·ness** *n.*

dai·qui·ri /dákəree/ (*plural* **-ris**) *n.* an iced cocktail made from rum, lemon or lime juice, and sugar or syrup [Early 20thC. Named for *Daiquiri*, a Cuban rum-producing district.]

dair·y /dáiree/ *n.* (*plural* **-ies**) **1. FARM FOR MILK PRODUCTION** a farm that produces milk and milk products **2. ESTABLISHMENT THAT SELLS OR PROCESSES MILK** a commercial establishment that processes, sells, or distributes milk and milk products **3. PLACE TO MAKE BUTTER AND CHEESE** a room or building where butter and cheese are made **4. PLACE TO STORE MILK AND CREAM** a room or building where milk and cream are stored **5. DAIRY PRODUCTS** dairy products collectively ■ *adj.* **1. RELATING TO MILK PRODUCTS** relating to, producing, or containing milk or milk products **2. CONCERNING FOODS IN JEWISH DIETARY LAW** relating to those foods, including milk products, eggs, fish, and vegetables, that Jewish dietary law allows on occasions when milk is consumed [13thC. Via *deie* "woman servant" (hence "place where she works") from Old English *dæge*, "kneader (of bread)" (source of English *lady*).]

WORD KEY: REGIONAL NOTE

In the southeastern sense "storage house or shed for storing milk and other perishables," ***dairy*** competes with *dairy house, milk house, safe, spring,* and *spring house.* In the Highlands, as in East Tennessee, the term ***dairy*** may signal a dugout space in the side of a hill.

dair·y cat·tle *npl.* cattle bred and raised for milk production

dair·y farm *n.* a farm that produces milk and milk products

dair·y·ing /dáiree ing/ *n.* the business of operating a dairy or dairy farm

dair·y·man /dáirimən, -màn/ (*plural* **-men** /dáirimən, -mèn/) *n.* somebody who owns or works in a dairy (*dated*)

da·is /dáy iss, dī́-/ *n.* a raised platform at the end of a hall or large room [13thC. Via Old French *deis* from Latin.]

dai·shi·ki *n.* CLOTHES = **dashiki**

Daisy

dai·sy /dáyzee/ (*plural* **-sies**) *n.* **1. TALL PLANT** a tall plant of Europe, Asia, and North America that has flowers with white petals radiating from a round yellow center. Latin name: *Chrysanthemum leucanthemum.* **2. LOW-GROWING FLOWERING PLANT** a plant of European origin that has short stems and flowers with white or pinkish-white petals radiating from a round yellow center. Latin name: *Bellis perennis.* Also called **English daisy 3. YOUNG GIRL SCOUT** a preschool-age member of the Girl Scouts **4. EXCELLENT PERSON OR THING** a person or thing regarded as first-rate or excellent (*slang*) [Old English *dæges eage*, literally "day's eye." Because the flower opens in daylight and closes at night.]

dai·sy chain *n.* **1. GARLAND OF DAISIES** a garland made by threading the stems of daisies together **2. SERIES** a series of connected things, events, or people (*slang*)

dai·sy·cut·ter /dáyzi kùttər/ *n.* **1.** MIL **FRAGMENTATION BOMB** a bomb that detonates just above ground level, used against personnel and to destroy vegetation in order to create a landing zone for helicopters **2.** BASEBALL **BALL THAT SKIMS GROUND** a batted baseball that skims the ground (*dated*)

dai·sy ham *n.* a small cut of pork shoulder that has been boned, salted, and smoked

dai·sy wheel *n.* a wheel with type elements at the ends of spokes radiating from a central hub, used in some electronic typewriters and printers

Dak. *abbr.* Dakota

Da·kar /dá kaár, də kaár/ capital and largest city of Senegal. It is situated on Cape Verde Peninsula, close to the westernmost tip of mainland Africa, and is one of western Africa's leading ports. Population: 1,729,823 (1992).

da·koit *n.* = **dacoit**

da·koi·ty *n.* = **dacoity**

Da·ko·ta /də kṓtə/ (*plural* **-tas** *or* **-ta**) *n.* **1. MEMBER OF NATIVE AMERICAN PEOPLE** a member of a Native North American people who originally lived in the upper Mississippi River valley **2. DAKOTA LANGUAGE** a Siouan language spoken in the United States and the Canadian province of Manitoba. Dakota is spoken by between 10,000 and 20,000 people. [Early 19thC. From Dakota *Dakhōta*, literally "allies."] —**Da·ko·ta** *adj.*

dal[1] /daal/ *n.* = **dahl**

dal[2] *symbol.* decaliter

Da·lai La·ma /daá lī laámə/ *n.* the highest priest of Tibetan Buddhism and, until the Chinese occupation of Tibet in 1959, the traditional spiritual and secular ruler of Tibet [Late 17thC. From Mongolian, literally "ocean lama." See LAMA.]

da·la·si /daa laássee/ (*plural* **-sis**) *n.* the basic monetary unit of Gambia, divided into 100 bututs. See table at **currency** [Late 20thC. From the name of an earlier Gambian coin.]

dale /dayl/ *n.* a broad lowland valley ○ *walked over hill and dale* [Old English *dæl*. Ultimately from an Indo-European word meaning "bend, curve," which is also the ancestor of English *dell* and *dollar*.]

Dale /dayl/, **Sir Henry Hallett** (1875–1968) British physiologist and pharmacist. With Otto Loewi, he established the role of the chemical acetylcholine in the transmission of nerve impulses. He and Loewi were joint Nobel laureates in 1936.

da·leth /daá lèth, daálət/, **da·led** /-lèd, -ləd/, **da·let** /-lèt, -lət/ *n.* the fourth letter of the Hebrew alphabet, transliterated into English as "d." See table at **alphabet**

Da·ley /dáylee/, **Richard J.** (1902–76) U.S. politician. He was the Democratic mayor of Chicago (1955–76) and noted for exerting strong personal control over local Democratic Party politics. Full name **Richard Joseph Daley**

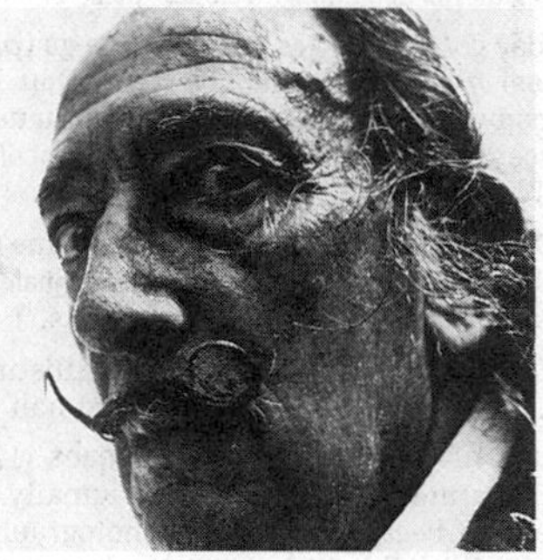

AKG London

Salvador Dali

Da·li /daálee/, **Da·lí, Salvador** (1904–89) Spanish surrealist painter. He is known for the dreamlike imagery and almost photographic realism of his work. After settling in New York (1940), he adopted other styles and wrote *The Secret Life of Salvador Dalí* (1942). —**Da·li·esque** *adj.*

Dal·ian /daálee ən/ industrial seaport on the southern peninsula in Liaoning Province, northeastern China. Population: 2,416,000 (1991).

Dal·las /dálləss/ city in northeastern Texas, on the Trinity River, east of Fort Worth. It is an important commercial, financial, and distribution center. Population: 1,053,292 (1996).

Dal·las, George (1792–1864) U.S. statesman. He was vice president of the United States (1845–49) under James K. Polk. The city of Dallas, Texas, is named for him. Full name **George Mifflin Dallas**

dalles /dalz/ *npl.* **1. CANYON WALLS** the steep walls of a canyon or ravine **2. RAPIDS** rapids where a river flows between the steep narrow walls of a canyon or gorge [Late 18thC. From French, literally "tubes, conduits."]

dal·li·ance /dállee əns/ *n.* (*literary*) **1. AFFAIR** a flirtation or flirtatious episode or affair **2. TRIFLING** frivolous or idle wasting of time [14thC. Coined from DALLY + -ANCE.]

Dal·lis grass /dálləss-/ *n.* a tall perennial grass native to South America, grown as a pasture grass in the southern United States. Latin name: *Paspalum dilatatum.* [Early 20thC. *Dallis* of uncertain origin: perhaps a variant of *Dallas*, Texas.]

Dall sheep /dáwl-/, **Dall's sheep** *n.* a wild sheep of mountainous regions of Alaska and Canada, with curved horns and a coat varying from white to black. Latin name: *Ovis dalli.*

dal·ly /dállee/ (**-lied, -ly·ing, -lies**) *v.* **1.** *vi.* **FLIRT** to act in an amorous, flirtatious, or playful manner **2.** *vi.* **TOY WITH SOMETHING OR SOMEBODY** to trifle or deal lightly with something or somebody **3.** *vti.* **WASTE TIME** to dawdle, loiter, or waste time [14thC. From Anglo-Norman *dalier*, "to amuse yourself," of ultimately unknown origin. The modern meaning, "to flirt," evolved from "to talk, converse" through "to chat idly."] —**dal·li·er** *n.*

Dal·ma·ti·a /dal máyshə/ region of Croatia, consisting of a coastal area and offshore islands. It is bordered inland by the Dinaric Alps and includes the major cities of Dubrovnik and Split. Area: 5,000 sq. mi./12,950 sq. km.

Dal·ma·tian /dal máysh'n/ *n.* **1. Dal·ma·tian, dal·ma·tian** ZOOL **SPOTTED DOG** a dog belonging to a breed that has a white coat with black or brown spots **2.** PEOPLES **SOMEBODY FROM DALMATIA** somebody who was born in or who lives in the Adriatic coastal region of Dalmatia **3.** LANG **EXTINCT ROMANCE LANGUAGE** an extinct language once spoken along the Adriatic coast in the region of Dubrovnik. It belongs to the Romance group of Indo-European languages and became extinct at the end of the 19th century. [Late 16thC. In the meaning of "dog," named for *Dalmatia*, because the breed supposedly originated there.] —**Dal·ma·tian** *adj.*

Dal·ma·tian coast *n.* GEOG a coastline characterized by chains of islands close to the mainland, formed when rising sea levels flood a series of valleys and ridges parallel to the coast

dal·mat·ic /dal máttik/ *n.* **1.** CHR **VESTMENT WORN BY PRIEST** a vestment with slit sides and wide sleeves, worn by a priest or deacon of the Roman Catholic Church **2.** HIST **CORONATION ROBE** a robe with slit sides and wide sleeves, worn by British sovereigns at their coronation [15thC. From Old French *dalmatique* or Latin *dalmatica*, "(robe) made of Dalmatian wool," formed from *Dalmaticus* "of Dalmatia," from *Dalmatia*.]

dal se·gno /daál sáynyō/ *adv.* to be played or sung again from the point marked with the sign 𝄋; to the point marked "fine" (*used as a musical direction*) ◊ **da capo** [Late 19thC. From Italian, literally "from the sign."]

dal·ton /dáwlt'n/ *n.* = **atomic mass unit** [Mid-20thC. Named for John *Dalton*.]

Dal·ton /dáwlt'n/, **John** (1766–1844) British physicist and meteorologist. His experiments with gases (1803) laid the foundations for modern atomic theory. He also first described color blindness (1794).

dal·ton·ism /dáwlt'n ìzzəm/, **Dal·ton·ism** *n.* color blindness, especially an inability to distinguish between red and green [Mid-19thC. From French *daltonisme*, named for John *Dalton*, who was affected by this.] —**dal·ton·ic** /dawl tónnik/ *adj.*

Dal·ton's law *n.* the principle that mixed gases in a given volume exert a pressure equal to the sum of the pressures they would exert individually in the same volume [Named for John *Dalton*]

Da·ly Cit·y /dàylee-/ city in western California, on the Pacific Ocean, south of San Francisco. Population: 97,649 (1996).

Barnaby's

Dam: Hoover Dam (completed 1936), Arizona/Nevada

dam[1] /dam/ *n.* **1. BARRIER CONTROLLING FLOW OF WATER** a barrier of concrete or earth that is built across a river or stream to obstruct or control the flow of water, especially in order to create a reservoir **2. SOMETHING RESEMBLING DAM** a barrier that resembles or acts as a dam **3. RESERVOIR CONFINED BY DAM** a reservoir of water created, confined, or controlled by a dam ■ *vt.* (**dammed, dam·ming, dams**) **1. CONFINE WITH DAM** to confine, provide, or restrain something with a dam **2. OBSTRUCT** to block, obstruct, or restrict something [14thC. From Middle Dutch, ultimately of unknown origin.]

dam[2] /dam/ *n.* the female parent of an animal, especially of four-legged domestic livestock [14thC. Variant of DAME.]

dam[3] *symbol.* decameter

Dam /dam, daam/, **Henrik** (1895–1976) Danish biochemist. Working with Edward A. Doisy, he isolated vitamin K, a fat-soluble substance necessary for blood coagulation. The pair shared a Nobel Prize in 1943. Full name **Carl Peter Henrik Dam**

dam·age /dámmij/ *n.* **1. HARM OR INJURY** physical harm or injury that makes something less useful, valuable, or able to function ○ *Damage to the vehicle was slight* ○ *The scandal did considerable damage to his reputation.* **2. ADVERSE EFFECT** a harmful effect on somebody or something **3. COST** the cost or price of something (*informal*) ○ *What's the damage?* ■ **dam·ag·es** *npl.* LAW **MONEY PAID AS COMPENSATION** money paid or claimed as compensation for harm, loss, or injury ■ *v.* (**-aged, -ag·ing, -ag·es**) **1.** *vt.* **CAUSE HARM** to cause damage to something or somebody **2.** *vi.* **BE HARMED** to suffer damage ○ *Soft fruit damages easily.* [13thC. Via Old French, "loss through injury," from *dam*, "loss, damage," from Latin *damnum* (source of English *damn* and *indemnity*).] —**dam·age·a·bil·i·ty** /dàmmijə bíllətee/ *n.* —**dam·age·a·ble** /dámmijəb'l/ *adj.* —**dam·a·ger** *n.*

WORD KEY: SYNONYMS

See Synonyms at ***harm***.

dam·age con·trol *n.* **1.** NAVY **QUICK CONTAINMENT OF PHYSICAL DAMAGE** shipboard measures to control, contain, and offset damages to a vessel by, e.g., collision, attack, fire, or an explosion **2. CONTAINMENT OF NONPHYSICAL DAMAGE** containment and neutralization of, e.g., public relations problems caused by a scandal, legal case, or other controversial matter (*informal*) ○ *As soon as the scandal broke, the Party's damage control kicked in.*

dam·ag·ing /dámmijing/ *adj.* causing or capable of causing harm, injury, or loss ○ *a damaging report* —**dam·ag·ing·ly** *adv.*

dam·ar *n.* = **dammar**

Dam·ar·a /də máarə/ (*plural* **-as** *or* **-a**) *n.* **1.** PEOPLES **MEMBER OF AFRICAN PEOPLE** a member of a people living in southwestern Africa, mainly in the Republic of Namibia **2.** LANG = **Nama** [Early 19thC. From Nama.] —**Dam·ar·a** *adj.*

dam·as·cene /dámmə seén, dàmmə seén/ *vt.* (**-cened, -cen·ing, -cenes**) **DECORATE METAL WITH WAVY PATTERNS** to decorate metal such as iron or steel with wavy patterns of etching or inlay of precious metals, especially gold or silver ■ *n.* **DESIGN OR OBJECT CREATED BY DAMASCENING** a design or object created by the process of damascening ■ *adj.* **1. RELATING TO DAMASCENING** relating to the art or process of damascening metal **2. OF OR LIKE DAMASK** made of or resembling damask [From Latin *Damascenus* "of Damascus," a city of Syria famous for its steel and silk fabrics, from Greek *damaskēnos*] —**dam·a·scen·er** *n.*

Da·mas·cus /də máskəss/ capital city of Syria on the Baradá River in the southwestern part of the country. Thought to have been inhabited since 2000 B.C., it is one of the oldest cities in the world. Population: 1,451,000 (1992). —**Da·mas·cene** /dámmə seén, dàmmə seén/ *n., adj.*

dam·ask /dáməsk/ *n.* **1. PATTERNED FABRIC** a reversible fabric, usually of cotton, linen, or silk, with a pattern woven into it. It is used especially for table linen. **2. TABLE LINEN** table linen made from damask **3.** COLORS **GRAYISH-PINK COLOR** a grayish-pink color, like that of the damask rose ■ *adj.* **PINK** pink or grayish-pink ■ *vt.* (**-asked, -ask·ing, -asks**) **DECORATE WITH PATTERN** to decorate or weave a fabric with an elaborate pattern [14thC. From Latin *Damascus*, named for that city because the fabric was originally produced there.]

dam·ask rose *n.* a large hardy rose native to Asia and cultivated for its fragrant pink or red flowers that are used to make a fragrant essential oil (**attar**). Latin name: *Rosa damascena.* [*Damask* from earlier English *Damask* "Damascus," from Latin *Damascus*]

Dam·a·vand /dámmə vànd/ mountain in Iran, northeast of Teheran, that is the highest point in the Elburz Mountains and in the country. Height: 18,934 ft./5,771 m.

dame /daym/ *n.* **1.** a term, often considered offensive, that refers to a woman or girl (*informal*) (*often offensive in context*) **2.** the woman in charge of a household (*archaic*) **3. SENIOR NUN** used as the formal title of the superior of a nunnery [13thC. Via Old French and late Latin *domna* from Latin *domina*, "woman in charge of the house."]

Dame *n.* **1. WOMAN AWARDED ORDER OF CHIVALRY** the title of a woman awarded any of various orders of chivalry or merit, e.g., the Order of the British Empire, by a sovereign or government **2. WIFE OF BARONET OR KNIGHT** the official title of the wife of a baronet or knight

dame's vi·o·let (*plural* **dame's vi·o·lets** *or* **dame's vi·o·let**) *n.* a perennial Eurasian plant of the mustard family, cultivated for its fragrant purple or white flowers. Latin name: *Hesperis matronalis.* [Translation of the Latin name in the old herbals, *Viola matronalis*]

da·mi·a·na /dàymee áanə, -ánnə/ *n.* a drug used as a stimulant and diuretic that is extracted from the leaves of a tropical American plant. Latin name: *Turnera diffusa.* [Late 20thC. From American Spanish.]

Da·mi·en /dáymee ən, daa myáN/, **Father** (1840–89) Belgian Roman Catholic priest. From 1873 until his death from leprosy, he lived among lepers isolated on Molokai Island, Hawaii, attending to their spiritual and material needs. Full name **Joseph Damien de Veuster**

dam·mar /dámmər/, **dam·ar, dam·mer** *n.* a hard resin obtained from various trees of Southeast Asia, used in inks, lacquers, oil paints, and varnishes [Late 17thC. From Malay *damar*, "resin."]

dam·mit /dámmit/ *interj.* used as a swearword to show annoyance (*informal*) [Mid-19thC. Variant of *damn it.*]

damn /dam/ *interj.* **EXCLAMATION OF ANNOYANCE** used as a swearword to emphasize irritation, displeasure, disappointment, or frustration ■ *adj., adv.* **USED TO EXPRESS ANNOYANCE** used emphatically or as a swearword to express annoyance, disappointment, or frustration with somebody or something ■ *v.* (**damned, damn·ing, damns**) **1.** *vt.* **DECLARE TO BE BAD** to express disapproval of something or somebody, especially in public **2.** *vt.* **DOOM TO FAILURE** to cause somebody or something to fail **3.** *vt.* **CONDEMN TO HELL** to condemn somebody to hell or to eternal punishment **4.** *vti.* **CURSE OR SWEAR AT** to curse or swear at somebody or something, using the word "damn" [13thC. Via Old French *damner*, "to condemn," from Latin *damnare*, from *damnum* "damage" (see DAMAGE).] —**damn·er** *n.* ◇ **not give** *or* **care a damn** to be not at all concerned or worried about something ◇ **not worth a damn** completely worthless

dam·na·ble /dámnəb'l/ *adj.* **1. DETESTABLE** detestable, hateful, or extremely bad (*informal*) **2. HEINOUS** deserving divine condemnation or damnation (*dated*) —**dam·na·bly** *adv.* —**dam·na·bil·i·ty** /dàmnə bíllətee/ *n.* —**dam·na·ble·ness** /dámnəb'lnəss/ *n.*

dam·na·tion /dam náysh'n/ *n.* **1. CONDEMNATION** condemnation to hell or eternal punishment **2. PUNISHMENT** eternal punishment in hell **3. SIN** something that causes condemnation to hell or eternal punishment ■ *interj.* **ANGRY EXCLAMATION** used as a swearword to express anger or disappointment

dam·na·to·ry /dámnə tàwree/ *adj.* causing, expressing, or threatening condemnation

damned /damd/ *adj.* **1. CONDEMNED** condemned to hell or to eternal punishment **2. EXPRESSION OF ANNOYANCE** used emphatically or as a swearword to express annoyance ■ *adv.* **VERY** extremely (*informal*) ○ *a damned good saxophone player* ■ *npl.* **THE CONDEMNED** those condemned to hell or doomed to suffer eternal punishment

damned·est /dámdəst/ *n.* **UTMOST** everything possible ○ *She did her damnedest to persuade them to stay.* ■ *adj.* **MOST AMAZING** most amazing or extraordinary ○ *It was the damnedest thing I'd ever seen.*

dam·ni·fy /dámni fì/ (**-fied, -fy·ing, -fies**) *vt.* in law, to cause damage or loss to somebody or something [Early 16thC. Via Old French *damnifier* from Latin *damnificare*, "injure, condemn," from *damnare.* See DAMN.] —**dam·ni·fi·ca·tion** /dàmnifi káysh'n/ *n.*

damn·ing /dámmig/ *adj.* **1. PROVING GUILTY, WRONG, OR BAD** proving or showing that somebody or something is guilty, wrong, or very bad **2. HIGHLY CRITICAL** very critical or unfavorable —**damn·ing·ly** *adv.* —**damn·ing·ness** *n.*

Dam·o·cle·an /dàmmə kleé ən, dámmə klee-/ *adj.* under the threat of imminent disaster [Late 19thC. Named for *Damocles.*]

Dam·o·cles /dámmə kleez/ (*fl.* 4th century B.C.) Syracusan Greek courtier. Dionysius of Syracuse, tired of his envious flattery, had him seated beneath a sword hanging from a hair, thus symbolizing the perils of the powerful.

damp /damp/ *adj.* **1. MOIST** slightly wet ○ *damp laundry* **2. HALF-HEARTED** unenthusiastic or indifferent **3. MELANCHOLY** dejected or melancholy (*archaic*) ■ *n.* **1. SLIGHT WETNESS** humidity, moisture, or slight wetness ○ *patches of damp* **2.** MINING **HARMFUL GAS** poisonous gas or rank air, especially in a mine **3. SOMETHING THAT DEPRESSES** a feeling of gloom or melancholy ○ *The host's low spirits cast a damp over the party.* ■ *vt.* (**damped, damp·ing, damps**) **1. DAMPEN** to make somebody or something slightly wet **2. EXTINGUISH** to extinguish a fire or make it burn more slowly by reducing its supply of air **3.** MUSIC **STOP** to stop the vibration of a string on a musical instrument **4. STIFLE** to discourage or stifle somebody or something ○ *Rain damped the picnickers' enthusiasm.* **5.** PHYS **REDUCE OSCILLATION** to decrease the amplitude of an oscillation or wave **6.** MUSIC **MUFFLE** to deaden or muffle the sound of a musical instrument [14thC. Via Middle Low German *damp* from prehistoric Germanic. "Moist" evolved from "vapor," through "noxious gas," "mist," and "moisture."] —**damp·ly** *adv.* —**damp·ness** *n.*

WORD KEY: SYNONYMS

See Synonyms at ***wet***.

damp down *vt.* **1. CAUSE TO BURN MORE SLOWLY** to cause a fire to burn more slowly by adding ash or by reducing the flow of air **2. REDUCE** to control, restrain, or reduce the intensity of something

damp course *n.* a layer of waterproof material near the ground in a brick wall that prevents damp from rising

damp·en /dámpən/ (**-ened, -en·ing, -ens**) *vti.* **1. MOISTEN** to make something slightly wet, or to become slightly wet **2. DEADEN** to deaden or stifle something, or to become deadened or stifled [14thC. Formed from DAMP.] —**damp·en·er** *n.*

damp·er /dámpər/ *n.* **1. SOMEBODY OR SOMETHING DISCOURAGING** somebody or something that causes discouragement or inhibition **2. PLATE TO CONTROL FIRE** a metal plate that controls the draft in a furnace or stove **3.** MUSIC **PIANO MUTE** a felt-covered block in a piano that stops the vibration of strings **4.** MUSIC **HORN OR WOODWIND MUTE** a mute to muffle the sound of a brass or woodwind instrument **5.** ELEC ENG **DEVICE TO CONTROL VIBRATION** a device for controlling the excessive vibration of a suspended magnetic needle **6.** ELEC ENG **DEVICE TO REDUCE HUNTING** a piece of copper embedded in or near the poles of an electric motor to reduce any tendency it might have to pulsate to speeds above or below its intended speed ◇ **put a damper on something** to make something less fun and more inhibited ○ *The sudden arrival of the adults put a damper on the kids' party.*

Dam·pi·er /dámpee ər/, **William** (1652–1715) English explorer. He was one of the first Europeans to visit Australia and published numerous surveys, logs, and charts of his voyages around the world.

damp·ing off *n.* a fatal disease of seedlings grown under very damp conditions that is caused by various fungi

damp-proof *adj.* **RESISTANT TO MOISTURE** impervious or resistant to damp or moisture ■ *vt.* (**damp-proofed, damp-proof·ing, damp-proofs**) **MAKE RESISTANT TO MOISTURE** to make something such as a building damp-proof

damp-proof course *n.* = **damp course**

Dam·rosch /dám ròsh/, **Walter Johannes** (1862–1950) German-born U.S. conductor and composer. He directed several noted orchestras, most notably the NBC Symphony Orchestra in New York (1928–42).

dam·sel /dámz'l/ *n.* a girl or young unmarried woman, originally one of noble birth (*archaic or literary*) [13thC. From Old French *dameisele*, by folk etymology (from *dame*) from *donsele*, from Vulgar Latin *dominicella*, "little lady," ultimately from Latin *domina*, "woman in charge of the house" (see DAME).]

dam·sel·fish /dámz'l fish/ (*plural* **-fish** *or* **-fish·es**) *n.* a small brightly colored marine fish that lives along coral reefs. Family: Pomacentridae.

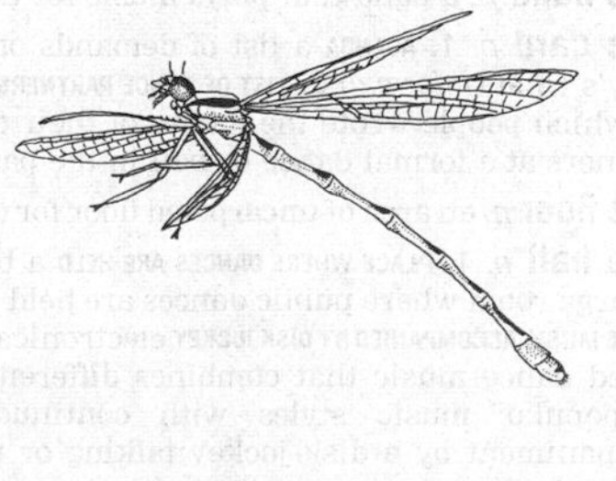

Damselfly

dam·sel·fly /dámz'l flì/ (*plural* **-flies**) *n.* a slender insect related to the dragonfly but smaller in size that folds its wings together above its body when resting. Damselflies are often brightly colored and have eyes that face sideways. Suborder: Zygoptera.

dam·son /dámz'n/ *n.* **1. PLUM TREE** a fruit tree related to the plum, cultivated for its edible dark purple fruit. Latin name: *Prunus insititia.* **2. SMALL PURPLE PLUM** the small sour dark purple fruit of the damson tree, usually eaten cooked or made into jelly [15thC. Alteration of DAMASCENE, translating Latin *(prunum) damascenus,* "(plum) from Damascus."]

dan[1] /dan/, **Dan** *n.* **1. PROFICIENCY LEVEL IN MARTIAL ARTS** any one of the numbered black-belt levels of proficiency in martial arts such as judo and karate **2. SOMEBODY PROFICIENT IN A MARTIAL ART** a person who has achieved a dan [Mid-20thC. From Japanese.]

dan[2] /dan/, **dan buoy** *n.* a small buoy, often with a flag attached, used as a marker [Late 17thC. Origin unknown.]

Dan *n.* a title of honor, equivalent to "Master" or "Sir," used in the past before the personal names of respected men such as clerics or poets (*archaic*) [13thC. Via Old French from Latin *dominus,* "master."]

Dan. *abbr.* **1.** BIBLE Daniel **2.** Danish

Da·na /dáynə/, **James Dwight** (1813–95) U.S. mineralogist. He was appointed professor of natural history (1849) and professor of geology and mineralogy (1864) at Yale University, and is known for his work *Manual of Mineralogy* (1848).

Da·na·i·des /də náyə deez/, **Da·na·ï·des** *npl.* in Greek mythology, the fifty daughters of Danaüs, who killed their bridegrooms

Da·na Point /dáynə-/ city in southwestern California on the shore of the Pacific Ocean, southeast of Los Angeles. Population: 33,875 (1996).

dan buoy *n.* = **dan**[2] [*Dan* from DAN[2]]

dance /dans/ *v.* **(danced, danc·ing, danc·es) 1.** *vi.* **MOVE RHYTHMICALLY TO MUSIC** to move the feet and body rhythmically, usually in time to music **2.** *vt.* **DO A DANCE** to perform or participate in a specified dance ○ *to dance a lively polka* **3.** *vi.* **JUMP UP AND DOWN** to leap or skip, especially in an emotional manner ○ *The children danced with glee.* **4.** *vi.* **MOVE ABOUT QUICKLY** to bob up and down or move quickly about ○ *The leaves danced across the lawn.* **5.** *vt.* **CAUSE TO DANCE** to make somebody dance or lead somebody in a dance ○ *He danced her across the floor.* **6.** *vi.* **EVADE AN ISSUE** to talk misleadingly so as to avoid facing an issue squarely (*informal*) ○ *They danced around on the issue of term limits.* **7.** *vt.* **REACH BY DANCING** to get to a particular state by dancing ○ *She danced her way to fame and fortune.* **8.** *vi.* BACKGAMMON **FAIL TO ROLL REENTRY NUMBER** to fail to roll a number that reenters a backgammon piece from the bar ○ *He rolled a 6-6 and danced.* ■ *n.* **1. RHYTHMICAL BODY MOVEMENTS TO MUSIC** a series of rhythmical steps and body movements, usually performed in time to music **2. ACTION OF DANCING** a session of dancing **3. OCCASION FOR DANCING** a party or social gathering for dancing **4. ART OF DANCING** dancing as a performance art **5.** MUSIC **MUSIC FOR DANCING** a piece of music in the rhythm of a particular type of dance **6. EVASION** evasive talk (*informal*) **7.** ZOOL **PATTERN OF ANIMAL MOVEMENTS** a pattern of animal movements used, e.g., in courtship by birds or by bees to give information about food ■ *adj.* **OF OR FOR DANCING** relating to, involving, or created for dancing [13thC. From Old French, of uncertain origin: perhaps via Vulgar Latin from Frankish.]

dance·a·ble /dánsəb'l/ *adj.* suitable for or conducive to dancing

dance band *n.* a band that plays music for dancing

dance card *n.* **1. AGENDA** a list of demands on somebody's time (*informal*) **2. LIST OF DANCE PARTNERS** a card on which people wrote the names of their dancing partners at a formal dance or ball in the past

dance floor *n.* an area of uncarpeted floor for dancing

dance hall *n.* **1. PLACE WHERE DANCES ARE HELD** a building or large room where public dances are held **2.** MUSIC **DANCE MUSIC ACCOMPANIED BY DISK JOCKEY** electronically produced dance music that combines different kinds of popular music styles with continuous accompaniment by a disk jockey talking or rapping to the rhythm

dance mu·sic *n.* **1. MUSIC FOR DANCING** any music suitable for dancing **2. ELECTRONIC POP MUSIC** pop music that is typically characterized by repeated electronic rhythms

dance of death, **Dance of Death** *n.* an allegorical representation in medieval art, literature, and music of a dance in which Death, personified as a skeleton, leads people to the grave

danc·er /dánsər/ *n.* **1. PERSON DANCING** a person who dances, usually in a specified way, or who is dancing **2. PERSON PAID TO DANCE** a person who dances as a professional artist

danc·er·cise /dánsər sīz/ *n.* aerobic exercise in the form of dance [Mid-20thC. Blend of DANCE and EXERCISE.]

dance·wear /dáns wàir/ *n.* clothing, such as leotards and leg warmers, worn for dance practice

danc·ing /dánsing/ *n.* the activity of performing or taking part in a dance

dan·cy /dánsee/ **(-ci·er, -ci·est)** *adj.* conducive to dancing, especially in a lively manner

D and C *n.* a gynecological surgical procedure in which the cervix is widened and some of the womb lining is scraped out, for diagnostic or treatment purposes or in an abortion. Full form **dilatation and curettage**

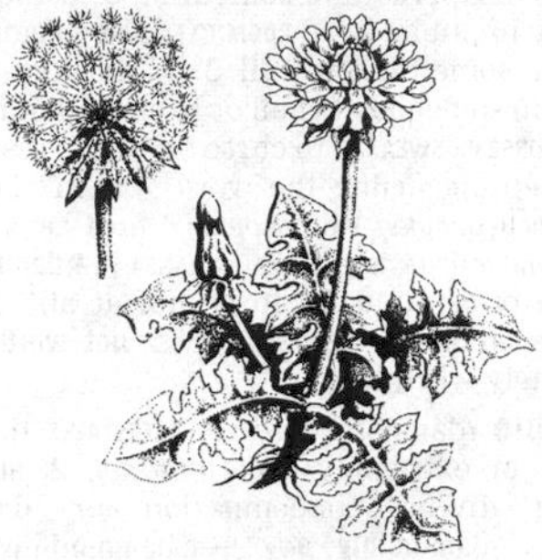

Dandelion

dan·de·li·on /dánd'l ī ən/ *n.* a common plant that has bright yellow flowers on a hollow stalk. Its seed head is white and fluffy and its leaves are used in salads, medicine, and winemaking. Latin name: *Taraxacum officinale.* [15thC. From French *dent de lion,* "lion's tooth," translating Latin *dens leonis.* Because of the plant's toothed leaves.]

dan·de·li·on greens *npl.* the tender leaves of young dandelion plants, eaten raw in salads or cooked as a vegetable

dan·der /dándər/ *n.* **1. SCALES OF HAIR OR FEATHERS** minute particles or scales that are shed from the feathers, hair, or skin of various animals. They may be the cause of some allergies, especially asthma. **2.** *Ireland* = **dandruff** [Late 18thC. Origin uncertain.] ◇ **get somebody's dander up** to make somebody angry

Dandie Dinmont

Dan·die Din·mont /dàndi dín mònt, -dínmənt/, **Dan·die Din·mont ter·ri·er** *n.* a small terrier of a breed from the Scottish borders with a long body, short legs, drooping ears, and a long wiry grayish or brownish coat [Early 19thC. Named for a character who owned six such dogs in *Guy Mannering,* a novel by Sir Walter Scott.]

dan·di·fy /dándə fī/ **(-fied, -fy·ing, -fies)** *vt.* to dress somebody as or cause somebody to resemble a dandy or fop —**dan·di·fi·ca·tion** /dàndəfi káysh'n/ *n.* —**dan·di·fied** /dándə fīd/ *adj.*

dan·dle /dánd'l/ **(-dled, -dling, -dles)** *vt.* **1. MOVE GENTLY UP AND DOWN** to move a baby or small child gently up and down in your arms or on your knees **2. FONDLE OR PET** to fondle or pet somebody or something [Mid-16thC. Origin uncertain: perhaps a variant of DANGLE.] —**dan·dler** *n.*

dan·druff /dándrəf/ *n.* loose dry scales of dead skin that are shed from the scalp [Mid-16thC. From *dand-,* of unknown origin, and *-ruff,* of uncertain origin: probably from English dialect *huff* "scab," from Scandinavian.] —**dan·druff·y** *adj.*

dan·dy /dándee/ *adj.* **(-di·er, -di·est) 1. EXCELLENT** very good, excellent, or first-rate (*informal*) **2. CHARACTERISTIC OF A DANDY** dressed or acting like a dandy ■ *n.* (*plural* **-dies**) **1. EXCELLENT PERSON OR THING** a person or thing considered to be very good or the best in its class (*informal*) **2. MAN TOO CONCERNED WITH APPEARANCE** a man who is much concerned with his elegant appearance (*dated*) **3.** SAILING **SAILBOAT** a ketch or yawl **4.** PAPER = **dandy roll** [Late 18thC. Shortening of Scottish *Jack-a-dandy,* "affected man," from *Dandy,* a Scots form of the name *Andrew.*] —**dan·di·ly** *adv.* —**dan·dy·ish** *adj.* —**dan·dy·ism** *n.*

dan·dy fe·ver *n.* = **dengue**

dan·dy roll, **dan·dy** (*plural* **-dies**), **dan·dy roll·er** *n.* a wire cylinder used in papermaking to produce a watermark

Dane /dayn/ *n.* **1. SOMEBODY FROM DENMARK** somebody who was born or raised in or is a citizen of Denmark **2. SOMEBODY OF DANISH DESCENT** a person of Danish descent [14thC. From Old Norse *Danir* (plural) "Danes."]

Dane·geld /dáyn gèld/, **Dane·gelt** /-gèlt/ *n.* **1.** HISTORY **HISTORICAL TAX** an annual tax first levied in the 10th century in England to buy off Danish invaders. It continued until the 12th century as a land tax. **2. PROTECTION MONEY** a payment made in order to avoid trouble or to prevent attack from a stronger enemy [Pre-12thC. From assumed Old Norse *Danagiald,* literally "payment of the Danes," from *Danir* (plural) "Danes" + *giald* "payment."]

Dane·law /dáyn làw/ *n.* **1. LAWS ENFORCED BY DANES IN ENGLAND** the body of laws established in the parts of England settled in the 9th century by Danish invaders **2. ANGLO-SAXON ENGLAND UNDER DANISH LAW** the parts of Anglo-Saxon England that came under Danish law and where Danish customs were observed [Old English *Dena lagu* "Danes' law"]

dang /dang/ *interj., adj., adv., vti.* **(danged, dang·ing, dangs)** = **damn** [Late 18thC. Euphemistic alteration.]

danged /dangd/ *adj., adv.* = **damned** [Late 19thC. Euphemistic alteration.]

dan·ger /dáynjər/ *n.* **1. EXPOSURE TO HARM** exposure or vulnerability to harm, injury, or loss ○ *Their lives were in danger.* **2. SOMEBODY OR SOMETHING THAT CAUSES HARM** somebody or something that may cause harm, injury, or loss (*often used in the plural*) [13thC. Via Anglo-Norman *daunger* from, ultimately, assumed Vulgar Latin *domniarium* "power to do harm," from Latin *dominium,* "sovereignty," which was in turn formed from *dominus,* "lord."]

dan·ger mon·ey *n. U.K.* = **hazard pay**

dan·ger·ous /dáynjərəss/ *adj.* **1. LIKELY TO CAUSE HARM** likely to cause or result in harm or injury **2. INVOLVING RISK** involving risk or difficulty ○ *The business is in a dangerous financial position.* —**dan·ger·ous·ly** *adv.* —**dan·ger·ous·ness** *n.*

dan·gle /dáng g'l/ *v.* **(-gled, -gling, -gles) 1.** *vti.* **HANG OR CAUSE TO HANG LOOSELY** to swing or hang loosely or cause something to swing or hang loosely ○ *The children dangled their legs over the side of the swimming pool.* **2.** *vt.* **OFFER AS INDUCEMENT** to offer or display something as an enticement or inducement ○ *The possibility of promotion was dangled before her.* **3.** *vi.* **HANG AROUND SOMEBODY** to hang around somebody ○ *The famous film director had many aspiring actors dangling after her.* ■ *n.* **1. DANGLING THING** something that dangles, especially a charm from a bracelet or necklace **2. ACT OF DANGLING** the act or an instance of dangling [Late 16thC. Thought to suggest the action.] —**dan·gler** *n.* —**dan·gly** *adj.*

dan·gling par·ti·ci·ple *n.* a participle that is not grammatically linked to the word it is intended to modify. In "Driving down the street, the house came into view," "driving" is a dangling participle.

WORD KEY: USAGE

Dangling participles: Also called "misplaced" or "unattached participles," these typically occur at the beginning of sentences and modify either the wrong thing or nothing in particular: *Startled by the noise, her book fell to the floor* (it was she, not her book, who was startled). *Lying in the sun, it was hard to imagine the winter back home* (who was lying in the sun?). Such mismatches should be corrected by rephrasing: *Startled by the noise, she dropped her book* and *lying in the sun, he found it hard to imagine the winter back home.* A number of dangling participles, however, are well established and idiomatic, for example, *given, granting,* and *speaking*: *Given that dividends depend on earnings, what determines earnings?* Other similar words, including *considering* and *regarding,* are so well established in such contexts that they are generally thought of as independent of the verbs from which they sprang and are now said to be prepositions.

dan grade *n.* = **dan**[1] *n.* **1**

Dan·iel /dánnyəl/ *n.* **1. BIBLICAL PROPHET** a biblical prophet whose faith in God protected him in the lion's den **2. BOOK OF BIBLE** the book of the Bible that tells the story of Daniel **3. WISE PERSON** somebody who is wise and honorable [Late 16thC. "Wise person" from the presentation of Daniel as a wise judge in the apocryphal Book of Susanna.]

Dan·iels /dánnyəlz/, **Josephus** (1862–1948) U.S. editor, publisher, and statesman. He served as secretary of the navy (1913–21) and U.S. ambassador to Mexico (1933–41).

da·ni·o /dáynee ō/ (*plural* **-os**) *n.* a brightly colored freshwater fish native to India and Sri Lanka that is kept as an aquarium fish. Genera: *Danio* and *Brachydanio.* [Late 19thC. From modern Latin, the genus name.]

Dan·ish /dáynish/ *adj.* **OF DENMARK** relating to or typical of Denmark or its people, culture, or language ■ *n.* LANG **LANGUAGE OF DANES** the language of Denmark, also an official language of the Faroe Islands and Greenland. It belongs to the North Germanic group of Indo-European languages. Danish is spoken by over five million people. ■ *npl.* PEOPLES **PEOPLE FROM DENMARK** people who were born or raised in or are citizens of Denmark ■ *n.* **Dan·ish, dan·ish** FOOD = **Danish pastry** [14thC. Formed from *Danes* (plural) "Danes," from Old Icelandic *Danir.*]

Dan·ish blue *n.* a blue-veined cheese with a strong taste, originally produced in Denmark

Dan·ish pas·try *n.* a rich puff pastry made from a yeast dough with a sweet filling containing fruit or nuts

Dan·ite /dá nīt/ *n.* in the Hebrew Bible, a member of the tribe descended from Dan —**Dan·ite** *adj.*

dank /dangk/ *adj.* unpleasantly damp and cold [14thC. Origin uncertain: probably from Scandinavian.] —**dank·ly** *adv.* —**dank·ness** *n.*

WORD KEY: SYNONYMS

See Synonyms at ***wet.***

danse ma·ca·bre /daàns mə kaábrə/ (*plural* **danses ma·ca·bres**) *n.* = **dance of death** [Late 19thC. From French, literally "macabre dance."]

dan·seur /dan súr, daaN súr/ *n.* a male ballet dancer [Early 19thC. From French, "male dancer."]

dan·seuse /dan so͞oz, daaN so͞oz/ *n.* a woman ballet dancer [Early 19thC. From French, "woman dancer."]

Dan·te A·li·ghi·e·ri /daàn tay alli gyérree/ (1265–1321) Italian poet. One of the greatest poets in world literature, he is best known for his epic masterpiece *The Divine Comedy,* which he began writing in 1307 and completed shortly before his death. He was involved in the political struggles of his time, which forced him to leave his native Florence. He finally settled in Ravenna.

Dan·te·an /dántee ən, daántee-/ *adj.* **1. OF OR BY DANTE** relating to Dante Alighieri or his works **2. DANTESQUE** in the style of the works of Dante Alighieri ■ *n.* **ADMIRER OR STUDENT OF DANTE ALIGHIERI** a person who admires, studies, or is an expert on Dante Alighieri

Dan·tesque /dan tésk, daan-/ *adj.* in the style of the works of Dante Alighieri

Dan·ton /daan táwN/, **Georges Jacques** (1759–94) French lawyer. Minister of Justice in Revolutionary France, he was overthrown in the Reign of Terror (1793) and guillotined the following year.

Dan·ube /dán yo͞ob/ the longest river in western Europe. It rises in the Black Forest in southwestern Germany and flows through Austria, the Czech Republic, Slovakia, Hungary, Croatia, Yugoslavia, Bulgaria, Romania, and Ukraine. It empties into the Black Sea. Length: 1,770 mi./2,850 km. —**Dan·u·bi·an** /də nyo͞obee ən/ *adj.*

Dan·vers /dánvərz/ town in northeastern Massachusetts, southwest of Gloucester and northeast of Boston. Population: 24,467 (1996).

Dan·ville /dán vìl/ **1.** city in Illinois, just east of the Illinois-Indiana border, east of Urbana. Population: 32,163 (1996). **2.** city in central Kentucky, east of Elizabethtown and southwest of Lexington. Population: 16,059 (1996).

Dan·zig /dánsig, daánt sik/ former name for **Gdansk**

dap /dap/ (**dapped, dap·ping, daps**) *v.* **1.** *vi.* ANGLING **FISH WITH BOBBING BAIT** to fish by bobbing the bait lightly on the surface of the water **2.** *vi.* **DIP QUICKLY** to dip gently or quickly into water **3.** *vti.* **BOUNCE OR SKIP** to bounce or skip, or cause something to bounce or skip, especially across the surface of water **4.** *vt.* WOODWORK **JOIN WITH A NOTCH** to cut a notch in timber in order to join it to another piece [Mid-17thC. Thought to suggest the action.]

daph·ne /dáfnee/ (*plural* **-nes** *or* **-ne**) *n.* a European and Asian shrub that is often cultivated as an ornamental garden plant for its glossy evergreen leaves and fragrant bell-shaped pink or purplish flowers. Genus: *Daphne.* [15thC. From Greek *daphnē,* "laurel, bay tree." Named for *Daphne,* a nymph in Greek mythology who was changed into such a tree to escape Apollo's attentions.]

daph·ni·a /dafnee ə/ (*plural* **-as** *or* **-a**) *n.* a tiny freshwater flea with a transparent shell and branched antennae for swimming. Some types are used as food for aquarium fish. Genus: *Daphnia.* [Mid-19thC. From modern Latin, where it was formed from *daphne,* genus name, named for *Daphne* (see DAPHNE).]

dap·per /dáppər/ *adj.* **1. TRIM** neat and elegant (*refers to men*) **2. LIVELY** alert and lively or brisk **3. NIMBLE** small and active or nimble [15thC. From Middle Dutch or Middle Low German *dapper,* "bold, heavy." The modern meanings, "elegant, nimble," evolved from "stolid, sturdy," perhaps ironically.] —**dap·per·ly** *adv.* —**dap·per·ness** *n.*

dap·ple /dápp'l/ *vti.* (**-pled, -pling, -ples**) **MARK WITH PATCHES OF COLOR** to mark something with patches or spots of a different color or with light and shade, or to be marked in this way ○ *Sunlight dappled the path through the trees.* ■ *adj.* = **dappled** ■ *n.* **1. COLORED MARKINGS** spots or patches of a different color, especially on a horse, or of light and shade **2. SPOT OF COLOR** an individual spot or patch of color, light, or shade **3.** ZOOL **DAPPLED ANIMAL** an animal, especially a horse, with a dappled coat [Late 16thC. Back-formation from DAPPLED.]

dap·pled /dápp'ld/, **dap·ple** *adj.* marked with spots or patches of a different color or with light and shade ○ *in the dappled shade of the chestnut tree* [15thC. Origin uncertain: perhaps formed from DAPPLE "blotch," or perhaps ultimately from APPLE (compare French *gris-pommelé* and German *apfelgrau* "dapple-gray," literally "apple-gray"), perhaps from the shape of the fruit.]

dap·ple-gray *adj.* **OF A LIGHT GRAY COLOR** used to describe a horse or pony of a light gray color with darker gray spots or patches ■ *n.* **HORSE** a dapple-gray horse or pony [14thC. Origin uncertain: perhaps from DAPPLED (of later date, but the dates are close enough to be ignored) + GRAY; or from assumed *apple-gray* (see DAPPLED).]

Dap·sang /dap saáng/ = **K2**

dap·sone /dáp sōn/ *n.* an antibacterial drug containing sulfur, used in the treatment of leprosy and some forms of dermatitis [Mid-20thC. Contraction of *di(para-amino-phenyl)sulfone,* its technical name.]

DAR *abbr.* **1.** MIL damage assessment routine **2.** Daughters of the American Revolution

Dar·by and Joan *n.* *U.K.* a contented and devoted couple who have long lived together in domestic harmony [Late 18thC. From the names of a contented long-married couple in a poem published in the *Gentleman's Magazine* in 1735.]

Dard /daard/ *n.* a member of any of the peoples who speak a Dardic language [Mid-19thC. From Dardic.]

Dar·dic /daárdik/ *n.* a subgroup of Indic languages spoken in the mountainous northern regions of India and Pakistan. Kashmiri is the best known of the Dardic languages, of which there are about seven million speakers. —**Dar·dic** *adj.*

dare /dair/ *vt.* (**dared, dar·ing, dares** *or* **dare**) **1. HAVE ENOUGH COURAGE FOR SOMETHING** to have the courage needed to do something (*sometimes used as an auxiliary*) ○ *wanted to ask but then didn't dare* ○ *"We must dare to think about 'unthinkable things' because when things have become unthinkable, thinking stops and action becomes mindless."* (William Fulbright *U.S. Senate Speech*; March 27, 1965) **2. HAVE AUDACITY TO DO SOMETHING** to do something that angers or outrages somebody (*sometimes used as an auxiliary*) ○ *Don't you dare do that!* ○ *How dare you?* **3. CHALLENGE SOMEBODY** to challenge somebody to do something, usually something dangerous or frightening ○ *daring each other to jump first* ■ *n.* **A CHALLENGE** a challenge to somebody to do something dangerous or frightening, or a response to such a challenge ○ *did it for a dare* [Old English *darr, dearr,* first and third person present singular forms of *durran* "to dare," from prehistoric Germanic] —**dar·er** *n.*

Dare /dair/, **Virginia** (1587–?) American colonist. She was the first child born to English colonists in North America. She had disappeared with the Roanoke Island colonists by 1590.

dare·dev·il /dáir dèvv'l/ *n.* **SOMEBODY WHO DOES RISKY THINGS** somebody who is daring and takes risks, especially somebody who performs dangerous stunts ■ *adj.* **1. UNMINDFUL OF DANGER** showing a carefree disregard for risk or danger, especially by performing dangerous stunts **2. DANGEROUS** with a high degree of risk or danger ○ *a daredevil stunt*

dare·dev·il·ry /dáir dèvv'lree/, **dare·dev·il·try** /-tree/ *n.* **1. FEARLESS ATTITUDE** a carefree disregard for danger **2. RISK-TAKING** dangerous acts or stunts performed by a daring person

dare·say /dáir sày/ ◇ **I daresay 1.** used, often in an irritable tone, to express the fact that the speaker considers something to be likely or possible **2.** used impatiently to dismiss something that is true but irrelevant

Dar es Sa·laam /daàr es sə laàm/ largest city, leading port, and former capital of Tanzania. The name means "haven of peace." Population: 1,360,850 (1988).

dar·ing /dáirring/ *adj.* **1. BRAVE AND ADVENTUROUS** showing a courageous or reckless disregard for danger ○ *The officer led a daring assault on the enemy machine-gun nest.* **2. RISKY** involving an element of risk or danger ○ *a daring move* **3. SHOCKING** unconventional or ahead of its time and therefore likely to shock, upset, or offend ■ *n.* **BOLDNESS** courage combined with a willingness to take risks or attempt difficult or unconventional things —**dar·ing·ly** *adv.* —**dar·ing·ness** *n.*

WORD KEY: SYNONYMS

See Synonyms at ***bold.***

dar·i·ole /dérri ōl/ *n.* **1. dar·i·ole, dar·i·ole mold COOKING MOLD** a small cup-shaped mold in which individual portions of savory or sweet dishes can be cooked and then served **2. DISH COOKED IN SMALL MOLD** a dish cooked and served in a dariole [14thC. From French, "custard tart."]

Da·ri·us I /də rī́ əss/, **King of Persia** (558–486 B.C.). He reorganized the administration of the Persian Empire during his reign (521–486 B.C.). His army invaded Greece in 490 but was defeated at the battle of Marathon.

Da·ri·us III, King of Persia (380?–330 B.C.). He was defeated by Alexander the Great at the battles of Issus (333 B.C.) and Guagamela (331 B.C.) and was assassinated by one of his own satraps.

Dar·jee·ling[1] /daar jéeling/ *n.* a high-quality black tea grown around Darjeeling in India, or the hot drink made from its leaves

Dar·jee·ling[2] /daar jéeling/ town in northern West Bengal, India, close to the border with Nepal. Under British rule it was the summer capital of the government of Bengal. It is famous for its tea plantations. Population: 73,078 (1991).

dark /daark/ *adj.* **1. NOT LIGHT OR LIT** with little or no light ○ *It's getting dark; do you mind if I put the light on?* ○ *It was a dark and stormy night.* **2. NOT LIGHT IN COLOR** reflecting less light than other colors or shades and therefore appearing deeper, richer, or more somber ○ *The curtains are dark green.* **3. BROWNISH OR BLACKISH** not pale or fair, but brown to black in hair or eye color ○ *She has darker eyes than her brother.* **4. MISERABLE** characterized by unhappiness, misfortune, or pessimism ○ *in the dark days of the Depression* **5. ANGRY** suggesting hostility or anger ○ *dark looks* **6. NASTY** evil or wicked ○ *the dark side of his character* **7. MYSTERIOUS** little known or kept hidden from others ○ *dark secrets* **8. UNENLIGHTENED** lacking enlightenment, learning, and artistic or scientific achievement (*formal*) **9.** THEATER **CLOSED** not presenting theatrical performances **10. MELLOW** deep and rich in sound ■ *n.* **1. LACK OF LIGHT** a place, time, or situation in which there is too little light to see properly ○ *I don't like driving in the dark.* **2. NIGHTFALL** the beginning of night ○ *We left early to be home before dark.* **3. SHADED AREA** a darker color or a darker-colored or shaded part ○ *the contrast between the darks and the lights in the picture* [Old English *deorc.* Ultimately from an Indo-European word that also produced German *tarnen* "to mask, screen," which is related via Old French to English *tarnish.*]

dark ad·ap·ta·tion, **dark a·dap·tion** *n.* the reflex changes, such as dilation of the pupil and increased sensitivity of the retina, that enable the eye to continue to see in dim light

dark-a·dapt·ed *adj.* ANAT having made the physical and chemical changes involved in dark adaptation and adjusted for seeing in relative darkness

Dark-Age *adj.* dating from, belonging to, or typical of the Dark Ages

Dark Ag·es *npl.* **1.** HIST **PERIOD BEFORE MIDDLE AGES** the period of European history between the fall of the Roman Empire in A.D. 476 and about A.D. 1000, for which there are few historical records and during which life was comparatively uncivilized **2. UNDEVELOPED STATE** an undeveloped state, way of life, or way of doing things (*informal*) ○ *Computers were in their Dark Ages a few decades ago.*

dark choc·o·late *n.* chocolate that has no added milk and is darker and less sweet than milk chocolate

Dark Con·ti·nent *n.* a term formerly used to refer to Africa before large areas of the continent had been explored (*archaic*) [Probably taken from the title of Henry M. Stanley's *Through the Dark Continent* (1878), most of central Africa being unknown and mysterious to Europeans of the time.]

dark·en /daárkən/ (**-ened, -en·ing, -ens**) *vti.* **1. GET DARKER OR COLOR SOMETHING DARKER** to become darker, or to make something darker ○ *I mixed a little blue and brown with the red to darken it.* **2. BECOME UNHAPPY OR MAKE SOMEBODY UNHAPPY** to become unhappy, less hopeful, or angry, or to cause such a change in somebody or something ○ *The outlook has darkened considerably since the last update.* —**dark·en·er** *n.*

dark-field il·lu·mi·na·tion *n.* the lighting of a specimen in a microscope from the side so that it can be seen against a dark background

dark-field mi·cro·scope *n.* = **ultramicroscope**

dark glass·es *npl.* eyeglasses with dark-tinted lenses, especially sunglasses

dark horse *n.* **1. UNKNOWN QUANTITY** somebody about whom very little is known or who tends to be reticent, especially somebody who subsequently reveals unexpected talents **2.** POL **UNEXPECTEDLY SUCCESSFUL CANDIDATE** a candidate who gains an unexpected amount of support in an electoral campaign **3.** SPORTS **UNEXPECTEDLY SUCCESSFUL CONTESTANT** a little-known competitor who achieves unexpected success in a race or other sports contest [From the image of a little-known racehorse who makes a surprisingly good showing in a race]

dark·ish /daárkish/ *adj.* fairly dark in color or shading ○ *a woman with darkish hair*

dark lan·tern *n.* a lantern with a sliding panel that is used to dim or hide its light

dar·kle /daárkəl/ (**-kled, -kling, -kles**) *vi.* (*archaic or literary*) **1. BECOME DARK** to grow dark **2. BE FAINT** to appear indistinctly [Early 19thC. Back-formation from DARKLING, adverb, mistaken for a present participle and adjective.]

dar·kling /daárkling/ *adv.* **IN DARKNESS** in the dark (*archaic literary*) ○ *"Darkling I listen, and full many a time... "* (John Keats, *Ode to a Nightingale*; 1820) ■ *adj.* (*archaic or literary*) **1. WITHOUT CLARITY** dark, dim, or obscure **2. OCCURRING IN DARKNESS** done or happening in the night [15thC. Formed from DARK + the obsolete adverbial suffix *-ling*, denoting position or condition.]

dar·kling bee·tle *n.* a beetle with a hard black or brown body whose larvae feed on decaying vegetable matter, living plants, and grain. Family: Tenebrionidae. [Probably from the beetle's habit of living in dark or hidden places]

dark·ly /daárklee/ *adv.* **1. THREATENINGLY** in a way that conveys a threat or a sense of foreboding **2. IN BLACK OR A DARK COLOR** in or with black, or as a dark-colored shape ○ *trees darkly outlined against the horizon*

dark mat·ter *n.* matter postulated to exist in the universe because of observed gravitational effects. It is thought to comprise a substantial part of the mass of the universe but remains as yet undetected by direct observation. [From the nonluminous and mysterious nature of the matter]

dark meat *n.* meat from the legs and thighs of poultry, which is a darker color than the meat of the breast

dark·ness /daárknəss/ *n.* **1. DARK** the absence or lack of light ○ *He flicked a switch and the room was plunged into darkness.* **2. NIGHT** nighttime **3. DEPTH OF COLOR** the comparative depth of a color or its closeness to black [Old English *deorcnes*]

dark re·ac·tion *n.* the second phase of photosynthesis, during which light is not required and carbon dioxide is reduced

dark·room /daárk room, -ro͝om/ *n.* a room from which natural light is excluded so that light-sensitive photographic materials can be safely handled and photographs can be developed

dark·some /daárksəm/ *adj.* without light and gloomy or unpleasant (*archaic or literary*) ○ *doomed to die in a darksome dungeon*

dark star *n.* a star that is not visible and is usually detectable only by its radio or infrared emissions or by its gravitational effect on other bodies. It is often a component of a binary star and can cause the brightness of its visible partner to vary periodically.

dar·ling /daárling/ *n.* **1. LOVING TERM OF ADDRESS** used as an affectionate form of address to a loved one, or as a general, informal, and sometimes slightly affected form of address to social acquaintances **2. SOMEBODY CONSIDERATE** a kind, helpful, or likable person **3. INFORMAL TERM OF ADDRESS** an extremely informal and typically suggestive term of address, often to a stranger (*informal*) **4. FAVORITE** somebody who is very popular with another person or with a particular group of people ○ *She's the darling of the literary reviews.* **5. BELOVED PERSON** a much-loved person or sweetheart (*dated*) ○ *She is my darling.* ■ *adj.* **1. DEARLY LOVED** loved very much **2. NICE** pretty and charming (*informal*) [Old English *deorling*, literally "dear person, dear one," formed from an earlier form of DEAR]

darn[1] /daarn/ *vti.* (**darned, darn·ing, darns**) **REPAIR SOMETHING WITH THREAD** to mend a hole in a piece of clothing or fabric using long interwoven stitches to fill the gap ○ *sat there darning socks.* ■ *n.* **REPAIR OF HOLE** a repair to a piece of clothing or fabric using long interwoven stitches [Early 17thC. Origin uncertain: probably from French dialect *darner* "to mend," from *darne* "piece," ultimately of Celtic origin.] —**darn·er** *n.*

darn[2] /daarn/ *interj.* **EXCLAMATION** used instead of a swearword to express irritation, displeasure, or surprise (*informal*) ■ *adj., adv.* **darn, darned EMPHATIC TERM** used instead of a swearword to give emphasis or to indicate irritation or displeasure with somebody or something (*informal*) ○ *a darn good movie* ■ *vt.* (**darned, darn·ing, darns**) **CONDEMN SOMETHING** used to express annoyance or frustration with something or somebody (*informal*) ○ *Darn it, I told you not to go in there.* [Late 18thC. Alteration of DAMN, perhaps influenced by regional "tarnal," alteration of ETERNAL.]

dar·na·tion /daar náysh'n/ *interj.* **EXCLAMATION** used instead of a swearword to express anger, disappointment, or frustration (*dated informal*) ○ *Darnation! I just hit my thumb again.* ■ *n.* **EXPRESSION OF ANNOYANCE** used to give emphasis to a question asked in irritation (*dated informal*) ○ *Where in darnation did I put that bag of corn?*

darned /daarnd/ *adj.* **TERM OF DENIAL** used instead of a swearword to express surprise, bafflement, disavowal, or refusal (*informal*) ○ *I'll be darned if I know.* ■ *adj., adv.* = **darn**[2] (*informal*)

darned·est /daárndəst/ *adj.* used to emphasize or draw to somebody's attention something that is unusual or out of the ordinary (*informal*)

darn·ing /daárning/ *n.* **1. MENDING HOLES IN CLOTHES** the work of repairing holes in clothes with long interwoven stitches **2. CLOTHING IN NEED OF MENDING** clothes that need to be darned

darn·ing nee·dle *n.* **1.** SEW **NEEDLE USED FOR DARNING** a long needle with a large eye, used in darning **2.** INSECTS **INSECT** a dragonfly (*regional*)

WORD KEY: REGIONAL NOTE

In the sense "dragonfly," ***darning needle*** is Northern, being found from New England to the Pacific states including California. The expanded form *devil's darning needle* occurs across the same territory, but less frequently. Neither term has currency in the Midlands, where *snake feeder* and *snake doctor* identify the dragonfly, as do *mosquito hawk* and *skeeter hawk* in the lower South.

Darn·ley /daárnlee/, **Henry Stewart, Lord** (1545–67) Scottish nobleman. He was the second husband of Mary, Queen of Scots, and father of James VI of Scotland, who later became James I of England.

DARPA /daárpə/ *abbr.* Defense Advanced Research Projects Agency

Dar·row /dérrō/, **Clarence** (1857–1938) U.S. lawyer. A defender of the "underdog" in controversial legal cases, he is best known for his defense of John T. Scopes, a schoolteacher charged in Tennessee with having violated a law banning the teaching of evolutionary theory in the public schools (1925). Full name **Clarence Seward Darrow**

dart /daart/ *n.* **1.** DARTS **MISSILE USED IN DARTS** a short weighted arrow with a long slender point, a tapered tubular body, and plastic or metal fins that is thrown at a dartboard in the game of darts **2.** ARMS **MISSILE USED AS WEAPON** a small arrow with a point at one end and feathers or fins at the other that can be thrown, shot from a blowgun, or scattered by an exploding bomb **3.** ZOOL **POINTED, PROJECTING PART OR ORGAN** a pointed, projecting part used, e.g., to penetrate tissue, or, in some species of snail, in mating **4. FAST MOVE** a sudden quick movement ○ *He made a dart for the door.* **5.** SEW **STITCHED TAPERING FOLD** a tapering fold sewn into a garment to make it fit, e.g., at the waist or bust ■ *v.* (**dart·ed, dart·ing, darts**) **1.** *vi.* **MOVE SWIFTLY** to move suddenly and quickly ○ *The little fish darted under a stone.* **2.** *vt.* **MAKE SOMETHING MOVE QUICKLY** to move, extend, or direct something quickly and suddenly ○ *She darted a meaningful glance at her husband across the table.* [14thC. Via Old French from a prehistoric Germanic word, from, ultimately, an Indo-European word meaning "sharp."]

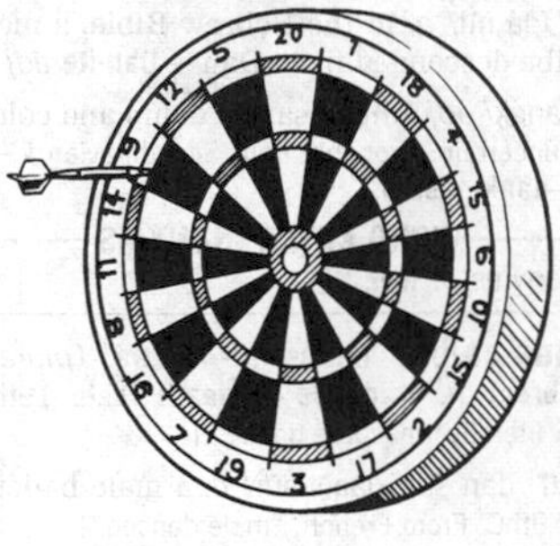

Dartboard

dart·board /daárt bàwrd/ *n.* a round piece of wood or similar material marked with twenty radiating numbered segments and a bull's eye in the center, used as a target in the game of darts

dart·er /daártər/ *n.* **1. N AMERICAN FISH** a small brightly colored fast-moving freshwater fish of the perch family, found in eastern North America. Family: *Percidae.* **2.** *U.K.* = **anhinga 3. SOMEBODY OR SOMETHING THAT DARTS** somebody or something that moves quickly and suddenly

dart·ing /daárting/ *adj.* swift and sudden, or making swift and sudden movements ○ *the darting movements of the dancers' feet* —**dart·ing·ly** *adv.*

Dart·mouth /daártməth/ town in southeastern Massachusetts, near Buzzards Bay, southwest of New Bedford. Population: 28,100 (1996).

darts /daarts/ *n.* an indoor game in which players take turns throwing arrow-shaped missiles (**darts**) from a set distance at a circular board (**dartboard**) placed at about eye level on a wall (*takes a singular verb*)

Dar·von *tdmk.* a trademark for propoxyphene hydrochloride

Dar·win /daárwən/ coastal city in northern Australia, capital of the Northern Territory. It was devastated by Cyclone Tracy in 1974. Population: 70,251 (1996).

Dar·win, Charles (1809–82) British scientist. He laid the foundation for modern evolutionary theory and wrote the highly controversial *On the Origin of Species by Means of Natural Selection* (1859). He wrote many other books on the natural sciences, including *The Volcanic Islands* (1844) and *The Descent of Man* (1871). Full name **Charles Robert Darwin**

Dar·win·i·an /daar wínnee ən/ *adj.* relating to the 19th-century British naturalist Charles Darwin or his theory of evolution —**Dar·win·i·an** *n.*

Dar·win·i·an the·o·ry *n.* the theory, first developed by the 19th-century British naturalist Charles Darwin, that species of living things originate, evolve, and survive through natural selection in response to environmental forces

Dar·win·ism /dáarwi nìzzəm/ *n.* **1.** = **Darwinian theory** **2. SUPPORT FOR DARWIN'S THEORY** belief in or advocacy of Charles Darwin's theory of evolution —**Dar·win·ist** *n., adj.*

Dar·win's finch·es *npl.* the birds of the Galapagos Islands on which Charles Darwin based his theory of evolution through observation of their feeding habits and corresponding differences in bill structure. Subfamily: Geospizinae.

dash /dash/ *n.* **1.** GRAM **PUNCTUATION MARK** a short horizontal line used as a punctuation mark, often in place of a comma or colon, or as a sign that certain letters or words have been omitted **2.** COMMUNICATION **MORSE SYMBOL** a short horizontal line representing a long sound or flash of light in written transcriptions of Morse code **3. RUSH** a quick purposeful movement by a person or a group of people in any direction ○ *There was a dash for the exit as soon as the alarm was raised.* **4.** SPORT **RACE** a short-distance running race **5. SMALL QUANTITY ADDED** a small quantity of something added to something else, e.g., to improve the flavor of food or drink or to enliven speech or writing ○ *A dash of common sense would make his arguments a lot more convincing.* **6. VIGOR AND VERVE** a combination of vigor, daring, and style in the way a person acts ○ *She carried it off with a certain amount of dash.* **7.** CARS **DASHBOARD** the instrument panel of a car (*informal*) **8. QUICK STROKE** a quick and often violent movement, blow, or stroke ○ *with a dash of her arm* ■ *v.* (**dashed, dash·ing, dash·es**) **1.** *vi.* **HURRY** to run, move, or travel fast or hastily ○ *He dashed off to catch his plane.* **2.** *vt.* **KNOCK OR THROW SOMETHING VIOLENTLY** to knock or throw something with a sudden violent sweep or blow (*formal*) ○ *She dashed the papers down on the desk in anger.* **3.** *vti.* **SMASH** to break or throw something or to be broken or thrown, usually against a hard surface (*formal*) ○ *The waves were dashing against the sea wall.* **4.** *vt.* **RUIN SOMETHING** to frustrate or destroy something (*often passive*) ○ *The new crisis has dashed all hopes of a speedy return to democratic government.* **5.** *vt.* **DISCOURAGE SOMEBODY** to make somebody feel discouraged or intimidated (*usually passive*) ○ *I felt more than a little dashed by the ease with which she had refuted my arguments.* **6.** *vt.* **ADD SMALL AMOUNT TO SOMETHING** to alter, improve, or flavor with a small amount of another substance (*often passive*) ○ *tonic water dashed with bitters* **7.** *vt.* **EXCLAIM AGAINST SOMETHING OR SOMEBODY** used to express annoyance or dissatisfaction with something or somebody (*dated informal*) ○ *Dash it, I've already paid the man!* [13thC. Origin uncertain: perhaps from Old Norse (compare Swedish *daska* "to slap, beat"). Originally a verb meaning "to smash to pieces"; the meaning evolved via the idea of quick movement.]

dash off *vt.* to write, draw, or compose something in a great hurry (*informal*) ○ *She dashed off a note to her secretary before leaving the office.*

dash·board /dásh bàwrd/ *n.* **1. PANEL IN FRONT OF DRIVER** a panel in front of the driver of a vehicle or the pilot of a small aircraft or boat that contains various indicator dials, switches, and controls **2. MUDGUARD ON CARRIAGE** a board, panel, or screen to protect the driver of a horse-drawn carriage from being splashed with mud [Mid-19thC. From DASH in the obsolete sense "to splash, spatter."]

da·sheen /da sheén/ *n. Carib* **1.** = **taro** **2. BOILED TUBERS** tubers of the dasheen plant, usually boiled for eating [Late 19thC. Origin uncertain: perhaps an alteration of French *(chou) de Chine* "Chinese (cabbage)."]

dash·er /dáshər/ *n.* a device that agitates or stirs the contents of a churn or ice-cream maker

da·shi /daáshee/ *n.* a clear broth or stock, usually made from fish [Mid-20thC. From Japanese.]

da·shi·ki /də sheékee/, **dai·shi·ki** /dī-/, **da·she·ki** /-shékee/ *n.* a man's brightly colored loose-fitting buttonless garment resembling a long shirt, worn mainly in Africa, the Caribbean, and the United States [Mid-20thC. Origin uncertain: probably from Yoruba *danshiki*.]

dash·ing /dáshing/ *adj.* **1. SPIRITED** confident and full of bravado and spirit (*dated*) ○ *a dashing young officer* **2. SMART** smart and stylish ○ *That's a rather dashing outfit, if I may say so.* —**dash·ing·ly** *adv.* —**dash·ing·ness** *n.*

dash·pot /dásh pòt/ *n.* a device consisting of a piston inside a fluid-filled cylinder that absorbs or dampens vibrations in a mechanism

das·sie /dássee/ *n.* ZOOL = **hyrax** [Late 18thC. Via Afrikaans from Dutch *dasje*, literally "small badger," from *das* "badger."]

das·tard /dástərd/ *n.* somebody who is cowardly, mean, and treacherous (*archaic*) [15thC. Origin uncertain: probably formed from Middle English *dast*, a form of the past participle of DAZE + -ARD. The original meaning was "unintelligent person."]

das·tard·ly /dástərdlee/ *adj.* used to refer humorously or melodramatically to somebody or something mean, treacherous, and cowardly ○ *a dastardly deed* —**das·tard·li·ness** *n.*

das·y·ure /dássi yoòr/ *n.* a small usually carnivorous marsupial found in Australia, Tasmania, and neighboring islands. Subfamily: Dasyurinae. [Mid-19thC. Via French from modern Latin *dasyurus*, from Greek *dasus* "rough, hairy" + *oura* "tail."]

DAT /deè ay teé, dat/ *abbr.* digital audiotape

dat. *abbr.* dative

da·ta[1] /dáytə, dáttə/ *n.* (*takes a singular or plural verb*) **1. FACTUAL INFORMATION** information, often in the form of facts or figures obtained from experiments or surveys, used as a basis for making calculations or drawing conclusions **2.** COMPUT **INFORMATION FOR COMPUTER PROCESSING** information, e.g., numbers, text, images, and sounds, in a form that is suitable for storage in or processing by a computer [Mid-17thC. From the plural of Latin *datum*, neuter past participle of *dare* "to give, grant" (source of English *condone* and *vendor*). The original English meaning was "accepted assumptions, premises."]

WORD KEY: USAGE

Singular or plural? Use of the term ***data*** has grown apace with the use of computer technology and of statistical methods. Because the word's meaning is much like that of the singular noun *information*, and because its Latin *-a* plural announces the word's plural status to us less plainly than a final *s* would, it is often treated as if it were singular. This use is extremely common, and few perceive it as wrong these days, especially given the word's connotation of a collection or single unit made up of many informational subunits. All the same, in highly formal English, use of ***data*** as a singular is best avoided. According to the traditional view, *Our data have been assembled over a number of years* would be correct, and constructions such as *very little data, The data shows. . .* , and *a great deal of data* would be regarded as incorrect.

da·ta[2] plural of **datum**

da·ta bank *n.* **1. STORE OF INFORMATION** a large store of information, especially one that is kept in or available to a computer, sometimes consisting of a number of databases **2.** = **database**

da·ta·base /dáytə bàyss/ (**-based, -bas·ing, -bas·es**) *n.* a systematically arranged collection of computer data, structured so that it can be automatically retrieved or manipulated

da·ta·base man·age·ment sys·tem *n.* a computer program devised to design, create, manipulate, update, control, and interrogate one or more databases, often containing a proprietary query language for extracting data

da·ta cap·ture *n.* the collecting of data and entering of it in a computer, or the conversion of data into a form that can be input into a computer

da·ta com·pres·sion *n.* the encoding of data so that it requires less disk space for storage and transmission

da·ta·glove /dáytə glùv, dáttə-/ *n.* a glove equipped with sensors that feed spatial and tactile data to a computer, allowing the wearer to manipulate and explore environments in virtual reality

da·ta min·ing *n.* the locating of previously unknown patterns and relationships within data using a database application, e.g., the locating of customers with common interests in a retail establishment's database

da·ta proc·ess·ing *n.* the entering, storing, updating, and retrieving of information, using a computer

da·ta pro·tec·tion *n.* **1. PREVENTION OF MISUSE OF COMPUTER DATA** legal safeguards to prevent the misuse of information stored on a computer, particularly information relating to individuals **2. INSTALLATION OF SAFEGUARDS FOR COMPUTER DATA** the adoption of administrative, technical, or physical deterrents to safeguard the privacy, integrity, and security of computer data

da·ta ware·house *n.* a database or collection of databases from different areas of a commercial organization used as a tool for analyzing overall business strategy as opposed to routine operations

date[1] /dayt/ *n.* **1.** TIME **DAY, MONTH, AND YEAR** a phrase or string of numbers that denotes a particular day of the month or year. It usually consists of the name or number of the month, the number of the day, and the number of the year. **2.** TIME **TIME OF AN EVENT** a date used to locate a past or future event in time ○ *The concert has been postponed to a later date.* **3. VISUAL REPRESENTATION OF DATE** the words or numbers of a date in the form of a written statement or inscription, e.g., on a document or coin ○ *There's no date on this letter.* **4. PERIOD** the period during which something such as a work of art was created ○ *This has much in common with other artifacts of that date.* **5. APPOINTMENT** an appointment to meet somebody for a social or business activity ○ *I've got a dinner date with a client.* **6. ROMANTIC APPOINTMENT** a social or romantic engagement with a person ○ *I thought we had a date tonight.* **7. PARTNER ON DATE** somebody with whom a date has been arranged ○ *My date stood me up.* **8.** ARTS **COMMITMENT TO PERFORM** an engagement to give a performance ○ *Our band has a date to play at the Coliseum.* ■ **dates** *npl.* **DATES OF BIRTH AND DEATH** the years of somebody's birth and death ○ *Do you happen to know Thomas Jefferson's dates?* ■ *v.* (**dat·ed, dat·ing, dates**) **1.** *vt.* **PUT DATE ON SOMETHING** to mark something with a date, usually the current date ○ *Please sign and date the contract.* **2.** *vt.* **ASSIGN DATE TO SOMETHING** to find out or state the time or period when something was made ○ *The early works of Shakespeare are rather difficult to date precisely.* **3.** *vi.* **ORIGINATE** to have an origin in a particular time in the past ○ *We have records dating back to the 16th century.* **4.** *vi.* **GO OUT OF STYLE** to become old-fashioned ○ *This is a classic style and won't date.* **5.** *vt.* **MAKE SOMEBODY OR SOMETHING SEEM OLD** to reveal the age of somebody or something, or to make somebody or something seem old-fashioned ○ *The shape of the headlights dates the car.* **6.** *vti.* **GO ON DATES WITH SOMEBODY** to go out regularly with somebody as a social or romantic partner ○ *We dated for a few months.* [14thC. Ultimately from medieval Latin *data*, literally "given," past participle of Latin *dare* (see DATA[1]); from "(epistola) data Romae," literally "(letter) given at Rome," with the day and month appended.] —**date·a·ble** *adj.* ◇ **to date** up to the present time

date[2] /dayt/ *n.* **1.** FOOD **SMALL OVAL FRUIT** the dark-colored oval edible fruit of the date palm tree. It has sweet flesh and a single hard narrow seed. **2.** TREES = **date palm** [13thC. Via Old French from, ultimately, Greek *daktulos* "finger or toe, date"; from the resemblance of dates to fingers or toes or of the date palm's leaves to a hand.]

dat·ed /dáytəd/ *adj.* **1. OLD-FASHIONED** no longer used or in vogue, often having been current or fashionable in the recent past **2. SHOWING A DATE** with a date marked or written on it

date·less /dáytləss/ *adj.* **1. TIMELESS** unlikely to become old-fashioned or obsolete **2. LIMITLESS** with no limit in time (*archaic or literary*) ○ *"For precious friends hid in death's dateless night"* (William Shakespeare, *Sonnets*; 1609)

date·line /dáyt lìn/ *n.* a line at the head of a newspaper article or similar item giving the date and place of writing

Date Line *n.* = **International Date Line**

date palm *n.* a tall palm tree with feathery fronds, originally from North Africa and West Asia, cultivated for its edible fruit. Latin name: *Phoenix dactylifera.*

date rape *n.* an act of rape committed on a person after a date —**date-rape** *vt.*

date rape drug *n.* a drug such as gamma hydroxy butyrate that causes unconsciousness and memory loss, thereby making identification of somebody's attacker more difficult (*informal*)

date stamp *n.* a rubber stamp used to mark the date on something, or the date marked by such a stamp —**date-stamp** *vt.*

dat·ing bar *n.* = **singles bar**

da·tive /dáytiv/ *n.* **1.** GRAMMATICAL FORM a grammatical form (**case**) of nouns, pronouns, and other parts of speech in some languages that indicates the indirect object of a verb or is used after certain prepositions **2.** WORD a word in the dative ■ *adj.* IN THE DATIVE in or relating to the dative [15thC. From Latin *dativus* "of giving" (formed from *dat-*, past participle stem of *dare* "to give"; see DATA[1]), used in the phrase *dativus casus* "dative case."]

da·tive bond *n.* CHEM = **coordinate bond** [From the fact that one of the atoms gives up or yields electrons to another atom to form the bond]

da·to·lite /dátt'l ìt/ *n.* a hydrated silicate of calcium and boron found in cavities in basalt and other igneous rocks. Formula: $CaBSiO_4(OH)$. [Early 19thC. Coined from Greek *dateisthai* "to divide" + -O- + -LITE; from the divisions between its crystals.]

da·tum /dáytəm, dáttəm/ (*plural* **-ta** /dáytə, dáttə/) *n.* **1.** ITEM OF INFORMATION a single piece of information **2.** LOGIC GIVEN FACT a known or assumed fact that is used as the basis for a theory, conclusion, or inference **3.** MAPS POINT OF REFERENCE a point, line, or surface used as a basis for measurement or calculation in mapping or surveying [Mid-18thC. From Latin (see DATA[1]).]

da·tum line, **da·tum lev·el**, **da·tum plane** *n.* the horizontal plane or line from which all other heights and depths are measured or calculated on a map or chart

DATV *abbr.* digitally assisted television

daub /dawb/ *v.* (**daubed, daub·ing, daubs**) **1.** *vt.* PUT SOMETHING ON BLOTCHILY to put or spread a semiliquid substance, e.g., mud, paint, or cream, on a surface in a crude, hurried, or irregular way ○ *They had daubed slogans all over the walls.* **2.** *vti.* PAINTING PAINT CRUDELY to paint or apply paint crudely and inexpertly ■ *n.* **1.** BLOTCH a crude patch, splash, or smear of a semiliquid substance on something **2.** BAD PAINTING a painting that is considered to be badly or inexpertly done ○ *"When he first came to Rome he painted worthless daubs and gave no promise of talent."* (Henry James, *Roderick Hudson*; 1876) **3.** CONSTR SUBSTANCE FOR DAUBING a mixture of clay, lime, and chopped straw plastered onto interwoven rods or twigs to make a wall. ◊ **wattle and daub** [14thC. Via Old French *dauber* from Latin *dealbare* "to whiten over, plaster," from *albare* "to whiten," from *albus* "white" (source of English *album*).] —**daub·y** *adj.*

daube /dōb/ *n.* a dish of braised meat or vegetables, especially a traditional French dish of beef braised in wine [Early 18thC. By folk etymology (from DAUB) from French *daube*, via Italian *dobba* from Catalan *a la adoba* "stewed," ultimately from a prehistoric Germanic word meaning "to strike."]

daub·er /dáwbər/ *n.* a very bad or inexpert painter

daugh·ter /dáwtər/ *n.* **1.** FEMALE CHILD somebody's female child **2.** WOMAN OR GIRL CONNECTED WITH PLACE a woman or girl considered as a product of a place or institution (*formal*) ○ *Daughters of the American Revolution* **3.** PRODUCT OF SOMETHING something produced by or issuing from something else (*literary*) ○ *Truth is the daughter of time.* **4.** DESCENDANT a woman or girl descendant (*literary*) ○ *a daughter of Eve* **5.** PHYS NUCLIDE FORMED BY RADIOACTIVE DECAY a nuclide formed from an element by radioactive decay ■ *adj.* **1.** FORMED FROM SOMETHING ELSE formed by or from a similar thing, usually retaining close links with it and sometimes remaining subordinate to it **2.** SCI BEING AN OFFSPRING produced by a process of reproduction, replication, or division [Old English *dohtor*. Via a prehistoric Germanic word, which also produced Dutch *dochter*, German *Tochter*, and Swedish *dotter*, from an Indo-European word with descendants in Sanskrit *duhitṛ* and Greek *thugatēr*.] —**daugh·ter·less** *adj.*

daugh·ter·board /dáwtər bàwrd/ *n.* a printed circuit board that plugs into the motherboard of a computer, usually to improve the performance of a system

daugh·ter cell *n.* either of the identical cells produced when a living cell divides

daugh·ter-in-law (*plural* **daugh·ters-in-law**) *n.* the wife of your son

daugh·ter·ly /dáwtərlee/ *adj.* typical or expected of a daughter ○ *She came to regard the distinguished professor with an almost daughterly affection.* —**daugh·ter·li·ness** *n.*

Daugh·ters of the A·mer·i·can Rev·o·lu·tion *npl.* a women's patriotic society founded in 1890 by descendants of those who fought in the American Revolution. It has about 200,000 members and is based in Washington.

daunt /dawnt/ (**daunt·ed, daunt·ing, daunts**) *vt.* to make somebody feel anxious, intimidated, or discouraged (*usually passive*) ○ *The scale of the task would have daunted even the most experienced organizer.* [13thC. Via Anglo-Norman *daunter* from Latin *domitare* "to tame."] —**daunt·er** *n.*

daunt·ing /dáwnting/ *adj.* likely to discourage, intimidate, or frighten somebody ○ *You'll find the task less daunting if you divide it up into manageable sections.* —**daunt·ing·ly** *adv.*

daunt·less /dáwntləss/ *adj.* unlikely or unable to be frightened or discouraged (*literary*) ○ *We remember with admiration their dauntless courage and optimism.* —**daunt·less·ly** *adv.* —**daunt·less·ness** *n.*

dau·phin /dō fèen/ *n.* in former times, the eldest son of the king of France and the direct heir to the throne [15thC. Via French, literally "dolphin," from Old French *daulphin* (see DOLPHIN).]

dau·phine /daw fèen, dō fèen/ *n.* the wife of the dauphin [Mid-19thC. From French, the feminine form of *dauphin* (see DAUPHIN).]

DAV *abbr.* Disabled American Veterans

dav·en /daávən/ (**-ened, -en·ing, -ens**) *vi.* JUDAISM **1.** RECITE JEWISH PRAYERS to recite prayers from the Jewish liturgies **2.** LEAD PRAYERS to lead Jewish prayers [Mid-20thC. From Yiddish *davnen* "to pray."]

dav·en·port /dávvən pàwrt/ *n.* **1.** LARGE SOFA a large well-upholstered sofa, especially one that can be converted into a bed **2.** WRITING DESK an ornamental writing desk with a sloping top and drawers in its sides [Mid-19thC. Origin uncertain: perhaps named for the craftsman who produced it, or one Captain *Davenport*, said by some to have ordered a writing desk with these features.]

Dav·en·port /dávvən pàwrt/ city in eastern Iowa, on the western bank of the Mississippi River. Population: 97,010 (1996).

Da·vid /dáy vid/, **King of Judah** (*d.* 961 B.C.). During his reign (1000 B.C.-962 B.C.), he defeated the Philistines, conquered Jerusalem, and became the ruler of Israel.

Da·vid·son /dáyvidsən/, **Jo** (1883–1952) U.S. sculptor. He is known for his busts of Woodrow Wilson and Albert Einstein.

Da·vies /dáyveez/, **Arthur B.** (1862–1928) U.S. painter. He was one of the early exponents of modern art, including cubism, and a member of an antiacademic group of artists known as The Eight. Full name **Arthur Bowen Davies**

Da·vies, Robertson (1913–95) Canadian novelist, essayist, and playwright. His books include *The Salterton Trilogy* (1951–58), *The Deptford Trilogy* (1970–75), and *The Cornish Trilogy* (1981–88). *What's Bred in the Bone* (1985) was shortlisted for the Booker Prize.

Da·vis /dáyviss/ city in central California, west of Sacramento and northeast of San Francisco. Population: 52,321 (1996).

Da·vis, Alexander Jackson (1803–92) U.S. architect. He was in the vanguard of the Greek Revival movement, designing many public buildings and state capitols in neoclassical style.

Da·vis, Benjamin Oliver, Jr. (*b.* 1912) U.S. pilot. He flew with the Tuskegee Airmen in World War II and became the first African American general in the U.S. air force (1954).

Bette Davis

Da·vis, Bette (1908–89) U.S. movie actor. She won the Academy Award for best actress for *Dangerous* (1935) and *Jezebel* (1938). Full name **Ruth Elizabeth Davis**

Da·vis[2], Jefferson (1808–89) U.S. statesman. He was the first and only president of the Confederate States of America (1861–65).

Da·vis, John (1550?–1605) English navigator. While searching for a northwestern route between Europe and the Indies, he sailed through the present-day Davis Strait (1587).

Popperfoto

Miles Davis

Da·vis, Miles (1926–91) U.S. trumpet player and band leader. A consummate improvisor, he pioneered a more understated form of bebop know as "cool jazz." He was also noted for incorporating electronic instruments into jazz and combining jazz and rock. Full name **Miles Dewey Davis III**

Da·vis, Ossie (*b.* 1917) U.S. actor and playwright. He starred in the movie *The Hill* (1964) and wrote the play *Purlie Victorious* (1961).

Da·vis, Stuart (1894–1964) U.S. painter. Known as the first abstract painter in the United States, he developed his distinctive style from Cubism and his love of jazz.

Da·vis Cup *n.* **1.** INTERNATIONAL MEN'S TENNIS COMPETITION an annual international men's tennis competition for which a trophy is awarded to the winning nation **2.** TROPHY GIVEN AS PRIZE the trophy awarded to the winning nation in the Davis Cup competition [Early 20thC. Named for Dwight Filley *Davis*, U.S. tennis player and government official, who donated the trophy.]

Da·vis Strait body of water separating Baffin Island, Canada, from Greenland, and forming the entrance to Baffin Bay. Depth: 11,900 ft./3,660 m.

dav·it /dávvit/ *n.* a small crane at the side of a ship's deck, especially one of a pair of curved metal posts with tackle attached for suspending and lowering a lifeboat [15thC. From Anglo-Norman *daviot, daviet*, literally "little David," from the male name *Davi* "David."]

Dav·os /daa vṓss/ mountain resort in Graubünden Canton, eastern Switzerland. Population: 10,500 (1992).

Da·vy Jones /dàyvee jṓnz/ *n.* the personification of the sea [Origin unknown]

Da·vy Jones's lock·er *n.* the bottom of the sea, especially considered as the final resting place of drowned sailors or sunken ships (*informal*) [Early 18thC. *Davy Jones* "Evil Spirit of the Sea" (in sailors' parlance); *locker* is a sea chest; the phrase "laid in the lockers" was a nautical metaphor for "dead."]

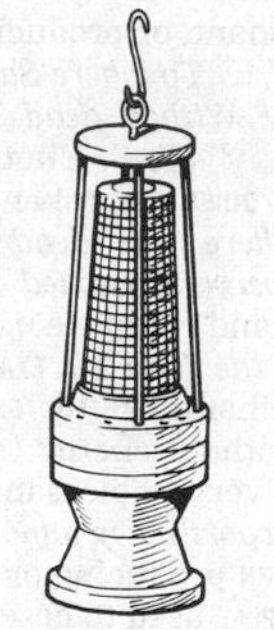

Davy lamp

Da·vy lamp *n.* *U.K.* MINING a portable oil-burning lamp, formerly used by miners, in which the flame is protected by metal gauze to prevent it from igniting explosive gases underground. [Early 19thC. Named for Sir Humphry DAVY, who invented it.]

daw /daw/ *n.* a jackdaw (*archaic or regional*) [15thC. Origin uncertain: probably from assumed Old English *dawe*, which came from a prehistoric Germanic word that also produced German *Dohle* "jackdaw."]

daw·dle /dáwd'l/ (**-dled, -dling, -dles**) *vi.* **1.** MOVE SLOWLY to walk or move slowly and reluctantly or idly ○ *We'll get there in time if you don't dawdle.* **2.** WASTE TIME to spend far more time than is necessary in doing something ○ *We dawdled over lunch and it was three o'clock before we left the restaurant.* [Mid-17thC. Origin uncertain: perhaps from a dialectal form of *daddle*, from *dadder* "to walk unsteadily, walk like a child, dawdle."] —**daw·dler** *n.* —**daw·dling** *n., adj.* —**daw·dling·ly** *adv.*

Dawes /dawz/, **Charles Gates** (1865–1951) U.S. financier and statesman. Originally a banker, he served as vice president (1925–29) under the Republican Calvin Coolidge.

dawn /dawn/ *n.* **1.** DAYBREAK the first appearance of light in the sky as the sun rises at the beginning of a new day **2.** BEGINNING the beginning of something, especially a period of time or history ○ *the dawn of the industrial era* ■ *vi.* (**dawned, dawn·ing, dawns**) **1.** BEGIN to begin, as the sun rises and light appears in the sky ○ *The day dawned cloudy and wet.* **2.** BECOME APPARENT to begin to be perceived ○ *The realization dawned that few of them would survive.* **3.** COMMENCE to begin to develop (*literary*) [15thC. The verb is a back-formation from DAWNING; the noun arose from the verb in the late 16thC.]

dawn on *vt.* to come into somebody's mind or consciousness ○ *It was some time before the seriousness of the situation dawned on them.*

dawn cho·rus *n.* **1.** BIRDSONG AT DAYBREAK the loud singing of many birds as the first light of day appears in the sky **2.** NOISE IN EARLY MORNING any loud sound, especially from a number of different sources, occurring very early in the morning (*humorous*) ○ *a dawn chorus of power drills and hammering*

dawn·ing /dáwnning/ *n.* BEGINNING OF DAY OR AGE the beginning of a new day or of a new period of time or history ○ *with the dawning of the computer age* ■ *adj.* DEVELOPING beginning to appear, develop, or be perceived [13thC. Alteration of obsolete *dawing*, from obsolete *daw* "to dawn," literally "to become day" (related to English *day*).]

dawn raid *n.* **1.** MIL SURPRISE ATTACK a surprise attack on enemy troops at dawn **2.** STOCK EXCH TAKEOVER STRATEGY a surprise attempt to buy a large number of a company's shares at the start of a day's trading, especially as a first stage in a takeover bid

dawn red·wood *n.* a deciduous tree with flat leaves and small round cones that is native to China and widely grown elsewhere as an ornamental. Latin name: *Metasequoia glyptostroboides.*

Daw·son /dáwss'n/, **Sir John William** (1820–99) Canadian geologist. He worked mainly with plant fossils and wrote *Acadian Geology* (1855).

Daw·son Creek city located on the British Columbia-Alberta border, Canada, and the starting point of the Alaska Highway. Population: 11,125 (1996).

DAX /daks/ *n.* a stock index on the Frankfurt Stock Exchange. Full form **Deutsche Aktienindex**

day /day/ *n.* **1.** TIME 24 HOURS a period of 24 hours, usually beginning and ending at midnight **2.** SUNRISE TO SUNSET the part of a 24-hour period when it is light, between sunrise and sunset **3.** TIME NOT ASLEEP the part of a 24-hour period when somebody is working or active ○ *I work an 8-hour day.* **4.** INDEFINITE PERIOD OR POINT IN TIME a time or period of time in the past, present, or future ○ *One of these days we'll get around to painting the house.* **5.** TIME OF FAME the time when a particular person or thing is well-known, popular, successful, or effective ○ *In her day she was one of our best-known Shakespearean actresses.* **6.** LIFE OR EXISTENCE the time when a particular person or thing is active or in existence ○ *In my day we had to work on Saturday mornings.* **7.** ASTRON, TIME PERIOD OF EARTH'S ROTATION ABOUT AXIS a unit of time equal to the Earth's period of rotation about its axis, measured either relative to the Sun (**solar day**) or the stars (**sidereal day**) **8.** ASTRON PERIOD OF PLANET'S ROTATION ABOUT AXIS the period of time in which a planet revolves once on its axis [Old English *dæg*. Ultimately from an Indo-European word that is also the ancestor of Latin *fovere* "to warm." The underlying sense is "time when the sun is hot."] ◇ **call it a day** to finish work or stop doing something ◇ **carry** *or* **win the day** to gain a victory ◇ **day after day** for several or many days in a row ◇ **day by day 1.** each consecutive day **2.** progressively ◇ **day in, day out** every day without exception and all day long ◇ **in this day and age** nowadays, as opposed to past times and customs ◇ **make somebody's day** to make somebody very happy ◇ **name the day** to set a date for something, typically a wedding ◇ **save the day** to prevent defeat or disaster ◇ **somebody's** *or* **something's days are numbered** somebody or something will not survive much longer

Day /day/, **Clarence** (1874–1935) U.S. humorist and essayist. He is known for the humorous autobiographical works *Life with Father* (1935) and *Life with Mother* (1937). Full name **Clarence Shepard Day**

Day, Doris (*b.* 1924) U.S. film actor and singer. She came to fame in the late 1950s with roles in light musicals and romantic comedies such as *Calamity Jane* (1953) and *Pillow Talk* (1959), for which she received an Academy Award nomination. Born **Doris von Kappelhoff**

Day, William Henry (1810–89) U.S. publisher. In 1883 he founded the *New York Sun*, the first penny daily newspaper in the United States.

Day·ak /dī àk/ (*plural* **-aks** *or* **-ak**), **Dy·ak** (*plural* **-aks** *or* **-ak**) *n.* a member of a Malaysian people who live in the interior of Borneo and are noted for their communal long houses [Mid-19thC. From Malay, literally "up-country."]

Da·yan /daa yaán/ *n.* the title of the judge of the Beth Din, a Jewish religious court [Late 19thC. From Hebrew, formed from *dān* "to judge."]

Da·yan /daa yaán/, **Moshe** (1915–81) Israeli general and statesman. He was chief of Israel's general staff (1953–58) and defense minister (1967 and 1969–74). He resigned after criticism over the Yom Kippur War (1973–74), but was foreign minister in 1977, resigning again in 1979 in protest over Menachem Begin's policies concerning the West Bank.

day bed *n.* **1.** PIECE OF FURNITURE FOR DAYTIME REST a couch or bed for reclining on during the day **2.** SOFA CONVERTIBLE INTO BED a sofa that can be converted into a bed

day blind·ness *n.* the inability to see clearly in bright light with comparatively good vision in dim light. Technical name **hemeralopia**

day·book /dáy bòök/ *n.* **1.** ACCT ACCOUNTS BOOK FOR DAILY RECORDS a book in which financial transactions are recorded day by day **2.** JOURNAL a diary or journal

day·break /dáy bràyk/ *n.* the time when light first appears in the sky at the beginning of a day

day camp *n.* a camp that provides activities and meals for children during the day but has no overnight accommodations

day·care /dáy kàir/ *n.* daytime supervision and recreational, training, or medical facilities for preschool children, physically challenged people, or seniors wishing special assistance

day·dream /dáy dreēm/ *n.* **1.** DREAM EXPERIENCED WHILE AWAKE a series of often distracting and usually pleasant thoughts and images that pass through the mind while awake **2.** UNREALIZABLE HOPE OR FANTASY a pleasant wish or hope that is unlikely to be fulfilled ■ *vi.* (**-dreamed** *or* **-dreamt, -dream·ing, -dreams**) THINK DISTRACTING THOUGHTS to have or indulge in daydreams —**day·dream·er** *n.* —**day·dream·ing** *n.* —**day·dream·y** *adj.*

day·flow·er /dáy flòwr/ *n.* a tropical plant with narrow pointed leaves and blue or purplish flowers that soon wilt. Genus: *Commelina.* [Late 17thC. From the fact that the flowers last for only one day.]

day·fly /dáy flī/ (*plural* **-flies**) *n.* = **mayfly** [Early 17thC. From the fact that the fly lives for only one day.]

Day-Glo /dáy glō/ *tdmk.* a trademark for fluorescent dyes and coloring agents

day·hop /dáy hòp/ *n.* (*informal*) **1.** DAY'S JOURNEY a journey or distance that can be traveled within a day **2.** EDUC DAY STUDENT somebody who studies at a boarding school or college but does not live there

day job *n.* a job that somebody does merely to earn an income while trying to achieve success in another field, especially the arts (*informal*)

day la·bor·er *n.* a manual worker who is hired and paid on a day-to-day basis

Day-Le·wis /day loō iss/, **Daniel** (*b.* 1957) British-born Irish stage and movie actor. He won an Academy Award for best actor in *My Left Foot* (1989).

day·light /dáy līt/ *n.* **1.** SUNLIGHT natural light from the sun ○ *Open the curtains and let in some daylight.* **2.** DAYTIME the part of the day when it is light **3.** DAYBREAK the time when light first appears in the sky at the beginning of a day **4.** PUBLIC AWARENESS public knowledge, notice, or scrutiny ○ *There are some secrets that they would prefer not to have exposed to daylight.* **5.** VISIBLE GAP a visible gap between competitors in a race, showing the lead that one has over the other ○ *There's definitely daylight now between the two boats as they approach the halfway mark.*

day·light rob·ber·y *n.* = **highway robbery** (*informal*) [From the idea that the price charged is outrageous enough to be considered a crime committed in full public view]

day·light-sav·ing time, **day·light time** *n.* an adjustment of clock time to allow more hours of normal daylight. Clocks are usually set one hour ahead of standard time to achieve this.

day lil·y *n.* a perennial plant with large yellow, red, or orange flowers resembling those of the lily. The individual flowers usually die after one day but are produced over a period of time. Genus: *Hemerocallis.*

day·long /dáy làwng/ *adj., adv.* throughout the entire day

day-neu·tral *adj.* used to describe plants that mature and flower unaffected by the length of the daylight period they grow in

day nurs·er·y *n.* a place where preschool children are looked after during the daytime, usually while their parents are at work

Day of A·tone·ment *n.* = **Yom Kippur**

day off (*plural* **days off**) *n.* a day on which somebody does not have to work

Day of Judg·ment *n.* = **Judgment Day**

day of reck·on·ing *n.* a time when somebody is made to answer for crimes or mistakes

day one *n.* the first day or the very beginning of something ○ *It's day one of the electoral campaign.*

day out (*plural* **days out**) *n.* a day of leisure spent away from home

day·pack /dáy pàk/ *n.* a small backpack or bag for carrying things needed during the day

day room *n.* a communal recreation room in an institution such as a hospital or barracks

days /dayz/ *adv.* during the day or every day ○ *I work days one week and nights the next.* [Old English *dæges*, the genitive singular of *dæg* "day," later reinterpreted as the plural of DAY]

day sail·er *n.* a small sailboat without sleeping accommodations

day school *n.* **1.** PRIVATE SCHOOL a private school that does not take boarders **2.** SCHOOL WITH DAYTIME CLASSES ONLY a school that holds classes during the daytime but not during the evening

day shift *n.* **1.** DAYTIME WORK PERIOD a shift that is worked during the day or part of the day **2.** WORKERS a group of employees who work during the day at a place where others work during the night

Days of Awe *npl.* JUDAISM = **High Holidays**

days of grace *npl.* the extra days, customarily three, allowed for the settlement of a note or bill after it falls due [From GRACE "favor shown by granting immunity from a penalty"]

day·spring /dáy spring/ *n.* the first light of day (*archaic or literary*)

day·star /dáy staar/ *n.* **1.** = **morning star** (*literary*) **2.** SUN the sun (*archaic or literary*) [Old English *dægsteorra*]

day stu·dent *n.* somebody who studies at a school, college, or university but who does not board there

day·time /dáy tīm/ *n.* SUNLIT PART OF DAY the part of the day when there is natural light ■ *adj.* OF OR FOR DAYTIME occurring, done, or used during the daytime

day-to-day *adj.* **1.** EVERYDAY occurring or tending to be the same every day ○ *the day-to-day business of earning a living* **2.** ONE DAY AT A TIME planning or providing for one day at a time ○ *We do everything on a day-to-day basis – we can never plan ahead.*

Day·ton /dáyt'n/ city in Ohio on the Great Miami River, southwest of Columbus and northeast of Cincinnati. Population: 172,947 (1996).

Day·ton Ac·cords *npl.* an agreement reached in November 1995 at Wright-Patterson Air Force Base among representatives for Bosnia, Croatia, and Serbia, containing measures to end hostilities in the former Yugoslavia. It was signed in Paris, France, on December 14, 1995, by the presidents of the three warring nations. [Mid-20thC. From *Dayton*, Ohio, where the agreement was reached.]

day trip *n.* a journey or outing to and from a place within a day

day trip·per *n.* somebody who goes on a day trip

day·wear /dáy wair/ *n.* clothes for wearing during the day

daze /dayz/ *n.* CONFUSED STATE a state of confusion and unclear thinking, often the result of a blow or shock ○ *Things happened so quickly I was left in a daze.* ■ *vt.* (**dazed, daz·ing, daz·es**) **1.** STUN SOMEBODY to leave somebody wholly or partly unconscious or unable to think clearly, especially as a result of a blow or shock ○ *The blow seemed to have dazed her.* **2.** BEWILDER SOMEBODY to leave somebody feeling confused or amazed [14thC. Back-formation from DAZED.]

dazed /dayzd/ *adj.* **1.** STUNNED not fully conscious or able to think clearly, often as a result of a blow or shock **2.** PUZZLED bewildered, confused, or amazed [14thC. From Old Norse *dasaðr* "weary from cold or exertion."] —**daz·ed·ly** /dáyzədlee/ *adv.*

daz·zle /dázz'l/ *vti.* (**-zled, -zling, -zles**) **1.** AMAZE SOMEBODY to amaze somebody with brilliance or skill or with a wonderful spectacle or display (*often passive*) ○ *She dazzled the spectators with a triple somersault.* **2.** DEPRIVE OF SIGHT TEMPORARILY to make somebody temporarily unable to see ○ *The glare of the oncoming headlights dazzled me.* ■ *n.* LIGHT THAT DAZZLES very bright light that deprives somebody of sight temporarily ○ *a lot of dazzle from the white-painted walls of the house* [15thC. Formed from DAZE, probably in the now obsolete sense "to become confused or stupefied."]

daz·zling /dázzling/ *adj.* **1.** STRIKING spectacularly skillful or impressive ○ *a dazzling lineup of stars* **2.** VERY BRIGHT bright enough to deprive somebody of sight temporarily —**daz·zling·ly** *adv.*

dB *symbol.* MEASURE decibel

Db *symbol.* dubnium

DB, D.B. *abbr.* ACCT daybook

d.b.a. *abbr.* doing business as

D.B.A. *abbr.* Doctor of Business Administration

D.B.E. *abbr.* Dame Commander of the Order of the British Empire

d.b.h. *abbr.* FORESTRY diameter at breast height

D.Bib. *abbr.* Douay Bible

dbl., dble. *abbr.* double

DBMS *abbr.* COMPUT database management system

DBS *abbr.* **1.** direct broadcasting by satellite **2.** direct broadcasting satellite

D.C. *abbr.* **1.** MUSIC da capo **2.** ELEC ENG direct current. ◊ **A.C.** **3.** District Commissioner **4.** District of Columbia

DCC *abbr.* digital compact cassette

DCD *abbr.* digital compact disk

dd. *abbr.* **1.** delivered **2.** dated

D.D. *abbr.* **1.** BANKING demand draft **2.** dishonorable discharge **3.** Doctor of Divinity

D-day *n.* **1.** HIST BEGINNING OF LIBERATION OF EUROPE June 6, 1944, the day on which Allied forces landed in northern France to begin the liberation of occupied Europe in World War II **2.** DAY WHEN OPERATION IS TO BEGIN a day chosen for the beginning of a military operation or other major venture [Origin uncertain; the initial "D" is perhaps from DAY, the phrase thus being modeled on H-HOUR; another possibility is that the "D" is from "designated"]

DDD *abbr.* direct distance dialing

D.D.R. *abbr.* HIST Deutsche Demokratische Republik

D.D.S. *abbr.* **1.** LIBRARIES Dewey Decimal System **2.** DENT Doctor of Dental Science **3.** DENT Doctor of Dental Surgery

D.D.Sc. *abbr.* Doctor of Dental Science

DDT *n.* an insecticide effective especially against malaria-carrying mosquitoes that has been banned in many countries since 1974 because of its toxicity, its persistence in the environment, and its ability to accumulate in living tissue. Formula: $C_{14}H_9Cl_5$. Full form **dichlorodiphenyltrichloroethane**

DE *abbr.* Delaware

de- *prefix.* **1.** opposite, reverse ○ *decertify* **2.** remove ○ *decaffeinate* ○ *delist* **3.** derived from ○ *denominative* **4.** reduce ○ *declass* **5.** to get off ○ *deplane* **6.** formed by removing one or more atoms from a particular element ○ *deoxy-* [Via Old French *de-* and *des-* from, ultimately, Latin *de-* "apart, away" and *dis-* (see DIS-)]

DEA *abbr.* Drug Enforcement Administration

de·ac·ces·sion /dee ak sésh'n/ (**-sioned, -sion·ing, -sions**) *vti.* to remove a book or work of art from the collection of a library or museum and sell it

de·a·cid·i·fy /dee ə síddə fī/ (**-fied, -fy·ing, -fies**) *vt.* to remove the acid from something or reduce the acid content of something —**de·a·cid·i·fi·ca·tion** /dee ə siddəfi káysh'n/ *n.*

dea·con /deékən/ *n.* **1.** ORDAINED PERSON RANKING BELOW A PRIEST in the Roman Catholic, Orthodox, and Episcopal Churches, an ordained member of the clergy with a rank immediately below that of a priest **2.** LAYPERSON ASSISTING MINISTER in many Protestant churches, a layperson who is appointed or elected to assist the minister [Pre-12thC. Via Latin *diaconus* from Greek *diakonos*, literally "servant, messenger."]

dea·con·ess /deékənəss/ *n.* a woman who ranks below a priest or who is appointed to assist a minister [Mid-16thC. Formed from DEACON on the model of medieval Latin *diaconissa* "deaconess."]

dea·con·ry /deékənree/ (*plural* **-ries**) *n.* **1.** POST OF DEACON the position or rank of a deacon **2.** DEACONS COLLECTIVELY deacons considered as a group

de·ac·ti·vate /dee ákti vayt/ (**-vat·ed, -vat·ing, -vates**) *vt.* **1.** MAKE SOMETHING INACTIVE OR HARMLESS to prevent something that is active or live, especially an explosive device, from operating **2.** BIOCHEM STOP ACTIVE COMPOUND FROM WORKING to render a biologically active compound, e.g., an enzyme, inactive or ineffective **3.** MIL END ACTIVE MILITARY STATUS to make a military unit no longer active —**de·ac·ti·va·tion** /dee àkti váysh'n/ *n.* —**de·ac·ti·va·tor** /dee ákti vaytər/ *n.*

dead /ded/ *adj.* **1.** NO LONGER ALIVE having passed from the living state to being no longer alive ○ *a dead bird* **2.** INANIMATE never having been alive and having none of the characteristics of a living thing **3.** WITHOUT LIVING THINGS IN IT having no living things, or unable to support life **4.** WITHOUT PHYSICAL SENSATION having lost normal sensitivity to touch or pain, e.g., from the effects of cold, disease, or anesthesia ○ *My fingers have gone completely dead.* **5.** INSENSITIVE unable or unwilling to respond to, understand, or appreciate something **6.** LACKING ANY SPARK OF LIFE showing little indication of feeling or vitality ○ *His eyes were dead.* **7.** LIKE A CORPSE having the appearance of a dead person **8.** LACKING ACTIVITY OR INTEREST without human activity or anything interesting or entertaining ○ *This town is dead after seven o'clock at night.* **9.** NO LONGER CURRENT no longer in use, or no longer relevant, appropriate, or important ○ *That issue is now well and truly dead, despite attempts to revive it.* **10.** TECH BROKEN DOWN no longer able to operate because of a fault, breakdown, or loss of power ○ *The phone went dead.* **11.** NOT BURNING no longer burning or able to burn **12.** ACOUSTICS NONRESONANT not resonant, or producing sounds that are not resonant ○ *"... To where Saint Mary Woolnoth kept the hours / With a dead sound on the final stroke of nine ..."* (T. S. Eliot, *The Waste Land*; 1922) **13.** TOTALLY QUIET unbroken by any sound or movement ○ *There was dead silence for a few seconds; then everyone started cheering.* **14.** TOTAL sudden, abrupt, and complete ○ *came to a dead stop in the middle of the road* **15.** EXACT precise or exact in position or character **16.** EXHAUSTED very tired or completely without energy (*informal*) **17.** DOOMED certain to face a very unpleasant fate (*informal*) ○ *If I don't get this report in by tomorrow, I'm dead.* **18.** COMM WITH NO RETURN producing or yielding no return **19.** SPORTS OUT OF PLAY used to describe a ball that has crossed the boundary of the playing area in some games **20.** GOLF LANDING CLOSE TO HOLE used to describe a golf shot in which the ball comes to rest so close to the hole that the next shot cannot miss ■ *npl.* DEAD PEOPLE people who have died or been killed (*takes a plural verb*) ○ *respect for the dead* ■ *adv.* **1.** PRECISELY used to emphasize that an approximate-sounding description or instruction, e.g., concerning a time, a position, or a straight line, is in fact precise or to be followed precisely ○ *Keep going dead ahead for another 300 yards.* **2.** ENTIRELY completely or absolutely ○ *You can be dead sure that he won't make the same mistake again.* **3.** WITH SUDDENNESS abruptly or immediately ○ *stopped dead in her tracks* [Old English *dēad*. Ultimately from the past participle of the prehistoric Germanic verb that is also the ancestor of English *die*, so the underlying meaning is "died."] ◇ **the dead of night** *or* **winter** the most extreme point of night *or* winter

WORD KEY: SYNONYMS

dead, deceased, departed, late, lifeless, defunct, extinct

CORE MEANING: no longer living, functioning, or in existence

dead the most general term, used of organisms that are no longer alive, physical objects that no longer function or exist, and abstract entities that are no longer valid or relevant; **deceased** a formal term restricted to people, most commonly used in legal or other technical contexts, or as a euphemism; **departed** a euphemistic term restricted to people, used to suggest that the dead person has gone away rather than died; **late** a term restricted to people, usually applied to somebody who has died fairly recently or whose death is within living memory. It is always followed by a proper name or a noun indicating a particular relationship or status; **lifeless** a literary term used to describe the body of a dead person or animal; **defunct** a neutral term used of something such as a machine or a system that has ceased to exist or function. In current usage, it is used to describe people only for comic effect; **extinct** a technical term used of animal and plant species that no longer exist, or of something such as a volcano that is no longer active. It is sometimes used to describe institutions, customs, or ways of life that no longer exist.

dead air *n.* an unintentional period of silence during a broadcast

dead-air space *n.* a space that is sealed or has no ventilation

dead·beat /déd beet/ *n.* **1.** SOMEBODY WHO DOES NOT PAY DEBTS somebody who does not pay money that is owed (*slang*) **2.** LOAFER somebody who is lazy and disreputable (*slang*) ■ *adj.* PHYS DAMPED AND NOT OSCILLATING used to describe an instrument that gives a true reading without oscillation

dead·beat dad *n.* a man who, upon divorce, separation, or desertion of his family, avoids or refuses payment of child support (*slang insult*)

dead·beat mom *n.* a woman who, upon divorce, separation, or desertion of her family, avoids or refuses payment of child support (*slang insult*)

dead bolt /déd bōlt/, **dead·bolt** *n.* a bolt that is operated directly by the turning of a key or knob and not by a spring mechanism

dead cat bounce *n.* FIN an apparent recovery from a major decline in stock prices resulting from speculators rebuying stock that they previously sold rather than from a genuine upturn in the market (*slang*)

dead cen·ter *n.* **1.** MIDDLE the exact center of something **2.** MECH ENG TOP OR BOTTOM OF A PISTON STROKE the position at the top or bottom of a piston stroke in a reciprocating engine or pump, at which point the piston and the connecting rod are in a straight line

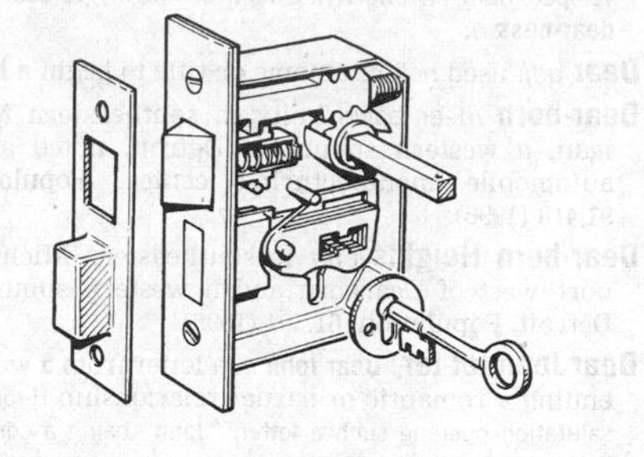

Dead bolt

3. TECH **POINTED ROD IN A LATHE** a nonrotating pointed shaft mounted at both ends or one end of a lathe to support the workpiece and hold it in place

dead duck *n.* something or somebody with no chance of success or survival (*slang*) [Origin uncertain: perhaps based on an early 19th-century U.S. proverb about the futility of shooting a duck that is already dead]

dead·en /dédd'n/ (**-ened, -en·ing, -ens**) *vt.* **1. MAKE SOMETHING LESS INTENSE** to lessen the intensity of something, such as pain or sound ○ *The snow deadened the sound of their footsteps.* **2. DESENSITIZE SOMEBODY OR SOMETHING** to make something or somebody less sensitive to pain or other stimuli ○ *A local anesthetic will deaden the nerves.* **3.** ACOUSTICS **MAKE SOMETHING LESS RESONANT** to make an area soundproof or less resonant —**dead·en·er** *n.*

dead end *n.* **1. POINT AT WHICH SOMETHING ENDS ABRUPTLY** an end of a street, path, road, or passage beyond which it is impossible to proceed **2. PASSAGE THAT ENDS ABRUPTLY** a street, path, or passage beyond which somebody or something cannot proceed **3. SITUATION THAT LEADS NOWHERE** a situation or course of action in which further progress or development is impossible ○ *a line of research that proved to be a dead end*

dead-end *adj.* **1. WITH CLOSED END** with no exit at one end **2. WITHOUT PROSPECTS** offering no prospects of progress, development, or improvement ○ *stuck in a dead-end job* **3. ROWDY AND TOUGH** used to describe young people, usually from underprivileged backgrounds, whose behavior makes them unlikely to succeed in life (*informal*) ■ *vi.* (**dead-end·ed, dead-end·ing, dead-ends**) **COME TO DEAD END** to have no exit or prospect of further progress or development ○ *A half a mile from here the road dead-ends.*

dead·en·ing /dédd'ning/ *n.* material used to make a room or building soundproof or less resonant

dead·eye /déd ì/ *n.* **1.** NAUT **WOODEN BLOCK WITH THREE HOLES** a rounded block of wood pierced by three holes that has a groove around its edge. Deadeyes are usually used in pairs to tighten stays or shrouds on sailing vessels. **2. EXPERT SHOT** somebody who always aims accurately and hits the target (*informal*)

dead·fall /déd fàwl/ *n.* a simple trap consisting of a heavy weight that falls on and crushes its victim when a support is removed

dead fin·gers *n.* a condition that can affect people who work with pneumatic drills, causing loss of sensation and reduced blood circulation in the fingers (*takes a singular verb*)

dead hand *n.* **1. OPPRESSIVE INFLUENCE** a negative or oppressive influence or control exerted over an activity or a group of people ○ *remove the dead hand of bureaucracy* **2.** = **mortmain**

dead·head /déd hèd/ *n.* **1. SOMEBODY INCOMPETENT** an unintelligent, useless, or ineffectual person (*informal insult*) **2.** TRANSP **SOMEBODY WITH A FREE TICKET** somebody who uses a free ticket for travel, accommodation, or some form of entertainment (*informal*) **3. VEHICLE WITH NO PASSENGERS** a vehicle or aircraft that is carrying no passengers or freight (*informal*) ■ *v.* (**-head·ed, -head·ing, -heads**) **1.** *vt.* **REMOVE DEAD FLOWERS FROM PLANT** to remove dead flower heads from a plant to improve its appearance or stimulate further flowering **2.** *vti.* **DRIVE EMPTY VEHICLE** to drive or pilot a vehicle or aircraft that is carrying no passengers or freight ○ *Williams deadheaded it from New Jersey to California last weekend.*

dead heat *n.* a race or other competition in which two or more contestants finish together or with the same score

dead-heat (**dead-heat·ed, dead-heat·ing, dead-heats**) *vi.* to finish a race or other competition together or with the same score

dead let·ter *n.* **1. MAIL LETTER THAT CANNOT BE DELIVERED** a letter that the postal service cannot deliver, usually because the address is inadequate or the addressee does not claim it **2. UNENFORCED OR INEFFECTIVE RULE** a law or regulation that still applies but is not enforced or uniformly obeyed **3. SOMETHING NOW IRRELEVANT OR UNIMPORTANT** something that is no longer considered relevant or important

dead let·ter box, dead let·ter drop *n.* a place where a message or other item can be left in secret by one person and collected later by another, so that the two people do not meet

dead lift *n.* a weightlifting event in which a weight is raised from the floor to the level of the hips and lowered again in a controlled manner [From the idea of lifting a dead weight]

dead·light /déd lìt/ *n.* **1. PROTECTIVE SHUTTER OVER PORTHOLE** a protective shutter or plate fastened over a porthole or cabin window in bad weather **2. THICK WINDOW IN DECK OR HULL** a thick glass window set in the deck or side of a ship to let light into a cabin

dead·line /déd lìn/ *n.* **1. TIME LIMIT** the time by which something must be done or completed **2. LINE MARKED IN PRISON** in former times, a line in a prison or prison camp marking a boundary beyond which prisoners were forbidden to go on pain of death

dead load *n.* the permanent weight of a structure, e.g., a bridge, exclusive of its load

dead·lock /déd lòk/ *n.* **1. BLOCK TO PROGRESS** a situation in which no further progress is possible in a dispute, usually because the people involved are unwilling to change their positions or to compromise ○ *try to break the deadlock in negotiations* **2.** BUILDING **TYPE OF LOCK** a type of lock that can be opened or closed only with a key ■ *vti.* (**-locked, -lock·ing, -locks**) **CAUSE DEADLOCK** to reach a situation in which no further progress is possible, or to bring something into such a situation ○ *The talks are deadlocked.*

dead loss *n.* a complete loss for which no form of compensation is available

dead·ly /dédlee/ *adj.* (**-li·er, -li·est**) **1. CAUSING DEATH** able or likely to cause death **2. PRECISE** very accurate, or able to aim or shoot very accurately **3. EXTREMELY HOSTILE** involving or having an intense desire for the defeat, downfall, or death of somebody ○ *deadly enemies* **4. CAUSING OFFENSE** causing or intended to cause great offense to another person **5. COMPLETE** used to emphasize the intensity of something (*informal*) ○ *in deadly earnest* **6. DULL** extremely boring (*informal*) ○ *back to the deadly routine of daily life* ■ *adv.* **1.** = **deathly 2. COMPLETELY** to the greatest extent possible ○ *I was being deadly serious when I made that suggestion.* [Old English *dēadlic*] —**dead·li·ness** *n.*

WORD KEY: SYNONYMS

deadly, fatal, mortal, lethal, terminal

CORE MEANING: causing death

deadly likely or designed to cause death, or having caused death; **fatal** a more commonly used term than *deadly*, used especially to describe accidents or illnesses that have resulted in death; **mortal** a more literary or formal term used to describe something that seems likely to cause death or that has already caused death; **lethal** a term used to describe something that is certain to cause death, especially something that is expressly intended to cause death; **terminal** used to describe illnesses that cause death.

dead·ly night·shade *n.* = **belladonna**

dead·ly sins *npl.* the sins that lead to damnation according to some Christian beliefs. The seven deadly sins are anger, avarice, envy, gluttony, lechery, pride, and sloth. [Translation of Latin *peccata mortalia*]

dead·man /déd màn/ (*plural* **-men** /-mèn/) *n.* a heavy block or plate buried in the ground and connected to another structure, e.g., a retaining wall, by means of a tie, thereby anchoring the structure firmly

dead man's float *n.* a floating position in which a swimmer is face down with arms extended forward and legs kept together

dead march *n.* a piece of solemn music played to accompany a procession at a funeral, especially a military funeral

dead men's shoes *npl.* a situation in which the only prospect of promotion is the death or retirement of more senior employees

dead·ness /dédnəss/ *n.* **1. DULLNESS** lack of activity, liveliness, or interest ○ *Young people complain about the deadness of the town.* **2. NUMBNESS** lack or loss of sensation in a part of the body **3. INABILITY TO OPERATE** lack of power or ability to operate

dead net·tle *n.* a flowering plant that resembles a nettle but does not have stinging hairs on its leaves. Genus: *Lamium.*

dead-on *adj.* very accurate or correct (*informal*) (*not hyphenated after verb*) ○ *a dead-on prediction*

dead·pan /déd pàn/ *adj.* **1. PURPOSELY INEXPRESSIVE** deliberately showing no expression or emotion **2. SAID EXPRESSIONLESSLY** spoken or delivered with no expression or emotion ■ *adv.* **EXPRESSIONLESS** without showing any expression or emotion ○ *delivered the line absolutely deadpan* ■ *n.* **EXPRESSIONLESS FACE OR PERFORMER** an expressionless face or somebody with an expressionless face ■ *vti.* (**-panned, -pan·ning, -pans**) **SPEAK OR ACT IN DEADPAN MANNER** to say something or do something in a deliberately expressionless way [Early 20thC. From U.S. slang PAN "face."]

dead reck·on·ing *n.* a simple method of determining the position of a ship or aircraft by charting its course and speed from a previously known position [Origin uncertain; probably from DEAD "absolute" or "exact," although "dead" may be by folk etymology from *ded.*, a shortening of DEDUCE or DEDUCTION.]

dead ring·er *n.* somebody who looks exactly like somebody else (*informal*)

Dead Sea salt lake on the border between Israel and Jordan, in southwestern Asia. Its surface, at 1,312 ft./400 m below sea level, marks the lowest point on earth. Area: 405 sq. mi./1,049 sq. km.

Dead Sea Scrolls *npl.* a collection of ancient manuscripts discovered in caves near the Dead Sea that provide important evidence for biblical scholars and historians. They were discovered between 1947 and 1956, and are generally held to have been written between 100 B.C. and A.D. 68.

dead set *n.* the rigid motionless position of a hunting dog pointing with its muzzle at game

dead shot *n.* somebody who always aims accurately and hits the target

dead sol·dier *n.* a bottle whose alcoholic contents have been drunk (*dated slang*) [Origin uncertain: perhaps from the former associations of liquor with liveliness and life itself (compare WHISKEY)]

dead spot *n.* an area within the range of a radio transmitter where reception of the signal is weak or dead

dead time *n.* an interval during which an electrical device or component, having just responded to one stimulus, is unable to respond to another

dead weight *n.* **1. HEAVY MASS** a heavy motionless mass or weight bearing down on something or somebody ○ *a foundation slab carrying the dead weight of the building* **2. OPPRESSIVE BURDEN** somebody or something that weighs somebody else down or hinders progress **3.** SHIPPING **TOTAL WEIGHT** the total weight of everything carried on a ship, equal to the difference between the laden and unladen weight **4.** CIV ENG = **dead load**

Dead White Eur·o·pe·an Male, Dead White Male *n.* a conventionally important historical figure, especially one of the writers and thinkers whose works have traditionally formed the basis of academic study in Europe and North America (*informal disapproving*)

dead·wood /déd wòod/ *n.* **1. DEAD TREE PARTS** dead trees and branches **2. SOMEBODY OR SOMETHING UNNECESSARY** useless or superfluous people or things **3.** NAUT **PLANKS BETWEEN KEEL AND STERN** vertical planks filling the gap between the keel and the stern of a sailing vessel

dead·zone *n.* an area of slow-moving or stagnant water close to the bank of a river

deaf /def/ *adj.* **1. HEARING-IMPAIRED** completely or partially unable to hear in one or both ears **2. UNRESPONSIVE OR INDIFFERENT** unwilling to respond to something as if unable to hear it ○ *They remained deaf to all our entreaties.* ■ *npl.* **HEARING-IMPAIRED PEOPLE** people who cannot hear (*takes a plural verb*) [Old English *dēaf*. Ultimately from an Indo-European word that also produced English *dumb* and Greek *taphlos* "sightless."]

deaf·en /déffən/ (**-ened, -en·ing, -ens**) *vt.* **1. MAKE SOMEBODY UNABLE TO HEAR** to make somebody temporarily or permanently unable to hear ○ *I was momentarily deafened by the noise of the explosion.* **2.** ACOUSTICS **SOUNDPROOF SOMETHING** to soundproof a room, wall, or building [Late 16thC]

deaf·en·ing /déffəning/ *adj.* extremely or unbearably loud ○ *She turned up the volume until the noise was absolutely deafening.* —**deaf·en·ing·ly** *adv.*

deaf-mute *adj.* **OFFENSIVE TERM FOR IMPAIRED CONDITION** an obsolete and now offensive term meaning unable to hear or speak ■ *n.* **OFFENSIVE TERM FOR PERSON WITH IMPAIRMENT** an obsolete and now offensive term meaning somebody who is unable to hear or speak

deaf·ness /défnəss/ *n.* a partial or total hearing impairment in one or both ears [Old English *dēafnis*]

deal[1] /deel/ *n.* **1.** BUSINESS **BUSINESS TRANSACTION** an agreement, arrangement, or transaction, usually one that has benefits for all the parties involved **2.** COMM **BARGAIN** something offered for sale on favorable terms (*informal*) (*often used in the plural*) **3. TREATMENT** the treatment given to somebody or received from somebody (*informal*) ○ *They got a pretty raw deal from their employer.* **4.** CARDS **DISTRIBUTION OF CARDS** the distribution of the cards needed to play a game **5.** CARDS **PLAYER'S TURN TO DISTRIBUTE CARDS** a particular player's right or turn to distribute the cards ○ *Whose deal is it?* **6.** CARDS **ROUND OF GAME** a round of a game following a particular distribution of the cards **7.** CARDS **CARDS DISTRIBUTED OR RECEIVED** the cards distributed or received for a particular round of a game ■ *v.* (**dealt, deal·ing, deals**) **1.** *vti.* CARDS **DISTRIBUTE CARDS** to distribute the cards for a round of a game ○ *You deal seven cards to each player.* **2.** *vti.* CARDS **GIVE OUT A PARTICULAR CARD** to give a particular card or cards to a player when distributing them ○ *I was dealt five clubs and no hearts.* **3.** *vti.* DRUGS **SELL ILLEGAL DRUGS** to sell something, especially illegal drugs **4.** *vt.* **MAKE SOMEBODY EXPERIENCE SOMETHING** to cause somebody to experience or suffer something, often as a reward or punishment ○ *The latest opinion poll has dealt a severe blow to her hopes of re-election.* [Old English *dǣl* "part, share, amount," and *dǣlan* "to divide," from a prehistoric Germanic word that also produced English *dole* and *ordeal*] ◇ **a done deal** something that has already been settled or finalized ◇ **make a big deal out of something** to make a fuss about something unimportant (*informal*)

deal in *vt.* **1. TRADE IN SOMETHING** to buy and sell something as a business ○ *We deal mainly in second-hand goods.* **2. INCLUDE SOMEBODY** to let somebody join in a card game or some other form of joint activity (*informal*) ○ *Deal me in.*

deal out *vt.* to give something, or a share of something, to each of a number of people ○ *She dealt out compliments to all the actors.*

deal with *vt.* **1. HANDLE SOMETHING** to take action with regard to something or somebody, e.g., to solve a problem or to help somebody **2. BE ABOUT SOMETHING** to write or speak about something or to have something as the subject of written or spoken material ○ *I was intending to deal with the Metaphysical poets in my next lecture.* **3. TREAT SOMEBODY IN PARTICULAR WAY** to treat or behave toward somebody in a specified way, especially in a business context ○ *People who break the regulations will be dealt with severely.* **4. HAVE BUSINESS DEALINGS WITH SOMEBODY** to do business with somebody or an organization

deal[2] /deel/ *n.* **1. SOFTWOOD LUMBER** fir or pine wood, especially when cut to a standard size **2. BOARD OF SOFTWOOD** a plank or board of deal [15thC. From Middle Low German or Middle Dutch *dele* "plank." Ultimately from a prehistoric Germanic word that also produced English *thill* "shaft."]

de·a·late /dee áy làyt, dee áylət/, **de·a·lat·ed** /dee áy làytəd/ *adj.* used to describe an insect such as an ant or termite that has lost or shed its wings, usually after mating [Early 20thC. Formed from ALATE.] —**de·a·la·tion** /dee ày láysh'n/ *n.*

de·al·co·hol·ize /dee álkə haw līz/ (**-ized, -iz·ing, -iz·es**) *vt.* to remove some or all of the alcohol from a drink —**de·al·co·hol·i·za·tion** /dee àlkə hawli záysh'n/ *n.*

deal·er /deélər/ *n.* **1.** COMM **SELLER OR TRADER** an individual or company whose business is buying and selling, especially in a particular commodity **2.** CARDS **SOMEBODY WHO DEALS CARDS** somebody who distributes the cards for a game or whose turn it is to distribute the cards **3.** DRUGS **SELLER OF DRUGS** somebody who sells illegal drugs [Old English *dǣlere* "distributor"]

deal·er·ship /deélər shìp/ *n.* **1. FRANCHISE TO SELL SOMETHING** a franchise to sell a particular brand of product or service **2. DEALER'S PREMISES** the premises from which a dealer, especially a car dealer, operates

deal·fish /deél fish/ (*plural* **-fish** *or* **-fish·es**) *n.* a deep-sea Atlantic fish with a long flat silvery body. Genus: *Trachipterus.* [Mid-19thC. *Deal* from the resemblance of the fish to a thin plank (see DEAL[2]).]

deal·ing /deéling/ *n.* **CONDUCT OR TREATMENT** conduct toward or treatment of other people, especially in business matters ○ *The firm's reputation for fair dealing is at stake.* ■ **dealings** *npl.* **TRANSACTIONS AND RELATIONS** contact and interaction with other people or organizations for business purposes

deal·mak·er /deél màykər/ *n.* somebody who makes deals, especially in business or politics —**deal·mak·ing** *n.*

dealt past tense, past participle of **deal**[1]

de·am·i·nase /dee ámmi nàyss, -nàyz/ *n.* an enzyme that breaks down amino compounds such as amino acids [Early 20thC. Coined from DE- + AMINE + -ASE.]

de·am·i·nate /dee ámmi nàyt/ (**-nat·ed, -nat·ing, -nates**), **de·am·i·nize** /dee ámmi nīz/ (**-nized, -niz·ing, -niz·es**) *v.* to remove an amino group from an organic compound in a chemical reaction [Early 20thC. Coined from DE- + AMINE + -ATE.] —**de·am·i·na·tion** /dee àmmi náysh'n/ *n.* —**de·am·i·ni·za·tion** /dee àmmini záysh'n/ *n.*

dean /deen/ *n.* **1.** EDUC **ACADEMIC ADMINISTRATOR** a senior member of the academic staff of a university or college who manages the whole institution or a department, faculty, or group of students **2.** EDUC **COLLEGE ADVISOR OR RULE ENFORCER** a member of the academic staff of a university, college or, sometimes, high school, responsible for the counseling and welfare of students, and sometimes for discipline **3.** CHR **SENIOR CLERIC** a senior member of the clergy who holds an administrative position in a cathedral or collegiate church, or in a division in a diocese [14thC. Via Old French *deien* from late Latin *decanus* "person in charge of ten others," from Latin *decem* "ten" (source of English *doyen*).] —**dean·ship** *n.*

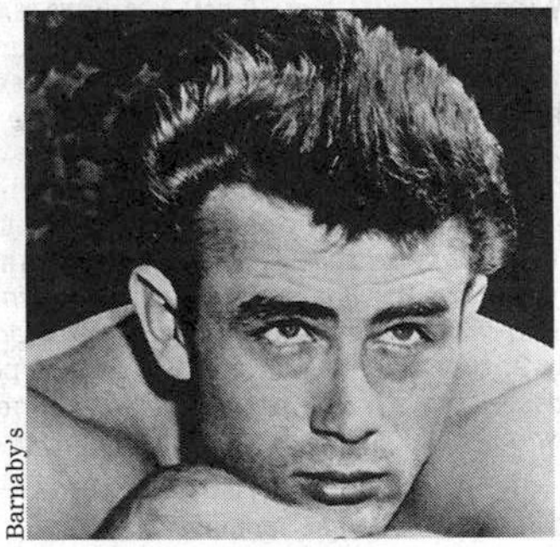
Barnaby's

James Dean

Dean /deen/, **James** (1931–55) U.S. movie actor. He became a symbol of misunderstood youth through his roles in *East of Eden* (1955) and *Rebel Without a Cause* (1955).

Deane /deen/, **Silas** (1737–89) U.S. diplomat. He negotiated a U.S. treaty with France (1778) during the Revolutionary War, but later denounced the war.

dean·er·y /deénəree/ (*plural* **-ies**) *n.* **1. OFFICE OF DEAN** a dean's jurisdiction, office, or residence **2. RURAL DEAN'S PARISHES** a group of parishes administered by a rural dean

Dean of Fac·ul·ty *n.* somebody who is in charge of a university or college faculty

dean's list *n.* a list of students who have achieved a high standard in their work at a high school, college, or university

dear /deer/ *adj.* **1. BELOVED** loved or especially valued ○ *a dear friend* **2. COSTLY** high in price **3. CHARGING A LOT** charging high prices ■ *n.* **1. SOMEBODY WHO IS LOVED** somebody who is loved and valued, especially for being a kind or thoughtful person **2. TERM OF ENDEARMENT** used as an affectionate term of address ■ *interj.* **USED TO EXPRESS SHOCK** used to express shock or consternation ■ *adv.* **DEARLY** at a high cost ○ *This will cost you dear.* [Old English *deore*, from prehistoric Germanic. The two senses "loved" and "expensive" developed from an underlying idea of "highly valued."] —**dear·ness** *n.*

Dear *adj.* used before a name or title to begin a letter

Dear·born /deér bàwrn/ city in southeastern Michigan, a western suburb of Detroit, noted as an automobile manufacturing center. Population: 91,418 (1996).

Dear·born Heights city in southeastern Michigan, northwest of Dearborn and a western suburb of Detroit. Population: 61,504 (1996).

Dear John let·ter, **Dear John** *n.* a letter from a woman ending a romantic or sexual relationship [From the salutation opening such a letter, "John" being a common male given name]

dear·ly /deérlee/ *adv.* **1. WITH STRONG FEELINGS** with great affection or intensity **2. AT GREAT COST** at a high cost ○ *He paid dearly for his mistake.*

dearth /durth/ *n.* a scarcity or lack of something ○ *a dearth of new ideas* [13thC. Formed from DEAR, probably originally with the idea of something being "expensive," which developed via "expensive because scarce" to "scarce."]

WORD KEY: SYNONYMS

See Synonyms at *lack.*

death /deth/ *n.* **1. END OF BEING ALIVE** the ending of all vital functions or processes in an organism or cell **2. WAY OF DYING** a way of dying ○ *an easy death* **3. SOMEBODY'S DYING** an instance of somebody's dying **4. END OF SOMETHING** the destruction or extinction of something **5. CONDITION OF BEING DEAD** the condition or quality of being dead ○ *In death she looked peaceful and composed.* [Old English *dēaþ*, from a prehistoric Germanic base that also produced English *die*] ◇ **at death's door** so ill or injured as to be almost dead ◇ **be the death of somebody** to cause somebody's death ◇ **bored to death with something** so bored as to be unable to stand it ◇ **catch your death (of cold)** to get a very bad cold ◇ **beat something to death** to continue arguing about something needlessly ◇ **like death warmed over** looking very ill ◇ **put somebody to death** to execute somebody ◇ **sick to death of something** tired of hearing about something or having to deal with it ◇ **to death** until somebody or something dies, or until something ends

Death *n.* a personification of death, usually represented as a ghostly form or skeleton holding a scythe

death ad·der *n.* a poisonous Australian snake with a body like an adder. Latin name: *Acanthopis antarcticus.*

death an·gel *n.* FUNGI = **death cap**

death·bed /déth bèd/ *n.* **BED WHERE SOMEBODY DIES** the bed on which somebody dies ■ *adj.* **WHILE DYING** said, done, or made by somebody while near death ○ *deathbed confessions*

death ben·e·fit *n.* a sum of money that is paid to the beneficiary of somebody's life insurance policy after the death of the insured

death·blow /déth blō/ *n.* **1. FATAL ACTION OR EVENT** an action or event that destroys or ends something **2. KILLING BLOW** a blow that kills somebody

death cam·as *n.* a plant of the lily family found in western North America. It has clusters of greenish-white flowers and roots that are poisonous to livestock. Genus: *Zigadenus.*

death camp *n.* a place where prisoners are systematically killed, or where harsh conditions make survival unlikely

death cap *n.* a poisonous fungus of North American and European woodlands that has a pale cap and a structure resembling a cup at its base. Latin name: *Amanita phalloides.*

death cell *n.* a prison cell in which somebody who has been sentenced to death is kept before execution

death cer·tif·i·cate *n.* an official document completed and signed by a doctor, stating that somebody is dead and giving the cause of death if known

death cham·ber *n.* a room where prisoners condemned to death are executed

death cup *n.* FUNGI = **death cap**

death-deal·ing *adj.* causing or liable to cause death (*literary*)

death-de·fy·ing *adj.* taking the risk of being killed

death fu·tures *npl.* a financial investment in the form of the purchase at a reduced rate of the life insurance of somebody who has a terminal illness, which provides necessary income for the dying person to meet medical costs and guarantees a good return for the purchaser (*hyphenated before a noun*) ○ *the growth in death-futures companies*

death grip *n.* a sudden powerful grip, especially one made by somebody who is dying

death house *n.* a building where prisoners condemned to death are housed prior to execution

death in·stinct *n.* an inherent and unconscious tendency, proposed in some theories of the mind, toward self-destruction

death knell *n.* 1. SIGNAL THAT SOMETHING IS DEAD a sign that something is dead, destroyed, or coming to an end ○ *The bankruptcy notice was the company's death knell.* 2. BELL ANNOUNCING A DEATH the ringing of a bell to announce that somebody has died

death·less /déthləss/ *adj.* immortal, usually because of being excellent ○ *deathless prose* —**death·less·ly** *adv.* —**death·less·ness** *n.*

death·ly /déthlee/ *adj.* LIKE DEATH resembling death or somebody who is dead ○ *deathly pale* ■ *adv.* EXTREMELY extremely or intensely —**death·li·ness** *n.*

Barnaby's

Death mask: "Mask of Agamemnon," discovered in a grave at Mycenae, Greece, in 1876

death mask *n.* a cast made of somebody's face soon after death

death met·al *n.* a type of heavy metal music characterized by satanic and horror film iconography

death no·tice *n. U.K.* an announcement of somebody's death published in a newspaper or journal

death pen·al·ty *n.* = **capital punishment**

death-qual·i·fy (**death-qual·i·fied, death-qual·i·fy·ing, death-qual·i·fies**) *vt.* to excuse somebody who rejects the death penalty from being on a jury whose verdict might entail a sentence of death —**death-qual·i·fi·ca·tion** *n.*

death rate *n.* the proportion of deaths to the population of a particular area or group

death rat·tle *n.* a rough gurgling noise that sometimes comes from somebody's throat at the moment of death, caused by breath passing through mucus

death ray *n.* an imaginary power beam that can kill

death row *n.* a row of prison cells, or an area in a prison, housing prisoners that have been sentenced to death

death seat *n. Aus, U.S.* the seat next to the driver in a motor vehicle, considered to be especially dangerous (*informal*)

death sen·tence *n.* 1. PUNISHMENT OF DEATH the punishment of death, received in a court of law 2. SOMETHING WITH FATAL RESULT an diagnosis or decision that has a fatal effect

death's head *n.* a human skull or its representation in art, often a symbol of mortality

death's head moth, death's head hawk·moth *n.* a large European hawkmoth with pale markings on the back of its thorax that look like a human skull. Latin name: *Acherontia atropos.*

death squad *n.* an unofficial but organized group of people who seek out and murder political opponents or other people they consider as enemies

death tax *n.* 1. = **estate tax** (*informal*) 2. = **inheritance tax**

death·trap /déth tràp/ *n.* a building, structure, or vehicle that is extremely unsafe (*informal*)

Death Val·ley Na·tion·al Park national park in southeastern California and southwestern Nevada. It contains the lowest point in the United States, 282 ft./86 m below sea level. Area: 8,554 sq. mi./13,765 sq. km.

death war·rant *n.* 1. LEGAL ORDER TO EXECUTE SOMEBODY an official document that authorizes somebody's execution 2. SOMETHING THAT IS FATAL something that ends hope or expectation

death·watch /déth wòch/ *n.* 1. TIME SPENT WATCHING AT DEATHBED a vigil near a dead or dying person, sometimes a traditional or religious custom 2. ZOOL = **deathwatch beetle**

death·watch bee·tle *n.* a small beetle whose larva bores into wood and makes a ticking sound. Latin name: *Xestobium rufovillosum.*

death wish *n.* a desire to die or, less commonly, a desire for the death of somebody else

de·at·tri·bu·tion /dee àttrə byóosh'n/ *n.* a change in an official or agreed opinion about the attribution of a work of art (*formal*)

deb /deb/ *n.* a debutante (*informal*) [Early 20thC. Shortening.]

deb. *abbr.* 1. FIN debenture 2. BANKING debit

de·ba·cle /də bák'l, də baák'l/ *n.* 1. CHAOTIC FAILURE something that becomes a disaster, defeat, or humiliating failure 2. BREAKUP OF RIVER ICE a sudden breakup of river ice in the spring thaw, causing a violent rush of flow water and ice [Early 19thC. From French, formed from *débâcler*, literally "to unbar" (used of ice breaking on a river), from, ultimately, Latin *bacculus* "stick" (source of English *bacillus* and *bacterium*).]

de·bag /dee bág/ (**-bagged, -bag·ging, -bags**) *vti.* to remove the testicles (*slang*) [Early 20thC. Formed from BAGS "trousers."]

De·Ba·key /də báykee/, **Michael Ellis** (*b.* 1908) U.S. cardiac surgeon. He performed the first coronary artery bypass operation (1966).

de·bar /di baár/ (**-barred, -bar·ring, -bars**) *vti.* to exclude somebody from entering or taking part in something [15thC. From Old French *desbarrer, barrer* "to bar."] —**de·bar·ment** *n.*

de·bark[1] /di baárk/ (**-barked, -bark·ing, -barks**) *v.* 1. *vi.* = **disembark** 2. *vt.* UNLOAD SOMETHING to take something off a vehicle after transporting it (*formal*) [Mid-17thC. From French *débarquer* "to get out of a boat."] —**de·bar·ka·tion** /dèe baar káysh'n/ *n.*

de·bark[2] /dee baárk/ (**-barked, -bark·ing, -barks**) *vt.* to remove the bark from wood

de·base /di báyss/ (**-based, -bas·ing, -bas·es**) *vt.* 1. MAKE SOMETHING INFERIOR to reduce something in value or quality 2. REDUCE IN RANK to reduce somebody in status, significance, or moral worth —**de·bas·ed·ness** *n.* —**de·bas·er** *n.*

de·base·ment /di báyssmənt/ *n.* a reduction in value, quality, or significance

de·bat·a·ble /di báytəb'l/ *adj.* liable to be questioned or disputed ○ *Whether it's actually an improvement is debatable.*

de·bate /di báyt/ *vti.* (**-bat·ed, -bat·ing, -bates**) 1. TALK OR ARGUE ABOUT SOMETHING to talk about something at length and in detail, especially as part of a formal exchange of opinion 2. THINK ABOUT SOMETHING to ponder something carefully ■ *n.* 1. PUBLIC MEETING FOR DISCUSSION an organized or public discussion of something 2. CONSIDERATION a prolonged consideration of something 3. ARGUMENT argument or prolonged discussion ○ *The matter is not open to debate.* [13thC. Via Old French *debat* from, ultimately, Latin *battere* "to fight."] —**de·bat·er** *n.*

de·bat·ing so·ci·e·ty *n.* an organization whose main purpose is to hold regular formal debates on various topics

de·bauch /di báwch/ *vt.* (**-bauched, -bauch·ing, -bauch·es**) (*formal*) 1. LEAD SOMEBODY INTO IMMORAL BEHAVIOR to persuade somebody to behave in an immoral way 2. SEDUCE SOMEBODY to seduce somebody ■ *n.* EPISODE OF DISSIPATION a period of indulgence in drunkenness or immoral behavior (*formal*) [Late 16thC. From French *débaucher*, of unknown origin.]

de·bauched /di báwcht/ *adj.* unrestrainedly and immorally self-indulgent —**de·bauch·ed·ly** /di báwchədlee, -báwcht-/ *adv.* —**de·bauch·ed·ness** /-báwchədnəss, -báwcht-/ *n.*

de·bauch·ee /di bàw chée, dèbbə shée/ *n.* somebody who leads an immoral, unrestrained, and self-indulgent life (*formal*)

de·bauch·er /di báwchər/ *n.* somebody who corrupts people by encouraging them to behave immorally, especially in an unrestrained and self-indulgent way (*formal*)

de·bauch·er·y /di báwchəree/ (*plural* **-ies**) *n.* unrestrained self-indulgent behavior, or an instance of this

de Beau·voir /də bò vwaár/, **Simone** ➧ **Beauvoir**

de·ben·ture /də bénchər/ *n.* 1. **de·ben·ture, de·ben·ture bond** BOND BACKED ONLY BY CREDIT RATING a bond backed only by the credit standing of the issuer, sometimes convertible into stock 2. CERTIFICATE OF DEBT a certificate that acknowledges the existence of a debt of a specified amount owed to somebody 3. CUSTOMS REFUND CERTIFICATE a certificate issued by customs officials to somebody providing for a refund of a duty previously paid [15thC. From Latin *debentur*, literally "they are owed," a form of the verb *debere* "to owe" (source of English *debt*). Probably originally used on certificates of indebtedness.] —**de·ben·tured** *adj.*

de·bil·i·tate /di bílli tàyt/ (**-tat·ed, -tat·ing, -tates**) *vt.* to sap strength of somebody or something [Mid-16thC. From Latin *debilitat-*, the past participle stem of *debilitare* "to weaken," from *debilitas* "weakness" (see DEBILITY).] —**de·bil·i·ta·tion** /-bìlli táysh'n/ *n.* —**de·bil·i·ta·tive** /-bílli tàytiv/ *adj.*

de·bil·i·tat·ed /di bílli tàytəd/ *adj.* with diminished strength and energy

WORD KEY: SYNONYMS

See Synonyms at ***weak***.

de·bil·i·tat·ing /di bílli tàyting/ *adj.* reducing somebody's strength or energy

de·bil·i·ty /di bíllətee/ (*plural* **-ties**) *n.* a general lack of energy and strength [15thC. Via French *débilité* from Latin *debilitas*, from *debilis* "weak."]

deb·it /débbit/ *n.* 1. RECORDED DEBT OR EXPENSE an entry showing a debt or expense in a record of accounts 2. SUM OF MONEY DEDUCTED an amount of money taken out of an account 3. TOTAL OF DEBTS OR EXPENSES the total of individual debit entries in an account 4. COLUMN FOR RECORDING DEBTS OR EXPENSES a column on the left of an accounting statement where debts and expenses are recorded 5. DRAWBACK something that is disadvantageous or unfavorable ○ *The pay's better, but on the debit side there's a lot more work to do.* ■ *vt.* (**-it·ed, -it·ing, -its**) 1. RECORD DEBIT to make, enter, or record a debit in an account 2. CHARGE SOMEBODY MONEY to remove a sum of money from somebody's account in payment for something [15thC. From Latin *debitum* "debt" (see DEBT).]

deb·it card *n.* a plastic card that the holder can use to pay for purchases, the money being transferred directly from the holder's account to the seller

deb·o·nair /dèbbə náir, débbə nàir/ *adj.* 1. ELEGANT looking well-dressed, sophisticated, and at ease 2. SHOWING ELEGANCE showing ease of manner, elegance, or sophistication [13thC. From Old French, from *de bon aire* "of good disposition."] —**deb·o·nair·ly** *adv.* —**deb·o·nair·ness** *n.*

de·bone /dee bṓn/ (**-boned, -bon·ing, -bones**) *vt.* to remove the bones from meat or fish

de Bo·no /də bṓ nō/, **Edward** (*b.* 1933) Maltese-born British psychologist. Director of the Cognitive Research Trust since 1971, he has published widely on thought processes and lateral thinking.

de·bouch /di bówch, di bóosh/ (**-bouched, -bouch·ing, -bouch·es**) *vi.* 1. MOVE INTO LESS CONFINED AREA to move from an enclosed or confined area into more open terrain 2. EMERGE INTO A WIDER PLACE to widen out, or flow out, from a valley or ravine into a wider area (*refers to a geographic feature such as a valley or a flow of water*) [Mid-18thC. From French *déboucher*, literally "to come out of the mouth," modeled on Italian *sboccare*, both ultimately from Latin *bucca* "cheek, mouth."]

dé·bou·ché /dày boo sháy/ *n.* an exit or outlet for troops in fortifications [Mid-18thC. From French, from the past participle of *déboucher* (see DEBOUCH).]

de·bouch·ment /di bówchmənt, di bóoshmənt/ *n.* an act of debouching, or a place where this happens

De·brett /də brét/, **De·brett's Peer·age** *n.* a publication that lists members of the British aristocracy [Mid-19thC. Named for John *Debrett* (1705–1822), a London publisher who wrote and published the first edition in 1803.]

dé·bride·ment /day brēedmənt, di brēedmənt, dày brēed maàN/ *n.* the removal of dead, damaged, or infected tissue from a wound in order to expose healthy tissue and allow the wound to heal [Mid-19thC. From French, literally "unbridling."]

de·brief /di brēef/ (**-briefed, -brief·ing, -briefs**) *v.* **1.** *vt.* INTERROGATE SOMEBODY AFTER SOMETHING HAS ENDED to question somebody closely after a task, mission, or event has ended **2.** *vi.* MAKE REPORT to supply information about a task, mission, or event after it has ended

de·brief·ing /di brēefing/ *n.* an interview in which somebody is asked about or reports on an event or mission after it has ended

de·bris /də brēe, day brēe, dáy brēe/ (*plural* **-bris**), **dé·bris** (*plural* **-bris**) *n.* **1.** FRAGMENTS fragments of something that has been destroyed or broken down **2.** BROKEN FRAGMENTS OF ROCK fragments of rock broken by a powerful or destructive natural force such as the action of a glacier [Early 18thC. Via French *débris*, literally "broken up," from, ultimately, Old French *brisier* "to break."]

de·bris flow *n.* a slow-moving body of sediment in which rock particles are suspended in a slurry of mud

de Bro·glie wave·length /də bràw glēe-/ *n.* the wavelength of the wave associated with the motion of an atomic or subatomic particle **(de Broglie wave)** that produces diffraction. The de Broglie wavelength is given by Planck's constant divided by the mass and velocity of the particle. [Early 20thC. Named for the French physicist Louis Victor *de Broglie* (1892–1987).]

Debs /debz/, **Eugene** (1855–1926) U.S. Socialist leader, pacifist, and labor organizer. He helped establish the Socialist Party of America and stood five times as Socialist candidate for U.S. president (1900–20). He was imprisoned from 1918 until 1921 for his pacifist beliefs. Full name **Eugene Victor Debs**

debt /det/ *n.* **1.** SOMETHING THAT IS OWED an amount of money, a service, or an item of property that is owed to somebody **2.** OBLIGATION an obligation or borrowing ○ *the criminal must repay his debt to society* **3.** STATE OF OWING SOMETHING the condition of owing something to somebody **4.** SIN a sin or trespass (*archaic*) [13thC. Via French *dette* from Latin *debitum* (which probably influenced the modern spelling of DEBT), from the past participle of *debere* "to owe" (source of English *due* and *duty*).] —**debt·less** *adj.*

debt of hon·or *n.* a debt that somebody is morally, but not legally, obliged to pay

debt·or /déttər/ *n.* **1.** SOMEBODY OR SOMETHING THAT OWES somebody who or something that owes a debt **2.** SINNER somebody who has sinned, especially against somebody (*archaic*)

debt swap *n.* an exchange of financial obligations with somebody or something in order to gain profit or a more convenient repayment schedule

de·bud /dee búd/ (**-bud·ded, -bud·ding, -buds**) *vt.* = **disbud**

de·bug /dee búg/ (**-bugged, -bug·ging, -bugs**) *vt.* **1.** COMPUT FIND AND REMOVE ERRORS to find and remove errors in something, especially in a computer program or system **2.** REMOVE SECRET LISTENING DEVICES to find and take away any electronic listening devices that are concealed in a place **3.** CLEAR PLACE OF INSECTS to remove or destroy insects that are in a place (*informal*)

de·bug·ger /dee búggər/ *n.* **1.** COMPUT COMPUTER PROGRAM THAT FINDS SOFTWARE ERRORS a computer utility program that helps to find software errors by allowing the user to access the source code as the program runs **2.** BUG REMOVER somebody who or something that removes bugs

de·bunk /dee búngk/ (**-bunked, -bunk·ing, -bunks**) *vt.* to show that something is wrong or false [Early 20thC. Formed from BUNK[2].] —**de·bunk·er** *n.*

de·burr /dee búr/ (**-burred, -bur·ring, -burrs**) *vt.* to remove rough edges (**burrs**) from a piece of machined metal

De·bus·sy /də byōōssee, dèbbyoo sēe/, **Claude** (1862–1918) French composer. His works include the opera *Pelléas et Mélisande* (1902) and the orchestral poem *La Mer* (1905). He developed a style known as musical impressionism.

de·but /day byōō, dáy byōō/ *n.* **1.** FIRST PUBLIC APPEARANCE the first public appearance or presentation of a performer, program, or performance **2.** YOUNG WOMAN'S FIRST OFFICIAL SOCIAL ENGAGEMENT a young woman's first appearance in public at a formal social event ■ *vti.* (**-buted, -but·ing, -buts**) MAKE FIRST FORMAL PUBLIC APPEARANCE to show or perform something formally and publicly for the first time [Mid-18thC. From French, formed from *débuter* "to lead off," from *de-* "from" + *but* "goal, target."]

deb·u·tante /débbyə taànt/ *n.* a young woman who is being introduced formally into society by appearing at a public event such as a dance or party [Early 19thC. From French, literally "leading off," from the present participle of *débuter* (see DEBUT).]

dec. *abbr.* **1. decd.** deceased **2.** declaration **3.** GRAMMAR declension **4.** declination **5.** decrease

Dec. *abbr.* December

dec- *prefix.* = **deca-**. symbol **da** (*used before vowels*)

deca- *prefix.* ten ○ *decagram.* Symbol **da** [From Greek *deka*. Ultimately from the Indo-European word for "ten," which is also the ancestor of English *ten* and *-teen*, and *decimal*.]

dec·ade /dé kàyd, de káyd/ *n.* **1.** TEN YEARS a period of ten years **2.** GROUP OF TEN a group, set, or series of ten [15thC. Via French from the late Latin stem *decad-*, from, ultimately, Greek *deka* "ten."] —**dec·a·dal** /dékəd'l/ *adj.*

dec·a·dence /dékəd'ns/, **dec·a·den·cy** /dékəd'nsee/ *n.* **1.** PROCESS OF CIVILIZATION'S DECLINE a process of decline or decay in a society, especially in its morals **2.** STATE OF DECLINE the condition of a civilization in decline **3.** IMMORALITY a state of uninhibited self-indulgence [Mid-16thC. Via French *décadence* from, ultimately, Latin *decadere* "to fall down or away," from *cadere* "to fall" (see DECAY).]

dec·a·dent /dékəd'nt/ *adj.* **1.** IN DECLINE in a process of decline or decay, especially in morals **2.** IMMORAL showing uninhibitedly self-indulgent behavior ■ *n.* DEGENERATE PERSON somebody who behaves in an immoral or uninhibitedly self-indulgent way [Mid-19thC. From French *décadent*, a back-formation from *décadence* (see DECADENCE).] —**de·ca·dent·ly** *adv.*

de·caf /dée kàf/ *n.* DECAFFEINATED DRINK a decaffeinated drink, especially coffee, tea, or a soft drink (*informal*) ■ *adj.* DECAFFEINATED decaffeinated (*informal*) [Late 20thC. Shortening.]

de·caf·fein·ate /dee káffə nàyt/ (**-at·ed, -at·ing, -ates**) *vt.* to remove all or most of the caffeine from a substance —**de·caf·fein·a·tion** /-kàffə náysh'n/ *n.*

de·caf·fein·at·ed /dee káffə nàytəd/ *adj.* WITHOUT CAFFEINE with all or most of the caffeine taken out ■ *n.* DRINK WITHOUT CAFFEINE a drink from which all or most of the caffeine has been removed

dec·a·gon /dékə gòn/ *n.* a polygon with ten straight sides and ten angles [Mid-17thC. Via medieval Latin from Greek *dekagōnos*, literally "ten-angled."] —**de·cag·o·nal** /də kággən'l/ *adj.* —**de·cag·o·nal·ly** /də kággənəlee/ *adv.*

dec·a·gram /dékə gràm/, **dek·a·gram** *n.* a unit of weight equal to ten grams. Symbol **dag, dkg** [Early 19thC. From French *décagramme*.]

dec·a·he·dron /dèkə hēedrən/ *n.* a solid geometric figure with ten flat outer surfaces [Early 19thC. Coined from DECA- + -HEDRON.] —**dec·a·he·dral** *adj.*

de·cal /dée kàl, di kál/ *n.* **1.** DECORATIVE STICKER a decorative paper or plastic sticker **2.** PICTURE FOR TRANSFER a picture or design on specially treated paper that allows it to be transferred to a surface such as glass, wood, or metal [Mid-20thC. Shortening of DECALCOMANIA.]

de·cal·ci·fi·ca·tion /dee kàlsəfi káysh'n/ *n.* the loss of calcium or calcium compounds from bone or teeth

de·cal·ci·fy /dee kálsə fì/ (**-fied, -fy·ing, -fies**) *vti.* to lose calcium or a calcium compound from the bones or teeth —**de·cal·ci·fi·er** *n.*

de·cal·co·ma·ni·a /di kàlkə máynee ə/ *n.* **1.** PROCESS OF TRANSFERRING PICTURE FROM PAPER the process of fixing a picture or design to the surface of something, e.g., glass, pottery, or textiles, by transferring it from a prepared type of paper **2.** = **decal** [Mid-19thC. From French *décalcomanie*, from *décalquer* "to transfer a tracing" + *-manie* "mania, craze," from its popularity in the 19thC.]

de·ca·les·cence /dèekə léss'ns/ *n.* the absorption of heat without temperature increase at specific conditions during the heating of a metal, caused by changes in the crystalline composition [Late 19thC. Formed from *calescence* "increasing warmth or heat."] —**de·ca·les·cent** *adj.*

dec·a·li·ter /dékə lèetər/, **dek·a·li·ter** *n.* a unit of volume equal to ten liters. Symbol **dal, dkl, dl** [Early 19thC. From French *décalitre*.]

Dec·a·logue /dékə lòg/ *n.* = **Ten Commandments** [14thC. Either directly or via French from ecclesiastical Latin *decalogus*, from Greek *dekalogos (biblos)* "(book of) ten pronouncements," from *deka* "ten" + *logos* "word, pronouncement."]

dec·a·me·ter /dékə mèetər/, **dek·a·me·ter** *n.* a unit of length equal to ten meters. Symbol **dam, dkm** [Early 19thC. From French *décamètre*.]

dec·a·met·ric /dèkə méttrik/ *adj.* having radio waves of high frequency, between 10 and 100 meters

de·camp /di kámp/ (**-camped, -camp·ing, -camps**) *vi.* **1.** SUDDENLY OR SECRETLY LEAVE to leave a place abruptly or secretly **2.** LEAVE A CAMP to pack up and leave a camp or camping site [Late 17thC. From French *décamper*, from *camp* "camp."] —**de·camp·ment** *n.*

de·ca·nal /di káyn'l, dékən'l/ *adj.* relating to a dean or deanery (*formal*) [Early 18thC. From medieval Latin *decanalis*, from late Latin *decanus* (see DEAN).]

de·ca·ni /di káy nì/ *adj.* connected with or sung by the half of a choir that sits on the south side of the chancel. ◊ **cantoris** [Mid-18thC. From Latin, literally "of the dean" (see DEAN), referring to the side of the church the dean usually sits on.]

dec·a·no·ic ac·id /dekə nō ik-/ *n.* = **capric acid**

de·cant /di kánt/ (**-cant·ed, -cant·ing, -cants**) *vt.* to pour a liquid gently and carefully from one container to another so as not to disturb sediment [Mid-17thC. From medieval Latin *decanthare*, from Latin *canthus* "lip of a jug," from Greek *kanthos* "corner of the eye" (from the supposed similarity in shape).]

Decanter

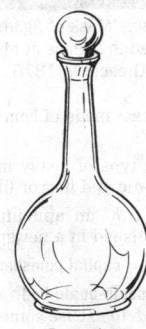

de·cant·er /di kántər/ *n.* a decorative bottle with a stopper, used for holding and serving drinks, especially wine

de·cap·i·tate /di káppi tàyt/ (**-tat·ed, -tat·ing, -tates**) *vt.* to cut off the head of somebody or something [Early 17thC. From late Latin *decapitat-*, the past participle stem of *decapitare*, from Latin *caput* "head" (source of English *capital, chieftain, mischief*, and *biceps*).] —**de·cap·i·ta·tor** *n.*

de·cap·i·ta·tion /di kàppi táysh'n/ *n.* the act, practice, or process of cutting the head off somebody or something

dec·a·pod /dékə pòd/ *n.* **1.** INVERTEBRATE ANIMAL WITH 10 LEGS an invertebrate animal with stalked eyes and five pairs of legs, one or more with pincers, attached to the thorax. Many decapods are marine crustaceans and they include shrimp, lobsters, and crabs. Order: Decapoda. **2.** MARINE INVERTEBRATE ANIMAL WITH 10 TENTACLES a marine mollusk with ten tentacles, e.g., the cuttlefish or squid. Class: Cephalopoda. [Early 19thC. Via French *décapode* from modern Latin, literally "ten legs."] —**de·cap·o·dal** /di káppəd'l/ *adj.* —**de·cap·o·dan** /-káppəd'n/ *adj.* —**de·cap·o·dous** /-káppədəss/ *adj.*

de·cap·su·late /dee kápsə làyt/ (**-lat·ed, -lat·ing, -lates**) *vt.* to remove a capsule from a body part or organ such as the kidney —**de·cap·su·la·tion** /dee kàpsə láysh'n/ *n.*

de·car·bon·ate /dee kaárbə nàyt/ (**-at·ed, -at·ing, -ates**) *vt.* to remove carbon dioxide or carbonic acid from something —**de·car·bon·a·tion** /-kaarbə náysh'n/ *n.* — **de·car·bon·a·tor** /-kaarbə nàytər/ *n.*

de·car·bon·ize /dee kaarbə nīz/ (**-ized, -iz·ing, -iz·es**) *vt.* to remove the carbon from something, e.g., the carbon deposits from an internal-combustion engine —**de·car·bon·i·za·tion** /-kaarbəni záysh'n/ *n.* — **de·car·bon·iz·er** /-kaarbə nīzər/ *n.*

de·car·box·yl·ase /dee kaar bóksə làyss, -làyz/ *n.* an enzyme that helps to remove a carboxyl group from an organic compound, e.g., an amino acid [Mid-20thC. Coined from DE- + CARBOXYL + -ASE.]

de·car·box·yl·a·tion /dee kaar bóksə làysh'n/ *n.* the removal or loss of a carboxyl group from an organic compound

de·car·bu·rize /dee kaarbə rīz/ (**-rized, -riz·ing, -riz·es**) *vt.* = **decarbonize**

dec·are /dé kaar/ *n.* a metric unit of area equal to ten ares [Early 19thC. From French *décare* "ten ares."]

de·ca·style /dékə stīl/ *n.* PORTICO WITH 10 COLUMNS a portico that has ten columns ■ *adj.* WITH 10 COLUMNS consisting of or having ten columns [Early 18thC. From Greek *dekastulos* "having ten columns."]

dec·a·syl·la·ble /dékə sìlləb'l/ *n.* a line of verse, or sometimes a word, made up of ten syllables — **dec·a·syl·lab·ic** /dèkə si lábbik/ *adj.*

de·cath·lete /di káthleet/ *n.* an athlete who competes in the decathlon

de·cath·lon /di káthlən, di káth lòn/ *n.* a contest for men in which the athletes compete in ten different events and are awarded points for each to find the best all-around athlete. The events are long jump, high jump, pole vault, shot put, discus, javelin, 110 meter hurdles, and running over 100 meters, 400 meters, and 1500 meters. ◊ **heptathlon, pentathlon, triathlon** [Early 20thC. Coined from DECA- + Greek *athlon* "contest."]

De·ca·tur /di káytər/ **1.** city in northern Alabama, on the southern bank of the Tennessee River, southwest of Huntsville. Population: 53,797 (1996). **2.** city in central Illinois, on the northern bank of the Sangamon River, southwest of Champaign and east of Springfield. Population: 81,369 (1996).

De·ca·tur, Stephen (1779–1820) U.S. naval officer. He commanded the *United States* in the War of 1812, defeating the British vessel *Macedonian*.

de·cay /di káy/ *v.* (**-cayed, -cay·ing, -cays**) **1.** *vti.* BIOL BECOME ROTTEN OR DETERIORATE to decompose, or make something decompose, and become soft, crumbly, or liquefied **2.** *vti.* DECLINE OR CAUSE SOMETHING TO DECLINE to decline in quality gradually and steadily, or cause something to undergo such a decline **3.** *vi.* NUCLEAR PHYS DISINTEGRATE to undergo spontaneous disintegration (*refers to radioactive material*) **4.** *vi.* PHYS DECREASE to decrease gradually in magnitude (*refers to a physical quantity or effect*) **5.** *vi.* ASTRON DESCEND to decrease gradually in altitude (*refers to an artificial satellite in orbit*) ■ *n.* **1.** DECLINE a decline in quality ○ *"A state too extensive in itself, or by virtue of its dependencies, ultimately falls into decay."* (Simón Bolivar, *Letter from Jamaica*; 1815) **2.** BIOL PROCESS OF BIOLOGICAL DETERIORATION the process of rotting and decomposition that affects plant material and the bodies of animals after they die and are invaded by bacteria or fungi **3.** BIOL ROTTEN OR SPOILED PART the areas of something that are decomposed or rotted ○ *cut out the decay* **4.** NUCLEAR PHYS DISINTEGRATION OF RADIOACTIVE MATERIAL the spontaneous disintegration of a radioactive material along with the emission of one or more elementary particles or radiation **5.** PHYS GRADUAL DECREASE a gradual decrease in the magnitude of a physical quantity or effect, such as current, stored charge, or phosphorescence **6.** ASTRON DESCENT OF ARTIFICIAL SATELLITE the gradual decrease in altitude of an orbiting artificial satellite **7.** MUSIC DECLINE IN SOUND OF NOTE the fading away of a musical note [15thC. Via French *decair* from, ultimately, Latin *decidere*, literally "to fall off or away" (source of English *deciduous*), from *cadere* "to fall" (source of English *case*, *accident*, and *chance*).] —**de·cay·a·ble** *adj.*

Dec·can /dékən/ triangular plateau that makes up much of southern India, south of the Sātpura Range. It is bordered by the mountainous Eastern and Western Ghats ranges.

decd. *abbr.* deceased

de·cease /di seess/ *n.* DEATH death, especially the death of somebody (*formal*) ■ *vi.* (**-ceased, -ceas·ing, -ceas·es**) DIE to die (*formal*) [14thC. Via French *décès* from Latin *decessus* "death, departure," from the past participle of *decedere* "to go away" (source of English *predecessor*), from *cedere* "to go" (see CEDE).]

de·ceased /di seest/ *adj.* DEAD no longer living (*formal*) ■ *n.* DEAD PERSON somebody who has died recently (*formal*)

WORD KEY: SYNONYMS

See Synonyms at ***dead***.

de·ceit /di seet/ *n.* **1.** DISHONEST PRACTICE the act or practice of deceiving or misleading somebody **2.** SOMETHING DONE TO MISLEAD something that is done to trick or mislead somebody [13thC. From Old French, formed from *deceveir* (see DECEIVE).]

de·ceit·ful /di seetfəl/ *adj.* intentionally misleading or fraudulent in lying to people or not telling them the whole truth —**de·ceit·ful·ly** *adv.*

de·ceit·ful·ness /di seetfəlnəss/ *n.* = **deceit** *n.* 1

de·ceive /di seev/ (**-ceived, -ceiv·ing, -ceives**) *v.* **1.** *vt.* INTENTIONALLY TRICK OR MISLEAD SOMEBODY to mislead somebody or hide the truth deliberately **2.** *vr.* FOOL YOURSELF to convince yourself of something that is not true **3.** *vt.* BE SEXUALLY UNFAITHFUL TO SOMEBODY to be sexually unfaithful to a spouse or sexual partner [13thC. Via Old French *deceveir* from, ultimately, Latin *decipere* "to ensnare, take in," from *capere* "to take, seize" (source of English *capture* and *receive*).] — **de·ceiv·a·bil·i·ty** /di seevə bíllətee/ *n.* —**de·ceiv·a·ble** /di seevəb'l/ *adj.* —**de·ceiv·er** *n.*

de·ceiv·ing /di seeving/ *adj.* liable or meant to mislead —**de·ceiv·ing·ly** *adv.*

de·cel·er·ate /dee séllə ràyt/ (**-at·ed, -at·ing, -ates**) *vti.* to reduce speed, or make something go more slowly [Late 19thC. Coined from DE- + ACCELERATE.] — **de·cel·er·a·tor** *n.*

de·cel·er·a·tion /dee sèllə ráysh'n/ *n.* the act or process of reducing speed or making something go more slowly

De·cem·ber /di sémbər/ *n.* the 12th month of the year in the Gregorian calendar. It is 31 days long. [13thC. Via French *décembre* from Latin *december*, from *decem* "ten," because it was the tenth month of the Roman year.]

De·cem·brist /di sémbrist/ *n.* a member of a group of Russian officers who tried unsuccessfully to overthrow Tsar Nicholas I of Russia in December 1825

de·cem·vir /di sémvər/ *n.* **1.** ROMAN LAW-MAKER any one of a group of ten ancient Roman magistrates, especially those who drew up the laws of the Twelve Tables in 451–450 B.C. **2.** ONE OF 10 OFFICIALS a member of an official body that consists of ten people (*archaic*) [15thC. From Latin *decem viri* (plural) "ten men."] —**de·cem·vi·ral** *adj.*

de·cem·vi·rate /di sémvərət, di sémvə ràyt/ *n.* a group of ten people who hold power or office together (*formal*)

de·cen·cy /deess'nsee/ *n.* (*plural* **-cies**) **1.** CONFORMITY WITH MORAL STANDARDS behavior or an attitude that conforms to the commonly accepted standards of what is right and respectable **2.** MODESTY modesty or propriety ■ **de·cen·cies** *npl.* MORAL BEHAVIOR the commonly accepted standards of good behavior (*formal*)

de·cen·na·ry /di sénnəree/ *n.* (*plural* **-ries**) DECADE a ten-year period (*formal*) ■ *adj.* = **decennial** [Early 19thC. Formed from DECENNIUM.]

de·cen·ni·al /di sénnee əl/ *adj.* IN OR EVERY 10 YEARS lasting for, consisting of, or happening every ten years ■ *n.* 10TH ANNIVERSARY an anniversary celebrated ten years after something or every ten years — **de·cen·ni·al·ly** *adv.*

de·cen·ni·um /di sénnee əm/ (*plural* **-ums** *or* **-a** /di sénnee ə/) *n.* a ten-year period (*formal*) [Late 17thC. From Latin, formed from *decennis*, from *decem* "ten" + *annus* "year."]

de·cent /deess'nt/ *adj.* **1.** MORAL conforming to accepted standards of moral behavior **2.** GOOD above average in quality or quantity ○ *one of the few decent restaurants around here* **3.** QUITE GOOD adequate or sufficient in quality ○ *did a decent job* **4.** SUFFICIENTLY DRESSED fully dressed, as opposed to being naked or in underwear only (*informal*) ○ *Don't come in; I'm not decent!* **5.** KIND kind, considerate, or generous [Mid-16thC. Either via French *décent* or directly from Latin *decent-*, the present participle stem of *decere* "to be fitting."] —**de·cent·ness** *n.*

de·cent·ly /deess'ntlee/ *adv.* in a way that conforms to accepted standards of conduct or appearance

de·cen·tral·ize /dee séntrə līz/ (**-ized, -iz·ing, -iz·es**) *vti.* to reorganize something such as a political unit so that power is shifted from a central or upper location to another, less central place — **de·cen·tral·i·za·tion** /dee sèntrəli záysh'n/ *n.*

de·cep·tion /di sépshən/ *n.* **1.** PRACTICE OF MISLEADING SOMEBODY the practice of deliberately making somebody believe things that are not true **2.** SOMETHING INTENDED TO MISLEAD SOMEBODY an act, trick, or device intended to deceive somebody [15thC. Either directly or via French from the Latin stem *deception-*, from *decept-*, the past participle stem of *decipere* (see DECEIVE).]

de·cep·tive /di séptiv/ *adj.* **1.** MISLEADING liable or meant to mislead somebody **2.** ABLE TO BE MISTAKEN capable of being mistaken for something else ○ *a deceptive barking noise* [Early 17thC. Either directly or via French from late Latin *deceptivus*, from Latin *decept-* (see DECEPTION).] —**de·cep·tive·ness** *n.*

de·cep·tive·ly /di séptivlee/ *adv.* in a way that misleads people or is contrary to appearances ○ *a deceptively easy task*

WORD KEY: USAGE

Although *deceptively simple* almost invariably means "complex despite apparent simplicity," that is not a model from which to generalize about the meaning of ***deceptively***. When people are asked whether, e.g., *a deceptively dangerous place to stand* is a place that is more or less dangerous than it appears, they respond variously, with a substantial minority admitting they have no idea what ***deceptively*** is intended to convey. Sometimes context clarifies the meaning: *It was a small house, but it had deceptively large rooms.* Where this is not the case, ***deceptively*** is best avoided.

de·cer·e·brate *adj.* /dee sérrə bràyt, -brət/ HAVING LOST CEREBRAL FUNCTION having lost all cerebral function, vision, hearing, and other sensations, and voluntary motor activity, e.g., as a result of a severe stroke ■ *vt.* /-bràyt/ (**-brat·ed, -brat·ing, -brates**) REMOVE CEREBRUM to remove the cerebrum or brainstem from an animal surgically [Late 19thC. Coined from DE- + CEREBRUM + -ATE.] —**de·cer·e·bra·tion** /dee sèrrə bráysh'n/ *n.*

de·cer·ti·fy /dee súrtə fī/ (**-fied, -fy·ing, -fies**) *vt.* to withdraw certification from somebody or something —**de·cer·ti·fi·ca·tion** /dee sùrtəfi káysh'n/ *n.*

de·chan·nel·ize (**de·chan·nel·ized, de·chan·nel·iz·ing, de·chan·nel·iz·es**) *vt.* /dee chánn'l īz/ to reroute a river to its original location and configuration of flow [Late 20thC]

deci- *prefix.* a tenth ○ *decigram*. Symbol **d** [Via French from Latin *decimus* (see DECIMAL)]

dec·i·are /déssee aar/ *n.* a metric unit of land area equal to ten square meters or one tenth of an are

de·ci·bel /déssəb'l, déssə bèl/ *n.* a unit of relative sound loudness, electric voltage, or current equal to ten times the common logarithm of the ratio of two readings. For sound, the decibel scale runs from zero for the least perceptible sound to 130 for sound that causes pain. Symbol **dB**

de·cide /di síd/ (**-cid·ed, -cid·ing, -cides**) *v.* **1.** *vti.* CHOOSE WHAT TO DO to make a choice or come to a conclusion about something ○ *We decided not to go in the end.* **2.** *vt.* LEAD SOMEBODY TO CHOOSE to make somebody choose what to do or come to a conclusion about something (*informal*) ○ *His encouraging letter decided me against dropping the course.* **3.** *vt.* END SOMETHING CLEARLY to bring something to an end in a definite or obvious way **4.** *vi.* ARRIVE AT A VERDICT to come to a verdict or judgment [14thC. Directly or via French *décider* from Latin *decidere*, literally "to cut off," from *caedere* "to cut" (source of English *chisel*); the underlying idea being to cut through a problem.] —**de·cid·a·ble** *adj.*

de·cid·ed /di sídəd/ *adj.* **1.** OBVIOUS clearly seen, felt, or noticed **2.** FIRM OR CERTAIN free of uncertainty or doubt —**de·cid·ed·ness** *n.*

de·cid·ed·ly /di sídədlee/ *adv.* without any doubt or question

de·cid·er /di sídər/ *n.* something that settles the outcome of a contest or argument, especially, in sport, a final scoring play or a game played to determine the ultimate winner

de·cid·ing /di síding/ *adj.* acting to settle the result of a contest or debate, or to make clear what must be done next

de·cid·u·a /di síjjoo ə/ (*plural* **-ae** /ee/) *n.* a specialized part of the mucous membrane (**endometrium**) that lines the womb during pregnancy and is shed with the placenta at birth [Late 18thC. From modern Latin *decidua (membrana)* "deciduous (membrane)," so called because it is shed (see DECIDUOUS).] —**de·cid·u·al** *adj.* —**de·cid·u·ate** /-síjjoo ət/ *adj.*

de·cid·u·ous /di síjjoo əss/ *adj.* **1.** SHEDDING LEAVES IN FALL used to describe trees and shrubs that shed their leaves in the fall **2.** WITH DECIDUOUS TREES used to describe a forest or wood that is composed mostly of deciduous trees **3.** SHED AFTER DEVELOPMENTAL STAGE shed after a stage of development, as are the teeth, antlers, or wings of mammals and birds, or shed easily or at intervals, as are the scales of fish [Mid-17thC. From Latin *deciduus*, from *decidere* "to fall down," from *cadere* "to fall, die" (see DECAY).] —**de·cid·u·ous·ly** *adv.* —**de·cid·u·ous·ness** *n.*

de·cid·u·ous tooth *n.* = **milk tooth**

dec·i·gram /déssi gràm/, **dec·i·gramme** *n.* a metric unit of weight or mass equal to one tenth of a gram [Early 19thC. From French *décigramme*.]

dec·ile /dé sīl, déss'l/ *n.* **1.** ANY OF 10 GROUPS any one of ten groups containing an equal number of the items that make up a frequency distribution **2.** VALUE DIVIDING UP A FREQUENCY DISTRIBUTION any of the nine values that divide the total number of items in a frequency distribution into ten groups, each containing an equal number of items [Late 19thC. Coined from DECI- + -ILE.]

dec·i·li·ter /déssə leètər/ *n.* a metric unit of volume equal to one tenth of a liter [Early 19thC. From French *décilitre*.]

dec·i·mal /déssəm'l/ *adj.* COUNTED IN GROUPS OF 10 using the number ten as a base and counted or ordered in units of ten, or belonging to a system organized in this way ■ *n.* NUMBER IN DECIMAL SYSTEM a number expressed in a counting system that uses units of ten, especially a decimal fraction [Early 17thC. From modern Latin *decimalis*, from Latin *decimus* "tenth," from *decem* "ten."] —**dec·i·mal·ly** *adv.*

dec·i·mal clas·si·fi·ca·tion *n.* = **Dewey decimal system**

dec·i·mal cur·ren·cy *n.* a type of currency based on units of ten or multiples of ten, now used in most countries

dec·i·mal frac·tion *n.* a numerical fraction with ten as its denominator, written showing the fractional elements after a decimal point

dec·i·mal·ize /déssəmə līz/ (**-ized, -iz·ing, -iz·es**) *vti.* to convert something, e.g., a country's currency or measurement system, into a decimal or metric system or convert to this —**dec·i·mal·i·za·tion** *n.*

dec·i·mal place *n.* the place or a specific number of digits to the right of the decimal point in a line of numbers

dec·i·mal point *n.* a printed or written dot in a decimal number that divides the whole numbers from the tenths, hundredths, and smaller divisions of ten

dec·i·mal sys·tem *n.* a numerical system that has the number ten as the basic unit from which the other counting units are formed as multiples. The metric system of measurement and most currency systems are based on a decimal system, using a basic unit of ten with larger units as multiples of it.

dec·i·mate /déssə màyt/ (**-mat·ed, -mat·ing, -mates**) *vt.* **1.** DESTROY LARGE PROPORTION OF SOMETHING to kill off or remove a large proportion of a group of people, animals, or things, or of the population of a place **2.** VIRTUALLY DESTROY SOMETHING to inflict so much damage on something that it is very nearly destroyed or rendered beyond repair **3.** KILL ONE PERSON IN 10 to kill one out of every ten people, especially in a body of mutinous soldiers (*archaic*) [Late 16thC. From Latin *decimat-*, the past participle stem of *decimare*, literally "to take a tenth," from *decimus* "tenth" (see DECIMAL).] —**dec·i·ma·tor** *n.*

WORD KEY: USAGE

Extension of meaning: No doubt *his cat decimated the neighborhood's mouse population* does not mean that the creature limited its destruction to one mouse in ten. The popular meaning of ***decimate*** is effectively the reverse of its historical meaning, and now predominates because the need for a word meaning "to kill one person in ten" has greatly diminished. Even so, the popular meaning is not accepted by everyone, and it is often better to use an alternative such as *annihilate*, *exterminate*, *destroy*, or *devastate*.

dec·i·ma·tion /dèssə máysh'n/ *n.* **1.** WIDESPREAD DESTRUCTION the act, process, or result of destroying, removing, or damaging a large proportion of something **2.** KILLING ONE IN 10 the execution of one person out of every ten, especially as a punishment on a body of mutinous soldiers (*archaic*)

dec·i·me·ter /déssə meètər/ *n.* a metric unit of length equal to one tenth of a meter

de·ci·pher /di sīfər/ (**-phered, -pher·ing, -phers**) *vt.* **1.** MAKE OUT WHAT SOMETHING SAYS to establish what a word or piece of writing says when it is difficult or almost impossible to read **2.** WORK OUT MEANING OF SOMETHING to study something that is written in code or in an unknown form of writing until it can be understood and read normally —**de·ci·pher·er** *n.* —**de·ci·pher·ment** *n.*

de·ci·pher·a·ble /di sīfərəb'l/ *adj.* capable of being read and understood —**de·ci·pher·a·bil·i·ty** /di sīfərə bìllətee/ *n.*

de·ci·sion /di sízh'n/ *n.* **1.** SOMETHING SOMEBODY HAS SETTLED ON something that somebody chooses or makes up his or her mind about, after considering it and other possible choices ○ *It was a tough decision to make.* **2.** FIRMNESS IN CHOOSING SOMETHING the ability to choose or decide about things in a clear and definite way without too much hesitation or delay ○ *a man of decision* **3.** PROCESS OF CHOOSING the process of coming to a conclusion or determination about something **4.** BOXING BOXING VICTORY DECIDED ON POINTS a win in a boxing match that is awarded to the fighter with the higher total of points given by a majority of one or more judges ○ *He won a 10-round decision.* [15thC. Either directly or via French from the Latin stem *decision-*, from the past participle stem of *decidere* "to decide" (see DECIDE).] —**de·ci·sion·al** *adj.*

de·ci·sion-mak·ing *n.* the process of making choices or reaching conclusions, especially on important political or business matters —**de·ci·sion-mak·er** *n.*

de·ci·sion the·o·ry *n.* the study of the best possible outcomes for decisions made under varying conditions

de·ci·sion tree *n.* a diagram set out like the branches of a tree that shows the consequences of a decision, each decision entailing a course of action that requires various other decisions

de·ci·sive /di sīssiv/ *adj.* **1.** SETTLING SOMETHING settling or ending something, e.g., a debate, controversy, or contest ○ *a decisive victory* **2.** ABLE TO MAKE DEFINITE DECISIONS showing an ability to make decisions quickly, firmly, and clearly [Early 17thC. Via French from, ultimately, Latin *decidere* "to decide" (see DECIDE).] —**de·ci·sive·ness** *n.*

de·ci·sive·ly /di sīssivlee/ *adv.* in a way that brings a clear and definite decision or a recognizable end

deck /dek/ *n.* **1.** NAUT FLOOR SURFACE ACROSS A SHIP a level surface that runs from one side of a ship to the other and along all or part of its length, forming a floor **2.** TRANSP VEHICLE SECTION ON ONE LEVEL a floored, self-contained area of a ship or of a passenger vehicle, e.g., a bus or tram **3.** ELEC AUDIO UNIT a wide, flat piece of audio equipment that contains a player for tapes, records, cassettes, or compact disks **4.** LEVEL OF A STRUCTURE any tier or level of a building or other structure **5.** CIV ENG FLOOR OF ROADWAY OR BRIDGE the floor or platform of a roadway or bridge **6.** CARDS PLAYING CARDS a pack of playing cards **7.** ARCHIT TERRACE OF HOUSE an open unroofed area of floor extending from the back of a house ○ *They had a barbecue on the deck.* **8.** GROUND the ground or floor (*informal*) ■ *vt.* (**decked, deck·ing, decks**) **1.** KNOCK SOMEBODY DOWN to strike and knock somebody down deliberately (*informal*) **2.** DECORATE SOMETHING OR SOMEBODY to decorate or ornament something or somebody (*literary*) ○ *deck the hall with boughs of holly* **3.** BUILD DECK FOR SOMETHING to make a deck for a ship or other structure [15thC. From Middle Dutch *dec* "roof, covering, cloak," ultimately from a prehistoric Germanic word that is the ancestor of English *thatch*.] —**deck·er** *n.* ◇ **clear the deck** *or* **decks** to get rid of all obstacles, especially pending work, prior to beginning a new task ◇ **hit the deck 1.** to fall on the floor or ground, often as self-protection (*informal*) **2.** to get out of bed ◇ **on deck 1.** NAUT on the top, external surface of a ship or boat **2.** prepared and available to take part in an event or activity (*informal*) **3.** scheduled to appear next

deck out *vt.* to decorate something, or dress somebody up in fancy clothes

deck over *vt.* to complete the construction of an upper deck on a ship or boat

deck bridge *n.* a bridge designed so that the roadway or track is supported by the upper horizontal part of the structural framework

deck chair *n.* a collapsible adjustable outdoor chair with a wooden framework and a seat made from a piece of strong fabric suspended between the top and bottom of the central frame. Deck chairs are usually made with striped or plain canvas in bright colors and used by the seashore, around a pool, or on the deck of a ship.

decked /dekt/ *adj.* **1.** DONE UP DECORATIVELY colorfully or attractively set out, draped, or decorated (*literary*) **2.** WITH A DECK having or equipped with a deck (*usually used in combination*)

deck hand *n.* somebody who does general manual work on a ship, yacht, or other vessel

deck·house /dék hòwss/ (*plural* **-hous·es** /-hòwzəz/) *n.* a structure built on the main deck of a ship or other vessel, used as a room or several rooms

deck·ing /déking/ *n.* any waterproof covering for the deck or roof of a house

deck·le /dék'l/ *n.* **1.** PAPER-MAKING FRAME a metal frame used to contain pulp in a mold during the making of handmade paper **2.** = **deckle edge** [Mid-18thC. From German *Deckel*, literally "little covering," from *Decke* "covering."]

deck·le edge *n.* a rough, irregular, or feathery edge on handmade paper —**deck·le-edged** *adj.*

deck of·fi·cer *n.* an officer responsible for tasks such as navigation that take place on a ship's main deck

deck ten·nis *n.* a game based on lawn tennis, using a small court with a net and a ring made of rubber or rope that the players throw back and forth

decl. *abbr.* GRAM declension

de·claim /di kláym/ (**-claimed, -claim·ing, -claims**) *v.* **1.** *vti.* SPEAK FORMALLY AND DRAMATICALLY to make a formal forceful speech about something, or say something in a formal and dramatic way **2.** *vi.* RECITE to deliver a recitation [14thC. Directly or via French *déclamer* from Latin *declamare* "to cry out," from *clamare* "to cry, call" (source of English *claim* and *clamor*).] —**de·claim·er** *n.*

dec·la·ma·tion /dèklə máysh'n/ *n.* **1.** FORMAL DRAMATIC SPEECH a speech or presentation spoken in a formal and theatrical style **2.** PROCESS OF DECLAIMING the art or process of declaiming ○ *"The air of the New World seems favorable to the art of declamation."* (Joseph Conrad, *Nostromo*; 1904)

de·clam·a·to·ry /di klámmə tàwree/ *adj.* **1.** DRAMATIC formal and dramatic in public speech **2.** RHETORICAL loud and rhetorical but without very meaningful content —**de·clam·a·to·ri·ly** *adv.*

de·clar·ant /di kláirənt/ *n.* **1.** SOMEBODY WHO FORMALLY DECLARES SOMETHING somebody who makes a formal, often legal, statement **2.** PROSPECTIVE U.S. CITIZEN a non-citizen of the United States who has formally declared the intention of becoming a U.S. citizen [Late 17thC. From French *déclarant*, the present participle of *déclarer* "to declare."]

dec·la·ra·tion /dèklə ráysh'n/ *n.* **1.** FORMAL STATEMENT a formal document giving explicit details, e.g., the terms of a business agreement or plan, or information on goods or assets for tax purposes **2.** OFFICIAL PROCLAMATION an emphatic formal public statement, especially by a government or public body **3.** PROCESS OF MAKING A DECLARATION the process or act of declaring something in an official or public way **4.** LAW UNSWORN BUT SOLEMN EVIDENCE a formal statement of facts that is allowed in a legal case in place of a statement made under oath **5.** LAW PLAINTIFF'S OFFICIAL WRITTEN CLAIM a formal document in which a plaintiff lays out precise details of the circumstances leading to the legal action being taken **6.** CARDS ANNOUNCEMENT OF BID the act of naming a particular suit as trump, or of declaring no-trump, by the player who makes the final bid of a hand of bridge

Dec·la·ra·tion of Hu·man Rights *n.* a United Nations document approved on December 10, 1948 by the General Assembly, affirming the dignity of all human beings. It proclaimed their right to free movement in search of truth and justice and their right to live their lives in dignity.

dec·la·ra·tion of in·de·pen·dence *n.* a proclamation by which a country, group, or people asserts firmly and publicly that it has become independent of a governing power

Dec·la·ra·tion of In·de·pen·dence *n.* a written statement issued and adopted by the Continental Congress in 1776 proclaiming that the 13 North American colonies henceforward would govern themselves rather than be ruled by Great Britain. The Declaration of Independence was adopted by the Congress on July 2, 1776 and formally endorsed on July 4. ○ *"If the American Revolution had produced nothing but the Declaration of Independence, it would have been worthwhile."* (Samuel Eliot Morison, *The Oxford History of the American People*; 1965)

de·clar·a·tive /di kláirətiv/ *adj.* containing a statement, or in the form of a statement —**de·clar·a·tive·ly** *adv.*

de·clar·a·to·ry /di kláirə tàwree/ *adj.* **1.** STATING A PRECISE LEGAL POSITION stating and clarifying something, especially a legal right, status, decree, or judgment **2.** = **declarative** —**de·clar·a·to·ri·ly** *adv.*

de·clare /di kláir/ (**-clared, -clar·ing, -clares**) *v.* **1.** *vti.* ANNOUNCE CLEARLY OR LOUDLY to state something in a plain, open, or emphatic way **2.** *vt.* STATE SOMETHING FORMALLY OR OFFICIALLY to make an official or public announcement about somebody or something, especially on a legal or medical matter ○ *The doctors declared her fit to work.* ○ *The chairperson declared the meeting open.* **3.** *vti.* REVEAL SOMETHING AS DUTIABLE OR TAXABLE to inform customs or tax authorities about goods on which duty is owed, or about income that is taxable **4.** *vt.* STATE AN INTENT OFFICIALLY to state an official intention to undertake a particular course of action or adopt a particular status ○ *to declare independence* **5.** *vi.* MAKE A DECISION KNOWN to announce a choice or decision formally and publicly (*formal*) **6.** *vti.* CARDS SAY WHICH SUIT IS TRUMPS to announce to the other players in bridge the suit that will be trumps for the hand or that there will be no trump suit **7.** *vti.* CARDS LAY CARDS ON THE TABLE to show that you have a particular score in bezique and other card games by displaying the cards face up on the table and claiming your score **8.** *vr.* PROPOSE MARRIAGE to make a formal or open statement of love for and a wish to marry somebody (*dated*) [14thC. From Latin *declarare* "to make clear," from *clarus* "clear" (source of English *clear* and *claret*).] —**de·clar·a·ble** *adj.* —**de·clar·er** *n.* ◇ **declare war 1.** to make a formal public announcement that the country represented is now at war with another country and will begin military action against it ○ *"Older men declare war, but it is the youth that must fight and die."* (Herbert Hoover, *Speech, Republican National Convention*; June 27, 1944) **2.** to begin a fierce campaign to get rid of or defeat something, or start fighting it in earnest

de·clar·er /di kláirər/ *n.* CARDS somebody who announces either no-trump or which suit is to be trumps in the next hand, and, in bridge, plays his or her own cards and those of the dummy for that hand

dé·clas·sé /dày klaa sáy/ *adj.* reduced to or having a low class or status in society [Late 19thC. From French, the past participle of *déclasser* "to declass."]

de·clas·si·fy /dee klássi fī/ (**-fied, -fy·ing, -fies**) *vt.* to remove something from an official list of confidential or top-secret material so that anyone may see it —**de·clas·si·fi·a·ble** /dee klàssi fī əb'l/ *adj.* —**de·clas·si·fi·ca·tion** /-fi káysh'n/ *n.*

de·claw /dee kláw/ (**-clawed, -claw·ing, -claws**) *vt.* **1.** REMOVE ANIMAL'S CLAWS to remove the claws from an animal's paws, often to prevent it from injuring or catching other animals, or from scratching or climbing **2.** DISABLE SOMEBODY OR SOMETHING to remove the power, authority, or force from somebody or something ○ *The Mayor's lack of support effectively declawed him.*

de·clen·sion /di klénshən/ *n.* **1.** GRAM SET OF WORDS THAT BEHAVE SIMILARLY a group of nouns, adjectives, or pronouns that all change their form or word endings in the same way according to gender, number, or grammatical case **2.** GRAM PROCESS OF ENDING WORDS the process by which some sets of nouns, adjectives, and pronouns vary in form to show gender, number, or grammatical case **3.** WORSENING OR FALLING AWAY the process of gradually declining or deteriorating (*formal*) **4.** GEOL DOWNWARD SLOPE a downward slope, especially of terrain [15thC. Via French *déclinaison* from the Latin stem *declination-*, from *declinare* "to fall away" (see DECLINE), from the idea that grammatical endings were a falling away from the pure form.] —**de·clen·sion·al** *adj.* —**de·clen·sion·al·ly** *adv.*

dec·li·na·tion /dèklə náysh'n/ *n.* **1.** ASTRON ANGULAR DISTANCE FROM CELESTIAL EQUATOR the angular distance of an astronomical body measured in degrees from the celestial equator along the great circle passing through it and the celestial poles **2.** PHYS, GEOG = **magnetic declination** —**dec·li·na·tion·al** *adj.*

de·cline /di klīn/ *v.* (**-clined, -clin·ing, -clines**) **1.** *vti.* REFUSE INVITATION to give a polite refusal to an invitation **2.** *vt.* REFUSE PARTICIPATION to refuse to respond or take part in something **3.** *vi.* DIMINISH to become fewer or less ○ *stocks declining in value* **4.** *vi.* GET WEAKER to become physically or mentally less vigorous, especially because of illness or mature years ○ *his health had declined* **5.** *vti.* GRAM SHOW VARIOUS FORMS to state the grammatical forms of a noun, adjective, or pronoun, or have various grammatical forms. ◊ **declension 6.** *vti.* SLOPE DOWN to bend something downward, or slope downward ■ *n.* **1.** DETERIORATION a deterioration in quality, strength, or degree, or a reduction in amount **2.** PERIOD NEAR END the terminal period of somebody or something, ending in death or disappearance ○ *at the decline of the empire* **3.** DOWNWARD SLOPE a downward slope or movement [14thC. Directly and via French *décliner* from Latin *declinare* "to turn aside," literally "to bend away," from *clinare* "to bend."] —**de·clin·er** *n.* ◇ **be on the decline 1.** show a gradual lessening of quality, amount, or degree **2.** show a gradual worsening of health

dec·li·nom·e·ter /dèklə nómmətər/ *n.* an instrument that measures the declination and inclination of the Earth's magnetic field [Mid-19thC. Coined from DECLINATION + METER.]

de·cliv·i·tous /di klívvətəss/ *adj.* sloping downward

de·cliv·i·ty /di klívvətee/ (*plural* **-ties**) *n.* **1.** SOMETHING SLOPING something, especially a piece of land, that slopes downward **2.** INCLINATION DOWNWARD a downward inclination, especially of a piece of land [Early 17thC. Via Latin *declivitas* from, ultimately, *clivus* "slope." Ultimately from an Indo-European word meaning "to lean, bend over," which is also the ancestor of English *client* and *ladder*.]

Dec·o /dékō/, **dec·o** *adj.* = **Art Deco**

de·coct /di kókt/ (**-coct·ed, -coct·ing, -cocts**) *vt.* to extract the essence or active ingredient from a substance by boiling it [15thC. From Latin *decoct-*, the past participle stem of *decoquere*, literally "to boil down," from *coquere* "to cook."]

de·coc·tion /di kókshən/ *n.* **1.** EXTRACTING PROCESS the extraction of an essence or active ingredient from a substance by boiling **2.** CONCENTRATED SUBSTANCE a concentrated substance that results from decoction

de·code /dee kṓd/ (**-cod·ed, -cod·ing, -codes**) *vt.* **1.** DECIPHER MESSAGE to transform an encoded message or signal into a usable form **2.** INTERPRET MESSAGE to find the direct meaning of cryptic or indirect language —**de·cod·a·ble** *adj.*

de·cod·er /dee kṓdər/ *n.* a person, device, or computer program that decodes something

de·col·late /dékə làyt, dee kṓ làyt/ (**-lat·ed, -lat·ing, -lates**) *vt.* to separate continuous paper into single sheets —**de·col·la·tion** /dèkə láysh'n, dèeko-/ *n.* —**de·col·la·tor** /dékə làytər/ *n.*

de·col·lec·tiv·ize /dèe kə léktə vīz/ (**-ized, -iz·ing, -iz·es**) *vti.* to modify a socialist production system or economy to work on free market principles —**de·col·lec·ti·vi·za·tion** /dèe kə lektəvi záysh'n/ *n.*

dé·colle·tage /dày kawl taázh, dày kollə taázh/ *n.* **1.** LOW NECKLINE the top front part of a woman's low-cut garment **2.** LOW-CUT GARMENT a piece of women's clothing with a décolletage [Late 19thC. From French, formed from *décolleté* (see DÉCOLLETÉ).]

dé·col·le·té /dày kawl táy, dày kollə táy/ *adj.* **1.** WITH LOW NECKLINE having a low-cut front neckline ○ *a décolleté dress* **2.** WEARING LOW-CUT GARMENT wearing a décolleté garment ■ *n.* CHEST AREA the upper part of a woman's chest, below the neck [Mid-19thC. From French, the past participle of *décolleter* "to lower the neckline," from *collet* "collar," from, ultimately, Latin *collum* "neck."]

de·col·o·nize /dee kóllə nīz/ (**-nized, -niz·ing, -niz·es**) *vt.* to grant a colony its independence —**de·col·o·ni·za·tion** /dee kòlləni záysh'n/ *n.*

de·col·or /dee kúllər/ (**-ored, -or·ing, -ors**) *vt.* = **decolorize** —**de·col·or·a·tion** /dee kùllə ráysh'n/ *n.*

de·col·or·ant /dee kúllərənt/ *n.* a chemical that removes the color from a fabric or other substance —**de·col·or·ant** *adj.*

de·col·or·ize /dee kúllə rīz/ (**-ized, -iz·ing, -iz·es**) *vt.* to remove the color from a fabric or other substance, e.g., by chemical means —**de·col·or·i·za·tion** /dee kùlləri záysh'n/ *n.*

de·com·mis·sion /dèe kə mísh'n/ (**-sioned, -sion·ing, -sions**) *vt.* to remove something, e.g., a ship, nuclear power station, machinery, or weapons, from service

de·com·pen·sa·tion /dèe kompən sáysh'n/ *n.* **1.** MED HEART CONDITION the failure of the heart to maintain adequate circulation because of various stresses upon it **2.** PSYCHIAT WORSENING PSYCHIATRIC CONDITION the deterioration of existing psychological defenses in a patient already exhibiting pathological behavior

de·com·pose /dèe kəm pṓz/ (**-posed, -pos·ing, -pos·es**) *vti.* **1.** BIOL ROT to break down organic matter from a complex to a simpler form, mainly through the action of fungi and bacteria, or undergo this process **2.** BREAK DOWN INTO PIECES to break something down, or be broken down, into smaller or simpler parts **3.** CHEM BREAK DOWN INTO CONSTITUENT PARTS to separate or cause something to separate into constituent parts —**de·com·pos·a·bil·i·ty** /dèe kəm pōzə bíllətee/ *n.* —**de·com·pos·a·ble** /-pṓzəb'l/ *adj.* —**de·com·po·si·tion** /dèe kompə zísh'n/ *n.*

de·com·pos·er /dèe kəm pṓzər/ *n.* an organism, especially a bacterium or fungus, that causes organic matter to rot or decay

de·com·press /dèe kəm préss/ (**-pressed, -press·ing, -press·es**) *v.* **1.** *vti.* REDUCE PRESSURE to cause or experience a reduction in the atmospheric pressure of an enclosed space **2.** *vti.* ALLOW EXPANSION to allow a substance to expand to normal dimensions or volume by the removal of pressure, or to undergo this process **3.** *vti.* COMPUT EXPAND DATA to expand compressed data to its normal extent, or to undergo this process **4.** *vi.* RELAX to relax or unwind, especially after being busy or stressed (*informal*) —**de·com·pres·sive** *adj.*

de·com·pres·sion /dèe kəm présh'n/ *n.* **1.** PRESSURE DECREASE a decrease in surrounding or inherent pressure, especially the controlled decrease in pressure that divers undergo to prevent decompression sickness **2.** COMPUT DATA EXPANSION the expansion to full size of compressed computer data **3.** SURG SURGERY TO REDUCE PRESSURE IN ORGAN a surgical procedure to reduce pressure in an organ or part of the body caused, e.g., by fluid on the brain, or to reduce the pressure of tissues on a nerve

de·com·pres·sion cham·ber *n.* a sealed room where decompression is carried out

de·com·pres·sion sick·ness, **de·com·pres·sion ill·ness** *n.* a condition marked by joint pain, nausea, loss of motion, and breathing difficulties experienced by divers and workers in caissons who emerge too quickly from a pressurized environment. It is caused by the formation of nitrogen bubbles in the blood and tissues.

de·con (**de·conned, de·con·ning, de·cons**) *vt.* /dee kón/ ♦ **decontaminate** (*informal*)

de·con·cen·trate /dee kónsən tràyt/ (**-trat·ed, -trat·ing, -trates**) *v.* **1.** *vti.* MAKE LESS CONCENTRATED to cause or experience a reduction in concentration or density **2.** *vt.* = **decentralize** —**de·con·cen·tra·tion** /dèe konsən tráysh'n/ *n.*

de·con·di·tion /dèe kən dísh'n/ (**-tioned, -tion·ing, -tions**) *vt.* PSYCHOL to cause or teach a person or animal to stop exhibiting a conditioned response

de·con·gest /dèe kən jést/ (**-gest·ed, -gest·ing, -gests**) *vt.* **1.** UNBLOCK NOSE to loosen mucus in the nasal passages, sinuses, or bronchi **2.** LOOSEN to increase the flow in something that is compacted or congested, especially with traffic

de·con·ges·tant /dèe kən jéstənt/ *n.* an agent that reduces or relieves nasal congestion, e.g., during a cold or chest infection —**de·con·ges·tant** *adj.*

de·con·se·crate /dee kónsə kràyt/ (**-crat·ed, -crat·ing, -crates**) *vt.* to convert a sacred place, building, or object to secular use —**de·con·se·cra·tion** /dee kònsə kráysh'n/ *n.*

de·con·struct /dèe kən strúkt/ (**-struct·ed, -struct·ing, -structs**) *vt.* to subject a text to critical analysis using the theories of deconstruction

de·con·struc·tion /dèe kən strúkshən/ *n.* a method of analyzing texts based on the ideas that language is inherently unstable and shifting and that the reader rather than the author is central in determining meaning. It was introduced by the French philosopher Jacques Derrida in the late 1960s. —**de·con·struc·tion·ism** *n.* —**de·con·struc·tion·ist** *n.*

de·con·tam·i·nate /dèe kən támmə nàyt/ (**-nat·ed, -nat·ing, -nates**) *vt.* to remove unwanted chemical, radioactive, or biological impurities or toxins from land or a person or object —**de·con·tam·i·na·tion** /dèe kən támmə náysh'n/ *n.*

de·con·trol /dèe kən trṓl/ *vt.* (**-trolled, -trol·ling, -trols**) REMOVE RESTRAINTS to remove official restraints or regulations on something, especially prices or rents ■ *n.* RESTRAINT REMOVAL the removal of restraints, especially by a government on prices or rents

de·cor /dáy kawr, day káwr/, **dé·cor** *n.* **1.** FURNISHING STYLE the style of furniture, wallpaper, carpeting, curtains, and accessories chosen for a room or house **2.** STAGE SCENERY the scenery of a stage [Late 19thC. From French, formed from *décorer* "to decorate," from Latin *decorare* (see DECORATE).]

dec·o·rate /dékə ràyt/ (**-rat·ed, -rat·ing, -rates**) *v.* **1.** *vt.* MAKE SOMETHING ATTRACTIVE to make something more attractive by adding nonfunctional elements to it ○ *decorated the hat with a couple of feathers* **2.** *vti.* CHANGE APPEARANCE OF ROOM to apply paint, wallpaper, and other accessories to a room or house **3.** *vt.* AWARD SOMEBODY A MEDAL to give a medal or other honor or award to somebody to acknowledge bravery, dedication, or achievement [Mid-16thC. From Latin *decoratus*, the past participle of *decorare* "to beautify," from *decus* "ornament."]

Dec·o·rat·ed ar·chi·tec·ture, **Dec·o·rat·ed style** *n.* the second, more ornate stage of English Gothic architecture that is characterized by an increased use of geometric tracery and floral motifs

dec·o·ra·tion /dèkə ráysh'n/ *n.* **1.** ORNAMENTATION the addition of ornaments to make something more attractive **2.** ATTRACTIVE ITEM an item, usually one of a group, attached to something to make it look more attractive or to mark a special occasion **3.** AWARD a medal or other honor or award given to somebody to acknowledge bravery, dedication, or achievement **4.** PAINTING AND PAPERING the application of paint, wallpaper, and accessories in a room or house

Dec·o·ra·tion Day *n.* = **Memorial Day** (*dated*)

dec·o·ra·tive /dékərətiv, dékə ràytiv/ *adj.* **1.** ORNAMENTAL serving to make something look more attractive, especially by adding nonfunctional embellishments **2.** OF DECORATION relating to the decoration of a room or home ○ *added some nice decorative touches* **3.** ATTRACTIVE serving merely to look attractive rather than having a functional purpose —**dec·o·ra·tive·ly** *adv.* —**dec·o·ra·tive·ness** *n.*

dec·o·ra·tive art *n.* **1.** DESIGN OF USEFUL THINGS any art concerned with the design and production of functional but decorative items for home use, e.g., ceramics, furniture, and fabrics (*often used in the plural*) **2.** DECORATIONS the products of decorative art, collectively

dec·o·ra·tor /dékə ràytər/ *n.* **1.** SOMEBODY WHO DECORATES somebody whose job is to decorate something (*often used in combination*) **2.** PAINTER OR WALLPAPERER somebody whose job is painting and wallpapering houses and other buildings ■ *adj.* FOR HOME DECOR used to describe colors, fabrics, and accessories suitable for use in home decor

dec·o·rous /dékərəss, di káwrəss/ *adj.* **1.** SEEMLY conforming to what is acceptable or expected in formal or solemn settings, especially in dress or behavior ○ *"They began to talk politely, in decorous half-completed sentences, with little gasps of agreement."* (William Faulkner, *Sanctuary*; 1931) **2.** DIGNIFIED understated and dignified [Mid-17thC. Formed from Latin *decorus*, "seemly," from *decor* "attractiveness." Ultimately from an Indo-European word meaning "to accept," which is also the ancestor of English *decent*, *docile*, *dogma*, and *disciple*.] —**dec·o·rous·ly** *adv.* —**dec·o·rous·ness** *n.*

de·cor·ti·cate *vt.* /dee káwrti kàyt/ (**-cat·ed, -cat·ing, -cates**) **1.** BOT REMOVE OUTER LAYER FROM A PLANT to remove an outer layer such as bark, rind, or a husk from a plant or part of a plant **2.** SURG REMOVE SOMETHING FROM AN ORGAN to remove surgically the outer layer of an organ or structure such as the brain or kidney ■ *adj.* /-kàyt, -kət/ MED WITHOUT CORTEX FUNCTION used to describe a brain that has lost the function of its cerebral cortex as a result of disease or surgery [Early 17thC. From Latin *decorticare*, from *cortex* (see CORTEX).] —**de·cor·ti·ca·tion** /dee kàwrti káysh'n/ *n.* —**de·cor·ti·ca·tor** /dee káwrti kàytər/ *n.*

de·co·rum /di káwrəm/ *n.* **1.** DIGNITY dignity or correctness that is socially expected **2.** APPROPRIATENESS OF ARTISTIC ELEMENT the compatibility of an element in a literary or artistic work, e.g., character, form, style, or plot, with the work as a whole **3.** CONVENTION a socially accepted or expected convention or requirement (*archaic*) [Mid-16thC. From Latin, formed from *decorus* (see DECOROUS).]

de·cou·page /dàykoo pàazh/, **dé·cou·page** *n.* **1.** PAPER DECORATION METHOD a technique for decorating something in which a design is made of pieces of printed paper cut out and stuck on a flat base, then coated with varnish **2.** DECOUPAGE PICTURE a picture or other form of decoration that is made using decoupage [Mid-20thC. From French, formed from *découper* "to cut up, cut out," from *couper* "to cut."]

de·cou·ple /dee kúpp'l/ (**-pled, -pling, -ples**) *vt.* **1.** ELEC REDUCE INTERDEPENDENCE to remove or weaken the interaction between two electronic circuits, subsystems, or systems so that there is little or no transfer or feedback of energy between them **2.** MIL LESSEN STRENGTH OF SHOCK WAVES to reduce or eliminate airborne shock waves from a nuclear or other explosion by detonating a device deep underground **3.** SEPARATE OBJECTS to separate or disengage one thing from another —**de·cou·pler** *n.*

de·coy /dèe kòy, di kóy/ *n.* **1.** HUNT HUNTING LURE a bird or animal, or a realistic replica, used by hunters to attract an animal or bird to a place for trapping or shooting **2.** DISTRACTER something or somebody used to deceive or divert attention, especially in order to lure somebody into a trap **3.** ENTRAPMENT AREA an enclosed area or stretch of water that game or fowl are driven or lured into so that they can be easily shot or captured ■ *vt.* (**-coyed, -coy·ing, -coys**) DECEIVE to deceive or entrap a person or animal by using a decoy [Mid-16thC. From Dutch *de kooi*, literally "the cage," ultimately from Latin *cavea* "cage" (source of English cage).] —**de·coy·er** *n.*

de·crease *vti.* /di krèess/ (**-creased, -creas·ing, -creas·es**) DIMINISH to lessen or cause something to lessen in size, strength, or amount ■ *n.* /dèe krèess/ **1.** PROCESS OF DECREASING the process of becoming less, fewer, or smaller ○ *street crime is on the decrease* **2.** REDUCTION a reduction in the amount or rate of something ○ *a 2% decrease in customers* [14thC. Via the Old French stem *decreiss-*, from, ultimately, Latin *decrescere*, from *crescere* "to grow."] —**de·creas·ing** *adj.* —**de·creas·ing·ly** /di krèesinglee/ *adv.*

de·cree /di krèe/ *n.* **1.** OFFICIAL ORDER an order with the power of legislation issued by a ruler or other person or group with authority **2.** LAW COURT RULING a ruling given by a court, especially a divorce, equity, or probate court **3.** RELIG DIVINE WILL the will or purpose of God, interpreted through events considered to be God's doing ■ *vt.* (**-creed, -cree·ing, -crees**) MAKE ORDER to make an official order, pronouncement, or legal ruling to effect something [14thC. Via Old French *decré* from Latin *decretum*, the neuter past participle of *decernere* "to decide, pronounce a decision."] —**de·cree·a·ble** *adj.* —**de·cre·er** *n.*

de·cree ni·si (*plural* **de·crees ni·si** /-nī́sī/) *n.* an interim ruling of a divorce court that will become absolute in the absence of objections arising

dec·re·ment /dékrəmənt/ *n.* **1.** AMOUNT OF DECREASE the amount by which a quantity or quality gradually decreases **2.** DECREASING the process of becoming less or fewer (*formal*) [Late 16thC. From Latin *decrementum*, from *decrescere* from *crescere* "to grow."] —**dec·re·ment·al** /dèkrə mént'l/ *adj.* —**dec·re·men·tal·ly** /-əlee/ *adv.*

de·cre·o·li·za·tion /dee krèe əli záysh'n/ *n.* the gradual adoption by speakers of a creole of a form of speech that is closer to the standard language from which the creole had originated

de·crep·it /di kréppit/ *adj.* **1.** OLD AND IN POOR CONDITION in poor condition, especially old, overused, or not working efficiently **2.** NOT YOUNG OR STRONG with strength lessened by the effects of age (*archaic or humorous*) [15thC. From Latin *decrepitus*, from *crepitus*, the past participle of *crepare* "to crack, creak." Ultimately from an imitative Indo-European base that is also the ancestor of English *raven* and *retch*.] —**de·crep·it·ly** *adv.*

WORD KEY: SYNONYMS

See Synonyms at ***weak***.

de·crep·i·tate /di kréppi tàyt/ (**-tat·ed, -tat·ing, -tates**) *vti.* to heat a substance, especially a salt, until it crackles or stops crackling, or to be heated in this way [Mid-17thC. Coined from DE- + Latin *crepitare* "to crackle," from *crepitus* "cracked" (see DECREPIT).] —**de·crep·i·ta·tion** /di krèppi táysh'n/ *n.*

de·crep·i·tude /di kréppi tood/ *n.* the condition of being old, worn out, or in poor working order

decresc. *abbr.* decrescendo

de·cre·scen·do /dày krə shéndō, dèe-/ *adv.* INCREASINGLY SOFTLY with decreasing loudness (*used as a musical direction*) ■ *n.* (*plural* **-dos**) PIECE OF MUSIC GROWING QUIETER a piece of music, or a section of a piece, played decrescendo [Early 19thC. From Italian, "decreasing."] —**de·cre·scen·do** *adj.*

de·cres·cent /di kréss'nt/ *adj.* used to describe the moon when it is waning (*technical*) [Early 17thC. Formed from Latin *decrescere*, from *crescere* "to grow."] —**de·cres·cence** *n.*

de·cre·tal /di krèet'l/ *n.* a papal decree or edict that relates to an aspect of church law or doctrine [14thC. Via late Latin *decretale*, from, ultimately, Latin *decret-*, the past participle stem of *decernere*, from *cernere* "to separate, sift."] —**de·cre·tal** *adj.*

dec·re·to·ry /dékrə tàwree, di krèetəree/ *adj.* relating to or having the force of a decree [Late 16thC. From Latin *decretorius*, from *decret-*, the past participle stem of *decernere* (see DECERN).]

de·crim·i·nal·ize /dee krímmənə lī̀z/ (**-ized, -iz·ing, -iz·es**) *vt.* to make legal an action or substance that was formerly illegal —**de·crim·i·nal·i·za·tion** /dee krìmmənəli záysh'n/ *n.*

WORD KEY: SYNONYMS

See Synonyms at ***legal***.

de·cry /di krī́/ (**-cried, -cry·ing, -cries**) *vt.* to express strong disapproval of or openly criticize somebody or something (*formal*) ○ *critics decrying lowered standards in education* [Early 17thC. Modeled on French *décrier* "to cry down."] —**de·cri·al** *n.* —**de·cri·er** *n.*

de·crypt /dee krípt/ (**-crypt·ed, -crypt·ing, -crypts**) *vt.* render an encoded text or message into plain language. = **decode** *v.* 1, **decode** *v.* 2 [Mid-20thC. Coined from DE- + CRYPT(OGRAM).] —**de·cryp·tion** *n.*

de·cu·bi·tus /di kyóobitəss/ *n.* the particular position of somebody's body when lying down, usually on the front, back, or side (*technical*) [Late 19thC. From modern Latin, formed from Latin *decumbere* "to lie down," on the model of *accubitus* "reclining at table."] —**de·cu·bi·tal** *adj.*

de·cu·bi·tus ul·cer *n.* a bedsore (*technical*)

de·cum·bent /di kúmbənt/ *adj.* **1.** BOT GROWING ALONG THE GROUND used to describe plants that lie along the ground but have a tip growing upward **2.** ZOOL GROWING FLAT used to describe hair or bristles that lie or grow flat along a surface [Early 17thC. From Latin *decumbere* "to lie down," from *cubare* "to lie down."] —**de·cum·bence** *n.* —**de·cum·bent·ly** *adv.*

dec·u·ple /dékyəp'l/ *adj.* increasing by ten times (*formal*) [15thC. From late Latin *decuplus* "tenfold," from Latin *decem* "ten" + *-plus* "-fold."]

de·cu·ri·on /di kyóoree ən/ *n.* **1.** ROMAN OFFICER in ancient Rome, an officer in command of ten soldiers **2.** ROMAN COUNCIL MEMBER a council member in the Roman Empire [14thC. From the Latin stem *decurion-*, from *decuria* (see DECURY) on the model of *centurion*.]

de·cur·rent /di kúrənt/ *adj.* used to describe plant leaves that curve down at the edges, or trees with a rounded shape [15thC. From Latin *decurrere*, literally "to run down," from *currere* "to run."] —**de·cur·rent·ly** *adv.*

dec·ur·y /dékyəree/ (*plural* **-ies**) *n.* in ancient Rome, a company of ten soldiers [Mid-16thC. From Latin *decuria*, from *decem* "ten," on the model of centuria "century."]

de·cus·sate /di kú sàyt, dékə sàyt/ *adj.* **1.** SHAPED LIKE A CROSS having the shape of a cross **2.** BOT FORMING OPPOSITE PAIRS used to describe leaves that form pairs opposite each other and at right angles to the pair above and the pair below, as in the horse chestnut [Early 19thC. From Latin *decussatus*, the past participle of *decussare* "to divide crosswise," from *decussis*, the numeral ten (written X), from *decem* "ten" + *assis*, a type of coin.] —**de·cus·sate·ly** *adv.* —**dec·us·sa·tion** /dèkə sáysh'n, dee kə sáysh'n/ *n.*

de·dans /də daaN/ *n.* (*plural* **-dans**) **SPECTATORS' AREA** in court tennis, the open end of the court just behind the serving area where spectators can watch the match ■ *npl.* **SPECTATORS** the spectators who watch from the dedans [Early 18thC. From French, "inside, interior."]

Ded·ham /déddəm/ town in eastern Massachusetts, on the southern bank of the Charles River, southwest of Boston. It was settled in 1635. Population: 23,741 (1996).

ded·i·cate /déddi kàyt/ (**-cat·ed, -cat·ing, -cates**) *vt.* **1. SET SOMETHING ASIDE AS SPECIAL** to set something aside for a particular purpose ○ *an entire TV series dedicated to birds* **2. ADDRESS WORK OF ART TO SOMEBODY** to associate a book, piece of music, or other art form with somebody as a token of friendship or esteem or as an acknowledgment of help received **3. COMMIT YOURSELF TO SOMETHING** to commit yourself or your life to something **4.** BROADCAST **PLAY MUSIC ADDRESSED TO SOMEBODY** to play a piece of music, or request the playing of a piece of music, as a tribute, especially on the radio **5. DEVOTE ATTENTION TO SOMETHING** to spend time or energy doing something **6.** RELIG **SET SOMETHING APART AS HOLY** to set something apart for a sacred purpose or to the memory of a holy person, saint, or god, especially in a ceremony for this purpose ○ *"We cannot dedicate – we cannot consecrate – we cannot hallow – this ground. The brave men... who struggled here have consecrated it."* (Abraham Lincoln, *Gettysburg Address*; November 19, 1863) [15thC. From Latin *dedicare* "to consecrate," from *dicare* "to proclaim."] —**ded·i·ca·tee** /dèddi kay tée/ *n.* —**ded·i·ca·tive** /déddi kàytiv/ *adj.* —**ded·i·ca·tor** /-kàyt ər/ *n.*

ded·i·cat·ed /déddi kàytəd/ *adj.* **1. DEVOTED** wholeheartedly devoted or committed to a goal, cause, or job **2. INTENDED ONLY FOR ONE PURPOSE** designed to carry out only one task, or set aside for a purpose ○ *relayed via a dedicated satellite link*

ded·i·ca·tion /dèddi káysh'n/ *n.* **1. DEVOTION** the quality of being devoted or committed to something ○ *her dedication to duty* **2. INSCRIPTION** a short printed text at the beginning of a written or musical work associating it with somebody esteemed by the author **3.** MUSIC **PIECE OF MUSIC** a piece of music played or requested as a tribute, especially on the radio **4. SETTING ASIDE** an act or process of setting something aside for a particular purpose, especially in a ceremony that achieves this —**ded·i·ca·tion·al** *adj.*

de·dif·fer·en·ti·a·tion /dee diffə renshee áysh'n/ *n.* CELL BIOL = **anaplasia**

de·duce /di dóoss/ (**-duced, -duc·ing, -duc·es**) *vt.* **1. REACH A CONCLUSION** to come to a conclusion, often without all the necessary or relevant information, but using what is known in a logical way **2.** LOGIC **INFER SOMETHING FROM A GENERAL PRINCIPLE** to come to a conclusion by inference from a general principle [15thC. From Latin *deducere*, literally "to lead out," from *ducere* "to lead."] —**de·duc·i·bil·i·ty** /di dòossə bíllətee/ *n.* —**de·duc·i·ble** /di dóossəb'l/ *adj.* —**de·duc·i·ble·ness** *n.*

WORD KEY: SYNONYMS

deduce, infer, assume, reason, conclude, work out, figure out

CORE MEANING: to reach a logical conclusion on the basis of information

deduce a general term for reaching a conclusion based on evidence; **infer** to draw a conclusion from specific circumstances or evidence; **assume** to take a premise or information as true without checking or confirming; **reason** to consider information and use it to reach a conclusion in a logical way; **conclude** a term used to suggest that a conclusion has been reached in a logical way after much consideration; **work out** an informal term suggesting some careful thought or reasoning, possibly working with limited information; **figure out** the most informal term, emphasizing the application of somebody's own intelligence to the solving of a problem.

de·duct /di dúkt/ (**-duct·ed, -duct·ing, -ducts**) *vt.* to subtract an amount for some purpose [15thC. From Latin *deduct-*, the past participle stem of *deducere*, literally "to lead out," from *ducere* "to lead."]

de·duct·i·ble /di dúktəb'l/ *n.* **UNINSURED AMOUNT** an agreed amount that must be paid by an insured person making a claim against an insurance policy before an insurer will pay any compensation ○ *a $500 deductible* ■ *adj.* **1. ALLOWABLE AGAINST TAX** allowed by tax authorities as a legitimate expense not subject to tax **2. LIABLE TO DEDUCTION** capable of being, or liable to be, subtracted from something for some purpose —**de·duct·i·bil·i·ty** /di dùktə bíllətee/ *n.*

de·duc·tion /di dúkshən/ *n.* **1. AMOUNT DEDUCTED** an amount that is subtracted from something, especially as an allowance against tax **2. SUBTRACTION OF AN AMOUNT** the subtracting of an amount for some particular purpose **3. CONCLUSION DRAWN** a conclusion drawn from available information **4. DRAWING A CONCLUSION** the process of drawing a conclusion from available information **5.** LOGIC **LOGICAL CONCLUSION** a conclusion reached by applying the rules of logic to a premise **6.** LOGIC **REASONING** the forming of conclusions by applying the rules of logic to a premise

de·duc·tive /di dúktiv/ *adj.* based on logical or reasonable deduction ○ *deductive reasoning* —**de·duc·tive·ly** *adv.*

deed /deed/ *n.* **1. SOMETHING DONE** an intentional act ○ *"The last temptation is the greatest treason / To do the right deed for the wrong reason."* (T.S. Eliot, *Murder in the Cathedral*; 1935) **2.** LAW **DOCUMENT** a signed document that outlines the terms of an agreement, especially one that details a change in ownership of property **3.** LAW = **title deed** ■ **deeds** *npl.* **ACTIONS** action in general, especially as contrasted with speech ■ *vt.* (**deed·ed, deed·ing, deeds**) LAW **TRANSFER PROPERTY TO SOMEBODY** to sign over or transfer something, especially real estate, to another person ○ *deeded her cabin to her grandson* [Old English *dēd*. From a prehistoric Germanic word meaning "a doing," ultimately from the same Indo-European ancestor as English *do*.]

deed·ed /déedəd/ *adj.* associated with a deed that shows clear ownership ○ *a ranch consisting of 640 deeded acres*

dee·jay /dée jày/ *n.* a disc jockey (*informal*) [Mid-20thC. Respelling.] —**deejay** *vi.*

deem /deem/ (**deemed, deem·ing, deems**) *vt.* to judge or consider something in a particular light (*formal*) (*often used in the passive*) ○ *a plan that was deemed impractical from the very start* [Old English *dēman*. Ultimately from a prehistoric Germanic word meaning "to judge," the ancestor of English *doom*.]

de·em·pha·size /dee émfə sìz/ (**de·em·pha·sized, de·em·pha·siz·ing, de·em·pha·sizes**) *vt.* to make something seem or be less important or central —**de·em·pha·sis** /dee émfəssiss/ *n.*

de·en·er·gize /dee énnər jìz/ (**de·en·er·gized, de·en·er·giz·ing, de·en·er·gizes**) *v.* **1.** *vt.* **CUT OFF POWER** to cut off an electrical circuit from its source of power **2.** *vti.* **LOSE ENERGY** to have or cause somebody to have less energy or vitality —**de·en·er·gi·za·tion** /dee ènnərji záysh'n/ *n.*

deep /deep/ *adj.* **1. DOWN FROM A SURFACE** extending from a surface downward or inward ○ *very deep mud* ○ *a deep wound* **2. FAR FROM TOP TO BOTTOM** extending a long way from top to bottom ○ *a deep well* ○ *"The deep dark-shining / Pacific leans on the land."* (Robinson Jeffers, *Night*; 1925) **3. FAR FROM FRONT TO BACK** extending a long way from front to back ○ *a cupboard with deep shelves* **4. FAR FROM AN EDGE** extending a long way from a surface or boundary inward ○ *deep woods* **5. MADE UP OF UNITS** standing or lining up in rows of a particular number ○ *people six deep on the sidewalk* **6. FAR DOWN OR IN** relatively far down, in, or inside something ○ *a nagging pain deep inside his chest* **7. COMING FROM OR REACHING FAR INSIDE** coming from or reaching far down inside the body ○ *take a deep breath* **8. LOW IN PITCH** low in pitch and rounded in tone ○ *a deep booming voice* **9. DARK IN COLOR** relatively dark, rich, or intense in color ○ *deep purple* **10. INTENSE** intensely held, kept, or experienced ○ *deep suspicion* ○ *deep discounts* **11. PROFOUND** intellectually profound ○ *no evidence of deep thinking* ■ *adj., adv.* SPORTS **1. NEAR OWN GOAL** nearer to the goal a team is defending than the goal it is attacking ○ *Chicago played with two deep defenders.* ○ *deep in their own territory* **2. NEAR BOUNDARY** playing or played near the boundary of the playing area or, in baseball, farther from home plate or one of the bases than is usual ○ *a fly ball to deep left field* ■ *adv.* **FAR** far, especially from a surface or point of entry ○ *The expedition went deep into the jungle.* ■ *n.* **1. SEA** the ocean depths **2. INTENSE PART** the middle or most intense part of something (*literary*) ○ *the deep of night* [Old English *dēop*. Ultimately from an Indo-European word meaning "deep, hollow," which is also the ancestor of English *dip* and *dive*.] —**deep·ness** *n.* ◇ **deep down (inside)** in your innermost being ◇ **deep in** completely overwhelmed by or absorbed in something ○ *deep in a new novel* ◇ **in deep** very involved

deep-dis·count bond *n.* FIN a bond sold at a large discount because it bears little or no interest. It will, however, provide a capital gain on redemption.

deep-dish *adj.* baked in a deep dish and so thicker than normal ○ *deep-dish pizza*

deep-dyed *adj.* **1.** TEXTILES **NONFADING** used to describe fabric that has been dyed with a concentrated fade-resistant dye **2.** = **dyed-in-the-wool**

deep·en /déepən/ (**-ened, -en·ing, -ens**) *vti.* **1. GET DEEPER** to become or make something deep or deeper **2. MAKE OR BECOME INTENSE** to become or make something more intense ○ *the recession was deepening* —**deep·en·er** *n.*

deep end *n.* the part of a swimming pool, lake, or other body of water where the water is deepest ◇ **be thrown in at the deep end** to have to learn something new or difficult with very little experience or warning ◇ **go off the deep end** to fly into a rage or lose your emotional equilibrium

deep-fat fry·er *n. U.K.* = **deep fryer**

deep·freeze /dèep fréez/ *n.* **1.** a large freezer for the storage of foods and other perishable items **2. STORAGE OF SOMETHING IN EXTREME CONDITIONS** the storage of something in very cold or hostile conditions **3. SUSPENSION OF ACTIVITY** the suspension or delay of further activity (*informal*)

Deepfreeze /dèep fréez/ *tdmk.* a trademark for a freezer

deep-freeze (**deep-froze, deep-fro·zen, deep-freez·ing, deep-freez·es**) *vt.* **1. FREEZE SOMETHING QUICKLY** to freeze something such as food quickly in order to prolong its freshness or nutritional value **2. KEEP SOMETHING VERY COLD** to store something at very low temperatures **3. SUSPEND ACTIVITY** to put off or suspend activity (*informal*) —**deep-fro·zen** *adj.*

deep-fry (**deep-fried, deep-fry·ing, deep-fries**) *vt.* to cook food in fat or oil that is deep enough to cover the food completely —**deep-fried** *adj.*

deep fry·er, deep-fat fry·er *n.* an electrical appliance for deep-frying food

deep kiss *n.* a French kiss (*dated*) —**deep-kiss** *vti.*

deep·ly /déeplee/ *adv.* **1. INTENSELY** profoundly or intensely ○ *deeply offended* **2. DEEP INSIDE** far down inside ○ *breathe deeply* ○ *deeply felt pain*

deep pock·et *n.* a seemingly unlimited supply of money (*informal*)

deep-root·ed *adj.* **1. FIRMLY HELD** firmly held or established, usually over a long period of time, and so unlikely to change **2.** BOT **WITH DEEP ROOTS** having roots that grow deep in the soil

deep-sea *adj.* relating to the deep waters of the ocean far away from land

deep-seat·ed *adj.* firmly established and difficult to change or eradicate ○ *deep-seated fear*

deep-set *adj.* used to describe eyes with deep sockets

deep six *n.* disposal of something in a way that makes its reappearance unlikely (*slang*) [From naval slang meaning "burial at sea," perhaps from the traditional depth of a grave, or from the phrase "by the deep, six," meaning "six fathoms" on the sounding line]

deep-six (**deep-sixed, deep-six·ing, deep-six·es**) *vt.* to discard or dispose of something irrevocably (*slang*)

deep soul *n.* soul music of the 1960s and 1970s that took the form of slow and emotionally sung ballads

deep space *n.* space beyond the Earth's gravitational influence or beyond the orbit of the Moon

deep struc·ture *n.* LING the underlying form of a language, conceived as containing all the information needed to make any sentence in that language

deep-wa·ter *adj.* **1. ACCOMMODATING LARGE SHIPS** used to describe a port or anchorage that is deep enough to accommodate large oceangoing vessels **2. SEAGOING** designed or trained to travel on the oceans (*regional*)

WORD KEY: REGIONAL NOTE

In the sense "seagoing," as in *deep-water ship* or *deep-water sailor*, **deep-water** is recorded in coastal Massachusetts and New York but is most common in coastal Maine.

deer /deer/ (*plural* **deer**) *n.* a mammal distinguished by the branched antlers on males. More than forty species of deer exist, of different sizes and with different markings, and they are found wild on all continents except Australia and Antarctica. Family: Cervidae. [Old English *dēor* "animal." From a prehistoric Germanic word meaning literally "breathing creature," ultimately from an Indo-European base denoting "breath, vapor," which is also the ancestor of English *fume, dust,* and *thyme.*]

Deere /deer/, **John** (1804–86) U.S. inventor. He founded a company that manufactured agricultural equipment, including a revolutionary steel plow.

Deer·field Beach /deer feeld-/ city in southeastern Florida, in Broward County, on the coast of the Atlantic Ocean. Population: 46,325 (1990).

deer fly *n.* a biting fly that infests deer and other animals, sucking blood and spreading the infectious disease tularemia. It also delivers a stinging bite to humans. Genus: *Chrysops.*

deer·grass /deer gràss/ (*plural* **-grass**) *n.* a perennial flowering grassy plant that grows in thick tufts in temperate peat bogs. Latin name: *Trichophorum caespitosum.*

deer·hound /deer hòwnd/ *n.* a large long-legged greyhound with a very shaggy coat, originally bred in Scotland as a hunting dog from a Mediterranean strain of greyhound

deer lick *n.* a naturally occurring or artificial salty patch of ground where deer come to lick salt

deer mouse *n.* an agile mouse native to North and Central America. Genus: *Peromyscus.*

Deer Park city in southwestern Texas, on Buffalo Bayou near Galveston Bay. It is a western suburb of Houston. Population: 30,220 (1996).

deer·skin /deer skìn/ *n.* the treated hide of a deer used as a fabric

deer·stalk·er /deer stàwkər/ *n.* **deer·stalk·er, deer·stalk·er hat** a type of tweed hat with bills at the front and back and earflaps that can either be tied together on its crown or fastened under the chin

deer tick *n.* a tick that is a parasite of humans and other mammals. It carries and transmits the bacterium causing Lyme disease. Latin name: *Ioxides dammini.*

de·es·ca·late /dee éskə làyt/ (**de·es·ca·la·ted, de·es·ca·la·ting, de·es·ca·lates**) *vt.* to reduce the level or intensity of a difficult or dangerous situation —**de·es·ca·la·tion** /dee èskə láysh'n/ *n.*

deet /deet/ *n.* an oily colorless insect repellent. Formula: $C_{12}H_{17}NO$. Full form **diethyl toluamide** [Mid-20thC. Probably from the initial letters of its chemical name.]

def. *abbr.* **1.** defense **2.** definition **3.** defendant **4.** deferred **5.** GRAM definite

de·face /di fáyss/ (**-faced, -fac·ing, -fac·es**) *vt.* to spoil the appearance of something, especially intentionally [14thC. From French *défacer,* from *face* (see FACE).] —**de·face·a·ble** *adj.* —**de·fac·er** *n.*

de·face·ment /di fáysmənt/ *n.* the deliberate spoiling of the appearance of something

de fac·to /di fáktō, day fáktō/ *adv.* **IN FACT** in fact, whether with a legal right or not ■ *adj.* **AS THOUGH RIGHTFUL** acting or existing in fact but without legal sanction ○ *the de facto rules of the country* [Early 17thC. From Latin, "in fact," literally "from what is done."]

de·fal·cate /di fál kàyt, -fáwl-, déff'l-/ (**-cat·ed, -cat·ing, -cates**) *vt.* to misuse something, especially money or property, that belongs to somebody else and is held in trust [Mid-16thC. From medieval Latin *defalcare* "to deduct," literally "to mow off," from Latin *falx* "scythe," of unknown origin.] —**de·fal·ca·tor** /di fál kàytər, -fáwl-/ *n.*

de·fal·ca·tion /dee fal káysh'n, -fawl-, déff'l-/ *n.* **1. EMBEZZLEMENT** the misuse of somebody else's money, property, or funds **2. SUM EMBEZZLED** an amount of money obtained by defalcation

def·a·ma·tion /dèffə máysh'n/ *n.* an attack on somebody's good name, character, or reputation

de·fam·a·to·ry /di fámmə tàwree/ *adj.* harmful to somebody's good name, character, or reputation —**de·fam·a·to·ri·ly** *adv.*

de·fame /di fáym/ (**-famed, -fam·ing, -fames**) *vt.* to attack somebody or somebody's reputation, character, or good name by making slanderous or libelous statements [14thC. Via Old French *deffamer* from Latin *diffamare* "to spread about as an insulting report," from *fama* (see FAME).] —**de·fam·er** *n.*

WORD KEY: SYNONYMS

See Synonyms at ***malign.***

de·fang /dee fáng/ (**-fanged, -fang·ing, -fangs**) *vt.* **1. WEAKEN** to weaken the power or harmful effect of something **2. REMOVE FANGS** to remove the fangs from a snake or other animal

de·fat /dee fát/ (**-fat·ted, -fat·ting, -fats**) *vt.* to remove the fat or fats from something

de·fault /di fáwlt/ *n.* **1.** COMPUT **PRESET OPTION** an option that will automatically be selected by a computer if the user does not choose one **2. FAILURE TO DO SOMETHING** a failure to meet an obligation, especially a financial one **3.** LAW **NONAPPEARANCE IN COURT** a failure to make a summoned court appearance **4.** SPORTS **NONPARTICIPATION IN COMPETITION** a failure to appear for or complete a competition ■ *vi.* (**-fault·ed, -fault·ing, -faults**) **1. FAIL TO PAY** to fail to pay a debt or other financial obligation **2.** LAW **FAIL TO APPEAR IN COURT** to fail to make an appearance in court although summoned to do so **3.** SPORTS **FAIL TO COMPETE** to fail to appear for a match or contest **4.** COMPUT **USE PRESET OPTION** to use a device, command, or file when no other is specified [13thC. From Old French *defaute,* the past participle of *defaillir* "to fail," from *faillir* (see FAIL).] ◇ **by default 1.** having come about because some other thing, often something expected, did not happen **2.** having come about because somebody failed to appear as expected **3.** according to a computer's preset configuration ◇ **in default of something** *or* **somebody** because of a lack of or the absence of something or somebody (*formal*)

de·fault·er /di fáwltər/ *n.* **1. NONPAYER** somebody who fails to comply with a financial obligation **2.** LAW **ABSENTEE FROM COURT** somebody who fails to appear when summoned to court **3.** SPORTS **ABSENTEE FROM COMPETITION** a person or team failing to appear for a match or contest

de·fea·sance /di feez'ns/ *n.* LAW **1. MAKING VOID** the declaration of something as null and void **2. LEGAL CLAUSE** a clause in a legal document that states that, in the event of a condition or conditions being fulfilled, the document will become null and void **3. LEGAL DOCUMENT** a document containing a defeasance [15thC. From Old French *defesance,* from *defaire,* from medieval Latin *disfacere* , literally "to unmake."]

de·fea·si·ble /di feezib'l/ *adj.* LAW **1. VOIDABLE** capable of being made or declared null and void **2. SUBJECT TO FORFEIT** liable to be forfeited —**de·fea·si·bil·i·ty** /di feezi bíllətee/ *n.* —**de·fea·si·ble·ness** /di feezib'lnəss/ *n.*

de·feat /di feet/ *vt.* (**-feat·ed, -feat·ing, -feats**) **1. BEAT A COMPETITOR** to win a victory over a competitor, e.g., in sports or business **2. WIN A VOTE** to win a victory over another in a debate or vote **3. BEAT AN ENEMY** to win a victory over enemy forces in a battle or war **4. CAUSE FAILURE** to cause something to fail or to fall short of realization ○ *The truck defeated all my attempts to get it to start.* **5. BAFFLE SOMEBODY** to leave somebody in a baffled or uncomprehending state ○ *His logic defeats me.* **6.** LAW **MAKE SOMETHING VOID** to make or declare something null and void ■ *n.* **1. LOSING TO AN OPPONENT** the fact or an instance of losing to an enemy in battle or an opponent in a competition ○ *our team's defeat of the visitors* **2. FAILURE** failure to win or to realize a goal ○ *She refused to admit defeat and appealed.* **3.** LAW = **annulment** [14thC. Via Anglo-Norman *defeter* "to disfigure, destroy" from, ultimately, medieval Latin *disfacere,* literally "to unmake," from Latin *facere* "to do, make" (see FACT).] —**de·feat·er** *n.* ◇ **defeat the object, defeat the purpose** make the desired outcome less likely or possible while appearing to have the intent of pursuing it

WORD KEY: SYNONYMS

defeat, beat, conquer, vanquish, overcome, triumph over, thrash, trounce

CORE MEANING: to win a victory

defeat the most general and wide-ranging term, used to talk about both real events and situations and abstract concepts; **beat** a slightly less formal term for *defeat,* commonly used to talk about real events or situations as well as successfully dealing with serious problems or surviving serious illnesses; **conquer** a term suggesting a convincing victory, often used in a military context, but also used with reference to abstract concepts; **vanquish** a formal or literary term for *conquer;* **overcome** a term suggesting that victory was gained after a struggle, often used with reference to abstract concepts; **triumph over** a fairly formal term suggesting decisive victory with cause for celebration; **thrash** an informal term used of an easy victory in a contest or athletic match, particularly one with a large margin of victory; **trounce** a more formal word for *thrash.*

de·feat·ist /di feetist/ *adj.* **EXPECTING FAILURE** showing a tendency to expect failure or accept it too readily ■ *n.* **SOMEBODY WHO EXPECTS FAILURE** somebody who expects or accepts failure as a matter of course —**de·feat·ism** *n.*

def·e·cate /déffə kàyt/ (**-cat·ed, -cat·ing, -cates**) *v.* **1.** *vi.* **EXPEL FECES** to expel feces from the bowel through the rectum (*formal or technical*) **2.** *vt.* CHEM **REMOVE IMPURITIES** to remove impurities from a solution, especially a solution that contains sugar [15thC. From Latin *defaecare* "to remove waste," from *faex* "dregs, waste" (source of English *feces*).] —**def·e·ca·tion** /dèffə káysh'n/ *n.* —**def·e·ca·tor** /déffə kàytər/ *n.*

de·fect *n.* /dee fèkt, di fékt/ **1. FLAW** a failing, blemish, or flaw, especially one that still allows the affected thing to function, however imperfectly **2. PERSONAL FLAW** a personal failing, weakness, or shortcoming, especially in character **3.** CRYSTALS **IMPERFECTION IN CRYSTAL** an imperfection in the internal structure of a crystal, e.g., an atom of a different substance ■ *vi.* /di fékt/ (**-fect·ed, -fect·ing, -fects**) **1. REJECT YOUR HOMELAND** to leave your native country or the country you are living in and refuse to return there, usually for political or moral reasons **2. ABANDON AN ALLEGIANCE** to abandon allegiance to a cause or party, especially when this also involves supporting something previously opposed [15thC. From Latin *defect-,* the past participle stem of *deficere* "to be wanting, desert," from *facere* "to do, make" (see FACT).] —**de·fec·tion** *n.*

WORD KEY: SYNONYMS

See Synonyms at ***flaw.***

de·fec·tive /di féktiv/ *adj.* **1. FAULTY** faulty, especially in having something missing or broken and so not functioning properly or at all **2. OFFENSIVE TERM FOR LEARNING DIFFICULTIES** highly objectionable term that means with learning difficulties or problems in coping with emotions (*offensive insult*) **3.** GRAM **INCOMPLETE** lacking the usual or expected range of grammatical inflections ■ *n.* **OFFENSIVE TERM REFERRING TO LEARNING DIFFICULTIES** highly objectionable term that means somebody who has learning difficulties or problems in coping with emotions (*offensive insult*) —**de·fec·tive·ly** *adv.* —**de·fec·tive·ness** *n.*

WORD KEY: USAGE

defective or **deficient**? ***Defective*** is normally used in reference to machines or to other functional things such as the human senses: *If the workmanship is defective, they'll replace the shoes with a new pair. Artillery officers sometimes have defective hearing.* ***Deficient*** is used to describe things that lack a quality or an attribute, without this amounting to actual failure to work or function: *Her voice is beautiful but a little deficient in power. Their diet is deficient in vitamin D.*

de·fec·tor /di féktər/ *n.* **1. POLITICAL EMIGRANT** somebody who rejects his or her native country in favor of another, usually for political or moral reasons **2. CONVERTED PERSON** somebody who, because of a clash in ideology, rejects one cause or political group in favor of another

de·fem·i·nize /dee fémmə nīz/ (**-nized, -niz·ing, -niz·es**) *vt.* to remove or diminish characteristics of somebody or something that are traditionally regarded as associated with women or girls

de·fence *n.* U.K. = **defense**

de·fend /di fénd/ (**-fend·ed, -fend·ing, -fends**) *v.* **1.** *vt.* **PROTECT SOMEBODY OR SOMETHING** to protect somebody or something from attack, harm, or danger **2.** *vti.* LAW **REPRESENT IN COURT** to represent and speak on behalf of an accused person in court **3.** *vt.* **SUPPORT A POSITION** to offer support for something or somebody, especially by arguing against the objections or criticism of others **4.** *vi.* **RESIST AN OPPONENT** to resist the attacks of an opposing player or team and try to prevent him or her from scoring **5.** *vt.* SPORTS **TRY TO KEEP A TITLE** to try to retain a title, especially a sporting one, by competing in the relevant competitions [13thC. Via French *défendre* from Latin *defendere* "to ward off." Ultimately from an Indo-European word meaning "to strike, kill," which is also the ancestor of English *bane* and *gun*.] —**de·fend·a·ble** *adj.*

WORD KEY: SYNONYMS

See Synonyms at ***safeguard***.

de·fen·dant /di féndənt/ *n.* a person, party, or company required to answer criminal or civil charges in a court

de·fend·er /di féndər/ *n.* **1.** SUPPORTER somebody who offers support, justification, or an explanation for something or somebody **2.** PROTECTOR somebody who protects a person or place against attack **3.** SPORTS HOLDER OF TITLE somebody who holds a title that is subject to recurring competition

De·fend·er of the Faith *n.* a title given by Pope Leo X in 1521 to King Henry VIII and held by British monarchs ever since

de·fend·ing /di fénding/ *adj.* SPORTS holding a title that is subject to recurring competition ○ *the defending champions*

de·fen·es·trate /dee fénnə strayt/ (**-trated, -trat·ing, -trates**) *vt.* to throw something or somebody out of a window (*formal or humorous*) [Early 17thC. Coined from DE- + Latin *fenestra* "window" (source of English *fenestrated*), of unknown origin.] —**de·fen·es·tra·tion** /dee fènnə stráysh'n/ *n.*

de·fense /di fénss/ *n.* **1.** PROTECTION the protection of something, especially from attack by an enemy **2.** SOMETHING THAT PROTECTS a method or object for protecting something ○ *a castle with strong defenses* **3.** MIL ARMED FORCES a country's armed forces **4.** JUSTIFICATION an excuse or justification for something ○ *spoke in defense of the motion* **5.** LAW REASONS OFFERED the set of reasons that a defendant offers in court in denial of a charge **6.** LAW DEFENDANT'S CASE the facts and their presentation as they relate to the defendant in a court case **7.** LAW COUNSEL AND DEFENDANT the counsel and the defendant in a court case **8.** /deé fènss/ SPORTS DEFENSIVE PLAY in sports, the method or maneuvers that prevent the other team from scoring **9.** /deé fènss/ SPORTS DEFENSIVE PLAYERS the sports team members who play defense ■ **de·fens·es** *npl.* **1.** PROTECTIVE QUALITIES the qualities of the body or mind that protect somebody from attack, injury, or illness **2.** FORTIFICATIONS the fortifications that protect a place from enemies or the forces of nature [14thC. Via Old French from, ultimately, Latin *defens-*, the past participle stem of *defendere* (see DEFEND).]

de·fense·less /di fénsləss/ *adj.* UNPROTECTED lacking any form of protection and therefore vulnerable ■ *npl.* UNPROTECTED PEOPLE people who are unable to defend themselves and their interests ○ *working as a shield for the defenseless* —**de·fense·less·ly** *adv.* —**de·fense·less·ness** *n.*

de·fense mech·a·nism *n.* **1.** PROTECTIVE MENTAL ACTIVITY any means of avoiding emotional distress, destructive impulses, or a threat to self-esteem, especially by the suppression of unwanted thoughts or memories **2.** PROTECTIVE PHYSICAL ACTIVITY any of the natural protective responses to danger or attack used by an organism, e.g., when faced with a predator or invaded by a disease agent

de·fense-mind·ed *adj.* giving emphasis to building a team with strong defensive skills

de·fen·si·ble /di fénsəb'l/ *adj.* **1.** ABLE TO BE PROTECTED capable of being protected from attack **2.** JUSTIFIABLE able to be explained, justified, or excused —**de·fen·si·bil·i·ty** /di fènsə bíllətee/ *n.* —**de·fen·si·ble·ness** /di fénsəb'lnəs/ *n.* —**de·fen·si·bly** *adv.*

de·fens·in /dee fénsin/ *n.* any of three peptides present in human white blood cells that appear to play a role in the prevention or elimination of infection

de·fen·sive /di fénsiv/ *adj.* **1.** QUICK TO JUSTIFY aiming to deflect or avoid perceived criticism **2.** SERVING TO PROTECT designed or intended for protection or defense **3.** FAVORING DEFENSE AS PLAYING STRATEGY concentrating more on preventing an opponent from gaining an advantage than on scoring **4.** OF A DEFENSE TEAM relating to the team that plays defense, especially in football —**de·fen·sive·ness** *n.* ◇ **on the defensive 1.** expecting criticism or aggression and prepared to respond **2.** having assumed a position that indicates readiness to play defensively

de·fen·sive med·i·cine *n.* medical treatment that involves carrying out extensive diagnostic testing in order to minimize the chances of a patient's suing the doctor or hospital for negligence

de·fens·man /deé fens màn/ (*plural* **-men** /-mèn/) *n.* a team member who plays a defensive position, especially in ice hockey

de·fer[1] /di fúr/ (**-ferred, -fer·ring, -fers**) *vti.* **1.** POSTPONE to put something off until a later time **2.** MIL POSTPONE MILITARY SERVICE to allow somebody to postpone conscription into the armed forces [14thC. From French *différer* "to put aside, differ."] —**de·fer·ment** *n.* —**de·fer·ra·ble** *adj.* —**de·fer·rer** *n.*

de·fer[2] /di fúr/ (**-ferred, -fer·ring, -fers**) *vi.* to give way to, and usually acknowledge the merit of, somebody else's judgment, opinion, wishes, or action ○ *I defer to your superior knowledge.* [15thC. Via French *déférer* from Latin *deferre*, literally "to carry away," from *ferre* "to carry" (see FERTILE).] —**de·fer·rer** *n.*

def·er·ence /déffərəns/ *n.* **1.** RESPECT polite respect, especially putting another person's interests first **2.** SUBMISSION submission to the judgment, opinion, or wishes of another person [Mid-17thC. Formed from DEFER[2].] ◇ **in deference to** out of respect or courtesy to somebody or something

def·er·ent[1] /déffərənt/ *adj.* = **deferential**

def·er·ent[2] *adj.* PHYSIOL used to describe a duct, nerve, or vessel in the body that is capable of carrying impulses or fluid away, down, or outward

def·er·en·tial /dèffə rénsh'l/ *adj.* showing or expressing polite respect or courtesy —**def·er·en·tial·ly** *adv.*

de·fer·ral /di fúrəl/ *n.* an instance or the process of putting something off, especially a trial or court hearing, until a later date

de·ferred an·nu·i·ty *n.* a type of investment that does not pay out until at least one year after the final premium has been paid

de·ferred sen·tence *n.* a sentence that is not passed until a specified period has elapsed in order to allow the court time to assess the behavior of the convicted person

de·fer·ves·cence /deé fər véss'ns/ *n.* **1.** DECREASE IN FEVER a decrease in a fever **2.** STAGE OF ILLNESS WHEN FEVER DECREASES the stage of an illness during which fever subsides [Early 18thC. Via Latin *defervescere* "to stop boiling" from, ultimately, *fervere* "to be hot, boil."] —**de·fer·vesce** *vti.* —**de·fer·ves·cent** *adj.*

de·fi·ance /di fí əns/ *n.* open, bold, or hostile refusal to obey or conform ◇ **in defiance of 1.** with complete disregard for a rule, law, or person in authority **2.** notwithstanding a rule or expectation

De·fi·ance /di fí əns/ city in northwestern Ohio southwest of Toledo and northwest of Lima. Population: 16,718 (1996).

de·fi·ant /di fí ənt/ *adj.* **1.** CHALLENGING AGGRESSIVELY tending to confront and challenge **2.** DISOBEDIENT deliberately and openly disobedient [Late 16thC. From French *défiant*, the present participle of *défier*, from assumed Vulgar Latin *disfidare* "to renounce your faith."] —**de·fi·ant·ly** *adv.*

de·fib·ril·late /dee fíbbrə làyt, -fíbrə-/ (**-lat·ed, -lat·ing, -lates**) *vt.* to apply an electric shock to the chest, or sometimes directly to the heart itself, in order to restore a regular heartbeat after a critically irregular beat has developed —**de·fib·ril·la·tion** /dee fìbbrə láysh'n, -fìbrə-/ *n.*

de·fib·ril·la·tor /dee fíbbrə làytər, -fíbrə-/ *n.* a machine that administers a controlled electric shock to the chest or heart to correct a fluttering heartbeat that cannot drive the circulation

de·fi·cien·cy /di físh'nsee/ (*plural* **-cies**) *n.* **1.** SHORTAGE a lack or shortage of something **2.** AMOUNT LACKING the amount by which something falls short of being complete

WORD KEY: SYNONYMS

See Synonyms at ***lack***.

de·fi·cien·cy dis·ease *n.* a disease resulting from lack of a nutrient or other substance required by a human or other animal or plant for growth, development, or general health. The deficiency may be caused either by an inadequate supply of the required substance or an inability to process it.

de·fi·cient /di físh'nt/ *adj.* **1.** LACKING lacking a particular quality, element, or ingredient, especially one that is expected or necessary **2.** INADEQUATE inadequate or not good enough [Late 16thC. From Latin *deficient-*, the present participle stem of *deficere* "to leave undone, fail," from *facere* "to do, make" (see FACT).] —**de·fi·cient·ly** *adv.*

WORD KEY: USAGE

See Usage note at ***defective***.

def·i·cit /déffissit/ *n.* **1.** EXCESSIVE AMOUNT SPENT the amount by which expenditures exceed income or budget **2.** SHORTFALL the amount by which a total is less than it should be [Late 18thC. Via French *déficit* from Latin *deficit* "it is lacking," from *deficere* "to leave undone, fail."]

WORD KEY: SYNONYMS

See Synonyms at ***lack***.

def·i·cit fi·nanc·ing *n.* the practice of deliberately allowing government spending to exceed its revenues in order to try to boost economic activity and lower unemployment

def·i·cit spend·ing *n.* government spending that is financed by borrowing money rather than through money raised by taxation

de·fi·er /di fír/ *n.* somebody who openly refuses to obey or conform to a rule, regulation, or authority

def·i·lade /déffi làyd, -laad/ *n.* DEFENSE CONFIGURATION fortifications or protection designed to guard against enemy gunfire that might be aimed at a line of troops. ◊ **enfilade** ■ *vt.* (**-lad·ed, -lad·ing, -lades**) PROTECT TROOPS to set up protective fortifications to protect troops or a position [Early 19thC. Formed from French *défiler* (see DEFILE[2]), on the model of "enfilade."]

de·file[1] /di fíl/ (**-filed, -fil·ing, -files**) *vt.* **1.** CORRUPT SOMETHING to corrupt or ruin something (*formal*) **2.** DAMAGE REPUTATION to damage somebody's reputation or good name **3.** DESTROY SANCTITY OF SOMETHING to make a holy or sacred thing or place no longer fit for ceremonial use **4.** POLLUTE SOMETHING to make something dirty or polluted (*formal*) **5.** DEPRIVE WOMAN OF VIRGINITY to be the first man to have sexual intercourse with a woman, usually outside marriage (*archaic*) [14thC. An alteration (influenced by an obsolete word meaning "to befoul") of French *defouler* "to trample," from *fouler* "to trample under foot."] —**de·file·ment** *n.* —**de·fil·er** *n.*

de·file[2] /di fíl/ *n.* **1.** NARROW MOUNTAIN PASS a narrow pass between mountains **2.** NARROW PASSAGE a passage only wide enough for people to pass single-file ■ *vi.* (**-filed, -fil·ing, -files**) MARCH SINGLE-FILE to march or go in single file, especially when the way is too narrow to march in any other formation [Late 17thC. From French *défiler* "to march in a line," from *file* "FILE[1]."]

de·fine /di fín/ (**-fined, -fin·ing, -fines**) *v.* **1.** *vti.* GIVE MEANING OF WORD to give the precise meaning of a word or expression **2.** *vt.* STATE to state or describe something clearly **3.** *vt.* CHARACTERIZE SOMEBODY OR SOMETHING to identify somebody or something by a distinctive characteristic quality or feature ○ *The age we live in is defined by a deep sense of uncertainty.* **4.** *vt.* SHOW SOMETHING CLEARLY to show something clearly, especially in shape or outline (*usually passive*) ○ *The tire marks were clearly defined in the snow.* **5.** *vt.* MARK to mark a boundary, edge, or limit ○ *That row of trees defines the eastern boundary of the estate.* [14thC. Via Old French *definer* from Latin *definire* "to limit, determine," from *finis* (see FINAL).] —**de·fin·a·bil·i·ty** /di fìnə bíllətee/ *n.* —**de·fin·a·ble** /di fínəb'l/ *adj.* —**de·fin·a·bly** *adv.* —**de·fin·er** *n.*

de·fin·i·en·dum /də finnee éndəm/ (*plural* **-da** /-də/) *n.* the word or expression defined by a definition, e.g., in a dictionary or glossary (*technical*) [Late 19thC. From Latin, literally "thing to be defined," formed from *definire* (see DEFINE).]

de·fin·i·ens /də finnee ènz/ (*plural* **-en·ti·a** /-énshə, -énshee ə/) *n.* the words used to define a particular word or expression, e.g., in a dictionary or glossary (*technical*) [Late 19thC. From medieval Latin, literally "something that defines," from the present participle of *definire* (see DEFINE).]

de·fin·ing /di fíning/ *adj.* giving a distinctive character to something, or encapsulating its character ○ *That was the defining moment of the election campaign.*

def·i·nite /déffənit/ *adj.* **1.** ABSOLUTELY SET ON SOMETHING certain about something and unlikely to have a change of plan ○ *I'm definite about this.* **2.** FIXED fixed, certain, and not to be altered ○ *Have we got a definite date for the meeting?* **3. OBVIOUS** unquestionable and unmistakable ○ *a definite turn for the better* **4. WITH CLEAR LIMITS** precise and distinct in describing the limits of something ○ *with a definite age range for the junior chess club* **5. WITH CLEAR OUTLINE** with a clearly distinct shape or outline ○ *the definite outline of a building among the trees* **6.** BOT **WITH TERMINAL FLOWER** used to describe a flower head in which the first-formed flower is at the stalk's end with subsequent flowers developing lower down on one or both sides of the stalk [Mid-16thC. From Latin *definitus*, the past participle of definire (see DEFINE).] —**def·i·nite·ness** *n.*

WORD KEY: USAGE

definite or **definitive**? ***Definite*** describes something as being clear or exact without making any strong judgment about it: *He has definite ideas on the subject.* ***Definitive*** denotes something that is authoritative, conclusive, or decisive, and is therefore a more judgmental word: *She wrote the definitive book on the subject.*

def·i·nite ar·ti·cle *n.* a word, e.g., "the" in English, that designates a noun as being specific and identifiable

def·i·nite in·te·gral *n.* a determination of the difference in values of an integral between two specified limits, expressed using symbols

def·i·nite·ly /déffənitlee/ *adv.* **1. CERTAINLY** without a doubt ○ *He definitely had a Swedish accent.* **2. FINALLY AND UNCHANGEABLY** as a conclusion after some thought or hesitation ○ *Once she had definitely decided to go, she started packing.* **3. EXACTLY** in a precise way ○ *Without knowing definitely what it was, he just felt that something was wrong.* **4. CLEARLY** in a distinct and unmistakable way ○ *Her attitude suddenly became more definitely critical.* **5. ABSOLUTELY** with no exceptions ○ *The sign read, "Definitely no admittance."* ■ *interj.* **YES** used to say "yes" in an emphatic and enthusiastic way ○ *"Are you going to come to the party?""Definitely!"*

def·i·ni·tion /dèffə nísh'n/ *n.* **1. MEANING OF WORD** a brief precise statement of what a word or expression means, e.g., in a dictionary **2. ACT OF DEFINING A WORD** the act or process of defining what a word or expression means, e.g., in writing a dictionary **3. MAKING SOMETHING CLEAR** the act of describing or stating something clearly and unambiguously **4.** TV, PHOTOGRAPHY **DEGREE OF CLARITY** the clarity of a photograph, television picture, or other reproduced image. It is related to the sharpness and degree of contrast in the image. **5.** RECORDING **CLARITY OF RECORDED SOUND** the degree of sharpness or clarity in recorded sound **6. EMBODIMENT OF SOMETHING** somebody or something believed to represent or embody a particular idea or quality (*formal*) ○ *His behavior has always seemed to me the very definition of courtesy.* [14thC. Via French from, ultimately, Latin *definire* (see DEFINE).] —**def·i·ni·tion·al** *adj.* ◇ **by definition** used to emphasize that somebody or something is considered to have a particular quality as part of his, her, or its nature

de·fin·i·tive /di fínnətiv/ *adj.* **1. CONCLUSIVE AND FINAL** providing a final decision that will not be questioned or changed ○ *We need a definitive answer.* **2. MOST AUTHORITATIVE** recognized as being the most authoritative and of the highest standard ○ *the definitive study of the subject* **3.** STAMPS **SOLD FOR LONG TIME** used to describe stamps sold for an extended or indefinite period and often part of a set sharing common design elements **4.** BIOL **FULLY GROWN** fully formed or completely developed ■ *n.* STAMPS **DEFINITIVE STAMP** a postage stamp sold for an extended or indefinite period [14thC. Via French *définitif* from, ultimately, Latin *definire* (see DEFINE).] —**de·fin·i·tive·ly** *adv.* —**de·fin·i·tive·ness** *n.*

WORD KEY: USAGE

See Usage note at ***definite***.

de·fin·i·tive host *n.* the plant or animal in or on which a parasitic organism reaches sexual maturity. ◊ **intermediate host**

de·fin·i·tude *n.* the quality of being exact and precise (*formal*) [Mid-19thC. Formed from DEFINITE, on the model of infinitude.]

def·la·grate /défflə gràyt/ (**-grat·ed, -grat·ing, -grates**) *vti.* to burn or make something burn violently (*literary or technical*) [Early 17thC. From Latin *deflagrare*, literally "to burn up," from *flagrare* (see FLAGRANT).] —**def·la·gra·tion** /dèfflə gráysh'n/ *n.*

de·flate /də fláyt/ (**-flat·ed, -flat·ing, -flates**) *v.* **1.** *vti.* **LET AIR OUT** to let out or lose air or gas from an inflatable object with the result that it shrinks or collapses **2.** *vt.* **MAKE SOMEBODY LESS CONFIDENT** to destroy somebody's confidence, or make somebody less self-assured or conceited **3.** *vt.* **DESTROY THEORY** to show that a theory or argument is wrong **4.** *vt.* ECON **CAUSE DEFLATION** to bring about deflation in the economy or the money supply [Late 19thC. Coined from DE- + INFLATE.] —**de·fla·tor** *n.*

de·fla·tion /di fláysh'n/ *n.* **1. COLLAPSE BECAUSE OF AIR LOSS** the releasing or escaping of air or gas from something, resulting in its shrinking or collapsing **2. LOSS OF SELF-ESTEEM** a sudden loss of confidence, self-assurance, or conceit **3.** ECON **REDUCED ECONOMIC ACTIVITY** the reduction of general economic activity, including lower prices and a reduced supply of money and credit **4.** GEOL **EROSION** the erosion of land by wind

de·fla·tion·ar·y /di fláysh'n èrree/ *adj.* undergoing or creating a lower level of general economic activity

de·fla·tion·ist /di fláysh'nist/ *adj.* **ADVOCATING DEFLATION** in favor of economic deflation ■ *n.* **SUPPORTER OF DEFLATION** somebody who advocates deflation of an economy

de·flect /di flékt/ (**-flect·ed, -flect·ing, -flects**) *v.* **1.** *vti.* **CHANGE COURSE** to change course because of hitting something, or change something's course by coming into contact with it ○ *The pitcher's arm deflected the ball into the outfield.* **2.** *vt.* **DIRECT ATTENTION AWAY** to direct people's attention or criticism away from a particular subject or issue to something else **3.** *vt.* **FORCE ALTERATION OF PLANS** to force somebody to change from what he or she usually does or planned to do [Mid-16thC. From Latin *deflectere*, literally "to bend away," from *flectere* (see FLEXIBLE).] —**de·flect·a·ble** *adj.* —**de·flec·tive** *adj.* —**de·flec·tor** *n.*

de·flec·tion /di flékshən/ *n.* **1. CHANGING OF COURSE** a change of course after hitting somebody or something, or a changing of something's course by being hit by it **2. AMOUNT SOMETHING DEFLECTS** the amount or distance by which something is deflected **3. DIVERTING OF ATTENTION** the act of directing people's attention or criticism away from something **4.** MEASURE **MOVEMENT OF NEEDLE AWAY FROM ZERO** the movement of a needle or pointer on a measuring instrument away from the zero position **5.** ENG **MOVEMENT OF STRUCTURE UNDER LOAD** the movement of a structure or a part of a structure when it is bearing a load

de·flexed /di flékst/ *adj.* BOT used to describe petals or leaves that bend sharply downward [Late 18thC. Formed from Latin *deflexus*, the past participle of *deflectere* (see DEFLECT).]

def·lo·ra·tion /dèfflə ráysh'n/ *n.* ending of a woman's or girl's virginity (*literary*) [14thC. Via French from, ultimately, late Latin *deflorare* (see DEFLOWER).]

de·flow·er /dee flówr/ (**-ered, -er·ing, -ers**) *vt.* to end the virginity of a girl or woman (*formal or literary*) [14thC. Via Old French *desflourer* from late Latin *deflorare*, from Latin *flos* (see FLOWER).] —**de·flow·er·er** *n.*

de·fo·cus /dee fṓkəss/ *v.* (**-cused, -cus·ing, -cus·es**) **1.** *vt.* PHOTOGRAPHY **SOFTEN PICTURE BY SHIFTING FOCUS** to soften or blur an image by focusing away from the exact plane of focus of the object in the image **2.** *vti.* **STOP FOCUSING** to stop focusing on something, or cause the eyes to stop focusing on something ■ *n.* **CONDITION OF DEFOCUSING** the condition or state caused by defocusing, e.g., the blurring of a photographic image

de·fog /dee fóg/ (**de·fogged, de·fog·ging, de·fogs**) *vti.* **1.** CARS **GET RID OF CONDENSATION FROM WINDSHIELD** to remove condensation from the windshield, mirror, and windows of a motor vehicle, or lose condensation **2.** PHOTOGRAPHY **GET RID OF CONDENSATION FROM LENS** to remove condensation from the lens of a camera or other optical equipment, especially by allowing it to warm up, or lose condensation in this way

de·fog·ger *n.* **1.** CARS **DEVICE THAT REMOVES CONDENSATION** device that clears condensation from the windshield of a motor vehicle, especially heating vents built into the dashboard or heating elements on or in the windshield glass **2.** SPORTS **LIQUID FOR REMOVING CONDENSATION** a liquid used to clean and remove condensation from goggles or eyeglasses

de·fo·li·ant /dee fṓlee ənt/ *n.* a chemical that strips trees and plants of their leaves and is sometimes used in warfare to deny cover to enemy forces

de·fo·li·ate /dee fṓlee àyt/ (**-at·ed, -at·ing, -ates**) *vti.* to strip trees and plants of their leaves, e.g., by using chemicals or through pollution or attack by pests, or to lose leaves in any of these ways [Late 18thC. From late Latin *defoliare*, from *folium* (see FOLIO).] —**de·fo·li·a·tion** *n.* —**de·fo·li·a·tor** *n.*

de·for·est /dee fáwrəst/ (**-est·ed, -est·ing, -ests**) *vt.* to remove the trees from an area of land —**de·for·es·ta·tion** /dee fàwrə stáysh'n/ *n.* —**de·for·est·er** *n.*

De For·est /di fáwrəst/, **Lee** (1873–1961) U.S. inventor. He invented the audion, a vacuum tube that revolutionized the radio industry (1906).

de·form /di fáwrm/ (**-formed, -form·ing, -forms**) *vti.* **1. MAKE OR BECOME DISTORTED** to become, or make something become, distorted, damaged, or disfigured **2. SPOIL SOMETHING OR BECOME SPOILED** to spoil the appearance of something and make it ugly, or become spoiled and ugly ○ *The new office buildings have deformed the whole area.* **3.** PHYS **CHANGE SHAPE BY STRESS** to change the shape of something through stress, or become changed in this way [15thC. Via Old French *deformer* from Latin *deformare*, literally "to un-form," from *forma* (see FORM).] —**de·form·a·bil·i·ty** /di fàwrmə bílllətee/ *n.* —**de·form·a·ble** *adj.* —**de·form·er** *n.*

de·for·mal·ize /dee fáwrm'l ìz/ (**-ized, -iz·ing, -iz·es**) *vt.* to make something such as a meeting or report less formal —**de·for·mal·i·za·tion** /dee f'awrməli záysh'n/ *n.*

de·for·ma·tion /dee fàwr máysh'n, dèffər-/ *n.* **1. ACT OF DEFORMING OR BEING DEFORMED** the act or process of damaging, disfiguring, or spoiling the look of something, or the condition of being damaged, disfigured, or spoiled **2. CHANGE IN SHAPE** a change in the shape of something, especially one that suggests damage or disfigurement **3. UNPLEASANT RESULT OF CHANGE** the harmful or disfiguring result of a change in form **4.** PHYS **CHANGE IN SHAPE BECAUSE OF STRESS** a change in shape resulting from the application of stress

de·formed /di fáwrmd/ *adj.* **1. BADLY FORMED** abnormal or unnatural in shape **2. NOT NORMAL** not normal in outlook or temperament, especially in a way that is considered dangerous or depraved **3.** PHYS **DISTORTED** changed in shape as a result of stress —**de·form·ed·ly** /di fáwrmədlee/ *adv.* —**de·form·ed·ness** /-nəss/ *n.*

de·for·mi·ty /di fáwrmətee/ (*plural* **-ties**) *n.* **1. DISFIGUREMENT** the condition of being disfigured or badly formed ○ *the deformity of the pine trees at such a high altitude in the mountains* **2.** ANAT **STRUCTURAL CHANGE FROM NORMAL** a permanent change from normal body structure **3. SOMETHING WITH SHAPE FAR FROM NORMAL** something that has a shape not normal for its kind or nature

de·frag /dee frág/ (**-fragged, -frag·ging, -frags**) *vt.* ◆ **defragment** (*informal*)

de·frag·ment /dee frág ment, dèe frag mént/ (**de·frag·ment·ed, de·frag·ment·ing, de·frag·ments**) *vt.* to reorganize the storage space on a hard disk by consolidating similar files thereby optimizing the performance of the hard disk

de·fraud /di fráwd/ (**-fraud·ed, -fraud·ing, -frauds**) *vt.* to deprive somebody of money or property by dishonest means [14thC. Directly or via Old French from Latin *defraudare*, from *fraudare* "to cheat."] —**de·fraud·a·tion** /di fràw dáysh'n/ *n.* —**de·fraud·er** *n.* —**de·fraud·ment** /-mənt/ *n.*

de·fray /di fráy/ (**-frayed, -fray·ing, -frays**) *vt.* to provide money to pay for part or all of the cost of something (*formal*) ○ *The company will defray the cost of your training.* [Mid-16thC. From French *défrayer*, from *frais* "expenses."] —**de·fray·a·ble** *adj.* —**de·fray·al** *n.* —**de·fray·er** *n.* —**de·fray·ment** *n.*

de·frock /dee frók/ (**-frocked, -frock·ing, -frocks**) *vt.* to take away the status, job, and authority of a priest or other member of the clergy, especially as a punishment for wrongdoing [Early 17thC. From French *défroquer*, from *froc* (see FROCK).]

de·frost /di fróst/ *vti.* (**-frost·ed, -frost·ing, -frosts**) **1. REMOVE ICE FROM** to remove frost or ice from something, or become free of frost or ice **2. THAW** to thaw frozen food, or become thawed ■ *n.* = **defroster**

de·frost·er /dee fróstər/ *n.* **1.** CARS **DEVICE FOR REMOVING ICE** a device that removes frost and ice or condensation from the windshield, windows, and mirror of a motor vehicle **2.** HOUSEHOLD **DEVICE FOR THAWING** a device used to thaw frozen foods

deft /deft/ *adj.* **1. QUICK AND SKILLFUL** moving or acting in a quick, smooth, and skillful way **2. CLEVER** showing good sense and skill in achieving or acquiring things [13thC. An early variant of DAFT.] —**deft·ly** *adv.* —**deft·ness** *n.*

de·funct /di fúngkt/ *adj.* **1. NOT OPERATING NOW** no longer operative, valid, or functional **2. DEAD** no longer alive or in existence [Mid-16thC. From Latin *defunctus*, the past participle of *defungi* "to finish," literally "to perform completely," from *fungi* "to perform" (source of English *function* and *perfunctory*).] —**de·funct·ness** *n.*

WORD KEY: SYNONYMS

See Synonyms at *dead*.

de·fuse /di fyóoz/ (**-fused, -fus·ing, -fus·es**) *vt.* **1.** ARMS **MAKE BOMB HARMLESS** to make a bomb or mine harmless by removing its detonating device **2. EASE DIFFICULT SITUATION** to make a situation less tense, dangerous, or uncomfortable ○ *The diplomats tried to defuse the escalating crisis.*

de·fy /di fí/ (**-fied, -fy·ing, -fies**) *vt.* **1. CHALLENGE AUTHORITY OR POWER** to challenge openly somebody's or something's authority or power by refusing to obey a command or regulation ○ *He defied all orders from headquarters* **2. CHALLENGE SOMEBODY TO DO SOMETHING** to challenge or dare somebody to do something ○ *I defy you to find a better deal than this.* **3. NOT BE EXPLAINED BY SOMETHING** to fail to be explained or clarified by something such as logic or analysis ○ *a decision that defies all logic* [14thC. Via French *défier* from assumed Vulgar Latin *disfidare* "to renounce your faith," from Latin *fides* (see FAITH).]

deg. *abbr.* degree

dé·ga·gé /dày gaa zháy/ *adj.* (*formal*) **1. RELAXED** casual and relaxed **2. NOT INVOLVED** detached and without emotional involvement [Late 17thC. From French, literally "disengaged."]

de·gas /dee gáss/ (**de·gassed, de·gas·sing, de·gas·es**) *vt.* to remove gas from a liquid or solid or from a vacuum system

Edgar Degas: Self-portrait (1854–5)

De·gas /də gaá/, **Edgar** (1834–1917) French painter and sculptor. A genius of modern art in the late 19th century, he often depicted the human figure in movement, particularly ballet dancers. Full name **Hilaire Germain Edgar Degas**

Charles De Gaulle

De Gaulle /də gáwl/, **Charles, General** (1890–1970) French general and statesman. He became leader of the Free French in London after the fall of France in World War II, taking over as head of the provisional government in 1945. He served as French President from 1959 to 1969. Full name **Charles André Joseph Marie de Gaulle**

de·gauss /dee gówss/ (**de·gaussed, de·gauss·ing, de·gauss·es**) *vt.* to remove or counteract a magnetic field in something, e.g., electrical equipment or a ship's hull. The hull of a ship can be degaussed as a protection against magnetic mines. —**de·gauss·er** *n.*

de·gen·der·ize /dee jéndə ríz/ (**-ized, -iz·ing, -iz·es**), **de·gen·der** /dee jéndər/ (**-dered, -der·ing, -ders**) *vt.* to remove references to people's gender from language or a text in order to make it more neutral or less biased —**de·gen·der·i·za·tion** /dee jèndəri záysh'n/ *n.*

de·gen·er·a·cy /di jénnərəsee/ *n.* **1. WORSENED CONDITION** a condition that is worse than normal or worse than before **2.** = **degeneration** *n.* 1 **3.** (*plural* **-cies**) **BAD BEHAVIOR** immoral, depraved, or corrupt behavior **4.** QUANTUM PHYS **STATE OF EQUAL ENERGY** the condition of two or more quantum states that have the same energy

de·gen·er·ate *vi.* /di jénnə ràyt/ (**-at·ed, -at·ing, -ates**) **1. BECOME WORSE** to develop into a condition that is worse than before, worse than normal, or not as good as it should be **2.** BIOL **BECOME USELESS** to become less specialized or lose the ability to function (*refers to organisms or body parts*) ■ *adj.* /di jénnərət/ **1. IN A WORSENED CONDITION** in a condition that is worse than normal or worse than before **2. INFERIOR** in a condition that is worse than an original or previous state **3.** PHYS **EQUAL IN ENERGY** used to describe a system in which different quantum states have equal energy **4.** BIOL **WITH REDUCED OR ABSENT PART** used to describe a part, or an organism with a part, that has become reduced in size or function, or lost completely, during the history of its species or compared to related species ■ *n.* /di jénnərət/ **SOMEBODY IMMORAL OR CORRUPT** somebody who is in a bad condition, especially as a result of immoral behavior [15thC. From Latin *degenerare*, literally "to depart from your own kind," from *genus* "kind."] —**de·gen·er·ate·ly** *adv.* —**de·gen·er·ate·ness** *n.*

de·gen·er·ate mat·ter *n.* PHYS highly compressed matter consisting of elementary particles that are not combined to form atoms, occurring in the final stage of a star's development into a white dwarf

de·gen·er·a·tion /di jènnə ráysh'n/ *n.* **1. WORSENING OF CONDITION** the process of becoming physically, morally, or mentally worse **2.** MED **DETERIORATION** a disease process that causes a gradual deterioration in the structure of a body part with a consequent loss of the ability to function **3.** BIOL **BIOLOGICAL LOSS OVER GENERATIONS** the gradual loss of the biological function, specialization, or adaptation of a part of the body over many generations

de·gen·er·a·tive /di jénnərətiv/ *adj.* causing or showing a gradual deterioration in the structure of a body part with a consequent loss of the part's ability to function

de·gen·er·a·tive joint dis·ease *n.* = **osteoarthritis**

de·glam·or·ize /dee glámmə ríz/ (**-ized, -iz·ing, -iz·es**), **de·glam·our·ize** (**-ized, -iz·ing, -iz·es**) *vt.* to make something less attractive or exciting than it sometimes appears —**de·glam·or·i·za·tion** /dee glàmməri záysh'n/ *n.*

de·glu·ti·nate /dee gloót'n àyt/ (**-nat·ed, -nat·ing, -nates**) *vt.* to remove the gluten from cereal or flour [Late 19thC. Coined from DE- + Latin *glutin-*, the stem of *gluten* "GLUTEN."] —**de·glu·ti·na·tion** /dee gloót'n áysh'n/ *n.*

de·glu·ti·tion /dèe gloo tísh'n/ *n.* the act or process of swallowing (*technical*) [Mid-17thC. Via French from, ultimately, Latin *deglutire*, literally "to swallow down," from *glutire* (see GLUTTON).]

de·grad·a·ble /di gráydəb'l/ *adj.* **1. ABLE TO ROT AWAY** able to undergo chemical or biological decomposition **2. ABLE TO BE DEGRADED** able to be degraded in any way —**de·grad·a·bil·i·ty** /di gràydə bíllətee/ *n.*

deg·ra·da·tion /dèggrə dáysh'n/ *n.* **1. GREAT HUMILIATION** great humiliation brought about by loss of status, reputation, or self-esteem ○ *suffered the degradation of overwhelming defeat at the polls* **2. HUMILIATING SOMEBODY** the humiliating of somebody, causing him or her a loss of status, reputation, or self-esteem ○ *the constant degradation and undermining of other members of the staff* **3. BAD LIVING CONDITIONS** way of life without dignity, health, or social comforts **4. LOSS OF QUALITY** a decline in something's quality or performance ○ *a rapid degradation in the engine's horsepower* **5. PROCESS OF DECLINE** the process by which a decline in quality or performance is brought about **6.** GEOL, GEOG **EROSION** erosion of the Earth's land surface by water, wind, or ice **7.** CHEM **BREAKDOWN OF COMPOUND** the breakdown of a chemical compound into atoms or simpler compounds **8.** PHYS **DECREASE OF ENERGY** the process by which the energy available for doing work is irreversibly decreased

de·grade /di gráyd/ (**-grad·ed, -grad·ing, -grades**) *v.* **1.** *vt.* **TREAT HUMILIATINGLY** to cause somebody or something a humiliating loss of status or reputation, or cause somebody a humiliating loss of self-esteem **2.** *vt.* **LOWER IN GRADE** to lower somebody or something in rank, grade, or level **3.** *vti.* **BECOME OR MAKE WORSE** to become worse, or make something become worse, especially in quality or performance ○ *Using the wrong fuel had significantly degraded the engine's power.* **4.** *vti.* GEOL, GEOG **ERODE LAND** to erode the land surface or a river bed, or be eroded by the action of wind, ice, or water. ◊ **aggrade 5.** ENVIRON **DESTROY ENVIRONMENT** to cause damage or destruction to part of the environment as a result of human activity **6.** *vti.* PHYS **REDUCE AVAILABLE ENERGY IN** to reduce irreversibly the energy available in matter, or be reduced irreversibly [14thC. Via French *dégrader* from ecclesiastical Latin *degradare* "to reduce in rank," from Latin *gradus* (see GRADE).] —**de·grad·er** *n.*

de·grad·ed /di gráydəd/ *adj.* **1. HUMILIATED** humiliated and suffering a loss of status, reputation, or self-esteem **2. SQUALID** existing in poverty and squalor **3. WITH POORER PERFORMANCE** showing a decline in quality, standard, or performance **4. OF LOWER RANK** made lower in rank, grade, or level —**de·grad·ed·ly** *adv.* —**de·grad·ed·ness** *n.*

de·grad·ing /di gráyding/ *adj.* causing somebody to feel shame and humiliation —**de·grad·ing·ly** *adv.*

de·grease /dee greéss/ (**-greased, -greas·ing, -greas·es**) *vt.* to remove grease from something such as an engine, especially using chemicals —**de·greas·er** *n.*

de·gree /di greé/ *n.* **1. EXTENT OR AMOUNT** the relative extent, amount, intensity, or level of something, especially when compared with other things **2.** EDUC **EDUCATIONAL QUALIFICATION** a qualification awarded by a university or college following successful completion of a course of study or period of research, or a similar qualification granted as an honor **3.** PHYS, MEASURE **TEMPERATURE UNIT** a unit of measurement for temperature on a scale such as Celsius or Fahrenheit. Symbol ° **4.** GEOM, MEASURE **UNIT FOR MEASURING ANGLES** a unit of measurement for angles, equal to 1/360 of the angle formed by a line when it makes a complete revolution around a fixed point. Symbol ° **5.** GEOG, MEASURE **UNIT OF LATITUDE OR LONGITUDE** a unit of latitude or longitude, equal to 1/360 of a circle ○ *27 degrees north.* Symbol ° **6.** LAW **CLASSIFICATION OF MURDER** a level of classification of murder according to its seriousness. First-degree murder is the most serious. **7.** MED **SEVERITY OF BURNS ON BODY** a level of classification of the seriousness of the damage to tissue caused by a burn. Third-degree burns are the most serious. **8.** MEASURE **UNIT OF MEASUREMENT ON SCALE** a unit of measurement on various scales, e.g., the one used to measure specific gravity or alcohol content **9.** GRAM **STATE OF ADJECTIVE OR ADVERB** any one of the three states that an adjective or adverb can exist in when used to describe something. "Red" and "quickly" are in the positive degree, "redder" and "more quickly" in the comparative degree, and "reddest" and "most quickly" in the superlative degree. **10.** SOC SCI **CLOSENESS OF RELATIONSHIP** an indication of the closeness of a relationship within a family **11.** SOC SCI **STATUS** rank, position, or status in society (*formal or literary*) ○ *of high degree* **12.** MUSIC **POSITION OF NOTE ON MUSICAL SCALE** the relative position of a note on a musical scale **13.** MATH **HIGHEST EXPONENT OF DERIVATIVE** in a differential equation, the exponent of the derivative of highest order, e.g., $4x^2y^2$ is of degree four **14.** MATH **SUM OF POLYNOMIAL VARIABLE EXPONENTS** in a polynomial equation, the sum of the exponents of the variables in the term with the highest power, e.g., $4x^3y^2 + 3y^2 + 2$ is of degree five [13thC. Via French *degré* from assumed Vulgar Latin *degradus*, literally "step down," from Latin *gradus* (see GRADE).]

de·gree-day *n.* a unit of measurement for heating systems, used to estimate fuel requirements and representing one degree of variation from the mean daily temperature outside

de·gree of free·dom *n.* **1.** STATS **INDEPENDENT VARIABLE** an independent variable in a statistical measure or frequency distribution **2.** PHYS, CHEM **VARIABLE SPECIFYING ENERGY** an independent variable needed to specify the energy state of an atom, molecule, or system **3.** CHEM **VARIABLE SPECIFYING STATE** any of the independent variables such as pressure that are needed to specify the state of a system according to the phase rule

de·gres·sion /di grésh'n/ *n.* **1.** DECREASE a gradual decrease or downward movement (*formal*) **2.** FIN GRADUAL DECREASE IN TAXATION a gradual lowering of the tax rate on sums below a specified amount [15thC. Via medieval Latin from Latin *degress-*, the past participle stem of *degredi*, literally "to step down," from *gradus* (see GRADE).] —**de·gres·sive** *adj.*

de·gust /di gúst/ (**-gust·ed, -gust·ing, -gusts**), **de·gus·tate** /di gú stàyt/ (**-tat·ed, -tat·ing, -tates**) *vt.* to taste food with great enjoyment and appreciation (*formal*) [Early 17thC. Directly and via French *déguster* from Latin *degustare*, literally "to taste thoroughly," from *gustare* "to taste."] —**de·gus·ta·tion** /di gù stáysh'n/ *n.*

De Ha·vil·land /də hávvilənd/, **Sir Geoffrey** (1882–1965) British aviation pioneer and aircraft designer. Aircraft designed by him include the Tiger Moth (1930), Mosquito (1941), and Comet airliner (1952).

De Ha·vil·land, Olivia (*b.* 1916) British-born U.S. movie actor. She won Academy Awards for *To Each His Own* (1946) and *The Heiress* (1949). Full name **Olivia Mary De Havilland**

de·hire /dee hír/ (**-hired, -hir·ing, -hires**) *vt.* to dismiss somebody from employment (*used euphemistically*)

de·hisce /di híss/ (**-hisced, -hisc·ing, -hisc·es**) *vi.* **1.** BOT BURST OPEN to burst open, releasing seeds, pollen, or spores (*refers to dry fruits, seed pods, anthers, or spore-bearing structures*) **2.** MED BREAK OPEN to open along the joined edges (*technical*) (*refers to a wound that has been stitched*) [Mid-17thC. From Latin *dehiscere*, literally "to open up," from *hiscere*, literally "to begin opening," from *hiare* (see HIATUS).] —**de·his·cence** *n.* —**de·his·cent** *adj.*

de·horn /dee háwrn/ (**-horned, -horn·ing, -horns**) *vt.* VET to remove or prevent the growth of an animal's horns by surgery or cauterization —**de·horn·er** *n.*

de·hu·man·ize /dee hyoómə nìz, -yoómə-/ (**-ized, -iz·ing, -iz·es**) *vt.* **1.** MAKE LESS HUMAN to take away somebody's individuality, the creative and interesting aspects of his or her personality, or his or her compassion and sensitivity toward others **2.** TAKE AWAY PEOPLE-FRIENDLY FEATURES OF to take away the qualities or features of something that make it able to meet human needs and desires or enhance people's lives **3.** MAKE ROUTINE to take away all creativity and interest from some process and make it dull, routine, and mechanical —**de·hu·man·i·za·tion** /dee hyoómənì záysh'n, dee yoómənì-/ *n.* —**de·hu·man·ized** *adj.* —**de·hu·man·iz·ing** *adj.*

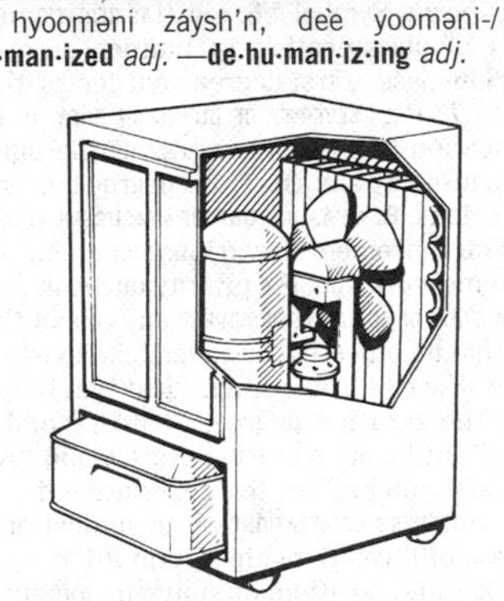

Dehumidifier: Cutaway view showing filters for removal of moisture from the air

de·hu·mid·i·fi·er /dee hyoo míddə fìr, -yoo-/ *n.* an electrical appliance for removing excess humidity from the air in a room or building

de·hu·mid·i·fy /dee hyoo míddə fì, -yoo-/ (**-fied, -fy·ing, -fies**) *vt.* to remove moisture from the air in a room or building

de·hy·drate /dee hí dràyt/ (**-drat·ed, -drat·ing, -drates**) *v.* **1.** *vt.* FOOD TECH PRESERVE FOOD BY DRYING to remove moisture from food as a way of preserving it **2.** *vti.* MED LOSE BODY FLUIDS to remove or lose water or fluids from the body or its tissues **3.** *vti.* CHEM TAKE AWAY WATER FROM to deprive a chemical compound of water or of the proportion of hydrogen and oxygen atoms that are present in water

de·hy·dra·tion /dee hì dráysh'n, dee hì-/ *n.* **1.** FOOD TECH REMOVAL OF MOISTURE FROM FOOD the removal of moisture from food as a way of preserving it **2.** MED LOSS OF BODY FLUID a dangerous lack of water in the body resulting from inadequate intake of fluids or excessive loss through sweating, vomiting, or diarrhea **3.** CHEM LOSS OF WATER BY CHEMICAL COMPOUND the process by which a chemical compound loses water molecules or the proportion of hydrogen and oxygen atoms that would be present in water

de·hy·dra·tor /dee hí dràytər/ *n.* HOUSEHOLD, FOOD TECH an electrical appliance for drying food, consisting of a stack of interlocking trays through which heated air is circulated

de·hy·dro·chlo·rin·ase /dee hìdrə kláwrə nàyss, -nàyz/ *n.* an enzyme that removes hydrogen and chlorine from chlorinated hydrocarbons. Its presence accounts for the resistance shown by some insects to DDT.

de·hy·dro·chlo·rin·ate /dee hìdrə kláwrə nàyt/ (**-at·ed, -at·ing, -ates**) *vt.* to chemically remove hydrogen and chlorine or hydrogen chloride from a substance —**de·hy·dro·chlo·ri·na·tion** /dee hìdrə klawrə náysh'n/ *n.*

de·hy·dro·gen·ase /dee hídrəjə nàyz, dee hì drójjə-, dee hídrəjə nàyss, dee hì drójjə-/ *n.* an enzyme that speeds up the removal and transfer of hydrogen atoms between organic compounds

de·hy·dro·gen·ate /dee hídrəjə nàyt, dee hì drójjə-/ (**-at·ed, -at·ing, -ates**) *vt.* to remove hydrogen from a compound, e.g., by means of a catalyst or in an enzyme-controlled process in cells —**de·hy·dro·gen·a·tion** /dee hì drojjə náysh'n/ *n.*

de·hy·dro·gen·ize /dee hídrəjə nìz, dee hì drójjə-/ (**-ized, -iz·ing, -iz·es**) *vt.* = **dehydrogenate** —**de·hy·dro·gen·i·za·tion** /dee hì drójjənì záysh'n/ *n.*

de·hyp·no·tize /dee hípnə tìz/ (**de·hyp·no·tized, de·hyp·no·tiz·ing, de·hyp·no·tiz·es**) *vt.* to bring somebody out of a hypnotic state —**de·hyp·no·sis** /dee hip nóssiss/ *n.* —**de·hyp·no·ti·za·tion** /di hìpnəti záysh'n/ *n.*

de·ice /dee íss/ (**de·iced, de·ic·ing, de·ic·es**) *vt.* to remove ice from something such as a windshield, or prevent ice from forming on it

de·ic·er /dee íssər/ *n.* a device or chemical substance that removes ice or prevents it forming, e.g., on the windshield of a motor vehicle or the wings of an aircraft. One of the commonest deicers is ethylene glycol, which is used in antifreeze.

de·i·cide /dee i sìd/ *n.* LITERAT **1.** KILLING A GOD OR GODDESS the act of killing a god or goddess **2.** SOMEBODY WHO KILLS A GOD OR GODDESS somebody who kills a god or goddess [Early 17thC. Partly from ecclesiastical Latin *deicida* "god-killer," and partly coined from Latin *deus* "god" + -CIDE.] —**de·i·ci·dal** /dee i sìd'l/ *adj.*

deic·tic /díktik/ *adj.* depending for its full meaning on the context in which it is used. Words such as "you," "this," "now," and "there" are deictic. [Early 19thC. From Greek *deiktikos*, from *deiknunai* "to show." Ultimately from an Indo-European word meaning "to point out" that is also the ancestor of English *dictate*, *index*, *digit*, and *token*.] —**deic·ti·cal·ly** *adv.*

de·if·ic /dee íffik/ *adj.* (*formal*) **1.** MAKING SOMEBODY A GOD OR GODDESS making somebody divine or giving him or her the status of a god or goddess **2.** LIKE A GOD OR GODDESS with a divine nature or the status of a god or goddess [15thC. From ecclesiastical Latin *deificus*, from Latin *deus* (see DEITY).]

de·i·fi·ca·tion /dee ifi káysh'n/ *n.* (*formal*) **1.** MAKING SOMEBODY A GOD OR GODDESS the action or process of making somebody a god or goddess **2.** STATE OF HAVING BEEN MADE A GOD OR GODDESS the condition of having been made a god or goddess

de·i·fy /dee i fì/ (**-fied, -fy·ing, -fies**) *vt.* **1.** MAKE DIVINE to make somebody into a god **2.** ADORE to honor or adore somebody or something as if he, she, or it were divine [14thC. Via French *déifier* from, ultimately, Latin *deus* (see DEITY).] —**de·i·fi·er** *n.*

Deigh·ton /dáyt'n/, **Len** (*b.* 1929) British writer. He is best known for spy thrillers, including *The Ipcress File* (1962). He has also written on cooking and military history. Full name **Leonard Cyril Deighton**

deign /dayn/ (**deigned, deign·ing, deigns**) *vti.* to do something in a way that shows that you consider it a great favor and almost beneath your dignity to do it ○ *I don't suppose he'll deign to accept our invitation.* [13thC. Via Old French *deignier* from Latin *dignare* "to deem worthy," from *dignus* "worthy."]

De·i gra·ti·a /dày i graatee ə/ *adv.* by the grace of God (*formal*) [From Latin, "by the grace of God"]

de·in·dus·tri·al·i·za·tion /dee in dùstree əli záysh'n/ *n.* the removal or reduction of industrial activity in a country or region, especially heavy industry or manufacturing industry

de·in·dus·tri·al·ize /dee in dústree ə lìz/ (**de·in·dus·tri·al·ized, de·in·dus·tri·al·iz·ing, de·in·dus·tri·al·iz·es**) *vti.* to take away or lose industries, especially the heavy industries and manufacturing industries, that a particular country or region has

de·in·sti·tu·tion·al·ize /dee instə toóshən'l ìz, -shnə lìz/ (**-ized, -iz·ing, -iz·es**) *vt.* to discharge somebody from institutional care, often in order to treat him or her in the community where he or she lives —**de·in·sti·tu·tion·al·i·za·tion** /dee instə toóshən'li záysh'n, -shnəli-/ *n.*

de·i·on·ize /dee í ə nìz/ (**de·i·on·ized, de·i·on·iz·ing, de·i·on·iz·es**) *v.* to remove ions from a solution —**de·i·on·i·za·tion** /dee ì əni záysh'n/ *n.* —**de·i·on·iz·er** /dee í ə nìzər/ *n.*

de·ism /dee ìzzəm/ *n.* a belief in God based on reason rather than revelation, and involving the view that God has set the universe in motion but does not interfere with how it runs. Deism was especially influential in the 17th and 18th centuries. [Late 17thC. Formed from Latin *deus* "god" (see DEITY).] —**de·ist** *n.* —**de·is·tic** /dee ístik/ *adj.* —**de·is·ti·cal·ly** /-əlee/ *adv.*

de·i·ty /dee itee/ (*plural* **-ties**) *n.* **1.** GOD OR GODDESS a god, goddess, or other divine being **2.** SOMEBODY OR SOMETHING LIKE GOD somebody or something that is treated like a god **3.** DIVINE STATE the condition or status of a god or goddess [14thC. Via French *déité* from ecclesiastical Latin *deitas* "divine nature," from Latin *deus* "god."]

De·i·ty /dee itee/ *n.* God in monotheistic belief [14thC]

deix·is /díksiss/ *n.* the use of a word such as "he," "that," "now," or "here," whose full meaning depends on the context in which it is used [Mid-20thC. From Greek, "reference," formed from *deiknunai* "to show" (see DEICTIC).]

dé·jà vu /dày zhaa voó/ *n.* **1.** PSYCHOL FEELING OF RELIVING SOMETHING a feeling of having experienced something before although in fact it is the first time that it has been experienced **2.** BOREDOM boredom resulting from something that has happened many times before [Early 20thC. From French, literally "already seen."]

WORD KEY: USAGE

Extension of meaning: ***déjà vu*** once referred exclusively to the illusion of having been somewhere before or done something before: *As she entered the house, so far from any place she had ever been, she had an eerie sense of déjà vu.* Recently, however, it has come to encompass as well the reality of repetitiveness in events or actions: *The opening of yet another Italian restaurant in that spot gave her a distinct sense of déjà vu.* This sense of the word has been extended still further, until the turnaround from the original meaning is almost complete and **déjà vu** is sometimes also used to describe tedium: *Gray winter days bring on déjà vu.*

de·ject /di jékt/ (**-ject·ed, -ject·ing, -jects**) *vt.* to make somebody or something miserable or disheartened (*archaic*) ○ *"Nor once deject the courage of our minds"* (William Shakespeare, *Troilus and Cressida*; 1601) [15thC. From Latin *deject-*, the past participle stem of *dejicere*, literally "to throw down," from *jacere* "to throw."]

de·ject·ed /di jéktəd/ *adj.* feeling or showing sadness and lack of hope, especially because of disappointment —**de·ject·ed·ly** *adv.* —**de·ject·ed·ness** *n.*

de·jec·tion /di jékshən/ *n.* **1.** GREAT UNHAPPINESS unhappiness and lack of hope, especially caused by disappointment **2.** MED DEFECATION the act of passing solid waste matter out of the anus (*technical*) **3.** MED EXCREMENT solid waste matter that is passed out through the anus (*technical*)

de ju·re /dee joóree, day yoó rày/ *adv., adj.* by right according to the law [Mid-16thC. From Latin, literally "from the law."]

deka- *prefix.* = **deca-**

dek·a·gram *n.* = **decagram**

De Kalb /di kálb/ city in northern Illinois, west of Chicago and southeast of Rockford. Population: 35,554 (1996).

dek·a·li·ter *n.* = **decaliter**

dek·a·me·ter *n.* = **decameter**

deke /deek/ *vt.* (**deked, dek·ing, dekes**) DECEIVE SOMEBODY IN ICE HOCKEY to deceive an opponent in ice hockey by making a fake move (*informal*) ○ *He deked two defencemen as he crossed the blue line.* ■ *n.* DECEPTIVE MOTION IN ICE HOCKEY in ice hockey, a deceptive move that lures a player out of position (*informal*) [Mid-20thC. Shortening of DECOY.]

de Klerk /də klúrk/, **F. W.** (*b.* 1936) South African politician. He introduced reforms during his presidency (1989–94) that led to the end of apartheid. He shared the Nobel Peace Prize with Nelson Mandela in 1993. Full name **Frederick Willem de Klerk**

de Koo·ning /də kṓning/, **Elaine** (1920–89) U.S. artist. She is known for her portraits of John F. Kennedy. Full name **Elaine Marie Catherine Fried de Kooning**

de Koo·ning, Willem (1904–97) Dutch-born U.S. artist. He is known for his abstract expressionist paintings, including the series of six paintings entitled *Woman* (1953).

del. *abbr.* **1.** delegate **2.** delegation **3.** delete

Del. *abbr.* Delaware

De·la·croix /də laa krwaá, dèllə-/, **Eugène** (1798–1863) French painter and lithographer. His romantic works, such as *Liberty Guiding the People* (1830), are characterized by Byronic melodrama and vivid color. Full name **Ferdinand Victor Eugène Delacroix**

Del·a·go·a Bay /dèllə gṓ ə-/ bay on the southern Mozambique coast. Mozambique's capital, Maputo, is situated near the head of the bay.

de·laine /də láyn/ *n.* a fine fabric resembling muslin but made of wool or wool and cotton [Mid-19thC. Shortening of MOUSSELINE DE LAINE.]

de·lam·i·nate /dee lámmə nàyt/ (**de·lam·i·nat·ed, de·lam·i·nat·ing, de·lam·i·nates**) *vti.* to separate or peel off in thin layers, or cause something to do this

de·lam·i·na·tion /dee làmmə náysh'n/ *n.* the process of separating something into, or peeling off in, thin layers, or the state of being separated into thin layers

de la Roche /də laa rṓsh, dèllə-/, **Mazo** (1885–1961) Canadian writer. She is known for her series of novels about the Whiteoak family, the first being *Jalna* (1927).

Del·a·ware[1] /déllə wàir/ (*plural* **-ware** *or* **-wares**) *n.* **1.** PEOPLES **MEMBER OF NATIVE AMERICAN PEOPLE** a member of a group of Native North American peoples who used to live between the Delaware and Hudson rivers, and who now live mostly in Oklahoma, Ontario, Wisconsin, and Kansas **2.** AGRIC **RED GRAPE** a sweet, light red variety of grape [Early 18thC. Named for the *Delaware* River in the eastern United States.]

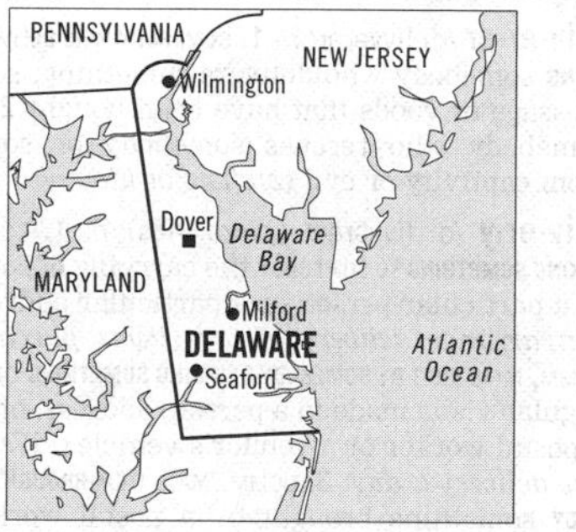

Delaware

Del·a·ware[2] /déllə wàir/ **1.** the first U.S. state, bordered by the Atlantic Ocean, Maryland, Pennsylvania, and New Jersey. Capital: Dover. Population: 731,581 (1997). Area: 2,396 sq. mi./6,206 sq. km. **2.** major river of the eastern United States, with its source in southern New York. Length: 280 mi./451 km. —**Del·a·war·e·an** /dèllə wáiree ən/ *n., adj.*

Del·a·ware Wa·ter Gap scenic gorge on the Delaware River, cutting through the Kittatinny Mountains. Length: 2 mi./3 km.

De La Warr /déllə waár/, **Thomas West,** 3rd Baron (1577–1618) English-born governor of the colony of Virginia. In 1610 he arrived at Jamestown in time to save the settlement from being disbanded. The state of Delaware is named for him. Known as **Lord Delaware**.

de·lay /di láy/ *v.* (**-layed, -lay·ing, -lays**) **1.** *vti.* **PUT SOMETHING OFF TILL LATER** to postpone something or wait until later before doing something **2.** *vt.* **MAKE LATE** to make somebody or something late by slowing or stopping him, her, or it ○ *I was delayed at the office.* ■ *n.* **1. LATENESS** a situation in which something does not happen or start at the time it was meant to ○ *All services are subject to delay or cancelation.* **2. EXTENT OF LATENESS** the extent of the period of time by which somebody or something is made late or slowed down ○ *long delays on the beltway* **3. PROCRASTINATION** procrastination, or failure to do something quickly enough ○ *This must be done without delay.* [13thC. From Anglo-Norman *delaier* "to leave off," from *laier* "to leave," of uncertain origin: probably from prehistoric Germanic.] —**de·lay·er** *n.*

de·lay ac·tion *n.* = **delayed action** *n.* 1

de·layed /di láyd/ *adj.* **1. MADE LATE** made to happen, start, arrive, or leave later than intended or later than usual **2. LATER THAN USUAL** happening at some time after the usual or expected time ○ *delayed language development* **3. HAPPENING LATER** happening after a period of time ○ *causing delayed damage to the kidneys*

de·layed ac·tion *n.* **1. EFFECT DEFERRED FOR A PERIOD** the activation of a mechanism a short time after it has been set (*hyphenated when used before a noun*) **2. DELAY MECHANISM** a mechanism used to produce delayed action

de·layed neu·tron *n.* a neutron emitted after a measurable time delay in the process of nuclear fission

de·lay·er·ing /dee láy əring/ *n.* the process of simplifying the structure of an organization to make it more efficient —**de·lay·er** *vti.*

de·lay·ing ac·tion, de·lay·ing op·er·a·tion *n.* a maneuver used to gain time or allow a retreat when there are not enough resources to confront an opponent directly

de·lay·ing tac·tic *n.* a deliberate attempt to delay something in order to gain time or some other advantage

de·lay line *n.* a device designed to cause a delay in transmitting an electronic signal

Del·brück /déll brŏŏk/, **Max** (1906–81) German-born U.S. biologist. In 1969 he shared the Nobel Prize in physiology or medicine for his work on the replication of viruses and their genetic structure.

Del City /dél-/ city in central Oklahoma. It is an eastern suburb of Oklahoma City. Population: 23,990 (1996).

de·le /deélee/ *n.* **MARK TO SHOW DELETION** a mark used in the margin of printed material to show that something is to be deleted (*informal*) ■ *vt.* (**-led, -le·ing, -les**) **MARK MATERIAL FOR DELETION** to mark a passage of printed material for deletion (*informal*) [Early 18thC. From Latin, "delete!", from *delere* (see DELETE).]

de·lec·ta·ble /di léktəb'l/ *adj.* **1. DELICIOUS** with a delicious taste **2. DELIGHTFUL** absolutely delightful, very pleasing, or very attractive ■ *n.* **SOMETHING VERY TASTY** an appetizing food or dish [14thC. Via French *délectable* from, ultimately, Latin *delectare* "to please" (see DELIGHT).] —**de·lec·ta·bil·i·ty** /di lèktə bíllətee/ *n.* —**de·lec·ta·ble·ness** /di léktəbəlnəss/ *n.* —**de·lec·ta·bly** /-di léktəblee/ *adv.*

de·lec·ta·tion /dee lek táysh'n/ *n.* pleasure or enjoyment (*formal*) [14thC. Via Old French from, ultimately, Latin *delectare* (see DELIGHT).]

del·e·gate *n.* /délləgət, déllə gàyt/ **1. REPRESENTATIVE OR DEPUTY** somebody chosen to represent or given the authority to act on behalf of another person, group, or organization, e.g., at a meeting or conference **2.** POL **MEMBER OF HOUSE OF DELEGATES** a member of a House of Delegates, the lower house of the legislature in Maryland, Virginia, or West Virginia **3.** POL **REPRESENTATIVE OF U.S. TERRITORY** a representative of a territory in the U.S. House of Representatives, who may speak on issues but not vote ■ *v.* /déllə gàyt/ (**-gat·ed, -gat·ing, -gates**) **1.** *vti.* **GIVE TASK TO** to give a task to somebody else with responsibility to act on your behalf **2.** *vti.* **GIVE POWER OR AUTHORITY TO** to give somebody the power to act, make decisions, or allocate resources on your behalf ○ *an executive who was unafraid to delegate* **3.** *vt.* LAW, FIN **SEND DEBTOR TO CREDITOR** to appoint one of your debtors to represent you to your creditor [15thC. From Latin *delegare*, literally "to send away," from *legare* "to send."] —**del·e·ga·ble** *adj.* —**del·e·ga·tor** *n.*

del·e·ga·tion /dèllə gáysh'n/ *n.* **1. GROUP REPRESENTING OTHERS** a group of people chosen to represent or act on behalf of others **2. GIVING OF RESPONSIBILITY TO SOMEBODY ELSE** the giving of some power, responsibility, or work to somebody else **3. BEING GIVEN TO SOMEBODY ELSE** the condition of being given to somebody else as a duty or responsibility **4.** POL **STATE REPRESENTATIVES** all the members of the U.S. Congress who represent one state

de·le·git·i·mize /deèlə jíttə mīz/ (**-mized, -miz·ing, -miz·es**) *vt.* to take away the legitimacy or legal status of somebody or something —**de·le·git·i·mi·za·tion** /deèlə jittəmi záysh'n/ *n.*

de·lete /di leét/ *vt.* (**-let·ed, -let·ing, -letes**) **REMOVE OR ERASE** to remove or score out something that is printed or written, or erase something from a computer file or disk ■ *n.* **KEY FOR REMOVAL OF DATA** a key on a computer keyboard that is depressed in order to erase or destroy files of previously keyed material ○ *Click on the icon for that file and then hit delete.* [15thC. From Latin *delere* "to blot out, efface," of unknown origin.]

del·e·te·ri·ous /dèllə teéree əss/ *adj.* with a harmful or damaging effect on somebody or something (*formal*) [Mid-17thC. Via medieval Latin from Greek *dēlētērios* "noxious."] —**del·e·te·ri·ous·ly** *adv.* —**del·e·te·ri·ous·ness** *n.*

de·le·tion /di leésh'n/ *n.* **1. REMOVING SOMETHING OR SCORING SOMETHING OUT** the action or process of removing or erasing something or scoring something out **2. SOMETHING REMOVED OR SCORED OUT** something removed or scored out from a text, or erased from a computer file **3.** GENETICS **ABSENCE OF GENETIC MATERIAL** the loss or absence of part of a chromosome, ranging from a pair of chemicals (**base pair**) to a whole arm. Some medical conditions are the result of deletion.

de·lev·er·age (**de·lev·er·aged, de·lev·er·ag·ing, de·lev·er·ag·es**) /dee lévvərij/ *vti.* to reduce the amount of debt that a company owes, usually by laying off workers, selling off unprofitable divisions, and other cost-cutting measures

delft /delft/, **Delft, delft·ware, Delft·ware** *n.* earthenware with an opaque white glaze, usually with blue decoration [Late 17thC. Named for the town of DELFT where such pottery was originally made.]

Delft /delft/ city in the province of Zuid-Holland, in the western Netherlands, known as a center of production of glazed earthenware. Population: 92,241 (1994).

delft·ware /délft wàir/, **Delft·ware** *n.* = **delft**

Del·ga·do /del gaádō/, **Cape** cape in northeastern Mozambique, just south of the border with Tanzania

Del·hi /déllee/ city in northern India and capital of the Union Territory of Delhi. It is a major transportation, commercial, and industrial center. Population: 8,375,188 (1991). ◊ **New Delhi**

del·i /déllee/ (*plural* **-is**) *n.* (*informal*) **1. FOOD SHOP** a delicatessen **2. FOOD FROM DELI** prepared food purchased from a delicatessen [Mid-20thC. Shortening.]

Del·i·an /deélyən/ **1.** *n.* somebody who lives on or was born or raised on the Greek island of Delos **2.** *adj.* relating to the Greek island of Delos, its people, or its culture

De·li·an League, De·li·an Con·fed·er·a·cy *n.* an alliance of Greek states set up in 478 B.C. to oppose Persia

de·lib·er·ate *adj.* /di líbbərət/ **1. INTENTIONAL** carefully thought out and done intentionally **2. CAREFUL** slow, careful, and methodical ■ *vti.* /di líbbə ràyt/ (**-at·ed, -at·ing, -ates**) **THINK** to consider something carefully and in detail [15thC. From Latin *deliberare*, literally "to weigh carefully," from *librare* "to weigh," from *libra* "balance" (source of English *level* and *equilibrium*).] —**de·lib·er·ate·ness** *n.* —**de·lib·er·a·tor** *n.*

de·lib·er·ate·ly /di líbbərətlee/ *adv.* **1. INTENTIONALLY** in a way that is intentional and thought out in advance ○ *The police believe that the fire was started deliberately.* **2. CAREFULLY** with care and thought ○ *He spoke slowly and deliberately.*

de·lib·er·a·tion /di lìbbə ráysh'n/ *n.* (*formal*) **1. CAREFUL THOUGHT** long careful consideration of something **2. DISCUSSION** formal or official discussion or debate ○ *The planning committee's deliberations seemed to last all night.* **3. CARE** slowness and methodical carefulness

de·lib·er·a·tive /di líbbə ràytiv, -rətiv/ *adj.* (*formal*) **1.** POL **INVOLVED IN DISCUSSION** involved in or organized for careful discussion and debate **2. RESULTING FROM DISCUSSION** relating to or resulting from discussion and debate —**de·lib·er·a·tive·ly** *adv.* —**de·lib·er·a·tive·ness** *n.*

De·libes /di leéb/, **Léo** (1836–91) French composer. His grand operas include *Lakmé* (1883), and his masterpiece ballet is *Coppélia* (1870). Full name **Clément Philibert Léo Delibes**

del·i·ca·cy /déllikəssee/ (*plural* **-cies**) *n.* **1.** FOOD **SOMETHING NICE TO EAT** a delicious, rare, or highly prized item of food **2. SENSITIVITY** sensitivity to the feelings of others **3. NEED FOR TACT** the quality of requiring great tact or sensitivity ○ *a matter of extreme delicacy* **4. GREAT SENSITIVITY IN FEELINGS** extreme and perhaps unnecessary fussiness or squeamishness in the way somebody responds to something offensive or embarrassing ○ *his delicacy on matters of a medical nature* **5. SUBTLETY AND REFINEMENT** pleasing subtlety in something, e.g., taste, smell, or color ○ *the delicacy of her perfume* **6. FINENESS** fineness and subtlety of feeling, observation, or execution ○ *the delicacy of the brushwork in his later paintings* **7. FRAGILITY** the quality of being easily damaged or broken **8. LACK OF PHYSICAL STRENGTH** lack physical strength or health **9. SENSITIVITY OF RESPONSE IN EQUIPMENT** sensitivity in the way something e.g., scientific equipment or a musical instrument, responds to use

del·i·cate /déllikət/ *adj.* **1. FRAGILE** easily damaged or broken **2. FRAIL** without much resistance to illness or injury ○ *in delicate health* **3. SUBTLE** mild, gentle, pale, or soft, and pleasant to the senses ○ *a delicate shade of blue.* **4. FINE** finely made and with small parts or detail in its design **5. SKILLFUL** showing somebody's skill or craft, especially in producing finely detailed intricate work or gentle or adroit movements ○ *a filigree of delicate, shimmering brush-strokes* **6. NEEDING TACT** needing to be dealt with using tact and sensitivity ○ *The negotiations were at a delicate stage.* **7. REFINED** having or showing a refined and sensitive taste **8. EASILY OFFENDED** easily shocked or upset by offensive or embarrassing things **9.** TECH **ACCURATE** used to describe instrumentation that is very precise and able to give exact readings ■ **del·i·cates** *npl.* CLOTHES **CLOTHES NEEDING SPECIAL WASHING AND DRYING** clothes that need careful washing and drying, e.g., using a special washing machine program cycle [14thC. Directly or via French *délicat* from Latin *delicatus*, related to *delicere* (see DELIGHT).] — **del·i·cate·ness** *n.*

WORD KEY: SYNONYMS

See Synonyms at ***fragile***.

del·i·cate·ly /déllikətlee/ *adv.* **1. FINELY** in a way that shows skill in producing fine detail **2. SUBTLY** in a pleasingly mild and subtle way ○ *delicately flavored* **3. GENTLY AND CAREFULLY** gently and carefully, with no rough or sudden movements **4. WITH TACT** tactfully and sensitively ○ *a matter that must be handled very delicately* **5. UNSTABLY** in a way that seems precarious or sensitive to even a slight change or disturbance ○ *delicately balanced on its edge*

del·i·ca·tes·sen /dèllikə téss'n/ *n.* **1.** FOOD, COMM **SPECIALIZED FOOD STORE** a store specializing in imported or unusual foods and ingredients, e.g., cooked meats, cheeses, and pickles **2. PREPARED FOOD SOLD IN DELICATESSEN** prepared food sold in a delicatessen, e.g., cooked meats, cheeses, pickles, and salads [Late 19thC. Via German and French from Italian *delicatezza* "delicacy," from Latin *delicatus* "pleasing, choice."]

de·li·cious /di líshəss/ *adj.* **1. GOOD TO EAT** with an appealing or enjoyable taste or smell **2. DELIGHTFUL** highly amusing, pleasing, or enjoyable [13thC. Via Old French from, ultimately, Latin *delicia* "pleasure," from *delicere* "to allure" (see DELIGHT).] —**de·li·cious·ness** *n.*

de·li·cious·ly /di líshəsslee/ *adv.* **1. TASTILY** in a way that appeals to the sense of taste or smell ○ *a deliciously sweet and crunchy apple* **2. APPETIZINGLY** in an appetizing way ○ *steaks sizzling away deliciously on the grill* **3. VERY SATISFYINGLY** to a great and very satisfying degree ○ *a deliciously ironic twist of fate* **4. ENJOYABLY** in an enjoyable and pleasant way

de·lict /di líkt/ *n.* LAW in civil and criminal law, a wrong or injury done to somebody [Early 16thC. From Latin *delictum*, the neuter past participle of *delinquere* "to offend" (see DELINQUENT).]

de·light /di lít/ *n.* **1. JOY** great joy and pleasure ○ *To my delight, he accepted.* **2. SOMEBODY OR SOMETHING GIVING JOY** somebody or something that brings somebody great joy and pleasure ○ *That's one of the delights of having children.* ■ *v.* (**-light·ed, -light·ing, -lights**) **1.** *vti.* **GIVE SOMEBODY JOY** to give somebody great joy and pleasure **2.** *vi.* **GAIN ENJOYMENT FROM SOMETHING** to gain great enjoyment or pleasure from something ○ *She delighted in outwitting her competitors.* [13thC. Via Old French *delit* from, ultimately, Latin *delectare*, literally "to keep enticing" (source of English *delectable*), from *delicere* "to allure," from *lacere* "to entice."] —**de·light·er** *n.*

de·light·ed /di lítəd/ *adj.* extremely pleased or filled with delight ○ *I was delighted to hear about your good news!* —**de·light·ed·ly** *adv.* —**de·light·ed·ness** *n.*

de·light·ful /di lítfəl/ *adj.* giving great pleasure and joy, especially by being pleasant, good to look at, or amusing —**de·light·ful·ly** *adv.* —**de·light·ful·ness** *n.*

de·light·some /di lítsəm/ *adj.* very pleasing and enjoyable (*literary*) —**de·light·some·ly** *adv.*

De·Lil·lo /də léelō/, **Don** (*b.* 1936) U.S. novelist. One of the foremost postmodernist writers in the United States, he is author of *White Noise* (1985), which won the National Book Award for Fiction, and *Underworld* (1997).

de·lim·it /di límmit/ (**-it·ed, -it·ing, -its**), **de·lim·i·tate** /di límmə tàyt/ (**-tat·ed, -tat·ing, -tates**) *vt.* to set out or establish the limits or boundaries of something (*formal*) [Mid-19thC. Via French *délimiter* from Latin *delimitare*, from *limit-*, the stem of *limes* (see LIMIT).] — **de·lim·i·ta·tion** /di lìmmə táysh'n/ *n.* —**de·lim·i·ta·tive** /di límmə tàytiv/ *adj.*

de·lim·it·er /di límmitər/ *n.* COMPUT a character or blank space that marks the beginning or end of a data element

de·lin·e·ate /di línnee àyt/ (**-at·ed, -at·ing, -ates**) *vt.* **1. DESCRIBE** to describe or explain something in detail (*formal*) **2.** DRAWING **DRAW** to sketch or draw something in outline **3. PORTRAY VISUALLY** to represent something visually using something such as a chart or graph [Mid-16thC. From Latin *delineare*, literally "to sketch out," from *linea* (see LINE).] —**de·lin·e·a·ble** *adj.* — **de·lin·e·a·tion** /di lìnnee áysh'n/ *n.* —**de·lin·e·a·tive** /di línnee àytiv/ *adj.*

de·lin·e·a·tor /di línnee àytər/ *n.* **1.** TEXTILES **TAILOR'S ADJUSTABLE PATTERN** an adjustable pattern that a tailor uses to cut garments of different sizes **2. SOMEBODY OR SOMETHING THAT DELINEATES** somebody or something that outlines or describes something

de·lin·quen·cy /di língkwənsee/ *n.* **1.** LAW, CRIMINOL **UNLAWFUL BEHAVIOR** antisocial or illegal behavior or acts, especially by young people **2. NEGLECT OF OBLIGATION** failure to fulfill an obligation, commitment, or pledge (*formal*) **3.** FIN **SOMETHING OVERDUE** something that is overdue, e.g., a debt or tax (*formal*)

de·lin·quent /di língkwənt/ *n.* LAW, CRIMINOL **LAWBREAKER, ESPECIALLY YOUNG OFFENDER** somebody, especially a young person, who has acted antisocially or broken the law ■ *adj.* **1.** LAW, CRIMINOL **ANTISOCIAL OR UNLAWFUL** relating to antisocial behavior or lawbreaking **2. IGNORING DUTY** neglecting a duty, commitment, or responsibility (*formal*) **3.** FIN **UNPAID** with unpaid sums of money due [15thC. From Latin *delinquere* "to offend," from *linquere* "to leave." Ultimately from an Indo-European base that is also the ancestor of English *lend* and *eclipse*.] — **de·lin·quent·ly** *adv.*

WORD KEY: SYNONYMS

See Synonyms at ***bad***.

del·i·quesce /dèlli kwéss/ (**-quesced, -quesc·ing, -quesc·es**) *vi.* **1.** CHEM **ABSORB MOISTURE** to dissolve gradually by absorbing moisture from the air **2.** BOT **FORM BRANCHES** to form many branches without a main stem **3.** FUNGI **BECOME LIQUID** to become soft or liquid after the release of spores [Mid-18thC. From Latin *deliquescere*, literally "to start melting away," from *liquere* "to be liquid."] —**del·i·ques·cence** *n.* —**del·i·ques·cent** *adj.*

de·lir·i·ous /di léeree əss/ *adj.* **1.** MED **IRRATIONAL THROUGH ILLNESS** irrational as a temporary result of a physical condition, e.g., fever, poisoning, or brain injury. ◊ **delirium 2. EXCITED** extremely excited or emotional ○ *delirious with joy* [Late 16thC. Formed from DELIRIUM.] —**de·lir·i·ous·ly** *adv.* —**de·lir·i·ous·ness** *n.*

de·lir·i·um /di léeree əm/ *n.* **1.** MED **TEMPORARY MENTAL DISTURBANCE** a state marked by extreme restlessness, confusion, and sometimes hallucinations, caused by fever, poisoning, or brain injury **2. GREAT EXCITEMENT** a condition of extreme excitement or emotion [Mid-16thC. From Latin, formed from *delirare* "to be deranged," literally "to be out of your track," from *lira* "ridge between furrows."]

de·lir·i·um tre·mens /di léeree əm trémmənz/ *n.* agitation, tremors, and hallucinations caused by alcohol dependence and withdrawal [From Latin, literally "trembling delirium"]

de·lish /di lísh/ *adj.* very delicious (*slang*) [Early 20thC. Shortening.]

de·list /dee líst/ (**-list·ed, -list·ing, -lists**) *vt.* **1. TAKE OFF LIST** to remove somebody or something from a list **2.** STOCK EXCH **REMOVE SECURITY FROM LISTING** to remove a security from a listing on a stock exchange

de·liv·er /di lívvər/ (**-ered, -er·ing, -ers**) *v.* **1.** *vti.* COMM, MAIL **CARRY SOMETHING TO SOMEBODY** to take something, e.g., mail, goods that have been bought, or a message, to a particular person or address **2.** *vt.* OBSTET, VET **ASSIST DURING BIRTH** to give medical help when a baby or other offspring is being born **3.** *vt.* GYN **PRODUCE BABY** to give birth to a baby (*often passive*) **4.** *vt.* **MAKE SPEECH** to make a speech or give a talk to an audience **5.** *vt.* **ANNOUNCE** to announce something formally, e.g., an opinion, decision, or judgment ○ *The jury delivered its verdict.* **6.** *vt.* SPORTS **THROW BALL OR PUNCH** to toss or throw a ball or aim a punch at somebody or something **7.** *vti.* **DO AS PROMISED** to do what has been promised ○ *He has yet to deliver anything that was promised in his speeches.* **8.** *vt.* POL **ACHIEVE SUPPORT FOR SOMEBODY** to organize and produce the support of a place or people for somebody (*informal*) **9.** *vt.* **PRODUCE** to provide or produce something ○ *Note the total dosage of antibiotics delivered.* **10.** *vt.* **RELEASE** to free or save somebody from captivity or hardship (*literary*) **11.** *vt.* **GIVE SOMEBODY SOMETHING** to hand somebody or something over to somebody else ○ *You have 48 hours to deliver the payment.* [13thC. Via French *délivrer* from Latin *deliberare*, literally "to free completely," from *liberare* (see LIBERATE).] —**de·liv·er·a·bil·i·ty** /də lìvvərə bíllətee/ *n.* —**de·liv·er·a·ble** *adj.*

de·liv·er·ance /di lívvərəns/ *n.* **1. RESCUE FROM SOMETHING** rescue from captivity, hardship, or domination by evil (*formal*) ○ *He sought deliverance from his imprisonment.* **2. ANNOUNCEMENT** a formal announcement of a decision, judgment, or opinion

WORD KEY: CULTURAL NOTE

Deliverance, a movie by British director John Boorman (1972) Based on the novel by James Dickey (1972), it is the story of a canoe trip through the Appalachian Mountains undertaken by four city businessmen. The journey turns into a struggle for survival when the men are exposed to unexpected dangers and harried by sinister mountain people. In the famous "Dueling Banjos" sequence, one of the men and a boy attempt to outplay each other on their banjos.

de·liv·er·er /di lívvərər/ *n.* **1. SOMEBODY WHO DELIVERS SOMETHING** somebody who delivers something, such as a message or goods that have been bought **2. RESCUER** somebody who rescues somebody or something from captivity or evil (*archaic or literary*)

de·liv·er·y /di lívvəree/ (*plural* **-ies**) *n.* **1.** COMM, MAIL **TAKING SOMETHING TO SOMEBODY** the carrying of something to a particular person or a particular address ○ *We can arrange delivery of any items purchased.* **2.** COMM, MAIL **VISIT BY SOMEBODY BRINGING SOMETHING** one of the regular visits made to a person, address, or area by a postal worker or a vendor's vehicle ○ *We only get one delivery a day.* **3.** COMM, MAIL **ITEM BROUGHT TO SOMEBODY** something brought by a postal worker or a vendor, e.g., mail or goods that have been bought **4.** OBST **GIVING BIRTH** the process of giving birth to a baby **5. MANNER OF SPEAKING** the action or manner in which somebody speaks to an audience ○ *She needs to work on her vocal delivery.* **6. RESCUE** the rescue or saving of somebody from captivity, hardship, or evil ○ *He prayed for delivery from his oppressors.* **7.** SPORTS **WAY OF PUTTING BALL IN MOTION** the action or manner of throwing, tossing, or rolling a ball or aiming a punch **8.** LAW **ACTION NEEDED TO EFFECT PROPERTY TRANSFER** a formal action needed to accomplish a transfer of property

de·liv·er·y room *n.* a specially equipped room in a hospital where women give birth

dell /del/ *n.* a small usually wooded valley or hollow (*literary*) [Old English. Ultimately from the same prehistoric Germanic word that was the ancestor of DALE.]

Del·la Rob·bi·a /dèllə róbee ə/, **Luca** (1400?–82) Italian sculptor and ceramist. He is best known for his early Renaissance panels in Florence Cathedral. He invented a technique for making glazed terracotta figures.

Del·mar·va Pen·in·su·la /del maarvə-/ peninsula in the states of Delaware, Maryland, and Virginia. Length: 180 mi./290 km.

Del·mon·i·co steak /del mònni kō/ *n.* a small steak cut from the front end of the short loin of beef [Early 20thC. Named for the *Delmonico* Restaurant in New York City, which in turn was named for the Swiss-born U.S. restaurateur Lorenzo Delmonico 1813–81.]

de·lo·cal·ize /di lṓkə līz/ (**-ized, -iz·ing, -iz·es**) *vt.* **1.** MOVE FROM LOCAL AREA to remove something from its locality **2.** TAKE SOMETHING BEYOND LOCAL SPHERE to remove something from influences that surround it, and broaden its range or scope —**de·lo·cal·i·za·tion** /dee lōkəli záysh'n/ *n.*

De·los island of Greece, the smallest island of the Cyclades group in the southern Aegean Sea, now almost uninhabited. Area: approximately 1 sq mi./3 sq km.

de·louse /dee lówss/ (**-loused, -lous·ing, -lous·es**) *vt.* to give a person or animal treatment to remove lice

Del·phi /dél fī/ ancient Greek town on the southern slopes of Mount Parnassus, about 6 mi./9.5 km north of the Gulf of Corinth. It is the site of the Temple of Apollo and the Delphic oracle.

Del·phic /délfik/, **Del·phi·an** /délfee ən/ *adj.* **1.** RELATING TO DELPHI relating to Delphi, or its temple or oracle **2. Del·phic, del·phic** AMBIGUOUS obscure and open to more than one interpretation —**Del·phi·cal·ly** *adv.*

Del·phic or·a·cle *n.* the oracle of great authority and notorious ambiguity at Delphi, where it was believed the god Apollo spoke through a priestess

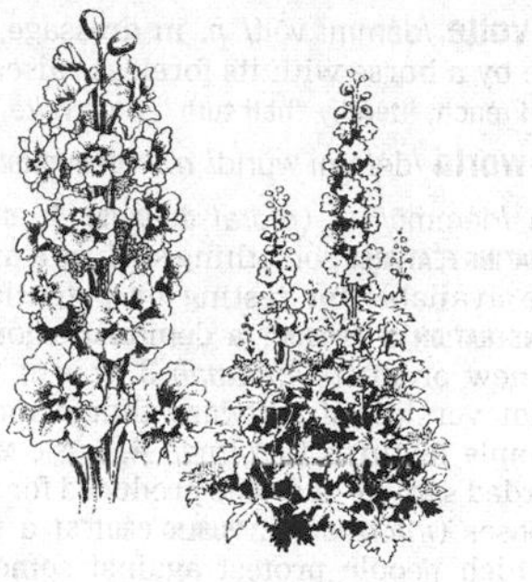

Delphinium

del·phin·i·um /del fínnee əm/ *n.* a plant cultivated for its variously colored flower spikes, especially those species with tall blue or white flower spikes. Genus: *Delphinium.* [Early 17thC. Via modern Latin from Greek *delphinion* "larkspur," literally "little dolphin," from *delphis* "dolphin" (because of the shape of the flower).]

Del·ray Beach /dèl ray-/ city on the Atlantic coast in southeastern Florida. Population: 47,181 (1990).

delt /delt/ *n.* a deltoid (*informal*) [Shortening of DELTOID]

del·ta /déltə/ *n.* **1.** GEOG TRIANGULAR LAND AREA AT RIVER MOUTH a triangular deposit of sand and soil at the mouth of a river or inlet **2. delta, Delta** GEOG AREA IN RIVER DELTA an area in or around the delta of a river **3.** 4TH LETTER OF GREEK ALPHABET the fourth letter of the Greek alphabet, represented in the English alphabet as "d." See table at **alphabet 4.** SOMETHING LIKE DELTA something shaped like a triangle or delta **5.** MATH CHANGE IN VARIABLE an increase or decrease in the value of a variable. Symbol Δ [Pre-12thC. Via Latin from Greek; ultimately of Phoenician origin.]

Del·ta /déltə/ *n.* **1.** COMMUNICATION CODE WORD FOR LETTER "D" a code word for the letter "D," used in international radio communications **2.** SPACE TECH U.S. ROCKET a rocket used by the United States to launch satellites into orbit above the Earth **3.** ASTRON FOURTH BRIGHTEST STAR the fourth brightest star in a constellation

Del·ta Force *n.* the U.S. Army 1st Special Forces Operational Detachment, a military and counter-terrorist force

del·ta ray *n.* a low-energy particle such as an electron, emitted by matter when subjected to ionizing radiation

del·ta wave, del·ta rhythm *n.* a brain wave that is produced by adults in deep sleep. Delta waves are produced in the front of the brain and are slow waves with a frequency of 3.5 cycles per second.

del·ta wing *n.* an airplane wing that has a triangular, swept-back shape

del·ti·ol·o·gy /dèltee óllajee/ *n.* the collection and study of postcards [Mid-20thC. Formed from Greek *deltion*, literally "little writing tablet," from *deltos* "writing tablet."] —**del·ti·ol·o·gist** *n.*

del·toid /dél tòyd/ *n.* SHOULDER MUSCLE a thick triangular muscle that covers the shoulder joint ■ *adj.* TRIANGULAR triangular in shape (*technical*) [Mid-18thC. Directly or via French *deltoïde* from modern Latin *deltoides*, literally "delta-shaped," from Greek *delta* (see DELTA).]

Del·to·na /del tṓnə/ city in Volusia County, Florida, situated southwest of Daytona Beach. Population: 50,828 (1990).

de·lude /di lóod/ (**-lud·ed, -lud·ing, -ludes**) *vt.* **1.** LEAD INTO FALSE BELIEF to persuade somebody to believe in something that is untrue or unreal **2.** FRUSTRATE HOPES to frustrate somebody's hopes or expectations (*archaic*) [15thC. From Latin *deludere*, literally "to play to your detriment," from *ludere* "to play" (see LUDICROUS).] —**de·lud·a·ble** *adj.* —**de·lud·er** *n.* —**de·lud·ing·ly** *adv.*

de·lud·ed /di lóodəd/ *adj.* firmly believing in something that is untrue or unreal

del·uge /déllyooj/ *n.* **1.** SUDDEN HEAVY DOWNPOUR a sudden heavy downpour of rain or torrent of water **2.** VAST QUANTITY an overwhelming amount of something ■ *vt.* (**-uged, -ug·ing, -ug·es**) **1.** OVERWHELM WITH SOMETHING to inundate somebody suddenly with a large amount of something **2.** OVERWHELM WITH WATER to flood or soak somebody or something with heavy rain or a sudden torrent of water [15thC. From Old French, from, ultimately, Latin *diluere* "to wash away" (source of English *dilute*), from *lavare* "to wash" (see LAVATORY).]

Del·uge *n.* BIBLE = **Flood**

de·lu·sion /di lóozh'n/ *n.* **1.** PSYCHOL FALSE BELIEF a persistent false belief held in the face of strong contradictory evidence, especially as a symptom of psychiatric disorder **2.** MISTAKEN NOTION a false or mistaken belief or idea about something [15thC. From the Latin stem *delusion-*, from the past participle stem of *deludere* (see DELUDE).] —**de·lu·sion·al** *adj.*

WORD KEY: USAGE

See Usage note at ***allusion***.

de·lu·sions of gran·deur *npl.* gross and false overestimation of personal worth, importance, powerfulness, or attractiveness

de·lu·sive /di lóossiv/ *adj.* leading to a belief in something untrue or unreal [Early 17thC. Formed from Latin *delus-*, past participle stem of *deludere* (see DELUDE).] —**de·lu·sive·ly** *adv.* —**de·lu·sive·ness** *n.*

de·lu·so·ry /di lóossəree/ *adj.* so deceptive in nature or character as to be likely to mislead or delude somebody [15thC. From late Latin *delusorius*, from the past participle stem of Latin *deludere* (see DELUDE).]

de·luxe /di lúks/, **de luxe** *adj.* of a luxurious standard and surpassing all others in its class [Early 19thC. From French *de luxe*, literally "of luxury."]

delve /delv/ *v.* (**delved, delv·ing, delves**) **1.** *vi.* DIG FOR INFORMATION to investigate or research something thoroughly to obtain information **2.** *vt.* EXCAVATE to dig something such as a ditch, hole, or burrow (*archaic*) ■ *n.* RUMMAGING FOR SOMETHING a rummaging or a digging into something to find something that is hidden or difficult to reach [Old English *delfan* "to dig," from prehistoric Germanic] —**delv·er** *n.*

dely. *abbr.* delivery

Dem /dem/ *n.* a member of the Democratic Party (*informal*) [Late 19thC. Shortening.]

dem. *abbr.* GRAM demonstrative

Dem. *abbr.* **1.** Democrat **2.** Democratic

de·mag·net·ize /dee mágnə tīz/ (**-ized, -iz·ing, -iz·es**) *vt.* to remove the magnetic properties from something —**de·mag·net·i·za·tion** /dee màgnəti záysh'n/ *n.* —**de·mag·net·iz·er** *n.*

dem·a·gog *n.*, *vti.* (**-gogs**) = **demagogue**

dem·a·gog·ic /dèmmə gójjik, -góggik/, **dem·a·gog·i·cal** /dèmmə gójjik'l, -góggik'l/ *adj.* making an appeal to people's emotions, instincts, and prejudices in a way that is considered to be politically manipulative and dangerous [Mid-19thC. From Greek *demagōgikos*, from *dēmagōgos* (see DEMAGOGUE).] —**dem·a·gog·i·cal·ly** *adv.*

dem·a·gog·ism, dem·a·gogu·ism *n.* = **demagoguery**

dem·a·gogue /démmə gòg/ *n.* **1.** EMOTIVE DICTATOR a political leader who gains power by appealing to people's emotions and prejudices rather than their rationality **2.** POPULAR LEADER IN ANCIENT TIMES in ancient times, a popular leader who represented the ordinary people ■ *v.* (**-gogued, -gogu·ing, -gogues**) **1.** *vi.* ENGAGE IN DEMAGOGUERY to act like a demagogue in gaining power by appealing to people's emotions and prejudices **2.** *vt.* ELICIT EMOTIVE BIAS ON ISSUES to elicit people's emotional and prejudicial biases on an issue [Mid-17thC. From Greek *dēmagōgos*, literally "leader of the people," from *agōgos* "leader," from *agein* "to lead" (source of English *stratagem*).]

dem·a·gogu·er·y /démmə gòggəree/, **dem·a·gog·y** /démmə gòjjee, -gòggee, -gōjee/, **dem·a·gog·ism** /démmə gògizzəm/ *n.* the character, behavior, tactics, or rhetoric of a demagogue

de·mand /di mánd/ *n.* **1.** FORCEFUL REQUEST a clear and firm request that is difficult to ignore or deny **2.** ECON CUSTOMER INTEREST IN ACQUIRING SOMETHING the level of desire or need that exists for particular goods or services ○ *Demand for that particular model is outstripping supply.* **3.** NEED FOR RESOURCES OR ACTION an urgent requirement for time, facilities, resources, or action **4.** LAW LEGALLY ENFORCEABLE REQUEST a formal request that must be complied with by law ■ *v.* (**-mand·ed, -mand·ing, -mands**) **1.** *vt.* ASK FORCEFULLY to request something firmly in a way that is difficult to ignore or deny **2.** *vt.* ASK TO KNOW AT ONCE to ask a question in an extremely forceful way **3.** *vti.* CALL FOR RESOURCES to require something such as time, resources, facilities, or action in order to function or succeed [14thC. Via Old French *demander* from Latin *demandare*, literally "to entrust completely," from *mandare* "to entrust, order" (see MANDATE).] —**de·mand·a·ble** *adj.* —**de·mand·er** *n.* ◇ **in demand** wanted or sought by many people ◇ **on demand** promptly, whenever a request is received

de·mand de·pos·it *n.* a bank deposit that can be withdrawn at any time without notice

de·mand draft *n.* FIN = **sight bill**

de·mand feed·ing *n.* the practice of feeding a baby when it cries to be fed, rather than at set times

de·mand·ing /di mánding/ *adj.* requiring a lot of time, attention, energy, or resources

de·mand·ing·ly /di mándinglee/ *adv.* in a highly insistent manner

de·mand loan *n.* FIN = **call loan**

de·mand note *n.* a bill or draft stating that a particular amount of money will be paid when it is asked for

de·mand-pull, de·mand-pull in·fla·tion *n.* inflation caused by demand for goods and services outstripping supply. ◊ **cost-push**

de·mand-side *adj.* relating to an economic policy that emphasizes the importance of demand and consumption

de·man·toid /di mán tòyd/ *n.* a transparent green variety of garnet used as a gemstone [Late 19thC. From German, literally "diamond-shaped," from *Demant* "diamond."]

de·mar·cate /di maár kàyt, deé maar kàyt/ (**-cat·ed, -cat·ing, -cates**) *vt.* **1.** DETERMINE AND SET OFFICIAL BORDERS to decide on and fix land boundaries **2.** SET DOWN NONPHYSICAL BOUNDS to state in a clear way where something begins and ends [Early 19thC. Back-formation from DEMARCATION.] —**de·mar·ca·tor** *n.*

de·mar·ca·tion /dee maar káysh'n/ *n.* **1.** SETTING OF BORDERS the process of deciding on and fixing land boundaries **2.** IDENTIFIABLE SEPARATION OF THINGS the division of something so that its divided parts are separate and identifiable [Early 18thC. From Spanish *demarcación*, literally "marking off," from *marcar* "to mark," from, ultimately, a prehistoric Germanic word that is also the ancestor of English *margin*.]

de·mar·ca·tion dis·pute *n.* a disagreement over where a land boundary lies

dé·marche /day maársh/ (*plural* **-march·es**) *n.* **1.** DIPLOMATIC REPRESENTATION a diplomatic representation, especially a move, maneuver, or protest made orally **2.** CITIZENS' PROTEST STATEMENT a statement of protest made by or on behalf of the citizens of a nation to their government or to a controlling authority **3.** MOVE OR COUNTERMOVE a move, step, or countermove [Mid-17thC. From French *démarcher* "to take steps," from *marcher* "to march."]

de·ma·te·ri·al·ize /deemə teéree ə līz/ (**-ized, -iz·ing, -izes**) *vti.* to disappear or cause something to disappear physically or apparently —**de·ma·te·ri·al·i·za·tion** /deemə teeree əli záysh'n/ *n.*

deme /deem/ *n.* **1.** HIST **TOWNSHIP IN ATTICA** a township in Attica in ancient Greece **2.** ECOL **POPULATION OF RELATED SPECIES** a local population of closely related interbreeding species [Mid-19thC. From Greek *dēmos* "district," hence, "people living in a district" (see DEMOS).]

de·mean[1] /di meen/ (**-meaned, -mean·ing, -means**) *vt.* to reduce somebody to a much lower status in a humiliating way [Early 17thC. Coined from DE- "down" + MEAN "inferior in rank."] —**de·mean·ing** *adj.*

de·mean[2] /di meen/ (**-meaned, -mean·ing, -means**) *vr.* to behave in a particular way (*dated*) [14thC. From Old French *demener*, literally "to lead away," from, ultimately, Latin *minare* "to drive a herd of animals."]

de·mean·or /di meenər/ *n.* somebody's behavior, manner, or appearance, especially as it reflects on character

de·mean·our *n.* U.K. = **demeanor**

de·ment·ed /di méntəd/ *adj.* **1.** **ENTIRELY IRRATIONAL** completely unreasonable or without any sense of consequences (*informal*) **2.** PSYCHIAT **AFFECTED WITH DEMENTIA** affected by the loss of intellectual functions that is associated with dementia [Mid-17thC. Originally the past participle of obsolete *dement* "to deprive of reason," from Latin *dementare*, literally "to take the mind away," from, ultimately, the stem *ment-* "mind" (see MENTAL).] —**de·ment·ed·ly** *adv.* —**de·ment·ed·ness** *n.*

de·men·tia /di ménshə/ *n.* PSYCHIAT the usually progressive deterioration of intellectual functions such as memory that can occur while other brain functions such as those controlling movement and the senses are retained. ◊ **senile dementia** [Late 18thC. From Latin, from the stem *dement-*, literally "mind away," from *ment-* "mind" (see MENTAL).]

de·men·tia prae·cox /-preé kòks/ *n.* schizophrenia (*archaic*) [From Latin, literally "premature loss of mind"]

de·merge /dee múrj/ (**-merged, -merg·ing, -merg·es**) *vti.* *U.K.* to separate a company from a larger company so that it becomes an individual concern, or divide a large company into a number of smaller companies

de·merg·er /dee múrjər/ *n.* *U.K.* a merger between two or more companies that is dissolved, or the separation of one company from a larger company or group

de·mer·it /di mérrit/ *n.* **1.** MIL, EDUC **MARK FOR DEFICIENCY OR MISCONDUCT** a mark against somebody such as a student or cadet for a deficiency or misconduct **2.** **NEGATIVE FEATURE** a negative feature or disadvantage of something, especially when contrasted with its positive features or advantages (*often used in the plural*) [14thC. Directly or via Old French *desmerite* from Latin *demeritum*, from, ultimately, *demereri*, literally "to deserve thoroughly," from *mereri* "to deserve." The original English meaning was "merit, worth." The modern meanings are derived from the negative connotations of DE-.] —**de·mer·i·to·ri·ous** /di mèrrə táwree əss/ *adj.* —**de·mer·i·to·ri·ous·ly** /-lee/ *adv.*

Dem·er·ol /démmə ròl/ *tdmk.* a trademark for a medicinal preparation of the painkiller meperidine

de·mer·sal /di múrs'l/ *adj.* living or found in the deepest part of a body of water [Late 19thC. Formed from Latin *demersus*, the past participle of *demergere* "to submerge," from *mergere* "to plunge" (see MERGE).]

de·mesne /di máyn/ *n.* **1.** **POSSESSION OF OWN LAND** possession and use of your own land, as opposed to ownership of land that is occupied by tenants (*formal*) **2.** **PRIVATE GROUNDS WITH MANSION** the grounds attached to a mansion for the private use of the owner (*archaic*) **3.** HIST **FEUDAL MANORIAL LAND** manorial land that a feudal lord kept for his own private use (*formal*) **4.** **ESTATE** an extensive landed property (*formal*) **5.** **REALM OF MONARCH** the realm under the rule of a monarch (*formal*) [14thC. Via Old French *demeine* "belonging to a lord" from Latin *dominicus* "of a lord" (source of English *domain*).]

De·me·ter /də meetər/ *n.* in Greek mythology, the goddess of corn and the harvest, daughter of Cronus and Rhea and mother of Persephone. Roman equivalent **Ceres**

dem·e·ton /démmə tòn/ *n.* either of two highly toxic chemicals that are pale yellow in color and used as systemic insecticides. Formula: $C_6H_{15}O_3PS_2$ *or* $C_6H_{15}O_4PS_2$.

demi- *prefix.* **1.** half ○ *demirep* **2.** partly ○ *demigod* [Via Old French from, ultimately, Latin *dimidius* "split in two," from *dis-* "apart" and *medius* "half"]

dem·i·bas·tion /dèmmi báschən, -bástee ən/ *n.* a two-sided fortification that consists of a wall facing forward and a wall facing a flank

dem·i·god /démmi gòd/ *n.* **1.** **SOMEBODY TREATED LIKE GOD** somebody who is very important or highly revered and is treated like a god **2.** **HUMAN WITH POWERS OF A GOD** a mythological being who is half human and half god **3.** **MINOR GOD** a god regarded as minor in a hierarchy of other gods [Mid-16thC. Translation of Latin *semideus*.]

dem·i·god·dess /démmi gòddəss/ *n.* **1.** **SOMEBODY TREATED LIKE A GOD** somebody who is very important or highly revered and is treated like a god **2.** **WOMAN WITH POWERS OF A GODDESS** a mythological being who is half woman and half goddess **3.** **SOMEBODY TREATED LIKE A GOD** somebody who is very important or highly revered and is treated like a god

dem·i·john /démmi jòn/ *n.* a large bottle that has a short narrow neck and is often used for making wine [Mid-18thC. By folk etymology from French *dame-jeanne*, literally "Lady Jane," its popular name in France.]

de·mil·i·ta·rize /dee míllitə rīz/ (**-rized, -riz·ing, -riz·es**) *vt.* to remove or prohibit the presence of soldiers, weapons, and military installations in an area after an agreement has been made to stop fighting —**de·mil·i·ta·ri·za·tion** /dee millitəri záysh'n/ *n.*

de·mil·i·ta·rized zone *n.* an officially recognized area from which all soldiers, weapons, and military installations have been removed after an agreement to stop fighting

De Mille /də míl/, **Agnes George** (1909–93) U.S. dancer and choreographer. She was known for integrating popular dance styles with ballet in classical productions and musicals.

DeMille /də míl/, **Cecil B.** (1881–1959) U.S. movie director and producer. He was known for lavish epics and movies dealing with contemporary social issues. Full name **Cecil Blount DeMille**

dem·i·mon·daine /dèmmi mon dáyn/ *n.* a woman who is financially supported by a wealthy lover (*literary*) [Late 19thC. From French, from *demi-monde* (see DEMIMONDE).]

dem·i·monde /démmi mònd, dèmmi mónd/ *n.* (*literary*) **1.** **PEOPLE OF QUESTIONABLE RESPECTABILITY** people who are not considered to be completely respectable **2.** **WOMEN SUPPORTED BY LOVERS** a class of women who were financially supported by wealthy lovers, especially in the 19th and early 20th centuries [Mid-19thC. From French *demi-monde*, literally "half world."]

de·min·er·al·i·za·tion /dee mìnnərəli záysh'n/ *n.* the loss of mineral salts from the body, especially in the teeth and bones

de·min·er·al·ize /dee mínnərə līz/ (**-ized, -iz·ing, -iz·es**) *vt.* to remove minerals or mineral salts from something such as bone or a liquid —**de·min·er·al·i·zer** *n.*

Dem·ing /démming/ city in southwestern New Mexico, west of Las Cruces. Population: 14,155 (1996).

dem·i·pen·sion *n.* *U.K.* = **half board**

De·mir·el /dèmmi rél/, **Süleyman** (*b.* 1924) Turkish statesman. He served four terms as prime minister (1965–93) and became the ninth president of Turkey in 1993.

dem·i·re·lief /démmiri leef/ *n.* sculptural relief made of modeled forms that are half-raised from the background

dem·i·rep /démmi rèp/ *n.* somebody who is disreputable, especially a woman who acts in a way considered sexually improper (*archaic*) [Mid-18thC. Coined from DEMI- + *rep*, shortening of REPUTABLE.]

de·mise /di mīz/ *n.* (*formal*) **1.** **SOMEBODY'S DEATH** the death of a person, especially when it happens slowly and predictably **2.** **END OF SOMETHING** the end of something that used to exist, especially when it happens slowly and predictably ■ *v.* (**-mised, -mis·ing, -mis·es**) (*formal*) **1.** *vi.* **DIE** die, especially slowly and predictably **2.** *vti.* LAW **BE LEGALLY TRANSFERRED** to transfer something or undergo transfer through a line of descent or according to a will [15thC. Via Anglo-Norman from Old French *demis* "sent away," from, ultimately, Latin *dimittere* (see DEMIT).] —**de·mis·a·ble** *adj.*

dem·i·sec /-sék/ *adj.* used to describe champagne or sparkling wine that is more sweet than dry [From French, literally "half-dry"] —**dem·i·sec** *n.*

dem·i·sem·i·qua·ver /dèmmi semmi kwáyvər/ *n.* *U.K.* = **thirty-second note**

de·mis·sion /di mísh'n/ *n.* resignation from an important official post [Mid-16thC. Via French *démission* from, ultimately, the Latin stem *dimission-* "dismissal," from the past participle of *dimittere* (see DEMIT).]

de·mist /dee míst/ *vti.* *U.K.* = **defog**

de·mist·er /dee místər/ *n.* *U.K.* = **defogger**

de·mit /di mít/ (**-mit·ted, -mit·ting, -mits**) *vti.* to resign from or give up an important official post [15thC. Via Old French *desmettre*, from, ultimately, Latin *dimittere* "to send away," from *mittere* "to send."]

dem·i·tasse /démmi taass, -tàss/ *n.* a small cup of strong black coffee, or the cup in which such coffee is served [Mid-19thC. From French, literally "half-cup," from *tasse* "cup," from, ultimately, Persian *tāsht*.]

dem·i·urge /démmee ùrj/ *n.* **1.** **POWERFUL FORCE OR PERSONALITY** a very strong, driving, and influential force or personality (*formal*) **2.** HIST **ANCIENT GREEK MAGISTRATE** a public magistrate in some ancient Greek states [Early 17thC. Via ecclesiastical Latin *demiurgus* from Greek *dēmiourgos* "skilled person," from *dēmios* "of the people" + *-ergos* "working."] —**dem·i·ur·geous** *adj.* —**dem·i·ur·gic** *adj.* —**dem·i·ur·gi·cal** *adj.* —**dem·i·ur·gi·cal·ly** *adv.*

Dem·i·urge *n.* PHILOS in Gnostic and Platonic philosophies, the creator and controller of the material world

dem·i·volte /démmi vòlt/ *n.* in dressage, a half turn made by a horse with its forelegs raised [Mid-17thC. From French, literally "half turn," from *volte* "turn."]

dem·i·world /démmi wùrld/ *n.* = **demimonde** *n.* 1

dem·o /démmō/ *n.* (*plural* **de·mos**) **1.** **SOMETHING DEMONSTRATING FEATURES** something such as a motor vehicle made available for testing by potential buyers **2.** **DEMONSTRATION OF PRODUCT** a demonstration, especially of a new product (*informal*) **3.** COMPUT **TRIAL SOFTWARE** a trial version of software that demonstrates its principle features (*informal*) **4.** MUSIC **MUSIC SAMPLE** a recorded sample of music produced for promotional purposes (*informal*) **5.** **PUBLIC PROTEST** a public event in which people protest against something, often by marching through the streets (*informal*) ■ *vt.* (**de·moed, de·mo·ing, de·mos**) **SHOW HOW SOMETHING WORKS** to explain, describe, or give a demonstration of how something works or how to do something (*informal*) [Mid-20thC. Shortening of DEMONSTRATION.]

de·mob /dee mób/ (**-mobbed, -mob·bing, -mobs**) *vti.* *U.K.* to demobilize armed forces (*informal*) [Early 20thC. Shortening of DEMOBILIZE.]

de·mo·bil·ize /di mōbi līz/ (**-ized, -iz·ing, -iz·es**) *vti.* to discharge personnel from the armed forces and send them home, usually after a war —**de·mo·bil·i·za·tion** /di mōbili záysh'n/ *n.*

de·moc·ra·cy /di mókrəssee/ (*plural* **-cies**) *n.* **1.** **FREE AND EQUAL REPRESENTATION OF PEOPLE** the free and equal right of every person to participate in a system of government, often practiced by electing representatives of the people by the people ○ *"Democracy is like the experience of life itself – always changing, infinite in its variety, sometimes turbulent and all the more valuable for having been tested for adversity."* (Jimmy Carter, *Speech to Parliament of India*; June 2, 1978) **2.** **DEMOCRATIC NATION** a country with a government that has been elected freely and equally by all its citizens **3.** **DEMOCRATIC GOVERNMENTAL SYSTEM** a system of government based on the principle of majority decision-making **4.** **ORGANIZATIONAL CONTROL BY MEMBERS** the control of an organization by its members, who have a free and equal right to participate in decision-making processes [Late 16thC. Directly and via Old French *democratie* from medieval Latin *democratia*, from, ultimately, Greek *dēmokratia*, literally "rule of the people," from *dēmos* "people" (see DEMOS) + *kratos* "rule."]

dem·o·crat /démmə kràt/ *n.* somebody who believes in democracy and the democratic system of government and argues in favor of them

Dem·o·crat /démmə kràt/ *n.* a member of the Democratic Party, one of the two major political parties in the United States

dem·o·crat·ic /dèmmə kráttik/ *adj.* characterized by free and equal participation in government or in the decision-making processes of an organization or group —**dem·o·crat·i·cal·ly** *adv.*

Dem·o·crat·ic *adj.* belonging or relating to or associated with the Democratic Party of the United States

Dem·o·crat·ic Par·ty *n.* one of the two major political parties in the United States. It was formed after a split in the former Democratic-Republican Party under Andrew Jackson in 1828.

Dem·o·crat·ic-Re·pub·li·can Par·ty *n.* a U.S. political party that was founded by Thomas Jefferson in 1792 and was dissolved in 1828 under Andrew Jackson. Its main opponent was the Federalist Party, originally led by Alexander Hamilton.

de·moc·ra·tize /di mókrə tīz/ (**-tized, -tiz·ing, -tiz·es**) *vt.* **1. GIVE GOVERNMENT CONTROL TO CITIZENRY** to put a country under the control of its citizens by allowing them to participate in government or decision-making processes in a free and equal way **2. INTRODUCE DEMOCRACY TO STATE** to take steps toward establishing the features of liberal democracy in a state **3. GIVE ORGANIZATIONAL CONTROL TO MEMBERS** to put an organization under the control of its members by giving them free and equal decision-making powers **4. GIVE SOMETHING POPULAR APPEAL** to make something accessible to everybody —**de·moc·ra·ti·za·tion** /di mòkrəti záysh'n/ *n.*

De·moc·ri·tus /di mókritəss/ (460?–370? B.C.) Greek philosopher. A prolific writer, he first propounded the atomic theory of the universe. Only a few fragments of his work remain.

dé·mo·dé /dày mō dáy/ *adj.* no longer fashionable [Late 19thC. From French, the past participle of *démoder* "to go out of fashion," from *mode* "fashion" (see MODE).]

de·mod·u·late /dee mójjə làyt/ (**-lat·ed, -lat·ing, -lates**) *vt.* to extract a signal carrying information from a radio wave **(carrier)** —**de·mod·u·la·tor** *n.*

de·mog·ra·pher /di móggrəfər/ *n.* somebody who studies human populations, including their size, growth, density, and distribution, and statistics regarding birth, marriage, disease, and death

dem·o·graph·ic /dèmmə gráffik/ *adj.* relating to demography or demographics —**dem·o·graph·i·cal** *adj.* —**dem·o·graph·i·cal·ly** *adv.*

dem·o·graph·ics /dèmmə gráffiks/ *npl.* the characteristics of a human population or part of it, especially its size, growth, density, distribution, and statistics regarding birth, marriage, disease, and death (*takes a plural verb*)

de·mog·ra·phy /di móggrəfee/ *n.* the study of human populations, including their size, growth, density, and distribution, as well as statistics regarding birth, marriage, disease, and death [Late 19thC. Coined from Greek *dēmos* "people" + -GRAPHY.] —**de·mog·ra·phist** *n.*

dem·oi·selle /dèmmwə zél/ *n.* **1. YOUNG WOMAN** a young woman or girl (*formal*) **2.** = **damselfish** (*formal*) **3.** = **damselfly** [Early 16thC. From French, "damsel," from Old French *dameisele* (see DAMSEL).]

Demoiselle crane

dem·oi·selle crane *n.* a small crane of North Africa and Asia that has a slender gray body, black plumes, and white ear tufts. Latin name: *Anthropoides virgo.* ["Demoiselle" from its ladylike form]

de·mol·ish /di móllish/ (**-ished, -ish·ing, -ish·es**) *vt.* **1. WRECK A BUILDING** to destroy a building or other structure completely **2. DAMAGE IRREPARABLY** to damage something so severely that it cannot be repaired or restored **3. BEAT OPPONENT SOUNDLY** to beat an opponent very convincingly, especially in sports or debate (*informal*) **4. EAT FAST AND GREEDILY** to eat a lot of food very quickly (*informal*) [Mid-16thC. From Old French *démoliss-*, a stem of *démolir*, from Latin *demolire*, literally "to undo construction of a mass," from, ultimately, *moles* "mass" (see MOLECULE).] —**de·mol·ish·er** *n.*

WORD KEY: USAGE

See Usage note at ***destroy.***

dem·o·li·tion /dèmmə lísh'n/ *n.* **1. WRECKING OF BUILDING** the total destruction of a building or other structure ○ *The old hospital is scheduled for demolition.* **2. DESTRUCTION OR ANNIHILATION** the destruction or annihilation of something or somebody ■ **dem·o·li·tions** *npl.* **EXPLOSIVES** explosives, especially those used by the military [Mid-16thC. Via French *démolition* from the Latin stem *demolition-*, from *demolire* (see DEMOLISH).]

dem·o·li·tion der·by (*plural* **dem·o·li·tion der·bies**) *n.* an entertainment and sporting event held at a fair or on a speedway, during which drivers crash old cars, the winner being the driver of the last car running

dem·o·li·tion·ist /dèmmə lísh'nist/ *n.* a person or company whose job it is to demolish buildings

de·mon /deéman/ *n.* **1. EVIL SPIRIT** an evil supernatural being such as a ghost or spirit **2. PERSONAL FEAR OR ANXIETY** a fear or anxiety that torments somebody **3. EXPERT** somebody who is extremely good at something (*informal*) [13thC. Via Latin *daemon* and medieval Latin *demon* "evil spirit" from Greek *daimōn* "divine power, guiding spirit" (see DAEMON).]

de·mon·e·tize /dee mónnə tīz/ (**-tized, -tiz·ing, -tiz·es**) *vt.* **1. CEASE MINTING COINS IN SPECIFIC METAL** to stop using a particular metal to make coins **2. WITHDRAW MONEY FROM CIRCULATION** to withdraw units of money from circulation [Mid-19thC. From French *démonétiser*, literally "to refrain from using money," from Latin *moneta* "money" (see MONEY).] —**de·mon·e·ti·za·tion** /dee mònnəti záysh'n/ *n.*

de·mo·ni·ac /di mṓnee àk/ *adj.* **1. de·mo·ni·a·cal RESEMBLING A DEMON** resembling or characteristic of an evil spirit **2. de·mo·ni·ac, de·mo·ni·a·cal EVIL OR WICKED** evil or wicked in character or nature **3. de·mo·ni·ac, de·mo·ni·a·cal INTENSE OR FRANTIC** intense, frantic, or wild, as if driven or possessed by a demon ■ *n.* **SOMEBODY INFLUENCED BY DEMON** somebody believed to be possessed by an evil supernatural being (*archaic*) [14thC. From late Latin *daemoniacus*, from, ultimately, Greek *daimōn* (see DEMON).]

de·mon·ic /di mónnik/ *adj.* **1. OF OR RESEMBLING DEMON** relating to or resembling a demon, especially in wickedness **2. INTENSE OR FRANTIC** intense, frantic, or wild, as if driven or possessed by a demon —**de·mon·i·cal·ly** *adv.*

de·mon·ize /deémə nīz/ (**-ized, -iz·ing, -iz·es**) *vt.* to cause somebody or something to appear evil or wicked in the eyes of others —**de·mon·i·za·tion** /deèməni záysh'n/ *n.*

de·mon·o·la·try /deèmə nóllətree/ *n.* worship of demons or of the devil —**de·mon·o·lat·er** *n.*

de·mon·ol·o·gy /deèmə nólləjee/ *n.* the study of demons, especially those that are frequent in folklore of certain societies —**de·mon·o·log·i·cal** /deèmənə lójjik'l/ *adj.* —**de·mon·ol·o·gist** /deèmə nólləjist/ *n.*

de·mon·stra·ble /di mónstrəb'l/ *adj.* **1. EASILY SHOWN TO BE SO** so obvious as to be readily provable **2. PROVABLE** capable of being shown to exist or be true [14thC. Directly or via Old French from Latin *demonstrabilis*, from *demonstrare* (see DEMONSTRATE).] —**de·mon·stra·bil·i·ty** /di mònstrə bíllətee/ *n.* —**de·mon·stra·ble·ness** /di mónstrəb'lnəss/ *n.* —**de·mon·stra·bly** /di mónstrəblee/ *adv.*

dem·on·strate /démmən stràyt/ (**-strat·ed, -strat·ing, -strates**) *v.* **1.** *vt.* **EXPLAIN WORKINGS** to explain or describe how something works or how to do something **2.** *vt.* **SHOW CONVINCINGLY** to show or prove something clearly and convincingly **3.** *vi.* **PROTEST OR SUPPORT SOMEBODY OR SOMETHING** to make a public show as a group for or against an issue, cause, or person, often by marching through the streets [Mid-16thC. From Latin *demonstrat-*, the past participle stem of *demonstrare*, from *monstrare* "to show," from *monstrum* "omen" (source of English *monster*).]

dem·on·stra·tion /dèmmən stráysh'n/ *n.* **1. DISPLAY SHOWING HOW TO DO SOMETHING** a display given to others of how something is done or how something works **2. CONCLUSIVE PROOF** evidence or proof that allows no doubt as to its validity or soundness **3. GROUP DISPLAY OF OPINION** a public show as a group for or against an issue, cause, or person **4. ATTACK OR SHOW OF FORCE** a show of military force or a movement toward an enemy —**dem·on·stra·tion·al** *adj.* —**dem·on·stra·tion·ist** *n.*

dem·on·stra·tion sport *n.* a sport that is contested in the Olympics on a trial basis even though it is not a permanent medal sport

de·mon·stra·tive /di mónstrətiv/ *adj.* **1. OBVIOUSLY AFFECTIONATE** unrestrained in showing love and affection toward somebody **2. PROVING** serving to show proof of truth **3.** GRAM **SPECIFYING WHICH PERSON OR THING** referring to a particular person or thing, e.g., "this," "that," "these," and "those" ■ *n.* GRAM **WORD SPECIFYING WHICH PERSON OR THING** a demonstrative word or phrase, e.g., "this," "that," "these," or "those" —**de·mon·stra·tive·ly** *adv.* —**de·mon·stra·tive·ness** *n.*

dem·on·stra·tor /démmən stràytər/ *n.* **1. SUPPORTER OR PROTESTER** somebody who protests or supports something publicly, usually as a member of a group **2. EXPLAINER OF DEVICES** somebody who shows people how do something or explains how something works **3.** = **demo** *n.* 5

de·mor·al·ize /di máwrə līz/ (**-ized, -iz·ing, -iz·es**) *vt.* **1. ERODE ANOTHER'S MORALE** to erode or destroy the courage, confidence, or hope of a person or group **2. MAKE DISORDERED** to throw something into disorder or chaos **3. CORRUPT SOMEBODY'S MORALS** to corrupt somebody's morals —**de·mor·al·i·za·tion** /di màwrəli záysh'n/ *n.* —**de·mor·al·iz·er** /di máwrə līzər/ *n.*

de·mos /démmōz/ *n.* **1. POPULACE** the ordinary people of a community or nation (*formal*) **2.** HIST **GREEK CITY-STATE POPULACE** the common people in an ancient Greek city-state [Late 18thC. From Greek *dēmos* "district," hence "people living in a district."]

de·mote /dee mṓt/ (**-mot·ed, -mot·ing, -motes**) *vt.* to reduce somebody or something to a lower rank, status, or position [Late 19thC. Blend of DE- and PROMOTE.]

de·mot·ic /di móttik/ *adj.* **1. OF THE POPULACE** relating to or involving ordinary people (*formal*) **2. USING SIMPLIFIED HIEROGLYPHICS** relating to a simplified form of hieroglyphics, the writing system used in ancient Egypt [Early 19thC. From Greek *dēmotikos* "popular, common," literally "of the people," from *dēmos* (see DEMOS).]

De·mot·ic *n.* **1. MODERN SPOKEN GREEK** the colloquial form of modern Greek, used in conversation and in literature and now adopted as the official variety of the language. ◊ **Katharevusa 2. LATE EGYPTIAN LANGUAGE** the later form of the ancient Egyptian language, written in demotic script, which was current in the first millennium B.C. —**De·mot·ic** *adj.*

de·mo·tion /di mṓsh'n/ *n.* a reduction in the rank, status, or position of somebody or something

de·mount /dee mównt/ (**-mount·ed, -mount·ing, -mounts**) *vt.* **1. REMOVE DEVICE FROM SUPPORTS** to take a piece of equipment away from its supports **2. DISMANTLE SOMETHING** to take something apart, usually with the intention of reassembling it later

de·mount·a·ble /dee mówntəb'l/ *adj.* **1. REMOVABLE FROM SUPPORTS** used to describe a piece of equipment that can be removed from its supports **2. REMOVABLE FROM CAB OF TRUCK** relating to the storage part of a truck that can be removed from the cab without the use of a crane

Demp·sey /démpsee/, **Jack** (1895–1983) U.S. professional boxer. He won the world heavyweight title in 1919, which he lost to Gene Tunny in 1926. Full name **William Harrison Dempsey**. Known as **The Manassa Mauler**

de·mul·cent /di múlsənt/ *n.* a substance that is used to soothe irritated or inflamed skin or internal parts of the nose, mouth, or throat. Lanoline and glycerine are demulcents. [Mid-18thC. From Latin *demulcent-*, present participle stem of *demulcere*, literally "to soothe down," from *mulcere* "to soothe."] —**de·mul·cent** *adj.*

de·mul·si·fy /di múlsi fī/ (**-fied, -fy·ing, -fies**) *vti.* to break an emulsion down permanently into its components, or be broken down permanently —**de·mul·si·fi·ca·tion** /di mùlsifi káysh'n/ *n.* —**de·mul·si·fi·er** /di múlsi fīr/ *n.*

de·mur /di múr/ (**-murred, -mur·ring, -murs**) *v.* **1.** *vi.* **SHOW RELUCTANCE TO DO SOMETHING** to delay or try to avoid doing something because of personal reservations or objections ○ *"While I acknowledged it might come to that (the use of force in the Persian Gulf), I demurred, saying it was too early to contemplate such action."* (George Bush, *A World Transformed*;

1998) **2.** *vi.* **OBJECT MILDLY** to object mildly to something that you do not want to do but have been asked to do **3.** *vti.* LAW **MAKE LEGAL OBJECTION** to admit the facts of an opposing argument, but object that those facts alone are not by themselves adequate to make the case [13thC. From Old French *demorer* "to delay, stay," from Latin *demorare.*] —**de·mur·ra·ble** *adj.*

WORD KEY: SYNONYMS

See Synonyms at ***object.***

de·mure /di myŏŏr/ (**-mur·er, -mur·est**) *adj.* **1. LOOKING SHYLY MODEST** looking or behaving in a modest manner with reserve or seriousness **2. AFFECTEDLY SHY OR MODEST** acting in an affectedly shy or modest way [14thC. From the past participle of Old French *demorer* (see DEMUR). The modern meaning evolved via the sense of "calmness."] —**de·mure·ly** *adv.* —**de·mure·ness** *n.*

de·mur·rage /di múrrij/ *n.* **1. DETENTION OF CARGO CARRIER** detention or delay of a cargo carrier during its loading or unloading process, beyond its scheduled time of departure **2. COMPENSATION FOR LOADING OR UNLOADING DELAY** compensation paid when there is a delay in loading or unloading a carrier causing a delay in the carrier's departure [Mid-17thC. From Old French *demo(u)rage,* from *demorer* (see DEMUR).]

de·mur·ral /di múrral/ *n.* a mild indication of hesitation, refusal, or objection

de·mur·rer /di múrrar/ *n.* LAW a legal objection that admits the facts of an opposing argument but asserts that those facts alone are not adequate to make the case [Early 16thC. From French *demorer* (see DEMUR).]

De·muth /di mōōth/, **Charles** (1883–1935) U.S. painter. He was known for his still-life watercolors, and his oil-and-tempera architectural scenes such as *Business* (1921).

de·my /di mī/ *adj.* used to describe printing paper that is 17.5 in./444.5 mm by 22.5 in./571.5 mm or writing paper that is 16 in./406.4 mm by 21 in./533.4 mm [15thC. Alteration of DEMI-.]

de·my·e·lin·a·tion /dee mī əli náysh'n/ *n.* loss of the fatty covering (**myelin**) of nerve fibers, which is characteristic of multiple sclerosis and other neurological disorders —**de·my·e·lin·ate** /di mī əli nàyt/ *vt.*

de·mys·ti·fy /dee místi fī/ (**-fied, -fy·ing, -fies**) *vt.* to remove the mystery surrounding something, e.g., by explaining it in simple language —**de·mys·ti·fi·ca·tion** /di mìstifi káysh'n/ *n.* —**de·mys·ti·fi·er** /dee místi fīr/ *n.*

de·my·thol·o·gize /deemi thólla jīz/ (**-gized, -giz·ing, -giz·es**) *vt.* to reveal and understand the true character, nature, or meaning of something by ridding it of all mythical or mysterious aspects —**de·my·thol·o·gi·za·tion** /deemi thòllaji záysh'n/ *n.* —**de·my·thol·o·giz·er** /deemi thólla jīzar/ *n.*

den /den/ *n.* **1. WILD ANIMAL'S LAIR** the hidden home of a wild animal **2. ROOM FOR RELAXING** a room in a house where family members and guests relax **3. PLACE OF CRIME** a place where illegal or secret activities take place **4. CUB SCOUT GROUP** a group of Cub Scouts that is typically made up of eight to ten youths **5. SQUALID ROOM** a squalid small room or place to live **6. CHILDREN'S HIDEOUT** a secret place where children play [Old English *denn* "wild animal's lair," from, ultimately, an Indo-European word meaning "flat surface"]

Den. *abbr.* Denmark

De·na·li Na·tion·al Park and Pre·serve /də naalee-/ park in central Alaska that contains Mount McKinley, the highest point in North America, at 20,320 ft./6,194 m. It was combined with Denali National Monument in 1980. Area: 6,076,528 acres/2,459,083 hectares.

de·nar·i·us /di náiree əss/ (*plural* **-i** /-ī/) *n.* **1. OLD ROMAN SILVER COIN** an ancient Roman silver coin originally worth ten asses **2. OLD ROMAN GOLD COIN** an ancient Roman gold coin worth 25 silver denarii [14thC. From Latin, literally "containing ten," from *deni* "ten at a time."]

den·a·ry /dénnaree/ *adj.* relating to a number system, or a number belonging to it, that has ten as its base, as in the decimal system [Mid-19thC. From Latin *denarius* (see DENARIUS).]

de·na·tion·al·ize /dee náshən'l īz, dee náshna līz/ (**-ized, -iz·ing, -iz·es**) *vt.* **1. SELL STATE-OWNED ASSETS** to sell industries or other major assets owned by the state to private buyers **2. DEPRIVE OF NATIONAL RIGHTS** to deprive a people or nation of national rights and characteristics —**de·na·tion·al·i·za·tion** /dee nàshən'li záysh'n, -nəli-/ *n.*

de·nat·u·ral·ize /dee náchəra līz/ (**-ized, -iz·ing, -iz·es**) *vt.* **1. REVOKE CITIZENSHIP OF** to take away a naturalized citizen's citizenship, e.g., for illegal entry into the country **2. MAKE UNNATURAL** to take away the original nature of something ○ *once verdant jungles that were denaturalized by defoliants* —**de·nat·u·ral·i·za·tion** /dee nàchərəli záysh'n/ *n.*

de·na·ture /dee náychər/ (**-tured, -tur·ing, -tures**) *vt.* **1. MAKE UNPALATABLE** to make food or drink, especially alcohol, unsuitable for human consumption, by adding poison, dye, or unpleasant flavors **2.** BIOCHEM **MODIFY MOLECULAR STRUCTURE** to change the molecular structure of a protein or nucleic acid by chemical or physical means, so that some of its original biological properties are reduced or lost **3.** PHYS **REMOVE WEAPON POTENTIAL OF NUCLEAR MATERIAL** to make nuclear material unsuitable for use in a weapon by adding an isotope that cannot be split —**de·na·tur·ant** *n.* —**de·na·tur·a·tion** /dee nàychə ráysh'n/ *n.*

de·naz·i·fy /dee naatsi fī/ (**-fied, -fy·ing, -fies**) *vt.* to remove connection with or hint of Nazism from something, or to remove Nazis from official positions [Mid-20thC. Coined from DE- + NAZI + -FY.] —**de·naz·i·fi·ca·tion** /dee naatsifi káysh'n/ *n.*

Dench /dench/, **Dame Judi** (*b.* 1934) British actor. She has played leading roles with Britain's major stage companies and in award-winning films such as *Mrs. Brown* (1997). She won an Academy Award for her performance in *Shakespeare in Love* (1999). Full name **Dame Judith Olivia Dench**

dendr- *prefix.* = **dendro-**

dendri- *prefix.* = **dendro-**

den·dri·form /déndri fàwrm/ *adj.* shaped like a tree

den·drite /dén drīt/ *n.* **1.** ANAT **BRANCHED EXTENSION OF NERVE CELL** a branched extension of a nerve cell (**neuron**) that receives electrical signals from other neurons and conducts those signals to the cell body **2.** MINERALS **TREE-SHAPED MINERAL** a mineral that crystallizes in the shape of a tree or branch [Early 18thC. Directly or via French from Greek *dendritēs* "of a tree," from *dendron* "tree."] —**den·drit·ic** /den dríttik/ *adj.* —**den·drit·i·cal** /-tik'l/ *adj.* —**den·drit·i·cal·ly** /-əlee/ *adv.*

dendro- *prefix.* tree, treelike ○ *dendrology* ○ *dendrite* [From Greek *dendron.* Ultimately from an Indo-European base meaning "to be solid," which is also the ancestor of English *tree, deodar,* and *druid.*]

den·dro·chro·nol·o·gy /dèndrōkrə nóllajee/ *n.* the study of the annual growth rings in trees or wooden objects, especially as a way of dating wooden remains or determining past climatic conditions —**den·dro·chron·o·log·i·cal** /dèndrō kronnə lójjik'l/ *adj.* —**den·dro·chro·nol·o·gist** /dèndrōkrə nóllójist/ *n.*

den·dro·gram /déndrə gràm/ *n.* a diagram showing the relationships of items arranged like the branches of a tree

den·droid /dén dròyd/, **den·droid·al** /den dróyd'l/ *adj.* **1. WITH STEM RESEMBLING TREE TRUNK** used to describe plants with an erect main stem like a tree trunk **2. MULTIBRANCHED** used to describe plants with many branches, like a tree **3. RESEMBLING A TREE** generally resembling a tree in shape or form

den·drol·o·gy /den drólləjee/ *n.* the study of trees and other woody plants —**den·dro·log·ic** /dèndrə lójjik/ *adj.* —**den·dro·log·i·cal** /-jik'l/ *adj.* —**den·drol·o·gist** /den drólləjist/ *n.* —**den·drol·o·gous** *adj.*

den·dron /dén dròn/ *n.* = **dendrite** *n.* 1 (*dated*) [Late 19thC. Coined from DENDRITE + -ON.]

Dene /day náy/ *npl.* the First Nations people of the Northwest Territories in Canada [Late 19thC. Via Canadian French from Athabaskan.]

den·e·ga·tion /dènni gáysh'n/ *n.* a refusal to accede to or grant something that is asked for (*archaic*) [15thC. Via French *dénégation* from the late Latin stem *denegation-,* from *negare* (see NEGATE).]

de·ner·vate /dee núr vàyt/ (**-vat·ed, -vat·ing, -vates**) *vt.* to deprive an organ or body part of nerves, either by cutting them or by blocking them with drugs, e.g., to control pain

de·ner·va·tion /deenər váysh'n/ *n.* interruption in nerve supply to muscles or skin, with loss of motion and sensation, caused by surgical or drug treatment, e.g., to control pain

De·neuve /də nŏŏv, də nőv/, **Catherine** (*b.* 1943) French movie actor. Her movies include *Repulsion* (1965) and *Belle de Jour* (1967). Born **Catherine Dorléac**

D.Eng. *abbr.* Doctor of Engineering

den·gue /déng gee, déng gày/, **den·gue fe·ver** *n.* a tropical disease caused by a virus that is transmitted by mosquitoes and marked by high fever, rash, headache, and severe muscle and joint pains [Early 19thC. From West Indian Spanish, of uncertain origin: perhaps from, ultimately, Kiswahili.]

Popperfoto

Deng Xiaoping

Deng Xiao·ping /dèng show píng, dùng-/ (1904–97) Chinese Communist leader. Despite a turbulent relationship with the Communist Party, he became its leader in 1978. He introduced reforms that led to greater economic freedom in China.

de·ni·a·ble /di nī əb'l/ *adj.* referring to something that can be disclaimed or declared untrue —**de·ni·a·bil·i·ty** /di nī ə bíllətee/ *n.* —**de·ni·a·bly** /di nī əblee/ *adv.*

de·ni·al /di nī əl/ *n.* **1. DISAVOWAL** a statement saying that something is not true or not correct **2. REFUSAL TO GRANT SOMETHING** a refusal to allow people to have something that they want or that they believe they have a right to **3. REFUSAL TO ACKNOWLEDGE EXISTENCE OF SOMETHING** an inability or a refusal to admit that something exists **4.** PSYCHOL **REFUSAL TO FACE UNPLEASANT FACTS** a state of mind marked by a refusal or an inability to recognize and deal with a serious personal problem ○ *She's in denial.* **5.** LAW **OPPOSITION TO AN ALLEGATION** in a court of law, saying that you did not do something that you are accused of

de·ni·er[1] /dénnyər/ *n.* **1. MEASURE OF FIBER FINENESS** a unit of fineness of silk and some artificial fibers, based on a mass of one gram per 9,000 meters of yarn **2. OLD SILVER COIN** a small silver coin used in several European countries between the 8th and 18th centuries [15thC. Via Old French from Latin *denarius* (see DENARIUS).]

de·ni·er[2] /di nīr/ *n.* somebody who asserts that something did not happen or does not exist

den·i·grate /dénni gràyt/ (**-grat·ed, -grat·ing, -grates**) *vt.* **1. DEFAME** to defame somebody's character or reputation **2. DISPARAGE AND BELITTLE** to disparage or criticize somebody or something, to lower somebody's self-esteem or to make something seem unimportant **3. CRITICIZE HARSHLY** to criticize something harshly, while attempting to make others think it has no importance [15thC. From Latin *denigrat-,* the past participle of stem *denigrare,* literally "to blacken completely," from *niger* "black."] —**den·i·gra·tion** /dènni gráysh'n/ *n.* —**den·i·gra·tor** /dénni gràytər/ *n.*

WORD KEY: USAGE

Denigrate In its best-established sense ***denigrate*** means "ruin a reputation" or "defame." However, it is now often found in sentences like *I don't mean to denigrate the problem,* where its meaning is more like "belittle". In this, it is following in the footsteps of *deprecate,* whose traditional meaning is "express disapproval of", but which, particularly in *self-deprecating,* has taken on the additional sense of "belittle".

den·im /dénnim/ *n.* **JEANS FABRIC** a hard-wearing woven cotton cloth that is typically used to make jeans ■ **den·ims** *npl.* **DENIM GARMENTS** clothes made of denim, especially jeans, jackets, shirts, or skirts [Late 17thC. From French *(serge) de Nîmes,* literally "(serge) of Nîmes," the town in France where it was primarily manufactured.]

De Ni·ro /də neér ō/, **Robert** (*b.* 1943) U.S. actor. He has won Academy Awards for *The Godfather II* (1974) and *Raging Bull* (1980).

Den·i·son /dénniss'n/ city in northeastern Texas, near the Red River and the Texas-Oklahoma border, north of Dallas. Population: 22,136 (1996).

den·i·trate /dee nī tràyt/ (**-trat·ed, -trat·ing, -trates**) *vti.* to remove a nitro or nitrate group, nitrogen compound, or nitrous acid from a chemical compound, or lose such components —**de·ni·tra·tion** /dèe nī tráysh'n/ *n.*

de·ni·tri·fy /dee nītrə fì/ (**-fied, -fy·ing, -fies**) *vt.* **1.** REMOVE NITROGEN FROM SUBSTANCE to remove nitrogen or a nitrogen compound from a substance **2.** CONVERT NITRATES to convert nitrates into nitrites, ammonia, and nitrogen —**de·ni·tri·fi·ca·tion** /dee nītrəfi káysh'n/ *n.*

den·i·zen /dénnizən/ *n.* **1.** RESIDENT OF PLACE somebody who lives in a particular country or area **2.** HABITUAL VISITOR TO PLACE a habitual visitor to a place ○ *denizens of cyberspace chat rooms* **3.** NONNATIVE PLANT OR ANIMAL a nonnative plant or animal that grows or lives in an area **4.** FOREIGNER WITH RIGHTS OF RESIDENCE somebody who has taken up permanent residence in a foreign country and is given some rights there [15thC. From Anglo-Norman *deinzein*, from Old French *deinz* "inside," from Latin *de intus*, literally "from inside."]

Denmark

Den·mark /dén maàrk/ smallest country in Scandinavia, comprising the Jutland peninsula and about 480 islands. Language: Danish. Currency: krone. Capital: Copenhagen. Population: 5,305,048 (1997). Area: 16,639 sq. mi./43,094 sq. km. Official name **Kingdom of Denmark**

den moth·er *n.* **1.** WOMAN CUB SCOUT LEADER a woman who is in charge of a den of Cub Scouts **2.** WOMAN IN CHARGE OF GROUP a woman who has responsibility for a group of people

Den·nis /dénniss/ resort town in southeastern Massachusetts, on the north shore of Cape Cod on Cape Cod Bay, northeast of Yarmouth. Population: 14,423 (1996).

denom. *abbr.* RELIG denomination

de·nom·i·nal /di nómmən'l/ *adj.* used to describe parts of speech that are formed from or have the same form as a noun, e.g., the verb "to butter"

de·nom·i·nate /di nómmə nàyt/ (**-nat·ed, -nat·ing, -nates**) *vt.* **1.** EXPRESS IN MONETARY UNITS to define something in terms of a specific unit of currency **2.** GIVE NAME TO to give something a particular name or description (*formal*) [Mid-16thC. From Latin *denominat-*, the past participle stem of *denominare*, literally "to name completely," from *nominare* "to name."] —**de·nom·i·na·ble** /di nómmənəb'l/ *adj.*

de·nom·i·na·tion /di nòmmə náysh'n/ *n.* **1.** RELIG RELIGIOUS GROUPING a religious grouping within a faith, e.g., a section of the Christian church that has specific beliefs and practices that differ from those of other groupings and its own system of organization **2.** UNIT OF MONETARY VALUE a unit of value, especially monetary value **3.** NAME OR DESIGNATION a name or designation given to a class, group, or type

de·nom·i·na·tion·al /di nòmmə náyshən'l, -shnəl/ *adj.* relating to a religious grouping within a faith —**de·nom·i·na·tion·al·ly** *adv.*

de·nom·i·na·tive /di nómmə nàytiv, di nómmənətiv/ *adj.* denominal (*dated*) —**de·nom·i·na·tive** *n.* —**de·nom·i·na·tive·ly** *adv.*

de·nom·i·na·tor /di nómmə nàytər/ *n.* **1.** MATH NUMBER BELOW LINE IN FRACTION the number below the line in a fraction, which indicates the number of parts making up the whole **2.** COMMON CHARACTERISTIC something held in common **3.** AVERAGE LEVEL an average standard, degree, or level of quality or taste

Den·on·ville /də nawN veél/, **Jacques-René de Brisay, Marquis de** (1642–1710) French-born Canadian colonial administrator. He was Governor-General of New France from 1685 to 1689, leading expeditions against the Iroquois in 1687 and 1689.

de·no·ta·tion /dèenō táysh'n/ *n.* **1.** LING BASIC MEANING the most specific or literal meaning of a word, as opposed to its figurative senses or connotations **2.** LOGIC REFERENCE OF TERM the reference of a term in logic

de·no·ta·tive /deé nō tàytiv, di nṓtətiv/ *adj.* designating or showing something —**de·no·ta·tive·ly** *adv.*

de·note /di nṓt/ (**-not·ed, -not·ing, -notes**) *vt.* **1.** MEAN to have something as a specified meaning ○ *The name actually denotes "lightning bolt" in Italian.* **2.** REFER TO to designate or refer to somebody or something specified ○ *The term "caregiver" will be used to denote those providing unpaid family care.* **3.** SIGNIFY to be a sign or representation of something ○ *The specks of light denote planets.* [Late 16thC. Via French *dénoter* from Latin *denotare* "to mark completely," from *notare* "to mark" (see NOTATION).] —**de·no·tive** *adj.*

de·noue·ment /dàynoo maáN/ (*plural* **-ments**) *n.* a final part in which everything is made clear and no questions or surprises remain (*formal*) [Mid-18thC. From French, from *dénouer* "to untie," from *nouer* "to tie," from, ultimately, Latin *nodus* "knot" (see NODE).]

de·nounce /di nówns/ (**-nounced, -nounc·ing, -nounc·es**) *vt.* **1.** CRITICIZE PUBLICLY AND HARSHLY to express harsh criticism or condemnation of something or somebody, usually in public **2.** ACCUSE PUBLICLY to accuse somebody publicly of something such as disloyalty, or inform against somebody **3.** ANNOUNCE TERMINATION OF to make a formal announcement of the end of a treaty or other agreement (*formal*) [14thC. Via Old French *denoncier* from Latin *denuntiare*, from *nuntiare* "to proclaim, announce," from *nuntius* "messenger," of uncertain origin.] —**de·nounce·ment** *n.* —**de·nounc·er** *n.*

WORD KEY: SYNONYMS

See Synonyms at ***disapprove***.

de nov·o /də nṓ vō, day-/ *adv.* LAW anew, afresh, or over again from the beginning ○ *Having found the lower court's analysis wrong, the appellate court undertook a review de novo.* [Mid-16thC. From Latin, literally "from new."]

Den·pa·sar /den paá saàr/ city in Indonesia and capital of the island province of Bali, located near Bali's southernmost point. Population: 367,000 (1993).

dense /dens/ (**dens·er, dens·est**) *adj.* **1.** TIGHTLY PACKED so close together that there is not much sense of room or open space **2.** VERY THICK so thick that it is difficult or impossible to see through **3.** SLOW TO LEARN OR UNDERSTAND lacking the ability to learn and understand quickly (*disapproving*) **4.** HARD TO PENETRATE INTELLECTUALLY so complex and intricate that it is difficult to assimilate and understand **5.** PHYS WITH HIGH MASS with a relatively high mass per unit volume [15thC. Directly or via French from Latin *densus* "thick."] —**dense·ly** *adv.* —**dense·ness** *n.*

den·sim·e·ter /den símmətər/ *n.* an instrument that measures density or specific gravity [Mid-19thC. Coined from Latin *densus* "dense" + -METER.] —**den·si·met·ric** /dènsi méttrik/ *adj.* —**den·sim·e·try** /den símmətree/ *n.*

den·si·tom·e·ter /dènsi tómmətər/ *n.* **1.** DEVICE MEASURING OPTICAL DENSITY an instrument for measuring optical density, e.g., that of a photographic negative **2.** = **densimeter** [Early 20thC. Coined from DENSITY + -METER.] —**den·sit·o·met·ric** /dènsitə méttrik/ *adj.* —**den·si·tom·e·try** /-tómmətree/ *n.*

den·si·ty /dénsitee/ (*plural* **-ties**) *n.* **1.** HOW FULL AN AREA IS concentration of people or things within an area in relation to its size **2.** PHYS RELATIVE MASS a measure of a quantity such as mass or electric charge per unit volume. Symbol **d 3.** ELEC = **charge density 4.** ELEC = **current density**

den·si·ty func·tion *n.* STATS = **probability density function** *n.* 2

dent /dent/ *v.* (**dent·ed, dent·ing, dents**) **1.** *vti.* MAKE DEPRESSION BY HITTING to make a shallow depression in the surface of something by hitting it or putting pressure on it **2.** *vt.* HARM SOMETHING ABSTRACT to do nonphysical, usually minor, damage to something ○ *His reputation was somewhat dented.* ■ *n.* **1.** BENT AREA IN SOMETHING a shallow depression in the surface of something that is made by hitting it or putting pressure on it **2.** ADVANCE progress in reaching a goal (*informal*) ○ *a dent in the team's lead* **3.** REDUCTION a reduction in an amount of something such as resources (*informal*) ○ *a dent in the budget* **4.** NONPHYSICAL DAMAGE nonphysical, usually minor, damage, e.g., to somebody's reputation [13thC. Variant of DINT "stroke, blow"; hence, "indentation made by blow."]

dent. *abbr.* **1.** dental **2.** dentistry

dent- *prefix.* = **denti-** (*used before vowels*)

den·tal /dént'l/ *adj.* **1.** OF DENTISTRY relating to or used in dentistry **2.** OF TEETH relating or belonging to the teeth **3.** DENT NEAR TOOTH affecting or located in or near a tooth ○ *dental abscess* **4.** PHON MADE BY TONGUE AND TEETH used to describe a consonant that is formed by placing the tongue against the back of the top front teeth [Late 16thC. From late Latin *dentalis*, from the Latin stem *dent-* "tooth" (see DENTIST).]

den·tal car·ies *n.* decay of teeth that is caused by the action of acid-forming bacteria and improper dental care

den·tal floss *n.* thread that is used to remove food and plaque from between the teeth

den·tal hy·giene *n.* the care people take of their teeth and gums to prevent tooth and gum diseases

den·tal hy·gien·ist *n.* somebody licensed to provide certain kinds of dental care under the supervision of a dentist, e.g., cleaning and scaling teeth and taking X-rays

den·tal sur·geon *n.* a dentist who is trained and licensed to practice oral surgery such as tooth extractions, and who is usually licensed to use general anesthesia

den·tal tech·ni·cian *n.* somebody trained to make dental appliances such as caps, dentures, and bridges

den·tate /dén tàyt/ *adj.* edged with pointed or tooth-shaped projections [15thC. From Latin *dentatus*, from the stem *dent-* "tooth" (see DENTIST).] —**den·tate·ly** *adv.*

den·ta·tion /den táysh'n/ *n.* a pointed or tooth-shaped projection on something such as a leaf

dent corn *n.* a type of corn with kernels that contain soft starch at the tip and are indented in this area when mature. Dent corn is the most widely grown type in the U.S. Latin name: *Zea mays.* ◊ **flint corn**

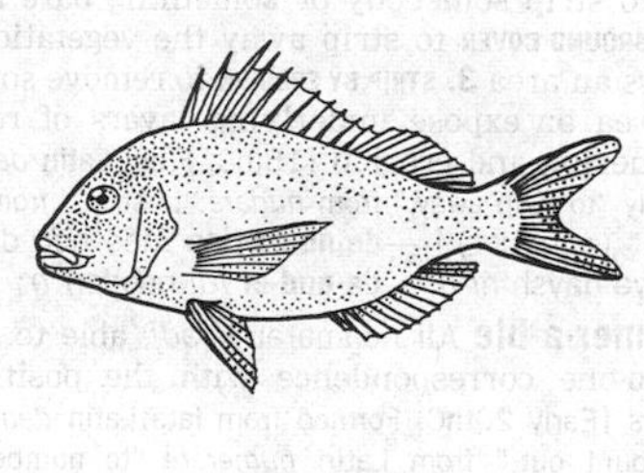

Dentex

den·tex /dén tèks/ (*plural* **-tex·es** *or* **-tex**) *n.* a red game fish, about 4 ft./1.2 m long, that is found in seas off the Cape of Good Hope, South Africa. Latin name: *Dentex rupestris.* [Mid-19thC. Via modern Latin from Latin, name of a type of fish.]

denti- *prefix.* tooth, dental ○ *dentiform* [From Latin *dent-*, the stem of *dens*. Ultimately from an Indo-European word that is also the ancestor of English *tooth, tusk, indent,* and *dandelion*.]

den·ti·cle /déntik'l/ *n.* **1.** BIOL SMALL TOOTH-SHAPED PART a small tooth or tooth-shaped projection **2.** ZOOL SMALL FISH SCALE a small tooth-shaped scale with a projecting spine, typical of cartilaginous fish [15thC. From Latin *denticulus*, literally "small tooth," from the stem *dent-* "tooth" (see DENTIST).] —**den·tic·u·lar** /den tíkyələr/ *adj.*

den·tic·u·late /den tíkyə làyt/ *adj.* **1.** WITH FINE TOOTH-SHAPED PROJECTIONS with fine teeth or pointed projections **2.** ARCHIT DECORATED WITH TOOTH-SHAPED BLOCKS decorated with small rectangular blocks (**dentils**) that look like a row of teeth [Mid-17thC. From Latin *denticulatus*, from *denticulus* (see DENTICLE).] —**den·tic·u·late·ly** *adv.*

den·ti·form /déntə fàwrm/ *adj.* shaped like a tooth

den·ti·frice /déntə frìss/ *n.* a paste or similar compound for cleaning teeth [15thC. Via French from Latin *dentifricium*, from the stem *dent-* "tooth" (see DENTIST) + *fricare* "to rub."]

den·til /dént'l, dén tìl/ *n.* ARCHIT a rectangular block that is arranged with others to look like a row of teeth, used as a form of architectural decoration [Late 16thC. Via either Italian *dentello* or obsolete French *dentille*, literally "small tooth," from, ultimately, the Latin stem *dent-* "tooth" (see DENTIST).]

den·ti·lin·gual /dènti líng gwəl/ *adj.* pronounced or articulated with the tongue touching the teeth on the top jaw

den·tine /dén teen/, **den·tin** /-tin/ *n.* the part of a tooth that is hard, contains calcium, lies underneath the enamel, and surrounds the pulp and root canals [Mid-19thC. Coined from the Latin stem *dent-* "tooth" (see DENTIST) + -INE.] —**den·tin·al** /den téen'l, déntən'l/ *adj.*

den·tist /déntist/ *n.* somebody trained and licensed to practice general dentistry or a specialty such as orthodontics or dental surgery [Mid-18thC. From French *dentiste*, from *dent* "tooth," from the Latin stem *dent-*. Ultimately from an Indo-European word that is also the ancestor of English *tooth*.]

den·tist·ry /déntistree/ *n.* the medical science concerned with the prevention and treatment of tooth and gum disorders and diseases, requiring graduation from dental school and appropriate licensing

den·ti·tion /den tísh'n/ *n.* **1.** ARRAY OF TEETH the type, number, and arrangement of a set of teeth **2.** DEVELOPING OF TEETH the process of developing and cutting new teeth [Late 16thC. From the Latin stem *dent-* "tooth" (see DENTIST).]

den·ture /dénchər/ *n.* a partial or complete set of artificial teeth for the upper or lower jaw, usually attached to a plate [Late 19thC. From French, from *dent* "tooth" (see DENTIST).]

den·tur·ist *n.* a dental technician who makes and fits dentures that are sold directly to the public rather than through a dentist

de·nu·cle·ar·ize /dee nóoklee ə rìz/ (**-ized, -iz·ing, -iz·es**) *vt.* to remove, ban, or eliminate nuclear weapons or nuclear power sources from a place, industry, or organization —**de·nu·cle·ar·i·za·tion** /dee nóoklee əri záysh'n/ *n.*

de·nude /di nóod/ (**-nud·ed, -nud·ing, -nudes**) *vt.* **1.** STRIP BARE to strip somebody or something bare **2.** STRIP AWAY GROUND COVER to strip away the vegetation that covers an area **3.** STRIP BY EROSION to remove soil from an area or expose underlying layers of rock by weathering and erosion [15thC. From Latin *denudare*, literally "to strip away," from *nudare* "to strip," from *nudus* "nude" (see NUDE).] —**de·nu·da·tion** /dee noo dáysh'n, dènnyə dáysh'n/ *n.* —**de·nud·er** /di nóodər/ *n.*

de·nu·mer·a·ble /di nóomərəb'l/ *adj.* able to form a one-to-one correspondence with the positive integers [Early 20thC. Formed from late Latin *denumerare* "to count out," from Latin *numerare* "to number" (see NUMERATION).] —**de·nu·mer·a·bil·i·ty** /di nòomərə bíllətee/ *n.* —**de·nu·mer·a·bly** /di nóomərəblee/ *adv.*

de·nun·ci·ate /di núnsee àyt/ (**-at·ed, -at·ing, -ates**) *vt.* to accuse or condemn somebody or something publicly (*formal*) [Late 16thC. From the medieval Latin stem *denunciat-*, from, ultimately, Latin *denuntiare* "to denounce" (see DENOUNCE).]

de·nun·ci·a·tion /di nùnsee áysh'n/ *n.* a public accusation or condemnation of something or somebody

Den·ver /dénvər/ capital city and commercial center of the state of Colorado, in the Rocky Mountains. Population: 467,610 (1990).

Den·ver, John (1943–97) U.S. country and pop singer. He is known for the songs *Rocky Mountain High* (1973) and *Annie's Song* (1974).

Den·ver boot *n.* a locking device fastened to one of the wheels of a vehicle parked illegally or on private property so that it cannot be moved until a fine or other charge has been paid [Named for DENVER, one of the first cities to adopt the boot]

de·ny /di nī/ (**-nied, -ny·ing, -nies**) *v.* **1.** *vt.* SAY SOMETHING IS NOT TRUE to declare that something is not true or not the case **2.** *vt.* REFUSE to refuse something to somebody **3.** *vt.* REFUSE TO ACKNOWLEDGE to refuse to acknowledge somebody **4.** *vr.* NOT ALLOW YOURSELF to refuse to gratify your needs or desires [13thC. Via Old French *deneier* from Latin *denegare*, literally "to negate completely," from *negare* "to deny."]

de·o·dar /dée ə daar/ (*plural* **-dars** *or* **-dar**) *n.* **1.** HIMALAYAN CEDAR TREE a Himalayan cedar with dark blue-green leaves and drooping branches, that is highly valued as a timber tree in India. Latin name: *Cedrus deodara*. **2.** DEODAR WOOD the hard sweet-smelling wood of the deodar [Early 19thC. Via Hindi *deodār* from Sanskrit *devadāru*, literally "divine wood" (perhaps because of its durability).]

de·o·dor·ant /dee ṓdərənt/ *n.* **1.** BODY ODOR MASK a spray, cream, or liquid that people apply under their arms to mask body odor **2.** SUBSTANCE TO DISGUISE SMELLS a substance that is used to disguise unpleasant smells

de·o·dor·ize /dee ṓdə rìz/ (**-ized, -iz·ing, -iz·es**) *vt.* to disguise or eliminate unpleasant smells —**de·o·dor·i·za·tion** /dee ṑdəri záysh'n/ *n.* —**de·o·dor·iz·er** /dee ṓdə rìzər/ *n.*

De·o gra·tias /dày ō graatee əss/ *interj.* thanks be to God, used in various Christian choral and liturgical contexts [From Latin, literally "thanks to God"]

de·on·tic /dee óntik/ *adj.* relating to the concept of moral obligation [Mid-19thC. Formed from Greek *deont-*, the present participle stem of *dein* "to be wanting, be needful."]

de·on·to·log·i·cal /dee òntə lójjik'l/ *adj.* relating to philosophical theories that state that the moral content of an action is not wholly dependent on its consequences —**de·on·to·log·i·cal·ly** *adv.*

de·on·tol·o·gy /dèe on tólləjee/ *n.* the study of what is obligatory, permissible, right, or wrong, in moral terms [Early 19thC. Coined from Greek *deont-*, the present participle stem of *dein* "to be wanting, be needful" + -LOGY.] —**de·on·tol·o·gist** *n.*

de·or·bit /dee áwrbit/ (**-bit·ed, -bit·ing, -bits**) *vti.* to put something out of orbit or go out of orbit

De·o vo·len·te /dày ō və léntee, dày ō vō lén tày/ *interj.* God willing [From Latin, "God willing"]

de·ox·i·dize /dee óksi dìz/ (**-dized, -diz·ing, -diz·es**) *vt.* **1.** REMOVE OXYGEN FROM MOLECULE to remove the oxygen from a compound or molecule **2.** = **reduce** —**de·ox·i·di·za·tion** /dee òksidi záysh'n/ *n.* —**de·ox·i·diz·er** /dee óksi dìzər/ *n.*

deoxy- *prefix.* containing less oxygen than a related compound ○ *deoxyribose* [From DE- + OXY-]

de·ox·y·gen·ate /dee óksijə nàyt/ (**-at·ed, -at·ing, -ates**) *vt.* to remove dissolved oxygen from a substance —**de·ox·y·gen·a·tion** /dee òksəjə náysh'n/ *n.*

de·ox·y·gen·ize /dee óksijə nìz/ (**-ized, -iz·ing, -iz·es**) *vt.* = **deoxygenate**

de·ox·y·ri·bo·nu·cle·ase /dee òksi rìbō nóoklee àyss, -àyz/ *n.* full form of **DNAase** [Mid-20thC. Formed from DEOXYRIBONUCLEIC ACID.]

de·ox·y·ri·bo·nu·cle·ic ac·id /dee oksi rìbō noo klée ik-/ *n.* full form of **DNA** [Mid-20thC. Coined from DEOXYRIBOSE + NUCLEIC.]

de·ox·y·ri·bo·nu·cle·o·tide /dee òksi rìbō nóoklee ə tìd/ *n.* a nucleotide composed of deoxyribose, a phosphate group and a base, that is a component of DNA [Mid-20thC. Coined from DEOXYRIBOSE + NUCLEOTIDE.]

de·ox·y·ri·bose /dee òksi rí bōss/ *n.* a five-carbon simple sugar that is a structural component of DNA [Mid-20thC. Coined from *deoxy-* "having fewer oxygen atoms" (from DE- + OXY-) + RIBOSE.]

DEP *abbr.* Department of Environmental Protection

dep. *abbr.* **1.** department **2.** departs **3.** departure **4.** GRAM deponent **5.** deposed **6.** deposit **7.** depot **8. dep., Dep.** deputy

De·par·dieu /də paar djṓ/, **Gérard** (*b.* 1948) French actor. His films include *The Last Metro* (1980), *Cyrano de Bergerac* (1990), and *Green Card* (1990).

de·part /di paart/ (**-part·ed, -part·ing, -parts**) *v.* **1.** *vi.* SET OFF to leave, especially at the beginning of a journey **2.** *vt.* LEAVE PLACE to leave from a place **3.** *vi.* CHANGE to change or vary from a pattern **4.** *vt.* DIE to end your life (*formal*) ○ *depart this life* [13thC. From French *départir* "to end your life," from, ultimately, Latin *partire* "to divide into parts" (the original sense of English *depart*), from *pars* "part."]

de·part·ed /di paartəd/ *adj.* DEAD having died (*formal or literary*) ■ *n.* (*plural* **-ed**) DEAD PERSON somebody who has died especially recently (*formal or literary*)

WORD KEY: SYNONYMS

See Synonyms at *dead*.

de·part·ment /di paartmənt/ *n.* **1.** SECTION OF ORGANIZATION a specialized section of a large organization such as a university or store **2.** POL PART OF GOVERNMENT a major division of government that is responsible for dealing with a particular area of policy or administration **3.** SPECIALTY somebody's specialty or particular area of responsibility (*informal*) **4.** CATEGORY a specified quantifiable or qualifiable category (*informal*) **5.** POL FRENCH DISTRICT an administrative district in France

de·part·men·tal /di paart mént'l/ *adj.* relating to or for a department in a government or an organization —**de·part·men·tal·ly** *adv.*

de·part·men·tal·ism /di paart mént'l ìzzəm/ *n.* **1.** POLICY OF MAKING DEPARTMENTS the division of organizations into departments, particularly as a deliberate policy that is taken to excess **2.** TENDENCY TO CONSIDER ONLY OWN DEPARTMENT the tendency of government departments to follow their own interests

de·part·men·tal·ize /di paart mént'l ìz/ (**-ized, -iz·ing, -iz·es**) *vt.* to divide an organization into departments, especially as a policy or to an excessive extent —**de·part·men·tal·i·za·tion** /di paart mént'li záysh'n/ *n.*

de·part·ment store *n.* a large store that sells a wide range of goods in separate departments

de·par·ture /di paarchər/ *n.* **1.** SETTING OFF the action of setting off on a journey **2.** CHANGE FROM USUAL a change from the usual or expected way **3.** COURSE a course of action or the beginning of one **4.** SAILING EAST OR WEST TRAVEL the distance traveled due east or west by a ship

de·par·ture lounge *n.* an area where departing passengers can wait until their aircraft or other transport is ready

de·pas·ture /di páschər/ (**-tured, -tur·ing, -tures**) *vt.* to allow animals to graze on a particular area

de·pau·pe·rate /di páwpə ràyt/ *adj.* **1.** NOT FULLY GROWN less than fully grown or developed **2.** LACKING SPECIES VARIETY lacking or depleted in the variety of plant or animal species [Mid-19thC. From medieval Latin *depauperatus*, the past participle of *depauperare* "to impoverish," from Latin *pauper* (see PAUPER).] —**de·pau·pe·ra·tion** /di pàwpə ráysh'n/ *n.*

de·pend /di pénd/ (**-pend·ed, -pend·ing, -pends**) *vi.* **1.** BE CONTINGENT to be affected or decided by other factors **2.** VARY to vary according to the circumstances **3.** HANG DOWN to hang down or be suspended from something (*archaic*) [15thC. Via French *dépendre* from Latin *dependere*, literally "to hang down," from *pendere* "to hang."]

depend on, de·pend up·on *vt.* **1.** REQUIRE to need something in order to exist or survive **2.** RELY ON to have complete confidence in somebody or something

de·pend·a·ble /di péndəb'l/ *adj.* able to be trusted to act in the way required or expected —**de·pend·a·bil·i·ty** /di pèndə bíllətee/ *n.*

de·pend·a·bly /di péndəblee/ *adv.* **1.** AS EXPECTED used to indicate that the way somebody or something is behaving as expected **2.** RELIABLY in a way that inspires confidence that whatever is required or promised will be done

de·pend·ance *n.* = **dependence**

de·pend·an·cy *n.* = **dependency**

de·pend·ant *n. U.K.* = **dependent**

de·pend·ence /di péndəns/, **de·pend·ance** *n.* **1.** NEED FOR SOMETHING a need for something or somebody to be available in order to exist or survive ○ *financial dependence* ○ *dependence on public transport* **2.** PHYSICAL OR PSYCHOLOGICAL NEED a physical or psychological need to use a drug or other substance regularly, despite the fact that it is likely to have a damaging effect

de·pend·en·cy /di péndənsee/ (*plural* **-cies**), **de·pend·an·cy** (*plural* **-cies**) *n.* **1.** POL TERRITORY a country or state that belongs to another non-adjacent country **2.** ARCHIT LESSER BUILDING a building near to and associated with a larger main building **3.** = **dependence**

de·pend·en·cy the·o·ry *n.* POL a theory of international relations that major states influence other states though their economic power

de·pend·ent /di péndənt/ *n.* FAMILY MEMBER a family member or other person who is supported financially by another, especially one living in the same house ■ *adj.* **1.** PSYCHOL NEEDING SOMETHING needing to use something, especially a drug (*usually used in combination*) **2.** NOT SELF-RELIANT not able to live without support from other people, especially financial support from a parent or child **3.** CONTINGENT affected or decided by stated factors or circumstances (*often used in combination*) ○ *age-dependent* **4.** SUSPENDED hanging down (*archaic or literary*) —**de·pend·ent·ly** *adv.*

de·pend·ent clause *n.* = **subordinate clause**

de·pend·ent var·i·a·ble *n.* an element in a mathematical expression that changes its value according to the value of other elements present

de·per·son·al·i·za·tion /di pùrsən'li záysh'n, -snəli-/ *n.* **1.** MAKING IMPERSONAL a process or act of depersonalizing somebody or something **2.** PSYCHOL ALIENATED STATE a psychological state in which somebody loses a sense of personal identity and of the reality of the world

de·per·son·al·ize /di púrsən'l ìz, -snə-/ (**-ized, -iz·ing, -iz·es**) *vt.* **1.** MAKE IMPERSONAL to take away or omit personal qualities from somebody or something **2.** PSYCHOL ALIENATE SOMEBODY to make somebody lose a sense of personal identity and of the reality of the world

de·pict /di píkt/ (**-pict·ed, -pict·ing, -picts**) *vt.* **1.** PORTRAY to describe or portray something in words **2.** ARTS SHOW IN A PICTURE to show something in a picture, painting, or sculpture [15thC. From Latin *depict-*, the past participle stem of *depingere* "to portray," from *pingere* "to paint."] —**de·pict·er** *n.* —**de·pic·tive** *adj.*

de·pic·tion /di píkshən/ *n.* a picture, description, or other representation of something

de·pic·ture /di píkchər/ (**-tured, -tur·ing, -tures**) *vt.* to depict (*archaic*) [Late 16thC. Formed from DE- + PICTURE.]

de·pig·men·ta·tion /dee pìgmən táysh'n/ *n.* partial or total absence of the body coloring pigment melanin, especially in the skin, hair, and eyes

dep·i·late /déppi làyt/ (**-lat·ed, -lat·ing, -lates**) *vti.* to remove hair from the body, usually from the legs or underarms [Mid-16thC. From Latin *depilare*, from *pilus* "hair."] —**dep·i·la·tor** *n.*

dep·i·la·tion /dèppi láysh'n/ *n.* the removal of hair, including its roots, from the body or from hides or leather

de·pil·a·to·ry /di píllə tàwree/ *adj.* HAIR-REMOVING used for removing hair from the body ■ *n.* (*plural* **-ries**) HAIR REMOVER an agent or substance that can be used to remove hair from the body

de·plane /dee pláyn/ (**-planed, -plan·ing, -planes**) *vi.* to disembark from an airplane

de·plete /di pleét/ (**-plet·ed, -plet·ing, -pletes**) *vt.* **1.** REDUCE to use up or reduce something, e.g., supplies, resources, or energy **2.** EMPTY to empty something [Early 19thC. From Latin *deplet-*, the past participle stem of *deplere* "to empty out," literally "to un-fill," from *plere* "to fill."] —**de·plet·a·ble** *adj.* —**de·ple·tion** *n.* —**de·ple·tive** *adj.*

de·plet·ed u·ra·ni·um *n.* uranium containing an abnormally low amount of the U-235 isotope, usually as a result of having been used as fuel in a nuclear reactor

de·ple·tion lay·er *n.* a layer in a semiconductor that has few charge carriers transporting electric charge between zones of different conductivity

de·plor·a·ble /di pláwrəb'l/ *adj.* **1.** EXTREMELY UNACCEPTABLE worthy of severe condemnation **2.** WRETCHED wretched because of neglect, poverty, or other misfortune —**de·plor·a·bil·i·ty** /di plàwrə bíllətee/ *n.* —**de·plor·a·ble·ness** /di pláwrəb'lnəss/ *n.* —**de·plor·a·bly** /-blee/ *adv.*

de·plore /di pláwr/ (**-plored, -plor·ing, -plores**) *vt.* **1.** FIND EXTREMELY UNACCEPTABLE to condemn something or disapprove of it strongly **2.** REGRET to regret or feel grief about something [Mid-16thC. Via French *déplorer* or Italian *deplorare* from Latin *deplorare* "to lament, regret," from *plorare* "to wail" (source also of English *implore*).] —**de·plor·er** *n.* —**de·plor·ing·ly** *adv.*

WORD KEY: SYNONYMS

See Synonyms at ***disapprove***.

de·ploy /di plóy/ (**-ployed, -ploy·ing, -ploys**) *v.* **1.** *vti.* MIL READY MILITARY FORCE to position troops, weapons, or resources in a specific area in readiness for action, or take up position in this way **2.** *vt.* USE to put something to use [15thC. Via French *déployer* from Latin *displicare*, literally "to unfold," from *plicare* (see PLY[2]).] —**de·ploy·a·ble** *adj.* —**de·ploy·er** *n.*

de·ploy·ment /di plóymənt/ *n.* the act of deploying troops, resources, or equipment

de·plume /dee plóom/ (**-plumed, -plum·ing, -plumes**) *vt.* to remove the feathers from a bird [15thC. Via French *déplumer* from medieval Latin *deplumare*, from Latin *pluma* (see PLUME).] —**de·plu·ma·tion** /dèe ploo máysh'n/ *n.*

de·po·lar·ize /dee pṓlə rìz/ (**-ized, -iz·ing, -iz·es**) *vti.* to remove or lose polarization or polarity —**de·po·lar·i·za·tion** /dee pṑləri záysh'n/ *n.* —**de·po·lar·iz·er** /dee pṓlə rìzər/ *n.*

de·po·lit·i·cize /dèepə lítti sìz/ (**-cized, -ciz·ing, -ciz·es**) *vt.* to remove the political aspect of something —**de·po·lit·i·ci·za·tion** /dèepə littissi záysh'n/ *n.*

de·pol·lu·tion /dèepə lóosh'n/ *n.* the removal of pollution from something —**de·pol·lute** *vt.*

de·pol·y·mer·ize /dee póllәmə rìz/ (**-ized, -iz·ing, -iz·es**) *vti.* to break down a polymer into simpler monomers or to undergo this process —**de·pol·y·mer·i·za·tion** /dee pòllәməri záysh'n/ *n.*

de·pone /di pṓn/ (**-poned, -pon·ing, -pones**) *vti.* LAW to testify or declare something under oath [15thC. From medieval Latin *deponere* "to testify" from Latin, "to put down" from *ponere* (see DEPOSE).]

de·po·nent /di pṓnənt/ *n.* **1.** LAW TESTIFYING WITNESS somebody who makes an affidavit or who testifies under oath **2.** GRAM DEPONENT VERB a deponent verb ■ *adj.* GRAM PASSIVE AND ACTIVE inflecting like a passive verb but active in meaning

de·pop·u·late /dee póppyə làyt/ (**-lat·ed, -lat·ing, -lates**) *vt.* to cause a reduction in the number of residents in an area through, e.g., disease, war, famine, or enforced relocation [Mid-16thC. From Latin *depopulare*, "to ravage completely," later "to reduce in population," from *populari* "to lay waste," from *populus* (see PEOPLE).] —**de·pop·u·la·tion** /dee pòppyə láysh'n/ *n.* —**de·pop·u·la·tor** /di póppyə làytər/ *n.*

de·port[1] /di páwrt/ (**-port·ed, -port·ing, -ports**) *vt.* **1.** FORCIBLY REPATRIATE to force a foreign national to leave a country **2.** BANISH to expel or banish somebody from their own country [Mid-17thC. Via French *déporter* from Latin *deportare*, literally "to carry off," from *portare* "to carry."]

de·port[2] /di páwrt/ (**-port·ed, -port·ing, -ports**) *vr.* to conduct yourself in a particular way [15thC. From Old French *deporter* "to behave, conduct oneself," from *porter*, from Latin *portare* "to carry."]

de·port·a·ble /di páwrtəb'l/ *adj.* **1.** RESULTING IN DEPORTATION liable to result in deportation **2.** LIABLE TO DEPORTATION liable to be deported

de·por·ta·tion /dèe pawr táysh'n/ *n.* **1.** EXPULSION OF FOREIGNER the forcible expulsion of a foreign national from a country **2.** EXPELLING NATIONAL the banishment or expulsion of somebody from his or her own country

de·port·ee /dèe pawr teé/ *n.* somebody who has been or is waiting to be deported

de·port·ment /di páwrtmənt/ *n.* the way that you stand, sit, or move, especially whether you have a straight back, move smoothly, and carry yourself well (*formal*) [Early 17thC. From French *déportement*, from Old French *deporter* (see DEPORT[2]).]

de·pos·al /di pṓz'l/ *n.* the deposing of somebody from office or power

de·pose /di pṓz/ (**-posed, -pos·ing, -pos·es**) *v.* **1.** *vt.* REMOVE FROM OFFICE to remove somebody from office or from a position of power **2.** *vti.* LAW GIVE EVIDENCE to give evidence or testify on oath, either in a written or verbal form **3.** *vt.* TAKE EVIDENCE to request and record evidence from a witness [13thC. From French *déposer*, an alteration (influenced by *poser* "to put") of Latin *deponere* "to put down," later "to testify," from *ponere* (see POSITION).] —**de·pos·a·ble** *adj.* —**de·pos·er** *n.*

de·pos·it /di pózzit/ *v.* (**-it·ed, -it·ing, -its**) **1.** *vt.* BANKING PUT MONEY IN BANK to pay money into a bank or other financial institution **2.** *vt.* COMM GIVE AS SECURITY to give a sum of money as part-payment or security ○ *deposited $1000 as a down payment* **3.** *vt.* PUT SOMETHING SOMEWHERE to put or drop something somewhere ○ *She deposited her coat on the couch.* **4.** *vt.* LEAVE SAFELY to leave something somewhere for safekeeping ○ *deposit valuables in the hotel safe* **5.** *vti.* GEOG FORM LAYER to form a layer of sand, sediment, or other substance, as a gradual process in one place ○ *layers of silt deposited by the river* ■ *n.* **1.** BANKING PUTTING MONEY IN BANK an act of placing money or a valuable item in a bank or other institution ○ *make a monthly deposit* **2.** BANKING MONEY IN BANK an amount of money or a valuable item that is paid into or left in a bank or other institution ○ *Deposits made after 2 pm are credited the following day.* **3.** COMM SECURITY MONEY a partial payment or security on something you wish to buy ○ *You need to pay a deposit.* **4.** SURETY MONEY money that is given as security against possible damage or loss, e.g., on something rented **5.** DEPOSITED THING something put or left in a place **6.** GEOG ACCUMULATION OF NATURAL MATERIALS an accumulation of sand, sediment, minerals, or other substances that has built up over a period of time through a natural process ○ *a land rich in mineral deposits* **7.** COATING a coating or crust that is left on a surface by a process such as evaporation or electrolysis [Late 16thC. From Latin *depositum*, from *deposit-*, the past participle stem of *deponere* (see DEPOSE).]

de·pos·it ac·count *n.* a bank account that earns interest

de·pos·i·tar·y /di pózzi tèrree/ (*plural* **-ies**) *n.* **1.** SAFE-KEEPER a person or institution that is entrusted with something for safekeeping **2.** = **depository** *n.* 1

dep·o·si·tion /dèppə zísh'n/ *n.* **1.** WITNESS'S TESTIMONY testimony that is given under oath, especially a statement given by a witness that is read out in court in the witness's absence **2.** OUSTING FROM OFFICE the act of removing somebody from high office or power **3.** SOMETHING DEPOSITED something that has been deposited somewhere **4.** BUILD-UP OF DEPOSITS the accumulation of natural materials by a gradual process [14thC. Via French *déposition* from the Latin stem *deposition-*, from, ultimately, *deponere* (see DEPOSE).] —**dep·o·si·tion·al** *adj.*

de·pos·i·tor /di pózzitər/ *n.* somebody who deposits or has money in a bank or similar institution

de·pos·i·to·ry /di pózzi tàwree/ (*plural* **-ries**) *n.* **1.** STOREHOUSE a place where something is kept for safekeeping or storage, such as a warehouse or store for furniture or valuables **2.** = **depositary** *n.* 1

de·pos·it slip *n.* a form for listing the contents of a bank deposit

de·pot /deépō, déppō/ *n.* **1.** WAREHOUSE a warehouse or other place used for storing things **2.** TRANSP STATION a railroad or bus station **3.** MIL MILITARY STORAGE a place where military supplies are stored **4.** MIL MILITARY TRAINING BASE a place where military recruits are gathered together and trained [Late 18thC. Via French *dépôt* from, ultimately, Latin *depositum* (see DEPOSIT). The underlying sense is "a place where things are deposited."]

de·prave /di práyv/ (**-praved, -prav·ing, -praves**) *vt.* to have a morally bad influence on somebody (*often passive*) [14thC. Directly or via French from Latin *depravare* "to corrupt," literally "to distort completely," from *pravus* "crooked," of unknown origin.] —**de·prav·er** *n.*

de·praved /di práyvd/ *adj.* showing great moral corruption or wickedness —**de·prav·ed·ly** /di práyvədlee, -práyvd-/ *adv.* —**de·praved·ness** /di práyvədnəss, -práyvd-/ *n.*

de·prav·i·ty /di právvitee/ (*plural* **-ties**) *n.* **1.** CORRUPTION a state of moral corruption **2.** CORRUPT ACT a morally corrupt or wicked act [Mid-17thC. Alteration (by association with DEPRAVE), of earlier *pravity*, from Latin *pravitas*, from *pravus* "crooked."]

dep·re·cate /déppṛə kàyt/ (**-cat·ed, -cat·ing, -cates**) *vt.* to express condemnation of something or somebody [Early 17thC. From Latin *deprecari*, literally "to pray against," from *precari* (see PRAY).] —**dep·re·ca·tion** /dèpprə káysh'n/ *n.* —**dep·re·ca·tor** *n.*

WORD KEY: USAGE

deprecate or **depreciate**? These two words are easily confused, but those who use English carefully try to maintain the distinction between them. To ***deprecate*** something is to deplore or condemn it as wrong in itself: *We deprecate the use of public money for nonessential purposes.* To ***depreciate*** something is to belittle or disparage it, although it may not be wrong or bad in itself: *They were constantly depreciating our attempts to speak Italian.* Admittedly, *self-deprecate* goes a long way toward blurring the distinction, for it means "belittle yourself," not "condemn yourself"; in this sense it is well established, but it may be best regarded as an exception rather than a precursor. Both words have more common synonyms: *condemn, deplore,* and *disapprove of* for ***deprecate***, and *belittle, disparage,* and *decry* for ***depreciate***. ***Depreciate*** is also used intransitively, in financial contexts: *The value of the yen depreciated 20 percent in real terms.*

dep·re·cat·ing /déppra kàyting/ *adj.* 1. EXPRESSING DISAPPROVAL showing or expressing disapproval 2. EXPRESSING APOLOGY showing or expressing apology —**dep·re·cat·ing·ly** *adv.*

dep·re·ca·to·ry /déppraka tàwree/, **dep·re·ca·tive** *adj.* 1. CRITICAL disapproving and critical 2. APOLOGETIC showing or expressing apology —**dep·re·ca·to·ri·ly** *adv.*

de·pre·cia·ble /di préeshee ab'l/ *adj.* capable of being or becoming depreciated

de·pre·ci·ate /di préeshee àyt/ (**-at·ed, -at·ing, -ates**) *v.* 1. *vti.* LOSE VALUE to lessen in value or to become less valuable 2. *vt.* ACCT DECREASE FOR TAX PURPOSES to consider something as having less value each year over a fixed period, for the calculation of income tax 3. *vt.* BELITTLE to speak critically or disparagingly about something or somebody [15thC. From late Latin *depreciare*, an alteration of Latin *depretiare* "to lower the price of," from *pretium* (see PRICE).] —**de·pre·ci·at·ing·ly** *adv.* —**de·pre·ci·a·tor** *n.*

WORD KEY: USAGE

See Usage note at ***deprecate***.

de·pre·ci·a·tion /di préeshee áysh'n/ *n.* 1. DROP IN VALUE the decrease in value of an item over time 2. AMOUNT OF DECREASE the amount or percentage by which something decreases in value over time, usually one year 3. BELITTLEMENT critical commentary or strong disparagement of somebody or something

de·pre·cia·tive /di préeshee àytiv/ *adj.* 1. REDUCING IN VALUE reducing or tending to reduce something in value 2. LOSING VALUE losing or tending to lose value

de·pre·cia·to·ry /di préeshee a tàwree/ *adj.* 1. = **depreciative** 2. CRITICAL belittling or critical

dep·re·date /déppra dàyt/ (**-dat·ed, -dat·ing, -dates**) *vti.* to ransack or plunder a place after attacking and overrunning it (*formal*) [Early 17thC. From Latin *depraedari*, literally "to plunder thoroughly," from *praedari* (see PREDATORY).] —**dep·re·da·tor** *n.* —**de·pred·a·to·ry** /di préddə tàwree, déppradə tàwree/ *adj.*

dep·re·da·tion /dèppra dáysh'n/ *n.* an attack involving plunder and pillage

de·press /di préss/ (**-pressed, -press·ing, -press·es**) *vt.* 1. MAKE SAD to make somebody feel very sad or hopeless ○ *"There's nothing that depresses me more than seeing a planet being destroyed."* Douglas Adams, *Life, the Universe, and Everything*; 1982) 2. WEAKEN to weaken something or make something less active 3. REDUCE to decrease the value of something 4. PRESS to press something, e.g., a button or lever [14thC. Via Old French from, ultimately, Latin *depress-*, the past participle stem of *deprimere* "to press down," from *premere* "to press."] —**de·press·i·ble** *adj.*

de·pres·sant /di préss'nt/ *n.* SEDATIVE a drug or agent that has the effect of slowing the rate of the body's vital functions ■ *adj.* WITH SLOWING EFFECT able to sedate or lower the rate of the body's vital functions

de·pressed /di prést/ *adj.* 1. UNHAPPY unhappy or hopeless 2. PSYCHIAT HAVING DEPRESSION having the psychiatric disorder depression 3. ECON ECONOMICALLY LACKING lacking economic resources or activities 4. WEAK less active or strong than usual 5. LOWER lower than the surrounding area 6. BIOL FLATTENED flattened, as if from downward pressure

de·press·ing /di préssing/ *adj.* making somebody feel sad or disheartened —**de·press·ing·ly** *adv.* —**de·press·ing·ness** *n.*

de·pres·sion /di présh'n/ *n.* 1. UNHAPPINESS a state of unhappiness and hopelessness 2. PSYCHIAT PSYCHIATRIC DISORDER a psychiatric disorder showing symptoms such as persistent feelings of hopelessness, dejection, poor concentration, lack of energy, inability to sleep, and, sometimes, suicidal tendencies 3. ECON ECONOMIC SLUMP a period in which an economy is greatly affected by unemployment, low output, and poverty 4. REDUCED ACTIVITY a lowering of activity, quality, vitality, or force 5. HOLLOW an area on the surface of something that is lower than the surface surrounding it 6. METEOROL LOW PRESSURE AREA an area of low barometric pressure that often brings rain

De·pres·sion glass *n.* decorative colored glassware that was produced in large quantities in the United States during the 1920s and 1930s

de·pres·sive /di préssiv/ *adj.* 1. CAUSING DEPRESSION relating to or causing depression ○ *the depressive atmosphere of a gray, cold marshland* 2. PSYCHIAT HAVING DEPRESSION experiencing or with a history of depression ■ *n.* PSYCHIAT DEPRESSED PERSON somebody who regularly experiences periods of depression —**de·pres·sive·ly** *adv.* —**de·pres·sive·ness** *n.*

de·pres·sor /di présser/ *n.* 1. MED MEDICAL INSTRUMENT a medical or surgical instrument that is used to move aside or press down an organ or part of the body 2. ANAT PULLING MUSCLE a muscle that acts to pull down a part of the body 3. SOMEBODY OR SOMETHING THAT PRESSES DOWN somebody or something that presses down

de·pres·sor nerve *n.* a nerve that, when stimulated, decreases activity in an organ, lowers blood pressure, or slows the heart

de·pres·sur·ize /dee présha rīz/ (**-ized, -iz·ing, -iz·es**) *vt.* 1. REDUCE PRESSURE to reduce the pressure of air or gas within a container, cabin, or other enclosed space 2. MAKE LESS TENSE to make a situation less tense —**de·pres·sur·i·za·tion** /di prèshari záysh'n/ *n.*

dep·ri·va·tion /dèppra váysh'n/ *n.* 1. STATE OF POVERTY the state of being without or denied something, especially of lacking adequate food or shelter 2. TAKING AWAY the act of taking something away from somebody or preventing somebody from having something

WORD KEY: SYNONYMS

See Synonyms at ***poverty***.

de·prive /di prív/ (**-prived, -priv·ing, -prives**) *vt.* 1. NOT ALLOW TO HAVE to prevent somebody from having something 2. TAKE AWAY to take something away from somebody ○ *They have no right to deprive you of your own property.* 3. DEPOSE to depose somebody from high rank or office (*archaic*) [14thC. Via Old French from medieval Latin *deprivare*, literally "to deprive completely," from Latin *privare* (see PRIVATION).] —**de·priv·a·ble** *adj.* —**de·priv·er** *n.*

de·prived /di prívd/ *adj.* lacking adequate food and shelter

de pro·fun·dis /dày pra fóondiss/ *adv.* out of the depths of misery or despair (*literary*) [13thC. From Latin, literally "out of the depths," the first words of Psalm 130 in the Bible.]

de·pro·gram /dee pró gràm/ (**-grammed** *or* **-gramed, -gram·ming** *or* **-gram·ing, -grams**) *vt.* to undo the effects of indoctrination on an individual, especially somebody under the influence of a religious group —**de·pro·gram·mer** /dee pró gràmmar/ *n.*

de·pro·gramme *vt.* U.K. = **deprogram**

dept. *abbr.* 1. department 2. deputy

depth /depth/ *n.* 1. HOW DEEP SOMETHING IS the distance or measurement from the top of something to its bottom, from front to back, or from the outside in 2. BEING DEEP the quality of being deep 3. INTENSITY the intensity or strength of a feeling or emotion 4. COMPLEXITY complexity or profundity of character ○ *a woman of great depth* ○ *hidden depths of knowledge* 5. BREADTH wideness in scope 6. COLOR QUALITY the intensity or richness of a color 7. LOWNESS the low tone or pitch of a sound ■ *npl.* 1. **depths** LOWEST POINT the lowest or worst point or moment ○ *the depths of despair* 2. **depths** DEEP PART a deep or remote part of something ○ *the ocean depths* 3. **depths** MIDDLE PART the middle part of something long, monotonous, and possibly unpleasant ○ *in the depths of tedious research* 4. DEBASEMENT a state of great moral debasement ○ *having fallen to such depths* [14thC. Formed from DEEP.] ◇ **out of your depth** 1. unable to understand or do something because it is outside the range of your knowledge or skills 2. unable to stand because the water is too deep

depth charge *n.* a bomb that is designed to explode at a particular depth under water, often used against submarines

depth gauge, **depth find·er** *n.* an instrument that measures the depth of water or other liquid

depth of field *n.* the total focused area in front of and behind an object held in the focus of a camera or lens

depth of fo·cus *n.* the distance that a camera lens can be moved closer to or further from the film, without the resulting image being blurred

depth per·cep·tion *n.* the ability to perceive objects and their spatial relationship in three dimensions

depth psy·chol·o·gy *n.* 1. STUDY OF UNCONSCIOUS the study and psychology of the unconscious mind 2. = **psychoanalysis**

depth sound·er *n.* an ultrasonic instrument that measures the depth of water under a ship

dep·u·rate /déppya ràyt/ (**-rat·ed, -rat·ing, -rates**) *vt.* to cleanse or purify something, especially by removing toxins [Early 17thC. From medieval Latin *depurare*, from Latin *purus* "pure."] —**dep·u·ra·tion** /dèppya ráysh'n/ *n.* —**dep·u·ra·tor** /déppya ràytar/ *n.*

dep·u·ra·tive /déppya ràytiv/ *adj.* purifying something by the removal of toxins (*technical*)

dep·u·ta·tion /dèppya táysh'n/ *n.* 1. REPRESENTATIVES a group of people who have been chosen to represent a larger group of people and act on their behalf 2. APPOINTMENT OF DEPUTY the act of appointing a deputy or deputation

de·pute /di pyóot/ (**-put·ed, -put·ing, -putes**) *v.* (*formal*) 1. *vt.* CHOOSE REPRESENTATIVE to choose somebody to be your agent, substitute, or representative 2. *vt.* DELEGATE to delegate one's work, authority, or duties to somebody else 3. *vi.* ACT AS DEPUTY to act as deputy for somebody [14thC. Via French *députer* from, ultimately, Latin *deputare* "to assign," from *putare* "to consider."]

dep·u·tize /déppya tīz/ (**-tized, -tiz·ing, -tiz·es**) *v.* 1. *vi.* BE DEPUTY to act as somebody's deputy 2. *vt.* SELECT DEPUTY to choose somebody to act as a deputy to somebody —**dep·u·ti·za·tion** /dèppyati záysh'n/ *n.*

dep·u·ty /déppyatee/ (*plural* **-ties**) *n.* 1. SOMEBODY'S REPRESENTATIVE somebody who has been authorized or appointed to act on behalf of somebody else with full authority 2. SECOND-IN-COMMAND an assistant who is authorized to act in a superior's place 3. MEMBER OF PARLIAMENT a parliamentary representative in some countries, e.g., France, Germany, or Italy 4. LAW = **deputy sheriff** [15thC. From French *député*, the past participle of *députer* (see DEPUTE).]

WORD KEY: SYNONYMS

See Synonyms at ***assistant***.

dep·u·ty min·is·ter *n.* *Can* the most senior civil servant in a Canadian government department

dep·u·ty sher·iff *n.* a sheriff's assistant, authorized to take charge when the sheriff is absent

de·rac·i·nate /di ráss'n àyt/ (**-nat·ed, -nat·ing, -nates**) *vt.* to remove somebody or something from a natural environment, especially people from their native culture (*formal*) [Late 16thC. Formed from French *déraciner*, from *racine* "root," which came via late Latin *radicina* from Latin *radix* "root" (see RADIX).] —**de·rac·i·na·tion** /di ràss'n áysh'n/ *n.*

de·raign /di ráyn/ (**-raigned, -raign·ing, -raigns**) *vt.* (*archaic*) 1. LAW CONTEST CASE to dispute a claim or suit 2. MIL ARRANGE SOLDIERS to line soldiers up ready for battle [14thC. Via Anglo-Norman *derainer* from assumed Vulgar Latin *disrationare* "to settle an account," from Latin *ratio* "reckoning" (see RATIO).] —**de·raign·ment** *n.*

de·rail /di ráyl/ (**-railed, -rail·ing, -rails**) *vti.* 1. COME OFF RAILS to make a train or tram come off the rails, or to come off the rails 2. SEND OR GO OFF COURSE to send something off course, or to go off course [Mid-19thC. From French *dérailler*, from *rail* "rail" (see RAIL[1]).] —**de·rail·ment** *n.*

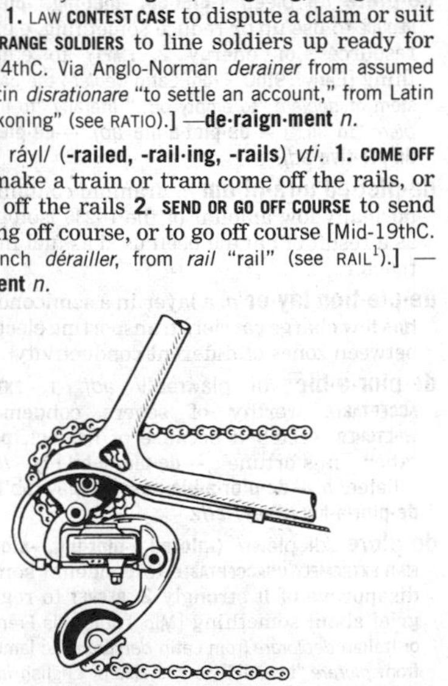

Derailleur

de·rail·leur /di ráylar/ *n.* a device for changing gears on a bicycle that lifts the chain from one sprocket wheel to another [Mid-20thC. From French *dérailleur*, literally "derailer," from *dérailler* (see DERAIL).]

de·range /di ráynj/ (**-ranged, -rang·ing, -rang·es**) *vt.* **1. MAKE IRRATIONAL** to make somebody irrational or extraordinarily angry **2. DISTURB** to disturb the normal way in which something works **3. THROW INTO DISORDER** to throw something into disorder and confusion [Late 18thC. From French *déranger,* literally "to put out of line," from *rang* "line."]

de·ranged /di ráynjd/ *adj.* completely unreasonable, especially as a result of great emotional excitement

de·range·ment /di ráynjmənt/ *n.* **1. COMPLETE IRRATIONALITY** a complete lack of rationality, especially with great emotional excitement **2. DISORDER** disorder and confusion **3. ACT OF DERANGING** the act of disturbing or confusing something

de·rate /dee ráyt/ (**-rat·ed, -rat·ing, -rates**) *vt.* ELEC ENG to lower the rated capability of an electrical apparatus

de·ra·tion /dee rásh'n/ (**-tioned, -tion·ing, -tions**) *vt.* to stop rationing a commodity, usually because the supply has become adequate

der·by /dúrbee/ (*plural* **-bies**) *n.* **1.** HORSERACING **HORSERACE** any of a number of horseraces run annually, usually for three year olds **2. RACE** a race or contest, open to qualified competitors **3.** CLOTHES **ROUND FELT HAT** a stiff felt hat with a round crown and a small, curved brim [Late 19thC. Named for DERBY. In sense 3, supposedly from the wearing of such hats at the Derby horserace.]

Der·by *n.* a flat horserace held each spring at Churchill Downs in Louisville, Kentucky, or one run annually at Epsom Downs, Surrey, England [Early 19thC. Named for Edward Stanley 1752–1834, 12th Earl of *Derby,* who founded the English race in 1780.]

de·rec·og·nize /dee rékəg nīz/ (**-nized, -niz·ing, -niz·es**) *vt.* to stop accepting the legitimacy of something, especially a diplomatic mission —**de·rec·og·ni·tion** /dee rèkəg nísh'n/ *n.*

de·reg·is·ter /dee réjjistər/ (**-tered, -ter·ing, -ters**) *vti.* to remove something or somebody from a register or official list —**de·reg·is·tra·tion** /dee rèjji stráysh'n/ *n.*

de·reg·u·late /dee réggyə layt/ (**-lat·ed, -lat·ing, -lates**) *vt.* to free something such as an organization or industry from regulation —**de·reg·u·la·tion** /dee règgyə láysh'n/ *n.* —**de·reg·u·la·tor** /dee réggyə làytər/ *n.* —**de·reg·u·la·to·ry** /dee réggyələ tàwree/ *adj.*

der·e·lict /dérrə likt/ *adj.* **1. DESERTED** no longer lived in **2. NEGLECTED** in poor condition because of neglect **3.** LAW **ABANDONING DUTY** neglectful of your duty or obligations ■ *n.* **1. HOMELESS PERSON** somebody who has no home, employment, or family care (*formal*) **2. ABANDONED BUILDING** a building, ship, or other property that has been abandoned or deserted **3.** LAW **NEGLECTFUL PERSON** a person who is neglectful of duty or obligations [Mid-17thC. From Latin *derelictus,* the past participle of *derelinquere,* literally "to abandon utterly," from *relinquere* (see RELINQUISH).]

der·e·lic·tion /dèrrə líkshən/ *n.* **1.** LAW **NEGLECT OF DUTY** deliberate neglect of duty or obligations **2. ABANDONMENT** the act of abandoning or deserting a building **3. STATE OF NEGLECT** a state of abandonment or neglect **4.** LAW **LAND GAINED FROM THE SEA** land gained because water has receded from it

de·re·press /dèe ri préss/ (**-pressed, -press·ing, -press·es**) *vt.* to activate a gene by deactivating the repressor —**de·re·pres·sion** /dèe ri présh'n/ *n.*

de·req·ui·si·tion /dee rèkwi zísh'n/ (**-tioned, -tion·ing, -tions**) *vt.* to return something to civilian use that was earlier requisitioned by the military or a government

de·re·strict /dèe ri stríkt/ (**-strict·ed, -strict·ing, -stricts**) *vt.* to remove the restrictions from something —**de·re·stric·tion** /dèe ri stríkshən/ *n.*

de·ride /di ríd/ (**-rid·ed, -rid·ing, -rides**) *vt.* to ridicule or show contempt for somebody or something [Mid-16thC. From Latin *deridere,* literally "to laugh down," from *ridere* "to laugh."] —**de·rid·er** *n.* —**de·rid·ing·ly** *adv.*

WORD KEY: SYNONYMS

See Synonyms at ***ridicule.***

de ri·gueur /də ri gúr/ *adj.* strictly required by the current fashion or by etiquette (*formal*) [Mid-19thC. From French, literally "of strictness."]

de·ris·i·ble /di rízəb'l/ *adj.* deserving contempt or ridicule (*formal*) [Mid-17thC. From late Latin *derisibilis,* from, ultimately, Latin *deridere* (see DERIDE).]

de·ri·sion /di rízh'n/ *n.* **1. MOCKING SCORN** contempt and mockery **2. STATE OF BEING DERIDED** the state of being derided [14thC. Via French *dérision* from, ultimately, Latin *deridere* (see DERIDE).]

de·ri·sive /di ríssiv/ *adj.* showing contempt or ridicule [Mid-17thC. Formed from DERISION.] —**de·ri·sive·ly** *adv.* —**de·ri·sive·ness** *n.*

WORD KEY: USAGE

derisive or **derisory**? ***Derisive*** means "showing derision" (that is, scornful, contemptuous): *He gave a derisive laugh.* ***Derisory*** means "deserving derision" (that is, ridiculous, contemptible): *a derisory offer.*

de·ri·so·ry /di ríssəree, -rízə-/ *adj.* **1. RIDICULOUSLY SMALL** so small or inadequate for the purpose intended that it is ridiculous **2.** = **derisive** [Early 17thC. From late Latin *derisorius* from, ultimately, Latin *deridere* (see DERIDE).]

WORD KEY: USAGE

See Usage note at ***derisive.***

deriv. *abbr.* **1.** derivation **2.** derivative

der·i·vate /dérrivət, -vàyt/ *n., adj.* = **derivative** [15thC. From Latin *derivatus,* the past participle of *derivare* (see DERIVE).]

der·i·va·tion /dèrri váysh'n/ *n.* **1. SOURCE** the origin or source of something, e.g., a word or someone's name **2.** LING **WORD FORMATION** the formation of a word or term from another, or from a base form **3.** MATH, LOGIC **PROOF** a mathematical or logical argument whose steps show that a conclusion follows necessarily from initial assumptions **4. ACT OF DERIVING SOMETHING** the act of obtaining something from a source or issuing from a source —**der·i·va·tion·al** *adj.*

WORD KEY: SYNONYMS

See Synonyms at ***origin.***

de·riv·a·tive /di rívvətiv/, **der·i·vate** *adj.* **UNORIGINAL** copied from somewhere and not original ■ *n.* **1. DERIVED THING** an idea, language, term, or other thing that has developed from something else that is similar to it **2.** LING **DERIVED WORD** a word that is formed from another word, e.g., "quickly" from "quick" **3.** CHEM **RELATED CHEMICAL PRODUCT** a chemical substance that is formed from a related substance **4.** MATH **CHANGE OF FUNCTION** the limit approached in the ratio of a function and its variable, as the variable is changed ever more infinitesimally **5.** FIN **FINANCIAL PRODUCT** a tradable financial product whose value depends on the value of some other asset or combination of assets —**de·riv·a·tive·ly** *adv.* —**de·riv·a·tive·ness** *n.*

de·rive /di rív/ (**-rived, -riv·ing, -rives**) *v.* **1.** *vti.* LING **COME FROM SOURCE** to develop from another word or a source word or term **2.** *vti.* **GET OR COME FROM SOMETHING** to obtain something or come from a source **3.** *vt.* LOGIC **DEDUCE** to reach a conclusion about something by reasoning **4.** *vt.* CHEM **MAKE COMPOUND** to create a chemical substance from another **5.** *vt.* MATH **OBTAIN FUNCTION** to obtain a function by differentiation [14thC. Directly or via French *dériver* from Latin *derivare* "to draw off water through a channel," from *rivus* "stream" (see RIVAL).] —**de·riv·a·ble** *adj.* —**de·riv·er** *n.*

derm- *prefix.* = **derma-** (*used before vowels*)

-derm *suffix.* skin ○ *ectoderm* [From Greek *derma* (see DERMA-)]

der·ma *n.* COOK = **kishke** [Origin uncertain: probably via Yiddish *gederem* "intestines" from, ultimately, Old High German *darm* "gut"]

derma- *prefix.* skin ○ *dermatome* [Early 18thC. Via modern Latin from Greek, "skin." Ultimately from an Indo-European word meaning "to peel," which is also the ancestor of English *tear*[1].]

der·ma·bra·sion /dùrmə bráyzh'n/ *n.* a surgical process that removes scars or other imperfections of the skin by scraping the skin's surface with wire brushes or very fine sandpaper [Mid-20thC. Coined from Greek *derma* "skin" + ABRASION.]

der·mal /dúrm'l/, **der·mic** *adj.* involving, located in, or made up of skin or its main layer (**dermis**) [Early 19thC. Formed from Greek *derma* "skin."]

der·map·ter·an /dər máptərən/ *n.* an insect, e.g., an earwig, that has strong sharp sensory appendages coming from the end of its abdomen [Late 19thC. Formed from modern Latin *Dermaptera,* order name, from Greek *derma* "skin" + *pteron* "wing." So called because of their membranous wings.] —**der·map·ter·an** *adj.*

dermat- *prefix.* = **dermato-** (*used before vowels*)

der·ma·ti·tis /dùrmə títiss/ *n.* inflammation of the skin from any cause, resulting in a range of symptoms such as redness, swelling, itching, or blistering

dermato- *prefix.* skin ○ *dermatoplasty* [From Greek *dermat-,* the stem of *derma* (see DERMA-)]

der·mat·o·glyph·ics /dùrmətə glíffiks/ *npl.* **SKIN PATTERNS** the lines that form a pattern on the skin, e.g., on the fingers and palms of the hands ■ *n.* **STUDY OF SKIN PATTERNS** the study of dermatoglyphics (*takes a singular verb*) [Early 20thC. Coined from DERMATO- + Greek *gluphē* "carving, inscription" (see GLYPH).] —**der·mat·o·glyph·ic** *adj.*

der·ma·toid /dúrmə tòyd/ *adj.* resembling skin

der·ma·tol·o·gy /dùrmə tólləjee/ *n.* the branch of medicine that deals with the skin and diseases affecting the skin —**der·ma·to·log·i·cal** /dùrmətə lójjik'l/ *adj.* —**der·ma·tol·o·gist** /dùrmə tólləjist/ *n.*

der·ma·tome /dúrmə tōm/ *n.* **1.** ANAT **SKIN SERVED BY ONE SPINAL NERVE** an area of skin that has nerve fibers coming from a single spinal nerve **2.** MED **SURGICAL INSTRUMENT** an instrument used to slice thin layers of skin for skin grafting [Late 19thC. Coined from DERMATO- + -TOME.] —**der·ma·tom·ic** /dùrmə tómmik/ *adj.*

der·mat·o·phyte /dur máttə fīt, dúrmətə fīt/ *n.* a parasitic fungus that affects the skin, hair, or nails —**der·mat·o·phyt·ic** /dur màttə fíttik, dùrmətə fíttik/ *adj.*

der·ma·to·phy·to·sis /dùrmə tō fī tóssiss/ *n.* a fungal infection of the skin, hair, or nails

der·ma·to·plas·ty /dúrmə tō plàstee/ *n.* any operation on the skin, especially skin grafting (*technical*) —**der·ma·to·plas·tic** /dùrmə tō plástik/ *adj.*

der·ma·to·sis /dùrmə tóssiss/ (*plural* **-ses** /dùrmə tó seez/) *n.* any disease affecting the skin

-dermatous *suffix.* having a particular kind of skin ○ *sclerodermatous* [Formed from Greek *dermat-,* the stem of *derma* (see DERMA-)]

der·mes·tid /dur méstid/ *n.* a beetle that has clubbed antennae and eats and destroys organic materials such as meat, fur, wool, fabric, or museum specimens. Cabinet and carpet beetles are dermestids. Family: Dermestidae. [Late 19thC. From modern Latin *Dermestidae,* family name, from Greek *derma* "skin" + *esthiein* "to eat."]

der·mic /dúrmik/ *adj.* = **dermal** [Mid-19thC. Formed from Greek *derma* "skin."]

der·mis /dúrmiss/ *n.* the thick sensitive layer of skin or connective tissue beneath the epidermis that contains blood, lymph vessels, sweat glands, and nerve endings [Mid-19thC. From modern Latin, back-formation from EPIDERMIS.]

-dermis *suffix.* skin ○ *endodermis* [Back-formation from EPIDERMIS]

der·moid /dúr mòyd/, **der·moid cyst** *n.* a benign tumor that contains skin or skin derivatives, found in the ovaries or on the face, especially around the eyes [Early 19thC. Formed from Greek *derma* "skin."]

der·nier cri /dèr nyay kreé/ *n.* the latest thing in fashion [Late 19thC. From French, literally "latest cry."]

der·o·gate /dérrə gàyt/ (**-gat·ed, -gat·ing, -gates**) *v.* **1.** *vi.* **DEVIATE FROM CONDITIONS** to deviate from a norm, rule, law, or set of conditions, e.g., by refusing to be bound by part of a treaty **2.** *vi.* **MAKE SEEM INFERIOR** to make something seem inferior or less significant (*formal*) ○ *conduct that will derogate from your good name* **3.** *vt.* **CRITICIZE** to criticize somebody or something negatively **4.** *vt.* LAW **REPEAL PARTIALLY** to repeal or abolish part of a law or decree [15thC. From Latin *derogare* "to repeal a law," later "to detract from, impair," from *rogare* "to ask, propose a law" (see ROGATION).]

der·o·ga·tion /dèrrə gáysh'n/ *n.* **1.** LAW **DEVIATION** a deviation from a rule or law, especially one specifically provided for **2.** RELIG **EXEMPTION FROM RULE** an exemption from a law or ruling given to a state **3. DISPARAGEMENT** the act of belittling or negatively criticizing somebody or something

de·rog·a·tive /di róggətiv, dérrə gàytiv/ *adj.* **1.** = **derogatory 2. RELATING TO DEROGATION** relating to a derogation —**de·rog·a·tive·ly** *adv.*

de·rog·a·to·ry /di róggə tàwree/ *adj.* expressing a low opinion or negative criticism —**de·rog·a·to·ri·ly** /di rògga táwrilee/ *adv.* —**de·rog·a·to·ri·ness** /di róggə táwrinəss/ *n.*

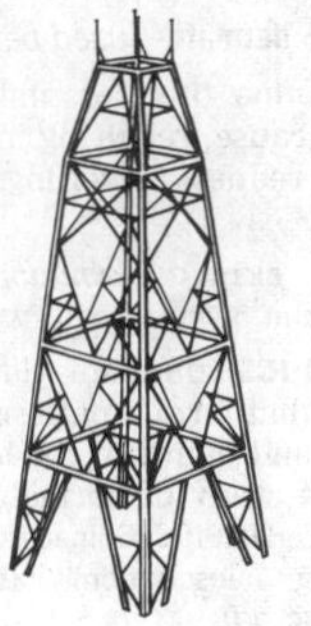

Derrick

der·rick /dérrik/ *n.* **1. LOADING CRANE** a simple crane that is often used for moving cargo onto or from a ship **2.** INDUST **OIL STRUCTURE** a structure placed over an oil well that is used to raise and lower piping, drills, and other boring equipment [Early 17thC. From an earlier sense "hangman, gallows," after a London hangman called *Derrick* who was working at Tyburn at about this time.]

Der·ri·da /dèrri daá/, **Jacques** (*b.* 1930) Algerian-born French philosopher. He introduced deconstruction, a controversial technique for textual analysis.

der·ri·ère /dèrree áir/ *n.* somebody's buttocks (*humorous*) [Late 18thC. Via French, literally "behind," from, ultimately, Latin *de retro*.]

der·ring-do /dèrring dóo, dérring dóo/ *n.* boldness, or acts of great daring (*literary*) [Late 16thC. Alteration of earlier *dorring don* "daring to do," which was erroneously printed in 16th-century editions of medieval works as *derrynge do* and interpreted as a noun.]

der·rin·ger /dérrinjər/ *n.* a pocket-sized short-barreled large-calibre pistol [Mid-19thC. Named for the U.S. gunsmith Henry *Deringer*, 1786–1868, who designed it.]

der·ris /dérriss/ *n.* **1.** PLANTS **E INDIAN CLIMBING PLANT** a woody climbing plant that grows in East India. Genus: *Derris*. **2.** GARDENING **INSECTICIDE** an insecticide made from the powdered roots of the derris plant, that contain the natural insecticide rotenone [Mid-19thC. Via modern Latin, genus name, from Greek, literally "leather covering." So called because of its leathery pod.]

der·vish /dúrvish/ *n.* **1. MEMBER OF MUSLIM RELIGIOUS GROUP** a member of any of several ascetic Muslim religious groups, some of which are known for their practices of very energetic dancing, whirling, chanting, or singing **2. FRENZIED PERSON** somebody who behaves very energetically [Late 16thC. Via Turkish *derviş* from Persian *darvīš* "poor, mendicant."]

DES *abbr.* **1.** diethylstilbestrol **2.** data encryption standard

de·sa·cral·ize /dee sákrə līz/ (**-ized, -iz·ing, -iz·es**) *vt.* to remove the sacred, religious, or supernatural qualities or status from something

de·sal·i·nate /dee sállə nàyt/ (**-nat·ed, -nat·ing, -nates**) *vt.* to remove the salt from something —**de·sal·i·na·tor** *n.*

de·sal·i·na·tion /dee sàllə náysh'n/ *n.* the process of removing salt from something, especially from seawater to produce drinking water. The main methods used are distillation and reverse osmosis.

de·sal·i·nize /dee sállə nīz/ (**-nized, -niz·ing, -niz·es**) *vt.* = **desalinate** —**de·sal·i·ni·za·tion** /dee sàlləni záysh'n/ *n.*

de·salt /dee sáwlt/ (**-salt·ed, -salt·ing, -salts**) *vt.* = **desalinate** —**de·salt·er** *n.*

de·sat·u·ra·tion /dee sàchə ráysh'n/ *n.* the addition of white to a saturated color in order to achieve a paler shade

desc. *abbr.* descendent

des·cant /dé skànt/, **dis·cant** /dí-/ *n.* **1.** MUSIC **HIGH MELODY** a melody that is sung or played above the basic melody of a piece of music **2. COMMENT** a comment, remark, or criticism on a particular subject (*archaic*) ■ *adj.* MUSIC **HIGH-TONED** highest in range of a family of musical instruments ○ *descant recorder* ■ *vi.* (**-cant·ed, -cant·ing, -cants**) **1.** MUSIC **MAKE MUSIC** to sing, play, or compose a descant part for a piece of music **2. DISCOURSE ON SOMETHING** to comment at length on a particular subject (*literary*) [14thC. Via Anglo-Norman *descaunt* from medieval Latin *discantus* "part-song, refrain," from Latin *cantus* "song" (see CANTO).] —**des·cant·er** *n.*

Des·cartes /day kaárt/, **René** (1596–1650) French philosopher and mathematician. He is often called the father of modern philosophy, and his *Discourse on Method* (1637) introduced his technique of philosophical enquiry. His work on analytical geometry resulted in the Cartesian system of coordinates.

de·scend /di sénd/ (**-scend·ed, -scend·ing, -scends**) *v.* **1.** *vti.* **GO DOWN** to go down a staircase, hill, valley, or other downward incline **2.** *vi.* **COME NEARER GROUND** to come nearer the ground, especially in an aircraft in preparation for landing **3.** *vi.* **SLOPE** to slope downwards **4.** *vti.* **BE RELATED** to be connected by blood to an ancestor ○ *Our family descends from French royalty.* ○ *be descended from* **5.** *vi.* **BE INHERITED** to be inherited from or passed down by parents or ancestors **6.** *vi.* **LOWER ONESELF** to behave in a way that is disappointing and below somebody's normal standards **7.** *vi.* **ARRIVE SUDDENLY** to arrive at a place suddenly, especially in large numbers ○ *tourists descending on unspoilt areas* **8.** *vi.* **BECOME ESTABLISHED** to become more evident or established, suddenly or by degrees ○ *An atmosphere of gloom descended on the assembled crowd.* [14thC. Via French *descendre* from Latin *descendere*, literally "to climb down," from *scandere* "to climb."] —**de·scend·a·ble** *adj.*

de·scen·dant /di séndənt/ *n.* **1. SOMEBODY OR SOMETHING RELATED TO ANCESTOR** a person, animal, or plant related to one that lived in the past **2. RELATED MODEL** something that is based in design, form, or concept on an earlier thing ■ *adj.* = **descendent**

de·scen·dent /di séndənt/, **de·scen·dant** *adj.* **1. MOVING DOWN** moving downward **2. DESCENDING FROM ANCESTOR** descending from an ancestor

de·scend·er /di séndər/ *n.* **1.** PRINTING **BOTTOM PART OF LETTER** the tail part of a letter, e.g., on a "y" or "g," that extends below the baseline of other letters **2. SOMETHING DESCENDING** somebody or something that descends

de·scen·deur /dè saaN dúr/ *n.* a mechanical device that can be tightened or loosened on a rope, enabling a climber to control the speed of his or her descent [Late 20thC. From French, literally "descender," from *descendre* (see DESCEND).]

de·scend·i·ble /di séndəb'l/ *adj.* **1.** LAW **HERITABLE** able to be inherited **2. ALLOWING DESCENT** allowing descent or downward movement

de·scend·ing /di sénding/ *adj.* going or arranged from highest to lowest, greatest to smallest, or latest to earliest ○ *in descending order*

de·scent /di sént/ *n.* **1. GOING DOWN** an act of going from the top to the bottom, or from a higher position to a lower position **2. WAY DOWN** a path or other way down something, e.g., a mountain **3. DECLINE** a decline or change from something better to something worse **4. ANCESTRAL BACKGROUND** the connection somebody has to an ancestor or group of ancestors **5. INHERITED DEVELOPMENT** characteristics or developments that can be traced to an earlier source **6. SUDDEN ARRIVAL** the sudden arrival of a person or group of people **7. ONE GENERATION** a step of one generation in a lineage **8.** LAW **INHERITANCE** the transmission of property by inheritance [13thC. From French *descente*, from *descendre* (see DESCEND).]

de·school /dee skóol/ (**-schooled, -school·ing, -schools**) *vti.* to reduce somebody's involvement with education within the school system, or to undergo this process —**de·school·ing** *n.*

Des·chutes /day shóot, də shóots/ river in northern Oregon that rises in the Cascade Range and flows northeastward to the Columbia River. Length: 250 mi./402 km.

de·scram·ble /dee skrámb'l/ (**-bled, -bling, -bles**) *vt.* to make intelligible a message transmitted in code form

de·scram·bler /dee skrámblər/ *n.* a device that decodes scrambled messages or signals

de·scribe /di skrīb/ (**-scribed, -scrib·ing, -scribes**) *vt.* **1. EXPLAIN** to give an account of something by giving details of its characteristics **2. LABEL** to label or typify somebody or something **3. DRAW SHAPE** to make a shape or outline in the air (*formal*) ○ *The plane described a perfect figure eight.* **4. REPRESENT** to represent something pictorially or with a model [15thC. From Latin *describere*, literally "to write down," from *scribere* "to write."] —**de·scrib·a·ble** *adj.* —**de·scrib·er** *n.*

de·scrip·tion /di skrípshən/ *n.* **1. EXPLANATION** a written or verbal account, representation, or explanation of something **2. PROCESS OF DESCRIBING** the process of giving an account or explanation of something **3. SORT** a kind or variety of something ○ *cars of every description* [14thC. Via French from the Latin stem *description-* from *descript-*, the past participle stem of *describere* (see DESCRIBE).]

de·scrip·tive /di skríptiv/ *adj.* **1. BEING DESCRIPTION** containing or consisting of description **2. CLASSIFYING** serving mainly to label, describe, or classify **3.** GRAM **ATTRIBUTIVE** expressing an attribute or quality of a noun [Mid-18thC. From late Latin *descriptivus*, from, ultimately, Latin *describere* (see DESCRIBE).] —**de·scrip·tive·ly** *adv.* —**de·scrip·tive·ness** *n.*

de·scrip·tive clause *n.* = **nonrestrictive clause**

de·scrip·tive lin·guis·tics *n.* the study of a language limited to a comprehensive account of its grammar at a given time, omitting historical or comparative features and not attempting to formulate prescriptive rules

de·scrip·tiv·ism /di skrípti vìzzəm/ *n.* **1.** LING **SUPPORT FOR DESCRIPTIVE LINGUISTICS** adherence to the practices and tenets of descriptive linguistics **2.** PHILOS **BELIEF IN DESCRIPTION** the notion or thesis that descriptive statements can be true and accurate reflections of phenomena —**de·scrip·tiv·ist** *n., adj.*

de·scrip·tor /di skríptər/ *n.* COMPUT something, e.g., a word or phrase, used as a key to categorize records in a database so that all records containing the key can be retrieved together [Mid-20thC. From Latin, literally "describer," formed from *describere* (see DESCRIBE).]

de·scry /di skrī/ (**-scried, -scry·ing, -scries**) *vt.* **1. SEE** to catch sight of something (*archaic or formal*) **2. DISCOVER** to detect or discover something (*archaic or humorous*) [14thC. From Old French *descrier* "to cry out, proclaim" (source also of English *decry*), from *crier* (see CRY). Its modern meaning developed by association with obsolete *descry* "to describe, perceive" which came via Old French *descrire* from Latin *describere* (see DESCRIBE).] —**de·scri·er** *n.*

des·e·crate /déssə kràyt/ (**-crat·ed, -crat·ing, -crates**) *vt.* to damage something sacred, or do something that is offensive to the religious nature of something [Late 17thC. Coined from DE- + CONSECRATE.] —**des·e·crat·er** *n.* —**des·e·cra·tion** /dèssə kráysh'n/ *n.* —**des·e·cra·tor** /déssə kràytər/ *n.*

de·seg·re·gate /dee séggrə gàyt/ (**-gat·ed, -gat·ing, -gates**) *vti.* to put an end to a customary or enforced separation of ethnic or racial groups, e.g., in a workplace or school —**de·seg·re·ga·tion** /dee sèggrə gáysh'n/ *n.* —**de·seg·re·ga·tion·ist** *n.*

de·seg·re·ga·tion /dee sèggrə gáysh'n/ *n.* the act of desegregating ethnic or racial groups

de·se·lect /dèe sə lékt/ (**-lect·ed, -lect·ing, -lects**) *vt.* **1.** COMPUT **REMOVE SELECTION** to remove selection status from an option or data on a menu or list on a computer monitor **2.** MANAGEMT **LET TRAINEE GO** to end the training of an unsuitable trainee before the training program is completed —**de·se·lec·tion** /dèe sə lékshən/ *n.*

de·sen·si·tize /dee sénsə tīz/ (**-tized, -tiz·ing, -tiz·es**) *vt.* **1. MAKE LESS SENSITIVE** to make somebody or something insensitive or less sensitive **2. MAKE LESS ALLERGIC** to make somebody less sensitive to a known allergen by injecting increasing amounts of the allergen over time, building up resistance **3. MAKE LESS SENSITIVE TO FEAR** to make somebody less responsive to an overwhelming fear by repeated exposure to the feared situation or object, either in natural or artificial circumstances —**de·sen·si·ti·za·tion** /dee sènsəti záysh'n/ *n.* —**de·sen·si·tiz·er** /dee sénsə tīzər/ *n.*

des·ert[1] /dézzərt/ *n.* **1. ARID AREA** an area of land, usually in very hot climates, that consists only of sand, gravel, or rock with little or no vegetation, no permanent bodies of water, and erratic rainfall **2. DEPRIVED PLACE** a place or situation that is devoid of some desirable thing, or overwhelmed by an undesirable thing ○ *a cultural desert* **3. LIFELESS PLACE** a place devoid of life **4. BARREN LAND** a wild, bleak, and uncultivated place (*archaic*) [12thC. Via French *désert* from late Latin *desertum* "abandoned place," from the past participle of Latin *deserere* (see DESERT[2]).]

de·sert[2] /di zúrt/ (**-sert·ed, -sert·ing, -serts**) *v.* **1.** *vt.* **ABANDON PLACE** to leave a place with no one staying behind **2.** *vt.* **ABANDON PERSON** to leave or abandon

WORLD'S LARGEST DESERTS

1		Sahara Desert
	Area	[3.5 million sq. mi. / 9.1 million sq. km]
	Location	*North Africa*
2		Rub' al-Khali Desert
	Area	[0.9 million sq. mi. / 2.3 million sq. km]
	Location	*Southwestern Asia / Arabia*
3		Gobi Desert
	Area	[0.5 million sq. mi. / 1.3 million sq. km]
	Location	*Central Asia / Mongolia*
4		Patagonian Desert
	Area	[0.3 million sq. mi. / 0.8 million sq. km]
	Location	*South America / Argentina*
5		Kalahari Desert
	Area	[0.27 million sq. mi. / 0.71 million sq. km]
	Location	*Southwestern Africa*
6		Great Victoria Desert
	Area	[0.25 million sq. mi. / 0.65 million sq. km]
	Location	*Australia*
7		Great Basin Desert
	Area	[0.2 million sq. mi. / 0.5 million sq. km]
	Location	*North America*
8		Great Sandy Desert
	Area	[0.15 million sq. mi. / 0.4 million sq. km]
	Location	*Australia*
9		Sonoran Desert
	Area	[0.12 million sq. mi. / 0.31 million sq. km]
	Location	*North America*
10		Garagum Desert
	Area	[0.11 million sq. mi. / 0.28 million sq. km]
	Location	*Central Asia / Turkmenistan*

somebody, especially when you have some kind of duty or obligation toward him or her **3.** *vti.* MIL **LEAVE ARMY WITHOUT PERMISSION** to run away from an armed force or military post without permission and intending never to go back **4.** *vt.* **LEAVE** to be absent when needed ○ *Her sense of humor appeared to have deserted her.* [14thC. Via French *déserter* from, ultimately, Latin *desert-*, the past participle stem of *deserere* "to abandon," from *serere* "to join."]

de·sert[3] /di zúrt/ *n.* something deserved, either punishment or reward (*usually used in the plural*) ○ *He'll get his just deserts.* [13thC. From Old French, literally "what is deserved," from the past participle of *deservir* (see DESERVE).]

WORD KEY: USAGE

desert or **dessert**? ***Dessert*** is a noun, is pronounced with the stress on the second syllable, and has only one meaning: "a sweet course of a meal." ***Desert*** is pronounced with the stress on the first syllable when it is a noun meaning "a dry barren area of land," and with the stress on the second syllable when it is a noun meaning "what somebody deserves," in *just deserts* and similar expressions. The stress is also on the second syllable when ***desert*** is used as a verb, meaning "abandon" or "abscond."

de·sert·ed /di zúrtəd/ *adj.* empty after being abandoned by people

de·sert·er /di zúrtər/ *n.* a member of the armed forces who leaves his or her post without permission and does not intend to go back

de·sert·i·fi·ca·tion /di zùrtəfi káysh'n/ *n.* a process by which land becomes increasingly dry until almost no vegetation grows on it, making it a desert

de·ser·tion /di zúrsh'n/ *n.* the act or an instance of deserting from the armed forces

des·ert is·land *n.* a small isolated unpopulated tropical island

des·ert lynx *n.* = **caracal**

des·ert pave·ment *n.* GEOG a layer of gravel that remains when the finer-grained particles of a desert soil have been blown away

des·ert rat *n.* **1.** ZOOL **DESERT RODENT** any rodent that lives in a desert **2.** *Southwest U.S.* **DESERT DWELLER** somebody who lives in the desert and attempts to earn a living there, e.g., a prospector

des·ert var·nish *n.* GEOG a very thin dark surface coating of iron and manganese oxides that forms on exposed rock surfaces in deserts

de·serve /di zúrv/ (**-served, -serv·ing, -serves**) *vt.* to have earned or be worthy of something [13thC. Via Old French *deservir* from Latin *deservire* "to serve well," from *servire* (see SERVE).] —**de·serv·er** *n.*

de·served /di zúrvd/ *adj.* justly earned or merited —**de·serv·ed·ness** /di zúrvədnəss/ *n.*

de·serv·ed·ly /di zúrvədlee/ *adv.* in a way that is justly and fully earned or merited ○ *She was deservedly popular as a teacher.*

de·serv·ing /di zúrving/ *adj.* **QUALIFIED OR ELIGIBLE TO RECEIVE SOMETHING** worthy to receive something because of need, merit, or justice ○ *I can think of no more deserving cause.* ■ *npl.* **PEOPLE QUALIFIED TO RECEIVE SOMETHING** people who have earned something justly through merit or need —**de·serv·ing·ly** *adv.* —**de·serv·ing·ness** *n.*

De Se·ver·sky /də sə vúrskee/, **Alexander Procofieff** (1894–1974) Russian-born U.S. aeronautical engineer. He manufactured war planes (1922–39) and invented the automatic bombsight.

de·sex /dee séks/ (**-sexed, -sex·ing, -sex·es**) *vt.* **1.** VET, MED **REMOVE SEX ORGANS** to remove the sex organs from an animal or person **2.** = **desexualize**

de·sex·u·al·ize /dee sékshoo ə lìz/ (**-ized, -iz·ing, -iz·es**) *vt.* **1. SUPPRESS SEXUAL CHARACTERISTICS** to suppress or diminish the sexual characteristics of an animal or person **2. REMOVE SEXIST MATERIAL** to remove sexist elements from something —**de·sex·u·al·i·za·tion** /dee sèkshoo əli záysh'n/ *n.*

des·ha·bille /dèssə beél, dèssə beé/ *n.* = **dishabille**

des·ic·cant /déssikənt/ *n.* a substance that absorbs water and can be used to remove moisture [Late 17thC. From Latin *desiccant-*, the present participle stem of *desiccare* (see DESICCATE).] —**des·ic·cant** *adj.*

des·ic·cate /déssi kàyt/ (**-cat·ed, -cat·ing, -cates**) *v.* **1. REMOVE OR LOSE MOISTURE** to remove the moisture from something or become free of moisture **2.** *vt.* **PRESERVE FOOD BY DRYING** to preserve food by removing its moisture **3.** *vt.* **MAKE UNINTERESTING** to remove vitality from something [Late 16thC. From Latin *desiccat-*, the past participle stem of *desiccare* "to dry out," from *siccus* "dry."] —**des·ic·ca·tion** /dèssi káysh'n/ *n.* —**des·ic·ca·tive** /déssi kàytiv/ *adj.*

des·ic·cat·ed /déssi kàytəd/ *adj.* **1. DRIED** dried and often pulverized **2. WITHOUT VITALITY** used to describe something, especially a literary work, lacking in energy or vitality

WORD KEY: SYNONYMS

See Synonyms at ***dry***.

des·ic·ca·tor /déssi kàytər/ *n.* an airtight apparatus that removes water from a substance either by heat or vacuum, or by using a chemical agent

de·sid·er·a·ta plural of **desideratum**

de·sid·er·ate /di síddə ràyt/ (**-at·ed, -at·ing, -ates**) *vt.* to wish or long for something (*archaic*) [Mid-17thC. From Latin *desiderat-*, the past participle stem of *desiderare* (see DESIRE).] —**de·sid·er·a·tion** /di sìddə ráysh'n/ *n.*

de·sid·er·a·tive /disíddə ràytiv, di síddərətiv/ *adj.* **1. DESIRING** having a desire for something (*formal*) **2.** GRAM **EXPRESSING DESIRE TO DO SOMETHING** used to describe a verb that, in some languages, expresses a desire to perform the action indicated by a related verb

de·sid·er·a·tum /di sìddə raátəm, -ráytəm/ (*plural* **-ta** /-raátə, -ráytə/) *n.* something that is desired or felt to be essential (*formal*) [Mid-17thC. From Latin, a form of the past participle of *desiderare* (see DESIRE).]

de·sign /di zín/ *v.* (**-signed, -sign·ing, -signs**) **1.** *vti.* **CREATE DETAILED PLAN OF SOMETHING** to work out or create the form or structure of something **2.** *vti.* **PLAN AND MAKE SOMETHING** to plan and make something in a skillful or artistic way **3.** *vt.* **INTEND FOR A USE** to intend something for a particular purpose ○ *The scholarship was designed to aid foreign students.* **4.** *vt.* **INVENT** to contrive, devise, or plan something ■ *n.* **1. WAY SOMETHING IS MADE** the way in which something is planned and made **2. PICTURE OF SOMETHING'S FORM AND STRUCTURE** a drawing or other graphical representation of something that shows how it is to be made **3. DECORATIVE PATTERN** a pattern or shape, sometimes repeated, used for decoration **4. PROCESS OF DESIGNING** the process and techniques of designing things **5. SCHEME** a plan or scheme for something **6. SOMETHING PLANNED** something that is planned or intended ■ **de·signs** *npl.* **SELFISH OR DISHONEST PLAN** a secretive plan undertaken for selfish or dishonest motives ○ *They had designs on her job.* [14thC. From, ultimately, Latin *designare* (see DESIGNATE).] —**de·sign·a·ble** *adj.* ◇ **by design** intentionally or on purpose

des·ig·nate *vt.* /dézzig nàyt/ (**-nat·ed, -nat·ing, -nates**) **1. DESCRIBE FORMALLY** to give somebody or something a formal description or name (*often passive*) **2. CHOOSE FOR A USE** to choose something for a particular purpose (*usually passive*) **3. NAME TO A POSITION** to formally choose somebody for a job, position, or duty **4. MARK** to mark or indicate something ○ *Colored pins on the map designated the new buildings* ■ *adj.* /dézzignət/ **CHOSEN FOR FUTURE POST** chosen for a particular position, while not yet actually in office [Late 18thC. From Latin *designat-*, the past participle stem of *designare* "to mark out," from, ultimately, *signum* "mark."] —**des·ig·na·tive** *adj.* —**des·ig·na·to·ry** *adj.* —**des·ig·na·tor** *n.*

des·ig·nat·ed driv·er *n.* somebody who goes to a social occasion and decides in advance not have any alcoholic drinks so as to be able to drive other people safely

des·ig·nat·ed hit·ter *n.* a player in baseball who does not play defensively but substitutes for a pitcher in the batting order

des·ig·na·tion /dèzzig náysh'n/ *n.* **1. NAME** a name, label, or description given to something or somebody **2. FACT OF BEING SPECIFIED** the act or process of being named or specified

de·sign·ed·ly /di zínədlee/ *adv.* intentionally or on purpose

des·ig·nee /dèzzig neé/ *n.* somebody chosen to perform a job, duty, or task

de·sign·er /di zínər/ *n.* **SOMEBODY WHO DESIGNS** somebody who makes and executes designs ■ *adj.* **1. TRENDY** used to describe something to suggest that it is trendy and popular ○ *designer foods* **2. DESIGNED BY SOMEBODY FAMOUS** created or produced by a famous designer ○ *designer jeans*

de·sign·er drug *n.* a drug that has been chemically altered to enhance its properties or to evade a legal prohibition

de·sign·er gene *n.* a gene that is introduced into an organism to control the presence or absence of a specific characteristic

de·sign·er stub·ble *n.* beard growth that is kept deliberately short to look as if the person has not shaved recently rather than as if trying to grow a beard (*informal*)

de·sign·ing /di zíning/ *adj.* tending to scheme and make secret plans for personal benefit —**de·sign·ing·ly** *adv.*

des·i·nence /déssinəns, dézz-/ *n.* an ending or suffix of a word (*technical*) [Late 16thC. Via French *désinence* from medieval Latin *desinentia*, from Latin *desinere* "to leave off, end," from *sinere* "to leave."] —**des·i·nen·tial** /dèssi nénshəl, dèzz-/ *adj.*

de·sir·a·ble /di zírəb'l/ *adj.* **1. WORTHY OF DESIRE** worth having or doing **2. ATTRACTIVE** sexually attractive or pleasing ■ *n.* **SOMEBODY OR SOMETHING DESIRED** somebody who or something that is desired —**de·sir·a·bil·i·ty** /di zìrə bíllətee/ *n.* —**de·sir·a·bly** /-blee/ *adv.*

de·sire /di zír/ *vt.* (**-sired, -sir·ing, -sires**) **1. WISH FOR** to want something very strongly **2. FIND SEXUALLY ATTRACTIVE** to want to have sexual relations with somebody **3. REQUEST** to wish for and request something (*formal*) ■ *n.* **1. CRAVING** a wish, craving, or longing for something **2. SOMETHING WISHED FOR** something that or somebody who is wished for (*formal*) **3. SEXUAL CRAVING** a strong wish for sexual relations with somebody [13thC. Via Old French from Latin *desiderare*, perhaps originally "to wish upon a star," from the stem *sider-* "star" (source of English *consider* and *sidereal*).] —**de·sir·er** *n.*

WORD KEY: SYNONYMS

See Synonyms at ***want***.

de·sir·ous /di zírəss/ *adj.* seeking or wishing for something very much (*formal*) —**de·sir·ous·ly** *adv.* —**de·sir·ous·ness** *n.*

de·sist /di síst, -zíst/ (**-sist·ed, -sist·ing, -sists**) *vi.* to cease or stop doing something [15thC. Via Old French from Latin *desistere*, from *sistere* "to bring to a standstill," from *stare* "to stand" (source of English *stance*).] —**de·sis·tance** *n.*

desk /desk/ *n.* **1.** FURNITURE **TABLE USED FOR WORK** a table with a broad flat or sloping top, often with drawers and compartments, used for writing, reading, drawing, or computing **2. COUNTER OFFERING SERVICE TO CUSTOMERS** a counter where a service is provided, e.g., in a hotel or an airport **3. DEPARTMENT OF ORGANIZATION** a division of a communications company or other organization that specializes in a particular area of interest **4.** MUSIC **STAND FOR SUPPORTING MUSIC** a stand for supporting a musical score that is shared by two players in an orchestra, or the two players who share it **5.** CHR **BOOK STAND IN CHURCH** a stand for the book from which a service is read in church ■ *adj.* **OF A DESK** at, for, done on, or taking place at a desk [14thC. Via medieval Latin *desca* from, ultimately, Latin *discus* "disk, dish, tray" (see DISH). The underlying idea is of a tray set on legs.]

desk·bound /désk bòwnd/ *adj.* working at a desk rather than at a physically active or practical task

desk clerk *n.* a hotel receptionist

de·skill /dee skíl/ (**-skilled, -skil·ling, -skills**) *vt.* to remove the need for skill or judgment in the performance of a task, often because of increasingly sophisticated production methods

desk·man /désk màn, -mən/ (*plural* **-men** /désk mèn, -mən/) *n.* somebody who works at a desk, especially one who edits copy at a newspaper desk

desk ser·geant *n.* a police sergeant who works in administration at a station

desk·top /désk tòp/ *n.* **1. SURFACE OF DESK** the working surface of a desk **2. GRAPHICAL COMPUTER REPRESENTATION OF OFFICE DESK** a visible portion of a software program that forms a background on which icons representing equipment, programs, and files are displayed ■ *adj.* **USABLE ON TOP OF DESK** small and compact enough to be used on the top of a desk, especially as a piece of computer equipment

desk·top pub·lish·ing *n.* the use of a personal computer and specialist software to design, lay out, and produce typeset-quality documents for output on a computer printer or for commercial printing

desm- *prefix.* = **desmo-** (*used before vowels*)

des·man /désmən/ *n.* **1. PYRENEAN AMPHIBIOUS MAMMAL** an amphibious mammal resembling a mole that has dense fur, webbed feet, and a flat scaly tail and lives in the Pyrenees. Latin name: *Galemys pyrenaicus.* **2. RUSSIAN AMPHIBIOUS MAMMAL** an amphibious mammal related to the Pyrenean desman that is found in Russia. Latin name: *Desmana moschata.* [Late 18thC. Shortening of Swedish *desmanråtta* "muskrat," from *desman* "musk" (from, ultimately, medieval Latin *bisamum*) + *råtta* "rat."]

De Smet /də smét/, **Pierre Jean** (1801–73) Belgian-born U.S. Jesuit missionary. He was known for mediating between Native American peoples and European settlers. Nickname **Blackrobe**

des·mid /désmid, déz-/ *n.* a green, usually one-celled, freshwater alga composed of two symmetrical half-cells. It forms branching matlike colonies and is found in unpolluted water. Family: Desmidiaceae. [Mid-19thC. From modern Latin *Desmidium*, genus name, which was coined from Greek *desmos* "bond, chain."] —**des·mid·i·an** /des míddee ən, dez-/ *adj.*

desmo- *prefix.* ligament, bond ○ *desmosome* [From Greek *desmos*, from *dein* "to bind" (source of English *diadem*)]

Des Moines /di móyn/ **1.** the longest river in Iowa, formed by the junction of its east and west branches near Humboldt. Length: 327 mi./526 km. **2.** capital, largest city, and commercial center of Iowa, situated where the Raccoon River meets the Des Moines River in the south central part of the state. Population: 193,422 (1996).

des·o·late *adj.* /déssələt/ **1. EMPTY** bare, uninhabited, and deserted **2. ALONE** solitary, joyless, and without hope **3. GRIM** dismal and gloomy ■ *vt.* /déssə làyt/ (**-lat·ed, -lat·ing, -lates**) **1. DEVASTATE PLACE** to make a place barren or deserted **2. MAKE WRETCHED** to make somebody feel sad and lonely [14thC. From Latin *desolatus*, the past participle of *desolare*, literally "to leave alone," from *solus* "alone" (source of English *solitary*).] —**des·o·la·ter** *n.* —**des·o·lat·ed** *adj.* —**des·o·late·ly** *adv.* —**des·o·late·ness** *n.*

des·o·la·tion /dèssə láysh'n/ *n.* **1. WRETCHED FEELING** a feeling of loneliness and despair **2. DESOLATE CONDITION** a condition of devastation or ruin in a place **3. ACT OF DEVASTATING PLACE** the act or process of devastating or laying waste to a place

de·sorp·tion /di sáwrpshən, di záwrpshən/ *n.* the action or process of releasing an absorbed substance from something, e.g., gas from rocks [Early 20thC. Coined from DE- + ABSORPTION.]

De So·to /də sṓtō/ city in northeastern Texas. It is a southern suburb of Dallas. Population: 34,993 (1996).

De So·to, Hernando (1500?–42?) Spanish explorer. He explored parts of South America (1519–32) and southeastern North America (1539–42).

de·spair /di spáir/ *n.* **1. FEELING OF HOPELESSNESS** a profound feeling that there is no hope **2. CAUSE OF HOPELESSNESS** somebody or something that makes somebody feel hopeless or exasperated ○ *He was the despair of his soccer coach.* ■ *vi.* (**-spaired, -spair·ing, -spairs**) **LOSE HOPE** to feel that there is no hope [13thC. Via Old French from Latin *desperare*, literally "to stop hoping," from *sperare* "to hope," from *spes* "hope."]

de·spair·ing /di spáiring/ *adj.* feeling or showing loss of hope —**de·spair·ing·ly** *adv.*

des·patch *vti., n.* = **dispatch**

des·per·a·do /dèspə ráa dō/ (*plural* **-does** *or* **-dos**) *n.* a reckless and violent criminal, especially in the early settlement of the western United States (*literary*) [Early 17thC. Alteration of obsolete *desperate* "desperate person," modeled on Spanish *desesperado*.]

des·per·ate /déspərət/ *adj.* **1. DESPAIRING** overwhelmed with urgency and anxiety, to the point of losing hope **2. AS LAST RESORT** so drastic or reckless as to be suitable only for a last resort **3. EXTREME** extremely difficult, serious, or dangerous ○ *a desperate shortage of food and water* **4. IN GREAT NEED** wanting or needing something very much ○ *Desperate for an answer, she phoned again.* **5. BEYOND HOPE** so wicked as to allow no hope of redemption **6. AWFUL** extremely bad or deplorable [14thC. From Latin *desperatus*, past participle of *desperare* (see DESPAIR).] —**des·per·ate·ly** *adv.* —**des·per·ate·ness** *n.*

des·per·a·tion /dèspə ráysh'n/ *n.* **1. RECKLESSNESS** recklessness brought on by great urgency and anxiety **2. HOPELESSNESS** a condition of being without hope

des·pi·ca·ble /di spíkəb'l/ *adj.* fully deserving of contempt [Mid-16thC. From late Latin *despicabilis*, from Latin *despicari* "to look down on."] —**des·pi·ca·bil·i·ty** /di spìkə bíllətee/ *n.* —**des·pi·ca·ble·ness** /di spíkəb'lnəss/ *n.* —**des·pi·ca·bly** /-blee/ *adv.*

de·spise /di spíz/ (**-spised, -spis·ing, -spis·es**) *vt.* to dislike somebody or something intensely and with contempt [13thC. From Old French *despis-*, the stem of *despire*, from Latin *despicere*, literally "to look down on," from *specere* "to look" (source of English *spectacle*).] —**de·spis·er** *n.*

de·spite /di spít/ *prep.* **1. REGARDLESS OF** notwithstanding or regardless of something ○ *A mission to investigate the rings of Saturn blasted off today despite bad weather.* **2. CONTRARY TO** indicates that something is done unexpectedly or unintentionally ○ *She blushed deeply despite herself.* [13thC. Via Old French *despit* "spite" from Latin *despect-*, the past participle stem of *despicere* (see DESPISE).] ◇ **in despite of** in spite of or notwithstanding (*archaic*)

de·spite·ful /di spítfəl/ *adj.* spiteful (*archaic*)

Des Plaines /dess pláynz/ city in northeastern Illinois, on the Des Plaines River. It is a northwestern suburb of Chicago. Population: 54,836 (1996).

de·spoil /di spóyl/ (**-spoiled, -spoil·ing, -spoils**) *vt.* to rob a place, often using force, of everything of value [13thC. Via Old French *despoillier* from Latin *despoliare* "to strip entirely of booty," from *spolium* "booty."] —**de·spoil·er** *n.* —**de·spoil·ment** *n.*

de·spo·li·a·tion /di spòlee áysh'n/ *n.* the plundering of everything of value in a place

de·spond /di spónd/ *vi.* (**-spond·ed, -spond·ing, -sponds**) **GIVE UP HOPE** to become discouraged or lose hope (*archaic or literary*) ○ *began to despond in their minds* ■ *n.* **HOPELESSNESS** a feeling of extreme unhappiness and hopelessness (*archaic or literary*) ○ *a slough of despond* [Mid-17thC. From Latin *despondere* "to give up (one's vitality)," literally "to promise away," from *spondere* "to promise" (source of English *sponsor*).] —**de·spond·ing·ly** *adv.*

de·spon·dent /di spóndənt/ *adj.* extremely unhappy and discouraged —**de·spon·dence** *n.* —**de·spon·den·cy** *n.* —**de·spon·dent·ly** *adv.*

des·pot /dés pòt, déspət/ *n.* **1.** POL **ABSOLUTE RULER** a tyrant or ruler with absolute powers **2. TYRANNICAL PERSON** somebody who acts in a tyrannical way towards people **3.** HIST **ROMAN, BYZANTINE, OR OTTOMAN RULER** a minor emperor or prince of the later Roman, Byzantine, or Ottoman empires [Mid-16thC. Via French *despote* from, ultimately, Greek *despotēs* "absolute ruler."]

des·pot·ic /di spóttik/, **des·pot·i·cal** /-k'l/ *adj.* relating to, typical of, or behaving like a despot — **des·pot·i·cal·ly** *adv.*

des·pot·ism /déspə tìzzəm/ *n.* **1. RULE BY DESPOT** rule by a despot or tyrant **2. ABUSE OF POWER** cruel and arbitrary use of power

de·spu·mate /déspyə màyt, di spyóo-/ (**-mated, -mat·ing, -mates**) *v.* **1.** *vi.* CHEM **FORM FROTH** to form froth or scum on the surface of a liquid **2.** *vt.* INDUST **REMOVE FROTH OR SCUM** to remove the scum or froth on the surface of a liquid [Mid-17thC. From Latin *despumat-* the past participle stem of *despumare* "to skim off (scum)," from *spuma* "foam, scum" (source of English *spume*).] — **de·spu·ma·tion** /dèspyə máysh'n/ *n.*

des·qua·mate /déskwə màyt/ (**-mat·ed, -mat·ing, -mates**) *v.* **1.** *vi.* PHYSIOL **SCALE OR PEEL OFF** to flake or peel off naturally in small pieces (*refers especially to skin*) **2.** *vt.* DERMAT **REMOVE LAYER OF SKIN** to remove a thin layer of skin, especially as a treatment for acne [Early 18thC. From *desquamat-*, the past participle stem of Latin *desquamare* "to scale off," from *squama* "scale."] — **des·qua·ma·tion** /dèskwə máysh'n/ *n.*

des·sert /di zúrt/ *n.* **1. SWEET DISH CONCLUDING MEAL** a sweet course eaten at the end or toward the end of a meal **2.** *U.K.* **FRUIT AND NUTS** fresh or dried fruit and nuts served at the end of a meal (*dated*) [Mid-16thC. From French, literally "(course following) clearing the table," from the past participle of *desservir*, literally "to remove what has been served," from *servir* (see SERVE).]

WORD KEY: USAGE

See Usage note at ***desert***.

des·sert·spoon /di zúrt spòon/ *n.* **1. MEDIUM-SIZED SPOON FOR EATING DESSERT** a medium-sized spoon, larger than a teaspoon but smaller than a tablespoon and used for eating dessert **2. des·sert·spoon, des·sert·spoon·ful AMOUNT HELD BY DESSERTSPOON** the amount a dessertspoon contains

des·sert wine *n.* a sweet wine served with dessert or after a meal

de·sta·bi·lize /dee stáybə lìz/ (**-lized, -liz·ing, -liz·es**) *vt.* to make something, particularly a government or economy, unstable in order to impair its functioning or bring about its collapse — **de·sta·bi·li·za·tion** /dee stàybəli záysh'n/ *n.*

des·ti·na·tion /dèsti náysh'n/ *n.* **1. PREDETERMINED END OF TRIP** the place to which somebody or something is going or must go **2. INTENDED OR DESTINED END** a purpose for which somebody or something is intended [14thC. From the Latin stem *destination-* "appointment," literally "something determined," from *destinare* (see DESTINE).]

des·tine /déstin/ (**-tined, -tin·ing, -tines**) *vt.* to preordain or intend somebody or something for a particular fate or use (*formal*) [14thC. Via French from Latin *destinare* "to set up, decree, determine," from the base *-stinare* "to cause to stand."]

des·tined /déstind/ *adj.* **1. SURE** sure, preordained, or intended ○ *She seemed destined for great things.* **2. HEADING TOWARD** bound or traveling toward a particular destination

des·ti·ny /déstinee/ (*plural* **-nies**) *n.* **1. SOMEBODY'S PREORDAINED FUTURE** the apparently predetermined and inevitable series of events that happen to somebody or something **2. INNER REALIZABLE PURPOSE OF A LIFE** the inner purpose of a life that can be discovered and realized **3. des·ti·ny, Des·ti·ny SOMETHING THAT PRETERMINES EVENTS** a force or agency that predetermines what will happen [14thC. From Old French *destinee*, from, ultimately, Latin *destinare* (see DESTINE).]

des·ti·tute /désti tòot/ *adj.* **1. LACKING THE NECESSITIES OF LIFE** lacking all money, resources, and possessions necessary for subsistence **2. LACKING SOMETHING** lacking or without something ○ *destitute of ideas* [14thC. From Latin *destitutus*, the past participle of *destituere* "to set down, abandon," from *statuere* "to set," from *status* "position."] —**des·ti·tute·ness** *n.*

des·ti·tu·tion /dèsti tóosh'n/ *n.* lack of the necessary means of subsistence

WORD KEY: SYNONYMS
See Synonyms at *poverty.*

des·tri·er /déstree ər, di streér/ *n.* a warhorse or charger, especially of a medieval knight (*archaic*) [14thC. Via Anglo-Norman *destrer* and Old French *destrier* from, ultimately, Latin *dexter* "right" (because the horse was led by the squire's right hand).]

de·stroy /di stróy/ (**-stroyed, -stroy·ing, -stroys**) *v.* **1.** *vti.* DEMOLISH to demolish or reduce something to fragments **2.** *vti.* RUIN to ruin or make something useless **3.** *vti.* ABOLISH to abolish, rescind, or end something **4.** *vt.* DEFEAT to defeat somebody in a crushing way **5.** *vt.* KILL ANIMAL to kill something or somebody, especially an animal (*usually passive*) ○ *Afterward, the dog could not be cured and so had to be destroyed.* [12thC. Via Old French *destruire* from, ultimately, Latin *destruere*, literally "to undo results of building" from *struere* "to build" (source of English *structure*).] —**de·stroy·a·ble** *adj.*

de·stroy·er /di stróyər/ *n.* **1.** NAVY SMALL FAST WARSHIP a fast highly maneuverable warship, smaller than a cruiser and bigger than a frigate, that is used to escort convoys and attack submarines **2.** SOMEBODY OR SOMETHING THAT DESTROYS somebody or something that causes destruction

de·stroy·er es·cort *n.* a small, slow form of destroyer that is mainly used to escort convoys of merchant ships

de·stroy·ing an·gel *n.* a highly poisonous large white mushroom with a frill near the top of its stalk. It grows in moist woodlands in temperate regions. Latin name: *Amanita virosa.*

de·struct /di strúkt/ *n.* INTENTIONAL DESTRUCTION OF ROCKET OR MISSILE the intentional destruction of a malfunctioning missile or rocket after its launch ■ *vti.* (**-struct·ed, -struct·ing, -structs**) DESTROY MALFUNCTIONING MISSILE OR ROCKET to intentionally destroy a malfunctioning missile or rocket after its launch, or be destroyed in this way [Mid-20thC. Back-formation from DESTRUCTION.]

de·struc·ti·ble /di strúktəb'l/ *adj.* capable of being destroyed or liable to be destroyed [Mid-18thC. Via French from late Latin *destructibilis*, from Latin *destruct-* (see DESTRUCTION).] —**de·struc·ti·bil·i·ty** /di strùktə bíllətee/ *n.*

de·struc·tion /di strúkshən/ *n.* **1.** PROCESS OF DESTROYING the act or process of destroying something **2.** DESTROYED STATE the condition of having been destroyed **3.** MEANS OF DESTROYING a cause or means of destroying something [13thC. From the Latin stem *destruction-*, from *destruct-*, the past participle stem of *destruere* (see DESTROY).]

de·struc·tive /di strúktiv/ *adj.* **1.** DESTROYING causing or capable of causing destruction **2.** MEANT TO DAMAGE intended to damage or hurt rather than be helpful or instructive [15thC. Via French from late Latin *destructivus*, from Latin *destruct-* (see DESTRUCTION).] —**de·struc·tive·ly** *adv.* —**de·struc·tiv·i·ty** /dee struk tívvətee, di strùk tívvətee/ *n.* —**de·struc·tive·ness** /di strúktivnəss/ *n.*

de·struc·tive dis·til·la·tion *n.* the process of heating solid substances in the absence of air to decompose them in order to obtain useful products from the vapor and residues

de·struc·tor /di strúktər/ *n.* **1.** *U.K.* INDUST INCINERATOR an incinerator used to burn garbage **2.** AEROSP EXPLOSIVE DEVICE FOR MISSILE OR ROCKET an onboard explosive device used to destroy a missile or rocket if it malfunctions dangerously after its launch

des·ue·tude /désswi tood/ *n.* the condition of not being in use (*formal*) [Early 17thC. Via French *désuétude* from, ultimately, Latin *desuescere* "to become unaccustomed," from *suescere* "to be accustomed" (source of English *custom*).]

de·sul·fur·ize /dee súlfə rīz/ (**-ized, -iz·ing, -iz·es**) *vti.* to remove sulfur and its compounds from something, typically from petroleum products or from flue gases when coal or another fuel is burned, or to lose sulfur in this way —**de·sul·fur·i·za·tion** /dee sùlfəri záysh'n/ *n.* —**de·sul·fur·iz·er** /dee súlfə rīzər/ *n.*

des·ul·to·ry /déss'l tàwree/ *adj.* **1.** PASSING FROM ONE THING TO ANOTHER aimlessly passing from one thing to another ○ *conversing in a desultory fashion* **2.** RANDOM happening in a random, disorganized, or unmethodical way ○ *The soldiers were subject to desultory fire from the enemy position.* [Late 16thC. From Latin *desultorius* "leaping," from *desilire* "to leap down," from *salire* "to leap" (source of English *salient*).] —**des·ul·to·ri·ly** *adv.* —**des·ul·to·ri·ness** *n.*

det., **det** *abbr.* **1.** MIL detachment **2.** detached **3.** detail **4.** GRAM determiner

Det. *abbr.* detective (*used in titles*)

de·tach /di tách/ (**-tached, -tach·ing, -tach·es**) *v.* **1.** *vti.* SEPARATE to separate, disconnect, or unfasten something, or become separated, disconnected, or unfastened **2.** *vt.* MIL SEND ON SPECIAL ASSIGNMENT to separate a military unit or an individual from the normal, larger unit for special duties [Late 17thC. Via French *détacher* from Old French *destachier*, from *attachier* "to attach" (see ATTACH).] —**de·tach·er** *n.*

de·tach·a·ble /di táchəb'l/ *adj.* capable of being taken off, disconnected, or removed —**de·tach·a·bil·i·ty** /di tàchə bíllətee/ *n.* —**de·tach·a·bly** /di táchəblee/ *adv.*

de·tached /di tácht/ *adj.* **1.** NOT ATTACHED not attached to something **2.** BUILDING SEPARATE standing on its own and not joined to another building **3.** FREE FROM EMOTIONAL INVOLVEMENT unaffected by emotional involvement or any form of bias —**de·tach·ed·ly** /di táchədlee, di táchtlee/ *adv.* —**de·tach·ed·ness** /di táchtnəss/ *n.*

de·tached ret·i·na *n.* an eye condition in which the retina becomes separated from the eyeball, causing loss of vision

de·tach·ment /di táchmənt/ *n.* **1.** ALOOFNESS AND INDIFFERENCE lack of interest in or involvement with other people, or indifference to worldly concerns **2.** DISINTERESTEDNESS a lack of bias, prejudice, or emotional involvement **3.** CONDITION OR PROCESS OF SEPARATION the condition of being separated from something, or the process of separating one thing from another **4.** MIL MILITARY UNIT SENT ON SPECIAL ASSIGNMENT a military unit separated from its normal, larger unit for special duties **5.** SPECIALIZED GROUP any specialized and separately employed unit of a group or organization **6.** *Can* CANADIAN POLICE UNIT an organizational unit of the Royal Canadian Mounted Police

de·tail *n.* /di táyl, deé tàyl/ **1.** INDIVIDUAL PART an individual separable part of something, especially one of several items of information ○ *No details of the proposed legislation are available yet.* **2.** EACH AND EVERY ELEMENT all of the individual elements that together make up a whole ○ *attention to detail* **3.** INCLUSION OF ALL ELEMENTS treatment of and inclusion of all of the individual elements that make up something ○ *Your description of the item needs more detail.* **4.** INSIGNIFICANT PART something that is insignificant or a minor part of something else ○ *Safety in the sport is not a mere detail.* **5.** ARTS, ARCHIT SMALL ELEMENT OF ART OR STRUCTURE a small element of a work of art or building structure, considered separately **6.** GROUP WITH SPECIAL TASK a group of people, especially in the armed services, given a specific task ■ **de·tails** *npl.* PERSONAL FACTS facts about somebody, e.g., his or her name and address ■ *vt.* /di táyl/ (**-tailed, -tail·ing, -tails**) **1.** LIST THINGS to list or enumerate a series of items or events **2.** DECORATE to add refinements or decorations to something, especially a motor vehicle **3.** MIL GIVE MILITARY UNIT SPECIALIZED ASSIGNMENT to assign a military unit to a specialized task (*often passive*) [Early 17thC. From French *détail*, literally "piece cut off," from *détaillir* "to cut up," from *taillier* "to cut."] —**de·tail·er** /di táylər, deé tàylər/ *n.* ◇ **go into detail** to be very specific and include all of the particulars ◇ **in detail** covering every item or particular

de·tail draw·ing *n.* a large-scale drawing that shows part of a machine, device, or building

de·tailed /di táyld, deé tàyld/ *adj.* including all or many of the particular elements of something

de·tain /di táyn/ (**-tained, -tain·ing, -tains**) *vt.* **1.** DELAY PROGRESS to hold back or delay somebody or something **2.** LAW HOLD IN CUSTODY to restrain or keep somebody or something in custody [15thC. Via Old French *detenir* from, ultimately, Latin *detinere*, literally "to hold back," from *tenere* "to hold" (see TENANT).] —**de·tain·a·ble** *adj.* —**de·tain·ment** *n.*

de·tain·ee /deé tay neé, di-/ *n.* somebody who is held in custody

de·tain·er /di táynər/ *n.* **1.** WRIT AUTHORIZING EXTENDED DETENTION a writ authorizing that somebody in custody may be confined for a further period **2.** WRONGFUL DETENTION the wrongful withholding of somebody's property or freedom

de·tect /di tékt/ (**-tect·ed, -tect·ing, -tects**) *v.* **1.** *vt.* PERCEIVE THE EXISTENCE OF to notice or discover the existence of something **2.** *vt.* ELECTRON ENG = **demodulate 3.** *vti.* CRIMINOL WORK ON CRIMES to investigate crimes or other matters as a detective [15thC. From Latin *detect-*, the past participle stem of *detegere* "to uncover," from *tegere* "to cover."] —**de·tect·a·ble** *adj.* —**de·tect·a·bil·i·ty** /di tèktə bíllətee/ *n.*

de·tec·tion /di tékshən/ *n.* **1.** PERCEPTION OF SOMETHING'S EXISTENCE the act of noticing or discovering the existence of something, or the state of having been detected **2.** CRIMINOL DETECTIVE WORK the work of a detective in investigating crime or wrongdoing **3.** ELECTRON ENG = **demodulation**

de·tec·tive /di téktiv/ *n.* SOMEBODY WHO INVESTIGATES WRONGDOING somebody who investigates and gathers evidence about crimes or possible wrongdoing, either for a police force or privately for a client ○ *I became a detective last year.* ■ *adj.* DETECTING SOMETHING acting to detect something ○ *detective devices*

de·tec·tor /di téktər/ *n.* **1.** TECH SENSING DEVICE a device for sensing the presence of or changes in something, e.g., radiation or pressure **2.** SOMEBODY OR SOMETHING THAT DETECTS somebody who or something that detects

de·tent /di tént/ *n.* a locking device, e.g., a lever or spring-loaded catch, that permits movement of a machine part in one direction only [Late 17thC. From French *détente* "release," literally "opposite of stretching," from, ultimately, Latin *tendere* "to stretch" (source of English *tension*).]

dé·tente /day taánt, day taáNt/, **de·tente** *n.* a relaxation of tension or hostility between nations [Early 20thC. From French, "relaxation" (see DETENT).]

de·ten·tion /di ténshən/ *n.* **1.** CRIMINOL PROCESS OF BEING DETAINED the act keeping somebody in custody, or the state of being kept in custody **2.** EDUC PUNISHMENT BY BEING DETAINED AFTER SCHOOL a form of punishment for school students in which they are made to stay in class at a break or at school after normal hours [15thC. From the late Latin stem *detention-*, from, ultimately, Latin *detinere* (see DETAIN).]

de·ten·tion home *n.* a place where young people are held in custody, usually while awaiting disposition of their cases by a juvenile court

de·ter /di túr/ (**-terred, -ter·ring, -ters**) *vti.* to discourage somebody from taking action or prevent something happening, especially by making people feel afraid or anxious [Mid-16thC. From Latin *deterrere*, literally "to scare off," from *terrere* "to scare" (source of English *terror*).] —**de·ter·ment** *n.* —**de·ter·ra·ble** *adj.*

de·terge /di túrj/ (**-terged, -terg·ing, -terg·es**) *vt.* to cleanse something, especially a wound (*technical*) [Early 17thC. Directly or via French *déterger* from Latin *detergere*, literally "to wipe off," from *tergere* "to wipe."]

de·ter·gen·cy /di túrjənsee/, **de·ter·gence** /di túrjəns/ *n.* the ability of a substance to cleanse (*technical*)

de·ter·gent /di túrjənt/ *n.* CLEANSING SUBSTANCE a cleansing substance, especially a synthetic liquid that dissolves dirt and oil ■ *adj.* CLEANSING with the properties of a detergent

de·te·ri·o·rate /di teéree ə ràyt/ (**-rat·ed, -rat·ing, -rates**) *vti.* to become or make something worse in quality, value, or strength [Late 16thC. From *deteriorat-*, the past participle stem of late Latin *deteriorare*, from Latin *deterior* "worse," from, ultimately, *de* "down."] —**de·te·ri·o·ra·tive** /di teéree ə ràytiv/ *adj.*

de·te·ri·o·ra·tion /di teéree ə ráysh'n/ *n.* **1.** DECLINE a decline in quality, value, or strength **2.** PROCESS OF DETERIORATING the act or process of deteriorating **3.** DETERIORATED CONDITION the condition of having deteriorated

de·ter·min·a·ble /di túrminəb'l/ *adj.* **1.** CAPABLE OF BEING DETERMINED able to be worked out, decided, or found **2.** ABLE TO BE ENDED subject to being terminated —**de·ter·min·a·bil·i·ty** /di tùrminə bíllətee/ *n.* —**de·ter·min·a·bly** /di túrminəblee/ *adv.*

de·ter·mi·na·cy /di túrmeenəssee/ *n.* the quality or condition of being determinate

de·ter·mi·nant /di túrminənt/ *n.* **1.** CAUSE a factor that causes or influences something **2.** MATH SQUARE ARRAY OF MATHEMATICAL ELEMENTS a square array of elements that is used in various mathematical processes, e.g., solving simultaneous equations and studying linear transformations, and which itself has a numerical value ■ *adj.* CAUSAL influencing or causing something

de·ter·mi·nate /di túrminət/ *adj.* 1. LIMITED with exact and definite limits 2. DETERMINED determined (*formal*) 3. BOT WITH STEMS ENDING IN A BUD used to describe a pattern of flowering in which primary and secondary stems end in a flower bud and stop growing. ◊ **indeterminate** —**de·ter·mi·nate·ly** *adv.* —**de·ter·mi·nate·ness** *n.*

de·ter·mi·na·tion /di tùrmi náysh'n/ *n.* 1. FIRMNESS OF PURPOSE firmness of purpose, will, or intention ○ *full of ambition and determination* 2. FIXED PURPOSE a fixed purpose or resolution ○ *her determination to succeed* 3. ACT OF DISCOVERING SOMETHING an act of finding out or ascertaining something, especially as a result of investigation or research (*formal*) ○ *determination of the cause of death* 4. DECISION ON COURSE OF ACTION decision-making on, or the establishment of, a course of action (*formal*) ○ *They were entrusted with the determination of future policy.* 5. SETTLEMENT OF DISPUTE OR CONTEST the authoritative settlement of a dispute, especially by a judicial body 6. LAW END OF ESTATE, INTEREST, OR RIGHT the conclusion or termination of an estate, interest, or right 7. LOGIC QUALIFYING OF CONCEPT the qualifying of a concept or proposition by defining its attributes 8. EMBRYOL STAGE IN DEVELOPMENT OF EMBRYONIC TISSUE the stage in the development of embryonic tissue after which it can only develop as one specific type of tissue and no longer has the potential to develop into different types

de·ter·mi·na·tive /di túrmi nàytiv, di túrminətiv/ *adj.* ACTING TO DETERMINE able to determine something ■ *n.* 1. DETERMINING FACTOR a factor that determines something 2. GRAM = **determiner** —**de·ter·mi·na·tive·ly** *adv.* —**de·ter·mi·na·tive·ness** *n.*

de·ter·mine /di túrmin/ (**-mined, -min·ing, -mines**) *v.* 1. *vt.* FIND OUT to find out or ascertain something, usually after investigation 2. *vt.* DECIDE to decide or settle something conclusively 3. *vt.* INFLUENCE to influence or give form to something 4. *vt.* FIX LIMITS to fix the limits or form of something 5. *vti.* ADOPT OR CAUSE TO ADOPT PURPOSE to adopt a set purpose, or make somebody do this ○ *determined to leave as soon as possible* 6. *vti.* LAW END to end something, or come to an end [14thC. Via Old French from Latin *determinare*, literally "to set the limits of," from *terminus* "limit, boundary." Originally in the sense "to bring to an end."]

de·ter·mined /di túrmind/ *adj.* feeling or showing firmness or a fixed purpose —**de·ter·mined·ly** *adv.* —**de·ter·mined·ness** *n.*

de·ter·min·er /di túrminər/ *n.* 1. GRAM WORD THAT DETERMINES NOUN USE a word such as "a," "the," "this," "each," "some," "either," "my," and "your" that appears before any descriptive adjective and decides the kind of reference that a noun has 2. SOMETHING OR SOMEBODY THAT DETERMINES something that or somebody who determines

de·ter·min·ing /di túrmining/ *adj.* causing or deciding something ○ *the determining factor*

de·ter·min·ism /di túrmi nìzzəm/ *n.* the doctrine or belief that everything, including every human act, is caused by something and that there is no real free will —**de·ter·min·ist** *n.*

de·ter·min·is·tic /di tùrmi nístik/ *adj.* 1. PHILOS RELATING TO DETERMINISM relating to the doctrine or belief that everything, including every human act, is caused by something and that there is no real free will 2. OF KNOWABLE OUTCOME having an outcome that can be predicted because all of its causes are either known or the same as those of a previous event —**de·ter·min·is·ti·cal·ly** *adv.*

de·ter·rence /di túrəns, di túrrəns/ *n.* 1. ACT OF DETERRING the act of deterring somebody or something 2. SOMETHING THAT DETERS a means of deterring somebody or something 3. DEFENSIVE POLICY the policy of discouraging enemy attack by maintaining sufficient military force to retaliate

de·ter·rent /di túrənt, di túrrənt/ *n.* 1. SOMETHING THAT DETERS something that deters somebody or something 2. WEAPONS THAT DETER AN ATTACK weapons, particularly nuclear weapons, held as a retaliatory threat ■ *adj.* ACTING TO DETER capable of deterring somebody or something

de·ter·sive /di túrsiv/ *adj.* with the properties of a detergent (*technical*) [Late 16thC. From French *détersif*, from Latin *deters-*, the past participle stem of *detergere* (see DETERGE).]

de·test /di tést/ (**-test·ed, -test·ing, -tests**) *vt.* to dislike somebody or something very much [15thC. Via French *détester* from Latin *detestari* "to bear witness against, denounce," from *testis* "witness" (source of English *testify*).] —**de·test·er** *n.*

de·test·a·ble /di téstəb'l/ *adj.* causing or deserving intense dislike —**de·test·a·bil·i·ty** /di tèstə bíllətee/ *n.* —**de·test·a·ble·ness** /di téstəb'lnəss/ *n.* —**de·test·a·bly** /-blee/ *adv.*

de·tes·ta·tion /dèe te stáysh'n/ *n.* 1. GREAT DISLIKE an intense loathing or hatred 2. DETESTED PERSON OR THING something that or somebody who is detested ○ *Neckties are a real detestation for him.*

de·throne /dee thrṓn/ (**-throned, -thron·ing, -thrones**) *vt.* 1. POL REMOVE RULER FROM POWER to remove a ruler, especially a monarch, from power 2. REMOVE FROM POSITION to remove somebody from a high or powerful position, especially a champion in a sport —**de·throne·ment** *n.* —**de·thron·er** *n.*

det·i·nue /détt'noo/ *n.* a legal action to reclaim wrongfully withheld personal property [15thC. From Old French, "detention," formed from *detenir* (see DETAIN).]

det·o·nate /détt'n àyt/ (**-nat·ed, -nat·ing, -nates**) *vti.* to explode, or make something explode [Early 18thC. From *detonat-*, the past participle stem of Latin *detonare* "to thunder down," from *tonare* "to thunder" (source of English *stun*).] —**det·o·na·tive** *adj.*

det·o·na·tion /dètt'n áysh'n/ *n.* 1. EXPLOSION an explosion, or an act of making something explode 2. AUTOMOT PREMATURE COMBUSTION INSIDE ENGINE a premature spontaneous burning of a fuel-air mixture inside an internal-combustion engine

det·o·na·tor /détt'n àytər/ *n.* a device or small quantity of explosive used to make a bomb or larger quantity of explosive explode

de·tour /dée toor, di toór/ *n.* 1. DEVIATION FROM MORE DIRECT ROUTE a deviation from a shorter, more direct route 2. TRANSP ALTERNATIVE ROUTE a route to be taken by traffic as an alternative to the normal route when the normal route cannot be used ○ *We encountered many detours.* 3. INDIRECT PATH OR PROCEDURE a deviation from a direct, expected, or previously decided course of action ■ *vti.* (**-toured, -tour·ing, -tours**) DEVIATE OR MAKE DEVIATE to deviate or make somebody or something deviate from a shorter route [Mid-18thC. From French *détour*, from, ultimately, Old French *destorner* "to turn away," from *torner* "to turn" (see TURN).]

de·tox /dée tòks/ *n.* = **detoxification** ■ *vti.* (**-toxed, -tox·ing, -tox·es**) = **detoxify** [Late 20thC. Shortening of DETOXIFICATION and DETOXIFY.]

de·tox·i·cate /dee tóksi kàyt/ (**-cat·ed, -cat·ing, -cates**) *vt.* = **detoxify** —**de·tox·i·cant** /dee tóksikənt/ *n., adj.*

de·tox·i·fi·ca·tion /dee tòksəfi káysh'n/, **de·tox·i·ca·tion** /dee tòksi káysh'n/ *n.* 1. BIOCHEM PROCESS OF REMOVING OR TRANSFORMING POISON the process of removing toxic substances or transforming them into something harmless 2. MED TREATMENT FOR ADDICT the treatment of an alcoholic or drug addict by controlled withdrawal of the toxic addictive substance

de·tox·i·fy /dee tóksi fī/ (**-fied, -fy·ing, -fies**) *v.* 1. *vti.* MED RID SOMEBODY OF TOXIC SUBSTANCES to subject somebody to or undergo the withdrawal of a toxic or addictive substance such as alcohol or a drug 2. *vt.* BIOCHEM REMOVE OR TRANSFORM TOXIC SUBSTANCE to remove a poison from something or counteract its toxic effects [Early 20thC. Coined from DE- + TOXIC + -FY.]

de·tract /di trákt/ (**-tract·ed, -tract·ing, -tracts**) *v.* 1. *vti.* TAKE SOMETHING AWAY to reduce the quality, value, or importance of something by taking something away 2. *vt.* DISPARAGE to disparage somebody or something (*archaic*) [15thC. From Latin *detract-*, the past participle stem of *detrahere* "to take or pull away," from *trahere* "to pull" (see TRACTOR).] —**de·trac·tive** *adj.* —**de·trac·tive·ly** *adv.*

de·trac·tion /di trákshən/ *n.* 1. LESSENING a reduction or taking away of quality, value, or importance from something 2. SLANDERING the act of damaging somebody's reputation, especially by making discrediting comments (*formal*) 3. DETRACTING PERSON OR THING somebody or something that detracts from the quality, value, or importance of something

de·trac·tor /di tráktər/ *n.* somebody who disparages or devalues something or somebody

de·train /dee tráyn/ (**-trained, -train·ing, -trains**) *vti.* to get out of or remove people from a railroad train —**de·train·ment** *n.*

de·trib·al·ize /dee tríb'l īz/ (**-ized, -iz·ing, -iz·es**) *vti.* to abandon or make people abandon tribal practices, usually by exposure to another culture —**de·trib·al·i·za·tion** /dee trìb'li záysh'n/ *n.*

det·ri·ment /déttrimənt/ *n.* 1. DISADVANTAGE damage, harm, or disadvantage 2. HARMFUL THING something that causes harm or injury (*formal*) [15thC. Via French from Latin *detrimentum*, from *deterere* "to wear away," from *terere* "to rub, wear" (source of English *attrition*).]

det·ri·men·tal /dèttri mént'l/ *adj.* causing harm or damage —**det·ri·men·tal·ly** *adv.*

de·tri·tion /di trísh'n/ *n.* the process of wearing something away by friction [Late 17thC. From the medieval Latin stem *detrition-*, from Latin *deterere* (see DETRIMENT).]

de·tri·tus /di trítəss/ *n.* 1. DEBRIS debris or discarded material 2. GEOL ROCK FRAGMENTS fragments of rock that have been worn away 3. ECOL ORGANIC MATTER organic debris formed by the decomposition of plants and animals [Late 18thC. From Latin, from the past participle of *deterere* (see DETRIMENT).] —**de·tri·tal** *adj.*

De·troit /də tróyt/ largest city in southeastern Michigan, on the Detroit River and Lake St. Clair. Population: 1,000,272 (1996).

De·troit tech·no *n.* a type of techno music with a warm emotional feel, often using strings, that originated in Detroit in the late 1980s

de trop /də trṓ/ *adj.* superfluous or excessive [Mid-18thC. From French, literally "excessive."]

de·trude /di troód/ (**-trud·ed, -trud·ing, -trudes**) *vt.* to force something down, out, or away (*formal*) [Mid-16thC. From Latin *detrudere* "to thrust down," from *trudere* "to thrust."] —**de·tru·sion** /di troózh'n/ *n.*

de·tu·mes·cence /dèe too méss'ns/ *n.* a gradual reduction in a swelling, especially of a penis [Late 17thC. Formed from Latin *detumescere* "to stop swelling," from *tumere* "to swell" (source of English *tumor*). —**de·tu·mesce** *vi.*]

de·tu·mes·cent /dèe too méss'nt/ *adj.* flaccid and no longer erect

deuce[1] /dooss/ *n.* 1. CARDS CARD WITH TWO SPOTS a playing card or the face of a dice that has two spots 2. RACKET GAMES TIE-BREAKING SITUATION in tennis, badminton, and other racket games, a situation in which a player must score two successive points to win after the score is tied 3. NUMBER 2 the number 2 (*slang*) 4. MONEY TWO DOLLARS two dollars, or a two-dollar bill (*slang*) [15thC. Via Old French *deus* "two" from Latin *duos*. Ultimately from an Indo-European word that is also the ancestor of English *two*.]

deuce[2] /dooss/ *n.* BAD THING something that is bad or unpleasant (*dated slang*) ■ *interj.* USED TO SHOW DISPLEASURE used instead of a swearword to show displeasure, irritation, or surprise (*dated slang*) [Mid-17thC. Via Dutch or Low German *duus* "throw of two on two dice" (the lowest score) from, ultimately, Latin *duus* "two" (see DEUCE[1]).]

deuc·ed /doóssəd, doost/ *adj.* USED FOR EMPHASIS used instead of a swearword to give emphasis or to show irritation or displeasure (*dated slang*) ■ *adv.* VERY decidedly or extremely (*dated slang*) —**deuc·ed·ly** *adv.*

deuc·es wild *n.* a form of poker or another card game in which a deuce can represent a card of any suit and denomination a player chooses

De·us /dáy əss/ *n.* God [13thC. From Latin. From an Indo-European word that is also the ancestor of *deity*, *divine*, and *July*.]

de·us ex ma·chi·na /dày əss eks maákinə/ *n.* 1. UNCONVINCING CHARACTER WHO RESOLVES PLOT an improbable character or unconvincing event used to resolve a plot 2. GOD WHO RESOLVES PLOT in ancient Greek and Roman theater, a god introduced to resolve a complicated plot [From modern Latin, literally "god from the machinery"; the *machina* was a device used in Greek theater to lower actors onto the stage]

Deut. *abbr.* Deuteronomy

deuter- *prefix.* = **deutero-** (*used before vowels*)

deu·ter·ag·o·nist /dootə rággənist/ *n.* a character second in importance to the leading character (**protagonist**) in ancient Greek drama [Mid-19thC. From Greek *deuteragōnistēs*, from *deuteros* "second" + *agōnistēs* "actor" (see PROTAGONIST).]

deu·ter·a·no·pi·a /dootərə nṓpee ə/ *n.* colorblindness in which red and green are confused [Early 20thC. Coined from DEUTERO- + AN- + -OPIA. From the fact that green is regarded as the second component of color vision.] —**deu·ter·a·nop·ic** /dootərə nóppik, dootərə nṓpik/ *adj.*

deu·ter·ate /do͞otə ràyt/ (**-at·ed, -at·ing, -ates**) *vt.* to add deuterium, an isotope of hydrogen with double the normal mass, to a chemical compound [Mid-20thC. Coined from DEUTERIUM + -ATE.] —**deu·te·ra·tion** /do͞otə ráysh'n/ *n.*

deu·ter·ide /do͞otə rīd/ *n.* a compound of hydrogen (**hydride**) in which hydrogen has been replaced by its heavier isotope deuterium [Mid-20thC. Coined from DEUTERIUM + -IDE.]

deu·te·ri·um /doo teéree əm/ *n.* an isotope of hydrogen that has double the mass of ordinary hydrogen because it contains a neutron in its nucleus. It is often used as a tracer in experiments. Symbol **D** [Mid-20thC. Coined from Greek *deuteros* "second" (see DEUTERO-) + -IUM. From the fact that it is second in the series of possible hydrogen isotopes.]

deu·te·ri·um ox·ide *n.* heavy water, used as a moderator in some nuclear reactors. Formula: D_2O. (*technical*) = **heavy water**

deutero- *prefix.* second, secondary ○ *deuteroplasm* [From Greek *deuteros*]

deu·ter·o·ca·non·i·cal /do͞otə rō kə nónnik'l/ *adj.* part of secondary, less well regarded, or disputed collection of religious scripture, especially the Apocrypha and the Antilegomena, or constituting or relating to one of these secondary canons

deu·ter·on /do͞otə ròn/ *n.* the nucleus of a deuterium atom, consisting of one proton and one neutron. It is mainly used as a bombarding particle in particle accelerators such as cyclotrons. Symbol D^+ [Mid-20thC. Formed from DEUTERO-, on the model of PROTON.]

Deu·ter·on·o·mist /do͞otə rónnəmist/ *n.* one of the authors of Deuteronomy, the fifth book of the Bible

Deu·ter·on·o·my /do͞otə rónnəmee/ *n.* the fifth book of the Bible [14thC. Via late Latin from Greek *Deuteronomion*, literally "second law" (because the book contains a repetition of the Decalogue and of parts of *Exodus*).] —**Deu·ter·o·nom·ic** /do͞otərə nómmik/ *adj.*

deu·to·plasm /do͞otə plàzzəm/ *n.* nutrient matter contained in certain reproductive cells, e.g., the yolk in a bird's egg [Late 19thC] —**deu·to·plas·mic** /do͞otə plázmik/ *adj.*

deut·sche mark, **deut·sche·mark** *n.* the standard currency unit of Germany. Symbol **DM**. See table at **currency** [Mid-20thC. From German, "German mark," from *deutsch* "German" (see DUTCH) + *Mark* MARK.]

deut·zi·a /do͞otsee ə, dóytsee ə/ (*plural* **-as** *or* **-a**) *n.* a shrub in the saxifrage family, native to Asia and Central America, that has clusters of white to pink or lavender flowers. Genus: *Deutzia*. [Mid-19thC. From modern Latin, genus name; named for Johann van der *Deutz*, 18th century Dutch patron of botany.]

dev. *abbr.* deviation

de·va /dáyvə/ *n.* a Hindu or Buddhist god [Early 19thC. From Sanskrit, "god," originally "bright or shining one." Ultimately from an Indo-European word meaning "to shine," which is also the ancestor of English *divine*.]

Eamon De Valera

De Va·le·ra /dèvvə lérrə/, **Eamon** (1882–1975) U.S.-born Irish statesman. He was a key figure in establishing the Irish Republic. He formed a dissident faction of Sinn Fein, the Fianna Fáil party (1926), was prime minister (1937–48, 1951–54, and 1957–59), and served as president (1959–73).

de·val·u·ate /dee vályoo àyt/ (**-at·ed, -at·ing, -ates**) *vti.* = **devalue** *v.* 1

de·val·u·a·tion /dee vàllyoo áysh'n/ *n.* **1. LOWERING OF CURRENCY'S VALUE** a lowering by the government of the value of a nation's currency relative to that of foreign currencies **2. REDUCTION IN IMPORTANCE** a reduction in the importance or value of something

de·val·ue /dee vállyoo/ (**-ued, -u·ing, -ues**) *v.* **1.** *vti.* **LOWER CURRENCY'S VALUE** to lower the value of a nation's currency by a governmental action, or to become lowered in value **2.** *vt.* **MAKE OR BECOME LESS VALUABLE** to cause the value or importance of somebody or something to be reduced, or to become reduced in value or importance

De·va·na·ga·ri /dàyvə naágəree/ *n.* the alphabet that is used to write many of the modern languages of India as well as ancient Sanskrit [Late 18thC. From Sanskrit, from *deva* DEVA + *Nāgarī*, an earlier name for the script, apparently literally "of the city, urbane."]

dev·as·tate /dévvə stàyt/ (**-tat·ed, -tat·ing, -tates**) *vt.* **1. DAMAGE SEVERELY** to cause severe or widespread damage to something ○ *an area devastated by floods* **2. UPSET ENORMOUSLY** to shock or upset somebody enormously, producing a feeling of being overwhelmed or helpless (*often passive*) [Mid-17thC. From Latin *devastat-*, the past participle stem of *devastare*, literally "to lay waste completely," from *vastare* "to lay waste," from *vastus* "waste" (source of English *waste* and *vast*).] —**dev·as·ta·tion** /dèvvə stáysh'n/ *n.* —**dev·as·ta·tive** /dévvə stàytiv/ *adj.* —**dev·as·ta·tor** /-tər/ *n.*

dev·as·tat·ing /dévvə stàyting/ *adj.* **1. DAMAGING** causing severe or widespread damage ○ *policies that have a devastating effect on economic growth* **2. VERY UPSETTING** causing enormous shock or upset ○ *The news was devastating.* **3. SHARPLY CRITICAL** containing criticism that is very sharp and very effective or damaging, often as a result of its precise detail or caustic wit **4. REMARKABLE** startlingly impressive or attractive (*informal*) ○ *the devastating speed of her forehand return* —**dev·as·tat·ing·ly** *adv.*

de·vein /dee váyn/ (**-veined, -vein·ing, -veins**) *vt.* to remove the dark threadlike gut (**vein**) from the back of the tail meat of a shrimp

de·vel·op /di véllәp/ (**-oped, -op·ing, -ops**) *v.* **1.** *vti.* **CHANGE AND GROW** to change, or cause to change, and become larger, stronger, or more impressive, successful, or advanced **2.** *vi.* **ARISE AND INCREASE** to arise and then increase or progress to a more complex state ○ *Tension was developing between the two nations.* **3.** *vt.* **ACQUIRE FEATURE, HABIT, OR ILLNESS** to acquire a particular feature, habit, or illness that then becomes more marked or extreme ○ *The baby is developing a cold.* **4.** *vt.* **ENLARGE ON** to add details to a basic plan or idea **5.** *vt.* **BECOME CLEAR** to become apparent and thus resolve a question or clarify a situation ○ *It developed that we didn't need reservations.* **6.** *vti.* **PRESENT OR BE REVEALED IN STAGES** to present the sequential events or successive stages of a story or argument, or to have such events or stages revealed ○ *The theory is developed at length in her new book.* **7.** *vt.* **USE RESOURCES FOR HUMAN PURPOSES** to use or make available land, minerals, or other natural resources for human purposes such as housing **8.** *vt.* **BUILD STRUCTURES** to plan and construct buildings, roads, or other technological structures ○ *develop a global communications system* **9.** *vt.* **TURN FILM INTO NEGATIVES OR PRINTS** to treat photographic film with chemicals in order to produce a negative or print (*often passive*) ○ *Send the rolls off to be developed.* **10.** *vi.* **ACHIEVE SEXUAL MATURITY** to become sexually mature **11.** *vt.* CHESS **BRING PIECE INTO PLAY** to bring a chess piece into play **12.** *vt.* MUSIC **VARY MUSICAL THEME** to add to a musical theme by using variation or ornamentation, especially by breaking it down into motifs and using other musical techniques [Mid-17thC. From French *développer*, literally "to unwrap" (the original sense in English), from, ultimately, Old French *voloper* "to wrap" (source of English *envelope*).] —**de·vel·op·a·ble** *adj.*

de·vel·oped /di vélləpt/ *adj.* ECON wealthy and technologically advanced, with sophisticated manufacturing and service industries

de·vel·op·er /di vélləpər/ *n.* **1. SOMEBODY WHO DEVELOPS** somebody who or something that develops something ○ *the developer of a new manufacturing process* **2. BUYER OF LAND FOR BUILDING** a person or company that buys land in order to build on it or sell it to others who want to build on it **3.** PHOTOGRAPHY **CHEMICAL FOR MAKING NEGATIVES OR PRINTS** a chemical used to turn exposed film into negatives or prints

de·vel·op·ing /di vélləping/ *adj.* ECON using or involving small-scale agriculture and industry of the kind that characterized the earlier economic stages of technologically advanced nations

de·vel·op·ment /di vélləpmənt/ *n.* **1. EVENT CAUSING CHANGE** an incident that causes a situation to change or progress (*often used in the plural*) ○ *Have there been any political developments since last week?* **2. DEVELOPING OF SOMETHING** the process of developing, developing something, or of being developed, e.g., by growth, change, or elaboration ○ *sustained economic development* **3. BEING DEVELOPED** a state in which the developing of something is not yet completed ○ *The prototype is in development.* **4. HOUSES OR OTHER BUILDINGS** a group of houses or other buildings that are built as a single construction project **5.** MUSIC **ELABORATION OF MUSICAL THEME** the process of varying and elaborating the rhythm and melody of a musical theme **6.** MUSIC **MUSICAL SECTION WHERE THEME IS DEVELOPED** one of the three main sections of the sonata form, in which the musical themes presented in the exposition are rhythmically and melodically elaborated

de·vel·op·men·tal /di vèlləp mént'l/ *adj.* **1. INVOLVING DEVELOPMENT** representing or involving a development of some kind **2. TYPICAL OF DEVELOPMENT** characteristic of or resulting from the way something develops **3. CONCERNED WITH DEVELOPMENT** concerned with development or a development **4.** EDUC, PSYCHOL **DEVELOPING AS CHILD GROWS** changing or growing as a child grows ○ *an educational program that takes into account a student's developmental capacity* **5.** EDUC **REFLECTING AGE-RELATED ABILITIES** taking into account the age-related capacities of children ○ *a developmental approach to the education of children* —**de·vel·op·men·tal·ly** *adv.*

de·vel·op·men·tal psy·chol·o·gy *n.* the branch of psychology that deals with the ways that personality, cognitive ability, and behavior change during a person's lifespan, concentrating particularly on childhood development

dé·vel·op·pé /di vèllə páy, dàyvə lō páy/ *n.* a ballet movement in which the foot of one leg is drawn up to the knee of the other and then extended slowly out into the air [Early 20thC. From French, the past participle of *développer* (see DEVELOP).]

de·verb·a·tive /dee vúrbətiv/, **de·ver·bal** /dee vúrb'l/ *adj.* GRAM derived from a verb, such as the noun "driver," which is derived from the verb "drive," and the adjective "clingy," from the verb "cling" [Early 20thC. Coined from DE- + VERB + -ATIVE.]

De·vi /dáyvee/ *n.* the supreme Hindu goddess, wife of the god Shiva, manifested in the different forms and characters of Durga, Kali, Parvati, and Sati [Late 20thC. From Sanskrit, the feminine of *deva* (see DEVA).]

de·vi·ance /deévee əns/, **de·vi·an·cy** /deévee ənsee/ *n.* behavior that is sharply different from the norm or the accepted standard

de·vi·ant /deévee ənt/ *adj.* **DIFFERENT FROM TRADITIONAL NORM** diverging sharply from a customary or traditional norm or accepted standard, or displaying sharply divergent behavior ○ *abstract paintings, once thought deviant, now worth millions* ■ *n.* **SOMEBODY BEHAVING DIFFERENTLY OR UNACCEPTABLY** somebody whose behavior is different from the norm or from accepted standards [14thC. From late Latin *deviant-*, the present participle stem of *deviare* (see DEVIATE).]

de·vi·ate *vi.* /deévee àyt/ (**-at·ed, -at·ing, -ates**) **1. BE DIFFERENT** to be different or behave differently **2. TURN FROM** to turn off from a course or path ■ *adj.* /deévee ət/ **BEHAVING DIFFERENTLY OR UNACCEPTABLY** exhibiting behavior that diverges sharply from a norm or accepted standards ■ *n.* /deévee ət/ **SOMEBODY BEHAVING DIFFERENTLY FROM TRADITIONAL NORM** somebody whose behavior differs sharply from the customary or traditional norm or accepted standards [Mid-17thC. From late Latin *deviat-*, the past participle stem of *deviare* "to depart from the way," from Latin *via* "way, road."] —**de·vi·a·tor** *n.* —**de·vi·a·to·ry** /deévee ə tàwree/ *adj.*

de·vi·a·tion /deévee áysh'n/ *n.* **1. CHANGE OR DIFFERENCE** a change or difference from what is normal, accepted, expected, or planned ○ *These rituals represented a deviation from established practices.* **2. UNACCEPTABLE BEHAVIOR OR ATTITUDE** behavior or an attitude that is sharply different from what is normal or acceptable **3.** STATS **DIFFERENCE FROM STATISTICAL AVERAGE** the difference between any particular value and a fixed value, such as the average of all the other values in its series **4.** NAVIG **COMPASS ERROR** an error in a compass reading caused by local magnetic fields, especially on a ship at sea

de·vi·a·tion·ism /dèevee áysh'n ìzzəm/ *n.* departure from accepted or established political views, especially from orthodox communism —**de·vi·a·tion·ist** *n., adj.*

de·vice /di vīss/ *n.* **1. TOOL OR MACHINE** a tool or machine designed to perform a particular task or function **2. PLOY** a way of achieving something, especially a clever or dishonest way **3. BOMB** a bomb or something that causes an explosion or fire **4. LITERARY OR DRAMATIC TOOL** something designed to create a particular effect in a story or drama or to evoke a particular response from a reader, listener, or viewer ○ *a familiar cinematic device* **5. EMBLEM OR MOTTO** an emblem, motto, or combination of the two, especially when used in heraldry ○ *a heraldic device* **6. ORNAMENTAL DESIGN** an ornamental pattern or design, e.g., in embroidery [13thC. From Old French *devis* "division, contrivance" and *devise* "plan," both from, ultimately, Latin *dividere* (see DIVIDE). The sense "simple machine" evolved in the 16thC.] ◇ **leave somebody to his** *or* **her own devices** to let somebody do as he or she wishes, instead of giving the person direction or assistance

dev·il /dévv'l/ *n.* **1. dev·il, Dev·il GOD'S ENEMY** in Christianity and some other religions, the enemy of God, who rules Hell, tempts people to sin, and as Satan personifies the spirit of evil **2. EVIL SPIRIT** an evil spirit, particularly a subordinate of Satan **3. EVIL PERSON OR ANIMAL** an unpleasant, violent, or evil person or animal **4. MISCHIEVOUS PERSON OR ANIMAL** a mischievous, troublesome, or high-spirited person or animal **5. PERSON OR ANIMAL** a person or animal of the sort described ○ *You lucky devil!* **6. NAME FOR TOOL** a name given to various tools or machines, especially ones that cut or tear **7.** = **dust devil 8. DIFFICULT OR UNPLEASANT CASE** an extremely difficult or unpleasant instance of something (*informal*) **9. INTENSIFIER** used as an intensifier in questions and exclamations (*slang*) ○ *Who the devil does he think he is, talking to his boss like that?* **10.** PRINTING = **printer's devil** (*archaic*) ■ *vt.* (**-iled, -il·ing, -ils**) **1. MAKE FOOD SPICY** to cook or prepare a food with spicy seasonings **2. PESTER** to annoy, worry, or pester somebody, especially by making repeated requests for something (*informal*) ○ *He's been deviling me with requests for an interview.* [Old English *dēofol*, from, ultimately, Greek *diabolus* "the Devil, Satan" (see DIABOLIC)] ◇ **between the devil and the deep blue sea** faced with two equally undesirable choices

dev·il·fish /dévv'l fìsh/ (*plural* **-fish** *or* **-fish·es**) *n.* a fish that is thought to have an evil or frightening appearance, such as a manta ray or octopus

dev·il·ish /dévvlish/ *adj.* **1. SINISTER OR CRUEL** so sinister, cruel, or evil as to be considered like or worthy of the devil ○ *some devilish scheme to get what they want* **2. MISCHIEVOUS** full of or indicating mischievousness ○ *a devilish grin* **3. GREAT** extremely great or intense (*informal*) ○ *the devilish midday heat* ■ *adv.* **VERY** extremely (*informal*) —**dev·il·ish·ly** *adv.* —**dev·il·ish·ness** *n.*

dev·il-may-care *adj.* **1. RECKLESS** foolishly nonchalant about risk or danger **2. CHEERFULLY UNCONCERNED** tending to enjoy the present and not think or worry about the future

dev·il·ment /dévv'lmənt/ *n.* troublesome, mischievous, or devilish behavior ○ *always getting up to some devilment or other*

dev·il·ry /dévv'lree/ *n.* = **deviltry**

dev·il's ad·vo·cate *n.* **1. OPPONENT FOR THE SAKE OF IT** somebody who criticizes or opposes something purely in order to provoke a discussion or argument **2. CATHOLIC OFFICIAL OPPOSING CANONIZATION** a Roman Catholic official appointed to argue against the canonization or beatification of a candidate [Translation of Latin *advocatus diaboli*]

dev·il's club *n.* a prickly shrub of western North America that has greenish white flowers and clusters of red berries. Latin name: *Oplopanax horridus.* [From its prickles]

dev·il's darn·ing needle *n.* (*informal*) **1. DRAGONFLY** a dragonfly (*regional*) **2.** = **damselfly** [From its long, needlelike body]

dev·il's food cake *n.* a rich dark chocolate cake [From the contrast with the paleness of ANGEL FOOD CAKE]

Dev·il's Is·land /dévvəlz-/ rocky islet off the coast of French Guiana in the Atlantic Ocean. It was used as a penal colony from 1852 to 1946.

dev·il's paint·brush (*plural* **dev·il's paint·brush·es**) *n.* = **orange hawkweed** [From the fiery color of the flowers, the devil being associated with fire]

dev·il's walk·ing stick *n.* = **Hercules' club** *n.* 1 [From its prickly leaves]

dev·il·try (*plural* **-tries**) *n.* **1. EVIL BEHAVIOR** cruel or evil behavior or actions **2. BLACK MAGIC** evil act or acts supposedly performed by calling on the powers of the devil or evil spirits **3. MISCHIEF** mischief or a mischievous act (*archaic*) ○ *the endearing deviltry of young puppies*

dev·il·wood /dévv'l wòod/ *n.* a tree of the southern United States that has hard wood, whitish bark, and fragrant greenish flowers. Latin name: *Osmanthus americanus.* [Early 19thC. From the fact that it is extremely difficult to cut.]

de·vi·ous /deévee əss/ *adj.* **1. SECRETIVE AND CALCULATING** not straightforward, sincere, and honest in or about your intentions or motives **2. UNFAIR OR UNDERHAND** not adhering to the right or usual course, procedures, or standards **3. RAMBLING** circuitous and roundabout, usually changing direction many times ○ *got here by a devious route* [Late 16thC. From Latin *devius* "out of the way," from *via* "way, road" (see DEVIATE).] —**de·vi·ous·ly** *adv.* —**de·vi·ous·ness** *n.*

de·vis·al /di vīz'l/ *n.* **1. CONTRIVING** the inventing or contriving of something **2.** LAW **PROPERTY TRANSFER BY WILL** the handing down of property through a will

de·vise /di vīz/ *vt.* (**-vised, -vis·ing, -vis·es**) **1. THINK UP** to conceive of the idea for something and figure out how it will work **2.** LAW **PASS ON PROPERTY** to pass on property through a will ■ *n.* LAW **1. WILL CLAUSE BEQUEATHING PROPERTY** a clause in a will stating that an item of property is to be given to somebody or something **2. BEQUEATHING PROPERTY** the bequeathing of an item of property **3. PROPERTY BEQUEATHED** an item of property bequeathed through a will [13thC. From French *deviser* "to divide, order" (the first senses in English), hence "to form a plan," from, ultimately, Latin *dividere* (see DIVIDE).] —**de·vis·a·ble** *adj.*

de·vi·see /di vī zeé/ *n.* LAW somebody to whom property has been bequeathed in a will

de·vis·er /di vīzər/ *n.* somebody who conceives of something and figures out how it will work

de·vi·sor /di vīzər/ *n.* LAW somebody who leaves property to another in a will [15thC. From Anglo-Norman *devisour* and Old French *deviseor,* both from Old French *deviser* (see DEVISE).]

de·vi·tal·ize /dee vīt'l ìz/ (**-ized, -iz·ing, -iz·es**) *vt.* to deprive something of its strength or vigor (*formal*) —**de·vit·al·i·za·tion** /dee vīt'li záysh'n/ *n.*

DeVi·to /də veé tō/, **Danny** (*b.* 1944) U.S. movie actor and director. He starred as Louie De Palma in the television series *Taxi* (1978–83). Full name **Daniel Michael DeVito**

de·vit·ri·fy /dee víttrə fī/ (**-fied, -fy·ing, -fies**) *vti.* to change, or cause a material to change, from a glassy to a crystalline state and become brittle and opaque —**de·vit·ri·fi·ca·tion** /dee vìttrəfi káysh'n/ *n.*

de·vo·cal·ize /dee vōkə lìz/ (**-ized, -iz·ing, -iz·es**) *vt.* = **devoice** —**de·vo·cal·i·za·tion** /di vōkəli záysh'n/ *n.*

de·voice /dee vóyss/ (**-voiced, -voic·ing, -voic·es**) *vt.* to make a usually voiced speech sound without vibration of the vocal cords

de·void /di vóyd/ *adj.* completely lacking in or without something ○ *a house devoid of charm* [14thC. From the past participle of obsolete *devoid* "to remove, vacate," from Old French *devoidier,* literally "to empty out," from *vuidier* "to empty," from, ultimately, Latin *vacare* (see VACATION).]

de·voirs /dev waár/ *npl.* expressions or acts of courtesy and respect (*archaic or literary*) [15thC. From Old French *deveir,* literally "to owe," from Latin *debere* "to owe" (source of English *debt* and *duty*).]

de·vol·a·til·ize /dee vóllət'l ìz/ (**-ized, -iz·ing, -iz·es**) *vt.* to remove volatile material from a substance, usually by means of heat or a vacuum and sometimes by both —**de·vol·a·til·i·za·tion** /di vòllət'li záysh'n/ *n.*

dev·o·lu·tion /dèvvə loósh'n/ *n.* **1. DELEGATING OF RESPONSIBILITIES** the delegation of responsibilities from a superior to a subordinate, deputy, or substitute **2. DELEGATING POWER** the transfer of power from a central to a subordinate level or organization, particularly from a central government to regional or local governments **3. INHERITANCE OF PRIVILEGES** the transfer or inheritance of authority, rights, or property, e.g., from a monarch to his or her successors **4.** = **degeneration** *n.* 3 [15thC. From the late Latin stem *devolution-* from, ultimately, Latin *devolvere* (see DEVOLVE).] —**dev·o·lu·tion·ar·y** /dèvvə loósh'n èrree/ *adj.*

dev·o·lu·tion·ist /dèvvə loósh'nist/ *n.* somebody who favors transferring power from a central government to regional or local governments —**devolutionist** *adj.*

de·volve /di vólv/ (**-volved, -volv·ing, -volves**) *v.* **1.** *vti.* **TRANSFER OR BE TRANSFERRED TO ANOTHER** to transfer power, responsibility, or rights to somebody or something, e.g., from a central government to a regional government, or to be transferred in this manner **2.** *vi.* **BECOME ANOTHER PERSON'S OBLIGATION** to become the duty or responsibility of another person **3.** *vi.* **DETERIORATE** to deteriorate slowly over time ○ *Order has devolved into anarchy.* **4.** *vi.* LAW **BE GIVEN OR BEQUEATHED** to be given to somebody under the terms of a will or other legal instruction [15thC. From Latin *devolvere;* literally "to roll down" (the original sense in English), from *volvere* "to roll" (source of English *involve* and *volume.*] —**de·volve·ment** *n.*

De·vo·ni·an /də vṓnee ən/ *n.* **1. De·vo·ni·an, De·vo·ni·an pe·ri·od GEOLOGIC PERIOD** the geologic period that extended from 410 to 360 million years ago, when forests and amphibians first appeared and fish became abundant **2. SOMEBODY FROM DEVON** somebody who was born in or resides in the English county of Devon ■ *adj.* **1. BELONGING TO GEOLOGIC PERIOD** belonging or relating to the geologic period that extended from 410 to 360 million years ago **2. CHARACTERISTIC OF DEVON** typical of or relating to the English county of Devon, its people, or its culture [Early 17thC. Formed from medieval Latin *Devonia,* from Old English *Defenascīr* "Devonshire," the former name of the county of Devon, U.K. Originally, the name given to a geologic formation of rocks particularly prevalent there.]

dé·voré *n.* the use of a chemical paste to create patterns in specially structured fabrics such as velvet by dissolving the natural fibers and revealing the synthetic warp and weft threads [From French *dévorer* (see DEVOUR)]

de·vote /di vṓt/ (**-vot·ed, -vot·ing, -votes**) *vt.* to commit yourself to, or allot or use something for, a particular activity, aim, or purpose ○ *She devoted her whole life to the cause.* [Late 16thC. From Latin *devot-,* the past participle stem of *devovere* "to dedicate by a vow," from *vovere* "to vow" (source of English *vow* and *vote*).]

de·vot·ed /di vṓtəd/ *adj.* **1. LOVING AND COMMITTED** feeling or showing great love, commitment, or loyalty to somebody or something, especially over a long period of time **2. DEDICATED** feeling or showing great dedication to something —**de·vot·ed·ly** *adv.* —**de·vot·ed·ness** *n.*

dev·o·tee /dèvvə teé, dè vō teé/ *n.* **1. ARDENT ENTHUSIAST** a very ardent enthusiast or follower of something **2. RELIGIOUS PERSON** a dedicated member of a religious or spiritual group

de·vo·tion /di vṓsh'n/ *n.* **1. COMMITTED LOVE** deep love and commitment **2. DEDICATION** great dedication and loyalty **3. ENTHUSIASM** strong enthusiasm and admiration for somebody or something **4. RELIGIOUS FERVOR** fervent religious or spiritual feeling (*formal*) **5. ACT OF DEVOTING** the act of devoting something or being devoted to a particular purpose ■ **de·vo·tions** *npl.* **PRAYERS** prayers or other religious observances, especially somebody's private prayers or observances

de·vo·tion·al /di vṓshən'l, -shnəl/ *n.* **SHORT RELIGIOUS SERVICE** a short religious service usually consisting of special prayers (*often used in the plural*) ■ *adj.* **EXPRESSING RELIGIOUS DEVOTION** expressing or relating to religious feeling, prayer, or worship —**de·vo·tion·al·ly** *adv.*

De·Vo·to /də vō tō/, **Bernard Augustine** (1897–1955) U.S. historian and critic. He was known for his articles for *Harper's Magazine* (1935–55) and his three-volume work on the American West (1943–52).

de·vour /di vówr/ (**-voured, -vour·ing, -vours**) *vt.* **1. EAT QUICKLY** to eat something quickly and hungrily ○ *They devour in minutes what it's taken you all afternoon to prepare.* **2. TAKE IN EAGERLY** to read, look at, watch, or listen to something eagerly ○ *Young children seem to devour her stories.* **3. DESTROY** to destroy something rapidly and completely (*literary*) (*often passive*) ○ *a house devoured by the flames* **4. WASTE** to use up something unwisely or wastefully (*literary*)

5. OVERWHELM to become an overwhelming and destructive passion or obsession for somebody (*literary*) (*usually passive*) [14thC. Via Old French *devour-*, the stressed stem of *devorer*, from Latin *devorare*, literally "to swallow down," from *vorare* "to swallow" (source of English *voracious*).] —**de·vour·er** *n.* —**de·vour·ing** *adj.* —**de·vour·ing·ly** *adv.*

de·vout /di vówt/ *adj.* **1. VERY RELIGIOUS** deeply and faithfully religious **2. VERY SINCERE** deeply and sincerely felt or meant (*formal*) **3. DEVOTED TO SOMETHING** devoted to a particular personal interest or cause ○ *a devout Red Sox fan* [12thC. Via French *dévot* from Latin *devotus*, the past participle of *devovere* (see DEVOTE).] —**de·vout·ly** *adv.* —**de·vout·ness** *n.*

dew /doo/ *n.* **1. WATER DROPLETS ON COOL OUTDOOR SURFACES** moisture from the air that has condensed as tiny drops on outdoor objects and surfaces that have cooled, especially during the night **2. SMALL DROPS** drops of moisture of any kind, e.g., tears or sweat (*literary*) **3. FRESHNESS AND PURITY** a fresh and pure or refreshing quality in something (*literary*) ■ **dews** *npl.* **DEWDROPS** drops of dew (*literary*) ■ *vt.* (**dewed, dew·ing, dews**) **COAT WITH DEW** to coat or moisten something with drops of dew (*literary*) [Old English *dēaw*]

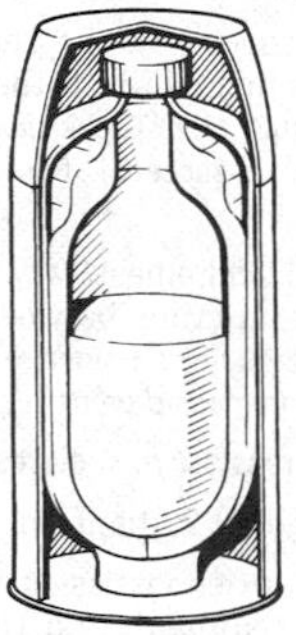

Dewar flask

Dew·ar flask /dóoər/, **Dew·ar vac·u·um flask** *n.* a double walled silvered glass or metal flask with a vacuum between the walls, providing thermal insulation. It is frequently used to store liquefied gases. [Mid-20thC. Named for Sir James *Dewar* (1824–1923), British physicist and chemist, who invented it.]

de·wat·er /dee wàwtər, dee wóttər/ (**-ered, -er·ing, -ers**) *vt.* to remove water from a substance, especially sewage or crude oil, or from a place

dew·ber·ry /dóo bèrree/ (*plural* **-ries**) *n.* **1. TRAILING BLACKBERRY PLANT** a variety of the blackberry bramble with trailing stems and bluish-black fruit. Genus: *Rubus.* **2. BLUISH BLACK BERRY** the edible bluish black fruit of a dewberry plant

dew·claw /dóo klàw/ *n.* a functionless shorter digit or claw on the foot of a dog or other mammal [Late 16thC. Origin uncertain: perhaps from the fact that while the other claws touch the soil, or press the grass to the ground, this only brushes the dewy surface.] —**dew·clawed** *adj.*

dew·drop /dóo dròp/ *n.* a drop of water that has condensed on a cool outdoor surface

Dew·ey /dóo ee/, **George** (1837–1917) U.S. naval officer. He defeated the Spanish fleet at the Battle of Manila Bay (1898) in the Philippines.

Dew·ey, John (1859–1952) U.S. philosopher, psychologist, and educator. He developed the philosophy of pragmatism and was a leading educational theorist.

Dew·ey, Melvil (1851–1931) U.S. librarian and educator. He formulated the Dewey Decimal System (1876), which revolutionized the way books were catalogued.

Dew·ey, Thomas Edmund (1902–71) U.S. lawyer and political leader. He was governor of New York State (1942, 1946, and 1950) and the Republican nominee for U.S. president in 1944 and 1948.

Dew·ey dec·i·mal sys·tem, Dew·ey dec·i·mal clas·si·fi·ca·tion *n.* a system of classifying library books that divides them into ten main classes, divided in turn into categories with three-digit numbers and subcategories with numbers after a decimal point [Late 19thC. Named for Melvil DEWEY.]

dew·fall /dóo fàwl/ *n.* **1. TIME DEW FORMS** the formation of dew, or the time when dew begins to form **2. AMOUNT OF DEW** the amount of dew that has condensed on objects and surfaces

dew·lap /dóo làp/ *n.* **1. HANGING FLAP OF SKIN ON ANIMAL'S NECK** a loose fold of skin hanging from the neck of certain animals such as cows **2. LOOSE SKIN ON PERSON'S THROAT** a loose fold of skin on the throat of a person, often forming later in life [14thC. From obsolete English *dewe*, of uncertain meaning and origin + LAP "loose piece." The first element was associated by folk etymology with DEW, from the idea that the "lap" touches the dewy ground.] —**dew·lapped** /dóo lapt/ *adj.*

DEW line *n.* a line of radar stations across the Arctic regions of North America, designed to give an early warning of approaching enemy aircraft and missiles [*DEW* is an acronym formed from *Distant Early Warning*]

de·worm /dee wúrm/ (**-wormed, -worm·ing, -worms**) *vt.* to cure an animal of an infestation of worms —**de·worm·er** *n.*

dew point *n.* the temperature at which the air cannot hold all the moisture in it and dew begins to form. If objects and surfaces have cooled to below freezing point when the moisture in the air begins to condense, frost is formed instead.

dew worm *n.* a common earthworm used as fishing bait [Origin uncertain: perhaps from the fact that the worm comes out when the earth is moist]

dew·y /dóo ee/ (**-i·er, -i·est**) *adj.* **1. COVERED WITH DEW** covered with dew or characterized by the presence of dew **2. MOIST** moist or moist-looking **3. LIKE DEW** like dew, especially in having a fresh, pure, or refreshing quality (*literary*) **4. NAIVE** childishly pure or innocent (*literary*) ○ *a dewy outlook on life* —**dew·i·ly** *adv.* —**dew·i·ness** *n.*

dew·y-eyed *adj.* childishly innocent, inexperienced, or trusting ○ *full of dewy-eyed optimism*

dex /deks/ *n.* dextroamphetamine or a tablet containing it (*slang*) [Mid-20thC. Shortening.]

dex·a·meth·a·sone *n.* a synthetic steroid used to treat inflammatory conditions and hormonal imbalances [Mid-20thC. Coined from *dexa-* (a blend of HEXA- and DECA-) + METHYL + CORTISONE.]

Dex·e·drine /déksə drèen/ *tdmk.* a trademark for a sulfate of dextroamphetamine used as a pharmaceutical drug

dex·ie /déksee/ *n.* a tablet containing dextroamphetamine (*slang*) [Mid-20thC. Shortening.]

dex·ter /dékstər/ *adj.* placed on the right-hand side of a coat of arms, that is, on the left from the point of view somebody looking at it (*technical*) (*usually used after the noun*) [Mid-16thC. From Latin, "on the right side" (see DEXTEROUS).]

dex·ter·i·ty /dek stérrətee/ *n.* **1. PHYSICAL SKILL** ease and skill in physical movement, especially in using the hands and manipulating objects ○ *manual dexterity* **2. QUICK WITS** sharpness or quickness of mind

dex·ter·ous /dékstərəss, dékstrəss/, **dex·trous** /dékstrəss/ *adj.* **1. PHYSICALLY SKILLFUL** characterized by ease and skill in movement, especially in the use of the hands to carry out tasks **2. QUICK-WITTED** mentally sharp or quick [Early 17thC. From Latin *dexter* "skillful," literally "on the right side" (source of English *ambidextrous* and *destrier*). The right hand was viewed as the stronger, hence the meaning "skillful."] —**dex·ter·ous·ly** *adv.* —**dex·ter·ous·ness** *n.*

dextr- *prefix.* = **dextro-** (*used before vowels*)

dex·tral /dékstrəl/ *adj.* (*technical*) **1. ON THE RIGHT** on or relating to the right-hand side, especially of the body **2. RIGHT-HANDED** right-handed **3. SPIRALING TO THE RIGHT** used to describe the clockwise spiraling of the shell of a marine invertebrate animal [Mid-17thC. Via medieval Latin *dextralis* from Latin *dextra* "right hand," from *dexter* (see DEXTEROUS).] —**dex·tral·i·ty** /dek strállətee/ *n.* —**dex·tral·ly** /dékstrəlee/ *adv.*

dex·tran /dék stràn, dékstrən/ *n.* a glucose polymer (**polysaccharide**) produced by the action of bacteria on sucrose and used as a blood plasma substitute, food additive, and in confections and lacquers [Late 19thC. Coined from DEXTRO- + -AN.]

dex·trin /dékstrin/, **dex·trine** /dék strèen, dékstrin/ *n.* a product formed from the heating of starch that is an intermediate in the formation of maltose, and is used as an adhesive and a sizing, and in syrups and beers. Formula: $(C_6H_{10}O_5)_n$. [Mid-19thC. Coined from DEXTRO- + -IN.]

dex·tro /dék strō/ *adj.* = **dextrorotatory** [Early 20thC. Shortening.]

dextro- *prefix.* **1.** right, on the right ○ *dextrocardia* **2.** dextrorotatory ○ *dextroglucose* [From Latin *dexter* "on the right" (source of English *dexterity* and *ambidextrous*)]

dex·tro·am·phet·a·mine /dèk strō am féttə mèen/ *n.* a form of amphetamine sulfate, used as a stimulant and antidepressant

dex·tro·car·di·a /dèk strō kaárdee ə/ *n.* a medical condition in which the heart inclines to the right side of the center of the chest instead of the left, often with a similar reversal of all abdominal organs

dex·tro·glu·cose /dèk strō glóo kòss/ *n.* = **dextrose**

dex·tro·ro·ta·ry /dèk strō rṓtəree/ *adj.* = **dextrorotatory**

dex·tro·ro·ta·tion /dèkstrə rō táysh'n/ *n.* a rotation to the right, particularly of the plane of polarization of light passing through a crystal or solution. Substances that cause dextrorotation are said to be optically active.

dex·tro·ro·ta·to·ry /dèkstrərṓtə tàwree/, **dex·tro·ro·ta·ry** *adj.* rotating the plane of polarization of light passing through it to the right or clockwise

dex·trose /dék stròss/ *n.* a sugar produced during cellular metabolism in plant and animal tissue. It is found in many fruits, especially grapes, and is a major component of honey and corn syrup.

dex·trous *adj.* = **dexterous**

dey /day/ (*plural* **deys**) *n.* **1. GOVERNOR OF ALGIERS** the governor of Algiers under the Ottoman Empire **2. RULER OF TUNIS OR TRIPOLI** a title sometimes used for ruling officials in Tunis and Tripoli in North Africa under the Ottoman Empire [Mid-17thC. Via French from Turkish *dayi* "maternal uncle," also a courtesy title.]

DF *abbr.* TELECOM direction finder

D.F. *abbr.* **1.** Defender of the Faith **2.** Federal District

D/F *abbr.* TELECOM direction finder

D.F.A. (*plural* **D.F.A.s**) *abbr.* Doctor of Fine Arts

DFC *abbr.* Distinguished Flying Cross

dg *abbr.* decigram

D.G. *abbr.* Deo gratias

DH *abbr.* **DH, dh** designated hitter

D.H. (*plural* **D.H.'s**) *abbr.* Doctor of Humanities

Dha·ka /daákə, dákə/, **Dac·ca** capital and largest city of Bangladesh. It is situated in the center of the country, on the Buriganga, one of the tributary rivers of the Ganges delta. Population: 3,397,190 (1991).

dhan·sak /dún saák/ *n.* an Indian curry that is made from meat or vegetables mixed with lentils [Late 20thC. From Gujarati.]

dhar·ma /daármə/ *n.* **1. PERFORMING OF DUTIES OF HINDUISM** in Hinduism, a person's duty to behave according to strict religious and social codes, or the righteousness earned by performing religious and social duties **2. ETERNAL TRUTH IN BUDDHISM** in Buddhism, the truth about the way things are, and will always be, in the universe or in nature, especially when contained in scripture [Late 18thC. From Sanskrit, "something established, decree, custom."] —**dhar·mic** *adj.*

dhar·na /daárnə/, **dhur·na** /dúrnə/ *n.* in India, the practice of protesting against an injustice by sitting and fasting outside the door of the offender [Late 18thC. From Hindi, "placing, act of sitting in restraint."]

Dhau·la·gi·ri /dòwlə gèeree/ one of the world's highest mountains. It is situated in the Himalayas in northern Nepal. Height: 26,811 ft./8,163 m.

dhole /dōl/ *n.* a wild dog found in South Asia that has a reddish coat and bushy tail, and hunts large animals in packs. Latin name: *Cuon alpinus.* [Early 19thC. Origin uncertain: perhaps from Canarese *tōla* "wolf."]

dho·ti /dṓtee/, **dhoo·tie, dho·tie, dhu·ti** *n.* **1. INDIAN MAN'S LOINCLOTH** a loincloth worn by some men in India **2. COTTON CLOTH** the cotton cloth used in India to make the loincloths called dhotis [Early 17thC. From Hindi.]

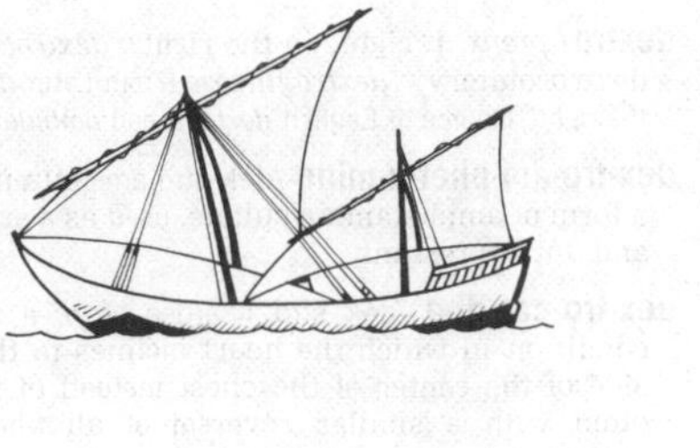

Dhow

dhow /dow/ *n.* a low-sided, one- or two-masted ship with triangular curving sails, used by Arab sailors in the Indian Ocean [Late 18thC. Origin uncertain: probably from Persian.]

Dhu al-Hij·jah /dool hí jaá/, **Dhu'l-Hij·jah** *n.* in the Islamic calendar, the 12th lunar month of the year during which the holiday of Yom Arafat is celebrated [Late 18thC. From Arabic, literally "the one of the pilgrimage."]

Dhu al-Qa·dah /dool kaá daá/, **Dhu'l-Qa·dah** *n.* in the Islamic calendar, the 11th lunar month of the year [Late 18thC. From Arabic, literally "the one of the sitting."]

dhur·na *n.* = **dharna**

dhur·rie /dúrree/, **dur·rie** *n.* a flat-woven cotton rug made in India [Late 19thC. From Hindi *darī*.]

dhu·ti /dóotee/ *n.* = **dhoti**

di. *abbr.* diameter [Shortening]

di-[1] *prefix.* **1.** two, twice, double: dicephalous ○ *dicephalous* **2.** containing two atoms, radicals, or groups ○ *dimethyl* [From Greek. Ultimately from a form of the Indo-European word for "two" that is also the ancestor of English *twin, twilight,* and *bi-*.]

di-[2] *prefix.* = **dia-** (*used before vowels*)

dia. *abbr.* diameter

dia- *prefix.* through, across ○ *diachronic* ○ *diadromous* [From Greek *dia*]

di·a·base /dí ə bàyss/ *n.* an igneous rock of fine to medium grain size [Mid-19thC. From French, of uncertain origin: probably from Greek *diabasis* "act of crossing over," from, ultimately, *bainein* "to go."] —**di·a·ba·sic** /dí ə báyssik/ *adj.*

di·a·be·tes /dí ə beé teez, dí ə beétiss/ *n.* a medical disorder that causes the body to produce an excessive amount of urine, especially diabetes mellitus [Mid-16thC. Via Latin from Greek, literally "passer through, siphon," from *diabainein*, literally "to go through." The underlying idea, from the symptomatic excessive urination, is "passing through."]

di·a·be·tes in·sip·i·dus *n.* a disorder of the pituitary gland that causes the body to produce large amounts of urine [From modern Latin, literally "bland diabetes"]

di·a·be·tes mel·li·tus *n.* a disorder in which there is no control of blood sugar, through inadequate insulin production (Type 1) or decreased cellular sensitivity to insulin (Type 2), causing kidney, eye, and nerve damage. Type 1 develops in childhood and requires lifelong injection of insulin, while Type 2 develops in middle age and can usually be controlled by diet and drugs. [From modern Latin, literally "honey-sweet diabetes"]

di·a·bet·ic /dí ə béttik/ *adj.* **1.** HAVING DIABETES having diabetes, especially diabetes mellitus **2.** RELATING TO DIABETES relating to or caused by diabetes, especially diabetes mellitus **3.** INTENDED FOR DIABETICS made without sugar and therefore suitable for people who have diabetes mellitus ■ *n.* SOMEBODY WITH DIABETES somebody who has diabetes, especially diabetes mellitus

di·a·ble·rie /dee aábləree/ *n.* **1.** MAGIC witchcraft or magic **2.** THINGS CONNECTED WITH WITCHCRAFT OR EVIL stories, traditions, and practices associated with magic or devil worship **3.** MISCHIEF mischief (*literary*) [Mid-18thC. From French, from *diable* "devil," from Latin *diabolic* (see DEVIL).]

di·ab·lo /dyaá blō, dee aá blō/ *adj.* used to describe a food that is seasoned with hot pepper (*usually used after a noun*) [Late 20thC. From French *diable* "flavored with hot spices," literally "devil," from Latin *diabolus* (see DEVIL).]

di·a·bol·i·cal /dī ə bóllik'l/, **di·a·bol·ic** /dī ə bóllik/ *adj.* **1.** OF DEVIL connected with the devil or devil worship **2.** EVIL extremely cruel or evil [14th c. Via French *diabolique* from late Latin *diabolicus*, from, ultimately Greek *diabolos* (see DEVIL).] —**di·a·bol·i·cal·ly** *adv.* —**di·a·bol·i·cal·ness** *n.*

di·ab·o·lism /dī ábbə lìzzəm/ *n.* **1.** DEVIL WORSHIP worship of the devil or devils **2.** EVIL BEHAVIOR evil behavior or character (*literary*) —**di·ab·o·list** *n.*

di·ab·o·lize /dī ábbə līz/ (**-lized, -liz·ing, -liz·es**) *vt.* **1.** CAUSE TO SEEM EVIL to cause somebody or something to appear evil **2.** MAKE EVIL to make somebody or something evil

di·a·chron·ic /dī ə krónnik/ *adj.* involving, or relating to the study of, the development of something, especially a language, through time ○ *diachronic linguistics* [Mid-19thC. Coined from DIA- + Greek *khronos* "time" (source of English *chronic, chronicle,* and *chronological*).] —**di·a·chron·i·cal·ly** *adv.*

di·ach·ro·nism /dī ákrə nìzzəm/ *n.* the existence within a single geological formation of regions of rock that were laid down at different times, e.g., by a sea that gradually covered a landmass —**di·ach·ro·nous** *adj.*

di·ach·ro·ny /dī ákrənee/ *n.* change or development over time (*formal*)

di·ac·id /dī ássid/ *adj.* HAVING TWO ACIDIC HYDROGEN ATOMS having two acidic hydrogen atoms that may be replaced by metal or acid ions to form a salt or an ester ■ *n.* ACID WITH TWO ACIDIC HYDROGEN ATOMS an acid that has two acidic hydrogen atoms [Mid-19thC. Coined from DI- + ACID, on the model of DIBASIC.]

di·ac·o·nal /dī ákən'l, dee ákən'l/ *adj.* relating to a deacon or deaconess or to the position of deacon or deaconess [Early 17thC. From late Latin *diaconalis*, from *diaconus* (see DEACON).]

di·ac·o·nate /dī ákənət, dee ákənət/ *n.* the position of deacon or deaconess, or the period of time during which it is held by a particular person [Early 18thC. From late Latin *diaconatus*, from *diaconus* (see DEACON).]

COMMON DIACRITICAL MARKS

Name	Mark	Word/Phrase
grave	À à	à la mode
acute	Á á	Cádiz
circumflex	Â â	château
tilde	Ã ã	São Paulo
umlaut	Ä ä	fräulein
angstrom	Å å	smörgåsbord
cedilla	Ç ç	façade
grave	È è	crèche
acute	É é	purée
circumflex	Ê ê	fête
umlaut	Ë ë	noël
grave	Ì ì	Forlì
acute	Í í	Valparaíso
circumflex	Î î	maître d'hôtel
umlaut	Ï ï	faïence
eth	Ð ð	Hamðir
tilde	Ñ ñ	mañana
acute	Ó ó	Kraków
circumflex	Ô ô	maître d'hôtel
umlaut	Ö ö	danke schön
Danish/ Norwegian O	Ø ø	øre
acute	Ú ú	Setúbal
circumflex	Û û	croûtons
umlaut	Ü ü	führer
thorn	Þ þ	þ ingeyrar

di·a·crit·ic /dī ə kríttik/ *adj.* = **diacritical** ■ *n.* PHONETIC MARK ADDED TO LETTER a mark above or below a printed letter that indicates a change in the way it is to be pronounced or stressed. Acute and grave accents, tildes, and cedillas are examples of diacritics. [Late 17thC. From Greek *diakritikos* "that distinguishes or separates," from, ultimately, *krinein* "to separate, decide" (source of English *crisis, critic,* and *hypocrisy*).]

di·a·crit·i·cal /dī ə kríttik'l/, **di·a·crit·ic** /dī ə kríttik/ *adj.* indicating a change or modification in something, especially in the way a printed letter is to be pronounced or stressed —**di·a·crit·i·cal·ly** *adv.*

di·a·crit·i·cal mark *n.* = **diacritic**

di·a·del·phous /dī ə délfəss/ *adj.* used to describe stamens or flowers that have the stamen filaments grouped into two bundles [Early 19thC. Coined from DI- + Greek *adelphos* "brother."]

di·a·dem /dī ə dèm, dī ədəm/ *n.* **1.** CROWN a jeweled headband used as a royal crown **2.** JEWELED HEADBAND any jeweled headband **3.** REGAL POWER royal power or dignity (*literary*) [14thC. Via Old French from, ultimately, Greek *diadēma* "headband," especially the regal headband of Persian kings, adopted by Alexander the Great, from *diadein* "to bind around," from *dein* "to bind."]

Di·ad·o·chi /dī áddəkee/ *npl.* the six Macedonian generals who divided up and then fought over the empire of Alexander the Great after his death

di·ad·o·chy /dī áddəkee/ *n.* the replacement of one element by another within the structure of a crystal [Early 18thC. From Greek *diadokhē* "succession," from *diadekhesthai* "to succeed," from *dekhesthai* "to take, accept."]

di·ad·ro·mous /dī áddrəməss/ *adj.* ZOOL used to describe fish that migrate between fresh and salt water [Mid-20thC. Coined from DIA- + "running," from, ultimately, Greek *-dromous dromos*.]

di·aer·e·sis /dī érrəssiss/ *n.* = **dieresis**

diag. *abbr.* **1.** diagonal **2.** diagram

di·a·gen·e·sis /dī ə jénnəssiss/ *n.* the changes that take place in a sediment as a result of increased temperatures and pressures, causing solid rock to form, e.g., as sand becomes sandstone —**di·a·ge·net·ic** /dī əjə néttik/ *adj.*

di·a·ge·ot·ro·pism /dī ajee óttrə pìzzəm/ *n.* a response of a plant to gravity in which a part of the plant adopts a horizontal position —**di·a·ge·o·trop·ic** /-əjee ə tróppik/ *adj.*

di·ag·nose /dī əg nōz, -nōss/ (**-nosed, -nos·ing, -nos·es**) *vt.* **1.** IDENTIFY ILLNESS IN PATIENT to identify an illness or disorder in a patient through an interview, physical examination, and medical tests and other procedures **2.** IDENTIFY CAUSE OF SOMETHING to identify the nature or cause of something, especially a problem or fault [Mid-19thC. Back-formation from DIAGNOSIS.] —**di·ag·nos·a·ble** /-nōzəb'l, -nōssəb'l/ *adj.*

WORD KEY: USAGE

Diagnose means "discover" or "identify." Thus *flu was diagnosed* is correct, and *she was diagnosed with flu* is not correct.

di·ag·no·sis /dī əg nōssiss/ (*plural* **-ses** /-seez/) *n.* **1.** IDENTIFICATION OF ILLNESS the identifying of an illness or disorder in a patient through an interview, physical examination, and medical tests and other procedures **2.** IDENTIFICATION OF PROBLEM the identifying of the nature or cause of something, especially a problem or fault **3.** DECISION REACHED BY DIAGNOSIS a decision or conclusion reached by medical or other diagnosis ○ *The diagnosis is flu.* [Late 17thC. Via modern Latin from Greek *diagnōsis*, from *diagignōskein* "to distinguish," literally "to know apart," from *gignōskein* "to know, perceive" (source of English *physiognomy* and *gnostic*).]

di·ag·nos·tic /dī əg nóstik/ *adj.* FOR IDENTIFYING ILLNESSES OR PROBLEMS identifying, or used in identifying, the nature or cause of an illness, disorder, or problem ■ *n.* TEST TO IDENTIFY SOMETHING a test, procedure, or instrument used to identify the nature or cause of an illness, disorder, or problem —**di·ag·nos·ti·cal·ly** /-nóstikəlee/ *adv.*

di·ag·nos·ti·cian /dī əg nos tísh'n/ *n.* **1.** DOCTOR SKILLED AT DIAGNOSIS a doctor with special skills in identifying illnesses or disorders **2.** PROBLEM IDENTIFIER somebody with special skills in identifying the cause or nature of a problem

di·ag·nos·tics /dī əg nóstiks/ *n.* the art of, or procedures for, identifying illnesses or disorders in patients through diagnosis (*takes a singular verb*)

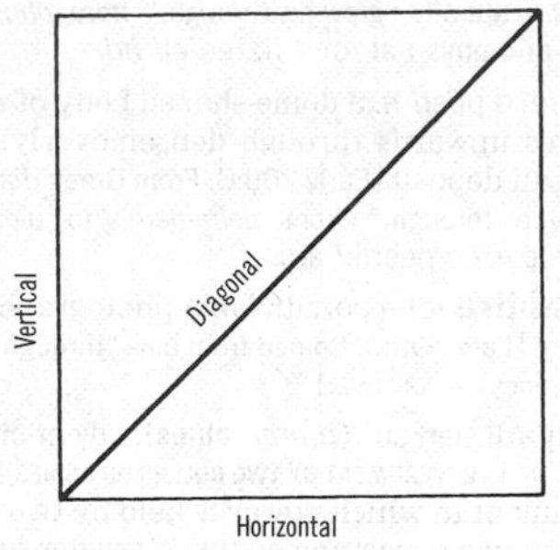

Diagonal

di·ag·o·nal /dī ággən'l, dī ággn'l/ *adj.* **1. SLANTING OR OBLIQUE** running from one side to another in a slanting or oblique way **2. WITH SLANTING LINES** having slanting lines or markings **3.** GEOM **JOINING ANGLES OR CORNERS** used to describe a line that joins two opposite or nonadjacent angles or corners of a straight-sided geometric figure ■ *n.* **1. SLANTING LINE** a slanting line or direction **2. LINE JOINING ANGLES** a line that joins two opposite or nonadjacent angles or corners of a straight-sided geometric figure **3.** PRINTING = **slash** [Mid-16thC. From Latin *diagonalis*, from Greek *diagōnios* "from angle to angle," from *gōnia* "angle" (source of English *polygon* and *amblygonite*).] —**di·ag·o·nal·ly** /dī ággən'lee, dī ággnəlee/ *adv.*

di·a·gram /dī ə gràm/ *n.* **1. SIMPLE EXPLANATORY DRAWING** a simple drawing showing the basic shape, layout, or workings of something **2. CHART** a chart or graph that illustrates something such as a statistical trend **3. MATHEMATICAL DRAWING** a line drawing that presents mathematical information ■ *vt.* (**-grammed, -gram·ing, -gram·ming, -grams**) **ILLUSTRATE SOMETHING** to make a diagram that represents or illustrates something [Early 17thC. Via Latin from Greek *diagramma* "geometrical figure, written list, scale in music," from *diagraphein* "to mark out by lines, draw," from *graphein* "to write" (see GRAPH).] —**di·a·gram·ma·ble** *adj.*

di·a·gram·mat·ic /dī əgrə máttik/, **di·a·gram·mat·i·cal** *adj.* in the form of an explanatory drawing or chart —**di·a·gram·mat·i·cal·ly** *adv.*

di·a·graph /dī ə gràf/ *n.* a mechanical instrument used for producing scale copies of diagrams and maps [Late 19thC. Via French from Greek *diagraphein* (see DIAGRAM).]

di·a·ki·ne·sis /dī əki neessiss/ *n.* the final stage in cell reduction division (**meiosis**) during which the paired chromosomes begin to shorten, thicken, and separate [Early 20thC. Via modern Latin from German *Diakinese*, from Greek *kinēsis* "motion" (see KINESIOLOGY).] —**di·a·ki·net·ic** /dī əki néttik/ *adj.*

di·al /dī əl/ *n.* **1. INDICATOR WITH MOVEABLE POINTER** an instrument with a movable pointer that displays a measurement, e.g., the current speed of a vehicle or the level of steam pressure inside a boiler **2. CONTROL KNOB** a round control knob or disk turned with the fingers to adjust a piece of electrical or mechanical equipment, e.g., a radio **3. STATION INDICATOR ON RADIO** a numbered panel with a movable pointer on a radio that is used for tuning in to different stations **4. CLOCK FACE** the round face of a traditional clock **5. DISK WITH HOLES ON TELEPHONE** a disk with numbered finger holes on the front of an old telephone, turned with a finger to select the required telephone number **6. SUNDIAL** a sundial or its face (*dated or literary*) ■ *vti.* (**-aled, -al·ing, -als**) **1. CALL BY TELEPHONE** to call a number or a person on the telephone **2. SELECT RADIO OR TELEVISION STATION** to tune in a radio or television station or program using a dial [14thC. Via Old French, "wheel in clockwork that makes a revolution once a day," from, ultimately, Latin *dies* "day." The underlying idea is "recording a day's passage."] —**di·al·er** *n.*

dial. *abbr.* 1. dialect 2. dialectal 3. dialectic 4. dialectical 5. dialogue

di·a·lect /dī ə lèkt/ *n.* **1. REGIONAL VARIETY OF LANGUAGE** a regional variety of a language, with differences in vocabulary, grammar, and pronunciation **2. LANGUAGE SPOKEN BY CLASS OR PROFESSION** a form of a language spoken by members of a particular social class or profession **3. NONSTANDARD SPEECH** nonstandard spoken language **4. MEMBER OF LANGUAGE FAMILY** one of a family of related languages ○ *Romance dialects such as French and Italian* [Mid-16thC. Directly or via French from Latin *dialogus*, "way of speaking, dialect," from Greek *dialektos* "conversation, language, local speech," from *dialegesthai* (see DIALOGUE).] —**di·a·lec·tal** /dī ə lékt'l/ *adj.* —**di·a·lec·tal·ly** /-léktəlee/ *adv.*

di·a·lect at·las *n.* = **linguistic atlas**

di·a·lect ge·og·ra·phy *n.* = **linguistic geography** — **di·a·lect ge·og·ra·pher** *n.*

di·a·lec·tic /dī ə léktik/ *n.* **1. TENSION BETWEEN CONFLICTING IDEAS** the tension that exists between two conflicting or interacting forces, elements, or ideas **2. INVESTIGATION OF TRUTH THROUGH DISCUSSION** the investigation of the truth through discussion, or the art of investigating truths through discussion **3. di·a·lec·tic, di·a·lec·tics DEBATE RESOLVING CONFLICT** debate intended to resolve a conflict between two contradictory or apparently contradictory ideas or elements logically, establishing truths on both sides rather than disproving one argument (*takes a singular verb*) **4. HEGELIAN PROCESS** the process, in Hegelian and Marxist thought, in which two apparently opposed ideas, the thesis and antithesis, become combined in a unified whole, the synthesis **5. SOCRATIC METHOD FOR REVEALING TRUTH** the methods used in Socratic philosophy to reveal truth through disputation [Late 16thC. Via Latin *dialectica* from Greek *dialektikē (tekhnē)* "(art) of discussion or debate," from *dialektikos* "of conversation," from *dialektos* (see DIALECT).]

di·a·lec·ti·cal /dī ə léktik'l/ *adj.* **1. ACHIEVED BY DIALECTIC** achieved or attempted by dialectic **2. INVOLVING DIALECTIC** involving or depending upon dialectic **3. RELATING TO DIALECT** relating to or belonging to a dialect — **di·a·lec·ti·cal·ly** *adv.*

di·a·lec·ti·cal ma·te·ri·al·ism *n.* the Marxian concept of reality in which material things are in the constant process of change brought about by the tension between conflicting or interacting forces, elements, or ideas —**di·a·lec·ti·cal ma·te·ri·al·ist** *n.*

di·a·lec·ti·cian /dī ə lek tísh'n/ *n.* **1. STUDENT OF DIALECTS** somebody who studies or is a specialist in language dialects **2. PHILOSOPHER SKILLED AT DIALECTIC** a person who practises dialectic or has special skills in dialectic

di·a·lec·tics *n.* = **dialectic** *n.* 3

di·a·lec·tol·o·gy /dī ə lek tólləjee/ *n.* the study of language dialects —**di·a·lec·to·log·i·cal** /dī ə lektə lójjik'l/ *adj.* —**di·a·lec·to·log·i·cal·ly** /-kəlee/ *adv.* — **di·a·lec·tol·o·gist** /dī ə lek tólləjist/ *n.*

di·al gauge *n.* a sensitive measuring device that indicates small displacements of a plunger by means of a pointer moving over a circular scale. It is usually used for measuring pressure or a vacuum.

di·al·ling tone *n. U.K.* = **dial tone**

di·a·log *n., vi.* = **dialogue**

di·a·log box *n.* a small rectangular window displayed on a computer screen that conveys information to, or requires a response from, the user

di·a·log·ic /dī ə lójjik/, **di·a·log·i·cal** /dī ə lójjək'l/ *adj.* **1. WRITTEN AS CONVERSATION** written in the form of a conversation **2. ABOUT DIALOGUES** relating to dialogues

di·al·o·gist /dī álləjist/ *n.* **1. WRITER OF DIALOGUE** somebody who writes dialogue for films, television, or radio **2. SOMEBODY WHO TAKES PART IN DIALOGUE** somebody who engages in a dialogue —**di·a·lo·gis·tic** /dī ələ jístik/ *adj.*

di·a·logue /dī ə lòg/, **di·a·log** /dī ə lòg/ *n.* **1. CHARACTERS' WORDS** the words spoken by characters in a book, a film, or a play, or a section of a work that contains spoken words **2. FORMAL DISCUSSION** a formal discussion or negotiation, especially between opposing sides in a political or international context **3. CONVERSATION** talk of any kind between two or more people (*formal*) **4. LITERARY WORK IN CONVERSATION FORM** a work of literature in the form of a conversation ■ *vi.*-**logued** *or* **-loged, -logu·ing** *or* **-log·ing -logues** *or* **-logs TAKE PART IN TALK** to take part in a conversation, discussion, or negotiation [12thC. Via Old French from, ultimately, Greek *dialogos*, from *dialegesthai*, literally "to speak with each other," from *legein* "to speak" (source of English *dialect* and *eclectic*).] —**di·a·log·uer** *n.*

di·al tone *n.* a continuous sound that you hear when you lift a telephone receiver. It indicates that you can dial a number.

di·al-up *adj.* COMPUT requiring the use of a computer modem and telephone line to establish communication with another computer or a network

di·al·y·sis /dī álləssiss/ *n.* **1. MEDICAL FILTERING PROCESS** the process of filtering the accumulated waste products of metabolism from the blood of a patient whose kidneys are not functioning properly, using a kidney machine **2.** CHEM **SEPARATION OF SUBSTANCES FROM SOLUTION** the separation of dissolved substances from a solution by allowing the solution to diffuse through a semipermeable membrane [Mid-19thC. Via Latin, "set of propositions without a connecting conjunction" (the original sense in English), from Greek *dialusis* "separation, loosening" from, ultimately, *luein* "to loosen."] — **di·a·lyt·ic** /dī ə líttik/ *adj.* —**di·a·lyt·i·cal·ly** /-kəlee/ *adv.*

di·a·lyze /dī ə līz/ (**-lyzed, -lyz·ing, -lyz·es**) *vti.* **1.** MED **REMOVE WASTE PRODUCTS** to remove the accumulated waste products of metabolism from the blood of a patient whose kidneys are not functioning, or to undergo such a procedure **2.** CHEM **SEPARATE SUBSTANCES FROM SOLUTION** to separate dissolved substances from a solution by diffusing it through a semipermeable membrane, or to be subjected to this process [Mid-19thC. Formed from DIALYSIS, on the model of ANALYZE.] — **di·a·lyz·a·bil·i·ty** /-bíllətee/ *n.* —**di·a·lyz·a·ble** /-līzəb'l/ *adj.* —**di·a·ly·za·tion** /dī əli záysh'n/ *n.*

di·a·lyz·er /dī ə līzər/ *n.* **1.** MED **KIDNEY MACHINE** a machine used to carry out dialysis of the blood of a patient whose kidneys are not functioning **2.** CHEM **MEMBRANE SEPARATING SUBSTANCES FROM SOLUTION** an apparatus used in chemical dialysis, especially a semipermeable membrane used to separate dissolved substances from a solution

diam. *abbr.* diameter

di·a·mag·net /dī ə mágnət/ *n.* a substance that is repelled by magnetic fields, such as noble gases, halogens, and alkali and alkaline earth metals — **di·a·mag·net·ic** /dī ə mag néttik/ *adj.* — **di·a·mag·net·i·cal·ly** /-néttikəlee/ *adv.*

di·a·mag·ne·tism /dī ə mágnə tìzzəm/ *n.* a tendency in materials with a relative permeability of less than one to be repelled by a magnetic field and align themselves at right angles to it

di·a·man·té /dèe ə maán tày/ *adj.* **RHINESTONE-COVERED** decorated with colorless imitation gems (**rhinestones**) that look like diamonds ■ *n.* **RHINESTONES** colorless imitation gems that look like diamonds, used for costume jewelry and decorating clothing [Early 20thC. From French, originally the past participle of *diamanter* "to set with diamonds," from *diamant* (see DIAMOND).]

di·a·man·tine /dī ə mán tīn, dī ə mán teen, dī ə mánt'n/ *adj.* **1. LOOKING LIKE DIAMONDS** resembling diamonds **2. MADE OF DIAMONDS** made of diamond or consisting of diamonds [Early 17thC. From French *diamantin*, from *diamant* (see DIAMOND).]

di·am·e·ter /dī ámmətər/ *n.* **1. LINE THROUGH CENTER OF CIRCLE** a straight line running from one side of a circle or other rounded geometric figure through the center to the other side, or the length of this line **2. WIDTH** the width or thickness of something, especially something circular or cylindrical ○ *in diameter* **3.** OPTICS **MAGNIFYING POWER OF LENS** the unit of measurement for the magnifying power of a lens [14thC. Via Old French *diametre* from Latin, from Greek *diametros (grammē)*, literally "(line) which measures through" from *metron* "measure" (source of English *meter* and *geometry*).]

di·am·e·tral /dī ámmətrəl/ *adj.* GEOM relating to or forming a diameter —**di·am·e·tral·ly** *adv.*

di·a·met·ric /dī ə méttrik/, **di·a·met·ri·cal** /dī ə méttrik'l/ *adj.* complete (refers to opposites, differences, etc.)

di·a·met·ri·cal·ly /dī ə méttrikəlee/ *adv.* used to emphasize that a difference or contrast is as great as it can be ○ *diametrically opposite concepts*

di·am·ine /dī ə meen, dī á meen/ *n.* an organic chemical compound that contains two amino (**nitrogen-containing**) groups [Mid-19thC. Coined from DI- + AMINE.]

di·a·mond /dī əmənd, dīmənd/ *n.* **1.** MINERALS **HARD COLORLESS MINERAL** a transparent form of carbon that is the hardest known mineral, with many applications in cutting tools and abrasives. It is also the most highly prized gemstone. **2. SHAPE LIKE SQUARE RESTING ON CORNER** a four-sided shape like a square standing on one of its corners **3.** CARDS **CARD WITH DIAMOND-SHAPED SYMBOL** a playing card with a diamond-shaped symbol on it. ◊ **diamonds 4.** BASEBALL **INFIELD** the area of a baseball field bounded by the home plate and the three bases **5.** BASEBALL **BASEBALL**

PLAYING AREA an area for playing baseball including the infield and the outfield ■ *vt.* (-mond·ed, -mond·ing, -monds) DECORATE WITH DIAMONDS to decorate something with diamonds or similar gemstones [13thC. Via Old French *diamant* "hardest metal" from the medieval Latin stem *diamant-*, an alteration of the Latin stem *adamant-* (see ADAMANT).]

di·a·mond an·ni·ver·sa·ry *n.* an anniversary celebrating 60, or sometimes 75, years of something, e.g., marriage [From the custom of marking the occasion with gifts containing diamonds]

di·a·mond·back /dī əmənd bàk, dīmənd bàk/ *n.* **1.** RATTLESNAKE WITH DIAMOND-SHAPED MARKINGS a large poisonous rattlesnake found in the southwestern United States and Mexico that has diamond-shaped markings on its back. Latin name: *Crotalus adamantus* and *Crotalus atrox*. **2.** TERRAPIN WITH DIAMOND-SHAPED MARKINGS a terrapin with diamond-shaped markings on its shell that lives in the salt marshes of the Atlantic and the Gulf coasts of North America. Genus: *Malaclemys*.

di·a·mond·back moth *n.* a brightly colored moth with diamond-shaped markings on the underside of the front wings, visible when the wings are folded. Family: Plutellidae.

Di·a·mond Head /dīmənd hèd/ landmark promontory and extinct volcano in Hawaii, at the southeastern tip of Oahu Island. Height: 760 ft./232 m.

di·a·mond·if·er·ous /dī əmən dífférəss, dīmən dífférəss/ *adj.* containing diamond or diamonds

di·a·mond in the rough *n.* somebody whose rough manners often hide his or her admirable or undeveloped qualities

di·a·mond ju·bi·lee *n.* = **diamond anniversary**

di·a·mond point *n.* a cutting tool in which two cutting edges meet at an acute angle, forming a diamond shape

di·a·monds /dī əməndz, dīməndz/ *n.* one of the four suits used in cards, with a red diamond shape as its symbol (*takes a singular or plural verb*)

di·a·mond wil·low *n.* *Can* willow wood with a diamond pattern in the grain

di·a·mor·phine /dī ə máwr feen/ *n.* heroin (*technical*) [Early 20thC. Contraction of *diacetylmorphine*, its chemical name.]

Barnaby's

Diana, Princess of Wales

Di·an·a /dī ánnə/, **Princess of Wales** (1961–97) British princess. She married Prince Charles in 1981, had two sons, and was divorced in 1996. She was killed in a car crash in Paris. Born **Diana Frances Spencer**

Di·an·a *n.* in Roman mythology, the goddess of hunting, virginity and the moon. Greek equivalent **Artemis**

di·an·drous /dī ándrəss/ *adj.* used to describe flowers that have two stamens, or fungi and non-seeding plants that have two antheridia [Late 18thC. Coined from DI- + the Greek stem *andr-* "man" + -OUS.]

di·an·thus /dī ánthəss/ *n.* a flowering plant belonging to the group that includes carnations, pinks, and sweet william. Genus: *Dianthus*. [Late 18thC. From modern Latin, genus name, from Greek *Dios* "of Zeus" + *anthos* "flower."]

di·a·pa·son /dī ə páyz'n, -páyss'n/ *n.* **1.** PIPE ORGAN'S MAIN STOP either of the two main stops on a pipe organ that control the organ's tone and give the instrument its characteristic sound **2.** RANGE OF SINGER OR MUSICAL INSTRUMENT the complete range of a musical instrument or a person's singing voice (*technical*) **3.** TUNING DEVICE a tuning fork or pitch pipe (*technical*) [14thC. Via Latin from, ultimately, Greek *dia pasōn khordōn*, literally "across all the notes of the scale."] —**di·a·pa·son·al** /dī ə páyzən'l, -páyssən'l, -páyznəl, -páyssnəl/ *adj.* —**di·a·pa·son·ic** /dī əpə zónnik/ *adj.*

di·a·pause /dī ə pàwz/ *n.* a period during which the metabolism of certain animals or insects slows down, temporarily suspending their bodily development and growth. Such periods are linked to seasonal or environmental changes.

di·a·pe·de·sis /dī əpə deéssiss/ *n.* a condition in which blood leaks through the apparently unruptured walls of blood vessels into surrounding tissue, as a reaction to severe inflammation or injury [Early 17thC. From modern Latin, formed from Greek *dia-* "through" + *pēdan* "to leap."] —**di·a·pe·det·ic** /dī əpə déttik/ *adj.*

di·a·pente /dī ə péntee/ *n.* in ancient Greek music, the interval of a perfect fifth [14thC. Via Old French from, ultimately, Greek *dia pente*, literally "through five."]

di·a·per /dī əpər, dīpər/ *n.* **1.** ABSORBENT BABY CLOTHING a piece of soft, absorbent material that is worn by a baby as underwear to absorb bodily waste **2.** CRAFT PATTERN OF SMALL MOTIFS a pattern, especially woven into or printed on fabric, consisting of a small motif, often a diamond, repeated over and over to cover an entire surface **3.** TEXTILES FABRIC WITH DIAPER PATTERN cotton or linen fabric with a diaper pattern woven into or printed on it ■ *vt.* (-pered, -per·ing, -pers) **1.** TEXTILES DECORATE WITH DIAPER PATTERN to decorate something, especially fabric, with a diaper pattern **2.** PUT DIAPER ON BABY to put a diaper on a baby [14thC. Via Old French *diapre* "ornamental cloth," from, ultimately, medieval Greek *diaspros* "thoroughly white," originally applied to silver coins, from, ultimately, Latin *asper* "rough," used for the surface of coins.]

di·a·per rash *n.* a sensitive red area or spotted rash on a baby's bottom, usually caused by irritation from urine, feces, or chemical irritants in diapers

di·aph·a·nous /dī áffənəss/ *adj.* **1.** TRANSPARENT delicate or gauzy, so as to be transparent ○ *the insect's diaphanous wings* **2.** INSUBSTANTIAL fragile or insubstantial because extremely faint or slight (*literary*) ○ *diaphanous imaginings* [Early 17thC. Via Latin *diaphanus* from Greek *diaphanēs*, literally "shown through," from *phainein* "to show" (source of English *fantasy*).] —**di·a·pha·ne·i·ty** /dī àffə neé itee/ *n.* —**di·aph·a·nous·ly** *n.* —**di·aph·a·nous·ness** *adv.*

di·a·phone /dī ə fōn/ *n.* **1.** PHON SET OF PRONUNCIATION VARIANTS a set of all the different ways that a particular speech sound is pronounced in all the dialects of a language, or a member of this set **2.** FOGHORN SOUNDING TWO NOTES a foghorn with a two-note sound

di·a·pho·re·sis /dī əfə reéssiss/ *n.* sweating, especially sweating induced for medical reasons (*technical*) [Late 17thC. Via late Latin from, ultimately, Greek *diaphorein* "to dissipate by sweating," literally "to carry away," from *phorein* "to carry."]

di·a·pho·ret·ic /dī əfə réttik/ *adj.* used to describe drugs, herbs, or other substances that induce sweating, or their effect —**di·a·pho·ret·ic** *n.*

di·a·phragm /dī ə fràm/ *n.* **1.** ANAT MUSCULAR WALL BELOW RIB CAGE a curved muscular membrane in humans and other mammals that separates the abdomen from the area around the lungs. Hiccups are caused by the diaphragm going into spasms. **2.** GYN DOME-SHAPED CONTRACEPTIVE a dome-shaped rubber or plastic contraceptive device for women, placed inside the vagina over the entrance to the womb to prevent sperm from entering **3.** OPTICS CAMERA'S MECHANISM CONTROLLING OPENING FOR LIGHT a disk with a fixed or variable opening that controls the amount of light that enters a camera or other optical instrument **4.** COMMUNICATION VIBRATING DISK IN SOUND EQUIPMENT a thin disk in a microphone, telephone receiver, or other sound device that vibrates in response to sound waves or electrical signals, converting one into the other **5.** ANY THIN MEMBRANE any thin separating membrane, e.g., the porous plate dividing the sections of an electrolytic cell or the plate of cells across the stems of some water plants [14thC. From late Latin *diaphragma*, from, ultimately, Greek *diaphrassein* "to barricade," literally "to fence across," from *phrassein* "to fence in."] —**di·a·phrag·mat·ic** /dī ə frag máttik, dī əfrə máttik/ *adj.* —**di·a·phrag·mat·i·cal·ly** /-máttikəlee, -máttikəlee/ *adv.*

di·aph·y·sis /dī áffississ/ (*plural* **-ses** /-seèz/) *n.* the central section of a long bone, between the growth areas at each end. ◊ **epiphysis** [Mid-19thC. From Greek *diaphusis*, literally "growing through," from *phusis* "growth."] —**di·a·phys·i·al** /dī ə fízzee əl/ *adj.*

di·a·pir /dī ə peèr/ *n.* a dome-shaped body of rock that migrates upwards through denser overlying rock, e.g., a salt deposit [Early 20thC. From Greek *diapeirainein* "to pierce through," from *peirainein* "to pierce."] —**di·a·pir·ic** /dī ə peèrik/ *adj.*

di·a·pos·i·tive /dī ə pózzitiv/ *n.* a photographic transparency [Late 19thC. Coined from DIA- "through" (from its transparency) + POSITIVE.]

di·ar·chy /dī aàrkee/ (*plural* **-chies**), **dy·ar·chy** (*plural* **-chies**) *n.* **1.** GOVERNMENT BY TWO RULERS OR BODIES a form of government in which power is held by two supreme rulers or two governing bodies **2.** COUNTRY RULED BY TWO RULERS a country ruled or run by two supreme rulers or two governing bodies [Mid-19thC. Formed from DI- on the model of MONARCHY.] —**di·ar·chal** /dī aàrk'l/ *adj.* —**di·arch·ic** *adj.* —**di·arch·i·cal** *adj.*

di·a·rist /dī ərist/ *n.* somebody who writes a diary, especially one that is published

di·ar·rhe·a /dī ə reé ə/ *n.* **1.** FREQUENT AND EXCESSIVE BOWEL MOVEMENTS frequent and excessive discharging of the bowels producing abnormally thin watery feces, usually as a symptom of gastrointestinal upset or infection **2.** WATERY FECES abnormally thin watery feces [Early 16thC. Via Latin *diarrhoea*, from Greek *diarrhoia*, from *diarrhein* "to flow through," from *rhein* "to flow."] —**di·ar·rhe·al** *adj.* —**di·ar·rhe·ic** *adj.*

di·ar·thro·sis /dī aar thróssiss/ *n.* the ability of some joints of the body to move in several directions [Late 16thC. From Greek, formed from *diarthroun* "to fasten by a joint," which in turn was formed from *arthroun* "to fasten."] —**di·ar·thro·di·al** *adj.*

di·a·ry /dī əree/ (*plural* **-ries**) *n.* **1.** PERSONAL RECORD OF LIFE'S EVENTS a personal record of events in somebody's life, often including personal thoughts and observations **2.** BLANK BOOK a book with blank or lined paper for keeping a diary in **3.** *U.K.* = **appointment book** [Late 16thC. From Latin *diarium*, from *dies* "day." The Latin word originally meant "daily allowance of food or pay."]

di·as·po·ra /dī áspərə/ *n.* a dispersion of a people, language, or culture that was formerly concentrated in one place ○ *the African diaspora* [Late 19thC. From Greek, formed from *diaspeirein* "to disperse," from *speirein* "to sow, scatter" (source of English *sperm*).]

Di·as·po·ra *n.* JUDAISM **1.** EXILE OF THE JEWS FROM ISRAEL the dispersion of the Jews from Palestine following the Babylonians' conquest of the Judean Kingdom in the 6th century B.C. and again, following the Romans' destruction of the Second Temple in A.D. 70 **2.** JEWS LIVING OUTSIDE ISRAEL the Jewish communities living outside either the present-day state of Israel or the ancient biblical kingdom of Israel

di·a·spore /dī ə spàwr/ *n.* **1.** MINERALS WHITE OXIDE OF ALUMINUM a white, gray, or pink form of aluminum oxide that is found in bauxite and corundum. It is useful for its abrasive and heat-resistant properties. **2.** BOT REPRODUCTIVE STRUCTURE a seed or spore that is dispersed from a plant [Early 19thC. From Greek *diaspora* (see DIASPORA); from its dispersion when heated.]

di·a·stase /dī ə stàyss, -stàyz/ *n.* BIOCHEM now called **amylase** [Mid-19thC. Coined from modern Latin *diastasis* (see DIASTASIS) + -ASE.] —**di·a·sta·sic** /dī ə stáyzik, -stáyssik/ *adj.*

di·as·ta·sis /dī ástəssiss/ (*plural* **-ses** /dī ástə seèz/) *n.* MED the dislodging of the end (**epiphysis**) of a long bone from its shaft without a fracturing of the bone itself (*technical*) [Early 18thC. Via modern Latin from Greek, "separation," from *stasis* "placing."] —**di·a·stat·ic** /dī ə státtik/ *adj.*

di·a·ste·ma /dī ə steémə/ (*plural* **-ma·ta** /-steémətə/) *n.* DENT a larger than usual gap between two adjacent teeth (*technical*) [Mid-19thC. Via late Latin from Greek, "gap," from *diistanai* "to place apart," from *histanai* "to place."] —**di·a·ste·mat·ic** /dī əstə máttik/ *adj.*

di·a·ste·re·o·i·so·mer /dī ə sterri ō ísəmər/, **di·a·ste·re·o·mer** *n.* CHEM a molecule that has the same formula and structure as another (**stereoisomer**), but is arranged differently in space and is therefore not a mirror image of the other (**enantiomer**)

di·as·to·le /dī ástəlee/ *n.* the rhythmic expansion of the chambers of the heart at each heartbeat, during which they fill with blood [Late 16thC. Via late Latin from Greek, "separation, expansion," from *diastellein*, literally "to place apart," from *stellein* "to place."] —**di·a·stol·ic** /dī ə stóllik/ *adj.*

di·a·style /dī ə stīl/ *adj.* HAVING WIDELY SPACED COLUMNS used to describe classical buildings with columns set at intervals equal to three, or sometimes four times the diameter of a column, slightly farther apart than in the Doric order ■ *n.* DIASTYLE STRUCTURE a diastyle building or colonnade [Mid-16thC. Directly or via Latin from Greek *diastulos,* literally "between columns," from *stulos* "column."]

di·a·tes·sa·ron /dī ə téssərən, dī ə téssə ròn/ *n.* **1.** BIBLE GOSPELS AS ONE STORY the combination of all four Gospels of the Bible to make a single narrative **2.** MUSIC ANCIENT GREEK INTERVAL OF A FOURTH in ancient Greek music, the interval of a perfect fourth [Late 16thC. Via late Latin from Greek *dia tessarōn,* literally "composed of four."]

di·a·ther·mi·a *n.* MED = **diathermy** [Early 20thC. From modern Latin, literally "heat across," formed from Greek *thermē* "heat."]

di·a·ther·mic /dī ə thúrmik/ *adj.* **1.** MED RELATING TO DIATHERMY relating to diathermy **2.** PHYS CONDUCTING HEAT able to conduct or transmit heat or infrared radiation [Early 20thC. From French *diathermique,* from Greek *thermē* "heat."]

di·a·ther·my /dī ə thùrmee/, **diather·mia** *n.* MED the treatment of organs or tissues by passing high-frequency electric currents through them in order to generate heat, thus increasing circulation [Early 20thC. From modern Latin *diathermia* (see DIATHERMIA).]

di·ath·e·sis /dī áthəssiss/ (*plural* **-ses** /-seez/) *n.* a susceptibility to a particular disease or set of diseases, e.g., allergies or gout [Mid-17thC. Via modern Latin from, ultimately, Greek *diatithenai* "to arrange, dispose," literally "to put in different directions," from *tithenai* "to put."] —**di·a·thet·ic** /-ə théttik/ *adj.*

di·a·tom /dí ə tòm/ *n.* a microscopic one-celled alga that has silica-filled cell walls or shells divided into two halves. Diatoms are responsible for the formation of diatomite in water. Class: Bacillariophyceae. [Mid-19thC. From modern Latin *Diatoma,* genus name, from Greek *diatomos* "cut in two," from *diatemnein* "to cut through," from *temnein* "to cut."]

di·a·to·ma·ceous /dí ətə máyshəss/ *adj.* containing diatoms or their skeletal remains

di·a·to·ma·ceous earth *n.* **1.** POWDERED ROCK USED AS NONTOXIC INSECTICIDE a form of unrefined diatomite that is used as an insecticide. It is used indoors as an alternative to chemical insecticides because it is virtually nontoxic to humans, although it can be a lung irritant if inhaled. **2.** = **diatomite**

di·a·tom·ic /dì ə tómmik/ *adj.* having two atoms per molecule [Mid-19thC. Coined from DI- "two" + ATOMIC.] —**di·a·tom·ic·ity** /dì attə míssitee/ *n.*

di·at·o·mite /dī áttə mīt/ *n.* a soft powdery porous rock made from the accumulated shells of diatoms. It is resistant to heat and chemical action and has many industrial uses, e.g., as an ingredient in fireproof cements and insulating materials, as well as in dynamite. [Late 19thC. Coined from DIATOM + -ITE.]

di·a·ton·ic /dì ə tónnik/ *adj.* RELATING TO SIMPLE MUSICAL SCALES relating to or based on musical scales consisting of five tones and two semitones, e.g., the major or minor scale, with no sharps or flats added ■ *n.* INTERVAL IN A DIATONIC SCALE the interval between any two notes of a diatonic scale [Early 17thC. Via French *diatonique* or late Latin *diatonicus,* from Greek *diatonikos* "at intervals of a tone," from *tonos* "tone."] —**di·a·ton·i·cal·ly** *adv.* —**di·a·ton·i·cism** /-tónni sìzzəm/ *n.*

di·a·tribe /dí ə trīb/ *n.* a bitter verbal or written attack on somebody or something ○ *a diatribe against falling standards* [Late 16thC. Via French from, ultimately, Greek *diatribē* "act of spending time (in discourse)." Originally, in English, "learned discourse"; its connotations of "bitter resentment" date from the 19thC.]

di·at·ro·pism /dī áttrə pìzzəm/ *n.* the tendency of a plant or plant part to grow at right angles in response to an external stimulus, e.g., light —**di·a·trop·ic** /dì ə tróppik/ *adj.*

Dí·az /dée àz, dée àass/, **Porfirio** (1830–1915) Mexican soldier and statesman. President of Mexico (1876–80, 1884–1911), he was forced out of office during the Mexican revolution. Full name **José de la Cruz Porfirio Díaz**

diaz- *prefix.* = **diazo-** (*used before vowels*)

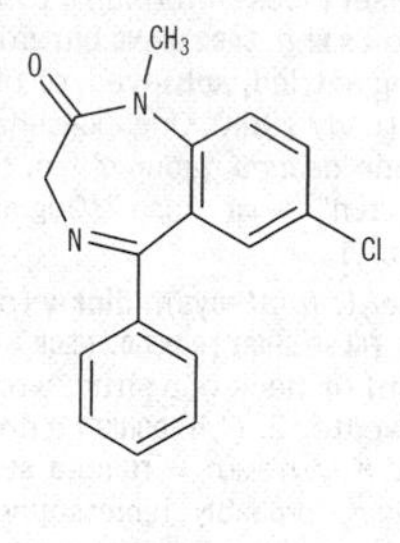

Diazepam

di·az·e·pam /dī ázzə pàm/ *n.* a tranquilizing drug used to reduce anxiety and tension, and as a muscle relaxant and sedative. Formula: $C_{16}H_{13}ClN_2O$. [Mid-20thC. Coined from a shortening of BENZODIAZEPINE + a shortening of AMIDE.]

di·a·zine /dí ə zeen, dī ázzin/ *n.* CHEM a chemical compound in which the molecules contain a hexagonal ring of four carbon atoms and two nitrogen atoms. It has three different molecular structures (**isomers**). Formula: $C_4N_2H_4$. [Early 20thC. Coined from DI- "two" + AZINE.]

Di·az·i·non *tdmk.* a trademark for an organophosphate insecticide

di·az·o /dī ázzō, dī áyzō/ *adj.* CHEM CONTAINING TWO ADJACENT NITROGEN ATOMS used to describe any organic compound containing two adjacent nitrogen atoms, e.g. an azo compound or a diazonium salt. ◊ **azo** ■ *n.* (*plural* **-a·zos** *or* **-a·zoes**) PRINTING, PHOTOGRAPHY DOCUMENT COPY MADE WITH DIAZO COMPOUND a photograph or photocopy made using a diazo compound or the diazotype process [Late 19thC. Coined from DI- + AZO-. The noun is a shortening of DIAZOTYPE.]

diazo- *prefix.* containing a pair of carbon atoms bonded to an aromatic hydrocarbon ○ *diazonium* [Coined from DI-[1] + AZO-]

di·a·zole /dì ə zól, dì á zòl/ *n.* CHEM an organic chemical compound with a five-sided ring structure containing three carbon atoms and two nitrogen atoms

Dí·az Or·daz /dée az áwr dàz, dée aass áwr dàass/, **Gustavo** (1911–79) Mexican statesman. He served as senator (1946–52), minister of the interior (1958–63), and president (1964–70).

di·a·zo·tize /dī ázzə tīz/ (**-tized, -tiz·ing, -tiz·es**) *v.* CHEM to use nitrous acid to transform an amine into a diazo compound —**di·a·zo·ti·za·tion** /dī àzzəti záysh'n/ *n.*

di·a·zo·type /dī ázzə tīp/ *n.* a printing or photographic process that exploits the light-sensitive properties of diazo compounds

di·ba·sic /dī báyssik/ *adj.* CHEM **1.** WITH TWO REPLACEABLE HYDROGEN ATOMS used to describe an acid that has two replaceable hydrogen atoms **2.** FORMED WITH TWO ATOMS OF METAL used to describe a salt or an acid that is formed with two atoms of a univalent metallic element —**di·ba·sic·i·ty** /dī bay síssitee/ *n.*

dib·ber /díbbər/ *n.* a small pointed gardening tool used to make holes in the soil for planting seeds, bulbs, or seedlings [Mid-18thC. Formed from DIB, in the dialect sense "to dibble."]

dib·ble /díbb'l/ *n.* = **dibber** ■ *vt.* (**-bled, -bling, -bles**) MAKE HOLES IN SOIL to make planting holes in soil with a pointed tool, or put plants or seeds in such holes [14thC. Origin uncertain: possibly formed from Old English *dyppan* "to dip."] —**dib·bler** /díbblər/ *n.*

di·bran·chi·ate /dī brángkee ət/ *n.* a mollusk with two gills. Octopus, squid, and cuttlefish are dibranchiates. Order: Dibranchiata. [Mid-19thC. Coined from DI- "two" + Greek *bragkhia* "gills" + -ATE.]

di·bro·mide /dī brṓ mīd/ *n.* a chemical compound whose molecules contain two bromine atoms

dibs /dibz/ *npl.* **1.** MONEY money, especially in small amounts (*dated informal*) **2.** CLAIM OF RIGHTS a claim of exclusive rights to take or use something (*informal*) ○ *called dibs on the front seat* ■ *interj.* EXPRESSION OF CLAIM used to express a claim to take or use something (*informal*) ○ *Dibs on the red bike!* [Early 19thC. From *dibs* "game played with pebbles," hence "counters used in a game," shortening of *dibstones,* probably from DIB in the obsolete sense "to tap."]

di·car·box·yl·ic ac·id /dī kaar bok sìllik-/ *n.* any acid that contains two carboxyl groups

di·cast /dī kàst, dí kàst/ *n.* in ancient Athens, a citizen who was among the six thousand chosen by lot each year to act as jurors and judges in the popular law courts [Early 19thC. From Greek *dikastes* "judge, juryman," from *dikazein* "to judge."] —**di·cas·tic** /dī kástik, di kástik/ *adj.*

dice /dīss/ *npl.* **1.** GAME GAMBLING GAME PLAYED WITH DICE a gambling game played with dice, e.g., craps (*often takes a singular verb*) **2.** CHUNKS cube-shaped pieces, especially of meat ■ *v.* (**diced, dic·ing, dic·es**) **1.** *vt.* CUT INTO CUBES to cut food into cubes ○ *diced carrots* **2.** *vti.* GAME GAMBLE WITH DICE to gamble using dice, or win or lose something playing dice **3.** *vi.* TAKE RISKS to challenge or take risks with somebody or something dangerous ○ *dicing with death* **4.** *vt.* DECORATE WITH SQUARE PATTERN to decorate something with a pattern of squares or cubes [14thC. Plural of DIE[2], from French *dé* (plural *dés*), from Latin *datum,* past participle of *dare* "to give," also "to play."] —**dic·er** *n.* ◇ **load the dice** to manipulate a situation unfairly in order to obtain a desired result ◇ **no dice** used to indicate that there is no chance of something happening

WORD KEY: USAGE

Dice – singular or plural? *Dice,* used with a plural verb, means "small cubes marked with one to six dots, used in gambling games." ***Dice,*** used with a singular verb, means a gambling game in which these cubes are used. *Dice* (plural) can also refer to any small cubes, especially cube-shaped pieces of food (*Cut the cheese into dice*).

di·cen·tra /dī séntrə/ *n.* a perennial plant with arching sprays of small drooping flowers that grows best in shade. Genus: *Dicentra.* [Mid-19thC. Via modern Latin, genus name, from Greek *dikentros,* literally "two-pointed," from *kentron* "center, point"; from the shape of its leaves.]

dic·ey /dīssee/ (**-i·er, -i·est**), **dic·y** (**-i·er, -i·est**) *adj.* uncertain and involving danger or risk (*informal*) [Mid-20thC. From the riskiness of gambling with dice.]

dich- *prefix.* = **dicho-** (*used before vowels*)

di·cha·si·um /dī káy zhee əm, -káyzhəm/ (*plural* **-a** /ə, -káyzhə/) *n.* a flowering stem that has a single flower growing on the end (**cyme**) and later sprouts two single-flower branches, one on each side of and below the first flower [Late 19thC. Coined from Greek *dikhasis* "division" formed from *dikha* "apart" + -IUM.] —**di·cha·si·al** *adj.* —**di·cha·si·al·ly** *adv.*

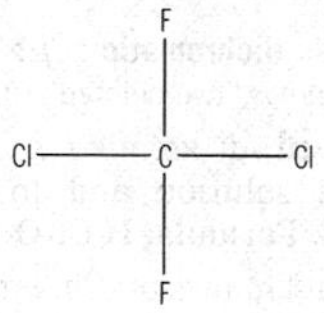

Dichloromethane

di·chlo·ro·di·fluor·o·meth·ane /dī klàw rō dī floor ō mé thàyn, dī klàw rō dī flawrō mé thàyn/ *n.* a colorless, nonflammable, gaseous CFC. It is easily liquified under pressure and is therefore used as a propellant in aerosols, as a refrigerant, and in fire extinguishers. Formula: CCl_2F_2.

di·chlo·ro·di·phen·yl·tri·chlo·ro·eth·ane /dī klàw rō dī fenn'l trī klaw rō é thàyn, trī kláw rō é thàyn/ *n.* full form of **DDT**

di·chlo·ro·meth·ane /dī klàw rō mé thàyn/ *n.* a colorless, nonflammable, toxic gas used in paint strippers, degreasing, and in plastics processing. Formula: CH_2Cl_2. [Mid-20thC]

dicho- *prefix.* having two parts ○ *dichogamy* [From Greek *dikha* "in two"; related to *di-* "two"]

di·chog·a·my /dī kóggəmee/ *n.* a plant's production of male and female parts at different times, in order to prevent self-pollination and ensure cross-fertilization [Mid-19thC. Coined from Greek *dikho-* "apart" + *gamos* "marriage."] —**di·cho·gam·ic** /dī kō gámmik/ *adj.* —**di·chog·a·mous** /dī kóggəməss/ *adj.*

di·chon·dra /dī kóndrə/ *n.* a low-growing plant of the morning glory family that is often planted in place of lawn grass in warm parts of the United States. Genus: *Dichondra.* [Mid-20thC. From modern Latin, genus name, literally "two grains," formed from Greek *dikho-* "apart" + *khondros* "grain."]

di·chop·tic /dī kóptik/ *adj.* with eyes clearly separated from each other [Late 19thC. Coined from Greek *dikho-* "apart" + OPTIC.]

di·chot·ic /dī kóttik/ *adj.* involving or relating to the simultaneous stimulation of each ear with different sounds [Mid-20thC. Coined from Greek *dikho-* "apart" + the Greek stem *ōt-* "ear" + -IC.]

di·chot·o·mize /dī kóttə mīz/ (**-mized, -miz·ing, -miz·es**) *vti.* to divide something, or become divided, into two classes or groups (*formal*) —**di·chot·o·mi·za·tion** /dī kòttəmi záysh'n/ *n.*

di·chot·o·my /dī kóttəmee/ (*plural* **-mies**) *n.* **1.** SEPARATION OF DIFFERENT OR CONTRADICTORY THINGS a separation into two divisions that differ widely from, or contradict each other **2.** BOT BRANCHING OF PLANTS the division of each of a plant's branches into two more branches **3.** ASTRON MOON PHASE WHEN HALF VISIBLE the phase of the moon or a planet when half of its surface appears illuminated by the sun [Late 16thC. Via modern Latin from Greek *dikhotomia*, literally "cutting in two," from *dikho-* "apart, in two" + *temnein* "to cut."] —**di·chot·o·mic** /dīkə tómmik/ *adj.* —**di·chot·o·mous** /dī kóttəmist/ *adj.* —**di·chot·o·mous·ly** /-məsslee/ *adv.*

di·chro·ic /dī krṓ ik/, **di·chro·it·ic** /dì krō íttik/ *adj.* used to describe a crystal that appears to be a different color when viewed along a different axis [Mid-19thC. Formed from Greek *dikhroos* "two-colored," from *khrōs* "colour."] —**di·chro·ism** *n.*

di·chro·ite /dī krṓ īt/ *n.* = **cordierite**

di·chro·mate /dī krṓ màyt/ *n.* a salt of dichromic acid. Dichromates are a characteristic orange-red color.

di·chro·mat·ic /dī krō máttik/ *adj.* **1.** WITH TWO COLORS having two colors **2. di·chro·mat·ic, di·chro·mic** /dì krómik/ OPHTHALMOL PARTIALLY COLORBLIND able to distinguish only two of the three primary colors and their combinations **3.** ZOOL WITH DIFFERENT COLOR PHASES used to describe animals, especially birds, that have two different colors in phases that are not associated with the normal variations in color that occur with sex and age

di·chro·ma·tism /dī krṓmə tìzzəm/ *n.* **1.** COLORING WITH TWO COLORS ONLY the presence of only two colors in something **2.** OPHTHALMOL PARTIAL COLORBLINDNESS a type of colorblindness in which only two of the three primary colors and their combinations can be distinguished

di·chro·mic *adj.* = **dichromatic** *adj.* 2 [Mid-19thC. Formed from Greek *dikhrōmos* "two-colored" (from *khrōma* "color.")]

di·chro·mic ac·id /dī krṓmik-/ *n.* an unstable acid found only in solution and in the form of dichromate salts. Formula: $H_2Cr_2O_7$.

di·chrom·ism /dī krṓ mìzzəm/ *n.* = **dichromatism** *n.* 2

dick[1] /dik/ *n.* offensive term for the penis (*slang offensive*) [Mid-16thC. From the male first name *Dick.*]

dick[2] /dik/ *n.* a detective (*dated slang*) [Early 20thC. Origin uncertain: perhaps a shortening of DETECTIVE, or from slang *dick* "look."]

Dick and Jane *npl.* the stereotypes of middle-class Caucasian Americans (*informal*) (*hyphenated when used before a noun*)

Dick·ens /díkənz/, **Charles** (1812–70) British novelist. His career began with magazine sketches, written under the pseudonym "Boz," before *Pickwick Papers* (1837) brought him greater popularity. His many subsequent novels, appearing in monthly installments and often depicting poverty and social injustice in Victorian England, have remained popular. Full name **Charles John Huffam Dickens**

Dick·en·si·an /di kénzee ən/ *adj.* **1.** OF CHARLES DICKENS relating to the 19th-century British author, Charles Dickens, his writing, or the times he lived in **2.** FULL OF TWISTS AND AMAZING COINCIDENCES full of twists and remarkable coincidences, like the plots of some of the novels of Dickens ○ *an episode too Dickensian for most modern audiences to swallow* **3.** REMINISCENT OF POVERTY-STRICKEN VICTORIAN BRITAIN typical or reminiscent of the harsh poverty-stricken living conditions described in the works of Dickens **4.** JOLLY AND GENIAL jolly and cordial, like some of the scenes and characters featured in the novels of Dickens

dick·er /díkər/ *vi.* (**-ered, -er·ing, -ers**) HAGGLE to bargain for goods or services (*informal*) ○ *collectors dickering at antique sales* ■ *n.* BARGAINING bargaining in general, or something settled, achieved, or obtained through bargaining [Early 19thC. Origin uncertain: probably from, ultimately, Latin *decuria* "group of ten, ten hides for sale," from *decem* "ten" + *vir* "man." Originally in English "a quantity of ten."]

dick·ey /díkee/ (*plural* **-eys**), **dick·y** (*plural* **-ys**), **dick·ie** *n.* **1.** CLOTHES FALSE SHIRT FRONT OR NECK a garment that is only the front or neck of a shirt, worn under a shirt, jacket, or sweater **2.** *U.K.* DONKEY a donkey, especially a male **3.** *U.K.* AUTOMOT = **rumble seat** [Mid-18thC. Of uncertain origin; probably representing different words, some of which may have been inspired by the male name *Dicky*, a pet form of *Richard.*]

Dick·ey /díkee/, **James** (1923–97) U.S. writer. He is known for his poetry and the novel *Deliverance* (1970). Full name **James Lafayette Dickey**

dick·head /dík hèd/ *n.* an offensive term for an unintelligent or inattentive man (*slang insult*)

dick·ie *n.* = **dickey**

Emily Dickinson

Dick·in·son /díkinsən/, **Emily** (1830–86) U.S. poet. She is considered one of America's greatest writers. Most of her poems were published posthumously. Full name **Emily Elizabeth Dickinson**

Dick·in·son, John (1732–1808) American founding father. He led opposition to British tax policy and wrote *Letters from a Farmer in Pennsylvania* (1767–68).

Dick test *n.* a skin test used to determine whether somebody is immune or susceptible to scarlet fever [Early 20thC. Named for George Frederick *Dick* (1881–1967), the U.S. biologist who invented the test.]

dick·y[1] /díkee/ (**-ier, -i·est**) *adj. U.K.* (*informal*) **1.** UNWELL not well in health **2.** NOT RELIABLE faulty or unreliable [Late 18thC. Origin unknown.]

dick·y[2] /díkee/ *n.* = **dickey**

di·cli·nous /dī klī́nəss/ *adj.* used to describe plants that have stamens and pistils in separate flowers, rather than in the same flower [Early 19thC. Formed from modern Latin *diclines*, literally "two beds," from Greek *klinē* "bed."] —**di·clin·ism** *n.* —**di·cli·ny** *n.*

di·cot·y·le·don /dī kott'l eéd'n/ *n.* a flowering plant with two seed leaves (**cotyledons**) that appear from the seed at germination and subsequent leaves with a network of veins. Most herbaceous plants, trees, and shrubs are dicotyledons. Subclass: Dicotyledonae. [Early 18thC. From modern Latin *Dicotyledonae*, subclass name, literally "two cotyledons."] —**di·cot·y·le·don·ous** *adj.*

di·cro·tism /díkrə tìzzəm/ *n.* a physiological condition in which each heartbeat produces a double pulse, as occurs, e.g., in typhoid fever [Mid-19thC. Formed from Greek *dikrotos* "double-beating."] —**di·cro·tal** /dī krṓt'l/ *adj.* —**di·crot·ic** /dī króttik/ *adj.*

dict. *abbr.* **1.** dictation **2.** dictator **3.** dictionary

dic·ta plural of **dictum**

Dic·ta·phone /díktə fōn/ *tdmk.* a trademark for a small hand-held tape recorder used for dictation

dic·tate /dík tàyt/ *v.* (**-tat·ed, -tat·ing, -tates**) **1.** *vti.* SPEAK ALOUD WORDS TO BE WRITTEN to speak the words of a text or letter to be written, either to somebody writing it down as it is spoken, or into a tape recorder for later transcription **2.** *vti.* RULE OR CONTROL OTHER PEOPLE to rule over or make decisions for others with absolute authority, or attempt to do so ○ *dictates their every move* **3.** *vt.* CONTROL to have control over something (*usually passive*) ■ *n.* **1.** COMMAND GIVEN an order telling people what they must do ○ *dictates received from their superiors* **2.** GOVERNING PRINCIPLE a rule or principle that governs how people behave ○ *the dictates of fashion* [Late 16thC. From Latin *dictat-*, the past participle stem of *dictare* "to say often," from *dicere* "to say" (see DICTION).]

dic·ta·tion /dik táysh'n/ *n.* **1.** ACT OF DICTATING the act of dictating a text or letter, or of writing down what is being dictated **2.** EDUC STUDENTS' WRITING OF WORDS SPOKEN a test or exercise of language comprehension in which students write down words spoken aloud by a teacher ○ *a Spanish dictation* **3.** WORDS WRITTEN DOWN words written down that have been dictated —**dic·ta·tion·al** *adj.*

dic·ta·tor /dík tàytər/ *n.* **1.** POL TYRANT a leader who rules a country with absolute power, usually by force **2.** BOSSY PERSON somebody who behaves in a tyrannical way **3.** AUTHORITY ON A SUBJECT somebody whose opinions on a subject are listened to and followed by society at large ○ *one of the great dictators of modern music* **4.** SOMEBODY WHO GIVES DICTATION somebody who speaks the words of a letter or text out loud so that somebody else can transcribe them **5.** HIST TEMPORARY ROMAN RULER in ancient Rome, a temporary appointed leader with absolute power to deal with a crisis or an emergency

dic·ta·to·ri·al /dìktə táwree əl/ *adj.* **1.** IMPOSING WILL ON OTHERS fond of telling others what to do, or of using power or authority to make them do it **2.** POL OF DICTATORS relating to or ruled by dictators —**dic·ta·to·ri·al·ly** *adv.*

dic·ta·tor·ship /dik táytər shìp/ *n.* **1.** DICTATOR'S POWER OR RULE a dictator's power or authority, or the period of time during which a dictator rules **2.** GOVERNMENT BY DICTATOR government by a dictator **3.** COUNTRY RULED BY DICTATOR a country ruled by a dictator **4.** ABSOLUTE AUTHORITY absolute power or authority

dic·tion /díkshən/ *n.* **1.** SPOKEN CLARITY the clarity with which somebody pronounces words when speaking or singing **2.** CHOICE OF WORDS choice of words to fit their context ○ *"a tendency to identify the poetic impulse with melancholy moods and sonorous diction"* (Northrop Frye, *The Bush Garden*; 1972) [Mid-16thC. From the Latin stem *diction-*, from *dicere* "to say."] —**dic·tion·al** *adj.* —**dic·tion·al·ly** *adv.*

dic·tion·ar·y /díkshə nèrree/ (*plural* **-ies**) *n.* **1.** BOOK OF WORD MEANINGS a reference book that contains words listed in alphabetical order and gives explanations of their meanings, often with additional information about grammar, pronunciation, and etymology **2.** FOREIGN-LANGUAGE REFERENCE BOOK OF WORDS a reference book that gives equivalents of words and phrases in two or more languages, often with translations from each language to the other in separate sections ○ *a Spanish-English dictionary* **3.** SPECIALIZED REFERENCE BOOK a reference book that gives the meanings of, and often other information about, terms relating to a particular subject or field, arranged alphabetically ○ *a dictionary of music* **4.** LIST OF INFORMATION a book that contains a list of examples or information arranged either alphabetically or in some other way, e.g., by author ○ *a dictionary of quotations* **5.** COMPUT ALPHABETICAL LIST OF COMPUTER CODES an alphabetized list of keys or code names used in a program, together with a brief description of the meaning of each **6.** COMPUT WORD-PROCESSING REFERENCE a file used as a reference by a word-processing program for correct spelling and hyphenation [Early 16thC. From medieval Latin *dictionarius* "of words," from the Latin stem *diction-* (see DICTION).]

dic·tum /díktəm/ (*plural* **-tums** *or* **-ta** /-tə/) *n.* **1.** PRONOUNCEMENT an authoritative saying, statement, or pronouncement (*formal*) **2.** LAW = **obiter dictum** [Late 16thC. From Latin, from the past participle of *dicere* (see DICTION).]

dic·ty·op·ter·an /dìktee óptərən/ *n.* an insect with, typically, a flattened body, long legs, and leathery front wings held flat over the membranous hind wings. Dictyopterans include cockroaches and mantises. Order: Dictyoptera.

dic·y *adj.* = **dicey**

di·cyn·o·dont /dī sínnə dònt/ *n.* an extinct plant-eating reptile with teeth like tusks. Suborder: Dicynodontia. [Mid-19thC. From modern Latin *Dicynodontia*, suborder name, literally "two canine teeth," from the Greek stems *kun-* "dog" and *odont-* "tooth."]

did past tense of **do**

di·dact /dī dàkt/ *n.* somebody who speaks or writes in a didactic way (*formal*) [Mid-20thC. Back-formation from DIDACTIC.]

di·dac·tic /dī dáktik/ *adj.* **1. WITH MESSAGE** containing a political or moral message ○ *didactic theater* **2. FOND OF INSTRUCTING OR ADVISING OTHERS** tending to give instruction or advice, even when it is not welcome or not needed [Mid-17thC. From Greek *didaktikos*, from *didaskein* "to teach."] —**di·dac·ti·cal·ly** *adv.*

di·dac·ti·cism /dī dákti sìzzəm/ *n.* the instructional quality of something, e.g., a piece of writing, or the attitude of somebody who likes to instruct others or give them advice ○ *the welcome absence of didacticism in modern poetry*

di·dac·tics /dī dáktiks/ *n.* the science or profession of teaching (*formal*) (*takes a singular verb*)

did·dle[1] /dídd'l/ (**-dled, -dling, -dles**) *vt.* **1. CHEAT** to cheat or swindle somebody (*slang*) (*often passive*) **2. COMPUT MANIPULATE DATA ILLEGALLY** to manipulate computer data illegally (*informal*) **3. COMPUT MANIPULATE PROGRAM** to manipulate a computer program in an informal or a not particularly serious manner (*informal*) [Early 19thC. Origin uncertain: perhaps a back-formation from *Diddler*, the surname of a swindler in *Raising the Wind*, a play by James Kenney (1803).] —**did·dler** *n.*

did·dle[2] /dídd'l/ (**-dled, -dling, -dles**) *v.* **1.** *vt.* **OFFENSIVE TERM** to have sexual intercourse with a woman (*slang offensive*) **2.** *vti.* **OFFENSIVE TERM** to masturbate (*slang offensive*) **3.** *vi.* **TOUCH OR PLAY WITH SOMETHING REPEATEDLY** to spend time touching, fiddling with, or adjusting something repeatedly (*slang*) **4.** *vt.* **JERK REPEATEDLY** to jerk something up and down or back and forth (*informal*) **5.** *vi.* **SPEND TIME IDLY** to spend time doing nothing in particular (*slang*) ○ *spent the morning diddling around* [Mid-17thC. Origin uncertain: perhaps formed from dialect *didder* "to quiver."] —**did·dler** *n.*

did·dly·squat /díddli skwàwt/, **did·dly** *n.* nothing at all (*informal*) ○ *And what did I get? Diddlysquat!* [Mid-20thC. Origin uncertain: probably alteration of *doodlysquat*.]

did·ger·i·doo /dìjjəri dóo/ (*plural* **-doos**), **did·jer·i·doo** (*plural* **-doos**) *n.* an Australian Aboriginal musical instrument consisting of a long thick wooden pipe that the player blows into, creating a deep reverberating humming sound [Early 20thC. An Aboriginal word imitating the sound of the instrument.]

did·n't /díd'nt/ *contr.* did not ○ *I didn't want to go.*

Di·do /dī dō/ in Roman mythology, the queen and founder of Carthage who killed herself when abandoned by her lover, Aeneas

didst /didst/ *contr.* second person present singular of "did," used with "thou" (*archaic*)

di·dym·i·um /dī dímmee əm/ *n.* a mixture of metallic elements from the rare-earth, or lanthanide, series of elements, consisting chiefly of neodymium and praseodymium, used in the production of colored glass and optical filters [Mid-19thC. Coined from Greek *didumos* "twin" + -IUM.]

die[1] /dī/ (**died, dy·ing, dies**) *v.* **1.** *vi.* **STOP LIVING** to cease to be alive (*refers to a person, plant, or animal*) **2.** *vi.* **STOP EXISTING** to cease to exist, especially gradually ○ *feelings I thought had died long ago* **3.** *vi.* **STOP WORKING** to stop functioning ○ *The engine suddenly died.* **4.** *vti.* **DIE AS STATED** to cease to live in a particular way ○ *The villain, of course, dies a gruesome death.* [12thC. Origin uncertain: probably from Old Norse *deyja* "to die," from, ultimately, an Indo-European base that also produced English *death* and *dead*.] ◇ **to die for** highly desirable and hence worth sacrificing something to obtain ◇ **die hard** give up or come to an end only after long, difficult, and sustained resistance. ◊ **diehard**

die away *vi.* to fade or grow faint

die back *vi.* to wither or die from the tips of new shoots back to the established stem or old wood of the plant, as a result of disease, seasonal change, or poor conditions

die down *vi.* to become quieter, weaker, or less intense

die off *vi.* to die gradually one by one, till none are left (*refers to plants or animals*)

die out *vi.* **1. CEASE GRADUALLY TO EXIST** to become extinct or cease to exist gradually ○ *entire species that have died out in our century* **2. DISAPPEAR GRADUALLY** to fade and finally disappear gradually ○ *Over the years, opposition to the plan had died out.*

die[2] /dī/ *n.* **1.** (*plural* **dice**) **GAME NUMBERED CUBE USED IN GAMES** a small cube with the numbers 1 to 6 marked in dots on the sides, used in gambling and in a wide variety of games of chance ○ *throw each die once* **2. ENG STAMPING OR PRESSING TOOL** the metal tool on a stamping or pressing machine that gives the finished article its shape and design **3. ENG MOLD** tool for molding substances such as metal or plastic **4. ENG TOOL FOR CUTTING** a tool that cuts screw threads on metal rods, consisting of a metal block with an internally threaded hole into which blank rods are screwed to cut external threads **5. ARCHIT PART OF PEDESTAL** the part of a pedestal that lies between the base and the cornice, especially when it is cubic in shape [12thC. From French *dé* (see DICE).]

die·back /dī bàk/ *n.* gradual decay that sets in at a plant's young shoots then works back to established stems or old wood, as a result of disease, seasonal change, or poor conditions

die-cast (**die-cast, die-cast·ing, die-casts**) *vt.* to make a metal or plastic object by pouring or forcing molten metal or plastic into a mold —**die-cast** *adj.*

die cast·ing *n.* a manufacturing process in which objects are formed by pouring or forcing molten metal or plastic into a die

di·e·cious *adj.* = **dioecious**

Die·fen·ba·ker /deéfən bàykər/, **John George** (1895–1979) Canadian statesman. He headed the Progressive Conservative Party (1956–67) and served as prime minister (1957–63).

di·ef·fen·bach·i·a /deèfən baákee ə, -bákee ə, deéfən baákee ə, -bàkee ə/ *n.* an evergreen plant with poisonous sap, native to tropical America but widely cultivated as a house plant for its large many-colored leaves. Dumb cane is a type of dieffenbachia. Genus: *Dieffenbachia.* [Late 19thC. From modern Latin, genus name, named for Ernst *Dieffenbach* (1794–1855), a German botanist.]

die·hard /dī haàrd/ *adj.* **STUBBORNLY RESISTANT TO CHANGE** resistant to any kind of change, and reluctant to give up beliefs, positions, or attitudes ○ *diehard team fans* ■ *n.* **STUBBORNLY RESISTANT PERSON** somebody who resists change or who clings to a belief, attitude, or position in the face of all opposition ○ *with the old diehards holding out to the bitter end* —**die·hard·ism** *n.*

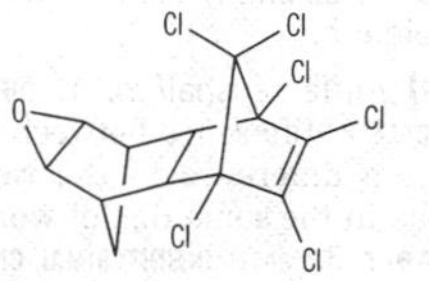

Dieldrin

diel·drin /deéldrin/ *n.* a contact insecticide based on a chlorinated naphthalene derivative. Its effects are cumulative and long lasting in humans and animals, therefore it is now widely banned. Formula: $C_{12}H_{10}OCl_6$. [Mid-20thC. Named for Otto *Diels* (1876–1954), German chemist + ALDRIN.]

di·e·lec·tric /dī i léktrik/ *adj.* **NOT CONDUCTING DIRECT ELECTRIC CURRENT** not able to conduct direct electric current and therefore useful as an insulator ■ *n.* **DIELECTRIC SUBSTANCE** a dielectric substance [Mid-19thC. Coined from DIA- "through" + ELECTRIC.] —**di·e·lec·tri·cal·ly** *adv.*

di·e·lec·tric con·stant *n.* PHYS = **relative permittivity**

di·e·lec·tric heat·ing *n.* ELEC ENG the heating of an insulating material by placing it in a rapidly changing electric field. The technique is used in the manufacture of foam rubber, plastics, and other materials.

di·e·lec·tric lens *n.* a lens made of insulating material that deflects radio waves passing through it in the way that a glass lens deflects light. It is used to shape the beams emitted from radar and microwave antennas.

Diels-Al·der re·ac·tion /deélz aáldər-/ *n.* a chemical reaction in which an organic compound with two double bonds between carbon atoms (**diene**) and a compound containing a double or triple bond, combine to form a ring compound [Mid-20thC. Named for the German chemists Otto *Diels* (see DIELDRIN) and Kurt *Alder* (see ALDRIN).]

Di·em /dee ém, dyem/, **Ngo Dinh** (1901–63) Vietnamese politician. He was supported by the United States as the first president of South Vietnam (1955–63). He was assassinated after large antigovernment demonstrations.

di·en·ceph·a·lon /dī en séffə lòn/ *n.* the area in the center of the brain just above the brain stem that includes the thalamus and hypothalamus [Late 19thC. Coined from DIA- "across" + Greek *enkephalos* "brain."] —**di·en·ce·phal·ic** /dī ensə fállik/ *adj.*

di·ene /dī een/ *n.* an unsaturated hydrocarbon (**alkene**) containing two carbon-to-carbon double bonds [Early 20thC. Coined from DI- + -ENE.]

Di·eppe /dee ép/ seaport and resort on the English Channel in the Seine-Maritime Department, Haute-Normandie Region, in northwestern France. It is situated about 60 mi./97 km west of Amiens. Population: 36,600 (1990).

di·er·e·sis /dī érrəssiss/ (*plural* **-ses** /dī érrə seez/), **di·aer·e·sis** (*plural* **-ses**) *n.* **1. LING MARK MAKING ADJACENT VOWEL SEPARATE SYLLABLE** a mark consisting of two dots, printed above the second of two adjacent vowels to show that it should be pronounced as a separate syllable, as in the word "naïve" **2. LANG MARK CHANGING PRONUNCIATION OF VOWEL** a mark consisting of two dots, placed above certain vowels in some languages to show that they are to be pronounced in a particular way **3. POETRY PAUSE IN POETRY** a pause in a line of poetry that occurs when the end of a metrical foot coincides with the end of a word [Late 16thC. Via Latin from, ultimately, Greek *diairein* "to separate, divide," literally "to take apart," from *hairein* "to take" (source of English *heresy*).] —**di·e·ret·ic** /dī ə réttik/ *adj.*

die·sel /deéz'l, deéss'l/ *n.* **1.** = **diesel engine 2. VEHICLE WITH DIESEL ENGINE** a vehicle such as a car or train that is powered by a diesel engine **3.** = **diesel fuel** [Late 19thC. Named for Rudolf *Diesel* (1858–1913), the German engineer who designed the engine.]

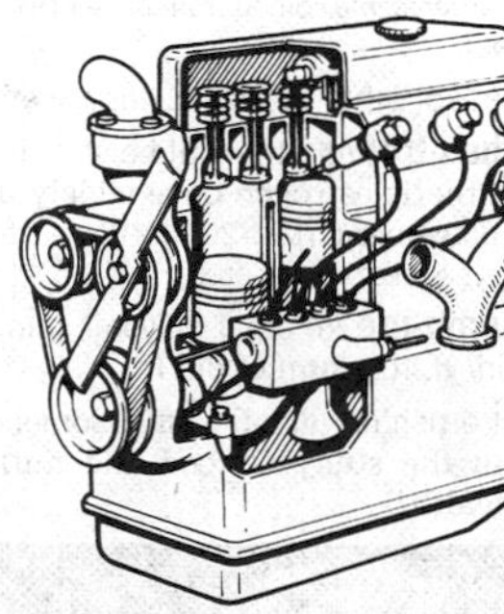

Diesel engine: Cutaway view showing compression chambers

die·sel en·gine, **die·sel** *n.* an internal combustion engine that ignites diesel fuel using compression alone, rather than using an electrical spark

die·sel fu·el *n.* a thick oily fuel that is obtained from the distillation of petroleum. It has an ignition temperature of 540°C and is ignited by the heat of compression.

die·sel oil *n. U.K.* = **diesel fuel**

Di·es I·rae /deé ayss eé rày/ *n.* **1. CHR CHRISTIAN HYMN FOR DEAD IN LATIN** a thirteenth-century Latin hymn that describes the Day of Judgment, used in a Requiem Mass **2. MUSIC PART OF REQUIEM MASS** a musical setting of the Dies Irae, usually as part of a Requiem Mass [From Latin, literally "day of wrath"]

di·e·sis /dī əssis/ (*plural* **-ses** /dī ə seez/) *n.* PRINTING = **double dagger**

die·stock /dī stòk/ *n.* a device for holding the dies that are used for cutting threads on screws

di·es·trus /dī éstrəss/ *n.* a stage of the estrous cycle, following estrus, in which the ovary is functional and the predominant ovarian hormone produced is progesterone [Early 20thC. Coined from DI- "twice, doubly" + ESTRUS.] —**di·es·trous** *adj.*

di·et[1] /dī ət/ *n.* **1. WHAT A PERSON OR ANIMAL EATS** the food that a person or animal usually consumes **2. CONTROLLED INTAKE OF FOOD** a controlled intake of food and drink designed for weight loss, for health or religious reasons, or to control or improve a medical condition ○ *a wheat-free diet* **3.** REGULAR INTAKE OF SOMETHING a continuous or daily experience of, or indulgence in, something other than food ○ *living on a diet of soap operas and game shows* ■ *adj.* DESIGNED OR PROMOTED FOR WEIGHT LOSS used to describe a food or drink that is intended for people trying to lose weight, usually because it is low in calories or fat, or contains a sugar substitute ○ *a diet soda* ■ *vi.* (**-et·ed, -et·ing, -ets**) EAT LESS to follow a restricted pattern of eating or drinking in order to lose weight [Pre-12thC. Via Old French *diete* from, ultimately, Greek *diaita* "course of life."]

di·et² /dī ət/ *n.* **1.** POL LEGISLATIVE ASSEMBLY a legislative assembly in certain countries, e.g., Japan **2.** HIST ASSEMBLY IN HOLY ROMAN EMPIRE a general assembly of the estates of the Holy Roman Empire **3.** LAW COURT SESSION IN SCOTLAND in Scotland, a session of a court, or the date fixed for a court hearing [15thC. From medieval Latin *dieta* "day's journey, work," associated with Latin *dies* "day," hence "day for a meeting (of legislators)," probably from, ultimately, Greek *diaita* (see DIET¹).]

di·e·tar·y /dī ə tèrree/ *adj.* OF EATING HABITS relating to what people or animals eat ■ *n.* (*plural* **-ies**) DIET a diet or system of dieting (*archaic*)

di·e·tar·y fi·ber *n.* = **fiber** *n.* 7

di·e·tar·y laws *npl.* the rules governing which items of food observant Jewish people are permitted to eat, derived from Leviticus 11 and Deuteronomy 14

di·et·er /dī ətər/ *n.* somebody who is on a diet, particularly somebody who is trying to lose weight

di·e·tet·ic /dī ə téttik/ *adj.* **1.** RELATING TO DIETS relating to what people eat and drink **2.** PREPARED WITH SPECIAL DIETS IN MIND specially prepared to suit the requirements of a particular diet —**di·e·tet·i·cal·ly** *adv.*

di·e·tet·ics /dī ə téttiks/ *n.* the study of food and nutrition and its relation to people's health (*takes a singular verb.*)

di·eth·yl·car·bam·a·zine cit·rate /dī ethəl kaar bammə zeen-/ *n.* a drug used to treat intestinal worms in humans, and roundworm in dogs and cats [*Diethylcarbamazine* coined from DI- + ETHYL + CARBO- + AMIDE + AZINE]

di·eth·yl eth·er /dī èthəl eethər/ *n.* CHEM = **ether**

di·eth·yl·stil·bes·trol /dī èthəl stil bé strawl/ *n.* PHARM a form of synthetic estrogen once widely used as a hormone replacement [Mid-20thC. Coined from DI- + ETHYL + STILBENE + OESTRUS + -OL.]

di·eth·yl tol·u·am·ide /dī èthəl tollyoo á mīd, dī èthəl tollyoo ámmid/ *n.* full form of **DEET**

di·e·ti·tian /dī ə tísh'n/, **di·e·ti·cian** *n.* somebody who specializes in the study of food and nutrition in relation to health

Marlene Dietrich

Die·trich /deetrik/, **Marlene** (1901–92) German-born U.S. singer and movie actor. She starred in movies from the 1930s to the 1970s, including *The Devil Is a Woman* (1935) and *Witness for the Prosecution* (1957). Full name **Maria Magdalene Dietrich von Losch**

diff. *abbr.* **1.** difference **2.** different

dif·fer /díffər/ (**-fered, -fer·ing, -fers**) *vi.* **1.** BE UNLIKE to be dissimilar or unlike ○ *new models that differ greatly from the early prototypes* **2.** DISAGREE to have different opinions about something ○ *We agreed to differ.* [14thC. Via French *différer* "to differ, defer" from Latin *differre* "to differ," literally "to carry apart," from *ferre* "to carry" (see -FER).]

WORD KEY: SYNONYMS

See Synonyms at ***disagree.***

dif·fer·ence /díffərəns, díffrəns/ *n.* **1.** STATE OF BEING UNLIKE OTHERS the quality of being different from or unlike something or somebody else ○ *There's no real difference between going by train and going by car.* **2.** DISTINGUISHING FEATURE a feature that distinguishes one person or thing from another ○ *Can you spot the differences between the two?* **3.** SIGNIFICANT CHANGE a change that has an effect ○ *a noticeable difference in her moods* **4.** DISAGREEMENT a disagreement, argument, or divergence of opinions ○ *settle our differences* **5.** MATH ANSWER TO SUBTRACTION EQUATION the amount by which one quantity is greater or smaller than another ○ *What's the difference between 16 and 6?* **6.** LOGIC DEFINING FEATURE a distinguishing feature that marks out a thing that is being defined or discussed, from others that are more general ○ *being divisible by two is the difference between even numbers and other whole numbers* ◇ **make all the difference** have an enormous, usually positive, effect or influence ◇ **make no difference** be of no importance or not matter ◇ **split the difference** take the average of two amounts, or agree on something that is halfway between two extremes ◇ **tell the difference** distinguish or figure out the particular features that make things unlike each other

dif·fer·ent /díffərənt, díffrənt/ *adj.* **1.** UNLIKE SOMETHING OR SOMEBODY ELSE not the same as something or somebody else ○ *The two places are very different from each other.* **2.** DISTINCT separate or distinct from another or others ○ *She wears a different pair of shoes every day.* **3.** UNUSUAL contrary to norms or expectations ○ *What do you think of my hat? – Well, it's certainly different.* [14thC. Via French from the Latin stem *different-*, present participle stem of *differre* (see DIFFER).]

WORD KEY: USAGE

Different from or **different than?** ***Different from*** and ***different than*** are both common in U.S. English, though critics for 300 years have objected to *different than.* If you are drawing distinctions directly between two people or items, then *from* is the safest choice: *Their attitudes are very different from those of their contemporaries.*

dif·fer·en·ti·a /dìffə rénshee ə, -rénshə/ (*plural* **-ae** /dìffə rénshee ee/) *n.* an element that separates one thing from another, especially a trait that distinguishes one subclass from another, e.g., one species from another in the same genus

dif·fer·en·tia·ble /diffə rénshee əb'l, -rénshəb'l/ *adj.* recognizable as different or distinct from something else —**dif·fer·en·tia·bil·i·ty** /dìffə renshee ə bíllətee, -renshə bíllətee/ *n.*

dif·fer·en·tial /dìffə rénshəl/ *n.* **1.** DIFFERENCE BETWEEN POINTS ON A SCALE a difference between two values on a scale, e.g., a difference in the rates of pay for different jobs in the same line of work **2.** AUTOMOT = **differential gear** **3.** MATH INFINITESIMAL CHANGE IN VARIABLE an infinitesimal change in a variable ■ *adj.* **1.** OF DIFFERENCES relating to or based on differences **2.** MATH RELATING TO INFINITESIMAL CHANGES relating to a function of one or more variables that exhibits an infinitesimal change as a consequence of a small change in the variables

dif·fer·en·tial cal·cu·lus *n.* the branch of mathematics dealing with continuously varying quantities, with applications in the determination of maximum and minimum points, and with rates of change through the use of derivatives and differentials

dif·fer·en·tial co·ef·fi·cient *n.* MATH = **derivative**

dif·fer·en·tial e·qua·tion *n.* a mathematical equation that relates functions and their derivatives

dif·fer·en·tial gear *n.* an arrangement of gears that allows two shafts driven by a third to turn at different speeds, e.g., in a motor vehicle

dif·fer·en·ti·ate /dìffə rénshee àyt/ (**-at·ed, -at·ing, -ates**) *v.* **1.** *vti.* SEE DIFFERENCES BETWEEN THINGS to see or show the differences between two or more things **2.** *vt.* BE A DIFFERENCE to establish a difference between two things or among several things **3.** *vti.* MAKE OR BECOME DIFFERENT to make something different or specialized by modifying it, or to become different or specialized by being modified **4.** *vi.* EMBRYOL BECOME SPECIALIZED to change from a generalized form into a form specialized for a certain tissue, organ, or other body part (*refers to embryo cells*) **5.** *vt.* MATH CALCULATE DERIVATIVE to calculate the mathematical derivative of a function [Early 19thC. From medieval Latin *differentiat-*, the past participle stem of *differentiare*, from, ultimately, Latin *differre* (see DIFFER).] —**dif·fer·en·tia·bil·i·ty** /dìffə renshə bíllətee, -renshee ə bíllətee/ *n.* —**dif·fer·en·ti·a·ble** /dìffə rénshəb'l, diffə rénshee əb'l/ *adj.* —**dif·fer·en·ti·a·tion** /dìffə renshee áysh'n/ *n.* —**dif·fer·en·ti·a·tor** /dìffə rénshee àytər/ *n.*

dif·fi·cult /díffikəlt/ *adj.* **1.** HARD TO DO requiring a lot of planning or effort to accomplish ○ *a difficult job* **2.** FULL OF PROBLEMS full of problems, trouble, or aspects that are hard to endure ○ *a difficult birth* **3.** HARD TO UNDERSTAND hard to understand, learn, or solve ○ *a difficult subject* **4.** HARD TO ANSWER hard to answer, deal with, or fulfill ○ *a difficult question* **5.** HARD TO MANAGE hard to cope with or control ○ *a difficult plant to grow indoors* **6.** HARD TO PLEASE hard to please or satisfy ○ *a difficult audience* **7.** HARD TO CONVINCE hard to convince or persuade ○ *If they're difficult, offer them more.* **8.** FULL OF HARDSHIP containing great hardship, especially of a financial kind [14thC. Back-formation from DIFFICULTY.] —**dif·fi·cult·ness** *n.*

WORD KEY: SYNONYMS

See Synonyms at ***hard.***

dif·fi·cul·ty /díffikəltee/ *n.* (*plural* **-ties**) **1.** QUALITY OF BEING DIFFICULT the quality of being hard to do, understand, or deal with **2.** SOMETHING NOT EASILY DONE something that is hard to do, understand, or deal with **3.** EFFORT a great effort or struggle to do something **4.** A DISPUTE a dispute or controversy ■ **difficulties** *npl.* **1.** TROUBLE a situation full of trouble, danger, or embarrassment ○ *Even a strong swimmer can get into difficulties in this river.* **2.** OBJECTIONS objections, or attempts to prevent the progress of something ○ *You're supposed to be here to help, not make difficulties.* [14thC. From Latin *difficultas*, from *difficilis*, literally "not easy," from *facilis* "easy" (see FACILE).]

dif·fi·dence /díffid'ns/ *n.* **1.** LACK OF SELF-CONFIDENCE a lack of self-confidence or hesitation caused by lack of confidence **2.** RESERVED MANNER a reserved or restrained manner

dif·fi·dent /díffid'nt/ *adj.* **1.** LACKING SELF-CONFIDENCE lacking self-confidence and rather shy **2.** RESERVED OR RESTRAINED reserved or restrained in the way you behave [15thC. From Latin *diffident-*, the present participle stem of *diffidere* "to distrust," from *fidere* "to trust." The original English meaning was "distrustful."] —**dif·fi·dent·ly** *adv.*

dif·fract /di frákt/ (**-fract·ed, -fract·ing, -fracts**) *vti.* to produce or undergo diffraction [Early 19thC. From Latin *diffract-*, the past participle stem of *diffringere*, literally "to break apart," from *frangere* "to break."] —**dif·frac·tive** *adj.* —**dif·frac·tive·ly** *adv.* —**dif·frac·tive·ness** *n.*

dif·frac·tion /di fráksh'n/ *n.* the bending or spreading out of waves, e.g., of sound or light, as they pass around the edge of an obstacle or through a narrow aperture

dif·frac·tion grat·ing *n.* a glass plate or metal mirror engraved with a large number of parallel lines or grooves, used to produce a spectrum by diffraction or interference

dif·frac·tom·e·ter /dì frak tómmətər/ *n.* an instrument that uses diffraction, typically of X-rays or electrons by crystals, to investigate the atomic structure of a material

dif·fuse¹ (**-fused, -fus·ing, -fus·es**) *v.* /di fyóoz/ **1.** *vti.* SPREAD THROUGH to spread something throughout something else, or to become spread throughout something else **2.** *vti.* SCATTER OR BECOME SCATTERED to scatter something over an area, or become scattered over an area **3.** *vt.* MAKE LESS INTENSE to make something, especially light, less bright or intense **4.** *vti.* PHYS UNDERGO OR SUBJECT TO DIFFUSION to undergo or subject something to diffusion [14thC. From Latin *diffus-*, the past participle stem of *diffundere*, literally "to pour in every direction," from *fundere* "to pour" (see FOUND).]

WORD KEY: SYNONYMS

See Synonyms at ***wordy.***

dif·fuse² /di fyóoss/ *adj.* **1.** SPREAD THROUGHOUT AREA spread throughout a wide area **2.** LACKING CONCISENESS lacking organization and conciseness, especially in writing or speech [15thC. Directly or via French *diffus* from Latin *diffusus* "spread out," from the past participle of *diffundere* (see DIFFUSE¹).] —**dif·fuse·ly** *adv.* —**dif·fuse·ness** *n.*

dif·fus·er /də fyóozər/, **dif·fu·sor** *n.* **1.** PERSON OR THING THAT DIFFUSES somebody or something that diffuses **2.** HOUSEHOLD DEVICE THAT DIFFUSES LAMP LIGHT a piece of translucent or reflective material fixed to a light source, such as a lamp, in order to soften or spread the light over a wide area **3.** PHOTOGRAPHY, CINEMA **DEVICE THAT SOFTENS LIGHT** a cloth screen, piece of frosted glass, or other material that is used to soften the brightness of the lighting in photography or cinematography **4.** HAIR **HAIRDRYER ATTACHMENT** an attachment for a hairdryer that slows down and spreads the air flow, making the drying action gentler **5.** ACOUSTICS **CONE TO DISPERSE SOUND WAVES** a device, such as a cone or wedge, fixed inside a loudspeaker to diffuse sound waves

dif·fus·i·ble /di fyóozəb'l/ *adj.* capable of being diffused —**dif·fus·i·bil·i·ty** /di fyóozə bíllətee/ *n.*

dif·fu·sion /də fyóozh'n/ *n.* **1. PROCESS OF DIFFUSING** a process during which something diffuses or is diffused **2. RESULT OF DIFFUSING** the result of something diffusing or being diffused, or a situation where something is diffused **3.** ANTHROP **SPREAD OF CULTURAL FEATURES** the spread of tools, practices, or other features from one culture to another **4.** PHYS **SCATTERING OF LIGHT** the scattering of light in many directions as the result of reflection from an uneven surface or passage though a translucent material **5.** PHYS **INTERMINGLING OF SUBSTANCES** the random movement of atoms, molecules, or ions from one site in a medium to another, resulting in complete mixing —**dif·fu·sion·al** *adj.*

dif·fu·sion·ism /də fyóozhə nìzzəm/ *n.* the theory that similarities in tools, practices, or other features between cultures, result from their being spread from one culture to another rather than being arrived at independently —**dif·fu·sion·ist** *adj., n.*

dif·fu·sive /də fyóossiv/ *adj.* **1. INVOLVED IN DIFFUSION** involved in diffusion **2. SPREADING** in which diffusion is important or characteristic **3.** = **diffuse**[2] *adj.* **2** —**dif·fu·sive·ly** *adv.* —**dif·fu·sive·ness** *n.*

dif·fu·sor *n.* = **diffuser**

dig /dig/ *v.* (**dug, dug** /dug/, **dig·ging, digs**) **1.** *vti.* **BREAK UP OR REMOVE EARTH** to break up, overturn, or remove something, especially earth, with the hands, paws, a tool, or a machine ○ *The excavator dug the rock out of the hole.* **2.** *vt.* **CREATE BY DIGGING** to make something by removing material, especially earth, with the hands, paws, a tool, or a machine ○ *digging a hole* **3.** *vti.* **OBTAIN OR FREE BY DIGGING** to obtain, uncover, or free something by removing the material covering it using a shovel, the hands, paws, a tool, or a machine **4.** *vi.* **SEARCH BY DIGGING** to try to find something by digging ○ *dig for buried treasure* **5.** *vi.* **MOVE THROUGH SOMETHING BY DIGGING** to move through something by digging a way through it **6.** *vt.* **DISCOVER BY RESEARCH** to find out something by research or questioning ○ *See what you can dig up about her past.* **7.** *vi.* **SEARCH CAREFULLY** to search something carefully or persistently ○ *digging through the papers in a file* **8.** *vti.* **PUSH INTO SOMETHING FORCEFULLY** to push something into something else with force, or be pushed forcefully into something ○ *He dug his teeth into the steak.* **9.** *vti.* **POKE** to push somebody with something fairly sharp ○ *She dug her elbow into my side.* **10.** *vti.* **UNDERSTAND** to understand something fully or with sympathy (*dated slang*) ○ *I dig what you're saying.* **11.** *vt.* **LIKE** to like or appreciate something (*dated slang*) ○ *They don't dig jazz.* **12.** *vt.* **LOOK AT** to look at, notice, or pay attention to something (*dated slang*) ○ *Now dig this, honey.* ■ *n.* **1. PROD** a push with something fairly sharp ○ *a dig in the ribs* **2. CUTTING REMARK** a remark that is meant to hurt or make fun of somebody ○ *a dig about her new hairstyle* **3.** ARCHEOL **ARCHEOLOGICAL EXCAVATION** an archeological or paleontological excavation ○ *a dig in Egypt* **4. ACT OF DIGGING** the act of digging or excavating something ■ **digs** *npl. U.K.* **LODGINGS** a room or rooms that somebody rents in another person's house (*dated informal*) [12thC. Origin uncertain: perhaps literally "to make a ditch," formed from Old English *dīc*, an earlier form of DITCH.]

dig in *v.* **1.** *vti.* MIL **TAKE UP POSITIONS** to prepare trenches or other defensive structures, or to establish a force or equipment in a defensive position **2.** *vi.* MIL **RESIST ATTACK** to put up a stubborn resistence to an attack **3.** *vi.* **FIGHT STUBBORNLY** to stick to an established position, e.g., in an argument, and fight stubbornly to maintain it **4.** *vi.* **START EATING** to start eating, especially in an enthusiastic way (*informal*) **5.** *vt.* AGRIC, GARDENING **BURYPLANTS** to cover plants or the remains of a crop by turning over the soil in which they are growing and burying them

dig out *vt.* **1. UNCOVER** to obtain, uncover, or free something by removing the material covering it using a shovel, the hands, paws, a tool, or a machine **2. RETRIEVE** to retrieve something from where it is kept, or find out something by research or questioning (*informal*)

dig up *vt.* **1. TAKE OUT OF GROUND** to dig for something that is buried in the ground and remove it **2. TURN OVER EARTH** to dig into and turn over the earth in an area **3. INVESTIGATE** to find out something by research or investigation (*informal*)

dig. *abbr.* PUBL digest

di·gam·ma /dī gámmə/ *n.* a letter of the ancient Greek alphabet, Ϝ, that was already obsolete in the classical period [Late 17thC. Via Latin from Greek, literally "double gamma," from *gamma* "gamma"; from its resemblance to two capital gammas, set one above the other.]

dig·a·my /díggəmee/ (*plural* **-mies**) *n.* a second marriage that, unlike bigamy, is legal because the first husband or wife is dead or has been divorced (*formal*) [Early 17thC. Via late Latin *digamia* from Greek, from *digamos* "married to two people," from *gamos* "marriage."] —**dig·a·mous** *adj.*

di·gas·tric /dī gástrik/ *adj.* used to describe a muscle, especially the muscle on either side of the lower jaw, in which two fleshy parts are connected by a tendon [Early 18thC. From modern Latin *digastricus*, from *gastricus* "gastric" (see GASTRIC); from an analogy between "fleshy parts" and "bellies."]

di·ge·ra·ti /dìjjə raátee/ *npl.* people who have or claim to have a sophisticated expertise in the area of computers, the Internet, and the World Wide Web [Late 20thC. Formed from DIGITAL on the model of LITERATI.]

di·gest *v.* /dī jést, di jést/ (**-gest·ed, -gest·ing, -gests**) **1.** *vti.* **PROCESS FOOD** to process food in the body into a form that can be absorbed and used or excreted **2.** *vt.* **ABSORB MENTALLY** to think about something and come to understand or appreciate what it means **3.** *vt.* **ORGANIZE SYSTEMATICALLY** to organize something into a system, often through selective condensing of the various items, so that essential information is readily available **4.** *vt.* **ABRIDGE** to make a summary of something, often a written work **5.** *vti.* CHEM **BREAK DOWN** to soften or break down a substance through exposure to heat, water, or chemicals, or to be broken down in this way **6.** *vt.* **BEAR PATIENTLY** to put up with something without reacting (*archaic*) ■ *n.* /dí jèst/ **1. SUMMARY** a shortened version of a work that contains the most important or interesting information from the original version **2. COLLECTION OF ABRIDGED PIECES** a magazine, book, or broadcast that contains shortened versions of articles or stories originally from different sources **3.** LAW **COLLECTION OF LEGAL OPINIONS** a systematic compilation of laws or legal opinions [14thC. From Latin *digest-*, the past participle stem of *digerere*, literally "to carry apart," from *gerere* "to carry."]

Di·gest /dí jèst/ *n.* a 50-volume compilation of Roman civil law, created by the order of Emperor Justinian in the 6th century

di·gest·er /dī jéstər, di-/ *n.* **1. SOMEBODY OR SOMETHING THAT DIGESTS** somebody or something that digests something **2. PERSON WHO MAKES DIGESTS** a person or organization that makes digests of written works **3.** CHEM **VESSEL FOR CHEMICAL DIGESTION** a vessel or device in which chemical digestion takes place

di·gest·i·ble /dī jéstəb'l, di-/ *adj.* easily digested —**di·gest·i·bil·i·ty** /dī jèstə bíllətee, di jèstə bíllətee/ *n.* —**di·gest·i·bly** /-əblee/ *adv.*

di·ges·tif /dee zhe stéef/ *n.* an alcoholic drink, e.g., a brandy or liqueur, drunk after a meal supposedly to help the digestion of food [Early 20thC. From French, literally "digestive," from Latin *digestivus*, from, ultimately, *digerere* (see DIGEST).]

di·ges·tion /dī jésch'n/ *n.* **1.** PHYSIOL **PROCESSING OF FOOD IN BODY** the breaking down of foodstuffs in the body into a form that can be absorbed and used or excreted **2.** PHYSIOL **ABILITY TO DIGEST FOOD** the ability to process food in the body into a form that can be absorbed and used or excreted **3. ABILITY TO ABSORB IDEAS** the ability to think about something and come to understand or appreciate its content, or the process of doing so **4.** CHEM **BREAKING DOWN** the softening or breaking down of a substance through exposure to heat, water, chemicals, enzymes, or bacteria —**di·ges·tion·al** *adj.*

di·ges·tive /də jéstiv/ *adj.* **RELATING TO DIGESTION** associated with or aiding in the digestion of food ■ *n.* **SOMETHING THAT AIDS DIGESTION** something that aids or promotes the digesting of food —**di·ges·tive·ly** *adv.*

di·ges·tive gland *n.* any gland that secretes digestive enzymes, e.g., the pancreas in vertebrates

di·ges·tive tract *n.* ANAT = **alimentary canal**

dig·ger /díggər/ *n.* **1. SOMEBODY OR SOMETHING THAT DIGS** somebody or something that digs **2. TOOL FOR DIGGING** a tool, machine, or part of a machine that is used for digging or excavation

Dig·ger[1] *n.* member of the English Puritan religious group, the Diggers, active in 1649 and 1650, that believed in communal land ownership [Mid-17thC. From the group's cultivation of land.]

Dig·ger[2], **dig·ger** *n.* **1.** PEOPLES **NATIVE AMERICAN PERSON** a member of any of various Native American peoples who gathered food mainly by digging for roots (*sometimes used disparagingly*) **2.** MIL **SOMEBODY FROM AUSTRALIA OR NEW ZEALAND** somebody from Australia or New Zealand, especially a soldier who served in World War I (*informal*) [Mid-19thC. In sense 1, from DIGGER "miner," reinforced by the idea of trench-digging in World War I.]

dig·gings /díggingz/ *n.* **MINING LOCATION** a place where something is mined, especially precious metals or gems ■ *npl.* **MATERIAL EXCAVATED** material that has been dug out of a hole or mine

dight /dīt/ (**dight·ed** *or* **dight, dight·ing, dights**) *vt.* to equip, dress, or adorn somebody (*archaic*) [Old English *dihtan*. From a prehistoric Germanic word borrowed from Latin *dictare* "to say often," (see DICTATE).]

dig·it /díjjit/ *n.* **1.** ANAT **HUMAN FINGER OR TOE** a finger or toe of a human **2.** ZOOL **ANIMAL TOE OR FINGER** a finger, toe, or similar part on a terrestrial vertebrate **3.** MEASURE **FINGER WIDTH** the width of a finger used as a unit of length, equal to approximately $\frac{3}{4}$ in./2 cm **4.** MATH **NUMERAL USED IN DECIMAL SYSTEM** any of the ten Arabic numerals, 0 through 9, that are used to represent numbers in the decimal system **5.** MATH **NUMERAL IN ANY NUMBER SYSTEM** a symbol that represents a number in any number system, such as the hexadecimal system [14thC. From Latin *digitus* "finger, toe," from assumed *dicitus* "pointer." The numerical senses come from the counting of numbers on the fingers.]

Digital: Clock displaying the time in numerical form

dig·i·tal /díjjit'l/ *adj.* **1. LIKE A FINGER** like a finger or toe **2. DONE WITH THE FINGERS** using the fingers, or operated by a finger or fingers **3. REPRESENTING DATA AS NUMBERS** processing, operating on, storing, transmitting, representing, or displaying data in the form of numerical digits, as in a digital computer. ◊ **analog** *adj.* **4. REPRESENTING SOUND/LIGHT WAVES AS NUMBERS** representing a varying physical quantity, such as sound or light waves, by means of discrete signals interpreted as numbers, usually in the binary system, as in a digital recording or digital television [15thC. From Latin *digitalis*, from *digitus* (see DIGIT.] —**dig·i·tal·ly** *adv.*

dig·i·tal au·di·o·tape *n.* a magnetic tape used in the digital recording of music

dig·i·tal com·put·er *n.* a computer that stores and performs a series of mathematical and logical operations on data expressed as discrete signals interpreted as numbers, usually in the form of binary notation

dig·i·tal im·age·ry, **dig·i·tal im·ag·ing** *n.* the process of transforming or altering a digital image by manipulating it on a computer

dig·i·tal·ize /díjjit'l īz/ (**-ized, -iz·ing, -iz·es**) *vt.* **1.** = **digitize 2.** MED **TREAT WITH DIGITALIS** to treat somebody with digitalis —**dig·i·tal·i·za·tion** /dìjjit'li záysh'n/ *n.*

dig·i·tal re·cord·ing *n.* **1. SOUND STORED AS DIGITS** a form of audio recording in which sounds are stored as numbers, producing a purer sound **2.** RECORDING MADE DIGITALLY a recording made using the digital method

dig·i·tal sig·na·ture *n.* a digital signal or pattern that serves to identify the user or the habits of the user

Dig·i·tal Sub·scrib·er Line *n.* a high-speed telephone line that can supply television, video, Internet access, and video telephoning, often over standard copper wire

dig·i·tal tab·let *n.* COMPUT = **graphics tablet**

dig·i·tal tel·e·vi·sion *n.* **1.** TELEVISION USING DIGITAL TRANSMISSION television broadcasting in which the picture is transmitted as a digital signal that is decoded by a device in or attached to the viewer's television set **2.** BROADCASTING SIGNALS INTERPRETED AS NUMBERS a system of broadcasting pictures and sounds as discrete signals represented as numbers, or a television set specially constructed or adapted for receiving such signals

dig·i·tal vid·e·o disk, dig·i·tal ver·sa·tile disk *n.* full form of **DVD**

dig·i·tal vid·e·o disk-ROM *n.* full form of **DVD-ROM**

dig·i·tal watch *n.* a watch that shows the time in numerical form, rather than by hands on a dial

dig·i·tate /díjji tàyt/, **dig·i·tat·ed** *adj.* **1.** HAVING FINGERS OR TOES having fingers or toes, or having parts that are like fingers or toes **2.** BOT SPREADING FROM CENTER having divisions or parts arrayed from a central point like the spread fingers of a hand, e.g., in the leaves of certain trees —**dig·i·tate·ly** *adv.* —**dig·i·ta·tion** /dìjji táysh'n/ *n.*

digiti- *prefix.* finger or toe ○ *digitigrade* [From Latin *digitus* (see DIGIT)]

dig·i·ti·form /díjjitə fàwrm/ *adj.* shaped or looking like a finger

dig·i·ti·grade /díjjitə gràyd/ *adj.* WALKING ON THE TOES used to describe the gait of those animals that walk with only the tips of the digits touching the ground, the rest of the foot being raised, e.g., cats and deer ■ *n.* ANIMAL THAT WALKS ON ITS TOES an animal, such as a deer or cat, that walks with its weight on its digits and the back of its foot raised [Mid-19thC. From French, literally "toe-stepping," from Latin *digitus* (see DIGIT) + *gradus* "step" (see GRADE).]

dig·i·tize /díjji tīz/ (**-tized, -tiz·ing, -tiz·es**) *vt.* to convert an image, graph, or other data into digital form for processing on a computer —**dig·i·ti·za·tion** /dìjjiti záysh'n/ *n.* —**dig·i·tiz·er** /díjji tīzər/ *n.*

dig·i·zine /díjji zeen/ *n.* a magazine that is delivered in digital form either on the Internet or on a CD-ROM (*informal*) ◊ **e-zine** [Combination of DIGITAL + MAGAZINE]

di·glos·si·a /dī glóssee ə/ *n.* the existence of a formal literary form of a language, considered higher and more prestigious, along with a colloquial form used by most speakers and considered of lower status [Mid-20thC. Formed from Greek *diglōssos* "bilingual," from *glōssa* "language."]

dig·ni·fied /dígnə fīd/ *adj.* showing self-respect or behaving in a proper and respectable way —**dig·ni·fied·ly** *adv.*

dig·ni·fy /dígnə fī/ (**-fied, -fy·ing, -fies**) *vt.* **1.** GIVE DISTINCTION TO to give honor or a sense of importance to something **2.** GIVE UNDESERVED ATTENTION TO to treat somebody or something as honorable or worthy of attention when this treatment is undeserved **3.** MAKE NOBLE to award an honor to somebody, or raise a person to noble rank [15thC. Via obsolete French *dignifier* from late Latin *dignificare*, literally "to make worthy," from Latin *dignus* (see DIGNITY).]

dig·ni·tar·y /dígnə tèree/ (*plural* **-ies**) *n.* a person who holds a high rank or position

dig·ni·ty /dígnətee/ (*plural* **-ties**) *n.* **1.** PRIDE AND SELF-RESPECT a proper sense of pride and self-respect **2.** SERIOUSNESS IN BEHAVIOR seriousness, respectfulness, or formality in a person's behavior and bearing **3.** WORTHINESS the condition of being worthy of respect, esteem, or honor **4.** DUE RESPECT the respect or honor that a high rank or position should be shown **5.** HIGH OFFICE a high rank, position, or honor **6.** DIGNITARY a dignitary (*archaic*) [12thC. Via Old French *digneté* from Latin *dignitas*, from *dignus* "worthy."]

dig·ox·in /dī góksin/ *n.* a glycoside extracted from foxglove leaves and used as a heart stimulant. Formula: $C_{41}H_{64}O_{14}$. [Mid-20thC. Contraction of *digitoxin*, name of a glycoside similar to digoxin, coined from DIGITALIS + TOXIN.]

di·graph /dī gràf/ *n.* **1.** TWO LETTERS REPRESENTING ONE SOUND a pair of letters that represents a single speech sound, such as "ng" in "ring" or "ch" in "child" **2.** = **ligature** —**di·graph·ic** /dī gráffik/ *adj.* —**di·graph·i·cal·ly** /dī gráffikəlee/ *adv.*

di·gress /dī gréss/ (**-gressed, -gress·ing, -gress·es**) *vi.* to move away from the central topic or line of argument in speaking or writing, usually temporarily [Early 16thC. From Latin *digress-*, past participle stem of *digredi*, literally "to step aside," from, ultimately, *gradus* "step" (see GRADE).]

di·gres·sion /dī grésh'n/ *n.* **1.** DEPARTURE FROM CENTRAL TOPIC an act or instance of departing from the central topic or line of argument while speaking or writing **2.** TEXT OR SPEECH OFF THE SUBJECT a part of something spoken or written that departs from the central topic or line of argument —**di·gres·sion·al** *adj.* —**di·gres·sion·ar·y** *adj.*

di·gres·sive /dī gréssiv/ *adj.* tending to depart from the main subject or line of argument —**di·gres·sive·ly** *adv.* —**di·gres·sive·ness** *n.*

di·he·dral /dī heédrəl/ *n.* **1. di·he·dral, di·he·dral an·gle** MATH ANGLE MADE BETWEEN SURFACES the angle contained between two planes that intersect, measured by the angle made by any two lines at right angles to the two planes **2.** AEROSP ANGLE OF AN AIRCRAFT WING the angle between an upwardly inclined aircraft wing and a horizontal line ■ *adj.* MATH TWO-SIDED made by intersecting planes and having two sides or two faces [Late 18thC. Coined from DI- + Greek *hedra* "seat" (see -HEDRON).]

di·hy·brid /dī hībrid/ *n.* an organism that is heterozygous for two genes, so that each gene is represented by two variant forms (**alleles**) —**di·hy·brid·ism** *n.*

di·hy·dric /dī hīdrik/ *adj.* containing two hydroxyl groups

Di·jon /di zháwN/ capital of the Côte d'Or Department on the Bourgogne Canal in east central France. It is situated at the foot of the Côte d'Or hills, about 155 mi./249 km southeast of Paris. Population: 151,636 (1990).

Dik-dik

dik-dik /dík dik/ (*plural* **dik-diks** *or* **dik-dik**) *n.* a small long-muzzled antelope that lives in arid regions of eastern Africa. Genus: *Madoqua*. [Late 19thC. From an East African language; an imitation of the animal's cry.]

dike /dīk/ *n.* **1.** EMBANKMENT TO PREVENT FLOODS an embankment built along the shore of a sea or lake or beside a river to hold back the water and prevent flooding **2.** BARRIER a barrier or obstacle meant to keep something out **3.** CAUSEWAY a raised roadway across a swamp or body of water **4.** DITCH a drainage ditch or other artificial watercourse **5.** GEOL LONG MASS OF IGNEOUS ROCK a vertical or near-vertical mass of igneous rock that has forced its way upward through overlying strata ■ *vt.* (**diked, dik·ing, dikes**) **1.** PROTECT WITH DIKES to enclose or protect an area of land with a dike or series of dikes **2.** DRAIN WITH DITCHES to drain an area of land using ditches [13thC. Origin uncertain: probably from Old Norse *dík*, from a prehistoric Germanic word meaning "hole and mound resulting from digging," which is also the ancestor of English *ditch*.] —**dik·er** *n.*

dik·tat /dik taát/ *n.* **1.** DICTATORIAL STATEMENT a statement or order that cannot be opposed **2.** HARSH IMPOSED SETTLEMENT a harsh settlement imposed on a defeated opponent or enemy [Mid-20thC. From German, from Latin *dictatum*, from the past participle of *dictare* (see DICTATE).]

di·lap·i·date /di láppə dàyt/ (**-dat·ed, -dat·ing, -dates**) *vti.* to become or make something become partially ruined or decayed, especially through neglect [Early 16thC. From Latin *dilapidat-*, past participle stem of *dilapidare* "to squander," literally "to scatter like stones," from, ultimately, *lapis* "stone."] —**di·lap·i·da·tion** /di làppi dáysh'n/ *n.*

di·lap·i·dat·ed /dəláppi dàytəd/ *adj.* in a condition of disrepair or partial decay

di·la·tan·cy /dī láyt'nsee, di-/ *n.* CHEM the tendency of a substance to become more viscous or solid when affected by an outside force or agitation

di·la·tant /dī láyt'nt, di-/ *adj.* **1.** ABLE TO EXPAND able or likely to expand **2.** CHEM BECOMING MORE VISCOUS tending to become more viscous or solid when affected by an outside force or agitation ■ *n.* SUBSTANCE CAUSING EXPANSION a substance that causes another to expand

dil·a·ta·tion /dìlə táysh'n, dìllə-/ *n.* **1.** PROCESS OF EXPANDING the act or process of widening or being widened, stretching or being stretched, or enlarging or being enlarged **2.** EXPANDED CONDITION a condition in which something is enlarged, expanded, or stretched **3.** DILATED THING something, especially a part of something else, that has become enlarged, expanded, or stretched **4.** LENGTHY EXPLANATION a lengthy detailed explanation or discussion of a subject by a speaker or writer **5.** MED = **dilation** *n.* 3 —**dil·a·ta·tion·al** *adj.*

dil·a·ta·tor /dílə tàytər, díllə tàytər/ *n.* = **dilator** *n.* 2

di·late /dī láyt, di-, dī làyt/ (**-lat·ed, -lat·ing, -lates**) *v.* **1.** *vti.* EXPAND OR MAKE EXPAND to become or cause something to become wider or larger **2.** *vi.* TALK OR WRITE AT LENGTH to talk or write about something at great length [14thC. Via French *dilater* from Latin *dilatare*, literally "to spread widely apart," from *latus* "wide."] —**di·lat·a·bil·i·ty** /dī làytə bíllətee, di làytə bíllətee, dī laytə bíllətee/ *n.* —**di·lat·a·ble** /dī láytəb'l, di-/ *adj.* —**di·la·tive** /dī láytəv, di-/ *adj.*

di·la·tion /dī láysh'n, di-/ *n.* **1.** EXPANDING OF SOMETHING the act or process of widening or being widened, stretching or being stretched, or enlarging or being enlarged **2.** DILATED CONDITION a condition in which something is enlarged, expanded, or stretched **3.** MED ENLARGEMENT OF BODY PART the stretching or enlargement of a hollow organ or body cavity

di·la·tion and cu·ret·tage *n.* full form of **D and C**

dil·a·tom·e·ter /dìllə tómmətər, dìlə tómmətər/ *n.* an instrument used to measure expansion, e.g., in the volume of a liquid —**dil·a·to·met·ric** /dìllətə méttrik/ *adj.* —**dil·a·tom·e·try** /dìllə tómmətree/ *n.*

di·la·tor /dī láytər, di-/ *n.* **1.** ANAT MUSCLE THAT DILATES SOMETHING a muscle or muscle group that expands a part of the body **2.** MED THING THAT DILATES something that makes something else wider or larger, especially a medical instrument used to widen a body passage

dil·a·to·ry /díllə tàwree/ *adj.* **1.** SLOW tending to waste time or move slowly **2.** INTENDED TO DELAY intended to cause a delay or waste time [15thC. From late Latin *dilatorius*, from, ultimately, Latin *dilat-*, the past participle stem of *differre* "to delay" (see DEFER).] —**dil·a·to·ri·ly** /dìllə táwrilee/ *adv.* —**dil·a·to·ri·ness** /díllə tàwreenəss/ *n.*

dil·do /díl dō/ (*plural* **-dos**), **dil·doe** (*plural* **-does**) *n.* an object shaped like a penis, used in sexual activity [Late 16thC. Origin uncertain: perhaps an alteration of Italian *diletto* "delight," from, ultimately, Latin *delectare* "to allure, delight" (see DELIGHT).]

di·lem·ma /di lémmə/ *n.* **1.** SITUATION WITH UNSATISFACTORY CHOICES a situation in which somebody must choose one of two or more unsatisfactory alternatives **2.** LOGIC ARGUMENT LEADING TO UNDESIRABLE CHOICE in logic, a form of reasoning that, though valid, leads to two undesirable alternatives [Early 16thC. From, ultimately, Greek *dilēmma*, literally "double proposition," from *lēmma* "proposition" (see LEMMA).]

dil·et·tante /dìllə taánt/ *n.* (*plural* **-tantes** *or* **-tan·ti** /-taántee/) **1.** DABBLER IN ART OR KNOWLEDGE somebody who is interested in an art or a specialized field of knowledge but who has only a superficial understanding of it **2.** ART LOVER somebody who has a passionate interest in the fine arts (*dated*) ■ *adj.* SUPERFICIAL typical of somebody who has only a superficial understanding of something [Mid-18thC. From Italian, from *dilettare* "to delight," from Latin *delectare* (see DELIGHT).] —**dil·et·tan·tish** *adj.* —**dil·et·tan·tism** *n.*

dil·i·gence[1] /díllәjәns/ *n.* **1. PERSISTENT EFFORT** persistent and hard-working effort in doing something **2. LEGAL CAREFULNESS** the care or attention expected by the law in doing something, such as fulfilling the terms of a contract [14thC. Via French from Latin *diligentia*, from *diligent-* (see DILIGENT).]

dil·i·gence[2] /díllәjәns/ *n.* a stagecoach, especially in France (*literary*) [Late 17thC. From French, a shortening of *carrosse de diligence*, literally "coach of speed" (see DILIGENCE[1]).]

dil·i·gent /díllәjәnt/ *adj.* showing persistent and hard-working effort in doing something [14thC. Via French from Latin *diligent-*, the present participle stem of *diligere* "to value highly, love" (literally "to single out"), from *legere* "to choose."] —**dil·i·gent·ly** *adv.*

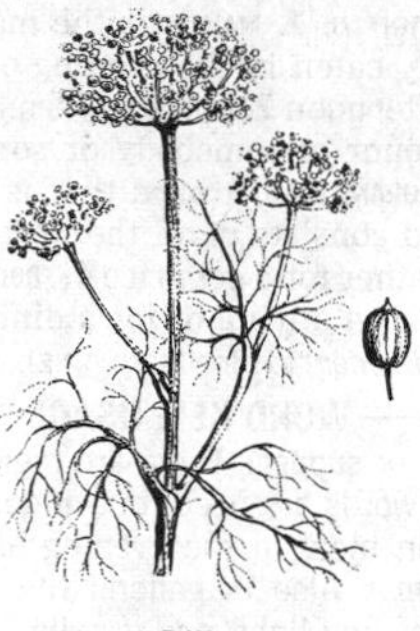

Dill

dill[1] /dil/ *n.* **1. AROMATIC PLANT** an aromatic plant with fine feathery leaves and flat flowerheads, grown as an herb. Latin name: *Anethum graveolens.* **2. DILL LEAVES OR SEEDS** the feathery leaves or seeds of the dill plant, used as a flavoring in foods [Old English *dile*] —**dilled** *adj.* —**dil·ly** *adj.*

dill[2] /dil/ *n. ANZ* a fool or idiot (*informal*) [Mid-20thC. Back-formation from *dilly* "fool," of uncertain origin: perhaps a blend of DAFT and SILLY.]

dill pick·le *n.* a cucumber that has been pickled in dill-flavored vinegar or brine, or a portion of such a pickled cucumber. ◊ **gherkin**

dil·ly /díllee/ (*plural* **-lies**) *n.* a remarkable thing or a person (*slang*)

dil·ly bag *n. Aus* a bag traditionally made of braided grass or reeds, used by Aborigines for carrying food and other belongings [From Aboriginal *dili* "coarse grass"]

dil·ly-dal·ly (**dil·ly-dal·lied, dil·ly-dal·ly·ing, dil·ly-dal·lies**) *vi.* to waste time by being too slow, doing nothing, or being unable to decide what to do [Doubled form (with alteration) of DALLY]

dil·u·ent /díllyoo әnt/ *adj.* **USED TO DILUTE** used for diluting something ■ *n.* **DILUTING SUBSTANCE** a substance that dilutes another substance [Early 18thC. From Latin *diluent-*, the present participle stem of *diluere* (see DILUTE).]

di·lute /dī lóot, di lóot/ *vti.* (**-lut·ed, -lut·ing, -lutes**) **1. MAKE THINNER** to make something thinner or weaker by adding water or another liquid, or to become thinner or weaker by the addition of water or another liquid **2. LESSEN STRENGTH** to lessen the strength or effect of something, or to become weaker in strength or effect ■ *adj.* **THINNED** thinner or weaker than at full concentration because of the addition of water or another liquid [Mid-16thC. From Latin *dilut-*, the past participle stem of *diluere* "to wash away," from *lavare* "to wash."] —**di·lute·ness** *n.* —**di·lut·er** *n.* —**di·lu·tive** *adj.*

di·lu·tion /dī lóosh'n, di lóosh'n/ *n.* **1. A THINNING OR WEAKENING** a thinning or weakening of a substance, usually a liquid, by the addition of another substance, such as water **2. LESSENING OF STRENGTH** a lessening of the strength or effect of something **3. THINNED OR WEAKENED STATE** a thinned or weakened condition **4. LESS CONCENTRATED LIQUID** a substance, especially a liquid, that has been made thinner or weaker by the addition of water or another liquid

di·lu·vi·al /di lóovee әl/, **di·lu·vi·an** /-ee әn/ *adj.* about, involving, typical of, deposited by, or caused by the great Flood described in the Bible [Mid-17thC. *Diluvial* from late Latin *diluvialis*, from Latin *diluvium* "flood" (source of English *deluge*, from *diluere* (see DILUTE).]

dim /dim/ *adj.* (**dim·mer, dim·mest**) **1. NOT WELL LIT** not easy to see in or into because of inadequate light **2. PRODUCING LITTLE LIGHT** not producing very much light, or less bright than is usual **3. DULL IN COLOR** dull or subdued in color or brightness **4. NOT CLEARLY VISIBLE** not clearly visible or distinct **5. NOT EASY TO PERCEIVE** difficult to understand or perceive with the senses **6. NOT CLEAR TO THE MIND** not clearly recalled or perceived **7. NOT SEEING CLEARLY** not able to see clearly **8. IMPROBABLE** unlikely to be successful or fulfilled **9. UNINTELLIGENT** lacking in intelligence or mental sharpness (*informal*) ■ *v.* (**dimmed, dim·ming, dims**) **1.** *vti.* **MAKE OR BECOME DIM** to make or become less bright, clear, or keen **2.** *vt.* **SWITCH TO LOW BEAMS** to switch the headlights of a motor vehicle from high beams to low beams ■ **dims** *npl.* **LOW BEAMS** the low beams of a motor vehicle's headlights [Old English, from a prehistoric Germanic word that is also the ancestor of English *damp*] —**dim·ly** *adv.* —**dim·ma·ble** *adj.* —**dim·ness** *n.*

dim. *abbr.* **1.** dimension **2.** MUSIC diminuendo **3.** diminutive

Di·Mag·gio /dә máazhi ō, dә májji ō/, **Joe** (1914–99) U.S. baseball player. Considered one of the greatest hitters and center fielders of all time, he played with the New York Yankees from 1936 and was elected to the Baseball Hall of Fame in 1955. Full name **Joseph Paul DiMaggio**. Known as **Joltin' Joe, The Yankee Clipper**

dime /dīm/ *n.* a U.S. or Canadian coin worth ten cents [14thC. Via French, "tithe, tenth part," from Latin *decima*, a form of *decimus* "tenth," from *decem* "ten" (source of English *decimal*).] ◇ **a dime a dozen** very common and not worth much ◇ **one thin dime** a very small amount of money

dime bag *n.* a quantity of an illegal drug sold for a set price, originally ten dollars (*slang*)

di·men·hy·dri·nate /dī men hídrә nàyt, -mәn-/ *n.* a white bitter antihistamine drug used to treat motion sickness. Formula: $C_{24}H_{28}ClN_5O_3$. [Mid-20thC. Coined from DIMETHYL + AMINE + HYDR- + AMINE + -ATE.]

dime nov·el *n.* a cheap paperback novel with a melodramatic or romantic story, especially one published in the United States from the mid-1800s to the early 1900s

di·men·sion /dә ménshәn/ *n.* **1. MEASUREMENT OF THE SIZE OF SOMETHING** a measurement of something in one or more directions, e.g., its length, width, or height **2. SIZE** the size or extent of something (*usually used in plural*) **3. ASPECT** a feature or distinctive part of something **4. LIFELIKE QUALITY** a fullness that gives a convincingly lifelike quality **5. LEVEL OF REALITY** a level of consciousness, existence, or reality **6.** MATH **COORDINATE FOR SPACE AND TIME** a coordinate used with others to locate a point in space and time **7.** PHYS **PROPERTY DEFINING PHYSICAL QUANTITY** any of a group of properties or magnitudes, such as mass or time, that collectively define a physical quantity ■ *vt.* (**-sioned, -sion·ing, -sions**) **1. MAKE TO REQUIRED DIMENSIONS** to cut or make something to a specified size **2. INDICATE THE DIMENSIONS OF** to specify the size of something [14thC. Via Old French from the Latin stem *dimension-*, from, ultimately, *dimetiri* "to measure out," from *metiri* "to measure."] —**di·men·sion·al** *adj.* —**di·men·sion·al·i·ty** /dә mènshә nállәtee/ *n.* —**di·men·sion·al·ly** /dә ménshәn'lee/ *adv.* —**di·men·sion·less** /-sh'nlәss/ *adj.*

di·mer /dímәr/ *n.* a molecule made up of two simpler identical molecules [Early 20thC. Coined from DI- + -MER.] —**di·mer·ic** /dī mérrik/ *adj.*

di·mer·cap·rol /dìmәr ká pràwl/ *n.* a clear thick compound used as an antidote to poisoning by heavy metals such as arsenic and mercury, or by substances containing such toxic metals. Formula: $C_3H_8OS_2$. [Mid-20thC. Coined from DI- + MERCAPTAN + PROPANE + -OL.]

dime store *n.* a shop that sells a range of inexpensive goods [From the maximum price of goods sold there being, originally, one dime]

dime-store *adj.* **1. INEXPENSIVE** not costing very much money **2. SECOND-RATE** of low or second-rate quality

dim·e·ter /dímmәtәr/ *n.* **1. LINE OF POETRY** a line of poetry consisting of two metrical feet **2. TYPE OF VERSE** verse made up of lines consisting of two metrical feet [Late 16thC. Via late Latin from Greek *dimetros* "having two measures," from *metron* "measure, poetic meter" (see METER[2]).]

di·meth·o·ate /dī méthō àyt/ *n.* a crystalline compound used as an insecticide. Formula: $C_5H_{12}NO_3PS_2$. [Mid-20thC. Coined from DIMETHYL + THIO- + -ATE.]

di·meth·yl /dī méthәl/ *adj.* with two methyl groups in a molecule

di·meth·yl·ni·tros·a·mine /dī mèthәl nītrōssә méen, dī mèthәl nītrō sá méen/ *n.* a carcinogenic compound found in tobacco smoke and some foods. Formula: $C_2H_6N_2O$.

di·meth·yl·sulf·ox·ide /dī mèthәl sul fók sīd/ *n.* full form of **DMSO**

dimin. *abbr.* **1.** MUSIC diminuendo **2.** diminutive

di·min·ish /di mínish/ (**-ished, -ish·ing, -ish·es**) *v.* **1.** *vti.* **MAKE OR BECOME SMALLER** to make something smaller or less important, or to become smaller or less important **2.** *vti.* **APPEAR SMALLER** to appear smaller or to make something appear smaller **3.** *vti.* ARCHIT **TAPER FROM BOTTOM TO TOP** to taper or make something taper from the lower part to the upper part **4.** *vt.* MUSIC **CONTRACT AN INTERVAL** to contract a perfect or minor interval by one semitone [15thC. Blend of obsolete *diminue* (literally "to lessen completely," from, ultimately, Latin *minuere* "to lessen") and *minish* "to diminish" (from, ultimately, Latin *minutia* "smallness").] —**di·min·ish·a·ble** *adj.* —**di·min·ish·ment** *n.* —**di·min·ish·ing·ly** *adv.*

di·min·ished /di mínisht/ *adj.* MUSIC used to describe a musical interval or chord reduced by one semitone

di·min·ished re·spon·si·bil·i·ty *n.* a partial defense in criminal law where the defendant seeks to argue reduced culpability on the grounds that a psychiatric disorder reduced responsibility for his or her actions

di·min·ish·ing re·turns *npl.* additional increases in something produced, e.g., profits or benefits, that do not rise in proportion to the additional effort or investment necessary to produce them

di·min·u·en·do /di mìnnyoo éndō/ *adv.* = **decrescendo** (*used as a musical direction*) ■ *n.* (*plural* **-dos**) = **decrescendo** [Late 18thC. From Italian, present participle of *diminuire* "to diminish," from Latin *deminuere*, literally "to lessen completely," from *minuere* "to lessen."] —**di·min·u·en·do** *adj.*

dim·i·nu·tion /dìmmә nóosh'n/ *n.* **1. REDUCTION** a lessening, decreasing, or reduction of something, or the result of such a reduction **2.** MUSIC **REPETITION OF MUSICAL PHRASE** the repetition of a musical phrase, using notes that are of a shorter duration than in the original phrase [14thC. From, ultimately, Latin *diminut-*, the past participle stem of *diminuere* "to break into small pieces," from *minuere* "to lessen."] —**dim·i·nu·tion·al** *adj.*

di·min·u·tive /di mínnyәtiv/ *adj.* **1. VERY SMALL** very small or much smaller than is usual **2.** GRAM **INDICATING SMALLNESS** used to describe a suffix that indicates small size, youth, familiarity, or fondness, e.g., "-ette" or "let" ■ *n.* **1. WORD INDICATING SMALLNESS OR FONDNESS** a word or name that indicates small size, youth, familiarity, or fondness, e.g., "kitchenette" or "booklet" **2.** GRAM **SUFFIX INDICATING SMALLNESS OR FONDNESS** a suffix, e.g., "-ette," or "let" that indicates small size, youth, familiarity, or fondness **3. VERY SMALL PERSON OR THING** a person or thing that is very small or much smaller than is usual [14thC. From French *diminutif*, from, ultimately, Latin *diminut-* (see DIMINUTION).] —**di·min·u·tive·ly** *adv.* —**di·min·u·tive·ness** *n.*

dim·i·ty /dímmәtee/ (*plural* **-ties**) *n.* a thin cotton fabric with a striped or checked texture produced by weaving together yarn of different thicknesses [15thC. Alteration of *demyt*, which came via medieval Latin *dimitum* from Greek *dimitos*, literally "of double thread," from *mitos* "warp thread."]

dim·mer /dímmәr/ *n.* **1. dim·mer, dim·mer switch DEVICE FOR VARYING LIGHT'S BRIGHTNESS** a device, such as a variable resistor, that can be used to vary the brightness of a light by regulating the amount of current supplied to it **2. SWITCH FOR DIMMING HEADLIGHTS** a control used to lower a car's headlights or raise them to full beam ■ **dim·mers** *npl.* **LOW BEAMS** the low beams of a motor vehicle's headlights

di·mor·phism /dī máwr fìzzәm/ *n.* **1.** BIOL **DIFFERENT FORMS WITHIN SINGLE BIOLOGICAL SPECIES** the existence of two or more different forms within a biological species. In sexual dimorphism, male and female may vary in color, size, or some other trait. **2.** BOT **DIFFERENT FORMS OF THE SAME ORGAN** the existence of two different forms of the same organ or part in a plant, such as leaves or flower forms **3.** CHEM **DIFFERENT CRYSTALLINE FORMS** the existence of a substance in two different crystalline forms —**di·mor·phic** *adj.* —**di·mor·phous** *adj.*

dim-out *n.* **1.** RESTRICTION ON USE OF LIGHTS a restriction on the use of lights at night, ordered by a government or the military, in order to make a city less visible to nighttime air raids. ◊ **black-out 2.** PARTIAL DARKNESS the partial darkness caused when the use of lights at night is restricted, e.g., for military reasons

dim·ple /dímpəl/ *n.* **1.** INDENTED AREA IN SKIN a naturally occurring slightly indented area in the skin and flesh of the cheek, chin, or other part of the body **2.** INDENTED SURFACE AREA an indented, hollowed, or depressed area in the surface of something ■ *v.* **(-pled, -pling, -ples) 1.** *vti.* FORM DIMPLE to form or have a dimple ○ *This mold dimples the surface of the golf ball.* **2.** *vt.* PRODUCE DIMPLES IN to smile, causing dimples to appear in the cheeks [14thC. From assumed Old English *dympel*, from a prehistoric Germanic base that may also be the ancestor of English *deep* and *dip*.] —**dim·ply** *adj.*

dim sum /dìm sŏŏm/ *n.* dumplings, spring rolls, and various other traditional Chinese dishes served in small portions as a meal [From Chinese (Cantonese) *tím sam*, literally "small center"]

dim·wit /dím wìt/ *n.* somebody who is unintelligent or slow to understand (*informal insult*) —**dim·wit·ted** *adj.* —**dim·wit·ted·ly** *adv.* —**dim·wit·ted·ness** *n.*

din /din/ *n.* LOUD PERSISTENT NOISE a loud persistent noise, especially one composed of confused sounds ■ *v.* **(dinned, din·ning, dins) 1.** *vi.* MAKE LOUD NOISE to make a loud persistent noise **2.** *vt.* SUBJECT TO LOUD NOISE to subject somebody to a loud persistent noise **3.** *vt.* INSTILL THROUGH REPETITION to fix something in somebody's mind by repeating it over and over again [Old English *dyne*. Ultimately from an Indo-European word meaning "loud noise."]

din *symbol.* dinar

di·nar /di náar, dée naar/ *n.* **1.** IRANIAN CURRENCY UNIT a subunit of currency in Iran, 100 of which are worth one rial. See table at **currency 2.** BILL OR COIN WORTH DINAR a bill or coin worth a dinar **3.** OLD MIDDLE EASTERN COIN a coin, especially gold, used in the past in the Middle East [Mid-17thC. From, ultimately, late Greek *dēnarion*, from Latin *denarius* "DENARIUS."]

dine /dīn/ **(dined, din·ing, dines)** *v.* **1.** *vi.* EAT DINNER to eat dinner ○ *We dine early.* **2.** *vi.* EAT to eat or have a particular food or type of food in a meal ○ *We dined on vegetables and rice.* **3.** *vt.* PROVIDE DINNER FOR to provide dinner for somebody or take somebody out to dinner (*informal*) ○ *wined and dined their guests* [13thC. From Old French *di(s)ner*, of uncertain origin: probably ultimately from assumed Vulgar Latin *disjejunare* "to break a fast," from, ultimately, Latin *jejunus* "fasting" (source of English *jejune*).]

dine out *vi.* to eat dinner somewhere other than at home, especially in a restaurant

din·er /dínər/ *n.* **1.** PERSON WHO EATS a person eating a meal, especially dinner **2.** INEXPENSIVE RESTAURANT a small inexpensive restaurant, often resembling a railroad dining car, where customers eat at the counter or in booths

Din·es·en /déenəss'n/, **Isak** (1885–1962) Danish writer. A much-traveled author, she is best known for her short stories, such as *Seven Gothic Tales* (1934), and her semi-autobiographical work, *Out of Africa* (1938). Real name **Karen Blixen-Finecke, Baroness Karen Christence**. Born **Karen Christence Dinesen**

di·nette /dī nét/ *n.* **1.** SMALL DINING AREA an alcove or part of a room where meals are eaten, especially in or near a kitchen **2.** KITCHEN TABLE AND CHAIRS a table and chairs used while eating in a dinette

ding[1] /ding/ *v.* **(dinged, ding·ing, dings) 1.** *vti.* RING OR MAKE RING to ring or make something ring with a high-pitched sound **2.** *vt.* = **din** *v.* 3 **3.** *vi.* TALK REPEATEDLY to talk repeatedly or wearyingly about something ■ *n.* RINGING a ringing sound, especially made by a bell [Mid-16thC. Partly an imitation of the sound of metal ringing, and partly an alteration of DIN; influenced by DING[2].]

ding[2] /ding/ *vt.* **(dinged, ding·ing, dings)** *U.S., Aus* MAKE A DENT IN to make a dent or other surface damage in something (*informal*) ■ *n. U.S., Aus* DENT a dent or other surface damage in something (*informal*) [14thC. Origin uncertain: probably from an Old Norse source.]

ding[3] /ding/ *n. Aus* an offensive term for an Italian or Greek person (*slang offensive*) [Mid-20thC. Shortening of DINGBAT.]

ding-a-ling *n.* **1.** TINKLE OF BELL the sound of a bell, especially a small hand-held bell, being rung **2.** SILLY PERSON a person with very odd, irrational ideas or behavior (*insult*) [Late 19thC. An imitation of the sound of a bell.]

ding·bat /díng bàt/ *n.* **1.** SILLY PERSON a person with very odd, irrational ideas or behavior (*informal*) **2.** PRINTER'S SYMBOL a symbol or ornamental character, such as a star or pointing hand, used in a printed work **3.** OBJECT USED AS MISSILE a brick, rock, or other object that is thrown as a missile [Mid-19thC. Origin uncertain: perhaps from DING[2] + BAT.]

ding-dong *n.* **1.** SOUND OF BELL a sound of a bell being struck two or more times **2.** SOUND IMITATIVE OF BELL SOUND any ringing or repeated sound that is similar to that made by a bell **3.** SILLY PERSON a person with very odd, irrational ideas or behavior (*insult*) ■ *adj.* FIERCELY CONTESTED fiercely contested, with advantage shifting continually from one side to another (*informal*) ○ *a ding-dong battle of wills* ■ *vi.* **(ding-donged, ding-dong·ing, ding-dongs)** MAKE RINGING SOUND to make a ringing sound like a bell [Mid-16thC. An imitation of the sound.]

dinge[1] /dinj/ *n.* a condition of dirtiness, shabbiness, or dullness [Early 19thC. Origin uncertain: probably a back-formation from DINGY.]

dinge[2] /dinj/ *n.* a highly offensive term formerly used to refer to a Black person (*archaic taboo insult*)

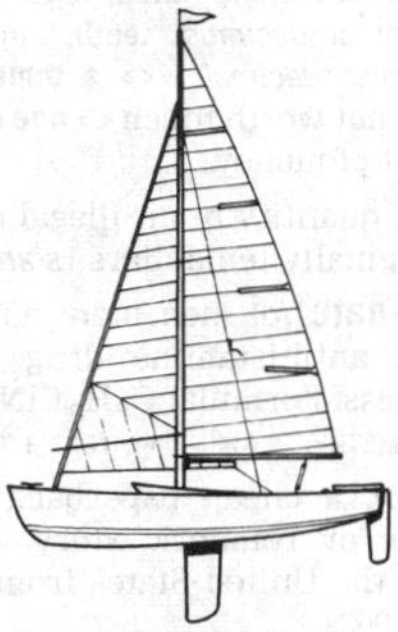

Dinghy

din·ghy /díngee/ (*plural* **-ghies**) *n.* **1.** SMALL BOAT any small boat, especially one that is towed behind or carried on a larger boat **2.** INFLATABLE LIFE RAFT an inflatable life raft [Early 19thC. From Hindi *dīgī*, literally "small boat," from *dēgā* "boat."]

din·gle /díng g'l/ *n.* a wooded valley (*literary*) [13thC. Origin uncertain. The original sense was "abyss."]

din·gle·ber·ry /díng g'l bèree/ (*plural* **-ries**) *n.* a small piece of dried feces that clings to the hair or fur near the anus (*slang*) [Mid-20thC. *Dingle* of unknown origin.]

din·go /díng gō/ (*plural* **-goes**) *n.* an Australian wild dog with a reddish brown coat. Latin name: *Canis dingo.* [Late 18thC. From Aboriginal *dingu*.]

din·gus /díng gəss/ (*plural* **-gus·es**) *n.* anything whose name you have forgotten or do not know (*informal*) [Late 19thC. From Dutch *Dinges* "what's-his-name," from German, literally "of the thing," a form of *Ding* "thing."]

din·gy /dínjee/ **(-gi·er, -gi·est)** *adj.* **1.** DIRTY OR FADED dirty looking, discolored, or faded **2.** SHABBY shabby, dirty, and uninviting [Mid-18thC. Origin uncertain: perhaps an alteration of DUNGY; or perhaps ultimately from Old English *dynge* "dung, manured land," from *dung* "DUNG."] —**din·gi·ly** *adv.* —**din·gi·ness** *n.*

din·ing car *n.* a railroad carriage where meals are served to a train's passengers

din·ing room *n.* a room where meals are eaten, especially in a home or hotel

di·ni·tro·ben·zene /dī nī trō bén zeen/ *n.* a yellow crystalline compound that occurs in three isomeric forms and is used in making dyes and plastics. Formula: $C_6H_4(NO_2)_2$. [Late 19thC. Coined from DI- + NITROBENZENE.]

dink /dingk/ *n.* SPORT = **drop shot** [Mid-20thC. An imitation of the sound of the ball being hit.]

DINK /dingk/, **dink** *n.* a member of a couple who both have careers, usually in well-paid fields, and have no children [Late 20thC. Acronym formed from *dual* (or *double*) *income, no kids*.]

Din·ka /díngkə/ (*plural* **-kas** or **-ka**) *n.* **1.** PEOPLES MEMBER OF AFRICAN PEOPLE a member of a tall people who live as herders in the Nile Valley in southern Sudan **2.** LANG NILO-SAHARAN LANGUAGE a language of the Nilo-Saharan family, spoken in southern Sudan. About 1,350,000 people speak Dinka. [Mid-19thC. From Dinka *Jieng* "people."] —**Din·ka** *adj.*

din·key /díngkee/ (*plural* **-keys**), **din·ky** (*plural* **-kies**) *n.* a small locomotive, used for tasks like shunting rather than long-distance journeys [Mid-19thC. Origin uncertain: probably from DINGHY. Originally "small boat."]

din·ky[1] /díngkee/ *adj.* **(-ki·er, -ki·est)** SMALL OR UNIMPORTANT small in size, or of almost no importance (*informal*) ■ *n.* (*plural* **-kies**) = **dinkey** [Late 18thC. Formed from Scots dialect *dink* "finely dressed, trim," of unknown origin. The original sense was "neat, dainty."]

din·ky[2] /díngkee/ (*plural* **-kies**), **din·kie** *n. U.K.* = **DINK** [Late 20thC. Formed from DINK.]

din·ner /dínnər/ *n.* **1.** MAIN MEAL the main meal of the day, usually eaten in the evening or sometimes in the early afternoon **2.** BANQUET a formal evening meal given in honor of somebody or something **3.** FULL-COURSE RESTAURANT MEAL a meal that is eaten in a restaurant and consists of all the usual courses often offered together for a set price **4.** FOOD SERVED FOR DINNER the food served during or for a dinner [13thC. From Old French *di(s)ner* "to dine" (see DINE), used as a noun.]

WORD KEY: USAGE

dinner, lunch, or **supper?** There are regional differences in how these words are used, but in general Americans eat their main meal in the evening and call it either ***dinner*** or ***supper.*** Also in general the midday meal is relatively quick and light, and is called ***lunch.*** A midday meal may be called ***dinner,*** however, if it is the main meal of the day; and then the evening meal will be ***supper.***

din·ner dance *n.* a formal social occasion at which dancing follows a dinner

din·ner jack·et *n. U.K.* = **tuxedo**

din·ner the·a·ter *n.* a restaurant where a play is performed for customers during or after their dinner

din·ner·ware /dínnər wàir/ *n.* dishes used for serving or eating a meal, or a specific set of these dishes

di·no·flag·el·late /dī nō flájjə làyt, dī nō flájjələt/ *n.* a tiny single-celled marine organism with two long slender appendages (**flagella**) that lie in surface grooves at right-angles to each other. Most are constituents of plankton. Some types are luminescent and some are toxic, especially when multiplying prolifically to cause colorful blooms (**red tide**). Latin name: *Dinoflagellata.* [Late 19thC. From modern Latin *Dinoflagellata*, order name, from Greek *dinos* "a whirling" + Latin *flagellum* "whip" (see FLAGELLUM).]

di·no·saur /dīnə sàwr/ *n.* **1.** EXTINCT REPTILE an extinct, chiefly terrestrial reptile that lived in the Mesozoic Era. Some dinosaurs were the largest known land animals. Order: Ornithischia and Saurischia. **2.** OUTMODED PERSON OR THING a person or thing that is hopelessly out of date or incapable of adapting to change [Mid-19thC. From modern Latin *dinosaurus*, from Greek *deinos* "terrible" (ultimately from an Indo-European word that is also the ancestor of English *dire*) + *sauros* "lizard" (source of English *saurian*).] —**di·no·sau·ri·an** /dīnə sáwree ən/ *adj.*

dint /dint/ *n.* DENT a dent ■ *vt.* **(dint·ed, dint·ing, dints) 1.** MAKE A DENT IN to make a dent in something **2.** DRIVE SOMETHING IN WITH FORCE to drive something in forcefully [Old English *dynt* "blow, stroke (especially of a weapon)"; influenced by related Old Norse *dyntr*] ◇ **by dint of** using something, or by the force of something

dioc. *abbr.* diocese

di·oc·e·san /dī óssəss'n/ *adj.* RELATING TO DIOCESE relating to, belonging to, or established by a diocese, its bishop, or its churches ■ *n.* BISHOP OF DIOCESE the bishop in charge of a diocese

di·o·cese /dī əssiss, dī ə seez/ *n.* the churches that are under the authority of one bishop, or the district containing those churches [14thC. From, ultimately, Greek *dioikēsis* "administration," from *dioikein* "to manage," literally "to inhabit a house thoroughly," from *oikos* "house."]

Di·o·cle·tian /dī ə kléesh'n/, **Emperor of Rome** (245–313). Proclaimed emperor in 284, his administrative reforms succeeded, but his attempt to restore traditional religion by persecuting Christians failed. He abdicated in 305. Full name **Gaius Aurelius Valerius Diocletianus**

di·ode /dī ŏd/ *n.* an electronic device that has two electrodes and is used to convert alternating current to direct current. The older vacuum tube diodes have been replaced by more reliable semiconductor devices. [Early 20thC. Coined from DI- + -ODE, the underlying sense being "double way."]

di·oe·cious /dī ée̲shəss/, **di·e·cious** *adj.* having male and female flowers on different plants of the same species [Mid-18thC. Formed from modern Latin *Dioecia*, class name, literally "two houses," from Greek *oikos* "house."] —**di·oe·cious·ly** *adv.* —**di·oe·cious·ness** *n.* —**di·oe·cism** *n.*

di·oe·strus *n., adj.* U.K. = **diestrus**

Di·og·e·nes /dī ójjə neez/ (412?–323 B.C.) Greek philosopher. He was a founder of Cynicism, an ancient school of philosophy. He is said to have lived in a tub in Athens and to have wandered the streets with a lamp, seeking an honest man.

di·ol /dī àwl/ *n.* an alcohol with two hydroxyl groups in each molecule [Early 20thC. Coined from DI- + -OL.]

Di·o·nys·i·a /dì ə nízhə, -nízhee ə, -níssee ə/ *npl.* the celebrations held in ancient Greece in honor of the god Dionysus, which included the performance of plays [Early 19thC. From Greek *Dionusia*, from *Dionusos* "Dionysus."]

Di·o·nys·i·ac *adj.* = **Dionysian** [Early 19thC. From Latin *Dionysiacus*, from, ultimately, Greek *Dionusos* "Dionysus."]

di·o·nys·i·an /dì ə nísh'n, -nízh'n, dì ə níssee ən/ *adj.* **1.** ORGIASTIC involving drunkenness and sexual activity **2.** PHILOS NOT RATIONAL in the philosophical writings of Nietzsche, spontaneous and intuitive rather than rational

Di·o·nys·i·an /dì ə nísh'n, -nízh'n, dì ə níssee ən/, **Di·o·nys·i·ac** /dì ə níssee àk, -nízzee àk/ *adj.* **1.** RELATING TO DIONYSUS relating to the Greek god Dionysus **2.** RELATING TO DIONYSIA connected with the worship of the Greek god Dionysus [Early 17thC. Formed from Greek *Dionusos* "Dionysus."]

Di·o·ny·si·us Ex·ig·u·us /dī ə nìshəss eg zíggyoo əss, dī ə níssee əss-/ (500?–556) Scythian Roman scholar. He introduced the Christian era of dating in his *Cyclus Paschalis* (525). He adopted the name *Exiguus* "little" as a token of humility.

Di·o·ny·sus /dì ə níssəss/ *n.* MYTHOL ➧ **Bacchus**

Di·o·phan·tine e·qua·tion /dì ə fán tīn-, dì ə fántin-/ *n.* an algebraic equation that contains two or more variables, has only whole number (**integral**) coefficients and has integral solutions for the variables [Named for DIOPHANTUS the 3rd-century Greek mathematician, who invented these equations]

di·op·side /dī óp sīd/ *n.* a pale green mineral calcium magnesium silicate that is a common component of some types of igneous rock. Formula: $CaMgSi_2O_6$. [Early 19thC. Coined from DI- + Greek *opsis*, literally "two aspects," later interpreted as a derivative of Greek *diopsis* "a view through."]

di·op·ter /dī óptər/ *n.* a unit of measurement for the refractive power of a lens, based on a convergent lens with a focal length of 1 m. The power of a lens is equivalent to the reciprocal of the focal length of the lens in meters, and a divergent lens is shown with a negative sign. [Late 19thC. Via French from Latin *dioptra* "instrument for measuring angles," from Greek, from *dia-* "through" + *optos* "visible" (see OPTIC).] —**di·op·tral** /dī óptrəl/ *adj.*

di·op·tric /dī óptrik/, **di·op·tri·cal** /-óptrik'l/ *adj.* **1.** RELATING TO BRANCH OF OPTICS relating to the study of how images are formed by lenses **2.** RELATING TO LIGHT'S REFRACTIVE POWERS relating to the refractive powers of light or the measurement of the refractive power of a lens [Mid-17thC. From Greek *dioptrikos* "of the dioptre," from *dioptra* (see DIOPTER).] —**di·op·tri·cal·ly** *adv.*

di·op·trics /dī óptriks/ *n.* the branch of optics that studies the refraction of light by lenses or within the eye

Di·or /dee áwr/, **Christian** (1905–57) French couturier. In 1946 he founded the fashion house bearing his name. He achieved worldwide fame by introducing the "New Look" in 1947, featuring narrow shoulders and calf-length skirts.

di·o·ram·a /dì ə rámmə, dì ə raámə/ *n.* **1.** DISPLAY CASE a three-dimensional representation of a scene, e.g., in a museum, in which objects or models are arranged in a natural setting against a realistic background **2.** MINIATURE REPLICA OF SCENE a representation of a scene that is made to appear three-dimensional, e.g., one in which the viewer looks through a hole at objects painted on layers of translucent material [Early 19thC. From French, literally "sight through"; formed from Greek *dia-* "through" on the model of *panorama*.] —**di·o·ram·ic** /dì ə rámmik/ *adj.*

di·o·rite /dī ə rīt/ *n.* a dark granular igneous rock that consists of plagioclase and a ferromagnesian mineral such as hornblende. Diorite is used in materials for surfacing roads. [Early 19thC. Formed from Greek *diorizein* "to distinguish," literally "to limit through," from *orizein* "to limit."] —**di·o·rit·ic** /dī ə ríttik/ *adj.*

Di·os·cu·ri /dì ə skyoŏr ī/ *npl.* the twin gods Castor and Polydeuces, or Pollux, who in Greek mythology were the sons of Zeus and Leda [Early 20thC. From Greek *Dioskouroi*, from *Dios* "of Zeus" + *kouros* "boy, son."]

di·ox·ane /dī ók sàyn/ *n.* a toxic flammable colorless liquid used as a solvent for waxes and resins, paints, lacquers, cosmetics, and deodorants, and in textile manufacture. Formula: $C_4H_8O_2$. [Early 20thC. Coined from DI- + OX- + -ANE.]

di·ox·ide /dī ók sīd/ *n.* an oxide that has two oxygen atoms in each molecule

di·ox·in /dī óksin/ *n.* any derivative of dibenzo-*p*-dioxin, produced as a toxic byproduct of combustion processes, the manufacture of some herbicides and bactericides, and in chlorine bleaching of paper. The best-known dioxin is the extremely carcinogenic and mutagenic 2,3,7,8-tetrachlorodibenzo-*p*-dioxin (TCDD). [Early 20thC. Coined from DI- + OX- + -IN.]

dip /dip/ *v.* (**dipped, dip·ping, dips**) **1.** *vt.* PUT BRIEFLY IN LIQUID to put something briefly into a liquid or soft mixture and take it out again ○ *She dipped her fingers in the water.* **2.** *vi.* MOVE DOWNWARD to sink to a lower level ○ *The plane dipped and then flew on.* **3.** *vt.* LOWER to lower something and raise it again ○ *The horse dipped its head.* **4.** *vt.* LOWER SOMEBODY OVER ONE ARM while dancing, to lower your partner toward the floor over one arm **5.** *vi.* BECOME LESS to fall to a lower amount, especially for a short time ○ *Prices dipped at the beginning of October.* **6.** *vti.* PUT YOUR HAND IN to put your hand into something in order to take something out ○ *He dipped his hand into his pocket.* **7.** *vt.* SCOOP to take up liquid or small pieces of a substance with something such as a spoon or cup ○ *She was dipping soup from the pot.* **8.** *vt. U.K.* = **dim 9.** *vt.* DISINFECT ANIMAL to put an animal, such as a sheep or dog, into a bath of disinfectant in order to clear or prevent infection by insects, parasites, or fungi **10.** *vi.* SLOPE DOWNWARD to slope downward from the horizontal **11.** *vt.* MAKE FROM WAX to make a candle by repeatedly putting a wick into melted wax ○ *dip a candle* ■ *n.* **1.** LOWERING an act of sinking lower, of lowering something, or of putting something in liquid ○ *She acknowledged him with a dip of her head.* **2.** PUTTING HAND IN the action of putting the hand into something to take something out, or of scooping up liquid or small pieces of a substance **3.** SWIM a quick swim ○ *There's time for a dip before lunch.* **4.** SLIGHT DECREASE a temporary decrease in the amount or level of something ○ *a dip in sales* **5.** LOWER PLACE a place where the ground slopes, especially to form a hollow ○ *We came to a dip in the road.* **6.** FOOD MIXTURE FOR DIPPING FOOD INTO a creamy mixture into which pieces of food can be dipped, often served with crackers or chips ○ *sour cream and onion dip* **7.** AGRIC DISINFECTANT FOR ANIMALS a mixture of chemicals used to disinfect animals ○ *sheep dip* **8.** INDUST LIQUID CHEMICAL PREPARATION a chemical mixture in which something can be immersed, such as a dye or preservative **9.** UNINTELLIGENT PERSON an unintelligent or unsophisticated person (*slang insult*) **10.** GEOG ANGLE OF MAGNETIC NEEDLE the angle that a magnetic needle makes with the horizontal plane **11.** GEOL ANGLE OF ROCK LAYER the angle a sloping rock layer makes to the horizontal ○ *The rock bed has a dip of ten degrees.* **12.** CANDLE a candle made by dipping a wick repeatedly in wax **13.** GYMNASTICS PARALLEL BARS EXERCISE an exercise on parallel bars in which the elbows are bent until the gymnast's chin is level with the bars, and the body is raised by straightening the arms **14.** PICKPOCKET a pickpocket (*slang*) [Old English *dyppan*, from a prehistoric Germanic word that is also the ancestor of English *deep*]

dip into *vt.* **1.** READ PARTS OF BOOK to read parts of a text, such as a book or magazine, rather than the whole of it **2.** USE SAVED MONEY to use some of the money that has been saved

Dip., **dip.** *abbr.* diploma

di·pep·ti·dase /dī pépti dàyss, -dàyz/ *n.* an enzyme that aids the breakdown of proteins as part of the process of protein digestion

di·pep·tide /dī pép tīd/ *n.* a chemical compound consisting of two linked amino acids

di·pha·sic /dī fáyzik/, **di·phase** /dī fàyz/ *adj.* relating to parasites that have an independent stage in their life cycle

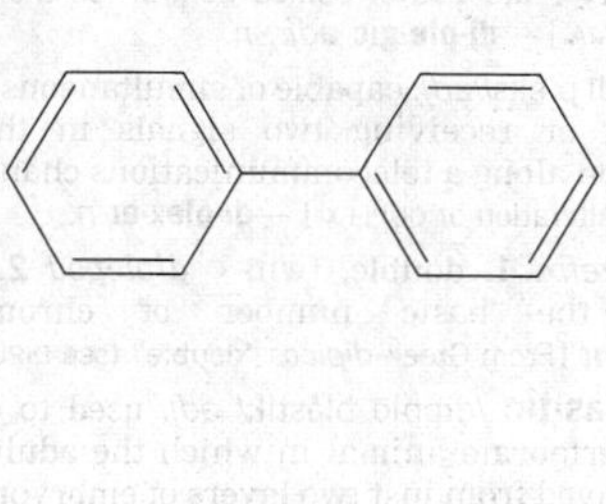

Diphenyl

di·phen·yl /dī fénn'l, dī féen'l/ *n.* a white crystalline substance used as a fungicide, in organic synthesis, and as a heat transfer agent. Formula: $C_{12}H_{10}$.

di·phen·yl·a·mine /dī fénn'lə meen, dī féen'l-/ *n.* a colorless toxic crystalline substance used in solid rocket propellants, dyes, and the manufacture of plastics. Formula: $(C_6H_5)_2NH$.

di·phen·yl·ke·tone /dī féen'l kée tōn, dī fènn'l-/ *n.* CHEM = **benzophenone**

di·phos·gene /dī fóz jeen/ *n.* a colorless oily liquid with an extremely poisonous vapor, used in gas warfare during World War I. Formula: $ClCOOCCl_3$.

di·phos·phate /dī fóss fàyt/ *n.* a chemical compound that contains two phosphate groups per molecule

di·phos·pho·gly·cer·ic ac·id /dī fòsfə gli sérrik ássid/ *n.* an abundant compound found in the red blood cells of most mammals that decreases the affinity of hemoglobin for oxygen

diph·the·ri·a /dif théeree ə, dip-/ *n.* a serious infectious disease, caused by a bacterium *Corynebacterium diphtheriae*, that attacks the membranes of the throat and releases a toxin that damages the heart and the nervous system. The main symptoms are fever, weakness, and severe inflammation of the affected membranes. [Mid-19thC. From modern Latin, ultimately from Greek *diphthera* or *diphtheris* "hide, skin," indicating the tough membrane developed in the throat.] —**diph·the·ri·al** *adj.* —**diph·ther·ic** *adj.* —**diph·the·rit·ic** /dìfthə ríttik, dìpthə-/ *adj.* —**diph·ther·oid** /dífthə ròyd, dípthə-/ *adj.*

diph·thong /díf thàwng, díp thàwng/ *n.* **1.** TWO VOWELS AS ONE SYLLABLE a complex vowel sound in which the first vowel is gradually raised by a second vowel so that both vowels form one syllable, such as "a" and "i" in "rail" **2.** JOINED LETTERS a character formed by joining the two letters "a" and "e" as "æ" or the two letters "o" and "e" as "œ" [15thC. Via French from Latin *diphthongus*, literally "two sounds," from, ultimately, Greek *phthoggos* "sound."] —**diph·thon·gal** /dif tháwng'l, dip tháwng'l/ *adj.*

diph·thong·ize /díf thawng īz, díp-/ (**-ized, -iz·ing, -iz·es**) *vti.* to become a diphthong or make a vowel into a diphthong —**diph·thong·i·za·tion** /díf thawngi záysh'n, díp-/ *n.*

diph·y·cer·cal /diffi súrk'l/ *adj.* used to describe a

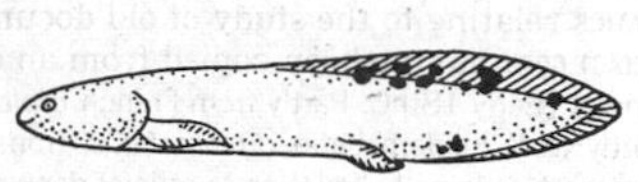

Diphycercal

fish's tail fin that is divided into two equal parts [Mid-19thC. From the Greek stem *diphu-* "of double form" + *kerkos* "tail."]

di·phy·o·dont /dī fī ə dònt/ *adj.* used to describe a mammal that grows two sets of teeth in a lifetime [Mid-19thC. Coined from the Greek stem *diphu-* "double form" + the Greek stem *odont-* "tooth."]

dipl. *abbr.* **1.** diplomat **2.** diplomatic

dipl- *prefix.* = **diplo-** (*used before vowels*)

di·ple·gia /dī plēejə, -jee ə/ *n.* inability to move corresponding parts on both the right and left sides of the body [Late 19thC. Coined from DI- on the model of PARAPLEGIA.] —**di·ple·gic** *adj., n.*

di·plex /dī plèks/ *adj.* capable of simultaneously transmitting or receiving two signals in the same direction along a telecommunications channel [Late 19thC. Alteration of DUPLEX.] —**di·plex·er** *n.*

diplo- *prefix.* **1.** double, twin ○ *diplopod* **2.** having twice the basic number of chromosomes ○ *diplont* [From Greek *diploos* "double" (see DIPLOMA)]

dip·lo·blas·tic /dìpplō blástik/ *adj.* used to describe an invertebrate animal in which the adult tissues are derived from just two layers of embryonic germ tissue, endoderm and ectoderm. Cnidarians are diploblastic.

di·plod·o·cus /di plóddəkəss/ *n.* a large herbivorous dinosaur of the late Jurassic Period that had four legs and a very long neck and tail. It had nostrils near the top of the head, indicating that it spent time in deep water. Genus: *Diplodocus.* [Late 19thC. From modern Latin, genus name, from Greek *diploos* "double" + *dokos* "beam." The underlying sense is of a creature twice as large as the widest part of anything.]

dip·lo·ë /dípplō ēe/ *n.* a layer of spongy bone tissue found between the harder inside and outside bone layers of the cranium [Late 16thC. From Greek *diploē* "doubling," from *diploos* "double."]

dip·loid /díp lòyd/ *adj.* possessing two matched sets of chromosomes in the cell nucleus, one set from each parent. There is a characteristic diploid number of chromosomes for each species. —**dip·loid·ic** /di plóydik/ *adj.* —**dip·loi·dy** *n.*

di·plo·ma /di plṓmə/ *n.* **1.** COURSE CERTIFICATE a certificate given by a high school, college, university, or professional organization, indicating that somebody has completed a course of education or training and reached the required level of competence **2.** OFFICIAL PAPER DESCRIBING RIGHTS AND PRIVILEGES a written document or charter, especially one that confers specific rights or privileges [Mid-17thC. Via Latin from Greek, "folded paper," from *diploun* "to fold, make double," from *diploos* "double."]

di·plo·ma·cy /di plṓməssee/ *n.* **1.** INTERNATIONAL RELATIONS the management of communication and relationships between nations by members and employees of each nation's government **2.** SKILL IN INTERNATIONAL DEALINGS skill in managing communication and relationships between nations **3.** TACT skill and tact in dealing with other people

dip·lo·mat /dípplə màt/ *n.* **1.** GOVERNMENT REPRESENTATIVE ABROAD a member or employee of a government who represents his or her country in dealings with other nations, especially by working in an embassy or consulate abroad **2.** TACTFUL PERSON somebody who is tactful and good at dealing with people [Early 19thC. From French *diplomate*, back-formation from *diplomatique* "diplomatic."]

dip·lo·mate /dípplə màyt/ *n.* somebody who holds a diploma granted by a professional organization (*formal*) ○ *a diplomate of the National Organization of Neuropsychologists*

dip·lo·mat·ic /dìpplə máttik/ *adj.* **1.** INVOLVING DIPLOMACY concerned with or involving international diplomacy or the work of diplomats **2.** TACTFUL showing tact and skill in dealing with people **3.** RELATING TO DIPLOMATICS relating to the study of old documents **4.** BEING EXACT COPY having been copied from an original document [Early 18thC. Partly from French *diplomatique*, and partly from modern Latin *diplomaticus*, from *diploma* (see DIPLOMA). Originally "relating to official documents."]

dip·lo·mat·ic bag *n.* a bag in which official correspondence travels between a government office and an embassy of that government in another country. The case is carried by a special messenger and is not subject to the regulations governing ordinary mail.

dip·lo·mat·ic corps *n.* all the diplomats from other countries who reside in another nation

dip·lo·mat·ic im·mu·ni·ty *n.* the legal status of diplomats, who are not subject to the legal and taxation systems of a country in which they are resident as accredited representatives

dip·lo·mat·ics /dìpplə máttiks/ *n.* the study and verification of very old documents (*takes a singular verb*)

di·plo·ma·tist /di plṓmətist/ *n.* a professional diplomat

dip·lont /dí plònt/ *n.* an organism whose cells, other than reproductive cells, have a diploid number of chromosomes in their nuclei [Early 20thC. Coined from DIPLO- + -ONT.] —**dip·lont·ic** /di plóntik/ *adj.*

dip·lo·pi·a /di plṓpee ə/ *n.* double vision (*technical*) [Early 19thC. Coined from DIPLO- + -OPIA.] —**dip·lo·pic** /di plóppik, di plṓpik/ *adj.*

dip·lo·pod /dípplə pòd/ *n.* a millipede that has two pairs of legs on each body segment. Class: Diplopoda. [Mid-19thC. From modern Latin *Diplopoda*, class name, from Greek *diploos* "double" + the stem *pod-* "foot."] —**dip·lop·o·dous** /di plóppədəss/ *adj.*

dip·lo·tene /dípplō tēen/ *n.* a stage in the first part of reproductive cell division (**meiosis**) in which paired chromosomes start to move apart from one another but remain connected at points. At these connecting points, genetic information is exchanged. [Early 20thC. Coined from DIPLO- + *-tene*, from Greek *tainia* "band, ribbon."]

dip·o·dy /díppədee/ (*plural* **-dies**) *n.* a unit of poetry that consists of two stressed units or feet [Late 19thC. Formed from the Greek stem *dipod-* "two-footed."]

di·pole /dī pōl/ *n.* two equal and opposite magnetized or electrically charged poles that are separated by a short distance —**di·pol·ar** /dī pṓlər/ *adj.*

di·pole mo·ment *n.* **1.** PRODUCT OF EQUAL BUT OPPOSITE CHARGES the product of one of the equal but opposite charges on two atoms in a molecule, and the distance separating them **2.** RESULT OF MAGNETIC DIPOLE the product of two equal and opposite magnetic poles or electric charges that are separated by a short distance

dip·per /díppər/ *n.* **1.** SCOOP a cup or ladle for dipping into liquid **2.** BIRDS SMALL WATER BIRD a small plain-colored bird that lives beside rivers and can swim and dive. Family: Cinclidae. **3.** SOMETHING THAT DIPS somebody or something, such as a machine, that dips objects in a liquid, e.g., in an industrial process

di·pro·pel·lant /dī prə péllənt/ *n.* SPACE TECH = **bipropellant**

di·prot·ic /dī próttik/ *adj.* with two transferable hydrogen protons [Coined from DI- + PROTON + -IC]

di·pro·to·dont /dī prṓtə dònt/ *adj.* WITH ENLARGED INCISORS used to describe a mammal that has the first pair of incisor teeth in each jaw enlarged ■ *n.* MARSUPIAL WITH ENLARGED INCISORS a marsupial that has enlarged incisors. Kangaroos and wallabies are diprotodonts. Order: Diprotodontia. [Late 19thC. Coined from DI- + PROTO- + -ODONT.]

dip·shit /díp shìt/ *n.* an offensive term for a person (*slang insult*) [20thC. Origin unknown.]

dip·so /díp sō/ (*plural* **-sos**) *n.* a dipsomaniac (*slang insult*) [Late 19thC. Shortening.]

dip·so·ma·ni·a /dìpsə máynee ə/ *n.* a habitual and uncontrollable craving for alcohol (*dated*) [Mid-19thC. From Greek *dipsa* "thirst" + MANIA.]

dip·so·ma·ni·ac /dìpsə máynee àk/ *n.* somebody with a habitual and uncontrollable craving for alcohol (*dated*) —**dip·so·ma·ni·a·cal** /dìpsō mə nī ək'l/ *adj.*

dip·stick /díp stìk/ *n.* a measuring rod that is dipped into a container to indicate the depth of liquid in it, especially one used to measure the amount of oil in a car's engine [20thC. The sense meaning "fool" is said to be a euphemism for DIPSHIT.]

dip switch *n.* **1.** *U.K.* = **dimmer 2.** = **DIP switch**

DIP switch, dip switch *n.* one or more tiny switches used to turn optional settings on or off on a computer component [Late 20thC. *DIP* an acronym formed from *dual in-line package.*]

dip·ter·an /díptərən/, **dip·ter·on** /-ròn/ *n.* a two-winged fly. Order: Diptera. [Mid-19thC. Formed from modern Latin *Diptera*, order name, from Greek *dipteros* "two winged."] —**dip·ter·al** *adj.*

dip·ter·ous /díptərəss/ *adj.* characteristic of or relating to the order Diptera of two-winged insects that includes flies, gnats, mosquitoes, and midges

dip·tych /díptik/ *n.* **1.** PAIRED PAINTINGS a pair of paintings, especially religious paintings on two hinged panels **2.** WRITING TABLETS a pair of writing tablets joined by a hinge and having wooden backs and waxed writing surfaces, used especially in ancient Greece and Rome [Early 17thC. Via late Latin *diptycha* from late Greek *diptukha* "pair of writing tablets," plural of *diptukhos* "folded in two," from *ptukhē* "fold."]

di·pyr·id·a·mole /dī pēeridə mōl, dīpə rídda mōl/ *n.* a vasodilator drug used to treat angina pectoris and to prevent clots in blood vessels. Formula: $C_{24}H_{40}N_8O_4$. [Mid-20thC. Coined from DI- + PYRIMIDINE + PIPERIDINE + AMINO- + -OL.]

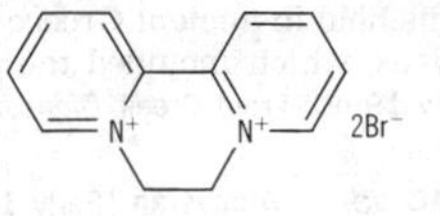

Diquat

di·quat /dī kwòt/ *n.* a biodegradable herbicide used to control weeds in water [Mid-20thC. Coined from DI- + QUATERNARY; from its being based on a quaternary amine.]

dir. *abbr.* director

Di·rac /di rák/, **Paul** (1902–84) British theoretical physicist. He worked on quantum theory and predicted the existence of the positron. He shared the Nobel Prize in physics (1933). Full name **Paul Adrien Maurice Dirac**

Di·rac con·stant *n.* a constant used in quantum mechanics that is Planck's constant divided by 2π [Named for Paul DIRAC]

Di·rac e·qua·tion *n.* an equation in quantum mechanics that describes the wave behavior of an electron in an electromagnetic field, in a manner consistent with special relativity [Named for Paul DIRAC]

dire /dīr/ (**dir·er, dir·est**) *adj.* **1.** VERY BAD characterized by severe, serious, or desperate circumstances **2.** THREATENING DISASTER warning of a future disaster or serious consequences [Mid-16thC. From Latin *dirus* "fearful, awful, boding ill." Ultimately from an Indo-European word that is also the ancestor of English *dinosaur.*] —**dire·ly** *adv.* —**dire·ness** *n.*

di·rect /di rékt, dī-/ *v.* (**-rect·ed, -rect·ing, -rects**) **1.** *vt.* SUPERVISE to organize and control the work of an organization or a group of people ○ *I found her directing the efforts of a team of rescue workers.* **2.** *vt.* INSTRUCT to tell somebody to do something (*formal*) ○ *The medicine should be taken only as directed.* **3.** *vt.* FOCUS ATTENTION ON SOMETHING to focus attention or concentrate activities on something ○ *Please direct your attention toward the figures at the right of the screen.* **4.** *vt.* AIM to aim, point, or send something or somebody in a particular direction ○ *Direct the extinguisher at the base of the flames.* **5.** *vt.* ADDRESS LETTER to write an address on something to be delivered ○ *The envelope was directed to our offices.* **6.** *vt.* GIVE DIRECTIONS to tell somebody how to get to a place ○ *Can you direct me to the station?* **7.** *vt.* ADDRESS to say something to somebody specifically ○ *The remarks were directed to his sister.* **8.** *vti.* ARTS SUPERVISE MOVIES OR PLAYS to be responsible for supervising the creative aspects of a movie, play, or television program, giving instructions and guidance to the actors and other people involved ○ *He has directed several movies.* **9.** *vt.* MUSIC = **conduct** *v.* 1 ■ *adj.* **1.** NOT STOPPING OR DEVIATING going straight from one place or point to another ○ *a direct flight from Paris to Miami* **2.** IMMEDIATE lacking the influence of any other factors ○ *No direct link between the two events has been established.* **3.** PERSONAL not having a person, action, or process intervene ○ *We are in direct contact with them.* **4.** STRAIGHTFORWARD easy to understand or respond to ○ *The author makes a direct appeal to* *our emotions.* **5.** PRECISE having the characteristics of accuracy and precision ○ *a direct quotation* **6.** IMMEDIATELY RELATED connected by a straight and unbroken line of descent from parent to child ○ *a direct descendant of George Washington* **7.** COMPLETE OR EXACT showing complete contradiction or opposition ○ *Their conclusions were in direct contradiction to ours.* **8.** POL DIRECTLY INVOLVING THE ELECTORATE involving participation in government from the electorate rather than through electoral representatives ○ *direct democracy* **9.** MATH, LOGIC WORKING FROM PREMISE TO CONCLUSION working immediately from the premise to the conclusion in proving something **10.** ASTRON MOVING WEST TO EAST moving from west to east as observed from celestial north ■ *adv.* **1.** STRAIGHT WITHOUT DIVERSION straight from one place or person to another, without a stop or diversion ○ *You can fly direct from Amsterdam to Chicago.* **2.** DIRECTLY by an immediate connection, without somebody or something intervening ○ *You can dial Calcutta direct.* [14thC. From Latin *directus*, past participle of *dirigere* "to set straight, guide."] —**di·rect·ness** *n.*

WORD KEY: SYNONYMS

See Synonyms at ***guide***.

di·rect ac·cess *n.* the ability to retrieve information directly from any part of a storage device without referring to the preceding data

di·rect ac·tion *n.* a political or industrial action, such as a strike, a boycott, or civil disobedience, intended to have an immediate and noticeable effect that will influence a government or employer

di·rect cou·pling *n.* direct connection of one part of a circuit to another without the use of transformers or capacitors, allowing both direct current and alternating current to flow along the connection —**di·rect-cou·pled** *adj.*

di·rect cur·rent *n.* electrical current that flows in only one direction and has a fairly constant average value. ◊ **alternating current**

di·rect deb·it *n.* an arrangement by which sums of varying amounts that are owed at regular intervals, such as bills, are payed to the creditor directly from the payer's bank account

di·rect dis·course *n.* GRAM the repeating of speech by giving the exact words that were spoken, in writing conventionally inside quotation marks

di·rect dye *n.* a dye that can be used directly on a fabric without needing an extra chemical (**mordant**) to fix the color

di·rect ev·i·dence *n.* evidence, such as a photograph, a document, or a witness's account, that provides direct factual information in a trial

di·rect free kick *n.* a free kick in soccer that is awarded as compensation for a foul and can be taken as a direct shot at the opponent's goal

di·rect in·jec·tion *n.* the injection of fuel in liquid form into the cylinders of an internal-combustion engine, without previously passing it through a carburetor

di·rec·tion /di rékshən, dī-/ *n.* **1.** MANAGEMENT the management or control of somebody or something by providing instructions **2.** WAY the way in which somebody or something goes, points, or faces ○ *They shook hands and walked off in opposite directions.* **3.** SUPERVISION OF SOMETHING the control and supervision of a group, person, or organization **4.** DEVELOPMENT the way in which something develops ○ *The organization has begun to take a new direction.* **5.** ARTS ART OF DIRECTING the art or practice of directing a movie or play **6.** SENSE OF PURPOSE a feeling of having a definite goal or purpose ○ *He's a nice boy, but seems to lack a sense of direction.* **7.** MUSIC INSTRUCTION IN MUSIC an instruction in a piece of music that shows how it should be played **8.** MUSIC CONDUCTING PERFORMERS the process of conducting an orchestra or choir ■ **di·rec·tions** *npl.* INSTRUCTIONS instructions on how to get to a place or how to do something ○ *I need to stop the car and ask for directions.*

di·rec·tion·al /di rékshən'l, dī-/ *adj.* **1.** RELATING TO DIRECTION showing, concerned with, or dependent on direction ○ *Use your directional lights to indicate the way you plan to turn.* **2.** ELECTRON ENG MORE EFFICIENT IN ONE DIRECTION more efficient in a specific direction for transmitting and receiving sound waves, nuclear particles, light, or radio waves **3.** RELATING TO CONTROL OF SOMETHING showing or relating to the management or control of somebody's work, behavior, or way of thinking **4.** INDICATING TREND showing the future direction in which something might go —**di·rec·tion·al·i·ty** /di rèkshə nálləte, dī-/ *n.*

di·rec·tion·al an·ten·na *n.* an antenna in which the transmitting and receiving characteristics are concentrated in certain directions, used when transmitting or receiving over very long distances, e.g., when receiving signals from space

di·rec·tion·al drill·ing *n.* a method of drilling for oil or gas in which special assemblies are used to turn a drill hole in the required direction

di·rec·tion find·er *n.* a device used especially in navigation to determine the direction of a transmitted radio signal —**di·rec·tion find·ing** *n.*

di·rec·tive /di réktiv, dī-/ *n.* ORDER an order or official instruction ■ *adj.* **1.** PROVIDING GUIDANCE giving explicit guidance or instructions ○ *directive utterances* **2.** SHOWING DIRECTION indicating a direction ○ *directive signals*

di·rect la·bor *n.* labor that is directly involved in the production of goods or the provision of services rather than, e.g., in administration or sales

di·rect light·ing *n.* a method of lighting in which a large percentage, usually not less than 90 percent, of the emitted light is directed downward

di·rect·ly /di réktlee, dī-/ *adv.* **1.** STRAIGHT straight to a place or a person, or straight in a direction ○ *She went directly to the filing cabinet.* ○ *Your letter was sent directly to me.* **2.** WITH NOTHING IN BETWEEN without any person, thing, or event intervening ○ *I prefer to deal directly with senior management.* ○ *I hold you directly responsible for what has happened.* **3.** COMPLETELY in every respect ○ *I am directly opposed to everything that they stand for.* **4.** CLEARLY in a clear and unambiguous manner ○ *She refuses to say directly what the trouble is.* **5.** IMMEDIATELY at once (*formal*) ○ *I'll deal with it directly.* **6.** SOON in a short while (*regional*) ○ *Please take a seat, and I'll be with you directly.*

di·rect mail *n.* the use of mail addressed to potential customers as a way of advertising, or the promotional material that is mailed —**di·rect mail·er** *n.*

di·rect mar·ket·ing, **di·rect sell·ing** *n.* methods of marketing by which a company deals directly with its end customers, including mail order by catalog, direct mail, telephone sales, or the advertising of goods

di·rect ob·ject *n.* the word or phrase in a sentence that indicates somebody or something directly affected by the action of the verb, such as "cat" in "she fed the cat"

di·rec·tor /di réktər, dī-/ *n.* **1.** BUSINESS HEAD OF MANAGEMENT somebody who is at the head of an organized group, such as a government department, or in charge of a program of activity, e.g., in social services **2.** BUSINESS SOMEBODY WHO RUNS A COMPANY a member of the board that controls the affairs of a company. A board may be made up of executive directors, who manage the company, and nonexecutive directors, who contribute advice. **3.** CINEMA, TV FILMMAKER somebody who has control over, and responsibility for, the actual making of a movie or television program, and its artistic and technical content **4.** MUSIC MUSICAL CONDUCTOR somebody who is responsible for the work of a group of musicians, especially the conductor of an orchestra [15thC. From Anglo-Norman *directour*, from, ultimately, Latin *direct-*, past participle stem of *dirigere* (see DIRECT).] —**di·rec·to·ri·al** /di rèk táwree əl, dī-/ *adj.* —**di·rec·to·ri·al·ly** *adv.* —**di·rec·tor·ship** /di réktər ship, dī-/ *n.*

di·rec·tor·ate /di réktərət, dī-/ *n.* a board of directors, e.g., of a company

di·rec·tor's chair *n.* **1.** CHAIR FOR MOVIE DIRECTOR the chair used by the director on the set of a movie **2.** FOLDING CHAIR a light folding chair with a wooden or metal frame with arms, and a canvas back and seat

di·rec·to·ry /di réktəree, dī-/ *n.* (*plural* **-ries**) **1.** BOOK OF NAMES a book containing the names of people and organizations, usually with telephone numbers, addresses, and other information about them, arranged alphabetically for reference **2.** LIST OF TENANTS a listing in the lobby of a building of the building's tenants and their floor or room numbers **3.** COMPUT INDEX OF COMPUTER FILES an index of files stored on a computer disk. A disk may have many separate directories containing different types of files. **4.** RULE BOOK a book of rules or instructions ■ *adj.* GIVING DIRECTION providing direction or advice

di·rec·to·ry as·sis·tance *n.* = **information**

di·rect pri·mar·y *n.* a primary election in which the candidates who will seek office as nominees of a political party are chosen directly by popular vote

di·rect ques·tion *n.* **1.** QUESTION THAT MUST BE ANSWERED a question directed to a specific person and requiring a response **2.** GRAM QUESTION IN DIRECT SPEECH a question repeated in the exact words that were spoken, placed inside quotation marks in writing

di·rect-read·ing *adj.* allowing the immediate reading of a measurement, without intervening calculations

di·rec·trix /di réktriks, dī-/ (*plural* **-trix·es** *or* **-tri·ces** /di réktri sèez, dī rek trī-/) *n.* a fixed line used in constructing a curve or conic section, the distance from the line divided by the distance from a fixed point being identical for all points on the figure [Early 16thC. From medieval Latin, feminine form of late Latin *director*, from Latin *direct-*, past participle stem of *dirigere* (see DIRECT).]

di·rect sell·ing *n.* = **direct marketing**

di·rect speech *n. U.K.* = **direct discourse**

di·rect tax *n.* a tax that is levied directly on the income or capital of a person or organization rather than as part of the price of goods or services

dire·ful /dírf'l/ *adj.* being extremely threatening or ominous (*archaic*) —**dire·ful·ly** *adv.* —**dire·ful·ness** *n.*

dire straits *npl.* a situation of emergency or desperate need

dire wolf *n.* a large extinct mammal similar to a wolf, found in North America during the Pleistocene Epoch. Latin name: *Canis dirus.* [*Dire*, a translation of *(Canis) dirus*, Latin name]

dirge /durj/ *n.* **1.** FUNERAL HYMN a song of mourning or lament, especially one about death or intended for a funeral **2.** MOURNFUL MUSIC a song or piece of music that sounds sad or depressing **3.** FUNERAL SERVICE a funeral service that is sung [Early 15thC. From Latin *dirige* (first word of the antiphon in the funeral service, Psalm 5:8), imperative singular of *dirigere* "to guide" (see DIRECT).]

dir·ham /də rám, dər hám/ *n.* **1.** CURRENCY UNIT IN MOROCCO AND U.A.E. a basic unit of currency in Morocco and the United Arab Emirates and a minor unit of currency in Libya. See table at **currency** **2.** BILL WORTH A DIRHAM a bill worth a dirham **3.** COIN WORTH A DIRHAM a coin worth a dirham, 100 of which are worth a riyal in Qatar and 1000 of which are worth a dinar in Libya [Late 18thC. From Arabic, from Greek *drachmē*, literally "number of coins one hand can hold."]

dir·i·gi·ble /dírrijəb'l, di ríjjəb'l/ *n.* AIR = **airship** ■ *adj.* STEERABLE able to be steered or navigated [Late 16thC. From Latin *dirigere* "to direct, guide" (see DIRECT) + -IBLE; from the fact that an airship (in contrast to a balloon) can be steered.] —**dir·i·gi·bil·i·ty** /dìrrəjə bíllətee, di rìjjə bíllətee/ *n.*

di·ri·gis·me /dìrri zhéezmə/ *n.* full and direct government control of a country's economy and social institutions [Mid-20thC. From French, where it was formed from *diriger* "to direct," from Latin *dirigere* (see DIRECT).] —**di·ri·giste** /dìrri zhéest/ *adj.*

dirk /durk/ *n.* DAGGER a dagger with a long straight blade, especially one that was formerly used by Scottish Highlanders ■ *vt.* (**dirked, dirk·ing, dirks**) STAB to stab somebody with a dagger [Mid-16thC. Origin unknown.]

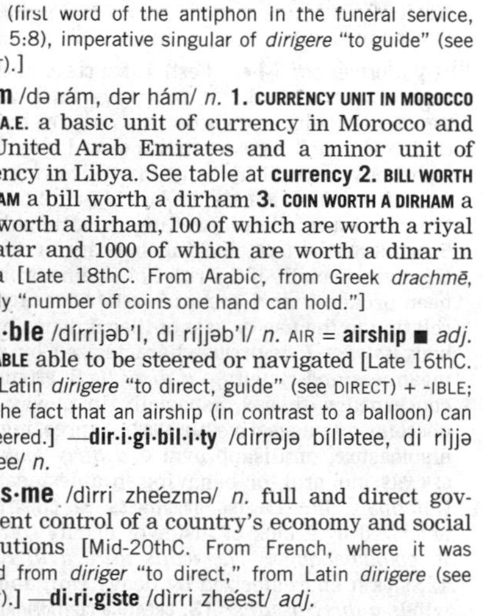

Dirndl

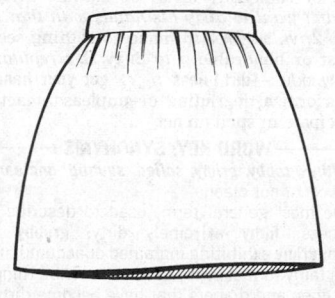

dirn·dl /dúrnd'l/ *n.* **1.** **dirn·dl, dirn·dl skirt** FULL SKIRT a full skirt that is gathered at the waist **2.** TRADITIONAL DRESS a dress with a full gathered skirt and a tight, low bodice that is worn over a short-sleeved blouse and is part of German and Austrian national costume [Mid-20thC. From German *Dirndlkleid* "dirndl dress": *Dirndl* from German dialect, literally "little girl," from *Dirne* "maid."]

dirt /durt/ *n.* **1. UNCLEAN SUBSTANCE** a substance that spoils the cleanness of somebody or something ○ *There was a smear of dirt on his shirt.* **2. EARTH** earth, soil, or mud ○ *Children were playing in the dirt by the side of the road.* **3. HARD-PACKED EARTH** earth packed down to make a firm surface, especially to form a road, track, or path ○ *We live on a dirt road.* **4. SCANDALOUS FACTS** scandalous or damaging facts about somebody ○ *The local paper may have some dirt on the candidates.* **5. CORRUPTING INFLUENCE** something such as pornography or foul language that is considered to have a corrupting influence [13thC. By transposition of *r* and *i* from Old Norse *drit* "excrement," from prehistoric Germanic.] —**dirt·i·ly** *adv.* —**dirt·i·ness** *n.* ◇ **dig the dirt on somebody** *or* **something** to search for scandalous information about somebody or something in order to reveal it

dirt bike *n.* a motorcycle designed to be ridden across country or on dirt roads

dirt-cheap *adj., adv.* extremely cheap or cheaply (*informal*)

dirt daub·er *n.* = **potter wasp**

WORD KEY: REGIONAL NOTE

With scattered instances in the Midwest, ***dirt dauber*** prevails across the entire South, and across Oklahoma and Texas. The potter wasp is also called *mud dauber* and *mud wasp*.

dirt farm·er *n.* a farmer with a little land who farms it alone or with family help —**dirt farm·ing** *n.*

dirt-poor *adj.* having so little money that the basic needs of life can scarcely be satisfied

dirt track *n.* **1. UNSURFACED TRACK** a road or path that is not surfaced, but consists of earth **2. RACE TRACK** a track of earth mixed with gravel and cinders that is used for horse racing or motorcycle racing

dirt·y /dúrtee/ *adj.* (**-i·er, -i·est**) **1. NOT CLEAN** marked by dirt or covered in dirt ○ *dirty fingernails* **2. CAUSING DIRT** creating dirt or pollution ○ *a battered truck with a dirty engine* **3. MAKING SOMEBODY GRIMY** likely to cause somebody to be filthy or grimy ○ *Working on cars is a dirty job.* **4. NOT KEPT UP** lacking care and maintenance, especially of dwellings in a neighborhood **5. NOT HONEST OR LEGAL** lacking honesty or moral integrity, especially if the rules of a game or law have been broken ○ *dirty tactics* **6. RELATING TO ILLEGAL DRUGS** relating to the use or sale of illegal drugs by somebody (*slang*) **7. MALICIOUS** characterized by extreme meanness and cruelty ○ *a dirty lie* **8. RELATING TO SEX** concerned with sex, especially in a way that is obscene or suggestive **9. ANGRY** expressing anger, displeasure, or disapproval ○ *a dirty look* **10. DESPICABLE** immoral, or behaving in a despicable way (*informal*) **11. LACKING BRIGHTNESS OR CLARITY** characterized by a lack of luster or clarity (*often used in combination*) ○ *The walls were a dirty green.* **12. STORMY** characterized by heavy rain and strong winds ○ *dirty weather* **13. CREATING CONTAMINATION** producing a lot of radioactive contamination ■ *adv.* (**-i·er, -i·est**) **1. UNFAIRLY** in an unfair or dishonest way ○ *You have to fight dirty if you want to win.* **2. SUGGESTIVELY** in a sexually suggestive or indecent way ■ *v.* (**-ied, -y·ing, -ies**) **1.** *vti.* **MAKE DIRTY** to make something or somebody dirty, or become dirty ○ *He wouldn't want to dirty his hands with that kind of work.* **2.** *vt.* **DISHONOR** to make something seem less honest or honorable ○ *to dirty sb's reputation* —**dirt·i·ly** *adv.* —**dirt·i·ness** *n.* ◇ **get your hands dirty** to perform a degrading or unpleasant act, or to participate in such an act

WORD KEY: SYNONYMS

dirty, filthy, grubby, grimy, soiled, squalid, unclean

CORE MEANING: not clean

dirty the most general term, used to describe lack of cleanliness; **filthy** extremely dirty; **grubby** slightly unclean; **grimy** exhibiting ingrained or accumulated dirt; **soiled** a fairly formal term, used to describe things such as bed linen and diapers that have become dirty in the course of normal use; **squalid** a term used to describe extremely dirty houses and living areas, usually with a suggestion of poor conditions; **unclean** a fairly formal term, frequently used in a moral or religious context.

WORD KEY: CULTURAL NOTE

Dirty Harry, a movie by Don Siegel (1971), is the story of San Francisco policeman Harry Callahan (Clint Eastwood), known as "Dirty" because he always gets the worst jobs, and his attempts to apprehend a serial killer, Scorpio. This and subsequent movies centering on the Callahan character resulted in *Dirty Harry* being used as an adjective meaning police who use unnecessary force, as in *Dirty Harry syndrome.* Famous lines spoken by the Callahan character also made their way into mainstream U.S. English. An example is "Go ahead, make my day!" from *Sudden Impact* (1983).

dirt·y dog *n.* somebody who takes advantage of other people in small, dishonest or unpleasant ways (*dated*)

dir·ty drug *n.* a drug used in treating a psychiatric condition that has effects on the functions of the brain that are not entirely understood by scientists (*informal*)

dirt·y lin·en, **dirt·y laun·dry** *n.* personal matters that it would be embarrassing or disadvantageous to let other people know about ○ *Don't wash your dirty linen in public.*

dirt·y old man *n.* an older man who shows an interest in sex that is perceived as immoral, perverted, or generally unpleasant (*informal insult*)

dirt·y pool *n.* unfair or dishonest tactics used to gain an advantage (*informal*)

dirt·y trick *n.* **UNFAIR ACTION** something unfair or dishonest that is done to gain an advantage ■ **dirt·y tricks** *npl.* **1. UNFAIR POLITICAL TACTICS** tactics used in a political campaign to discredit an opponent in a way that is not completely fair or honest **2. SPY TACTICS** secret activities carried out by the spies of one government in order to disrupt or destroy the internal functioning of another nation (*informal*) **3. COMMERCIAL ESPIONAGE** the activity of stealing secret products or processes from one company and selling them to rival companies (*informal*)

dirt·y trick·ster *n.* somebody who helps a politician by finding or using unfair or dishonest ways to discredit an opponent ○ *The dirty tricksters on both sides have overreached themselves this time.*

dirt·y word *n.* **1. OFFENSIVE WORD** a swearword or offensive word **2. UNPOPULAR THING** something that is disapproved of ○ *Delay seems to be a dirty word in this office!*

dirt·y work *n.* something that somebody wants to be done that is unpleasant, unfair, unkind, dishonest, or illegal

dis /diss/ (**dissed, diss·ing, diss·es**), **diss** *vt.* (*slang*) **1. TREAT DISRESPECTFULLY** to treat somebody without respect, e.g., by talking back to somebody in authority, or by being purposely rude or inconsiderate ○ *Don't you dis me!* ○ *Don't be dissing me!* **2. CRITICIZE** to criticize somebody or something [Late 20thC. Origin uncertain: perhaps a shortening of DISRESPECT.]

Dis /diss/ *n.* in Roman mythology, the underworld, or region of the dead. Greek equivalent **Hades**

dis- *prefix.* **1.** to undo, do the opposite ○ *disapprove* **2.** opposite or absence of ○ *discourtesy* **3.** to deprive of, remove from ○ *dishonor* **4.** not ○ *disobedient* **5.** to free from ○ *disburden* **6.** completely ○ *dissever* [Directly and via Old French *des-* from Latin *dis-*, from *dis* "apart," of unknown origin]

dis·a·bil·i·ty /dìssə bíllətee/ (*plural* **-ties**) *n.* **1. RESTRICTED CAPABILITY TO PERFORM PARTICULAR ACTIVITIES** an inability to perform some or all of the tasks of daily life **2. MEDICAL CONDITION RESTRICTING ACTIVITIES** a medically diagnosed condition that makes it difficult to engage in the activities of daily life **3. PAYMENT TO PERSON WITH INABILITY** a sum of money paid to somebody, usually on a monthly basis, by a government agency or insurance company because he or she is unable to work **4. LEGAL DISQUALIFIER** something that causes somebody to be regarded in law as ineligible to perform a particular transaction

dis·a·bil·i·ty clause *n.* a clause in a life insurance policy, indicating the conditions that will apply if the holder becomes unable to work, including release from payment of further premiums

dis·a·ble /di sáyb'l/ (**-bled, -bling, -bles**) *vt.* **1. RESTRICT IN CERTAIN ACTIVITIES** to make somebody unable to perform the activities needed to earn a living or to carry out the basic tasks of daily life without difficulty **2. STOP FROM WORKING** to prevent a machine, weapon, system, or device from working by disconnecting a part of it **3. DISQUALIFY LEGALLY** to make somebody ineligible in law to perform a particular transaction —**dis·a·ble·ment** *n.*

dis·a·bled /di sáyb'ld/ *adj.* **1. UNABLE TO PERFOM PARTICULAR ACTIVITIES** used to describe somebody with a condition that makes it difficult to perform some or all the basic tasks of daily life **2. UNABLE TO OPERATE** incapable of performing or functioning ■ *n.* **DISABLED PEOPLE** people who are disabled

disabled list *n.* a list of the players of a particular sports team who are unable to play because of an injury

dis·a·buse /dìssə byóoz/ (**-bused, -bus·ing, -bus·es**) *vt.* to tell somebody or make somebody realize that an idea is not true ○ *I was quickly disabused of my idealistic notions about the campaign.* ○ *She disabused him of many old prejudices.* [Early 17thC. Formed from ABUSE in the obsolete sense "a delusion."] —**dis·a·bus·al** *n.*

di·sac·cha·ride /dī sákə rīd/ *n.* a sugar formed from two single sugar molecules, e.g., the disaccharide sucrose, which is composed of glucose and fructose. Lactose and maltose are also disaccharides.

dis·ac·cord /dìssə káwrd/ *n.* **DISAGREEMENT** lack of harmony or agreement (*formal*) ■ *vi.* (**-cord·ed, -cord·ing, -cords**) **NOT AGREE** to disagree or not be in accordance with one another (*formal*)

dis·ac·cred·it /dìssə kréddit/ (**-it·ed, -it·ing, -its**) *vt.* to take away somebody's authorization or credentials

dis·ac·cus·tom /dìssə kústəm/ (**-tomed, -tom·ing, -toms**) *vt.* to make somebody break a habit, or to make somebody become unused to something that was familiar (*formal*)

dis·ad·van·tage /dìssəd vántij/ *n.* **1. BAD THING** something that makes a situation worse, or that makes somebody or something less effective or desirable **2. BAD SITUATION** a situation in which somebody is weaker or less effective in relation to other people **3. LOSS** injury, loss, or damage (*formal*) ■ *vt.* (**-taged, -tag·ing, -tag·es**) **COUNT AGAINST** to put somebody or something at a disadvantage

dis·ad·van·taged /dìssəd vántijd/ *adj.* **1. BADLY OFF** in a worse position than somone else or other people **2. LACKING COMPETITIVE ABILITY** unable to perform well in a competitive or military endeavor

dis·ad·van·ta·geous /diss àdvən táyjəss, dìss advən táyjəss/ *adj.* not helpful or favorable —**dis·ad·van·ta·geous·ly** *adv.* —**dis·ad·van·ta·geous·ness** *n.*

dis·af·fect /dìssə fékt/ (**-fect·ed, -fect·ing, -fects**) *vt.* to make somebody dissatisfied with somebody or something, especially somebody to whom respect or loyalty is owed —**dis·af·fect·ed** *adj.* —**dis·af·fect·ed·ly** *adv.* —**dis·af·fect·ed·ness** *n.* —**dis·af·fec·tion** *n.*

dis·af·fil·i·ate /dìssə fíllee àyt/ (**-at·ed, -at·ing, -ates**) *vti.* to end the connection or affiliation of one group with another, or to withdraw a personal association from a group or organization formally ○ *The group was formally disaffiliated from its parent body at the end of 1985.* —**dis·af·fil·i·a·tion** /dìssə fillee áysh'n/ *n.*

dis·af·firm /dìssə fúrm/ (**-firmed, -firm·ing, -firms**) *vt.* **1. DENY OR CONTRADICT** to say that something is not true or that the opposite is true (*formal*) **2. CHANGE DECISION** to alter a legal decision or to refuse to recognize or acknowledge something formally —**dis·af·fir·mance** *n.* —**dis·af·fir·ma·tion** /diss àffər máysh'n/ *n.*

dis·ag·gre·gate /diss ággrə gàyt/ (**-gat·ed, -gat·ing, -gates**) *vti.* to separate something into its component parts or to break apart —**dis·ag·gre·ga·tion** /diss àggrə gáysh'n/ *n.*

dis·a·gree /dìssə grée/ (**-greed, -gree·ing, -grees**) *v.* **1.** *vt.* **NOT AGREE** to have or put forward a different view or opinion from somebody or from each other **2.** *vi.* **NOT MATCH** to fail to be in accordance with something, or to show a different result **3.** *vi.* **AFFECT BADLY** to have an unpleasant effect on somebody ○ *I love oysters, but they disagree with me.* [15thC. From French *desagréer*, from *agréer* "to agree."]

WORD KEY: SYNONYMS

disagree, differ, argue, dispute, take issue with, contradict, agree to differ, be at odds

CORE MEANING: to have or express a difference of opinion with somebody

disagree the most general and wide-ranging term; **differ**

a somewhat more formal term for *disagree;* **argue** to give reasons for or against something, usually in opposition to somebody else; **dispute** to debate something, often suggesting a heated argument; **take issue with** to disagree strongly with somebody or something; **contradict** to make a statement that shows or suggests that something somebody has just said is wrong; **agree to differ** to stop arguing and accept that the opposing viewpoints are irreconcilable; **be at odds** a term used to refer to people who are disagreeing or arguing with each other, especially over a period of time or about a particular issue.

dis·a·gree·a·ble /dìssə greé əb'l/ *adj.* **1.** UNPLEASANT causing feelings that are not enjoyable **2.** RUDE OR QUARRELSOME lacking courtesy or constantly finding a reason to disagree with somebody —**dis·a·gree·a·bil·i·ty** /dìssə gree ə bíllətee/ *n.* —**dis·a·gree·a·ble·ness** /dìssə greé əb'lnəss/ *n.* —**dis·a·gree·a·bly** *adv.*

dis·a·gree·ment /dìssə greémənt/ *n.* **1.** FAILURE TO AGREE ABOUT SOMETHING the fact of having or expressing a different opinion and failing to agree about something **2.** SLIGHT ARGUMENT a situation in which a number of people or groups argue **3.** DIFFERENCE failure to be in accordance with something

dis·al·low /dìssə lów/ (**-lowed, -low·ing, -lows**) *vt.* **1.** REJECT to refuse to accept something because it is not true, valid, or correctly done (*formal*) **2.** CANCEL SOMETHING PREVIOUSLY ALLOWED to cancel a privilege or entitlement, or refuse to allow something that was previously allowed —**dis·al·low·a·ble** *adj.* —**dis·al·low·ance** *n.*

dis·am·big·u·ate /dìss am bíggyoo àyt/ (**-at·ed, -at·ing, -ates**) *vt.* to establish the true meaning of an expression, regulation, or ruling that is confusing or that could be interpreted in more than one way —**dis·am·big·u·a·tion** /dìss am biggyoo áysh'n/ *n.*

dis·an·nul /dìssə núl/ (**-nulled, -null·ing, -nuls**) *vt.* to annul or cancel a law, rule, or privilege [15thC. Formed from DIS- in the sense "completely" + ANNUL.] —**dis·an·nul·ment** *n.*

dis·ap·pear /dìssə peér/ (**-peared, -pear·ing, -pears**) *v.* **1.** *vi.* VANISH FROM SIGHT to cease to be seen, e.g., by moving away, or going behind or into something **2.** *vi.* NOT BE FOUND to be gone from or no longer be seen in a place without any explanation **3.** *vi.* CEASE TO EXIST to no longer exist **4.** *vt.* CAUSE OPPONENT TO DISAPPEAR to make a political opponent disappear by arresting or killing the person without any process of law —**dis·ap·pear·ance** *n.*

dis·ap·peared /dìssə peérd/ *npl.* people who have been arrested by a regime that they opposed and whose fate is not known [Late 20thC. Translation of the Spanish past participle *desaparecido.* Originally "those who disappeared" in Argentina during the military dictatorship (1976–83).]

dis·ap·point /dìssə póynt/ (**-point·ed, -point·ing, -points**) *v.* **1.** *vi.* BE NOT GOOD ENOUGH to be not as good, attractive, or satisfactory as was hoped or expected **2.** *vt.* FAIL SOMEBODY to let somebody down by not doing something, or by something not happening as hoped or expected [15thC. From French *désappointer,* literally "to deprive of an appointment."]

dis·ap·point·ed /dìssə póyntəd/ *adj.* unhappy because something was not as good, attractive, or satisfactory as expected, or because something hoped for or expected did not happen —**dis·ap·point·ed·ly** *adv.*

dis·ap·point·ing /dìssə póynting/ *adj.* not as good, attractive, or satisfactory as was expected or hoped —**dis·ap·point·ing·ly** *adv.*

dis·ap·point·ment /dìssə póyntmənt/ *n.* **1.** FEELING OF BEING LET DOWN a feeling of sadness or frustration because something was not as good, attractive, or satisfactory as expected, or because something hoped for did not happen **2.** SOMETHING DISAPPOINTING something or somebody that disappoints somebody, or an occasion when somebody is disappointed **3.** FRUSTRATION the failure to attain somebody's hopes or wishes

dis·ap·pro·ba·tion /diss àpprə báysh'n/ *n.* the expression of moral or social disapproval (*formal*)

dis·ap·prov·al /dìssə proóv'l/ *n.* dislike or condemnation of somebody or something immoral or bad in some way

dis·ap·prove /dìssə proóv/ (**-proved, -prov·ing, -proves**) *v.* **1.** *vi.* NOT APPROVE to dislike, look down on, or condemn somebody or something as being immoral or bad in some way **2.** *vt.* REFUSE TO SANCTION to refuse to give approval or agree to something (*formal*) —**dis·ap·prov·ing** *adj.* —**dis·ap·prov·ing·ly** *adv.*

WORD KEY: SYNONYMS

disapprove, frown on, object to, criticize, condemn, deplore, denounce, censure

CORE MEANING: to have an unfavorable opinion of something or somebody

disapprove a general term meaning to judge something negatively based on personal standards; **frown on** a term indicating mild disapproval; **object to** a somewhat stronger term, usually implying verbal expression of disapproval; **criticize** to identify specific flaws or faults in something; **condemn** to express very strong disapproval of something, usually publicly; **deplore** a fairly formal term expressing strong disapproval, often for moral reasons; **denounce** to issue a strong public criticism of somebody or something, usually formally or for the record; **censure** to condemn somebody or something strongly and publicly.

dis·arm /diss aárm/ (**-armed, -arm·ing, -arms**) *v.* **1.** *vti.* MIL GIVE UP WEAPONS to give up a supply of weapons or reduce the strength of armed forces, or to force another nation to do this **2.** *vt.* MIL DEFUSE BOMB to make a bomb unable to explode, or to make a weapon incapable of being fired **3.** *vt.* WIN OVER to make somebody less hostile or suspicious and more inclined to act in a friendly way ○ *They disarmed us with their confidence and skill.* —**dis·arm·er** *n.*

dis·ar·ma·ment /diss aárməmənt/ *n.* **1.** REDUCTION IN ARMS the process of reducing a nation's supply of weapons or the strength of its armed forces ○ *a believer in negotiated mutual disarmament* **2.** GIVING UP ARMS the condition of having given up weapons ○ *Disarmament brought peace to the troubled region.* [Late 18thC. Modeled on French *désarmement.*]

dis·arm·ing /diss aárming/ *adj.* making somebody feel more friendly or trusting —**dis·arm·ing·ly** *adv.*

dis·ar·range /dìssə ráynj/ (**-ranged, -rang·ing, -rang·es**) *vt.* to disturb or spoil the order or arrangement of something —**dis·ar·range·ment** *n.*

dis·ar·ray /dìssə ráy/ *n.* **1.** DISORGANIZED STATE a disorganized and confused state ○ *The meeting was thrown into disarray by the surprise announcement.* **2.** UNTIDINESS a state of untidiness, especially in dress ■ *vt.* (**-rayed, -ray·ing, -rays**) **1.** MAKE DISORGANIZED to make something confused and disorganized **2.** UNDRESS to remove somebody's clothes (*archaic*) [14thC. Probably modeled on Old French *disareer* "to put in disorder."]

dis·ar·tic·u·late /diss aar tíkyə làyt/ (**-lat·ed, -lat·ing, -lates**) *vti.* to separate something at the joints, or to become separated at the joints —**dis·ar·tic·u·la·tion** /diss aar tikyə láysh'n/ *n.* —**dis·ar·tic·u·la·tor** /diss aar tikyə làytər/ *n.*

dis·as·sem·ble /dìssə sémb'l/ (**-bled, -bling, -bles**) *vt.* to take something apart, e.g., a piece of machinery —**dis·as·sem·bly** *n.*

dis·as·so·ci·ate /dìssə sṓshee àyt/ (**-at·ed, -at·ing, -ates**) *vt.* **1.** END ASSOCIATION WITH to end an association or relationship with another person or group ○ *She had disassociated herself from that clique years ago.* **2.** DISTANCE SELF to deny any connection or involvement with somebody or something ○ *In a press conference, the spokesperson attempted to disassociate himself from the scandal*

dis·as·so·ci·a·tion /dìssə sōshee áysh'n/ *n.* **1.** ENDING OF RELATIONSHIP the termination of an association or relationship with another person or group **2.** DISTANCING OF SELF the denial of any connection or involvement with somebody or something else

dis·as·ter /di zástər/ *n.* **1.** DAMAGING OR DESTRUCTIVE EVENT an event that causes serious loss, destruction, hardship, unhappiness, or death **2.** SOMEBODY OR SOMETHING UNSUCCESSFUL somebody or something that fails completely, especially in a way that is distressing, embarrassing, or laughable (*informal*) [Late 16thC. Via French *désastre* from Italian *disastro,* literally "ill-starred," from Latin *astrum* "star," from Greek *astron* (source of English *astronomy*).]

dis·as·ter ar·e·a *n.* **1.** PLACE NEEDING GOVERNMENT ASSISTANCE a place that is officially declared to be in a state of emergency and in need of special assistance such as federal relief money after a natural disaster ○ *The southern half of the state has been declared a disaster area.* **2.** MESS a very messy or disorganized place or situation (*informal*)

dis·as·ter mov·ie *n.* a movie that deals with a disaster such as an earthquake or plane crash in a dramatic and spectacular way

dis·as·trous /di zástrəss/ *adj.* **1.** CALAMITOUS having seriously damaging results **2.** COMPLETELY UNSUCCESSFUL performed in an incompetent or awkward way [Late 16thC. Via French *désastreux* from, ultimately, Italian *disastro* (see DISASTER).] —**dis·as·trous·ly** *adv.* —**dis·as·trous·ness** *n.*

dis·a·vow /dìssə vów/ (**-vowed, -vow·ing, -vows**) *vt.* to deny any knowledge of or responsibility for something, or any association with somebody or something (*formal*) —**dis·a·vow·a·ble** *adj.* —**dis·a·vow·al** *n.* —**dis·a·vow·ed·ly** /dìssə vówədlee/ *adv.* —**dis·a·vow·er** /dìssə vówr/ *n.*

dis·band /diss bánd/ (**-band·ed, -band·ing, -bands**) *vti.* to break up as a group or organization, or to cause a group or organization to break up —**dis·band·ment** *n.*

dis·bar /diss baár/ (**-barred, -bar·ring, -bars**) *vt.* to take away officially the right of an attorney to practice law [Mid-17thC. Literally "to remove from the bar," formed from BAR.] —**dis·bar·ment** *n.*

dis·be·lief /dìss bi leéf/ *n.* the feeling of not believing or of not being able to believe somebody or something

dis·be·lieve /dìss bi leév/ (**-lieved, -liev·ing, -lieves**) *v.* **1.** *vt.* NOT BELIEVE to think that something somebody has said is untrue **2.** *vi.* HAVE NO FAITH to have no belief in something, especially in God or religion —**dis·be·liev·er** *n.* —**dis·be·liev·ing** *adj.* —**dis·be·liev·ing·ly** *adv.*

dis·bud /diss búd/ (**-bud·ded, -bud·ding, -buds**) *vt.* **1.** GARDENING REMOVE BUDS to remove buds or shoots from a plant so that the remaining ones will be larger and stronger **2.** AGRIC REMOVE ANIMAL'S HORNS to remove the horns from a young animal, especially from cattle

dis·bur·den /diss búrd'n/ (**-dened, -den·ing, -dens**) *v.* **1.** *vt.* SHARE TROUBLES WITH SOMEBODY to gain relief by telling somebody about something that is causing anxiety or guilt **2.** *vt.* TAKE OFF A LOAD to relieve a person or animal of a load **3.** *vti.* UNLOAD to unload goods or luggage (*archaic*) —**dis·bur·den·ment** *n.*

dis·burse /diss búrs/ (**-bursed, -burs·ing, -burs·es**) *vt.* to pay out money, especially from a fund [Mid-16thC. From Old French *desbourser,* literally "to remove from the purse," from *bourse* "purse."] —**dis·burs·a·ble** *adj.* —**dis·burse·ment** *n.* —**dis·burs·er** *n.*

disc *n.* **1.** U.K. = **disk 2.** record

disc. *abbr.* **1.** discount **2.** discovered

disc- *prefix.* = **disco-** (*used before vowels*)

dis·calced /diss kálst/ *adj.* wearing sandals or going barefoot as part of the rules of some orders of monks, friars, or nuns [Mid-17thC. Shortening of obsolete *discalceated,* literally "with shoes removed," ultimately from Latin *calceare* "to shoe," from *calceus* "shoe."]

dis·cant /díss kànt/ *n., vi.* (**-cant·ed, -cant·ing, -cants**) MUSIC = **descant** —**dis·cant·er** *n.*

dis·card *v.* /diss kaárd/ (**-card·ed, -card·ing, -cards**) **1.** *vt.* THROW AWAY to get rid of something that is not wanted or needed **2.** *vt.* CARDS REJECT CARD to put down a card from a hand and not play it **3.** *vti.* CARDS PLAY CARD to play a card so that it has no value, because it is neither in the required suit nor a trump ■ *n.* /díss kaàrd/ **1.** CARDS ACT OF DISCARDING the act of discarding a card **2.** SOMETHING DISCARDED somebody or something that has been discarded [Mid-18thC. Literally "to throw out a card (from a hand)," formed from CARD; hence "to cast aside."] —**dis·card·a·ble** *adj.* —**dis·card·er** *n.*

dis·car·nate /diss kaárnət, diss kaár nàyt/ *adj.* RELIG lacking a physical body [Mid-17thC. Coined from DIS- + the Latin stem *carn-* "flesh" + -ATE.]

disc brake, disk brake *n.* a brake that works by the friction of a caliper or pads against a rotating disk

dis·cern /di súrn/ (**-cerned, -cern·ing, -cerns**) *v.* **1.** *vt.* SEE OR NOTICE SOMETHING UNCLEAR to see something that is not very clear or obvious **2.** *vt.* UNDERSTAND to understand something that is not immediately obvious **3.** *vti.* DISTINGUISH to be able to tell the difference between two or more things [14thC. Directly or via French *discerner* from Latin *discernere,* literally "to separate off," from *cernere* "to separate, determine" (source of English *certain*).] —**dis·cern·er** /di súrnər/ *n.*

dis·cern·i·ble /di súrnəb'l/, **dis·cern·a·ble** *adj.* able to be seen, recognized, or understood

dis·cern·i·bly /di súrnəblee/ *adv.* in an obvious way or to a noticeable extent ○ *not discernibly different*

dis·cern·ing /di súrning/ *adj.* showing good judgment and good taste —**dis·cern·ing·ly** *adv.*

dis·cern·ment /di súrnmənt/ *n.* good taste and judgment

dis·charge *v.* /diss chaárj/ (**-charged, -charg·ing, -charg·es**) **1.** *vti.* **EMIT OR DUMP LIQUID OR GAS** to emit, give off, or dispose of a gas or liquid **2.** *vt.* **DISMISS FROM INSTITUTIONAL SETTING** to allow or write the orders for somebody to leave an institution, especially a hospital, or to make the decision yourself to leave such a place after being an inpatient **3.** *vt.* MIL **BE RELEASED FROM ARMED FORCES** to be formally released from service in the armed forces **4.** *vt.* **CARRY OUT** to carry out a duty, responsibility, or promise (*formal*) **5.** *vt.* **FREE OR RELEASE FROM DUTY** to excuse or release somebody from a duty or obligation **6.** *vt.* COMM **FIRE EMPLOYEE** to dismiss somebody from a job (*formal*) **7.** *vt.* FIN **PAY DEBT** to pay a debt in full (*formal*) **8.** *vti.* ARMS **SHOOT OR BE SHOT FROM** to fire a weapon or to be fired from a weapon (*formal*) **9.** *vt.* LAW **RELEASE OR ACQUIT** to release a prisoner or aquit somebody in a court of law **10.** *vt.* LAW **CANCEL COURT ORDER** to cancel or annul a court order **11.** *vti.* FREIGHT, SHIPPING **OFFLOAD SHIP'S CARGO** to unload cargo from a ship **12.** *vti.* ELEC **LOSE ELECTRIC CHARGE** to lose or release electric charge by the addition or loss of electrons from a stationary body, such as in static electricity **13.** *vi.* ELEC **SPARK** to give off electricity suddenly in the form of a spark or arc, such as occurs in the release of stored energy in a capacitator **14.** *vti.* ELEC **DRAIN ELECTRICITY** to drain slowly, or make the electricity in a battery drain slowly **15.** *vt.* ARCHIT **RELEASE PRESSURE ON BUILDING** to release the pressure on part of a building by spreading it over adjacent parts **16.** *vt.* TEXTILES **BLEACH FABRIC** to remove the color from fabric by bleaching it **17.** *vi.* TEXTILES **RUN OR BLUR** to undergo a running or blurring of dyes ■ *n.* /diss chaárj/ **1. DISMISSAL FROM INSTITUTION** permission or orders to leave an institution, especially a hospital, after being a patient **2.** MIL **SEPARATION FROM ARMED FORCES** formal and official release of somebody from the armed forces, or a document certifying this **3.** MED **MUCUS** a flow of fluid from the body, especially an unusual or large flow of mucus from the bodily orifices or pus from a wound **4. EMISSION OF SUBSTANCES** the emission, giving off, or dumping of gases, liquids, or chemicals **5. RATE OF EMISSION** the rate at which a gas or liquid is being emitted **6. PERFORMANCE OF DUTY** the carrying out of a duty, obligation, responsibility, or promise (*formal*) **7.** FIN **DEBT PAYMENT** the payment of a debt (*formal*) **8.** ARMS **FIRING** the firing of a gun (*formal*) **9.** LAW **PRISONER'S RELEASE** the release of a prisoner from custody **10.** ELEC ENG **PRODUCTION OF ELECTRICITY** the process of converting chemical energy into electrical energy, e.g., in a battery **11.** ELEC ENG **CONTINUOUS FLOW OF ELECTRICITY THROUGH AIR** the continuous flow of electric energy through air or a gas as a result of ionization, as occurs when a spark jumps a gap, or at a reduced pressure, as in a fluorescent lamp **12.** FREIGHT **CARGO OFFLOADING** the unloading of cargo **13.** GEOG **VOLUME OF RIVER WATER FLOW** the volume of water in a river flowing past a particular point during a specific time interval [14thC. Via Old French *descharger* from late Latin *discar(r)icare* "to unload," from *car(r)icare* "to load."] —**dis·charge·a·ble** /dis chaárjəb'l/ *adj.* —**dis·charg·er** /diss chaárjər/ *n.*

WORD KEY: SYNONYMS

See Synonyms at ***perform***.

dis·charge lamp *n.* an electric lamp that glows as a result of electricity passing through a gas

dis·charge tube *n.* a tube filled with low-pressure gas that glows when it conducts electricity at a given voltage. Discharge tubes are used in neon and fluorescent lights.

dis·ci plural of **discus**

disci- *prefix.* = **disco-** (*used before vowels*)

dis·ci·ple *n.* **1. FOLLOWER OF PERSON OR IDEA** somebody who strongly believes in the teachings of a leader, a philosophy, or a religion, and tries to act according to them **2. dis·ci·ple, Dis·ci·ple ORIGINAL FOLLOWER OF JESUS** one of the 12 original followers of Jesus Christ, according to the Bible [Pre-12thC. From Latin *discipulus* "learner," from *discere* "to learn." Ultimately from an Indo-European word that is also the ancestor of English *doctrine*.] —**dis·ci·ple·ship** *n.* —**dis·cip·u·lar** /di síppyələr/ *adj.*

Dis·ci·ple *n.* a member of the Disciples of Christ

Dis·ci·ples of Christ *n.* a Protestant denomination of the Christian Church, founded in the United States in 1809 by Thomas and Alexander Campbell. Its congregations regard the Bible as the sole rule of faith and living, and practice baptism by total immersion.

dis·ci·plin·ant /díssəplinənt, di sípplinənt/ *n.* somebody who belonged to a now defunct Spanish Roman Catholic group whose members whipped themselves in public as a religious penance [Early 17thC. Via Spanish *disciplinantes* or Italian *disciplinanti*, both plural, from medieval Latin *disciplinare* "to discipline," from Latin *disciplina* (see DISCIPLINE).]

dis·ci·pli·nar·i·an /dìssəplə náiree ən/ *n.* somebody who insists that rules are obeyed strictly, and who punishes people who break them

dis·ci·pli·nar·y /díssəplə nèrree/ *adj.* **1. RELATING TO ENFORCEMENT AND PUNISHMENT** relating to the enforcing of rules and the punishing of people who break them **2.** EDUC **RELATING TO ACADEMIC SUBJECT** relating to an academic subject ○ *Teachers tried to cut across traditional disciplinary boundaries in their lessons.* —**dis·ci·pli·nar·i·ly** *adv.* —**dis·ci·pli·nar·i·ty** /dìssəplə nérrətee/ *n.*

dis·ci·pli·nar·y bar·racks *n.* MIL a military prison (*formal*)

dis·ci·pline /díssəplin/ *n.* **1. MAKING PEOPLE OBEY RULES** the practice or methods of ensuring that people obey rules by teaching them to do so and punishing them if they do not **2. ORDER AND CONTROL** a controlled orderly state, especially in a class of schoolchildren **3. CALM CONTROLLED BEHAVIOR** the ability to behave in a controlled and calm way even in a difficult or stressful situation **4. CONSCIOUS CONTROL OVER LIFESTYLE** mental self-control used in directing or changing behavior, learning something, or training for something **5.** EDUC **ACTIVITY OR SUBJECT** a subject or field of activity, e.g., an academic subject **6. PUNISHMENT** punishment designed to teach somebody to obey rules **7.** CHR **CHURCH RULES** the system of rules and punishment used in a particular religious denomination ■ *v.* (**-plined, -plin·ing, -plines**) **1.** *vr.* **MAKE YOURSELF DO SOMETHING REGULARLY** to make yourself act or work in a controlled or regular way **2.** *vt.* **PUNISH** to punish somebody because he or she has broken the rules **3.** *vt.* **TEACH OBEDIENCE OR ORDER TO** to teach somebody to obey rules or to behave in an ordered or controlled way [13thC. Directly or via French *descepline* from Latin *disciplina* "instruction given to a disciple," from *discipulus* (see DISCIPLE).] —**dis·ci·plin·a·ble** *adj.* —**dis·ci·pli·nal** /díssəplin'l, di sípplin'l/ *adj.* —**dis·ci·plin·er** /díssəplinər/ *n.*

dis·ci·plined *adj.* showing orderliness and control in the way something is done or somebody behaves ○ *a well disciplined child* ○ *a disciplined organization*

disc jock·ey, disk jock·ey *n.* = **DJ**

dis·claim /diss kláym/ (**-claimed, -claim·ing, -claims**) *v.* **1.** *vt.* **DENY A CONNECTION WITH** to deny that you know about something or that you are responsible for something **2.** *vt.* **DENY VALIDITY OF** to refuse to accept the validity or authority of something **3.** *vti.* **RENOUNCE LEGAL RIGHT** to renounce a legal claim or right to something [15thC. Via Anglo-Norman *disclaimer* from Old French *desclamer*, literally "not to claim," from *clamer* "to claim."] —**dis·cla·ma·tion** /dìsklə máysh'n/ *n.*

dis·claim·er /diss kláymər/ *n.* **1. REFUSAL TO ACCEPT RESPONSIBILITY** a statement refusing to accept responsibility for something, e.g., a written warning stating a possible hazard associated with a product or service and denying legal liability for any injury **2.** LAW **STATEMENT RENOUNCING LEGAL RIGHT** a statement saying that somebody gives up a legal right or claim to something, e.g., damages arising from an accident **3. DENIAL OF KNOWLEDGE** a statement denying knowledge of something

dis·close /diss klṓz/ (**-closed, -clos·ing, -clos·es**) *vt.* **1. TELL SOMETHING PREVIOUSLY SECRET** to reveal something that has been kept a secret **2. SHOW SOMETHING PREVIOUSLY COVERED** to reveal something that has been covered or hidden (*formal*) [15thC. From Old French *desclos-*, present stem of *desclore*, from medieval Latin *disclaudere* "to open," from Latin *claudere* "to close."] —**dis·clos·a·ble** *adj.* —**dis·clos·er** *n.*

dis·clos·ing a·gent *n.* a dye in liquid or tablet form that colors something, especially the teeth to show plaque

dis·clo·sure /diss klṓzhər/ *n.* **1. SECRET INFORMATION MADE PUBLIC** the revealing of information that was previously kept secret, or the information that is revealed **2.** LAW **PROCESS OF SHARING INFORMATION BETWEEN SIDES** in a lawsuit, the legal requirement, or the process of fulfilling it, that each side must provide copies of all documents to the other side before trial. This is done so that there are no surprises. ○ *We discovered her medical history only after disclosure.*

dis·co /dískō/ *n.* **1. dis·co, dis·co·theque CLUB OR PARTY WITH DANCING** a club or party where people dance to recorded pop music, often introduced by a DJ **2. STEADY-BEAT POP MUSIC FOR DANCING** a style of pop music, popular in the 1970s for dancing, with a steady, pronounced beat. It developed from soul music, in response to the growing popularity of discos. **3. STYLE OF DANCING TO DISCO MUSIC** a style of popular dancing designed to accompany the steady repetitive beat of disco music, typified by free and flamboyant swinging movements with the hips and arms ■ *vi.* (**-coed, -co·ing, -cos**) **TAKE PART IN DISCO DANCING** to dance to disco music (*informal*) [Mid-20thC. Shortening of DISCOTHEQUE.]

disco- *prefix.* **1.** disk ○ *discoid* **2.** phonograph record ○ *discography* [Via Latin from, ultimately, Greek *diskos* (see DISK)]

dis·cob·o·lus /diss kóbbələss/ (*plural* **-li** /-ī, -/), **dis·cob·o·los** (*plural* **-li**) *n.* HIST a discus thrower in ancient Greece [Early 18thC. Via Latin from Greek *diskobolos*, literally "disk-throwing," from *diskos* "disk," + *-bolos* "throwing," from *ballein* "to throw."]

dis·cog·ra·phy /diss kóggrəfee/ (*plural* **-phies**) *n.* a list of the recordings made by a performer or a group, or of the recordings of a particular category of music —**dis·cog·ra·pher** *n.* —**dis·co·graph·ic** /dìskə gráffik/ *adj.*

dis·coid /díss kòyd/ *n.* **FLAT ROUND OBJECT** a disk-shaped object or part ■ *adj.* **dis·coid, dis·coi·dal DISC-SHAPED** shaped like a disk [Late 18thC. From Greek *diskoeidēs*, from *diskos* (see DISCUS).] —**dis·coid** *adj.*

dis·col·or /diss kúllər/ (**-ored, -or·ing, -ors**) *vti.* to change, or make something change, from the original or desired color and take on an unpleasant, faded, darkened, or dirty appearance [14thC. Directly or via Old French *descolorer* from medieval Latin *discolorare*, from Latin *colorare* "to color."] —**dis·col·ored** *adj.* —**dis·col·or·ment** *n.*

dis·col·or·a·tion /diss kùllə ráysh'n/ *n.* a change in the original or desired color of something that gives it an unpleasant, faded, darkened, or dirty appearance

dis·com·bob·u·late /dìskəm bóbbyə làyt/ (**-lat·ed, -lat·ing, -lates**) *vt.* to throw somebody into a state of disconcerting confusion (*informal*) (*often passive*) [Mid-19thC. Origin uncertain: probably an alteration of DISCOMPOSE or DISCOMFIT.] —**dis·com·bob·u·la·tion** /dìskəm bobbyə láysh'n/ *n.*

dis·com·fit /diss kúmfit/ (**-fit·ed, -fit·ing, -fits**) *vt.* **1. MAKE UNSETTLED OR CONFUSED** to make somebody feel confused, uneasy, or embarrassed (*formal*) **2. THWART PLANS** to frustrate somebody's plans (*formal*) **3.** MIL **DEFEAT ENEMY** to defeat an enemy in battle (*archaic*) [13thC. From Old French *desconfit*, past participle of *desconfire* "to destroy," literally "not to make," from *confire* "to make," from Latin *conficere* (see CONFECT).] —**dis·com·fit·er** *n.*

dis·com·fi·ture /diss kúmfichər/ *n.* frustrating feelings of embarrassment or awkwardness (*formal*)

dis·com·fort /diss kúmfərt/ *n.* **1. STATE OF PHYSICAL UNEASE** very mild pain or a feeling of being physically uncomfortable **2. EMBARRASSMENT** feelings of awkwardness and embarrassment **3. CAUSE OF UNEASE** something that causes physical or mental uneasiness **4. CAUSE OF LACK OF COMFORT** something that makes somebody feel physically uncomfortable or inconvenienced ■ *vt.* (**-fort·ed, -fort·ing, -forts**) **MAKE UNCOMFORTABLE** to make somebody feel physically or mentally uncomfortable (*formal*) [14thC. From Old French *desconfort*, from *desconforter*, literally "to deprive of comfort," from *conforter* "to comfort."] —**dis·com·fort·a·ble** *adj.* —**dis·com·fort·ing** *adj.* —**dis·com·fort·ing·ly** *adv.*

dis·com·mode /dìskə mṓd/ (**-mod·ed, -mod·ing, -modes**) *vt.* to cause problems or inconvenience to somebody (*formal*) [Early 18thC. From obsolete French *discommoder,* literally "to deprive of convenience," ultimately from Latin *commodus* "suitable."] —**dis·com·mo·di·ous** *adj.* —**dis·com·mo·di·ous·ly** *adv.*

dis·com·pose /dìskəm pṓz/ (**-posed, -pos·ing, -pos·es**) *vt.* to make somebody lose his or her composure (*formal*) —**dis·com·pos·ed·ly** /dìskəm pṓzədlee/ *adv.*

dis·com·po·sure /dìskəm pṓzhər/ *n.* the state of being anxious, confused, or physically disordered

dis·con·cert /dìskən súrt/ (**-cert·ed, -cert·ing, -certs**) *vt.* 1. **CAUSE TO FEEL UNEASY** to make somebody feel ill at ease, slightly confused, or taken aback 2. **UPSET OR FRUSTRATE PLANS** to prevent somebody from carrying out plans or arrangements and therefore create confusion [Mid-17thC. From French *desconcerter,* literally "to bring out of agreement," ultimately from Old Italian *concertare* "to bring into agreement," of unknown origin (source of English *concert*).] —**dis·con·cer·tion** *n.* —**dis·con·cert·ment** *n.*

dis·con·cert·ed /dìskən súrtəd/ *adj.* ill at ease, slightly confused, or taken aback

dis·con·cert·ing /dìskən súrting/ *adj.* making somebody feel uneasy confusion and dismay —**dis·con·cert·ing·ly** *adv.*

dis·con·firm /dìskən fúrm/ (**-firmed, -firm·ing, -firms**) *vt.* to show that something such as a theory cannot be right (*formal*) —**dis·con·fir·ma·tion** /dìss konfər máysh'n/ *n.*

dis·con·form·i·ty /dìskən fáwrmətee/ (*plural* **-ties**) *n.* 1. **NONCONFORMITY** nonconformity (*archaic*) 2. GEOL **BREAK IN CONTINUITY IN SEDIMENTARY ROCKS** a break in the sedimentary record in which the rock layers remain parallel

dis·con·nect /dìskə nékt/ *v.* (**-nect·ed, -nect·ing, -nects**) 1. *vti.* **DETACH POWER SOURCE FROM APPLIANCE** to break the connection between an appliance and its source of power 2. *vt.* **SHUT OFF SUPPLY OF PUBLIC UTILITY** to shut off the telephone line or the supply of water, gas, or electricity to a building 3. *vt.* **BREAK TELEPHONE CONNECTION** to break or lose the connection between two people who were speaking on the telephone (*usually passive*) 4. *vt.* **DETACH ONE PART FROM ANOTHER** to detach something that was connected to something else 5. *vti.* **BREAK OFF EMOTIONAL OR SPIRITUAL RELATIONSHIP** to end, forget, or lose an emotional or spiritual connection with something or somebody ■ *n.* 1. **EMOTIONAL DISINTEREST AND ISOLATION** a state of emotional isolation and disinterest that may be voluntary or involuntary ○ *She's in a state of utter disconnect as far as her old school is concerned.* 2. **DISCONNECTION** a disconnection of joined parts or things ○ *a disconnect betweeen his words and his acts* —**dis·con·nect·er** *n.* —**dis·con·nec·tive** *adj.*

dis·con·nect·ed /dìskə néktəd/ *adj.* showing no logical connection or relationship ○ *rambling disconnected prose* —**dis·con·nect·ed·ly** /dìskə néktədlee/ *adv.* —**dis·con·nect·ed·ness** *n.*

dis·con·nec·tion /dìskə nékshən/ *n.* 1. **BREAK IN UTILITIES OR POWER CONNECTION** the disconnecting of a telephone line or a supply of gas, water, or electricity 2. **SEPARATION** the separation of things that were formerly linked or connected

dis·con·so·late /diss kónsələt/ *adj.* miserable or disappointed and unable to be cheered up [15thC. From medieval Latin *disconsolatus* "comfortless," from Latin *consolatus,* past participle of *consolare* (see CONSOLE).] —**dis·con·so·late·ly** *adv.* —**dis·con·so·late·ness** *n.* —**dis·con·so·la·tion** /diss kònsə láysh'n/ *n.*

dis·con·tent /dìskən tént/ *n.* 1. **DISSATISFIED UNHAPPINESS** unhappiness or dissatisfaction 2. **RESTLESS LONGING FOR BETTER THINGS** a restless desire for something better (*literary*) 3. **SOMEBODY WHO IS DISCONTENTED** somebody who is dissatisfied and unhappy with a situation (*literary or formal*) ■ *adj.* = **discontented**

dis·con·tent·ed /dìskən téntəd/ *adj.* feeling unhappy or dissatisfied with a situation —**dis·con·tent·ed·ness** *n.*

dis·con·tent·ed·ly /dìskən téntədlee/ *adv.* with moody dissatisfaction or unhappiness

dis·con·tent·ment /dìskən téntmənt/ *n.* sad or moody dissatisfaction

dis·con·tin·ue /dìskən tínnyoo/ (**-ued, -u·ing, -ues**) *v.* 1. *vti.* **STOP** to come to an end after happening regularly, or end something that has been happening regularly 2. *vt.* **STOP MANUFACTURING** to stop manufacturing something, usually a particular model or type of product [15thC. Via French *discontinuer* from medieval Latin *discontinuare,* literally "not to continue," from Latin *continuare* "to continue."] —**dis·con·tin·u·ance** *n.* —**dis·con·tin·u·a·tion** /dìskən tinnyoo áysh'n/ *n.* —**dis·con·tin·u·er** /dìskən tínnyoo ər/ *n.*

dis·con·tin·ued /dìskən tínnyood/ *adj.* no longer manufactured and distributed (*refers to a product*)

dis·con·ti·nu·i·ty /diss kòntə nóo itee/ (*plural* **-ties**) *n.* 1. **BREAK IN OTHERWISE CONTINUOUS PROCESS** a break or gap in a process that would normally be continuous 2. MATH **POINT OF CHANGE** the point or value of a variable at which a curve or mathematical function shows an abrupt change as the variable smoothly increases or decreases 3. MATH **LACK OF MATHEMATICAL CONTINUITY** the characteristic of being discontinuous 4. MATH **MATHEMATICAL VALUE** a value of a variable for which a function is not continuous 5. GEOL **BOUNDARY BETWEEN ROCK TYPES** a boundary between rock types deep within the earth's crust that is detected as a change in the speed of seismic waves

dis·con·tin·u·ous /dìskən tínnyoo əss/ *adj.* 1. **PROCEEDING INTERMITTENTLY** having breaks or gaps in an otherwise continuous process or line 2. MATH **HAVING MATHEMATICAL DISCONTINUITY** with a mathematical discontinuity (*refers to variables and functions*) —**dis·con·tin·u·ous·ly** *adv.* —**dis·con·tin·u·ous·ness** *n.*

dis·cord /díss kàwrd/ *n.* 1. **LACK OF AGREEMENT** disagreement or strife between people, things, or situations 2. MUSIC **UNPLEASANT MUSICAL SOUNDS** unpleasant or harsh sounds clashing with each other, usually musical notes that produce a disagreeable combination [13thC. Via Old French *discorde* from Latin *discordia,* from *discord-,* stem of *discors,* literally "heart apart," from *cors* "heart."]

dis·cor·dance /diss káwrd'ns/, **dis·cor·dan·cy** /-d'nsee/ *n.* 1. = **discord** 2. GENETICS **GENETIC TRAIT IN ONE SIBLING** the occurrence of a genetic trait in just one twin or sibling

dis·cor·dant /diss káwrd'nt/ *adj.* 1. **DISAGREEING** in disagreement 2. MUSIC **SOUNDING UNPLEASANT** consisting of sounds, usually musical notes, that are harsh, unpleasant, or clashing —**dis·cor·dant·ly** *adv.*

dis·co·theque /dískə tèk/ *n.* = **disco** *n.* 1 [Mid-20thC. From French *discothèque,* from *disque* "disk, record" (via Latin from Greek *diskos;* see DISCUS) + *-thèque* "library" (from *bibliothèque*).]

dis·count *n.* /dìss kòwnt/ 1. **REDUCTION IN PRICE** a reduction in the usual price of something 2. FIN = **discount rate** 3. BANKING = **discount rate** *n.* 2 4. FIN **INTEREST DEDUCTED FROM FINANCIAL INSTRUMENT** the interest deducted from the face value of a financial instrument or promissory note before a sale or loan is completed 5. STOCK EXCH **DEDUCTION FROM PAR VALUE OF STOCK** the amount by which the (**par value**) of stock exceeds the market price actually paid by purchasers ■ *v.* /diss kównt, díss kòwnt/ (**-count·ed, -count·ing, -counts**) 1. *vt.* **DISMISS AS UNTRUE OR TRIVIAL** to decide that something can be disregarded as unimportant, irrelevant, or untrue ○ *We had already discounted the theory that they were involved.* 2. *vt.* **ANTICIPATE THEN ADJUST** to foresee something and make adjustments to lessen or absorb its impact 3. *vt.* BUSINESS **REDUCE IN PRICE** to reduce the price of something by a particular amount or percentage 4. *vt.* FIN **TRADE INVESTMENT AT REDUCED PRICE** to buy or sell a financial instrument at a reduced price that is calculated according to the interest rate and risk on the investment 5. *vti.* FIN **MAKE SECURED LOAN AT REDUCED RATE** to lend money on a negotiable long-term financial instrument at a reduced price that is calculated according to the instrument's risk and the interest due before its maturity ■ *adj.* **WITH REDUCED PRICE** less than the usual price, or selling goods for less than the usual price ○ *a discount warehouse* [Early 17thC. Partly from French *descompte;* partly from Italian *discontare;* both from, ultimately, medieval Latin *discomputare,* literally "to count away," from Latin *computare* (see COMPUTE).] —**dis·count·a·ble** /díss kòwntəb'l, diss kówntəb'l/ *adj.* —**dis·count·er** /díss kòwntər, diss kówntər/ *n.*

dis·count bro·ker *n.* 1. **STOCKBROKER WITH LOW COMMISSIONS** a stockbroker who executes trades for customers, but who in exchange for low commissions offers little advice or investment research 2. FIN **AGENT WHO DISCOUNTS COMMERCIAL PAPER** an agent who buys and sells bills or other commercial paper at a discount —**dis·count bro·ker·age** *n.*

dis·count·ed cash flow *n.* a method of valuing an investment by calculating what future cash returns will be worth at the time they are received, based on estimates of future inflation and interest rates

dis·coun·te·nance /diss kówntənəns/ *vt.* (**-nanced, -nanc·ing, -nanc·es**) (*formal*) 1. **EMBARRASS** to make somebody embarrassed 2. **DISAPPROVE OF** to discourage or disapprove of somebody or something ■ *n.* **DISFAVOR** disapproval of somebody or something (*formal*)

dis·count·er /díss kòwntər/ *n.* = **discount store**

dis·count house /díss kownt-/ *n.* = **discount store**

dis·count mar·ket /díss kownt-/ *n.* the part of the financial market trading in discounted commercial bills, including banks, brokers, and discount houses

dis·count rate *n.* 1. FIN **DIFFERENCE BETWEEN PRICE AND FUTURE RETURNS** the rate at which expected cash returns from a security are converted into the security's market price 2. BANKING **FEDERAL RESERVE INTEREST RATE** the rate of interest at which member banks may borrow money from the Federal Reserve Bank

dis·count store *n.* a store that sells goods at prices that are reduced from those recommended by the manufacturers

dis·cour·age /diss kúr ij/ (**-aged, -ag·ing, -ag·es**) *vt.* 1. **TEND TO STOP** to tend to prevent something from happening by making it more difficult or unpleasant ○ *dirty beaches that discourage sunbathing* 2. **TRY TO STOP SOMEBODY'S ACTIONS** to try to stop somebody from doing something 3. **MAKE LESS OPTIMISTIC** to make somebody feel less motivated, confident, or optimistic [15thC. From Old French *descoragier,* literally "to deprive of courage," from *corage* "courage."] —**dis·cour·ag·er** *n.*

dis·cour·aged /diss kúr ijd/ *adj.* feeling less motivated, confident, or optimistic about something

dis·cour·age·ment /diss kúr ijmənt/ *n.* 1. **LOSS OF OPTIMISM** feelings of lost motivation, confidence, or optimism 2. **ATTEMPTS TO STOP SOMETHING** the process of attempting to stop somebody from doing something or to prevent something from happening 3. **SOMETHING THAT CAUSES LOSS OF OPTIMISM** something that makes somebody lose motivation, confidence, or optimism

dis·cour·ag·ing /diss kúr ijing/ *adj.* making somebody feel less motivation, confidence, or optimism about something —**dis·cour·ag·ing·ly** *adv.*

dis·course *n.* /díss kàwrs/ 1. **SERIOUS SPEECH OR PIECE OF WRITING** a serious and lengthy speech or piece of writing about a topic 2. **SERIOUS CONVERSATION** serious discussion about something between people or groups 3. LING **LANGUAGE** language, especially the type of language used in a particular context or subject 4. LING **MAJOR UNIT OF LANGUAGE** a unit of language, especially spoken language, that is longer than the sentence. The term is used by linguists when investigating features of language that extend beyond sentences. 5. **REASONING ABILITY** reasoning or the ability to reason (*archaic*) ■ *vi.* /diss káwrs/ (**-coursed, -cours·ing, -cours·es**) 1. **SERIOUSLY SPEAK OR WRITE ON TOPIC** to speak or write about a subject in a formal context and at length ○ *In the second part, the author discourses on ethics.* 2. **CONVERSE** to have a conversation (*formal*) [15thC. From Latin *discursus* "running to and fro," from *discurrere,* literally "to run apart," from *currere* "to run" (see CURRENT).] —**dis·cours·er** /diss káwrsər/ *n.*

dis·cour·te·ous /diss kúrtee əss/ *adj.* lacking in politeness or good manners —**dis·cour·te·ous·ly** *adv.* —**dis·cour·te·ous·ness** *n.*

dis·cour·te·sy /diss kúrtəssee/ (*plural* **-sies**) *n.* behavior or an action that is bad-mannered or impolite

dis·cov·er /diss kúvvər/ (**-ered, -er·ing, -ers**) *vt.* 1. **FIND OUT ABOUT** to find out information that was not previously known ○ *We discovered she'd known all along.* 2. **BE FIRST TO FIND OR LEARN** to be the first person to find or learn something previously unknown ○ *researchers discovered a new genetic link to the causes of the disease* 3. **FIND** to find somebody or something unexpectedly or after a search ○ *The missing child was finally discovered downtown.* 4. **FIRST NOTICE INTEREST IN** to realize for the first time that you enjoy or have a talent for a particular thing ○ *Having discovered painting in her 50s, she ended up making a living by it.* 5. **RECOGNIZE SOMEBODY'S TALENT OR BEAUTY** to realize that a musician, actor, performer, or everyday citizen has exceptional talent or unusual beauty, and help to bring him or her to prominence [14thC. Via Old French *descovrir* from late

Latin *discooperire*, literally "to uncover," from Latin *cooperire* "to cover."] —**dis·cov·er·a·ble** *adj.*

dis·cov·ered check *n.* a move in chess that creates a check previously blocked by the piece moved

dis·cov·er·er /diss kúvvərər/ *n.* the person who is the first to find out something new or to find a new place or thing ○ *Gay-Lussac was the discoverer of boron.*

dis·cov·er·y /diss kúvvəree/ (*plural* **-ies**) *n.* **1. SOMETHING LEARNED OR FOUND** something new that has been learned or found ○ *These dinosaur remains were one of the most important discoveries of the century.* **2. PROCESS OF LEARNING SOMETHING PREVIOUSLY UNKNOWN** the fact or process of finding out about something for the first time ○ *the discovery of DNA* ○ *a voyage of discovery* **3. PROCESS OF FINDING SOMETHING** the finding of somebody or something new or unexpected, or after a search **4. RECOGNITION OF UNUSUAL TALENT OR BEAUTY** the recognition of somebody's exceptional talent or beauty, leading to that person's fame, or the person who is recognized in this way **5.** LAW **MUTUAL DISCLOSING OF DATA OR DOCUMENTS** the stage of a legal proceeding during which each side must provide data and documents to the other side **6.** LAW **DISCLOSABLE DATA AND DOCUMENTS** data or materials that a party in a legal proceeding must disclose to another party before or during the proceeding

dis·cred·it /diss kréddit/ *vt.* (**-it·ed, -it·ing, -its**) **1. HARM REPUTATION OF** to make somebody or something appear untrustworthy or wrong **2. CAUSE TO SEEM DOUBTFUL** to cast doubt on the validity or accuracy of something **3. NOT BELIEVE** to not accept that something is accurate or true ○ *Scientists generally discredit the theory of canals on Mars.* ■ *n.* **1. LOSS OF REPUTATION** the loss of somebody's or something's good name or reputation, or the person or thing that causes its loss ○ *Their conduct is regarded as a discredit to the whole industry.* **2. DOUBT OR SUSPICION** doubt about the validity or accuracy of something

dis·cred·it·a·ble /diss krédditəb'l/ *adj.* bringing shame or dishonor to somebody's good name or reputation —**dis·cred·it·a·bly** *adv.*

dis·creet /diss kreét/ *adj.* **1. CAREFUL TO AVOID OFFENDING PEOPLE** careful to avoid embarrassing or upsetting others **2. GOOD AT KEEPING SECRETS** careful not to speak about anything that should be secret or confidential **3. CIRCUMSPECTLY SUBTLE AND CAREFUL** subtle and circumspect, ensuring that no undue attention is attracted **4. MODEST** modest, and not ostentatious or flashy [14thC. Via French *discret* from Latin *discretus* "distinct," past participle of *discernere* "to distinguish" (see DISCERN).] —**dis·creet·ness** *n.*

dis·creet·ly /diss kreétlee/ *adv.* taking care to avoid upsetting or embarrassing people, giving away anything confidential, or appearing immodest or flashy

dis·crep·an·cy /diss kréppənsee/ (*plural* **-cies**) *n.* a distinct difference between two things, e.g., sets of figures, that should match or correspond

dis·crep·ant /diss kréppənt/ *adj.* differing where a match or correspondence is expected [15thC. From Latin *discrepant-*, present participle stem of *discrepare* "to differ," literally "to rattle apart," from *crepare* "to rattle."] —**dis·crep·ant·ly** /diss kréppəntlee/ *adv.*

dis·crete /diss kreét/ *adj.* **1. COMPLETELY SEPARATE** completely separate and unconnected **2.** MATH **FINITE** used to describe elements or variables that are distinct, unrelated, and have a finite number of values [14thC. From Latin *discretus* (see DISCREET).] —**dis·crete·ly** *adv.*

dis·cre·tion /diss krésh'n/ *n.* **1. ABILITY TO AVOID OFFENSE** the good judgment and sensitivity needed to avoid embarrassing or upsetting others **2. FREEDOM TO DECIDE** the freedom or authority to judge something or make a decision about it ○ *Tipping is left to the customer's discretion.* **3. CONFIDENTIALITY** the ability to keep sensitive information secret [14thC. Via French *discrétion* from the Latin stem *discretion-* "separation," later "discernment," from *discret-*, past participle stem of *discernere* (see DISCERN).]

dis·cre·tion·ar·y /diss krésh'n èrree/ *adj.* **1. GIVING SOMEBODY AUTHORITY TO DECIDE** giving somebody the freedom to make a decision according to individual circumstances **2. GIVEN OR REFUSED ACCORDING TO CIRCUMSTANCES** given according to the merits of an individual case, rather than being provided or awarded automatically **3. USABLE AS WANTED** able to be used as desired without any stipulations —**dis·cre·tion·ar·i·ly** *adv.*

dis·cre·tion·ar·y ac·count *n.* a securities account in which the broker has been given the authority to make decisions about buying and selling without the customer's prior permission

dis·cre·tion·ar·y in·come *n.* FIN income that is left over after necessary expenditure and is therefore available to be spent however you wish

dis·crim·i·na·ble /diss krímmənəb'l/ *adj.* able to be perceived as different or distinct [Mid-18thC. Coined from DISCRIMINATE + -ABLE.] —**dis·crim·i·na·bil·i·ty** /diss krìmmənə bíllətee/ *n.* —**dis·crim·i·na·bly** /diss krímmənəblee/ *adv.*

dis·crim·i·nant /diss krímmənənt/ *n.* MATH a relation between the coefficients *a*, *b* and *c* of a mathematical expression of the form $ax^2 + bx + c = 0$, used in the study of roots and other properties of the expression [Mid-19thC. From Latin *discriminant-*, present participle stem of *discriminare* (see DISCRIMINATE).]

dis·crim·i·nant func·tion *n.* a statistical method used to place an item that could belong to any of two or more sets of variables in the correct set, with a minimal probability of error

dis·crim·i·nate (**-nat·ed, -nat·ing, -nates**) *v.* /diss krímmə nàyt/ **1.** *vi.* **TREAT GROUP UNFAIRLY BECAUSE OF PREJUDICE** to treat one person or group worse than others or better than others, usually because of a prejudice about race, ethnic group, age group, religion, or gender **2.** *vti.* **DISCERN DIFFERENCE** to recognize or identify a difference ○ *could not discriminate between red and green* **3.** *vi.* **BE AWARE OF DIFFERENCES** to pay attention to subtle differences and exercise judgment and taste [Early 17thC. From Latin *discriminat-*, the past participle stem of *discriminare* "to divide," from the stem *discrimin-* "division," from *discernere* (see DISCERN).] —**dis·crim·i·nate·ly** *adv.*

dis·crim·i·nat·ing /diss krímmə nàyting/ *adj.* **1. RECOGNIZING DISTINCTIONS AND VALUING QUALITY** able to identify subtle differences and appreciate good quality or taste ○ *Discriminating customers prefer these handmade linens.* **2.** FIN **DIFFERENTIAL** used to describe tariffs that are set at different rates for different importers —**dis·crim·i·nat·ing·ly** *adv.*

dis·crim·i·na·tion /diss krìmmə náysh'n/ *n.* **1. TREATING PEOPLE DIFFERENTLY THROUGH PREJUDICE** unfair treatment of one person or group, usually because of prejudice about race, ethnic group, age group, religion, or gender **2. ABILITY TO NOTICE AND VALUE QUALITY** the ability to appreciate good quality or taste **3. ATTUNEMENT TO SUBTLE DIFFERENTIATION** the ability to notice subtle differences **4.** ELECTRON ENG **SIGNAL SELECTION** the selection of a transmitted signal with a particular characteristic, such as frequency, by elimination of signals with other characteristics, using a discriminator —**dis·crim·i·na·tion·al** /diss krìmmə náyshən'l, -shnəl/ *adj.*

dis·crim·i·na·tive /diss krímmə nàytiv, -nətiv/ *adj.* **1.** = **discriminatory** *adj.* 1 **2. RECOGNIZING DISTINCTIONS** recognizing and acknowledging distinctions and differences —**dis·crim·i·na·tive·ly** *adv.*

dis·crim·i·na·tor /diss krímmə nàytər/ *n.* ELECTRON ENG a device or circuit that translates phase or frequency variations into amplitude variations in a modulated signal, e.g., a radio signal, and is used to select signals with particular characteristics

dis·crim·i·na·to·ry /diss krímmənə tàwree/ *adj.* **1.** SOCIOL **UNFAIRLY TREATING** treating a person or group unfairly, especially because of prejudice about race, ethnicity, age, or gender **2.** STATS **STATISTICALLY UNBIASED** used to describe a statistical test that is unbiased because the sampling procedure avoided the systematic distortion that could be introduced by an unrepresentative population —**dis·crim·i·na·to·ri·ly** *adv.*

dis·cur·sive /diss kúrsiv/ *adj.* **1. LENGTHY WITH DIGRESSIONS** lengthy and including extra material that is not essential to what is being written or spoken about ○ *One book is concise and snappy, while the other has a more relaxed, discursive style.* **2.** PHILOS **RATIONAL** using logic rather than intuition to reach a conclusion [Late 16thC. From medieval Latin *discursivus*, from *discurs-*, the past participle stem of *discurrere* (see DISCOURSE).] —**dis·cur·sive·ly** *adv.* —**dis·cur·sive·ness** *n.*

dis·cus /dískəss/ (*plural* **-cus·es** *or* **-ci** /dí skī/) *n.* **1.** SPORT **DISK THROWN IN ATHLETICS** a weighted disk thrown in track-and-field competitions by an athlete who spins with outstretched arms to launch it from the flat of his or her hand. The ancient Greek Olympic games included the throwing of a bronze discus. **2.**

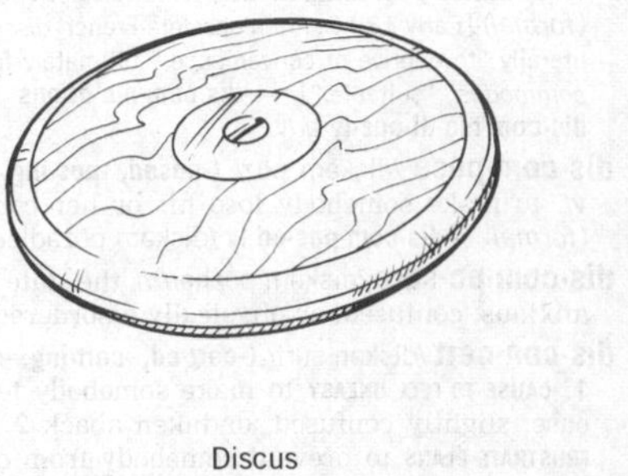

Discus

SPORT **EVENT OF THROWING DISCUS** the event or sport in which athletes compete to throw a discus as far as possible **3.** ZOOL **COLORFUL AQUARIUM FISH** a small colorful South American freshwater fish that has a compressed disk-shaped body and is popular as an aquarium fish. Latin name: *Symphysodon discus.* [Mid-17thC. Via Latin from Greek *diskos* "disk, quoit, platter" (source of English *disc* and *dish*).]

dis·cuss /diss kúss/ (**-cussed, -cuss·ing, -cuss·es**) *vt.* **1. TALK OVER** to talk about a subject with others ○ *need to discuss it with them first* **2. WRITE OR SPEAK ABOUT TOPIC FORMALLY** to consider a particular topic in speaking or writing ○ *Chapter 3 discusses the events leading up to the Revolutionary War.* [14thC. From Latin *discuss-*, past participle stem of *discutere* "to dash to pieces," literally "to shake apart," from *quatere* "to shake."] —**dis·cuss·er** *n.* —**dis·cuss·a·ble** *adj.*

dis·cus·sant /diss kúss'nt/ *n.* somebody who participates in a formal discussion or seminar (*formal*)

dis·cus·sion /diss kúsh'n/ *n.* **1. TALK BETWEEN PEOPLE** talk or a talk between two or more people about a subject **2. SPOKEN OR WRITTEN EXAMINATION OF TOPIC** a detailed consideration or examination of a topic in writing or speech —**dis·cus·sion·al** /diss kúshən'l, diss kúshnəl/ *adj.*

dis·dain /diss dáyn/ *n.* **INTENSE SCORN** extreme contempt or disgust for something or somebody ■ *vt.* (**-dained, -dain·ing, -dains**) **LOOK DOWN ON** to regard somebody or something as not worthy of respect [14thC. Origin uncertain: probably ultimately from Old French *desdeignier*, literally "to treat as unworthy," from late Latin *dedignare*, from *dignare* "to treat as worthy."]

dis·dain·ful /diss dáynfəl/ *adj.* showing or feeling contempt or disrespect for somebody or something —**dis·dain·ful·ly** *adv.* —**dis·dain·ful·ness** *n.*

dis·ease /di zeéz/ *n.* **1.** MED **MEDICAL CONDITION IN HUMANS** a condition that results in medically significant symptoms in a human **2.** BOT, VET **MEDICAL CONDITION IN PLANTS OR ANIMALS** a condition in plants or animals that causes medically significant symptoms **3. SPECIFIC DISORDER** a disorder with recognizable signs and often having a known cause **4. PROBLEM IN SOCIETY** a serious problem in society or with a particular group of people [14thC. From Old French *desaise*, literally "lack of ease," from *aise* "ease."]

dis·eased /di zeézd/ *adj.* **1.** MED, BOT, VET **HAVING DISEASE** affected by a disease **2. CORRUPT OR UNBALANCED** affected, or seemingly affected by corruption or psychiatric disorder

dis·e·con·o·my /dìssi kónnəmee/ (*plural* **-mies**) *n.* ECON something that contributes to increased costs

dis·em·bark /dìssəm baárk/ (**-barked, -bark·ing, -barks**) *v.* **1.** *vi.* **GET OFF PASSENGER VEHICLE** to get off a passenger vehicle, especially a ship, aircraft, or train **2.** *vt.* **PUT PASSENGERS OR CARGO OFF VEHICLE** to let passengers off a ship, bus, train, or aircraft, or to unload cargo (*formal*) [Late 16thC. From French *désembarquer*, Spanish *desembarcar*, or Italian *disimbarcare*, which were formed from French *embarquer* or the equivalent (see EMBARK).] —**dis·em·bar·ka·tion** /diss èm baar káysh'n/ *n.* —**dis·em·bark·ment** /dìssəm baárkmənt/ *n.*

dis·em·bar·rass /dìssəm bérrəss/ (**-rassed, -rass·ing, -rass·es**) *vt.* to free somebody from something embarrassing, unpleasant, or burdensome (*formal*) —**dis·em·bar·rass·ment** *n.*

dis·em·bod·ied /dìssəm bóddeed/ *adj.* coming from somebody who cannot be seen, often regarded as eerie or frightening ○ *a disembodied voice whispering in the darkness*

dis·em·bod·y /dìssəm bóddee/ (-ied, -y·ing, -ies) *vt.* to free the soul or spirit from the body —**dis·em·bod·i·ment** *n.*

dis·em·bow·el /dìssəm bówl/ (-eled, -el·ing, -els) *vt.* 1. REMOVE SOMEBODY'S INTERNAL ORGANS to cut open the stomach of a person or animal and remove the internal organs, especially the intestines 2. CUT OUT SUBSTANCE to remove the internal substance, elements, or parts of something (*literary*) —**dis·em·bow·el·ment** *n.*

dis·em·broil /dìssəm bróyl/ (-broiled, -broil·ing, -broils) *vt.* to free yourself or somebody else from a difficult situation

dis·em·ploy /dìssəm plóy/ (-ployed, -ploy·ing, -ploys) *vt.* to stop somebody or something from working (*formal*) —**dis·em·ploy·ment** *n.*

dis·em·pow·er /dìssəm pówr/ (-ered, -er·ing, -ers) *vt.* to take power or influence away from somebody or from yourself

dis·em·pow·er·ment /dìssəm pówərmənt/ *n.* the loss of personal worth, self-esteem, or power, or the process of losing these

dis·en·a·ble /dìssi náyb'l/ (-bled, -bling, -bles) *vt.* to prevent something or make something unable to operate or perform a function ○ *disenabled the weapons system on the aircraft prior to landing* —**dis·en·a·ble·ment** *n.*

dis·en·chant /dìssən chánt/ (-chant·ed, -chant·ing, -chants) *vt.* 1. CAUSE TO LOSE INTEREST to make somebody stop believing that something or somebody is worthwhile, right, or deserving of support 2. FREE FROM MAGIC SPELL to free somebody from an enchantment or magic spell [Late 16thC. From French *désenchanter,* literally "to undo enchantment," from *enchanter* "to enchant."] —**dis·en·chant·er** *n.* —**dis·en·chant·ing** *adj.* —**dis·en·chant·ing·ly** *adv.*

dis·en·chant·ed /dìssən chántəd/ *adj.* no longer happy, supportive, or enthusiastic about something or somebody —**dis·en·chant·ed·ly** *adv.*

dis·en·chant·ment /dìssən chántmənt/ *n.* the loss of happiness about, satisfaction with, or enthusiasm for something or somebody ○ *a growing disenchantment with the new government*

dis·en·cum·ber /dìssən kúmbər/ (-bered, -ber·ing, -bers) *vt.* to relieve somebody or something of a burden or problem —**dis·en·cum·ber·ment** *n.*

dis·en·dow /dìssən dów/ (-dowed, -dow·ing, -dows) *vt.* to withdraw an endowment, especially a gift of money —**dis·en·dow·er** *n.* —**dis·en·dow·ment** *n.*

dis·en·fran·chise /dìssən frán chīz/ (-chised, -chis·ing, -chis·es) *vt.* to deprive a person or organization of a privilege, immunity, or legal right, especially the right to vote —**dis·en·fran·chise·ment** /dìssən frán chīzmənt, dìssən fránchizmənt/ *n.*

dis·en·gage /dìssən gáyj/ (-gaged, -gag·ing, -gag·es) *v.* 1. *vti.* ENG PHYSICALLY DISCONNECT OR BECOME DISCONNECTED to disconnect one thing from another, or to become disconnected from something 2. *vt.* MENTALLY DISCONNECT OR BECOME UNINVOLVED to mentally separate yourself or somebody else from, or to become uninvolved in, a situation or difficulty 3. *vti.* MIL STOP FIGHTING IN WAR to bring troops out of, or end involvement in, a war or combat 4. *vti.* FENCING MOVE SWORD IN FENCING to move the point of your sword around an opponent's sword in order to open a new line of attack

dis·en·gage·ment /dìssən gáyjmənt/ *n.* 1. RELEASE FROM SOMETHING the process or action in which something or somebody is released from a physical or mental attachment 2. MIL WITHDRAWAL OF ARMY the withdrawal of troops or an army from a war or combat

dis·en·tail /dìssən táyl/ (-tailed, -tail·ing, -tails) *vt.* FIN, LAW to lift the restrictions on who may inherit a person's property —**dis·en·tail·ment** *n.*

dis·en·tan·gle /dìssən táng g'l/ (-gled, -gling, -gles) *vt.* 1. UNTANGLE to untangle and free things that are muddled, tied, or knotted together 2. DISTINGUISH, ANALYZE, OR UNDERSTAND to clarify something confusing, or to separate and analyze a confusion of ideas ○ *It was hard to disentangle fact from fiction in his account.* 3. BREAK OFF RELATIONSHIP to free somebody or yourself from a relationship or connection —**dis·en·tan·gle·ment** *n.*

dis·en·thrall /dìssən thráwl/ (-thralled, -thral·ling, -thralls) *vt.* to set somebody free from a situation of harsh control, or a condition resembling servitude (*formal*) —**dis·en·thrall·ment** *n.*

dis·en·ti·tle /dìssən tīt'l/ (-tled, -tling, -tles) *vt.* to take away somebody's title or somebody's right to something (*formal*)

dis·en·tomb /dìssən tóom/ (-tombed, -tomb·ing, -tombs) *vt.* to take a body out of a tomb or from a place like a tomb. ◊ **exhume**

dis·en·twine /dìssən twīn/ (-twined, -twin·ing, -twines) *vti.* to become untangled or to untangle things that have become twisted or tangled together (*formal*)

dis·e·quil·i·brate /dìssə kwíllə bràyt/ (-brat·ed, -brat·ing, -brates) *vt.* to put something into a state of unbalance (*formal*) —**dis·e·quil·i·bra·tion** /dìssə kwíllə bráysh'n/ *n.*

dis·e·qui·lib·ri·um /dìss eekwə líbbree əm/ *n.* a state of instability or imbalance, usually in the economy

dis·es·tab·lish /dìssə stábblish/ (-lished, -lish·ing, -lish·es) *vt.* 1. STOP LONG ESTABLISHED CUSTOM to undo or change something that has been established for a long time 2. END CONNECTION BETWEEN CHURCH AND STATE to end the official relationship between the state and a nation's official church or religion

dis·es·tab·lish·ment /dìssə stábblishmənt/ *n.* the act or process of separation between the state and a nation's official church or religion

dis·es·tab·lish·men·tar·i·an /dìssə stabblishmən táiree ən/ *n.* somebody who is opposed to having a church that is connected to and supported by the state

dis·es·teem /dìssə stéem/ *vt.* (-teemed, -teem·ing, -teems) THINK BADLY OF to have a low opinion of somebody or something (*formal*) ■ *n.* NO RESPECT lack of respect or esteem (*formal*) ○ *held in disesteem*

di·seur /dee zúr/ *n.* ARTS a man, usually an actor, who is an accomplished reciter of dramatic monologues. Such recitals, often accompanied by music, were once a popular form of theatrical entertainment. [From French, literally "talker," from *dire* "to say," from Latin *dicere* (see DICTION)]

di·seuse /dee zóoz/ *n.* ARTS a woman, usually an actor, who is an accomplished reciter of dramatic monologues. Such recitals, often accompanied by music, were once a popular theatrical entertainment. [Late 19thC. From French, feminine of *diseur* (see DISEUR).]

dis·fa·vor /diss fáyvər/ *n.* 1. CONDITION OF DISAPPROVAL the state of being disapproved of ○ *This fell into disfavor years ago.* 2. NO RESPECT OR APPROVAL disapproval or lack of respect ○ *They were looked on with disfavor.* ■ *vt.* (-vored, -vor·ing, -vors) NOT LIKE OR APPROVE OF to dislike or disapprove of something (*formal*)

dis·fea·ture /diss féechər/ (-tured, -tur·ing, -tures) *vt.* = **disfigure** —**dis·fea·ture·ment** /diss féechərmənt/ *n.*

dis·fig·u·ra·tion /diss fìggyə ráysh'n/ *n.* = **disfigurement** *n.* 2

dis·fig·ure /diss fíggyər/ (-ured, -ur·ing, -ures) *vt.* to mar the appearance of somebody or something [14thC. From Old French *desfigurer,* literally "to deprive something of its figure," from Latin *figura* "figure."]

dis·fig·ured /diss fíggyərd/ *adj.* partially or totally made worse in appearance

dis·fig·ure·ment /diss fíggyərmənt/ *n.* 1. SOMETHING THAT WORSENS SOMEBODY'S APPEARANCE something, e.g., a very bad haircut, that spoils the appearance of somebody or something 2. ACT, PROCESS, OR STATE OF DISFIGURING the worsening of the appearance of somebody or something

dis·fran·chise /diss frán chīz/ (-chised, -chis·ing, -chis·es) *vt.* POL = **disenfranchise** —**dis·fran·chise·ment** /diss frán chīzmənt, diss fránchizmənt/ *n.*

dis·frock /diss frók/ (-frocked, -frock·ing, -frocks) *vt.* CHR = **defrock**

dis·gorge /diss gáwrj/ (-gorged, -gorg·ing, -gorg·es) *vt.* 1. POUR SUBSTANCES OUT to pour out liquid, gas, or other contents in a gushing stream 2. LET PEOPLE OUT to let a large number of people come out of a building or vehicle at the same time ○ *a cruise ship disgorging thousands of passengers* 3. REGURGITATE OR VOMIT to vomit or regurgitate food that has been eaten or partly eaten, as some birds and mammals do to feed their young [15thC. From Old French *desgorger,* literally "to expel from the throat," from *gorge* "throat" (source of English *gorge*).] —**dis·gorge·ment** *n.*

dis·grace /diss gráyss/ *n.* 1. STATE OF BEING DISAPPROVED OF shame or loss of respect arising from bad behavior ○ *She was sent home in disgrace.* 2. CAUSE OF SHAME OR DISRESPECT somebody who or something that causes shame or loss of respect ○ *She's a disgrace to the family.* ■ *vt.* (-graced, -grac·ing, -grac·es) CAUSE FEELINGS OF SHAME TO SOMEBODY to bring shame on yourself or others who are associated with you by bad behavior ○ *He disgraced himself by forgetting the wedding.* [Mid-16thC. Via French *disgracier* from, ultimately, Italian *disgrazia,* literally "disfavor," from Latin *gratia* (see GRACE).] —**dis·grac·er** *n.*

dis·graced /diss gráyst/ *adj.* regarded with disrespect or contempt because of bad behavior ○ *The disgraced players returned to a somewhat muted reception from the fans back home.*

dis·grace·ful /diss gráysfəl/ *adj.* so bad or unacceptable that it is something to be ashamed of ○ *The way they were treated was disgraceful.* —**dis·grace·ful·ly** *adv.* —**dis·grace·ful·ness** *n.*

dis·grun·tle /diss grúnt'l/ (-tled, -tling, -tles) *vt.* to make somebody feel dissatisfied and irritated [Mid-17thC. Literally "to grumble greatly," formed from obsolete *gruntle* "to grumble, grunt," literally "to grunt repeatedly," from GRUNT.] —**dis·grun·tle·ment** *n.*

dis·grun·tled /diss grúnt'ld/ *adj.* in a state of resentful dissatisfaction, anger, and irritation

dis·guise /diss gīz/ *vt.* (-guised, -guis·ing, -guis·es) 1. CHANGE SOMEBODY'S APPEARANCE FOR CONCEALMENT to make changes in the appearance of somebody or something to avoid being recognized ○ *He fled the besieged city disguised as a woman.* 2. HIDE SOMETHING TO PREVENT OTHERS KNOWING to hide feelings or facts from other people ○ *She couldn't disguise her horror.* 3. CHANGE SOMETHING TO PREVENT RECOGNITION to change something so that it cannot be recognized ○ *His voice has been disguised during the interview to conceal his identity.* ■ *n.* 1. SOMETHING DONE TO PREVENT RECOGNITION something worn or done in order to change somebody's appearance and prevent recognition ○ *Anyone would have seen through such a flimsy disguise.* 2. ALTERATION OR CONCEALMENT TO PREVENT RECOGNITION the alteration or concealment of something in order to prevent it being seen or recognized by others ○ *a plot that relies on disguise* 3. STATE OF ALTERED APPEARANCE an altered appearance intended to conceal somebody's identity or make somebody look like somebody else ○ *The film star must be traveling in disguise.* [14thC. From Old French *desguis(i)er,* literally "to remove your appearance," from *guise* "appearance" (source of English *guise*).] —**dis·guis·a·ble** *adj.* —**dis·guis·er** *n.*

dis·guised /diss gīzd/ *adj.* 1. CHANGED TO PREVENT RECOGNITION changed in appearance so as to prevent recognition 2. CONCEALED concealed in an attempt to prevent recognition —**dis·guis·ed·ly** /diss gīzədlee/ *adv.*

dis·gust /diss gúst/ *n.* 1. STRONG DISAPPROVAL OR REVULSION a feeling of horrified or sickened distaste for something ○ *viewed the tawdry scandal with unconcealed disgust* 2. IMPATIENT IRRITATION a feeling of impatient irritation ○ *Much to my disgust, I was compelled to hand over the documents.* ■ *vt.* (-gust·ed, -gust·ing, -gusts) MAKE SOMEBODY FEEL REVOLTED to make somebody feel sickened or revolted [Late 16thC. Via either French *desgoust* or Italian *disgusto,* literally "to have a distaste for," from, ultimately, Latin *gustus* "taste" (source of English *gusto*).] —**dis·gust·ed** *adv.* —**dis·gust·ed·ness** *adj.*

WORD KEY: SYNONYMS

See Synonyms at ***dislike.***

dis·gust·ing /diss gústing/ *adj.* 1. REPELLENT AND SICKENING tending to repel and sicken people ○ *a disgusting smell* 2. DISGRACEFUL completely unacceptable or disgraceful ○ *a disgusting waste of money* —**dis·gust·ing·ly** *adv.* —**dis·gust·ing·ness** *n.*

dish /dish/ *n.* 1. HOUSEHOLD CONTAINER FOR SERVING FOOD a container for serving food, usually a bowl 2. FOOD SERVING OF FOOD a serving or plateful of food, especially one that forms only part of a larger meal 3. FOOD FOOD PREPARED TO RECIPE OR STYLE food prepared to a particular recipe or in a particular style 4. SCI SHALLOW OPEN CONTAINER a shallow open container used, e.g., in laboratories or hospitals 5. ELECTRON ENG RADIO OR TELEVISION ANTENNA a dish-shaped antenna transmitting and receiving radio or television signals, used, e.g., in radar and satellite broadcasting 6. GEOL HOLLOW PLACE a shallow depression, e.g., in rock 7. GOOD-LOOKING PERSON a good-looking person (*slang*) ■ **dish·es** *npl.* HOUSEHOLD DIRTY PLATES, CUTLERY, AND PANS the plates, eating utensils, and pans that are dirtied during the cooking and eating of a meal ○ *my turn to wash the dishes* ■ *vt.* (dished, dish·ing, dish·es) HOLLOW OUT to make or form a concave shape in something [Pre-12thC. Via Latin *discus* "dish, platter" from Greek *diskos* "disk, platter," from *dikein* "to throw" (source of English *discus*).]

dish out *vt.* **1.** HAND OUT FREELY to give something out freely, especially criticism, money, punishment, or advice (*informal*) **2.** SERVE FOOD to serve food to people ○ *dishing out mashed potatoes* ◇ **to dish it out but not be able to take it** to criticize others freely while not being able to accept criticism (*informal*) ○ *She can really dish it out but she surely can't take it*

dis·ha·bille /dìssə beél, dìssə beé/, **des·ha·bille** /dèssə beél, dèssə beé/ *n.* **1.** STATE OF CASUAL DRESS a state in which somebody is partially undressed or dressed very casually or incompletely (*formal*) **2.** CASUAL CLOTHING very casual clothes or clothes worn very casually (*archaic*) [Late 17thC. From French *déshabillé*, past participle of *déshabiller* "to undress," from *habiller* "to dress."]

dish aer·i·al *n. U.K.* = **dish antenna**

dish an·ten·na (*plural* **dish an·ten·nas** *or* **dish an·ten·nae**) *n.* a transmitting and receiving antenna in the form of a bowl-shaped reflector, used, e.g., in radar and in satellite television broadcasting

dis·har·mo·ny /diss haármənee/ *n.* **1.** CONFLICT BETWEEN PEOPLE disagreement or conflict between people or groups who cannot get along with each other **2.** MUSIC LACK OF MUSICAL HARMONY lack of agreement in music or sounds, resulting in unpleasant sound combinations **3.** IMBALANCE lack of balance in something such as the body or the environment —**dis·har·mo·ni·ous** /dìss haar mṓnee əss/ *adj.* —**dishar·mo·ni·ous·ly** /-əsslee/ *adv.*

dish·cloth /dísh klòth/ *n.* **1.** = **dish towel 2.** CLOTH FOR WASHING DISHES a cloth used for washing dishes

dis·heart·en /diss haárt'n/ (**-ened, -en·ing, -ens**) *vt.* to make somebody lose hope and enthusiasm —**dis·heart·en·ment** *n.*

dis·heart·en·ing /diss haárt'ning/ *adj.* making somebody lose hope or enthusiasm —**dis·heart·en·ing·ly** *adv.*

dished /disht/ *adj.* hollowed out in a shape like a dish

di·shev·el /di shévv'l/ (**-eled** *or* **-elled, -el·ing** *or* **-el·ling, -els**) *vt.* **1.** MUSS CLOTHES OR HAIR to disarrange somebody's clothes or hair **2.** MESS SOMETHING UP to disarrange something, making it messy [Late 16thC. Origin uncertain: probably a back-formation from DISHEVELED.] —**di·shev·el·ment** *n.*

di·shev·eled /di shévv'ld/, **di·shev·elled** *adj.* **1.** WITH MESSED-UP HAIR OR CLOTHES with messed-up hair or clothes **2.** UNTIDY disordered and untidy [14thC. From Old French *deschevelé*, past participle of *descheveler* "to disarrange the hair," from *des-* "apart" (from Latin *dis-*) + *chevel* "hair" (from Latin *capillus*).]

dis·hon·est /diss ónnəst/ *adj.* meaning or meant to deceive, defraud, or trick people [14thC. Via Old French *deshoneste* from Latin *dehonestus*, from *honestus* "honorable."]

dis·hon·est·ly /diss ónnəstlee/ *adv.* in a lying or deceitful way

dis·hon·es·ty /diss ónnəstee/ (*plural* **-ties**) *n.* **1.** DECEITFUL BEHAVIOR the use of lies or deceit, or the tendency to be deceitful **2.** DISHONEST DEED a dishonest act or action

dis·hon·or /diss ónnər/ *n.* **1.** LOSS OF OTHER PEOPLE'S RESPECT the loss of a good reputation **2.** CAUSE OF SHAME a cause of shame or loss of respect **3.** FIN FAILURE TO PAY CHECK failure or refusal by a bank or other financial institution to pay a check, bill of exchange, or other financial instrument ■ *vt.* (**-ored, -or·ing, -ors**) **1.** BRING SHAME ON SOMEBODY to do something that brings shame on yourself or on people associated with you **2.** BREAK AGREEMENT to fail to keep a promise or agreement **3.** TREAT DISRESPECTFULLY to treat somebody without any respect (*formal*) **4.** FIN FAIL TO PAY CHECK to fail to pay a check, bill of exchange, or other financial instrument (*formal*) **5.** DISGRACE WOMAN BY SEDUCTION OR RAPE to bring shame on a woman by seducing her before marriage, or by raping her (*archaic*) [14thC. Via Old French *deshonorer* from medieval Latin *dishonorare*, literally "not to honor," from *honorare* "honor."] —**dis·hon·or·er** *n.*

dis·hon·or·a·ble /diss ónnərəb'l/ *adj.* **1.** SHAMEFUL AND TO SOMEBODY'S DISCREDIT morally unacceptable and liable to make somebody lose the respect of others **2.** WITHOUT MORALS OR INTEGRITY behaving in a dishonest or morally unacceptable way —**dis·hon·or·a·ble·ness** *n.* —**dis·hon·or·a·bly** *adv.*

dis·hon·or·a·ble dis·charge *n.* MIL dismissal from the armed forces as punishment for a serious offense such as desertion

dish·pan /dísh pàn/ *n.* a large pan or plastic tub used for washing the dishes

dish·pan hands *npl.* a condition of the hands in which the skin is dry, scaly, and reddened because of sensitivity or overexposure to cleaning materials such as detergent (*takes a singular or plural verb*)

dish·rag /dísh ràg/ *n.* = **dishcloth**

dish·tow·el /dísh tòwəl/ *n.* a cloth used for drying dishes

dish·ware /dísh wàir/ *n.* dishes used for serving food

dish·wash·er /dísh wàwshər/ *n.* **1.** MACHINE FOR WASHING DISHES an electrically operated machine that washes, rinses, and dries dishes and utensils **2.** SOMEBODY WHO WASHES DISHES somebody who washes dishes, especially in a restaurant

dish·wash·ing liq·uid *n.* a liquid detergent used for washing dishes

dish·wa·ter /dísh wòttər/ *n.* **1.** WATER USED FOR WASHING DISHES water that is or has been used for washing dishes or utensils **2.** WEAK DRINK a weak or tasteless drink

dish·wa·ter blond, **dish·wa·ter blonde** *adj.* DULL YELLOW used to describe hair that is dull blond or yellow in color (*informal insult*) ■ *n.* SOMEBODY WITH DULL BLOND HAIR somebody whose hair is dishwater blond (*informal insult*)

dish·y /díshee/ (**-i·er, -i·est**) *adj.* good-looking (*informal*)

dis·il·lu·sion /dìssi lóozh'n/ *vt.* (**-sioned, -sion·ing, -sions**) DESTROY ILLUSION to destroy or undermine an ideal, illusion, or mistaken belief that is held by somebody (*often passive*) ■ *n.* = **disillusionment** —**dis·il·lu·sive** *adj.*

dis·il·lu·sioned /dìssi lóozh'nd/ *adj.* disappointed by a frustrated ideal or belief

dis·il·lu·sion·ment /dìssi lóozh'nmənt/ *n.* disappointment caused by a frustrated ideal or belief

dis·in·cen·tive /dìssin séntiv/ *n.* something that deters somebody from taking a particular action

dis·in·cli·na·tion /dìssinklə náysh'n/ *n.* a reluctance to do something

dis·in·cline /dìssin klī́n/ (**-clined, -clin·ing, -clines**) *vt.* to make somebody reluctant or unwilling to do something (*often passive*)

dis·in·cor·po·rate /dìssin káwrpə ràyt/ (**-rat·ed, -rat·ing, -rates**) *vti.* **1.** BUSINESS END CORPORATE STATUS to remove the corporate status of a company or organization, or to undergo such a process **2.** POL END MUNICIPAL STATUS to end the corporate status of a community, or to undergo such a process —**dis·in·cor·po·ra·tion** /dìssin kawrpə ráysh'n/ *n.*

dis·in·fect /dìssin fékt/ (**-fect·ed, -fect·ing, -fects**) *vt.* to clean something so as to destroy disease-carrying microorganisms and prevent infection [Late 16thC. From French *désinfecter*, from *dés-* "dis-" and *infecter* "to infect."] —**dis·in·fec·tion** /dìssin féksh'n/ *n.* —**dis·in·fec·tor** *n.*

dis·in·fec·tant /dìssin féktənt/ *n.* a chemical that destroys or inhibits the growth of microorganisms that cause disease

dis·in·fest /dìssin fést/ (**-fest·ed, -fest·ing, -fests**) *vt.* to free a place, person, or animal of small pests such as rodents or insects —**dis·in·fes·ta·tion** /dìssin fe stáysh'n/ *n.*

dis·in·fla·tion /dìssin fláysh'n/ *n.* a slowdown in the rate at which prices increase, e.g., during a recession —**dis·in·fla·tion·ar·y** *adj.*

dis·in·form /dìssin fáwrm/ (**-formed, -form·ing, -forms**) *vt.* to supply somebody with false or misleading information [Late 20thC. Back-formation from DISINFORMATION.]

dis·in·for·ma·tion /dìssinfər máysh'n/ *n.* false or deliberately misleading information, often put out as propaganda [Mid-20thC. Modeled on Russian *dezinformatsiya.*]

dis·in·gen·u·ous /dìssin jénnyoo əss/ *adj.* **1.** WITHHOLDING INFORMATION withholding or not taking account of known information **2.** NOT GENUINELY SINCERE giving a false impression of sincerity or simplicity —**dis·in·gen·u·ous·ly** *adv.* —**dis·in·gen·u·ous·ness** *n.*

dis·in·her·it /dìssin hérrit/ (**-it·ed, -it·ing, -its**) *vt.* **1.** DEPRIVE OF INHERITANCE to change a will so as to deprive somebody of an inheritance **2.** DEPRIVE OF RIGHT to deprive somebody of a natural or established right or privilege —**dis·in·her·i·tance** *n.*

dis·in·hib·it /dìssin híbbit/ (**-it·ed, -it·ing, -its**) *vt.* PSYCHOL to free somebody from inhibitions (*technical*)

dis·in·hi·bi·tion /dìssin hi bísh'n/ *n.* **1.** LOSS OF INHIBITION a loss of inhibition, e.g., through the influence of alcohol or drugs (*technical*) **2.** PSYCHOL TEMPORARY LOSS OF INHIBITION a temporary loss of inhibition caused by an outside stimulus, e.g. , a loud noise **3.** CHEM REMOVAL OF INHIBITOR the removal of a substance that slows or stops a chemical reaction

dis·in·te·grate /diss íntə gràyt/ (**-grat·ed, -grat·ing, -grates**) *v.* **1.** *vti.* BREAK INTO FRAGMENTS to break into components or fragments, or break something into small pieces or constituent parts **2.** *vti.* LOSE WHOLENESS to destroy the cohesion, unity, or wholeness of something, or undergo such destruction **3.** NUCLEAR PHYS SPLIT ATOMS to split the nuclei of atoms, or cause the nuclei of atoms to split —**dis·in·te·gra·ble** *adj.* —**dis·in·te·gra·tive** *adj.*

dis·in·te·gra·tion /diss ìntə gráysh'n/ *n.* **1.** BREAKING INTO PIECES irreversible breaking into components or fragments **2.** LOSS OF UNITY the loss of unity, cohesion, or integrity **3.** NUCLEAR PHYS BREAKUP OF NUCLEUS the breakup of an atomic nucleus or an unstable elementary particle into smaller parts, either by radioactive decay or through bombardment with high-energy particles

dis·in·te·gra·tor *n.* **1.** NUCLEAR PHYS ATOM-SPLITTING MACHINE a machine in which atoms are split as a result of being hit by accelerated particles **2.** DISINTEGRATING AGENT a person, machine, or force that destroys or disintegrates something

dis·in·ter /dìssin túr/ (**-terred, -ter·ring, -ters**) *vt.* **1.** DIG UP BODY to dig up or remove a dead body from a grave or tomb **2.** EXPOSE SOMETHING HIDDEN to expose something that was hidden (*formal*) [Early 17thC. From French *désenterrer*, from *dés-* "dis-" and *enterrer* "to inter."] —**dis·in·ter·ment** *n.*

dis·in·ter·est /diss íntərəst, diss íntrəst/ *vt.* (**-est·ed, -est·ing, -ests**) FREE FROM INTEREST to cause somebody to lose interest or partiality ■ *n.* IMPARTIALITY lack of bias or self-interest

dis·in·ter·est·ed /diss íntərəstəd, diss íntrəstəd/ *adj.* **1.** IMPARTIAL free from bias or self-interest **2.** NOT INTERESTED indifferent, not interested, or no longer interested (*considered incorrect by many people*) —**dis·in·ter·est·ed·ly** *adv.* —**dis·in·ter·est·ed·ness** *n.*

dis·in·ter·me·di·a·tion /dìssintər meedee áysh'n/ *n.* **1.** COMM REMOVAL OF INTERMEDIARIES the elimination of intermediaries, e.g., wholesalers or retailers, in business transactions between producers and consumers **2.** FIN MOVING MONEY the diversion of invested funds from low-yield to higher-yield areas, e.g., from depository accounts to stocks

dis·in·tox·i·cate /dìssin tóksi kàyt/ (**-cat·ed, -cat·ing, -cates**) *vt.* = **detoxify** *v.* 1 —**dis·in·tox·i·ca·tion** *n.*

dis·in·vent /dìssin vént/ (**-vent·ed, -vent·ing, -vents**) *vt.* to undo the invention of something ○ *Nuclear weapons cannot be disinvented.*

dis·in·vest /dìssin vést/ (**-vest·ed, -vest·ing, -vests**) *vti.* to withdraw an investment in something

dis·in·vest·ment /dìssin véstmənt/ *n.* **1.** WITHDRAWING INVESTMENT the withdrawal of an investment **2.** REDUCTION OF INVESTMENT a reduction of investment caused by a selling of or deterioration in assets

dis·in·vite /dìssin vī́t/ (**-vit·ed, -vit·ing, -vites**) *vt.* to withdraw an invitation to somebody (*humorous*)

dis·join /diss jóyn/ (**-joined, -join·ing, -joins**) *vti.* to disconnect parts, things, or ideas, or become separated [15thC. Via Old French *desjoign-*, the stem of *desjoindre*, from Latin *disjungere*, from *jungere* (see JOIN).] —**dis·join·a·ble** *adj.*

dis·joint /diss jóynt/ (**-joint·ed, -joint·ing, -joints**) *v.* **1.** *vti.* SEPARATE AT JOINTS to separate something at the joints, or be separated in this way **2.** *vti.* DISLOCATE to force or move something out of its usual position, or undergo such a change **3.** *vt.* DESTROY UNITY to destroy the unity or coherence of something **4.** *vt.* = **disjoin** [15thC. From Old French *desjoint*, the past participle of *desjoindre* (see DISJOIN).] —**dis·joint** *adj.* —**dis·joint·ed** *adj.* —**dis·joint·ed·ness** *n.*

dis·joint·ed·ly /diss jóyntədlee/ *adv.* in a way that makes connections or order unclear

dis·junct /diss júngkt/ *adj.* **1.** SEPARATED discontinuous or separated in time or space **2.** MUSIC DESCRIBING NOTES A SECOND APART relating to two consecutive notes that are separated by an interval of a second **3.** MUSIC DESCRIBING A LEAPING MELODY relating to a melody in which leaps are the dominant feature rather than smooth progression ■ *n.* LOGIC CLAUSE either the p clause or the q clause in a logical proposition of the form "p or q" [15thC. From Latin *disjunctus*, the past participle of *disjungere* (see DISJOIN).]

dis·junc·tion /diss júngkshən/ *n.* **1.** DISCONNECTION a disconnection of joined parts or things **2.** LOGIC PROPOSITION WITH "OR" a proposition of the form "p or q" that is false if both p and q are false, but true if at least one of them is true **3.** LOGIC = **disjunct** *n.* **4.** GENETICS CHROMOSOME SEPARATION the separation of like chromosomes during cell division

dis·junc·tive /diss júngktiv/ *adj.* **1.** DIVIDING serving to divide, or having the effect of dividing (*technical*) **2.** GRAM SHOWING CONTRAST used to describe a word, e.g., "or," that establishes a contrast between two words or linguistic elements **3.** LOGIC CONTAINING OR RELATED TO A DISJUNCTION relating to or having the form of a proposition of the type "p or q" ■ *n.* **1.** GRAM CONTRAST WORD a conjunction or other word that establishes a contrast **2.** LOGIC = **disjunction** *n.* 2 —**dis·junc·tive·ly** *adv.*

dis·junc·ture /diss júngchər/ *n.* = **disjunction** *n.* 1

disk /disk/, **disc** *n.* **1.** ROUND FLAT OBJECT object that is, or appears to be, thin, flat, and circular **2.** COMPUT COMPUTER STORAGE DEVICE a device consisting of one or more thin magnetically or optically etched plates, used in a computer to store information **3.** ANAT, ZOOL PART BETWEEN BONES OF SPINE a flat round structure in the skeleton of a person or animal that separates the bones of the spine **4.** CARS BRAKE PART a circular piece of metal around the hub of a vehicle wheel, against which the pads of a disc brake press **5.** AGRIC STEEL BLADE a circular steel blade with a sharpened edge that is used on a disk harrow or plow **6.** BOT CENTER OF FLOWERHEAD the central part of the flowerhead of a composite plant, made up of tiny tubular flowers [Mid-17thC. Directly or via French *disque* from Latin *discus* "dish, quoit," from Greek *diskos* (see DISH).]

disk cam·er·a *n.* a camera that uses film in a disk rather than a roll or cartridge

disk drive *n.* a device that a computer uses to read data from and write data to magnetic or optical disks

disk·ette /di skét/ *n.* = **floppy disk**

disk flow·er, disk flo·ret *n.* a tiny tubular flower that is one of the group that forms the center disk of the flowerhead of certain composite plants, e.g., the daisy

disk har·row *n.* a harrow with a series of disks set at an angle on one or more axles that loosen the soil when moved over plowed land

disk op·er·at·ing sys·tem *n.* an operating system for personal computers that uses disks and diskettes for storage of programs and data

disk pack *n.* a removable data storage device for use in minicomputers and mainframes, consisting of several magnetic or optical disks stacked one on top of another and handled as a unit

disk plow *n.* an agricultural implement with a cutting disk fixed in a frame that is drawn by a tractor that cuts furrows in the soil and turns it up

disk sand·er *n.* an electrically powered tool with a revolving abrasive disk, used for sanding, grinding, and polishing irregular surfaces

disk wheel *n.* an automobile wheel with a continuous flat outer surface instead of spokes

dis·lik·a·ble /diss líkəb'l/, **dis·like·a·ble** *adj.* hard to like because of being disagreeable or unpleasant

dis·like /diss lík/ *vt.* (**-liked, -lik·ing, -likes**) CONSIDER DISAGREEABLE to consider something or somebody disagreeable or unpleasant ■ *n.* **1.** DISAPPROVING FEELING an attitude or feeling of aversion, disapproval, or distaste **2.** SOMETHING PERSONALLY DISAGREEABLE something that you do not like

WORD KEY: SYNONYMS

dislike, distaste, hatred, hate, disgust, loathing, repugnance, abhorrence, animosity, antipathy, aversion

CORE MEANING: not liking somebody or something

dislike the most general term; **distaste** mild dislike, used especially of behavior and activities; **hatred** extremely strong dislike; **hate** a more informal term for *hatred*; **disgust** very strong dislike and disapproval; **loathing** strong dislike and disgust, often referring to people; **repugnance** a fairly formal term for strong dislike and disgust, often referring to behavior and activities; **abhorrence** a more formal term for repugnance; **animosity** intense dislike and hostility, usually used to refer to people; **antipathy** a deep-seated dislike that is often instinctive or intuitive; **aversion** strong, possibly unreasonable, dislike of a particular thing.

dis·like·a·ble *adj.* = **dislikable**

dis·lo·cate /dísslō kàyt/ (**-cat·ed, -cat·ing, -cates**) *vt.* **1.** PUT OUT OF PLACE to put or force something out of its usual place or position **2.** MED DISPLACE BODY PART to move or force a bone, out of the joint into which it fits **3.** THROW INTO CONFUSION to disrupt, upset, or disturb the order of something [Late 16thC. Origin uncertain: probably a back-formation from DISLOCATION.] —**dis·lo·cat·ed** *adj.*

dis·lo·cat·ed work·er *n.* somebody who has lost his or her job because of the employer's moving, shutting down, or permanently reducing its workforce

dis·lo·ca·tion /dìss lō káysh'n/ *n.* **1.** DISLOCATING OR BEING DISLOCATED the displacement of something from its usual or proper position **2.** MED DISPLACEMENT OF BODY PART the displacement of a body part, especially of a bone, from its usual fitting in a joint **3.** CHEM IMPERFECTION IN CRYSTAL an irregularity in the fine structure (**lattice**) of an otherwise normal crystal [14thC. Via Old French from, ultimately, Latin *dislocare*, from *locare* (see LOCATE).]

dis·lodge /diss lój/ (**-lodged, -lodg·ing, -lodg·es**) *vti.* to force something or somebody from a previously fixed or secure position, or leave such a position [15thC. From Old French *dislogier*, from *des-* "dis-" and *logier* (see LODGE).] —**dis·lodg·ment** *n.*

dis·loy·al /diss lóy əl/ *adj.* showing a lack of faith in or loyalty to somebody or something [15thC. From Old French *desloial*, from *des-* "dis-" and *loial* (see LOYAL).] —**dis·loy·al·ly** *adv.*

dis·loy·al·ty /diss lóy əltee/ (*plural* **-ties**) *n.* **1.** BEING DISLOYAL a lack of loyalty to a person, vow, organization, or state **2.** DISLOYAL ACT a disloyal or unfaithful act

dis·mal /dízməl/ *adj.* **1.** DEPRESSING depressing to the spirit or outlook **2.** HOPELESS showing a lack or failure of hope **3.** OF POOR QUALITY very poor or inadequate ○ *a dismal performance* [14thC. Via Anglo-Norman *dismal* "unlucky days" from medieval Latin *dies mali*.] —**dis·mal·ly** *adv.* —**dis·mal·ness** *n.*

dis·mal sci·ence *n.* *U.K.* political economy (*humorous*) [Coined by the Scottish essayist Thomas Carlyle (1795–1881)]

Dis·mal Swamp /dìzməl-/ former name for **Great Dismal Swamp**

dis·man·tle /diss mánt'l/ (**-tled, -tling, -tles**) *v.* **1.** *vt.* TAKE APART to take something apart in a way that causes it to stop working **2.** *vi.* COME APART to be able to be separated into components **3.** *vt.* DESTROY SOMETHING BY REMOVING KEY ELEMENTS to destroy something, e.g., an institution or system, by removing essential elements **4.** *vt.* REMOVE EQUIPMENT to strip a room or building of furniture or equipment [Late 16thC. From Old French *desmanteler* "to tear down a fortress wall," from *des-* "dis-" and *emmanteler* "to shelter, fortify," from *mantel* "cloak" (see MANTLE).] —**dis·man·tle·ment** *n.* —**dis·man·tler** *n.*

dis·mast /dìss mást/ (**-mast·ed, -mast·ing, -masts**) *vt.* to break off or remove the mast or masts of a boat or ship —**dis·mast·ment** *n.*

dis·may /diss máy/ *vt.* (**-mayed, -may·ing, -mays**) (*usually passive*) **1.** DISCOURAGE SOMEBODY to cause somebody to feel discouraged or disappointed **2.** ALARM SOMEBODY to fill somebody with alarm, apprehension, or distress ■ *n.* **1.** FEELING OF DISCOURAGEMENT a feeling of hopelessness, disappointment, or discouragement **2.** LOSS OF COURAGE a sudden loss of courage or confidence [14thC. From assumed Anglo-Norman *desmaiier*, of uncertain origin: ultimately a negative form of a prehistoric Germanic word meaning "to be able," which is also the ancestor of English *may*.]

disme /dīm/ *n.* a United States coin first minted in 1792, worth a tenth of a dollar [Late 18thC. From obsolete French, a variant of *dime* (see DIME).]

dis·mem·ber /diss mémbər/ (**-bered, -ber·ing, -bers**) *vt.* **1.** REMOVE LIMB FROM BODY to cut off or remove a limb or other part of a person or animal **2.** DIVIDE SOMETHING UP to cut or tear something into pieces **3.** DESTROY SOMETHING BY TAKING IT APART to destroy something by taking it apart so that its parts no longer work together ○ *dismembered the alliance* [14thC. Via Old French from assumed Vulgar Latin *dismembrare*, from Latin *membrum* (see MEMBER).] —**dis·mem·ber·er** *n.* —**dis·mem·ber·ment** *n.*

dis·miss /diss míss/ (**-missed, -miss·ing, -miss·es**) *vt.* **1.** END EMPLOYMENT OF SOMEBODY to stop employing somebody, e.g., because of unsatisfactory work or wrongdoing **2.** SEND AWAY to send somebody away, or give somebody formal permission to leave **3.** LAW REFUSE FURTHER HEARING IN COURT to refuse to give further hearing to a case in court **4.** REFUSE TO CONSIDER to refuse to give consideration to something **5.** REJECT WITH REASON to consider somebody or something as unsuitable for a particular reason ○ *dismissed the idea as ridiculous* [15thC. From medieval Latin *dismiss-*, the past participle stem of *dismittere*, literally "to send away," from Latin *mittere* (see MISSION).] —**dis·miss·i·ble** *adj.*

dis·miss·al /diss míss'l/ *n.* **1.** ENDING OF SOMEBODY'S EMPLOYMENT the removal of somebody from employment **2.** SENDING AWAY the formal sending away of a person or group **3.** REJECTION the rejection of something from consideration

dis·mis·sive /diss míssiv/ *adj.* indicating rejection, especially showing contempt or indifference —**dis·mis·sive·ly** *adv.* —**dis·mis·sive·ness** *n.*

dis·mount /diss mównt/ *v.* (**-mount·ed, -mount·ing, -mounts**) **1.** *vi.* GET OFF ANIMAL to get down from the back of an animal, e.g., a horse or camel **2.** *vi.* GET OFF CYCLE to get off a bicycle or motorcycle **3.** *vt.* REMOVE FROM FRAME to remove something from a frame, mounting, stand, or support **4.** *vt.* THROW SOMEBODY OFF to remove somebody from a mounted position ○ *The horse dismounted its rider.* ■ *n.* ACT OF DISMOUNTING an act of dismounting or of being dismounted [Mid-16thC. Origin uncertain: probably modeled on obsolete French *désmonter*, literally "to unseat," from *monter* (see MOUNT).] —**dis·mount·a·ble** *adj.*

CORBIS/Bettmann

Walt Disney

Dis·ney /dízneе/, **Walt** (1901–66) U.S. animator and producer. He created Mickey Mouse and Donald Duck, and originated the feature-length cartoon with *Snow White and the Seven Dwarfs* (1937). Full name **Walter Elias Disney**

Dis·ney·esque /dìznee ésk/ *adj.* reminiscent of, or in the style of, the sometimes whimsical movies and cartoons created by Walt Disney or the Disney studios

dis·o·be·di·ence /dìssə beédee əns/ *n.* refusal or failure to obey

dis·o·be·di·ent /dìssə beédee ənt/ *adj.* refusing or failing to obey, especially habitually [15thC. Via Old French from assumed Vulgar Latin *desobedient-*, from Latin *oboedient-*, the present participle stem of *oboedire* (see OBEY).] —**dis·o·be·di·ent·ly** *adv.*

dis·o·bey /dìssə báy/ (**-beyed, -bey·ing, -beys**) *vti.* to refuse or fail to obey a rule, instruction, or authority, or somebody giving an instruction or in authority [14thC. Via French *désobéir* from assumed Vulgar Latin *desobedir*, from Latin *oboedire* (see OBEY).] —**dis·o·bey·er** *n.*

dis·o·blige /dìssə blíj/ (**-bliged, -blig·ing, -blig·es**) *vt.* to be unwilling to help somebody (*formal*) [Late 16thC. Via French *désobliger* from, ultimately, Latin *obligare* (see OBLIGE).]

dis·o·blig·ing /dìssə blī́jing/ *adj.* selfishly or rudely unwilling to help —**dis·o·blig·ing·ly** *adv.* —**dis·o·blig·ing·ness** *n.*

di·som·ic /dī sṓmik/ *adj.* GENETICS with chromosomes occurring in pairs [Early 20thC. Coined from DI- + -SOME + -IC.] —**di·som·y** *n.*

dis·or·der /diss áwrdər/ *n.* **1. LACK OF ORDER** a lack of systematic or orderly arrangement **2. MESSINESS** a state of messiness ○ *found the room in complete disorder* **3.** LAW **UNRULY BEHAVIOR** a public disturbance or breach of peace **4.** MED **ILLNESS** a medical condition involving a disturbance to the normal functioning of the mind or body ■ *vt.* (**-dered, -der·ing, -ders**) **UPSET ARRANGEMENT** to disarrange or disturb the order of something [15thC. Origin uncertain: possibly an alteration of obsolete *disordain*, under the influence of ORDER and French *désordre*.]

dis·or·dered /diss áwrdərd/ *adj.* **1. MESSY OR CONFUSED** marked by confusion or disarray **2. NOT FUNCTIONING NORMALLY** having lost normal physical functioning or thought processes ○ *disordered sleep*

dis·or·der·ly /diss áwrdərlee/ *adj.* **1. LACKING ORDER** lacking order or organization **2. UNRULY** unruly and resisting authority **3.** LAW **DISTURBING PEACE** disturbing the peace or violating public order —**dis·or·der·li·ness** *n.*

dis·or·der·ly con·duct *n.* any one of several minor offenses likely to cause a breach of the peace

dis·or·gan·i·za·tion /diss àwrgəni záysh'n/ *n.* **1. LACK OF ORGANIZATION** a lack of organization or orderly arrangement **2. DESTRUCTION OF ORDER** the destruction of an order or system

dis·or·gan·ize /diss áwrgə nīz/ (**-ized, -iz·ing, -iz·es**) *vt.* to destroy or disrupt the organization, system, or unity of something [Late 18thC. From French *desorganiser*, from *dés-* "not" and *organiser* (see ORGANIZE).] —**dis·or·gan·iz·er** *n.*

dis·or·gan·ized /diss áwrgə nīzd/ *adj.* lacking order and coherence

dis·o·ri·ent /diss áwree ènt/ (**-ent·ed, -ent·ing, -ents**), **dis·o·ri·en·tate** /diss áwree ən tàyt/ (**-tated, -tat·ing, -tates**) *vt.* **1. MAKE SOMEBODY LOSE BEARINGS** to cause somebody to feel lost or confused, especially with regard to direction or position **2. CONFUSE SOMEBODY** to confuse somebody by giving misleading information —**dis·o·ri·en·ta·tion** /diss àwree ən táysh'n/ *n.*

dis·o·ri·ent·ed /diss áwree èntəd/, **dis·ori·en·tat·ed** /-ən tàytəd/ *adj.* **1. HAVING LOST BEARINGS** feeling lost or confused, especially with regard to direction or position **2. CONFUSED** not understanding clearly

dis·own /diss ṓn/ (**-owned, -own·ing, -owns**) *vt.* to refuse or no longer acknowledge a connection with somebody or something —**dis·own·er** *n.* —**dis·own·ment** *n.*

disp. *abbr.* dispensary

dis·par·age /di sperrij/ (**-aged, -ag·ing, -ag·es**) *vt.* to refer disapprovingly to somebody or something —**dis·par·ag·er** *n.*

dis·par·age·ment /di spérrijmənt/ *n.* **1. NEGATIVE CRITICISM** negative or adverse criticism **2. ACT OF DISPARAGING** the act of criticizing or discrediting somebody or something **3. LOWERING OF ESTEEM** a lowering of esteem (*archaic*)

dis·par·ag·ing /di spérrijing/ *adj.* showing or expressing contempt or disapproval —**dis·par·ag·ing·ly** *adv.*

dis·pa·rate /di spérrət/ *adj.* used to describe things or people so completely unlike each other that they cannot be compared [15thC. From Latin *disparatus*, the past participle of *disparare* "to separate," from *parare* "to prepare" (see PARE).] —**dis·pa·rate·ly** *adv.* —**dis·pa·rate·ness** *n.*

dis·par·i·ty /di spérrətee/ (*plural* **-ties**) *n.* **1. LACK OF EQUALITY** lack of equality between things or people **2. UNLIKENESS** dissimilarity or incongruity [Mid-16thC. Via French *disparité* from late Latin *disparitas*, from *paritas* (see PARITY).]

dis·pas·sion /diss pásh'n/ *n.* absence of prejudicial feeling ○ *viewed the chaos around her with dispassion*

dis·pas·sion·ate *adj.* not influenced by emotion or personal feelings —**dis·pas·sion·ate·ly** *adv.* —**dis·pas·sion·ate·ness** *n.*

dis·patch /di spách/, **des·patch** *vt.* (**-patched, -patch·ing, -patch·es**) **1. SEND SOMETHING** to send off something, e.g., a letter or package, to a particular destination **2. SEND SOMEBODY AWAY TO DO SOMETHING** to instruct somebody to go somewhere to carry out a task **3. DEAL WITH SOMETHING QUICKLY** to complete or deal with something quickly or efficiently **4. KILL SOMEBODY** to kill a person or animal ■ *n.* **1.** MAIL **SENDING OFF** the sending of something or somebody such as a letter or a messenger **2. CARRYING OUT** the carrying out of an activity **3. SPEED** speed and efficiency ○ *carried out her duties with dispatch* **4. OFFICIAL MESSAGE** a message or report, especially an official communication from a diplomat or an officer in the armed forces **5.** PRESS **NEWS REPORT** a news item or report sent by a journalist or news agency ○ *dispatches from the scene of the fire* **6. ACT OF KILLING** the killing of a person or animal [Early 16thC. Via Italian *dispacciare* from, ultimately, a negative form of assumed Vulgar Latin *impactare* "to impede," from Latin *impact-*, the past participle stem of *impingere* (see IMPINGE).]

dis·patch·er /di spáchər/ *n.* somebody whose job is to control a fleet of vehicles, e.g., taxis, by radio communication

dis·pel /di spél/ (**-pelled, -pel·ling, -pels**) *vt.* **1. RID MIND OF SOMETHING** to rid somebody's mind of a particular thought or idea, especially an erroneous one **2. DISPERSE SOMETHING** to disperse or drive away something ○ *clouds and mist that the sun soon dispelled* [15thC. From Latin *dispellere*, literally "to drive away," from *pellere* (see PULSE).] —**dis·pel·ler** *n.*

dis·pen·sa·ble /di spénsəb'l/ *adj.* able to be dispensed with or replaced —**dis·pen·sa·bil·i·ty** /di spènsə bíllətee/ *n.* —**dis·pen·sa·ble·ness** /-b'lnəss/ *n.*

dis·pen·sa·ry /di spénsəree/ (*plural* **-ries**) *n.* **1.** **MEDICINE STORE** a place where medical supplies are stored and distributed to patients by a pharmacist **2. TEMPORARY MEDICAL CENTER** a place where temporary or provisional medical treatment is provided

dis·pen·sa·tion /dìspən sáysh'n/ *n.* **1. EXEMPTION** exemption or release from a rule or obligation, especially a religious one **2. DOCUMENT GIVING EXEMPTION** an official document authorizing dispensation, especially religious dispensation **3.** RELIG **RELIGIOUS SYSTEM** in Christian belief, a divinely ordained religious system **4.** CHR **DIVINE ORDERING** in Christian belief, a divine ordering or management of affairs and events in the world **5.** RELIG **RELIGIOUS EPOCH** the time during which a religious doctrine or practice is believed to be in force **6. DISPENSING** the distribution or giving out of something ○ *dispensation of emergency supplies* —**dis·pen·sa·tion·al** *adj.*

dis·pen·sa·to·ry /di spénsə tàwree/ *adj.* relating to or granting dispensation, especially religious dispensation

dis·pense /di spéns/ (**-pensed, -pens·ing, -pens·es**) *v.* **1.** *vt.* **PROVIDE SOMETHING** to distribute something to several recipients **2.** *vt.* **SELL SOMETHING** to sell something at more than one location or to more than one customer **3.** *vt.* PHARM **SUPPLY MEDICINES** to supply medicine according to a prescription **4.** *vt.* LAW **ADMINISTER JUSTICE** to be an agent of the administration of justice **5.** *vi.* CHR **GRANT DISPENSATION** to grant a religious dispensation [14thC. Via Old French from Latin *dispensare*, from *dispendere*, literally "to weigh out," from *pendere* "to weigh" (see PENSIVE).]

dispense with *vt.* **1. DO WITHOUT** to manage without something ○ *Since it's sunny, we can dispense with the rain gear.* **2. GET RID OF** to get rid of something not wanted or needed ○ *Let's dispense with all these convoluted rules and regulations.*

dis·pens·er /di spénsər/ *n.* **1. DEVICE FOR DISPENSING GOODS** a device that releases its contents in convenient or measured quantities when operated (*usually used in combination*) **2. PROVIDER OF SOMETHING** somebody who or something that distributes something **3.** PHARM **MEDICINE SUPPLIER** somebody who supplies medicine according to a prescription

dis·per·sal /di spúrs'l/ *n.* **1. DISTRIBUTION** the distribution or scattering of people or things over an area **2.** BIOL **NATURAL SPREAD OF SEED** the natural distribution of plant seeds and the offspring of non-mobile organisms over a wide area by various methods **3.** BIOL **MOVEMENT OF ORGANISMS** the movement of organisms away from their place of birth or from centers of population density **4. DISAPPEARANCE** disappearance as a result of scattering or going away in different directions

dis·per·sant /di spúrs'nt/ *n.* a liquid or gas that facilitates or improves the dispersion of small particles or droplets, e.g., in an aerosol —**dis·per·sant** *adj.*

dis·perse /di spúrs/ (**-persed, -pers·ing, -pers·es**) *vti.* **1. SCATTER** to cause something to scatter, or go away in different directions **2. DISTRIBUTE** to distribute something over a wide area, or become widespread **3. CAUSE TO DISAPPEAR** to cause something to disappear, or disappear **4.** CHEM **DISTRIBUTE EVENLY** to distribute particles evenly throughout a medium, or become distributed in this way **5.** PHYS **SEPARATE INTO COLORS** to separate white light into the component colors of the spectrum, or undergo this process [14thC. Via Old French from Latin *dispers-*, the past participle stem of *dispergere*, literally "to scatter around," from *spargere* (see SPARSE).] —**dis·pers·er** *n.*

dis·per·sion /di spúrsh'n/ *n.* **1. DISPERSING** the scattering or distribution of something within an area or space **2. BEING DISPERSED** the fact or state of being spread, scattered, or distributed **3. STATS DISTRIBUTION OF VALUES** the distribution of a statistical frequency distribution about an average or median **4.** CHEM **MEDIUM WITH DISPERSED PARTICLES** a chemical system consisting of a gas, liquid, or colloid containing dispersed particles

Dis·per·sion /di spúrsh'n/ *n.* = **Diaspora**

dis·per·sive *adj.* tending to cause dispersion —**dis·per·sive·ly** *adv.* —**dis·per·sive·ness** *n.*

dis·pir·it /di spírrit/ (**-it·ed, -it·ing, -its**) *vt.* to discourage or dishearten somebody

dis·pir·it·ed /di spírritəd/ *adj.* affected by lack of energy and a loss of enthusiasm —**dis·pir·it·ed·ly** *adv.* —**dis·pir·it·ed·ness** *n.*

dis·pir·it·ing /di spírriting/ *adj.* depressing or disheartening —**dis·pir·it·ing·ly** *adv.*

dis·place /dis pláyss/ (**-placed, -plac·ing, -plac·es**) *vt.* **1. MOVE FROM USUAL PLACE** to move something from its usual or correct place **2. FORCE TO LEAVE HOME** to force somebody to leave his or her home or country, e.g., because of war **3. REMOVE FROM POST** to discharge or remove somebody from an office, position, or job **4. REPLACE** to take the place of somebody or something **5.** CHEM **TAKE PLACE OF ATOM** to take the place of another atom or group in a compound **6.** PHYS **REPLACE FLUID WITH OBJECT** to replace a volume of fluid with a floating or submerged object, forcing the original fluid to move elsewhere —**dis·place·a·ble** *adj.* —**dis·plac·er** *n.*

dis·placed per·son (*plural* **dis·placed per·sons** *or* **dis·placed peo·ple**) *n.* somebody who has been forced to leave his or her home or country, especially because of war or political oppression

dis·place·ment /dis pláyssmənt/ *n.* **1. DISPLACING OR BEING DISPLACED** the moving or movement of something from its usual or correct place **2.** PHYS, SHIPPING **FLUID DISPLACED** the fluid, e.g., water, that is forced to move by an object floating or submerged in it. It is often used as a measure of a ship's size. **3.** PSYCHOL **TRANSFER OF EMOTIONS OR BEHAVIOR** transfer of emotion from the original focus to another less threatening object or person, or the substitution of one response or piece of behavior for another **4.** PHYS **AMOUNT OF MOVEMENT IN PARTICULAR DIRECTION** the amount of movement of an object measured in a particular direction **5.** CHEM **CHEMICAL REPLACEMENT** a chemical reaction in which one atom or chemical group takes the place of another in a compound **6.** GEOL **MOVEMENT OF GEOLOGIC FAULT** the distance that a point on one side of a geologic fault has moved, relative to a corresponding point on the other side **7.** AUTOMOT **ENGINE VOLUME** the total volume displaced by the pistons in an internal combustion engine

dis·place·ment ton *n.* a unit of measure for the displacement of a floating ship, equivalent to 2240 lb

dis·play /di spláy/ *v.* (**-played, -play·ing, -plays**) **1.** *vt.* **MAKE VISIBLE** to make something visible or available for others to see **2.** *vt.* **MAKE EVIDENT** to reveal or make evident a quality or feeling **3.** *vti.* COMPUT **SHOW DATA** to show messages, data, or graphics on a monitor, or appear on a monitor **4.** *vti.* ZOOL **SHOW STYLIZED BEHAVIOR** to show a particular pattern of animal behavior, e.g., to attract a mate or defend a territory ■ *n.* **1. VISUAL ARRANGEMENT** a collection of things arranged or done for others to see, especially something considered attractive, interesting, or entertaining (*often used in combination*) **2. BEING VISIBLE OR ARRANGED FOR VIEWING** the act of being clearly and easily visible or placed for people to view ○ *new work on display* **3. EVIDENT FEELING OR QUALITY** an evident feeling or quality ○ *a display of courage* **4.** PRINTING **GRAPHIC ADVERTISING** printed advertising that uses attractive pictures, typography, and other features **5.** COMPUT **ELECTRONIC SCREEN** an electronic device that presents visual information **6.** COMPUT **INFORMATION ON A SCREEN** the information shown on a computer monitor or other electronic device **7.** ZOOL **STYLIZED BEHAVIOR** a particular pattern of animal behavior used to produce a response in other animals, especially of the same species, e.g., when courting or defending territory ■ *adj.* PRINTING **FOR ADVERTISING** relating to typefaces that are designed for prominent use in advertising [Late 16thC. Via Old French *despleier* from Latin *displicare*, literally "to unfold," from *plicare* (see PLY²).] —**dis·play·er** *n.*

dis·play cab·i·net, **dis·play case** *n.* a case or stand with glass panels, used for showing items of interest

dis·please /dis plẽez/ (**-pleased, -pleas·ing, -pleas·es**) *vti.* to annoy or dissatisfy somebody [14thC. Via Old French *desplais-*, the stem of *desplaire*, from assumed Vulgar Latin *displacere*, from Latin *placere* (see PLACID).]

dis·pleased /diss plẽezd/ *adj.* annoyed or dissatisfied

dis·pleas·ing /diss plẽezing/ *adj.* causing annoyance or dissatisfaction —**dis·pleas·ing·ly** *adv.*

dis·pleas·ure /diss plézhər/ *n.* a feeling of annoyance or dissatisfaction [15thC. From Old French *desplaisir* "to displease," used as a noun, from *des-* "dis-" and *plaisir* "pleasure" (see PLEASURE).]

dis·plode (**-plod·ed, -plod·ing, -plodes**) *vti.* to explode (*archaic*)

dis·port /di spáwrt/ *v.* (**-port·ed, -port·ing, -ports**) (*archaic or humorous*) **1.** *vr.* **SHOW OFF** to show off or try to draw attention to yourself **2.** *vi.* **BEHAVE PLAYFULLY** to behave in a playful manner ■ *n.* **FORM OF ENTERTAINMENT** a form of lively entertainment or diversion [14thC. From Old French *desporter* "to divert," from *des-* "apart" and *porter* "to carry."]

dis·pos·a·ble /di spṓzəb'l/ *adj.* **1.** **THROWAWAY** designed to be thrown away after use **2.** **AVAILABLE FOR USE** used to describe money or assets that are available for use ■ *n.* **SOMETHING TO BE USED ONLY ONCE** something that is designed to be thrown away after use, e.g., a paper cup (*often used in the plural*) —**dis·pos·a·bil·i·ty** /di spṑzə bíllətee/ *n.* —**dis·pos·a·ble·ness** /-b'lnəss/ *n.*

dis·pos·a·ble in·come *n.* **1.** **INCOME AFTER TAX** income that remains available for spending after deductions for taxes and other obligations **2.** FIN **MONEY AVAILABLE FOR SPENDING** the total amount of money that a country or community has available for spending

dis·pos·al /di spṓz'l/ *n.* **1.** **PROCESS OF GETTING RID OF SOMETHING** the process of throwing away or getting rid of something **2.** **ORDERLY ARRANGEMENT** an orderly arrangement, distribution, or placement **3.** **TRANSFERRING SOMETHING TO ANOTHER** the transferring of something valuable to another by sale or gift **4.** **GARBAGE DISPOSAL** a garbage disposal (*informal*)

dis·pose /di spṓz/ *v.* (**-posed, -pos·ing, -pos·es**) **1.** *vt.* **MAKE WILLING** to make somebody willing or receptive to something (*often passive*) **2.** *vt.* **PUT IN PLACE** to arrange or position something for use or for a particular purpose (*formal*) (*often passive*) **3.** *vti.* **SETTLE** to settle a matter by putting it into its correct or definitive form **4.** *vt.* **INCLINE** to make somebody likely to experience something **5.** *vt.* **BESTOW** to bestow (*archaic*) ■ *n.* **DISPOSAL** disposal (*archaic*) [14thC. From French *disposer*, an alteration (under the influence of *poser* "to place") of Latin *disponere*, literally "to set out," from *ponere* (see POSITION).] —**dis·pos·er** *n.*

dispose of *vt.* **1.** **GET RID OF SOMETHING** to throw away or get rid of something **2.** **TRANSFER** to transfer something to another's ownership, by sale or other means **3.** **KILL** to kill a person or animal **4.** **ATTEND TO SOMETHING** to deal with a matter in order to settle it (*formal*)

dis·po·si·tion /dìspə zísh'n/ *n.* **1.** **PERSONALITY** somebody's usual mood or temperament **2.** **BEHAVIORAL TENDENCY** an inclination or tendency to act in a particular way **3.** **SETTLEMENT** settlement of a business or legal matter **4.** = **disposal** *n.* **2**, **disposal** *n.* **3** [14thC. Via French from, ultimately, Latin *disponere* (see DISPOSE).] —**dis·po·si·tion·al** *adj.*

dis·pos·i·tive /diss pózzitiv/ *adj.* effecting the final outcome of a court case [Early 17thC. Directly or via French from medieval Latin *dispositivus*, from *disposit-*, the past participle stem of *disponere* (see DISPOSE).]

dis·pos·sess /dìspə zéss/ (**-sessed, -ses·sing, -sess·es**) *vt.* to take away possession or occupancy of something, especially property (*archaic or formal*) [15thC. From Old French *despossesser*, from *des-* "dis-" and *possesser* (see POSSESS).] —**dis·pos·ses·sor** *n.* —**dis·pos·ses·so·ry** *adj.*

dis·pos·sessed /dìspə zést/ *adj.* **DEPRIVED OF POSSESSION** deprived of property or rights ■ *npl.* **DISPOSSESSED PEOPLE** people who have been deprived of their property or rights

dis·praise /diss práyz/ *vt.* (**-praised, -prais·ing, -prais·es**) **EXPRESS DISAPPROVAL** to express disapproval of somebody (*archaic literary*) ■ *n.* **DISAPPROVAL** the expression of disapproval (*archaic*) —**dis·prais·er** *n.*

dis·prize /diss príz/ (**-prized, -priz·ing, -priz·es**) *vt.* to be unwilling to appreciate the worth of somebody or something (*archaic*)

dis·proof /diss próof/ *n.* **1.** **PROVING WRONG** the disproving of a legal argument or point **2.** **EVIDENCE PROVING SOMETHING WRONG** evidence that disproves something

dis·pro·por·tion /dìsprə páwrsh'n/ *n.* **SOMETHING OUT OF PROPORTION** something that is out of proportion or unequal ■ *vt.* (**-tioned, -tion·ing, -tions**) **MAKE SOMETHING DISPROPORTIONATE** to make something disproportionate —**dis·pro·por·tion·a·ble** *adj.* —**dis·pro·por·tion·a·ble·ness** *n.* —**dis·pro·por·tion·a·bly** *adv.*

dis·pro·por·tion·ate, **dis·pro·por·tion·al** *adj.* /dìsprə páwrsh'nət/ unequal or out of proportion in quantity, shape, or size —**dis·pro·por·tion·ate·ly** *adv.* —**dis·pro·por·tion·ate·ness** *n.*

dis·pro·por·tion·a·tion /dìsprə pawrsh'n áysh'n/ *n.* a chemical reaction in which a single substance acts as both oxidizing and reducing agent, resulting in the production of dissimilar substances

dis·prove /dis próov/ (**-proved, -prov·ing, -proves**) *vt.* to show that something is incorrect [14thC. From Old French *desprover*, from *des-* "dis-" and *prover* (see PROVE).] —**dis·prov·a·ble** *adj.* —**dis·prov·al** *n.*

dis·put·a·ble /di spyóotəb'l/ *adj.* not definitely true or valid and therefore debatable or open to argument —**dis·put·a·bil·i·ty** /di spyóotə bíllətee/ *n.* —**dis·put·a·ble·ness** /-b'lnəss/ *n.*

dis·put·a·bly /di spyóotəblee/ *adv.* used to suggest that the speaker or writer thinks something is true and could defend that view against those who disagree

WORD KEY: USAGE

See Usage note at ***arguably.***

dis·pu·tant /di spyóot'nt, díspyət'nt/ *n.* **PARTY TO CASE** somebody involved in an argument or a legal dispute ■ *adj.* **IN A CASE** engaged in an argument or a legal dispute

dis·pu·ta·tion /dìspyə táysh'n/ *n.* **1.** **ARGUMENT** arguing or disagreement (*formal*) **2.** EDUC **FORMAL ACADEMIC DEBATE** a formal academic debate in defense of a thesis

dis·pu·ta·tious /dìspyə táyshəss/, **dis·pu·ta·tive** /di spyóotətiv/ *adj.* tending to argue or disagree without adequate cause (*formal*) —**dis·pu·ta·tious·ly** *adv.* —**dis·pu·ta·tious·ness** *n.*

dis·pute /di spyóot/ *v.* (**-put·ed, -put·ing, -putes**) **1.** *vti.* **QUESTION** to question or doubt the truth or validity of something **2.** *vi.* **DISAGREE** to disagree or argue about something **3.** *vt.* **CONTEST** to fight for or strive to win something (*formal*) **4.** *vt.* **OPPOSE** to strive against or resist something (*formal*) ■ *n.* **1.** **ARGUMENT** serious argument or disagreement **2.** **INDUSTRIAL DISAGREEMENT** a prolonged disagreement between management and workers or a labor union, often involving a strike [Late 16thC. Via Old French from Latin *disputare*, literally "to argue out," from *putare* "to consider."] —**dis·put·er** *n.*

WORD KEY: SYNONYMS

See Synonyms at ***disagree.***

dis·qual·i·fi·ca·tion /diss kwòlləfi káysh'n/ *n.* **1.** **INELIGIBILITY** being or becoming ineligible to do or take part in something **2.** **ACT OF BEING DISQUALIFIED** an instance of being disqualified **3.** **SOMETHING THAT DISQUALIFIES** something that makes somebody ineligible to do or take part in something

dis·qual·i·fied /diss kwóllə fīd/ *adj.* ineligible to compete or take part in something, or deprived of the right to do something

dis·qual·i·fy /diss kwóllə fī/ (**-fied, -fy·ing, -fies**) *vt.* **1.** **DECLARE UNFIT** to make or declare somebody unfit, unqualified, or ineligible to do or take part in something **2.** **TAKE AWAY LEGAL RIGHT** to deprive somebody of a legal or other right or privilege —**dis·qual·i·fi·able** *adj.* —**dis·qual·i·fi·er** *n.*

dis·qui·et /diss kwī ət/ *n.* **LACK OF PEACE** a lack of peace resulting from anxiety ■ *vt.* (**-et·ed, -et·ing, -ets**) **MAKE ANXIOUS** to make somebody anxious or uneasy (*archaic or literary*) —**dis·qui·et·ly** *adv.* —**dis·qui·et·ness** *n.*

dis·qui·et·ed /diss kwī ətəd/ *adj.* anxious, worried, or uneasy (*archaic or literary*) —**dis·qui·et·ed·ly** *adv.* —**dis·qui·et·ed·ness** *n.*

dis·qui·et·ing /diss kwī əting/ *adj.* causing discomfort, worry, or doubt to arise —**dis·qui·et·ing·ly** *adv.*

dis·qui·e·tude /diss kwī ə tood/ *n.* = **disquiet**

dis·qui·si·tion /dìskwi zísh'n/ *n.* a long formal essay or discussion on a subject (*formal*) [Early 17thC. Via French from, ultimately, Latin *disquirere* "to inquire," from *quaerere* (see QUERY).] —**dis·qui·si·tion·al** *adj.*

Benjamin Disraeli

Dis·rae·li /diz ráylee/, **Benjamin, 1st Earl of Beaconsfield** (1804–81) British statesman and novelist. He was Conservative prime minister (1868, 1874–80), and author of *Coningsby* (1844) and *Sybil* (1845).

dis·rate /diss ráyt/ (**-rat·ed, -rat·ing, -rates**) *vt.* to demote somebody in the military to a lower rank

dis·re·gard /dìssri gárd/ *vt.* (**-gard·ed, -gard·ing, -gards**) **1.** **IGNORE** to ignore or pay no attention to somebody or something **2.** **TREAT WITHOUT RESPECT** to treat somebody or something with contempt or without respect ■ *n.* **NEGLECT** lack of attention or respect —**dis·re·gard·er** *n.* —**dis·re·gard·ful** *adj.* —**dis·re·gard·ful·ly** *adv.* —**dis·re·gard·ful·ness** *n.*

dis·re·la·ted /dìss ri láytəd/ *adj.* not related ○ ***a series of disrelated arguments leading nowhere***

dis·rel·ish /diss réllish/ *vt.* (**-ished, -ish·ing, -ish·es**) **DISLIKE** to dislike something, or find something distasteful (*archaic*) ■ *n.* **AVERSION** dislike or aversion (*archaic*)

dis·re·mem·ber /dìssri mémbər/ (**-bered, -ber·ing, -bers**) *vti.* to forget or fail to remember something (*informal*)

dis·re·pair /dìssri páir/ *n.* poor working order or condition as a result of neglect

dis·rep·u·ta·ble /diss réppyətəb'l/ *adj.* lacking respectability on the basis of past or present actions —**dis·rep·u·ta·bil·i·ty** /diss rèppyətə bíllətee/ *n.* —**dis·rep·u·ta·ble·ness** /diss réppyətəb'lnəss/ *n.* —**dis·rep·u·ta·bly** /-blee/ *adv.*

dis·re·pute /dìssri pyóot/ *n.* a lack or loss of good reputation or respect

dis·re·spect /dìssri spékt/ *n.* **TOTAL CONTEMPT** a lack of respect ■ *vt.* (**-spect·ed, -spect·ing, -spects**) **SHOW NO RESPECT** to show a lack of respect for somebody or something. ◊ **dis**

dis·re·spect·a·ble /dìssri spéktəb'l/ *adj.* not deserving or getting respect or social approval —**dis·re·spect·a·ble·ness** *n.*

dis·re·spect·ful /dìssri spéktfəl/ *adj.* showing a lack of respect —**dis·re·spect·ful·ly** *adv.* —**dis·re·spect·ful·ness** *n.*

dis·robe /diss rṓb/ (**-robed, -rob·ing, -robes**) *v.* **1.** *vti.* **UNDRESS** to remove your own or somebody else's clothing (*formal*) **2.** *vt.* **DIVEST OF AUTHORITY** to strip somebody of authority or office (*archaic*) [Late 16thC. From Old French *desrober*, from *des-* "dis-" and *robe* "ROBE."] —**dis·robe·ment** *n.* —**dis·rob·er** *n.*

dis·rupt /diss rúpt/ (**-rupt·ed, -rupt·ing, -rupts**) *vt.* **1.** **INTERRUPT** to interrupt the normal course of a process or activity **2.** **DESTROY ORDER** to destroy the order or orderly progression of something **3.** **SPLIT** to break or burst something (*archaic*) [15thC. From Latin *disrupt-*, the past participle stem of *disrumpere*, literally "to break apart," from *rumpere* (see RUPTURE).] —**dis·rupt·er** *n.*

dis·rup·tion /diss rúpshən/ *n.* **1. UNWANTED BREAK** an unwelcome or unexpected break in a process or activity **2. SUSPENSION** the interruption or suspension of normal activity or progress **3. STATE OF DISORDER** a state of disorder caused by outside influence

dis·rup·tive /diss rúptiv/ *adj.* interrupting normal order or progress —**dis·rup·tive·ly** *adv.*

dis·rup·tive col·or·a·tion *n.* a coloration pattern in an animal that confuses or disrupts the perception of its body outline, thus providing a means of protection

diss. *abbr.* dissertation

dis·sat·is·fac·tion /diss sàttiss fákshən/ *n.* **1. DISCONTENT** a state or feeling of not being satisfied **2. SOMETHING CAUSING DISCONTENT** something that causes discontent or disappointment

dis·sat·is·fac·to·ry /diss sàttiss fáktəree/ *adj.* not satisfactory

dis·sat·is·fied /diss sáttiss fīd/ *adj.* not pleased or contented —**dis·sat·is·fied·ly** *adv.*

dis·sat·is·fy /diss sáttiss fī/ (**-fied, -fy·ing, -fies**) *vt.* to displease or fail to satisfy

dis·sect /di sékt/ (**-sect·ed, -sect·ing, -sects**) *v.* **1.** *vti.* BIOL **CUT AND EXAMINE** to cut and separate the parts of animal or plant specimens for scientific study **2.** *vt.* **EXAMINE IN DETAIL** to examine or analyze a person or subject in detail [Late 16thC. From Latin *dissect-*, the past participle stem of *dissecare*, literally "to cut apart," from *secare* (see SECTION).] —**dis·sec·ti·ble** *adj.* —**dis·sec·tor** *n.*

dis·sect·ed /di séktəd/ *adj.* **1.** BOT **DIVIDED INTO PARTS** used to describe a leaf that is divided into narrow lobes or segments **2.** GEOL **WITH HILLS AND VALLEYS** used to describe a landscape that has been eroded into hills and valleys

dis·sec·tion /di sékshən/ *n.* **1.** BIOL **CUTTING AND EXAMINING** the cutting and separating of the constituent parts of animal or plant specimens for scientific study **2.** BIOL **DISSECTED SPECIMEN** something that has been dissected, e.g., an anatomical specimen **3. EXAMINATION** a thorough and detailed analysis or examination

dis·seize /diss séez/ (**dis·seized, dis·seiz·ing, dis·seiz·es**) *vi.* to deprive somebody wrongfully of possession of land [14thC. From Anglo-Norman *disseisir*, a variant of Old French *dessaisir* "to dispossess," from *des-* "dis-" and *saisir* (see SEIZE).] —**dis·sei·sor** *n.*

dis·sei·zee /dìss see zée/ (*plural* **dis·sei·zees**) *n.* wrongful deprivation of somebody of his or her land

dis·sei·zin /diss séezin/ *n.* the act of wrongfully depriving somebody of land [14thC. From Anglo-Norman *disseisine*, a variant of Old French *dessaisine*, from *dessaisir* (see DISSEIZE).]

dis·sem·ble /di sémb'l/ (**-bled, -bling, -bles**) *v.* **1.** *vi.* **PUT ON FALSE APPEARANCE** to put on a false appearance in order to conceal facts, feelings, or intentions **2.** *vt.* **GIVE APPEARANCE** to put on the appearance of something not actually felt or true (*formal*) **3.** *vt.* **HIDE BY PRETENSE** to hide real beliefs or intentions through misleading speech or behavior (*formal*) [15thC. From Old French *dessembler* "to be different," from *des-* "dis-" and *sembler* "to seem" (see SEMBLANCE).] —**dis·sem·blance** *n.* —**dis·sem·bler** *n.*

dis·sem·bling /di sémbling/ *n.* **ADOPTION OF FALSE APPEARANCE** creation or adoption of a false appearance so as to elicit a false impression on the part of somebody else ■ *adj.* **FEIGNING** feigning or pretending —**dis·sem·bling·ly** *adv.*

dis·sem·i·nate /di sémmi nàyt/ (**-nat·ed, -nat·ing, -nates**) *vti.* to distribute or spread something, especially information, or become widespread [15thC. From Latin *disseminat-*, the past participle stem of *disseminare*, literally "to sow abroad," from *semin-*, the stem of *semen* "seed" (see SEMEN).] —**dis·sem·i·na·tion** /di sèmmi náysh'n/ *n.* —**dis·sem·i·na·tive** /di sémmi nàytiv/ *adj.* —**dis·sem·i·na·tor** /-nàytər/ *n.*

WORD KEY: SYNONYMS

See Synonyms at ***scatter***.

dis·sen·sion /di sénshən/ *n.* disagreement or difference of opinion, especially when leading to open conflict [14thC. Via French from, ultimately, Latin *dissentire* (see DISSENT).]

dis·sen·sus /di sénsəss/ *n.* a preponderance of disagreement [Mid-20thC. Blend of DISSENT and CONSENSUS.]

dis·sent /di sént/ *vi.* (**-sent·ed, -sent·ing, -sents**) **1. DISAGREE** to disagree with a widely held or majority opinion **2.** CHR **NOT SUPPORT RELIGIOUS PRACTICES** to refuse to conform to the authority, doctrines and practices of an established church **3. WITHHOLD ASSENT** to withhold assent or approval ■ *n.* **1. DISAGREEMENT** disagreement from a widely held or majority opinion **2.** CHR **RELIGIOUS NONCONFORMITY** refusal to conform to the authority, doctrines, or practices of an established church **3.** LAW **MINORITY OPINION** an opinion of a judge that is not in agreement with that of other judges **4.** POL **REFUSAL TO ACCEPT POLITICAL RULES** opposition to the laws, norms, and structures of a political regime, especially on moral grounds [15thC. From Latin *dissentire*, literally "to feel differently," from *sentire* (see SENTIENT).]

dis·sent·er /di séntər/ *n.* somebody who disagrees with the beliefs or opinions of a majority

Dis·sent·er *n.* somebody who refuses to accept the authority, doctrines, or practices of an established church, especially a Protestant who dissented from the Church of England in the 17th and 18th centuries

dis·sen·tient /di sénshee ənt/ *adj.* **DISSENTING** showing or expressing disagreement with the beliefs or opinions of a majority ■ *n.* **DISSENTER** somebody who disagrees with the beliefs or opinions of a majority [Early 17thC. From Latin *dissentient-*, the present participle stem of *dissentire* (see DISSENT).] —**dis·sen·tience** *n.* —**dis·sen·tien·cy** *n.* —**dis·sen·tient·ly** *adv.*

dis·sent·ing /di sénting/ *adj.* **1. EXPRESSING OR SHOWING DISAGREEMENT** disagreeing with the beliefs or opinions of a majority **2. dis·sent·ing, Dis·sent·ing** CHR **OF DISSENTERS** relating or belonging to a group of religious nonconformists, especially an English Protestant denomination of the 17th or 18th centuries **3.** LAW **DISAGREEING WITH OTHER JUDGES** disagreeing with the majority verdict or opinion of other judges —**dis·sent·ing·ly** *adv.*

dis·sep·i·ment /di séppəmənt/ *n.* BOT a dividing wall or membrane separating an organ, e.g., a plant ovary, into distinct chambers [Early 18thC. From Latin *dissaepimentum*, from *dissaepire* "to make separate," from *saepire* "to divide off," from *saepes* "hedge" (source of English *septum*).] —**dis·sep·i·men·tal** /di sèppə mént'l/ *adj.*

dis·ser·tate /díssər tàyt/ (**-tat·ed, -tat·ing, -tates**), **dis·sert** /di súrt/ (**-sert·ed, -sert·ing, -serts**) *vi.* to write or present a dissertation (*formal*) —**dis·ser·ta·tor** *n.*

dis·ser·ta·tion /dìssər táysh'n/ *n.* **1. LONG ESSAY** a lengthy and formal written treatment of a subject, especially a long paper submitted as a requirement for a degree **2. FORMAL DISCOURSE** a formal spoken or written discourse —**dis·ser·ta·tion·al** *adj.* —**dis·ser·ta·tion·ist** *n.*

dis·serve /di súrv/ (**-served, -serv·ing, -serves**) *vt.* to harm or to mistreat another (*formal*)

dis·serv·ice /di súrviss/ *n.* an action that causes harm or difficulty

dis·sev·er /di sévvər/ (**-ered, -er·ing, -ers**) *v.* (*formal*) **1.** *vt.* **SEPARATE** to separate or sever something **2.** *vt.* **BREAK UP** to break up or divide something **3.** *vi.* **COME APART** to come apart or become disunited [13thC. Via Anglo-Norman *deseverer* from, ultimately, late Latin *disseparare*, literally "to split apart," from Latin *separare* (see SEPARATE).] —**dis·sev·er·ance** *n.* —**dis·sev·er·a·tion** /di sèvvə ráysh'n/ *n.* —**dis·sev·er·ment** /di sévvərmənt/ *n.*

dis·si·dence /díssidənss/ *n.* disagreement with authority or with prevailing opinion

dis·si·dent /díssidənt/ *n.* **SOMEBODY WHO DISAGREES** somebody who publicly disagrees with an established political or religious system or organization ■ *adj.* **EXPRESSING DISAGREEMENT** expressing or showing disagreement with authority or with prevailing opinion [Mid-16thC. From Latin *dissident-*, the present participle stem of *dissidere*, literally "to sit apart," from *sedere* (see SEDENTARY).] —**dis·si·dent·ly** *adv.*

dis·sim·i·lar /di símmələr/ *adj.* differing in one or more respects —**dis·sim·i·lar·ly** *adv.*

dis·sim·i·lar·i·ty /dìssimə lérrətee/ (*plural* **-ties**) *n.* **1. FACT OF DIFFERENCE** the fact or state of being different in one or more respects **2. POINT OF DIFFERENCE** a point of difference or distinction

dis·sim·i·late /di símmə làyt/ (**-lat·ed, -lat·ing, -lates**) *vti.* **1. LOSE SIMILARITY** to make something dissimilar, or become dissimilar **2.** PHON **CHANGE TO DIFFERENT CONSONANT SOUND** to undergo linguistic dissimilation, or to change a consonant or consonants by this process [Mid-19thC. Formed from DIS- + ASSIMILATE.] —**dis·sim·i·la·tive** /di símmə làytiv/ *adj.* —**dis·sim·i·la·tory** /di símmələ tàwree/ *adj.*

dis·sim·i·la·tion /di sìmmi láysh'n/ *n.* **1. LOSS OF SIMILARITY** the process of becoming dissimilar **2.** PHON **SOUNDS BECOMING DISSIMILAR** the development of a dissimilarity between two consonant sounds in a word that are originally identical

dis·si·mil·i·tude /dìssi mílli to͝od/ *n.* the condition or quality of differing or of being different from something else or others (*formal*) [15thC. From Latin *dissimilitudo*, from *dissimilis*, literally "unlike," from *similis* (see SIMILAR).]

dis·sim·u·late /di símmyə làyt/ (**-lat·ed, -lat·ing, -lates**) *vti.* to disguise or hide your true feelings, thoughts, or intentions (*formal*) [15thC. From Latin *dissimulat-*, the past participle stem of *dissimulare*, literally "to disguise completely," from *simulare* (see SIMULATE).] —**dis·sim·u·la·tion** /di sìmmyə láysh'n/ *n.* —**dis·sim·u·la·tive** /di símmyə làytiv/ *adj.* —**dis·sim·u·la·tor** /-tər/ *n.*

dis·si·pate /díssə pàyt/ (**-pat·ed, -pat·ing, -pates**) *v.* **1.** *vti.* **CAUSE TO DIMINISH** to cause something to fade or disappear, or to undergo such a process **2.** *vt.* **WASTE** to spend or use something wastefully [15thC. From Latin *dissipat-*, the past participle stem of *dissipare*, literally "to scatter around."] —**dis·si·pat·er** *n.* —**dis·si·pa·tive** *adj.* —**dis·si·pa·tor** *n.*

dis·si·pat·ed /díssə pàytəd/ *adj.* **1. OVERINDULGING** overindulging in the pursuit of pleasure by physical methods **2. SQUANDERED** lost through squandering, as money sometimes is ○ *a dissipated inheritance* —**dis·si·pat·ed·ly** *adv.* —**dis·si·pat·ed·ness** *n.*

dis·si·pa·tion /díssə páysh'n/ *n.* **1. OVERINDULGENCE** overindulgence in the pursuit of pleasure by physical methods **2. WASTEFUL USE** the use or squandering of resources, e.g., money or fuel (*formal*) **3. DISAPPEARANCE** disappearance through being scattered or dispersed **4. REMOVAL** the disappearing of a feeling or emotion, e.g., anger or anxiety

dis·so·cia·ble /di sṓshəb'l/ *adj.* capable of being distinguished [Early 17thC. Via French from Latin *dissociabilis* "separating, incompatible," from *dissociare* (see DISSOCIATE).] —**dis·so·cia·bil·i·ty** /di sṑshə bíllətee/ *n.* —**dis·so·cia·ble·ness** /-əb'lnəss/ *n.* —**dis·so·cia·bly** /-blee/ *adv.*

dis·so·ci·ate /di sṓshee àyt/ (**-at·ed, -at·ing, -ates**) *v.* **1.** *vt.* **REGARD SOMETHING OR SOMEBODY AS DISTINCT** to treat somebody or something as distinct from or unconnected with somebody or something else **2.** *vt.* = **disassociate** *v.* 2 **3.** *vt.* = **disassociate** *v.* 1 **4.** *vti.* CHEM **SPLIT SOMETHING INTO SIMPLER PARTS** to cause the molecules of a compound to break down into simpler molecules, atoms, ions, or radicals, usually in a reversible reaction, or to break down in this way **5.** *vi.* PSYCHIAT **SEPARATE OFF AREAS OF THE MIND** to separate a group of mental processes from the rest of the mind, causing them to lose their normal relationship with it [Mid-16thC. From, ultimately, Latin *dissociare*, literally "to separate from fellowship," from *sociare* "to join together," from *socius* "companion" (see SOCIAL).] —**dis·so·ci·a·tive** *adj.*

dis·so·ci·a·tion /di sṑshee áysh'n/ *n.* **1. TREATMENT OF SOMETHING AS UNCONNECTED** the treatment of somebody or something as distinct or unconnected, or the fact of being regarded in this way **2.** = **disassociation** *n.* 2 **3.** = **disassociation** *n.* 1 **4.** CHEM **DIVISION OF MOLECULE** a breaking up of a molecule into simpler components **5.** PSYCHIAT **SEPARATION OF EMOTIONS** the separation of a group of normally connected mental processes, e.g., emotion and understanding, from the rest of the mind as a defense mechanism

dis·sol·u·ble /di sóllyəb'l/ *adj.* = **soluble** [Mid-16thC. Directly or via French from Latin *dissolubilis*, from *dissolvere* (see DISSOLVE).] —**dis·sol·u·bil·i·ty** /di sòllyə bíllətee/ *n.* —**dis·sol·u·ble·ness** /di sóllyəb'lnəss/ *n.*

dis·so·lute /díssə lo͞ot/ *adj.* overindulging in physical pleasures in a way or to an extent that is considered immoral or harmful [14thC. From Latin *dissolutus*, originally the past participle of *dissolvere* (see DISSOLVE). The underlying idea is of something loosened or disconnected from accepted standards of behavior.] —**dis·so·lute·ly** *adv.* —**dis·so·lute·ness** *n.*

dis·so·lu·tion /dìssə lo͞osh'n/ *n.* **1.** BREAKDOWN OF SOMETHING INTO PARTS the separating, decomposing, or disintegrating of something into smaller or more basic constituents **2.** BREAKUP OF SOMETHING the breaking up or destruction of an organization or institution ○ *the dissolution of parliament* **3.** FORMAL CLOSING the bringing to an end of a meeting or assembly **4.** LAW ENDING OF LEGAL RELATIONSHIP the termination of a legal relationship, e.g., a business partnership or a marriage **5.** DEMISE somebody's death (*formal*)

dis·solve /di zólv/ *v.* (**-solved, -solv·ing, -solves**) **1.** *vti.* BECOME ABSORBED IN LIQUID to become absorbed in a liquid solution, or cause this process to occur to a solid ○ *Dissolve two tablets in a glass of water.* **2.** *vti.* DISAPPEAR to fade away gradually and disappear, or make something gradually fade away and disappear ○ *All his fears dissolved.* **3.** *vti.* BREAK UP to break up, or break something up, into smaller or more basic parts **4.** *vi.* START LAUGHING OR CRYING to begin to laugh or cry uncontrollably **5.** *vt.* CLOSE FORMALLY to bring something such as a meeting or a political assembly to a formal close **6.** *vt.* LAW END LEGAL RELATIONSHIP to bring a legal relationship, e.g., a business partnership or a marriage, formally to an end **7.** *vi.* CINEMA, TV, VIDEO SIMULTANEOUSLY FADE OUT AND IN to fade out slowly as a second image fades in, briefly merging one with the other ■ *n.* CINEMA, TV, VIDEO SIMULTANEOUS FADING OUT AND IN a change from one scene to another, with the first scene gradually fading out and the next one gradually fading in over it [14thC. From Latin *dissolvere*, literally "to loosen asunder," from *solvere* "to loosen."] —**dis·solv·a·bil·i·ty** *n.* —**dis·solv·a·ble** *adj.* —**dis·solv·a·ble·ness** *n.* —**dis·solv·er** *n.*

dis·sol·vent /di zólvənt/ *adj.* CAPABLE OF DISSOLVING SOMETHING able to dissolve another substance ■ *n.* = **solvent** *n.*

dis·so·nance /díssənəns/ *n.* **1.** UNPLEASANT NOISE a combination of sounds that is unpleasant to listen to **2.** INCONSISTENCY lack of consistency or compatibility between actions or beliefs **3.** MUSIC UNSTABLE COMBINATION OF MUSICAL NOTES a combination of notes that, when played simultaneously, sounds displeasing and needs to be resolved to a consonance

dis·so·nant /díssənənt/ *adj.* **1.** UNPLEASANT TO HEAR making or involving a combination of sounds that is unpleasant to listen to **2.** CONFLICTING incompatible or inconsistent (*formal*) **3.** MUSIC CONTAINING UNSTABLE CHORDS containing unstable chords or harmonies that need to be resolved to a consonance [15thC. From, ultimately, the Latin present participle stem *dissonant-* of *dissonare*, literally "to be apart in sound," from *sonare* "to sound."] —**dis·so·nant·ly** *adv.*

dis·suade /di swáyd/ (**-suad·ed, -suad·ing, -suades**) *vt.* to persuade somebody not to do something or not to believe, think, or feel something [Early 16thC. From Latin *dissuadere*, literally "to advise against," from *suadere* "to advise, persuade."] —**dis·suad·a·ble** *adj.* —**dis·suad·er** *n.*

dis·sua·sion /di swáyzh'n/ *n.* persuasion not to do something or not to believe, think, or feel something [15thC. Directly or via French from the Latin stem *dissuasion-*, from the past participle stem *dissuas-* of *dissuadere* (see DISSUADE).]

dis·sua·sive /di swáyssiv/ *adj.* convincing enough to persuade somebody not to do something or not to believe, think, or feel something [Early 16thC. Formed from the Latin past participle stem *dissuas-* of *dissuadere* (see DISSUADE).] —**dis·sua·sive·ly** *adv.* —**dis·sua·sive·ness** *n.*

dis·syl·la·ble *n.* = **disyllable**

dis·sym·met·ric /dìssi méttrik/, **dis·sym·met·ri·cal** /dìssi méttrik'l/ *adj.* = **asymmetrical** [DISSYMMETRIC, mid-19thC; DISSYMMETRICAL, late 19thC] —**dis·sym·met·ri·cal·ly** *adv.*

dis·sym·me·try /di símmətree/ (*plural* **-tries**) *n.* = **asymmetry**

dist. *abbr.* **1.** distance **2.** district

dis·taff /dí stàf/ (*plural* **-taffs** *or* **-taves** /-stàvz/) *n.* **1.** WOMEN'S CONCERNS women's work or any other matters traditionally considered to be the concern of women (*literary*) **2.** CRAFT ROD FOR UNSPUN THREAD a rod on which a fiber, e.g., wool or flax, is wound for somebody to use when spinning by hand, or the corresponding rod on a spinning wheel [Old English *distæf*, from a prehistoric Germanic base meaning "bunch of flax" (ancestor of English *dizen*) + an earlier form of STAFF]

dis·taff side *n.* a wife's or mother's side of a family

dis·tal /díst'l/ *adj.* ANAT used to describe a body part situated away from a point of attachment or origin. For example, the elbow is distal to the shoulder. ◊ **proximal** [Early 19thC. Coined from DISTANT + -AL.] —**dis·tal·ly** *adv.*

dis·tance /dístəns/ *n.* **1.** LENGTH BETWEEN TWO THINGS the length of the space separating two people, places, or things ○ *What's the distance between Paris and New York?* **2.** FAR-OFF PLACE a place or position far away, or not very close ○ *It's best seen from a distance.* **3.** CLOSENESS ALLOWING SOME ACTIVITY the space between two people, places, or things with regard to activity carried on between the two ○ *We can do nothing until they're within hailing distance.* **4.** AMOUNT OF SEPARATION the amount by which two places are separated, especially when thought of in terms of the time or inconvenience of a journey between the two ○ *She lives some distance away.* **5.** COOLNESS OR ALOOFNESS a cool or slightly aloof response to another person or group ○ *He suddenly felt the need to put some distance between himself and his friends.* **6.** INTERVAL OF TIME the interval between one point in time and another, especially a long interval ○ *You can't expect to remember all the details at a distance of more than 20 years.* **7.** AMOUNT OF PROGRESS the amount of progress that has been made or that is still to be made ○ *still some distance to go before we can reach an agreement* **8.** IDEOLOGICAL GULF difference of opinion or ideology ○ *There's still some distance between us with regard to the basic issues.* **9.** DIFFERENCE IN RANK difference in social status, or the extent of such a difference (*archaic*) **10.** HORSERACING SPACE GREATER THAN 20 LENGTHS a space of more than twenty lengths between two racehorses, usually the winner and the horse finishing second ○ *win by a distance* ■ *v.* (**-tanced, -tanc·ing, -tanc·es**) **1.** *vr.* AVOID EMOTIONAL INVOLVEMENT to avoid becoming emotionally involved in something, or encourage somebody to feel less close emotionally to something ○ *Try to distance yourself from past experiences.* **2.** *vt.* AVOID SUPPORTING to avoid giving any support to or having any involvement with somebody or something, or deny that you support or have any involvement with somebody or something ○ *He was trying to distance himself from the allegations.* **3.** *vt.* HORSERACING WIN BY A DISTANCE to beat another racehorse by more than twenty lengths [13thC. Directly or via French from Latin *distantia*, from *distant-* "standing apart" (see DISTANT).] ◇ **go the distance** to continue until you have completed something

dis·tance learn·ing *n.* education for students working at home, with little or no face-to-face with teachers and with material provided remotely, e.g., by e-mail, television, or correspondence

dis·tant /dístənt/ *adj.* **1.** FAR AWAY situated, living, or happening far away ○ *a distant galaxy* **2.** FAR AWAY IN TIME remote in time, either in the future or the past ○ *They hope to meet again in the distant future.* **3.** ALOOFLY RESERVED showing that somebody does not want to be friendly or intimate **4.** FAINT so slight as to be hard to discern ○ *a distant resemblance* [14thC. Directly or via French from the Latin present participle stem *distant-* of *distare* "to stand apart," from *stare* "to stand."]

dis·tant·ly /dístəntlee/ *adv.* **1.** FAR AWAY far away or from far away ○ *We could distantly make out figures dancing in the village square.* **2.** FAR AWAY MENTALLY not concentrating on the immediate surroundings **3.** ALOOFLY in a detached, cold, or formal way ○ *He smiled at her distantly as she walked past.* **4.** NOT CLOSELY not closely in terms of family or blood relations ○ *distantly related*

dis·taste /diss táyst/ *n.* a feeling of dislike, disapproval, or mild disgust [Late 16thC. From DIS- + TASTE; modeled on Old French *desgoust*, literally "distaste."]

WORD KEY: SYNONYMS

See Synonyms at ***dislike***.

dis·taste·ful /diss táystf'l/ *adj.* **1.** UNPLEASANT provoking dislike, disapproval, or mild disgust **2.** DISAPPROVING showing that you dislike or disapprove of something (*archaic*) —**distastefully** *adv.* —**dis·taste·ful·ness** *n.*

Dist. Atty. *abbr.* district attorney

dis·tem·per[1] /diss témpər/ *n.* a viral disease that affects various animals, especially dogs and cats. ◊ **canine distemper, feline distemper** [Mid-16thC. Ultimately from late Latin *distemperare*, literally "to combine awry" (referring to an imbalance of humors), from Latin *temperare* "to combine" (see TEMPER).]

dis·tem·per[2] /diss témpər/ *n.* **1.** PAINT a type of paint in which the coloring material is mixed with water and a substance such as glue, size,or egg yolk or white, instead of with oil. Distemper is often used for painting walls, theatrical scenery, and posters. **2.** PAINTING WITH DISTEMPER the use of distemper in painting posters and murals ■ *vt.* (**-pered, -per·ing, -pers**) PAINT SOMETHING WITH DISTEMPER to paint or cover something, e.g., a wall, with distemper [14thC. Directly or via Old French *destremper* "to soak, mix" from late Latin *distemperare*, literally "to mix thoroughly," from Latin *temperare* "to mix."]

dis·tend /di sténd/ (**-tend·ed, -tend·ing, -tends**) *vti.* to expand, swell, or inflate as if by pressure from within [14thC. From Latin *distendere*, literally "to stretch apart," from *tendere* "to stretch."] —**dis·ten·der** *n.* —**dis·ten·si·bil·i·ty** /di stènsə bíllətee/ *n.* —**dis·ten·si·ble** /di sténsəb'l/ *adj.* —**dis·ten·sion** /-shən/ *n.*

dis·tich /dí stik/ *n.* two lines of poetry, sometimes rhyming, that form a complete unit in themselves [Early 16thC. Via Latin *distichon* from Greek *distikhon*, originally a form of *distikhos* "of two rows or verses," from *stikhos* "row, line of verse."] —**dis·tich·al** *adj.*

dis·ti·chous /dístəkəss/ *adj.* used to describe leaves that grow in vertical rows on opposite sides of a stem —**dis·ti·chous·ly** *adv.*

dis·till /di stíl/ (**-tilled, -till·ing, -tills**), **dis·til** (**-tilled, -till·ing, -tils**) *v.* **1.** *vti.* PURIFY LIQUID WITH HEAT to purify a liquid by heating it and then condensing its vapor, or to undergo purification in this way **2.** *vt.* MAKE ALCOHOLIC SPIRITS to produce alcoholic spirits using the process of heating liquid and condensing its vapor **3.** *vt.* CREATE FROM ESSENTIAL ELEMENTS to create something from the essential or most important elements of something larger or longer **4.** *vi.* EMERGE SLOWLY to be emitted slowly or in small quantities ○ *"Then slowly from the silence there distilled drops of music"* (John Buchan, *Greenmantle*; 1916) [14thC. From, ultimately, Latin *distillare*, alteration of *destillare*, literally "to drip apart," from *stillare* "to drip," from *stilla* "drop."] —**dis·till·a·ble** *adj.*

dis·til·late /díst'l àyt, díst'lət/ *n.* **1.** CHEM LIQUID PRODUCED BY DISTILLATION a concentrated liquid produced by heating a liquid mixture and condensing the vapor **2.** ESSENCE the concentrated essence of something

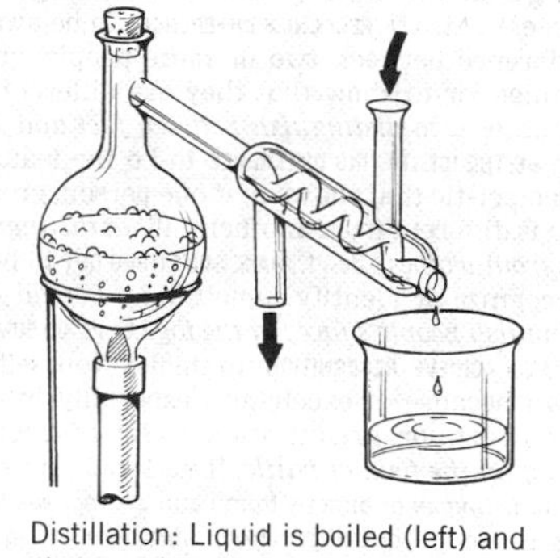

Distillation: Liquid is boiled (left) and the resulting vapor condensed (right)

dis·til·la·tion /dìst'l áysh'n/ *n.* **1.** BOILING AND CONDENSING OF LIQUID the process of separating, concentrating, or purifying liquid by boiling it and then condensing the resulting vapor. Alcoholic liquors, e.g., whiskey and vodka, are made in this way. **2.** CONDENSED VERSION OF SOMETHING something that consists of the essential points, aspects, or implications of something larger or longer **3.** CHEM = **distillate** *n.* 1 —**dis·til·la·to·ry** /di stíllə tàwree/ *adj.*

dis·til·la·tion col·umn *n.* CHEM a hollow vertical column, fitted inside with perforated trays or packing material, in which liquid mixtures are separated into their components by heating the mixture and condensing the vapor produced

dis·tilled /di stíld/ *adj.* **1.** SUMMING SOMETHING UP derived from or encapsulating a wider experience or larger set of ideas **2.** CHEM RESULTING FROM DISTILLATION used to describe liquids that have been purified or concentrated by distillation

dis·till·er /di stíllər/ *n.* a company that or person who produces hard liquor such as whiskey, vodka, and gin

dis·till·er·y /di stíllәree/ (*plural* **-ies**) *n.* a place where strong alcoholic liquors such as whiskey, vodka, and gin are made by distilling

dis·tinct /di stíngkt/ *adj.* **1. SEPARATE** clearly different and separate ○ *The word has two distinct senses.* **2. APPARENT TO THE SENSES** easy to hear, see, smell, or understand ○ *I have a very distinct memory of that day.* **3. CERTAIN** definite or undeniable ○ *I had the distinct impression they'd been arguing.* **4. NOTICEABLE** strong enough, large enough, or definite enough to be noticed ○ *There's a distinct smell of gasoline in the car.* **5. EMPHATIC** very great in degree, e.g., as an honor felt or experienced ○ *a distinct privilege* [14thC. Directly or via French from the Latin past participle *distinctus* of *distinguere* "to separate" (see DISTINGUISH).] —**dis·tinct·ness** *n.*

dis·tinc·tion /di stíngkshәn/ *n.* **1. DIFFERENCE** a difference, or the recognition of a difference, between two or more things or people **2. HIGH QUALITY** excellence in quality or talent ○ *tailors of distinction* **3. SOMETHING TO BE PROUD OF** something done or given as a mark of respect or honor ○ *I had the distinction of giving the opening address.* **4. DISTINGUISHING FEATURE** something that characterizes or singles out something or somebody ○ *She has the dubious distinction of being the administration's most slavish defender.* **5.** EDUC **MARK OF HIGH ACHIEVEMENT** recognition of high achievement or a grade that signifies this ○ *graduated from the university with distinction*

dis·tinc·tive /di stíngktiv/ *adj.* **1. DIFFERENT FROM OTHERS** uniquely characteristic of a particular person, group, or thing **2.** PHON **RELATING TO PHONEME'S DISTINGUISHING FEATURE** relating to the features of a phoneme that distinguish it from other similar phonemes, e.g., the fact that it is labial, fricative, or nasal

dis·tinct·ly /di stíngktlee/ *adv.* **1. CLEARLY** clearly or obviously enough to be easily seen, heard, remembered, identified, or understood ○ *I distinctly recall the incident.* ○ *I wasn't able to see what was going on very distinctly as I didn't have my glasses with me.* **2. UNDENIABLY** to a marked extent ○ *She was distinctly angry*

dis·tin·gué /di stìng gáy/ *adj.* having the confidence and dignity of somebody who is used to being respected (*formal*) [Early 19thC. From French, the past participle of *distinguer* "to distinguish" (see DISTINGUISH).]

dis·tin·guish /di stíng gwish/ (**-guished, -guish·ing, -guish·es**) *v.* **1.** *vti.* **RECOGNIZE DIFFERENCES** to be aware of a difference between two or more people, groups, or things, or to show that they are different from each other ○ *to distinguish between fact and fiction* **2.** *vt.* **BE THE IDENTIFYING DIFFERENCE** to be the feature or characteristic that shows that one person, group, or thing is different from another ○ *What distinguishes dogs from wolves?* **3.** *vt.* **MAKE SOMETHING OUT** to be able to recognize or identify something ○ *I could barely distinguish people's faces in the fog.* **4.** *vr.* **DO SOMETHING WELL AND ACHIEVE RECOGNITION** to make yourself well known because of excellence, especially in a profession, art, or organization ○ *He distinguished himself on the field of battle.* [Late 16thC. Formed from French *distinguer* or directly from Latin *distinguere*, literally "to separate by pricking," from *stinguere* "to quench" (presumed earlier "to prick").] —**dis·tin·guish·er** *n.*

dis·tin·guish·a·ble /di stíng gwishәb'l/ *adj.* **1. DIFFERENT** recognizably different **2. DETECTABLE** capable of being seen, heard, tasted, or detected in some way —**dis·tin·guish·a·bly** *adv.*

dis·tin·guished /di stíng gwisht/ *adj.* **1. RECOGNIZED FOR EXCELLENCE** well known and respected for a particular achievement, skill, knowledge, or talent ○ *a distinguished composer* **2. CONFIDENT AND DIGNIFIED** showing the confident and dignified appearance and manners of somebody who is used to respect **3. SUCCESSFUL** showing or involving a great deal of skill, talent, or success

Dis·tin·guished Fly·ing Cross *n.* **1. U.S. FLYING MEDAL** a U.S. military medal awarded for extraordinary achievement or for heroism in air combat **2. BRITISH AIR FORCE MEDAL** a Royal Air Force medal awarded to noncommissioned and warrant officers for distinguished conduct when flying in action

Dis·tin·guished Ser·vice Cross *n.* **1. U.S. ARMY MEDAL** a U.S. Army medal awarded for extraordinary heroism against an enemy. It is the U.S. Army's second highest award for bravery, the highest being the Congressional Medal of Honor. **2. BRITISH ARMED SERVICES MEDAL** a British medal awarded in all branches of the armed forces for distinguished service in action

Dis·tin·guished Ser·vice Or·der *n.* a British medal awarded to commissioned officers in all armed forces for distinguished service in action

dis·tin·guish·ing /di stíng gwishing/ *adj.* allowing one person, group, or thing to be told apart from another ○ *distinguishing characteristics*

dis·tort /di stáwrt/ (**-tort·ed, -tort·ing, -torts**) *v.* **1.** *vt.* **GIVE AN INACCURATE REPORT OF SOMETHING** to describe or report something in a way that is inaccurate or misleading **2.** *vti.* **ALTER SHAPE** to bend, twist, stretch, or change from a normal or natural shape, or make something do this **3.** *vt.* **MAKE SOMETHING UNNATURAL OR UNCLEAR** to change something such as an image in such a way that it becomes unclear or unrecognizable **4.** *vt.* ELECTRON ENG **REPRODUCE INACCURATELY** to amplify or reproduce something, e.g., a radio signal, inaccurately [15thC. From the Latin past participle stem *distort-* of *distorquere*, literally "to twist completely," from *torquere* "to twist."] —**dis·tort·er** *n.* —**dis·tor·tive** *adj.*

dis·tort·ed /di stáwrtәd/ *adj.* **1. INACCURATELY REPORTED** described or reported in a way that is inaccurate or misleading ○ *a distorted version of events* **2. OUT OF SHAPE** bent or twisted out of shape **3. UNNATURAL OR UNCLEAR** changed in such a way as to become unclear or unrecognizable ○ *a distorted face in the mirror* —**dis·tort·ed·ly** *adv.* —**dis·tort·ed·ness** *n.*

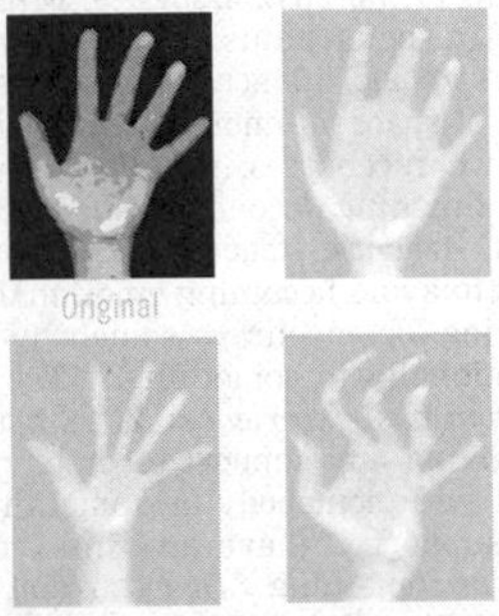

Distortion: Electronically manipulated images of a hand

dis·tor·tion /di stáwrsh'n/ *n.* **1. MISLEADING ALTERATION** the altering of information in such a way that people are misinformed or misled **2. CHANGING FROM CORRECT SHAPE** the bending or twisting of something out of its normal or natural shape **3. MISSHAPEN PART** a part of something that has been bent, twisted, stretched, or forced out of its normal or natural shape **4. MAKING SOMETHING UNCLEAR** the altering of something, e.g., a radio or television signal, to the extent that it becomes unclear or unrecognizable **5.** OPTICS **ALTERATION IN OPTICAL IMAGE** an alteration in an image in which the original proportions are changed, resulting from a defect in a lens or optical system —**dis·tor·tion·al** *adj.* —**dis·tor·tion·ar·y** *adj.*

distr. *abbr.* **1.** distribution **2.** distributor

dis·tract /di strákt/ (**-tract·ed, -tract·ing, -tracts**) *vt.* **1. CATCH SOMEBODY'S ATTENTION** to take somebody's attention away from what he or she is doing or thinking, or from what is happening **2. AMUSE SOMEBODY** to amuse or entertain somebody, especially as a means of taking his or her mind off something unpleasant **3. MAKE SOMEBODY UNEASY** to unsettle somebody's mind with disturbing, confusing, or conflicting emotions (*archaic*) ○ *"O Husband, Husband, my Heart long'd to see thee; but to see thee thus distracts me."* (John Gay, *The Beggar's Opera*; 1728) [14thC. From the Latin past participle stem *distract-* of *distrahere*, literally "to draw away," from *trahere* "to draw, drag."] —**dis·tract·er** *n.* —**dis·tract·i·bil·i·ty** /di stràktә bíllәtee/ *n.* —**dis·tract·i·ble** /-stráktәb'l/ *adj.* —**dis·trac·tive** /-tiv/ *adj.* —**dis·trac·tive·ly** /di stráktivlee/ *adv.*

dis·tract·ed /di stráktәd/ *adj.* **1. PREOCCUPIED** showing a lack of concentration **2. ANXIOUS** so worried or upset as to be unable to think clearly or act sensibly —**dis·tract·ed·ness** *n.*

dis·tract·ing /di strákting/ *adj.* **1. DIVERTING SOMEBODY'S ATTENTION** taking somebody's attention away from what he or she wants to do or ought to be doing **2. RELAXING** helping somebody to relax and forget work or worries —**dis·tract·ing·ly** *adv.*

dis·trac·tion /di strákshәn/ *n.* **1. SOMETHING THAT DIVERTS ATTENTION** something that interferes with concentration or takes attention away from something else **2. AMUSEMENT** something providing entertainment or amusement, especially something that takes the mind off work or worries and helps relaxation **3. EMOTIONAL UPSET** a state of great mental or emotional upset

dis·train /di stráyn/ (**-trained, -train·ing, -trains**) *vt.* to take and hold somebody's property as a pledge for something such as unpaid rent [14thC. From the Old French present stem *destreign-* of *destreindre*, from Latin *distringere* "to draw asunder."] —**dis·train·a·ble** *adj.* —**dis·train·ee** /di stràyníe/ *n.* —**dis·train·er** /di stráynәr/ *n.* —**dis·train·ment** /-mәnt/ *n.*

dis·traint /di stráynt/ *n.* LAW = **distress** *n.* 5 [Mid-18thC. Formed from DISTRAIN; modeled on CONSTRAINT.]

dis·trait /di stráy/ *adj.* **1. INATTENTIVE** inattentive and slightly distracted or absent-minded (*literary*) **2. DISTRAUGHT** upset or perturbed (*archaic*) [14thC. Via French from the Old French past participle of *destraire* "to distract," from Latin *distrahere* (see DISTRACT).]

dis·traught /di stráwt/ *adj.* **1. EXTREMELY UPSET** extremely upset and distressed **2. NOT IN MENTAL HEALTH** experiencing psychiatric disorder (*archaic*) [14thC. Alteration of archaic *distract* "perplexed," from Latin *distractus*, past participle of *distrahere* (see DISTRACT); influenced by *straught*, former past participle of STRETCH.]

dis·tress /di stréss/ *n.* **1. MENTAL SUFFERING** mental suffering, e.g., that caused by grief, anxiety, or unhappiness **2. HARDSHIP OR DIFFICULTY** difficulty or hardship caused by a lack of basic necessities **3. PHYSICAL PAIN** physical pain or discomfort **4. DANGER OR DIFFICULTY** great danger or difficulty, with a need for immediate assistance ○ *a ship in distress* **5.** LAW **SEIZURE OF BAD DEBTOR'S PROPERTY** the seizing of somebody's movable property either in lieu of payment of a debt or in order to force the person to pay ■ *vt.* (**-tressed, -tress·ing, -tress·es**) **1. UPSET SOMEBODY** to make somebody extremely upset, anxious, or alarmed **2. MAKE FURNITURE OR FABRIC LOOK OLD** to give a new piece of furniture or fabric an old or worn appearance [13thC. Via Old French *destresce* from assumed Vulgar Latin *districtia*, from the Latin past participle stem *district-* of *distringere*, literally "to draw asunder" (see STRINGENT).]

dis·tressed /di strést/ *adj.* **1. VERY UPSET** extremely upset, anxious, or unhappy **2. MADE TO LOOK OLDER** artificially given an old or worn appearance **3.** LAW, FIN **REPOSSESSED FROM BAD DEBTOR** repossessed by a bank or other lender from the borrower and offered for sale at a reduced price ○ *a distressed loan* **4. OF DAMAGED GOODS** damaged or used ○ *They had a sale of distressed goods.*

dis·tress·ing /di stréssing/, **dis·tress·ful** /-fәl/ *adj.* causing somebody to feel extremely upset —**dis·tress·ing·ly** *adv.*

dis·tress mer·chan·dise *n.* goods that have been repossessed by a bank or other lender from a borrower who has failed to repay a loan and are offered for sale at below-market prices

dis·tress sig·nal *n.* a signal, e.g., a radio message or a flare, sent by a ship or aircraft in urgent need of assistance

dis·trib·u·tar·y /di stríbbyә tèree/ (*plural* **-ies**) *n.* a channel leading water away from a main single channel

dis·trib·ute /di strí byoot/ (**-ut·ed, -ut·ing, -utes**) *v.* **1.** *vt.* **GIVE SOMETHING OUT** to deliver or share things out to people ○ *distribute prizes* **2.** *vt.* **DIVIDE AND SHARE SOMETHING** to divide something into shares and give the shares to a number of people **3.** *vt.* **SPREAD SOMETHING** to scatter something or spread it throughout a particular area or place **4.** *vt.* **DIVIDE INTO CLASSES** to divide something up into different classes or categories **5.** *vt.* COMM **SELL AND DISPATCH GOODS** to sell and deliver merchandise, especially wholesale goods to a retailer **6.** *vt.* LOGIC **MAKE TERM APPLY TO ALL** to apply a term to all the members of the class it designates **7.** *vti.* MATH **MAKE OPERATION APPLY THROUGHOUT** to apply or make an operation, e.g., multiplication or division, apply to each part of a mathematical expression [15thC. From the Latin past participle stem *distribut-* of *distribuere*, literally "to assign separately," from *tribuere* "to assign" (see TRIBUTE).] —**dis·trib·ut·a·ble** *adj.*

WORD KEY: SYNONYMS
See Synonyms at *scatter.*

dis·trib·ut·ed /di stríbbyətəd/ *adj.* used to describe computer systems in which two or more computers have a telecommunications link to each other but can also operate independently

dis·trib·u·tee /di strìbbyoo tee/ *n.* somebody entitled to a share of the estate of a person who has died without making a will

dis·trib·ut·er /di stríbbyətər/ *n.* = **distributor**

dis·tri·bu·tion /dìstrə byoosh'n/ *n.* **1. GIVING OUT** the sharing out or delivery of things to a number of people **2. SHARING** the process of dividing up and giving out something, e.g., money, when it is shared by a number of people **3. SCATTERING** the scattering or spreading of something over an area **4.** ECOL **ENTIRE AREA WHERE SPECIES IS FOUND** the area or areas taken together where something is located or where a species lives and reproduces **5.** STATS **SPREAD OF STATISTICS** the spread of statistics within known or possible limits, especially in relation to the norm or to expectations **6.** LAW **SHARING OUT OF SOMEBODY'S ESTATE** the dividing up of the estate of somebody who has died intestate among people who are entitled to receive a share **7.** LOGIC **RECOMBINING OF TWO PROPOSITIONS** the recombining of two operations from one proposition in another equivalent proposition, e.g., "p and (q or r)" is equivalent to "(p and q) or (p and r)" —**dis·tri·bu·tion·al** *adj.*

dis·trib·u·tive /di stríbbyətiv/ *adj.* **1. INVOLVING DISTRIBUTION** relating to or involving the handing out, sharing out, or scattering about of things **2.** COMM **INVOLVED WITH DELIVERIES** relating to or involved in the delivery of merchandise **3.** GRAM **REFERRING TO EACH MEMBER OF GROUP** referring to each member of a set or group individually and separately. "Each,""every," and "either" are examples of distributive words in English. **4.** LOGIC **REFERRING TO INDIVIDUALS, NOT CLASSES** referring to an individual member of a class, or to each member individually **5.** MATH **PRODUCING EQUAL RESULTS** used to describe a mathematical expression with two operators whose expansion produces the same results whether operated on as a whole or as a sum of the parts ■ *n.* GRAM **DISTRIBUTIVE WORD** a word that refers to every member of a set or group individually and separately —**dis·trib·u·tive·ly** *adv.* —**dis·trib·u·tive·ness** /di stríbbyətivnəss/ *n.*

dis·trib·u·tive ed·u·ca·tion *n.* EDUC educational courses in vocational subjects that combine classroom teaching with on-the-job training

dis·trib·u·tor /di stríbbyətər/, **dis·trib·ut·er** *n.* **1. SOMEBODY WHO DISTRIBUTES SOMETHING** a person who or an organization or thing that distributes something **2.** COMM **WHOLESALER** a wholesaler who sells merchandise to retailers, usually within a specified geographic area **3.** AUTOMOT **DEVICE CONVEYING ELECTRICITY TO SPARK PLUGS** the device in a motor vehicle's engine that transfers electric current from the induction coil to the spark plugs **4.** CINEMA **ORGANIZATION ARRANGING SCREENING OF MOTION PICTURES** an organization that advertises movies and arranges with exhibitors, who own the movie theaters, to have them shown

dis·trict /dístrikt/ *n.* **AREA** an area of a town or country, especially one with a particular distinguishing feature or one that is an administrative division ○ *a fruit-growing district* ■ *vt.* (**-trict·ed, -trict·ing, -tricts**) **DIVIDE INTO GEOPOLITICAL AREAS** to divide an area into distinct geopolitical or cultural sectors ○ *hard at work districting the huge county for voting purposes* [Early 17thC. Via French from medieval Latin *districtus* "(area of) jurisdiction," literally "restraining (of offenders)," from the Latin stem *district-* (see DISTRESS).]

dis·trict at·tor·ney *n.* the prosecuting officer of a particular jurisdiction

dis·trict court *n.* the trial court in either a state or a federal district in the United States

Dis·trict of Co·lum·bi·a /-kə lúmbee ə/ federal district of the United States, situated on the Potomac and Anacostia rivers, coextensive with the city of Washington, D.C., the nation's capital. It was created in 1790–91. Area: 68 sq. mi./177 sq. km.

dis·trust /diss trúst/ *n.* **LACK OF TRUST** a feeling that somebody or something is dishonest or unreliable ■ *vt.* (**-trust·ed, -trust·ing, -trusts**) **HAVE NO CONFIDENCE IN SOMEBODY** to have a feeling that somebody or something is dishonest or unreliable —**dis·trust·er** *n.*

dis·trust·ful /diss trústfəl/ *adj.* showing lack of trust in somebody or something —**dis·trust·ful·ly** *adv.* —**dis·trust·ful·ness** *n.*

dis·turb /di stúrb/ (**-turbed, -turb·ing, -turbs**) *vt.* **1. INTERRUPT SOMEBODY** to interrupt or distract somebody when he or she is busy **2. UPSET SOMEBODY** to make somebody feel anxious or slightly troubled **3. CHANGE SHAPE OR POSITION** to move something so that it is not in its normal, expected, or correct shape or position ○ *Nothing had been disturbed.* **4. SPOIL PEACE AND QUIET** to spoil the quietness, stillness, or peacefulness of something **5. AWAKEN** to waken somebody or something [12thC. Directly or via Old French *desto(u)rber* from Latin *disturbare*, literally "to disturb completely," from *turbare* "to disturb."] —**dis·turb·er** *n.*

WORD KEY: SYNONYMS
See Synonyms at *bother.*

dis·tur·bance /di stúrbəns/ *n.* **1. DISRUPTION OF PEACE** the disruption of a peaceful or ordered environment, or something that causes such disruption **2. DISRUPTION OF CONCENTRATION** the disruption of somebody's concentration, or something that disrupts somebody's ability to continue with a task in hand **3. COMMOTION** noisy and violent behavior in a public place, or an incident involving such behavior **4. MENTAL UPSET** psychological or emotional upset **5.** GEOL **EARTH TREMOR** a minor movement of the earth that falls short of an earthquake **6.** LAW **INTERFERENCE WITH SOMEBODY'S RIGHTS** any act that causes disruption to others or hinders them from pursuing normal legal activities **7.** METEOROL **LOW-PRESSURE AREA** a small area of low pressure

dis·turbed /di stúrbd/ *adj.* **1. ANXIOUS** worried or concerned **2. TROUBLED** unsettled and unhappy, with many troubles and upsets **3. NOT IN MENTAL HEALTH** affected by or displaying symptoms of psychiatric disorder

dis·turb·ing /di stúrbing/ *adj.* causing worry, or emotional or physical upset —**dis·turb·ing·ly** *adv.*

di·sul·fide /dī súl fīd/ *n.* a chemical compound that has two atoms of sulfur combined with one or more other elements

di·sul·fi·ram /dī súlfə ràm/ *n.* a chemical compound used in the treatment of alcoholism for its deterrent effect. It causes nausea, vomiting, and other extreme effects when alcohol is consumed. Formula: $C_{10}H_{20}N_2S_4$. [Mid-20thC. From DISULFIDE + THIOUREA + AMYL.]

di·sul·fo·ton /dī súlfə tòn/ *n.* a systemic organophosphate insecticide used in agriculture [Mid-20thC. Coined from DI- + SULFO- + *-ton* (of uncertain origin: probably a contraction of *thion-* "sulfur," from Greek *theion*; see THIO-).]

dis·un·ion /diss yoonee ən/ *n.* **1. DIVISION INTO SMALLER PARTS** the splitting up of something into separate smaller parts or groups **2. DISCORD** disagreement or discord

dis·u·nite /dìssyoo nít/ (**-nit·ed, -nit·ing, -nites**) *v.* **1.** *vt.* **CAUSE DISAGREEMENT BETWEEN PEOPLE** to create or be a source of disagreement between different people or factions within a group **2.** *vti.* **DIVIDE SOMETHING** to divide something, or become divided, into smaller parts or groups —**dis·u·nit·er** *n.*

dis·u·nit·ed /dìssyoo nítəd/ *adj.* divided into separate groups or factions because of a disagreement or difference of opinion

dis·u·ni·ty /diss yoonitee/ *n.* a lack of unity within a group, especially one caused by a disagreement or a difference of opinion

dis·use /diss yooss/ *n.* the fact or condition of not being used, applied, or followed, especially for a long time

dis·used /diss yoozd/ *adj.* no longer in use, or no longer used for its original purpose ○ *a disused airfield*

dis·val·ue /diss vályoo/ *vt.* (**-ued, -u·ing, -ues**) = **undervalue** ■ *n.* **NEGATIVE VALUE** negative worth or value

di·syl·la·ble /dī síllәb'l, di-/, **dis·syl·la·ble** *n.* **1.** LING **TWO-SYLLABLE WORD** a word composed of two syllables **2.** POETRY **TWO-SYLLABLE POETIC UNIT** a two-syllable unit of rhythm in poetry —**di·syl·lab·ic** /dìssi lábbik, dìssi-/ *adj.*

dit /dit/ *n.* the spoken form of the short sound used in Morse and other telegraphic codes. ◊ **dah** [Mid-20thC. An imitation of the sound.]

ditch /dich/ *n.* **1. NARROW CHANNEL** a long narrow channel dug in the ground, usually used for drainage or irrigation but sometimes used as a boundary marker **2.** *U.K.* **SMALL BROOK** a small natural stream or brook ■ *v.* (**ditched, ditch·ing, ditch·es**) **1.** *vt.* **ABANDON SOMETHING OR SOMEBODY** to abandon something or somebody as no longer wanted, liked, or needed (*informal*) **2.** *vti.* **MAKE EMERGENCY LANDING ON WATER** to land, or make an aircraft land, on water in an emergency (*informal*) **3.** *vti.* **DIG DITCHES** to enclose, drain, or irrigate an area with ditches, or dig ditches for this purpose [Old English *dīc*, from a prehistoric Germanic word meaning "hole and mound produced by digging," which is also the ancestor of English *dig* and *dike*] —**ditch·er** *n.*

ditch·wa·ter /dích wòttər/ *n.* the dirty stagnant water found in ditches

di·the·ism /dīthee ìzzəm, dī thee-/ *n.* **1. BELIEF IN TWO GODS** belief in two equal gods **2. BELIEF IN GOOD AND EVIL GODS** the belief that the world is ruled by two equal and opposing forces or gods, one good and one evil —**di·the·ist** *n.* —**di·the·is·tic** /dìthee ístik/ *adj.*

dith·er /díthər/ *vi.* (**-ered, -er·ing, -ers**) **1. BE AGITATED AND INDECISIVE** to behave in a nervous and indecisive way **2. SHIVER** to tremble or quiver, e.g., with cold (*archaic*) ■ *n.* **AGITATED OR INDECISIVE STATE** a state of nervous agitation or indecisiveness [Mid-17thC. Alteration of obsolete *didder* "to tremble, shake," of uncertain origin, but thought to suggest the action.] —**dith·er·er** *n.*

dith·er·ing /díthəring/ *n.* **1. NERVOUS INDECISIVENESS** nervously confused indecisiveness in the face of alternative possible actions **2.** COMPUT **SIMULATION OF COLORS** a technique of mixing pixels of several colors on a computer display to create the illusion of extra colors or shading

dith·y·ramb /díthə ràm/ *n.* **1. FERVENT SPEECH** a passionately emotional speech or piece of writing (*formal*) **2. IMPASSIONED GREEK CHORUS** in ancient Greece, a wild and impassioned choral hymn, originally directed to the god Dionysus [Early 17thC. Via Latin *dithyrambus* from Greek *dithurambos*, of unknown origin.]

dith·y·ramb·ic /dìthə rámbik/ *adj.* passionately emotional or wildly enthusiastic (*formal*) —**dith·y·ramb·i·cal·ly** *adv.*

dit·sy /dítsee/ (**-si·er, -si·est**), **dit·zy** (**-zi·er, -zi·est**) *adj.* silly or scatterbrained (*informal*) [Late 20thC. Origin uncertain: perhaps a blend of DOTTY and DIZZY.]

dit·ta·ny /dítt'nee/ (*plural* **-nies** *or* **-ny**) *n.* **1. PINK-FLOWERED PLANT OF S EUROPE** an aromatic pink-flowered plant found in southern Europe and related to oregano and marjoram. It is cultivated as an ornamental and for its medicinal properties. Latin name: *Origanum dictamnus.* **2. CULINARY HERB** an aromatic plant, cultivated as a kitchen herb. Latin name: *Cunila origanoides.* **3.** = **gas plant** [12thC. From Old French *ditain* and medieval Latin *ditaneum*, both ultimately from Greek *diktamnon*, of uncertain origin: perhaps named after *Diktē*, mountain on Crete where it grows.]

dit·to /díttō/ *interj.* **SAME HERE** used instead of repeating something that has just been said to indicate that the same thing applies to you (*informal*) ■ *adv.* **THE SAME THING APPLIES ELSEWHERE** indicating that whatever has just been said about one person or thing applies equally to somebody or something else ○ *The car will need to be cleaned; ditto the children.* ■ *n.* (*plural* **-tos**) **SYMBOLS REPRESENTING REPEATED MATTER** a pair of symbols (") that together represent matter that is repeated directly from what appears above them but that is unstated ■ *vt.* (**-toed, -to·ing, -tos**) **REPEAT SOMETHING** to repeat or imitate something that somebody else has said or done [Early 17thC. Via a Tuscan dialect variant of Italian *detto* "said," from the Latin past participle *dictus*. Originally used to avoid repeating the name of a month.]

dit·ty /díttee/ (*plural* **-ties**) *n.* a short simple popular song [14thC. Via Old French *dité* "composition" from Latin *dictatum* "thing dictated," from the past participle of *dictare* "to dictate" (see DICTATE).]

dit·ty bag *n.* a small canvas or leather bag used by men for holding small personal belongings [*Ditty* of unknown origin]

ditz /dits/ *n.* somebody considered to be silly in a scatterbrained sort of way (*slang insult*) [Late 20thC. Back-formation from DITZY.]

dit·zy *adj.* = **ditsy**

di·u·re·sis /dī ə reessiss/ *n.* abnormally increased excretion of urine caused by excessive intake of fluids, a drug, or a disease [Late 17thC. From modern

Latin, literally "urination through," from Greek *ourēsis* "urination."]

di·u·ret·ic /dī̀ ə réttik/ *adj.* CAUSING INCREASED URINE OUTPUT causing increased flow of urine ■ *n.* DRUG INCREASING URINE OUTPUT a medication or other agent that increases urine output [14thC. From, ultimately, late Latin *diureticus*, from Greek *diourētikos*, from *diourein*, literally "to urinate through," from *ourein* "to urinate."] —**di·u·ret·ic·al·ly** *adv.*

di·ur·nal /dī úrn'l/ *adj.* **1.** IN THE DAYTIME happening during the day as opposed to at night. ◊ **nocturnal 2.** EVERY DAY happening every day **3.** SCI VARYING WITHIN A DAY varying within the course of a single day **4.** BOT OPEN ONLY IN DAYTIME used to describe flowers that open during the day and close at night. ◊ **nocturnal 5.** ZOOL ACTIVE IN DAYTIME used to describe animals that are active during the day rather than at night. ◊ **nocturnal** ■ *n.* CHR WORSHIP BOOK in the Roman Catholic Church, a book containing the prayer and worship material for all of the set daily services except matins [14thC. From late Latin *diurnalis*, from Latin *diurnus* "daily," from *dies* "day" (source of English *diary*).] —**di·ur·nal·ly** *adv.*

di·ur·nal par·al·lax *n.* the change in a celestial body's apparent position caused by the change in the observer's position because of the motion of the Earth in a day

di·u·ron /dī́ ə ròn/ *n.* a long-lasting agricultural herbicide used especially to kill annual weeds. Formula: $C_9H_{10}Cl_2N_2O$. [Mid-20thC. Coined from DICHLOR- + UREA + -ON.]

div. *abbr.* **1.** divergence **2.** divergency **3.** diversion **4.** divide **5.** dividend **6.** division **7.** divorced

di·va /déevə/ (*plural* **-vas** *or* **-ve** /-vay/) *n.* **1.** WOMAN OPERA SINGER a distinguished woman singer, especially one who sings in operas **2.** TEMPERAMENTAL WOMAN an extremely arrogant or temperamental woman [Late 19thC. Via Italian from Latin, "goddess," from the feminine of *divus* "divine" (see DIVINE).]

di·va·gate /dī́və gàyt, dívvə-/ (**-gat·ed, -gat·ing, -gates**) *vi.* (*literary*) **1.** DIGRESS to wander off the subject under discussion **2.** WANDER to wander around somewhere [Mid-16thC. From the Latin past participle stem *divagat-* of *divagari*, literally "to wander around," from *vagari* "to wander."] —**di·va·ga·tion** /dī̀və gáysh'n, divvə-/ *n.*

di·va·lent /dī váylənt/ *adj.* CHEM having a valence of 2

Di·va·li /di vaálee/ *n.* INDIAN RELIG = **Diwali**

di·van /dī́ vàn, di ván/ *n.* **1.** FURNITURE BACKLESS SOFA a sofa without a back, and sometimes without arms **2.** SMOKING ROOM in former times, a smoking room attached to a coffee shop or cigar shop **3.** POETRY ARABIC POEMS a collection of poems written in Persian or Arabic, often by a single poet [Late 16thC. Via French or Italian *divano* from Turkish *dīvān*, from Persian *dīvān*.]

di·var·i·cate /dī vérrə kàyt, di-/ *vi.* (**-cat·ed, -cat·ing, -cates**) BRANCH OR FORK to branch or fork at a wide angle ■ *adj.* BIOL BRANCHING branching or forking at a wide angle [Early 17thC. From the Latin past participle stem *divaricat-* of *divaricare*, literally "to stretch apart," from, ultimately, *varicus* "straddling."] —**di·var·i·cate·ly** *adv.* —**di·var·i·cat·ing·ly** *adv.*

di·var·i·ca·tion /dī vèrri káysh'n, di vèrri káysh'n/ *n.* **1.** ANAT WIDE BRANCHING separation into widely spread parts or branches, or the point at which something forks or branches **2.** DIFFERING IN OPINION a difference of opinion (*formal*)

dive /dīv/ *v.* (**dived** *or* **dove** /dōv/, **dived, div·ing, dives**) **1.** *vi.* JUMP INTO WATER to jump or throw yourself into water, usually head first, especially with your arms stretched out above your head **2.** *vi.* SWIM UNDER WATER to swim below the surface of a stretch of water, often with special breathing apparatus **3.** *vi.* GO TOWARD BOTTOM OF WATER to go down steeply and quickly in the direction of the bottom of a body of water, sometimes in search of something ○ *dive for treasure* **4.** *vi.* DESCEND STEEPLY AND RAPIDLY to fly or make an aircraft fly steeply and rapidly in the direction of the ground or the sea **5.** *vi.* THROW YOURSELF TO THE GROUND to jump quickly to one side or throw yourself forward or sideways to the ground ○ *dive out of the way* **6.** *vi.* MOVE FAST to move quickly and in a rush in a particular direction ○ *dive for the door* **7.** *vti.* PUT HAND IN SOMETHING to put your hand or hands quickly into something, e.g., a pocket, a bag, or a cupboard, in order to get something out of it **8.** *vi.* BEGIN SOMETHING ENTHUSIASTICALLY to undertake or start on some activity with great enthusiasm ○ *He dived into the project.* **9.** *vi.* SWIMMING PERFORM JUMPS INTO WATER AS SPORT to perform a pattern of acrobatic movements in the air ending in a usually headfirst plunge into water, or do this regularly as a sport **10.** *vi.* NAVY GO UNDER WATER to cause something such as a submarine to go below the surface of the sea **11.** *vi.* FIN DROP IN VALUE to fall sharply in value ■ *n.* **1.** HEADLONG JUMP INTO WATER a jump into water, usually head first, especially with your arms stretched out above your head **2.** SWIMMING ACT OF SWIMMING UNDER WATER a swim below the surface of a stretch of water, often with special breathing apparatus **3.** DESCENT TOWARD BOTTOM OF WATER a steep and usually rapid descent in the direction of the bottom of a body of water **4.** AIR STEEP DESCENT a bird's or aircraft's rapid and steep fall or flight in the direction of the ground or the sea **5.** QUICK MOVEMENT SIDEWAYS OR DOWN a quick jump or movement to one side, or forward or sideways to the ground **6.** FAST MOVEMENT a rapid movement in a particular direction **7.** DISREPUTABLE BAR OR CLUB a dirty, shabby, or disreputable bar or club (*informal*) **8.** SWIMMING ACROBATIC PLUNGE an acrobatic plunge into water performed as a sport or in a competition **9.** NAVY SUBMARINE'S DESCENT a submarine's descent below the surface of the sea **10.** FIN SHARP FINANCIAL DROP a sharp fall in value **11.** FOOTBALL PLAYER'S DRIVE FORWARD TO MAKE GROUND an offensive play in which the ball carrier gains a little yardage by driving into the opposing line of players instead of passing the ball or running with it **12.** SOCCER SOCCER PLAYER'S FALL a feigned dramatic fall by a player to try to gain a free kick or penalty, or a goalkeeper's attempt to stretch horizontally to save a shot (*informal*) **13.** BOXING BOXER'S FEIGNED FALL a fall or injury feigned by a boxer in order to lose a fight dishonestly (*slang*) [Old English *dūfan* "to sink" and *dȳfan* "to dip," from a prehistoric Germanic base that is also the ancestor of English *deep* and *dip*]

WORD KEY: USAGE

Dived or **dove**? Both forms are acceptable as past tenses of ***dive***. ***Dived*** is actually an earlier past tense form, but ***dove*** has become a standard alternative. This is anomalous in light of the general tendency of verbs to form their past tense with *-ed*, as opposed to a change in their vowel, which was more frequently the case in the Old English period. The past participle is nonetheless *dived*.

dive in *vi.* to begin eating quickly and with gusto (*informal*)

dive-bomb (**dive-bombed, dive-bomb·ing, dive-bombs**) *vt.* to descend steeply in a military aircraft and deliver bombs onto a target —**dive-bomb·er** *n.* —**dive-bomb·ing** *n.*

dive brake *n.* AIR FORCE = **air brake** *n.* 2

Di·ve·hi /dívve ee/ *n.* a dialect of Sinhalese spoken in the Republic of Maldives. Divehi is spoken by about 260,000 people. —**Di·ve·hi** *adj.*

div·er /dī́vər/ *n.* **1.** SOMEBODY WHO DIVES IN WATER somebody who dives in water, e.g., somebody trained to carry out underwater work or exploration, or a sportsperson performing acrobatic dives **2.** BIRDS WATER BIRD any water bird noted for its diving skills **3.** *U.K.* BIRDS = **loon**

di·verge /di vúrj, dī-/ (**-verged, -verg·ing, -verg·es**) *vi.* **1.** SEPARATE to separate and go in a different direction or different directions **2.** DIFFER to differ to some extent **3.** NOT MATCH to deviate from or not fit in with or conform to something, e.g., a typical pattern or expressed wish [Mid-17thC. From medieval Latin *divergere*, literally "to bend apart," from Latin *vergere* "to bend" (see VERGE[2]).] —**di·verg·ing** *adj.*

di·ver·gence /di vúrjənss, dī vúrjənss/, **di·ver·gen·cy** /-jənsee, -jənsee/ (*plural* **-cies**) *n.* **1.** DIFFERENCE OR DISPARITY a difference between two or more things, e.g., opinions or attitudes **2.** FAILURE TO CONFORM OR MATCH deviation from something, e.g., a typical pattern or expressed wish **3.** MOVING APART the process of separating or moving apart to follow different paths or different courses **4.** AMOUNT OF DIFFERENCE the amount by which something differs from something else, especially where such a difference is not expected **5.** OPHTHALMOL DEVIATION OF EYE FROM SIGHT LINE a condition in which only one eye is directed at the object of interest and the other is directed outward **6.** BIOL DIFFERENT DEVELOPMENT the development of different characteristics by organisms that come from the same ancestor, caused by the influence of different environments. ◊ **convergence 7.** MATH SEQUENCE OF NUMBERS WITHOUT LIMIT the characteristic of a series or sequence of numbers in which the value of the last term and the sum of the series are without limit. ◊ **convergence**. Symbol **div 8.** METEOROL MOVEMENT OF AIR CURRENTS a set of meteorological conditions in a given area in which the air expands and the net flow of air is out of the area, usually resulting in fair, dry conditions

di·ver·gent /di-, dī vúrjənt/ *adj.* **1.** MOVING APART following paths or courses that become increasingly different or separate **2.** DIFFERING showing or having differences **3.** NOT MATCHING SOMETHING deviating from something, e.g., a typical pattern or an expressed wish **4.** MATH INCREASING WITHOUT LIMIT used to describe a series or sequence of numbers in which each term is equal to or greater than the preceding term, and the value of the last term and the sum of the series are without limit **5.** GEOM RADIATING FROM A POINT used to describe lines radiating from a single point —**di·ver·gent·ly** *adv.*

di·verg·ing lens *n.* a lens, usually concave, that causes a parallel beam of light to spread

di·vers /dī́vərz/ *adj.* more than one, and of various types (*formal*) [13thC. Via French from Latin *diversus*, the past participle of *divertere* "to separate" (see DIVERT).]

di·verse /di vúrs, dī́-/ *adj.* **1.** CONSISTING OF DIFFERENT THINGS made up of many different elements or kinds of things **2.** DIFFERING FROM EACH OTHER very different or distinct from one another **3.** SOCIALLY INCLUSIVE composed of many ethnic, as well as socioeconomic and gender, groups ○ *sought a more diverse population of students* [13thC. Variant of DIVERS.] —**di·verse·ness** *n.*

di·verse·ly /di vúrslee, dī-/ *adv.* in different or various ways ○ *diversely colored*

di·ver·si·fi·ca·tion /di vùrsəfi káysh'n, dī vùrsəfi káysh'n/ *n.* **1.** PROVISION OF VARIETY the provision or development of greater variety **2.** COMM DEVELOPMENT OF NEW BUSINESS the expansion of a commercial organization or enterprise into new areas of business

di·ver·si·form /di vúrsə fàrm, dī-/ *adj.* occurring in various forms (*formal*) [Early 18thC. From, ultimately, Latin *diversus* (see DIVERS) + -FORM.]

di·ver·si·fy /di vúrsə fī, dī-/ (**-fied, -fy·ing, -fies**) *vti.* **1.** MAKE OR BECOME VARIED to become more varied, or make something more varied **2.** COMM EXPAND INTO NEW AREAS OF BUSINESS to expand, or expand a commercial organization, into new areas of business [15thC. Via Old French *diversifier* from medieval Latin *diversificare* "to make unlike," from the Latin past participle *diversus* (see DIVERS).] —**di·ver·si·fi·a·bil·i·ty** /di vùrsə fī ə bíllətee, dī-/ *n.* —**di·ver·si·fi·a·ble** /di vúrsə fī əb'l, dī vúrsə fī əb'l/ *adj.* —**di·ver·si·fied** /di vúrsə fīd, dī-/ *adj.* —**di·ver·si·fi·er** /di vúrsə fīr, dī vúrsə fīr/ *n.*

di·ver·sion /di vúrzh'n, dī-/ *n.* **1.** DISTRACTION something that takes somebody's attention away from something else, especially from more routine activities ○ *a welcome diversion from housework* **2.** CHANGE OF PURPOSE OR USE a change in the purpose or use of something from what was intended or from what something was previously **3.** CHANGE OF DIRECTION OR PATH a change in the direction or path of something **4.** PASTIME OR HOBBY an activity or interest that takes somebody's mind off more routine or serious things **5.** MIL MOCK ATTACK a mock attack aimed at drawing enemy attention and troops away from the place of the intended main attack **6.** *U.K.* TRANSP = **detour** [15thC. Directly or via French from the late Latin stem *diversion-* "turning away," from the Latin past participle stem *divers-* (see DIVERS).] —**di·ver·sion·al** *adj.*

di·ver·sion·ar·y /di vúrzh'n èrree, dī-/ *adj.* designed or carried out to divert somebody's attention away from something

di·ver·sion·ist /di vúrzh'nist, dī-/ *n.* somebody such as an irregular soldier, guerrilla, or political operative who engages in disruptive actions or sabotage in order to thwart an enemy or government

di·ver·si·ty /di vúrsətee, dī-/ (*plural* **-ties**) *n.* **1.** VARIETY a variety of something such as opinion, color, or style ○ *a city of great cultural diversity* **2.** SOCIAL INCLUSIVENESS ethnic variety, as well as socioeconomic and gender variety, in a group, society, or institution ○ *a company committed to diversity* **3.** DIFFERENCE OR DISCREPANCY discrepancy, or a difference from what is normal or expected [14thC. Via French *diversité* from Latin *diversitas*, from *diversus* (see DIVERS).]

di·vert /di vúrt, dī-/ (**-vert·ed, -vert·ing, -verts**) *vt.* **1. CHANGE SOMETHING'S PATH** to change the route or path taken by something, e.g., traffic or a river **2. DRAW ATTENTION FROM SOMETHING** to take somebody's mind off something and draw attention to something else **3. CHANGE PURPOSE OR USE** to change the purpose or use of something from what it was previously **4. AMUSE SOMEBODY** to amuse or entertain somebody or yourself [15thC. Via French *divertir* from Latin *divertere*, literally "to turn aside," from *vertere* "to turn."] —**di·vert·er** *n.* —**di·vert·i·ble** *adj.* —**di·ver·tive** *adj.*

di·ver·tic·u·la plural of **diverticulum**

di·ver·tic·u·li·tis /dìvərtikyə lítiss/ *n.* inflammation of abnormal protrusions (**diverticula**) of the lining of the large intestine, causing severe abdominal pain, often with fever and constipation

di·ver·tic·u·lo·sis /dìvərtikyə lóssiss/ *n.* the presence of abnormal protrusions (**diverticula**) in the bowel, caused when the bowel muscles rupture the bowel wall

di·ver·tic·u·lum /dìvər tíkyələm/ (*plural* **-la** /-lə/) *n.* a pouch or sac in the lining of the mucous membrane of a hollow organ, especially one produced in the bowel when the bowel muscle ruptures the bowel wall. ◊ **hernia** [Mid-17thC. From medieval Latin, "byway," variant of Latin *deverticulum*, literally "turning from," from, ultimately, *vertere* "to turn."] —**di·ver·tic·u·lar** *adj.*

di·ver·ti·men·to /di vùrtə méntō/ (*plural* **-ti** /-tee/ *or* **-tos**) *n.* a piece of light classical instrumental music composed in several movements for an ensemble [Mid-18thC. From Italian, "diversion," from *divirtire* "to divert," from, ultimately, Latin *divertere* (see DIVERT).]

di·vert·ing /di vúrting, dī vúrting/ *adj.* amusing or entertaining, and acting as a temporary distraction from more routine or serious matters —**di·vert·ing·ly** *adv.*

di·ver·tisse·ment /di vúrtismənt, dī vúrtismənt/ *n.* **1.** BALLET **SERIES OF UNTHEMED DANCES** in ballet, a series of dances lacking a unifying theme **2.** DANCE **DANCE INTERLUDE** a dance interlude in a play or opera **3.** MUSIC **TUNES DERIVED FROM FAMOUS MELODIES** a set of tunes that are based on well-known melodies [Early 18thC. From French, from the stem *divertiss-* of *divertir* "to divert," from Latin *divertere* (see DIVERT).]

di·vest /di vést, dī vést/ (**-vest·ed, -vest·ing, -vests**) *vt.* **1. TAKE AWAY FROM SOMEBODY** to take away something, especially status or power, from somebody or something (*often passive*) **2. TAKE SOMETHING OFF** to remove something, usually clothes (*formal or humorous*) **3. GIVE UP SOMETHING** to give up or get rid of something, especially a belief or idea **4.** LAW **GIVE AWAY PROPERTY RIGHTS** to lose or give away rights to the possession of property, or deprive somebody of them [Early 17thC. Alteration of obsolete *devest* "deprive of something," from Old French *de(s)vester*, literally "to undress," from *vestir* "to clothe," from Latin *vestire*.] —**di·ves·ti·ble** *adj.* —**di·vest·ment** *n.* —**di·ves·ture** /di vés choor, dī-, -véschər/ *n.*

di·ves·ti·ture /di vésti choor, dī-, -véstichər/ *n.* **1. DISPOSSESSION** the removal or deprivation of something **2. SALE OF PROPERTY** the sale of one or more of a company's subsidiaries, divisions, or holdings, or of its stock in those holdings

di·vide /di víd/ *v.* (**-vid·ed, -vid·ing, -vides**) **1.** *vti.* **SPLIT INTO PARTS** to separate or split something, or be separated or split, into two or more parts ○ *a dormitory divided into cubicles* **2.** *vi.* **SEPARATE AND GO IN DIFFERENT DIRECTIONS** to split into two or more parts that go off in different directions **3.** *vti.* **SHARE SOMETHING** to share something, or be shared, between two or more people or groups ○ *Her inheritance was divided equally among the children.* **4.** *vti.* **SEPARATE TWO PLACES** to be a barrier or boundary between one place or thing and another ○ *The river divides the north of the island from the south.* **5.** *vt.* **CAUSE DISAGREEMENT BETWEEN PEOPLE** to be the cause or subject of disagreement between people **6.** *vt.* MEASURE **MARK SOMETHING OFF** to mark units or sections of a particular size on a measuring instrument, e.g., a ruler **7.** *vti.* MATH **CALCULATE OCCURRENCE OF ONE NUMBER IN ANOTHER** to calculate how many times one number contains another ■ *n.* **1. BOUNDARY OR GAP** a boundary or gap that stands between two things, conditions, or groups **2.** GEOG **RIDGE SEPARATING WATERSHEDS** a long ridge separating watersheds [14thC. From Latin *dividere*, literally "to separate apart," from *-videre* "to separate." Ultimately from an Indo-European word that is also the ancestor of English *widow*.] —**di·vid·a·ble** *adj.*

di·vid·ed /di vídəd/ *adj.* **1. SEPARATED** separated into two or more parts or groups **2. OF TWO MINDS** drawn toward two or more different and often incompatible purposes or groups **3. IN DISAGREEMENT** in a state of internal discord, strife, or disagreement **4.** BOT **SEPARATED INTO SECTIONS** used to describe leaves that are divided into separate sections —**di·vid·ed·ly** *adv.* —**di·vid·ed·ness** *n.*

di·vid·ed high·way *n.* a highway that has a median strip or a barrier separating the lanes going in opposite directions, usually with two or more lanes on either side

di·vid·ed skirt *n.* = **culottes**

div·i·dend /dívvi dènd, dívvidənd/ *n.* **1. BONUS** something good or desirable that is gained as a bonus along with something else **2.** FIN **STOCKHOLDER'S SHARE OF PROFIT** company profits paid pro rata to stockholders, either in cash or in more shares **3.** MATH **NUMBER DIVIDED BY ANOTHER** a number or quantity that is to be divided by another number or quantity. ◊ **divisor 4.** LAW **PROPORTION OF A BANKRUPT'S ESTATE** the proportion of a bankrupt party's estate that is to be divided among the creditors [15thC. Via Anglo-Norman *dividende* from Latin *dividendum* "thing to be divided," a form of *dividere* (see DIVIDE).]

di·vid·er /di vídər/ *n.* a device that separates something into sections, e.g., a screen that partitions a room or a sheet of card that separates the sections of a loose-leaf binder

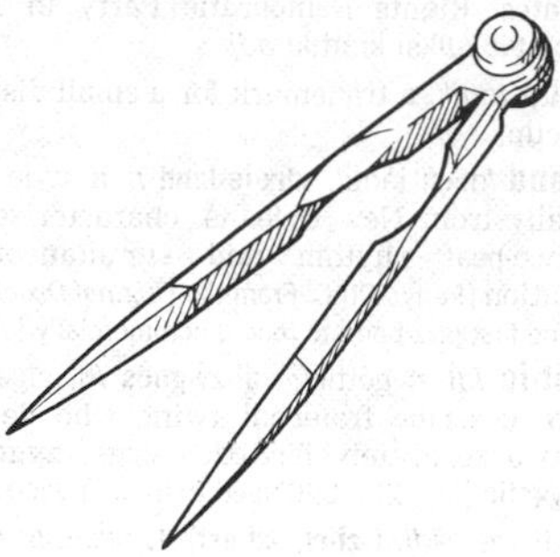

Dividers

di·vid·ers /di vídərz/ *npl.* an instrument with two movable pointed legs hinged at one end, used for measuring distances on maps and charts and for transferring measurements from one chart to another

di·vid·ing line *n.* something that marks a change or distinction between two states or qualities

di·vi-di·vi /dìvvi dívvee/ *n.* **1. TROPICAL TREE** a small tropical American tree with long seed pods. Latin name: *Caesalpinia coriaria*. **2. POD OF DIVI-DIVI TREE** the pod of the divi-divi tree, which has a high tannin content and is used for tanning leather [Mid-19thC. Via American Spanish from Carib.]

div·i·na·tion /dìvvi náysh'n/ *n.* **1. SEEKING KNOWLEDGE BY SUPERNATURAL MEANS** the methods or practice of attempting to foretell the future or discovering the unknown through omens, oracles, or supernatural powers **2. PROPHECY** a prophecy or prediction **3. PREMONITION** a premonition or feeling of foreboding about something that is going to happen —**di·vin·a·to·ry** /di vínnə tàwree/ *adj.*

di·vine /di vín/ *adj.* **1.** RELIG **HAVING GODLIKE NATURE** being God or a god or goddess **2.** RELIG **RELATING TO GOD, GODS, OR GODDESSES** connected with, coming from, or caused by God or a god or goddess **3.** RELIG **CONNECTED WITH WORSHIP** connected with the worship or service of God or a god or goddess **4. LOVELY** pleasing or attractive (*informal or humorous*) ■ *v.* (**-vined, -vin·ing, -vines**) **1.** *vt.* **REALIZE SOMETHING** to come to understand or realize something **2.** *vt.* **DISCOVER AS IF SUPERNATURALLY** to learn or discover something by intuition, inspiration, or other apparently supernatural means **3.** *vt.* **PREDICT SOMETHING AS IF SUPERNATURALLY** to predict something by apparently supernatural means **4.** *vti.* **SEARCH WITH DIVINING ROD** to search for underground water, metal, or minerals using something such as a divining rod ■ *n.* RELIG **1. THEOLOGIAN** a member of the clergy, especially one who is knowledgeable about theology **2. Di·vine, di·vine GOD** God, or whatever else is believed to be the underlying creative and sustaining force in the universe [14thC. Via Old French *devin* from Latin *divinus*, from *divus* "god" (source of English *diva*). Ultimately from an Indo-European word meaning "shining."] —**di·vin·a·ble** *adj.* —**di·vine·ness** /di vín nəss/ *n.*

Di·vine /di vín/, **Father** (1882?–1965) U.S. religious leader. He advocated communal living and racial equality, and his Peace Mission Movement, founded in the 1910s, attracted many African Americans in New York City and Philadelphia. Born **George Baker**

di·vine·ly /di vínlee/ *adv.* **1. WONDERFULLY** well, pleasingly, or attractively (*informal or humorous*) **2.** RELIG **BY GOD, A GOD, OR GODDESS** by God or a god or goddess

di·vin·er /di vínər/ *n.* somebody who searches for underground water, metal, or minerals using something such as a divining rod

di·vine right *n.* the belief that the monarch's authority comes directly from God rather than from the people

div·ing beetle *n.* a predatory water beetle adapted for swimming that has flattened hind legs and the capacity to breathe air trapped under its wings. Family: Dytiscidae.

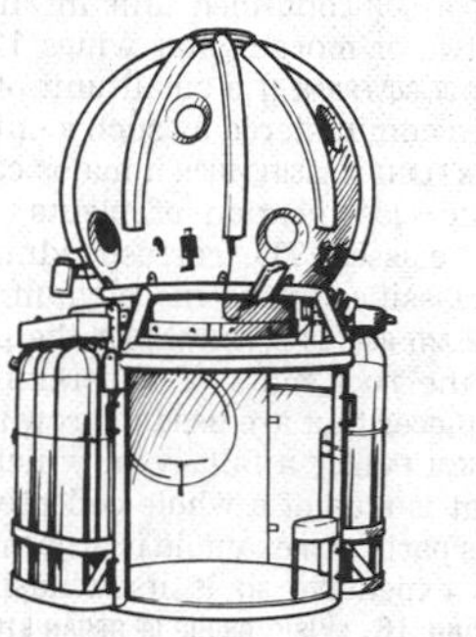

Diving bell

div·ing bell *n.* a metal bell-shaped device used for working underwater. It has an open bottom and is supplied with compressed air.

div·ing board *n.* a raised board at the edge of a swimming pool from which to dive into the water

div·ing duck *n.* a duck, e.g., the bufflehead, pochard, or scaup, that dives for food and swims under water

div·ing re·flex *n.* a reflex in mammals in which the heart rate slows and skin blood vessels narrow on immersion in cold water, so as to help them to conserve oxygen. The reflex is strongest in aquatic animals such as seals, but is still present to a minor extent in nonaquatic animals, including human beings.

div·ing suit *n.* a waterproof suit, often including a helmet and an air supply, worn by divers

di·vin·ing rod *n.* a forked stick used as a device for sensing underground water sources or minerals. The diviner holds an end of the rod in each hand, and the rod is said to dip sharply downward when the diviner walks over a water source or minerals.

di·vin·i·ty /di vínnətee/ (*plural* **-ties**) *n.* **1. QUALITY OF BEING GOD, A GOD, OR GODDESS** the quality associated with being God, a god, or a goddess **2. THEOLOGY** the study of religion, especially the Christian religion **3. di·vin·i·ty, Di·vin·i·ty GOD** God, a god or a goddess **4. CANDY** a fluffy white candy, usually made with egg white and nuts [13thC. From French *divinité*, from the Latin stem *divinitat-* "godhead, divinity," from *divinus*, from *divus* "god."]

di·vin·i·ty school *n.* a college for students training to be ministers

di·vis·i·bil·i·ty /di vìzzə bíllətee/ *n.* the capability of being divided exactly by a particular number

di·vis·i·ble /di vízzəb'l/ *adj.* **1. ABLE TO BE DIVIDED** able to be divided, especially without leaving a remainder **2. ABLE TO BE SEPARATED** capable of being separated into different parts [15thC. Directly or via French from late Latin *divisibilis*, from the Latin past participle stem *divis-* of *dividere* "to separate apart."] —**di·vis·i·ble·ness** *n.* —**di·vis·i·bly** *adv.*

di·vi·sion /di vízh'n/ *n.* **1. ACT OF SPLITTING INTO PARTS** the act of separating or splitting something into parts, or an instance of this ○ *the division of the region into smaller administrative districts* **2. SHARING OF SOMETHING** the separation of something into parts to be shared among people or groups ○ *The division of work between members of the group should be equal.* **3.**

MATH **OPERATION OF DIVIDING ONE NUMBER BY ANOTHER** an operation used to calculate the number of times one number is contained in another **4. DISAGREEMENT** a disagreement or strong difference of opinion, especially when this leads to a split in a group ○ *Deep divisions exist within senior management itself as to the best way of dealing with the problem.* **5. SOMETHING SEPARATING** something that separates things by forming a boundary between them **6. SEPARATE PART** one of the parts created when something is split **7. SECTION OF ORGANIZATION** a section of a large organization that has a particular task or function ○ *the sales division of a large firm* **8.** SPORTS **GROUP OF TEAMS IN SPORTS LEAGUE** a group of teams, usually those representing cities close to one another or of roughly similar standard in a sports league, conference, or association **9.** MIL **ARMY UNIT** a self-contained military unit in an army capable of sustained operations, including a headquarters and two or more brigades or, in the Marines, several regiments **10.** NAVY **NAVAL UNIT** a self-contained unit in a navy including a group of ships of the same class **11.** AIR FORCE **AIR FORCE UNIT** a self-contained unit in an air force including two or more fighter wings **12.** PUBLIC ADMIN **SMALL UNIT OF GOVERNMENT** a small unit of government, or an area administered by such a unit **13.** BOT **MAJOR CATEGORY IN PLANT CLASSIFICATION** a major category in the taxonomic classification of plants, comprising a group of classes. The corresponding category in animal classification is the phylum. **14.** GARDENING **SPLITTING PLANT ROOTS FOR PROPAGATION** the process of separating the root mass of a perennial plant into smaller pieces that are used to grow new plants **15.** LOGIC **LOGICAL FALLACY** a fallacy in which it is argued that what is true of a whole collectively is true of any of its parts. An example is arguing that because a car is expensive so is its windshield wiper. ◊ **composition 16.** MUSIC **GROUP OF ORGAN STOPS** a group of organ stops played on the same manual [14thC. Via Old French *devisiun* from the Latin stem *division-*, from the past participle stem *divis-* of *dividere* "to separate apart."] —**di·vi·sion·al** *adj.* —**di·vi·sion·al·ly** *adv.* —**di·vi·sion·ar·y** *adj.*

di·vi·sion of la·bor *n.* a system of organizing production by giving separate tasks to separate workers or groups of workers

di·vi·sion sign *n.* a sign (÷) placed between two numbers to show that the first number is divided by the second

di·vi·sive /di vɪ́ssiv/ *adj.* causing disagreement or hostility within a group so that it is likely to split [Late 16thC. From late Latin *divisivus*, from the Latin past participle stem *divis-* of *dividere* "to separate apart."] —**di·vi·sive·ly** *adv.* —**di·vi·sive·ness** *n.*

di·vi·sor /di vɪ́zər/ *n.* a number divided into another number. ◊ **dividend** [15thC. Directly or via French *diviseur* from Latin *divisor*, from the past participle stem *divis-* of *dividere* "to separate apart."]

di·vor·ce /di váwrs/ *n.* **1.** LAW **OFFICIAL ENDING OF A MARRIAGE** the ending of a marriage by an official decision in a court of law **2. SEPARATION** a complete separation or split ■ *v.* (**-vorced, -vorc·ing, -vor·ces**) **1.** *vti.* LAW **OFFICIALLY END A MARRIAGE** to end a marriage to somebody by an official decision in a court of law **2.** *vt.* **SEPARATE SOMETHING** to separate or distinguish something from something else [14thC. Via French from Latin *divortium*, from *divortere*, variant of *divertere* "to part, turn aside."] —**di·vorce·a·ble** *adj.* —**di·vorc·er** *n.* —**di·vor·cive** *adj.*

di·vor·cé /di vàwr sáy/ *n.* a man who is divorced [Late 19thC. From French, originally the past participle of *divorcer* "to divorce," from, ultimately, Latin *divortium* (see DIVORCE).]

di·vorced /di váwrst/ *adj.* no longer married because the marriage has been ended by a divorce

di·vor·cée /di vàwr sáy/ *n.* a woman who is divorced [Early 19thC. Partly from French, from the feminine of the past participle of *divorcer* "to divorce," from, ultimately, Latin *divortium* (see DIVORCE); partly from DIVORCE + -EE.]

div·ot /dívvət/ *n.* a small lump of grass and earth accidentally dug out of the ground while playing a sport, especially golf [Early 16thC. Origin unknown. Originally Scots dialect "piece of turf (especially for roofing cottages)"; the current sense dates from the late 19thC.]

di·vulge /di vúlj/ (**-vulged, -vulg·ing, -vulg·es**) *vt.* to reveal information, especially information that was previously secret [15thC. From, ultimately, Latin *divulgare*, literally "to make widely known to the masses," from *vulgus* "masses."] —**di·vulge·ment** *n.* —**di·vul·gence** *n.* —**di·vulg·er** *n.*

div·vy /dívvee/ *vt.* (**-vied, -vy·ing, -vies**) **DIVIDE SOMETHING UP** to divide something up and share it among a group of people (*informal*) ■ *n.* (*plural* **-vies**) **PORTION** a person's share of something (*informal*) [Late 19thC. Shortening of DIVIDEND.]

Di·wa·li /di wàalee/, **Di·va·li** /di vàalee/ *n.* an important Hindu festival associated with Lakshmi, the goddess of prosperity, held in the autumn [Late 17thC. Via Hindi *diwālī* from Sanskrit *dīpāvalī* "row of lights," from *dīpa* "light, lamp."]

Dix /diks/, **Dorothea** (1802–87) U.S. philanthropist and reformer. She investigated conditions in prisons, almshouses, and asylums, securing legislation for their improvement. During the Civil War she was superintendent of women nurses with the Union army. Full name **Dorothea Lynde Dix**

Dix·ie /díksee/ *n.* **1. SOUTHERN U.S. STATES** the southern states that were members of the Confederacy during the Civil War (*informal*) **2. CIVIL WAR SONG** the popular name for a song used as a Confederate marching tune during the Civil War [Mid-19thC. Origin uncertain: perhaps an alteration of *Dixon*, from *Mason-Dixon Line*; or from assumed *Dixies* "Louisiana banknotes," from French *dix* "ten."]

Dix·ie·crat /díksi kràt/ *n.* a member of a group of southern Democrats who disagreed with the Democratic Party's civil rights programs and left to form the States' Rights Democratic Party in 1948 —**Dix·ie·crat·ic** /dìksi kráttik/ *adj.*

Dix·ie cup *tdmk.* a trademark for a small disposable paper cup

Dix·ie·land /díksi lànd/, **dix·ie·land** *n.* a style of jazz, originally from New Orleans, characterized by a fast two-beat rhythm and simultaneous improvisation [Early 20thC. From the *Original Dixieland Jazz Band*, the first jazz band to record commercially.]

di·zy·got·ic /dì zī góttik/, **di·zy·gous** /dī zígəss/ *adj.* used to describe fraternal twins who developed from two separately fertilized eggs (**zygotes**). ◊ **monozygotic** [Mid-20thC. Coined from DI- + ZYGOTE + -IC.]

diz·zy /dízzee/ *adj.* (**-zi·er, -zi·est**) **1. UNSTEADY AND GIDDY** unsteady, as if about to lose balance, and slightly giddy **2. CONFUSED AND BEWILDERED** confused, overwhelmed, and unable to think clearly **3. FUN-LOVING BUT THOUGHTLESS** fun-loving and somewhat silly or empty-headed (*informal*) **4. FAST** extremely fast ○ *dizzy speeds* **5. EXTREME** so high as to make somebody giddy ○ *the dizzy height of the tower* ■ *vt.* (**-zied, -zy·ing, -zies**) **CAUSE SOMEBODY TO FEEL DIZZY** to cause somebody to feel unsteady and slightly giddy, or confused and bewildered [Old English *dysig* "foolish, stupid," from a prehistoric Germanic base that is also the ancestor of English *doze*] —**diz·zi·ly** *adv.* —**diz·zi·ness** *n.*

DJ *n.* somebody who plays records or other recorded music for the entertainment of others, whether at a live dance or on the radio

D.J. *abbr.* district judge

djel·la·ba /jə làabə/, **djel·la·bah** *n.* a long loose-fitting robe with sleeves and a hood, worn especially in Islamic countries [Early 19thC. From Moroccan Arabic *jellāb(a)* or *jellābiyya*.]

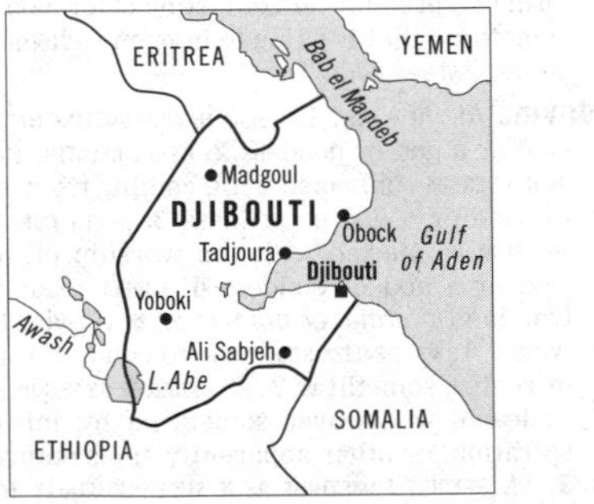

Dji·bou·ti /ji bóotee/ **1.** republic in the Horn of Africa, bounded by the Gulf of Aden, Somalia, Ethiopia, and Eritrea. Language: Arabic, French. Currency: Djibouti franc. Capital: Djibouti. Population: 434,116 (1997). Area: 8,958 sq. mi./23,200 sq. km. **2.** the capital of the Republic of Djibouti. Population: 383,000 (1995).

djinn, **djin·ni** *n.* ◊ **jinni**

dk. *abbr.* **1.** dark **2.** deck **3.** dock

dkg *symbol.* decagram

dkl *symbol.* decaliter

dkm *symbol.* decameter

dl *symbol.* deciliter

DL *abbr.* disabled list

D/L *abbr.* BANKING demand loan

D lay·er *n.* **1.** = **D region 2. LOWER LAYER OF EARTH'S MANTLE** the lower layer of the Earth's mantle, from 450 mi./720 km deep down to the boundary with the core

D.Litt. /di lít/, **D.Lit.** *abbr.* **1.** Doctor of Letters **2.** Doctor of Literature

DLO *abbr.* dead letter office

dlvy. *abbr.* delivery

dm *symbol.* decimeter

DM *symbol.* deutsche mark

D.M.A. *abbr.* Doctor of Musical Arts

D-mark, **D-Mark** *abbr.* deutsche mark

D.M.D. *abbr.* Doctor of Dental Medicine

DMK *n.* a political party in Tamil Nadu, India. Full form **Dravida Munnetra Kazgham**

DMSO *n.* a clear odorless liquid compound used as a solvent and in medicine to enable drugs applied to the skin to penetrate. Formula: $(CH_3)_2SO$. Full form **dimethylsulfoxide**

D.Mus. *abbr.* Doctor of Music

DMV *abbr.* Department of Motor Vehicles

DMZ *abbr.* demilitarized zone

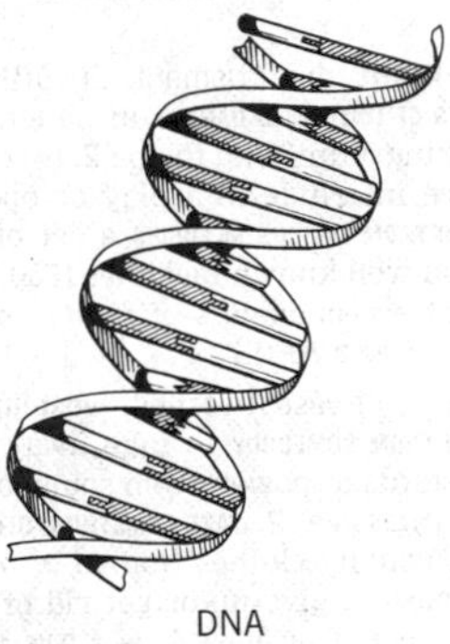

DNA

DNA *n.* a nucleic acid molecule in the form of a twisted double strand (**double helix**) that is the major component of chromosomes and carries genetic information. DNA, which is found in all living organisms except some viruses, is self-replicating and is responsible for passing along hereditary characteristics from one generation to the next. Full form **deoxyribonucleic acid**

DNAase /dée en áy àyss, -àyz/, **DNase** /dée en áyss, -áyz/ *n.* an enzyme that aids the hydrolysis of DNA into smaller molecules. Full form **deoxyribonuclease**

DNA fin·ger·print·ing *n.* = **genetic fingerprinting**

DNA i·den·ti·fi·ca·tion *n.* a forensic method of identifying somebody on the basis of a DNA analysis

DNA pol·y·mer·ase *n.* an enzyme that uses single-stranded DNA to reproduce and repair DNA

DNase *n.* = **DNAase**

DNA vi·rus *n.* a virus with a genome containing DNA

do[1] /doo/ (**did** /did/, **done** /dun/, **do·ing, does** /duz/) CORE MEANING: a verb indicating that somebody performs an action, an activity, or a task. It is often used as an informal equivalent of more specific and less frequent verbs, e.g., "do your nails" instead of "paint your nails." ○ *He usually did the cleaning on a Sunday morning.* ○ *Why won't you let me do your hair for you?* ○ *Assuming that your terminal is properly set up, here is what you have to do to connect it.*

1. *vt.* **USE SOMETHING** to use something in a particular way ○ *She's done absolutely nothing with the money she inherited.* **2.** *vt.* **TAKE ACTION** to take action in a particular situation in order to change it or solve a problem ○ *Companies must decide what to do about their chemical waste.* **3.** *vt.* **CAUSE SOMETHING** to cause or produce a particular effect or result ○ *These* *disputes do little to help the peace process.* **4.** *vt.* **WORK AT SOMETHING** to work at something, particularly as a job or profession, or as a course of study ○ *What does your mother do at the bank?* **5.** *vt.* **BE OCCUPIED WITH SOMETHING** to be occupied or busy with something ○ *Are you doing anything this evening?* **6.** *vt.* **CONDUCT SELF** to behave in a particular manner ○ *Do what you want.* **7.** *vi.* **FARE** to be successful or unsuccessful to a particular extent ○ *Automobile insurance companies are doing well this year.* **8.** *vt.* **PROVIDE SOMETHING** to prepare or provide something ○ *I'm sorry but we don't do a lunch menu.* **9.** *vt.* **ACHIEVE A SPEED OR RATE** to achieve a particular speed or rate ○ *We were doing 55 down the freeway.* ○ *We did about 400 miles a day.* **10.** *vt.* **STUDY SOMETHING** to study or work at doing something ○ *Have you done Nabokov yet?* ○ *I've never been able to do algebra.* **11.** *vt.* **PERFORM SOMETHING** to perform or act a particular play, role, or accent ○ *They're doing "Macbeth" at the Hippodrome next month.* ○ *I'm not very good at doing accents.* **12.** *vt.* **VISIT OR EXPLORE PLACE** to visit or explore a country or city as a tourist (*informal*) ○ *We're doing London tomorrow.* **13.** *v. vti.* **BE ADEQUATE** to be adequate in quantity or quality ○ *A paper cup does just as well.* ○ *Just an orange juice will do me.* **14.** *vt.* **SERVE TIME IN PRISON** to serve a period of time in prison (*slang*) ○ *He's doing time for cheating on his taxes.* **15.** *vt.* **EXHAUST SOMEBODY** to wear somebody out (*informal*) ○ *After slaving in the garden for six hours, I'm done!* **16.** *vt.* **ADAPT SOMETHING** to translate or adapt a play, book, or other work ○ *The novel was done into a feature film.* **17.** *vt.* **CHEAT SOMEBODY** to cheat or trick somebody (*informal*) ○ *They did her out of her lunch money.* **18.** *vt.* **ROB SOMEBODY** to rob a person or place (*slang*) ○ *They got caught while they were doing the local bank.* **19.** *vt.* **TAKE DRUGS** to take or use a narcotic drug (*slang*) **20.** *vt.* **HAVE SEX WITH SOMEBODY** to have sexual intercourse with somebody (*slang*) **21.** *vt.* **MURDER** to kill somebody deliberately (*slang*) **22.** *vt.* **FORMS QUESTIONS AND NEGATIVES** used with simple present and simple past tenses in the formation of questions and negative sentences. "Do" and "did" are often contracted to "don't" and "didn't" in negative structures. ○ *What did he want?* ○ *Don't sit there!* ○ *It doesn't matter if you can't come.* **23.** *vi.* **GIVES EMPHASIS** used to emphasize a positive statement or command, often as a way of politely inviting or persuading somebody to do something ○ *Yes, I do realize you can't finish the work today.* ○ *Please do be quiet!* **24.** *vt.* **CHANGES THE EMPHASIS** used to form inverted sentences in order to change the emphasis of a statement ○ *I want to have a break just as much as you do.* **25.** *vt.* **REPLACES ANOTHER VERB** used to replace an earlier verb or verb phrase to avoid repetition, usually when comparing two things ○ *She hopes to go to college, as do her brothers.* **26.** *n. NZ, U.K.* **SOCIAL GATHERING** a formal social gathering, e.g., a wedding reception (*informal*) **27.** *n.* **EXCREMENT** excrement (*informal*) (*used euphemistically*) ○ *a pile of doggy do* [Old English *dōn*. Ultimately from an Indo-European word meaning "to place"that is also the ancestor of English *deed*, *theme*, and *fashion*.] ◇ **could do with** be sure to benefit from something ○ *I could do with some help.* ◇ **have to do with somebody** *or* **something 1.** be connected with somebody or something **2.** concern somebody or something **3.** involve contact or a relationship with something or somebody

WORD KEY: USAGE

did you or **have you**? A distinction that arises in connection with questions and negative statements is represented by the types *Did you see the show*/*Have you seen the show? I didn't see the show*/*I haven't seen the show.* In informal conversation, the two are used almost interchangeably. In strict usage, however, there is a difference in time perspective: the first type in each pair refers to a particular point in the past, whereas the second type has to do with any time in the past (thus, *ever* could be added to the second sentence in each pair without substantially changing its meaning).

WORD KEY: USAGE

do have or **have got**? Both these constructions are used in questions and in negative statements: *Do you have change for a dollar? / Have you got change for a dollar? I don't have any change / I haven't got any change.* Some consider the first type in each pair to be more proper, perceiving *have got* as colloquial and even redundant, and pointing out that *have* alone is sufficient to signify possession. But *Have you change?* and *I haven't any change* are not idiomatic, and *do have* has just as many syllables as *have got.* Therefore it is hard to see what reasonable basis exists for preferring *do have* to *have got.*

WORD KEY: SYNONYMS

See Synonyms at ***perform***.

do away with *vt.* **1. ABOLISH SOMETHING** to abolish something so that it no longer happens or exists **2. KILL SOMEBODY** to kill somebody (*informal*)

do for *vt.* to provide for or take care of somebody ○ *You'll have to do for yourself this week – I won't be here.*

do in *vt.* (*informal*) **1. KILL SOMEBODY** to kill or severely beat somebody **2. TIRE OUT** to make somebody feel exhausted

do up *vt.* **1. GIVE SOMETHING DECORATIVE WRAPPING** to wrap or cover something in something decorative (*often passive*) **2. DRESS FASHIONABLY** to dress somebody or yourself in fashionable clothes (*informal*) **3. FASTEN SOMETHING** to fasten something, e.g., with string or ribbons **4. MAKE SOMETHING USABLE AGAIN** to make something fit to use again by repairing or decorating it

do without *vti.* to manage or survive without something that you want, need, or normally have

do[2] /dō/ *n.* a syllable that represents the first note in a scale, used for singing solfeggio. In fixed solfeggio it represents the note C, while in solfeggio with movable do it is used to represent the tonic of the key being sung. [Mid-18thC. From Italian *do*, a replacement for the less singable medieval Latin syllable *ut* (source of English *gamut*).]

D.O. *abbr.* **1.** Doctor of Optometry **2.** Doctor of Osteopathy

D/O *abbr.* COMM **1.** delivery order **2.** direct order

DOA *abbr.* dead on arrival

do·a·ble /dóo əb'l/ *adj.* able to be done or achieved

DOB, **d.o.b** *abbr.* date of birth

dob·bin /dóbbin/, **Dob·bin** *n.* a horse, especially a large heavy working horse [Late 16thC. From *Dobbin*, personal name, an alteration of *Robin*, literally "little Robert," from *Robert*.]

dob·by /dóbbee/ (*plural* **-bies**) *n.* a part of a loom that allows small figures to be woven on it [Late 17thC. Origin uncertain; perhaps from *Dobbie*, personal name, literally "little Dob," from *Dob*, an alteration of *Rob*. Originally "unintelligent person," later "household spirit."]

Doberman pinscher

Do·ber·man pin·scher /dṓbərmən pínshər/, **Do·ber·man** *n.* a medium-sized to large powerful dog with a smooth black or dark brown coat, often used as a guard dog or for police work and belonging to a breed originating in Germany [Early 20thC. Named for Ludwig *Dobermann*, 19th-C German dog breeder who bred it; *pinscher* from German, breed name.]

do·bra /dṓbrə/ *n.* **1. UNIT OF CURRENCY OF SÃO TOMÉ AND PRINCIPE** the main unit of currency of São Tomé and Principe. See table at **currency 2. COIN WORTH A DOBRA** a coin worth one dobra [Late 20thC. Via Portuguese from, ultimately, Latin *duplus* "double" (source of English *double*).]

dob·son·fly /dóbsən flī/ (*plural* **-flies**) *n.* a very large winged North American insect that has long slender mandibles in the male and is noted for its large aquatic larva. Genus: *Corydalus cornutus.*

Dob·zhan·sky /dəb zhánskee/, **Theodosius** (1900–75) Russian-born U.S. geneticist and zoologist. He made important discoveries about genetics and adaptation from his studies of fruit flies.

doc /dok/ *n.* a doctor (*informal*)

DOC *n.* a certification for Italian wine that guarantees its origin [From Italian *Denominazione di Origine Controllata*]

doc. *abbr.* document

do·cent /dṓss'nt, dō sént/ *n.* **1. U.S. UNIVERSITY LECTURER** a lecturer or teacher in a U.S. university, especially one who is not a full-time member of the faculty **2. TOURIST GUIDE** a tourist guide working in some museums or cathedrals [Late 19thC. Via obsolete German *Docent* from the Latin present participle stem *docent-* of *docere* "to teach" (see DOCTOR).]

Do·ce·tism /dō sée tìzzəm, dṓssə-/ *n.* in Christianity, an early heresy that claimed that Jesus Christ was not a real person [Mid-19thC. Formed from *Docete* "Docetist," via medieval Latin *Docetae* (plural) "Docetists" from patristic Greek *Dokētai*, from Greek *dokein* "to seem, appear."] —**Do·ce·tist** *n.*

DOCG *n.* a certification for Italian wine that guarantees its origin and verifies that it meets production regulations [From Italian *Denominazione di Origine Controllata e Garantita*]

doc·ile /dóss'l/ *adj.* **1. QUIET AND EASY TO CONTROL** quiet, easy to control, and unlikely to cause trouble **2. EASILY TAUGHT** easy to teach (*archaic*) [15thC. From Latin *docilis*, from *docere* "to teach" (see DOCTOR). "Easy to control" is not attested until the late 18thC.] —**doc·ile·ly** *adv.* —**do·cil·i·ty** /do sílləte e/ *n.*

dock[1] /dok/ *n.* **1. PLACE FOR SHIPS TO MOOR** an area of water between two piers or next to a pier, where ships can be moored safely for loading and repair **2. GROUP OF PIERS FOR SHIPS** a group of piers on a protected area of water used as a general landing area for ships **3. PIER OR WHARF** a long narrow structure stretching out into a body of water, or a raised area of land alongside water where ships can load and unload **4. ENCLOSED AREA OF WATER FOR SHIP** an enclosed area of water for a ship in which the water level can be adjusted **5.** = **dry dock 6.** TRANSP **LOADING PLATFORM FOR TRAINS OR TRUCKS** a raised platform where trains or trucks can load and unload **7.** *U.K.* = **dockyard** ■ *vti.* (**docked, dock·ing, docks**) **1. MOOR** to steer a ship into a dock and tie it up, or be steered in and tied up there **2.** SPACE TECH **LINK UP WITH SPACECRAFT** to link up with another spacecraft in space [14thC. From either Middle Low German *docke* or Middle Dutch *docke*, of uncertain origin: perhaps from Latin *ductio* "leading," from Latin *ducere* "to lead."]

dock[2] /dok/ *vt.* (**docked, dock·ing, docks**) **1. REDUCE WAGES** to deduct a sum of money from somebody's wages, especially as a punishment **2. REMOVE TAIL** to remove the tail of a dog, sheep, or other animal, leaving a short stump ■ *n.* **1. SOLID PART OF TAIL** the solid part of an animal's tail **2. STUMP OF TAIL** the stump left when an animal's tail has been docked [14thC. The verb came from the noun, of uncertain origin: perhaps from assumed Old English *docca* "muscle," from a prehistoric Germanic base meaning "round thing."]

dock[3] /dok/ *n.* LAW the area in a lawcourt where the accused person stands during a trial [Late 16thC. Origin uncertain: probably originally thieves' slang, from Flemish *dok* "fowl pen, rabbit hutch," of unknown origin.]

dock[4] /dok/ (*plural* **docks** *or* **dock**) *n.* **1. PLANT IN BUCKWHEAT FAMILY** a plant of the buckwheat family with greenish or reddish flowers, long broad leaves, and a long taproot. Genus: *Rumex.* **2. BROAD-LEAFED WEED** any broad-leafed weedy plant [Old English *docce*, from prehistoric Germanic]

dock·age /dókij/ *n.* **1. MOORING CHARGE** a charge payable for mooring at a dock **2. FACILITIES FOR MOORED SHIPS** the facilities for ships moored at a dock **3. DOCKING PROCESS** the process of docking a ship

dock·er /dókər/ *n.* = **longshoreman**

dock·et /dókət/ *n.* **1.** LAW **LIST OF FUTURE COURT CASES** a list of pending cases in a court **2.** LAW **BOOK OF UPCOMING CASES** a book in which pending court cases are kept **3. LIST OF THINGS TO DO** a list of things to do **4. DOCUMENT SUMMARY** a summary of a document **5. CUSTOMS CERTIFICATE** a customs certificate confirming payment of duty ■ *vt.* (**-et·ed, -et·ing, -ets**) **1.** LAW **PUT A LEGAL CASE IN THE CALENDAR** to enter a legal case in the calendar of future cases **2.** LAW **SUMMARIZE A COURT CASE** to summarize a court case and enter the summary in the appropriate register **3. LABEL A PACKAGE** to label a package with a document giving the contents or delivery details **4. SUMMARIZE SOMETHING** to attach or give a summary of something [15thC. Origin uncertain: perhaps formed from DOCK[2].]

dock·hand /dók hànd/ *n.* = **longshoreman**

dock·land /dók lànd/ *n. U.K.* the area surrounding a city's docks or port (*often used in the plural*)

dock·mack·ie /dók màkee/ (*plural* **-mack·ies** *or* **-mak·ie**) *n.* a tall deciduous shrub that produces clusters of white flowers followed by reddish-black berries. The shrub originally came from China and Japan but is now grown in Europe and North America. Genus: *Viburnum acerifolium.* [Origin uncertain: perhaps via American Dutch from Mahican]

dock·o·min·i·um /dòkō mínnee əm/ *n.* a harbor with several jetties providing permanent moorings for boats used as homes [Late 20thC. Blend of DOCK[1] and CONDOMINIUM.]

dock·side /dók sīd/ *n.* the area of ground alongside the moorings in a dock or harbor

dock·yard /dók yaàrd/ *n.* an area of workshops, offices, and docks where ships are repaired and built

doc·tor /dóktər/ *n.* **1.** MED **SOMEBODY MEDICALLY QUALIFIED** somebody qualified and licensed to give people medical treatment **2.** DENT, VET, MED **DENTIST, VETERINARIAN, OR OSTEOPATH** a title used before the names of health professionals such as dentists, veterinarians, and osteopaths **3. SOMEBODY WHO CAN FIX THINGS** somebody who is good at doing something, especially fixing or improving something **4.** EDUC **SOMEBODY WITH THE HIGHEST UNIVERSITY DEGREE** a title given to somebody who has been awarded a doctorate, the highest level of degree awarded by a university **5.** CHR **ROMAN CATHOLIC THEOLOGIAN** in the earlier history of the Roman Catholic Church, an eminent and influential theologian **6.** EDUC **TEACHER OR SCHOLAR** a teacher, or somebody very knowledgeable (*archaic*) ■ *v.* (**-tored, -tor·ing, -tors**) **1.** *vt.* **CHANGE SOMETHING TO DECEIVE** to change something in order to make it appear different from the facts or the truth ○ *doctored the figures* **2.** *vt.* **ADD SOMETHING TO A SUBSTANCE** to add something, especially a drug, alcohol, or poison, to food or drink **3.** *vti.* **TREAT ILL PEOPLE** to treat people when they are ill **4.** *vt.* **FIX SOMETHING** to fix something, especially in a rough or hurried way [14thC. Via Old French *doctour* from Latin *doctor* "teacher," from the past participle stem *doct-* of *docere* "to teach" (source of English *docile*).] —**doc·tor·ly** *adj.*

doc·tor·al /dóktərəl/, **doc·tor·i·al** /dok táwree əl/ *adj.* **1. DONE TO OBTAIN A DOCTORATE** written or done in order to obtain a doctorate, the highest degree awarded by a university ○ *a doctoral thesis* **2. FOR A DOCTORATE** relating to or aiming for a doctorate ○ *doctoral candidate*

doc·tor·ate /dóktərət/ *n.* the highest level of university degree, usually awarded for a lengthy piece of original research but sometimes for other outstanding achievements

doc·to·ri·al *adj.* = **doctoral**

Doc·tor of Phi·los·o·phy *n.* **1. HIGHEST UNIVERSITY DEGREE** the highest level of university degree that can be studied for, awarded to somebody who has successfully completed a lengthy piece of original research. A Doctor of Philosophy may be awarded in any subject except law, theology, or medicine. **2. SOMEBODY WITH DOCTOR OF PHILOSOPHY DEGREE** somebody who has been awarded the degree of Doctor of Philosophy

Doc·tor·ow /dóktə rō/, **E. L.** (*b.* 1931) U.S. writer. He is known for his novel *Ragtime* (1975), a critical look at turn-of-the-century America, later made into a Broadway musical. Full name **Edgar Laurence Doctorow**

doc·tri·naire /dòktrə náir/ *adj.* **DETERMINED TO USE A THEORY** determined to use a particular theory or method and refusing to accept that there might be a better approach ■ *n.* **SOMEBODY WITH FIXED IDEAS** somebody who is determined to follow a particular theory or method and refuses to consider alternate approaches —**doc·tri·nair·ism** *n.* —**doc·tri·nar·i·an** /dòktrə náiree ən/ *n.*

doc·trine /dóktrin/ *n.* **1. RULE OR PRINCIPLE** a rule or principle that forms the basis of a belief, theory, or policy **2. IDEAS TAUGHT AS TRUTH** a body of ideas, particularly in religion, taught to people as truthful or correct **3. SOMETHING TAUGHT** something taught to people (*archaic*) [14thC. Directly or via French from Latin *doctrina* "teaching, learning," from *doctor* (see DOCTOR).] —**doc·tri·nal** /dóktrin'l/ *adj.* —**doc·tri·nal·i·ty** /dòktrə nállətee/ *n.* —**doc·tri·nal·ly** /dóktrinəlee/ *adv.*

doc·u·dra·ma /dókyə draàmə/ *n.* a dramatized movie or television version of a true story [Mid-20thC. Blend of DOCUMENTARY and DRAMA.] —**doc·u·dra·mat·ic** /dòkyə drə máttik/ *adj.*

doc·u·ment /dókyəmənt/ *n.* **1. FORMAL PIECE OF WRITING** a formal piece of writing that provides information or that acts as a record of events **2. OBJECT CONTAINING INFORMATION** an object such as a movie, photograph, or audio recording that contains information and can be used as evidence **3.** COMPUT **COMPUTER FILE** a computer file created using an applications program, e.g., a database, spreadsheet, illustration, or text file ■ *vt.* (**-ment·ed, -ment·ing, -ments**) **1. RECORD INFORMATION IN OR ON MEDIA** to make a record of something by writing about it or by filming or photographing it **2. SUPPORT A CLAIM WITH EVIDENCE** to provide evidence for a statement or claim by supplying supporting information [15thC. Via French from Latin *documentum* "lesson, example" (in medieval Latin "instruction, official paper"), from *docere* "to teach" (see DOCTOR).] —**doc·u·ment·al** /dòkyə mént'l/ *adj.* —**doc·u·ment·er** /dókyə mèntər/ *n.*

doc·u·ment·a·ble /dòkyə méntəb'l/ *adj.* able to be verified or proved by evidence

doc·u·ment·al·ist /dòkyə mént'list/ *n.* somebody who specializes in documentation

doc·u·men·ta·ry /dòkyə méntəree/ *n.* (*plural* **-ries**) **FACTUAL MOVIE OR TV PROGRAM** a movie or TV program presenting facts and information, especially about a political, historical, or social issue ■ *adj.* **1. CONSISTING OF DOCUMENTS** in the form of documents, or collected from documents **2. GIVING FACTS** giving facts and information rather than telling a fictional story —**doc·u·men·tar·i·ly** /dòkyəmən térrilee/ *adv.*

doc·u·men·ta·tion /dòkyəmən táysh'n/ *n.* **1. EVIDENTIAL OR REFERENCE DOCUMENTS** documents provided or collected together as evidence or as reference material **2. PROCESS OF PROVIDING WRITTEN INFORMATION** the process of providing written details or information about something **3.** COMPUT **COMPUTER SOFTWARE INFORMATION** the instructions, tutorials, and reference information provided to explain how to install and use software or a computer system

doc·u·ment feed·er *n.* the part of a printer, scanner, or fax machine that holds a stack of papers and feeds them through the machine to be printed

doc·u·ment hold·er *n.* a stand that holds papers in a vertical position so that they can be read easily by somebody working at a desk

do·cu·soap /dòkyə sōp/ *n.* a television program that combines documentary style with elements of soap opera, e.g., by showing the personal lives of people at their workplace [Combination of DOCUMENTARY + SOAP OPERA]

DOD *abbr.* Department of Defense

dod·der[1] /dóddər/ (**-dered, -der·ing, -ders**) *vi.* **1. SHAKE OR TREMBLE** to tremble or shake slightly as a result of age **2. WALK UNSTEADILY** to walk slowly and unsteadily with shaking limbs as a result of age [Early 17thC. Alteration of or related to obsolete (except for dialect) *dadder* "to quake, tremble," of unknown origin.] —**dod·der·er** *n.*

dod·der[2] /dóddər/ (*plural* **-ders** *or* **-der**) *n.* a leafless rootless parasitic plant of the morning glory family that lacks chlorophyll and has a reddish twining stem and small white flowers. Genus: *Cuscuta.* [14thC. Origin uncertain: perhaps from prehistoric Germanic.]

dod·dered /dóddərd/ *adj.* **1. HAVING THE TOP BRANCHES MISSING** having the top branches missing as a result of age or disease **2. UNSTEADY** weak and unsteady [Late 17thC. Origin uncertain: probably ultimately from *dod* "to lop (a tree)," of unknown origin; influenced by DODDER[1].]

dod·der·ing /dóddəring/, **dod·der·y** /-ree/ *adj.* walking unsteadily, especially as a result of age —**dod·der·ing·ly** *adv.*

dodeca- *prefix.* phonograph record (*discography*) [From Greek *dōdeka*, from *duō* "two" + *deka* "ten"]

do·dec·a·he·dron /dō dekə heédrən/ (*plural* **-drons** *or* **-dra** /-drə/) *n.* a solid figure with 12 equal pentagonal faces meeting in threes at 20 vertices [Late 16thC. From Greek *dōdekaedron*, from *dōdeka* "twelve" + *hedra* "seat, face."] —**do·dec·a·he·dral** *adj.*

do·de·ca·no·ic ac·id /dō dekə nō ik-/ *n.* = **lauric acid** [Mid-20thC. Formed from *dodecane* "(a kind of) paraffin," from DODECA- + -ANE.]

do·dec·a·phon·ic /dō dekə fónnik/ *adj.* = **twelvetone** —**do·dec·a·phon·ism** /dō dékə fō nìzzəm, -fònnizzəm, dōdə káffə-/ *n.* —**do·dec·a·phon·ist** /-fōnist, -fònnist, dōdə káffənist/ *n.* —**do·dec·a·phon·y** /-fōnee, -fònnee, dōdə káffənee/ *n.*

do·dec·a·syl·la·ble /dō dekə síllәb'l/ *n.* a line of verse of 12 syllables —**do·dec·a·syl·lab·ic** /dō dekə si lábbik/ *adj.*

dodge /doj/ *v.* (**dodged, dodg·ing, dodg·es**) **1.** *vti.* **MOVE QUICKLY TO AVOID SOMETHING** to move quickly and suddenly to one side to avoid being caught or hit ○ *He dodged the punch.* **2.** *vt.* **AVOID SOMETHING UNPLEASANT** to avoid doing something regarded as unpleasant **3.** *vt.* PHOTOGRAPHY **MASK AREA OF PRINT** to mask an area of a print during exposure to prevent light reaching it ■ *n.* **1. TRICK TO AVOID DOING SOMETHING** a clever trick or tactic to avoid doing something ○ *a tax dodge* **2. QUICK AVOIDING MOVEMENT** a sudden quick movement to one side to avoid being caught or hit [Mid-16thC. Origin uncertain. Originally "to go this way and that, haggle."]

dodge ball *n.* a children's game in which opponents try to avoid being hit by a large rubber ball

Dodge Cit·y /dój-/ city in southern Kansas, on the northern bank of the Arkansas River, southwest of Great Bend. Population: 22,430 (1996).

dodg·er /dójjər/ *n.* **1. SOMEBODY AVOIDING DUTY** somebody who avoids a duty or responsibility, especially by using dishonest or deceitful methods **2. SOMEBODY DISHONEST** somebody cunning and untrustworthy **3.** *U.S., Aus* **HANDBILL** a small leaflet or notice **4. SHELTERING SCREEN ON SHIP** a canvas screen on a ship or yacht to protect the person at the helm from spray **5.** *Southern U.S.* = **corndodger**

dodg·y /dójjee/ (**-i·er, -i·est**) *adj. U.K., ANZ* (*informal*) **1. SUSPECT OR DISHONEST** suspect, dishonest, or untrustworthy **2. RISKY** dangerous or risky —**dodg·i·ly** *adv.* —**dodg·i·ness** *n.*

Dodo

do·do /dṓ dō/ (*plural* **-dos** *or* **-does**) *n.* **1. EXTINCT BIRD** a large extinct flightless bird of the pigeon family that once inhabited Mauritius and neighboring islands in the Indian Ocean. The dodo, which was heavyset with short legs and a hooked bill, became extinct in the late 17th century. Latin name: *Raphus cucullatus.* **2. SOMEBODY THOUGHTLESS** somebody thoughtless or unintelligent (*informal insult*) **3. OLD-FASHIONED PERSON** somebody who is regarded as old-fashioned, conservative, and out of date [Early 17thC. From Portuguese *doudo* "fool, simpleton."] —**do·do·ism** *n.* ◇ **(as) dead as a dodo** no longer existing, functioning, flourishing, or popular

doe /dō/ *n.* a mature female of several mammals, including the deer, kangaroo, rabbit, hare, and goat [Old English *dā*, of unknown origin]

DOE *abbr.* Department of Energy

do·er /dóo ər/ *n.* **1. SOMEBODY WHO DOES SOMETHING** somebody who does a particular thing (*often used in combination*) ○ *wrongdoer* **2. SOMEBODY ACTIVELY DOING THINGS** somebody who is active in doing things rather than just thinking or talking about them

doe·skin /dṓ skin/ *n.* **1. SKIN OF DEER** the skin of various animals, including a doe, deer, and goat **2. LEATHER** light supple leather made from doeskin that is particularly suitable for gloves **3. SMOOTH WOOLEN CLOTH** a densely woven smooth woolen cloth

does·n't /dúzz'nt/ *contr.* does not

do·est /dóo əst/ 2nd person present singular of **do**[1] (*archaic*)

do·eth /dóo əth/ 3rd person present singular of **do**[1] (*archaic*)

doff /dof/ (**doffed, doff·ing, doffs**) *vt.* **1. TAKE OFF OR LIFT HAT** to take off a hat, or lift and tilt it as a greeting or a mark of respect **2. TAKE OFF CLOTHING** to take off a coat or another piece of clothing [14thC. Contraction of archaic *do off* "to take off."] —**dof·fer** *n.*

dog /dawg, dog/ *n.* **1.** ZOOL **DOMESTIC ANIMAL THAT BARKS** a domestic carnivorous animal that typically has a long muzzle, pointed ears, a fur coat, and a long fur-covered tail, and whose characteristic call is a bark. Latin name: *Canis familiaris.* **2.** ZOOL **WILD ANIMAL RESEMBLING DOMESTIC DOG** any wild animal that resembles a domestic dog and belongs to the same family, e.g., a wolf, fox, dingo, or coyote. Family: Canidae. **3.** ZOOL **MALE DOG** a male dog, wolf, fox, or other member of the dog family **4. CONTEMPTIBLE PERSON** somebody who is regarded as unpleasant or contemptible (*informal insult*) **5. OFFENSIVE TERM** somebody who is regarded as not good to look at (*slang insult*) **6. MAN** a man of the particular type described (*informal*) ○ *You lucky dog!* **7. SOMETHING USELESS OR INFERIOR** something useless or of a very poor standard (*informal*) **8.** HOUSEHOLD = **andiron 9.** METEOROL = **seadog 10.** MECH ENG **GRIPPING TOOL** a device for gripping or holding things ■ *vt.* **(dogged, dog·ging, dogs) 1. BOTHER SOMEBODY PERSISTENTLY** to bother or trouble somebody persistently (*often passive*) ○ *dogged by bad luck* **2. FOLLOW SOMEBODY CLOSELY** to follow somebody closely in a determined way ○ *dogging her footsteps* **3.** MECH ENG **GRIP SOMETHING WITH MECHANICAL DEVICE** to grip or hold something firmly with a mechanical device [Old English *docga*, of uncertain origin: probably originally "powerful breed of dog." *Dog* did not supplant *hound* as the general English term for the animal until the 16thC.] ◇ **a dog in the manger** *U.K.* somebody who cannot have or does not want something, but who tries to prevent somebody else from having or doing it ◇ **a dog's life** a wretched existence ◇ **dog eat dog** ruthlessly competitive ◇ **go to the dogs** be in the final stages of a gradual decline in standards (*informal*) ◇ **let sleeping dogs lie** to take no action in a situation that is currently peaceful but potentially troublesome ◇ **put on the dog** *U.S., Aus* make a display of wealth or knowledge ostentatiously or pretentiously (*dated informal*)

dog-and-po·ny show *n.* an elaborate business presentation or promotional event (*informal*)

dog·bane /dáwg bàyn, dóg-/ *n.* a plant with pungent milky juice, a bitter root, and small bell-shaped white or pink flowers. Genus: *Apocynum.*

dog·ber·ry[1] /dáwg bèrree, dóg-/ (*plural* **-ries**) *n.* **1. PLANT WITH BERRIES** any one of various plants with berries, including mountain ash, bearberry, gooseberry, chokeberry, and dogwood **2. BERRY OF DOGBERRY PLANT** a berry of any dogberry plant

dog·ber·ry[2] /dáwg bèrree, dóg-/ (*plural* **-ries**), **Dog·ber·ry** (*plural* **-ries**) *n.* an unintelligent but self-important official [Mid-19thC. Named for *Dogberry*, an unintelligent constable in *Much Ado About Nothing* by Shakespeare.] —**dog·ber·ry·ism** *n.*

dog bis·cuit *n.* a hard biscuit made for dogs to eat

dog·cart /dáwg kaàrt, dóg-/ *n.* a two-wheeled vehicle drawn by a horse and seating two people back to back

dog·catch·er /dáwg kàchər, dóg-/ *n.* somebody who is employed to catch stray dogs

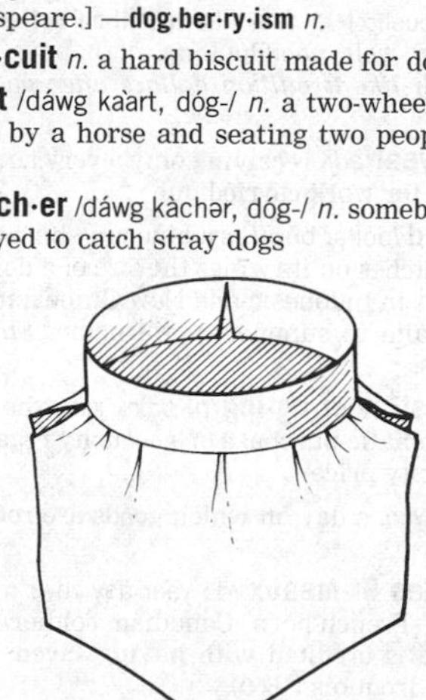

Dog collar

dog col·lar *n.* **1. COLLAR FOR DOG** a piece of leather or fabric worn around a dog's neck, often with the dog's name attached to it **2.** *U.K.* CHR **CLERICAL COLLAR** a clerical collar (*informal*) **3. CLOSE-FITTING NECKLACE** a necklace that fits closely around the neck

dog days *npl.* **1. HOTTEST PERIOD OF THE SUMMER** the hottest period of the summer, roughly between early July and early September in the northern hemisphere. In ancient times the beginning of the dog days was heralded by the simultaneous rising of the Dog Star (**Sirius**) and the sun. **2. LAZY PERIOD** a lazy or inactive period of time [Mid-16thC. Translation of Latin *dies caniculares*, literally "Dog Star days."]

doge /dōj/ *n.* the chief magistrate in Renaissance Venice and Genoa [Mid-16thC. Via French from, ultimately, Venetian Italian *doze*, ultimately from the Latin stem *ducem* "leader" (source of English *duke*).] —**doge·ship** *n.*

dog-eared *adj.* **1. HAVING WORN AND WELL-THUMBED PAGES** having worn and well-thumbed pages that have been creased or folded over to mark the place reached in reading **2. WORN OR SHABBY** shabby or well-used

do·gey *n.* = **dogie**

dog·face /dáwg fàyss, dóg-/ *n.* a U.S. infantryman (*slang*) [Mid-20thC. Perhaps from the downcast or "hang dog" expression of some enlisted men.]

dog fen·nel *n.* PLANTS = **mayweed** [So called from its fetid smell, and from its leaves being likened to those of fennel]

dog·fight /dáwg fìt, dóg-/ *n.* **1.** AIR **COMBAT BETWEEN FIGHTER PLANES** an aerial combat involving two or more fighter planes **2. FIERCE FIGHT** a fierce violent fight **3. FIGHT INVOLVING DOGS** a fight between dogs —**dog·fight·ing** *n.*

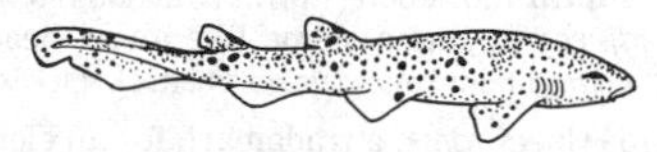

Dogfish

dog·fish /dáwg fìsh, dóg-/ (*plural* **-fish·es** *or* **-fish**) *n.* **1. SMALL SHARK** a small, long-tailed shark, either spiny or smooth-skinned, found in the Pacific, Atlantic, and Mediterranean. Families: Squalidae and Carcharhinidae and Scyliorhinidae. **2.** = **bowfin**

dog·ged /dáwgəd, dóggəd/ *adj.* determined to continue without giving up in spite of difficulties —**dog·ged·ly** *adv.* —**dog·ged·ness** *n.*

dog·ger[1] /dáwgər, dóggər/ *n.* a Dutch fishing vessel [14thC. From Middle Dutch.]

dog·ger[2] /dáwgər, dóggər/ *n.* GEOL a large mass of calcium-containing sandstone or ironstone occurring in sedimentary rock [Late 17thC. Origin uncertain: perhaps formed from DOG.]

dog·ger·el /dáwgərəl, dóggərəl/, **dog·grel** /dáwgrəl, dógrəl/ *n.* **1.** POETRY **POETRY WITH IRREGULAR RHYTHM** poetry that does not scan well and is often not intended to be taken seriously **2. POOR-QUALITY COMPOSITION** something that is badly written or makes no sense at all [14thC. Origin uncertain: probably formed from DOG (with its pejorative connotations).]

dog·gie *n.* = **doggy**

dog·gish /dáwgish, dóggish/ *adj.* **1. RESEMBLING A DOG** resembling a dog, or possessing the qualities of a dog **2. BAD-TEMPERED** bad-tempered and aggressive **3. SHOWY** ostentatiously stylish —**dog·gish·ly** *adv.* —**dog·gish·ness** *n.*

dog·go /dáwgō, dóggō/ *adv. U.K.* not moving or making any sound in order not to be discovered ○ *lying doggo* [Late 19thC. Formed from DOG, dogs having the capacity to lie in this manner.]

dog·gone /dáwg gàwn, dóg gòn/, **dog·goned** *adv., adj.* **ANNOYING** used to emphasize how bad or annoying something is (*informal*) ■ *interj.* **EXPRESSING ANNOYANCE** used to express annoyance or irritation (*informal*) [Early 19thC. Origin uncertain: probably (perhaps via Scots dialect *dagone*) ultimately from GODDAMN.]

dog·grel *n.* = **doggerel**

dog·gy /dáwgee, dóggee/, **dog·gie** *n.* (*plural* **-gies**) **DOG** a dog (*babytalk*) ■ *adj.* **1. RESEMBLING A DOG** resembling or typical of a dog's behavior or appearance **2. FOND OF DOGS** fond of or interested in dogs (*informal*)

dog·gy bag, dog·gie bag *n.* a bag that can be used by a customer at a restaurant to take home any leftover food from his or her meal [*Doggy* from giving the food in it to a dog]

dog·gy pad·dle *n., vi.* (**dog·gy pad·dled, dog·gy pad·dling, dog·gy pad·dles**) *U.K.* = **dog paddle**

dog han·dler *n.* a police officer or security guard who is in charge of a specially trained working dog

dog·hanged /dáwg hàngd, dóg-/ *adj. Southern U.S.* hangdog

dog·house /dáwg hòws, dóg hòws/ (*plural* **-hous·es** /-zəz, -zəz/) *n.* a small enclosed shelter for a dog ◇ **in the doghouse** in disgrace (*informal*)

do·gie /dṓgee/, **do·gy** (*plural* **-gies**), **do·gey** (*plural* **-geys**) *n.* a calf with no mother [Late 19thC. Origin unknown.]

dog i·ron *n. Southern U.S.* an andiron

WORD KEY: REGIONAL NOTE

Dog iron is the dominant term in the Southwest Midland and Interior South, where it competes with Coastal and Piedmont *fire iron* and *fire dog.*

dog Lat·in *n.* Latin that is incorrect in some way, especially a word or phrase that is falsely made to look or sound like Latin for humorous or satiric effect. ◊ **pig Latin**

dog·leg /dáwg lèg, dóg lèg/ *n.* **1.** GOLF **GOLF HOLE WITH BEND** a hole in golf in which the fairway contains a gentle or sharp bend **2. SHARP BEND** a sharp bend or angle in something, especially in a road ■ *vi.* (**-legged, -leg·ging, -legs**) **FORM A SHARP BEND** to form a sharp bend or angle [From being likened to the bent form of a dog's hind leg] —**dog·leg·ged** /dawg léggəd, -légd, dog-/ *adj.*

dog·ma /dáwgmə, dógmə/ (*plural* **-mas** *or* **-ma·ta** /-tə, -tə/) *n.* **1.** RELIG **RELIGIOUS BELIEF** a belief or set of beliefs that a religion holds to be true **2. GROUP BELIEF** a belief or set of beliefs that a political, philosophical, or moral group holds to be true [Mid-16thC. Via late Latin from Greek *dogma* (stem *dogmat-*) "opinion, tenet," from *dokein* "to seem good, think" (source of English *orthodox* and *paradox*).]

dog·mat·ic /dawg máttik, dog-/, **dog·mat·i·cal** /-k'l/ *adj.* **1. EXPRESSING RIGID OPINIONS** prone to expressing strongly held beliefs and opinions **2. RELATING TO DOGMA** relating to or expressing a religious, political, philosophical, or moral dogma —**dog·mat·i·cal·ly** *adv.*

dog·mat·ics /dawg máttiks, dog-/, **dog·mat·ic the·ol·o·gy** *n.* RELIG the study of religious dogmas, especially Christian dogmas (*takes a singular verb*)

dog·ma·tism /dáwgmə tìzzəm, dógmə-/ *n.* the tendency to express strongly held opinions in a way that suggests they should be accepted without question

dog·ma·tist /dáwgmətist, dógmə-/ *n.* **1. SOMEBODY DOGMATIC** somebody who expresses strongly held opinions, expecting them to be accepted without question **2. SOMEBODY DEVISING DOGMA** somebody who devises a new religious, political, philosophical, or moral dogma

dog·ma·tize /dáwgmə tìz, dógmə-/ (**-tized, -tiz·ing, -tiz·es**) *vi.* to express strongly held opinions in a way that suggests they should be accepted without question —**dog·ma·ti·za·tion** /dàwgməti záysh'n, dògməti-/ *n.* —**dog·ma·tiz·er** /dáwgmə tìzər, dógmə-/ *n.*

dog·nap /dáwg nàp, dóg-/ (**-napped, -nap·ping, -naps**) *vt.* to steal a dog, especially in order to sell it for use in medical research —**dog·nap·per** *n.*

dog of·fi·cer *n.* = **dogcatcher**

Do·gon /dṓ gòn/ (*plural* **-gon** *or* **-gons**) *n.* **1.** PEOPLES **MEMBER OF A VOLTAIC PEOPLE** a member of a Voltaic people living on the plateaus of southeastern Mali in western Africa **2.** LANG **LANGUAGE OF W AFRICA** a language of Mali and Burkina Faso, belonging to the Niger-Congo family and perhaps to the Gur group. Dogon is spoken by over 500,000 people. —**Do·gon** *adj.*

do-good·er *n.* somebody who tries to help others, with the best intentions, but who can be perceived as unwelcome or even interfering (*informal*) —**do-good·ing** *n., adj.*

dog pad·dle *n.* **SWIMMING STROKE** a swimming stroke in which the swimmer lies face down and makes rapid downward movements with the arms and legs underneath the body. This stroke is often used by children learning to swim and is not used in competitions. ■ *vi.* (**dog pad·dled, dog pad·dling, dog pad·dles**) **SWIM USING DOG PADDLE** to swim using the dog paddle

dog rac·ing *n.* the sport of greyhound racing in which dogs chase a mechanical rabbit around a track and spectators may bet on which dog will win

dog rose *n.* a European wild rose with delicate pink or white flowers. Latin name: *Rosa canina.* [Ultimately from an account in the ancient Roman Pliny's *Historia Naturalis* in which a soldier with rabies contracted from a dog bite is cured with the root of this plant]

dogs·bod·y /dáwgz boddee, dógz-/ (*plural* **-ies**) *n. U.K.* somebody who does all the boring menial jobs that others do not want to do (*informal*) [Early 19thC. First attested as British naval slang for a pudding made of peas.]

dog show *n.* a competitive event in which dogs are judged on the qualities considered to be characteristic of the breed or type, e.g., appearance, obedience, and agility

dog·sled /dáwg slèd, dóg-/ *n.* a vehicle mounted on runners and pulled by dogs, designed to travel over snow and ice —**dog·sled** *vi.* —**dog·sled·der** *n.*

Dog Star *n.* ASTRON = **Sirius**

dog tag *n.* **1.** MIL **IDENTIFICATION TAG FOR SOLDIERS** a metal identification tag for a member of the military, worn on a chain around the neck (*informal*) **2.** **IDENTIFICATION DISK FOR DOG** a metal disk, attached to a dog's collar, that gives the name and address of the dog's owner and often the name of the dog

dog team *n.* a team of dogs for pulling a dog sled

dog·teeth plural of **dogtooth**

dog-tired *adj.* completely exhausted (*informal*)

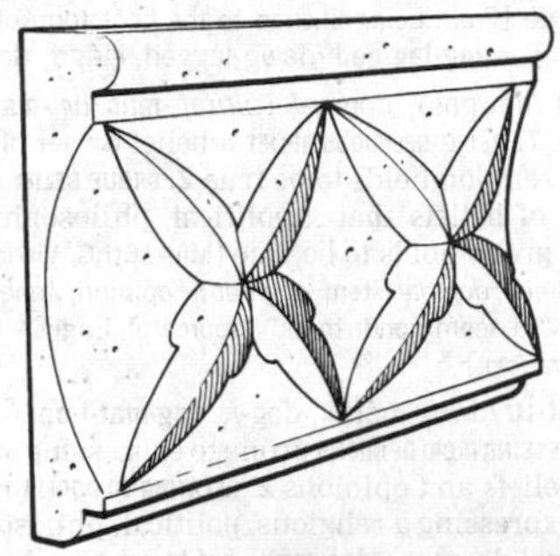

Dogtooth

dog·tooth /dáwg toòth, dóg-/ (*plural* **-teeth** /dáwg teèth, dóg-/) *n.* **1.** DENT **CANINE** a canine tooth (*informal*) **2.** ARCHIT **LATE MEDIEVAL ARCHITECTURAL FEATURE** in 13th-century English architecture, a small raised ornamental feature on a building consisting of four leaf-shaped parts arranged to form an X-shape

dog·tooth vi·o·let *n.* a small bulbous plant of the lily family that flowers in the spring and has red-speckled leaves and nodding yellow or purple flowers resembling lilies. Genus: *Erythronium.* [From the toothed inner segments of the perianth]

dog·trot /dáwg tròt, dóg-/ *n.* a gentle trot at a steady pace

dog war·den *n. U.K.* = **dogcatcher**

dog·watch /dáwg wàwch, dóg-/ *n.* NAUT on a ship, the late afternoon watch from 4:00 P.M. to 6:00 P.M. or the early evening watch from 6:00 P.M. to 8:00 P.M.

dog·wood /dáwg woòd, dóg-/ (*plural* **-woods** *or* **-wood**) *n.* a tree or shrub that has clusters of small white flowers surrounded by four large white or reddish leaves (**bracts**). Genus: *Cornus.*

do·gy *n.* = **dogie**

doh /dō/ *n.* MUSIC = **do**²

Do·ha /dṓ hə, -haà/ capital and largest city of Qatar, on the Persian Gulf. Population: 296,821 (1991).

doi·ly /dóylee/ (*plural* **-lies**) *n.* **1.** **LACY MAT FOR PLATE** a decorative lacy mat, usually made of lace, linen, or paper, that is put on plates under cakes or party food to display the food attractively **2.** **SMALL NAPKIN** a small table napkin [Late 18thC. Named for *Doiley* or *Doyley,* surname of a 17th-C London draper.]

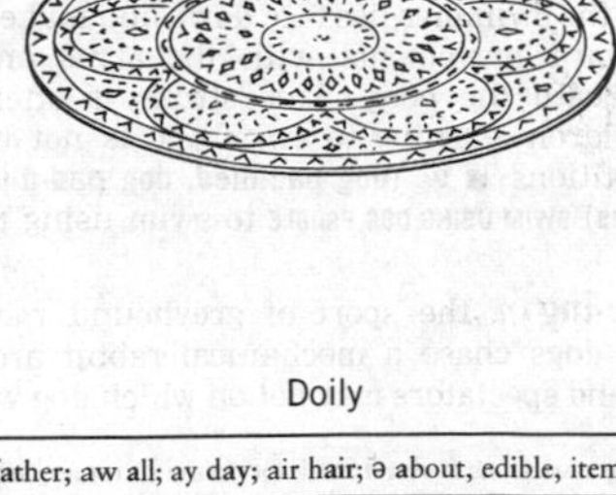

Doily

do·ing¹ /doò ing/ present participle of **do**¹

do·ing² /doò ing/ *n.* **CARRYING OUT OF SOMETHING** the act of performing or carrying out something ○ *It's all your doing.* ■ **do·ings** *npl.* **SOCIAL ACTIVITIES** social activities

Doi·sy /dóyzee/, **Edward Adelbert** (1893–1986) U.S. biochemist. He shared a Nobel Prize with Henrik Dam for discovering the chemical structure of vitamin K (1943).

doit /doyt/ *n.* **1.** MONEY **OLD DUTCH UNIT OF CURRENCY** a small low-value silver coin that was a Dutch unit of currency between the 15th and 17th centuries **2.** **JOT** something that is very small and unimportant (*archaic*) [Late 16thC. From Middle Low German *doyt.*]

do-it-your·self *n.* the activity of doing repairs and alterations in the home yourself, especially as a hobby, instead of employing tradespeople to do the work —**do-it-your·self·er** *n.*

do·jo /dṓ jō/ (*plural* **-jos**) *n.* a school or room for practicing judo [Mid-20thC. From Japanese, literally "way ground, pursuit place," from *dō* "way, art" (source of English *kendo*) + *-jō* "ground."]

dol. *abbr.* dollar

do·lab·ri·form /dō lábbrə fàwrm/, **do·lab·rate** /dō láb ràyt/ *adj.* BOT having a shape like an ax head [Mid-18thC. Formed from Latin *dolabra* "mattock, pickax."]

Dol·by /dáwlbee/ *tdmk.* a trademark for an electronic circuit that reduces noise on an audio tape recording

dol·ce /dól chày/ *adv.* sweetly and gently (*used as a musical direction*) [Early 19thC. Via Italian, "sweet," from Latin *dulcis* (source of English *dulcet*).] —**dol·ce** *adj.*

dol·ce far ni·en·te /-faar nee éntee/ *n.* pleasant idleness and relaxation [Early 19thC. From Italian, literally "sweet doing nothing."]

Dol·ce·lat·te /dōl chay laà tày/ *n.* a soft creamy Italian blue cheese with a mild flavor, made from cow's milk

dol·ce vi·ta /-veétə/ *n.* a life of luxury and idle self-indulgence [Mid-20thC. From Italian, literally "sweet life."]

dol·drums /dṓldrəmz, dóldrəmz/ *npl.* **1.** **STAGNATION** a sluggish state in which something fails to develop or improve **2.** **GLOOMINESS** a state of gloominess or very low energy **3.** METEOROL, SHIPPING **AREA OF WINDS NORTH OF EQUATOR** an area with no wind or light variable winds just north of the equator in the Atlantic and Pacific oceans, situated between the trade winds **4.** METEOROL, SHIPPING **WEATHER CONDITIONS IN DOLDRUMS** the weather conditions prevailing in the doldrums. These formerly caused problems for sailing ships, which could become becalmed there. [Late 18thC. Origin uncertain: perhaps formed (on the model of TANTRUM) from *dold* "stupid, inactive," ultimately from Old English *dol* "foolish."]

dole¹ /dōl/ *n.* **1.** *U.K.* SOC WELFARE **GOVERNMENT UNEMPLOYMENT PAYMENT** a regular sum of money paid by the government to people who are unemployed (*informal*) **2.** **CHARITY** the giving of clothes, money, or food to people who are in need **3.** **SOMEBODY'S FATE** somebody's fate in life (*archaic*) ■ *vt.* (**doled, dol·ing, doles**) **DISTRIBUTE SOMETHING AS CHARITY** to distribute something as charity to people who are in need [Old English *dāl* "portion," from a prehistoric Germanic base that is also the ancestor of English *deal* and *ordeal*]

dole out *vt.* to give something to each of a group of people (*informal*)

dole² /dōl/ *n.* grief, sadness, or misery (*archaic*) [13thC. Via Old French *dol* "mourning" from popular Latin *dolus,* from Latin *dolere* "to grieve, suffer pain" (source of English *condolence*).]

Dole, Bob (*b.* 1923) U.S. statesman and lawyer. He was the Republican nominee for U.S. president in 1996, running against Bill Clinton after many years in the U.S. Senate. Full name **Robert Joseph Dole**

Dole, Elizabeth (*b.* 1936) U.S. attorney and public official. A former cabinet member, she was appointed director of the American Red Cross in 1990. In 1999 she announced plans to run for president. Born **Elizabeth Hanford**

Dole, Sanford Ballard (1844–1926) U.S. politician. He was first and only president of the Republic of Hawaii (1894–1900) and territorial governor (1900–03).

dole·ful /dṓlfəl/ *adj.* very sad and mournful —**dole·ful·ly** *adv.* —**dole·ful·ness** *n.*

do·len·te /dō léntee, dō lén tày/ *adv.* in a sorrowful manner (*used as a musical direction*) [From Italian, present participle of *dolere* "to feel grief," from Latin *dolere* (see DOLE²)] —**do·len·te** *adj.*

dol·er·ite /dóllə rīt/ *n. U.K.* = **diabase** [Mid-19thC. From French *dolérite,* from Greek *doleros* "deceptive," from *dolos* "deceit" (from its being difficult to distinguish from diorite).] —**dol·er·it·ic** /dòllə ríttik/ *adj.*

dol·i·cho·ce·phal·ic /dòlli kō sə fállik/, **dol·i·cho·ceph·a·lous** /-séffələss/ *adj.* having a head disproportionately longer than it is wide, specifically one with a cephalic index of less than 75 [Mid-19thC. Coined from *dolicho-* "narrow" (from Greek *dolikhos*) + -CEPHALIC.] —**dol·i·cho·ceph·a·lism** /dòlli kō séffəl ìzzəm/ *n.*

do·li·cho·saur·us /dòlli kō sáwrəss/ *n.* an extinct aquatic long-necked reptile that was common 65 million years ago [Coined from *dolicho-* "narrow" (from Greek *dolikhos*) + -SAURUS, from their long necks and bodies]

do·line /də leénə/, **do·li·na** *n.* a large, often roughly circular basin of valley-sized proportions formed as a result of water dissolving surface limestone [Late 19thC. Via German from Slovene *dolina* "valley."]

do-lit·tle *n.* somebody who is lazy (*informal*)

doll /dol/ *n.* **1.** **CHILD'S TOY** a child's toy in the shape of a person or baby **2.** **WOMAN PLEASANT TO LOOK AT** a woman or girl who is pleasant to look at and described in that sense (*informal*) (*sometimes offensive*) **3.** **HELPFUL PERSON** a nice or helpful person (*informal*) [Mid-16thC. From the pet form of the female name *Dorothy* (compare the formation of *Moll* from *Mary*). Originally "man's woman lover."] —**dol·lish** *adj.* —**dol·lish·ly** *adv.* —**dol·lish·ness** *n.*

doll up *vt.* to make yourself or somebody else, e.g., a child, look particularly elegant and stylish, usually for a special occasion (*informal*)

dol·lar /dóllər/ *n.* **1.** **COMMON UNIT OF CURRENCY** a unit of currency used in the United States, Canada, Australia, and some other countries all around the world. See table at **currency** **2.** **BILL WORTH A DOLLAR** a bill worth one dollar **3.** *U.K.* **FORMER FIVE-SHILLING COIN** formerly in the United Kingdom, a five-shilling coin (*informal*) [Mid-16thC. Via early Flemish *daler* or Low German from German *Taler,* shortening of *Joachimst(h)aler,* named for the silver mine of *Joachimsthal,* now Jáchymov, Czech Republic.] ◇ **feel like a million dollars** to feel extremely well, good-looking, or happy (*informal*) ○ *She felt like a million dollars after passing the exam.*

dol·lar-a-year *adj.* receiving only a very small token payment for work carried out

dol·lar·bird /dóllər bùrd/ *n.* a blue-gray bird with pale round patches on its wings the size of a dollar coin. It winters in Indonesia and New Guinea, migrating to Australia in summer. Latin name: *Eurystomus orientalis.*

dol·lar cost av·er·ag·ing *n.* STOCK EXCH the periodic and systematic purchase of a security regardless of the security price

dol·lar day *n.* a day on which goods are reduced for sale

Dol·lard des Or·meaux /dō yaàr day zawr mṓ/, **Adam** (1635–60) French-born Canadian soldier and colonist. He is credited with having saved Montreal from the Iroquois (1660).

dol·lar di·plo·ma·cy *n.* **1.** **USE OF FINANCIAL POWER IN DIPLOMACY** the use of financial resources to facilitate foreign relations **2.** **U.S. POLICY PROTECTING OVERSEAS INVESTMENT** in the United States, a policy aimed at encouraging and protecting American investment abroad

dol·lars-and-cents *adj.* considering finance as the determining factor

dol·lar sign *n.* the symbol ($) that represents a dollar

dol·lar store *n.* a retail establishment selling inexpensive items, many at one dollar or less

doll·house /dól hòws/ (*plural* **-hous·es** /-hòw zəz/) *n.* a toy house containing miniature furniture

dol·lop /dólləp/ *n.* **SMALL AMOUNT OF SOMETHING** a spoon-sized quantity of a thick liquid or a soft solid such as ice cream or cream (*informal*) ■ *vt.* **(-loped, -lop·ing, -lops) SPOON SOMETHING** to spoon a quantity of a thick liquid or a soft solid (*informal*) [Late 16thC. Origin uncertain: perhaps from Scandinavian. Originally "clump of grass or weeds."]

doll's house *n. U.K.* = **dollhouse**

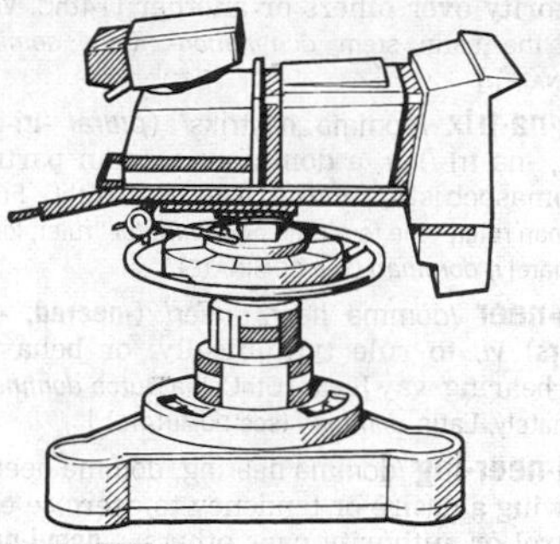

Dolly: Television camera on pedestal dolly

dol·ly /dóllee/ *n.* (*plural* **-lies**) **1. DOLL** a toy doll (*babytalk*) **2.** TV, CINEMA **MOVING PLATFORM FOR CAMERA OPERATOR** a platform with wheels on which a camera operator and camera are placed in order to film moving shots for a movie or television program **3.** MECH ENG **PLATFORM ON WHEELS FOR MOVING THINGS** a platform on wheels used to move heavy weights **4.** CIV ENG **WEIGHT DROPPED ON A PILE** a heavy weight dropped on a pile to force it into the ground **5.** CONSTR **TOOL FOR HOLDING RIVET** an anvil that holds one end of a rivet while the other end is being hammered **6.** METALL **HEAVY BLOCK HELD BEHIND HAMMERED METAL** a heavy block held behind sheet metal that is being hammered ■ *vti.* **(-lied, -ly·ing, -lies) MOVE CAMERA ON A DOLLY** to move a camera on a dolly

dol·ly shot *n.* a shot filmed from a camera mounted on a wheeled platform

Dol·ly Var·den /dòlli vaárd'n/ *n.* (*plural* **Dol·ly Var·den** *or* **Dol·ly Var·den trout** *or* **Dol·ly Var·den trouts** *or* **Dol·ly Var·den trout**) a trout or char with red spots found in lakes and streams of western North America and eastern Asia. Latin name: *Salvelinus malma.* [Late 19thC. Named for *Dolly Varden*, a woman of colorful dress in the novel *Barnaby Rudge* by Charles Dickens.]

dol·ma /dáwlmə, dáwl maá/ (*plural* **-mas** *or* **-ma·des** /-maá deéz/) *n.* a grape or cabbage leaf with a savory stuffing usually containing meat and rice, a specialty of Greek and Turkish cooking [Late 17thC. From Turkish, literally "something stuffed."]

dol·man /dólmən, dṓl-/ *n.* **1. WOMAN'S WIDE-SLEEVED COAT** a woman's coat with large sleeves cut in one piece with the body of the garment **2. LONG ROBE** a long Turkish robe [Late 16thC. Via French *dol(i)man* from, ultimately, Turkish *dolama(n)* "robe."]

dol·man sleeve *n.* a sleeve cut in one piece with the body of a garment such as a jacket or dress, particularly one fitting tightly at the wrist and wide at the armhole

Dolmen

dol·men /dólmən, dṓl-/ *n.* a prehistoric structure that consists of a large horizontal slab of stone supported by two or more vertical slabs and is thought to have been used as a tomb [Mid-19thC. From French, of uncertain origin: probably from Cornish *tolmen*, literally "hole (of) stone" (from the aperture formed by the slabs).]

dol·o·mite /dṓlə mìt, dóllə-/ *n.* **1.** MINERALS **PALE-COLORED MINERAL** a white, reddish, or greenish mineral consisting of calcium magnesium carbonate, found in sedimentary rocks. It is used as a building stone and in the manufacture of cement and fertilizers. Formula: $CaMg(CO_3)_2$. **2.** GEOL **SEDIMENTARY ROCK** a sedimentary rock consisting mainly of the mineral dolomite [Late 18thC. From French, named for Déodat de *Dolomieu* (1750–1801), a French geologist, who first described it.]

Do·lo·mi·tes /dṓlə mìts, dóllə-/ mountain group in the eastern part of the northern Italian Alps. The highest peak is Marmolada, 10,964 ft./3,342 km.

do·lor /dṓlər/ *n.* intense sadness (*literary*) [13thC. Via Old French *dolo(u)r* from Latin *dolor* "pain, grief, sorrow," from *dolere* "to feel pain."]

do·lor·i·me·try /dòlə rímmətree, dòllə-/ *n.* a technique by which somebody's tolerance of pain is measured by applying heat to the skin [Mid-20thC. Coined from Latin *dolor* (see DOLOR) + -METRY.]

do·lo·ro·so /dòlə rṓssō/ *adv.* to be played with sadness (*used as a musical direction.*) [Early 19thC. Via Italian from late Latin *dolorosus* (see DOLOROUS).] —**do·lo·ro·so** *adj.*

do·lor·ous /dṓlərəss, dóll-/ *adj.* showing, causing, or involving sorrow or pain (*literary*) [14thC] —**do·lor·ous·ly** *adv.* —**do·lor·ous·ness** *n.*

do·lour *n.* U.K. = **dolor**

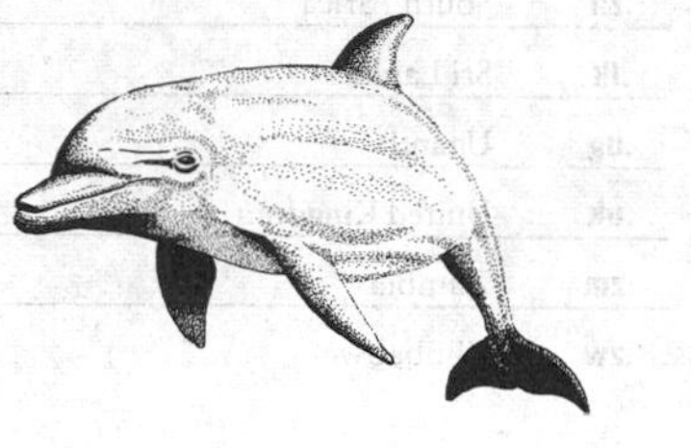

Dolphin

dol·phin /dólfin/ (*plural* **-phins** *or* **-phin**) *n.* ZOOL **1. SEA ANIMAL RELATED TO WHALES** an intelligent marine mammal (**cetacean**) that resembles a large fish and has teeth and a snout similar to a beak. Found almost worldwide, dolphins are related to whales but are smaller. Family: Delphinidae. **2. LARGE MARINE GAME FISH** a large sea fish of the perch family, popular as a game fish, that has a long dorsal fin, high blunt forehead, and a brilliant green, blue, and yellow body. Latin name: *Coryphaena hippurus* and *Coryphaena equisetis.* [14thC. Via Old French *daulphin* (source of English *dauphin*) from, ultimately, Greek *delphin* (source of English *delphinium*).]

dol·phi·nar·i·um /dòlfi náiree əm/ (*plural* **-ums** *or* **-a** /-ə/) *n.* a large pool in which dolphins are kept, either for research or for public displays [Mid-20thC. Blend of DOLPHIN and AQUARIUM; modeled on OCEANARIUM.]

dol·phin·fish /dólfin fish/ (*plural* **-fish** *or* **-fish·es**) *n.* = **dolphin** *n.* **2**

dol·phin strik·er *n.* a strut that helps to prevent upward movement of a spar extending from the front of a sailing vessel

dolt /dōlt/ *n.* somebody thought of as being without intelligence (*informal insult*) [Mid-16thC. Origin uncertain: perhaps ultimately *dulled*, past participle of DULL.]

dolt·ish /dṓltish/ *adj.* of low intelligence or showing lack of intelligence (*informal insult*) —**dolt·ish·ly** *adv.* —**dolt·ish·ness** *n.*

Dol·ton /dṓlt'n/ village in northeastern Illinois, just west of the Illinois-Indiana border, a southern suburb of Chicago. Population: 24,102 (1996).

DOM *abbr.* dirty old man (*slang insult*)

dom. *abbr.* 1. domestic 2. MUSIC dominant

Dom. *abbr.* Dominican

D.O.M. *abbr.* Deo Optimo Maximo

-dom *suffix.* **1.** status, condition ○ *martyrdom* **2.** people associated with a particular status or rank ○ *fandom* **3.** office, rank, domain ○ *dukedom* [Old English *-dōm*. Ultimately from an Indo-European base meaning "to put, place," which is also the ancestor of English *doom*.]

do·main /dō máyn, də-/ *n.* **1. PURVIEW** the scope of a subject **2. SPHERE OF INFLUENCE** an area of activity over which somebody has influence **3. TERRITORY GOVERNED** territory ruled by a government or a leader **4. LAND OWNED** an area of land owned and controlled by a person, family, or organization **5.** LAW **RIGHTS OF OWNERSHIP** rights relating to the ownership of land. ◊ **demesne 6.** PHYS **REGION OF UNIFORM MAGNETISM** a region in a ferromagnetic material within which all the atoms are magnetically oriented in the same direction. Increasing the magnetic field increases the size and number of the domains. **7.** MATH **SET OF VALUES OF VARIABLE** the set of possible values specified for a given mathematical function **8.** COMPUT = **domain name** [15thC. From French *domaine*, an alteration of *demeine* "demesne" (source of English *demesne*), from, ultimately, Latin *dominus* "lord" (see DON[1]), the underlying sense being "land belonging to a lord."]

do·main name *n.* the sequence of words, phrases, abbreviations, or characters that identifies a specific computer or network on the Internet and serves as its address

do·main of quan·ti·fi·ca·tion *n.* the set of objects to which the quantifiers "all" and "some" apply

dome /dōm/ *n.* **1.** ARCHIT **HEMISPHERICAL ROOF** a hemispherical roof, e.g., on a palace or cathedral **2. HEMISPHERICAL TOP** something that resembles a dome in shape and position, e.g., the cover of a furnace or the top of somebody's head ○ *the dome of the sky* **3. HEMISPHERICAL BUILDING STRUCTURE** a hemispherical or convex structure, especially a building ○ *a sports dome* **4. CRYSTAL FORMATION RESEMBLING A ROOF** a crystal form in which two inclined surfaces intersect to form an edge like a roof **5. LARGE STATELY BUILDING** a large grand building (*archaic*) **6.** GEOL **CURVED ROCK LAYER** a semispherical topographic feature that slopes in all directions from a central point, formed by upward folding of sediments **7.** GEOL **LAVA MASS** a mass of solidified viscous lava formed above the vent of a volcano by the buildup of magma ■ *v.* **(domed, dom·ing, domes) 1.** *vti.* **FORM A HEMISPHERICAL SHAPE** to rise in a hemispherical shape, or form something into this shape **2.** *vt.* **COVER WITH A DOME** to cover something with a dome [Mid-17thC. Via French *dôme* from Italian *duomo* "house, house of God, cathedral" (source of English *duomo*), from Latin *domus* "house."]

domed /dōmd/ *adj.* **1. HAVING A DOME** with a dome or many domes **2. LOOKING LIKE A DOME** with a shape or structure resembling a dome ○ *"His brow is deeply lined with thought, his head is highly domed"* (T. S. Eliot, *Macavity: The Mystery Cat*; 1939)

domes·day /doómz dày/ *n.* doomsday (*archaic*)

Domes·day Book, Dooms·day Book *n.* a record of all the land in England, its value and its ownership, commissioned by William the Conqueror in 1085 [*Domesday* reflecting the book's status as the ultimate authority on matters within its compass]

do·mes·tic /də méstik/ *adj.* **1. RELATING TO HOME** relating to or used in the home or everyday life within a household **2.** DOMESTIC **RELATING TO FAMILY** relating to or involving the family or people living together within a household **3.** AGRIC **NOT WILD** kept as a farm animal or as a pet **4.** COMM **NOT FOREIGN** produced, distributed, sold, or occurring within a country ○ *domestic oil producers* **5.** POL **OF A NATION'S INTERNAL AFFAIRS** relating to the internal affairs of a nation or country ○ *domestic issues such as elections* **6. ENJOYING HOME** enjoying home and family life ■ *n.* **1. HOUSEHOLD SERVANT** somebody employed to do housework in somebody else's home or other duties in a large household **2.** COMM **PRODUCT NOT ORIGINATING ABROAD** a product manufactured within a country [15thC. Via French *domestique* from Latin *domesticus*, from *domus* "house."] —**do·mes·ti·cal·ly** *adv.*

do·mes·ti·cate /də mésti kàyt/ **(-cat·ed, -cat·ing, -cates)** *vt.* **1.** AGRIC **TAME AN ANIMAL** to accustom an animal to living with or near people, usually as a farm animal or pet **2. ACCUSTOM TO HOUSEHOLD LIFE** to accustom somebody to home life or housework (*humorous*) **3.** BIOL **ADAPT PLANTS AND ANIMALS FOR HUMANS** to cultivate plants or raise animals, selectively breeding them to increase their suitability for human requirements [Mid-17thC. From medieval Latin *domesticat-*, the past participle stem of *domesticare*, from Latin *domesticus* (see DOMESTIC).] —**do·mes·ti·ca·ble** *adj.* —**do·mes·ti·ca·tion** /də mèsti káysh'n/ *n.* —**do·mes·ti·ca·tor** /-kàytər/ *n.*

INTERNET DOMAIN NAMES

The Domain Name System (DNS) is a method of translating Internet addresses from systematic alphabetical sequences to numeric codes so that messages can be transmitted from one computer or network to another. A DNS name appears in the form:

username@computer (or Internet provider).domain

Domains indicate the country — except for the United States, where no country code is used — or type of organization or both country and organization.

Selected Organization Domains

Domain	Organization
.ac	Educational Organization outside US
.co	Commercial Organization outside US
.com	Commercial Organization
.edu	Educational Organization
.gov	Government Organization
.int	International Organization
.mil	Military Organization
.net	Network Organization
.org	Private Organization

For countries other than the United States country domains can be combined with organization domains, e.g.:

.co.uk	UK Commercial Organization
.edu.au	Australian Educational Organization

Selected Country Domains

Domain	Country
.au	Australia
.bd	Bangladesh
.ca	Canada
.gh	Ghana
.hk	Hong Kong
.id	Indonesia
.ie	Ireland
.in	India
.ke	Kenya
.my	Malaysia
.nz	New Zealand
.ng	Nigeria
.pk	Pakistan
.sg	Singapore
.za	South Africa
.lk	Sri Lanka
.ug	Uganda
.uk	United Kingdom
.zm	Zambia
.zw	Zimbabwe

do·mes·ti·cat·ed /də mésti kàytəd/ *adj.* **1.** AGRIC **NOT WILD** accustomed to living near people, usually on a farm or in a home **2.** BIOL **RAISED FOR HUMANS** cultivated, raised, or bred for human requirements **3. ACCUSTOMED TO HOUSEWORK** accustomed to doing domestic chores in the home (*humorous*)

do·mes·tic court *n.* LAW a court having jurisdiction at the location of a party's residence or domicile

do·mes·tic·i·ty /dō me stíssətee/ *n.* **1. HOME LIFE** life as it is lived at home **2. FONDNESS FOR HOME LIFE** a liking for or familiarity with home life ■ **do·mes·tic·i·ties** *npl.* **HOUSEHOLD MATTERS** the concerns of the home and family

do·mes·tic part·ner *n.* a sexual partner living in the same house

do·mes·tic prel·ate *n.* a Roman Catholic priest with honorary membership in the papal household

do·mette /dō mét/ *n.* a soft fleecy fabric made from wool and acrylic fibers, used as lightweight interlining [Early 19thC. Origin unknown.]

do·mi·cal /dṓmik'l, dómm-/ *adj.* **1. DOME-SHAPED** shaped like a dome **2. WITH A DOME** having a dome or domes

dom·i·cile /dómmi sīl, dómmiss'l/ *n.* **1. SOMEBODY'S HOME** the house, apartment, or other place where somebody lives (*formal*) **2.** LAW **SOMEBODY'S PLACE OF RESIDENCE** somebody's true, fixed, and legally recognized place of residence, especially in cases of prolonged absence that require the person to prove a continuing and significant connection with the place ■ *vt.* (**-ciled, -cil·ing, -ciles**) **GIVE A HOME** to establish somebody in or provide somebody with a place of residence [15thC. Directly or via French from Latin *domicilium*, from *domus* "house."]

dom·i·cil·i·ar·y /dòmmə síllee èrree/ *adj.* **1. OF HOME** relating to a home or homes **2. FOR PEOPLE AT HOME** provided for or attending to people in their own homes ○ *domiciliary care* [Late 19thC. Via French *domiciliare* from medieval Latin *domiciliarius*, from *domicilium* (see DOMICILE).]

dom·i·cil·i·ate /dòmmə síllee àyt/ (**-at·ed, -at·ing, -ates**) *vt.* = **domicile** *v.* [Late 18thC. From Latin *domicilium* (see DOMICILE).]

dom·i·nance /dómmənəns/ *n.* **1. POWER EXERTED OVER OTHERS** control or command wielded over others **2. FIRST IMPORTANCE** prime importance, effectiveness, or prominence **3.** GENETICS **PRODUCTION OF GENETIC FEATURE** the property of a gene that causes a parental characteristic it controls to occur in any offspring **4.** ECOL **PREPONDERANCE OF ONE SPECIES** the preponderance of a single plant or animal species in a specific community or over a specific period

dom·i·nant /dómmənənt/ *adj.* **1. IN CONTROL** in control or command over others **2. MORE IMPORTANT** more important, effective, or prominent than others **3.** GENETICS **PRODUCING SAME CHARACTERISTIC IN OFFSPRING** used to describe a gene that causes a parental characteristic it controls to occur in any offspring, or the characteristic itself **4.** ECOL **PREPONDERANT IN A COMMUNITY OR PERIOD** relating to a single plant or animal species that is preponderant within a specific community or over a specific period **5.** MUSIC **RELATING TO 5TH NOTE OF SCALE** relating to the fifth note of a musical scale or the harmony based around that note ■ *n.* MUSIC **1. 5TH NOTE OF SCALE** the 5th note of a musical scale **2. CHORD BASED ON FIFTH NOTE** a chord or key based on the fifth note of a musical scale [15thC. Via French from Latin *dominant-*, present participle stem of *dominari* (see DOMINATE).] —**dom·i·nant·ly** *adv.*

dom·i·nant es·tate *n.* property that gives its owner certain rights over other property, e.g., the right to cross land belonging to somebody else in order to reach your own house

dom·i·nant hem·i·sphere *n.* the half of the brain that tends to exercise greater control over certain functions, e.g., language or movement of the left or right side of the body

dom·i·nant sev·enth chord *n.* MUSIC a chord containing, in its most common form, the dominant as root and the major third, perfect fifth, and minor seventh above the root. It often resolves to a chord on the tonic.

dom·i·nant ten·e·ment *n. U.K.* = **dominant estate**

dom·i·nate /dómmə nàyt/ (**-nat·ed, -nat·ing, -nates**) *vti.* **1. CONTROL** to have control, power, or authority over somebody or something **2. BE PROMINENT** to be the most important aspect or element of something **3. BE INFLUENTIAL** to have a prevailing influence on somebody or something **4. TOWER ABOVE** to overlook an area from a prominent and usually elevated position [Early 17thC. Partly from Latin *dominat-*, past participle stem of *dominari* "to be lord, rule," from *dominus* "lord" (see DON[1]); partly a back-formation from DOMINATION.] —**dom·i·na·tive** *adj.* —**dom·i·na·tor** *n.*

dom·i·na·tion /dòmmə náysh'n/ *n.* control, power, or authority over others or another [14thC. Via French from the Latin stem *domination-*, from *dominari* (see DOMINATE).]

dom·i·na·trix /dòmmə náytriks/ (*plural* **-tri·ces** /-trə seez, -nə trī-/) *n.* a dominant woman partner in a sadomasochistic relationship [Mid-16thC. From Latin, "woman ruler," the feminine of *dominator* "ruler, lord," from, ultimately, *dominari* (see DOMINATE).]

dom·i·neer /dòmmə néer, -néer/ (**-neered, -neer·ing, -neers**) *vi.* to rule tyrannically, or behave in an overbearing way [Late 16thC. Via Dutch *domineren* from, ultimately, Latin *dominari* (see DOMINATE).]

dom·i·neer·ing /dòmmə néering, dómmə néering/ *adj.* showing a desire or tendency to exercise excessive control or authority over others —**dom·i·neer·ing·ly** *adv.*

Do·min·go /də míng gō/, **Plácido** (*b.* 1941) Spanish opera singer. He is widely regarded as the greatest tenor voice of his time. Since 1990, he has often appeared with José Carreras and Luciano Pavarotti as one of the "Three Tenors."

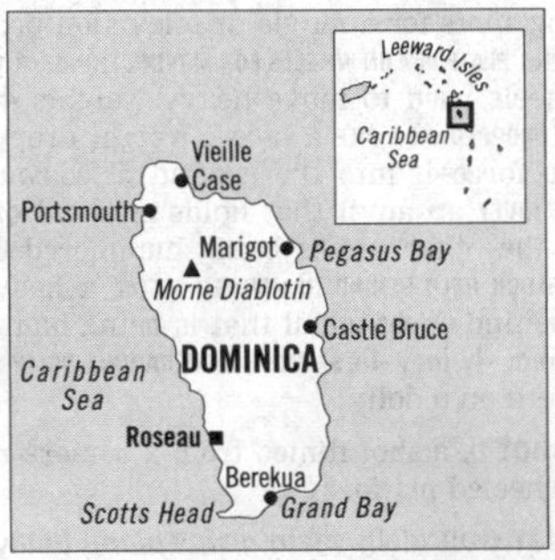

Dominica

Dom·i·ni·ca /dòmmə néekə, də mínnikə/ independent island republic in the West Indies, lying in the Caribbean Sea. Language: English. Currency: Eastern Caribbean dollar. Capital: Roseau. Population: 666,633 (1997). Area: 290 sq. mi./751 sq. km. Length: 29 mi./47 km. Official name **Commonwealth of Dominica**

do·min·i·cal /də mínnik'l/ *adj.* CHR (*formal*) **1. OF JESUS CHRIST** relating to Jesus Christ as the Lord **2. RELATING TO SUNDAY** relating to Sunday as the day of the Lord [15thC. Directly or via French from late Latin *dominicalis*, from, ultimately, Latin *dominus* "lord, master" (see DON[1]).]

do·min·i·cal let·ter *n.* any of the letters A to G used in the church calendar to denote all the Sundays of a given year. For example, if January 4 falls on a Sunday, the dominical letter for the year is D.

Do·min·i·can[1] /də mínnikən, dòmmə níkən/ *n.* PEOPLES **1. SOMEBODY FROM DOMINICAN REPUBLIC** somebody who was born or raised in the Dominican Republic, or who is a citizen of the Dominican Republic **2. SOMEBODY FROM DOMINICA** somebody who lives on or was born or raised on the island of Dominica —**Do·min·i·can** *adj.*

Do·min·i·can[2] /də mínnikən/ *n.* CHR **MEMBER OF A RELIGIOUS ORDER** a member of the order of friars founded by St. Dominic in 1215. ■ *adj.* **OF ST. DOMINIC OR HIS ORDER** relating or belonging to St. Dominic or his order of friars. [Late 16thC. From medieval Latin *Dominicanus*, from the founder's name.]

Dom·i·ni·can Re·pub·lic /də mìnnikən-/ independent republic on Hispaniola Island, off the coast of Puerto Rica in the Caribbean Sea. It was proclaimed a republic in 1844. Language: Spanish. Currency: Dominican peso. Capital: Santo Domingo. Population: 7,868,731 (1997). Area: 18,816 sq. mi./48,734 sq. km. Length: 235 mi./380 km.

do·min·ion /də mínnyən/ *n.* **1. RULING CONTROL** ruling power, authority, or control **2. SPHERE OF INFLUENCE** somebody's area of influence or control **3. LAND RULED** the land governed by a ruler (*often used in the plural*) ○ *the monarch's dominions beyond the sea* **4.**

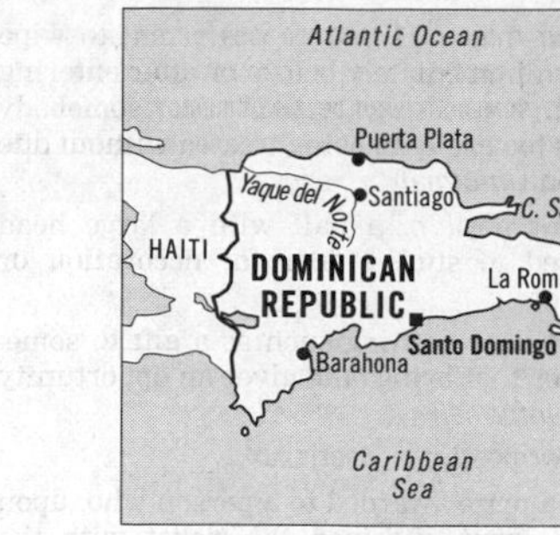

Dominican Republic

do·min·ion, Do·min·ion SELF-GOVERNING TERRITORY a self-governing part of the British Commonwealth or, formerly, the British Empire [15thC. Via Old French from the medieval Latin stem *dominion-*, from Latin *dominium* "property, right of ownership," from *dominus* "lord" (see DON[1]).]

Do·min·ion Day *n.* former name for **Canada Day**

dom·i·no /dómmə nō/ (*plural* **-noes**) *n.* **1.** BOARD GAMES **SMALL OBLONG TILE** any one of a set of small oblong blocks with its face divided into two sections, each section either blank or marked with a number of dots **2.** CLOTHES, LEISURE **HOODED CLOAK AND MASK** a hooded cloak and eye mask formerly worn as a disguise at a party (**masquerade**), the cloak or mask alone, or the wearer of any of these **3.** POL **COUNTRY AFFECTED BY DOMINO THEORY** a country thought likely to be affected by political events in another country, particularly by the spread of Communism [Late 17thC. From French, "priest's winter hood," also "masked cloak worn at masquerades" (the original sense in English), of uncertain origin: perhaps ultimately from Latin *dominus* "lord" (see DON[1]).]

dom·i·no ef·fect *n.* an inevitable succession of related and usually undesirable events, each caused by the preceding one. ◊ **domino theory** [So called because dominoes set up in a row fall in sequence once the first has fallen]

dom·i·no the·o·ry *n.* POL a theory that political events are interrelated and that one can trigger off a chain of others. The theory was developed by U.S. President Dwight D. Eisenhower to warn of the spread of Communism in Southeast Asia. ◊ **domino effect**

don[1] /don/ *n.* **1.** CRIMINOL **LEADER OF ORGANIZED CRIME FAMILY** a head of an organized crime family, especially in the Mafia **2.** *U.K.* UNIV **UNIVERSITY OR COLLEGE TEACHER** a university or college teacher, especially one at the universities of Oxford or Cambridge in England **3.** **SPANISH MAN OF RANK** a Spanish gentleman or aristocrat **4.** **PERSONAGE** an important person (*archaic*) [Late 16thC. Via Spanish from Latin *dominus* "lord" (source of English *domain, dominate, domino,* and *dungeon*).]

don[2] /don/ (**donned, don·ning, dons**) *vt.* to put on a garment (*formal*) [14thC. Contraction of *do on* "to put on" (see DO). The word became largely obsolete in the 17thC, but was revived in the 19thC.]

Don[1] *n.* a title used before a man's name in Spain and other Spanish-speaking countries [Early 16thC. From Spanish (see DON[1]).]

Don[2] river rising southeast of Moscow, Russia, flowing through Volgograd and into the Sea of Azov. Length: 1,160 mi./1,870 km.

Do·na /dṓnə/ *n.* a title used before a married woman's name in Portugal and other Portuguese-speaking countries [Early 17thC. Via Portuguese from Latin *domina* "lady," the feminine of *dominus* "lord" (see DON[1]).]

Do·ña /dṓnyə/ *n.* a title used before a married woman's name in Spain and other Spanish-speaking countries [Early 17thC. Via Spanish from Latin *domina* (see DONA).]

do·nate /dṓ nàyt, dō náyt/ (**-nat·ed, -nat·ing, -nates**) *v.* **1.** *vt.* **GIVE OR PRESENT** to give or present something, especially to a charitable organization or other good cause **2.** *vt.* MED **GIVE BODY PART** to give your own blood, tissue, organs, or reproductive material to be used in the treatment of another person, either while you are alive or after your death **3.** CHEM **TRANSFER ELECTRONS** to transfer electrons to another atom or molecule in a chemical reaction [Late 18thC. Back-formation from DONATION.]

WORD KEY: SYNONYMS

See Synonyms at ***give***.

Don·a·tel·lo /dònnə téllō/ (1386?–1466) Italian sculptor. In his bronze statue *David* (1430–35) and other works he revived the classical art of portraying independent functional human figures. Full name **Donato di Niccolò di Betto Bardi**

do·na·tion /dō náysh'n/ *n.* **1.** **GIFT OR CONTRIBUTION** a gift or contribution, especially a sum of money given to a charity ○ *All donations will be gratefully accepted.* **2.** **ACT OF GIVING** the act of giving something, especially money to a charity [15thC. Via French from the Latin stem *donation-*, from, ultimately, Latin *donare* "to give," from *donum* "gift."]

Don·a·tism /dṓnə tìzzəm, dónn-/ *n.* the beliefs of the Donatists

Don·a·tist /dṓnətist, dónn-/ *n.* a member of a Christian group of the 4th and 5th centuries, originating in North Africa, that placed great emphasis on sanctity [Late 16thC. From late Latin *Donatista*, named for *Donatus*, the second Bishop of Carthage after Caecilian (whose consecration the Donatists did not recognize).]

don·a·tive /dṓnətiv, dónn-/ *n.* **1.** **OFFICIAL DONATION** a donation, especially a formal or official one **2.** CHR **CHURCH POSITION GIVEN AS GIFT** a church office (**benefice**) that is or can be presented as a gift without reference to the bishop, as opposed to one received as a right ■ *adj.* **MADE AS GIFT** given or presented as a gift (*formal*) [15thC. Via Latin *donativum* from, ultimately, *donare* "to give" (see DONATION).]

do·na·tor /dṓ nàytər/ *n.* somebody who gives or presents something, especially money to a charity (*formal*) [15thC. Originally directly or via French *donateur* from Latin *donator*, from, ultimately, *donare* "to give" (see DONATION); in modern use formed from *donate.*]

done /dun/ past participle of **do**[1] ■ *v. Carib, Southern U.S.* **ALREADY** used as an auxiliary verb to express the sense of "already" (*nonstandard*) ○ *He done leave.* ■ *adj.* **1.** **CONCLUDED** completed or finished **2.** COOK **COOKED THROUGH** cooked as thoroughly as required **3.** **PREORDAINED** having been decided already, therefore permitting no alterations or changes (*slang*) ○ *It's a done deal, and you can't fight it.* **4.** **SOCIALLY ACCEPTABLE** acceptable to the established rules and expectations of a society ■ *interj.* **AGREED** used to confirm acceptance of a deal ◇ **have done with something** to be finished with or have had enough of something ○ *Why don't we just sell the house and have done with it?*

WORD KEY: USAGE

done or **finished?** It is sometimes maintained that ***done*** is the wrong word to indicate that one has completed something. Certainly, *I have finished reading the newspaper* is more formal than *I'm done with the paper.* Not only does one of these sentences use ***finished*** instead of ***done*** but also it uses ***finished*** as a past participle, whereas ***done*** in the example is being used as an adjective. ***Finished,*** too, can be an adjective: *I'm finished with the paper.* Such adjectival uses are very common in casual speech and writing. For clarity's sake, the adjective ***done*** should not be used where it might be interpreted as the participle (*The work wasn't done well, but it least it was done before the deadline*). In formal contexts ***finished*** is preferable, and either it or ***done*** should modify what has been completed (*The job is finished*), rather than the one who has completed something (*I am done*).

WORD KEY: REGIONAL NOTE

The emphatic perfective, *I done told you* extends to adverbial usage *He's done dead* in folk speech across the Southern states and into the Caribbean.

do·nee /dō neé/ *n.* the recipient of a gift (*formal*) [Early 16thC. Formed from DONOR.]

done for *adj.* (*informal*) **1.** **NEAR DEATH** close to the point of dying **2.** **EXHAUSTED** extremely tired **3.** **ABOUT TO BE RUINED** facing defeat, ruin, or destruction

Don·e·gal /dónnə gàwl/ county in northwestern Ireland. The Atlantic Ocean lies to the west, Northern Ireland to the east. Population: 129,435 (1996). Area: 1865 sq. mi./4830 sq. km. Irish **Dœn Na nGall**

Don·e·gal tweed *n.* a rough tweed characterized by a white lumpy effect [Early 20thC. Named for County *Donegal* in Ireland, where it was first produced.]

Do·nets /də néts, də nyéts/ river in Russia and Ukraine that flows into the Don River northeast of Rostov in southwestern Russia. Length: 631 mi./1,020 km.

Do·nets Ba·sin major coalfield and industrial region in southeastern Ukraine. The basin extends across the Russian border into the Rostov region.

dong[1] /dawng/ *n.* **DEEP TOLL** a deep ringing sound ■ *vi.* (**donged, dong·ing, dongs**) **TOLL DEEPLY** to make a deep ringing sound [Late 16thC. An imitation of the sound.]

dong[2] /dawng/ *n.* a penis (*slang taboo*) [Mid-20thC. Origin uncertain.]

dong[3] /dawng/ *n.* MONEY a Vietnamese coin. See table at **currency** [Early 19thC. From Vietnamese.]

don·gle /dóng g'l, dáw-/ *n.* a small hardware device that, when plugged into a computer, enables a specific copy-protected program to run, the program being disabled on that computer if the device is not present. The device is effective against software piracy. [Late 20thC. Origin uncertain: probably an arbitrary formation.]

Dong Yu·an /dàwng yoo áan/ (*fl.* late 10th century) Chinese artist. He is noted for his monumental, richly colored landscapes.

Don·i·zet·ti /dònni zéttee/, **Gaetano** (1797–1848) Italian composer. He wrote 65 operas, ranging from dramas such as *Lucia di Lammermoor* (1835) to comic works such as *Don Pasquale* (1843).

don·jon /dónjən, dúnj-/ *n.* a fortified central tower in a medieval castle [14thC. An early form of DUNGEON.]

Don Juan /dòn wáan, -hwáan/ *n.* a man who has a reputation for having casual sexual relationships with numerous women [Mid-19thC. Named for *Don Juan* Tenorio, a legendary Spanish nobleman known for his seduction of women.]

Donkey

don·key /dáwngkee, dóng-/ (*plural* **-keys**) *n.* **1.** **ANIMAL RESEMBLING A SMALL HORSE** a small domesticated member of the horse family with a gray or brown coat, long ears, and a large head. Latin name: *Equus asinus.* **2.** **UNINTELLIGENT PERSON** somebody thought of as lacking intelligence (*informal insult*) [Late 18thC. Origin uncertain: perhaps from DUN (the word originally rhymed with MONKEY); or perhaps a pet form of the name *Duncan.*]

don·key en·gine *n.* a small auxiliary engine used either to start a larger engine or independently, e.g., for pumping water on steamships

don·key's tail *n.* PLANTS = **burro's tail**

don·key·work /dáwngki wùrk, dóngki-/ *n.* hard or boring work (*informal*)

Don·leav·y /don leévee/, **J. P.** (*b.* 1926) U.S.-born Irish novelist, short-story writer, and playwright. His first novel, *The Ginger Man* (1955), was hailed as a comic masterpiece. Among his other novels are *A Singular Man* (1963) and *The Beastly Beatitudes of Balthazar B* (1968). Full name **James Patrick Donleavy**

Don·na /dónnə/ *n.* a title used before a married woman's name in Italy [Early 17thC. Via Italian from Latin *domina* "lady" (see DONA).]

Don·ne /dun/, **John** (1572–1631) English poet, prose writer, and clergyman, considered the greatest of the Metaphysical poets. An author of passionate love poetry, he was later ordained and appointed Dean of St. Paul's (1621). His verse includes the love poems *Songs and Sonnets*, his *Satires* (both dating from the 1590s), *Divine Poems* (1607), and *Epithalamion* (1613).

don·née /daw náy/ *n.* **1.** **BASIC ASSUMPTION** a basic fact or assumption on which something else, e.g., a literary or theatrical work, is based and from which it develops or moves forward **2.** **THEME** a theme or subject, e.g., of a literary or theatrical work [Late

19thC. From French, the feminine past participle, used as a noun, of *donner* "to give."]

don·nish /dónnish/ *adj. U.K.* resembling the stereotypical image of a university professor, e.g., in displaying erudition or being absent-minded

don·ny·brook /dónni broŏk/ *n.* a riotous brawl [Mid-19thC. Named for *Donnybrook* Fair, an annual event known for its brawls, which was formerly held in Donnybrook, a suburb of Dublin in the Republic of Ireland.]

do·nor /dṓnər/ *n.* **1. SOMEBODY WHO GIVES SOMETHING** somebody who gives something, especially money **2.** MED **SOMEBODY GIVING BLOOD OR BODY ORGAN** somebody who voluntarily gives part of his or her body for the treatment of another person, e.g., blood for transfusion, during life or after death, or an organ or tissue for transplantation **3.** ELECTRON ENG **IMPURITY ADDED TO SEMICONDUCTOR** an impurity (**dopant**), e.g., antimony, that is deliberately added to a pure semiconductor material, e.g., silicon, in order to increase its conductivity by increasing the number of free electrons, carriers of negative electrical charge **4.** CHEM **ATOM PROVIDING ELECTRONS FOR A BOND** an atom, molecule, or group that provides the pair of electrons necessary to form a chemical bond. ◊ **acceptor** [15thC. Via Anglo-Norman *donour* and Old French *doneur* from Latin *donator*, from, ultimately, *donare* "to give" (see DONATION).] —**do·nor·ship** *n.*

do·nor card *n.* a card stating that specified organs, or sometimes the entire body, of the person carrying it may be used for the treatment of others after the donor's death

do·nor in·sem·i·na·tion *n.* the introduction into a woman's vagina of sperm from a man who is not the woman's sexual partner. The procedure is performed as a method of assisted conception with the intention of making the woman pregnant.

do-noth·ing *adj.* **DISINCLINED TO PRODUCTIVITY OR CHANGE** not inclined to engage in productive activities or to change ○ *a do-nothing committee* ■ *n.* **IDLER** a lazy or idle person (*informal*) —**do-noth·ing·ism** *n.*

Don Qui·xo·te /dòn kee hṓtee, -kwíksət/ *n.* an impractical idealist who champions hopeless causes [Mid-17thC. Named for *Don Quixote*, the naively idealistic hero of the satirical romance *Don Quixote de la Mancha* (1605, 1615) by the Spanish author Cervantes.]

don't /dōnt/ *contr.* **DO NOT** do not ■ *n.* **SOMETHING NOT TO BE DONE** something that should not be done

don't-care con·di·tion *n.* ELECTRON ENG a state or part of an electronic circuit that has no influence on the circuit's output

don't know *n.* somebody who has not made a decision one way or the other about a specific issue, e.g., before an election or in a market research survey (*informal*)

do·nut *n.* = **doughnut**

doo·dad /doó dàd/ *n.* (*informal*) **1. THING** a thing whose name you cannot remember or do not know **2. INCIDENTAL DECORATION** a decoration incidentally added to clothing or some other product [Early 20thC. Origin unknown.]

doo·dah /doó daa/ *n. U.K.* = **doodad** (*informal*) [Early 20thC. Origin uncertain: probably from *dooda(h)* in the refrain to the song *Camptown Races*.]

doo·dle /doód'l/ *vti.* (**-dled, -dling, -dles**) **SCRIBBLE DRAWINGS OR DESIGNS** to draw aimlessly or absentmindedly, usually while doing something else such as having a telephone conversation or attending a meeting ■ *n.* **DRAWING OR DESIGN** a drawing or abstract design produced aimlessly or absentmindedly while doing something else [Early 17thC. From Low German *dudel-* in *dudeltopf* "fool" (the original English sense). The senses "idle drawing" and "to draw aimlessly" date from the mid-20thC.] —**doo·dler** *n.*

doo·dle·bug /doód'l bùg/ *n.* **1.** INSECTS **INSECT LARVA** the large-jawed larva of an antlion, or any similar insect larva **2.** MINERALS **DEVICE USED TO FIND MINERALS** a device used by prospectors to help them to locate minerals

doo-doo /doó doò/ *n.* human or animal excrement (*slang humorous*) [Mid-20thC. Origin uncertain: probably an alteration and repetition of DO.]

doof·er /doófər/ *n.* an object or gadget whose name you cannot remember or do not know (*slang*) [Mid-20thC. Origin uncertain: probably from *do for* in phrases such as *that will do for now*.]

doo·fus /doófəss/ *n.* an unintelligent or thoughtless person (*slang insult*) [Late 20thC. Origin uncertain: perhaps an alteration of GOOF.]

doo·hick·ey /doó hikee/ (*plural* **-eys**) *n.* an unspecified gadget (*informal*) [Early 20thC. Blend of DOODAD and HICKEY.]

Doo·lit·tle /doó litt'l/, **Hilda** (1886–1961) U.S. poet. Known for her imagist poetry, she wrote *Sea Garden* (1916) and *Bid Me to Live* (1960). Pen name **H. D., Imagiste**

Doo·lit·tle, James H. (1896–1993) U.S. aviator. He set many flight records after World War I and returned to military duty in 1940. Full name **James Harold Doolittle**

doom /doom/ *n.* **1. DISASTROUS DESTINY** a dreadful fate, especially death or utter ruin **2. OFFICIAL JUDGMENT** an official judgment on somebody (*formal*) **3. doom, Doom** RELIG **LAST JUDGMENT** the Last Judgment (*archaic*) ■ *vt.* (**doomed, doom·ing, dooms**) **DESTINE TO DISASTER** to condemn somebody or something to a dreadful fate [Old English *dōm* "judgment, sentence, law." Ultimately, from an Indo-European base meaning "to set, put" that is also the ancestor of English *deed, deem, defeat*, and *do*.]

doomed /doomd/ *adj.* **1. DESTINED TO DISASTER** condemned to suffer a dreadful fate, especially one that is imminent and inescapable ○ *With our best player hurt, we were doomed to lose.* **2. DESTINED TO FAILURE OR MISFORTUNE** bound to fail or suffer something unpleasant ○ *The partnership was doomed from the start.*

doom palm *n.* BOT = **doum** [Early 18thC. *Doum* from Arabic *dūm*.]

doom·say·er /doóm sàyr/ *n.* somebody who frequently prophesies disaster

dooms·day /doómz dày/ *n.* **1. dooms·day, Dooms·day DAY OF FINAL JUDGMENT** a day of final reckoning, especially, in Christian theology, the day of the Last Judgment **2. END OF WORLD** the final destruction or dissolution of the world

Dooms·day Book *n.* = **Domesday Book**

door /dawr/ *n.* **1. MOVABLE PANEL AT AN ENTRANCE** a movable barrier used to open and close the entrance to a building, room, closet, or vehicle. It is usually a solid panel, hinged to or sliding in a frame. **2. GAP FORMING AN ENTRANCE** the gap that forms the entrance to a building or room **3. BUILDING OR ROOM** a building or room considered in relation to those on either side ○ *Does she live two doors down the street or one?* [Old English *duru* "door" and *dor* "gate," both from, ultimately, an Indo-European word meaning "entrance to the enclosure around the house" that is also the ancestor of English *thyroid*] ◇ **close** *or* **shut the door on something** to disallow the possibility of something happening ◇ **Katie bar the door** used as a warning that you should brace yourself for impending calamity (*regional*) ◇ **lay something at somebody's door** to blame something on somebody ◇ **out of doors** in the open air ◇ **show somebody the door** to tell somebody to leave

door·bell /dáwr bèl/ *n.* a bell placed on or beside a door, to be rung by visitors as a sign of their arrival

door bun·dle *n.* a bundle of equipment pushed out of an aircraft by hand before parachutists exit

do-or-die *adj.* involving the determination to risk everything in an effort to succeed

door·frame /dáwr fràym/ *n.* the frame constructed around the entrance to a building or room and into which a door is set

door·jamb /dáwr jàm/ *n.* either of the vertical side pieces of a doorframe

door·keep·er /dáwr keèpər/ *n.* **1. SOMEBODY ON DUTY AT DOOR** somebody on duty at a door or gate, especially somebody who guards the entrance **2. door·keep·er, Door·keep·er** POL **LEGISLATIVE OFFICER** an officer of a legislature whose job it is to control access to the floor and the visitors' galleries

door·knob /dáwr nòb/ *n.* a round handle used to open or close a door

door·man /dáwr màn, -mən/ (*plural* **-men** /dáwr mèn, -mən/) *n.* somebody on duty at the door of a building such as a nightclub, hotel, or apartment building, usually employed to assist customers, e.g., by calling cabs

door·mat /dáwr màt/ *n.* **1. MAT BY DOOR** a mat to wipe your shoes on immediately before or after entering a building **2. SOMEBODY WHO DOES NOT RESIST** somebody who submits too easily to being treated without due consideration (*informal*)

door·nail /dáwr nàyl/ *n.* a nail with a large head formerly used to stud a door for decoration or reinforcement

door o·pen·er *n.* something such as a gift to somebody in power that brings the giver an opportunity for success (*informal*)

door·post /dáwr pōst/ *n.* = **doorjamb**

door prize *n.* a prize awarded to a person who, upon entry to an event, received the ticket with the winning number [From the ticket having been handed out at the entrance to the function]

door·sill /dáwr sìl/ *n.* = **threshold** *n.* 1

door·step /dáwr stèp/ *n.* a step at the entrance to a building ◇ **on your (own) doorstep** very near where you live

door·stop /dáwr stòp/ *n.* **1. SOMETHING USED TO KEEP DOOR OPEN** a movable device such as a wedge or heavy object used to hold a door open **2. DEVICE TO PROTECT WALL FROM DOOR** a rubber stud or rubber-tipped projection on a wall, floor, or door that prevents damage to the wall when the door is opened

door to door *adv.* **1. TO ALL HOUSES IN AREA** going from one house to the next, usually in order to sell things, to collect money for charity, or to solicit support in an election **2. OVER WHOLE TRIP** from the place of departure to the place of arrival ○ *The trip took three hours door to door.*

door-to-door *adj.* (*not hyphenated after a verb*) **1. COVERING ALL HOUSES IN AREA** done or going from one house to the next **2. COVERING WHOLE JOURNEY** from the point of departure to the point of arrival

door·way /dáwr wày/ *n.* **1. ENTRANCE TO BUILDING** an entrance to a building or room, especially one that has a door **2. OPPORTUNITY** a means of achieving or escaping from something

doo-wop /doó wòp/ *n.* harmonized singing of nonsense syllables, with a rhythm-and-blues melody on top, popularized by street singers in the 1950s [Mid-20thC. An imitation of the sound.]

doo·zy /doózee/ (*plural* **-zies**) *n.* a remarkable or excellent thing (*slang*) [Early 20thC. Origin uncertain: perhaps an alteration of DAISY (perhaps blended with *Duesenberg* (a type of luxury car).]

do·pa /dṓpə/ *n.* a substance that occurs naturally in the body and is involved in the synthesis of epinephrine, dopamine, and the pigment melanin. It is also used in the form levodopa as a drug to treat Parkinson's disease. Formula: $C_9H_{11}NO_4$. [Early 20thC. Acronym formed from DI- + OXY- + PHENYL + ALANINE.]

do·pa·mine /dṓpə meen/ *n.* a chemical compound, found in the brain, that transmits nerve impulses and is involved in the formation of epinephrine [Mid-20thC. Blend of DOPA and AMINE.]

dop·ant /dṓpənt/ *n.* a substance, e.g., arsenic or antimony, that is added in small quantities to a semiconductor material in order to change its electrical characteristics. Dopants are added during the manufacture of semiconducting diodes and transistors.

dope /dōp/ *n.* **1.** DRUGS **ILLEGAL DRUG** an illegal drug, especially marijuana (*slang*) **2. DRUG AFFECTING PERFORMANCE** a drug given illegally, e.g., to racehorses or athletes, to affect performance **3. INSIDE INFORMATION** confidential information about somebody or something (*slang*) **4.** CHEM **VISCOUS LIQUID** a viscous liquid used for lubrication, waterproofing and strengthening fabrics, coating aircraft wings, or improving the combustion of engine fuels **5.** CHEM **ABSORBENT MATERIAL** an absorbent material used in the manufacture of dynamite **6.** ELECTRON ENG = **dopant** ■ *vt.* (**doped, dop·ing, dopes**) **1.** DRUGS **ADD DRUG TO FOOD OR DRINK** to add a drug to somebody's food or drink secretly in order to affect the person's performance or consciousness adversely **2.** ELECTRON ENG **ADD IMPURITY TO SEMICONDUCTOR** to add a substance, e.g., arsenic or antimony to a semiconductor material like silicon or germanium during the manufacturing process in order to increase its conductivity [Early 19thC. From Dutch *doop* "thick dipping sauce," from *doopen* "to dip, mix."] —**dop·er** *n.*

dope out *vt.* to gain an understanding of something puzzling through analysis (*slang*)

dope up *vt.* to make somebody drowsy or semiconscious by administering a drug such as an anesthetic or an illegal narcotic (*slang*)

dope dog *n.* a dog specially trained to locate by scent contraband narcotics hidden in luggage or packages, or concealed on somebody's body (*informal*)

dope sheet *n.* a booklet that gives information about the horses entered for races (*slang*)

dop·ey /dṓpee/ (**-i·er, -i·est**), **dop·y** (**-i·er, -i·est**) *adj.* showing a lack of good sense or intelligence (*informal insult*) —**dop·i·ly** *adv.* —**dop·i·ness** *n.*

dop·ing a·gent *n.* ELECTRON ENG = **dopant**

dop·pel·gäng·er /dópp'l gàngər/, **dop·pel·gang·er** *n.* **1.** **SOMEBODY SIMILAR TO ANOTHER PERSON** somebody who looks very like another person **2.** **GHOST IDENTICAL TO LIVING PERSON** an apparition in the form of a double of a living person [Mid-19thC. From German, literally "double-goer."]

Dop·pler ef·fect /dópplər-/, **Dop·pler shift** *n.* a perceived change in the frequency of a wave as the distance between the source and the observer changes. For example, the sound of a siren on a moving vehicle appears to change as it approaches and passes an observer. ◊ **blueshift, redshift** [Early 20thC. Named for Christian J. *Doppler* (1803–53), the Austrian mathematician and physicist who first explained it.]

Dop·pler ra·dar *n.* a means of detecting a moving target that uses electromagnetic radiation and relies on a change in the frequency of microwave signals reflected from the target [Mid-20thC. From its use of the DOPPLER EFFECT.]

Dop·pler shift *n.* = **Doppler effect**

dop·y *adj.* = **dopey** (*informal*)

dor /dawr/ *n.* a European dung beetle that makes a droning sound as it flies. Latin name: *Geotrupes stercorarius.* [Old English *dora* "bumblebee," of uncertain origin: probably an imitation of its buzzing sound]

Dor. *abbr.* Doric

do·ra·do /də raádō/ (*plural* **-dos** *or* **-do**) *n.* **1.** = **dolphin** *n.* 2 **2.** **S AMERICAN FISH** a South American fish resembling a salmon. Genus: *Salminus.* [Early 17thC. Via Spanish, "dolphinfish," literally "gilded" (from its iridescent colors), from, ultimately, late Latin *deaurare* (see DORY[2]).]

Do·rá·ti /daw raátee/, **Antal** (1906–88) Hungarian-born U.S. conductor and composer. He was music director of several major orchestras and made over 500 recordings.

dor·bee·tle /dáwr beet'l/ *n.* = **dor**

Dor·dogne /dawr dáwnyə/ river in southwestern France. It rises in the Massif Central and flows generally westward to join the Garonne north of Bordeaux. Length: 300 mi./483 km.

Do·ri·an /dáwree ən/ *n.* **MEMBER OF ANCIENT GREEK PEOPLE** a member of a Greek-speaking people who overthrew the Mycenaean civilization in mainland Greece around 1100 B.C. They subsequently colonized Peloponnesos and other parts of the Mediterranean area. ■ *adj.* PEOPLES **OF DORIANS** relating to the Dorians or their culture [Mid-16thC. Via Latin *Dorius* "of Doris" (a region of ancient Greece) from Greek *Dōrios*, from *Dōris* "Doris."]

Do·ri·an mode *n.* a scale of notes originating in ancient Greek music and consisting of the eight notes of the diatonic scale rising from D to D

Dor·ic /dáwrik/ *n.* LANGUAGE **1.** **ANCIENT GREEK DIALECT** a dialect of ancient Greek spoken mainly in the area of modern Peloponnesos **2.** **DIALECT OF ENGLISH** a rural dialect of English, especially the dialect of Scots spoken in parts of northeastern Scotland ■ *adj.* **1.** ARCHIT **IN SIMPLE CLASSICAL ARCHITECTURAL STYLE** relating to or built in a style of architecture characterized by fluted columns with a rounded molding at the top and no base **2.** PEOPLES **OF DORIANS** relating to or typical of the Dorians of ancient Greece or their culture **3.** LANGUAGE **OF DORIC DIALECT** relating to a Doric dialect [Mid-16thC. Via Latin *Doricus* "of Doris" (a region of ancient Greece) from Greek *Dōrikos*, from *Dōris* "Doris."]

Dor·ic or·der *n.* the first of the five classical orders of architecture, characterized by fluted columns with a rounded molding at the top and no base. It was developed in Greece in the 7th century B.C.

dork /dawrk/ *n.* **1.** **OFFENSIVE TERM** an offensive term used to refer to somebody who is seen as unattractive or socially inept (*slang insult*) **2.** **PENIS** a penis (*taboo slang*) [Mid-20thC. Origin uncertain: perhaps a variant of DIRK or an alteration of DICK. The original sense was "penis."]

Dor·king /dáwrking/ *n.* a heavy domestic fowl belonging to a breed originating in England and raised mostly for eating [Late 18thC. Named for *Dorking*, a town in Surrey, England.]

dork·y /dáwrkee/ (**-i·er, -i·est**) *adj.* unintelligent or useless (*slang insult*)

dorm /dawrm/ *n.* a dormitory (*informal*) [Early 20thC. Shortening.]

dor·mant /dáwrmənt/ *adj.* **1.** BIOL **NOT ACTIVELY GROWING** in an inactive state, when growth and development slow or cease, in order to survive adverse environmental conditions **2.** **TEMPORARILY INACTIVE** temporarily inactive or not in use **3.** GEOL **NOT ERUPTING** used to describe a volcano that is not erupting, but not extinct **4.** **LATENT** latent and able to be aroused ○ *dormant feelings of uneasiness* **5.** HERALDRY **SLEEPING** in a heraldic device, portrayed in a sleeping posture [14thC. From French, literally "sleeping," present participle of *dormir* "to sleep," from Latin *dormire* (source of English *dormer* and *dormitory*).] —**dor·man·cy** *n.*

Dormer

dor·mer /dáwrmər/, **dor·mer win·dow** *n.* a window for a room within the roof space that is built out at right angles to the main roof and has its own gable [Late 16thC. From Old French *dorméor* "sleeping room," from *dormir* "to sleep" (see DORMANT). The original English sense was "dormitory or bedroom window."]

dor·mice plural of **dormouse**

dor·mie /dáwrmee/ *adj.* in golf, as many holes up on an opponent as there are holes left to play ○ *dormie four* [Mid-19thC. Origin unknown.]

dor·mi·to·ry /dáwrmi tàwree/ (*plural* **-ries**) *n.* **1.** **ROOM WITH MANY BEDS** a large room in which many people sleep, e.g., at a boarding school or in a hostel **2.** **BUILDING WHERE STUDENTS LIVE** a building used as living and sleeping quarters by college students [15thC. Via Latin *dormitorium* from, ultimately, *dormire* "to sleep" (see DORMANT).]

dor·mi·to·ry town *n. U.K.* = **bedroom community**

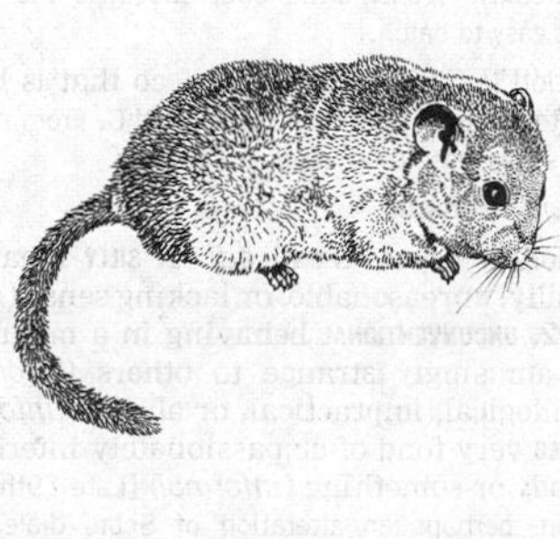

Dormouse

dor·mouse /dáwr mòwss/ (*plural* **-mice** /-mìss/) *n.* a small nocturnal rodent resembling a mouse with reddish-brown fur and a bushy tail. Dormice feed on nuts, berries, and seeds, and hibernate during the winter. Family: Gliridae. [15thC. Origin uncertain: perhaps an alteration, by association with MOUSE, of Anglo-Norman *dormeus* "sleepy," from French *dormir* (see DORMANT).]

dor·nick[1] /dáwrnik/ *n.* a heavy damask cloth [Named for *Doornik*, the Flemish name for the town of Tournai in Belgium, where it was first made]

dor·nick[2] /dáwrnik/ *n.* a small stone (*regional*) [Mid-19thC. Origin uncertain: probably from Irish *dornóg.*]

dors- *prefix.* = **dorso-**

dor·sa plural of **dorsum**

dor·sad /dáwr sàd/ *adv., adj.* toward the back of the body [Early 19thC. From Latin *dorsum* (see DORSUM).]

dor·sal /dáwrs'l/ *adj.* **1.** ANAT **OF OR ON THE BACK** relating to or situated on the back of the body **2.** BOT = **abaxial** [15thC. Directly or via French from late Latin *dorsalis*, which was formed from Latin *dorsum* (see DORSUM).] —**dor·sal·ly** *adv.*

dor·sal fin *n.* a single fin on the back of a fish or other aquatic animal e.g., a dolphin that gives it stability while swimming. ◊ **ventral fin**

Dor·set Down /dáwrsət-/ *n.* a sheep belonging to a sturdy domestic breed with dense wool and a broad head, kept for lamb production [Named for *Dorset*, a county in southwestern England, where it was bred]

Dor·set Horn *n.* a sheep belonging to a domestic breed with large horns and dense fine-textured wool [Early 19thC. Named for *Dorset*, a county in southwestern England, where it was bred.]

dor·si·flex·ion /dàwrsi flékshən/ *n.* the bending back of a hand or foot, or of the fingers or toes

dor·si·ven·tral /dàwrsi véntrəl/ *adj.* **1.** BOT **FLAT** flat, with distinct upper and lower surfaces **2.** BIOL = **dorsoventral** *adj.* 1 —**dor·si·ven·tral·i·ty** /-ven trállətee/ *n.* —**dor·si·ven·tral·ly** /-véntrəlee/ *adv.*

dorso- *prefix.* back, upper surface ○ *dorsolateral* [From Latin *dorsum*]

dor·so·lat·er·al /dàwrsō láttərəl/ *adj.* relating to or involving both the back and the side —**dor·so·lat·er·al·ly** *adv.*

dor·so·ven·tral /dàwrsō véntrəl/ *adj.* **1.** BOT = **dorsiventral** *adj.* 1 **2.** BIOL **EXTENDING FROM BACK TO FRONT** extending from the back of the body to the front

dor·sum /dáwrsəm/ (*plural* **-sa** /-sə/) *n.* the back or upper surface of a part of the body, e.g., the hand or foot (*technical*) [Late 18thC. From Latin, "the back" (source also of English *dorsal, dossier*, and *endorse*).]

do·ry[1] /dáwree/ (*plural* **-ries**) *n.* **1.** **SMALL BOAT** a small boat used for various purposes e.g., patrolling a harbor or transporting people from a larger vessel to the shore **2.** **FISHING BOAT** a narrow flat-bottomed fishing boat with high sides [Early 18thC. Origin uncertain: perhaps from Miskito *dóri*, literally "dugout."]

do·ry[2] /dáwree/ (*plural* **-ries**) *n.* a fish with a deep flattened body, spiny fins, and an extendable mouth, found near the ocean bottom. Family: Zeidae. [14thC. From French *dorée*, the feminine past participle, used as a noun, of *dorer* "to gild," from late Latin *deaurare* "to gild over," from Latin *aurum* "gold."]

dos-à-dos /dṑzə dṓ, dṑs-/ *n., interj.* DANCE = **do-si-do** [Mid-19thC. From French, literally "back to back" (the original English sense), from *dos* "back" (source of English *dossier*), from, ultimately, Latin *dorsum* (see DORSUM).]

dos·age /dṓssij/ *n.* **1.** PHARM **DOSE OF DRUG** the amount of a drug to be taken at any one time and the intervals at which it should be taken ○ *Do not exceed the recommended dosage.* **2.** MED **ADMINISTRATION OR DETERMINATION OF DOSE** the administration of a drug in measured amounts, or the determination of the correct or required amount **3.** **ADDING EXTRA INGREDIENT** the addition of an extra ingredient to something, especially wine

dose /dṑss/ *n.* **1.** PHARM, MED **PRESCRIBED AMOUNT OF MEDICATION** a measured quantity of medication, e.g., drugs or radiotherapy, administered at any one time or at stated intervals **2.** MED **VENEREAL DISEASE** an infection with a sexually transmitted disease (*slang*) **3.** MED, SCI **EXPOSURE TO RADIATION** the amount of radiation to which somebody or something is exposed during a specified time, either accidentally or as part of an experiment or medical treatment **4.** **EXTRA INGREDIENT** an additional ingredient, e.g., syrup added to wine to fortify it ■ *vt.* (**dosed, dos·ing, dos·es**) **1.** MED **GIVE MEDICINE TO** to administer medication to somebody ○ *I've been dosing myself up with flu remedies all week.* **2.** PHARM, MED **MEASURE OUT MEDICATION** to prescribe or administer the correct or required amount of medication **3.** **ADD EXTRA INGREDIENT** to add an extra ingredient to something [15thC. Via French from, ultimately, Greek *dosis* "prescribed portion" (literally "a giving"), from *didonai* "to give" (source of English *anecdote* and *antidote*).]

do·sem·e·ter /dóss meetər/ *n.* = **dosimeter**

do-si-do /dòssi dṓ/ *n.* (*plural* **do-si-dos**) **FIGURE IN SQUARE DANCING** a movement in square dancing in which two dancers pass each other and circle back to back ■ *interj.* **CIRCLE BACK TO BACK** used to instruct dancers to perform a do-si-do [Early 20thC. Alteration of DOS-À-DOS.] —**do-si-do** *vi.*

do·sim·e·ter /dō símmətər/ *n.* an instrument for measuring the amount of radiation absorbed by somebody or something, often fixed in a working area or worn by personnel who might be exposed to radiation [Late 19thC. Coined from DOSE + -METER.] —**do·si·met·ric** /dòssi méttrik/ *adj.* —**do·sim·e·trist** *n.* —**do·sim·e·try** *n.*

Dos Pas·sos /dōss pássōss/, **John** (1896–1970) U.S. writer. He is best known for his *U.S.A.* trilogy (1930–36), a critical portrait of U.S. life. Full name **John Roderigo Dos Passos**

doss /doss/ *vi.* (**dossed, doss·ing, doss·es**) *U.K.* **SLEEP ON MAKESHIFT BED** to sleep or settle down to sleep, especially on an improvised bed (*slang*) ○ *Can I doss down on your floor tonight?* ■ *n. U.K.* **IMPROVISED OR BASIC BED** a bed for the night or a place to sleep, especially a makeshift one or one in a doss-house [Late 18thC. Origin uncertain: perhaps via obsolete *dorse, doss* "the back" from, ultimately, Latin *dorsum* (see DORSUM). If so, the underlying notion is probably "to lie on your back."]

dos·sal /dóss'l/, **dos·sel** *n.* a rich hanging for the back of an altar or the sides of a chancel in a church [Mid-17thC. Via medieval Latin *dossale* from, ultimately, Latin *dorsum* (see DORSUM).]

doss·house /dóss hòwss/ (*plural* **-hous·es** /-zəz/) *n. U.K.* = **flophouse** (*slang*)

dos·si·er /dóssee ày/ *n.* a collection of documents relating to a particular person or topic [Late 19thC. From French (originally "bunch of papers with a label on the back"), from *dos* "the back," from, ultimately, Latin *dorsum* (see DORSUM).]

dost /dust/ 2nd person present singular of **do** (*archaic*)

AKG London

Fyodor Dostoyevsky

Dos·toy·ev·sky /dòstə yéfskee/, **Fyodor** (1821–81) Russian novelist. He is author of *Crime and Punishment* (1866) and *The Brothers Karamazov* (1879–80). Full name **Fyodor Mikhaylovich Dostoyevsky**

dot[1] /dot/ *n.* 1. **WRITTEN OR PRINTED POINT** a small round written or printed mark, e.g., that placed above the body of the lowercase letter "i" or one of a set of three replacing missing text 2. **SPOT OR SPECK** a small round mark, spot, or speck ○ *The ship was just a dot on the horizon.* 3. **SMALL AMOUNT** a very small amount, especially of butter used for basting 4. COMPUT **E-MAIL PUNCTUATION MARK** a punctuation mark used to separate the various components of an internet address 5. COMMUNICATION **MARK USED IN MORSE CODE** the shorter of the two signaling elements used in Morse code, represented as a small round mark 6. MUSIC **SYMBOL PLACED AFTER NOTE IN MUSIC** in written or printed music, a small round mark placed after a note or rest to increase its value by half 7. LOGIC **MARK INDICATING LOGICAL CONJUNCTION** a small round mark used in logic to join compound sentences when both elements are true ■ *v.* (**dot·ted, dot·ting, dots**) 1. *vt.* **MARK WITH DOT** to mark something with a dot ○ *dot your i's* 2. *vt.* **SPRINKLE WITH DOTS** to scatter or sprinkle something with spots, specks, or small amounts of something ○ *Dot the surface with butter.* 3. *vi.* **MAKE SMALL ROUND MARK** to make a small round mark [Old English *dott* "head of a boil." Probably from, ultimately, a prehistoric Germanic word meaning "lump, plug."] —**dot·ter** *n.* ◇ **dot the i's and cross the t's** to be careful with the details of something ○ *We've drawn up the basis of the agreement but we have yet to dot the i's and cross the t's.* ◇ **on the dot (of)** exactly at the specified time ○ *arrived on the dot* ○ *was expected to get here on the dot of nine*

dot[2] /dot/ *n.* in law, a woman's dowry [Mid-19thC. Via Old French from Latin *dot-*, the stem of *dos* "dowry" (see DOWER).] —**do·tal** /dṓt'l/ *adj.*

DOT *abbr.* Department of Transportation

dot·age /dṓtij/ *n.* 1. **WEAKNESS ASSOCIATED WITH AGE** the lack of strength or concentration sometimes believed to be characteristic of old age (*offensive*) 2. **DANGEROUS INFATUATION** infatuation leading to folly (*archaic*) ○ *"Nay, but this dotage of our general's O'erflows the measure"* (William Shakespeare, *Anthony & Cleopatra*; 1606) [14thC. From DOTE.]

do·ta·tion /dō táysh'n/ *n.* in law, the giving of a dowry (*formal*) [14thC. From DOT[2].]

dote /dōt/ (**dot·ed, dot·ing, dotes**) *vi.* 1. **SHOW EXTREME FONDNESS** to be excessively fond of somebody or something ○ *They dote on their grandchildren.* 2. **LACK CLEAR THOUGHT** to lack clear thought in a way sometimes associated with old age (*archaic*) [12thC. Origin uncertain: perhaps from Middle Low German or Middle Dutch *doten* "to be foolish" (the original English sense), of unknown origin.] —**dot·er** *n.*

doth /duth/ 3rd person present singular of **do** (*archaic*)

Do·than /dṓthən/ city in southeastern Alabama, southwest of Phenix City. Population: 55,944 (1996).

dot·ing /dṓting/ *adj.* expressing and demonstrating great love and fondness for somebody or something ○ *doting parents of two new babies* —**dot·ing·ly** *adv.*

dot ma·trix *n.* a grid of dots selectively lighted or colored to display or print letters, numbers, and other symbols

dot pitch *n.* a measure of the clarity or sharpness of an image on a computer screen, based on the amount of white space between the pixels or dots that form the image

dot prod·uct *n.* MATH = **scalar product**

dots per inch *n.* full form of **dpi**

dot·ted /dóttəd/ *adj.* 1. **WITH DOTS** marked or patterned with dots 2. MUSIC **INCREASED IN VALUE BY HALF** used to describe a note or rest increased in value by half 3. **COVERED WITH SPECKS** scattered or sprinkled with small things or larger things seen from a distance ○ *a sky dotted with stars* 4. **RANDOMLY ARRAYED** spread randomly over a wide area ○ *a lawn dotted with hoop-skirted belles.*

dot·ted line *n.* a printed line formed from dots or dashes, especially one on which somebody is to write something such as a signature

dot·ted swiss *n.* a cotton fabric patterned with raised dots [Shortening of *Swiss muslin*]

dot·ter·el /dóttrəl/ (*plural* **-els** *or* **-el**), **dot·trel** (*plural* **-trels** *or* **-trel**) *n.* a reddish-brown Eurasian bird of the plover family with white markings on the head and neck. Latin name: *Eudromias morinellus.* [15thC. Formed from DOTE + the suffix *-rel* (from Old French *-erel*), literally "foolish little one," because the Eurasian plover is easy to catch.]

dot·tle /dótt'l/ *n.* the plug of tobacco that is left in a pipe after it has been smoked [15thC. From DOT[1]. The original sense was "plug, stopper."]

dot·trel *n.* = **dotterel**

dot·ty /dóttee/ (**-ti·er, -ti·est**) *adj.* 1. **SILLY** regarded as being silly, unreasonable, or lacking sense (*informal insult*) 2. **UNCONVENTIONAL** behaving in a manner that seems amusingly strange to others (*informal*) 3. **ABSURD** illogical, impractical, or absurd (*informal*) 4. **INFATUATED** very fond of or passionately interested in somebody or something (*informal*) [Late 19thC. Origin uncertain: perhaps an alteration of Scots dialect *dottle* "fool," from DOTE, or perhaps directly from DOTE. First recorded in the sense "walking unsteadily."] —**dot·ti·ly** *adv.* —**dot·ti·ness** *n.*

Dou·ay Bi·ble /dóo ay-/, **Dou·ay Ver·sion** *n.* 1. **TRANSLATION OF LATIN BIBLE** a Roman Catholic translation of the Latin Vulgate version of the Bible into English, written in the early 17th century 2. **COPY OF DOUAY BIBLE** a copy of the Douay Bible [Mid-19thC. Named for *Douay* (modern DOUAI), where it was completed in 1609.]

dou·ble /dúbb'l/ *adj.* 1. **BEING TWICE AS MUCH OR MANY** being twice as much in size, number, or value 2. **HAVING TWO LIKE PARTS** consisting of two identical, similar, or equal parts 3. **MEANT FOR TWO PEOPLE** designed or intended for two people ○ *reserved a double hotel room* 4. **FITTING A DOUBLE BED** used to describe bedding of a size that will fit onto a double bed 5. **TWO-LAYERED** consisting of two layers 6. **FOLDED OVER ONCE** folded in two, or bent over 7. **OF TWO ELEMENTS** consisting of two different elements 8. **ACTING IN CONTRASTING OR OPPOSING WAYS** acting one way while feeling very differently, especially when this involves hypocrisy or deceit 9. BOT **HAVING EXTRA PETALS** used to describe flowers that have more petals than normal, or plants that have flowers of this type 10. MUSIC **SOUNDING AN OCTAVE BELOW** used to describe a musical instrument sounding an octave lower than the written music indicates ■ *adv.* 1. **TWICE AS MUCH** twice as much as normal ○ *had to pay double to get in* 2. **IN TWO LAYERS** so as to form two layers ■ *n.* 1. **TWO TOGETHER** two viewed or regarded together 2. **TWICE THE NORMAL AMOUNT** twice the normal or standard amount ○ *He offered me double.* 3. BEVERAGES **TWO MEASURES OF DRINK** a drink containing two single measures, especially of spirits (*informal*) 4. **DUPLICATE IN APPEARANCE** somebody or something that looks very like another, especially a living person bearing a strong resemblance to somebody else 5. **GHOST IDENTICAL TO LIVING PERSON** an apparition that closely resembles a living person 6. CINEMA **STAND-IN FOR MOVIE STAR** somebody who replaces a movie actor in certain scenes, e.g., those that involve danger, special skill, or nudity 7. HORSERACING **BET ON TWO RACES** a bet on two races, in which any winnings from the first become the stake for the second (*informal*) 8. SPORTS **SUCCESS IN TWO EVENTS** success in two events or competitions in the same or successive years or series, or against the same opponent 9. BRIDGE **CALL INCREASING SCORE OR BID** in an auction at bridge, a call that increases the score for succeeding or failing in a contract 10. TENNIS **DOUBLE FAULT** a double fault (*informal*) 11. BASEBALL = **two-base hit** 12. MIL **FAST MARCHING PACE** a fast marching pace at twice the usual speed 13. **ABRUPT DIRECTIONAL CHANGE** a sharp change of direction 14. PRINTING = **doublet** *n.* 3 ■ **dou·bles** *npl.* RACKET GAMES **RACKET GAME BETWEEN PAIRS OF PLAYERS** a racket game played between two pairs of players ■ *v.* (**-bled, -bling, -bles**) 1. *vti.* **INCREASE TWOFOLD** to make something twice as large or numerous, or become twice as much or many ○ *We doubled our profits the following year.* 2. *vt.* **FOLD IN TWO** to fold or bend something in two 3. *vi.* **HAVE SECOND FUNCTION** to have a second or secondary function ○ *His felt hat doubles as a water pail.* 4. *vi.* CINEMA **ACT AS STAND-IN** to replace a movie actor in certain scenes 5. *vi.* THEATER **PLAY SECOND ROLE** to play an additional part in the same performance 6. *vt.* MUSIC **DUPLICATE A MUSICAL PART** to duplicate a part, either at the same pitch or an octave above or below 7. *vi.* MUSIC **PLAY MORE THAN ONE MUSICAL INSTRUMENT** to play one or more musical instruments, in addition to the principal one ○ *a violinist who doubles on cello* 8. *vi.* BRIDGE **ANNOUNCE BRIDGE DOUBLE** to announce a double as a bid in an auction at bridge 9. *vt.* CHESS **PLACE PIECES NEXT TO EACH OTHER** to place two chess pieces of the same type and color together ○ *double your opponent's pawns* 10. *vi.* BASEBALL **MAKE TWO-BASE HIT** to make a hit that gives the batter time to run to second base 11. *vt.* BASEBALL **ADVANCE WITH TWO-BASE HIT** to advance a teammate on the bases by making a two-base hit ○ *double a runner home* [12thC. Via Old French *do(u)bler* from Latin *duplare*, from *duplus*, literally "twofold" (source of English *duplicate*) from *duo* "two."] —**doubleness** /dúbb'lnəss/ *n.* ◇ **on the double** right away and as quickly as possible ○ *told the children to get into lines on the double*

double back *vi.* to turn around and retrace your steps

double over *vi.* to bend from the waist in response to pain or laughter

double up *vi.* 1. **SHARE WITH SOMEBODY ELSE** to share something with another person ○ *There weren't enough beds, so some of the children had to double up.* 2. **BEND BODY SHARPLY** to bend the body over sharply

dou·ble-act·ing *adj.* 1. ENG **WITH PISTONS ACTING BOTH WAYS** with one or more pistons that move in both directions, giving two strokes per cycle 2. CONSTR **ACTING IN OPPOSITE DIRECTIONS** acting in opposite directions from a central point

dou·ble a·gent *n.* somebody who works as a spy for one government but supplies secret information about that government to another

dou·ble bar *n.* a symbol, ‖, that marks the end of a piece of music or the end of its principal sections

dou·ble-bar·reled *adj.* **1.** ARMS **WITH TWO BARRELS** used to describe a gun that has two barrels **2. WITH TWO PURPOSES OR INTERPRETATIONS** serving two purposes, or open to two possible interpretations

dou·ble bass *n.* the largest and lowest in pitch of the instruments of the violin family, used in the modern symphony orchestra. It is also commonly found in jazz and dance bands, where it is usually plucked rather than bowed.

dou·ble-bass *adj.* used to describe an instrument that is larger and lower in pitch than others of its group

dou·ble bas·soon *n.* = **contrabassoon**

dou·ble bed *n.* a bed intended for two people

dou·ble bind *n.* **1. DILEMMA WITH NO GOOD ALTERNATIVES** an unresolvable situation from which there is no escape without undesirable consequences **2. DILEMMA CAUSED BY CONTRADICTORY DEMANDS** a situation in which conflicting demands make it impossible to do the right thing

dou·ble-blind *adj.* used to describe an experiment in which neither the experimenters nor the subjects know which of two similar treatments is genuine and which is a control procedure

dou·ble boil·er *n.* a pair of cooking pots, one fitting on top of and partly inside the other. Food cooks gently in the upper pot while water simmers in the lower pot.

dou·ble bond *n.* a chemical bond in which two atoms share two pairs of electrons

dou·ble-breast·ed *adj.* used to describe a coat or jacket that has a large overlap at the front, usually with two sets of buttons

dou·ble bri·dle *n.* a bridle with four reins and a bit with two rings on each side

dou·ble-ceil·ing *n.* the housing of two prisoners in a space designed for only one

dou·ble check *n.* **1. SECOND CHECK OF SOMETHING** a second examination to make sure **2.** CHESS **CHECK FROM TWO PIECES SIMULTANEOUSLY** a situation in chess in which a king is in check from two pieces at once

dou·ble-check (**dou·ble-checked, dou·ble-check·ing, dou·ble-checks**) *vti.* to check something twice or for a second time ○ *I double-checked that the windows were locked.*

dou·ble chin *n.* a fold of flesh or loose skin under the chin —**dou·ble-chinned** *adj.*

dou·ble-click (**dou·ble-clicked, dou·ble-click·ing, dou·ble-clicks**) *vti.* to press and release a mouse button twice in rapid succession. Double-clicking is used in many programs to invoke specific commands.

dou·ble-clutch *vi.* to use the clutch twice when changing gear in a motor vehicle, first to put the gear lever into neutral and rev the engine, second to engage the new gear. U.K. = **double-declutch**

dou·ble co·co·nut *n.* = **coco-de-mer**

dou·ble con·cer·to *n.* a concerto for two solo instruments

dou·ble cream *n. U.K.* cream with a high fat content that can be whipped to make it thicker

dou·ble cross *n.* a genetic cross in which a new hybrid is produced from parents each of which is a first-generation hybrid of pure strains

dou·ble-cross *vt.* (**dou·ble-crossed, dou·ble-crossing, dou·ble-cross·es**) **BETRAY ASSOCIATE** to betray or cheat somebody who believes that he or she is a partner or associate in the same, often criminal, enterprise ■ *n.* **BETRAYAL OF ASSOCIATE** an act of double-crossing a partner or associate —**dou·ble-cross·er** *n.* —**double-cross·ing** *adj.*

dou·ble dag·ger *n.* the printed character (‡), used to mark a cross-reference, especially to a footnote

dou·ble date *n.* an arrangement for two couples to go out together socially as a foursome

dou·ble-date (**dou·ble-dat·ed, dou·ble-dat·ing, dou·ble-dates**) *vi.* to go out socially as a couple with another couple

Dou·ble·day /dúbb'l dày/, **Abner** (1819–93) U.S. army officer. He fought in the Mexican War (1846–48) and for the Union in the Civil War (1861–65). He is traditionally thought of as the creator of baseball, even though a similar game antedated his lifetime.

dou·ble-deal·ing *n.* deliberately deceitful behavior, especially involving the betrayal of a partner or associate —**dou·ble-deal·er** *n.* —**double-deal·ing** *adj.*

Double-decker

dou·ble-deck·er *n.* **1. SOMETHING WITH TWO LAYERS** something that has two layers, levels, or tiers ○ *a double-decker sandwich* **2.** TRANSP **BUS WITH TWO DECKS** a bus with an upper and a lower deck

dou·ble-de·clutch *vi. U.K.* = **double-clutch**

dou·ble de·com·po·si·tion *n.* a chemical reaction in which two compounds exchange one or more of their components so that two new compounds are formed

dou·ble de·scent *n.* the use in some societies of sometimes mother's and sometimes father's ancestry in establishing different features of social identity or status

dou·ble dig·ging *n.* AGRIC the process of digging a plot of ground to twice the normal depth and transferring soil from the lower level to the top in order to revitalize it before planting

dou·ble-dig·it *adj.* being between 10 and 99 ○ *double-digit inflation*

dou·ble dip·ping *n.* the fraudulent receipt of two incomes from the government, e.g., by holding a government job and collecting a government pension at the same time (*informal*) —**dou·ble dip·per** *n.*

dou·ble doors *npl.* two full-length doors that meet in the middle of the doorway when closed

dou·ble-dot·ted *adj.* MUSIC used to describe a musical note that has two dots following it to indicate that the length of the note is to be increased by three quarters

dou·ble drib·ble *n.* an illegal move in basketball, in which the player dribbles the ball with both hands simultaneously or, having stopped, starts to dribble again

dou·ble Dutch *n.* **1.** GAME **SKIPPING GAME** a skipping game in which players jump over two ropes that are swung crossing over each other by two turners **2.** *U.K.* LANGUAGE **INCOMPREHENSIBLE TALK OR WRITING** speech or writing that cannot be understood at all (*informal*)

dou·ble-du·ty *adj.* designed to do two different jobs

dou·ble-edged *adj.* **1. AMBIGUOUS** having two possible meanings or interpretations, especially one that is apparently innocuous and another that is intentionally cutting or malicious **2. DOING TWO THINGS** achieving two purposes or having two effects **3. HAVING TWO CUTTING EDGES** having a blade sharpened on both edges

dou·ble ef·fect *n.* the ethical principle that intentionally doing wrong is impermissible, even if the action has good consequences, and that intentionally doing right is permissible, even if the action has bad consequences

dou·ble en·ten·dre /-aan taándrə, -aaN taáNdrə/ *n.* **1. SEXUALLY AMBIGUOUS REMARK** a remark that is ambiguous and sexually suggestive **2. AMBIGUITY WITH SEXUALLY SUGGESTIVE MEANING** ambiguity in which one meaning is sexually suggestive [Late 17thC. From obsolete French, literally "double understanding."]

dou·ble en·try *n.* a bookkeeping system that records each transaction as a credit to one account and a debit from another

dou·ble ex·po·sure *n.* **1. SUPERIMPOSING OF PHOTOGRAPHIC IMAGES** the exposure of two separate images on a single piece of photographic film **2. PHOTOGRAPH WITH TWO SUPERIMPOSED IMAGES** a photograph that contains one image superimposed on another

dou·ble-faced *adj.* **1. FINISHED ON BOTH SIDES** used to describe fabrics that are finished on both sides **2. TWO-FACED** behaving insincerely or deceitfully **3. HAVING TWO USABLE SIDES** having two faces or sides that can both be used ○ *a double-faced tape*

dou·ble fault *n.* in tennis, two consecutive serves that land outside the service box or in the net, with the result that the server loses a point

dou·ble-fault (**dou·ble-fault·ed, dou·ble-fault·ing, dou·ble-faults**) *vi.* in tennis, to make two consecutive faulty serves, and lose a point as a result

dou·ble fea·ture *n.* a program consisting of two full-length movies shown consecutively

dou·ble fig·ures *npl. U.K.* the numbers with two digits, from 10 to 99

dou·ble flat *n.* MUSIC **1. SYMBOL LOWERING NOTE TWO HALF TONES** a symbol, 𝄫, placed in front of a musical note to indicate that the pitch of the note is to be lowered by two half tones **2. NOTE WITH DOUBLE FLAT** a musical note marked with a double flat

dou·ble-head·er *n.* **1.** SPORTS **TWO CONSECUTIVE GAMES** two games played consecutively by the same teams, especially in baseball **2. TRAIN WITH TWO LOCOMOTIVES** a train pulled by two locomotives coupled together

dou·ble he·lix *n.* the molecular structure of DNA, consisting of a pair of polynucleotide strands connected by a series of hydrogen bonds and wound in opposing spirals

dou·ble-hung *adj.* used to describe a window that has two sashes, each sliding vertically in its own grooves

dou·ble in·dem·ni·ty *n.* the guaranteed payout of double the face value of a life insurance policy if the policyholder dies in an accident

dou·ble jeop·ard·y *n.* LAW the prosecution of somebody a second time for something that he or she has already been tried for. It is prohibited by the U.S. Constitution.

dou·ble-joint·ed *adj.* used to describe a joint or limb that has unusual flexibility and can bend in the opposite direction to the normal one, or somebody with such joints —**dou·ble-joint·ed·ness** *n.*

dou·ble knit *n.* a knitted fabric of double thickness

dou·ble life *n.* a situation in which somebody is simultaneously involved in two sets of circumstances or relationships and keeps each completely separate, and usually secret, from the other

dou·ble ne·ga·tion *n.* the principle that a proposition and the negation of its negation mean one and the same thing

dou·ble neg·a·tive *n.* a phrase containing two negatives

WORD KEY: USAGE

Double negatives of the type *I don't know nothing*, in which two negatives close together are intended to reinforce each other, are considered illiterate in current standard English, acceptable though they were in earlier usage. These are to be distinguished from the acceptable, if somewhat uncommon, type *That's not a good idea, I don't think*, in which the reinforcing negatives appear in different clauses. The more usual type of acceptable double negative is seen in *It is not impossible* (= it is distinctly possible), in which the negatives are intended to cancel each other out. This is thought of as a figure of speech called litotes.

dou·ble oc·cu·pan·cy *n.* the use of a hotel room or other accommodation by two people (*hyphenated when used before a noun*)

dou·ble or noth·ing *n.* a bet in gambling where a player who owes money has the debt doubled or canceled depending on the outcome of the next play

dou·ble or quits *n.* U.K. = **double or nothing**

dou·ble-page spread *n.* a feature or article that fills two facing pages of a newspaper or magazine

dou·ble-park (**dou·ble-parked, dou·ble-park·ing, dou·ble-parks**) *vti.* to park a vehicle alongside another already parked and so cause an obstruction —**dou·ble-park·er** *n.* —**dou·ble-park·ing** *n.*

dou·ble play *n.* a baseball play in which two players are put out

dou·ble pneu·mo·nia *n.* pneumonia affecting both lungs

dou·ble quote *n.* a quotation mark that consists of two marks ("), not one

dou·bler /dúbblər/ *n.* an electronic device that doubles an input frequency or voltage

dou·ble reed *n.* 1. REED IN WOODWIND INSTRUMENTS a reed in the oboe, English horn, or bassoon consisting of two halves that vibrate against each other when air passes through them (*hyphenated when used before a noun*) 2. WOODWIND INSTRUMENT WITH DOUBLE REED a woodwind instrument that has a double reed

dou·ble re·frac·tion *n.* = **birefringence**

dou·ble rhyme *n.* a two-syllable rhyme e.g., "cooking" and "looking"

dou·bles /dúbb'lz/ (*plural* **-bles**) *n. Carib* a popular and cheap East Indian fast food consisting of a sandwich of curried chickpeas in two "baras," or fried seasoned batter patties (*informal*)

dou·ble salt *n.* a salt such as alum that dissolves in solution as two substances but crystallizes as one

dou·ble sauce·pan *n. U.K.* = **double boiler**

dou·ble sculls *n.* a race between boats for two rowers who sit one behind the other and pull two oars each

dou·ble sharp *n.* MUSIC 1. SYMBOL RAISING NOTE TWO HALF TONES a symbol, 𝄪 placed in front of a musical note to indicate that the pitch of the note is to be raised by two half tones 2. NOTE WITH DOUBLE SHARP a musical note marked with a double sharp

dou·ble-sid·ed *adj.* used or usable on both sides

dou·ble-space (**dou·ble-spaced, dou·ble-spac·ing, dou·ble-spac·es**) *vt.* to type or print text with a blank line between typed or printed lines

dou·ble·speak /dúbb'l spēek/ *n.* = **double talk** *n.* 1

dou·ble stan·dard *n.* a principle, rule, or expectation that is applied unfairly to different groups, one group usually being condemned for the slightest offense while the other is treated far more leniently

dou·ble star *n.* 1. = **binary star** 2. = **optical double star**

dou·ble-stop *vi.* (**dou·ble-stopped, dou·ble-stop·ping, dou·ble-stops**) PLAY TWO STRINGS TOGETHER to draw the bow of a stringed instrument simultaneously across two strings, producing two tones ■ *n.* TWO-NOTE CHORD ON STRINGED INSTRUMENT a musical chord of two notes played on a stringed instrument —**dou·ble-stop·ping** *n.*

dou·blet /dúbblət/ *n.* 1. CLOTHES MAN'S JACKET a man's close-fitting jacket, with or without sleeves, popular in Europe between the 15th and 17th centuries 2. LING WORD WITH SAME ROOT AS ANOTHER either of two similar words in a language that have the same historical root but have arrived at their current forms via different languages, e.g., "mood" and "mode" 3. PRINTING REPEATED PRINTED LETTER, WORD, OR LINE a repeated letter, word, or line that is printed in error 4. OPTICS PAIR OF LENSES USED TOGETHER a pair of lenses designed to be used together so that one lens cancels out the distortions in the other 5. MINERALS FAKE GEM a fake gem made by sticking two pieces of glass together with a colored layer between them or by sticking a thin layer of a gem on a base ■ **dou·blets** *npl.* 1. GAMBLING DICE WITH SAME NUMBER THROWN a pair of dice thrown simultaneously each showing the same number of spots 2. GAME WORD GAME a word game in which one word is transformed into another by substituting letters, the object being to achieve this in the minimum number of substitutions [14thC. From French, literally "something doubled."]

dou·ble tack·le *n.* a pair of double pulleys for lifting or pulling

dou·ble take *n.* a reaction of surprise or astonishment after an initial hesitation

dou·ble talk *n.* 1. TALK INTENDED TO CONFUSE OR DECEIVE intentionally ambiguous or confusing talk 2. MIXTURE OF WORDS AND NONSENSE SYLLABLES speech that includes a mixture of real words and nonsense syllables

dou·ble-team (**dou·ble-teamed, dou·ble-team·ing, dou·ble-teams**) *vt.* in various team games, to use two players to guard an opponent

dou·ble teeth *npl. U.K.* back teeth; teeth from the canines back (*regional*) ○ *She's only two. She hasn't got her double teeth yet.* [From their having two points or cusps]

dou·ble·think /dúbb'l thìnk/ *n.* the conscious or unconscious holding of two opposing beliefs at the same time [Coined by George Orwell in *1984* (1949)]

dou·ble time *n.* 1. FIN DOUBLE PAY double the usual rate of pay 2. MUSIC DOUBLY FAST MUSICAL TEMPO a tempo twice as fast as the basic tempo of a piece of music, or a passage played at that speed 3. MIL FAST MARCHING PACE a fast marching pace of 180 steps per minute

dou·ble-time (**dou·ble-timed, dou·ble-tim·ing, dou·ble-times**) *vi.* MIL to march at the fast pace of 180 steps per minute

dou·ble·ton /dúbb'ltən/ *n.* two cards of the same suit that are the only cards of that suit dealt to a player [Early 20thC. Modeled on SINGLETON.]

dou·ble-tongu·ing *n.* the production of a rapid series of staccato notes on a wind or brass instrument by using rapid movements of the tongue —**dou·ble-tongue** *vi.*

dou·ble·tree /dúbb'l trēe/ *n.* a bar used to harness two horses to a carriage or other vehicle [Modeled on SINGLETREE]

dou·ble-u *n.* the letter w

dou·ble vi·sion *n.* a condition in which two images of the same object are seen simultaneously because the eyes are not focusing properly. Technical name **diplopia**

dou·ble wham·my *n.* two setbacks or unpleasant experiences occurring very close together (*slang*)

dou·ble·wide /dúbb'l wīd/ *n.* a manufactured or mobile home that is twice the width of a standard mobile home

dou·bloon /də blóon/ *n.* a former Spanish gold coin [Early 17thC. From Spanish *doblón*, from *dobla* "double," from, ultimately, Latin *duplus* "double."]

dou·blure /də blóor/ *n.* a lining, especially one made of leather or highly decorated, inside the cover of a book [Late 19thC. From French, literally "lining."]

dou·bly /dúbblee/ *adv.* 1. IN TWO WAYS in two different ways 2. TO DOUBLE DEGREE to twice the usual degree or extent

doubt /dowt/ *vt.* (**doubt·ed, doubt·ing, doubts**) 1. THINK SOMETHING UNLIKELY to feel unconvinced or uncertain about something, or think that something is unlikely 2. NOT TRUST SOMEBODY OR SOMETHING to suspect that something is not true, likely, or genuine, or that somebody is not sincere or trustworthy ■ *n.* 1. UNCERTAINTY OR MISTRUST a feeling or state of uncertainty, especially as to whether something is true, likely, or genuine, or as to whether somebody is sincere or trustworthy 2. PHILOS METHOD OF PHILOSOPHICAL QUESTIONING the method of questioning claims to knowledge, especially in the philosophy of Descartes 3. FEAR fear (*archaic*) [13thC. Via Old French *doter* from Latin *dubitare* "to be uncertain," from *dubius* "uncertain" (source of English *dubious*). Earlier also "to fear."] —**doubt·a·ble** *adj.* —**doubt·a·bly** *adv.* —**doubt·ing·ly** *adv.* ◇ **beyond doubt** completely certain ◇ **no doubt** almost definitely ◇ **open to doubt, in doubt** not certain, settled, foreseeable with confidence, or finally proved

WORD KEY: SYNONYMS

See Synonyms at ***doubtful***.

doubt·er /dówtər/ *n.* somebody who is skeptical or unsure about something, especially a religion or a political system

doubt·ful /dówtfəl/ *adj.* 1. UNSURE unsure or undecided about something 2. UNLIKELY not likely to happen or be successful 3. INVITING SUSPICION probably not true, honest, reputable, or genuine —**doubt·ful·ness** *n.*

WORD KEY: SYNONYMS

doubtful, uncertain, unsure, in doubt, have doubts, have reservations, dubious, skeptical

CORE MEANING: feeling doubt or uncertainty

doubtful a general term suggesting uncertainty or hesitancy; **uncertain** a less strong term than "doubtful," suggesting that somebody is hesitant or undecided; **unsure** another term for "uncertain"; **in doubt** a term used to emphasize that somebody or something is in a state of uncertainty or indecision; **have doubts** a term suggesting uncertainty or lack of confidence; **dubious** a term suggesting strong doubt and, often, suspicion; **skeptical** a term used to suggest that somebody doubts something is true or that something will happen.

doubt·ful·ly /dówtfəlee/ *adv.* with or expressing doubt

doubt·ing Thom·as (*plural* **doubt·ing Thom·as·es**) *n.* somebody who is generally doubtful or skeptical about things or refuses to believe something until given proof [From Jesus Christ's apostle who doubted in the Bible (John 20:24–9)]

doubt·less /dówtləss/ *adv.* 1. CERTAINLY certainly or almost certainly ○ *That was doubtless their intention, as these documents show.* 2. PROBABLY probably or presumably ○ *You would doubtless have been informed in due course.* ■ *adj.* (*formal*) 1. CERTAIN impossible to doubt or deny 2. HAVING NO DOUBT having no doubts or suspicions —**doubt·less·ly** *adv.* —**doubt·less·ness** *n.*

douc /dook/ *n.* a rare yellow-faced monkey of the langur family that lives in Southeast Asia. Latin name: *Pygathrix nemaeus.* [Late 18thC. From Vietnamese *douc.*]

dou·ceur /doo súr/ *n.* something given as a tip or a bribe [14thC. From French *douceur* "sweetness favor," from *douce* "sweet" (see DOUCE).]

douche /doosh/ *n.* 1. CLEANING BODY BY SQUIRTING WATER a cleaning of part of the body, with a jet of water or air 2. EQUIPMENT PRODUCING CLEANSING WATER JET a piece of equipment that produces a jet of water or air for a douche ■ *vti.* (**douched, douch·ing, douch·es**) CLEAN BODY WITH WATER JET to clean a part of the body or body cavity with a jet of water or air [Mid-18thC. Via French from Italian *doccia* "water pipe," from, ultimately, the Latin stem *duction-* "leading (through a pipe)."]

dough /dō/ *n.* 1. COOK MIXTURE OF FLOUR AND WATER a soft elastic mixture of flour and water, often with other ingredients such as yeast, oil, butter, salt, and sugar, that becomes bread or pastry when baked 2. MONEY cash and other financial assets (*slang*) [Old English *dāg*. Ultimately from an Indo-European word meaning "to form" that is also the ancestor of English *effigy, faint,* and *lady.*]

dough·boy /dṓ bòy/ *n.* 1. FOOD BREAD DUMPLING a ball of bread dough boiled, steamed, or fried as a dumpling 2. **dough boy, Dough boy** MIL U.S. SOLDIER a U.S. infantryman in World War I

dough·face /dṓ fàyss/ *n.* a Northerner who sided with the South during the Civil War, especially a Northern congressman who refused to condemn slavery

dough·nut /dṓ nùt/, **do·nut** *n.* 1. FOOD ROUND CAKE WITH HOLE OR FILLING a small sugar-coated cake of sweet dough, fried or baked, and either spherical with a filling of cream or jam, or ring-shaped with no filling 2. MECH ENG RING-SHAPED OBJECT an object in the shape of an inflated ring, e.g., an accelerating tube in a nuclear reactor or an undersized spare tire 3. MOTOR SPORTS 360-DEGREE TURN IN VEHICLE a tight 360-degree turn made in a motor vehicle or motor boat

dough·ty /dówtee/ (**-ti·er, -ti·est**) *adj.* brave and determined (*literary*) [Old English *dohtig*, from earlier *dyhtig* "worthy, virtuous." Ultimately from an Indo-European word meaning "to be fit, prosper."] —**dough·ti·ly** *adv.* —**dough·ti·ness** *n.*

dough·y /dṓ ee/ (**-i·er, -i·est**) *adj.* 1. RESEMBLING DOUGH IN CONSISTENCY soft, sticky, and elastic, like dough 2. PALE AND FLABBY unhealthily pale and flabby —**dough·i·ness** *n.*

Doug·las, Kirk (*b.* 1916) U.S. movie actor. He has starred in over 70 Hollywood films, including *The Bad and the Beautiful* (1952). In 1995, he received a special Academy Award for his contribution to motion pictures. Real name **Issur Danielovitch**

Doug·las, Michael (*b.* 1944) U.S. television and movie actor. He won an Academy Award for *Wall Street* (1987). His father is Kirk Douglas.

Doug·las, Stephen A. (1813–61) U.S. politician. He lost the presidential election to Abraham Lincoln (1860), whom he then supported in the Civil War. Full name **Stephen Arnold Douglas**

Doug·las, Thomas Clement (1904–86) Scottish-born Canadian politician. He led the New Democratic Party from 1961 to 1971.

Doug·las, William Orville (1898–1980) U.S. associate justice of the Supreme Court. Of strongly held liberal views, he championed individual rights, especially free speech. He wrote a number of books, including *An Almanac of Liberty* (1954), and *Points of Rebellion* (1970).

Doug·las fir *n.* 1. TALL CONIFER a very tall pine tree that grows in northwestern North America and has distinctive rough bark and shaggy-looking cones. It is used for its timber and as a Christmas tree. Latin name: *Pseudotsuga menziesii.* 2. WOOD OF DOUGLAS FIR TREE the strong durable wood of the Douglas fir tree [Named for Scottish botanist David *Douglas* (1798–1834)]

Doug·lass /dúgglәss/, **Frederick** (1817–95) U.S. abolitionist, orator, and writer. He escaped from slavery (1838) and campaigned against slavery and racism in the United States. He wrote *Narrative of the Life of Frederick Douglass, an American Slave* (1845).

Doug·las spruc·e *n.* = **Douglas fir** *n.* 1

Dou·kho·bor /dóokә bàwr/, **Du·kho·bor** *n.* a member of an 18th-century Russian Christian group that rejected state and church authority and emigrated to western Canada at the end of the century to escape persecution [Late 19thC. From Russian *Dukhobar*, from *dukh* "spirit, Holy Ghost" + *-bor* "fighter."]

dou·la (*plural* **dou·las**) *n.* a woman who is experienced in childbirth and who provides physical, emotional, and informational assistance and support to a mother before, during, or after childbirth [From Greek, "most important woman servant" (who would have helped the woman of the house in childbearing)]

doum /doom/, **doum palm** *n.* = **doom palm**

dou·ma *n.* = **duma**

dour /dowr, door/ *adj.* **1.** SEVERE OR UNFRIENDLY severe or gloomy, and unfriendly and unresponsive toward other people **2.** *U.K.* DETERMINED grimly and stubbornly determined [14thC. Origin uncertain: probably via Gaelic *dūr* "obstinate," from Latin *durus* "hard" (source also of English *endure*).] —**dour·ly** *adv.* —**dour·ness** *n.*

dou·ra *n.* = **durra**

dou·rine /dŏo reén, dŏo reén/ *n.* a sexually transmitted disease of horses and related animals that causes swollen genitals [Late 19thC. From French.]

dou·rou·cou·li /dòorә kóolee/ (*plural* **-lis**) *n.* a fairly small, large-eyed, nocturnal South American monkey with an inflatable sac under its neck that amplifies its calls. Genus: *Aotus*. [Mid-19thC. Origin uncertain: probably from the language of the Rio Negro people in southern Venezuela.]

douse[1] /dowss, dowz/, **dowse** *vt.* (**doused** *or* **dowsed, dous·ing** *or* **dows·ing, dous·es** *or* **dows·es**) **1.** IMMERSE SOMETHING IN WATER to plunge or submerge somebody or something in water **2.** PUT LIQUID ON SOMETHING to put a lot of water or other liquid on somebody or something **3.** EXTINGUISH SOMETHING to put out a light, fire, or flame, especially with water ■ *n.* DRENCHING a thorough wetting or soaking [Early 17thC. Origin uncertain: perhaps from DOUSE[2] "to strike."] —**dous·er** *n.*

douse[2] /dowss, dowz/ *vt.* (**doused, dous·ing, dous·es**) **1.** LOWER SAIL to lower a sail, especially at speed **2.** TAKE OFF A HAT to take off a hat or other item of clothing (*archaic*) **3.** PUNCH OR STRIKE SOMEBODY to punch or strike somebody or something (*archaic*) ■ *n.* A BLOW a punch or blow (*archaic*) [Mid-16thC. Origin uncertain.]

DO·VAP /dō vàp/ *n.* a system for measuring the speed and position of objects in flight that is based on the frequency of sound waves. Full form **Doppler velocity and position**

dove[1] /duv/ *n.* **1.** BIRDS BIRD OF PIGEON FAMILY a bird of the pigeon family that has a heavy body, a small head, and a cooing call. Family: Columbidae. **2.** POL SUPPORTER OF PEACE somebody who supports peaceful measures and resists confrontation or war. ◊ **hawk 3.** TERM OF ENDEARMENT used as an affectionate name for a loved one ■ *adj., n.* = **dove-gray** [Assumed Old English *dūfe*, originally "dark-colored bird." Ultimately from an Indo-European word meaning "to darken."]

dove[2] /dōv/ past tense of **dive**

Dove *n.* in Christianity, a manifestation or representation of the Holy Spirit

Dove /duv/, **Rita** (*b.* 1952) U.S. poet and novelist. Her third collection of poetry, *Thomas and Beulah* (1986), won the 1987 Pulitzer Prize in poetry, and she served as poet laureate of the United States (1993–94).

dove·cote /dúv kŏt/, **dove·cot** /dúv kòt/ *n.* a building or structure, e.g., mounted on a pole or set into a wall, with many separate entrances and compartments, used for housing domestic pigeons

dove-gray *adj.* of a mid-gray color with a slight tinge of pink or blue —**dove -gray** *n.*

dove·kie /dúv kee/ (*plural* **-kies**), **dove·key** (*plural* **-keys**) *n.* a small squat northern sea bird of the auk family with a strong bill. Its dark-colored throat and breast change to white in winter. Latin name: *Alle alle*. [Early 19thC. Literally "small dove," formed from DOVE.]

dove pri·on *n.* a sea bird of the petrel family with a blueish gray back and black and white markings on its underparts, found in cool southern regions. Latin name: *Pachyptila desolata*.

Do·ver, Strait of /dṓvәr/ the narrowest part of the English Channel, between Dover, England, and Calais, France. Length: 21 mi./34 km.

Do·ver sole *n.* **1.** FLATFISH OF N AMERICAN PACIFIC a brownish mottled flat-bodied fish of the Pacific coast of North America that is a popular food fish. Latin name: *Microstomus pacificus*. **2.** EUROPEAN FLATFISH a flat-bodied European fish that is a popular food fish. Latin name: *Solea solea*. [Early 20thC. Origin uncertain: probably named for *Dover*, England.]

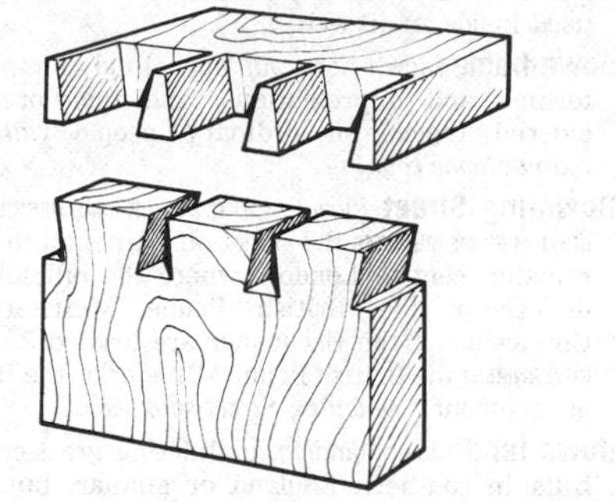

Dovetail

dove·tail /dúv tàyl/ *v.* (**-tailed, -tail·ing, -tails**) **1.** *vti.* FIT TOGETHER to fit neatly together or combine smoothly and efficiently, or to fit or combine things in this way **2.** *vt.* JOIN PIECES OF WOOD to join wooden boards with interlocking V-shaped tenons ■ *n.* **1.** V-SHAPED TENON a V-shaped projection on the end of a piece of wood that fits into a similarly shaped opening in another piece to form a strong joint **2. dove·tail, dove·tail joint** JOINT WITH DOVETAILS a joint made using dovetails [From its shape]

dove·tail saw *n.* a small saw with a reinforced back, slightly smaller than a tenon saw and used for fine woodworking

dov·ish /dúvvish/ *adj.* advocating peaceful solutions and the avoidance of confrontation or war. ◊ **hawkish** —**dov·ish·ness** *n.*

Dow /dow/, **Herbert Henry** (1866–1930) Canadian-born U.S. chemist. He discovered a way to process pure chlorine in 1895 and founded a major chemical company in 1897 to market his product.

dow·a·ger /dówәjәr/ *n.* **1.** WIDOW WITH HUSBAND'S TITLE OR PROPERTY a woman who has inherited a title or property from her deceased husband **2.** WOMAN OF STATUS a rich-looking or respected woman of advanced years [Mid-16thC. From Old French *douagere*, from, ultimately, Latin *dos* "dowry."]

dow·a·ger's hump *n.* a marked abnormal curving of the spine around the area of the shoulder blades, caused by osteoporosis and found among women, often as the result of age

dow·dy /dówdee/ (**-di·er, -di·est**) *adj.* **1.** PLAIN AND UNFASHIONABLE IN STYLE unattractively plain and unfashionable in style **2.** DRESSED PLAINLY wearing plain unfashionable clothes [Late 16thC. Origin uncertain: probably literally "little poorly dressed woman," formed from *doue* "poorly dressed woman."] —**dow·di·ly** *adv.* —**dow·di·ness** *n.*

dow·el /dów әl/ *n.* **dow·el, dow·el pin** JOINING PEG a short wooden or metal peg used to join two pieces of wood or metal by fitting tightly at each end into specially drilled holes in the two pieces to be joined ■ *vt.* (**-eled, -el·ing, -els**) JOIN WOOD OR METAL WITH DOWELS to join pieces of wood or metal using dowels [13thC. Origin uncertain.]

dow·er /dowr/ *n.* **1.** WIDOW'S INHERITANCE a dead man's estate, or part of his estate, inherited by his widow **2.** DOWRY a dowry (*archaic*) **3.** NATURAL GIFT something, especially a skill or talent, with which somebody is endowed (*literary*) ■ *vt.* (**-ers**) ENDOW to endow somebody with something (*literary*) [13thC. From Old French *douaire*, from Latin *dotare* "to endow," from *dos* "marriage portion."]

Dow Jones Av·er·ag·es *tdmk.* a trademark for an index of the prices of selected industrial, transportation, and utilities stocks that is based on a formula developed and revised periodically by Dow Jones & Company, Inc.

down[1] /down/ (**downed, downing, downs**) CORE MEANING: a grammatical word used to indicate movement or position toward a lower level or the ground ○ (prep) *He ran down the stairs and opened the door.* ○ (prep) *The sheep was caught in brambles 50 ft. down the hillside.* ○ (prep) *Tears were pouring down her cheeks.* ○ (adv) *I was numb from the waist down.* ○ (adv) *They all watched the sun go down.* ○ (adv) *She pressed a button and the window slid down.*

1. *prep.* TO LOWER LEVEL IN SOMETHING toward or at a lower level in something ○ *I dropped my keys down a hole.* **2.** *prep.* ALONG toward or at a position further along the length of something and usually at a somewhat lower level ○ *halfway down the street* **3.** *adv.* AT OR TO LOWER LEVEL at or to a physically lower level or position ○ *down in the basement* **4.** *adv.* ONTO SURFACE out of the hand and onto a surface ○ *She calmly put her fork down.* **5.** *adv.* AWAY FROM PRESENT LOCATION to another place away from your present location or base **6.** *adv.* TO MORE SOUTHERLY PLACE to a place in the south or to the south of your present location ○ *going down to Florida for the winter* **7.** *adv.* TO OR AT LOWER AMOUNT to or at a lower amount or price ○ *to get interest rates down* **8.** *adv.* SHORT BY SPECIFIED AMOUNT short of, having lost, or losing by a specified amount ○ *They were two goals down at halftime.* **9.** *adv.* HAVING ONLY SPECIFIED AMOUNT LEFT having only a specified amount left ○ *I'm down to my last dollar.* **10.** *adv.* IN PART PAYMENT in part payment for something or as a deposit ○ *You put 5% down, and pay the rest in installments.* **11.** *adv.* INCLUDING EVERYONE OR EVERYTHING including everyone or everything, from highest to lowest, within a specified group or hierarchy of people or things, or even including the particular person or thing mentioned ○ *everyone from the managing editor down* ○ *account for everything down to the last cent* **12.** *adv.* TO LATER PERIOD from an earlier to a later time or person ○ *The piano had been handed down to him by his grandmother.* **13.** *adv.* IN INFERIOR POSITION in or to an inferior, less free, or privileged position or condition ○ *holding political opponents down* **14.** *adv.* TO REDUCED CONDITION to a lower level of intensity or activity ○ *wind down after work* **15.** *adv.* INTO LESS SOLID STATE into a different and less solid state **16.** *adv.* ON PAPER in writing on paper, as a record **17.** *adv.* CHOSEN OR ARRANGED chosen or detailed for something, or arranged or scheduled for a particular time or date ○ *We're down for two sessions next month.* **18.** *adv.* LEISURE VERTICALLY IN A CROSSWORD PUZZLE in a vertical position in a crossword puzzle ○ *still need the solution to 10 down.* ◊ **across 19.** *adv. U.K.* UNIV AWAY FROM UNIVERSITY away from, or no longer at, a university ○ *down from Cambridge* **20.** *adv.* NAUT TO WINDWARD having the rudder to windward **21.** *adj.* UNHAPPY unhappy and gloomy **22.** *adj.* COMPUT NOT IN OPERATION temporarily not in operation **23.** *adj.* MADE IN PART PAYMENT made or given in part payment for something or as a deposit ○ *a down payment on the car* **24.** *adj.* FOOTBALL NOT IN PLAY no longer in play **25.** *adj.* BASEBALL PUT OUT eliminated from a game **26.** *adj.* ON THE GROUND lying on the ground ○ *a down tree* **27.** *interj.* INSTRUCTION TO DOG used as an instruction to a dog to stop jumping up, or to lie or sit ○ *Down boy!* **28.** *vt.* EAT OR DRINK to eat food or drink liquid, especially quickly or greedily **29.** *vt.* MAKE FALL TO THE GROUND to cause somebody or something to fall to the ground through being hurt or damaged **30.** *n.* FOOTBALL A PLAY MADE IN FOOTBALL one of four consecutive plays within which a team must either score or advance the ball at least ten yards **31.** *n.* FOOTBALL DECLARE BALL OUT OF PLAY to declare a ball as no longer in play [Old English *dūn* "hill," literally "from the hill," of uncertain origin: perhaps ultimately from a Celtic word that is also the source of *dune*] ◇ **be down on somebody** to show dislike or hostility toward somebody or something, often giving him, her, or it unfair treatment (*informal*) ◇ **be down to somebody** to be the responsibility of somebody ◇ **be down to something** to be the result of something ◇ **come down with something** to be or become ill with something ◇ **down under** to or in Australia or New Zealand (*informal*) ◇ **down with somebody** *or* **something!** used to express disapproval of, opposition to, or a desire to get rid of somebody or something

down[2] /down/ *n.* **1.** SOFT FLUFFY FEATHERS the soft fluffy feathers that are a young bird's first plumage, or that lie beneath the outer feathers in some adult birds **2.** FEATHERS AS STUFFING the soft breast feathers of a duck or goose, especially the female eider duck, used to fill pillows and quilts. ◊ **eiderdown 3.** COVERING OF SOFT HAIRS a covering of fine fluffy hairs, e.g., on a child's skin or on the skin of some kinds of fruit [14thC. From Old Norse *dúnn* "grassland," from Old English *dūn*, ultimately from an Indo-European word meaning "to fly around like dust, whirl."]

down³ /down/ *n. U.K.* TREELESS HILL a grassy treeless hill or ridge (*often used in place names*) ■ **downs** *npl.* ROLLING GRASSLAND an area of gently rolling, treeless, grassy upland, used mainly as pasture [Old English *dūn* (see DOWN¹)]

Down *n.* SOUTHERN ENGLISH SHEEP a sheep belonging to a southern English breed, such as the South Down or Dorset Down ■ **Downs** *npl.* HILLS IN SOUTHERN ENGLAND any of several ranges of low chalk hills in southern England [Named for the English *downs*, origin of the breeds]

down-and-dirt·y *adj.* crude and often unpleasant (*slang*) ○ *the down-and-dirty truth*

down-and-out *adj.* **1.** JOBLESS AND POOR having no money or job, often no home, and little hope of things getting better **2.** UNABLE TO CARRY ON completely incapacitated and unable to carry on ■ *n.* JOBLESS POOR PERSON somebody who has no job, money, or hope, especially a homeless person

down-at-heel, down-at-the-heel *adj.* shabbily dressed through poverty

down·beat /dówn bèet/ *adj.* PESSIMISTIC showing or expressing pessimism and hopelessness ■ *n.* **1.** FIRST BEAT IN BAR the first beat in a bar of music **2.** CONDUCTOR'S DOWNWARD GESTURE INDICATING DOWNBEAT the downward movement made by a conductor to indicate the downbeat of a bar of music

down-bow *n.* the action of drawing a bow from its heel toward its point across a stringed instrument

down·burst /dówn bùrst/ *n.* a powerful downward wind, often part of a thunderstorm system, that creates strong horizontal winds in all directions when it strikes the earth and is a danger to aircraft

down·cast /dówn kàst/ *adj.* **1.** SAD sad and pessimistic **2.** LOOKING DOWN looking or directed toward the ground ○ *with downcast eyes*

down·court /down káwrt/ *adj., adv.* SPORTS in, to, or toward the opposite end of a basketball or similar court

down·draft /dówn dràft/ *n.* a downward movement of air, e.g., on the lee side of a mountain range or down a chimney

Down East, down East *n.* New England, or more specifically, the U.S. state of Maine (*informal*) —**Down East·er** *n.* —**Down East·ern** *adj.*

downed /downd/ *adj.* brought to the ground, especially by force ○ *downed power lines*

down·er /dównər/ *n.* **1.** SEDATIVE DRUG a drug, especially a barbiturate, that induces calmness or sleepiness (*slang*) **2.** GLOOMY PERSON OR THING a gloomy person, situation, or experience (*informal*)

Dow·ners Grove /dòwnərz-/ village in northeastern Illinois, southeast of Wheaton, that is a western suburb of Chicago. Population: 50,089 (1996).

Dow·ney /dównee/ city in southern California, southeast of Los Angeles. Population: 93,073 (1996).

down·fall /dówn fàwl/ *n.* **1.** FAILURE OR RUIN the failure or ruin of a previously successful person, group, or organization **2.** CAUSE OF RUIN an action or situation responsible for the failure or ruin of a previously successful person, group, or organisation **3.** METEOROL FALL OF RAIN OR SNOW a sudden heavy fall of rain or snow

down·fall·en /dówn fàwlən/ *adj.* **1.** NO LONGER SUCCESSFUL fallen from a position of fame, power, or wealth **2.** NEGLECTED in a seriously neglected or ruined condition

down·field /dówn fèeld/ *adj., adv.* SPORTS in, to, or toward the opponents' half of a field of play

down·grade /dówn gràyd/ *vt.* (**-grad·ed, -grad·ing, -grades**) **1.** LOWER STATUS to lower the status, value, or rating of something ○ *The hurricane was downgraded to a tropical storm.* **2.** MOVE SOMEBODY TO LESS IMPORTANT JOB to move somebody from one post or job to another with less responsibility, status, or pay **3.** DISPARAGE to speak or write about somebody or something disparagingly ■ *n.* DOWNWARD SLOPE a downward slope on a road

down·haul /dówn hàwl/ *n.* a rope for pulling down or holding down a sail or a spar

down·heart·ed /dòwn haártəd/ *adj.* discouraged and unhappy —**down·heart·ed·ly** *adv.* —**down·heart·ed·ness** *n.*

down·hill *adv.* /down híl/ TOWARD BOTTOM OF HILL toward the bottom of a slope or hill ■ *adj.* /dówn hìl/ SLOPING DOWN sloping down, or taking place on a downward slope ■ *n.* /dówn hìl/ SKIING RACE DOWN LONG MOUNTAINSIDE COURSE a skiing race against the clock down a long mountainside course with several hundred yards between marker flags ◇ **go downhill** to decline or deteriorate

down·hole /down hṓl/ *adj.* used to describe equipment used inside an oil well

down·home /down hṓm/ *adj.* appealingly simple, informal, and unpretentious, and therefore considered typical of ordinary people (*informal*) ○ *downhome cooking*

Down·ing Street /dówning-/ *n.* **1.** OFFICIAL RESIDENCE OF BRITISH PRIME MINISTER the street off Whitehall in Westminster, central London, where the official residences of the British Prime Minister and Chancellor of the Exchequer are located **2.** BRITISH GOVERNMENT the British Prime Minister or the British government ○ *Downing Street sources*

down·land /dówn lànd/ *n.* undulating grass-covered hills in southern England or similar, but often flatter grassland in Australia and New Zealand

down·light /dówn lìt/ *n.* a lamp or bulb whose light is directed straight downward

down·link /dówn lìngk/ *n.* a path for the transmission of signals and data between a vehicle or satellite in space and the Earth —**down·link** *vti.*

down·load /dówn lṑd/ *vti.* (**-load·ed, -load·ing, -loads**) **1.** COMPUT TRANSFER DATA to transfer or copy data from one computer to another, or to a disk or peripheral device, or be transferred or copied in this way **2.** TRANSP UNLOAD to unload cargo or passengers ■ *n.* COMPUT **1.** INSTANCE OF DOWNLOADING an instance or the process of downloading data **2.** DOWNLOADED DATA data that has been downloaded in a single operation

down·mar·ket /dówn maàrkət/ *adj.* = **downscale** ■ *adv.* TOWARD LESS DISCRIMINATING SECTOR OF MARKET toward the part of the market that deals in cheaper, lower-quality goods for mass consumption

down pay·ment *n.* a part of the full price of something paid at the time it is bought, with the remaining part to be paid later

down·pipe /dówn pìp/ *n. U.K.* = **downspout**

down·play /dówn plày/ (**-played, -play·ing, -plays**) *vt.* to make something seem less important, significant, or serious than it really is

down·pour /dówn pàwr/ *n.* a heavy and sustained fall of rain

down·range /down ráynj/ *adj., adv.* away from where a missile was fired

down·rig·ger /dówn riggər/ *n.* a fishing line attached to a weighted cable allowing the baited line to be trailed at or near the bottom of the water

down·right /dówn rìt/ *adj.* **1.** ABSOLUTE complete and utter ○ *a downright lie* **2.** STRAIGHTFORWARD frank in expressing opinions **3.** POINTING DOWN pointing straight down (*archaic*) ■ *adv.* POSITIVELY positively and undeniably ○ *downright unfair* —**down·right·ly** *adv.* —**down·right·ness** *n.*

down·riv·er /down rívvər/ *adv., adj.* toward or nearer the mouth of a river, or following the direction of its current

down·scale /down skáyl/ *adj.* CHEAP AND OF LOW QUALITY cheap, appealing to mass taste, and regarded as being of low quality ■ *vti.* (**-scaled, -scal·ing, -scales**) MAKE OR BECOME SMALLER to reduce the scale or extent of something, especially a business

down·shift /dówn shìft/ (**-shift·ed, -shift·ing, -shifts**) *vi.* **1.** CARS CHANGE TO LOWER GEAR to change to a lower gear in a motor vehicle **2.** CHANGE LIFESTYLE to change a highly paid but stressful job for one that makes it possible to improve quality of life in other respects —**down·shift** *n.*

down·side /dówn sìd/ *n.* a negative side to something that also has positive aspects

down·size /dówn sìz/ (**-sized, -siz·ing, -siz·es**) *v.* **1.** *vti.* BUSINESS MAKE BUSINESS SMALLER to reduce the size of a business or organization, especially by cutting the workforce **2.** *vt.* MAKE SOMETHING SMALLER to make something physically smaller or produce something in a smaller size

down·slide /dówn slìd/ *n.* a downward trend or course

down·spin /dówn spìn/ *n.* a very sudden and sharp reduction

down·spout /dówn spòwt/ *n.* a pipe that carries rainwater from a roof gutter down to a drain or to the ground

Down's syn·drome *n.* = **Down syndrome** [Mid-20thC. Named for J. H. L. *Down*.]

down·stage /down stáyj/ *adv., adj.* TO OR AT STAGE'S FRONT toward or at the front of a theater stage ■ *n.* FRONT HALF OF STAGE the front half of a theater stage

down·stairs /down stáirz/ *adv.* TO LOWER FLOOR down the stairs or to a lower floor ■ *adj.* ON LOWER FLOOR on a lower or the lowest floor ○ *a downstairs bathroom* ■ *n.* LOWER FLOOR the lower floor of a building

down·state /down stáyt/ *adj., adv.* **1.** IN OR TO SOUTH OF STATE in or to the southerly part of a state **2.** AWAY FROM CITIES away from the big cities and in or into the more rural parts of a state whose major metropolitan area is to the north ○ *downstate Illinois* ■ *n.* SOUTHERLY OR RURAL PART OF STATE the southerly part of a U.S. state, or the more rural part when the major metropolitan area is to the north —**down·stat·er** *n.*

down·stream /down strèem/ *adv., adj.* TOWARD MOUTH OF RIVER toward or nearer the mouth of a river, or following the direction of the current ■ *adj.* INDUST OF LATER PRODUCTION STAGES relating to or occurring in the later stages of production ■ *adv.* GENETICS FURTHER FORWARD ON DNA MOLECULE further forward on a DNA molecule, in the direction in which the sequence is being read during replication. ◊ **upstream** ■ *n.* TRANSMISSION AWAY FROM CENTRAL NETWORK transmission of data on a network that is traveling away from a central distribution point. Downstream network capacity is generally greater than upstream capacity.

down·swing /dówn swing/ *n.* **1.** DOWNWARD TREND a downward trend or course **2.** GOLF DOWNWARD SWING OF GOLF CLUB the downward part of a golfer's swing

Down syn·drome /down-/ *n.* a genetic disorder characterized by a broad skull, blunt facial features, short stature, and learning difficulties. It is caused by the presence of an extra copy of a particular chromosome. [Mid-20thC. Named for J. H. L. *Down* (1828–96), an English physician.]

down-the-line *adj.* unwavering in support of or adherence to rules or policy

down·throw /dówn thrṑ/ *n.* the relative vertical displacement of rocks on one side of a fault

down·tick /dówn tìk/ *n.* **1.** SMALL DECREASE a very small decrease or reduction **2.** STOCK EXCH STOCK MARKET TRANSACTION a stock market transaction that is lower than the previous transaction in the same stock

down·time /dówn tìm/ *n.* **1.** TIME SPENT NOT WORKING OR PRODUCING time during which work or production is stopped, e.g., because machinery is not working **2.** TIME FOR RELAXATION a period of relaxation or play between periods of work

down-to-earth *adj.* practical and realistic

down·town /down tówn, dówn tòwn/ *adj., adv. U.S., Can, NZ* IN OR TO TOWN'S CENTER in or to the center of a city, especially its business center ■ *n.* **1.** CITY CENTER the center of a city, especially its business center **2.** LOWER MANHATTAN in New York City, the lower or southern end of Manhattan. ◊ **uptown** —**down·town·er** *n.*

down·trend /dówn trènd/ *n.* a downward trend or tendency

down·trod·den /dówn tròdd'n/ *adj.* made submissive by constant harsh treatment

down·turn /dówn tùrn/ *n.* a period or trend in which business or economic activity is reduced or is less successful

down·ward /dównwərd/, **down·wards** *adj.* **1.** MOVING LOWER IN SPACE moving or directed to the ground or to a lower place **2.** MOVING TO LOWER LEVEL moving to a lower level or condition **3.** COMING FROM ORIGIN OR SOURCE descending from a source, origin, or beginning ■ *adv.* **1.** TOWARD LOWER PLACE toward the ground or a lower place **2.** TO LOWER LEVEL to a lower level or condition **3.** TO AND INCLUDING EVERYONE to and including all the members of an organization, even the most junior ○ *everyone from the general manager downward* **4. TO LATER TIME** to a later time or generation —**down·ward·ly** *adv.* —**down·ward·ness** *n.*

down·ward·ly mo·bile *adj.* moving to a lower status, social class, or income bracket

down·ward mo·bil·i·ty *n.* movement to a lower status, social class, or income bracket

down·wards /dównwərdz/ = **downward**

down·wash /dówn wòsh/ *n.* a downward wind, e.g., the wind created by an aircraft wing

down·wind /down wínd/ *adv., adj.* **1. WITH THE WIND** in the direction that the wind is blowing **2. FURTHER IN DIRECTION OF WIND** in or into a position further along the line of the direction of the wind

down·y /dównee/ (**-i·er, -i·est**) *adj.* **1. SOFT** soft and fluffy **2. COVERED WITH SOFT HAIRS** covered with soft fine hairs **3. FEATHER-FILLED** filled with feathers —**down·i·ness** *n.*

down·y mil·dew *n.* a disease of plants that produces gray velvety patches on lower leaf surfaces, caused by various fungi Family Peronosporaceae

down·y wood·peck·er *n.* a small black and white North American woodpecker with a white back. The male also has a red head patch. Latin name: *Picoides pubescens.*

down·zone /dówn zṑn/ (**-zoned, -zon·ing, -zones**) *vti.* to restrict or reduce the number of buildings in an area ○ *plans to downzone urban districts*

dow·ry /dówree/ (*plural* **-ries**) *n.* **1. BRIDE'S FAMILY'S GIFT TO BRIDEGROOM** an amount of money or property given in some societies by a bride's family to her bridegroom or his family when she marries **2. MAN'S GIFT TO BRIDE** an amount of money or property transferred by a man to his bride when they marry **3.** CHR **MONEY PAID TO ENTER NUNS' ORDER** a sum of money required for a woman to enter some monastic orders **4. TALENT** a natural talent (*literary*) [14thC. Via Anglo-Norman *dowarie* from Old French *douaire* (see DOWER).]

dows·a·bel /dówssə bèl, dówzə-/ *n.* a woman or girl sweetheart (*archaic*) [Late 16thC. From French, an alteration of the name *Dulcibella.*]

dowse[1] /dowss, dowz/ (**dowsed, dows·ing, dows·es**) *vi.* to use a divining rod to search for underground water or minerals [Late 17thC. Origin unknown.]

dowse[2] /dowss, dowz/ *vt., n.* = **douse**[1]

dowse[3] /dows/ *vt., n.* = **douse**[2]

dows·er /dówsər/ *n.* somebody who uses a divining rod to dowse

dows·ing rod *n.* = **divining rod**

Dow the·o·ry /dów-/ *n.* a theory that states that stock market prices can be forecast on the basis of the movements of a selected group of stocks

dox·as·tic /dok sástik/ *n.* **LOGIC OF BELIEF** the branch of logic that deals with belief ■ *adj.* **OF BELIEF** relating to belief [Early 19thC. Coined from Greek *doxa* "opinion" + -ASTIC.]

dox·ie *n.* RELIG = **doxy**[1]

dox·ol·o·gy /dok sóllәjee/ (*plural* **-gies**) *n.* in Christian religious services, a hymn, prayer, or formula of worship in praise of God [Mid-17thC. From medieval Latin *doxologia*, literally "science of opinion," from Greek *doxa* "opinion."] —**dox·o·log·i·cal** /dòksə lójjik'l/ *adj.* —**dox·o·log·i·cal·ly** /-lójjəkəlee/ *adv.*

dox·o·ru·bi·cin /dòksə ro͝obissin/ *n.* an antibiotic, obtained from a bacterium, that is used to treat many types of tumors [Late 20thC. Coined from DE + OXY + Latin *rubus* "red" + MYCIN.]

dox·y[1] /dóksee/ (*plural* **-ies**), **dox·ie** *n.* RELIG a set of beliefs, especially religious beliefs (*informal*) [Mid-18thC. From *-doxy*, in such words as ORTHODOXY and HETERODOXY.]

dox·y[2] /dóksee/ (*plural* **-ies**) *n.* a man's woman lover, a woman who has many men lovers, or prostitute (*archaic slang*) [Mid-16thC. Origin unknown.]

dox·y·cy·cline /dòksi sī́ kleen, -klin/ *n.* an antibiotic derived from tetracycline that is used to treat many diseases, especially diarrhea in travelers and acne [Mid-20thC. Contraction of *deoxytetracycline.*]

doy·en /dóy ən, doy én/ *n.* a man who is the most experienced and respected member of a group or profession [15thC. Via French from Old French *deien*, from Latin *decanus* "one set over ten persons" (see DEAN).]

doy·enne /doy én/ *n.* a woman who is the most experienced and respected member of a group or profession [Mid-19thC. From French, feminine form of *doyen* "DOYEN."]

Doyle /doyl/, **Sir Arthur Conan** (1859–1930) Scottish-born British writer and physician. He was author of the Sherlock Holmes detective novels, including *The Hound of the Baskervilles* (1902).

D'Oy·ly Carte /dòylee kaárt/, **Richard** (1844–1901) British agent, manager, and producer. He founded an eponymous opera company in 1875 to perform the operettas of W. S. Gilbert and Arthur Sullivan. From 1881 these operettas were staged at his own Savoy Theatre, London.

doz. *abbr.* dozen

doze[1] /dṓz/ *vi.* (**dozed, doz·ing, doz·es**) **1. HAVE SHORT LIGHT SLEEP** to sleep lightly for a short time, especially during the day **2. LAZE OR DAYDREAM** to spend time lazily or in a daydream ■ *n.* **LIGHT SLEEP** a short light sleep [Mid-17thC. Origin uncertain: probably from Scandinavian.] —**doz·er** *n.*

doze off *vi.* to fall into a light sleep, especially unintentionally

doze[2] /dṓz/ (**dozed, doz·ing, doz·es**) *vt.* = **bulldoze** (*slang*) [Mid-20thC. Back-formation from DOZER.]

doz·en /dúzz'n/ *n.* (*plural* **-en**), *det.* **GROUP OF 12** a group of 12 objects or people ■ *det.* (*informal*) **1. MANY** a large number of ○ *I've told you a dozen times already!* **2. doz·ens LOTS** a large quantity or a great many [13thC. Via Old French *dozeine* from Latin *duodecim* "twelve," from *duo* "two" + *decem* "ten."] —**doz·enth** *adj.* ◇ **by the dozen** in large quantities

doz·er /dṓzər/ *n.* a bulldozer (*slang*) [Mid-20thC. Shortening of BULLDOZER.]

do·zy /dṓzee/ (**-zi·er, -zi·est**) *adj.* **1. DROWSY** half asleep or tending to fall asleep or doze **2.** *U.S., ANZ* FORESTRY **ROTTEN** rotten in the middle —**doz·i·ly** *adv.* —**doz·i·ness** *n.*

dp *abbr.* BASEBALL double play

DP *abbr.* **1. DP, dp** COMPUT data processing **2. DP, dp** PHYS dew point **3. DP, D.P.** displaced person

D/P *abbr.* **1.** COMM documents against presentation **2.** documents against payment

DPH *abbr.* **1.** Department of Public Health **2.** Doctor of Public Health

D.Phil., D.Ph. *abbr.* Doctor of Philosophy

dpi *n.* a measure of the density of the image produced by a computer screen or printer. Full form **dots per inch**

DPN *abbr.* diphosphopyridine nucleotide (*dated*)

DPT *abbr.* diphtheria, pertussis, tetanus (vaccine)

dpt. *abbr.* **1.** department **2.** GRAM deponent

dr *abbr.* **1.** MEASURE dram **2. dr, DR** dining room (*used in advertisements*)

Dr *abbr.* drachma

DR *abbr.* NAVIG dead reckoning

dr. *abbr.* **1.** FIN debit **2.** MONEY drachma **3.** MEASURE dram

Dr. *abbr.* **1.** MED doctor **2.** TRANSP Drive (*used in addresses*)

drab[1] /drab/ *adj.* (**drab·ber, drab·best**) **1. LACKING COLOR OR BRIGHTNESS** uninteresting to look at because of a lack of color or brightness **2. BORING** lacking interest, enthusiasm, or excitement **3. OF PALE GRAYISH BROWN COLOR** of a dull pale grayish brown color ■ *n.* **1. PALE GRAYISH BROWN COLOR** a dull pale grayish brown color **2.** TEXTILES **DULL-COLORED FABRIC** a gray or brown fabric [Early 16thC. From Old French *drap* "cloth" (source of English *drape* and *trappings*). Originally "cloth," then "natural, undyed cloth," hence "dull grayish brown."] —**drab·ly** *adv.* —**drab·ness** *n.*

drab[2] /drab/ *n.* **1. OFFENSIVE TERM FOR DIRTY WOMAN** a dirty, lazy, and messy woman (*archaic insult*) **2. PROSTITUTE** a prostitute (*archaic*) ■ *vi.* (**drabbed, drab·bing, drabs**) **USE PROSTITUTES** to use prostitutes (*archaic*) [Early 16thC. Origin uncertain: perhaps from Dutch.]

drab·ble /drább'l/ (**-bled, -bling, -bles**) *vti.* to become, or make something, wet and dirty [14thC. From Low German *drabbeln* "to splash in water," of uncertain origin: probably an imitation of the sound.]

Drab·ble /drább'l/, **Margaret** (*b.* 1939) British novelist, editor, and critic. Her novels explore the dilemmas of women in contemporary society and include *The Needle's Eye* (1972) and *The Radiant Way* (1987). She edited *The Oxford Companion to English Literature* (1985).

dra·cae·na /drə seénə/, **dra·ce·na** *n.* **1. TROPICAL EVERGREEN PLANT** a member of a genus of tropical evergreen plants that have long, strap-shaped, often variegated leaves and are popular as house plants. Genus: *Dracaena.* **2. PLANT LIKE DRACAENA** a plant with long narrow leaves resembling a true dracaena. Genus: *Cordyline.* [Early 19thC. Via modern Latin from Greek *drakaina*, feminine of *drakōn* "dragon," from the supposed resemblance of the juice of one of the species to dragon's blood.]

drachm /dram/ *n.* **1.** = **dram** *n.* 2 **2.** *U.K.* = **fluid dram 3.** MONEY = **drachma** *n.* 2 [14thC. Via Old French *drachme* from, ultimately, Greek *drakhmē*, literally "number of coins one hand can hold," from the assumed stem *drakh-* "to grasp."]

drach·ma /drákmə/ (*plural* **-mas** *or* **-mae**) *n.* **1.** MONEY **GREEK CURRENCY UNIT** the main unit of currency of modern Greece. See table at **currency 2.** MONEY **COIN WORTH ONE DRACHMA** a coin worth one drachma **3.** MEASURE = **dram** *n.* 2 **4.** MONEY **ANCIENT GREEK SILVER COIN** a silver coin used in ancient Greece **5.** MEASURE **ANCIENT GREEK UNIT OF WEIGHT** a unit of weight in ancient Greece [Early 16thC. Via Latin from Greek *drakhmē* (see DRACHM).]

Dra·co /dráykō/ *n.* a constellation in the sky of the northern hemisphere that partially encircles the celestial North Pole and lies close to Ursa Major

dra·co liz·ard *n.* = **flying lizard**

Dra·co·ni·an /drə kṓnee ən/, **dra·co·ni·an, Dra·con·ic** /drə kónnik/, **dra·con·ic** *adj.* **1. TOO HARSH** unjustly harsh or severe **2. OF DRACO** relating to the Athenian statesman Draco of the 7th century B.C., or to his wide-ranging and harsh code of laws [Late 19thC. From the Greek stem *Drakōn-* "Draco."] —**Dra·co·ni·an·ism** *n.* —**Dra·con·i·cal·ly** *adv.*

dra·con·ic /drə kónnik/ *adj.* relating to or like a dragon or dragons —**dra·con·i·cal·ly** *adv.*

Dra·cut /dráy kət/ town in northeastern Massachusetts, just south of the New Hampshire border, and a suburb of Lowell. Population: 27,769 (1996).

draff /draf/ *n.* a residue left in brewing after the grain has been fermented, used as food for cattle [13thC. Origin uncertain.] —**draff·y** *adj.*

draft /draft/ *n.* **1. CURRENT OF COLD AIR** a current of uncomfortably cold air penetrating a room or other space **2. CURRENT OF AIR IN ENCLOSED SPACE** a current of air, especially one that is moving through an enclosed space such as a chimney or tunnel **3.** MIL **CONSCRIPTION** the order to join the armed services in time of war **4. PRELIMINARY SKETCH** a preliminary sketch or plan **5. PRELIMINARY VERSION** a preliminary version of something written, such as a speech or report **6.** ENG **REGULATING DEVICE** a valve that regulates the flow of air to or from a pipe, e.g., a chimney **7.** FIN **CHECK** a written order to pay money from an account to an individual or to another account **8.** BUILDING **LEVELING LINE ON STONE** a line chiseled on the surface of a building stone as a guide to laying it level **9. PULLING ALONG OR DRAWING IN** the act of pulling something along, of drawing something in, or of breathing or drinking something **10. MOUTHFUL OF AIR, LIQUID, OR SMOKE** the amount of air, liquid, or smoke taken in in a single breath or swallow **11.** MED **DOSE OF LIQUID MEDICINE** a dose of medicine in liquid form (*dated*) **12.** BEVERAGES **BEER IN BARRELS** beer that is stored in and served from barrels or casks rather than bottles **13.** SAILING **DEPTH NEEDED BY SHIP TO FLOAT** the distance between the waterline of a ship and the lowest part of its hull, which is the minimum depth of water it requires in order to float ■ *v.* (**draft·ed, draft·ing, drafts**) **1.** *vt.* MIL **CALL FOR MILITARY SERVICE** to select somebody for compulsory service in the armed forces **2.** *vt.* **TRANSFER SOMEBODY SOMEWHERE FOR DUTY** to move or send somebody somewhere to carry out a particular task or general work and duties **3.** *vt.* POL **COMPEL TO RUN FOR OFFICE** to compel somebody to run for elective office **4.** *vt.* **MAKE PLAN** to make a preliminary plan or sketch of something, before all required information is in hand **5.** *vt.* **WRITE PRELIMINARY VERSION OF** to write a preliminary version of something such as a speech or report **6.** *vt.* FIN **WITHDRAW MONEY** to move money from one account to another as a way of effecting payment for something **7.** *vi.* TRANSP **FOLLOW CLOSELY** to follow another vehicle closely, taking advantage of the reduced resistance to movement ■ *adj.* **1.** BEVERAGES **SERVED FROM BARREL** stored in and served from a barrel rather than a bottle **2.** AGRIC **PULLING HEAVY LOADS** used to pull heavy loads ○ *a draft* *animal* [12thC. From Old Norse *dráttr,* of prehistoric Germanic origin (related to English *draw.*] —**draft·er** *n.* ◇ **on draft** available for serving from the barrel

draft board *n.* a board of civilians responsible for registering, classifying, and selecting people for compulsory military service

draft dodg·er *n.* somebody who tries to avoid doing compulsory military service

draft·ee /draf tée/ *n.* somebody who has been drafted for military service

draft·er /dráftər/ *n.* **1.** ARCHIT, ENG = **draftsperson 2.** DESIGNER OF SOMETHING somebody who devises and designs something such as a document ○ *tried to understand the full intent of the drafters of the Constitution* [Early 19thC]

drafts·man /dráftsmən/ (*plural* **-men**) *n.* **1.** TECHNICAL DESIGNER a man who makes detailed plans or drawings for buildings, ships, aircraft, or machines before they are built. This job is now done mainly by computer-aided design. **2.** MAN WHO DRAWS WELL a man who draws well or is considered from the point of view of his skill at drawing ○ *He's an excellent draftsman.*

drafts·man·ship /dráftsmən shìp/ *n.* skill in drawing or drafting shown by a person or in a piece of work

drafts·per·son /dráfts pùrs'n/ *n.* somebody who makes detailed drawings for buildings, ships, aircraft, or machines before they are built. This job is now done mainly by computer-aided design.

drafts·wom·an /dráfts wòommən/ (*plural* **-en** /-wìmmən/) *n.* **1.** TECHNICAL DESIGNER a woman who makes detailed plans or drawings for buildings, ships, aircraft, or machines before they are built. This job is now done mainly by computer-aided design. **2.** WOMAN WHO DRAWS WELL a woman who draws well, or a woman considered from the point of view of her skill at drawing

draft·y /dráftee/ (**draft·i·er, draft·i·est**) *adj.* chilly and uncomfortable because of flowing currents of cold air —**draft·i·ly** *adv.* —**draft·i·ness** *n.*

drag /drag/ *v.* (**dragged, drag·ging, drags**) **1.** *vt.* PULL SOMETHING ALONG WITH EFFORT to move something, especially something that is too large, heavy, or cumbersome to carry, by pulling it along the ground or across a surface **2.** *vt.* PULL BY FORCE to move or remove somebody or something that resists, usually by pulling at the person or object with considerable force or violence ○ *They dragged the fallen tree out of the road.* **3.** *vt.* PERSUADE SOMEBODY TO COME AWAY to cause, persuade, or force somebody to stop doing something or to leave a place unwillingly ○ *I'm sorry to drag you away from your work.* **4.** *vti.* TRAIL SOMETHING ALONG THE GROUND to be in continuous contact with the ground while moving across it, or allow something such as the foot or the bottom of a garment to do this ○ *He dragged his feet as he walked.* **5.** *vti.* MOVE to move, or move yourself or your feet, slowly and with difficulty or great reluctance ○ *I was so tired that I could scarcely drag myself up the stairs.* **6.** *vi.* PASS OR PROCEED SLOWLY to pass or proceed at a very slow and boring pace ○ *The afternoon was beginning to drag.* **7.** *vt.* COMPUT MOVE ICON WITH MOUSE to move an icon or other selected item on a computer screen by clicking on it with the mouse and pulling it to a new location **8.** *vt.* SEARCH to search a river bed, pond, or other area of water using a net or hook in an attempt to find something that or somebody who is missing **9.** *vi.* PUFF ON SMOKING MATERIAL to put a cigarette, pipe, or cigar to the mouth and suck in the smoke (*informal*) **10.** *vi.* MOTOR SPORTS TAKE PART IN DRAG RACE to take part in a drag race ■ *n.* **1.** HINDRANCE somebody who or something that slows down movement in any direction or progress in a particular area or activity ○ *These measures have been a drag on our economy.* **2.** AEROSP, PHYS RESISTANCE TO MOTION the resistance experienced by a body moving through a fluid medium, especially by an aircraft when traveling through the air. Symbol **D 3.** SOMEBODY OR SOMETHING BORING a person, task, duty, or event that is held to be extremely boring and irritating (*informal*) ○ *It was such a drag having to take our heavy coats and hats with us.* **4.** SLOW AND LABORIOUS MOVEMENT OR ACTION an action or movement carried out slowly and with great effort or difficulty **5.** DRAGGING MOVEMENT a sound, movement, or act of dragging **6.** CLOTHING OF OPPOSITE SEX clothing characteristic of one sex worn by a member of the other, especially women's clothing when worn by men (*slang*) **7.** PUFF a puff on a cigarette, pipe, or cigar (*informal*) **8.** STREET OR ROAD a street or road (*slang*) ○ *the main drag* **9.** LINE USED FOR DRAGGING RIVER a line, chain, or hook that is used for searching or dredging the bottom of an area of water such as a river or pond **10.** TRANSP MACHINE OR VEHICLE THAT IS DRAGGED a vehicle such as a cart that is pulled along the surface of the ground **11.** TRANSP BRAKING DEVICE a braking device, especially a horseshoe-shaped piece of metal attached to the underside of the wheel of a horse-drawn vehicle **12.** HUNT FOX SCENT the scent left by a fox or other animal that is hunted by dogs **13.** HUNT ARTIFICIAL SCENT an artificial scent put on the ground for hunting dogs to follow **14.** HUNT = **drag hunt 15.** MOTOR SPORTS = **drag race 16.** TRANSP HORSE-DRAWN COACH a large coach, similar to a stagecoach but privately owned, with seats inside and on top and usually drawn by four horses [14thC. From either Old English *dragan,* an earlier form of DRAW, or Old Norse *draga,* both from a common prehistoric Germanic ancestor.] ◇ **drag your feet** *or* **heels** to be slow to act, usually because you would prefer to avoid doing anything if possible ○ *The Administration has been dragging its feet on the new budget proposals.*

WORD KEY: SYNONYMS

See Synonyms at ***pull.***

drag down *vt.* **1.** BRING TO LOWER LEVEL to reduce somebody or something to a lower level or an inferior status by force or pressure of some kind ○ *Don't allow yourself to be dragged down by a timid banker.* **2.** MAKE SOMEBODY LISTLESS OR TIRED to make somebody feel listless, uninterested, or physically weak and tired ○ *Sitting at home all week really dragged me down.*

drag in *vt.* to involve somebody or something in something when it is not necessary or appropriate to do so, especially to insist on mentioning something that is not relevant in a conversation ○ *Mention music and he's bound to drag in a reference to the song he's just written.*

drag into *vt.* to involve somebody in something dishonest, disreputable, or otherwise undesirable ○ *What are you trying to drag me into?* ○ *They were dragged into the scandal.*

drag on *vi.* to continue for a very long time, especially past the expected or desired finishing time

drag out *vt.* to make something last longer than is necessary or desirable

drag out of *vt.* to force somebody to reveal or admit something ○ *Are you going to tell me, or do I have to drag it out of you?*

drag up *vt.* to mention something that somebody does not want to be discussed or known because it is unpleasant, upsetting, or embarrassing, especially something from that person's past

drag and drop *vt.* COMPUT to perform tasks on a computer by clicking onto items, moving them across the screen with the mouse, and releasing them on a particular icon

drag bunt *n.* BASEBALL a bunt made by a batter moving toward first base

dra·gée /dra zháy/ *n.* **1.** HARD-COATED CANDY a candy consisting of a nut, piece of fruit, or other center covered in a hard sugar coating **2.** TINY CONFECTIONERY BALL a tiny silver-coated ball used for decorating cakes **3.** SWEETENED PILL a medicinal pill covered with a sugar coating to make it taste better [Late 17thC. From French, from Old French *dragie* (see DREDGE).]

drag·ger /drággər/ *n.* a fishing boat that uses a trawl or dragnet

drag·gle /drágg'l/ (**-gled, -gling, -gles**) *v.* **1.** *vti.* MAKE OR BECOME WET AND DIRTY to make something wet and dirty by trailing it along the ground, or become wet and dirty by being trailed along the ground **2.** *vi.* TRAIL ALONG BEHIND SOMEBODY to follow along behind somebody else in a slow and usually undisciplined or slovenly fashion [Early 16thC. Origin uncertain: probably literally "to drag repeatedly," formed from DRAG.]

drag·gy /drággee/ (**-gi·er, -gi·est**) *adj.* (*informal*) **1.** SLUGGISH slow-moving ○ *a draggy musical* **2.** TIRESOME boring or otherwise annoying ○ *spent a draggy afternoon weeding the garden*

drag·hound /drág hòwnd/ *n.* a hound used in a drag hunt to follow an artificial scent trail

drag·lift /drág lìft/ *n.* a ski lift with metal bars or ropes that people hold onto as they are pulled up to the top of a slope on their skis

drag·line /drág lìn/ *n.* **1.** EXCAVATOR an excavating machine with a digging bucket attached by cables to a long jib and operated by being dragged back toward the machine by another cable **2.** LINE USED FOR DRAGGING a line that is used for dragging, e.g., when hauling a load or dragging a river or pond

drag link *n.* a link that conveys motion from one point to another. In motor vehicles, it is used to connect the steering gear to the steering arm.

drag·net /drág nèt/ *n.* **1.** CRIMINOL POLICE HUNT FOR A CRIMINAL a systematic and coordinated search for a wanted person made by police **2.** ANGLING WEIGHTED NET a net with weights on it used when trawling for fish at sea or when searching for something at the bottom of a river or pond **3.** HUNT GAME NET a net that is drawn across the ground and used to trap small game

drag·o·man /drággəmən/ (*plural* **-mans** *or* **-men** /-mən/) *n.* a guide or interpreter in certain Arabic-, Turkish-, or Persian-speaking countries (*archaic*) [16thC. Via French, Italian, and medieval Greek, from Arabic *targumān,* from Aramaic *tūrgemānā,* from Akkadian *targumānu* "interpreter."]

Dragon

drag·on /drággən/ *n.* **1.** MYTHOL SCALY GREEN MONSTER a large and usually ferocious fire-breathing creature in myths, legends, and fairy tales that has green scaly skin, a long tail, and wings **2.** ZOOL LARGE LIZARD a large lizard, e.g., the Komodo dragon **3.** INSULT FOR FORMIDABLE WOMAN a woman who is regarded as fierce and formidable (*insult*) [13thC. Via Old French from Latin *draco,* from Greek *drákōn* "snake," literally "one with a deadly glance." Ultimately from an Indo-European word meaning "to look."] ◇ **chase the dragon** to take heroin by heating it and breathing in the fumes (*slang*)

Drag·on /drággən/ *n.* = **Draco**

drag·on ar·um *n.* = **dragonroot** *n.* **2**

drag·on boat *n.* a long narrow boat decorated like a dragon, used especially by Chinese people when taking part in the boat races held during a particular festival. The festival is held every May 5th of the lunar year.

drag·on·et /drággənət/ (*plural* **-ets** *or* **-et**) *n.* a small brightly colored spiny marine fish belonging to a family with flat heads, narrow bodies, and large pectoral fins, living near the bottom of warm shallow waters. Family Callionymidae. [14thC. Formed from DRAGON.]

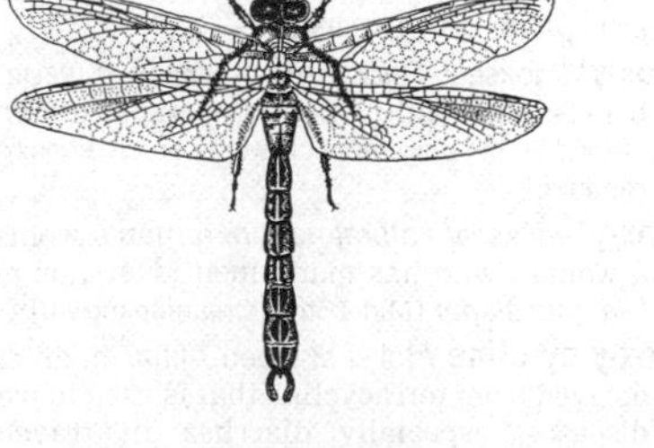

Dragonfly

drag·on·fly /drággən flì/ (*plural* **-flies**) *n.* an insect with a large head and eyes, a long thin body, and two pairs of iridescent wings that usually remain outstretched when the insect is at rest. Suborder Anisoptera.

drag·on·head /drággən hèd/ (*plural* **-heads** *or* **-head**), **drag·on's head** *n.* a plant of the mint family grown for its spikes of double-lipped, white, pink, or purplish flowers. Genus: *Dracocephalum* and *Physostegia.*

drag·on·root /dr ággən ro͝ot/ (*plural* **-roots** *or* **-root**) *n.* **1.** = **green dragon 2.** LARGE FOUL-SMELLING ARUM a tuberous, foul-smelling, and poisonous perennial plant belonging to the arum family. Latin name: *Dracunculus vulgaris.*

drag·on's blood *n.* a red resinous substance used to color varnishes and lacquers. It comes from the fruit of various trees including the dragon tree.

drag·on's teeth *npl.* rows of short wedge-shaped concrete posts implanted in the ground as an antitank barrier, especially in World War II (*slang*) ◇ **sow dragon's teeth** to take action that is, either deliberately or accidentally, the cause of future quarreling and conflict (*literary*) ○ *a troublemaker known for her ability to sow dragon's teeth within the department*

drag·on tree *n.* an evergreen tree native to the Canary Islands with a trunk that grows very thick clusters of spiky leaves and orange fruit. Its resin is a source of dragon's blood. Latin name: *Dracaena draco.*

dra·goon /drə go͞on/ *n.* **1.** MOUNTED INFANTRYMAN in European armies of the 17th and 18th centuries, a mounted infantryman armed with a carbine **2.** CAVALRYMAN in armies of the late 18th and 19th centuries, a cavalryman, especially a heavily armed cavalryman. The word is retained in the names of some modern regiments that were originally cavalry regiments. ■ *vt.* (**-gooned, -goon·ing, -goons**) **1.** FORCE SOMEBODY to involve somebody in an activity, or force somebody to do something, against his or her will ○ *He was dragooned into joining the chorus for the show.* **2.** SUBJUGATE SOMEBODY to persecute or subjugate somebody using military troops [Early 17thC. From French *dragon* "carbine or musket," literally "dragon" because the soldier carried a carbine or musket that "breathed fire" like a dragon.]

drag queen *n.* a man who dresses as a woman, especially a performer who dresses in a flamboyant women's costume and traditionally affects feminine mannerisms for comic effect (*slang*)

drag race *n.* a race between cars with specially modified bodies and engines on a straight track over a distance of a quarter of a mile to discover which has the fastest acceleration —**drag rac·er** *n.* —**drag rac·ing** *n.*

drag·ster /drággstər/ *n.* **1.** DRAG-RACING CAR a car that is specially designed for and used in drag racing **2.** DRIVER OF DRAG-RACING CAR a driver who takes part in a drag race

drag strip *n.* a short straight track, usually a quarter of a mile in length, used for drag racing

drain /drayn/ *n.* **1.** SEWAGE PIPE a pipe or channel that carries water or sewage away from a place **2.** SOMETHING THAT USES UP RESOURCES something that diminishes or uses up resources or energy ○ *a serious drain on our financial resources* **3.** PROCESS OF LOSS OR DIMINISHING the gradual loss, withdrawal, or diminishing of something regarded as an important resource ○ *the drain of trained personnel from the industry* **4.** MED DEVICE TO REMOVE FLUID FROM WOUND a tube or other device placed in a wound or incision to draw off fluids such as blood, pus, or water **5.** AGRIC ARTIFICIAL WATERWAY an artificial waterway that allows for land drainage ■ *v.* (**drained, drain·ing, drains**) **1.** *vti.* FLOW OR ALLOW TO FLOW OUT to flow out of something, often leaving it empty or dry, or allow a liquid to do this **2.** *vti.* EMPTY OR DRY to empty or dry something by allowing the water to flow out of or off it, or become empty or dry in this way ○ *The water drained slowly from the bathtub.* **3.** *vt.* AGRIC DRY OUT LAND to make marshy land drier by laying pipes, digging ditches or channels, or by any other means that removes the excess water **4.** *vt.* GEOG CHANNEL WATER AWAY FROM to be a channel for leading water off land ○ *The river Loire drains most of central France.* **5.** *vi.* GEOG DISCHARGE INTO SOMETHING to discharge water from its surface or channel into a river or lake (*refers to a geographic area or a smaller watercourse*) **6.** *vt.* DRINK SOMETHING UP to empty a cup, glass, or other container by drinking all its contents ○ *He drained his tea in one gulp and left.* **7.** *vt.* USE SOMETHING UP to use up or deplete something gradually, especially somebody's energy and resources, by making constant demands on it ○ *These payments are draining the country dry.* **8.** *vi.* WANE to disappear gradually, or become less strong or intense ○ *The color drained from her cheeks.* **9.** *vt.* EXHAUST SOMEBODY to leave somebody feeling physically or emotionally exhausted ○ *It drains me to care for six active youngsters five days a week.* [Old English *drēahnian* "to strain," literally "to dry out," from a prehistoric Germanic word that is also the ancestor of English *drought* and *dry*] —**drain·a·ble** *adj.* ◇ **down the drain 1.** wasted or squandered with no hope of retrieval (*informal*) **2.** toward or in a state of total failure or ruin, especially financial failure (*informal*)

drain·age /dráynij/ *n.* **1.** DRAINING PROCESS the process of draining liquid from something **2.** SEWAGE SYSTEM a system of pipes or channels that carries water or sewage away from a place **3.** MED FLUID REMOVAL FROM BODY the removal of fluid such as water, blood, or pus from a wound or part of the body, usually by means of a tube **4.** FLUID REMOVED BY DRAINING water, sewage, or any other fluid removed by draining

drain·age ba·sin, drain·age ar·e·a *n.* = **catchment area**

drain·age well *n.* a shaft sunk in waterlogged land, designed to draw water away from the surface soil layers

drain·board /dráyn bàwrd/ *n.* a slightly sloping metal or plastic surface with shallow grooves on it, next to a sink, that allows water to drain off wet dishes into the sink

drain·er /dráynər/ *n.* a rack or container in which things are put so that liquid can drain off them

drain·ing board *n. U.K.* = **drainboard**

drain·pipe /dráyn pīp/ *n.* a pipe that carries off rainwater, waste water, or sewage to or through drains, especially a downspout attached to the side of a house

drake /drayk/ *n.* a male duck [13thC. Origin uncertain: probably ultimately from prehistoric Germanic.]

dram /dram/ *n.* **1.** MEASURE UNIT OF WEIGHT a unit of weight equal to 1/16 of an ounce/1.77 grams **2.** MEASURE U.S. UNIT OF WEIGHT a unit of apothecaries' weight equal to 1/8 of an ounce or 60 grains/3.89 grams **3.** BEVERAGES SMALL ALCOHOLIC DRINK a small amount of an alcoholic drink, particularly whiskey or brandy **4.** VERY SMALL AMOUNT a very small amount of something ○ *not a dram of remorse* [15thC. Via Old French *drame* or medieval Latin *drama* from Greek *drakhmē* "handful."]

DRAM /dee ràm/ *abbr.* dynamic random access memory

dram. *abbr.* dramatic

dra·ma /dra̋amə, drámmə/ *n.* **1.** THEATER PERFORMED PLAY a serious play written for performance on stage, television, or radio **2.** ARTS PLAYS AS GENRE works written for performance on the stage, radio, or television considered as a literary genre ○ *17th-century French drama* **3.** THEATER PRODUCING OR PERFORMING PLAYS the performance, production, or writing of plays considered as a job, activity, or subject to be studied **4.** EXCITING EVENT a real-life event or situation that is particularly exciting or emotionally involving **5.** DRAMATIC EVENTS OR QUALITY exciting, tense, and gripping events and actions, or an exciting, tense, and gripping quality, either in a work of art or in a real-life situation ○ *an evening full of drama* [Early 16thC. Via late Latin from Greek, "play, deed," from *dran* "to do" (source of English *drastic*).]

dra·ma school *n.* a college of higher education specifically devoted to the practical and theoretical study of acting, stage management, and direction, mainly for the theater, but also for films and broadcasting

dra·ma ther·a·py *n.* a form of therapy that encourages people to use acting, role-playing, and improvisation to deal with psychological and emotional problems

dra·mat·ic /drə máttik/ *adj.* **1.** THEATER FOR THE THEATER written for the theater, or relating to the theater, plays, or acting **2.** EXCITING AND INTENSE characterized, in real life or in art, by the kind of intense and gripping excitement, startling suddenness, or larger-than-life impressiveness associated with drama and the theater ○ *the dramatic sequence of events leading to his escape* **3.** SUDDEN AND MARKED large in degree or scale, and often occurring with surprising suddenness ○ *a dramatic jump in prices* **4.** STRIKING bold, vivid, or strikingly impressive in appearance, color, or effect ○ *a dramatic view of the Alps* **5.** MUSIC HAVING POWERFUL EXPRESSIVE VOICE having a powerful singing voice especially suited to the expression of intense emotion, e.g., in tragic or villainous roles in opera [Late 16thC. Via Late Latin *dramaticus* from Greek *drāmatikos*, from *drama* (see DRAMA).]

dra·mat·i·cal·ly /drə máttikəlee/ *adv.* **1.** IN A STARTLING AND ATTENTION-GRABBING WAY in a way that grabs the attention and causes an excited, shocked, or startled reaction **2.** MARKEDLY to a very noticeable degree and often with surprising suddenness ○ *Things have improved dramatically since your last visit.*

dra·mat·ic i·ro·ny *n.* a situation, or the irony arising from a situation, in which the audience has a fuller knowledge of what is happening in a drama than a character does

dra·mat·ic mon·o·logue *n.* a poem or other literary work consisting of words supposedly spoken by a character, often in a specfic situation, either directly to the reader or to a listener. Among the best-known dramatic monologues in English literature are those of Robert Browning, e.g., "My Last Duchess" and "Porphyria's Lover."

dra·mat·ics /drə máttiks/ *n.* PRODUCTION OF PLAYS the performance and production of plays for the theater, especially in a nonprofessional context (*takes a singular or plural verb*) ■ *npl.* MELODRAMATIC BEHAVIOR theatrical and exaggerated behavior (*takes a plural verb*) ○ *Spare us the dramatics, for goodness sake, and tell us what happened!*

dra·ma·tis per·so·nae /drə ma̋atiss pər sṓnee, -nī, dra̋amətiss-, dra̋amətiss-/ *n.* LIST OF CHARACTERS a list of the names of the characters that appear in a play, usually printed at the beginning of the text of a play or, sometimes, in a theater program ■ *npl.* CHARACTERS IN A DRAMA the characters who appear in a drama, or the people involved in a situation (*formal*) [From Latin, "persons of the drama"]

dram·a·tist /drámmətist, dra̋amətist/ *n.* somebody who writes plays for the stage, television, or radio

dram·a·ti·za·tion /dràmməti záysh'n, dra̋aməti záysh'n/ *n.* **1.** THEATER PLAY ADAPTED FROM FICTION an adaptation of a work of fiction or a presentation of a real event that is intended for performance on the stage, television, or radio **2.** THEATER PROCESS OF ADAPTING the act, art, or process of turning a literary work or a real event into a drama for performance on the stage, television, or radio **3.** EXAGGERATION the act of making something appear more dramatic or of exaggerating its importance

dram·a·tize /drámmə tīz, dra̋amə tīz/ (**-tized, -tiz·ing, -tiz·es**) *v.* **1.** *vt.* THEATER ADAPT SOMETHING FOR STAGE to turn a literary work or a real event into a drama for presentation on the stage, television, or radio **2.** *vti.* EXAGGERATE to make something more dramatic, especially to exaggerate the importance or seriousness of a situation in an attention-seeking and theatrical way —**dram·a·ti·za·ble** *adj.* —**dra·ma·tiz·er** *n.*

dram·a·turge /drámmə tùrj, dra̋amə tùrj/ *n.* **1.** **dram·a·turge, dra·mat·ur·gist** PLAYWRIGHT a playwright, particularly one who works with a specific theater or company **2.** **dram·a·turge, dra·ma·turg** LITERARY ADVISOR IN THEATER a member of the staff of a theater with mainly literary responsibilities such as choosing the plays for performance, editing and adapting texts where necessary, and writing program notes [Mid-19thC. Via French from, ultimately, Greek *dramatourgos*, literally "worker in drama," from *drama* (see DRAMA).]

dram·a·tur·gy /drámmə tùrjee, dra̋amə tùrjee/ *n.* the art of the theater, especially with regard to the techniques involved in writing plays —**dram·a·tur·gic** /drámə túrjik, dra̋amə-/ *adj.* —**dram·a·tur·gi·cal** /-túrjik'l, -/ *adj.* —**dra·ma·tur·gi·cal·ly** /-əlee, -/ *adv.*

Dram·bu·ie /dram bo͞o ee/ *tdmk.* a trademark for a sweet whiskey-based liqueur made in Scotland

drank past tense of **drink**

drape /drayp/ *v.* (**draped, drap·ing, drapes**) **1.** *vt.* PLACE FABRIC OVER SOMETHING to hang or place a piece of fabric over something so that it falls in folds around it or covers it ○ *draped a scarf over her shoulders* **2.** *vt.* COVER OVER WITH FABRIC to cover something over with a piece of fabric, usually so that the fabric hangs down around it in folds ○ *a chair draped in a dust sheet* **3.** *vi.* HANG IN FOLDS to hang or be able to hang in loose folds on or over something ○ *a heavy fabric that will drape well* **4.** *vt.* **LAY SOMETHING CASUALLY** to place part of the body on or over something, e.g., the back of a chair, in a relaxed and casual way ○ *She draped herself elegantly over the sofa.* ■ *n.* **1.** = **curtain 2. PIECE OF DRAPING FABRIC** a piece of fabric used to drape over something **3.** MED **STERILE COVER** a piece of cloth placed over a patient's body during an examination or operation to provide a sterile area around the part of the body that is being treated **4. WAY FABRIC HANGS** the way in which fabric hangs and forms folds, especially when made into a garment ○ *adjusting the drape of the dress* [15thC. From Old French *draper,* from *drap* "cloth," from late Latin *drappus,* from, ultimately, a Celtic word (source of English *drab* and *trappings*).]

drap·er /dráypər/ *n. U.K.* somebody who sells fabric and sewing materials in a shop (*dated*) [14thC. From Old French *drapier,* from *drap* (see DRAPE).]

Dra·per city in northern Utah on the the Jordan River. It is a southern suburb of Salt Lake City. Population: 12,478 (1996).

drap·er·y /dráypə ree/ (*plural* **-ies**) *n.* **1. CLOTH ARRANGED TO HANG IN FOLDS** cloth or clothing that has been arranged to hang in elegant or decorative folds **2. PIECE OF ELEGANTLY HANGING FABRIC** a piece of fabric used as a decorative cover or garment and usually hanging in loose elegant folds **3.** = **curtain 4.** *U.K.* = **dry goods** [14thC. From Old French *draperie,* from *drap* (see DRAPE).]

dras·tic /drástik/ *adj.* **1. POWERFUL IN EFFECT** having a powerful effect or far-reaching consequences ○ *a crisis calling for drastic remedies* **2. VERY MARKED** very noticeable, significant, and usually worrying because of its amount or degree [Late 17thC. From Greek *drastikos* "effective, active," from *dran* "to do" (source of English *drama*).]

dras·ti·cal·ly /drástikəlee/ *adv.* to a very great and usually very worrying degree

drat /drat/ *interj.* used to express annoyance or frustration (*informal*) [Early 19thC. Alteration of *od rot,* a shortening of *God rot.*]

draught /draft/ *n., adj.* U.K. = **draft** ■ *n. U.K.* BOARD GAMES = **checker**

draughts *n. U.K.* = **checkers** [12thC. From DRAUGHT in the obsolete sense "act of drawing a piece across the board in chess and similar games."]

Dra·vid·i·an /drə víddee ən/ *n.* **1.** LANG **FAMILY OF INDIAN LANGUAGES** a family of over twenty languages spoken in southern India and northeastern Sri Lanka, including Tamil, Telugu, Kannada, and Malayalam. Over 200 million people speak a Dravidian language. **2.** PEOPLES **MEMBER OF ABORIGINAL INDIAN PEOPLE** a member of an ancient people who were the aboriginal inhabitants of India and who moved southward during the influx of Indo-European peoples from the North [Mid-19thC. From Sanskrit *drāvida* "relating to the Tamils," from *Dravida* "Tamil."] —**Dra·vid·i·an** *adj.*

draw /draw/ *v.* (**drew** /droo/, **drawn** /drawn/, **draw·ing, draws**) **1.** *vti.* ARTS **MAKE A PICTURE** to make a line, picture, or plan on a surface using a pencil, pen, or crayon rather than paints ○ *She drew a picture of a flower.* **2.** *vt.* **DESCRIBE SOMETHING** to depict or describe something in words ○ *He drew a vivid picture of life in 18th-century Philadelphia.* **3.** *vi.* **MOVE** to move in a particular direction, often alongside, toward, or away from something else, and with a smooth steady motion ○ *Another car drew alongside ours.* **4.** *vi.* **APPROACH** to approach through time, or move toward a particular point or stage in something, especially its end ○ *The meeting was drawing to a close.* **5.** *vt.* **PULL SOMEBODY OR SOMETHING TOWARD OR AWAY** to pull something or lead or pull somebody in a particular direction, especially toward or away from something ○ *She drew him toward the door.* **6.** *vt.* TRANSP **PULL A VEHICLE** to pull a vehicle along ○ *a carriage drawn by six white horses* **7.** *vt.* **OPEN OR CLOSE A CURTAIN** to pull a curtain or blind across a window so that it covers or uncovers it **8.** *vt.* **PULL ON A STRING, ROPE, OR CORD** to pull on a string, rope, or cord, usually in order to tighten it around something **9.** *vt.* ARCHERY **PULL BACK THE STRING OF A BOW** to pull back the string of a bow prior to shooting an arrow **10.** *vt.* **TAKE SOMETHING OUT** to take or pull an object out of something in which it has been enclosed or embedded ○ *He drew his hand from his pocket.* **11.** *vti.* **PULL WEAPON FROM HOLSTER OR SHEATH** to pull a weapon from a holster or sheath in order to use it **12.** *vt.* **REMOVE LIQUID** to remove liquid from a large container such as a barrel by means of a tap **13.** *vt.* MED **DRAIN A WOUND** to drain a liquid such as blood, pus, or water from a wound or incision **14.** *vt.* **HAUL UP WATER** to haul up water from a well or other source using a bucket on a rope **15.** *vt.* **ELICIT A RESPONSE** to cause somebody or something to make a particular type of response or sound ○ *The speech had drawn hoots of derision from the crowd.* **16.** *vt.* **OBTAIN SOMETHING FROM SOURCE** to obtain a physical or a moral resource from a particular place or thing ○ *They drew courage from our example.* **17.** *vt.* **OBTAIN INFORMATION FROM SOMEBODY** to obtain information, a secret, or an opinion from somebody by questioning or persuasion (*often passive*) ○ *She refused to be drawn on the subject.* **18.** *vt.* **CAUSE TO BE DIRECTED TOWARD SOMETHING** to cause somebody's attention, eye, or interest to be directed toward somebody or something **19.** *vt.* **ATTRACT PEOPLE** to attract somebody or arouse people's interest or curiosity so that they come to see something or somebody ○ *The performance had drawn a huge crowd of onlookers.* **20.** *vt.* **SUCK SOMETHING IN** to suck something in, especially air into the lungs ○ *I drew a long breath.* **21.** *vi.* **ALLOW A CURRENT OF AIR THROUGH** to allow a current of air to flow through, removing smoke or gases **22.** *vt.* FIN **WITHDRAW MONEY** to take money out of a bank or savings account, or a similar source ○ *He drew $600 from the bank.* **23.** *vt.* FIN **RECEIVE MONEY** to receive money regularly from a particular source **24.** *vt.* FIN **WRITE A CHECK** to write a check, bill of exchange, or promissory note on an account so that somebody can receive money from that account **25.** *vt.* LAW **WRITE OUT A LEGAL DOCUMENT** to compose or write out a legal document in the proper form **26.** *vt.* **ARRIVE AT A CONCLUSION OR INFERENCE** to arrive at a particular conclusion or inference by examining the evidence for something ○ *You'll have to draw your own conclusions.* **27.** *vt.* **FORMULATE SOMETHING** to formulate or state a distinction, comparison, or parallel between two or more different things ○ *There are certain parallels that may be drawn between the two cases.* **28.** *vt.* **CHOOSE SOMETHING AT RANDOM** to choose or be given something at random, usually in order to ensure that all participants are treated fairly ○ *They drew lots to see who would have to go.* **29.** *vt.* CARDS **TAKE A CARD** to take a card from a stack, the deck, or the dealer during a card game **30.** *vt.* CARDS **MAKE PLAYERS PLAY PARTICULAR SUIT** to make the other players in a card game play the cards they have in a particular suit by repeatedly leading that suit ○ *drew all the trumps early in the hand* **31.** *vti.* SPORTS **FINISH EQUAL** to finish a game with the scores for the opposing sides level or with neither side having won ○ *Finland and Holland drew 1–1 in the soccer semifinals.* **32.** *vt.* SHIPPING **NEED PARTICULAR DEPTH OF WATER** to need a particular depth of water in which to float **33.** *vti.* COOK **STEEP IN BOILING WATER** to steep tea leaves, or allow tea leaves to steep, in boiling water ○ *Let the tea draw for five minutes.* **34.** *vt.* INDUST **MAKE WIRE** to make wire by pulling a length of metal through a conical hole **35.** *vt.* **REMOVE INNARDS FROM CARCASS** to remove the innards from a carcass before cooking it **36.** *vt.* **DISEMBOWEL SOMEBODY** to disembowel a hanged person, especially in former times **37.** *vt.* CUE GAMES **GIVE BACKSPIN TO A BALL** to give a backward spin to a ball when making a stroke, especially in billiards **38.** *vt.* GOLF **MAKE THE BALL CURVE** to hit the ball so that it curves in flight following the direction of the golfer's swing (to the left for a right-handed player) instead of traveling straight ■ *n.* **1. ACT OF DRAWING** the act of pulling or sucking on something or otherwise drawing something **2.** GAMBLING **LOTTERY** a lottery, raffle, or other competition where the winner is decided by selecting a ticket at random **3.** GAMBLING **CHOOSING LOTTERY WINNER** the choosing of a winner in a lottery, raffle, or other competition by selecting a ticket at random **4.** SPORTS **SELECTION OF OPPONENTS** the act of selecting at random which contestants are to play each other in a sports contest, or the resulting list of games to be played ○ *the draw for the third round of the competition* **5.** CARDS, GAMBLING **SOMETHING CHOSEN AT RANDOM** something chosen at random, e.g., a ticket in a lottery or a card or cards taken from a stack or the dealer **6. ATTRACTION** something or somebody that interests a lot of people and attracts them as spectators, visitors, or customers ○ *The rock band will be a huge draw for the local fair.* **7.** SPORTS **CONTEST THAT NEITHER SIDE WINS** a contest that ends with both sides having the same score or with neither side having won **8. DRAWING A GUN** the action of pulling a gun from its holster in order to fire it, especially in a gunfight **9.** GEOG **SHALLOW GULLY** a shallow natural channel into which rainwater drains **10. MOVABLE PART OF DRAWBRIDGE** the movable part of a drawbridge **11.** CARDS **SECOND OR FURTHER DEAL** in draw poker, the deal made to improve the players' hands after they have discarded [Old English *dragan,* from a prehistoric Germanic word meaning "to carry," which is also the ancestor of English *drag*] —**draw·a·ble** *adj.*

WORD KEY: SYNONYMS

See Synonyms at ***pull.***

draw back *vi.* to decide not to continue with some contemplated, planned, or agreed action ○ *They drew back from the deal at the last moment.*

draw in *v.* **1.** *vt.* **INVOLVE SOMEBODY** to get somebody involved in something unwillingly (*often passive*) ○ *I got drawn in before I realized what the argument was really about.* **2.** *vi. U.K.* **BECOME SHORTER** to become shorter, so that it gets dark sooner (*refers to days in fall*) **3.** *vi. U.K.* **BEGIN EARLIER** to begin earlier, causing it to become darker sooner (*refers to nights or evenings in fall*)

draw off *vt.* to remove a small amount of liquid from a larger amount by means of a tube or pipe

draw on *v.* **1.** *vt.* **USE SOMETHING** to make use of a resource of some kind for personal benefit ○ *The novel draws on her experiences in Alaska.* **2.** *vi.* **ENTER A LATER STAGE** to enter a later stage or move toward its end ○ *As the day drew on I grew worried that they would not come.* **3.** *vt.* **TAKE IN SMOKE** to inhale the smoke from a cigarette or pipe ○ *He drew on his pipe.*

draw out *v.* **1.** *vt.* **PROLONG SOMETHING** to make something continue longer than is usual, necessary, or desirable ○ *I drew the conversation out as long as I could.* **2.** *vi.* **GROW LONGER** to have more hours of daylight (*refers to days in spring*) **3.** *vt.* **GET SOMEBODY TO TALK** to encourage a shy, hostile, or reserved person to talk at length or in detail, or to become more forthcoming in a social or legal situation ○ *The prosecutor took great pains to draw the hostile witness out during cross-examination.*

draw up *v.* **1.** *vt.* **WRITE SOMETHING OUT** to prepare or write out a plan, list, or other document ○ *The lawyers are drawing up the terms of the contract as we speak.* **2.** *vti.* **COME TO A STOP** to arrive at a particular point or place in a vehicle or on a horse and stop, or bring a vehicle or horse to a halt ○ *A car drew up outside.* **3.** *vt.* **BRING SOMETHING NEARER** to place a chair or seat near something or somebody and sit down on it **4.** *vr.* **STRAIGHTEN SOMETHING** to straighten the body in order to reach full height and look as imposing or dignified as possible ○ *She drew herself up to her full height, then spoke.*

draw·back /dráw bàk/ *n.* something that causes problems or is a disadvantage or hindrance ○ *The only drawback is the size of the machine.*

draw·bar /dráw baar/ *n.* a strong metal bar attached across the back of a tractor, locomotive, or other vehicle, with a coupling on it to which machinery or a trailer can be hitched

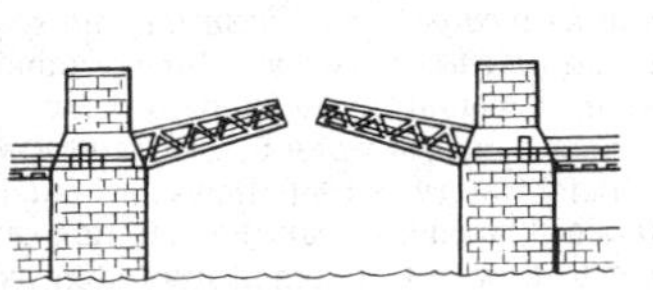

Drawbridge

draw·bridge /dráw brìj/ *n.* a bridge that is hinged at one end or in the middle and can be lifted up to cut off access to a place or allow something to pass beneath it. Drawbridges are often built across water, either outside medieval castles that have a moat or along rivers or near harbors.

draw·down /dró dòwn/ *n.* **1. DEPLETION** the process of reducing or using up a supply or store of something **2. LOWERING OF WATER LEVEL** a lowering of the level of the water in a reservoir

draw·ee /draw ée/ *n.* the person or organization from whose account money is taken when a check or other order for payment is drawn

draw·er /drawr/ *n.* **1.** HOUSEHOLD **PLACE TO STORE THINGS** a storage compartment in a piece of furniture such as a desk, chest, or table that slides in and out and is usually shaped like a shallow rectangular box **2.** FIN **SOMEBODY WHO WRITES A CHECK** somebody who draws a check or money order **3. SOMEBODY OR SOMETHING THAT DRAWS** somebody or something that draws, especially somebody who draws pictures or plans **4. SERVER IN AN INN** somebody who draws beer or serves customers in an inn (*archaic*)

draw·ers /drawrz/ *npl.* large old-fashioned underpants with short legs, worn by men or women (*dated*)

draw·gate /dráwgàyt/ *n.* a barrier that can be raised or lowered to control the flow of water in a sluice

draw·ing /dráw ing/ *n.* **1.** ARTS **OUTLINE PICTURE** a picture of something made with a pencil, pen, or crayon, usually consisting of lines, often with shading, but generally without color **2.** ARTS **MAKING PICTURES** the art, activity, or practice of making pictures using a pencil, crayon, or pen ○ *I never was very good at drawing.* **3.** GAMBLING = **draw** *n.* 2 **4.** GAMBLING = **draw** *n.* 3

draw·ing ac·count *n.* a company account from which a company employee can draw money for expenses or as an advance against a future salary payment

draw·ing board *n.* a large flat board used for drawing and design work, usually attached to a frame with legs and adjustable to different heights and angles ◇ **back to the drawing board** back to the beginning or the planning stage of a failed operation or project, ready to start all over again (*informal*) ○ *Since all else has failed, we're now back to the drawing board.*

draw·ing card *n.* = **draw** *n.* 6

draw·ing pin *n. U.K.* = **thumbtack**

draw·ing room *n.* **1. ROOM TO ENTERTAIN GUESTS** a large formal room in a house, in which guests are entertained **2.** RAIL **ROOM IN A RAILROAD SLEEPING CAR** a large private room with berths in a railroad sleeping car (*dated*) [Mid-17thC. Shortening of *withdrawing-room.*]

draw·knife /dráw nīf/ (*plural* **-knives** /-nīvz/) *n.* a tool for shaving the surface of wood, consisting of a narrow rectangular blade with a handle at either end set at right angles to it

drawl /drawl/ *vti.* (**drawled, drawl·ing, drawls**) **SPEAK SLOWLY** to draw out the vowel sounds and pronounce words with a slow inflection when speaking ■ *n.* **SLOW WAY OF SPEAKING** a way of speaking in which the speaker draws out the vowel sounds and pronounces words slowly [Late 16thC. Origin uncertain: probably from Middle Dutch *dralen* "to linger, delay," from *dragan* "to draw."] —**drawl·er** *n.* —**drawl·ing·ly** *adv.* —**draw·ly** *adj.*

drawn[1] /drawn/ *adj.* appearing tired and careworn, usually as a result of anxiety, grief, or illness ○ *He looked pale and drawn.*

drawn[2] past tense of **draw**

drawn but·ter *n.* melted butter that has had the solids removed, served as a sauce, sometimes with herbs and seasoning

drawn-out *adj.* continuing longer than is intended or desired

drawn-thread work, drawn work *n.* a type of embroidery in which selected threads are pulled from the fabric and stitches are worked on the remaining threads to produce decorated open areas

draw·plate /dráw plàyt/ *n.* a plate pierced by conical holes through which metal is drawn in wiremaking

draw pok·er *n.* a form of poker in which each player is dealt five cards face down and after the first round of betting can draw replacements for any discards

draw·shave /dráw shàyv/ *n.* = **drawknife**

draw shot *n.* in cue games, a shot in which the cue ball is hit below center so that the backspin makes it bounce back when it hits another ball

draw·string /dráw strìng/ *n.* a cord threaded through a hem, piping, or eyelets around the opening in a bag or a garment so that it can be drawn tight and the opening closed

draw·tube /dráw tòob/ *n.* a tube that slides inside another tube, e.g., one of the extending tubes in a telescope

dray /dray/ *n.* a large low horsedrawn cart with no fixed sides, designed for heavy loads [From Old English *dragan* "to draw"]

dray·horse /dráy hàwrs/ *n.* a large horse used for pulling a dray

dread /dred/ *vti.* (**dread·ed, dread·ing, dreads**) **1. FEEL EXTREMELY FRIGHTENED** to feel extremely frightened or worried about something that may happen in the future **2. BE RELUCTANT** to be reluctant or frightened to do something because it is unpleasant, upsetting, or annoying ■ *n.* **1. TERROR** a feeling of great fear or terror, especially at the thought of experiencing or encountering something unpleasant **2. SOURCE OF DREAD** something that is dreaded **3. AWE** a feeling of awe and reverence (*archaic*) ■ *adj.* (*literary*) **1. FEARED** causing fear and extreme anxiety ○ *The dread day arrived.* **2. AWE-INSPIRING** inspiring fear and respect or awe in equal measure [12thC. Shortening of *adreden*, from Old English *adrǣdan*, from *ondrǣdan* "to counsel against," from *rǣdan* "to counsel."]

dread·ed /dréddəd/ *adj.* inspiring great fear (*sometimes used humorously*)

dread·ful /drédfəl/ *adj.* **1. EXTREMELY BAD** extremely unpleasant, harmful, or serious in its effects ○ *a dreadful mistake* **2. EXTREME** extreme in character or degree ○ *a dreadful shame* **3. AWE-INSPIRING** inspiring awe (*literary*) —**dread·ful·ness** *n.*

dread·ful·ly /drédfəlee/ *adv.* **1. BADLY** in a very unsatisfactory or unpleasant way ○ *He behaved dreadfully.* **2.** *U.K.* **VERY** to a very great extent

Dreadlocks: Bob Marley

dread·locks /dréd lòks/ *npl.* long strands of hair that have been twisted closely from the scalp down to the tips in a style made popular by Rastafarians [Mid-20thC. From DREAD + LOCK, because of the supposed fear on the part of non-Rastafarians of the power of faithful Rastafarians.]

dread·nought /dréd nàwt/ *n.* a heavily armed battleship whose main guns are all of the same caliber [Early 20thC. Named for the British battleship *Dreadnought*, the first of its kind, from DREAD + NOUGHT, literally "fear nothing."]

dreads /dredz/ *npl.* = **dreadlocks** [Late 20thC. Contraction.]

dream /dreem/ *n.* **1. IMAGININGS WHILE ASLEEP** a sequence of images that appear involuntarily to the mind of a sleeping person, often a mixture of real and imaginary characters, places, and events **2. WAKING IMAGININGS** a series of images, usually pleasant ones, that pass through the mind of somebody who is awake **3. SOMETHING HOPED FOR** something that somebody hopes, longs, or is ambitious for, usually something difficult to attain or far removed from present circumstances **4. IDLE HOPE** an idea or hope that is impractical or unlikely ever to be realized **5. VAGUE STATE** a state of inattention owing to preoccupation with thoughts or fantasies **6. SOMETHING BEAUTIFUL** somebody or something that seems particularly good-looking or wonderful ■ *v.* (**dreamed** /dremt/ *or* **dreamt, dreamed** *or* **dreamt, dream·ing, dreams**) **1.** *vti.* **HAVE A DREAM WHILE SLEEPING** to experience vivid mental images of events while sleeping **2.** *vi.* **DAYDREAM** to let the mind dwell on pleasant scenes and images while awake, often resulting in inattention **3.** *vi.* **WISH** to want something very much and imagine having or doing it, though it may be unlikely ○ *For years I'd dreamed of living abroad.* **4.** *vi.* **CONSIDER** to think of or consider doing something regarded as wrong or inappropriate ○ *How could you even dream of doing such a thing?* ■ *adj.* **1. OCCURRING IN A DREAM** occurring in or reminiscent of a dream ○ *a dream sequence* **2. IDEAL** perfect and wonderful in every way [13thC. Origin uncertain: perhaps from an assumed Old English word (influenced by Old Norse *draumr*). Ultimately from an Indo-European word meaning "deception."] —**dream·ful** *adj.* ◇ **in your dreams** used to indicate that somebody's hope or expectation is completely unrealistic (*informal*)

dream up *vt.* to devise or invent something, especially a complicated, ingenious, or ridiculous plan

dream·boat /dréem bṑt/ *n.* somebody considered to be very good-looking (*dated informal*)

dream·er /dréemər/ *n.* **1. SOMEBODY WHO DREAMS** somebody who dreams or is dreaming **2. SOMEBODY WHO DAYDREAMS** somebody who is preoccupied with fantasies or unrealistic plans and is out of touch with reality

dream·i·ly /dréemilee/ *adv.* in a vague and absent-minded way that suggests a preoccupation with pleasant thoughts and fantasies ○ *He smiled dreamily.*

dream·land /dréem lànd/ *n.* **1. FANTASY WORLD** an imaginary, very pleasant or perfect sphere of existence that exists only in dreams **2. SLEEP** a state of sleep or unconsciousness (*informal*)

dream·less /dréemləss/ *adj.* deep, peaceful, and undisturbed by dreams ○ *a dreamless sleep* —**dream·less·ly** *adv.* —**dream·less·ness** *n.*

dream·like /dréem lìk/ *adj.* resembling a dream or the images in a dream, especially in seeming unreal and strange

dream·scape /dréem skàyp/ *n.* a scene, setting, or picture that has the unreal or strange qualities usually associated with images in dreams

dreamt past tense, past participle of **dream**

dream team *n.* (*informal*) **1.** SPORTS **WINNING GROUP OF ATHLETES** an exceptionally good team of athletes who regularly win medals or championships **2.** LAW **EXCEPTIONALLY GOOD GROUP OF LAWYERS** a powerful, exceptionally well qualified team of attorneys, whether defense or prosecution **3. SUCCESSFUL PARTNERSHIP** the best possible combination of people to perform a task [The nickname of the 1992 U.S. Olympic basketball team that included Michael Jordan, Magic Johnson, and Larry Bird]

dream tick·et *n.* candidates running as a team for associated political offices, especially those of President and Vice President, who seem to have between them all the qualities needed for electoral success (*informal*)

dream world *n.* a world that bears little resemblance to reality and exists only in the mind

dream·y /dréemee/ (**dream·i·er, dream·i·est**) *adj.* **1. VAGUE** caused by dreaming or by thinking about something very pleasant and absorbing **2. GIVEN TO DAYDREAMING** having a tendency to spend time daydreaming or lost in thought **3. UNREAL** strange, vague, or ethereal, like an image in a dream **4. SOOTHING** gently soothing and relaxing

drear /dreer/ *adj.* dark, foreboding, and gloomy (*literary*) ○ *It was a cold, drear day.* [Mid-16thC. Back formation from DREARY.]

drea·ry /dréeree/ (**drea·ri·er, drea·ri·est**) *adj.* gloomy, unexciting, and certain to have a wearying and depressing influence ○ *the dreary routine of prison life* [Old English *drēorig* "dripping with blood," from a prehistoric Germanic word that is probably also the ancestor of English *drowsy* and *drizzle*] —**drea·ri·ly** *adv.* —**drea·ri·ness** *n.*

dreck /drek/ *n.* worthless trashy stuff, especially low-quality merchandise [Early 20thC. From Yiddish *drek* "filth, dung," from Middle High German *drec.*] —**dreck·y** /drékee/ *adj.*

dredge[1] /drej/ *n.* **1. MACHINE FOR DIGGING UNDERWATER** a machine equipped with a continuous revolving chain of buckets, a scoop, or a suction device for digging out and removing material from under water **2.** SHIPPING = **dredger**[1] *n.* 1 **3.** AGRIC **SHELLFISH NET** a net on a frame dragged along the bottom of the sea or a river to gather shellfish ■ *v.* **1.** *vt.* **DIG SOMETHING UP WITH A DREDGE** to remove or recover material from under water by means of a dredge **2.** *vti.* SHIPPING **CLEAR A CHANNEL** to clear, deepen, or widen a waterway, especially one intended for shipping, using a dredge **3.** *vti.* **SEARCH WITH A DREDGE** to search something, or search for something, using a dredge or a similar device [Early 16thC. Origin uncertain: perhaps formed from Old English *dragan* "to draw" or Middle Dutch *dregghe* "drag-net."]

dredge up *vt.* to bring something to light from an obscure source, e.g., to recall something bad that happened long ago or unearth some scandalous information

dredge[2] /drej/ (**dredged, dredg·ing, dredg·es**) *vt.* to sprinkle or cover food with a coating of confectioner's sugar, flour, or sugar [Late 16thC. Via Old French *dragie* "sugarplum, sugar almond," from Latin *tragemata*, from Greek *tragēmata* "spices, sweetmeats."]

dredg·er[1] /dréjjər/ *n.* **1.** SHIPPING **BOAT WITH DREDGE** a boat or barge with a dredge on it, used mainly for clearing or deepening waterways **2.** = **dredge**[1] *n.* 1

dredg·er[2] /dréjjər/ *n.* a container with small holes in the top used for sprinkling confectioner's sugar, flour, or sugar onto food

dreg /dreg/ *n.* a small amount, especially a small remainder of something ○ *not a dreg of sympathy for them* [14thC. Origin uncertain: probably from Old Norse *dregg* "sediment."]

D re·gion *n.* **1.** METEOROL **LOWEST PART OF IONOSPHERE** the lowest part of the ionosphere above the Earth's surface **2.** BIOCHEM **SHORT SEQUENCE OF AMINO ACIDS** a short sequence of amino acids at the end of an immunoglobulin chain that allows for variations and thus contributes to antibody diversity

dregs /dregz/ *npl.* **1. GRITTY PARTICLES IN LIQUID** small solid particles found in liquids such as coffee or wine that sink to the bottom of a container and are most in evidence when the container is nearly empty **2. LEAST VALUABLE PART** the least valuable or most unpleasant part of something, especially a group of people ○ *the dregs of society* **3. LAST REMAINING PART** the last remaining, and often least attractive part of something (*literary*) ○ *sat through the dregs of a long boring evening*

drei·del /dráyd'l/, **drei·dl** *n.* a toy that looks like a spinning top used to play games during Hanukkah [Mid-20thC. From Yiddish *dreydl*, from Middle High German *dræhen* "to turn."]

Drei·ser /drīssər, -zər/, **Theodore** (1871–1945) U.S. novelist and journalist. He was known for his naturalist novels, including *An American Tragedy* (1925). Full name **Theodore Herman Albert Dreiser**

drench /drench/ *vt.* (**drenched, drench·ing, drench·es**) **1. SOAK SOMEBODY OR SOMETHING** to make somebody or something completely wet ○ *I got absolutely drenched going out in the storm.* **2.** VET **GIVE AN ANIMAL LIQUID MEDICINE** to give an animal a large dose of medicine in liquid form by mouth ■ *n.* VET **DOSE OF ANIMAL MEDICINE** a large oral dose of medicine given to an animal in liquid form by mouth [Old English *drencan* "to give to drink," from a prehistoric Germanic word that is also the ancestor of English *drink*. The underlying idea is of making something drink.] —**drench·er** *n.* —**drench·ing** *adj., n.*

Dres·den /drézdən/ capital of the state of Saxony in east-central Germany. Almost completely destroyed during World War II, it has been largely rebuilt and restored. Population: 477,600 (1994).

Dres·den chi·na *n.* = **Meissen**

dress /dress/ *v.* (**dressed, dress·ing, dress·es**) **1.** *vti.* **PUT CLOTHES ON** to put clothes on somebody **2.** *vi.* **WEAR** to wear clothes of a particular type, or wear them in a particular way ○ *She usually dresses in black.* **3.** *vi.* **PUT ON APPROPRIATE CLOTHES** to put on clothes appropriate to a particular occasion, especially formal clothes ○ *We need to dress for the theater.* **4.** *vt.* **DECORATE SOMETHING** to make a place or thing look festive by putting special decorations on it ○ *They dressed the big house for the holidays.* **5.** *vt.* COMM **ARRANGE GOODS IN A WINDOW DISPLAY** to arrange goods in a store window so that they look attractive ○ *windows that were dressed for spring* **6.** *vt.* MED **COVER A WOUND** to put a bandage or other protective covering on a wound **7.** *vt.* COOK **PUT SAUCE ON SALAD** to put mayonnaise, vinaigrette, or a similar type of sauce on a salad **8.** *vt.* COOK, HUNT **CLEAN FISH AND GAME** to clean and prepare fish, poultry, or meat for cooking or selling **9.** *vt.* **ARRANGE HAIR** to arrange hair, e.g., by combing, clipping, or oiling it **10.** *vti.* MIL **COME INTO ALIGNMENT** to come, or bring troops, into a correct alignment with one another for a parade formation **11.** *vt.* AGRIC **SPREAD MANURE OR FERTILIZER ON SOIL** to spread manure or fertilizer over the surface of an area of land **12.** *vt.* **FINISH A MATERIAL** to apply a finishing process to a material such as stone or lumber, usually in order to give it a smooth and good-looking surface ■ *n.* **1. WOMAN'S ONE-PIECE GARMENT** a one-piece garment for women and girls combining a bodice, with or without sleeves, and a skirt and covering most of the body **2. TYPE OF CLOTHES** clothes of a particular type or style **3. CLOTHES** clothes and clothing in general, considered, e.g., as an item in a budget or from the point of view of somebody's taste in them ○ *He has no interest in matters of dress.* **4. CLOTHING REQUIRED FOR PARTICULAR OCCASION** the clothing required for a particular occasion **5. OUTWARD APPEARANCE** the outward appearance or covering of a thing, especially a living thing, or the way in which something is presented (*literary*) **6.** THEATER **DRESS REHEARSAL** a dress rehearsal (*informal*) ■ *adj.* **1. FORMAL** worn on formal occasions ○ *dress uniform* **2. REQUIRING FORMAL ATTIRE** requiring formal clothes to be worn ○ *a dress banquet* [14thC. Via Old French *dresser* "arrange, prepare" from Vulgar Latin *directiare*, from Latin *directus* "straight" (source of English *direct*).] ◇ **dressed to kill** dressed in very glamorous clothes, especially when intending to impress somebody (*slang*)

dress down *v.* **1.** *vi.* **LOOK CASUAL** to dress in a deliberately understated or casual way for an occasion (*informal*) **2.** *vt.* **REPRIMAND SOMEBODY** to scold somebody severely

dress up *v.* **1.** *vi.* **DRESS FORMALLY** to put on formal or especially elegant clothes, usually for a special occasion such as a party **2.** *vi.* **PUT ON COSTUMES** to put on a special costume or different clothes from those normally worn so as to look like or pretend to be somebody else **3.** *vt.* **DISGUISE SOMETHING** to disguise something unpleasant and try to make it look more pleasant

dres·sage /drə saázh/ *n.* **1. TRAINING A HORSE TO EXECUTE PRECISE MOVEMENTS** the training of a horse to carry out a series of precise controlled movements in response to minimal signals from its rider **2. DRESSAGE EVENT** a competitive event in which horse and rider are judged on the elegance, precision, and discipline of the horse's movements [Mid-20thC. From French, literally "training," from *dresser* (see DRESS).]

dress cir·cle *n.* a separate raised section of the auditorium in a theater, concert hall, or opera house, usually the first seating gallery above ground level

dress coat *n.* a coat, forming part of a man's full evening dress, that is usually black with a cutaway skirt and tails

dress code *n.* a set of requirements as to how people should dress when attending a function or visiting a place

dress-down day *n.* a day, typically a Friday, or days during the summer months, on which office workers wear casual clothing to work

dress·er[1] /dréssər/ *n.* **1. BEDROOM CHEST OF DRAWERS** a chest of drawers used in a bedroom for storing clothes sometimes with a mirror on top **2. SHELVES AND A CHEST** a piece of furniture consisting of a set of shelves on top of a chest containing cupboards and drawers, often used for storing crockery and cutlery in traditional kitchens [Early 15thC. From Old French *dresseur*, from *dresser* (see DRESS).]

dress·er[2] /dréssər/ *n.* **1. SOMEBODY WHO DRESSES IN PARTICULAR WAY** somebody who dresses in a particular way **2. ACTOR'S ASSISTANT** somebody who helps an actor to put on or change a costume before and during a performance **3. PERSONAL GROOMING ASSISTANT** somebody whose job it is to ensure that another person's wardrobe is in order

dress form *n.* an adjustable tailor's dummy

dress·ing /dréssing/ *n.* **1.** MED **WOUND COVERING** a bandage or other sterile covering that is put on a wound to protect it from infection or further damage **2. SALAD SAUCE** a sauce used on salads, usually with an oil and vinegar or mayonnaise base **3. STUFFING** stuffing for poultry or meat **4.** AGRIC **FERTILIZER** natural or artificial fertilizer for spreading on the soil

dress·ing-down *n.* a scolding or severe reprimand, often in public

dress·ing gown *n.* a coat made of soft light material that is worn over nightclothes, before or after taking a bath, or in the early stages of getting dressed

dress·ing room *n.* **1.** THEATER **ACTORS' ROOM TO PUT ON COSTUMES** a room in a theater where actors can prepare for a performance by putting on their makeup and costumes **2. ROOM TO CHANGE CLOTHES IN** a small room or alcove in a house, hotel suite, or other place that people can use when putting on or changing their clothes

dress·ing ta·ble *n.* a low table with drawers and a mirror attached to the top, usually placed in a bedroom so that a woman can sit at it when putting on her makeup

Dress·ler /dréssler/, **Marie** (1869–1934) Canadian-born U.S. stage and movie actor. She won an Academy Award for her performance in *Min and Bill* (1930). Real name **Leila von Koerber**

dress·mak·er /dréss màykər/ *n.* somebody who makes women's clothes, especially somebody who makes a living by doing this —**dress·mak·ing** *n.*

dress pa·rade *n.* a military parade in which the soldiers wear formal dress uniform

dress re·hears·al *n.* **1.** THEATER **FINAL REHEARSAL** the final rehearsal of a play, in full costume and with lights, music, and effects, before it is given its first public performance **2. FULL-SCALE PRACTICE BEFORE EVENT** a full-scale practice before any important event

dress sense *n.* the ability to choose clothes well and coordinate colors and styles effectively

dress shield *n.* a small fabric pad worn around the armpits of a piece of clothing to prevent sweat from showing or staining it

dress shirt *n.* **1. MAN'S FORMAL SHIRT** a man's shirt worn with formal evening wear, usually white and with either a stiff collar or a ruffle down the front **2. SHIRT WORN WITH A SUIT** a shirt that is not casual and is suitable for wearing with a suit, e.g., at work

dress suit *n.* a man's suit worn as part of formal evening wear, especially with a tailcoat

dress u·ni·form *n.* a ceremonial uniform worn by members of the armed forces for formal occasions

dress·y /déssee/ (**-i·er, -i·est**) *adj.* **1. ELEGANT** stylish and elegant **2. AT WHICH GUESTS DRESS IN STYLE** at which stylish and elegant clothes are worn ○ *a very dressy buffet luncheon* **3. OVERDRESSED** dressed in an inappropriately elaborate or showy way —**dress·i·ly** *adv.* —**dress·i·ness** *n.*

drew past tense of **draw**

Drex·el /dréks'l/, **Anthony Joseph** (1826–93) U.S. banker and philanthropist. He worked in investment banking and founded Philadelphia's Drexel Institute of Technology (1891).

Drex·el Hill city in Delaware County, Pennsylvania, situated southwest of Philadelphia. Population: 29,744 (1990).

drey /dray/ (*plural* **dreys**) *n.* a squirrel's nest [Early 17thC. Origin unknown.]

drib /drib/ *n.* a very small amount, usually a tiny drop of liquid or a fragment of material ○ *just a drib of paint on the porch floor* [Early 18thC. Origin uncertain: perhaps from *drib* "to drip," alteration of DRIP; or shortening of DRIBBLE or DRIBLET.] ◇ **in dribs and drabs** in very small amounts or stages, and usually in a rather haphazard way ○ *Wedding presents are beginning to arrive in dribs and drabs.*

drib·ble /dríbb'l/ *v.* (**-bled, -bling, -bles**) **1.** *vi.* **PRODUCE SALIVA** to let saliva spill out of the mouth **2.** *vti.* **SPILL DROPS** to flow, or allow a liquid to flow or spill out, in drops or a small stream **3.** *vti.* SPORTS **MOVE BALL** to move a ball along using small repeated movements of the foot, the hand, or a stick **4.** *vti.* BASKETBALL **BOUNCE A BALL ON COURT** to propel the ball in any direction on the court by bouncing it with the hands ■ *n.* **1. TINY AMOUNT OF LIQUID** a small amount of liquid that is falling or has fallen in drops or a thin stream **2.** SPORTS **MOVEMENT WHILE DRIBBLING BALL** a movement or run made while dribbling the ball, especially in basketball or soccer ○ *a hard, fast dribble to midcourt* [Mid-16thC. Literally "to drip frequently," formed from *drib* "to drip," alteration of DRIP.] —**drib·bler** *n.* —**drib·bly** *adj.*

drib·let /dríbblət/, **drib·blet** *n.* a tiny amount of a liquid [Late 16thC. Coined from *drib* "to drip," alteration of DRIP, + -LET.]

dri·er /drīər/, **dry·er** comparative of **dry** ■ *n.* **1. DRYING DEVICE** a machine or device for drying things **2. SUBSTANCE TO AID DRYING** a substance added to paint or ink to speed up the drying process

dri·est /drī ist/, **dry·est** superlative of **dry**

drift /drift/ *v.* (**drift·ed, drift·ing, drifts**) **1.** *vi.* **BE CARRIED ALONG** to be, or allow something to be, carried along by the flow of water or air **2.** *vi.* **MOVE AIMLESSLY** to move in a slow, smooth, gentle, and unforced way, usually without any direction or purpose ○ *The crowd gradually drifted away.* **3.** *vi.* **WANDER FROM PLACE TO PLACE AIMLESSLY** to go from one place to another, never staying anywhere for very long and seemingly with little purpose **4.** *vi.* NAVIG **WANDER FROM A SET COURSE OR POSITION** to deviate from a set course, or move gradually away from a fixed position **5.** *vi.* **CHANGE GRADUALLY** to change or develop gradually, or move slowly from one point or position to another ○ *Prices have drifted downwards in recent weeks.* **6.** *vti.* **FORM HEAPS** to build up and form heaps as a result of the action of the wind or water currents, or cause something such as snow, sand, or leaves to form heaps ■ *n.* **1. PILED-UP DEPOSITS** a heap, pile, or bank of something such as snow, sand, or leaves created by the action of the wind or water currents **2. DRIFTING MOVEMENT** a slow gentle movement in which something is, or seems to be, carried along on a current of air or water **3. MATERIAL CARRIED ALONG** an amount of something carried along by the flow of air or water ○ *drifts of smoke coming from the chimneys* **4. MOVEMENT OF PEOPLE** a gradual movement over a period of time of groups of people or animals toward or away from a place ○ *the drift of young people away from rural areas* **5. GRADUAL CHANGE** a broad and gradual change or development, e.g., in people's opinions or behavior ○ *a drift back to larger cars* ○ *a downward drift in prices* **6. GENERAL MEANING** the general meaning of an argument, opinion, or statement **7. STATE OF INACTIVITY** a state of inactivity or indecision in which a person or group is carried along by events **8.** NAVIG **DEVIATION FROM COURSE** the distance or extent to which a ship or aircraft deviates from its set course due to the action of wind or currents **9.** GEOL **DEPOSIT OF GRAVEL** a loose deposit of sand, gravel, or rock left by a glacier or ice sheet **10.** GEOG **CURRENT** the motion of a river or broad ocean current **11.** MINING **HORIZONTAL MINESHAFT** a horizontal or virtually horizontal mineshaft that follows a vein of ore **12.** MINING **CONNECTING PASSAGE IN MINE** a small passage in a mine connecting two main shafts or tunnels **13.** ELEC ENG **UNCONTROLLED CHANGE IN A SETTING** a slow uncontrolled change in a previously adjusted setting, e.g., in the frequency to which an electronic device has been set **14.** MECH ENG **TAPERING STEEL TOOL FOR ENLARGING HOLES** a tapering steel tool used to enlarge or align holes in pieces of metal before they are bolted or riveted **15.** SPORTS **CONTROLLED SKID IN RACING CAR** a controlled slide used by racing drivers as a method of cornering at high speed [14thC. From Old Norse *drift* "snowdrift," from a prehistoric Germanic word that is also the ancestor of English *drive*. The underlying idea is of something driven.] —**drift·y** *adj.*

drift·age /dríftij/ *n.* **1. DRIFTED MATERIAL** material that has drifted along on, and been deposited by, air or water currents **2.** NAVIG **DEVIATION FROM SET COURSE** the distance by which a ship or aircraft has deviated from its set course owing to winds or currents

drift·er /dríftər/ *n.* **1. WANDERER** somebody who does not stay in the same place or job for long but is always moving on, apparently aimlessly, from place to place **2.** SAILING, ANGLING **FISHING BOAT WITH DRIFT NET** a fishing vessel that fishes with a drift net

drift ice *n.* large areas of ice that float in the open sea

drift net *n.* a large fishing net supported by floats that is allowed to drift along with the current or is attached to a vessel

drift·wood /dríft wòod/ *n.* broken pieces of wood that are found washed up on a beach or riverbank or floating in the sea or a river

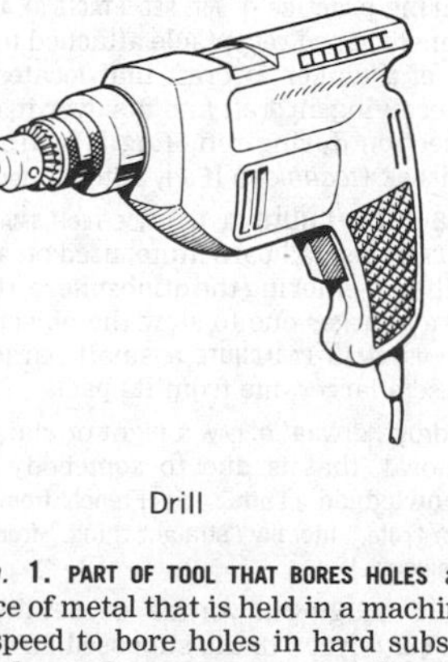

Drill

drill[1] /dril/ *n.* **1. PART OF TOOL THAT BORES HOLES** a long pointed piece of metal that is held in a machine and rotated at speed to bore holes in hard substances such as wood, metal, masonry, or rock **2. BORING TOOL WITH DRILL** a tool or machine that holds, drives, and bores holes with a drill **3.** MIL **TRAINING BY REPETITION** a type of military training, particularly in marching maneuvers and weapons handling, that involves the constant repetition of a set pattern of movements or tasks **4.** EDUC **REPEATED EXERCISE** a sequence of tasks, exercises, or words repeated over and over until they can be performed faultlessly, as used in teaching military skills, languages, or basic arithmetic **5. SAFETY ROUTINE** a sequence of actions practiced repeatedly so that people know what to do in an emergency to ensure their safety **6. ROUTINE** a set procedure or routine for doing something (*informal*) **7.** ZOOL **PREDATORY MOLLUSK** a marine mollusk that preys on oysters by boring into their shells. Latin name: *Urosalpinx cinerea.* ■ *v.* (**drilled, drill·ing, drills**) **1.** *vti.* **BORE A HOLE WITH A DRILL** to bore a hole in something with a drill **2.** *vti.* MIL **PRACTICE MARCHING** to practice marching maneuvers repeatedly on a parade ground as a form of military training and discipline **3.** *vt.* EDUC **TEACH A SUBJECT BY ROTE** to make somebody repeat a sequence of exercises or procedures over and over again in order to learn it **4.** *vt.* **SHOOT SOMEBODY OR SOMETHING** to shoot somebody with bullets, or shoot bullets into something (*informal*) **5.** *vt.* SPORTS **THROW OR HIT A BALL HARD** to throw or hit a ball with great force in a straight line toward somebody or something (*informal*) [Early 16thC . From Middle Dutch *drillen* "to make a hole, whirl." Ultimately from an Indo-European word meaning "to turn," which is also the ancestor of English *trite* and *threshold*.] —**drill·a·ble** *adj.*

WORD KEY: SYNONYMS

See Synonyms at ***teach***.

drill[2] /dril/ *n.* AGRIC **1. FURROW FOR SEEDS** a shallow furrow in which seeds are sown **2. SEED-PLANTING MACHINE** a machine for planting seeds in furrows **3. PLANTED ROW OF SEEDS** a row of seeds planted along a small furrow ■ *vt.* (**drilled, drill·ing, drills**) AGRIC **PLANT WITH DRILL** to plant seeds with a drill [Early 18thC. Origin uncertain: perhaps from DRILL[1].]

drill[3] /dril/ *n.* a tough cotton twill used especially for making workclothes and uniforms [Mid-18thC. From German *Drillich*, from Latin *trilix*, literally "with three threads," from *licium* "thread" (source of English *trellis*).]

drill[4] /dril/ *n.* a West African baboon with a black face and brown fur, similar to a mandrill though smaller in size. Latin name: *Papio leucophaeus.* [Mid-17thC. From a West African name for the baboon.]

drill·ing mud *n.* a mixture of clay, water, and chemicals pumped into a well as it is being bored to lubricate the drill, remove debris, and prevent gas or oil escaping

drill·ing plat·form *n.* a structure used in offshore oil drilling that supports drilling equipment and is either fixed to the seabed or floats independently

drill in·struc·tor *n.* MIL a noncommissioned officer responsible for giving recruits their basic training

drill·mas·ter /dríl màstər/ *n.* **1.** *U.K.* MIL = **drill instructor 2. STRICT TRAINER** somebody who trains people in a very strict and militaristic way

drill pipe *n.* = **drill string**

drill press *n.* a machine consisting of a powered drill on a vertical stand that is brought down onto the work automatically or by a hand lever

drill ser·geant *n.* MIL = **drill instructor**

drill·stock /dríl stòk/ *n.* the part of a drilling tool or machine that holds the shank of the drill

drill string *n.* a long metal pipe, progressively built up from lengths of steel tubing, that is attached above the drill when drilling for oil or gas and eventually forms the bore of the well

dri·ly /drîlee/, **dry·ly** *adv.* with subtle and almost imperceptible irony or humor

drink /dringk/ *vti.* (**drank** /drangk/, **drunk** /drungk/, **drink·ing, drinks**) **1. SWALLOW LIQUID** to take in liquid through the mouth **2. DRINK ALCOHOL** to drink an alcoholic beverage, especially habitually ○ *Don't drink and drive.* **3. TOAST SOMEBODY BY RAISING A GLASS** to raise a glass and then drink from it as a sign that you wish somebody or something happiness, luck, success, or good health ■ *n.* **1. DRINKABLE LIQUID** liquid that can be drunk, usually in a container ○ *There isn't much food or drink in the house.* **2. AMOUNT OF LIQUID** an amount of liquid that somebody drinks ○ *Could I have a drink of water?* **3. ALCOHOLIC BEVERAGE** alcoholic drink, especially an individual serving in a glass, bottle, or can **4. EXCESSIVE CONSUMPTION OF ALCOHOL** excessive consumption of alcohol **5. BODY OF WATER** the sea or a large body of water, e.g., a lake or swimming pool (*informal*) ○ *in the drink* ■ **drinks** *npl.* **INFORMAL PARTY WITH DRINKS SERVED** an informal party with alcoholic or other drinks served but not a meal [Old English *drincan*. Ultimately from a prehistoric Germanic word that is also the ancestor of English *drench* and *drown*.]

drink down *vt.* to consume a liquid quickly and completely ○ *Drink your coffee down before it gets cold.*

drink in *vt.* **1. ABSORB LIQUID** to absorb as much liquid as is available ○ *The plants drank in the welcome rain.* **2. ABSORB SOMETHING WITH MIND AND SENSES** to absorb eagerly every aspect of something with the mind and senses ○ *She stood silently on the beach, drinking in the beauty.*

drink up *vt.* **1. FINISH A DRINK** to drink all of something **2. ABSORB LIQUID COMPLETELY** to absorb a liquid completely ○ *The dry earth drank up the rain.*

drink·a·ble /dríngkəb'l/ *adj.* **1. SAFE TO DRINK** safe for humans or animals to drink **2. NICE TO DRINK** pleasant or enjoyable to drink ○ *a very drinkable local fruit juice* —**drink·a·bil·i·ty** /dringkə bíllətee/ *n.* —**drink·a·ble·ness** /dríngkəb'lnəss/ *n.*

drink·er /dríngkər/ *n.* **1. SOMEBODY WHO DRINKS SOMETHING PARTICULAR** somebody who drinks a particular type of beverage (*used in combination*) ○ *I'm not a coffee drinker.* **2. SOMEBODY WHO DRINKS ALCOHOLIC BEVERAGES** somebody who drinks alcoholic beverages, especially to excess

drink·ing foun·tain *n.* a device attached to a wall that produces a jet of water that people can drink

drink·ing song *n.* a song, often rowdy or suggestive, sung by people drinking alcohol together

drink·ing wa·ter *n.* water intended for people to drink, especially when free of harmful elements such as industrial waste, chemicals, or animal waste

drip /drip/ *v.* (**dripped, drip·ping, drips**) **1.** *vti.* **FALL OR LET FALL IN DROPS** to fall as drops of liquid, or let liquid fall as drops ○ *The faucet is dripping.* **2.** *vt.* **LET SOMETHING OUT COPIOUSLY** to let out something, particularly an emotion, in great quantity ○ *His voice positively dripped malice.* ■ *n.* **1. SMALL AMOUNT OF LIQUID** a drop of liquid or moisture ○ *a bucket to catch the drips* **2. DRIPPING OF LIQUID** an instance or the process of a liquid falling in drops ○ *Our ceiling has developed a drip.* **3. SOUND OF FALLING DROPS** the sound of drops of liquid falling onto something ○ *the steady drip of a leaking faucet* **4.** *U.K.* MED = **drip feed 5. SOCIALLY INEPT PERSON** somebody regarded by others as socially inept, inadequate, or uninteresting (*slang*) **6.** ARCHIT **PROTECTIVE GROOVE** a protective groove cut in a sill or other overhang of a wall or building to cause water to drip freely **7.** FOOD **REGULAR COFFEE** a regular cup of coffee (*slang*) ○ *The guy in the corner wants a drip.* [Old English *dryppan*. Ultimately from an Indo-European base meaning "to drop," which is also the ancestor of English *drop, droop,* and *drizzle*.]

drip with *vt.* **1. HAVE DROPS FALLING CONTINUOUSLY** to have liquid falling in a continuous stream of drops ○ *dripping with sweat* **2. HAVE TOO MUCH OF SOMETHING** to have too much of something, especially some kind of adornment, usually in a way that is considered to be bad taste **3. GIVE VENT TO EMOTION** to give continuous expression to an emotion, especially a negative one such as spite, malice, or sarcasm ○ *Her voice dripped with sarcasm.*

drip cof·fee *n.* coffee made by pouring hot water over ground coffee beans held in a filter above a pot so that it drips into the pot

drip-dry *adj.* **REQUIRING NO IRONING** not wrinkling or creasing as it dries, and thus not needing ironing ○ *a drip-dry shirt* ■ *vti.* (**drip-dried, drip-dry·ing, drip-dries**) **1. DRY WITHOUT CREASES** to dry without creases when hung up wet, or cause something to dry in this way **2. DRY HAIR NATURALLY** to dry hair merely by exposing it to the air, without using a hairdrier, or to become dry in this way

drip feed *n.* MED **1. MEDICAL PROCEDURE FOR INJECTING LIQUID** injection of quantities of a therapeutic fluid, such as blood, plasma, saline, or glucose, directly into somebody's vein at an adjustable rate. A plastic bag containing the fluid is hung above the patient on a stand. ○ *They put her on a drip feed* **2. FLUID USED IN DRIP FEED** the therapeutic fluid used in a drip feed ○ *Add antibiotic to the drip feed.* **3. EQUIPMENT USED TO ADMINISTER A DRIP FEED** the equipment used to administer a drip feed (*informal*)

drip-feed (**drip-fed, drip-feed·ing, drip-feeds**) *vt.* **1.** MED **ADMINISTER A DRIP FEED TO** to pass a liquid, especially a sugar solution, directly into somebody's vein using a drip feed **2.** GARDENING, AGRIC **PROVIDE PLANTS WITH A CONTINUOUS WATER SUPPLY** to provide water, and sometimes nutrients, to indoor plants or field crops continuously in small quantities

drip·less /drípplәss/ *adj.* designed or made not to drip ○ *This teapot has a dripless spout.*

drip pan *n.* a shallow pan or cookie sheet used in the oven to catch the juices of roasting meat

drip·ping /drípping/ *npl.* **drippings** FOOD **JUICES FROM COOKING MEAT** the juices, including fat, produced by roasting or frying meat ■ *adj.* **THOROUGHLY WET** thoroughly wet ○ *She hurried in, cold and dripping from the storm.*

drip·pings /drípping*z*/ *npl.* the juices, including fat, produced by roasting or frying meat

drip·py /drípee/ (**-pi·er, -pi·est**) *adj.* **1. INEPT OR BORING** socially inept, inadequate, or uninteresting (*slang insult*) **2. TOO SENTIMENTAL** silly and extremely sentimental (*slang*) **3.** METEOROL **WITH RAIN** drizzly or tending to rain ○ *This is our fifth drippy day in a row.* [Early 19thC. From the notion of "dripping with tears or sentiment."] —**drip·pi·ly** *adv.* —**drip·pi·ness** *n.*

drip·stone /dríp stōn/ *n.* **1.** ARCHIT **PROTECTIVE STONE DRIP** a stone drip used to protect a projection over a door or window **2.** GEOL **FORM OF CALCIUM CARBONATE** calcium carbonate deposits in the form of stalactites or stalagmites

driv·a·ble /drívәb'l/ *adj.* **1. NICE TO DRIVE** easy, comfortable, or pleasant to drive **2. IN A CONDITION TO BE DRIVEN** in good enough condition to be driven safely —**driv·a·bil·i·ty** /drìvә bíllәtee/ *n.*

drive /drīv/ *v.* (**drove** /drōv/, **driv·en** /drívv'n/, **driv·ing, drives**) **1.** *vti.* TRANSP **CONTROL MOVEMENT OF A VEHICLE** to operate a vehicle, controlling its speed and direction, or be operated so as to move in a particular direction ○ *He's learning to drive.* **2.** *vti.* TRANSP **TRAVEL OR CONVEY IN VEHICLE** to travel somewhere in a vehicle, or take somebody somewhere in a vehicle ○ *I'll drive you to the airport.* **3.** *vt.* ENG **PROVIDE POWER FOR SOMETHING** to supply the power that makes something work (*often passive*) ○ *The lawn mower is driven by a gasoline engine.* **4.** *vt.* **STEER THE PROGRESS OF SOMETHING** to provide momentum toward the successful operation or functioning of something ○ *This company is driven by a concern for quality.* **5.** *vt.* **FORCE INTO A CONDITION** to force somebody or something into a particular state or condition, often an extremely negative one ○ *Her son's behavior drove her to despair.* **6.** *vt.* **COMPEL SOMEBODY TO DO SOMETHING** to supply the emotional or physical energy that leads somebody to act or behave in an extreme way ○ *Driven by fear, the elephants stampeded.* **7.** *vr.* **FORCE YOURSELF TO WORK TOO HARD** to force yourself to work too hard or too long hours at something ○ *You drive yourself too hard.* **8.** *vt.* **FORCE PEOPLE OR ANIMALS TO MOVE** to force people or animals to go somewhere ○ *Rain drove them indoors.* **9.** *vt.* **FORCE SOMETHING IN OR OUT** to push, knock, or hammer something forcefully into a particular position ○ *He drove the stakes into the ground.* **10.** *vti.* **MOVE OR PROPEL FORCEFULLY** to move or be blown or thrown with great force against something, or provide the force that does this ○ *The wind drove the snow into huge drifts.* **11.** *vt.* **MAKE A HOLE** to make a hole or tunnel in something using great force **12.** *vt.* SPORTS **HIT A BALL HARD** to kick or hit a ball or puck forcefully when playing a sport ○ *The clean-up batter drove the ball past the shortstop.* **13.** *vti.* GOLF **HIT A LONG SHOT** to hit a long shot in golf, from either a tee or a fairway, when covering the principal distance between holes ○ *He drove into the rough.* **14.** *vti.* BASKETBALL **DRIBBLE DIRECTLY TOWARD THE BASKET** in basketball, to dribble the ball through a particular area of the court toward the basket ○ *She's unstoppable when she drives the baseline.* **15.** *vt.* HUNT **CHASE GAME INTO THE OPEN** to chase a hunted animal into the open where it can be killed ■ *n.* **1.** TRANSP **RIDE TAKEN IN A VEHICLE** a trip in a car or other vehicle ○ *go for a drive* **2.** TRANSP = **driveaway 3.** TRANSP **WIDE ROAD** any street or road that can be used for vehicles, especially one that has more than two lanes or has pleasant views (*often used in place names*) **4.** ENG **TRANSMISSION OF POWER** the means of converting power into motion in a machine, e.g., a motor vehicle (*often used in combination*) ○ *a car with four-wheel drive* **5.** COMPUT = **disk drive 6.** SPORTS **HARD HIT OF BALL** in some sports, a forceful shot or stroke in hitting a ball ○ *His drive to left field scored two runners.* **7.** GOLF **LONG SHOT** a long shot in golf, played from either a tee or fairway, when covering the main portion of the distance between the tee and green **8.** BASKETBALL **FAST MOVEMENT TOWARD BASKET** in basketball, a fast direct run toward the basket while dribbling the ball ○ *Our players are having trouble scoring off drives.* **9.** FOOTBALL **CONTINUOUS MOVEMENT TOWARD GOAL** in football, steady movement toward a goal line, usually achieved in one or more series of downs ○ *They've been unable to manage a sustained drive in this quarter.* **10. FOCUSED ENERGY** energy and determination that helps somebody achieve what he or she wants to do ○ *Do you have the drive to achieve your ambitions?* **11.** PSYCHOL **MOTIVATING NEED** a powerful need or instinct, e.g., hunger or sex, that motivates behavior **12. MAJOR PLANNED EFFORT** an organized effort made by a lot of people working together to achieve a particular goal ○ *a recruitment drive* **13.** MIL **SUSTAINED MILITARY ATTACK** a major sustained attack on an enemy, usually including armored vehicles and large guns **14.** AGRIC **ROUNDUP OF LIVESTOCK** a gathering and herding of cattle, sheep, or horses to a new pasture or to be sold for slaughter ○ *This will be my first cattle drive.* **15.** ELECTRON ENG **VOLTAGE** voltage applied to the grid of a transmitting or amplifying valve or to the base of a transistor **16.** AUTOMOT **FORWARD POSITION IN AUTOMATIC TRANSMISSION** in an automatic transmission, the principal shift position that moves the vehicle forward [Old English *drīfan*. Ultimately from an Indo-European word that is also the ancestor of English *drift* and *drove*.]

drive-by *n.* (*plural* **drive-bys**) **DRIVE-BY SHOOTING** a drive-by shooting (*informal*) ■ *adj.* **BRIEF AND NEGLIGENT** performed very quickly and with a lack of care or purpose ○ *a drive-by washing up that left the dishes only half clean*

drive-by shoot·ing *n.* an act of firing a firearm from a moving vehicle

drive-in *n.* a commercial establishment, e.g., a movie theater, that provides services or products to customers while they remain in their cars in a parking lot (*often used before a noun*) —**drive-in** *n.*

driv·el *n.* **1. SILLY TALK** silly and irrelevant or inaccurate talk ○ *They're talking drivel.* **2. DROOLED SALIVA** saliva dribbling from the mouth ■ *vi.* (**-eled, -el·ing, -els**) **1. TALK NONSENSE** to talk silly and irrelevant or inaccurate nonsense **2. DROOL** to let saliva dribble from the mouth [Old English *dreflian*, of uncertain origin] —**driv·el·er** *n.* —**driv·el·ing** *n.*

drive·line /drív līn/ *n.* = **drive train**

driv·en[1] /drívvn'n/ past participle of **drive**

driv·en[2] /drívvn'n/ *adj.* **1. COMPELLED BY PERSONAL NEED** striving to achieve because of a strong need or inner compulsion ○ *Driven people are often overachievers.* **2. CAUSED BY** having a particular thing as its principal cause (*used in combination*) ○ *a demand-driven economy*

driv·er /drívәr/ *n.* **1.** TRANSP **SOMEBODY WHO CAN DRIVE** somebody who operates a motor vehicle, or who is capable of operating one **2.** TRANSP **CHAUFFEUR** somebody who drives a car or limousine for other people **3.** GOLF **GOLF CLUB** a golf club with a wide wooden head, deep face, and a long shaft, used to drive the ball from the tee down the fairway **4.** ENG **PART THAT TRANSMITS SOMETHING** a part of a machine that causes another part to move **5.** TECH **TOOL THAT APPLIES PRESSURE** a tool, e.g., a screwdriver or drill, that exerts heavy pressure on something else **6.** ELECTRON ENG **ELECTRONIC CIRCUIT** an electronic circuit that produces an output used to control another circuit **7.** COMPUT **CONTROLLING SOFTWARE** computer software that controls the input and output of a particular device ○ *a printer driver* **8. STRONG FORCE** something that provides impetus or motivation, e.g., within an organization

driv·er ant *n.* = **army ant** [So called because they appear to herd other insects and small animals while on the march]

driv·er·less /drívәrlәss/ *adj.* **1. LACKING A DRIVER WHILE MOVING** moving out of control because the driver is missing **2. NEEDING NO DRIVER** having no driver because of being automatically operated

driv·er's li·cense *n.* a small card that somebody must carry whenever driving, obtained after a person has passed a test and demonstrating that he or she knows the laws that apply to good driving

driv·er's seat *n.* the seat in which the driver sits when operating a motor vehicle. = **driver's seat** ◇ **in the driver's seat** in a position to determine the course or direction of something

driv·er's side *n.* the side of a car on which the steering wheel is located, where the driver sits when operating a vehicle

drive shaft *n.* **1.** MECH ENG **ROTATING SHAFT TRANSMITTING ENGINE POWER** a rotating shaft that transmits the power from a motor or engine to another part of the machine, e.g., from the engine to the propellor of an aircraft **2.** AUTOMOT **SHAFT TRANSFERRING POWER TO REAR WHEELS** the shaft that transmits power from the transmission to the differential in a rear-wheel drive automobile or truck

drive-through *n.* a business, e.g., a fast-food restaurant or bank, that provides goods or services through a special window to customers who remain in their cars (*often used before a noun*)

drive time *n.* **1. COMMUTERS' RUSH HOURS** a time during the morning or afternoon when commuters are driving to and from work in their cars and listening to the radio **2. TIME FROM ONE PLACE TO ANOTHER** the amount of time that it takes to drive between two places

drive train *n.* a mechanical part of a vehicle, including the drive shaft and universal joint, that connects the transmission with the axles and transmits power, torque, and motion

drive-up *n.* a place in a commercial establishment such as a restaurant or bank where customers are served while remaining in their cars (*often used before a noun*)

drive·way /drív wày/ *n.* a private road that enables vehicles to travel from a public road to the entrance of a building such as a house or hotel

driv·ing /dríving/ *adj.* **1. FALLING HARD** falling or being blown very hard and forcefully ○ *driving rain* **2. ABLE TO MAKE SOMETHING HAPPEN** having the ability or influence to make something new or different happen ○ *She is the driving force behind the new development.* ○ *driving ambition* ■ *n.* TRANSP **PROCESS OF OPERATING A VEHICLE** the act or process of operating a motor vehicle, especially with regard to how skillful somebody is ○ *Your driving is even worse than usual today.* —**driv·ing·ly** *adv.*

driv·ing gloves *npl.* gloves worn while driving a vehicle, often a sports car. They are usually made of leather or have leather palms and knitted fabric backs.

driv·ing i·ron *n.* an iron golf club that can be used instead of a driver

driv·ing test *n.* a test of driving skills and knowledge, usually consisting of both a written and a road test that people must pass before driving without supervision on public roads

driv·ing time *n.* = **drive time** *n.* 1

driz·zle /drízz'l/ *n.* METEOROL **LIGHT RAIN** light steady rain ■ *v.* (**-zled, -zling, -zles**) **1.** *vi.* METEOROL **RAIN LIGHTLY** to rain lightly and steadily **2.** *vt.* COOK **DRIBBLE LIQUID OVER FOOD** to pour very small quantities of a liquid in a thin stream over food ○ *Lightly drizzle the dressing over the vegetables.* [Mid-16thC. Origin uncertain: perhaps ultimately from Old English *drēosan* "to fall," from a prehistoric Germanic word.] —**driz·zly** *adj.*

drogue /drōg/ *n.* **1.** NAUT = **sea anchor 2.** SPACE TECH, AIR = **drogue parachute 3.** MIL **TARGET TOWED BY AN AIRCRAFT** a cylindrical target towed behind an aircraft, used for firing practice **4.** AIR **RECEPTACLE ON A TANKER AIRCRAFT** a funnel-shaped receptacle attached to the refueling hose of a tanker aircraft that locates the probe of the receiving aircraft and fits over it, ensuring firm connection during refueling **5.** METEOROL **WINDSOCK** a windsock (*technical*) [Early 18thC. Origin uncertain.]

drogue par·a·chute *n.* **1.** SPACE TECH **SMALL PARACHUTE FOR SPACECRAFT** a small parachute, used on a spacecraft or satellite re-entering the atmosphere, that is released before a larger one to slow the object and stabilize it **2.** AIR **SMALL PARACHUTE** a small parachute used to release a larger one from its pack

droit /droyt, drwaa/ *n.* LAW a right or claim, either legal or moral, that is due to somebody and must be acknowledged [15thC. Via French from late Latin *directum* "rule," literally "straight thing," from Latin *directus* (see DIRECT).]

droit de seign·eur /drwaà dә say nyúr/, **droit du seign·eur** /-dyoo-/ *n.* the supposed former legal right of a feudal lord to have sexual intercourse with the bride or daughter of an inferior, usually a serf, on the night of her wedding [From French, literally "lord's right"]

droll /drōl/ *adj.* amusing in a wry or odd way ○ *Don't you enjoy his droll asides?* [Early 17thC. From French *drôle* "buffoon, comical," of uncertain origin: perhaps ultimately from Middle Dutch *drol* "imp, goblin."] —**drol·ly** *adv.* —**droll·ness** *n.*

WORD KEY: SYNONYMS

See Synonyms at ***funny***.

droll·er·y /drṓləree/ (*plural* **-ies**) *n.* **1. QUIRKY HUMOR** slightly odd or wry humor **2. TALKING OR BEHAVING AMUSINGLY** talking or acting in a wryly or oddly amusing way ○ *Such drollery is inappropriate in a formal context.* **3. SOMETHING FUNNY** an act or story that is wryly funny ○ *Whoever would have guessed that he was capable of such drolleries?*

-drome *suffix.* racecourse, field ○ *hippodrome* ○ *cosmodrome* [Via Latin from Greek *dromos* "racecourse." Ultimately from an Indo-European base meaning "to walk, run," which is also the ancestor of English *tread, trip,* and *dromedary.*]

Dromedary

drom·e·dar·y /drómmə dèree, drúmmə dèree/ (*plural* **-ies**) *n.* a camel with one hump, native to northern Africa and southwestern Asia where it is now domesticated and bred for working and racing. Latin name: *Camelus dromedarius.* [13thC. Via Old French *dromedaire* and late Latin *dromedarius* from, ultimately, Greek *dromad*, the stem of *dromas* "running."]

drom·ond /drómmənd, drúmm-/, **drom·on** /-mən, -mən/ *n.* a sailing galley used during the Middle Ages [14thC. Via Anglo-Norman *dromund* from, ultimately, Greek *dromō* "swift ship," from *dromos* "running, race" (see -DROME).]

-dromous *suffix.* moving, migrating ○ *catadromous* [Formed from modern Latin *-dromus*, from Greek *dromos* 'running, race' (see -DROME)]

drone[1] /drōn/ *v.* (**droned, dron·ing, drones**) **1.** *vi.* **MAKE A LOW HUMMING SOUND** to make a continuous low humming sound **2.** *vti.* **TALK IN A BORING VOICE** to talk for a long time in a boring voice ○ *I could hear his voice droning on in the background.* ■ *n.* **1. HUMMING SOUND** a continuous low sound **2.** MUSIC **UNCHANGING NOTE HELD DURING MELODY** a single note or chord that is held through a melodic part **3.** MUSIC **PIPE IN BAGPIPES PRODUCING CONTINUOUS NOTE** one of the pipes in a bagpipe that produces a single continuous note [Early 16thC. From DRONE[2].] —**dron·ing·ly** *adv.*

drone[2] /drōn/ *n.* **1.** INSECTS **NONWORKER MALE BEE** a male bee that has no sting, does not gather pollen, and exists only to mate with the queen bee **2. LAZY PERSON** somebody who does not work or contribute anything, instead relying on the work or energy of other people **3.** AIR **PILOTLESS AIRCRAFT** an aircraft whose flight is controlled from the ground [Old English *drān*. Ultimately from an Indo-European word meaning "to buzz," which is also the ancestor of English *threnody.*] —**dro·nish** /drṓnish/ *adj.*

dron·go /dróng gō/ (*plural* **-gos** *or* **-go**), **dron·go shrike** *n.* a tropical bird found in Africa, Asia, and Australia that is usually black with a strong beak, glossy feathers, and a long forked tail. Family: Dicruridae. [Mid-19thC. From Malagasy.]

drool /drool/ *v.* (**drooled, drool·ing, drools**) **1.** *vi.* **SHOW EXAGGERATED APPRECIATION** to show excessive appreciation of something or somebody really liked or wanted **2.** *vi.* **DRIBBLE SALIVA** to let saliva dribble from the mouth ○ *The dog lay drooling at his feet.* **3.** *vti.* **TALK NONSENSE** to talk nonsense or foolishness ■ *n.* **SALIVA DRIBBLING FROM THE MOUTH** saliva dribbling from the mouth [Early 19thC. Origin uncertain: possibly an alteration of DRIVEL.] —**drool·ing·ly** *adv.*

droop /droop/ *v.* (**drooped, droop·ing, droops**) **1.** *vti.* **HANG OR BEND DOWN LIMPLY** to move lower, hang down, or sag limply, or make something sag limply ○ *Her eyelids drooped with weariness.* **2.** *vi.* **BE DISPIRITED** to become discouraged or dejected ○ *His spirits drooped at the prospect of the long and arduous journey.* ■ *n.* **SAGGING** a lowered, sagging, or slumped position ○ *The droop of her shoulders suggested her disappointment.* [13thC. From Old Norse *drūpa.*] —**droop·i·ly** *adv.* —**droop·i·ness** *n.* —**droop·ing·ly** *adv.* —**droop·y** *adj.*

droop nose, droop snoot *n.* an aircraft nose section that can be tilted downward to increase the pilot's range of vision during landing and takeoff

drop /drop/ *v.* (**dropped, drop·ping, drops**) **1.** *vt.* **LET GO OF SOMETHING** to allow something to fall, sometimes intentionally ○ *somebody had dropped a glove in the street.* **2.** *vi.* **FALL** to fall from a higher place to a lower place **3.** *vti.* **MOVE TO A LOWER POSITION** to move into a lower position, or move the body or part of the body lower ○ *He dropped into a chair.* **4.** *vti.* **FALL IN DROPS** to fall or make something fall in drops of liquid ○ *We listened to the rain dropping on the roof.* **5.** *vti.* **LESSEN** to decrease, or reduce something, to a lower level, rate, or number ○ *The temperature dropped sharply overnight.* **6.** *vi.* **SLOPE DOWNWARD** to slope downward, often in a particular way **7.** *vti.* **LOWER THE VOICE** to lower the voice to a quieter level, or become quieter ○ *She dropped her voice to a whisper.* **8.** *vt.* **TAKE SOMEBODY OR SOMETHING SOMEWHERE** to take somebody or something to a place, usually by car, and leave the person or thing there ○ *Can you drop me at the bus station?* **9.** *vt.* **WRITE TO SOMEBODY** to write and send a message or greeting to somebody ○ *Drop me a line.* **10.** *vt.* **STOP DOING OR PLANNING SOMETHING** to abandon a plan or course of action ○ *We've dropped our plans to remodel the kitchen.* **11.** *vti.* **STOP TALKING ABOUT SOMETHING** to stop talking about something, or stop being talked about ○ *Can we drop the subject please?* **12.** *vt.* **END RELATIONSHIP WITH SOMEBODY** to end a close or intimate relationship with somebody (*informal*) **13.** *vt.* **REMOVE SOMEBODY** to remove somebody from a group of which she or he was formerly a member ○ *She may be dropped from the team.* **14.** *vt.* **OMIT LETTER OR WORD** to leave out a letter, word, or phrase ○ *You can drop the "Sir": just call me Max.* **15.** *vi.* **COLLAPSE FROM EXHAUSTION** to collapse in a state of complete exhaustion ○ *I'm ready to drop.* **16.** *vi.* **COLLAPSE** to lose consciousness or die, especially suddenly or unexpectedly (*informal*) ○ *People were dropping like flies from the extreme heat.* **17.** *vt.* SPORTS **LOSE A MATCH OR GAME** to lose a match, game, or part of a game ○ *He got through to the finals without dropping a set.* **18.** *vt.* **SAY SOMETHING CASUALLY** to say something with an air of pretended casualness ○ *She's dropping hints about what she wants for her birthday.* **19.** *vt.* **HIT OR SHOOT SOMEBODY** to hit or shoot somebody so that he or she falls down (*informal*) **20.** *vt.* **SPEND OR LOSE MONEY** to spend or lose a particular amount of money on something expensive or in gambling (*informal*) **21.** *vti.* SPORTS **HIT A BALL INTO THE TARGET HOLE** to make the ball go into a target, e.g., a hole or net, or go into a target hole or net **22.** *vt.* VET **GIVE BIRTH TO** to give birth to young, especially a foal **23.** *vt.* DRUGS **TAKE ILLEGAL DRUGS** to take an illegal drug by mouth, especially LSD or pills (*slang*) **24.** *vt.* SEW **LOWER A HEM** to lower the hem of something, e.g., a garment or curtain **25.** *vt.* AIR **DELIVER SOMETHING BY PARACHUTE** to deliver somebody or something by parachute from an aircraft, e.g., soldiers or supplies **26.** *vt.* **UNLOAD SOMETHING** to unload something from a ship or vehicle ■ *n.* **1. SMALL ROUND PORTION OF LIQUID** a very small amount of liquid that becomes a rounded or pear shape as it falls **2. SMALL AMOUNT OF LIQUID** any small amount of a liquid ○ *There's not a drop of milk in the house.* **3. TINIEST AMOUNT** the least amount of sympathy or other feeling (*used in negative statements*) ○ *I swear there isn't a drop of sympathy in that man.* **4. DECREASE IN SOMETHING** a decrease in quantity or amount ○ *a drop in salary* **5. DISTANCE BETWEEN A HIGH POINT AND THE GROUND** the distance between a higher level and a lower level or the ground **6. DESCENT** a slope or discontinuity in ground level, usually sharp or sudden **7.** FOOD **SMALL ROUND PIECE OF CANDY** a small round or oval piece of candy (*used in combination*) ○ *cough drops* **8.** ACCESSORIES **ROUND EARRING OR PENDANT** a roundish or pear-shaped earring or pendant **9.** MIL **DESCENT BY PARACHUTE** a descent from an aircraft by parachute **10. DELIVERY** a delivery ○ *make a drop every two weeks* **11. GOODS DELIVERED BY PARACHUTE** goods, e.g., equipment, that an aircraft delivers by parachute, or people dropped by parachute (*often used in combination*) **12. SECRET REPOSITORY FOR DANGEROUS MESSAGES** a secret place where somebody leaves dangerous letters or messages to be picked up by somebody else **13. ACT OF LEAVING SECRET COMMUNICATION** the act of leaving a dangerous letter, message, or goods at a prearranged location ○ *It's too dangerous to make the drop tonight.* **14.** MAIL = **mail drop 15.** THEATER = **drop curtain** *n.* 1 **16.** ELECTRON ENG **CONNECTION ON LINE** a point on a transmission line where data can be put in or taken out **17. DELIVERY SLOT IN A RECEPTACLE** a slot in something or a special outside container through which letters and borrowed or rented items, such as videotapes and books, can be inserted (*often used in combination*) ○ *Return the videotapes to the drop outside the store.* **18.** TV **SHORT SPUR** a short line that feeds signals to an individual house from a cable television trunk line **19. TRAP DOOR UNDER GALLOWS** a trap door on which somebody who is to be hanged stands under the gallows **20.** SEW **CURTAIN LENGTH** the measured length for a curtain, from the top of a window to its sill or to the floor ■ **drops** *npl.* PHARM **LIQUID MEDICINE APPLIED IN SMALL QUANTITIES** liquid medicine that is applied to the ear, nose, or eye using a device that produces a droplet each time it is squeezed [The noun is from Old English *dropa*, the verb from Old English *droppian*. Both ultimately from an Indo-European base that is also the ancestor of English *droop, drip,* and *drizzle.*] ◇ **a drop in the bucket** just a tiny part of the full quantity that is required, and thus insignificant ◇ **at the drop of a hat** without needing persuasion or prompting ◇ **get** *or* **have the drop on somebody** to catch somebody by surprise before he or she can surprise you (*informal*) ◇ **let something drop** to reveal information to somebody, often casually or accidentally

drop away *vi.* **1.** = **drop** *v.* 6 **2. LEAVE GRADUALLY** to leave a group or formation gradually, either on purpose or not ○ *One by one, each jet banked and dropped away from the formation.* **3. DISAPPEAR GRADUALLY** to disappear gradually

drop back, drop be·hind *vi.* to move more slowly than other people and gradually fall farther behind them

drop by *v.* **1.** *vi.* **VISIT SOMEBODY CASUALLY** to visit somebody casually or without having agreed on a time **2.** *vt.* **DELIVER SOMETHING OR SOMEBODY SOMEWHERE** to deliver something or somebody to a specific place ○ *Just drop the laundry by some time this afternoon.*

drop into *vt.* to go from a more active into a less active state of consciousness

drop off *v.* **1.** *vi.* **DOZE OFF** to fall asleep (*informal*) **2.** *vi.* **DECREASE** to decline or fall to a lower level (*informal*) ○ *Sales tend to drop off during the summer.* **3.** *vt.* **TAKE SOMEBODY OR SOMETHING SOMEWHERE** to take somebody or something to a place, usually by car, and leave the person or thing there

drop out *vi.* **1. LEAVE WITHOUT FINISHING SOMETHING** to abandon a project or activity without finishing it ○ *He dropped out of college in his final year.* **2. REJECT SOCIETY** to reject conventional society and live in an alternative way (*informal*)

drop over, drop a·round *vi.* to visit somebody casually and without agreeing on a time ○ *Drop around any time.*

drop cloth *n.* a large cloth used to cover surfaces, such as floors and furniture, to protect them from paint or dust

drop cur·tain *n.* **1. UNFRAMED CURTAIN** an unframed curtain that can be lowered to a theater stage from the flies. It usually provides background scenery. **2. LOWERABLE CURTAIN** a theater curtain that is raised or lowered on stage, rather than being opened or closed by moving sideways

drop forge *n.* a machine used to shape or stamp molten metal by placing it between two dies and dropping a weight on it —**drop-forge** *vt.*

drop front *n.* a part of a writing desk that can be lowered to provide a writing surface and then raised to conceal the inner part of the desk (*hyphenated before a noun*) ○ *a drop-front desk*

drop goal *n.* a goal in rugby scored by dropping the ball and then kicking it

drop ham·mer *n.* = **drop forge**

drop han·dle·bars *npl.* on a racing bicycle, handlebars that curve downward, enabling the rider to adopt a more aerodynamic posture

drop-in *n.* **1. CASUAL VISITOR** a casual visitor or client who has not made a previous arrangement to visit **2. SOCIAL EVENT** an informal party that does not require an invitation

drop-in cen·ter *n.* a place that people can visit without an appointment to get advice, information, or an opportunity to meet others

drop kick *n.* **1.** FOOTBALL, RUGBY **METHOD OF KICKING A BALL** a way of kicking a football by dropping it first and then kicking it just as it bounces up from the ground **2.** WRESTLING **ILLEGAL WRESTLING MOVE** in amateur wrestling, an illegal move in which one wrestler attacks another by leaping into the air and striking an opponent with both feet —**drop-kick** *vti.*

drop leaf *n.* an extension on the end of a table that can be folded down when not needed (*hyphenated before a noun*) ○ *a drop-leaf table*

drop·let /dróppləṭ/ *n.* a very small drop of liquid

drop·light /dróp lìt/ *n.* an electric light that can be raised or lowered by using a rope, cord, or pulley

drop lock *n.* in international financial markets, a variable-rate bank loan that is automatically converted to a fixed-rate bond when long-term interest rates fall to a specified level

drop·mas·ter *n.* a noncommissioned officer trained to prepare, load, tie down, and eject materials from a plane during an airdrop operation

drop-off *n.* **1. SLOPE IN THE GROUND** a steep slope where the ground descends abruptly **2. DECREASE** a fall in the level of something

drop·out /dróp òwt/ *n.* **1.** EDUC **SOMEBODY WHO LEAVES WITHOUT COMPLETING A COURSE** somebody who fails to complete an educational course, usually at a college or school **2. UNCONVENTIONAL PERSON** somebody who prefers to live an unconventional way of life (*informal*) **3.** COMPUT **SECTION WITHOUT DATA** a small section on a magnetic tape or disk that is missing data

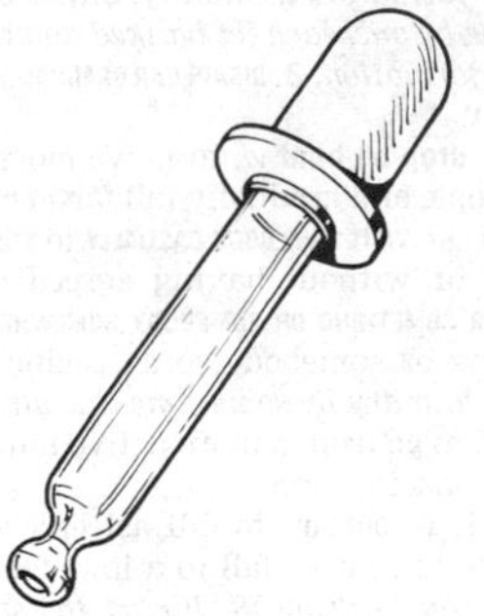

Dropper

drop·per /dróppər/ *n.* a small glass or plastic tube with a rubber bulb at one end that is used to suck up liquid and release it one drop at a time (*often used in combination*) ○ *an eye dropper*

drop·pings /dróppingz/ *npl.* animal or bird excrement left on the ground or another surface

drop ship·ment *n.* a load of a product shipped directly from the manufacturer to the retailer but billed to a third party

drop shot *n.* a shot in a racket game in which the ball drops abruptly to the ground just after crossing over the net or hitting the wall

drop·sy /drópsee/ *n.* edema (*dated*) [13thC. Shortening of earlier *hydropsy*, via Old French *idropisie* from, ultimately, Greek *hudrōps*, "somebody with dropsy," from *hudōr* "water" (see HYDRO-).]

drop tank *n.* on fighter and bomber planes, an extra tank of fuel that enables the aircraft to fly longer and farther. When the tank is empty or the plane enters combat it can be jettisoned.

drop·wort /dróp wàwrt, dróp wùrt/ (*plural* **-worts** *or* **-wort**) *n.* a Eurasian plant that produces odorless clusters of small white or red flowers and has finely divided leaves. Latin name: *Filipendula vulgaris.* [Coined from DROP + WORT; so called because of the plant's tuberous root fibers]

drop zone *n.* an area where troops or goods such as military equipment or medical supplies are to be landed, usually by parachute

drosh·ky /dróshkee/ (*plural* **-kies**), **dros·ky** /dróskee/ (*plural* **-kies**) *n.* an open four-wheeled carriage drawn by horses, formerly used in Russia and Poland [Early 19thC. From Russian *drozhki*, literally "small wagon," from *drogi* "wagon." Ultimately from an Indo-European word that is also the ancestor of English *drag* and *draw*.]

dro·som·e·ter /dro sómmətər/ *n.* a device for measuring how much dew there is [Early 19thC. Coined from Greek *drosos* "dew" + -METER.]

dro·soph·i·la /drō sóffələ, drə-/ (*plural* **-las** *or* **-la** /-lee/ *or* **-lae**) *n.* a small two-winged fruit fly that is frequently used in genetic research. Genus: *Drosophila.* [Early 19thC. From modern Latin, genus name, from Greek *drosos* "dew" and *-philos* "loving."]

dross /dross, drawss/ *n.* **1. SOMETHING WORTHLESS** something that is worthless or of a low standard or quality ○ *I considered her early fiction to be pure dross.* **2.** METALL **SCUM ON METAL** the scum formed on molten metals, usually caused by oxidation [Old English *drōs*. Ultimately from an Indo-European base denoting "dark, muddy," which is also the ancestor of English *dregs* and *dark*.]

dross·y /dróssee, dráwssee/ (**-i·er, -i·est**) *adj.* worthless, or very low in quality —**dross·i·ness** *n.*

drought *n.* **1.** METEOROL **PERIOD OF DRY WEATHER** a long period of extremely dry weather when there is not enough rain for the successful growing of crops or the replenishment of water supplies **2. LACK OF SOMETHING** a lengthy serious lack of something ○ *She experienced a period of creative drought.* [Old English *drūgaþ*, literally "dryness." From a prehistoric Germanic base meaning "dry," which is also the ancestor of English *dry* and *drain*.] —**drought·y** *adj.*

drove[1] past tense of **drive**

drove[2] /drōv/ *n.* **1.** AGRIC **GROUP OF ANIMALS MOVING** a large number of animals, especially cattle, moving in the same direction, especially when being driven **2.** BUILDING **TYPE OF STONE CHISEL** a broad-edged chisel used for dressing stone ■ **droves** *npl.* **CROWDS OF PEOPLE** very large numbers of people ○ *They came out of the football stadium in droves.* ■ *vti.* (**droved, drov·ing, droves**) AGRIC **MOVE ANIMALS ALONG** to move a herd or flock of animals from one place to another, usually over long distances, e.g., to new pastures or to market [Old English *drāf*, from *drīfan* (see DRIVE)]

drov·er /drṓvər/ *n.* somebody whose job is to move herds or flocks of animals from one place to another, e.g., to new pastures or to market

drown /drown/ (**drowned, drown·ing, drowns**) *v.* **1.** *vti.* PHYSIOL **DIE BY IMMERSION IN WATER** to die, or kill a person or animal, by immersion and usually suffocation in a liquid, normally water. Death occurs either from lack of oxygen or as a result of cardiac arrest from the lowered body temperature. ○ *death by drowning* **2.** *vt.* = **drown out 3.** *vt.* **COVER WITH TOO MUCH LIQUID** to cover or soak something, usually an item of food, with too much liquid ○ *He served us pancakes drowned in syrup.* [13thC. Origin uncertain: probably from a Scandinavian source. Ultimately from a prehistoric Germanic base that is also the ancestor of English *drink* and *drench*.] —**drown·er** *n.*

drown out *vt.* to make so much noise that it is impossible to hear another sound (*often passive*)

drowned /drownd/ *adj.* **1. HAVING DIED BY IMMERSION** having died by immersion in water **2. THOROUGHLY SOAKED** thoroughly soaked with water or another liquid

drowse /drówz/ *vi.* (**drowsed, drows·ing, drows·es**) **BE HALF ASLEEP** to be in a state partway between sleeping and waking ■ *n.* **SLIGHTLY SLEEPY STATE** a state partway between sleeping and waking [Late 16thC. Back-formation from DROWSY.]

drows·y /drówzee/ (**-i·er, -i·est**) *adj.* **1. ALMOST ASLEEP** almost asleep or very lightly asleep **2. CAUSING SLEEPINESS** tending to make somebody feel sleepy ○ *a drowsy summer afternoon* **3. SLUGGISH** sluggish and dull [15thC. Origin uncertain: ultimately from Old English *drūsian* "to be sluggish," from a prehistoric Germanic word that is also the ancestor of English *drop* and *droop*.] —**drows·i·ly** *adv.* —**drows·i·ness** *n.*

drub /drub/ *vt.* (**drubbed, drub·bing, drubs**) **1. BEAT SOMEBODY WITH A STICK** to beat somebody using a heavy stick or club **2. DEFEAT AN OPPONENT** to defeat an opponent comprehensively ○ *Their baseball team really drubbed us last year.* **3. STAMP YOUR FEET** to stamp the feet hard on the ground ■ *n.* **BLOW WITH A STICK** a blow made using a heavy stick or club [Early 17thC. Origin uncertain: possibly from Arabic *ḍaraba* "to beat."] —**drub·ber** *n.*

drudge /druj/ *n.* **SOMEBODY WHO DOES MENIAL WORK** somebody who does work that is both boring and strenuous ■ *vi.* (**drudged, drudg·ing, drudg·es**) **DO MENIAL WORK** to do boring or exhausting work [15thC. From an obsolete word meaning "to work hard."] —**drudg·er** *n.* —**drudg·ing·ly** *adv.*

drudg·er·y /drújjəree/ *n.* exhausting, boring, unpleasant work

WORD KEY: SYNONYMS

See Synonyms at ***work***.

drudge·work /drúj wùrk/ *n.* work that is boring and unpleasant ○ *We had to do hours of drudgework before we were happy with the garden.*

drug /drug/ *n.* **1.** PHARM **SUBSTANCE GIVEN AS MEDICINE** a natural or artificial substance that is given to treat, prevent, or diagnose a disease or to lessen pain **2.** DRUGS **ILLEGAL SUBSTANCE** an often illegal and sometimes addictive substance that causes changes in behavior and perception and is taken for the effects **3.** PHARM **MEDICAL SUBSTANCE** a substance given to treat or prevent illness as defined in the U.S. Food, Drug, and Cosmetic Act ■ *vt.* (**drugged, drug·ging, drugs**) **1. GIVE SOMEBODY A DRUG** to give a drug to somebody **2. ADD DRUG TO FOOD OR DRINK** to mix a drug with food or a drink and give it to somebody to make him or her fall asleep or become unconscious [14thC. From French *drogue*, of uncertain origin: possibly from Dutch *droog* "dry," in a phrase meaning "dry goods" or "goods packed in barrels."]

drug a·buse *n.* deliberate use of an illegal drug or of too much of a prescribed drug

drug bar·on *n.* = **drug lord** (*informal*)

drugged /drugd/ *adj.* **1.** PHARM **AFFECTED BY DRUGS** heavily asleep, unconscious, or unable to function after being given drugs **2. TIRED AND STUPEFIED** extremely tired and unable to concentrate ○ *drugged with sleep*

drug·get /drúggət/ *n.* **1.** TEXTILES **CARPETING FABRIC** a thick heavy fabric made of wool, or cotton and wool, used to cover floors **2.** HOUSEHOLD **RUG** a coarse rug made of wool or cotton and wool **3.** TEXTILES **WOOLEN FABRIC** a woolen or wool-blend fabric formerly used to make clothing [Mid-16thC. From French *droguet*, of uncertain origin: perhaps from *drogue* "drug, worthless stuff."]

drug·gie /drúggee/, **drug·gy** (*plural* **-gies**) *n.* somebody who regularly takes illegal drugs (*slang*)

drug·gist /drúggist/ *n.* **1. SOMEBODY WHO SELLS MEDICINES** a pharmacist who owns or manages a drugstore **2. PHARMACIST** a pharmacist

drug·gy /drúggee/ *adj.* (**-gi·er, -gi·est**) **TYPICAL OF HABITUAL DRUG-TAKER** typical of somebody who takes drugs regularly and often (*slang*) ○ *a druggy stupor.* ■ *n.* = **druggie** (*slang*)

drug lord *n.* somebody who controls a large international network engaged in the production, processing, and sale of illegal drugs (*informal*)

drug·o·la /drug ṓlə/ *n.* the use of illegal drugs as a form of bribery (*slang*) [Late 20thC. Coined from DRUG, on the model of PAYOLA.]

drug push·er *n.* somebody who sells illegal drugs

drug run·ner *n.* somebody who transports illegal drugs, usually by ship or airplane

drug·store /drúg stàwr/ *n.* a store where prescription and over-the-counter drugs are sold along with a wide variety of other goods and often including snacks

Dru·id /drṓō id/ *n.* **1.** HIST **PRIEST IN ANCIENT CELTIC RELIGION** a priest in an ancient religion practiced in Britain, Ireland, and Gaul until the people of those areas were converted to Christianity **2.** RELIG **MODERN FOLLOWER OF ANCIENT CELTIC RELIGION** somebody who worships the forces of nature by means of meditation, prayer, and celebration of the Earth, seen as a modern-day representative of the ancient Celtic religion [Mid-16thC. Directly or via French from Latin *druides* "druids," of prehistoric Celtic origin. Probably from an Indo-European compound, "tree, strength," (the ancestor of English *tree* and *true*) and "seer."] —**dru·id·ic** /droo íddik/ *adj.* —**dru·id·i·cal** /-íddik'l/ *adj.*

Dru·id·ess /drṓō idəss/ *n.* **1. PRIEST IN ANCIENT CELTIC RELIGION** a woman priest in an ancient religion practiced in Britain, Ireland, and Gaul until the people of those areas were converted to Christianity **2.** RELIG **MODERN FOLLOWER OF ANCIENT CELTIC RELIGION** somebody who worships the forces of nature by meditation, prayer, and celebration of the earth, seen as a modern-day representative of the ancient Celtic religion

Dru·id·ism /droō i dìzzəm/ *n.* an ancient Celtic religion in which the forces of nature were worshiped, and the priests were also prophets and poets, or the modern religion said to derive from it

drum /drum/ *n.* **1.** MUSIC **PERCUSSION INSTRUMENT** a musical instrument usually consisting of a membrane stretched across a hollow frame and played by striking the stretched membrane. Other hollow objects are also used as drums. **2. TAPPING SOUND** a regular tapping sound made by something striking a surface ○ *the drum of rain on the roof* **3. LARGE CYLINDRICAL CONTAINER** a large cylindrical container used for storing liquids, e.g., oil or chemicals **4. SPOOL ON WHICH SOMETHING IS WOUND** a large spool around which wire, cable, or rope is wound for storage **5. PART IN A MACHINE** a cylindrical hollow part in a machine, e.g., a clothes drier **6.** ANAT = **eardrum 7.** ZOOL **FISH THAT MAKES A RHYTHMIC SOUND** a large bony saltwater or freshwater fish that emits a repeated rhythmic sound. Family: Sciaenidae. **8.** ARCHIT **CYLINDRICAL STONE BLOCK** one of the cylindrical stone blocks used to make a column **9.** ARCHIT **SUPPORT FOR A DOME** a band or other structure around the bottom of a dome or circular ceiling that supports it ■ *vi.* **(drummed, drum·ming, drums) 1.** MUSIC **PLAY A DRUM OR DRUMS** to play a drum or drums **2. TAP A SURFACE** to tap repeatedly and rhythmically on a surface ○ *The rain was drumming on the roof.* **3.** BIRDS **MAKE SOUND WITH THE BILL OR WINGS** to make a repeated sound with the bill or wings (*refers to birds*) [Mid-16thC. Origin uncertain, probably from Middle Dutch *tromme*, literally "instrument making a loud noise," ultimately of imitative origin.] ◇ **bang** *or* **beat the drum (for somebody** *or* **something)** to try to attract support and favorable attention for somebody or something that you favor (*informal*)

drum into *vt.* to tell somebody something repeatedly and persistently until the person has learned it or will always remember it (*often passive*)

drum out *vt.* to force somebody to leave a group or an organization, usually in disgrace (*usually passive*)

drum up *vt.* **1. TRY TO ELICIT** to try actively to get more of something such as business or support **2. INVENT AN EXPLANATION** to create or think up an explanation ○ *What excuse can I drum up this time?*

drum and bass *n.* a type of popular music originating in the U.K. in the 1990s that has a fast rhythm, complex percussion, and very low bass lines. It is influenced by hardcore and reggae.

drum and bu·gle corps *n.* a type of marching band whose instruments are limited to percussion and bugles or fifes, that performs precisely choreographed field drills

drum·beat /drúm beet/ *n.* **1.** MUSIC **SOUND OF DRUM** a sound made by somebody beating a drum **2. PASSIONATELY SUPPORTED CAUSE** a cause that attracts passionate support **3. INCESSANT CRITICISM** heavy unending criticism, typically public criticism ○ *a steady drumbeat of accusations* —**drum·beat·er** *n.* —**drum·beat·ing** *n.*

drum brake *n.* a type of brake on vehicles that operates by applying pressure to the inner part of the wheel (**brake drum**)

drum corps *n.* a type of marching band whose instruments are limited to percussion and sometimes bugles or fifes that performs precisely choreographed field drills

drum·ette /dru mét/ *n.* the meaty part of a chicken wing separated from the rest of the wing [So called because it resembles a small drumstick]

drum·fire /drúm fìr/ *n.* **1. HEAVY GUNFIRE** continuous heavy gunfire **2. INTENSE ROUND OF SOMETHING** a continuous intense sequence or round of something

drum·fish /drúm fish/ (*plural* **-fish** *or* **-fish·es**) *n.* = **drum** *n.* 7

drum·head /drúm hèd/ *n.* **1.** MUSIC **MEMBRANE ON A DRUM** the membrane, usually made of calfskin or plastic, that is stretched over the frame of a drum **2.** NAUT **PART OF A CAPSTAN** the round topmost part of a capstan that holds the capstan bars in position for turning

drum·head court-mar·tial *n.* an informal brief trial held during military operations to hear charges of serious offenses committed by soldiers while in action [So called because an upturned drum serves as the magistrate's bench]

drum kit *n.* = **drum set**

drum·lin /drúmmlin/ *n.* a long narrow ridge of gravel and rock deposited by a moving glacier, one end of which is blunt and the other end tapering [Mid-19thC. Formed from earlier *drum* "ridge," from Irish *druim* "back, ridge," of unknown origin.]

drum ma·chine *n.* an electronic synthesizer that can reproduce drum and percussion sounds in various rhythms and combinations

drum ma·jor *n.* somebody who leads a marching band and conducts it by moving a baton up and down and twirling it rhythmically

drum ma·jor·ette *n.* = **majorette**

drum·mer /drúmmər/ *n.* **1.** MUSIC **DRUM PLAYER** somebody who plays the drums **2.** (*plural* **-mers** *or* **-mer**) ZOOL **AUSTRALIAN FISH** an Australian fish that frequents rocky shores. Family: Kyphosidae.

drum·roll /drúm rōl/ *n.* a very fast regular beating on a drum that sounds like one long sound

drum set *n.* a set of percussion instruments used in bands, usually consisting of one or more snare drums, tom-toms, bass drums, and various cymbals

drum·stick /drúm stìk/ *n.* **1.** MUSIC **STICK FOR BEATING A DRUM** the stick used to beat a drum **2.** FOOD **LOWER HALF OF A POULTRY LEG** the lower half of the leg of a bird such as a chicken when prepared for eating, so called because of its shape

drunk /drungk/ past participle of **drink** ■ *adj.* **1. INTOXICATED WITH ALCOHOL** having drunk too much alcohol and lost control over behavior, movement, and speech **2. EMOTIONALLY INTOXICATED** overwhelmed with and judgmentally impaired by an intense emotion ○ *drunk with power* **3.** COOK **LONG-SOAKED** used to describe a meat dish in Chinese cooking in which the meat, usually chicken, has been immersed in a liquid and boiled or marinated overnight ○ *drunk chicken* ■ *n.* **1. SOMEBODY WHO DRINKS ALL THE TIME** somebody who habitually drinks too much alcohol or who is in a drunken state **2. DRINKING BOUT** a bout of drinking too much alcohol (*slang*) ○ *One more drunk, and I divorce you.*

drunk·ard /drúngkərd/ *n.* somebody who habitually drinks too much alcohol

drunk-driv·ing *n.* the offense of driving a vehicle while having a higher blood alcohol content than the law allows ○ *Drunk-driving cost him his driver's license.* —**drunk-driv·er** *n.*

drunk·en /drúngkən/ *adj.* **1. INVOLVING ALCOHOL** involving too much alcohol or occurring while people have had too much alcohol ○ *a drunken quarrel* **2. INTOXICATED** overly excited by or as if by having consumed too much alcohol **3. AFFECTED BY ALCOHOL** drunk or frequently drunk [Old English, old past participle of DRINK] —**drunk·en·ly** *adv.* —**drunk·en·ness** *n.*

drunk tank *n.* a special cell in a jail or police station where people who have been arrested for public drunkenness are kept (*slang*)

drupe /droop/ *n.* a fruit with a thin outer skin, soft pulpy middle, and hard stony central part that encloses a seed. Apricots, plums, cherries, and almonds are drupes. [Mid-18thC. Via modern Latin from Latin *drupa* "overripe olive," from Greek *druppa* "olive," of uncertain origin.]

drupe·let /droōplət/, **dru·pel** /droōp'l/ *n.* a small fruit enclosing a single seed that with many other small sections makes up a compound fruit such as a blackberry or raspberry

Druse *n.* = **Druze**

druth·ers /drúthərz/ *npl.* somebody's own free choice or preference (*informal*) ○ *If I had my druthers, I'd be lying on a beach somewhere.* [Late 19thC. Alteration of "would rather."]

Druze /drooz/ (*plural* **Druze** *or* **Druz·es**), **Druse** (*plural* **Druse** *or* **Drus·es**) *n.* a member of a religion similar to Islam that is found mainly in Israel, Lebanon, and Syria [Late 18thC. Directly or via French from Arabic *durūz*, plural of *durzī*, from the name of the religion's founder, Muḥammad ibn Ismā'īl *ad-Darazī* (d. 1019).] —**Dru·ze·an** /droōzee ən/ *adj.*

dry /drī/ *adj.* **(dri·er, dri·est) 1. NOT WET** not wet, or no longer wet **2.** METEOROL **LACKING MOISTURE IN THE AIR** having very little or no rain or moisture in the air **3. NOT WET AND THUS COMFORTABLE** not wet and therefore comfortable to wear ○ *dry clothes* **4. LACKING IN APPROPRIATE MOISTURE** lacking in normal levels of natural oiliness or moisture ○ *dry skin* **5. DRAINED OF WATER** no longer having water because it has evaporated or been exhausted ○ *The spring has been dry for years.* **6. LACKING CUSTOMARY MOISTURE** not producing or accompanied by associated moisture, in the form of phlegm, tears, or vomit ○ *a dry cough* **7. NOT REQUIRING LIQUID FOR USE** manufactured so as to be usable without water ○ *dry shampoo* **8. WITHOUT FLESH ATTACHED** no longer having the meat attached ○ *dry bones* **9. THIRSTY** thirsty and dehydrated **10.** BEVERAGES **LACKING SWEETNESS** not sweet because the sugar has been broken down during the process of fermentation ○ *dry sherry* **11.** FOOD **SERVED WITHOUT FAT OR LIQUID** lacking the usual moist spread or sauce such as butter, preserves, or gravy ○ *dry toast* **12.** FOOD **UNAPPETIZINGLY LACKING MOISTNESS** lacking in appetizing moistness, e.g., because of being stale or overcooked **13. SHREWDLY AMUSING** witty in a shrewd, subtle, or sarcastic way **14. BORING AND ACADEMIC** dense and academic in style **15. MATTER-OF-FACT** plain and without unnecessary ornamentation ○ *a dry, matter-of-fact account of the incident* **16. UNPRODUCTIVE** unable to produce expected or creative results ○ *They've looked for him everywhere, and come up dry.* **17.** LAW **NOT ALLOWING ALCOHOL SALES** not allowing legal sale of alcoholic beverages ○ *a dry county* **18.** ZOOL **NO LONGER GIVING MILK** used to describe a female animal that no longer produces milk **19. CONTAINING NO MOISTURE** from which the liquid or moisture has been removed ○ *Dry fruit has become popular as a snack.* ○ *dry weight* **20.** ELECTRON ENG **NOT CONDUCTING ELECTRICITY** used to describe a current-carrying path that cannot conduct electricity because the solder at the joint has not completely adhered to a surface ○ *a dry joint* ■ *v.* **(dried, dry·ing, dries) 1.** *vti.* **MAKE SOMETHING DRY** to make something dry, or become dry ○ *It's your turn to dry the dishes.* **2.** *vt.* FOOD TECH **PRESERVE FOOD BY EXTRACTING MOISTURE** to preserve food, especially fruit, vegetables, and meat, by extracting most of the moisture from it ■ *n.* **1. DRY PLACE** a place that is dry or sheltered from the rain (*informal*) ○ *stay in the dry* **2. dry** (*plural* **dries**) POL **PROHIBITIONIST** somebody who supports the legal prohibition of alcoholic beverages (*archaic*) [Old English *drȳge*. Ultimately from a prehistoric Germanic word that is also the ancestor of English *drought* and *drain*.] —**dry·a·ble** *adj.* —**dry·ness** *n.*

WORD KEY: SYNONYMS

dry, dehydrated, desiccated, arid, parched, shriveled, sere

CORE MEANING: lacking moisture

dry the most general term used to describe something containing little or no moisture; **dehydrated** a term for something from which water has been removed, also used to describe a person or animal whose body does not contain enough fluids; **desiccated** a formal term for *dehydrated*. It is not used to refer to people or animals; **arid** dry because of a lack of rain; **parched** dry because of excessive heat; **shriveled** dry and shrunken; **sere** a somewhat literary term meaning withered and dry, used especially of plants.

dry off *vti.* to become drier, or make something drier

dry out *vti.* **1. MAKE OR BECOME COMPLETELY DRY** to become completely dry, or make something completely dry ○ *It will take a while for the plaster to dry out.* **2.** DRUGS **STOP USING ALCOHOL OR DRUGS** to purge alcohol or other drugs from the body, or put somebody through such a process (*informal*)

dry up *v.* **1.** *vti.* **LOSE OR REMOVE MOISTURE** to lose water or moisture over a period, or make a river or pool lose its water over a period ○ *The river dried up centuries ago.* **2.** *vi.* **STOP BEING AVAILABLE** to stop being available as a resource ○ *Our project ended because our sources of funding dried up.* **3.** *vt.* *U.K.* **DRY DISHES** to dry plates, dishes, pans, and cutlery with a cloth after they have been washed **4.** *vi.* **STOP TALKING** to stop talking, or forget lines during a performance or rehearsal (*informal*) (*often used as a command*) ○ *Oh, just dry up, will you? I'm trying to think!* **5.** *vi.* **RUN OUT OF IDEAS** to be unable to perform as usual or as expected ○ *His ideas have dried up.*

dry·ad /drī əd, -ad/ (*plural* **-ads** *or* **-ades** /-ə deez/) *n.* in Greek mythology, a spiritual being believed to live in trees and forests [14thC. Via Latin from Greek *Druad-*, the stem of *Druas*, from *drus* "tree." Ultimately from an Indo-European word that is also the ancestor of English *tree*.] —**dry·ad·ic** /drī áddik/ *adj.*

dry·as·dust /drī əz dùst/ *n.* somebody who bores audiences with tedious speeches (*dated*) [Late 19thC. From the name of the fictitious Dr. Jonas *Dryasdust*, to whom Sir Walter Scott dedicated some of his novels.]

dry bat·ter·y (*plural* **dry bat·ter·ies**) *n.* an electric battery that has more than one dry cell

dry-bone ore *n.* a kind of smithsonite that has many holes, found near the surface of the Earth's crust

dry-bulb ther·mom·e·ter *n.* a normal air thermometer used in conjunction with a wet-bulb thermometer to determine relative humidity

dry cell *n.* a current-generating electric cell that cannot be regenerated and contains an electrolyte in the form of a paste or within a porous material to keep it from spilling. ◊ **wet cell**

dry-clean (**dry-cleaned, dry-clean·ing, dry-cleans**) *vt.* to clean clothes or other fabrics with a chemical solvent instead of water

dry clean·ing *n.* **1. COMMERCIAL METHOD OF CLEANING CLOTHES** the professional cleaning of clothes and other fabrics using a chemical solvent rather than water **2. DRY-CLEANED ITEMS** clothes and other fabrics that require dry-cleaning or have just been dry-cleaned

Dry·den /drĭd'n/, **John** (1631–1700) English poet, dramatist, and critic. His works include the play *Marriage à la Mode* (1672) and the verse satire *Absalom and Achitophel* (1681). He was made poet laureate by Charles II (1668), but having become a Catholic in 1685, was deprived of the office on the accession of William of Orange.

dry dis·til·la·tion *n.* = **destructive distillation**

dry dock *n.* an enclosed dock from which the water can be removed so that construction or repairs can be carried out below the waterline of a boat or ship —**dry-dock** *vti.*

dry·er *n.* = **drier** ■ comparative of **dry**

dry-eyed *adj.* unable or unwilling to shed tears ○ *He remained dry-eyed throughout the trial.*

dry farm·ing *n.* a method of growing crops in dry areas by selecting plants that are drought-resistant and using mulch to retain moisture in the soil, so making irrigation unnecessary —**dry farm·er** *n.*

dry fly *n.* a kind of artificial lure used in fly-fishing that remains on the surface of the water instead of sinking. ◊ **wet fly**

Dry·gas /drī́gàs/ *tdmk.* a trademark for a gasoline additive

dry goods *npl.* goods such as fabrics, clothing, and notions, as distinct from hardware, food, and other products

dry hole *n.* an oil well that has been drilled but that produces no oil, or not enough to make it economically profitable

dry ice *n.* cold solid carbon dioxide at the temperature of −78.5°C/−110°F, used to keep other things very cold or to produce an artificial fog effect

dry·ing oil *n.* an organic oil e.g., linseed or cottonseed oil, used as a base in paints and varnishes because it reduces drying time. Such oils form a tough thin film when exposed to air.

dry kiln *n.* a large oven used to season cut lumber

dry land *n.* the land as distinct from the sea or a body of water

dry law *n.* in some U.S. states and counties, a law that forbids the sale of alcohol

dry·ly *adv.* = **drily**

dry mar·ti·ni *n.* a cocktail that contains a little dry vermouth mixed with gin or vodka

dry meas·ure *n.* a system of units used to measure dry products such as grains and fruits by volume, or a unit in such a system

dry nurse *n.* a nurse employed to look after somebody's young baby but not to breastfeed it (*archaic*) ◊ **wet nurse** —**dry-nurse** *vt.*

dry·o·pith·e·cine /drī ō pĭthə seen/ (*plural* **-cines** *or* **-cine**) *n.* an extinct ape of the Miocene and Pliocene epochs, believed by some scientists to be the ancestor of modern apes and humans. Genus: *Dryopithecus.* [Mid-20thC. Formed from modern Latin *Dryopithecus*, genus name, from Greek *drus* "tree" and *pithēkos* "ape."]

dry point *n.* **1. METHOD OF ENGRAVING** a technique of engraving in intaglio on a metal, usually copper, plate that produces a feathery effect in the lines of the print **2. STEEL NEEDLE** a hard steel needle used to engrave a metal plate **3. PRINT MADE BY DRY POINT** an engraving or print made by using dry point

dry rot *n.* **1.** BUILDING **CRUMBLING DECAY IN WOOD** dry crumbling decay in wood caused by various fungi **2.** BOT **PLANT DISEASE** a disease caused by various fungi that invade plant stems, bulbs, and fruits, causing them to dry out and decay **3.** FUNGI **DESTRUCTIVE FUNGUS** a fungus that causes dry rot. Genus: *Merulius.*

dry run *n.* a rehearsal of a planned action or activity ○ *Let's have a dry run to make sure it's going to work.*

dry-salt (**dry-salt·ed, dry-salt·ing, dry-salts**) *vt.* to use salt to dry and preserve food

dry sock·et *n.* a painful condition caused when the blood left by an extracted tooth fails to clot or the clot is dislodged

Dry Tor·tu·gas Na·tion·al Park /-tawr to͞ogəz-/ national park in southwestern Florida that contains Fort Jefferson and Shark Island. Area: 100 sq. mi./262 sq. km.

dry·wall /drī́ wàwl/, **dry wall** *n.* **1.** = **plasterboard 2. WALL MADE OF PLASTERBOARD** a wall constructed with sheets of plasterboard **3. WALL MADE WITHOUT MORTAR** a wall constructed of stone or masonry without mortar —**dry-wall** *vt.*

dry wash *n.* laundry that has been washed and dried but has not been ironed

d.s. *abbr.* **1. d.s., D.S.** MUSIC dal segno **2.** days after sight **3.** document signed

D.Sc., DSc *abbr.* Doctor of Science

D.S.C., DSC *abbr.* Distinguished Service Cross

DSL *abbr.* Digital Subscriber Line

D.S.O., DSO *abbr.* Distinguished Service Order

d.s.p. *abbr.* died without issue [Latin *decessit sine prole*]

DSS *abbr.* Director of Social Services

DST, D.S.T. *abbr.* daylight-saving time

DT, D.T. *abbr.* daylight time

Dt. *abbr.* BIBLE Deuteronomy

D.T. *abbr.* Doctor Theologiae

DTP *abbr.* desktop publishing

d.t.'s, D.T.'s *abbr.* delirium tremens

du·al /do͞o əl/ *adj.* **1. HAVING TWO SIMILAR ELEMENTS** having two parts, functions, aspects, or items of a similar kind ○ *dual citizenship* **2. HAVING TWO DISTINCT ASPECTS** made up of two distinct, often opposite, elements ○ *serve a dual purpose* **3.** GRAM **SPECIFYING TWO** in various languages, used to describe or relating to a grammatical number category, in addition to singular and plural, that specifies two people or things ■ *n.* GRAM **DUAL NUMBER OR INFLECTED FORM** dual number, or, in various languages, the inflected form of a noun, pronoun, adjective, or verb that refers to dual number [Early 17thC. From Latin *dualis*, from *duo* "two." Ultimately from the Indo-European word for "two," which is also the ancestor of English *two* and *binary*).] —**du·al·ly** *adv.*

Du·a·la /doo àalə/ (*plural* **-la** *or* **-las**) *n.* **1.** PEOPLES **MEMBER OF AN AFRICAN ETHNIC GROUP** a member of an African ethnic group that lives in Cameroon **2.** LANG **LANGUAGE OF THE DUALA** the language of the Duala, belonging to the Bantu group of Niger-Congo languages. = **Douala** —**Du·a·la** *adj.*

du·al-hat·ted *adj.* holding two military commands at the same time

du·al in-line pack·age *n.* a package consisting of a printed circuit board and a series of switches, used to control optional settings for electronic devices

du·al·ism /do͞o ə lìzzəm/ *n.* **1. STATE OF HAVING TWO PARTS** a state in which something has two distinct parts or aspects, which are often opposites **2.** PHILOS **THEORY OF TWO OPPOSING CONCEPTS** a philosophical theory based on the idea of opposing concepts, especially the theory that human beings are made up of two independent constituents, the body and the mind or soul **3.** RELIG **DOCTRINE OF OPPOSING PRINCIPLES** the religious doctrine that two opposed and antagonistic forces of good and evil determine the course of events **4.** RELIG **DUAL NATURE OF PEOPLE** the religious idea that people are inherently dual in nature, both spiritual and physical —**du·al·ist** *n.* —**du·al·is·tic** /do͞o ə lístik/ *adj.* —**du·al·is·ti·cal·ly** *adv.*

du·al·i·ty /doo állətee/ (*plural* **-ties**) *n.* **1. SOMETHING CONSISTING OF TWO PARTS** a situation or nature that has two states or parts that are complementary or opposed to each other **2.** PHYS **THEORY OF MATTER** in microphysics, the theory that both wave and particle theory account for the behavior of matter and energy under different conditions **3.** GEOM **MATHEMATICAL SYMMETRY OF OBJECTS OR OPERATIONS** a mathematical symmetry in which certain objects or operations to be interchanged without invalidating a relationship, e.g., the interchange of points and lines in a plane in projective geometry

du·al-pur·pose *adj.* capable of performing two functions satisfactorily ○ *a dual-purpose cleaner*

Duar·te /dwaártee/ city in southwestern California below the San Gabriel Mountains, east of Los Angeles. Population: 21,318 (1996).

Duar·te, José Napoleón (1925–90) Salvadorean politician. He was twice president of El Salvador (1980–82, 1984–89).

dub[1] /dub/ *vt.* (**dubbed, dub·bing, dubs**) **1. GIVE DESCRIPTIVE NICKNAME** to give a descriptive nickname to somebody or something ○ *The press dubbed him the King of Chess.* **2. HONOR SOMEBODY BY RENAMING** to honor somebody by giving him or her a new name or description **3.** POL **CONFER A KNIGHTHOOD ON SOMEBODY** to give somebody a knighthood by tapping the person on the shoulder with a sword as part of a formal ceremony **4.** INDUST **MAKE SOMETHING SMOOTH OR EVEN** to dress a material, e.g., leather or timber, to make it smooth or even **5.** FOOD **CLEAN MEAT** to clean meat, especially fish or poultry, in preparation for sale or eating **6.** SPORTS **PERFORM POORLY** to perform something, such as a golf stroke, ineptly ■ *n.* **CLUMSY UNSKILLFUL PERSON** somebody who is clumsy, awkward, or lacking in skill (*informal dated*) [Pre-12thC. From Anglo-Norman *duber*, a variant of Old French *adober* "to equip with armor," of unknown origin.] —**dub·ber** *n.*

dub[2] /dub/ *vt.* (**dubbed, dub·bing, dubs**) **1.** CINEMA, TV **ADD A SOUNDTRACK IN A DIFFERENT LANGUAGE** to add a new soundtrack to a movie or television show with the dialogue in a different language but synchronized as closely as possible with the actors' lips ○ *The movie was dubbed into Italian.* **2.** RECORDING **COPY SOMETHING ONTO NEW MEDIUM** to copy something already recorded onto a different recording medium **3.** RECORDING **COPY** to make a copy of a record or tape **4.** RECORDING **ADD SOUNDS TO A MOVIE** to add sounds that have been recorded separately to a movie soundtrack ■ *n.* **1. SOMETHING ADDED BY DUBBING** new sounds added by dubbing **2. COPY OF RECORDING** a copy made of a tape or recording **3. STYLE OF MUSIC** a style of popular music, originating in reggae in the 1970s, involving remixing records to bring certain instruments into the foreground and causing others to echo (*informal*) [Early 20thC. Shortening of DOUBLE.] —**dub·ber** *n.*

dub[3] /dub/ *v.* (**dubbed, dub·bing, dubs**) **1.** *vt.* **POKE AT SOMEBODY OR SOMETHING** to make a thrust at somebody or something **2.** *vti.* MUSIC **DRUM** to beat drums or a drum ■ *n.* **1. ACT OF THRUSTING** the act of poking at somebody or something **2.** MUSIC **DRUMMING** the sound of drumming or a drummer [Late 20thC. Origin uncertain.]

dub[4] /dub/ *n.* a style of popular music, originating with reggae in the 1970s, that involves remixing records to bring some instruments into the foreground while causing others to echo

Du·bai /doo bī́/, **Dubayy** city in the northeastern United Arab Emirates, and the capital city of Dubai state. Population: 674,100 (1995).

dub·bing /dúbbing/ *n.* **1. PROCESS OF ADDING NEW SOUNDTRACK** the process of providing a new soundtrack for a movie or television show with the dialogue in a different language but synchronized as closely as possible with the actors' lips **2. SOUNDTRACK** a soundtrack recorded for a movie or television show after the photography is finished **3. FINAL SOUNDTRACK** a final mix of all the soundtracks for a movie [Formed from DUB[2]]

Dub·ček /do͝ob chèk, do͝op-/, **Alexander** (1921–92) Czech statesman. His liberal reforms as leader of the Communist party led to Soviet invasion in 1968. Shortly afterward, he was ousted from power. He reemerged as a popular leader in 1989.

du·bi·e·ty /doo bī́ ətee/ (*plural* **-ties**) *n.* (*formal*) **1. UNCERTAINTY ABOUT SOMETHING** a feeling of uncertainty about something **2. SOMETHING DOUBTFUL** something about which you are unsure [Mid-18thC. From late Latin *dubietas*, from Latin *dubius* "doubtful" (see DUBIOUS).]

Du·bin·sky /do͞o bínskee/, **David** (1892–1982) Russian-born U.S. labor leader. He was president of the

International Ladies' Garment Workers' Union (1932–66).

du·bi·ous /do͞obee əss/ *adj.* **1. UNSURE ABOUT AN OUTCOME** uncertain about an outcome or conclusion ○ *I was a little dubious about whether or not to trust him.* **2. POSSIBLY DISHONEST OR IMMORAL** likely to be dishonest, untrustworthy, or morally worrisome in some way ○ *It's a dubious proposition.* **3. OF UNCERTAIN QUALITY** of uncertain quality, intention, or appropriateness ○ *The thesis is based on several dubious theories.* [Mid-16thC. Formed from Latin *dubius* "doubtful." The underlying meaning was "split between two choices."] —**du·bi·ous·ly** *adv.* —**du·bi·ous·ness** *n.*

WORD KEY: SYNONYMS

See Synonyms at ***doubtful.***

du·bi·ta·ble /do͞obitəb'l/ *adj.* causing or leading to doubt or uncertainty (*formal*) [Early 17thC. From Latin *dubitabilis*, from *dubitare* "to be uncertain."] —**du·bi·ta·bly** *adv.*

Dub·lin 1. city and capital of the Republic of Ireland. It is situated on the Liffey River in east central Ireland, at the head of Dublin Bay on the Irish Sea. Population: 480,996 (1996). **2.** city in western California east of San Francisco Bay and southeast of Oakland. Population: 25,231 (1996). —**Dub·lin·er** *n.*

dub·ni·um /dúbnee əm/ *n.* an extremely rare, unstable chemical element produced in high-energy atomic-ion collisions. Symbol **Db**

Du Bois /doo bóyss/, **W. E. B.** (1868–1963) U.S. historian, sociologist, and civil rights leader. He conducted the first research on the experience of Blacks in the United States and fought for racial equality, becoming the most influential African American intellectual of his time. Full name **William Edward Burghardt Du Bois**

Du·bon·net /do͞o bə náy/ *tdmk.* a trademark for a wine used as an apéritif

Du·bos /doo báwss, -bóss/, **René** (1901–82) French-born U.S. bacteriologist. He discovered tyrothricin (1939), the first commercially produced antibiotic. His writings on the environment include *So Human an Animal* (1968). Full name **René Jules Dubos**

Du·brov·nik city, port, and vacation resort on the Dalmatian coast in southeastern Croatia. It suffered much damage during ethnic conflict in the 1990s. Population: 49,728 (1991).

Du·buque /də byo͞ok/ city and port in northeastern Iowa, on the Mississippi River, that forms Iowa's border with Wisconsin northeast of Cedar Rapids. Population: 57,312 (1996).

du·cal /do͞ok'l/ *adj.* belonging to, relating to, or like a duke or dukedom ○ *a ducal palace* [15thC. Via French from, ultimately, Latin *duc-*, the stem of *dux* "leader."] —**du·cal·ly** *adv.*

duc·at /dúkət/ *n.* **1. OLD EUROPEAN COIN** a gold or silver coin formerly used in some European countries, e.g., Italy and the Netherlands **2. TICKET** a ticket for a performance (*dated informal*) ■ **duc·ats** *npl.* **CASH** money or cash (*dated informal*) [14thC. Via Old French from, ultimately, medieval Latin *ducatus* "duchy" (see DUCHY); so called because the word appeared on early coins.]

du·ce /do͞o chày/ *n.* an Italian term for "leader." The Italian Fascist leader Mussolini was called "Il Duce." [Early 20thC. Via Italian from, ultimately, Latin *dux* "leader."]

Du·champ /doo shaáN/, **Marcel** (1887–1968) French-born U.S. artist. He displayed everyday objects as works of art, and helped to introduce Cubism to the United States. He became a citizen of the United States in 1954, and later his work became an inspiration for the pop art movement.

Du·chenne mus·cu·lar dys·tro·phy /doo shèn-/, **Du·chenne's mus·cu·lar dys·tro·phy, Du·chenne dys·tro·phy, Du·chenne's dys·tro·phy** *n.* a form of muscular dystroph that attacks the muscles of the upper respiratory and pelvic areas, usually affecting boys and causing death before maturity [Late 19thC. Named for the French neurologist G. B. A. *Duchenne* (1806–75), who first described it.]

duch·ess /dúchəss/ *n.* **1. HIGH-RANKING NOBLEWOMAN** a noblewoman of high rank. In the British Isles this is the highest hereditary title of nobility. **2. WIFE OR WIDOW OF A DUKE** the wife or widow of a duke [14thC. Via Old French *duchesse* from medieval Latin *ducissa*, feminine form of *dux* "leader."]

duch·esse sat·in /doo shéss-/ *n.* a firm heavy satin with a glossy finish, used often for formal gowns

duch·ess po·ta·toes /doo shèss-/ *npl.* a mixture of mashed potatoes, eggs, and butter that is made into a patty and baked [*Duchesse* from French, "duchess"]

duch·y /dúchee/ (*plural* **-ies**) *n.* the territory over which a duke or duchess has jurisdiction [14thC. Via Old French *duche* from medieval Latin *ducatus*, from Latin *duc-*, the stem of *dux* "leader."]

duck[1] /duk/ *n.* **1.** (*plural* **ducks** *or* **duck**) BIRDS **COMMON WATER BIRD** a common water bird with webbed feet, short legs, and a broad flat bill. It is found all over the world, with the exception of Antarctica. Order: Anseriformes. **2. FEMALE DUCK** a female duck. ◊ **drake 3.** FOOD **DUCK AS FOOD** the flesh of a duck when it is eaten as a food [Old English *dūce*, of uncertain origin: probably from assumed *dūcan* "to dive" (see DUCK[2])] ◇ **get** *or* **have your ducks all in a row** to have organized your life or a specific task so that it runs smoothly ◇ **take to something like a duck to water** to have a natural talent for something

duck[2] /duk/ *v.* (**ducked, duck·ing, ducks**) **1.** *vti.* **BEND QUICKLY** to bend or move the head down quickly, especially to avoid being hit by something **2.** *vi.* **MOVE QUICKLY** to move somewhere very quickly, often to avoid being seen ○ *I ducked behind a desk and kept as still as possible.* **3.** *vti.* **PLUNGE UNDER WATER** to push somebody under water, or move quickly so as to go below the surface of the water ○ *No ducking.* **4.** *vt.* **AVOID SOMETHING** to avoid dealing with something that ought to be dealt with ○ *The candidate ducked all the questions about her past* **5.** *vi.* BRIDGE **DELIBERATELY LOSE A TRICK** to play a card lower than an opponent's on purpose in order to lose a trick ■ *n.* **QUICK DOWNWARD MOVEMENT** a movement downward with the head, especially to avoid being hit by something [13thC. Origin uncertain: probably from assumed Old English *dūcan*, ultimately from a prehistoric West Germanic word meaning "to dive, dip."] —**duck·er** *n.* ◇ **duck and run** to avoid meeting somebody face to face

duck out *vi.* to avoid or dodge doing something ○ *She's trying to duck out of paying her part of the bill.*

duck[3] /duk/ *n.* TEXTILES **STRONG CLOTH** strong, fairly stiff, closely woven cloth, usually of cotton or canvas, used to make protective clothing and furnishings ■ **ducks** *npl.* CLOTHES **PAIR OF WHITE PANTS** a pair of pants, usually white, or like those worn by sailors

Duck-billed platypus

duck-billed plat·y·pus *n.* an Australian egg-laying aquatic mammal with a snout shaped like a duck's bill and webbed feet. Latin name: *Ornithorynchus anatinus.*

duck blind *n.* a camouflaged shelter from which hunters shoot ducks

duck·board /dúk bàwrd/ *n.* a temporary walkway made of wooden boards laid over a wet or muddy area to form a raised path

duck call *n.* a device similar to a whistle that a duck hunter blows into in order to attract ducks

duck·ie *n., adj.* = **ducky** (*dated informal*)

duck·ing stool *n.* formerly, in Europe and New England, a chair or stool in which an offender was tied and then immersed in water as a punishment

duck·ling /dúkling/ *n.* a duck that has not reached maturity

duck·pin /dúk pìn/ *n.* a bowling pin smaller in size than a tenpin [Early 20thC. *Duck* from the shape of the pin, which resembles a duck.]

duck·pins /dúk pìnz/ *n.* a bowling game played with a small ball and pins smaller than tenpins (*takes a singular verb*)

ducks *n.* ➧ **duck**[1]

ducks and drakes *n.* a game in which flat stones are skipped across water by throwing them almost parallel to its surface (*takes a singular verb*) [So called because of the game's similarity to a waterfowl's movements] ◇ **play ducks and drakes with** to use something recklessly and wastefully

duck's ass *n.* full form of **DA** (*slang*)

duck soup *n.* a task or feat done or accomplished easily (*slang*)

duck·tail /dúk tàyl/ *n.* = **DA** [Mid-20thC. So called because of the haircut's similarity to a duck's tail.]

duck·weed /dúk weēd/ *n.* a stemless free-floating aquatic plant with small rounded leaves that is found on still temperate waters and eaten by waterfowl. Genus: *Lemna.*

duck·y /dúkee/ (*plural* **-ies**), **duck·ie** *adj.* charmingly pretty (*dated informal*) ○ *a ducky little cottage*

duct /dukt/ *n.* **1. CHANNEL THROUGH WHICH SOMETHING FLOWS** a tube, pipe, or channel through which something can flow or be carried, e.g., in air-conditioning equipment **2.** ANAT **TUBE IN A BODY ORGAN** a narrow tubular exit passageway in a gland or bladder through which fluid passes **3.** ELEC ENG **TUBE FOR CABLES** a tube or channel containing electrical cables ■ *vt.* (**duct·ed, duct·ing, ducts**) **1. SUPPLY WITH DUCTING** to supply or equip something such as a building with a duct or a system of ducts **2. CAUSE TO PASS THROUGH CHANNEL** to make a fluid or gas pass through a tube, pipe, or channel ○ *Exhaust fumes are ducted out of the workshop.* [Mid-17thC. From Latin *ductus*, from *ducere* "to lead."] —**duct·al** *adj.* —**duct·less** *adj.*

duc·tile /dúkt'l/ *adj.* **1. MALLEABLE ENOUGH TO BE WORKED** able to be drawn out into wire or hammered into very thin sheets ○ *ductile metal* **2. READILY SHAPED OR MOLDED** able to be molded or shaped without breaking **3. READILY INFLUENCED** easily persuaded or influenced [14thC. Directly or via Old French *ductile* from Latin *ductilis* "something that may be led or conducted," from *ducere* "to lead."] —**duc·tile·ly** *adv.* —**duc·tile·ness** *n.* —**duc·til·i·ty** /duk tíllətee/ *n.*

WORD KEY: SYNONYMS

See Synonyms at ***pliable.***

duct·ing /dúkting/ *n.* **1. SYSTEM OF DUCTS** a duct or system of ducts **2. MATERIAL FOR DUCTS** materials such as pipes and tubing that can be used as ducts

duct tape *n.* a very strong, wide, adhesive tape, typically silver in color, used especially in making temporary repairs to pipes

duct·work /dúkt wùrk/ *n.* a system of ducts that has been constructed, or its design

dud /dud/ *n.* **1. SHELL THAT DOES NOT EXPLODE** a munition that fails to fire or explode **2. FAILURE AT SOMETHING** somebody or something considered ineffective or a failure (*informal*) [Early 19thC. Origin uncertain: perhaps from DUDS via "somebody in rags," hence "useless thing," hence "shell that failed to explode," hence "failure."]

dude /dood/ *n.* (*slang*) **1. MAN** a man or boy ○ *He's one cool dude.* ○ *Hey, dude, what's up?* **2. CITY DWELLER VACATIONING OUT WEST** a resident of the urban eastern seaboard who vacations on a dude ranch in the west, or who moves out west to work or live ○ *"A new word has been coined. It is d-u-d-e ... It has sprung into popularity within the last two weeks."* (*Brooklyn Daily Eagle*; February 15, 1883) **3. FLASHILY DRESSED MAN** a man who wears flashy, highly stylish clothes [Late 19thC. Origin uncertain: perhaps from a German dialect word meaning "fool."]

dude up *v.* to wear flashy, very stylish clothes (*slang*) (*refers to a male*)

du·deen /doo deēn/ *n.* a clay tobacco pipe with a short stem [Mid-19thC. From Irish *dúidín*, literally "small pipe," from *dúd* "pipe."]

dude ranch *n.* a vacation resort offering outdoor activities that is or resembles a typical western ranch

dudg·eon /dújjən/ *n.* **1. PIQUE** a fit of anger and irritation **2. DAGGER HANDLE** the handle of a dagger (*archaic*) [Late 16thC. Origin unknown.] ◇ **in high dudgeon** in a very angry or irritated mood

duds /dudz/ *npl.* (*dated informal*) **1. CLOTHES** articles of clothing and accessories **2. SMALL BELONGINGS** small, portable personal possessions [15thC. Of uncertain origin.]

due /doo/ *adj.* **1.** **EXPECTED TO ARRIVE** expected to arrive imminently ○ *The baby is due in three weeks.* **2.** **READY FOR SOMETHING** awaiting an event, as part of a normal chain or progression of other events ○ *due for a long-awaited promotion* **3.** **PROPER AND APPROPRIATE** meeting all the necessary requirements and thus proper and appropriate to the situation ○ *after due consideration* **4.** **OWED** owed as a debt because of a right or an obligation ○ *Our deep gratitude is due to all those who have helped over the last few months.* **5.** FIN **PAYABLE** payable at once and on demand, or at a stipulated time ○ *Payment is due in 30 days.* **6.** **BECAUSE OF SOMEBODY OR SOMETHING** caused by or attributable to somebody or something ○ *The delay was due to bad weather.* ■ *n.* **SOMEBODY'S RIGHT** something that somebody has deserved or is owed ○ *I'll give you your due–you were absolutely right.* ■ **dues** *npl.* **MEMBERSHIP FEES** fees for membership in an organization ■ *adv.* **DIRECTLY AND EXACTLY** in a direct exact way or course ○ *due west* [13thC. Via Old French *deu* "owed" from Latin *debitus*, from *debere* "to owe" (source of English *debit* and *debt*.]

due bill *n.* a document that acknowledges one party's indebtedness to another, exchangeable for merchandise or services

du·el /do͝o əl/ *n.* **1.** **FORMAL FIGHT OVER MATTER OF HONOR** a prearranged combat, especially in former times, between two people with lethal weapons, usually to settle a disagreement over a matter of honor. The combatants were usually accompanied by seconds or supporters. **2.** **STRUGGLE BETWEEN TWO PARTIES** a struggle or conflict between two people or groups ■ *vi.* **(-eled, -el·ing, -els) 1.** **ENGAGE IN ONE-ON-ONE COMBAT** to fight somebody one-on-one, typically with firearms or sabers and usually over a matter of honor **2.** **OPPOSE** to be involved in a conflict or struggle with somebody [15thC. From medieval Latin *duellum* "combat between two persons," from (by folk etymology from Latin *duo* "two") Latin *duellum*, an archaic form of *bellum* "war."] —**du·el·er** *n.*

du·el·ing pis·tol *n.* a pistol specifically designed for fighting a duel, usually more finely manufactured than a normal pistol and often made in sets of two

du·el·ist /do͝o əlist/ *n.* **1.** **FIGHTER OF DUELS** somebody who fights in a duel **2.** **PARTY TO A CONFLICT** a person or entity taking part in a dual-party conflict or competition ○ *corporate duelists struggling for market share*

du·en·na /doo énnə/ *n.* a woman acting as a chaperone or governess to a younger woman, especially in Spain and Portugal in former times [Mid-17thC. Via Spanish, "married lady," from late Latin *domna*, from Latin *domina* "lady" (source of English *dame*).]

due proc·ess *n.* **1.** **FUNDAMENTAL PRINCIPLES OF JUSTICE** fundamental principles of justice as opposed to a specific rule of law **2.** **CITIZEN'S RIGHT TO JUSTICE** the entitlement of a citizen to proper legal procedures and natural justice

du·et /doo ét/ *n.* **1.** **COMPOSITION FOR TWO PERFORMERS** an instrumental or vocal composition written for two performers of equal importance **2.** **PAIR** a pair of people, animals, or things [Mid-18thC. Via Italian *duetto*, literally "little duo" from *duo* "two musicians," from Latin *duo* "two" or perhaps via German *Duett*.] —**du·et·tist** *n.*

duff[1] /duf/ **(duffed, duff·ing, duffs)** *vt.* to play a bad shot in golf by hitting the ground behind the ball (*informal*) [Mid-19thC. Origin uncertain: perhaps a back-formation from DUFFER.]

duff[2] /duf/ *n.* the buttocks (*slang offensive*) [Late 19thC. Origin uncertain.]

duf·fel, **duf·fle** *n.* **1.** TEXTILES **WOOLEN FABRIC** woolen material with a nap on both sides **2.** **CAMPING GEAR** gear, including clothing and equipment, used by campers and hikers [Late 17thC. From Dutch *duffel*, named for *Duffel*, town in Belgium where the cloth was originally made.]

duf·fel bag *n.* a cylindrical bag for personal belongings that is fastened with a drawstring

duff·er /dúffər/ *n.* **1.** **UNINTELLIGENT PERSON** somebody who is thought of as slow to learn or incompetent at something (*dated informal insult*) **2.** **SOMETHING WORTHLESS** something worthless or useless (*dated informal*) **3.** **PEDDLER** somebody who peddles goods, especially cheap or worthless merchandise (*regional or archaic*) [Mid-18thC. Origin uncertain: perhaps an alteration of Scottish *dowfart* "dull, inactive fellow," or from Old Norse *daufr* "deaf."]

duf·fle *n.* = **duffel**

Duffle coat

duf·fle coat, **duf·fel coat** *n.* TEXTILES a heavy medium-length coat with a hood and toggles for fastening it that is made from duffel

dug[1] past participle, past tense of **dig**

dug[2] /dug/ *n.* an udder, teat, nipple, or breast of a female mammal [Mid-16thC. Origin uncertain.]

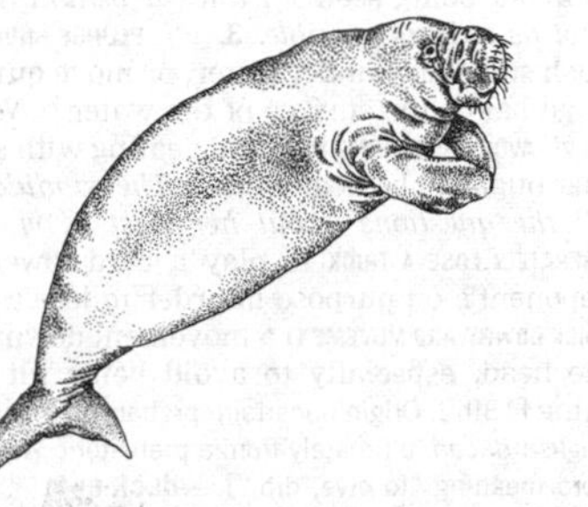

Dugong

du·gong /do͝o gàwng/ *n.* a large plant-eating mammal of shallow tropical coastal waters, related to the manatee. It has a two-lobed tail, cleft upper lip, forelimbs resembling flippers, and tusks in the male. Latin name: *Dugong dugon.* [Early 19thC. Ultimately from Malay *duyung*.]

dug·out /dúg òwt/ *n.* **1.** **CANOE MADE FROM A HOLLOWED LOG** a canoe or boat hollowed out from a log or tree trunk **2.** MIL **SOLDIERS' SHELTER** a hole dug in the ground that is covered and used as a shelter, especially by soldiers **3.** BASEBALL **BASEBALL SHELTER** either of two shelters, one for each team, on opposite sides of a baseball field where team members wait while not playing **4.** SOCCER **SOCCER SHELTER** either of two shelters beside a sports field, especially a soccer field, for team officials, e.g., the manager and trainer and team members who are not on the field

duh *interj.* (*slang*) **1.** **RESPONSE TO SOMETHING ALREADY KNOWN** said as an ironic response to a simple question or statement to show that somebody already knows the truth of something that he or she has just been told ○ *"Billy asked me to the party, I think he really likes me!""Duh!"* **2.** **HUMOROUS EXPRESSION OF STUPIDITY** said slowly in a humorous manner to suggest stupidity by imitating the hesitant noise somebody might make to indicate that he or she does not know the answer to something ○ *"What did you do with the keys?"—"Duh."*

DUI *abbr.* driving under the influence

dui·ker /dĭkər/, **duy·ker** *n.* a small African antelope with short backward-pointing horns. Genera: *Cephalophus* and *Sylvicapra.* [Late 18thC. Via Afrikaans, "diver," from, ultimately, Middle Dutch *dūken* "to dive."]

dui·ker·bok /dĭkər bòk/ *n.* a duiker that is the most widespread in Africa and is often found close to human settlements. Latin name: *Silvicapra grimma.* [Late 18thC. From Afrikaans, from *duiker* "diver" + *bok* "buck."]

du jour /doo zho͝or/ *prep.* offered or served today ○ *Let's ask what the soup du jour is.* [From French, literally "of the day"]

Du·ka·kis /do͝o kaákəss/, **Michael** (*b.* 1933) U.S. politician. He was Democratic governor of Massachusetts (1975–79 and 1983–91) and ran for the U.S. presidency in 1988. Full name **Michael Stanley Dukakis**

duke /dook/ *n.* **1.** **HIGH-RANKING NOBLEMAN** a nobleman of very high rank. In the British Isles this is the highest hereditary title of the nobility. **2.** **RULER OF PRINCIPALITY** a prince who rules a duchy, principality, or other small state **3.** **FIST** a hand or fist, especially a fist clenched for fighting or a boxer's fist raised as an indication of victory (*slang*) (*often used in the plural*) [12thC. Via Old French *duc* from Latin *dux* "leader," from *ducere* "to lead." "Fist" from *Duke of Yorks*, rhyming slang for "forks," that is, "fingers, fists."] ◇ **duke it out** to be in a highly aggressive competitive situation with somebody (*slang*)

Duke /dook/, **James Buchanan** (1856–1925) U.S. industrialist. He dominated the U.S. tobacco industry by 1889 and formed the American Tobacco Co. in 1890.

duke·dom /do͝okdəm/ *n.* **1.** **RANK OF DUKE** the rank, position, or title of a duke **2.** = **duchy**

Du·kho·bor *n.* = **Doukhobor**

dul·cet /dúlsət/ *adj.* pleasant to hear, especially by being soft or soothing [15thC. From Old French *doucet*, literally "small sweet (thing)," from *doux* "sweet," from Latin *dulcis*.]

dul·ci·a·na /dùlsee ánnə, dùlsee aánə/ *n.* an organ stop or pipe of the diapason type, characterized by a soft sweet tone [Late 18thC. From medieval Latin, from Latin *dulcis* "sweet."]

dul·ci·fy /dúlsə fī/ **(-fied, -fy·ing, -fies)** *vt.* to make something agreeable, especially to the senses (*literary*) [Late 16thC. From Latin *dulcificare*, literally "to make sweet," from *dulcis* "sweet."] —**dul·ci·fi·ca·tion** /dùlsəfi káysh'n/ *n.*

dul·ci·mer /dúlsəmər/ *n.* a zither played with lightweight hammers or sometimes by plucking. ◊ **hammer dulcimer** [15thC. From French *doulcemer*, of uncertain origin: perhaps from Latin *dulcis* "sweet" + *melos* "song."]

dul·cin·e·a /dùlsə nee ə, dul sínnee ə/ *n.* a woman who is the object of somebody's love, especially one who is idealized (*literary*) [Mid-17thC. From *Dulcinea*, the name of Don Quixote's love.]

dul·fer /dúlfər, do͝olfər/ *n.* in mountaineering, a classic method of rappelling using a rope wrapped around the body

du·li·a /doo lī ə/ *n.* the veneration of saints and angels, as in the Roman Catholic and Eastern churches [Early 17thC. Via medieval Latin, "service, work done," from Greek *douleia* "slavery."]

dull /dul/ *adj.* **1.** **BORING** arousing no interest or excitement **2.** **OVERCAST** not bright because of weather conditions such as thick clouds or mist **3.** **NOT VIVID** lacking vividness or brightness of hue **4.** **NOT INTENSELY FELT** not acutely or intensely felt or experienced, but prolonged ○ *a dull ache* **5.** **MUFFLED** muffled and not resonant ○ *a dull thud* **6.** **BLUNT** lacking sharpness or the ability to cut cleanly **7.** **UNINTELLIGENT** slow to understand or learn **8.** **SLOW TO RESPOND** lacking in alertness or speedy responsiveness ○ *dull reflexes* **9.** **LISTLESS** lacking in energy or enthusiasm ○ *dull, scattered applause* ■ *vti.* **(dulled, dull·ing, dulls) 1.** **BECOME OR MAKE LESS ACUTE** to become, or cause something to become, less acute or intensely felt ○ *Sleepiness had dulled his hunger.* **2.** **REDUCE IN LOUDNESS** to become, or cause something to become, quieter **3.** **BECOME OR MAKE BLUNT** to become, or cause something to become, less sharp **4.** **BECOME OR MAKE LESS BRIGHT** to become, or cause something to become, less bright or intense [Old English *dol* "slow-witted," from a prehistoric Germanic word that is also the ancestor of English *dolt* and *doldrums*] —**dull·ish** *adj.* —**dull·ness** *n.* —**dul·ly** *adv.*

WORD KEY: SYNONYMS

See Synonyms at ***boring***.

dull·ard /dúllərd/ *n.* somebody regarded as unintelligent or slow to comprehend (*dated insult*) [15thC. Coined from DULL + -ARD.]

Dul·les /dúlliss/, **Allen Welsh** (1893–1969) U.S. government official. Director of the Central Intelligence Agency (1953–61), he resigned after the disastrous Bay of Pigs landing in Cuba and subsequent rout.

Dul·les, John Foster (1888–1959) U.S. statesman and diplomat. He was secretary of state (1953–59), and delegate to the United Nations, which he helped to form.

dulls·ville /dúlz vìl/, **Dulls·ville** *n.* (*slang*) **1.** **SOMETHING BORING** a place, thing, or activity that is boring or unexciting ○ *This town is dullsville in the evening.* **2.** **BOREDOM** the condition of being bored or uninterested ○ *I sat there in dullsville during the entire eight-hour flight.* [Mid-20thC. Modeled on place names.]

dulse /duls/ (*plural* **duls·es** *or* **dulse**) *n.* a red alga with edible fronds that grows in the intertidal zone and near the low-water mark in northern temperate seas. Latin name: *Palmaria palmata.* [Early 17thC. From Irish and Gaelic *duileasg.*]

Du·luth /də lóoth/ major port and city in northeastern Minnesota, at the southern end of Lake Superior, northeast of Minneapolis. Population: 83,699 (1996).

du·ly /dóolee/ *adv.* **1.** **PROPERLY AND SUITABLY** in a proper, correct, or suitable way ○ *duly grateful* **2.** **AS EXPECTED** at the proper or expected time ○ *A signal was given and our coach duly departed.* [14thC. Coined from DUE + -LY.]

du·ma /dóomə, dóo maà/, **dou·ma** *n.* **1.** **MODERN RUSSIAN PARLIAMENT** the parliament of modern Russia, established in 1993 after the dissolution of the former Soviet Union **2.** **TSARIST RUSSIAN PARLIAMENT** a Russian council or parliament during the time of tsarist rule, set up around 1905 but quickly deprived of power [Late 19thC. From Russian, from Old Russian, "council, thought," of uncertain origin: probably from a prehistoric Germanic word meaning "to judge."]

Du·mas /doo maà, dyoo-/, **Alexandre** (1802–70) French novelist and dramatist. He wrote the celebrated novels *The Three Musketeers* (1844) and *The Count of Monte Cristo* (1844). Known as **Dumas père**

Du·mas, Alexandre (1824–95) French playwright and novelist. He wrote *The Lady of the Camellias* (1848), on which Verdi based *La Traviata*. Known as **Dumas fils**

du Mau·rier /doo máwree ày/, **Dame Daphne** (1907–89) British novelist. Her books include *Jamaica Inn* (1936), *Rebecca* (1938), and *My Cousin Rachel* (1951).

dumb /dum/ *adj.* **1.** **UNINTELLIGENT** having or characterized by a low level of intelligence (*informal insult*) **2.** **OFFENSIVE TERM MEANING UNABLE TO SPEAK** unable to speak (*offensive*) **3.** **TEMPORARILY SPEECHLESS** temporarily unable to speak because of shock, fear, surprise, or anger **4.** **DONE WITHOUT SPEECH** performed or expressed without using speech **5.** **INTENTIONALLY SILENT** deliberately not speaking or refusing to speak **6.** COMPUT **NOT PROGRAMMABLE** able only to transmit information to or receive information from a computer, and not able to process data ○ *a dumb terminal* **7.** **PRODUCING NO SOUND** designed or adapted to produce no sound **8.** **LACKING HUMAN SPEECH** lacking the power of speech because not human ■ *vt.* (**dumbed, dumb·ing, dumbs**) **MAKE TEMPORARILY SPEECHLESS** to make somebody temporarily unable to speak, especially by using shock or surprise (*literary*) [Old English. Ultimately from an Indo-European word meaning "sensory or mental impairment" that is also the ancestor of English *dull* and *doldrums*.] —**dumb·ly** *adv.* —**dumb·ness** *n.*

dumb down *vti.* to make something less intellectually challenging (*informal*) ○ *parents and teachers who were adamantly opposed to dumbing down science courses*

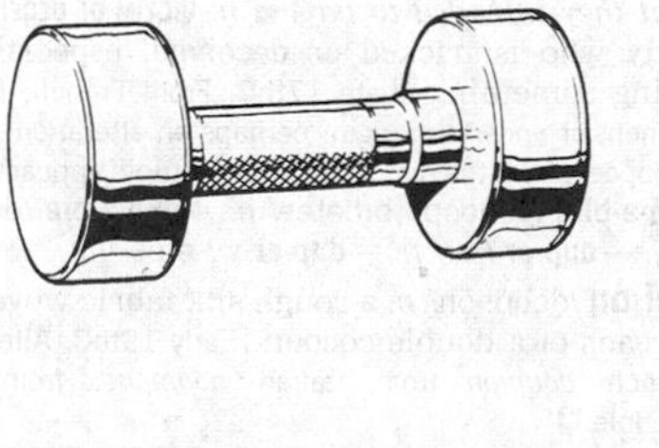

Dumbbell

dumb·bell /dúm bèl/ *n.* **1.** **WEIGHT FOR EXERCISING** an exercise weight in the form of a metal bar with a metal disk or ball at each end **2.** **UNINTELLIGENT PERSON** somebody regarded as lacking in intelligence and common sense (*slang insult*)

dumb blond, **dumb blonde** *n.* a blonde woman stereotyped as being good-looking but unintelligent (*offensive*)

dumb cane *n.* a poisonous tropical American plant that if chewed can lead to loss of speech in adults or death in children and small animals. Latin name: *Dieffenbachia seguine.*

dumb cluck *n.* somebody regarded as very unintelligent or thoughtless (*dated insult*)

dumb·found /dùm fównd, dúm fòwnd/ (**-found·ed, -found·ing, -founds**), **dum·found** (**-found·ed, -found·ing, -founds**) *vti.* to make somebody temporarily speechless with astonishment [Mid-17thC. From DUMB + CONFOUND.]

dum·bo /dúm bō/ (*plural* **-bos**) *n.* somebody unintelligent or very silly (*slang insult*) [Mid-20thC. Modeled on JUMBO.]

dumb show *n.* THEATER **1.** **ACTORS' PANTOMIME** communication without words by actors using gesture or facial expressions **2.** **PLAY IN MIME** a play or part of a play presented in mime form

dumb·struck /dúm strùk/ *adj.* made temporarily speechless by astonishment or shock

dumb·wait·er /dúm wàytər/ *n.* **1.** **SMALL ELEVATOR** a small elevator used for moving food and tableware between the floors of a building **2.** **MOVABLE FOOD STAND** a movable stand for food, often with revolving shelves, that is placed near a table

dum·dum bul·let, **dum·dum** *n.* a bullet with a soft core or vertical cuts made in its point that expands on impact and inflicts a severe wound. Dumdum bullets are contrary to the Geneva Convention. [Late 19thC. Named for *DumDum*, town and arsenal near Calcutta, India, where the bullets were first produced.]

dum·found *vti.* = **dumbfound**

dumm·kopf /dúm kàwpf, dúm kàwf/ *n.* a person who is regarded as unintelligent and clumsy (*slang insult*) [Early 19thC. From German, from *dumm* "stupid" + *Kopf* "head."]

dum·my /dúmmee/ *n.* (*plural* **-mies**) **1.** **MANNEQUIN IN A STORE** a model of a human used for making or displaying clothes **2.** **MODEL USED BY A VENTRILOQUIST** a large, sometimes stuffed, model of a human used, e.g., by a ventriloquist **3.** **UNINTELLIGENT PERSON** somebody regarded as being unintelligent or silly (*informal insult*) **4.** FOOTBALL **BAG USED IN TACKLING PRACTICE** a stuffed bag, usually mounted on a frame, that represents an opposing player and is used in blocking and tackling practice **5.** **IMITATION OF SOMETHING** an imitation of something, especially one lacking a feature or function of the original and deceivingly substituted for it ○ *A lot of the system's switches are just dummies.* **6.** SPORTS **FEIGNED PASS IN BALL GAMES** a feigned pass or other move intended to deceive an opponent, especially a tackler, in soccer, rugby, or a similar game **7.** **PERSON OR ORGANIZATION ACTING AS FRONT** a person or organization serving as a front for another while pretending to be independent ○ *a dummy corporation* **8.** ARMS **NONEXPLOSIVE FORM OF MUNITION** a nonexplosive form of an explosive munition **9.** BRIDGE **EXPOSED HAND IN BRIDGE** an exposed hand of cards in bridge played by the player who is the first bidder of the suit in the final contract (**declarer**), or a player of this hand **10.** *U.K.* = **pacifier** **11.** PUBL **MODEL PAGE** a page that looks like the final product but is a computer-generated or pasted-up facsimile showing general design specifications **12.** PUBL **MODEL BOOK** a set of model pages, often blank or containing only one signature, that have been bound and jacketed to give an idea of the final book. Dummies are used in preselling books. ■ *vt.* (**-mied, -my·ing, -mies**) PUBL **MAKE INTO PAGE OR BOOK FACSIMILE** to make up pages into page or book facsimiles ○ *dummied several pages for the sales conference* [Late 16thC. Coined from DUMB + -Y.]

dum·my var·i·a·ble *n.* a mathematical variable that can be replaced by another arbitrarily

Du·mont /doo máwnt/, **Gabriel** (1838–1906) Canadian military leader. He commanded rebels against government forces and settlers in Saskatchewan (1885).

du·mor·ti·er·ite /doo máwrtee ə rìt/ *n.* a hard fibrous bright blue, bluish-green, or pink mineral consisting of a silicate of aluminum and boron [Late 19thC. From French, named for Eugène *Dumortier*, a French paleontologist.]

dump /dump/ *vt.* (**dumped, dump·ing, dumps**) **1.** **DROP OR PUT DOWN CARELESSLY** to deposit something on a surface in a careless and usually noisy manner ○ *dumped the reports on my desk* **2.** **THROW OUT AS UNWANTED** to get rid of something that is unwanted, especially by taking it and leaving it somewhere **3.** **DISPOSE OF WASTE** to dispose of waste by moving it to a prearranged site **4.** **TERMINATE RELATIONSHIP** to end a romantic or sexual relationship with somebody, especially abruptly and hurtfully (*informal*) **5.** **REMOVE SOMEBODY UNDESIRABLE** to remove somebody deemed undesirable or a liability from a position such as leadership in a group, especially abruptly and unceremoniously (*informal*) **6.** COUNSELLING **CONFIDE** to offload negative feelings by talking about them to somebody, especially a friend or therapist ○ *I'm sorry to dump all this on you, but I've got no one else to talk to.* **7.** COMM **FLOOD MARKET WITH CHEAP MERCHANDISE** to flood a market with cheaply priced merchandise **8.** **RELEGATE SOMEBODY TO CUSTODIAL CARE** to entrust somebody, e.g., a child or a person of advanced years, to custodial care (*informal disapproving*) **9.** STOCK EXCH **GET RID OF STOCKS** to sell off large quantities of stock all at once, thereby driving the price down **10.** COMPUT **TRANSFER DATA WITHOUT PROCESSING** to transfer computer data from one site to another without processing it ■ *n.* **1.** MIL **MUNITIONS AND SUPPLY AREA** a place for the temporary storage of munitions, food, water, fuel, and other supplies for distribution to troops **2.** **WASTE DISPOSAL SITE** a place where waste materials can be left **3.** **UNPLEASANT PLACE** an unpleasant or dirty place (*informal*) ○ *The hotel was a real dump.* **4.** **ACT OF DEFECATING** an act of evacuating the bowels (*slang offensive*) **5.** **ACT OF THROWING SOMETHING AWAY** an act of discarding something [14thC. Origin uncertain: perhaps from Scandinavian, from, ultimately, an Indo-European word meaning "to hit," or from Dutch *dumpen* "to immerse, topple."]

dump on *vi.* to insult, criticize, or otherwise denigrate somebody else severely (*slang*)

dump·er /dúmpər/ *n.* **1.** **DISPOSER OF WASTE** a person who or machine that disposes of waste by taking it to a prearranged site **2.** **SOMEBODY WHO THROWS THINGS OUT** somebody who throws things out, littering in the process

dump·er truck *n. U.K.* = **dump truck**

dump·ing /dúmping/ *n.* the activity of depositing waste in an area or place

dump·ling /dúmpling/ *n.* **1.** **SMALL BALL OF COOKED DOUGH** a small dough ball cooked and served with a stew or soup **2.** **PASTRY AND FRUIT DESSERT** a baked dessert consisting of pastry wrapped around fruit **3.** **SOMEBODY SHORT AND PLUMP** somebody who is endearingly short and plump (*informal insult*) [Early 17thC. Origin uncertain: perhaps formed from Low German *dump* "damp, moist, heavy."]

dump or·bit *n.* an orbit that a communications satellite is moved into at the end of its useful life in which it will not collide with operational satellites

dumps /dumps/ *npl.* a state of sadness and hopelessness (*informal*) ○ *feeling down in the dumps* [Early 16thC. Plural of obsolete *dump*, of uncertain origin: perhaps from Dutch *domp* "haze."]

Dump·ster /dúmpstər/ *tdmk.* a trademark for large trash-and-garbage containers and hoisting units

dump truck *n.* a heavy truck with an open bed that can be tilted up and back to unload cargo such as gravel, dirt, or refuse from construction sites

dump·y[1] /dúmpee/ (**-i·er, -i·est**) *adj.* having a short and plump build or shape (*insult*) [Mid-18thC. Origin uncertain: perhaps formed from Low German *dump* "damp, heavy, lump" (possible source of English *dumpling*).] —**dump·i·ly** *adv.* —**dump·i·ness** *n.*

dump·y[2] /dúmpee/ (**-i·er, -i·est**) *adj.* messy, cheap, and usually dirty (*informal*) ○ *a dumpy little airless apartment* [Mid-18thC. See DUMPY[1].]

dump·y lev·el *n.* a surveying instrument for taking levels with a short fixed horizontal telescope

dun[1] /dun/ *n.* **1.** COLORS **BROWNISH-GRAY COLOR** a brownish-gray color **2.** EQU **BROWNISH-GRAY HORSE** a horse whose coat is brownish gray ■ *adj.* (**dun·ner, dun·nest**) **1.** COLORS **BROWNISH-GRAY** of a brownish-gray color **2.** **GLOOMY** gloomily and darkly bleak and depressing (*literary*) ○ *a dun and bare prairie* [Old English *dunn*. Ultimately from an Indo-European word that is also the ancestor of English *dusk*.]

dun[2] /dun/ *vt.* (**dunned, dun·ning, duns**) **HARASS FOR DEBT PAYMENT** to press or harass somebody persistently for the settlement of a debt ■ *n.* **1.** **PAYMENT DEMAND** a pressing, usually written, demand for payment **2.** **DEBT COLLECTOR** somebody whose job is to collect other people's debts [Early 17thC. Origin uncertain: perhaps a shortening of *dunkirk* "privateer sailing from Dunkirk in France"; or named for Joe *Dun*, bailiff of Lincoln, England, famous for catching debtors.]

Du·nant /doo naáN/, **Jean Henri** (1828–1910) Swiss philanthropist. He founded the International Red Cross (1862–64) and shared the first Nobel Peace Prize (1901).

Dun·a·way /dúnnə wày/, **Faye** (*b.* 1941) U.S. movie actor. She has acted in various Hollywood films and won an Academy Award for *Network* (1976).

Dun·bar /dún baàr/, **Paul Laurence** (1872–1906) U.S. poet. The son of former slaves, he was known for his poems, written in dialect, about the experiences of African Americans.

Dun·can /dúngkən/ city in southern Oklahoma, south of Oklahoma City and southeast of Lawton. Population: 22,057 (1996).

AKG London

Isadora Duncan

Dun·can, Isadora (1877–1927) U.S. dancer. She laid the foundation for modern dance, basing her ideas on the dances of the ancient Greeks. Full name **Dora Angela Duncan**

Dun·can·ville /dúngkən vìl/ city in northeastern Texas, southeast of Mountain Creek Lake. It is a southwestern suburb of Dallas. Population: 36,008 (1996).

dunce /duns/ *n.* somebody who is felt to be unintelligent or a slow learner, especially somebody with no aptitude for a particular subject (*insult*) [Mid-16thC. From *Duns* in the name of John DUNS SCOTUS. Originally "follower of Duns Scotus" (a contemptuous term).]

dunce cap, **dunc·e's cap** *n.* a conical paper hat formerly worn as a punishment by a pupil who was slow to learn or lazy in school

dun·der·head /dúndər hèd/ *n.* somebody regarded as unintelligent or slow to learn (*informal insult*) [Early 17thC. Origin uncertain: perhaps from Dutch *dunderkop*, from *dunder* "thunder" + *kop* "head."] —**dun·der·head·ed** *adj.* —**dun·der·head·ed·ness** *n.*

dun·drear·ies /dun dreériz/ *npl.* long sideburns worn in conjunction with a clean-shaven chin [Mid-19thC. Named for Lord *Dundreary* in Tom Taylor's comedy *Our American Cousin*, from the whiskers worn by actor E. A. Sothern, who played the part.]

dune /doon/ *n.* a mound or ridge of sand formed by wind or water action, typically seen on coasts and in deserts [Late 18thC. Via French from Middle Dutch *dūne*.]

Dune buggy

dune bug·gy *n.* a motorized beach vehicle, usually with no top and with oversized tires to prevent it from getting mired in sand

dung /dung/ *n.* **1. ANIMAL EXCREMENT** the solid excrement of animals, especially large animals such as cattle or horses **2.** = **manure** ■ *vt.* (**dunged, dung·ing, dungs**) **COVER WITH DUNG** to cover land with dung or manure [Old English, of uncertain origin: perhaps originally "material for covering the earth," and ultimately from an Indo-European word meaning "to cover," which may also be the ancestor of English *dingy*] —**dung·y** *adj.*

dun·ga·ree /dùng gə reé, dúng gə reè/ *n.* a sturdy hard-wearing blue-denim fabric [Late 17thC. From Hindi *dungrī* "kind of coarse cloth," named after the village near Mumbai (Bombay) where it was first made.]

dun·ga·rees /dùng gə reéz, dúng gə reèz/ *npl.* pants made from strong material, usually blue denim

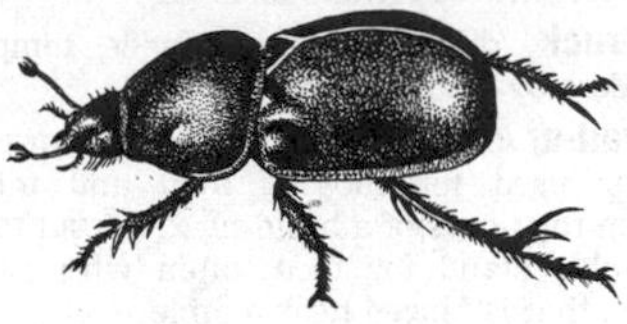

Dung beetle

dung bee·tle *n.* a scarab beetle that rolls large balls of dung into tunnels to feed the larvae that hatch from the eggs it lays there. Subfamily: Coprinae.

Dun·ge·ness crab /dùnjə ness-/ *n.* a large edible crab native to the Pacific coast, especially to the area around Dungeness, Washington. Latin name: *Cancer magister*.

dun·geon /dúnjən/ *n.* **1. PRISON CELL** a prison cell, often underground, especially beneath a castle **2. CASTLE KEEP** the secure main tower of a castle (*archaic*) [14thC. Via Old French *donjon* "castle keep" (later "secure underground cell") from, ultimately, Latin *dominus* "lord" (source of English *danger* and *dominion*).]

dung·hill /dúng hìl/, **dung·heap** /dúng heèp/ *n.* a pile of solid animal excrement

Dun·ham /dúnnəm/, **Katherine** (*b.* 1910) U.S. dancer, choreographer, and scholar. She introduced Black and Caribbean themes into modern dance.

du·nite /doo nìt, dú nīt/ *n.* a coarse-grained dark igneous rock consisting mainly of a magnesium-rich olivine. It is an important source of magnesium, chromium, and platinum. [Mid-19thC. Named for Mt. *Dun* in New Zealand, where it is found.] —**du·nit·ic** /doo níttik, də níttik/ *adj.*

dunk /dungk/ *v.* (**dunked, dunk·ing, dunks**) **1.** *vt.* **DIP FOOD IN LIQUID** to dip food into a liquid before eating it **2.** *vt.* **QUICKLY SUBMERGE IN LIQUID** to submerge something in liquid, especially quickly and for a short time **3.** *vi.* **IMMERSE SELF IN WATER** to immerse yourself in water for a short period (*informal*) ○ *a huge swimming pool to dunk in every morning* **4.** *vt.* **SHOVE SOMEBODY'S HEAD UNDER WATER** to push somebody's head beneath the surface of water **5.** *vt.* BASKETBALL **SLAM BASKETBALL INTO BASKET FROM ABOVE** to slam or jam a basketball through the hoop from above by jumping and arcing the ball-carrying arm over the head ■ *n.* BASKETBALL = **dunk shot** [Early 20thC. Via Pennsylvanian German *dunke* "to dip" from, ultimately, Old High German *dunkōn*.] —**dunk·er** *n.*

Dunk·er /dúngkər/, **Dunk·ard** /-ərd/ *n.* a member of a group of German-American Baptists, the German Baptist Brethren, who baptize by total immersion and oppose military service and official oath-taking. They also dress plainly and believe in living a simple life unencumbered by materialism. [Mid-18thC. From Pennsylvanian German, from *dunke* "to dip."]

Dun·kirk /dún kùrk, dun kúrk/ seaport and town in northern France, in the Nord Department, Nord-Pas-de-Calais Region, near Calais. In World War II over 330,000 Allied troops were evacuated from the town by sea, under constant enemy fire. Population: 71,071 (1990).

dunk shot *n.* BASKETBALL a shot in basketball made by jamming or slamming the ball through the hoop from above

dun·lin /dúnlin/ (*plural* **-lins** *or* **-lin**) *n.* a small wading bird with a slightly downcurved bill and a black belly, found in North America, Europe, Africa, and Asia. Latin name: *Calidris alpina*. [Mid-16thC. Formed from DUN[1].]

dun·nage /dúnnij/ *n.* packing material used to cushion cargo on a ship [14thC. Origin unknown.]

Dunne /dun/, **Finley Peter** (1867–1936) U.S. journalist and humorist. He created the character of Mr. Dooley, an Irish barman and social commentator.

dun·nite /dú nīt/ *n.* an explosive that contains ammonium picrate [Early 20thC. Named for its inventor U.S. Army Col. B. W. *Dunn* (1860–1936).]

dun·no /də nṓ/ *contr.* (I) don't know (*nonstandard*) ○ *'Who broke the glass'? 'Dunno'.*

Dun·wood·y /dun wŏŏdee/ city in DeKalb County, Georgia, north of Atlanta. Population: 26,302 (1990).

du·o /dóo ō/ (*plural* **-os**) *n.* **1. PAIR OF CLOSELY ASSOCIATED PEOPLE** two people who are considered to be closely connected in some way **2. DUET** a duet, especially one for two instruments **3. PLAYERS OF A DUET** a pair of musicians who play together **4. SET OF TWO CLOSELY RELATED THINGS** a set of two items considered as closely connected [Late 16thC. Via Italian *duo* "two" from, ultimately, Latin.]

duo- *prefix.* two ○ *duopoly* [From Latin. Ultimately from the Indo-European word for "two," which is also the ancestor of English *two* and *bi-*.]

du·o·dec·i·mal /dòo ə déssəm'l/ *adj.* **BASED ON 12** using the number 12 as a base and counted or ordered in units of 12 or 12ths, or belonging to a sytem organized in this way. Although no longer commonly used, vestiges of a duodecimal system remain in such units as the foot being equal to 12 inches. ■ *n.* **1. DUODECIMAL NUMBER** a number in a counting system that uses units of 12 **2. 12TH** a 12th part [Early 18thC. Formed from Latin *duodecimus* "twelfth."] —**du·o·dec·i·mal·ly** *adv.*

du·o·de·num /dòo ə deénəm, doo ódd'nəm/ (*plural* **-na** /-ə deénə, -ódd'nə/ *or* **-nums**) *n.* the first short section of the small intestine immediately beyond the stomach [14thC. From medieval Latin *intestinum duodenum digitorum*, literally "12 finger-breadths long," from, ultimately, Latin *duodecim* "twelve."] —**du·o·de·nal** *adj.*

du·o·logue /dóo ə lòg/ *n.* **1. PIECE FOR TWO SPEAKING ACTORS** a play or part of a play in which only two actors speak **2. DIALOGUE BETWEEN TWO** a dialogue between two actors, or a conversation between two people [Mid-18thC. Blend of DUO and MONOLOGUE.]

duo·mo /dwáw mō, dwṓ mō/ (*plural* **-mos**) *n.* a cathedral in Italy [Mid-16thC. Via Italian from Latin *domus* "house."]

du·op·o·ly /doo óppəlee/ (*plural* **-lies**) *n.* an economic situation in which two powerful groups or organizations concentrate or dominate commerce in one business market or commodity [Early 20thC. Modeled on MONOPOLY.] —**du·op·o·lis·tic** /dòo oppə lístik/ *adj.*

du·op·so·ny /doo ópsənee/ (*plural* **-nies**) *n.* a situation in which two competing buyers exert controlling influence over many sellers [Blend of DUO and *-opsony*, from Greek *opsōnía* "purchasing of food"]

dup. *abbr.* duplicate

dupe /doop/ *vt.* (**duped, dup·ing, dupes**) **TRICK SOMEBODY** to persuade or induce somebody to do something by trickery or deception ○ *He was duped into thinking that they intended to pay.* ■ *n.* **VICTIM OF DECEIT** somebody who is tricked or deceived, especially into doing something [Late 17thC. From French, from Old French, of uncertain origin: perhaps an alteration of *huppe* "hoopoe"; from the bird's supposedly stupid appearance.] —**dup·a·bil·i·ty** /dòopə bíllətee/ *n.* —**dup·a·ble** /dóopəb'l/ *adj.* —**dup·er** /-ər/ *n.* —**dup·er·y** /-əree/ *n.*

du·pi·on /dóopi òn/ *n.* a rough silk fabric woven from threads of a double cocoon [Early 19thC. Alteration of French *doupion* from Italian *doppione*, from *doppio* "double."]

du·ple /dóop'l/ *adj.* MUSIC consisting of two beats to the bar or measure [Mid-16thC. From Latin *duplus* "double."]

Du·ples·sis /dòo play seé/, **Maurice Le Noblet** (1890–1959) Canadian statesman. He was premier of Quebec (1936–39 and 1944–59) with the Union Nationale Party.

du·plet /dóoplət/ *n.* **1.** MUSIC **GROUP OF 2 NOTES** a group of 2 notes played in the time usually required by three **2.** CHEM **2 SHARED ELECTRONS** a pair of electrons shared between two atoms that are joined in a chemical bond [Mid-17thC. Formed from DUPLE, modeled on DOUBLET.]

du·ple time *n.* a musical meter in which there are two beats to the measure, e.g., 2/4 or 6/8

du·plex /dŏŏ plèks, dyŏŏ-/ *n.* **1.** ARCHIT **2-FAMILY DWELLING WITH 2 ENTRANCES** a house that is divided into two halves and is inhabited by two separate families or tenants with separate entrances and exits **2.** ELECTRON ENG **SIMULTANEOUS TRANSMISSION IN BOTH DIRECTIONS** transmission of signals along a communications channel in both directions at the same time, e.g., over a telephone line ■ *adj.* **1. TWOFOLD** consisting of two parts, especially two identical or equivalent parts **2.** ENG **HAVING TWO PARTS PERFORMING ONE OPERATION** consisting of pairs of units or components that perform the same machine function but operate independently [Mid-16thC. From Latin *duplex*, literally "twofold," from *plicare* "to fold."] —**du·plex·i·ty** /doo pléksitee/ *n.*

du·plex a·part·ment *n.* an apartment that is on two floors with an inside stairway connecting the two levels

du·pli·ca·ble /dŏŏplikəb'l/ *adj.* able to be copied exactly or repeated —**du·pli·ca·bil·i·ty** /dŏŏplikə bíllətee/ *n.*

du·pli·cate *vt.* /dŏŏpli kàyt, dyŏŏpli-/ (**-cat·ed, -cat·ing, -cates**) **1. COPY SOMETHING** to make an exact copy of something **2. REPEAT SOMETHING** to do something more than once, especially unknowingly or unnecessarily ■ *n.* /dŏŏplikət, dyŏŏ-/ **1. COPY OF SOMETHING** an exact copy, especially of a document **2. ANOTHER OF THE SAME** a spare of the same kind **3. REPEAT OF SOMETHING** a repeat of an earlier action or achievement ■ *adj.* /dŏŏplikət, dyŏŏ-/ **1. COPIED EXACTLY** being an exact copy of something ○ *a duplicate key* **2. HAVING 2 CORRESPONDING PARTS** consisting of or existing in two corresponding parts [15thC. From Latin *duplicare* "to make twofold, double," from *duplus* "twofold."] —**du·pli·cate·ly** *adv.* —**du·pli·ca·tive** *adj.* ◇ **in duplicate** so as to create or consist of two exact copies

WORD KEY: SYNONYMS

See Synonyms at ***copy***.

du·pli·cate bridge *n.* contract bridge in which the same hand is played by different consecutive players

du·pli·ca·tion /dŏŏpli káysh'n, dyŏŏpli-/ *n.* **1. REPEATING OR COPYING** the action or an act of duplicating something **2. EXACT COPY** an exact copy of something **3.** GENETICS **REPETITION OF GENES** a chromosome mutation in which a section of a chromosome, along with the genes it carries, occurs twice

du·pli·ca·tor /dŏŏpli kàytər, dyŏŏpli-/ *n.* something that makes copies, especially a machine for copying printed matter

du·plic·i·tous /doo plíssitəss, dyoo-/ *adj.* deceptive, dishonest, or misleading —**du·plic·i·tous·ly** *adv.* —**du·plic·i·tous·ness** *n.*

du·plic·i·ty /doo plíssətee, dyoo-/ *n.* **1. DECEITFULNESS** the fact of being deceptive, dishonest, or misleading **2. CONDITION OF BEING DOUBLE** the state of being double or in a pair (*formal*) ○ *the duplicity of the stars of the constellation* [15thC. Directly or via French *duplicité* from late Latin *duplicitas*, from Latin *duplic-*, stem of *duplex* (see DUPLEX).]

Du Pont de Ne·mours /doo pònt də nə mŏŏr/, **Eleuthère Irénée** (1771–1834) U.S. industrialist. He founded a gunpowder mill (1802) that became the largest factory of its kind in the United States.

Du Pont de Ne·mours, Pierre Samuel (1739–1817) French economist. A friend and disciple of the French economist, François Quesnay, he was imprisoned for his royalist views and later immigrated to the United States, where he played an important role in the negotiations for the Louisiana Purchase.

dup·py /dúppee/ (*plural* **-pies**) *n. Carib* a ghost or spirit [Late 18thC. Origin uncertain: perhaps of West African origin.]

du Pré /doo práy/, **Jacqueline** (1945–87) British cellist and teacher. She is particularly famous for her interpretations of cello concertos. Her playing, though not her teaching, was halted in 1972 by multiple sclerosis.

du·ra·ble /dŏŏrəb'l/ *adj.* lasting for a long time, especially without sustaining damage or wear ○ *durable materials* ○ *a durable peace* [14thC. Via Old French *durable* from Latin *durabilis*, from *durare* "to last, harden" (source of English *endure*).] —**du·ra·bil·i·ty** /dŏŏrə bíllətee/ *n.* —**du·ra·ble·ness** /dŏŏrəb'lnəss/ *n.* —**du·ra·bly** /-blee/ *adv.*

du·ra·ble goods *npl.* = **durables**

du·ra·bles /dŏŏrəb'lz/ *n.* long-lasting products, e.g., motor vehicles and large appliances such as stoves and refrigerators

Du·rack Range /dyŏŏrak-/ mountain range in Western Australia, in the Kimberley region, west of Lake Argyle

du·ral /dŏŏrəl/ *adj.* relating to the dura mater, the outermost membrane around the brain and spinal cord [Late 19thC. Formed from *dura* (see DURA MATER).]

du·ra ma·ter /dŏŏrə màatər, dŏŏrə máytər/ *n.* the tough outermost membrane of the three that cover the brain and spinal cord [14thC. From medieval Latin, literally "hard mother," translation of Arabic *al-'umm al-jāfiya* "coarse mother."]

du·rance /dŏŏrəns/ *n.* **1. DURATION** the period of duration of something (*literary*) **2. IMPRISONMENT** forcible confinement or imprisonment (*archaic or literary*) [15thC. Via Old French from, ultimately, Latin *durare* "to last, harden."]

Du·rand /də ránd/, **Asher B.** (1796–1886) U.S. engraver and painter. He was known for his engravings and for cofounding the Hudson River School of painting. Full name **Asher Brown Durand**

Du·ran·go /doo ráng gō/ city in central Mexico and the capital of Durango State, in the Sierra Madre Mountains. Population: 413,835 (1990). Full name **Victoria de Durango**

Du·rant /də ránt/ city in southern Oklahoma on the Blue River, southeast of Oklahoma City and Ardmore. Population: 13,075 (1996).

Du·rant, Will (1885–1981) U.S. historian. After publication of *The Story of Philosophy* (1926), he and his wife, Ariel, wrote *The Story of Civilization* (1935–75), an enormously popular series covering history from before Jesus Christ to the Napoleonic age. Full name **William James Durant**

Du·ran·te /də rántee/, **Jimmy** (1893–1980) U.S. comic entertainer. Known for his prominent nose and raspy voice, he performed in cabaret, movies, and television. Full name **James Francis Durante**

du·ra·tion /də ráysh'n/ *n.* the period of time that something lasts or exists ○ *an intermission of 15 minutes' duration* [14thC. Via Old French *duracioun* from, ultimately, Latin *durare* "to last, harden."] —**du·ra·tion·al** *adj.* ◇ **for the duration** for the entire period of time that something is going on or will continue to go on

du·ra·tive /dŏŏrətiv/ *adj.* GRAM used to describe a verb in a continuous tense or aspect, or a verb indicating a continuous action

Dur·ban /dúrbən/ city, seaport, and tourist resort in KwaZulu-Natal Province in eastern South Africa. Population: 715,699 (1991).

dur·bar /dúr baar/ *n.* formerly, an official reception held by a local prince or British governor in colonial India, or by a local chief or British official in colonial Africa [Early 17thC. Alteration of Urdu *darbār* from Persian *dar* "door" + *bār* "court."]

Dur·bin /dúrbin/, **Deanna** (*b.* 1921) Canadian-born U.S. singer and actor. She became a teenage singing star in film musicals of the 1930s. Full name **Deanna Edna Mae Durbin**

Dür·er /dŏŏrər, dyŏŏrər/, **Albrecht** (1471–1528) German painter and engraver. The clarity of his paintings, e.g., in *Self Portrait* (1498) made him one of the most influential artists of the Reformation.

du·ress /dŏŏ réss/ *n.* **1. USE OF FORCE** the use of force or threats to make somebody do something **2.** LAW **ILLEGAL COERCION** illegal force or coercion used, e.g., against a criminal suspect or a prisoner in lawful custody before trial [14thC. Via Old French *duresse* from Latin *duritia*, literally "hardness," from *durus* "hard" (source of English *during*).]

Dur·ga /dúrgə/ *n.* a goddess who is one of the most important Hindu deities, embodying for many the supreme manifest form of godhead

Dur·ham[1] /dúrrəm/ *n.* a shorthorn beef or dairy cow belonging to a hardy breed originating in northeastern England [Named for the city of *Durham*, in northern England]

Dur·ham[2] /dúrrəm/ city in central North Carolina, east of Greensboro, site of Duke University. Population: 143,439 (1994).

du·ri·an /dŏŏree ən, dŏŏree aan/ (*plural* **-ans** *or* **-an**) *n.* **1. TREE WITH FOUL-SMELLING FRUIT** a tree found in the tropical rain forests of Southeast Asia that has foul-smelling but deliciously flavored fruits. Latin name: *Durio zibethinus*. **2. FRUIT OF DURIAN TREE** the fruit of the durian tree [Late 16thC. From Malay *durian*, from *duri* "thorn, prickle."]

du·ri·crust /dŏŏri krùst/ *n.* a hard crust formed on the surface of the soil by the precipitation of soluble minerals from mineral waters, particularly during the dry season in semiarid climates [Early 20thC. Coined from Latin *durus* "hard" + CRUST.]

dur·ing /dŏŏring/ *prep.* **1. THROUGHOUT** throughout a particular period or event, either continuously or several times between the beginning and the end ○ *There was not even a whisper during the service.* **2. AT SOME POINT IN A PERIOD** at some point or moment within a particular period or event ○ *I can't remember the date, but it was during the winter.* [14thC. Present participle of obsolete *dure* "to last," from Old French *durer*, from, ultimately, Latin *durus* "hard," perhaps originally "oak" (source of English *endure*).]

dur·mast oak /dúr mast-/, **dur·mast** *n.* an oak tree native to Europe and Asia Minor that has lobed leaves and yields a heavy flexible wood used in cabinetry. Latin name: *Quercus petraea*. [Late 18thC. Perhaps an error for *dunmast*, from DUN + MAST "acorns."]

durn /durn/ *interj., adj., adv., vt.* (**durned, durn·ing, durns**) *Southern U.S.* = **darn** (*informal*) [Variant of DARN]

durned /durnd/ (*superlative* **durned·est**) *adj. Southern U.S.* = **darned** (*informal*)

du·ro /dŏŏ rō/ (*plural* **-ros**) *n.* in some Latin American countries and formerly in Spain, a coin worth a peso or a dollar [Late 18thC. From Spanish *peso duro* "hard or solid piastre."]

Du·ro·cher /də rṓshər/, **Leo** (1905–91) U.S. baseball player. During his career in baseball he became manager of four national teams, retiring in 1973. Full name **Leo Ernest Durocher**. Known as **Leo the Lip**

dur·ra /dŏŏrə/, **dour·ra** *n.* a race of sorghum grown for its grain and as animal feed, especially in tropical and warm arid areas. Latin name: *Sorghum bicolor*. [Late 18thC. From Arabic *dura*.]

durst /durst/ past tense of **dare** (*archaic*)

du·rum wheat /dúrrəm-/, **du·rum** *n.* a wheat that produces glutinous flour, used in making pasta. Latin name: *Triticum durum*. [Early 20thC. From Latin, a form of *durus* "hard."]

Dur·yea /dŏŏryay, dŏŏr ee ày/, **Charles Edgar** (1861–1938) U.S. automaker and inventor. Together with his brother, he built one of the first cars in the United States (1893).

Du·shan·be /doo shámbə, -shaam-/ capital city of Tajikistan, in the west of the country in the Gissar Valley. Population: 602,000 (1990).

dusk /dusk/ *n.* **1. PERIOD AFTER DAY BUT BEFORE NIGHT** the period of the day after the sun has gone below the horizon but before the sky has become dark **2. ABSENCE OF DAYLIGHT** partial or almost complete darkness (*literary*) ■ *adj.* **DIM** having little or insufficient light (*literary*) ■ *vti.* (**dusked, dusk·ing, dusks**) **DARKEN** to become or make something dark (*literary*) [Old English *dox* "dark in color." Ultimately from an Indo-European word that is also the ancestor of English *obfuscate*.]

dusk·y /dúskee/ (**-i·er, -i·est**) *adj.* **1. DARK-COLORED** somewhat dark in color **2. DIM** having little or insufficient light **3. OFFENSIVE TERM MEANING DARK-SKINNED** having a somewhat dark skin or complexion (*dated offensive*) —**dusk·i·ly** *adv.* —**dusk·i·ness** *n.*

Düs·sel·dorf /dŏŏss'l dàwrf/ capital of North Rhine-Westphalia, west central Germany. Situated on the Rhine River, about 20 mi./32 km north of Cologne, it is the commercial and cultural center of the greater Ruhr area. Population: 573,100 (1994).

dust /dust/ *n.* **1. SMALL DRY PARTICLES** very small dry particles of a substance such as sand or coal, either in the form of a deposit or a cloud **2. HOUSEHOLD DIRT** the small pieces of dirt that accumulate in a layer on horizontal surfaces in buildings **3. REMAINS FROM**

THE DECAY OF A BODY the small particles that something, especially a human body, is thought to be reduced to by decay after death **4.** EARTH AS A BURIAL PLACE dirt or soil, particularly that of somebody's grave (*literary*) **5.** MED MINERS' DISEASE silicosis or another respiratory disease affecting miners (*informal*) ■ *v.* (**dust·ed, dust·ing, dusts**) **1.** *vti.* CLEAN OFF DIRT PARTICLES to remove small particles of dirt and lint from something, usually by wiping with a cloth **2.** *vt.* SPRINKLE to sprinkle something with a powdery substance, or sprinkle a powdery substance over something ○ *Dust the board with flour to keep the dough from sticking to it.* [Old English *dūst*, from a prehistoric Germanic word that is also the ancestor of English *fumigate* and *perfume*] —**dust·less** *adj.* ◇ **(as) dry as dust** so scholarly and devoid of humor as to be arid in tone and content ◇ **bite the dust 1.** to die, especially in or as a result a fight (*informal*) **2.** to suffer total failure (*informal*) ◇ **gather dust** to remain unused over a period of time ◇ **kick up dust, raise dust** to cause a controversy or loud disturbance (*informal*) ◇ **make the dust fly** to set about doing something energetically and aggressively (*informal*)

dust bath *n.* a form of grooming behavior in animals, especially birds, that consists in rolling or making agitated movements in the dust on the ground in order to remove parasites

dust·bin /dúst bìn/ *n. U.K.* = **garbage can**

dust bowl *n.* an area in a semiarid environment in which the topsoil is exposed and dust storms are likely to occur

Dust Bowl *n.* a large area in the southern part of the central United States that suffered badly from wind erosion during the 1930s

dust cloth *n.* a piece of cloth used for removing dust, especially from household objects and surfaces

dust cov·er *n.* **1.** COVER FOR EQUIPMENT a cover, often made from transparent plastic, for protecting a piece of equipment **2.** PUBL = **dust jacket**

dust dev·il *n.* a rising or traveling funnel of dust, dirt, or sand that occurs on hot days, especially in desert or arid areas. Dust devils are smaller than tornadoes and are generally not dangerous.

dust·er /dústər/ *n.* **1.** *U.K.* = **dust cloth 2.** AGRIC DEVICE FOR SPREADING AGROCHEMICALS a machine or device for spreading powdered fungicide, insecticide, or fertilizer over crops or other plants **3.** DUST REMOVER a cloth or pad that removes household dust **4.** CLOTHES HOUSECOAT a woman's loose housecoat **5.** CLOTHES WOMAN'S LONG LOOSE COAT a woman or girl's long loose coat, sometimes one without buttons or lapels

dust·i·ness /dústeenəss/ *n.* the state of being covered with or containing dust

dust·ing /dústing/ *n.* **1.** THIN POWDERY COVERING a thin, sometimes patchy covering of a powdery substance ○ *a dusting of snow on the ground* **2.** DEFEAT a defeat or setback (*slang*) ○ *a candidate who took a real dusting at the polls*

dust·ing pow·der *n.* fine powder such as talcum powder, especially for use on the skin

dust jack·et *n.* a paper book cover that protects the hardbound binding and that can be discarded

dust-off *adj.* used to describe an aircraft such as a helicopter that is used to medevac wounded troops from a combat zone ○ *dust-off choppers*

dust·pan /dúst pàn/ *n.* a container with a flat base and an open front into which dirt and dust can be swept

dust·sheet /dúst sheet/ *n. U.K.* = **drop cloth**

dust storm *n.* a strong hot dry wind laden with dust

dust·up /dúst ùp/ *n.* a violent argument or physical altercation, often one that starts and stops quickly (*slang*)

dust·y /dústee/ (**-i·er, -i·est**) *adj.* **1.** FULL OF DUST covered with or containing dust **2.** COLORS TINGED WITH GRAY containing tinges of gray with other colors ○ *dusty pink* **3.** BORING boring, especially because of being obscure or outdated ○ *dusty political slogans* **4.** LIKE DUST resembling dust ○ *a dusty gold powder*

dust·y mill·er *n.* PLANTS a plant with gray or white leaves covered with a down resembling dust. Latin name: *Artemisia stelleriana.*

Dutch /duch/ *n.* OFFICIAL LANGUAGE OF THE NETHERLANDS the official language of the Netherlands and the Republic of Surinam, and one of the West Germanic group of Indo-European languages. Dutch is spoken by about 20 million people. ■ *npl.* PEOPLE OF THE NETHERLANDS the people of the Netherlands collectively ■ *adj.* **1.** OF THE NETHERLANDS relating to or typical of the Netherlands, or its people or culture **2.** OF THE DUTCH LANGUAGE relating to Dutch [14thC. From Middle Dutch *dutsch*, from a prehistoric Germanic word meaning "people," which is also the ancestor of English *Deutschmark* and *Teuton*.] ◇ **go Dutch** to pay for your own part of the cost of a meal or entertainment ◇ **in Dutch** in a state of disfavor, difficulty, or trouble (*slang*)

Dutch auc·tion *n.* an auction in which the price is lowered gradually until somebody makes a bid

Dutch cap *n. U.K.* = **diaphragm** *n.* 2

Dutch clo·ver *n.* = **white clover**

Dutch cour·age *n.* the temporary confidence supposedly obtained from drinking alcohol (*informal*) [Derogatory expressions containing *Dutch* stem from the rivalry between the Dutch and the English in the 17th and 18th centuries]

Dutch door *n.* a door that is divided into two horizontal sections above and below so that each section can be opened and closed independently

Dutch East In·dies the islands of Indonesia from late 18th-century Dutch rule until Indonesian independence in 1949

Dutch elm *n.* a cultivated hybrid elm tree introduced to Great Britain from the Netherlands in the 17th century and now common in northeastern France and parts of western Great Britain and Ireland. Latin name: *Ulmus x hollandica.*

Dutch elm dis·ease *n.* a disease of elm trees that eventually kills the tree. It is caused by a fungus *Ceratocystis ulmi* carried by a bark beetle. [*Dutch* from the identification of the disease by Dutch scientists]

Dutch hoe *n.* a hoe used for weeding that is pushed instead of pulled

Dutch·man /dúchmən/ (*plural* **-men**) *n.* **1.** MAN FROM THE NETHERLANDS a man who was born in or is a citizen of the Netherlands **2.** CONSTR PIECE USED TO REPAIR BUILDING a piece of building material used to repair or conceal a fault in a construction

Dutch·man's breech·es *n.* a woodland plant of the eastern United States that has creamy white flowers with two spurs. Latin name: *Dicentra cucullaria.* (*takes a singular or plural verb*)

Dutch·man's pipe *n.* a woody climbing vine of the eastern United States that has mottled greenish-brown flowers shaped like the bowl and stem of an old-fashioned tobacco pipe. Latin name: *Aristolochia sipho.*

Dutch ov·en *n.* **1.** HEAVY COOKING POT an iron or earthenware container with a lid, used for cooking stews or casseroles **2.** OUTDOOR OVEN a metal box with an open front placed beside an open fire so that food can be cooked inside it

Dutch treat *n.* an outing, e.g., to a restaurant or theater, at which each person pays for himself or herself (*informal*)

Dutch un·cle *n.* somebody, typically a mentor, who criticizes or advises in a frank, sometimes harsh manner (*informal*)

Dutch·wom·an /dúch wòommən/ (*plural* **-en** /-wìmmən/) *n.* a woman who was born in or is a citizen of the Netherlands

du·te·ous /dóotee əss, dyóo-/ *adj.* obedient or submitting to duty (*literary*) —**du·te·ous·ly** *adv.* —**du·te·ous·ness** *n.*

du·ti·a·ble /dóotee əb'l, dyóo-/ *adj.* subject to tax, especially as an import —**du·ti·a·bil·i·ty** /dóotee ə bíllətee, dyóo-/ *n.*

du·ti·ful /dóotif'l, dyóo-/ *adj.* **1.** MEETING OBLIGATIONS done to fulfill obligations, often with little enthusiasm ○ *made a dutiful attempt at conversation* **2.** OBEDIENT acting according to obligations ○ *a dutiful and hardworking employee* —**du·ti·ful·ly** *adv.* —**du·ti·ful·ness** *n.*

du·ty /dóotee, dyóo-/ (*plural* **-ties**) *n.* **1.** OBLIGATION something that somebody is obliged to do for moral, legal, or religious reasons ○ *your duties as a parent* **2.** NEED TO MEET OBLIGATIONS the urge to meet moral or religious obligations ○ *a strong sense of duty* **3.** ALLOCATED TASK a task or service allocated to somebody, especially in the course of work **4.** ECON TAX a tax on goods, especially imports and exports **5.** RESPECT OWED TO OTHERS the respect owed to people because of their age or status (*archaic*) **6.** QUALITY suitability for a particular grade of use (*usually used in combination*) ○ *heavy-duty shoes* ○ *medium-duty carpet* **7.** MECH ENG MACHINE'S DESIGNATED WORKLOAD the amount of work that a machine is designed to do, or a measure of a machine's efficiency **8.** AGRIC VOLUME OF WATER NEEDED FOR IRRIGATION the volume of water that is needed in order to irrigate an area of land so as to cultivate a crop from planting to harvest time [13thC. Via Anglo-Norman *dueté* from Old French *deu* "owed," from Latin *debitus*, from *debere* "to owe."]

du·ty-free *adj.* EXEMPTED FROM EXCISE DUTIES on or at which no customs or excise duties have to be paid ■ *adv.* WITHOUT CUSTOMS AND EXCISE DUTIES without paying or charging customs or excise duties ■ *n.* STORE SELLING DUTY-FREE GOODS a store, especially at an airport or on board a ship, that sells duty-free goods (*informal*) ■ **du·ty-frees** *npl.* DUTY-FREE GOODS duty-free goods, especially the allowance of duty-free goods that an individual is allowed to bring into his or her own country (*informal*)

du·ty of·fi·cer *n.* an officer who is present in an office or headquarters and responsible for handling situations that may arise during a given period, especially a period when others are off duty

du·um·vir /doo úmvər/ (*plural* **-virs** *or* **-vi·ri** /-və rèe/) *n.* **1.** POL ONE OF TWO PEOPLE SHARING AUTHORITY either of two people who share a position of authority equally between them **2.** ANCIENT ROMAN HOLDER OF JOINT OFFICE a joint holder of any of the paired posts in the ancient Roman government or judiciary [Early 17thC. From Latin, from *duo* "two" + *vir* "man."] —**du·um·vi·rate** /doo úmvərət/ *n.*

Du·va·lier /dòo vaal yáy/, **François** (1907–71) Haitian politician and doctor. He was elected president in 1957 and declared himself president for life in 1964, instituting a dictatorial regime known for its violent purges and mass executions. Known as **Papa Doc**

Du·va·lier, Jean-Claude (*b.* 1951) Haitian political leader. He succeeded his father François Duvalier as president (1971–86). Known as **Baby Doc**

du·vet /doo váy, dòo vày/ *n. U.K.* = **comforter** [Mid-18thC. Via French, "down," from, ultimately, Old Norse *dūnn* (also the source of English *down*).]

du·ve·tyn /dóovə tèen/, **du·ve·tyne, du·ve·tine** *n.* a soft velvety fabric with a nap, made of silk, cotton, wool, or rayon [Early 20thC. From French *duvetine*, from *duvet* "down."]

du Vi·gneaud /doo vèenyō, dyoo-/, **Vincent** (1901–78) U.S. biochemist. For his work on pituitary hormones, he won the Nobel Prize (1955).

Dux·bur·y /dúks bèrree, -bəree/ town in eastern Massachusetts, on the northwestern shore of Plymouth Bay, north of Plymouth and southeast of Boston. Population: 15,007 (1996).

duy·ker *n.* = **duiker**

D.V. *abbr.* Deo volente

DVD a type of high-capacity optical compact disk that can store a much larger quantity of video, audio, or other information than can a conventional compact disk. Full form **digital video disc**

DVD-ROM a high-capacity digital video disk on which data can be stored but cannot be altered. Full form **digital versatile disc read only memory**

DVI *abbr.* digital video imaging

D.V.M. *abbr.* Doctor of Veterinary Medicine

Dvo·řák /dváwr zhaak, dváwr zhàk/, **Antonín** (1841–1904) Bohemian Czech composer. An ardent nationalist, he based many themes on Czech or, e.g., his ninth symphony, *From the New World* (1893), U.S. folk music.

DW *abbr.* **1.** dead weight **2.** distilled water

dwarf /dwawrf/ *n.* (*plural* **dwarves** /dwawrvz/ *or* **dwarfs**) **1.** PHYSIOL PERSON SMALL FOR MEDICAL REASONS a person of small stature for medical reasons, usually somebody with an average-sized body but unusually short limbs, or somebody with growth hormone deficiency **2.** BIOL SMALL PLANT OR ANIMAL a plant or animal that is much smaller than others of its species, usually as a result of selective breeding (*often used before a noun*) ○ *a dwarf conifer* **3.** LITERAT SMALL HUMANOID CREATURE IN FOLKLORE in fairy tales and folklore, a small creature with a mainly human appearance, associated with mountains, mines, and buried treasures. Fictional dwarves were often believed to have magic powers and to be sometimes malevolent. **4.** ASTRON = **dwarf star** ■ *vt.* **(dwarfed, dwarf·ing, dwarfs) 1. MAKE SOMEBODY OR SOMETHING SEEM SMALL** to make somebody or something else seem very small or very unimportant, by comparison ○ *The cathedral is dwarfed by the enormous tower blocks surrounding it.* **2. STUNT SOMEBODY'S OR SOMETHING'S GROWTH** to stunt the growth of somebody or something [Old English *dweorg,* of prehistoric Germanic origin] —**dwarf·ish** *adj.* —**dwarf·ish·ly** *adv.* —**dwarf·ish·ness** *n.*

dwarf bean *n. U.K.* = **bush bean**

dwarf chest·nut *n.* = **chinquapin**

dwarf·ism /dwáwr fìzzəm/ *n.* BIOL, PHYSIOL the condition of being a dwarf

dwarf star, dwarf *n.* a star with relatively low mass, size, and luminosity. The Sun is a dwarf star. ◊ **giant star**

dwarves plural of **dwarf**

dweeb /dweeb/ *n.* somebody who is considered to be boring, silly, or socially inept (*slang insult*) [Late 20thC. Origin unknown.]

dwell /dwel/ *vi.* **(dwelt** *or* **dwelled, dwelt** /dwelt/ *or* **dwelled, dwell·ing, dwells** /dwelt/) **RESIDE** to live and have a home in a particular place (*literary*) ■ *n.* MECH ENG **REGULAR PAUSE** a regular pause in the operation of a machine [Old English *dwellan* "to lead astray." Ultimately from an Indo-European base meaning "to rise in a cloud," which is also the ancestor of English *dust* and *typhus.*] —**dwell·er** *n.*

dwell on, dwell up·on *vt.* to think, write, or talk about something at considerable length

dwell·ing /dwélling/ *n.* a house or other building or place in which somebody lives (*formal*)

dwelt past tense, past participle of **dwell**

DWEM /dwem/, **dwem** *abbr.* dead white European male (*slang offensive*)

DWI *abbr.* driving while intoxicated

Dwight /dwīt/, **Timothy** (1752–1817) U.S. clergyman and educator. He left the Congregational ministry in 1795 to become president of Yale (1795–1817).

dwin·dle /dwínd'l/ **(-dled, -dling, -dles)** *vti.* to decrease little by little in size, number, or intensity and approach zero, or reduce something in this way ○ *Supplies were dwindling.* [Late 16thC. Formed from the obsolete verb *dwine* "to waste away." Ultimately from an Indo-European base meaning "to become exhausted," which is also the ancestor of English *dead.*]

dwt. *abbr.* **1.** deadweight tonnage **2.** pennyweight (*archaic*)

Dy *symbol.* dysprosium

dy. *abbr.* **1.** delivery **2.** duty

dy·ad /dí àd/ *n.* **1. COUPLE** two individual units, things, or people linked as a pair (*formal*) **2.** CHEM **DIVALENT ATOM** an atom or chemical group with a valence of two **3.** MATH **VECTOR OPERATOR** a mathematical operator consisting of two vectors expressed without a multiplication sign between them **4.** MUSIC **TWO-NOTE CHORD** a musical chord consisting of two notes [Late 17thC. Via late Latin from the stem of Greek *duas,* from *duo* "two."] —**dy·ad·ic** /dī áddik/ *adj.* —**dy·ad·i·cal·ly** /-áddikəlee/ *adv.*

Dy·ak (*plural* **-ak** *or* **-aks**) *n.* = **Dayak**

dy·ar·chy *n.* = **diarchy**

dyb·buk /díbbək/ (*plural* **-buks** *or* **-buk·im** /díbbəkim/) *n.* in Jewish folklore, a malevolent spirit of a dead person, believed able to take over a living person's body and control his or her behavior unless exorcised [Early 20thC. Via Yiddish *dibek* from Hebrew *dibbūq,* from *dābaq* "to cling."]

dye /dī/ *v.* **(dyed, dye·ing, dyes) 1.** *vt.* **COLOR SOMETHING BY SOAKING** to color or stain something, e.g., fabric or hair, by soaking it in a coloring solution so that it takes on the new color permanently or semipermanently **2.** *vi.* **COLOR WELL OR BADLY** to respond to being treated with a coloring agent and take its color in a particular way ■ *n.* **1. COLORING AGENT** a natural or synthetic substance that can be used to color something such as a textile or hair and is most often applied in liquid form **2. COLORING SOLUTION** a coloring solution containing a dye **3. COLOR PRODUCED BY A DYE** the color produced on something by a dye [Old English *dēah* "color, a color that hides." The distinction in spelling between the verbs DIE and DYE is relatively recent.] —**dy·a·ble** *adj.* —**dy·er** *n.*

dyed-in-the-wool *adj.* **1. WHOLEHEARTEDLY AND STUBBORNLY ATTACHED TO SOMETHING** wholeheartedly and stubbornly attached to a set of beliefs, political party, or philosophy and totally convinced of its merits **2.** TEXTILES **DYED BEFORE WEAVING** dyed before weaving into cloth

dye·line /dí lìn/ *adj.* CHEM = **diazo**

Dy·er /díər/, **Mary** (1610?–60) English-born U.S. Quaker martyr. Twice banished from Boston for her religious beliefs, she was finally hanged after defying the ruling for a second time.

dy·er's green·weed *n.* a small Eurasian shrub similar to broom that produces clusters of flowers formerly used to produce a yellow dye. It is now naturalized in North America. Latin name: *Genista tinctoria.* [From the yellowish green color of the flowers]

dy·er's rock·et *n.* a Eurasian plant of the mignonette family that has spikes of pale yellowish-green flowers formerly used to produce a yellow dye. Latin name: *Reseda luteola.*

dy·er's-weed *n.* any plant that yields a dye, especially dyer's greenweed and dyer's rocket

dye·stuff /dí stùf/ *n.* = **dye** *n.* 1

dye·wood /dí wòod/ *n.* any wood that can be used as a dye

dy·ing /dí ing/ *adj.* **1. ABOUT TO DIE** on the point of death **2. OCCURRING JUST BEFORE DEATH** carried out, spoken, or occurring at or just before the point of death **3. FINAL** occurring as something is about to reach its end ○ *in the dying seconds of the game*

dyke /dīk/ *n.* a highly offensive term for a lesbian (*slang offensive*)

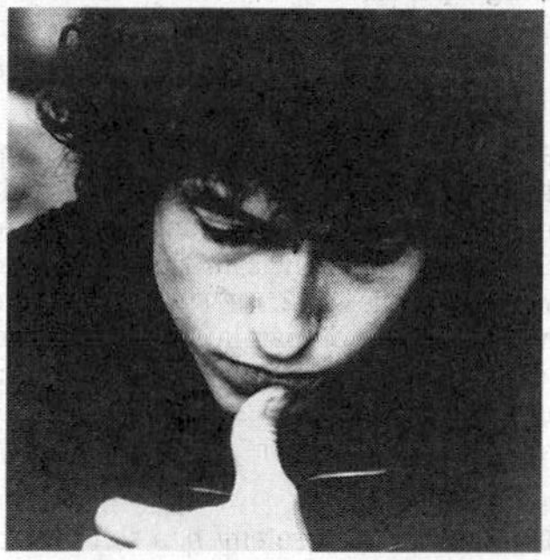

Bob Dylan

Dy·lan /díllən/, **Bob** (*b.* 1941) U.S. folk singer. He wrote protest songs such as *"Blowin' in the Wind"* (1962) and *"The Times They Are A-Changin'"* (1964). Real name **Robert Zimmerman**

dyn *symbol.* PHYS dyne

dy·nam·ic /dī námmik/ *adj.* **1. VIGOROUS AND PURPOSEFUL** full of energy, enthusiasm, and a sense of purpose and able both to get things going and to get things done **2. ACTIVE AND CHANGING** characterized by vigorous activity and producing or undergoing change and development ○ *a dynamic economy* **3. RELATING TO ENERGY** involving or relating to energy and forces that produce motion **4. RELATING TO DYNAMICS** involved in or connected with the study of dynamics **5.** MUSIC **RELATING TO LOUDNESS IN MUSIC** relating to or indicating variations in the loudness of musical sounds **6.** PHYS **CHANGING OVER TIME** used to describe any system that changes over time ■ *n.* **DRIVING FORCE** a driving or energizing force, especially one involved in a process of social or psychological change [Early 19thC. Via French *dynamique* from, ultimately, Greek *dunamis* "force," from *dunasthai* "to be able."] —**dy·namical** /dī námmik'l/ *adj.* —**dy·nam·i·cal·ly** *adv.*

dy·nam·ic mark·ings, dy·nam·ic marks *npl.* MUSIC the symbols and words that indicate the degree of loudness or softness with which a piece, passage, or note of music should be played

dy·nam·ic range *n.* **1.** MUSIC **VOLUME RANGE OF PIECE OF MUSIC** the range of volume used within a single piece of music **2.** ELECTRON ENG **RANGE OF REPRODUCIBLE SOUND** the range over which an electronic audio system can operate to a set standard of performance based on given limits for noise and distortion

dy·nam·ics /dī námmiks/ *n.* **1. CHANGE-PRODUCING FORCES** the forces that tend to produce activity and change in any situation or sphere of existence (*takes a plural verb*) **2.** MUSIC **LOUDNESS AND SOFTNESS IN MUSICAL PIECE** the different levels of loudness and softness in a piece of music, and the way in which a performer reproduces them in performance (*takes a plural verb*) **3.** MUSIC **DYNAMIC MARKINGS** dynamic markings symbols and words (*takes a plural verb*) **4.** PHYS **STUDY OF MOTION** the study of motion and the way in which forces produce motion (*takes a singular verb*)

dy·na·mism /dínə mìzzəm/ *n.* **1. VIGOROUSLY ACTIVE, FORCEFUL, AND ENERGIZING QUALITY** a vigorously active, forceful, and energizing quality, especially as the hallmark of somebody's personality or approach to a task **2. THEORY OF FORCES** a philosophical or scientific theory stressing the role of dynamic forces in explaining phenomena, especially by interpreting events as an expression of forces residing within the object or person involved —**dy·na·mist** *n.* —**dy·na·mis·tic** /dìnə místik/ *adj.*

dy·na·mite /dínə mīt/ *n.* **1. POWERFUL EXPLOSIVE** a powerful explosive used for blasting consisting of a porous material e.g., wood pulp or sawdust combined with ammonium or sodium nitrate, or nitroglycerine, and an antacid e.g., calcium carbonate **2. VERY EXCITING OR POWERFUL THING** something that or somebody who is exceptionally exciting or has an extremely powerful effect (*slang*) ○ *This music is absolute dynamite.* **3. VERY DANGEROUS OR HARMFUL THING** something that or somebody who is potentially very dangerous or harmful (*slang*) ○ *news stories that were political dynamite* ■ *vt.* **(-mit·ed, -mit·ing) dy·na·mites BLAST SOMETHING WITH DYNAMITE** to blast or explode something with dynamite [Mid-19thC. Coined from Greek *dunamis* "force" + -ITE by its inventor, Swedish chemist Alfred NOBEL.] —**dy·na·mit·er** *n.*

dy·na·mo /dínə mō/ (*plural* **-mos**) *n.* **1.** ELEC ENG **GENERATOR OF ELECTRICITY FROM MECHANICAL ENERGY** a machine that converts mechanical energy into electrical energy, usually in the form of direct current **2. ENERGETIC PERSON** a hard-working, tirelessly energetic person [Late 19thC. Shortening of *dynamo-electric machine.*]

dynamo- *prefix.* power, energy ○ *dynamometer* [From Greek *dunamis* (see DYNAMIC)]

dy·na·mo·e·lec·tric /dìnəmō i léktrik/, **dy·na·mo·e·lec·tri·cal** /-k'l/ *adj.* involved in or relating to the production of electrical energy from mechanical energy, and vice versa

dy·na·mom·e·ter /dìnə mómmətər/ *n.* an instrument used to measure mechanical force or power, e.g., the power output of an engine —**dy·na·mo·met·ric** /dìnəmō méttrik/ *adj.* —**dy·na·mom·e·try** /dìnə mómmətree/ *n.*

dy·na·mo·tor /dínə mōtər/ *n.* an electrical device combining a motor and generator and used to convert alternating current to direct current, and vice versa [Early 20thC. Coined from Greek *dunamis* "force" (see DYNAMIC) + MOTOR.]

dy·nast /dí nàst, dínəst/ *n.* **1. RULER** a ruler, especially a hereditary monarch (*literary*) **2. MEMBER OR FOUNDER OF DYNASTY** a member of a dynasty, or the founder of one [Mid-17thC. Via Latin from Greek *dunastēs* "lord," from *dunasthai* "to be able."]

dy·nas·ty /dínəstee/ (*plural* **-ties**) *n.* **1. SUCCESSION OF HEREDITARY RULERS** a succession of rulers from the same family **2. PROMINENT AND POWERFUL FAMILY** a prominent and powerful family or group of people whose members retain their power and influence through several generations [14thC. Via French *dynastie* or directly from late Latin *dynastia,* from, ultimately, Greek *dunastēs* "lord" (see DYNAST).] —**dy·nas·tic** /dī nástik, di-/ *adj.* —**dy·nas·ti·cal·ly** /-kəlee/ *adv.*

dyne /dīn/ *n.* the unit of force in the centimeter-gram-second system equal to the force that will accelerate a mass of one gram one centimeter per second per second [Late 19thC. Formed from Greek *dunamis* "force" (see DYNAMIC).]

Dy·nel /dī nél/ *tdmk.* a trademark for a copolymer used in making fire- and insect-resistant textile fiber and derived from vinyl chloride and acrylonitrile

dys- *prefix.* bad, impaired, abnormal ○ *dysplasia* [Via Latin from Greek *dus-*]

dys·ar·thri·a /dis áarthree ə/ *n.* difficulty in speech articulation due to lack of muscle control caused by damage to the central nervous system [Late 19thC. From modern Latin, formed from DYS- + Greek *arthron* "joint."]

dys·cra·sia /dis kráyzhə/ *n.* any abnormal condition of blood cells [14thC. Via late Latin from Greek *dyskrasia,* literally "bad mixture," from *krasis* "mixing" (source of English *idiosyncrasy*).]

dys·en·ter·y /dìss'n térree/ *n.* the disease of the lower intestine caused by infection with bacteria, protozoa, or parasites and marked by severe diarrhea, inflammation, and the passage of blood and mucus [14thC. Via Old French *dissenterie* or directly from Latin *dysenteria*, from, ultimately, Greek *dusenteros*, literally "bad intestines," from *enteron* "intestine."] —**dys·en·ter·ic** /dìss'n térrik/ *adj.*

dys·func·tion /dis fúngkshən/ *n.* a medical abnormality in the functioning of an organ or other part or system of the body

dys·func·tion·al /dis fúngkshənəl/ *adj.* **1.** NOT PERFORMING ITS FUNCTION PROPERLY failing to perform the function that is normally expected ○ *counseling a dysfunctional family* **2.** SOCIOL RELATING BADLY unable to function emotionally as a social unit **3.** MED NOT FUNCTIONING NORMALLY unable to function normally as a result of disease or impairment

dys·gen·ic /dis jénnik/ *adj.* involving or causing the inheriting of detrimental characteristics

dys·gen·ics /dis jénniks/ *n.* the study of factors relating to or causing a decrease in the survival of the hereditarily well-adapted members of a line of descent (*takes a singular verb*)

dys·graph·ia /dis gráffee ə/ *n.* impairment of writing ability, arising from brain injury or disease

dys·ki·ne·sia /dìski néezhə, dìs kī néezhə/ *n.* impairment of the control over ordinary muscle movement, often resulting in spasmodic movements or tics [Early 18thC. Via modern Latin from Greek *duskinēsia*, literally "difficulty in moving," from *kinēsis* "movement" (see -KINESIS).]

dys·lex·i·a /diss léksee ə/ *n.* a learning disorder marked by a severe difficulty in recognizing and understanding written language, leading to spelling and writing problems. It is not caused by low intelligence or brain damage. [Late 19thC. Coined from DYS- + Greek *lexis* "speech," from *legein* "to speak."] —**dys·lex·ic** *adj., n.*

dys·men·or·rhe·a /dìss mennə rée ə/, **dys·men·or·rhoe·a** *n.* severe pain or cramps in the lower abdomen during menstruation —**dys·men·or·rhe·al** *adj.* —**dys·men·or·rhe·ic** *adj.*

dys·pa·reu·ni·a /dìspar yóonee ə/ *n.* pain occurring during sexual intercourse

dys·pep·sia /dis pépsee ə, dis pépshə/ *n.* acid indigestion (*technical*) [Early 18thC. Via Latin from Greek *duspepsia*, literally "difficult digestion," from *peptein* "to cook, digest."]

dys·pep·tic /diss péptik/ *adj.* **1.** HAVING INDIGESTION having acid indigestion **2.** BAD-TEMPERED in a bad temper, or having a bad-tempered disposition ■ *n.* BAD-TEMPERED PERSON an irritable bad-tempered person [Late 17thC. From Greek *duspeptos*, literally "difficult of digestion," from *peptein* "to cook, digest."]

dys·pha·gia /dis fáyjə/ *n.* difficulty in swallowing, with a variety of possible causes —**dys·phag·ic** /dis fájjik/ *adj.*

dys·pha·sia /dis fáyzhə, -fáyzee ə/ *n.* difficulty in speaking and understanding spoken or written language, caused by brain injury or disease —**dys·pha·sic** /dis fáyzik/ *adj.*

dys·phe·mism /dísfə mìzzəm/ *n.* **1.** SUBSTITUTION OF A COARSER WORD the deliberate substitution of an offensive expression for a neutral one **2.** OFFENSIVE SUBSTITUTE FOR NEUTRAL WORD an offensive expression deliberately substituted for a neutral one [Late 19thC. Formed from DYS- on the model of *euphemism*.] —**dys·phe·mis·tic** /dìsfə místik/ *adj.*

dys·pho·ni·a /diss fṓnee ə/ *n.* hoarseness or difficulty in speaking as a result of dysfunction of the vocal cords caused by brain injury, brain disease, or chemical poisoning [Early 18thC. Via modern Latin from Greek *dusphōnia*, literally "roughness of sound," from *phōnē* "sound."] —**dys·phon·ic** /-fónnik/ *adj.*

dys·pho·ri·a /diss fáwree ə/ *n.* a state of feeling acutely hopeless, uncomfortable, and unhappy [Mid-19thC. From Greek *dusphoria*, literally "discomfort," from, ultimately, *pherein* "to bear."] —**dys·phor·ic** *adj.*

dys·pla·sia /diss pláyzhə, -pláyzhee ə/ *n.* medically abnormal development or growth of a part of the body, e.g., an organ, bone, or cell, including the total absence of such a part —**dys·plas·tic** /-plástik/ *adj.*

dysp·ne·a /disp née ə, dísp née ə/ *n.* difficulty in breathing caused, e.g., by heart disease or overexertion [Mid-17thC. Via Latin from Greek *duspnoia*, literally "difficulty of breathing," from, ultimately, *pnein* "to breathe."] —**dysp·ne·al** *adj.* —**dysp·ne·ic** *adj.*

dys·prax·i·a /dis práksee ə/ *n.* **1.** POOR COORDINATION poor coordination displayed by some children, diagnosed by illegible handwriting and inability to catch a ball and clap while the ball is in the air. It sometimes accompanies dyslexia. **2.** IMPAIRMENT OF THE MOTOR SYSTEM an impairment in or partial loss of control of the body's motor system, resulting from brain damage. = **apraxia** [From Greek *duspraxia*, literally "ill success," from *praxis* "action" (see PRAXIS)] —**dys·prax·ic** *adj.*

dys·pro·si·um /dis prṓzee əm/ *n.* a soft silvery chemical element of the rare earth group that is paramagnetic, highly reactive, and used in laser materials and nuclear research. Symbol **Dy** [Late 19thC. Coined from Greek *dusprositos*, literally "difficult to approach," from, ultimately, *ienai* "to go" (source of English *ion*).]

dys·rhyth·mi·a /dis ríthmee ə/ *n.* an irregularity in an otherwise normal rhythm, especially of heartbeats or brainwaves [Early 20thC. From modern Latin, literally "bad rhythm," from, ultimately, Greek *rhuthmos* "rhythm."]

dys·to·ci·a /diss tṓshə/ *n.* abnormally difficult childbirth [Early 18thC. From Greek *dustokia*, literally "difficult childbirth," from *tokos* "childbirth."] —**dys·to·ci·al** *adj.*

dys·to·pi·a /diss tṓpee ə/ *n.* an imaginary place where everything is as bad as it possibly can be, or a vision or description of such a place [Mid-20thC. Coined from DYS- + UTOPIA.] —**dys·to·pi·an** *adj.*

dys·troph·ic /dis trófik/ *adj.* **1.** AFFECTED BY DYSTROPHY relating to or affected by dystrophy **2.** ECOL CONTAINING EXCESS HUMUS used to describe a pond or lake containing water that is brown in color, abnormally acidic, and lacking in oxygen. Such water is unable to support much plant or animal life because of the amount of humus dissolved in it.

dys·tro·phin /dístrəfin/ *n.* a protein found in normal muscle that is missing in muscle affected by some forms of muscular dystrophy

dys·tro·phy /dístrəfee/ (*plural* **-phies**), **dys·tro·phi·a** /də strṓfee ə/ *n.* **1.** MED PROGRESSIVE DEGENERATION OF TISSUE progressive degeneration of a body tissue, e.g., muscle, as a result of inadequate nourishment of the affected part, due to some unknown cause **2.** ENVIRON EXCESSIVE HUMUS IN WATER a condition in which pond or lake water is unable to support thriving animal or plant life because of excessive humus content

dys·u·ri·a /diss yóoree ə, di shóoree ə/ *n.* pain or difficulty in urinating —**dys·u·ric** *adj.*

dy·tis·cid /dī tíssid, di tíssid/ *n.* a carnivorous freshwater diving beetle. Family: Dytiscidae. [Mid-19thC. From modern Latin, formed from Greek *dutikos* "able to dive," from *duein* "to dive."] —**dy·tis·cid** *adj.*

Dy·u·la /dee óola, dyóolə/ (*plural* **-la** *or* **-las**) *n.* **1.** PEOPLES MEMBER OF AN AFRICAN PEOPLE a member of an African people who live mainly in the rain forests of the Ivory Coast **2.** LANG MANDE LANGUAGE a Mande language spoken in parts of the Ivory Coast, Burkina Faso, and Ghana. Dyula is spoken by just over one million people. —**Dy·u·la** *adj.*

dz. *abbr.* dozen

Dzer·zhinsk /dur zhínsk/ city in central European Russia on the Oka River. It is a chemical-manufacturing center. Population: 286,000 (1990).

dzo /zō, dzō/ (*plural* **dzos** *or* **dzo**), **zo** (*plural* **zos** *or* **zo**), **zho** (*plural* **zhos** *or* **zho**) *n.* an animal belonging to a breed developed from a hybrid between a cow and a yak [Mid-19thC. From Tibetan *mdso*.]

Dzong·kha /zóngkə, dzóngkə/, **Dzong·ka** *n.* the official language of Bhutan, a dialect of Tibetan. Dzongkha is spoken by just under one million people. [Early 20thC. From Tibetan, literally "language of the fortress."] —**Dzong·kha** *adj.*

Dzun·gar·ia /zòong gáiree ə, dzòong-/ region in northwestern China, west of the Republic of Mongolia and east of Kazakhstan, in Xinjiang Uygur Autonomous Region

Ee

e[1] /ee/ (*plural* **e's**), **E** (*plural* **E's** *or* **Es**) *n.* **1. 5TH LETTER OF THE ENGLISH ALPHABET** the fifth letter of the modern English alphabet **2. SPEECH SOUND CORRESPONDING TO THE LETTER "E"** the speech sound that corresponds to the letter "E" **3. LETTER "E" WRITTEN** a written representation of the letter "E"

e[2] *symbol.* **1.** MATH the transcendental number 2.718 282... **2.** CHESS the fifth vertical row of squares from the left on a chessboard **3.** PHYS electron

e[3] *abbr.* BASEBALL error

E[1] *symbol.* **1.** PHYS energy **2.** PHYS electric field strength **3.** PHYS electromotive force (*usually written italicized*) **4.** LOGIC negative categorical proposition **5.** PHYS internal energy **6.** MEASURE exa- **7.** energy *n.* 5.

E[2] /ee/ (*plural* **Es** *or* **E's**) *n.* **1.** MUSIC **3RD NOTE OF SCALE IN C** the third note of a scale in C major **2.** MUSIC **SOMETHING THAT PRODUCES AN E** a string, key, or pipe tuned to produce the note E **3.** MUSIC **SCALE BEGINNING ON E** a scale or key that starts on the note E **4.** MUSIC **WRITTEN SYMBOL OF E** a graphic representation of the tone of E **5.** DRUGS **ECSTASY** the drug ecstasy or a tablet of the drug (*slang*)

E[3] *abbr.* **1.** east **2.** eastern **3.** ELEC earth **4.** English

e. *abbr.* **1.** engineer **2.** engineering **3.** BASEBALL error

E. *abbr.* earl

e- *prefix.* **1.** electronic ○ *e-mail* **2.** electronic data transfer via the internet ○ *e-commerce* [Shortening]

ea. *abbr.* each

EAC *abbr.* East African Community

eace·worm /eés wurm/ *n.* an earthworm (*regional*) [*Eace-* ultimately from Old English *æs* "bait," related to Latin *esca* "food, bait" and English *eat*]

WORD KEY: REGIONAL NOTE

Often thought of as typical of a Northern or New England term, ***eaceworm*** most clearly marks northern Rhode Island speech. Other forms are *easterworm* and *eastworm*.

each /eech/ *adj., pron., adv.* used to refer to every member of a group of people or things, considered individually ○ *With each victory we get closer to the championship.* ○ *Is a VCR that can be connected to more than one TV better than buying one for each?* ○ *Environmental health officers were supervising an average of 40 cases each.* [Old English *ælc.* From a prehistoric Germanic compound meaning "ever alike."]

WORD KEY: USAGE

each or **every**? In some contexts these two words are nearly interchangeable, as in *I adore each puppy in the litter* and *I adore every puppy.* Here the only difference is a slight shift in perspective from considering the animals individually, with ***each***, to considering them collectively, with ***every***. Either of the words, placed before the noun, requires the noun and the verb to be singular: *each puppy is affectionate every puppy is affectionate.* ***Each,*** though not ***every,*** may also be placed after a plural noun, and then the plural governs the verb: *The puppies each have their own toys.* Also ***each*** can refer to two or more, whereas ***every*** must refer to three or more. ***Each*** can be an adjective (*each puppy*), a pronoun (*each of them*), and an adverb (*Give them a bowlful each*), whereas ***every*** is an adjective only.

each oth·er *pron.* each one of two or more persons or things reciprocally

WORD KEY: USAGE

each other or **one another**? The traditional rule is that ***each other*** refers to two items and ***one another*** refers to more than two: *Joe and Lee respect each other deeply. All the people at the party knew one another already.* However, this distinction is not supported by the weight of usage, and there is no good reason to reject the alternatives *Joe and Lee respect one another deeply* and *All the people at the party knew each other already,* although the last example sounds somewhat less natural than the others.

EACSO *abbr.* East African Common Services Organization

ea·ger /eégər/ *adj.* **1. ENTHUSIASTIC AND EXCITED ABOUT DOING SOMETHING** enthusiastic and excited about something and impatiently waiting to do or get it ○ *eager to help* ○ *eager for praise* **2. FULL OF ENTHUSIAM AND IMPATIENCE** expressing enthusiastic interest and expectation or an impatient desire to do something ○ *eager face* [13thC. Via Anglo-Norman *egre* from, ultimately, Latin *acer* "sharp" (source of English *acrid* and *vinegar*).] —**ea·ger·ly** *adv.* —**ea·ger·ness** *n.*

ea·ger bea·ver *n.* somebody who is exceptionally, or even excessively, ready and willing to work hard, carry out tasks, or volunteer (*informal*) [From the perceived industriousness of beavers. Originally a World War II expression in the United States for an overzealous recruit.]

ea·gle /eég'l/ *n.* **1.** BIRDS **LARGE BIRD OF PREY** a large and powerful bird of prey with a hooked bill and broad wingspan that hunts by day and is noted for its keen eyesight and majestic soaring flight. Subfamily: Buteoninae. **2. FIGURE OF AN EAGLE AS A SYMBOL** the figure of an eagle used as a symbol of military or political power, e.g. on the standards carried by the Roman legions **3.** GOLF **SCORE OF 2 UNDER PAR** a score of two under par for a single hole in golf **4.** COINS **FORMER U.S. 10-DOLLAR GOLD COIN** a gold coin worth ten dollars, current in the United States until 1934 ■ *vti.* (**-gled, -gling, -gles**) GOLF **SCORE 2 UNDER PAR** to complete a hole in two strokes under par in golf [14thC. Via Anglo-Norman *egle* from Latin *aquila*.]

ea·gle eye *n.* extremely keen eyesight, especially over long distances, or the ability to notice what other people might miss —**ea·gle-eyed** *adj.*

ea·gle owl *n.* a large Eurasian owl, the largest species of owl in the world, with brownish plumage and tufts of feathers on its head that look like horns. Latin name: *Bubo bubo.*

ea·gle ray *n.* a large ray found in tropical and subtropical seas that has a projecting snout, massive jaws, and pectoral fins shaped like wings that propel it with a soaring motion. Family: Myliobatidae.

Ea·gle Scout *n.* a Boy Scout who has reached the highest level of attainment in the various tests of skill and endurance set by the Boy Scout movement [*Eagle* with reference to the hierarchy of birds]

ea·glet /eéglət/ *n.* a young eagle, especially before it leaves the nest

ea·gre /eégər/ *n.* GEOG = **bore**[3] *n.* [Early 17thC. Origin unknown.]

Ea·kins /áykinz/, **Thomas** (1844–1916) U.S. artist. He is known for his realist paintings drawn from life, such as *The Gross Clinic* (1875).

eal·dor·man /áwldərmən/ (*plural* **-men** /-mən/) *n.* the principal magistrate and commander of the military forces of a shire in Anglo-Saxon England [Old English *ealdormann*, from *ealdor* "an elder" + MAN]

Eames /eemz/ *tdmk.* a trademark for chairs, especially and originally ones of molded plywood, whose seats and backs are shaped to accommodate human body contours

Eames /eemz/, **Charles** (1907–78) U.S. designer. He is known for the prototype of the molded plywood chair that bears his name.

E. & O.E. *abbr.* errors and omissions excepted (*used on invoices*)

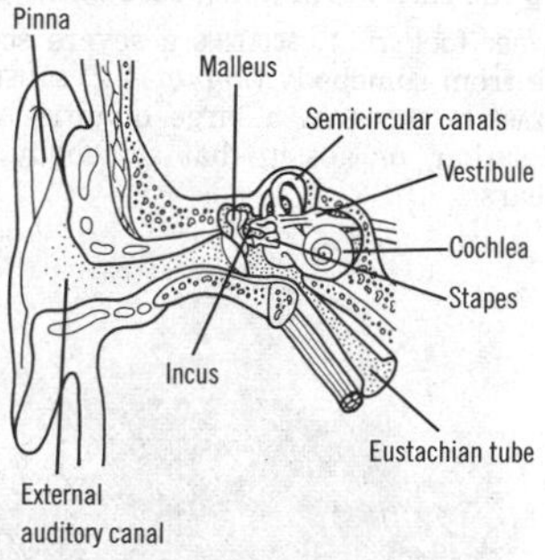

Ear

ear[1] /eer/ *n.* **1.** BIOL **ORGAN OF HEARING** the organ of hearing and balance in vertebrates that, in mammals, is divided into three parts, the external, middle, and inner ear. The external ear collects sound, the middle ear contains small bones that amplify and transmit it, while the inner ear maintains balance and contains sensory nerve endings for detecting sound. **2.** BIOL **EXTERNAL PART OF HEARING ORGAN** the external part of an ear, visible in humans and most mammals on each side of the head as a flap of cartilage with skin surrounding or covering it **3.** BIOL **INVERTEBRATE SENSORY ORGAN SIMILAR TO AN EAR** any sensory organ in invertebrates that is able to sense vibrations and perform a similar function to a vertebrate ear **4.** BIRDS = **ear tuft** **5. EAR SHAPE** something shaped like an ear, especially a handle on a jug or jar **6. ABILITY TO TELL SOUNDS APART** the ability to distinguish accurately between different sounds, e.g., in speech or music ○ *She has an ear for other languages.* **7. ATTENTION** somebody's attention, especially somebody's sympathetic or favorable attention **8.** PRESS **SECTION AT TOP CORNER OF NEWSPAPER** a small section at the top corner of the front page of a newspaper for advertising or a weather forecast [Old English *ēare.* Ultimately from an Indo-European word meaning "ear," which is also the ancestor of English *aural.*] ◇ **all ears** listening, or ready to listen, attentively or enthusiastically to something (*informal*) ◇ **go in one ear and out the other** to be forgotten as soon as heard and so have absolutely no effect on somebody ◇ **have somebody's ear** to be a trusted adviser to somebody, especially somebody powerful or influential ◇ **have** *or* **keep your ear to the ground** to remain continuously alert to discover new developments or information ◇ **out on your ear** unceremoniously thrown out or dismissed from a place or position you previously occupied (*informal*) ○ *You'll be out on your ear if you're late again.* ◇ **play it by ear** to improvise or adapt your response to a situation as it occurs rather than make plans in advance ◇ **set something** *or* **somebody on its** *or* **somebody's ear** to send something or somebody into a state of excited agitation, shock, or confusion ◇ **wet behind the ears** very inexperienced or naive

ear[2] /eer/ *n.* BOT **PLANT PART CONTAINING GRAIN** the grain-bearing part at the top of the stalk of a cereal plant such as wheat or corn, or the grain-bearing part of corn ■ *vi.* (**eared, ear·ing, ears**) BOT **FORM EARS** to form the part of a corn plant that contains the grains [Old

English *ēar.* Ultimately from an Indo-European base meaning "sharp" (see EAGER).]

ear·ache /éer àyk/ *n.* pain in the middle or inner ear. Technical name **otalgia**

ear clip *n.* **1.** ORNAMENT CLIPPED TO THE UPPER EAR an ornament, e.g., a metal band, clipped to the upper part of the ear **2.** CLIP-ON EARRING a clip-on earring

ear·drop /éer dròp/ *n.* PENDANT EARRING a pendant earring ■ **ear·drops** *npl.* LIQUID EAR MEDICINE liquid medicine for the ear, usually inserted with a dropper

ear·drum /éer drùm/ *n.* a membrane of thin skin and fibrous tissue that vibrates in response to sound waves, located between the external and the middle ear. Technical name **tympanic membrane**

eared /eerd/ *adj.* with ears, or with ears of a particular type (*usually used in combination*) ○ *long-eared*

eared seal *n.* a seal with conspicuous external ears and independent hind limbs or flippers that are used to walk on land. Sea lions and fur seals are eared seals. Family: Otariidae.

ear·flap /éer flàp/ *n.* either of two extra pieces of fabric or fur attached to a hat that can be let down to keep the ears warm (*often used in the plural*)

ear·ful /éer fŏŏl/ *n.* **1.** SCOLDING a severe scolding or lecture from somebody (*informal*) **2.** SOMETHING SOMEBODY HEARS OR OVERHEARS a large quantity of sound, conversation, or gossip that somebody hears or overhears

Barnaby's

Amelia Earhart

Ear·hart /áir haàrt/, **Amelia** (1898–1937) U.S. aviator. She was the first woman to fly solo over both the Atlantic (1932) and the Pacific (1935). She disappeared in the Pacific Ocean in 1937 while attempting an around-the-world flight.

ear·ing /éering/ *n.* SAILING a small rope that attaches the upper corner of a sail to a yard [Early 17thC. Origin uncertain: perhaps from EAR[1].]

earl /url/ *n.* a British nobleman ranked above a viscount and below a marquess. The title corresponds to "count" in Europe, and Great Britain and Europe both use "countess" for a woman's equivalent rank. [Old English *eorl* "warrior, nobleman," of unknown origin]

earl·dom /úrldəm/ *n.* **1.** RANK OF EARL the rank or position of an earl or countess **2.** TERRITORY the territory belonging to or administered by an earl or countess

ear·less seal *n.* a seal that does not have conspicuous external ears and has short front and hind flippers that are adapted for swimming rather than walking on land. Family: Phocidae.

Earl Grey *n.* a tea flavored with bergamot to produce a lighter-colored brew with a musky taste [Said to be named for Charles *Grey,* the second Earl Grey (1764–1845), British statesman and prime minister]

ear·lobe /éer lòb/ *n.* the soft fleshy lower part of the outer ear

ear·ly /úrlee/ *adv.* (**-li·er, -li·est**) **1.** BEFORE THE EXPECTED TIME before the expected or arranged time ○ *they arrived early* **2.** NEAR THE BEGINNING at or near the beginning of a specified period, process, or event that is experienced over a period of time ○ *early in the interview* **3.** DURING THE FIRST STAGES at a time when something was not far advanced or developed or when somebody was at a comparatively young age ○ *She decided early that she wanted to become a teacher.* **4.** SOON promptly or soon ○ *Buy your tickets early, for seating is limited.* ■ *adj.* (**-li·er, -li·est**) **1.** OCCURRING NEAR THE BEGINNING occurring at or near the beginning of a period of time, process, or sequence of events ○ *early reports indicate a high level of interest* **2.** OCCURRING BEFORE THE EXPECTED TIME occurring before the expected or arranged time ○ *early retirement* **3.** PRODUCED NEAR THE BEGINNING OF SOMETHING produced at, characteristic of, or representing a not very advanced stage in the development of something or somebody ○ *looking forward to an early end to the deadlock* **4.** IN THE VERY NEAR FUTURE due, expected, or requested to happen in the very near future **5.** BOT RIPENING BEFORE OTHERS ripening before other varieties of the same type ○ *early peaches* [Old English *ǣrlīce.* Ultimately from an Indo-European word meaning "day," which is also the ancestor of English *erst.*] —**early on** *adv.* ◇ **early on** at an early stage

Ear·ly /úrlee/, **Jubal Anderson** (1816–94) U.S. Confederate general. He interrupted his career as a lawyer to serve during the Mexican War (1846–48) and Civil War (1861–65).

ear·ly bird *n.* (*informal*) **1.** SOMEBODY WHO GETS UP EARLY somebody who gets up early in the morning **2.** SOMEBODY WHO ARRIVES EARLY somebody who arrives earlier than the expected or arranged time [From the proverb *The early bird gets the worm*]

ear·ly mu·sic *n.* MEDIEVAL AND RENAISSANCE MUSIC music written during the Medieval and Renaissance periods, sometimes also including the music of the Baroque and early Classical periods ■ *adj.* PERFORMED IN THE STYLE OF THE TIME typical of a way of performing early music that aims to be as authentic as possible, using period instruments, the contemporary performing style, and a carefully researched score

ear·ly warn·ing sys·tem *n.* a network of radar, satellites, or other sensing devices designed to give advance warning of an enemy attack, especially in time to take countermeasures

ear·mark /éer maàrk/ *vt.* (**-marked, -mark·ing, -marks**) **1.** DESIGNATE SOMETHING FOR PARTICULAR PURPOSE to select and reserve something to be used for a particular purpose ○ *That money's already been earmarked for upgrading the computer system.* **2.** AGRIC PUT AN IDENTIFICATION MARK ON AN ANIMAL'S EAR to mark the ear of a farm animal with an identifying symbol, notch, or hole ■ *n.* **1.** IDENTIFYING CHARACTERISTIC something enabling recognition of the nature or origins of something (*often used in the plural*) ○ *The crime seemed to have all the earmarks of an inside job.* **2.** AGRIC IDENTIFICATION MARK ON AN ANIMAL'S EAR an identifying symbol, hole, or notch in the ear of a farm animal [Early 16thC. The earliest meaning is that of marking an animal's ear.]

ear·muffs /éer mùfs/ *npl.* ear covers attached to an adjustable headband, worn in cold weather

earn /urn/ (**earned, earn·ing, earns**) *v.* **1.** *vti.* MAKE MONEY BY WORKING to receive money or payment of some other kind in return for work done ○ *earn enough to live on* **2.** *vt.* DESERVE SOMETHING to acquire something as a reward for, or as a result of your actions or behavior ○ *earn praise* ○ *the remark earned him a stern rebuke* **3.** *vt.* FIN PRODUCE INTEREST OR DIVIDENDS to produce interest or dividends from money invested [Old English *earnian.* From a prehistoric Germanic base meaning "to harvest," which is also the ancestor of German *Ernte* "harvest."]

earned in·come *n.* income from paid employment as opposed to income from investments

earned run *n.* BASEBALL a run scored without the benefit of an error or a wild pitch

earned run av·er·age *n.* BASEBALL the number of earned runs allowed by a pitcher per every nine innings, used as a measure of the pitcher's performance

ear·nest[1] /úrnəst/ *adj.* **1.** INTENSELY SERIOUS AND SINCERE intensely, or even excessively, serious and sincere in manner or attitude **2.** DONE IN A DEEPLY SINCERE WAY undertaken or made in a spirit of deep seriousness and sincerity, or with deep feeling **3.** DESERVING SERIOUS ATTENTION of a serious nature or worthy of serious attention (*formal*) [Old English *eornost,* from a prehistoric Germanic base of uncertain origin] —**ear·nest·ly** *adv.* —**ear·nest·ness** *n.* ◇ **in earnest 1.** serious and sincere in your actions, words, or intentions **2.** more intensely, or in a determined and purposeful way

ear·nest[2] /úrnəst/ *n.* **1. ear·nest, ear·nest mon·ey** COMM DOWN PAYMENT a small advance payment that confirms a contract **2.** TOKEN OF SOMETHING TO COME a sign, foretaste, or pledge of something to come (*literary*) [13thC. Origin uncertain: probably an alteration of Old French *erres* "pledges," from Latin *arra* from, ultimately, Greek *arrabōn* "pledge," from Hebrew *'ērābhôn,* from *'ārab* "to pledge."]

earn·ings /úrningz/ *npl.* money earned, either through paid employment, as profit, or from investments

Earp /urp/, **Wyatt** (1848–1929) U.S. frontiersman and law enforcement officer. He was based in Dodge City, Kansas, from 1876 and in Tombstone, Arizona (1879–82), and he participated in the gunfight at the O.K. Corral (1881). Full name **Wyatt Berry Stapp Earp**

ear·phone /éer fòn/ *n.* a device that converts electric signals into audible sound and is worn on or held close to the ear (*often used in the plural*)

ear·piece /éer peèss/ *n.* **1.** THE PART OF A DEVICE HEARD THROUGH the part of a device such as a telephone, radio, or hearing aid that is held in, or close to, the ear **2.** PART OF GLASSES FRAME AROUND THE EAR the part of the frame of a pair of eyeglasses that fits over and around the ear

ear·pierc·ing *adj.* extremely or painfully loud and shrill

ear·plug /éer plùg/ *n.* a piece of something soft such as wax or foam rubber that is placed in the ear to keep out noise, water, or cold (*often used in the plural*)

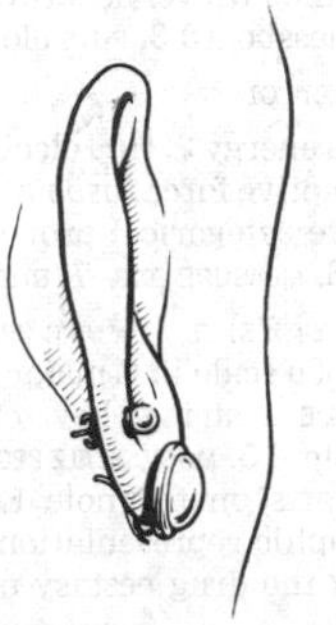

Earring

ear·ring /éer rìng/ *n.* ACCESSORIES a piece of jewelry worn on the ear, usually either clipped to the earlobe or attached through a hole pierced in it (*often used in the plural*)

ear shell *n.* = **abalone**

ear·shot /éer shòt/ *n.* the distance within which sound is audible to somebody ○ *within earshot* [Early 17thC. Modeled on words such as *bowshot* "distance to which an arrow can be shot from a bow."]

ear·split·ting /éer splìtting/ *adj.* extremely loud or shrill

earth /urth/ *n.* **1. Earth, earth** 3RD PLANET FROM SUN the third planet in order from the Sun with an orbital period of 365.26 days, a diameter of 7,926 mi./12,756 km, and an average distance from the sun of 93,000,000 mi./149,600,000 km. Surrounded by an atmosphere composed primarily of nitrogen and oxygen, it is the only planet in the universe known to support life. **2.** LAND the solid dry land surface of the Earth, as opposed to the sea or sky **3.** SOIL the soft, workable material in which plants grow **4.** HUMAN INHABITANTS OF EARTH all the human inhabitants of the Earth (*formal*) **5.** PURSUITS OF EVERYDAY LIFE the pursuits of everyday human life, especially as opposed to matters of the spirit **6.** *U.K.* ZOOL BURROW the hole or underground lair of a fox, or sometimes a badger **7.** *U.K.* ELEC ENG = **ground 8.** PHILOS, HIST ONE OF THE FOUR ELEMENTS in ancient and medieval philosophy, one of the four elements, earth, air, fire, and water, from which it was believed everything was made ■ *vt.* (**earthed, earth·ing, earths**) *U.K.* ELEC ENG = **ground** [Old English *eorþe,* from a prehistoric Germanic word] ◇ **come** *or* **be brought back (down) to earth** to become or be made aware of the usually unglamorous realities of your situation again ◇ **on earth** used to add intensity to a question, often indicating surprise or disbelief on the part of the questioner (*informal*) ○ *What on earth have you done to the computer now?*

earth·born /úrth bàwrn/ *adj.* born on or originating from the Earth, and therefore human, mortal, or earthly (*literary*)

earth·bound /úrth bòwnd/ *adj.* **1.** MUNDANE AND UNIMAGINATIVE exclusively concerned with or confined to ordinary everyday or wordly matters and lacking in imagination or spirituality **2.** HEADING TOWARD EARTH heading or moving toward Earth

earth col·or *n.* COLORS any of a number of pigments, e.g., umber or ocher, that are obtained from the earth

earth·en /úrthən/ *adj.* **1.** MADE OF EARTH made of earth or baked clay **2.** EARTHLY being from Earth and having human or mortal qualities

earth·en·ware /úrthən wàir/ *n.* pottery made of fairly coarse-textured baked clay that is fired at a very low temperature

earth·light /úrth lìt/ *n.* ASTRON = **earthshine**

earth·ling /úrthling/ *n.* **1.** HUMAN BEING especially in science fiction, a human being as contrasted with an extraterrestrial or supernatural being **2.** WORLDLING somebody who is concerned with the affairs of the everyday world

earth·ly /úrthlee/ (**-li·er, -li·est**) *adj.* **1.** CHARACTERISTIC OF THIS WORLD belonging to or characteristic of this world, especially as opposed to the spiritual realm or heaven **2.** POSSIBLE imaginable or possible

earth·man /úrth màn/ (*plural* **-men** /-mèn/) *n.* especially in science fiction, resident of Earth as referred to by an extraterrestrial

earth moth·er *n.* **1.** SENSUAL AND MOTHERLY WOMAN a woman who conveys a warm earthy combination of sensuality and motherliness **2.** THE EARTH PERSONIFIED AS MOTHER the Earth personified as a mother **3.** GODDESS SYMBOLIZING EARTH a goddess symbolizing earth and worshiped as a source of life and fertility

earth·mov·er /úrth mòovər/ *n.* a vehicle such as a bulldozer that is designed to move earth, especially in large quantities —**earth·mov·ing** *adj.*

earth·nut /úrth nùt/ *n.* a plant, e.g., the peanut, that has underground pods

earth pil·lar *n.* a pillar of soft material capped by a boulder of more resistant rock that protects it from erosion

earth·quake /úrth kwàyk/ *n.* **1.** SHAKING OF THE EARTH'S CRUST a violent shaking of the Earth's crust that may cause destruction to buildings and installations and results from the sudden release of tectonic stress along a fault line or volcanic activity **2.** DISRUPTIVE EVENT an event that causes an upheaval in society, politics, or somebody's life

earth·rise /úrth rìz/ *n.* the rising of the Earth above the Moon's horizon, as seen from space or from the Moon itself

earth sci·ence *n.* a science that deals with the Earth's physical properties, structure, or development, e.g., geology

earth·shak·ing /úrth shàyking/, **earth·shat·ter·ing** /úrth shàttəring/ *adj.* extremely great or important, or having an extremely powerful effect —**earth·shak·ing·ly** *adv.*

earth·shine /úrth shìn/ *n.* sunlight reflected from the Earth that illuminates the part of the Moon not receiving light directly from the Sun

earth sign *n.* any of the three signs of the zodiac, Taurus, Virgo, or Capricorn, all associated with stability and consistency

earth·star /úrth staàr/ *n.* a woodland fungus with a round outer surface that splits open in a star-shaped pattern to release spores. Genus: *Geastrum.*

earth sta·tion *n.* a sytem for relaying radio signals between one or more satellites and other communications networks. Earth stations may be on the ground, at sea, or in aircraft.

earth tone *n.* a color that has an element of deep rich brown in it, e.g., gold or russet

earth·ward /úrthwərd/ *adj.* DIRECTED TOWARD THE EARTH directed or facing toward the Earth ■ *adv.* **earth·ward, earth·wards** TOWARD THE EARTH in the direction of the Earth or the ground

earth·work /úrth wùrk/ *n.* **1.** MIL EARTH FORTIFICATION a fortification made of earth **2.** CONSTR EXCAVATION AND EARTHMOVING WORK construction work involving excavating, earthmoving, and building embankments

earth·worm /úrth wùrm/ *n.* a worm that burrows in the soil and helps to aerate and improve it. Family: Lumbricidae.

earth·y /úrthee/ (**-i·er, -i·est**) *adj.* **1.** LIKE SOIL relating to or consisting of soil **2.** NOT SQUEAMISH OR PRETENTIOUS having or showing a hearty, cheerful, no-nonsense acceptance of the realities and facts of life **3.** CRUDE crude and coarse —**earth·i·ly** *adv.* —**earth·i·ness** *n.*

ear trum·pet *n.* an early type of hearing aid consisting of a trumpet-shaped device that was held to the ear

ear tuft /éer tùft/ *n.* a tuft of feathers above the eyes of some owls and other birds, causing the bird to look larger or blend in with foliage but not used in hearing

ear·wax /éer wàks/ *n.* a yellowish waxy substance secreted by glands in the external ear to protect the delicate lining of the outer ear. Technical name **cerumen**

ear·wig /éer wìg/ *n.* a common insect with a slender shiny body, small forewings, antennae, and pincers at the end of its abdomen. Order: Dermaptera. [Old English *ēarwicga*. Literally "ear-insect," from *ēare* "ear" + *wicga* "insect." The insect received its name from the belief that it creeps into people's ears.]

ease /eez/ *n.* **1.** LACK OF DIFFICULTY lack of difficulty in doing or achieving something ○ *defeated the challenger with ease* **2.** LACK OF AWKWARDNESS lack of awkwardness, stiffness, or self-consciousness in social situations ○ *He felt totally at ease with her.* **3.** COMFORT AND AFFLUENCE a comfortable and leisured state free from problems and restrictions, especially those caused by poverty ○ *a life of ease* **4.** RELAXATION a state of comfort and relaxation **5.** RELIEF FROM WORRY OR PAIN freedom or relief from worry or pain ■ *v.* (**eased, eas·ing, eas·es**) **1.** *vt.* MAKE SOMETHING LESS UNPLEASANT to make something less unpleasant, difficult, or restrictive **2.** *vt.* RELIEVE THE MIND OR BODY FROM PAIN to relieve somebody's mind or body from pain or discomfort **3.** *vi.* ABATE to become less strong or intense ○ *The rain eased.* **4.** *vti.* MANEUVER GENTLY to maneuver gently and carefully, especially in a tight space, or maneuver something in this way ○ *eased the truck into the space* **5.** *vt.* LOOSEN SOMETHING to slacken something that is tied or fitted tightly **6.** *vt.* MAKE SOMETHING EASIER to enable something to take place more easily [12thC. From Old French *aise* "comfort," of uncertain origin: perhaps from Latin *adjacens* "lying near."]

ease·ful /éezfəl/ *adj.* giving relief from pain, suffering, or distress (*literary*) —**ease·ful·ly** *adv.* —**ease·ful·ness** *n.*

ea·sel /éez'l/ *n.* a freestanding upright support for a painter's canvas or a blackboard, usually made of wood and having movable clamps [Late 16thC. Via Dutch *ezel* "donkey," from, ultimately, Latin *asinus* "ass" (source of English *ass*).]

ease·ment /éezmənt/ *n.* LAW a limited right to make use of a property owned by another, e.g., a right of way across the property [14thC. Via Old French *aisement* from, ultimately, *aise* "comfort" (see EASE).]

eas·i·ly /éezilee, éezlee/ *adv.* **1.** WITHOUT DIFFICULTY in an easy manner and without difficulty or strain ○ *We can easily be there by lunchtime.* **2.** BY FAR without doubt and by a large margin ○ *she's easily the best* **3.** AT LEAST certainly not less and probably far more than a particular number or amount ○ *There were easily 200 people at the meeting.*

east /eest/ *n.* **1.** DIRECTION IN WHICH THE SUN RISES the direction that lies directly ahead of somebody facing the rising sun or that is located toward the right-hand side of a conventional map of the world **2.** COMPASS POINT OPPOSITE WEST the compass point that lies directly opposite west **3. east, East** AREA IN THE EAST the part of an area, region, or country that is situated in or toward the east **4.** CHR ALTAR END OF CHURCH the end of a church where the altar is situated **5. east, East** GAMES POSITION EQUIVALENT TO EAST the position equivalent to east in any diagram consisting of four points at 90 degree intervals ■ *adj.* **1.** IN THE EAST situated in, facing, or coming from the east of a place, region, or country **2.** BLOWING FROM THE EAST blowing from the east ■ *adv.* TOWARD THE EAST in or toward the east [Old English *ēast-*. Ultimately from an Indo-European word meaning "to shine," which also produced English *aurora*. The underlying idea is of the point at which the sun rises.]

East Af·ri·ca region in east central Africa, usually taken to comprise Burundi, Kenya, Rwanda, Somalia, Tanzania, and Uganda —**East Af·ri·can** *n., adj.*

East A·sia *n.* the countries of the Far East

East Ben·gal former name for **Bangladesh** (1947–55)

East Ber·lin capital of East Germany from 1949 until 1990, when both Berlin and Germany were reunified —**East Ber·lin·er** *n.*

east·bound /éest bòwnd/ *adj.* going or leading toward the east

East Bruns·wick town in central New Jersey. Population: 43,548 (1990).

east by north *n.* the direction or compass point midway between east and east-northeast —**east by north** *adv., adj.*

east by south *n.* the direction or compass point midway between east and east-southeast —**east by south** *adj., adv.*

East·ches·ter /éest chèstər/ town in southeastern New York State, between Yonkers and New Rochelle. Population: 22,600 (1992).

East Chi·ca·go industrial city in northwestern Indiana, on the south shore of Lake Michigan. It is a southeastern suburb of Chicago. Population: 31,761 (1996).

East End *n.* a densely populated area in the east of London

East·er /éestər/ *n.* **1.** CHRISTIAN FESTIVAL the Christian festival commemorating the resurrection of Jesus Christ **2.** DAY OF THE EASTER FESTIVAL the day on which Easter is celebrated, the Sunday following the full moon on or after March 21 **3.** EASTER WEEKEND the period from Good Friday to Easter Monday [Old English *Ēastre*, from the name of a prehistoric Germanic dawn-goddess whose festival was celebrated at the vernal equinox. Ultimately from an Indo-European base meaning "to shine" (see EAST).]

East·er cac·tus *n.* a cactus with flattened branches that is cultivated as an ornamental plant for its clusters of large red flowers. Latin name: *Rhipsalidopsis gaertneri.* [*Easter* from the fact that it blooms in the spring]

East·er Day *n.* = **Easter** *n.* 2

East·er egg *n.* **1.** COLORED HEN'S EGG FOR EASTER a hen's egg that has been dyed, painted, or decorated for Easter, often hidden for children to find in an Easter egg hunt **2.** COMPUT HIDDEN ELEMENT OF A COMPUTER PROGRAM a secret message, graphic, animation, or sound effect hidden in a computer program and activated by a specific undocumented sequence of keystrokes. An Easter egg is typically intended as a harmless joke or as a way to display the credits of the program's development team.

Barnaby's

Easter Island

Eas·ter Is·land island in the South Pacific Ocean belonging to Chile. It is noted for its huge carved stone heads and hieroglyphic tablets. Population: 2,095 (1989). Area: 45 sq. mi./117 sq. km. —**East·er Is·land·er** *n.*

East·er lil·y *n.* **1.** LILY BLOOMING IN SPRING a cultivated lily with large white flowers that bloom in the spring **2.** TRILLIUM a trillium, which has three flowers (*regional*)

WORD KEY: REGIONAL NOTE

Although the term ***Easter lily*** is used of many U.S. plants, including the Bermuda lily and the Madonna lily, the trillium sense characterizes the speech of Washington state.

east·er·ly /éestərlee/ *adj.* **1.** IN THE EAST situated in or toward the east **2.** BLOWING FROM THE EAST used to describe a wind that blows from the east ■ *n.* (*plural* **-lies**) WIND FROM THE EAST a wind blowing from the east —**east·er·ly** *adv.*

East·er Mon·day *n.* the Monday after the Christian festival of Easter

east·ern /éestərn/ *adj.* **1.** IN THE EAST situated in the east of a region or country **2.** FACING EAST situated in or facing the east **3.** BLOWING FROM THE EAST used to describe a wind that blows from the east **4. east·ern, East·ern** TYPICAL OF THE EAST typical of or native to the east of a geographic region

East·ern *adj.* **1.** RELIG OF THE EASTERN ORTHODOX CHURCH relating to the Eastern Orthodox Church **2.** OF THE COUNTRIES OF ASIA relating or belonging to the countries of Asia as viewed from Europe or North America

East·ern Em·pire *n.* = **Byzantine Empire**

east·ern·er /éestərnər/ *n.* somebody who comes from the eastern part of a country or region, especially somebody from the East Coast of the United States

east·ern hem·i·sphere *n.* the half of the Earth that lies east of the Greenwich meridian and contains Asia, Australasia, and most of Europe and Africa

east·ern·most /éestərn mōst/ *adj.* **1.** FARTHEST TO THE EAST farthest to the east **2.** AT THE MOST EASTERN EXTREME located at the most eastern extreme of a county, state, or country

East·ern Or·tho·dox Church *n.* the self-governing Orthodox Christian churches that originated in the Byzantine Empire and recognize the Patriarch of Constantinople as primate. They now comprise the churches of Eastern Europe, Russia, and Greece.

East·ern Stan·dard Time *n.* the standard time in the time zone centered on longitude 75° W, which includes the eastern part of North America. It is five hours earlier than Universal Coordinated Time.

East·er Ris·ing *n.* an armed rebellion against British rule that took place in Dublin, Ireland, on Easter Day in 1916

East·er Sun·day *n.* = **Easter** *n.* 2

East Ger·man·ic *n.* a group of extinct languages that were formerly spoken in parts of eastern Europe. It is one of the three groups that form the Germanic branch of Indo-European. Gothic is the only language in this group that has any known written form. —**East Ger·man·ic** *adj.*

East Ger·ma·ny common name of a former republic of central Europe, reunited with the rest of Germany in 1990. It was founded under the influence of the Soviet Union in 1949 and recognized as an independent state in 1955. Area: 41,768 sq. mi./108,178 sq. km. —**East Ger·man** *n., adj.*

East Green·wich town and summer resort in central Rhode Island, southwest of Providence. Population: 11,865 (1990).

East·hamp·ton /eest hámptən/ town in west central Massachusetts, on the Manhan River, northwest of Springfield and southwest of Northampton. Population: 15,744 (1996).

East Hart·ford town in central Connecticut, on the east side of the Connecticut River, opposite Hartford. Population: 50,452 (1990).

East Ha·ven town and summer resort in southern Connecticut, on Long Island Sound. Population: 26,144 (1990).

East In·di·a Com·pa·ny *n.* a trading company established in England in 1600 to trade with the East Indies, and later with India, which it effectively governed for many years. Similar companies were also founded in the Netherlands and France.

East In·di·an *adj.* relating to or typical of the East Indies, or their peoples or cultures

East In·dies /eest índeez/ collective name formerly applied to India, Southeast Asia, and the Malay Archipelago, especially Indonesia

east·ing /éesting/ *n.* **1.** DISTANCE TRAVELED EAST the net distance eastward that a vessel travels when making for the east **2.** PART OF A MAP REFERENCE the first part of a map reference that shows how far east a point lies from a reference line running from north to south **3.** NORTH-SOUTH GRID LINE ON MAP a grid line on a map running north to south

East Los An·ge·les town in southwestern California, adjoining the city of Los Angeles. Population: 126,379 (1990).

East·man /éestmən/, **George** (1854–1932) U.S. inventor and philanthropist. He perfected the box camera (1888), the first camera designed specifically for roll film.

East·man, Max Forrester (1883–1969) U.S. writer and editor. His work concentrated on radical politics and he edited the revolutionary magazine *The Masses* (1913–18).

East Mo·line /-mo léen/ city in northwestern Illinois, just east of the Mississippi River on the Illinois-Iowa border. Population: 20,214 (1996).

east-north·east *n.* COMPASS POINT BETWEEN E AND NE the direction or compass point midway between east and northeast ■ *adj., adv.* IN THE EAST-NORTHEAST in, from, facing, or toward the east-northeast —**east-north·east·er·ly** *adv.*

East·on /éestən/ **1.** city in east central Maryland, on the Delmarva Peninsula, west of the Choptank River. It is southeast of Annapolis across the Chesapeake Bay. Population: 10,195 (1996). **2.** town in southeastern Massachusetts, directly southwest of Brockton and north of Taunton. Population: 20,970 (1996).

East Or·ange city in northeastern New Jersey, northwest of Newark. Population: 77,690 (1992).

East Pak·i·stan former name for **Bangladesh** (1955–71)

East Pe·or·i·a /eest pay óree ə/ city in central Illinois, on the eastern bank of the Illinois River, east of Peoria. Population: 22,201 (1996).

East Prov·i·dence /eest próvidəns/ city in eastern Rhode Island, a suburb of Providence. Population: 48,389 (1996).

East Prus·sia former German province on the Baltic Sea that was divided between Poland and Russia in 1945 —**East Prus·sian** *n., adj.*

East Rid·ing of York·shire council area in northeastern England, established in 1996, covering largely the same area as the historic division

East Riv·er strait in southeastern New York State, separating Manhattan Island from Long Island. Length: 15 mi./24 km.

East Saint Lou·is city in southwestern Illinois, east of the Mississippi River, across from Saint Louis, Missouri. Population: 38,595 (1996).

East Sea ◆ **Japan, Sea of**

east-south·east *n.* COMPASS POINT BETWEEN E AND SE the direction or compass point midway between east and southeast. ■ *adj., adv.* IN EAST-SOUTHEAST in, from, facing, or toward the east-southeast —**east-south·east·er·ly** *adv.*

east·ward /éestwərd/ *adv.* TOWARD THE EAST in an easterly direction ■ *n.* POINT IN THE EAST a direction toward or a point in the east [Old English *ēastwærde*] —**east·ward** *adj.* —**east·ward·ly** *adj., adv.*

WORD KEY: USAGE

eastward or **eastwards**? ***Eastward*** is the only form available for the adjective: *in an eastward direction.* ***Eastward*** is more common than ***eastwards*** for the adverb: *The ship was moving slowly eastward / eastwards.*

East·wood /éest wŏŏd/, **Clint** (*b.* 1930) U.S. movie actor and director He is known for his action movies such as *A Fistful of Dollars* (1964) and *Dirty Harry* (1971).

eas·y /éezee/ *adj.* (**-i·er, -i·est**) **1.** NOT DIFFICULT not causing problems or difficulty or requiring much effort, work, or thought ○ *Answer the easy questions first.* ○ *It's easy to see why they chose him.* **2.** INAPPROPRIATELY EFFORTLESS requiring less effort, thought, or emotional involvement than is appropriate or right ○ *always taking the easy way out* ○ *easy answers* **3.** RELAXED AND INFORMAL relaxed, informal, and without awkwardness or self-consciousness, especially in social situations ○ *has an easy manner* **4.** GOOD-NATURED good-natured and tolerant ○ *has an easy disposition* **5.** FINANCIALLY PROSPEROUS characterized by financial prosperity and security and the comfort and peace of mind that goes with them ○ *dreams of selling her invention and living the easy life* **6.** NOT HARSH not severe or harsh ○ *She's always claiming that easy discipline makes people soft.* **7.** EASY TO TAKE ADVANTAGE OF not difficult to catch, acquire, take advantage of, or exploit ○ *unscrupulous sellers looking for easy targets* **8.** LOOSE not tight or close-fitting ○ *jeans that are an easy fit* **9.** UNHURRIED comfortable, unhurried, and not too fast ○ *took an easy pace up the trail* **10.** NOT STEEP not steep or difficult to climb up or down ○ *It's an easy slope to the top.* **11.** PLEASANT TO EXPERIENCE pleasant to experience through one of the senses, especially good to look at or soothing to listen to ○ *easy on the eyes* **12.** LACKING PREFERENCES having no strong preferences (*informal*) ○ *We can do either; I'm easy.* **13.** ECON READILY OBTAINABLE readily obtainable, because demand is lower than usual **14.** ECON MARKED BY LOW DEMAND AND PRICES characterized by low demand or overproduction and hence low prices **15.** PROMISCUOUS sexually promiscuous or too willing to become sexually involved (*slang*) ■ *adv.* **1.** EASILY without difficulty or the need for hard work ○ *Everything comes easy to her.* **2.** AT LEAST certainly not less than a particular amount ○ *cost $400 easy* ■ *adj.* (**-i·er, -i·est**) NOT ANXIOUS free from unpleasant feelings such as anxiety, guilt, or worry ○ *Rest easy; we'll be there soon.* ■ *adv.* WITHOUT PUNISHMENT without punishment or suffering ○ *Considering what they did, they got off easy.* ■ *interj.* USED TO CALM SOMEBODY OR SOMETHING used to try to make a person or animal calm down or slow down (*informal*) [12thC. From Old French *aisié*, the past participle of *aisier* "to put at ease," from *aise* "comfort" (see EASE).] ◇ **easy on something** an instruction or recommendation to somebody not to use too much of something (*informal*) ○ *Hey, easy on the whipped cream!* ◇ **go easy on somebody** to treat or deal with somebody gently, leniently, or without harsh criticism or reproaches (*informal*) ◇ **go easy on something** to avoid using, eating, or drinking too much of something (*informal*) ◇ **take it easy 1.** to relax, avoid effort, or not work too hard **2.** to calm down and avoid becoming upset or angry ◇ **take it easy on something** to avoid using, eating, or drinking too much of something (*informal*) ○ *You'd better take it easy on that greasy food–you know what the doctor said.*

WORD KEY: SYNONYMS

easy, simple, straightforward, uncomplicated

CORE MEANING: not difficult to do or achieve

easy a general word indicating the lack of effort required to do, achieve or understand something; **simple** emphasizing something that is not at all complicated and so can be done or understood quickly or with very little effort; **straightforward** used especially to suggest that a process or action is easy to carry out; **uncomplicated** used to suggest that something is not especially difficult, but usually suggesting a greater degree of effort or thought than *easy* or *simple.*

eas·y chair *n.* a comfortably upholstered chair, especially an armchair

eas·y·go·ing /éezi gṓ ing, éezi gō ing/ *adj.* **1.** RELAXED, INFORMAL, AND TOLERANT relaxed, informal, and tolerant in attitude and reluctant to make heavy demands or enforce strict discipline on people **2.** UNHURRIED unhurried and comfortable

eas·y lis·ten·ing *n.* popular music in an undemanding style, usually with a lyrical or romantic tune, gentle rhythms, and soft soothing orchestration

eas·y mark *n.* somebody who or something that is easy to deceive or exploit (*informal*)

eas·y mon·ey *n.* money made with little effort, and often dishonestly

eas·y vir·tue *n.* lax sexual morals and promiscuous sexual habits (*literary*)

eat /eet/ (**ate** /ayt/, **eat·en** /éet'n/, **eat·ing, eats**) *v.* **1.** *vti.* CONSUME AS SUSTENANCE to take something into the mouth as food and swallow it ○ *They hadn't eaten for three days.* **2.** *vi.* DINE to have a meal ○ *Are you ready to eat?* **3.** *vt.* CONSUME USUALLY to include something as a usual or fundamental part of a diet ○ *Do dogs eat fish?* **4.** *vt.* BOTHER to bother or annoy somebody (*slang*) ○ *What's eating her?* **5.** *vt.* USE A LOT OF SOMETHING to use or consume something in large quantities (*slang*) ○ *a car that eats gas* **6.** *vt.* ABSORB THE COST OF SOMETHING to absorb the cost of something (*slang*) ○ *You're going to have to eat that traffic fine.* **7.** *vti.* PENETRATE to penetrate the surface of something by corrosive or mechanical action ○ *Rust had eaten into the chrome.* **8.** *vt.* OFFENSIVE TERM to perform fellatio or cunnilingus on somebody (*taboo slang*) **9.** *vt.* VANQUISH to attack and subdue, e.g., in a competition ○ *ate us in the second half* [Old English *etan.* Ultimately from an Indo-European base that also produced English *edible, etch,* and *tooth.*]

eat away *vt.* to consume or destroy something gradually ○ *eaten away in parts by acid rain*

eat away at *vt.* **1.** WORRY to worry or be a continual source of distress to somebody ○ *Guilt had been eating away at him all day.* **2.** CONSUME GRADUALLY to deplete or use up something gradually by taking small amounts regularly ○ *medical expenses eating away at our income*

eat in *vi.* to consume a meal at home ○ *Would you rather eat in or go to a restaurant?*
eat into *vt.* to use up part of something, especially in a wasteful or nonproductive way
eat out *vi.* to consume a meal away from home, usually in a restaurant or similar establishment ○ *Let's eat out tonight.*
eat up *v.* **1.** *vti.* EAT COMPLETELY to consume food completely or with great appetite **2.** *vt.* OBSESS SOMEBODY to absorb or obsess somebody (*usually passive*) ○ *eaten up by envy* **3.** *vt.* RECEIVE ENTHUSIASTICALLY to receive something with enthusiasm or pleasure (*informal*) ○ *The reading public eats up everything she writes.* **4.** *vt.* CONSUME QUICKLY to consume or deal with something quickly (*informal*)

eat·a·ble /eétəb'l/ *adj.* FIT TO BE EATEN fit, suitable, or pleasant to eat ■ *n.* FOOD ITEM something that is fit or suitable for eating (*informal*) (*usually used in the plural*) ○ *buy some bread and other eatables*

eat·en past participle of **eat**

eat·er /eétər/ *n.* a person who or animal that eats a particular food or eats in a particular way (*often used in combination*)

eat·er·y /eétəree/ (*plural* **-ies**) *n.* a restaurant or other establishment where food is cooked and sold (*informal*)

eat·ing /eéting/ *n.* FOOD food, especially of a particular quality ○ *These apples are good eating.* ■ *adj.* **1.** SUITABLE FOR EATING suitable for human consumption, especially uncooked **2.** INVOLVING FOOD relating to or used for the consumption of food

eat·ing dis·or·der *n.* MED any emotional disorder, e.g., bulimia, that manifests itself in an irrational craving for or avoidance of food

eats /eets/ *npl.* food (*slang*) ○ *What do you do for eats around here?* [Late 19thC. Formed from the verb *eat*.]

EAU *abbr.* (East Africa) Uganda (*international vehicle registration*)

Eau Claire /ō kláir/ **1.** river in west central Wisconsin that flows into the Chippewa River at the town of Eau Claire. Length: 70 mi./113 km. **2.** city in western Wisconsin, at the confluence of the Chippewa and Eau Claire rivers. Population: 56,856 (1990).

eau de co·logne /ō də kə lṓn/ *n.* = **cologne** [Early 19thC. From French, literally "water of Cologne."]

eau de nil /ō də neél/ *adj.* of a pale yellowish-green color [Late 19thC. From French, literally "water of the Nile." The pale greenish color supposedly resembles the color of the Nile.] —**eau de nil** *n.*

eau de toi·lette /ō də twaa lét/ *n.* = **toilet water** [From French, literally "toilet water"]

eau de vie /ō də veé/ *n.* a strong alcoholic liquor, especially brandy [Mid-18thC. From French, literally "water of life."]

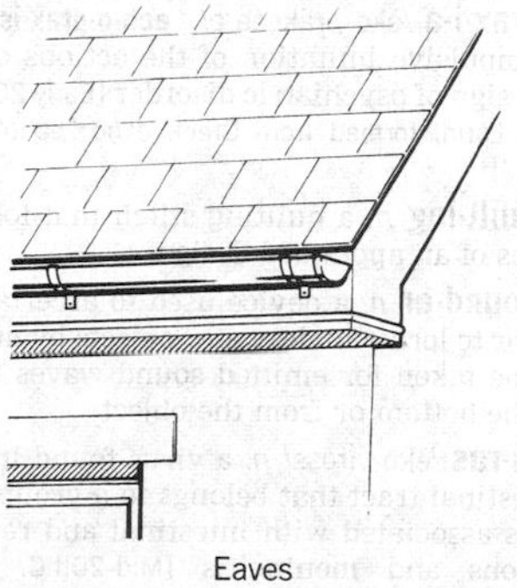

Eaves

eaves /eevz/ *npl.* the part of a roof that projects beyond the wall that supports it [Old English *efes*. Probably formed from the same prehistoric Germanic base as English *over*.]

eaves·drop /eévz dròp/ (**-dropped, -drop·ping, -drops**) *vi.* to listen to a conversation without the speakers being aware of it [Early 17thC. Probably a back-formation from EAVESDROPPER.]

eaves·drop·per /eévz dròppər/ *n.* somebody who secretly listens to or overhears a conversation between others [15thC. From obsolete *eavesdrop* "ground on which rainwater thrown off by eaves falls"; from the idea of somebody standing in this area trying to hear private conversations.]

eaves spout *n.* a gutter, or the downspout of a gutter (*regional*)

WORD KEY: REGIONAL NOTE

See Regional note at ***eaves trough.***

eaves trough *n.* a gutter on a building (*regional*)

WORD KEY: REGIONAL NOTE

The Northern terms ***eaves trough*** and ***eaves spout*** extend from New England through the Midwest. In the earlier part of the 20th century, the ***eaves trough*** form was general currency in New England and New York state, from Albany westward. At that time, ***eaves spout*** prevailed in the western reserve of Ohio. Indeed, that term was recorded for *rain gutter* as early as 1846 in Randolph county, North Carolina. Both terms have currency across the Western states to the Pacific coast, from Washington to California, where they survive as less common alternatives. Today they have been challenged or overtaken by the general currency terms *rain gutter* or *gutter* and *downspout* respectively. In the Southern states, with the exception of the occasional occurrence of *trough*, the terms have been generally replaced by *gutter*.

E·ban /eébən/, **Abba** (*b.* 1915) South African-born Israeli statesman. He worked for the United Nations in Palestine (1946) and later held diplomatic and ministerial posts in Israel. These include being Israel's ambassador to the UN (1948–59) and to the United States (1950–59), and deputy prime minister (1963–66). Born **Aubrey Solomon**

ebb /eb/ *vi.* (**ebbed, ebb·ing, ebbs**) **1.** RECEDE FROM THE SHORE to recede from the land, as the tide falls (*refers to the sea or tidal water*) **2.** DIMINISH to diminish or lessen in intensity ○ *the pain gradually ebbed away* ■ *n.* **1.** TIDAL MOVEMENT AWAY FROM LAND the movement of a receding tide away from the land **2.** DIMINUTION diminution or lessening ○ *the ebb and flow of the company's fortunes* [Old English *ebbian*. Formed from the prehistoric Germanic ancestor of English *off*; the underlying meaning is "going away, departure."] ◇ **at a low ebb** lacking hope and energy, or in a depleted condition

ebb tide *n.* a receding tide, or the time when this happens

EBCDIC /ébseedik/ *n.* a binary computer character code, used to represent 256 standard letters, numbers, symbols, and control characters by means of eight binary digits. Full form **Extended Binary Coded Decimal Interchange Code**

EbN *abbr.* east by north

E-boat *n.* a fast torpedo boat used by the German navy in World War II [*E* a shortening of ENEMY]

Eb·o·la /i bṓlə/, **Eb·o·la vi·rus** *n.* a contagious virus transmitted by blood and body fluids that causes the linings of bodily organs and vessels to leak blood and fluids, usually resulting in death [Late 20thC. Named for the *Ebola* River in Zaire, in the area of which the virus was first identified following an outbreak in 1976.]

eb·on /ébbən/ *n., adj.* ebony (*literary*) [14thC. Via Old French *eban* from, ultimately, Greek *ebenos*, of Semitic origin.]

E·bon·ics /ee bónniks/ *n.* Black American English considered as a language in its own right. The most scholars prefer the term AAVE (African American Vernacular English).

eb·on·ite /ébbə nīt/ *n.* MANUF = **vulcanite**

eb·on·ize /ébbə nīz/ (**-ized, -iz·ing, -iz·es**) *vt.* to stain something black so as to resemble ebony

eb·on·y /ébbənee/ *n.* (*plural* **-ies**) **1.** ASIAN TREE a tree of tropical Asia that yields a hard wood. Genus: *Diospyros*. **2.** DARK HARD WOOD the blackish hard wood of an ebony tree **3.** BROWNISH-BLACK COLOR black with a tinge of olive or brown ■ *adj.* BROWNISH-BLACK of a black color tinged with olive or brown [15thC. Formed from EBON, perhaps on the model of IVORY.]

e·brac·te·ate /i bráktee àyt/ *adj.* used to describe plants that have no bracts [Mid-19thC. From modern Latin *ebracteatus*, literally "without bracts."]

Eb·ro /ébbrō/ river in northeastern Spain. It rises in the Cantabrian Mountains near Reinosa and flows to its delta on the Mediterranean coast, south of Tarragona. Length: 565 mi./909 km.

EbS *abbr.* east by south

e·bul·lient /i búllyənt, i bóollyənt/ *adj.* **1.** LIVELY AND ENTHUSIASTIC full of cheerful excitement or enthusiasm **2.** BOILING boiling vigorously (*formal*) [Late 16thC. From Latin *ebullient-*, the present participle stem of *ebullire*, literally "to bubble out," from *bullire* "to bubble" (source of English *boil*).] —**e·bul·lience** *n.*

eb·ul·li·tion /èbbə lísh'n/ *n.* **1.** BOILING a state of bubbling up or boiling (*formal*) **2.** OUTBURST a sudden outbreak of violent emotion (*literary*) [14thC. Via French from, ultimately, Latin *ebullire* (see EBULLIENT).]

e·bur·na·tion /eèbər náysh'n, èbbər náysh'n/ *n.* an abnormal hardening of the surfaces of bones in a joint that have lost their cartilage covering, as occurs in such conditions as osteoarthritis [Mid-19thC. Formed from Latin *eburnus* "made of ivory."]

EBV *abbr.* Epstein-Barr virus

EB vi·rus *n.* = **Epstein-Barr virus**

EC *abbr.* HIST European Community

é·car·té[1] /ày kaar táy/ *n.* a card game for two people played with 32 cards in which cards may be discarded in exchange for others [Early 19thC. From French, literally "discarded."]

é·car·té[2] /ày kaar táy/ *n.* a ballet position in which the arm and leg on one side of the body are extended [Early 20thC. From French, literally "spread out."]

ec·ce ho·mo /échay hṓmō, èksee-, èkə-/ *n.* a portrayal of Jesus Christ crowned with thorns [From Latin, literally "behold the man" (John 19: 5), the words spoken by Pontius Pilate to Jesus Christ's accusers after Jesus Christ had been crowned with thorns]

ec·cen·tric /ik séntrik, ek-/ *adj.* **1.** UNCONVENTIONAL unconventional, especially in a whimsical way ○ *an eccentric mode of dress* **2.** TECH AWAY FROM THE CENTER away from the center or axis **3.** GEOM HAVING DIFFERENT CENTERS used to describe circles with different centers **4.** ASTRON ELLIPTICAL used to describe an orbit that is elliptical rather than circular ■ *n.* **1.** UNCONVENTIONAL PERSON somebody who is unconventional, especially in a whimsical way **2.** MECH ENG MECHANICAL DEVICE a mechanical device with an off-center axis of revolution that converts the rotary motion of one component of a mechanism to reciprocating motion in another [Mid-16thC. Via late Latin *eccentricus* from Greek *ekkentros*, literally "out of center," from *kentron* (see CENTER).] —**ec·cen·tri·cal·ly** *adv.*

ec·cen·tric·i·ty /èk sen tríssitee/ (*plural* **-ties**) *n.* **1.** ECCENTRIC QUALITY unconventionality, especially of a whimsical sort **2.** ECCENTRIC ACT an example or instance of unconventional, whimsical behavior **3.** MECH ENG DISTANCE BETWEEN A MAIN AND SECONDARY AXIS the distance between the axis about which an object rotates and a secondary axis on the object at which a device such as a rod could be attached **4.** ASTRON DEVIATION the deviation of the path of an orbiting body from a true circle **5.** GEOM GEOMETRIC CONSTANT a constant that describes the shape of a conic section. It is equal to the ratio of the distance from a fixed point of any point on the curve to the distance of that point from the corresponding fixed straight line.

ec·chy·mo·sis /èki mṓssiss/ (*plural* **-moses** /-mṓseez/) *n.* bleeding into surrounding tissue caused by bruising (*technical*) [Mid-16thC. Via modern Latin from, ultimately, Greek *ekkhumonothai*, literally "to pour out."]

eccl., **eccles.** *abbr.* **1.** ecclesiastic **2.** ecclesiastical

Eccl., **Eccles.** *abbr.* BIBLE Ecclesiastes

Ec·cles /ék'lz/, **Sir John** (1903–97) Australian physiologist. He was joint winner of the 1963 Nobel Prize in physiology or medicine for his studies of the transmission of impulses between nerve cells. Full name **Sir John Carew Eccles**

ec·cle·si·a /i kleézyə/ (*plural* **-ae** /-zyee/) *n.* **1.** CHR CONGREGATION OR CHURCH a church or congregation (*formal*) **2.** HIST ANCIENT GREEK ASSEMBLY in ancient Greece, an assembly of the citizens of a state [Late 16thC. Via Latin from Greek *ekklēsia* "assembly," from *ekkalein* "to call to come out, summon," from *kalein* "to call."]

Ec·cle·si·as·tes /i kleèzee ásteez/ *n.* a book in the Bible that discusses the futility of life and how to be a God-fearing person

ec·cle·si·as·tic /i kleèzee ástik/ *n.* a member of the clergy

ec·cle·si·as·ti·cal /i kleèzee ástik'l/ *adj.* belonging to, involving, or typical of the Christian church or clergy —**ec·cle·si·as·ti·cal·ly** *adv.*

ec·cle·si·as·ti·cism /i kleèzee ásti sìzzəm/ *n.* **1.** ALL-ABSORBING REGARD FOR THE CHURCH all-absorbing regard for the principles and customary practices of the

Christian Church **2.** CHURCH PRINCIPLES the principles or body of thought constituting organized Christianity

Ec·cle·si·as·ti·cus /i kleezee ástikəss/ *n.* a book of teachings in the Jerusalem Version of the Bible

ec·cle·si·ol·o·gy /i kleezee óllәjee/ *n.* **1.** STUDY OF THE CHRISTIAN CHURCH the study of the history and theology of the Christian Church **2.** STUDY OF CHURCH ARCHITECTURE the study of the architecture and decoration of Christian churches

ec·cre·mo·car·pus /ékrəmə kaárpəss/ *n.* a climbing evergreen plant native to Chile and Peru that is widely cultivated for its decorative leaves and brightly colored tubular flowers. Genus: *Eccremocarpus.* [From modern Latin, genus name, formed from Greek *ekkremēs* "suspended" + *karpos* "fruit"]

ec·crine /é krīn, ékrin/ *adj.* used to describe sweat glands that are distributed all over the body, especially on the hands and feet, that do not secrete organic matter, and that are important in regulating body temperature [Mid-20thC. From German *Ekkrin*, from Greek *ekkrinein* "to secrete."]

ec·dys·i·ast /ek dízee àst/ *n.* a performer of striptease (*humorous*) [Mid-20thC. Coined by H. L. Mencken from ECDYSIS, on the model of *gymnast.*]

ec·dy·sis /ékdississ/ *n.* ZOOL the regular molting of an outer layer by arthropods, e.g., insects and crustaceans, and by reptiles [Mid-19thC. From Greek *ekdusis*, from *ekduein* "to put off, shed."]

ec·dy·sone /ékdi sōn/ *n.* a hormone that promotes metamorphosis and ecdysis in insects and crustaceans

e·ce·sis /i séessiss/ *n.* the successful establishment of a plant or animal species in a new environment [Early 20thC. From Greek *oikēsis* "an inhabiting," from *oikos* "house."]

ECG *abbr.* **1.** electrocardiogram **2.** electrocardiograph **3.** echocardiograph

E·che·ga·ray y Ei·za·guir·re /áychəgə rī ee ayssə géer ày, -gweér ày/, **José** (1832–1916) Spanish playwright and politician. His poetic dramas won him a shared Nobel Prize in 1904, and he also held ministerial office (1868–74 and 1905).

ech·e·lon /éshə lòn/ *n.* **1.** LEVEL IN A HIERARCHY a level of authority or rank in an organization or system ○ *the lower echelons of society* **2.** MIL FORMATION WITH OFFSET POSITIONS a formation in which individuals or units are positioned behind and to one side of those in front to give a stepped effect and allow each a clear view ahead **3.** AIR FORCE AIRCRAFT FORMATION WITH OFFSET POSITIONS a group of aircraft flying in positions behind and to one side of the aircraft in front **4.** PHYS DEVICE FOR STUDYING SPECTRA a series of glass plates of equal thickness arranged like steps, used in spectroscopy for studying the fine structure of spectral lines ■ *vti.* **(-loned, -lon·ing, -lons)** FORM AN ECHELON to arrange something in or form an echelon [Late 18thC. From French, "rung," formed from *échelle* "ladder," from Latin *scala* "stair."]

ech·e·ve·ri·a /èchə və reé ə/ *n.* a usually stemless plant that is native to tropical America and cultivated for its rosettes of fleshy leaves and its tubular or bell-shaped flowers. Genus: *Echeveria.* [Mid-19thC. From modern Latin, genus name, named for Atanasio *Echeverría*, a Mexican botanical illustrator.]

e·chid·na /i kídnə/ *n.* a spiny insect-eating mammal of Australia, Tasmania, and New Guinea, with a long snout and strong claws. Echidnas lay their eggs in burrows. Family: Tachyglossidae. [Mid-19thC. Via modern Latin, "viper," from Greek, from *ekhis* "viper."]

echin- *prefix.* = **echino-** (*used before vowels*)

ech·i·na·ce·a /èkə náyssee ə/ *n.* **1.** BOT = **coneflower 2.** HERBAL REMEDY an herbal remedy prepared from the pulverized leaves and stems of purple coneflowers, thought to bolster the immune system [Via modern Latin, genus name, from, ultimately, Greek *ekhinos* "hedgehog, sea urchin"]

ech·i·nate /ékə nàyt/, **echi·nat·ed** /-təd/ *adj.* used to describe plant and animal parts that have spines or similar outgrowths [Late 17thC. From Latin *echinatus*, from Greek *ekhinos* "hedgehog, sea urchin."]

e·chi·ni plural of **echinus**

echino- *prefix.* **1.** spine ○ *echinoderm* **2.** echinoderm ○ *echinoid* [From Latin *echinus* "sea urchin" (see ECHINUS)]

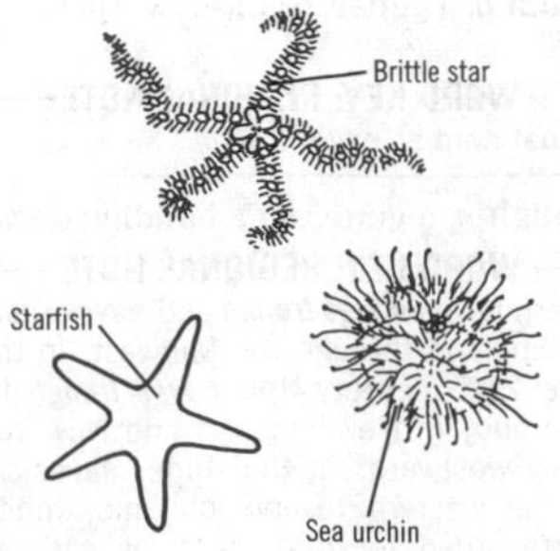

Echinoderm

e·chi·no·derm /i kīnə dùrm/ *n.* a marine invertebrate animal that has a radially symmetrical body, tube feet, and a system of calcareous plates under the skin. Starfish, sea urchins, sea lilies, and sea cucumbers are echinoderms. Phylum: Echinodermata. [Mid-19thC. Coined from ECHINO- + Greek *derma* "skin."] —**e·chi·no·der·mal** /i kīnə dúrməl/ *adj.* —**e·chi·no·der·ma·tous** /-təss/ *adj.*

e·chi·noid /i kī nòyd, ékə nòyd/ *n.* a marine invertebrate with a hard ovoid body and movable spines. Sea urchins and sand dollars are echinoids. Class: Echinoidea. —**e·chin·oid** *adj.*

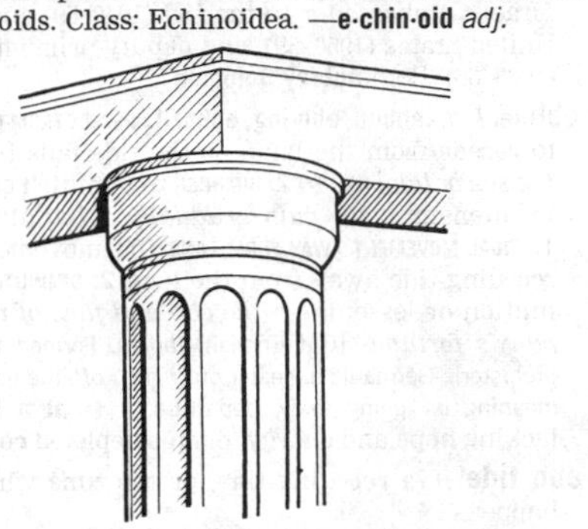
Echinus

e·chi·nus /i kīnəss/ (*plural* **-ni** /-nī/) *n.* **1.** ARCHIT ROUNDED MOLDING a rounded molding beneath the flat upper part (**abacus**) of a Doric or Tuscan column **2.** MARINE BIOL = **sea urchin** [14thC. Via Latin from Greek *ekhinos* "hedgehog, sea urchin."]

ech·i·um /ékee əm/ *n.* a plant of the borage family, native to Europe, western Asia, and Africa, that has oblong or lance-shaped leaves and spikes of funnel-shaped flowers. Genus: *Echium.* [Late 19thC. From modern Latin, genus name, formed from Greek *ekhis* "viper"; from the spotted markings on the plant's stem.]

ech·o /ékō/ *n.* (*plural* **-oes**) **1.** REPEATED SOUND the repetition of a sound caused by the reflection of sound waves from a surface **2.** SYMPATHETIC REACTION a reaction of agreement or sympathy ○ *Her songs found an echo in the hearts of thousands.* **3.** SOMETHING REPEATED something repeated or imitated rather than original ○ *echoes of the boss's ideas* **4.** REMINDER something that looks back to an earlier period or is reminiscent of it ○ *the current style with its echoes of the 1920s* **5.** EFFECT a lingering effect of an earlier event **6.** IMITATOR somebody who imitates another, especially in slavish repetition of his or her opinions (*literary*) **7.** PHYS RETURNED SIGNAL the signal reflected by an object struck by a radar transmission, or the image of this on a radar screen **8.** LITERAT REPETITION OF SOUNDS the repetition of sounds within a sequence of verse or prose **9.** MUSIC REPEATED MUSIC the repetition, usually quieter, of a phrase or note in music **10.** MUSIC ELECTRONIC SOUND REPETITION the repetition of sound created electronically for effect or by accident ○ *The echo on the guitar riff was added in the studio.* **11.** MUSIC ORGAN CONTROL a device on some organs that gives the effect of an echo coming from a distance ■ *v.* **(-oed, -o·ing, -oes) 1.** *vt.* MAKE SOMETHING REPEAT to make a sound repeat by the reflection of sound waves ○ *The surrounding peaks echoed the eagle's cry.* **2.** *vt.* REPEAT to repeat a statement or opinion, especially in agreement or imitation ○ *The completed report echoed the initial assessment.* **3.** *vt.* IMITATE to imitate or incorporate elements of something earlier ○ *The building's design echoes the surrounding brownstone rowhouses.* **4.** *vi.* RESOUND to resound by the reflection of sound waves ○ *Their footsteps echoed down the tunnel.* **5.** *vi.* BE FULL OF SOUND to be full of echoes of a sound ○ *The auditorium echoed with cheering.* **6.** *vt.* COMPUT DISPLAY AS A CHECK to return a character back to its source after a computer or communications device receives it, as an accuracy check. A common example is when a character is displayed on a computer monitor after it has been entered from a keyboard. [14thC. Via Old French or Latin from Greek *ēkhō* "echo," also the mythological Echo, who faded away for love of Narcissus until only her voice remained.]

Ech·o *n.* a code word for the letter "E," used in international radio communications

ech·o·car·di·o·gram /èkō kaárdee əgràm/ *n.* the visual record produced by an echocardiograph

ech·o·car·di·o·graph /èkō kaárdee ə gràf/ *n.* an ultrasound device used to examine the working heart and display moving images of its action —**ech·o·car·di·o·graph·ic** /èkō kaardee ə gráffik/ *adj.* —**ech·o·car·di·o·graph·i·cal·ly** /-gráffikəlee/ *adv.* —**ech·o·car·di·og·ra·phy** /èkō kaardee óggrəfee/ *n.*

ech·o cham·ber *n.* a room with sound-reflecting walls, used in making acoustic measurements or generating sound effects

ech·o·en·ceph·a·lo·gram /èkō en séfələ gràm/ *n.* the visual record produced by an echoencephalograph

ech·o·en·ceph·a·lo·graph /èkō en séffələ gràf/ *n.* an ultrasound device used to examine the structures of the brain —**ech·o·en·ceph·a·lo·graph·ic** /èkō en seffələ gráffik/ *adj.* —**ech·o·en·ceph·a·lo·graph·ic·al·ly** /-gráffikəlee/ *adv.* —**ech·o·en·ceph·a·log·ra·phy** /èkō en seffə lóggrəfee/ *n.*

ech·o·gram /ékō gràm/ *n.* PHYS = **sonogram**

e·chog·ra·phy /e kóggrəfee/ *n.* PHYS = **ultrasonography**

e·cho·ic /e kō ik/ *adj.* **1.** OF OR LIKE AN ECHO resembling or relating to an echo **2.** POETRY = **onomatopoeic**

e·cho·ic mem·o·ry *n.* the ability to remember and reproduce a sound in the two or three seconds after it is heard

ech·o·ism /ékō ìzzəm/ *n.* **1.** POETRY = **onomatopoeia 2.** LING CHANGE OF VOWEL SOUND a process by which the sound of a vowel changes to imitate the sound of a preceding vowel

ech·o·la·li·a /èkō láylee ə/ *n.* the compulsive repetition of words spoken by somebody else, often a sign of psychiatric disorder

ech·o·lo·ca·tion /èkō lō káysh'n/ *n.* a means of locating an object using an emitted sound and the reflection back from it, used naturally by animals such as bats and electronically by humans

ech·o plate *n.* an electromechanical device used in broadcasting or recording to create the effect of reverberation or echo

ech·o·prax·i·a /èkō práksee ə/, **ech·o·prax·is** /-siss/ *n.* the compulsive imitation of the actions of others, often a sign of psychiatric disorder [Early 20thC. From modern Latin, formed from Greek *ēkhō* "echo" + *praxis* "action."]

ech·o quilt·ing *n.* a quilting stitch that follows the outlines of an appliquéd design

ech·o sound·er *n.* a device used to ascertain water depth or to locate underwater objects by measuring the time taken for emitted sound waves to return from the bottom or from the object

ech·o·vi·rus /ékō vīrəss/ *n.* a virus found in the gastrointestinal tract that belongs to a group of retroviruses associated with intestinal and respiratory infections and meningitis [Mid-20thC. *Echos* an acronym formed from *entericcytopathogenichuman orphan.*]

é·clair /ay kláir, áy klàir/ *n.* a long thin cream puff filled with whipped cream or custard and topped with chocolate frosting [Mid-19thC. From French, literally "lightning."]

é·clair·cisse·ment /ay klàirseess maáN/ *n.* a clearing up of something puzzling (*literary*) [Mid-17thC. From French, literally "clearing up."]

e·clamp·si·a /i klámpsee ə/ *n.* an illness that sometimes occurs during the later stages of pregnancy and involves high blood pressure and convulsions sometimes followed by a coma [Mid-19thC. Via modern Latin from French *éclampsie*, from Greek *eklampsis* "sudden development," from *eklampein* "to shine out."] —**e·clamp·tic** /i klámptik/ *adj.*

é·clat /ay klaá, áy klaà/ *n.* **1.** SUCCESS brilliant success ○ *The show came off with éclat.* **2.** DISPLAY ostentatious display (*literary*) **3.** RENOWN renown based on achievement (*literary*) [Late 17thC. From French, literally "splinter, fragment."]

e·clec·tic /i kléktik/ *adj.* **1.** CHOOSING FROM VARIOUS SOURCES choosing what is best or preferred from a variety of sources or styles ○ *an eclectic taste in music* **2.** VARIED made up of elements from various sources ○ *an eclectic collection of paintings* ■ *n.* ECLECTIC PERSON somebody who selects what is best or preferred from a variety of sources or styles [Late 17thC. From Greek *eklektikos*, literally "picking out, selecting," from *eklegein* "to pick out," from *legein* "to choose."] —**e·clec·ti·cal·ly** *adv.*

e·clec·ti·cism /i klékti sìzzəm/ *n.* the theory or use of an eclectic approach

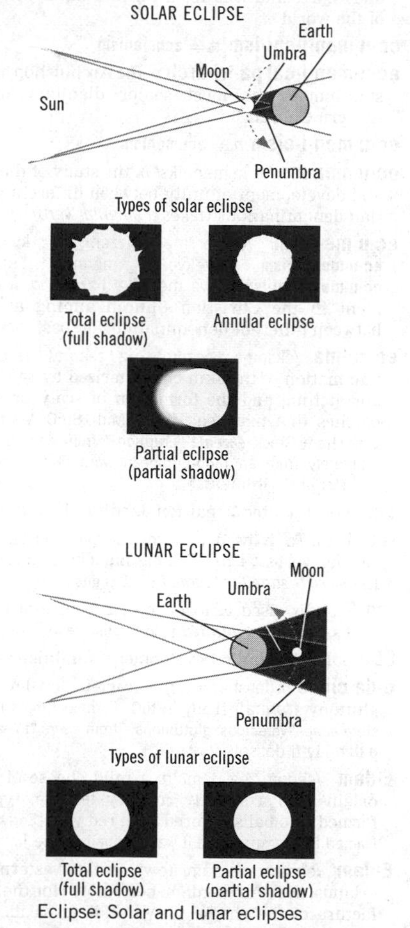

Eclipse: Solar and lunar eclipses

e·clipse /i klíps/ *n.* **1.** ASTRON OBSCURING OF A CELESTIAL BODY the partial or complete hiding from view of a celestial body, e.g., the Sun or Moon, when another celestial body comes between it and the observer **2.** LOSS OF LIGHT a loss or blocking of light **3.** DECLINE a loss of status, power, or favor ○ *the eclipse of supply-side economics* ■ *vt.* (**e·clipsed, e·clips·ing, e·clips·es**) **1.** ASTRON OBSCURE CELESTIAL BODY to cause a total or partial obscuring of another celestial body **2.** SHADOW to block the light falling on something, or cast a shadow on it **3.** OUTDO to outdo in achievement or become more powerful or popular than something or somebody ○ *a performance that eclipsed all the others* [13thC. Via Old French and Latin from Greek *ekleipsis*, from *ekleipein* "no longer to appear or be present," from *leipein* "to leave."] —**eclips·er** *n.*

e·clipse plum·age *n.* dull plumage grown for a short period by some birds, especially male ducks, after the brightly colored breeding plumage has been shed

e·clips·ing bi·na·ry, e·clips·ing var·i·a·ble *n.* a system in which one star's orbit periodically brings it between Earth and the other star of the pair

e·clip·tic /i klíptik/ *n.* PATH OF THE SUN'S ANNUAL MOTION the apparent path of the Sun's annual motion relative to the stars, shown as a circle passing through the center of the imaginary sphere (**celestial sphere**) containing all the celestial bodies ■ *adj.* OF AN ECLIPSE relating to, involving, or typical of an eclipse [14thC. Via Latin from, ultimately, Greek *ekleipein* (see ECLIPSE); from the fact that eclipses of the Sun or Moon can occur only when the Moon crosses the ecliptic.]

ec·logue /ék làwg, ék lòg/ *n.* a pastoral poem, usually in the form of a dialogue between shepherds [15thC. Via Latin *ecloga* from Greek *eklogē* "selection (of poems)," from *eklegein* (see ECLECTIC).]

e·clo·sion /i klṓzh'n/ *n.* the emergence of an insect from its pupal case, or the hatching of a larva from an egg [Late 19thC. From French *éclosion*, from *éclore* "to hatch, open," from, ultimately, Latin *excludere* "to hatch" (source of English *exclude*).]

Ec·o /ékō/, **Umberto** (*b.* 1932) Italian novelist and academic. He wrote the novels *The Name of the Rose* (1981) and *Foucault's Pendulum* (1989), and has written numerous critical works on literature and aesthetics.

eco- *prefix.* environment, ecology ○ *ecofriendly* [Shortened from ECOLOGY]

ec·o·ca·tas·tro·phe /ékō kə tástrəfee, éekō-/ *n.* an event, usually caused by human actions, that results in very severe damage to the environment

e·co·freak /ékō freek, éekō-/ *n.* somebody who is obsessed or preoccupied with the state of the environment (*slang insult*)

e·co·friend·ly /ékō fréndlee, éekō-/ *adj.* intended or perceived to have no harmful effect on the natural environment and its inhabitants

ecol. *abbr.* **1.** ecology **2.** ecological

E. coli *n.* a species of bacterium normally inhabiting the intestines of humans and other vertebrates, especially the colon, but commonly causing infection in other parts of the body. New and highly virulent strains of this bacterium that have recently evolved are particularly dangerous and can cause serious illness or death. Full form **Escherichia coli** [Late 20thC. Shortening of modern Latin *Escherichia coli*, named for the German physician T. *Escherich* (1857–1911). *Coli* "of the colon" was formed from Latin *colon* (see COLON).]

ec·o·log·i·cal /ékə lójjik'l, éekə-/, **ec·o·log·ic** /-lójjik/ *adj.* **1.** RELATING TO ORGANISMS AND THE ENVIRONMENT relating to the interrelationships of organisms and their environment **2.** ENVIRONMENTAL relating to the environment ○ *an ecological disaster* **3.** PROTECTIVE OF THE ENVIRONMENT concerned with the protection and preservation of the natural environment ○ *an ecological product* —**ec·o·log·i·cal·ly** *adv.*

e·col·o·gy /i kólləjee/ (*plural* **-gies**) *n.* **1.** STUDY OF ORGANISMS AND THE ENVIRONMENT the study of the relationships and interactions between living organisms and their natural or developed environment ○ *"A land ethic...should be as honest as Thoreau's Walden, and as comprehensive as the sensitive science of ecology."* (Stewart Udall, *The Quiet Crisis*; 1963) **2.** RELATIONSHIP BETWEEN AN ORGANISM AND THE ENVIRONMENT the relationships between individual organisms and between organisms and their environment **3.** = **human ecology** [Late 19thC. Coined from Greek *oikos* "house, habitation" + -LOGY.] —**e·col·o·gist** *n.*

econ. *abbr.* **1.** economy **2.** economics **3.** economist

e·con·o·met·rics /i kònnə méttriks/ *n.* the application of mathematical and statistical techniques to economic data and problems (*takes a singular verb*) —**e·con·o·met·ric** *adj.* —**e·con·o·met·ri·cal·ly** *adv.* —**e·con·o·me·tri·cian** /i kònnəmə trísh'n/ *n.*

ec·o·nom·ic /ékə nómmik, éekə-/ *adj.* **1.** OF ECONOMY OR ECONOMICS relating to economics, the economy of a country, or money in general **2.** PROFITABLE producing or capable of producing a profit **3.** MATERIAL relating to or affecting material goods and resources **4.** = **economical** *adj.* **3** [Late 16thC. Directly or via French from Latin *oeconomicus* from Greek *oikonomikos* from *oikonomos* (see ECONOMY).]

WORD KEY: USAGE

economic or **economical**? The adjective ***economic*** denotes economics or the economy, and is concerned with "aspects of the supply of goods and structure of wealth": *a Nobel Laureate's economic theories.* The adjective ***economical***, on the other hand, has to do with economy specifically in its senses "making the best and most frugal use of resources" and "inexpensiveness": *It is much more economical to buy in bulk. Public transportation is economical, compared with hiring a limousine.* But the two adjectives can overlap in one sense, "efficient in terms of contributing to thrift": *an economical* [*or economic*] *use of electricity.*

ec·o·nom·i·cal /ékə nómmik'l, éekə-/ *adj.* **1.** RESOURCEFULLY FRUGAL careful in making the best use of resources ○ *an economical cook* **2.** INEXPENSIVE costing relatively little in comparison with other things in the same class ○ *a home that's economical to run* **3.** EFFICIENT efficient in terms of avoiding unnecessary expenditure of time or energy ○ *an economical gesture*

WORD KEY: USAGE

See Usage note at ***economic.***

ec·o·nom·i·cal·ly /ékə nómmikəlee, éekə-/ *adv.* **1.** WITH REGARD TO ECONOMY OR ECONOMICS with regard to economics, the economy of a country, or financial matters in general ○ *economically and socially developing societies* **2.** PROFITABLY in such a way as to produce a profit **3.** FRUGALLY in a thrifty, sparing, or careful manner

ec·o·nom·ic de·ter·min·ism *n.* the belief that the economic organization of a society determines the nature of all other aspects of its life

ec·o·nom·ic ge·og·ra·phy *n.* a branch of geography that deals with the distribution and use of an area's economic resources

ec·o·nom·ic ge·ol·o·gy *n.* the study of geologic deposits from the viewpoint of their value as resources

ec·o·nom·ic in·di·ca·tor *n.* a quantity expressed statistically and taken as a measure of an economic variable

ec·o·nom·ic mi·grant *n.* somebody who travels or migrates to an area where work or a better standard of living is available, especially when this involves entering another country

ec·o·nom·ic rent *n.* a payment for use of a factor of production that is enough to make it profitable for the owner

ec·o·nom·ics /ékə nómmiks, éekə-/ *n.* **1.** STUDY OF GOODS AND SERVICES the study of the production, distribution, and consumption of goods and services (*takes a singular verb*) **2.** FINANCIAL ASPECTS the financial element of something (*takes a plural verb*) ○ *the economics of running a business* [Late 18thC. Probably from French *économique* + *-s*, based on the Latin plural *oeconomica*, translating Greek *ta oikonomika*, a treatise title on the duties of domestic life by Aristotle.]

ec·o·nom·ic un·ion *n.* a merging of the economies of two or more states to function as a unit that shares a common financial policy and currency

e·con·o·mism /i kónnə mìzzəm/ *n.* **1.** IMPORTANCE OF ECONOMICS the belief that economics is the most important element in a society **2.** IMPROVING OF LIVING STANDARDS the belief that bringing about an improvement in the living standards of its members is the chief goal of a political organization or labor union organization

e·con·o·mist /i kónnəmist/ *n.* **1.** SPECIALIST IN ECONOMICS somebody who studies, works, or is an expert in the field of economics **2.** FRUGAL PERSON a frugal person (*archaic*)

e·con·o·mist·ic /i kònnə místik/ *adj.* showing bias toward economic factors

e·con·o·mize /i kónnə mīz/ (**-mized, -miz·ing, -miz·es**) *vi.* to reduce expenditure, or use resources less wastefully ○ *We had to economize on fuel.* —**e·con·o·miz·er** *n.*

e·con·o·my /i kónnəmee/ *n.* (*plural* **-mies**) **1.** ECON FINANCIAL AFFAIRS the production and consumption of goods and services of a community regarded as a whole ○ *a gradual shift from an agricultural to an industrial economy* **2.** ECON THRIFT the prudent managing of resources to avoid extravagant expenditure or waste **3.** ECON, FIN SPARING USE a sparing, controlled, or efficient use of something ○ *a graceful economy of effort* **4.** SAVING a saving or attempt to reduce expenditure **5.** TRANSP = **economy class 6.** SYSTEM a system of interacting elements, especially when seen as being harmonious ○ *the economy of the natural world* **7.** HOUSEHOLD MANAGEMENT the management of a household (*archaic*) ■ *adj.* ECON, FIN CHEAPER intended to be cheaper or give better value [15thC. Via French or Latin from Greek *oikonomia*, from *oikonomos* "steward of a household," from *oikos* "house" + *nemein* "to manage" (source of English *antinomian* and *nomad*).]

e·con·o·my class *n.* a class of travel, especially on airlines, that is relatively low in price and caters for the majority of passengers

e·con·o·my class syn·drome *n.* thrombosis believed to be caused by a prolonged period of restricted movement and dehydration, such as occurs during air travel

e·con·o·my drive *n.* an organized attempt to reduce expenditure and waste

e·con·o·my of scale *n.* a reduction in unit cost achieved by increasing the amount of production

é·cor·ché /ày kawr sháy/ (*plural* **-chés**) *n.* an anatomical model of part or all of the human body with the skin removed, to allow study of the muscle structure [Mid-19thC. From French, the past participle of *écorcher* "to flay."]

ec·o·spe·cies /ékō spe̅e̅sheez, -seez, e̅e̅kō-/ (*plural* **-cies**) *n.* a species made up of several subgroups **(ecotypes)** and characterized by its ecological traits

ec·o·sphere /ékō sfe̅e̅r, e̅e̅kō-/ *n.* = **biosphere**

ec·o·sys·tem /ékō sìstəm, e̅e̅kō-/ *n.* a localized group of interdependent organisms together with the environment that they inhabit and depend on

ec·o·ter·ror·ism /ékō térrə rìzzəm, e̅e̅kō-/ *n.* the sabotage of the activities of individuals or corporations, e.g., industrial companies, considered to be polluting or destroying the natural environment —**ec·o·ter·ror·ist** *n.*

ec·o·tone /ékə tōn, e̅e̅kə tōn/ *n.* a zone of transition between two different ecosystems, e.g., where the sea meets the land [Early 20thC. Coined from ECO- + Greek *tonos* "tension."]

ec·o·tour·ism /ékō to͝or rìzzəm, e̅e̅kō-/ *n.* a form of tourism that strives to minimize ecological or other damage to areas visited for their natural or cultural interest

ec·o·tox·i·col·o·gy *n.* the study of how organisms are affected by chemicals released into the environment by human activities

ec·o·type /ékō tīp, e̅e̅kō-/ *n.* a subgroup of a species of plant or other organism whose members show genetically determined adaptations to certain environmental conditions in their habitat

ec·o·war·ri·or /ékō wàwree ər, e̅e̅kō-/ *n.* an activist who takes direct, often unlawful action on an environmental issue

ec·ru /é kro͞o, áy kro͞o/ *adj.* of a pale brown color, like unbleached linen [Mid-19thC. Via French, "raw, unbleached," from, ultimately, Latin *crudus* "raw" (source of English *crude*).] —**ec·ru** *n.*

ec·sta·sy /ékstəsee/ (*plural* **-sies**) *n.* **1. INTENSE DELIGHT** a feeling of intense delight **2. ecstasy, Ecstasy** DRUGS **ILLEGAL DRUG** a drug used illicitly as a stimulant and relaxer of inhibitions. Formula: $C_{11}H_{15}NO_2$. **3.** PSYCHOL **LOSS OF SELF-CONTROL** a mental state, usually caused by intense religious experience, sexual pleasure, or drugs, in which somebody is so dominated by an emotion that self-control and sometimes consciousness are lost **4. INTENSE FEELING OR ACTIVITY** a feeling or activity characterized by its extreme intensity ○ *an ecstasy of remorse* [14thC. Via Old French from, ultimately, Greek *ekstasis*, from *existanai* "to displace, drive out (of your mind)," from *histanai* "to put." The sense "delight" developed in the 17thC.]

WORD KEY: CULTURAL NOTE

The Ecstasy of St. Theresa, a sculpture by Italian artist Gianlorenzo Bernini (1645–52). An altarpiece in the Cornaro Chapel in the church of Santa Maria Della Vittoria in Rome, it depicts a vision experienced by the Spanish saint Theresa during which an angel pierced her heart with a golden arrow, causing pain but also intense religious rapture.

ec·stat·ic /ik státtik, ek-/ *adj.* **1. DELIGHTED** showing or feeling great pleasure or delight **2. DOMINATED BY EMOTION** completely dominated by an intense emotion ■ *n.* **SOMEBODY SUBJECT TO A TRANCE** somebody who undergoes spells of intense emotion —**ec·stat·i·cal·ly** *adv.*

ECT *abbr.* electroconvulsive therapy

ec·ta·si·a /ek táyzhə, -zhee ə/, **ec·ta·sis** /éktəssiss/ *n.* a swelling or dilation of a part of the body (*technical*) [Late 19thC. From modern Latin, from Greek *ektasis*, from *ekteinein* "to stretch out."]

ecto- *prefix.* external, outside ○ *ectotherm* [From Greek *ektos*, from *ek* "out" (see EXO-)]

ec·to·com·men·sal /éktə kə méns'l/ *n.* a harmless parasitic plant or animal that lives on the outer surface or skin of another organism

ec·to·derm /éktə dùrm/ *n.* the outermost of three cell layers of an embryo, from which the epidermis, nervous tissue, and sense organs develop

ec·to·gen·e·sis /èktō jénnəssiss/ *n.* the development of an organism in an artificial environment, outside the body in which it would normally be found

ec·tog·e·nous /ek tójjənəss/ *adj.* used to describe an organism, e.g., a parasitic bacterium, that grows or is able to grow outside the body of a host

ec·to·mere /éktə me̅e̅r/ *n.* a cell **(blastomere)** produced during the division of a fertilized egg that develops with others into the outer cell layer **(ectoderm)** of an embryo

ec·to·morph /éktə màwrf/ *n.* somebody belonging to a physiological type that is tall with long lean limbs. ◊ **endomorph, mesomorph** —**ec·to·mor·phic** /èktə máwrfik/ *adj.*

-ectomy *suffix.* surgical removal of a part of the body ○ *iridectomy* [From modern Latin *-ectomia*, literally "cutting out," from Greek *ek-* "out" + *-tomia* "-tomy"]

ec·to·par·a·site /èktə pérrə sīt/ *n.* a parasite that lives on the outside of its host, e.g., on the skin or in the hair. Fleas are ectoparasites. —**ec·to·par·a·sit·ic** /èktə perrə síttik/ *adj.* —**ec·to·par·a·sit·ism** /èktə pérrəssi tìzzəm/ *n.*

ec·to·phyte /éktə fīt/ *n.* a parasitic plant that lives on the outer surface of its host —**ec·to·phyt·ic** /èktə fíttik/ *adj.*

ec·to·pi·a /ek tōpee ə/ *n.* a change from the normal positioning of an organ or body part [Mid-19thC. From modern Latin, from Greek *ektopos* "out of place," from *topos* "place."]

ec·top·ic /ek tóppik/ *adj.* used to describe an organ or body part occurring in a position or form that is not usual or normal

ec·top·ic preg·nan·cy *n.* the development of a fertilized egg outside the womb, e.g., in a fallopian tube

ec·to·plasm /éktə plàzzəm/ *n.* **1.** CELL BIOL **OUTER LAYER OF CELL CONTENTS** the dense outer layer of the substance **(cytoplasm)** that surrounds the nucleus of a cell **2.** PARANORMAL **GHOSTLY SUBSTANCE** the substance believed by spiritualists to issue from a medium who is communicating with spirits —**ec·to·plas·mic** /èktə plázmik/ *adj.*

ec·to·therm /éktə thùrm/ *n.* an animal that maintains its body temperature by absorbing heat from its environment. All animals other than birds and mammals are ectotherms. ◊ **poikilotherm** [Mid-20thC. Coined from ECTO- + Greek *thermē* "heat."] —**ec·to·ther·mic** /èktə thúrmik/ *adj.*

ec·to·troph·ic /éktə tróffik/ *adj.* used to describe an association **(mycorrhiza)** between a fungus and the roots of a plant, in which the fungus obtains its nourishment by enveloping the roots in a sheath. ◊ **endotrophic**

é·cu /ay kyo͞o/ *n.* any one of several former French silver or gold coins [Late 16thC. Via French from Latin *scutum* "shield"; from the shield that was part of the design of such coins.]

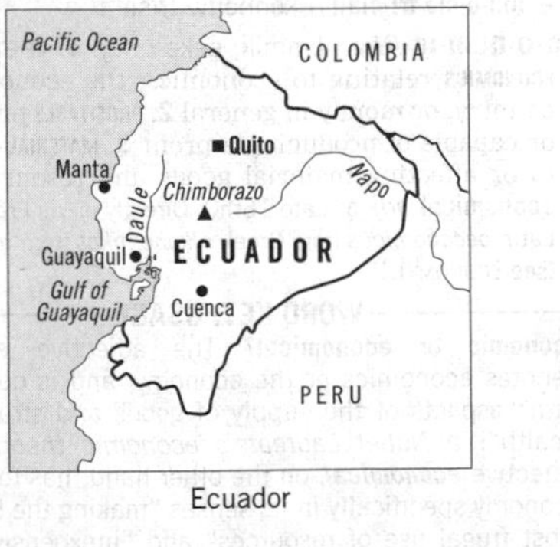

Ecuador

Ec·ua·dor /ékwə dàwr/ equatorial republic in northwestern South America, bounded on the north by Colombia, on the south and east by Peru, and on the west by the Pacific Ocean. Language: Spanish. Currency: sucre. Capital: Quito. Population: 12,105,124 (1997). Area: 107,037 sq. mi./272,045 sq. km. Official name **Republic of Ecuador** —**E·cua·dor·i·an** /èkwə dáwree ən/ *n.*, *adj.*

ec·u·men·i·cal /èkyə ménnik'l/, **ec·u·men·ic** /èkyə ménnik/ *adj.* **1.** CHR **CONCERNING CHURCH UNITY** relating to, involving, or promoting the unity of Christian Churches around the world **2. INVOLVING FRIENDSHIP BETWEEN RELIGIONS** involving or promoting friendly relations between different religions [Late 16thC. Formed from late Latin *oecumenicus* "general, universal," from Greek *oikoumenikos*, from *oikoumenē (gē)* "inhabited (world)," from *oikos* "house, habitation."] —**ec·u·men·i·cal·ly** *adv.*

ec·u·men·i·cal coun·cil *n.* a gathering of leaders and representatives from the Christian Churches of the world

ec·u·men·i·cal·ism *n.* = **ecumenism**

ec·u·men·i·cal pa·tri·arch *n.* the Archbishop of Constantinople, the most senior dignitary of the Eastern Church

ec·u·men·i·cism *n.* = **ecumenism**

ec·u·men·ics /èkyə ménniks/ *n.* the study of the goals and development of unity between different Christian denominations (*takes a singular verb*)

ec·u·me·nism /ékyə mə nìzzəm, i kyo͞omə-/, **ec·u·men·i·cism** /èkyə ménni sìzzəm/, **ec·u·men·i·cal·ism** /èkyə ménnikə lìzzəm/ *n.* a movement in the Christian Church aiming at unity between different denominations on basic issues

ec·ze·ma /éksəmə, égzəmə, ig ze̅e̅mə/ *n.* an inflammation of the skin characterized by reddening and itching and the formation of scaly or crusty patches that may leak fluid [Mid-18thC. Via modern Latin from Greek *ekzema* "eruption," from *zein* "to boil," ultimately from an Indo-European word that is also the ancestor of English *yeast*.]

ed. *abbr.* **1.** edited **2.** edition **3.** editor **4.** education

-ed 1 *suffix.* **1.** used to form the past participle of regular verbs ○ *wasted* **2.** having, characterized by, like ○ *redheaded* ○ *bigoted* [Old English *-ed, -od*]

-ed 2 *suffix.* used to form the past tense of regular verbs ○ *nicked* ○ *landed* [Old English *-ede, -ode*]

EDA *abbr.* Economic Development Administration

e·da·cious /i dáyshəss/ *adj.* voracious, or devoted to gluttony (*formal*) [Early 19thC. Formed from the Latin stem *edac-* "voracious, gluttonous," from *edere* "to eat."] —**e·dac·i·ty** /i dássətee/ *n.*

E·dam[1] /e̅e̅dəm, e̅e̅ dàm/ *n.* a mild cheese of Dutch origin with a slightly rubbery texture, typically formed into balls covered with red wax [Early 19thC. Named for EDAM[2], where it was originally made.]

E·dam[2] /e̅e̅dəm, e̅e̅ dàm/ town in the western Netherlands, near Amsterdam, best known for the manufacture of the cheese to which it gives its name. Population: 25,603 (1994).

e·daph·ic /i dáffik/ *adj.* ECOL used to describe the effect of soil characteristics, especially chemical or physical properties, on plants and animals [Late 19thC. Formed from Greek *edaphos* "floor, ground, soil."]

e·daph·ic cli·max *n.* a stable ecological community **(climax)** that results from the content or properties of the soil rather than the climate

Ed·berg /éd bùrg/, **Stefan** (*b.* 1966) Swedish tennis player. He progressed from a junior grand slam in 1983 to winning both Wimbledon and the U.S. Open singles championships (1988, 1990, 1991, and 1992).

Ed·da /éddə/ *n.* **1. 12THC NORSE POEM COLLECTION** a 12th-century collection of Old Norse poems **2. 13THC NORSE POEM COLLECTION** a 13th-century collection compiled by Snorri Sturluson containing Norse myths, poems, and a treatise on poetry [Late 17thC. Origin uncertain, probably from Old Norse *ō-r* "spirit, mind, passion, song, poetry."] —**Ed·dic** *adj.*

ed·do /éddō/ (*plural* **-does**) *n.* PLANTS = **taro** [Late 17thC. Of West African origin.]

ed·dy /éddee/ *n.* (*plural* **-dies**) **1. SMALL WHIRL** a movement in a flowing stream of liquid or gas in which the current doubles back to form a small whirl ○ *a pleasing pattern of eddies in the river* **2. DIVERGENCE** a relatively unimportant divergence from or movement contrary to the mainstream of something

○ *negotiated a few political eddies* ■ *vti.* **(-died, -dy·ing, -dies)** FLOW CONTRARY to flow or make something flow contrary to the main current ○ *He waded out, the stream eddying around his legs.* [15thC. Origin uncertain, perhaps from Old Norse *iða* "whirlpool," or from assumed Old English *edwæg*, literally "back wave."]

Ed·dy /éddee/, **Mary Baker** (1821–1910) U.S. religious leader. She founded the Church of Christ, Scientist, and the associated Christian Science movement, in Boston in 1879. Born **Mary Baker**

ed·dy cur·rent *n.* an electric current set up by an alternating magnetic field

Ed·dy·stone Rocks /édistən-/ dangerous rocks in the English Channel, near Plymouth, England. Four lighthouses have successively been built on or near the rocks since 1698.

Edelweiss

e·del·weiss /áyd'l vīss, -wīss/ *n.* a small plant with white woolly leaves and small flowers, native to the Alps and mountains of Asia. Latin name: *Leontopodium alpinum.* [Mid-19thC. From German, literally "noble white."]

e·de·ma /i deémə/ (*plural* **-mas** *or* **-ma·ta** /-mətə/) *n.* **1.** MED EXCESS FLUID an abnormal buildup of serous fluid between tissue cells **2.** BOT EXCESS FLUID IN PLANT an abnormal swelling in a plant, chiefly caused by a buildup of excess water [15thC. From Greek *oidēma* "swelling tumor," from *oidein* "to swell."] —**e·dem·a·tous** /i démmətəss, i deémətəss/ *adj.*

E·den /éed'n/ *n.* **1.** ADAM AND EVE'S GARDEN in the Bible, the garden where Adam and Eve first lived **2.** PERFECT PLACE any place seen as being perfect, highly pleasing, or happy ○ *The first explorers saw America as an Eden.* —**E·den·ic** /ee dénnik/ *adj.*

e·den·tate /ee dén tàyt/ *n.* any placental mammal found in tropical America that has few or no teeth. Sloths and armadillos are edentates. Order: Edentata. [Early 19thC. Via Latin *edentatus* from, ultimately, the stem *dent-* "tooth."]

e·den·tu·lous /ee dénchələss/, **e·den·tu·late** /-lət, -làyt/ *adj.* ZOOL, MED without any teeth [Early 18thC. From Latin *edentulus*, from the stem *dent-* "tooth."]

E·der·le /áydərlee/, **Gertrude Caroline** (*b.* 1906) U.S. swimmer. She became the first woman to swim across the English Channel (1926).

Ed·gar /édgər/ *n.* a small statuette awarded annually to authors for achievement in mystery fiction [Mid-20thC. Named for *Edgar* Allan Poe.]

edge /ej/ *n.* **1.** BORDER a line or area that is the outermost part or the part farthest away from the center of something ○ *a tablecloth with embroidered edges* **2.** PART ABOVE A DROP the area where land suddenly falls away steeply ○ *the cliff edge* **3.** BRINK OR THRESHOLD the point or moment just before a marked change or event ○ *on the edge of victory* **4.** MEETING SURFACES the line where two surfaces of something solid meet ○ *A cube has 6 faces and 12 edges.* **5.** SHARP SIDE the cutting side of a blade ○ *a razor's edge* **6.** SHARPNESS sharpness of a blade ○ *a knife with a fine edge* **7.** SHARP QUALITY a piercing, cutting, or wounding quality, e.g., of language or expression ○ *There was an unmistakable edge to her remarks.* **8.** VIGOR noticeable vigor and energy ○ *After the timeout there was a new edge to the team's play.* ■ *vi.* **(edged, edg·ing, edg·es)** MOVE GRADUALLY to move gradually sideways, or make something move in this direction by pushing it ○ *just room enough to edge through* ■ *n.* ADVANTAGE an advantage over, e.g., a competitor (*informal*) ■ *vt.* **(edged, edg·ing, edg·es) 1.** ADD A BORDER to add a border to something, especially a decorative one ○ *a handkerchief edged with lace* **2.** TRIM to cut, shape, or trim the border of something ○ *a tool for edging the lawn* **3.** SHARPEN to sharpen or give a sharp edge to a blade **4.** SKIING LEAN A SKI to lean a ski over so that its edge cuts the snow [Old English *ecg* "corner, edge, sword." Ultimately from an Indo-European base meaning "to be sharp or pointed," which also produced English *acid, acute, alacrity,* and *oxygen.*] ◇ **live on the edge** to be habitually in highly stressful and demanding situations, often involving physical risk and danger ◇ **on edge** in or into an irritated or nervous state ◇ **take the edge off something 1.** to reduce the intensity or strength of something ○ *the snack took the edge off my hunger* **2.** to do something that makes a tense situation less so

edge in *vt.* to accommodate with effort, e.g., because of lack of time, space, or opportunity ○ *edge in a swim after work*

edge out *vt.* **1.** MOVE OUT to move somebody or something gradually out of position ○ *trying to edge him out of the presidency* **2.** DEFEAT to defeat a competitor by a narrow margin (*informal*) ○ *She was edged out of the championship.*

edge cit·y[1] *n.* a highly urbanized, yet officially unincorporated, community adjacent to a major established city, with residences, varied businesses, entertainment districts, and large shopping areas (*informal*) ○ *"Edge City... is the creation of a new world, being shaped by the free in a constantly reinvented land."* (Joel Garreau, *Washington Post*; September 19, 1991) [Late 20thC. Coined by Joel *Garreau*, author of *Edge City on the New Frontier.*]

edge cit·y[2] *n.* a state of great psychological or physical danger (*slang*) [Perhaps modeled on the idea of *fat city* or *city* as used with various modifiers or attributives such as *car* and *sin*]

edg·er /éjjər/ *n.* somebody who or something that edges something, especially a gardening tool for edging

edge tool *n.* an implement that has at least one cutting edge

Edge·wa·ter /éj wàwtər, -wòttər/ **1.** town in central Colorado, west of Denver. Population: 4,613 (1990). **2.** town in eastern Florida. Population: 15,337 (1990). **3.** borough in northeastern New Jersey, situated on the Hudson River. Population: 5,001 (1990).

edge·wise /éj wīz/ *adv., adj.* with the edge or side leading or forward ○ *fit in edgewise* ○ *with an edgewise motion* ◇ **get a word in edgewise** to succeed in speaking when other people are talking nonstop (*usually used in negative statements*)

Edge·wood /éj wŏŏd/ **1.** city in northern Kentucky. Population: 8,143 (1990). **2.** town in northeastern Maryland, northeast of Baltimore. Population: 23,903 (1990). **3.** borough in southwestern Pennsylvania, east of Pittsburgh. Population: 3,581 (1990).

edg·ing /éjjing/ *n.* **1.** BORDER something used as a border or trim, usually for decoration or protection **2.** FORMING OF AN EDGE the formation of an edge ■ *adj.* USED TO FORM EDGES used in forming an edge

edg·y /éjjee/ **(-i·er, -i·est)** *adj.* **1.** ON EDGE nervous and irritable **2.** INTENSE having an intense or energetic quality or atmosphere ○ *an edgy neighborhood* **3.** STYLISH unusually smart or stylish ○ *edgy clothes* —**edg·i·ly** *adv.* —**edg·i·ness** *n.*

edh /eth/ (*plural* **edhs**), **eth** (*plural* **eths**) *n.* a printed or written character (ð) used in the runic alphabet and in modern phonetics to represent the "th" sound in the English words "this" and "other" [Mid-19thC. From Danish, perhaps originally representing the sound of the letter.]

ed·i·ble /éddib'l/ *adj.* ABLE TO BE EATEN able to be eaten by human beings, or fit or suitable for eating ■ **ed·i·bles** *npl.* FOOD things to eat [Early 17thC. From Latin *edibilis* "eatable," from *edere* "to eat" (source of English *obese*).] —**ed·i·bil·i·ty** /èddi bíllətee/ *n.* —**ed·i·ble·ness** /éddib'lnəss/ *n.*

e·dict /ée dìkt/ *n.* **1.** DECREE a formal proclamation, especially one issued by a government, ruler, or other authority **2.** AUTHORITATIVE COMMAND a formal or authoritative command [15thC. From Latin *edictum*, from the past participle of *edicere* "to proclaim," from *dicere* "to say."]

ed·i·fi·ca·tion /èddəfi káysh'n/ *n.* instruction or enlightenment, especially when it is morally or spiritually uplifting

ed·i·fice /éddəfiss/ *n.* **1.** BUILDING a building, especially a large or impressive one **2.** STRUCTURE a large or complex structure or organization ○ *the edifice of government* [14thC. Via French from Latin *aedificium*, from *aedificare* "to build" (see EDIFY).]

ed·i·fy /éddə fī/ **(-fied, -fy·ing, -fies)** *vt.* to improve the morals or knowledge of somebody [14thC. Via French *édifier* from Latin *aedificare* "to build, construct," later "to instruct," from *aedis* "building, temple" + *facere* "to make."] —**ed·i·fi·er** *n.*

ed·i·fy·ing /éddə fī ing/ *adj.* providing morally useful knowledge or information

Ed·in·burgh /éd'nbərə, éd'n bùr ə/ capital city of Scotland, situated on the southern shore of the Firth of Forth. It is home to a cathedral, a castle, the royal Palace of Holyroodhouse, three universities, and the headquarters of the Scottish Assembly. Population: 447,600 (1995).

Ed·in·burgh, Duke of ➧ **Prince Philip**

E·dir·ne /e dérnə/ city of northwestern Turkey, northwest of Istanbul. Population: 102,300 (1990).

Ed·i·son /éddiss'n/ town in central New Jersey, southwest of Elizabeth. Population: 88,680 (1990).

Library of Congress

Thomas Alva Edison

Ed·i·son, Thomas Alva (1847–1931) U.S. inventor. He invented the light bulb, the microphone (1877), and the phonograph (1877), and many other devices.

ed·it /éddit/ *vt.* **(-it·ed, -it·ing, -its) 1.** PUBL PREPARE FOR PUBLICATION to prepare a text for publication by correcting errors and ensuring clarity and accuracy **2.** PUBL DECIDE THE CONTENT OF A PUBLICATION to be in overall charge of the publication of a newspaper or magazine **3.** BROADCAST DECIDE THE CONTENT OF A PROGRAM to be in overall charge of the content of a broadcast program **4.** CINEMA CUT A MOVIE OR TAPE to cut and arrange a movie or recording, deciding its final order and content ○ *The show was edited down from hours of live recording.* **5.** PUBL, BROADCAST CUT MATERIAL to remove material from something, such as a publication or broadcast item, e.g., because it is lengthy or offensive ■ *n.* PUBL EDITING the preparation of a text for publication or release, or a stage in this process ○ *Look out for errors missed in the first edit.* [Late 18thC. Back-formation from EDITOR.]

edit out *vt.* to delete or remove an unwanted part of a text, movie, or recording ○ *Her walk-on part was eventually edited out.*

edit. *abbr.* **1.** edited **2.** edition **3.** editor

ed·it·ed /éddited/ *adj.* **1.** READY TO PUBLISH prepared for publication, broadcast, or release by having errors corrected and other refinements made **2.** WITH UNWANTED PARTS REMOVED used to describe something such as a text or broadcast that has had unwanted material removed ○ *an edited version of the original movie*

e·di·tion /i dísh'n/ *n.* **1.** PUBL PRINTED VERSION one version of a publication issued serially, periodically, or in multiple formats ○ *the morning edition of the newspaper* **2.** BROADCAST BROADCAST VERSION a version or installment of a broadcast for a particular time or purpose ○ *last week's edition of the show* **3.** PRINTING PRINTED BATCH a batch of identical copies of a publication all printed at the same time **4.** BATCH OF ITEMS a batch or number of items all produced at the same time **5.** SIMILAR THING a version or copy of something [15thC. From the Latin stem *edition-*, from *edit-*, the past participle stem of *edere* "to give out," from *dare* "to give."]

e·di·ti·o prin·ceps /i dìshee ō prín sèps/ (*plural* **e·di·ti·o·nes prin·ci·pes** /i dishee ōneez prínsə peez/) *n.* the first printed edition of a piece of writing (*literary*) [From modern Latin, literally "first edition"]

ed·i·tor /éddìtər/ *n.* **1.** PUBL **PUBLISHING SUPERVISOR** somebody who is in overall charge of the publication of a book, newspaper, or magazine **2.** PUBL **CHIEF JOURNALIST** somebody who is in charge of a particular part of a newspaper or magazine **3.** PUBL **TEXT CORRECTOR** somebody who prepares a text for publication by correcting errors and improving accuracy and clarity **4.** BROADCAST **SOMEBODY CONTROLLING PROGRAM CONTENT** somebody who is in overall charge of the content of a broadcast program **5.** CINEMA **SOMEBODY WHO EDITS FILM** somebody who prepares the final version of a movie, deciding its length and the order of shots and scenes **6.** COMPUT = **text editor** [Mid-17thC. From late Latin, "producer, publisher," from the Latin stem *edit-* (see EDITION).] —**ed·i·tor·ship** *n.*

ed·i·to·ri·al /èddi táwree əl/ *adj.* PUBL, BROADCAST **OF EDITING** relating to, involving, or concerned with the editing of something such as a text or broadcast ○ *made lots of editorial comments in the margins* ■ *n.* PUBL **OPINION PIECE** an article in a newspaper or magazine that expresses the opinion of its editor or publisher —**ed·i·to·ri·al·ist** *n.* —**ed·i·to·ri·al·ly** *adv.*

ed·i·to·ri·al·ize /èddi táwree ə̀lìz/ (**-ized, -iz·ing, -iz·es**) *vi.* **1.** PUBL **WRITE EDITORIALS** to express an opinion or view in an editorial **2. WRITE SUBJECTIVELY** to introduce personal opinions or views, especially inappropriately ○ *He couldn't resist the opportunity, when reporting on a burglary, to editorialize on security systems.*

ed·i·tor in chief (*plural* **ed·i·tors in chief**) *n.* the executive editor of a publication, publishing house, or set of publications

Ed.M. *abbr.* Master of Education [Latin, *Educationis Magister*]

Ed·monds /édməndz/ city in northwestern Washington State, north of Seattle. Population: 30,744 (1990).

Ed·mon·ton /édməntən/ capital city of Alberta, Canada, located in the center of the province, on the North Saskatchewan River. Population: 862,597 (1996).

Ed·mund /édmənd/, **St. and King of East Anglia** (841?–870). After defeat in battle by the Danes, he is said to have been martyred for refusing to deny Christianity.

Ed·mund I, King of the English (921–946). He made war on the Vikings, expelling them from England, and carried out legal reforms.

Ed·mund II, King of the English (981?–1016). He reigned for only a few months in 1016, until defeated in battle by Canute. He was allowed to keep control of the south of England, but died a month later. Known as **Edmund Ironside**

Ed·munds·ton /édməndstən/ city in northwestern New Brunswick, Canada, across the U.S.-Canadian border from Maine. Population: 11,033 (1996).

E·dom·ite /éedə mìt/ *n.* **1.** PEOPLES **SOMEBODY FROM EDOM** a member of an ancient ethnic group who lived in the kingdom of Edom in pre-Christian times and who were noted for their longstanding hostility toward the Israelites **2.** LANG **EXTINCT LANGUAGE** an extinct language formerly spoken in the ancient kingdom of Edom in the Middle East. It is one of the Semitic group of Afro-Asian languages and is related to Hebrew. —**E·dom·it·ic** /èedə míttik/ *adj.*

EDP *abbr.* electronic data processing

EDT, E.D.T. *abbr.* Eastern Daylight Time

EDTA *n.* a colorless compound that reacts with metals and is used in food preservation, as an anticoagulant, and to treat lead poisoning. Formula: $C_{10}H_{16}N_2O_8$. Full form **ethylene diamine tetra-acetate**

edu *abbr.* educational institution (*used as an Internet suffix*)

educ. *abbr.* **1.** education **2.** educational

ed·u·ca·ble /éjjəkəb'l/, **ed·u·cat·a·ble** /éjjə káytəb'l/ *adj.* able to learn or be taught [Mid-19thC. Formed from EDUCATE.] —**ed·u·ca·bil·i·ty** /èjjəkə bíllətee/ *n.*

ed·u·cate /éjjə kàyt/ (**-cat·ed, -cat·ing, -cates**) *v.* **1.** *vti.* **TEACH** to give knowledge to or develop the abilities of somebody by teaching ○ *educated at a public school* **2.** *vt.* **ARRANGE SCHOOLING** to arrange schooling for somebody ○ *They educated their daughters* **3.** *vt.* **DEVELOP** to develop or improve a faculty or sense **4.** *vt.* **TRAIN** to train or instruct somebody in a particular field [15thC. From Latin *educat-*, the past participle stem of *educare* "to bring up, rear," related to *educere* "to lead out," from *ducere* "to lead."]

WORD KEY: SYNONYMS

See Synonyms at ***teach.***

ed·u·cat·ed /éjjə kàytəd/ *adj.* **1. WELL TAUGHT** having had a good education ○ *This is the writing of an educated person.* **2. CULTURED** showing good taste, expert knowledge, or cultivation ○ *cast an educated eye over the antiques* **3. KNOWLEDGEABLE** having the benefit of experience or knowledge

ed·u·cat·ed guess *n.* a guess that is based on a degree of experience, knowledge, or information

ed·u·ca·tion /èjjə káysh'n/ *n.* **1. EDUCATING** the imparting and acquiring of knowledge through teaching and learning, especially at a school or similar institution ○ *"After all, what is education but a process by which a person begins to learn how to learn?"* (Peter Ustinov, *Dear Me*; 1977) **2. KNOWLEDGE** the knowledge or abilities gained through being educated **3. INSTRUCTION** training and instruction in a particular subject, e.g., health matters **4. LEARNING EXPERIENCE** an informative experience ○ *Spending a weekend in their house was a real education.* **5. STUDY OF TEACHING** the study of the theories and practices of teaching ○ *a degree in education* **6. SYSTEM FOR EDUCATING PEOPLE** the system of educating people in a community or society ○ *jobs in education*

ed·u·ca·tion·al /èjjə káyshən'l, -shnəl/ *adj.* **1. INSTRUCTIVE OR INFORMATIVE** giving knowledge, instruction, or information **2. RELATING TO TEACHING AND LEARNING** relating to, involving, or concerned with education —**ed·u·ca·tion·al·ly** *adv.*

ed·u·ca·tion·al·ist /èjjə káyshən'list, -shnəlist/, **ed·u·ca·tion·ist** /-shnist/ *n.* an expert in the theories or administration of education

ed·u·ca·tion·al psy·chol·o·gy *n.* a branch of applied psychology that studies children in an educational setting and is concerned with the assessment of ability and aptitude and the evaluation of teaching and learning methods. Educational psychologists also deal with problems experienced by some children at school and in other learning situations. —**ed·u·ca·tion·al psy·chol·o·gist** *n.*

ed·u·ca·tion·ist *n.* **1.** = **educationalist 2. EDUCATIONAL THEORIST** somebody who espouses and propounds educational theories (*disapproving*)

ed·u·ca·tive /éjjə kàytiv/ *adj.* giving or concerned with education

ed·u·ca·tor /éjjə kàytər/ *n.* **1. SOMEBODY WHO EDUCATES** a professional teacher **2. SPECIALIST IN EDUCATION** an expert in the theories or administration of education

ed·u·ca·tor·y /éjjəkə tàwree/ *adj.* giving or concerned with education

e·duce /i dóoss/ (**e·duced, e·duc·ing, e·duc·es**) *vt.* (*formal*) **1. ELICIT** to elicit or derive something, e.g., a conclusion **2. DEVELOP** to make something latent develop or appear [15thC. From Latin *educere* "to lead out," from *ducere* "to lead."]

e·duct /ée dùkt/ *n.* a substance extracted from another substance without chemical alteration [Late 17thC. From Latin *eductum*, from the past participle of *educere* (see EDUCE).]

e·duc·tion /i dúkshən/ *n.* **1. DERIVATION** the derivation or development of something, or something derived or developed (*formal*) **2.** TECH **EXHAUST OF AN ENGINE** the exhaust of an engine, especially an internal-combustion or steam engine (*technical*) [Mid-17thC. From the Latin stem *eduction-*, from *educere* (see EDUCE).]

e·dul·co·rate /i dúlkə ràyt/ (**-rat·ed, -rat·ing, -rates**) *vt.* to remove soluble impurities from something by washing (*technical*) [Mid-17thC. From medieval Latin *edulcorat-*, the past participle stem of *edulcorare* "to sweeten," from Latin *dulcis* "sweet."]

ed·u·tain·ment /èjjə táynmənt/ *n.* television programs, computer software, or other media content intended to entertain and educate the user at the same time [Late 20thC. A blend of EDUCATION and ENTERTAINMENT.]

Ed·ward I /éd wərd/, **King of England** (1239–1307). His reign (1272–1307) was marked by the development of parliamentary government and by conflicts with the Welsh, the Scots, and France. Known as **Edward Longshanks**

Ed·ward II, King of England (1284–1327). Defeated by the Scots at the Battle of Bannockburn in 1314, his reign (1307–27) ended in his forced abdication and murder. He was the first future king to be styled Prince of Wales (1301). Known as **Edward of Caernarvon**

Ed·ward III, King of England (1312–77). He ruled from 1327 until 1377. Through his mother, Isabella of France, he claimed the French throne, starting the Hundred Years War.

Ed·ward IV, King of England (1442–83). As an outcome of the Wars of the Roses (1455–85), he became the first king of the House of York (1461–83). He was briefly deposed in 1470–71 by Lancastrian supporters of Henry VI.

Ed·ward V, King of England (1470–83?). On his accession in 1483, he was imprisoned by the future Richard III in the Tower of London and is thought to have been assassinated. With his brother he is often referred to as one of the "Princes in the Tower."

Ed·ward VI, King of England (1537–53). He was the son of Henry VIII and Jane Seymour. His reign (1547–53) saw rapid advancement of Protestantism in England.

Ed·ward VII, King of the United Kingdom (1841–1910). Son of Queen Victoria, he was an avid sportsman and traveler, promoting good relations abroad. His reign (1901–10) is known as the Edwardian period.

Ed·ward VIII, King of the United Kingdom (1894–1972). His brief reign (January-December 1936) ended in abdication after the British Government refused to agree to his marrying U.S. divorcée Wallis Simpson.

Ed·ward (the Con·fes·sor), St. and King of the English (1002?–66). He was canonized in 1161, but his reign (1042–66) was troubled by political conflict between Norman and English groups.

Ed·ward (the Mar·tyr), St. and King of the English (963?–978). He reigned from 975. His murder in 978 was possibly at the instigation of his stepmother Elfrida.

Ed·ward, Lake lake in east central Africa straddling the border between the Democratic Republic of Congo and Uganda. Area: 830 sq. mi./2,150 sq. km.

Ed·ward·i·an /ed wáwrdee ən, ed waárdee ən/ *adj.* **OF THE REIGN OF EDWARD VII** relating to, belonging to, or typical of British society during the reign of Edward VII in the first decade of the 20th century ■ *n.* **SOMEBODY OF OR STUDYING THE EDWARDIAN ERA** somebody who was alive or active during the reign of Edward VII or who is a specialist in this period of history

Ed·wards /éddwərdz/, **Jonathan** (1703–58) American colonial theologian and clergyman. A stern Calvinist, he was a leading figure in the religious revival known as the Great Awakening.

e.e. *abbr.* errors excepted

E.E. *abbr.* **1.** electrical engineer **2.** electrical engineering

-ee[1] *suffix.* **1.** one who receives or benefits from an action ○ *consignee* **2.** one who receives a thing ○ *biographee* **3.** one who performs an action ○ *attendee* [Via Anglo-Norman from, ultimately, Latin *-atus*]

-ee[2] *suffix.* **1.** one that resembles ○ *coatee* **2.** a kind of, especially a small one ○ *vestee* **3.** one connected with ○ *bargee* [Variant of -Y]

E.E. & M.P. *abbr.* Envoy Extraordinary and Minister Plenipotentiary

EEC *abbr.* HIST European Economic Community

EEG *abbr.* **1.** echoencephalograph **2.** electroencephalogram **3.** electroencephalograph

eel /eel/ (*plural* **eels** *or* **eel**) *n.* **1. LONG THIN FISH** a fish that has a long thin body resembling that of a snake, smooth skin without scales, and reduced fins. Most eels live in shallow marine waters. Order: Apodes. **2. FISH RESEMBLING AN EEL** any fish similar to a true eel in appearance, e.g., an electric eel [Old English *ǣl*, from a prehistoric Germanic word of unknown origin]

eel·grass /éel gràss/ *n.* **1. MARINE PLANT RESEMBLING GRASS** a perennial plant with long narrow dark green leaves that grows submerged in shallow seawater. Genus: *Zostera.* **2.** = **tape grass**

eel·pout /éel pòwt/ (*plural* **-pouts** *or* **-pout**) *n.* **1.** ZOOL **FISH RESEMBLING AN EEL** a marine fish with a long thin body like an eel. Family: Zoarcidae. **2.** = **burbot**

eel·worm /éel wùrm/ (*plural* **-worms** *or* **-worm**) *n.* ZOOL = **nematode**

e'en /een/ *n.* evening (*literary*) ■ *adv.* even (*literary*)

EEO *abbr.* equal employment opportunity

EEOC *abbr.* Equal Employment Opportunity Commission

e'er /air/ *adv.* ever (*literary*) [Late 16thC. Contraction.]

-eer *suffix.* a person engaged in or concerned with ○ *auctioneer* ○ *charioteer* [Via Old French *-ier* from, ultimately, Latin *-arius*]

ee·rie /éeree/ (**-ri·er, -ri·est**) *adj.* unnerving or unusual in a way that suggests a connection with the supernatural ○ *an eerie old house* [13thC. Probably from, ultimately, Old English *earg* "cowardly." Originally in Scottish and northern English meaning "fearful"; the sense "causing fear" developed in the 18thC, becoming standard in the 19thC.] —**ee·ri·ly** *adv.* —**ee·ri·ness** *n.*

eff. *abbr.* efficiency

ef·face /i fáyss/ (**-faced, -fac·ing, -fac·es**) *v.* **1.** *vt.* **RUB OUT** to remove or obliterate something by or as if by wearing away or rubbing out **2.** *vr.* **BEHAVE HUMBLY** to act in an inconspicuous manner, especially because of shyness or modesty [15thC. From French *effacer* "to wipe out, destroy," literally "to remove the face," from *face* "face, appearance."] —**ef·face·a·ble** *adj.* —**ef·face·ment** *n.* —**ef·fac·er** *n.*

ef·fect /i fékt/ *n.* **1. RESULT** a change or changed state occurring as a direct result of action by somebody or something else ○ *showing the effects of prolonged malnutrition* **2. POWER TO INFLUENCE** success in bringing about a change in somebody or something, or the ability to achieve this ○ *I've told her again and again, but it has no effect on her.* **3. BEING IN FORCE OR OPERATION** the state of being in force, in operation, or the case, often from a particular point in time ○ *The new law doesn't come into effect until next month.* **4. IMPRESSION** an impression produced in the mind of somebody who sees, hears, or reads something, especially one that is deliberately intended or engineered **5. CAUSE OR PRODUCTION OF AN IMPRESSION** something that produces an impression, or the actual process of causing a special feeling or impression ○ *a grand little speech made merely for effect* **6.** ARTS **SPECIAL SOUND, LIGHTING IN PLAY, MOVIE** something done to produce a desired response or to add to the realism or theatricality of a movie, play, or broadcast (*often used in the plural*) **7. MEANING OR INTENT** the intent or essential meaning conveyed, often in other words, by a statement, or words to that effect **8. SCIENTIFIC PHENOMENON** a scientifically observed and described phenomenon ■ **ef·fects** *npl.* **BELONGINGS** somebody's personal belongings, or the things that somebody is carrying about him or her (*formal*) ○ *Her personal effects consisted of not much more than the clothes on her back.* ■ *vt.* (**-fect·ed, -fect·ing, -fects**) **DO OR MAKE SOMETHING** to carry something out, or succeed in making or doing something (*formal*) ○ *They effected their escape through a rear window.* [14thC. Directly or via Old French from Latin *effectus*, from *efficere* "to accomplish," literally "to work out" (source of English *efficient*), from *facere* "to make or do."] —**ef·fect·er** *n.* —**ef·fect·i·ble** *adj.* ◇ **in effect** used to indicate that what is being said represents the truth of the matter, even though the words used may not be those that other people would choose ○ *In effect, this means that the program is shut down.*

WORD KEY: USAGE

See Usage note at ***affect.***

ef·fec·tive /i féktiv/ *adj.* **1. PRODUCING A RESULT** causing a result, especially the desired or intended result ○ *an effective remedy for headaches* **2. HAVING A STRIKING RESULT** successful, especially in producing a strong or favorable impression on people ○ *The painting had the characteristics of a winner, including effective color use.* **3. ACTUAL** actual or in practice, even if not officially or theoretically so ○ *he was effective ruler during the monarch's last illness* **4. OFFICIALLY IN FORCE** officially in force, operative, or applicable ○ *a regulation effective as from next month* **5. TRUE AS A RATE OF INTEREST** used to describe the true or actual rate of interest that is paid on an interest-bearing account ○ *The effective rate of interest will change next quarter.* **6.** MIL **READY FOR ACTION** fully equipped and ready for action ■ *n.* MIL **MILITARY PERSONNEL OR EQUIPMENT** a soldier, military unit, or piece of military equipment that is ready for action —**ef·fec·tive·ness** *n.* —**ef·fec·tiv·i·ty** /è fek tívvətee/ *n.*

WORD KEY: USAGE

effective, effectual, efficacious, or **efficient?** All these words are about having some kind of *effect.* The main difficulty is in choosing between ***effective*** and ***effectual.*** ***Effective*** means "having or producing the desired effect" and refers to what actually happens or what (on the basis of experience, for example) might be expected to happen: *Exercise is an effective way of keeping healthy.* ***Effectual*** is a more formal word and refers to potential capability rather than known performance: *Publicizing stringent penalties is an effectual deterrent against illegal parking.* ***Efficacious*** is also a more formal word, is applied only to things or processes and not to people, and refers to the power something has to produce a result: *Professional counseling proved more efficacious in the long term than medication.* ***Efficient*** has to do with the means or resources used in achieving a result in an economical manner: *efficient office communication procedures.* It also denotes the idea of being able to work directly to produce a given effect: *efficient causes of an early and highly successful space launch.*

WORD KEY: SYNONYMS

effective, efficient, effectual, efficacious

CORE MEANING: producing a result

effective suggesting the ability to produce the required result or the actual achievement of the result; **efficient** suggesting that something or somebody is capable of achieving the desired result with the minimum use of resources, time and effort; **effectual** a more formal word than "efficient" suggesting the achievement of a desired result, especially when this has already taken place; **efficacious** a formal word, used especially to suggest that something has the power to achieve the desired result.

ef·fec·tive·ly /i féktivlee/ *adv.* **1. WELL** in a way that produces a desired result **2. ESSENTIALLY** in fact or in practical terms, though not usually directly or technically ○ *She was effectively barred from seeking another position with the firm.*

ef·fec·tor /i féktər/ *n.* **1.** PHYSIOL **RESPONDING ORGAN OR MUSCLE** a body part, e.g., a muscle or organ, that is activated by a stimulus, particularly a nerve impulse **2. AGENT CAUSING AN EFFECT** a substance, procedure, or agent that produces an effect, e.g., a nerve ending activating a muscle or a molecule affecting enzyme activity

ef·fec·tu·al /i fékchoo əl/ *adj.* potentially successful in producing a desired or intended result (*formal*) [14thC. From medieval Latin *effectualis*, from Latin *effectus* (see EFFECT).] —**ef·fec·tu·al·i·ty** /i fèkchoo állətee/ *n.* —**ef·fec·tu·al·ly** /-əlee/ *adv.* —**ef·fec·tu·al·ness** /i fékchoo əlnəss/ *n.*

WORD KEY: USAGE

See Usage note at ***effective.***

ef·fec·tu·ate /i fékchoo àyt/ (**-at·ed, -at·ing, -ates**) *vt.* to do, cause, or accomplish something (*formal*) [Late 16thC. From medieval Latin *effectuat-*, past participle stem of *effectuare*, from Latin *effectus* (see EFFECT).] —**ef·fec·tu·a·tion** /i fèkchoo áysh'n/ *n.*

ef·fem·i·nate /i fémmənət/ *adj.* (*disapproving*) **1. LIKE A GIRL OR WOMAN** similar to or imitating a woman or girl, or the behavior, appearance, or speech traditionally associated with women and girls (*refers to men*) **2. OVERREFINED AND LACKING STRENGTH** weak through overrefinement or an absence of vigorous qualities [14thC. From Latin *effeminatus*, past participle of *effeminare* "to make feminine," from *femina* "woman" (source of English *feminine*).] —**ef·fem·i·na·cy** *n.* —**ef·fem·i·nate** *n.* —**ef·fem·i·nate·ly** *adv.* —**ef·fem·i·nate·ness** *n.*

ef·fen·di /i féndee/ (*plural* **-dis**) *n.* **1. IMPORTANT MAN** in Middle Eastern countries, an important or well-educated man **2. TITLE OF RESPECT** a title of respect that is the Turkish equivalent of such terms as "Mr." and "Sir." [Early 17thC. Via Turkish *efendi* from modern Greek *aphentēs*, from Greek *authentēs* "lord, master."]

ef·fer·ent /éffərənt/ *adj.* PHYSIOL conducting outward or directing away from an organ, especially the brain or spinal cord. ◊ **afferent** [Mid-19thC. From Latin *efferent-*, present participle stem of *efferre* "to bring out," from *ferre* "to bring or carry."] —**ef·fer·ent** *n.*

ef·fer·ent neu·ron *n.* ANAT = **motor neuron**

ef·fer·vesce /èffər véss/ (**-vesced, -vesc·ing, -vesc·es**) *vi.* **1. TO PRODUCE TINY GAS BUBBLES** to give off gas in small bubbles, often producing foam and a hissing sound (*refers to a liquid such as carbonated water or sparkling wine.*) **2. ESCAPE AS TINY BUBBLES** to be given off by a liquid in the form of small bubbles (*refers to gas*) **3. BE LIVELY OR EXCITED** to behave in a lively, high-spirited, or highly excited way [Early 18thC. From Latin *effervescere*, from *fervescere* "to come to the boil," from *fervere* "to be hot, to boil" (source of English *fervent*).] —**ef·fer·ves·cence** *n.*

ef·fer·vesc·ent /èffər véss'nt/ *adj.* **1. BUBBLY** producing gas in the form of tiny bubbles **2. VIVACIOUS** lively and excited —**ef·fer·vesc·ent·ly** *adv.*

ef·fete /i féet/ *adj.* **1. DECADENT** characterized by decadence, overrefinement, or overindulgence **2. WEAK** lacking or having lost the strength or ability to get things done (*archaic*) **3. BARREN** no longer able to reproduce [Early 17thC. From Latin *effetus* "worn out by bearing young," from *fetus* "breeding" (source of English *fetus*).] —**ef·fete·ly** *adv.* —**ef·fete·ness** *n.*

ef·fi·ca·cious /èffi káyshəss/ *adj.* having the power to produce the desired result, especially a cure or an improvement in somebody's physical condition (*formal*) [Early 16thC. From Latin *efficac-*, stem of *efficax*, from *efficere* (see EFFECT).] —**ef·fi·ca·cious·ly** *adv.* —**ef·fi·ca·cious·ness** *n.*

WORD KEY: USAGE

See Usage note at ***effective.***

ef·fi·ca·cy /éffikəsee/, **ef·fi·cac·i·ty** /èffi kássətee/ *n.* ability to produce the necessary or desired results [Early 16thC. From Latin *efficacia*, from *efficax* (see EFFICACIOUS).]

ef·fi·cien·cy /i fish'nsee/ (*plural* **-cies**) *n.* **1. COMPETENCE** the ability to do something well or achieve a desired result without wasted energy or effort, or the degree to which this ability is used **2.** TECH **MEASURE OF A MACHINE'S ENERGY EFFECTIVENESS** the ratio of the amount of energy used by a machine to the amount of work done by it. For example, the measurement of the amount of heat produced per unit of fuel when all of a fuel has been burned is a measure of a heating unit's efficiency. **3.** = **efficiency apartment**

ef·fi·cien·cy a·part·ment *n.* a small, usually furnished, apartment consisting of one room that includes kitchen facilities, and a bathroom

ef·fi·cien·cy ex·pert *n.* somebody who is proficient in increasing the productivity of a process, e.g., by eliminating waste or improving technology

ef·fi·cient /i fish'nt/ *adj.* **1. WELL-ORGANIZED** performing tasks in an organized and capable way **2. ABLE TO FUNCTION WITHOUT WASTE** able to function well or achieve a desired result without waste ○ *an efficient use of fuel* **3.** PHILOSOPHY **ACTING DIRECTLY TO PRODUCE AN EFFECT** acting directly to bring something into being or produce changes in it ○ *efficient cause* [14thC. From Latin *efficient-*, present participle stem of *efficere* (see EFFECT).] —**ef·fi·cient·ly** *adv.*

WORD KEY: USAGE

See Usage note at ***effective.***

ef·fi·gy /éffəjee/ (*plural* **-gies**) *n.* **1. DUMMY REPRESENTING SOMEBODY DISLIKED** a dummy, often roughly made and intentionally amusing or insulting, representing somebody or something disliked or despised **2. CARVING** a carved representation of somebody, used, e.g. as an architectural decoration or a monument [Mid-16thC. From Latin *effigies*, from *effingere* "to portray or form," from *fingere* "to fashion or shape."]

ef·flo·resce /èfflə réss/ (**-resced, -resc·ing, -resc·es**) *vi.* **1.** CHEM **LOSE WATER FROM CRYSTAL** to lose water (**water of crystallization**) from a crystal **2. BLOOM** to bloom or develop, like a flower coming into blossom (*literary*) **3. PRODUCE FINE POWDER** to become covered with a layer of fine powder **4.** CHEM **BECOME ENCRUSTED WITH POWDERY DEPOSIT** to become encrusted with a powdery deposit or crystals as a result of a process of chemical change or the evaporation of a solution [Late 18thC. From Latin *efflorescere*, from *florescere* "to come into flower," ultimately from *flos* "flower."]

ef·flo·res·cence /èfflə réss'ns/ *n.* **1.** CHEM **LOSS OF WATER FROM CRYSTAL** the loss of water (**water of crystallization**) from a crystal **2. UNFOLDING AND FLOURISHING** a process or time of development and unfolding, or the culmination of this (*literary*) **3.** GEOL **POWDERY SUBSTANCE ON ROCK SURFACE** a powdery substance that forms on the surface of some rocks —**ef·flo·res·cent** *adj.*

ef·flu·ence /éffloo əns/ *n.* **1. FLOWING OUT** the act or process of flowing out **2. SOMETHING THAT FLOWS OUT** something, often an immaterial substance or intangible influence, that flows out from a source (*literary*)

ef·flu·ent /éffloo ənt/ *n.* **1.** LIQUID WASTE liquid waste discharged from a sewage system, factory, nuclear power station, or other industrial plant **2.** STREAM OR RIVER a stream or river that flows out of a larger body of water such as a lake or a larger stream [15thC. From Latin *effluent-*, present participle stem of *effluere* "to flow out," from *fluere* "to flow" (source of English *fluent* and *fluid*).]

ef·flu·vi·um /i floovee əm, e-/ (*plural* **-a** /-ə/) *n.* an unpleasant smell or harmful fumes given off by something, usually waste or decaying matter (*often used in the plural*) [Mid-17thC. From Latin, formed from *effluere* (see EFFLUENT).] —**ef·flu·vi·al** *adj.*

ef·flux /é flùks/ *n.* **1.** INSTANCE OR ACT OF FLOWING OUT the act or process of flowing out **2.** SOMETHING THAT FLOWS OUT something that flows out of something else (*formal*) **3.** PASSING AWAY OF SOMETHING a passing away of something, e.g., time (*formal*) [Mid-16thC. From medieval Latin *effluxus*, from Latin *efflux-*, past participle stem of *effluere* (see EFFLUENT).] —**ef·flux·ion** /i flúkshən, e-/ *n.*

ef·fort /éffərt/ *n.* **1.** ENERGY OR EXERTION mental or physical energy that is exerted in order to achieve a purpose ○ *I wish they'd put a little more effort into it.* **2.** USE OF PHYSICAL OR MENTAL ENERGY the use of physical or mental energy, often in considerable quantities, in order to achieve a particular goal or overcome a particular difficulty ○ *With an effort, he managed to get himself out of the bed.* **3.** ATTEMPT an attempt to do something, especially one that involves a considerable amount of exertion, work, or determination ○ *He can at last make an effort to improve things.* **4.** SOMETHING DONE something that somebody has made or done, especially for the first time ○ *It's not bad for a first effort.* **5.** PHYS APPLIED FORCE the force (**input force**) applied to a simple machine that produces an effect (**output force**) on the load [15thC. From French, formed from Old French *esforcier* "to exert power," ultimately from Latin *fortis* "strong."] —**ef·fort·ful** *adj.* —**ef·fort·ful·ly** *adv.*

ef·fort·less /éffərtləss/ *adj.* involving or appearing to involve little or no effort —**ef·fort·less·ly** *adv.* —**ef·fort·less·ness** *n.*

ef·front·er·y /ə frúntəree/ (*plural* **-ies**) *n.* behavior or an attitude that is so bold or arrogant as to be insulting [Late 17thC. Via French *effronterie* from, ultimately, late Latin *effrons* "barefaced," from *frons* "forehead."]

ef·ful·gence /i fóoljəns, i fúljəns/ *n.* brightness or a brilliant light radiating from something (*literary*) [Mid-17thC. From late Latin *effulgentia*, from Latin *effulgere* "to shine brightly," from *fulgere* "to shine."] —**ef·ful·gent** *adj.*

ef·fuse *v.* /i fyóoz/ (**-fused, -fus·ing, -fus·es**) **1.** *vti.* POUR OUT to flow out, or produce a flow of something such as a liquid, gas, or light (*formal*) **2.** *vi.* RADIATE to spread out or radiate from something ■ *adj.* /i fyóoss/ BOT IRREGULARLY SPREAD tending to spread loosely or irregularly ○ *effuse lichens* [15thC. From Latin *effus-*, past participle stem of *effundere* "to pour out," from *fundere* "to pour" (source of English *futile*).]

ef·fu·sion /i fyóozh'n/ *n.* **1.** UNRESTRAINED OUTPOURING OF FEELINGS an extravagant and sometimes excessive expression of feelings in speech or writing **2.** ACT OF POURING OUT the pouring out of something such as a liquid or light **3.** SOMETHING POURED OUT something, e.g., a liquid, that is poured out **4.** MED MOVEMENT OF BODY FLUIDS the oozing of fluids from blood or lymph vessels into body cavities or intercellular tissue spaces as a result of inflammation, or the presence of excess blood or tissue fluid **5.** PHYS FLOW OF GAS THROUGH A SMALL APERTURE the flow of a gas through a small aperture under pressure, particularly when the aperture is so small that the distance between molecules is significant. The relative rates of effusion of gases are inversely proportional to the square roots of their densities in such a case.

ef·fu·sive /i fyóossiv/ *adj.* giving or involving an extravagant and sometimes excessive expression of feelings in writing or speech ○ *effusive thanks* —**ef·fu·sive·ly** *adv.*

Ef·ik /éffik/ (*plural* **-ik** *or* **-iks**) *n.* **1.** PEOPLES MEMBER OF A NIGERIAN PEOPLE a member of an Ibibio people who live in southeastern Nigeria **2.** LANG LANGUAGE SPOKEN IN PARTS OF NIGERIA a language spoken in parts of Nigeria that is one of the Niger-Congo family of African languages and is used by about four million people. Some linguists classify it with the Kwa branch of the Niger-Congo family, while others think of it as a non-Bantu language, forming part of the Benue-Congo branch. [Mid-19thC. From Efik.] —**Ef·ik** *adj.*

EFM *abbr.* electronic fetal monitor

eft /eft/ *n.* an immature newt in the terrestrial phase, usually reddish-orange in colour. Latin name: *Notophthalmus viridescens.* [Old English *efta*, of unknown origin]

EFT·POS /éft pòss/ *abbr.* electronic funds transfer at point of sale

EFTS /éfts/ *n., abbr.* electronic funds transfer system

e.g. *abbr.* for or as an example [From Latin "for example"]

EGA *abbr.* COMPUT enhanced graphics adapter

e·gad /i gád/ *interj.* used as an exclamation, generally to express surprise (*archaic*) [Late 17thC. From an alteration of AH + *gad*, a euphemism for GOD.]

e·gal·i·tar·i·an /i gàllə táiree ən/ *adj.* maintaining, relating to, or based on a belief that all people are, in principle, equal and should enjoy equal social, political, and economic rights and opportunities [Late 19thC. From French *égalitaire*, from *égal* "equal," from Latin *aequalis* (see EQUAL).] —**e·gal·i·tar·i·an** *n.* —**e·gal·i·tar·i·an·ism** *n.*

E·ge·ri·a /i jéeree ə/ *n.* a woman who acts as a trusted adviser or loyal companion (*literary*) [Early 17thC. From the Roman goddess who acted as adviser to the early Roman king Numa Pompilius.]

e·gest /i jést/ (**e·gest·ed, e·gest·ing, e·gests**) *vt.* to excrete something from a cell or organism (*formal*) [15thC. From Latin *egest-*, past participle stem of *egerere*, literally "to carry out," from *gerere* "to carry."] —**e·ges·tion** *n.* —**e·ges·tive** *adj.*

e·ges·ta /i jéstə/ *npl.* waste materials excreted from a cell or organism [Early 18thC. From Latin, neuter plural of *egestus*, past participle of *egerere* (see EGEST).]

egg[1] /eg/ *n.* **1.** BIOL ANIMAL REPRODUCTIVE STRUCTURE a large sex cell produced by birds, fish, insects, reptiles, or amphibians, enclosed in a protective covering that allows the fertilized embryo to continue developing outside the mother's body until it hatches **2.** BIRDS, FOOD HARD-SHELLED OBJECT LAID BY HEN the hard-shelled, oval, cream- or light-brown egg produced by a hen or similar fowl, used as food **3.** SOMETHING SHAPED LIKE A HEN'S EGG something that resembles a hen's egg in shape, e.g., a carved or molded ornament or an egg-shaped piece of candy **4.** BIOL FEMALE REPRODUCTIVE CELL a female reproductive cell **5.** PERSON a person (*dated informal*) ○ *All in all, he's not a bad egg.* ■ *vt.* THROW EGGS AT SOMEBODY to throw eggs at somebody or something (*informal*) [14thC. From Old Norse. Ultimately from an Indo-European word that is also the ancestor of English *ovary*.] —**egg·y** *adj.* ◇ **have egg on your face** to be left in an embarrassing or humiliating situation, especially because of having made an obvious mistake ◇ **put all your eggs in one basket** to rely entirely on one thing or person, or on the outcome of one plan or course of action

egg[2] /eg/ (**egged, egg·ing, eggs**) *vt.* to encourage somebody to do something, especially something wrong, foolish, or dangerous ○ *She never would have done it herself, but the girls were egging her on.* [12thC. From Old Norse *eggja* "to urge," from a prehistoric Germanic word that is also the ancestor of English *edge*.]

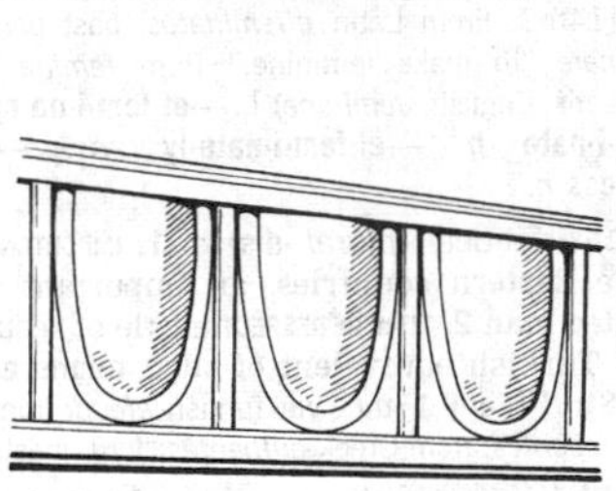

Egg-and-dart

egg-and-dart *n.* an ornamental pattern, commonly used in moldings on buildings or furniture, in which egg-shaped figures alternate with slightly tapered bars, arrows, or anchors

eg·gar *n.* ZOOL = **egger**

egg·beat·er /ég bèetər/ *n.* **1.** HOUSEHOLD UTENSIL FOR BEATING EGGS a kitchen utensil used for beating or blending such ingredients as raw eggs or cream, especially one with two sets of spaced vertical blades rotated by turning a handle **2.** AIR HELICOPTER a rotary-wing aircraft (*slang*)

egg bread *n.* a soft cake of cornmeal and eggs, baked in a pan (*regional*)

WORD KEY: REGIONAL NOTE

The term ***egg bread*** is used in the Carolinas and southern Maryland for the Virginia and Northern Maryland term *batter bread.* Elsewhere in the South today, the term has a high frequency of occurrence in Upper and Lower Georgia, with its highest use in Lower Alabama.

egg·case *n.* a protective covering containing eggs, especially one produced by insects and mollusks

egg cream *n.* a carbonated drink made by mixing milk, chocolate syrup, and seltzer water

WORD KEY: REGIONAL NOTE

The soda fountain drink ***egg cream*** is probably so called for its white froth that resembles an egg white. This popular and inexpensive drink is associated with New York residents, like the even more economical *two-cents plain* (seltzer) and *chocolate phosphate* (seltzer syrup). Of these, only the *chocolate phosphate* has much currency in other American cities.

egg·cup /ég kùp/ *n.* a small bowl-shaped container, often with a short neck and wide base below the bowl, used for holding a boiled egg while it is being eaten

eg·ger /éggər/, **eg·gar** *n.* a moth with a brown body and wings whose larvae spin egg-shaped cocoons in the branches of trees. Family: Lasiocampidae. [Early 18thC. Origin uncertain: probably from EGG, because of its egg-shaped cocoon.]

egg foo yung /èg foo yúng/ *n.* a Chinese dish that combines beansprouts, onions, meat, and eggs

egg·head /ég hèd/ *n.* somebody who is very intelligent and whose interests are mainly intellectual and bookish (*informal*) [Early 20thC. From the idea that a high forehead indicates brains.] —**egg·head·ed** *adj.*

egg·nog /ég nòg/ *n.* a drink made of milk or cream, eggs, sugar, spice, and sometimes an alcoholic beverage such as brandy, bourbon, rye, or rum, traditionally served in the winter, especially at Christmas [Early 19thC. *Nog* was a kind of strong beer (origin unknown).]

egg·plant /ég plànt/ *n.* **1.** PLANT WITH LARGE EDIBLE FRUIT a plant of the nightshade family that comes originally from southern and eastern Asia, and is closely related to the potato. Latin name: *Solanum melongena.* **2.** FRUIT OF EGGPLANT the large, oval, fleshy, edible fruit of the eggplant, usually purple-skinned but also occurring in other colors, and widely used in dishes of Mediterranean origin **3.** BLACKISH PURPLE a very dark purple color

egg roll *n.* a roughly cylindrical casing of thin egg dough enclosing a mixture of minced vegetables, often with meat or seafood, usually eaten deep-fried, and common in Chinese-American cuisine

egg sac *n.* the pouch or cocoon that a female spider spins to protect its eggs

eggs Ben·e·dict *n.* ham and a poached egg in hollandaise sauce on top of a slice of toast or a split toasted English muffin, usually served for breakfast or brunch (*takes a singular or plural verb*) [Late 19thC. Origin uncertain: perhaps named for Samuel *Benedict*, a New York socialite, who together with a maître d' supposedly created the dish as a cure for his hangover.]

egg·shell /ég shèl/ *n.* **1.** BIOL HARD COVER OF AN EGG the hard brittle protective outer cover of the egg of a bird, or the similar tough outer covering of the eggs of animals such as crocodiles and turtles **2.** COLORS PALE WHITISH COLOR a pale yellowish-white color ■ *adj.* **1.** COLORS YELLOWISH-WHITE of a pale yellowish-white color **2.** COLORS SLIGHTLY GLOSSY having a slight sheen, giving a finish between that of gloss and matt paint **3.** FRAGILE, THIN, OR DELICATE as fragile, thin, or delicate as an eggshell ◇ **walk on eggshells** to proceed with extreme wariness, caution, and tact

egg·shell blue *adj.* of a delicate pale blue color —**egg·shell blue** *n.*

egg tim·er *n.* a small hourglass or clockwork timing device used to time the boiling of an egg, usually capable of timing intervals of three to five minutes

egg tooth *n.* a small projection on the beak of a baby bird or the upper jaw of a baby reptile, used to cut through the eggshell when hatching and later shed

egg white *n.* the clear viscous liquid found between the yolk and the shell of an egg that turns solid and white when cooked

e·gis *n.* = **aegis**

eg·lan·tine /égglən tìn, égglən tèen/ (*plural* **-tines** *or* **-tine**) *n.* PLANTS = **sweetbrier** [14thC. Via French *églantine* from, ultimately, Latin *aculentus* "spiny," ultimately from *acus* "needle."]

e·go /éegō, éggō/ (*plural* **e·gos**) *n.* **1. APPROPRIATE SELF-ESTEEM** somebody's idea of his or her own importance or worth, usually of an appropriate level **2. INFLATED OPINION OF YOURSELF** an exaggerated sense of your own importance and a feeling of superiority to other people **3.** PSYCHOANAL **PART OF THE MIND CONTAINING CONSCIOUSNESS** in Freudian psychology, one of three main divisions of the mind, containing consciousness and memory and involved with control, planning, and conforming to reality ○ *"The poor ego has a still harder time of it; it has to serve three harsh masters, and has to do its best to reconcile the claims and demands of all three."* (Sigmund Freud, *The Anatomy of the Mental Personality, Lecture 31*) ◊ **id, superego 4.** PHILOS **THE SELF** the individual self, as distinct from the outside world and other selves [Early 19thC. From Latin, "I."]

e·go·cen·tric /èegō séntrik, èggō-/ *adj.* **1. SELFISH** interested only in the needs and wants of the self and not caring about other people **2. LIMITED OR CONFINED IN OUTLOOK** limited in outlook to things mainly relating to yourself, or confined to your own affairs or activities **3. MORE CONCERNED WITH THE INDIVIDUAL THAN SOCIETY** concerned with the individual rather than, or at the expense of, society as a whole **4.** PHILOS **CENTERED ON THE SELF** centered on the individual self, and considering it to be the hub of all experience —**e·go·cen·tric** *n.* —**e·go·cen·tric·al·ly** *adv.* —**e·go·cen·tric·i·ty** /èegō sen trìssətee, èggō-/ *n.* —**e·go·cen·trism** /èegō sén trìzzəm, èggō-/ *n.*

e·go i·de·al *n.* an ideal image of what you could or should be, built up from observation of parents or other admired people

e·go·ism /éegō ìzzəm, éggō-/ *n.* **1.** = **egotism** *n.* 1 **2.** PHILOS **PURSUIT OF YOUR OWN WELFARE AND INTERESTS** making personal welfare and interests your primary or only concern, sometimes at the expense of others **3.** ETHICS **MORALITY DERIVED FROM SELF-INTEREST** the belief that the correct basis for a moral code is every person's concern for his or her own best interests, or the doctrine supporting this belief

WORD KEY: USAGE

egoism or **egotism**? It is difficult to distinguish between these two words, which are equally common and are often used interchangeably, although there is a theoretical difference between them. ***Egoism*** refers, in terms of philosophy, to ethical and metaphysical theories in which self-interest is regarded as the principal motivating factor. And so an *egoist* believes an individual should seek as an end only his or her own welfare: *His conduct was characterized by ruthless egoism.* ***Egotism*** implies a vain and selfish absorption with the self as a matter of behavior rather than an ethical principle, and an *egotist* is somebody who behaves in a selfish or self-centered way: *Her egotism makes her oblivious to other people's concerns.*

e·go·ist /éegō ist, éggō-/ *n.* **1.** ETHICS **BELIEVER IN EGOISM** somebody who believes that the correct basis for a moral code is every person's concern for his or her own best interests **2.** = **egotist** —**e·go·is·tic** /èegō ístik, èggō-/ *adj.* —**e·go·is·ti·cal** /-ístik'l/ *adj.* —**e·go·is·ti·cal·ly** /-ístikəlee/ *adv.*

e·go·ma·ni·a /èegō máynee ə, èggō-/ *n.* a dangerously obsessive preoccupation with the self —**e·go·ma·ni·ac** *n.* —**e·go·ma·ni·a·cal** /-mə nī́ ək'l/ *adj.* —**e·go·ma·ni·a·cal·ly** /-mə nī́ əkəlee/ *adv.*

e·go·tism /éegə tìzzəm, éggə-/ *n.* **1. INFLATED SENSE OF SELF-IMPORTANCE** the possession of an exaggerated sense of self-importance and superiority to other people **2. PREOCCUPATION WITH SELF** the tendency to speak or write too much about the self **3. SELFISHNESS** selfishness or self-centeredness [Early 18thC. Coined from EGO + "t" + -ISM.]

WORD KEY: USAGE

See Usage note at ***egoism.***

e·go·tist /éegətist, éggə-/ *n.* **1. CONCEITED PERSON** somebody with an exaggerated sense of his or her self-importance, especially somebody who tends to speak or write about himself or herself all the time **2. SELFISH PERSON** somebody who is selfish, self-absorbed, and self-centered —**e·go·tis·tic** /èegə tístik, èggə-/ *adj.* —**e·go·tis·ti·cal·ly** /-tístikəlee/ *adv.*

e·go trip *n.* a course of action or an experience the main effect of which is to boost somebody's own sense of self-importance (*slang*) —**e·go-trip** *vi.* —**e·go-trip·per** *n.*

e·gre·gious /i grèejəss, -jee əss/ *adj.* bad, blatant, or ridiculous to an extraordinary degree (*formal*) [Mid-16thC. Formed from Latin *egregius* "illustrious" (literally "outside the flock," from *greg-*, stem of *grex* "flock.") The original sense was "remarkably good."] —**e·gre·gious·ly** *adv.* —**e·gre·gious·ness** *n.*

e·gress /ée grèss/ *n.* **1. ACT OF COMING OR GOING OUT** the act of coming or going out from or of leaving a place (*formal*) **2. RIGHT TO LEAVE** the right to leave or go out from a place (*formal*) **3. EXIT OR PATH OUT** an exit from a place (*formal*) **4.** ASTRON = **emersion** *n.* 2 ■ *vi.* (**e·gressed, e·gress·ing, e·gress·es**) **COME OUT** to come out from or leave a place (*formal*) [Mid-16thC. From Latin *egressus*, from *egredi* "to go out," from *gradi* "to proceed, to step."]

e·gres·sion /i grésh'n/ *n.* = **egress** *n.* 1

e·gret /éegrət, éggrət/ *n.* a heron that produces long drooping ornamental feathers on the lower part of the back at the start of the breeding season. Egrets' feathers were once popular as decorations for women's hats, causing the birds to be hunted almost to extinction. Family: Ardeidae. [14thC. Via Anglo-Norman *egrette* from, ultimately, Provençal *aigreta*, from *aigron* "heron," ultimately from a prehistoric Germanic word that is also the ancestor of English *heron*.]

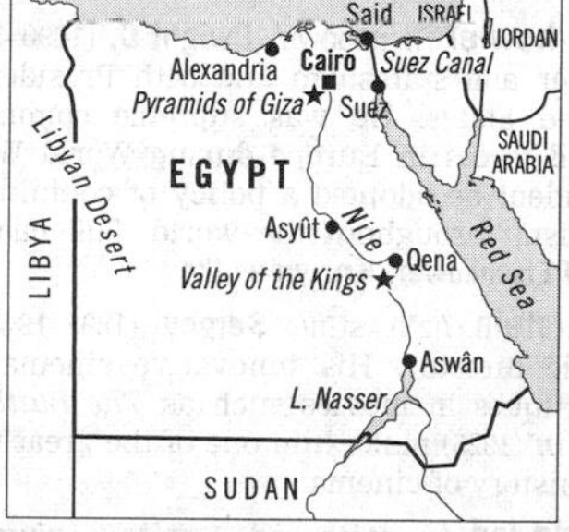

Egypt

E·gypt /éejipt/ country in northeastern Africa bordering the Mediterranean Sea and the Red Sea. It became a republic in 1952. Language: Arabic. Currency: Egyptian pound. Capital: Cairo. Population: 63,575,100 (1996). Area: 385,229 sq. mi./997,738 sq. km. Official name **Arab Republic of Egypt**

E·gyp·tian /i jípshən/ *n.* **1. NATIVE OR CITIZEN OF EGYPT** somebody who was born in or is a citizen of Egypt **2. LANGUAGE OF ANCIENT EGYPT** the language of ancient Egypt, a now extinct branch of the Afro-Asiatic family of African languages dating from roughly 3000 B.C. that developed into Coptic around A.D. 200 **3. DIALECT OF ARABIC SPOKEN IN EGYPT** the dialect of Arabic spoken in modern Egypt. Egyptian is spoken by about 65 million people. ■ *adj.* **1. RELATING TO EGYPT AND THE EGYPTIANS** relating to or typical of Egypt, its people, or their culture **2. RELATING TO THE LANGUAGE OF ANCIENT EGYPT** characteristic of or relating to the language of ancient Egypt **3. RELATING TO THE ARABIC DIALECT OF EGYPT** relating to the dialect of Arabic spoken in modern Egypt

E·gyp·tol·o·gy /èejip tólləjee/ *n.* the study of the history, archaeology, culture, and language of ancient Egypt —**E·gyp·tol·o·gist** *n.*

eh /ay, e/ *interj.* (*informal*) **1. PARDON ME?** used to ask somebody to repeat something **2. WHAT?** used to express surprise at something that has been said **3. ISN'T THAT SO?** used to invite somebody to respond to something that has been said, especially to agree with it or confirm that it is correct or accurately sums up a previous statement [Mid-16thC. Natural exclamation.]

EHF *abbr.* extremely high frequency

Ehr·lich /áirlik, -likh/, **Paul** (1854–1915) German bacteriologist and immunologist. His work on immunology won him a shared Nobel Prize in 1908. He also pioneered chemotherapy, developing Salvarsan as a treatment for syphilis.

EHV *abbr.* extra-high voltage

EIA *abbr.* environmental impact assessment

Eich·mann /íkmən, íkh maan/, **Adolf** (1906–62) German Nazi official and war criminal. Nazi official, responsible for carrying out anti-Semitic policy during World War II. He was captured in Argentina in 1960 by Israeli agents, tried in Israel for "crimes against humanity," and hanged two years later. Full name **Karl Adolf Eichmann**

Eid /eed/ *n.* ISLAM **1.** = **Eid-ul-Adha 2.** = **Eid-ul-Fitr** [Late 17thC. From Arabic *'īd* "festival," from Aramaic.]

ei·der /ídər/ (*plural* **-ders** *or* **-der**), **ei·der duck** *n.* a large sea duck of the northern hemisphere, the male of which has distinctive black-and-white plumage while the female, the source of eiderdown, has mottled brown plumage. Genus: *Somateria.* [Late 17thC. Via Icelandic *æður* from Old Norse *æðr.*]

ei·der·down /ídər dòwn/ *n.* **1. EIDER DUCK'S FEATHERS** the soft fluffy breast feathers of the female eider duck, used to fill pillows and bed coverings **2. BED COVERING** a bed covering in the form of a quilt or duvet stuffed with the soft feathers of the eider duck

ei·det·ic /ī déttik/ *adj.* PSYCHOL (*formal*) **1. RECALLED WITH STARTLING ACCURACY** recalled or reproduced with startling accuracy, clarity, and vividness ○ *eidetic images* **2. ABLE TO RECALL WITH STARTLING ACCURACY** able to recall or reproduce things previously seen with startling accuracy, clarity, and vividness ○ *an eidetic memory* [Early 20thC. From Greek *eidētikos*, from *eidos* "form."] —**ei·det·i·cal·ly** *adv.*

ei·do·lon /ī dōlən/ (*plural* **-lons** *or* **-la** /-lə/) *n.* (*literary*) **1. PHANTOM** a ghostly figure or image **2. AN IDEAL IMAGE** an idealized image of something or somebody [Mid-17thC. From Greek *eidōlon* "idol" (see IDOL).]

Eid-ul-Ad·ha /èed ŏol aadə/ *n.* a Muslim festival, the festival of the sacrifice, that marks the end of the annual pilgrimage to Mecca but is celebrated everywhere, especially by the sacrifice of sheep

Eid-ul-Fitr /èed ŏol féetər/ *n.* a Muslim festival that marks the end of Ramadan, the period of fasting

Eif·fel /íf'l/, **Gustave** (1832–1923) French engineer. A specialist in metal structures, he is best known as the designer of the Eiffel Tower (1889) and architect of the inner structure of the Statue of Liberty (1885). Full name **Alexandre Gustave Eiffel**

AKG London

Eiffel Tower, Paris, France

Eif·fel Tow·er *n.* a 984-foot/300-meter-high iron tower in central Paris, France. It was designed by Gustave Eiffel for the 1889 Paris Exposition.

Ei·ger /ígər/ mountain peak in the Bernese Alps, southeast of Bern, Switzerland. The north face of the mountain is notorious for the number of mountaineers who have died attempting to climb it. Height: 13,025 ft./3,970 m.

eight /ayt/ *n.* **1. NUMBER 8** the number 8, which is one more than 7 and one fewer than 9 **2. SOMETHING WITH A VALUE OF 8** something in a numbered series, e.g., a playing card, with a value of eight **3. GROUP OF 8** a group of eight objects or people **4. SOMETHING WITH 8 PARTS** something composed of eight parts or members, e.g., an eight-cylinder engine **5.** ROWING **ROWING CREW** a crew of eight rowers **6.** ROWING **RACING SHELL** a long narrow racing shell crewed by eight rowers [Old English *e(a)hta.* Ultimately from an Indo-

European word that is also the ancestor of English *octave*, *October*, and *octo-*.] —**eight** *adj., pron.*

eight ball *n.* **1.** BLACK BALL IN POOL in pool, the black ball, because it has the number 8 on it **2.** FORM OF POOL a form of pool in which a player must pocket a given 7 of the 15 balls, and then pocket the eight ball, before his or her opponent does ◇ **behind the eight ball** in a difficult or awkward position (*slang*)

eight·een /ay tee'n, áy tee'n/ *n.* **1.** NUMBER 18 the number 18, which is one more than 17 and one fewer than 19 **2.** SOMETHING WITH A VALUE OF 18 something in a numbered series with a value of 18 **3.** GROUP OF 18 a group of 18 objects or people [Old English *e(a)hatēne*, ultimately from prehistoric Germanic words that are also the ancestors of English *eight* and *ten*] —**eight·een** *adj., pron.*

eight·een·mo /ay tee'n mō/ (*plural* **-mos**) *n.* PRINTING = **octodecimo**

eight·eenth /ay tee'nth/ *n.* **1.** ONE OF 18 PARTS OF SOMETHING one of 18 equal parts of something **2.** BIRTHDAY OF AN 18-YEAR-OLD the birthday of somebody who has just reached 18 years of age —**eight·eenth** *adj., adv.*

eight·een-wheel·er *n.* a large truck used to haul heavy loads and having a tractor, or cab and engine, and a large trailer, or box-shaped container, and usually 18 wheels

eight·fold /áyt fōld/ *adj.* **1.** MULTIPLYING BY 8 multiplying the original figure by eight **2.** CONSISTING OF 8 PARTS consisting of eight parts ■ *adv.* BY A FACTOR OF 8 by eight, or to an amount eight times greater than the original

eighth /aytth, ayth/ *n.* one of eight equal parts of something —**eighth** *adj., adv.*

eighth note *n.* in music, a note with a time value of one-eighth of a whole note

eighth rest *n.* a rest equal in length to an eighth note

eight·i·eth /áytee əth/ *n.* **1.** ONE OF 80 PARTS OF SOMETHING one of 80 equal parts of something **2.** BIRTHDAY OF AN 80-YEAR-OLD the birthday of somebody who has just reached 80 years of age —**eight·i·eth** *adj., adv.*

eight·pen·ny nail /áyt pènnee-/ *n.* a nail that is usually 2 1/2 in./6.4 cm in length

eight·vo /áyt vō/ (*plural* **-vos**) *n.* = **octavo** [From *8vo*, a written abbreviation for "octavo"]

eight·y /áytee/ *n.* (*plural* **-ies**) **1.** NUMBER 80 the number 80, which is 8 times 10 **2.** GROUP OF 80 a group of 80 objects or people ■ **eight·ies** *npl.* **1.** NUMBERS 80 TO 89 the numbers 80 to 89, particularly as a range of temperature **2.** YEARS 1980 TO 1989 the years 1980 to 1989, or the years numbered 80 to 89 in any century **3.** PERIOD FROM AGE 80 TO 89 the period of somebody's life from the age of 80 to 89 [13thC. Shortening of Old English *hundeahtatig*, from *hund-*, literally "hundred" + *e(a)hta* "eight" + *-tig* "group of ten."] —**eight·y** *adj., pron.*

eight·y-six (**eight·y-sixed, eight·y-six·ing, eight·y-six·es**), **86** (**86ed, 86ing, 86es**) *vt.* (*slang*) **1.** GET RID OF SOMEBODY to dispose of somebody or something **2.** REFUSE TO SERVE A CUSTOMER to refuse to serve somebody in a restaurant or bar [Mid-20thC. Origin uncertain: perhaps rhyming slang for *nix* or from Chumley's bar and grill, 86 Bedford Street, Greenwich Village, New York City.]

Eijk·man /ík maan, áyk maan/, **Christiaan** (1858–1930) Dutch physician. His research on diet-deficiency diseases, particularly beriberi, revealed the importance of vitamins in human physiology. He shared the Nobel Prize in 1929.

Eil·at /ay laat/, **Elat** seaport, tourist resort, and leading oil port in southern Israel, situated at the head of the Gulf of Aqaba. Population: 33,300 (1993).

-ein *suffix.* a chemical compound related to one whose name ends in "-in" or "-ein" ○ *fluorescein* [Alteration of -IN]

Ein·stein /ín stīn/, **Albert** (1879–1955) German-born U.S. physicist. His theory of general relativity revolutionized scientific thought and served as the theoretical foundation for later exploitation of atomic energy. He won a Nobel Prize in 1921 for his work explaining the photoelectric effect. He became a Swiss (1905) and later a U.S. citizen (1940). He joined other physicists in writing to President Franklin Roosevelt to warn him that Germany could possibly make an atomic bomb.

ein·stein·i·um /īn stínee əm/ *n.* a synthetic radioactive chemical element, first identified in 1952. It is usually produced by irradiating plutonium and other elements. Symbol **Es** [Named for Albert EINSTEIN]

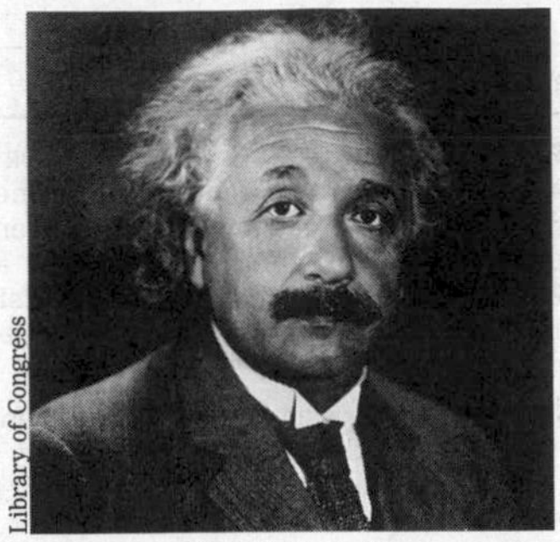

Albert Einstein

Eint·ho·ven /ínt hōv'n/, **Willem** (1860–1927) Dutch physiologist. His most important invention was the string galvanometer, which recorded precise measurements of electrical activity in the heart. He won the Nobel Prize in 1924.

EISA *abbr.* COMPUT extended industry standard architecture

Dwight D. Eisenhower

Ei·sen·how·er /íz'n hòwr/, **Dwight D.** (1890–1969) U.S. soldier and statesman and 34th President of the United States. He was supreme commander of Allied forces in Europe during World War II. As president he adopted a policy of containing Communism throughout the world. Full name **Dwight David Eisenhower**. Known as **Ike**

Ei·sen·stein /íz'n stīn/, **Sergey** (1898–1948) Soviet movie director. His innovative cinematographic techniques in movies such as *The Battleship Potemkin* (1925) make him one of the great figures in the history of cinema.

eis·tedd·fod /ay stéth vòd, ī stéth-/ (*plural* **-fods** *or* **-fod·au** /ày steth vóddī, ī steth-/) *n.* a traditional Welsh festival at which competitions are held for performers and composers of music and poetry [Early 19thC. From Welsh, literally "session, sitting."]

eis·wein /íss wīn/ *n.* a sweet white wine produced in Germany and Austria from grapes that have frozen on the vine, concentrating the sugar content

ei·ther /eéthər, íthər/ CORE MEANING: a grammatical word that introduces two situations, one of which may include or exclude the other ○ (adj) *It won't make much difference either way.* ○ (pron) *I refuse to meet either of them.* ○ (conj) *Either there's a problem or there isn't.* See Usage note below.

1. *adj., pron.* ONE OR THE OTHER one or the other, when it does not matter which ○ (adj) *You can execute commands on either machine.* ○ (pron) *If either fell behind, the other would help him to catch up.* ○ (pron) *You can get this information from either of the two addressees.* **2.** *adj., pron.* INDICATES A NEGATIVE used to refer negatively to each of two situations where the negative includes them both ○ (adj) *You cannot send e-mails to either address at the moment.* ○ (pron) *I'm not interested in either of them.* **3.** *adj.* BOTH both of two things ○ *The red and yellow patches on either side of the sun are radiation from the dust ring.* **4.** *conj.* INDICATES ALTERNATIVES used to indicate that there is a choice between two or more options ○ *The only way to get around the city was either by the super freeways or by the canals and the gondolas.* ○ *Data sources may be either digital or analog.* **5.** *adv.* INDICATES CONNECTION used in a negative statement that indicates a connection or a partial agreement with a previous statement (*used at the end of a second statement*) ○ *You won't find really bad conditions, but you won't find luxury hotels either.* [Old English *ægþer*, contraction of *æg(e)hwæþer*, from a prehistoric Germanic phrase meaning "always each of two," which contained the ancestors of English *aye* and *whether*]

WORD KEY: USAGE

Singular or plural after **either**? ***Either*** is normally used with a singular verb: *Has either of you been to Paris? Either Lee or David is responsible.* Informally, however, the plural is used when the choices are regarded collectively rather than individually, and it is quite natural to say *Have either of you been to Paris?*, which permits the possibility that both the people addressed have done so. When ***either* ... *or* ...** occurs with a mixture of singular and plural subjects, the verb traditionally agrees with the one that is closer to it: *Either David or his parents are at home.*

ei·ther-or *adj.* offering a choice strictly limited to two options ○ *It's an either-or situation – either you accept or you refuse.*

e·jac·u·late *v.* /i jákyə làyt/ (**-lat·ed, -lat·ing, -lates**) **1.** *vti.* EJECT SEMEN DURING ORGASM to eject semen from the penis during an orgasm **2.** *vt.* EXCLAIM SOMETHING SUDDENLY to exclaim something suddenly and usually forcefully (*literary*) ■ *n.* /i jákyələt/ EJACULATED SEMEN semen that has been ejected from the penis during orgasm [Late 16thC. From Latin *ejaculat-*, past participle stem of *ejaculari* "to throw out," ultimately from *jacere* "to throw" (source of English *inject* and *project*).]

e·jac·u·la·tion /i jàkyə láysh'n/ *n.* **1.** EJECTING OF SEMEN FROM PENIS the ejecting of semen from the penis during an orgasm **2.** SUDDEN EXCLAMATION a sudden, usually loud or forceful exclamation (*literary*)

e·jac·u·la·to·ry /i jákyələ tàwree/ *adj.* **1.** RELATING TO EJACULATION involved in or related to the structures involved in ejaculation ○ *ejaculatory ducts* **2.** CHARACTERIZED BY SUDDEN BURSTS OF SPEECH spoken in or characterized by short bursts of loud or forceful speech (*formal*)

e·ject /i jékt/ (**e·ject·ed, e·ject·ing, e·jects**) *v.* **1.** *vt.* PUSH SOMETHING OUT WITH FORCE to cause something to burst out from something else with considerable force **2.** *vt.* REMOVE SOMEBODY FROM A PLACE OR POSITION to force somebody to leave a place or give up a position, e.g., a job or membership ○ *They were forcibly ejected from the meeting.* **3.** *vi.* AIR LEAVE AN AIRCRAFT IN AN ESCAPE DEVICE to escape from an aircraft in an emergency by means of an ejection seat or special capsule **4.** *vt.* LAW EVICT SOMEBODY to remove somebody, especially a tenant, from a property by taking legal action [15thC. From Latin *eject-*, past participle stem of *e(j)icere*, from *jacere* "to throw."] —**e·ject·a·ble** *adj.* —**e·jec·tion** *n.* —**e·jec·tive** *adj.*

e·jec·ta /i jéktə/ *n.* substances ejected from something, especially the material thrown out by a volcanic eruption or from a star (*formal*) (*takes a singular or plural verb*) [Late 19thC. From Latin, a plural form of the past participle of *e(j)icere* (see EJECT).]

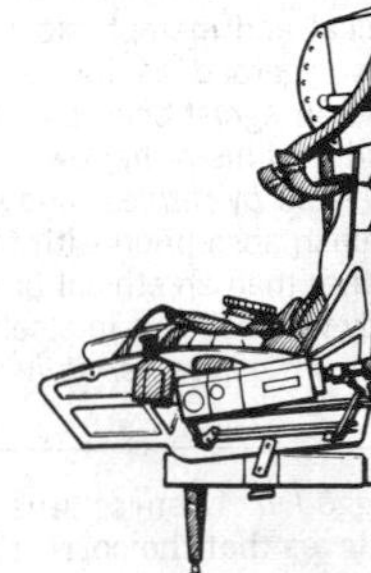
Ejection seat

e·jec·tion seat *n.* AIR a seat in the cockpit of an aircraft that in an emergency propels the occupant clear of the craft by means of a rocket or explosive device

e·ject·ment /i jéktmənt/ *n.* **1.** EJECTING OR BEING EJECTED the process of ejecting somebody or something, or of being ejected from somewhere (*formal*) **2.** LAW RECOVERY OF REAL PROPERTY a legal action brought by somebody to recover possession of land that is being held by somebody else

e·jec·tor /i jéktər/ *n.* **1.** DEVICE FOR EJECTING SOMETHING a device for ejecting something from something else, especially a mechanism for ejecting an empty cartridge or shell from a gun **2.** PUMP USED TO WITHDRAW SOMETHING a jet pump device that uses water, steam, or air to remove a gas, fluid, or powder from a space

e·jec·tor seat *n. U.K.* = **ejection seat**

eke out **(eked out, ek·ing out, ekes out)** *vt.* **1.** MAKE SOMETHING LAST WITH SPARING USE to make a supply of something last by using it as slowly and economically as possible **2.** SUPPLEMENT SOMETHING INSUFFICIENT OR INADEQUATE to supplement something that is insufficient or inadequate, usually with difficulty and by hard work **3.** GET SOMETHING ONLY WITH EFFORT to manage to get or achieve something but only on a small scale and with a great deal of effort ○ *eked out a bare existence* [Late 16thC. Later form of Old English *ēacan, ēacian*, from a prehistoric Germanic base related to Latin *augere* "to increase."]

EKG *abbr.* **1.** electrocardiogram **2.** electrocardiograph

e·kis·tics /i kístiks/ *n.* the study of human settlements in all their aspects, including, e.g., the origin and development of cities and city planning (*takes a singular verb*) [Mid-20thC. From Greek *oikistikos*, from *oikizein* "to settle," from *oikos* "house" (source of English *economy* and *parish*).] —**e·kis·tic** *adj.* —**ek·is·ti·cian** /èki stísh'n/ *n.*

el /el/ *n.* an elevated railroad in a city (*informal*)

e·lab·o·rate *adj.* /i lábbərət/ **1.** COMPLEX having many different parts or a lot of detail and being organized in a complicated way **2.** FINELY OR RICHLY DECORATED made with a lot of intricate detail or extravagant ornamentation ○ *an elaborate headdress* **3.** DETAILED AND THOROUGH thought out or organized with thoroughness and careful attention to detail ■ *v.* /i lábbə ràyt/ **(-rat·ed, -rat·ing, -rates) 1.** *vi.* GIVE MORE DETAIL ABOUT SOMETHING to go into greater detail about something that has already been spoken about or described in broad terms ○ *Would you care to elaborate on that?* **2.** *vt.* WORK SOMETHING OUT IN DETAIL to work out the details of something **3.** *vti.* MAKE OR BECOME MORE COMPLEX to make something more complex or ornate, or become more complex or ornate [15thC. From Latin *elaborat-*, past participle stem of *elaborare* "to produce by effort or labor," from *labor* "labor."] —**e·lab·o·rate·ly** *adv.* —**e·lab·o·rate·ness** *n.* —**e·lab·o·ra·tion** /i làbbə ráysh'n/ *n.* —**e·lab·o·ra·tor** /i lábbə ràytər/ *n.*

E·lam /éeləm/ ancient state in southwestern Iran, east of the Tigris River. It was established before 4000 B.C. and corresponds to the present-day Khuzistan Province, Iran.

E·la·mite /éelə mìt/ *n.* **1.** PEOPLES SOMEBODY FROM ANCIENT ELAM somebody who was born or who lived in the ancient Middle Eastern kingdom of Elam **2.** LANG ANCIENT LANGUAGE OF ELAM an extinct language formerly spoken in the ancient kingdom of Elam. Elamite has been attested by important discoveries of pictographic and cuneiform inscriptions dating from the third millennium B.C. through to the first millennium A.D. ■ *adj.* RELATING TO ELAM relating to or typical of Elam, or its people, language, or culture —**E·la·mit·ic** /èelə míttik/ *adj.*

é·lan /ay láan, ay láaN/, **e·lan** *n.* vigor and enthusiasm, often combined with self-confidence and style (*literary*) [Mid-19thC. From French *élan*, formed from *élancer* "to dart, throw," ultimately from *lance* "LANCE."]

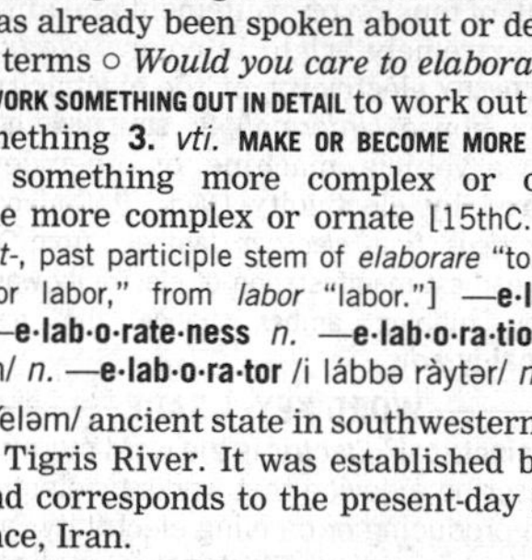
Eland

e·land /éelənd/ (*plural* **e·lands** *or* **e·land**) *n.* the largest of living antelopes, found in central and southern Africa and distinguished by its humped shoulders, dewlap, and tightly spiraling horns. Genus: *Taurotragus.* [Late 18thC. Via Afrikaans from Dutch, "elk," ultimately from Lithuanian *élnis*.]

é·lan vi·tal /ay láan vee táal, ay láaN-/ *n.* according to the philosophy of Henri Bergson, a creative life force present in all living things and responsible for evolution [From French]

el·a·pid /élləpid/ *n.* a venomous snake that has its short fangs at the front of the upper jaw. Cobras, coral snakes, and mambas are elapids. Family: Elapidae. [Late 19thC. From modern Latin *Elapidae*, family name, ultimately from Greek *elaps*, variant of *el(l)ops*, a kind of fish, also a kind of sea serpent.] —**el·a·pid** *adj.*

e·lapse /i láps/ *vi.* **(e·lapsed, e·laps·ing, e·laps·es)** GO BY to pass or go by, especially in a gradual, slow, or imperceptible way ○ *several hours elapsed* ■ *n.* PASSING OF A PERIOD OF TIME the passing of a certain period of time (*formal*) [Late 16thC. From Latin *elaps-*, past participle stem of *elabi* "to slip away," from *labi* "to glide, fall" (source of English *lapse*).]

e·las·mo·branch /i lásmə bràngk, i lázmə-/ *n.* a fish with a cartilaginous skeleton. Sharks, rays, and skates are elasmobranchs. Subclass: Elasmobranchii. [Late 19thC. From modern Latin *Elasmobranchii*, subclass name, from Greek *elasmos* "beaten metal" + *bragkhia* "gills."] —**e·las·mo·branch** *adj.*

e·las·tic /i lástik/ *n.* **1.** STRETCHY MATERIAL a strip or thread of rubber or similar stretchable material, or a fabric or tape with a stretchy material woven into it so that it can fit tightly around something **2.** = **rubber band** ■ *adj.* **1.** STRETCHY AND FLEXIBLE able to return quickly to its original shape and size after being bent, stretched, or squashed **2.** EASILY CHANGED able to incorporate changes or adapt to new circumstances easily **3.** MADE OF ELASTIC made of elastic **4.** SPRINGY having a light springy or bouncy quality, especially in movement **5.** PHYS RETURNING TO ITS ORIGINAL SHAPE AFTER STRESS used to describe a substance that is capable of returning to its original shape after undergoing stress or deformation [Mid-17thC. Via modern Latin *elasticus* from Greek *elastikos* "driving, propelling," from *elaunein* "to drive." Originally used in describing the way gas expands.] —**e·las·ti·cal·ly** *adv.*

WORD KEY: SYNONYMS

See Synonyms at ***pliable.***

e·las·ti·cate /i lásti kàyt/ **(-cat·ed, -cat·ing, -cates)** *vt. U.K.* = **elasticize** *v.* 1

e·las·tic col·li·sion *n.* a collision between two perfectly elastic bodies such that the final kinetic energy of the system is the same as the initial kinetic energy of the system

e·las·tic fi·ber *n.* a smooth, long, thin, branching fiber in connective tissue, composed mainly of the fibrous protein elastin

e·las·tic·i·ty /i làss tíssətee, ee-/ *n.* **1.** ABILITY TO RETURN TO SHAPE the ability of an object or substance to return quickly to its original shape and size after being bent, stretched, or squashed **2.** FLEXIBILITY the ability to incorporate changes or adapt to new circumstances easily **3.** PHYS ABILITY TO REGAIN DIMENSIONS AFTER STRESS the property that makes a material return to its original dimensions after being stressed or deformed, or the degree to which this is exhibited **4.** ECON RELATIVE CHANGE IN AN ECONOMIC VARIABLE the relative change in an economic variable, e.g., demand, that occurs in reaction to changes in other variables, e.g., price or advertising input

e·las·ti·cize /i lásti sìz/ **(-cized, -ciz·ing, -ciz·es)** *vt.* **1.** PUT ELASTIC INTO SOMETHING to put strips or threads of rubber or similar material into a fabric or item of clothing in order to make it stretchy and tight-fitting **2.** MAKE SOMETHING ELASTIC to make something elastic or more elastic

e·las·tic lim·it *n.* the maximum stress that can be applied to a material without the material's becoming permanently deformed

e·las·tin /i lástin/ *n.* a fibrous protein resembling collagen that is the main constituent of the elastic fibers of connective tissue [Late 19thC. Coined from ELASTIC + -IN.]

e·las·to·mer /i lástəmər/ *n.* a natural material, e.g., rubber, or a synthetic material, e.g., polyvinyl, that has elastic properties [Mid-20thC. Coined from ELASTIC + -MER.] —**e·las·to·mer·ic** /i làstə mérrik/ *adj.*

e·late /i láyt/ **(e·lat·ed, e·lat·ing, e·lates)** *vt.* to make somebody very happy and excited [Late 16thC. From Latin *elat-* (source of English *translate*), used as the past participle stem of *efferre* "to carry up," from *ferre* "to carry."] —**e·late** *adj.*

e·lat·ed /i láytəd/ *adj.* very happy and excited —**e·lat·ed·ly** *adv.* —**e·lat·ed·ness** *n.*

el·a·ter /éllətər/ *n.* a beetle that belongs to the click beetle family. Family: Elateridae. [Mid-17thC. From Greek *elatēr* "driver," from *elaunein* "to drive" (source of English *elastic*).]

e·lat·er·id /i láttərid/ *n.* = **elater** ■ *adj.* OF THE CLICK BEETLE FAMILY belonging or relating to the click beetle family

e·la·tion /i láysh'n/ *n.* a feeling of extraordinary happiness and excitement

Elba

El·ba /élbə/ mountainous island off the western coast of Italy, the place of Napoleon's first period of exile (1814–15)

El·be /elb/ river in central Europe that rises in the northern Czech Republic and flows about 725 mi./1,167 km northwest to the North Sea

El·bert, Mount /él bùrt/ mountain in central Colorado that is the highest peak in the state and in the Rocky Mountains. Height: 14,433 ft./4,399 m.

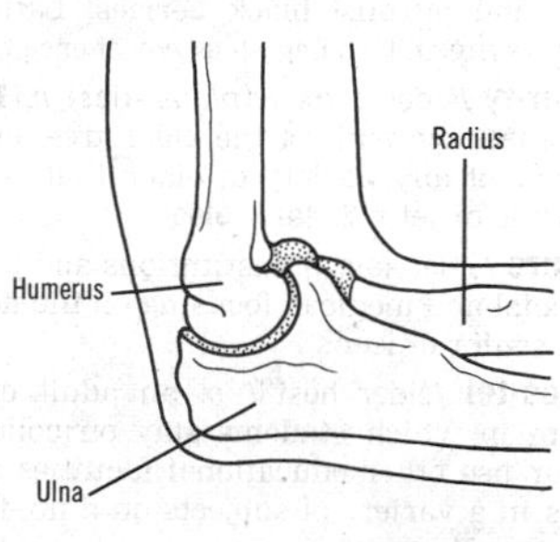

Elbow

el·bow /élbō/ *n.* **1.** ANAT JOINT IN THE ARM the joint between the upper and lower parts of the human arm **2.** CLOTHES PART OF A SLEEVE COVERING THE ELBOW the part of a sleeve that covers the elbow **3.** ZOOL JOINT IN AN ANIMAL LEG the joint in an animal's forelimb corresponding to the elbow in humans **4.** CONSTR BEND a bend in something such as a river, road, or pipe **5.** CONSTR SOMETHING BENT something, especially a piece of pipe, made with a bend in it ■ *vti.* **(-bowed, -bow·ing, -bows)** PUSH SOMETHING WITH THE ELBOW to push or hit somebody or something with the elbow, or progress through a crowd by pushing with the elbow or elbows [Old English *el(n)boga*, literally "arm bend," from the prehistoric Germanic ancestors of English *ell* and *bow*] ◇ **bend the** *or* **your elbow** to drink alcohol often (*informal*) ◇ **get the elbow, be given the elbow** *U.K.* to be dismissed or rejected (*informal*) ◇ **out at elbow, out at the elbows** poorly dressed, or short of money

el·bow grease *n.* hard physical effort or work with the arms, especially scrubbing or polishing (*informal*)

el·bow·room /élbō ròom, -rŏom/ *n.* (*informal*) **1.** SPACE TO MOVE AROUND IN COMFORTABLY space to move around or work in comfortably **2.** FREEDOM TO TRY SOMETHING NEW freedom from restriction for a time, especially to move or develop in a new area or direction

El·brus, Mount /el bróoss/, **El'brus** the highest mountain in Europe, in the Caucasus Mountains in southern Russia, near the border with Georgia. Height: 18,510 ft./5,642 m.

El·burz Moun·tains /él bóorz-/ mountain range in northern Iran, near the southern shore of the Caspian Sea. The highest peak is Damāvand, 18,386 ft./5,604 m.

El Ca·jon /èl kə hṓn/ city in southern California, a suburb of San Diego. Population: 92,057 (1996).

El Cen·tro /el séntrō/ city in southeastern California near the Mexican border. Population: 37,369 (1996).

El Cer·ri·to /èl sə reétō/ city in western California on the northeastern shore of San Francisco Bay, northwest of Oakland. Population: 23,567 (1996).

eld·er[1] /éldər/ *adj.* **1.** BORN EARLIER born before others, especially within a family, or having more seniority. See Usage note below. **2.** SUPERIOR superior to others, either by rank or experience ■ *n.* **1.** PERSON BORN EARLIER somebody who was born before somebody else ○ *She is five years my elder.* **2.** CHR SENIOR MEMBER OF A CHURCH a senior lay member in some Christian churches with responsibility for some aspects of church administration, the pastoral care of church members, and sometimes for teaching and preaching **3.** ANTHROP SENIOR MEMBER OF A COMMUNITY a member of a family, tribal group, or village who is respected for advanced years and has some influence and authority within the community **4.** *Can* RESPECTED ADVISER a respected senior member of a First Nations group who acts as an adviser [Old English *(i)eldra*, from a prehistoric Germanic word that is also the ancestor of English *eldest* and *old*] —**el·der·ship** *n.*

WORD KEY: USAGE

elder or **older**? ***Elder*** and *eldest* are used only of people, and usually in the context of family relationships: *She is the elder of Ruth's daughters. Mark is my eldest son.* ***Older*** and *oldest* can apply to things as well as people and can be used in a wider range of grammatical constructions: *I am older than David. It is the oldest church in Paris.* When **elder** is used after a verb (for example, *be*), it has to be preceded by *the*: *Who is the eldest?* not *Who is eldest?*

el·der[2] /éldər/ *n.* a common shrub or small tree of the honeysuckle family that has flat clusters of white flowers and purplish-black berries. Latin name: *Sambucus nigra.* [Old English *ellærn*, of uncertain origin]

el·der·ber·ry /éldər bèrree/ (*plural* **-ries**) *n.* **1.** FRUIT OF THE ELDER TREE the fruit of the elder tree, especially the berry of any variety of elder that is used to make wine or jelly **2.** BOT = **elder**[2]

eld·er·care /éldər kàir/ *n.* institutions and programs, both social and medical, focusing on the needs and care of senior citizens

El·der·hos·tel /éldər hòst'l/ *n.* an adult education program in which students stay on college campuses or use other educational facilities and take courses in a variety of subjects on a not-for-credit basis

eld·er·ly /éldərlee/ *adj.* **1.** PAST MIDDLE AGE past middle age and approaching the rest of life (*sometimes considered offensive*) **2.** CHARACTERISTIC OF LIFE AFTER MIDDLE AGE characteristic of or relating to life after middle age **3.** OLD-FASHIONED old and somewhat old-fashioned ■ *npl.* PEOPLE PAST MIDDLE AGE people who have lived past middle age, considered as a group (*sometimes considered offensive*) —**el·der·li·ness** *n.*

eld·er states·man *n.* a person, advanced in years and experience, especially a politician or former politician, who is respected for his or her wisdom and whose advice is still valued and unofficially sought

eld·est /éldəst/ *adj.* first, either in age or seniority [Old English *(i)eldest*, from a prehistoric Germanic word that is also the ancestor of English *elder*[1] and *old*]

WORD KEY: USAGE

See Usage note at ***elder.***

ELDO /éldō/ *abbr.* SPACE TECH European Launch Development Organization

El Do·ra·do[1] /èl də raádō, -ráydō/ *n.* **1.** LEGENDARY PLACE OF FABULOUS WEALTH a legendary place in South America where the streets were said to be paved with gold and wealth and riches were to be had in abundance **2.** PLACE OF RICHES a place that has great wealth or where great riches can be acquired [From Spanish, literally "the gilded"]

El Do·ra·do[2] /èl də raádō, -ráydō/ city in southern Arkansas, southeast of Texarkana, directly north of the Louisiana border. Population: 22,419 (1996).

El·e·at·ic /èllee áttik/ *adj.* relating to an ancient Greek school of philosophy founded by Xenophanes or Parmenides that flourished in the 5th and 6th centuries B.C. It advocated philosophical reflection over sensory observation. [Late 19thC. From Latin *Eliaticus*, from *Elea*, an ancient Greek city in southwestern Italy where the school flourished.] —**El·e·at·ic** *n.* —**El·e·at·i·cism** /-sìzzəm/ *n.*

elec. *abbr.* **1.** electric **2.** electrical **3.** electricity

el·e·cam·pane /èlli kam páyn/ (*plural* **-panes** *or* **-pane**) *n.* a tall perennial flowering plant that is related to daisies and dandelions and has yellow flowers and large toothed hairy leaves. It is a natural antibiotic and digestive stimulant, and the roots are used to make a herbal remedy that is effective in the treatment of coughs and fevers. Latin name: *Inula helenium.* [14thC. Ultimately a contraction of medieval Latin *enula campana*, literally "elecampane of the fields," from *enula* "elecampane," via Latin *inula* from Greek *helenion*.]

e·lect /i lékt/ *v.* (**e·lect·ed, e·lect·ing, e·lects**) **1.** *vt.* CHOOSE SOMEBODY BY VOTE to choose somebody by a vote, e.g., for public office, an official role, or membership of some group ○ *She was elected leader of the commission.* **2.** *vt.* DECIDE TO DO SOMETHING to make a decision to do something **3.** *vti.* CHOOSE SOMETHING to choose or select something, particularly a subject or course to study at college **4.** *vt.* RELIG CHOOSE SOMEBODY FOR SALVATION to choose somebody by divine will for salvation ■ *adj.* **1.** CHOSEN BUT NOT YET IN OFFICE chosen by a vote but not yet formally installed in office (*used after a noun, usually in combination*) ○ *the president elect* **2.** RELIG CHOSEN BY GOD specially chosen by God for favor, salvation, or a task ○ *"Samson has assumed that, as an elect instrument, he must be always actively engaged in God's service."* (John Spencer Hill, *John Milton: Poet, Priest and Prophet*; 1979) ■ *npl.* **1.** RELIG PEOPLE CHOSEN BY GOD people specially chosen or favored by God, e.g., those chosen by God for salvation **2.** SELECT GROUP a specially privileged or gifted group (*literary*) ○ *World-class opera singers are among today's elect.* [15thC. From Latin *electus*, from *eligere* "to choose," from *legere* (source of English *collect, neglect,* and *lecture*).]

e·lect·a·ble /i léktəb'l/ *adj.* worthy to be elected, or having a good chance of being elected, especially to a public office —**e·lect·a·bil·i·ty** *n.*

e·lec·tion /i lékshən/ *n.* **1.** EVENT FOR CHOOSING BY VOTE an organized event at which somebody is chosen for something, especially a public office, by vote **2.** CHOOSING OR BEING CHOSEN BY VOTE the process of choosing somebody or of being chosen by vote ○ *he stood for election* **3.** SELECTION OF SOMETHING the act or process of choosing something, e.g., a course of action or subject (*formal*) **4.** RELIG SELECTION BY GOD FOR SOMETHING the fact of being chosen by God, or God's act of choosing somebody for salvation, a task, or special favor

Elec·tion Day *n.* a day designated by law for the election of people to public office. In the United States, Election Day for national elections is designated by law as the Tuesday after the first Monday in November in even-numbered years.

e·lec·tion·eer /i lèkshə neér/ (**-eered, -eer·ing, -eers**) *vi.* **1.** CAMPAIGN IN AN ELECTION to take an active part in an election campaign, especially as, or on behalf of, a candidate for political office **2.** DO SOMETHING JUST TO WIN VOTES to attempt to win votes in an election by being insincere and unscrupulous (*disapproving*) —**e·lec·tion·eer** *n.* —**e·lec·tion·eer·ing** *n.*

e·lec·tive /i léktiv/ *adj.* **1.** POL RELATING TO VOTING involving or concerned with voting **2.** POL REQUIRING ELECTION chosen by a vote, or whose holder is chosen by a vote ○ *The monarchy at that time was elective not hereditary.* **3.** EDUC NOT COMPULSORY optional rather than essential or compulsory ■ *n.* EDUC OPTIONAL SUBJECT OF STUDY an optional course that a student may select from among several alternatives —**e·lec·tive·ly** *adv.* —**e·lec·tive·ness** *n.*

e·lec·tor /i léktər/ *n.* **1.** SOMEBODY WHO VOTES somebody who votes or is entitled to vote in an election **2.** MEMBER OF AN ELECTORAL COLLEGE a member of an electoral college or the Electoral College

E·lec·tor *n.* any one of the rulers of the German states within the Holy Roman Empire who was entitled to vote in the election of the emperor

e·lec·tor·al /i léktərəl/ *adj.* relating to or involving elections, electors, or voters —**e·lec·tor·al·ly** *adv.*

e·lec·tor·al col·lege *n.* a select body of people who elect somebody to an office

E·lec·tor·al col·lege *n.* in the United States, the formal body elected by voters to choose the President and Vice President. Although U.S. voters in effect choose a President and Vice President, they are formally voting for members of the Electoral College, who make the choice on their behalf.

e·lec·tor·ate /i léktərət/ *n.* all the officially qualified voters within a given country or area or for a given election

electr- *prefix.* = **electro-** (*used before vowels*)

E·lec·tra /i léktrə/ *n.* in Greek mythology, the daughter of Agamemnon and Clytemnestra. She helped her brother Orestes to avenge their father's murder by killing their mother and Clytemnestra's lover. [From Greek *Ēlektra*, literally "bright, beaming," from *ēlektōr* "sun"; from her beauty]

E·lec·tra com·plex *n.* PSYCHOANAL a daughter's unconscious unresolved sexual attraction to her father. The term itself has now been rejected by most theorists.

E·lec·tra par·a·dox *n.* a logical paradox arising from the possibility of somebody knowing that something is true when it is described in one way but not when it is described in another [From a Greek myth in which Electra is said to know her brother Orestes when he is described but not when she encounters him as a stranger]

e·lec·tret /i léktrət/ *n.* a piece of insulating material that is permanently polarized and has a permanent electric field, used in microphones and telephones [Late 19thC. A blend of ELECTRICITY and MAGNET.]

e·lec·tric /i léktrik/ *adj.* **1.** INVOLVING OR CAUSED BY ELECTRICITY involving, relating to, or caused by electricity. See Usage note below. **2.** FOR ELECTRICITY carrying or conveying electricity **3.** USING ELECTRICITY powered or operated by electricity ○ *an electric guitar* **4.** TENSE OR EXCITED full of tension or excitement and anticipation **5.** BRIGHT extremely bright in color ○ *electric blue* ■ *n.* **1.** ELECTRICITY electricity, or the electricity supply, e.g., to a house (*informal*) **2.** SOMETHING OPERATED BY ELECTRICITY a vehicle, machine, or other device that is powered by electricity [Mid-17thC. From modern Latin *electricus*, from *electrum* "amber," from Greek *ēlektron*. The earliest manifestation of electricity was that produced by rubbing amber, hence the name.] —**e·lec·tri·cal·ly** *adv.*

WORD KEY: USAGE

electric or **electrical**? ***Electric*** is the word more commonly used to describe a device that works by electricity or is involved in producing or carrying electricity: *an electric oven; an electric socket.* ***Electrical*** is applied to more general things and to areas of study or activity that are concerned with electricity: *electrical appliances; electrical engineering.* ***Electric*** is more usual in the figurative meaning "tense or excited": *The atmosphere at the meeting was electric.*

e·lec·tri·cal /i léktrik'l/ *adj.* **1.** = **electric** *adj.* 1 **2.** = **electric** *adj.* 2 **3.** INVOLVING THE APPLICATION OF ELECTRICITY involved in or involving the application of electricity in technology **4.** RELATING TO ELECTRIC FUNCTIONING involving or concerned with electric cables or circuits, or parts powered by electricity ○ *You'll need an electrician for the electrical work.* **5.** CAUSED BY ELECTRICITY caused by electricity or something that uses or conveys electricity

WORD KEY: USAGE

See Usage note at ***electric.***

e·lec·tri·cal en·gi·neer·ing *n.* a branch of engineering that studies the practical applications of electricity in science and technology —**e·lec·tri·cal en·gi·neer** *n.*

e·lec·tric blan·ket *n.* a blanket containing an insulated electric heating element, used to warm a bed

e·lec·tric chair *n.* **1.** CHAIR FOR EXECUTING PEOPLE BY ELECTRICITY a specially designed chair used to execute people sentenced to death by electrocuting them **2.** SENTENCE OF DEATH BY ELECTROCUTION a sentence of death by electrocution in an electric chair

e·lec·tric eel *n.* a long air-breathing fish resembling a true eel that is found in South American rivers and can release a strong discharge of electricity from specialized organs in the tail region. Electric eels can produce a discharge of up to 650 volts, enough to stun a human being. Latin name: *Electrophorus electricus.*

e·lec·tric eye *n.* a device that converts light into electrical energy or uses it to regulate a flow of current, often incorporated into automatic control systems for doors and lighting

e·lec·tric field *n.* a field of force surrounding a charged body or associated with a fluctuating magnetic field, with which charged particles interact

e·lec·tric fire *n. U.K.* a heater for a room with an element that is made hot by an electric current passing through it

e·lec·tric gui·tar *n.* an electrically operated guitar, often with a solid body, that has a device for picking up sound fitted below the strings and connected to an amplifier and loudspeaker

e·lec·tri·cian /i lèk trísh'n, ee lek-/ *n.* somebody licensed to install, maintain, repair, or approve electrical wiring or electrical goods

e·lec·tric·i·ty /i lèk tríssətee, ee lek-/ *n.* **1.** PHYS **ENERGY CREATED BY MOVING CHARGED PARTICLES** a fundamental form of kinetic or potential energy created by the free or controlled movement of charged particles such as electrons, positrons, and ions **2.** ELEC ENG **ELECTRIC CURRENT** electric current, especially when used as a source of power **3. ANTICIPATION OR TENSION** a feeling or atmosphere of excited anticipation or tension

e·lec·tric jazz *n.* jazz produced using electronic instruments or other electronic devices

e·lec·tric light *n.* **1. ELECTRIC LIGHTING DEVICE** a light operated by electricity, e.g., one with an electric bulb or a fluorescent tube **2.** the illumination produced by electricity

e·lec·tric mo·tor *n.* a machine that converts energy from electricity into mechanical energy

e·lec·tric or·gan *n.* **1.** MUSIC **ORGAN POWERED BY ELECTRICITY** an organ whose sound is produced or amplified by means of electricity **2.** ZOOL **ELECTRICITY-PRODUCING MUSCLE IN FISH** specialized muscle tissue in some fish that creates an electric field used for finding enemies, obstacles, and food in murky water, and, in some species, for defense against attack

e·lec·tric pi·a·no *n.* an electronic keyboard instrument that produces sounds resembling those of the piano

e·lec·tric po·ten·tial *n.* PHYS the work required to bring a unit of positive electric charge from infinity to a specified point in an electric field. Symbol **V**

e·lec·tric ray *n.* a fish that lives in tropical or temperate seas and can emit a strong electric discharge from electric organs in its enlarged pectoral fins. Family: Torpedinidae.

e·lec·tric ra·zor *n.* a small electrically powered device used for shaving hair on the face or body

e·lec·tric shock *n.* a sudden painful physical reaction consisting of nerve stimulation and muscle contraction caused by an electric current flowing through the body

e·lec·tri·fy /i léktrə fī/ (**-fied, -fy·ing, -fies**) *vt.* **1. CONVERT TO USING ELECTRICITY** to convert something, e.g., a railroad line or a piece of machinery, so that it can operate on electric power **2.** PHYS **CHARGE ELECTRICALLY** to charge something with electricity **3. THRILL SOMEBODY** to cause somebody to feel a sudden and surprising shock, thrill, or sense of excitement **4.** MUSIC **ELECTRICALLY AMPLIFY A MUSICAL INSTRUMENT** to amplify the sounds produced by a musical instrument by electrical means —**e·lec·tri·fi·a·ble** *adj.* —**e·lec·tri·fi·ca·tion** /i lèktrəfi káysh'n/ *n.* —**e·lec·tri·fi·er** /i léktrə fīr/ *n.*

e·lec·tri·fy·ing·ly /i léktrə fī inglee/ *adv.* in an excitingly stimulating way

electro- *prefix.* **1.** electricity, electric, electronic ○ *electromyogram* **2.** electrolysis ○ *electrometallurgy* **3.** electron ○ *electropositive* [Via modern Latin from, ultimately, Greek *ēlektron* "amber"]

e·lec·tro·a·cous·tic *adj.* used to describe a device that converts sound into electrical signals or vice versa

e·lec·tro·a·cous·tics /i lèktrō ə kóostiks/ *n.* a branch of electronics that is concerned with how electricity is converted into sound (*takes a singular verb*) —**e·lec·tro·a·cous·tic·al·ly** *adv.*

e·lec·tro·a·nal·y·sis /i lèktrō ə nálləssiss/ (*plural* **-ses** /-nállə seez/) *n.* the use of electrolysis to perform chemical analysis —**e·lec·tro·an·a·lyt·ic** /i lèktrō ann'l íttik/ *adj.* —**e·lec·tro·an·a·lyt·i·cal** /-íttik'l/ *adj.* —**e·lec·tro·an·a·lyt·i·cal·ly** /-íttikəlee/ *adv.*

e·lec·tro·car·di·o·gram /i lèktrō kaárdee ə gràm/ *n.* a visual record of the heart's electrical activity made using an electrocardiograph

e·lec·tro·car·di·o·graph /i lèktrō kaárdee ə gràf/ *n.* a device that records the electrical activity of the heart muscle via electrodes placed on the chest, and displays it as a visual record —**e·lec·tro·car·di·o·graph·ic** /-kaardee ə gráffik/ *adj.* —**e·lec·tro·car·di·o·graph·i·cal·ly** /-gráffikəlee/ *adv.* —**e·lec·tro·car·di·og·ra·phy** /-óggrəfee/ *n.*

e·lec·tro·cau·ter·y /i lèktrō kóttəree/ *n.* the process of destroying unwanted tissue, e.g., warts and polyps, or sealing blood vessels, by means of an electrically heated needle

e·lec·tro·chem·i·cal se·ries *n.* a series in which the chemical elements are arranged in order of decreasing tendency to lose electrons

e·lec·tro·chem·is·try /i lèktrō kémmistree/ *n.* a branch of chemistry that studies chemical change associated with electrons and electricity —**e·lec·tro·chem·i·cal** *adj.* —**e·lec·tro·chem·i·cal·ly** *adv.* —**e·lec·tro·chem·ist** *n.*

e·lec·tro·co·ag·u·la·tion /i lèktrō kō aggyə láysh'n/ *n.* the use of an electrical device that burns tissue to stop bleeding from small blood vessels during surgery or to destroy small tumors

e·lec·tro·con·vul·sive ther·a·py *n.* the passing of a small electric current through the brain to induce a seizure, used in the treatment of severe psychiatric disorders

e·lec·tro·cute /i léktrə kyoot/ (**-cut·ed, -cut·ing, -cutes**) *vt.* **1. INJURE OR KILL WITH ELECTRIC SHOCK** to cause injury or death with an electric shock **2.** CRIMINOL **EXECUTE IN THE ELECTRIC CHAIR** to execute somebody by means of the electric chair [Late 19thC. A blend of ELECTRO- and EXECUTE.] —**e·lec·tro·cu·tion** /i léktrə kyóosh'n/ *n.*

e·lec·trode /i lék trōd/ *n.* either of the two conductors through which electricity enters or leaves something such as a battery or a piece of electrical equipment

e·lec·tro·de·pos·it /i lèktrō di pózzit/ *vt.* (**-it·ed, -it·ing, -its**) **DEPOSIT METAL BY ELECTROLYSIS** to deposit a substance, especially a metal, on an electrode by using electrolysis ■ *n.* **DEPOSITED SUBSTANCE** a substance deposited by using electrolysis —**e·lec·tro·dep·o·si·tion** /i lèktrō deppə zísh'n, -deepə-/ *n.*

e·lec·tro·dy·nam·ics /i lèktrō dī námmiks/ *n.* a branch of physics that studies how electric currents interact with magnetic and mechanical forces (*takes a singular verb*) —**e·lec·tro·dy·nam·ic** *adj.*

e·lec·tro·dy·na·mom·e·ter /i lèktrō dīnə mómmətər/ *n.* a device for measuring the strength of an electric current by the magnetic force it induces in a coil

e·lec·tro·en·ceph·a·lo·gram /i lèktrō en séffələ gràm/ *n.* the record of the electrical activity of the brain that is produced by an electroencephalograph

e·lec·tro·en·ceph·a·lo·graph /i lèktrō en séffələ gràf/ *n.* a machine that uses electrodes placed on the scalp to monitor the electrical activity of different parts of the brain, recording these as complex tracings. Irregularities recorded in the tracings may help in the diagnosis of a range of organic brain disorders such as tumors and epilepsy and in establishing brain death. —**e·lec·tro·en·ceph·a·lo·graph·ic** /i lèktrō en seffələ gráffik/ *adj.* —**e·lec·tro·en·ceph·a·log·ra·phy** /i lèktrō en seffə lóggrəfee/ *n.*

e·lec·tro·fish·ing /i léktrō fishing/ *n.* fishing that employs an electric current to attract or stun fish [Mid-20thC]

e·lec·tro·form /i léktrə fawrm/ *vt.* (**-formed, -form·ing, -forms**) **FORM BY DEPOSITING METAL USING ELECTRICITY** to form something, e.g., a medal, by using electrolysis to coat the surface of the mold or matrix with a metal ■ *n.* **ELECTROFORMED OBJECT** an object made by electroforming

e·lec·tro·graph /i léktrə gràf/ *n.* **1.** PHYS **ELECTROMETER** an electrometer that produces a graphic record of the measurements it makes, or the record it produces **2.** PHYS **GRAPH FROM AN ELECTROMETER** the visual record produced by an electrometer **3. ELECTRICAL ENGRAVING DEVICE** an electrical device for engraving a design on a metal plate for use in printing patterns for fabrics or wallpaper **4.** TELECOM **ELECTRICAL PICTURE TRANSMISSION DEVICE** an apparatus used to transmit pictures by electrical means, e.g., by fax **5.** TELECOM **TRANSMITTED PICTURE** a printed picture produced by an electrograph

e·lec·tro·hy·drau·lic /i lèktrō hī dróllik/ *adj.* using, or relating to the use of, electrical and hydraulic components —**e·lec·tro·hy·drau·li·cal·ly** *adv.*

e·lec·tro·ki·net·ic /i lèktrō ki néttik, -kī-/ *adj.* relating to or involving the motion of electrically charged particles and its effects —**e·lec·tro·ki·net·i·cal·ly** *adv.*

e·lec·tro·ki·net·ics /i lèktrō ki néttiks/ *n.* a branch of physics that deals with the motion of electrically charged particles (*takes a singular verb*) —**e·lec·tro·ki·net·i·cist** /i lèktrō ki néttissist/ *n.*

e·lec·trol·o·gist /i lèk tróllәjist, ee lek-/ *n.* somebody who removes moles, warts, or body hair by electrolysis

e·lec·tro·lu·mi·nes·cence /i lèk trō loomə néss'ns/ *n.* the emission of light by something such as a gas or phosphor resulting from a high-frequency electric discharge —**e·lec·tro·lu·mi·nes·cent** *adj.*

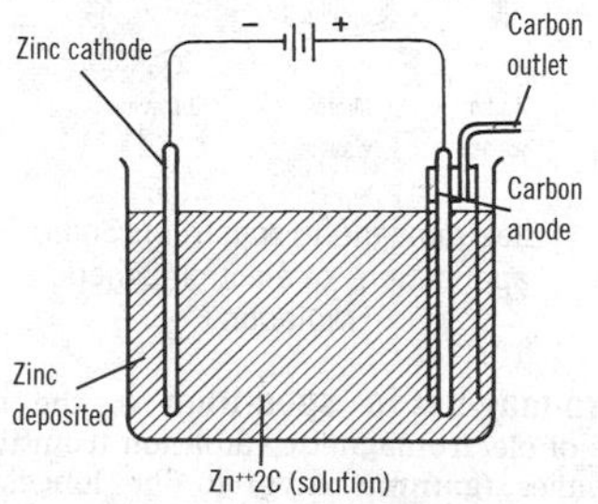

Electrolysis: Separation of zinc carbonate by electrolysis

e·lec·trol·y·sis /i lèk tróllisiss, ee lek-/ *n.* **1.** CHEM **CHEMICAL SEPARATION BY ELECTRICITY** the conduction of electricity through something melted or dissolved in order to induce decomposition of the melted or dissolved chemical into its components **2.** MED, COSMETICS **REMOVAL TECHNIQUE USING ELECTRICITY** the use of an electric current applied though a needle to remove body hair for cosmetic purposes, or to destroy warts, moles, or tumors for medical reasons

e·lec·tro·lyte /i léktrə līt/ *n.* **1.** CHEM **COMPOUND SEPARABLE INTO IONS IN SOLUTION** a chemical compound that separates into ions in a solution or when molten and is able to conduct electricity **2.** CHEM **ION** an ion in an electrolyte **3.** PHYSIOL **ION NEEDED BY CELL** any ion in cells, blood, or other organic material. Electrolytes help to control fluid levels in the body, maintain normal pH levels, and ensure the correct electric potential between nerve cells that enables the transmission of nerve signals.

e·lec·tro·lyt·ic /i léktrə líttik/ *adj.* **1. RELATING TO ELECTROLYSIS** involved in or relating to electrolysis **2. RELATING TO ELECTROLYTES** relating to, containing, or consisting of electrolytes —**e·lec·tro·lyt·i·cal·ly** *adv.*

e·lec·tro·lyt·ic cell *n.* **1. DEVICE PRODUCING ELECTROLYSIS BY ELECTRICITY** a device in which electrolysis can be produced, usually consisting of an electrolyte, its container, and electrodes **2. DEVICE PRODUCING ELECTRICITY BY CHEMICAL REACTION** a device consisting of an electrolyte, its container, and two electrodes, in which a chemical reaction between the electrolyte and the electrodes produces electricity

e·lec·tro·lyze /i léktrə līz/ (**-lyzed, -lyz·ing, -lyz·es**) *vt.* to use electrolysis to decompose a chemical compound [Mid-19thC. A blend of ELECTROLYSIS and ANALYZE.]

e·lec·tro·mag·net /i lèktrō mágnət/ *n.* a magnet consisting of a core, often made of soft iron, that is temporarily magnetized by an electric current in a coil that surrounds it

e·lec·tro·mag·net·ic /i lèktrō mag néttik/ *adj.* created by or relating to electromagnetism —**e·lec·tro·mag·net·i·cal·ly** *adv.*

e·lec·tro·mag·net·ic field *n.* a field of force associated with a moving electric charge and consisting of electric and magnetic fields that are generated at right angles to each other

e·lec·tro·mag·net·ic force *n.* the force resulting from the interaction of charged particles and their electric and magnetic fields

e·lec·tro·mag·net·ic in·ter·fer·ence *n.* the interference in a circuit, e.g., disturbance on a television set, caused by the radiation of an electric or magnetic field or the operation of a nearby electric motor

e·lec·tro·mag·net·ic ra·di·a·tion *n.* electromagnetic energy such as gamma rays, X-rays, ultraviolet light, visible light, infrared radiation, microwaves, and radio waves. The radiation is characterized by having magnetic and electric fields that are perpendicular to one another and to the direction of propagation, and travels without a supporting medium.

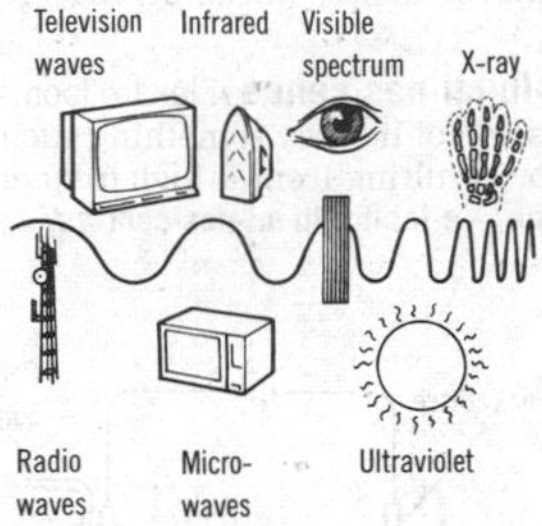

Electromagnetic spectrum: Some applications of electromagnetic radiation

e·lec·tro·mag·net·ic spec·trum *n.* the complete range of electromagnetic radiation from the shortest waves **(gamma rays)** to the longest **(radio waves)**

e·lec·tro·mag·net·ic u·nit *n.* any unit in the centimeter-gram-second system of units for measuring electricity and magnetism that gives a value of 1 to the magnetic constant, e.g., the abampere or the abvolt

e·lec·tro·mag·net·ic wave *n.* a wave of energy with a frequency within the electromagnetic spectrum, generated by the periodic fluctuation of an electromagnetic field resulting from the acceleration or oscillation of an electric charge. Electromagnetic waves can be reflected, refracted, and polarized, and exhibit interference and diffraction effects.

e·lec·tro·mag·net·ism /i lèktrō mágnə tìzzəm/ *n.* **1.** MAGNETISM FROM ELECTRIC CURRENTS magnetism produced by an electric current **2.** INTERACTION OF ELECTROMAGNETIC FORCES the branch of physics concerned with the interaction of electric and magnetic fields and with electromagnetism

e·lec·tro·mech·an·i·cal /i lèktrō mə kánnik'l/ *adj.* relating to or used to describe a mechanical device that is powered or controlled by electricity —**e·lec·tro·mech·an·i·cal·ly** *adv.*

e·lec·tro·met·al·lur·gy /i lèktrō métt'l ùrjee/ *n.* the range of metallurgical processes in which electricity has a key role, e.g., electroplating and the use of arc furnaces

e·lec·trom·e·ter /i lek trómmətər, èelek-/ *n.* a sensitive device for measuring extremely low voltages by means of the forces of attraction and repulsion between charged bodies on plates or wires

e·lec·tro·mo·tive /i lèktrō mṓtiv/ *adj.* relating to or producing an electric current

e·lec·tro·mo·tive force *n.* **1.** FORCE CAUSING ELECTRICITY FLOW a force that causes the flow of electricity from one point to another. Symbol *E* **2.** ENERGY CONVERTIBLE INTO ELECTRICITY the energy available in a source such as a battery for conversion into electricity from a chemical, mechanical, or other nonelectric form, measured in volts per unit of electric charge. Full form of **EMF, emf**

e·lec·tro·my·o·gram /i lèktrō mī ə gràm/ *n.* a graphical tracing of the electrical activity in a muscle at rest or during contraction, used to diagnose nerve and muscle disorders

e·lec·tro·my·o·graph /i lèktrō mī ə gràf/ *n.* a machine for producing an electromyogram from electrical activity picked up via electrodes inserted into muscle tissue. It consists of an amplifier, an electrically activated trace-drawing pen, and a moving strip of paper. —**e·lec·tro·my·o·graph·ic** /i lèktrō mī ə gráffik/ *adj.* —**e·lec·tro·my·o·graph·i·cal·ly** /-gráffikəlee/ *adv.* —**e·lec·tro·my·og·ra·phy** /-mī óggrəfee/ *n.*

e·lec·tron /i lék tròn/ *n.* a stable negatively charged elementary particle with a small mass that is a fundamental constituent of matter and orbits the nucleus of an atom

e·lec·tro·neg·a·tive /i lèktrō néggətiv/ *adj.* ◊ **electropositive 1.** POSSESSING NEGATIVE ELECTRIC CHARGE with a negative electric charge, and so tending to move toward a positive electric pole **2.** GAINING ELECTRONS IN CHEMICAL REACTION tending to gain electrons to form a bond in a chemical reaction

e·lec·tro·neg·a·tiv·i·ty *n.* a measure of the tendency of an atom in a molecule to attract the electrons in a chemical bond

e·lec·tron gun *n.* a device such as one used in a cathode-ray tube that directs a steady stream of electrons in a desired direction

e·lec·tron·ic /i lèk trónnik, èe lek-/ *adj.* **1.** ELECTRON ENG INVOLVING A CONTROLLED FLOW OF ELECTRONS relating to, or produced or operated by, the controlled flow of electrons through a semiconductor, a gas, or free space **2.** ELECTRON ENG USING VALVES, TRANSISTORS, OR SILICON CHIPS relating to devices, systems, or circuits that employ components such as vacuum tubes, integrated circuits, or transistors in their design **3.** COMPUT BY COMPUTER using or controlled by a computer or computer network, or relating to the use of computers in an activity ○ *electronic banking* **4.** PHYS ELECTRONS relating to electrons ○ *electronic spectrum* —**e·lec·tron·i·cal·ly** *adv.*

e·lec·tron·ic church *n.* radio and television broadcasting devoted to religious services, especially Protestant ones, and their pastors and audience

e·lec·tron·ic da·ta proc·ess·ing *n.* computer-based tasks that involve the input of data such as invoices or payrolls and its subsequent manipulation, usually using database programs

e·lec·tron·ic flash *n.* a flash device used in high-speed photography that produces a very bright light by passing an electric charge through a gas-filled tube

e·lec·tron·ic jour·nal·ism *n.* news coverage that is transmitted electronically, e.g., by television or over the Internet

e·lec·tron·ic mail *n.* full form of **e-mail**

e·lec·tron·ic mu·sic *n.* music produced or modified by electronic means, often with the aid of a computer

e·lec·tron·ic news·gath·er·ing *n.* televison news coverage made at the time and place of the event or incident by means of video equipment

e·lec·tron·ic of·fice *n.* an office in which traditional office equipment such as typewriters, telephones, and fax machines are replaced by integrated programs running on computers (*dated*)

e·lec·tron·ic or·gan *n.* an electric organ (*dated*)

e·lec·tron·ic pub·lish·ing *n.* the production of documents in computer-readable form for distribution over a computer network or in other formats such as CD-ROMs

e·lec·tron·ics /i lèk trónniks, èe lek trónniks/ *n.* TECHNOLOGY OF ELECTRONIC DEVICES the branch of technology concerned with the design, manufacture, and maintenance of electronic devices (*takes a singular verb*) ■ *npl.* ELECTRONIC PARTS the electronic parts of a piece of equipment, or electronic devices and equipment generally

e·lec·tron·ic shop·ping *n.* the ordering and purchase of goods and services over a computer network, especially over the Internet

e·lec·tron·ic smog *n.* nonionizing radiation produced in the atmosphere by sources such as radar, radio and television broadcasting, and considered by some people to pose a general health risk

e·lec·tron·ic su·per·high·way *n.* = **information superhighway**

e·lec·tron·ic sur·veil·lance *n.* the gathering of information, especially in crime detection and prevention or in espionage, using electronic devices such as video cameras and wiretaps

e·lec·tron·ic town hall *n.* communication and discussion over television or the Internet between members of the governing bodies, e.g., states, towns, or schools, and members of the public

e·lec·tron lens *n.* a device that creates an electric or magnetic field around the path of an electron beam so that the beam may be focused

e·lec·tron mi·cro·graph *n.* a photograph of a specimen taken using an electron microscope

e·lec·tron mi·cro·scope *n.* a high-powered microscope that uses beams of electrons focused by an electron lens to create a magnified image on a fluorescent screen or photographic plate —**e·lec·tron mi·cros·co·py** *n.*

e·lec·tron mul·ti·pli·er *n.* a device for amplifying a very small current using the effects of secondary emission. Electrons from the original current strike an anode, producing secondary electrons that are directed to the next anode in a multi-stage process until the desired level of current is obtained.

e·lec·tron op·tics *n.* the science that deals with the direction, deflection, or focusing of beams of electrons by electric and magnetic fields, e.g., in electron lenses (*takes a singular verb*)

e·lec·tron shell *n.* PHYS = **shell** *n.* **19**

e·lec·tron trans·port *n.* the process in cells by which electrons are gradually transferred from compounds rich in energy to molecular oxygen by a series of chemical reactions, resulting in the release of energy subsequently used in the production of ATP

e·lec·tron tube *n.* a device that consists of a sealed glass vessel containing a gas or a vacuum, within which electrons flow between electrodes

e·lec·tron volt *n.* **1.** UNIT OF ENERGY a unit of energy equal to the energy gained by an electron accelerated through a potential difference of one volt and equal to 1.602 x 10^{-19} joule. Symbol **eV 2.** UNIT OF MASS the unit of mass of elementary particles, measured as a function of energy and usually expressed in terms of mega electron volts **(MeV)**

e·lec·tro·os·mo·sis *n.* the movement of a liquid through a membrane under the effect of an electric field

e·lec·tro·paint /i léktrə pàynt/ (**-paint·ed, -paint·ing, -paints**) *vt.* to apply paint to something by means of electrolysis [Mid-20thC]

e·lec·tro·phile /i léktrə fìl/ *n.* an atom, molecule, or chemical group that is attracted to electrons or accepts them —**e·lec·tro·phil·ic** /i lèktrə fíllik/ *adj.*

e·lec·tro·phon·ic /i lèktrə fónnik/ *adj.* producing sound by means of electronic equipment

e·lec·tro·pho·re·sis /i lèktrō fə réesiss/ *n.* the movement of charged particles in a colloid or suspension when an electric field is applied to them [Early 20thC. Coined from ELECTRO + Greek *phorēsis* "being carried" (see -PHORE).] —**e·lec·tro·pho·ret·ic** /i lèktrō fə réttik/ *adj.*

e·lec·troph·o·rus /i lèk tróffərəss, èe lek-/ (*plural* **-ri** /-rì/) *n.* a device that produces electric charges from the friction between a disk and a metal plate [Late 18thC. Coined from ELECTRO + *-phorus*, a Latinization of -PHORE.]

e·lec·tro·pho·tog·ra·phy /i lèktrō fə tóggrəfee/ *n.* any form of photography, e.g., xerography, that uses electricity to transfer an image onto paper —**e·lec·tro·pho·to·graph·ic** /i lèktrō fōtə gráffik/ *adj.*

e·lec·tro·phys·i·ol·o·gy /i lèktrō fìzzee ólləjee/ *n.* the branch of medicine or biology dealing with the study of electric activity in human or animal bodies —**e·lec·tro·phys·i·o·log·ic** /i lèktrō fìzzee ə lójjik/ *adj.* —**e·lec·tro·phys·i·o·log·i·cal** /-lójjik'l/ *adj.* —**e·lec·tro·phys·i·o·log·i·cal·ly** /-lójjikəlee/ *adv.* —**e·lec·tro·phys·i·ol·o·gist** /i lèktrō fìzzee óllәjist/ *n.*

e·lec·tro·plate /i léktrə plàyt/ *vt.* (**-plat·ed, -plat·ing, -plates**) COAT A SURFACE WITH METAL BY ELECTROLYSIS to use electrolysis to coat the surface of an object with metal ■ *n.* ELECTROPLATED OBJECTS objects coated with metal by means of electrolysis

e·lec·tro·pos·i·tive /i lèktrō pózzitiv/ *adj.* ◊ **electronegative 1.** PHYS POSSESSING POSITIVE ELECTRIC CHARGE with a positive electric charge, and so tending to move toward a negative electric pole **2.** CHEM RELEASING ELECTRONS TO FORM A CHEMICAL BOND tending to release electrons to form a bond in a chemical reaction

e·lec·tro·re·cep·tor /i lèktrō ri séptər/ *n.* an organ in fish such as sharks, electric eels, and catfish that detects electric charges

e·lec·tro·scope /i léktrə skṑp/ *n.* a device that detects and measures an electric charge, usually consisting of a rod holding two strips of gold foil that separate when a like charge is applied to each —**e·lec·tro·scop·ic** /i lèktrə skóppik/ *adj.*

e·lec·tro·sen·si·tiv·i·ty /i lèktrō sensə tívvətee/ *n.* the ability in an animal to detect naturally occurring electric currents and use them to navigate or locate objects

e·lec·tro·shock /i léktrō shòk/ *n.* = **electroconvulsive therapy** ■ *vt.* (**-shocked, -shock·ing, -shocks**) **GIVE ELECTROCONVULSIVE THERAPY TO SOMEBODY** to administer electroconvulsive therapy to a patient

e·lec·tro·shock ther·a·py *n.* PSYCHIAT = **electroconvulsive therapy**

e·lec·tro·stat·ic /i lèktrō státtik/ *adj.* **1. RELATING TO STATIC ELECTRICITY** produced by or relating to static electricity **2. OF ELECTROSTATICS** relating to electrostatics —**e·lec·tro·stat·i·cal·ly** *adv.*

e·lec·tro·stat·ic gen·er·a·tor *n.* PHYS = **Van de Graaff generator**

e·lec·tro·stat·ic pre·cip·i·ta·tor *n.* a device that removes small particles of smoke, dust, or oil from air by electrostatically charging them and then attracting them to an oppositely charged collector plate or surface —**e·lec·tro·stat·ic pre·cip·i·ta·tion** *n.*

e·lec·tro·stat·ic print·ing *n.* a photocopying or printing process in which images are reproduced on a surface using electrostatic charges

e·lec·tro·stat·ics /i lèktrō státtiks/ *n.* a branch of physics dealing with electric charges at rest (**static electricity**) (*takes a singular verb*)

e·lec·tro·stat·ic u·nit *n.* a unit for measuring the magnitude of forces of repulsion between static electric charges in the centimeter-gram-second system, e.g., the statampere and the statvolt

e·lec·tro·sur·ger·y /i lèktrō súrjəree/ *n.* the use of an electric device or current during surgery, e.g., to cut or cauterize tissue —**elec·tro·sur·gi·cal** /i lèktrō súrjik'l/ *adj.* —**e·lec·tro·sur·gi·cal·ly** *adv.*

e·lec·tro·ther·a·py /i lèktrō thérrəpee/ *n.* any form of medical treatment that uses electricity as a cure or relief, e.g., as a way of stimulating nerves and the muscles they are connected to —**e·lec·tro·ther·a·peu·tic** /i lèktrō therrə pyṓotik/ *adj.*

e·lec·tro·ther·mal /i lèktrō thúrm'l/ *adj.* involving or relating to electricity and heat, or the production of heat by electricity ○ *electrothermal energy conversion* —**e·lec·tro·ther·mal·ly** *adv.*

e·lec·tro·type /i léktrə tīp/ *n.* **1. DUPLICATE PRINTING PLATE MADE BY ELECTROPLATING** a duplicate of a block of type or engraving made by electroplating a wax, lead, or plastic mold of the original **2. PRINTED ITEM** something printed from an electrotype ■ *vt.* (**-typed, -typ·ing, -types**) **PRINT USING AN ELECTROTYPE** to print something from an electrotype —**e·lec·tro·typ·er** *n.* —**e·lec·tro·typ·ic** /i lèktrō típpik/ *adj.*

e·lec·tro·va·lence /i lèktrō váyləns/ *n.* the combining power of an element, measured by the number of electrons one atom of it acquires from or transfers to another atom during the formation of a chemical compound —**e·lec·tro·va·lent** *adj.*

e·lec·tro·va·lent bond *n.* a chemical bond that is created during the formation of a compound by transfer of one or more electrons from one atom to another, the resulting oppositely charged ions being held together by attraction

e·lec·tro·weak /i léktrō wḗk/ *adj.* PHYS used to describe a type of fundamental interaction uniting electromagnetic forces with the weak interaction

e·lec·trum /i léktrəm/ *n.* a pale-colored alloy of silver and gold used in jewelry and ornaments [14thC. Via Latin, "amber," from Greek *ēlektron.*]

e·lec·tu·ar·y /i lékchoo èrree/ (*plural* **-ies**) *n.* a sweet-tasting paste made by mixing a drug with syrup or honey, administered by being applied to the teeth, tongue, or gums [14thC. Via late Latin *electuarium*, of uncertain origin: probably from Greek *eleikton*, from *eleikhein* "to lick up."]

el·ee·mos·y·nar·y /èllə móss'n èrree, èllee ə-/ *adj.* (*formal*) **1. OF OR FOR CHARITY** relating to or given as charity **2. SUPPORTED BY CHARITY** supported by or depending on charitable gifts [Late 16thC. Via medieval Latin *eleemosynarius*, from *eleemosyna* "alms," from, ultimately, Greek *eleos* "mercy."]

el·e·gance /élləgəns/ *n.* **1. GRACE AND DIGNITY** a combination of graceful stylishness, distinction, and good taste in appearance, behavior, or movement ○ *leaning in a pose of studied elegance against the mantelpiece* **2. CONCISENESS** a satisfying or admirable neatness, ingenious simplicity, or precision in something ○ *the elegance of the solution* **3. SOMETHING ELEGANT** an elegant thing or quality [Early 16thC. Via French *élégance* from, ultimately, Latin *elegans* "choice" (see ELEGANT).]

el·e·gant /élləgənt/ *adj.* **1. STYLISH AND GRACEFUL** stylishly graceful, and showing sophistication and good taste in appearance or behavior ○ *A suit can be as expensive as you like; it's the wearer who makes it look elegant.* **2. SHOWING SKILL AND GRACE** executed or made with a combination of skill, ease, and grace ○ *an elegant forehand return* **3. CONCISE** satisfyingly and often ingeniously neat, simple, or concise ○ *an equation elegant in its simplicity* [15thC. Via French from Latin *elegans* "choice," from, ultimately, *eligire* "to pick out" (source of English *elect*).] —**el·e·gant·ly** *adv.*

el·e·gi·ac /èllə jī ək/, **el·e·gi·a·cal** /èllə jī ək'l/ *adj.* **1. MOURNFUL** expressing sorrow or regret (*formal*) ○ *"The same elegiac and lonely tone continues to haunt the later poetry."* (Northrop Frye, *The Bush Garden*; 1972) **2.** LITERAT **LIKE AN ELEGY** resembling or characteristic of a poetic elegy in form or content [Late 16thC. Via French *élégiaque* or late Latin *elegiacus* from, ultimately, Greek *elegos* "song."] —**el·e·gi·a·cal·ly** *adv.*

el·e·gi·ac cou·plet *n.* a two-line unit of classical Greek and Latin poetry in which the first line comprises six dactylic feet and the second line five

el·e·gi·ac stan·za *n.* a four-line unit of verse in which each line comprises five iambic feet and alternate lines rhyme

el·e·gist /élləjist/ *n.* somebody who writes, reads, or recites an elegy

e·le·git /i lḗejit/ *n.* a writ against a debtor's property that permits a creditor to keep it until the debt is paid [Early 16thC. From medieval Latin, formed from Latin *eligire* "to choose."]

el·e·gize /éllə jīz/ (**-gized, -giz·ing, -giz·es**) *v.* **1.** *vti.* **COMMEMORATE SOMEBODY OR SOMETHING SORROWFULLY** to write or speak about somebody or something in a mournful, sorrowful way ○ *He elegized his lost comrade.* **2.** *vi.* **WRITE OR DELIVER AN ELEGY** to write, read, or recite an elegy

el·e·gy /élləjee/ (*plural* **-gies**) *n.* **1. MOURNFUL POEM** a mournful or reflective poem **2. POEM IN ELEGIAC COUPLETS OR STANZAS** a poem written in elegiac couplets or stanzas **3.** MUSIC **MUSICAL FOR LAMENT FOR DEAD PERSON** an instrumental piece, or setting for a song, composed as a lament for somebody who has died [Early 16thC. Via French *élégie* or directly from Latin *elegia* from, ultimately, Greek *elegos* "song."]

WORD KEY: CULTURAL NOTE

Elegy Written in a Country Churchyard, a poem by English writer Thomas Gray (1750). Inspired by a churchyard at Stoke Poges, Buckinghamshire, England, it is a reflection on rural life, human ambitions, friendship, and mortality. It is considered the masterpiece of the "graveyard" school of literature, which was popular in the 1740s and 1750s.

elem. *abbr.* elementary

el·e·ment /élləmənt/ *n.* **1. SEPARATE PART OR GROUP** a separate, identifiable part of something, or a distinct group within a larger group ○ *Landowners were the most stable element of society.* **2. LITTLE BIT** a small amount of something ○ *There was an element of revenge in what she did.* **3. FACTOR** a cause or factor leading to something ○ *Surprise was the key element in ensuring the success of the operation.* **4.** CHEM **BASIC UNIT OF MATTER** any substance that cannot be broken down into a simpler one by a chemical reaction. Elements consist of atoms with the same number of protons in their nuclei, and 92 occur naturally on earth. **5.** HIST **SUPPOSED BASIC UNIT OF MATTER** any one of the four primary substances, earth, air, fire, and water, that were formerly thought to be the materials from which all matter is constructed **6. SOMETHING'S HABITAT** a natural habitat or environment **7.** ELEC, HOUSEHOLD **HEATING PART OF AN APPLIANCE** a part of an electric heater, stove, or other appliance that heats up when an electric current is passed through it **8.** GEOM **CONSTITUENT OF GEOMETRIC FIGURE** a point, line, plane, or other part of which a geometric figure is composed **9.** ELEC **COMPONENT OF ELECTRIC CIRCUIT** any component of an electric circuit **10.** MATH **PART OF MATHEMATICAL QUANTITY** a part of a given mathematical or geometric quantity, e.g., a number in an array or an angle in a triangle **11.** LOGIC, MATH **MEMBER OF SET** a member of a set **12.** OPTICS **COMPONENT OF AN OPTICAL SYSTEM** any lens or other component of an optical system **13.** ASTRON **PARAMETER DEFINING AN ORBIT** any one of the parameters required to define the nature of an orbit and to determine the position of a planetary body within it ■ *npl.* **1.** METEOROL **FORCES OF WEATHER** the forces of the weather, e.g., wind, cold, rain, or sunshine, especially when thought of as harsh and damaging ○ *We're pretty exposed to the elements up here on the hilltop.* **2. BASIC PRINCIPLES** the basic and most important things to be learned when studying a subject ○ *She was endeavoring to teach us the elements of a good prose style.* **3.** CHR **BREAD AND WINE IN CHRISTIAN CEREMONY** the bread and wine used by Christians to celebrate the ceremony known as the Eucharist, Communion, or the Lord's Supper [14thC. Via Old French from Latin *elementum* "rudiment," of uncertain origin.] ◇ **in your element** in the situation or environment to which you feel most suited or where you feel particularly happy

el·e·men·tal /èllə mént'l/ *adj.* **1. FUNDAMENTAL** basic and essential **2. RELATING TO NATURAL FORCES** relating to or caused by powerful natural forces ○ *elemental passions* **3.** reduced to, or reducing something to, a stark simplicity ○ *classic, elemental sculptures* **4.** CHEM **OF CHEMICAL OR ANCIENT ELEMENTS** relating to the chemical elements, or to the elements of earth, air, fire, and water that were once supposed to be the basic units of matter —**el·e·men·tal·ly** *adv.*

el·e·men·ta·ry /èllə méntəree, èllə méntree/ *adj.* **1. RUDIMENTARY** involving or encompassing only the most simple and basic facts or principles ○ *Anyone with an elementary knowledge of computing could have pointed that out to you.* **2. SIMPLE TO DO OR UNDERSTAND** requiring little skill or knowledge **3.** EDUC **OF AN ELEMENTARY SCHOOL** relating to an elementary school or the education provided there —**el·e·men·ta·ri·ly** /èllə men térrilee/ *adv.* —**el·e·men·ta·ri·ness** /-térreenəss/ *n.*

el·e·men·ta·ry par·ti·cle *n.* any one of the basic constituents of which matter and energy are composed, e.g., electrons, leptons, photons, or hadrons, held to be indivisible. They are elementary particles.

el·e·men·ta·ry school *n.* a school that provides the first four to eight years of basic education

el·e·mi /éllәmee/ *n.* CHEM a fragrant resin obtained from various tropical trees and used in making varnishes, inks, ointments, and perfumes [Mid-16thC. Via modern Latin from Arabic *al-lāmī*.]

e·len·chus /i léngkəss/ (*plural* **-chi** /-kī/) *n.* an argument that refutes a proposition by proving the opposite of its conclusions [Mid-17thC. Via Latin from Greek *elegkhos* "refutation."] —**e·lenc·tic** /i léngtik/ *adj.*

Elephant

el·e·phant /élləfənt/ (*plural* **-phants** *or* **-phant**) *n.* **1.** ZOOL **LARGE GRAYISH ANIMAL WITH LONG TRUNK** a large gray or grayish-brown animal with a long flexible trunk, prominent ears, thick legs, and pointed tusks. Elephants are the largest living land animals. Three species of elephants remain in existence today: the African elephant, African forest elephant, and Asian or Indian elephant. Latin name: *Loxodonta africana* and *Loxodonta cyclotis* and *Elephas maximus.* **2.** PALEONT **EXTINCT ANIMAL** an extinct animal that is related to living elephants **3. SOMETHING VERY LARGE** somebody or something that is extremely large or much larger than average [13thC. Via Old French *olifant* from Latin *elephantus* from, ultimately, Greek *elephās* "elephant, ivory."]

El·e·phan·ta Is·land /éllәfәntә-/ island in Bombay harbor, western India, approximately 6 mi./10 km east of Bombay. Area: 2 sq. mi./5 sq. km.

el·e·phant fo·li·o *n.* a book size from 24 to 25 in./61 to 63.5 cm in height

el·e·phant gar·lic *n.* a mild-flavored variety of garlic with very large bulbs, often roasted as a vegetable. Latin name: *Allium ampeloprasum.*

el·e·phant grass *n.* any of a number of tall coarse grasses or plants resembling grasses of tropical Africa and southern Asia. Genera: *Typha* and *Pennisetum.*

el·e·phant gun *n.* a large-caliber gun, typically .410 or more, used in hunting big game.

el·e·phan·ti·a·sis /èllәfәn tī́ әsiss/ *n.* **1.** MED **DISFIGURING ILLNESS CAUSING SWELLING** a chronic disease in which parasitic worms obstruct the lymphatic system, causing enlargement of parts of the body such as the legs and scrotum and hardening of the surrounding skin. It is transmitted by mosquitoes. **2. UNREASONABLE GROWTH** excessive and unreasonable growth or development of something [Mid-16thC. Via Latin from Greek, from *elephās* "elephant."]

ele·phan·tine /èllә fán teen, -tīn, éllәfәn-/ *adj.* **1. SLOW AND HEAVY** moving in a slow, heavy, and often clumsy or awkward way ○ *the heavy, elephantine tread of his feet* **2. ENORMOUS** very large or very great **3. LIKE AN ELEPHANT'S** resembling that of an elephant [Early 16thC. Via Latin from Greek *elephantinos*, from *elephās* "elephant."]

el·e·phant seal *n.* a large earless seal, the male of which has a long inflatable snout resembling an elephant's trunk. Elephant seals were hunted almost to extinction in the 19th century. Latin name: *Mirounga angustirostris* and *Mirounga leonina.*

el·e·phant's foot (*plural* **el·e·phant's foots**) *n.* an ornamental southern African climbing or trailing plant of the yam family with a large above-ground tuber that is sometimes used for food. Latin name: *Dioscorea elephantipes.*

El·eu·sin·i·an mys·ter·ies /ellyә sínnee әn-/ *npl.* an ancient Greek festival held annually at Eleusis and Athens that honored and celebrated Persephone, Demeter, and Dionysus

elev. *abbr.* elevation

el·e·vate /éllә vàyt/ (**-vat·ed, -vat·ing, -vates**) *vt.* **1. RAISE SOMETHING UP** to raise something to a higher level or position **2. RAISE SOMEBODY TO HIGHER RANK** to raise or promote somebody or something to a high or higher status, rank, or office ○ *elevated to the rank of bishop* **3. INCREASE SOMETHING** to increase the amount or intensity of something ○ *This was one factor that elevated interest rates higher than they otherwise would have been.* **4. RAISE SOMEBODY'S MIND OR SPIRIT** to lift somebody's mind or spirit to a more enlightened or exalted level (*formal*) **5.** ARMS **MAKE A GUN BARREL POINT HIGHER** to make the barrel of a field gun point at a higher angle [14thC. Via Latin *elevatus* from, ultimately, *levare* "to lighten."]

WORD KEY: SYNONYMS

See Synonyms at ***raise.***

el·e·vat·ed /éllә vàytәd/ *adj.* **1. AT A HIGH LEVEL OR POSITION** raised above ground level, or situated at a higher level than something else ○ *elevated track* **2. HIGH OR HIGHER IN RANK** high or higher in rank or status **3. INCREASED** increased in amount ○ *elevated levels of cholesterol* **4. AT A HIGH MORAL OR INTELLECTUAL LEVEL** set at a high moral or intellectual level ○ *Milton's elevated conception of the role of the poet*

el·e·vat·ed rail·road *n.* a rail system operating on a raised structure, usually above or over a street

el·e·va·tion /èllә váysh'n/ *n.* **1.** GEOG **HEIGHT ABOVE A LOCATION** the height above a specific reference point, especially sea level ○ *at an elevation of 1,000 feet above sea level* **2. RAISING SOMETHING, OR BEING RAISED** the act of raising somebody or something in height or status, or the process of being raised in height or status ○ *They congratulated him on his elevation to the cardinalship.* **3. DEGREE OF BEING RAISED** the degree or amount by which somebody or something is raised or elevated ○ *a figure skater who is able to get tremendous elevation in her triple jumps* **4. INCREASE** an increase in something (*technical*) ○ *Among the effects was an elevation in the level of dopamine.* **5.** ARCHIT **ARCHITECTURAL DRAWING OF A SIDE OF BUILDING** a scale drawing of any side of a building or other structure ○ *the front elevation of the proposed new wing* **6.** CIV ENG **ANGLE IN SURVEYING** the angle between a horizontal line and the line from a surveying instrument to a point above the horizontal, e.g., between eye level and a line to a nearby rooftop **7.** ARMS **ANGLE OF A GUN BARREL ABOVE HORIZONTAL** the angle to which the barrel of a large gun is raised above the horizontal **8.** CHR **RAISING OF THE HOST AND CHALICE** the raising up and showing to the people of the Host or chalice by a priest immediately after their consecration in a Mass **9.** ASTRON = **altitude** *n.* 4 **10.** BALLET **ABILITY TO JUMP, OR THE HEIGHT REACHED** the ability of a ballet dancer to jump high and hold the position briefly, or the height a dancer can reach in jumping — **el·e·va·tion·al** *adj.*

el·e·va·tor /éllә vàytәr/ *n.* **1.** TRANSP, BUILDING **PLATFORM FOR TAKING UP OR DOWN** a platform, cage, or enclosed compartment that is raised or lowered mechanically and used to take people or things to a higher or lower level in a building **2.** AGRIC **GRAIN STOREHOUSE** a storehouse for grain, equipped with a mechanism for taking in, lifting, and discharging the grain **3.** TECH **HOISTING MACHINE** a machine with scoops or similar devices for hoisting something to a higher level **4.** AIR **AIRCRAFT DEVICE CONTROLLING CLIMB AND DESCENT** a hinged flap, either of a pair on the rear portion of the horizontal stabilizing surface or tail plane of an aircraft, used to control the aircraft's up and down movement **5.** AIR **AIRCRAFT PLATFORM ON CARRIER** on an aircraft carrier, a mechanized platform that transports aircraft from a below-the-deck hangar up to the flight deck and vice versa **6.** ANAT **MUSCLE THAT LIFTS PART OF THE BODY** a muscle that contracts to lift a part of the body

el·e·va·tor mu·sic *n.* bland instrumental background music played over loudspeakers in elevators, stores, and other public places (*informal disapproving*)

e·lev·en /i lévәn/ *n.* **1. NUMBER 11** the number 11, which is one more than 10 and one fewer than 12 **2. SOMETHING WITH A VALUE OF 11** something in a numbered series with a value of 11 **3. GROUP OF 11** a group of 11 objects or people **4.** SPORTS **TEAM OF 11** a team of 11 players, e.g., a football team or a field hockey team [Old English *endleofan*, literally "one over (ten)"] — **e·lev·en** *adj., pron.*

e·lev·ens·es *n. U.K.* a snack, usually including a drink, taken in the middle of the morning, especially by children (*takes a singular or plural verb*)

e·lev·enth /i lévәnth/ *n.* one of 11 equal parts of something [Old English *endleofeþa*. See ELEVEN.] — **e·lev·enth** *adj., adv.*

e·lev·enth hour *n.* the last moment before something happens ○ *"Time after time you'll find solutions are reached at the 59th minute of the eleventh hour."* (John Major, *Guardian Weekly*; April 3, 1994)

el·e·von /éllә vòn/ *n.* a hinged flap on an aircraft, especially one with a delta wing or no tail, that functions both as an elevator and an aileron [Mid-20thC. A blend of ELEVATOR and AILERON.]

elf /elf/ (*plural* **elves** /elvz/) *n.* **1.** MYTHOL **SMALL SUPERNATURAL MISCHIEF-MAKER** a small lively creature resembling a human being, often considered to have a mischievous nature and magical powers **2. SMALL MISCHIEVOUS PERSON** any small person, especially a child, who plays pranks or tricks [Old English, of prehistoric Germanic origin]

ELF *abbr.* extremely low frequency

elf·in /élfin/ *adj.* **1. OF OR LIKE AN ELF** like, characteristic of, or associated with elves **2. BY ELVES** caused or made by elves **3. DELICATE** small and delicate ○ *elfin features* **4. SMALL AND LIVELY** small, delicate, and charmingly spritely, lively, or mischievous **5. MAGICAL OR CHARMING** having a magical or delicately charming quality

elf·ish /élfish/, **elv·ish** /élvish/, **elf·like** /élf līk/ *adj.* **1. OF OR LIKE AN ELF** like or relating to an elf **2. MISCHIEVOUS** full of lively mischief —**elf·ish·ly** *adv.*

elf·lock /élf lòk/ *n.* a tangled coil of hair (*often used in the plural*)

El·gar /él gaar, élgәr/, **Sir Edward** (1857–1934) British composer. He was a major figure of late romanticism in music, writing both choral and orchestral works. His *Enigma Variations* (1899) and the patriotic *Pomp and Circumstance Marches* (1901–30) are among his most popular pieces.

AKG London

Sir Edward Elgar

El·gin /élgin/ city in northeastern Illinois, on the Fox River, north of Aurora and west of Chicago. Population: 86,034 (1996).

el·hi /él hī/ *adj.* used to describe educational material relating to or designed for use in grades 1 to 12 ○ *elhi textbooks and software* [Mid-20thC. Shortening and blend of ELEMENTARY + HIGH.]

e·lic·it /i líssit/ (**-it·ed, -it·ing, -its**) *vt.* **1. PROVOKE A REACTION** to cause or produce something as a reaction or reponse to a stimulus of some kind ○ *His jokes failed to elicit even the faintest of smiles from her.* **2. DRAW OUT SOMETHING HIDDEN** to bring to light, or cause somebody to disclose, something hidden or not immediately obvious, especially by a process of questioning or research ○ *What were their chances of eliciting any worthwhile information from such an obstinately uncooperative witness?* [Mid-17thC. Formed from Latin *elicitus* "drawn out," from, ultimately, *lacere* "to deceive."] —**e·lic·i·ta·tion** /i lìssi táysh'n/ *n.* —**e·lic·i·tor** /i líssitәr/ *n.*

e·lide /i līd/ (**e·lid·ed, e·lid·ing, e·lides**) *vt.* **1.** LANG **OMIT ELEMENT OF WORD OR PHRASE** to omit a vowel, consonant, or syllable of a word, or leave out part of a sentence or phrase **2. OMIT SOMETHING** to omit, delete, or ignore something (*formal*) [Late 16thC. From Latin *elidere* "to strike out," from *laedere* "to strike."]

el·i·gi·ble /éllijәb'l/ *adj.* **1. QUALIFIED** entitled or qualified to do, be, or get something ○ *She is eligible to run for office.* **2. MARRIAGEABLE** considered a good candidate for marriage ○ *the most eligible bachelor in town* **3.** FOOTBALL **ALLOWED BY RULES TO CATCH A FOOTBALL** permitted by the rules to catch a forward pass during a play in football ■ *n.* **SOMEBODY OR SOMETHING ELIGIBLE** somebody who or something that meets a set of requirements ○ *We've separated the eligibles from the nonstarters.* [15thC. Via middle French *éligible* "fit to be chosen" from late Latin *eligibilis* "that may be chosen," from Latin *eligere* "to choose" (see ELECT).] —**el·i·gi·bil·i·ty** /èllijә bíllәtee/ *n.* —**el·i·gi·bly** /éllijәblee/ *adv.*

e·lim·i·nate /i límmә nàyt/ (**-nat·ed, -nat·ing, -nates**) *vt.* **1. TAKE SOMEBODY OR SOMETHING AWAY** to remove something or somebody from a list or group, or decide to disregard somebody or something as irrelevant or unimportant ○ *The police eliminated him from the list of suspects.* **2. END SOMETHING** to put an end to something, usually something undesirable ○ *They are pledged to eliminate poverty by the end of the century.* **3.** SPORTS **PUT SOMEBODY OUT OF A COMPETITION** to defeat and put a player or team out of a competition ○ *The local team was eliminated in the first round.* **4. DESTROY SOMEBODY** to kill somebody, destroy something, or make somebody or something ineffective ○ *The pills eliminated the dog's worms.* **5.** PHYSIOL **DEFECATE OR URINATE** to expel waste from the body (*technical*) **6.** MATH **REMOVE A MATHEMATICAL VARIABLE** to remove variables from two or more simultaneous mathematical equations by combining the equations [Mid-16thC. From Latin *eliminare*, literally "to turn out of doors," from *limen* "threshhold" (source of English *subliminal* and probably *sublime*).] —**e·lim·i·na·tion** /i lìmmә náysh'n/ *n.* —**e·lim·i·na·tive** /i límmә nàytiv/ *adj.* —**e·lim·i·na·to·ry** /i límmәnә tàwree/ *adj.* —**e·lim·i·na·tor** /i límmә nàytәr/ *n.*

E·LINT /ée lìnt/, **e·lint** *n.* the gathering of information by electronic means, e.g., from aircraft or ships, or the section of the military intelligence service involved in this [Mid-20thC. Shortening and blend of ELECTRONIC + INTELLIGENCE.]

El·i·ot /éllee әt/, **George** (1819–80) British novelist. One of the greatest English novelists, she wrote works including *Adam Bede* (1854) and *Middlemarch* (1871–72). Real name **Mary Ann Evans**

Barnaby's

George Eliot

El·i·ot, John (1604–90) English-born American colonial clergyman. As a missionary, he preached to the Native Americans in Massachusetts in their own language and published a Native American translation of the Bible (1661–63). Known as **Apostle to the Indians**

U.S. Office of War Information

T. S. Eliot

El·i·ot, T. S. (1888–1965) U.S.-born British poet, critic, and dramatist. His poem *The Waste Land* (1922) represents a landmark in modern English poetry. He won a Nobel Prize in literature in 1948. Later works include *Four Quartets* (1935–42) and the verse drama *Murder in the Cathedral* (1935). Full name **Thomas Stearns Eliot**

E·LI·SA /i lízə, i líssə/ *n.* a widely used technique for determining the presence or amount of protein in a biological sample, using an enzyme that bonds to an antibody or antigen and causes a color change. Full form **enzyme-linked immunosorbent assay**

e·li·sion /i lízh'n/ *n.* **1.** LANGUAGE **OMISSION OF ELEMENT OF WORD** the omission of a vowel, consonant, or syllable while pronouncing or writing something, sometimes as a natural shortening, as in "He's," sometimes for literary or poetic effect, as in "t'is" **2. ANY OMISSION OR DELETION** the suppression, omission, or deletion of something, or what has been suppressed, omitted, or deleted (*formal*) [Late 16thC. Via Latin *elisio* from, ultimately, *elidere* "to strike out" (see ELIDE).]

e·lite /i léet, ay léet/ *n.* **1. PRIVILEGED MINORITY** a small group of people within a larger group who have more power, social standing, wealth, or talent than the rest of the group (*takes a singular or plural verb*) ○ *They belonged to a privileged elite who were being groomed for the top posts in the administration.* **2.** PRINTING **SIZE OF PRINTING TYPE** a 10-point type that has about 12 characters to the inch, or just under 5 characters to the centimeter ■ *adj.* **1. RICHEST, BEST, OR MOST POWERFUL** belonging to an elite, especially in being more talented, privileged, or highly trained than the rest ○ *elite troops* **2. FOR RICH OR PRIVILEGED PEOPLE** with a membership that is restricted, especially to the rich or privileged [Late 18thC. Via French from, ultimately, Latin *eligere* "to choose" (see ELECT).]

e·lit·ism /i lée tìzzəm, ay lée-/ *n.* **1. BELIEF IN CONCEPT OF SUPERIORITY** the belief that some people or things are inherently superior to others and deserve preeminence, preferential treatment, or higher rewards because of their superiority **2.** POL, SOC SCI **BELIEF IN CONTROL BY SMALL GROUP** the belief that government or control should be in the hands of a small group of privileged, wealthy, or intelligent people, or the active promotion of such a system **3.** POL, SOC SCI **CONTROL BY SMALL GROUP** government or control by a small, specially qualified or privileged group —**e·lit·ist** *n., adj.*

e·lix·ir /i líksər/ *n.* **1.** PHARM **SWEETENED DRUG** a sweetened flavored solution of alcohol and water that acts as a medium for a drug and masks its taste **2.** HIST **MIRACULOUS SUBSTANCE** a substance once believed to prolong life indefinitely, or to transform base metals into gold **3. CURE-ALL** a panacea or a quick or magical cure [14thC.Via medieval Latin from Arabic *al-iksir,* from Greek *xērion* "dry powder for treating wounds," from *xēros* "dry."]

E·liz·a·beth /i lízzəbəth/, **Queen consort of the United Kingdom** (*b.* 1900). She married the second son of George V, who came to the throne as George VI in 1936, and is the mother of Queen Elizabeth II. Born **Lady Elizabeth Bowes-Lyon**

E·liz·a·beth city in northeastern New Jersey, situated on Newark Bay. Population: 110,002 (1990).

E·liz·a·beth I, Queen of England and Ireland (1533–1603). The daughter of Henry VIII and Anne Boleyn, she established the Protestant church in England and presided over a period of domestic political stability and global exploration.

E·liz·a·beth II, Queen of the United Kingdom (*b.* 1926). Daughter of George VI and queen since 1952, she married Prince Philip in 1947 and has four children, Prince Charles, Princess Anne, Prince Andrew, and Prince Edward. Born **Princess Elizabeth Alexandra Mary**

E·liz·a·be·than /i lìzzə béethən, -béthən/ *adj.* relating to or characteristic of the life and times of Elizabeth I, Queen of England and Ireland, who reigned from 1558 to 1603

E·liz·a·be·than son·net *n.* = **Shakespearean sonnet**

E·liz·a·beth·town /i lízzə bəth tòwn/ city in north central Kentucky, northeast of Bowling Green and south of Louisville. Population: 19,434 (1996).

elk /elk/ (*plural* **elk** *or* **elks**) *n. U.K.* = **moose** [Old English *eolh*]

Elk *n.* a member of a men's social and charitable organization, the Benevolent and Protective Order of Elks

Elk Grove /élk grōv/ village in northern California, a southern suburb of Sacramento. Population: 34,370 (1996).

Elk Grove Vil·lage village in northeastern Illinois, southwest of Des Plaines, that is a western suburb of Chicago. Population: 34,470 (1996).

Elk·hart /élk haàrt/ city in northern Indiana, at the confluence of the Saint Joseph and Elkhart rivers, near the border with Michigan. Population: 44,224 (1996).

elk·hound /élk hòwnd/ *n.* = **Norwegian elkhound**

Elk Is·land Na·tion·al Park national park in central Alberta, Canada, 20 mi./48 km east of Edmonton, established in 1913. Area: 75 sq. mi./194 sq. km.

Elk·ton /élktən/ city in northeastern Maryland, on the Elk River at the northern end of Chesapeake Bay. Population: 10,308 (1996).

ell /el/ *n.* **1.** ARCHIT **BUILDING EXTENSION** an extension of a building, usually at right angles to the main part **2. SOMETHING L-SHAPED** something L-shaped or with a right-angled bend [Late 18thC. Variant spelling of the letter *L*.]

el·lag·ic ac·id /ə làjjik-/ *n.* a crystalline compound obtained from oak galls and tannins. It has some capacity for reducing bleeding. Formula: $C_{14}H_6O_8$.

El·lef Ring·nes Is·land /è lef ríng nayss-/ one of the Canadian Sverdrup Islands, located in the Arctic Ocean, in the Northwest Territories. Area: 5,139 sq. mi./13,310 sq. km.

El·le·ry /éllərее/, **William** (1727–1820) U.S. politician. He was elected to the Second Continental Congress from Rhode Island (1776) and was a signatory of the Declaration of Independence.

Elles·mere Is·land /élzmeer-/ island in Nunavut Territory, northern Canada, close to the northwestern coast of Greenland. Area: 82,120 sq. mi./212,690 sq. km.

Elles·mere Is·land Na·tion·al Park Re·serve national park, established in 1980, in the northern part of Ellesmere Island situated in the Arctic Ocean, Nunavut, northeastern Canada. Area: 14,585 sq. mi./37,775 sq. km.

El·lice Is·lands /élliss-/ former name for **Tuvalu** (until 1975)

El·li·cott Cit·y /élli kot-/ town in central Maryland. Population: 41,396 (1990).

Barnaby's

Duke Ellington

El·ling·ton /éllingtən/, **Duke** (1899–1974) U.S. jazz pianist, composer, and band leader. He came to fame in the early 1930s and is known for compositions such as "Sophisticated Lady" (1933). Real name **Edward Kennedy Ellington**

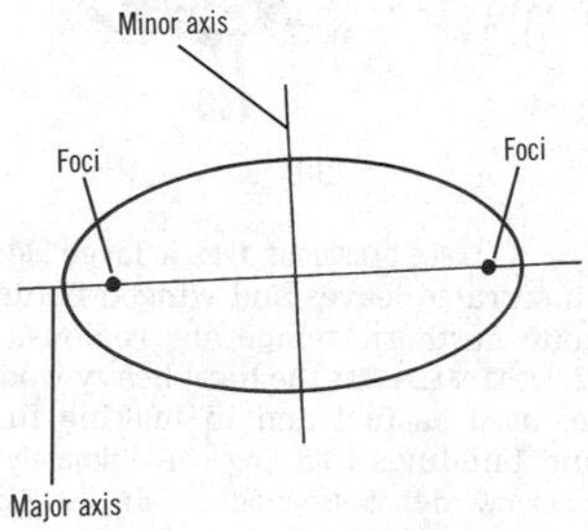

Ellipse

el·lipse /i líps/ *n.* **1.** GEOM **SHAPE RESEMBLING OVAL** a shape like a stretched circle with slightly longer, flatter sides **2.** GEOM **INTERSECTION OF CONE AND OBLIQUE PLANE** the shape formed by the intersection of a right cone and an oblique plane that does not intersect the base of the cone **3.** GRAM, PRINTING = **ellipsis** [Mid-18thC. Via French from Latin *ellipsis,* from Greek *elleipsis* "defect, omission," from *elleipein* "to leave out, fall short."]

el·lip·sis /i lípsiss/ (*plural* **-ses** /-seèz/) *n.* **1.** GRAM **OMISSION OF IMPLIED WORD** the omission of one or more words from a sentence, especially when what is omitted can be understood from the context. The omission of "go" in "I went but my wife didn't" (= "didn't go") is an example of ellipsis. **2.** PRINTING **MARK INDICATING OMITTED TEXT** a printed mark, usually three dots (...) or, less often, asterisks (***), used to indicate that something has been omitted from a text [Early 17thC. From Latin (see ELLIPSE).]

el·lip·soid /i líp sòyd/ *n.* GEOM **OVAL SHAPE** a geometric surface or a solid figure shaped like an oval. Any section through an ellipsoid is either an ellipse or a circle. ■ *adj.* **OVAL-SHAPED** in the shape of an ellipsoid —**el·lip·soid·al** *adj.*

el·lip·ti·cal /i líptək'l/, **el·lip·tic** /i líptik/ *adj.* **1.** GEOM **LIKE ELLIPSE** in the shape or pattern of a geometric ellipse **2.** GRAM **RELATING TO ELLIPSIS** relating to ellipsis or containing an example of ellipsis **3. HIGHLY ECONOMICAL IN SPEECH OR WRITING** extremely concise in speech or writing, sometimes so concise as to be difficult or impossible to understand —**el·lip·ti·cal·ly** *adv.*

el·lip·tic·i·ty /i lìp tíssitee/ (*plural* **-ties**) *n.* the deviation or degree of deviation of an ellipse or ellipsoid from a perfect circle or sphere. Ellipticity is measured as the ratio of the major axis to the minor axis of the ellipse or ellipsoid.

El·lis /élliss/, **Havelock** (1859–1939) British psychologist. His *Studies in the Psychology of Sex* (1897–1928) was a landmark in the analysis of sexual behavior. Full name **Henry Havelock Ellis**

El·lis Is·land complex of one natural and two artificial islands in upper New York Bay, eastern New Jersey and southeastern New York State, near Manhattan. From 1892 to1954 it served as a chief entry point for immigrants to the United States. Area: 27 acres/11 hectares.

El·li·son /élliss'n/, **Ralph** (1914–94) U.S. writer. He is best known for his novel about U.S. racial issues, *Invisible Man* (1952). Full name **Ralph Waldo Ellison**

Ells·worth /élz wùrth/, **Lincoln** (1880–1951) U.S. explorer. He was the first person to fly over the Arctic (1926) and Antarctica (1935).

Ells·worth, Oliver (1745–1807) U.S. judge and politician. He helped to shape the U.S. Constitution and was chief justice from 1796 to1799.

Ells·worth Land high plateau in western Antarctica, south of the Antarctic Peninsula. It rises at the Vinson Massif, the highest point in Antarctica, to 16,863 ft./5,140 m.

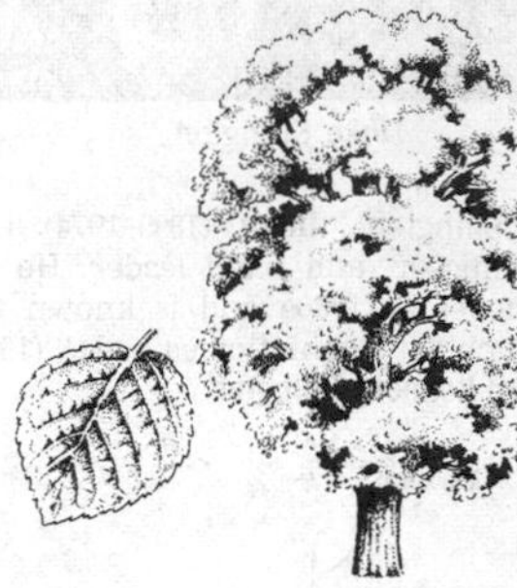

Elm

elm /elm/ *n.* **1. LARGE DECIDUOUS TREE** a large deciduous tree with serrated leaves and winged fruits, found throughout northern temperate regions. Genus: *Ulmus*. **2. WOOD OF ELM TREE** the hard heavy wood of the elm tree, used as fuel and in making furniture, boats, and buildings [Old English. Ultimately from an Indo-European word that also produced English *alder*.]

elm bark bee·tle *n.* the beetle that spreads the fungus causing Dutch elm disease. Family: Scolytidae.

Elm·hurst /élm hùrst/ city in northeastern Illinois, a residential and industrial suburb of Chicago. Population: 43,290 (1996).

El·mi·ra /el mīrə/ city in southern New York on the Chemung River, west of Binghamton. Population: 32,009 (1996).

El Mon·te /el móntee/ city in California south of the San Gabriel Mountains, an eastern suburb of Los Angeles. Population: 110,026 (1996).

Elm·wood Park /élm wŏŏd-/ village in northeastern Illinois, west of Chicago. Population: 22,760 (1996).

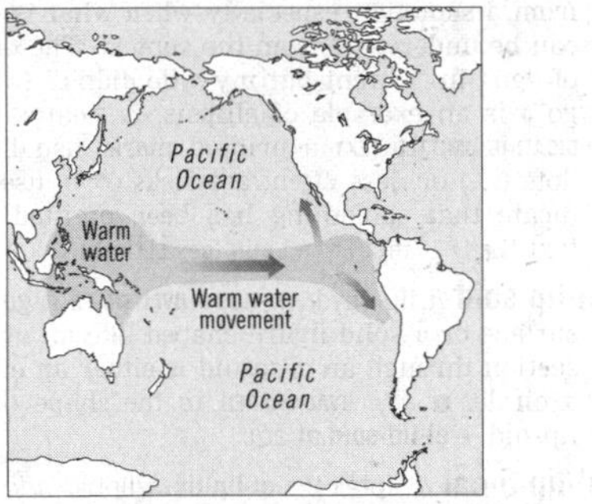

El Niño: Map showing movement of warm water currents across the Pacific Ocean

El Ni·ño /el neényō/ *n.* METEOROL a periodic change occurring every 5 to 8 years in Pacific Ocean currents off South America, often bringing severe climate disruption to countries in and beside the Pacific [From Spanish, shortening of *El Niño de Navidad* "the Christmas Child"; from the time of year when the currents change]

e·lo·de·a /i lṓdee ə/ *n.* a plant that grows submerged in ponds and ditches or is used in aquariums as an oxygenating plant. Canadian pondweed is a type of elodea. Genus: *Elodea*. [Late 19thC. From modern Latin, genus name, formed from Greek *helōdēs* "marshy."]

E·lo·him /e lṓ hìm, i lṓ hìm, èllō hím/ *n.* in the Bible, a Hebrew word for God [Late 16thC. From Hebrew *ĕlōhīm*, the plural of *ĕlōah* "God."]

e·lon·gate /i láwng gàyt/ *vti.* (**-gat·ed, -gat·ing, -gates**) **LENGTHEN** to make something longer, or become longer ■ *adj.* **1. LONG** long and narrow or slender (*technical*) **2. MADE LONGER** lengthened or stretched out (*formal*) [Mid-16thC. From late Latin *elongat-*, the past participle stem of *elongare* "to lengthen," from Latin *longus* "long."] —**e·lon·gat·ed** *adj.*

e·lon·ga·tion /i làwng gáysh'n/ *n.* **1. LENGTHENING** the act of lengthening something, or the condition of being lengthened **2. SOMETHING LENGTHENED** something that has become or been made longer **3.** ASTRON **ANGLE BETWEEN SUN AND CELESTIAL OBJECT** the angle between the Sun and either the Moon or a planet, as seen from Earth or a point in space

e·lope /i lṓp/ (**e·loped, e·lop·ing, e·lopes**) *vi.* to go away suddenly without telling anyone, especially in order to get married without the knowledge or consent of parents or guardians, or to live with a lover [Late 16thC. From Anglo-Norman *aloper*, literally "to run away," which was perhaps formed from a Middle English word meaning "run."] —**e·lope·ment** *n.* —**e·lop·er** *n.*

el·o·quence /élləkwəns/ *n.* **1. NOTABLE SPEAKING ABILITY** the ability to speak forcefully, expressively, and persuasively **2. EFFECTIVE LANGUAGE** forceful, expressive, and persuasive language

el·o·quent /élləkwənt/ *adj.* **1. SPEAKING OR SPOKEN BEAUTIFULLY AND FORCEFULLY** said or saying something in a forceful, expressive, and persuasive way **2. EXPRESSING EMOTION CLEARLY** expressing a feeling or thought clearly, memorably, or movingly [14thC. Via French from Latin *eloquent-*, the present participle stem of *eloqui* "to speak out," from *loqui* "to speak."] —**el·o·quent·ly** *adv.* —**el·o·quent·ness** *n.*

El Pas·o /el pássō/ city in western Texas on the Rio Grande, a port of entry from Mexico. Population: 579,307 (1994).

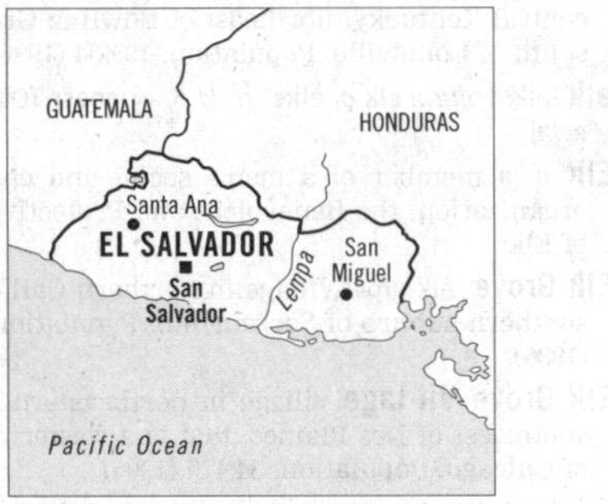

El Salvador

El Sal·va·dor /el sálvə dàwr/ republic on the Pacific coast of Central America, bordered by Guatemala and Honduras. Language: Spanish. Currency: colón. Capital: San Salvador. Population: 5,661,827 (1997). Area: 8,124 sq. mi./21,041 sq. km. Official name **Republic of El Salvador** —**Sal·va·do·ran** *n.*, *adj.*

else /els/ *adj.*, *adv.* **1. IN ADDITION** used to refer in a vague way to another person, place, or thing ○ (adj) *Something else I'd like to see is more jobs for skilled manual workers.* ○ (adj) *What else did she say?* ○ (adv) *Try to shop around and go somewhere else apart from your usual stores.* **2. DIFFERENT** used to refer in a vague way to somebody or something other or different ○ (adj) *Let's try something else.* ○ (adv) *He was unhappy and considered working somewhere else.* [Old English *elles*. Ultimately from an Indo-European word that also produced English *alter* and *alien*.]

El Se·gun·do /èl si gŏŏndō/ city in southern California on the southeastern shore of Santa Monica Bay, south of Los Angeles. Population: 15,607 (1996).

else·where /éls wàir, -hwàir/ *adv.* at, in, or to another place ○ *If you're calling from elsewhere, please press 2 to contact reception.* ○ *They stock used books, and they have their own imprint that may be hard to find elsewhere.* [Old English *elles hwǣr*, literally "other where"]

ELT *n.* the teaching of English to people whose first language is not English. Full form **English Language Teaching**

el·u·ant /éllyoo ənt/, **el·u·ent** *n.* a solvent used to remove something from a substance [Mid-20thC. From Latin *eluent-*, the present participle stem of *eluere* (see ELUTE).]

el·u·ate /élloo àyt, élloo ət/ *n.* CHEM the liquid left after the process of elution, consisting of dissolved matter and the solvent used [Mid-20thC. Coined from Latin *eluere* (see ELUTE) + -ATE.]

e·lu·ci·date /i lŏŏssə dàyt/ (**-dat·ed, -dat·ing, -dates**) *vti.* to explain or clarify something (*formal*) [Mid-16thC. From late Latin *elucidat-*, the past participle stem of *elucidare* "to make clear," from Latin *lucidus* "clear" (source of English *lucid*).] —**e·lu·ci·da·tion** /i lŏŏssə dáysh'n/ *n.* —**e·lu·ci·da·tive** *adj.* —**e·lu·ci·da·tor** *n.*

e·lude /i lŏŏd/ (**e·lud·ed, e·lud·ing, e·ludes**) *vt.* **1. ESCAPE OR AVOID** to escape from or avoid somebody or something by cunning, skill, or resourcefulness **2. ESCAPE SOMEBODY'S UNDERSTANDING OR MEMORY** to be beyond somebody's understanding, or be unable to be recalled [Mid-16thC. From Latin *eludere* "to deceive, escape from, win from somebody at play," from *ludere* "to play."]

WORD KEY: USAGE

See Usage note at ***avoid.***

E·lul /é lùl/ *n.* in the Jewish calendar, the 12th month of the civil year and the 6th month of the religious year. It is 29 days long. [Mid-16thC. From Hebrew *elūl*.]

e·lu·sion /ə lŏŏzh'n/ *n.* the act of avoiding or escaping from somebody or something (*formal*) [Mid-16thC. From the late Latin stem *elusion-*, from Latin *elus-*, the past participle stem of *eludere* (see ELUDE).]

e·lu·sive /ə lŏŏssiv, i-/ *adj.* **1. HARD TO FIND** difficult to find or catch **2. HARD TO PIN DOWN** difficult to understand, define, or identify **3. HARD TO REMEMBER** not easily called to mind or memory —**e·lu·sive·ly** *adv.* —**e·lu·sive·ness** *n.*

e·lu·so·ry /ə lŏŏssəree, ə lŏŏzəree/ *adj.* **1. HARD TO FIND** difficult to find or catch (*formal*) **2. EVASIVE** avoiding the issue in an evasive or deceitful way

e·lute /i lŏŏt/ (**e·lut·ed, e·lut·ing, e·lutes**) *vt.* CHEM to remove one substance from another, usually an adsorbed material from an adsorbent surface, by washing it out with a solvent (*technical*) [Mid-18thC. From Latin *elut-*, the past participle stem of *eluere* "to wash out," from *luere* "to wash" (source of English *ablution*).] —**e·lu·tion** /i lŏŏsh'n/ *n.*

e·lu·tri·ate /ə lŏŏtree àyt/ (**-at·ed, -at·ing, -ates**) *vt.* to purify or separate something from a mixture by washing, decanting, or straining it (*technical*) [Mid-18thC. From Latin *elutriat-*, the past participle stem of *elutriare* "to wash out," from *lutriare* "to wash."] —**e·lu·tri·a·tion** /ə lŏŏtree áysh'n/ *n.*

e·lu·vi·a plural of **eluvium**

e·lu·vi·al de·pos·it *n.* a concentration of an ore deposit formed as a result of the removal of less dense host material

e·lu·vi·a·tion /ə lŏŏvee áysh'n/ *n.* GEOL a process by which material dissolved or suspended in water within soil moves down or sideways as rainwater moves through the soil

e·lu·vi·um /ə lŏŏvee əm/ (*plural* **-a** /-ə/) *n.* GEOL an accumulated mass of soil, sand, silt, or rock debris resulting from weathering or drifting [Late 19thC. Coined from Latin *eluere* (see ELUTE) on the model of ALLUVIUM.] —**e·lu·vi·al** *adj.*

el·ver /élvər/ *n.* a young freshwater eel, especially one that migrates from salt water [Mid-17thC. From English dialect *elffare*, literally "eel-journey," because they migrate into streams from the ocean.]

elves plural of **elf**

elv·ish /élvish/ *adj.* = **elfish**

E·ly·si·an /i lízh'n/ *adj.* **1. RELATING TO ELYSIUM** relating to or typical of Elysium **2. BLISSFUL** full of or giving great pleasure and delight (*literary*) [Mid-16thC. Formed from Latin *Elysium*, from Greek *Elusion pedion* "Elysian field," of unknown origin.]

E·ly·si·an Fields *npl.* = **Elysium** *n.* 1

E·ly·si·um /i lízhee əm, ə lízzee-/ *n.* **1. HEAVEN** in Greek mythology, the home of the blessed after death **2. IDEAL PLACE OR CONDITION** any ideally delightful or blissful place or condition **3.** ASTRON **BULGE ON SURFACE OF MARS** an extensive shallow bulge on the surface of Mars in the northern hemisphere gently rising to a height of approximately 3 mi./5 km, supporting the volcanoes Hecate Tholus and Elysium Mons

el·y·tron /éllə tròn/ (*plural* **-tra** /-trə/), **el·y·trum** /-trəm/ (*plural* **-tra**) *n.* a tough front wing, occurring in pairs on beetles and some other insects, that acts as a protective covering for the rear wings [Mid-18thC. From Greek *elutron* "sheath."]

em /em/ *n.* PRINTING **1. VARIABLE MEASURE OF TYPE** a unit of measurement of print size, equal to the point size of the typeface being used **2.** = **pica**[2] *n.*

'em /əm/ *contr.* them (*informal*) [14thC. Originally a variant of Old English *hem* "them"; now regarded as a shortening of THEM.]

EM *abbr.* **1.** electromagnetic **2.** electron microscope **3.** enlisted man

em- *prefix.* = **en-** (*used before m, b, or p*)

e·ma·ci·ate /i máyshee àyt/ (**-at·ed, -at·ing, -ates**) *vti.* to become, or make somebody or something become, extremely thin [Early 17thC. From Latin *emaciat-*, the past participle stem of *emaciare* "to make lean, waste away," from *macer* "lean" (source of English *meagre*).] — **e·ma·ci·a·tion** /i màyshee áysh'n/ *n.*

e·ma·ci·at·ed /i máyshee àytəd/ *adj.* extremely thin, especially because of starvation or illness

WORD KEY: SYNONYMS

See Synonyms at ***thin.***

e-mail /ée màyl/, **e·mail** *n.* **1.** COMPUTER-TO-COMPUTER COMMUNICATION SYSTEM a system for transmitting messages and data from one computer to another, using a telephone connection and modems. Full form **electronic mail 2.** E-MAIL MESSAGE a communication sent by e-mail ■ *vt.* (**e-mailed, e-mail·ing, e-mails; e·mailed, e·mail·ing, e·mails**) COMMUNICATE SOMETHING BY E-MAIL to send a message to somebody by e-mail

em·a·lan·ge·ni plural of **lilangeni**

em·a·nate /émmə nàyt/ (**-nat·ed, -nat·ing, -nates**) *v.* **1.** *vi.* COME FROM to come from or come out of somebody, something, or somewhere **2.** *vt.* SEND OUT to emit, send out, or give out something such as rays or information (*formal*) [Mid-18thC. From Latin *emanat-*, the past participle stem of *emanare* "to flow out, arise," from *manare* "to flow."] —**em·a·na·tive** *adj.*

em·a·na·tion /èmmə náysh'n/ *n.* **1.** ACT OF SENDING OUT the act of emitting, sending out, or giving out something **2.** SOMETHING SENT OUT something that issues or is sent out or given out from somebody or something **3.** PHYS RADIOACTIVE GAS any gas produced by radioactive decay, e.g., radon —**em·a·na·tion·al** *adj.*

e·man·ci·pate /i mánsə pàyt/ (**-pat·ed, -pat·ing, -pates**) *vt.* **1.** SET SOMEBODY FREE to free somebody from slavery, serfdom, or bondage **2.** FREE SOMEBODY FROM RESTRICTIONS to free somebody from restrictions or conventions (*often passive*) [Early 17thC. From Latin *emancipat-*, the past participle stem of *emancipare* "to free from parental power," from *mancipium* "ownership."] —**e·man·ci·pa·tive** *adj.* —**e·man·ci·pa·tor** *n.* —**e·man·ci·pa·to·ry** *adj.*

e·man·ci·pa·tion /i mànsə páysh'n/ *n.* **1.** ACT OF FREEING the act or process of setting somebody free or of freeing somebody from restrictions **2.** BEING FREED the condition or fact of being set free or freed from some restriction

E·man·ci·pa·tion Proc·la·ma·tion *n.* a proclamation, effective on January 1, 1863, that was issued by President Abraham Lincoln and declared freedom for all enslaved people in states still in rebellion against the federal government

e·mar·gi·nate /i máarjə nàyt/ *adj.* BOT, BIOL with a notch at the tip [Late 18thC. From Latin *emarginatus*, the past participle of *emarginare* "to remove the edges of."] —**e·mar·gi·na·tion** /i màarjə náysh'n/ *n.*

e·mas·cu·late (**-lat·ed, -lat·ing, -lates**) *vt.* /i máskyə làyt/ **1.** PHYSIOL CASTRATE to remove the testicles of a male human being or animal (*formal or literary*) **2.** WEAKEN SOMEBODY OR SOMETHING to deprive somebody or something of effectiveness, spirit, or force (*formal*) (*sometimes considered offensive*) **3.** BOT REMOVE STAMENS FROM to remove the male reproductive organs (**stamens**) from a flower, e.g., to prevent self-pollination [Early 17thC. From Latin *emasculat-*, the past participle stem of *emasculare* "to remove the male glands of, castrate," from *masculus* "male."] —**e·mas·cu·la·tion** /i màskyə láysh'n/ *n.* —**e·mas·cu·la·tive** /i máskyələtiv/ *adj.* —**e·mas·cu·la·tor** /-làytər/ *n.* —**e·mas·cu·la·to·ry** /-tàwree/ *adj.*

em·balm /əm báam/ (**-balmed, -balm·ing, -balms**) *vt.* **1.** PRESERVE DEAD BODY to treat a dead body with a preservative substance in order to stop it decaying **2.** KEEP SOMETHING INTACT to preserve something from change or oblivion (*formal*) **3.** PERFUME SOMETHING to give a sweet scent to something (*literary*) [14thC. From French *embaumer*, from *baume* "balm."] — **em·balm·er** *n.* —**em·balm·ment** *n.*

em·bank /em bángk/ (**-banked, -bank·ing, -banks**) *vt.* to surround or line a road, canal, or other area with an embankment

em·bank·ment /em bángkmənt/ *n.* a ridge or raised platform built of earth or stone to confine a waterway or support a road or railroad line

em·bar·ca·der·o /em baàrkə dérrō/ (*plural* **-os**) *n.* *Southwestern U.S.* a landing place on a waterway [Mid-19thC. From Spanish, formed from *embarcar* "to embark."]

em·bar·go /em baárgō/ *n.* (*plural* **-goes**) **1.** POL ORDER STOPPING TRADE a government restriction or restraint on commerce, especially an order that prohibits trade in a given commodity or with a particular nation **2.** PROHIBITION any official restraint or prohibition **3.** POL ORDER HALTING MOVEMENT OF SHIPS a government order that prohibits commercial ships from entering or leaving its ports, often as a measure during war ■ *vt.* (**-goed, -go·ing, -goes**) **1.** PROHIBIT OR FORBID SOMETHING to place an embargo on something **2.** SEIZE SOMETHING to confiscate or seize something for government use [Late 16thC. From Spanish, formed from *embargar* "to restrain, seize, embargo," probably from assumed Vulgar Latin *imbarricare* "to restrain, impede," from, ultimately, Latin *barra* "bar."]

em·bark /em baárk/ (**-barked, -bark·ing, -barks**) *vti.* to go on board, or put or take somebody or something on board a ship or aircraft [Mid-16thC. From French *embarquer*, from *barque* "ship" (source of English *bark*^{3}).] — **em·bar·ka·tion** /èm baar káysh'n/ *n.* —**em·bark·ment** *n.*

embark on, em·bark up·on *vti.* to start or engage in or involve somebody or something in an undertaking

em·bar·ras de ri·chesses /aambaa raà də ree shéss/ *n.* an overabundance of desirable things that makes choice among them difficult [From French, literally "embarrassment of wealth"]

em·bar·rass /em bérrəss/ (**-rassed, -rass·ing, -rass·es**) *v.* **1.** *vti.* MAKE OR BECOME SELF-CONSCIOUS to become or cause somebody to become painfully self-conscious, ashamed, humiliated, or ill at ease **2.** *vt.* HOLD SOMEBODY OR SOMETHING UP to hinder or impede somebody or something (*often passive*) [Late 17thC. Via French *embarrasser* "to impede, disconcert" from, ultimately, Portuguese *embaraçar*, from *baraço* "halter."] — **em·bar·rass·a·ble** *adj.*

WORD KEY: USAGE

Spelling trap: Note the spelling with *-rr-* and *-ass.* ***Harass*** has only one *r.*

em·bar·rassed /em bérrəst/ *adj.* **1.** SELF-CONSCIOUS painfully self-conscious, ill at ease, ashamed, or humiliated **2.** SHORT OF MONEY in financial difficulties because of a lack of money —**em·bar·rassed·ly** /em bérrəstlee, em bérrəssədlee/ *adv.*

em·bar·rass·ing /em-/ *adj.* causing painful self-consciousness, uncomfortableness, shame, or humiliation —**em·bar·rass·ing·ly** *adv.*

em·bar·rass·ment /em bérrəsmənt/ *n.* **1.** ACUTE SELF-CONSCIOUSNESS a feeling of painful self-consciousness, uncomfortableness, shame, or humiliation **2.** SOMETHING THAT CAUSES SELF-CONSCIOUSNESS something that causes a feeling of painful self-consciousness, uncomfortableness, shame, or humiliation **3.** LACK OF MONEY a state of financial difficulty

em·bas·sy /émbəsee/ (*plural* **-sies**) *n.* **1.** AMBASSADOR'S HEADQUARTERS the residence and place of business of an ambassador **2.** EMBASSY STAFF an ambassador with his or her ambassadorial staff **3.** AMBASSADOR'S POSITION AND RESPONSIBILITIES the mission, rank, or function of an ambassador [Late 16thC. Via Old French *ambassé* from, ultimately, assumed Vulgar Latin *ambactiare* "to go on a mission."]

em·bat·tle /em bátt'l/ (**-tled, -tling, -tles**) *vt.* **1.** MIL POSITION FORCES to arrange forces in readiness for battle **2.** MIL FORTIFY SOMETHING to fortify something such as a building, village, or position in battle (*archaic*) (*usually passive*) **3.** ARCHIT BUILD SOMETHING WITH BATTLEMENTS to provide a building with battlements (*archaic*) (*usually passive*) [14thC. From Old French *embataillier*, from *bataille* "battle."]

em·bat·tled /em bátt'ld/ *adj.* **1.** UNDER ASSAULT under attack or subject to controversy **2.** MIL FIGHTING OR READY TO FIGHT ready for or engaged in battle **3.** ARCHIT WITH BATTLEMENTS with battlements provided (*archaic*)

em·bat·tle·ments /em bátt'lmənts/ *n.* = **battlements**

em·bay·ment /em báymənt/ *n.* **1.** BAY a bay in a coastline (*technical*) **2.** BAY FORMATION the process by which a bay is formed in a coastline

em·bed /em béd/ (**-bed·ded, -bed·ding, -beds**), **im·bed** (**-bed·ded, -bed·ding, -beds**) *v.* **1.** *vti.* PLACE OR BE PLACED SOLIDLY to fix something or become fixed in a surrounding mass **2.** *vt.* SURROUND SOMETHING to surround or cover something closely (*usually passive*) **3.** *vt.* FIX SOMETHING IN MIND to fix something deeply in the mind or memory (*often passive*) **4.** *vi.* BECOME LODGED to become deeply and solidly lodged in something

em·bel·lish /em béllish/ (**-lished, -lish·ing, -lish·es**) *vt.* **1.** BEAUTIFY SOMETHING to increase the beauty of something by adding ornaments or decorations **2.** ADD FICTITIOUS OR EXAGGERATED DETAILS TO to make an account or description more interesting by inventing or exaggerating details **3.** MUSIC ADD TO MELODY to add extra notes, accents, or trills to a melody to make it more beautiful or interesting [14thC. From Old French *embellir*, literally "to make beautiful," from *bel* "beautiful," from Latin *bellus* (source of English *beauty*).]

em·bel·lish·ment /em béllishmənt/ *n.* **1.** BEAUTIFICATION OF SOMETHING the act or process of adding ornaments or decorations to something to make it more beautiful **2.** SOMETHING ADDED FOR BEAUTIFICATION something added to increase beauty or interest **3.** MUSIC ADDITION TO MELODY the addition of notes, accents, or trills to a melody to make it more beautiful or interesting, or an added note, accent, or trill. ◊ **fioritura**

em·ber /émbər/ *n.* BURNING FRAGMENT a small piece of glowing or smoldering material from a dying fire ■ **em·bers** *npl.* **1.** REMAINS OF FIRE the glowing or smoldering remains of a dying fire **2.** REMAINS OF PASSION the dying but not yet extinguished remains of a great emotion, especially love (*literary*) [Old English *æmyrge*. Ultimately from an Indo-European word meaning "to burn" that also produced English *combustion*.]

Em·ber Days, em·ber days *npl.* days of prayer and fasting in Roman Catholic and Anglican Churches, comprising the Wednesday, Friday, and Saturday following Pentecost, the first Sunday after Lent, September 14, and December 13 [*Ember* from Old English *ymbryne* "circuit," literally "running around," from *ryne* "course, running"; from the fact that these days "come around" four times a year]

em·bez·zle /em bézz'l/ (**-zled, -zling, -zles**) *vti.* to take for personal use money or property that has been given on trust by others, without their knowledge or permission [15thC. From Anglo-Norman *embesiler* "to steal," from Old French *besillier* "to gouge, destroy," of unknown origin.] —**em·bez·zle·ment** *n.* —**em·bez·zler** *n.*

WORD KEY: SYNONYMS

See Synonyms at ***steal.***

em·bit·ter /em bíttər/ (**-tered, -ter·ing, -ters**) *vt.* **1.** MAKE SOMEBODY BITTER to make somebody feel bitter or aggrieved **2.** MAKE SOMETHING WORSE to make something more bitter or acrimonious —**em·bit·ter·ment** *n.*

em·bit·tered /em bíttərd/ *adj.* having become bitter, e.g., because of hardship, injustice, or neglect

em·blaze^{1} /em bláyz/ (**-blazed, -blaz·ing, -blaz·es**) *vt.* (*archaic*) **1.** LIGHT SOMETHING UP to light up or illuminate something **2.** SET SOMETHING ALIGHT to kindle something or set it on fire [15thC. Formed from BLAZE^{1}.]

em·blaze^{2} /em bláyz/ (**-blazed, -blaz·ing, -blaz·es**) *vt.* = **emblazon** (*archaic*) [Early 16thC. Formed from BLAZE^{2}.]

em·bla·zon /em bláyz'n/ (**-zoned, -zon·ing, -zons**) *vt.* **1.** HERALDRY DECORATE FLAG OR SHIELD in heraldry, to decorate or adorn a shield or flag by depicting something, especially a coat of arms **2.** ADD DESIGN TO SOMETHING to decorate or adorn something such as clothing with bright colors or a symbol or picture **3.** MAKE SOMEBODY OR SOMETHING FAMOUS to celebrate somebody or something, or make somebody or something famous (*literary*) (*often passive*) —**em·bla·zon·er** *n.* — **em·bla·zon·ment** *n.*

em·bla·zon·ry /em bláyz'nree/ (*plural* **-ries**) *n.* **1.** ACT OF EMBLAZONING the act or process of putting heraldic decorations on something such as a shield or flag **2.** DECORATION heraldic decorations on such things as shields and flags

em·blem /émbləm/ *n.* **1.** SYMBOL something that visually symbolizes an object, idea, group, or quality **2.** BADGE a badge or sign that represents a person, group, or organization **3.** PAINTING ALLEGORICAL IMAGE an allegorical picture, often with a motto, used to illustrate a moral lesson [15thC. Via Latin *emblema* "inlaid design" from, ultimately, Greek *emballein* "to throw in, insert," from *ballein* "to throw."]

em·blem·at·ic /èmblə máttik/, **em·blem·at·i·cal** /èmblə máttik'l/ *adj.* relating to, consisting of, or acting as an emblem or symbol —**em·blem·at·i·cal·ly** *adv.*

em·blem·a·tize /em blémmə tīz/ (**-tized, -tiz·ing, -tiz·es**) *vt.* to serve as a symbol of something (*formal*)

em·bod·i·ment /em bóddimənt/ *n.* **1.** CONCRETE EXPRESSION OF SOMETHING somebody who or something that is the tangible or visible expression of an idea or quality **2.** EMBODYING OF SOMETHING the act or process by which something is made tangible or visible

em·bod·y /em bóddee/ (**-ied, -y·ing, -ies**) *vt.* **1.** MAKE SOMETHING TANGIBLE to give a tangible or visible form to something abstract **2.** PERSONIFY SOMETHING to express or exemplify something abstract in bodily form **3.** INCORPORATE THINGS INTO ORGANIZED WHOLE to gather and organize a number of things into a whole

em·bold·en /em bṓld'n/ (**-ened, -en·ing, -ens**) *vt.* to give somebody courage or boldness

em·bo·lec·to·my /èmbə léktəmee/ (*plural* **-mies**) *n.* the surgical removal of an embolus, usually a blood clot or other obstruction in a blood vessel

em·bo·li plural of **embolus**

em·bol·ic /em bóllik/ *adj.* relating to or caused by an embolus or embolism

em·bo·lism /émbə lìzzəm/ *n.* **1.** MED BLOCKAGE OF ARTERY a condition in which an artery is blocked by an embolus, usually a blood clot formed at one place in the circulation and then lodging in another **2.** MED EMBOLUS an embolus (*informal*) **3.** CALENDAR INSERTION OF DAY OR DAYS the insertion of a day or days into a calendar **4.** CHR PRAYER DURING ROMAN CATHOLIC MASS in the Roman Catholic Church, a prayer for deliverance from evil inserted in a Mass after the Lord's Prayer [14thC. Via late Latin *embolismus* from Greek *embolismos*, from *emballein* "to insert" (see EMBLEM).]

em·bo·li·za·tion /èmbəli záysh'n/ *n.* the process or condition in which a blood vessel is blocked by a blood clot or other obstruction (**embolus**)

em·bo·lus /émbələss/ (*plural* **-li** /-lī/) *n.* an abnormal mass, most commonly a blood clot, that becomes lodged in a blood vessel and obstructs it [Mid-17thC. Via Latin from Greek *embolos* "peg, stopper, wedge," from *emballein* "to insert" (see EMBLEM).]

em·bon·point /aàN bawN pwáN/ *n.* ABOVE-AVERAGE BODY WEIGHT a body weight that is above average and causes an impression of roundness (*humorous*) ○ *"She was slightly inclined to embonpoint."* (J. M. Barrie, *Peter Pan*; 1904) ■ *adj.* ABOVE AVERAGE BODY WEIGHT having a body weight that is above average and causes the impression of roundness (*humorous dated*) (*sometimes considered offensive*) [Late 17thC. From French, literally "in good condition."]

em·bos·om /em bóozəm/ (**-omed, -om·ing, -oms**) *vt.* (*archaic*) **1.** SURROUND SOMEBODY OR SOMETHING PROTECTIVELY to surround or envelop somebody or something, especially in a protective way **2.** EMBRACE SOMEBODY to take somebody into your arms and hold him or her to your bosom **3.** CHERISH SOMEBODY to cherish, foster, or care about somebody

em·boss /em báwss/ (**-bossed, -boss·ing, -boss·es**) *vt.* **1.** DECORATE SOMETHING WITH RAISED PATTERN to decorate or mark a surface with a slightly raised design or lettering **2.** MAKE RAISED PATTERN OF SOMETHING to make something as a raised pattern on a surface ○ *the title was embossed in gold lettering on the cover* [14thC. From Old French *embocer*, from *boce* "protuberance, knoblike mass" (source of English *boss*[2]).] —**em·boss·er** *n.*

em·boss·ment /em báwsmənt/ *n.* **1.** ACT OF EMBOSSING SOMETHING the act, process, or condition of making something as or decorating something with a slightly raised pattern **2.** RAISED DECORATION slightly raised decoration on a surface

em·bou·chure /aàm boo shoor/ *n.* **1.** GEOG RIVER MOUTH the mouth of a river **2.** GEOG VALLEY MOUTH the mouth of a valley where it becomes a plain **3.** MUSIC POSITION OF LIPS AND TONGUE the adjustment of the lips and tongue in playing a wind instrument **4.** MUSIC MOUTHPIECE the mouthpiece of a wind instrument [Mid-18thC. From French, formed from *emboucher* "to put to your mouth," from *bouche* "mouth."]

em·bour·geoise·ment /èm boor zhwaàzmaant, èm boor zhwaàz maànt/ *n.* the process by which a social group becomes middle-class in manners and attitudes [Mid-20thC. From French, formed from *bourgeois* (see BOURGEOIS).]

em·bowed /em bṓd/ *adj.* shaped like a vault or arch

em·bow·el /em bówəl/ (**-eled, -el·ing, -els**) *vt.* (*archaic*) **1.** PUT DEEP IN SOMETHING to enclose, embed, or bury something deeply **2.** = **disembowel**

em·bow·er /em bówər/ (**-ered, -er·ing, -ers**) *vt.* to shelter or enclose somebody or something in a bower or a place or structure resembling a bower (*archaic or literary*) [Late 16thC. Coined from EM- + BOWER.]

em·brace /em bráyss/ *v.* (**-braced, -brac·ing, -brac·es**) **1.** *vti.* HUG SOMEBODY to hug somebody in your arms fondly, or hug each other fondly **2.** *vt.* MAKE USE OF SOMETHING to welcome and take advantage of something eagerly or willingly **3.** *vt.* ADOPT SOMETHING to adopt or take up something, especially a belief or way of life **4.** *vt.* COMPRISE SOMETHING to include something as part of a whole **5.** *vt.* SURROUND SOMETHING to surround or enclose something (*literary*) (*often passive*) ■ *n.* HUG GIVEN an affectionate or passionate hug [14thC. Via Old French *embracer*, literally "to take into your arms," from, ultimately, Latin *bracchium* "arm" (source of English *brace, bracelet*, and *bra*).] —**em·brace·able** *adj.* —**em·brace·ment** *n.* —**em·brac·er** *n.*

em·brac·er·y /em bráyssəree/ *n.* LAW, CRIMINOL the offense of trying to influence a judge or jury, e.g., by bribery, threats, or promises

em·branch·ment /em bránchmənt/ *n.* **1.** BRANCHING OUT OF GEOGRAPHIC FEATURE an act of branching out by a feature of the natural landscape, e.g., a river or mountain range **2.** BRANCH OF GEOGRAPHIC FEATURE a branch of something such as a river or mountain range [Mid-19thC. From French *embranchement*, from *branche* (source of English *branch*).]

em·bran·gle /em bráng g'l/ (**-gled, -gling, -gles**) *vt.* to confuse, perplex, or entangle somebody or something (*archaic*) [Mid-17thC. Formed from obsolete *brangle* "to shake, squabble," from French *branler* "to shake."] —**em·bran·gle·ment** *n.*

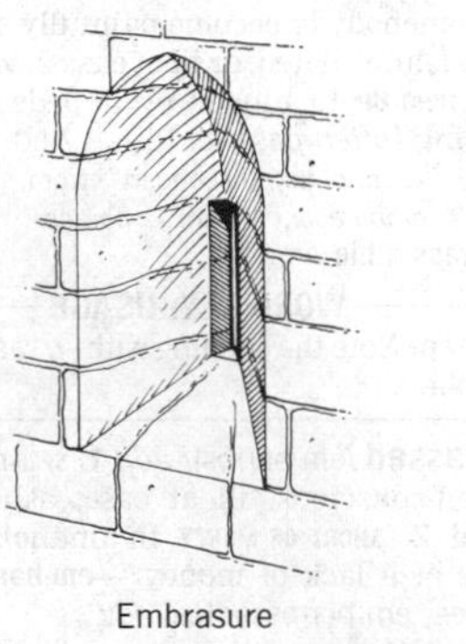

Embrasure

em·bra·sure /em bráyzhər/ *n.* **1.** INDUST SLANTED OPENING IN FORTIFICATION a slanted opening in the wall or parapet of a fortification, designed so that a defender can fire through it on attackers **2.** ARCHIT TAPERED OPENING an opening in the wall of a building for a door or window, tapered so as to be wider on the inside than on the outside [Early 17thC. From French, formed from obsolete *embraser* "to widen (a door or window)," of unknown origin.]

em·brit·tle /em brítt'l/ (**-tled, -tling, -tles**) *vti.* to become or make something become brittle

em·bro·cate /émbrə kàyt/ (**-cat·ed, -cat·ing, -cates**) *vt.* to rub lotion or liniment onto a part of the body [Early 17thC. From Latin *embrocat-*, the past participle stem of *embrocare* "to treat with healing liquid," from late Latin *embroc(h)a*, from Greek *embrokhē* "lotion."]

em·bro·ca·tion /èmbrə káysh'n/ *n.* a liniment or lotion for rubbing onto the body, usually to relieve muscle or joint pain

em·broi·der /em bróydər/ (**-dered, -der·ing, -ders**) *v.* **1.** *vti.* CRAFT SEW PATTERN INTO SOMETHING to decorate something with needlework **2.** *vt.* CRAFT MAKE SOMETHING BY SEWING to use needlework to make a decoration **3.** *vti.* EMBELLISH STORY to add exaggerated or fictitious details to an account of something to make it more interesting [14thC. From Anglo-Norman *enbrouder*, from Old French *brouder* "to embroider," of prehistoric Germanic origin.] —**em·broi·der·er** *n.*

em·broi·der·y /em bróydəree/ (*plural* **-ies**) *n.* **1.** CRAFT ACT OF MAKING DECORATIVE NEEDLEWORK the craft of using needlework to make decorative designs **2.** CRAFT SOMETHING WITH DECORATIVE NEEDLEWORK something produced by or ornamented with decorative needlework **3.** ADDITION OF FICTITIOUS DETAILS elaboration or embellishment in somebody's account of something to make it more interesting

Barnaby's

Embroidery

em·broil /em bróyl/ (**-broiled, -broil·ing, -broils**) *vt.* **1.** INVOLVE SOMEBODY IN CONFLICT to involve somebody or yourself in trouble, disagreement, or conflict **2.** MUDDLE OR MIX UP SOMETHING to make something confused or overly complicated [Early 17thC. From French *embrouiller* "to confuse, confound," from *brouiller* "to mix confusedly," ultimately of prehistoric Germanic origin.]

em·brown /em brówn/ (**-browned, -brown·ing, -browns**) *vt.* to make something darker, especially brown (*literary*)

em·brue /em bróo/ *vt.* = **imbrue**

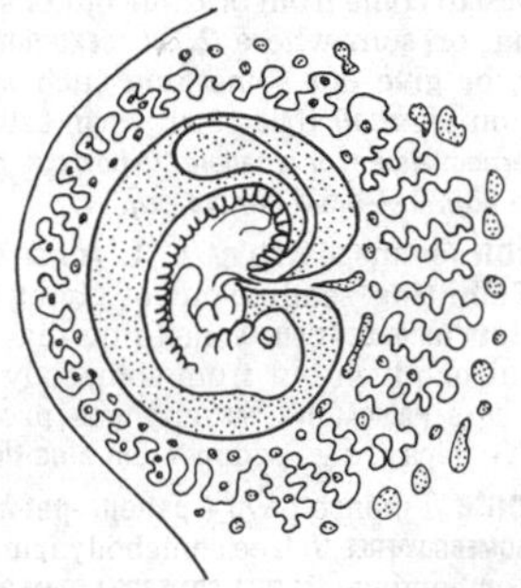

Embryo: Human embryo

em·bry·o /émbree ṑ/ (*plural* **-os**) *n.* **1.** MED HUMAN OFFSPRING IN INITIAL DEVELOPMENTAL STAGE a human offspring in the early stages following conception up to the end of the eighth week, after which it is classified as a fetus **2.** ZOOL ANIMAL IN INITIAL DEVELOPMENTAL STAGE the developing young of an animal from the earliest stages after conception up to birth or hatching **3.** BOT PLANT IN INITIAL DEVELOPMENTAL STAGE a plant in its earliest stages of development. In seed-bearing plants, the embryo is contained within the seed. **4.** EARLY FORM an early form or rudimentary stage of something ○ *the embryo of an exciting new invention* [14thC. Via Latin from Greek *embruon*, from *bruein* "to swell, grow"; the underlying idea is "something growing inside the body."]

em·bry·o·gen·e·sis /èmbree ō jénnəssiss/, **em·bry·og·e·ny** /-ójjənee/ *n.* EMBRYOL the formation and growth of an embryo —**em·bry·o·ge·net·ic** *adj.* —**em·bry·o·gen·ic** /èmbree ə jə néttik/ *adj.*

em·bry·ol·o·gy /èmbree óllәjee/ *n.* **1.** STUDY OF EMBRYOS the scientific study of embryos and their development **2.** MED STUDY OF DEVELOPMENT OF HUMAN OFFSPRING the study of the growth and development of the human embryo and fetus from conception to birth —**em·bry·o·log·ic** /èmbree ə lójjik/ *adj.* —**em·bry·o·log·i·cal·ly** *adv.* —**em·bry·ol·o·gist** *n.*

em·bry·on·ic /èmbree ónnik/, **em·bry·on·al** /em brée ən'l, émbree-/, **em·bry·ot·ic** /èmbree óttik/ *adj.* **1.** RELATING TO EMBRYO relating to or characteristic of an embryo **2.** **em·bry·on·ic, em·bry·ot·ic** IN EARLY DEVELOPMENTAL STAGE in an initial or rudimentary stage of development —**em·bry·on·ic·al·ly** *adv.*

em·bry·on·ic mem·brane *n.* any membranous structure, e.g., the amnion, chorion, or yolk sac, that comes from a fertilized ovum but does not become part of the embryo

em·bry·o sac *n.* BOT a large oval cell found inside a female reproductive organ (**ovule**) of a flowering plant, that contains the egg cell, which gives rise to the embryo and the endosperm nuclei

em·bry·ot·ic *adj.* = **embryonic**

em·bry·o trans·fer *n.* EMBRYOL the transplanting of an embryo from one female animal into the womb of a surrogate mother

em·cee /em sée/ *n.* **MASTER OF CEREMONIES** a master of ceremonies (*informal*) ■ *vti.* (**-ceed, -cee·ing, -cees**) **BE MASTER OF CEREMONIES** to act as a master of ceremonies for an event (*informal*) [Mid-20thC. Represents the pronunciation of *MC*, shortening of *Master of Ceremonies*.]

em dash *n.* in printing, a dash that is one em long

-eme *suffix.* a distinctive unit of linguistic structure ○ *lexeme* [From French *-ème*, from *phonème* (see PHONEME)]

e·mend /i ménd/ (**e·mend·ed, e·mend·ing, e·mends**), **e·mend·ate** (**-at·ed, -at·ing, -ates**) *vt.* to make corrections or alterations to improve a text [15thC. From Latin *emendare*, literally "to take out a fault," from *menda* "fault, blemish."] —**e·mend·er** *n.*

WORD KEY: USAGE

See Usage note at ***amend.***

e·men·da·tion /èemən dáysh'n, èmmən-, i mèn-/ *n.* **1. CORRECTION MADE** a correction or alteration made to a text **2. ACT OR PROCESS OF TEXT CORRECTION** the act or process of correcting a text

em·er·ald /émmərəld, émmrəld/ *n.* MINERALS **GREEN GEMSTONE** a form of beryl colored green by chromium that is highly valued as a gemstone ■ *adj., n.* COLORS = **emerald green** [13thC. Directly or via Old French *emeraude* from medieval Latin *esmeraldus*, alteration of Latin *smaragdus*, which came via Greek *smaragdos* "green gem" from a Semitic word meaning "to shine."]

em·er·ald cut *n.* a rectangular multifaceted cut for gemstones, epecially emeralds and diamonds

em·er·ald green *n.* a bright green color, like that of an emerald —**emerald-green** *adj.*

Em·er·ald Isle /émmərald-/ *n.* Ireland, so called because of its vividly green countryside and because the wearing of green was associated with the struggle for national sovereignty (*literary*)

e·merge /i múrj/ (**e·merged, e·merg·ing, e·merg·es**) *v.* **1.** *vi.* **COME OUT** to appear out of or from behind something **2.** *vi.* **SURVIVE** to come out of an experience, condition, or situation, especially a difficult one **3.** *vti.* **BECOME KNOWN** to become known or apparent ○ *It emerged that I had been wrong all along.* **4.** *vi.* **APPEAR OR HAPPEN** to arise, appear, or occur [Late 16thC. From Latin *emergere* "to rise out or up," from *mergere* "to dive, plunge."]

e·mer·gence /i múrjəns/ *n.* **1. ACT OF EMERGING** the act or process of coming out, appearing, or coming about **2.** INSECTS **APPEARANCE IN ADULT FORM** the appearance of the adult form (**imago**) of an insect on the completion of the change (**metamorphosis**) from the larval stage **3.** BOT **OUTGROWTH FROM PLANT** an outgrowth that lacks sap-conducting tissue, e.g., a thorn, coming from the body surface of a plant

e·mer·gen·cy /i múrjənsee/ *n.* (*plural* **-cies**) **SUDDEN CRISIS REQUIRING ACTION** an unexpected and sudden event that must be dealt with urgently ■ *adj.* **1. USED IN EMERGENCY** used or suitable for use in an emergency **2.** MED **FOR IMMEDIATE TREATMENT** requiring, providing, or given immediate medical attention [The underlying idea is of something that suddenly "emerges" or arises]

e·mer·gen·cy brake *n.* **1. SECONDARY BRAKE ON VEHICLE** a brake on a vehicle intended to be used when the main brakes have failed or when a sudden halt is required, or to prevent a parked vehicle from moving **2.** INDUST, TECH **DEVICE TO STOP MACHINERY** a mechanical device on a piece of machinery that is used to bring the machinery to a halt when a dangerous condition arises

e·mer·gen·cy cord *n.* a chain, cord, or handle in a railroad car that a passenger can pull in order to stop a train in an emergency

e·mer·gen·cy ex·it *n.* an exit from a building or vehicle that is designed and designated as an escape route in an emergency such as a fire

e·mer·gen·cy pow·ers *npl.* special powers given to a government or other authority to take extraordinary actions in order to cope with a crisis

e·mer·gen·cy room *n.* a part of a hospital for patients who need immediate urgent attention, e.g., because of heart attacks

e·mer·gen·cy ser·vic·es *npl.* the fire department, the police, and the ambulance services collectively, especially when mobilized to deal with emergencies

e·mer·gen·cy ve·hi·cle *n.* an ambulance, fire engine, police car, or other vehicle used by the emergency services

e·mer·gent /i múrjənt/ *adj.* **1.** POL = **emerging** *adj.* 2 **2. NEW** appearing, arising, occurring, or developing, especially for the first time ■ *n.* **1.** PLANTS **PLANT WITH UPPER PARTS ABOVE WATER** a plant that has its roots under water but its upper part above the surface **2.** TREES **TALL TREE** a forest tree that stands taller than the trees around it

e·mer·gent ev·o·lu·tion *n.* the theory of evolution in which new organisms and characteristics appear at crises not predictable from those already in existence

e·merg·ing /i múrjing/ *adj.* **1. NEW** starting to appear, arise, occur, or develop **2.** POL **NEWLY INDEPENDENT** newly or recently independent as a nation

e·mer·i·ta /i mérritə/ *adj.* **RETIRED BUT RETAINING PROFESSIONAL TITLE** retired but retaining professional title, especially as a woman professor ○ *She's a professor emerita of biology.* ■ *n.* (*plural* **-tae** /-tee/) **WOMAN RETAINING FORMER PROFESSIONAL TITLE** a woman who has retired from a post but retains her former professional title, especially as a professor [Early 20thC. From Latin, the feminine form of *emeritus* (see EMERITUS).]

e·mer·i·tus /i mérritəss/ *adj.* **RETIRED BUT RETAINING PROFESSIONAL TITLE** retired but retaining a professional title, especially as a professor ○ *He's a professor emeritus of chemistry.* ■ *n.* (*plural* **-ti** /-tī/) **MAN RETAINING FORMER PROFESSIONAL TITLE** a man who has retired from a post but retains his former professional title, especially as a professor [Early 17thC. From Latin, the past participle of *emerere* "to serve out, earn, deserve," from *merere* "to serve, earn" (source of English *merit*).]

e·mersed /i múrst/ *adj.* used to describe the stems, leaves, or other parts of an aquatic plant that stand above the water surface [Late 17thC. Formed from Latin *emersus*, the past participle of *emergere* (see EMERGE).]

e·mer·sion /i múrzh'n/ *n.* **1. ACT OF EMERGING** the act or process of emerging **2.** ASTRON **REAPPEARANCE OF CELESTIAL BODY** the reappearance of a celestial body after it has been eclipsed or occulted

Ralph Waldo Emerson

Em·er·son /émmərsən/, **Ralph Waldo** (1803–82) U.S. essayist, lecturer, and poet. He was a main figure in the philosophical movement known as transcendentalism. His landmark works include *Nature* (1836). —**Em·er·so·ni·an** /èmmər sónee ən/ *adj.*

em·er·y /émməree/ *n.* a variety of the mineral corundum, that can be crushed and used as an abrasive for polishing hard surfaces [15thC. Via French *émeri* from Italian *smeriglio*, from, ultimately, Greek *smuris* "abrasive powder."]

em·er·y board *n.* a small strip of card or thin wood coated with powdered emery and used for filing the fingernails

em·er·y pa·per *n.* a strong paper coated with powdered emery and used as an abrasive and for polishing

em·er·y wheel *n.* a wheel coated with powdered emery and used as an abrasive and for polishing

em·e·sis /émməssiss/ *n.* vomiting (*technical*) [Late 19thC. From Greek, formed from *emein* (see EMETIC).]

e·met·ic /i méttik/ *adj.* **CAUSING VOMITING** causing a person or animal to vomit ■ *n.* **SOMETHING CAUSING VOMITING** a substance that causes vomiting [Mid-17thC. From Greek *emetikos*, from, ultimately, *emein* "to vomit." Ultimately from an Indo-European word that also produced English *vomit*.] —**e·met·i·cal·ly** *adv.*

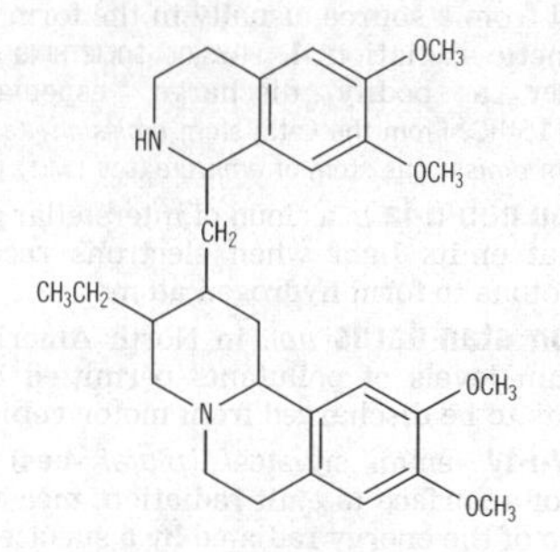

Emetine

em·e·tine /émmə teen/ *n.* an alkaloid extracted from a South American shrub (**ipecacuanha**) that was formerly used as an emetic. Formula: $C_{29}H_{40}O_4N_2$.

emf, EMF *abbr.* PHYS electromotive force

EMG *abbr.* **1.** electromyogram **2.** electromyograph

em·ic /éemik/ *adj.* **1.** LING, SOC SCI **ANALYZING STRUCTURAL AND FUNCTIONAL ELEMENTS** relating to the analysis of structural and functional elements of language or behavior **2.** ANTHROP **USING CATEGORIES OF PEOPLE STUDIED** relating to the organization and interpretation of data that makes use of the categories of the people being studied [Mid-20thC. Shortening of PHONEMIC.]

em·i·grant /émmigrənt/ *n.* **SOMEBODY WHO MOVES TO ANOTHER COUNTRY** somebody who leaves a place, especially his or her native country, to go and live in another country ■ *adj.* **MOVING TO ANOTHER COUNTRY** relating to those who have left a place, especially their native country, to go and live in another country

em·i·grate /émmi gràyt/ (**-grat·ed, -grat·ing, -grates**) *vi.* to leave a place, especially a native country, to go and live in another country [Late 18thC. From Latin *emigrat-*, the past participle stem of *emigrare* "to move away, depart from a place," from *migrare* (see MIGRATE).]

em·i·gra·tion /èmmi gráysh'n/ *n.* the act of leaving a native country to live in another country

em·i·nence /émminəns/ *n.* **1. HIGH POSITION** a position or rank of distinction or superiority **2. HILL** a high or raised area of ground (*formal*) **3.** ANAT **BODY PROJECTION** a projecting area of the body, especially a bone

Em·i·nence *n.* in the Roman Catholic Church, a title and form of address for a cardinal

é·mi·nence grise /ày mi naaNs gréez/ (*plural* **é·mi·nences grises** /ày mi naaNs gréez/) *n.* somebody who exercises great power or influence secretly or unofficially [From French, literally "gray eminence," originally the nickname of Père Joseph, secretary to Cardinal Richelieu, known as *Éminence Rouge* "Red Eminence"; their respective habits were gray and red]

em·i·nen·cy /émmənənsee/ *n., adj.* = **eminence** *n.* 1

em·i·nent /émminənt/ *adj.* **1. OF HIGH STANDING** superior in position, fame, or achievement **2. CLEAR** easy to see or notice **3. HIGH** in a high or raised position [15thC. From Latin *eminent-*, the present participle of *eminere* "to stand out, project," from *minere* "to stand, project" (source also of English *imminent* and *prominent*).]

em·i·nent do·main *n.* the power of a government to take private property for public use, usually with compensation paid to the owner

em·i·nent·ly /émminəntlee/ *adv.* **1. VERY** to a great degree ○ *is eminently qualified to be a corporate officer* **2. OBVIOUSLY** obviously or apparently (*archaic*)

e·mir /ə méer/ *n.* **1. ISLAMIC RULER** an independent ruler, commander, or governor in some Islamic countries **2. DESCENDANT OF MUHAMMAD** a title for a descendant of the prophet Muhammad [Early 17thC. Via French from Arabic *amīr* "commander."]

e·mir·ate /émmi ràyt, -ət, i méerət/ *n.* **1.** POL **STATUS OF EMIR** the rank or office of an emir **2.** POL, GEOG **PLACE UNDER EMIR'S RULE** an area ruled by an emir

em·is·sar·y /émmi seree/ (*plural* **-ies**) *n.* **1. REPRESENTATIVE** an agent or representative sent on a particular mission **2. SPY** a secret agent or spy (*dated*) [Early 17thC. From Latin *emissarius*, literally "somebody who is sent out," from *emiss-*, the past participle stem of *emittere* (see EMIT).]

e·mis·sion /i mísh'n/ *n.* **1. LETTING SOMETHING OUT** the act or process of letting something out or giving something out **2. SOMETHING GIVEN OUT** something that is produced or given out **3.** PHYS **RELEASED ENERGY** energy released from a source, usually in the form of electromagnetic radiation **4.** PHYSIOL **SOMETHING RELEASED FROM BODY** a bodily discharge, especially of semen [15thC. From the Latin stem *emission-* "a sending out," from *emiss-*, the stem of *emittere* (see EMIT).]

e·mis·sion neb·u·la *n.* a cloud of interstellar gas and dust that emits light when electrons recombine with protons to form hydrogen atoms

e·mis·sion stan·dards *npl.* in North America, the maximum levels of pollutants permitted by governments to be discharged from motor vehicles

em·is·siv·i·ty /èmmi sívvətee/ (*plural* **-ties**) *n.* the ability of a surface to emit radiation, measured as the ratio of the energy radiated by a surface to that radiated by a black body at the same temperature

e·mit /i mít/ (**e·mit·ted, e·mit·ting, e·mits**) *vt.* **1. PRODUCE SOMETHING** to send or give out something **2. UTTER SOMETHING** to utter something as a sound **3.** FIN **PUT MONEY INTO CIRCULATION** to put currency in circulation [Early 17thC. From Latin *emittere* "to send out," from *mittere* "to send."]

e·mit·ter /i míttər/ *n.* **1. SOMEBODY OR SOMETHING THAT EMITS SOMETHING** somebody who or something that lets out or gives out something **2.** ELECTRON ENG **SEMICONDUCTOR MATERIAL IN TRANSISTOR** a layer of semiconductor material in a transistor from which charge carriers, such as electrons, originate and control the current flow

Em·men·tha·ler /émmən taalər/, **Em·men·ta·ler, Em·men·thal** /émmən taal/, **Em·men·tal** *n.* a hard cheese of Swiss origin with large holes and a mild nutty flavor [Early 20thC. From obsolete German, named for *Emmental*, a region in Switzerland.]

em·mer /émmər/ *n.* a Eurasian wheat grown chiefly for fodder. Latin name: *Triticum dicoccum.* [Early 20thC. From German.]

em·met /émmət/ *n.* an ant (*regional archaic*) [Old English *æmete* (source also of English *ant*)]

em·me·tro·pi·a /èmmə trṓpee ə/ *n.* the normal condition of the eye in which vision is accurate [Mid-19thC. Coined from Greek *emmetros* "in measure" + *ōps* "eye" + -IA.] —**em·me·trop·ic** /èmmə tróppik/ *adj.*

Em·my /émmee/ (*plural* **-mys**) *n.* a statuette awarded annually by the American Academy of Television Arts and Sciences for excellence in television programming, production, or performance [Mid-20thC. Origin uncertain: perhaps an alteration of *Immy*, engineering slang for "image-orthicon camera," on the model of *Oscar* and other first names used for awards.]

e·mol·lient /i móllyənt/ *adj.* **1. SOOTHING TO SKIN** softening or soothing, especially to the skin **2. CALMING** trying to avoid anger and argument by using a calming manner ■ *n.* **SOOTHING SUBSTANCE** a substance that softens or soothes something, especially the skin [Mid-17thC. From Latin *emollient-*, the present participle stem of *emollire* "to soften," from *mollis* "soft."]

e·mol·u·ment /i móllyəmənt/ *n.* any payment for work (*formal or humorous*) [15thC. From Latin *emolumentum* "profit, gain," literally "fee paid to a miller for grinding grain," from *emolere* "to grind out."]

WORD KEY: SYNONYMS

See Synonyms at ***wage.***

e·mote /ə mṓt/ (**e·mot·ed, e·mot·ing, e·motes**) *vi.* to make an exaggerated show of emotions, e.g., in the playing of a dramatic part (*literary or humorous*) [Early 20thC. Back-formation from EMOTION.]

:-) Happy
:-(Sad
|-| Asleep
;-) Winking
:-)) Very happy
:-~) User has a cold
:-* Blowing a kiss
:-& Tongue tied
(:+(Scared
(-D Laughing
:-() Talking
:-O Shocked
:-X Mute
~:-) Baby
|-O Yawning
@->- Rose
{:V Duck
3:-) Cow
<:3 Mouse
:8) Pig

Emoticon

e·mo·ti·con /i mṓtə kòn/ *n.* a symbolic picture used in computer communications to convey emotions, constructed by arranging standard keyboard characters that are usually to be viewed sideways. A smile might be represented as :-). [Late 20thC. Blend of EMOTION and ICON.]

e·mo·tion /i mṓsh'n/ *n.* **1. HEIGHTENED FEELING** a strong feeling about somebody or something **2. AGITATION CAUSED BY STRONG FEELINGS** agitation or disturbance caused by strong feelings [Late 16thC. From French, formed from *émouvoir* "to stir up the feelings of," from Latin *emovere*, literally "to move out," from *movere* (see MOVE).]

e·mo·tion·al /i mṓshən'l, i mṓshnəl/ *adj.* **1. EXPRESSING EMOTION** relating to or expressing emotion **2. EASILY AFFECTED BY EMOTIONS** being by nature easily affected by or quick to express emotions **3. AFFECTED BY EMOTION** openly affected by emotion, especially sadness **4. STIRRING EMOTIONS** arousing or affecting the emotions **5. INSPIRED BY EMOTION** inspired or governed by emotion rather than reason or will-power ○ *one of the more emotional issues before the public this decade* —**e·mo·tion·al·i·ty** *n.* —**e·mo·tion·al·ly** *adv.*

e·mo·tion·al·ism /i mṓshən'l ìzzəm, i mṓshnə lìzzəm/ *n.* **1. OPENNESS TO EMOTION** a tendency to be easily swayed by the emotions **2. DISPLAY OF EMOTION** an exaggerated or undue display of strong feelings

e·mo·tion·al·ist /i mṓshən'list, i mṓshnəlist/ *n.* **1. EMOTIONAL PERSON** somebody whose thoughts or actions are greatly influenced by the emotions **2. OVERLY DEMONSTRATIVE PERSON** somebody who is prone to undue displays of strong feelings

e·mo·tion·a·lize /i mṓshən'l ìz, i mṓshnə lìz/ (**-al·ized, -al·iz·ing, -al·iz·es**) *vt.* to present or treat something emotionally

e·mo·tion·less /i mṓsh'nləss/ *adj.* not having or showing emotions —**e·mo·tion·less·ly** *adv.* —**e·mo·tion·less·ness** *n.*

e·mo·tive /i mṓtiv/ *adj.* **1. CAUSING EMOTION** causing or intended to cause emotion ○ *The actor gave an emotive delivery of the last lines of the play.* **2. INVOLVING EMOTION** showing or characterized by emotion ○ *an emotive plea for outlawing land mines* [Mid-18thC. Formed from Latin *emotus*, past participle of *emovere* "to move out, remove."] —**e·mo·tive·ly** *adv.* —**e·mo·tive·ness** *n.*

e·mo·tiv·ism /i mṓti vìzzəm/ *n.* the theory that ethical terms are not statements but instead reflect the feelings of the user

EMP *abbr.* electromagnetic pulse

Emp. *abbr.* **1.** Emperor **2.** Empire **3.** Empress

em·pale /em páyl/ (**-paled, -pa·ling, -pales**) *vt.* = **impale**

em·pa·na·da /èmpə naadə/ *n.* a Spanish, Filipino, or Latin American turnover with a spicy or sweet filling [Mid-20thC. From Spanish, from the past participle of *empanar* "to bake or roll in pastry," literally "to put into bread," from *pan* "bread."]

em·pan·el /em pánn'l/ *vt.* = **impanel**

em·pa·thize /émpə thìz/ (**-thiz·es, -thiz·ing, -thized**) *vi.* to identify with and understand another person's feelings or difficulties

em·pa·thy /émpəthee/ *n.* **1. UNDERSTANDING OF ANOTHER'S FEELINGS** the ability to identify with and understand another person's feelings or difficulties **2. ATTRIBUTION OF FEELINGS TO AN OBJECT** the transfer of your own feelings and emotions to an object such as a painting [Early 20thC. From Greek *empatheia* "affection, passion"; translation of German *Einfühlung.*] —**em·pa·thet·ic** /èmpə thétik/ *adj.* —**em·pa·thet·i·cal·ly** *adv.* —**em·path·ic** /empáthik/ *adj.* —**em·path·i·cal·ly** *adv.*

em·pen·nage /aampə naazh, èmpə naazh, émpənij/ *n.* the tail portion of an aircraft, including the stabilizer, elevator, vertical fin, and rudder [Early 20thC. From French, "feathering (of an arrow)," from *empenner*, literally "to feather in," from *penne* "feather."]

em·per·or /émpərər, -rər/ *n.* **1. RULER OF EMPIRE** a man who rules an empire **2.** = **emperor moth 3.** = **emperor butterfly** [12thC. From, ultimately, Latin *imperator* "commander," from *imperare* "to command," literally "to prepare in relation to," from *parare* "to prepare."]

em·per·or but·ter·fly *n.* a brightly colored butterfly that typically has mottled purple and brownish markings. Family: Nymphalidae. [*Emperor* from the imperial associations of the color purple]

em·per·or moth *n.* a large brightly colored Eurasian moth with distinctive markings resembling eyes on its wings. It is the largest European moth. Latin name: *Saturnia pyri.* [*Emperor* from the moth's large size]

em·per·or pen·guin *n.* an Antarctic penguin that has bluish-gray and black plumage, a white chest, and yellowish-orange neck markings. The largest of the penguins, the emperor penguin nurtures its eggs and young between its feet and a pouch-shaped fold in its abdomen. Latin name: *Aptenodytes forsteri.* [*Emperor* from the large size of the penguin]

em·pha·sis /émfəssiss/ (*plural* **-ses** /-seez/) *n.* **1. IMPORTANCE** special importance, significance, or stress **2. FORCEFULNESS OF EXPRESSION** forcefulness of expression to indicate the importance of something **3.** GRAM **EXTRA SPOKEN STRESS ON IMPORTANT WORD** extra stress of voice put on a syllable, word, or phrase, usually to show its significance [Late 16thC. From, ultimately, Greek *emphasis* "significance, appearance," from *emphainein* "to show, indicate," literally "to show in," from *phainein* "to show."]

em·pha·size /émfə sìz/ (**-sized, -siz·ing, -siz·es**) *vt.* to stress or give importance to something

em·phat·ic /em fáttik/ *adj.* **1. WITH EMPHASIS** expressed, thought, or done with emphasis **2. DEFINITE** forcible and definite **3.** GRAM **SHOWING EMPHASIS GRAMMATICALLY** used to describe a grammatical form that shows emphasis, e.g. the auxiliary "do" in the statement "I do like apples" [Early 18thC. From, ultimately, Greek *emphatikos*, from *emphasis* "appearance" (see EMPHASIS).]

em·phat·i·cal·ly /em fáttikəlee/ *adv.* **1. FORCEFULLY** with great force or definiteness **2. USED FOR EMPHASIS** used to reinforce the accuracy or appropriateness of a description

em·phy·se·ma /èmfə seemə, -zeemə/ *n.* **1. LUNG CONDITION CAUSING BREATHING IMPAIRMENT** a chronic medical disorder of the lungs in which the air sacs are dilated or enlarged and lack flexibility, resulting in breathing impairment and sometimes infection **2. ABNORMAL ENLARGEMENT CAUSED BY RETAINED GAS** an abnormal enlargement of an organ or body tissue caused by retention of air or other gas [Mid-17thC. From, ultimately, Greek *emphusēma* "swelling," from *emphusan* "to inflate, blow in," from *phusan* "to blow."] —**em·phy·sem·a·tous** /èmfə sémmətəss, -zémmətəss/ *adj.* —**em·phy·se·mic** /èmfə seemik, -zeemik/ *adj.*

em·pire /ém pìr/ *n.* **1. LANDS RULED BY SINGLE AUTHORITY** a group of nations, territories, or peoples ruled by a single authority, especially an emperor or empress **2. MONARCHY HEADED BY EMPEROR OR EMPRESS** a monarchy that has an emperor or empress as its ruler **3. PERIOD OF EMPIRE'S EXISTENCE** the period during which an empire exists **4. LARGE FARFLUNG BUSINESS** a very large, powerful, and extensive industrial or commercial organization **5. PART OF ORGANIZATION SOMEBODY PERSONALLY CONTROLS** a part of an organization controlled by a single person, especially somebody who is keenly protective of personal power **6. ABSOLUTE POWER** supreme or absolute power (*formal or literary*) [13thC. Via Old French from Latin *imperium* "command," from *imperare* (see EMPEROR).]

Em·pire *adj.* ARTS, ARCHIT **FRENCH FIRST EMPIRE STYLE** relating to a style of architecture, furniture, and clothing popular during the French First Empire (1804–15) during the reign of Napoleon I ○ *a dress with an Empire waist* ■ *n.* BOT **RED EATING APPLE** a variety of red eating apple that is a cross between the Delicious and the Macintosh

em·pire-build·ing *n.* the tendency to acquire power and authority within an organization, especially by adding extra subordinates —**em·pire-build·er** *n.*

Em·pire Day *n.* *U.K.* the former name for Commonwealth Day, used before 1958

Em·pire gown *n.* a woman's dress popular during the French First Empire, characterized by a low-cut neckline and a high waist from which the skirt hangs straight and loose

Em·pire State *n.* the U.S. state of New York (*informal*) [From the affluence and importance of the state]

Em·pire State Build·ing *n.* a skyscraper on Fifth Avenue in New York City built between 1930 and 1931. It has 102 stories and was the tallest building in the world for several years.

Em·pire State of the South *n.* the U.S. state of Georgia (*informal*)

em·pir·ic /em pírrik/ *n.* **1. SOMEBODY GUIDED BY EXPERIENCE NOT THEORY** somebody who relies upon observation and experiment rather than theory to determine the truth about something **2. CHARLATAN OR IMPOSTOR** a charlatan or quack, especially in medicine (*archaic*) [Mid-16thC. From, ultimately, Greek *empeirikos* "experienced," from *empeiros* "skilled," literally "tried in," from *peira* "try" (source of English *pirate*).]

em·pir·i·cal /em pírrik'l/ *adj.* **1.** **BASED ON OBSERVATION AND EXPERIMENT** based on or characterized by observation and experiment rather than theory **2.** MED **BASED ON PRACTICAL MEDICAL EXPERIENCE** based on practical experience in the medical treatment of real cases rather than on applied theory or scientific proof **3.** PHILOS **DERIVED SOLELY FROM EXPERIENCE** derived as knowledge from experience, particularly from sensory observation, rather than from the application of logic —**em·pir·i·cal·ly** *adv.*

em·pir·i·cal for·mu·la *n.* a chemical formula showing the relative proportion of elements in a compound instead of their structural arrangement or molecular weights, e.g., the formula H_2O

em·pir·i·cism /em pírri sìzz'm/ *n.* **1.** PHILOS **PHILOSOPHICAL BELIEF REGARDING SENSE-DERIVED KNOWLEDGE** the philosophical belief that all knowledge is derived from the experience of the senses **2.** **APPLICATION OF OBSERVATION AND EXPERIMENT** the application of observation and experiment, rather than theory, in determining something **3.** MED **MEDICINE BASED SOLELY ON EXPERIENCE** medicine that is based on practical experience rather than on theory and scientific proof —**em·pir·i·cist** *n.*

em·place /em pláyss/ (**-placed, -plac·ing, -plac·es**) *vt.* to put something into place or position [Mid-19thC. Back-formation from EMPLACEMENT.]

em·place·ment /em pláysmənt/ *n.* **1.** MIL **POSITION FOR LARGE WEAPONRY** a position that is specially prepared for a large gun or group of guns **2.** **POSITIONING OF SOMETHING** the act of putting something into place, or the condition of being in place [Early 19thC. From French, literally "placing in," from *place* "place."]

em·plane /em pláyn/ *vti.* = **enplane**

em·ploy /em plóy/ *vt.* (**-ployed, -ploy·ing, -ploys**) **1.** **GIVE PAID WORK TO SOMEBODY** to hire somebody to work in exchange for money **2.** **KEEP BUSY** to keep somebody occupied doing something **3.** **USE SOMETHING** to make use of something ■ *n.* **1.** **EMPLOYED STATE** the condition of working for pay (*formal*) ○ *I was in his employ.* **2.** **JOB** a job or occupation (*archaic*) [15thC. Via French *emploier* "to apply" from Latin *implicare* "to involve, enfold," from *plicare* "to fold" (source of English *ply, pliant,* and *display*).] —**em·ploy·a·bil·i·ty** /em plòy ə bíllətee/ *n.* —**em·ploy·a·ble** /em plóy əb'l/ *adj.*

WORD KEY: SYNONYMS

See Synonyms at ***use.***

em·ploy·ee /em plóy ee, èm ploy ée/, **em·ploy·e** *n.* somebody who is paid by somebody else to do work

em·ploy·er /em plóy ər/ *n.* **1.** **PERSON OR GROUP THAT HIRES WORKERS** a person, business, or organization that hires and pays one or more workers **2.** **SOMEBODY WHO USES SOMETHING** somebody who uses or makes use of something

em·ploy·ment /em plóymənt/ *n.* **1.** **WORKING FOR PAY** the condition of working for pay **2.** **WORK OR JOB DONE BY SOMEBODY** the work, especially paid work, that somebody does **3.** **NUMBER OF PAID WORKERS IN POPULATION** the total number or level of people that work for pay in a given population **4.** **USE OF SOMETHING** the use or practice of something

em·ploy·ment a·gen·cy *n.* a commercial organization that finds jobs for people or people for jobs

em·poi·son /em póyz'n/ (**-soned, -son·ing, -sons**) *vt.* to make somebody resentful or bitter (*formal*) [14thC. From Old French *empoisoner,* literally "to poison in," from *poison* "POISON."]

Em·po·ri·a /em páwree è/ city in eastern Kansas, on the Neosho River, northeast of Wichita and southwest of Topeka. Population: 24,866 (1996).

em·po·ri·um /em páwree əm/ (*plural* **-ums** *or* **-a** /-ə/) *n.* **1.** **STORE OFFERING WIDE SELECTION OF GOODS** a store, usually a large store, that offers a wide selection of goods **2.** **TRADE CENTER** a marketplace or center of trade [Late 16thC. From, ultimately, Greek *emporion,* from *emporos* "merchant, traveler," literally "journeyer in," from *poros* "journey."]

em·pow·er /em pówər/ (**-ered, -er·ing, -ers**) *vt.* **1.** **GIVE AUTHORITY TO SOMEBODY** to give somebody power or authority (*often passive*) **2.** **INSPIRE SOMEBODY WITH CONFIDENCE** to give somebody a sense of confidence or self-esteem —**em·pow·er·ment** *n.*

em·press /émprəss/ *n.* **1.** **RULER OF EMPIRE** a woman who rules an empire **2.** **EMPEROR'S WIFE** the wife or widow of an emperor

em·presse·ment /em préssmənt, aaN press maaN/ *n.* great attentiveness or cordiality (*formal*) [Early 18thC. From French, from *empresser* "to urge, be eager," literally "to press in," from *presser* "to press" (see PRESS).]

em·prise /em príz/ *n.* (*formal*) **1.** **BOLD ADVENTURE** a chivalrous, brave, or daring undertaking **2.** **CHIVALROUS DARING** chivalrous skill or daring [13thC. From French, from Old French *emprendre,* literally "to seize into," from Latin *prendere* "to seize."]

emp·ty /émptee, émtee/ *adj.* (**-ti·er, -ti·est**) **1.** **CONTAINING NOTHING** not containing or holding anything ○ *a heap of empty bags* **2.** **UNOCCUPIED** unoccupied or uninhabited ○ *There's an empty office next door.* **3.** **WITH NO PASSENGERS OR LOAD** without passengers, a load, or cargo ○ *The bus goes back to the depot empty.* **4.** **INSINCERE** lacking sincerity or truthfulness ○ *another empty promise* **5.** **MEANINGLESS** without value, meaning, or purpose ○ *contemplating his empty existence* **6.** **DULL** devoid of vitality ○ *an empty look* **7.** **UNFED** hungry or lacking food ○ *can't work on an empty stomach* **8.** MATH, LOGIC **WITHOUT MEMBERS OF SET** used to describe a set that has no elements or members ■ *v.* (**-tied, -ty·ing, -ties**) **1.** *vti.* **REMOVE CONTENTS OF SOMETHING** to remove or pour out the contents of something **2.** *vti.* **DISCHARGE OR TRANSFER** to discharge or transfer something, or be discharged and transferred **3.** *vr.* **UNBURDEN YOURSELF** to unburden or free yourself of something ■ *n.* (*plural* **-ties**) **CONTAINER WITHOUT CONTENTS** a bottle or other container that has nothing in it [Old English *æmtig* "unoccupied, at leisure," from *æmetta* "rest, leisure," of uncertain origin; perhaps from *æ-* "not" + METE. The underlying idea would be of not being assigned.] —**emp·ti·a·ble** *adj.* —**emp·ti·ly** *adv.* —**emp·ti·ness** *n.*

WORD KEY: SYNONYMS

See Synonyms at ***vacant*** and ***vain.***

emp·ty-hand·ed *adj.* **1.** **HAVING GAINED NOTHING** with nothing gained or achieved **2.** **WITH NOTHING IN HANDS** holding nothing in the hands

emp·ty-head·ed *adj.* silly or lacking in intelligence

emp·ty nest·er *n.* a parent whose children have grown up and moved away from home (*informal*)

emp·ty-nest syn·drome *n.* distress, especially a lack of energy or an emotional letdown experienced by parents whose grown children have moved away from home [*Empty-nest* in reference to birds' nests]

em·py·e·ma /èm pī éemə/ *n.* an accumulation of pus in a body cavity, e.g., the chest [Early 17thC. From, ultimately, Greek *empuēma,* from *empuein,* literally "to put pus in," from *puon* "pus."] —**em·py·e·mic** *adj.*

em·pyr·e·al /èm pī rée əl, -pírree-/ *adj.* **1.** **OF THE SKY** relating to the sky, the celestial sphere, or heaven **2.** **SUBLIME** glorious and sublime (*literary*) [15thC. Formed from medieval Latin *empyreus* (see EMPYREAN).]

em·py·re·an /èm pī rée ən, -pírree-/ *n.* **1.** **THE SKY OR HEAVENS** the sky, heavens, or celestial sphere (*literary*) **2.** **HIGHEST PART OF HEAVEN** the highest part of heaven, believed in ancient Greek and Roman times to contain pure fire or light and believed by some Christians to be the dwelling place of God (*archaic*) ■ *adj.* = **empyreal** *adj.* 2 [15thC. Formed from medieval Latin *empyreus,* from Greek *empurios,* literally "in fire," from, ultimately, *pur* "fire."]

EMS *abbr.* **1.** European Monetary System **2.** electrical muscle stimulation

EMT *abbr.* emergency medical technician

Emu

e·mu[1] /ée myoo/ (*plural* **e·mus** *or* **e·mu**) *n.* a large flightless bird native to Australia that is related to the ostrich and has three-toed feet and loose shaggy feathers. Latin name: *Dromaius novaehollandiae.* [Early 17thC. Shortening of Portuguese *ema di gei* "crane of the ground," of uncertain origin; probably from Moluccan *emeu.*]

emu[2], **EMU** *abbr.* electromagnetic unit

EMU /ée em yoo, ée myoo/ *abbr.* European Monetary Union

em·u·late /émmyə làyt/ (**-lat·ed, -lat·ing, -lates**) *vt.* **1.** **TRY TO EQUAL SOMEBODY OR SOMETHING** to try hard to equal or surpass somebody or something, especially by imitation **2.** **COMPETE SUCCESSFULLY WITH SOMEBODY OR SOMETHING** to be successful in competing with or rival somebody or something **3.** COMPUT **MAKE BEHAVE LIKE ANOTHER COMPUTER SYSTEM** to modify a computer system so that it appears to behave like another computer system, and can thereby accept data and run programs that are designed for the system being emulated [Late 16thC. From, ultimately, Latin *aemulari* "to rival," from *aemulus* "rival." Ultimately from a word that is also the ancestor of English *imitate* and *image.*] —**em·u·la·tive** *adj.* —**em·u·la·tive·ly** *adv.*

WORD KEY: SYNONYMS

See Synonyms at ***imitate.***

em·u·la·tion /èmmyə láysh'n/ *n.* **1.** **RIVALRY BY IMITATION** the attempt to equal or surpass somebody or something, usually by means of imitation **2.** COMPUT **PROCESS OF IMITATING COMPUTER SYSTEM** the process of successfully duplicating the performance of a computer device or program

em·u·la·tor /émmyə làytər/ *n.* **1.** **SOMEBODY WHO EMULATES** somebody or something that emulates another person or thing **2.** COMPUT **HARDWARE OR SOFTWARE IMITATING ANOTHER SYSTEM** hardware or software that permits a computer system to run programs written for and process data originating from a different type of computer system. ◊ **simulator**

em·u·lous /émmyələss/ *adj.* **1.** **EAGER TO RIVAL SOMEBODY OR SOMETHING** seeking to match or rival another's achievement or performance **2.** **MOTIVATED BY RIVALRY** motivated or characterized by rivalry or imitation [14thC. From Latin *aemulus* (see EMULATE).] —**em·u·lous·ly** *adv.* —**em·u·lous·ness** *n.*

e·mul·si·fi·a·ble /i múlsə fī əb'l, i-/, **e·mul·si·ble** /i múlsəb'l/ *adj.* capable of forming an emulsion

e·mul·si·fy /i múlsə fī/ (**-fied, -fy·ing, -fies**) *vt.* to disperse something in an emulsion, or convert two or more liquids into an emulsion —**e·mul·si·fi·ca·tion** /i mùlsəfi káysh'n/ *n.*

e·mul·sion /i múlshən/ *n.* **1.** **SUSPENSION OF LIQUID WITHIN ANOTHER LIQUID** a suspension of one liquid in another, e.g., oil in water or fat in milk **2.** PHOTOGRAPHY **LIGHT-SENSITIVE PHOTOGRAPHIC COATING** a thin light-sensitive coating of silver bromide or other silver halide in a medium such as gelatin on a photographic plate, paper, or film **3.** **WATER-BASED PAINT WITH MATTE FINISH** a water-based paint that is mainly used for interior decorating and usually has a matt finish [Early 17thC. From, ultimately, Latin *emuls-,* the past participle stem of *emulgere* "to milk out," from *mulgere* "to milk."] —**e·mul·sive** *adj.*

e·munc·to·ry /i múngktəree/ (*plural* **-ries**) *n.* a body part or organ that removes waste products from the body, e.g. the kidneys, lungs, or skin [14thC. From medieval Latin *emunctorius,* from, ultimately, Latin *emungere,* literally "to blow the nose thoroughly," from *mungere* "to blow the nose."]

en /en/ *n.* a measure of printing width, half that of an em

en- *prefix.* **1.** to put or go into, cover with ○ *entomb* ○ *encamp* ○ *enfold* **2.** to provide with **3.** to cause to be ○ *enlarge* **4.** thoroughly ○ *enmesh* **5.** in, within, into ○ *enzootic* [Via Old French from, ultimately, Latin *in* "in" (see IN)]

-en *suffix.* **1.** to cause to be or have ○ *brighten* ○ *strengthen* **2.** to come to be or have ○ *taughten* ○ *lengthen* **3.** made of or resembling ○ *wooden* [Via Latin from, ultimately, Greek *en.* Ultimately from an Indo-European word that is also the ancestor of English *in, en-,* and *internal.*]

en·a·ble /in áyb'l, en-/ (**-bled, -bling, -bles**) *vt.* **1.** **PROVIDE SOMEBODY WITH MEANS** to provide somebody with the resources, authority, or opportunity to do something **2.** **MAKE SOMETHING POSSIBLE** to make something possible or feasible [15thC. Coined from EN- + ABLE.] —**e·nab·ler** *n.*

en·a·bling /in áybling, en-/ *adj.* conferring new legal powers

en·act /in ákt, en-/ (**-act·ed, -act·ing, -acts**) *vt.* **1.** POL **MAKE SOMETHING LAW** to make proposed legislation into law **2.** THEATER **ACT SOMETHING OUT** to perform or relate something using acting [15thC. Coined from EN- + ACT, modeled on Anglo-Latin *inactitare.*] —**en·act·a·ble** *adj.* —**en·ac·tive** *adj.* —**en·ac·tor** *n.*

en·act·ment /in áktmənt, en-/ *n.* **1. PROCESS OF ENACTING** the act or process of enacting something **2. SOMETHING ENACTED** something that is enacted, especially a law

e·nam·el /i námm'l/ *n.* **1.** INDUST **GLASSY DECORATIVE OR PROTECTIVE COATING** a glassy decorative or protective coating, usually colored and opaque, that is fused onto metal, glass, or ceramics **2. SOMETHING WITH ENAMEL COATING** something that is coated with enamel **3.** INDUST **PAINT WITH A HARD SHINY FINISH** a paint that gives a shiny smooth finish when dry **4.** DENT **HARD LAYER ON TOOTH CROWN** a hard thin calcium-containing layer that covers and protects the crown of a tooth ■ *vt.* (**-eled, -el·ing, -els**) **1. COAT SOMETHING WITH ENAMEL** to decorate or coat all or part of an object with enamel **2. APPLY BRIGHT SHINY SURFACE TO SOMETHING** to apply a shiny brightly colored surface to something [14thC. From Anglo-Norman *enamailler*, literally "to enamel in," from, ultimately, Old French *esmail* "enamel," from a prehistoric Germanic base meaning "melting" that is also the ancestor of English *schmaltz.*] —**e·nam·el·er** *n.*

e·nam·el·ing /i námm'ling/ *n.* **1. APPLICATION OF ENAMEL** the process of applying enamel to something **2. SURFACE COATED WITH ENAMEL** the surface of something coated with enamel

e·nam·el·ware /i námm'l wàir/ *n.* household utensils coated with enamel

e·nam·el·work /i námm'l wùrk/ *n.* = **enameling** *n.* 2

en·am·or /in ámmər, en-/ (**-ored, -or·ing, -ors**) *vt.* (*formal or literary*) **1. INSPIRE SOMEBODY WITH LOVE** to inspire somebody with love or passion **2. CHARM SOMEBODY** to charm, fascinate, or captivate somebody [13thC. From Old French *enamourer*, from *en-* "to cause to" + *amour* "love."]

en·am·our *vt.* U.K. = **enamor**

en·an·ti·o·morph /i nántee ə màwrf/, **en·an·ti·o·mer** /i nántee əmər/ *n.* either of a pair of molecules that are a mirror image of each other in structure but cannot be superimposed [Late 19thC. Coined from Greek *enantios* "opposite" + -MORPH.] —**en·an·ti·o·mor·phic** /i nàntee ə máwrfik/ *adj.* —**en·an·ti·o·morph·ism** /-máwrfəss/ *n.* —**en·an·ti·o·mor·phous** /-máwr fìzzəm/ *adj.*

e·nate /ée nàyt/ *adj.* **MATERNALLY RELATED** related through the mother ■ *n.* **SOMEBODY MATERNALLY RELATED** somebody related on the mother's side [Mid-17thC. From Latin *enatus*, past participle of *enasci* "to issue out, be born."]

e·nat·ic /i náttik/ = **enate** *adj.*

e·na·tion /i náysh'n/ *n.* a small outgrowth on an organ, especially on a leaf, caused by a virus infection [Mid-19thC. From the Latin stem *enation-*, from, ultimately, *enasci* "to issue out, be born."]

enc, **enc.** *abbr.* **1.** enclosed **2.** enclosure

en·cage /in káyj, en-/ (**-caged, -cag·ing, -cag·es**) *vt.* to confine somebody or something in or in something resembling a cage (*formal*)

en·camp /in kámp, en-/ (**-camped, -camp·ing, -camps**) *vti.* to lodge in a camp, or provide somebody with a camp

en·camp·ment /in kámpmənt, en-/ *n.* **1. CAMPSITE** a place occupied by a camp **2. STAYING IN A CAMP** residence in a camp, or the setting up of a camp

en·cap·su·late /in kápsə làyt, en-/ (**-lat·ed, -lat·ing, -lates**), **in·cap·su·late** (**-lat·ed, -lat·ing, -lates**) *v.* **1.** *vt.* **CONDENSE SOMETHING** to express something in concise form **2.** *vti.* **ENCLOSE** to enclose something or be enclosed completely [Late 19thC. Coined from EN- + CAPSULE + -ATE.] —**en·cap·su·la·tion** /in kàpsə láysh'n, en-/ *n.* —**en·cap·su·la·tor** *n.*

en·cap·su·lat·ed /in kápsə làytəd, en-/ *adj.* used to describe an organ or tumor covered by a thin protective membrane

en·cap·sule /in káps'l, -káp so͞ol, en-/ (**-suled, -sul·ing, -sules**) *vt.* to encapsulate something (*formal*) ○ *fruit encapsuled in a large, hard shell*

en·case /in káyss, en-/ (**-cased, -cas·ing, -cas·es**), **in·case** (**-cased, -cas·ing, -cas·es**) *vt.* to surround something completely with a case or cover —**en·case·ment** *n.*

en·caus·tic /en káwstik/ *adj.* **HAVING FUSED COLORS** having wax colors fused to a surface by heat ■ *n.* **SOMETHING WITH FUSED COLORS** an object or work of art whose colors are fused to a surface by the application of heat, especially an earthenware tile decorated with an inlaid design in the style of medieval floor tiles [Late 16thC. Via Latin *encausticus* from Greek *egkaustikos*, from *egkaiein* "to burn in."]

en·ceinte[1] /en sáynt, aan sánt/ *adj.* having a child developing in the womb (*formal*) (*used euphemistically*) [Early 17thC. Via French from medieval Latin *incincta* "ungirded," from *cincta* "girded."]

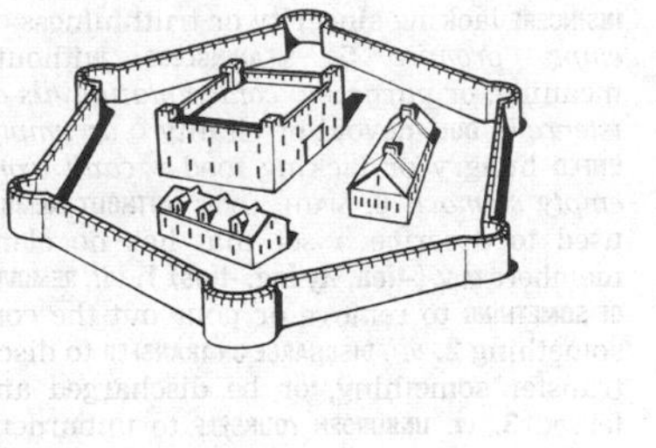

Enceinte

en·ceinte[2] /en sáynt, aan sánt/ *n.* MIL **1. DEFENSIVE ENCLOSURE** a defensive wall or enclosure **2. AREA ENCLOSED BY DEFENSIVE STRUCTURE** a place protected by a defensive wall or enclosure [Early 18thC. Via French from Latin *incincta*, past participle of *incingere* "to gird in."]

encephal- *prefix.* = **encephalo-** (*used before vowels*)

en·ce·phal·ic /èn sə fállik/ *adj.* related to the brain, or located within the cranium [Mid-19thC. Formed from Greek *egkephalos* "brain."]

en·ceph·a·li·tis /en sèffə lítiss/ *n.* inflammation of the brain, usually caused by a viral infection [Mid-19thC.] —**en·ceph·a·lit·ic** /-líttik/ *adj.*

en·ceph·a·li·tis le·thar·gi·ca /-lə tháarjikə/ *n.* sleeping sickness (*technical*) [From modern Latin: *lethargica* from Latin, a form of *lethargicus* "sleepy"]

encephalo- *prefix.* brain ○ *encephalogram* [Via modern Latin from Greek *(muelos) enkephalos* "(marrow) in the head," from *en* "in" + *kephalē* "head" (see CEPHALIC)]

en·ceph·a·lo·gram /en séffələ gràm/ *n.* **1. BRAIN X RAY** an X-ray photograph of the brain **2.** = **electroencephalogram**

en·ceph·a·lo·graph /en séffələ gràf/ *n.* **1.** = **encephalogram** *n.* 1 **2.** = **electroencephalograph**

en·ceph·a·log·ra·phy /en sèffə lóggrəfee/ *n.* X-raying photography of the brain —**en·ceph·a·lo·graph·ic** /en sèffələ gráffik/ *adj.* —**en·ceph·a·lo·graph·i·cal·ly** *adv.*

en·ceph·a·lo·my·e·li·tis /en sèffəlō mī ə lítiss/ *n.* inflammation of the brain and spinal cord —**en·ceph·a·lo·my·e·lit·ic** /en sèffəlō mī ə líttik/ *adj.*

en·ceph·a·lon /en séffə lòn/ (*plural* **-la** /-lə/) *n.* the brain of a vertebrate [Mid-18thC. From Greek *egkephalon*, literally "inside the head," from *kephalē* "head."] —**en·ceph·a·lous** *adj.*

en·ceph·a·lop·a·thy /en sèffə lóppəthee/ *n.* any disease of the brain —**en·ceph·a·lo·path·ic** /en sèffələ páthik/ *adj.*

en·chain /in cháyn, en-/ (**-chained, -chain·ing, -chains**) *vt.* **1. PUT SOMEBODY OR SOMETHING IN CHAINS** to bind somebody or something with chains (*formal or literary*) **2. CAPIVATE SOMEBODY'S ATTENTION** to dominate somebody's attention or thoughts (*literary*) [14thC. From French *enchainer*, from, ultimately, Latin *catenare* "to chain."] —**en·chain·ment** *n.*

en·chant /in chánt, en-/ (**-chant·ed, -chant·ing, -chants**) *vt.* **1. DELIGHT SOMEBODY** to charm, delight, or captivate somebody **2. PUT SOMEBODY OR SOMETHING UNDER SPELL** to cast a spell on somebody or something [14thC. Via Old French *enchanter* from Latin *incantare*, literally "to chant a magic formula upon," from *cantare* "to sing."]

en·chant·ed /in chántəd, en-/ *adj.* **1. DELIGHTED** charmed, delighted or captured by somebody or something **2. UNDER SPELL** put under a magic spell

en·chant·er /in chántər, en-/ *n.* **1. CHARMING OR DELIGHTFUL PERSON** somebody who is charming or delightful **2. MAGICIAN** somebody who casts spells

en·chant·er's night·shade *n.* a plant that is found in cool woodland regions and has small white flowers and bristly fruits. Genus: *Circaea.*

en·chant·ing /in chánting, en chánting/ *adj.* captivating or delightful —**en·chant·ing·ly** *adv.*

en·chant·ment /in chántmənt, en-/ *n.* **1. STATE OF BEING ENCHANTED** the act or condition of being enchanted **2. CHARM** something that delights or captivates **3. SPELL** a magic spell

en·chant·ress /in chántrəss, en-/ *n.* **1. CHARMING WOMAN** a woman who is charming or delightful **2. WOMAN MAGICIAN** woman who casts spells

en·chase /in cháyss, en-/ (**-chased, -chas·ing, -chas·es**) *vt.* **1. SET JEWELRY WITH GEMS** to set jewelry or other decorative objects with gems **2. DECORATE METAL** to emboss, engrave, or carve designs on metal [15thC. From French *enchasser* "to set (gems), encase," from *chasse* "case, box."]

en·chi·la·da /ènchi laáadə/ *n.* a fried tortilla rolled around a mixture of poultry, meat, or vegetables and served hot with a usually spicy sauce [Late 19thC. From Mexican Spanish, a form of the past participle of *enchilar* "to season with chili."] ◇ **the big enchilada** somebody important or dominant in an organization (*slang*) ◇ **the whole enchilada** the entirety of something (*slang*)

en·chi·rid·i·on /èn kī ríddee ən/ (*plural* **-ons** *or* **-a** /-ə/) *n.* a manual or handbook (*archaic*) [Mid-16thC. Via late Latin from Greek *egkheiridion*, literally "small thing in the hand," from *kheir* "hand."]

en·cho·ri·al /en káwree əl/, **en·cho·ric** /-rik/ *adj.* belonging to or used in a particular country, especially as a writing system [Early 19thC. Formed from Greek *egkōrios* "in the country," from *khōra* "country."]

-enchyma *suffix.* cellular tissue ○ *aerenchyma* [From PARENCHYMA]

en·ci·na /en séénə/ *n.* *Southwestern U.S.* live oak [Early 20thC. From Spanish, "holm oak," from late Latin *ilicina*, from, ultimately, the Latin stem *ilic-* "ilex" (see ILEX).]

En·ci·ni·tas /ènsi neétəss/ city in southern California on the Gulf of Santa Catalina, northwest of San Diego. Population: 57,873 (1996).

en·ci·pher /in sífər, en-/ (**-phered, -pher·ing, -phers**) *vt.* to convert a text into code or cipher —**en·ci·pher·er** *n.* —**en·ci·pher·ment** *n.*

en·cir·cle /in súrk'l, en-/ (**-cled, -cling, -cles**) *vt.* **1. SURROUND SOMEBODY OR SOMETHING** to form a circle around somebody or something **2. MAKE CIRCUIT OF SOMEBODY OR SOMETHING** to go in a circle around somebody or something —**en·cir·cle·ment** *n.* —**en·cir·cling** *adj.*

WORD KEY: USAGE

See Usage note at ***surround.***

encl. *abbr.* **1.** enclosed **2.** enclosure

en·clasp /in klásp, en-/ (**-clasped, -clasp·ing, -clasps**) *vt.* to embrace or hold somebody or something tightly (*literary*)

en·clave /én klàyv, óN-/ *n.* **1.** POL **REGION SURROUNDED BY FOREIGN TERRITORY** a small country or territory that is culturally or ethnically different from a surrounding larger and distinct political unit. ◊ **exclave** **2. DISTINCT GROUP IN LARGER COMMUNITY** a distinct group that lives or operates together within a larger community [Mid-19thC. From French, from Old French *enclaver* "to enclose," from Latin *in* "in" + *clavis* "key" (source of English *clavicle*).]

en·clit·ic /en klíttik/ *adj.* depending on a preceding word for its formation or pronunciation [Mid-17thC. Via late Latin *encliticus* from Greek *egklitikos*, from *egklinein* "to lean on."]

en·close /in klṓz, en-/ (**-closed, -clos·ing, -clos·es**), **in·close** /in-/ (**-closed, -clos·ing, -clos·es**) *vt.* **1. SURROUND SOMETHING** to surround something, or shut something in **2. SURROUND LAND OR BUILDING WITH BOUNDARY** to surround land or a building with a fence, wall, or other boundary **3. INSERT SOMETHING IN ENVELOPE OR PACKAGE** to add something to the contents of an envelope or package **4. HOLD SOMETHING** to hold or contain something [14thC. From Old French *enclos*, the past participle of *enclore*, from Latin *includere* "to shut in" (see INCLUDE).] —**en·clos·a·ble** *adj.*

WORD KEY: USAGE

See Usage note at ***surround.***

en·closed or·der *n.* a Christian religious community whose members remain physically within it

en·clo·sure /in klṓzhər, en-/, **in·clo·sure** /in-/ *n.* **1.** SOMETHING INSIDE A LETTER something added to a letter or package **2.** LAND SURROUNDED BY A BOUNDARY an area of land surrounded by a fence, wall, or other boundary **3.** BOUNDARY FENCE a fence, wall, or other boundary surrounding something **4.** *U.K.* SPORTS RESERVED AREA AT SPORTS EVENT an area of ground at a sports event set aside for particular spectators or competitors **5.** ACT OF ENCLOSING the act or process of enclosing something **6.** CHR RESTRICTED PART OF CONVENT OR MONASTERY the part of a convent or monastery, especially the living quarters, that is restricted to members

en·code /in kṓd, en-/ (**-cod·ed, -cod·ing, -codes**) *vt.* **1.** CONVERT TEXT TO CODE to convert a message from plain text into code **2.** COMPUT CONVERT COMPUTER CHARACTERS INTO DIGITAL FORM to convert input data, e.g., analog signals, characters, and commands, into a digital form recognizable by a computer **3.** GENETICS PROVIDE GENETIC INFORMATION to provide the genetic information that enables a polypeptide, RNA molecule, or one of their constituent groups to be produced (*refers to codons and genes*) —**en·code·ment** *n.*

en·co·mi·ast /en kṓmee àst, -mee əst/ *n.* somebody who speaks or writes an encomium (*formal*) [Early 17thC. From Greek *egkōmiastēs*, from *egkōmiazein* "to praise," from *egkōmion* "eulogy."]

en·co·mi·um /en kṓmee əm/ (*plural* **-ums** *or* **-a** /-mee ə/) *n.* (*formal*) **1.** TEXT EXPRESSING HIGH PRAISE a formal text that expresses high praise for somebody **2.** HIGH PRAISE an expression of high praise [Mid-16thC. Via Latin from Greek *egkōmion* "eulogy," literally "revel in," from *kōmos* "revel" (source of English *comedy*).]

en·com·pass /in kúmpəss, en-/ (**-passed, -pass·ing, -pass·es**) *vt.* **1.** INCLUDE IN ENTIRETY to include the entirety of something **2.** ENCIRCLE SOMETHING to surround, envelop, or encircle something **3.** CAUSE SOMETHING TO OCCUR to cause something, or bring something about (*formal*) —**en·com·pass·ment** *n.*

en·core /ón kàwr/ *n.* EXTRA OR REPEATED PERFORMANCE OF SOMETHING an additional or repeated performance of something in response to a demand from an audience ■ *interj.* USED TO DEMAND REPEAT PERFORMANCE used to demand an additional or repeated performance of something ■ *vti.* (**-cored, -cor·ing, -cores**) ADD TO OR REPEAT PERFORMANCE OF to give an additional or repeated performance of something [Early 18thC. From French "still, again."]

en·coun·ter /in kówntər, en-/ *vt.* (**-tered, -ter·ing, -ters**) **1.** MEET SOMEBODY OR SOMETHING UNEXPECTEDLY to meet somebody or something, usually unexpectedly **2.** MEET SOMEBODY OR SOMETHING IN CONFLICT to confront somebody or something with hostility or aggression **3.** COME UP AGAINST SOMEBODY OR SOMETHING to be faced with somebody or something, or come up against somebody or something ■ *n.* **1.** UNEXPECTED MEETING a meeting with somebody or something, usually unexpected and brief **2.** CONFRONTATION a hostile confrontation or contest [13thC. Via Old French *encontrer* "to confront" from late Latin *incontra* "in front of," from Latin *in-* "in" + *contra* "against."]

en·coun·ter group *n.* a small group of people, often guided by a leader, who meet in order to achieve personal growth, self-awareness, and social skills by means of emotional expression and interaction

en·cour·age /in kúr ij, en-/ (**-aged, -ag·ing, -ag·es**) *vt.* **1.** GIVE SOMEBODY HOPE OR COURAGE TO to give somebody hope, confidence, or courage **2.** BE SUPPORTIVE OF SOMEBODY to urge somebody in a helpful way to do or be something **3.** FOSTER SOMETHING to assist something to occur or increase [15thC. From French *encoragier*, from *en-* "to cause" + *corage* "courage."] —**en·cour·ag·er** *n.*

en·cour·age·ment /in kúr ijmənt, en-/ *n.* **1.** SUPPORT THAT INSPIRES CONFIDENCE support of a kind that inspires confidence and a will to continue or develop **2.** SOMETHING THAT ENCOURAGES somebody who or something that encourages

en·cour·ag·ing /in kúr ijing, en-/ *adj.* giving hope, confidence, or courage —**en·cour·ag·ing·ly** *adv.*

en·croach /in krṓch, en-/ (**-croached, -croach·ing, -croach·es**) *vi.* **1.** TRESPASS ON SOMETHING to intrude gradually or stealthily, often taking away somebody's authority, rights, or property **2.** EXCEED PROPER LIMITS to exceed the proper limits of something [14thC. From Old French *encrochier* "to seize," literally "to hook in," from, ultimately, *croc* "hook," from Old Norse *krókr* (source of English *crook*).] —**en·croach·er** *n.* —**en·croach·ing·ly** *adv.* —**en·croach·ment** *n.*

en·crust /in krúst, en-/ (**-crust·ed, -crust·ing, -crusts**), **in·crust** /in-/ (**-crusted, -crust·ing, -crusts**) *vt.* (*often passive*) **1.** COVER SOMETHING WITH HARD COATING to cover something with a hard thick coating **2.** DECORATE SOMETHING RICHLY to embellish something richly, especially with jewels [Early 17thC. Via French *incruster* from Latin *incrustare*, from *in-* "upon" + *crusta* "crust."]

en·crust·a·tion *n.* = **incrustation**

en·crypt /in krípt, en-/ (**-crypt·ed, -crypt·ing, -crypts**) *vt.* **1.** CONVERT TEXT INTO CODE to convert a text into code or cipher **2.** COMPUT ENCODE COMPUTER DATA to convert computer data and messages to something incomprehensible by means of a key, so that it can be reconverted only by an authorized recipient holding the matching key —**en·cryp·tion** /in krípshən, en-/ *n.*

en·cul·tu·ra·tion /in kùlchə ráysh'n, en-/ *n.* = **socialization** [Mid-20thC. Coined from EN- + CULTURE + -ATION.] —**en·cul·tu·ra·tive** /in kúlchə ràytiv, en-/ *adj.*

en·cum·ber /in kúmbər, en-/ (**-bered, -ber·ing, -bers**), **in·cum·ber** (**-bered, -ber·ing, -bers**) *vt.* **1.** HINDER SOMEBODY OR SOMETHING to hamper or impede somebody or something **2.** LOAD SOMEBODY OR SOMETHING DOWN to burden or weigh down somebody or something (*often passive*) **3.** FILL SOMETHING WITH SUPERFLUOUS THINGS to fill something with superfluous matter or objects (*often passive*) [14thC. From Old French *encombrer* "to obstruct," literally "to put in a barrier," from *combre* "barrier."]

en·cum·brance /in kúmbrəns, en-/ *n.* **1.** BURDEN OR HINDRANCE somebody who or something that hinders or burdens somebody **2.** LAW BURDEN OR CLAIM ON PROPERTY a lien, charge, or claim on property, especially a mortgage

en·cum·branc·er /in kúmbrənsər, en-/ *n.* somebody who has a legal claim on property, especially a mortgage

ency., **encyc.**, **encycl.** *abbr.* encyclopedia

en·cyc·li·cal /in síklik'l, en-/ *n.* CHR in the Roman Catholic Church, a formal statement issued by the Pope to bishops, often on matters of doctrine [Mid-17thC. From, ultimately, Greek *egkuklios* "circular, general," literally "in a circle," from *kuklos* "circle" (see CYCLE).]

en·cy·clo·pe·di·a /in sìklə péedee ə, en-/, **en·cy·clo·pae·di·a** *n.* a reference work offering comprehensive information on all or specialized areas of knowledge [Mid-16thC. From, ultimately, Greek *egkuklopaideia* "general education," from *egkuklios* "general" (see ENCYCLICAL) + *paideia* "education," from *pais* "boy, child" (source of English *pediatrician*).]

en·cy·clo·pe·dic /in sìklə péedik, en-/, **en·cy·clo·pae·dic** *adj.* covering or including a broad range of detailed knowledge such as is found in an encyclopedia —**en·cy·clo·pe·di·cal·ly** *adv.*

en·cy·clo·pe·dism /in sìklə pée dìzzəm, en-/, **en·cy·clo·pae·dism** *n.* comprehensive learning or knowledge

en·cy·clo·pe·dist /in sìklə péedist, en-/, **en·cy·clo·pae·dist** *n.* somebody who compiles or contributes to an encyclopedia

En·cy·clo·pe·dist /in sìklə péedist, en-/ *n.* a writer or editor of the *Encyclopédie* (1751–72), a French reference work in which the advanced secular, technical, and political ideas of the period were articulated

en·cyst /en síst/ (**-cyst·ed, -cyst·ing, -cysts**) *vti.* to enclose or be enclosed in a cyst —**en·cys·ta·tion** /èn sis táysh'n/ *n.* —**en·cyst·ed** /en sístəd, in-/ *adj.* —**en·cyst·ment** /en sístmənt/ *n.*

end /end/ (**end·ed, end·ing, ends**) CORE MEANING: a noun indicating the last part of something, either physically or in the abstract, and a verb indicating that something finishes or stops ○ (n) *At the far end lay a vacant lot.* ○ (n) *bound with a red rubber band at one end* ○ (n) *closed down at the end of 1991* ○ (n) *listened until the end* ○ (v) *We want to end discrimination.* ○ (v) *the weeks before school ends* ○ (v) *The reef ends in a perpendicular wall.*

1. *n.* FINAL PART the final part of a period of time, of an event, or of a book, film or other work ○ *The goal was to bring the information superhighway to even the most remote reaches of the globe by the end of the century.* ○ *His e-mail address is at the end of the article.* **2.** *n.* EXTREMITY OF OBJECT the tip or extremity of a long narrow object ○ *I'm surprised he knows which end of the mike to hold.* **3.** *n.* LIMIT OR BOUNDARY the limit, extent, or boundary of something ○ *They walked the valley from end to end.* **4.** *n.* STOPPING OF SOMETHING the act or result of stopping something ○ *call for an unconditional end to the pollution* **5.** *n.* EXTREMITY OF A SCALE either of the extreme points on a scale ○ *at both ends of the political spectrum* ○ *those at the high end of the income range* **6.** *n.* GOAL a goal, object, or purpose ○ *for purely political ends* **7.** *n.* PART OF COMMUNICATIONS LINK either of the places connected by a communications link ○ *Pick up the phone and find out who's on the other end.* **8.** *n.* DEATH the experience of death ○ *an untimely end* **9.** *n.* LEFTOVER PIECE a piece or part of something that is left over **10.** *n.* SHARE OF JOINT RESPONSIBILITY a part or portion of shared responsibility ○ *Are you sure they'll honor their end of the deal?* **11.** *n.* SPORTS AREA ON PLAYING FIELD the area at either end of a playing field **12.** *n.* FOOTBALL PLAYER POSITIONED AT END OF LINE in football, a player positioned at either end of the offensive or defensive line **13.** *v. vti.* STOP to reach, or bring something to, a close or a final point ○ *She abruptly ended the meeting.* ○ *The meeting ended without an agreement being made.* **14.** *vi.* RESULT to have an ultimate consequence or result ○ *The vacation ended in tragedy.* **15.** *vi.* STOP AT A PLACE to reach a particular place and stop there ○ *The road ends at a little village called Moneta.* **16.** *vi.* HAVE A TIP to have a particular kind of tip or extremity ○ *The dog's tail ends in a tuft of hair.* [Old English *ende*. Ultimately from an Indo-European word meaning "front" that is also the ancestor of English *advance*, *antique*, and *until*.] ◇ **an end in itself** indicates that something is worth having or doing although it may not lead to anything ○ *A friendship should be satisfying; it is an end in itself, and not a means to an end.* ◇ **at loose ends** having no purpose or occupation ○ *With all her work done she found herself at loose ends.* ◇ **at wit's end** totally perplexed and not knowing what to do ○ *I've tried everything to solve the problem; I'm at wit's end.* ◇ **end it all** commit suicide ◇ **end on 1.** with the end facing or next to something ○ *The plane crash-landed on the runway, its tail section end on to the tarmac.* **2.** in such a way that an object's end piece or section is flush with a flat surface ○ *Set the heavy crate end on near the loading dock.* ◇ **end to end** in a row with the ends adjacent ○ *The beds of flowers were arranged end to end.* ◇ **go off the deep end** to behave furiously or irrationally (*informal*) ◇ **in the end** finally ○ *In the end, I had to admit he was right.* ◇ **no end of something** a great deal of something (*informal*) ○ *The old photocopier gave us no end of trouble.* ◇ **on end 1.** for an uninterrupted period ○ *The rain continued for weeks on end.* **2.** in a vertical position ○ *We left the table standing on end against the wall.* ◇ **the end of the line, the end of the road** the point beyond which somebody or something can no longer continue or survive ○ *The coming of the supermarkets was the end of the line for many small independent grocers.* ◇ **the ... to end all ...** something that is so impressive or important that nothing else of the same kind will ever rival it ○ *the war to end all wars* ○ *the movie to end all movies* ◇ **to the bitter** *or* **to the very end** for as long as is possible, however unpleasant the situation becomes ○ *The company's policy was to fight to the bitter end all consequent damage suits.* ◇ **until the end of time** forever

end up *vi.* **1.** TURN OUT TO BE to become something eventually **2.** ARRIVE AT LAST to arrive at a destination at long last

end- *prefix.* = **endo-** (*used before vowels*)

-end *suffix.* person or thing to be treated in a particular way ○ *adherend* [From Latin *-endus, -endum*]

en·dam·age /in dámmij, en-/ (**-aged, -ag·ing, -ag·es**) *vt.* to cause injury or harm to somebody or something (*archaic*)

en·da·moe·ba /èndə meébə/ (*plural* **-moe·bas** *or* **-moe·bae** /-bee/ *or* **-me·bae**) *n.* a parasitic protozoan found in the digestive tracts of some invertebrates, especially cockroaches and termites. Genus: *Endamoeba.*

en·dan·ger /in dáynjər, en-/ (**-gered, -ger·ing, -gers**) *vt.* to expose somebody or something to danger —**en·dan·ger·ment** *n.*

en·dan·gered /in dáynjərd, en-/ *adj.* in danger or at risk, especially of ceasing to exist

en·dan·gered spe·cies *n.* a species of animal, plant or other organism, whose numbers are so few, or declining so quickly, that it may soon become extinct. Endangered species are sometimes protected under national or international law.

end a·round *n.* **1. end-a-round play** FOOTBALL **PLAY WITH END CARRYING BALL** a play in which an end on one side carries the ball around the opposite side of the field **2. INDIRECT WAY OF GETTING RESULT** an indirect attack on a problem that avoids opponents instead of confronting them (*informal*)

end·ar·te·rec·to·my /èn daartə réktəmee/ (*plural* **-mies**) *n.* the surgical removal of material that is wholly or partially obstructing blood flow in an artery [Mid-20thC. Coined from END- + ARTERY + -ECTOMY.]

en dash *n.* in printing, a dash that is one en in length

en·dear /in déer, en-/ (**-deared, -dear·ing, -dears**) *vt.* to make somebody or something affectionately loved or greatly liked [Late 16thC. Coined from EN- + DEAR, modeled on French *enchérir.*]

en·dear·ing /in déering, en-/ *adj.* producing feelings of affection or fondness —**en·dear·ing·ly** *adv.*

en·dear·ment /in déermənt, en-/ *n.* **1. EXPRESSION OF AFFECTION** an expression of affection, especially if spoken ○ *terms of endearment* **2. ACT OF BEING ENDEARED** the act or condition of being endeared

en·deav·or /in dévvər, en-/ *vt.* (**-ored, -or·ing, -ors**) **TRY TO DO SOMETHING** to make an effort to achieve something (*formal*) ■ *n.* **1. EFFORT** an earnest exertion in order to achieve something **2. ENTERPRISE** an enterprise or directed activity [15thC. From *put in dever,* partial translation of French *mettre en devoir,* literally "to put in duty"; *devoir* from, ultimately, Latin *debere* "to owe" (source of English *debt*).] —**en·deav·or·er** *n.*

en·deav·our *vt.* U.K. = **endeavor**

en·dem·ic /en démmik/ *adj.* **1.** MED **OCCURRING IN PARTICULAR PLACE** used to describe a disease occurring within a specific area, region, or locale ○ *Typhoid fever used to be endemic in the Deep South.* **2.** ECOL **RESTRICTED TO PARTICULAR AREA** used to describe a species of organism that is confined to a particular geographical region, e.g., an island or river basin **3. CHARACTERISTIC OF AREA** characteristic of a particular place or among a particular group or area of interest or activity ■ *n.* MED **ENDEMIC DISEASE** an endemic disease [Mid-17thC. From, ultimately, Greek *endēmos* "native," literally "in the people," from *dēmos* "people."] —**en·dem·i·cal·ly** *adv.* —**en·de·mic·i·ty** /èndə míssətee/ *n.* —**en·dem·ism** /éndə mìzzəm/ *n.*

end·er·gon·ic /èndər gónnik/ *adj.* used to describe a chemical or biochemical reaction in which energy is absorbed [Mid-20thC. Coined from END- + Greek *ergon* "work" + -IC.]

En·ders /éndərz/, **John Franklin** (1897–1985) U.S. microbiologist. He shared a Nobel Prize (1954) for research that led to the development of vaccines against viral diseases such as poliomyelitis, mumps, and measles.

end·game /énd gàym/ *n.* **1.** CHESS **LAST STAGE OF CHESS GAME** the final stage of a chess game in which only a few pieces are left on the board **2. ULTIMATE STAGE OF SOMETHING** the final stage of a process or contest ○ *As the trial neared its close, reporters watched closely to see what the prosecutors' endgame would be.*

En·di·cott /éndi kòt/ village in southern New York, on the Susquehanna River. Population: 13,531 (1990).

end·ing /énding/ *n.* **1. FINAL PART OF SOMETHING** the final or concluding part of something, e.g., a book or movie **2. WAY SOMETHING IS FINISHED** the manner in which something is ended **3.** LING **END PART OF WORD** the terminating part of a word, e.g., an inflection or suffix **4.** CHESS = **endgame** *n.* 1 **5.** PSYCHOL **PROCESS OF CONCLUDING A RELATIONSHIP** the process of concluding a relationship with another person, especially a therapist. An ending may offer somebody an opportunity to explore feelings about separation and loss.

en·dive /én dīv, aaN déev/ (*plural* **-dives** *or* **-dive**) *n.* **1. LEAFY PLANT USED IN SALADS** a plant grown for its tightly packed curly leaves that are used in salads and as a garnish. Latin name: *Cichorium endivia.* **2. CHICORY USED IN SALADS** a chicory grown for its mainly white, succulent leaves that are used in salads. Latin name: *Cichorium intybus.* [14thC. From, ultimately, Latin *endivia* from medieval Greek *entubia,* of uncertain origin; perhaps ultimately from Semitic.]

end·less /éndləss/ *adj.* **1. WITHOUT END** having no end or limit **2. CONTINUOUS** made continuous by joining the ends —**end·less·ly** *adv.* —**end·less·ness** *n.*

end line *n.* a line at the end of a court or field that marks the boundary of a playing area

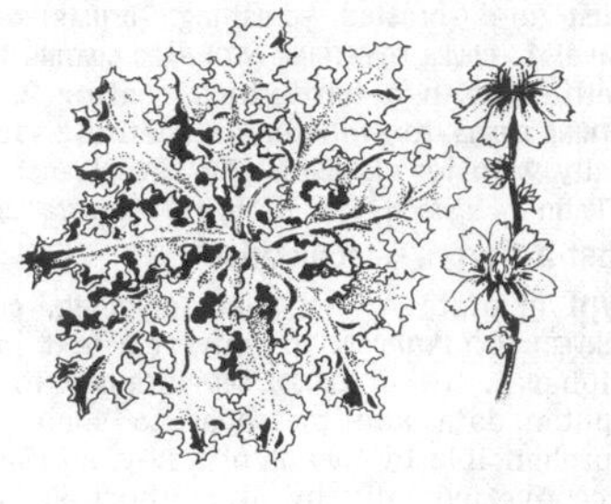

Endive

end man *n.* a man at the end of a line in a minstrel show. ◊ **interlocutor**

end mat·ter *n.* PUBL = **back matter**

end·most /énd mōst/ *adj.* **1. NEAREST END** nearest or at the end **2.** last or most distant

end·note /énd nōt/ *n.* a note of comment or reference placed at the end of an article, chapter, book, or essay instead of the bottom of a page. ◊ **footnote**

endo- *prefix.* in, within, inside ○ *endotracheal* [From Greek *endo.* Ultimately from an Indo-European base meaning "in," which is also the ancestor of English *in, industry,* and *indigent.*]

en·do·car·di·al /èndō kaárdee əl/ *adj.* **1. IN HEART** located within the heart **2. OF MEMBRANE OF HEART** concerned with the membranous lining of the heart's cavities (**endocardium**)

en·do·car·di·tis /èndō kaar dítiss/ *n.* inflammation of the membranous lining of the heart's cavities (**endocardium**) —**en·do·car·dit·ic** /èndō kaar díttik/ *adj.*

en·do·car·di·um /èndō kaárdee əm/ (*plural* **-a** /-ə/) *n.* the thin membranous lining of the heart's cavities

en·do·carp /éndə kaàrp/ *n.* the innermost of the three layers of the wall (**pericarp**) of a fruit. It may be toughened or hardened, as in a cherry stone or peach pit. (*technical*) —**en·do·car·pal** /èndə kaárp'l/ *adj.*

en·do·cra·ni·um /èndō kráynee əm/ (*plural* **-a** /-ə/) *n.* = **dura mater** —**en·do·cra·ni·al** *adj.*

en·do·crine /éndəkrin, -kreen, éndəkrīn/ *adj.* relating to glands that secrete hormones internally directly into the lymph or bloodstream. ◊ **exocrine** [Early 20thC. Coined from ENDO- + Greek *krinein* "to separate."]

en·do·crine gland *n.* any gland of the body that secretes hormones directly into the blood or lymph, e.g. the thyroid, pituitary, pineal, and adrenal glands

en·do·cri·nol·o·gist /èndəkrə nólləjist/ *n.* a medical specialist who treats endocrine disorders

en·do·cri·nol·o·gy /èndəkrə nólləjee/ *n.* a branch of medicine dealing with disorders of the endocrine glands —**en·do·cri·no·log·ic** /èndə krinə lójjik/ *adj.* —**en·do·crin·o·log·i·cal** /-lójjik'l/ *adj.*

en·do·cy·to·sis /èndō sī tṓssiss/ *n.* the process by which a cell membrane folds inward to take in substances bound to its surface [Mid-20thC. Coined from ENDO- + -CYTE + -OSIS.]

en·do·derm /éndə dùrm/ *n.* the innermost layer of an animal embryo that develops into the lining of the respiratory and digestive tracts [Mid-19thC. Coined from ENDO- + Greek *derma* "skin."] —**en·do·der·mal** /èndə dúrm'l/ *adj.*

en·do·der·mis /èndə dúrmiss/ *n.* a layer of cells that marks the boundary between the inner core (**stele**) and outer surrounding tissue (**cortex**) of a plant root. It is also evident in the stems of certain plants, notably ferns and some flowering plants. [Late 19thC. Formed from ENDODERM, modeled on *epidermis.*]

en·do·don·tics /èndə dóntiks/, **en·do·don·tia** /-dónshə, -shee ə/ *n.* the branch of dentistry that deals with diseases of the dental pulp (*takes a singular verb*) [Mid-20thC. Coined from ENDO- + ORTHODONTICS.] —**en·do·don·tic** *adj.* —**en·do·don·tist** *n.*

en·do·en·zyme /èndō én zīm/ *n.* an enzyme that functions inside the cell where it is found or produced

en·do·er·gic /èndō úrjik/ *adj.* NUCLEAR PHYS relating to a nuclear reaction in which energy is consumed. [Mid-20thC. Coined from ENDO- + Greek *ergon* "work."]

end of steel *n. Can* **1. END OF RAILROAD LINE** the furthest point to which the rails of a railroad line have been laid **2. TOWN AT END OF RAILROAD LINE** the town at the end of a railroad line ○ *Dawson was the end of steel in the Yukon region.*

en·dog·a·my /en dóggəmee/ *n.* **1.** ANTHROP **MARRIAGE WITHIN GROUP** the social practice of marrying another member of the same clan, people, or other kinship group **2.** BOT **SELF-POLLINATION** pollination between the flowers of the same plant —**en·dog·a·mous** *adj.*

en·dog·e·nous /en dójjənəss/ *adj.* **1. WITHOUT EXTERNAL CAUSE** with no apparent external cause ○ *endogenous depression* **2.** BIOL **PRODUCED INSIDE ORGANISM** originating or growing within an organism or tissue ○ *endogenous secretions.* ◊ **exogenous** —**en·dog·e·nous·ly** *adv.* —**en·dog·e·ny** *n.*

en·do·lymph /éndə lìmf/ *n.* the fluid inside the membranous labyrinth of the ear —**en·do·lym·phat·ic** /èndə lim fáttik/ *adj.*

en·do·me·tri·a plural of **endometrium**

en·do·me·tri·o·sis /èndō meetri ṓssiss/ *n.* a medical condition in which the mucous membrane (**endometrium**) that normally lines only the womb is present and functioning in the ovaries or elsewhere in the body

en·do·me·tri·um /èndō méetree əm/ (*plural* **-a** /-ə/) *n.* the mucous membrane that lines the womb and increases in thickness in the latter part of the menstrual cycle [Late 19thC. Coined from ENDO- + Greek *mētra* "womb."] —**en·do·me·tri·al** *adj.*

en·do·mi·to·sis /èndō mī tṓssiss/ *n.* a process by which chromosomes divide within a cell but the nucleus does not, so that an increase in chromosome number results —**en·do·mi·tot·ic** /èndō mī tóttik/ *adj.*

en·do·morph /éndə màwrf/ *n.* **1.** PHYSIOL **STOCKY PERSON** somebody whose body has a stocky build and a prominent abdomen **2.** MINERALS **MINERAL INSIDE ANOTHER** a mineral that is found within another mineral. An example of this is tourmaline, often found enclosed in quartz. ◊ **perimorph** —**en·do·mor·phic** /èndə máwrfik/ *adj.* —**en·do·mor·phy** /éndə màwrfee/ *n.*

en·do·nu·cle·ase /èndō nóoklee àyss, -àyz/ *n.* an enzyme that splits a DNA or RNA molecule by aiding the breakdown of bonds between nucleotides

en·do·par·a·site /èndō pérrə sìt/ *n.* a parasite, e.g., a tapeworm, that lives inside its host —**en·do·par·a·sit·ic** /-perrə síttik/ *adj.* —**en·do·par·a·sit·ism** /-pérrəssi tìzzəm, -sī tìzzəm/ *n.*

en·do·pep·ti·dase /èndō pépti dàyss, -dàyz/ *n.* an enzyme, e.g., pepsin that aids the breakdown of peptide bonds in proteins

en·do·phyte /éndə fìt/ *n.* a plant or fungus that lives inside another plant. It may or may not be a parasite of its host plant. —**en·do·phyt·ic** /èndə fíttik/ *adj.*

en·do·plasm /éndə plàzzəm/ *n.* the inner, more fluid layer of cytoplasm in a cell —**en·do·plas·mic** /èndə plázmik/ *adj.*

en·do·plas·mic re·tic·u·lum *n.* an intricate system of tubular membranes in the cytoplasm of a cell. It is responsible for the synthesis and transport of materials to and from cells.

end or·gan *n.* the specialized end of a sensory or motor nerve

en·dor·phin /en dáwrfin/ *n.* a substance in the brain that attaches to the same cell receptors that morphine does. Endorphins are released when severe injury occurs, often abolishing all sensation of pain. [Late 20thC. Blend of ENDOGENOUS and MORPHINE.]

en·dorse /in dáwrs, en-/ (**-dorsed, -dors·ing, -dors·es**), **in·dorse** /in-/ (**-dorsed, -dors·ing, -dors·es**) *vt.* **1. APPROVE FORMALLY** to give formal approval or permission for something ○ *This practice is not endorsed by headquarters.* **2. SUPPORT** to give public support to somebody or something, especially during an election ○ *decided to endorse the mayor as a candidate for higher office* **3.** COMM **PROMOTE** to give public approval of a product for advertising purposes ○ *a brand endorsed by a popular TV star* **4.** FIN **SIGN CHECK TO OBTAIN CASH** to sign the back of a check or money order in order to cash it **5.** FIN **SIGN SOMETHING TO ASSIGN PAYMENT** to sign the back of a negotiable document in order to make it payable to a specified payee **6.** FIN **SIGN RECEIPT** to sign a document to acknowledge receipt of a payment **7. WRITE ON BACK OF DOCUMENT** to write a comment on the back of a document ○ *a* *fitness report that had been endorsed on the back by its recipient* [15thC. From medieval Latin *indorsare*, from Latin *dorsum* "back" (source of English *dorsal* and *dossier*).] —**en·dors·a·ble** *adj.* —**en·dor·see** /èn dawr seé, in dàwr seé/ *n.* —**en·dors·er** /in dáwrsər, en dáwrsər/ *n.*

en·dorse·ment /in dáwrsmənt, en dáwrsmənt/, **in·dorse·ment** /in dáwrsmənt/ *n.* **1.** FIN **ACT OF ENDORSING** an act or instance of endorsing something or somebody ○ *make an endorsement of a check* **2. SIGNATURE OR WRITTEN COMMENT** something, especially a signature, written on the back of a document to make it payable, approve it, or comment on it **3. OFFICIAL APPROVAL OR PERMISSION** official approval of or permission for something **4. PUBLIC SUPPORT** public support for somebody or something **5.** COMM **ADVERTISING TESTIMONIAL** an instance of public approval of a product for advertising purposes **6.** INSUR **POLICY ALTERATION** a clause added to an insurance policy that changes the coverage

en·do·scope /éndə skōp/ *n.* a medical instrument consisting of a long tube inserted into the body, usually through a small incision. It is used for diagnostic examination and surgical procedures. —**en·do·scop·ic** /èndə skóppik/ *adj.* —**en·do·scop·i·cal·ly** /-skóppikəlee/ *adv.* —**en·dos·co·py** /en dóskəpee/ *n.*

en·do·skel·e·ton /èndō skéllət'n/ *n.* the internal skeleton of an animal, especially of a vertebrate —**en·do·skel·e·tal** *adj.*

en·dos·mo·sis /èn daws mṓssiss/ *n.* osmosis in which fluid is absorbed from a surrounding fluid into a cell —**en·dos·mot·ic** /èn daws móttik/ *adj.* —**en·dos·mot·i·cal·ly** /-móttikəlee/ *adv.*

en·do·sperm /éndə spùrm/ *n.* the tissue that surrounds the embryo inside a plant seed and provides nourishment for it —**en·do·sper·mic** *adj.*

en·do·spore /éndə spáwr/ *n.* **1. ASEXUAL SPORE** an asexual spore that is formed inside the cells of certain bacteria and algae **2. INNER SPORE WALL** the inner layer of the wall of a spore —**en·do·spor·ous** /éndə spáwrəss, en dóspərəss/ *adj.*

en·dos·te·um /en dóstee əm/ (*plural* **-a** /-ə/) *n.* a layer of vascular tissue lining the inside of certain bones, e.g., the femur [Late 19thC. Coined from ENDO- + Greek *osteon* "bone."] —**en·dos·te·al** *adj.*

en·do·sul·fan /èndō súlfən/ *n.* an organochlorine insecticide and acaricide used to control insects, e.g., aphids and mites, on farm and garden crops. Its use is now restricted because of its toxic side effects. Formula: $C_9H_6Cl_6O_3S$. [Mid-20thC. Coined from ENDO- + SULFUR.]

en·do·sym·bi·o·sis /èndō sìm bī ṓssiss/ *n.* symbiosis in which one organism lives inside the body of another

en·do·the·ci·um /èndō theésheé əm, -theéssee əm/ (*plural* **-a** /-shee ə/) *n.* **1. MOSS TISSUE** the inner tissue of the spore-producing capsule of a moss **2. ANTHER TISSUE** the tissue of the inner wall of an anther in a flower [Mid-19thC. Coined from ENDO- + Greek *thēkion* "little case," a diminutive of *thēkē* "chest."]

en·do·the·li·a plural of **endothelium**

en·do·the·li·o·ma /èndō theelee ṓmə/ (*plural* **-mas** *or* **-ma·ta** /-ṓmətə/) *n.* a tumor of cells that line internal body surfaces

en·do·the·li·um /èndə theélee əm/ (*plural* **-a** /-ə/) *n.* a layer of cells that lines the inside of certain body cavities, e.g., blood vessels [Late 19thC. From modern Latin, formed from Greek *endon* "within" + *thēlē* "nipple."] —**en·do·the·li·al** *adj.* —**en·do·the·li·oid** *adj.*

en·do·therm /éndə thùrm/ *n.* an animal that is able to maintain a constant body temperature despite changes in the temperature of its environment [Mid-20thC. Coined from ENDO- + Greek *thermē* "heat."]

en·do·ther·mic /èndə thúrmik/, **en·do·ther·mal** /èndə-thúrm'l/ *adj.* **1.** CHEM, PHYS **ABSORBING HEAT** used to describe a reaction that absorbs heat (*the preferred term in nuclear physics is "endoergic"*) **2.** ZOOL **WARM-BLOODED** maintaining a constant body temperature despite changes in the temperature of the environment —**en·do·ther·my** /éndə thùrmee/ *n.*

en·do·tox·in /éndə tòksin/ *n.* a toxin produced within certain bacteria that is released only when the bacteria disintegrate —**en·do·tox·ic** /éndə tóksik/ *adj.*

en·do·tra·che·al /èndō trákee əl/ *adj.* located in or passed through the windpipe ○ *an endotracheal tube*

en·do·troph·ic /èndō tróffik/ *adj.* used to describe an association (**mycorrhiza**) between a fungus and a plant in which the fungus obtains its nourishment from inside its plant host. ◊ **ectotrophic**

en·dow /in dów, en-/ (**-dowed, -dow·ing, -dows**) *vt.* **1.** FIN **PROVIDE WITH MONEY** to provide a person or institution with income or property **2. PROVIDE WITH SOMETHING DESIRABLE** to provide somebody or something with desirable qualities, abilities, or characteristics ○ *Nature has endowed the area with a perfect climate.* **3. GIVE DOWER** to provide somebody with a dower (*archaic*) [14thC. Via Anglo-Norman *endouer* from, ultimately, Latin *dotare* "to provide with a dowry" (the original sense in English), from *dos* "dowry."]

en·dow·ment /in dówmənt, en-/ *n.* **1.** FIN **FUNDS OR PROPERTY** an amount of income or property that has been provided to a person or institution, especially an educational institution **2.** FIN **GIVING OF ENDOWMENT** the giving of an endowment, or an instance of this **3. NATURAL QUALITY** a natural ability or quality ○ *A sharp mind was one of her many endowments.*

en·do·zo·ic /èndə zṓ ik/ *adj.* **1. LIVING IN ANIMAL** used to describe organisms that live inside an animal **2. DISPERSED THROUGH ANIMAL'S GUT** related to or being a method of seed dispersal in which the seeds are eaten by an animal and then passed out in the animal's feces

end·pa·per /énd pàypər/ *n.* a sturdy sheet of paper pasted to the inside of a book's front or back cover and to the spine edge of the first or last page

end·pin /énd pìn/ *n.* the adjustable spike-shaped leg at the bottom of a cello or double bass that the instrument rests on while being played

end·play /énd plày/ *n.* **BRIDGE TACTIC FORCING LOSS OF TRICK** a play in bridge in which an opponent is forced to lead near the end of the hand, with the result that he or she loses a trick that would otherwise have been won ■ *vt.* (**-played, -play·ing, -plays**) **FORCE BRIDGE OPPONENT TO LEAD** to force an opponent in bridge to lead near the end of a hand of bridge so that he or she will lose a trick

end point *n.* **1. COMPLETION** the point at which something is complete or comes to an end **2.** CHEM **COMPLETION OF TITRATION** the point, marked by a color change or other indicator, at which a titration is complete

end·point /énd pòynt/ *n.* MATH the point located at either end of a line segment or at the end of a ray

end prod·uct *n.* the final result of a process or series of events or operations

end rhyme *n.* the use of rhyme at the ends of lines of poetry, or an example of this

en·drin /éndrin/ *n.* a poisonous white crystalline compound that is used as an insecticide. A chlorinated hydrocarbon, it is an isomer of dieldrin. Formula: $C_{12}H_8Cl_6O$. [Mid-20thC. Coined from ENDO- + DIELDRIN.]

end run *n.* **1. ATTEMPT TO BYPASS** an attempt to get around an obstacle or difficulty, often by using deceitful methods (*informal*) **2.** FOOTBALL **OUTFLANKING RUNNING PLAY** a play in which the player with the ball attempts to run around the defensive line of the opposing team

end-run (**end-ran, end-run, end-run·ning, end-runs**) *vt.* to get around an obstacle or difficulty, often by using deceitful methods (*informal*)

end-stopped *adj.* used to describe poetry containing a pause in meaning at the end of a line or couplet, instead of continuing into the next line or couplet

end ta·ble *n.* a small table placed at the side of a couch or armchair, often with a lamp on top

en·due /in dóo, en dóo/ (**-dued, -du·ing, -dues**), **in·due** /in dóo/ (**-dued, -du·ing, -dues**) *vt.* to endow somebody or something with an ability or quality ○ *His successes have endued him with an aura of invincibility.* [14thC. Via French *enduire* from, ultimately, Latin *ducere* "to lead" (source of English *induce* and *duct*).]

en·dur·a·ble /in dóorəb'l, en-/ *adj.* able to be borne or tolerated ○ *The level of noise was barely endurable.* —**en·dur·a·bil·i·ty** /in dòorə bíllətee, en-/ *n.* —**en·dur·a·bly** /in dóorəblee, en-/ *adv.*

en·dur·ance /in dóorəns, en-/ *n.* **1. ABILITY TO BEAR PROLONGED HARDSHIP** the ability or power to bear prolonged exertion, pain, or hardship ○ *an endurance race* **2. TOLERATION OF HARDSHIP** an act or example of toleration of prolonged suffering or hardship ○ *an unflinching endurance of pain* **3. PERSISTENCE OVER TIME** the survival or persistence of something despite the ravages of time ○ *the endurance of ancient traditions* [15thC. From French, formed from *endurer* (see ENDURE).]

en·dure /in dóor, en-/ (**-dured, -dur·ing, -dures**) *v.* **1.** *vti.* **BEAR HARDSHIP** to experience exertion, pain, or hardship without giving up ○ *The nation endured years of war to create a lasting peace.* **2.** *vt.* **TOLERATE DISAGREEABLE THINGS** to tolerate or accept somebody or something that is extremely disagreeable (*formal*) ○ *I cannot endure that song.* **3.** *vi.* **SURVIVE** to last or survive over a period of time, especially when faced with difficulties ○ *The philosophical ideas of the ancient Greeks endure to this day.* [14thC. Via French *endurer* from Latin *indurare* "to harden," from *durus* "hard."]

en·dur·ing /in dóoring, en-/ *adj.* **1. PERSISTING OR SURVIVING** persisting or surviving in the face of difficulties **2. LONG-SUFFERING** patient or tolerant despite many difficulties —**en·dur·ing·ly** *adv.* —**en·dur·ing·ness** *n.*

en·dur·o /en dóorō/ (*plural* **-os**) *n.* a long race, especially one involving motorcycles or carts, that is intended to be won through endurance rather than speed [Mid-20thC. Alteration of ENDURANCE.]

end us·er *n.* a person or group that is one of the ultimate consumers or users that a product has been designed for ○ *a survey that is designed to assess what the end user really needs*

end·wise /énd wīz/, **end·ways** /énd wàyz/ *adv.* **1. WITH END UP** with an end up or forward **2. TOWARD ENDS** toward the ends **3. WITH ENDS TOUCHING** with one end next to another end

En·dym·i·on /en dímmee ən/ *n.* in Greek mythology, a handsome man loved by the moon goddess Selene

end zone *n.* either of the two areas at the ends of a football field between the goal line and the end line where a touchdown is scored

ENE *abbr.* east-northeast

-ene *suffix.* an unsaturated organic compound ○ *butene* [From Greek *-ēnē*, feminine of *-ēnos*, an adjective suffix]

en·e·ma /énnəmə/ *n.* **1. INSERTION OF LIQUID INTO RECTUM** the insertion of a liquid into the bowels via the rectum as a treatment, especially for constipation, or as an aid to diagnosis **2. LIQUID USED IN ENEMA** the liquid used in an enema ○ *a barium enema* [Late 17thC. Via late Latin from Greek, formed from *enienai* "to send or put in," from *hienai* "to send."]

en·e·my /énnəmee/ (*plural* **-mies**) *n.* **1. UNFRIENDLY OPPONENT** somebody who hates and seeks to harm or cause trouble for somebody else **2.** MIL **A MILITARY OPPONENT** a person or group, especially a military force, that fights against another in combat or battle **3.** POL **HOSTILE POWER** a hostile nation or power **4. HARMFUL THING** something that harms or opposes something else ○ *In a case like this, time is the enemy.* [13thC. Via Old French *enemi* from Latin *inimicus* "unfriendly," from *amicus* "friend" (source of English *amicable*).]

en·er·get·ic /ènnər jéttik/ *adj.* **1. FORCEFUL** displaying great vigor or force **2. REQUIRING STAMINA** requiring great vigor or stamina [Mid-17thC. Via Greek *energētikos* "active" from, ultimately, *ergon* "work" (see ENERGY).] —**en·er·get·i·cal·ly** *adv.*

en·er·get·ics /ènnər jéttiks/ *n.* the branch of physics that studies energy and its transformations (*takes a singular verb*)

en·er·gize /énnər jīz/ (**-gized, -giz·ing, -giz·es**) *v.* **1.** *vt.* **GIVE SOMEBODY OR SOMETHING ENERGY** to supply somebody or something with strength or power ○ *He felt energized by his nap.* **2.** *vti.* **MAKE OR BECOME ACTIVE** to become or cause something to become vigorously active **3.** *vt.* ELEC **SUPPLY WITH ELECTRICAL POWER** to supply something with a source of electrical power —**en·er·gi·za·tion** /ènnərji záysh'n/ *n.* —**en·er·giz·er** /énnər jīzər/ *n.*

en·er·gy /énnərjee/ (*plural* **-gies**) *n.* **1. VIGOR** liveliness and forcefulness ○ *She gave a speech that was full of energy.* **2. ABILITY TO DO THINGS** the ability or power to work or make an effort ○ *His illness left him feeling drained of energy.* **3. FORCEFUL EFFORT** a vigorous effort or action ○ *We must concentrate our energies on the task in hand.* **4.** PHYS **POWER SUPPLY OR SOURCE** a supply or source of electrical, mechanical, or other form of power **5.** PHYS **CAPACITY TO DO WORK** the capacity of a body or system to do work. Symbol *E* [Mid-16thC. Via French *énergie* from, ultimately, Greek *energeia*, from *ergon* "work."]

WORD KEY: ORIGIN

The Indo-European word from which *energy* ultimately comes is also the ancestor of English *irk, liturgy, organ, orgy, surgeon,* and *work.*

en·er·gy au·dit *n.* a survey of the use of energy in a building or organization, undertaken in order to make energy use as efficient as possible

en·er·gy bal·ance *n.* a mathematical relationship, using the principle of the conservation of energy, that shows the energy inputs and outputs of a process or system

en·er·gy band *n.* PHYS = **band**² *n.* 7

en·er·gy-band the·o·ry *n.* PHYS = **band theory**

en·er·gy cri·sis *n.* a situation in which available sources of energy are not sufficient to meet the demand

en·er·gy ef·fi·cient *adj.* using electrical or other energy in an economical way (*hyphenated when used before a noun*)

en·er·gy lev·el *n.* one of the discrete stable energy values that can be assumed by a physical system, e.g., the electrons in an atom or an atomic nucleus

en·er·gy tax *n.* a tax on an energy source intended to discourage environmentally unfriendly sources and encourage energy conservation or use of alternative sources

en·er·vate /énnər vàyt/ *vt.* (**-vat·ed, -vat·ing, -vates**) WEAKEN to weaken somebody's physical, mental, or moral vitality ○ *I was feeling quite enervated by the strain of moving.* ■ *adj.* = **enervated** [Early 17thC. From Latin *enervare* "to extract the sinews of, weaken," from *nervus* "sinew" (source of English *nerve*).] —**en·er·va·tion** /ènnər váysh'n/ *n.*

en·face /in fáyss, en-/ (**-faced, -fac·ing, -fac·es**) *vt.* to mark something on the face of a document by writing, stamping, or printing [Mid-19thC. From EN- + FACE, modeled on ENDORSE.] —**en·face·ment** *n.*

en fa·mille /aaN fa meé/ *adv.* 1. WITH THE FAMILY with the members of your family, especially at home 2. INFORMALLY in an informal, relaxed, or casual way [Early 18thC. From French, literally "in the family."]

en·fant ter·ri·ble /aaN faaN te reéblə/ (*plural* **en·fants ter·ri·bles** /aaN faaN te reéblə/) *n.* 1. SHOCKING PERSON somebody whose unconventional behavior, attitudes, or remarks are shocking to others 2. AVANT-GARDE YOUNG ARTIST a young person, especially in the arts, who has become successful because of work that is radically innovative or extremely avant-garde [From French, literally "terrible child"]

en·fee·ble /in feéb'l, en-/ (**-bled, -bling, -bles**) *vt.* to reduce the strength of somebody or something to the point of weakness [14thC. From Old French *enfiblir*, from *feble* (see FEEBLE).] —**en·fee·ble·ment** *n.*

en·feoff /in feéf, en-/ (**-feoffed, -feoff·ing, -feoffs**) *vt.* 1. GIVE SOMEBODY LAND FREEHOLD to invest somebody with the freehold possession of a piece of land 2. MAKE SOMEBODY VASSAL to make somebody a feudal vassal by giving that person a fief or fee (*archaic*) [14thC. From Anglo-Norman *enfeoffer*, from Old French *fief* (see FIEF).] —**en·feoff·ment** *n.*

En·field¹ /én feeld/ city in northern Connecticut, situated on the eastern bank of the Connecticut River, near the Massachusetts border. Population: 45,532 (1990).

En·field² /én feeld/ *n.* = **Enfield rifle** *n.* 1

En·field mus·ket *n.* a muzzle-loading rifled musket used by British forces in the 19th century and by American troops in the Civil War [Named for the English town of *Enfield*, where it was made]

En·field ri·fle *n.* 1. U.S. RIFLE a .30-caliber bolt-action breech-loading rifle used by U.S. forces in World War I. 2. BRITISH RIFLE a .303-caliber bolt-action breech-loading rifle, used by British forces in World War I and until the 1930s. 3. = **Enfield musket** [Named for the English town of *Enfield*, where the British rifle was made]

en·fi·lade /énfə làyd, -laad/ *n.* 1. VULNERABLE POSITION a position in which troops are exposed to gunfire along the length of their formation 2. RAKING FIRE gunfire that strikes a body of troops along its whole length ■ *vt.* (**-lad·ed, -lad·ing, -lades**) 1. FIRE AT SOMETHING ALONG ITS LENGTH to attack a position or body of troops with fire along its whole length 2. FIRE ALONG WHOLE LENGTH OF ENEMY to place guns or troops in a position from which they can fire on the whole length of an enemy position or body of troops [Early 18thC. Via French, from, ultimately, *fil* "thread," from Latin *filum* (source of English *filament* and *fillet*).]

en·fleu·rage /aaNflə raazh/ *n.* a process used in making perfume in which oils acquire fragrance by being exposed to the scent of flowers [Mid-19thC. From French, formed from *enfleurer* "to saturate with the scent of flowers," from *fleur* "flower."]

en·fold /in fṓld, en-/ (**-fold·ed, -fold·ing, -folds**), **in·fold** /in fṓld/ (**-fold·ed, -fold·ing, -folds**) *vt.* 1. ENVELOP to wrap, or wrap something, completely around somebody or something 2. EMBRACE to hold somebody or something in an embrace 3. ENCLOSE OR SURROUND to enclose or surround somebody or something ○ *enfold a child in your love* —**en·fold·er** *n.*

en·force /in fáwrs, en-/ (**-forced, -forc·ing, -forc·es**) *vt.* 1. MAKE PEOPLE OBEY SOMETHING to compel obedience to a law, regulation, or command 2. IMPOSE to impose something by force 3. STRENGTHEN to give strength or emphasis to something ○ *enforce an argument* [13thC. Via French *enforcir* from, ultimately, Latin *fortis* "strong" (source of English *fort* and *fortify*).] —**en·force·a·bil·i·ty** /in fàwrsə bíllətee, in-/ *n.* —**en·force·a·ble** /in fáwrsəb'l, en-/ *adj.* —**en·force·ment** *n.*—**en·forc·er** /in fáwrsər, en-/ *n.* 1. LAW SOMEBODY WHO ENFORCES LAW somebody who enforces a rule, law, or other order 2. CRIMINOL CRIMINAL WHO INTIMIDATES a member of a criminal gang who uses physical violence to intimidate and enforce compliance (*slang*) 3. HOCKEY INTIMIDATING PLAYER a player whose job it is to intimidate opposing players or retaliate for rough play or violence

en·fran·chise /in frán chīz, en-/ (**-chised, -chis·ing, -chis·es**) *vt.* 1. GIVE SOMEBODY RIGHT TO VOTE to give somebody the right to vote in an election 2. SET FREE to set somebody free, especially from slavery 3. ALLOW REPRESENTATION TO to grant political representation to a town or city [Early 16thC. From Old French *enfranchir*, from *franc* "free" (source of English *frank*), from Latin *francus*.] —**en·fran·chise·ment** *n.*

ENG *abbr.* electronic newsgathering

eng. *abbr.* 1. engine 2. engineer 3. engineering

Eng. *abbr.* 1. England 2. English

en·gage /in gáyj, en-/ (**-gaged, -gag·ing, -gag·es**) *v.* 1. *vti.* INVOLVE OR BECOME INVOLVED to involve somebody in an activity, or become involved or take part in an activity 2. *vt.* HIRE SOMEBODY to hire somebody for a job or to do some work 3. *vti.* MIL FIGHT SOMEBODY to fight or begin a battle with an enemy 4. *vti.* ACTIVATE OR BECOME ACTIVATED to activate something or bring something into operation, or become activated or operational 5. *vt.* RESERVE SOMETHING to reserve or rent something for personal use (*dated*) 6. *vt.* REQUIRE USE OF SOMETHING to require the use or devotion of something 7. *vt.* HOLD SOMEBODY'S ATTENTION to attract and hold somebody's attention 8. *vt.* BECOME BETROTHED to promise to marry ○ *The couple have become engaged at last.* 9. *vt.* ATTRACT SOMEBODY BY PLEASING to attract or win the affection of somebody by pleasing that person ○ *He was engaged by the child's charm.* 10. *vti.* MECH ENG INTERLOCK to become interlocked, or bring something together and cause something to interlock [Early 16thC. From French *engagier*, from *gage* "pledge." Ultimately from a prehistoric Germanic word that is also the ancestor of English *wage*.] —**en·gag·er** *n.*

en·ga·gé /aaNgə zháy/ *adj.* committed to a political cause or ideology, usually a left-wing one [Mid-20thC. From French, the past participle of *engager* (see ENGAGE).]

en·gaged /in gáyjd, en-/ *adj.* 1. HAVING AGREED TO MARRY having agreed to get married ○ *the newly engaged couple* 2. OCCUPIED busy doing something ○ *The senator is otherwise engaged this afternoon.* 3. MIL FIGHTING BATTLE fighting a military battle 4. MECH ENG WITH PARTS INTERLOCKED with teeth or other parts interlocked and often in operation 5. *U.K.* TELECOM = **busy** *adj.* 4 6. BUILDING BUILT INTO OR ATTACHED TO WALL used to describe a part of a building that is built into or attached to a wall

WORD KEY: SYNONYMS

See Synonyms at *busy*.

en·gaged tone *n.* *U.K.* = **busy signal**

en·gage·ment /in gáyjmənt, en-/ *n.* 1. AGREEMENT TO MARRY an agreement to get married ○ *announce our engagement* 2. COMMITMENT TO ATTEND an arrangement to be present at an event, especially a business or social appointment 3. PLEDGE FOR SOMETHING something, e.g., a promise, that is freely made and that carries an obligation to do something 4. SHORT JOB a job that lasts for a short period of time, especially one for an entertainer in a club or theater ○ *a week-long engagement in Las Vegas* 5. MIL BATTLE a battle or other conflict involving military forces ○ *a minor engagement on the frontier* 6. ACTIVE OR OPERATIONAL STATE an act or condition of being activated or becoming operational

WORD KEY: SYNONYMS

See Synonyms at *fight*.

en·gage·ment r·ing *n.* a ring, often a diamond solitaire, given by a man to his fiancée to mark their engagement to marry. It is worn on the ring finger of the left hand.

en·gag·ing /in gáyjing, en-/ *adj.* charming or pleasing in a way that attracts and holds the attention —**en·gag·ing·ly** *adv.*

en garde /aaN gaard/ *interj.* used to warn a fencer to assume the prescribed stance for the start of a match [From French, literally "on guard"]

En·gel·mann spruce /éng g'lmən-/ *n.* a large spruce tree found in western North America. Latin name: *Picea engelmannii.* [Mid-19thC. Named for the U.S. botanist George *Engelmann* (1809–84).]

Popperfoto

Friedrich Engels

En·gels /éng g'lz/, **Friedrich** (1820–95) German political thinker and revolutionary. He co-wrote the *Communist Manifesto* (1848) with Karl Marx and supported Marx financially. He lived mainly in England.

en·gen·der /ən jéndər/ (**-dered, -der·ing, -ders**) *v.* 1. *vti.* CREATE OR ARISE to arise or come into existence, or cause something to do so ○ *Secrecy engenders suspicion.* 2. *vt.* HAVE OFFSPRING to cause offspring to be conceived or born (*formal*) [14thC. Via French from Latin *ingenerare*, from *generare* "to produce."] —**en·gen·der·er** *n.*

en·gine /énjin/ *n.* 1. MECH ENG MACHINE FOR POWERING EQUIPMENT a machine that converts energy into mechanical power or motion ○ *a gasoline-powered engine* 2. RAIL RAILROAD LOCOMOTIVE a railroad locomotive 3. DRIVING FORCE OR ENERGY SOURCE something that supplies the driving force or energy to a movement, system, or trend ○ *a political movement that was seen as a great engine of social change* 4. MIL, HISTORY BATTLEFIELD MACHINE a battering ram, catapult, or other device used in warfare (*archaic*) ○ *a siege engine* [14thC. Via French *engin* from Latin *ingenium* "talent, clever device" (source of English *ingenious*).]

en·gine block *n.* the heavy metal casing that houses the cylinders in an internal-combustion engine

en·gined /énjind/ *adj.* powered by an engine or engines, often of a specified make or number (*usually used in combination*)

en·gine driv·er *n.* *U.K.* RAIL = **engineer** *n.* 2

en·gi·neer /ènjə neér/ *n.* 1. ENG ENGINEERING PROFESSIONAL somebody who is trained in a branch of professional engineering 2. RAIL LOCOMOTIVE DRIVER somebody who operates a railroad locomotive 3. MECH ENG MECHANIC somebody who operates or services machines 4. SHIPPING, NAVY SHIP'S OFFICER an officer on a ship who is in charge of the engines 5. MIL CONSTRUCTION SOLDIER a member of a unit of the armed forces that specializes in building and sometimes destroying bridges, fortifications, and other large structures 6. PLANNER somebody who plans, oversees, or brings about something, especially something that is achieved with ingenuity or secretiveness ○ *the engineer of the overthrow of the government* ■ *vt.* (**-neered, -neer·ing, -neers**) 1. CONTRIVE SOMETHING to plan something or bring it about, especially in an ingenious or secretive manner **2.** ENG **USE ENGINEERING SKILL TO DESIGN SOMETHING** to use professional engineering skill to design or create something ○ *This car was engineered in Italy.* **3.** GENETICS **USE GENETIC ENGINEERING ON SOMETHING** to use the techniques of genetic engineering on something [14thC. Via Old French *engigneor* "contriver" from, ultimately, Latin *ingenium* (see ENGINE).]

en·gi·neer·ing /ènjə neéring/ *n.* **1.** ENG **APPLICATION OF SCIENCE TO DESIGNING THINGS** the application of science in the design, planning, construction, and maintenance of buildings, machines, and other manufactured things ○ *leading the world in engineering* **2.** ENG **PROFESSION INVOLVING TECHNICAL DESIGNING** any one of various branches of engineering pursued as a profession, e.g., civil engineering or electronic engineering **3. CONTRIVANCE** the planning or bringing about of something, especially when done with ingenuity or secretiveness

en·gine room *n.* the place on board a ship where the engines are housed

en·gird /in gúrd, en-/ (**-gird·ed** *or* **-girt** /-gúrt/, **-gird·ing, -girds**) *vt.* to encircle something (*literary*)

en·gird·le /in gúrd'l, en-/ (**-gir·dled, -gird·ling, -gir·dles**) *vt.* to surround or encircle something (*literary*)

en·girt past tense, past participle of **engird**

en·gla·cial /in gláysh'l, en-/ *adj.* used to describe material or processes occurring within a glacier

Eng·land /íngglənd/ country forming the southern and largest part of Great Britain and of the United Kingdom. Capital: London. Population: 48,903,000 (1995). Area: 50,351 sq. mi./130,410 sq. km.

En·gle·wood /éng'l wòod/ **1.** city in north central Colorado, a suburb of Denver. Population: 29,387 (1990). **2.** city in northeastern New Jersey, near the Hudson River. Population: 24,850 (1990).

Eng·lish /íng glish/ *n.* **1.** LANG **LANGUAGE OF U.S. AND CANADA** the language of the U.S., Canada, the United Kingdom of Great Britain and Northern Ireland, the Republic of Ireland, Australia, New Zealand, South Africa, and several other countries. There are about 350 million native speakers of English, and approximately 375 million people use it as a second language. **2.** PEOPLES **PEOPLE FROM ENGLAND** people who are born in England or are U.K. citizens living in England **3.** EDUC **STUDY OF ENGLISH** the English language, together with literature written in it, as a subject of scholarly or educational study ○ *major in English* **4. UNDERSTANDABLE ENGLISH** clear, understandable spoken or written English, as distinct from technical jargon, dialect or nonstandard or incomprehensible speech or writing **5. ENGLISH TRANSLATION** a translation of something from another language into English ○ *Do you have the English of Dante?* **6. Eng·lish, eng·lish** CUE GAMES **SPIN** spin applied to a billiard ball by striking it off-center ■ *adj.* **1. OF THE LANGUAGE ENGLISH** relating to, expressed in, or typical of, the English language **2. OF THE ENGLISH** relating to, belonging to, or typical of the English or England ■ *vt.* (**-lished, -lish·ing, -lish·es**) LANG (*archaic*) **1. TRANSLATE SOMETHING INTO ENGLISH** to translate something into English **2. ANGLICIZE SOMETHING** to convert a word or phrase to an English spelling or pronunciation [Old English *Englisc*, from *Engle* "the Angles"] —**Eng·lish·ness** *n.*

WORD KEY: WORLD ENGLISH

English, a language originating in northwestern Europe, is the most widely used member of the Germanic language family. Anglo-Saxon settlers whose dialects were collectively known as "Englisc" arrived in Britain in the 5th century and in due course their language became identified as the main one of the kingdom of England. This early English was a homogeneous tongue, and the characteristic hybrid vocabulary of the present-day language is the result, successively, of Scandinavian, Norman-French, and Greco-Latin influence. For convenience, English is usually divided into four historical phases: Old English (around 500–1150), Middle English (around 1150–1450), Early Modern English (around 1450–1700), and Modern English (around 1700 onward). However, the distance and difference between Old and Modern English is as great as that between Latin and its descendant French. After 1707, English became the primary language of first the United Kingdom and Ireland, then the British Empire at large, from which the United States broke away in the 1770s. The world's primary English-speaking countries today are the United States, the United Kingdom, Canada, Australia, Ireland, South Africa, New Zealand, and Singapore, and the many other nations and territories using English include Bangladesh, Ghana, Guyana, India, Hong Kong, Kenya, Jamaica, Malta, Malaysia, Nigeria, Pakistan, and the Philippines. All territories using the language tend to have distinctive pronunciations, grammatical features, and items of vocabulary, and, increasingly, subvarieties of the standard international language. English is a primary working language of the United Nations and the European Union and the sole working language of the Commonwealth, NATO, Caricom, and ASEAN. It is also learned as a second language for purposes of education, employment, entertainment, electronic communication, and travel by a rapidly increasing number of people worldwide, approaching between one and two billion people. Since the 1960s the already immense literature of the language, primarily in the United States and United Kingdom, was markedly extended throughout the English-speaking world, with English becoming overwhelmingly the primary language of global communication and the media. See also the introductory essay on ***World English***.

Eng·lish bond *n.* an arrangement of bricks in a wall in which layers (**courses**) of bricks laid end to end (**stretchers**) alternate with layers of bricks laid side to side (**headers**). The stretchers of all layers are aligned vertically, and the headers are centered on the stretchers and the mortar joints between them.

Eng·lish bull·dog *n.* = **bulldog**

Eng·lish Can·a·da *n. Can* those regions of Canada where English is the dominant language

Eng·lish Ca·na·di·an *n. Can* a Canadian whose first language is English or who is of English ancestry —**Eng·lish-Ca·na·di·an** *adj.*

Eng·lish Chan·nel area of water linking the North Sea with the Atlantic Ocean. It lies between England and France. Length: 350 mi./560 km.

Eng·lish dai·sy *n.* = **daisy** *n.* **1**

Eng·lish fox·hound *n.* a medium-sized hunting dog of a breed originally developed in England, with a smooth, short-haired coat that may be black, tan, and white or a mixture of these

Eng·lish horn *n.* a woodwind instrument that resembles an oboe but is larger, has a double reed, and is lower-pitched

Eng·lish i·vy *n.* = **ivy** *n.* **1**

Eng·lish·man /íng glishmən/ (*plural* **-men** /-mən/) *n.* a man who was born in England or is a British citizen living in England

Eng·lish muf·fin *n.* a small flat round type of bread made with yeast dough and cooked on a griddle. It is split and toasted before serving.

Eng·lish sad·dle *n.* a light hornless saddle with long side flaps and a low cantle and pommel

Eng·lish set·ter *n.* a hunting dog of a medium-sized breed of setters having a silky white coat with brown or black markings

Eng·lish sheep·dog *n.* = **Old English sheepdog**

Eng·lish son·net *n.* = **Shakespearean sonnet**

Eng·lish spar·row *n.* = **house sparrow**

Eng·lish spring·er span·iel *n.* a hunting dog of a medium-sized breed of spaniels that originated in England, with a silky coat that may be a mixture of white, black, liver, or tan

Eng·lish toy span·iel *n.* a toy dog with a thick wavy coat, belonging to a small breed of spaniels that originated in Eastern Asia. King Charles and Blenheim are types of toy spaniels.

Eng·lish wal·nut *n.* **1. EURASIAN TREE** a Eurasian tree grown in Europe and the United States for its large edible nuts and hard wood. Latin name: *Juglans regia*. **2. NUT OF ENGLISH WALNUT TREE** the large edible nut of an English walnut tree

Eng·lish·wom·an /íng glish wòomən/ (*plural* **-en** /-wimmən/) *n.* a woman who was born in England or is a British citizen living in England

en·gobe /én gōb/ *n.* liquid clay used to decorate a ceramic piece before it has been fired and usually applied before the piece has dried [Mid-19thC. From French.]

en·gorge /in gáwrj, en-/ (**-gorged, -gorg·ing, -gorg·es**) *v.* **1.** *vti.* **FILL WITH BLOOD** to fill something with blood until it is congested, or become filled with blood **2.** *vti.* **EAT GREEDILY** to eat something greedily **3.** *vr.* **GORGE YOURSELF** to gorge or fill yourself with food [15thC. Via French *engorger* from, ultimately, Old French *gorge* "throat"(see GORGE).] —**en·gorge·ment** *n.*

engr. *abbr.* **1.** engineer **2.** engraved **3.** engraver **4.** engraving

en·graft /in gráft, en-/ (**-graft·ed, -graft·ing, -grafts**), **in·graft** /ən-/ (**-graft·ed, -graft·ing, -grafts**) *vt.* **1. GRAFT PLANT PART** to graft a bud or other plant part from one plant onto another (*technical*) **2. GRAFT ANIMAL TISSUE** to graft animal tissue from one part of the body onto another part or onto another animal (*technical*) **3. ATTACH SOMETHING PERMANENTLY** to attach something permanently to something else by a process resembling grafting **4. IMPLANT SOMETHING PERMANENTLY** to implant something permanently or deeply in something else —**en·graft·ment** *n.*

en·grailed /in gráyld, en-/ *adj.* **1. EDGED WITH CONCAVE INDENTATIONS** edged with a series of concave indentations **2. EDGED WITH DOTS** edged with a row of raised dots ○ *an engrailed gold coin* [14thC. From Old French *engresler* "to make thin," from *gresle* "thin," from Latin *gracilis* (source of English *gracile*).]

en·grain /in gráyn, en-/ (**-grained, -grain·ing, -grains**) *vt.* = **ingrain**

en·grave /in gráyv, en-/ (**-graved, -grav·ing, -graves**) *vt.* **1.** ARTS **CARVE OR ETCH MATERIAL** to carve or etch a hard surface with a design or lettering for decoration or printing ○ *engraved a silver cup* **2.** ARTS **CARVE OR ETCH DESIGN** to carve or etch a design or lettering into a hard surface for decoration or printing ○ *engraving a dedication on a watch* **3.** PRINTING **PRINT IMAGE** to print an image, especially a raised image, from an engraved printing plate **4. IMPRESS SOMETHING** to impress something deeply, e.g., a memory on the mind —**en·grav·er** *n.*

en·grav·ing /in gráyving, en-/ *n.* **1.** PRINTING **ENGRAVED PRINT** a print of an image that was made using an engraved plate or block **2.** ARTS **ENGRAVED DESIGN** a design or lettering engraved into a hard surface for decoration or printing **3.** ARTS **CUTTING OR ETCHING OF IMAGES** the art or process of cutting or etching images into a hard surface **4.** PRINTING **PRINTING SURFACE** a plate, block, or other hard surface on which an image has been engraved for printing

en·gross[1] /in grṓss, en-/ (**-grossed, -gross·ing, -gross·es**) *vt.* **1. OCCUPY SOMEBODY'S ATTENTION** to take up somebody's whole attention ○ *The children were engrossed by the story.* **2.** STOCK EXCH **BUY ALL OF SOMETHING** to buy all of a commodity, or enough of it to control the market [14thC. Via Old French *en gros* or medieval Latin *in grosso*; literally "in bulk, wholesale," both from late Latin *grossus* (see GROSS).] —**en·gross·er** *n.*

en·gross[2] /in grṓss, en-/ (**-grossed, -gross·ing, -gross·es**) *vt.* **1.** LAW **MAKE FINAL COPY OF DOCUMENT** to write or print the final version of a legal document **2. COPY DOCUMENT** to copy a document in large clear handwriting (*dated*) [14thC. Via Anglo-Norman *engrosser* or medieval Latin *ingrossare* from, ultimately, late Latin *grossus* "bulky, coarse."] —**en·gross·er** *n.*

en·gross·ing /in grṓssing, en-/ *adj.* engaging somebody's whole attention —**en·gross·ing·ly** *adv.*

en·gross·ment /in grṓssmənt, en-/ *n.* **1. COMPLETELY ABSORBED STATE** the complete absorption of somebody's attention with something **2.** LAW **FINAL LEGAL COPY** a formally prepared copy of a deed or other document for legal use **3.** LAW **DOCUMENT PREPARATION** the preparation of the final legal copy or a clean copy of a document (*dated*) **4.** STOCK EXCH **CORNERING OF MARKET** the purchasing of enough of a commodity to control the market in it

en·gulf /in g-lf, en-/ (**-gulfed, -gulf·ing, -gulfs**), **in·gulf** /in gúlf/ (**-gulfed, -gulf·ing, -gulfs**) *vt.* **1. SWALLOW SOMETHING UP** to surround, cover over, and swallow up somebody or something, as floodwaters do **2. OVERWHELM** to overwhelm somebody or something with a great amount or number of something (*often passive*) ○ *The attacking hordes engulfed the undefended town.* —**en·gulf·ment** *n.*

en·hance /in háns, en-/ (**-hanced, -hanc·ing, -hanc·es**) *vt.* **1. IMPROVE** to improve or add to the strength, worth, beauty, or other desirable quality of something **2.** COMPUT **INCREASE CLARITY OF IMAGE** to increase the clarity, degree of detail, or another quality of an electronic image by using a computer program

EF

[13thC. Via Anglo-Norman *enhauncer* "to raise up" (the original sense in English) from, ultimately, Latin *altus* "high."] —**en·hance·ment** *n.* —**en·hanc·er** *n.* —**en·hanc·ive** *adj.*

en·har·mon·ic /in haar mónnik, en-/ *adj.* MUSIC used to describe notes, e.g., A♯ and B♭, that are spelled differently in a score but have the same pitch in a tempered scale, e.g., on the piano. In other scales or on other instruments, enharmonic notes may actually have different pitches. —**en·har·mon·i·cal·ly** *adv.*

e·nig·ma /i nígmə, e nígmə/ *n.* somebody or something that is not easily explained or understood [Mid-16thC. Via Latin *aenigma* from Greek *ainigma*, from, ultimately, *ainos* "fable."]

WORD KEY: SYNONYMS

See Synonyms at ***problem***.

WORD KEY: CULTURAL NOTE

The Enigma Variations, an orchestral work by English composer Edward Elgar (1899). Elgar's most popular and widely performed work, it was originally entitled *Variations on an Original Theme*. Each of the variations is a musical portrait of a friend of Elgar, identified in the score only by his or her initials or nickname. The title of Elgar's piece influenced the Berlin engineer who built the now-famed German military cipher machine, a typewriter-like device capable of of producing an infinite number of ciphers: the engineer called the machine *Enigma* because he had been struck by Elgar's musical ciphers.

en·ig·mat·ic /ènnig máttik/, **en·ig·mat·i·cal** /-máttik'l/ *adj.* difficult to interpret, understand, or explain —**en·ig·mat·i·cal·ly** *adv.*

WORD KEY: SYNONYMS

See Synonyms at ***obscure***.

en·isle /in íl, en-/ (**-isled, -isl·ing, -isles**) *vt.* (*literary*) **1.** ISOLATE to isolate somebody or something from other people or things **2.** MAKE SOMETHING INTO ISLAND to make something into an island

En·i·we·tok /ènnə wé tòk, ə néewə tòk/ circular atoll in the northwestern Marshall Islands in the Northern Pacific Ocean, a former testing ground for nuclear weapons. Population: 715 (1988).

en·jamb·ment /in jám mənt, en-, in jámb mənt, en-/, **en·jambe·ment** *n.* the continuation of meaning, without pause or break, from one line of poetry to the next [Mid-19thC. Via French *enjambement* from, ultimately, *jambe* "leg" (see JAMB).] —**en·jambed** /in jámd, en-, in jámbd, en-/ *adj.*

en·join /in jóyn, en-/ (**-joined, -join·ing, -joins**) *vt.* **1.** COMMAND SOMEBODY to command somebody to do something or behave in a certain way (*formal*) **2.** IMPOSE SOMETHING to urge or impose a condition or course of action upon others ○ *She enjoined secrecy upon all of us.* **3.** FORBID SOMETHING to forbid or prohibit something forcefully ○ *a deed universally enjoined by religions* **4.** LAW FORBID OR COMMAND SOMEBODY LEGALLY to forbid or command somebody to do something by means of a legal injunction —**en·join·er** *n.* —**en·join·ment** *n.*

en·joy /in jóy, en-/ *v.* (**-joyed, -joy·ing, -joys**) **1.** *vt.* FIND SOMETHING PLEASING to take pleasure in something ○ *She really enjoys ballet.* **2.** *vt.* HAVE USE OF SOMETHING to have the full and satisfying use or benefit of something ○ *He enjoys sole possession of the estate.* **3.** *vt.* BENEFIT FROM DESIRABLE CONDITION OR SITUATION to benefit from a desirable condition or situation ○ *The resort enjoys months of uninterrupted sunshine.* **4.** *vr.* HAVE GOOD EXPERIENCE to have a pleasurable experience ○ *They all enjoyed themselves at the party.* **5.** *vt.* HAVE SEX WITH SOMEBODY to have sexual intercourse with somebody (*archaic*) ■ *interj.* HAVE GOOD TIME used to express a wish for somebody to have a pleasurable experience [14thC. Via Old French *enjoïr* from, ultimately, Latin *gaudere* "to rejoice" (source of English *joy* and *gaudy*).] —**en·joy·er** *n.*

en·joy·a·ble /in jóyəb'l, en-/ *adj.* providing pleasure, or capable of providing pleasure ○ *The food is always enjoyable.* —**en·joy·a·ble·ness** *n.* —**en·joy·a·bly** *adv.*

en·joy·ment /in jóymənt, en-/ *n.* **1.** PLEASURE pleasure that results from using or experiencing something ○ *eating with great enjoyment* **2.** EXPERIENCING OF SOMETHING THAT PROVIDES PLEASURE the experiencing of something that provides pleasure ○ *He wished his enjoyment of the concert would never end.* **3.** SOURCE OF PLEASURE something that gives pleasure ○ *Fishing is one of her chief enjoyments.* **4.** USE OR BENEFIT the use or benefit of something, especially as a legal right ○ *the enjoyment of his rights as a landowner*

en·keph·a·lin /en kéffəlin, -leen/ *n.* either of two chemicals with opiate qualities that are secreted in the brain and spinal cord and act to relieve pain [Mid-20thC. From Greek *enkephalos* "brain," from *kephalē* "head."]

en·kin·dle /in kínd'l, en-/ (**-dled, -dling, -dles**) *v.* **1.** *vti.* BURN SOMETHING to set something on fire, or start burning **2.** *vt.* AROUSE RESPONSE IN SOMEBODY to spark an emotional or intellectual response in somebody —**en·kin·dler** *n.*

enl. *abbr.* **1.** enlarged **2.** enlisted

en·lace /in láyss, en-/ (**en·laced** *or* **in·laced, en·lac·ing** *or* **in·lac·ing, en·lac·es** *or* **in·lac·es**) *v.* **1.** *vt.* WRAP WITH LACES to wrap something around with laces or something similar **2.** *vti.* INTERTWINE WITH SOMETHING to intertwine with something, or become intertwined —**en·lace·ment** *n.*

en·large /in laarj, en-/ (**-larged, -larg·ing, -larg·es**) *v.* **1.** *vti.* MAKE OR BECOME LARGER to increase the size, amount, or extent of something, or become larger **2.** *vt.* PHOTOGRAPHY MAKE LARGER PHOTOGRAPH to make a photographic print or image that is larger than the original negative, print, or slide **3.** *vti.* BROADEN IN SCOPE to broaden the scope of something, or become broader in scope ○ *the need for the investigation to be enlarged* **4.** *vi.* GIVE MORE DETAIL to speak or write at greater length or in more detail about something

WORD KEY: SYNONYMS

See Synonyms at ***increase***.

en·large·ment /in laarjmənt, en-/ *n.* **1.** PROCESS OF ENLARGING OR BEING ENLARGED the process of increasing, broadening, or enlarging something, or of being increased, broadened, or enlarged **2.** ADDITION TO SOMETHING something added to something else to make it larger ○ *an enlargement to a house* **3.** ENLARGED CONDITION the increased, broadened, or enlarged state of something **4.** PHOTOGRAPHY ENLARGED PHOTOGRAPH a photographic print or image that is larger than the negative, print, or slide from which it was made

en·larg·er /in laarjər, en-/ *n.* **1.** PHOTOGRAPHY DEVICE THAT ENLARGES PHOTOGRAPHS a device for projecting an enlarged image of a photographic negative onto a sheet of sensitized paper **2.** SOMEBODY OR SOMETHING THAT ENLARGES somebody or something that increases, broadens, or enlarges something

en·light·en /in lít'n, en-/ (**-ened, -en·ing, -ens**) *vt.* **1.** GIVE INFORMATION TO SOMEBODY to give clarifying information to somebody ○ *Let me enlighten you about our problems.* **2.** FREE SOMEBODY FROM IGNORANCE to free somebody from ignorance, prejudice, or superstition ○ *an article written to enlighten his critics* **3.** RELIG TEACH SOMEBODY RELIGION to teach religious beliefs to an unbeliever —**en·light·en·er** *n.* —**en·light·en·ing** *adj.*

en·light·ened /in lít'nd, en-/ *adj.* **1.** RATIONAL free of ignorance, prejudice, or superstition ○ *an enlightened age* **2.** WELL-INFORMED having a sound and open-minded understanding of all the facts, or based on such an understanding ○ *an enlightened piece of legislation* **3.** HAVING ACHIEVED GREAT SPIRITUALITY having achieved the realization of a spiritual or religious understanding, especially when it results in the transcendence of human suffering and desire

en·light·en·ment /in lít'nmənt, en-/ *n.* **1.** ENLIGHTENING OF SOMEBODY the enlightening of somebody or a cause of the enlightening of somebody **2.** ENLIGHTENED STATE the condition of somebody who has been enlightened **3.** BUDDHISM TRANSCENDENCE OF DESIRE AND SUFFERING a state attained when the cycle of reincarnation ends and desire and suffering are transcended, or the achievement of this state

En·light·en·ment *n.* an 18th-century intellectual movement in western Europe that emphasized reason and science in philosophy and in the study of human culture and the natural world

en·list /in líst, en-/ (**-list·ed, -list·ing, -lists**) *vti.* **1.** MIL ENROLL IN MILITARY to enroll somebody in a branch of the armed forces, or join the armed forces **2.** GAIN SUPPORT to gain the cooperation or support of somebody or something, or become actively involved in an effort ○ *May I enlist your help in this?* [Mid-16thC. Formed from EN- + LIST, perhaps modeled on Dutch *inlijsten* "to put on a list."] —**en·list·ment** *n.*

en·list·ed per·son *n.* a member of the U.S. armed forces who is lower in rank than a commissioned or warrant officer

en·list·ee /en lìs teé/ *n.* somebody who has enlisted in the armed forces

en·liv·en /in lív'n, en-/ (**-ened, -en·ing, -ens**) *vt.* **1.** INVIGORATE to make somebody or something more lively or interesting ○ *We felt enlivened after our walk in the fresh air.* **2.** MAKE BRIGHTER to make something brighter or more cheerful ○ *A few more pictures on the wall would enliven this room.* —**en·liv·en·er** *n.* —**en·liv·en·ment** *n.*

en masse /on máss, aaN maáss/ *adv.* as a body or in a group ○ *people rising from their seats en masse, starting to cheer* [Late 18thC. From French, literally "in a mass."]

en·mesh /in mésh, en-/ (**-meshed, -mesh·ing, -mesh·es**), **in·mesh** /in mésh/ (**-meshed, -mesh·ing, -mesh·es**) *vt.* **1.** CATCH IN ENTANGLEMENT to entangle somebody or something in something from which it is difficult to be extricated or separated ○ *a government enmeshed in scandal* **2.** CATCH IN NET to catch somebody or something in the mesh of a net —**en·mesh·ment** *n.*

en·mi·ty /énmitee/ (*plural* **-ties**) *n.* the extreme ill will or hatred that exists between enemies ○ *trying to resolve age-old enmities* [Via Old French *enemistie* from, ultimately, Latin *inimicus* "enemy" (see ENEMY)]

en·ne·ad /énnee àd, -əd/ *n.* a set of nine persons or things (*formal*) [Mid-16thC. Via the Greek stem *ennead-* from *ennea* "nine."]

En·ni·us /énnee əss/, **Quintus** (239–169? B.C.) Roman poet and dramatist, called the founding father of Roman poetry. He introduced the hexameter into Roman verse, invented the literary miscellany, and wrote an epic of Roman history, of which only fragments survive.

en·no·ble /i nṓb'l, e-/ (**-bled, -bling, -bles**) *vt.* **1.** MAKE SOMEBODY OR SOMETHING NOBLE to make somebody or something noble or more dignified (*formal*) ○ *Your presence ennobles this gathering.* **2.** ELEVATE SOMEBODY TO NOBILITY to confer a noble title on somebody ○ *ennobled for his services to his country* —**en·no·ble·ment** *n.* —**en·no·bler** *n.*

en·nui /on weé/ *n.* weariness and dissatisfaction with life that results from a loss of interest or sense of excitement [Mid-18thC. Via French from, ultimately, Latin *in odio*, in the phrase *in odio est* "it is hateful" (source of English *annoy*).]

e·no·ki /e nṓkee/, **e·no·ki mush·room** *n.* a white edible mushroom native to eastern Asia and North America that has a small cap and long thin stem. Latin name: *Flammulina velutipes.* [Late 20thC. From Japanese.]

e·nol /eé nàwl/ *n.* an organic compound that has a hydroxyl group bonded to a carbon atom that is attached to another carbon atom by a double bond [Mid-20thC. Coined from -ENE + -OL.] —**e·nol·ic** /ee nóllik/ *adj.*

e·no·lase /eénō làyss, -làyz/ *n.* an enzyme that occurs in muscle tissue and in yeasts and is active in the metabolism of carbohydrates

e·nol·o·gy /ee nólləjee/, **oe·nol·o·gy** *n.* the scientific study of wine and the making of wine [Early 19thC. Coined from Greek *oinos* "wine" + -LOGY.]

e·nor·mi·ty /ə náwrmitee/ (*plural* **-ties**) *n.* **1.** EVIL extreme evil or moral offensiveness ○ *the enormity of his crimes against humanity.* See Usage note below. **2.** VERY EVIL ACT a very evil or morally offensive deed [15thC. Via French *énormité* from Latin *enormitas*, from *enormis* "irregular" (see ENORMOUS).]

WORD KEY: USAGE

enormity or **enormousness**? ***Enormity*** is the older word, and after several changes in usage over several centuries it settled down in the 19th century in the meaning associated with evil. It is used in this way both as a concept or attribute and as a concrete word with a plural form: *We were shocked by the enormity of the crime. The regime committed many enormities to suppress opposition.* ***Enormousness*** is the only word in this pair that refers, in correct usage, to significant size: *We were daunted by the enormousness of the task.*

e·nor·mous /ə náwrməss/ *adj.* **1.** UNUSUALLY LARGE unusually large or great in size, amount, or degree **2.** EVIL extremely evil or morally offensive (*archaic*) [Mid-16thC. From Latin *enormis* "irregular," from *norma* "rule" (source of English *normal*).] —**e·nor·mous·ly** *adv.*

e·nor·mous·ness /ə náwrməssnəss/ *n.* the quality of being huge in size, scope, or significance

WORD KEY: USAGE

See Usage note at ***enormity.***

e·nough /i núf/ *det.* **1.** ADEQUATE as much as is needed ○ *enough time to go shopping* **2.** AS MUCH AS BEARABLE as much or as many as can be tolerated ○ *in enough trouble already* ■ *adv.* **1.** IN THE RIGHT AMOUNT to an extent that is as much as is needed ○ *I couldn't run fast enough to catch the cat.* **2.** USED FOR EMPHASIS used to give emphasis to adverbs ○ *Oddly enough, our husbands had met each other just the day before.* **3.** SUFFICIENTLY to an extent that is as much as can be tolerated ○ *She was arrogant enough before the promotion.* **4.** PASSABLY to a moderate or satisfactory extent ○ *speaks the language well enough* ■ *pron.* NEEDED OR TOLERATED AMOUNT the amount that is needed or that can be tolerated ○ *take more cash because we never have enough* ■ *interj.* STOP THAT! used to tell somebody firmly to stop doing something (*informal*) ○ *Enough! There will be no more teasing in the car.* [Old English *ġenōg*, from prehistoric Germanic] ◇ **enough is enough** used by a speaker to indicate that he or she will tolerate no more of something ○ *All right, enough is enough; I am not entertaining any more argumentation from counsel.*

WORD KEY: SYNONYMS

enough, sufficient, adequate, ample, plenty

CORE MEANING: equal in quantity to what is needed

enough a general word used to indicate that an amount or quantity is equal to what it needed; **sufficient** a fairly formal word used to indicate that there is enough of something for a particular purpose; **adequate** a fairly formal word meanind the same as "enough." It is often used to indicate that there is only just enough of something; **ample** used to indicate that there is more than enough of something; **plenty** used to indicate that there is a large amount of something and so there will be enough of it to meet requirements.

e·nounce /i nównss/ (**e·nounced, e·nounc·ing, e·nounc·es**) *vt.* **1.** SAY CLEARLY to pronounce a word clearly and definitely **2.** STATE FORMALLY to state something in an official way (*formal*) [Early 19thC. Via French *énoncer* from Latin *enuntiare*, "to tell" (see ENUNCIATE).] —**e·nounce·ment** *n.*

e·now /i nów/ *adv., adj.* enough (*archaic*) ○ *"there are liars and swearers enow to beat the honest men and hang up them"* (William Shakespeare, *Macbeth*; 1606) [Old English. Via Middle English *inow* from Old English *ġenōge*, a plural form of *ġenōg* (see ENOUGH).]

en pas·sant /ôN paa sa̋aN/ *adv.* **1.** IN PASSING in passing rather than as the full focus of somebody's attention (*formal*) ○ *He mentioned it en passant.* **2.** CHESS UNDER RULE FOR PAWN CAPTURE used when a pawn that has moved two squares is captured by an enemy pawn as if it had only moved one square ○ *capture a pawn en passant* [Mid-17thC. From French, literally "in passing."]

en·plane /in pláyn, en-/ (**-planed, -plan·ing, -planes**) *vti.* to board or to allow somebody to board an aircraft

en prise /ôn préez/ *adj.* used to describe a chess piece positioned in such a way that it could be captured if it is not moved [Early 19thC. From French, literally "in (position for) capture."]

en·quire *vti.* = **inquire**

en·quir·y *n.* = **inquiry**

en·rage /in ráyj, en-/ (**-raged, -rag·ing, -rag·es**) *vt.* to make somebody furiously angry —**en·rage·ment** *n.*

en rap·port /aaN rə páwr/ *adv.* in harmony or sympathy with somebody or something (*formal*) [Early 19thC. From French, literally "in agreement."]

en·rapt /in rápt, en-/ *adj.* in a state of delight or ecstasy (*formal*)

en·rap·ture /in rápchər, en-/ (**-tured, -tur·ing, -tures**) *vt.* to fill somebody with delight (*formal*) —**en·rap·ture·ment** *n.*

en·rich /in rích, en-/ (**-riched, -rich·ing, -rich·es**) *vt.* **1.** IMPROVE to improve the quality of something **2.** FOOD TECH IMPROVE NUTRITIONAL CONTENT OF FOOD to add substances such as vitamins or minerals to a food to improve its nutritional value ○ *calcium-enriched orange juice* **3.** MAKE WEALTHIER to increase the amount of wealth that somebody or something has ○ *economic systems that existed to enrich the settlers* **4.** PHYS ADD MORE OF CONSTITUENT TO SUBSTANCE to boost the amount of an active substance in a mixture, e.g., in a fuel **5.** AGRIC IMPROVE SOIL to improve the nutrient value of soil by adding natural or artificial fertilizers **6.** MAKE MORE BEAUTIFUL to add to the beauty of something with decoration (*literary*) —**en·rich·er** *n.*

en·rich·ment /in ríchmənt, en-/ *n.* **1.** SOMETHING THAT IMPROVES an added feature or quality that improves something **2.** IMPROVING OF SOMEBODY OR SOMETHING the addition of characteristics or elements that improve somebody or something ○ *the enrichment of the cultural experience* **3.** INCREASE IN WEALTH increase in a person's or organization's wealth

en·robe /in rṓb, en-/ (**-robed, -rob·ing, -robes**) *v.* **1.** *vti.* DRESS GRANDLY to put ceremonial robes on somebody (*formal*) **2.** *vt.* MAKE SOMEBODY GRAND OR NOBLE to invest somebody with a grand or noble quality (*literary*)

en·roll /in rṓl, en-/ (**-rolled, -roll·ing, -rolls**), **en·rol** (**-rolled, -roll·ing, -rols**) *v.* **1.** *vti.* ENTER ON REGISTER to enter your own or somebody else's name on an official register or list of members ○ *enroll the children in school* **2.** *vt.* MAKE SURE OF AVAILABILITY OF to make sure that something, especially somebody's help, will definitely be available **3.** *vt.* ROLL OR WRAP UP to form something into a roll **4.** *vt.* WRITE OUT OFFICIAL COPY OF SOMETHING to produce the final version of something, usually a formal document or record [14thC. From Old French *enroller*, literally "to put on a roll," from *rolle* "roll, register" (see ROLL).] —**en·roll·ee** /en rō lée, in rō lée/ *n.*

en·roll·ment /in rṓlmənt, en-/, **en·rol·ment** *n.* **1.** SIGNING UP FORMALLY the official act or process of entering your own or another person's name on a register or membership list ○ *The insurance plan has a two-week open enrollment period once each year.* **2.** NUMBER OF REGISTERED the number of people registered for something, e.g., a class ○ *a sharp increase in student enrollments* **3.** LIST OF REGISTERED a list of people registered for or enrolled in something

en·root /in ro͞ot, en-/ (**-root·ed, -root·ing, -roots**) *vt.* to fix or establish something firmly (*literary*)

en route /aan ro͞ot/ *adv.* during the trip to a destination [Late 18thC. From French, literally "on (the) way."]

ens /enz/ (*plural* **en·tia** /énshee ə, éntee ə/) *n.* PHILOS an actual entity, as distinct from a quality or characteristic [Mid-16thC. From medieval Latin, present participle (on the model of Latin *absens* "absent") of Latin *esse* "to be."]

ENS, Ens. *abbr.* NAVY ensign

en·san·guine /in sánggwin, en-/ (**-guined, -guin·ing, -guines**) *vt.* to stain, smear, or cover something with blood (*archaic or literary*) (*often passive*) ○ *"yet millions of men have supinely allowed the nerveless limbs of the posterity of such rapacious prowlers to rest quietly on their ensanguined thrones"* (Mary Wollstonecraft, *A Vindication of the Rights of Woman*; 1792)

en·sconce /in skóns, en-/ (**-sconced, -sconc·ing, -sconc·es**) *vt.* **1.** SETTLE IN COMFORTABLY to make somebody or yourself comfortably established, as though ready to stay a long while (*often passive*) ○ *ensconced on the sofa* **2.** HIDE AWAY to hide something somewhere, for safety or secrecy (*archaic or literary*) [Literally "to put into a sconce"]

en·sem·ble /on sómb'l/ *n.* **1.** ARTS GROUP OF PERFORMERS a group of musicians, dancers, or actors who perform together with roughly equal contributions from all members **2.** FASHION OUTFIT OF CLOTHES a number of different items of clothing and accessories, put together to create an outfit **3.** SOMETHING FORMED BY SEVERAL ITEMS something created from a number of individual parts put together deliberately **4.** MUSIC PART PERFORMED BY WHOLE GROUP a section of a larger work, e.g., a ballet or opera, that all the cast perform together ■ *adj.* ARTS COLLABORATIVE performed collaboratively, with no performer given prominence [Mid-18thC. From French, "together," from Latin *insimul*, literally "in at the same time," from *simul* "at the same time" (source of English *simultaneous*).]

En·se·na·da /ènsə nàddə/ major deep-sea port city on the Pacific Ocean in Baja California, northwestern Mexico. Population: 169,426 (1990).

en·shrine /in shrī́n, en-/ (**-shrined, -shrin·ing, -shrines**), **in·shrine** (**-shrined, -shrin·ing, -shrines**) *vt.* **1.** GIVE SPECIAL PROTECTION TO SOMETHING to protect something from change, e.g., in a formal constitution ○ *principles enshrined in law* **2.** PUT SOMETHING INTO A SHRINE to keep or cherish something in a shrine or other special place —**en·shrine·ment** *n.*

en·shroud /in shrówd, en-/ (**-shroud·ed, -shroud·ing, -shrouds**) *vt.* **1.** OBSCURE to cover or obscure something (*usually passive*) ○ *mountains enshrouded in mist* **2.** WRAP IN SHROUD to cover somebody in a shroud

en·si·form /énsə fàwrm/ *adj.* BIOL long and narrow with a pointed tip ○ *ensiform leaves* [Mid-16thC. Via French from modern Latin *ensiformis*, formed from *ensi-* "sword" + *forma* "FORM."]

en·sign (*flag*) /énsən, én sīn/; (*rank*) /énsən/ *n.* **1.** FLAG INDICATING ALLEGIANCE a flag that shows the nationality of the ship or aircraft flying it or what military unit it belongs to **2.** NAVY U.S. NAVY RANK a commissioned officer of the lowest rank in the United States Navy or Coast Guard **3.** BADGE OF OFFICE an emblem or sign that indicates an authority or command **4.** FLAG BEARER somebody who carries a standard or national emblem (*dated*) [14thC. Via Old French *enseigne* from Latin *insignia* (plural) "badges," literally "marks on," ultimately from *signum* "mark" (source of English *insignia*).]

en·si·lage /énsəlij/ *n.* **1.** MAKING OF SILAGE the harvesting and preservation of green fodder crops for future use by fermentation in a silo **2.** STORED FODDER green fodder preserved in a silo ■ *vt.* (**-laged, -laging, -lages**) = **ensile**

en·sile /in sī́l, en-/ (**-siled, -sil·ing, -siles**) *vt.* to preserve green fodder, e.g., grass, as silage by allowing it to ferment and become acidified in a silo [Late 19thC. Via French *ensiler* from Spanish *ensilar*, formed from *en* "in" + *silo* "SILO."]

en·slave /in sláyv, en-/ (**-slaved, -slav·ing, -slaves**) *vt.* **1.** SUBJECT TO CONTROLLING INFLUENCE to subject somebody to a dominating influence that takes away his or her freedom **2.** TO CLAIM OWNERSHIP OF SOMEBODY to take somebody prisoner and claim legal ownership of that person and his or her labor —**en·slave·ment** *n.* —**en·slav·er** *n.*

en·snare /in snáir, en-/ (**-snared, -snar·ing, -snares**), **in·snare** (**-snared, -snar·ing, -snares**) *vt.* **1.** TRAP IN UNPLEASANT SITUATION to lure somebody into a bad situation from which it is difficult to escape **2.** TRAP to catch an animal in a trap —**en·snare·ment** *n.* —**en·snar·er** *n.*

en·snarl /in sna̋arl, en-/ (**-snarled, -snarl·ing, -snarls**) *vt.* to involve somebody or something in a situation that causes delay (*often passive*)

en·soul /in sṓl, en-/ (**-souled, -soul·ing, -souls**), **in·soul** (**-souled, -soul·ing, -souls**) *vt.* (*literary*) **1.** GIVE A SOUL TO to endow somebody with a soul **2.** KEEP DEEP WITHIN to cherish deeply something such as a feeling or memory

en·sphere /in sféer, en-/ (**-sphered, -spher·ing, -spheres**), **in·sphere** (**-sphered, -spher·ing, -spheres**) *vt.* **1.** SURROUND to enclose something in a sphere or in something like a sphere (*literary*) **2.** MAKE SPHERICAL to make something sphere-shaped (*formal*)

en·sta·tite /énstə tī̀t/ *n.* a brown, gray, or yellowish form of the mineral pyroxene, consisting of magnesium silicate. It is often found in igneous rock and meteorites and may contain up to 10% ferrous iron silicate. [Mid-19thC. From German *Enstatit*, coined from the Greek stem *enstat* "-adversary" (from the refractoriness of the mineral).]

en·sue /in so͞o, en-/ (**-sued, -su·ing, -sues**) *vi.* **1.** FOLLOW to follow closely after something **2.** RESULT to be a consequence of something [14thC. From Old French *ensu-*, stem of *ensuivre*, from assumed Vulgar Latin *insequere*, literally "to follow in," from Latin *sequi* "to follow" (see SUE).]

en·su·ing /in so͞o ing, en-/ *adj.* happening next or as a result

en suite /aaN swéet/ *adj., adv.* (*formal*) **1.** LEADING OFF forming part of a larger unit or set of rooms ○ *an en suite bathroom* ○ *with a bathroom en suite* **2.** FORMING PART OF SET forming part of a series or set [Late 18thC. From French, literally "in succession."]

en·sure /in sho͝or, en-/ (**-sured, -sur·ing, -sures**), **in·sure** (**-sured, -sur·ing, -sures**) *vt.* **1.** MAKE SOMETHING CERTAIN to make sure that something will happen **2.** SAFEGUARD to protect something or somebody from harm

WORD KEY: USAGE

See Usage note at *assure.*

en·swathe /in swáyth, en-/ (**-swathed, -swath·ing, -swathes**) *vt.* to wrap somebody or something in bandages or cloth (*literary*)

ENT *abbr.* MED ear, nose, and throat

-ent *suffix.* **1.** performing a particular action ○ *acquiescent* **2.** one that performs a particular action ○ *respondent* [From Latin *-ent-*, the stem of *-ens*, a present participle ending] —**-ence** *suffix.* —**-ency** *suffix.*

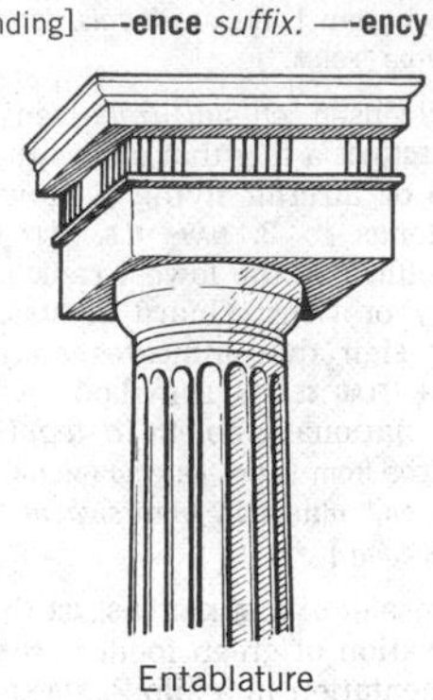

Entablature

en·tab·la·ture /in tábblə chòor, en-/ *n.* in classical architecture, the section that lies between the columns and the roof. It comprises, from bottom to top, the architrave, frieze, and cornice. [Early 17thC. Via obsolete French from Italian *intavolatura* "boarding," from *intavolare* "to board up, put on a table," from *tavola* "table."]

en·ta·ble·ment /in táyb'lmənt, en-/ *n.* a plinth (*technical*) [Mid-17thC. From French, from *table* "table."]

en·tail *vt.* /in táyl, in-/ (**-tailed, -tail·ing, -tails**) **1.** HAVE AS CONSEQUENCE to involve or result in something inevitably **2.** LAW RESTRICT OWNERSHIP OF BEQUEST to restrict the future ownership of real estate to particular descendants, through instructions written into a will ■ *n.* /én tàyl/ LAW **1.** = **entailment** *n.* 2 **2.** ENTAILED PIECE OF REAL ESTATE a piece of real estate that has been entailed **3.** FUTURE OWNERS OF ENTAILED REAL ESTATE the line of descendants who own an entailed real estate [14thC. Literally "to put under limitation," formed from Old French *taille* "limitation," from *taillier* "to cut" (see TAILOR).]

en·tail·ment /in táylmənt, en-/ *n.* **1.** LOGIC ONE PROPOSITION'S IMPLYING OF ANOTHER the relationship between one proposition and another that is a logically necessary consequence of it **2. en·tail·ment, en·tail** LAW RESTRICTION OF FUTURE OWNERSHIP the limiting of the future ownership of bequeathed real estate to particular descendants

en·tan·gle /in táng g'l, en-/ (**-gled, -gling, -gles**) *vt.* **1.** TANGLE UP to make something become twisted up in a mass of strands, e.g., netting or hair (*usually passive*) **2.** PUT INTO DIFFICULT SITUATION to involve somebody or something in a problem that will be difficult to escape from (*usually passive*) ○ *entangled in corporate politics* **3.** COMPLICATE SOMETHING to make something complicated

en·tan·gle·ment /in táng g'lmənt, en-/ *n.* **1.** COMPLICATED PERSONAL SITUATION a complicated situation involving two or more people **2.** CONFUSION confusion or a confused situation ○ *"He sat with his mouth full of toast and his eyes sparkling with mischief, watching my intellectual entanglement."* (Arthur Conan Doyle, *The Valley of Fear*; 1915) **3.** TANGLED THING a mass of tangled objects

en·ta·sis /éntəssiss/ *n.* a slight bulge in the shaft of a column, designed to counter the visual impression of concavity that a perfectly straight column would give [Mid-18thC. From Greek, "straining," literally "stretching in," ultimately from *teinein* "to stretch."]

en·tel·e·chy /en téllәkee/ *n.* **1.** FULL EXISTENCE the real existence of a thing, not merely its theoretical existence **2.** LIFE-GIVING FORCE in some philosophies, a life-giving force believed to be responsible for the development of all living things [Early 17thC. Via late Latin from Greek *entelekheia*, literally "having completeness," from *entelēs* "complete," literally "in the end," from *telos* "end."]

en·tente /aaN taaNt/ *n.* **1.** FRIENDLY UNDERSTANDING BETWEEN COUNTRIES a state of friendly agreement or understanding that exists or is declared between two or more countries **2.** PARTIES IN AGREEMENT the parties involved in an entente [Mid-19thC. From French, literally "understanding," from *entendre* (see INTEND).]

en·tente cor·di·ale /-kàwrdee aál/ (*plural* **en·tentes cor·di·ales**) *n.* amicable relations between countries or states, especially the agreement formed between France and Britain in 1904 [From French, literally "friendly understanding"]

en·ter /éntər/ *v.* (**-tered, -ter·ing, -ters**) **1.** *vti.* GO IN to go or come into a place **2.** *vt.* COMPUT WRITE OR TYPE IN to write or type something in a book or on a computer ○ *The names and addresses are entered into a database.* **3.** *vt.* PUT IN FOR FORMAL CONSIDERATION to submit something, e.g., a proposal, complaint, or bid, officially **4.** *vti.* BECOME COMPETITOR to take part in a competition **5.** *vt.* BECOME MEMBER OF to join or become officially involved in something, especially a body such as a school or company **6.** *vi.* THEATER WALK ON to come on stage during a play ○ *She enters stage right.* **7.** *vti.* MAKE HOLE IN SOMETHING to force a way into something, or be pushed or inserted into something, especially the human body ○ *The bullet entered through the anterior abdominal wall.* **8.** *vt.* LAW TAKE OWNERSHIP OF LAND LEGALLY to go onto land and take legal possession of it ■ *n.* COMPUT = **enter key** [13thC. Via Old French *entrer* from Latin *intrare* "to go in, enter," formed from *intra* "inside, within."] —**en·ter·a·ble** *adj.*

enter into *v.* **1.** *vi.* TAKE PART IN to become involved in something **2.** *vt.* TAKE PART ENTHUSIASTICALLY to get actively involved in something ○ *Enter into the spirit of things.* **3.** *vt.* BE RELEVANT TO to be one of the factors that are relevant to something ○ *Money doesn't enter into it.* **4.** *vt.* SIGN UP FOR to become one of the parties bound by a contract **5.** *vt.* CONSIDER FORMALLY to go into a discussion or investigation about something ○ *I do not propose to enter into the issue of who is responsible.*

enter on, en·ter up·on *vt.* to start out on something, e.g., an important task or a significant period

en·ter·al feed·ing *n.* direct infusion into the intestines of nutrients in liquid form [*Enteral* partly formed from ENTERIC and partly a back-formation from PARENTERAL]

en·ter·ic /en térrik/ *adj.* relating to or situated in the intestine [Mid-19thC. From Greek *enterikos*, from *enteron* "intestine."]

en·ter·ic fe·ver *n.* = **typhoid**

en·ter·i·tis /éntə rítiss/ *n.* inflammation of the intestine, most commonly of the small intestine

en·ter key *n.* a key on a computer keyboard that executes an instruction or begins a new line in text

en·ter·o·bi·a·sis /èntə rō bí əssiss/ *n.* infestation of the large intestine with pinworms, especially in children [Early 20thC.]

en·ter·o·coele /éntə rō seel/ *n.* a body cavity (**coelom**) formed from an outgrowth in the wall of an embryonic intestine, especially in invertebrate marine organisms such as starfish and sea urchins

en·ter·o·co·li·tis /èntə rō kə lítiss/ *n.* inflammation of the small and large intestine as a result of infection

en·ter·o·ki·nase /èntə rō kí nàyss, -kí-/ *n.* an enzyme produced in the mucous membrane of the upper intestine that converts trypsinogen to trypsin

en·ter·on /éntə ròn/ *n.* ZOOL **1.** DIGESTIVE SYSTEM the alimentary canal, especially of an embryo **2.** INTESTINE OF MARINE INVERTEBRATE the intestine of marine invertebrates, e.g., sea anemones and jellyfish, with one opening that serves as both mouth and anus [Mid-19thC. From Greek, "intestine."]

en·ter·op·a·thy /èntə róppəthee/ (*plural* **-thies**) *n.* any disease of the intestines

en·ter·os·to·my /èntə róstəmee/ (*plural* **-mies**) *n.* the surgical creation of a permanent opening into the intestine through the abdominal wall —**en·ter·os·to·mal** /èntə róstəm'l/ *adj.*

en·ter·ot·o·my /èntə róttəmee/ (*plural* **-mies**) *n.* a surgical incision into the intestine

en·ter·o·tox·in /èntə rō tóksin/ *n.* any toxin produced by bacteria that causes the vomiting and diarrhea associated with food poisoning

en·ter·prise /éntər prīz/ *n.* **1.** ENERGETIC CONFIDENCE readiness to put effort into new, often risky, ventures or activities **2.** DARING PROJECT a new, often risky venture that involves confidence and initiative **3.** COMM BUSINESS a commercial company or firm **4.** COMM HIGHLY MOTIVATED INDUSTRY organized business activities aimed specifically at growth and profit [15thC. From Old French *entreprise*, from the past participle of *entreprendre* "to undertake," literally "to take between," from *prendre* "to take" (see PRIZE[2]).]

En·ter·prise /éntər prīz/ city in southeastern Alabama, southeast of Montgomery. Population: 21,253 (1996).

en·ter·prise zone *n.* an economically depressed urban area where the government encourages new business ventures by offering financial incentives

en·ter·pris·ing /éntər prīzing/ *adj.* showing initiative and a willingness to undertake new, often risky projects —**en·ter·pris·ing·ly** *adv.*

en·ter·tain /èntər táyn, éntər tàyn/ (**-tained, -tain·ing, -tains**) *v.* **1.** *vti.* AMUSE OR INTEREST to engage a person or audience by providing amusing or interesting material **2.** *vti.* OFFER HOSPITALITY to offer hospitality, especially by providing food and drink for people in your home **3.** *vt.* CONSIDER to turn something over in your mind, looking at it from various points of view ○ *He would never entertain such an idea!* [15thC. From Old French *entretenir* "to hold together, support," from Latin *tenere* "to hold."]

en·ter·tain·er /èntər táynər, éntər tàynər/ *n.* somebody who amuses or interests others by telling jokes, singing, dancing, or acting, especially somebody who does this for a living

en·ter·tain·ing /èntər táyning, éntər tàyning/ *adj.* enjoyable to watch, read, or listen to —**en·ter·tain·ing·ly** *adv.*

en·ter·tain·ment /èntər táynmənt/ *n.* **1.** ARTS ART OF KEEPING PEOPLE ENTERTAINED the various ways of amusing people, especially by performing for them **2.** ENJOYMENT the amount of pleasure or amusement you get from something **3.** THEATER PERFORMANCE OR EXHIBITION something that is produced or performed for an audience ○ *chief among the evening's entertainments*

en·thal·py /én thàlpee, en thálpee/ *n.* a thermodynamic property equal to the sum of the internal energy of a system and the product of its pressure and volume. Symbol *H* [Early 20thC. From Greek *enthalpein* "to warm within," from *thalpein* "to heat."]

en·thrall /in thráwl, en-/ (**-thralled, -thrall·ing, -thralls**), **en·thral** (**-thralled, -thrall·ing, -thrals**), **in·thrall** /in thráwl/ (**-thralled, -thrall·ing, -thralls**) *vt.* **1.** DELIGHT to delight or fascinate somebody thoroughly, engaging that person's attention completely **2.** ENSLAVE to make somebody a prisoner and claim legal ownership of that person (*literary*) [Late 16thC. Literally "to enslave, make someone a thrall," formed from THRALL.] —**en·thrall·ment** *n.*

en·thrall·ing /in thráwlling/ *adj.* so interesting, delightful, or beautiful as to hold the attention completely —**en·thrall·ing·ly** *adv.*

en·throne /in thrṓn, en-/ (**-throned, -thron·ing, -thrones**), **in·throne** *vt.* **1.** PUT ON THRONE to install a monarch or bishop, especially in a ceremony that involves seating the person on a throne (*formal*) **2.** REGARD AS IMPORTANT to regard somebody as being worthy of adoration (*literary*) —**en·throne·ment** *n.*

en·thuse /in thóoz, en-/ (**-thused, -thus·ing, -thus·es**) *vti.* to have, or make somebody feel, great excitement or interest. See Usage note below. [Early 19thC. Back-formation from ENTHUSIASM.]

WORD KEY: USAGE

"You've won a prize," the caller enthuses. Unlike such other back-formations as *diagnose, edit,* and *reminisce,* ***enthuse*** has yet to win universal acceptance. Although it has been in use since the early 1800s, it continues to irritate many people.

en·thu·si·asm /in thóozee àzzəm, en-/ *n.* **1.** EXCITED INTEREST passionate interest in or eagerness to do something **2.** ENGROSSING INTEREST something that arouses a consuming interest [Late 16thC. Via late Latin from Greek *enthousiasmos* "possession by (a) god," formed from *enthous* "inspired," literally "with (a) god in," from *theos* "god."]

en·thu·si·ast /in thóozee àst, en-/ *n.* somebody who is very interested or involved in something, especially somebody with a particular hobby [Early 17thC. From Greek *enthousiastēs* "one inspired (by a god)," from *enthous* (see ENTHUSIASM).]

en·thu·si·as·tic /in thóozee ástik, en-/ *adj.* showing passionate interest in something or eagerness about something —**en·thu·si·as·ti·cal·ly** *adv.*

en·thy·meme /énthə meèm/ *n.* LOGIC an argument that assumes the truth of one or more premises and therefore omits them from the logical sequence [Late 16thC. Via Latin from Greek *enthumēma*, literally "(something) in mind," ultimately from *thumos* "mind."]

en·tia PHILOS plural of **ens**

en·tice /in tı́ss, en-/ (**-ticed, -tic·ing, -tic·es**) *vt.* to make a person or animal do something by offering something desirable [13thC. Via Old French *enticier* from assumed Vulgar Latin *intitiare* "to set on fire," from Latin *titio* "firebrand."] —**en·tic·er** *n.*

en·tic·ing /in tı́ssing, en-/ *adj.* very desirable and hard to resist —**en·tic·ing·ly** *adv.*

en·tire /in tı́r, en-/ *adj.* **1. WHOLE** as a whole, from beginning to end or including everything **2. ABSOLUTE** in every way, without doubt or question ○ *The day was an entire fiasco.* **3. IN ONE PIECE** not damaged or broken up (*literary*) ○ *"with strength entire, and free Will arm'd"* (John Milton, *Paradise Lost*; 1667) **4.** VET **UNGELDED** used to describe a male animal, especially a stallion or dog, that has not been castrated **5.** BOT **SMOOTH-EDGED** used to describe leaves with smooth edges that are not lobed or indented ■ *n.* **EVERYTHING** everything (*formal*) ○ *A three-judge panel has rejected our appeal in its entire.* [14thC. Via Old French *entier* from Latin *integrum*, a form of *integer* "whole, intact" (see INTEGER).] —**en·tire·ness** *n.*

en·tire·ly /in tı́rlee, en-/ *adv.* **1. IN EVERY WAY** in every sense **2. ONLY** exclusively or individually

en·tire·ty /in tı́rtee, en-/ *n.* the whole extent of something

en·ti·tle /in tı́t'l/ (**-tled, -tling, -tles**) *vt.* **1. ALLOW TO CLAIM** to give somebody the right to have or to do something (*often passive*) **2. GIVE TITLE TO** to assign a title to something such as a book (*usually passive*) **3. GIVE SPECIAL TITLE TO** to confer an official position or honor on somebody that brings a particular title with it [14thC. Via Old French *entiteler* from late Latin *intitulare*, from *titulus* (see TITLE).]

en·ti·tle·ment /in tı́t'lmənt, en-/ *n.* **1. RIGHT TO SOMETHING** the right somebody has to do or receive something ○ *"I'd like us to shift [our programs] from entitlement to empowerment. In the end, we want people not to need us anymore."* (William Jefferson Clinton, *State of the Union Address*; February 17, 1993) **2. SOMETHING YOU HAVE A RIGHT TO** a thing to which somebody is entitled

en·ti·tle·ment pro·gram *n.* a government program that targets a particular section of the population to receive certain benefits

en·ti·ty /éntitee/ (*plural* **-ties**) *n.* **1. OBJECT** something that exists as or is perceived as a single separate object **2.** PHILOSOPHY **EXISTENCE** the state of having existence **3.** PHILOSOPHY **ESSENTIAL NATURE OF SOMETHING** the essence or character of something [Late 16thC. From medieval Latin *entitas*, from late Latin *ent-*, stem of *ens* (see ENS).]

en·to·derm *n.* = **endoderm**

en·toil /in tóyl, en-/ (**-toiled, -toil·ing, -toils**) *vt.* to capture or entangle something or somebody (*archaic*) [Late 16thC. Literally "to place in a "toil"," formed from *toil* "net," from Old French *toile* "cloth, web," from Latin *tela*.]

entom. *abbr.* entomology

en·tomb /in toóm, en-/ (**-tombed, -tomb·ing, -tombs**) *vt.* **1. PUT IN TOMB** to put a corpse into a tomb **2. PUT IN DEEP PLACE** to put something in a place that is hidden or very deep ○ *the secret vaults where the treasures were entombed* **3. SERVE AS TOMB** to serve as a tomb for somebody or something ○ *the collapsed mine that entombed them*

entomol. *abbr.* entomology

en·to·mol·o·gy /èntə móllәjee/ *n.* the branch of zoology that deals with the study of insects [Mid-18thC. From French *entomologie* or modern Latin *entomologia*, literally "science of insects," formed from Greek *entomon* (see ENTOMO-).] —**en·to·mo·log·i·cal** /èntəmə lójjik'l/ *adj.* —**en·to·mo·log·i·cal·ly** *adv.* —**en·to·mol·o·gist** *n.*

en·to·moph·a·gous /èntə móffәgәss/ *adj.* ZOOL feeding on insects

en·to·moph·i·lous /èntə móffәlәss/ *adj.* BOT used to describe flowering plants that are pollinated by insects —**en·to·moph·i·ly** /èntə móffәlee/ *n.*

en·tou·rage /óntə raázh, óntə raàzh/ *n.* **1. PEOPLE ACCOMPANYING VIP** a group of special employees who go with a high-ranking or famous person on visits and engagements **2. ENVIRONMENT** the surroundings or environment (*literary*) [Mid-19thC. From French, where it was formed from *entourer* "to surround," literally "to make a circuit around," from *tour* "circuit" (see TOUR).]

en·tr'·acte /on trákt/ (*plural* **-actes**) *n.* **1. BREAK BETWEEN ACTS OF PLAY** an interval between the acts of a play or opera **2. PERFORMANCE BETWEEN ACTS** an additional piece of entertainment during the break between the acts of a play or opera [Mid-18thC. From obsolete French, literally "between the act(s)," from *acte* "act."]

en·trails /éntrәlz, én tràylz/ *npl.* **1. INTERNAL ORGANS** an animal's or person's internal organs **2. SOMETHING'S INSIDES** the various working parts inside something, especially something complex **3.** HIST **ANIMAL'S INSIDES USED FOR ROMAN DIVINATION** the internal organs of a sacrificial animal, used by the ancient Romans to try to determine the will of the gods [13thC. Via Old French *entrailles* from medieval Latin *intralia*, alteration of Latin *interanea* "intestines, guts," literally "internal things," ultimately from *inter* "between."]

en·train[1] /in tráyn, en-/ (**-trained, -train·ing, -trains**) *vti.* TRANSP to board or to put somebody or something aboard a train —**en·train·er** *n.* —**en·train·ment** *n.*

en·train[2] /in tráyn, en-/ (**-trained, -train·ing, -trains**) *v.* **1.** *vt.* **CAUSE TO HAPPEN** to cause something to happen as a consequence of an action **2.** CHEM, PHYS **TRAP IN GAS OR LIQUID** to draw solid particles, air bubbles, or liquid drops into a moving fluid and carry them along in the flow [Mid-16thC. From Old French *entraîner*, literally "to drag away," from *traîner* "to drag" (see TRAIN).] —**en·train·ment** *n.*

en·trance[1] /éntrәns/ *n.* **1. WAY IN** a door or gate that people enter through **2. COMING ONTO THE SCENE** the occasion or act of entering a place ○ *a highly theatrical entrance* **3. RIGHT OF ENTRY** the right to go into a place or to enter an institution [15thC. From Old French, where it was formed from *entrer* (see ENTER).]

en·trance[2] /en tráns/ (**-tranced, -tranc·ing, -tranc·es**) *vt.* **1. FASCINATE** to hold somebody's attention and produce a sense of wonder in that person **2. PUT SPELL ON** to make somebody go into a trance

en·trance·way /éntrәns wày/ *n.* = **entryway**

en·trant /éntrәnt/ *n.* somebody who enters a competition or contest [Mid-17thC. From French, present participle of *entrer* (see ENTER).]

WORD KEY: SYNONYMS

See Synonyms at ***candidate***.

en·trap /in tráp, en-/ (**-trapped, -trap·ping, -traps**) *vt.* **1. TRICK INTO SOMETHING BAD** to lead somebody into doing something wrong or into danger **2.** HUNT **TRAP** to catch something such as an animal in a trap

en·trap·ment /in trápmәnt, en-/ *n.* the act of tricking somebody into committing a crime in order to obtain a prosecution

en·treat /in treét, en-/ (**-treat·ed, -treat·ing, -treats**), **in·treat** (**-treat·ed, -treat·ing, -treats**) *vti.* to beg somebody for something, often repeatedly (*formal*) [14thC. From Old French *entraitier*, literally "to treat in (a certain way)," from *traitier* "to treat" (see TREAT).] —**en·treat·ing·ly** *adv.*

en·treat·y /in treétee, en-/ (*plural* **-ies**) *n.* a serious and passionate request

en·tre·chat /óntrə shaá/ *n.* in ballet, a leap in which the dancer's legs are crossed rapidly in the air and the heels are beaten together [Late 18thC. Via French from Italian *(capriola) intrecciata* "intricate (caper)."]

en·tre·côte /óntrə kòt, óNtrə-/, **en·tre·côte steak** *n.* a piece of beef without any bone, cut from between the ribs [Mid-19thC. From French, literally "between (the) rib(s)."]

en·trée /ón tràу, on tráy/, **en·tree** *n.* **1.** FOOD **MAIN COURSE** a dish served as the main part of a meal **2.** FOOD **DISH BEFORE MAIN COURSE** in a formal dinner, a light dish served before the main course **3. RIGHT OF ENTRY** something that permits entry into something, especially to an exclusive group or place [Late 18thC. From French (see ENTRY).]

en·tre·mets /óntrə máy/ (*plural* **-mets**) *n.* **1. DISH BETWEEN MAIN COURSE AND DESSERT** in a formal dinner, a light dish served between the main course and the dessert **2. DESSERT** a sweet dish, especially one served after cheese in a multicourse dinner [15thC. From Old French, literally "between the course(s)," from *mes* "course."]

en·trench /in trénch, en-/ (**-trenched, -trench·ing, -trench·es**), **in·trench** /in-/ (**-trenched, -trench·ing, -trench·es**) *v.* **1.** *vt.* **DIG DITCH AROUND** to defend something by surrounding it with trenches **2.** *vt.* **PROTECT** to take action to protect an argument or position **3.** *vi.* **ENCROACH** to encroach upon or trespass on somebody else's property or things (*archaic*) —**en·trench·ment** *n.*

en·trenched /in tréncht, en-/ *adj.* **1. FIRMLY HELD** firmly held and hard to change ○ *deeply entrenched political views* **2. FIRMLY ESTABLISHED** firmly established and unlikely to change

en·tre nous /òntrə noó/ *adv.* in confidence (*formal*) [Late 17thC. From French, literally "between ourselves."]

en·tre·pre·neur /òntrәprə noór, -núr/ *n.* somebody who sets up and finances new commercial enterprises to make a profit [Late 19thC. From French, literally "one who undertakes," from *entreprendre* "to undertake" (see ENTERPRISE).] —**en·tre·pre·neu·ri·al** *adj.* —**en·tre·pre·neur·i·al·ism** *n.* —**en·tre·pre·neur·ism** *n.* —**en·tre·pre·neur·ship** *n.*

en·tre·sol /óntrə sàwl/ *n.* = **mezzanine** [Early 18thC. From Via French from Spanish *entresuelo*, literally "between-level," from *suelo* "level," ultimately from Latin *solea* "sole" (see SOLE).]

en·tro·py /éntrәpee/ (*plural* **-pies**) *n.* **1. MEASURE OF DISORDER** a measure of the disorder that exists in a system **2.** PHYS **MEASURE OF UNAVAILABLE ENERGY** a measure of the energy in a system or process that is unavailable to do work. In a reversible thermodynamic process, entropy is expressed as the heat absorbed or emitted divided by the absolute temperature. Symbol **S** **3.** COMMUNICATION **MEASURE OF COMMUNICATIONS SYSTEM EFFICIENCY** a measure of the random errors (**noise**) occurring in the transmission of signals, and from this a measure of the efficiency of transmission systems [Mid-19thC. Literally "turning or change toward," formed from Greek *tropē* "change," literally "turning," on the model of ENERGY.] —**en·tro·pic** /en tróppik/ *adj.* —**en·tro·pi·cal·ly** *adv.*

en·trust /in trúst, en-/ (**-trust·ed, -trust·ing, -trusts**), **in·trust** /in-/ (**-trust·ed, -trust·ing, -trusts**) *vt.* to give something to another person to be responsible for

en·try /éntree/ (*plural* **-tries**) *n.* **1. GOING IN** an act or instance of somebody entering **2.** = **entrance**[1] *n.* 3 **3. SINGLE WRITTEN ITEM** an item or piece of data included in a list or a book **4.** COMPUT **INCLUDING AN ITEM ON LIST** the process of recording something in writing or on a computer ○ *data entry* **5. WAY IN** a way into a place **6. SOMEBODY OR SOMETHING ENTERED IN CONTEST** a person, animal, or item entered in a contest ○ *the winning entry* **7.** THEATER **APPEARANCE ON STAGE** the occasion when an actor comes on stage **8.** CARDS **WINNING CARD** in some games, a card that can win a trick and thus gain the lead for a player [13thC. Via French *entrée* from Latin *intrata*, a form of the past participle of *intrare* "to enter" (see ENTER).]

en·try-lev·el *adj.* at the lowest level and suitable for somebody who is new to a job, field, or subject

en·try·way /éntri wày/ *n.* a way into a place, such as a doorway or passageway

en·twine /in twı́n, en-/ (**-twined, -twin·ing, -twines**), **in·twine** /in-/ (**-twined, -twin·ing, -twines**) *vti.* to twist things together, or to twist something around something else (*often passive*) —**en·twine·ment** *n.*

en·twist /in twíst, en-/ (**-twist·ed, -twist·ing, -twists**), **in·twist** /in-/ (**-twist·ed, -twist·ing, -twists**) *vti.* = **entwine**

e·nu·cle·ate /i noóklee àyt/ *vt.* (**-at·ed, -at·ing, -ates**) **1.** CELL BIOL **TAKE OUT THE NUCLEUS** to remove the nucleus of a cell **2.** SURG **SURGICALLY REMOVE WITHOUT DAMAGE** to remove something surgically, such as a tumor, from its capsule while keeping it intact ■ *adj.* CELL BIOL **WITHOUT A NUCLEUS** used to describe a cell without a nucleus [Mid-16thC. From Latin *enucleat-*, past participle stem of *enucleare* "to remove the pit from (olives, fruit)," from *nucleus* "kernel" (see NUCLEUS).] —**e·nu·cle·a·tion** /i noòklee áysh'n/ *n.*

e·nu·mer·a·ble /i noómәrәb'l/ *adj.* = **denumerable** [Late 19thC. Formed from ENUMERATE + -ABLE.]

e·nu·mer·ate /i noómə ràyt/ (**-at·ed, -at·ing, -ates**) *vt.* **1. LIST INDIVIDUALLY** to name a number of things on a list one by one **2. COUNT THE NUMBER OF** to count how many things there are in something **3.** *Can* POL **PUT A VOTER'S NAME ON LIST** to put a voter's name on an official list used in elections [Mid-17thC. From Latin *enumerat-*, the past participle stem of *enumerare* "to count out," from *numerus* "number" (see NUMBER).] —**e·nu·mer·a·tion** /i no͞omə ráysh'n/ *n.* —**e·nu·mer·a·tive** /-ràytiv, i no͞omərativ/ *adj.* —**e·nu·mer·a·tor** /-ràytər/ *n.*

e·nun·ci·ate /i núnsee àyt/ (**-at·ed, -at·ing, -ates**) *v.* **1.** *vti.* SPEAK CLEARLY to pronounce something distinctly **2.** *vt.* STATE CLEARLY to give a speech or statement that explains something clearly [Early 17thC. From Latin *enuntiare* "to announce," from *enuntiat-*, the past participle stem of *nuntius* "message, messenger."] —**e·nun·ci·a·tion** /i nùnsee áysh'n/ *n.* —**e·nun·ci·a·tive** /i núnsee àytiv, -ətiv/ *adj.* —**e·nun·ci·a·tive·ly** /-àytivlee/ *adv.* —**e·nun·ci·a·tor** /i núnsee àytər/ *n.*

en·ure *vt.* = **inure**

en·u·re·sis /ènnyə réessiss/ *n.* involuntary discharge of urine, especially while asleep (*technical*) [Late 18thC. From modern Latin, from Greek *enourein* "to urinate in," from *ouron* "urine."] —**en·u·ret·ic** /ènnyə réttik/ *adj.*

en·vel·op /in véləp, en-/ (**-oped, -op·ing, -ops**) *vt.* **1.** WRAP UP to enclose somebody or something completely (*often passive*) **2.** HIDE to conceal something or somebody (*often passive*) **3.** MIL SURROUND AN ENEMY to surround an enemy completely [14thC. From Old French *envoluper* "to wrap in," of unknown origin.] —**en·vel·op·er** *n.* —**en·vel·op·ment** *n.*

en·ve·lope /énvə lòp, ónvə lòp/ *n.* **1.** PAPER COVER FOR A LETTER a flat pocket of paper with a sealable flap for holding letters **2.** ENCLOSING CASE something that surrounds or encloses something else ○ *seafood sauce in phyllo pastry envelopes* **3.** BIOL ENCLOSING STRUCTURE a covering that encloses and protects an animal's body or a biological structure, such as a shell or membrane **4.** MATH CURVE FORMING A TANGENT a curve or surface that forms a tangent to each of the members of a set of curves or surfaces, such as circles with a common center but different radii **5.** AEROSP BALLOON the bag of an airship or balloon that contains the gas **6.** AEROSP PERFORMANCE LIMITS OF AN AIRCRAFT the performance limits of a piece of equipment, particularly of an aircraft [Early 18thC. From French *enveloppe*, from *envelopper* "to wrap in" from Old French *envoluper* (see ENVELOP).] ◇ **push the envelope** to try to accomplish more than is theoretically possible (*informal*)

en·ven·om /in vénəm/ (**-omed, -om·ing, -oms**) *vt.* **1.** MAKE POISONOUS to make something poisonous (*technical*) **2.** MAKE ANGRY AND BITTER to cause somebody to become malicious or hostile (*formal*) —**en·ven·om·i·za·tion** /in vènnəmi záysh'n/ *n.*

en·vi·a·ble /énvee əb'l/ *adj.* likely to evoke feelings of envy ○ *in the enviable position of having two job offers to choose from* —**en·vi·a·bly** *adv.*

en·vi·ous /énvee əss/ *adj.* wanting to have somebody's else's success, good fortune, qualities, or possessions —**en·vi·ous·ly** *adv.* —**en·vi·ous·ness** *n.*

en·vi·ron /in vírən, in ví ərn/ (**-roned, -ron·ing, -rons**) *vt.* to surround somebody or something. ◊ **environs** [14thC. From Old French *environer*, literally "to make a circle around," ultimately from *viron* "circle," from *virer* "to turn" (see VEER).]

en·vi·ron·ment /in vírənmənt, -víərn-/ *n.* **1.** ENVIRON NATURAL WORLD the natural world, within which people, animals, and plants live. It is regarded by many as being at risk from the harmful influences of industrialized societies. **2.** ENVIRON, ECOL SURROUNDING INFLUENCES all the external factors influencing the life of organisms, such as light or food supply **3.** SOC SCI SOCIAL AND PHYSICAL CONDITIONS the conditions that surround people and affect the way they live ○ *the nurturing environment a child needs*

en·vi·ron·men·tal /in vìrən mént'l, -víərn-/ *adj.* **1.** OF THE NATURAL WORLD relating to the natural world, especially to its conservation ○ *environmental groups* **2.** OF YOUR SURROUNDINGS relating to, or caused by, a person's or animal's surroundings

en·vi·ron·men·tal art *n.* creative art, usually on a grand scale, that is meant to invite the viewer's participation by interacting with it

en·vi·ron·men·tal as·sess·ment *n.* *U.K.* = **environmental impact statement**

en·vi·ron·men·tal health *n.* the impact on human health of the environment, especially as safeguarded by government agencies dealing with areas such as water quality, food hygiene, and pest control

en·vi·ron·men·tal im·pact *n.* the indirect and direct consequences of human actions on the natural environment

en·vi·ron·men·tal im·pact state·ment *n.* *U.S., ANZ* the identification of the likely environmental effects of a proposed development

en·vi·ron·men·tal·ism /in vìrən mént'l ìzzəm, -vìərn-/ *n.* **1.** POL CONCERN FOR THE ENVIRONMENT the movement, especially in politics and consumer affairs, that works toward protecting the natural world from harmful human activities **2.** PSYCHOL THEORY OF ENVIRONMENTAL INFLUENCE a theory stating that a person's environment is more influential than heredity in determining his or her development

en·vi·ron·men·tal·ist /in vìrən mént'list, -vìərn-/ *n.* **1.** POL SOMEBODY WORKING TO PROTECT THE ENVIRONMENT somebody involved in issues relating to the protection of the natural world, especially a member of a political group campaigning against the perceived harmful effects of industrialized societies **2.** PSYCHOL BELIEVER IN THE DEVELOPMENTAL IMPORTANCE OF ENVIRONMENT a supporter of the theory that a person's environment is more influential than heredity in determining his or her development

en·vi·ron·men·tal·ly /in vìrən mént'lee, -vìərn-/ *adv.* with regard to the natural world and its vulnerability to destructive influences ○ *the environmentally aware consumer*

en·vi·ron·men·tal·ly friend·ly, **en·vi·ron·ment-friend·ly** *adj.* designed to minimize harmful impact on the natural world, e.g., by using biodegradable ingredients

en·vi·ron·men·tal stud·ies *n.* a course of academic study including a range of disciplines that relate to the environment (*takes a singular or plural verb*)

en·vi·rons /in vírənz, in ví ərnz/ *npl.* the land or area surrounding a place [Mid-17thC. From French, plural of *environ* "surroundings, around," literally "in a circle," from *viron* (see ENVIRON).]

en·vis·age /in vízzij, en-/ (**-aged, -ag·ing, -ag·es**) *vt.* (*formal*) **1.** FORESEE to conceive of and contemplate a future possibility ○ *Do you envisage being able to avert a crisis?* **2.** IMAGINE to form a mental picture of something or somebody **3.** CONSIDER to regard something in a particular way [Early 19thC. From French *envisager*, literally "(to cause to be) in the face," from *visage* "face" (see VISAGE).]

en·vi·sion /in ví<u>zh</u>'n, en-/ (**-sioned, -sion·ing, -sions**) *vt.* to form a mental picture of something, typically something that may occur or be possible in the future

en·voi *n.* = **envoy** *n.* 2

en·voy /én vòy/ *n.* **1.** POL OFFICIAL REPRESENTATIVE somebody acting as a diplomat on behalf of a national government or sent as an official messenger on behalf of a higher authority **2. en·voy, en·voi** LITERAT CONCLUDING PART OF A POEM the final section of a book or play, or a short stanza at the end of a poem, used for summing up or as a dedication [Mid-17thC. From French *envoyé*, past participle of *envoyer*, "to send," from assumed Vulgar Latin *inviare* "to put on the way" from Latin *via* "way."]

en·vy /énvee/ *n.* WANTING WHAT SOMEBODY ELSE HAS the resentful or unhappy feeling of wanting somebody else's success, good fortune, qualities, or possessions ■ *vt.* (**-vied, -vy·ing, -vies**) WANT WHAT SOMEBODY ELSE HAS to desire something possessed by somebody else ○ *It would be churlish of me to envy them their success.* [13thC. Via Old French *envie* from Latin *invidia*, from *invidere* "to look askance at," from *videre* "to see" (see VIDEO).] —**en·vy·ing·ly** *adv.* ◇ **be the envy of somebody** to be the object of somebody's envy

en·wind /in wínd, en-/ (**-wound, -wound** /in wównd, en-/, **-wind·ing, -winds**), **in·wind** /in-/ (**-wound** /in wównd/, **-wound, -winds** *or* **-wind·ing**) *vt.* to wind or coil something around somebody or something (*literary*)

en·womb /in wo͞om, en-/ (**-wombed, -womb·ing, -wombs**) *vt.* **1.** ENCLOSE WARMLY to hold something or somebody in a warm safe place (*literary*) **2.** CAUSE WOMAN TO BE PREGNANT to make a woman pregnant or be the child in a woman's womb (*archaic*) ○ *"I say, I am your mother; and put you in the catalogue of those that were enwombed mine."* (William Shakespeare, *All's Well That Ends Well*; 1602)

en·wound past participle, past tense of **enwind**

en·wrap /in ráp, en-/ (**-wrapped, -wrap·ping, -wraps**), **in·wrap** /in-/ (**-wrapped, -wrap·ping, -wraps**) *vt.* **1.** HOLD THE ATTENTION to involve or engross somebody or something thoroughly (*formal*) (*often passive*) **2.** WRAP to wrap something or somebody up

en·wreathe /in reéth, en-/ (**-wreathed, -wreath·ing, -wreathes**), **in·wreathe** /in-/ (**-wreathed, -wreath·ing, -wreathes**) *vt.* to encircle something, especially with decorations (*literary*)

en·zo·ot·ic /èn zō óttik/ *adj.* ZOOL AFFECTING ANIMALS IN A RESTRICTED AREA used to describe an animal disease that occurs only within a specific geographic area ■ *n.* ZOOL DISEASE OF ANIMALS a disease that affects animals in a specific area, locale, or region [Late 19thC.]

en·zyme /én zìm/ *n.* a complex protein produced by living cells that promotes a specific biochemical reaction by acting as a catalyst [Late 19thC. Via German *Enzym* from modern Greek *enzumos* "leavened," literally "with leaven in," from Greek *zumē* "leaven."] —**en·zy·mat·ic** /ènzə màttik/ *adj.* —**en·zy·mic** /en zímik, -zímmik/ *adj.* —**en·zy·mi·cal·ly** /en zímikəlee, en zímm-/ *adv.*

en·zy·mol·o·gy /ènzə mólləjee/ *n.* the branch of biochemistry that deals with enzymes

EO *abbr.* LAW executive order (*followed by a number*)

e.o. *abbr.* ex officio

eo- *prefix.* oldest, earliest ○ *eolithic* [From Greek *ēōs* "dawn." Ultimately from an Indo-European word that is also the ancestor of English *aurora*.]

E·o·cene /ée ə seen/ *n.* the epoch of geologic time when mammals first appeared, 56.5 to 35.4 million years ago. —**E·o·cene** *adj.*

EOF *abbr.* COMPUT end of file

e·o·hip·pus /ée ō híppəss/ (*plural* **-pus·es**) *n.* a small prehistoric horse that lived in North America. It was dog-sized and had four toes on the forefeet and three on the hind. [Late 19thC. From modern Latin, literally "dawn horse," from Greek *hippos* "horse."]

e·o·li·an /ee ólee ən, -ólyən/, **ae·o·li·an** *adj.* GEOL carried or produced by the wind ○ *eolian deposits* [Early 20thC. Formed from "Aeolus," Greek god of the winds.]

E·o·li·an *n., adj.* = **Aeolian**

e·o·lith /ée ə lìth/ *n.* one of the oldest stone tools used by humans, believed by some scientists to have formed naturally

e·o·lith·ic /ée ə líthik/ *adj.* relating to the earliest part of the Stone Age, during which time simple stone tools began to be used

e.o.m. *abbr.* COMM end of the month

e·on /ée òn, ée ən/ *n.* **1.** VAST AMOUNT OF TIME a length of time that is too long to measure **2.** GEOL LONGEST UNIT OF GEOLOGIC TIME a division of geologic time comprising two or more eras [Mid-17thC. Via late Latin from Greek *aiōn*, "age, lifetime."] —**e·o·ni·an** /ee ónee ən/ *adj.*

e·o·sin /ée əssin/ *n.* a red crystalline solid used as a biological stain and as a dye in cosmetics. Formula: $C_{20}H_6Br_4O_5K_2$. [Mid-19thC. Coined from Greek *ēōs* "dawn" + -IN; so called because of its color.]

e·o·sin·o·phil /ée ə sínnə fil/ *n.* a granular white blood cell that stains with the dye eosin and is thought to play a part in allergic reactions and the body's response to parasitic diseases [Late 19thC. Coined from EOSIN + -PHIL.] —**e·o·sin·o·phil·ic** /ée ə sinnə fíllik/ *adj.* —**e·o·si·noph·i·lous** /ée ō si nóffiləss/ *adj.*

e·o·sin·o·phil·i·a /ée ə sinnə fíllee ə/ *n.* an increase in the number of granular white blood cells that stain with the dye eosin, occurring in some allergies and parasitic diseases

-eous *suffix.* ◆ **-ous** [Formed from Latin *-eus*, a suffix forming adjectives of material, such as *aureus*, "golden," from *aurum*, "gold"]

EP[1] *n.* a phonograph record that is the size of a single but contains a longer recording on it and is designed to be played at 33 1/3 revolutions per minute rather than 45 [Mid-20thC. Shortening of EXTENDED PLAY.]

EP[2] *abbr.* European Plan

Ep. *abbr.* BIBLE **1.** Ephesians **2.** Epistle

e.p. *abbr.* CHESS en passant

ep- *prefix.* = **epi-** (*used before vowels or h*)

EPA *abbr.* Environmental Protection Agency

e·pact /ée pàkt/ *n.* a period of about 11 days that represents the difference between the lunar year and the solar year [Mid-16thC. Via Old French from late Latin, from Greek *epaktē (hēmera)*, "added (day)," literally "(day) led in," from *agein* "to lead."]

e·pan·a·lep·sis /èppənə lépsiss/ (*plural* **-ses** /-seez/) *n.* a phrase or words repeated later on in a speech or text as a rhetorical device [Late 16thC. From Greek "repetition," literally "taking up again," from epana- "again" + *lēpsis* "taking."] —**e·pan·a·lep·tic** /èppənə léptik/ *adj.*

e·pan·or·tho·sis /èppə nawr thóssiss/ (*plural* **-orth·o·ses** /-thó seez/) *n.* the immediate rephrasing of something said or written in order to emphasize or correct it [Late 16thC. From Greek "correction," literally "setting straight again," from *epana-* "again" + *orthōsis* "making straight," ultimately from *orthos* "straight."] —**e·pan·or·tho·tic** *adj.*

ep·arch /é paark/ *n.* **1.** CHR **BISHOP** a bishop in the Greek Orthodox Church **2.** POL **GREEK GOVERNOR** the governor of a modern Greek province [Mid-17thC. From Greek *eparkhos*, literally "ruler over," from *arkhos* "ruler" (see -ARCH).]

ep·ar·chy /é paarkee/ (*plural* **-chies**) *n.* **1.** CHR **DIOCESE** a bishop's diocese in the Greek Orthodox Church **2.** POL **PART OF A GREEK PROVINCE** a political subdivision of a province in modern Greece [Late 18thC. From Greek *eparkhia* "prefecture, province," from *eparkhos* (see EPARCH).]

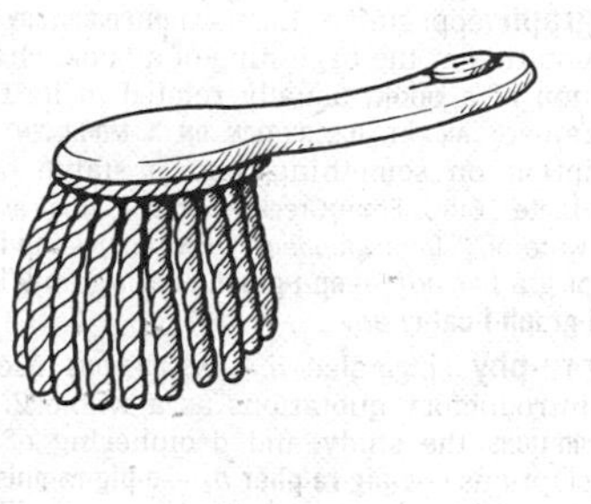

Epaulet

ep·au·let /éppə lèt, èppə lét/, **ep·au·lette** *n.* a decoration on the shoulder of a jacket, especially on a military uniform. Epaulets are worn on the shoulders of a uniform jacket or coat, and in officers' dress are usually made of gold or silver braid. [Late 18thC. From French, literally "small shoulder," from *épaule* "shoulder," from, ultimately, Latin *spatula* "broad piece, shoulder blade" (see SPATULA).]

é·pée /e páy/ (*plural* **é·pées**) *n.* **1.** **FENCING SWORD** a fencing sword that has a narrow triangular blade with a blunted end and a large handguard, heavier than a foil. It derives from the type of sword formerly used in dueling. **2.** **FENCING WITH ÉPÉES** the sport of fencing using épées [Late 19thC. From French, literally "sword," from Latin *spatha* "broad double-edged sword" (see SPATHE).] —**é·pée·ist** *n.*

ep·ei·rog·e·ny /è pī rójjənee/, **ep·ei·ro·gen·e·sis** /i pīrə jénnəssiss/ *n.* the slow movements of the Earth's crust that lead to the formation of features such as continents [Late 19thC. Coined from Greek *ēpeiros* "mainland, continent" + -GENY.] —**ep·ei·ro·gen·ic** /i pīrō jénnik/ *adj.* —**ep·ei·ro·gen·i·cal·ly** /-jennikəlee/ *adv.*

e·pen·the·sis /i pénthəssiss/ *n.* insertion of an extra sound into a word, as happens in some dialect pronunciations or in a word's development over time. The "b" in "crumble" is an example of epenthesis. [Mid-17thC. Via late Latin from Greek, where it was formed from *epentithenai*, literally "to place in also," ultimately from *tithenai* "to place."] —**e·pen·thet·ic** /èppən théttik/ *adj.*

e·pergne /i púrn, ày-/ *n.* a large elaborate centerpiece for a table with containers for fruit or flowers [Mid-18thC. Origin uncertain: probably from French *épergne* "savings, treasury," from Old French *espargnier*, from a prehistoric Germanic word that is also the ancestor of English *spare*.]

ep·ex·e·ge·sis /e pèksə jéessiss/ (*plural* **-ses** /-seez/) *n.* **1.** **ADDITIONAL WORDS EXPLAINING A TEXT** the addition of words or phrases to a text to clarify its meaning **2.** **WORD ADDED FOR CLARIFICATION** a word or phrase added to help explain the sense of a text [Early 17thC. From, literally "explaining in addition," from *exēgēsis* (see EXEGESIS).] —**ep·ex·e·get·ic** /e pèksə jéttik/ *adj.* —**ep·ex·e·get·i·cal** /-jéttik'l/ *adj.* —**ep·ex·e·get·i·cal·ly** /-kəlee/ *adv.*

Eph. *abbr.* BIBLE Ephesians

eph- *prefix.* = **epi-**

e·phah /éefə, éffə/, **e·pha** *n.* an ancient Hebrew unit of dry measure, roughly equivalent to a bushel or 33 liters [14thC. From Hebrew *ēpāh*.]

e·phebe /é feeb, i féeb/, **e·phe·bus** /i féebəss/ (*plural* **-bi** /i fée bī/), **ephe·bos** (*plural* **e·phe·bi**) *n.* in ancient Greece, a young man aged between 18 and 20 who had just reached manhood or full citizenship and was undergoing military training [Mid-19thC. Via Latin *ephebus* from Greek *ephēbos*, literally "one approaching manhood," from *hēbē* "early manhood."] —**e·phe·bic** *adj.*

e·phed·rine /i féddrin, éffə dreen/ *n.* a white odorless alkaloid that is used to enlarge air passages in asthma attacks, relieve allergic nasal congestion, and dilate the pupils, and as a central nervous system stimulant. It can be manufactured synthetically or obtained from a shrub. [Late 19thC. Formed from modern Latin *Ephedra*, from Latin *ephedra* "horsetail," from the Greek name of a genus of plants, some of which contain this substance.]

e·phem·er·a[1] /i fémmərə/ plural of **ephemeron**

e·phem·er·a[2] /i fémmərə/ *n.* (*plural* **-ae** /-ee/ *or* **-as**) **1.** **SOMETHING SHORT-LIVED** something that is transitory and without lasting significance **2.** INSECTS = **mayfly** *n.* 1 ■ *npl.* **COLLECTABLE ITEMS** a range of collectable items that were originally designed to be short-lived ○ *He's a collector of ticket stubs, movie passes, and other ephemera.* [14thC. From medieval Latin, feminine of late Latin *ephemerus* "lasting only a day," from Greek *ephēmeros*, from *hēmera* "day."]

e·phem·er·al /i fémmərəl/ *adj.* **SHORT-LIVED** lasting for only a short period of time ○ *the ephemeral nature of slang* ■ *n.* **SHORT-LIVED ORGANISM** a plant or insect that lives for only a short period of time. Groundsel and mayflies are ephemerals. —**e·phem·er·al·i·ty** /i fèmmə rálləteel/ *n.* —**e·phem·er·al·ly** /i fémmərəlee/ *adv.* —**e·phem·er·al·ness** /-əlnəss/ *n.*

e·phem·er·id /i fémmərid/ *n.* an insect of the mayfly family that emerges in the summer from a long aquatic larval stage and lives only a matter of hours as an adult. Family: Ephemeridae. [Late 19thC. From modern Latin *Ephemeridae*, family name, from, ultimately, Greek *ephēmeros* (see EPHEMERA[2]).]

e·phem·er·is /i fémməriss/ (*plural* **eph·e·mer·i·des** /èefə mérrə deez/) *n.* a table listing the future positions of the Sun, Moon, and planets over a given period of time [Early 16thC. Via Latin from Greek, where it was formed from *ephēmeros* (see EPHEMERA[2]).]

e·phem·er·is time *n.* a system of time measurement based on the Earth's orbit around the Sun and therefore independent of the irregularities of the Earth's rotation

e·phem·er·on /i fémmə ròn/ (*plural* **-a** /-rə/ *or* **-ons**) *n.* a short-lived thing (*usually used in the plural*) [Late 16thC. From Greek *ephēmeron*, a form of *ephēmeros* (see EPHEMERA[2]).]

E·phe·sians /i féezh'nz/ *n.* one of the books of the Bible, consisting of a letter from the Apostle Paul to the early Christians (*used with a singular verb*) [15thC. Formed from Latin *ephesius* "of Ephesus," from Greek *ephesios*, from *Ephesos* "Ephesus," a Greek city in Asia Minor.]

Eph·e·sus /éffəsəss/ ancient Greek city on the western coast of Asia Minor, in present-day Turkey. An important center for early Christianity, it was the site of the temple of Artemis, one of the Seven Wonders of the World.

eph·od /é fòd, ée-/ *n.* an embroidered garment, believed to be like an apron with shoulder straps, worn by Hebrew priests in ancient Israel [14thC. From Hebrew *ēpōd*.]

eph·or /é fàwr, éffər/ (*plural* **-ors** *or* **-o·ri** /-rī/) *n.* in ancient Greece, one of five magistrates elected in any of various Dorian states, especially Sparta, to supervise the king [Late 16thC. Directly or via Latin *ephorus* from Greek *ephoros* "overseer," from *horan* "to see."] —**eph·or·al** /éffərəl/ *adj.* —**eph·or·ate** /-ràyt, -rət/ *n.*

E·phra·im·ite /éefree ə mīt/ *n.* **1.** **MEMBER OF THE TRIBE OF EPHRAIM** a member of the Hebrew tribe of Ephraim **2.** **SOMEBODY FROM THE KINGDOM OF ISRAEL** somebody born in the northern kingdom of Israel

epi- *prefix.* **1.** on, over, above ○ *epiphyte* ○ *epipelagic* **2.** around, near ○ *epicalyx* **3.** after, in addition ○ *epiphenomenon* [From Greek *epi* "upon"]

ep·i·blast /éppi blàst/ *n.* the outer layer of cells in an early embryo (**blastula**). It develops into ectoderm. —**ep·i·blast·ic** /èppi blástik/ *adj.*

e·pib·o·ly /i píbbəlee/ *n.* the growth of a layer of rapidly dividing cells over a layer of more slowly dividing cells during embryo development. This process occurs in the eggs of birds and reptiles. [Late 19thC. From Greek *epibolē* "throwing on," from *epiballein* "to throw on," from *ballein* "to throw" (see BALLISTIC).] —**ep·i·bol·ic** /èppi bóllik/ *adj.*

ep·ic /éppik/ *n.* **1.** POETRY **LONG NARRATIVE POEM** a lengthy narrative poem in elevated language celebrating the adventures and achievements of a legendary or traditional hero, e.g., Homer's *Odyssey* **2.** POETRY **EPIC POETRY** epic poetry as a genre ○ *This term we'll cover epic, romance, and allegory.* **3.** ARTS **LARGE-SCALE PRODUCTION** a work of literature, cinema, television, or theater that is large-scale and expensively produced and often deals with a historical theme **4.** **LONG SERIES OF EVENTS** a long series of events characterized by adventures or struggle ○ *Our trek across town turned out to be an epic.* ■ *adj.* **1.** POETRY **ABOUT AN EPIC** relating to or being an epic ○ *Milton's "Paradise Lost" is an epic poem.* **2.** **LIKE AN EPIC** having some of the characteristics of an epic ○ *an epic story of true love and adventure* **3.** **VERY LARGE OR HEROIC** impressive by virtue of greatness of size, scope, or heroism ○ *a scandal of epic proportions* [Late 16thC. Via Latin *epicus* from Greek *epikos*, from *epos* (see EPOS).] —**ep·i·cal** *adj.* —**ep·i·cal·ly** *adv.*

ep·i·ca·lyx /èppi káyliks, -kálliks/ (*plural* **-lyx·es** /-li seez/ *or* **-ly·ces**) *n.* a ring of modified leaves (**bracts**) at the base of a flower that resemble an extra calyx, found in the carnation, hibiscus, and mallow

ep·i·can·thic fold /èppi kànthik-/ *n.* a fold of skin from the eyelid that partially covers the part of the eye nearest the nose

ep·i·can·thus /èppi kánthəss/ (*plural* **-thi** /-thī/) *n.* = **epicanthic fold** [Mid-19thC. Coined from EPI- + CANTHUS.]

ep·i·carp /éppi kaarp/ *n.* = **exocarp**

ep·i·cene /éppi seen/ *adj.* **1.** **HAVING CHARACTERISTICS OF BOTH SEXES** having both male and female characteristics **2.** **NEITHER MALE NOR FEMALE** of neither male nor female sex **3.** **WITH FEMALE CHARACTERISTICS** having typically female characteristics (*literary*) (*used of a male*) **4.** **WEAK** lacking vigor and strength **5.** GRAM **SAME FOR MASCULINE AND FEMININE** having only one grammatical form for both masculine and feminine, in languages where nouns have genders ■ *n.* **1.** **SOMEBODY OR SOMETHING EPICENE** an epicene person or thing (*literary*) **2.** GRAM **NOUN WITH SAME MASCULINE AND FEMININE FORM** a noun with the same grammatical form for both masculine and feminine in languages where nouns have genders [15thC. Via late Latin *epicoenus* from Greek *epikoinos*, literally "in common," from *koinos* "common."] —**ep·i·cen·ism** /éppissi nìzzəm/ *n.*

ep·i·cen·ter /éppi sèntər/ *n.* **1.** GEOL **EARTH'S SURFACE ABOVE THE FOCUS OF AN EARTHQUAKE** the exact location on the Earth's surface directly above the focus of an earthquake or underground nuclear explosion **2.** **FOCAL POINT** the very center or focal point ○ *Paris is the epicenter of the fashion world.* [Mid-19thC. From Greek *epikentron*, neuter of *epikentos* "situated on a center," from *kentros* "center" (see CENTER).] —**ep·i·cen·tral** /èppi séntrəl/ *adj.*

ep·i·cot·yl /éppi kòtt'l/ *n.* the tip of a plant embryo above the embryonic leaves (**cotyledons**) that gives rise to the stem of the new plant [Late 19thC. Coined from EPI- + Greek *kotulē* (see COTYLEDON).]

ep·ic sim·i·le *n.* a lengthy simile developed over a number of lines of verse in narrative poetry

ep·i·cure /éppi kyoor/ *n.* **1.** **GOURMET** somebody who has developed a refined taste for food **2.** **SENSUAL PERSON** somebody who is dedicated to sensual pleasure and luxury [14thC. From medieval Latin *epicurus*, from EPICURUS. Originally "follower of Epicurus."] —**ep·i·cur·ism** *n.*

ep·i·cu·re·an /èppikyə rée ən, èppi kyooree ən/ *adj.* **1.** **DEVOTED TO SENSUAL PLEASURE** devoted to sensual pleasures and luxury, especially good food **2.** **PLEASING TO AN EPICURE** suitable for or pleasing to an epicure ○ *led an epicurean life* ■ *n.* = **epicure** *n.* 2 [14thC. Directly or via French *épicurien* from Latin *epicureus*, from EPICURUS.] —**ep·i·cu·re·an·ism** *n.*

Ep·i·cu·re·an *adj.* **OF EPICURUS** relating to the philosophy of Epicureanism ■ *n.* **ADHERENT OF EPICUREANISM** a follower of Epicureanism

Ep·i·cu·re·an·ism /èppikyə rée ə nìzzəm, éppi kyŏŏree-/ *n.* the school of philosophy founded by Epicurus and its teachings

Ep·i·cu·rus /èppi kyŏŏrəss/ (341–270 B.C.) Greek philosopher. His philosophy, Epicureanism, taught that the greatest good is freedom from pain and emotional disturbance.

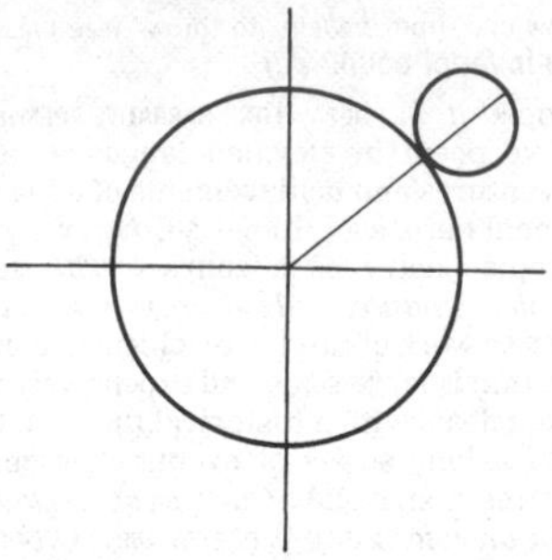

Epicycle

ep·i·cy·cle /éppi sĭk'l/ *n.* **1.** PLANET'S CIRCULAR MOTION in the Ptolemaic theory of the solar system, a circle that is followed by a planet, the circle itself being centered on a larger circle within which is the Earth. The epicycle accounts for irregularities of planetary motion in geocentric astronomy. **2.** GEOM CIRCLE THAT ROLLS AROUND ANOTHER a circle that rolls around the circumference of another circle, either inside or outside [14thC. Via French *épicycle* or late Latin *epicyclus* from Greek *epikuklos,* literally "on a circle," from *kuklos* "circle" (see CYCLE).] —**ep·i·cy·clic** /èppi sĭklik, -síklik/ *adj.* —**ep·i·cy·cli·cal** /-sĭklik'l, -síklik'l/ *adj.*

ep·i·cy·clic train *n.* a system of gears arranged such that one or more gears engage with and revolve around a fixed or moving part

ep·i·cy·cloid /èppi sī klòyd/ *n.* a mathematical curve traced by a point on the circumference of a circle that rolls around the outside of the circumference of another circle —**ep·i·cy·cloid·al** /èppi sī klóyd'l/ *adj.*

ep·i·dem·ic /èppi démmik/ *n.* **1.** MED FAST-SPREADING DISEASE an outbreak of a disease that spreads more quickly and more extensively among a group of people than would normally be expected **2.** RAPID DEVELOPMENT a rapid and extensive development or growth, usually of something unpleasant ○ *an epidemic of civil unrest and rioting* ■ *adj.* SPREADING UNUSUALLY QUICKLY AND EXTENSIVELY spreading more quickly and more extensively among a group of people at the same time than would normally be expected ○ *Influenza was epidemic.* [Early 17thC. From French *épidémique,* from *épidémie* "an epidemic," from, ultimately, Greek *epidēmia* "disease prevalent among the people," from *dēmos* "people."] —**ep·i·dem·i·cal·ly** *adv.* —**ep·i·de·mic·i·ty** /èppidə míssətee/ *n.*

WORD KEY: SYNONYMS

See Synonyms at ***widespread.***

ep·i·de·mi·ol·o·gy /èppi deemee ólləjee, -demmee-/ *n.* **1.** STUDY OF DISEASE ORIGIN AND SPREAD the scientific and medical study of the causes and transmission of disease within a population **2.** PATTERN OF DISEASE DEVELOPMENT the origin and development characteristics of a particular disease [Late 19thC. Coined from Greek *epidēmia* (see EPIDEMIC) + -OLOGY.] —**ep·i·de·mi·o·log·ic** /èppi deemee ə lójjik, -demmee-/ *adj.* —**ep·i·de·mi·o·log·i·cal·ly** /èppi deemee ə lójjikəlee, -demmee-/ *adv.* —**ep·i·de·mi·ol·o·gist** /èppi deemee ólləjist, -demmee-/ *n.*

ep·i·der·mis /èppi dúrmiss/ *n.* **1.** ANAT OUTER LAYER OF THE SKIN the thin outermost layer of the skin, itself made up of several layers, that covers and protects the underlying dermis **2.** BIOL OUTER LAYER OF INVERTEBRATES' CELLS the outer layer of cells of invertebrates that secretes the protective waxy cuticle **3.** BOT OUTER CELL LAYER OF A PLANT the outermost layer of cells on a plant. In woody plants the epidermis is usually replaced by corky protective tissue (**periderm**). [Early 17thC. Via late Latin from Greek, literally "above skin," from *derma* "skin" (see DERMATO-).] —**ep·i·der·mal** *adj.* —**ep·i·der·mic** *adj.* —**ep·i·der·moid** *adj.*

ep·i·di·a·scope /èppi dī ə skōp/ *n.* **1.** ENLARGING PROJECTOR a device for projecting an enlarged image of an opaque or transparent object onto a screen **2.** = **episcope** [Early 20thC. Coined from EPI- + DIA- + -SCOPE.]

ep·i·did·y·mis /èppi díddimiss/ (*plural* **-mi·des** /-mə deez/) *n.* a coiled tube attached to the back and upper side of the testicle that stores sperm and is connected to the vas deferens [Early 17thC. From Greek *epididumis,* from *didumis* "testicle, twin," from *duo* "two."] —**ep·i·did·y·mal** *adj.*

ep·i·dote /éppi dōt/ *n.* a shiny green, yellow, or black mineral occurring in metamorphic rocks. Formula: $Ca_2(Al,Fe)_3(SiO_4)_3(OH)$. [Early 19thC. From French *épidote,* from Greek *epididonai* "to give in addition," from *didonai* "to give"; from its very long crystals.] —**ep·i·dot·ic** /èppi dóttik/ *adj.*

ep·i·du·ral /èppi dŏŏrəl/ *n.* MED ANESTHETIC INJECTION INTO SPINE a local anesthetic injected into the space between the outer membrane covering the spinal cord and the overlying bones of the spine. It is often used in childbirth. ■ *adj.* ANAT ON THE DURA MATER located on or outside the outermost membrane covering the brain and spinal cord (**dura mater**) [Late 19thC. Coined from EPI- + *dura,* from DURA MATER + -AL.]

ep·i·fau·na /éppi fàwnə/ *npl.* ECOL animals that live on the sea floor, or attached to other animals or objects under water —**ep·i·fau·nal** /èppi fáwn'l/ *adj.*

epi·fo·cal *adj.* located or occurring at the point on the Earth's surface directly above the focus (**epicenter**) of an earthquake or underground nuclear explosion

ep·i·gam·ic /èppi gámmik/ *adj.* ZOOL used to describe a trait or behavior that attracts a mate, such as large antlers or bright colors [Late 19thC. Formed from EPI- + Greek *gamos* "marriage."]

ep·i·gas·tri·um /èppi gástree əm/ (*plural* **-a** /-ə/) *n.* ANAT the upper middle part of the abdomen [Late 17thC. Via late Latin from Greek *epigastrion,* a form of *epigastrios* "over the belly," from *gaster* "belly" (see GASTRIC).]

ep·i·ge·al /èppi jée əl/ *adj.* **1.** BIOL, BOT LIVING ON SURFACE OF GROUND living or growing on or right above the surface of the ground. ◊ **hypogeal 2.** BOT GERMINATING WITH SEED LEAVES HELD ALOFT used to describe seed germination in which the embryo elongates so that the seed leaves (**cotyledons**) are carried above the soil to form the first leaves of the new plant [Mid-19thC. Formed from Greek *epigeios* "on the earth," from *gē* "earth."]

ep·i·gene /éppi jeen/ *adj.* GEOL formed or occurring at the Earth's surface, especially with reference to weathering, erosion, and deposition [Early 19thC. Via French *épigène* from Greek *epigenēs* "born on or after," from *-genes* (see -GEN).]

ep·i·gen·e·sis /èppi jénnəsiss/ *n.* **1.** EMBRYOL EMBRYONIC DEVELOPMENT BY GRADUAL CHANGE the theory that the development of tissues and organs during embryonic development proceeds by successive gradual change **2.** GEOL CHANGE IN THE MINERAL CONTENT OF ROCK change in the mineral content or structure of a rock through external influences, such as the injection of a vein of ore into existing rock —**ep·i·gen·e·sist** *n.* —**ep·i·ge·net·ic** /èppəjə néttik/ *adj.* —**ep·i·ge·net·i·cal·ly** /-kəlee/ *adv.* —**e·pig·e·nist** /i píjjənist/ *n.*

e·pig·e·nous /i píjjənəss/ *adj.* BOT growing on the upper surface of an organism

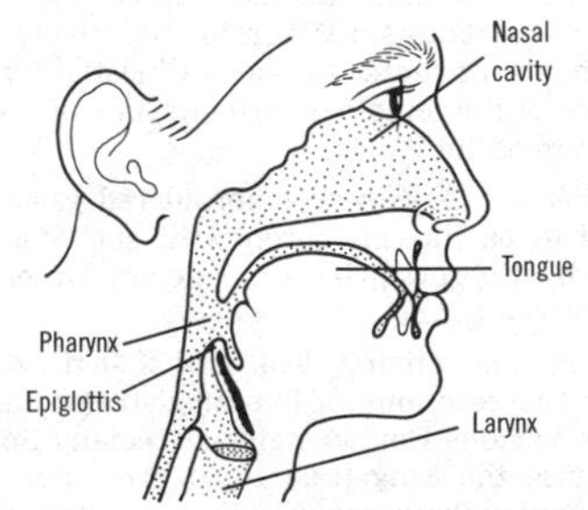

Epiglottis

ep·i·glot·tis /èppi glóttiss/ (*plural* **-ti·ses** *or* **-tid·es** /-deez/) *n.* a flap of cartilage situated at the base of the tongue that covers the opening to the air passages when swallowing, preventing food or liquids from entering the windpipe (**trachea**) [Early 16thC. From Greek *epiglōttis,* literally "on the tongue," from *glōtta* "tongue."] —**ep·i·glot·tal** *adj.* —**ep·i·glot·tic** *adj.*

ep·i·gone /éppi gòn/, **ep·i·gon** *n.* a follower, especially of an important artist or philosopher, who is a mediocre imitator (*formal or literary*) [Mid-18thC. Singular of *epigones* "epigones," which came via French from, ultimately, Greek *epigonoi,* plural of *epigonos* "offspring," literally "one born after," from *gignesthai* "to be born."] —**ep·i·gon·ic** /èppi gónnik/ *adj.* —**ep·i·gon·ous** /i píggənəss/ *adj.* —**ep·i·gon·ism** /-nìzzəm/ *n.*

ep·i·gram /éppi gràm/ *n.* **1.** WITTY SAYING a concise, witty, and often paradoxical remark or saying **2.** POETRY SHORT POEM a short poem, often expressing a single idea, that is usually satirical and has a witty ending **3.** WITTY EXPRESSION a written or spoken mode of expression that is witty or concise like an epigram [15thC. Directly or via French *épigramme* from Latin *epigramma,* from Greek, literally "writing upon," from *graphein* "to write."] —**ep·i·gram·ma·tism** /èppi grámmə tìzzəm/ *n.* —**ep·i·gram·ma·tist** /-grámmətist/ *n.*

ep·i·gram·mat·ic /èppigrə máttik/, **ep·i·gram·mat·i·cal** /-máttik'l/ *adj.* **1.** LIKE AN EPIGRAM containing or in the form of an epigram **2.** USING EPIGRAMS tending to use epigrams —**ep·i·gram·mat·i·cal·ly** *adv.*

ep·i·gram·ma·tize /èppi grámmə tīz/ (**-mat·ized, -mat·iz·ing, -mat·iz·es**) *vti.* to create a short and witty poem or saying about something

ep·i·graph /éppi gràf/ *n.* **1.** LITERAT INTRODUCTORY QUOTATION a quotation at the beginning of a book, chapter, or section of a book, usually related to its theme **2.** SCULPTURE, ARCHIT INSCRIPTION ON A MONUMENT an inscription on something, e.g., a statue or building [Late 16thC. From Greek *epigraphē,* from *epigraphein* "to write on," from *graphein* "to write."] —**ep·i·graph·ic** /èppi gráffik/ *adj.* —**ep·i·graph·i·cal** /-gráffik'l/ *adj.* —**ep·i·graph·i·cal·ly** *adv.*

e·pig·ra·phy /i píggrəfee/ *n.* **1.** INSCRIPTIONS inscriptions or introductory quotations as a whole **2.** STUDY OF INSCRIPTIONS the study and deciphering of ancient inscriptions —**e·pig·ra·pher** *n.* —**e·pig·ra·phist** *n.*

e·pig·y·nous /i píjjənəss/ *adj.* BOT used to describe a flower in which the sepals, petals, and stamens arise from the enlarged tip of the flower axis (**receptacle**) above the ovary [Mid-19thC. From modern Latin *epigynus,* from Greek *gunē* "woman" (used to mean "pistil").] —**e·pig·y·ny** *n.*

ep·i·la·tion /èppi láysh'n/ *n.* = **depilation** [Late 19thC. From French *épilation,* from *épiler* "to remove hair," from Latin *pilus* "hair."]

ep·i·lep·sy /éppi lèpsee/ (*plural* **-sies**) *n.* a medical disorder involving episodes of abnormal electrical discharge in the brain and characterized by periodic sudden loss or impairment of consciousness, often accompanied by convulsions [Mid-16thC. Via French *épilepsie* from, ultimately, Greek *epilēpsia,* literally "seizure," from *epilambanein* "to seize," from *lambanein* "to grasp."]

ep·i·lep·tic /èppi léptik/ *adj.* CONCERNING EPILEPSY relating to or affected by epilepsy ■ *n.* SOMEBODY WITH EPILEPSY somebody who has epilepsy (*offensive*) [Early 17thC. Via French *épileptique* from, ultimately, Greek *epilēptikos,* from *epilēpsia* (see EPILEPSY).] —**ep·i·lep·ti·cal·ly** *adv.*

ep·i·lep·ti·form /èppi lépti fàwrm/ *adj.* resembling epilepsy

ep·i·lep·to·gen·ic /èppi leptə jénnik/ *adj.* causing or able to cause an epileptic episode

ep·i·lep·toid /èppi lép tòyd/ *adj.* **1.** = **epileptiform 2.** SHOWING SYMPTOMS LIKE EPILEPSY showing symptoms similar to those of epilepsy

ep·i·lim·ni·on /èppi límnee òn, -límnee ən/ *n.* the uppermost circulating layer of warm water in a lake with different temperatures at different levels in summer [Early 20thC. Coined from EPI- + Greek *limnion,* literally "small lake," from *limnē* "lake."]

ep·i·logue /éppi lòg/, **ep·i·log** *n.* **1.** LITERAT SHORT SECTION AT THE END OF A BOOK a short chapter or section at the end of a literary work, sometimes detailing the fate of its characters **2.** THEATER CONCLUDING SPEECH a short speech, usually in verse, that an actor addresses directly to the audience at the end of a play **3.** THEATER ACTOR GIVING A SHORT SPEECH the actor who addresses a short speech, usually in verse, directly to the audience at the end of a play [15thC. Via French *épilogue* from, ultimately, Greek *epilogos,* literally "additional speech," from *logos* "speech."]

ep·i·mys·i·um /èppi mízee əm, -mízhee-/ (*plural* **-a** /-ə/) *n.* the covering of connective tissue surrounding a muscle [Early 20thC. From modern Latin, from Greek *mus* "muscle" (see MUSCLE).]

ep·i·nas·ty /éppi nàstee/ (*plural* **-ties**) *n.* the outward and downward bending of a plant part resulting from different growth rates on the upper and lower sides [Late 19thC. Coined from EPI- + Greek *nastos* "pressed together."] —**ep·i·nas·tic** /éppi nástik/ *adj.*

ep·i·neph·rine /éppi néffrin/, **ep·i·neph·rin** *n.* **1.** ADRENALINE the hormone adrenaline (*technical*) **2.** SYNTHETIC ADRENALINE a synthetic form of adrenaline that relaxes the airways and constricts blood vessels, used to treat asthma and to reduce blood loss. Formula: $C_9H_{13}NO_3$. [Late 19thC. Coined from EPI- + -INE + Greek *nephros* "kidney."]

ep·i·neu·ri·um /èppi nóoree əm/ (*plural* **-a** /-ə/) *n.* a sheath of connective tissue around a nerve [Late 19thC. From modern Latin, from Greek *neuron* "nerve."] —**ep·i·neu·ri·al** *adj.*

ep·i·pe·lag·ic /èppipə lájjik/ *adj.* relating to or living in the upper zone of the ocean, from the surface to a depth of about 200 m

Epiph. *abbr.* Epiphany

e·piph·a·ny /i píffənee/ (*plural* **-nies**) *n.* **1.** APPEARANCE OF A GOD the manifestation of a divine being **2.** SUDDEN REALIZATION a sudden intuitive leap of understanding, especially through an ordinary but striking occurrence ○ *It came to him in an epiphany what his life's work was to be.* [17thC. Via French *épiphanie* from, ultimately, Greek *epiphaneia* "manifestation," from *epiphanein* "to manifest," from *phanein* "to show."] —**ep·i·phan·ic** /èppi fánnik/ *adj.* —**e·piph·a·nous** /i píffənəss/ *adj.*

E·piph·a·ny *n.* CHR a Christian festival observed on January 6, celebrating the divine manifestation of Jesus Christ through the Three Wise Men's visit, or, in the Eastern Orthodox Church, the baptism of Jesus Christ

ep·i·phe·nom·e·nal·ism /èppifə nómmən'l ìzzəm/ *n.* the view that consciousness is merely an aftereffect of physical processes in the brain and nervous system —**ep·i·phe·nom·e·nal·ist** *n.*

ep·i·phe·nom·e·non /èppifə nómmə nòn/ (*plural* **-na** /-ənə/) *n.* **1.** SECONDARY PHENOMENON a secondary phenomenon resulting from another **2.** MED ADDITIONAL SYMPTOM a secondary incidental condition or symptom that appears during the course of an illness —**ep·i·phe·nom·e·nal** *adj.* —**ep·i·phe·nom·e·nal·ly** *adv.*

e·piph·y·sis /i píffississ/ (*plural* **-ses** /-seez/) *n.* **1.** END OF A LONG BONE the end of a long bone that fuses with the shaft of the bone at the point where it was previously separated by cartilage. This is to allow bone growth during development. Once the epiphyses fuse, no further growth of long bones is possible. **2.** PINEAL GLAND a pineal gland (*archaic*) [Mid-17thC. Via modern Latin from Greek *epiphusis*, literally "growing on," from *phusis* "growth."] —**ep·i·phys·e·al** /èppi fízzee əl/ *adj.*

ep·i·phyte /éppi fìt/ *n.* a plant that grows on top of or is supported by another plant but does not depend on it for nutrition. Mosses, tropical orchids, and many ferns are epiphytes. —**ep·i·phyt·ic** /èppi fíttik/ *adj.* —**ep·i·phyt·i·cal·ly** /-fíttikəlee/ *adv.*

ep·i·phy·tot·ic /èppi fì tóttik/ *adj.* RELATING TO EPIDEMIC OF PLANT DISEASE used to describe an outbreak of disease that rapidly affects many plants in a given area ■ *n.* SUDDEN PLANT DISEASE OUTBREAK a plant disease that suddenly and rapidly affects many plants in a given area

Epis. *abbr.* **1. Epis., Episc.** CHR Episcopal **2. Epis., Episc.** CHR Episcopalian **3.** BIBLE Epistle

e·pi·sci·a /i píshə, i píshee ə/ *n.* a tropical American plant with showy flowers and hairy leaves that is related to African violets. Genus: *Episcia.* [Mid-19thC. Via modern Latin from Greek *episkios* "shaded," literally "with shadow on," from *skia* "shadow."]

e·pis·co·pa·cy /i pískəpəsee/ (*plural* **-cies**) *n.* **1.** CHURCH GOVERNMENT BY BISHOPS church government by bishops, as in the Roman Catholic, Eastern and Episcopal Churches **2.** = **episcopate** *n.* 3 [Mid-17thC. Formed from ecclesiastical Latin *episcopatus* (see EPISCOPATE), modeled on PRELACY.]

e·pis·co·pal /i pískəpəl/ *adj.* **1.** OF BISHOPS relating to a bishop or bishops **2.** GOVERNED BY BISHOPS involving or recognizing church government by bishops [15thC. From French *épiscopal* or ecclesiastical Latin *episcopalis*, from *episcopus* (see BISHOP).] —**e·pis·co·pal·ly** *adv.*

E·pis·co·pal *adj.* relating to or being the Protestant Episcopal Church

E·pis·co·pal Church *n.* an independent branch of the Anglican Church in North America and Scotland

e·pis·co·pa·lian /i pìskə páylee ən/ *adj.* BELIEVING IN CHURCH GOVERNMENT BY BISHOPS adhering to or practicing church government by bishops ■ *n.* BELIEVER IN GOVERNMENT BY BISHOPS a supporter of church government by bishops —**e·pis·co·pa·lian·ism** *n.*

E·pis·co·pa·lian *adj.* BELONGING TO THE EPISCOPAL CHURCH relating to or belonging to the Episcopal Church ■ *n.* MEMBER OF THE EPISCOPAL CHURCH a member of the Episcopal Church of North America or Scotland —**E·pis·co·pal·ian·ism** *n.*

e·pis·co·pal·ism /i pískəpə lìzzəm/ *n.* the belief that authority in a church government should lie in a group of bishops

e·pis·co·pate /i pískəpət, i pískə pàyt/ *n.* **1.** OFFICE OR POSITION OF BISHOP the office, position, or term of office of a bishop **2.** DIOCESE a bishop's diocese or jurisdiction **3.** BISHOPS bishops as a group [Mid-17thC. From ecclesiastical Latin *episcopatus*, from *episcopus* (see BISHOP).]

e·pis·cope /éppi skōp/ *n.* a device for projecting an enlarged image of an opaque object such as a printed page or a photograph onto a screen using reflected light

e·pi·si·ot·o·my /i peezee óttəmee/ (*plural* **-mies**) *n.* an incision sometimes made to enlarge the vaginal opening in the late stages of labor to prevent tearing and facilitate the birth [Late 19thC. Coined from Greek *epision* "pubic region" + -TOMY.]

ep·i·sode /éppi sōd/ *n.* **1.** SIGNIFICANT INCIDENT an event that is a part of but distinct from a greater whole and that often has some kind of significance ○ *Let's try to put this unfortunate episode behind us, OK ?* **2.** LITERAT, TV, RADIO PART OF SERIALIZED WORK a part of a serialized work that is published or broadcast separately ○ *Find out what happens in next week's thrilling episode.* **3.** LITERAT EVENT IN A NARRATIVE an incident, description, or series of events in a narrative that is part of the whole but may digress from the main plot ○ *The episode in the library reveals a lot about the main character.* **4.** MED an occurrence of a particular illness or symptom of an illness, usually one of a connected series, often repeated over a period of time ○ *episodes of breathlessness and chest pain* **5.** THEATER SECTION OF GREEK TRAGEDY a section of an ancient Greek tragedy between two choruses **6.** MUSIC DIGRESSIVE MUSICAL PASSAGE a digressive passage between two musical themes, e.g., in a rondo or fugue [Late 17thC. From Greek *epeisodion* "addition," a form of *epeisodios* "coming in besides," from *eisodos* "coming in," from *hodos* "road."]

ep·i·sod·ic /èppi sóddik/, **ep·i·sod·i·cal** /-sóddik'l/ *adj.* **1.** OF AN EPISODE in the form of an episode, or resembling an episode in nature **2.** DIVIDED INTO EPISODES divided into or composed of closely connected but independent sections **3.** SPORADIC happening at irregular intervals ○ *episodic pain in the lower back* **4.** TEMPORARY of a limited duration ○ *episodic wind squalls* —**ep·i·sod·i·cal·ly** *adv.*

ep·i·some /éppi sōm/ *n.* a genetic unit that can multiply independently in host cells or when integrated with a chromosome. Bacterial plasmids are examples of episomes. [Mid-20thC. Coined from EPI- + Greek *sōma* "body."] —**ep·i·so·mal** /èppi sṓm'l/ *adj.* —**ep·i·so·mal·ly** *adv.*

Epist. *abbr.* BIBLE Epistle

e·pis·ta·sis /i pístəsiss/ (*plural* **-ses** /-seez/) *n.* the nonappearance of a characteristic determined by one gene because it has been suppressed or masked by the activity of another gene [Early 19thC. From Greek, literally "stoppage," from *ephistanai* "to stop," literally "to put on," from *histanai* "to put."] —**ep·i·stat·ic** /èppi státtik/ *adj.*

ep·i·stax·is /èppi stáksiss/ (*plural* **-stax·es** /-seez/) *n.* a bleeding from the nose (*technical*) [Late 18thC. Via modern Latin from Greek, where it was formed from *epistazein*, literally "to drip at (the nose)," from *stazein* "to drip."]

ep·i·ste·mic /èppi steemik, -stémmik/ *adj.* involving or relating to knowledge (*formal*) [Early 20thC. Formed from Greek *epistēmē* "knowledge," from *epistasthai* "to know," literally "to stand over," from *histasthai* "to stand."] —**ep·i·ste·mi·cal·ly** *adv.*

ep·i·ste·mics /èppi steemiks, -stémmiks/ *n. U.K.* the use of logic, philosophy, psychology, and linguistics to study knowledge and how it is processed by humans (*takes a singular verb*)

e·pis·te·mol·o·gy /i pìstə mólləjee/ *n.* the branch of philosophy that studies the nature of knowledge, in particular its foundations, scope, and validity [Mid-19thC. Coined from Greek *epistēmē* (see EPISTEMIC) + -OLOGY.] —**e·pis·te·mo·log·i·cal** /i pìstəmə lójjik'l/ *adj.* —**e·pis·te·mo·log·i·cal·ly** /-lójjikəlee/ *adv.* —**e·pis·te·mol·o·gist** /i pìstə mólləjist/ *n.*

e·pis·tle /i píss'l/ *n.* **1.** LETTER a long formal letter that often serves to instruct (*formal*) **2.** LITERAT BOOK IN LETTER FORM a literary work in the form of a letter [12thC. Directly or via Old French from Latin *epistola*, from Greek *epistolē*, literally "something sent," from *stellein* "to send."]

E·pis·tle *n.* **1.** BIBLE LETTER FROM THE APOSTLE PAUL OR OTHERS any of the letters written by the apostle Paul or other early Christian writers and included as books of the Bible **2.** CHR EXCERPT FROM EPISTLE an excerpt from one of the Epistles read as part of the service in a Christian church

e·pis·tle side, E·pis·tle Side *n.* the right side of a Christian church, as you face the altar [So called because it is the side from which an extract from one of the Epistles is traditionally read as part of the Communion service]

e·pis·to·lar·y /i pístə lèrree/, **e·pis·to·la·to·ry** /i pístələ tàwree/ *adj.* **1.** ASSOCIATED WITH CORRESPONDENCE BY LETTER associated with, conducted by, or suitable for letters (*formal*) **2.** LITERAT IN THE FORM OF A LETTER OR LETTERS taking the form of a letter or a series of letters [Mid-17thC. *Epistolary* directly or via French *épistolaire* from Latin *epistolaris*, from *epistola* (see EPISTLE).]

e·pis·tro·phe /i pístrəfee/ *n.* repetition of a word, phrase, or other expression at the end of consecutive clauses or sentences for rhetorical effect, as occurs in the expression "of the people, by the people, for the people" [Late 16thC. From Greek, from *epistrephein* "to turn around," from *strephein* "to turn."]

ep·i·style /éppi stìl/ *n.* ARCHIT = **architrave** [Mid-16thC. Directly or via French *épistyle* from Latin *epistylium*, from Greek *epistulion*, literally "on a column," from *stulos* "column."]

ep·i·taph /éppi tàf/ *n.* LITERAT **1.** INSCRIPTION ON A TOMBSTONE an inscription on a tombstone or monument commemorating the person buried there **2.** SPEECH OR WRITING COMMEMORATING A DEAD PERSON a short speech or piece of writing celebrating the life of a recently deceased person [14thC. Via French *épitaphe* from, ultimately, Greek *epitaphion* "something above a tomb or burial," from *taphos* "funeral ceremonies, tomb."]

e·pit·a·sis /i píttəsiss/ (*plural* **-ses** /-seez/) *n.* in classical drama, the middle part of a play that develops the main action [Late 16thC. Via modern Latin from Greek, where it was formed from *epiteinein* "to intensify, stretch upon," from *teinein* "to stretch."]

ep·i·tax·y /éppi tàksee/ *n.* growth of a layer of crystal on a single crystal of another substance [Mid-20thC. From French *épitaxie*, literally "growth on," from Greek *taxis* "growth."] —**ep·i·tax·i·al** /èppi táksee əl/ *adj.*

ep·i·tha·la·mi·um /èppithə laymee əm/ (*plural* **-a** /-ə/), **ep·i·tha·la·mi·on** /èppithə láymee ən, -òn/ (*plural* **-a**) *n.* a poem or song written or performed in celebration of a wedding [Late 16thC. From, ultimately, Greek *epithalamion*, literally "(song sung) at the bridal chamber," a form of *epithalamios*, literally "at the bridal chamber," from *thalamos* "bridal chamber."] —**ep·i·tha·la·mic** /èppithə lámmik/ *adj.*

ep·i·the·li·a plural of **epithelium**

ep·i·the·li·al /èppi theelee əl/ *adj.* used to describe tissue that forms a thin protective layer on exposed bodily surfaces and forms the lining of internal cavities, ducts, and organs

ep·i·the·li·al·i·za·tion /èppi theelee əli záysh'n/ *n.* the covering of a surface by the development of epithelial tissue, as in the healing of a wound

ep·i·the·li·al·ize /èppi theelee ə lìz/ (**-ized, -iz·ing, -iz·es**), **ep·i·thel·ize** /èppi thee lìz/ (**-ized, -iz·ing, -iz·es**) *vti.* to become or cause to become covered with epithelial tissue, as in the healing of a wound

ep·i·the·li·um /èppi theelee əm/ (*plural* **-a** /-ə/ *or* **-ums**) *n.* a thin layer of tightly packed cells lining internal cavities, ducts, and organs of animals and covering exposed bodily surfaces, especially in healing wounds [Mid-18thC. From modern Latin, where it was formed from Greek *thēlē* "teat, nipple"; from its originally being applied to tissue with a nipple-like surface.]

ep·i·the·lize *vti.* = **epithelialize** —**ep·i·the·li·za·tion** /èppi theeli záysh'n/ *n.*

ep·i·ther·mal /èppi thúrm'l/ *adj.* used to describe veins of gold or silver originally formed deep within the Earth's crust from ascending hot solutions

ep·i·thet /éppi thèt/ *n.* **1.** LANG **OFFENSIVE TERM** an abusive insulting word or phrase **2.** LING **DESCRIPTIVE WORD ADDED TO SOMEBODY'S NAME** a descriptive word or phrase added to or substituted for the name of a person or thing, highlighting a characteristic feature or quality ○ *easy to see how she earned herself the epithet "The All-Knowing"* **3.** BIOL **PART OF A TAXONOMIC NAME** in biological classification, the specific name that follows the generic name, e.g., "sapiens" in "Homo sapiens" [Late 16thC. Directly or via French *épithète* from Latin *epitheton* "something added," from Greek *epitheto*, past participle of *epitithenai* "to put on," from *tithenai* "to place."] —**ep·i·thet·ic** /èppi théttik/ *adj.* —**ep·i·thet·i·cal** /-théttik'l/ *adj.*

e·pit·o·me /i píttəmee/ *n.* **1. TYPICAL EXAMPLE** a highly representative example of a type, class, or characteristic ○ *Isn't she just the epitome of elegance?* **2.** LITERAT **SUMMARY OF A WRITTEN WORK** a brief summary of a piece of written work (*formal*) [Early 16thC. Via Latin from Greek, from *epitemnein* "to cut short," from *temnein* "to cut."]

e·pit·o·mize /i píttə mīz/ (**-om·ized, -om·iz·ing, -om·iz·es**) *vt.* **1. EXEMPLIFY** to be a highly representative example of something ○ *This incident epitomizes all that is wrong with modern society.* **2.** LITERAT **SUMMARIZE** to write a brief summary of a piece of writing (*formal*) —**e·pit·o·mi·za·tion** /i pìttəmi záysh'n/ *n.* —**e·pit·o·mist** /-mist/ *n.*

ep·i·zo·ic /èppi zṓ ik/ *adj.* **1.** BIOL **LIVING ON THE EXTERIOR OF ANIMAL** used to describe a nonparasitic animal or plant that lives on the external surface of a living animal **2.** BOT **DISPERSED BY ANIMALS** used to describe plants whose seeds or spores are dispersed by being attached to the coats of animals —**ep·i·zo·ism** *n.*

ep·i·zo·on /èppi zṓ òn/ (*plural* **-a** /-ə/), **ep·i·zo·ite** /-zṓ īt/ *n.* an organism that lives on the external surface of a living animal [Mid-19thC. From modern Latin, literally "on an animal," from Greek *zōion* "animal."] —**ep·i·zo·an** *adj.*

ep·i·zo·ot·ic /èppi zō óttik/ *adj.* **RELATING TO AN EPIDEMIC OF ANIMAL DISEASE** used to describe an outbreak of disease that rapidly affects many animals in a given area at the same time ■ *n.* **DISEASE SIMULTANEOUSLY AFFECTING MANY ANIMALS** a disease that rapidly affects a large number of animals in a given area at the same time [Late 18thC. From French *épizootique*, literally "at animals," ultimately from Greek *zōion* "animal."] —**ep·i·zo·ot·i·cal·ly** *adv.*

e plu·ri·bus u·num /i plòori booss óonəm, -yóonəm/ one out of many (*used as the motto of the United States*) [Latin]

EPNS *abbr.* electroplated nickel silver

ep·och /éppək, ée pòk/ *n.* **1.** HISTORY, TIME **SIGNIFICANT PERIOD** a significant period in history or in somebody's life ○ *The invention of the telephone marked an epoch in the development of international communication.* **2. START OF A HISTORICALLY SIGNIFICANT PERIOD** the beginning of a long period of history considered particularly significant ○ *His accession to the throne marked the beginning of a new epoch.* **3.** GEOL **UNIT OF GEOLOGIC TIME** a unit of geologic time that is a division of a period and is characterized by rock formation ○ *the Holocene and Pleistocene epochs of the Quaternary period* **4.** ASTRON **MOMENT IN TIME AS A REFERENCE POINT** a precise moment in time arbitrarily chosen as a reference point for defining the position of celestial bodies [Early 17thC. Via modern Latin *epocha* from Greek *epokhē* "pause (in time)," literally "holding back," from, ultimately, *ekhein* "to hold."]

ep·och·al /éppək'l, é pòk'l/ *adj.* **1. VERY SIGNIFICANT** highly significant or momentous ○ *Her resignation had an epochal impact on the company.* **2. CHARACTERISTIC OF AN EPOCH** characteristic of or relating to a long period of history considered particularly significant (*formal*)

ep·och-mak·ing *adj.* having great importance or momentous significance ○ *Galileo's epoch-making discoveries*

ep·ode /é pṑd/ *n.* **1.** THEATER **PART OF A LYRIC ODE** the part of a lyric ode in classical Greek drama that follows the strophe and the antistrophe **2.** POETRY **TYPE OF LYRIC ODE** a type of lyric ode characterized by couplets made up of a long line followed by a shorter one [Early 17thC. Directly or via French *épode* from Latin *epodos*, from Greek *epōidos* "sung after," from *ōidē* "song."]

ep·o·nym /éppə nìm/ *n.* **1. PERSON FOR WHOM SOMETHING IS NAMED** the name of a person or mythical character from which another name or term is derived **2.** MED **MEDICAL NAME FROM A PERSON** a medical name, e.g., of a disease, coming from the name of a person **3.** LANGUAGE **NAME DERIVED FROM A PERSON** a name derived from the name of a person or mythical character. For example, "Rome" is an eponym coming from "Romulus." [Mid-19thC. From Greek *epōnumos* "given as a name," literally "name on," from *onuma* "name."] —**ep·o·nym·ic** /èppə nímmik/ *adj.*

e·pon·y·mous /i pónnəməss/ *adj.* having the name that is used as the title or name of something else, especially the title of a book, play, or film ○ *the eponymous hero* —**e·pon·y·mous·ly** *adv.*

EPOS /ée pòss/ *abbr.* electronic point of sale

ep·ox·ide /e pók sīd, i-/ *n.* a chemical compound containing a three-membered ring consisting of an oxygen atom bonded to each of two carbon atoms [Mid-20thC. Coined from EPI- + OXIDE.]

ep·ox·y /e póksee, i-/ *adj.* **RELATING TO EPOXIDE** relating to an epoxide or epoxy resin ■ *n.* (*plural* **-ies**) = **epoxy resin** ■ *vt.* (**-ied, -y·ing, -ies**) **STICK WITH EPOXY RESIN** to stick one thing to another using epoxy resin [Mid-20thC. Coined from EPI- + OXY-.]

ep·ox·y res·in, **ep·ox·ide res·in** *n.* a tough synthetic resin that sets after the application of heat or pressure, contains epoxy groups, and is used in adhesives and surface coatings

EPROM /ée pròm/ *n.* an integrated circuit that can be programmed by a manufacturer and subsequently erased and reprogrammed by a user to correct an error in the original program or to add a function. Full form **erasable-programmable read-only memory**

eps *abbr.* earnings per share

ep·si·lon /épsilòn, -lən/ *n.* the fifth letter of the Greek alphabet, represented in the English alphabet as "e." See table at **alphabet** [Early 18thC. From Greek *e psilon* "short e" (literally "bare e").]

Ep·som /épsəm/ town in Surrey, southeastern England. There is a racecourse on Epsom Downs, where the Derby horse race is run. Population: 69,200 (1995).

Ep·som salts *n.* a bitter-tasting medicinal preparation of hydrated magnesium sulfate formerly widely used as a purgative or to help reduce swelling. Formula: $MgSO_4.7H_2O$. (*takes a singular verb*) [Mid-18thC. Named for EPSOM, southern England: the salts were originally obtained from the water of a mineral spring there.]

Ep·stein /ép stīn/, **Sir Jacob** (1880–1959) U.S.-born British sculptor. His massively powerful, usually nude figures, including *Genesis* (1930), caused an uproar. His later portrait bronzes and monumental works were more immediately popular and less controversial.

Ep·stein-Barr vi·rus /épstīn baar-/ *n.* a virus believed to cause infectious mononucleosis and associated with Burkitt's lymphoma and some carcinomas [Mid-20thC. Named for the British virologists M.A. *Epstein* (born 1921) and Y.M. *Barr* (born 1932), who discovered it.]

eq. *abbr.* **1.** equal **2.** equation **3.** equivalent

E.Q. *n.* the ratio of educational attainment to chronological age. Full form **educational quotient**

eq·ua·ble /ékwəb'l, éekwəb'l/ *adj.* **1. CALM** calm and not easily disturbed ○ *She maintained the most equable of temperaments despite her financial problems.* **2. NOT EXTREME** free from variation and marked extremes [Mid-16thC. From Latin *aequabilis*, from *aequare* (see EQUATE).] —**eq·ua·bil·i·ty** /èkwə bíllətee, èekwə-/ *n.* —**eq·ua·ble·ness** /ékwəb'lnəss, éekwə-/ *n.* —**eq·ua·bly** /ékwəblee, éekwə-/ *adv.*

e·qual /éekwəl/ *adj.* **1. IDENTICAL** identical in size, quantity, value, or standard ○ *equal quantities of flour and sugar* **2. WITH THE SAME RIGHTS** having the same privileges, rights, status, and opportunities as others ○ *with all citizens equal under the law* **3. WITH AN EVEN BALANCE** evenly balanced between opposing sides ○ *hoping for a more equal match in the second game* **4. EQUIPPED WITH THE NECESSARY QUALITIES** equipped with the necessary qualities or means to accomplish something (*formal*) ○ *didn't think he would be equal to the task* **5. TREATING IMPARTIALLY** treating or affecting all things impartially ○ *marked all the students' papers with an equal pen* **6. EQUIVALENT** having the same effect, value, or meaning as another ■ *n.* **SOMEBODY OR SOMETHING EQUAL** somebody or something equal in quality to another ○ *The computers are equals in speed and this one costs less.* ■ *v.* (**e·qualed, e·qual·ing, e·quals**) **1.** *vt.* MATH **HAVE SAME VALUE AS** to be equal to, usually in value ○ *Two plus two equals four.* **2.** *vt.* **DO SOMETHING EQUAL TO SOMETHING ELSE** to do, produce, or achieve something to the same standard or of the same value as something else ○ *And with that jump, she has equaled the world record.* **3.** *vi.* **BECOME EQUAL** to become identical or the same ○ *It will all equal out in the end.* [14thC. From Latin *aequalis*, from *aequus* (see EQUATE).] ◇ **first among equals** the most powerful or influential person in a group whose members are supposed to have equal status

e·qual-ar·e·a *adj.* on a map projection, accurately representing the relative sizes of regions that are of equal area, although distorting shape and direction

e·qual·i·tar·i·an /i kwòlli táiree ən/ *n., adj.* = **egalitarian** —**e·qual·i·tar·i·an·ism** *n.*

e·qual·i·ty /i kwóllitee, ee-/ (*plural* **-ties**) *n.* **1. STATE OF BEING EQUAL** rights, treatment, quantity, or value equal to all others in a given group ○ *full equality under the law* **2.** MATH **EQUATION WITH EQUAL QUANTITIES** an equation in which the quantities on either side of an equal sign are the same

E·qual·i·ty State *n.* the state of Wyoming (*informal*)

e·qual·ize /éekwə līz/ (**-ized, -iz·ing, -iz·es**) *v.* **1.** *vt.* **MAKE EQUAL** to make things uniform or equal ○ *You must equalize the liquid levels in each bottle.* **2.** *vt.* ELECTRON ENG **ADJUST AN ELECTRONIC SIGNAL** to adjust the amplitude of an electronic signal **3.** *vi.* *U.K.* SPORTS **ACHIEVE SAME SCORE** to score a point or goal that brings a score level with that of an opponent ○ *They equalized just before halftime.* —**e·qual·i·za·tion** /èekwəli záysh'n/ *n.*

e·qual·iz·er /éekwə līzər/ *n.* **1. SOMEBODY OR SOMETHING THAT EQUALIZES** somebody or something that makes things uniform or equal **2.** ELECTRON ENG **ELECTRONIC SOUND ADJUSTER** an electronic device used to reduce distortion in a sound system by internally adjusting the system's response to different audio frequencies **3.** *U.K.* SPORTS **GOAL OR POINT THAT LEVELS SCORES** a goal or point that brings a person or team's score level with that of an opponent **4.** ARMS **WEAPON** a dangerous weapon, e.g., a knife or gun (*slang*)

e·qual·ly /éekwəlee/ *adv.* **1. IN SAME WAY** in an identical or uniform way ○ *treat people equally* **2. TO SAME EXTENT** to the same degree or extent ○ *This issue is equally important.* See Usage note below. **3. IN SAME SIZED AMOUNTS** in parts or amounts of the same size ○ *Divide it equally between four people.* **4. AT THE SAME TIME** used to introduce a second statement that is of equal importance to the first but may contrast or balance it ○ *I want the business to succeed, but equally, I don't want to be working all the time.*

WORD KEY: USAGE

equally or **as?** You can say *She is a brilliant pianist, and her brother is equally talented* or *She is a brilliant pianist, and her brother is as talented*, but not *She is a brilliant pianist, and her brother is equally as talented.*

e·qual op·por·tu·ni·ty *n.* the availability of the same rights, position, and status to all people, regardless of gender, sexual preference, age, race, ethnicity, or religion ○ *the implementation of a more comprehensive equal opportunity policy*

e·qual sign *n.* a mathematical symbol (=) used to indicate that two or more numbers, symbols, or terms have the same value as each other

e·qual tem·per·a·ment *n.* MUSIC the division of a musical octave into 12 equal half steps in the tuning of an instrument

e·qual time *n.* a broadcasting policy that gives opposing political candidates equal air time for radio and television campaigning

e·qua·nim·i·ty /éekwə nímmitee, èkwə-/ *n.* evenness of temper even under stress (*formal*) ○ *faced his critical constituents with equanimity* [Early 17thC. From Latin *aequanimitas*, from *aequus* "even" (see EQUATE) + *animus* "mind" (source of English *magnanimous*).] —**e·quan·i·mous** /i kwánnəməss/ *adj.*

e·quate /i kwáyt/ (**e·quat·ed, e·quat·ing, e·quates**) *v.* **1.** *vt.* CONSIDER AS EQUIVALENT to treat, show, or consider something as equivalent to something else ○ *equating money with happiness* **2.** *vt.* REDUCE SOMETHING TO THE SAME LEVEL to reduce something to the same level or value as something else **3.** *vt.* MATH FORM AN EQUATION to form an equation involving an equality **4.** *vi.* APPEAR TO BE EQUAL to be or appear to be the same (*formal*) ○ *Their two accounts of the incident seem to equate.* [15thC. From Latin *aequat-*, the past participle stem of *aequare* "to make equal," from *aequus* "equal, even" (source of English *egalitarian, adequate,* and *iniquity*).] —**e·qua·ta·bil·i·ty** /i kwàytə bíllətee/ *n.* —**e·qua·ta·ble** /i kwáytəb'l/ *adj.*

e·qua·tion /i kwáyzh'n, i kwáysh'n/ *n.* **1.** MATH STATEMENT OF EQUALITY a mathematical statement that two expressions, usually divided by an equal sign, are of the same value **2.** ACT OF REGARDING AS EQUAL the act or process of making things equal or considering them to be equal **3.** STATE OF BEING EQUAL the state of being the same or equivalent ○ *bring the balance of power into equation* **4.** SITUATION INVOLVING MANY VARIABLE FACTORS a situation that has two or more variable elements to be considered ○ *The selling option just does not enter into the equation.* **5.** CHEM REPRESENTATION OF A CHEMICAL REACTION a written representation of the reactants and products in a chemical reaction —**e·qua·tion·al** *adj.* —**e·qua·tion·al·ly** *adv.*

e·qua·tion of state *n.* CHEM an equation that states the relationship between the pressure, temperature, and volume of a gas or liquid

e·qua·tion of time *n.* the difference between apparent solar time and mean solar time, usually expressed as a correction to the apparent time, and varying in a complex annual pattern between maxima of about fifteen minutes in February and November

e·qua·tor /i kwáytər/ *n.* **1.** GEOG IMAGINARY CIRCLE AROUND EARTH the imaginary great circle around the Earth that is the same distance from the North and South Poles and divides the Earth into the northern and southern hemispheres **2.** ASTRON IMAGINARY CIRCLE AROUND A CELESTIAL BODY the imaginary great circle around a celestial body that is everywhere the same distance from the poles **3.** GEOM CIRCLE DIVIDING A SPHERE INTO TWO a circle that divides a sphere or other surface into two equal parts **4.** ASTRON = **celestial equator** [14thC. Directly or via French *équator* from medieval Latin *aequator*, in the phrase *aequator diei et noctis* "equalizer of day and night," from *aequare* (see EQUATE).]

e·qua·to·ri·al /èekwə táwree əl, èkwə-/ *adj.* **1.** OF EQUATOR relating to or present near the equator **2.** IN EQUATOR'S PLANE situated in the plane of an equator —**e·qua·to·ri·al·ly** /èekwə táwree -əlee/ *adv.*

e·qua·to·ri·al cur·rent *n.* a current that moves in a westerly direction near the surface of an ocean at the equator

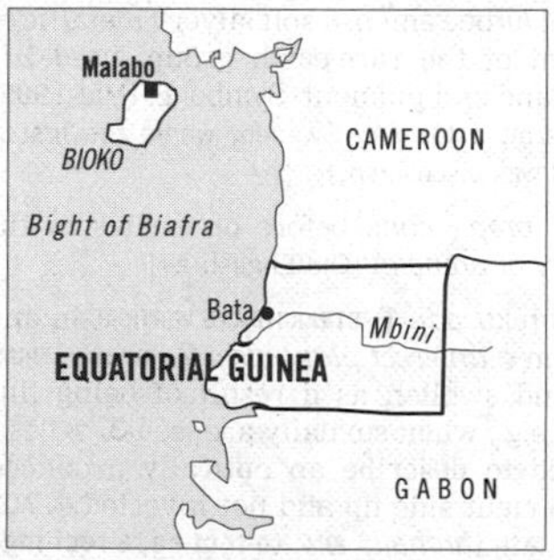

Equatorial Guinea

E·qua·to·ri·al Guin·ea /èekwə táwree əl/ independent republic in western Africa comprising a mainland section, Río Muni, and several islands. Language: Spanish. Currency: CFA franc. Capital: Malabo. Population: 442,516 (1997). Area: 10,831 sq. mi./28,051 sq. km. Official name **Republic of Equatorial Guinea**

e·qua·to·ri·al plate *n.* the plane midway between the poles of the spindle of a dividing cell, where chromosomes are aligned

e·qua·to·ri·al tel·e·scope *n.* an astronomical telescope mounted so that it allows a celestial body to be kept in view without adjustment as the Earth rotates. This is accomplished by mounting it on two axes at right angles to each other, the one about which it rotates being parallel to the Earth's axis.

eq·uer·ry /ékwəree/ (*plural* **-ries**) *n.* **1.** MIL PERSONAL ATTENDANT OF BRITISH SOVEREIGN an officer who is the personal attendant of the British monarch or a member of the royal family **2.** MIL, EQU OFFICER RESPONSIBLE FOR ROYAL HORSES in the past, an officer in an aristocratic or royal household who was responsible for the supervision of the horses [Early 16thC. Via obsolete French *escurie* (source of French *écurie* "stable") from Old French *esquierie* "company of squires, prince's stables," from *esquier* "squire" (see ESQUIRE), perhaps influenced by Latin *equus* "horse."]

e·ques·tri·an /i kwéstree ən/ *adj.* **1.** OF HORSES relating to horses or horseback riding **2.** DEPICTING SOMEBODY ON HORSEBACK depicting somebody mounted on a horse ○ *an equestrian statue* **3.** OF MOUNTED SOLDIERS composed of soldiers on horseback ■ *n.* SKILLED RIDER somebody who is skilled at riding horses or performing on horseback [Mid-17thC. Formed from Latin *equester* "belonging to a horseman," from *eques* "horseman, knight," from *equus* "horse."] —**e·ques·tri·an·ism** *n.*

e·ques·tri·enne /i kwèstree én/ *n.* a woman who is skilled at riding horses or performing on horseback [Mid-19thC. Formed from EQUESTRIAN on the model of French feminine nouns ending in *-enne*.]

equi- *prefix.* equal ○ *equimolar* [From Latin *aequus* (source of English *equal*)]

e·qui·an·gu·lar /èekwee áng gyələr, èkwee-/ *adj.* used to describe a geometric figure in which all the angles are equal [Mid-17thC. Formed from late Latin *equiangulus*, from Latin *angulus* "corner" (see ANGLE).]

e·qui·dis·tant /èekwi dístənt, èkwi-/ *adj.* situated at the same distance from two or more places or points ○ *Baltimore is almost equidistant from Washington and Philadelphia.* [Late 16thC. From French *équidistant* or the medieval Latin stem *equidistant-*, from the Latin stem *distant-* (see DISTANT).] —**e·qui·dis·tance** *n.* —**e·qui·dis·tant·ly** *adv.*

e·qui·lat·er·al /èekwə láttərəl, èkwə-/ *adj.* WITH EQUAL SIDES used to describe a geometric figure in which all the sides are of equal length ■ *n.* **1.** EQUILATERAL FIGURE a geometric figure with all of its sides of equal length **2.** SIDE OF AN EQUILATERAL FIGURE any side of a geometric figure that is the same length as the other sides [Late 16thC. Directly or via French *équilateral* from late Latin *aequilateralis*, from Latin *lateralis* (see LATERAL).] —**e·qui·lat·er·al·ly** *adv.*

e·quil·i·brant /i kwíllibrənt/ *n.* a force able to balance out another force and produce an equilibrium [Late 19thC. Via French *équilibrant* from, ultimately, *équilibre* "balance," from Latin *aequilibrium* (see EQUILIBRIUM).]

e·quil·i·brate /i kwíllə bràyt/ (**-brat·ed, -brat·ing, -brates**) *vti.* to be evenly balanced, or counterbalance something, or bring something into a state of balance [Mid-17thC. From late Latin *aequilibrare*, from *libra* (see EQUILIBRIUM).] —**e·quil·i·bra·tion** /i kwìlli bráysh'n/ *n.* —**e·quil·i·bra·tor** /i kwílli bràytər/ *n.* —**e·quil·i·bra·to·ry** /i kwìllibrə táwree/ *adj.*

e·quil·i·brist /i kwíllibrist/ *n.* a performer skilled in the art of balancing, especially tightrope walking (*dated or formal*)

e·qui·lib·ri·um /èekwə líbbree əm, èkwə-/ (*plural* **-ums** *or* **-a** /-ə/) *n.* **1.** BODILY BALANCE a physical state or sense of being able to maintain bodily balance **2.** EMOTIONAL STABILITY a mental state of calmness and composure **3.** SITUATION OF BALANCE a state or situation in which opposing forces or factors balance each other out and stability is attained **4.** PHYS, CHEM BALANCE BETWEEN FORCES a static or dynamic state in which all forces or processes are in balance and there is no resultant change [Early 17thC. From Latin *aequilibrium* "equal balance," from *libra* "balance" (source of English *deliberate*, and of the abbreviation *lb.* and the symbol *£*.)]

e·qui·mo·lar /èekwə mṓlər, èkwə-/ *adj.* CHEM with an equal concentration of moles in one liter of solution

e·qui·mo·lec·u·lar /èekwəmə lékyələr, èkwəmə-/ *adj.* CHEM used to describe a substance or mixture that has the same number of molecules as another

e·quine /ée kwìn, é-/ *adj.* **1.** ZOOL OF HORSES relating to, belonging to, or affecting horses **2.** RESEMBLING A HORSE characteristic of or similar to a horse in appearance or behavior **3.** ZOOL BELONGING TO THE HORSE FAMILY belonging to or characteristic of the family of mammals that includes horses, zebras, and donkeys ■ *n.* ZOOL HORSE OR THEIR RELATIVES a horse or other member of the horse family [Late 18thC. From Latin *equinus*, from *equus* "horse."]

e·qui·noc·tial /èekwə nókshəl, èkwə-/ *adj.* **1.** TIME OCCURRING AT AN EQUINOX happening at or near either of the two equinoxes **2.** BOT WITH FLOWERS OPEN AT DEFINITE TIMES used to describe a plant whose flowers open and close at specific times of day **3.** ASTRON OF THE CELESTIAL EQUATOR relating to the celestial equator ■ *n.* **1.** METEOROL STORM AT AN EQUINOX a storm or strong wind that occurs at a time when day and night are the same length (**equinox**) **2.** ASTRON = **celestial equator** [14thC. From French *équinoctial*, from, ultimately, Latin *aequinoctium* (see EQUINOX).]

e·qui·noc·tial cir·cle *n.* ASTRON = **celestial equator**

e·qui·noc·tial point *n.* either of the two points on the celestial sphere where the Sun crosses the celestial equator. The points are called respectively the First Point of Aries and the First Point of Libra.

e·qui·noc·tial year *n.* = **solar year**

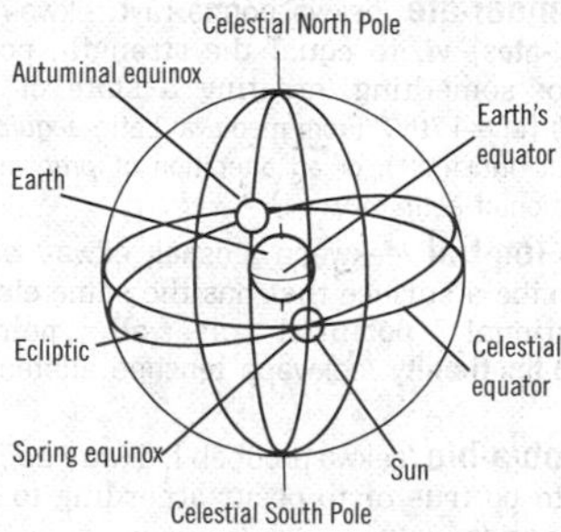

Equinox: Diagram showing positions of Sun and Earth at spring and autumnal equinoxes

e·qui·nox /éekwə nòks, ékwə-/ *n.* **1.** TIME OF EQUAL DAY AND NIGHT either of the two annual crossings of the equator by the Sun, once in each direction, when the length of day and night are approximately equal everywhere on Earth. The equinoxes occur around March 21 and September 23. **2.** = **equinoctial point** [14thC. Directly or via French *équinoxe* from Latin *aequinoctium*, literally "equal night," from *nox* "night."]

e·quip /i kwíp/ (**e·quipped, e·quip·ping, e·quips**) *vt.* **1.** PROVIDE WITH NECESSITIES to provide somebody or something with what is needed for a particular activity or purpose, e.g., with the appropriate tools, supplies, parts, or clothing ○ *a computer equipped with a modem and a CD-ROM drive* **2.** PREPARE TO ACCOMPLISH SOMETHING to prepare somebody with the necessary education, training, or experience to succeed at a task or role in life (*often passive*) ○ *I'm sorry, but I don't feel equipped to answer that question.* **3.** DRESS UP to dress yourself or another person in clothes suitable for a particular occasion, task, or environment ○ *The children were equipped with wool hats, scarves, and mittens for playing in the snow.* [Early 16thC. From French *équiper*, probably formed from Old Norse *skipa* "to fit out a ship," from *skip* "ship."] —**e·quip·per** *n.*

equip. *abbr.* equipment

eq·ui·page /ékwəpij/ *n.* **1.** TRANSP, EQU WELL-EQUIPPED CARRIAGE a horse-drawn carriage, especially a luxurious one, or a carriage together its with horses and attendants **2.** EQUIPMENT AND SUPPLIES FOR EXPEDITIONS the necessary equipment and supplies for an undertaking, especially a military expedition or ship's journey [Mid-16thC. Originally denoting the crew, later the equipping of a ship, hence the equipment provided.]

e·qui·par·ti·tion /èekwə paar tísh'n, èkwə-/ *n.* the equal distribution of energy among the components of motion, such as linear movement and rotation, of the gas molecules in a system

e·quip·ment /i kwípmənt/ *n.* **1.** NECESSARY ITEMS the tools, clothing, or other items needed for a particular purpose or activity ○ *camping equipment* **2.** PERSONAL RESOURCES FOR SUCCESS the intellectual and emotional resources that enable a person to succeed at a task or role in life **3.** PROVIDING SOMEBODY WITH EQUIPMENT the equipping of somebody or something with what is necessary for a particular purpose or activity **4.** TRANSP TRANSPORTATION VEHICLES the rolling stock necessary to carry passengers or goods

e·qui·poise /éekwə pòyz, ékwə-/ *n.* (*formal*) **1. BALANCED STATE** a condition where weights are in balance or there is a balance between different social, emotional, or intellectual influences **2. SOMETHING CAUSING BALANCE** something that creates a balanced state, usually by counterbalancing some other force or thing ■ *vt.* (**-poised, -pois·ing, -pois·es**) **COUNTERBALANCE** to counterbalance a weight or influence (*formal*)

e·qui·pol·lent /éekwə póllənt, èkwə-/ *adj.* having the same weight, influence, validity, or effect as another, or as each other (*formal*) [14thC. From Old French *equipolent,* from, ultimately, Latin *pollere* "to be strong."] —**e·qui·pol·lence** *n.* —**e·qui·pol·len·cy** *n.* —**e·qui·pol·lent·ly** *adv.*

e·qui·pon·der·ant /éekwə póndərənt, èkwə-/ *adj.* equal, or evenly balanced, in weight, influence, or effect (*formal*) [Mid-17thC. From medieval Latin *aequiponderant-,* the present participle stem of *aequiponderare* "to weigh the same," from *ponderare* "to weigh" (source of English *ponder*).] —**e·qui·pon·der·ance** *n.* —**e·qui·pon·der·an·cy** *n.*

e·qui·pon·der·ate /éekwə póndə ràyt, èkwə-/ (**-at·ed, -at·ing, -ates**) *vt.* to equal the strength, power, or effect of something, creating a state of balance (*formal*) [Mid-17thC. From medieval Latin *aequiponderare* (see EQUIPONDERANT), or an alteration of *preponderate* by substitution of *equi-* for *pre-*.]

e·qui·po·ten·tial /éekwəpə ténshəl, èkwə-/ *adj.* used to describe a surface that has the same electric or gravitational potential at all points —**e·qui·po·ten·ti·al·i·ty** /éekwəpə tenshee állətee, èkwə-/ *n.*

e·qui·prob·a·ble /éekwə próbbəb'l, èkwə-/ *adj.* equally likely to be true or to occur according to logic or mathematics

eq·ui·ta·ble /ékwitəb'l/ *adj.* **1. FAIR** characterized by justice or fairness and impartiality toward those involved (*formal*) **2.** LAW **RELATING TO THE LAW OF EQUITY** applicable under the law of equity as distinguished from common or statute law [Mid-16thC. From French *équitable,* from *équité* (see EQUITY).] —**eq·ui·ta·ble·ness** *n.* —**eq·ui·ta·bly** *adv.*

eq·ui·ta·tion /èkwi táysh'n/ *n.* the skill and theory of riding horses (*formal*) [Mid-16thC. Directly or via French *équitation* from the Latin stem *equitation-,* from *equitare* "to ride on horseback," from, ultimately, *equus* "horse."]

eq·ui·tes /ékwi tàyss, -tàyz/ *npl.* **1. ANCIENT ROMAN CAVALRY** the cavalry of ancient Rome **2. PRIVILEGED ROMANS** the privileged class of ancient Romans, ranking just below the senators, whose members served as cavalry [Early 17thC. From Latin, plural of *eques* "horse-rider," from *equus* "horse."]

eq·ui·ty /ékwitee/ *n.* (*plural* **-ties**) **1. FAIRNESS** actions, treatment of others, or a general condition characterized by justice, fairness, and impartiality **2.** LAW **MODIFICATION OF COMMON LAW** the system of jurisprudence that supplements common and statutory law, when those bodies of law are inadequate in the attainment of justice **3.** LAW **JUSTICE TEMPERED BY ETHICS** justice applied in conformity with the law, but influenced at the same time by principles of ethics and fair play **4.** LAW **FAIR CLAIM** a claim that is judged to be just and fair **5.** FIN **PART OF THE VALUE PAID FOR** the value of a piece of property over and above any mortgage or other liabilities relating to it ■ **eq·ui·ties** *npl.* STOCK EXCH **STOCK ENTITLING HOLDER TO PROFITS** shares of stock in a corporation that pay the holder some of the company's profits [14thC. Via French *équité* from, ultimately, Latin *aequus* "fair" (see EQUATE).]

eq·ui·ty cap·i·tal *n.* funds for a business raised by selling stock or by retaining earnings

eq·ui·ty of re·demp·tion *n.* the right of a mortgagor to redeem mortgaged property by paying the sum owed within a reasonable time after the date on which payment was due

equiv. *abbr.* equivalent

e·quiv·a·lence /i kwívvələns/, **e·quiv·a·len·cy** /-lənsee/ *n.* **1. BEING THE SAME OR SIMILAR** the fact of being the same, effectively the same, or interchangeable with something else **2.** MATH, LOGIC **RELATIONSHIP BETWEEN STATEMENTS** the relationship between two statements, both of which are either true or false, and each of which can be proved from the other

e·quiv·a·lence re·la·tion *n.* the relation between members of a set that is reflexive, symmetrical, and transitive, e.g., if "a" equals "b" and "b" equals "c," then "a" equals "c"

e·quiv·a·len·cy *n.* = **equivalence**

e·quiv·a·lent /i kwívvələnt/ *adj.* **1. EQUAL** being the same, or effectively the same, in effect, value, or meaning as something and usually interchangeable with it ○ *That's equivalent to the amount of energy needed to power a single light bulb.* **2.** GEOM **OF THE SAME SIZE BUT DIFFERENT SHAPE** used to describe geometric figures that have different shapes but equal areas, e.g., a circle and a square, or equal volumes, e.g., a cylinder and a cube **3.** MATH, LOGIC **IN AN EQUIVALENCE RELATION** used to describe members of a set that are in a reflexive, symmetrical, and transitive relation with each other **4.** MATH **WITH THE SAME SOLUTION** used to describe equations that share a common solution or solutions, e.g., for both $2x\text{-}3 = x\text{+}2$ and $x\text{-}5 = 0$ the solution is $x = 5$ ■ *n.* **1. SOMETHING CONSIDERED THE SAME** something that is considered to be equal to or have the same effect, value, or meaning as something else ○ *He's the Italian equivalent of a district attorney.* **2.** CHEM = **equivalent weight** [15thC. From French *équivalent,* from, ultimately, late Latin *aequivalere* "to be of equal value," from Latin *valere* "to be strong" (see VALENCY).] —**e·quiv·a·lent·ly** *adv.*

e·quiv·a·lent weight *n.* CHEM a measure of the ability of a substance to react chemically, defined as the mass of a substance that will combine with or is chemically equivalent to one gram of hydrogen or eight grams of oxygen

e·quiv·o·cal /i kwívvək'l/ *adj.* **1. AMBIGUOUS** open to more than one interpretation, especially in being deliberately expressed in an ambiguous way in an attempt to mislead somebody ○ *an equivocal reply to a tough question* **2. DIFFICULT TO INTERPRET** difficult to interpret, understand, or respond to ○ *Their stance on this issue is equivocal and nobody knows how they are likely to react.* **3. RAISING DOUBTS** arousing doubts and suspicions, especially about somebody's honesty or sincerity ○ *To arrive at the peace talks with an armed guard was an equivocal gesture.* [Mid-16thC. Formed from late Latin *aequivocus* (see EQUIVOCATE).] —**e·quiv·o·cal·i·ty** /i kwìvvə kállitee/ *n.* —**e·quiv·o·cal·ness** /i kwívvəkəlnəss/ *n.* —**e·quiv·o·cal·ly** /-kəlee/ *adv.*

e·quiv·o·cate /i kwívvə kàyt/ (**-cat·ed, -cat·ing, -cates**) *vi.* to speak vaguely or ambiguously, especially in order to mislead ○ *When pressed for a firm answer, she equivocated.* [15thC. From late Latin *aequivocare,* from *aequivocus* "ambiguous," literally "equal-voiced," from Latin *vox* "voice" (see VOICE).] —**e·quiv·o·cat·ing·ly** *adv.* —**e·quiv·o·ca·tor** *n.* —**e·quiv·o·ca·to·ry** /i kwívvəkə tàwree/ *adj.*

e·quiv·o·ca·tion /i kwìvvə káysh'n/ *n.* **1. USE OF AMBIGUITY** the use of vague or ambiguous and sometimes misleading language ○ *What we ask for is facts: what we get is equivocation or downright lies.* **2. AMBIGUOUS STATEMENT** an expression or statement that is vague or ambiguous and often deliberately misleading ○ *Their equivocations could not disguise the fact that corruption was rife in the committee.* **3.** LOGIC **WRONG LOGICAL CONCLUSION** an invalid conclusion based on statements in which one term has two different meanings

eq·ui·voque /ékwi vōk, éekwi-/, **eq·ui·voke** *n.* (*formal*) **1. PLAY ON WORDS** an amusing use of an ambiguous word **2. AMBIGUOUS WORD OR PHRASE** a word or phrase with a double meaning **3. AMBIGUITY** ambiguity, double meaning, or misleading words and expressions [Early 17thC. Directly or via French *équivoque* from late Latin *aequivocus* (see EQUIVOCATE).]

er /ur/ *interj.* used to express hesitation [Mid-19thC. An imitation of the sound.]

Er *symbol.* erbium

ER *abbr.* **1.** emergency room **2.** BASEBALL earned runs

-er[1] *suffix.* **1.** one that performs or undergoes a particular action ○ *adjuster* ○ *fryer* **2.** a person connected with, often as an occupation ○ *trucker* **3.** a person from a particular place ○ *Londoner* ○ *foreigner* [Partly Old English *-ere,* partly via Anglo-Norman from, ultimately, Latin *-arius,* and partly from Old French *-eor* (see -OR[1])]

-er[2] *suffix.* more ○ *greener* ○ *slower* [Old English *-re, -ra*]

e·ra /éerə, érrə/ *n.* **1.** TIME **DISTINCTIVE PERIOD OF HISTORY** a period of time made distinctive by a significant development, feature, event, or personality ○ *during the postwar era* **2.** TIME **PERIOD WITH OWN CHRONOLOGICAL SYSTEM** a time period within which years are consecutively numbered from a particular significant event that provides its starting point ○ *the Christian era* **3.** PREHIST **DIVISION OF EARTH'S HISTORY** a division of geologic time composed of several periods **4.** TIME **DATE THAT BEGINS PERIOD** a significant date or event that is regarded as the beginning of a new period of time ○ *The agreement marked an era in U.S.-Soviet relations.* [Mid-17thC. From late Latin *aera* "number used as a basis for counting."]

ERA /ée aar áy/ *abbr.* **1.** BASEBALL earned run average **2.** Equal Rights Amendment

e·rad·i·cate /i ráddi kàyt/ (**-cat·ed, -cat·ing, -cates**) *vt.* to destroy or get rid of something completely, so that it can never recur or return [15thC. From Latin *eradicat-,* the past participle stem of *eradicare* "to pull up by the roots" (the original sense in English), from *radix* "root" (source of English *radish*).] —**e·rad·i·ca·ble** *adj.* —**e·rad·i·ca·bly** *adv.* —**e·rad·i·ca·tion** /i ràddi káysh'n/ *n.* —**e·rad·i·ca·tive** /i ráddi kàytiv/ *adj.* —**e·rad·i·ca·tor** /-kàytər/ *n.*

e·rase /i ráyss/ (**e·rased, e·ras·ing, e·ras·es**) *vt.* **1. REMOVE WRITTEN MATERIAL** to remove written, typed, or printed material by rubbing it out, or to obliterate it with something such as correction fluid **2.** COMPUT, RECORDING **DELETE RECORDED DATA** to delete data or recorded material from a computer's memory, a magnetic tape, or other storage media **3. REMOVE OR DESTROY** to remove or destroy something completely ○ *an ancient civilization, all traces of which had been erased over time* [Late 16thC. From Latin *eras-,* the past participle stem of *eradere* "to scrape out," from *radere* "to scrape" (see RAZE).] —**e·ras·a·bil·i·ty** /i ràyssə bíllətee/ *n.* —**e·ras·a·ble** /i ráyssəb'l/ *adj.*

e·ras·er /i ráyssər/ *n.* something used to rub out written, typed, or printed material, such as a piece of rubber for pencil markings or a felt pad used on a chalkboard

E·ras·mus /i rázməss/, **Desiderius** (1466?–1536) Dutch scholar and writer. His works, combining a Christian outlook with Renaissance humanism, influenced both sides during the Reformation. Among his many other works was a new edition of the Greek New Testament (1516).

e·ra·sure /i ráyshər/ *n.* **1. REMOVAL** the complete removal or destruction of something ○ *an erasure of data from a hard drive* **2. ERASED PLACE OR MARK** the place where something has been rubbed out, or the mark left behind

Er·a·to /érrə tō/ *n.* in Greek mythology, the muse of lyric poetry. ◊ **Muse**

E·ra·tos·the·nes /èrrə tósthə neez/ (276?–196?B.C.) Greek astronomer and mathematician. He is best known for his calculation of the Earth's circumference, which was the most accurate until the 17th century. ■ *n.* ASTRON **CRATER ON MOON** a prominent deep crater on the Moon with a distinctive central peak, located at the southern edge of Mare Imbrium, 36 mi./58 km in diameter

er·bi·um /úrbee əm/ *n.* a soft silvery metallic chemical element of the rare-earth group, used in certain alloys and as a pigment. Symbol **Er** [Mid-19thC. Named for *Ytterby,* a town in Sweden, where the first rare-earth mineral was discovered.]

ere /air/ *prep., conj.* before or earlier in time than (*literary or archaic*) [Old English *ǣr*]

e·rect /i rékt/ *adj.* **1. STRAIGHT AND VERTICAL** in an upright position ○ *an erect plant stem* **2.** PHYSIOL **FIRM AND RIGID** stiff and swollen as a result of being filled with blood, e.g., when sexually aroused **3.** OPTICS **RIGHT SIDE UP** used to describe an optically produced image that is right side up and not inverted **4. ALERT** in an alert state (*archaic*) ■ *v.* (**e·rect·ed, e·rect·ing, e·rects**) **1.** *vt.* **CONSTRUCT** to build a structure from basic parts and materials ○ *The building was erected in 1885.* **2.** *vt.* **PUT TOGETHER** to fit something together and put it into position so that it is ready for use **3.** *vt.* **SET UPRIGHT** to fix something in an upright position **4.** *vt.* **ESTABLISH** to bring an organization, system, or theory into being ○ *The corporation erected a new legal department just to deal with mergers and acquistions.* **5.** *vt.* GEOM **DRAW FIGURE ON BASE** to draw or construct a line or figure on a given base **6.** *vti.* PHYSIOL **BECOME OR MAKE RIGID** to become, or cause an organ to become, stiff and swollen by being filled with blood [14thC. From Latin *erectus,* past participle of *erigere* "to set up," from *regere* "to direct or rule" (see REGENT).] —**e·rect·a·ble** *adj.* —**e·rect·ly** *adv.* —**e·rect·ness** *n.*

WORD KEY: SYNONYMS

See Synonyms at ***build.***

e·rec·tile /i rékt'l, i rék tīl/ *adj.* capable of filling with blood under pressure, swelling, and becoming stiff —**e·rec·til·i·ty** /i rèk tílləteel *n.*

e·rec·tion /i rékshən/ *n.* **1. PUTTING SOMETHING UP** the construction or setting up of something **2.** PHYSIOL **SWELLING OF TISSUE** the swollen and stiffened state of erectile tissue, especially that of the penis, usually as a result of sexual arousal **3. STRUCTURE** something that has been built or constructed (*formal*)

e·rec·tor /i réktər/ *n.* **1. MUSCLE** a muscle that is capable of raising or holding up a body part **2. SOMEBODY WHO ERECTS THINGS** somebody or something that erects things, generally things made elsewhere

E re·gion *n.* the middle part of the ionosphere, lying approximately 50 to 70 mi./80 to 110 km above the Earth's surface, that reflects medium-length radio waves

ere·long /air láwng/ *adv.* soon or in a short time (*archaic or literary*)

er·e·mite /érrə mīt/ *n.* somebody who lives in solitude, especially for religious reasons (*literary*) [13thC. From Old French *eremite* or late Latin *eremita* (see HERMIT).] —**er·e·mit·ic** /èrrə míttik/ *adj.* —**er·e·mit·i·cal** /-míttik'l/ *adj.* —**er·e·mit·ism** /érrə mī tìzzəm/ *n.*

ere·now /air nów/ *adv.* previously (*archaic or literary*)

er·e·thism /érrə thìzzəm/ *n.* excessive sensitivity of a body part to stimuli (*technical*) [Early 19thC. From French *éréthisme,* from, ultimately, Greek *erethizein* "to irritate."] —**er·e·this·mic** /èrrə thízmik/ *adj.* —**er·e·this·tic** /-thístik/ *adj.* —**er·e·thit·ic** /-thíttik/ *adj.*

ere·while /air wīl/, **ere·whiles** /air wīlz/ *adv.* some time ago (*archaic or literary*)

erg[1] /urg/ *n.* the unit of energy or work in the centimeter- gram-second system equal to the work done by a force of one dyne acting through a distance of one centimeter. 1 erg is equivalent to 10^7 joule. [Late 19thC. From Greek *ergon* "work."]

erg[2] /urg/ (*plural* **ergs** *or* **a·reg** /áa règ/) *n.* a large, relatively flat area of desert covered with shifting wind-swept sand, especially in the Sahara [Late 19thC. Via French from Arabic *'irk, 'erg.*]

er·ga·tive /úrgətiv/ *adj.* GRAM **1. ALLOWING OBJECT TO BE SUBJECT** used to describe a class of verbs in which the object of the transitive form can be used as the subject of the intransitive form with an equivalent meaning. "Open" is an example of an ergative verb, in that "I opened the door" and "The door opened" have equivalent meanings. **2. WITH DOER OF ACTION AS OBJECT** used to describe a case of nouns in languages such as Inuit and Basque in which the object of the verb acts, while the subject is affected by the action ■ *n.* GRAM **ERGATIVE WORD** an ergative verb or a noun in the ergative case [Mid-20thC. Formed from Greek *ergatēs* "worker."]

er·go /áirgō, úrgō/ *adv., conj.* therefore (*formal*) [14thC. From Latin.]

er·go·cal·cif·er·ol /ùrgō kal síffə ràwl/ *n.* = **vitamin D_2** [Mid-20thC. Coined from ERGOSTEROL + CALCIFEROL.]

er·gom·e·ter /ur gómmətər/ *n.* an instrument for measuring muscle power or work done by muscles, e.g., when exercising [Late 19thC. Coined from Greek *ergon* "work" + -METER.] —**er·go·met·ric** /ùrgə méttrik/ *adj.*

er·go·no·met·ric /ùrgənə méttrik/ *adj.* relating or conforming to ergonomics —**er·go·no·met·ri·cal·ly** /-méttrikəlee/ *adv.*

er·go·nom·ic /ùrgə nómmik/ *adj.* designed for maximum comfort, efficiency, safety, and ease of use, especially in the workplace —**er·go·nom·i·cal·ly** *adv.*

er·go·nom·ics /ùrgə nómmiks/ *n.* **STUDY OF WORKPLACE DESIGN** the study of how a workplace and the equipment used there can best be designed for comfort, safety, efficiency, and productivity (*takes a singular verb*) ■ *npl.* **DESIGN OF WORKPLACE OR EQUIPMENT** those factors or qualities in the design of something, especially a workplace or equipment used by people at work, that contribute to comfort, safety, efficiency, and ease of use [Mid-20thC. Coined from Greek *ergon* "work" on the model of ECONOMICS.] —**er·gon·o·mist** /ur gónnəmist/ *n.*

er·gos·ter·ol /ur góstə ràwl/ *n.* a crystalline steroid alcohol that is found mainly in yeast and molds and is converted to vitamin D_2 by ultraviolet light. Formula: $C_{28}H_{44}O$. [Early 20thC. Coined from ERGOT + STEROL.]

er·got /úrgət, úr gòt/ *n.* **1. FUNGUS ATTACKING CEREALS** a disease of cereals caused by a parasitic fungus that grows in dense black masses (**sclerotia**) in the grains of the ear. Latin name: *Claviceps purpurea.* **2. FUNGAL BODIES USED IN MEDICINE** the dried sclerotia of an ergot fungus that yield substances used in drugs to treat migraine and to induce uterine contractions in childbirth [Late 17thC. From French, literally "rooster's spur" (of unknown origin), because the diseased grain resembles a rooster's claw.] —**er·got·ic** /ur góttik/ *adj.*

er·got·a·mine /ur góttə meen, ur góttəmin/ *n.* an alkaloid drug derived from ergot that causes constriction of blood vessels and is used to treat migraines. Formula: $C_{33}H_{35}N_5O_5$.

er·got·ism /úrgə tìzzəm/ *n.* a severe toxic reaction to food containing ergot-contaminated grains or excessive amounts of drugs containing ergot derivatives. The toxin produces neurological and gastrointestinal symptoms and, if not properly treated, gangrene.

Er·hard /áir haàrd/, **Ludwig** (1897–1977) German statesman. As finance minister, he achieved West Germany's postwar economic revival and was the Christian Democratic Chancellor from 1963 until 1966.

er·i·ca /érrikə/ (*plural* **-cas** *or* **-ca**) *n.* an evergreen shrub or small tree of the heath family with small leathery leaves and bell-shaped flowers. All the heaths and several heathers are types of erica. Genus: *Erica.* [Early 17thC. Via modern Latin, genus name, from Greek *ereikē* "heath."]

er·i·ca·ceous /èrri káyshəss/ *adj.* belonging or relating to the heath family, a group of evergreen shrubs and small trees that includes the heath, heather, blueberry, rhododendron, azalea, and arbutus

Er·ic·son /érriksən/, **Leif** (975–1020) Icelandic explorer. He is traditionally believed to be the first European to have reached the North American mainland.

Er·ics·son /érriksən/, **John** (1803–89) Swedish-born U.S. inventor and engineer. After work on steam locomotives, he built the warship *Monitor,* which fought the Confederacy's warship *Merrimack,* in the Civil War (1862).

Er·ic the Red /èrrik-/ (950?–1000?) Norwegian explorer. He was the father of Leif Ericson. Banished from Scandinavia for manslaughter, he explored Greenland (982–86), where he established the first European settlement. Real name **Eric Thorvaldson**

E·rie /éeree/ *n.* an extinct language formerly spoken in an area along the southern shores of Lake Erie. It was one of the Iroquoian group of the Hokan-Siouan family of North American languages. —**E·rie** *adj.*

E·rie, Lake /éeree/ lake in the United States and Canada. It is one of the five Great Lakes of North America. Area: 9,910 sq. mi./25,667 sq. km.

E·rie Ca·nal artificial inland waterway between Buffalo, on Lake Erie, and Albany, New York, where it links with the Hudson River. Length: 363 mi./584 km.

er·i·ger·on /i ríjjə ròn/ (*plural* **-ons** *or* **-on**) *n.* a plant of the daisy family, many species of which are cultivated as ornamentals. Fleabane is a type of erigeron. Genus: *Erigeron.* [Early 17thC. Via Latin from Greek, literally "early old man," from its former application to the groundsel, an early-flowering plant with fluffy white seed heads.]

Er·ik·son /érriksən/, **Erik** (1902–94) German-born U.S. psychoanalyst. He developed the concept of the identity crisis, as well as making major contributions to the area of child psychology. Full name **Erik Homburger Erikson**

Er·in /érrin/ *n.* the country of Ireland (*literary*)

Er·in go bragh /èrrin gō braá/ *interj.* *Ireland* an expression meaning "Ireland forever" [From ERIN + Irish *go brách, go bráth,* literally "till doomsday"]

E·rin·yes /i réenee èz/ *npl.* = **Furies**

ERISA /i ríssə/ *abbr.* Employee Retirement Income Security Act

e·ris·tic /i rístik/ *adj.* **e·ris·tic, e·ris·ti·cal ARGUMENTATIVE** fond of or characterized by argument or controversy (*formal*) ■ *n.* (*formal*) **1. ART OF DISPUTING** the skill or practice of debating, especially in a manner involving subtle logic and specious argument **2. DEBATER** somebody who is an expert or delights in argument and controversy [Mid-17thC. From Greek *eristikos,* from, ultimately, *eris* "strife."] —**e·ris·ti·cal·ly** *adv.*

Eritrea

Er·i·tre·a /èrri trée ə/ republic on the Red Sea coast in northeastern Africa. A former Italian colony, it became part of Ethiopia in 1952 and fully independent in 1993. Language: Tigrinya, Tigre, Arabic. Currency: nakfa. Capital: Asmara. Population: 3,714,963 (1997). Area: 46,774 sq. mi./121,144 sq. km. Official name **State of Eritrea** —**Er·i·tre·an** *n., adj.*

Er·lang·er /úr làngər/ city in northern Kentucky, northwest of Independence, a southern suburb of Cincinnati, Ohio. Population: 16,717 (1996).

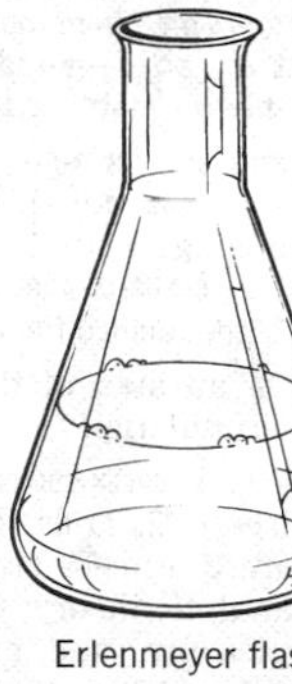

Erlenmeyer flask

Er·len·mey·er flask /úrlən mīr-, érrlən-/ *n.* a cone-shaped laboratory flask with a narrow neck and broad flat bottom [Late 19thC. Named for the German chemist Emil *Erlenmeyer* 1825–1909.]

Ermine

er·mine /úrmin/ (*plural* **-mines** *or* **-mine**) *n.* **1. SMALL NORTHERN WEASEL** a small northern weasel, with dark fur whose silky winter coat is white except for a black-tipped tail. Latin name: *Mustela erminea.* **2. WHITE FUR OF ERMINE** the white fur of an ermine, once valued as a symbol of wealth, nobility, or high rank [12thC. From Old French *(h)ermine,* probably from medieval Latin (mus) *Armenius* "Armenian (mouse)."]

erne /urn/ (*plural* **ernes** *or* **erne**), **ern** (*plural* **erns** *or* **ern**) *n.* a long-winged European sea eagle. Latin name: *Haliaetus albicilla.* [Old English *earn.* Ultimately from an Indo-European word that is also the ancestor of Greek *ornis* "bird" (source of English *ornithology*).]

Max Ernst

Ernst /airnst, urnst/, **Max** (1891–1976) German-born French artist. A co-founder of Dada and surrealism, he is known for the startling and violent imagery of his works.

e·rode /i rṓd/ (**e·rod·ed, e·rod·ing, e·rodes**) *v.* **1.** *vti.* GEOL **WEAR AWAY LAND** to wear away outer layers of rock or soil, or to be gradually worn away by the action of wind or water **2.** *vt.* GEOL **FORM BY WEATHERING** to form a land feature such as a valley or gully by the action of wind or water ○ *The runoff from the rain eroded a gully.* **3.** *vti.* **BREAK DOWN GRADUALLY** to diminish or destroy something such as a relationship or feeling gradually over time, or to be gradually diminished or destroyed ○ *Deceit will erode any friendship.* **4.** *vti.* CHEM **EAT AWAY** to eat into or destroy something by corrosion or chemical action, or to be damaged or destroyed in this way ○ *The acid eroded the copper.* **5.** *vt.* MED **WEAR TISSUE AWAY** to cause tissue to wear away as a result of decay, cancer, ulceration, or the chemical processes associated with inflammation [Early 17thC. Directly or via French *éroder* from Latin *erodere* "to gnaw off," from *rodere* "to gnaw" (see RODENT).] —**e·ro·dent** *n., adj.* —**e·rod·i·bil·i·ty** /i rṓdə bíllətee/ *n.* —**e·rod·i·ble** /i rṓdəb'l/ *adj.*

e·rog·e·nous /i rójjənəss/, **er·o·gen·ic** /i rójjənnik/, **er·o·to·ge·nic** /i ròttə jénnik/ *adj.* **1. SEXUALLY SENSITIVE** sensitive and arousing sexual feelings when touched or stroked **2. SEXUALLY AROUSING** stimulating sexual desire [Late 19thC. Coined from EROS + -GENOUS.]

e·rog·e·nous zone *n.* an area of the body that is sensitive to sexual stimulation

Er·os /é ròss, èe ròss/ *n.* **1. GREEK GOD OF LOVE** the god of love in ancient Greece **2. Er·os, er·os SEXUAL LOVE** sexual love or desire **3.** PSYCHOL **INSTINCT FOR SELF-PRESERVATION** in psychoanalytic theory, the instincts for self-preservation, pleasure, and procreation considered as a group [Late 17thC. Via Latin from Greek, "sexual love."]

e·ro·sion /i rṓzh'n/ *n.* **1.** GEOL **WEARING AWAY OF ROCK** the gradual wearing away of rock or soil by physical breakdown, chemical solution, and transportation of material, as caused, e.g., by water, wind, or ice **2. GRADUAL BREAKING DOWN** the gradual destruction or reduction and weakening of something such as a relationship or somebody's power ○ *The erosion of profits was due to careless management.* **3.** DENT **LOSS OF TOOTH ENAMEL** loss of tooth enamel caused by excessive intake of acidic citrus juices or through repeated contact with stomach acid, as in bulimia **4.** MED **WEARING AWAY OF TISSUE** the wearing away of surface tissue by disease, ulceration, cancer, or the chemical processes associated with inflammation [Mid-16thC. From French *érosion*, from, ultimately, Latin *eros-*, the past participle stem of *erodere* (see ERODE).] —**e·ro·sion·al** *adj.* —**e·ro·sion·al·ly** *adv.*

e·ro·sive /i rṓssiv/ *adj.* causing the gradual breaking down or wearing away of something, especially rock or soil —**e·ro·sive·ness** *n.* —**e·ro·siv·i·ty** /i rō sívvətee/ *n.*

e·rot·ic /i róttik/ *adj.* **1. AROUSING SEXUAL FEELINGS** arousing, or designed to arouse, feelings of sexual desire **2. MARKED BY SEXUAL DESIRE** characterized by or arising out of sexual desire [Mid-17thC. Via French *érotique* from Greek *erōtikos*, from *erōs* "sexual love."] —**e·rot·i·cal·ly** *adv.*

e·rot·i·ca /i róttikə/ *n.* art or literature intended to arouse sexual desire by portraying sex in an explicit way. ◊ **pornography** [Mid-19thC. From Greek *erōtika*, neuter plural of *erōtikos* (see EROTIC).]

e·rot·i·cism /i rótti sìzzəm/, **er·o·tism** /érrə tìzzəm/ *n.* **1. EROTIC QUALITY** an erotic quality in something, especially an erotic style or subject in literature or art ○ *the eroticism of her poetry* **2. SEXUAL DESIRE** feelings of sexual desire **3. EXCESSIVE SEXUAL EXCITEMENT** unusually persistent or frequent sexual interest or desire —**e·rot·i·cist** *n.*

e·rot·i·cize /i rótti sīz/ (**-cized, -ciz·ing, -ciz·es**), **er·o·tize** /érrə tīz/ (**-tized, -tiz·ing, -tiz·es**) *vt.* to make something erotic, especially by giving a sexual quality to something not usually regarded in that way ○ *The paintings were thought to eroticize flowers.* —**e·rot·i·ci·za·tion** /i ròttissi záysh'n/ *n.*

er·o·tism *n.* = **eroticism**

er·o·tize *vt.* = **eroticize** —**er·o·ti·za·tion** /èrrəti záysh'n/ *n.*

e·ro·to·gen·ic *adj.* = **erogenous**

e·ro·to·ma·ni·a /i ròttə máynee ə/ *n.* **1. EXCESSIVE SEXUAL DESIRE** excessive and insatiable feelings of sexual desire **2.** PSYCHIAT **BELIEF IN NONEXISTENT ROMANCE** the delusion of being loved by and romantically involved in a relationship with a person, especially somebody famous or of high social position —**e·ro·to·ma·ni·ac** *n.*

err /ur, air/ (**erred, err·ing, errs**) *vi.* **1. MAKE MISTAKE** to make a mistake or do an incorrect thing ○ *The committee erred in interpreting the contract in this way.* **2. BEHAVE BADLY** to behave badly and do something that is morally wrong (*formal*) ○ *"To err is human, to forgive, divine."* (Alexander Pope, *Essay On Criticism*; 1711) [13thC. Via Old French *errer* from Latin *errare* "to wander." The underlying sense is of wandering from the right path.] ◇ **err on the side of something** to show a particular quality, e.g., caution or generosity, to a greater extent than is strictly necessary in order to avoid the risks involved in its opposite

er·ran·cy /érrənsee/ *n.* (*formal*) **1. INCORRECT BEHAVIOR** incorrect or morally wrong behavior **2. TENDENCY TO DO WRONG** the propensity for making mistakes or acting improperly

er·rand /érrənd/ *n.* **1. SHORT TRIP FOR SOMEBODY ELSE** a short trip somewhere to do something on behalf of somebody else, e.g., to buy something or deliver a message ○ *She sometimes runs errands for me if I'm not well enough to go out.* **2. PURPOSE OF ERRAND** the task that somebody goes on an errand to carry out ○ *My errand was to collect her suit from the dry cleaners.* [Old English *ǣrende* "message, mission," of unknown origin]

er·rant /érrənt/ *adj.* **1. BEHAVING BADLY** behaving in an unacceptable manner **2. GOING ASTRAY** wandering from an intended course or not reaching an intended destination **3. LOOKING FOR ADVENTURE** wandering in search of adventure and romance (*literary*) **4. MOVING IRREGULARLY** with no regular or purposeful pattern of motion [14thC. From Latin *errant-*, the present participle stem of *errare* (see ERR).] —**er·rant·ly** *adv.*

er·rant·ry /érrəntree/ *n.* the wandering, romantic, and adventurous life of a knight errant

er·ra·ta plural of **erratum** ■ *npl.* **LIST OF PRINTING ERRORS** a list of mistakes noticed after a book was printed, often included as a separate sheet in the book

er·rat·ic /i ráttik/ *adj.* **1. INCONSISTENT** not predictable, regular, or consistent, especially in being likely to depart from or fall below expected standards at any time ○ *His driving tends to be rather erratic.* **2. OFTEN CHANGING DIRECTION** often changing direction and not following any definite course **3.** GEOL **CARRIED AND DEPOSITED BY ICE** used to describe a rock or boulder that was carried from its source by ice and deposited when the ice melted ■ *n.* **1. SOMEBODY BEHAVING UNPREDICTABLY** somebody who does not behave predictably **2.** GEOL **ROCK MOVED BY ICE** a piece of rock that was carried from its source by ice and deposited when the ice melted [14thC. From Old French *erratique*, from, ultimately, Latin *errare* (see ERR).] —**er·rat·i·cal·ly** *adv.* —**er·rat·i·cism** /i rátti sìzzəm/ *n.*

er·ra·tum /e raátəm, i-/ (*plural* **-ta** /-tə/) *n.* a mistake in printing or writing, especially one on a list that is included with a printed book [Mid-16thC. From Latin, neuter past participle of *errare* (see ERR).]

er·ro·ne·ous /i rṓnee əss/ *adj.* incorrect, based on an incorrect assumption, or containing something that is incorrect [14thC. From Old French *erroneus*, from, ultimately, the Latin stem *erron-* "truant," from *errare* (see ERR).] —**er·ro·ne·ous·ly** *adv.* —**er·ro·ne·ous·ness** *n.*

er·ror /érrər/ *n.* **1. MISTAKE** something unintentionally done wrong, e.g., as a result of poor judgment or lack of care ○ *The report blames the crash on human error.* **2. WRONG BELIEF** a belief or opinion that is contrary to fact or to established doctrine ○ *Errors and superstitions were to be banished by the pure light of science.* **3. STATE OF BELIEVING OR ACTING WRONGLY** a state in which somebody holds incorrect beliefs or opinions or acts wrongly or misguidedly **4. BEING WRONG** incorrectness, inappropriateness, or unacceptability ○ *He's seen the error of his ways and has decided to apologize.* **5.** BASEBALL **MISPLAY IN BASEBALL** a fielding misplay in baseball when, in the judgment of the official scorer, play should have either led to an out or prevented a runner from advancing **6.** COMPUT **PROBLEM DETECTED BY PROGRAM** the failure of a computer program, subroutine, or system to produce an anticipated result, such as the result of a calculation not falling within an expected range **7.** MATH **MATHEMATICAL DIFFERENCE** a variation between the true value of a mathematical quantity and a calculated or measured value **8.** LAW **MISTAKE IN COURT PROCEEDINGS** a mistake either in law or in fact in court proceedings [13thC. From Old French *err(o)ur*, from, ultimately, Latin *errare* (see ERR).] —**er·ror·less** *adj.* ◇ **in error 1.** by mistake **2.** mistaken or acting on the basis of a false assumption or belief

WORD KEY: SYNONYMS

See Synonyms at ***mistake***.

er·ror code *n.* a unique combination of characters printed or displayed by a computer or communicated between parts of a program indicating an error or specific problem in software or hardware operation

er·ror mes·sage *n.* a message indicating that a computer has encountered a problem and often suggesting alternative action. The message may take the form of a display on a monitor, text on a printer, a computer-generated voice, or a sequence of audio signals.

er·satz /ér zaàts/ *adj.* imitating or presented as a substitute for something of superior quality (*disapproving*) [Late 19thC. From German, literally "replacement."]

Erse /urss/ *n.* LANG = **Gaelic** *n.* ■ *adj.* **OF GAELIC LANGUAGE** relating or belonging to the Gaelic language, especially Irish Gaelic [14thC. Early Scots variant of IRISH.]

erst /urst/ *adv.* in the past or a long time ago (*archaic*) [Old English *ǣrest* "first"]

erst·while /úrst hwīl/ *adj.* **FORMER** who in the past was something, e.g., a friend or supporter, but now no longer is ○ *Since leaving the bank, she has been ostracized by her erstwhile colleagues.* ■ *adv.* **FORMERLY** at a time in the past (*archaic*) ◊ **erewhile**

er·ub *n.* = **eruv**

e·ru·cic ac·id /i ròossik-/ *n.* a soft, colorless, solid fatty acid derived from rape seeds. It is used primarily in the manufacture of plastics. [*Erucic* formed from Latin *eruca* "rape plant"]

e·ruct /i rúkt/ (**e·ruct·ed, e·ruct·ing, e·ructs**), **e·ruc·tate** /i rúk tàyt/ (**-tat·ed, -tat·ing, -tates**) *vti.* to expel stomach gases through the mouth (*technical*) [Mid-17thC. From Latin *eructare* "to belch or vomit up," from *ructare* "to belch."] —**e·ruc·ta·tion** /i rùk táysh'n, èe ruk-/ *n.*

er·u·dite /érryə dīt, érrə-/ *adj.* having or showing great knowledge gained from study and reading ○ *scholars erudite in Sanskrit* [15thC. From Latin *eruditus*, past participle of *erudire* "to instruct," from *rudis* "untrained" (source of English *rude*).] —**er·u·dite·ly** *adv.* —**er·u·dite·ness** *n.*

er·u·di·tion /èrryə dísh'n, èrrə-/ *n.* knowledge acquired through study and reading ○ *a work of great erudition*

WORD KEY: SYNONYMS

See Synonyms at ***knowledge***.

e·rupt /i rúpt/ (**e·rupt·ed, e·rupt·ing, e·rupts**) *v.* **1.** *vti.* **VIOLENTLY RELEASE MATERIAL** to eject material such as gas, steam, ash, or lava, usually violently, from within ○ *The volcano last erupted in 1935.* **2.** *vi.* **BURST OUT** to burst out suddenly or violently ○ *Tired of her comments, he suddenly erupted in a fit of temper.* **3.** *vi.* MED **APPEAR ON SKIN** to appear as a rash or blemish on the skin or a mucous membrane **4.** *vi.* DENT **COME THROUGH GUM** to break through and emerge from a gum (*technical*) (*refers to growing teeth*) [Mid-17thC. From Latin *erupt-*, past participle stem of *erumpere*, literally "to break out," from *rumpere* "to break" (source of English *rupture*).] —**e·rupt·i·ble** *adj.* —**e·rup·tive** *adj.* —**e·rup·tive·ly** *adv.*

e·rup·tion /i rúpshən/ *n.* **1. VIOLENT RELEASE OF MATERIAL** the violent ejection of material, such as gas, steam, ash, or lava from a volcano **2. OUTBURST** a sudden outburst or occurrence of something **3.** MED **RASH OR BLEMISH ON SKIN** a rash or blemish, or the appearance of a rash or blemish on the skin or a mucous membrane **4.** DENT **EMERGENCE OF TOOTH** an emergence of a growing tooth from a gum

er·uv /ay róov, áy rùv/, **er·ub** *n.* the physical boundary within which certain relaxations of the rules concerning the Jewish Sabbath are allowed. It may be the walls of a town, a natural barrier, or a special construction. [Early 18thC. From Hebrew *'ērūbh*, literally "mixture."]

Er·ving /úrving/, **Julius** (*b.* 1950) U.S. basketball player He is widely regarded as one of the greatest and most exciting scorers in basketball history. Full name **Julius Winfred Erving II**. Known as **Dr. J**

-ery, **-ry** *suffix.* **1.** place for ○ *brewery* **2.** activity or behavior ○ *trickery* **3.** collection of ○ *crockery* **4.** qualities or character of ○ *buffoonery* **5.** state, condition ○ *drudgery* [From Old French *-erie*, from *-er* "-er, -or" + *-ie* "-y"]

er·y·sip·e·las /èrri síppələss/ *n.* a severe skin rash accompanied by fever and vomiting and caused by a streptococcal bacterium [14thC. Via Latin from Greek *erusipelas*, literally "red skin."] —**er·y·si·pel·a·tous** /èrrissi péllətəss/ *adj.*

er·y·the·ma /èrri théemə/ *n.* redness of the skin as a result of a widening of the small blood vessels near its surface. It has various causes, including fever and inflammation. [Late 18thC. From Greek *eruthēma*, from, ultimately, *eruthros* "red."] —**er·y·them·a·tous** /èrri thémmətəss, -théemə-/ *adj.* —**er·y·the·mic** /-théemik/ *adj.*

erythr- *prefix.* = **erythro-** (*used before vowels*)

er·y·thrism /érrə thrìzzəm/ *n.* unusual redness of plumage or hair, often accompanied by a ruddy complexion in humans [Late 19thC. Coined from Greek *eruthros* "red" + -ISM.] —**er·y·thris·mal** /èrrə thrízməl/ *adj.*

er·y·thrite /érrə thrìt/ *n.* pale red cobalt arsenate that occurs as crystals on cobalt minerals and is used as a glass pigment [Mid-19thC. Coined from Greek *eruthros* "red" + -ITE.]

erythro- *prefix.* **1.** red ○ *erythrocyte* **2.** erythrocyte ○ *erythroblast* [From Greek *eruthros* "red." Ultimately from an Indo-European base that is also the ancestor of English *red* and *ruddy*.]

e·ryth·ro·blast /i ríthrə blàst/ *n.* ANAT an immature red blood cell that is found in bone marrow and eventually develops into a mature red blood cell. Unlike a mature red blood cell, an erythroblast has a nucleus. —**e·ryth·ro·blas·tic** /i rìthrə blástik/ *adj.*

e·ryth·ro·blas·to·sis /i rìthrō bla stṓssiss/ *n.* the abnormal presence of immature red blood cells in the bloodstream that occurs especially in erythroblastosis fetalis

e·ryth·ro·blas·to·sis fe·tal·is /i rìthrō bla stṓssiss fi tálliss/ *n.* a serious blood disease of fetuses and newborn babies, in which the antibodies produced by a rhesus-negative mother destroy the red blood cells of a rhesus-positive fetus [*Fetalis* from modern Latin, "fetal"]

e·ryth·ro·cyte /i ríthrə sìt/ *n.* = **red blood cell** —**e·ryth·ro·cyt·ic** /i rìthrə síttik/ *adj.*

e·ryth·ro·my·cin /i rìthrə míssin/ *n.* an antibiotic used in treating a broad range of bacterial infections. It is derived from cultures of a bacterium *Streptomyces erythreus*.

e·ryth·ro·poi·e·sis /i rìthrō poy éessiss/ *n.* the formation of red blood cells, a process that begins with stem cells in the bone marrow and ends with the release of mature red blood cells (**erythrocytes**) into circulation [Early 20thC. Coined from ERYTHROCYTE+ Greek *poiēsis* "creation" (see POESY).] —**e·ryth·ro·poi·et·ic** /i rìthrō poy éttik/ *adj.*

e·ryth·ro·poi·e·tin /i rìthrō poy éetin/ *n.* a hormone produced in the kidneys that stimulates increased development of red blood cells in the bone marrow. The kidneys produce erythropoietin in response to lowered oxygen levels in body tissues. [Mid-20thC. Coined from ERYTHROPOIESIS + -IN.]

Es *symbol.* einsteinium

ES *abbr.* El Salvador (*international vehicle registration*)

-es *suffix.* = **-s**

ESA *abbr.* European Space Agency

Esc *abbr.* COMPUT escape (key)

es·ca·drille /éskə drìl, -dreél/ *n.* a squadron of usually six aircraft, especially a French air squadron of World War I [Early 20thC. Via French from Spanish *escuadrilla*, literally "little squadron," from *escuadra* "squadron."]

es·ca·lade /éskə làyd, -laád/ *n.* **CLIMBING WALL WITH LADDERS** an attack involving the use of ladders to scale the walls of a fortified place ■ *vt.* (**-lad·ed, -lad·ing, -lades**) **CLIMB WALL WITH LADDERS** to scale the walls of a fortification using ladders [Late 16thC. Directly or via French from Spanish *escalada*. Ultimately from medieval Latin *scalare* "to climb" (source of English *scale*).] —**es·ca·lad·er** *n.*

es·ca·late /éskə làyt/ (**-lat·ed, -lat·ing, -lates**) *vti.* to become or cause something to become greater, more serious, or more intense. See Usage note below. [Early 20thC. Back-formation from ESCALATOR. Originally, "to travel on an escalator."] —**es·ca·la·tion** /èskə láysh'n/ *n.* —**es·ca·la·to·ry** /éskələ tàwree/ *adj.*

WORD KEY: USAGE

His claims are certain to escalate into a big political scandal. No one uses ***escalate*** now to mean "ride on an escalator," and the figurative meaning has taken over completely. Its earliest and still most common uses are in connection with military activity and conflicts: *Officials killed by mine as terrorist attacks escalate.* It is used most effectively when it describes a development that proceeds in stages, rather than as a simple synonym for *increase* or *mount.*

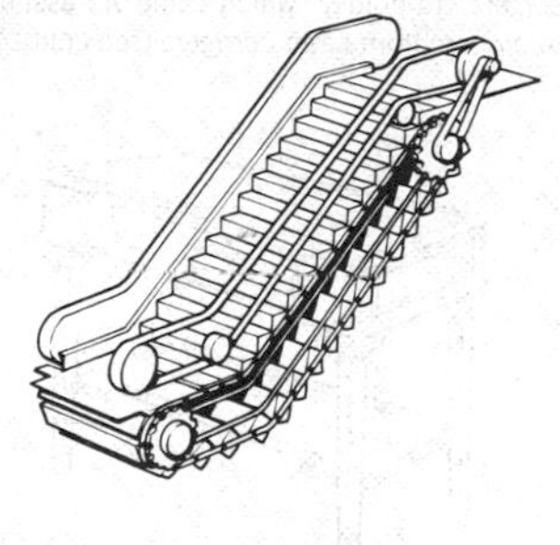

Escalator

es·ca·la·tor /éskə làytər/ *n.* a set of moving steps attached to a continuously circulating belt, that carries people up or down between different levels in a building [Early 20thC. From ESCALADE, modeled on ELEVATOR.]

es·ca·la·tor /éskə làytər/, **es·ca·la·tor clause** *n.* a stipulation in a contract that conditions an increase or decrease in something on a change in something else. It might, e.g., relate compensation to cost of living or prices to sales.

es·cal·lop /i skóllәp, i skálləp/ *n.* = **scallop** *n.* **6** [15thC. From Old French *escalope* "shell" (see SCALLOP).]

es·cal·ope /éskə lòp, -lóp/ *n. U.K.* FOOD = **scallop** *n.* **6** [Early 19thC. Via French from Old French, "shell" (see ESCALLOP); probably from its curling into a shell shape in cooking.]

es·ca·pade /éskə pàyd/ *n.* something exciting or adventurous that somebody does or is involved in, especially something showing recklessness or disregard for authority [Mid-17thC. Via French from Spanish *escapada* "an escape," from, ultimately, assumed Vulgar Latin *excappare* (see ESCAPE).]

es·cape /i skáyp/ *v.* (**-caped, -cap·ing, -capes**) **1.** *vti.* **BREAK FREE FROM CAPTIVITY** to free yourself and get away from captivity or confinement ○ *prisoners who attempted to escape* **2.** *vt.* **AVOID BAD SITUATION** to avoid danger, harm, or involvement in an unpleasant situation ○ *There's no escaping the fact that the house needs painting.* **3.** *vi.* **LEAK OUT** to leak out from a container **4.** *vt.* **BE TEMPORARILY UNKNOWN TO** to fail to be noticed, remembered, or understood by somebody ○ *a little village whose name escapes me for the moment* **5.** *vti.* **BE UTTERED** to be uttered by somebody unintentionally ○ *A muffled curse escaped his lips.* **6.** *vi.* BOT **SPREAD FROM GARDEN INTO THE WILD** to spread from a garden or other cultivated area and become established in the wild (*refers to cultivated plants*) **7.** *vi.* COMPUT **EXIT COMPUTER PROCEDURE** to exit from a computer program or file, cancel a command or operation, or return from the currently active menu to a previous one ■ *n.* **1. BREAKING FREE FROM CAPTIVITY** an act of getting free from captivity or confinement ○ *He made his escape while the guard was asleep.* **2. AVOIDANCE OF BAD SITUATION** the avoidance of a dangerous, harmful, or unpleasant situation ○ *an escape from danger* **3. MEANS OF GETTING AWAY** a method, means, or route by which somebody can escape from a place or situation **4. GAS OR LIQUID LEAK** a leak of gas or liquid from a container **5.** BOT **WILD PLANT ONCE CULTIVATED** a plant that has spread from a garden or other cultivated area and is growing wild **6.** COMPUT **COMPUTER KEY** the key on a computer keyboard that allows a user to exit a program, cancel a command, or return to a previous menu ○ *Press escape to exit the program.* **7.** COMPUT = **escape code** [13thC. Via Old Northern French *escaper* from, ultimately, assumed Vulgar Latin *excappare*, literally "to throw off your cloak," from *cappa* "cloak" (source of English *cape*).] —**es·cap·a·ble** *adj.* —**es·cap·er** *n.*

es·cape art·ist *n.* **1. PERFORMER SKILLED AT ESCAPING** a performer who is skilled at escaping from restraints or confinement **2. SOMEBODY ADEPT AT ESCAPING DIFFICULTIES** somebody who is skilled at getting out of difficulties or apparently very dangerous or compromising situations

es·cape clause *n.* a clause in a contract that sets out the conditions under which a party to the contract can be released from his or her obligations under it

es·cape code *n.* a sequence of one or more characters instructing a device that what follows is not part of the regular data but rather a command. For example, an escape code might instruct a printer to print in italics the text that follows the code.

es·cap·ee /i skày peé, ès kay-/ *n.* somebody who has escaped from captivity

es·cape hatch *n.* **1. EMERGENCY EXIT** a small opening providing a way out of an enclosed space, such as a submarine, through which people can escape in an emergency **2. WAY OUT OF TROUBLE** a way of avoiding an anticipated problem (*informal*)

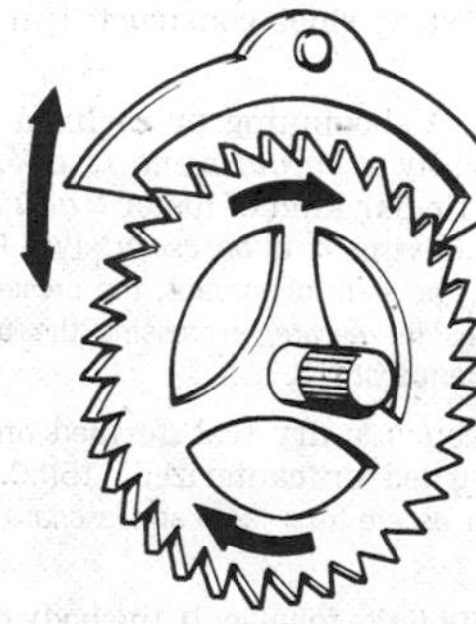

Escapement: Pallets on arm (top) engage teeth on wheel, driving gears in the movement

es·cape·ment /i skáypmənt/ *n.* **1. CLOCK MECHANISM** a mechanism in a clock or watch that allows power from a spring or falling weight to turn gears connected to the hands **2. PIANO MECHANISM** a mechanism in a piano that allows the hammer to rebound from a string after striking it **3. TYPEWRITER MECHANISM** a mechanism in a typewriter or printer that regulates the relative movement between the paper carrier and the typing or printing position on a line [Late 18thC. From its allowing a cogwheel to "escape" or be released repeatedly.]

es·cape ve·loc·i·ty *n.* the minimum speed at which an object must travel to escape a planet's or moon's gravitational field in order to orbit around it or move off into space. At or near the Earth's surface, the escape velocity is about 25,000 mph/40,000 kph.

es·cape wheel *n.* a toothed wheel in the mechanism of a watch or clock, designed to regulate the movement of the pendulum or balance wheel and so move the hands at regular intervals

es·cap·ism /i skáy pìzzəm/ *n.* **1. ESCAPE FROM EVERYDAY REALITY** something such as fantasy or entertainment that makes it possible to forget about the ordinary or unpleasant realities of life for a while **2. INDULGENCE IN FANTASIES TO ESCAPE REALITY** the act of indulging in daydreams or fantasies to escape from everyday reality

es·cap·ist /i skáypist/ *adj.* HELPING TO FORGET providing a means of forgetting about everyday or unpleasant realities for a while ■ *n.* SOMEBODY AVOIDING REALITY somebody who tries to avoid reality by indulging in daydreams or fantasies

es·cap·ol·o·gist /ès kay póllǝjist/ *n.* = **escape artist**

es·cap·ol·o·gy /ès kay póllǝjee/ *n.* the skill of escaping from restraints or confinement as a form of entertainment

es·car·got /ès kaar gṓ/ *n.* a snail that is cooked and eaten, especially served in its shell with melted garlic butter [Late 19thC. Via French from, ultimately, Old Provençal *escaragol*, of unknown origin.]

es·ca·role /éskǝ rṑl/ *n.* = **endive** *n.* 1 [Early 20thC. Via French from Italian *scariola*, from, ultimately, Latin *esca* "food" (see ESCULENT).]

es·carp /ǝ skaárp/ *n.* the inner side of a ditch dug as a fortification [Late 17thC. Via French *escarpe* from Italian *scarpa* "slope" (see SCARP).]

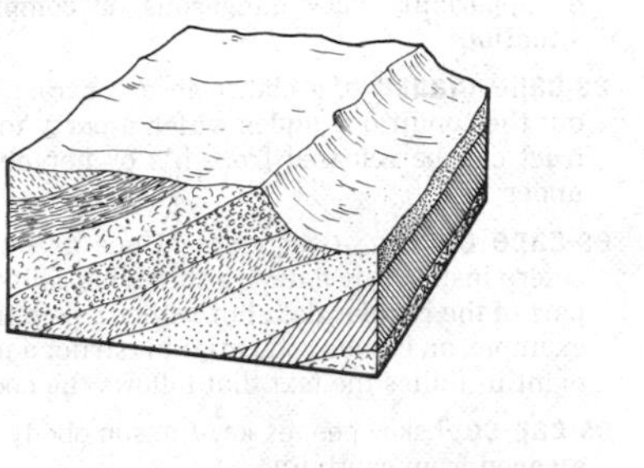

Escarpment

es·carp·ment /ǝ skaárpmǝnt/ *n.* **1.** STEEP RIDGE a steep slope or cliff that marks the boundary of a flat or gently sloping upland area such as a plateau, often formed by faulting or erosion. ◊ **scarp 2.** SLOPE IN FORTIFICATION a steep slope constructed in front of a fortification

-escent *suffix.* **1.** beginning or inclined to be, becoming, slightly ○ *acquiescent* ○ *alkalescent* **2.** having a particular kind of luster ○ *adularescent* **3.** resembling, having ○ *arborescent* [Via French from Latin *-escent-*, the stem of *-escens*, the present participle ending of verbs in *-escere*, expressing the beginning of action] —**-escence** *suffix.*

es·char /és kaar/ *n.* a dry scab formed on skin that has been burned or cauterized [15thC. Directly or via Old French *escare* from late Latin *eschara* "scab" (see SCAR[1]).]

es·cha·tol·o·gy /èskǝ tóllǝjee/ *n.* the body of religious doctrines concerning the human soul in its relation to death, judgment, heaven, and hell [Mid-19thC. Coined from Greek *eskhatos* "last" + -LOGY.] —**es·chat·o·log·i·cal** /èskǝtǝ lójjik'l, i skàttǝ-/ *adj.* —**es·chat·o·log·i·cal·ly** /-lójjikǝlee/ *adv.* —**es·cha·tol·o·gist** /èskǝ tóllǝjist/ *n.*

es·cheat /ǝss cheét/ *n.* **1.** REVERSION OF PROPERTY TO STATE the reversion of the property of a deceased person to the state in the United States, or to the Crown in England before 1926, when there are no legal heirs **2.** HIST REVERSION OF PROPERTY TO FEUDAL LORD in medieval England, the reversion to a feudal overlord of the property of a deceased person when there was no legal heir or when a tenant was outlawed **3.** PROPERTY AFFECTED BY ESCHEAT property that reverts by escheat [13thC. From Old French *eschete* and Anglo-Latin *escheta*, from assumed Vulgar Latin *excadere*, literally "to fall away," from Latin *cadere* (see CADENCE).] —**es·cheat·a·ble** *adj.*

Esch·er /éshǝr/, **M. C.** (1898–1972) Dutch graphic artist. He is known for his distinctive prints depicting intricate interlocking patterns and optical illusions based on mathematical concepts. Full name **Maurits Cornelis Escher**

es·chew /ǝss choó/ (**-chewed, -chew·ing, -chews**) *vt.* to avoid doing or using something on principle or as a matter of course [14thC. From Old French *eschiver*. Ultimately from a prehistoric Germanic word that is also the ancestor of English *shy*.] —**es·chew·al** *n.*

Es·cof·fier /es kóffee ày/, **Auguste** (1846–1935) French chef and cookbook author. Master of the haute cuisine style of French cookery, he gained an international reputation while working in London at the Savoy (1890–99) and Carlton (1899–1919) hotels. Full name **Georges Auguste Escoffier**

es·co·lar /èskǝ laár/ *n.* a deepwater fish of tropical and temperate seas with a slim bony body, jutting lower jaw, and sharp teeth. Family: Gempylidae. [Late 19thC. Via Spanish, "student" (because of the rings around its eyes resembling spectacles), from late Latin *scholaris* (see SCHOLAR).]

Es·con·di·do /èss kon deédō/ city in southwestern California, north of San Diego and east of Carlsbad. Population: 116,184 (1996).

es·cort *n.* /éss kàwrt/ **1.** SOMEBODY ACCOMPANYING SOMEBODY OR SOMETHING one or more persons accompanying somebody or something as a guard or guide, or as a mark of honor **2.** MIL ACCOMPANYING MILITARY VESSEL OR AIRCRAFT one or more warships or fighter aircraft accompanying a larger, more vulnerable ship or aircraft as protection ○ *The bombers were joined by their fighter escort when they reached the coast.* **3.** MAN AS SOCIAL PARTNER a man accompanying a woman on a social occasion **4.** HIRED SOCIAL PARTNER a man or woman who is hired to accompany another person as a companion, especially to a social event or entertainment **5.** PROTECTION OR SECURITY FOR JOURNEY protection or restraint provided by an escort ○ *The prisoner will proceed under escort to the guardhouse.* ■ *vt.* /ǝss káwrt, éss kàwrt/ (**-cort·ed, -cort·ing, -corts**) GO WITH AS ESCORT to accompany somebody or something as an escort ○ *The butler will escort you to the door.* [Late 16thC. Via French *escorte* from Italian *scorta*, from *scorgere* "to guide," which came via assumed Vulgar Latin *excorrigere* from Latin *corrigere* (see CORRECT).]

Escritoire

es·cri·toire /èskri twaár/ *n.* a writing desk, often with a hinged flap that conceals drawers and pigeonholes [Late 16thC. Via Old French, "writing box," from medieval Latin *scriptorium* (see SCRIPTORIUM).]

es·crow /és krṑ, e skrṓ/ *n.* **1.** SOMETHING HELD INDEPENDENTLY UNTIL CONDITION MET an amount of money or property granted to somebody but held by a third party and only released after a condition has been met **2.** STATE OF BEING AN ESCROW the condition of being held as an escrow ■ *vt.* (**-crowed, -crow·ing, -crows**) PUT IN ESCROW to place something in escrow [Mid-17thC. From Anglo-Norman *escrowe* "scroll," a variant of Old French *escroe* (see SCROLL).]

es·cu·do /ǝ skoó dō/ (*plural* **-dos**) *n.* **1.** UNIT OF PORTUGESE CURRENCY a unit of currency used in Portugal. See table at **currency 2.** OLD UNIT OF CURRENCY any one of various units of currency that were formerly used in Spain and countries of South America **3.** COIN WORTH ONE ESCUDO a coin worth one escudo [Early 19thC. Via Spanish and Portugese from Latin *scutum* "shield" (see SCUTUM), because early coins resembled heraldic shields.]

es·cu·lent /éskyǝlǝnt/ *adj.* EDIBLE fit to be eaten (*formal*) ■ *n.* EDIBLE SUBSTANCE something edible, especially a plant (*formal*) [Early 17thC. From Latin *esculentus*, from *esca* "food," from *edere* "to eat" (see EDIBLE).]

es·cutch·eon /ǝ skúchǝn/ *n.* **1.** HERALDRY HERALDIC SHIELD a shield, especially one used in heraldry to display a coat of arms **2.** PROTECTIVE SHIELD a plate or shield fixed around something, e.g., a light switch or keyhole, as an ornament or to protect the surrounding surface **3.** NAUT NAME PLATE ON VESSEL a panel on the stern of a vessel on which the vessel's name is shown [15thC. Via Anglo-Norman *escuchon* from, ultimately, Latin *scutum* "shield" (see SCUTUM).] —**es·cutch·eoned** *adj.*

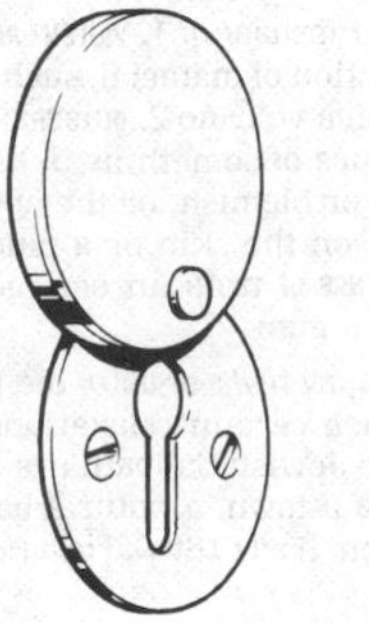

Escutcheon

Esd. *abbr.* BIBLE Esdras

Es·dras /ézdrǝss/ *n.* **1.** BOOK OF APOCRYPHA either of two books in the Apocrypha **2.** BOOK OF ROMAN CATHOLIC BIBLE either of two books of the Roman Catholic version of the Bible (**Douay Bible**), equivalent to the books of Ezra and Nehemiah in the Authorized Version

ESE *abbr.* east-southeast

-ese *suffix.* **1.** from, of, native to, or inhabiting a particular place ○ *Taiwanese* **2.** the language of a particular place ○ *Faeroese* **3.** style or jargon ○ *officialese* [Via Old French *-eis* and Italian *-ese* from Latin *-ensis* "originating in"]

es·er·ine /éssǝ reén/ *n.* = **physostigmine** [Mid-19thC. From French *ésérine*, from Efik *esere* "Calabar bean."]

Esh·kol /ésh kawl, esh káwl/, **Levi** (1895–1969) Russian-born Israeli statesman. He was prime minister of Israel from 1963 to his death in 1969. Born **Levi Shkolnik**

es·ker /éskǝr/, **es·kar** *n.* a long narrow winding ridge of sand or gravel, deposited by a stream flowing under a glacier [Mid-19thC. From Irish *eiscir*, from Old Irish *escir*, of unknown origin.]

Es·ki·mo /éskǝ mṑ/ *adj., n.* (*plural* **-mos** *or* **-mo**) = **Inuit.** See Usage note below. [Late 16thC. From French *Esquimaux*, ultimately of Algonquian origin.]

WORD KEY: USAGE

Sensitivity trap: The Inuit Circumpolar Conference, held in 1977 in Barrow, Alaska, chose officially to replace the term ***Eskimo*** with ***Inuit*** (which means "the real people"). ***Eskimo*** nonetheless remains in common use, appearing even in academic contexts. Because some may find it offensive, care should be exercised in using this word.

Es·ki·mo-A·leut *n.* a family of languages spoken in Greenland, Alaska, Canada, Siberia, and the Aleutian Islands

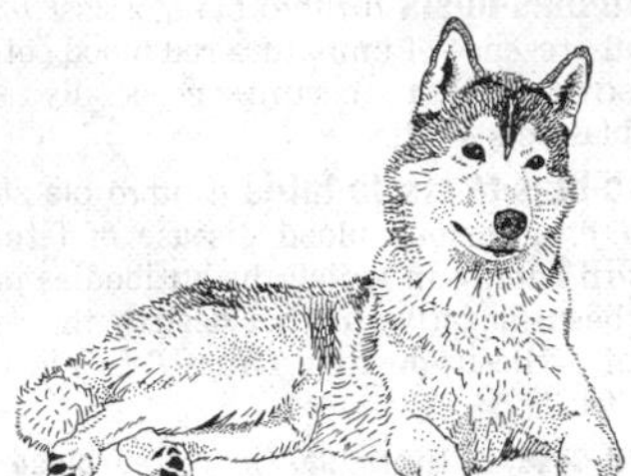

Eskimo dog

Es·ki·mo dog *n.* a large powerful thick-coated dog with erect ears that is used to pull sleds in Arctic regions

Es·ki·mo roll *n.* a process or procedure by which a capsized kayak is rolled over underwater in order to come up righted

Es·ki·şe·hir /éski shǝ heér/ city in western Turkey, west of Ankara. Population: 413,300 (1990).

ESL *abbr.* English as a second language

ESOL /eé sàwl/ *abbr.* English for speakers of other languages

ESOP /eé sòp/ *n.* a plan in which employees acquire stock of the company they work for by making tax-deductible contributions [Late 20thC. Acronym formed from *employee stock ownership plan*.]

e·soph·a·gus /i sóffəgəss/ (*plural* **-guses** *or* **-gi** /-jī, -gī/), **oe·soph·a·gus** (*plural* **-guses** *or* **-gi**) *n.* the passage down which food moves between the throat and the stomach [14thC. Via medieval Latin *isophagus* from Greek *oisophagos*.]

es·o·ter·ic /èssə térrik/ *adj.* **1. RESTRICTED TO INITIATES** intended for or understood by only an initiated few **2. ABSTRUSE** difficult to understand **3. SECRET** secret or highly confidential [Mid-17thC. From Greek *esōterikos* "belonging to an inner circle," from *esōterō* "inner," from *esō* "within."] —**es·o·ter·i·cal·ly** *adv.*

es·o·ter·i·ca /èssə térrikə/ *npl.* things that are for initiates only, or are difficult or secret [Early 20thC. From Greek *esōterika*, from *esōterikos* (see ESOTERIC).]

es·o·ter·i·cism /èssə térrə sìzzəm/ *n.* **1. ESOTERIC BELIEFS OR PRACTICES** beliefs or practices that are arcane, mysterious, or secret **2. STATE OF BEING ESOTERIC** the condition or quality of being esoteric

ESP *abbr.* **1.** English for special purposes **2.** extrasensory perception

esp. *abbr.* especially

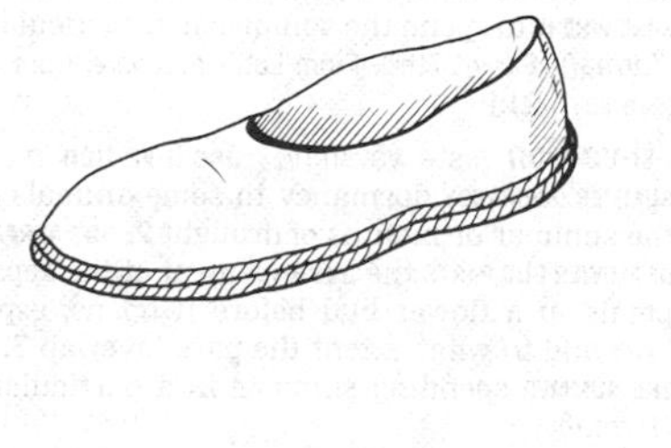

Espadrille

es·pa·drille /éspə drìl/ *n.* a light shoe with a fabric or canvas upper and a sole made of twisted cord, sometimes tied with lacing around the ankle [Late 19thC. Via French from Provençal *espardilho*, from *espart* "esparto" (from which it was originally made), from Latin *spartum* (see ESPARTO).]

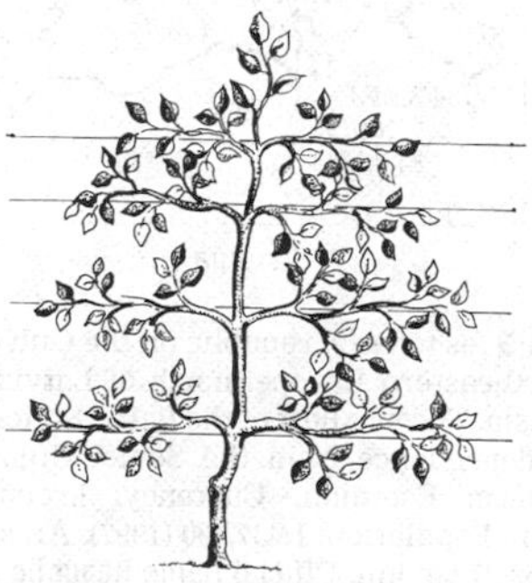

Espalier

es·pal·ier /əss pállyər, -pál yày/ *n.* a plant, especially a fruit tree, trained to grow flat against an upright surface, e.g., a wall or fence, or on wires [Mid-17thC. Via French from Italian *spalliera* "shoulder support," from *spalla* "shoulder," from Latin *spatula* (see SPATULA).]

es·par·to /ə spaár tō/ (*plural* **-tos**), **es·par·to grass** *n.* a long coarse grass found in southern Europe and North Africa whose fibers are used in making paper, ropes, and mats. Latin name: *Stipa tenacissima.* [Mid-19thC. Via Spanish from Latin *spartum*, from Greek *sparton* "rope."]

es·pe·cial /ə spésh'l/ *adj.* (*formal*) **1. NOTABLE** unusual or exceptional **2. PARTICULAR** particular or specific [13thC. Via Old French from Latin *specialis*, literally "of a specific kind," from *species* (see SPECIES).]

es·pe·cial·ly /ə spésh'lee/ *adv.* **1. EXCEPTIONALLY** to an unusual or exceptional degree **2. PARTICULARLY** used to single out one among a range **3. CHIEFLY** in most cases **4. EXPRESSLY** for a particular or specific purpose

Es·pe·ran·to /èspə rán tō, -raán-/ *n.* an artificial language invented in 1887 as a means of making international communication easier. It is based on the root forms of certain words common to the major European languages. In general, the word order is similar to that of English, although the grammar is more highly inflected. [Late 19thC. Named for Doctor *Esperanto*, literally "one who hopes," the Esperanto pseudonym of the Polish philologist Ludwik Zamenhof 1859–1917, who invented the language.] —**Es·pe·ran·tist** *n.*

es·pi·al /ə spí əl/ *n.* (*archaic*) **1. ACT OF SIGHTING SOMETHING** the action of sighting or discovering something **2. ACT OF NOTICING SOMETHING** the action of noticing or detecting something **3. ACT OF SPYING** the action of secretly watching somebody or something [14thC. From Old French *espialle*, from *espier* (see SPY).]

es·pi·o·nage /éspee ə naàzh/ *n.* the use of spying or spies to gather secret information [Late 18thC. From French *espionnage*, from *espionner* "to spy," from *espion* "spy." Ultimately of prehistoric Germanic origin.]

es·pla·nade /éspla naàd, -nàyd/ *n.* **1.** TRANSP **OPEN WALKWAY** a long level area, especially by the sea, for walking or driving along **2.** MIL **LEVEL AREA OUTSIDE FORTIFICATION** a wide level area outside a fortification, where attackers will be exposed to fire from defenders [Late 17thC. From French, from, ultimately, Latin *explanare*, literally "to flatten out" (see EXPLAIN).]

Es·pos·i·to /èspə zéetō/, **Phil** (*b.* 1942) Canadian ice hockey player. A center noted for his goal scoring, he played professionally between 1963 and his retirement in 1981. Full name **Philip Anthony Esposito**

es·pous·al /əss pówz'l/ *n.* **1. ADOPTION AS BELIEF** the adoption of something as a belief or cause **2. MARRIAGE** a betrothal or wedding (*formal*) (*often used in the plural*)

es·pouse /əss pówz/ (**-poused, -pous·ing, -pous·es**) *vt.* **1. ADOPT** to adopt or support something as a belief or cause **2. MARRY OR GIVE IN MARRIAGE** to marry somebody or give somebody in marriage (*archaic*) [15thC. Via Old French *espouser* from Latin *sponsare*, from *spons-*, the stem of *spondere* (see SPONSOR).] —**es·pous·er** *n.*

es·pres·si·vo /èsprə sée vō/ *adv.* played in a expressive way (*used as a musical direction*) [Late 19thC. From Italian, "expressively."]

es·pres·so /ə spréssō/ *n.* **1. STRONG COFFEE MADE IN A SPECIAL MACHINE** dark strong-tasting coffee made by using a special machine to pass steam under pressure or boiling water through finely ground coffee beans **2. CUP OF ESPRESSO** a serving of espresso coffee, usually in a small cup ○ *Two espressos and a cappuccino.* **3. MACHINE FOR MAKING ESPRESSO** a machine for making espresso coffee ○ *the hiss of the espresso* [Mid-20thC. From Italian *(caffè) espresso*, literally "pressed-out (coffee)," from the past participle of *esprimere* "to press out," from Latin *exprimere* (see EXPRESS).]

es·prit /e sprée/ *n.* lively intelligence or wit [Late 16thC. From French (see SPIRIT).]

es·prit de corps *n.* a feeling of pride in belonging to a group and a sense of identification with it [From French, literally "group spirit"]

es·py /ə spí/ (**-pied, -py·ing, -pies**) *vt.* to catch sight of or detect something (*formal*) [14thC. From Old French *espier* (see SPY).]

Esq. *abbr.* Esquire (*in correspondence*)

-esque *suffix.* in the style of, like ○ *Pythonesque* [Via French from, ultimately, assumed Vulgar Latin *-iscus*, of Germanic origin (ultimately related to English *-ish*)]

Es·qui·malt /éski màwlt/ seaport and naval station on southeastern Vancouver Island, British Columbia, Canada. It is a suburb of the city of Victoria. Population: 16,192 (1991).

es·quire /ə skwír/ *n.* a youth serving as an attendant or shield-bearer to a medieval knight, especially as a stage in his own training for knighthood [14thC. Via Old French *escuier* from late Latin *scutarius* "shield bearer," from Latin *scutum* "shield" (see SCUTUM).]

Es·quire /es kwír, ə skwír/ *n.* a courtesy title placed after a man's full name, especially in correspondence

Es·qui·vel /éski vél/, **Manuel** (*b.* 1940) Belizean statesman. He was prime minister from 1984 to 1989 and again from 1993.

ESR *abbr.* **1.** PHYS electron spin resonance **2.** MED erythrocyte sedimentation rate

ess /ess/ *n.* **1. S** the letter s or S **2. SOMETHING S-SHAPED** something shaped like an S [Mid-16thC. From Latin *es*.]

-ess *suffix.* woman or girl ○ *heiress* [Via Old French and Latin from, ultimately, Greek *-issa*]

es·say *n.* /éssày, ə sáy/ **1. SHORT NONFICTION PROSE PIECE** a short analytical, descriptive, or interpretive piece of literary or journalistic prose dealing with a particular topic, especially from a personal and unsystematic viewpoint **2. SET WRITTEN PIECE** a short piece of written work assigned to a student **3. WORK RESEMBLING A WRITTEN ESSAY** an artistic or journalistic work resembling a written essay but in another medium ○ *not so much a short film as a cinematographic essay* **4. ATTEMPT AT SOMETHING** an attempt to accomplish something (*formal*) **5. TEST OF SOMETHING** a test or trial of something (*formal*) ■ *vt.* /ə sáy, éssay/ (**-sayed, -say·ing, -says**) **1. ATTEMPT** to try out or attempt something (*formal*) ○ *Shall we essay a walk on the promenade?* **2. TEST** to make a test of something ○ *essay his theory* [15thC. Via Old French *essaier* "to try" from assumed Vulgar Latin *exagiare*, literally "to weigh out," from *agere* (see ACT).]

es·say·ist /é sàyist/ *n.* a writer of literary or journalistic essays

es·say·is·tic /èssay ístik/ *adj.* resembling or styled like a literary or journalistic essay

es·say ques·tion *n.* a question on an examination that must be answered in a prose piece of a specified length

Es·sen /éss'n/ industrial city in the Ruhr valley, North Rhine-Westphalia State, west central Germany. Population: 626,100 (1990).

es·sence /éss'ns/ *n.* **1. IDENTIFYING NATURE** the quality or nature of something that identifies it or makes it what it is **2. BASIC FEATURE** the most basic element or feature of something ○ *Lack of time is the essence of the problem.* **3. PERFECT FORM** the perfect or idealized form of something, especially when embodied in a person ○ *She is the essence of tact.* **4.** PHILOS **IDEAL NATURE OF SOMETHING** the ideal nature of something, independent of and prior to its existence **5.** RELIG **SPIRITUAL ENTITY** a spiritual entity **6.** BIOCHEM **CHEMICAL CONSTITUENT OF PLANT** an extract or derivative of a plant that contains its characteristic or special chemical constituents **7.** COOK, COSMETICS **CONCENTRATED PLANT EXTRACT** a concentrated substance extracted from a plant that retains the plant's essential properties, such as flavor and fragrance ○ *peppermint essence* [14thC. Via French from Latin *essentia*, from *essent-*, the present participle stem of *esse* "to be" (source of English *entity*). Ultimately from an Indo-European word meaning "to be."] ◇ **in essence** fundamentally or intrinsically ◇ **of the essence** of the highest importance for achieving something

es·sen·tial /i sénshəl/ *adj.* **1. NECESSARY** of the highest importance for achieving something ○ *It is essential that we arrive on time.* **2. BASIC** being the most basic element or feature of something or somebody ○ *We wanted the biography to tell us the essential nature of the man.* **3. PERFECT** being the pure or perfect form or embodiment of something **4.** BIOCHEM **REQUIRED IN DIET** used to describe a nutrient such as a fatty acid that is required in the diet for the health and growth of an organism but not synthesized in the body **5. DEFINING** constituting the property or characteristic of something that makes it what it is ○ *Being three-sided is essential to being a triangle.* **6.** MED **WITHOUT KNOWN CAUSE** used to describe a disease that has no known cause ■ *n.* **SOMETHING ESSENTIAL** something that is necessary or fundamental ○ *Having your own computer is an essential for this kind of work.* ○ *She soon picked up the essentials of the subject.* [14thC. From late Latin *essentialis*, from Latin *essentia* (see ESSENCE).] —**es·sen·ti·al·i·ty** /i sènshee állətee/ *n.* —**es·sen·tial·ly** /i sénshəlee/ *adv.* —**es·sen·tial·ness** /-nəss/ *n.*

WORD KEY: SYNONYMS

See Synonyms at ***necessary.***

es·sen·tial a·mi·no ac·id *n.* any amino acid needed by the body to maintain growth but not synthesized by the body and usually obtained from food

es·sen·tial el·e·ment *n.* a chemical element that is necessary to the healthy growth of an organism

es·sen·tial·ism /ə sénshə lìzzəm/ *n.* the doctrine that things have an essence or ideal nature that is independent of and prior to their existence —**es·sen·tial·ist** *n.*

es·sen·tial oil *n.* an oil made from an extract of a plant or substance that preserves its fundamental properties such as flavor and fragrance

Es·sex /éssiks/ town in central Maryland, east of Baltimore. Population: 40,872 (1990).

es·so·nite /éssə nīt/ *n.* a type of garnet ranging in color from yellow to brown [Early 19thC. Coined from Greek *hēssōn* "inferior" (because it is less hard than other garnets) + -ITE.]

EST *abbr.* **1. EST, E.S.T.** Eastern Standard Time **2.** electric shock treatment

est. *abbr.* **1.** established **2.** estimated **3.** estuary

Est. *abbr.* BIBLE Esther

-est *suffix.* most ○ *hardest* ○ *sloppiest* [Old English]

es·tab·lish /ə stábblish/ (**-lished, -lish·ing, -lish·es**) *v.* **1.** *vt.* FIX PERMANENTLY to place something securely and permanently in a position, situation, or condition ○ *A settlement was established here two hundred years ago.* **2.** *vt.* INAUGURATE to start or set up something that is intended to continue or be permanent ○ *The firm was established in 1954.* **3.** *vt.* PROVE to investigate something and prove or confirm its truth or validity ○ *Have we established who gave the instruction?* **4.** *vt.* CAUSE TO BE RECOGNIZED to cause something or somebody to become generally accepted or recognized ○ *The victory established his superiority.* ○ *Her first novel established her on the literary scene.* **5.** *vt.* RELIG MAKE A CHURCH NATIONAL AND OFFICIAL to make a church an official national institution **6.** *vti.* GARDENING CAUSE A PLANT TO GROW SUCCESSFULLY to grow, or cause a plant to grow, successfully in a new place ○ *The new owners established an avenue of poplars.* ○ *Keep the area weeded to allow the seedlings to establish.* [14thC. From Old French *establiss-*, the stem of *establir*, from Latin *stabilire*, literally "to make stable," from *stabilis* (see STABLE).] —**es·tab·lish·er** *n.*

es·tab·lished *adj.* **1.** ACCEPTED AS TRUE generally recognized as being true or valid ○ *an established fact* **2.** SUCCESSFUL having gained public recognition in a particular sphere of activity ○ *an established author* **3.** GROWING SUCCESSFULLY growing strongly ○ *an established garden* **4.** LEGALLY RECOGNIZED legally recognized and sometimes financially supported as an official national institution ○ *an established church*

es·tab·lish·ing shot *n.* a shot in a movie that introduces a new scene

es·tab·lish·ment /ə stábblishmənt/ *n.* **1.** ESTABLISHING SOMETHING the act of establishing something or the condition of being established ○ *the establishment of new guidelines for users* **2.** COMM SOMETHING ESTABLISHED something that is established as a business, institution, or successful undertaking ○ *The establishment hired several new managers.* **3.** COMM BUSINESS PREMISES a place of business ○ *The restaurant manager told them they were now banned from the establishment.* **4. es·tab·lish·ment, Es·tab·lish·ment** PEOPLE IN POWER a group of people who hold power in a society or social group and dominate its institutions ○ *One period's avantgarde becomes the next's artistic establishment.* **5.** VETERAN STAFF the staff of a permanent organization, institution, or department, especially in the military or government. Used particularly in relation to the size and deployment of staff. **6.** HOUSEHOLD a place of residence, or the household that occupies it

es·tab·lish·men·tar·i·an /ə stàbblishmən térree ən/ *n.* **1.** MEMBER OF THE SOCIAL ESTABLISHMENT a supporter or member of the establishment in a society or social group **2.** MEMBER OF ESTABLISHED CHURCH a supporter or member of an established church —**es·tab·lish·men·tar·i·an·ism** *n.*

es·ta·mi·net /es tàmmi náy/ *n.* a small and simple café, bar, or bistro, especially in France [Early 19thC. From French, of uncertain origin: possibly from Walloon *staminé* "cowshed," from *stamo* "hitching post," probably of prehistoric Germanic origin.]

es·tan·cia /e staán syaá/ *n.* a large landed estate, especially a cattle ranch, in South America [Mid-17thC. Via Spanish, literally "station," from medieval Latin *stantia*, from Latin *stant-*, the present participle stem of *stare* "to stand" (see STATION).]

es·tate /ə stáyt/ *n.* **1.** RURAL PROPERTY WITH A RESIDENCE an area of rural, privately owned property that includes a large residence **2.** ALL OF SOMEBODY'S PROPERTY the whole of somebody's property, possessions, and capital **3.** PROPERTY OF A DEAD OR BANKRUPT PERSON the assets and liabilities of somebody who is dead or bankrupt **4.** SOMEBODY'S OVERALL SITUATION the circumstances, period, or condition in which somebody lives **5.** POL, HIST ONE OF 3 TRADITIONAL RANKS especially formerly in Europe, any of three traditional ranks or sectors of society with some political power, broadly the clergy, the nobility, and the middle class **6.** *U.K.* COMMERCIAL OR INDUSTRIAL AREA a large area set aside for industrial or commercial use [13thC. From Old French *estat* (see STATE). The underlying meaning is "condition in which somebody lives."]

es·tate a·gent *n. U.K.* = **real estate agent**

es·tate-bot·tled *adj.* bottled by the same vineyard at which the wine was made

es·tate car *n. U.K.* = **station wagon** [From its ability to hold the owner's possessions]

es·tate tax *n.* a tax on the right to bequeath property, assessed on the value of the bequeather's property before it is passed on to the heirs

estd., **est'd.** *abbr.* established

es·teem /ə steém/ *vt.* (**-teemed, -teem·ing, -teems**) **1.** VALUE HIGHLY to value somebody or something highly **2.** REGARD AS SOMETHING to consider or regard something or somebody as being in a particular category ○ *I esteem him a friend.* ■ *n.* **1.** HIGH REGARD high valuation of somebody or something ○ *It was a relationship founded on mutual esteem.* **2.** VALUATION judgment or estimation of the worth of somebody or something [Early 16thC. Via Old French *estimer* "to value" from Latin *aestimare* (see ESTIMATE).]

WORD KEY: SYNONYMS

See Synonyms at ***regard***.

Es·te·fan /éstə fàn/, **Gloria** (*b.* 1957) Cuban-born U.S. singer and songwriter. She established herself first as a Spanish-language pop singer with the group Miami Sound Machine (1985–89) before gaining an international following as a solo artist. Born **Gloria Maria Fajardo**

es·ter /éstər/ *n.* an organic often fragrant compound formed in a reaction between an acid and an alcohol with the elimination of water [Mid-19thC. From German, a contraction of *Essigäther* "acetic ether."]

es·ter·ase /éstə ràyss, -ràyz/ *n.* any enzyme that acts as a catalyst in the hydrolysis of an ester

es·ter·i·fy /ə stérrə fī/ (**-fied, -fy·ing, -fies**) *vti.* to change or make a substance change into an ester —**es·ter·i·fi·ca·tion** /es tèrrəfi káysh'n/ *n.*

Esth. *abbr.* BIBLE Esther

Es·ther /éstər/ *n.* **1.** JEWISH QUEEN IN THE BIBLE in the Bible, the Jewish Queen of Persia who is described as having rescued her Jewish subjects from massacre **2.** BOOK OF BIBLE a book in the Bible that tells the story of Esther

es·the·sia *n.* = **aesthesia**

es·thete *n.* = **aesthete**

es·thet·ic *adj., n.* = **aesthetic**

es·thet·i·cize *vt.* = **aestheticize**

es·thet·ics *n.* = **aesthetics**

Es·ti·gar·ri·bi·a /ésti gə ríbbee ə, -gaa-/, **Jose Felix** (1888–1940) Paraguayan general and politician. He was president from 1939 until his death in an airplane crash.

es·ti·ma·ble /éstəməb'l/ *adj.* **1.** ADMIRABLE deserving respect or admiration **2.** ABLE TO BE ESTIMATED able to be estimated (*archaic*) [15thC. From Old French, from, ultimately, Latin *aestimare* (see ESTEEM).] —**es·ti·ma·ble·ness** *n.* —**es·ti·ma·bly** *adv.*

es·ti·mate *vti.* /éstə màyt/ (**-mat·ed, -mat·ing, -mates**) **1.** CALCULATE ROUGHLY to make an approximate calculation of something ○ *Can you estimate the time it will take?* See Usage note below. **2.** SUBMIT A PRICE to assess something, such as an item to be bought or a job to be done, and to state a likely price for it ○ *Ask at least two contractors to estimate the job.* **3.** ASSESS to form an opinion or judgment about somebody or something ○ *How would you estimate that performance?* ■ *n.* /éstəmət/ **1.** ROUGH CALCULATION an approximate calculation ○ *At least a thousand people attended, by my estimate.* ○ *Here are the estimates for next month's sales figures.* **2.** APPROXIMATE PRICE an assessment of the likely price of something, such as an item to be bought or a job to be done ○ *Their estimate is the lowest.* [Late 16thC. From Latin *aestimare* "to value" (source also of English *esteem*), of unknown origin.] —**es·ti·ma·tive** /éstə màytiv/ *adj.* —**es·ti·ma·tor** /-màytər/ *n.*

WORD KEY: USAGE

estimate or **estimation**? Broadly speaking, ***estimation*** refers to "a thinking or valuing process" and ***estimate*** to "the result of such a process." *An estimate of the time needed* is the figure produced by working out how long something will take, whereas *an estimation of the time needed* is the calculation process that produces that figure. ***Estimation*** also has the special meaning "opinion or regard," which ***estimate*** does not have: *What, in your estimation, is the cause of the problem? She went down in their estimation when the truth came out.*

es·ti·ma·tion /èstə máysh'n/ *n.* **1.** ASSESMENT a judgment or opinion about somebody or something ○ *Her behavior bore out his estimation of her.* **2.** ACT OF ESTIMATING the act of estimating something, or the result of this

WORD KEY: USAGE

See Usage note at ***estimate***.

es·ti·val /éstəv'l/, **aes·ti·val** *adj.* relating to or happening during summer [14thC. Via Old French from, ultimately, Latin *aestivus*, from *aestas* "summer." Ultimately from an Indo-European word meaning "to burn."]

es·ti·vate /éstə vàyt/ (**-vat·ed, -vat·ing, -vates**), **aes·ti·vate** (**-vat·ed, -vat·ing, -vates**) *vi.* **1.** BE DORMANT IN SUMMER to be dormant during the summer or during months of drought (*refers to animals, especially some amphibians, reptiles, and insects*) **2.** SPEND SUMMER SOMEWHERE to spend the summer in a particular place (*formal*) [Early 17thC. From Latin *aestivare*, from *aestivus* (see ESTIVAL).]

es·ti·va·tion /èstə váysh'n/, **aes·ti·va·tion** *n.* **1.** ZOOL SUMMER DORMANCY dormancy in some animals during the summer or months of drought **2.** BOT ARRANGEMENT OF FLOWER BUD PARTS the arrangement of the sepals and petals in a flower bud before it opens, especially how and to what extent the parts overlap **3.** PASSING THE SUMMER spending summer in a particular place (*formal*)

Estonia

Es·to·ni·a /es tṓnee ə/ republic on the Gulf of Finland in northeastern Europe, north of Latvia and west of Russia. The smallest of the Baltic States, it gained its independence from the Soviet Union in 1991. Language: Estonian. Currency: kroon. Capital: Tallinn. Population: 1,437,000 (1997). Area: 17,462 sq. mi./45,227 sq. km. Official name **Republic of Estonia**

Es·to·ni·an /es tṓnee ən/ *n.* **1.** SOMEBODY FROM ESTONIA somebody who was born or raised in Estonia, or who has Estonian citizenship **2.** LANGUAGE OF ESTONIA the official language of Estonia. It is one of the Finnic group of the Finno-Ugric branch of the Uralic family of languages. About 1.7 million people speak Estonian. ■ *adj.* OF ESTONIA relating to or typical of Estonia or its people, language, or culture

es·top /ə stóp/ (**-topped, -top·ping, -tops**) *vt.* **1.** PREVENT BY LEGAL RULE to use the legal rule of estoppel to prevent something **2.** PREVENT to stop or prevent something (*archaic*) [15thC. From Anglo-Norman and Old French *estopper*, literally "to plug up," from, ultimately, Latin *stuppa* "tow, broken flax," used for plugging gaps.] —**es·top·page** *n.*

es·top·pel /e stópp'l/ *n.* a legal rule that prevents somebody from stating a position inconsistent with one previously stated, especially when the earlier representation has been relied upon by others [Mid-16thC. From Old French *estouppail* "stopper," from *estopper* (see ESTOP).]

es·tra·di·ol /èstrə dī àwl/ *n.* an estrogenic hormone produced in the ovaries and synthesized for use in treating estrogen deficiency and breast cancer. Formula: $C_{18}H_{24}O_2$. [Mid-20thC. Coined from ESTR(US) + DI- + -OL.]

es·tral *adj.* ZOOL = **estrous**

es·trange /ə stráynj/ (**-tranged, -trang·ing, -trang·es**) *vt.* to cause somebody to stop feeling friendly or affectionate toward somebody else or sympathetic toward a tradition or belief (*usually passive*) ○ *He managed to become estranged from all of his friends.* [15thC. Via Old French *estrangier* "to alienate" from Latin *extraneare* "to treat as a stranger," from *extraneus* (see STRANGE).] —**es·trang·er** *n.* —**es·trange·ment** *n.*

es·tranged /i stráynjd/ *adj.* no longer living with a husband or wife

es·tray /ə stráy/ *n.* in law, a domestic animal that has strayed and has no obvious owner (*formal*) [Early 16thC. Via Anglo-Norman from Old French *estraier* (see STRAY).]

es·tri·ol /éstree àwl/ *n.* an estrogen hormone produced in the ovaries, secreted in the urine during pregnancy, and synthesized for use in treating estrogen deficiency. Formula: $C_{18}H_{24}O_3$. [Early 20thC. Coined from ESTRUS + TRI- + -OL.]

es·tro·gen /éstrəjən/ *n.* any of several steroid hormones, produced mainly in the ovaries, that stimulate estrus and the development of female secondary sexual characteristics [Early 20thC. Coined from ESTR(US) + -GEN.]

es·tro·gen-re·place·ment ther·a·py *n.* treatment to maintain levels of the hormone estrogen in women after menopause to avoid bone fragility **(osteoporosis)** and protect against heart attacks

es·trone /és trōn/ *n.* an estrogenic hormone produced in the ovaries and synthesized for use in treating estrogen deficiency and breast cancer. Formula: $C_{18}H_{22}O_2$. [Early 20thC. Coined from ESTR(US) + -ONE.]

es·trous /éstrəss/, **es·tral** /éstrəl/ *adj.* ZOOL relating to, involving, or in estrus. ◊ **anestrus** [Early 20thC]

es·trous cy·cle *n.* a hormonally controlled reproductive cycle occurring in many female mammals, marked by a period of sexual activity, ovulation, and changes in the womb lining

es·trus /éstrəss/, **oes·trus** *n.* a regular period of sexual excitement in many female mammals during which the animal seeks to mate [Late 19thC. Via Latin *oestrus*, "frenzy," from Greek *oistros* "gad-fly," the underlying sense being "sting, irritation" and hence "stimulus to action," from, ultimately, an Indo-European word denoting "passion" that is also the ancestor of English *irate*.]

es·tu·a·rine /éschoo ə rīn, éschoo ə reèn/ *adj.* relating to, formed in, or found in an estuary

es·tu·ar·y /éschoo èrree/ (*plural* **-ies**) *n.* the wide lower course of a river where the tide flows in, causing fresh and salt water to mix [Mid-16thC. From Latin *aestuarium*, from *aestus* "heat, surge, tide."] —**es·tu·ar·i·al** /éschoo érree əl/ *adj.*

Es·tu·ar·y Eng·lish *n.* a variety of standard English influenced by Cockney spoken by people in London and southeastern England along the Thames estuary

esu, ESU *abbr.* electrostatic unit

e·su·ri·ent /i sóoree ənt/ *adj.* very hungry or greedy (*archaic or formal*) [Late 17thC. From Latin *esurient-*, the present participle stem of *esurire* "to be hungry," literally "to want to eat," from *edere* (see EDIBLE).] —**e·su·ri·ence** *n.* —**e·su·ri·en·cy** *n.*

ET *abbr.* extraterrestrial

-et *suffix.* **1.** small one ○ *falconet* **2.** something worn on ○ *anklet* [Via Old French from assumed Vulgar Latin *-ittum*, of unknown origin]

e·ta[1] /áytə, eétə/ *n.* the seventh letter of the Greek alphabet, represented in the English alphabet as "e" or "ē" [15thC. From Greek *ēta*.]

e·ta[2] /áytə/ (*plural* **e·tas** *or* **e·ta**) *n.* in former times, a member of a Japanese class that was restricted to doing menial and disagreeable tasks [Late 19thC. From Japanese.]

ETA[1], **e.t.a.** *abbr.* estimated time of arrival

ETA[2], **Eta** *n.* a Basque nationalist guerrilla group that seeks separation and independence from Spain for the Basque region [Mid-20thC. From Basque, an acronym for *Euzkadi ta Askatsuna* "Basque Nation and Liberty."]

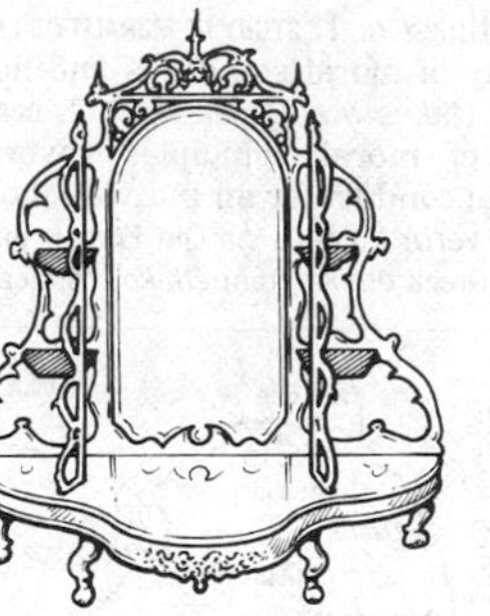

Étagère

é·ta·gère /ày taa zháir/ *n.* a piece of furniture made up of open shelves, used to hold small objects [Mid-19thC. Via French from Old French *estagiere* "scaffold," from *estage* (see STAGE).]

et al. *adv.* and elsewhere [Shortening of Latin et alibi "and elsewhere"]

et·a·lon /áyt'l òn, étt'l òn/ *n.* a spectroscopic device that has two flat parallel reflecting surfaces and is used to measure wavelengths [Early 20thC. From French *étalon* "standard," from Old French *estal* "standing place" (see STALE).]

et·a·mine /éttə meèn/ *n.* a light, loosely woven cotton or worsted fabric [Early 18thC. Via French from, ultimately, Latin *stamineus* "made of threads," from *stamen* "thread" (see STAMEN).]

etc. *abbr.* et cetera

et cet·er·a /et séttərə, et séttrə/, **et·cet·er·a** *adv.* AND SO ON used to indicate that a list contains other unspecified items ○ *an urgent request for clothes, food, medicines, etc* ■ *n.* SOMETHING OR SOMEBODY UNSPECIFIED one of several or many unspecified things or people [From Latin, literally "and the rest"]

etch /ech/ (**etched, etch·ing, etch·es**) *v.* **1.** *vti.* DESIGN CUT A DESIGN INTO SOMETHING WITH ACID to create a design or drawing on the surface of something, especially a printing plate, by the action of an acid **2.** *vti.* CUT MARKS WITH SOMETHING SHARP to cut a design or mark into the surface of something using a sharp point or laser beam **3.** *vt.* MAKE CLEARLY VISIBLE to leave a clear and distinct impression of something (*usually passive*) ○ *His sorrow was etched on his face.* [Mid-17thC. Via Dutch *etsen* from, ultimately, Old High German *ezzen* "to eat away." Ultimately from an Indo-European word that is also the ancestor of English *eat* and *edible*.] —**etch·er** *n.*

etch·ing /éching/ *n.* **1.** CREATION OF CUT DESIGNS the art or process of creating etched designs or making prints from etched surfaces **2.** PRINT FROM AN ETCHED PLATE a print made from an etched plate **3.** PRINTING PLATE FOR ETCHING a printing plate with an etched design

ETD, e.t.d. *abbr.* estimated time of departure

e·ter·nal /ə túrn'l/ *adj.* **1.** EXISTING THROUGH ALL TIME lasting for all time without beginning or end ○ *eternal life* **2.** UNCHANGING unaffected by the passage of time ○ *eternal truths* **3.** SEEMINGLY EVERLASTING seeming to go on for ever or recur incessantly (*informal*) ○ *an eternal student* ■ *n.* WHAT LASTS FOR EVER something that exists everlastingly [14thC. From Old French, from, ultimately, Latin *aeternus*.] —**e·ter·nal·i·ty** /eètər nállətee/ *n.* —**e·ter·nal·ly** /ə túrn'lee/ *adv.*

E·ter·nal *n.* God as a universal spirit

E·ter·nal Cit·y *n.* Rome, the capital of Italy (*literary*)

e·ter·nal·ize /ə túrn'l īz/ (**-ized, -iz·ing, -iz·es**) *vt.* **1.** MAKE ETERNAL to make something eternal **2.** MAKE IMMORTAL to make something so famous as to become immortal

e·ter·nal tri·an·gle *n.* a sexual or romantic relationship among three persons that involves jealousy or other emotional conflicts [From the notion that such relationships have been known throughout history]

e·ter·ni·ty /ə túrnitee/ *n.* **1.** INFINITE TIME time without beginning or end ○ *lost for all eternity* **2.** TIMELESSNESS the condition, quality, or fact of being without beginning or end **3.** RELIG TIMELESSNESS AFTER DEATH a timeless state conceived as being experienced after death **4.** VERY LONG TIME a very long or seemingly very long period of time ○ *It will take an eternity to put it together again.* ■ **e·ter·ni·ties** *npl.* TRUTHS SAID TO BE ETERNAL beliefs or ideas about life that are conceived as being timeless [14thC. Via Old French *eternite* from Latin *aeternitas*, from *aeternus* (see ETERNAL).]

WORD KEY: CULTURAL NOTE

From Here to Eternity, a movie by director Fred Zinnemann (1953). Based on James Jones's 1951 novel of the same name, it depicts the lives of U.S. military personnel in Hawaii immediately prior to the attack on Pearl Harbor. It is perhaps best remembered for a scene in which Burt Lancaster and Deborah Kerr embrace in the surf.

e·ter·ni·ty ring *n.* a ring with gemstones set around its whole circumference, intended to symbolize everlasting love

e·ter·nize /ə túr nīz/ (**-nized, -niz·ing, -niz·es**) *vt.* = **eternalize** [Mid-16thC. From French *éterniser*, from, ultimately, Latin *aeternus* (see ETERNAL).]

e·te·sian wind /ə teézh'n-/ *adj.* an annual summer wind that blows from the northwest in the Aegean Sea and other parts of the eastern Mediterranean [Early 17thC. *Etesian* formed from Latin *etesius* "annual," from Greek *etēsios*, from *etos* "year." Ultimately from an Indo-European word meaning "year."]

eth *n.* = **edh**

eth·am·bu·tol /e thámbyə tàwl/ *n.* an antimicrobial substance used in combination with other drugs in the treatment of tuberculosis. Formula: $C_{10}H_{24}N_2O_2$. [Mid-20thC. Coined from ETHYL + AMINE + BUTANOL.]

eth·a·nal /éthə nàl/ *n.* = **acetaldehyde**

e·tha·na·mide /i thánnə mīd/ *n.* = **acetamide**

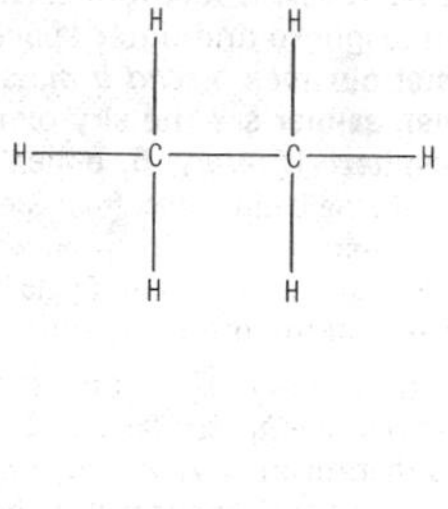

Ethane

eth·ane /é thàyn/ *n.* a colorless odorless gas that is highly flammable and occurs naturally in petroleum and natural gas. It is used as a fuel and in refrigeration. Formula: C_2H_6. [Late 19thC. Coined from ETHYL + -ANE.]

eth·ane·di·o·ic acid /ethayn dī ōik-/ *n.* CHEM = **oxalic acid**

eth·a·no·ic ac·id /ethə nō ik-/ *n.* = **acetic acid**

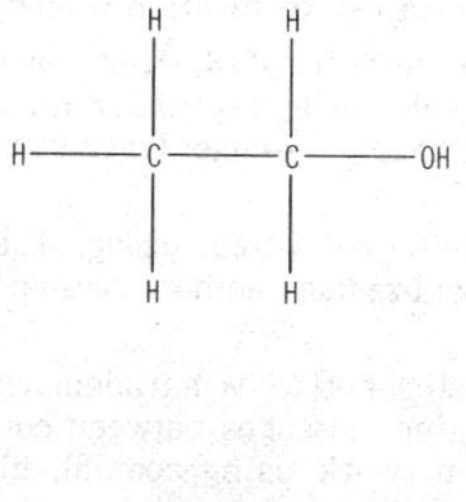

Ethanol

eth·a·nol /éthə nàwl/ *n.* a colorless liquid with a pleasant smell that is produced naturally from fermentation by yeasts and other microorganisms. It is used in alcoholic beverages, as a solvent, and in the manufacture of other chemicals. Formula: C_2H_5OH. [Early 20thC. Coined from ETHANE + -OL.]

eth·a·nol·a·mine /éthə nóllə meèn/ *n.* any of three colorless solid or viscous substances. They are used widely in industry, e.g., in manufacturing antibiotics, cosmetics, detergents, and herbicides.

Eth·el·bert /éth'l bùrt/, **King of Kent** (552?–616). He dominated southern England during his reign (560–616) and was the first Christian Anglo-Saxon monarch, being baptized in 597 by St. Augustine of Canterbury.

Eth·el·red I /éth'l rèd/, **King of the West Saxons and Kentishmen** (830?–871). His reign (866–71) saw continual struggle with Danish invaders, whom he defeated at Ashdown in 871.

Eth·el·red II, King of the English (968–1016). His reign was marked by bitter military struggles. Known as **Ethelred the Unready**

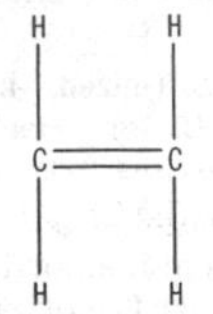

Ethene

eth·ene /é thèen/ *n.* ethylene (*technical*) [Mid-19thC. Coined from ETHYL + -ENE.]

e·ther /éethər/ *n.* **1.** CHEM **LIQUID SOLVENT AND ANESTHETIC** a volatile colorless liquid with a pleasant smell. It is used as a solvent and was formerly used as an anesthetic. Formula: $C_2H_5OC_2H_5$. **2.** CHEM **ORGANIC COMPOUND WITH LINKED HYDROCARBON GROUPS** any organic compound containing two hydrocarbon groups linked by an oxygen atom **3. e·ther, ae·ther** PHYS **HYPOTHETICAL ELECTRO-MAGNETIC MEDIUM** a medium formerly believed to fill the atmosphere and outer space and to carry electromagnetic waves ○ *send a message across the ether* **4. e·ther, ae·ther SKY** the sky or upper reaches of the atmosphere (*literary*) **5. e·ther, ae·ther AIR** air (*literary*) [14thC. Via Latin *aether* from Greek *aithēr* "upper air." Ultimately from an Indo-European word meaning "to burn," which is also the ancestor of English *estival, edifice,* and *estuary.*] —**e·ther·ic** /i thérrik/ *adj.*

e·the·re·al /ə thèeree əl/ *adj.* **1. EXQUISITE** very delicate or highly refined ○ *ethereal beauty* **2. AIRY** very light, airy, or insubstantial ○ *Her fragrance lingered in the room, an ethereal reminder of her presence.* **3. HEAVENLY** belonging to the heavens or the celestial sphere **4.** CHEM **OF ETHER** consisting of, containing, or relating to ether [Early 16thC. Via Latin *aetherius* from, ultimately, Greek *aithēr* (see ETHER).] —**e·the·re·al·i·ty** /ə thèeree állətee/ *n.* —**e·the·re·al·ly** /ə thèeree əlee/ *adv.* —**e·the·re·al·ness** /-əlnəss/ *n.*

e·the·re·al·ize /ə thèeree ə līz/ (**-ized, -iz·ing, -iz·es**) *vt.* **1. MAKE ETHEREAL** to make something very delicate or refined **2.** CHEM **MAKE INTO ETHER** to turn something into ether —**e·the·re·al·i·za·tion** /ə thèeree əli záysh'n/ *n.*

Eth·er·ege /éthərij/, **Sir George** (1635?–91) English playwright. His witty and mildly risqué plays, such as *The Man of Mode* (1676), established the style for what is now called Restoration comedy.

e·ther·i·fy /ə thérrə fī/ (**-fied, -fy·ing, -fies**) *vt.* CHEM to convert a substance, especially an alcohol, into ether (*technical*) —**e·ther·i·fi·ca·tion** /ə thèrrəfi káysh'n/ *n.*

e·ther·ize /éethə rīz/ (**-ized, -iz·ing, -iz·es**) *vt.* = **etherify** —**e·ther·i·za·tion** /éethəri záysh'n/ *n.* —**e·ther·iz·er** *n.*

Eth·er·net /éethər nèt/ *tdmk.* a trademark for a system for exchanging messages between computers on a local area network using coaxial, fiber optic, or twisted-pair cables

eth·ic /éthik/ *n.* a system of moral standards or principles ○ *the Protestant work ethic.* ◊ **ethics** [Late 19thC. Via French *éthique* from, ultimately, Greek *ēthikē,* from *ēthikos* "ethical," from *ēthos* "character, nature" (see ETHOS).]

eth·i·cal /éthik'l/ *adj.* **1. CONFORMING TO ACCEPTED STANDARDS** consistent with agreed principles of correct moral conduct ○ *While such activities are not strictly illegal, they are certainly not ethical.* **2. OF ETHICS** relating to or involving ethics **3.** PHARM **AVAILABLE BY PRESCRIPTION ONLY** used to describe a drug that is available only through a doctor's prescription —**eth·i·cal·i·ty** /èthi kállətee/ *n.* —**eth·i·cal·ly** /éthikəlee/ *adv.* —**eth·i·cal·ness** /éthik'lnəss/ *n.*

eth·i·cist /éthissist/ *n.* somebody who studies ethics or is devoted to ethical ideals

eth·ics /éthiks/ *n.* **1. STUDY OF MORALITY'S EFFECT ON CONDUCT** the study of moral standards and how they affect conduct (*takes a singular verb*) **2. CODE OF MORALITY** a system of moral principles governing the appropriate conduct for an individual or group (*takes a plural verb*) [15thC. Via Old French *ethiques* from, ultimately, Greek *ēthika,* from *ēthikos* "ethical" (see ETHIC).]

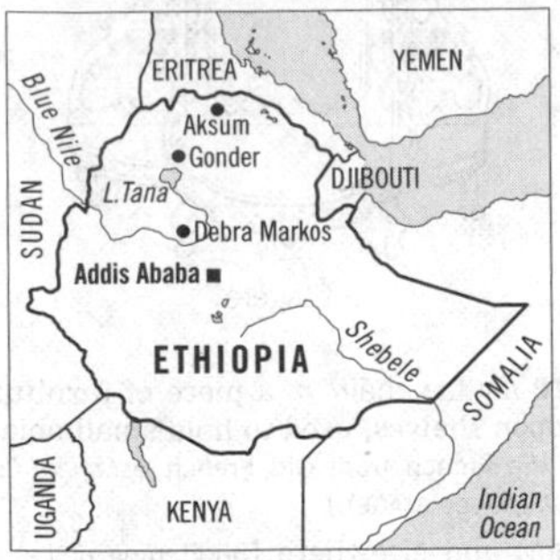

Ethiopia

E·thi·o·pi·a /èethee ópee ə/ landlocked country in northeastern Africa, separated from the Red Sea by Eritrea and Djibouti, and from the Gulf of Aden by Somalia. It is the oldest independent country in Africa. Language: Amharic. Currency: birr. Capital: Addis Ababa. Population: 57,098,762 (1997). Area: 437,600 sq. mi./1,133,380 sq. km. Official name **Federal Democratic Republic of Ethiopia**

E·thi·o·pi·an /èethee ópee ən/ *n.* **1. SOMEBODY FROM ETHIOPIA** somebody who was born or raised in Ethiopia, or who has Ethiopian citizenship **2. OLD TERM FOR BLACK PERSON** a term, now considered offensive, for a Black person (*archaic*) ■ *adj.* **1. OF ETHIOPIA** relating to or typical of Ethiopia or its people or culture **2.** ZOOL **OF AFRICA SOUTH OF THE SAHARA** used to describe Africa south of the Sahara as a biogeographical area

E·thi·op·ic /èethee óppik, -ópik/ *n.* LANG = **Geez** [Mid-17thC. Via Latin from Greek *aithiopikos,* from the stem *Aithiop-* "Ethiopian," from *aithein* "to burn" + *ōps* "face."]

eth·moid bone /éth mòyd-/ *n.* a perforated bone in the skull whose outer surfaces form part of the outer wall of the nasal cavity and the inner wall of the eye socket [Mid-18thC. From Greek *ēthmoeidēs* "sievelike," from *ēthmos* "sieve."] —**eth·moid·al** /eth móyd'l/ *adj.*

eth·narch /éth naark/ *n.* **1. RULER** a ruler of a province or people **2. RULER IN THE ROMAN EMPIRE** a ruler of a province or people in the Roman Empire [Mid-17thC. From Greek *ethnarkhēs,* from *ethnos* "nation" (see ETHNIC) and *-arkhēs* "ruler" (see -ARCH).] —**eth·nar·chy** *n.*

eth·nic /éthnik/ *adj.* **1. SHARING CULTURAL CHARACTERISTICS** sharing distinctive cultural traits as a group in society ○ *ethnic minorities* **2. OF A GROUP SHARING CULTURAL CHARACTERISTICS** relating to a group or groups in society with distinctive cultural traits ○ *ethnic origins* **3. OF SPECIFIED ORIGIN OR CULTURE** belonging to a particular group by descent or culture rather than by nationality **4. CULTURALLY TRADITIONAL** belonging to or typical of the traditional culture of a social group ○ *ethnic clothing* ■ *n.* **MEMBER OF AN ETHNIC GROUP** a member of an ethnic group within a society [14thC. Via late Latin *ethnicus* "heathen" from Greek *ethnikos,* from *ethnos* "people, nation." Ultimately from an Indo-European base denoting "self."] —**eth·ni·cal·ly** *adv.*

eth·nic cleans·ing *n.* the violent elimination or removal from an area of people attacked because of their ethnic backgrounds, by means of genocide or forced expulsion

eth·nic·i·ty /eth níssətee/ (*plural* **-ties**) *n.* ethnic affiliation or distinctiveness

eth·nic mi·nor·i·ty *n.* an ethnic group that is a minority within a nation or society

ethno- *prefix.* people, culture ○ *ethnohistory* [From Greek *ethnos* 'people, nation' (see ETHNIC)]

eth·no·bot·a·ny /èthnō bótt'nee/ *n.* the scientific study of the traditional classification and uses of plants in different human societies —**eth·no·bo·tan·i·cal** /èthnō bə tánnik'l/ *adj.* —**eth·no·bo·tan·i·cal·ly** /-kəlee/ *adv.* —**eth·no·bot·a·nist** /èthnō bótt'nist/ *n.*

eth·no·cen·trism /èthnō sén trìzzəm/ *n.* a belief in or assumption of the superiority of your own social or cultural group (*disapproving*) —**eth·no·cen·tric** *adj.* —**eth·no·cen·tri·cal·ly** *adv.* —**eth·no·cen·tric·i·ty** /èthnō sen tríssətee/ *n.*

eth·no·gen·e·sis /èthnō jénnəssiss/ *n.* the creation of a new ethnic group identity

eth·nog·ra·phy /eth nóggrəfee/ *n.* a branch of anthropology concerned with the description of ethnic groups —**eth·nog·ra·pher** *n.* —**eth·no·graph·ic** /èthnə gráffik/ *adj.* —**eth·no·graph·i·cal·ly** /-kəlee/ *adv.*

eth·no·his·to·ry /èthnō hístəree/ *n.* the scientific study of how cultures have developed through history —**eth·no·his·to·ri·an** /èthnō his táwree ən/ *n.* —**eth·no·his·to·ric** *adj.*

eth·no·lin·guis·tics /èthnō ling wístiks/ *n.* the scientific study of the relationship between language and culture (*takes a singular verb*) —**eth·no·lin·guist** /èthnō líng gwist/ *n.* —**eth·no·lin·guis·tic** /-ling gwístik/ *adj.* —**eth·no·lin·guis·ti·cally** /-tikəlee/ *adv.*

eth·nol·o·gy /eth nóllajee/ *n.* **1. STUDY OF ETHNIC GROUPS** the comparison of different cultures, or the study of how and why cultures differ. Ethnology can focus on one culture through time, or several cultures at the same time. **2.** = **cultural anthropology** —**eth·no·log·ic** /èthnə lójjik/ *adj.* —**eth·no·log·i·cal·ly** /-kəlee/ *adv.* —**eth·nol·o·gist** /eth nólləjist/ *n.*

eth·no·meth·od·ol·o·gy /èthnō methə dólləjee/ *n.* the study of how people interact in ways that maintain the social structure of the situations in which they find themselves —**eth·no·meth·od·ol·o·gist** *n.*

eth·no·mu·si·col·o·gy /èthnō myoozi kólləjee/ *n.* the study of the music of non-Western cultures —**eth·no·mu·si·co·log·i·cal** /èthnō myoozikə lójjik'l/ *adj.* —**eth·no·mu·si·col·o·gist** /èthnō myoozi kólləjist/ *n.*

e·thol·o·gy /ee thólləjee, i-/ *n.* **1. STUDY OF ANIMAL BEHAVIORAL PATTERNS** the study of the behavior of animals in their natural habitat, usually proposing evolutionary explanations **2.** = **human ethology** [Mid-17thC. From Latin *ethologia,* from, ultimately, Greek *ēthos* (see ETHOS).] —**eth·o·log·i·cal** /èethə lójjik'l, èthə-/ *adj.* —**e·thol·o·gist** /ee thólləjist, i-/ *n.*

e·thos /ée thòss/ *n.* the fundamental and distinctive character of a group, social context, or period of time, typically expressed in attitudes, habits, and beliefs [Mid-19thC. From Greek *ēthos* "custom, disposition." Ultimately from an Indo-European base denoting "self," which is also the ancestor of English *self, suicide, idiom,* and *custom.*]

eth·ox·y /i thóksee/ *adj.* forming or containing a chemical group composed of ethyl and oxygen. Formula: CH_3CH_2O. [Late 19thC. Coined from ETHYL + OXY-.]

eth·ox·y·eth·ane /ithòksi éethayn/ *n.* ether (*technical*)

eth·ox·yl /i thóksəl/ *adj.* = **ethoxy**

eth·yl /éthəl/ *n.* a chemical group containing carbon and hydrogen, deriving from ethane. Formula: CH_3CH_2. [Mid-19thC. Coined from ETHER + -YL.]

eth·yl ac·e·tate *n.* a volatile colorless liquid with a pleasant fruity smell. It is used in making perfumes and as a solvent. Formula: $C_4H_8O_2$.

eth·yl al·co·hol *n.* = **ethanol**

eth·yl·a·mine /èthələ méen, éthələ méen/ *n.* a colorless liquid used in petroleum refining and detergents. Formula: $C_2H_5NH_2$.

eth·yl·ate /éthə làyt/ (**-at·ed, -at·ing, -ates**) *vt.* to attach an ethyl group to a molecule or to one of the molecules of a compound —**eth·yl·a·tion** /èthə láysh'n/ *n.*

eth·yl·ene /éthə lèen/ *n.* a colorless flammable gas occurring in petroleum and natural gas and produced by ripening fruit. It is used in the manufacture of polymers and other chemicals, in metallurgy, and to ripen and color harvested fruit. Formula: C_2H_4. —**eth·yl·e·nic** /èthə léenik/ *adj.*

eth·yl·ene gly·col *n.* a viscous colorless liquid with a sweet taste. It is used as an antifreeze and in the manufacture of polyester. Formula: $C_2H_6O_2$.

eth·yl mer·cap·tan *n.* a strong-smelling colorless liquid that is added to odorless fuels to give them an odor so that leaks can be detected. Formula: C_2H_5SH.

e·thyne /é thīn, e thín/ *n.* = **acetylene**

et·ic /éttik/ *adj.* ANTHROP making use of preestablished categories for organizing and interpreting anthropological data, rather than categories recognized within the culture being studied. ◊ **-emic** [Mid-20thC. From PHONETIC.]

-etic *suffix.* used to form adjectives from nouns ending in *-esis* ○ *geodetic* [Via Latin from Greek *-ētikos*, from *-etos*]

e·ti·o·lat·ed /éetee ə làytəd/ *adj.* used to describe a plant that is abnormally tall and spindly and deficient in green pigment chlorophyll owing to lack of light [Late 18thC. Formed from *etiolate*, from French *étioler*, of uncertain origin: perhaps from Norman French *étieuler* "to grow into stalks," ultimately from Latin *stipula* "straw."] —**e·ti·o·la·tion** /èetee ə láysh'n/ *n.*

e·ti·ol·o·gy /èetee óllәjee/ (*plural* **-gies**), **ae·ti·ol·o·gy** (*plural* **-gies**) *n.* **1. STUDY OF CAUSES** the philosophical investigation of causes and origins **2. MEDICAL SPECIALTY** the branch of medicine that investigates the causes and origins of disease **3. CAUSE OF A DISEASE** the set of factors that contributes to the occurrence of a disease [Mid-16thC. Via Latin *aetiologia* from Greek *aitiologia* "statement of the cause," from *aita* "cause."] —**e·ti·o·log·ic** /èetee ə lójjik/ *adj.* —**e·ti·o·log·i·cal·ly** /-lójjikəlee/ *adv.* —**e·ti·ol·o·gist** /èetee óllәjist/ *n.*

et·i·quette /éttikət, étti kèt/ *n.* the rules and conventions governing correct or polite behavior in society in general or in a particular social or professional group or situation ○ *Etiquette dictates that wedding invitations should be acknowledged in writing.* [Mid-18thC. From French, "ticket," also "etiquette" (probably from the custom of giving rules for behavior either on a soldier's lodging ticket or on cards given out at court).]

Et·na, Mount /étnə/ volcano in eastern Sicily. It is the highest active volcano in Europe and has had over ninety recorded eruptions. Height: 10,902 ft./3,323 m.

ETO *abbr.* European theater of operations

E·ton /éet'n/ town in Buckinghamshire, England, on the Thames River opposite Windsor. Eton College is a leading independent school. Population: 3,523 (1991).

E·ton col·lar *n.* a broad stiff white collar turned down over the collar and lapels of a coat or jacket, especially one worn as part of the Eton College uniform

E·ton Col·lege /éet'n-/, **E·ton** *n.* a private school in the town of Eton, in Buckinghamshire, southeastern England. It was founded in 1440 by Henry VI. —**E·to·ni·an** /ee tṓnee ən/ *n., adj.*

E·ton jack·et *n.* a short black jacket with wide lapels and an open front, formerly worn by the pupils of Eton College

E·to·sha Na·tion·al Park /i tṓshə-/ national park in Namibia, southwestern Africa. Established in 1958, it contains the Etosha Pan, a salt desert that was once a lake. Area: 8,000 sq. mi./20,700 sq. km.

E·tru·ri·a /i tròoree ə/ ancient region on the northwestern coast of peninsular Italy, where the Etruscan civilization flourished in the first millennium B.C. The region occupied roughly the same area as present-day Tuscany and part of Umbria, and at its greatest extent stretched from the Alps to the Tiber River. —**E·tru·ri·an** *n., adj.*

Etruscan: Gable end from Villa Giulia, Rome, Italy (4th century B.C.)

E·trus·can /i trúskən/ *n.* **1. MEMBER OF AN ANCIENT PEOPLE FROM ETRURIA** a member of an ancient people who lived in Etruria. Their civilization flourished during the period from the eighth to the sixth centuries B.C., although they survived until overcome by the Romans during the second century B.C. **2. ANCIENT LANGUAGE OF ETRURIA** an extinct language spoken in ancient Etruria that has no relation to the languages of the Indo-European family [Early 18thC. Formed from Latin *Etruscus* "of Etruria."] —**E·trus·can** *adj.*

ETS *abbr.* Educational Testing Service

et seq. 1. AND THE FOLLOWING ONE and another following, especially the next page in a book. Full form **et sequens, et sequentia 2. et seq., et seqq. AND THOSE THAT FOLLOW** and others following, especially the next pages in a book. Full form **et sequentia** [Shortening of Latin et sequens (or sequentia) "and the following one (or ones)"]

-ette *suffix.* **1.** small ○ *diskette* **2.** female ○ *usherette* **3.** imitation ○ *leatherette* [From Old French, feminine of *-et*]

é·tude /áy tòod, ay tóod/, **e·tude** *n.* a short musical composition for a solo instrument intended to develop a point of technique or to display the performer's skill, but often played for its artistic merit [Mid-19thC. From French, "study," via Old French *estudie* (source of English *study*) from Latin *studium*.]

é·tui /ay twée, e twée/ *n.* a small ornamental case for needles or other small items [Early 17thC. From French, from Old French *estui* "prison," from *estuier* "to keep."]

ETV *abbr.* Educational Television

ety., etym. *abbr.* **1.** etymology **2.** etymological

et·y·ma plural of **etymon**

etymol. *abbr.* **1.** etymological **2.** etymology

et·y·mol·o·gize /èttə mólla jīz/ (**-gized, -giz·ing, -giz·es**) *vti.* to study, trace, or describe the origin and development of a word, or make a suggestion as to its possible origin and development

et·y·mol·o·gy /èttə mólləjee/ (*plural* **-gies**) *n.* **1. STUDY OF WORD ORIGINS** the study of the origins of words or parts of words and how they have arrived at their current form and meaning **2. HISTORY OF A WORD** the origin of a word or part of a word, or a statement of this and how it has arrived at its current form and meaning. An etymology often shows the different forms the word has taken in passing from one language to another, and sometimes shows related words in other languages. ○ *The words have the same spelling but different etymologies.* [14thC. Via Old French *ethimologie* from, ultimately, Greek *etumologia*, from *etumon* (see ETYMON).] —**et·y·mo·log·i·cal** /èttəmə lójjik'l/ *adj.* —**et·y·mo·log·i·cal·ly** /-lójjikəlee/ *adv.* —**et·y·mol·o·gist** /èttə mólləjist/ *n.*

et·y·mon /éttə mòn/ (*plural* **-ma** /-mə/ *or* **-mons**) *n.* **1. ORIGIN OF A WORD** an earlier form of a word or part of a word, especially the first recorded form in any language **2. ROOT OF A WORD** a word or part of a word from which another word is derived [Late 16thC. Via Latin from Greek *etumon* "true sense of a word," from *etumos* "true," hence "original."]

Eu *symbol.* europium

eu- *prefix.* good, well, true, easily ○ *euphonious* ○ *euplastic* [Via Latin from Greek *eus*]

eu·bac·te·ri·a /yòo bak téeree ə/ *npl.* in modern biological classification, all those bacteria considered to be the true bacteria, characterized by their rigid cell walls

eu·ca·lypt *n.* = **eucalyptus** [Late 19thC. Shortening.]

Eucalyptus

eu·ca·lyp·tus /yòokə líptəss/ (*plural* **-tus·es** *or* **-ti** /-tī/), **eu·ca·lypt** /yóokə lìpt/ *n.* a tall evergreen tree mainly native to Australia that has tough aromatic leaves and flowers in clusters and provides good timber, resin, and an oil with medicinal properties. There are more than 600 species. Genus: *Eucalyptus.* [Early 19thC. From modern Latin, genus name, from Greek *eu-* "well" + *kaluptos* "covered," from the covering on the tree's buds.]

eu·car·y·ote *n.* BIOL = **eukaryote**

Eu·cha·rist /yóokərist/ *n.* **1. CEREMONY WITH SYMBOLIC BREAD AND WINE** a ceremony in many Christian churches during which symbolic or consecrated bread and wine are consumed, to commemorate the last meal of Jesus Christ with his disciples before his death **2. SYMBOLIC BREAD AND WINE** the symbolic or consecrated bread and wine eaten and drunk during the ceremony of the Eucharist [14thC. Via Old French *eucariste* from, ultimately, Greek *eukharistia* "giving of thanks," from *eukharistos* "grateful," from *kharizesthai* "to show favor" (source of English *charisma*).] —**Eu·cha·ris·tic** /yòokə rístik/ *adj.*

eu·chre /yóokər/ *n.* **1. CARD GAME OF WINNING TRICKS** a card game played with the highest 32 cards in the deck in which each player receives five cards and must take at least three tricks to win **2. THWARTING OF AN OPPONENT AT EUCHRE** an instance of preventing another player from making the three tricks needed to win a game of euchre ■ *vt.* (**-chred, -chring, -chres**) **1. THWART AN OPPONENT AT EUCHRE** to prevent another player from taking the three tricks needed to win a game of euchre **2.** *ANZ, Can, U.S.* **TRICK** to cheat, trick, or deceive somebody [Early 19thC. Origin uncertain: perhaps from German dialect *Jucker(spiel)*.]

eu·chro·ma·tin /yoo krṓmətin/ *n.* an expanded form of the material of which chromosomes are composed, occurring when DNA is being actively copied. It stains lightly only with basic dyes. —**eu·chro·mat·ic** /yòo krō máttik/ *adj.*

Eu·clid /yóoklid/ (*fl.* 300 B.C.) Greek mathematician. He taught in Alexandria and compiled the 13-volume *Elements* (300? B.C.), the standard text on geometry until the 19th century.

Eu·clid·e·an /yoo klíddee ən/, **Eu·clid·i·an** *adj.* relating to Euclid or his system of geometry

Eu·clid·e·an ge·om·e·try *n.* geometry according to the principles of Euclid, as described in his *Elements*, in which only one line parallel to another given line may pass through a given point

eu·de·mon /yoo déemən/, **eu·dae·mon** *n.* PARANORMAL a benevolent supernatural being [Early 17thC. From Greek *eudaimōn* "having a guardian spirit," hence "fortunate, happy," from *daimōn* "spiritual being, guardian" (source of English *demon*).]

eu·de·mon·ism /yoo déemə nìzzəm/, **eu·dae·mon·ism** *n.* an ethical doctrine that characterizes the value of life in terms of happiness —**eu·de·mo·nist** *n.* —**eu·de·mon·is·tic** /yoo dèemə nístik/ *adj.*

eu·di·om·e·ter /yòodee ómmətər/ *n.* an instrument used to measure the volume changes that take place in chemical gas reactions [Late 18thC. Formed from Greek *eudios* "fine (weather)" (from *eu-* "good" + *Zeus* "god of the sky"), because an increase in the oxygen content of air supposedly forecast good weather.] —**eu·di·o·met·ric** /yòodee ə méttrik/ *adj.* —**eu·di·o·met·ri·cal·ly** *adv.* —**eu·di·om·e·try** *n.*

eu·gen·i·cist /yoo jénnəssist/, **eu·gen·ist** /yóojənist/ *n.* somebody who studies proposed ways of improving the human species, especially by selective breeding, or who advocates the principles or practice of eugenics

eu·gen·ics /yoo jénniks/ *n.* the proposed improvement of the human species by encouraging or permitting reproduction of only those individuals with genetic characteristics judged desirable. It has been regarded with disfavor since the Nazi period. (*takes a singular verb*) [Late 19thC.] —**eu·gen·ic** *adj.* —**eu·gen·i·cal·ly** *adv.*

eu·gen·ist *n.* = **eugenicist**

eu·ge·nol /yóojə nàwl/ *n.* a colorless oily liquid obtained from cloves and used in dentistry to reduce pain and in perfumes. Formula: $C_{10}H_{12}O_2$. [Late 19thC. Formed from *eugenia*, genus name of the clove tree, ultimately named for Prince *Eugene* of Savoy (1663–1736), Austrian general.]

eu·gle·na /yoo gléenə/ *n.* a single-celled freshwater organism that has appendages (**flagella**) for locomotion and produces its food by photosynthesis. Genus: *Euglena.* [Mid-19thC. From modern Latin, genus name, from Greek *eu-* "well" + *glēnē* "eyeball," perhaps from its reddish eyespot.] —**eu·gle·noid** /yoo gléen òyd/ *adj.*

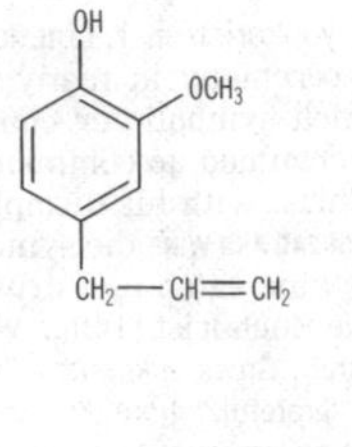

Eugenol

eu·he·mer·ism /yoo hēəmə rìzzəm, -hémmə rìzzəm/ *n.* the theory that mythology has its origins in history, the gods being deified heroes of the past [Mid-19thC. Formed from Latin *Euhemerus*, from Greek *Euēmeros* (4thC B.C.), name of a Greek writer who maintained that the deities of Greek mythology were deified men and women.] —**eu·he·mer·ist** *n.* —**eu·he·mer·is·tic** /yoo hēəmə rístik, -hèmmə-/ *adj.* —**eu·he·mer·is·ti·cal·ly** *adv.*

eu·he·mer·ize /yoo hēəmə rīz, -hémmə-/ (**-ized, -iz·ing, -iz·es**) *vti.* to explain a myth or myths using the theory that the gods were originally historical heroes

eu·kar·y·ote /yoo kérree ōt/, **eu·car·y·ote** *n.* any organism with one or more cells that have visible nuclei and organelles. The group contains all living and fossil cellular organisms except bacteria and blue-green algae. [Mid-20thC. Coined from EU- + Greek *karuōtos* "having nuts," from *karuon* "nut," from, ultimately, an Indo-European word that is also the ancestor of English *cancer*.] —**eu·kar·y·ot·ic** /yoo kèrree óttik/ *adj.*

eu·la·chon /yoōlə kòn/ (*plural* **-chons** *or* **-chon**) *n.* = **candlefish** [Mid-19thC. From Lower Chinook *úłxan*.]

Eu·ler /óylər/, **Leonhard** (1707–83) Swiss mathematician. With Joseph Lagrange, he was the foremost mathematician of his century. In some 800 publications he laid the foundations of modern analytical mathematics.

eu·lo·gi·a[1] /yoo lṓdZee ə, -lṓdZə/ *n.* bread blessed and given after the liturgy in the Eastern Orthodox Church to those not present at the Eucharist [Mid-18thC. Via late Latin, "consecrated bread," from, ultimately, Greek (see EULOGIUM).]

eu·lo·gi·a[2] plural of **eulogium**

eu·lo·gis·tic /yoōlə jístik/ *adj.* full of praise for somebody or something (*formal*) —**eu·lo·gis·ti·cal·ly** *adv.*

eu·lo·gi·um /yoo lṓjee əm/ (*plural* **-a** /-jee ə/ *or* **-ums**) *n.* a eulogy (*formal*) [Early 17thC. From medieval Latin, probably a blend of *eulogia* "praise" (from Greek, formed from *eu-*"well" + *-logia* "speaking") and Latin *elogium* "epitaph."]

eu·lo·gize /yoōlə jīz/ (**-gized, -giz·ing, -giz·es**) *vti.* to praise somebody or something very highly (*formal*) —**eu·lo·giz·er** *n.*

eu·lo·gy /yoōləjee/ (*plural* **-gies**) *n.* **1. SPOKEN OR WRITTEN TRIBUTE** a speech or piece of writing that praises somebody or something very highly, especially a tribute to somebody who has recently died **2. HIGH PRAISE** great praise (*formal*) [15thC. From medieval Latin *eulogium* (see EULOGIUM).] —**eu·lo·gist** *n.*

Eu·men·i·des /yoo ménni dēez/ *n.* three sister goddesses in Greek mythology. They were originally fertility goddesses, but were later identified with the Furies. [Late 17thC. Via Latin from Greek, from eumenēs "kindly, friendly," from menos "spirit."]

eu·nuch /yoōnək/ *n.* **1. CASTRATED HUMAN MALE** a man or boy whose testicles have been removed or do not function. Eunuchs were formerly employed in Islamic countries to guard the women of a harem or as court officials. **2. INEFFECTUAL MAN** a man who lacks power or effectiveness (*informal insult*) [15thC. Via Latin *eunuchus* from Greek *eunoukhos* "attendant of a bedroom or harem," from *eunē* "bed" + *ekhein* "to keep."] —**eu·nuch·ism** *n.*

eu·nuch·oid /yoōnə kòyd/ *adj.* lacking fully developed male sexual organs or characteristics

eu·on·y·mus /yoo ónnəməss/ *n.* a tree or shrub of northern temperate regions cultivated for its decorative evergreen foliage and clusters of orange or red fruits. The spindle tree is a type of euonymus. Genus: *Euonymus.* [Mid-19thC. Via modern Latin, genus name, from, ultimately, Greek *euōnumos*, literally "of good name," hence "lucky" (perhaps euphemistic, since the flowering of the tree was taken to be an omen of disease).]

eu·pat·rid /yoo páttrid/ (*plural* **-ri·dae** /-dee/ *or* **-rids**) *n.* somebody belonging to the hereditary class of nobles and landowners in ancient Athens [Mid-19thC. From Greek *eupatridēs* "somebody of noble ancestry," literally "having a good father," from *patēr* "father."]

eu·pep·si·a /yoo pépshə, -pépsee ə/ *n.* good or efficient digestion [Early 18thC. From Greek, "digestibility," from *eupeptos* "easy to digest" (see EUPEPTIC).]

eu·pep·tic /yoo péptik/ *adj.* **1.** PHYSIOL **OF GOOD DIGESTION** relating to or producing good digestion **2. CHEERFUL** with a cheerful manner or disposition [Late 17thC. Formed from Greek *eupeptos* "easy to digest, having good digestion," from *peptein* "to digest."] —**eu·pep·ti·cal·ly** *adv.*

eu·phe·mism /yoōfə mìzzəm/ *n.* **1. LESS OFFENSIVE SYNONYM** a word or phrase used in place of a term that might be considered too direct, harsh, unpleasant, or offensive. A wide range of euphemisms is used in connection with death, sex, and excretion. ○ *The phrase "collateral damage" is a euphemism for injury to civilians during a military operation.* **2. USE OF INOFFENSIVE WORDS** the use of a word or phrase that is more neutral, vague, or indirect to replace a direct, harsh, unpleasant, or offensive term [Late 16thC. From Greek *euphēmismos*, from *euphēmizein* "to speak with pleasing words," from, ultimately, *phēmē* "speech."] —**eu·phe·mist** *n.* —**eu·phe·mis·tic** /yoōfə místik/ *adj.*

eu·phe·mize /yoōfə mīz/ (**-mized, -miz·ing, -miz·es**) *vti.* to avoid saying or writing something direct, harsh, unpleasant, or offensive by using milder or more indirect language —**eu·phe·miz·er** *n.*

eu·pho·ni·ous /yoo fṓnee əss/ *adj.* having a pleasant sound —**eu·pho·ni·ous·ly** *adv.* —**eu·pho·ni·ous·ness** *n.*

Euphonium

eu·pho·ni·um /yoo fṓnee əm/ *n.* a brass instrument similar to, but smaller than, a tuba, used mainly in military and brass bands [Mid-19thC. Coined from Greek *euphōnos* "well-sounding" (see EUPHONY) + -IUM.]

eu·pho·nize /yoōfə nīz/ (**-nized, -niz·ing, -niz·es**) *vt.* to make something sound pleasant

eu·pho·ny /yoōfənee/ (*plural* **-nies**) *n.* a pleasant sound, especially in speech or pronunciation [15thC. From French *euphonie*, from, ultimately, Greek *euphōnos* "sweet-voiced," from *phōnē* "sound."] —**eu·phon·ic** /yoo fónnik/ *adj.* —**eu·phon·i·cal·ly** *adv.*

eu·phor·bi·a /yoo fáwrbee ə/ *n.* a plant with milky juice and green flowers. Spurges and poinsettia are euphorbias. Genus: *Euphorbia.* [12thC. Alteration of Latin *euphorbea*, from *Euphorbus* (1stC B.C.), a physician to Juba, king of Mauretania, who supposedly discovered the plant.] —**eu·phor·bi·a·ceous** /yoo fàwrbee áyshəss/ *adj.*

eu·pho·ri·a /yoo fáwree ə/ *n.* a feeling of great joy, excitement, or well-being ○ *She was in a state of euphoria after her win.* [Late 17thC. Via modern Latin from, ultimately, Greek *euphoros*, literally "borne well," hence "healthy." Originally in the meaning "happiness brought about by relief from pain."]

eu·phor·i·ant /yoo fáwree ənt/ *n.* a drug or other substance that induces euphoria —**eu·phor·i·ant** *adj.*

eu·phor·ic /yoo fáwrik/ *adj.* extremely happy or excited ○ *She'll be euphoric when she hears these results.* —**eu·phor·i·cal·ly** *adv.*

eu·phot·ic /yoo fóttik/ *adj.* used to describe the upper layer of a body of water that allows the penetration of enough light to support photosynthetic, or green, plants [Early 20thC. Coined from EU- + the Greek stem *phōt-* "light" + -IC.]

Eu·phra·tes /yoo fráyteez/ river in southwestern Asia, rising in Turkey and flowing through Syria and Iraq before joining the Tigris River near the Persian Gulf. Length: 1,700 mi./2,700 km.

Eu·phros·y·ne /yoo fróssənee/ *n.* MYTHOL in Greek mythology, one of the three Graces who lived on Mount Olympus and were attendants of the goddess Aphrodite

eu·phu·ism /yoō fyoo ìzzəm/ *n.* **1.** LITERAT **AFFECTED LITERARY STYLE** a literary style of the 16th and 17th centuries characterized by excessive use of devices such as alliteration, antithesis, and simile **2.** LANG **AFFECTED LANGUAGE OR EXPRESSION** an affected or pompous expression or use of language (*formal*) [Late 16thC. Named for *Euphues*, a fictional character in the works of John LYLY. The name itself was based on Greek *euphuēs* "shapely."] —**eu·phu·ist** *n.* —**eu·phu·is·tic** /yoōfyoo ístik/ *adj.* —**eu·phu·is·ti·cal·ly** /-ístikəlee/ *adv.*

eu·plas·tic /yoo plástik/ *adj.* healing readily

eu·ploid /yoō plòyd/ *adj.* **WITH AN EVEN CHROMOSOME NUMBER** with a chromosome number that is an even multiple of the basic chromosome set for the species ■ *n.* **A EUPLOID CELL OR ORGANISM** a euploid cell or organism —**eu·ploi·dy** /yoō plòydee/ *n.*

Eur. *abbr.* **1.** Europe **2.** European

Eur- *prefix.* = **Euro-** (*used before vowels*)

Eur·a·sian /yoo ráyzh'n, -sh'n/ *n.* somebody of both European and Asian descent [Mid-19thC] —**Eur·a·sian** *adj.*

Eur·at·om /yoo ráttəm/ *n.* a body formed in 1957 to coordinate the development and use of atomic energy in Europe, later incorporated into the European Community [Mid-20thC. Contraction of the first two words of its full name, European Atomic Energy Commission.]

eu·re·ka /yoo rēekə/ *interj., n.* used to express delight on finding, discovering, or solving something or finally succeeding in doing something ○ *I rolled back the carpet and eureka – there it was!* [Early 17thC. From Greek *heurēka*, literally "I have found (it)," from *heuriskein* "to find," supposedly exclaimed by Archimedes when he discovered the principle of water displacement.]

Eu·re·ka port city in northwestern California on Humboldt Bay, on the Pacific Ocean, northwest of Santa Rosa. Population: 26,202 (1996).

eu·rhyth·mic, **eu·rhyth·mi·cal** *adj.* = **eurythmic**

eu·rhyth·mics *n.* **1. RHYTHMICAL MOVEMENT TO MUSIC** a system of physical excercise, therapy, and musical training in which the body moves rhythmically and gracefully in interpretation of a piece of music. It was invented by Rudolf Steiner. **2.** = **eurythmics**

eu·rhyth·my *n.* = **eurythmy**

Eu·rip·i·des /yoo ríppi dēez/ (480?–406? B.C.) Greek dramatist. After Aeschylus and Sophocles, he was the third of the great dramatists of the classical period in Athens. His works have been revived through the centuries and have influenced many writers, from Milton and Racine to those of the present day.

Eu·ro /yoōrō/ (*plural* **-ros**) *n.* the currency unit of 11 countries in the European Union, introduced in 1999 as part of economic and monetary union, which by 2002 will have replaced local currency in the participating member states. ◊ **Ecu** [Late 20thC. Shortening of EUROPEAN.]

Euro- *prefix.* Europe, European ○ *Eurocurrency* [From EUROPE]

Eu·ro·bond /yoōrō bònd/ *n.* a bond measured in dollars or other currency and sold to investors from a country other than that whose currency is specified in the bond

Eu·ro·cen·tric /yoōrə séntrik/, **Eu·ro·po·cen·tric** /yoo rōpə-/ *adj.* focusing on Europe or its people, institutions, and cultures, sometimes in an arrogant way (*disapproving*) —**Eu·ro·cen·trism** /yoōrə sén trìzzəm/ *n.*

Eu·ro·cur·ren·cy /yoōrō kùrənsee/ (*plural* **-cies**) *n.* money deposited by companies and governments in banks outside the home country

Eu·ro·dol·lar /yoōrō dòllər/ *n.* a United States dollar on deposit in a bank outside the United States, especially a European bank (*usually used in the plural*)

Eu·ro·land /yŏŏrō lànd/, **eu·ro·land** *n.* the countries in the European Union committed to adopting the common European currency, the **Euro**

Eu·ro·mar·ket /yŏŏrō maàrkət/ *n.* **1. EUROPE AS A MARKET** the European Union considered as a single market **2. EUROPEAN FINANCIAL MARKETS** the European financial markets collectively, especially when considered as a finance source for international trade

Eu·ro-MP *n.* a member of the European Parliament

Eu·rope /yŏŏrəp/ the second smallest continent after Australia, lying west of Asia, north of Africa, and east of the Atlantic Ocean. Population: 728 million. Area: 4,065,000 sq. mi./10,525,000 sq. km.

Eu·ro·pe·an /yŏŏrə peé ən/ *adj.* **1. OF EUROPE** relating to or typical of Europe or its peoples, languages, or cultures **2. OF THE EUROPEAN UNION** belonging to, relating to, or connected with the European Union ■ *n.* **1. SOMEBODY FROM EUROPE** somebody who was born or raised in a European country, is a citizen of a European country, or is of European descent **2. ADVOCATE OF EUROPEAN UNION** somebody who supports the principles and ideals of the European Union

Eu·ro·pe·an Com·mu·ni·ty *n.* an economic and political union of 12 European countries that developed from the European Economic Community and was itself replaced in 1993 by the European Union

Eu·ro·pe·an E·co·nom·ic Com·mu·ni·ty *n.* the alliance of six European countries begun in 1957 to promote free trade in Europe, and subsequently expanded in both numbers and areas of interest, and called the European Union

Eu·ro·pe·an Free Trade As·so·ci·a·tion *n.* a union of western European countries, established in 1960 to eliminate trade tariffs between member states. The original members were Austria, Denmark, Great Britain, Norway, Portugal, Sweden, and Switzerland. Abbr of **EFTA**

Eu·ro·pe·an·ize /yŏŏrə peé ə nīz/ (**-ized, -iz·ing, -iz·es**) *vt.* **1. MAKE EUROPEAN** to make somebody or something part of European culture, or change somebody or something to fit in with European life, customs, or ideas **2. MAKE PART OF EUROPEAN UNION** to make a country part of the European Union, or make something conform to the regulations or specifications of the European Union —**Eu·ro·pe·an·i·za·tion** /yŏŏrə pee əni záysh'n/ *n.*

Eu·ro·pe·an plan *n.* a rate system for hotel accommodation in which only the cost of the room and service are covered, not meals

European Union: Map showing member states

Eu·ro·pe·an Un·ion *n.* the economic and political alliance of 15 European nations, including the United Kingdom. Its goals include a single economic community and social and political cooperation.

eu·ro·pi·um /yoo rṓpee əm/ *n.* a soft silvery-white metallic chemical element of the rare-earth group that is used in lasers. Symbol **Eu** [Early 20thC. From modern Latin, from Latin *Europa* "Europe."]

eury- *prefix.* wide, broad ○ *euryphagous* [From Greek *eurus* (source of English *aneurysm*)]

eu·ry·bath·ic /yŏŏri báthik/ *adj.* used to describe aquatic organisms that tolerate a wide range of depths [Early 20thC. Coined from EURY- + Greek *bathos* "depth" + -IC.] —**eu·ry·bath** /yŏŏri bàth/ *n.*

Eu·ryd·i·ce /yoo ríddissee/ in Greek mythology, the wife of Orpheus. When she died, Orpheus pursued her to Hades. His lyre-playing won her release, but his failure to observe its conditions resulted in her irrevocable loss.

eu·ry·ha·line /yŏŏri háy līn/ *adj.* used to describe aquatic organisms that tolerate a wide range of salinity [Late 19thC. Coined from EURY- + Greek *halinos* "of salt."]

eu·ryph·a·gous /yoo ríffəgəss/ *adj.* used to describe organisms that feed on a variety of different things

eu·ryp·ter·id /yoo ríptərid/ *n.* an extinct invertebrate animal, some types of which were very large, that was common in fresh or brackish water during the Paleozoic era. It was related to the ancestors of the horseshoe crab. Order: Eurypterida. [Late 19thC. Formed from modern Latin *Eurypterida*, order name, from Greek *eury-* "wide" + *pteron* "wing."]

eu·ry·ther·mal /yŏŏrə thúrm'l/, **eu·ry·ther·mic** /yŏŏrə thúrmik/, **eu·ry·ther·mous** /-thúrməss/ *adj.* used to describe organisms that tolerate a wide range of temperatures —**eu·ry·therm** *n.*

eu·ryth·mic /yoo ríthmik/, **eu·rhyth·mic, eu·ryth·mi·cal** /yoo ríthmik'l/, **eu·rhyth·mi·cal** *adj.* **1. HARMONIOUS** having an aesthetically pleasing rhythm or structure **2. OF EURYTHMICS** relating to eurythmics or eurythmy

eu·ryth·mics /yoo ríthmiks/, **eu·rhyth·mics** *n.* a system of physical exercise, therapy, and musical training in which the body moves rhythmically and gracefully in interpretation of a piece of music (*takes a singular or plural verb*) [Early 20thC. Coined from EU- + RHYTHM + -ICS.]

eu·ryth·my /yoo ríthmee/, **eu·rhyth·my** *n.* **1. STRUCTURAL HARMONY** harmony of proportion or structure **2. RHYTHMICAL MOVEMENT TO VERSE OR MUSIC** a system of rhythmical movement performed to verse or music for artistic or therapeutic purposes. It was invented by Rudolf Steiner. [Late 16thC. Via Latin from Greek *eurythmia* "good proportion," from *rhuthmos* "proportion, rhythm" (source of English *rhythm*).]

eu·ry·top·ic /yŏŏrə tóppik/ *adj.* used to describe organisms that tolerate a wide range of environmental conditions [Mid-20thC. Coined from EURY- + Greek *topos* "place" + -IC.] —**eu·ry·to·pic·i·ty** /yŏŏrə to píssətee/ *n.*

Eu·se·bi·us of Cae·sa·re·a /yoo seébee əss-/ (260?–340?) Palestinian bishop and Christian scholar. He was bishop of Caesarea and worked on texts with his teacher, Pamphilus of Caesarea, as well as writing his *Ecclesiastical History*, a history of the Church until 324. Alternate name **Eusebius Pamphili**

Eu·se·bi·us of Nic·o·me·di·a (*d.* 342?) Syrian bishop and Christian theologian. He helped to spread Arianism, which denies Jesus Christ's divinity. He was patriarch of Constantinople (339–42).

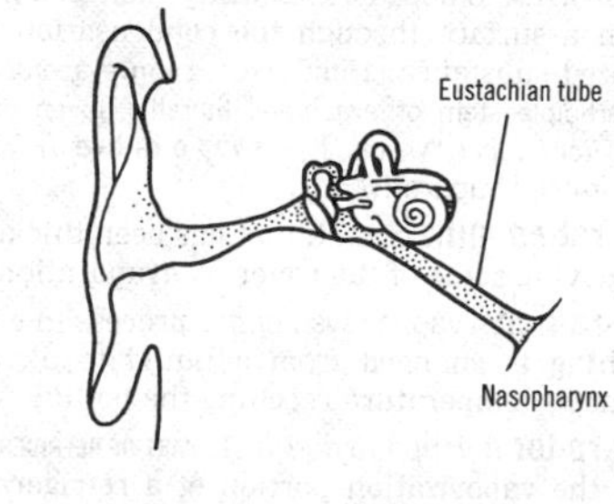

Eustachian tube

eu·sta·chian tube /yoo stáysh'n-/, **Eu·sta·chian tube** *n.* a bony passage extending from the middle ear to the nasopharynx that has a role in equalizing air pressure on both sides of the eardrum [Mid-18thC. Named for Bartolomeo *Eustachio* (1520–74), an Italian anatomist known for his descriptions of the human ear and heart.]

eu·sta·sy /yŏŏstəssee/ (*plural* **-sies**) *n.* a worldwide change in sea level, as a result of melting glaciers or earth movements [Mid-20thC. Back-formation from EUSTATIC (from German, from Greek *eu* "well" + *statikos* "static"), as if an anglicization of hypothetical modern Latin *eustasis*.] —**eu·stat·ic** /yoo státtik/ *adj.*

eu·tec·tic /yoo téktik/ *adj.* **FORMED AT THE LOWEST FREEZING POINT** used to describe a mixture, especially an alloy, that has the lowest freezing point of all combinations or constituents, or to refer to the temperature at which this occurs ■ *n.* **EUTECTIC SUBSTANCE** a substance or mixture that is eutectic [Late 19thC. Formed from Greek *eutēktos* "easily melting," from *tēkein* "to melt."]

Eu·ter·pe /yoo túrpee/ *n.* MYTHOL in Greek mythology, the muse of lyric poetry and music. ◊ **Muse**

eu·tha·na·sia /yŏŏthə náyzhə/ *n.* the act or practice of killing somebody who has an incurable illness or injury, or allowing or assisting that person to die. Euthanasia is illegal in most countries. [Early 17thC. From Greek, "easy death," from *thanatos* "death."]

eu·than·ize /yŏŏthə nīz/ (**-ized, -iz·ing, -iz·es**), **eu·than·a·tize** /yoo thánnə tīz/ (**-tized, -tiz·ing, -tiz·es**) *vt.* to kill an incurably ill or injured person or animal to relieve suffering

eu·then·ics /yoo thénniks/ *n.* the study of ways of improving people's environment and living standards in order to improve their health and well-being (*takes a singular verb*) [Early 20thC. Coined from Greek *euthēnein* "to thrive" + -ICS.] —**eu·then·ist** /yŏŏthənist/ *n.*

eu·ther·i·an /yoo theéree ən/ *adj.* **HAVING A PLACENTA** used to describe a mammal whose young develop to an advanced stage within the womb surrounded by a placenta ■ *n.* **PLACENTAL MAMMAL** a mammal whose young develop within the womb surrounded by a placenta. Subclass: Eutheria. (*technical*) [Late 19thC. Formed from modern Latin *Eutheria*, subclass name, from, ultimately, Greek *thērion* "wild animal."]

eu·troph·ic /yoo tróffik, -trṓfik/ *adj.* ECOL used to describe a body of water whose oxygen content is depleted by organic nutrients (**eutrophication**) [Mid-20thC. Formed from Greek *eutrophia*, literally "good nutrition," from *trephein* "to nourish." Applied earlier to medicine that promotes good nutrition.] —**eu·tro·phy** /yŏŏtrəfee/ *n.*

eu·troph·i·ca·tion /yoo tròffi káysh'n, -trṓfi-/ *n.* the process by which a body of water becomes rich in dissolved nutrients, thereby encouraging the growth and decomposition of oxygen-depleting plant life and resulting in harm to other organisms. The problem occurs in freshwater lakes or shallow seas when human sewage or nitrates and phosphates from fertilizers drain into them.

eV *symbol.* electron volt

EV *abbr.* BIBLE English Version

EVA *abbr.* extravehicular activity

e·vac·u·ant /i vákyoo ənt/ *adj.* **CAUSING DISCHARGE FROM BODY** used to describe a drug or treatment that causes a discharge, especially an emptying of the bowels ■ *n.* **DRUG CAUSING DISCHARGE** a drug or other substance that brings about a discharge, especially an emptying of the bowels

e·vac·u·ate /i vákyoo àyt/ (**-at·ed, -at·ing, -ates**) *v.* **1.** *vt.* **MAKE EVERYONE LEAVE A PLACE** to empty a dangerous or potentially dangerous place of people ○ *Towns near the nuclear plant were evacuated as a precautionary measure.* **2.** *vti.* **MOVE TO SAFETY** to leave or cause people to leave a place of danger and go somewhere safer ○ *The government has evacuated all its embassy officials from the city.* **3.** *vti.* PHYSIOL **EMPTY BOWELS OR BLADDER** to discharge feces or urine from the body (*technical*) **4.** *vt.* **EMPTY** to empty something by removing all its contents (*formal*) **5.** *vt.* PHYS **CREATE VACUUM IN** to remove a gas from something, leaving a vacuum [14thC. From Latin *evacuat-*, the past participle stem of *evacuare* "to empty (the bowels)" and, in late Latin, "to clear out," from *vacuus* "empty" (source of English *vacuum*).] —**e·vac·u·a·tive** *adj.* —**e·vac·u·a·tor** *n.*

e·vac·u·a·tion /i vàkyoo áysh'n/ *n.* **1. CLEARING OF A DANGEROUS PLACE** an emptying of a dangerous or potentially dangerous place **2. MOVING PEOPLE TO SAFETY** a removal of people from a dangerous or potentially dangerous place **3.** PHYSIOL **DISCHARGE OF BODILY WASTE** elimination of feces or urine from the body (*technical*) **4.** PHYSIOL **BODILY WASTE** feces or urine eliminated from the body (*technical*) **5.** PHYS **CREATION OF A VACUUM** the making of a vacuum by the removal of gas from something

e·vac·u·ee /i vàkyoo eé/ *n.* somebody who is removed from a place of danger and sent somewhere safer, especially during a war [Early 20thC. Anglicization of French *évacué*, from the past participle of *évacuer* "to cease to occupy," from Latin *evacuare* (see EVACUATE).]

e·vade /i váyd/ (**e·vad·ed, e·vad·ing, e·vades**) *v.* **1.** *vt.* **CLEVERLY ESCAPE** to escape or avoid somebody or something, usually by ingenuity or guile **2.** *vt.* **AVOID SOMETHING UNPLEASANT** to avoid doing something unpleasant, especially something that is a moral or legal obligation 3. *vti.* GIVE INDIRECT RESPONSE TO to avoid dealing with or responding directly to something 4. *vt.* BE UNATTAINABLE to be difficult or impossible for somebody to find, obtain, or achieve (*formal*) [Early 16thC. Via French *évader* from Latin *evadere* "to escape," literally "to go away," from *vadere* "to go, walk" (source of English *invade*).] —**e·vad·a·ble** *adj.* —**e·vad·er** *n.*

WORD KEY: USAGE

See Usage note at ***avoid.***

e·vag·i·nate /i vájjə nàyt/ (**-nat·ed, -nat·ing, -nates**) *vt.* to turn a hollow structure or bodily organ inside out [Mid-17thC. From Latin *evaginat-* the past participle stem of *evaginare* "to unsheathe," from *vagina* "sheath" (source of English *vagina*).] —**e·vag·i·na·tion** /i vàjjə náysh'n/ *n.*

e·val·u·ate /i vállyoo àyt/ (**-at·ed, -at·ing, -ates**) *vt.* 1. EXAMINE AND JUDGE to consider or examine something in order to judge its value, quality, importance, extent, or condition ○ *We evaluated the situation carefully.* 2. PUT A VALUE ON to estimate the monetary value of something ○ *The appraiser evaluated the property at $100,000* 3. MATH FIND NUMERICAL VALUE to calculate a numerical value for a mathematical expression ○ *evaluate an expression* [Mid-19thC. Back-formation from EVALUATION.] —**e·val·u·a·tor** *n.*

e·val·u·a·tion /i vàllyoo áysh'n/ *n.* 1. ASSESSMENT OF VALUE the act of considering or examining something in order to judge its value, quality, importance, extent, or condition 2. STATEMENT OF VALUE a spoken or written statement of the value, quality, importance, extent, or condition of something [Mid-18thC. From French *évaluation*, from *évaluer* "to find the value of," from *value* "VALUE."]

e·val·u·a·tive /i vállyoo àytiv, -ətiv/ *adj.* 1. DETERMINED BY ASSESSMENT relating to or based on examination and judgment of the value, quality, or importance of something 2. PHILOS NORMATIVE expressing a judgment about something, or assigning a value to it, as opposed to describing a fact

evan. *abbr.* 1. evangelical 2. evangelist

ev·a·nesce /èvvə néss/ (**-nesced, -nesc·ing, -nesc·es**) *vi.* to grow less until completely gone (*literary*) ○ *His cares evanesced.* [Mid-19thC. From Latin *evanescere* "to vanish" ultimately from *vanus* "empty," from, ultimately, an Indo-European word that is also the ancestor of English *want*.]

ev·a·nes·cent /èvvə néss'nt/ *adj.* disappearing after only a short time ○ *an evanescent moment* —**ev·a·nes·cence** *n.* —**ev·a·nes·cent·ly** *adv.*

evang. *abbr.* 1. evangelical 2. evangelist

e·van·gel /i vánjəl/ *n.* 1. CHR CHRISTIAN GOSPEL the Christian gospel (*archaic*) 2. **e·van·gel, E·van·gel** CHR ANY OF FOUR CHRISTIAN GOSPELS any of the four Christian Gospels: Matthew, Mark, Luke, or John (*archaic*) 3. BASIC DOCTRINE a basic doctrine or set of moral or political principles or teachings (*formal*) 4. = **evangelist** [14thC. Via Old French *evangile* from, ultimately, Greek *euaggelion* "good news," from *euaggelos* "bringing good news," from *eu* "good" + *aggelein* "to announce."]

e·van·gel·ic /ee van jéllik, èvvən-/, **E·van·gel·ic** *adj.* = **evangelical**

e·van·gel·i·cal /ee van jéllik'l, èvvən-/ *adj.* 1. **e·van·gel·i·cal, E·van·gel·i·cal, e·van·gel·ic, E·van·gel·ic** CHR OF PARTICULAR PROTESTANT CHURCHES relating or belonging to any Protestant Christian church whose members believe in the authority of the Bible and salvation through the personal acceptance of Jesus Christ 2. **e·van·gel·i·cal, e·van·gel·ic** WITH STRONG BELIEFS enthusiastic or zealous in support of a particular cause and very eager to make other people share its beliefs or ideals 3. **e·van·gel·i·cal, e·van·gel·ic** CHR RELATING TO THE CHRISTIAN GOSPELS relating to or based on the Christian Gospels: Matthew, Mark, Luke, or John ■ *n.* **e·van·gel·i·cal, E·van·gel·i·cal** MEMBER OF EVANGELICAL CHRISTIAN CHURCH a member of an evangelical Christian church or movement —**e·van·gel·i·cal·ly** *adv.*

e·van·gel·i·cal·ism /ee van jéllik'l izzəm, èvvən-/, **E·van·gel·i·cal·ism** *n.* a Protestant movement of the Christian church whose members believe in the authority of the Bible and salvation through the personal acceptance of Jesus Christ

e·van·gel·ism /i vánjə lìzzəm/ *n.* 1. CHR SPREADING OF CHRISTIANITY the spreading of Christianity, especially through the activities of evangelists 2. CRUSADING ZEAL great enthusiasm, fervor, or zeal for a particular cause

e·van·gel·ist /i vánjəlist/ *n.* 1. CHRISTIAN WHO CONVERTS OTHERS somebody who tries to persuade other people to become Christians, especially one who travels around speaking at public meetings or making radio or television broadcasts 2. **e·van·gel·ist, E·van·gel·ist** WRITER OF CHRISTIAN GOSPEL any of the writers of the first four Christian Gospels: Matthew, Mark, Luke, or John —**e·van·gel·is·tic** /i vànjə lístik/ *adj.* —**e·van·gel·is·ti·cal·ly** /-lístiklee/ *adv.*

e·van·gel·ize /i vánjə lìz/ (**-ized, -iz·ing, -iz·es**) *vti.* 1. CHR CONVERT TO CHRISTIANITY to convert somebody or the people of an area to Christianity, especially by preaching or missionary work 2. BE ADVOCATE FOR A CAUSE to try to persuade other people to share enthusiasm for particular beliefs and ideals —**e·van·gel·i·za·tion** /i vànjəli záysh'n/ *n.* —**e·van·gel·iz·er** *n.*

Ev·ans /évv'nz/, **Dame Edith** (1888–1976) British actor. She is remembered for her Shakespearean roles and also for her performance as Lady Bracknell in the 1951 movie of *The Importance of Being Earnest.* Full name **Dame Edith Mary Evans**

Ev·ans, Maurice (1901–89) British-born U.S. actor and producer. He began his career playing Shakespearean characters on stage and later became a character actor in movies and television productions.

Ev·ans, Mount mountain in north central Colorado, site of a high-altitude laboratory. Height: 14,264 ft./4,348 m.

Ev·ans, Walker (1903–75) U.S. photographer. He is known for his records of everyday life in the United States from the Great Depression onward.

Ev·ans·ton /évvənstən/ city in northeastern Illinois on Lake Michigan and a northern suburb of Chicago. Population: 71,593 (1996).

Ev·ans·ville /évvənz vìl/ city in southwestern Indiana, on the northern bank of the Ohio River, southwest of Bloomington. Population: 123,456 (1996).

e·vap·o·ra·ble /i váppərəb'l, -vápprə-/ *adj.* subject to evaporation —**e·vap·o·ra·bil·i·ty** /i vàppərə bíllətee, -vàpprə-/ *n.*

e·vap·o·rate /i váppə ràyt/ (**-rat·ed, -rat·ing, -rates**) *v.* 1. *vti.* CHANGE LIQUID TO VAPOR to change a liquid into a vapor, usually by heating to below its boiling point, or to change from a liquid to vapor in this way ○ *The water evaporates, increasing the moisture in the air.* 2. *vt.* REMOVE LIQUID FROM to remove liquid from something, usually by heating, to produce a more concentrated or solid substance 3. *vi.* VANISH to disappear gradually or fade away to nothing 4. *vt.* PHYS TO DEPOSIT A FILM to deposit something such as a metal film on a surface through the condensation of a vaporized substance [15thC. From Latin *evaporat-*, the past participle stem of *evaporare*, literally "to go out in vapor," from *vapor* "VAPOR."] —**e·vap·o·ra·tive** /i váppə ràytiv, -rətiv, i vápprətiv/ *adj.*

e·vap·o·rat·ed milk *n.* milk that has been thickened by removing some of the water by evaporation

e·vap·o·ra·tion /i vàppə ráysh'n/ *n.* a process in which something is changed from a liquid to a vapor without its temperature reaching the boiling point

e·vap·o·ra·tor /i váppə ràytər/ *n.* 1. PART OF REFRIGERATION SYSTEM the vaporization portion of a refrigeration system 2. WATER-REMOVING DEVICE a vaporizing device that removes water or other solvents to obtain the dried or concentrated residue, as in the preparation of powdered milk from milk

e·vap·o·rite /i váppə rìt/ *n.* a sedimentary rock or deposit that results from the evaporation of salt water in lagoons and saline lakes. Gypsum and rock salt are evaporites. [Early 20thC. Coined from EVAPORATION + -ITE.] —**e·vap·o·rit·ic** /i vàppə ríttik/ *adj.*

e·vap·o·tran·spi·ra·tion /i vàppō transpi ráysh'n/ *n.* the return of moisture to the air through both evaporation from the soil and transpiration by plants [Mid-20thC. Coined from EVAPORATION.]

e·va·sion /i váyzh'n/ *n.* 1. AVOIDANCE OF SOMETHING avoidance of something unpleasant, especially a moral or legal obligation 2. MEANS OF AVOIDANCE a means of escaping or avoiding something, especially one that involves cunning or deceit 3. AVOIDING AN ISSUE not giving a direct answer to a direct question, usually in order to conceal the truth [15thC. Via Old French *évasion* from, ultimately Latin *evadere* (see EVADE).]

WORD KEY: USAGE

See Usage note at ***avoidance.***

e·va·sive /i váyssiv/ *adj.* 1. AVOIDING AN ISSUE not giving a direct answer to a direct question 2. AVOIDING TROUBLE intended to avoid something unpleasant, e.g., trouble or an attack ○ *took evasive action* [Early 18thC] —**e·va·sive·ly** *adv.* —**e·va·sive·ness** *n.*

eve /eev/ *n.* 1. **eve, Eve** DAY BEFORE FESTIVAL the day, evening, or night before a religious festival or public holiday 2. PERIOD BEFORE EVENT the day or days immediately before an important event or special occasion ○ *He died on the eve of his 100th birthday.* 3. EVENING an evening (*literary*) ○ *on a cold winter's eve* [12thC. Originally a variant of EVEN[2].]

Eve /eev/ *n.* in the Bible, the first woman created by God, and Adam's companion in the Garden of Eden

e·vec·tion /i vékshən/ *n.* a periodic irregularity in the motion of the Moon caused by the variation in the gravitational attraction of the Sun as the Moon orbits the earth [Mid-17thC. From the Latin stem *evection-*, from *evect-*, the past participle stem of *evehere* "to carry out, elevate," from *vehere* "to carry" (source of English *inveigh*, *vehicle*, and *vex*).] —**e·vec·tion·al** *adj.*

e·ven[1] /éevən/ *adj.* 1. NOT SLOPING, ROUGH, OR IRREGULAR having no slope, roughness, or irregularities 2. AT THE SAME HEIGHT at the same distance above the ground or other point of reference 3. ALIGNED lining up along the same horizontal or vertical line and usually with equal spaces between 4. NOT CHANGING OR FLUCTUATING not changing or fluctuating in level or strength 5. THE SAME THROUGHOUT the same all over or throughout ○ *an even consistency* 6. EQUAL IN AMOUNT equal in amount, number, or extent ○ *At the end of the first round, the score was even.* 7. WELL-BALANCED between competitors of equal strength or skill, and therefore fair or well-balanced 8. NOT OWING ANYTHING not or no longer owing anything to each other (*informal*) ○ *Give me five dollars, and we'll call it even.* 9. MATH EXACTLY DIVISIBLE BY TWO used to describe a number or quantity that can be exactly divided by two with nothing left over, e.g., 2, 6, 30, or 518. ◊ **odd** 10. WITH AN EVEN NUMBER having a number that can be exactly divided by two ○ *on the even pages* 11. CALM AND STEADY calm and controlled 12. EXACT IN AMOUNT exact in amount, number, or extent ○ *an even dozen* ■ *vti.* (**e·vened, e·ven·ing, e·vens**) LEVEL OR EQUALIZE to make something more level or equal, or become more level or equal ○ *Atlanta scored three quick runs to even the score.* [Old English *efen*, from a prehistoric Germanic word meaning either "flat, level" or "equal, alike"] —**e·ven·ness** *n.* ◇ **get even (with somebody)** to take revenge on somebody ○ *They took advantage of me, and I was determined to get even.*

even out *vti.* 1. FLATTEN OR LEVEL SOMETHING to become or make something more flat, smooth, or level 2. EQUALIZE THINGS to make two or more different things more equal, or become more equal

even up *vti.* to become or make something more equal, fair, or well-balanced

e·ven[2] /éevən/ *n.* evening (*literary*) ○ *at even, when the sun was set* [Old English *æfen* (see EVENING)]

e·ven[3] /éevən/ CORE MEANING used for emphasis to indicate something surprising, unlikely, or extreme ○ *Even I know how to repair a flat!*

1. SO MUCH AS used after a negative for emphasis to indicate something unexpected and usually annoying or disappointing ○ *She couldn't even remember my name.* 2. TO A GREATER EXTENT used for emphasis in comparisons to indicate the degree to which something exists ○ *His writing is even messier than hers, and hers is barely legible.* 3. FURTHERMORE used to indicate that the description that follows applies in addition to and more strongly or precisely than the preceding one ○ *She is careful with her money, even miserly.* 4. THAT IS TO SAY used to emphasize a statement (*archaic*) 5. ALL THE WAY used to emphasize that something is true completely and fully (*archaic*) ○ *I will follow thee even unto the ends of the earth.* [Old English *efne*, from a prehistoric Germanic base that also produced English *even*[1]]

e·ven break *n.* an equal opportunity for winning or losing

e·ven chance *n.* an equal likelihood that something will or will not happen

e·ven·er /éevənər/ *n.* 1. SOMETHING THAT EQUALIZES something or somebody that makes something even 2. PIVOTING BAR ON HORSE-DRAWN VEHICLE a pivoting bar or set of bars on a horse-drawn carriage or other vehicle that equalizes the force of two or more singletrees (*regional*)

WORD KEY: REGIONAL NOTE

Elsewhere an ***evener*** on a carriage or cart is called *doubletree* and *equalizer.* Most common in New England and the Midwest, ***evener*** contrasts with *doubletree* in the South. The old-fashioned *equalizer* is most common in the Midwest. Where it has currency, ***evener*** is often used to mean the singletree itself.

e·ven·fall /éevən fàwl/ *n.* the beginning of evening (*archaic*)

e·ven·hand·ed /éevən hándəd/ *adj.* treating everyone fairly, without favoritism or discrimination ○ *an evenhanded distribution of the profits* —**e·ven·hand·ed·ly** *adv.* —**e·ven·hand·ed·ness** *n.*

eve·ning /éevning/ *n.* **1. LATE PART OF DAY** the part of the day between afternoon and night, as daylight begins to fade **2. TIME BEFORE BEDTIME** the part of the day between sunset or the last main meal of the day and bedtime ○ *We went out for the evening.* **3. EVENING'S ACTIVITY** a social gathering, meeting, or entertainment held in the evening ○ *Thank you for the enjoyable evening.* **4. PERIOD AT END** the final part of a period of time, e.g., somebody's life or a historical era (*literary*) ○ *the evening of the British Empire* **5.** *Southern U.S.* **AFTERNOON** the afternoon, especially middle to late afternoon ■ *interj.* **GOOD EVENING** good evening (*informal*) [Old English *æfnung,* from *æfen* (source of English *even*[2]), from, ultimately, an Indo-European word meaning "lateness"]

eve·ning dress *n.* **1. FORMAL CLOTHING** clothing worn by men or women for formal social events held in the evening. A man in evening dress usually wears a dinner jacket and black tie, and a woman usually wears a full-length dress of elegant design. **2.** = **evening gown**

eve·ning gown *n.* a woman's dress suitable for formal social events held in the evening, usually a full-length dress of elegant design

eve·ning prayer, Eve·ning Prayer *n.* = **evensong** *n.* 1

Evening primrose

eve·ning prim·rose *n.* a biennial plant with hairy leaves and yellow flowers that open in the evening. Its seeds yield an oil used especially in treatments for menstrual problems. Genus: *Oenothera.*

eve·nings /éevningz/ *adv.* in the evening, especially regularly

eve·ning star *n.* a bright planet that can be seen in the western sky around sunset, usually Venus but occasionally Mercury

E·ven·ki /i véngkee, i wéngkee/ (*plural* **-ki** *or* **-kis**), **E·wen·ki** /i wéngkee/ (*plural* **-ki** *or* **-kis**) *n.* **1.** PEOPLES **MEMBER OF ASIAN ETHNIC GROUP** a member of an ethnic group that lives mainly in eastern parts of Asiatic Russia and the northwest of China **2.** LANG **LANGUAGE SPOKEN IN ASIATIC RUSSIA** a language spoken in eastern parts of Asiatic Russia and the northwest of China that belongs to the Manchu-Tungus group of the Mongolian branch of Altaic. Evenki is spoken by about 30,000 people. [Via Russian, "Evenki people," from Evenki] —**E·ven·ki** *adj.*

e·ven·ly /éevənlee/ *adv.* **1. EQUALLY** in equal amounts, numbers, parts, or shares **2. UNIFORMLY** with the same thickness, consistency, amount, or degree over or throughout something **3. WITH EQUAL SPACING** with gaps of the same size between each item **4. IN BALANCE** having the same weight, strength, or skill as another **5. STEADILY** in an unchanging, regular, or rhythmical way **6. CALMLY AND UNEMOTIONALLY** in a calm unemotional way

e·ven mon·ey *n.* **EQUAL ODDS** a betting situation in which the odds of winning or losing are equal and the winnings equal the stake ■ *adj.* **AS LIKELY AS NOT** equally likely or unlikely ○ *It's even money she'll forget.*

e·ven·song /éevən sàwng/ *n.* **1. EVENING SERVICE IN ANGLICAN CHURCH** the daily evening worship service of the Anglican Church **2. VESPERS** vespers (*archaic*) **3. EVENING** evening (*archaic*)

e·ven-ste·ven, e·ven Ste·ven *adj.* (*informal*) **1. SETTLED EQUALLY AND FAIRLY** with all debts or grievances mutually settled **2. EQUAL IN SCORE** with equal scores or chances of winning ○ *At the end of the first round the two teams were even-steven.* [Origin uncertain: probably an arbitrary rhyming formation, although *Steven* is obsolete slang for "money"]

e·vent /i vént/ *n.* **1. IMPORTANT INCIDENT** an occurrence, especially one that is particularly significant, interesting, exciting, or unusual ○ *the events leading up to the strike* **2. ORGANIZED OCCASION** an organized occasion such as a social function or sports competition ○ *She has competed in many international events.* **3.** SPORTS **INDIVIDUAL SPORTS CONTEST** any of the races or other competitions that form part of a larger sports occasion, e.g., the Olympic Games ○ *The 100 meters is his best event.* **4.** PHILOS **OCCURRENCE** a happening or occurrence **5.** PHYS **SINGLE POINT IN SPACE-TIME** an occurrence defined in the theory of relativity as a single point in space-time **6.** COMPUT **OCCURRENCE AFFECTING COMPUTER PROGRAM** an occurrence or happening of significance to a computer program, e.g., the clicking of a mouse button or the completion of a write operation to a disk [Late 16thC. From Latin *eventus,* from the past participle of *evenire* "to happen," literally "to come out" from *venire* "to come" (see VENTURE).] ◇ **be wise after the event** to know with hindsight what should have been done or said in a situation ◇ **in the event of something** if something should happen

e·vent-driv·en *adj.* used to describe a computer program with a main loop that waits for an event, e.g., the pressing of a mouse button, and then passes the details of it along

e·ven-tem·pered *adj.* not easily angered or upset

e·vent·ful /i véntfəl/ *adj.* **1. INTERESTING OR EXCITING** full of important, interesting, or exciting occurrences **2. MEANINGFUL** having a major effect on a somebody's life —**e·vent·ful·ly** *adv.* —**e·vent·ful·ness** *n.*

e·vent ho·ri·zon *n.* the theoretical boundary surrounding a black hole, within which gravitational attraction is so great that nothing, not even radiation, can escape because the escape velocity is greater than the speed of light

e·ven·tide /éevən tìd/ *n.* evening (*literary*)

e·vent·less /i véntləss/ *adj.* having no significant events

e·ven·tu·al /i vénchoo əl, i vénchəl/ *adj.* **1. ULTIMATE** happening in the course of time or events, usually much later ○ *her eventual fall from power* **2. CONTINGENT** depending on circumstances or unknown future events (*archaic*) [Early 17thC. From French *éventuel,* from, ultimately, Latin *eventus* "outcome" (see EVENT).]

e·ven·tu·al·i·ty /i vènchoo állətee/ (*plural* **-ties**) *n.* a possible occurrence or result, especially something undesirable or unexpected (*formal*) ○ *We must be prepared for all eventualities.*

e·ven·tu·al·ly /i vénchoo əlee, i vénchəlee/ *adv.* **1. IN THE END** after a long time, especially after many problems or setbacks ○ *We eventually managed to open the door.* **2. ULTIMATELY** at some later time after a series of events ○ *She hopes eventually to study.*

e·ven·tu·ate /i vénchoo àyt/ (**-at·ed, -at·ing, -ates**) *vi.* to happen as a final result (*formal*)

eventuate in *vt.* to cause or result in something, especially after an extended period of time (*formal*) ○ *The oil spill eventuated in the destruction of wildlife habitats along the coast.*

e·ven·weave /éevən wèev/ *n.* a fabric with warp and weft threads of the same thickness and tension, and with an equal number of warp and weft threads in any square measurement

ev·er /évvər/ *adv.* **1. AT ANY TIME** used for emphasis in indicating any time in the past or future ○ *This is the most fascinating book I've ever read.* ○ *Have you ever been skiing?* See Usage note below. **2. USED TO INDICATE SURPRISE** used for emphasis to indicate surprise, shock, or incomprehension at something ○ *Where ever can it be?* **3. INCREASINGLY** to an increasing degree (*formal*) ○ *The questions were becoming ever more technical.* **4. USED AS INTENSIFIER** used to emphasize a particular quality, especially to express enthusiasm (*informal*) ○ *Was I ever glad to get home!* **5. ALWAYS** showing at all times a particular quality ○ *He is ever anxious to please.* [Old English *æfre.* Ultimately from an Indo-European word meaning "eternity" that is also the ancestor of English *age.*]

WORD KEY: USAGE

The best dictionary **ever***:* Some people object to this use of ***ever*** because they maintain that ***ever*** should include the future as well as the past. However, the future can rarely be accounted for, and the idiom is well established in conversational use, although it would not normally be used in more formal spoken or in written English.

Barnaby's

Mount Everest: West shoulder of the mountain

Ev·er·est, Mount /évvərist/ mountain in the Himalayas on the border between Nepal and the Tibet Autonomous Region of China. It is the highest mountain in the world. Height: 29,028 ft./8,848 m.

Ev·er·ett /évvərət/ **1.** city in eastern Massachusetts on the Mystic River, near Boston. Population: 35,006 (1996). **2.** city and seaport in northwestern Washington, near Seattle. Population: 69,961 (1990).

Ev·er·ett, Edward (1794–1865) U.S. statesman, educator, and orator. He delivered the oration at Gettysburg prior to Lincoln's address.

ev·er·glade /évvər glàyd/ *n.* a stretch of marshy grassland usually covered with water for at least part of the year [Early 19thC. Back-formation from the EVERGLADES.]

Ev·er·glade kite *n.* = **snail kite**

Barnaby's

Everglades National Park

Ev·er·glades Na·tion·al Park /èvvər glaydz-/ national park in southern Florida, established in 1947. It contains the largest subtropical wilderness in the United States. Area: 2,356 sq. mi./6,102 sq. km.

ev·er·green /évvər grèen/ *adj.* **1.** BOT **WITH LEAVES THROUGHOUT THE YEAR** used to describe a tree or shrub that retains its foliage throughout the year **2. REMAINING FRESH OR POPULAR** used to describe people or things that always seem fresh, lively, or interesting, and that remain popular despite their age ■ *n.* **1.** BOT **EVERGREEN TREE** a tree or shrub that keeps its foliage throughout the year **2. EVERGREEN PERSON OR THING** somebody or something that remains fresh, lively, interesting, or popular ■ **ev·er·greens** *npl.* **DECORATIVE BRANCHES** twigs or branches cut from evergreen trees or shrubs and used for decoration

Ev·er·green Park /évvər green-/ village in northeastern Illinois that is a residential suburb of Chicago. Population: 20,584 (1996).

Ev·er·green State *n.* the state of Washington (*informal*)

ev·er·last·ing /évvər lásting/ *adj.* **1.** LASTING FOR EVER never failing or coming to an end **2.** LASTING A LONG TIME continuing indefinitely or for a long time **3.** INCESSANT going on for too long and becoming tedious or annoying ○ *everlasting grumbling* ■ *n.* **1.** INFINITY infinite time **2. ev·er·last·ing, ev·er·last·ing flow·er** PLANTS FLOWER THAT LOOKS FRESH WHEN DRIED a plant with flowers that keep their shape and color when dried, e.g., helichrysum —**ev·er·last·ing·ly** *adv.* —**ev·er·last·ing·ness** *n.*

Ev·er·last·ing *n.* God (*literary*)

ev·er·more /évvər máwr, évvər màwr/ *adv.* from now until the end of time or the end of somebody's life (*literary*) ○ *I will be evermore in your debt.*

Ev·ers /évvərz/, **Medgar** (1925–63) U.S. civil rights leader. He was a major figure in the National Association for the Advancement of Colored People (NAACP) until his murder in 1963.

e·ver·sion /i vúrzh'n, i vúrsh'n/ *n.* MED, BIOL **1.** TURNING INSIDE OUT the process or condition of being turned inside out ○ *eversion of the bladder* **2.** TURNING OUTWARD a condition of being turned outward ○ *an eversion of the feet* [Mid-18thC. Directly or via French from the Latin stem *eversion-*, from *evers-*, the past participle stem of *evertere* (see EVERT).] —**e·ver·si·ble** *adj.*

e·vert /i vúrt/ (**e·vert·ed, e·vert·ing, e·verts**) *vt.* to turn an organ or other body part outward or inside out [Mid-16thC. From Latin *evertere*, literally "to turn out," from *vertere* "to turn" (see VERSE).]

Chris Evert

Ev·ert /évvərt/, **Chris** (*b.* 1954) U.S. tennis player. She won 16 grand slam singles championships during her career (1972–89). Full name **Christine Marie Evert**

ev·er·where /évvər wàir, èvvər wáir, -hwàir, -hwáir/ *adv.* *Southern U.S.* **1.** EVERYWHERE everywhere **2.** WHEREVER wherever

ev·er·which /évvər wìch, èvvər wích, -hwìch, -hwích/ *adv. Southern U.S.* whichever

eve·ry /évvree/ CORE MEANING: used to indicate each member of a group without exception ○ *Every life has value.*

adj. **1.** THE UTMOST used to emphasize that there is all there could be of a particular quality ○ *The committee has every intention of exploring this issue.* **2.** EACH, OCCURRING INTERMITTENTLY OR PROPORTIONATELY used to indicate each occurrence in recurrent or intermittent groups of things, or to indicate a ratio ○ *We intend to meet every two weeks.* ○ *Take this medicine every three hours.* [13thC. From the Old English phrase _æfre _ælc "ever each."] ◇ **every now and then, every now and again** occasionally

WORD KEY: USAGE

See Usage note at ***each.***

eve·ry·bod·y *pron.* = **everyone**

eve·ry·day /évvree dày/ *adj.* **1.** ORDINARY AND UNREMARKABLE having no remarkable feature to set it apart ○ *an everyday story of city life* **2.** HAPPENING OR DONE EACH DAY happening or done each day ○ *an everyday occurrence* **3.** USED ON ORDINARY OCCASIONS suitable for use on ordinary days or for routine tasks, rather than on special occasions ■ *n.* ORDINARY OCCASIONS routine or daily life —**eve·ry·day·ness** *n.*

WORD KEY: USAGE

everyday or **every day**? When you intend either an adjective (for the most part this will come before a noun, as in *everyday life* or a noun that means "ordinary occasions" *part of the everyday,* the one-word version is correct. Adverbial uses *We should eat fruit every day* and the noun use that means "each day" *Every day is different* call for the two-word version. Thus *everyday in every way* means "ordinary in all respects," whereas *every day in every way* means "daily and completely."

Eve·ry·man /évvri màn/ *n.* **1. Eve·ry·man, eve·ry·man** ORDINARY PERSON somebody, usually a man, considered to be typical or representative of all human beings **2.** HERO OF MORALITY PLAY the hero of a medieval morality play who represents the whole of the human race

eve·ry·one /évvri wùn/, **eve·ry·bod·y** /évvri bòddee/ *pron.* every person, whether of a defined group or in general ○ *Everyone is going to come to the office party.* ○ *This is not just for one area; it will affect everyone around the country.*

eve·ry·place /évvri plàyss/ *adv.* everywhere (*informal*) ○ *I've looked everyplace.*

eve·ry·thing /évvri thing/ *pron.* **1.** THE ENTIRETY all the items, actions, or facts in a given situation ○ *Everything I do is for my family.* ○ *Is everything all right?* **2.** SOMETHING ALL-IMPORTANT used to emphasize that somebody or something is the most important person or thing there is ○ *To them, family is everything.*

eve·ry·where /évvri wàir, -hwàir/ *adv.* in or to all conceivable places ○ *Children everywhere play these games.* ○ *Her cat followed her everywhere she went.*

Eve·ry·wom·an /évvri wòommən/, **eve·ry·wom·an** *n.* a woman considered to be typical or representative of woman generally [Mid-20thC. Modeled on EVERYMAN.]

evg. *abbr.* evening

Ev·i·an /évvee àwN, évvee àn/ *tdmk.* a trademark for a bottled mineral water from Evian, France

e·vict /i víkt/ (**e·vict·ed, e·vict·ing, e·victs**) *vt.* **1.** EJECT SOMEBODY FROM A PROPERTY to force a tenant to leave a property, especially the tenant's residence, usually because he or she has failed to comply with the terms of the lease **2.** THROW OUT OF A PLACE to force somebody to leave a place, usually because of bad behavior ○ *She was evicted from the game for insulting the referee* **3.** GET BACK PROPERTY to recover property or title to property from somebody by legal means [(see EVINCE)] —**e·vic·tion** *n.* —**e·vic·tor** *n.*

e·vict·ee /i vìk tée/ *n.* somebody who is evicted from a property

ev·i·dence /évvid'ns/ *n.* **1.** SIGN OR PROOF something that gives a sign or proof of the existence or truth of something, or that helps somebody to come to a particular conclusion ○ *There is no evidence that the disease is related to diet.* **2.** PROOF OF GUILT the objects or information used to prove or suggest the guilt of somebody accused of a crime ○ *The police have no evidence.* **3.** STATEMENTS OF WITNESSES the oral or written statements of witnesses and other people involved in a trial or official inquiry ■ *vt.* (**-denced, -denc·ing, -denc·es**) DEMONSTRATE OR PROVE to demonstrate or prove something (*usually passive*) ○ *Their unwillingness to participate is evidenced by their failure to contact us.*

ev·i·dent /évvid'nt/ *adj.* easy or clear to see or understand ○ *The full extent of her injuries did not become evident until they tried to move her.* [See VISION.]

ev·i·den·tial /èvvi dénshəl/ *adj. U.K.* = **evidentiary** —**ev·i·den·tial·ly** *adv.*

ev·i·den·tia·ry /èvvi dénsharee, -dénshee èrree/ *adj.* relating to, consisting of, or based on evidence ○ *statements with no evidentiary value*

ev·i·dent·ly /évvidəntlee/ *adv.* **1.** CLEARLY used to indicate that something is undoubtedly true, often because it is there to be seen ○ *Evidently, you have not grasped all the ramifications of this proposal.* **2.** APPARENTLY used to indicate that something may be true based on available evidence ○ *He then completely ignored her, evidently intent on hurting her feelings even more.*

e·vil /éev'l/ *adj.* **1.** MORALLY BAD profoundly immoral or wrong **2.** HARMFUL deliberately causing great harm, pain, or upset ○ *This evil act is clearly the work of terrorists.* **3.** DEVILISH connected with the Devil or other powerful destructive forces ○ *evil spirits* **4.** CAUSING MISFORTUNE characterized by, bringing, or signifying bad luck ○ *an evil omen* **5.** MALICIOUS characterized by a desire to cause hurt or harm ○ *an evil mood* **6.** DISAGREEABLE very unpleasant ○ *What an evil smell!* ■ *n.* **1.** WICKEDNESS the quality of being profoundly immoral or wrong **2. e·vil, E·vil** FORCE CAUSING HARMFUL EFFECTS the force held to bring about harmful, painful, or unpleasant events ○ *a struggle between good and evil* **3.** SOMETHING EVIL a situation or thing that is very unpleasant, harmful, or morally wrong [Old English *yfel.* Ultimately from an Indo-European word meaning "exceeding due limits."] —**e·vil·ly** *adv.* —**e·vil·ness** *n.*

e·vil·do·er /éev'l dòo ər, èev'l dóo ər/ *n.* somebody who does evil things —**e·vil·do·ing** *n.*

e·vil eye *n.* **1.** LOOK OF STRONG DISLIKE a piercing look that conveys strong feelings of hatred, disapproval, jealousy, or malice, or that supposedly can cause harm **2.** SUPPOSED HARMFUL MAGICAL POWER a supernatural or magical power that some people believe can bring harm or cause bad luck ○ *an amulet to protect children from the evil eye*

E·vil One *n.* the Devil

e·vince /i víns/ (**e·vinced, e·vinc·ing, e·vinc·es**) *vt.* **1.** SHOW CLEARLY to show a feeling or a quality clearly ○ *She evinced her disapproval of the production by leaving the auditorium.* **2.** REVEAL to indicate something by action or implication [Late 16thC. From Latin *evincere*, literally "to win out" (source also of English *evict*), from *vincere* "to conquer" (see VICTOR).] —**e·vinc·i·ble** *adj.*

e·vis·cer·ate /i víssə ràyt/ (**-at·ed, -at·ing, -ates**) *vt.* **1.** DISEMBOWEL to remove the internal organs or entrails of a person or an animal **2.** REMOVE IMPORTANT PART OF to remove an essential part of something and so weaken it **3.** SURG REMOVE THE CONTENTS OF AN ORGAN to remove the contents of the eyeball or another organ or body cavity [Late 16thC. From Latin *eviscerare*, from *viscera* (see VISCERA).] —**e·vis·cer·a·tion** /i vìssə ráysh'n/ *n.* —**e·vis·cer·a·tor** /i víssə ràytər/ *n.*

ev·o·ca·tion /èvvə káysh'n, èe vō káysh'n/ *n.* **1.** EVOKING a recreation of something not present, especially an event or feeling from the past ○ *an accurate evocation of that period* **2.** LAW TRANSFER OF COURT CASE the transfer of a case from a lower to a higher court for review

e·voc·a·tive /i vókətiv/ *adj.* prompting vivid memories or images of things not present, especially things from the past ○ *an outfit evocative of the 1960s* —**e·voc·a·tive·ly** *adv.* —**e·voc·a·tive·ness** *n.*

e·voke /i vṓk/ (**e·voked, e·vok·ing, e·vokes**) *vt.* **1.** STIMULATE MEMORIES FROM PAST to bring to mind a memory or feeling, especially from the past ○ *evoke childhood memories* **2.** CAUSE REACTION OR FEELING to provoke a particular reaction or feeling ○ *Her question evoked a bitter retort.* **3.** CAUSE TO APPEAR to make beings appear who are normally invisible ○ *evoke a spirit* [Early 17thC. From Latin *evocare*, literally "to call out," from *vocare* "to call" (see VOCAL).] —**ev·o·ca·ble** /évvəkəb'l, i vṓkəb'l/ *adj.* —**ev·o·ca·tor** /évvə kàytər/ *n.* —**e·vo·ker** *n.*

ev·o·lute /évvə lòot/ *n.* MATH the curve formed by the set of points that are the centers of curvature of another geometric curve (**involute**) [Mid-18thC. From Latin *evolutus*, the past participle of *evolvere* (see EVOLVE).]

ev·o·lu·tion /èvvə lóosh'n, èevə-/ *n.* **1.** BIOL THEORY OF DEVELOPMENT FROM EARLIER FORMS the theoretical process by which all species develop from earlier forms of life. On this theory, natural variation in the genetic material of a population favors reproduction by some individuals more than others, so that over the generations all members of the population come to possess the favorable traits. **2.** BIOL DEVELOPMENTAL PROCESS the natural or artificially induced process by which new and different organisms develop as a result of changes in genetic material **3.** GRADUAL DEVELOPMENT the gradual development of something into a more complex or better form ○ *the evolution of democracy in Western Europe* **4.** PHYS GIVING OFF HEAT OR GAS the emission of heat, gas, or vapor **5.** PATTERN CAUSED BY MOVEMENT a pattern formed by a series of movements **6.** MATH FINDING ROOT OF NUMBER an algebraic operation in which the root, e.g., the square root or cube root, of a number is found. ◊ **involution 7.** MIL MILITARY EXERCISE a military exercise or maneuver carried out according to a plan [Early 17thC. Formed from Latin *evolut-*, the past participle stem of *evolvere* (see EVOLVE).] —**ev·o·lu·tion·al** *adj.* —**evo·lu·tion·al·ly** *adv.*

ev·o·lu·tion·ar·y /èvvə lóosh'n èrree, èevə-/ *adj.* **1.** BIOL OF EVOLUTION relating to the theory of evolution **2.** FROM EVOLUTION resulting from or conferred by evolution ○ *evolutionary advantage* **3.** GRADUAL developing in small increments that accumulate to bring about significant change ○ *an evolutionary process* —**ev·o·lu·tion·ar·i·ly** *adv.*

ev·o·lu·tion·ism /èvvə lo͞osh'n ìzzəm, èevə-/ *n.* **1.** BIOL **EVOLUTIONARY THEORY** the theory of biological evolution **2. BELIEF IN EVOLUTION** belief in the theory of biological evolution —**ev·o·lu·tion·ist** *n.*

e·volve /i vólv/ (**e·volved, e·volv·ing, e·volves**) *v.* **1.** *vti.* **DEVELOP GRADUALLY** to develop something gradually, often into something more complex or advanced, or undergo such development **2.** *vti.* BIOL **DEVELOP VIA EVOLUTIONARY CHANGE** in evolutionary theory to develop from an earlier biological form, or to develop a characteristic in this way **3.** *vt.* PHYS **EMIT HEAT OR GAS** to give off heat, gas, or vapor [Early 17thC. From Latin *evolvere*, literally "to roll out," from *volvere* "to roll" (source of English *volume* and *revolver*; see VOLUTE).] —**e·volv·a·ble** *adj.* —**e·volve·ment** *n.* —**e·volv·er** *n.*

E·wa Beach /áy vaa-, -waa-/ town on Oahu Island, Hawaii, west of Honolulu. Population: 14,315 (1990).

ewe /yoo/ *n.* a female sheep, especially when fully grown [Old English *ēowu*. Ultimately from an Indo-European word meaning "sheep," which is also the ancestor of English *ovine*.]

E·we /áy wày, áy vày/ (*plural* **E·we** *or* **E·wes**) *n.* **1. MEMBER OF A W AFRICAN PEOPLE** a member of a West African people living in coastal regions of Ghana, Togo, and Benin **2. LANGUAGE OF THE EWE** the language of the Ewe, belonging to the Kwa branch of the Niger-Congo family. Ewe is spoken by about three million people. [Mid-19thC. From *Ewe*.] —**E·we** *adj.*

Ew·ell /yo͞o əl/, **Richard Stoddert** (1817–72) U.S. soldier. He led the Confederate army after Stonewall Jackson's death.

ewe-neck *n.* a thin concave neck in a horse or dog, considered to be a defect —**ewe-necked** *adj.*

Ewer

ew·er /yo͞o ər/ *n.* a large jug or pitcher with a wide spout [15thC. Via Anglo-Norman from Old French *aiguière*, from, ultimately, Latin *aquarius* "of water," from *aqua* "water" (see AQUA).]

ex[1] /eks/ *n.* the letter X [Late 19thC. From the pronunciation of the letter X.]

ex[2] /eks/ *n.* a former spouse, boyfriend, or girlfriend (*informal*) [Early 19thC. From EX-[1].]

ex[3] /eks/ *prep.* **1.** FIN **EXCLUDING** not including or participating in ○ *ex dividend* **2.** COMM **SOLD FROM** sold directly from with no charge before collection ○ *ex works* [Mid-19thC. From Latin (see EX-[1]).]

ex. *abbr.* **1.** example **2. ex., exc.** except **3. ex., exch.** exchange **4.** examination **5.** executive **6.** express **7.** extra

Ex. *abbr.* BIBLE Exodus

ex-[1] *prefix.* **1.** out, outside, away ○ *exclave* ○ *explant* **2.** not, without ○ *exstipulate* **3.** former ○ *ex-convict* [From Latin "out of." Ultimately from an Indo-European word meaning "out," which is also the ancestor of English *external*.]

ex-[2] *prefix.* = **exo-** (*used before vowels*)

exa- one million million million, or 10^{18}. Symbol **E** [From HEXA-]

ex·ac·er·bate /ig zássər bàyt/ (**-bat·ed, -bat·ing, -bates**) *vt.* to make an already bad or problematic situation worse. ○ *Her silence merely exacerbated the problem.* [Mid-17thC. From Latin *exacerbat-*, the past participle stem of *exacerbare*, literally "to make thoroughly harsh," from *acerbare* "to make harsh," from *acerbus* "bitter" (see ACERBIC).] —**ex·ac·er·ba·tion** /ig zàssər báysh'n/ *n.*

ex·act /ig zákt/ *adj.* **1. CORRECT** accurate and correct in all important details ○ *an exact account* **2. PRECISE** precise and not allowing for any variation ○ *a check for the exact amount* **3. THIS AND NO OTHER** used to emphasize that what is being referred to is one precise and often significant thing and not any other ○ *on this exact spot* **4. STRICT** rigorous and thorough ○ *an exact argument* **5. FUNCTIONING ACCURATELY** characterized by precise measurements ○ *exact instruments* ■ *vt.* (**-act·ed, -act·ing, -acts**) **1. GET** to demand and obtain something, especially payment ○ *exacted a heavy tribute from their defeated enemies* **2. INFLICT AS SUFFERING** to make somebody endure something unpleasant (*formal*) ○ *I was already thinking how I could exact revenge for what he had done.* **3. REQUIRE** to call for something as a matter of necessity or urgency [15thC. From Latin *exactus*, the past participle of *exigere* "to demand," literally "to drive out" (source of English *essay*), from *agere* "to drive" (see AGENT).] —**ex·act·a·ble** *adj.* —**ex·act·ness** *n.* —**ex·ac·tor** *n.*

ex·act·a /ig záktə/ (*plural* **-as**) *n.* a type of bet, especially on dogs or horses, that pays if the two entries chosen come in first and second in the order predicted [Mid-20thC. From American Spanish *quiniela exacta* "exact quinella," a game of chance.]

ex·act·ing /ig zákting/ *adj.* **1. DEMANDING ATTENTION** requiring concentration and strict attention to detail ○ *an exacting task* **2. DEMANDING** demanding hard work and great effort ○ *an exacting boss* —**ex·act·ing·ly** *adv.* —**ex·act·ing·ness** *n.*

ex·ac·tion /ig zákshən/ *n.* **1. ACT OF DEMANDING AND OBTAINING SOMETHING** the act of forcing somebody to give something, especially payment **2. UNFAIR DEMAND** an unfair or excessive demand for something, especially money (*formal*) **3. PAYMENT OBTAINED BY FORCE** a sum of money or a payment that has been forcibly demanded and obtained (*formal*)

ex·ac·ti·tude /ig zákti to͞od/ *n.* the quality or state of being exact, precise, or accurate ○ *"The children were drilled in their parts with a military exactitude; obedience and punctuality became cardinal virtues."* (Frank Norris, *McTeague – A Story of San Francisco*; 1899)

ex·act·ly /ig záktlee/ *adv.* **1. PRECISELY** used to emphasize that a particular quality or quantity is stated precisely ○ *One lap around the park is exactly two miles.* **2. FULLY** used to emphasize that what is stated is true in all details or to the fullest extent ○ *He did exactly what I said he would.* **3. SHOWING AGREEMENT** used to indicate agreement that what has just been said is true or correct ○ *"We need to give this more thought." "Exactly."* **4. SHOWING DISAPPROVAL** used in questions to ask for precise information, often implying suspicion or disapproval ○ *So exactly what are you doing?*

ex·act sci·ence *n.* a science such as physics that deals with precise quantifiable measurements

ex·ag·ger·ate /ig zájjə ràyt/ (**-at·ed, -at·ing, -ates**) *v.* **1.** *vti.* **OVERSTATE SOMETHING** to state that something is better, worse, larger, more common, or more important than is true or usual **2.** *vt.* **MAKE MORE NOTICEABLE** to make something appear more noticeable or prominent than is usual or desirable [Mid-16thC. From Latin *exaggerat-*, the past participle stem of *exaggerare*, "to heap up," from *agger* "heap," from, *gerere* "to carry" (see GESTURE).] —**ex·ag·ger·at·ed·ly** *adv.* —**ex·ag·ger·at·ing·ly** *adv.* —**ex·ag·ger·a·tive** *adj.* —**ex·ag·ger·a·tor** *n.*

ex·ag·ger·a·tion /ig zàjjə ráysh'n/ *n.* **1. EXAGGERATING** the act or activity of exaggerating something ○ *a personality given to exaggeration* **2. EXAGGERATED STATEMENT** behavior or a statement that exaggerates something

ex·alt /ig záwlt/ (**-alt·ed, -alt·ing, -alts**) *vt.* **1. PROMOTE** to raise somebody or something in rank, position, or esteem (*formal*) ○ *exalted to the rank of major* **2. PRAISE** to praise or worship somebody or something (*formal*) **3. INTENSIFY** to increase the intensity or effect of something (*formal*) **4. STIMULATE** to stimulate a mental quality or faculty (*archaic*) ○ *"Of Lorna, of my lifelong darling, of my more and more loved wife, I will not talk; for it is not seemly that a man should exalt his pride."* (R. D. Blackmore, *Lorna Doone, A Romance of Exmoor*; 1869) **5. RAISE** to raise somebody or something physically (*archaic*) [15thC. From Latin *exaltare*, literally "to put up high," from *altus* "high" (see ALTO.] —**ex·alt·er** *n.*

ex·al·ta·tion /èg zawl táysh'n/ *n.* **1. FEELING OF EXTREME HAPPINESS** a feeling of intense or excessive happiness or exhilaration (*formal*) ○ *the miseries and exaltations of romance* **2. RAISING UP** the act of raising or holding something up (*formal*) **3. FLOCK** a flock of larks (*literary*)

ex·alt·ed /ig záwltəd/ *adj.* (*formal*) **1. ELEVATED** high in rank, position, or esteem **2. NOBLE** grand or noble in character **3. HIGH-SPIRITED** in very high spirits —**ex·alt·ed·ly** *adv.* —**ex·alt·ed·ness** *n.*

ex·am /ig zám/ *n.* **1. TEST OF KNOWLEDGE OR ABILITY** a test designed to assess somebody's ability or knowledge in a particular subject or field ○ *a chemistry exam* **2.** MED **MEDICAL INSPECTION OF A PATIENT** a medical inspection of a particular kind carried out on a patient [Mid-19thC. Shortening of EXAMINATION.]

ex·a·men /ig záymən/ *n.* in the Roman Catholic Church, an examination of conscience [Early 17thC. From Latin (see EXAMINE).]

ex·am·i·na·tion /ig zàmmə náysh'n/ *n.* **1. INSPECTION** the process of looking at and considering something carefully with the aim of learning something ○ *Their applications are currently under examination.* **2.** EDUC full form of **exam** *n.* 1 **3.** *U.K.* MED = **exam 4.** MED **STUDY OF SAMPLES FOR MEDICAL DIAGNOSIS** the study of laboratory samples from a patient in order to diagnose an illness **5.** LAW **INTERROGATION IN LAW COURT** an interrogation of a witness or party to a case in a court of law

ex·am·ine /ig zámmin/ (**-ined, -in·ing, -ines**) *vt.* **1. STUDY** to inspect or study somebody or something in detail ○ *examine the scene for fingerprints* **2. INVESTIGATE** to analyze something in order to understand or expose it ○ *examine your conscience* **3.** EDUC **TEST** to test the knowledge or ability of somebody by giving written, oral, or practical examinations **4.** MED **INSPECT CONDITION OF A PATIENT** to inspect a patient in order to determine his or her condition or health ○ *examined by a qualified physician* **5.** LAW **INTERROGATE A WITNESS** to ask questions of a witness or other party to a case in a court of law [14thC. Via French from Latin *examinare* "to weigh," from *examen* "weighing out," from *exigere* (see EXACT).] —**ex·am·in·a·ble** *adj.* —**ex·am·in·ee** /ig zàmmə née/ *n.* —**ex·am·in·er** /ig zámminər/ *n.*

ex·am pa·per, ex·am·i·na·tion pa·per *n. U.K.* the printed set of questions used to test somebody's knowledge in an exam

ex·am·ple /ig zámp'l/ *n.* **1. SAMPLE** something that is representative by virtue of having typical features of the thing it represents ○ *a fine example of Baroque carving* **2. MODEL** a person, action, or thing taken as a model to be copied or avoided by others ○ *Her achievement is an example to us all.* **3. ILLUSTRATION SUPPORTING SOMETHING** an illustration that supports or provides more information on an opinion, theory, or principle ○ *The prosecutor then listed several examples of the accused's mismanagement of funds.* **4. LEARNING AID** an exercise or description that illustrates a principle, method, or problem ○ *Each chapter contains easy-to-follow examples.* **5. PERSON PUNISHED** somebody punished as a warning to others who may be inclined to offend in the same way ■ *vt.* (**-pled, -pling, -ples**) **EXEMPLIFY** to exemplify (*archaic*) (*usually passive*) [14thC. Via Old French from Latin *exemplum*, originally "something taken out, sample," from *eximere* "to take out," from *emere* "to take."] ◇ **for example** used to introduce a typical instance of somebody or something ◇ **make an example of somebody** to punish somebody as a warning to others who might be inclined to offend in the same way

ex·an·the·ma /èg zan théemə/ (*plural* **-them·a·ta** /-tə/ *or* **-the·mas**), **ex·an·them** /ig zánthəm/ *n.* **1. SKIN RASH** a skin rash appearing as a sign of some infectious diseases, such as measles **2. DISEASE WITH RASH** a disease characterized by the appearance of a skin rash, e.g., measles or scarlet fever [Mid-17thC. Via late Latin from Greek *exanthēma* "eruption," literally "blossoming out," from *anthein* "to blossom," from *anthos* "flower."] —**ex·an·the·mat·ic** /ig zànthə máttik/ *adj.* —**ex·an·them·a·tous** /èg zan thémmətəss/ *adj.*

ex·arch /ék saark/ *n.* **1.** CHR **EASTERN ORTHODOX BISHOP** a bishop in the Eastern Orthodox Church, ranked above a metropolitan and below a patriarch **2.** HIST **PROVINCIAL BYZANTINE RULER** the ruler of a province in the Byzantine Empire [Late 16thC. Via ecclesiastical Latin *exarchus* from Greek *exarkhos* "leader," from *exarkhein* "to lead," from *arkhein* "to rule."] —**ex·arch·al** /ek saark'l/ *adj.*

ex·ar·chate /ék saar kayt/, **ex·ar·chy** /ék saarkee/ (*plural* **-chies**) *n.* the office, domain, or term of an exarch

ex·as·per·ate (**-at·ed, -at·ing, -ates**) *vt.* /ig záspə ràyt/ **1. MAKE ANGRY** to make somebody very angry or frustrated, often by repeatedly doing something annoying (*usually passive*) ○ *Guests were exasperated* *by their hosts' constant bickering.* **2. WORSEN** to make an unpleasant condition or feeling worse (*literary*) [Mid-16thC. From Latin *exasperat-*, the past participle stem of *exasperare* "to irritate, roughen," literally "to make thoroughly rough," from *asper* "rough."] —**ex·as·per·at·ed·ly** *adv.* —**ex·as·per·at·ing** *adj.* —**ex·as·per·at·ing·ly** *adv.*

WORD KEY: SYNONYMS

See Synonyms at ***annoy.***

ex·as·per·a·tion /ig zàspə ráysh'n/ *n.* annoyance and frustration, often caused by an irritation that cannot be overcome or stopped

exc. *abbr.* **1.** excellent **2.** except **3. exc., ex.** excepted **4. exc., ex.** exception **5.** excursion

Exc. *abbr.* Excellency

Ex·cal·i·bur /ek skállәbәr/ *n.* in Arthurian legend, King Arthur's magic sword that was given to him by the mysterious Lady of the Lake [15thC. Alteration of medieval Latin *Caliburnus*, from Middle Welsh *Caletuwlch* or Middle Irish *Caladbolg*, the name of a sword of Irish legend.]

ex ca·the·dra /èks kә theédrә/ *adj., adv.* with the authority of status or rank (*formal*) ○ *imposed the decisions ex cathedra* [From Latin, literally "from the (teacher's) chair"]

ex·ca·vate /ékskә vàyt/ (**-vat·ed, -vat·ing, -vates**) *v.* **1.** *vti.* **REMOVE EARTH** to remove earth or soil by digging or scooping out ○ *Before the foundations can be laid, they will have to excavate about six feet of soil.* **2.** *vti.* **HOLLOW SOMETHING OUT** to make a hole or cavity in something by removing the material inside ○ *excavate a tooth* **3.** *vti.* ARCHEOL **DIG FOR ARTIFACTS** to dig in a place carefully and methodically, taking notes about procedures, conditions, and finds, with a view to uncovering objects of archeological interest **4.** *vt.* **FORM BY HOLLOWING** to form a shape or cavity by hollowing ○ *excavates a hollow in the sand as its nest* **5.** *vti.* **UNCOVER SOMETHING WITH DIFFICULTY** to discover or uncover something valuable by effort [Late 16thC. From Latin *excavat-*, the past participle stem of *excavare* "to hollow out," from *cavare* "to hollow," from *cavus* "hollow" (see CAVE).]

ex·ca·va·tion /èkskә váysh'n/ *n.* **1. EXCAVATING** the act or process of digging, removing earth, hollowing something out, or excavating an archeological site ○ *recent excavations in Sumatra* **2. HOLE MADE BY DIGGING** a hole that has been made by digging or hollowing something out, or part of an archeological site that has been excavated

ex·ca·va·tor /ékskә vàytәr/ *n.* **1. MECHANICAL DIGGER** a large machine with a hinged metal bucket attached to a hydraulic arm, used to move large quantities of earth or soil or for lifting **2. DIGGER** a person or animal that digs or hollows something out, especially somebody engaged in archeological excavation

ex·ceed /ik seéd/ (**-ceed·ed, -ceed·ing, -ceeds**) *vt.* **1. BE GREATER THAN** to be greater than something in quantity, degree, or scope ○ *The cost of the movie is reported to exceed 20 million dollars.* **2. GO BEYOND LIMITS** to go beyond the limits of something in quantity, degree, or scope ○ *He was fined for exceeding the speed limit.* ○ *You've exceeded your authority.* **3. OUTDO** to be better than something or somebody ○ *descriptions of nature that far exceed anything else we've heard* [14thC. Via Old French *exceder* from Latin *excedere* "to go beyond, depart," literally "to go out," from *cedere* "to go" (see CEDE).]

ex·ceed·ance /ik seéd'ns/ *n.* **1. GOING BEYOND** an instance of going beyond a limit ○ *fined $50 for each exceedance* **2. EXCESSIVE AMOUNT** the amount by which something exceeds a limit ○ *an exceedance of 50 parts per million*

ex·ceed·ing /ik seéding/ *adj.* **ENORMOUS** very great (*literary*) ○ *exceeding joy* ■ *adv.* **EXCEEDINGLY** to an unusually high degree (*archaic*)

ex·ceed·ing·ly /ik seédinglee/ *adv.* to an unusually high degree ○ *You've been exceedingly generous.*

ex·cel /ik sél/ (**-celled, -cel·ling, -cels**) *v.* **1.** *vti.* **DO WELL OR BETTER** to do very well, or do better than all others or than a given standard **2.** *vi.* **BE VERY GOOD** to be outstanding or have a particular talent in something ○ *excels in marketing* [15thC. From Latin *excellere*, literally "to rise above," from assumed *cellere* "to rise." Ultimately from an Indo-European word meaning "hill," which is also the ancestor of English *hill* and *culminate*.]

ex·cel·lence /éksәlәns/ *n.* **1. SUPERIORITY** the quality or state of being outstanding and superior ○ *an award for excellence in photography* **2. OUTSTANDING FEATURE** a feature or respect in which somebody or something is superior and outstanding

Ex·cel·len·cy /éksәlәnsee/ (*plural* **-cies**), **Ex·cel·lence** /éksәlәns/ *n.* a title and form of address for some high officials, e.g., governors, ambassadors, and high-ranking Roman Catholic clergy

ex·cel·lent /éksәlәnt/ *adj.* **EXTREMELY GOOD** of a very high quality or standard ■ *interj.* **AGREED** used to show wholehearted approval or agreement —**ex·cel·lent·ly** *adv.*

ex·cel·si·or /ik sélsee әr/ *n.* packing material made from wood shavings [Late 18thC. From Latin, literally "higher," from *excelsus* "high," from the past participle of *excellere* (see EXCEL); in the noun usage, from a proprietary name.]

ex·cept /ik sépt/ (**-cept·ed, -cept·ing, -cepts**) CORE MEANING: a grammatical word indicating the only person or thing that does not apply to a statement just made, or a fact that modifies the truth of that statement ○ (prep) *Every house in the street except ours is painted white.* ○ (prep) *I like all vegetables except cabbage.* ○ (conj) *The fires that annually sweep over the prairies prevent the growth of timber, except along the river courses.* ○ (conj) *He dislikes the game except when he wins.*

1. *vt.* **OMIT** to leave out or exclude somebody or something (*formal*) (*usually passive*) ○ *"Hazel eyes excepted, two years more might make her all that he wished."* (Jane Austen, *Emma*; 1816) **2.** *conj.* unless (*archaic*) [14thC. From Latin *exceptus*, the past participle of *excipere* "to take out," from *capere* "to take" (see CAPTURE).] ◇ **except for** apart from ○ *He had always been healthy except for an irregular heartbeat.*

ex·cept·ed /ik séptәd/ *adj.* with the exception of a particular person or thing ○ *present company excepted*

ex·cept·ing /ik sépting/ *prep., conj.* used to indicate the only person or thing excluded from statement just made (*formal*)

WORD KEY: USAGE

See Usage note at ***except.***

ex·cep·tion /ik sépshәn/ *n.* **1. SOMEBODY OR SOMETHING EXCLUDED** somebody or something that is not included in or does not fit into a general rule, pattern, or judgment ○ *make an exception for family members* **2. EXCLUSION** the act or condition of being excluded **3. CRITICISM** a criticism, usually a negative one (*formal*) **4.** LAW **LEGAL CLAUSE** a clause in a legal document that limits the effect of a part or the whole of it ○ *read through and approved all the exceptions* **5. FORMAL OBJECTION USED IN COURT** a formal objection formerly used in court proceedings ◇ **the exception that proves the rule** something that, by being an exception, shows that a general rule exists

ex·cep·tion·a·ble /ik sépshәnәb'l/ *adj.* causing or liable to cause objection or offense (*formal*)

WORD KEY: USAGE

See Usage note at ***exceptional.***

ex·cep·tion·al /ik sépshәn'l/ *adj.* **1. UNUSUAL** not conforming to a general rule or pattern ○ *exceptional circumstances.* See Usage note below. **2. OUTSTANDING** having or showing intelligence or ability well above average ○ *an exceptional talent* —**ex·cep·tion·al·i·ty** /ik sèpshә nállәtee/ *n.* —**ex·cep·tion·al·ly** *adv.* —**ex·cep·tion·al·ness** *n.*

WORD KEY: USAGE

exceptional or **exceptionable**? ***Exceptional*** is the more common word and refers, often favorably, to "something or somebody unusual in some way": *She has exceptional powers of concentration.* Occasionally, ***exceptional*** is used in a factual or neutral way that is not meant to be a compliment: *Expenses can only be reimbursed in exceptional cases.* ***Exceptionable***, despite its similar sound, has a quite different meaning, "something to which exception can be taken": *There was something in his manner that we found exceptionable.* More often, it is used in the negative form *unexceptionable*, meaning "acceptable, satisfactory, adequate."

ex·cep·tive /ik séptiv/ *adj.* relating to or of the nature of an exception

ex·cerpt *n.* /ék sùrpt/ **EXTRACTED PART** a section or passage taken from a longer work, e.g., a book, film, musical composition, or document ■ *vt.* /ik súrpt/ (**-cerpt·ed, -cerpt·ing, -cerpts**) **TAKE A PART FROM LONGER WORK** to select a section or passage from a longer work (*usually passive*) [Mid-16thC. From Latin *excerptus*, the past participle of *excerpere*, literally "to pluck out," from *carpere* "to pluck" (source of English *carpet*).] —**ex·cerpt·i·ble** /ik súrptәb'l/ *adj.* —**ex·cerp·tion** /ik súrpshәn/ *n.* —**ex·cerp·tor** /ik súrptәr/ *n.*

ex·cess *n.* /ik séss, ék sèss/ **1. SURPLUS** an amount or quantity beyond what is considered normal or sufficient ○ *leaped up in an excess of enthusiasm* **2. EXTRA** the amount by which one quantity exceeds another **3. UNRESTRAINED BEHAVIOR** behavior or activity that goes beyond what is socially or morally acceptable, or beyond what is good for somebody's health or well-being ○ *led a life of excess* **4.** *U.K., Carib* INSUR = **deductible** ■ *adj.* /ék sèss, ik séss/ **1. MORE THAN ENOUGH** more than is usual, required, or allowed ○ *excess capacity* **2. REQUIRED IN ADDITION** that constitutes or is required as an additional payment ○ *excess postage* ■ *vt.* /ik séss, ék sèss/ (**-cessed, -cess·ing, -cess·es**) **DISMISS FROM EMPLOYMENT** to dismiss an employee as part of a program of layoffs ○ *excessed in the most recent downsizing* [14thC. Via French *excès* from Latin *excessus*, from the past participle of *excedere* (see EXCEED).]

ex·cess bag·gage *n.* **1. HEAVIER LUGGAGE THAN ALLOWED** luggage that is heavier than the amount a passenger is allowed to take on a flight without an extra charge **2. ANYTHING UNWANTED** something somebody would rather not have (*informal*)

ex·cess de·mand *n.* demand for a product or service that outstrips the supply and so pushes the price up

ex·ces·sive /ik séssiv/ *adj.* beyond what is considered acceptable, proper, usual, or necessary (*disapproving*) ○ *excessive hilarity* —**ex·ces·sive·ly** *adv.* —**ex·ces·sive·ness** *n.*

ex·cess sup·ply *n.* supply of a product or service that outstrips the demand and so pushes the price down

exch. *abbr.* **1. exch., ex.** exchange **2. exch., Exch.** exchequer

ex·change /iks cháynj/ *v.* (**-changed, -chang·ing, -chang·es**) **1.** *vt.* **GIVE SOMETHING AND GET SOMETHING** to give something and receive something different in return ○ *exchange land for peace* ○ *exchange tokens for cash* **2.** *vti.* **SWAP** to give something and receive another of the same or an equivalent in return ○ *exchange glances* **3.** *vt.* **REPLACE SOMETHING** to hand something over and receive as a replacement something more suitable or more satisfactory ○ *exchanged her coat for one a size smaller* **4.** *vt.* CHESS **TAKE A PIECE OF SIMILAR VALUE** in chess, to take a piece in return for a piece of your own, usually of similar value, that your opponent has just taken or will soon take ■ *n.* **1. GIVING AND RECEIVING** the action or process or an instance of exchanging something for something else or for something the same ○ *an exchange of compliments* **2.** COMM **BUILDING USED FOR COMMERCIAL ACTIVITIES** a building formerly or still used as a center for the trading of commodities, securities, or other assets, or the market operating there **3. ARGUMENT** a short conversation, usually between two people or groups who are angry ○ *a bitter exchange* **4.** UTIL = **telephone exchange** **5. SOMETHING GIVEN OR RECEIVED** something given or received in place of another **6.** FIN **MONEY TRANSFER BETWEEN TWO CURRENCIES** the transferring or a transfer of equal amounts of money between two currencies **7.** FIN **SYSTEM OF PAYMENTS** a system of payments in which commercial documents, e.g., bills of exchange, are used instead of money **8.** COMM **FEE FOR PAYMENT** the percentage or fee that is charged when paying in commercial documents instead of money **9.** CHESS **TAKING OF CHESS PIECES** the taking of chess pieces of similar value by each player in consecutive or nearly consecutive moves **10. TRANSFER OF PARTICLE** the transfer of a particle between two others **11.** CHESS **TRADE OF A ROOK FOR A MINOR PIECE** taking a rook just before or after your opponent takes your knight or bishop, or vice-versa. The player taking the rook wins the exchange. [14thC. Via Old French *eschangier* from assumed Vulgar Latin *excambiare*, from late Latin *cambiare* "to barter" (see CHANGE).] —**ex·change·a·bil·i·ty** /iks chàynjә bíllәtee/ *n.* —**ex·change·a·ble** /iks cháynjәb'l/ *adj.* —**ex·chang·er** /-cháynjәr/ *n.*

ex·change force *n.* a force existing between particles due to the transfer of another particle

ex·change rate *n.* the rate at which a unit of the currency of one country can be exchanged for a unit of the currency of another country

ex·change stu·dent *n.* a student who studies in another country as part of a program in which students trade places for a year or more

ex·cheq·uer /iks chékər/ *n.* **1. ex·cheq·uer, Ex·cheq·uer** GOVERNMENT DEPARTMENT COLLECTING TAXES formerly in the United Kingdom, and in some other countries, the government department responsible for collecting taxes and managing public spending **2. ex·cheq·uer, Ex·cheq·uer** GOVERNMENT FUNDS a national treasury or account, especially the U.K. government's account at the Bank of England, or the assets in it **3.** PERSONAL FUNDS private funds or finances (*archaic*) [13thC. From Old French *eschequier* "counting table, chessboard," from *eschec* "check," from the custom of counting royal revenue on a checked tablecloth.]

ex·ci·mer /éksəmər/ *n.* CHEM a stable atomic pair **(dimer)** in which one of the two bound atoms is in a higher energy state [Mid-20thC. Blend of EXCITED and DIMER.]

ex·cip·i·ent /ik síppee ənt/ *n.* an inert substance, e.g., starch or gum arabic, that is combined with a drug to make it easier to administer [Early 18thC. From Latin *excipient-*, the present participle stem of *excipere* "to receive, take out" (see EXCEPT).]

ex·cise[1] *n.* /ék sīz/ **1.** TAX ON GOODS FOR THE DOMESTIC MARKET taxation of or a tax imposed on goods for a domestic market only **2.** LICENSING CHARGE a tax paid for a license, e.g., one required to use a vehicle on public roads or to engage in certain commercial activities ■ *vt.* /ik sīz/ **(-cised, -cis·ing, -cis·es)** TAX to impose an excise on somebody or something [15thC. Via Middle Dutch *excijs* from Old French *acceis*, partly from assumed Vulgar Latin *accensum*, from Latin *census* (see CENSUS), and partly from Old French *assise* (see ASSIZE).] —**ex·cis·a·ble** /ik sízəb'l/ *adj.*

ex·cise[2] /ik síz/ **(-cised, -cis·ing, -cis·es)** *vt.* **1.** DELETE to edit or delete a part of something, e.g., a text (*formal*) **2.** REMOVE SURGICALLY to remove something by cutting, especially in surgery [Late 16thC. From Latin *excis-*, the past participle stem of *excidere* "to cut out," from *caedere* "to cut" (see CAESURA).] —**ex·ci·sion** /ik sízh'n/ *n.*

ex·cise du·ty *n.* tax imposed on goods intended for a domestic market only

ex·cit·a·ble /ik sítəb'l/ *adj.* **1.** EASILY STIMULATED nervous and liable to become quickly excited **2.** PHYSIOL ABLE TO RESPOND TO STIMULUS used to describe a nerve or tissue that is able to respond to a stimulus —**ex·cit·a·bil·i·ty** /ik sìtə bíllətee/ *n.* —**ex·cit·a·ble·ness** /ik sítəb'lnəss/ *n.* —**ex·cit·a·bly** /ik sítəblee/ *adv.*

ex·ci·tant /ik sít'nt/ *n.* (*plural* **-tants**) STIMULANT a drug or other agent that stimulates or augments a response ■*adj.* STIMULATING tending to excite or stimulate something

ex·ci·ta·tion /èk sī táysh'n, èksi táysh'n/ *n.* **1.** EXCITING the act or process of exciting something (*formal*) **2.** BEING EXCITED the state of being excited **3.** PHYSIOL ACTIVITY CAUSED BY STIMULATION the activity or altered condition produced in a cell, tissue, or organ as a result of stimulation **4.** ELEC ENG PRODUCTION OF MAGNETIC FIELD the production of a magnetic field in a generator or motor by passing electricity through the coil **5.** PHYS RAISING ENERGY OF ATOM FROM LOWEST the addition of sufficient energy to an electron, atom, atomic nucleus, or molecule, to raise it from its lowest energy level **(ground state)** to a higher energy level **6.** ELECTRON ENG APPLICATION OF SIGNAL MAKING TRANSISTOR OPERATE the application of an electrical signal to a device such as a transistor causing it to operate

ex·cite /ik sít/ **(-cit·ed, -cit·ing, -cites)** *v.* **1.** *vti.* STIMULATE FAVORABLY to cause somebody to feel enjoyment or pleasurable anticipation ○ *an exciting story* **2.** *vt.* STIMULATE UNFAVORABLY to make a person or animal feel nervous apprehension or an unpleasant state of heightened emotion ○ *Don't excite the dog or he'll bite.* **3.** *vt.* AROUSE PHYSICALLY to cause somebody to feel physical desire **4.** *vt.* AROUSE AN EMOTION to cause somebody to feel a particular emotion or reaction ○ *excite suspicion* **5.** *vt.* PHYS RAISE A PARTICLE TO A HIGHER ENERGY LEVEL to raise a particle or system of particles, e.g., an electron, atom, atomic nucleus, or molecule, above its lowest energy level **(ground state)** to a higher energy level **6.** *vt.* EVOKE to cause a memory, thought, or other response to form in the mind ○ *an image that excited a memory* **7.** *vt.* PHYSIOL INCEASE SOMETHING'S ACTIVITY to stimulate or increase the rate of activity of an organ, tissue, or other body part **8.** *vt.* ELEC ENG PRODUCE MAGNETIC FIELD IN ELECTRIC MACHINE to produce a magnetic field in a generator or motor by supplying electricity to the coil **9.** *vt.* ELECTRON ENG APPLY SIGNAL CAUSING DEVICE TO OPERATE to apply an electrical signal that will cause a device, such as a transistor, to operate [14thC. Directly or via French from Latin *excitare* "to rouse," literally "to call forth repeatedly," from, ultimately, *ciere* "to call, set in motion" (see CITE).]

ex·cit·ed /ik sítəd/ *adj.* **1.** HAPPY AND ENTHUSIASTIC happy and enthusiastic about something pleasant that is happening or is about to happen **2.** PHYSICALLY AROUSED in a state of physical arousal **3.** AGITATED nervous, agitated, and unable to relax —**ex·cit·ed·ly** *adv.* —**ex·cit·ed·ness** *n.*

ex·cit·ed state *n.* PHYS the condition of a physical system, especially of atoms and atomic nuclei, that has an energy level higher than the lowest possible level **(ground state)**

ex·cite·ment /ik sítmənt/ *n.* **1.** BEING EXCITED the feeling or condition of lively enjoyment or pleasant anticipation ○ *finding it difficult to contain her excitement* **2.** EXCITING SOMETHING the act or process of exciting something ○ *excitement of electrons* **3.** EXCITING EVENT something that engages people's attention or emotions in a lively and compelling way ○ *Going in a helicopter was a great excitement for the children.*

ex·cit·er /ik sítər/ *n.* **1.** CAUSE OF EXCITEMENT somebody or something that causes excitement **2.** ELEC ENG SMALL AUXILIARY GENERATOR a small generator or transmitter that provides the necessary energy to run a larger device or amplifier **3.** RADIO ELECTRICAL OSCILLATOR an oscillator for supplying a radio transmitter with the basic wave that is modified to carry a radio signal

ex·cit·ing /ik síting/ *adj.* causing feelings of happiness and enthusiasm or nervousness and tension —**ex·cit·ing·ly** *adv.*

ex·ci·ton /éksi tòn/ *n.* PHYS a mobile neutral combination of an electron in an excited state and a hole in a crystal. Exciton activity is important in semiconductors. [Mid-20thC. Coined from EXCITATION + -ON.]

excl. *abbr.* **1.** exclamation **2.** exclusive

ex·claim /ik skláym/ **(-claimed, -claim·ing, -claims)** *vti.* to speak or cry out loudly and suddenly, often through surprise, anger, or excitement [Late 16thC. Directly or via French *exclamer* from Latin *exclamare*, literally "to call out," from *clamare* "to call" (see CLAIM).] —**ex·claim·er** *n.*

ex·cla·ma·tion /èksklə máysh'n/ *n.* **1.** SUDDEN CRY a word, phrase, or sentence that is shouted out suddenly, often through surprise, anger, or excitement ○ *an exclamation of horror* **2.** EXCLAIMING the act of crying out suddenly —**ex·cla·ma·tion·al** *adj.*

ex·cla·ma·tion point, ex·cla·ma·tion mark *n.* **1.** PUNCTUATION FOR EXCLAMATION a punctuation mark (!) used after an exclamation or interjection, and sometimes after a command **2.** MARK INDICATING HAZARD OR MISTAKE a mark (!) used to indicate a road hazard or a mistake or point of note in a text, or as a mathematical or logical symbol

ex·clam·a·to·ry /ik sklámmə tàwree/ *adj.* using, of the nature of, or relating to an exclamation or exclamations (*formal*) —**ex·clam·a·to·ri·ly** *adv.*

ex·clave /ék sklàyv/ *n.* a part of a country that is isolated from the main body of the country, being surrounded by foreign territory [Late 19thC. Coined from EX- + ENCLAVE.]

ex·clo·sure /ik sklózhər/ *n.* an area fenced in to keep out animals or intruders [Early 20thC. Coined from EX- + CLOSURE on the model of ENCLOSURE.]

ex·clude /ik sklóod/ **(-clud·ed, -clud·ing, -cludes)** *vt.* **1.** KEEP OUT to prevent somebody or something from entering or participating ○ *I felt excluded from the family celebrations.* **2.** REJECT to prevent somebody or something from being considered or accepted ○ *cannot exclude the possibility of treason* **3.** OMIT to fail to include something or somebody ○ *Three names were inadvertently excluded from the list.* [14thC. From Latin *excludere*, literally "to shut out," from *claudere* "to shut" (see CLOSE).] —**ex·clud·a·bil·i·ty** /ik sklóodə bíllətee/ *n.* —**ex·clud·a·ble** /ik sklóodəb'l/ *adj.* —**ex·clud·er** /-sklóodər/ *n.*

ex·clu·sion /ik sklóozh'n/ *n.* **1.** EXCLUDING the act of excluding something or somebody **2.** BEING EXCLUDED the state of being excluded, especially from mainstream society and its advantages ○ *addressing the issue of social exclusion* **3.** EXCLUDED PERSON OR THING somebody or something that has been excluded [15thC. From the Latin stem *exclusion-*, from *exclus-*, the past participle stem of *excludere* (see EXCLUDE).] —**ex·clu·sion·ar·y** *adj.*

ex·clu·sion·ar·y rule *n.* a law that prevents illegally obtained evidence from being used in a criminal trial

ex·clu·sion·ist /ik sklóozh'nist/ *adj.* **1.** DISCRIMINATORY used to describe a policy that excludes individuals or groups from areas or rights and privileges **2.** PROTECTIONIST used to describe a policy that excludes specific imports or forms of commerce ■ *n.* EXCLUSION ADVOCATE somebody who supports exclusionist policies —**ex·clu·sion·ism** *n.* —**ex·clu·sion·is·tic** /ik sklòozh'n ístik/ *adj.*

ex·clu·sion prin·ci·ple *n.* PHYS = **Pauli exclusion principle**

ex·clu·sion zone *n.* **1.** AREA OF BAN an area where an authority has banned a particular activity **2.** HAZARDOUS AREA an area that is off-limits to people because a hazardous substance has been released ○ *the Chernobyl exclusion zone*

ex·clu·sive /ik sklóossiv/ *adj.* **1.** HIGH-CLASS limited to a group of people, especially one considered fashionable or wealthy ○ *an exclusive club* **2.** SELECTIVE excluding or intending to exclude many from participation or consideration **3.** RESTRICTED IN USE only available to or used by one person, group, or organization ○ *Members have exclusive use of the pool.* **4.** APPEARING IN ONE PLACE published or broadcast in only one place ○ *exclusive coverage* **5.** SOLE being the only one ○ *A proposal has been put forward to make bicycles the exclusive means of transport in the city center.* **6.** CONFINED TO ONE THING limited to one thing and excluding everything else ○ *exclusive attention* **7.** NOT INCLUDING THE STATED NUMBERS not including the numbers, dates, or other series members mentioned immediately before ○ *from July 8 to July10 exclusive* **8.** COMM RESTRICTING TRADE restricting trade in certain goods or services only to those who have signed the contract or agreement **9.** LOGIC WHERE BOTH CANNOT BE TRUE used to describe a proposition **(disjunction)** where one alternative rules out the other, e.g., being an odd number rules out the possibility of being an even number. ◊ **inclusive** ■ *n.* REPORT IN ONE PUBLICATION OR PROGRAM a news report or article that is printed in only one publication or broadcast on only one channel ○ *an exclusive on the wedding* [15thC. From medieval Latin *exclusivus*, from Latin *exclus-*, the past participle stem of *excludere* (see EXCLUDE).] —**ex·clu·sive·ly** *adv.* —**ex·clu·sive·ness** *n.* —**ex·clu·siv·i·ty** /èk skloo sívvətee/ *n.* ◇ **exclusive of** not including ○ *The price covers all your vacation costs, exclusive of travel insurance.*

ex·clu·siv·ism /ik sklóossi vìzzəm/ *n.* the practice or policy of being exclusive or excluding others —**ex·clu·siv·ist** *n., adj.*

ex·cog·i·tate /ek skójji tàyt/ **(-tat·ed, -tat·ing, -tates)** *vt.* to consider or think about something carefully and thoroughly (*formal*) [Early 16thC. From Latin *excogitat-*, the past participle stem of *excogitare*, literally "to think out," from *cogitare* "to think" (see COGITATE).] —**ex·cog·i·ta·ble** /ek skójji təb'l/ *adj.*

ex·com·mu·ni·cate *vt.* /èkskə myóoni kàyt/ **(-cat·ed, -cat·ing, -cates)** EXCLUDE SOMEBODY FROM THE CHRISTIAN COMMUNITY to exclude a baptized Christian from taking part in Communion because of doctrine or moral behavior that is adjudged to offend against God or the Christian community ■ *adj.* /-kət, -kàyt/ EXCOMMUNICATED having been officially excluded from taking part in the Eucharist ■ *n.* /-kət/ EXCOMMUNICATED PERSON somebody who has been officially excluded from taking part in the Eucharist [15thC. From late Latin *excommunicare*, literally "to put out of the community," from Latin *communis* "common."] —**ex·com·mu·ni·ca·ble** *adj.* —**ex·com·mu·ni·ca·tive** /-kàytiv/ *adj.* —**ex·com·mu·ni·ca·tor** /-kàytər/ *n.*

ex·com·mu·ni·ca·tion /èkskə myooni káysh'n/ *n.* **1.** EXCLUSION FROM THE CHRISTIAN COMMUNITY the act of excommunicating a baptized member of the Christian church 2. BEING EXCOMMUNICATED the condition of being excommunicated

ex·con *n.* somebody who has served time in prison, having been convicted of a crime (*informal*) [Early 20thC. Shortening of *ex-convict*.]

ex·co·ri·ate /ik skáwree àyt/ (**-at·ed, -at·ing, -ates**) *vt.* **1.** DENOUNCE to criticize somebody or something very strongly (*formal*) ○ *The paper excoriated the governor's conduct in this case.* **2.** TEAR SOMEBODY'S SKIN OFF to tear the skin off a person or animal (*formal*) **3.** MED REMOVE SKIN LAYER to destroy or remove an area of skin, often through abrasion or chemical action [15thC. From Latin *excoriat-*, the past participle stem of *excoriare* "to strip off the hide," from *corium* "hide, skin."] —**ex·co·ri·a·tion** /ik skàwree áysh'n/ *n.* —**ex·co·ri·a·tor** /ik skáwree àytər/ *n.*

ex·cre·ment /ékskrəmənt/ *n.* waste material, particularly feces, discharged from the body (*technical*) [Mid-16thC. From Latin *excrementum*, from *excretus*, the past participle of *excernere* "to discharge" (see EXCRETE).] —**ex·cre·ment·al** /èkskrə mént'l/ *adj.* —**ex·cre·men·ti·tious** /èkskrəmən tíshəss/ *adj.*

ex·cres·cence /ik skréss'ns/ *n.* **1.** BIOL OUTGROWTH a growth that sticks out from the body of a human, animal, or plant, especially an abnormal or diseased one **2.** UNSIGHTLY ADDITION an ugly addition or extension to something, e.g., a building

ex·cres·cent /ik skréss'nt/ *adj.* **1.** SUPERFLUOUS added or growing out unnecessarily (*formal*) **2.** BIOL RELATING TO AN OUTGROWTH relating to or like an outgrowth on an organism **3.** LING ADDED IN SPEAKING used to describe a speech sound that occurs in a word to allow ease of pronunciation [15thC. From Latin *excrescent-*, the present participle stem of *excrescere* "to grow out," from *crescere* "to grow" (see CRESCENT).] —**ex·cres·cent·ly** *adv.*

ex·cre·ta /ik skre̅e̅tə/ *npl.* any waste matter discharged from the body, e.g., feces, or urine (*technical*) [Mid-19thC. From Latin, literally "things excreted," from a form of the past participle of *excernere* (see EXCRETE).] —**ex·cre·tal** *adj.*

ex·crete /ik skre̅e̅t/ (**-cret·ed, -cret·ing, -cretes**) *vt.* **1.** PHYSIOL EXPEL WASTE FROM THE BODY to isolate and discharge waste matter generated during metabolism, e.g., through urinating or defecating (*formal*) ◊ **secrete 2.** PHYSIOL, BOT EXPEL WASTE FROM TISSUES to eliminate waste matter from leaves and roots [Early 17thC. From Latin *excret-*, the past participle stem of *excernere*, literally "to separate out," from *cernere* "to separate" (source of English *discern*).] —**ex·cre·to·ry** /ékskrə tàwree/ *adj.*

ex·cre·tion /ik skre̅e̅sh'n/ *n.* **1.** EXCRETING OF WASTE MATTER the act or process of discharging waste matter from the tissues or organs **2.** WASTE MATTER waste matter that has been discharged from an animal or a plant

ex·cru·ci·ate /ik skro͞oshee àyt/ (**-at·ed, -at·ing, -ates**) *vt.* (*formal*) **1.** TORMENT SOMEBODY to inflict severe mental and emotional distress on somebody **2.** TORTURE SOMEBODY to inflict physical pain on somebody [Late 16thC. From, ultimately, Latin *excruciare*, literally "to torture thoroughly," from *cruciare* "to torture, crucify," from the stem *cruc-* "cross" (see CROSS).] —**ex·cru·ci·a·tion** /ik skro͞oshee áysh'n/ *n.*

ex·cru·ci·at·ing /ik skro͞oshee àyting/ *adj.* **1.** EXTREMELY PAINFUL extremely painful, physically or emotionally **2.** HARD TO BEAR intolerably embarrassing, tedious or irritating ○ *The first act was bad enough, but the second was just excruciating.* —**ex·cru·ci·at·ing·ly** *adv.*

ex·cul·pate /ékskəl pàyt, ik skúl pàyt/ (**-pat·ed, -pat·ing, -pates**) *vt.* to free somebody from blame or accusation of guilt (*formal*) [Mid-17thC. From medieval Latin *exculpare*, literally "to remove from blame," from Latin *culpa* "blame" (see CULPABLE).] —**ex·cul·pa·ble** /ik skúlpəb'l/ *adj.* —**ex·cul·pa·tion** /èkskəl páysh'n/ *n.*

ex·cul·pa·to·ry /ik skúlpə tàwree/ *adj.* tending to prove that somebody is free from guilt or blame (*formal*) ○ *exculpatory evidence*

ex·cur·sion /ik skúrzh'n/ *n.* **1.** SHORT TRIP a short trip to a place and back, for pleasure or a purpose **2.** GROUP ON A SHORT TRIP a group of people who are on an excursion **3.** DIGRESSION a temporary change of direction (*formal*) ○ *After an unsuccessful excursion into banking, he returned to public life.* **4.** MIL SORTIE a military raid or attack (*archaic*) **5.** PHYS ALTERNATING MOTION an oscillating or alternating motion away from a point of equilibrium and back **6.** PHYS DISTANCE COVERED the distance traversed by an oscillating excursion away from a point of equilibrium and back **7.** PHYSIOL MOVEMENT OF A BODY PART the movement of a part or organ of the body, e.g., the lungs, from the resting position to another position [Late 16thC. From the Latin stem *excursion-*, from *excurs-*, the past participle stem of *excurrere* "to run out," from *currere* (see CURRENT).]

ex·cur·sion fare *n.* a reduced fare on a common carrier, typically carrying various restrictions

ex·cur·sion·ist /ik skúrzhənist/ *n.* somebody who goes on an excursion, especially for pleasure (*dated*)

ex·cur·sive /ik skúrsiv/ *adj.* tending to digress from the main topic, often in a rambling and wordy manner (*formal*) [Late 17thC. Formed from obsolete *excurse* "to digress," from the Latin stem *excurs-* (see EXCURSION); perhaps modeled on DISCURSIVE.] —**ex·cur·sive·ly** *adv.* —**ex·cur·sive·ness** *n.*

ex·cur·sus /ik skúrsiss/ (*plural* **-sus·es** *or* **-sus**) *n.* a lengthy digression from the main topic (*formal*) [Early 19thC. From Latin, "excursion," from the past participle of *excurrere* "to run out," from *currere* "to run" (see CURRENT).]

ex·cus·a·to·ry /ik skyo͞ozə tàwree/ *adj.* tending or serving to excuse somebody or something (*formal*)

ex·cuse *v.* /ik skyo͞oz/ (**-cused, -cus·ing, -cus·es**) **1.** *vt.* FORGIVE SOMETHING to release somebody from blame or criticism for a mistake or wrongdoing ○ *excuse their tardiness* **2.** *vt.* OVERLOOK SOMETHING to make allowances for somebody or something ○ *Please excuse my spelling.* **3.** *vt.* RELEASE SOMEBODY FROM AN OBLIGATION to release somebody from an obligation or responsibility ○ *excused from games because of a sprained ankle* **4.** *vt.* JUSTIFY SOMETHING to provide a reason or explanation for somebody's behavior that makes it appear more acceptable or less offensive ○ *That doesn't excuse the way he acted last night.* **5.** *vt.* ALLOW SOMEBODY TO LEAVE to allow somebody to leave, or say politely that somebody should leave ○ *asked if he could be excused* **6.** *vr.* APOLOGIZE FOR LEAVING to leave with a polite apology or explanation ○ *excused herself and left the room* ■ *n.* /ik skyo͞oss/ **1.** JUSTIFICATION a reason or explanation, not necessarily true, given in order to make something appear more acceptable or less offensive ○ *There can be no excuse for laziness.* **2.** FALSE REASON a false reason that enables somebody to do something he or she wants to do or avoid something he or she does not want to do ○ *the perfect excuse to do nothing* **3.** BAD EXAMPLE somebody who is not very good at what he or she does (*informal*) ○ *a poor excuse for a cook* **4.** NOTE JUSTIFYING ABSENCE a note from a doctor or parent confirming that somebody is not well enough to go to work or attend school [15thC. Via Old French *escuser* from Latin *excusare*, literally "to remove from accusation," from *causa* "accusation" (see CAUSE).] —**ex·cus·a·ble** *adj.* —**ex·cus·a·ble·ness** *n.* —**ex·cus·a·bly** *adv.* —**ex·cus·er** *n.*

ex·di·rec·to·ry *adj.* *U.K.* TELECOM = **unlisted**

ex div·i·dend *adv., adj.* without the right to the current dividend on purchase

exe *suffix.* COMPUT used after the period in a computer file to show that the file is a program

ex·ec /ig zék/ *n.* an executive or executive officer (*informal*) [Late 19thC. Shortening.]

exec. *abbr.* executor

ex·e·cra·ble /éksəkrəb'l/ *adj.* (*formal*) **1.** VERY BAD extremely bad or of very low quality ○ *has execrable taste* **2.** DETESTABLE deserving to be detested ○ *execrable behavior* [14thC. Via Old French from Latin *execrabilis*, from *execrari* (see EXECRATE).] —**ex·e·cra·ble·ness** *n.* —**ex·e·cra·bly** *adv.*

ex·e·crate /éksə kràyt/ (**-crat·ed, -crat·ing, -crates**) *v.* (*literary or formal*) **1.** *vt.* DETEST SOMEBODY OR SOMETHING to feel loathing for somebody or something **2.** *vt.* DENOUNCE SOMEBODY OR SOMETHING to declare somebody or something to be loathsome **3.** *vti.* CURSE SOMEBODY OR SOMETHING to curse or put a curse on somebody or something [Mid-16thC. From Latin *execrari*, literally "to unconsecrate," from *sacrare* (see CONSECRATE).] —**ex·e·cra·tive** *adj.* —**ex·e·cra·tor** *n.*

ex·e·cra·tion /éksə kráysh'n/ *n.* (*literary or formal*) **1.** CURSE a curse ○ *"With an execration the thoroughly terrified robber threw down the pocketbook, and the relieved owner hastened forward to pick it up."* (Horatio Alger, Jr., *Struggling Upward*; 1868) **2.** SOMETHING CURSED something that is cursed or detested **3.** EXECRATING the act of execrating somebody or something, or the state of being execrated

ex·e·cut·a·ble /éksə kyo͞otəb'l/ *adj.* ABLE TO BE RUN AS A PROGRAM used to describe a file that is capable of being run as a program on a computer ■ *n.* EXECUTABLE FILE a computer file that can be run as a program and that often carries the extension .exe

ex·ec·u·tant /ig zékyət'nt/ *n.* somebody who performs a piece of music, dance, or theater, usually to a very high standard (*formal*)

ex·e·cute /éksə kyo͞ot/ (**-cut·ed, -cut·ing, -cutes**) *v.* **1.** *vt.* LAW KILL SOMEBODY to put somebody to death as part of a legal or extralegal process **2.** *vt.* PERFORM SOMETHING to complete or perform an action or movement, especially one requiring skill **3.** *vt.* CARRY SOMETHING OUT to put an instruction or plan into effect **4.** *vti.* COMPUT RUN ON COMPUTER to run a computer file or program in response to a command or instruction **5.** *vt.* CREATE SOMETHING to produce or create something, usually a work of art, to a specific design ○ *execute a drawing* **6.** *vt.* LAW CARRY OUT TERMS OF A LEGAL DOCUMENT to carry out the terms laid out in a will, legal document, or legal decision ○ *execute a sentence* **7.** *vt.* LAW SIGN A LEGAL DOCUMENT BEFORE WITNESSES to sign a will or other legal document in the presence of witnesses in order to make it binding [14thC. From, ultimately, Latin *exsecut-*, the past participle stem of *exsequi*, literally "to follow out," from *sequi* "to follow" (see SEQUENCE).] —**ex·e·cut·er** *n.*

WORD KEY: SYNONYMS

See Synonyms at ***kill*** and ***perform***.

ex·e·cu·tion /éksə kyo͞osh'n/ *n.* **1.** LAW KILLING the killing of somebody as part of a legal or extralegal process **2.** PERFORMING OF SOMETHING the carrying out of an action, instruction, command, or movement ○ *a plan that failed in execution* **3.** MANNER OF PERFORMANCE the style or manner in which something is carried out or accomplished **4.** LAW CARRYING OUT OF LEGAL PROVISIONS the carrying out of the provisions of a legal document such as a will or contract **5.** LAW SIGNING OF A DOCUMENT the formal signing of a legal document in the presence of witnesses in order to make it binding (*formal*) **6.** LAW ENFORCEMENT OF A COURT JUDGMENT the carrying out or enforcing of a judgment made in court **7.** LAW WRIT a legal writ that orders the carrying out of a judgment or decision

ex·e·cu·tion·er /éksə kyo͞osh'nər/ *n.* **1.** LAW OFFICIAL WHO CARRIES OUT AN EXECUTION somebody who puts to death somebody who has been sentenced to capital punishment **2.** CRIMINOL ASSASSIN a hired assassin

ex·e·cu·tion time *n.* the amount of time needed for a complete run of a computer program

ex·ec·u·tive /ig zékyətiv/ *n.* **1.** MANAGEMT SENIOR MANAGER a senior manager in a company or organization, whose job it is to make and implement major decisions **2.** POL GOVERNMENT SECTION RESPONSIBLE FOR DECISIONS the section of a country's government responsible for implementing legislative decisions **3.** POL COMMITTEE THAT MAKES DECISIONS a committee or group in a political organization that makes decisions and has the authority to implement them ■ *adj.* **1.** MANAGEMT, POL OF POLICYMAKING responsible for or relating to the making and implementing of general decisions in a company, organization, or government ○ *a meeting of the executive committee* **2.** BUSINESS FOR BUSINESSPEOPLE restricted to or designed to be used by business executives ○ *an executive toy* **3.** VERY EXPENSIVE very expensive and so only affordable by those who earn high salaries ○ *executive homes* [15thC. From Old French *executif*, from *executer* "to carry out," ultimately from Latin *execut-* (see EXECUTE).] —**ex·ec·u·tive·ly** *adv.*

ex·ec·u·tive a·gree·ment *n.* an agreement between a U.S. president and a foreign head of state that has not been given approval by the Senate

Ex·ec·u·tive Coun·cil *n.* in Canada, the cabinet of a provincial government

ex·ec·u·tive di·rec·tor *n.* a director of a company who is employed by the company in a senior management position

ex·ec·u·tive jet *n.* a small jet aircraft designed for private use, especially one used to transport corporate executives

ex·ec·u·tive of·fi·cer *n.* **1.** MIL SECOND-IN-COMMAND an officer who is second in command of a military or naval unit **2.** MANAGEMT SENIOR MANAGER somebody in a senior management position in an organization

ex·ec·u·tive or·der *n.* a rule or order that has been issued by a government department in the executive branch, giving it the status of a law

ex·ec·u·tive priv·i·lege *n.* the right of the President and other government officials in the executive branch to refuse to reveal confidential material if this would interfere with the administration's ability to govern

ex·ec·u·tive pro·duc·er *n.* **1.** CINEMA, TV **HEAD PRODUCER AT A STUDIO** the head producer in charge of other producers at a movie or television studio **2.** CINEMA **A PRODUCER CONTROLLING FINANCES FOR MOVIE** the producer who handles the finances for a movie

ex·ec·u·tive sec·re·tar·y *n.* **1. SOMEBODY RUNNING BUSINESS OPERATIONS** a senior official who handles an organization's business operations **2. TOP-LEVEL SECRETARY** a secretary who reports to a senior manager or executive in a company

ex·ec·u·tive ses·sion *n.* a meeting of the U.S. Senate, closed to the public, to discuss confidential government business such as judicial appointments or the ratification of treaties

ex·ec·u·tor /ig zékyətər, éksə kyo͞otər/ *n.* **1.** LAW **SOMEBODY IMPLEMENTING A WILL** somebody named in a will or appointed by a court to carry out the instructions contained in a will **2. SOMEBODY WHO DOES SOMETHING** somebody who carries something out, e.g., an order [13thC. Via Anglo-Norman *execut(o)ur* from Latin *executor*, from *execut-* (see EXECUTE).] —**ex·ec·u·to·ri·al** /ig zèkyə táwree əl/ *adj.* —**ex·ec·u·tor·ship** /ig zékyətər shìp, eg-/ *n.*

ex·ec·u·to·ry /ig zékyə tàwree/ *adj.* **1.** LAW **COMING INTO EFFECT LATER** coming into effect at a future time or in accordance with circumstances **2. ADMINISTRATIVE** relating to the task or process of carrying out laws, policies, or instructions [15thC. From late Latin *executorius*, from Latin *executor* (see EXECUTOR). First recorded in the sense "operative, in force (of a law)."]

ex·e·dra /éksədrə, ek seédrə/ *n.* **1.** ARCHIT, HIST **CONVERSATION ROOM** a room for relaxation or conversation in ancient Greece and Rome, especially a semicircular recess in a larger hall with a continuous bench along the wall **2.** FURNITURE **LONG CURVED OUTDOOR BENCH** a long curved or semicircular outdoor bench, usually with a high back **3.** ARCHIT **RECESS** any kind of recess or niche (*technical*) [Early 18thC. Via Latin from Greek, literally "outside seat," from *hedra* "seat" (source of English *-hedron*).]

ex·e·ge·sis /èksə jeéssiss/ (*plural* **-ses** /-seéz/) *n.* the explanation or interpretation of texts, especially from the Bible, or an explanation or interpretation of a particular text [Early 17thC. From Greek *exēgēsis*, from *exēgeisthai* "to interpret," literally "to lead or guide out," from *hēgeisthai* "to guide."]

ex·e·gete /éksə jeèt/ *n.* somebody who studies and interprets texts, especially religious writings [Mid-18thC. From Greek *exēgētes*, from *exēgeisthai* (see EXEGESIS).]

ex·e·get·ic /èksə jéttik/, **ex·e·get·i·cal** /-jéttik'l/ *adj.* **1. OF TEXTUAL STUDY** relating to the study and interpretation of texts, especially religious writings **2. EXPLANATORY** intended to explain or interpret something, especially a written text (*formal*) [Early 17thC. From Greek *exēgetikos*, from *exēgeisthai* (see EXEGESIS).] —**ex·e·get·i·cal·ly** *adv.*

ex·e·get·ics /èksə jéttiks/ *n.* the branch of theology dealing with the study and interpretation of scripture (*takes a singular verb*)

ex·e·ge·tist /èksə jéttist/ *n.* = **exegete**

ex·em·pla plural of **exemplum**

ex·em·plar /ig zém plaàr, ig zémplər/ *n.* **1. IDEAL** an ideal example of something, worthy of being copied or imitated (*literary*) ○ *Michelangelo's David is an exemplar of Renaissance sculpture.* **2. TYPICAL EXAMPLE** a typical example or instance of something (*literary*) **3.** PUBL **COPY OF A BOOK** a copy of a book or text, especially one from which further copies have originated [15thC. Directly or via French *exemplaire* from late Latin *exemplarium*, from Latin *exemplum* (see EXAMPLE).]

ex·em·pla·ry /ig zémpləree/ *adj.* **1. SETTING AN EXAMPLE** so good or admirable that others would do well to copy it ○ *the child's exemplary conduct* **2. SERVING AS AN EXAMPLE** designed to serve as a warning to others ○ *exemplary punishment* **3. GIVING AN EXAMPLE** serving as an illustration or example of something (*formal*) [Late 16thC. From late Latin *exemplaris*, from Latin *exemplum* (see EXAMPLE).] —**ex·em·plar·i·ly** *adv.* —**ex·em·pla·ri·ness** *n.* —**ex·em·plar·i·ty** /ègzəm pláirətee/ *n.*

ex·em·pli·fi·ca·tion /ig zèmpləfi káysh'n/ *n.* **1. EXAMPLE** a thing that acts as an example or illustration of something **2. GIVING EXAMPLES** the process of giving examples to illustrate or explain something **3.** LAW **OFFICIAL COPY** an official copy of a legal document [Directly or via Anglo-Norman from the medieval Latin stem *exemplification-*, from *exemplificare* (see EXEMPLIFY)]

ex·em·pli·fy /ig zémplə fì/ (**-fied, -fy·ing, -fies**) *vt.* **1. BE AN EXAMPLE OF SOMETHING** to show or illustrate something by being a typical or model example of it ○ *He exemplified all the qualities of a natural leader.* **2. GIVE AN EXAMPLE OF SOMETHING** to give an example or examples in order to make something clearer or more convincing ○ *Perhaps you could exemplify your point with a few statistics.* **3.** LAW **MAKE A COPY OF DOCUMENT** to make an official copy of a legal document [15thC. From medieval Latin *exemplificare*, from Latin *exemplum* (see EXAMPLE).] —**ex·em·pli·fi·a·ble** /ig zèmplə fíəb'l/ *adj.* —**ex·em·pli·fi·er** *n.*

ex·em·pli gra·ti·a /ig zèmpli gráyshee ə, ik sèmpli graàtee aà/ *adv.* full form of **e.g.** (*literary*) [Mid-17thC. From Latin, literally "for example's sake."]

ex·em·plum /ig zémpləm/ (*plural* **-pla** /-plə/) *n.* **1. ILLUSTRATIVE STORY** a brief story told to illustrate a moral point or support an argument **2. EXAMPLE** an example or illustration (*literary*) [Late 19thC. From Latin (see EXAMPLE).]

ex·empt /ig zémpt/ *adj.* **NOT SUBJECT TO SOMETHING** freed from or not subject to something such as a duty, tax, or military service that others have to do or pay ○ *tax-exempt savings accounts* ■ *vt.* (**-empt·ed, -empt·ing, -empts**) **1. FREE SOMEBODY FROM AN OBLIGATION** to allow or entitle somebody not to do something that others are obliged to do **2. RELEASE SOMETHING FROM A RULE** to release something from a rule that applies to others ○ *a law that exempts certain capital gains from taxes* ■ *n.* **EXEMPT PERSON OR THING** somebody or something that is exempt from something [14thC. Directly or via French from Latin *exemptus*, past participle of *eximere* (see EXAMPLE).] —**ex·empt·i·ble** *adj.*

ex·emp·tion /ig zémpshən/ *n.* **1. FREEDOM FROM AN OBLIGATION** permission or entitlement not to do something that others are obliged to do ○ *an exemption from jury duty* **2. EXEMPT PERSON OR THING** somebody who or something that is exempt from something, especially an amount of money that is not subject to taxation ○ *a range of tax exemptions*

ex·en·ter·ate /ig zéntə ràyt/ (**-at·ed, -at·ing, -ates**) *vt.* to remove surgically all the organs and other contents of a body cavity, usually to minimize the spread of cancer [Early 17thC. From the Latin *exenterat-*, past participle stem of *exenterare*, which was modeled on Greek *exenterizein*, literally "to remove the intestine," from *enteron* "intestine."] —**ex·en·ter·a·tion** /ig zèntə ráysh'n/ *n.*

ex·er·cise /éksər sìz/ *n.* **1.** FITNESS, VET **PHYSICAL ACTIVITY** physical activity and movement, especially when intended to keep a person or animal fit and healthy ○ *regular exercise is important* **2.** FITNESS, GYMNASTICS **PHYSICAL MOVEMENT** a physical movement or action, or a series of them, designed to make the body stronger and fitter or to show off gymnastic skill (*often used in the plural*) ○ *warmup exercises* **3. PRACTICE OF A SKILL OR PROCEDURE** a series of actions, movements, or tasks performed repeatedly or regularly as a way of practicing and improving a skill or procedure (*often used in the plural*) ○ *voice exercises for singers* **4.** EDUC **PIECE OF WORK** a piece of work intended to test somebody's knowledge or skill ○ *Test yourself by doing the exercises at the back of the book.* **5.** MIL **MILITARY TRAINING OPERATIONS OR MANEUVERS** a set of extensive operations or maneuvers, usually under simulated combat conditions, intended to train military personnel, test their equipment, and assess their capabilities **6. ACTIVITY INTENDED TO ACHIEVE A PARTICULAR PURPOSE** an action, activity, or undertaking intended to achieve a particular purpose ○ *The object of the exercise is to make money fast.* **7. CARRYING OUT OR USING SOMETHING** the carrying out or making use of something such as a choice, duty, responsibility, or right (*formal*) ○ *We urge the exercise of patience and restraint.* ■ *v.* (**-cised, -cis·ing, -cis·es**) **1.** *vi.* FITNESS **GET EXERCISE** to undertake physical exercise in order to keep fit and healthy **2.** *vt.* FITNESS **SUBJECT TO PHYSICAL EXERTION** to subject the body, or part of it, to repetitive physical exertion or energetic movement in order to strengthen it or improve its condition ○ *a routine designed to exercise your back and thigh muscles* **3.** *vt.* VET **EXERT AN ANIMAL PHYSICALLY** to make an animal exert itself physically in order to keep it healthy and fit **4.** *vt.* **DO EXERCISES TO DEVELOP A SKILL** to develop a particular faculty or skill by carrying out specific tasks or procedures repeatedly or systematically **5.** *vt.* **PUT SOMETHING TO PRACTICAL USE** to make use of a right or responsibility ○ *They have the power to prevent the merger, if they choose to exercise it.* **6.** *vt.* **SHOW A TYPE OF BEHAVIOR** to adopt a type of behavior or quality of character when dealing with a situation ○ *Exercise extreme care in your dealings with them.* **7.** *vt.* **OCCUPY OR WORRY SOMEBODY** to be a cause for serious thought, worry, or anxiety to somebody (*formal*) ○ *It is not a question that has exercised me greatly in the past.* **8.** *vti.* MIL **TAKE PART IN MILITARY TRAINING OPERATIONS** to take part in, or make troops take part in, large-scale operations or maneuvers as part of combat training [14thC. Via French *exercice* from Latin *exercitium*, from *exercere* "to keep busy," literally "to drive on or out, let loose," from *arcere* "to restrain" (source of English *arcane*).] —**ex·er·cis·a·ble** *adj.*

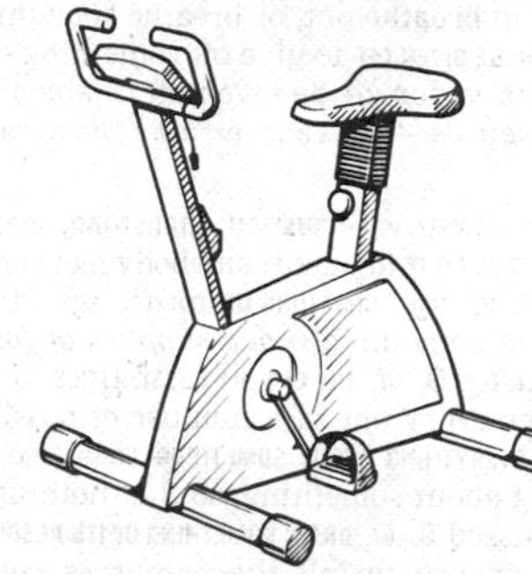

Exercise bike

ex·er·cise bike, ex·er·cise bi·cy·cle *n.* an exercise machine in the form of a stationary bicycle that is pedaled vigorously for exercise

ex·er·cise book *n.* a book containing exercises in a particular subject for students to complete

ex·er·cise price *n.* STOCK EXCH = **striking price**

ex·er·cis·er /éksər sìzər/ *n.* **1. APPARATUS FOR PHYSICAL FITNESS** a piece of equipment used to exercise all or part of the body **2. SOMEBODY WHO EXERCISES** somebody who does physical exercises or who exercises something, especially somebody employed to exercise racehorses

ex·er·gon·ic /èksər gónnik/ *adj.* used to describe a biochemical reaction in which energy is released and that can therefore take place spontaneously, without being started by energy from another source [Mid-20thC. Coined from EX- + Greek *ergon* "work" (source of English *energy*) + -IC.]

ex·ergue /ék sùrg, ég zùrg/ *n.* the part of a coin or medal that carries details such as the date and place of minting [Late 17thC. Via French from medieval Latin *exergum*, from Greek *ex-* "outside" + *ergon* "work." The underlying sense is "something outside the (main) work."]

ex·ert /ig zúrt/ (**-ert·ed, -ert·ing, -erts**) *v.* **1.** *vt.* **BRING SOMETHING TO BEAR** to apply influence, pressure, or authority in an attempt to have a powerful effect on a situation **2.** *vr.* **MAKE AN EFFORT** to make a strenuous physical or mental effort [Mid-17thC. From Latin *ex(s)ert-*, past participle stem of *ex(s)erere* "to thrust out, put forth," from *serere* "to join, braid, entwine" (source of English *series*).]

ex·er·tion /ig zúrsh'n/ *n.* **1. STRENUOUS EFFORT** strenuous physical exercise or effort **2. STRENUOUS ACTION** an action that involves strenuous physical effort (*often used in the plural*) ○ *After his exertions in the garden, he felt he deserved a rest.* **3. BRINGING SOMETHING TO BEAR** the application of pressure or influence ○ *the exertion of pressure on unsuspecting clients*

Ex·e·ter /éksətər/ **1.** town in southeastern New Hampshire, settled in 1638. Population: 12,481 (1990). **2.** historic cathedral city on the Exe River in Devon, southwestern England. Population: 106,600 (1995).

ex·e·unt /éksee ənt/ *vi.* used as a stage direction in a text in place of "exit" when more than one person is to leave the stage. ◊ **exit** [15thC. From Latin, literally "they go out," 3rd person plural of *exire* (see EXIT).]

ex·fo·li·ate /eks fólee àyt/ (**-at·ed, -at·ing, -ates**) *v.* **1.** *vi.* SCI **FALL OFF IN FLAKES** to come off the outer surface of something in thin flakes, scales, or layers **2.** *vti.* SCI **REMOVE THIN OUTER LAYER** to remove or shed a thin outer layer from something, e.g., skin, a mineral, or a bone in surgery **3.** *vti.* COSMETICS, DERMAT **SCRUB SKIN** to scrub skin with a gritty substance to remove the dead surface layer **4.** *vti.* MINERALS **SPLIT INTO THIN LAYERS** to split, or split a mineral, into thin layers [Mid-17thC. From late Latin *exfoliat-*, past participle stem of *exfoliare*, literally "to take leaves from," from Latin *folium* "leaf" (source of English *foliage*).] —**ex·fo·li·a·tion** /eks fōlee áysh'n/ *n.* —**ex·fo·li·a·tive** /eks fōlee àytiv/ *adj.* —**ex·fo·li·a·tor** /-àytər/ *n.*

ex gra·ti·a /eks gráyshə, -graátee aa/ *adj., adv.* given as a gift, favor, or gesture of goodwill, rather than because it is owed ○ *an ex gratia payment* [Mid-18thC. From Latin, literally "out of kindness."]

ex·ha·la·tion /èkshə láysh'n, èksə-/ *n.* **1.** PHYSIOL **BREATH FROM THE LUNGS** a breath exhaled from the lungs **2.** PHYSIOL **BREATHING OUT** the act of breathing out **3. SCENT OR VAPOR GIVEN OFF** a scent, a vapor, or fumes given off by something (*literary*)

ex·hale /eks háyl/ (**-haled, -hal·ing, -hales**) *vti.* **1.** PHYSIOL **BREATHE OUT** to breathe out, or breathe something out **2. GIVE OFF OR BE GIVEN OFF** to give off something such as a smell or a vapor, or be given off (*literary*) [14thC. Via French *exhaler* from Latin *exhalare*, from *halare* "to breathe."]

ex·haust /ig záwst/ *v.* (**-haust·ed, -haust·ing, -hausts**) **1.** *vt.* **TIRE SOMEBODY OUT** to make somebody feel very tired or weak **2.** *vt.* **USE SOMETHING UP** to use up all that is available of something ○ *our supplies of fuel were now exhausted* **3.** *vt.* **TRY OUT ALL POSSIBILITIES** to try out or consider every one of a number of possibilities **4.** *vt.* **SAY EVERYTHING ABOUT SOMETHING** to say or write everything about something, so that nothing is left to be discussed **5.** *vt.* **DRAIN SOMETHING OF ITS RESOURCES** to draw off or use up all the resources contained within something ○ *overgrazing that has exhausted the pasture* **6.** *vti.* TECH **LET OUT WASTE GASES** to escape, or allow steam or waste gases to escape, at the end of an industrial process ○ *Waste gases are exhausted through the flue.* **7.** *vt.* SCI **REMOVE GAS TO CREATE A VACUUM** to remove all of the air or gas from a container in order to create a vacuum inside it ■ *n.* TECH **1. DISCHARGE OF WASTE GASES** the discharge of waste gases, vapor, and fumes created by and released at the end of a process, especially from the working of an internal-combustion engine **2. ESCAPE SYSTEM FOR WASTE GASES** a pipe or other piece of apparatus through which waste gases escape [Mid-16thC. From Latin *exhaust-*, past participle stem of *exhaurire* "to draw out," from *haurire* "to draw (water) out or up, to drain."] —**ex·haust·er** *n.* —**ex·haust·i·bil·i·ty** /ig zàwstə bíllətee/ *n.* —**ex·haust·i·ble** /ig záwstəb'l/ *adj.*

ex·haust·ed /ig záwstəd/ *adj.* **1. WORN OUT** extremely tired or weak **2. USED UP** completely used up —**ex·haust·ed·ly** *adv.*

ex·haus·tion /ig záwschən/ *n.* **1.** MED **EXTREMELY TIRED OR WEAK STATE** a state of extreme physical or mental tiredness or collapse ○ *he was close to exhaustion* **2. ACT OF EXHAUSTING SOMETHING** the process of using up the entire stock or contents of something (*formal*) [Early 17thC. From the Latin stem *exhaustion-*, from the past participle stem *exhaust-* of *exhaurire* "to draw out, exhaust" (see EXHAUST).]

ex·haus·tive /ig záwstiv/ *adj.* involving or dealing with everything relevant to the matter in hand ○ *an exhaustive account of the author's life* —**ex·haus·tive·ly** *adv.* —**ex·haus·tive·ness** *n.* —**ex·haus·tiv·i·ty** /ig zàwss tívvətee/ *n.*

ex·haust pipe *n.* = **tailpipe**

ex·hib·it /ig zíbbit/ *v.* (**-it·ed, -it·ing, -its**) **1.** *vti.* **DISPLAY ART** to display something, especially a work of art, in a public place such as a museum or gallery **2.** *vt.* **SHOW SOMETHING TO OTHERS** to show something off for others to look at or admire ○ *She decided it was a good time to exhibit her skills as a solver of business disputes.* **3.** *vt.* **REVEAL A QUALITY** to show the outward signs of something, especially an emotion or a physical or mental condition ○ *The wings exhibited signs of metal fatigue.* **4.** *vt.* LAW **GIVE SOMETHING AS EVIDENCE** to present something to be used as evidence in a court of law ■ *n.* **1. OBJECT ON DISPLAY** an object displayed in public, especially in a gallery or museum or for a show or competition **2. ACT OF EXHIBITING** the act of displaying something ○ *an impressive exhibit of strength* **3.** = **exhibition** *n.* 1 **4.** LAW **PIECE OF EVIDENCE** an object or document presented or identified as evidence in a court of law [15thC. Partly from Latin *exhibere* "to hold out, display," from *habere* "to hold"; partly a back-formation from EXHIBITION.] —**ex·hib·i·to·ry** *adj.*

ex·hib·it·er *n.* = **exhibitor**

ex·hi·bi·tion /èksə bísh'n/ *n.* **1. PUBLIC DISPLAY OF WORKS OF ART** a public display, usually for a limited period, of a collection of works of art or objects of special interest **2. DISPLAYING OF SOMETHING** the displaying of something in public ○ *one or two of the works on exhibition* **3. DEMONSTRATION OF SKILL** a demonstration of a particular skill or craft ○ *a karate exhibition* **4. DISPLAY OF BEHAVIOR** a display of a particular type of behavior, usually bad behavior ○ *What did she mean by that little exhibition, I wonder?* [14thC. Directly or via French from the late Latin stem *exhibition-* "handing over, display," from Latin *exhibere* (see EXHIBIT). Originally in the sense "maintenance, support."]

WORD KEY: CULTURAL NOTE

Pictures at an Exhibition, a suite of piano pieces by the Russian composer Modest Mussorgsky (1874). The compositions were written in memory of the architect and painter Victor Alexandrovich Hartmann and inspired by paintings and drawings displayed at a memorial exhibition of the artist's work.

ex·hi·bi·tion game *n.* a sports contest played purely as a display of skill and an entertainment for spectators, having no bearing on team or individual standings

ex·hi·bi·tion·ism /èksə bísh'n ìzzəm/ *n.* **1. ATTENTION-SEEKING** loud, exaggerated, or boastful behavior designed to attract attention **2.** PSYCHIAT **EXPOSING OF THE GENITALS** a psychological disorder causing a compulsion to show the genitals in public —**ex·hi·bi·tion·ist** *n.* —**ex·hi·bi·tion·is·tic** /èksə bìsh'n ístik/ *adj.*

ex·hi·bi·tion match *n.* = **exhibition game**

ex·hib·i·tive /ig zíbbitiv/ *adj.* displaying or demonstrating something (*formal*) —**ex·hib·i·tive·ly** *adv.*

ex·hib·i·tor /ig zíbbitər/, **ex·hib·it·er** *n.* **1. SOMEBODY WITH WORK ON DISPLAY** somebody who exhibits something, especially somebody whose artistic work is included in an exhibition **2.** CINEMA **SOMEBODY WHO SCREENS A MOVIE** a person who or company that screens a movie

ex·hil·a·rate /ig zíllə ràyt/ (**-rat·ed, -rat·ing, -rates**) *vt.* to make somebody feel happy, excited, and more than usually vigorous and alive [Mid-16thC. From Latin *exhilarat-*, past participle stem of *exhilarare*, literally "to gladden thoroughly," from *hilarare* "to gladden," ultimately from Greek *hilaros* "cheerful, glad" (source of English *hilarious*).] —**ex·hil·a·rat·ing·ly** *adv.* —**ex·hil·a·ra·tive** *adj.* —**ex·hil·a·ra·tor** *n.*

ex·hil·a·ra·tion /ig zìllə ráysh'n/ *n.* a feeling of happiness and excitement combined with a heightened sense of being alive

ex·hort /ig záwrt/ (**-hort·ed, -hort·ing, -horts**) *v.* (*formal*) **1.** *vt.* **URGE TO DO SOMETHING** to urge somebody strongly and earnestly to do something **2.** *vi.* **GIVE EARNEST ADVICE** to give somebody urgent or earnest advice [14thC. Directly or via French *exhorter* from Latin *exhortari*, literally "to encourage thoroughly," from *hortari* "to encourage, urge."] —**ex·hort·er** *n.*

ex·hor·ta·tion /èg zawr táysh'n/ *n.* (*formal*) **1. SOMETHING INTENDED TO URGE OR PERSUADE** something said or written in order to urge somebody strongly to do something **2. GIVING OF ADVICE** the giving of earnest advice or encouragement

ex·hor·ta·tive /ig záwrtətiv/, **ex·hor·ta·to·ry** /-təwree/ *adj.* intended to urge or inspire somebody to do something (*formal*)

ex·hume /ig zoóm, -zyoóm/ (**-humed, -hum·ing, -humes**) *vt.* **1. DIG UP A BODY** to dig up a corpse from a grave **2. REINTRODUCE SOMETHING** to reveal, reestablish, or refer again to something long forgotten or neglected ○ *Cultures are reinvented and dead traditions exhumed for the tourists.* [15thC. From medieval Latin *exhumare*, from *humare* "to bury," from *humus* "ground, earth" (source of English *humus, humiliate*, and *humble*).] —**ex·hu·ma·tion** /èksyoo máysh'n, èksoo-, ègzoo-, ègzyoo-/ *n.* —**ex·hum·er** /ig zoómər, -zyoómər/ *n.*

ex·i·gen·cy /éksəjənsee, égzə-, ig zíjj-/ (*plural* **-cies**), **ex·i·gence** /éksəjəns, égzə-/ *n.* (*formal*) **1. URGENT NEED** something that a situation demands or makes urgently necessary and that puts pressure on the people involved (*often used in the plural*) ○ *unable to cope with the exigencies of political life* **2. SOMETHING NEEDING IMMEDIATE ACTION** a difficult situation requiring urgent action [Late 16thC. From late Latin *exigentia*, from the Latin present participle stem *exigent-* of *exigere* "to demand, require" (see EXACT).]

ex·i·gent /éksəjənt, égzə-/ *adj.* (*formal*) **1. REQUIRING ACTION** needing immediate action **2. DEMANDING** making heavy demands on somebody ○ *suffered at the hands of an exigent boss* [Early 17thC. From Latin *exigent-* (see EXIGENCY).] —**ex·i·gent·ly** *adv.*

ex·ig·u·ous /ig zíggyoo əss, ik sígg-/ *adj.* scanty or meager (*formal*) ○ *barely surviving on their exiguous supplies* [Mid-17thC. Formed from Latin *exiguus*, from *exigere* "to weigh precisely, measure" (see EXACT).] —**ex·i·gu·i·ty** /ègzi gyoó ətee, èksi-/ *n.* —**ex·ig·u·ous·ly** /ig zíggyoo əsslee, ik sígg-/ *adv.* —**ex·ig·u·ous·ness** *n.*

ex·ile /ég zīl, ék sīl/ *n.* **1. ABSENCE FROM YOUR OWN COUNTRY** unwilling absence from your own country or home, whether enforced by a government or court as a punishment, or imposed for political or religious reasons **2. SOMEBODY LIVING OUTSIDE HIS OR HER OWN COUNTRY** somebody who is forced to live in another country, either for personal or political reasons or after being ordered to leave as a punishment **3. BANISHMENT FROM HOME OR COUNTRY** official expulsion from a home country or area, sometimes to a specified place, as a punishment ■ *vt.* (**-iled, -il·ing, -iles**) **BANISH SOMEBODY FROM HOME OR COUNTRY** to order somebody to leave and stay away from his or her own country or home as a punishment [14thC. Via French *exil* from Latin *exilium* "banishment," from *exul* "banished person."] —**ex·il·ic** /ig zíllik, ik síllik/ *adj.*

Ex·im·bank /éksimbàngk/ *n.* = **Export-Import Bank**

ex·ine /ék seen, -sīn/ *n.* the outer layer of a pollen grain or other spore. The surface patterns vary among different plant groups, allowing the makeup of former plant populations to be deduced from preserved pollen samples. [Late 19thC. Origin uncertain; perhaps formed from EX- + modern Latin *in-* "fibrous tissue" (from Greek *in-*, *is* "fiber, sinew").]

ex·ist /ig zíst/ (**-ist·ed, -ist·ing, -ists**) *vi.* **1. BE** to be, especially to be a real, actual, or current thing, not merely something imagined or written about ○ *Does life exist on other planets?* **2. LIVE** to be alive or continue to live ○ *Humans need water and food to exist.* **3. OCCUR** to be present or found in a particular place or situation ○ *Shortages on products in high demand exist.* **4. SURVIVE** to manage to survive or stay alive ○ *The lost hikers existed for two days on berries.* **5. LIVE AN UNSATISFACTORY LIFE** to live an unsatisfactory, joyless, or humdrum life, as opposed to an exciting or meaningful one [Early 17thC. Origin uncertain; probably a back-formation from EXISTENCE.]

ex·is·tence /ig zíst'ns/ *n.* **1. BEING REAL** the state of being real, actual, or current, rather than imagined, invented, or obsolete ○ *evidence for the existence of other worlds* **2. PRESENCE IN A PLACE OR SITUATION** the presence or occurrence of something in a particular place or situation ○ *discovered the existence of the bacterium in sheep* **3. WAY OF LIVING** a way of living, especially a life of severe hardship ○ *scratch out a pitiable existence* **4. EVERYTHING** all living things (*literary*) ○ *hymns that celebrate the wonder of existence* **5. SINGLE LIVING THING** something that lives or exists (*literary or archaic*) [14thC. Directly or via French from late Latin *existentia*, from Latin *ex(s)istere* "to emerge, come into being," from *sistere* "to cause to stand firm."]

ex·is·tent /ig zíst'nt/ *adj.* (*formal*) **1. REAL** real or actual, not imagined or invented **2. CURRENT** currently existing or in operation ■ *n.* **REAL THING** a real or living thing (*formal*)

ex·is·ten·tial /ègzi sténshəl, èksi-/ *adj.* **1. RELATING TO HUMAN EXISTENCE** concerned with or relating to existence, especially human existence **2.** PHILOS **CRUCIAL IN SHAPING INDIVIDUAL DESTINY** in the context of existentialism, involved in or vital to the shaping of an individual's self-chosen mode of existence and moral stance with respect to the rest of the world **3.** LOGIC **GOVERNED BY THE EXISTENTIAL QUANTIFIER** governed by the existential quantifier and thus asserting the existence of something by saying that there is at least one object that possesses the properties specified ■ *n.* LOGIC **EXISTENTIAL PROPOSITION** a proposition governed by the existential quantifier —**ex·is·ten·tial·ly** *adv.*

ex·is·ten·tial·ism /ègzi sténshə lìzzəm, èksi-/ *n.* a 20th-century philosophical movement that denies that the universe has any intrinsic meaning or purpose and requires individuals to take responsibility for their own actions and shape their own destinies [Mid-20thC. From German *Existentialismus*, a translation of Danish *existents-forhold* "condition of existence."] —**ex·is·ten·tial·ist** *adj., n.*

ex·is·ten·tial quan·ti·fi·er *n.* the logical constant, frequently symbolized as "Ex," that is a prefix to another clause and that is read as saying "there is at least one object such that." ◊ **universal quantifier**

ex·ist·ing /ig zísting/ *adj.* currently present, in operation, or available ○ *Existing legislation is inadequate to cover these cases.*

ex·it /égzit, éksit/ *n.* **1.** MEANS OF LEAVING A PLACE a door or other means of leaving a room or building **2.** DEPARTURE an act of leaving a room, building, or gathering **3.** DEATH departure from life (*formal*) **4.** THEATER ACTOR'S LEAVING OF THE STAGE an actor's departure from the stage **5.** TRANSP PLACE FOR LEAVING AN EXPRESSWAY any of the slip roads by which a vehicle can leave a expressway or other main road with limited access **6.** COMPUT TERMINATION OF A COMPUTER OPERATION an act of terminating a computer operation ■ *v.* (**-it·ed, -it·ing, -its**) **1.** *vti.* LEAVE to leave something such as a room, building, or gathering ○ *In the event of a fire, exit the building at the rear.* **2.** *vi.* DIE to cease to live (*literary*) **3.** *vi.* THEATER GO OFFSTAGE to leave the stage during a performance of a play (*refers to an actor*) ◊ **exeunt 4.** *vti.* COMPUT TERMINATE A COMPUTER PROGRAM to terminate the running of a computer operating system, program, or routine in a program [Mid-16thC. From Latin *exitus* "a departure," past participle, used as a noun, of *exire* "to go out," from *ire* "to go."]

ex·it poll *n.* a poll designed to give an early indication of the result of an election, conducted by asking people how they voted as they leave the place of voting

ex li·bris /eks leébriss/ (*plural* **ex li·bris**) *adv.* from the library of the person whose name follows (*used on bookplates*) [From Latin, literally "from the books (of)," in reference to the owner's library]

ex ni·hi·lo /eks neé ə lō, -neéhi-/ *adv., adj.* from or out of nothing (*formal*) [Late 16thC. From Latin.]

exo- *prefix.* outside, external ○ *exothermic* [From Greek *exō*, from *ex* "out." Ultimately from an Indo-European base that is also the ancestor of English *ex-, extra-,* and *extreme.*]

ex·o·bi·ol·o·gy /èksō bī óllәjee/ *n.* a branch of biology concerned with the possibility that life forms exist on other planets and with the problems of adapting the Earth's life forms to alien environments —**ex·o·bi·o·log·i·cal** /èksō bī ə lójjik'l/ *adj.* —**ex·o·bi·ol·o·gist** /-bī óllәjist/ *n.*

ex·o·carp /éksō kaàrp/ *n.* the outer layer of the fruit wall (**pericarp**)

Ex·o·cet /éksə sèt/ *tdmk.* a trademark for a French-manufactured surface-to-surface guided missile with a high-explosive warhead

ex·o·crine /éksəkrin, éksə kreèn, éksə krīn/ *adj.* used to describe or relating to glands such as sweat glands or salivary glands that release a secretion through a duct to the surface of an organ. ◊ **endocrine** [Early 20thC. Coined from *exo-* + Greek *krinein* "to separate" (source of English *crisis* and *hypocrite*).]

ex·o·cy·clic /èksō síklik, -síklik/ *adj.* situated outside a chemical ring structure ○ *an exocyclic bond*

ex·o·cy·to·sis /èksō sī tṓssiss/ *n.* the release of substances contained in a sac (**vesicle**) within a cell by a process in which the membrane surrounding the sac unites with the membrane forming the outer wall of the cell —**ex·o·cy·tot·ic** /èksō sī tóttik/ *adj.*

Exod. *abbr.* BIBLE Exodus

ex·o·don·tics /èksə dóntiks/, **ex·o·don·tia** /-dónshə/ *n.* the branch of dentistry concerned with extracting teeth (*takes a singular verb*) [Early 20thC. Coined from EXO- + Greek *odont-*, stem of *odous* "tooth."] —**ex·o·don·tist** *n.*

ex·o·dus /éksədəss/ *n.* a departure or going out or away from a place that involves large numbers of people [Pre-12thC. Via ecclesiastical Latin "(biblical Book of) Exodus" from Greek, literally "way out," from *hodos* "way, road."]

Ex·o·dus *n.* **1.** 2ND BOOK OF THE BIBLE the second book of the Bible, which describes the flight of the Israelites from Egypt and Moses receiving the Ten Commandments on Mount Sinai **2.** FLIGHT OF ISRAELITES FROM EGYPT the flight of Moses and the Israelites from Egypt, as described in the second book of the Bible [Pre-12thC. See EXODUS.]

ex·o·en·zyme /èksō én zīm/ *n.* an enzyme that operates outside the cell in which it was produced, e.g., a digestive enzyme

ex·o·er·gic /èksō úrjik/ *adj.* NUCLEAR PHYS = **exothermic** [Mid-20thC. Coined from EXO- + Greek *ergon* "work" (source of English *energy*) + -IC.]

ex off. *abbr.* ex officio

ex of·fi·ci·o /èks ə físhi ō/ *adv., adj.* as a result of the official position somebody holds ○ *Heads of state are often ex officio heads of the armed forces* [Mid-16thC. From Latin, literally "out of duty, on account of office."]

ex·og·a·my /ek sóggəmee/ *n.* **1.** ANTHROP MARRIAGE TRADITION the custom in some societies of marrying outside their people's own tribe, clan, or social group **2.** BIOL FUSION OF UNRELATED CELLS the fusion of sex cells (**gametes**) of organisms not closely related, as occurs in cross pollination and outbreeding —**ex·og·a·mous** *adj.*

ex·og·e·nous /ek sójjənəss/ *adj.* originating outside an organism or system. ◊ **endogenous** [Mid-19thC. Formed from modern Latin *exogena* "growing on the outside," from Greek *genēs* "born."] —**ex·og·e·nous·ly** *adv.*

ex·on /ék sòn/ *n.* a discontinuous sequence of DNA that codes for protein synthesis and carries the genetic code for the final messenger RNA molecule. ◊ **intron** [Late 20thC. Coined from *expressed* (past participle of EXPRESS) + -ON.]

ex·on·er·ate /ig zónnə ràyt/ (**-at·ed, -at·ing, -ates**) *vt.* **1.** FREE SOMEBODY FROM BLAME OR GUILT to declare officially that somebody is not to blame, or is not guilty of a crime **2.** FREE SOMEBODY FROM AN OBLIGATION to relieve somebody from an obligation or responsibility [15thC. From Latin *exonerat-*, past participle stem of *exonerare*, literally "to take off a burden," from *onus* "burden" (source of English *onerous* and *onus*).] —**ex·on·er·a·tion** /ig zònnə ráysh'n/ *n.* —**ex·on·er·a·tive** /ig zónnə ràytiv/ *adj.*

ex·oph·thal·mos /èk səf thálməss/, **ex·oph·thal·mus** *n.* abnormal protrusion of the eyeball resulting, e.g., from an aneurysm [Early 17thC. Directly or via modern Latin *exophthalmus* from Greek *exophthalmos*, literally "(condition of) the eye being outside," from *ophthalmos* "eye" (source of English *ophthalmic*).] —**ex·oph·thal·mic** *adj.*

ex·or·bi·tant /ig záwrbit'nt/ *adj.* **1.** UNREASONABLY HIGH OR LARGE far greater or higher than is reasonable ○ *exorbitant* **2.** EXTREME going beyond what is reasonable, proper, or manageable [15thC. Ultimately from Christian Latin *exorbitare* "to go out of the track," from Latin *orbita* "track," from *orbis* "circle" . Originally "not within the intended scope of a law."] —**ex·or·bi·tant·ly** *adv.*

ex·or·cise /ék sawr sīz, éksər-/ (**-cised, -cis·ing, -cis·es**), **ex·or·cize** (**-cized, -ciz·ing, -ciz·es**) *vt.* **1.** RELIG FREE A PERSON OR PLACE FROM EVIL to use prayers and religious rituals with the intention of ridding a person or place of the presence or influence of evil spirits **2.** RELIG SEND EVIL AWAY to use prayers and religious rituals with the intention of driving away an evil spirit believed to have been possessing a person or place **3.** GET RID OF AN OPPRESSIVE FEELING to clear the mind of a painful or oppressive feeling or memory [15thC. Directly or via French *exorciser* from ecclesiastical Latin *exorcizare*, from Greek *exorkizein*, literally "to swear out (an evil spirit)," from *orkos* "oath."] —**ex·or·cis·er** *n.*

ex·or·cism /ék sawr sìzzəm, éksər-/ *n.* **1.** RELIG DRIVING OUT OF EVIL SPIRITS the use of prayer or religious ritual to drive out evil spirits **2.** RELIG CEREMONY TO DRIVE OUT EVIL SPIRITS a religious ceremony in which somebody attempts to drive out an evil spirit believed to be possessing a person or place **3.** RELIG THING DONE TO EXPEL EVIL a special ritual or spoken formula used with the intention of driving out evil spirits **4.** CLEARING THE MIND OF OPPRESSIVE FEELINGS the act of ridding the mind of oppressive feelings or memories [14thC. Via ecclesiastical Latin *exorcismus* from ecclesiastical Greek *exorkismos*, from *exorkizein* (see EXORCISE).] —**ex·or·cist** *n.*

ex·or·cize *vt.* = **exorcise**

ex·or·di·um /eg záwrdee əm/ (*plural* **-ums** *or* **-a** /-dee ə/) *n.* an opening section, especially of a lecture or a piece of scholarly writing (*formal*) [Late 16thC. From Latin, formed from *exordiri* "to begin."] —**ex·or·di·al** *adj.*

ex·o·skel·e·ton /èksō skéllət'n/ *n.* a hard covering on the outside of many organisms such as crustaceans, insects, turtles, and armadillos that provides support and protection —**ex·o·skel·e·tal** *adj.*

ex·os·mo·sis /èks oz mṓssiss, -os-/ *n.* movement of fluid toward a solution of lower concentration, as is the case when water percolates through a cell membrane into the medium surrounding the cell [Mid-19thC. An alteration of obsolete *exosmose*, from French, literally "a pushing out," from Greek *ōsmos* "act of pushing" (source of English *osmosis*).] —**ex·os·mot·ic** /èks oz móttik, -os-/ *adj.*

ex·o·sphere /éksō sfeèr/ *n.* the outermost region of the atmosphere of the Earth or another planet —**ex·o·spher·ic** /èksō sfeèrik, -sférrik/ *adj.*

ex·o·spore /éksə spàwr/ *n.* a spore that is formed outside a parent cell, e.g. by partitioning of parental material, or outside a spore-bearing organ

ex·os·to·sis /èk so stṓssiss/ (*plural* **-ses** /-seez/) *n.* an abnormal benign bony growth on the surface of a bone or a tooth root, caused by inflammation or repeated trauma [Late 16thC. From Greek, "bony outgrowth," formed from *osteon* "bone" (source of English *osteo-*).]

ex·o·ter·ic /èksə térrik/ *adj.* capable of being understood by most people, not just an informed or select minority (*formal*) [Mid-17thC. Via Latin *exotericus* from Greek *exōterikos*, from *exōterō* "outer," from *exō* "outside."] —**ex·o·ter·i·cal·ly** *adv.*

ex·o·ther·mic /èksō thúrmik/, **ex·o·ther·mal** /èksō thúrm'l/ *adj.* CHEM, PHYS used to describe a reaction that produces heat (*preferred term in nuclear physics is "exoergic"*) [Late 19thC. From French *exothermique*, from Greek *thermē* "heat" (source of *thermometer*).] —**ex·o·ther·mi·cal·ly** *adv.*

ex·ot·ic /ig zóttik/ *adj.* **1.** STRIKINGLY DIFFERENT strikingly unusual and often very colorful and exciting or suggesting distant countries and unfamiliar cultures **2.** ECOL FROM ELSEWHERE introduced from another place or region ○ *an exotic species* ■ *n.* EXOTIC PERSON OR THING somebody who or something that is exotic, especially a plant or animal [Late 16thC. Via Latin *exoticus* from Greek *exōtikos*, from *exō* "out, outside," the underlying notion being "foreign, out of the ordinary."] —**ex·ot·i·cal·ly** *adv.* —**ex·ot·i·cism** *n.* —**ex·ot·ic·ness** *n.*

ex·ot·i·ca /ig zóttikə/ *npl.* exotic or extraordinary things, especially when forming a collection [Late 19thC. From Latin, neuter plural of *exoticus* (see EXOTIC).]

ex·ot·ic dancer *n.* a striptease dancer

ex·o·tox·in /èksō tóksin/ *n.* a highly potent soluble toxin produced by a bacterium and released into its infected host, often affecting the central nervous system. Exotoxins are produced in diphtheria, botulism, and tetanus and are among the most potent known toxins.

exp *symbol.* MATH exponential function

exp. *abbr.* **1.** experiment **2.** experimental **3.** expiration **4.** expired **5.** expires **6.** export **7.** exported **8.** express

ex·pand /ik spánd/ (**-pand·ed, -pand·ing, -pands**) *v.* **1.** *vti.* MAKE OR BECOME LARGER to become or cause something to become larger in size, scope, or extent, or greater in number or amount ○ *We need to expand our client base.* **2.** *vti.* PHYS INCREASE IN SIZE OR VOLUME to increase or cause something to increase in size or volume as a result of a rise in temperature or decrease in pressure **3.** *vti.* OPEN OUT to open out or open something out wider after being kept folded in **4.** *vti.* DESCRIBE SOMETHING MORE FULLY to explain or describe something more fully, usually by giving more detail ○ *If you expanded that argument a little, it would fill another chapter.* **5.** *vt.* GIVE THE FULL FORM OF SOMETHING to give the full form of something such as the abbreviation of a word **6.** *vi.* RELAX to relax and become friendlier and more talkative **7.** *vt.* MATH REWRITE A MATHEMATICAL EXPRESSION to rewrite a mathematical expression as the sum or product of its terms, e.g., $(x+1)(x-1)+2x$ expands to x^2+2x-1 [15thC. Directly or via Anglo-Norman *espaundre* from Latin *expandere* "to spread out," from *pandere* "to spread."] —**ex·pand·a·bil·i·ty** /ik spàndə bíllətee/ *n.* —**ex·pand·a·ble** /ik spándəb'l/ *adj.* —**ex·pand·er** /-spándər/ *n.*

WORD KEY: SYNONYMS

See Synonyms at ***increase***.

ex·pand·ed /ik spándəd/ *adj.* **1.** MADE LARGER extended, unfolded, or outstretched **2.** INDUST MADE INTO FOAM used to describe plastics made into a lightweight solid foam by the introduction of gas during the manufacturing process ○ *expanded polyurethane* **3.** PRINTING WIDER THAN USUAL used to describe typefaces or printed characters that are wider than usual in relation to their height

ex·pand·ed met·al *n.* strong metal mesh made by cutting slits in sheet metal and stretching it out of shape, used as a reinforcing material in construction

ex·panse /ik spáns/ *n.* a wide area or surface, especially of sea, land, or sky [Mid-17thC. From modern Latin *expansum* "firmament," neuter past participle (used as a noun) of Latin *expandere* (see EXPAND).]

ex·pan·si·ble /ik spánsəb'l/ *adj.* able to expand or be expanded —**ex·pan·si·bil·i·ty** /ik spànsə bíllətee/ *n.*

ex·pan·sile /ik spánsəl/ *adj.* **1.** RELATING TO EXPANSION relating to expansion or the ability to expand **2.** EXPANSIBLE able to expand or be expanded

ex·pan·sion /ik spánshən/ *n.* **1.** PROCESS OF BECOMING ENLARGED the process of increasing, or increasing something, in size, extent, scope, or number ○ *This site does not give us enough room for expansion.* **2.** INCREASE an increase, or the amount by which something increases, in size, extent, or scope ○ *Geologists measured the expansion of the volcanic island.* **3.** PHYS INCREASE IN DIMENSIONS an increase in the dimensions of something as a result of a rise in temperature or decrease in pressure **4.** GROWTH BY ACQUISITION the increase of a country's size by the acquisition of new territory ○ *westward expansion* **5.** ACT OF EXPANDING the act or state of expanding, opening, or spreading out **6.** FULLER TREATMENT a fuller or more detailed treatment or version of something ○ *The expansion of "Dr." is "Doctor."* **7.** ENG COMBUSTION STAGE IN AN ENGINE a stage in an engine cycle during which the fuel and air mixture explodes, thereby increasing in volume and providing power **8.** MATH EXPANDED MATHEMATICAL EXPRESSION the result of expanding a mathematical expression

ex·pan·sion·ar·y /ik spánshə nèrree/ *adj.* bringing about expansion, especially economic or territorial expansion

ex·pan·sion board *n.* COMPUT = **expansion card**

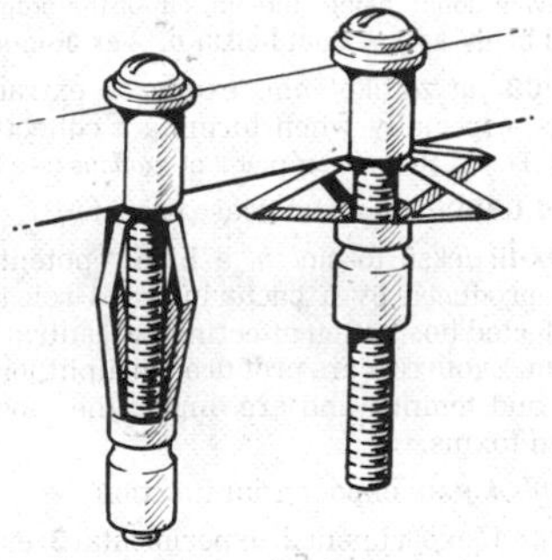

Expansion bolt

ex·pan·sion bolt *n.* a bolt with an attachment on the screw end that expands as the bolt is tightened, thereby securing it

ex·pan·sion card *n.* a printed circuit board inserted into a computer to add features or capability

ex·pan·sion·ism /ik spánshə nìzzəm/ *n.* a policy of expanding a country's economy or territory —**ex·pan·sion·ist** *n., adj.* —**ex·pan·sion·is·tic** /ik spànshə nístik/ *adj.*

ex·pan·sion joint *n.* a gap between adjacent parts or surfaces, e.g., between the concrete sections that form the road surface of a bridge, to prevent buckling when they expand under heat

ex·pan·sion slot *n.* a receptacle connected to and interfacing with a computer's internal circuitry and designed to hold an expansion card

ex·pan·sive /ik spánsiv/ *adj.* **1.** COMMUNICATIVE willing to talk openly and at some length, usually in a relaxed and jovial way ○ *He gradually became more expansive once he got to know us.* **2.** EXTENSIVE covering a wide area or broad in scope ○ *a large house with expansive grounds* **3.** EXPANDING capable of, having a tendency to, or typically undergoing expansion ○ *polymers with expansive capability* **4.** WITH OUTSTRETCHED ARMS with the arms stretched out and open wide ○ *an expansive gesture* **5.** LAVISH generous, lavish, or extravagant in scale ○ *an expansive lifestyle* **6.** PSYCHIAT HAVING EXAGGERATED FEELINGS OF SELF-WORTH characterized by extreme feelings of euphoria and delusions of grandeur or self-importance —**ex·pan·sive·ly** *adv.* —**ex·pan·sive·ness** *n.* —**ex·pan·siv·i·ty** /èk span sívvətee/ *n.*

ex par·te /eks paártee/ *adj., adv.* made or undertaken on behalf of only one of the parties involved in a court case [Early 17thC. From Latin, literally "from a (or the) side."]

ex·pat /èks pát/ *n.* an expatriate (*informal*) [Mid-20thC. Shortening.]

ex·pa·ti·ate /ek spáyshee àyt/ (**-at·ed, -at·ing, -ates**) *vi.* **1.** SPEAK OR WRITE AT LENGTH to speak or write about something at length ○ *We had to listen to him expatiating on the shortcomings of our system.* **2.** WANDER to wander or roam at will (*archaic*) [Mid-16thC. From Latin *ex(s)patiat-*, past participle stem of *ex(s)patiari*, literally "to walk out," from *spatiari* "to walk," from *spatium* "space" (source of English *space*). Originally "to roam freely."] —**ex·pa·ti·a·tion** /ek spàyshee áysh'n/ *n.*

ex·pa·tri·ate *n.* /eks páytree ət, -àyt/ **1.** SOMEBODY WHO HAS MOVED ABROAD somebody who has left his or her homeland to live or work in another country, usually for a long period of time **2.** SOMEBODY WITHOUT CITIZENSHIP somebody who has renounced his or her citizenship or whose citizenship has been revoked ■ *adj.* /eks páytree ət, -àyt/ RELATING TO THOSE LIVING ABROAD relating to or typical of people who live outside their own country ■ *v.* /eks páytree àyt/ (**-at·ed, -at·ing, -ates**) **1.** *vi.* SETTLE ABROAD to settle in another country **2.** *vti.* TAKE AWAY SOMEBODY'S CITIZENSHIP to deprive somebody of native citizenship, or renounce native citizenship voluntarily **3.** *vt.* EXPEL SOMEBODY FROM HIS OR HER OWN COUNTRY to send somebody away from his or her own country as a punishment [Mid-18thC. From Latin *expatriat-*, past participle stem of *expatriare*, literally "to leave your native land," from *patria* "native land," from *pater* "father."] —**ex·pa·tri·a·tion** /eks pàytree áysh'n/ *n.*

ex·pect /ik spékt/ (**-pect·ed, -pect·ing, -pects**) *v.* **1.** *vti.* CONFIDENTLY BELIEVE to believe with confidence, or think it likely, that an event will happen in the future ○ *A few setbacks along the way were only to be expected.* **2.** *vt.* WAIT FOR AN ANTICIPATED THING to wait for, or look forward to, something that you believe is going to happen or arrive ○ *I'm expecting a visit from them any day now.* **3.** *vt.* DEMAND SOMETHING AS A RIGHT OR DUTY to demand or anticipate receiving something because of a perceived right to it or because it is somebody's duty to give it ○ *They expect you to abide by their rules.* **4.** *vti.* BE GOING TO HAVE A BABY to be pregnant with or look forward to the birth of a child (*informal*) (*used only in progressive tenses*) ○ *She is expecting her third in July.* [Mid-16thC. From Latin *ex(s)pectare* "to look out for," from *spectare* "to look at", from *specere* "to look, look at."] —**ex·pect·a·ble** *adj.* —**ex·pect·a·bly** *adv.* —**ex·pect·ed·ly** *adv.* —**ex·pect·ed·ness** *n.*

ex·pec·tan·cy /ik spéktənsee/ (*plural* **-cies**), **ex·pec·tance** /-təns/ *n.* **1.** EXCITED ANTICIPATION excited awareness that something is about to happen ○ *An air of expectancy hung over the crowd.* **2.** STATS SOMETHING EXPECTED something expected, especially an amount or length of time expected on the basis of statistical calculations

ex·pec·tant /ik spéktənt/ *adj.* **1.** EXCITEDLY ANTICIPATING SOMETHING excitedly aware that something is about to happen **2.** EXPECTING A BABY expecting the birth of a baby **3.** EXPECTING SOMETHING FAVORABLE expecting something, especially something that will bring success or wealth (*formal*) [14thC. Directly or via French from Latin *ex(s)pectant-*, present participle stem of *ex(s)pectare* (see EXPECT).]

ex·pec·ta·tion /èk spek táysh'n/ *n.* **1.** ANTICIPATION OF SOMETHING HAPPENING a confident belief or strong hope that a particular event will happen **2.** NOTION OF SOMETHING a mental image of something expected, often compared to its reality (*often used in the plural*) ○ *All our expectations of a quiet evening at home were dashed by the arrival of guests.* **3.** EXPECTED STANDARD a standard of conduct or performance expected by or of somebody (*often used in the plural*) ○ *Her work wasn't up to expectations so she was dismissed.* **4.** = **expectancy** *n.* 1 ■ **ex·pec·ta·tions** *npl.* PROSPECTS FOR THE FUTURE somebody's likely prospects of wealth or success in the future

ex·pect·ed val·ue *n.* the value of a random variable that is most likely to occur, calculated by taking the sum of every possible value multiplied by a factor representing the probability of its occurrence

ex·pec·to·rant /ik spéktərənt/ *adj.* PRODUCING AND GETTING RID OF PHLEGM causing phlegm to be produced or liquefied and coughed up ■ *n.* MEDICINE FOR COUGHS a medicine that stimulates the production and secretion of phlegm, used to treat coughs

ex·pec·to·rate /ik spéktə ràyt/ (**-rat·ed, -rat·ing, -rates**) *vti.* to cough up and spit out phlegm, thus clearing the bronchial passages [Early 17thC. From Latin *expectorat-*, past participle stem of *expectorare*, literally "to get out of the chest," from *pectus* "chest, breast" (source of English *pectoral*).] —**ex·pec·to·ra·tion** /ik spèktə ráysh'n/ *n.*

ex·pe·di·en·cy /ik speédee ənsee/ (*plural* **-cies**), **ex·pe·di·ence** /ik speédee əns/ *n.* **1.** USE OF SHORT-TERM EFFECTIVE METHODS the use of methods that bring the most immediate benefits, based on practical rather than moral considerations (*disapproving*) **2.** APPROPRIATENESS the usefulness, appropriateness, or advisability of something, especially of a particular action or type of behavior in a particular situation ○ *doubts about the expediency of such a course in the present crisis* **3.** = **expedient** *n.*

ex·pe·di·ent /ik speédee ənt/ *adj.* **1.** APPROPRIATE appropriate, advisable, or useful in a situation that requires action **2.** ADVANTAGEOUS advantageous for practical rather than moral reasons (*disapproving*) ○ *She changed her vote because it was expedient for her to do so.* ■ *n.* SOMETHING ACHIEVING AIMS QUICKLY something done or a method used to achieve an aim quickly, regardless of whether it is fair, right, or wise in the long term [14thC. Directly or via French from Latin *expedient-*, present participle stem of *expedire* (see EXPEDITE).] —**ex·pe·di·ent·ly** *adv.*

ex·pe·dite /ékspə dìt/ (**-dit·ed, -dit·ing, -dites**) *vt.* (*formal*) **1.** SPEED UP THE PROGRESS OF SOMETHING to ensure that something takes place or is dealt with more quickly than usual **2.** DEAL WITH QUICKLY AND EFFICIENTLY to deal with something, especially a business transaction, swiftly and efficiently [15thC. From Latin *expedit-*, past participle stem of *expedire* "to set free," literally "to free the feet," from ultimately, *pes* "foot" (source of English *pedal*).] —**ex·pe·dit·er** *n.*

ex·pe·di·tion /ékspə dísh'n/ *n.* **1.** ORGANIZED TRIP BY A GROUP a trip made by a group of people for a specific purpose, e.g., to explore unknown territory, to do scientific study, or to achieve a military objective ○ *a scientific expedition to the ocean floor* **2.** PEOPLE MAKING AN EXPEDITION a group of people who go on an expedition together ○ *The expedition returned at the end of the month.* **3.** OUTING a short outing, usually for a pleasurable purpose **4.** PROMPTNESS speed, promptness, or efficiency in doing something ○ *carried out our errand with expedition* [15thC. Directly or via French from the Latin stem *expedition-*, from *expedire* (see EXPEDITE).]

ex·pe·di·tion·ar·y /èkspə dísh'n èrree/ *adj.* sent to fight or do military service in another country ○ *an expeditionary force*

ex·pe·di·tious /èkspə díshəss/ *adj.* speedy or carried out promptly and efficiently —**ex·pe·di·tious·ly** *adv.* —**ex·pe·di·tious·ness** *n.*

ex·pel /ik spél/ (**-pelled, -pel·ling, -pels**) *vt.* **1.** DISMISS SOMEBODY FROM AN ORGANIZATION to compel somebody to leave or give up membership in an institution such as a school, political party, or club ○ *expel a child from school* **2.** DRIVE OUT to push or drive something out with force ○ *Air is expelled under pressure from outlets under the hovercraft's apron.* [14thC. From Latin *expellere*, literally "to drive out," from *pellere* "to beat, drive" (source of English *appeal* and *pulse*).] —**ex·pel·la·ble** *adj.* —**ex·pel·ler** *n.*

ex·pel·lant /ik spéllənt/, **ex·pel·lent** *adj.* MED ABLE TO EXPEL SOMETHING capable of expelling something, especially from the body ■ *n.* MED MEDICINE TO REMOVE WORMS a medicine that causes the body to get rid of something undesirable, especially intestinal worms

ex·pel·lee /èk spe leé, ik spè leé/ *n.* somebody who has been expelled from an organization

ex·pel·lent *adj., n.* MED = **expellant**

ex·pend /ik spénd/ (**-pend·ed, -pend·ing, -pends**) *vt.* **1.** USE UP to use up time, energy, effort, or some other resource **2.** SPEND MONEY to spend money or an amount of money (*formal*) [15thC. From Latin *expendere* "to weigh out (especially money in payment)," from *pendere* "to weigh, weigh out" (source of English *dispense, pendant, pendulum,* and *spend*).] —**ex·pen·der** *n.*

ex·pend·a·ble /ik spéndəb'l/ *adj.* **1.** NOT WORTH PRESERVING not worth preserving or saving for reuse **2.** DISPENSABLE easily sacrificed or dispensed with if the need arises or in order to achieve an aim ■ *n.* EXPENDABLE ITEM an expendable person or thing —**ex·pend·a·bil·i·ty** /ik spèndə bíllətee/ *n.*

ex·pen·di·ture /ik spéndəchər/ *n.* **1. MONEY SPENT** an amount of money spent, as a whole or on a particular thing ○ *when income exceeds expenditure* **2. USING UP** the consuming or using up of something ○ *the huge expenditure of time and human resources on this project* [Mid-18thC. From EXPEND; modeled on *expenditor* "somebody in charge of expenditure."]

ex·pense /ik spéns/ *n.* **1. MONEY SPENT ON SOMETHING** the amount of money spent in order to buy or do something **2.** ACCT **VALUE OF RESOURCE USED** the value of a resource that has been used during the current accounting period and can be charged against revenues for that period **3. SOMETHING EXPENSIVE TO BUY** something that costs money, usually a lot of money, to buy, keep, or run **4. USING UP** the using up or loss of something ○ *preserved his integrity at the expense of his job* ■ **ex·pens·es** *npl.* **BUSINESS EXPENDITURES** an amount of money that somebody spends for business purposes that is reimbursable by an employer or deductible from income tax ■ *vt.* **(-pensed, -pens·ing, -pens·es) 1. TREAT SOMETHING AS CHARGEABLE OR DEDUCTIBLE** to identify something as an expense for tax, accounting, or expense-account purposes ○ *expensed our moving costs* **2. CHARGE SOMEBODY FOR EXPENSES** to charge your expenses to somebody [14thC. Via Anglo-Norman from, ultimately, Latin *expendere* (see EXPEND). The verb uses are 20th-century developments.]

ex·pense ac·count *n.* **1. AGREEMENT TO REPAY AN EMPLOYEE'S WORK COSTS** a benefit given by an employer that entitles an employee to be repaid for some or all of the expenses incurred in the course of his or her employment **2. AMOUNT OR RECORD OF EXPENSES** the amount or a record of an employee's expenses during a particular period

ex·pen·sive /ik spénsiv/ *adj.* **1. COSTING A LOT** costing a lot of money **2. CHARGING A LOT** charging high prices **3. VERY DISADVANTAGEOUS** involving serious losses or disadvantage to a particular person or group ○ *an expensive first quarter for the home team* —**ex·pen·sive·ly** *adv.* —**ex·pen·sive·ness** *n.*

ex·pe·ri·ence /ik spéeree əns/ *n.* **1. INVOLVEMENT IN SOMETHING OVER TIME** active involvement in an activity or exposure to events or people over a period of time, leading to an increase in knowledge and skill **2. KNOWLEDGE AND SKILL ACQUIRED** the knowledge of and skill in something gained through being involved in it or exposed to it over a period of time ○ *Paper qualifications are no substitute for real-life experience.* **3. SOMETHING THAT HAPPENS TO SOMEBODY** something that happens to somebody, or an event that somebody is involved in ○ *an experience that changed his life* **4. DIRECT PERSONAL AWARENESS OF SOMETHING** direct personal awareness of or contact with a particular thing ○ *Very few of us remember our first experience of pain.* **5. SUM TOTAL OF AN INDIVIDUAL'S EXPERIENCES** the sum total of the things that have happened to an individual and of his or her past thoughts and feelings ○ *Nothing quite like this has ever been done before, at least not in my experience.* **6.** PHILOS **KNOWLEDGE FROM OBSERVATION** knowledge acquired through the senses rather than through abstract reasoning ■ *vt.* **(-enced, -enc·ing, -enc·es) 1. HAVE EXPERIENCE OF SOMETHING** to be exposed to, involved in, or affected by something ○ *the most thrilling ride I've ever experienced* **2. FEEL SOMETHING** to feel a particular sensation or emotion ○ *You might experience a tingling sensation in your face.* [14thC. Via French from Latin *experientia*, from *experiri* "to try out" (source of English *experiment*). Ultimately from an Indo-European word that also produced English *fear* and *pirate*. Originally "testing."]

WORD KEY: CULTURAL NOTE

Songs of Experience, a collection of poems by the English writer William Blake (1794). Blake's *Songs of Innocence* (1789) described the world from the optimistic viewpoint of an innocent child. In this, its adult counterpart, he portrays a world of disease, poverty, and irredeemable corruption. The collection includes perhaps his best-known poem, "The Tyger.".

ex·pe·ri·enced /ik spéeree ənst/ *adj.* possessing knowledge and skill acquired through involvement in or exposure to something over a period of time ○ *an experienced pilot*

ex·pe·ri·en·tial /ik spèeree énshəl/ *adj.* derived from or relating to experience as opposed to other methods of acquiring knowledge [Mid-17thC. From EXPERIENCE; modeled on a word such as INFERENTIAL.] —**ex·pe·ri·en·tial·ly** *adv.*

ex·per·i·ment *n.* /ik spérrəmənt/ **1.** SCI **SCIENTIFIC TEST** a test, especially a scientific one, carried out in order to discover whether a theory is correct or what the results of a particular course of action would be ○ *experiments in parapsychology* **2. DOING SOMETHING NEW** an attempt to do something new, or a trying out of something to see what will happen ○ *We switched to decaffeinated coffee as an experiment.* **3. USING OF REPEATED TRIALS AND TESTS** the use of tests and trials in order to make discoveries ○ *The most efficient way of working was developed by experiment.* ■ *vi.* /ik spérrə mènt, ik spérrəmənt/ **(-ment·ed, -ment·ing, -ments) 1. TRY NEW THINGS** to try out new methods of doing or using things ○ *a reluctance to experiment with new ingredients* **2.** SCI **CARRY OUT A SCIENTIFIC TEST** to carry out a scientific test of a theory or process [14thC. Directly or via Old French from Latin *experimentum* "trial, test," from *experiri* (see EXPERIENCE).] —**ex·per·i·ment·er** *n.*

ex·per·i·men·tal /ik spèrrə mént'l/ *adj.* **1. RELATING TO SOMETHING NEW AND UNTRIED** employing ideas, methods, or materials that have not been tried before ○ *a new, experimental form of treatment* **2.** SCI **RELATING TO SCIENTIFIC EXPERIMENTS** relating to, involving, or based on scientific experiments **3. BASED ON EXPERIENCE AND EVIDENCE** based on experience and practical evidence rather than on ideas —**ex·per·i·men·tal·ly** *adv.*

ex·per·i·men·tal·ism /ik spèrrə mént'l ìzzəm/ *n.* the use of new techniques in artistic, literary, and musical works —**ex·per·i·men·tal·ist** *n.*

ex·per·i·men·tal psy·chol·o·gy *n.* the branch of psychology that studies the basic mechanisms of the mind, e.g., perception, thinking, learning, and memory, often using experiments with individuals in controlled situations

ex·per·i·men·ta·tion /ik spèrrəmən táysh'n/ *n.* **1. USING SCIENTIFIC TESTS** the conducting or use of scientific tests **2. USING NEW METHODS** the use of new and untried methods

ex·pert *n.* /ék spùrt/ **1. SKILLED OR KNOWLEDGEABLE PERSON** somebody with a great deal of knowledge about, or skill, training, or experience in, a particular field or activity ○ *a medical expert* **2.** SPORTS **HIGHEST-RANKED SHOOTER** the highest grade of marksmanship in shooting, or somebody who has achieved this grade ■ *adj.* /ék spùrt, ik-/ **1. SKILLFUL OR KNOWLEDGEABLE** having a great deal of knowledge about, or skill, training, or experience in, a particular field or activity ○ *an expert pizza maker* **2. GIVEN OR DONE BY AN EXPERT** given or done by somebody who is very knowledgeable or highly skilled, trained, or experienced [14thC. Via French from Latin *expertus*, the past participle of *experiri* (see EXPERIENCE). The underlying meaning is "somebody who knows from experience."] —**ex·pert·ly** *adv.* —**ex·pert·ness** *n.*

ex·per·tise /èkspər téez/ *n.* the skill, knowledge, or opinion of somebody who is an expert [Mid-19thC. From French, formed from *expert* (see EXPERT).]

ex·pert sys·tem *n.* a computer program that applies artificial-intelligence methods to the task of problem-solving by using detailed knowledge and attempting to simulate the reasoning processes of an expert

ex·pert wit·ness *n.* an expert called to answer questions on the stand in a court of law in order to provide specialized information relevant to the case being tried

ex·pi·ate /ékspee àyt/ **(-at·ed, -at·ing, -ates)** *vt.* to make amends, show remorse, or suffer punishment for having done something wrong [Late 16thC. From Latin *expiat-*, the past participle stem of *expiare*, literally "to atone completely," from *pius* (see PIOUS).] —**ex·pi·a·tor** *n.* —**ex·pi·a·to·ry** /ékspee ətàwree/ *adj.*

ex·pi·a·tion /èkspee áysh'n/ *n.* **1. ATONING OR SUFFERING PUNISHMENT FOR WRONGDOING** making amends, showing remorse, or suffering punishment for a wrongdoing **2. SOMETHING DONE OR GIVEN AS ATONEMENT** something done or given to make up for a wrongdoing

ex·pi·ra·tion /èkspə ráysh'n/ *n.* **1. ENDING** the act of coming to an end, or the fact of having come to an end **2.** PHYSIOL **EXHALATION** the act or process of breathing out (*technical*) **3. DYING** the act or fact of dying (*archaic*)

ex·pi·ra·tion date *n.* **1. DATE SOMETHING SHOULD BE USED BY** a date printed on the packaging of food and drug products that indicates the time after which they should not be used **2. DATE SOMETHING IS VALID TO** the date after which something such as a credit card or raincheck is no longer valid

ex·pi·ra·to·ry /ik spírə tàwree/ *adj.* relating to the process of breathing out, or used in breathing out

ex·pire /ik spír/ **(-pired, -pir·ing, -pires)** *vi.* **1. END OR BE NO LONGER VALID** to come to an end, or be no longer valid or in operation ○ *my visa has expired* **2.** PHYSIOL **BREATHE OUT** exhale (*technical*) **3. DIE** to die or release a last breath [14thC. Via French from Latin *exspirare*, literally "to breathe out," from *spirare* "to breathe" (source of English *spirit*). The underlying meaning is "to breathe your last, die."]

ex·pi·ry /ik spíree/ (*plural* **-ries**) *n.* **1. ENDING OR CEASING TO BE VALID** the fact of coming to an end and being no longer valid after a certain period of time ○ *two weeks before the date of expiry* **2. DEATH** death, especially the death of a person (*formal or literary*)

ex·pi·ry date *n. U.K.* = **expiration date**

ex·plain /ik spláyn/ **(-plained, -plain·ing, -plains)** *v.* **1.** *vti.* **GIVE DETAILS ABOUT SOMETHING** to give an account of something with enough clarity and detail to be understood by somebody else ○ *I explained to him that we had no option.* **2.** *vt.* **CLARIFY SOMETHING'S MEANING** to make the meaning of something clear to somebody ○ *can you explain this sentence to me?* **3.** *vti.* **GIVE REASON FOR SOMETHING** to give the reason for something, often as justification for something that has happened **4.** *vr.* **OFFER JUSTIFICATION** to give reasons to justify personal behavior or actions ○ *You'll have to explain yourself to the principal.* **5.** *vr.* **CLARIFY IDEAS** to express ideas or thoughts in a way that is easily understood ○ *I'm sorry, I'm not explaining myself very well.* [Early 16thC. From Latin *explanare*, literally "to flatten out, unfold," from *planus* "flat, clear" (see PLANE).] —**ex·plain·a·ble** *adj.* —**ex·plain·er** *n.*

explain away *vt.* to give excuses, reasons, or explanations for something in an attempt to show that it is less serious, important, or problematic than it seems

ex·pla·na·tion /èksplə náysh'n/ *n.* **1. STATEMENT EXPLAINING SOMETHING** a statement giving reasons for something or details of something ○ *an explanation of how the machine works* **2. GIVING OF DETAILS OR REASONS** the giving of details about something or reasons for something ○ *There's probably a perfectly simple explanation for all this.* **3. DISCUSSION TO END A MISUNDERSTANDING** a mutual discussion or clarification of something that removes misunderstandings or reconciles the parties [14thC. From the Latin stem *explanation-*, from *explanare* (see EXPLAIN).]

ex·plan·a·to·ry /ik splánnə tàwree/, **ex·plan·a·tive** /ik splánnətiv/ *adj.* giving reasons or details that explain something ○ *an explanatory leaflet is enclosed* [Early 17thC. From late Latin *explanatorius*, from Latin *explanare* (see EXPLAIN).] —**ex·plan·a·to·ri·ly** *adv.*

ex·plant /ek splánt/ *vt.* **(-plant·ed, -plant·ing, -plants) REMOVE TISSUE FROM AN ORGANISM FOR CULTURING** to remove living tissue from an organism and place it in a culture medium ■ *n.* **TISSUE REMOVED FOR CULTURING** tissue removed from an organism and placed in a culture medium [Early 20thC. Modeled on IMPLANT.] —**ex·plan·ta·tion** /èks plan táysh'n/ *n.*

ex·ple·tive /éksplətiv/ *n.* **1.** LING **SWEARWORD** an exclamation, especially a swearword **2.** GRAM **WORD WITH NO MEANING** a word that carries no meaning but has a grammatical function in a sentence. In the sentence "There are three books on the table," "there" is an expletive. **3.** POETRY **MEANINGLESS WORD IN A LINE OF POETRY** a word added to a line of verse in order to fill it out, usually for the sake of the meter. In the line from a folksong "When and that I was a little tiny lad," the words "and that" are expletives. ■ *adj.* GRAM, POETRY **USED AS AN EXPLETIVE** functioning as an expletive in a sentence or poem [Early 17thC. From late Latin *expletivus*, from *explet-*, the past participle stem of *explere*, literally "to fill up," from *plere* "to fill" (see COMPLETE).]

ex·ple·to·ry /éksplə tàwree/ *adj.* GRAM, POETRY = **expletive** [Late 17thC. Formed from Latin *explet-*, the past participle stem of *explere* (see EXPLETIVE).]

ex·pli·ca·ble /éksplikəb'l, ik splíkəb'l/ *adj.* able to be explained —**ex·pli·ca·bly** *adv.*

ex·pli·cate /ékspli kàyt/ **(-cat·ed, -cat·ing, -cates)** *vt.* **1. EXPLAIN SOMETHING** to explain something, especially a literary text, in a detailed and formal way **2. DEVELOP A THEORY** to explain and develop an idea or theory and show its implications [Early 16thC. From Latin *explicat-*, the past participle stem of *explicare*, literally "to unfold," from *plicare* "to fold" (see PLY[2]).] —**ex·pli·ca·tion** /èkspli káysh'n/ *n.* —**ex·pli·ca·tive** *adj.* —**ex·pli·ca·tive·ly** *adv.* —**ex·pli·ca·tor** /ékspli kàytər/ *n.*

ex·plic·it /ik splíssit/ *adj.* 1. CLEAR AND OBVIOUS expressing all details in a clear and obvious way, leaving no doubt as to the intended meaning ○ *explicit instructions* 2. DEFINITE definite and unqualified rather than implied or guessed at ○ *I didn't have explicit knowledge of what was going on, but I knew something was up.* 3. SEX portraying nudity or sexual activity in an open and direct way 4. MATH WITH ONLY INDEPENDENT VARIABLES used to describe a mathematical function that contains only variables whose value is independent of the value of the other variables in the function [Early 17thC. Directly or via French, from Latin *explicitus*, the past participle of *explicare* (see EXPLICATE).] —**ex·plic·it·ly** *adv.* —**ex·plic·it·ness** *n.*

ex·plode /ik splṓd/ (-**plod·ed**, -**plod·ing**, -**plodes**) *v.* 1. *vti.* BLOW UP OR BURST to blow up or burst with a sudden release of chemical or nuclear energy and a loud noise, or cause something to blow up or burst explosively 2. *vti.* BURST OR SHATTER to burst like a bomb or shatter into many pieces, or cause something to burst or shatter 3. *vi.* EXPRESS EMOTION to give vent to an emotion, suddenly or violently ○ *He exploded into roars of laughter.* 4. *vi.* INCREASE DRAMATICALLY to increase suddenly in extent or severity in an uncontrolled way ○ *The growth rate in home ownership exploded.* 5. *vi.* PRODUCE A VIVID DISPLAY to produce a vivid, often sudden display of light or color ○ *Her late paintings explode with intense reds and oranges.* 6. *vi.* COME SUDDENLY to appear or start as suddenly and forcefully as an explosion ○ *The band exploded onto the pop scene late last year.* 7. *vt.* DISPROVE A THEORY to show that a belief or theory is completely wrong [Mid-16thC. From Latin *explodere* "to drive off the stage by clapping," from *plaudere* "to clap" (source of English *applaud* and *plaudit*). The modern meaning developed from "drive off noisily."] —**ex·plod·er** *n.*

ex·plod·ed /ik splṓdəd/ *adj.* showing the parts of something as separate items in a diagram, but with their relative positions maintained ○ *an exploded diagram*

ex·ploit *vt.* /ik splóyt/ (-**ploit·ed**, -**ploit·ing**, -**ploits**) 1. TAKE ADVANTAGE OF SOMEBODY to take selfish or unfair advantage of a person or situation, usually for personal gain 2. USE SOMETHING FOR BENEFIT to use or develop something in order to gain a benefit ■ *n.* /ék splòyt, ik-/ NOTABLE ACT an interesting or daring action or achievement [Mid-16thC. Via Old French *esploit* "accomplishment," from Latin *explicitum*, the past participle of *explicare* "to unfold" (see EXPLICATE). The underlying meaning is "to make progress, be successful."] —**ex·ploit·a·ble** *adj.* —**ex·ploit·er** *n.*

ex·ploi·ta·tion /èk sploy táysh'n/ *n.* 1. UNFAIR TREATMENT OR USE unfair treatment or use of somebody or something, usually for personal gain 2. DEVELOPMENT OF SOMETHING FOR BENEFIT the use or development of something to produce a benefit

ex·ploit·ive /ik splóytiv/, **ex·ploit·a·tive** /-tətiv/ *adj.* making use of somebody or something unfairly —**ex·ploit·ive·ly** *adv.* —**ex·ploit·ive·ness** *n.*

ex·plo·ra·tion /èksplə ráysh'n/ *n.* 1. TRAVEL FOR DISCOVERY traveling to discover what a place is like or where it is ○ *polar exploration* 2. STUDY OR CONSIDERATION OF SOMETHING an investigation or the study of something such as data, or the consideration and testing of something such as possible courses of action 3. SEARCHING FOR NATURAL RESOURCES the testing of a number of places for natural resources, e.g., drilling or boring for samples that will be examined for possible mineral deposits 4. MED EXAMINATION FOR DIAGNOSIS the examination of a part of the body for the purpose of diagnosis

ex·plor·a·to·ry /ik splàwrə tàwree/ *adj.* involving exploration ○ *an exploratory mission* ○ *exploratory surgery*

ex·plore /ik splàwr/ (-**plored**, -**plor·ing**, -**plores**) *v.* 1. *vti.* TRAVEL FOR DISCOVERY to travel to a place to discover what it is like or what is there 2. *vti.* INVESTIGATE OR STUDY SOMETHING to make a careful investigation or study of something ○ *the committee is exploring all possible avenues of research* 3. *vti.* SEARCH A PLACE FOR NATURAL RESOURCES to make a search of an area for natural resources such as mineral deposits 4. *vt.* MED EXAMINE SOMETHING FOR DIAGNOSIS to examine a part of the body in order to make a diagnosis [Mid-16thC. Via French, from Latin *explorare* "to search out," from *plorare* "to cry out," perhaps as in hunting for game.]

ex·plor·er /ik splàwrər/ *n.* somebody who travels to places that were previously unknown or unnavigated

ex·plo·sion /ik splṓzh'n/ *n.* 1. SUDDEN NOISY RELEASE OF ENERGY the sudden loud release of energy and a rapidly expanding volume of gas that occurs when a bomb detonates or gas explodes 2. BURSTING OR SHATTERING OF SOMETHING a bursting with a loud noise, or a shattering of something into many pieces 3. SUDDEN BURST OF EMOTION a sudden release of intense feeling such as anger ○ *an explosion of rage* 4. DRAMATIC INCREASE a sudden and dramatic increase in the extent or severity of something, e.g., a population or an activity ○ *the explosion in e-mail subscriptions* 5. SUDDEN APPEARANCE the sudden and forceful appearance of somebody or something, or sudden and forceful beginning of something 6. INTENSE DISPLAY a vivid, often sudden display of light or color 7. PHON = **plosion** [Early 17thC. From the Latin stem *explosion-*, from *explos-*, the past participle stem of *explodere* (see EXPLODE).]

ex·plo·sive /ik splṓssiv, -splṓz-/ *adj.* 1. LIABLE TO EXPLODE capable of exploding, or likely to explode 2. OPERATED BY EXPLODING designed to explode, or operated by means of something that explodes 3. LIKELY TO GENERATE VIOLENT ANGER likely to cause or erupt suddenly into angry disagreement or violence ○ *an explosive temperament* 4. SUDDEN AND DRAMATIC happening or appearing suddenly and dramatically ○ *The company capitalized on the explosive increase in the popularity of their new game.* 5. PHON = **plosive** *n.* ■ *n.* 1. SOMETHING THAT EXPLODES any substance or device that suddenly produces a volume of rapidly expanding gas 2. PHON = **plosive** —**ex·plo·sive·ly** *adv.* —**ex·plo·sive·ness** *n.*

ex·po /ék spṑ/ *n.* a large exhibition or internationally sanctioned exposition [Mid-20thC. Shortening of EXPOSITION.]

ex·po·nent /ik spṓnənt, ék-/ *n.* 1. ADVOCATE somebody who supports a cause and speaks in favor of it 2. EXPLAINER OF SOMETHING somebody who explains or interprets something ○ *an exponent of Kant's philosophy* 3. PRACTITIONER OF AN ART OR SKILL a performer or practitioner of some art or skill, especially somebody who is regarded as an excellent example of how something should be done 4. MATH INDICATOR OF THE TIMES TO MULTIPLY A NUMBER a number or variable placed to the upper right of a number or mathematical expression that indicates the number of times the number or expression is to be multiplied by itself, as in 2^3, which equals 8 [Late 16thC. From Latin *exponent-*, the present participle stem of *exponere* (see EXPOUND).]

ex·po·nen·tial /èkspə nénshəl/ *adj.* 1. MATH RELATING TO EXPONENT used to describe a mathematical entity such as a curve, function, equation, or series that contains, is expressed as, or involves numbers or quantities raised to an exponent 2. MATH USING A BASE OF NATURAL LOGARITHMS used to describe a mathematical entity that involves the transcendental number *e*, the base of natural logarithms, raised to an exponent 3. RAPIDLY DEVELOPING rapidly becoming greater in size ○ *an exponential increase in sales* —**ex·po·nen·tial·ly** *adv.*

ex·po·nen·tial func·tion *n.* a mathematical expression with the formula e^x, in which *e* is the base of natural logarithms. Symbol **exp**

ex·po·nen·ti·a·tion /èkspə nenshee áysh'n/ *n.* the multiplication of a number or quantity by itself a given number of times, the number of times being the power to which the number or quantity is to be raised

ex·port *v.* /ik spáwrt/ (-**port·ed**, -**port·ing**, -**ports**) 1. *vti.* COMM SEND GOODS ABROAD to send goods for sale or exchange to other countries 2. *vt.* SOC SCI SPREAD A SOCIETY'S CULTURE TO ANOTHER SOCIETY to cause the spread of ideas, values, or a way of life from one society, culture, or nation to another 3. *vt.* COMPUT ALTER THE FORMAT OF COMPUTER DATA to convert data from a computer program into a form suitable for use by a different program ■ *n.* /ék spàwrt/ COMM 1. SELLING OF GOODS ABROAD the selling of goods to other countries 2. PRODUCT SOLD ABROAD a product sold and transported to another country [15thC. From Latin *exportare*, literally "to carry away," from *portare* (see PORT[1]).] —**ex·port·a·bil·i·ty** /ik spàwrtə bílləte e/ *n.* —**ex·port·a·ble** /ik spáwrtəb'l/ *adj.* —**ex·por·ta·tion** /èk spàwr táysh'n/ *n.* —**ex·port·er** /ik spáwrtər/ *n.*

Ex·port-Im·port Bank *n.* a U.S. bank established in 1934 to facilitate the exporting and importing of U.S. goods by extending long-terms loans to foreign buyers

ex·pose /ik spṓz/ (-**posed**, -**pos·ing**, -**pos·es**) *v.* 1. *vt.* LET SOMETHING BE SEEN to uncover something or turn it over in order for it to be seen or with the result that it can be seen ○ *expose the wound to the air* 2. *vt.* PUT SOMEBODY IN AN UNPROTECTED SITUATION to put somebody or something in a vulnerable or potentially dangerous situation ○ *financially exposed* 3. *vt.* MAKE SOMEBODY EXPERIENCE SOMETHING to cause somebody to have a personal and often enlightening experience of something 4. *vt.* REVEAL SOMEBODY'S WRONGDOINGS to reveal that somebody has done something wrong, especially by publishing or broadcasting the information 5. *vr.* REVEAL THE BODY INDECENTLY to uncover a part of the body, especially the genitals, in public in an indecent way 6. *vt.* PHOTOGRAPHY ALLOW LIGHT ONTO A FILM to allow light to fall on light-sensitive material such as photographic film 7. *vt.* ANTHROP LEAVE A BABY TO DIE OUTSIDE especially in earlier societies, to abandon a baby to die in the open air, e.g., because it was not healthy 8. *vt.* CHR SHOW SOMETHING TO BE REVERED to display something for religious veneration, e.g., the Eucharist in a Roman Catholic service [15thC. Via French (influenced by *poser* "to place") from Latin *exponere*, literally "to set out" (see EXPOUND).] —**ex·pos·al** *n.* —**ex·pos·er** *n.*

ex·po·sé /èks pō záy/ (*plural* -**sés**) *n.* 1. PUBLICATION OF WRONGDOING a book or article that reveals details of a scandal or crime 2. DECLARATION OF FACTS a formal and systematic statement giving facts about something [Early 19thC. From French, the past participle of *exposer* (see EXPOSE).]

ex·posed /ik spṓzd/ *adj.* 1. VISIBLE OR UNPROTECTED uncovered and therefore visible or without protection ○ *Cover any exposed areas of skin liberally with sunscreen.* 2. WITH NO SHELTER unprotected from wind and weather by shelter from trees or higher ground 3. UNPROTECTED FROM HARM vulnerable to danger or harm 4. MOUNTAINEERING CARRIED OUT ON OPEN ROCK FACE carried out on a high, sheer, and open rock face ○ *an exposed ascent* —**ex·posed·ness** *n.*

ex·po·si·tion /èkspə zísh'n/ *n.* 1. EXHIBITION OR FAIR a large exhibition, e.g., of industrial achievements, sometimes international in scope 2. DETAILED DESCRIPTION OR DISCUSSION a detailed description of a theory, problem, or proposal discussing the issues involved, or a commentary on a written text discussing its meaning and implications 3. ACT OF DESCRIBING OR DISCUSSING SOMETHING the act of describing and discussing a theory, problem, or proposal or commenting on a written text 4. MUSIC OPENING SECTION OF A PIECE OF MUSIC the opening section of a piece of music, especially of a sonata or fugue, in which the principal themes are introduced 5. DISPLAYING SOMETHING TO THE PUBLIC the act of showing or displaying something for veneration 6. LITERAT, THEATER REVELATION OF A STORY'S BACKGROUND the part of a literary or dramatic work in which the basic facts of setting and character are made known [14thC. Directly or via French, from the Latin stem *exposition-*, from *exposit-*, the past participle stem of *exponere* (see EXPOUND).] —**ex·pos·i·tive** /ik spózzitiv/ *adj.* —**ex·pos·i·tor** /ik spózzitər/ *n.* —**ex·pos·i·to·ry** /ik spózzi tàwree/ *adj.*

ex post fac·to /èks pōst fák tṑ/ *adj., adv.* applying to events that have already occurred as well as to subsequent events [Mid-17thC. From Latin *ex postfacto*, literally "from what is done afterward."]

ex·pos·tu·late /ik spóschə làyt/ (-**lat·ed**, -**lat·ing**, -**lates**) *vi.* to express disagreement or disapproval, or attempt to dissuade somebody from doing something [Late 16thC. From Latin *expostulat-*, the past participle stem of *expostulare*, literally "to demand from," from *postulare* (see POSTULATE).] —**ex·pos·tu·la·tion** /ik spòschə láysh'n/ *n.* —**ex·pos·tu·la·tor** /ik spóschə làytər/ *n.* —**ex·pos·tu·la·to·ry** /ik spóschələ tàwree/ *adj.*

WORD KEY: SYNONYMS

See Synonyms at ***object***.

ex·po·sure /ik spṓzhər/ *n.* 1. CONTACT WITH OR EXPERIENCE OF SOMETHING the experience of coming into contact with some environmental condition or social influence that has an effect, either harmful or beneficial 2. MED HARMFUL EFFECTS OF WEATHER the harmful effects of cold or other extreme weather conditions 3. BROADCAST, PRESS PUBLICITY reporting of events by the broadcast or print media 4. REVELATION OF A SCANDAL

OR IDENTITY the revelation of a scandal or of somebody's secrets or private information **5.** PHOTOGRAPHY **TIME AND INTENSITY OF LIGHT** an amount of light permitted to fall on light-sensitive material such as film or paper coated with emulsion **6.** PHOTOGRAPHY **TAKING OF A PHOTOGRAPH** the act or process of taking a photograph **7.** PHOTOGRAPHY **FILM OR PLATE EXPOSED FOR PHOTOGRAPH** a section of film or a photographic plate exposed to light in taking a photograph **8.** BUILDING **POSITION OF A ROOM OR BUILDING** the direction something faces or the way it is sited relative to sunlight or wind direction ○ *This room has a southern exposure.* **9.** FIN **RISK OF FINANCIAL LOSS** the state of being at risk of financial loss or the amount of possible financial loss involved **10.** MOUNTAINEERING **DEGREE EXPOSED TO THE WEATHER** the extent to which a rock face is exposed to the weather **11.** ANTHROP **LEAVING OF A BABY TO DIE OUTDOORS** the former practice in some societies of leaving a baby in the open to die, e.g., because it was not healthy **12.** GEOL **ROCKY OUTCROPPING** the outcropping of bare rock in a landscape, enabling mapping of the underlying geology

ex·po·sure me·ter *n.* a device for measuring the intensity of light for photography, often giving the value as a combination of shutter speed and lens aperture

ex·pound /ik spównd/ (**-pound·ed, -pound·ing, -pounds**) *vti.* to give a detailed description and explanation of a theory or viewpoint or an explanation of the meaning and implications of a written text [13thC. Via Old French *espondre*, from Latin *exponere* "to explain," literally "to set forth," from *ponere* "to place" (see POSITION).] —**ex·pound·er** *n.*

ex·press /ik spréss/ *v.* (**-pressed, -press·ing, -press·es**) **1.** *vt.* **SAY SOMETHING** to state thoughts or feelings in words ○ *I'd like to express my gratitude to everyone* **2.** *vt.* **SHOW MEANING SYMBOLICALLY** to convey meaning by gesture, behavior, representation in art or drama, or in some other symbolic way **3.** *vr.* **REVEAL THOUGHTS** to make thoughts and feelings known to others ○ *able to express herself through her music* **4.** *vt.* **REPRESENT SOMETHING AS A SYMBOL** to use a symbol, figure, or formula to represent something such as a quantity in a different way ○ *Express the fractions as decimal numbers.* **5.** *vt.* **SQUEEZE SOMETHING OUT** to force a liquid out of something by squeezing or pressing ○ *to express juice from lemons and limes* **6.** *vt.* MAIL **SEND SOMETHING BY SPECIAL FAST DELIVERY** to send a package or message using a special rapid-delivery service **7.** *vt.* GENETICS **PRODUCE AN INHERITED CHARACTERISTIC** to produce an observable inherited characteristic (*refers to genes*) ○ *Some genes are only expressed in adults.* ■ *adj.* **1.** TRANSP, MAIL **DONE OR TRAVELING VERY QUICKLY** traveling, moving, or delivered quickly and directly to the destination ○ *Take the express train.* **2.** COMM **OF BRIEF TRANSACTIONS** relating to purchases or other transactions that can be completed quickly and easily because, e.g., only one item or cash is involved **3. EXPLICIT** stated in a clear, unambiguous way ○ *it was his express wish* **4. SPECIFIC** definitely, and usually exclusively, intended or specified ○ *formed for the express purpose of making a profit* ■ *adv.* MAIL, TRANSP **BY EXPRESS DELIVERY OR TRANSPORTATION** by a special high-speed delivery service or an express train, bus, or similar mode of transportation ■ *n.* **1.** TRANSP **FAST TRAIN OR BUS** a fast train or bus that travels to its destination directly, making few or no stops on the way **2.** MAIL **FAST DELIVERY SERVICE** a special fast delivery service or the organization providing it [14thC. Ultimately from medieval Latin *expressare*, literally "to press out" (verb) and Latin *expressus* "clearly evident" (adjective), both from, ultimately, Latin *exprimere*, literally "to press out," from *premere* (see PRESS).] —**ex·press·er** *n.* —**ex·press·i·ble** *adj.*

ex·pres·sion /ik sprésh'n/ *n.* **1. LOOK ON SOMEBODY'S FACE** a look on somebody's face, conveying a thought or feeling ○ *She listened with a puzzled expression.* **2.** LANG **WORD OR PHRASE** a word or group of words that communicates an idea **3. CONVEYING OF THOUGHTS OR FEELINGS** the communication of thoughts or feelings, e.g., directly to another person or through a work of art ○ *a heart-rending expression of sorrow* **4. WAY OF COMMUNICATING SOMETHING** something done or given as a means of communicating a feeling or thought to somebody else **5. INFLECTION IN THE VOICE** somebody's intonation or tone of voice **6.** MUSIC **INTERPRETIVE ELEMENT OF MUSIC** the interpretive element of music, including tempo, dynamics, articulation, and phrasing, by which a player or singer draws out its emotional content, or its emotion stirs the feelings **7.** MATH **MATHEMATICAL REPRESENTATION** any combination of constants, operators, and variables representing numbers or quantities, e.g., (5 + x) **8. EXTRACTION OF LIQUID** the pressing out of a liquid from a substance using pressure **9.** GENETICS **EFFECT OR ACTION OF A GENE** the effect or action produced by a particular gene —**ex·pres·sion·al** *adj.*

ex·pres·sion·ism /ik sprésh'n ìzzəm/ *n.* **1.** PAINTING **ART MOVEMENT CONCENTRATING ON EXPRESSING EMOTION** an artistic movement that flourished in Germany between 1905 and 1925 whose adherents sought to represent feelings and moods rather than objective reality, often distorting color and form. The term is also used more loosely to apply to the work of Matisse and the Fauves. **2.** THEATER, LITERAT **LITERARY MOVEMENT PRESENTING STYLIZED REALITY** a literary movement of the early 20th century, especially in the theater, that represented external reality in a highly stylized and subjective manner, attempting to convey a psychological or spiritual reality rather than a record of actual events. Typical expressionists are the playwrights August Strindberg, Georg Wedekind, and Eugene O'Neill. —**ex·pres·sion·ist** *n., adj.* —**ex·pres·sion·is·tic** /ik sprèshə'n ístik/ *adj.* —**ex·pres·sion·is·ti·cal·ly** *adv.*

ex·pres·sion·less /ik sprésh'nləss/ *adj.* showing no emotion or interest by the tone of voice or by the look on the face —**ex·pres·sion·less·ly** *adv.*

ex·pres·sion mark (*plural* **ex·pres·sion mark·ings**) *n.* a symbol or written direction, often in Italian, that indicates the expression to be used in performing a piece of music

ex·pres·sive /ik spréssiv/ *adj.* **1. FULL OF EXPRESSION** expressing a great deal of feeling and meaning ○ *an expressive face* **2. CONVEYING SOMETHING** communicating a particular meaning ○ *a gesture expressive of the utmost contempt* **3. OF SPEAKING AND WRITING** relating to disorders involving the expression of ideas in speech and writing as opposed to the interpretation of what is heard or read —**ex·pres·sive·ly** *adv.*

ex·pres·siv·i·ty /èk spre sívvətee/ (*plural* **-ties**) *n.* **1. ABILITY TO EXPRESS FEELING OR THOUGHT** the ability or the extent to which somebody has the ability to communicate emotion or meaning **2.** GENETICS **GENE'S EFFECT ON AN ORGANISM** the extent to which a gene affects the observable characteristics (**phenotype**) of an organism

ex·press lane *n.* the lane on a multilane limited-access highway designated for fast-traveling vehicles, located on the left

ex·press·ly /ik spréssle/ *adv.* **1. SPECIFICALLY** having a deliberate and specific intention or purpose or somebody specific in mind **2. UNAMBIGUOUSLY** in a clear and unambiguous way ○ *He expressly rejected my offer.*

Ex·press Mail *tdmk.* a trademark for the overnight delivery service of the United States Postal Service

ex·pres·so *n.* = **espresso**

ex·press·way /ik spréss wày/ *n.* a limited-access road with several lanes in each direction, designed for fast direct travel especially through or round a city

ex·pro·pri·ate /ik sprópree àyt/ (**-at·ed, -at·ing, -ates**) *vti.* to take property or money from somebody, either legally for the public good or illegally by theft or fraud [Late 16thC. From medieval Latin *expropriat-*, the past participle stem of *expropriare*, literally "to take away and make your own," from Latin *proprius* "your own" (see PROPER).] —**ex·pro·pri·a·tion** /ik spròpree áysh'n/ *n.* —**ex·pro·pri·a·tor** /ik sprópree àytər/ *n.* —**ex·pro·pri·a·to·ry** /ik spróprее ə tàwree/ *adj.*

expt. *abbr.* experiment

exptl. *abbr.* experimental

ex·pul·sion /ik spúlshən/ *n.* **1. DISMISSAL FROM A PLACE OR MEMBERSHIP** the act of compelling somebody to give up membership in or leave an institution such as a school, political party, or club, usually as a punishment **2. FORCING SOMEBODY OR SOMETHING OUT** the forcing out of something or somebody from something ○ *expulsion of air from the lungs* [15thC. From the Latin stem *expulsion-*, from *expuls-*, the past participle stem of *expellere* (see EXPEL).] —**ex·pul·sive** *adj.*

ex·punge /ik spúnj/ (**-punged, -pung·ing, -pung·es**) *vt.* **1. GET RID OF SOMETHING COMPLETELY** to delete something unwanted from a written record, or blot out something unpleasant from the memory **2. DO AWAY WITH SOMETHING** to destroy or put an end to something [Early 17thC. From Latin *expungere*, literally "to prick out," from *pungere* "to mark with a point" (see PUNGENT); from the placing of points next to the text to be deleted.] —**ex·punc·tion** /ik spúngkshən/ *n.* —**ex·pung·er** /ik spúnjər/ *n.*

ex·pur·gate /ékspər gàyt/ (**-gat·ed, -gat·ing, -gates**) *vt.* to remove words or passages considered offensive or unsuitable from a book before publication [Late 17thC. From the Latin *expurgat-*, the past participle stem of *expurgare*, literally "to cleanse out," from *purgare* (see PURGE).] —**ex·pur·ga·tion** /èkspər gáysh'n/ *n.* —**ex·pur·ga·tor** /ékspər gàytər/ *n.* —**ex·pur·ga·to·ri·al** /ik spùrgə táwree əl/ *adj.* —**ex·pur·ga·to·ry** /ik spúrgə tàwree/ *adj.*

expy *abbr.* expressway

ex·qui·site /ik skwízzit, ékskwizit/ *adj.* **1. FINELY BEAUTIFUL** very beautiful and delicate or intricate ○ *exquisite workmanship* **2. EXCELLENT** perfect and delightful **3. SENSITIVE AND DISCRIMINATING** sensitive and capable of detecting subtle differences ○ *exquisite taste in dress* **4. INTENSE** felt with a sharp intensity ○ *exquisite pain* [Mid-16thC. From Latin *exquisitus*, the past participle of *exquirere*, literally "to seek out," from *quaerere* (see QUERY). The underlying meaning is "sought after, choice, perfect."] —**ex·qui·site·ly** *adv.* —**ex·qui·site·ness** *n.*

ex·sert /ik súrt/ *vt.* (**-sert·ed, -sert·ing, -serts**) BIOL **EXTEND SOMETHING OUT** to thrust out or project something ○ *A bee exserts its sting.* ■ *adj.* **ex·sert, ex·sert·ed** BIOL **PROJECTING** projecting beyond an enclosing or adjoining part ○ *an exsert stamen* [Early 19thC. From Latin *exsert-*, the past participle stem of *exserere* (see EXERT).] —**ex·ser·tion** *n.*

ext. *abbr.* **1.** extension **2.** exterior **3.** external **4.** PHARM extract

ex·tant /ékstənt, ek stánt/ *adj.* still in existence ○ *Three copies of the document are extant.* [Mid-16thC. From Latin *exstant-*, the present participle stem of *exstare*, "to exist," literally "to stand out," from *stare* "to stand" (see STATION).]

WORD KEY: SYNONYMS

See Synonyms at ***living***.

ex·tem·po·ra·ne·ous /ik stèmpə ráynee əss/, **ex·tem·po·rar·y** /ik stémpə ràiree/, **ex·tem·po·ral** /ik stémpərəl/ *adj.* **1. DONE UNREHEARSED** performed without any preparation **2. PREPARED BUT SAID WITHOUT NOTES** prepared in advance but delivered without notes **3. SPEAKING UNREHEARSED** speaking without preparation or notes **4. MAKESHIFT** done as a temporary measure [Mid-17thC. Formed from late Latin *extemporaneus*, from *ex tempore*, literally "out of the moment."] —**ex·tem·po·ra·ne·i·ty** /ik stèmpərə née ətee/ *n.* —**ex·tem·po·ra·ne·ous·ly** /-ráynee əsslee/ *adv.* —**ex·tem·po·ra·ne·ous·ness** /-əssnəss/ *n.*

ex·tem·po·re /ik stémpəree/ *adj., adv.* with little or no preparation [Mid-16thC. From Latin *ex tempore*, literally "out of the moment," from *tempor-*, the stem of *tempus* "time" (source of English *tempo* and *temporary*).]

ex·tem·po·rize /ik stémpə rìz/ (**-rized, -riz·ing, -riz·es**) *vti.* **1. PERFORM SOMETHING WITHOUT PREPARATION** to perform or speak without having made any preparation **2.** MUSIC **IMPROVISE MUSIC** to compose or perform a piece of music by improvising **3. HANDLE IN A MAKESHIFT WAY** to do or devise something in a makeshift fashion [Mid-17thC. Formed from EXTEMPORE.] —**ex·tem·po·ri·za·tion** /ik stèmpəri záysh'n/ *n.* —**ex·tem·po·riz·er** /ik stémpə rìzər/ *n.*

ex·tend /ik sténd/ (**-tend·ed, -tend·ing, -tends**) *v.* **1.** *vi.* **OCCUPY DISTANCE OR SPACE** to continue for a distance or occupy a space, often within a particular range ○ *the city center extends for another mile in both directions* **2.** *vi.* **CONTINUE FOR A TIME** to last or continue for a period of time, usually a particular one **3.** *vti.* **APPLY TO SOMEBODY OR SOMETHING** to affect or apply to somebody or something, or make something affect or apply ○ *the offer extends to new readers too* **4.** *vt.* **INCREASE SOMETHING'S SIZE** to make something larger or longer ○ *extend the driveway* **5.** *vt.* **INCREASE TIME SPAN** to increase the length of time something lasts or the length of time before something applies or ceases to apply **6.** *vt.* **INCREASE LIMITS** to broaden or expand the range, influence, or scope of something ○ *a vital research project that will extend our knowledge of the disease* **7.** *vt.* **INCREASE AN AMOUNT BY ADDING SOMETHING** to increase the amount of something by adding something else to it ○ *There's not much stew left, but we could always extend it by adding more potatoes and vegetables.* **8.** *vti.* **OPEN OUT INTO SPACE** to stretch out into space, or stretch something out **9.**

vt. **OFFER OR GIVE SOMETHING** to offer or provide something to somebody ○ *to extend the hand of friendship* **10.** *vt.* **MAKE AN EXTRA EFFORT TO DO SOMETHING** to work or make somebody or something work as hard as possible to achieve the best possible result ○ *They had to extend themselves to finish on time* **11.** *vt.* FIN **CALCULATE THE LINE TOTAL ON INVOICE** to calculate the total on the line of an invoice by multiplying quantity by price [14thC. From Latin *extendere*, literally "to stretch out," from *tendere* (see TENDER²).] —**ex·tend·a·bil·i·ty** /ik stèndə bíllətee/ *n.* —**ex·tend·a·ble** /ik sténdəb'l/ *adj.*

WORD KEY: SYNONYMS

See Synonyms at ***increase***.

ex·tend·ed /ik sténdəd/ *adj.* **1. LENGTHIER THAN USUAL** lasting longer than is normal or typical **2. MADE LONGER OR LARGER** stretched or pulled out, lengthened, enlarged, or expanded **3. HAVING A WIDER RANGE** having wider influence, effect, or application **4.** CLOTHES **EXTRA LARGE OR SMALL** larger or smaller than those in the usual range ○ *We carry suits in extended sizes – both talls and bigs.* —**ex·tend·ed·ly** /ik sténdədlee/ *adv.*

Ex·tend·ed Bi·na·ry Cod·ed Dec·i·mal In·ter·change Code *n.* COMPUT full form of **EBCDIC**

ex·tend·ed fam·i·ly *n.* the family as a unit embracing parents and children together with grandparents, aunts, uncles, cousins, and sometimes more distant relatives. ◊ **nuclear family**

ex·tend·ed-play *adj.* **1. RECORDING FOR A LONGER TIME** used to describe a videotape format that can record four or six hours of material on a two-hour tape (*not hyphenated after a verb*) **2. WITH A LONGER RECORDING ON EACH SIDE** used to describe a vinyl record of the same size as a single but with two tracks on each side rather than one (*not hyphenated when used after a verb*)

ex·tend·er /ik sténdər/ *n.* **1.** INDUST **SUBSTANCE ADDED TO MODIFY A PRODUCT** a substance that is added to a product to dilute it, add body to it, or modify it in other ways **2.** PRINTING **PROJECTING PART OF LETTER** the part of a lower-case letter such as "p" or "h" that projects above or below the body of the letter

ex·ten·si·ble /ik sténsəb'l/, **ex·ten·sile** /ik sténsəl/ *adj.* having the capability of being extended [Early 17thC. Directly or via French, from medieval Latin *extensibilis*.] —**ex·ten·si·bil·i·ty** /ik stènsə bíllətee/ *n.* —**ex·ten·si·bly** /ik sténsəblee/ *adv.*

ex·ten·sim·e·ter *n.* = **extensometer**

ex·ten·sion /ik sténshən/ *n.* **1.** BUILDING **ADDITION TO A BUILDING** a room or area added to an existing building ○ *We're having an extension built onto the kitchen.* **2. ADDITIONAL PIECE** a piece that has been or can be added, or that can be pulled out, to enlarge or lengthen something **3.** UTIL **ADDITIONAL TELEPHONE LINE** an additional telephone line or telephone connected to the main line in a building or organization, often having its own number **4.** UTIL **TELEPHONE NUMBER OF AN EXTENSION** the number used to contact a telephone extension within a building or organization **5.** ELEC = **extension cord 6. ADDITIONAL PERIOD OF TIME** an additional period of time allowed for completion of work or payment of a debt ○ *You'll never finish that essay on time; why don't you ask for an extension?* **7. EXTENDING OR BEING EXTENDED** the act or process of increasing the size, scope, range, or application of something, or the fact of being increased in size, scope, range, or application **8. RANGE** the range or sphere over which something extends **9.** EDUC **OFF-CAMPUS UNIVERSITY TEACHING PROGRAM** courses or facilities provided by a college or university for people who are unable to attend classes on the campus or during scheduled class periods **10.** MED = **traction 11.** ANAT **STRAIGHTENING OF A LIMB** the stretching out of a limb after it has been bent, or the position attained by a limb after stretching it **12.** LOGIC **BROADER SENSE OF AN EXPRESSION** the broad range of meaning of an expression, as opposed to its precise meaning. The extension of the term "man" is the set comprising all men, whereas the meaning of the word "man" is "an adult male human being." **13.** MATH **SET INCLUDING TWO SIMILAR SETS** a mathematical set that includes as subsets all the members of a given set and of another similar set **14.** COMPUT = **file extension** ■ **ex·ten·sions** *npl.* HAIR **EXTRA HAIR ATTACHED TO YOUR OWN HAIR** lengths of real or synthetic hair attached to the hair to create longer hairstyle [Early 16thC. From the late Latin stem *extension-*, from Latin *extens-*, the past participle stem of *extendere* (see EXTEND).] —**ex·ten·sion·al** *adj.* —**ex·ten·sion·al·ly** *adv.*

ex·ten·sion a·gent *n.* somebody employed by federal and state governments to provide information to the public about agriculture, health, and home economics

ex·ten·sion cord *n.* a length of electrical cord with a plug at one end and a socket at the other, used to connect an appliance when the electrical supply is some distance away

ex·ten·sive /ik sténsiv/ *adj.* **1. VAST** covering a large area ○ *a hotel set in extensive grounds* **2. BROAD IN SCOPE** great in extent, range, or application ○ *extensive research into a subject* **3. LARGE IN AMOUNT** great in amount or number **4.** AGRIC **USING LOW TECHNOLOGICAL INPUT** relating to a farming practice in which a large area of land is cultivated using little labor and expense, resulting in a relatively small crop. ◊ **intensive** [Early 17thC. Directly or via French from late Latin *extensivus*, from the Latin *extens-*, the past participle stem of *extendere* (see EXTEND).] —**ex·ten·sive·ly** *adv.* —**ex·ten·sive·ness** *n.*

ex·ten·som·e·ter /èk sten sómmətər/, **ex·ten·sim·e·ter** /-símmətər/ *n.* a device for measuring small changes of length in a sample, especially those caused by stress or thermal expansion in a metal [Late 19thC. Coined from Latin *extens-*, the past participle stem of *extendere* (see EXTEND) + -METER.]

ex·ten·sor /ik sténsər/ *n.* a muscle that straightens or extends a part of the body such as an arm or leg [Early 18thC. From modern Latin, formed from Latin *extens-*, the past participle stem of *extendere* (see EXTEND).]

ex·tent /ik stént/ *n.* **1. RANGE OR SCOPE** the area or range covered or affected by something ○ *a technique for determining the location and extent of brain damage* **2. DEGREE** the degree to which something applies ○ *To what extent should we allow newspaper reporters into people's private lives?* **3. REGION** an area of land or water ○ *a vast extent of fertile land* **4.** LAW **WRIT ALLOWING SEIZURE OF PROPERTY** a writ that authorizes somebody to take possession of the property of somebody who owes him or her money [Late 16thC. Via Anglo-Norman *extente* "valuation of land" from, ultimately, Latin *extendere* (see EXTEND).]

ex·ten·u·ate /ik sténnyoo àyt/ (**-at·ed, -at·ing, -ates**) *vt.* to make a mistake or wrongdoing seem less serious than it first appeared, or to provide a mitigating excuse for something that has happened [Early 16thC. From Latin *extenuat-*, the past participle stem of *extenuare*, literally "to thin out," from *tenuis* "thin" (see TENUOUS).] —**ex·ten·u·at·ing** *adj.* —**ex·ten·u·at·ing·ly** *adv.* —**ex·ten·u·a·tion** /ik stènnyoo áysh'n/ *n.* —**ex·ten·u·a·tive** /-àytəv/ *adj.* —**ex·ten·u·a·tor** /-aytər/ *n.* —**ex·ten·u·a·to·ry** /-sténnyooə tàwree/ *adj.*

ex·te·ri·or /ik steéree ər/ *adj.* **1. ON THE OUTSIDE** on or for the outside of something ○ *added protection for the exterior walls of the building* **2. COMING FROM OUTSIDE** coming from outside or beyond something or somebody ○ *There must be some exterior cause for this.* **3.** CINEMA **OUTDOOR** taken out of doors or depicting an outdoor scene ○ *an exterior shot* ■ *n.* **1. OUTSIDE** the outside surface, appearance, or coating of something **2. OUTWARD APPEARANCE** somebody's outward appearance as distinct from his or her inner thoughts **3.** CINEMA, ARTS **SCENE OUTSIDE** an outdoor scene, especially as represented in the visual arts [Early 16thC. From Latin, literally "more outward," from *exter* (see EXTERNAL).] —**ex·te·ri·or·i·ty** /ik steèree áwrətee/ *n.*

ex·te·ri·or an·gle *n.* **1. ANGLE ON THE OUTSIDE OF A POLYGON** an angle on the outside of a polygon, formed between a side and an extension of an adjacent side **2. ANGLE FORMED BY A LINE CROSSING LINES** any of the four angles formed on the outside of a pair of lines that are crossed by a third line

ex·te·ri·or·ize /ik steéree ə rīz/ (**-ized, -iz·ing, -iz·es**) *vt.* **1.** = **externalize 2.** SURG **REMOVE AN INTERNAL ORGAN** to remove an internal organ from the body, e.g., to perform surgery on it —**ex·te·ri·or·i·za·tion** /ik steèree əri záysh'n/ *n.*

ex·ter·mi·nate /ik stúrmə nàyt/ (**-nat·ed, -nat·ing, -nates**) *vt.* to kill or destroy somebody or something completely ○ *a species nearly exterminated by hunting* [Late 16thC. From Latin *exterminat-*, the past participle stem of *exterminare*, literally "to drive beyond the boundaries," from *termen* "boundary," a variant of *terminus* (see TERMINUS).] —**ex·ter·mi·na·tion** /ik stùrmə náysh'n/ *n.* —**ex·ter·mi·na·to·ry** /ik stúrmənə tàwree/ *adj.*

ex·ter·mi·na·tor /ik stúrmə nàytər/ *n.* **1. SOMEBODY PAID TO KILL VERMIN** somebody who kills insects, rodents, and other vermin **2. EXTERMINATING PERSON OR THING** somebody or something that kills or destroys somebody or something else [14thC]

ex·tern /ék stùrn/, **ex·terne** *n.* a nonresident doctor or other staff member attached to a hospital [Early 17thC. Via French *externe* from Latin *externus* (see EXTERNAL).] —**ex·tern·ship** *n.*

ex·ter·nal /ik stúrn'l/ *adj.* **1. OUTSIDE** situated on, happening on, or coming from the outside ○ *The sudden collapse of the empire should not be laid to external forces alone.* **2. FOR USE ON THE OUTSIDE** suitable or designed for use only on the outside or surface of something, especially the body **3. OUTSIDE SOMETHING'S SCOPE** existing outside the body or mind, or the limits of something ○ *What real evidence is there for the existence of the external world?* **4. VISIBLE FROM OUTWARD APPEARANCE** conveyed by somebody's or something's outward appearance, as opposed to what is inside or underneath **5. OUTSIDE AN ORGANIZATION** relating to, forming, or from a separate or independent organization ○ *The investigation must be carried out by members of an external body.* **6.** POL **RELATING TO FOREIGN COUNTRIES** dealing with or involving relations with foreign countries ■ *n.* **SOMETHING'S EXTERIOR** the outer surface of something ■ **ex·ter·nals** *npl.* **1. OUTWARD APPEARANCES** the outward appearance of somebody or something, especially when it is not considered to be a true indication of the person's or thing's real nature **2. SURROUNDINGS** somebody or something's circumstances or environment [Late 16thC. Partly formed from French *externe* and partly from Latin *externus*, both ultimately from *exter* "outward, on the outside."] —**ex·ter·nal·ly** *adv.*

ex·ter·nal-com·bus·tion en·gine *n.* an engine that converts into power heat generated from fuel consumed outside the engine. A steam engine is a type of external-combustion engine. ◊ **internal-combustion engine**

ex·ter·nal de·gree *n.* a university degree awarded to a candidate who, instead of taking traditional courses to fulfill degree requirements, works and studies off campus

ex·ter·nal ear *n.* the outside part of the ear, consisting of the auricle and auditory canal

ex·ter·nal·ism /ik stúrn'l ìzzəm/ *n.* **1. EXCESSIVE CONCERN ABOUT OUTWARD APPEARANCES** excessive concern about outward forms and appearances, especially in religious matters **2.** PHILOSOPHY **VIEW THAT THOUGHTS DEPEND ON EXTERNALS** the view that the content of thoughts depends at least partly on relationships with objects outside the mind —**ex·ter·nal·ist** *n.*

ex·ter·nal·i·ty /èkstər nállətee/ (*plural* **-ties**) *n.* **1. QUALITY OF BEING EXTERNAL** the fact or quality of being external **2. SOMETHING OUTSIDE OR EXTERNAL** an outward form or appearance, or anything that is outside or external to somebody or something **3.** ECON **CONSEQUENCE OF PRODUCTION IGNORED IN PRICING** a factor, e.g., environmental damage, that results from the way something is produced but is not taken into account in establishing the market price of the goods or materials concerned

ex·ter·nal·ize /ik stúrn'l īz/ (**-ized, -iz·ing, -iz·es**) *vt.* **1. GIVE OUTWARD EXPRESSION TO SOMETHING** to express ideas or feelings in some visible or perceptible way in order to communicate them to others **2. PERCEIVE SOMETHING AS EXTERNAL** to attribute something to causes in the outside world **3.** PSYCHOL **ATTRIBUTE FEELINGS TO OUTSIDE CAUSES** to attribute emotions or inner conflicts to outside causes, sources, or surroundings —**ex·ter·nal·i·za·tion** /ik stùrn'li záysh'n/ *n.*

ex·ter·nal res·pi·ra·tion *n.* the exchange of gases between an organism's respiratory system, e.g., the lungs in vertebrates, and the outside environment

ex·terne *n.* = **extern**

ex·ter·o·cep·tor /ékstərō séptər/ *n.* a body part or sensory organ such as the eye, ear, or any of the nerve endings in the skin that is able to receive outside stimuli [Early 20thC. Coined from Latin *exter* (see EXTERNAL) + RECEPTOR.] —**ex·ter·o·cep·tive** *adj.*

ex·ter·ri·to·ri·al *adj.* = **extraterritorial**

ex·tinct /ik stíngkt/ *adj.* **1.** BIOL **HAVING NO LIVING MEMBERS** having no members of the species or family in existence, as is the case with many organisms known only from fossils **2. NO LONGER IN EXISTENCE** having died out or ceased to exist ○ *relics of extinct* *and forgotten civilizations* **3.** GEOL **NO LONGER ERUPTING** no longer active or likely to erupt ○ *an extinct volcano* **4.** SOC SCI, LAW **NOT NOW VALID** no longer valid or practiced ○ *This custom has for many years been almost extinct.* **5.** **EXTINGUISHED** extinguished, quenched, or no longer burning [15thC. From Latin *exstinctus*, the past participle of *exstinguere* (see EXTINGUISH).]

WORD KEY: SYNONYMS

See Synonyms at ***dead***.

ex·tinc·tion /ik stíngkshən/ *n.* **1.** BIOL **THE FACT OF BECOMING EXTINCT** the death or ceasing to exist of all members of a species or family of organisms **2.** **OBSOLESCENCE** the process or fact of disappearing completely from use ○ *"Dominant languages and dialects spread widely, and lead to the gradual extinction of other tongues."* (Charles Darwin, *The Descent of Man*; 1871) **3.** GEOL **PROCESS OF BECOMING INACTIVE** the permanent ceasing of eruptions in a volcano **4.** SOC SCI, LAW **BEING NO LONGER USED** the state of no longer being valid or practiced, or the process of ceasing to be valid or practiced **5.** **DESTRUCTION** the destruction or killing off of somebody or something ○ *the extinction of self and ego through meditation* **6.** PHYS, ASTRON **LOWERING OF RADIATION INTENSITY** reduction of radiation intensity because of absorption or scattering as it passes through matter. This effect is observed in the reduction in the intensity of electromagnetic radiation reaching Earth from celestial bodies because of the interference of interstellar gas and dust. **7.** PSYCHOL **REDUCTION IN RESPONSE** the decreasing or dying out of a behavioral response created by conditioning because of lack of reinforcement —**ex·tinc·tive** *adj.*

ex·tin·guish /ik stíng gwish/ (**-guished, -guish·ing, -guish·es**) *vt.* **1.** **PUT OUT A FIRE OR LIGHT** to put out something that is burning or giving off light ○ *The lamps along the terrace had not been extinguished.* **2.** **END SOMETHING** to take away or bring to an end something such as a hope, feeling, custom, or practice ○ *As the days went by, hope for more survivors was extinguished.* **3.** **DESTROY SOMEBODY OR SOMETHING** to kill or destroy somebody or something completely ○ *They came with a large army in order to be certain of extinguishing the enemy by force of numbers.* **4.** **OUTSHINE** to outshine or eclipse something or somebody by having greater brilliance ○ *Beauty that extinguishes all others by comparison.* **5.** LAW **PAY DEBT** to pay off a debt **6.** LAW **MAKE SOMETHING INVALID** to make something no longer valid or applicable **7.** PSYCHOL **DECREASE RESPONSE** to cause a decrease in a conditioned response through lack of reinforcement [Early 16thC. Formed from Latin *exstinguere*, literally "to quench completely," from *stinguere* "to quench, prick" (source of English *distinguish* and *instinct*).] —**ex·tin·guish·a·ble** *adj.* —**ex·tin·guish·ment** *n.*

ex·tin·guish·er /ik stíng gwishər/ *n.* **1.** = **fire extinguisher** **2.** **SOMETHING THAT ENDS OR REMOVES SOMETHING** somebody or something that puts an end to something else or eliminates its effects

ex·tir·pate /ékstər pàyt/ (**-pat·ed, -pat·ing, -pates**) *vt.* **1.** **COMPLETELY REMOVE SOMETHING UNDESIRABLE** to completely get rid of, kill off, or destroy something or somebody considered undesirable (*formal*) **2.** SURG **REMOVE BY SURGERY** to remove something surgically [Mid-16thC. From Latin *exstirpat-*, the past participle stem of *exstirpare*, literally "to root out," from *stirps* "stem, root," of unknown origin.] —**ex·tir·pa·tion** /èkstər páysh'n/ *n.* —**ex·tir·pa·tive** /ékstər pàytiv/ *adj.* —**ex·tir·pa·tor** /-pàytər/ *n.*

extn. *abbr.* extension

ex·tol /ik stṓl/ (**-tolled, -tol·ling, -tols**), **ex·toll** (**-tolled, -toll·ing, -tolls**) *vt.* to praise somebody or something with great enthusiasm and admiration [Early 16thC. From Latin *extollere*, literally "to raise up," from *tollere* "to raise." Ultimately from an Indo-European word that also produced English *elate* and *toll*.] —**ex·tol·ler** *n.* —**ex·tol·ment** *n.*

ex·tort /ik stáwrt/ (**-tort·ed, -tort·ing, -torts**) *vt.* to obtain something such as money or information, from somebody by using force, threats, or other unacceptable methods ○ *I wouldn't want to speculate about what means were used to extort the confessions.* [15thC. From Latin *extort-*, the past participle stem of *extorquere*, literally "to twist out," from *torquere* "to twist" (see TORQUE[1]).] —**ex·tort·er** *n.* —**ex·tor·tive** *adj.*

ex·tor·tion /ik stáwrsh'n/ *n.* **1.** LAW **OBTAINING SOMETHING BY ILLEGAL THREATS** the crime of obtaining something such as money from somebody using illegal methods of persuasion **2.** **EXCESSIVE CHARGING** the charging of an excessive amount of money for something (*informal*) **3.** **GETTING SOMETHING BY FORCE** the acquiring of anything through the use of force or threats —**ex·tor·tion·ar·y** *adj.* —**ex·tor·tion·er** *n.* —**ex·tor·tion·ist** *n.*

ex·tor·tion·ate /ik stáwrsh'nət/ *adj.* **1.** **EXCESSIVE** highly excessive, especially in price **2.** **INVOLVING EXTORTION** involving or using extortion —**ex·tor·tion·ate·ly** *adv.*

ex·tra /ékstrə/ *adj.* **1.** **MORE THAN USUAL** added to, or over and above, the usual, original, or necessary amount ○ *Take extra precautions when traveling in bad weather.* **2.** **MORE AND BETTER** greater in degree and of better quality than is normal **3.** **CHARGED FOR IN ADDITION** charged for in addition to the basic cost ○ *You get one free drink with the meal; further drinks are extra.* ■ *adv.* **EXCEPTIONALLY** to a greater extent than is usual or expected ○ *Be extra careful at that crossing.* ■ *pron.* **MORE** more than the usual amount or price ○ *The hotel charges extra for cable television.* ■ *n.* **1.** **SOMETHING ADDITIONAL** something additional or unexpected ○ *The books at the end of the list are optional extras that you can read if you have time.* **2.** **SOMETHING CHARGED IN ADDITION** something for which an additional charge is made, or the additional charge itself ○ *This is the guaranteed full price and there are no hidden extras.* **3.** CINEMA **NONSPEAKING MOVIE ACTOR** somebody employed in a minor, usually nonspeaking, part in a movie, e.g., in a crowd scene **4.** PRESS **SPECIAL EDITION OF A NEWSPAPER** a special edition of a newspaper or magazine, often reporting later news or concentrating on a particular subject ○ *a sports extra* **5.** something of exceptionally high quality [Mid-17thC. Origin uncertain: probably shortening of EXTRAORDINARY, whose prefix comes from Latin *extra* (see EXTRA-).]

extra-, **extro-** *prefix.* beyond or outside something ○ *extraterrestrial* ○ *extracurricular* [From Latin *extra* "outside, beyond," from *exter* "outer" (source of English *exterior*)]

ex·tra-base hit *n.* BASEBALL a hit that allows the batter to take more than one base, that is, a double, triple, or home run

ex·tra·cel·lu·lar /èkstrə séllyələr/ *adj.* situated or happening outside a cell or cells —**ex·tra·cel·lu·lar·ly** *adv.*

ex·tra·chro·mo·so·mal /èkstrə krōmə sṓm'l/ *adj.* used to describe an inheritance of characteristics that is controlled by factors that are not carried on chromosomes

ex·tra·cor·po·re·al /èkstrə kawr páwree əl/ *adj.* situated or happening outside the body —**ex·tra·cor·po·re·al·ly** *adv.*

ex·tra·cra·ni·al /èkstrə kráynee əl/ *adj.* situated or happening outside the skull

ex·tract *vt.* /ik strákt/ (**-tract·ed, -tract·ing, -tracts**) **1.** **PULL SOMETHING OUT** to pull something out, often using force ○ *have a tooth extracted* **2.** **OBTAIN SOMETHING FROM SOURCE** to obtain something from a source, usually by separating it out from other material ○ *a few snippets of information that I managed to extract from the conversation* **3.** **GET SOMETHING BY FORCE** to obtain something from somebody who is unwilling to give it, often by using force or threats ○ *After a lengthy interrogation the police extracted a confession from him.* **4.** **COPY SOMETHING OUT FROM SOMETHING** to copy or remove a passage from a text ○ *This passage is extracted from the author's memoirs.* **5.** **DERIVE PLEASURE FROM** to obtain pleasure or enjoyment from something **6.** CHEM, INDUST **TAKE SOMETHING OUT OF COMPOUND** to obtain a substance from a compound, in solid, liquid, or gas form, by using an industrial or chemical process **7.** MATH **FIND THE ROOT OF NUMBER** to calculate the value of the root, e.g., the square root or cube root, of a number ■ *n.* /ék stràkt/ **1.** **PASSAGE** a passage taken from a publication, movie, or play ○ *The novelist read a few extracts from her forthcoming book.* **2.** CHEM, INDUST **SOMETHING SEPARATED FROM A COMPOUND** a substance obtained from a compound by an industrial or chemical process ○ *mineral extracts* **3.** **PURIFIED SUBSTANCE** a concentrated or purified substance obtained by first using a solvent to dissolve this substance when present in a mixture and then evaporating the solvent ○ *vanilla extract* **4.** **CONCENTRATED SOLUTION** a preparation, usually in alcohol, containing the pharmaceutically active components of a natural product such as a plant [15thC. From Latin *extract-*, the past participle stem of *extrahere* "to pull out," from *trahere* "to pull."] —**ex·tract·a·ble** *adj.*

ex·trac·tion /ik strákshən/ *n.* **1.** **TAKING OUT OF SOMETHING** the process of extracting something or of being extracted, or a thing that has been extracted **2.** **REMOVAL OF A TOOTH** the removal of a tooth or teeth **3.** **SEPARATION OF SUBSTANCES** the separation of a substance from a mixture by dissolving one or more of the components in a solvent

ex·trac·tive /ik stráktiv/ *adj.* **1.** **EXTRACTABLE** capable of being extracted **2.** **USED IN AN EXTRACTION PROCESS** used in the process of extraction **3.** **OBTAINED BY EXTRACTION** obtained as a result of extraction ■ *n.* **1.** **SOMETHING EXTRACTABLE** something that can be extracted **2.** CHEM **PART OF A CHEMICAL EXTRACT** the insoluble part of a chemical extract —**ex·trac·tive·ly** *adv.*

ex·tract·or /ik stráktər/ *n.* **1.** **SOMEBODY OR SOMETHING THAT EXTRACTS** somebody who or something that extracts something **2.** **DEVICE FOR TAKING OUT LIQUID** a device that removes a liquid from a solid, e.g., the juice out of a fruit **3.** ARMS **PART OF GUN** a part of a firearm that removes spent cartridges from the chamber

ex·tra·cur·ric·u·lar /èkstrə kə ríkyələr/ *adj.* **1.** EDUC **OUTSIDE CURRICULUM** done or happening outside the normal curriculum of a school, college, or university **2.** **OUTSIDE NORMAL DUTIES** not part of the normal duties of a job or profession **3.** **WITH SOMEBODY OTHER THAN A PARTNER** involving somebody other than a spouse or partner (*informal*)

ex·tra·dit·a·ble /èkstrə dītəb'l/ *adj.* **1.** **WITHIN THE TERMS OF AN EXTRADITION AGREEMENT** used to describe a crime for which somebody may be extradited, or a person who has committed such a crime **2.** **ABLE TO BE EXTRADITED** able to be extradited

ex·tra·dite /ékstrə dīt/ (**-dit·ed, -dit·ing, -dites**) *vt.* to return somebody accused of a crime by a different legal authority to that authority for trial or punishment [Mid-19thC. Back-formation from EXTRADITION, probably on the model of *expedition* and *expedite*.]

ex·tra·di·tion /èkstrə dísh'n/ *n.* the handing over by a government of somebody accused of a crime in a different country for trial or punishment there [Mid-19thC. From French, formed from Latin *ex-* "out" + the stem *tradition-* "deliverance" (see TRADITION).]

ex·tra·dos /èkstrə dòss, ékstrə dṑss/ (*plural* **-dos** /ékstrə dṑz/ *or* **-dos·es**) *n.* the outer curve of an arch [Late 18thC. From French, formed from Latin *extra* "outside" + French *dos* "back."]

ex·tra·ga·lac·tic /èkstrə gə láktik/ *adj.* existing, originating, or happening outside the Milky Way, the galaxy that contains the solar system

ex·tra·ju·di·cial /èkstrə joo dísh'l/ *adj.* **1.** **OUTSIDE NORMAL LEGAL PROCEEDINGS** happening or originating outside the normal course of legal proceedings **2.** **OUTSIDE A COURT'S JURISDICTION** outside the jurisdiction of a court —**ex·tra·ju·di·cial·ly** *adv.*

ex·tra·le·gal /èkstrə leég'l/ *adj.* not permitted by or subject to the law —**ex·tra·le·gal·ly** *adv.*

ex·tra·lim·i·tal /èkstrə límmit'l/ *adj.* used to describe a species or group of organisms found outside a given area, e.g., a population of bears outside a national park

ex·tra·mar·i·tal /èkstrə mérrit'l/ *adj.* involving sexual relations with somebody other than a marriage partner

ex·tra·mun·dane /èkstrə mun dáyn, -mún dàyn/ *adj.* not belonging to the physical world [Mid-17thC. From late Latin *extramundanus*, from *extra mundum* "outside the world or universe."]

ex·tra·mu·ral /èkstrə myóorəl/ *adj.* **1.** EDUC **OUTSIDE USUAL STUDY COURSES** outside or additional to the usual courses of study at a university, college, or other educational institution, though usually connected with them **2.** **OUTSIDE WALLS** outside the walls or boundaries of something, e.g., a castle, town, or organization [Mid-19thC. Formed from Latin *extra muros* "outside the walls."]

ex·tra·ne·ous /ik stráynee əss/ *adj.* **1.** **NOT RELEVANT** not relevant or applicable **2.** **NOT ESSENTIAL** not essential or important **3.** **COMING FROM OUTSIDE** existing or coming from outside [Mid-17thC. Formed from Latin *extraneus* "foreign, strange" (source of English *strange*), from *extra* "outside" (see EXTRA-).] —**ex·tra·ne·ous·ly** *adv.* —**ex·tra·ne·ous·ness** *n.*

ex·tra·net /ékstrə nèt/ *n.* an extension of the intranet of a company or organization. An extranet gives authorized outsiders, e.g., customers, suppliers, or business partners, controlled access to parts of the intranet.

ex·tra·nu·cle·ar /ékstrə nóoklee ər/ *adj.* **1.** BIOL **OUTSIDE CELL NUCLEUS** existing in or affecting parts of a cell outside the nucleus **2.** PHYS **OUTSIDE ATOM NUCLEUS** existing, happening, or originating outside the nucleus of an atom

ex·tra·or·di·naire /èkstrə awrd'n áir, ik stràwd'n-/ *adj.* excellent or outstanding ○ *a piano player extraordinaire* [Mid-20thC. Via French from Latin *extraordinarius* (see EXTRAORDINARY).]

ex·traor·di·nar·y /ik stráwrd'n èrree, èkstrə áwrd'n-/ *adj.* **1.** **VERY UNUSUAL** very unusual and deserving attention and comment because of being wonderful, excellent, strange, or shocking ○ *For a ten-year-old, her mathematical abilities are quite extraordinary.* **2.** **ADDITIONAL** additional and having a special purpose ○ *an extraordinary general meeting* **3.** **EMPLOYED FOR SPECIAL PURPOSE** employed for a special purpose or to do additional work ○ *ambassador extraordinary* **4.** **ADDITIONAL AND GREATER** additional to and going beyond the scope of something in ordinary or established use ○ *Extraordinary measures are necessary in these highly unusual circumstances.* [15thC. From Latin *extraordinarius*, from *extra ordinem* "out of order, exceptionally."] —**ex·traor·di·nar·i·ly** *adv.* —**ex·traor·di·nar·i·ness** *n.*

ex·tra point *n.* FOOTBALL a point scored by kicking the field goal awarded after a touchdown

ex·trap·o·late /ik stráppə làyt/ (**-lat·ed, -lat·ing, -lates**) *v.* **1.** *vti.* **INFER** to use known facts as the starting point from which to draw inferences or draw conclusions about something unknown ○ *If we extrapolate from the data, we can come up with a reasonable prediction.* **2.** *vt.* MATH **ESTIMATE A VALUE** to estimate a value that falls outside a range of known values, e.g., by extending a curve on a graph [Mid-19thC. Coined from EXTRA- + INTERPOLATE. In early use, it denoted the insertion of intermediate terms in a mathematical series.] —**ex·trap·o·la·tion** /ik stràppə láysh'n/ *n.* —**ex·trap·o·la·tive** /-làytəvər/ *adj.* —**ex·trap·o·la·tor** /ik stráppə làytər/ *n.*

ex·tra·sen·so·ry /èkstrə sénsəree/ *adj.* relating to or involving powers of perception other than the normal five senses

ex·tra·sen·so·ry per·cep·tion *n.* the apparent ability of some people to become aware of things by means other than the normal senses, e.g., through clairvoyance or telepathy

ex·tra·ter·res·tri·al /èkstrə tə réstree əl/ *adj.* **OUTSIDE THE EARTH** existing or coming from somewhere outside the Earth and its atmosphere ■ *n.* **ALIEN** a supposed living creature that comes from outside the Earth

ex·tra·ter·ri·to·ri·al /èkstrə terri táwree əl/, **ex·ter·ri·to·ri·al** /èks terri tawree əl/ *adj.* **1.** POL **OUTSIDE TERRITORIAL BOUNDARY** situated or coming from outside a country's territorial boundary **2.** INTERNAT LAW **RELATING TO EXTRATERRITORIALITY** relating to or involving exemption from the legal jurisdiction of a country of residence —**ex·tra·ter·ri·to·ri·al·ly** *adv.*

ex·tra·ter·ri·to·ri·al·i·ty /èkstrə terrə tawree állətee/ *n.* exemption from the legal jurisdiction of a country of residence, as granted e.g., to foreign diplomats

ex·tra time *n. U.K.* = **overtime** *n.* 3

ex·tra·u·ter·ine /èkstrə yóotərin, -rìn/ *adj.* occurring or situated outside the womb ○ *extrauterine pregnancy*

ex·trav·a·gance /ik strávvəgəns/, **ex·trav·a·gan·cy** /-gənsee/ (*plural* **-cies**) *n.* **1.** **WASTEFUL SPENDING** excessive or wasteful spending of money ○ *condemned to poverty by their father's extravagance* **2.** **EXPENSIVE THING** something that is expensive or wasteful ○ *A car like that is an extravagance in today's economic climate.* **3.** **EXTRAVAGANT NATURE** the exaggerated, excessive, or extremely flamboyant nature of something, e.g., a wild unreasonableness in somebody's speech or behavior

ex·trav·a·gant /ik strávvəgənt/ *adj.* **1.** **SPENDING TOO MUCH** characterized by spending excessively or wastefully ○ *I think it's extravagant to spend $500 on a shirt.* **2.** **BEYOND WHAT IS REASONABLE** exaggerated or unreasonable ○ *The scientific community has dismissed these claims as wildly extravagant.* **3.** **UNREASONABLY HIGH IN PRICE** unreasonably high in price or cost ○ *can't afford their extravagant asking price* **4.** **FLAMBOYANT** profusely or exaggeratedly decorated, decorative, or showy ○ *hair dyed pink and done in the most extravagant coiffure* **5.** **ABUNDANT** extremely abundant ○ *The fire produced extravagant quantities of smoke and very little heat.* [14thC. From medieval Latin, from Latin *extra* "outside" + *vagari* "to wander" (source of English *vagabond* and *vagrant*). An early meaning is "uncodified," referring to papal decrees.] —**ex·trav·a·gant·ly** *adv.* —**ex·trav·a·gant·ness** *n.*

ex·trav·a·gan·za /ik stràvvə gánzə/ *n.* **1.** **LAVISH ENTERTAINMENT** a lavish and spectacular entertainment **2.** **SPECTACULAR DISPLAY** any spectacular or fanciful display [Mid-18thC. From Italian *estravaganza* "peculiar behavior," from *estravagante* "extravagant." The English spelling with "x" was influenced by *extravagance*.]

ex·trav·a·sate /ik strávvə sàyt/ (**-sat·ed, -sat·ing, -sates**) *vti.* to leak, or cause blood or other fluid to leak, from a vessel into the surrounding tissue, following injury, burns, or inflammation [Mid-17thC. Coined from EXTRA- + Latin *vas* "vessel" + -ATE.] —**ex·trav·a·sa·tion** /ik stràvvə sáysh'n/ *n.*

ex·tra·vas·cu·lar /èkstrə váskyələr/ *adj.* not contained in the body's blood vessels or lymph vessels

ex·tra·ve·hic·u·lar ac·tiv·i·ty /èkstrə vi hìkyələr-/ *n.* an activity undertaken by an astronaut outside the spacecraft during a mission, e.g., a repair to the craft, or an experiment on the surface of the Moon

ex·tra·ver·sion *n.* = **extroversion**

ex·tra·vert *n., adj.* = **extrovert**

ex·tra vir·gin ol·ive oil *n.* the highest quality of olive oil, made from the first cold pressing of ripe olives

ex·treme /ik stréem/ *adj.* **1.** **HIGH IN DEGREE OR INTENSITY** highest in intensity or degree ○ *will withstand extreme pressure* **2.** **NOT REASONABLE** going far beyond what is reasonable or normal ○ *an extreme reaction* **3.** **FARTHEST OUT** farthest out, especially from the center ○ *They live in the extreme north of the country.* **4.** **SEVERE** very strict or severe ○ *A government must take extreme measures during wartime.* **5.** LEISURE **SENSATION-SEEKING** denoting an activity in which participants actively seek out dangerous or even life-threatening experiences ■ *n.* **1.** **FURTHEST LIMIT** the furthest limit or highest degree of something ○ *the extreme of bad taste* **2.** **END OF SCALE** something or somebody that represents either of the two ends of a scale or range, e.g., the highest or lowest degree of something, or a quality and its polar opposite ○ *Beween these two extremes there must be a middle way.* **3.** MATH **FIRST OR LAST TERM** the first or last term in a mathematical proportion or series ■ **ex·tremes** *npl.* **DRASTIC MEASURES** drastic or unreasonable measures ○ *The authorities have been driven to extremes by the widespread popular unrest.* [15thC. Via French *extrême* from Latin *extremus* "farthest, last," literally "most out," a superlative form of *ex* "out."] —**ex·treme·ness** *n.*

ex·treme·ly /ik stréemlee/ *adv.* very, or to a very high degree ○ *She plays the violin extremely well.*

ex·treme·ly high fre·quen·cy *n.* a radio frequency in the range between 30,000 and 300,000 megahertz

ex·treme·ly low fre·quen·cy *n.* a radio frequency below 30 hertz

ex·treme unc·tion *n.* the sacrament of anointing the sick in the Roman Catholic Church (*dated*)

ex·trem·ist /ik stréemist/ *n.* **SOMEBODY WITH EXTREME OPINIONS** somebody who holds extreme or radical political or religious beliefs ■ *adj.* **BEYOND THE MODERATE** involving, typical of, or motivated by extreme opinions, especially in politics or religion

ex·trem·i·ty /ik strémmətee/ *n.* (*plural* **-ties**) **1.** **FARTHEST POINT** a point that is the farthest out, especially from the center ○ *the southernmost extremity of the continent* **2.** **HIGHEST DEGREE** the highest degree or greatest intensity of something ○ *in the extremity of her grief* **3.** **DANGER** a situation of great danger or distress ○ *They prayed for help in their extremity.* **4.** **LIMB** a limb of a person or animal, or the part of a limb that is farthest from the body, especially somebody's hand or foot ○ *Frostbite attacks the extremities first.* **5.** **STATE OF BEING EXTREME** the state of being extreme, especially extremely dangerous or severe ○ *You don't seem to understand the extremity of the situation.* ■ **ex·trem·i·ties** *npl.* **DRASTIC MEASURES** drastic or unreasonable measures (*formal*) ○ *There was no need for such extremities.*

ex·tri·cate /ékstri kàyt/ (**-cat·ed, -cat·ing, -cates**) *vt.* to release somebody or something with difficulty from a physical constraint or an unpleasant or complicated situation ○ *It took an hour to extricate the vehicle from the mud.* ○ *He hoped their intervention might extricate him from his embarrassing predicament.* [Early 17thC. From Latin *extricat-*, past participle stem of *extricare*, literally "to remove from perplexities," from *tricae* (plural) "perplexities."] —**ex·tri·ca·ble** /ékstrikəb'l, ik stríkəb'l/ *adj.* —**ex·tri·ca·tion** /èkstri káysh'n/ *n.*

ex·trin·sic /ik strínsik, -zik/ *adj.* **1.** **INESSENTIAL** that is not an essential part of something ○ *It's a good point, but extrinsic to the argument.* **2.** **COMING FROM OUTSIDE** coming or operating from outside something ○ *the importance of extrinsic influences on a nation's literature* [Mid-16thC. From late Latin *extrinsecus* "outer," from Latin *exter* "external" + adverb-forming ending *-im* + *secus* "alongside of."] —**ex·trin·si·cal·ly** *adv.*

extro- *prefix.* = **extra-** [Alteration of EXTRA-, on the model of its antonym *intro-*]

ex·trorse /ék stràwrs, ik stráwrs/ *adj.* facing or turning outward or away from a center [Mid-19thC. From late Latin *extrorsus* "in an outward direction," from Latin *extra* "outside" + *versus* "toward," past participle of *vertere* "to turn."]

ex·tro·ver·sion /ékstrə vùrzh'n, èkstrə vúrzh'n/, **ex·tra·ver·sion** *n.* **1.** PSYCHOL **INTEREST IN THINGS OUTSIDE THE SELF** interest in and involvement with people and things outside the self **2.** MED **TURNING INSIDE OUT** the turning inside out of an organ or other body part, especially the womb [Mid-17thC. Coined from EXTRO- + the Latin stem *version* "turning," from *vertere* "to turn."] —**ex·tro·ver·sive** *adj.* —**ex·tro·ver·sive·ly** *adv.*

ex·tro·vert /ékstrə vùrt/, **ex·tra·vert** *n.* **1.** **OUTGOING PERSON** somebody who is sociable, self-confident, and uninhibited when with other people **2.** **SOMEBODY WITH INTEREST OUTSIDE SELF** somebody who goes beyond self-interest and is involved with other people and things ■ *adj.* **1.** **OUTGOING** typical of a sociable or outgoing person **2.** **TYPICAL OF SOMEBODY WITH OUTWARD INTEREST** characteristic of somebody who is interested in and involved with people and things outside the self [Early 20thC. Coined from EXTRO- + Latin *vertere* "to turn."] —**ex·tro·vert·ed** *adj.*

ex·trude /ik stróod/ (**-trud·ed, -trud·ing, -trudes**) *v.* **1.** *vt.* **FORCE SOMETHING OUT** to force or squeeze something out **2.** *vt.* INDUST **MAKE BY FORCING THROUGH MOLD** to make something by forcing a semisoft material such as plastic or molten metal through a specially shaped mold or nozzle **3.** *vi.* = **protrude** [Mid-16thC. From Latin *extrudere* , literally "to thrust out," from *trudere* "to thrust."]

ex·tru·sion /ik stróozh'n/ *n.* **1.** INDUST **SOMETHING FORMED BY BEING EXTRUDED** something formed by forcing semisoft material through a specially shaped mold or nozzle **2.** INDUST **PROCESS OF EXTRUDING** the process or an instance of making something by forcing semisoft material through a specially shaped mold or nozzle **3.** GEOL **IGNEOUS ROCK** an igneous rock formed by the emission of molten material (**magma**) through cracks in the earth's surface where it forms a lava flow **4.** GEOL **MOVEMENT OF MOLTEN ROCK** the movement of molten material (**magma**) from a volcano or through cracks in the earth's surface to form solidified igneous rock [Mid-16thC. From the medieval Latin stem *extrusion-*, from Latin *extrudere* (see EXTRUDE).]

ex·tru·sive /ik stróossiv/ *adj.* used to describe rock formed from molten material (**magma**) that has flowed out of cracks in the Earth's surface

ex·u·ber·ant /ig zóobərənt/ *adj.* **1.** **FULL OF ENTHUSIASM** full of happy high spirits and vitality **2.** **ABUNDANT** growing in great abundance or profusion **3.** **LAVISH** lavish or elaborate, often to the point of being excessive [15thC. Via French from Latin *exuberant-*, the present participle stem of *exuberare* "to be very fruitful," from *uberare* "to be fruitful," from *uber* "fertile."] —**ex·u·ber·ance** *n.* —**ex·u·ber·ant·ly** *adv.*

ex·u·date /éksyə dàyt/ *n.* a substance such as sweat or a cellular waste product that is exuded from a cell or organ

ex·u·da·tion /èksyə dáysh'n/ *n.* **1.** **RELEASE THROUGH PORES OR CUT** the release of a substance through pores or a surface cut, e.g., the release of sweat from the body or resin from a tree **2.** = **exudate** —**ex·u·da·tive** /éksyə dàytiv/ *adj.*

ex·ude /ig zóod/ (**-ud·ed, -ud·ing, -udes**) *v.* **1.** *vt.* **SHOW A PARTICULAR QUALITY CLEARLY** to communicate a particular quality or feeling in abundance and very clearly, usually through general behavior and body language ○ *a voice that exuded confidence* **2.** *vti.* **RELEASE SLOWLY** to release something such as a liquid or an odor slowly from a gland, pore, membrane, or cut, or ooze out slowly [Late 16thC. From Latin *exudare*, *exsudare*, literally "to ooze out like sweat," from *sudare* "to sweat."]

ex·ult /ig zúlt/ (**-ult·ed, -ult·ing, -ults**) *vi.* **1. BE VERY HAPPY** to be extremely happy or joyful about something ○ *exulted in his newfound freedom* **2. BE TRIUMPHANT** to be very happy or triumphant about something unpleasant that happens to somebody else ○ *The victors exulted over their enemies' annihilation.* [Late 16thC. Via French *exulter* from Latin *exsultare*, literally "to keep leaping up," from *exsalire*, literally "to leap out," from *salire* "to leap" (source of English *salient*).] —**ex·ul·tance** *n.* —**ex·ult·ing·ly** *adv.*

ex·ul·tant /ig zúlt'nt/ *adj.* extremely happy, joyful, or triumphant ○ *an exultant roar from the crowd* —**ex·ul·tant·ly** *adv.*

ex·ul·ta·tion /èksəl táysh'n, ègzəl-/ *n.* a feeling or the expression of great happiness, triumph, or joy ○ *jumping in exultation at the news*

ex·urb /ék sùrb/ *n.* a prosperous residential area outside a city, beyond the suburbs [Mid-20thC. Back-formation from EXURBAN (from Latin *ex* "out of" + urbs "city") on the model of *suburb*.] —**ex·ur·ban** /ek súrbən/ *adj.*

ex·ur·ban·ite /ek súrbə nìt, eg zúrbə-/ *n.* somebody who lives in a prosperous residential area outside a city, beyond the suburbs

ex·ur·bi·a /ek súrbee ə, eg zú-/ *n.* the prosperous residential area beyond the suburbs of a city [Mid-20thC. Coined from EX- + *-urbia*, on the model of *suburbia*.]

ex·u·vi·ae /ig zóovee èe/ *npl.* a skin, shell, or other body covering cast off by an animal [Mid-17thC. From Latin, "things cast off," formed from *exuere* "to divest oneself of."] —**ex·u·vi·al** *adj.*

-ey *suffix.* = **-y** [Variant]

ey·as /í əss/ *n.* a young hawk or falcon, especially one bred for falconry [15thC. Alteration of obsolete *nias*, from French *niais* "bird taken from the nest," from Latin *nidus* "nest." Initial "n" lost by misdivision ("an ias"), as in ADDER.]

Jan van Eyck: Portrait engraving by Joachim von Sandrart

Eyck /īk/, **Jan van** (1390?–1441) Flemish painter. He painted in vivid oil colors in a naturalistic style and is regarded as the greatest Flemish artist of the 15th century.

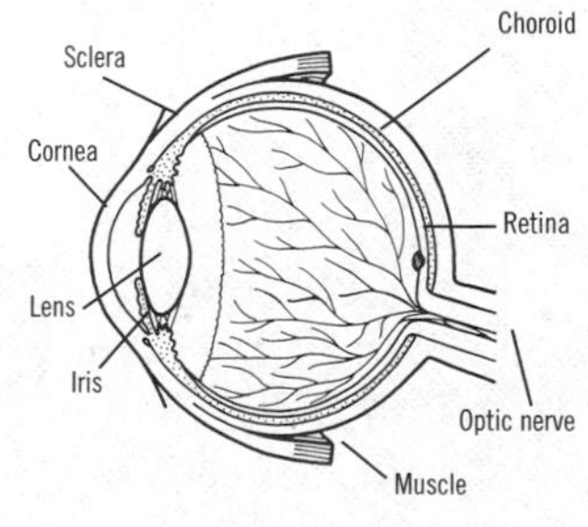

Cross section of a human eye

eye /ī/ *n.* **1.** ANAT **ORGAN OF VISION** the organ of sight or light sensitivity in vertebrates, usually occurring in pairs. The eye is an approximately spherical organ with light-sensitive rod and cone cells in the retina, which is responsible for converting light into impulses that are transmitted to the brain for interpretation. **2. VISIBLE AREA OF THE EYE** the externally visible part of the eye, and the area of face around it, including the orbit, eyelid, and eyelashes **3. POWER OF SIGHT** the ability to see (*often used in the plural*) ○ *If my eyes get any worse I'll have to wear glasses.* **4. ATTENTION** somebody's attention or gaze ○ *He took his eye off the prisoners at the wrong moment.* **5. EXPRESSION** a look, or the facial expression of a person looking ○ *She looked me over with a cold eye.* **6. APPRECIATION OF SOMETHING** an ability to recognize and appreciate something ○ *He's got a good eye for spotting a talent.* **7. OPINION** a point of view or way of thinking ○ *He can do no wrong in her eyes.* **8.** ZOOL = **eyespot** *n.* 2 **9.** BOT **NEW SHOOT ON POTATO** a dark round patch on a potato tuber, from which a new shoot grows **10.** SEW **HOLE IN NEEDLE** a hole in the top of a needle for passing a thread through **11.** CLOTHES **LOOP PART OF FASTENER** a loop, usually metal, into which a small hook fits, used as a means of fastening two parts of a garment together **12.** METEOROL **CENTER OF A STORM** a calm area at the center of a storm **13.** FOOD **TASTY CUT OF MEAT** a choice central cut of meat ■ *vt.* (**eyed, eye·ing** *or* **ey·ing, eyes**) **LOOK AT SOMETHING** to look at something or somebody inquisitively ○ *She quickly eyed the building up and down.* [Old English *eage*. Ultimately from an Indo-European base that produced the word for "eye" in all Indo-European languages and is also the ancestor of English *atrocious*, *inoculate*, and *window*.] ◇ **close** *or* **shut your eyes to something** to ignore or overlook something obvious ◇ **cry your eyes out** to cry bitterly ◇ **give somebody the eye** to look at somebody in a way that signals sexual interest ◇ **keep your eye on the ball 1.** to watch somebody or something closely **2.** to take care of somebody or something, especially for a short time ◇ **turn a blind eye to something** to pretend not to be aware of something ◇ **with an eye to something** having something as a purpose or objective ◇ **with your eyes (wide) open** fully aware of all that is involved in what you are doing

eye·ball /í bàwl/ *n.* **ROUND MASS OF THE EYE** the round mass of the eye within its bony socket ■ *vt.* (**-balled, -ball·ing, -balls**) **STARE AT SOMEBODY** to stare at somebody or something intently (*informal*)

eye bank *n.* a place where human corneas taken from people who have recently died are stored for use in corneal transplants

eye·bolt /í bòlt/ *n.* a bolt with an eye or ring at the end instead of the usual head, used for pulling, lifting, or fastening

eye·bright /í brìt/ *n.* a plant of the snapdragon family with small white and purple flowers, used in the past for treating eye diseases. Genus: *Euphrasia.*

eye·brow /í bròw/ *n.* **1. HAIR ABOVE EYE SOCKET** the arched line of hair above each eye socket **2. BONY RIDGE ABOVE THE EYE** the upper bony ridge of the eye socket. Technical name **supraorbital ridge**

eye·brow pen·cil *n.* a soft cosmetic pencil used to darken the eyebrows

eye can·dy *n.* something visually pleasing but intellectually undemanding (*slang*)

eye-catch·er *n.* somebody who or something that tends to attract people's attention

eye-catch·ing *adj.* that attracts people's attention easily

eye chart *n.* a sheet printed with different sizes of letters, used to test eyesight

eye con·tact *n.* the act of looking directly into the eyes of another person

eye·cup /í kùp/ *n.* a small container that fits over the eye and is used to apply liquid medical treatment to it or cleanse it

eyed /īd/ *adj.* having an eye or eyes, usually of a specified kind (*usually used in combination*) ○ *a sharp-eyed observer* ○ *a wide-eyed stare*

eye di·a·lect *n.* the use of spellings that represent the sound of dialectal or nonstandard forms, e.g., "enuff" or "wimmin"

eye drops *npl.* liquid medication for the eyes, usually applied with a dropper

eye·ful /í fòol/ *n.* **1. GOOD LOOK** a long steady look at something or somebody (*informal*) ○ *Get an eyeful of this!* **2. SOMEBODY OR SOMETHING BEAUTIFUL** somebody who or something that is very beautiful, especially an attractive woman (*slang offensive*)

eye·glass /í glàss/ *n.* **1. SINGLE LENS FOR CORRECTING VISION** a single framed lens for correcting defective vision, e.g., a monocle **2.** = **eyecup 3.** = **eyepiece** ■ **eye·glass·es** *npl.* **GLASSES** a pair of glasses (*formal*)

eye·hole /í hòl/ *n.* = **peephole** *n.* 2

eye·hook /í hòok/ *n.* a hook that is fixed to a ring at the end of a rope or chain

eye·lash /í làsh/ *n.* **1. HAIR AT EDGE OF EYELID** any of the short hairs that grow out of the edge of the eyelid **2. ROW OF HAIRS EDGING EYELID** the row of short hairs that grow out of the edge of the eyelid

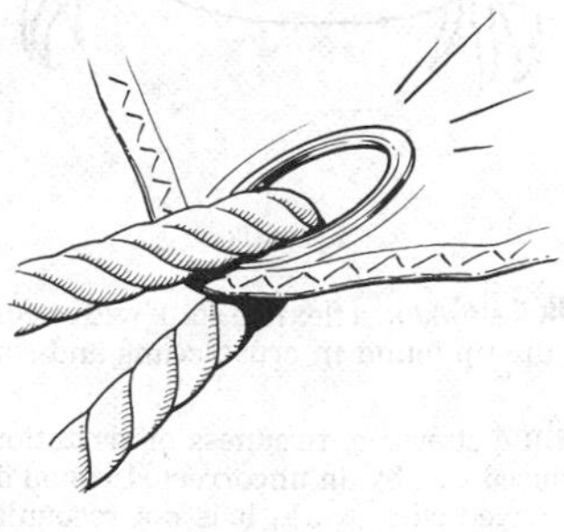

Eyelet

eye·let /ílət/ *n.* **1. HOLE FOR CORD** a small hole, especially in fabric, for a lace or cord to be passed through **2. METAL REINFORCEMENT FOR EYELET** a small ring of metal or stiff fabric fixed to an eyelet to strengthen its edges **3. ORNAMENTED HOLE IN EMBROIDERY** a small hole with ornamental stitched edges in embroidered fabric **4.** = **peephole** *n.* 2 [14thC. Anglicization of Old French *oillet*, literally "little eye," from *oil* "eye," from Latin *oculus*.]

eye·lid /í lìd/ *n.* a protective fold of skin and muscle that can be closed to cover the front of the eyeball ◇ **not bat an eyelid** to show no sign of emotion, especially of surprise or distress

eye·lift /í lìft/ *n.* a surgical operation to improve the appearance of the area around the eyes, e.g. by removing wrinkles

eye·lin·er /í lìnər/ *n.* a cosmetic worn along the edges of the eyelids to emphasize the eyes

eye o·pen·er *n.* **1. SOMETHING SURPRISING** a surprising or revealing experience or piece of information **2. MORNING DRINK** an alcoholic drink that is believed to help somebody to wake up, especially first thing in the morning —**eye-o·pen·ing** *adj.*

eye patch *n.* a covering worn over one eye to protect it or as concealment

eye·piece /í pèess/ *n.* the lens or group of lenses in an optical instrument on the side that the user looks through

eye-pop·ping *adj.* so striking or unusual that eyes widen in amazement (*informal*) ○ *an eye-popping crimson dress* —**eye-pop·per** *n.*

eye rhyme *n.* the use of rhymes as words that, because they are similarly spelled, look as if they rhyme but are in fact pronounced differently, e.g., "bough" and "enough"

eye·shade /í shàyd/ *n.* a tinted or opaque visor worn around the head above the eyes to protect them from glare

eye shad·ow *n.* a colored cosmetic for the area around the eyes, especially the eyelids

eye·shot /í shòt/ *n.* the range over which the eye can see

eye·sight /í sìt/ *n.* the power of sight

eye sock·et *n.* either of the two bony recesses in the skull that contain the eyeballs

eyes-on·ly *adj.* intended to be seen only by the person to whom it is addressed ○ *an eyes-only memo from the chief*

eye·sore /í sàwr/ *n.* an offensively ugly building or place ○ *That old office building is a real eyesore and ought to be pulled down.*

eye·spot /í spòt/ *n.* **1.** BIOL **LIGHT-SENSITIVE PART** a small pigmented area or organelle that is sensitive to light, found in some algae and simple multicellular organisms, including some flatworms, and jellyfish **2.** ZOOL **EYE-SHAPED MARKING** a marking shaped like an eye, e.g., on the wings of some butterflies or on a peacock's tail

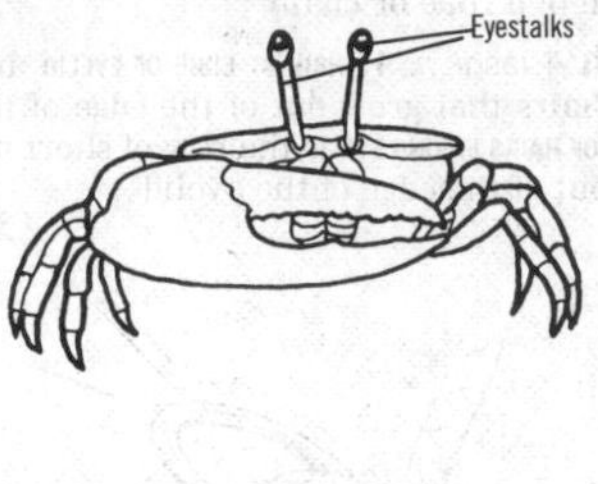

Eyestalk

eye·stalk /ī stàwk/ *n.* a flexible stalk with a compound eye at the tip found in crustaceans and some mollusks

eye·strain /ī stràyn/ *n.* tiredness or irritation in the eyes caused e.g., by an uncorrected visual defect or by prolonged close work. It is not recognized as a medical condition by ophthalmologists.

eye·tooth /ī to͝oth/ (*plural* **-teeth** /ī teèth/) *n.* a canine tooth found on each side of the upper jaw [From its being directly below the eye] ◇ **give your eyeteeth for something** to be prepared to do anything to be able to do or have something

eye·wash /ī wòsh, ī wàwsh/ *n.* **1.** CLEANSING LIQUID a liquid used to cleanse or soothe the eyes **2.** NONSENSE pretentious nonsense that is intended to flatter or deceive (*informal*) ○ *The official version is just so much eyewash.*

eye·wear /ī wàir/ *n.* something worn over the eyes to protect them or correct sight, e.g., glasses, goggles, or contact lenses

eye·wit·ness /ī wítnəss/ *n.* somebody who sees something happen and can give evidence about it

ey·ra /áirə, áyrə/ *n.* a jaguarundi in its reddish-brown seasonal color phase. Latin name: *Felis yagouaroundi.* [Early 17thC. Via Spanish from Tupi-Guarani *(e)irára.*]

Eyre, Lake /air/ the largest salt lake in Australia, located in central South Australia. Area: 3,658 sq. mi./9,475 sq. km.

Eyre Penin·sula peninsula in southern South Australia that separates the Great Australian Bight from the Spencer Gulf

ey·rie /áiree, eéree/ *n. U.K.* the brood of a bird of prey [15thC. From medieval Latin *aeria,* which probably came via Old French *aire* from Latin *area* "level ground, garden bed," later "bird of prey's nest" (source of English *area*). The spelling "eyrie" was introduced in the 17thC in the mistaken belief that the word was derived from Middle English *ey(e)* "egg."]

ey·rie *n.* = **aerie**

ey·rir /áy reèr/ (*plural* **au·rar** /ō raàr/) *n.* **1.** MINOR UNIT OF ICELANDIC CURRENCY a minor unit of currency in Iceland, 100 of which are worth a krona. See table at **currency 2.** COIN WORTH AN EYRIR a coin with a value of one eyrir [Early 20thC. From Icelandic, probably ultimately from Latin *aureus* "gold coin."]

eyr·y *n.* = **aerie**

Eys·enck /ī zèngk/, **H. J.** (1916–97) German-born British psychologist. He was an authority on personality studies and contributed to the controversial area of the links between genetics and intelligence.

EZ /eézee/, **E-Z** *abbr.* easy

Ez. *abbr.* BIBLE Ezra

Ezek. *abbr.* BIBLE Ezekiel

E·ze·ki·el /i zeékee əl/ *n.* **1.** HEBREW PROPHET a Hebrew priest and prophet who lived in the 6th century B.C. As the Jews' spiritual leader during the Babylonian captivity, he foretold the creation of a Jewish nation. **2.** BOOK OF BIBLE the book of the Bible that tells the story of the Jews' exile in Babylon in the 6th century B.C. It is traditionally attributed to Ezekiel and contains his prophecies of the destruction and subsequent rebuilding of Jerusalem and Judah. See table at **Bible**

e-zine /eé zeèn/ *n.* a web site with contents and layout modeled on those of a print magazine. Some more ambitious e-zines charge a subscription fee but many are devoted to a specific topic or field and are distributed free to their readership. [From *e(lectronic) (maga)zine*]

Ezr. *abbr.* BIBLE Ezra

Ez·ra /ézrə/ *n.* **1.** HEBREW PRIEST a Hebrew high priest who lived in the 5th century B.C. He led the Jews back to Jerusalem from their exile in Babylon and founded a Jewish nation. **2.** BOOK OF BIBLE the book of the Bible that tells the story of the rebuilding of the Jewish state in Palestine 536–432 B.C. after the Babylonian captivity. It is traditionally attributed to the prophet Ezra. See table at **Bible**

F f

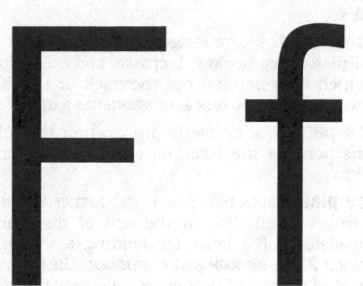

f[1] /ef/ (*plural* **f's**), **F** (*plural* **F's**) *n.* **1.** **6TH LETTER OF ENGLISH ALPHABET** the sixth letter of the modern English alphabet **2.** **SPEECH SOUND CORRESPONDING TO LETTER "F"** the speech sound that corresponds to the letter "F" **3.** **LETTER "F" WRITTEN** a written representation of the letter "F"

f[2] *symbol.* **1.** OPTICS f-number **2.** PHYS focal length **3.** PHYS frequency *n.* 4. **4.** MATH function **5.** femto- **6.** CHESS the sixth vertical row of squares from the left on a chessboard **7.** PHYS force

f[3] *abbr.* **1.** Fahrenheit **2.** fluorine **3.** franc **4.** MUSIC forte

F (*plural* **Fs** *or* **F's**) *n.* **1.** **4TH NOTE OF SCALE IN C** the 4th note of a scale in C major **2.** **SOMETHING THAT PRODUCES F** a string, key, or pipe tuned to produce the note F **3.** **SCALE BEGINNING ON F** a scale or key that starts on the note F **4.** **WRITTEN SYMBOL FOR F** a graphic representation of the tone of F

f. *abbr.* **1.** following (page) **2.** folio **3.** foul

F. *abbr.* **1.** fathom **2.** February **3.** female **4.** GRAM feminine **5.** METALL fine **6.** folio **7.** Friday

F- *abbr.* fighter (plane)

f/ *symbol.* PHOTOGRAPHY f-number

F2F *abbr.* face-to-face (*used in e-mail messages*)

fa /faa/ *n.* a syllable that represents the fourth note in a scale, used for singing solfege. In fixed solfege it represents the note C, while in solfege with movable do it is used to represent the tonic of the key being sung.

FA[1] *abbr.* **1.** Football Association **2.** field artillery **3.** financial adviser **4.** freight agent

FA[2], **F.A.** *abbr.* fine art

f.a. *abbr.* fire alarm

faa, **f.a.a.** *abbr.* INSUR, SHIPPING free of all average

FAA *abbr.* Federal Aviation Administration

fab /fab/ *adj.* fabulous (*dated informal*) ○ *It was a fab party!* [Mid-20thC. Shortening.]

Peter Carl Fabergé: Decorative jeweled egg (1901)

Fa·ber·gé /fàbber zháy/, **Peter Carl** (1846–1920) Russian goldsmith and jeweler. He designed and produced highly decorative gifts, notably gold-and-enamel Easter eggs, for European royalty. Born **Karl Gustavovich Fabergé**

Fa·bi·an /fáybee ən/ *adj.* **1.** **RELATING TO FABIAN SOCIETY** relating to, belonging to, or typical of the Fabian Society **2.** **CAUTIOUS** cautious, using delay, or avoiding direct confrontation ■ *n.* **MEMBER OF FABIAN SOCIETY** a member of the Fabian Society, or somebody who sympathizes with its political principles [Late 16thC. From Latin *Fabianus* "of Fabius"; from the cautious tactics of the Roman general Quintus Fabius Maximus.]

Fa·bi·an·ism /fáybee ə nìzzəm/ *n.* the beliefs or tactics of the Fabian Society —**Fa·bi·an·ist** *n.*

Fa·bi·an So·ci·e·ty *n.* a political organization founded in Britain in 1884 with the aim of bringing about socialism by gradual and lawful means rather than by revolution

Fa·bi·us Max·i·mus /fàybee əss máksiməss/, **Quintus** (?–203B.C.) Roman commander and statesman. As a result of his delaying tactics, Rome countered the invasion of Hannibal during the Second Punic War. Full name **Quintus Fabius Maximus Verrucosus**. Known as **Fabius Cunctator (the "Delayer")**

fa·ble /fáyb'l/ *n.* **1.** **STORY THAT TEACHES A LESSON** a short story with a moral, especially one in which the characters are animals **2.** **LEGEND** a story about supernatural, mythological, or legendary characters and events **3.** **FALSE ACCOUNT** a false or improbable account of something ○ *His version of events turned out to be a complete fable.* **4.** **MYTHS AND LEGENDS** myths and legends collectively ○ *a character out of fable* ■ *vt.* (**-bled, -bling, -bles**) **TELL IN FABLE** to tell the story of or describe something in a fable or similar type of fictional work (*usually passive*) ○ *Cerberus, the three-headed dog fabled to guard the entrance to the underworld* [13thC. Via Old French from Latin *fabula* "story," from *fari* "to speak." Ultimately from an Indo-European base that also produced English *affable, fairy,* and *profess.* Originally "falsehood, pretense."] —**fa·bler** *n.*

WORD KEY: CULTURAL NOTE

Fables, a collection of stories attributed to Greek writer Aesop (?6th century B.C.). Many of the tales feature animals as characters and each one illustrates a specific moral. Traditionally said to be the origin of the literary fable (although earlier examples have been found), they were used by the ancient Greeks for both educational and rhetorical purposes.

fa·bled /fáybəld/ *adj.* **1.** **LEGENDARY** famous from being described or recounted in legends **2.** **FICTITIOUS** made-up or fictitious

fab·li·au /fáblee ō/ (*plural* **-aux** /-ōz/) *n.* a comic and often bawdy story in verse, especially of a kind popular in 12th- and 13th-century France [Early 19thC. From French, from the plural of Old French *fablel,* literally "little story," from *fable* (see FABLE).]

fab·ric /fábbrik/ *n.* **1.** **CLOTH** cloth of any type made from thread or fibers, whether woven, knitted, or felted **2.** **TEXTURE** the particular texture or quality of a kind of cloth **3.** **SUBSTANCE** the fundamental structure or makeup of something ○ *the fabric of her being* **4.** BUILDING **STRUCTURAL MATERIAL** the material from which something is constructed, especially a building, or the physical structure of something ○ *Has there been any damage to the actual fabric of the church?* **5.** GEOL **ROCK COMPOSITION** the texture of a rock with respect to its macroscopic and microscopic arrangement of minerals and particles [15thC. Via Old French *fabrique* from Latin *fabrica* "trade, manufactured object, workshop," from *faber* "worker in metal or stone, artisan." The meaning "(manufactured) cloth" developed in the late 18thC.]

fab·ri·cate /fábbri kàyt/ (**-cat·ed, -cat·ing, -cates**) *vt.* **1.** **CONSTRUCT** to make something from different parts **2.** **INVENT** to make up something that is not true ○ *The evidence against him has been fabricated.* **3.** **FORGE** to make a fraudulent imitation of a signature or document [15thC. From Latin *fabricat-*, the past participle of *fabricare* "to make" (source also of English *forge*), from *fabrica* (see FABRIC).] —**fab·ri·ca·tor** *n.*

fab·ri·ca·tion /fàbbri káysh'n/ *n.* **1.** **ACT OF MAKING** the construction of something, or something that has been constructed or made **2.** **CONCOCTING LIES** the invention of something that is not true ○ *engaged in the fabrication of stories to discredit him* **3.** **UNTRUTH** something that is not true but has been made up ○ *This story is a mere fabrication.* **4.** **COUNTERFEIT** a fraudulent imitation of a signature or document

WORD KEY: SYNONYMS

See Synonyms at *lie.*

fab·u·list /fábbyəlist/ *n.* **1.** **FABLE WRITER** somebody who composes or recites fables **2.** **LIAR** somebody who tells fanciful lies

fab·u·lous /fábbyələss/ *adj.* **1.** **EXCELLENT** extremely good, pleasant, or enjoyable (*informal*) **2.** **AMAZING** amazingly or almost unbelievably great or wonderful **3.** **TYPICAL OF A FABLE** existing only in, described in, or typical of myths and legends [15thC. Directly or via French *fabuleux* from Latin *fabulosus* "celebrated in fable," from *fabula* (see FABLE). The meaning "extremely good" developed in the mid-20thC.] —**fab·u·lous·ly** *adv.* —**fab·u·lous·ness** *n.*

fac. *abbr.* **1.** facsimile **2.** MATH factor **3.** factory

Fac. *abbr.* Faculty

fa·çade /fə saád/, **fa·cade** *n.* **1.** ARCHIT **VISIBLE SURFACE** the face of a building, especially the principal or front face showing its most prominent architectural features **2.** **DECEPTIVE APPEARANCE** the way something or somebody appears on the surface, especially when that appearance is false or meant to deceive ○ *Her geniality is just a façade.* [Mid-17thC. From French, formed from *face* (source of English *face*) on the model of Italian *facciata.*]

face /fayss/ *n.* **1.** **FRONT OF HEAD** the front of the human head, where the eyes, nose, mouth, chin, cheeks, and forehead are **2.** **PERSON** a person being looked at (*informal*) ○ *It's nice to see so many familiar faces here today.* **3.** **COUNTENANCE** a facial expression or look of a specified kind ○ *Why the long face?* **4.** **UNPLEASANT FACIAL EXPRESSION** an expression in which the face is distorted, e.g., to show distaste or as a way of being rude to somebody ○ *The children made faces at him behind his back.* **5.** **WAY SOMETHING LOOKS** the general or outward appearance of something ○ *The arrival of the automobile changed the face of the modern city.* **6.** **FALSE APPEARANCE** an outward appearance that does not show the true nature of somebody's feelings or situation or is intended to deceive ○ *Even after a third defeat he was still putting on a brave face.* **7.** **REPUTATION** personal prestige, or the respect accorded to somebody by others ○ *a way of enabling her to back down without losing face* **8.** **BOLDNESS** impudence or self-assurance (*informal*) ○ *How can he have the face to come back here after what he said?* **9.** **FACE MAKEUP** makeup for the face (*informal*) **10.** GEOM **SURFACE OF OBJECT** a plane surface or side of a three-dimensional object, e.g., a geometric figure, or gem, that is presented towards a particular direction ○ *A cube has six faces.* **11.** **OUTSIDE OF BUILDING** the exterior of the front or side of a large building ○ *the evening sun shining on the west face* **12.** GEOG **SIDE OF CLIFF** the steep exposed side of a cliff **13.** GEOG **SIDE OF MOUNTAIN** any of the steep sides of a mountain, usually specified according to its orientation ○ *the north face of Mt. Rainier* **14.** MINING **WORKING AREA IN A MINE** an area in a mine from which a mineral such as coal is being extracted **15.** PRINTING **TYPEFACE** a typeface, or the area of a printing character that actually prints **16.** **DIAL ON CLOCK OR INSTRUMENT** the surface of a timepiece or similar instrument that displays the time or other data **17.** CARDS **SIDE OF CARD SHOWING VALUE** the side of a playing card that is marked with numbers and symbols **18. FUNCTIONAL SIDE OF AN IMPLEMENT** the side of something such as a tool or golf club that is most important in carrying out its function **19.** COINS **SIDE OF COIN** either surface of a coin, especially one with somebody's head on it ■ *v.* **(faced, fac·ing, fac·es) 1.** *vti.* **TURN TOWARD SOMEBODY OR SOMETHING** to be positioned or turn so that the face or front side is directed a particular way or toward something or somebody ○ *The largest bedroom faces south.* **2.** *vt.* **BE LOOKING AT SOMEBODY OR SOMETHING** to be in a position opposite somebody or something ○ *The boys faced each other.* **3.** *vt.* **COME UP AGAINST SOMEBODY OR SOMETHING** to meet or confront somebody or something directly and bravely ○ *Their retreat was cut off and they had no choice but to stand and face the enemy.* **4.** *vt.* **ACCEPT THE FACTS** to accept the reality of a difficult or unpleasant situation ○ *Let's face it, our chances of being on time are slim.* **5.** *vt.* **HAVE TO CONTEND WITH SOMETHING** to have to deal with or undergo something unpleasant or difficult ○ *She was faced with the task of breaking the news to her family.* **6.** *vt.* **BE ENCOUNTERED BY SOMEBODY** to be met and overcome by somebody ○ *the difficulties facing the new administration* **7.** *vt.* **EXPECT SOMETHING BAD** to have the prospect of experiencing something unpleasant, usually within a short period of time ○ *They face ruin if the bank calls in the loan.* **8.** *vt.* **LINE OR DECORATE SOMETHING** to line or trim the edge of something with a contrasting material ○ *The cuffs were faced with velvet.* **9.** *vt.* **SMOOTH** to put a smooth surface on a piece of stone **10.** *vti.* **ORDER TROOPS TO TURN** to order troops to turn in a specified direction, or to turn in a specified direction when ordered to do so ○ *The captain ordered her troops to face left.* [13thC. Via French (source also of English *façade* and *facet*) from Latin *facies* "appearance, aspect, form," hence "face."] —**face·a·ble** *adj.* ◇ **face to face 1.** in the actual presence of another person **2.** in direct contact with, or having first-hand knowledge of, an unpleasant fact or situation ◇ **fly in the face of** to defy something deliberately or recklessly ◇ **have a long face** to look miserable or disappointed ◇ **in (the) face of something** when confronted by or in spite of something (*slang*) ◇ **set your face against something** to oppose something with determination ○ *He won't dare show his face at her house again after her brother threw him out.* ◇ **show your face somewhere or at something** to put in an appearance somewhere

WORD KEY: ORIGIN

The Latin word *facies* from which ***face*** is derived is also the source of English *façade, facet, superficial*, and *surface*.

face down *vt.* to prevail against somebody in a direct confrontation

face off *v.* **1.** *vti.* SPORTS **BEGIN PLAY** to start or restart play in ice hockey, lacrosse, and other sports by dropping the puck or ball between two opposing players **2.** *vi.* **CONFRONT SOMEBODY** to confront each other, or confront somebody (*informal*)

face up to *vt.* **1. ACCEPT** to accept having to deal with something unpleasant **2. CONFRONT** to confront somebody or something bravely

face an·gle *n.* an angle between two flat surfaces on a polyhedron

face card *n.* a king, queen, or jack in a deck of cards

face-cen·tered *adj.* used to describe a crystal lattice with an atom in the center of each unit cell face as well as at the corners

face·cloth /fáyss klòth/ *n.* = **washcloth**

-faced *suffix.* **1. WITH SO MANY FACES** having a specified number of faces **2. WITH A CERTAIN KIND OF FACE** having a face of a specified kind

face·down /fáyss dòwn/ *n.* a determined confrontation between two adversaries

face·less /fáyssləss/ *adj.* lacking character or distinction as an individual —**face·less·ly** *adv.* —**face·less·ness** *n.*

face-lift *n.* **1.** SURG **COSMETIC SURGERY OF THE FACE** a surgical operation in which the skin of the face is pulled back and up to tighten it and remove wrinkles. Technical name **rhytidectomy 2. SPRUCING UP** a renovation or refurbishment of something e.g., an area or a building ○ *The whole harbor area could use a face-lift.*

face mask *n.* a covering for the whole head or the face alone, used either to protect or to disguise the face

face-off *n.* **1.** SPORTS **BEGINNING OF PLAY** a start or restart of play in ice hockey, lacrosse, and other sports in which the referee drops the puck or ball between two opposing players **2. CONFRONTATION** a direct conflict

face pack *n.* a cosmetic preparation that cleanses the pores of the face and removes dead layers of skin

face·plate /fáyss plàyt/ *n.* **1.** ENG **PART OF A LATHE** a perforated metal disk at the end of the spindle or headstock of a lathe for holding a workpiece in place **2. SEE-THROUGH PART OF HEADGEAR** the transparent part of a piece of protective headgear that protects the face while allowing the wearer to see **3. FRONT OF A CATHODE-RAY TUBE** the front of a cathode-ray tube, on which an image is seen

face pow·der *n.* a flesh-colored cosmetic powder applied to the face to make it look smoother or less shiny

fac·er /fáyssər/ *n.* **1. LATHE TOOL** a lathe tool used to smooth a surface **2.** *U.K.* **SOMETHING ASTONISHING** something that is astonishing or very difficult to deal with (*dated informal*) ○ *This latest development is a facer, and no mistake!*

face-sav·ing *adj.* intended to preserve somebody's reputation and dignity ○ *find a face-saving compromise* —**face-sav·er** *n.*

fac·et /fássət/ *n.* **1. AN ASPECT OF SOMETHING** any one of the several parts or possible aspects of something **2. FACE OF A GEMSTONE** any of the faces of a cut gemstone **3.** ZOOL, INSECTS **PART OF INSECT EYE** any of the separate lens segments in the compound eye of an insect or other arthropod **4.** ANAT **FLAT AREA** any smooth flat area on a hard surface such as a bone or a tooth ■ *vt.* **(fac·et·ed** *or* **fac·et·ted, fa·cet·ing** *or* **fa·cet·ting, fac·ets) CUT FACETS IN SOMETHING** to cut facets in something, especially a precious stone such as a diamond [Early 17thC. From French *facette*, literally "little face," from *face* (see FACE).]

fa·ce·ti·ae *npl.* witty or humorous remarks (*literary*) [Early 16thC. From Latin *facetiae* "jokes," the plural of *facetia* (see FACETIOUS).]

face time *n.* **1.** COMPUT **TIME SPENT FACE-TO-FACE** time spent dealing face-to-face with other people (*informal*) ○ *The schedule calls for the weekly e-mail reports as well as some actual face time between team members.* **2. TIME SPENT ON TELEVISION** the amount of time that somebody spends appearing on television ○ *We need more face time to sway public opinion on this issue.* **3. EXTRA TIME AT PLACE OF EMPLOYMENT** the amount of time somebody spends at his or her place of employment, especially beyond normal working hours ○ *What is she trying to prove with all this face time?*

fa·ce·tious /fə séeshəss/ *adj.* **1. SUPPOSED TO BE FUNNY** intended to be humorous but often silly or inappropriate **2. NOT IN EARNEST** not to be taken seriously ○ *a facetious suggestion* [Late 16thC. From French *facétieux*, from *facétie* "joke," from Latin *facetia*, from *facetus* "graceful, witty."] —**fa·ce·tious·ly** *adv.* —**fa·ce·tious·ness** *n.*

WORD KEY: SYNONYMS

See Synonyms at ***funny***.

face-to-face *adj., adv.* **1. IN EACH OTHER'S PRESENCE** in the physical presence of somebody else (*not hyphenated when used after a verb*) **2. HEAD-ON** in direct contact or confrontation ○ *We came face-to-face with the situation.*

face val·ue *n.* **1. STATED VALUE** the value that is stated on something, especially a note, coin, or stamp **2. SEEMING WORTH** what something seems to mean or be worth, which may be better than its true worth or meaning ○ *We'd be unwise to accept his promises at face value.*

Fa·cey /fáyzzee/, **Albert Barnett** (1894–1982) Australian writer. He is the author of *A Fortunate Life* (1981), his autobiography.

fa·cial /fáysh'l/ *adj.* **ON THE FACE** relating to the face ○ *an unhappy facial expression* ■ *n.* **BEAUTY TREATMENT FOR FACE** a beauty treatment for the face, usually consisting of a facial massage followed by cleansing and makeup —**fa·cial·ly** *adv.*

fa·cial nerve *n.* a nerve of the seventh cranial pair that controls the muscles of the face and jaw, and the sensory abilities of the palate, front of the tongue, and nose

-facient *suffix.* causing, making ○ *febrifacient* [From Latin *facient-*, the present participle stem of *facere* "to do, make" (see FACT)]

fa·ci·es /fáyshee èez, fáysheez/ (*plural* **-es**) *n.* **1.** BIOL **GENERAL APPEARANCE** the general characteristic appearance of something e.g., a plant or animal species **2.** GEOL **ROCK FEATURES INDICATING FORMATION** the combined physical and chemical features of a rock that indicate the manner of its formation or deposition **3.** MED **FACIAL APPEARANCE LINKED TO DISEASE** the appearance of somebody's face as a characteristic of a particular disease or condition [Early 18thC. From Latin, "face" (see FACE).]

fac·ile /fáss'l/ *adj.* **1. EASY TO DO** requiring little effort **2. FLUENT BUT INSINCERE** produced, spoken, or speaking so fluently and easily as to seem insincere or superficial **3. SUPERFICIAL** made or arrived at without any serious thought or depth of feeling and therefore of little value or significance **4. WORKING EASILY** working or acting smoothly and easily [15thC. Via French, "easy," from Latin *facilis* "easy to do, pliant, courteous," from *facere* "to do, make."] —**fac·ile·ly** *adv.* —**fac·ile·ness** *n.*

fac·il·e prin·ceps *n.* somebody who is the obvious leader of a group (*literary*) [From Latin, literally "easily first"]

fa·cil·i·tate /fə sílli tàyt/ **(-tat·ed, -tat·ing, -tates)** *vt.* to make something easy or easier to do [Early 17thC. Via French *faciliter* from Italian *facilitare* "to make easy," from *facile* "easy," from Latin *facilis* (see FACILE).] —**fa·cil·i·ta·tive** *adj.*

fa·cil·i·ta·tion /fə sìlli táysh'n/ *n.* **1. SIMPLIFICATION** the process of making something easy or easier **2.** MED **EASING OF NERVE TRANSMISSION** a decrease in the resistance to a nerve impulse in a neural pathway, brought about by prior or repeated stimulation

fa·cil·i·ta·tor /fə sílli tàytər/ *n.* **1. SOMEBODY ENABLING SOMETHING TO HAPPEN** somebody who aids or assists in a process, especially by encouraging people to find their own solutions to problems or tasks **2. MEETING ORGANIZER** somebody who organizes and provides the services for a meeting, seminar, or other event

fa·cil·i·ty /fə síllətee/ *n.* (*plural* **-ties**) **1. SKILL** an ability to do something easily **2. EFFORTLESSNESS** ease in doing something or in being done **3. SOMETHING WITH A FUNCTION** something designed or created to provide a service or fulfill a need (*often used in the plural*) ○ *A wide range of facilities is available at the sports center, including a weight room and saunas.* ■ **fa·cil·i·ties** *npl.* **TOILET** a toilet

fac·ing /fáyssing/ *n.* **1.** CLOTHES **LINING THAT FINISHES EDGE** a lining that finishes the edge of something, especially a piece of fabric sewn and turned in on a garment to finish the edges neatly **2.** CLOTHES **PROTECTIVE OR DECORATIVE COVERING** material, or a piece of it, applied to part of an item of clothing for decoration or protection **3.** BUILDING **WALL SURFACE** a layer of material that covers the outer surface of a wall, applied for decoration or protection ■ **fac·ings** *npl.* CLOTHES **CUFFS AND COLLAR OF JACKET** contrasting coverings on the cuffs and collar of a jacket, especially a military jacket

-facing *suffix.* pointing in the specified direction

fack /fak/ **(facked, fack·ing, facks)** *vi.* to speak truthfully about something (*slang*) [Alteration of FACT]

FACP, F.A.C.P. *abbr.* Fellow of the American College of Physicians

FACS *abbr.* **FACS, F.A.C.S.** Fellow of the American College of Surgeons

fac·sim·i·le /fak símməlee/ *n.* **1. COPY OF SOMETHING** an exact copy of something, e.g., a document, a coin, or somebody's handwriting **2. FAX** a fax ■ *vt.* **(-i·led, -il·ing, -i·les) MAKE COPY OF SOMETHING** to make an exact copy or reproduction of something [Late 16thC. From modern Latin, from Latin *facere* "to do, make" + *simile*, "similar."]

fact /fakt/ *n.* **1. SOMETHING KNOWN TO BE TRUE** something that can be shown to be true, to exist, or to have happened **2. TRUTH OR REALITY OF SOMETHING** the truth or actual existence of something, as opposed to the supposition of something or a belief about something **3. PIECE OF INFORMATION** a piece of information such as a statistic or a statement of the truth **4.** LAW **ACTUAL COURSE OF EVENTS** the circumstances of an event, motion, occurrence, or state of affairs, rather than an interpretation of its significance ○ *Matters of fact are issues for a jury, while matters of law are issues for the court.* **5.** LAW **SOMETHING BASED ON EVIDENCE** something that is based on or concerned with the evidence presented in a legal case [15thC. From Latin *factum* "deed," from the past participle of *facere* "to do."] ◇ **after the fact** after something, especially a criminal act, has been done ◇ **before the fact** before something, especially a criminal act, has been done ◇ **in (point of) fact** in truth or reality

WORD KEY: ORIGIN

The Latin word *facere* from which ***fact*** is derived is also the source of English *difficult, effect, factor, fashion, feasible, feat, feature,* and *fetish.*

fact-find·ing *adj.* **FOR GATHERING INFORMATION** intended to find out information about something ■ *n.* **1. GATHERING INFORMATION** activity that is intended to find out information about something **2.** LAW **FAMILY-COURT TRIAL** a trial in a family court —**fact-find·er** *n.*

fac·tic·i·ty /fak tíssətee/ *n.* the reality, truth, or truthfulness of something (*formal*) [Mid-20thC. Formed from FACT.]

fac·tion[1] /fákshən/ *n.* **1. DISSENTING MINORITY WITHIN LARGER GROUP** a group that is a minority within a larger group and has specific interests or beliefs that are not always in harmony with the larger group **2. CONFLICT WITHIN GROUP** conflict or dissension within a group [15thC. Via French from Latin *faction-*, literally "act of making," from *fact-*, past participle stem of *facere* (see FACT).] —**fac·tion·al** *adj.* —**fac·tion·al·ly** *adv.*

fac·tion[2] /fákshən/ *n.* **1. TECHNIQUE OF DRAMATIZING HISTORY** a type of writing or filmmaking that portrays real people or events by dramatizing the facts using the techniques of fiction **2. DRAMATIZED WORK BASED ON REAL LIFE** a piece of writing, a movie, or a television program that portrays real people or events in a dramatized way [Mid-20thC. Blend of FACT and FICTION.] —**fac·tion·al** *adj.*

-faction *suffix.* making, producing ○ *rarefaction* [Via Old French from, ultimately, Latin *facere* "to do, make" (see FACT)]

fac·tion·al·ism /fákshənə lìzzəm/ *n.* the existence of or conflict between groups within a larger group —**fac·tion·al·ist** *n.*

fac·tion·al·ize /fákshənə lìz/ (**-ized, -iz·ing, -iz·es**) *vti.* to split, or cause something to split, into factions

fac·tious /fákshəss/ *adj.* liable to cause, taking part in, or typical of conflict within a group [Mid-16thC. Directly or via French *factieux* from Latin *factiosus*, from *faction-* (see FACTION[1]).] —**fac·tious·ly** *adv.* —**fac·tious·ness** *n.*

fac·ti·tious /fak tíshəss/ *adj.* **1. INSINCERE** contrived and insincere rather than genuine **2. ARTIFICIAL** not real or natural but artificial or invented (*formal*) [Mid-17thC. From Latin, from *faction-* (see FACTION[1]).] —**fac·ti·tious·ly** *adv.* —**fac·ti·tious·ness** *n.*

fac·ti·tive /fáktitiv/ *adj.* used to describe a verb that takes a direct object and a complement. An example is "appoint" in "They appointed her Head of Department" where "her" is the direct object and "Head of Department" is a noun complement. [Mid-19thC. From Latin *factitivus*, from *factitare* "to frequent."] —**fac·ti·tive·ly** *adv.*

fact of life *n.* **UNAVOIDABLE TRUTH** an unavoidable truth, especially an unpleasant one ■ **facts of life** *npl.* **SEX EDUCATION** basic information on sexual matters and reproduction

fac·toid /fák tòyd/ *n.* **1. UNRELIABLE INFORMATION** something that may not be true but is widely accepted as true because it is repeatedly quoted, especially in the media **2. SINGLE FACT** a small and often unimportant bit of information

fac·tor /fáktər/ *n.* **1. INFLUENCE** something that contributes to or has an influence on the result of something ○ *Access to emergency exits is an important factor when planning the layout of a public building.* **2. LEVEL** a quantity or level of something **3.** MATH **QUANTITY MULTIPLIED WITH OTHERS** one of two or more numbers or quantities that can be multiplied together to give a specified number or quantity ○ *3 and 5 are factors of 15.* **4. AMOUNT BY WHICH SOMETHING IS MULTIPLIED** an amount by which something is multiplied to give a specific result ○ *The number of visitors to the museum has increased by a factor of three.* **5.** BUSINESS **SOMEBODY TRADING FOR COMMISSION** a person who or organization that buys and sells goods for a commission **6.** BUSINESS **BUSINESS AGENT** somebody who or an organization that carries out business for another **7.** FIN **FINANCING COMPANY** a business that makes loans to other businesses on the security of their accounts receivable, or that buys their accounts receivable at a discounted price **8.** BIOCHEM **BIOLOGICAL SUBSTANCE** a biological substance that promotes a physiological process, e.g., blood clotting. ◊ **factor VIII** ■ *v.* (**-tored, -tor·ing, -tors**) **1.** *vt.* MATH **WORK OUT FACTORS** to calculate the factors of a given number or expression **2.** *vi.* BUSINESS **ACT AS FACTOR** to work as a factor [15thC. Via French from Latin, from *fact-*, past participle stem of *facere* (see FACT).] —**fac·tor·a·bil·i·ty** /fàktərə bíllətee/ *n.* —**fac·tor·a·ble** /-tərəb'l/ *adj.*

factor in *vt.* to include or consider something as contributing to or influencing something else, e.g., when making a decision

fac·tor·age /fáktərij/ *n.* **1. MONEY CHARGED BY FACTOR** the fees or commission charged by a factor **2. WORK OF A FACTOR** the business of working as a factor

fac·tor a·nal·y·sis *n.* a statistical technique used to determine the relative strength of various influences on an outcome

fac·to·ri·al /fak táwree əl/ *n.* **PRODUCT OF MULTIPLICATION** the number resulting from multiplying a whole number by every whole number between itself and 1 inclusive. 6 factorial, or 6!, is 6 x 5 x 4 x 3 x 2 x 1 = 720. Symbol **!** ■ *adj.* **1. RELATING TO FACTORIAL** relating to or involving a factorial **2.** BUSINESS **INVOLVING FACTOR** involving or typical of a commercial factor or the work of such a factor —**fac·to·ri·al·ly** *adv.*

fac·tor·ing /fáktəring/ *n.* the business of buying debts at a discount so as to make a profit from collecting them

fac·tor·ize /fáktə rìz/ (**-ized, -iz·ing, -iz·es**) *vti.* = **factor** —**fac·tor·i·za·tion** /fàktəri záysh'n/ *n.*

fac·tor·ship /fáktər shìp/ *n.* the position or business of being a factor for another person or business

fac·tor VIII *n.* a protein substance, one of a number that promote clotting of blood. Its inherited absence causes hemophilia.

fac·to·ry /fáktəree/ (*plural* **-ries**) *n.* **1. BUILDING WHERE GOODS ARE MANUFACTURED** a building or complex of buildings where goods are manufactured on a large scale, e.g., an automobile assembly plant (*often used before a noun*) ○ *a factory worker* **2. PRODUCTIVE PLACE** a place where a lot of things of a particular kind are produced (*informal*) ○ *As far as popular music was concerned, it was a hit factory.* **3.** COMM **PLACE ABROAD WHERE AGENTS DID BUSINESS** in the past, a place where business was carried out abroad by commercial agents (**factors**), especially a trading station

fac·to·ry farm *n.* a farm where animals are raised by intensive methods and on a large scale using modern industrial equipment —**fac·to·ry farm·ing** *n.*

fac·to·ry floor *n.* = **shop floor**

fac·to·ry ship *n.* a large fishing vessel equipped to process and freeze its own catch, or a whole fleet's catch, of fish or whales

fac·to·tum /fak tṓtəm/ *n.* somebody employed to do a variety of jobs for somebody else [Mid-16thC. From Latin, literally "do everything!", from *fac* "do!", imperative of *facere* (see FACT), + *totum* "all" (source of English *total*).]

fac·tu·al /fák choo əl, fákchəl/ *adj.* **1. CONTAINING FACTS** involving, containing, or based on facts **2. TRUTHFUL** consisting of the truth, or including only those things that are real or actual [Mid-19thC. Modeled on ACTUAL.] —**fac·tu·al·i·ty** /fàk choo állətee/ *n.* —**fac·tu·al·ly** /fák choo əlee, -chəlee/ *adv.* —**fac·tu·al·ness** *n.*

fac·tu·al·ism /fák choo ə lìzzəm, fákchə lìzzəm/ *n.* a strict devotion to or adherence to facts —**fac·tu·al·ist** *n.*

fac·u·la /fákyələ/ (*plural* **-lae** /fákyə lèe/) *n.* a large bright extremely hot region on the sun's surface, usually occurring near a sunspot [Early 18thC. From Latin, literally "little torch."] —**fac·u·lar** *adj.*

fac·ul·ta·tive /fákəl tàytiv/ *adj.* **1. ALLOWING SOMETHING TO HAPPEN** enabling or capable of permitting something to happen or be done, but not able to force its occurrence **2. NOT REQUIRED** optional rather than obligatory **3.** BIOL **ASSOCIATED WITH A VARIETY OF CONDITIONS** able to live or take place under a range of external conditions ○ *a facultative parasite.* ◊ **obligate** —**fac·ul·ta·tive·ly** *adv.*

fac·ul·ty /fákəltee/ (*plural* **-ties**) *n.* **1. MENTAL ABILITY** a mental power or ability that somebody has, e.g., reason or memory **2. ABILITY** any capacity or ability that somebody is born with or learns ○ *have a great faculty for learning languages* **3. ENTIRE TEACHING STAFF** the entire teaching staff of a university, college, or school, including any administrators holding academic rank **4. TEACHING STAFF FOR PARTICULAR UNIVERSITY DIVISION** the teaching staff of a particular faculty in a university or college **5. DIVISION OF UNIVERSITY** a department or group of departments dealing with a particular subject in a university or college **6. ALL MEMBERS OF PROFESSION** all of the people who practice a particular profession, especially medicine **7. POWER GRANTED BY AUTHORITY** a power or right given by an authority [14thC. Via French *faculté* from Latin *facultas*, from *facilis*, "easy" (source of English *facility*).]

fad /fad/ *n.* something that is embraced very enthusiastically for a short time, especially by many people [Mid-19thC. Origin uncertain: perhaps a shortening of *fidfad*, a shortening of FIDDLE-FADDLE.] —**fad·dism** *n.* —**fad·dist** *n.*

Fad·den /fádd'n /, **Sir Arthur William** (1895–1973) Australian statesman. He was leader of the Country Party (1941–58) and was briefly prime minister of Australia in 1941.

fad·dish /fáddish/ *adj.* **1. BRIEFLY FASHIONABLE** very popular but only for a short time **2. GIVEN TO FADS** tending to have strongly held, but brief, enthusiasms —**fad·dish·ly** *adv.* —**fad·dish·ness** *n.*

fad·dy /fáddee/ *adj. U.K.* = **faddish** *adj.* **2**

fade /fayd/ *v.* (**fad·ed, fad·ing, fades**) **1.** *vti.* **GRADUALLY BECOME LESS** to lose or make something lose brightness, color, or loudness gradually ○ *The clothes had faded from months of washing.* **2.** *vi.* **BECOME TIRED** to lose strength, freshness, and vigor ○ *His concentration faded after about an hour.* **3.** *vi.* **DISAPPEAR SLOWLY** to die away or vanish gradually ○ *The movie ends with a closeup that gradually fades to black.* **4.** *vi.* **LOSE EFFECTIVENESS** to become less effective temporarily **5.** *vi.* **LEAVE** to leave or depart (*slang*) ○ *They faded sometime after midnight.* **6.** *vi.* FOOTBALL **DROP BACK TO PASS** to drop back from the line of scrimmage in a football game before passing the ball (*refers to the quarterback*) **7.** *vti.* SPORTS **CURVE OR CAUSE TO CURVE** to curve, or cause a ball to curve, from a straight path **8.** *vt.* GAMBLING **MATCH BET IN DICE GAME** to match the bet of an opponent in dice (*slang*) ■ *n.* **1. GRADUAL LESSENING** an instance of something gradually becoming quieter, less bright, or less distinct **2.** SPORTS **CURVING PATH OF BALL** the curve of a ball, especially a golf ball, away from a straight path or flight **3. GRADUAL DISAPPEARANCE OF IMAGE** a gradual disappearance of an image in a film or television show **4. BLACK PERSON WITH WHITE LIFESTYLE** a Black person who has adopted white friends and attitudes (*slang*) [14thC. From French *fade* "weak, pale," of uncertain origin: probably from a Vulgar Latin blend of Latin *fatuus* "insipid" and *vapidus* "flat."] —**fad·a·ble** *adj.* —**fad·ed·ness** *n.* —**fad·er** *n.*

fade away *vi.* **1. GRADUALLY DISAPPEAR** to become gradually fainter or weaker and finally disappear **2. WASTE AWAY** to become thin and unhealthy

fade in *vti.* to gradually make a sound audible or an image visible, or become gradually audible or visible

fade out *vti.* to gradually make an image or sound fainter until it disappears, or become gradually fainter before disappearing

fade·a·way /fáydə wày/ *n.* **1. GRADUAL DISAPPEARANCE** a gradual decrease in the brightness, color, or loudness of something until it disappears completely **2.** BASEBALL **SCREWBALL** a screwball (*dated*) **3.** BASEBALL **DODGE BY BASEBALL RUNNER** in baseball, a baserunner's slide to one side to avoid being tagged out

fade-in *n.* the gradual introduction of a sound until it is audible, or of an image until it is visible and clear

fade·less /fáydləss/ *adj.* not affected by fading from sunlight or washing —**fade·less·ly** *adv.*

fade-out *n.* **1. GRADUAL DECREASE IN LOUDNESS OR BRIGHTNESS** a gradual decrease in loudness or brightness as a sound or image becomes fainter and less distinct, and eventually disappears **2.** BROADCAST **WEAKENING OF TV OR RADIO SIGNAL** a gradual reduction in the strength of a broadcast television or radio signal, especially with temporary loss of reception, often because of interference in transmission

fa·do /fáa thòo/ (*plural* **-dos**) *n.* a type of sad Portuguese folk song [Early 20thC. From Portuguese, literally "fate."]

faeces *npl.* U.K. = **feces**

fa·e·na /faa áynə/ *n.* a series of maneuvers in the final stages of a bullfight, leading up to the killing of the bull by the matador [Early 20thC. From Spanish, literally "task."]

fa·er·ie /fáyəree, fáiree/, **fa·er·y** (*plural* **-ies**) *n.* (*literary*) **1.** FAIRYLAND the world of the fairies, or fairyland **2.** FAIRY a fairy [Late 16thC. A mock-medieval word based on French (source of English *fairy*) introduced by the author Edmund Spenser.]

Faer·oe Is·lands /fáirō-/, **Far·oe Is·lands** ISLANDS = **Faroe Islands**

Faer·o·ese /fàirō éez, -éess/ *n., adj.* = **Faroese**

FAF *abbr.* financial aid form

fag[1] /fag/ *n. U.K.* **1.** SOMETHING BORING something that is tedious or that makes somebody weary (*informal*) **2.** ERRAND BOY a schoolboy at a public school who in the past had to do menial jobs and run errands for an older schoolboy ■ *v.* (**fagged, fag·ging, fags**) **1.** *vti.* EXHAUST THROUGH WORK to tire out, or cause to become exhausted, through drudgery or hard labor **2.** *vi. U.K.* ACT AS ERRAND BOY to do menial jobs and run errands for an older schoolboy [Mid-16thC. Originally the verb, of uncertain origin: perhaps an alteration of FLAG. Current senses evolved from "to droop, decline" through "bent over by weariness."]

fag[2] /fag/ *n. U.K.* a cigarette (*informal*) [Late 19thC. Shortening of FAG END.]

fag[3] /fag/ *n.* an offensive term for a homosexual man (*slang offensive*) [Early 20thC. Shortening of FAGGOT.] — **faggy** *adj.*

fag end *n.* **1.** LAST AND WORST PART OF SOMETHING the last part of something after the best of it has been used ○ *the fag end of the day* **2.** REMNANT OF CLOTH the remaining part of a piece of cloth, most of which has been used [*Fag* of unknown origin. Originally "flap, something hanging down."]

fag·got[1] *n., vt.* = **fagot**

fag·got[2] /fággət/ *n.* an offensive term for a homosexual man (*slang offensive*) [Early 20thC. From an earlier use of FAGOT, "bundle of sticks," as an offensive term for a woman. Compare BAGGAGE.] —**fag·got·ry** *n.* — **fag·got·y** *adj.*

fag·got·ing /fággəting/ *n.* a decorative way of sewing two hemmed pieces of fabric together, leaving a gap between them that is filled with an insertion. = **fagoting**

fag hag *n.* an offensive term for a woman who enjoys socializing with homosexual men (*slang offensive*)

fag·ot /fággət/, **fag·got** *n.* **1.** BUNDLE OF STICKS FOR FIREWOOD a bundle of sticks or twigs, especially wood to be burned as fuel **2.** METALL BUNDLE OF PIECES OF METAL a bundle of pieces of metal, especially pieces of iron or steel for welding ■ *vt.* (**-ot·ed, -ots; -got·ed, -gots**) **1.** COLLECT SOMETHING AND TIE INTO BUNDLE to collect things, especially sticks, and tie them into a bundle or bundles **2.** SEW STITCH WITH FAGOTING to sew something using fagoting [13thC. Via Old French from Italian *faggotto*, ultimately from Greek *phakelos* "bundle."]

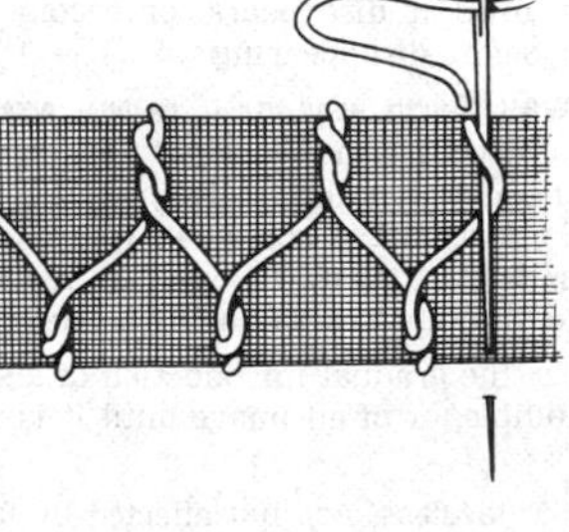

Fagoting

fag·ot·ing /fággəting/, **fag·got·ing** *n.* **1.** SEW DECORATIVE WAY OF JOINING FABRIC a decorative way of sewing two hemmed pieces of fabric together, leaving a gap between them that is filled with an insertion stitch **2.** CRAFT EMBROIDERY TECHNIQUE a technique of embroidery in which sections of lengthwise threads are pulled out and the cross threads tied into bundles, producing a decorative openwork effect [Mid-19thC]

Fah. *abbr.* Fahrenheit

Fahd /faad/, **King of Saudi Arabia** (*b.* 1922). He succeeded to the throne in 1982, and was instrumental in stabilizing the Middle East

Fahr. *abbr.* Fahrenheit

Fah·ren·heit /férrən hìt/ *adj.* using or measured on a temperature scale on which water freezes at 32°F and boils at 212°F under normal atmospheric conditions. In scientific and technical contexts temperatures are now usually measured in degrees (**Celsius**) rather than Fahrenheit. ◊ **Celsius, kelvin.** Symbol **F** [Mid-18thC. Named for Gabriel *Fahrenheit* (1686–1736), the German physicist who invented the thermometric Fahrenheit scale.]

WORD KEY: USAGE

See Usage note at ***centigrade.***

FAIA, F.A.I.A. *abbr.* Fellow of the American Institute of Architects

FAIC, F.A.I.C. *abbr.* Fellow of the American Institute of Chemists

fa·ience /fī áans, fay-/, **fa·ïence** *n.* earthenware decorated with colored opaque metallic glazes (*often used before a noun*) ○ *a faience bowl* [Late 17thC. From French, named after *Faïence* "Faenza," town in northern Italy where this type of pottery was first made.]

fail /fayl/ *v.* (**failed, fail·ing, fails**) **1.** *vi.* BE UNSUCCESSFUL to be unsuccessful in trying to do something ○ *This plan can't fail.* **2.** *vi.* BE UNABLE TO DO SOMETHING to be incapable of doing something, or choose not to do something ○ *She failed to see what the problem was.* **3.** *vti.* EDUC NOT PASS EXAM OR COURSE to fall short of the standard required to pass an examination or course ○ *He failed English.* **4.** *vt.* EDUC JUDGE STUDENT NOT GOOD ENOUGH to judge a student not good enough to pass an examination or a course **5.** *vi.* STOP FUNCTIONING OR GROWING to stop working, or not perform or grow as expected ○ *The brakes on the car failed.* **6.** *vi.* COMM COLLAPSE FINANCIALLY to collapse financially, becoming insolvent or bankrupt ○ *The business failed after six years.* **7.** *vt.* LET SOMEBODY DOWN to let somebody down by not doing what is expected or needed, or abandon or forsake somebody ○ *My courage failed me.* **8.** *vi.* BECOME WEAKER to lose strength, loudness, or brightness ○ *The light began to fail.* ■ *n.* STOCK EXCH STOCKBROKER'S DEFAULT the failure by a stockbroker to deliver stock to a purchaser within the normal delivery period [13thC. Via Old French *faillir* from Latin *fallere*, "to deceive somebody's hopes, disappoint."] ◇ **without fail** for certain, or without any possibility of something specified not happening

fail·ing /fáyling/ *n.* **1.** FAILURE the failure to do something, e.g., pass a course or work properly **2.** SHORTCOMING a fault or weakness ■ *prep.* WITHOUT if something does not happen ○ *Failing a resolution of the dispute by this afternoon, we will suspend you.*

WORD KEY: SYNONYMS

See Synonyms at ***flaw.***

faille /fīl/ *n.* a closely woven silk, cotton, or rayon fabric that is slightly ribbed [Mid-16thC. From French, of uncertain origin: probably via Old Northern French from Middle Dutch *falie* "scarf."]

fail-safe *adj.* **1.** SWITCHING TO SAFE CONDITION designed to switch equipment or a system to a safe condition if there is a fault or failure, e.g., as a thermostat turns something off if it overheats **2.** WITH FAIL-SAFE DEVICE protected by or using a fail-safe mechanism **3.** SURE TO SUCCEED not capable of failing ■ *v.* (**fail-safed, fail-saf·ing, fail-safes**) **1.** *vt.* MAKE SOMETHING FAIL-SAFE to safeguard something from failure through use of a fail-safe device or procedure **2.** *vi.* ENG SWITCH TO SAFE CONDITION to switch automatically to a safe condition in the event of a failure in the supply, control, or structural system of something ■ *n.* SOMETHING THAT SAFEGUARDS a fail-safe device or procedure

fail-soft *adj.* used to describe electronic equipment that can operate at a reduced level after the failure of a component or power supply

fail·ure /fáylyər/ *n.* **1.** LACK OF SUCCESS a lack of success in something, or an unsuccessful attempt at doing something **2.** SOMETHING LESS THAN THAT REQUIRED something that falls short of what is required or expected ○ *Failure will not be tolerated.* **3.** SOMETHING THAT FAILS somebody who or something that is unsuccessful **4.** BREAKDOWN OF SOMETHING a breakdown or decline in the performance of something, or an occasion when something stops working or stops working adequately ○ *engine failure* **5.** LACK OF DEVELOPMENT OR PRODUCTION inadequate growth, development, or production of something ○ *crop failure* **6.** BUSINESS BANKRUPTCY a financial collapse, usually leading to bankruptcy

fail·ure to thrive *n.* pronounced lack of growth in a child due to inadequate absorption of nutrients or a serious heart or kidney condition, resulting in below-average height and weight

fain /fayn/ *adv.* (*archaic*) **1.** HAPPILY with gladness or eagerness **2.** PREFERABLY in preference ■ *adj.* (*archaic*) **1.** EAGER willing or eager **2.** COMPELLED forced by an obligation or circumstances [Old English *faegen* "glad," from a prehistoric Germanic word that is also the ancestor of English *fawn* "to act slavishly"]

fai·né·ant /fáynee ənt/ *adj.* IDLE tending to do nothing, or unwilling to do anything (*literary*) ■ *n.* SOMEBODY LAZY somebody who is idle or unwilling to do anything (*literary*) [Early 17thC. From French, alteration of *fait-nient*, literally "does nothing," by folk etymology from *faignant* "shirker."]

faint /faynt/ *adj.* **1.** DIM not bright, clear, or loud **2.** UNENTHUSIASTIC feeble and done without conviction ○ *damned him with faint praise* **3.** DIZZY dizzy or weak, as if about to become unconscious ○ *All of a sudden he felt faint.* **4.** SLIGHT remote or slight ■ *vi.* (**faint·ed, faint·ing, faints**) **1.** MED LOSE CONSCIOUSNESS BRIEFLY to become unconscious, especially for a short time, because of a reduction in the flow of blood to the brain **2.** WEAKEN to become weak or lose courage (*archaic*) ■ *n.* MED SUDDEN LOSS OF CONSCIOUSNESS a sudden, usually brief, loss of consciousness, caused by a reduction in the flow of blood to the brain. Technical name **syncope** [13thC. From Old French, from *faindre* "to pretend, shirk." The meaning "not bright" evolved from "cowardly, lazy" through "feeble."] —**faint·er** *n.* —**faint·ly** *adv.* —**faint·ness** *n.*

faint-heart·ed *adj.* lacking courage, boldness, or enthusiasm —**faint-heart·ed·ly** *adv.* —**faint-heart·ed·ness** *n.*

WORD KEY: SYNONYMS

See Synonyms at ***cowardly.***

fair[1] /fair/ *adj.* **1.** REASONABLE OR UNBIASED not exhibiting any bias, and therefore reasonable or impartial **2.** DONE PROPERLY according to the rules ○ *fair and free elections* **3.** METEOROL NOT STORMY OR CLOUDY sunny or clear, and without much wind **4.** SAILING GOOD FOR SAILING favorable for sailing or travel by ship ○ *a fair wind* **5.** PLEASING TO LOOK AT beautiful or pleasing to the eye **6.** NOT BLOCKED clear and unobstructed ○ *a fair view of the enemy's forces* **7.** LIGHT-COLORED light-colored, or with light-colored hair or skin **8.** SIZEABLE reasonably large in size or quantity ○ *They had a fair number of responses to the advertisement.* **9.** BASEBALL IN FAIR TERRITORY constituting a fair ball according to the rules of baseball ○ *The ball's not going to stay fair* **10.** ACCEPTABLE no more than acceptable or average ○ *Your performance this year has only been fair.* **11.** BETTER THAN ACCEPTABLE quite good, or very reasonable ○ *a fair understanding* **12.** UNSULLIED not marred by any blemish or stain **13.** FALSE DESPITE APPEARANCES seemingly good or true, but actually false or insincere ■ *adv.* **1.** PROPERLY in accordance with the rules or what is expected ○ *He's always played fair with me.* **2.** BASEBALL IN FAIR TERRITORY in or into fair territory on a baseball field **3.** DIRECTLY in a direct or straight way, and squarely ○ *hit fair in the center of the board* ■ *v.* (**faired, fair·ing, fairs**) **1.** *vi. Scotland* METEOROL IMPROVE to become bright after cloud or rain (*refers to the weather or sky*) **2.** *vt.* MAKE SMOOTH AND EVEN to smooth or streamline the surface of something, e.g., of an airplane wing or tabletop [Old English *faeger* "beautiful," from a prehistoric Germanic word meaning "suitable," which is also the ancestor of English *fake*] —**fair·ish** *adj.* ◇ **fair and square** justly, or according to the rules ◇ **fair's fair** used to urge or appeal for just or even treatment (*informal*) ◇ **fair to middling** reasonably good or reasonably well (*informal*) (*hyphenated when used before a noun*) ◇ **for fair** utterly or completely (*informal*) ◇ **no fair** something that is unfair or against the rules (*informal*)

fair off, fair up *vi. Southern U.S.* to become bright after cloud or rain (*refers to the weather or sky*)

WORD KEY: REGIONAL NOTE

An essentially Southern term concerning the weather clearing, ***fair off*** is used alongside less frequent ***fair up*** and *fair*. Today, ***fair off*** recurs most frequently in the Lower South, especially in Georgia, Alabama, Mississippi, and Louisiana, beyond the New Orleans focal area. Taken together, the incidence of ***fair off*** and ***fair up*** surpasses all synonyms except *break, break off* and the general currency term *clear up*.

fair[2] /fair/ *n.* **1. EVENT WITH FARM COMPETITIONS AND AMUSEMENTS** an annual outdoor event, held especially for a state or county, with competitions for the best livestock, produce, and prepared foods and with entertainment, rides, and other amusements **2.** *U.K.* LEISURE = **carnival 3. LIVESTOCK MARKET** a large market selling a wide range of goods including livestock, sometimes with amusements and sideshows **4. COMMERCIAL EXHIBITION** an exhibition, often held annually, at which companies show their products to potential buyers or inform people of business and job opportunities ○ *a book fair* **5. SALE TO RAISE MONEY** a sale of goods to raise money for something, especially a charity [13thC. Via Old French *feire* from late Latin *feria* "holiday," from Latin *feriae* (plural) "holiday, religious festival."]

fair ball *n.* a baseball batted into the portion of the field within the foul lines, unless it subsequently crosses the foul line between home and first or third base before being fielded

Fair·banks /fáir bànks/ city in eastern Alaska, on the northern bank of the Tanana River, northeast of Anchorage. Population: 32,960 (1996).

Fair·banks, Charles (1852–1918) U.S. politician. He was a U.S. senator (1897–1905) before serving as vice president under Theodore Roosevelt (1905–09). Full name **Charles Warren Fairbanks**

Fair·banks, Douglas (1883–1939) U.S. silent movie actor. He is best known for his swashbuckling performances in movies such as *The Mark of Zorro* (1920). Real name **Douglas Elton Ulman**

fair catch *n.* a catch of a kicked football by the receiver who has signaled the he or she will not run. The receiver may not be tackled.

fair cop·y *n.* an unmarked version of a document that has been corrected and retyped or printed out again

Fair·fax /fáir fàks/, **John** (1804–77) English-born Australian newspaper proprietor. He was the owner of the *Sydney Morning Herald* and founder of the Fairfax media dynasty.

Fair·field /fáir feeld/ **1.** city in northern Alabama, a western suburb of Birmingham. Population: 11,490 (1996). **2.** city in western California, northeast of San Francisco and southwest of Sacramento. Population: 85,610 (1996). **3.** town in southeastern Fairfield County, southwestern Connecticut, situated on Long Island Sound. Population: 53,418 (1990).

fair game *n.* somebody who or something that it is considered permissible to pursue, ridicule, or attack

fair·ground /fáir gròwnd/ *n.* a large open outdoor space where fairs or exhibitions may be held ○ *fairground attractions*

fair-haired *adj.* with light-colored hair

fair-haired boy *n.* somebody who is the favorite of a person or a group

fair·ing[1] /fáiring/ *n.* a streamlined structure added to an aircraft, car, or other vehicle to reduce drag. ◊ **cowling**

fair·ing[2] /fáiring/ *n. U.K.* a gift, especially one brought back from, or given at, a fair (*archaic*)

fair·ish /fáirish/ *adj. U.K.* quite light in color — **fair·ish·ly** *adv.*

Fair Isle *n.* any traditional Shetland Islands knitting design, used especially for sweaters, that incorporates bands of repeated multicolored geometric motifs [Mid-19thC. Named for *Fair Isle*, one of the Shetland Islands off the Scottish coast, where garments in this pattern were first knitted.]

Fair Lawn /fáir làwn/ borough in Bergen county, northeastern New Jersey, situated 3 mi./5 km northeast of Paterson. Population: 30,548 (1990).

fair·lead /fáir leed/, **fair·lead·er** /-leedər/ *n.* a ring, hole, or other device through which a rope is guided in order to reduce friction and prevent chafing, or to keep it in place

fair·ly /fáirlee/ *adv.* **1. HONESTLY** in a just and honest, proper, or legitimate way **2. MODERATELY** to a reasonable or moderate degree ○ *a fairly easy decision* **3. COMPLETELY** in a complete, full, or utter way ○ *The ground fairly shook with the impact.*

fair-mar·ket val·ue *n.* a price for something that both buyer and seller willingly agree to when neither party is under undue pressure to complete the transaction

fair-mind·ed *adj.* able to make impartial and just judgments, or resulting from such a judgment — **fair-mind·ed·ness** *n.*

Fair·mont /fáir mònt/ city in northern West Virginia on the Monongahela River, southwest of Morgantown and northeast of Parkersburg. Population: 19,731 (1996).

fair·ness /fáirnəss/ *n.* **1. QUALITY OF BEING FAIR** the condition of being just or impartial **2. BEAUTY** beauty, or the condition of being pleasing to look at ◇ **in (all) fairness** being just and impartial

fair·ness doc·trine *n.* the principle that licensed broadcasters should give equal air time to opposing views on controversial issues

Fair Oaks /fáir ṓks/ area in northeastern Virginia, just east of Richmond, that was the site of the Battle of Fair Oaks and Seven Pines (1862)

fair play *n.* conduct that adheres to the rules or is just and equitable

fair sex *n.* women and girls (*dated*)

fair shake *n.* just treatment, or a reasonable chance to attempt something (*informal*)

fair-spo·ken *adj.* speaking in a pleasant and polite way —**fair-spo·ken·ness** *n.*

fair ter·ri·to·ry *n.* the area of a baseball field within the foul lines, including home plate, the foul poles, and the foul lines themselves

fair-trade a·gree·ment *n.* an agreement between a manufacturer of a product and distributors or retailers that the product will not be sold for less than a price set by the manufacturer —**fair-trade** *adj.*

fair·way /fáir wày/ *n.* **1.** GOLF **GRASS BETWEEN GOLF TEE AND GREEN** the closely mown area on a golf hole that forms the main avenue between a tee and a green **2.** SHIPPING **NAVIGABLE CHANNEL FOR BOATS** a navigable channel or the usual course followed by vessels in a river, harbor, or other body of water

fair-weath·er *adj.* **1. FOR OR IN GOOD WEATHER** suitable, done, or taking part only when the weather is fine **2. NOT STEADFAST** able to be relied upon only when things are going well

Fair·weath·er /fáir wəthər/, **Mount** mountain in the St. Elias Mountains on the border between Alaska and British Columbia, Canada. Part of Glacier Bay National Park and Preserve, it is the highest peak in southern Alaska. Height: 15,300 ft./4,663 m.

Fair·weath·er Cape cape on the southeastern coast of Alaska, approximately 35 mi./55 km south of Mount Fairweather

fair·y /fáiree/ *n.* (*plural* **-ies**) **1. SMALL SUPERNATURAL CREATURE** an imaginary supernatural being, usually resembling a small person, with magic powers. In folklore, fairies may be kindly or malicious. **2. OFFENSIVE TERM** an offensive term for a homosexual man (*slang offensive*) ■ *adj.* **OF FAIRIES** relating to, belonging to, or typical of fairies ○ *the fairy folk* [14thC. From Old French *faerie* "enchantment," from *fae* "fairy," from Latin *fata* "the Fates," plural of *fatum* "fate."] —**fair·y·like** *adj.*

fair·y god·moth·er *n.* **1. KIND FAIRY** in some fairy stories, a kind fairy in the form of a woman who gives vital help to somebody, especially to the hero or heroine. Perhaps the most famous fairy godmother is the one who appears to Cinderella and enables her to attend the prince's ball. **2. SOMEBODY VERY HELPFUL** somebody, especially a woman, who gives generous help, often anonymously

fair·y·land /fáiri lànd/ *n.* **1. LAND OF FAIRIES** the imaginary country where fairies live **2. ENCHANTING PLACE** any enchanting place, e.g., a fantasy world existing in somebody's imagination

fair·y ring *n.* a ring of mushrooms or grass darker than the surrounding grass, traditionally thought to be associated with dancing fairies but actually marking the outer edge of growth of various underground perennial fungi

fair·y shrimp *n.* a tiny soft-bodied crustacean found in fresh or brackish water, with an elongated body and eleven pairs of appendages. Order: Anostraca.

fair·y tale *n.* **1. STORY ABOUT FAIRIES** a story for children about fairies or other imaginary beings and events, often containing a moral message **2. UNLIKELY EXPLANATION** an improbable invented account of something, often a false excuse

WORD KEY: CULTURAL NOTE

Grimm's Fairy Tales, a collection of folk tales compiled and edited by German scholars Jacob and Wilhelm Grimm (1812–15). Based on written sources dating back to the 16th century and on German folk tales, it includes many stories now famous worldwide, including "Cinderella," "Hansel and Gretel," and "Rumpelstiltskin." With their universal themes the tales were seen by the Grimms as repositories of the hopes, passions, and fears of humankind.

fair·y-tale *adj.* **1. FROM FAIRY TALE** derived from or typical of a fairy tale **2. FORTUNATE AND HAPPY** like something from a fairy tale, especially in being fortunate, happy, or extravagantly beautiful

Fai·sal /fı́ss'l/, **King of Saudi Arabia** (1905–75). As absolute ruler and king (1964–75), he supported Middle Eastern nations in their conflict with Israel. Full name **Faisal ibn Abdul Aziz**

Fai·sal I, King of Iraq (1885–1933). An Arab nationalist leader, he was the first king of Iraq (1921–33), and founded the Hashemite dynasty.

Fai·sal II, King of Iraq (1935–58). A minor during most of his long reign (1939–58), he was assassinated during a military coup.

fait ac·com·pli /fèt ə kom plée, fàyt ə kawN plée/ (*plural* **faits ac·com·plis**) *n.* something that is already done or decided and seems unalterable [Mid-19thC. From French, literally "accomplished fact."]

faith /fayth/ *n.* **1. BELIEF OR TRUST** belief in, devotion to, or trust in somebody or something, especially without logical proof **2.** RELIG **RELIGION OR RELIGIOUS GROUP** a system of religious belief, or the group of people who adhere to it **3.** RELIG **TRUST IN GOD** belief in and devotion to God ○ *Her faith is unwavering.* **4. SET OF BELIEFS** a strongly held set of beliefs or principles ○ *people of different political faiths* **5. LOYALTY** allegiance or loyalty to somebody or something [13thC. Via Old French *feid* from Latin *fides* "trust, belief" (source of English *confide* and *fealty*). Ultimately from an Indo-European word that is also the ancestor of English *federal*.] ◇ **keep faith with** be loyal or true to a person or promise ◇ **on faith** without demanding proof

faith·ful /fáythfəl/ *adj.* **1. WITH UNWAVERING BELIEF** believing firmly in something or somebody, especially a religion **2. CONSISTENTLY LOYAL** consistently trustworthy and loyal, especially to a person, a promise, or duty **3. NOT PROMISCUOUS** not having sexual relations with somebody other than a spouse or partner **4. CONSCIENTIOUS** displaying or resulting from a sense of responsibility or devotion to duty **5. CORRECT** accurate and true ○ *a faithful account of the events* ■ *n.* **SOMEBODY OR SOMETHING RELIABLE** somebody who or something that can be trusted or depended on ■ **faith·ful, Faith·ful** *npl.* RELIG **RELIGIOUS BELIEVERS** the believers in a religion considered as a group, especially Muslims or Christians —**faith·ful·ly** *adv.* —**faith·ful·ness** *n.*

faith heal·er *n.* somebody who treats illness or disorders in other people through prayer, sometimes also laying his or her hands on the person being treated —**faith heal·ing** *n.*

faith·less /fáythləss/ *adj.* **1. DISHONEST** dishonest, or disloyal to somebody or something, e.g., in not keeping a promise or performing a duty **2. UNTRUSTWORTHY** not to be trusted or relied on **3.** RELIG **NOT RELIGIOUS** not believing in a religious faith — **faith·less·ly** *adv.* —**faith·less·ness** *n.*

fa·ji·ta /fə heétə/ *n.* a Mexican dish consisting of beef or other meat that has been marinated, grilled, cut into strips, and served in a soft flour tortilla [Late 20thC. From Mexican Spanish, literally "little strip, belt."]

fake[1] /fayk/ *n.* **1. SOMETHING NOT GENUINE** somebody who or something that is not genuine but is presented as, or appears to be, genuine **2.** SPORTS **MOVE TO MISLEAD SPORTS OPPONENT** a move made by a player in attempt to mislead a sports opponent about the player's intended play ○ *He made a fake to the right, and then charged to the hoop.* ■ *adj.* **NOT GENUINE** not genuine, but meant to be taken for genuine ■ *v.* **(faked, fak·ing, fakes) 1.** *vt.* **FALSELY PRESENT SOMETHING AS GENUINE** to make or produce something and claim it is genuine when it is not **2.** *vti.* **PRETEND FEELING OR KNOWLEDGE** to pretend to have, feel, or know something ○ *faked a knowledge of Italian* **3.** *vti.* SPORTS **PERFORM FAKE TO DECEIVE OPPONENT** to perform a fake in an attempt to deceive an opposing player in a sport ○ *The pitcher faked a throw to first base.* **4.** *vt.* ARTS **IMPROVISE WHILE PERFORMING** to improvise or ad-lib a piece of music or lines in a play during a performance [Late 18thC. From *feague*, 16th-century criminal slang for "to rob, tamper with," of uncertain origin; probably from German *fegen* "to polish, refurbish."]

fake out *vt.* to deceive or surprise somebody, especially by bluffing (*informal*)

fake² /fayk/ *vt.* **(faked, fak·ing, fakes) COIL ROPE** to coil or loop a rope so that it will not tangle when used ■ *n.* **COIL OF ROPE** a single coil or loop of a rope that has been faked [15thC. Origin unknown.]

fakeer *n.* = **fakir**

fak·er /fáykər/ *n.* somebody who pretends that something such as an emotion is genuine when it is not —**fak·er·y** *n.*

fa·kir /fə keér/, **fa·qir, fa·keer** *n.* **1.** ISLAM **MENDICANT MUSLIM** a religious Muslim, especially a Sufi, who lives by begging **2.** INDIAN RELIG **HINDU MENDICANT** a Hindu ascetic who lives by begging and whose religious practice often includes the performance of extraordinary feats of physical endurance [Early 17thC. Directly or via French from Arabic, literally "poor man."]

fa·la·fel /fə laáf'l/, **fe·la·fel** *n.* a deep-fried ball of ground chickpeas seasoned with onions and spices, often eaten in pita bread with lettuce and yogurt or tahini sauce. It was originally a Middle Eastern dish. [Mid-20thC. Via Egyptian Arabic *falāfil* from Arabic *fulful* "pepper."]

Fa·lange /fə lánj/ *n.* a Spanish fascist movement founded in 1933 and dissolved in 1977. It was the official ruling party of Spain under Francisco Franco. [Mid-20thC. From Spanish, "phalanx."] —**Fa·lan·gist** *n.*

Fa·la·sha /fə láshə/ (*plural* **-shas** *or* **-sha**) *n.* a member of an Ethiopian Jewish religious group now largely living in Israel [Early 18thC. From *Amharic*, "exile."]

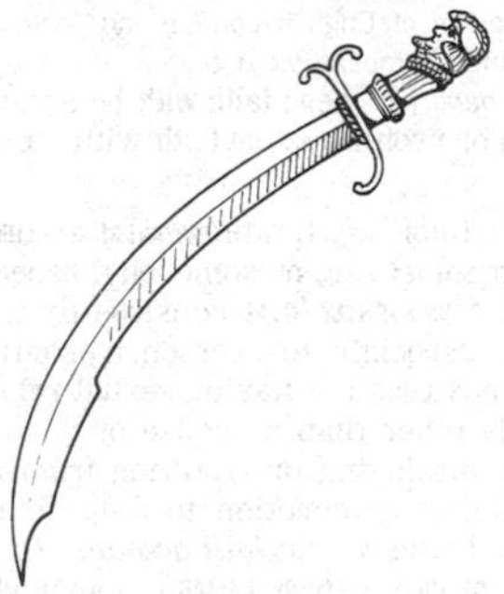

Falchion

fal·chion /fáwlchən/ *n.* a short sword with a broad slightly curved blade, used in medieval times [14thC. Via Old French *fauchon* from, ultimately, Latin *falc-* (see FALCATE).]

fal·con /fálkən/ *n.* **1.** BIRDS **FAST-FLYING BIRD OF PREY** a bird of prey related to the hawk that is fast and powerful and often catches birds as they fly. Family: Falconidae. **2.** HUNT **HAWK TRAINED TO HUNT** a hawk that is trained to hunt small birds and animals. In falconry the term is used only for female hawks. [13thC. Via Old French *fau(l)con* from the late Latin stem *falcon-*, of uncertain origin: perhaps formed from Latin *falc-*, stem of *falx* "sickle," because its talons resemble sickles.]

WORD KEY: CULTURAL NOTE

The Maltese Falcon, a movie by John Huston (1941). Based on Dashiell Hammett's 1930 detective novel, this is regarded as one of the finest examples of film noir. Private investigator Sam Spade's attempts to track down the murderer of his partner lead to a group of people who share a common interest in a priceless statuette of a falcon.

fal·con·er /fálkənər/ *n.* somebody who breeds falcons or trains or uses them to hunt small birds and animals

fal·con·et /fálkə nèt/ *n.* a small falcon, originally from Asia. Genus: *Microhierax.*

fal·con·i·form /fal kóni fàwrm/ *adj.* relating to or resembling birds of prey with strong and sharply hooked beaks, strong feet and sharp claws for grasping prey, and large wings

fal·co·nine /fálkə nīn/ *adj.* relating to, involving, or typical of a falcon

fal·con·ry /fálkənree/ *n.* the breeding, training, and use of falcons or other hawks to hunt small prey and return from flight at a falconer's direction

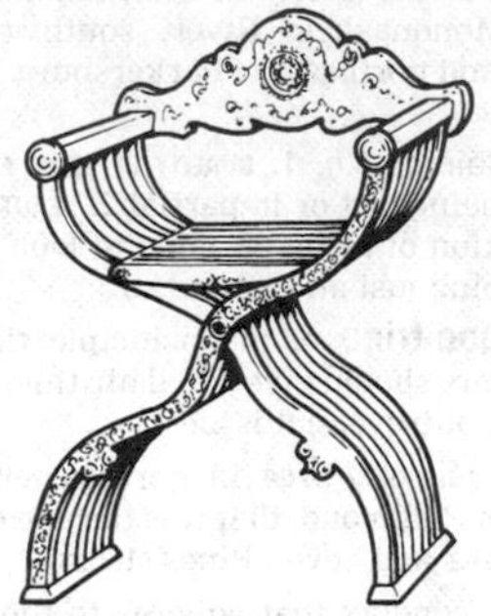

Faldstool

fald·stool /fáwld stōōl/ *n.* **1. FOLDING SEAT FOR BISHOP** a folding seat, especially one used by a bishop when officiating away from his throne or at another church **2. FOLDING STOOL FOR WORSHIPER** a small folding stool with a raised desklike attachment at which a worshiper kneels to pray **3. DESK IN CHURCH** a desk from which the liturgy is read during a church service [Old English *fældstōl*, from FOLD "to be collapsible" + STOOL "seat"; partly from medieval Latin *faldistolium*, ultimately from prehistoric Germanic]

Fa·lis·can /fə lískən/ *n.* an ancient language spoken in Italy before Latin, which was related to and replaced it [Late 17thC. Formed from Latin *Faliscus* "of Falerii," important city of Etruria.]

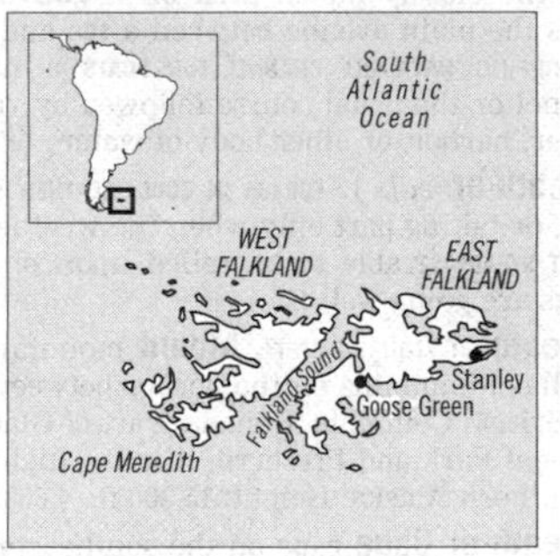

Falkland Islands

Falk·land Is·lands /fáwklənd-/ group of islands and British dependency in the South Atlantic Ocean, 300 mi./483 km east of the Strait of Magellan. Population: 2,100 (1993). Area: 4,700 sq. mi./12,173 sq. km.

fall /fawl/ *vi.* **(fell, fall·en, fall·ing, falls) 1. MOVE DOWNWARD** to come down freely from a higher to a lower position, moved by the force of gravity ○ *The vase fell to the ground and shattered.* **2. DROP OR BE LOWERED** to drop or be dropped or lowered ○ *The curtain fell at the end of the performance.* **3. COME DOWN SUDDENLY FROM UPRIGHT POSITION** to drop or come down suddenly from an upright position, especially by accident ○ *The horse fell at the first fence.* **4. BECOME LOWER** to become lower or be reduced in amount, value, or quality ○ *Prices have fallen in the last year.* **5.** ACOUSTICS **BECOME LOWER IN PITCH** to become lower in pitch or volume **6.** MIL **BE TAKEN BY FORCE** to be conquered or captured by a military force ○ *The city fell despite the best efforts of the army.* **7.** MIL **DROP TO GROUND IN BATTLE** to drop to the ground in battle after being wounded or having died ○ *He fell at the Battle of Waterloo.* **8.** POL **COLLAPSE POLITICALLY** to lose political power or be defeated ○ *The administration fell after 18 months in office.* **9. BE DRAPED** to hang down ○ *When her hair is down it falls across her shoulders.* **10. TAKE PLACE** to happen or occur as if falling on something and enveloping it ○ *Night fell suddenly.* **11. DISPLAY DISAPPOINTMENT** to show an expression of disappointment ○ *Their faces fell when they heard the result.* **12. GROW SAD** to become sad and gloomy or to lose hope ○ *Our hearts fell.* **13. STOP TO LOOK** to settle or come to rest ○ *His gaze fell on an open book.* **14. BE AVERTED** to look away or downward ○ *Her eyes fell.* **15. BEGIN TO BE IN SPECIFIED STATE** to begin to be in, or enter into, a specified state or condition ○ *The class eventually fell silent.* **16.** CHR **SIN** to sin, or give in to temptation (*archaic*) ◊ **Fall 17.** GEOG **SLOPE** to slope downward and away ○ *The land falls gradually to the lake.* **18. START** to begin doing something vigorously ○ *The laborers fell to work on the ditch.* ■ *n.* **1. ACT OF FALLING** the act of falling or moving down freely or suddenly ○ *She broke her arm in a fall.* **2. SOMETHING FALLEN** something that falls or has fallen, or the amount that has fallen ○ *a heavy fall of snow* **3. DISTANCE DOWN** the distance that something drops or could fall ○ *a ten-foot fall* **4. LOWERING OF SOMETHING** a decrease in the amount, size, quantity, or quality of something ○ *Even a slight fall in prices is welcome.* **5.** GEOG **SLOPE** a slope that heads downward and away **6. fall, Fall SEASON BETWEEN SUMMER AND WINTER** the season between summer and winter when leaves change color and fall to the ground **7.** GEOG **WATERFALL** a waterfall or steep rapids (*often used in the plural, often used in placenames*) ○ *Niagara Falls* **8.** MIL **MILITARY LOSS** a military defeat or collapse, or the loss of something to an enemy ○ *the fall of Leningrad* **9.** POL **POLITICAL COLLAPSE** a loss of political power or control ○ *the fall of the government* **10.** RELIG **SINNING** a giving in to temptation, or the commiting of a sin **11. END OF HOISTING ROPE** the end of a rope or chain to which power is applied when hoisting something **12.** WRESTLING **WRESTLING MOVE** a scoring move in wrestling in which one wrestler forces his or her opponent's shoulders to the floor for a specified period **13.** HAIR **HAIRPIECE** a hairpiece of long hair, usually attached to the top of the head and covered over in front by the wearer's own hair **14.** CLOTHES **ORNAMENTAL DECORATION OF LACE** an ornamental piece of lace, veiling, or other light fabric, usually attached to hang draped from a collar or hat **15.** CLOTHES = **falling band 16.** PLANTS **DOWNWARD FACING PART OF IRIS BLOSSOM** the outer part of an iris flower, resembling a petal that hangs down in front ■ *adj.* **FOR OR OF AUTUMN** appropriate for or associated with autumn [Old English *feallan*, from prehistoric Germanic] ◇ **fall flat** to fail to have the intended effect ◇ **fall foul of, fall afoul of 1.** to come into conflict with somebody or something **2.** SAILING to collide with something ◇ **fall short 1.** to be less than is needed **2. fall short of** to fail to meet a desired standard

fall among *vt.* to become associated unwittingly with somebody, something, or a group

fall apart *vi.* **1. BREAK DOWN** to collapse, fail, or break into pieces **2. BE DISTRESSED** to be in a state of great emotional distress (*informal*)

fall away *vi.* **1. DECREASE** to become smaller in number, quantity, or size ○ *Attendance fell away after the third week of the course.* **2. SLOPE** to slope downward **3. STOP ASSOCIATING WITH SOMEBODY** to withdraw friendship, devotion, or support

fall back *vi.* **1. RETREAT** to retreat or move back, e.g., during a battle **2. BE OVERTAKEN** to be overtaken by others in a race or contest

fall back on, fall back up·on *vt.* to resort to something, especially something familiar, if other plans do not work out

fall behind *v.* **1.** *vti.* **FAIL TO KEEP UP** to fail to keep up with somebody or something **2.** *vi.* **BE LATE** to be late in doing something, e.g., making a regular payment or completing a task ○ *He fell behind with the car payments.*

fall down *vi.* **1. COLLAPSE** to collapse or drop to the ground **2. FAIL** to be invalid or unsuccessful

fall down on *vt.* to be unsuccessful or negligent in something

fall for *vt.* **1. FALL IN LOVE WITH** to become infatuated with somebody or something, or fall in love **2. BE DUPED BY SOMETHING** to be deceived by something

fall in *v.* **1.** *vti.* ARMY **FORM RANKS** to join or form an organized rank ○ *The whistle blew and the soldiers fell in.* **2.** *vi.* **CAVE IN** to collapse inward

fall in with *vt.* **1. MEET AND JOIN** to meet and start associating with somebody or a group **2. AGREE WITH** to agree or comply with something or somebody

fall off *v.* **1.** *vi.* **DECLINE** to decrease in size, number, or quality ○ *Stock prices have fallen off in the last couple of days.* **2.** *vti.* SAILING **SAIL DOWNWIND** to deviate from a course to sail downwind, or make a vessel sail downwind

fall on *vt.* **1.** ATTACK to attack somebody vigorously, especially by surprise (*literary*) **2.** *U.K.* BEGIN SOMETHING EAGERLY to begin eating or doing something eagerly **3.** = **fall to** *v.* 1

fall out *v.* **1.** *vi.* QUARREL to have a quarrel with somebody, especially one that leads to strained relations **2.** *vi.* OCCUR to happen **3.** *vti.* BREAK RANKS to leave or break up an organized rank or position

fall through *vi.* to fail to work out successfully

fall to *v.* **1.** *vt.* BE DUTY OF SOMEBODY to be the responsibility, obligation, or duty of somebody or a group ○ *It falls to the council to decide the matter.* **2.** *vti.* START to begin doing something **3.** *vt.* BE GIVEN to be given by right or inheritance to somebody

fall upon *vt.* **1.** = **fall on 2.** = **fall to**

Fall[1] *n.* in Judaism and Christianity, the lapse of humankind into a sinful state as a result of Adam and Eve's sin in disobeying God

Fall[2] /fáwl/ city in southeastern Massachusetts, just north of the Rhode Island border, on the eastern shore of Mount Hope Bay, northwest of New Bedford. Population: 90,865 (1996).

Fall, Albert Bacon (1861–1944) U.S. politician. He was secretary of the interior (1921–23), and was convicted (1929) of accepting a bribe in connection with the leasing of naval oil reserves during his administration.

fal la *n.* = **fa-la**

fal·la·cious /fə láyshəss/ *adj.* **1.** CONTAINING MISTAKEN BELIEF containing or involving a mistaken belief or idea **2.** DECEPTIVE deceptive or liable to mislead people [Early 16thC. Via Old French *fallacieux* from Latin *fallaciosus*, from *fallacia* (see FALLACY.)] —**fal·la·cious·ly** *adv.* —**fal·la·cious·ness** *n.*

fal·la·cy /fálləssee/ (*plural* **-cies**) *n.* **1.** MISTAKEN BELIEF OR IDEA something that is believed to be truth but is erroneous **2.** LOGIC INVALID ARGUMENT an argument or reasoning in which the conclusion does not follow from the premises **3.** DECEPTIVENESS the condition of being misleading or deceptive **4.** LOGIC LOGICAL ERROR IN ARGUMENT a mistake made in a line of reasoning that invalidates it [15thC. Via Old French *fallace* from Latin *fallacia* "deception," from *fallere* "to deceive."]

fal·lal /fa lál, fa laál, fá làl/ *n.* a fancy ornament or piece of clothing [Early 18thC. Origin uncertain.] —**fal·lal·er·y** /fa lálləree/ *n.*

fall·a·way /fáwlə wày/ *adj.* occurring as a player moves away from the basket in a basketball game

fall·back /fáwl bàk/ *n.* **1.** REPLACEMENT OR ALTERNATIVE something that can be used as a replacement or substitute if something else does not or would not work **2.** MIL RETREAT a retreat or withdrawal

fall·board /fáwl bàwrd/ *n.* the hinged cover that protects a piano keyboard when it is not being played

fall·en /fáwllən/ *n.* those people killed in war, especially while fighting

fall·en arch *n.* a flattening of the arches of the foot (*usually used in the plural*)

fall·en wom·an *n.* a woman who is seen as sinful or disgraced because she has had sexual relations outside marriage (*dated disapproving*)

fall·er /fáwllər/ *n.* **1.** SOMEBODY OR SOMETHING THAT FALLS a person, animal, or thing that falls **2.** *Australian* FELLER OF TREES somebody who cuts down trees

fall·fish /fáwl fìsh/ (*plural* **-fish** *or* **-fish·es**) *n.* a large minnow native to eastern North America that is known for its substantial nests, made by piling up small pebbles. Latin name: *Semotilus corporalis.*

fall guy *n.* (*slang*) **1.** SOMEBODY WHO CAN BE FOOLED somebody who is easily tricked or deceived **2.** SCAPEGOAT somebody who takes the blame for something that somebody else has done

fal·li·ble /fálləb'l/ *adj.* **1.** TENDING TO ERR liable to make mistakes **2.** NOT TRUE liable to be wrong or misleading [15thC. From medieval Latin *fallibilis*, from *fallere* "to deceive."] —**fal·li·bil·i·ty** /fàllə bíllətee/ *n.* —**fal·li·ble·ness** /fálləb'lnəss/ *n.* —**fal·li·bly** /fálləblee/ *adv.*

fall·ing ac·tion *n.* the events that follow the climax and lead to the denouement in a work of fiction or drama

fall·ing band *n.* a large collar, often trimmed with lace, turned down flat onto the shoulders and worn by men in the 17th century

fall·ing-off *n.* a decline in quality or quantity

fall·ing-out (*plural* **fall·ings-out** *or* **fall·ing-outs**) *n.* a quarrel or disagreement, especially one that leads to strained relations with somebody

fall·ing rhythm *n.* poetic meter in which the stress falls consistently on the first syllable of a foot

fall·ing star *n.* = **meteor**

fall line *n.* **1.** GEOG LINE ALONG TOP OF SLOPE an imaginary line along the edge of higher land, marked by rapids and waterfalls, that indicates where rivers begin to descend more steeply from a highland region to a lowland one **2.** SKIING, GEOG NATURAL ROUTE OF DESCENT OF HILL the natural route of descent on a hill between two given points **3.** MOUNTAINEERING LINE CONNECTING HIGH AND LOW POINT vertical line connecting a high and low point on a mountain or cliff

fall·off /fáwl àwf, fáwl òf/ *n.* a decrease or decline, especially in prices of something or demand for something

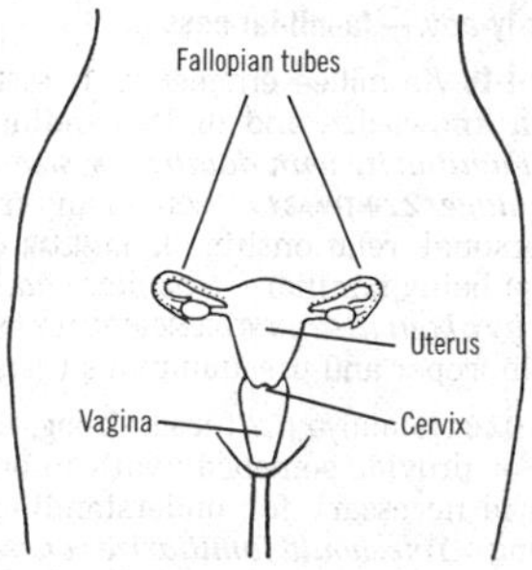

Fallopian tube

fal·lo·pi·an tube /fə lṓpee ən-/, **Fal·lo·pi·an tube** *n.* either of two narrow tubes through which a female mammal's eggs pass from either of the ovaries to the womb [Early 18thC. Named for Gabriele *Fallopio* (1523–62), the Italian anatomist who is reputed to have discovered the structures.]

fall·out /fáwl òwt/ *n.* **1.** PHYS RADIOACTIVE PARTICLES a cloud of radioactive dust that is created by a nuclear explosion and settles back down to the earth **2.** PHYS, METEOROL DESCENT OF RADIOACTIVE DUST the descent to the earth of particles from a cloud of radioactive dust **3.** INCIDENTAL CONSEQUENCES consequences, especially undesirable ones, that result incidentally from a situation or event

fall·out shel·ter *n.* a place of refuge built to protect people from the effects of a nuclear weapon

fal·low[1] /fállō/ *adj.* **1.** AGRIC LEFT UNSEEDED AFTER PLOWING left unseeded after plowing for a period of time in order to recover natural fertility **2.** CURRENTLY INACTIVE currently inactive but with the possibility of activity or use in the future ■ *n.* AGRIC FALLOW LAND land that has been left fallow [13thC. From Old English *fealh*, from *fealgian* "to break up land by plowing."] —**fal·low·ness** *n.*

fal·low[2] /fállō/ *adj.* of a light yellowish brown color [Old English *fealu*. Ultimately from an Indo-European word that is also the ancestor of English *appal*, *pale*, and *pallid*.] —**fal·low** *n.*

Fallow deer

fal·low deer *n.* a deer that lives in Europe and Asia, the male of which has broad flattened antlers and a variably colored coat spotted with white in summer. Latin name: *Dama dama.*

Fall Riv·er town in southeastern Massachusetts, 12 mi./19 km northwest of New Bedford. Population: 92, 703 (1990).

Fal·mouth /fálməth/ town on Cape Cod, in southeastern Massachusetts, where the land narrows between Buzzards Bay and Vineyard Sound. Population: 30,451 (1996).

false /fawls/ *adj.* (**fals·er, fals·est**) **1.** INCORRECT not conforming to facts or truth **2.** MISTAKEN resulting from a mistaken belief or misunderstanding **3.** ARTIFICIAL imitating, copying, or having the same function as the other thing named and replacing or used alongside it **4.** DELIBERATELY DECEPTIVE done with or having the intention of deceiving somebody **5.** NOT GENUINE intentionally made or adopted to deceive somebody **6.** TREACHEROUS disloyal and untrustworthy **7.** BIOL CONFUSABLE WITH NAMED PLANT OR ANIMAL superficially resembling and often mistaken for the plant or animal named ○ *false acacia* ■ *adv.* (**fals·er, fals·est**) DISHONESTLY in a dishonest and disloyal way (*literary*) [Pre-12thC. Directly or via Old French from Latin *falsus*, from *fallere* "to deceive" (source of English *fail* and *fault*).] —**false·ly** *adv.* —**false·ness** *n.*

false a·ca·cia *n.* = **locust**

false a·larm *n.* **1.** NEEDLESS ALARM a situation in which an alarm goes off unnecessarily **2.** SOMETHING CAUSING NEEDLESS WORRY something that appears to be a problem but is not ○ *The company's impending bankruptcy proved to be a false alarm.*

false ar·rest *n.* an arrest made without legal authority

false bed·ding *n.* = **cross-bedding**

false-card (**false-card·ed, false-card·ing, false-cards**) *vi.* to play a card in bridge to mislead an opponent about the cards held in the suit led

false dawn *n.* **1.** LIGHT OCCURRING BEFORE SUNRISE light that appears in the east just before dawn **2.** FAVORABLE SIGN HAVING EXPECTATIONS UNFULFILLED a sign that promises but does not deliver good results

false friend *n.* **1.** DECEPTIVE FOREIGN WORD a word in a second language that looks as if it could be translated by the corresponding word in the first language but actually has a different meaning **2.** TREACHEROUS FRIEND a friend proven to be disloyal and untrustworthy

false fruit *n.* = **pseudocarp**

false·hood /fáwls hòod/ *n.* **1.** LIE a lying or erroneous statement **2.** UNTRUTH something that is untrue **3.** TELLING OF LIES the telling of untruths

WORD KEY: SYNONYMS

See Synonyms at ***lie.***

false im·pris·on·ment *n.* the unlawful confinement of somebody

false keel *n.* an extension to a boat's keel, added to protect the main keel or to increase stability

false mem·o·ry syn·drome *n.* a situation in which examination, therapy or hypnosis has elicited apparent memories, especially of childhood abuse, that are disputed by family members and often traumatic to the patient

false mi·ter·wort *n.* = **foamflower**

false move *n.* an action showing an error of timing or judgment

false po·si·tion *n.* a situation in which somebody is forced to act in an inconsistent or uncharacteristic way

false preg·nan·cy *n.* a condition in which a woman has the delusional belief that she is pregnant and displays symptoms and signs of pregnancy. Technical name **pseudocyesis**

false pre·ten·ses *npl.* deception or misrepresentation in order to gain something from somebody ○ *He gained her trust under false pretenses and didn't tell her he was wanted by the police.*

false rib *n.* any of the lower ribs, the bottom five pairs in humans, not connected directly to the sternum

false start *n.* **1.** ABANDONED START OF RACE a situation in which a competitor in a race breaks a regulation governing the starting procedure and the race has to be restarted **2.** UNSUCCESSFUL START a failed attempt to begin something

false step *n.* **1.** CARELESS ACT an action showing an error of judgment **2.** STUMBLE an act of stumbling

false to·paz *n.* = **citrine**

fal·set·to /fawl séttō/ *n.* (*plural* **-tos**) **1. HIGH SINGING METHOD** a method used by male singers to sing at a very high pitch by using more air and a combination of vocal chord vibration and head resonance. It is used by countertenors in classical music and has been applied to pop music by groups such as the Beach Boys. **2. FALSETTO SINGER** a male singer who sings in a very high voice **3. FALSETTO VOICE** a very high voice used by a male singer ■ *adv.* **IN FALSETTO VOICE** in an artificially or unusually high voice [Late 18thC. From Italian, literally "little false (one)," from *falso* "false," from Latin *falsus* (see FALSE).]

false vam·pire *n.* a bat that hunts and feeds on smaller bats, and is therefore falsely believed to feed on blood. There are five species of false vampires in Europe and Asia and one in Central and South America. Families: Megadermatidae and Phyllostomatidae.

false·work /fáwls wùrk/ *n.* a structure or frame that supports something that is being built

fals·ie /fáwlsee/ *n.* either of two pads worn inside a bra to make the breasts look larger or more shapely (*informal*)

fal·si·fi·ca·tion /fàwlsəfi káysh'n/ *n.* **1. FRAUDULENT ALTERATION** the alteration of documents or evidence for the purposes of deception **2. LIE** a deliberate misrepresentation of the truth or facts

fal·si·fy /fáwlsə fī/ (**-fied, -fy·ing, -fies**) *vt.* **1. ALTER FRAUDULENTLY** to alter something in order to deceive somebody **2. DISPROVE** to prove that something is incorrect **3. MISREPRESENT** to misrepresent the facts in order to mislead ○ *They falsified every detail of their story.* [15thC. Directly or via French *falsifier* from medieval Latin *falsificare* "to act dishonestly," from, ultimately, Latin *falsus* (see FALSE) + Latin *facere* "to make, do" (source of FACT).] —**fal·si·fi·a·bil·i·ty** /fàwlsə fī ə bíllətee/ *n.* —**fal·si·fi·a·ble** /fáwlsə fī əb'l/ *adj.* —**fal·si·fi·er** /fáwlsə fīr/ *n.*

fal·si·ty /fáwlsətee/ (*plural* **-ties**) *n.* **1. BEING UNTRUE** the fact or condition of being untrue **2. SOMETHING UNTRUE** something that is incorrect or untrue [13thC. Directly or via French from Latin *falsitas*, from *falsus* (see FALSE).]

Fal·staff·i·an /fawl stáffee ən/ *adj.* typical of the Shakespearean character Sir John Falstaff in being bawdy, pleasure-loving, given to outlandish bragging, and of great size

falt·boat /fólt bōt, fáwlt-/ *n.* = **foldboat** [Early 20thC. From German *Faltboot*, literally "folding boat," from *falten* "to fold" + *Boot* "boat."]

fal·ter /fáwltər/ (**-tered, -ter·ing, -ters**) *v.* **1.** *vi.* **LOSE CONFIDENCE** to become unsure and hesitant **2.** *vi.* **BEGIN TO FAIL** to lose strength, power, or vitality **3.** *vi.* **STUMBLE** to move unsteadily **4.** *vti.* **HESITATE IN SPEECH** to speak or say something hesitatingly ○ *Trembling with shame, she faltered an apology.* [14thC. Origin uncertain: possibly from Scandinavian.] —**fal·ter·er** *n.* —**fal·ter·ing·ly** *adv.*

WORD KEY: SYNONYMS

See Synonyms at ***hesitate.***

fam. *abbr.* **1.** familiar **2.** family

F.A.M. *abbr.* Free and Accepted Masons

fame /faym/ *n.* **1. RENOWN** the condition of being very well known **2. REPUTATION** somebody's reputation (*archaic*) **3. RUMOR** rumor or report (*archaic*) [12thC. Via French from Latin *fama* "talk, report, reputation" (source of English *famous, infamous,* and *defame*).]

famed /faymd/ *adj.* very well known ○ *The restaurant was famed for its steaks.*

fa·mil·ial /fə míllyəl/ *adj.* relating to or involving a family

fa·mil·iar /fə míllyər/ *adj.* **1. OFTEN ENCOUNTERED** well known, commonly seen or heard, and easily recognized **2. ACQUAINTED WITH SOMETHING** with a thorough knowledge and good understanding of something ○ *Are you familiar with the theory?* **3. FRIENDLY** in or characteristic of a close personal relationship with somebody **4. IMPERTINENTLY INTIMATE** unduly friendly or intimate in a way that is seen as presumptuous or impertinent (*dated*) **5. FAMILIAL** relating to or involving a family (*archaic*) ■ *n.* **1.** RELIG **SPIRIT HELPING WITCH** the supposed aid or helper of a witch, usually supposed to be a spirit with supernatural powers that takes the form of an animal, e.g., a cat **2. INTIMATE FRIEND** a close friend and companion (*formal*) **3.** CHR **LAY MEMBER OF MONASTERY** somebody who lives and works in

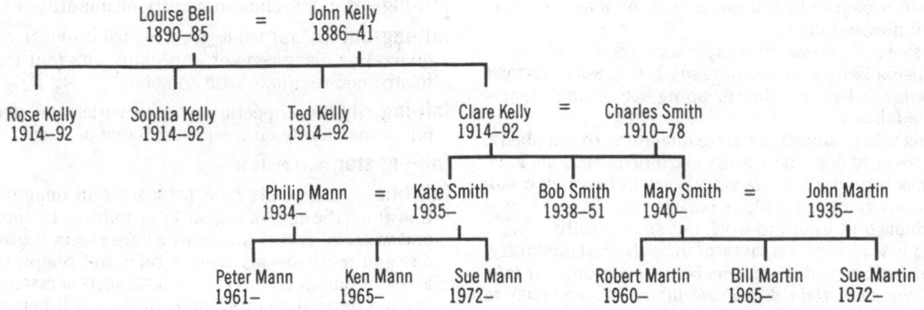

Family tree

a monastic community but has not taken a vow **4.** CHR **HOUSEHOLD ATTENDANT OF POPE OR BISHOP** somebody who undertakes domestic duties in the household of a pope or Roman Catholic bishop [13thC. Via French *familier* from Latin *familiaris*, from *familia* (see FAMILY).] —**fa·mil·iar·ly** *adv.* —**fa·mil·iar·ness** *n.*

fa·mil·iar·i·ty /fə mìllee érrətee/ *n.* **1. GOOD KNOWLEDGE** thorough knowledge and understanding of something ○ *Familiarity with database systems would be an advantage.* **2. INTIMACY** closeness and friendliness in a personal relationship **3. FAMILIAR QUALITY** the quality of being familiar ○ *The place had a strange familiarity about it.* **4. UNWELCOME INTIMACY** an intimacy that is improper and presumptuous (*dated*)

fa·mil·iar·ize /fə míllyə rīz/ (**-ized, -iz·ing, -iz·es**) *vt.* to acquire or provide somebody with information or experience necessary for understanding or doing something ○ *You should familiarize yourself with the emergency procedure.* —**fa·mil·iar·i·za·tion** /fə mìllyəri záysh'n/ *n.* —**fa·mil·iar·iz·er** /fə míllyə rīzər/ *n.*

fa·mil·iar spir·it *n.* = **familiar** *n.* **1**

fam·i·ly /fámmәlee/ *n.* (*plural* **-lies**) **1. PEOPLE LIVING TOGETHER** a group of people living together and functioning as a single household, usually consisting of parents and their children **2. GROUP OF RELATIVES** a group of people who are closely related by birth, marriage, or adoption. ◊ **extended family, nuclear family 3. OTHERS IN SOMEBODY'S FAMILY** the other members of the family to which somebody belongs ○ *He always spends Sunday afternoon with his family.* **4. LINEAGE** all the people who are descended from a common ancestor **5. OFFSPRING** a child or set of children born to somebody ○ *They're not ready to start a family.* **6. GROUP WITH SOMETHING IN COMMON** a group whose members are related in origin, characteristics, or occupation **7.** LING **RELATED LANGUAGES** a group of languages that have a common origin **8.** BIOL **SET OF RELATED ORGANISMS** a category in the taxonomic classification of related organisms, comprising one or more genera **9.** MATH **RELATED MATHEMATICAL SHAPES OR EXPRESSIONS** a set of related mathematical curves, surfaces, or functions, usually expressed as a single equation containing one or more parameters or arbitrary constants ○ *a family of concentric circles* **10.** CHEM **CHEMICAL ELEMENTS WITH SIMILAR PROPERTIES** a set of chemical elements that have similar properties. = **series 11. BRANCH OF MAFIA** a branch of the Mafia or of a similar large criminal group (*informal*) ■ *adj.* **1. USED BY FAMILY** used, owned, or employed by a family, or suitable for one **2. APPROPRIATE FOR CHILDREN** suitable to be experienced by families with children **3. SERVING FAMILIES** serving families not just businesses or institutions [15thC. From Latin *familia* "servants of a household, household, family," from *famulus* "servant."] ◇ **in the family way** pregnant (*dated informal*)

fam·i·ly Bi·ble *n.* a large Bible handed down in a family from one generation to another. A family Bible usually contains records of births, marriages, and deaths.

fam·i·ly cir·cle *n.* **1. CLOSE RELATIVES** the members of a family who are closely related and usually who live together **2. CHEAPER SEATS** an area or tier in a theater where the seats are less expensive

fam·i·ly court *n.* a court that rules on domestic disputes, especially those involving the care and custody of children

fam·i·ly doc·tor *n.* a general practitioner

family leave *n.* LAW a temporary leave of absence for an employee, usually unpaid, so that he or she can take care of family concerns such as emergency child care or a serious illness

fam·i·ly man *n.* a married man who enjoys family life and spends a lot of time with his wife and children

fam·i·ly name *n.* = **surname**

fam·i·ly plan·ning *n.* the use of birth control methods to choose the number and timing of children born into a family

fam·i·ly room *n.* a room in a family home used for relaxation, entertainment, or children's play

fam·i·ly style *adj., adv.* having food provided in serving dishes on the table, so that people can serve themselves (*hyphenated when used before a noun*)

fam·i·ly tree *n.* a chart that shows the relationships of members of a family over time, including dates of marriages, births, and deaths

fam·ine /fámmin/ *n.* **1. EXTREME FOOD SCARCITY** a severe shortage of food resulting in widespread hunger **2. DEFICIENCY OF SOMETHING** a severe shortage of something **3. EXTREME HUNGER** extreme hunger and starvation [14thC. From French, from *faim* "hunger," from, ultimately, Latin *fames* (source of English *famish*).]

fam·ish /fámmish/ (**-ished, -ish·ing, -ish·es**) *vti.* **1. STARVE** to be extremely hungry, or make somebody extremely hungry (*often passive*) **2. DIE OF HUNGER** to die or kill somebody by starvation (*archaic*) [14thC. Formed from earlier *fame*, from Old French *afamer*, from assumed Vulgar Latin *affamare*, literally "to hunger toward," from Latin *fames*.] —**fam·ish·ment** *n.*

fa·mous /fáyməss/ *adj.* **1. VERY WELL KNOWN** known and recognized by many people **2. EXCELLENT** excellent and satisfying (*dated*) [14thC. Via Old French *fameus* from Latin *famosus*, from *fama* (see FAME).] —**fa·mous·ly** *adv.* —**fa·mous·ness** *n.*

fam·u·lus /fámmyələss/ (*plural* **-li** /-lī/) *n.* a personal secretary or attendant, especially to a scholar or magician (*literary*) [Mid-19thC. From Latin, "servant" (see FAMILY).]

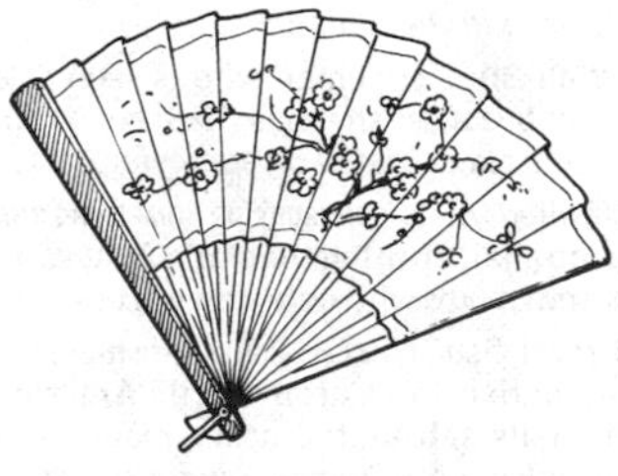

Fan

fan[1] /fan/ *n.* **1. DEVICE FOR MOVING AIR** a device to cool or circulate currents of air, especially one with rotating blades **2. PERSONAL COOLING DEVICE** a flat disk on a handle or a semicircular device of folding struts of paper, silk, or plastic for waving back and forth in order to cool the face **3. SOMETHING FAN-SHAPED** something in the shape of an open handheld fan, e.g., the tail of a peacock **4.** AGRIC **WINNOWING MACHINE** a series of revolving blades used to winnow or clean grain ■ *v.* (**fanned, fan·ning, fans**) **1.** *vt.* **BLOW ON SOMETHING** to blow a current of air steadily and lightly across or around something, either cooling or agitating it ○ *A cool breeze fanned the shore.* **2.** *vt.* **MOVE AIR USING FAN** to move air around using a fan **3.** *vt.* **STIR UP** to cause emotions to become more intense or a situation to become more volatile **4.** *vt.* AGRIC **SEPARATE GRAIN FROM CHAFF** to winnow grain by blowing away the chaff **5.** *vt.* ARMS **FIRE GUN WITH REPEATED CHOPPING MOVEMENT** to fire a gun repeatedly by holding the trigger back and chopping at the hammer with the open hand **6.** *vti.* **SPREAD ACROSS SOMETHING** to spread or spread something out in the shape of an open handheld fan **7.** *vti.* BASEBALL **STRIKE OUT** to strike out a batter in baseball, or while at bat (*slang*) [Pre-12thC. From Latin *vannus* "device for winnowing grain." The sense of cooling device developed in the 16thC as a metaphorical extension.] —**fan·ner** *n.*

fan out *vti.* to spread or spread something out in the shape of an open handheld fan

fan[2] /fan/ *n.* **1. ENTHUSIASTIC ADMIRER** an enthusiastic admirer of a celebrity or public performer **2.** = **fanatic** *n.* 2 [Late 19thC. Shortening of FANATIC. The word is first recorded from the 17thC, but it was not used regularly until the 19thC (referring to sports supporters).]

fa·nat·ic /fə náttik/ *n.* **1. EXTREMIST** somebody who has extreme and sometimes irrational enthusiasms or beliefs, especially in religion or politics **2. FAN OF SOMETHING** somebody who is very enthusiastic about a pastime or hobby ■ *adj.* = **fanatical** [Mid-16thC. Directly or via French from Latin *fanaticus* "inspired by a god, frenzied," from *fanum* "temple" (source of English *profane*).]

fa·nat·i·cal /fə náttik'l/ *adj.* excessively enthusiastic about a particular belief, cause, or activity —**fa·nat·i·cal·ly** *adv.* —**fa·nat·i·cal·ness** *n.*

fa·nat·i·cism /fə nátti sìzzəm/ *n.* an extreme and often irrational enthusiasm or belief

fa·nat·i·cize /fə nátti sīz/ (**-cized, -ciz·ing, -ciz·es**) *vti.* to make somebody fanatical about something, or become fanatical

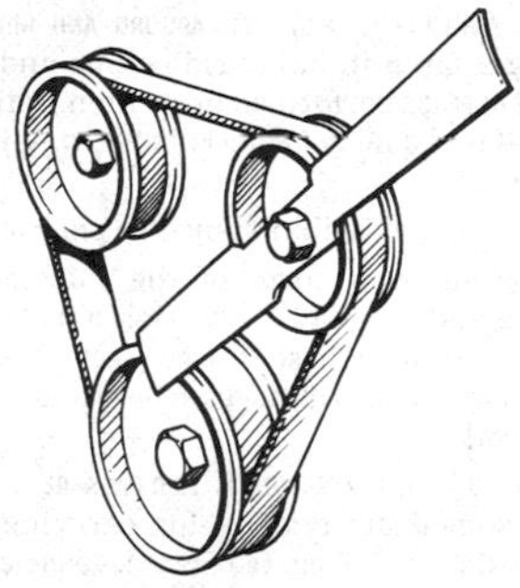

Fan belt

fan belt *n.* a continuous belt that turns a fan, especially one turning the cooling fan in the engine of a motor vehicle

fan·ci·er /fánsee ər/ *n.* **1. ENTHUSIAST** somebody especially interested in or enthusiastic about something **2. BREEDER OF PLANT OR ANIMAL** somebody with a special interest in the breeding of a particular animal or plant

fan·ci·ful /fánsif'l/ *adj.* **1. IMAGINARY** based on imagination or dreams **2. IMAGINATIVE AND IMPRACTICAL** led by imagination rather than realism and practicality **3. CURIOUSLY MADE** strangely and imaginatively designed or made —**fan·ci·ful·ly** *adv.* —**fan·ci·ful·ness** *n.*

fan club *n.* an organization whose members are devoted to a celebrity or public performer, providing information and sometimes organizing special events

fan·cy /fánsee/ *adj.* (**-ci·er, -ci·est**) **1. NOT PLAIN** elaborately and ornately decorated **2. INTRICATE** intricately and skillfully performed **3. HIGH QUALITY** having superior quality (*used especially of foods*) **4. EXPENSIVE** excessively priced or valued ○ *fancy prices* ○ *fancy restaurants charging high prices* **5. SELECTIVELY BRED** used to describe animals that have been bred for specific features and qualities ■ *vt.* (**-cied, -cy·ing, -cies**) **1. SUPPOSE** to be inclined to think that something is the case ○ *I fancy that it will be bright and sunny tomorrow.* **2. IMAGINE** to form the idea of something in the imagination **3.** *U.K.* **WISH FOR SOMETHING** to want to do or have something ○ *I fancy a walk this afternoon.* ○ *Do you fancy a coffee?* **4.** *U.K.* **DESIRE SOMEBODY** to find somebody sexually desirable (*informal*) ○ *I'm sure he fancies you!* **5.** *U.K.* **SELECT AS WINNER** to think that somebody will succeed ○ *Who do you fancy for the title?* ■ *interj.* *U.K.* **EXPRESSING SURPRISE** used to express surprise (*informal*) ○ *Fancy! All that money!* ○ *Fancy that! I would never have believed it!* ○ *Fancy them splitting up after all these years!* ■ *n.* (*plural* **-cies**) **1. SUDDEN LIKING** an impulsive desire for something ○ *The hat caught my fancy.* **2. NOTION** an unfounded belief about something **3. PLAYFUL IMAGINATIVENESS** the faculty of using the imagination playfully or inventively **4. SOMETHING IMAGINARY** something created by the imagination, especially something of a playful or superficial nature **5. LIKELY WINNER** something or somebody thought likely to succeed or win **6. GOOD TASTE** good critical taste and judgment (*formal*) **7. BOXING ENTHUSIASTS** enthusiasts of a sport or pastime, especially boxing (*archaic*) [15thC. A contraction of FANTASY. The adjective arose from the idea of something varied according to the fancy.] —**fan·ci·ly** *adv.* —**fan·ci·ness** *n.*

fancy up *vt.* to decorate something

fan·cy dress *n.* unusual clothing worn to a social gathering, often depicting a famous person, fictional character, or historical period [Because it is a costume arranged according to the wearer's fancy]

fan·cy-free *adj.* free to go anywhere and do anything ○ *footloose and fancy-free* [Literally "free from the power of love," from FANCY in an obsolete sense of the word, "love, amorous inclination"]

fan·cy man *n.* (*dated informal*) **1. WOMAN'S LOVER** the lover or boyfriend of a woman, especially a married woman **2. PIMP** a man who finds customers for prostitutes in return for part or all of their earnings

fan·cy wom·an *n.* (*dated informal*) **1. MAN'S LOVER** the lover or girlfriend of a man, especially a married man **2. PROSTITUTE** a prostitute

fan·cy·work /fánsi wùrk/ *n.* embroidery and other decorative needlework

fan dance *n.* an erotic dance in which large fans are used to mask and reveal parts of the dancer's nude body

fan·dan·go /fan dáng gō/ (*plural* **-gos**) *n.* **1.** DANCE **SPANISH DANCE** a vigorous Spanish or Latin American dance in triple time, traditionally performed by a man and woman as a courtship ritual **2.** MUSIC **DANCE MUSIC** a piece of music for the fandango, in triple time [Mid-18thC. From Spanish, of uncertain origin: perhaps African.]

fan·dom /fándəm/ *n.* fans collectively, especially of a public entertainer such a movie or TV star

fane /fayn/ *n.* a temple or shrine to a god or gods (*archaic*) [14thC. From Latin *fanum* "temple" (source of English *fanatic*).]

fan·fare /fán fàir/ *n.* **1. TRUMPET FLOURISH** a short dramatic series of notes played on trumpets or other brass instruments, especially to mark the arrival of somebody important **2. SHOWY DISPLAY** any dramatic and ostentatious event, especially an announcement or publicity stunt [Mid-18thC. From French, of uncertain origin: perhaps from, ultimately, Arabic *farfār* "chatterer"; or perhaps an imitation of the sound.]

fan·fold /fán fōld/ *adj.* folded into pleats by making alternate folds in opposite directions ○ *fanfold computer paper*

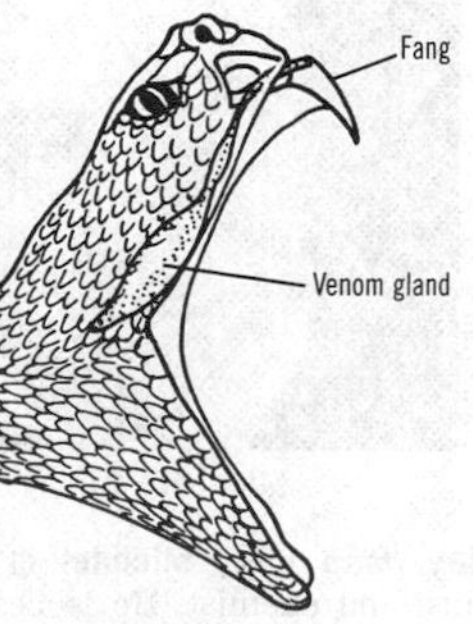

Fang

fang /fang/ *n.* **1. CANINE TOOTH** a long pointed tooth of a mammal on each side of the mouth toward the front **2. SNAKE'S TOOTH** a tooth of a venomous snake, with a hollow or grooves through which venom is injected **3. SPIDER'S MOUTHPART** either of the pair of mouthparts of a spider, from which poison is emitted ■ **fangs** *npl.* **TEETH** the teeth (*informal*) [Old English, "plunder, booty." In Middle English, the word also had the sense of "grasp" or "embrace," from which the meaning of "animal's tooth" presumably derives.]

Fang /fang, faang/ (*plural* **Fang** *or* **Fangs**) *n.* **1.** PEOPLES **MEMBER OF W AFRICAN PEOPLE** a member of a people who live mainly in the rain forests of Gabon, Equatorial Guinea, and Cameroon **2.** LANG **W AFRICAN LANGUAGE** the language spoken by the Fang. It is a Bantu language of the Benue-Congo branch of the Niger-Congo family of African languages. About two million people speak Fang. [Mid-19thC. From French *Fan*, of uncertain origin: probably from Fan *Pangwe*.] —**Fang** *adj.*

fanged /fangd/ *adj.* having fangs

fan·heat·er /fán hèetər/ *n.* *U.K.* an electric heater that blows out a current of warm air using a fan

fan·ion /fánnyən/ *n.* a small marking flag used by surveyors and soldiers [Early 18thC. From French, "small mancíple," from *fanon*, from assumed Frankish *fano* "piece of fabric." Ultimately from an Indo-European word that is also the ancestor of English *vane*.]

fan·jet /fán jèt/ *n.* **1. JET ENGINE WITH LARGE FRONTAL FAN** a jet engine with a large turbine-driven fan located in a forward duct that increases thrust and reduces noise by forcing air back around the exhaust **2. AIRCRAFT POWERED BY FANJETS** an aircraft powered by one or more fanjets

Fan Kuan /faán kwaán/ (*fl.* 990–1030) Chinese artist. He is noted for his landscapes of mountains and streams, which he painted while living alone in the mountains.

fan let·ter *n.* a letter written to a celebrity by a fan

fan·light /fán līt/ *n.* **1. FAN-SHAPED WINDOW** a semicircular window above a door or another window, often with struts forming the shape of an open handheld fan **2.** *U.K.* = **transom**

fan mail *n.* letters sent to celebrities by their fans

Fan·nie Mae /fànni máy/ *n.* the Federal National Mortgage Association, a private corporation sponsored by the U.S. government that supplies funds for mortgages, or a publicly traded security backed by it [Origin uncertain: perhaps from the acronym FNMA short for *Federal National Mortgage Association*]

fan·ny /fánnee/ (*plural* **-nies**) *n.* the buttocks (*informal*) [Early 20thC. Origin uncertain: perhaps from *Fanny*, the nickname of *Frances*.]

fan·ny pack *n.* a pouch for valuables, strapped around the waist

fan palm *n.* a palm tree such as the palmetto that has divided fan-shaped leaves

fan·tab·u·lous /fan tábbyələss/ *adj.* extremely good (*humorous*) [Mid-20thC. A blend of FANTASTIC and FABULOUS.]

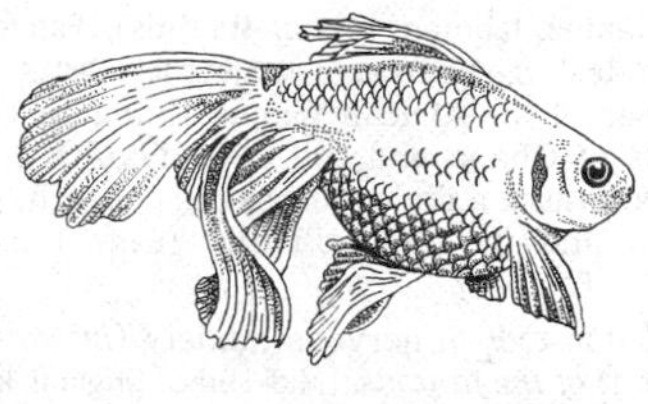

Fantail

fan·tail /fán tàyl/ *n.* **1. FAN-SHAPED TAIL OR END** a tail or the end of something shaped like an open handheld fan **2.** BIRDS **PIGEON WITH FAN-SHAPED TAIL** a breed of domestic pigeon with a broad fan-shaped tail **3.** BIRDS **BIRD WITH BROAD TAIL** a small flycatcher of Australia, New Zealand, and Asia with a fan-shaped tail. Genus: *Rhipidura*. **4.** ZOOL **GOLDFISH WITH BROAD TAIL** a goldfish with a broad double tail fin **5.** SHIPPING **ROUNDED PART OF STERN** a rounded overhanging part of a ship's stern **6. WINDMILL SAIL** a secondary sail on a windmill that keeps the main sails facing into the wind

fan-tan /fán tàn/ *n.* **1.** GAMBLING **GAMBLING GAME** a Chinese gambling game in which players bet on how many items that have been concealed under a bowl remain after being counted off in fours **2.** CARDS **CARD GAME** a card game in which players seek to discard all their cards in a sequence based on the same suit as a seven that has been led [Late 19thC. From Chinese, from *fān* "turn, chance" + *tān* "to spread out."]

fan·ta·sia /fan táyzhə, fan táyzhee ə/ *n.* an instrumental composition in a free and improvisatory style, sometimes based on well-known melodies [Early 18thC. From Italian, literally "fantasy, imagination," from Latin *phantasia* (see FANTASY).]

WORD KEY: CULTURAL NOTE

Fantasia, a movie produced by Walt Disney (1940). This ambitious attempt to popularize classical music consists of cartoon animation matched to eight famous musical compositions. Its best-known sequences include hippos dancing to Ponchielli's "Dance of the Hours" and Mickey Mouse as the protagonist of Dukas' "The Sorcerer's Apprentice."

fan·ta·sist /fántəssist/ *n.* somebody who imagines fantasies

fan·ta·size /fántə sīz/ (**-sized, -si·zing, -siz·es**) *vti.* to form or indulge in fantasies of the imagination

fan·tast /fán tàst/ *n.* somebody who has impractical daydreams [Late 16thC. Via German *Phantast* from Greek *phantastēs* "boaster," from *phantazein* or *phantazesthai* (see FANTASY).]

fan·tas·tic /fan tástik/, **fan·tas·ti·cal** /fan tástik'l/ *adj.* **1.** EXCELLENT extraordinarily good **2.** INCREDIBLE apparently impossible but real or true **3.** IMAGINARY existing only in the imagination **4.** ENORMOUS much larger than is usual, expected, or desirable **5.** BIZARRE extremely strange or weird in appearance **6.** UNLIKELY unusual and unlikely to be successful ■ *interj.* EXPRESSING PLEASURE used to express amazement at and approval of some event or piece of information (*informal*) ○ *You won the game? Fantastic!* [14thC. Via French from, ultimately, Greek *phantastikos*, from *phantazein* or *phantazesthai* (see FANTASY).] —**fan·tas·ti·cal·i·ty** /fan tàsti kállətee/ *n.* —**fan·tas·ti·cal·ness** /fan tástik'lnəss/ *n.*

fan·tas·ti·cal·ly /fan tástikəlee/ *adv.* **1.** VERY extremely **2.** VERY WELL in a superb way **3.** STRANGELY in a weird and strange way

fan·tas·ti·co /fan tástikō/ *interj.* = **fantastic** (*informal*) [Late 16thC. Via Italian, literally "fantastic," from, ultimately, Greek *phantazein* or *phantazesthai* (see FANTASY).]

fan·ta·sy /fántəssee/ *n.* (*plural* **-sies**) **1.** IMAGINATIVE POWER the creative power of the imagination **2.** MENTAL IMAGE OR DREAM an image or dream created by the imagination **3.** PSYCHOL CREATION OF MENTAL IMAGES the creation of exaggerated mental images in response to an ungratified need **4.** IMPRACTICAL IDEA an unrealistic and impractical idea **5.** LITERAT GENRE OF FICTION a type of fiction featuring imaginary worlds and magical or supernatural events **6.** MUSIC = **fantasia** ■ *vti.* (**-sied, -sy·ing, -sies**) = **fantasize** [14thC. Via Old French from Greek *phantasia*, "appearance, imagination," from, ultimately, *phainein* "to show" (source of English *phantom* and *phenomenon*).]

Fan·ti /fántee, faántee/ (*plural* **-ti** *or* **-tis**), **Fan·te** (*plural* **-te** *or* **-tes**) *n.* **1.** PEOPLES MEMBER OF AFRICAN PEOPLE a member of an African people living in the rain forests of Ghana and the Côte d'Ivoire **2.** LANG W AFRICAN LANGUAGE a dialect of Akan spoken in parts of Ghana and the Côte d'Ivoire [Early 19thC. From Fanti.] —**Fanti** *adj.*

fan·tod /fán tòd/ *n.* nervous anxiety (*informal*) ○ *He had a fit of the fantods.* [Mid-19thC. Origin unknown.]

fan vault·ing *n.* a form of vaulting in which ribs fan out from the four corners of a bay, like a fan

fan·wort /fán wùrt, -wàwrt/ *n.* an aquatic plant of the lily family that has fan-shaped submerged and floating leaves. Genus: *Cambomba.*

fan·zine /fán zeen/ *n.* an amateur magazine produced for fans of a pastime or celebrity [Mid-20thC. Coined from FAN^2 + MAGAZINE.]

FAO *abbr.* Food and Agricultural Organization (of the UN)

f.a.o. *abbr.* for the attention of

FAQ /fak, àf ay kyoō/ *abbr.* **1. FAQ, FAQs** frequently asked questions **2.** SHIPPING free alongside quay

f.a.q. *abbr.* COMM fair average quality

faqir *n.* = **fakir**

far /faar/ (**far·ther** /faárthər/ *or* **fur·ther** /fúrthər/, **far·thest** /faárthəst/ *or* **fur·thest** /fúr-/) CORE MEANING: an adverb and adjective indicating that something is a long way away in distance or time ○ *These vessels had been venturing as far as Iceland for cod.* ○ *They have been fishing in the area as far back as 1980.*

1. *adv.* A LONG WAY OFF at, to, or from a great distance ○ *We saw the first outline of the shore far away.* **2.** *adv.* A LONG TIME OFF at or to a long time distant from the point of reference ○ *The well was contaminated as far back as 1986.* **3.** *adv.* MUCH OR MANY to or by a considerable degree ○ *Keeping a dog healthy is far more complicated than it seems.* ○ *There are far fewer factory jobs available these days.* **4.** *adj.* DISTANT remote in space or time ○ *He stood there, gazing into the far distance.* **5.** *adj.* MORE DISTANT more distant from somebody or something ○ *Becky cowered in a far corner of the trailer.* **6.** *adj.* EXTREME having an extreme position in a particular direction ○ *His politics are far left of center.* [Old English *feor(r)*, from the comparative of the assumed Germanic word for "beyond." Ultimately from an Indo-European word that is also the ancestor of English *forth* and *prow.*] —**far·ness** *n.* ◇ **far and away** without a doubt and by a large margin ○ *She is far and away the best player that we have.* ◇ **far and near** everywhere ○ *Doctors from far and near flocked to his bedside.* ◇ **far and wide** covering a great distance ○ *The church bells will be heard far and wide.* ◇ **far from** indicates that something is not the case ○ *This upscale meat market is far from an old style butcher shop.* ◇ **far from it** on the contrary ○ *He was not the tallest boy in the class – far from it.* ◇ **far gone 1.** in a state of deterioration and unable to function ○ *These shoes can't be repaired – they're too far gone.* **2.** very drunk (*informal*) ○ *there's nothing pleasant about someone that far gone.* ◇ **go far 1.** to be very successful ○ *He is very talented and I am sure he will go far in his chosen career.* **2.** to last or be sufficient ○ *Three loaves of bread won't go far once my family gets going.* ◇ **go too far, take something too far** to do or say something that is unacceptable or that exceeds reasonable limits ○ *Harriet paused, and realized that she had gone too far.* ◇ **in so far as** to the extent that ◇ **so far 1.** up to this moment ○ *So far, 150 people have shown an interest in the product.* **2.** up to a certain point, extent, or degree ○ *Freedom of information can only go so far.* ◇ **so far so good** indicates satisfaction with progress made up to this point ○ *So far so good, but the last part of the climb is the hardest.* ◇ **thus far** up to this point ○ *The evidence thus far pointed clearly and conclusively against him.*

Fa·ra·bi /fə raábee/, **al-** (873?–950?) Arabian philosopher. He influenced Islamic philosophy with his studies of Plato and Aristotle.

far·ad /fé ràd, férrəd/ *n.* the SI unit of capacitance equal to that of a capacitor carrying one coulomb of charge when a potential difference of one volt is applied. Symbol **F** [Mid-19thC. Named for Michael FARADAY.]

far·a·da·ic *adj.* = **faradic**

far·a·day /férrə dày/ *n.* a unit of electricity equal to that needed to deposit a unit amount of singly-charged substance during electolysis, equivalent to 96,485 coulombs. Symbol *F* [Early 20thC. Named for Michael FARADAY.]

Michael Faraday

Far·a·day /fárrə dày/, **Michael** (1791–1867) British physicist and chemist. He is best known for his discoveries of electromagnetic induction and of the laws of electrolysis. He also showed how electromagnetic induction could be used in generators and transformers.

fa·rad·ic /fə ráddik/, **far·a·da·ic** /fèrrə dáy ik/ *adj.* relatng to an intermittent alternating current produced in the secondary winding of an induction coil [Late 19thC. From French *faradique*, named for Michael FARADAY.]

far·a·dism /férrə dìzzəm/ *n.* the therapeutic application of an alternating electric current to stimulate nerve and muscle function [Late 19thC. Named for Michael FARADAY. See -ISM.]

far·a·dize /férrə dīz/ (**-dized, -diz·ing, -diz·es**) *vt.* to use an alternating electric current to stimulate nerve and muscle function [Mid-19thC. Named for Michael FARADAY.] —**far·a·di·za·tion** /fèrrədi záysh'n/ *n.* —**far·a·diz·er** /férrə dīzər/ *n.*

far·an·dole /férrən dòl/ *n.* **1.** DANCE PROVENÇAL DANCE a lively dance from the Provence region of France in which dancers link hands to form a weaving line following the leader **2.** MUSIC MUSIC FOR FARANDOLE DANCE a piece of music for the farandole, in six-eight or four-four time [Mid-19thC. Via French from modern Provençal *farandoulo*, of unknown origin.]

far·a·way /faárə wày/ *adj.* **1.** REMOTE a great distance away **2.** SOUNDING DISTANT heard from a distance **3.** DREAMY having a dreamy, absent-minded expression or appearance —**far·a·way·ness** *n.*

farce /faars/ *n.* **1.** ABSURD SITUATION a ridiculous situation in which everything goes wrong or becomes a sham ○ *It was a complete farce – the bride changed her mind at the last minute and the two families ended up having a public shouting match.* **2.** COMIC PLAY a comic play in which authority, order, and morality are at risk and ordinary people are caught up in extraordinary goings on **3.** STYLE OF COMIC DRAMA the style of comic drama in which authority, order, and morality are at risk and ordinary people are caught up in extraordinary goings on [Early 16thC. Via French, literally "stuffing," from, ultimately, Latin *farcire*. In the Middle Ages comical interludes were often inserted into religious plays.]

far·ceur /faar súr/ *n.* **1.** SOMEBODY INVOLVED WITH FARCES an actor in or writer of farces **2.** JOKER somebody who is intentionally comical [Late 17thC. From French, from *farce* (see FARCE).]

far·ci·cal /faársik'l/ *adj.* **1.** ABSURD AND MIXED UP resembling a farce in being ridiculous and confused **2.** IN STYLE OF FARCE performed or written in the style of a farce —**far·ci·cal·i·ty** /faàrsi kállətee/ *n.* —**far·si·cal·ly** /faársik'l/ *adv.*

far cry *n.* a long way in distance or character

far·cy /faársee/ *n.* a form of the infectious horse disease glanders [14thC. Via French *farcin* from, ultimately, Latin *farcire* "to stuff" (see FARCE). The underlying idea is that of a swollen gland resembling a sausage or other stuffed food.]

far·del /faárd'l/ *n.* (*archaic*) **1.** TIED PACKAGE a bundle or pack of something tied up for carrying **2.** LOAD a heavy load [14thC. From Old French, "bundle, load," the diminutive of *farde* "bundle," of uncertain origin; perhaps ultimately from Arabic *fardah*, *farde* "load."]

fare /fair/ *n.* **1.** COST OF TRAVEL the amount charged for a journey **2.** PASSENGER a paying passenger in a taxi **3.** FOOD food that is provided, especially when simple and substantial **4.** ENTERTAINMENT the range of entertainment provided ■ *vi.* (**fared, far·ing, fares**) **1.** MANAGE IN DOING SOMETHING to get on in a specified way in doing or experiencing something ○ *How did she fare in the exam?* **2.** HAPPEN to turn out in a specified way for somebody **3.** EAT to dine or be given food **4.** TRAVEL to go on a journey [Old English *fær* or *faru* "journey," from prehistoric Germanic. The sense "food" seems to derive from the notion of "how well somebody is faring, how somebody is provided for."]

fare·well /fair wél/ *interj.* GOODBYE used to express good wishes at parting (*dated*) ○ *Farewell, my friend!* ■ *n.* EXPRESSION OF PARTING GOOD WISHES an expression of good wishes at parting ■ *adj.* SAYING GOODBYE marking an end, conclusion, or leavetaking [14thC. From the phrase *fare well*, originally addressed to somebody setting out on a journey.]

Fare·well, Cape /fáir wel, fair wél/ cape on the northern coast of the South Island, New Zealand. It is the northernmost point of the South Island.

far·fel /faárf'l/, **far·fal** *n.* pasta in the shape of small grains [Late 19thC. From Yiddish *farfl*, from Middle High German *varveln* "noodles, noodle soup."]

far-fetched *adj.* exaggerated and unconvincing [The first meaning of the word was "brought from far"]

far-flung *adj.* **1.** WIDESPREAD distributed over a wide area **2.** REMOTE at a great distance

Far·go /faárgō/ city in southeastern North Dakota, on the Minnesota border, south of Grand Forks. Population: 83,788 (1996).

Far·go, William George (1818–81) U.S. entrepreneur. In 1852, he cofounded an express delivery company that shipped goods by stagecoach.

fa·ri·na /fə reénə/ *n.* **1. FLOUR** flour or meal made from wheat, nuts, or vegetables, often used in pastries and soups **2.** *U.K.* **STARCH** starch, especially that made from potatoes [14thC. From Latin *farina* "ground corn, flour, meal," from *far* (see FARRAGO).]

far·i·na·ceous /fèrrə náyshəss/ *adj.* containing or consisting of starch [Mid-17thC. From late Latin *farinaceus*, from Latin *farina* "flour."]

far·i·nose /férrə nṑss/ *adj.* **1.** FOOD TECH **YIELDING STARCH** consisting of or yielding starch **2.** BOT **FLOURY IN APPEARANCE** with a powdery or floury appearance, especially because of a covering of fine whitish hairs [Early 18thC. From late Latin *farinosus*, from Latin *farina* "flour."]

far·kle·ber·ry /faárk'l bèrree/ (*plural* **-ries**) *n.* a shrub of the heath family, native to the southeastern United States, that has leathery leaves and hard black berries with stony seeds. Latin name: *Vaccinium arboreum*. [Mid-18thC. *Farkle* of uncertain origin.]

farm /faarm/ *n.* **1. AGRICULTURAL LAND AND BUILDINGS** an area of land where crops are grown or animals are reared for sale, for commercial purposes, together with appropriate buildings **2. PLACE PRODUCING PARTICULAR ANIMALS OR CROPS** an area of land or water where particular animals, birds, fish, or crops are raised for commercial purposes (*usually used in combination*) ○ *a trout farm* **3. FARM BUILDINGS** a farmhouse or group of farm buildings **4. LAND USED BY INDUSTRY** a piece of land on which something is stored, produced or processed, especially on an industrial scale (*usually used in combination*) ○ *an antenna farm* ■ *v.* (**farmed, farm·ing, farms**) **1.** *vti.* **USE LAND FOR AGRICULTURE** to use land for growing crops and rearing animals for sale **2.** *vt.* **REAR SOMETHING COMMERCIALLY** to rear animals, birds, or fish commercially **3.** *vt.* = **farm out** [14thC. Via French *ferme* "lease" from medieval Latin *firma* "fixed payment," from Latin *firmare* "to fix, settle, confirm," from *firmus* "firm."] —**farm·a·ble** *adj.* —**farm·ing** *n.*

WORD KEY: CULTURAL NOTE

Animal Farm, a novel by British writer George Orwell (1945). A satirical allegory of Stalinist Russia, it describes how a group of farm animals, led by pigs, overthrow their human owner and try to run the farm on egalitarian principles. Corrupted by power, the pigs distort their ideology to support their increasingly brutal tyranny, justifying their actions with slogans such as "All animals are equal, but some are more equal than others."

farm out *vt.* **1. SEND WORK OUT** to send work out to be done by somebody else **2. SEND ELSEWHERE FOR CARE** to send children or animals to be looked after by somebody else **3. REASSIGN PLAYER** to assign a major league player to a minor league team

farm·er /faármər/ *n.* somebody who owns or operates a farm

Far·mer /faármər/, **Fannie** (1857–1915) U.S. home economist. She edited *The Boston Cooking School Cook Book* (1896), out of which grew the classic *Fannie Farmer Cookbook*. Full name **Fannie Merritt Farmer**

Far·mer, James (*b.* 1920) U.S. civil rights leader. He founded the nonviolent Congress of Racial Equality (CORE) (1942) and served as its national director (1961–66). Full name **James Leonard Farmer**

farm·er cheese *n.* a mild cheese made from pressing together milk curds

farm·er's lung *n.* inflammation of the lungs marked by chronic shortness of breath and caused by an allergic reaction to fungal spores from moldy hay

farm·ers' mar·ket *n.* an area, usually outdoors, where farmers gather to sell fresh produce direct to the public

farmer's match *n.* *Midwest* a match that ignites on any surface, as opposed to a safety match

WORD KEY: REGIONAL NOTE

The term **farmer's match** is recurrent in the Upper Midwest, especially South Dakota.

farm hand *n.* somebody hired to work on a farm

farm·house /faárm hòwss/ *n.* (*plural* **-houses** /-zəz/) **FARMER'S HOUSE** a house on a farm, especially the main dwelling place of the farmer ■ *adj.* **MADE ON FARM** produced on a farm or of a similar style or quality as that produced on a farm

Far·ming·ton /faármingtən/ city in northwestern New Mexico, northeast of Gallup and northwest of Santa Fe. Population: 37,936 (1996).

farm·land /faárm lànd/ *n.* land that is suitable for farming or used by farmers

farm·stay /faárm stày/ *n.* *ANZ, Can* a stay on a farm as a paying guest, providing some experience of rural life

farm·stead /faárm stèd/ *n.* a farm and all its buildings, regarded as a unit

farm team *n.* a sports team in a minor league that is owned by or affiliated with a major league team

farm·wom·an /faárm wòomən/ (*plural* **-en** /-wìmmin/) *n.* a woman who lives or works on a farm

farm·work·er /faárm wùrkər/ *n.* = **farm hand**

farm·yard /faárm yaàrd/ *n.* an enclosed or surfaced area beside farm buildings

far·o /fáirō/ *n.* a card game in which players bet against the dealer on the order in which cards are turned up [Mid-18thC. Origin uncertain: probably an alteration of earlier *pharaoh*, modeled on Italian *faraone*.]

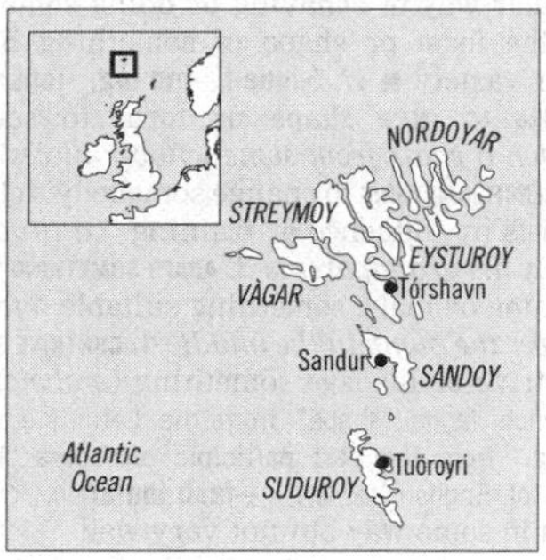

Faroe Islands

Far·oe Is·lands /fáirō-/, **Faer·oe Is·lands** ISLANDS group of islands in the North Atlantic Ocean, almost midway between Iceland and the Shetland Islands. The islands have been Danish territory since 1814. Capital: Tórshavn. Population: 43,382 (1995). Area: 540 sq. mi./1,399 sq. km.

Far·o·ese /fàirō éez, fàirō éess/ (*plural* **-ese**), **Faer·o·ese** (*plural* **-ese**) *n.* **1.** LANG **LANGUAGE OF FAROE ISLANDS** the language spoken in the Faroe Islands. It is a member of the North Germanic group of the Germanic branch of Indo-European. About 45,000 people speak Faroese. **2. SOMEBODY FROM FAROE ISLANDS** somebody who was born in, raised, or who lives in the Faroe Islands —**Far·o·ese** *adj.*

far-off *adj.* distant in location or time

fa·rouche /fə ròosh/ *adj.* **1. LACKING SOCIAL SKILLS** unsociable and lacking grace because of fierceness, sullenness, or shyness **2. MENACING** menacing in appearance or behavior [Mid-18thC. Via French from medieval Latin *forasticus*, from Latin *foras* "out of doors, outside" (source of English *foreign*).]

Fa·rouk I /fə ròok/, **King of Egypt** (1920–65). He was the last king of Egypt (1936–52), and after a coup lived in exile in Monaco.

far-out *adj.* (*slang*) **1. UNUSUAL** strange and unconventional **2. EXCELLENT** extremely good or enjoyable —**far-out·ness** *n.* ◇ **far out!** used to express amazement and approval (*slang*)

far·rag·i·nous /fə rájjənəss/ *adj.* consisting of many things mixed together (*formal*)

far·ra·go /fə raá gō, -ráy-/ (*plural* **-gos** *or* **-goes**) *n.* a confused mixture of things [Mid-17thC. From Latin, "mixed fodder for cattle, medley," from *far* "spelt, grain" (source of English *farina*).]

Far·ra·gut /férrəgət/, **David** (1801–70) U.S. admiral. He commanded Union ships during the Civil War and became a national hero after the Battle of Mobile Bay (1864). Full name **David Glasgow Farragut**

Far·ra·khan /férrə kaán/, **Louis Abdul** (*b.* 1933) U.S. religious leader. Long a member of the Nation of Islam, he led the organization after 1978 and broadened its base with calls for African American self-reliance. He organized the Million Man March in Washington, D.C., in 1995. Born **Louis Eugene Walcott**

far-reach·ing *adj.* with widespread implications, influences, or effects

Far·rell /férrəl/, **James T.** (1904–79) U.S. novelist. He is best known for his *Studs Lonigan* trilogy (1932–35). Full name **James Thomas Farrell**

Far·rer /férrər/, **William James** (1845–1906) English-born Australian agricultural scientist, who was a pioneer of wheat breeding in Australia. He developed domestic strains of wheat that produced greater yields than overseas strains.

far·ri·er /férree ər/ *n.* *U.K.* somebody who makes and fits horseshoes [Mid-16thC. Via French *ferrier* from Latin *ferrarius*, from *ferrum* "horseshoe, iron."] —**far·ri·er·y** /férree əree/ *n.*

far·row[1] /férrō/ *vi.* (**-rowed, -row·ing, -rows**) **PRODUCE PIGLETS** to give birth to a litter of piglets ■ *n.* **LITTER OF PIGS** a litter of young pigs [Old English *fearh* "young pig." Ultimately from an Indo-European word that is also the ancestor of Latin *porcus* "pig" (source of English *pork*, *porcelain*, and *porcupine*).]

far·row[2] /férrō/ *adj.* not pregnant with a calf [15thC. Origin uncertain; probably from Flemish *verwe-*, *varwe-*, in *verwekoe*, *varwekoe*, *verrekoe* "cow that has become barren."]

far·ru·ca /fə ròokə/ *n.* a form of flamenco dance [Early 20thC. From Spanish, "Galician or Asturian," from *Farruco*, a pet-name of *Francisco* "Francis."]

far·see·ing /faar sée ing/ *adj.* = **farsighted** *adj.* **2**, **farsighted** *adj.* **3**

Far·si /faársee/ *n.* the official language of Iran, also spoken in parts of Afghanistan, Bahrain, Tadzhikistan, and the United Arab Emirates. It belongs to the Indo-Iranian branch of Indo-European languages. Farsi is spoken by about 30 million native speakers and by around a further 55 million people who use it as a second language. [Late 19thC. Via Arabic, "Persia," modern-day Iran, from Persian *Pars*.] —**Far·si** *adj.*

far·sight·ed /faar sítəd/ *adj.* **1. UNABLE TO SEE NEARBY OBJECTS CLEARLY** able to see distant objects better than nearby ones **2. far·sight·ed, far·see·ing HAVING SOUND JUDGMENT** wise and able to anticipate the future **3. far·sight·ed, far·see·ing SEEING FAR** able to see a long way —**far·sight·ed·ly** *adv.* —**far·sight·ed·ness** *n.*

fart /faart/ *vti.* (**fart·ed, fart·ing, farts**) **OFFENSIVE TERM** to release intestinal gases through the anus, usually with an accompanying sound (*slang offensive*) ■ *n.* **1. OFFENSIVE TERM** a release of intestinal gases through the anus (*slang offensive*) **2. OFFENSIVE TERM** a highly offensive term for somebody who is unpleasant, boring, or irritating (*taboo insult*) [Old English *feortan*. Ultimately from an Indo-European word that is also the ancestor of Greek *perdix* "partridge" (named for the sharp whirring sound it makes when suddenly flushed).]

fart around *vi.* offensive term meaning to waste time by behaving foolishly (*slang offensive*)

far·ther /faárthər/ *adv.* ◊ **further 1. TO GREATER DISTANCE** to or at a point that is more distant in space or time **2. TO GREATER EXTENT** to a greater degree or extent ■ *adj.* **1. MORE DISTANT** more distant in space or time **2. ADDITIONAL** that is more than or adds to the quantity or extent of something (*archaic*) ◊ **further** [13thC. From earlier *ferther*, a variant of FURTHER, probably modeled on *ferthren* "to further."] —**far·ther·most** /-mōst/ *adj.*

far·thest /faárthəst/ *adv.* ◊ **furthest 1. TO GREATEST DISTANCE** to a more distant point in space or time than anything else **2. TO GREATEST EXTENT** to a greater degree or extent than anything else ■ *adj.* **MOST DISTANT** more distant in space or time than anything else. ◊ **furthest**

far·thing /faárthing/ *n.* **1. FORMER BRITISH COIN** a former British coin worth a quarter of the old penny **2. THE LEAST** the lowest value or smallest amount [Old English *fēorthung* "quarter of a penny," from *fēortha* "fourth" + *-ing* "fractional part." Ultimately from an Indo-European word that is also the ancestor of English *four* and *tessera*.]

far·thin·gale /faárthing gàyl/ *n.* a structure worn under the skirt by women in the late 16th and early 17th centuries to give it the shape of a cone, bell, or drum [Early 16thC. Via Old French *verdugale* from Spanish *verdugado*, from *verdugo* "rod, stick" (from the wooden hoops used to sustain the structure).]

fart·lek /faártlək/ *n.* = **interval training** [Mid-20thC. From Swedish, literally "speed-play," formed from *fart* "speed" + *lek* "play."]

Far West *n.* the area of the continental United States west of the Great Plains

FAS *abbr.* **1.** fetal alcohol syndrome **2.** SHIPPING free alongside ship

f.a.s. *abbr.* SHIPPING free alongside ship

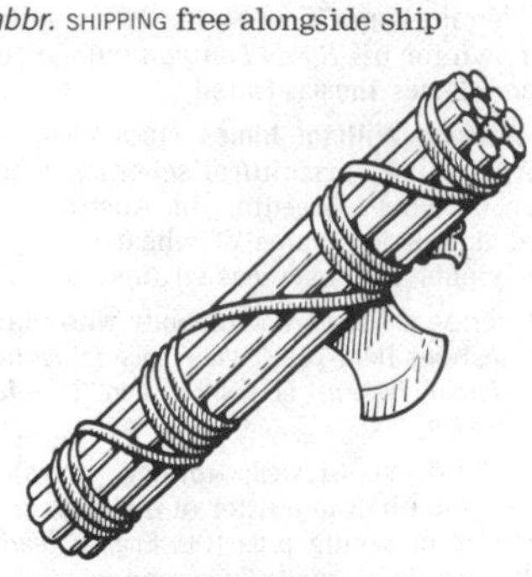

Fasces

fas·ces /fá seez/ *npl.* a bundle of rods containing an ax with a projecting blade, carried in front of magistrates in ancient Rome [Late 16thC. From Latin, plural of *fascis* (see FASCIST).]

fas·ci·a *(architecture)* /fáshee ə, fáyshee ə/; *(anatomy)* /fáshee ə/ (*plural* **-ci·ae** *(architecture)* /fáshee ee, fáyshee ee/; *(anatomy)* /fáshee ee/ *or* **-cias**) *n.* **1.** ARCHIT **FLAT SURFACE ON BUILDING** the flat horizontal surface immediately below the edge of a roof **2.** ANAT **CONNECTIVE TISSUE** a sheet or band of connective tissue covering or binding together parts of the body, e.g., muscles or organs **3.** **BAND OF COLOR** a broad band of color, e.g., on an insect [Mid-16thC. From Latin, "band, fillet, casing of a door" (source of English *fess*).] —**fas·ci·al** /fásh'l/ *adj.*

fas·ci·ate /fáshee àyt/, **fas·ci·at·ed** /-àytəd/ *adj.* used to describe plant stems or branches that have grown together and become abnormally flattened [Mid-17thC. From Latin *fasciare* "to swathe," from *fascia* (see FASCIA).] —**fas·ci·ate·ly** *adv.*

fas·ci·a·tion /fàshee áysh'n/ *n.* abnormal fusion and flattening of several plant stems

fas·ci·cle /fássik'l/ *n.* **1.** **BUNDLE** a small bunch or bundle of something **2.** BOT **PLANT PARTS BUNCHED TOGETHER** a cluster of plant parts such as branches, leaves, or stems **3.** ANAT **BUNDLE OF FIBERS** a bundle of nerve, muscle, or tendon fibers **4.** PUBL **PART OF BOOK PUBLISHED AS INSTALLMENT** a section of a book published in installments as a volume or pamphlet [15thC. From Latin *fasciculus* "small bundle," from *fascis* (see FASCIST).] —**fas·ci·cled** *adj.*

fas·cic·u·lar /fə síkyələr/ *adj.* forming a bundle or cluster

fas·cic·u·late /fə síkyələt, -làyt/ *adj.* = **fascicular** —**fa·sic·u·late·ly** *adv.* —**fas·cic·u·la·tion** /fə sìkyə láysh'n/ *n.*

fas·ci·cule /fássi kyool/ *n.* PUBL = **fascicle** *n.* 4 [Late 19thC. From Latin *fasciculus* (see FASCICLE).]

fas·ci·nate /fássə nàyt/ (**-nat·ed, -nat·ing, -nates**) *v.* **1.** *vti.* **CAPTIVATE** to hold somebody's attention completely or irresistibly **2.** *vt.* **IMMOBILIZE SOMEBODY OR SOMETHING** to make somebody or something unable to move, especially out of fear [Late 16thC. From Latin *fascinare* "to cast an evil eye on, bewitch," from *fascinum* "spell, witchcraft."] —**fas·ci·nat·ed·ly** *adv.* —**fas·ci·na·tor** *n.*

fas·ci·nat·ing /fássə nàyting/ *adj.* inspiring a great interest or attraction —**fas·ci·nat·ing·ly** *adv.*

fas·ci·na·tion /fàssə náysh'n/ *n.* **1.** **POWER TO CAPTURE ATTENTION** the power to hold somebody's attention completely or irresistibly **2.** **SOMETHING FASCINATING** something that inspires great interest **3.** **INTEREST IN SOMETHING** complete absorption in something interesting ○ *I can't understand his fascination with tarantulas.*

fas·cine /fə seen/ *n.* a long piece or bundle of wood used for engineering purposes to line or fill a trench [Late 17thC. Via French from Latin *fascina*, from *fascis* "bundle" (see FASCIST).]

fas·ci·o·li·a·sis /fə see ə lí əssiss, fə sì ə-/ *n.* a disease caused by an infestation of parasitic liver flukes [Late 19thC. From modern Latin *Fasciola hepatica* "liver fluke," from Latin *fasciola* "small bandage," from *fascia* (see FASCIA).]

Fas·cism /fá shizzəm/ *n.* **1.** **DICTATORIAL GOVERNMENT OF MUSSOLINI** a system of government practiced by Benito Mussolini in Italy between 1922 and 1943 that was characterized by dictatorship, centralized control of private enterprise, repression of opposition, and extreme nationalism **2.** **fas·cism, Fas·cism** **DICTATORIAL MOVEMENT** any movement, tendency, or ideology that favors dictatorial government, centralized control of private enterprise, repression of all opposition, and extreme nationalism [Early 20thC. From Italian *fascismo*, from *fascio* (see FASCIST).]

Fas·cist /fáshist/ *n.* **1.** **SUPPORTER OF FASCISM IN ITALY** somebody who belonged to Benito Mussolini's party or who supported Fascism in Italy between 1922 and 1943 **2.** **fas·cist, Fas·cist** **SUPPORTER OF FASCISM** somebody who supports or advocates a system of government characterized by dictatorship, centralized control of private enterprise, repression of all opposition, and extreme nationalism [Early 20thC. Via Italian *Fascista*, from *fascio* "group, bundle," from, ultimately, Latin *fascis* (see FASCES).] —**fas·cis·tic** /fə shístik/ *adj.*

fash /fash/ *n.* **FASHION** fashion (*slang*) ■ *adj.* **FASHIONABLE** fashionable (*slang*) [Late 19thC. Shortening.]

fash·ion /fásh'n/ *n.* **1.** **CLOTHING STYLES** style in clothing, hair, and personal appearance generally, or the business of creating, promoting, or studying the latest styles ○ *the latest in men's fashions* **2.** **CURRENT STYLE** the style of dress, behavior, way of living, or other expression that is popular at present ○ *a way of speaking that is no longer in fashion* **3.** **MANNER** a particular way of behaving or doing something **4.** **SHAPE** the form or shape of something **5.** **TYPE** a type or variety ■ *vt.* (**-ioned, -ion·ing, -ions**) **1.** **MAKE SOMETHING** to give shape or form to something ○ *fashion a chair from some leftover pieces of wood* **2.** **INFLUENCE SOMETHING** to change somebody's character or beliefs by influence or training ○ *attitudes fashioned by his grandparents* **3.** **ADAPT SOMETHING** to adapt something or make something suitable ○ *fashion it to fit over the bump in the middle* **4.** **CONTRIVE SOMETHING** to contrive or manage something (*archaic*) [14thC. Via French *façon* "shape" from the Latin stem *faction-* "making," from the past participle of *facere* "to make" (source of English *facile*).] —**fash·ion·er** *n.* ◇ **after a fashion** in some way but not very well

WORD KEY: SYNONYMS

See Synonyms at ***make.***

-fashion *suffix.* in the manner of

fash·ion·a·ble /fásh'nəb'l/ *adj.* **1.** **CURRENTLY POPULAR** following a style or fashion that is currently popular ○ *fashionable ideas* **2.** **TRENDY** popular with or frequented by rich, famous, or otherwise glamorous people ○ *a fashionable nightspot* —**fash·ion·a·bil·i·ty** /fàsh'nə bíllətee/ *n.* —**fash·ion·a·ble·ness** /fàsh'nəb'lnəss/ *n.* —**fash·ion·a·bly** /fàsh'nəblee/ *adv.*

fash·ion house *n.* a business that designs, makes, and sells fashionable clothes, typically associated with a named designer

fash·ion·ista /fàsh'n eestə/ *npl.* somebody who is a devoted enthusiast of the fashion industry (*informal*) [Coined from FASHION + Latin *-ista*]

fash·ion mod·el *n.* somebody who models clothes as a profession

fash·ion pho·tog·ra·phy *n.* the art or practice of taking photographs of models wearing clothes or clothing accessories, especially for fashion magazines

fash·ion plate *n.* **1.** **FASHIONABLE PERSON** somebody who wears the latest fashions or who is fashionably dressed **2.** **PICTURE SHOWING FASHION** an illustration showing a style of clothing, especially a current or new fashion

Fass·bind·er /faass bìndər/, **Rainer Werner** (1946–82) German movie director. He is renowned for politically controversial plays and films, such as *The Marriage of Maria Braun* (1979), that often criticize social institutions.

fast[1] /fast/ *adj.* **1.** **ACTING OR MOVING RAPIDLY** acting, functioning, or moving quickly, or capable of doing this ○ *a fast car* **2.** **DONE QUICKLY** lasting or taking a relatively short time ○ *a fast trip* **3.** **RUNNING AHEAD OF TIME** indicating a time that is later than the correct time **4.** **CONDUCIVE TO RAPID SPEED** adapted to or allowing rapid movement ○ *driving in the fast lane* **5.** **REQUIRING SPEEDY MOVEMENT** requiring agility and quickness of movement and reaction **6.** PHOTOGRAPHY **WITH SHORT EXPOSURE** used to describe photographic equipment that requires or permits a relatively short exposure time **7.** **DEBAUCHED** energetically pursuing excitement and enjoyment (*informal*) ○ *a fast crowd* **8.** **PROMISCUOUS** wanting or tending to start sexual relationships with people very soon after meeting them (*informal*) **9.** **TRICKY** using quick-wittedness to trick or cheat people (*informal*) ○ *a fast bargainer* **10.** **MADE EASILY** acquired very easily and sometimes dishonestly (*informal*) ○ *fast money* **11.** **UNFADING** not liable to fade or change color **12.** **STRONG AND CLOSE** strong, close, and steadfast, e.g., in a relationship ○ *fast friends* **13.** **FASTENED** firmly attached, fastened, or fixed **14.** **SHUT** firmly closed ■ *adv.* **1.** **RAPIDLY** at great speed ○ *You drive too fast.* **2.** **IMMEDIATELY** in quick succession **3.** **AT INCORRECT TIME** ahead of the correct time ○ *The clock is running a little fast.* **4.** **SOUNDLY** deeply in a state of sleep **5.** **FIRMLY** allowing no movement or no chance of slipping or escaping ○ *held fast by ice* **6.** **RECKLESSLY** without regard to consequences (*informal*) ○ *live fast and die young* **7.** **CLOSE** so as to be nearby (*archaic*) [Old English *fæst* "firm," from a prehistoric Germanic word that is also the ancestor of English *avast*] ◇ **pull a fast one** to trick or cheat somebody (*slang*)

fast[2] /fast/ *v.* (**fast·ed, fast·ing, fasts**) **1.** *vi.* **ABSTAIN FROM FOOD** to abstain from all or certain types of food, especially as an act of religious observance **2.** *vt.* **DEPRIVE OF FOOD** to deprive a person or animal of food ■ *n.* **PERIOD OF FASTING** a period of time spent abstaining from food [Old English *fæstan*, from a prehistoric Germanic word meaning "firm" (see FAST[1]). The underlying sense is of "holding fast" to an observance.] —**fast·er** *n.*

fast-act·ing *adj.* beginning to take effect soon after being used ○ *a fast-acting analgesic*

fast·back /fást bàk/ *n.* **1.** **CAR DESIGN FEATURE** a back of a car that forms a continuous curve downward from the rear edge of the roof **2.** **CAR** a car with a fastback

fast·ball /fást bàwl/ *n.* a baseball pitch at top speed

fast break *n.* in team sports, a swift counterattack made in an attempt to score before the opposing players have the chance to recover their defensive positions —**fast-break** *vi.*

fast-breed·er re·ac·tor *n.* a nuclear reactor in which the chain reaction is maintained mainly by fast neutrons. It is capable of producing more fissionable material than it consumes.

fas·ten /fáss'n/ (**-tened, -ten·ing, -tens**) *v.* **1.** *vti.* **SECURE SOMETHING** to attach something firmly, usually using parts or devices made to achieve this, or become firmly attached in this way ○ *These snaps won't fasten.* **2.** *vti.* **SHUT TIGHTLY** to close something firmly or securely, or become firmly or securely closed ○ *fasten the door shut* **3.** *vt.* **HOLD SOMETHING FIRMLY** to use a tool, device, or body part to hold somebody or something firmly **4.** *vti.* **CONCENTRATE ATTENTION** to focus the mind or eyes concentratedly on something, or become focused in this way ○ *His suspicions fastened upon the woman sitting opposite him.* **5.** *vi.* **BECOME A NUISANCE** to become associated closely with somebody in a persistent and usually unwelcome manner ○ *just some guy who fastened onto me in the street* [Old English *fæstnian*, literally "to make firm or fast," ultimately from a prehistoric Germanic word meaning "firm" (see FAST[1])]

fas·ten·er /fáss'nər/ *n.* a device, e.g., a button, hook, or zipper, used to close something, especially a piece of clothing

fas·ten·ing /fáss'ning/ *n.* a device that fastens something, e.g., a clasp, hook, or lock

fast food *n.* highly processed restaurant foods, e.g., burgers, that are prepared quickly or are available on demand (*hyphenated when used before a noun*) ○ *a fast-food diet*

fast-for·ward *n.* **1.** **FUNCTION FOR WINDING TAPE FORWARD** a function on an electronic recording device, e.g., a tape or videocassette recorder, that causes the tape to wind forward quickly **2.** **BUTTON FOR FAST-FORWARD FUNCTION** a mechanism, e.g., a button or switch, used to control the fast-forward function on an electronic recording device ■ *vti.* (**fast-for·ward·ed, fast-for·ward·ing, fast-for·wards**) **1.** **ADVANCE TAPE RAPIDLY** to wind a tape forward quickly on an electronic recording device **2.** **ADVANCE QUICKLY** to advance rapidly, or move something forward rapidly, e.g., in time or in rate of progress (*informal*) ○ *decided to fast-forward negotiations so as to avoid a strike*

fas·tid·i·ous /fa stíddee əss/ *adj.* **1.** **DEMANDING** concerned that even the smallest details should be just right ○ *fastidious about his appearance* **2.** **DELICATE** easily disgusted by things that are not perfectly clean **3.** **SCORNFUL** showing disdain or scorn (*archaic*) [15thC. From Latin *fastidiosus*, from *fastidium* "disgust."] —**fas·tid·i·ous·ly** *adv.* —**fas·tid·i·ous·ness** *n.*

fas·tig·i·a plural of **fastigium**

fas·tig·i·ate /fa stíjjee ət/, **fas·tig·i·at·ed** /-àytəd/ *adj.* used to describe a tree or other plant with upright clustering branches that taper toward the top, e.g., a Lombardy poplar —**fas·tig·i·ate·ly** *adv.*

fas·tig·i·um /fa stíjjee əm/ (*plural* **-ums** *or* **-a** /-ə/) *n.* a period during which an illness, often a fever, is at its most severe [Late 17thC. From Latin.]

fast·ing /fásting/ *n.* abstention from all or certain types of food, especially as an act of religious observance

fast lane *n.* **1.** TRANSP = **express lane 2.** HECTIC LIFESTYLE the kind of lifestyle that is busy, exciting, often highly stressful, and sometimes devoted to pleasure (*informal*) ○ *living life in the fast lane* **3.** ROUTE TO SUCCESS a rapid but extremely competitive route to progress, promotion, or success —**fast-lane** *adj.*

fast mo·tion *n.* filmed action that is faster than is naturally possible, achieved by shooting the film at a rate slower than that projected. It is often used for comic effect. (*hyphenated when used before a noun*) ○ *a fast-motion sequence*

fast·ness /fástnəss/ *n.* **1.** FIXEDNESS the state or quality of being firm, fixed, or secure ○ *deceived about the fastness of their friendship* **2.** UNFADING QUALITY the ability of a dye to retain its color and not to fade **3.** FORTRESS a fortress, stronghold, or other secure place (*archaic or literary*) **4.** REMOTE PLACE a remote and secluded or secret place (*archaic or literary*) **5.** RAPIDITY swiftness of movement or progress (*archaic*)

fast neu·tron *n.* a neutron that has energy in excess of 1.5 MeV, sufficient to produce fission in Uranium-238

fast-talk *vt.* to influence or deceive somebody with false but appealing arguments (*informal*) ○ *fast-talked them into parting with the car keys* —**fast-talk·er** *n.*

fast track *n.* **1.** RAPID ROUTE TO PROGRESS a rapid and sometimes highly competitive route to progress or advancement that exists alongside the slower conventional one (*informal*) ○ *a fast track to promotion for the brightest recruits* **2.** RAIL RAILROAD TRACK FOR FAST TRAINS a railroad track for fast trains alongside one for slower trains —**fast-track** *adj.*

fast-track *v.* **1.** *vti.* GO QUICKLY to advance, develop, or process something rapidly, or be handled rapidly ○ *fast-tracking the best of the new recruits* **2.** *vt.* DEAL WITH FIRST to give priority to somebody or something ○ *fast-track an application* —**fast-track·er** *n.*

fas·tu·ous /fáschoo əss/ *adj.* (*archaic*) **1.** CONCEITED excessively self-satisfied and disdainful of others **2.** OSTENTATIOUS designed to impress others [Mid-17thC. From late Latin *fastuosus*, from Latin *fastus* (see FASH).]

fat /fat/ *n.* **1.** BIOCHEM NUTRITIONAL COMPONENT OF FOOD a greasy water-insoluble solid or semisolid chemical compound that is among the chief nutritional components of food. Fats are esters of glycerol and fatty acids. ○ *a diet that is lower in fat* **2.** ANAT TISSUE CONTAINING FAT animal or vegetable tissue made up of cells that contain fat, especially the layer of cells under the skin that in excess make somebody overweight **3.** COOK COOKING MEDIUM a solid or liquid substance such as butter or sunflower oil that is derived from animals or plants and is used as a cooking medium or ingredient ○ *rub the fat into the flour* **4.** EXCESS amounts that are surplus to what is needed or wanted (*informal*) ○ *a budget with little fat* ■ *adj.* (**fat·ter, fat·test**) **1.** OVERWEIGHT having a bodyweight greater than is considered desirable or advisable **2.** CONTAINING FAT containing a lot of fat or too much fat ○ *pork that was rather fat* **3.** THICK very wide or large ○ *a fat book* **4.** PROFITABLE bringing large profits or financial rewards ○ *a fat construction contract* **5.** REWARDING providing good opportunities ○ *offered a fat part in a movie* **6.** RICH owning great wealth ○ *grown fat on the profits of illegal arms deals* **7.** PLENTIFUL with abundant contents, stocks, or supplies ○ *a fat savings account* **8.** AGRIC FERTILE land that is very productive for agricultural purposes (*archaic*) **9.** CHEM RICH IN CONTENT with a high content of a particular material or substance, e.g., resin in wood or volatile hydrocarbons in coal ■ *vti.* (**fat·ted, fat·ting, fats**) AGRIC FATTEN AN ANIMAL to fatten an animal, usually before slaughtering it [Old English *fǣt(t)*. Ultimately from an Indo-European word meaning "fat," which is probably also the ancestor of English *pine* and *pituitary*.] —**fat·ly** *adv.* —**fat·ness** *n.* ◇ **chew the fat** to have a leisurely conversation (*slang*) ◇ **the fat is in the fire** something irreversible has happened that will cause trouble

FAT /fat/ *n.* in the MS-DOS disk-operating system on a computer, an internal store of information about the structure of stored files on a disk (*often used before a noun*) Full form **file allocation table**

fa·tal /fáyt'l/ *adj.* **1.** LEADING TO DEATH causing death, or capable of causing death ○ *a fatal car crash* **2.** RUINOUS causing destruction, disaster, or ruin ○ *a fatal mistake in calculations* **3.** DECISIVE at which time important decisions or choices are made ○ *the fatal day of his first treasonous act* **4.** PREDESTINED arranged or controlled by fate ■ *n.* INSTANCE OF DEATH an instance of death, especially one caused by an auto, plane, train, or bus crash (*informal*) ○ *a fatal on the turnpike during rush hour* [14thC. Directly or via French from Latin *fatalis*, from *fatum* (see FATE).] —**fa·tal·ness** *n.*

WORD KEY: SYNONYMS

See Synonyms at ***deadly***.

WORD KEY: CULTURAL NOTE

Fatal Attraction, a movie by British director Adrian Lyne (1987). It portrays a married man's brief but passionate involvement with a single woman and her violent reaction when he attempts to end their relationship.The spurned lover attacks the man's family, and, having apparently been finally drowned by the husband, suddenly returns to life before being shot dead. This movie title quickly came to be used in the United States to indicate the wrath of a scorned woman: "There was no such attack rape, the defense will counter vehemently. The woman . . . will be proved to be a *Fatal Attraction* psychotic." *Washington Post* (December 1, 1991).

fa·tal·ism /fáyt'l ìzzəm/ *n.* **1.** PHILOSOPHY DOCTRINE OF FATE the philosophical doctrine holding that all events are fated to happen and that human beings cannot therefore change their destinies **2.** BELIEF IN FATE the belief that people are powerless against fate, or the attitude of resignation and passivity that sometimes results from this belief

fa·tal·ist /fáyt'list/ *n.* somebody who believes in the philosophical doctrine of fatalism

fa·tal·is·tic /fàyt'l ístik/ *adj.* **1.** SUBMITTING TO FATE feeling or demonstrating resignation in the face of events regarded as controlled by fate ○ *a fatalistic attitude* **2.** PHILOS OF FATALISM relating to the philosophical doctrine of fatalism —**fa·tal·is·ti·cal·ly** *adv.*

fa·tal·i·ty /fay tállətee, fə-/ (*plural* **-ties**) *n.* **1.** UNEXPECTED DEATH a death resulting from accident or disaster ○ *The traffic accident resulted in three fatalities.* **2.** DEADLINESS the ability to cause death, disaster, or destruction ○ *fatality associated with toxic waste exposure* **3.** PREDETERMINATION BY FATE the quality or state of being predetermined by fate **4.** EVENTS THOUGHT FATED an event or train of events thought to be determined by fate

fa·tal·i·ty rate *n.* = **death rate**

fa·tal·ly /fáyt'lee/ *adv.* **1.** SO AS TO CAUSE DEATH in a manner that results in death ○ *fatally wounded* **2.** SO AS TO CAUSE RUIN in a manner resulting in disaster or ruin ○ *fatally mistaken* **3.** INEVITABLY as a result of unalterable fate

fa·ta mor·ga·na /fàatə mawr gaánə/, **Fa·ta Mor·ga·na** *n.* a mirage or an illusion (*literary*) [From Italian, literally "fairy Morgan," in reference to the legendary magician MORGAN LE FAY; from the belief that a fairy caused the mirage frequently seen near the Strait of Messina]

fat·back /fát bàk/ *n.* fatty meat from the upper part of a side of pork, usually dried and cured by salt

WORD KEY: REGIONAL NOTE

The upper part of a side of bacon, usually without lean, is also called *fat meat, fat pork, boiling meat, dry salt meat, salt bacon, salt meat, seasoning meat, side meat, sowbelly*, and *white bacon*. The meat is used in the South and West primarily to season boiled and steamed vegetables. Because the substance so closely approximates ordinary bacon, in both its location on the hog and its applications in cooking, ***fatback*** often merges with *middling meat, streak of lean*, and other bacon synonyms, all of which invariably include lean.

fat bod·y *n.* **1.** FATTY TISSUE IN INSECTS a fatty tissue in the bodies of insects, especially larvae, used as a source of energy during metamorphosis and hibernation **2.** FATTY TISSUE IN AMPHIBIANS AND REPTILES a fatty tissue found near the genital glands of certain amphibians and reptiles

fat camp *n.* a residential camp that helps children to lose undesired weight (*slang*)

fat cat *n.* (*slang*) **1.** SOMEBODY RICH an extremely wealthy and privileged person (*hyphenated when used before a noun*) ○ *fees charged by fat-cat lawyers* **2.** CONTRIBUTOR TO POLITICAL CAMPAIGN somebody wealthy who contributes a substantial amount of money to a political campaign

fat cell *n.* any cell that is specialized for the synthesis and storage of fat

Fat City, **fat cit·y** *n.* prosperous circumstances (*slang*)

fate /fayt/ *n.* **1.** FORCE PREDETERMINING EVENTS the force or principle believed to predetermine events ○ *little knew what fate had in store for him* **2.** OUTCOME a consequence or final result ○ *What was the fate of the mission?* **3.** DESTINY something consequential that inevitably happens to somebody or something ○ *felt it was her fate to marry him* **4.** UNHAPPY CONSEQUENCE a disastrous or ruinous outcome ■ *vt.* (**fat·ed, fat·ing, fates**) MAKE SOMETHING INEVITABLE to predetermine something, usually with negative results (*usually passive*) [14thC. From, ultimately, Latin *fatum*, literally "something spoken (by the gods)," from the past participle of *fari* "to speak" (source of English *fable* and *fairy*).] ◇ **tempt fate** to do something risky that might end in misfortune or disaster, and depend too much on luck

fat·ed /fáytəd/ *adj.* believed to be controlled or predetermined by fate ○ *fated mishaps*

fate·ful /fáytfəl/ *adj.* **1.** CRITICALLY IMPORTANT after which an important, often dire consequence seems to have been made inevitable ○ *a fateful decision* **2.** DECIDED BY FATE predetermined or controlled by fate **3.** OMINOUS prefiguring what is to come, especially when it is something disastrous ○ *a fateful sign* —**fate·ful·ly** *adv.* —**fate·ful·ness** *n.*

Fates /fayts/ *npl.* GREEK GODDESSES OF DESTINY in Greek mythology, the three goddesses, Clotho, Lachesis, and Atropos, often depicted as women of advanced years spinning, who were believed to decree the events in and duration of somebody's life. The Greeks believed that Clotho spun the thread that represented somebody's life, Lachesis decided the extent of it, and Atropos was responsible for cutting it. Roman equivalent **Parcae**

fat face *n.* any typeface with wide main strokes and prominent serifs, producing a relatively heavy and dark image when set as text

fat farm *n.* a health spa dedicated to helping people lose weight (*slang*)

fath, **fath.** *abbr.* fathom

fat·head /fát hèd/ *n.* an unintelligent or thoughtless person who is extremely slow to understand things or makes very bad decisions (*slang insult*) —**fat·head·ed** /fàt héddəd/ *adj.* —**fat·head·ed·ly** /-lee/ *adv.* —**fat·head·ed·ness** /-nəss/ *n.*

fat hen *n. U.K.* = **pigweed** [Origin uncertain; perhaps from a fanciful likening of its seeds to hen's eggs because they contain fat and albumen and were formerly eaten as food]

fa·ther /faáthər/ *n.* **1.** MALE PARENT a male parent of a human being or animal ○ *been like a father to me* **2.** MAN ACTING AS PARENT a man who brings up and looks after a child as if he were its male parent **3.** MAN ANCESTOR a man who is an ancestor, especially the founder of a family or people ○ *the land of our fathers and mothers* **4.** FOUNDER a man who establishes, founds, or originates something ○ *the father of modern linguistics* **5.** PRECURSOR a precursor, prototype, or early version of something **6.** MAN LEADER a man who is a community or civic leader ○ *the town fathers* ■ *v.* (**-thered, -ther·ing, -thers**) **1.** *vt.* HAVE OFFSPRING to beget offspring as a male parent **2.** *vti.* ACT AS FATHER to act as a father to somebody, especially giving advice, comfort, and protection **3.** *vt.* ORIGINATE SOMETHING to create, found, or establish something ○ *father a plan* [Old English *fæder*. Ultimately from an Indo-European word that is also the ancestor of English *patriarch, paternal*, and *perpetrate*.]

WORD KEY: CULTURAL NOTE

Fathers and Sons, a novel by Russian writer Ivan Turgenev (1862). It deals with the conflicting attitudes toward social change (particularly the emancipation of serfs) among Russia's younger radical intelligentsia, represented by the novel's nihilistic protagonist, Bazarov, and the older liberal gentry, to which Turgenev himself belonged. The novel was seen as Turgenev's acknowledgment that Russia's future was now in the hands of a new generation.

Fa·ther *n.* **1. GOD** in the Christian religion, God, especially when considered as the first person of the Holy Trinity **2.** = **Church Father 3. TITLE FOR CHRISTIAN CLERGYMAN** a title and form of address used for Christian clergymen, especially in the Roman Catholic, Eastern Orthodox, and Episcopal churches **4. RESPECTFUL TITLE FOR MAN** a respectful term of address for a man who is past middle age **5. PERSONIFICATION** something personified as man of advanced years

Fa·ther Christ·mas *n. U.K.* = **Santa Claus**

fa·ther con·fes·sor *n.* a Roman Catholic priest who hears confessions and gives advice (*literary*)

fa·ther fig·ure *n.* a man whom other people look up to for advice, inspiration, or protection

fa·ther·hood /fáathər hòòd/ *n.* the status of a man who is somebody's father, or the fact that he is a father

fa·ther-in-law (*plural* **fa·thers-in-law**) *n.* **1. SPOUSE'S FATHER** the father of somebody's husband or wife **2. STEPFATHER** a stepfather (*archaic*)

fa·ther·land /fáathər lànd/ *n.* **1. HOMELAND** somebody's native land or country **2. ANCESTRAL COUNTRY** the native land of somebody's ancestors

fa·ther-lash·er *n.* a large sea scorpion with short spines, found in European and North Atlantic coastal waters. Latin name: *Myoxocephalus scorpius* and *Myoxocephalus bubalis.*

fa·ther·less /fáathərləss/ *adj.* having no father, or no one identified as father —**fa·ther·less·ness** *n.*

fa·ther·ly /fáathərlee/ *adj.* having or showing the qualities associated with a father, usually love, support, and protection ○ *fatherly affection* —**fa·ther·li·ness** *n.*

Fa·ther's Day *n.* the third Sunday in June, observed as a celebration of fatherhood in the United States, Britain, Canada, Australia, and some other Commonwealth countries

Fa·ther Time *n.* the personification of time as a bearded man or advanced years, usually wearing a robe and carrying a scythe and an hourglass

fath·om /fáthəm/ *n.* **MEASURE OF WATER DEPTH** a unit of length equal to 6 ft./1.83 m, used mainly in nautical contexts for measuring the depth of water ■ *vt.* (**-omed, -om·ing, -oms**) **1. MEASURE WATER DEPTH USING SOUNDING LINE** to measure the depth of water, especially using a sounding line **2. COMPREHEND** to understand something, usually something profound or mystifying ○ *couldn't fathom why he came back* [Old English *fæðm*, of uncertain origin: probably "length spanned by outstretched arms," ultimately from an Indo-European word meaning "to spread," which is also the ancestor of English *petal* and *patent*] —**fath·om·a·ble** *adj.* —**fath·om·er** *n.*

fath·om·less /fáthəmləss/ *adj.* **1. ENDLESSLY DEEP** too deep to be measured **2. MYSTIFYING** impossible to understand —**fath·om·less·ly** *adv.* —**fath·om·less·ness** *n.*

fa·tid·ic /fay tíddik, fə-/, **fa·tid·i·cal** /-ik'l/ *adj.* seeming to foretell the future (*archaic*) [Early 17thC. From Latin *fatidicus*, from *fatum* "fate" (see FATE) + *dicere* "to say" (source of English *diction*).] —**fa·tid·i·cal·ly** *adv.*

fat·i·ga·ble /fáttigəb'l/ *adj.* able or tending to become exhausted —**fat·i·ga·bil·i·ty** /fàttigə bíllətee/ *n.* —**fat·i·ga·ble·ness** /fáttigəb'lnəss/ *n.*

fa·tigue /fə teég/ *n.* **1. MENTAL OR PHYSICAL EXHAUSTION** extreme tiredness or weariness resulting from physical or mental activity ○ *The soldiers were weak with fatigue after the long march.* **2.** PHYSIOL **INABILITY TO RESPOND TO STIMULUS** temporary inability of an organ or part such as a muscle or nerve cell to respond to a stimulus and function normally, following continuous activity or stimulation **3. INABILITY TO RESPOND TO SITUATION** temporary inability of somebody to respond to a situation as a result of overexposure or excessive activity (*often used in combination*) ○ *compassion fatigue* **4. WEAKENING OF MATERIAL UNDER STRESS** the weakening or breakdown of a material subjected to prolonged or repeated stress **5.** MIL **NONMILITARY WORK** manual or menial work done by soldiers, often as a punishment (*often used before a noun*) ■ **fa·tigues** *npl.* MIL **BATTLEDRESS** informal military uniforms worn day to day and in battle, as distinct from formal uniforms ■ *vti.* (**-tigued, -tigu·ing, -tigues**) **1. MAKE OR BECOME TIRED** to tire somebody out, or become tired out, as a result of physical or mental activity **2. WEAKEN UNDER STRESS** to weaken or break something, or become weakened or broken, when subjected to prolonged or repeated stress [Mid-17thC. Via French *fatiguer*, from Latin *fatigare*, of uncertain origin: probably "to drive to the breaking point," from *ad fatim* "to bursting" + *agere* "to drive."]

fa·tigued /fə teégd/ *adj.* **1. EXHAUSTED** exhausted or weary as a result of physical or mental activity **2. WEAKENED UNDER STRESS** weakened or broken as a result of being subjected to prolonged or repeated stress

Fat·i·ma /fáttəmə/ (606?–632 B.C.) Arabian religious figure. The youngest daughter of the prophet Muhammad, she is revered especially by Shiite Muslims.

Fat·i·mid /fáttə mìd/, **Fat·i·mite** /-mìt/ *n.* **1. MEMBER OF MUSLIM DYNASTY** a member of a Muslim dynasty, descended from Muhammad's daughter Fatima and her husband Ali, that ruled North Africa and parts of Egypt and Syria from 909 to 1171 A.D. **2. FATIMA'S DESCENDANT** any descendant of Fatima and Ali [Mid-19thC. Formed from Arabic *Fāṭima* "Fatima."]

fat lip *n.* a lip swollen from having been hit in a fistfight (*slang*)

fat mouse *n.* a nocturnal short-tailed mouse found in dry regions of Africa and eaten as a delicacy because of its high stored fat content. Genus: *Steatomys.*

fat pine *n. Southern U.S.* rich pinewood used as kindling [From its resinous nature]

WORD KEY: REGIONAL NOTE

In the South, ***fat pine*** is also called *fatwood, fat lighterd,* and *lightwood.*

fats·hed·er·a /fàt séddərə, fàts héddərə/ *n.* a hybrid ornamental plant with glossy leaves and pale green flowers. Latin name: *Fatsia japonica* × *Hedera helix.* [Mid-20thC. From modern Latin *Fatsia* (genus of shrubs) + *Hedera* (genus of climbing plants, from Latin, "ivy").]

fat·si·a /fátsee ə/ *n.* a shrub with leaves divided like the fingers on a hand and clusters of white flowers, commonly grown as a houseplant. Latin name: *Fatsia japonica.* [From modern Latin, genus name]

fat·so /fát sō/ (*plural* **-soes**) *n.* an offensive term used to refer to or address somebody who is overweight (*slang insult*) [Mid-20thC. Origin uncertain: probably formed from *fats*, offensive term for an overweight person.]

fat-tailed sheep *n.* a sheep, found mostly in North Africa and the Middle East, that has coarse wool and large quantities of fat stored in the tail and rump, and is raised for meat and milk

fat·ten /fátt'n/ (**-tened, -ten·ing, -tens**) *v.* **1.** *vti.* **MAKE OR BECOME FAT** to become fat or fatter, or make somebody fat or fatter **2.** *vti.* **FEED ANIMAL** to make an animal fat by feeding it plentifully, usually for slaughter **3.** *vt.* **ENLARGE** to make something larger, richer, or fuller ○ *fatten your wallet* **4.** *vt.* **FERTILIZE** to make land or soil more fertile ○ *fatten the soil with manure* —**fat·ten·a·ble** *adj.* —**fat·ten·er** *n.*

fat·ten·ing /fátt'ning/ *adj.* **1. HIGH IN FAT** high in fat or calorie content, and so likely to make some people gain weight **2. GROWING FAT** becoming fat in readiness for slaughter —**fat·ten·ing·ly** *adv.*

fat·ty /fáttee/ *adj.* (**-ti·er, -ti·est**) **1. CONTAINING FAT** containing fat or grease, especially in large or distasteful amounts **2. DERIVED FROM FAT** derived from fat, or chemically related to fat ○ *fatty alcohol* **3. WITH ACCUMULATED FAT** containing accumulated fat, sometimes in undesirable amounts ○ *fatty tissue* ■ *n.* (*plural* **-ties**) **OFFENSIVE TERM** an offensive term used to refer to or address somebody who is overweight (*slang insult*) —**fat·ti·ness** *n.*

fat·ty ac·id *n.* an organic acid belonging to a group that may occur naturally as waxes, fats, and essential oils, and are found in animal and plant materials. Fatty acids consist of a straight chain of carbon atoms linked by single bonds and end in a carboxyl group. Formula: $C_nH_{n+1}COOH$.

fat·ty de·gen·er·a·tion *n.* deterioration in the function of an organ, e.g., the liver or heart, caused by the accumulation of abnormally high levels of fats in its cells

fat·ty oil *n.* = **fixed oil**

fa·tu·i·ty /fə tòò itee/ (*plural* **-ties**) *n.* (*formal*) **1. SELF-SATISFIED UNINTELLIGENCE** complacency combined with lack of intelligence or thought **2. UNINTELLIGENT ACTION** an action or remark that is unintelligent or thoughtless —**fa·tu·i·tous** *adj.*

fat·u·ous /fáchoo əss/ *adj.* showing lack of intelligence coupled with a lack of awareness ○ *a fatuous joke* [Early 17thC. Formed from Latin *fatuus* (source of English *infatuate*. Originally "tasteless, vapid.")] —**fat·u·ous·ly** *adv.* —**fat·u·ous·ness** *n.*

fat·wa /fáttwə/, **fat·wah** *n.* a formal legal opinion or religious decree issued by an Islamic leader [Early 17thC. From Arabic, from *aftā* "to decide a point of law" (source of English *mufti*).]

fatware /fát wàir/ *n.* COMPUT, COMPUT = **bloatware**

fat·wit·ted /fát wìttəd/ *adj.* tending to act in a thoughtless or unintelligent way (*dated insult*)

fat·wood /fát wòòd/ *n. Southern U.S.* wood used as kindling [From its resinous nature]

fau·bourg /fō bùrg, fō bòòr/ *n.* **1.** *Southern U.S.* **SUBURB OF NEW ORLEANS** a suburb or quarter situated just outside New Orleans **2. SUBURB** an inner suburb or quarter of a city, especially in France [15thC. From French, an alteration (influenced by *faux* "false") of Old French *forsborc*, from Latin *foris* "outside" and late Latin *burgus* "fat" (of prehistoric Germanic origin).]

Fau·bus /fōbəss/, **Orval E.** (*b.* 1910) U.S. politician. While governor of Arkansas, he used the National Guard to try to prevent the racial integration of Little Rock High School (1957). Full name **Orval Eugene Faubus**

fau·cal /fáwk'l/, **fau·cial** /fáwsh'l/ *adj.* **1.** ANAT **OF FAUCES** relating to the fauces **2.** PHON **FROM PHARYNX** used to describe speech sounds that originate in the pharynx [Early 19thC. Formed from Latin *fauces* "throat" (see FAUCES).]

fau·ces /fō seez/ *npl.* the passage between the back of the mouth and the pharynx [15thC. From Latin, "throat" (source of English *suffocate*), of unknown origin.]

fau·cet /fáwssit/ *n.* a valve operated by a handle that controls the flow of a liquid, especially from pipes supplying water [14thC. Via Old French *fausset* or Provençal *falset* from *falser* "to bore in," from late Latin *fausser* "to corrupt," from Latin *falsus* "false."]

fau·cial *adj.* = **faucal**

William Faulkner

Faulk·ner /fáwknər/, **William** (1897–1962) U.S. writer. He is regarded as one of the greatest American novelists for his stream-of-consciousness works about Southern life, including *The Sound and the Fury* (1929). He won the 1949 Nobel Prize in literature. Full name **William Cuthbert Faulkner** —**Faulk·ner·i·an** /fawk neéree ən/ *adj.*

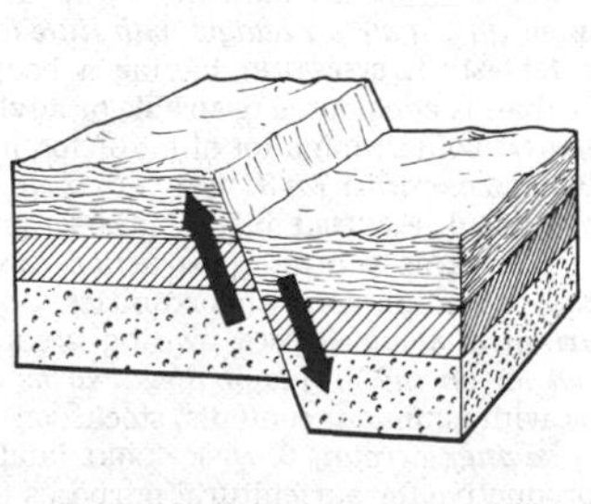

Fault: Displacement of rock layers in Earth's crust

fault /fawlt/ *n.* **1. RESPONSIBILITY** responsibility for a mistake, failure, or act of wrongdoing **2. PERSONAL**

SHORTCOMING a failing or character weakness in somebody ○ *My main fault is laziness.* **3.** DEFECT something that detracts from the integrity, functioning, or perfection of a thing **4.** MISTAKE an error, especially in calculation **5.** MISDEMEANOR a wrongful action **6.** GEOL DISPLACEMENT IN EARTH'S CRUST a displacement of rock layers in the earth's crust in response to stress, accompanied by a break in the continuity of the rocks on each side of the fault line **7.** RACKET GAMES INVALID SERVE IN RACKET GAMES a serve in certain racket games, e.g., tennis, that is invalid because it fails to land within a prescribed area **8.** SHOWJUMPING PENALTY MARK IN SHOW JUMPING a penalty mark awarded in show jumping for various errors such as a failure or refusal to clear a fence ■ *v.* **(fault·ed, fault·ing, faults) 1.** *vt.* BLAME SOMEBODY OR SOMETHING to blame, criticize, or find a defect in somebody or something ○ *He gave an excellent performance that could not be faulted.* **2.** *vi.* MAKE MISTAKE to commit a fault or make a mistake (*archaic*) **3.** *vi.* GEOL DISPLACE to respond to stress by becoming displaced and developing as a geologic fault (*refers to rock layers*) [13thC. Via Old French *faut(e)* "lack" from assumed Vulgar Latin *fallitum* "failing," from Latin *fallere* "to fail" (source of English *fail*).] ◇ **find fault with somebody** *or* **something** to criticize somebody or something, often unfairly ○ *She's always finding fault with the children's work.* ◇ **to a fault** excessively ○ *She was somewhat naive, and generous to a fault.*

WORD KEY: SYNONYMS

See Synonyms at ***flaw.***

fault·find·er /fáwlt fìndər/ *n.* somebody who constantly complains or is given to petty criticism

fault·find·ing /fáwlt fìnding/ *n.* CRITICISM constant and often petty complaining or criticism ■ *adj.* CRITICAL given to complaining or finding fault

fault·less /fáwltləss/ *adj.* having no faults or defects ○ *a faultless performance* —**fault·less·ly** *adv.* —**fault·less·ness** *n.*

fault line *n.* a linear feature on the earth's surface, occurring where displaced rock layers have broken through the earth's surface

fault plane *n.* the surface along which displacement of rock layers has taken place in a geologic fault

fault tol·er·ance *n.* the ability of an individual computer or computer network to preserve the integrity of data and continue operating when one or more components are malfunctioning

fault·y /fáwltee/ **(-i·er, -i·est)** *adj.* **1.** WITH FAULTS containing defects, especially ones that cause malfunctions ○ *faulty wiring* **2.** BLAMEWORTHY guilty or deserving blame (*archaic*) —**fault·i·ly** *adv.* —**fault·i·ness** *n.*

faun /fawn/ *n.* in Roman mythology, a rural god, often depicted as a creature with the body of a man and the legs and horns of a goat. Greek equivalent **satyr** [14thC. Directly or via French *faune* from Latin *Faunus* (see FAUNUS).]

fau·na /fáwnə/ (*plural* **-nas** *or* **-nae** /-nee/) *n.* **1.** ANIMAL LIFE IN GENERAL the animal life of a particular region or period, considered as a whole. ◊ **flora 2.** LIST OF ANIMALS a catalog or list describing the animals of a particular region or period [Late 18thC. Via modern Latin from late Latin *Fauna* "Fauna," an ancient Italian rural goddess, the sister of FAUNUS.] —**fau·nal** *adj.* —**fau·nal·ly** *adv.*

Fau·nus /fáwnəss/ *n.* in Roman mythology, the god of nature, farming, and fertility. He was the grandson of Saturn. Greek equivalent **Pan**

Fau·ré /faw ráy/, **Gabriel** (1845–1924) French composer and organist. His best known work is the *Requiem* (1887) for solo voices, choir, and orchestra. Full name **Gabriel Urbain Fauré**

Faust /fowst/ (1480?–1540?) German fortune-teller and magician. Reputed to have sold his soul to the devil, he is most noted for the legends concerning him that formed the basis for numerous literary and musical works. —**Faust·i·an** *adj.*

faute de mieux /fòt də myő/ *adv.* in the absence of something better (*literary*) ○ *the feeling that she had married him faute de mieux* [From French, literally "lack of better"]

fau·teuil /fō tő́y/ *n.* an upholstered armchair, usually with open sides (*literary or technical*) [Mid-18thC. Via French from Old French *faudestuel* "folding chair," from a prehistoric Germanic compound word formed from the ancestors of English *fold* + *stool*.]

fau·tor /fáwtər/ *n.* (*archaic*) **1.** SUPPORTER somebody who supports a person or cause **2.** PATRON somebody who gives protection or material support, e.g., in the form of funding [14thC. From Latin *fautor*, from *favere* (see FAVOR).]

Fauve /fōv/, **fauve** *n.* an artist belonging to a 20th-century movement in French painting **(Fauvism)** characterized by the use of simple forms and bright colors (*often used before a noun*) [Early 20thC. From French, literally "wild animal," via Old French *falve* "tawny" from prehistoric Germanic; from the vivid colors the painters used.]

Fau·vism /fṓ vìzzəm/, **fau·vism** *n.* an early 20th-century movement in painting, begun in about 1905 by a group of French artists, including Matisse, and characterized by the use of simple forms and vivid colors

Fau·vist /fṓvist/ *n.* = **Fauve** —**Fauv·ist** *adj.*

faux /fō/ *adj.* made in imitation of a natural material, e.g., leather or fur [Late 20thC. Via French from, ultimately, Latin *falsus* (see FALSE).]

faux a·mi /fō za mée/ (*plural* **faux a·mis**) *n.* LING = **false friend** *n.* 1 [From French, literally "false friend"]

faux-na·ïf /fō naa éef/ *adj.* FALSELY UNSOPHISTICATED pretending to be simple or without sophistication (*literary*) ■ *n.* FAUX-NAÏF PERSON somebody who affects innocence or lack of sophistication (*literary*) [From French, literally "falsely naive"]

faux pas /fō páa/ (*plural* **faux pas**) *n.* an embarrassing blunder that breaks a social convention of some kind (*literary*) [From French, literally "false step"]

WORD KEY: SYNONYMS

See Synonyms at ***mistake.***

fa·va bean /fáavə-/ *n.* = **broad bean** [Early 20thC. *Fava* via Italian from Latin *faba*.]

fave /fayv/ *n.*, *adj.* favorite (*dated slang*) [Mid-20thC. Shortening.]

fa·ve·la /fə véllə/ *n.* a shantytown or slum area, especially in Brazil [Mid-20thC. From Brazilian Portuguese, of uncertain origin; perhaps named for *Favela*, a hill near Rio de Janeiro where such towns were built.]

fa·ve·o·late /fə vée əlat, -làyt/ *adj.* with a honeycomb or pitted pattern (*formal*) [Mid-19thC. Formed from modern Latin *faveolus*, literally "little honeycomb," from Latin *favus* "honeycomb."]

fa·vism /fáa vìzzəm/ *n.* acute anemia caused by an allergic reaction to fava beans or the plant's pollen, usually as a result of a hereditary enzyme deficiency [Early 20thC. From Italian *favismo*, from *fava* "broad bean"(see FAVA BEAN).]

fa·vo·ni·an /fə vṓnee ən/ *adj.* LITERAT **1.** WESTERLY blowing from the west, or relating to the west wind (*literary*) **2.** FAVORABLE benign or kind [Mid-17thC. From Latin *favonianus*, from *Favonius* "west wind" (source of English *foehn*).]

fa·vor /fáyvər/ *n.* **1.** KIND ACT an act of kindness performed or granted out of good will ○ *lent me the car as a favor* **2.** ATTITUDE OR APPROVAL an approving, friendly, or supportive attitude ○ *They seem to be out of favor with the judges.* **3.** PREFERENCE preferential treatment shown to somebody **4.** TOKEN OF LOYALTY something given or worn as a token of love, allegiance, or good will **5.** SMALL GIFT a small gift given to each guest at a party **6.** APPEARANCE the way something or somebody looks to others (*archaic*) **7.** FACE a facial expression or feature (*archaic*) ■ **fa·vors** *npl.* SEX sexual intimacy, especially when consented to by a woman (*dated*) ■ *vt.* **(-vored, -vor·ing, -vors) 1.** PREFER SOMEBODY OR SOMETHING to show a preference for or to somebody or something ○ *He favored loud suits and colorful ties.* **2.** SUPPORT SOMEBODY OR SOMETHING to express support for somebody or something ○ *voters who favored reform* **3.** ASSIST SOMEBODY OR SOMETHING to be advantageous to somebody or something ○ *tax measures that favor the rich* **4.** SHOW SOMEBODY PREFERENTIAL TREATMENT to distinguish somebody by giving him or her something valuable ○ *favored him with a seat next to her* **5.** BE CAREFUL WITH SOMETHING to treat or use something gently ○ *favoring a bad knee* **6.** TREAT SOMEBODY OR SOMETHING WELL to treat somebody or something with particular approval or kindness ○ *She has been favoring him since he got a new car.* **7.** RESEMBLE SOMEBODY to resemble somebody, usually a parent, in appearance ○ *favors his uncle* [14thC. Via Old French "friendly regard," from Latin *favor*, from *favere* "to be well disposed toward."] —**fa·vor·er** *n.* ◇ **curry favor with somebody** to try to gain favor with a superior by flattery and obsequiousness ○ *They put more energy into currying favor with the principal than they ever put into their work.*

fa·vor·a·ble /fáyvərəb'l/ *adj.* **1.** ADVANTAGEOUS acting in a beneficial way ○ *favorable winds* **2.** PROMISING suggesting future improvement or good results ○ *a favorable outlook* **3.** APPROVING expressing approval or admiration ○ *a favorable reaction* **4.** GAINING APPROVAL winning approval or favor **5.** CONSENTING expressing agreement or consent ○ *a favorable response* —**fa·vor·a·ble·ness** *n.* —**fa·vor·a·bly** *adv.*

fa·vored /fáyvərd/ *adj.* **1.** CHOSEN preferred to any other ○ *The favored plan is unfortunately the costliest.* **2.** DISTINGUISHED enjoying the advantages of a particular thing ○ *a child favored with his mother's looks and father's good nature* **3.** PRIVILEGED enjoying advantages or privileges denied to others —**fa·vored·ness** *n.*

fa·vor·ite /fáyvərit, -vrit/ *adj.* MOST LIKED most liked, or preferred above all others ■ *n.* **1.** MOST LIKED PERSON OR THING somebody who or something that is especially liked or preferred above others ○ *Which author is your favorite?* **2.** ONE MOST LIKELY TO WIN a competitor considered to be the most likely to win, especially in a horserace **3.** SOMEBODY FAVORED BY SUPERIOR somebody who is treated with special favor by a superior ○ *a cherished position as one of the King's favorites* [Late 16thC. Via obsolete French *favorit* from, ultimately, Italian *favorito*, the past participle of *favorire* "to favor," from *favore* "favor," from Latin *favor* (see FAVOR).]

fa·vor·ite son *n.* **1.** MAN KNOWN TO COMMUNITY a successful man who is admired by the people of his hometown or home state **2.** PREFERRED PRESIDENTIAL CANDIDATE a politician preferred for nomination as a presidential candidate by delegates from his own state at a national convention

fa·vor·it·ism /fáyvəri tìzzəm, fáyvri-/ *n.* **1.** UNFAIRLY FAVORING PERSON OR GROUP the practice of giving special treatment or unfair advantages to a person or group ○ *The teacher was accused of showing favoritism toward certain students.* **2.** STATUS AS PREFERRED PERSON the state of being a favorite person ○ *basking in your favoritism*

fa·vour *n.*, *vt.* U.K. = **favor**

WORD KEY: SYNONYMS

See Synonyms at ***regard.***

fav·our·ite *adj.*, *n.* U.K. = **favorite**

fa·vus /fáyvəss/ *n.* an infectious skin disease that affects people, especially on the scalp, and some domestic animals, causing the formation of dry yellowish incrustations. It is caused by a fungus, *Trichophyton schoenleinii.* [Mid-16thC. From Latin, "honeycomb"; from the appearance of the skin lesions.]

Fawkes /fawks/, **Guy** (1570–1606) English conspirator. He was executed for his role in the Gunpowder Plot against James I on November 5, 1605.

fawn[1] /fawn/ *n.* **1.** YOUNG DEER a young deer, especially one that is unweaned or less than a year old **2.** YELLOWISH-BROWN COLOR a pale yellowish-brown color ■ *adj.* OF YELLOWISH-BROWN COLOR of a pale yellowish-brown color ■ *vi.* **(fawned, fawn·ing, fawns)** HAVE YOUNG to give birth to a fawn [14thC. Via French *faon* "young animal," from the assumed vulgar Latin stem *feton-*, from Latin *fetus* "offspring" (source of English *fetus*).]

fawn[2] /fáwn/ **(fawned, fawn·ing, fawns)** *vi.* **1.** SEEK FAVOR BY FLATTERY to seek attention or curry favor by flattery and obsequious behavior ○ *admirers fawning at his feet* **2.** TRY TO PLEASE to attempt to please somebody by showing enthusiastic affection ○ *started fawning all over me as soon as I walked in* [Old English *fagnian* "to rejoice," from *fægen* "glad" source also of English *fain*] —**fawn·er** *n.* —**fawn·ing·ly** *adv.* —**fawn·ing·ness** *n.*

fawn lil·y *n.* a North American plant with cream- or yellow-colored flowers and mottled leaves. Genus: *Erythronium.* [From its mottled leaves]

fax /faks/ *n.* **1.** MESSAGE SENT ELECTRONICALLY an image or document that is transmitted in digitized electronic form over telephone lines and reproduced in its original form on the receiving end **2.** SYSTEM FOR TRANSMITTING DOCUMENTS a system of transmitting documents and images electronically over telephone lines (*often used before a noun*) ○ *sent by fax* **3.** TRANSMITTING MACHINE a machine incorporating a telephone that sends and receives documents or images via fax ■ *vt.* (**faxed, fax·ing, fax·es**) SEND ELECTRONICALLY to send a message or document electronically using a fax machine [Mid-20thC. Shortening of FACSIMILE.]

fax-mo·dem *n.* a modem that enables a computer to send and receive faxes

fax-on-demand *n.* TECH, TELECOM technology that will send a facsimile automatically to somebody who telephones a particular number for information

fay[1] /fay/ *n.* a fairy, elf, or other small supernatural being from folklore (*literary*) ○ *"You are, upon the whole, a sort of fay, or sprite – not a woman!"* (Thomas Hardy, *Jude the Obscure*; 1895) [14thC. Via Old French *fa(i)e* "fairy" from Latin *Fata*, the goddess of fate, from *fatum* (source also of English *fairy*; see FATE).]

fay[2] /fay/ *n.* faith, religious or personal (*archaic*) ○ *"Ah, sirrah, by my fay, it waxes late: I'll to my rest."* (William Shakespeare, *Romeo and Juliet*; 1594) [14thC. From Old French *fei*, earlier *feid* (see FAITH).]

fay[3] /fay/ (**fayed, fay·ing, fays**) *vti.* to join pieces of wood together tightly, or fit tightly inside another piece of wood [Old English *fēgan*. Ultimately from an Indo-European base meaning "to fasten," which is also the ancestor of English *impale, compact*, and *peace*.]

fay[4] /fay/ *n.* = **ofay** (*slang insult*) [Early 20thC. Shortening.]

Fay·ette·ville /fáy ət vìl/ city in northwestern Arkansas, northeast of Fort Smith and west of the White River. Population: 52,360 (1996).

faze /fayz/ (**fazed, faz·ing, faz·es**) *vt.* to disconcert or disturb somebody ○ *News of the disaster didn't seem to faze her.* [Mid-19thC. Variant of dialectal *feeze* "to frighten," from Old English *fēsian* "to drive away," from prehistoric Germanic.]

fa·zen·da /fə zéndə/ *n.* a large estate, farm, plantation, or cattle ranch, especially in Brazil or Portugal [Early 19thC. Via Portuguese, originally "place with things to be done," from Latin *facienda* "things to be done," from *facere* "to do" (source also of English *hacienda*; see FACT).]

fb, f.b. *abbr.* fullback

F.B. *abbr.* **1.** foreign body **2.** freight bill

FBA *abbr.* LAW Federal Bar Association

fbd. *abbr.* SHIPPING freeboard

FBI, F.B.I. *n.* a bureau of the U.S. Department of Justice that deals with matters of national security, interstate crime, and crimes against the government. Full form **Federal Bureau of Investigation**

FBR *abbr.* fast-breeder reactor

f.c. *abbr.* PRINTING follow copy

FCA *abbr.* Farm Credit Administration

fcap. *abbr.* foolscap

FCC, F.C.C. *n.* the federal agency that oversees radio, television, and telecommunications in the United States. Full form **Federal Communications Commission**

F clef *n.* = **bass clef**

fcp. *abbr.* foolscap

fcy. *abbr.* fancy

FD, F.D. *abbr.* **1.** fatal dose **2.** Fidei Defensor **3.** Fire Department

FDA, F.D.A. *n.* the United States federal agency that oversees trade in and the safety of food and drugs. Full form **Food and Drug Adminstration**

FDIC, F.D.I.C. *n.* the U.S. federally chartered organization that insures deposits in banks. Full form **Federal Deposit Insurance Corporation**

F dis·tri·bu·tion *n.* a statistical measure of the spread or scattering of members of two observed random samples as a test of whether the samples have the same variability. The F-distribution is obtained by taking the ratio of the chi-square distributions of the samples divided by the number of their degrees of freedom. [Mid-20thC. Named for Sir Ronald Fisher (d. 1962), an English geneticist and statistician.]

FDR *abbr.* Franklin Delano Roosevelt

Fe *symbol.* iron [From Latin *ferrum* "iron"]

feal /feel/ *adj.* showing loyalty or faithfulness (*archaic*)

fe·al·ty /fée əltee/ (*plural* **-ties**) *n.* **1.** ALLEGIANCE TO FEUDAL LORD the loyalty sworn to a feudal lord by a vassal or tenant **2.** FAITHFULNESS loyalty or allegiance shown to anyone (*archaic or literary*) [13thC. Via Old French *feau(l)te* from Latin *fidelitas* (see FIDELITY.]

fear /feer/ *n.* **1.** FEELING OF ANXIETY an unpleasant feeling of apprehension or distress caused by the presence or anticipation of danger ○ *showed no signs of fear* **2.** FRIGHTENING THOUGHT an idea, thought, or other entity that causes feelings of fear ○ *irrational fears* **3.** REVERENCE awe or reverence, especially toward God **4.** WORRY a concern about something that threatens to bring bad news or results (*often used in the plural*) ○ *fears for their safe return* **5.** CHANCE chance or likelihood of an undesirable thing happening ○ *There's no fear that he'll misunderstand.* ■ *v.* (**feared, fear·ing, fears**) **1.** *vti.* BE AFRAID to be frightened of somebody or something, or frightened about doing something ○ *She fears going to the dentist.* **2.** *vt.* EXPRESS REGRETFULLY to be sorry to say something (*formal*) ○ *I fear that you have not been successful on this occasion.* **3.** *vt.* REVERE to show respect for or be in awe of somebody or something ○ *fear God* **4.** *vt.* FRIGHTEN to make somebody afraid (*archaic*) [Old English *fǣr* "calamity, danger" and *fǣran* "to frighten." Ultimately from an Indo-European base meaning "to try," which is also the ancestor of English *peril* and *experience*.]

fear for *vt.* to be worried or apprehensive about somebody who or something that appears to be at risk or in danger

fear·ful /féerfəl/ *adj.* **1.** FRIGHTENING causing or likely to cause fear ○ *a fearful storm* **2.** WORRIED feeling anxiety or apprehension ○ *fearful for the safety of her investment* **3.** TIMID nervous and easily frightened ○ *a fearful kitten* **4.** SHOWING FEAR arising from or expressing fear ○ *a fearful expression* **5.** REVERENTIAL feeling awe or reverence for somebody or something ○ *gazed in fearful wonder* **6.** VERY BAD extreme in degree, intensity, or badness (*informal*) ○ *had a fearful headache* —**fear·ful·ly** *adv.* —**fear·ful·ness** *n.*

fear·less /féerləss/ *adj.* courageous in the face of dangers or challenges —**fear·less·ly** *adv.* —**fear·less·ness** *n.*

fear·some /féersəm/ *adj.* **1.** FRIGHTENING inspiring fear ○ *a fearsome howling* **2.** IMPRESSIVE evoking awe and respect **3.** TIMID easily frightened ■ *adv.* VERY used to emphasize how severe something is (*regional dated*) ○ *It was fearsome cold.* —**fear·some·ly** *adv.* —**fear·some·ness** *n.*

fea·si·bil·i·ty /feezə bíllətee/ (*plural* **-ties**) *n.* **1.** FEASIBLE QUALITY the degree to which something can be carried out or achieved (*often used before a noun*) ○ *examining the feasibility of the proposed merger* **2.** SOMETHING FEASIBLE something that can be carried out or achieved ○ *That idea is not even a feasibility.*

fea·si·bil·i·ty stud·y *n.* a preliminary study undertaken to assess whether a planned project is likely to be practical and successful, and also estimating its cost

fea·si·ble /feezəb'l/ *adj.* **1.** POSSIBLE capable of being accomplished or put into effect **2.** PLAUSIBLE reasonable enough to be believed or accepted ○ *a feasible plan* [15thC. From French *faisable*, from *fais-*, the stem of *faire* "to do," from Latin *facere* (see FACT).] —**fea·si·bly** *adv.* —**fea·si·ble·ness** *n.*

feast /feest/ *n.* **1.** CELEBRATORY MEAL an elaborate meal for many people that celebrates an occasion ○ *a wedding feast* **2.** LARGE MEAL any large and elaborate meal **3.** SOMETHING VERY AGREEABLE something that provides a great deal of pleasure ○ *a feast for the eyes* **4.** RELIG RELIGIOUS CELEBRATION a periodic religious celebration, often marked by a special meal ■ *v.* (**feast·ed, feast·ing, feasts**) **1.** *vi.* ATTEND CELEBRATORY MEAL to be present at a celebratory meal **2.** *vi.* ENJOY EATING to eat heartily or with enjoyment ○ *feasting on strawberries and cream* **3.** *vt.* PROVIDE FEAST FOR to entertain somebody with a feast **4.** *vi.* TAKE DELIGHT to derive great pleasure from something, or enjoy something at length ○ *feast on the magnificent scenery* [12thC. Via Old French *feste* from, ultimately, Latin *festum* (source of English *festival* and *festoon*).] —**feast·er** *n.*

feast day *n.* **1.** RELIG DAY OF RELIGIOUS FESTIVAL a day on which a religious festival takes place **2.** DAY OF EATING a day on which an elaborate celebratory meal is enjoyed

Feast of Ded·i·ca·tion, Feast of Lights *n.* JUDAISM = **Hanukkah**

Feast of Lots *n.* JUDAISM = **Purim**

Feast of St. Mi·chael and All An·gels *n.* CHR = **Michaelmas**

Feast of Tab·er·na·cles *n.* JUDAISM = **Sukkoth**

Feast of the As·sump·tion *n.* CHR = **Assumption of the Virgin Mary**

Feast of the Ho·ly In·no·cents *n.* CHR = **Holy Innocents' Day**

Feast of Weeks *n.* JUDAISM = **Shavuoth**

feat[1] /feet/ *n.* **1.** NOTABLE ACT a remarkable act or achievement involving courage, skill, or strength ○ *She achieved the impressive feat of winning three gold medals.* **2.** ACTIVITY an art, skill, or profession (*archaic*) [14thC. Via Old French *fait* "deed" from Latin *factum* (see FACT).]

feat[2] /feet/ *adj.* (*archaic*) **1.** SKILLFUL possessing or demonstrating great skill **2.** STYLISHLY ELEGANT elegant or neat in appearance [Via Old French *fet* from Latin *factus*, literally "made (for something)," the past participle of *facere* (see FACT)] —**feat·ly** *adv.*

feath·er /féthər/ *n.* **1.** PART OF BIRD'S PLUMAGE an individual part of a bird's plumage, consisting of a hollow central shaft with numerous interlocking fine strands on either side **2.** SOMETHING RESEMBLING FEATHER something, e.g., the leaf of a plant, with light or wispy strands that give it a superficial resemblance to a feather **3.** FLAW IN PRECIOUS STONE a feather-shaped flaw, especially one found in a precious stone **4.** UNIMPORTANT THING something small, trivial, or of minimal value **5.** ARCHERY ARROW ATTACHMENT a piece of a feather attached to the end of an arrow or dart to make it fly straight **6.** ARCHERY BLUNT END OF ARROW the end of an arrow that has a feather fitted on it, as distinct from its head **7.** CONSTR PART OF WOOD JOINT a projecting strip of wood fitted into a groove in the edge of a board to form a joint **8.** NAVY TRACK MADE BY PERISCOPE the track made on the surface of the sea by a submarine's periscope **9.** ROWING HORIZONTAL OAR POSITION the horizontal position of an oar, after raising it from the water between strokes, that reduces wind resistance ■ *npl.* **1. feathers** ZOOL LONG HAIR ON ANIMAL'S LEGS fringes of hair on the legs or tails of certain dogs and horses **2. feath·ers** ATTIRE the clothes that somebody is wearing (*dated*) ■ *v.* (**-ered, -er·ing, -ers**) **1.** *vt.* HAIR CUT HAIR TO FORM LAYERS to style hair by cutting and thinning, giving a layered texture **2.** *vt.* FIT SOMETHING WITH FEATHERS to fit something, e.g., an arrow, with a feather or feathers **3.** *vti.* FRAY to fray a surface or end by cutting it or wearing it away, or become frayed in this way **4.** *vt.* COVER SOMETHING WITH FEATHERS to cover or decorate somebody or something with feathers **5.** *vi.* SPREAD to grow or move out at an angle from a central line, in a pattern resembling the structure of a feather **6.** *vi.* GROW FEATHERS to grow or form feathers (*refers to birds*) **7.** *vti.* ROWING TURN OAR BLADE HORIZONTAL to turn an oar with the blade face parallel to the water, after raising it from the water between strokes, in order to reduce wind resistance **8.** *vt.* AIR ALTER PROPELLER BLADES to change the angle of an aircraft's propeller so that the line of the blades is roughly parallel to the line of flight and air resistance is minimized **9.** *vt.* CONSTR CONNECT BOARDS WITH TONGUE-AND-GROOVE to join two boards or pieces of wood by using a tongue-and-groove joint [Old English *feðer*. Ultimately from an Indo-European word meaning "to fly," which is also the ancestor of English *pen, pterodactyl*, and *appetite*.] —**feath·er·y** *adj.* ◇ **a feather in somebody's cap** an act or achievement that gives somebody cause to be proud ○ *Being asked to give the after-dinner speech was a feather in my cap.*

feath·er·bed /féthər bèd/ (**-bed·ded, -bed·ding, -beds**) *v.* **1.** *vt.* PAMPER SOMEBODY to pamper somebody, or protect somebody from unpleasantness **2.** *vi.* OVERSTAFF OR LIMIT PRODUCTION to overstaff or limit production, especially in compliance with a union contract

feath·er·bed·ding /féthər bèdding/ *n.* the practice of overstaffing or limiting production, especially in compliance with a union contract, in order to save or create jobs

feath·er·brain /féthər brayn/ *n.* a forgetful, thoughtless, or inattentive person (*informal insult*) —**feath·er·brained** *adj.*

feather dust·er *n.* a brush used for dusting, made of long feathers attached to a stick

feath·ered /féthərd/ *adj.* **1.** WITH FEATHERS covered or decorated with feathers **2.** LIKE A FEATHER with many fine parallel strands ○ *a feathered lace border*

feath·er·edge /féthər èj/ *n.* **1.** JOINERY TAPERED BOARD a board or plank with a thin tapering edge **2.** JOINERY TAPERING EDGE OF BOARD the thinner tapering edge of a wedge-shaped board or plank **3.** PAPER = **deckle edge** ■ *vt.* (**-edged, -edg·ing, -edges**) JOINERY HONE TO AN EDGE to taper a side or end of a board to a very thin edge

feath·er grass *n.* a perennial grass plant that has feathery clusters of spikelets. Genus: *Stipa.*

feath·er·head /féthər hèd/ *n.* = **featherbrain** (*informal insult*) —**feath·er·head·ed** /fèthər héddəd/ *adj.*

feath·er·ing /féthəring/ *n.* **1.** PLUMAGE the feathers on a bird **2.** FEATHERS ATTACHED TO ARROW the feathers attached to an arrow or dart, or their arrangement **3.** ZOOL LONG HAIR ON ANIMAL'S LEGS fringes of hair on the legs or tails of certain dogs and horses **4.** PRINTING PRINTING DEFECT the spreading of ink in veiny lines through printed paper that is too absorbent

feath·er palm *n.* a palm tree with leaves that resemble feathers, e.g., a date palm

feath·er star *n.* a free-swimming marine invertebrate animal related to the starfish, with between five and ten feathery arms radiating from a central disk. Order: Comatulida.

feath·er·stitch /féthər stìch/ *n.* EMBROIDERY STITCH ornamental embroidery stitching with a zigzag pattern ■ *vt.* (**-stitched, -stitch·ing, -stitch·es**) SEW SOMETHING WITH FEATHERSTITCH to sew or decorate something with featherstitch

feath·er·weight /féthər wàyt/ *n.* **1.** LIGHT BOXER a professional boxer weighing not more than 126 pounds/57 kg, between bantamweight and lightweight **2.** SPORTSPERSON a competitor of light weight in other sports, e.g., wrestling **3.** SOMETHING LIGHT somebody or something that is very light, small, or insignificant

feath·er·y /féthəree/ *adj.* **1.** RESEMBLING FEATHERS similar to a feather or feathers, especially in lightness or softness **2.** CONSISTING OF FEATHERS made of or covered in feathers —**feath·er·i·ness** *n.*

fea·ture /féechər/ *n.* **1.** PART OF FACE a part of a face that contributes to its distinctiveness, especially the eyes, nose, or mouth **2.** DISTINCTIVE PART a part of something that distinguishes it **3.** CINEMA FULL-LENGTH MOTION PICTURE a full-length motion picture or, formerly, the main motion picture in a movie program **4.** PUBL REGULAR ARTICLE a regular item in a newspaper or magazine or on a broadcast **5.** PUBL MAIN ARTICLE an article that is given particular prominence in a newspaper or magazine **6.** BROADCAST MAIN PROGRAM a television or radio program that is considered especially important or popular **7.** SPECIAL ATTRACTION something offered as a special attraction, e.g., a particular aspect of something ○ *a refrigerator with several energy-saving features* **8.** LING PROPERTY OF LINGUISTIC UNIT a distinctive property of a linguistic unit. Voicing is a feature of the consonants *b, d,* and *g.* **9.** APPEARANCE the general appearance of somebody or something (*archaic*) ■ *v.* (**-tured, -tur·ing, -tures**) **1.** *vt.* CONTAIN SOMETHING AS IMPORTANT ELEMENT to have or present somebody or something as an important element of something ○ *This week's activities will feature horseback riding and golf.* **2.** *vti.* GIVE PROMINENCE TO IN PERFORMANCE to give prominence to somebody taking part in a performance or to something performed or portrayed in a performance, or be given prominence in this way ○ *a movie featuring two of the most popular actors* **3.** *vt.* IMAGINE OR VISUALIZE SOMETHING to imagine or visualize something mentally (*informal*) ○ *Feature this: You've just returned and can choose to live wherever you please.* **4.** *vi.* FIGURE IN SOMETHING to figure in or be a part of something ○ *Marriage doesn't feature in his plans.* **5.** *vt.* RESEMBLE SOMEBODY OR SOMETHING to resemble somebody or something (*archaic*) ○ *The baby features her father.* [14thC. Via Old French *faiture*, from, ultimately, Latin *facere* "to do, make" (see FACT). Originally in English, "shape or proportions," especially of the body.]

feature creature *n.* COMPUT somebody who adds excessive features to a design, software program, or Web site, often at the expense of coherence or utility (*slang*)

fea·tured /féechərd/ *adj.* **1.** GIVEN PROMINENCE given prominence or treated as a special attraction **2.** HAVING SPECIFIED FACIAL FEATURES having facial features of a specified kind (*often used in combination*) ○ *a sharp-featured man*

fea·ture film *n.* a full-length motion picture

fea·ture-length *adj.* being as long as a feature film ○ *a feature-length episode of a TV show*

fea·ture·less /féechərləss/ *adj.* lacking any characteristics or properties that can be considered distinctive

Feb., Feb *abbr.* February

fe·brif·ic /fə bríffik/ *adj.* **1.** CAUSING FEVER capable of causing somebody to have a fever **2.** HAVING FEVER affected by a fever [Early 18thC. From French *fébrifique* (now obsolete), from Latin *febris* "fever" (see FEVER).]

feb·ri·fuge /fébbrə fyo͞oj/ *n.* DRUG THAT REDUCES FEVER a drug or treatment that is capable of reducing a fever ■ *adj.* REDUCING FEVER capable of reducing a fever [Late 17thC. From French *fébrifuge*, from Latin *febris* "fever" (see FEVER).] —**feb·ri·fug·al** /fə bríffyəg'l, fébbrə fyo͞og'l/ *adj.*

fe·brile /fébbrəl, féebrəl/ *adj.* relating to, involving, or typical of fever [Mid-17thC. From French *fébrile* or medieval Latin *febrilis*, both formed from Latin *febris* "fever."]

Feb·ru·ar·y /fébroo èrree, fébbyoo-/ (*plural* **Febru·ar·ies**) *n.* the second month of the year in the Gregorian calendar, between January and March. It has 28 days, except in every fourth year, when it has 29. [14thC. Via Old French *feverier* from, ultimately, Latin *februarius (mensis)* "(month) of purification," from a Roman festival of purification held in this month.]

FEC *abbr.* Federal Election Commission

fec. *abbr.* fecit

fe·cal /féek'l/ *adj.* relating to or consisting of feces

fe·ces /féesseez/ *npl.* the body's solid waste matter, composed of undigested food, bacteria, water, and bile pigments and discharged from the bowel through the anus [14thC. From Latin *faeces*, plural of *faex* "sediment, dregs."] —**fe·cal** /féek'l/ *adj.*

feck·less /fékləss/ *adj.* **1.** INEFFECTIVE unable or unwilling to do anything useful **2.** UNLIKELY TO BE SUCCESSFUL lacking the thought or organization necessary to succeed ○ *feckless attempts at starting a business* [Late 16thC. From obsolete *feck* "value, efficacy," a shortening of EFFECT.] —**feck·less·ly** *adv.* —**feck·less·ness** *n.*

fec·u·la /fékyələ/ (*plural* **-lae** /-lee/) *n.* **1.** STARCH a starch extracted as sediment from a mixture of water and crushed plants **2.** INSECT DROPPING a piece of excrement, especially an insect dropping [Late 17thC. From Latin *faecula* "crust of wine," from *faex* "dregs, sediment" (source of English *feces*).]

fec·u·lent /fékyələnt/ *adj.* very dirty or foul, especially when polluted by excrement (*formal*) [15thC. Directly or via French *féculent* from Latin *faeculentus*, from *faeces* (see FECES).] —**fec·u·lence** *n.*

fe·cund /féekənd, fék-/ *adj.* **1.** FERTILE capable of producing much vegetation or many offspring (*formal*) **2.** HIGHLY PRODUCTIVE capable of producing many different works or works that are highly imaginative ○ *a fecund liar* [14thC. Directly or via French *fécond* from Latin *fecundus.*]

fe·cun·date /féekən dàyt, fék-/ (**-dat·ed, -dat·ing, -dates**) *vt.* (*formal*) **1.** MAKE SOMEBODY OR SOMETHING PRODUCTIVE to make somebody or something fruitful or productive **2.** MAKE SOMEBODY PREGNANT to fertilize something, or make somebody pregnant —**fe·cun·da·tion** /fèekən dáysh'n, fèk-/ *n.*

fe·cun·di·ty /fi kúndətee/ *n.* **1.** ABILITY TO PRODUCE OFFSPRING the ability to produce offspring, especially in large numbers **2.** CREATIVE PRODUCTIVITY the ability to produce many different and original ideas (*formal*)

fed past participle, past tense of **feed**

Fed /fed/, **fed** *n.* (*informal*) **1.** FEDERAL AGENT a Federal agent or official, especially an agent of one of the watchdog agencies such as the Federal Bureau of Investigation or the Environmental Protection Agency **2.** FEDERAL RESERVE BOARD the Federal Reserve Board **3.** FEDERAL RESERVE SYSTEM the Federal Reserve System

Fed., fed. *abbr.* **1.** Federal **2.** Federated

fe·da·yee /fe daa yee, -dà-/ (*plural* **fed·a·yeen** /-yeen, fe dà-/) *n.* an Arab commando or guerrilla, especially one who fights against Israel [Mid-20thC. From Arabic and Persian *fidā'ī* "somebody who sacrifices himself or herself."]

fed·er·a·cy /féddərəssee/ (*plural* **-cies**) *n.* an alliance of people or countries formed to achieve a shared purpose (*archaic*) [Mid-17thC. From FEDERATE, or a shortening of CONFEDERACY.]

fed·er·al /féddərəl, féddrəl/ *adj.* **1.** MADE UP OF ALLIES relating to a form of government in which several states or regions defer certain powers, e.g., in foreign affairs, to a central government while retaining some measure of self-government **2.** CENTRAL relating to a political unit established on a federal basis, especially its central government **3.** ASSOCIATED relating to or characteristic of a unified body with constituent elements that retain a measure of autonomy **4.** OF A U.S. ARCHITECTURAL STYLE relating to, involving, or typical of a classical style of architecture, decoration, and furniture popular in the United States in the late 18th and early 19th centuries ■ *n.* SUPPORTER OF ALLIANCE somebody who supports joining an alliance [Mid-17thC. From Latin *foeder-*, the stem of *foedus* "treaty." Ultimately from an Indo-European base meaning "to trust," which is also the ancestor of English *confide, faith,* and *abide*).]

Fed·er·al *adj.* OF UNION involving or supporting the Union during the Civil War in the United States ○ *Federal troops* ■ *n.* **1.** UNION SOLDIER a soldier or supporter of the Union during the United States Civil War **2.** = **federalist**

Fed·er·al Bu·reau of In·ves·ti·ga·tion *n.* full form of **FBI**

fed·er·al case *n.* a matter in law that comes under the jurisdiction of a federal court ◇ **make a federal case out of** to make a fuss about something trivial ○ *Why do you have to make a federal case out of everything?*

fed·eral dis·trict *n.* an area in which the seat of the national government of a federation, e.g., the United States, is located

Fed·er·al Funds *npl.* money lent overnight from one Federal Reserve bank to another. The rate of interest charged on such loans is a key economic indicator.

fed·er·al gov·ern·ment *n.* the central government of a federation

fed·er·al·ism /féddərə lìzzəm, féddrə-/ *n.* **1.** POLITICAL SYSTEM a political system in which several states or regions defer certain powers, e.g., in foreign affairs, to a central government while retaining a limited measure of self-government **2.** POLITICAL PRINCIPLE the principle of a federal system of government, or support for such a system

Fed·er·al·ism *n.* the political doctrine of the former Federalist Party

fed·er·al·ist /féddərəlist, féddrə-/ *n.* **1.** SUPPORTER OF FEDERALISM somebody who supports a federal system of government **2.** *Can* SUPPORTER OF CONFEDERATION in Canada, somebody who supports the federation of the Canadian provinces and opposes separatism

Fed·er·al·ist *n.* somebody who supported the former Federalist Party

Fed·er·al·ist Par·ty *n.* a former political party of the United States advocating a strong centralized government within the federal system. Founded in 1787, it declined in influence after 1800.

fed·er·al·ize /féddərə lìz, féddrə-/ (**-ized, -iz·ing, -iz·es**) *vt.* **1.** JOIN STATES IN FEDERAL UNION to bring various states together in a federal union **2.** PUT SOMETHING UNDER FEDERAL CONTROL to place something under the control of a federal government —**fed·er·al·i·za·tion** /fèddərəli záysh'n, fèddrəli-/ *n.*

Fed·er·al Re·serve Bank *n.* one of the 12 reserve banks responsible for regulating the affiliated banks in a Federal Reserve District in the United States

Fed·er·al Re·serve Board *n.* the group responsible for supervising the Federal Reserve System

Fed·er·al Re·serve note *n.* a bank note or certificate, sometimes used as money, issued by a Federal Reserve Bank

Fed·er·al Re·serve Sys·tem *n.* the United States banking system that regulates the money supply and interest rates, consisting of 12 Federal Reserve Districts in which a Federal Reserve Bank regulates the activities of affiliated banks

fed·er·ate /féddə ràyt/ (**-ated, -at·ing, -ates**) *vti.* to join, or cause various bodies to join together, in a federation [Late 17thC. From Latin *foederare*, from *foedus* (see FEDERAL).]

fed·er·a·tion /fèddə ráysh'n/ *n.* **1.** JOINING IN FEDERAL UNION an act of joining in a federal union or a federal system of government **2.** POLITICAL UNIT a political unit formed from smaller units on a federal basis **3.** ALLIANCE a group of various bodies or parties that have united to achieve a common goal

fe·do·ra /fə dáwrə/ *n.* a soft felt hat with a brim and a crease along the length of its crown [Late 19thC. From *Fédora*, title of a drama by Victorien Sardou (1831–1908).]

fed up *adj.* having reached the limits of tolerance or patience with somebody or something (*informal*) ○ *I know she's fed up with working all the time.*

fee /fee/ (**feed, fee·ing, fees**) *n.* **1.** PAYMENT FOR SERVICES a payment for professional services **2.** CHARGE MADE BY INSTITUTION a charge made by an institution, e.g., for membership, entrance, or the administering of an examination **3.** TIP an extra sum of money given to somebody, e.g., waitperson, for good service (*archaic*) **4.** LAW HERITABLE INTEREST IN LAND a right to land that can be passed on by inheritance **5.** = **fief** *n.* 1 [14thC. Via Anglo-Norman from medieval Latin *feudum* (see FEUD[2]).]

WORD KEY: SYNONYMS

See Synonyms at ***wage.***

WORD KEY: ORIGIN

The word ***fee*** and its close relatives *feudal* and *fief* take us back to the very beginnings of feudal society in Europe, when the ownership of cattle was symbolic of wealth. The Indo-European source of ***fee***, denoting "livestock," is also the source of the German word *Vieh*, meaning "cattle."

Feeb /feeb/, **Fee·bie** /fée bèe/ *n.* an agent of the F.B.I. (*slang*)

fee·ble /féeb'l/ (**-bler, -blest**) *adj.* **1.** PHYSICALLY OR MENTALLY WEAK lacking physical or mental strength or health **2.** UNCONVINCING unlikely to convince ○ *a feeble excuse* [12thC. Via Old French *fe(i)ble* from, ultimately, Latin *flebilis* "lamentable," later "weak," from *flere* "to weep."] —**fee·ble·ness** *n.* —**fee·bly** *adv.*

WORD KEY: SYNONYMS

See Synonyms at ***weak.***

fee·ble-mind·ed *adj.* **1.** OFFENSIVE TERM an offensive term for mentally challenged (*offensive*) **2.** UNINTELLIGENT unintelligent or thoughtless (*insult*) **3.** NOT WELL-THOUGHT-OUT done without forethought, or lacking a well-thought-out plan **4.** IRRESOLUTE lacking in will or resolution (*archaic*) —**fee·ble-mind·edly** *adv.* —**fee·ble-mind·ed·ness** *n.*

feed /feed/ *v.* (**fed, fed** /fed/, **feed·ing, feeds**) **1.** *vt.* GIVE FOOD TO SOMEBODY to give food to a person or an animal **2.** *vt.* GIVE SOMETHING AS FOOD to give something as food to a person or an animal **3.** *vt.* SERVE AS FOOD FOR SOMEBODY to serve as or be enough food for a person or an animal **4.** *vi.* EAT to eat food, or take in nourishment **5.** *vt.* SUPPORT SOMETHING to sustain or encourage a specific belief or behavior ○ *Compliments merely feed vanity.* **6.** *vt.* PROVIDE SOMETHING WITH NECESSARY MATERIAL to provide the necessary materials for something to operate **7.** *vti.* MOVE GRADUALLY to move something gradually into, through, or out of something, or be moved in this way **8.** *vt.* ARTS GIVE PERFORMER CUE to deliver a line or cue to a fellow performer **9.** *vti.* SPORTS PASS BALL TO FELLOW PLAYER to pass a ball to a teammate (*informal*) **10.** *vt.* UTIL SUPPLY SOMETHING WITH POWER to supply power or an electrical signal to a system, component, or station **11.** *vti.* BROADCAST SEND BROADCAST to provide a local television or radio broadcast to a larger audience by using a satellite or network ■ *n.* **1.** ACT OF FEEDING an act or occasion of feeding **2.** FOOD food, especially for animals or babies **3.** LARGE MEAL a meal, especially a large and satisfying one (*dated informal*) **4.** MATERIAL PROVIDER a device that supplies material to a machine, as does the paper tray on a printer **5.** BROADCAST NETWORK SIGNAL the signal a network broadcasts to local radio or television stations for broadcast ○ *The local television station lost the network's feed for a few minutes.* **6.** ARTS SOMEBODY WHO PROVIDES CUES somebody who delivers a line or cue to a fellow performer [Old English *fēdan*; related to *foda* (see FOOD)]

feed into *vt.* **1.** CONTRIBUTE TO SOMETHING to add weight and impetus to something **2.** JOIN WITH SOMETHING LARGER to connect with and contribute to something larger, e.g., a road or river

feed·back /féed bàk/ *n.* **1.** RETURN OF OUTPUT the return of part of the output of a machine, system, or circuit to the input in a way that affects its performance **2.** NOISE IN LOUDSPEAKER the high whistling or howling noise caused by feedback in a loudspeaker **3.** RESPONSE comments in the form of opinions about and reactions to something, intended to provide useful information for future decisions and development

feed·back cir·cuit *n.* a circuit in which a portion of the output signal is returned to the input, often in order to control or stabilize the circuit

feed·back con·trol loop *n.* the connection or path that forms an electrical loop from the output to the input of a feedback circuit

feed·back fac·tor *n.* a portion of an output signal that is returned to and combined with the input signal

feed·back in·hi·bi·tion *n.* an internal control on a hormone or enzyme that causes a reduction in activity once the end product reaches a certain concentration

feed·back loop *n.* a cycle in which two agents each act to reinforce the other's action

feed·bag /féed bàg/ *n.* **1.** *U.K.* BAG FOR ANIMAL FEED a bag or sack containing food for livestock **2.** HORSE'S FEEDING BAG a bag placed over the muzzle of a horse from which it can eat

feed·er /féedər/ *n.* **1.** EATER somebody who or something that eats, gives food to others, or is fed **2.** CONTAINER FOR ANIMAL'S FOOD a device that supplies food for animals and birds ○ *a bird feeder in the garden* **3.** AGRIC LIVESTOCK an animal that is fattened for sale or slaughter **4.** MACHINE PART a part of a machine that accepts or controls the input of material to be processed ○ *a document feeder* **5.** GEOG TRIBUTARY a stream or river that joins the flow of a larger one **6.** TRANSP CONNECTING CARRIER a road, railroad, or airline that carries traffic from a relatively small place to a city in order to connect with a larger carrier **7.** UTIL POWER LINE a power line that carries power from a generating station to a substation or network **8.** RADIO CONNECTION a line that connects an antenna to a receiver or transmitter **9.** EDUC PRIMARY SCHOOL a primary or middle school whose graduates go on to a particular secondary school **10.** GARDENING PLANT REQUIRING FERTILIZER a plant that requires a large amount of fertilizer to grow, and especially flower, well ○ *Fuchsias are gross feeders.*

feed·ing bot·tle *n.* a bottle with a plastic or rubber nipple used to give milk or other liquids to a baby or young animal

feed·ing fren·zy *n.* **1.** ZOOL VIOLENT FEEDING BY MANY ANIMALS an intense violent period of eating that occurs when a large number of animals of the same or related species, e.g., sharks or piranhas, converge on a food source **2.** INSTANCE OF FRANTIC ACTIVITY an instance of frantic activity centered on a person or organization that occurs when other people, especially journalists, sense an opportunity they can exploit (*informal*)

feed·ing ground *n.* an area where animals, birds, or fish regularly come to feed

feed·lot /féed lòt/ *n.* an area or building in which livestock are kept while being fattened for slaughter

feed·stock /féed stòk/ *n.* a raw material used in the industrial manufacture of a product

feed·stuff /féed stùf/ *n.* feed for livestock, especially consisting of processed and balanced ingredients

feed·through /féed thrōō/ *n.* an electrical conductor that connects two sides of a circuit board

feel /feel/ *v.* (**felt** /felt/, **felt, feel·ing, feels**) **1.** *vt.* TOUCH SOMETHING to perceive something using the sense of touch **2.** *vt.* TOUCH SOMEBODY SEXUALLY to touch somebody or a part of somebody's body for the purpose of sexual gratification **3.** *vt.* EXAMINE SOMETHING to test or examine something by touching it **4.** *vt.* ADVANCE HESITANTLY to make your way forward slowly, guided by the sense of touch or tentatively, because what is ahead is hard to see or uncertain **5.** *vi.* USE TOUCH IN SEARCHING to use the sense of touch to try to find something ○ *feel around for my keys* **6.** *vt.* HAVE SENSATION IN BODY PART to have physical sensation in a specified part of the body **7.** *vt.* EXPERIENCE SOMETHING to experience an emotion or physical sensation ○ *I feel no regret.* **8.** *vi.* SEEM TO YOURSELF to seem to yourself to be in a specified physical or emotional state ○ *Don't feel sad.* **9.** *vi.* CAUSE SPECIFIED SENSATION to cause a specified physical or emotional sensation ○ *The water feels cold.* **10.** *vt.* BE AWARE OF SOMETHING to be instinctively aware of something, usually an emotion, that is not visible or apparent **11.** *vt.* BE AFFECTED BY SOMETHING to be deeply affected emotionally by something painful **12.** *vt.* THINK SOMETHING IS TRUE to be convinced about something by instinct or intuition rather than concrete evidence ○ *I feel you're lying to me.* **13.** *vt.* BELIEVE SOMETHING to have the opinion or belief that something is the case ○ *She felt she could no longer carry on.* ■ *n.* **1.** ACT OF TOUCHING an act of touching something **2.** IMPRESSION GAINED FROM TOUCH an impression of something gained through touching or being touched by it ○ *the feel of wool against the skin* **3.** IMPRESSION SENSED FROM SOMETHING a specified impression, appearance, effect, or atmosphere sensed from something ○ *a hotel with a more traditional feel* **4.** SENSE OF TOUCH the sensation felt on touching something ○ *hot to the feel* **5.** INSTINCT FOR SOMETHING an instinctive understanding of, or talent for, something ○ *He has a feel for these things.* **6.** GROPE an uninvited sexual touch (*informal*) [Old English *fēlan*. Ultimately from an Indo-European base that is also the ancestor of English *palpable*.] ◇ **feel like 1.** to have an inclination or desire for something **2.** to have or acknowledge a physical or emotional condition that is considered comparable to something else

feel for *vt.* to experience sympathy or compassion for somebody

feel out *vt.* to try to establish, often in an indirect way, the nature of a situation or somebody's attitude or opinion about something

feel up *vt.* to touch somebody sexually, especially without permission (*informal*)

feel up to *vt.* to consider yourself ready for something or able to do something

feel·er /féelər/ *n.* **1.** SOMEBODY WHO FEELS somebody who or something that feels something **2.** ZOOL TOUCHING ORGAN an organ of touch in various animals, e.g., an insect's antenna **3.** ATTEMPT TO TEST OTHERS' REACTION something said or done to test the reaction of others to an idea, plan, or project

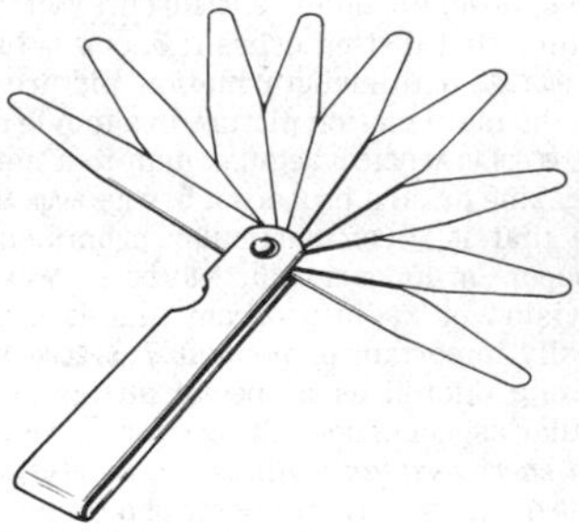

Feeler gauge

feel·er gauge *n.* a thin strip of metal of a specific size used to measure or set a gap between parts of a mechanism

feel-good *adj.* causing, involving, or typical of a sense of well-being or satisfaction

feel·ing /féeling/ *n.* **1.** SENSE OF TOUCH the sensation felt on touching something **2.** ABILITY TO HAVE PHYSICAL SENSATION the ability to perceive physical sensation in a part of the body ○ *Slowly the feeling returned to his fingers.* **3.** SOMETHING FELT PHYSICALLY OR MENTALLY a perceived physical or mental sensation **4.** SOMETHING FELT EMOTIONALLY a perceived emotion **5.** AFFECTION the emotional response of love, sympathy, or tenderness toward somebody **6.** ABILITY TO EXPRESS EMOTION the capacity to experience strong emotions **7.** IMPRESSION SENSED FROM SOMETHING a specified impression, appearance, effect, or atmosphere sensed from something ○ *There was a feeling of abandonment about the old house.* **8.** INSTINCTIVE AWARENESS an instinctive awareness or presentiment of something ○ *I have a feeling you're going to be disappointed.* **9.** INSTINCTIVE UNDERSTANDING OR TALENT an instinctive understanding of, or talent for, something ○ *has a real feeling for this kind of work* **10.** EXPRESSIVENESS the ability to express strong emotion, especially in performance ○ *Play the piece again with more feeling.* ■ **feel·ings** *npl.* SENSIBILITIES somebody's emotional susceptibilities ○ *I didn't want to hurt their feelings.* ■ *adj.* **1.** SENSITIVE TO TOUCH able to experience the sensation of touch **2.** EXPRESSIVE expressing or full of strong emotion **3.** HAVING STRONG EMOTIONS easily or strongly affected by emotion —**feel·ing·ly** *adv.*

fee sim·ple (*plural* **fees sim·ple**) *n.* a form of property ownership in which the owner has outright and unconditional disposal rights ○ *The deed transferred ownership in fee simple.* ◊ **fee tail**

fee split·ting *n.* the practice in which part of a client's fee is paid by one professional to another for having referred the client

feet plural of **foot** ◇ **drag your feet (on something)** to delay doing something

fee tail (*plural* **fees tail**) *n.* a form of property ownership in which the property may be inherited only by a specified line of heirs. ◊ **fee simple** [From TAIL]

Feh·ling's so·lu·tion /fáylingz-/ *n.* a solution of copper sulfate, sodium potassium tartrate, and sodium hydroxide used to detect the presence of aldehydes, including sugars [Late 19thC. Named for the German chemist Hermann von *Fehling* (1812–85).]

feign /fayn/ (**feigned, feign·ing, feigns**) *vt.* **1. PRETEND SOMETHING** to make a show or pretense of something ○ *She feigned ignorance.* **2. INVENT SOMETHING** to make up or fabricate something **3. COPY** to imitate or copy somebody or something [13thC. From French *feign-*, the present stem of *feindre* "to pretend, shirk" (source of English *faint*), from Latin *fingere* "to fabricate, form" (source of English *fiction, figure,* and *figment*).]

fei·jo·a /fay yṓ ə, -hṓ ə/ *n.* **1. AMERICAN TREE** a South American tree related to myrtle and cultivated for its edible fruit. Latin name: *Acca sellowiana.* **2. FRUIT TASTING LIKE PINEAPPLE** an edible green fruit of the feijoa tree that has a flavor similar to pineapple and is eaten raw or used in cooking or making jellies and preserves [Late 19thC. From modern Latin, genus name, named for the Brazilian naturalist J. da Silva *Feijó* (1760–1824).]

fei·jo·a·da /fàyzhṑ aá daá, fàyzhə waádə/ *n.* a Brazilian party dish consisting of meat with rice, black beans, green vegetables such as kale, sliced oranges, and a hot pepper sauce, all served on platters [Mid-20thC. From Portuguese, formed from *feijão*, any of various edible beans, from Latin *phaseolus*.]

Fei·ning·er /fíningər/, **Lyonel Charles Adrian** (1871–1956) U.S. artist. His work showed a strong cubist influence in its geometric style and translucent colors.

feint /faynt/ *n.* **1.** MIL **MOCK ATTACK** a mock attack by a military force, intended to draw the enemy's attention away from the true attack **2.** SPORTS **DECEPTIVE MOVE** a deceptive move in a competitive sport **3. DECEPTIVE ACTION** a deceptive action made to disguise what is really intended ■ *vti.* (**feint·ed, feint·ing, feints**) **MAKE FEINT** to carry out a feint [Late 17thC. From French *feinte* "sham, pretense," from the past participle of *feindre* (see FEIGN).]

feist /fīst/ *n.* a small dog (*regional*) [Late 18thC. Variant of *fist*, a shortening of *fisting cur*, from obsolete *fisten* "to break wind" (see FIZZLE).]

feist·y /fístee/ (**-i·er, -i·est**) *adj.* (*informal*) **1. SPIRITED** characterized by spirited, sometimes aggressive, behavior **2. IRRITABLE** likely to respond in an irritable or touchy way [Late 19thC. From FEIST (from the temperament of a small aggressive pet dog).]

Feke /feek/, **Robert** (1705?–50?) U.S. artist, noted for his colorful portraits of prominent colonial families. His first and largest portrait was *Family of Isaac Royall* (1741).

fe·la·fel *n.* = **falafel**

feld·spar /féld spaàr/, **fel·spar** /fél spaàr/ *n.* an extremely common aluminosilicate mineral found in most igneous and metamorphic rocks and many sediments. It contains varying proportions of calcium, sodium, potassium, and other minerals. Feldspar minerals are subdivided into two groups, orthoclase feldspars and plagioclase feldspars. [Late 18thC. Alteration of German *Feldspath*, literally "field mineral." Spelling variation *fels-* comes from a mistaken association with German *Fels* "rock."] —**feld·spath·ic** /feld spáthik/ *adj.*

feld·spath·oid /féld spà thòyd/ *n.* a rock-forming mineral found in silica-deficient alkaline igneous rocks [Literally "similar to feldspar"]

fe·li·cif·ic /feèli síffik/ *adj.* creating or intended to cause happiness (*formal*) [Mid-19thC. From Latin *felicificus*, from *felix* "happy" (see FELICITY).]

fe·lic·i·tate /fə líssi tàyt/ (**-tat·ed, -tat·ing, -tates**) *vt.* to congratulate somebody, or wish somebody happiness (*formal*) [Early 17thC. From late Latin *felicitare* "to make happy," from Latin *felix* "happy" (see FELICITY).] —**fe·lic·i·ta·tor** *n.*

fe·lic·i·ta·tion /fə lìssi táysh'n/ *n.* **ACT OF CONGRATULATING** an act of congratulating or wishing somebody happiness (*formal*) ■ **fe·lic·i·ta·tions** *npl.* **FRIENDLY GREETING** used as a greeting or to wish somebody happiness (*formal*)

fe·lic·i·tous /fə líssitəss/ *adj.* **1. APPROPRIATE** appropriate or highly suitable ○ *a felicitous choice of words* **2. PLEASANT** pleasing or agreeable **3. FORTUNATE** happy or fortunate [Mid-16thC. Formed from FELICITY.] —**fe·lic·i·tous·ly** *adv.* —**fe·lic·i·tous·ness** *n.*

fe·lic·i·ty /fə líssətee/ (*plural* **-ties**) *n.* **1. HAPPINESS** happiness or contentment **2. SOMETHING PRODUCING HAPPINESS** something that creates happiness **3. APPROPRIATENESS** an appropriate or pleasing manner **4. SOMETHING APPROPRIATE** something appropriate or pleasing [14thC. Via Old French *félicité* from, ultimately, Latin *felix* "fruitful, happy." Ultimately from an Indo-European base meaning "to suck, suckle," which is also the ancestor of English *female, fetus, fellatio,* and *fecund*.]

fe·lid /feélid/ (*plural* **-lids** *or* **-lid**) *n.* a feline (*technical*) [Late 19thC. Via modern Latin *Felidae*, family name, from, ultimately, Latin *feles* "cat."]

fe·line /feé līn/ *adj.* **1. OF CAT FAMILY** belonging to or typical of animals of the cat family, including lions, tigers, and domestic cats **2. RESEMBLING CAT** similar to a cat, especially in graceful movement or stealthiness ○ *feline suppleness* ■ *n.* **MEMBER OF CAT FAMILY** an animal belonging to the cat family. Domestic cats, lions, and tigers are felines. Family: Felidae. [Late 17thC. From Latin *felinus*, from *feles* "cat."] —**fe·line·ly** *adv.* —**fe·line·ness** *n.* —**fe·lin·i·ty** /fi línnətee/ *n.*

fe·line dis·tem·per *n.* an infectious viral disease of cats that causes vomiting and diarrhea and is often fatal

fell[1] past tense of **fall** [13thC. Via Old Norse *fjall* "hill" from, ultimately, an Indo-European base that is also the ancestor of German *fels* "rock."]

fell[2] /fel/ *vt.* (**felled, fell·ing, fells**) **1. CHOP TREE DOWN** to cut down a tree **2. KNOCK SOMEBODY DOWN** to knock somebody down, or cause somebody to fall **3.** SEW **SEW SEAM FLAT** to sew a seam by turning an edge over and sewing it down on the inside ■ *n.* **1.** FORESTRY **NUMBER OF TREES CUT DOWN** an amount of timber cut down at one time or over one period **2.** SEW **SEWN SEAM** a seam sewn by turning an edge over and sewing it down on the inside [Old English *fel(l)* "to cause to fall" from, ultimately, prehistoric Germanic] —**fell·a·ble** *adj.*

fell[3] /fel/ *adj.* (*archaic or literary*) **1. FIERCE** having an extremely cruel or vicious character **2. LETHAL** capable of killing somebody or destroying something **3. INAUSPICIOUS** having a bad or malign outcome [13thC. From Old French *fel*, a form of *felon* (see FELON[1]).]

fell[4] /fel/ *n.* **1. ANIMAL HIDE** the hide of an animal **2. THIN MEMBRANE** the thin membrane between an animal's hide and its flesh [Old English. Ultimately from an Indo-European base that is also the ancestor of English *pelt* and *film*.]

fel·la /féllə/ *n.* a man or boy (*informal*) [Mid-19thC. Alteration of FELLOW.]

fel·lah /féllə, fə laá/ (*plural* **-la·hin** /-heén/ *or* **-la·heen**) *n.* a member of the laboring class in an Arab country who lives off the land [Mid-18thC. From Arabic *fallah* "tiller of the soil," from *falahah* "to split, till the soil."]

fel·late /fə láyt/ (**-lated, -lat·ing, -lates**) *vti.* to perform oral sex for a man (*formal*) [Late 19thC. From Latin *fellare* "to suck." Ultimately from an Indo-European base meaning "to suck," which is also the ancestor of English *fetus, female,* and *felicity*.] —**fel·la·tion** *n.* —**fel·la·tor** *n.*

fel·la·ti·o /fə láyshi ō/ *n.* the act or practice of sucking or licking a man's penis to provide sexual stimulation (*formal*) [Late 19thC. From modern Latin, from Latin *fellat* the past participle stem of *fellare* (see FELLATE).]

fell·er[1] /féllər/ *n.* **1.** FORESTRY **TREE CUTTER** somebody who cuts down trees **2.** SEW **SOMEBODY WHO FELLS SEAMS** a person who or a machine attachment that fells seams

fel·ler[2] /féllər/ *n.* a man or boy (*informal*) [Early 19thC. Representing a nonstandard pronunciation of FELLOW.]

Fel·ler /féllər/, **Bob** (*b.* 1918) U.S. baseball player. A pitcher noted for his fastball, he pitched three no-hitters and struck out 2,581 batters in 18 seasons with the Cleveland Indians (1936–56). Full name **Robert William Andrew Feller**

Federico Fellini: Directing his *Satyricon* (1969)

Fel·li·ni /fə leénee/, **Federico** (1920–93) Italian movie director. He was known for his use of fantasy and satire, and won Academy Awards for *La Strada* (1954), *Nights of Cabiria* (1957), *8½* (1963), and *Amarcord* (1974).

Fel·li·ni·esque /fə leènee ésk/ *adj.* blending reality and fantasy as Federico Fellini does in his movies

fell·mon·ger /fél mùngər, -mòngər/ *n. U.K.* somebody who prepares and sells animal skins —**fell·mon·ger·ing** *n.*

fel·loe *n.* = **felly**

fel·low /féllō/ *n.* **1. MAN OR BOY** a man or boy **2. BOYFRIEND** somebody's boyfriend (*dated informal*) **3. ONE OF PAIR** either one of a pair of objects **4. COMPANION** a companion or colleague (*dated*) **5. EQUAL** somebody or something of the same rank or quality **6. LOW-CLASS PERSON** somebody considered to be socially inferior, especially in belonging to the working class or not having money (*archaic*) **7.** UNIV **GRADUATE STUDENT** a graduate student who is supported by a university department to teach or do research ○ *a research fellow* ■ *adj.* **BEING IN SAME GROUP** belonging to the same group, occupation, rank, or location [Old English *feolaga* "partner," from Old Norse *félagi*, from *fé* "money" and a prehistoric Germanic base meaning "to lay down." The underlying idea is "somebody laying down money in a joint venture."]

Fel·low *n.* a member of a learned or scientific society ○ *Fellow of the American College of Surgeons*

fel·low ser·vant *n.* an employee whose employer is not legally responsible for harm or injury done to him or her by another employee

fel·low·ship /féllō shìp/ *n.* **1. COMMUNION** a sharing of common interests, goals, experiences, or views **2. SOCIETY** a group of people who share common interests, goals, experiences, or views **3. COMPANIONSHIP** companionship or friendly association **4. SIMILARITY** membership in a group, or the sharing of characteristics with others **5.** UNIV **MEMBERSHIP OF UNIVERSITY STAFF** membership in the governing board of a university or college usually also involving teaching duties **6.** UNIV **GRADUATE POST** a university post awarded to a graduate student who is supported by a university department to teach or undertake research **7.** UNIV **FINANCIAL ENDOWMENT** a financial endowment set up to support graduate students

fel·low trav·el·er *n.* **1. SOMEBODY ON SAME JOURNEY** somebody who is making the same journey as another at the same time **2. COMMUNIST SYMPATHIZER** somebody who sympathizes with the cause of an organized group, especially the Communist Party, without becoming a member

fel·ly /féllee/ (*plural* **-lies**), **fel·loe** *n.* an outer rim of a wooden wheel, or a segment of this, with a metal tire shrunk around it [Old English]

fe·lo-de-se /fe lṑdə sáy/ (*plural* **fe·lo·nes-de-se** /fe lṑneez-/ *or* **fe·los-de-se**) *n.* **1. SOMEBODY WHO KILLS SELF** somebody who commits suicide **2. KILLING SELF** an act of committing suicide [Early 17thC. From Anglo-Latin, "crime against yourself."]

fel·on[1] /féllən/ *n.* **1. CRIMINAL** somebody who is guilty of a felony **2. SOMEBODY EVIL** somebody whose behavior and actions are evil or depraved (*archaic*) ■ *adj.* **EVIL** characterized by evil or depravity (*archaic*) [13thC. Via Old French from medieval Latin *fello* "evildoer" (source of English *fell*[3]), of uncertain origin.]

fel·on[2] /féllən/ *n.* a whitlow (*technical*) [14thC. Origin uncertain: perhaps from Latin *fel* "gall, bile."]

fe·lo·ni·ous /fə lṓnee əss/ *adj.* **1. RELATING TO FELONY** relating to felonies, or constituting a felony **2. EVIL** characterized by evil or depravity (*archaic*) —**fe·lo·ni·ous·ly** *adv.* —**fe·lo·ni·ous·ness** *n.*

fel·on·ry /féllənree/ (*plural* **-ries**) *n.* a group of felons, especially the criminals in a penal colony (*dated*)

fel·o·ny /féllənee/ (*plural* **-nies**) *n.* a serious crime, e.g., murder, that is punished more severely than a misdemeanor [13thC. From Old French *felonie.*]

fel·sic /félsik/ *adj.* used to describe igneous rocks or minerals that are light in color, indicating relatively high levels of quartz and feldspars [Early 20thC. Coined from FELDSPAR + SILICA.]

fel·site /fél sīt/ *n.* a light-colored igneous rock consisting chiefly of feldspar and quartz, that can only be precisely classifed by microscopic examination [Late 18thC. Formed from FELSPAR.] —**fel·sit·ic** /fel síttik/ *adj.*

fel·spar *n.* = **feldspar**

felt[1] past tense, past participle of **feel**

felt[2] /felt/ *n.* **1. WOOL OR ANIMAL-HAIR FABRIC** a fabric made from wool or animal hair by compressing, heating, or treating the natural fibers with chemicals **2. SYNTHETIC FABRIC** a synthetic fabric made by the process of matting, especially a heavy paper permeated with asphalt, used to seal roofs ○ *roofing felt* ■ *v.* (**felt·ed, felt·ing, felts**) **1.** *vt.* **MAKE INTO FELT** to make something into felt **2.** *vt.* **COVER WITH FELT** to cover something with felt ○ *felting the roof* **3.** *vi.* **BECOME MATTED** to become matted, or come to resemble felt [Old English. Ultimately from an Indo-European base meaning "to strike, beat, pound," which is also the ancestor of English *anvil, push, pelt*[2], and *polish.*] —**felt·y** *adj.*

felt·ing /félting/ *n.* **1. FELT FABRIC** felt, or any material made in a similar way **2. MAKING OF FELT** the process of making felt

felt pen *n.* = **felt-tipped pen**

felt tip *n.* **1. FELT PEN POINT** a pen point made from felt or a similar compressed fiber **2.** = **felt-tipped pen**

felt-tipped pen *n.* a pen with a point made from felt or a similar compressed fiber

Felucca

fe·luc·ca /fə lóokə, fə lúkə/ *n.* a small sailing boat with curving triangular sails (**lateen-rigged**), used in the Mediterranean Sea and on the Nile River [Early 17thC. Via Italian from, ultimately, Mediterranean Arabic *fluka.*]

fel·wort /fél wùrt, -wàwrt/ *n.* a plant of the gentian family that is native to Europe and China and has purple flowers. Latin name: *Gentianella amarella.* [Old English *feldwyrt*, literally "field plant"]

fem. *abbr.* **1.** GRAM feminine **2.** BIOL female

fe·male /fée màyl/ *adj.* **1.** BIOL **OF SEX CAPABLE OF CHILDBEARING** relating to, belonging to, or characteristic of the sex that produces eggs or young **2. RELATING TO WOMEN** relating to, belonging to, or considered typical of women or girls **3.** BOT **PRODUCING SEEDS** used to describe the part of a plant, e.g., a carpel, that produces the female sex cells **4.** BOT **HAVING CARPELS** used to describe flowers that have carpels but no stamens **5.** ENG **MADE WITH A RECESS** used to describe a component or part of a component , e.g., an electric socket, that has a recess designed to receive a corresponding projecting part ■ *n.* **1.** BIOL **FEMALE PERSON** a female person or animal **2. GIRL OR WOMAN** a girl or woman (*offensive*) **3.** BOT **PLANT WITH FEMALE FLOWERS** a plant that has only female flowers [14thC. Alteration (under the influence of MALE) of Old French *femelle* from Latin *femella*, from *femina* "woman" (see FEMININE).] —**fe·male·ness** *n.*

fe·male cir·cum·ci·sion, **fe·male gen·i·tal mu·ti·la·tion** *n.* the practice of circumcision of adolescent women in some cultures that generally involves the surgical removal of the clitoris or the sewing up of the vaginal opening

fe·male im·per·son·a·tor *n.* a man, often appearing as a solo thearical performer, who dresses as and imitates a woman

fe·male suf·frage *n.* = **women's suffrage**

feme /fem/ *n.* in law, a woman or wife [Mid-16thC. Via Anglo-Norman from Latin *femina* (see FEMININE).]

feme cov·ert (*plural* **femes cov·ert**) *n.* in law, a married woman [From Anglo-Norman, literally "covered woman"]

feme sole (*plural* **femes sole**) *n.* in law, a single woman, including women not married, widows, divorcées, and married women living independently and separately from their husbands [From Anglo-Norman]

Fem·i·dom /fémmədəm/ *tdmk.* a trademark for a contraceptive device consisting of a sheath of thin rubber that is inserted into a vagina before insertion of a penis

fem·i·ne·i·ty /fèmmə née itee/ *n.* the quality of looking and behaving in ways conventionally thought to be appropriate for a woman [Early 19thC. Formed from Latin *femineus* "womanish," from *femina* (see FEMININE).]

fem·i·nine /fémmənin/ *adj.* **1. CONVENTIONALLY CHARACTERISTIC OF WOMEN** conventionally believed to be typical of or appropriate for a woman or girl **2. ATTRIBUTED TO WOMEN** considered to be specific to women **3. EFFEMINATE** used to describe qualities, actions, or types of behavior in a man or boy that are conventionally associated with women or girls **4.** GRAM **CLASSIFIED GRAMMATICALLY AS FEMALE IN GENDER** used to describe or relating to a class of words or forms in various languages that includes the majority of words referring to females ■ *n.* GRAM **FEMININE WORD OR FORM** a word or form that in a particular language is classified grammatically as feminine [14thC. Via Old French from Latin *femininus*, from *femina* "woman," literally "she who suckles." Ultimately from an Indo-European base meaning "to suck," which is also the ancestor of English *fetus, fecund,* and *felicity.*] —**fem·i·nine·ly** *adv.* —**fem·i·nine·ness** *n.*

fem·i·nine cae·su·ra *n.* a pause in a line of scanned verse that does not come immediately after a stressed syllable

fem·i·nine end·ing *n.* **1.** GRAM **GRAMMATICALLY FEMININE LAST PART OF WORD** an inflectional morpheme attached to the end of a word that marks it as belonging to the feminine gender **2.** POETRY **UNSTRESSED LAST SYLLABLE OF LINE** an ending of a line of verse that ends with an extra unstressed syllable

fem·i·nine rhyme *n.* a rhyme scheme in which the lines containing rhyming words end in unstressed syllables

fem·i·nin·i·ty /fèmmə nínnətee/ *n.* **1. CONVENTIONALLY FEMININE QUALITY** the quality of looking and behaving in ways conventionally thought to be appropriate for a woman or girl **2. WOMEN** women as a group (*dated*) **3. CONVENTIONAL IDEA ABOUT WOMEN** a manner or feature commonly attributed to women **4. EFFEMINACY** the qualities, actions, or types of behavior in a man or boy that are conventionally associated with women or girls

fem·i·nism /fémmə nìzzəm/ *n.* **1. BELIEF IN WOMEN'S RIGHTS** belief in the need to secure, or a commitment to securing, rights and opportunities for women equal to those of men **2. MOVEMENT FOR WOMEN'S RIGHTS** the movement committed to securing and defending equal rights and opportunities for women equal to those of men [Mid-19thC. From French *féminisme.*]

fem·i·nist /fémmənist/ *n.* **BELIEVER IN WOMEN'S RIGHTS** somebody who believes in the need to secure rights and opportunities for women equal to those of men, or somebody who works to secure these rights and opportunities ■ *adj.* **RELATING TO WOMEN'S RIGHTS** relating to, believing in, or working for rights and opportunities for women equal to those of men [Late 19thC. From French *féministe.*]

fem·i·nize /fémmə nīz/ (**-nized, -niz·ing, -niz·es**) *vt.* **1. MAKE SOMETHING SUITABLE FOR WOMEN** to cause somebody or something to acquire characteristics considered suitable for women **2. MAKE SOMEBODY CONVENTIONALLY LIKE WOMAN** to make somebody behave in ways conventionally associated with women (*often passive*) **3.** MED **MAKE MALE DEVELOP FEMALE SEXUAL CHARACTERISTICS** to cause a man to develop secondary female sexual characteristics as a result of a hormone imbalance —**fem·i·ni·za·tion** /fèmməni záysh'n/ *n.*

femme /fem/ *n.* **1. WOMAN** a woman or girl (*dated informal*) **2. PERSON BEHAVING IN CONVENTIONALLY FEMININE WAY** a person who behaves in a conventionally feminine way (*slang*) ■ *adj.* **BEHAVING IN FEMININE WAY** used to describe a person, originally usually a lesbian, who behaving in a conventionally feminine way (*slang*) [Early 19thC. Originally borrowed from the French "woman," by Lord Byron (1788–1824), for inclusion in his *Journals.*]

femme fa·tale /fém fə tàl, -tàal, fám-/ (*plural* **femmes fa·tales**) *n.* a woman who is considered to be highly attractive and to have a destructive effect on those who succumb to her charms (*disapproving*) [Borrowed from the French, (literally "deadly woman"), by George Bernard Shaw (1856–1950), who used the term in his letters]

fem·o·ra plural of **femur**

fem·o·ral /fémmərəl/ *adj.* relating to, in, or involving the thigh or femur [Late 18thC. Formed from Latin *femor-*, the stem of *femur* "thigh."]

fe·mur /féemər/ *n.* **1.** ANAT **MAIN BONE IN HUMAN THIGH** the main bone in the human thigh, the strongest bone in the body **2.** ZOOL **LARGE BONE IN VERTEBRATE LEG** a bone equivalent to the human thighbone in other vertebrates **3.** INSECTS **INSECT LEG PART** the third and largest segment of an insect's leg, between the trochanter and the tibia [Mid-16thC. Originally an architectural term from Latin *femor-, femur* "thigh," of unknown origin. The anatomical sense was first used in the late 18thC.]

fen /fen/ *n.* low-lying, inland marshy area, now often drained and cultivated because of its nutrient-rich soil. ◊ **Fens** [Old English *fen(n)*, of prehistoric Germanic origin]

fence /fens/ *n.* **1. ENCLOSING STRUCTURE** a structure erected to enclose an area and act as a barrier, especially one made of wood or with posts and wire **2.** HORSE-RACING, SHOWJUMPING **OBSTACLE** a specially constructed obstacle that horses must jump over in a race or as part of a showjumping circuit **3.** CRIMINOL **BUYER OF STOLEN GOODS** somebody who buys stolen goods from thieves and then sells the goods (*slang*) **4.** FENCING **FENCING** the art or practice of fencing (*archaic*) ■ *v.* (**fenced, fenc·ing, fenc·es**) **1.** *vt.* **ENCLOSE AREA WITH FENCE** to enclose an area or close a gap by erecting a fence **2.** *vti.* CRIMINOL **DEAL IN STOLEN GOODS** to buy or sell stolen goods (*slang*) **3.** *vi.* FENCING **FIGHT WITH SWORD** to fight using a slender sword, formerly in combat, now as a competitive sport **4.** *vi.* **EVADE QUESTIONING** to avoid answering a question ○ *a candidate fencing with the press* **5.** *vi.* **ARGUE** to engage in repartee or witty argument with somebody [14thC. Originally a shortening of DEFENSE.] —**fence·less** *adj.* —**fenc·er** *n.* ◇ **mend fences** to restore good relations with a friend or neighbor after a dispute or quarrel ◇ **sit** *or* **be on the fence** to refuse to make a choice between sides in a dispute or contest

fence in *vt.* **1. ENCLOSE SOMETHING WITH FENCE** to enclose somebody or something inside a fence **2. RESTRICT SOMEBODY** to limit or restrain somebody's freedom of movement or action

fence off *vt.* to enclose or separate something with a fence

fence·row /féns rō/ *n.* the uncultivated strip of land on which a fence stands, including a narrow area on each side of it

fence sit·ter *n.* somebody who will not or cannot make a choice between sides in a dispute or contest

fenc·ing /fénsing/ *n.* **1. SWORD FIGHTING** the art or practice

Fencing: As one fencer lunges forward the other prepares to parry

of fighting with slender swords, formerly in combat, now as a competitive sport **2. FENCE MATERIALS** materials used in making fences, e.g., posts and wire **3. FENCES** fences considered collectively **4. EVASIVENESS** evasiveness in responding to questioning **5. REPARTEE** repartee or witty argument **6.** CRIMINOL **DEALING IN STOLEN GOODS** the business of buying and selling stolen goods (*slang*)

fend /fend/ (**fend·ed, fend·ing, fends**) *v.* **1.** *vt.* **PROTECT SOMEBODY OR SOMETHING** to defend somebody or something from harm (*archaic*) **2.** *vi. U.K.* **STRIVE** to strive or make an effort (*regional*) [13thC. Shortening of DEFEND.]

fend for *vt.* to support or provide for somebody, especially yourself ○ *He's used to fending for himself.*

fend off *vt.* **1. REPULSE SOMEBODY OR SOMETHING** to push somebody or something away, or turn somebody or something aside **2.** NAUT **PUSH OFF FROM** to push against an approaching vessel or object in order to prevent a collision

fend·er /féndər/ *n.* **1.** AUTOMOT **CORNER OF CAR** any of the corner parts of the body of a motor vehicle, that surround each wheel **2. BICYCLE WHEEL COVERING** a curved piece of metal or plastic fixed above the front and back wheels of a bicycle to protect the cyclist from being splashed with mud **3.** RAIL **METAL GUARD AT FRONT OF LOCOMOTIVE** a metal guard built onto the front of a locomotive to push away any obstruction and lessen injury to people or animals struck by the locomotive **4. FIRE GUARD** a metal guard built onto the front of an open fire to prevent coals from falling out **5.** NAUT **PROTECTIVE CUSHION** an inflatable cylinder, rubber tire, or something similar, hung over the side of the vessel to protect it from rubbing against a pier or another ship

fend·er-bend·er *n.* a collision between vehicles in which only minor damage occurs (*informal*)

fend·er pile *n.* a pile driven into the bottom of a body of water near a berth to protect the pier or wharf against damage by incoming vessels

fen·es·tel·la /fènnə stéllə/ (*plural* **-lae** /-lee/) *n.* **1. PART OF ALTAR** a small opening for holding relics at the south side of an altar in a Roman Catholic church **2. NICHE IN CHANCEL WALL** a niche in the wall of a chancel that houses the piscina and credence table **3.** ARCHIT **WINDOW** a small window or similar opening in a wall [Late 18thC. From Latin, diminutive of *fenestra* "window."]

fe·nes·tra /fə néstrə/ (*plural* **-trae** /-tree/) *n.* **1.** ANAT **SMALL ANATOMICAL OPENING** a small anatomical opening covered by a membrane, e.g., either of two cavities (**fenestra rotunda; fenestra ovalis**), inside the ear **2.** ZOOL **TRANSPARENT MARKING** a transparent marking on a moth's wing **3.** ARCHIT **WINDOW** a window or similar opening on the outer wall of a building [Early 19thC. From Latin, "window."] —**fe·nes·tral** *adj.*

fen·es·trat·ed /fénnə stràytəd/, **fen·es·trate** /fénnə stràyt, fə nés tràyt/ *adj.* **1.** ARCHIT **HAVING WINDOWS** made with windows or similar openings **2.** BIOL **WITH OPENINGS** with openings or perforations **3.** ZOOL **WITH TRANSPARENT MARKINGS** used to describe a moth's wing that has transparent markings

fen·es·tra·tion /fènnə stráysh'n/ *n.* **1.** ARCHIT **WINDOW DESIGN** the design and placing of windows in a building **2.** SURG **EAR OPERATION** the surgical cutting of an opening in the labyrinth of the inner ear to restore somebody's hearing

fen·flur·i·dine /fen flóorə deen/ *n.* an appetite-suppressant drug taken to help to lose weight [Fen- an alteration of PHEN-]

feng shui /fəng shwáy/ *n.* the Chinese system that studies people's relationships to the environment in which they live, especially their dwelling or workspace, in order to achieve maximum harmony with the spiritual forces perceived to influence all places [Late 18thC. From Chinese, literally "wind water."]

Fe·ni·an /féenee ən/ *n.* **1.** POL **IRISH REVOLUTIONARY** a member of a Irish revolutionary republican organization founded in the United States in 1857 to fight for Irish independence **2.** MYTHOL **LEGENDARY IRISH WARRIOR** a member of the legendary Irish warriors, the Fianna [Early 19thC. From Old Irish *féne*, a name for the ancient population of Ireland.] —**Fe·ni·an·ism** *n.*

fen·land /fén lànd, fénlənd/ *n.* a wide inland area of low-lying marshy land, especially in East Anglia

fen·nec /fénnik/ *n.* a small large-eared fox that lives in the deserts of North Africa and has light tan fur and big pointed ears. Latin name: *Vulpes zerda* and *Fennecus zerda.* [Late 18thC. Via Arabic *fanak* from Persian.]

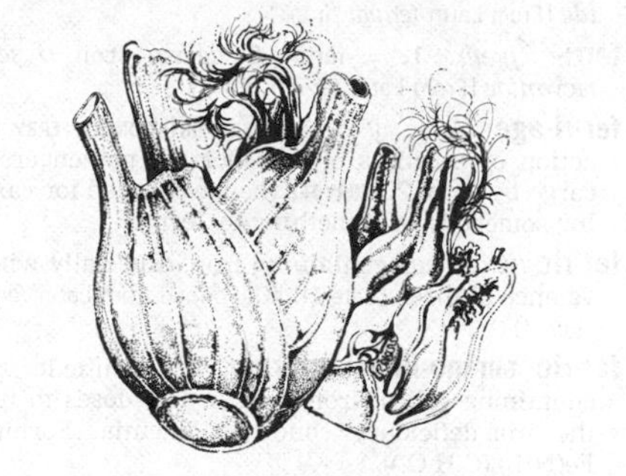

Fennel

fen·nel /fénn'l/ *n.* **1. AROMATIC PLANT** an aromatic plant of European origin, the seeds and feathery leaves of which have a light aniseed flavor and are used in cooking. Genus: *Foeniculum.* **2. EDIBLE PLANT** a type of fennel that produces a bulb and clump of short edible stalks resembling celery but with an aniseed flavor. It can be eaten raw or cooked. Latin name: *Foeniculum vulgare* var. *azoricum.* [Old English *finugle*, from Vulgar Latin *fenuculum*, diminutive of *faenum* "hay," said to be so called because of its appearance and sweet odor]

fen·ta·nyl /féntənil/ *n.* a narcotic drug used medicinally as a painkiller [An alteration of the drug's chemical name]

Fenugreek

fen·u·greek /fénnyə greek, fénnə-/ *n.* **1. EURASIAN PLANT** a Eurasian plant with white flowers and aromatic seeds. Latin name: *Trigonella foenum-graecum.* **2. AROMATIC SEEDS** the aromatic seeds of the fenugreek plant, used medicinally and to flavor food ○ *add a pinch of fenugreek* [Old English *fenogrecum*, superseded in Middle English by forms via Old French *fenugrec* from Latin *faenugraecum*, literally "Greek hay," dried and used by the Romans for fodder]

fen·u·ron /fénnyə ròn/ *n.* a compound used as a herbicide. Formula: $C_9H_{12}N_2O$. [Formed from fen-, an alteration of PHEN- + UREA + -ON]

feoff /feef/ *n.* = **fief** *n.* **1** ■ *vt.* (**feoffed, feoff·ing, feoffs**) **GRANT SOMEBODY FIEF** to grant a fief to somebody [13thC. Via Anglo-Norman *feoffer* from Old French *feu, fieu* "fee," from late Latin *feudum* (see FEUD²).]

feoff·ee /fe fée, fi fée/ *n.* a vassal holding a fief granted by a feudal lord

feoff·ment /féfmənt, féef-/ *n.* an act or the process of granting a fief to somebody

FEP *abbr.* front-end processor

FEPA *abbr.* Fair Employment Practices Act

-fer *suffix.* one that bears ○ *conifer* [From Latin, from *ferre* "to carry" (see FERTILE)]

fe·rae na·tu·rae /fèrrī nə tóoree, fèrree-, féerī-, féeree-/ *adj.* living in the wild (*technical*) [Mid-17thC. From Latin, literally "of wild nature."]

fe·ral /féerəl, férrəl/, **fe·rine** /fī rìn, fé-/ *adj.* **1. GONE WILD** used to describe animals that live or grow in the wild after having been domestically reared or cultivated **2. SAVAGE** similar to or typical of a wild animal [Early 17thC. From Latin *fera* "wild animal."]

fer-de-lance /fàirdə láns/ (*plural* **fer-de-lance** *or* **fer-de-lanc·es**) *n.* a large, highly venomous tropical American snake that belongs to the pit viper family. It is mottled brown and gray. Latin name: *Bothops atrox.* [Late 19thC. From French, "spear head."]

Fer·di·nand I /fúrd'n ànd/, **King of Spain** (1005?–65). He was king of Castile (1035–65) and León (1037–65), and reconquered much of Portugal from the Moors. Known as **Ferdinand the Great**

Fer·di·nand III, King of Hungary (1608–57). King of Bohemia (1627–57) and Holy Roman Emperor (1637–57), he commanded the imperial armies fighting the Thirty Years' War.

fere /feer/ *n.* (*archaic*) **1. FRIEND** a friend or companion **2. SPOUSE** a husband or wife [Old English *gefēra*, literally "fellow traveller"]

fer·e·to·ry /férrə tàwree/ (*plural* **-ries**) *n.* a container or an area in a church where relics are kept [14thC. Literally "(object or place) for the purpose of carrying." Via Old French *fiertre*, from, ultimately, Greek *pheretron* "bier," from *pherein* "to carry" (see -PHORE).]

Fer·ga·na /fur gáanə/ city in eastern Uzbekistan, about 260 mi./420 km east of the capital, Tashkent. Population: 226,500 (1991). Also known as **Farghona**. Formerly **Skobelev**

fe·ri·a /féeree ə, férree ə/ (*plural* **-as** *or* **-ae**) *n.* in the Roman Catholic Church, any weekday on which there is no feast [14thC. From Latin, "holiday."] —**fe·ri·al** *adj.*

Fer·mat /fer máa/, **Pierre de** (1601–65) French mathematician. One of the greatest 17th-century mathematical theorists, he was a pioneer in the fields of probability theory, analytic geometry, and differential calculus.

fer·ma·ta /fer máatə/ *n.* **1. TIME EXTENSION IN MUSIC** an act of holding a note, chord, or pause longer than the indicated time value **2.** = **pause** *n.* **4** [Late 19thC. From Italian.]

fer·ment *vti.* /fər mént/ (**-ment·ed, -ment·ing, -ments**) **1. SUBJECT TO FERMENTATION** to subject something to fermentation, or be subjected to fermentation **2. STIR UP** to stir up somebody or something, or be stirred up **3. DEVELOP** to cause, develop or evolve something, be developed or evolved ○ *Her brain was continually fermenting new schemes.* ■ *n.* /fúr mènt/ **1. COMMOTION** a state or situation of extreme agitation or commotion about something **2. SUBSTANCE CAUSING FERMENTATION** an agent, an enzyme or cell that causes fermentation [14thC. Via Old French *fermenter*, from, ultimately, Latin *fermentum* "yeast."] —**fer·ment·a·bil·i·ty** /fər mèntə bíllətee/ *n.* —**fer·ment·a·ble** /fər méntəb'l/ *adj.*

fer·men·ta·tion /fùrmən táysh'n, -men-/ *n.* the biochemical process in which a microorganism breaks down a substance into simpler ones, especially the creation of alcohol by the action of yeast on sugar. Many pharmaceuticals are produced by fermentation.

fer·men·ta·tion lock *n.* a valve used in winemaking to seal a container of fermenting wine, allowing gas to escape but no air to enter

fer·men·ta·tive /fər méntətiv/ *adj.* relating to or causing fermentation

fer·ment·er /fər méntər/ *n.* **1.** = **ferment** *n.* **2** **2. fer·ment·er, fer·men·tor FERMENTATION APPARATUS** an apparatus that maintains the ideal conditions for fermentation, e.g., the growing of microorganisms

fer·mi /fúrmee, fér-/ *n.* a unit of length used mainly for nuclear distances, equivalent to 10^{-15} meter [Early 20thC. Named for Enrico FERMI.]

Fer·mi /fúrmee/, **Enrico** (1901–54) Italian-born U.S. physicist. He received the 1938 Nobel Prize for his work on particle physics and nuclear fission. He constructed the first atomic pile at the University of Chicago (1942).

fer·mi·on /fúrmee òn, fér-/ *n.* an elementary particle with a half-integral spin that obeys the Pauli exclusion principle. Electrons, protons, and neutrons are types of fermion. [From the name of Enrico FERMI + -ON]

fer·mi·um /fúrmee əm, fér-/ *n.* a radioactive element produced artificially by the bombardment of plutonium with neutrons. Symbol **Fm** [From the name of Enrico FERMI + -IUM]

Fern

fern /furn/ (*plural* **ferns** *or* **fern**) *n.* a plant that has roots, stems, and fronds, but no flowers, and reproduces by means of spores. Order: Filicales. [Old English *fearn* from Indo-European] —**fern·y** *adj.*

Fer·nan·do de No·ro·nha /fər nàndō də nə rṓnyə/ island group in the Atlantic Ocean off the coast of Brazil, approximately 250 mi./400 km northeast of Cape São Roque. Population: 1,266 (1980). Area: 10 sq. mi./26 sq. km.

fern bar *n.* a bar or restaurant with ferns for decoration

fern·er·y /fúrnəree/ (*plural* **-ies**) *n.* **1. PLACE FOR GROWING FERNS** a container or cultivated area in which ferns are grown **2. FERN COLLECTION** a collection of growing ferns

fern seed *n.* a tiny spore by which a fern reproduces. Because their smallness makes them difficult to see, at one time it was believed that carrying fern seeds made somebody invisible. ○ *"We have the receipt of fern seed, we walk invisible"* (William Shakespeare, *Henry IV Pt I*; 1597)

fe·ro·cious /fə rṓshəss/ *adj.* **1. FIERCE** very fierce or savage **2. EXTREME** very intense [Mid-17thC. From Latin *ferox*, literally "wild-looking."] —**fe·ro·cious·ly** *adv.* —**fe·ro·cious·ness** *n.* —**fe·roc·i·ty** /fə róssətee/ *n.*

-ferous *suffix.* bearing, containing, producing ○ *diamondiferous* [Coined from -FER + -OUS]

ferr- *prefix.* = **ferro-**

Fer·ra·ri /fə raáree/, **Enzo** (1898–1988) Italian race car driver and automobile manufacturer. He designed and produced racing cars that have achieved success in Grand Prix competitions since the 1950s.

Fer·ra·ro /fə raá rō/, **Geraldine** (*b.* 1935) U.S. politician. A lawyer and Democratic member of the U.S. Congress from New York (1979–85), she was the first woman vice-presidential candidate of a major political party (1984). Full name **Geraldine Anne Ferraro**

fer·re·dox·in /fèrrə dóksin/ *n.* an iron-containing protein that occurs in plants and certain bacteria and is active in the process of photosynthesis [Mid-20thC. Coined from Latin *ferrum* "iron" + REDOX + -IN.]

fer·re·ous /férree əss/ *adj.* relating to or containing iron [Mid-17thC. Formed from Latin *ferreus* "of iron."]

fer·ret[1] /férrət/ *n.* (*plural* **-rets** *or* **-ret**) **1. DOMESTICATED POLECAT** a typically albino polecat bred for use in hunting rabbits or rats and kept as a pet. Latin name: *Mustela eversmanni.* **2.** = **black-footed ferret 3. PERSISTENT SEARCHER** somebody who searches persistently ■ *vti.* (**-ret·ed, -ret·ing, -rets**) **HUNT USING FERRET** to hunt rabbits or rats using a ferret [14thC. Via Old French *furet* from assumed Vulgar Latin *furittus*, literally "little thief," from Latin *fur* "thief" (see FURTIVE).] —**fer·ret·er** *n.* —**fer·ret·y** *adj.*

ferret about, fer·ret a·round *vi.* to search in an area persistently ○ *ferreting about in a drawer*

ferret out *vt.* **1. LOCATE SOMETHING BY PERSISTENT SEARCHING** to force somebody or something out of a hiding place by persistent searching **2. DISCOVER SOMETHING SECRET** to discover something hidden by persistent searching

fer·ret[2] /férrət/ *n.* a narrow silk tape used for edging or binding fabric [Mid-17thC. Origin uncertain: probably an alteration of Italian *fioretti* "floss silk" (the original sense in English), literally "little flowers," from *fiore* "flower" (see FLORIN).]

fer·ret-badg·er *n.* a small tree-climbing badger native to Southeast Asia. Genus: *Melogale.*

fer·ret·ing[1] /férrəting/ *n.* the practice of hunting rabbits or rats with ferrets

fer·ret·ing[2] /férrəting/ *n.* = **ferret**[2] *n.*

ferri-[1] *prefix.* indicating iron, especially in chemical combination with a valence of three ○ *ferric chloride* [From Latin *ferrum* "iron"]

ferri-[2] *prefix.* **1. ferro- 2.** ferric iron ○ *ferricyanide* [From Latin *ferrum* "iron"]

fer·ri·age /férree ij/ *n.* **1. TRANSPORTATION BY FERRY** the action or business of transporting passengers or cargo by ferry **2. FERRY FEE** the fee charged for carrying somebody or something by ferry

fer·ric /férrik/ *adj.* containing iron, especially with a valence of three [Late 18thC. Formed from Latin *ferrum* "iron."]

fer·ric am·mo·ni·um cit·rate *n.* a nontoxic iron-containing salt of iron used in low doses to treat the iron-deficiency condition anemia. Formula: $Fe(NH_4)_3(C_6H_5O_7)_2$.

fer·ric chlo·ride *n.* a dark-red iron-containing salt. It is used in medicine as an astringent and in industry as a coagulating agent. Formula: $FeCl_3$.

fer·ric ox·ide *n.* a reddish-brown solid containing iron and oxygen. It occurs in rust and the mineral hematite and is used as a pigment, in jeweler's rouge for polishing, and on magnetic recording tape. Formula: Fe_2O_3.

fer·ric sul·fate *n.* a pale yellow solid chemical containing iron, oxygen, and sulfur. It is used in pigments, water purification, dyeing, and in medicine. Formula: $Fe_2(SO_4)_3$.

fer·ri·cy·a·nide /fèrri sī́ ə nīd/ *n.* any salt containing iron and six cyanide groups. They are used to make pigments.

fer·rif·er·ous /fə ríffərəss/ *adj.* used to describe a rock or mineral deposit that contains iron, often at a level high enough to make extraction economically worthwhile [Early 19thC. Coined from Latin *ferrum* "iron" + -FEROUS.]

fer·ri·mag·ne·tism /fèrri mágnə tìzzəm/ *n.* a property of some substances, e.g., ferrites, in which two different types of ion having unequal magnetic moments occur aligned in antiparallel, giving an appreciable bulk magnetization —**fer·ri·mag·net** *n.* —**fer·ri·mag·net·ic** *adj., n.* —**fer·ri·mag·net·i·cal·ly** *adv.*

Ferris wheel

Fer·ris wheel /férris-, férris-/, **fer·ris wheel** *n.* a fairground ride consisting of a giant revolving wheel with seats that hang down from its rim and stay horizontal as the wheel rotates [Late 19thC. Named for the American engineer G. W. G. *Ferris* (1859–96), its inventor.]

fer·rite /fé rīt/ *n.* **1. MAGNETIC IRON OXIDE** a mixed oxide of iron and another metal such as cobalt or nickel. They are ceramic materials with magnetic properties and are used in the electronics industry and in magnets. **2. FORM OF IRON OCCURRING IN STEEL** a form of iron occurring in steel, cast iron, and pig iron **3. IRON MINERAL** iron oxide containing mineral, e.g., magnetite, found as small grains in various types of rock [Mid-19thC. Formed from Latin *ferrum* "iron."]

fer·ri·tin /férrət'n/ *n.* a spherical complex of iron and protein mainly found in the liver and spleen that is one of the forms in which iron is stored in the body. When required, iron is released and used in the production of hemoglobin in red blood cells. [Mid-20thC. Coined from FERRI- + -*t*- + -IN.]

ferro- *prefix.* **1.** iron ○ *ferroalloy* **2.** CHEM ferrous iron ○ *ferrocyanide* [From Latin *ferrum* "iron"]

fer·ro·al·loy /fèrrō á lòy/ *n.* an iron alloy, containing a large proportion of one or more other elements, that is added to molten metal during iron and steel production to give the required composition

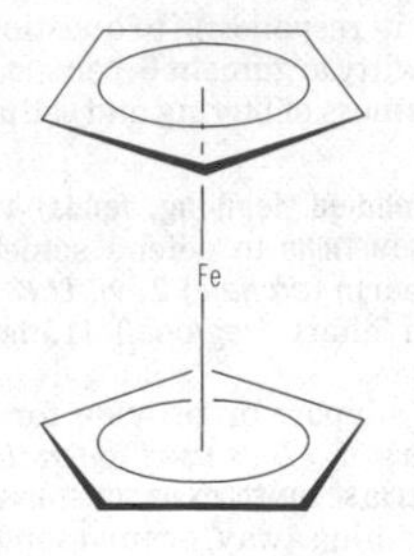

Ferrocene

fer·ro·cene /férrō seen/ *n.* an orange-red crystalline solid in which an atom of iron is situated between two rings that are composed of five carbon and five hydrogen atoms. Formula: $Fe(C_5H_5)_2$. [Mid-20thC. Coined from FERRO- + *cene*, a contraction of *cyclopentadiene*, a hydrocarbon obtained in the cracking of petroleum hydrocarbons.]

fer·ro·con·crete /fèrrō kóng kreet/ *n.* = **reinforced concrete**

fer·ro·cy·a·nide /fèrrō sī́ ə nīd/ *n.* any salt containing iron and six cyanide groups. They are used to make blue pigments.

fer·ro·e·lec·tric /fèrrō i léktrik/ *adj.* **WITH SPONTANEOUS ELECTRIC POLARIZATION** used to describe a crystalline compound that has a natural spontaneous electric polarization that can be reversed by the application of an electric field ■ *n.* **FERROELECTRIC SUBSTANCE** a substance that is ferroelectric —**fer·ro·elec·tri·cal·ly** *adv.* —**fer·ro·e·lec·tric·i·ty** /fèrrō i lek tríssətee/ *n.*

fer·ro·mag·ne·sian /fèrrō mag neézh'n/ *adj.* used to describe silicate minerals that contain high levels of iron and magnesium, e.g., olivines

fer·ro·mag·net·ic /fèrrō mag néttik/ *adj.* with the property of ferromagnetism. Iron, cobalt, and nickel are ferromagnetic metals.

fer·ro·mag·ne·tism /fèrrō mágnə tìzzəm/ *n.* a property of some substances, including iron and some alloys, in which application of a weak magnetic field within a certain temperature range induces high magnetism. Small discrete regions within the substance (**domains**) align with the direction of an applied magnetic field and produce the bulk magnetization. —**fer·ro·mag·net** *n.* —**fer·ro·mag·net·ic** *adj., n.* —**fer·ro·mag·net·ic·al·ly** *adv.*

fer·ro·man·ga·nese /fèrrō mángə neez/ *n.* an alloy of iron and manganese used to add manganese during the making of steel and cast iron

fer·ron·ner·ies *n.* a variety of ceramics that copies forms from metalwork, e.g., candlesticks (*takes a singular verb*) [Early 20thC. From French, "iron work, wrought iron."]

fer·ro·sil·i·con /fèrrō síllikən/ *n.* an alloy of iron and silicon, used in the production of steel and cast iron

fer·ro·type /férrō tīp/ *n.* a positive photograph made on a plate of sensitized iron

fer·rous /férrəss/ *adj.* containing iron with a valence of two [Mid-19thC. Formed from Latin *ferrum* "iron."]

fer·rous ox·ide *n.* a black solid containing iron and oxygen. It is used in the manufacture of steel and enamels. Formula: FeO.

fer·rous sul·fate *n.* a white or pale green salt containing iron, oxygen, and sulfur. It occurs naturally as the mineral copperas, and is used in inks, tanning, and in the treatment of iron-deficient anemia. Formula: $FeSO_4.7H_2O$.

fer·rous sul·fide *n.* a black solid containing iron and sulfur. It occurs naturally in pyrites and marcasite, and is used in making hydrogen sulfide. Formula: FeS.

fer·ru·gi·nous /fə roójənəss/ *adj.* **1. CONTAINING IRON** containing or resembling iron **2. RUST-COLORED** of a reddish-brown color, like rust [Mid-17thC. Formed from Latin *ferrugin*, the stem of *ferrugo* "iron rust," from *ferrum* "iron."]

fer·ru·gi·nous duck *n.* a common European diving duck with reddish-brown plumage that lives in fresh or blackish water. Latin name: *Aythya nyroca.*

fer·rule /férrəl/, **fer·ule** *n.* **1.** PROTECTIVE CAP ON SHAFT a usually metal cap or ring attached to the end of something long and thin, e.g., a walking stick, in order to strengthen it **2.** CYLINDRICAL JOINT a metal cylinder used to make a pipe joint **3.** ANGLING CONNECTION FOR FISHING ROD PIECES a connection that joins the pieces of a fishing rod, consisting of male and female couplings that fit together ■ *vt.* FIT WITH FERRULE to provide something with a ferrule [Early 17thC. Alteration of earlier *virolle* (influenced by Latin *ferrum* "iron"), from, ultimately, Latin *viriae* "bracelets."]

fer·ry /férree/ *n.* (*plural* **-ries**) **1.** BOAT MAKING REGULAR SHORT CROSSING a boat used to transport passengers, vehicles, or goods across water, especially one operating regularly across a river or narrow channel **2.** COMMERCIAL TRANSPORT SERVICE a commercial service transporting passengers, vehicles, or goods across water **3.** PLACE WHERE FERRY BERTHS a place where passengers, vehicles, or goods are transported across water by ferry **4.** RIGHT TO OPERATE FERRY a legal right to operate and charge for a ferry service ■ *v.* (**-ried, -ry·ing, -ries**) **1.** *vt.* TRANSPORT SOMEBODY OR SOMETHING BY FERRY to transport somebody or something across water by ferry **2.** *vi.* GO BY FERRY to travel by ferry **3.** *vt.* TRANSPORT PASSENGERS to transport passengers or goods back and forth by any vehicle ○ *He had to ferry his children to school every morning.* **4.** *vt.* AIR DELIVER AIRCRAFT to deliver an aircraft by flying it to its operator [14thC. From Old Norse *ferja*, or from *ferju-*, the stem of *ferjuskip* and *ferjukarl* "ferryman." Ultimately from a prehistoric Germanic word.]

fer·ry·boat /férri bōt/ *n.* = **ferry** *n.* 1

fer·ry·man /férri màn, -mən/ (*plural* **-men** /-mèn, -mən/) *n.* somebody who owns, operates, or works on a ferry

fer·tile /fúrt'l/ *adj.* **1.** BIOL ABLE TO PRODUCE OFFSPRING capable of breeding or reproducing **2.** BOT ABLE TO PRODUCE FRUITS OR SEEDS able to produce sex cells, seeds, spores, or fruit **3.** BIOL ABLE TO DEVELOP used to describe an egg or seed that has the capacity to grow and develop **4.** REPRODUCING OFTEN producing many offspring **5.** AGRIC PRODUCING GOOD CROPS used to describe an area that produces many plants, fruit, or crops **6.** AGRIC, GARDENING RICH IN PLANT NUTRIENTS used to describe soil or land that is rich in the nutrients needed to sustain the growth of healthy plants **7.** CREATIVE readily able to produce new ideas ○ *a fertile imagination* **8.** NUCLEAR PHYS CAPABLE OF BECOMING FISSILE capable of being converted into fissile or fissionable material, typically in a nuclear reactor [15thC. Directly or via French from Latin *fertilis*, from *ferre* "to bear." Ultimately from an Indo-European base meaning "to carry" which is also the ancestor of English *bear, bier, burden* and *-phore*.] —**fer·tile·ly** *adv.* —**fer·tile·ness** *n.* —**fer·til·i·ty** /fur tíllətee/ *n.*

Fer·tile Cres·cent *n.* an area of fertile land in the Middle East reaching from Israel to the Persian Gulf and incorporating the Tigris and Euphrates rivers in modern Iraq. The ancient Babylonian, Sumerian, Assyrian, Phoenician, and Hebrew civilizations arose here.

fer·til·i·ty /fur tíllətee/ *n.* **1.** BEING FERTILE the quality or condition of being fertile **2.** BIRTHRATE the birthrate of a population [15thC. Via French *fertilité* from Latin *fertilitas*, from *fertilis* (see FERTILE).]

fer·til·i·ty cult *n.* a form of religion using ceremonies meant to ensure the fertility of the people and agriculture of a community

fer·til·i·ty drug *n.* a synthetic chemical that enhances female fertility by stimulating the release of ova from the ovaries. Some fertility drugs are also used in in vitro fertilization programs.

fer·til·i·za·tion /fùrt'lə záysh'n/ *n.* **1.** BIOL STARTING REPRODUCTION the act or process of enabling reproduction by insemination or pollination **2.** BIOL UNION OF MALE AND FEMALE GAMETES the union of male and female reproductive cells (**gametes**) to produce a fertilized reproductive cell (**zygote**) l **3.** AGRIC, GARDENING APPLYING FERTILIZER the act or process of applying fertilizer to soil

fer·ti·lize /fúrt'l ìz/ (**-lized, -liz·ing, -liz·es**) *vt.* **1.** BIOL UNITE FEMALE AND MALE REPRODUCTIVE CELLS to unite a female gamete with a male gamete, thus enabling the development of a new individual to take place. Fertilization can take place inside the female's body, as in humans, or outside the body, as in fish. **2.** AGRIC, GARDENING APPLY FERTILIZER to apply fertilizer to soil or plants [Mid-17thC. Formed from FERTILE.] —**fer·ti·liz·a·ble** *adj.*

fer·til·iz·er /fúrt'l ìzər/ *n.* **1.** AGRIC, GARDENING SUBSTANCE AIDING PLANT GROWTH a substance usually added to or spread onto soil to increase its ability to support plant growth. Fertilizers include organic materials, e.g., manure, and synthetic chemicals, e.g., nitrates. **2.** BIOL FERTILIZING AGENT an agent that fertilizes plants or animals, e.g., an insect fertilizing a plant

fer·u·la /férrələ/ (*plural* **-las** *or* **-lae** /-lèe/) *n.* PLANTS a Mediterranean plant of the parsley family with thick stems and finely divided leaves from which strong-smelling resinous gums are extracted that can be used medicinally. Genus: *Ferula.* [14thC. From Latin, "fennel stalk, rod."] —**fer·u·la·ceous** /fèrrə láyshəss/ *adj.*

fer·ule[1] /férrəl/ *n.* a cane, rod, or flat piece of wood used to punish children by striking them, usually on the hand [15thC. From Latin *ferula* "fennel stalk," formerly used by schoolmasters to punish children.]

fer·ule[2] *n.*, *vt.* = **ferrule**

fe·rul·ic ac·id /fə rōōlik-/ *n.* a compound similar to the aromatic chemical vanillin that is obtained from some plants. Ferulic acid is a component of asafoetida, a bitter resin derived from a plant of the parsley family. Formula: $C_{10}H_{10}O_4$. [*Ferulic* formed from FERULA]

fer·ven·cy /fúrvənsee/ *n.* = **fervor**

fer·vent /fúrvənt/ *adj.* **1.** SHOWING PASSIONATE ENTHUSIASM showing ardent or extremely passionate enthusiasm **2.** GLOWINGLY HOT so hot as to glow (*archaic or literary*) [14thC. Via Old French from, ultimately, Latin *fervere* "to boil." Ultimately from an Indo-European word meaning "to bubble" which is also the ancestor of English *barm*.] —**fer·vent·ly** *adv.* —**fer·vent·ness** *n.*

fer·vid /fúrvid/ *adj.* = **fervent** [Late 16thC. From Latin *fervidus*, from *fervere* "to boil" (see FERVENT).] —**fer·vid·ly** *adv.* —**fer·vid·ness** *n.*

fer·vor /fúrvər/ *n.* **1.** INTENSITY extreme intensity of emotion or belief **2.** GREAT HEAT intense heat (*archaic or literary*) [14thC. Via Old French from Latin *fervor*, from *fervere* "to boil" (see FERVENT).]

fer·vour *n.* U.K. = **fervor**

fes·cen·nine /féssə nìn, -neen/, **Fes·cen·nine** *adj.* indecent, especially using coarse or vulgar language (*archaic or literary*) [Early 17thC. From Latin *Fescenninus*, "of Fescennia," a town in ancient Etruria known for its scurrilous verse.]

fes·cue /féskyoo/ *n.* **1.** BOT PASTURE GRASS a perennial grass that has narrow spiky leaves and is often grown for lawns or pasture. Several varieties have been developed that can be grown on soils contaminated with heavy metals. Genus: *Festuca.* **2.** EDUC POINTER a pointer, e.g., a stick or piece of straw, used to point out letters for children learning to read [14thC. Alteration of earlier *festu*, from Old French, "straw," from Latin *festuca*.]

fess /fess/, **fesse** *n.* a broad horizontal band crossing the middle section of a heraldic shield [15thC. Via Old French *fesse* from, ultimately, Latin *fascia* "band, sash."]

fess point *n.* the central point of a heraldic shield

fess up (**fessed up, fes·s·ing up, fesses up**) *vi.* to admit to something (*informal*) ○ *Come on, fess up, was it you?* [Early 19thC. Shortening of CONFESS.]

fest /fest/ *n.* a gathering of people for a specific activity, or an event where a lot of a particular activity goes on (*informal; usually used in combination*) ○ *a music fest* [Mid-19thC. Via German *Fest* from Latin *festum* "feast."]

-fest *suffix.* used in compounds such as "gore-fest" and "horror-fest" by fans to denote movies filled with horrific gory detail ○ *"Night of the Living Dead" is a real gore-fest.*

fes·tal /fést'l/ *adj.* festive (*dated or literary*) [15thC. Via Old French from, ultimately, Latin *festum* "festival."] —**fes·tal·ly** *adv.*

fes·ter /féstər/ *v.* (**-tered, -ter·ing, -ters**) **1.** *vi.* PRODUCE PUS to produce pus because of an infection or ulceration, usually of the skin **2.** *vi.* BECOME ROTTEN to decay or rot **3.** *vi.* DETERIORATE to be in or enter a state of decline **4.** *vti.* RANKLE to become, or make somebody become, increasingly bitter, irritated, or resentful ■ *n.* MED SORE DISCHARGING PUS a small sore or ulcer containing or discharging pus [14thC. Via Old French *festre* "pipe-like ulcer," from Latin *fistula*.]

fes·ti·na·tion /fèstə náysh'n/ *n.* an style of walking tottering that is characteristic of people with Parkinson's disease [Mid-16thC. Formed from Latin *festinare* "to hurry."]

fes·ti·val /féstəv'l/ *n.* **1.** TIME OF CELEBRATION a day or period of celebration, often one of religious significance **2.** PROGRAM OF CULTURAL EVENTS a program or series of performances or other cultural events, usually held at regular intervals, often in one place ■ *adj.* APPROPRIATE TO FESTIVAL typical of or appropriate to a festival [14thC. Via Old French from, ultimately, Latin *festivus* "festive," from *festum* "feast."]

fes·ti·val·go·er /féstəv'l gō ər/ *n.* somebody who attends a festival

fes·tive /féstiv/ *adj.* **1.** RELATING TO CELEBRATION relating to, suitable for, or typical of a feast, festival, or holiday **2.** CHEERFUL marked by cheerfulness and joy [Mid-17thC. From Latin *festivus* "festive," from *festum* "feast."] —**fes·tive·ly** *adv.* —**fes·tive·ness** *n.*

fes·tiv·i·ty /fe stívvətee/ *n.* (*plural* **-ties**) **1.** CELEBRATION a celebration, feast, or party **2.** ENJOYMENT the enjoyment or merrymaking typical of a celebration ■ **fes·tiv·i·ties** *npl.* CELEBRATIONS celebrations or merrymaking [14thC. Directly or via French from Latin *festivitas*, from, ultimately, *festum* "feast."]

Festoon

fes·toon /fe stōōn/ *n.* **1.** GARLAND an ornamental chain of flowers, leaves, or ribbons hanging in a loop or curve between two points **2.** ARTISTIC REPRESENTATION OF FESTOON a carved or painted representation of a festoon, e.g., on a building, in a painting, or in pottery ■ *vt.* (**-tooned, -toon·ing, -toons**) **1.** HANG FESTOONS ON SOMETHING to decorate something with festoons **2.** JOIN WITH FESTOONS to join things together with festoons **3.** SHAPE SOMETHING INTO FESTOONS to make something into festoons [Mid-17thC. Via French *feston* from Italian *festone*, originally "ornament for festivities," from assumed vulgate Latin *festa* "festivities" which was formed from Latin *festum* (see FESTIVE.]

fes·toon blind *n.* a blind for a window, made of cloth gathered into rows that can be drawn up to hang in curves

fes·tooned /fe stōōnd/ *adj.* covered with festoons or other things used as decorations ○ *The whole room was festooned with roses.*

fest·schrift /fést shrìft/, **Fest·schrift** (*plural* **-schrifts** *or* **-schrif·ten** /fést shrìftən/) *n.* a volume of writings by various people collected in honor of somebody, e.g., a writer or scholar [Early 20thC. From German, literally "celebration-writing."]

FET *abbr.* **1. FET, F.E.T.** federal excise tax **2.** field-effect transistor

fet·a /féttə/ *n.* a firm crumbly salty cheese, originally from Greece, made from sheep's or goat's milk and preserved in brine. It is now produced in other countries, though still most often used as an ingredient in Greek dishes. [Mid-20thC. From modern Greek *pheta*.]

fe·tal /féet'l/, **foe·tal** *adj.* relating to or characteristic of a fetus [Early 19thC. Formed from FETUS.]

fe·tal al·co·hol syn·drome *n.* a condition affecting babies born to women who drank excessive amounts of alcohol during pregnancy, characterized by a range of effects including facial abnormalities and learning difficulties

fe·tal he·mo·glo·bin *n.* a type of hemoglobin that is most common in the fetus and newborn, normally present only in small amounts in adults except in certain forms of anemia

fe·tal po·si·tion *n.* a body position in which the body lies curled up on one side with the head bowed and the legs and arms drawn in toward the chest. As well as being a comfortable position for relaxation, the fetal position is often assumed by people during intense emotional trauma.

fetch[1] /fech/ *v.* **(fetched, fetch·ing, fetch·es) 1.** *vt.* GO AND GET SOMETHING to go after and bring back somebody or something ○ *She went upstairs to fetch her car keys.* **2.** *vt.* CAUSE TO COME to make somebody or something appear or come **3.** *vt.* SELL FOR to sell for a certain price ○ *The painting fetched six hundred dollars at an auction.* **4.** *vti.* RETRIEVE SOMETHING to retrieve animals that have been shot or something that has been thrown, e.g., a stick or ball ○ *The boy threw the ball and told the dog to fetch it.* **5.** *vt.* UTTER to utter a sigh or groan with a deep breath **6.** *vt.* HIT SOMEBODY BLOW to hit somebody with a blow (*informal*) ○ *fetched the bully a slap on the face* **7.** *vt.* DRAW IN BREATH to draw in a breath **8.** *vt.* PLEASE to attract or charm somebody (*often passive*) ○ *fetched by the notion of going to New York* **9.** *vt.* NAUT ARRIVE SOMEWHERE BY BOAT to reach or arrive at a place by sailing ○ *fetched port at nightfall* ■ *n.* **1.** ACT OF FETCHING the act or an instance of fetching something or somebody **2.** STRATAGEM a dodge, trick, or stratagem ○ *They used cunning fetches to swindle money out of the gullible.* **3.** METEOROL DISTANCE WIND TRAVELS UNOBSTRUCTED the distance wind or waves can travel without obstruction [Old English *feccean*] —**fetch·er** *n.*
◇ **fetch and carry (for somebody)** to do menial tasks for somebody

fetch up *v.* **1.** *vi.* ARRIVE to arrive or come to a halt somewhere (*informal*) ○ *After a week on the road, we fetched up at a small coastal town.* **2.** *vi.* NAUT HALT SUDDENLY to come to a sudden halt ○ *The boat fetched up on a sandbar.* **3.** *vt.* CAUSE TO STOP to make somebody or something come to a stop ○ *His abrupt tone fetched me up short.* **4.** *vt.* RAISE SOMEBODY to raise children or animals (*regional dated*)

fetch[2] /fech/ *n.* a vision, apparition, or ghost appearing as the doppelgänger of a living person [Late 17thC. Origin uncertain: possibly from the verb, as somebody sent to fetch souls.]

fetch·ing /féching/ *adj.* **1.** GOOD LOOKING plasant, stylish, or becoming in appearance **2.** CHARMING having a charming or captivating quality —**fetch·ing·ly** *adv.*

fete /fayt/, **fête** *n.* **1.** HOLIDAY a holiday or day of celebration **2.** RELIGIOUS FESTIVAL a religious festival such as a saint's day ■ *vt.* **(fet·ed, fet·ing, fetes; fêt·ed, fêt·ed, fêt·ing)** HONOR SOMEBODY WITH FETE to entertain or honor somebody with a fete, feast, or other lavish entertainment (*usually passive*) [Mid-18thC. French from ultimately, Latin *festum*.]

fête cham·pê·tre /fàyt shaaN pétrə/ (*plural* **fêtes cham·pê·tres** /fàyt shaaN pétrə/) *n.* an outdoor party or festival [From French, literally "rural festival"]

fet·ich *n.* = **fetish**

fe·ti·cide /féetə sīd/, **foe·ti·cide** *n.* **1.** DESTRUCTION OF FETUS the act of destroying a fetus **2.** AGENT FOR DESTROYING FETUS an agent or drug used to destroy a fetus —**fe·ti·cid·al** /féetə sīd'l/ *adj.*

fet·id /féttid/, **foe·tid** *adj.* with a rotten or offensive smell ○ *fetid odor of rotten meat* [15thC. From Latin *fetidus*, from *fetere* "to stink."] —**fet·id·ly** *adv.* —**fet·id·ness** *n.*

fe·ti·pa·rous /fi típpərəss/, **foe·ti·pa·rous** *adj.* used to describe animals that give birth to incompletely developed young. Kangaroos and other marsupials are fetiparous. [Late 19thC. Coined from FETUS + -PAROUS.]

fet·ish /féttish/, **fet·ich** *n.* **1.** MAGICAL OBJECT something, especially an inanimate object, that some people revere or worship because they believe it has magical powers or is animated by a spirit **2.** OBJECT OF OBSESSION an object, idea, or activity that somebody is irrationally obsessed with or attached to ○ *make a fetish of neatness* **3.** PSYCHIAT OBJECT AROUSING SEXUAL DESIRE something, e.g., an inanimate object or nonsexual part of the body that arouses sexual excitement in some people [Early 17thC. Via French *fétiche* "charm, sorcery" from, ultimately, Latin *factitius* "made by art, artificial" (see FACTITIOUS).]

fet·ish·ism /fétti shìzzəm/ *n.* **1.** BELIEF IN FETISH belief in, use of, or worship of a magical fetish **2.** OBSESSION WITH SOMETHING excessive or obsessive attachment or devotion to something **3.** PSYCHIAT SEXUAL AROUSAL WITH FETISH the use of a fetish to produce sexual arousal

fet·ish·ist /féttishist/ *n.* somebody who uses a fetish for sexual arousal —**fet·ish·is·tic** /fètti shístik/ *adj.* —**fet·ish·is·ti·cal·ly** /-kəlee/ *adv.*

fet·ish·ize /fétti shīz/ (**-ized, -iz·ing, -iz·es**) *vt.* to make a fetish of something

fet·lock /fét lòk/ *n.* **1.** PROJECTION ON HORSE'S LEG a part of the lower leg of a horse or related animal situated above and behind the hoof and projecting down from the associated joint **2.** HAIR ON FETLOCK the tuft of hair growing on a fetlock **3. fet·lock, fet·lock joint** LEG JOINT the joint at the fetlock [14thC. Believed to be from an earlier form of FOOT + LOCK "hair."]

fe·tol·o·gy /fee tóllәjee/, **foe·tol·o·gy** *n.* a branch of medicine concerned with the study and treatment of the fetus [Mid-20thC. Coined from FETUS + -LOGY.] —**fe·tol·o·gist** *n.*

fe·tor /féetər/, **foe·tor** *n.* a strong offensive smell [15thC. From Latin, from *fetere* "to stink" (source of English *fetid*).]

fe·to·scope /féetə skōp/, **foe·to·scope** *n.* a fiber optic device that is passed through a woman's abdomen to view a fetus in the uterus, and sometimes also to remove material for examination —**fe·tos·co·py** /fee tóskəpee/ *n.*

fet·ter /féttər/ *n.* (*often used in the plural*) **1.** SHACKLE FOR ANKLES a chain or shackle fastened to somebody's ankles or feet **2.** RESTRAINT a means of confinement or restraint ○ *These harsh rules keep us in fetters.* ■ *vt.* (**-tered, -ter·ing, -ters**) **1.** PUT FETTERS ON SOMEBODY to shackle somebody with fetters **2.** RESTRAIN SOMEBODY OR SOMETHING to confine, restrict, or restrain somebody or something ○ *fettered by her own inhibitions* [Old English *feter*. Ultimately from a prehistoric Germanic word.]

fet·tle /fétt'l/ *n.* METALL = **fettling** ■ *vt.* (**-tled, -tling, -tles**) **1.** MANUF TRIM CASTING to remove molding or excess material from a ceramic or metal casting **2.** METALL LINE OR REPAIR FURNACE to line the hearth of a furnace with fettling, or repair the lining of a furnace [Old English *fetel* "girdle, strap"] —**fet·tler** *n.* ◇ **in fine** *or* **good fettle** in good health, condition, or spirits

fet·tling /fétt'ling/ *n.* loose refractory material, typically sand or ore, used to line the hearths of some types of furnace before adding the molten metal

fet·tuc·ci·ne /fèttə chéenee/, **fet·tuc·ci·ni** /fèttə chéenee/ *n.* **1.** NARROW FLAT PASTA a type of pasta made in narrow flat strips, slightly narrower and thicker than tagliatelle (*takes a singular or plural verb*) **2.** DISH MADE WITH FETTUCCINE a pasta dish made with fettuccine [Early 20thC. From Italian, literally "little ribbons."]

fet·tuc·ci·ne Al·fre·do /-al frédō/ *n.* a pasta dish made with fettuccine tossed in a cream sauce with Parmesan cheese and black pepper [Named for *Alfredo* all'Augusteo, a restaurant in Rome]

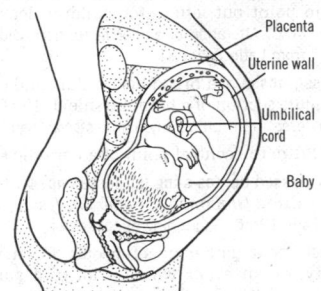

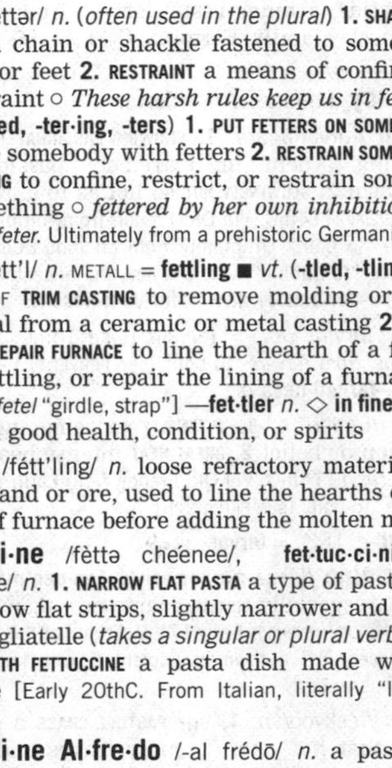

Fetus: Human fetus

fe·tus /féetəss/, **foe·tus** *n.* an unborn vertebrate at a stage when all the structural features of the adult are recognizable, especially an unborn human offspring after eight weeks of development [14thC. From Latin, "offspring" (source of English *fawn* "young deer").]

feud[1] /fyood/ *n.* **1.** LONG VIOLENT DISPUTE a bitter prolonged violent quarrel or state of hostility between families, clans, or other groups **2.** CONTINUOUS HOSTILITY any prolonged dispute or quarrel ■ *vi.* **(feud·ed, feud·ing, feuds)** PARTICIPATE IN FEUD to take part in or perpetuate a feud [13thC. From Old French *fe(i)de* "vendetta" (originally, "hostility"). Ultimately from a prehistoric Germanic word that is also the ancestor of English *foe*.]

feud[2] /fyood/ *n.* = **fief** *n.* 1 [Early 17thC. From medieval Latin *feudum*, "land or other property used as a reward for service." Ultimately from an Indo-European word denoting "wealth" or "cattle," which is also the ancestor of English *fee, pecuniary,* and *peculiar*.]

feud. *abbr.* **1.** feudal **2.** feudalism

feu·dal /fyood'l/ *adj.* **1.** RELATING TO FEUDALISM relating to, typical of, or resembling feudalism **2.** RELATING TO FIEF relating to a fief [Early 17thC. From medieval Latin *feudalis*, from *feudum* (see FEUD[2].] —**feu·dal·ly** *adv.*

feu·dal·ism /fyood'l izzəm/ *n.* **1.** MEDIEVAL SOCIAL SYSTEM the legal and social system that existed in medieval Europe, in which vassals held land from lords in exchange for military service **2.** SYSTEM LIKE FEUDALISM a system of economic, political, or social organization resembling European feudalism, e.g., in medieval Japan —**feu·dal·ist** *n.* —**feu·dal·is·tic** /fyood'l ístik/ *adj.*

feu·dal·i·ty /fyoo dállətee/ (*plural* **-ties**) *n.* **1.** BEING FEUDAL the quality or condition of being feudal **2.** FEUDAL REGIME a feudal holding or system

feu·dal·ize /fyood'l īz/ (**-ized, -iz·ing, -iz·es**) *vt.* to make something feudal in nature —**feu·dal·i·za·tion** /fyood'lə záysh'n/ *n.*

feu·da·to·ry /fyoodə tàwree/ *n.* (*plural* **-ries**) TENANT OF FEUDAL LAND somebody holding land by feudal tenure ■ *adj.* **1.** INVOLVING FEUDAL RELATIONSHIP relating to or typical of the relationship between a feudal lord and vassal **2.** SUBJECT TO OVERLORDSHIP owing feudal allegiance to an overlord or another state [Late 16thC. From medieval Latin *feudatorius*, from the past participle of *feudare* "to invest with feudal property."]

feuil·le·ton /fú i tàwn, fȯy taaN/ *n.* **1.** PART OF EUROPEAN NEWSPAPER a section of a European newspaper containing reviews, serial fiction, and articles of general interest **2.** SOMETHING IN FEUILLETON an article, review, or other piece published in a feuilleton [Mid-19thC. Via French *feuillet*, literally "little leaf" from, ultimately, Latin *folium* (see FOLIO).]

fe·ver /féevər/ *n.* **1.** ABNORMALLY HIGH BODY TEMPERATURE a body temperature that is abnormally high, usually caused by bacterial or viral infections and commonly accompanied by shivering, headache, and an increased pulse rate. Technical name **pyrexia 2.** DISEASE WITH FEVER a disease in which people typically have an abnormally high body temperature, e.g., typhoid fever, yellow fever, and scarlet fever **3.** CRAZE an intense and often brief enthusiasm or craze **4.** STATE OF EXCITEMENT a state of intense agitation, excitement, or emotion (*often used in combination*) ■ *v.* (**-vered, -ver·ing, -vers**) **1.** *vt.* AFFECT WITH FEVER to affect somebody or something with fever (*archaic*) (*usually passive*) **2.** *vi.* MED HAVE A FEVER to get or show the symptoms of a fever ○ *She fevered intermittently throughout the night.* **3.** *vt.* AGITATE SOMEBODY to throw somebody into a state of agitation or excitement [Pre-12thC. From Latin *febris*.]

fe·ver blis·ter *n.* = **cold sore**

fe·vered /féevərd/ *adj.* **1.** AFFECTED BY FEVER affected by fever **2.** EXCITED showing great activity, agitation, or excitement

Feverfew

fe·ver·few /féevər fyoo/ *n.* a perennial European plant with small white flowers, whose leaves are a popular remedy for headaches and migraine. Latin name: *Tanacetum parthenium.* [Pre-12thC. From Latin *febris* "fever" + -FUGE.]

fe·ver·ish /féevərish/ *adj.* **1.** HAVING FEVER affected by or having the symptoms of a fever **2.** RELATING TO FEVER relating to, causing, or caused by fever ○ *a feverish cold* **3.** AGITATED showing agitation, excitement, or restlessness —**fe·ver·ish·ly** *adv.* —**fe·ver·ish·ness** *n.*

fe·ver·ous /féevərəss/ *adj.* feverish (*archaic*) —**fe·ver·ous·ly** *adv.*

fe·ver pitch *n.* a state of intense activity, agitation, or excitement ○ *His grand slam brought the crowd to a fever pitch.*

fe·ver tree *n.* a tree whose leaves or bark have been used to treat fevers, especially a tree of the southeastern United States that was used to treat malaria. Latin name: *Pinckneya pubens.*

fe·ver·wort /fèevər wùrt, -wàwrt/ *n.* any plant used medicinally, especially horse gentian and boneset

few /fyoo/ CORE MEANING: a grammatical word used to indicate that there are not many or hardly any people or things ○ (adj) *There were few books on the shelves.* ○ (adj) *spending her few free hours relaxing in front of the television* ○ (pron) *Many people have entered the contest, but few will win prizes.* ○ (pron) *Few of the gardens had been cared for.*
1. *npl., pron.* LIMITED NUMBER a limited or exclusive number, e.g., an elite or minority of people ○ (n) *the fortunate few who managed to escape sickness this winter* ○ (n) *The needs of the many outweigh the needs of the few.* ○ (pron) *Few would have thought it.* **2.** *adj., pron.* **a few** SOME, THOUGH NOT MANY not very many people or things, but more than two, and sometimes more than might be expected ○ (adj) *We had a few meetings before signing the contract.* ○ (pron) *Only a few ever achieve real artistic success.* ○ (pron) *A few of the kids wanted to watch a video.* [Old English *fēawa.* Ultimately from an Indo-European base denoting smallness, which is also the ancestor of Latin *paucus* "little" (source of English *poor*).] —**few·ness** *n.* ◇ **few and far between** scarce or infrequent (*informal*) ◇ **quite a few** a fairly large number (*informal*)

fey /fay/ *adj.* **1.** IRRATIONAL AND EQUITABLE behaving or talking in very unusual, uninhibited ways that suggest possible psychiatric disorder ○ *Everyone was convinced he was fey because he rehearsed his lines in the park* **2.** SUPERNATURAL relating to or typical of magic or the supernatural **3.** CLAIRVOYANT supposedly able to see into the future **4.** *Scotland* DOOMED TO DIE doomed or destined to die, especially as indicated by peculiar, usually elated, behavior [Old English *fæge* "fated to die," of prehistoric Germanic origin] —**fey·ly** *adv.* —**fey·ness** *n.*

Feyn·man /fīnmən/, **Richard** (1918–88) U.S. physicist. He shared a Nobel Prize in physics in 1965 for work on quantum electrodynamics. Full name **Richard Phillips Feynman**

Feyn·man di·a·gram *n.* a diagrammatic representation of interactions between elementary particles [Named for Richard FEYNMAN]

fez /fez/ (*plural* **fez·zes**) *n.* a brimless felt hat shaped like a cone with a flat top, usually red with a black tassel, worn by men in eastern Mediterranean and North African countries. In the past it was the national headdress of Turkish men. [Early 19thC. Via French from Turkish *fes.* Probably named for FEZ, where they were originally made.]

Fez /fess/, **Fès** city in northern Morocco, northeast of Casablanca. The oldest of the country's four imperial cities, it is about 100 mi./161 km east of Rabat. Population: 564,000 (1993).

FF, ff. *symbol.* MUSIC fortissimo

ff. *abbr.* **1.** following (*used of lines or pages*) **2.** folios

ffa *abbr.* SHIPPING free from alongside

f.f.a., F.F.A. *abbr.* Future Farmers of America

FFV *abbr.* First Family of Virginia

FG *abbr.* **1.** FOOTBALL, BASKETBALL field goal **2.** fine grain

FGSA *abbr.* Fellow of the Geological Society of America

FGT *abbr.* federal gift tax

FHA *abbr.* **1.** Federal Housing Administration **2.** Future Homemakers of America

f.h.p *abbr.* friction horsepower

FHWA *abbr.* Federal Highway Administration

FIA *abbr.* Federal Insurance Administration

fi·a·cre /fee ákrə/ *n.* a small horse-drawn carriage with four wheels, used in the past for hire like a taxi [Late 17thC. From French, named for the Hôtel de St. *Fiacre*, where it was first hired out.]

fi·an·cé /fèe on sáy, fee ón sày/ *n.* the man to whom a woman is engaged to be married [Mid-19thC. From French, the past participle of *fiancer* "to betroth," from, ultimately, Old French *fiance* "a promise."]

fi·an·cée /fèe on sáy, fee ón sày/ *n.* the woman to whom a man is engaged to be married [Mid-19thC. From French, the feminine form of *fiancé* (see FIANCÉ).]

fi·an·chet·to /fèe ən chéttō, -kéttō/ *n.* (*plural* **-tos** *or* **-ti**) CHESS MOVE OF BISHOP in chess, the development of a bishop by moving it from its original position to the second square of the adjacent knight's file ■ *vt.* (**-toed, -to·ing, -tos**) MOVE BISHOP to move a bishop using a fianchetto [Mid-19thC. From Italian, literally "little flank," from *fianco* "flank."]

Fi·an·na /fèe ənə/ *npl.* a band of warriors in Irish mythology, led by the legendary Finn MacCool and celebrated for feats of heroism [Late 18thC. From Irish, "band of warriors and hunters."]

Fi·an·na Fáil /fèe ənə fáal/ *n.* an important Irish political party founded in 1926 [From Irish, literally "warriors of Ireland"]

fi·as·co /fee áskō/ (*plural* **-cos**) *n.* **1.** HUMILIATING FAILURE a total failure, especially a humiliating or ludicrous one **2.** STRAW-COVERED WINE BOTTLE a wine bottle having a round bottom and often in a basketlike straw covering [Mid-19thC. Via Italian, "bottle" from medieval Latin *flasco* "flask." The sense "failure" comes from *far fiasco*, literally "to make a bottle," used in theatrical slang for "to fail in a performance."]

fi·at /fèe ət, -àat/ *n.* **1.** OFFICIAL SANCTION a formal or official authorization of something **2.** ARBITRARY ORDER an authoritative and often arbitrary or unreasonable command [14thC. From Latin, literally "let it be done."]

fi·at mon·ey *n.* money that a government declares to be legal tender although it is not based on or convertible into coin and therefore depends on government decree to determine its value

fib /fib/ *n.* WHITE LIE an insignificant, harmless, or small lie (*informal*) ■ *vi.* (**fibbed, fib·bing, fibs**) TELL WHITE LIES to tell an insignificant, harmless, or small lie (*informal*) [Early 17thC. Origin uncertain: perhaps a shortening of earlier *fible-fable* "nonsense" (an alteration of FABLE).] —**fib·ber** *n.*

WORD KEY: SYNONYMS

See Synonyms at ***lie.***

fi·ber /fībər/, **fi·bre** *n.* **1.** THIN THREAD a long slender thread or filament **2.** INDUST THREAD FOR YARN a fine thread or filament of a natural or synthetic material, e.g., cotton or nylon, that can be spun into yarn **3.** TEXTILES CLOTH cloth or material made of fibers **4.** FIBROUS STRUCTURE the texture or structure of a material made of fibers **5.** ESSENTIAL CHARACTER the fundamental character, quality, or makeup of something **6.** STRENGTH OF CHARACTER somebody's strength of character or sense of right and wrong ○ *the moral fiber of the nation* **7.** HEALTH COARSE FIBROUS SUBSTANCES IN FOOD the coarse fibrous substances in grains, fruits, and vegetables that aid digestion and clean out the intestines. Primarily composed of cellulose, this largely indigestible plant matter is considered to play a role in the prevention of many diseases of the digestive tract. ○ *Whole wheat bread and brown rice are rich in fiber.* **8.** BOT LONG THICK-WALLED PLANT CELL a long narrow plant cell that has walls thickened with lignin and is a major component of the plant's supporting and strengthening tissue. Fiber cells are frequently found in the outer walls of plant stems. **9.** MANUF PLANT CELLS MAKING ROPE AND TEXTILES strands of fiber cells removed from the stems or leaves of some plants, e.g., flax, that can be separated and woven **10.** BOT THIN ROOT a thin narrow root of a plant **11.** ANAT THREAD-SHAPED BODY STRUCTURE a long thin structure of the body tissues, e.g., muscle cells and nerve cells [Mid-16thC. Via French from Latin *fibra* "filament," of uncertain origin.] —**fi·bered** *adj.*

fi·ber·board /fībər bàwrd/ *n.* building material made by compressing wood fibers into sheets

fi·ber bun·dle *n.* a flexible group of parallel optical fibers held in a fixed arrangement with respect to each other

fi·ber·fill /fībər fil/ *n.* synthetic material used for stuffing or insulation, e.g., in cushions, comforters, or clothing

Fi·ber·glas /fībər glàss/ *tdmk.* a trademark for a material made of glass fibers and plastic

fi·ber·glass /fībər glàss/ *n.* **1.** GLASS FIBERS glass fibers compressed to make materials such as insulation **2.** MATERIAL MADE FROM FIBERGLASS a material made from fiberglass and used in the construction of many things including boat hulls and car bodies

fi·ber op·tics *n.* the technology of transferring information, e.g., in communications or computer technology, through a number of thin flexible glass or plastic tubes (**optical fibers**) using modulated light waves. Information is transmitted in the form of coded pulses. (*takes a singular verb*) —**fi·ber-op·tic** *adj.*

fi·ber·scope /fībər skōp/ *n.* an instrument that uses fiber optics to transmit images from inaccessible places such as the interior of the body. Thin flexible fibers can be introduced into blood vessels, e.g., as a diagnostic tool or to assist in microsurgery.

Fi·bo·nac·ci num·ber *n.* a number in the unending Fibonacci sequence

Fi·bo·nac·ci se·quence *n.* the unending series of numbers 0,1,1,2,3,5,8 ... in which each number except for the first two is the sum of the preceding two. This sequence frequently occurs with applications in botany, psychology, and astronomy, e.g., providing a better correspondence for the distances between the sun and the planets than does Bode's law. [Named for Leonardo *Fibonacci*, the 13thC Italian mathematician who first described it]

fibr- *prefix.* = **fibro-** (*used before vowels*)

fi·bre *n.* = **fiber**

fibri- *prefix.* = **fibro-**

fi·bri·form /fíbbrə fàwrm/ *adj.* in the form of a fiber or fibers

fi·bril /fī brəl, fíbbrəl/ *n.* a small or delicate fiber or part of a fiber [Mid-17thC. From modern Latin *fibrilla*, literally "little fiber," from *fibra* "fiber."] —**fi·bril·lar** /fíbbrələr/ *adj.* —**fi·bril·lar·y** /-lèrree/ *adj.* —**fi·bril·li·form** /-ə fàwrm/ *adj.* —**fi·bril·lose** /-lōss/ *adj.* —**fib·ril·lous** /-ləss/ *adj.*

fi·bril·late /fíbbrə làyt/ (**-lat·ed, -lat·ing, -lates**) *vti.* to undergo, or make the heart or muscles undergo, rapid irregular beating or uncontrolled contraction (**fibrillation**) [Mid-19thC. Formed from modern Latin *fibrilla* (see FIBRIL).] —**fib·ril·la·tive** *adj.*

fib·ril·la·tion /fibbrə láysh'n/ *n.* **1.** RAPID IRREGULAR HEARTBEAT rapid chaotic beating of the heart muscles in a nonsynchronous way such that normal heartbeat is not maintained and the affected part of the heart may stop pumping blood **2.** RAPID CONTRACTION OF MUSCLE FIBERS rapid uncontrolled contraction of individual muscle fibers with little or no movement of the muscle as a whole **3.** FORMATION OF FIBERS the formation of fibers or fibrils

fi·brin /fíbrin/ *n.* an insoluble fibrous protein produced in the liver from the soluble protein fibrinogen during the blood clotting process. It forms a network of fibers in which blood cells become trapped, thus producing a clot. [Early 19thC. Coined from FIBER + -IN.]

fi·brin·o·gen /fī brínnəjən/ *n.* a soluble protein in the blood that is made in the liver and is converted to insoluble fibrin by the action of the enzyme thrombin in response to tissue damage. Fibrinogen is a clotting factor and is required to prevent major blood loss. —**fi·brin·o·gen·ic** /fībrənō jénnik/ *adj.* —**fi·brin·o·gen·i·cal·ly** /-jénnikəlee/ *adv.* —**fi·bri·nog·e·nous** /fībrə nójjənəss/ *adj.*

fib·ri·noid /fíbrə nòyd/ *adj.* RESEMBLING FIBRIN relating to or resembling the protein fibrin ■ *n.* MATERIAL RESEMBLING FIBRIN a naturally occurring material resembling the protein fibrin, normally found in the placenta and formed in connective tissue and blood vessel walls in some diseases

fi·bri·nol·y·sin /fībrə nólləsin/ *n.* any enzyme found in the blood that breaks down the protein fibrin found in blood clots and disperses them. Plasmin is a fibrinolysin.

fi·bri·nol·y·sis /fībrə nólləssiss/ *n.* the destruction of fibrin, especially its enzymatic breakdown by a fibrinolysin such as plasmin —**fi·bri·no·lyt·ic** /fībrənō líttik/ *adj.*

fi·bri·nous /fíbbrənəss/ *adj.* relating to or containing fibrin

fibro-[1] *prefix.* **1.** FIBRE used to mean fiber **2.** FIBROUS TISSUE used to mean fibrous tissue [From Latin *fibra* "fiber"]

fibro-[2] *prefix.* fiber, fibrous tissue ○ *fibrolite* ○ *fibrosarcoma* [From Latin *fibra*, of unknown origin]

fi·bro·blast /fîbrō blàst/ *n.* a large flat cell that secretes the proteins that form collagen and elastic fibers and the substance between the cells of connective tissue

fi·bro·car·ti·lage /fìbrō kaártəlij, -tlij/ *n.* a type of strong, relatively inelastic cartilage containing bundles of collagen fibers

fi·bro·cys·tic /fìbrō sístik/ *adj.* being an unusual growth of fibrous tissue that contains cystic spaces, occurring particularly in glandular tissue such as the breast. Fibrocystic disease of the pancreas is called cystic fibrosis.

fi·broid /fî bròyd/ *adj.* LIKE FIBERS resembling or consisting of fibers or fibrous tissue ■ *n.* FIBROUS TISSUE GROWTH a benign growth composed of fibrous and muscle tissue, especially one that develops in the wall of the womb and is associated with painful and excessive menstrual flow. Fibroids can be removed surgically and are not life-threatening, but fibroids in the womb reduce the chance of pregnancy.

fi·bro·in /fî brō in/ *n.* a tough insoluble white protein secreted by spiders and silkworms that quickly solidifies into a strong thread, used to form cocoons and webs

fi·bro·ma /fī brṓmə/ (*plural* **-mas** *or* **-ma·ta**) *n.* a nonmalignant tumor of fibrous connective tissue such as cartilage [Mid-19thC. Coined from Latin *fibra* "fiber" + -OMA.] —**fi·brom·a·tous** /fī brómmətəss/ *adj.*

fi·brose[1] /fîbrōss/ (**-brosed, -bros·ing, -bros·es**) *vi.* to form tissue consisting of or resembling fibres [Late 19thC. Back-formation from FIBROSIS.]

fi·brose[2] /fîbrōss/ *adj.* containing or resembling fibers (*technical*)

fi·bro·sis /fī brṓssiss/ *n.* an abnormal thickening and scarring of connective tissue most often following injury, infection, lack of oxygen, or surgery —**fi·brot·ic** /fī bróttik/ *adj.*

fi·bro·si·tis /fìbrə sîtiss/ *n.* pain and stiffness, especially in the back muscles

fi·brous /fîbrəss/ *adj.* **1.** CONSISTING OF FIBERS consisting of or resembling fibers **2.** GEOL IN ELONGATED THREADS used to describe a mineral that crystallizes in thin elongated threads, e.g., asbestos —**fi·brous·ly** *adv.* —**fi·brous·ness** *n.*

fi·brous root *n.* any of the fine roots of some plants, e.g., grasses, that are roughly the same length and branch in all directions

fi·bro·vas·cu·lar /fìbrō váskyələr/ *adj.* used to describe plant tissue that provides structural support and conducts sap

fi·bro·vas·cu·lar bun·dle *n.* = **vascular bundle**

fib·u·la /fíbbyələ/ (*plural* **-lae** /-lee/ *or* **-las**) *n.* **1.** HUMAN LEG BONE the outer and narrower of the two bones in the human lower leg, between the knee and the ankle **2.** ANIMAL LEG BONE the thinner outermost bone of the two bones that form the lower leg of terrestrial vertebrates between the knee and ankle, or the hind leg of a four-legged animal **3.** CLASP a brooch or clasp shaped like a modern safety pin, worn by the ancient Greeks and Romans to fasten cloaks [Late 16thC. From Latin, "brooch, clasp," perhaps formed from *figere* "to fasten." The sense "bone in the leg" comes from the two bones' similarity in shape to a Roman *fibula*.] —**fib·u·lar** *adj.*

-fic *suffix.* making, causing ○ *sudorific* [From Latin *-ficus*, from *facere* "to make, do" (see FACT)]

FICA *abbr.* Federal Insurance Contributions Act

-fication *suffix.* production, process ○ *versification* ○ *unification* [From the Latin stem *-fication-*, from *-ficatus*, the past participle stem of *-ficare* "to make," from *-ficus*, the past participle stem of *facere* (see FACT)]

fice /fīss/ *n.* = **feist** (*regional*) [Mid-19thC. Variant of FEIST.]

fiche /feesh/ *n.* (*informal*) **1.** MICROFICHE a microfiche **2.** ULTRAFICHE an ultrafiche [Mid-20thC. Shortening.]

fich·u /fí shoŏ, fee shoŏ/ *n.* a woman's triangular scarf made of a lightweight material such as muslin or lace, worn around the neck and shoulders, especially in the 18th and early 19th centuries [Mid-18thC. Via French, "knotted," from, ultimately, Latin *figere* "to fasten" (see FIX).]

fick·le /fík'l/ (**-ler, -lest**) *adj.* likely to change, especially in affections, intentions, loyalties, or preferences [Old English *ficol* "deceitful." Ultimately from an Indo-European word meaning "hostile."] —**fick·le·ness** *n.*

fic·tile /fíkt'l/ *adj.* **1.** MALLEABLE molded or capable of being molded, as, e.g., clay for making pottery can be **2.** MADE OF CLAY molded in earth or clay by a potter **3.** RELATING TO POTTERY MAKING relating to the making of earthenware or pottery [Early 17thC. Via Latin *fictilis* from, ultimately, *fingere* "to make, shape."]

fic·tion /fíkshən/ *n.* **1.** LITERARY WORKS OF IMAGINATION novels and stories that describe imaginary people and events **2.** WORK OF FICTION a novel, story, or other work of fiction **3.** UNTRUE STATEMENT something that is untrue and has been made up to deceive people ○ *The account she gave was pure fiction.* **4.** ACT OF PRETENDING the act of pretending or inventing something such as a story or explanation **5.** LAW SOMETHING ASSUMED TO BE TRUE something that is assumed in law to be true regardless of whether or not it is really true [14thC. Via Old French from Latin *fictio*, from *fingere* "to make, shape."]

WORD KEY: ORIGIN

The Latin word *fingere*, from which ***fiction*** is derived, is also the source of English *effigy, faint, feign, figment,* and *figure*.

fic·tion·al /fíkshən'l/ *adj.* **1.** NOT TRUE not real or true but made up by somebody **2.** RELATING TO FICTION occurring in, invented for, or relating to novels or stories —**fic·tion·al·i·ty** /fìkshə nállətee/ *n.* —**fic·tion·al·ly** /fíkshən'lee/ *adv.*

fic·tion·al·ize /fíkshən'l īz/ (**-ized, -iz·ing, -iz·es**) *vt.* to make something into fiction, or make a fictional version of something ○ *a fictionalized life of Shakespeare* —**fic·tion·al·i·za·tion** /fìkshənəli záysh'n/ *n.*

fic·ti·tious /fik tíshəss/ *adj.* **1.** FALSE not true or genuine, and intended to deceive ○ *He gave a fictitious name when confronted.* **2.** FICTIONAL invented by somebody's imagination, especially as part of a work of fiction **3.** LAW ASSUMED TO BE SO assumed to be true for legal purposes, regardless of whether or not it really is [Early 17thC. Formed from Latin *ficticius*, from, ultimately, *fingere* "to make, shape."] —**fic·ti·tious·ly** *adv.* —**fic·ti·tious·ness** *n.*

fic·tive /fíktiv/ *adj.* **1.** RELATING TO FICTION relating to fiction or imaginative invention **2.** NOT REAL not genuine or true [Late 15thC. Directly or via French from medieval Latin *fictivus*, from *fingere* "to make, shape."] —**fic·tive·ly** *adv.*

fid /fid/ *n.* **1.** TOPMAST SUPPORT a bar used to support a topmast on a ship **2.** TAPERED TOOL FOR SPLICING a tapered wooden implement used to separate the strands of a rope in splicing [Early 17thC. Origin unknown.]

-fid *suffix.* divided in parts ○ *multifid* [From Latin *-fidus*, from *fid-*, the stem of *findere* "to split" (see FISSI-)]

fid·dle /fídd'l/ *n.* **1.** MUSIC VIOLIN a musical instrument of the viol or violin family, especially the violin. Violins are often called fiddles in folk, bluegrass, or country music, but in classical music this can sometimes be disparaging. **2.** FRAUDULENT ACTIVITY a fraudulent or illegal way of getting money (*informal*) **3.** TRIVIAL MATTERS nonsensical or trivial matters or behavior **4.** NAUT GUARDRAIL ON SHIP'S TABLE a small guardrail on top of a table or stove on a ship, used to prevent things from sliding off in rough weather ■ *v.* (**-dled, -dling, -dles**) **1.** *vi.* MUSIC PLAY VIOLIN to play the fiddle **2.** *vt.* SWINDLE to cheat or swindle somebody (*informal*) **3.** *vt.* FALSIFY SOMETHING to falsify something, e.g., financial accounts, especially for dishonest personal gain (*informal*) **4.** *vi.* MOVE HANDS NERVOUSLY to move the hands or fingers nervously or restlessly, or play with something in the hands in this way ○ *The schoolboy fiddled nervously with his pencil.* **5.** *vti.* WASTE TIME to waste time doing unimportant things ○ *fiddle the day away* **6.** *vi.* TAMPER WITH SOMETHING to interfere, meddle, or tamper with something (*informal*) ○ *Who's been fiddling with my computer?* **7.** *vi.* TINKER WITH SOMETHING TO FIX IT to manipulate or tinker with something to try to make it work properly ○ *She fiddled with the controls on the video recorder.* [Pre-12thC. From medieval Latin *vitula* "instrument played at festivals," from *vitulari* "to hold celebrations" (source of English *violin*).]

fid·dle a·round *vi.* to waste time doing unimportant things (*informal*)

fid·dle·back /fídd'l bàk/, **fid·dle·back chair** *n.* a chair with a back shaped like the body of a fiddle

fid·dle-de-dee /fìdd'l dee deé/ *interj.* used to express mild annoyance, disagreement, or impatience (*dated informal*) [From FIDDLE and a nonsensical ending]

fid·dle-fad·dle /fídd'l fàdd'l/ *n.* NONSENSE nonsense or trifling matters (*informal*) ■ *interj.* NONSENSE! used to express the view that something is nonsense (*dated informal*) ■ *vi.* (**fid·dle-fad·dled, fid·dle-fad·dling, fid·dle-fad·dles**) WASTE TIME to waste time with unimportant matters (*informal*) [Late 16thC. From FIDDLE and earlier *faddle* "nonsense."] —**fid·dle-fad·dler** *n.*

fid·dle-foot·ed *adj.* **1.** SKITTISH showing excitability or nervousness **2.** WANDERING having a tendency to roam

Fiddlehead

fid·dle·head /fídd'l hèd/, **fid·dle·neck** /-nèk/ *n.* **1.** PLANTS EDIBLE FERN SHOOT the coiled frond of a young fern often cooked and eaten as a delicacy **2.** NAUT CARVING ON SHIP'S BOW an ornamental carving on a ship's bow, shaped like the scroll at the end of the fingerboard of a violin

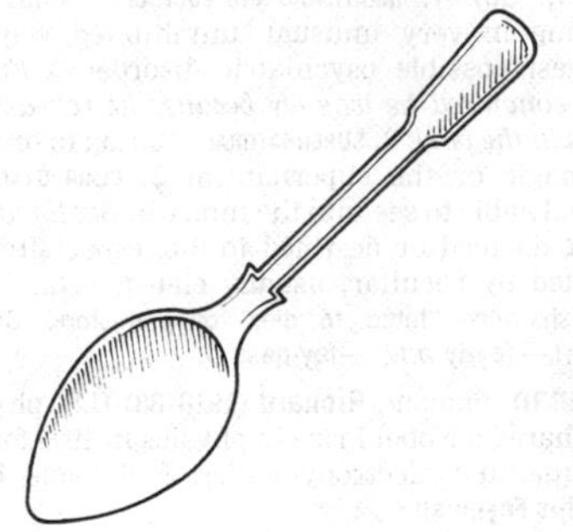

Fiddle pattern

fid·dle pat·tern *n.* the design of a fork or spoon with a handle that has a tapering wide end —**fid·dle-pat·tern** *adj.*

fid·dler /fíddlər/ *n.* **1.** MUSIC VIOLIN PLAYER somebody who plays the violin **2.** TIME WASTER somebody who idles or wastes time **3.** SOMEBODY WHO TOYS WITH SOMETHING somebody who plays or fidgets with something aimlessly **4.** SWINDLER somebody who cheats or swindles others (*informal*) **5.** ZOOL = **fiddler crab**

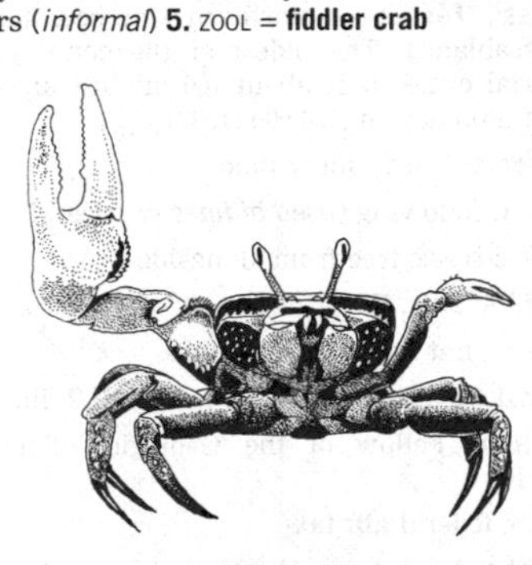

Fiddler crab

fid·dler crab *n.* a small marine burrowing crab. Males have one enlarged claw that they move like a violinist's arm as a signal during courtship. Genus: *Uca.*

fid·dle·stick /fídd'l stìk/ *n.* (*informal*) **1.** VIOLIN BOW a bow for playing a violin **2.** THING OF LITTLE VALUE something that is unimportant or worthless ○ *I don't care a fiddlestick what you think.*

fid·dle·sticks /fídd'l stiks/ *interj.* used to express mild annoyance, disagreement, or impatience (*dated informal*)

fid·dle·wood /fídd'l wòod/ *n.* **1.** TREES **TROPICAL TREE** a tropical American tree that yields a hard wood. Genus: *Citharexylum.* **2.** INDUST **WOOD OF FIDDLEWOOD TREE** the hard wood of the fiddlewood tree

fid·dling /fíddling/ *adj.* petty or unimportant

fid·dly /fíddlee/ (**-dli·er, -dli·est**) *adj. U.K.* difficult to do, handle, or use, usually because it involves small objects or intricate work with the hands (*informal*) ○ *Changing the battery in this type of watch can be quite a fiddly job.*

FIDE *abbr.* International Chess Federation [From French, an acronym formed from *Fédération Internationale des Échecs*]

fi·de·ism /fée day ìzzəm/ *n.* the view that religious knowledge depends on faith and revelation [Late 19thC. Formed from Latin *fides* "faith" (see FAITH.] —**fi·de·ist** *n.* —**fi·de·is·tic** /fée day ístik/ *adj.*

Fi·del·ism /fi dé lìzzəm/ *n.* the practice or policies of Castroism [Mid-20thC. Named for Fidel CASTRO.]

fi·del·i·ty /fi délləteе/ *n.* **1.** **LOYALTY** loyalty to an allegiance, promise, or vow **2.** **SEXUAL FAITHFULNESS** faithfulness to a sexual partner, especially a husband or wife **3.** **FACTUAL ACCURACY** accuracy in describing or reporting facts or details **4.** ELECTRON ENG **PRECISION OF REPRODUCTION** the extent to which an electronic device, e.g., a stereo system or television, accurately reproduces sound or images [15thC. Directly or via French from Latin *fidelitas* "faithfulness" from, ultimately, *fides* "faith" (see FAITH.]

fidg·et /fíjjət/ *vi.* (**-et·ed, -et·ing, -ets**) **1.** **MOVE AROUND NERVOUSLY** to move around in a restless, absent-minded, or uneasy manner ○ *The lecture was so boring we couldn't keep from fidgeting.* **2.** **FIDDLE NERVOUSLY** to fiddle or play with something in a restless, absent-minded, or uneasy manner ○ *He kept fidgeting with his glasses as he spoke to her.* ■ *n.* **SOMEBODY WHO FIDGETS** somebody who fidgets in a restless, absent-minded, or uneasy manner ■ **fidg·ets** *npl.* **UNEASINESS** a state of restlessness or unease expressed by continual nervous movements ○ *He seems to have a case of the fidgets.* [Late 17thC. Alteration of earlier *fidge* "to twitch, fidget."] —**fid·get·ing·ly** *adv.*

fidg·et·y /fíjjətee/ *adj.* **1.** **INCLINED TO FIDGET** tending to fidget **2.** **UNEASY** restless or ill at ease —**fidg·et·i·ness** *n.*

fi·do /fídō/ (*plural* **-dos**) *n.* a coin with a minting error [Mid-20thC. Acronym formed from *freaks, irregulars, defects,* and *oddities.*]

fi·du·cial /fi dóosh'l/ *adj.* **1.** **FOUNDED ON TRUST** founded on or relating to faith or trust (*formal*) **2.** **USED AS BASIS OF REFERENCE** accepted or used as a standard of comparison, measurement, or reference **3.** LAW **RESEMBLING LEGAL TRUST** resembling a legal trust [Late 16thC. Via late Latin *fiducialis* from, ultimately, Latin *fidere* "to trust."] —**fi·du·cial·ly** *adv.*

fi·du·ci·ar·y /fi dóoshee èrree, fi dóosharee/ *adj.* **1.** **RELATING TO A TRUST RELATIONSHIP** relating to the relationship between a trustee and the person or body for whom the trustee acts **2.** **RELATING TO A TRUST** relating to or based on a trust **3.** **TRUSTING GOVERNMENT TO STAND BEHIND MONEY** relating to or depending on confidence in a government for the value of fiat money ■ *n.* (*plural* **-ies**) **TRUSTEE** somebody who is entrusted with the management of property or with the power to act on behalf of and for the benefit of another [Late 16thC. Via Latin *fiduciarius* "(holding) in a trust" from, ultimately *fides* "trust" (see FAITH.] —**fi·du·ci·ar·i·ly** *adv.*

fie /fī/ *interj.* used to express disapproval, annoyance, or disgust with somebody or something (*archaic*) [14thC. Via French *fi* from Latin, an exclamation of disgust at a stench.]

Fied·ler /féedlər/, **Arthur** (1894–1979) U.S. conductor. As director of the Boston Pops Orchestra (1930–79), he arranged programs that were a mixture of light classics and popular tunes.

fief /feef/ *n.* **1.** **PIECE OF LAND GRANTED BY LORD** a piece of land, rather than money, formerly granted by a feudal lord to somebody in return for service **2.** = **fiefdom** [Early 17thC. Via French from Old French *fieu*, from medieval Latin *feudum* (see FEUD[2]).]

fief·dom /féefdəm/ *n.* **1.** **LANDS OF FEUDAL LORD** the lands controlled by a feudal lord **2.** **SOMETHING UNDER SOMEBODY'S INFLUENCE OR AUTHORITY** something such as territory or a sphere of activity that is controlled or dominated by a particular person or group

Library of Congress
Arthur Fiedler

field /feeld/ *n.* **1.** AGRIC **AREA OF AGRICULTURAL LAND** an area of open ground, especially an area used to grow crops or graze livestock **2.** SPORTS **PLAYING AREA** an open expanse of ground kept or marked off as a playing area for a particular sport **3.** GEOL **AREA RICH IN RESOURCES** an area of land or seabed that is rich in an exploitable natural resource **4.** GEOG **BROAD AREA OF SOMETHING** an expanse of something such as ice, snow, or lava **5.** **AREA OF ACTIVITY** an activity or subject, especially one that is somebody's particular responsibility, specialty, or interest **6.** **PLACE OUTSIDE INSTITUTION** the setting outside a workplace, office, school, or laboratory in which somebody has direct contact with clients, the public, or the phenomena being studied **7.** MIL **AREA OF MILITARY OPERATIONS** the scene or location of military operations or maneuvers **8.** MIL **BATTLEFIELD** an area where a battle is fought **9.** MIL **BATTLE** a battle (*archaic literary*) **10.** SPORTS **GROUP OF CONTESTANTS** all the participants in a race or other competitive event **11.** SPORTS **ALL PARTICIPANTS EXCEPT FAVORITE** all the participants in a race or competitive event except the favorite, winner, or leader ○ *five lengths ahead of the field* **12.** MATH **SET OF MATHEMATICAL ELEMENTS** a set of mathematical elements having two properties that are like addition and multiplication for ordinary numbers **13.** PHYS **AREA OF FORCE** an area or region within which a force exerts an influence at every point **14.** = **field of view** **15.** COMPUT **STORAGE AREA FOR INFORMATION** an area in a computer memory or program, or on a monitor screen, where information can be entered and manipulated **16.** HERALDRY **BACKGROUND FOR DESIGN** the background surface or color on which a design is displayed, e.g., on a flag, coin, or coat of arms ■ *v.* (**field·ed, field·ing, fields**) **1.** *vt.* SPORTS **RETRIEVE BALL** to retrieve, pick up, or catch a ball in play, usually after it has been struck by a batter in baseball or a batsman in cricket **2.** *vi.* SPORTS **BE A FIELDER** to act as a fielder in cricket or baseball **3.** *vt.* **SELECT SOMEBODY FOR A COMPETITION** to select a person, group, or team to participate in an event, especially a competitive event ○ *We did not have enough players to field a team* **4.** *vt.* **DEPLOY A GROUP** to send out a large number of people or things to accomplish a task, especially to deploy military forces for action **5.** *vt.* **DEAL WITH QUESTION OR COMPLAINT** to handle something such as a question or complaint [Old English *feld.* Ultimately from an Indo-European base meaning "flat," which also produced English *flat, plate,* and *place.*] ◇ **play the field** to avoid a romantic relationship with one person by dating many people

Field /feeld/, **Cyrus West** (1819–92) U.S. entrepreneur. He transmitted the first successful transatlantic telegraph cable (1856).

Field, David Dudley (1805–94) U.S. law reformer. His code of U.S. civil procedure was enacted in 1848.

Field, Eugene (1850–95) U.S. writer. He is best known for his witty newspaper columns and poetry for children such as *"Little Boy Blue"* (1892).

Field, Marshall (1834–1906) U.S. entrepreneur. After 1867 he headed the Chicago department store that was later to bear his name, and was noted for its innovative merchandising practices.

Field, Stephen J. (1816–99) U.S. jurist. He served on the U.S. Supreme Court (1863–97). His decisions were usually conservative. Full name **Stephen Johnson Field**

field ar·til·ler·y *n.* large guns mobile enough to be brought close to the front line of a battle

field coil *n.* the coil of wire that, when carrying current, produces the magnetization inside an electrical motor or generator needed for it to operate

field corn *n.* corn that is grown as feed for livestock

field day *n.* **1.** **TIME OF UNRESTRAINED ACTIVITY** an opportunity for unrestrained or rewarding activity ○ *If the slightest hint of this gets out, the press will have a field day.* **2.** **DAY FOR AMATEUR COMPETITIONS** a day devoted to amateur outdoor sports and competitions, especially at a school **3.** **DAY FOR OUTDOOR ACTIVITIES** a day spent in outdoor activities **4.** **DAY FOR MILITARY SHOW** a day devoted to military exercises and display, usually performed in front of spectators

field-ef·fect tran·sis·tor *n.* a transistor, with three or more electrodes, in which the output current is controlled by a variable electric field

field e·mis·sion *n.* the liberation of electrons from the surface of a metallic conductor subjected to a strong electric field

field·er /féeldər/ *n.* a player in cricket or baseball who is positioned on the field of play to catch or retrieve the ball when it is struck by the batter or batsman

field·er's choice *n.* an attempt by a fielder in baseball to put out a base runner when the ball is hit, allowing the batter to reach first base safely

field e·vent *n.* an athletic event in a track-and-field meet, e.g., the discus, javelin, long jump, or high jump, that takes place on an open area not on a track

field·fare /féeld fàir/ (*plural* **-fares** *or* **-fare**) *n.* a migratory Eurasian thrush with reddish-brown plumage and a gray head and rump and a noisy call. Latin name: *Turdus pilaris.* [Assumed Old English *feldefare* "field dweller"]

field glass·es *npl.* a pair of binoculars

field goal *n.* **1.** FOOTBALL **GOAL MADE WITH A KICK** in football, a score worth three points, made by kicking the ball over the crossbar from a point about ten yards behind the line of scrimmage **2.** BASKETBALL **GOAL IN NORMAL PLAY** in basketball, a goal made during normal play by throwing the ball through the basket. It is worth two points, or three points if scored from beyond a specified distance.

field-grade of·fi·cer *n.* = **field officer**

field guide *n.* an illustrated manual that is used to identify plants, animals, or birds in their natural habitats

field hand *n.* somebody who works on a farm cultivating or harvesting crops

field hock·ey *n.* a game played outdoors in which two teams of 11 players each use curved sticks to direct a ball into each other's netted goal

field hos·pi·tal *n.* a center for medical treatment on a battlefield or in an isolated place

field house *n.* **1.** **BUILDING FOR TEAMS** a building equipped with storage facilities and dressing rooms for the use of sports teams **2.** **INDOOR SPORTS ARENA** a building containing a large space for athletic events, often with seating for spectators

Field·ing /féelding/, **Henry** (1707–54) British novelist and dramatist. Of his 25 plays, the most popular was the farce *Tom Thumb* (1730). He is also considered to be a founder of the English novel.

field lens *n.* the lens that is farthest from the eye in the compound eyepiece of an optical instrument

field mag·net *n.* an electromagnet or permanent magnet that supplies the magnetic field in an electric machine

field mar·shal *n.* an officer holding the highest rank in the British army or in the armies of some other countries

field mouse *n.* **1.** *U.K.* **SMALL EURASIAN MOUSE** a small

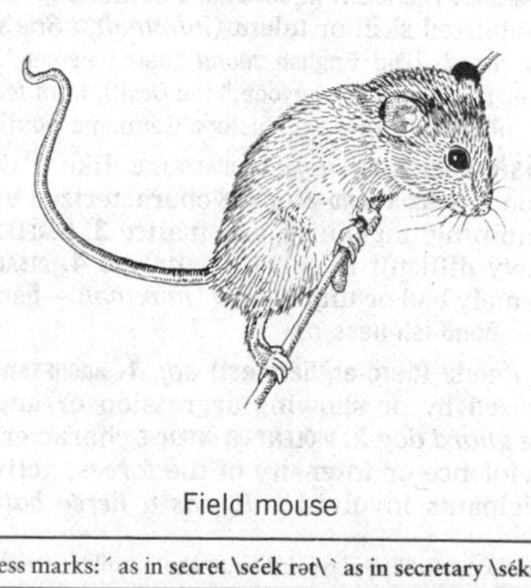
Field mouse

Eurasian mouse with large eyes and ears and a long tail that lives in fields and gardens. Genus: *Apodemus.* 2. **N AMERICAN VOLE** the most common North American vole. Genus: *Microtus.*

field of·fi·cer *n.* a military officer of the middle rank, e.g., a major or colonel

field of hon·or *n.* a battlefield, or the site of a duel (*archaic*)

field of view *n.* the area in the eyepiece of an optical instrument in which the image is visible

field of vi·sion *n.* the whole area that can be seen by the eyes when they are kept fixed in one direction

field pop·py *n.* = **corn poppy**

Fields /feeldz/, **Sally** (*b.* 1946) U.S. television and movie actor. She won Academy Awards for *Norma Rae* (1979) and *Places in the Heart* (1984).

W. C. Fields

Fields, W. C. (1880–1946) U.S. actor and comedian. He is best known for his portrayal of irascible, irresponsible characters struggling to keep one step ahead of the law. One of his most popular films is *My Little Chickadee* (1940). Real name **William Claude Dukenfield**

field·stone /feéld stōn/ *n.* a stone found in fields and used, often in unfinished form, for building

field·strip /feéld strìp/ (**-stripped, -strip·ping, -strips**) *vt.* to take apart a weapon for inspection or for cleaning, lubrication, or repair

field test *n.* a test carried out on a product under normal conditions of use

field-test *vt.* to test a device or product by using it under normal conditions

field tri·al *n.* 1. = **field test** 2. **CONTEST FOR HUNTING DOGS** a competition to determine how well hunting dogs perform

field trip *n.* a trip made by students or researchers to study something firsthand

field wind·ing *n.* = **field coil**

field·work /feéld wùrk/ *n.* 1. **WORK DONE OUTSIDE NORMAL PLACE OF WORK** work undertaken outside the school, office, or laboratory in order to gain knowledge through direct contact and observation 2. **SOCIAL RESEARCH AMONG POPULATION** social or anthropological research carried out among the subjects of the research, and done by observing and interviewing them 3. MIL **TEMPORARY FORTIFICATION** a temporary defensive earthwork or fortification —**field work·er** *n.*

fiend /feend/ *n.* 1. **DEVIL** an evil supernatural being, especially a devil from hell 2. **SOMEBODY EVIL** somebody who is extremely wicked or cruel 3. **TROUBLEMAKER** somebody who is mischievous or annoying ○ *Those little fiends ate all the cake!* 4. **PERSON WITH STRONG INTEREST** somebody who is keen and devotedly interested in a particular topic, occupation, or activity 5. **SOMEBODY PROFICIENT AT SOMETHING** somebody who has a specialized skill or talent (*informal*) ○ *She's a real math fiend.* [Old English *fēond* "hated person, enemy" (hence "the enemy of everyone," the Devil), from *fēogan* "to hate"; ultimately from a prehistoric Germanic word]

fiend·ish /feéndish/ *adj.* 1. **DIABOLICAL** like a devil or demon 2. **CUNNING AND MALICIOUS** characterized by devilish cunning, ingenuity, and malice 3. **PERPLEXING** extremely difficult to solve or analyze 4. **DISAGREEABLE** extremely bad or unpleasant (*informal*) —**fiend·ish·ly** *adv.* —**fiend·ish·ness** *n.*

fierce /feérs/ (**fierc·er, fierc·est**) *adj.* 1. **AGGRESSIVE** characterized by or showing aggression or anger ○ *a fierce guard dog* 2. **VIOLENT OR INTENSE** characterized by the violence or intensity of the forces, activity, or participants involved ○ *It was a fierce battle.* ○ *a fierce storm* 3. **PROFOUND** deeply and intensely felt and often aggressively expressed ○ *He felt a fierce loyalty to his family.* [13thC. Via Anglo-Norman *fers* "brave, proud, hostile" from, ultimately, Latin *ferus* "wild, untamed" (source of English *feral*).] —**fierce·ly** *adv.* —**fierce·ness** *n.*

fi·er·i fa·ci·as *n.* a legal document that authorizes a sheriff to sell enough of a debtor's property to settle the claim of a creditor [From Latin, literally "you should cause to be done"]

fier·y /fí əree, fíree/ (**-i·er, -i·est**) *adj.* 1. **GLOWING HOT** burning or full of fire 2. **RED** bright red in color 3. **SHOWING INTENSE EMOTION** full of or prone to sudden extremes of emotions 4. **SPICY** extremely hot or spicy to the taste 5. **INFLAMED** red and inflamed —**fier·i·ly** *adv.* —**fier·i·ness** *n.*

fier·y cross *n.* a burning wooden cross, originally carried by runners in the Scottish Highlands to call men to arms and later adopted by the Ku Klux Klan

fi·es·ta /fee éstə/ *n.* 1. **RELIGIOUS FESTIVAL** a celebration or festival linked to a religious holiday and held especially in Spanish-speaking countries 2. **FESTIVAL** any festival or celebration [Mid-19thC. Via Spanish from, ultimately, Latin *festum.*]

FIFA /feéfə/ *abbr.* the governing organisation of international soccer [From French, an acronym formed from *[Fédération Internationale de Football Association]*]

fife /fīf/ *n.* a small high-pitched flute without keys, often used in military and marching bands [Mid-16thC. Origin uncertain; via German *Pfeife*, or French *fifre* "fife, fife player" from, ultimately, assumed Vulgar Latin *pipa*, from Latin *pipare* "to peep, chirp" (source of English *pipe*).] —**fifer** /fífər/ *n.*

fife rail *n.* a low rail around the lower part of the mast of a sailing ship, with belaying pins to which running rigging is attached [Origin unknown]

FIFO /fí fō/ *abbr.* first in, first out

fif·teen /fif teén/ *n.* 1. **NUMBER 15** the number 15 2. **SOMETHING WITH VALUE OF 15** something in a numbered series with a value of 15 3. **GROUP OF FIFTEEN** a group of fifteen objects or people [Old English *fīftēne*, from *fīf* "five" + *-tēne* (from a prehistoric German word meaning "ten")] —**fif·teen** *adj., pron.*

fif·teenth /fif teénth/ *n.* 1. **ONE OF 15 PARTS OF SOMETHING** one of 15 equal parts of something 2. **15 IN A SERIES** the ordinal number assigned to item number 15 in a series —**fif·teenth** *adj., adv.*

fifth /fifth/ *n.* 1. **ONE OF 5 PARTS OF SOMETHING** one of five equal parts of something 2. **FIVE IN A SERIES** the ordinal number assigned to item number five in a series 3. **MEASURE OF LIQUOR** a fifth part of a gallon of alcoholic liquor 4. MUSIC **FIVE-NOTE INTERVAL** in a diatonic scale, an interval stretching from one note to another five notes higher, or the sound made when both these notes are played simultaneously 5. AUTOMOT **FIFTH GEAR** in some cars or motor vehicles, the fifth gear [Old English *fīfta*, from *fīf* (see FIVE)] —**fifth** *adj., adv.*

Fifth *n.* the Fifth Amendment (*informal*) ◇ **take the Fifth** refuse to answer an awkward or self-incriminating question (*informal*)

Fifth A·mend·ment *n.* an amendment to the U.S. Constitution stating, among other things, that defendants or witnesses in criminal trials need not testify against themselves and may not be subjected to double jeopardy

fifth col·umn *n.* a secret or subversive group that seeks to undermine the efforts of others and promote its own ends [Originally denoting the supporters that General Mola claimed to have inside Madrid during the Spanish Civil War, in addition to the four columns of his army besieging the city] —**fifth col·um·nist** *n.*

fifth-gen·er·a·tion *adj.* used to describe a highly advanced and as yet undeveloped level of computer technology, incorporating artificial intelligence

fifth·ly /fifthlee/ *adv.* used to introduce the fifth point in an argument or discussion

fifth wheel *n.* 1. **SOMEBODY OR SOMETHING UNNECESSARY** somebody or something whose presence is superfluous or unwanted 2. **SPARE WHEEL** a spare wheel for a four-wheeled vehicle 3. **ARTICULATED BEARING OR COUPLING** a horizontal bearing that allows a vehicle's front axle to swivel left or right relative to its body, or that allows a trailer attached to a tractor vehicle to pivot

fif·ti·eth /fíftee əth/ *n.* 1. **ONE OF 50 PARTS** one of 50 equal parts of something 2. **50 IN A SERIES** the ordinal number assigned to item number 50 in a series 3. **50TH BIRTHDAY** somebody's 50th birthday —**fif·ti·eth** *adj., adv.*

fif·ty /fíftee/ *n.* (*plural* **-ties**) 1. **NUMBER 50** the number 50, equal to 5 times 10 2. **GROUP OF 50** a group of 50 objects or people ■ *npl.* 1. **NUMBERS 50 TO 59** the numbers 50 to 59, particularly as a range of temperature ○ *in the low fifties* 2. **YEARS 1950 TO 1959** the years 1950 to 1959 3. **PERIOD FROM AGE 50 TO 59** the period of somebody's life from the age of 50 to 59 [Old English *fīftig*, from *fīf* (see FIVE)] —**fif·ty** *adj., pron.*

fif·ty-fif·ty *adj., adv.* **IN EXACTLY EQUAL SHARES** in two equally divided parts or shares ○ *We'll split the profits fifty-fifty.* ■ *adj.* **EQUAL** equally likely that either of two possibilities may come about ○ *a fifty-fifty chance*

Fig

fig[1] /fig/ *n.* 1. **SWEET-TASTING FRUIT** a pear-shaped fruit with sweet-tasting flesh and many seeds that is eaten fresh, preserved, or dried 2. **TREE** a small tropical or subtropical tree of the mulberry family that bears figs. Latin name: *Ficus carica.* [13thC. Via Old French *figue* from, ultimately, Latin *ficus.*] ◇ **not give** *or* **care a fig for somebody** *or* **something** not to care about somebody or something at all

fig[2] /fig/ *n.* the way somebody is dressed, usually in particularly grand or formal clothing (*archaic*) [Mid-19thC. From obsolete *feague* "to beat, to work at briskly," of uncertain origin; probably from German *fegen* "to polish."]

fig. *abbr.* 1. figurative 2. figure

fight /fīt/ *v.* (**fought, fight·ing, fights**) 1. *vti.* **USE VIOLENCE** to use violent physical means such as blows with fists or a weapon to try to overpower somebody 2. *vti.* **GO TO WAR** to go to war, or engage in armed conflict with another country, force, or group ○ *In the Civil War the Confederacy was fighting against the Union.* 3. *vi.* **TAKE PART IN WAR** to take part in a war or battle, e.g., as a member or unit of the armed forces involved in it 4. *vt.* **CARRY ON BATTLE OR CONTEST** to enter into or carry on a battle or other contest such as an election or court case 5. *vi.* **STRUGGLE DETERMINEDLY** to make a strenuous effort to do, obtain, achieve, or defend something 6. *vti.* **OPPOSE SOMETHING** to make vigorous efforts to oppose, resist, or overcome something or somebody ○ *fight injustice* 7. *vi.* **QUARREL** to argue or quarrel with somebody or with each other 8. *vti.* **BOX AGAINST SOMEBODY** to take part in a boxing match against somebody ■ *n.* 1. **VIOLENT ENCOUNTER** a conflict between individuals or groups in which each tries to do physical harm to, or defeat, the other 2. **STRUGGLE** a determined effort to achieve or gain something, or to resist or oppose something or somebody 3. **VERBAL CONFRONTATION** a verbal dispute or quarrel 4. **ABILITY OR WILLINGNESS TO FIGHT** the ability or willingness to continue a battle or struggle ○ *We've still got a lot of fight left in us.* 5. **BOXING MATCH** a boxing match or similar contest [Old English *feohtan* "to fight," ultimately from a prehistoric West Germanic word] —**fight·a·ble** *adj.* ◇ **fight it out** to fight or argue until a decisive result is obtained ◇ **fight shy of something** to try to avoid something

WORD KEY: SYNONYMS

fight, battle, war, conflict, engagement, skirmish, clash

CORE MEANING: a struggle between opposing forces

fight a general word used to talk about a physical struggle between opponents. It can be used both of individuals or groups of people, such as battalions or armies; **battle** used to describe a fight between large organized opposing forces that is part of an ongoing war or campaign; **war** a state of hostilities between nations, states or factions involving the use of arms and the occurrence of a series of fights or battles; **conflict** used to describe a situation in which opposing forces struggle for supremacy. It is often used to talk about a prolonged and bitter struggle; **engagement** a formal word used to describe a hostile encounter that is part of a continuing struggle such as a war and that suggests that the encounter has been anticipated and planned; **skirmish** used to describe a brief minor fight, usually one that is part of an ongoing conflict; **clash** used to describe a short, fierce encounter, usually involving physical combat and often forming part of an ongoing conflict.

fight back *v.* **1.** *vi.* **GET BACK AT SOMEBODY** to resist or retaliate when attacked **2.** *vi.* **COUNTERATTACK** to counterattack or make a determined effort to recover after initial defeat or difficulty ○ *They fought back from being down 15 points to win the game.* **3.** *vt.* **RESTRAIN TEARS OR EMOTION** to suppress something such as tears or the outward expression of an emotion or impulse

fight off *vt.* **1. FEND OFF AN ATTACKER** to drive away or resist an attacker **2. AVOID CATCHING SOMETHING** to make an effort not to succumb to something such as an illness or an unpleasant feeling

fight·er /fítər/ *n.* **1. ATTACKING AIRCRAFT** a fast armed military aircraft designed principally to attack enemy aircraft **2. VERY DETERMINED PERSON** somebody who is very determined and struggles hard to achieve or resist something **3. BOXER** somebody who takes part in boxing matches

fight·er-bomb·er *n.* an aircraft designed to combine the roles of fighter and bomber

fight·ing chair *n.* a chair attached to the deck of an oceangoing fishing boat for an angler to sit in while struggling to bring large game fish to the boat

fight·ing chance *n.* a possibility of success, but only with sustained effort

fight·ing cock *n. U.K.* = **gamecock**

Fighting fish

fight·ing fish *n.* a small brightly colored, highly aggressive freshwater fish with long flowing fins that is found in Southeast Asia and elsewhere and is also kept in aquariums. Genus: *Betta.*

fight-or-flight re·ac·tion *n.* a set of physiological changes, including an increase in heart rate, blood pressure, and the flow of adrenalin, that constitutes the body's instinctive response to impending danger or other stress

fig leaf *n.* **1.** ARTS **COVERING FOR GENITALS IN ART** a stylized representation of a leaf of the fig tree, formerly used as a covering for the genitals in painting or sculpture **2. SOMETHING MEANT TO HIDE SOMETHING ELSE** an unconvincing or inadequate attempt to conceal something considered shameful or wrong

fig·ment /fígmənt/ *n.* something produced by or only existing in somebody's imagination ○ *a figment of her imagination* [15thC. From Latin *figmentum* "formation, figure, creation," from *fingere* "to form or shape."]

Fi·gue·res Ol·sen /fi gàyrəss ṓls'n/, **José María** (*b.* 1954) Costa Rican government leader. A member of the Partido de Liberacion Nacional (PLN), he was elected president in 1994.

fig·ur·al /fíggyərəl/ *adj.* = **figurative** *adj.* 2

fig·u·rant /fíggyərənt/ *n.* a ballet dancer who performs in group numbers but does not dance solo [Late 18thC. From Frenchpresent participle of *figurer* "to represent," from, ultimately, Latin *figura* "FIGURE."]

fig·u·rante /fíggyə raánt, fíggyə raántee/ *n.* a woman ballet dancer who performs in group numbers but does not dance solo [Late 18thC. From French feminine form of *figurant* "FIGURANT."]

fig·u·ra·tion /fíggyə ráysh'n/ *n.* **1.** MUSIC **USE OF MUSICAL FIGURES AS EMBELLISHMENT** the use of musical figures or other ornaments to embellish or vary a theme **2.** ARTS **GIVING SOMETHING FIGURATIVE FORM** the process of giving allegorical or emblematic form to something abstract, especially by representing it using human or animal figures **3. FIGURATIVE REPRESENTATION OF SOMETHING** a depiction of something in emblematic or allegorical form

fig·u·ra·tive /fíggyərətiv/ *adj.* **1. NOT LITERAL** using or containing a nonliteral sense of a word or words **2. REPRESENTATIONAL** relating to or representing form in art by means of human or animal figures **3. REPRESENTING BY ALLEGORICAL FIGURES** using an allegorical or emblematic human or animal figure to represent an abstract idea or quality —**fig·u·ra·tive·ly** *adv.* —**fig·u·ra·tive·ness** *n.*

fig·ure /fíggyər/ *n.* **1. SYMBOL REPRESENTING NUMBER** a symbol representing something other than a letter of the alphabet, especially a number **2. AMOUNT EXPRESSED NUMERICALLY** an amount or value expressed as a number **3. SOMEBODY'S BODY SHAPE** the shape of an individual human body, especially with regard to its slimness or attractiveness **4.** ARTS **REPRESENTATION** a representation of a human being in a picture or sculpture **5. HUMAN SHAPE SEEN INDISTINCTLY** a human shape seen in outline or indistinctly or that is unidentified **6. SOMEBODY WITHIN PARTICULAR CONTEXT** an individual, especially with regard to status within a particular context, e.g., in history or in a community or profession ○ *She was a prominent figure in her community.* **7. SOMEBODY SERVING AS EXAMPLE** somebody regarded as having qualities that exemplify a particular role in life (*usually used in combination*) ○ *father figure* **8. WAY SOMEBODY APPEARS TO OTHERS** the general impression somebody makes on other people ○ *He cut a dashing figure on the morning of his wedding.* **9.** PUBL **ILLUSTRATIVE DRAWING OR DIAGRAM** an illustrative drawing or diagram in a book or article **10. SHAPE OR OUTLINE OF SOMETHING** something represented by a shape or outline **11.** GEOM **GEOMETRICAL FORM** any two- or three-dimensional geometrical form consisting of points, lines, curves, or planes **12.** CRAFT **PATTERN OR DESIGN** a pattern or design, especially on cloth or wood **13.** DANCE, ICE SKATING **DANCE OR SKATING ROUTINE** a particular sequence of movements carried out by dancers or ice skaters as part of a dance or routine **14.** MUSIC **GROUP OF MUSICAL NOTES** a short progression of musical notes that produces a single and distinct impression **15.** LOGIC **FORM OF SYLLOGISM** the form of an Aristotelian syllogism as determined by the position of the middle term ■ **fig·ures** *npl.* **MATHEMATICAL CALCULATIONS** calculations involving numbers (*informal*) ■ *v.* (**-ured, -ur·ing, -ures**) **1.** *vi.* **BE INCLUDED IN SOMETHING** to appear, take part, or be included in something ○ *did not figure in the outcome* **2.** *vt.* **BELIEVE OR CONCLUDE** to believe or come to the conclusion that something is the case (*informal*) ○ *She figured he must have meant something by it, but she didn't know what.* **3.** *vt.* **BELIEVE SOMEBODY TO BE SOMETHING** to believe somebody or something to be a particular type ○ *I had him figured for a lawyer or something like that.* **4.** *vt.* **IMAGINE SOMETHING** to form an idea about or envision something ○ *The way I figure it, she must have seen the guy somewhere before.* **5.** *vti.* **BE UNSURPRISING** to be or happen as expected ○ *It just figures she'd show up late.* **6.** *vti.* **CALCULATE** to do mathematical calculations, or calculate something using mathematical operations [13thC. Via French from Latin *figura* "form, shape, figure," from *fingere* "to make or shape" (source of English *effigy, faint,* and *fiction*).]

figure in *vt.* to take something into account ○ *She failed to figure in all the consequences.*

figure on *vt.* to plan that something should happen, or assume that it will happen ○ *We can figure on running a loss this year.*

figure out *vt.* **1. WORK SOMETHING OUT** to find a solution or explanation for something **2. DECIDE** to reach a decision or conclusion about something

WORD KEY: SYNONYMS

See Synonyms at ***deduce.***

fig·ured /fíggyərd/ *adj.* decorated with a design or pattern

fig·ured bass *n.* a bass part of a musical composition, typically baroque or classical, in which the notes have numbers written above them to indicate which chords to play

fig·ure eight *n.* an outline of the number eight formed with two loops and one continuous line, e.g., in figure skating or aerobatics

fig·ure·head /fíggyər hèd/ *n.* **1.** SHIPPING **CARVED FIGURE ON BOW OF SHIP** a carving, usually of a full or half-length human figure, built into the bow of a sailing ship **2. SOMEBODY NOMINALLY IN CHARGE** somebody who appears to be the head of an organization or institution but has no real responsibility or authority

fig·ure of mer·it *n.* a parameter or characteristic of a machine, component, or instrument that is used as a measure of its performance

fig·ure of speech *n.* an expression or use of language in a nonliteral sense in order to achieve a particular effect. Metaphors, similes, and hyperbole are all common figures of speech.

fig·ure skat·ing *n.* a form of competitive skating in which skaters trace patterns on the ice and perform spins, jumps, and other maneuvers —**fig·ure skat·er** *n.*

fig·u·rine /fíggyə reén/ *n.* a small ornamental figure, often of pottery or metal [Mid-19thC. Via French from Italian *figurina* "small figure," from, ultimately, Latin *figura* "FIGURE."]

fig wasp *n.* a wasp native to Europe that breeds in caprifigs and pollinates the flowers of wild fig trees. Each species of fig is believed to be pollinated by a different species of wasp. Genus: *Blastophaga.*

fig·wort /fíg wùrt, -wàwrt/ (*plural* **-worts** *or* **-wort**) *n.* a tall woodland plant of the snapdragon family that has clusters of small greenish flowers. Genus: *Scrophularia.* [Mid-16thC. From FIG[1], used as a dialect term for hemorrhoids, which it was used to treat.]

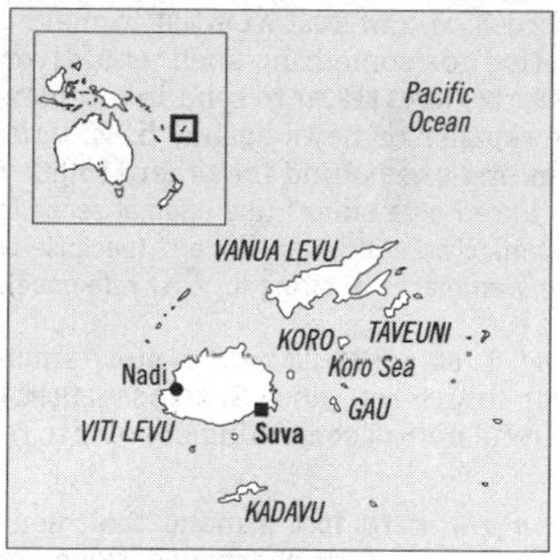

Fiji

Fi·ji /feéjee/ island nation in the southern Pacific Ocean north of New Zealand and east of northern Australia. A British colony from 1874, it gained its independence in 1970. Language: English. Currency: Fijian dollar. Capital: Suva. Population: 792,441 (1997). Area: 7,095 sq. mi./18,376 sq. km. Official name **Republic of Fiji**

Fi·ji·an /feéjee ən/ *n.* **1.** LANG **LANGUAGE SPOKEN IN FIJI** a language spoken on the islands of Fiji, belonging to the Eastern branch of the Austronesian family of languages. About 400,000 people speak Fijian. **2.** PEOPLES **SOMEBODY FROM FIJI** somebody who was born or raised on the islands of Fiji, or who has Fijian citizenship —**Fi·ji·an** *adj.*

fil·a·ment /fílləmənt/ *n.* **1. SLENDER STRAND OR FIBER** a slender strand or fiber of a material **2.** ELEC ENG **WIRE CONDUCTOR IN LIGHTBULB** a thin wire or ribbon that, when an electric current passes through it, acts as the light-producing element in an incandescent bulb or the electron-emitting element in a vacuum tube **3.** BOT **FLOWER PART** the stalk that supports the pollen-bearing anther in the male reproductive organ (**stamen**) of a flower. ◊ **anther 4.** BIOL **LONG STRAND OF CELLS** a long strand consisting of similar cells joined end to end, as found, e.g., in certain bacteria and algae [Late 16thC. Via French, or modern Latin *filamentum,* from, ultimately, Latin *filum* "thread."] —**fil·a·men·ta·ry** /fíllə méntəree/ *adj.* —**fil·a·men·tous** /-méntəss/ *adj.*

fi·lar·i·a /fi lérree ə/ (*plural* **-ae** *or* **-a**) *n.* a parasitic nematode worm that is carried as a larva by biting insects and lives as an adult in the blood or tissues of vertebrates, causing filariasis. Family: Filaridae. [Mid-19thC. From modern Latin *Filaria,* former genus name, from Latin *filum* "thread."] —**fi·lar·i·al** *adj.* —**fi·lar·i·an** *adj.*

fil·a·ri·a·sis /fíllə rí əssiss/ *n.* a disease caused by parasitic worms (**filaria**) that inflames and obstructs the lymphatic glands, sometimes resulting in elephantiasis

fil·a·ture /fíllə choòr, fílləchər/ *n.* **1. REELING OF SILK FROM COCOONS** the process of reeling silk fibers from cocoons **2. SILK REEL** a reel used in reeling silk fibers **3. SILK FACTORY** a factory for reeling silk fibers [Mid-18thC. Via French from Italian *filatura*, from *filare* "to spin," from, ultimately, Latin *filum* "thread."]

fil·bert /fílbərt/ (*plural* **-berts** *or* **-bert**) *n.* **1.** FOOD = **hazelnut 2.** = **hazel** [14thC. From Anglo-Norman *philbert*, named for St. *Philibert*, whose feast day falls on August 22, the month hazelnuts begin to ripen.]

filch /filch/ (**filched, filch·ing, filch·es**) *vt.* to steal something furtively, usually a small item or amount of little value (*informal*) [13thC. Origin uncertain, perhaps from Old English *fylcian* "to marshal troops," later changing meaning to "to attack, to take as booty."] —**filch·er** *n.*

WORD KEY: SYNONYMS

See Synonyms at ***steal.***

file[1] /fīl/ *n.* **1. STORAGE FOR PAPERS** a folder, cabinet, or other container that holds papers for convenient storage and reference **2. ORDERED COLLECTION** a collection of related documents or papers arranged so they can be consulted easily **3.** COMPUT **COMPUTER INFORMATION** a uniquely named collection of program instructions or data stored on a hard drive, disk, or other storage medium and treated as a single entity **4. LINE** a line of people or things standing or moving one behind the other ■ *v.* (**filed, fil·ing, files**) **1.** *vt.* **STORE SOMETHING IN ORDER** to arrange and store something in a file for future reference **2.** *vt.* LAW **SUBMIT SOMETHING** to submit something such as a claim or complaint to the appropriate authority so that it can be put on record **3.** *vi.* LAW **BRING A LAWSUIT** to make a formal application for something such as a divorce **4.** *vt.* PRESS **SEND IN A NEWS REPORT** to send in a report or story to a newspaper or news agency **5.** *vi.* **MOVE IN LINE** to move in line one behind the other [15thC. Via French *filer* "to thread on a string" (the original sense in English) from, ultimately, Latin *filum* "thread" (because documents were hung on pieces of string for easy reference).] —**fil·er** *n.*

file away *vt.* **1. PUT SOMETHING AWAY** to store something in a file for future reference **2. KEEP SOMETHING IN MIND** to take careful note of something in order to remember it

file[2] /fīl/ *n.* ENG **METAL TOOL** a metal tool, usually long and narrow and with sharpened ridges on one or more of its surfaces, that is used to smooth down or wear away wood or metal ■ *vti.* (**filed, fil·ing, files**) **MAKE SOMETHING SMOOTH USING A FILE** to smooth or wear away the surface of something using a file [Old English *fēol*. Ultimately via a prehistoric Germanic word from an Indo-European base meaning "to cut or carve," which also produced English *depict* and *pigment*.]

fi·lé /feè lày, fi láy/ *n.* a powder made from the ground leaves of the sassafras tree that is used in Cajun cooking to thicken and flavor soups, gumbos, and other dishes [Mid-19thC. From French, past participle of *filer* "to twist," from, ultimately, Latin *filum* "thread."]

file cab·i·net *n.* = **filing cabinet**

file ex·ten·sion *n.* a combination of characters following the period after the name of a file created with DOS-based software, certain combinations identifying the file as being of a standardized type

file·fish /fīl fìsh/ (*plural* **-fish** *or* **-fish·es**) *n.* a long bony tropical fish with rough-edged scales, a tiny mouth, and a sharp dorsal spine over the eye. Family: Balistidae.

Filegate /fīl gàyt/ *n.* a scandal in the Clinton White House involving the alleged improper acquisition and use by Clinton staffers of FBI background files of people with access to the White House property (*slang*)

file man·ag·er *n.* a computer program that helps to arrange and manipulate files and directories of files

file·name /fīl nàym/ *n.* a set of characters, sometimes restricted in number, serving as an identifying title for a computer file and often including a file extension

file serv·er *n.* a computer in a network that stores application programs and data files accessed by the other computers in the network

fi·let /fi láy, feèlày/ *n.* COOK = **fillet** *n.* 1 ■ *vt.* COOK = **fillet** *v.* 1 [Mid-19thC. French form of FILLET.]

fi·let cro·chet *n.* crochet in the form of a square mesh stitched with a double crochet stitch, in which the combination of holes and filled-in squares creates the pattern [From French]

fi·let mi·gnon *n.* a small round boneless beefsteak cut from the inside of the loin and usually grilled, fried, or broiled

fil·i·al /fíllee əl/ *adj.* **1. OF CHILDREN TO PARENTS** relating or appropriate to a child's relationship with, or feelings toward, his or her parents ○ *filial duty* **2.** GENETICS **DESCRIBING FIRST HYBRID GENERATION** used to describe the first generation that results from crossing two parental lines [15thC. Directly or via Old French from late Latin *filialis* "of a son or daughter," from Latin *filius* "son" and *filia* "daughter."] —**fil·i·al·ly** *adv.* —**fil·i·al·ness** *n.*

fil·i·a·tion /fíllee áysh'n/ *n.* **1. PROCESS OF ESTABLISHING PATERNITY** the process of determining legally who is the father of a child whose paternity is in dispute **2. BEING SOMEBODY'S CHILD** the condition of being the child of particular parents (*formal*)

fil·i·bus·ter /fílli bùstər/ *n.* **1.** POL **POLITICAL DELAYING TACTIC** a tactic such as a long irrelevant speech or several such speeches used to delay or prevent the passage of legislation **2.** POL **LEGISLATIVE OBSTRUCTOR** somebody who uses obstructive tactics to prevent the passage of legislation **3.** MIL **MILITARY ADVENTURER** somebody who is a mercenary or irregular in a revolutionary army of a foreign country ■ *v.* (**-tered, -ter·ing, -ters**) **1.** *vti.* **TRY TO BLOCK LEGISLATION WITH A FILIBUSTER** to try to stop legislation being passed by making long speeches **2.** *vi.* MIL **BE A MILITARY ADVENTURER ABROAD** to serve as a mercenary or irregular in a revolutionary army of a foreign country [Mid-19thC. Via Spanish *filibustero* from, ultimately, Dutch *vrijbuiter* "pirate" (source of English *freebooter*).] —**fil·i·bus·ter·er** *n.* —**fil·i·bus·ter·ism** *n.* —**fil·i·bus·ter·ous** *adj.*

fil·i·cide /fílli sīd/ *n.* (*formal*) **1. KILLING OF OWN CHILD** the killing by a parent of a son or daughter **2. KILLER OF OWN CHILD** a parent who kills his or her own son or daughter [Mid-17thC. From Latin *filius* "son" or *filia* "daughter."] —**fil·i·cid·al** /fílli sīd'l/ *adj.*

fil·i·form /fílli fàwrm, fīli-/ *adj.* BIOL long, thin, and fine like a thread [Mid-18thC. From Latin *filum* "thread" + FORM.]

AKG London

Filigree: Detail of decorative filigree and jeweled medieval book cover (1225–30)

fil·i·gree /fílli greè/ *n.* **1. LACY METAL ORNAMENTATION** delicate decorative openwork made from thin twisted wire in silver, gold, or another metal **2. DELICATE WORK** a delicate ornamental tracery ■ *adj.* **IN A DELICATE PATTERN** made in a delicate ornamental openwork design ■ *vt.* (**-greed, -gree·ing, -grees**) **FORM SOMETHING INTO A DELICATE PATTERN** to form something into a delicate ornamental openwork design [Late 17thC. An alteration of French *filigrane* "filigree" from Italian *filigrana*, from Latin *filum* "thread" + *granum* "grain."]

fil·ing /fíling/ *n.* a tiny particle or shaving of metal, such as might have been removed with a file (*often used in the plural*) ○ *iron filings*

fil·ing cab·i·net *n.* a piece of office furniture containing drawers for storing files

fil·i·o·pi·e·tis·tic /fíllee ō pī ə tístik/ *adj.* having great reverence for ancestors (*formal*) [Late 19thC. From Latin *filius* "son," *filia* "daughter" + PIETISTIC.]

Fil·i·pi·no /fíllə peè nō/, **Pil·i·pi·no** *adj.* **Fil·i·pi·no, Phil·ip·pine OF THE PHILIPPINES** relating to or typical of the Philippines or their people or culture ■ *n.* (*plural* **-nos**) **1.** LANG **OFFICIAL LANGUAGE OF THE PHILIPPINES** the official language of the Philippines, an Austronesian language based on Tagalog. Over 15,000,000 people speak Filipino. **2.** PEOPLES **SOMEBODY FROM THE PHILIPPINES** somebody who was born or raised in the Philippines, or who has Philippine citizenship

fill /fil/ *v.* (**filled, fill·ing, fills**) **1.** *vti.* **MAKE SOMETHING FULL OR BECOME FULL** to make a container full, or become full ○ *The bathtub filled rapidly.* **2.** *vt.* **TAKE UP ALL THE SPACE** to take up all or most of the space inside or cover the whole or most of the surface area of something ○ *the room was filled with light* **3.** *vt.* **COVER A BLANK AREA** to cover a page or a blank space on a page with writing or drawing **4.** *vt.* **BECOME ABUNDANT** to become present and very noticeable throughout something ○ *The scent of spring filled the air.* **5.** *vt.* **MAKE SOMEBODY FEEL SOMETHING POWERFULLY** to cause somebody to experience a strong emotion, usually to the exclusion of all others ○ *The news filled me with dread.* **6.** *vt.* **CLOSE UP A HOLE** to plug a hole, crack, or cavity in something **7.** *vt.* **MEET A NEED** to satisfy a need or requirement ○ *The retreat filled her need for solitude.* **8.** *vt.* **OCCUPY FREE TIME** to occupy a period of time with an activity ○ *They filled their days with busywork until she returned.* **9.** *vt.* **PROVIDE** to carry out somebody's instructions to supply something ○ *fill a prescription* **10.** *vt.* POL **HOLD OFFICE** to hold a job or office and carry out the duties associated with it **11.** *vt.* **CHOOSE SOMEBODY** to elect or appoint somebody to a job or position **12.** *vt.* COOK **PUT A FILLING INTO SOMETHING** to put a type of food into something such as a cake or sandwich as its filling **13.** *vt.* CONSTR **ADD SOMETHING TO RAISE A SURFACE LEVEL** to build up the surface of something with earth, stones, or other materials until it reaches a desired level **14.** *vti.* NAUT **POWER A SAIL WITH WIND** to stretch a sail and make it bulge out, or bulge out under the pressure of the wind ■ *n.* **1. PLENTY OF SOMETHING** a sufficient or excessive quantity of something ○ *I've had my fill of his complaints.* **2. ENOUGH TO MAKE A CONTAINER FULL** enough of something to fill a container, or the act of filling a container **3.** CONSTR **MATERIAL TO RAISE A SURFACE** material, e.g., earth or stones, used to build up the surface of something to a desired level **4.** MUSIC **IMPROVISED MUSIC** music improvised to fill designated spaces in a jazz or other musical score [Old English *fyllan*, ultimately from a prehistoric Germanic word]

fill in *v.* **1.** *vt.* **COLOR A BLANK SPACE ON SOMETHING** to cover a blank space on something with coloring or shading **2.** *vt.* **PLUG A CAVITY AND MAKE THE SURFACE LEVEL** to put material into a cavity in a surface to make the surface level **3.** *vt.* **OCCUPY TIME** to spend a period of time that would otherwise be unoccupied in an activity **4.** *vi.* **SUBSTITUTE FOR SOMEBODY** to act as a substitute for somebody **5.** *vt.* **GIVE SOMEBODY INFORMATION** to supply somebody with information about something **6.** *vt.* = **fill out** *v.* 1

fill out *v.* **1.** *vt.* **COMPLETE THE BLANK SPACES IN SOMETHING** to write information into the blank spaces on a form or document **2.** *vti.* **BECOME OR MAKE SOMETHING BIGGER** to become or make something larger and more substantial

fill up *v.* **1.** *vti.* **BECOME OR MAKE SOMETHING FULL** to become full, or make something full **2.** *vt.* **SATISFY SOMEBODY'S HUNGER** to give somebody the feeling of having eaten enough **3.** *vi.* CARS **MAKE FUEL TANK FULL** to fill a vehicle's tank with fuel

fille de joie (*plural* **filles de joie**) *n.* a woman prostitute (*used euphemistically*) [From French, literally "girl of pleasure"]

filled gold *n.* a thin layer of gold bonded to a backing layer of brass or other base metal

fill·er /fíllər/ *n.* **1. SOMETHING THAT FILLS** somebody who or something that fills something **2. PLUGGING OR COATING SUBSTANCE** a substance used to plug a crack or cavity or smooth a surface before painting or varnishing **3. SUBSTANCE ADDED FOR BULK** a substance such as sizing that is used to fill spaces or add bulk or strength to a material **4.** PRESS, BROADCAST **LESS IMPORTANT MATERIAL** something, often relatively unimportant, added to fill space, e.g., in a newspaper or between items in a broadcast or performance **5. TOBACCO FILLING** the tobacco inside a cigar or cigarette **6.** INDUST **PADDING** a material such as cotton or down that is used to stuff something such as a quilt or toy

fil·lér /fí làir/ *n.* **1. HUNGARIAN CURRENCY UNIT** a subunit of currency in Hungary one hundred of which make a forint. See table at **currency 2.** MONEY **COIN WORTH A FILLÉR** a coin worth one fillér [Early 20thC. From Hungarian.]

fil·let /fi láy/ *n.* **1.** COOK **BONELESS PORTION OF FISH OR MEAT** a boneless portion cut from a fish, a poultry breast, or the rib area of beef, lamb, or pork **2.** ACCESSORIES

RIBBON WORN AROUND THE HEAD a ribbon or narrow band of fabric worn around the head across the forehead, as an ornament or to hold back the hair **3.** ARCHIT FLAT NARROW MOLDING a raised or sunken ornamental surface set between larger surfaces **4.** PRINTING DECORATIVE LINE ON THE COVER OF BOOK a thin decorative line impressed onto the cover of a book, or the tool used to make it ■ *vt.* (**-let·ed, -let·ing, -lets**) **1.** FOOD CUT A FILLET FROM SOMETHING to cut and prepare boneless portions of fish, poultry, or meat **2.** USE A FILLET AS BINDING OR DECORATION to bind hair or decorate a surface with a fillet [14thC. Via Old French *filet* from, ultimately, Latin *filum* "thread."]

fill-in *n.* a temporary replacement or substitute for somebody

fill·ing /filling/ *n.* **1.** DENT PLUG FOR A DECAYED TOOTH a plug made of metal or composite material, used to fill a cavity in a decayed tooth **2.** GETTING SOMETHING FILLED the process or an instance of having something such as a cavity in a tooth filled **3.** SOMETHING USED TO FILL SOMETHING a substance or material used to fill the space inside something, pad it, or add bulk to it **4.** FOOD FOOD MIXTURE PUT INSIDE SOMETHING a food mixture that is put inside something else such as a pie, pastry case, or sandwich **5.** TEXTILES THREADS GOING ACROSS FABRIC the horizontal threads or yarn in a woven fabric ■ *adj.* SATISFYING HUNGER leaving somebody with the feeling of having eaten enough

fill·ing sta·tion *n.* a gas station

fil·lip /fillip/ *n.* **1.** FEELING OF ENCOURAGEMENT something that stimulates or encourages something or somebody **2.** SNAPPING MOVEMENT OF THE FINGERTIP AGAINST THE THUMB a snapping of the tip of one of the fingers against the ball of the thumb in order to make a sound or to propel a small object ■ *vt.* (**-liped, -lip·ing, -lips**) **1.** PROPEL SOMETHING WITH A FILLIP to strike or propel something by snapping the fingertip against the ball of the thumb **2.** GIVE SOMEBODY OR SOMETHING AN INCENTIVE to provide a stimulus or encouragement to somebody or something [15thC. An imitation of the sound of flicking or snapping the fingers.]

fill light *n.* in photography and filmmaking, a secondary source of light used to eliminate, reduce, or soften shadows

Fill·more /fil màwr/, **Millard** (1800–74) U.S. statesman and 13th president of the United States. A member of the Whig Party, he served as vice president (1849–50) before assuming the presidency (1850–53) upon the death of Zachary Taylor.

fill-up *n.* a filling of something, especially a vehicle's fuel tank

fil·ly /fillee/ (*plural* **-lies**) *n.* **1.** ZOOL YOUNG FEMALE HORSE a female horse under four years of age **2.** OFFENSIVE TERM an a offensive term for a young woman or girl (*dated informal offensive*) [15thC. From Old Norse *fylja*. Ultimately from a prehistoric Germanic word that is also the ancestor of English *foal*.]

film /film/ *n.* **1.** CINEMA = **movie 2.** CINEMA MOTION PICTURES COLLECTIVELY movies collectively, considered as a medium for recording events, a form of entertainment, or an art form **3.** PHOTOGRAPHY COATED STRIP FOR TAKING PICTURES a thin translucent strip or sheet of cellulose coated with an emulsion sensitive to light, used in a camera to take still or moving pictures **4.** INDUST VERY THIN SHEET OF SOMETHING material, especially a plastic, in the form of a very thin, flexible, and usually translucent or transparent sheet, often used for wrapping things **5.** THIN LAYER a thin coating of a substance such as dust, liquid, or ice covering the surface of something **6.** SOMETHING MAKING A VIEW HAZY a thin haze or mist, or something similar that blurs somebody's view ■ **films** *npl. U.K.* CINEMA MOVIE INDUSTRY the motion-picture industry (*informal*) ■ *v.* (**filmed, film·ing, films**) **1.** *vt.* PHOTOGRAPHY TAKE PICTURES OF SOMETHING to record somebody or something on film **2.** *vti.* CINEMA MAKE A MOTION PICTURE to make or be involved in the making of a motion picture **3.** *vt.* CINEMA MAKE MOVIE OF SOMETHING to make a motion picture of a book, story, or event **4.** *vi.* CINEMA BE GOOD FOR FILMING to be a suitable subject for cinematic treatment ○ *a story that would film well* **5.** *vt.* COVER WITH A THIN LAYER to cover the surface of something with a thin coating of a substance [Old English *filmen* "membrane, skin," ultimately via a prehistoric Germanic word from an Indo-European base that also produced English *pelt*]

film over *vi.* to become covered with a thin or misty layer of something

film badge *n.* a piece of photographic film incorporated into a badge and used to register the wearer's exposure to nuclear radiation

film·go·er /film gō ər/ *n. U.K.* = **moviegoer**

film·ic /filmik/ *adj.* characteristic or reminiscent of a movie, especially in the techniques used to tell a story or describe a scene —**film·i·cal·ly** *adv.*

film li·brar·y *n.* a large collection of motion pictures or newsreels used as an archive

film·mak·er /film màykər/ *n.* somebody who produces or directs movies —**film·mak·ing** *n.*

film noir (*plural* **films noirs**) *n.* a motion picture of a type popular in the 1940s and 1950s, often filmed in urban settings with extensive use of shadows, cynical in outlook and featuring antiheroes [Mid-20thC. From French, literally "black film."]

film·og·ra·phy /fil móggrəfee/ (*plural* **-phies**) *n.* **1.** LIST OF MOVIES a list of the motion pictures made by a particular actor or director, or on a particular subject **2.** WRITING ABOUT MOVIES writing about motion pictures [Mid-20thC. A blend of FILM and BIBLIOGRAPHY.]

film·set·ting /film sètting/ *n.* = **photocomposition** —**film·set** *vt.* —**film·set·ter** *n.*

film star *n. U.K.* = **movie star**

film·strip /film strip/ *n.* a length of developed photographic film containing a series of still images to be projected on a screen

film·y /filmee/ (**-i·er, -i·est**) *adj.* **1.** LIGHT AND AIRY consisting or made of very thin translucent material **2.** COVERED WITH A FILM covered or misted over with a thin layer of something —**film·i·ly** *adv.* —**film·i·ness** *n.*

fi·lo /fée lō/, **fi·lo pas·try** *n. U.K.* = **phyllo** [Mid-20thC. From Greek *phullo* "leaf."]

FILO /fī lō/ *abbr.* ACCT first in, last out

fils[1] /fils/ (*plural* **filses** *or* **fils**) *n.* MONEY **1.** ARAB CURRENCY UNIT a subunit of currency in Iraq, Bahrain, Jordan, Kuwait, and Yemen, one hundred of which are equivalent to one riyal. See table at **currency 2.** COIN WORTH A FILS a coin worth one fils [Late 19thC. From Arabic *fals*, a small copper coin.]

fils[2] /feess/ *n.* in France and French-speaking countries, a word used after a man's or boy's surname to distinguish him from his father of the same name ○ *Henri Dupont fils.* ◊ **père** [Late 19thC. From French, "son."]

fil·ter /filtər/ *n.* **1.** STRAINING DEVICE a device made of or containing a porous material used to collect particles from a liquid or gas passing through it **2.** POROUS MATERIAL USED FOR STRAINING any porous layer or material such as sand, paper, or cloth, used in or as a filter **3.** PHOTOGRAPHY TINTED SCREEN a tinted glass or dyed gelatin screen placed on a camera lens to reduce light intensity, exclude some types of light, control the rendering of color, or distort an image **4.** ELECTRON ENG DEVICE RESTRICTING THE PASSAGE OF FREQUENCIES an acoustic, electric, electronic, or optical device, instrument, or computer program that allows the passage of some frequencies or digital elements and blocks others **5.** = **filter tip** *n.* **1 6.** CHEM ENG DEVICE FOR REMOVING PARTICLES a separating medium or device for removing small particles from a gas or liquid by mechanical interception, based mainly on the difference between the size of the partcles and the openings in the filter medium, but sometimes also aided by electrostatic forces ■ *v.* (**-tered, -ter·ing, -ters**) **1.** *vt.* PASS SOMETHING THROUGH A FILTER to put something such as a fluid, light, or electrical impulses through a filter to remove or recover something **2.** *vi.* PASS THROUGH SOMETHING to seep or pass through a filter or something that is intended to act as a barrier ○ *The sunlight filtered in through the shutters.* **3.** *vi.* TRICKLE to move or pass slowly and gradually ○ *People filtered into the auditorium.* [14thC. Via Old French *filtre* "felt" (used for filtering liquids, the original sense in English), from medieval Latin *filtrum*. Ultimately, from a prehistoric Germanic word that also produced English *felt*.] —**fil·ter·er** *n.* —**fil·ter·less** *adj.*

fil·ter·a·ble /filtərəb'l, filtrəb'l/, **fil·tra·ble** /filtrəb'l/ *adj.* capable of being passed through a filter —**fil·ter·a·bil·i·ty** /filtərə bíllətee, filtrə-/ *n.*

fil·ter bed *n.* a thick layer of sand, gravel, charcoal, or other filtering material in a tank, used to remove sewage or other impurities from liquids

fil·ter cof·fee *n.* = **drip coffee**

fil·ter feed·er *n.* an aquatic animal such as a clam, sponge, or baleen whale that feeds on particles or small organisms that it filters from the water —**fil·ter feed·ing** *n.*

fil·ter pa·per *n.* a type of porous paper used as or in a filter

fil·ter tip *n.* **1.** FILTERING DEVICE ON A CIGARETTE a small cylindrical mouthpiece made of a dense porous material attached to the end of a cigarette to remove tar and other impurities from the smoke **2.** FILTERED CIGARETTE a cigarette with a filter tip —**fil·ter-tipped** *adj.*

filth /filth/ *n.* **1.** FOUL DIRT dirt or refuse that is disgusting or excessive **2.** MORALLY OBJECTIONABLE MATERIAL something considered extremely morally objectionable or obscene, e.g., coarse language or explicit descriptions or depictions of sexual activity [Old English *fȳlð*, ultimately from a prehistoric Germanic word that is also the ancestor of English *foul*]

filth·y /filthee/ *adj.* (**-i·er, -i·est**) **1.** EXTREMELY DIRTY extremely or disgustingly dirty ○ *your hands are filthy!* **2.** MORALLY OBJECTIONABLE considered extremely morally objectionable or obscene **3.** DESPICABLE used to express contempt or strong disapproval (*informal*) ○ *a filthy liar* ■ *adv.* VERY to an extreme degree (*informal*) ○ *filthy rich* —**filth·i·ly** *adv.* —**filth·i·ness** *n.*

WORD KEY: SYNONYMS

See Synonyms at *dirty*.

fil·tra·ble *adj.* = **filterable**

fil·trate /fil trayt/ *n.* FILTERED MATERIAL the material that emerges from a filtering process, usually a liquid or gas from which impurities have been removed ■ *vti.* (**-trat·ed, -trat·ing, -trates**) PASS THROUGH A FILTER to pass through or put something through a filter [Early 17thC. From modern Latin *filtrat-*, past participle stem of *filtrare* "to filter," from medieval Latin *filtrum* (see FILTER).]

fil·tra·tion /fil tráysh'n/ *n.* the process of passing through or putting something through a filter

fi·lum /fíləm/ (*plural* **-la** /-lə/) *n.* a fine part or structure of a living organism that is long and thin like a thread [Mid-19thC. From Latin, "thread, filament, fiber."]

fim·bri·a /fímbree ə/ (*plural* **-ae** /-ee/) *n.* ANAT a fringed border or part in the body, e.g., that found at the entrance to the fallopian tubes [Mid-18thC. From Latin, "border, fringe."] —**fim·bri·al** *adj.*

fim·bri·ate /fímbree ət/, **fim·bri·at·ed** /-àytəd/ *adj.* used to describe parts of organisms having a fringed border [15thC. From Latin *fimbriatus* "fringed," from *fimbria* "border, fringe."] —**fim·bri·a·tion** /fímbree áysh'n/ *n.*

fin[1] /fin/ *n.* **1.** ZOOL PART OF A FISH USED FOR MOTION a flexible organ, sometimes paddle-shaped, fan-shaped, or triangular, extending from the body of a fish or aquatic animal and helping to balance it or propel it through the water **2.** SHIPPING PART ATTACHED TO THE HULL OF SUBMARINE a wing-shaped often movable blade attached low on the hull of a vessel such as a submarine that helps to control and stabilize it **3.** AIR UPRIGHT PART OF AIRCRAFT'S TAIL a fixed vertical surface at the tail of an aircraft giving stability and to which the rudder is attached **4.** AIR, AEROSP STABILIZING STRUCTURE ON ROCKET OR MISSILE any small flat fixed structure extending from the body of a rocket, missile, or aircraft, often near the tail, to give stability in flight **5.** RIB ON A HEATING DEVICE a flat metal part projecting from a heating mechanism such as a radiator that helps to increase the transfer of heat to the surrounding air **6.** SWIMMING = **flipper 7.** CARS DECORATIVE EXTENSION ON AN AUTOMOBILE BODY an ornamental extension on the body of a motor vehicle, especially on the rear fender ■ *vi.* (**finned, fin·ning, fins**) SWIM USING FINS to swim or beat the water with fins, or show a fin above water [Old English *fin(n)*. Ultimately from a prehistoric Germanic word that probably came from Latin *pinna* "feather, wing" (source of English *pin, pinion*, and *pinnacle*).] —**finned** *adj.*

fin[2] /fin/ *n.* MONEY a five-dollar bill (*informal*) [Mid-19thC. Shortening of Yiddish *finef* "five," ultimately from a prehistoric Germanic word that is also the ancestor of English *five*.]

FIN *abbr.* Finland

fin. *abbr.* **1.** finance **2.** financial **3.** finish

Fin. *abbr.* **1.** Finland **2.** Finnish

fin·a·ble /fínəb'l/ *adj.* subject to or punishable by a fine

fi·na·gle /fi náyg'l/ (**-gled, -gling, -gles**) *vti.* to trick, cheat, or manipulate somebody in order to obtain or achieve something (*informal*) ○ *He finagled his way out of the difficulty.* [Early 20thC. Probably from dialectal *fainaigue*, of unknown origin.] —**fi·na·gler** *n.*

fi·nal /fín'l/ *adj.* **1.** LAST last of a number or series of similar things ○ *a final reminder* **2.** ALLOWING NO CHANGE conclusive and allowing no further discussion ○ *the editor's decision is final* **3.** ENDING occurring at the end of something ○ *the final curtain* ■ *n.* END OF A SERIES the last and most important in a series of sports or other contests that decides the winner of a tournament or competition ■ **fi·nals** *npl.* **1.** SPORTS LAST DECISIVE ROUNDS OF A TOURNAMENT the last decisive rounds of a tournament or competition during which the winners of previous rounds play each other **2.** EDUC EXAMINATIONS AT THE END OF A UNIVERSITY COURSE the examinations that take place at the end of a course of study or studies for a professional qualification [14thC. Directly or via French from Latin *finalis* "last," from *finis* "final moment, end" (source of English *finance* and *finish*).]

fi·nal ap·proach *n.* the last stage of an aircraft's descent before landing, from its turning into line with the runway to the procedures immediately preceding touchdown

fi·nal cut *n.* the approved and edited version of a movie prior to its being released for viewing by the public

fi·nal·e /fi nállee, -naálee/ *n.* **1.** THEATER FINAL THEATRICAL NUMBER a scene or number that brings a stage performance or an act of a performance to an end **2.** MUSIC FINAL MOVEMENT a final movement or section of a musical composition **3.** FINAL EVENT IN A SERIES an event that is the last or climactic event in a series [Mid-18thC. Via Italian from Latin *finalis* (see FINAL).]

fi·nal·ist /fín'list/ *n.* somebody who has qualified to take part in the finals of a tournament or competition

fi·nal·i·ty /fī nállətee, fi nállətee/ (*plural* **-ties**) *n.* **1.** QUALITY OF BEING FINAL the quality, state, or condition of being concluded or decided, permitting no further progress or development ○ *he spoke with an air of finality* **2.** FINAL ACTION an act, belief, or statement that is final

fi·nal·ize /fín'l īz/ (**-ized, -iz·ing, -iz·es**) *v.* **1.** *vti.* PUT SOMETHING INTO FINAL FORM to bring something to a point at which everything has been agreed upon and arranged **2.** *vt.* COMPLETE SOMETHING to complete an agreement, sale, or other transaction —**fi·nal·i·za·tion** /fín'li záysh'n/ *n.* —**fi·nal·iz·er** /fín'l īzər/ *n.*

WORD KEY: USAGE

finalize or **make final**? Though ***finalize*** has been in use for many years, even increasing in currency by the end of the 20th century, it is regarded with extreme disdain by many people in spite of its obvious utility in being a more concise way of saying "make final." Therefore, those people wanting their writing to be above reproach will avoid using it, substituting *finish*, *complete*, or *make final*.

fi·nal·ly /fín'lee/ *adv.* **1.** AT LAST after a long period of time or a long delay and often after previous unsuccessful attempts ○ *So you've finally decided to ask her out, right?* **2.** DEFINITIVELY in a way that rules out further continuance, change, or discussion ○ *The venue won't be finally decided until the next meeting.* **3.** AS LAST IN THE SERIES as the last in a series of things or actions ○ *We visited Belgium, Holland, Germany, and finally Switzerland.* **4.** AS THE LAST THING TO BE SAID used to introduce the last in a series of things said by somebody ○ *Finally, I'd like to thank all of you for coming here tonight.*

Fi·nal So·lu·tion, **fi·nal so·lu·tion** *n.* the plan to murder systematically all the Jews of Europe, conceived and put into action by the Nazis during World War II [Translation of German *Endlösung*]

fi·nance /fī nàns, fi náns/ *n.* **1.** CONTROL OF MONEY the business or art of managing the monetary resources of an organization, country, or individual ○ *high finance* **2.** MONEY NECESSARY TO DO SOMETHING the money necessary to do something, especially to fund a project ■ **fi·nanc·es** *npl.* THE MONEY SOMEBODY HAS the money at the disposal of a person, organization, or country ○ *It'll depend on the state of my finances at the end of the month.* ■ *vt.* (**-nanced, -nanc·ing, -nanc·es**) PROVIDE MONEY FOR SOMETHING to raise or provide the money required for something or by somebody [14thC. From French, from *finer* "to end, settle" (the original sense in English) from, ultimately, Latin *finis* "end." Its present-day monetary connotation derived from the notion of settling a debt.] —**fi·nance·a·ble** *adj.*

fi·nance bill *n.* an act passed by a legislature to raise or provide money for public expenditure

fi·nance com·pa·ny *n.* a business enterprise that loans money to individuals or companies against collateral, especially to buy homes or items on an installment plan

fi·nan·cial /fi nánshəl, fī nánshəl/ *adj.* relating to or involving money or finance —**fi·nan·cial·ly** *adv.*

Fi·nan·cial Times In·dus·tri·al Or·di·nar·y Share In·dex *n.* an index of prices on the London Stock Exchange based on the average price of thirty shares. It is produced by the *Financial Times*.

Fi·nan·cial Times Stock Ex·change 100 In·dex *n.* full form of **FTSE 100 Index**

fi·nan·cial year *n. U.K.* = **fiscal year**

fin·an·cier /fìnnən seér, fínnən seér/ *n.* somebody who is practiced or skilled in financial matters and considerable personal wealth [Early 17thC. From French, formed from *finance* (see FINANCE).]

fin·back /fín bàk/ *n.* a large baleen whale that has a prominent dorsal fin. Latin name: *Balaenoptera physalus.*

Finch

finch /finch/ *n.* a small songbird that has a short broad seed-eating bill and colorful plumage in males. Family: Fringillidae. [Old English *finc*, from prehistoric Germanic]

Finch /finch/, **Peter** (1916–77) British actor. A stage and screen performer, he received a posthumous Academy Award for his role in *Network* (1976). Full name **Peter George Frederick Ingle Finch**

find /fīnd/ *v.* (**found, found** /fownd/, **find·ing, finds**) **1.** *vt.* DISCOVER SOMETHING to discover something or somebody after a search ○ *He was found wandering a mile from his home.* **2.** *vt.* GET SOMETHING BACK to recover something after losing it ○ *I can't find my car keys.* **3.** *vt.* DISCOVER SOMETHING FOR FIRST TIME to realize, understand, or locate something for the first time, especially by studying or observing ○ *We have to find answers to the problem of global warming.* **4.** *vt.* DISCOVER SOMETHING ACCIDENTALLY to notice or come across somebody or something by chance ○ *I found my glasses under the table.* **5.** *vt.* EXPERIENCE SOMETHING to notice or experience something personally ○ *They found great comfort in their work.* ○ *I think you'll find them easy to get along with.* **6.** *vt.* MANAGE TO GET SOMETHING to make a special effort to gather something together or summon something up ○ *I don't know where we'll find the money.* **7.** *vt.* REACH GOAL to succeed in reaching something aimed for ○ *He has finally found his place as a world-class tennis player.* **8.** *vt.* SCI RECORD AS OCCURRING to observe something such as a natural species as existing or occurring (*often passive*) ○ *This species is found all across the continent.* **9.** *vti.* LAW REACH A VERDICT to decide about something or somebody at the end of a legal procedure, or announce the decision reached ○ *The jury found for the plaintiff.* **10.** *vt.* SUPPLY NEED to bring or provide something that is necessary for a process to occur ○ *You will need to find your own transportation and equipment for the job.* **11.** *vr.* BECOME CONSCIOUS OF YOUR OWN CONDITION to become aware of being in a particular place or state ○ *He found himself in an empty street.* **12.** *vr.* MAKE DECISIONS ABOUT YOUR OWN LIFE to become more self-aware and self-motivated (*informal*) ○ *She finally found herself and became a successful artist.* ■ *n.* DISCOVERY something noteworthy or valuable that has been found, or somebody who is talented and is brought to public attention ○ *a real find* [Old English *findan*. Ultimately from an Indo-European word meaning "to tread or go," which is also the ancestor of English *path*, *peripatetic*, and *pontiff*.] —**find·a·ble** *adj.*

find out *v.* **1.** *vti.* DISCOVER INFORMATION to get to know something, especially by asking somebody or searching in an appropriate source, or just by chance ○ *I don't know how they found out about the proposed merger.* **2.** *vt.* DETECT WRONGDOING to detect and expose an offense ○ *He was quickly found out and his lies exposed.*

find·er /fíndər/ *n.* **1.** SOMEBODY FINDING THINGS somebody who or something that locates something **2.** ASTRON SMALL TELESCOPE ATTACHED TO LARGER TELESCOPE a small wide-angle telescope attached parallel to the optical axis of a larger telescope to help locate celestial objects

fin de siè·cle *n.* the final years of the 19th century, characterized as being a time of decadence and self-doubt [From French, literally "end of the century"]

find·ing /fínding/ *n.* **1.** RESEARCH RESULT a piece of information obtained from an investigation, especially scientific research **2.** LAW VERDICT a conclusion that is reached and recorded at the end of a judicial or other formal inquiry ■ *npl.* MATERIALS FOR CRAFTWORK small articles or tools used in making craftwork, e.g., metal clips used on earrings

fine[1] /fīn/ *adj.* **1.** VERY WELL OR SATISFACTORY in a good, acceptable, or comfortable condition (*informal*) ○ *The patient is doing fine.* **2.** NOT COARSE made up of tiny particles ○ *fine sand* **3.** SUNNY with sunny and clear skies ○ *a fine morning* **4.** THIN very thin, sharp, or delicate ○ *fine features* ○ *fine hair* **5.** GOOD-LOOKING very good to look at ○ *a fine view of the valley* **6.** OUTSTANDING far better than the average ○ *a fine wine* **7.** UNPLEASANT extremely unsuitable or undesirable (*informal*) (*used ironically*) ○ *This is a fine mess!* **8.** SPURIOUSLY IMPRESSIVE sounding or looking good, but probably just for show (*used ironically*) ○ *nothing but fine gestures* **9.** DELICATELY FORMED showing special skill, detail, or intricacy, especially in artistic work ○ *fine detail* **10.** SMALL AND DELICATE set very closely and carefully together ○ *fine stitching* **11.** VERY SUBTLE so particular or small that it may hardly be noticeable ○ *a maze of fine legal detail* ○ *a fine distinction* **12.** EXTREMELY PURE with any or most impurities removed, especially in a precious metal ■ *adv.* **1.** WELL very well (*informal*) ○ *It works just fine.* **2.** INTO SMALL PIECES into tiny or delicate bits ○ *Chop the onions very fine.* ■ *v.* (**fined, fin·ing, fines**) **1.** *vt.* SHARPEN to make something thinner or sharper (*technical*) **2.** *vti.* PURIFY to purify beer or wine [13thC. From French *fin*, from, ultimately Latin *finire* "to finish" (see FINISH). The underlying sense is of something finished.]

WORD KEY: ORIGIN

The Latin word *finire* from which ***fine*** is derived is also the source of English *affinity*, *confine*, *define*, *final*, *finance*, *finesse*, *finish*, *finite*, *paraffin*, and *refine*.

fine[2] /fīn/ *n.* LAW CASH PAID AS PUNISHMENT a sum of money that somebody is ordered to pay for breaking a law or rule ■ *vt.* (**fined, fin·ing, fines**) LAW PUNISH BY IMPOSING A PAYMENT to take a fixed amount of money from somebody who has broken a rule or a law [13thC. Via French *fin* from Latin *finis* "end," used in medieval Latin to denote a sum to be paid on completion of legal proceedings.]

fine[3] /feen/ *n.* = **fine champagne**

fine[4] /feé nāy/ *n.* the place on a music score that shows where the piece finishes after a repeated section, or the symbol that marks the place [Late 18thC. From Italian, from Latin *finis* "end."]

fine art *n.* **1.** ARTS CREATION OF BEAUTIFUL OBJECTS artistic work that is meant to be appreciated for its own sake, rather than to serve some useful function **2.** EDUC COLLEGE COURSE IN ART a course of study designed to teach students practical artistic skills as well as the theory and history of art **3.** ARTS PURE ART any art form, e.g., painting, sculpture, architecture, drawing, or engraving, that is considered to have purely aesthetic value (*often used in the plural*) **4.** IMPRESSIVELY DETAILED TECHNIQUE something that requires great skill, talent, or precision (*informal*) ○ *the fine art of public speaking*

fine cham·pagne *n.* a liqueur brandy made in the Champagne region of France [Mid-19thC. From French *fine champagne* "fine (brandy from) Champagne."]

fine chem·i·cal *n.* a chemical product that is made in relatively small quantities and is typically high in cost, e.g., a flavoring or vitamin

fine-grained, **fine-grain** *adj.* formed with a smooth, even, or closely-patterned grain ○ *fine-grained wood*

fine·ly /fínlee/ *adv.* **1.** INTO SMALL PIECES into small, thin, or delicate pieces **2.** SKILLFULLY in a careful, delicate, or sensitive way ○ *an actor finely tuned to her audience's reactions* ○ *finely wrought*

fine print *n.* the detailed part of a document that is printed in small characters, often regarded with suspicion as containing unattractive conditions the author hopes the signer will not notice

fin·er·y /fínəree/ *n.* clothing, jewelry, or accessories that are especially dressy and stylish, usually worn on special occasions [Late 17thC. Formed from FINE, modeled on BRAVERY.]

fines herbes /feenz érb/ *npl.* a mixture of finely chopped herbs used to flavor a dish [From French, literally "fine herbs"]

fine·spun /fín spún/ *adj.* spun or stretched out thinly ○ *finespun yarn*

fi·nesse /fi néss/ *n.* **1.** PHYSICAL SKILL elegant ability and dexterity ○ *As a top-flight tennis star, she made up in finesse what she lacked in power.* **2.** TACTFUL TREATMENT a delicate and skillful approach in dealing with a troublesome situation **3.** BRIDGE TACTIC IN BRIDGE in bridge, an attempt to win a trick with a lower-value card while holding a higher card not in sequence, hoping that your left-hand opponent will not play a card of intervening value ■ *v.* (**-nessed, -ness·ing, -ness·es**) **1.** *vti.* BRIDGE TRY WINNING A TRICK WITH A LOWER CARD in bridge, to attempt to win a trick with a lower-value card while holding a higher card not in sequence, hoping that your left-hand opponent will not play a card of intervening value **2.** *vt.* CONTROL IN A DEVIOUS WAY to use subtle tricks or deception to manipulate something or somebody ○ *He finessed the competition by praising one course then doing quite the opposite.* [Mid-16thC. From French, literally "fineness," from *fin* (see FINE[1]). The word originally denoted purity, especially of metals, or delicacy.]

fine struc·ture *n.* the separation of light of particular wavelengths produced by atoms or molecules into two or more very similar wavelengths, caused by the interaction of particular quantum mechanical properties

fine-tooth comb, **fine-toothed comb** *n.* **1.** DETAILED APPROACH a thorough approach to an investigation or search, examining every detail ○ *went over the figures with a fine-tooth comb but failed to find the error* **2.** TOOL FOR COMBING THOROUGHLY a comb with very narrow tightly-set teeth

fine-tune (**fine-tuned, fine-tun·ing, fine-tunes**) *v.* **1.** *vt.* IMPROVE ENGINE PERFORMANCE OF to adjust the engine of a motor vehicle to improve its performance **2.** *vti.* GET SOMETHING JUST RIGHT to make tiny adjustments to something to achieve the best possible performance or appearance —**fine-tun·ing** *n.*

fin·foot /fín fòòt/ (*plural* **-foots** *or* **-foot**) *n.* BIRDS = **sungrebe**

Fingal's Cave

Fin·gal's Cave /fíng g'lz-/ cave on Staffa Island in the Inner Hebrides, off the western coast of Scotland. Height: 60 ft./18 m. Length: 228 ft./70 m.

fin·ger /fíng gər/ *n.* **1.** ANAT DIGIT OF THE HAND any of the digits of the hand, sometimes excluding the thumb (*often used before a noun*) **2.** CLOTHES PART OF GLOVE any of the long narrow parts of a glove that fits the finger **3.** NARROW STRIP something that resembles a finger in shape ○ *a finger of sand* **4.** FOOD LONG NARROW PORTION OF FOOD a small portion of food about as long and thick as a finger **5.** BEVERAGES APPROXIMATE QUANTITY OF ALCOHOL an approximate measure of alcoholic beverage in a glass, equal in depth to the width of a finger **6.** MEASURE APPROXIMATE UNIT OF LENGTH an approximate unit of measurement, equal to the width or length of a finger. = **digit** ■ *v.* (**-gered, -ger·ing, -gers**) **1.** *vt.* TOUCH to feel or move the fingers across something, often in a gentle, affectionate, or thoughtful way ○ *she fingered the fabric lovingly* **2.** *vt.* CRIMINOL GIVE UP TO POLICE to tell the police about the whereabouts or illegal activities of somebody (*slang*) **3.** *vti.* MUSIC PLAY INSTRUMENT USING THE FINGERS to handle the strings or keys of a musical instrument with the fingers **4.** *vt.* MUSIC MARK WITH INSTRUCTIONS FOR FINGERING to show on a musical score which fingers the musician should use **5.** *vt.* COMPUT LOCATE COMPUTER USERS to run a computer program that obtains and displays information about other users on the same computer or on other computers connected through a network or the Internet [Old English. Ultimately from an Indo-European word meaning "five," which is also the ancestor of English *five, fist, pentagon,* and *quintet.*] —**fin·ger·er** *n.* ◇ **cross your fingers** used to express a hope that things will turn out well ◇ **give (somebody) the finger** to make an aggressively obscene gesture with the middle finger extended upwards and held towards somebody (*slang*) ◇ **have a finger in every pie** to be involved in many advantageous or lucrative projects ◇ **have a finger in the pie** to be involved in a particular project, especially an advantageous or lucrative one ◇ **let something slip through your fingers** to fail to take advantage of something that would have been of benefit to you ◇ **put your finger on something** to identify something, especially something difficult or elusive ◇ **twist somebody around your little finger** to succeed in getting somebody to do exactly as you wish

fin·ger·board /fíng gər bàwrd/ *n.* a long strip of wood fixed on the neck of string instruments against which strings are pressed in order to vary the pitch

fin·ger bowl *n.* a small bowl of water set beside a place at a table so that fingers can be cleaned, e.g., after picking up food with the hands

fin·ger food *n.* small items of food made to be eaten with the fingers

fin·ger·fuck /fíng gər fùk/ (**-fucked, -fuck·ing, -fucks**) *vt.* to use the fingers to stimulate a woman's genitals (*slang taboo*)

fin·ger hole *n.* any one of a series of holes on a woodwind instrument that a player covers with the fingers in order to register a pitch

fin·ger·ing /fíng gəring/ *n.* **1.** MUSIC USE OF FINGERS ON MUSICAL INSTRUMENT the action or technique of using the fingers in playing a musical instrument **2.** USE OF FINGERS the use of the fingers to do something

Fin·ger Lakes /fíng gər làyks/ group of 11 glacial lakes in western New York, the center of the state's wine region.

fin·ger·ling /fíng gərling/ *n.* a small fish less than one year old, especially a salmon or trout

fin·ger·mark /fíng gər ma̍ark/ *n.* a smear or greasy mark left after somebody has touched something

fin·ger mil·let *n.* a short-stemmed millet with an ear divided into five parts, cultivated widely in southern India, Sri Lanka, and parts of Africa. Latin name: *Eleusine coracana.* [From its ears that resemble the fingers of a hand]

fin·ger·nail /fíng gər nàyl/ *n.* a flat protective layer of keratin that covers the end part of a finger's upper surface

fin·ger-paint (**fin·ger-paint·ed, fin·ger-paint·ing, fin·ger-paints**) *vti.* to put paint directly onto a surface with the fingers —**fin·ger-paint·ing** *n.*

fin·ger pick *n.* a musician's pick with a curved handle for attaching it to the finger

fin·ger·print /fíng gər prìnt/ *n.* **1.** PATTERN ON A FINGERTIP an impression of the curved lines of skin at the end of a finger that is left on a surface or made by pressing an inked finger onto paper **2.** DISTINGUISHING CHARACTERISTIC a unique characteristic, mark or pattern that can be used to identify somebody or something ■ *vt.* (**-print·ed, -print·ing, -prints**) RECORD THE FINGERPRINTS OF to press each of somebody's fingertips in ink and then onto paper to make a set of marks that can be used to identify the person

fin·ger·spell·ing /fíng gər spèlling/ *n.* a form of sign language communication using the fingers to gesture the spelling of words

fin·ger·stall /fíng gər stàwl/ *n.* a sheath-shaped protective covering worn over an injured finger

fin·ger·tip /fíng gər tìp/ *n.* FINGER'S END the tip of a finger ■ *adj.* USING THE FINGERTIPS involving the use of the fingertips and so very sensitive or delicate ○ *fingertip controls* ◇ **have something at your fingertips 1.** to know all the details of something thoroughly **2.** to have something available and nearby

fin·ger wave *n.* a wave made by shaping damp hair with the fingers and a comb

Fin·go /fíng gō/ (*plural* **-go** *or* **-gos**) *n.* a member of an African people who live among the Xhosa in the Eastern Cape province of South Africa [Early 19thC. From Xhosa *mfengu* "destitute wanderer."]

fin·i·al /fínnee əl/ *n.* **1.** ARCHIT ARCHITECTURAL DECORATION a carved decoration at the top of a gable, spire, or arched structure **2.** FURNITURE FURNITURE DECORATION an ornamental feature, e.g., a carved knob, on the top or end of a part of a piece of furniture **3.** PRINTING CURVE IN A TYPEFACE a curve that ends a main stroke in some italic typefaces [15thC. Via assumed Anglo-Norman or Anglo-Latin, literally "final," from, ultimately, Latin *finis* "end."] —**fin·i·aled** *adj.*

fin·ick·y /fínnikee/ (**-i·er, -i·est**), **fin·ick·ing** /fínniking/, **fin·i·cal** /-k'l/ *adj.* **1.** FUSSY concentrating too much on small unimportant details **2.** TOO DETAILED complicated by trivial details [Late 16thC. Earliest as *finical*, probably coined from FINE + -ICAL *Finicking* is recorded from the mid-17thC and *finicky* from the early 19thC.] —**fin·ick·i·ness** *n.*

WORD KEY: SYNONYMS

See Synonyms at ***careful.***

fin·ing /fíning/ *n.* **1.** CLARIFICATION OF LIQUID the process of clarifying a liquid, especially wine or beer **2.** INDUST REMOVING GAS FROM MOLTEN GLASS the process of removing undissolved gas from molten glass

fin·is /fínniss, finee/ *interj.* used to indicate that something has or must come to an end completely [14thC. From Latin, literally "end."]

fin·ish /fínnish/ *v.* (**-ished, -ish·ing, -ish·es**) **1.** *vti.* NO LONGER CONTINUE to come to an end, or bring something to an end ○ *we finished eating* **2.** *vt.* CONSUME to eat, drink, or use all of something ○ *Who finished the cake?* **3.** *vt.* DESTROY to kill, ruin, or exhaust somebody or something (*informal*) ○ *His dishonesty finished him in business.* **4.** *vt.* COMPLETE THE SURFACE EFFECT OF to treat something, especially wood or metal, in order to achieve a desired surface effect **5.** *vt.* MAKE JUST RIGHT to give something or somebody the final touches, qualities, or skills that are required to create a desired effect ■ *n.* **1.** END PART the terminating part of something **2.** SPECIAL TOP LAYER a surface texture or final coat applied to something, especially wood or metal ○ *a mirror with a gilt finish* **3.** SPORTS SPURT OF SPEED AT END a final part of a race, especially a sprint, acceleration, or challenge near the finish line **4.** CONSTR, MANUF QUALITY OF WORKMANSHIP the degree of care with which a product has been manufactured or a job of work has been carried out, judged by its final appearance ○ *The finish on the woodwork is poor.* [14thC. Via Old French *fenir* from Latin *finire*, from *finis* "end."]

finish off *vt.* **1.** COMPLETE to bring something to an end, e.g., by making it as complete as is wished or needed **2.** USE UP to eat, drink, or use up all of something **3.** DESTROY to kill, ruin, or exhaust somebody or something (*informal*)

finish up *v.* **1.** *vt.* USE UP to eat, drink, or use up all of something **2.** *vi.* *U.K.* ARRIVE FINALLY to be in a particular place or condition in the end, often not the planned one

finish up with *vt.* to be left with something ○ *We finished up with nothing.*

finish with *vt.* **1.** NO LONGER WANT TO SEE to end a relationship or partnership with somebody (*informal*) **2.** NOT NEED ANY MORE to stop using, wanting, or being interested in something

WORD KEY: USAGE

See Usage note at ***done.***

fin·ished /fínnisht/ *adj.* **1.** DONE WELL produced and completed with skill and professionalism **2.** OF NO FURTHER USE with no further prospect of success or development

fin·ish·er /fínnishər/ *n.* **1. SOMEBODY WHO COMPLETES SOMETHING** somebody who completes something, e.g., a task or a race **2. SOMEBODY WHO ADDS FINISHING TOUCHES** somebody who completes the final stage of a process in manufacturing or restoration

fin·ish·ing /fínnishing/ *n.* the tasks that complete the production process of a garment, fabric, or material

fin·ish·ing line *n. U.K.* = **finish line**

fin·ish·ing nail *n.* a slender nail with a small head that is used in carpentry

fin·ish·ing school *n.* a private school for girls close to school-leaving age in which social skills, the arts, and academic courses are taught

fin·ish·ing touch *n.* a final small change or addition made to something

fin·ish line *n.* a real or imaginary line that marks the end of a race

fi·nite /fī nīt/ *adj.* **1. LIMITED** with an end or limit ○ *we have only a finite amount of resources* **2.** MATH **COUNTABLE** having a countable number of elements **3. MEASURABLE** subject to measurable limitations **4.** GRAM **USING VERB** appearing in a verb form that limits person, number, and tense [14thC. From Latin *finitus*, past participle of *finire* (see FINISH).] —**fi·nite·ly** *adv.* —**fi·nite·ness** *n.*

fin·i·tude /fínni to͞od/ *n.* the condition of being finite (*formal*)

fink /fingk/ *n.* **1. SOMEBODY LOATHSOME** somebody who is thought to be obnoxious or loathsome (*dated slang insult*) **2.** CRIMINOL **INFORMER** somebody who gives an authority such as a police officer information about another's criminal or bad behavior (*dated slang disapproving*) **3. STRIKEBREAKER** somebody who continues to work when fellow workers are on strike (*dated slang*) ■ *vi.* (**finked, fink·ing, finks**) **1. INFORM ON OTHERS** to give an authority information about another's criminal or bad behavior (*dated slang disapproving*) **2. BE A STRIKEBREAKER** to continue to work in defiance of a strike (*dated slang*) [Late 19thC. Origin unknown.]

fink out *vi.* to fail to do something after previously agreeing or volunteering to do it (*dated slang*)

Fink /fingk/, **Mike** (1770?–1823) U.S. folk hero. His adventurous life as a scout and trapper on the frontier attracted numerous legends, and he became a popular hero.

fin keel *n.* a fin-shaped part that extends downward from the underside of a sailboat to give extra stability

Finland

Fin·land /fínnlənd/ republic in northern Europe on the Baltic Sea. Approximately a third of the country lies within the Arctic Circle. Language: Finnish, Swedish. Currency: markka. Capital: Helsinki. Population: 5,137,269 (1997). Area: 130,559 sq. mi./338,145 sq. km. Official name **Republic of Finland**

Fin·land, Gulf of arm of the Baltic Sea, extending about 250 mi./400 km east between Finland and Estonia. Area: 11,600 sq. mi./30,044 sq. km.

Fin·land·ize /fínnlən dīz/ (**-ized, -iz·ing, -iz·es**) *vt.* to make a small country or power act in an accommodating way toward a superpower rather than confronting it [Mid-20thC. So called because Finland was compelled to behave in this way toward the Soviet Union after World War II.] —**Fin·land·i·za·tion** /fínnləndi záysh'n/ *n.*

Fin·lay /fín lày/ river in north central British Columbia, Canada, that flows southeast into Williston Lake. Length: 250 mi./400 km.

Finn /fin/ *n.* **1. SOMEBODY FROM FINLAND** somebody who was born or raised in Finland, or who has Finnish citizenship **2. SPEAKER OF A FINNIC LANGUAGE** somebody who speaks a Finnic language [Old English *Finnas*]

fin·ner /fínnər/ *n.* = **finback**

Fin·nic /fínnik/ *n.* **N EUROPEAN LANGUAGE GROUP** a group of languages that includes Finnish, Estonian, Lapp, and some other northeastern European languages. The group is from the Finno-Ugric branch of the Uralic family of languages and has about seven million speakers. ■ *adj.* **1. OF FINNIC** relating to the Finnic group of languages **2.** = **Finnish** *adj.* 1

Finn·ish /fínnish/ *n.* **OFFICIAL LANGUAGE OF FINLAND** the official language of Finland, also spoken in parts of Estonia and European Russia. It is from the Finnic group of the Finno-Ugric branch of the Uralic family of languages. About six million people speak Finnish. ■ *adj.* **1. OF FINLAND** relating to or typical of Finland, or its people or culture **2. OF THE FINNISH LANGUAGE** relating to the language Finnish

Fin·no-U·gric /fínnō o͞ogrik, -yo͞ogrik/, **Fin·no-U·gri·an** /-o͞ogree ən, -yo͞ogree-/ *n.* a group of languages that includes Finnish, Estonian, Lapp, Hungarian, and some other northeastern European languages. It is one of the two major branches of the Uralic family of languages. About 22 million people speak one of the languages classified as Finno-Ugric. ◊ **Samoyed** —**Fin·no-U·gric** *adj.*

fi·no /féenō/ (*plural* **-nos**) *n.* a very pale dry sherry [Mid-19thC. From Spanish, literally "fine," from Latin *finire* (see FINISH).]

fi·noc·chi·o /fi nṓkee ō/ (*plural* **-o** *or* **-os**) *n.* = **fennel** *n.* 2 [Early 18thC. Via Italian from Vulgar Latin *feniculum* (see FENNEL).]

fin whale *n.* = **finback**

FIO *abbr.* for information only

f.i.o. *abbr.* for information only

fiord *n.* = **fjord**

fio·ri·tu·ra /fee àwrə to͞orə/ (*plural* **-re** /-ray/) *n.* an embellished vocal figure in opera of the 17th and 18th centuries, similar to a cadenza and often improvised. It was later applied to keyboard and violin music. ◊ **embellishment** [Mid-19thC. From Italian, from *fiorire* "to flower," from, ultimately, Latin *florere* (see FLOURISH).]

fip·ple /fípp'l/ *n.* a small wooden plug in a woodwind instrument or organ pipe that redirects air and creates vibrations [Early 17thC. Origin uncertain.]

fip·ple flute *n.* an end-blown flute containing a fipple

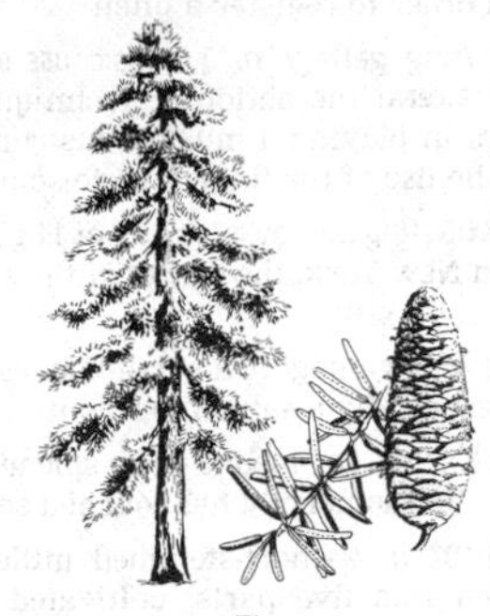

Fir

fir /fur/ (*plural* **firs** *or* **fir**) *n.* **1. EVERGREEN TREE WITH NEEDLE-SHAPED LEAVES** an evergreen tree with single flat needle-shaped leaves and erect female cones. Genus: *Abies.* **2. EVERGREEN RESEMBLING A FIR** an evergreen tree that resembles the true fir, e.g., the Douglas fir **3. WOOD OF THE FIR** the wood of the fir or a related tree [14thC. Origin uncertain.]

Fir·daw·si /feer dówssee/ (940?–1020?) Persian poet. He is best known for the epic *The Book of Kings* (1010), which traces the history of the Persian empire. Full name **Abu al-Qasim Firdawsi**

fire /fīr/ *n.* **1. DESTRUCTIVE BURNING OF SOMETHING** a situation in which something is destroyed or damaged by burning, e.g., a building or an area of land (*often used before a noun*) ○ *destroyed by fire* ○ *fire damage* **2. PILE OF BURNING FUEL** a collection of material such as logs or coal that is set alight and used as fuel for heating, cooking, or burning something ○ *a forest fire* **3. BLAZE** the light, heat, and flames caused by something that is burning ○ *sat at a roaring fire* **4. GAS STOVE FLAME** the flame on the burners or in the oven of a gas stove **5. PROCESS OF BURNING** the rapid production of light, heat, and flames from something that is burning, e.g., in the combustion of wood, coal, or petroleum **6.** ARMS **LAUNCH OF A PROJECTILE** the process or timing of sending off a missile or rocket **7.** ARMS **DISCHARGE FROM GUNS** a discharge of ammunition from one or more guns ○ *The troops advanced under heavy fire.* **8. CONTINUOUS ATTACK** a series of things that follow each other quickly and relentlessly, especially if hostile or intimidating ○ *She took heavy fire from her political opponents.* **9. GEM'S BRILLIANCE** the shine and sparkle of a diamond or similar gemstone **10. PASSION** energy, spirit, or intensity of feeling ○ *the composer's creative fire* ■ *v.* (**fired, fir·ing, fires**) **1.** *vti.* ARMS **DISCHARGE BULLET** to discharge ammunition or a projectile **2.** *vti.* **LAUNCH SOMETHING FORCEFULLY** to launch something powerfully through the air **3.** *vt.* **DISMISS SOMEBODY FROM WORK** to dismiss somebody from employment (*informal*) **4.** *vi.* **START UP** to begin to burn fuel and start working ○ *The engine fired and the racecar took off.* **5.** *vt.* **STOKE OR FILL WITH FUEL** to keep supplying fuel to something, e.g., a furnace, engine, or oven **6.** *vt.* CERAMICS **BAKE IN A KILN** to put pottery into a kiln to be baked hard **7.** *vt.* **STRIKE WITH FORCE** to hit or throw something forcefully **8.** *vt.* **EXCITE** to arouse strong emotion in somebody (*often passive*) ○ *She was fired with enthusiasm.* **9.** *vt.* **DESTROY WITH FIRE** to cause something to burn, especially in order to destroy it (*formal or dated*) ○ *Crossing the border, the invaders fired the first town they encountered.* ■ *interj.* **1. WARNING CRY** used to tell others that a dangerous fire has started **2.** ARMS **COMMAND TO SHOOT** used to command that guns or other weapons, missiles, or projectiles are to be discharged at somebody or something ○ *Ready, aim, and fire!* [Old English *fȳr*. Ultimately from an Indo-European word that is also the ancestor of English *pyre, pyrites*, and *empyreal*.] —**fir·er** *n.* ◇ **open fire (on somebody** *or* **something)** to begin attacking somebody or something ◇ **on fire 1.** in a condition of combustion in which flames, heat, and usually smoke are being produced **2.** full of eagerness or passion ◇ **play with fire** to do something dangerous or risky ◇ **set fire to something** to make something start burning ◇ **set the world on fire** to do something remarkable or very successful ◇ **under fire 1.** MIL shot at by weapons **2.** subject to severe criticism

WORD KEY: SYNONYMS

fire, blaze, conflagration, inferno

CORE MEANING: referring to burning and flames

fire a general word, used to describe flames that were started deliberately and are under control, for example a bonfire. It can also be used to describe uncontrolled flames, whether caused accidentally or on purpose; **blaze** used like ***fire*** but suggesting a greater degree of intensity and brightness, and more rapid burning; **conflagration** a fairly formal word, used to describe a fierce, destructive fire, especially one that affects a large building or area; **inferno** used especially in journalism to describe a fierce, destructive fire.

WORD KEY: CULTURAL NOTE

Pale Fire, a novel by Russian-born Vladimir Nabokov (1962). Partly an attack on parasitic critics, it is presented as a long poem by John Shade, with introduction, notes, and index by Charles Kinbote. Kinbote's commentary gradually reveals him to be an unscrupulous critic, ready to use the work of others to further his own career.

fire away *vi.* **1.** ARMS **BEGIN SHOOTING** to begin or keep on shooting **2. BEGIN** to begin doing something, especially asking questions (*informal*)

fire off *vt.* **1. DIRECT IN SHARP BURSTS** to deliver a series of things, especially questions or demands **2.** ARMS **SHOOT** to discharge a bullet or some other projectile

fire up *v.* **1.** *vt.* **GET GOING** to initiate the operation of something **2.** *vti.* **START TO BURN** to begin to burn, or set something burning **3.** *vti.* **MAKE ENTHUSIASTIC** to cause somebody to become enthusiastic (*informal*)

fire a·larm *n.* a bell or siren that is sounded if a fire starts

fire and brim·stone *n.* eternal punishment [From the use of fire and brimstone in the Bible (Genesis 19:24, Revelation 19:20) as instruments of God's punishment]

fire ant *n.* a predatory ant of tropical or temperate regions that inflicts a painful sting. Genus: *Solenopsis.* [So called because of the burning sensation its sting causes]

fire·arm /fír àarm/ *n.* a portable weapon such as a pistol or rifle that fires ammunition

fire·back /fír bàk/ *n.* a metal lining placed behind a fireplace, or the area of wall where it is placed

fire·ball /fír bàwl/ *n.* **1.** ASTRON, METEOROL **BRIGHT METEOR** an exceptionally bright meteor **2.** = **ball of fire** (*informal*) **3.** NUCLEAR PHYS **CENTER OF A NUCLEAR EXPLOSION** the highly ionized spherical region of bright hot gas and dust at the center of a nuclear explosion **4.** **BALL LIGHTNING** a discharge of ball lightning

fire blight *n.* an infectious disease of apples, pears, and other fruit trees that blackens leaves and kills branches and is caused by the bacterium *Erwinia amylovora*

fire·board /fír bàwrd/ *n. Southern U.S.* a mantel over a fireplace

WORD KEY: REGIONAL NOTE

The term ***fireboard*** is largely restricted to the South Midland highlands of Appalachia in West Virginia, Kentucky, Tennessee, the Carolinas, Georgia, and Alabama, and the Ozarks of Arkansas. In these places, ***fireboard*** contrasts with the general currency word *mantel*, with Southern *mantelpiece*, and with the Piney Woods blend *mantelboard*.

fire·boat /fír bōt/ *n.* a vessel equipped with high-pressure hoses and pumps that take in and shoot seawater, river water, or lake water onto other, burning vessels. Fireboats are also used to spray water in the air in a port as an official welcoming gesture to an important visiting vessel.

fire·bomb /fír bòm/ *n.* **BOMB STARTING FIRE** a bomb designed to start a fire ■ *vti.* (**-bombed, -bomb·ing, -bombs**) **PLACE DEVICE TO START FIRE** to attack a target with a device designed to start a fire —**fire·bomb·er** *n.* —**fire·bomb·ing** *n.*

fire·box /fír bòks/ *n.* an enclosure for a fire in a stove, furnace, or the engine of a steam locomotive

fire·brand /fír brànd/ *n.* **1.** **AGITATOR** somebody with a strong or aggressive personality who encourages unrest **2.** **BURNING STICK** a burning stick carried by somebody as a torch or a weapon

fire·brat /fír bràt/ *n.* a small wingless insect related to silverfish found in warm moist places. Latin name: *Thermobia domestica.*

fire·break /fír bràyk/ *n.* a strip of land that has been cleared of trees, bushes, and any other combustible material in order to prevent a fire from spreading

fire·brick /fír brìk/ *n.* a type of brick that can withstand very high temperatures, used to make fireplaces and furnaces

fire bri·gade *n. U.K.* = **fire department**

fire·bug /fír bùg/ *n.* somebody who causes deliberate damage or destruction by starting fires, especially repeatedly and for pleasure (*slang*)

fire chief *n.* somebody who leads a fire company or department

fire·clay /fír klày/ *n.* a durable clay that can withstand great heat, used to make firebricks, crucibles, and furnace linings

fire com·pa·ny *n.* a group of firefighters stationed in one location, along with their vehicles and equipment

fire con·trol *n.* the control of naval or artillery fire directed at a target

fire·crack·er /fír kràkər/ *n.* a small paper or cardboard cylinder filled with an explosive that makes one or several loud bangs when it is lit

fired /fírd/ *adj.* **1.** **FUELED** using a particular fuel to provide the heat or power (*used in combination*) ○ *a gas-fired turbine* **2.** **KILN-BAKED** baked hard in a kiln

fire·damp /fír dàmp/ *n.* a mixture of methane and other hydrocarbon gases that forms in coalmines. It becomes explosive when it mixes with air. [From an earlier sense of DAMP "noxious gas"]

fire de·part·ment *n.* an organization of people trained to prevent, control, and extinguish fires and to rescue people from fires and other dangerous situations

fire·dog /fír dòg/ *n. Southern U.S.* = **andiron**

fire door *n.* **1.** **DOOR CONFINING A FIRE** a fireproof door that is normally kept closed or locked, ensuring that any fire is confined to one area **2.** **EMERGENCY EXIT** an emergency exit opened from inside

fire·drake /fír dràyk/, **fire·drag·on** /fír dràg'n/ *n.* a dragon that breathes fire (*archaic or literary*) [*Drake* from *draca* "dragon," ultimately from Greek *drakōn* "serpent" (source of English *dragon*)]

fire drill *n.* a rehearsal for evacuating a building quickly and safely in the event of a fire or other emergency

fire-eat·er *n.* **1.** **ENTERTAINER USING FIRE** somebody who entertains by appearing to swallow flames from a burning stick **2.** **SOMEBODY EASILY PROVOKED** somebody who is aggressive, angry, or argumentative (*informal*) —**fire-eat·ing** *n.*

fire en·gine *n.* a large road vehicle equipped with ladders, hoses, and other equipment to fight fires and rescue people

fire es·cape *n.* a specially designed means of getting out of a building if it catches fire, especially an exterior metal stairway attached to the building

fire ex·tin·guish·er *n.* a cylindrical metal container holding a substance such as foam or vaporizing liquid that can be sprayed onto a fire

fire·fight /fír fìt/ *n.* MIL a fierce battle involving a heavy exchange of gunfire

fire·fight·er /fír fìtər/ *n.* somebody who helps to control and extinguish fires and rescue people trapped by fire or in other dangerous situations —**fire·fight·ing** *n.*

fire·fly /fír flì/ (*plural* **-flies**) *n.* a winged nocturnal beetle that, during courtship, produces an intermittent light from luminescent chemicals in its abdominal organs. Family: Lampyridae.

fire·guard /fír gaàrd/ *n.* **1.** **SCREEN PROTECTING FROM FIRE** a metal, usually meshed, screen that is put around the front of an open fire, mainly to stop sparks from flying out and to prevent people from going too close **2.** = **firebreak**

fire·house /fír hòwss/ *n.* = **fire station**

fire hy·drant *n.* an upright pipe, usually in a street, connected to a water main with a valve to which a hose can be attached, e.g., by firefighters

fire in·sur·ance *n.* insurance that offers coverage against damage or loss due to fire

fire i·rons *npl.* a set of implements used for tending a fire in a fireplace, especially a shovel, tongs, poker, and brush

Fire Is·land Na·tion·al Sea·shore sand barrier island off Long Island, southeastern New York, that is a popular summer resort area. Area: 19,579 acres/7,923 hectares.

fire·light /fír lìt/ *n.* the flickering light given off by an open fire

fire·lock /fír lòk/ *n.* in early firearms, a mechanism that struck a spark from flint or steel and caused a charge to explode

fire·man /fírmən/ (*plural* **-men** /-mən/) *n.* **1.** **MAN WHO IS FIREFIGHTER** a man who is firefighter, especially one who works for a fire company **2.** NAVY **SHIP'S ENGINEER** an enlisted man in the U.S. Navy who operates and services engines and similar machinery **3.** BASEBALL **RELIEVER** a relief pitcher in baseball (*slang*) **4.** RAIL, SHIPPING **STOKER** a man who stokes a furnace, especially on a steam locomotive or steamboat

fire mar·shal *n.* **1.** **FIRE INVESTIGATOR** a state or local official whose job it is to investigate suspicious fires and work in the areas of fire prevention and building inspection **2.** **FIRE SAFETY OFFICER** an employee of a plant or other industrial site who is responsible for firefighting equipment and fire safety procedures

Fi·ren·ze Italian **Florence**

fire o·pal *n.* a translucent reddish opal

fire pink *n.* a wild plant of the pink family with bright scarlet flowers. Latin name: *Silene virginica.*

fire·place /fír plàyss/ *n.* a recess, usually with a mantelpiece above it, built into the wall of a room as a place to light an open fire

fire·plug /fír plùg/ *n.* = **fire hydrant**

fire·pow·er /fír pòwr/ *n.* **1.** MIL **DESTRUCTIVE MILITARY POWER** the capability of a military unit or weapon to direct effective fire at an enemy **2.** **POWER TO ACHIEVE RESULTS** the capability or potential of an organization for effective action ○ *The new staff gave the company much-needed firepower.*

fire·proof /fír proòf/ *adj.* **UNBURNABLE OR VERY RESISTANT TO FIRE** treated or manufactured so as to be impossible or very difficult to burn and therefore destroy by fire ■ *vt.* (**-proofed, -proof·ing, -proofs**) **MAKE FIREPROOF** to make something such as a fabric fireproof

fire-re·sis·tant *adj.* treated or made so that it is very slow to catch fire and burn

fire-re·tar·dant *adj.* tending not to catch fire easily and therefore checking the spread of fire

fire sale *n.* a sale of goods or property damaged in a fire

fire screen *n.* = **fireguard** *n.* 1

fire ship *n.* HIST in former times, a ship loaded with explosives or combustibles that was set on fire and allowed to drift as a weapon among enemy ships

fire·side /fír sìd/ *n.* **PLACE BY A FIRE** the space around a fireplace or hearth ■ *adj.* **SAFE AND COMFORTABLE** of a cozy, familiar, or homey nature

fire·side chat *n.* an informal talk made to the nation on radio or television by the President of the United States. During the Great Depression Franklin D. Roosevelt gave fireside chats over the radio as a way of raising national morale and explaining his policies.

fire sign *n.* ZODIAC one of the three signs of the zodiac Aries, Leo, or Sagittarius, traditionally associated with a fiery, assertive, and dynamic temperament

fire sta·tion *n.* a building where professional firefighters are stationed and their vehicles and equipment are kept

fire·stone /fír stòn/ *n.* a form of sandstone that can withstand great heat, used to line kilns and furnaces

Fire·stone /fír stòn/, **Harvey Samuel** (1868–1938) U.S. entrepreneur. He became president of his own tire and rubber company (1900) and established rubber plantations in Liberia (1922).

fire·storm /fír stàwrm/ *n.* **1.** **INTENSE DISTURBANCE** a strong, sometimes violent, upheaval or outburst ○ *a firestorm of protest* **2.** **LARGE UNCONTROLLABLE BLAZE** a large extremely intense fire sustained by strong inwardly rushing winds that feed a rising column of hot air

fire thorn *n.* PLANTS a thorny evergreen shrub of Europe and Asia that is often cultivated for its bright orange or red fruits. Genus: *Pyracantha.*

fire·trap /fír tràp/ *n.* any building or structure regarded as a fire hazard, either because it is built of combustible materials or it lacks adequate means of escape

firetruck *n.* = **fire engine**

fire·walk·ing /fír wàwking/ *n.* the rite or practice of walking barefoot over hot coals, ashes, or stones —**fire·walk·er** *n.*

fire·wall /fír wàwl/ *n.* **1.** BUILDING **WALL PREVENTING THE SPREAD OF FIRE** a fireproof wall put in place to ensure that if a fire occurs it is confined to one area **2.** COMPUT **SECURITY SOFTWARE** a piece of computer software intended to prevent unauthorized access to system software or data ■ *vt.* (**-walled, -walling, -walls**) CARS, AIR **ACCELERATE TO TOP SPEED** to accelerate to the maximum speed (*slang*)

fire·wa·ter /fír wàwttər, -wòttər/ *n.* strong and harsh-tasting alcoholic liquor (*dated slang*)

fire·weed /fír weèd/ (*plural* **-weed** *or* **-weeds**) *n.* a perennial plant of the evening primrose family that grows on recently cleared land. It has spike-shaped clusters of purplish-red flowers. Genus: *Epilobium.* [So called because the plants are often the first to grow on land that has been burned]

fire·wood /fír wòod/ *n.* wood that is burned as fuel

fire·work /fír wùrk/ *n.* **BRIGHT EXPLODING OBJECT** a package of manufactured chemicals designed to make a loud and brilliant explosion when lit (*often used before a noun*) ○ *a firework party* ■ **fire·works** *npl.* **1.** **SHOW USING FIREWORKS** a display of many brilliant fireworks **2.** **ANGRY OUTBURST** a display of violent temper (*informal*) **3.** **SPECTACULAR DISPLAY** any impressive display of talent (*informal*)

fir·ing /fíring/ *n.* the application of great heat to a ceramic object in a kiln, to harden it or to fix an applied substance such as a glaze

fir·ing line *n.* **1.** MIL **FRONT POSITION IN BATTLE** an exposed position from which guns are fired at an enemy, or the troops who occupy it **2.** **VANGUARD OF ACTION** the forefront of a movement, operation, or activity, especially one that is controversial

fir·ing or·der *n.* the sequence of ignition of the cylinders in an internal-combustion engine

fir·ing pin *n.* a pin behind the barrel of a firearm that strikes the container of explosive (**primer**) to make the cartridge fire

fir·ing squad *n.* a group of soldiers with the task of carrying out an execution by gunfire or delivering a ceremonial volley over a grave

fir·kin /fúrkin/ *n.* 1. BREWING MEASURE a British unit of capacity used especially in the brewing industry, equal to nine U.K. gallonsl 2. WOODEN TUB a small wooden tub (*archaic*) [14thC. Origin uncertain: probably from assumed Middle Dutch *verdelkijn*, literally "small fourth," from *veerde* "fourth."]

firm[1] /furm/ *adj.* 1. NOT YIELDING TO THE TOUCH compact and solid when pressed ○ *a firm mattress* 2. SECURE fixed securely and unlikely to give way ○ *a firm hold* 3. DETERMINED showing certainty or determination ○ *You must be more firm with them.* 4. TRUSTWORTHY reliable and able to be trusted 5. STEADY showing no or few fluctuations ■ *adv.* WITH DETERMINATION in a determined and unshakable way ○ *They stood firm despite a wave of criticism.* ■ *vti.* (**firmed, firm·ing, firms**) MAKE OR BECOME FIRM to become firm or firmer, or make something firm or firmer [14thC. Via Old French from Latin *firmus*.] —**firm·ly** *adv.* —**firm·ness** *n.*

firm up *vt.* to make something more definite, clear, or less liable to change ○ *Let's firm up the date of the meeting.*

firm[2] /furm/ *n.* a group of people who form a commercial organization selling goods or services [14thC. From Italian *firma*, late Latin *firmare* "to confirm by signing," from Latin, "to strengthen" , from *firmus* "strong."]

fir·ma·ment /fúrməmənt/ *n.* 1. SKY the sky, considered as an arch (*literary*) 2. WHERE STARS ARE the world occupied by all the stars in a particular field such as the theater or sports ○ *a big name in the yachting firmament* [13thC. Via French from Latin *firmamentum*, from, ultimately, *firmus* "firm, strong."]

firm·ware /fúrm wàir/ *n.* a set of computer instructions used so frequently that it is stored on a memory chip in a computer rather than being part of a program. ◊ **software, hardware** [*Firm* from the fact that the instructions will not be lost when the power is shut off]

firn /furn/ *n.* GEOG = **névé** [Mid-19thC. Via German, literally "of last year," from Old High German *firni* "old."]

firn wind *n.* a summer wind that blows downhill off a glacier during the day

first /furst/ *adj.* 1. BEFORE THE REST preceding or ahead of any others in order 2. EARLIER THAN THE REST occurring before any others in a series 3. MOST IMPORTANT with a higher rank, significance, or authority than others in the same category 4. FUNDAMENTAL forming a basis or foundation for something 5. BEST best in quality or achievement ■ *n.* 1. ONE AHEAD OF ANY OTHER somebody who or something that is positioned before any other in achievement, rank, quality, or time 2. NEW THING something that has not been done before or has not occurred before (*informal*) 3. CARS FIRST GEAR the lowest gear in a motor vehicle (*informal*) 4. BASEBALL FIRST BASE first base on a baseball diamond ○ *He grounded out to first.* ■ *adv.* 1. BEFORE OTHERS earlier than something or somebody else 2. ORIGINALLY for the first time 3. INITIALLY at the start 4. MORE WILLINGLY used to indicate a preference [Old English *fyr(e)st*. Ultimately from an Indo-European word that is also the ancestor of English *fore, principal*, and *priest*.]

first aid *n.* emergency medical treatment for somebody who is ill or injured, given before more thorough medical attention can be obtained

First A·mend·ment *n.* an amendment to the U.S. Constitution that forbids Congress from interfering with a citizen's freedom of religion, speech, assembly, or petition

first base *n.* the initial base that a player attempts to reach in baseball ◇ **get to first base** to succeed in the initial phase of an activity, especially in making advances to a prospective girlfriend (*informal*)

first base·man *n.* a baseball fielder responsible for the area near first base

first-born *n.* OLDEST OFFSPRING the first offspring to be born to a set of parents ■ *adj.* BORN FIRST born first of all

First Cause *n.* in Christianity, God as the originator of everything

first class *n.* 1. BEST CLASS the highest rank, standard, or quality 2. BEST ACCOMMODATIONS the best accommodations offered on an airplane, ship, or train

first-class *adj.* 1. BEST of the highest standard of excellence 2. MOST LUXURIOUS most exclusive and expensive 3. MAIL GIVEN PRIORITY IN THE MAIL SERVICE costing more to mail and given priority in delivery ■ *adv.* 1. IN FIRST CLASS expensively and exclusively 2. MAIL WITH POSTAL PRIORITY more expensively and with higher priority as mail

first class·man *n.* a fourth-year student at a military college

first course *n.* a dish or selection of dishes served at the beginning of a meal

first cous·in *n.* = **cousin** *n.* 1

first-day cov·er *n.* an envelope, often specially designed, that bears a newly issued stamp and a postmark for the day of issue

first-de·gree burn *n.* a burn marked by pain and reddening of the skin but without blistering or charring of tissue

first-de·gree mur·der *n.* murder that is carried out with the planned and deliberate intention of killing somebody

first down *n.* 1. STAGE IN A FOOTBALL PLAY the first in a series of four plays in football, or three plays in Canadian football, by which the offensive team has to move the ball ten yards in order to maintain possession of it 2. GAIN IN FOOTBALL ten or more yards gained by an offensive football team during a series of plays from its starting point, entitling it to keep the ball for another series of plays

first e·di·tion *n.* 1. ORIGINAL COPY OF A BOOK a copy of a book in its original printed and published format 2. ORIGINAL PRINTING OF A PUBLICATION the total number of copies of a book issued by the original publisher in the first instance 3. FIRST NEWSPAPER OF DAY the first batch or copy of a newspaper on a day of publication

first es·tate *n.* in societies that date from feudal times, the social and political class that consists of senior members of the clergy

first fam·i·ly *n.* a family with great social prestige, especially one with a long history and residence in a place

First Fam·i·ly *n.* the U.S. President and the President's spouse and children

first fin·ger *n.* ANAT = **index finger**

first floor *n.* 1. = **ground floor** 2. *U.K.* = **second floor**

first fruits *npl.* 1. FIRST CROP HARVESTED the first harvest of the season or year 2. FIRST BENEFITS the first results of an activity

first-gen·er·a·tion *adj.* 1. SOC SCI WITH IMMIGRANT PARENTS relating to or being the children of parents who have left one country to settle in another 2. COMPUT OF THE EARLIEST KIND used to describe the earliest computers, which were based on vacuum tubes

first·hand /furst hánd/ *adj., adv.* obtained directly from an original source rather than via somebody else

first la·dy *n.* 1. **first la·dy, First La·dy** U.S. LEADER'S SPOUSE OR HOSTESS the wife or hostess of the President of the United States or of a U.S. state governor, or the woman appointed by him to act as his official hostess 2. GOVERNMENT LEADER'S PARTNER the wife or hostess of a high government official, especially of a country's leader 3. WOMAN AT THE TOP the most important or respected woman member of a profession or field of activity

first lan·guage *n.* 1. NATIVE LANGUAGE the language that somebody learned in infancy 2. MAIN LANGUAGE the principal language in a neighborhood, district, region, or country

first lieu·ten·ant *n.* 1. MIL RANK IN THE U.S. FORCES a commissioned officer in the U.S. Army, Marine Corps, and Air Force ranking immediately below captain and above second lieutenant 2. NAVY NAVAL OFFICER MAINTAINING A SHIP a naval officer in charge of the upkeep and maintenance of a ship

first light *n.* the earliest part or time of the day, when the sun begins to rise

first·ling /fúrstling/ *n.* the first of something, e.g., an offspring, product, or result (*archaic or literary*)

first love *n.* 1. FIRST RECIPIENT OF LOVE the first object of somebody's romantic love or affectionate admiration 2. FIRST EXPERIENCE OF LOVE the experience of being in love for the first time 3. FAVORITE the object of somebody's greatest interest or affection ○ *He enjoyed playing tennis, but sailing was always his first love.*

first·ly /fúrstlee/ *adv.* used to introduce the first point in an argument or discussion

first mate *n.* an officer on a merchant ship or any nonnaval vessel who ranks immediately below the captain

first name *n.* a personal name that accompanies a family name to identify somebody fully

First Na·tion, first na·tion *n. Can* in Canada, a community of indigenous people who are bound by treaty to the federal government

first night *n.* the first public performance of a new production of a play or show, or the day on which this takes place

first night·er *n.* somebody who regularly attends the first night of new plays or shows

first of·fend·er *n.* somebody with no previous criminal record who breaks the law and is convicted for the first time

first of·fi·cer *n.* 1. = **first mate** 2. AIRCRAFT COMMANDER the aircraft commander, or captain, of a commercial aircraft

first-past-the-post *adj. U.K., Can* used to describe a voting system in which the winning candidate needs to receive more votes than any other candidate but does not need to get an absolute majority of the votes cast

first per·son *n.* the style of verb and accompanying pronoun that is used when referring to the speaker or writer, or a group including the speaker or writer

first prin·ci·ple *n.* a fundamental rule underlying a theory, faith, or procedure

first quar·ter *n.* one of four phases of the Moon, during which one half of the Moon's visible surface is illuminated by the Sun

first-rate *adj.* of the best quality or the highest standard

first read·ing *n.* the introduction of a bill in a legislature prior to debate and a vote

first re·fus·al *n.* the right to decide whether or not to buy something before it is offered to other potential buyers

first ser·geant *n.* a noncommissioned officer who holds a senior position administering a unit of the U.S. Army, Air Force, or Marine Corps

first strike *n.* the use of nuclear weapons against an enemy that is similarly armed, intended to destroy its military capacity and prevent it from attacking first (*hyphenated before a noun*) ○ *first-strike capability*

first wa·ter *n.* the highest grade in gemstones

First World *n.* the principal industrialized countries of the world, including the United States, the United Kingdom, the nations of Western Europe, Japan, Canada, Australia, and New Zealand

First World War *n.* = **World War I**

firth /furth/ *n. Scotland* a river estuary, or a wide inlet of the sea (*often used in placenames*) [14thC. From Old Norse *fjörðr* (see FJORD).]

fisc /fisk/ *n.* 1. TREASURY a public treasury 2. ROYAL TREASURY royal funds, especially those belonging to a Roman emperor (*archaic*) [Late 16thC. Directly or via French from Latin *fiscus*, literally "rush basket," later "purse, treasury."]

fis·cal /fískəl/ *adj.* 1. FINANCIAL relating to financial matters in general 2. OF THE PUBLIC TREASURY relating to public revenues, especially the revenue from taxation ○ *fiscal prudence* [Mid-16thC. Directly or via French from Latin *fiscalis*, from *fiscus* (see FISC).]

fis·cal year *n.* a 12-month period at the end of which all accounts are completed in order to furnish a statement of a company's, organization's, or government's financial condition, or for tax purposes. A fiscal year does not necessarily correspond to a calendar year.

Fi·scher /físhər/, **Bobby** (*b.* 1943) U.S. chess player. In 1972, he became the first chess player from the United States to win the world championship, and he held the title until 1975. Full name **Robert James Fischer**

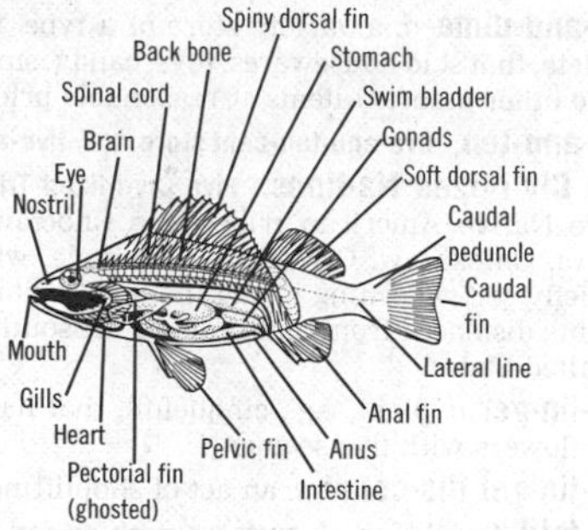

Fish: Anatomy of a fish

fish /fish/ *n.* (*plural* **fish** *or* **fish·es**) **1.** ZOOL **AQUATIC VERTEBRATE WITH GILLS** any cold-blooded aquatic vertebrate animal that typically has jaws, fins, scales, a slender body, a two-chambered heart, and gills for providing oxygen to the blood (*often used before a noun*) ○ *a fish tank* **2.** FOOD **FISH CONSUMED AS FOOD** the flesh of any edible fish consumed as food, either cooked or raw (*often used before a noun*) ○ *fish soup* **3. SOMEBODY UNUSUAL** somebody who is unusual or regarded as strange (*informal*) ○ *an odd fish* ■ *v.* (**fished, fish·ing, fish·es**) **1.** *vi.* **CATCH FISH** to use a rod, net, or some other method to bring fish out of the water **2.** *vt.* **CATCH FISH IN A PLACE** to try to get fish from a particular river, lake, or stream **3.** *vi.* **SEARCH** to feel around with the hands in order to find something (*informal*) [Old English *fisc*. Ultimately from an Indo-European word that is also the ancestor of English *Pisces* and *porpoise*.] ◇ **drink like a fish** to habitually drink a lot of alcoholic liquor (*informal*) ◇ **have other fish to fry** to have something else to do, usually something more interesting (*informal*) ◇ **like a fish out of water** ill at ease in a situation

fish for *vt.* to search, especially in an indirect way or in difficult circumstances ○ *fish for compliments*

fish out *vt.* to find something or take something out, especially after searching with the hands (*informal*) ○ *He fished out a coin from his pocket.*

Fish /fish/ *n.* ZODIAC = **Pisces**

Fish /fish/, **Hamilton** (1808–93) U.S. politician. He served as a member of the U.S. House of Representatives (1843–45), governor of New York (1849–50), U.S. senator (1851–57), and U.S. secretary of state (1869–77).

fish and chips *n.* a fillet of fish deep-fried in batter, served with French fries (*takes a singular or plural verb*)

fish·bowl /físh bòl/ *n.* **1. ROUND GLASS BOWL** a round clear open-topped container of water in which a pet goldfish is kept **2. PUBLIC LIFESTYLE** a place or condition of high public visibility and little or no personal privacy

fish cake *n.* a round flat individual cake made from cooked fish mixed with potato and other ingredients, coated with breadcrumbs, and fried, baked, or grilled

fish crow *n.* a small crow native to the Gulf and Atlantic coasts of North America that feeds on fish and mollusks. Latin name: *Corvus ossifragus.*

fish duck *n.* = **merganser**

fish ea·gle *n.* = **osprey**

fish·er /físhər/ *n.* a carnivorous mammal of northern North America, a species of marten, with dense dark brown fur. Latin name: *Martes pennanti.* [Old English]

fish·er·man /físhərmən/ (*plural* **-men** /-mən/) *n.* somebody who fishes as a sport or occupation

fish·er·man's bend *n.* a knot used to tie the end of a line to a ring or spar

fish·er·man's knot *n.* a knot for joining the ends of two ropes, consisting of one or two overhand knots that tighten with tension on the line

fish·er·y /físhəree/ (*plural* **-ies**) *n.* **1. PLACE FOR REARING FISH** a region of water or a tank in which fish are reared **2. REGION OF WATER FOR FISHING** a region of water where industrial fishing is practiced **3. FISH BUSINESS** a business that harvests, processes, or sells fish **4. FISHING INDUSTRY** the catching, processing, or selling of fish, including the industries and occupations involved in these activities **5.** LAW **RIGHT TO FISH** the right to fish in an area

Fish·es /físhəz/ *n.* ZODIAC = **Pisces**

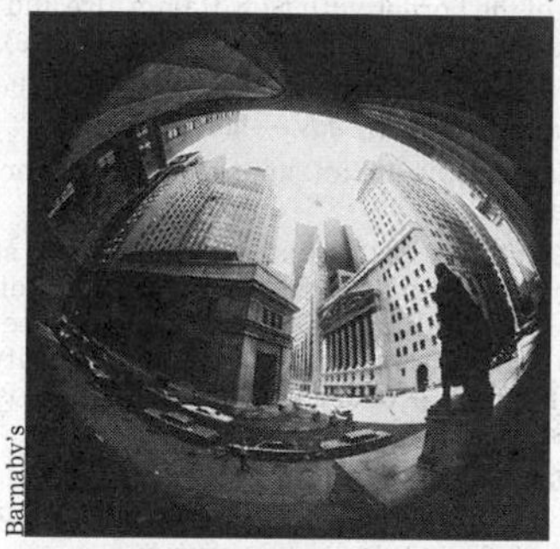

Fisheye lens: View from a fisheye lens of Wall Street, New York City

fish·eye lens *n.* a wide-angle lens that gives an extremely wide field of view, up to 180 degrees. Straight lines are curved and distorted by this type of lens.

fish farm *n.* a place with facilities for rearing fish commercially —**fish farm·er** *n.* —**fish farm·ing** *n.*

fish fin·ger *n. U.K.* = **fish stick**

fish fry *n.* a meal with deep-fried fish as the main course

fish·gig /físh gìg/ *n.* ANGLING a pole with barbs, used for spearing fish [Mid-16thC. By folk etymology from earlier FIZGIG, by association with FISH.]

fish hawk *n.* = **osprey**

fish·hook /físh hòok/ *n.* **1. HOOK FOR CATCHING FISH** a sharp metal hook used for catching fish **2.** LOGIC **SYMBOL IN LOGIC** a symbol used in logic to represent an "if-then" proposition

fish·ing /físhing/ *n.* **1. CATCHING FISH** the sport, industry, or occupation of catching fish **2. PLACE FOR FISHING** a place for fishing

fish·ing ex·pe·di·tion *n.* an investigation or line of questioning that strays from its ostensible purpose in order to uncover incriminating or damaging information

fish·ing rod *n.* a long flexible pole to which a fishing line and usually a reel are attached for catching fish

fish joint *n.* a connection in which two rails or beams are joined together by one or more fishplates [*Fish* of uncertain origin: probably from French *fiche* (see FISHPLATE]

fish ket·tle *n.* an oblong pan, often with a rack inside, for cooking a whole fish

fish knife *n.* a broad-bladed knife with blunt edges, used for eating fish

fish lad·der *n.* a series of pools on an incline separated by short increments so as to enable fish to swim up past a dam or other obstruction

fish louse *n.* a small flat rounded crustacean with sucking mouth parts that lives as a parasite on fish. Class: Branchiura.

fish·meal /físh mèel/ *n.* a substance prepared from ground dried fish, used as an animal feed and a fertilizer

fish·net /físh nèt/ *n.* **1. NET FOR FISHING** a net used to catch fish **2.** TEXTILES **FABRIC SIMILAR TO NETTING** an open mesh fabric that looks like netting and is often used to make stockings and pantyhose

fish·plate /físh plàyt/ *n.* a flat piece of metal bolted between two abutting rails or beams to join them, especially on railroad track [Mid-19thC. *Fish* of uncertain origin: probably from French *fiche* "peg," from *fichier* "to drive in, fasten," from, ultimately, Latin *figere* (source of English *fix*).]

fish·pond /físh pònd/ *n.* a pond where fish are found or kept

fish pro·tein con·cen·trate *n.* a food supplement that contains high concentrations of protein and is prepared from fish

fish·skin dis·ease *n.* ichthyosis (*informal*)

fish stick *n.* a rectangular piece of filleted or ground fish that is covered in breadcrumbs or batter

fish sto·ry *n.* an implausible story boasting about something that was nearly accomplished (*informal*) [From fishermen's traditional exaggeration of the size of fish almost caught]

fish·tail /físh tàyl/ *vi.* (**-tailed, -tail·ing, -tails**) **1.** CARS **SWING FROM SIDE TO SIDE** to swing from side to side, especially uncontrollably, while moving forward in a motor vehicle **2.** AIR **SWING AIRPLANE'S TAIL TO REDUCE SPEED** to move the tail of an airplane from side to side in order to reduce speed ■ *adj.* CLOTHES **GATHERED AND FLARED** used to describe the back of skirt or dress that has a section that is closely gathered or pleated and then flares out

fish·way /físh wày/ *n.* = **fish ladder**

fish·wife /físh wìf/ *n.* **1. COARSE AND LOUD WOMAN** a woman who is seen as coarse and loud-voiced (*insult*) **2. WOMAN FISH SELLER** a woman selling fish in former times (*archaic*)

fishworm /físhwùrm/ *n.* an earthworm (*regional*)

WORD KEY: REGIONAL NOTE

Fishworm has currency in most parts of the country, with the strongest concentrations in New England and the North Central States. In the South, *earthworm*, a general currency word elsewhere, is frequent in all types or speech and especially in folk speech.

fish·y /físhee/ (**-i·er, -i·est**) *adj.* **1. DUBIOUS** arousing suspicion (*informal*) **2. LIKE FISH** like fish, especially in taste, smell, or coldness or sliminess to the touch **3. EXPRESSIONLESS** cold and expressionless, like the eye of a fish ○ *He gave me a fishy look.* —**fish·i·ly** *adv.* —**fish·i·ness** *n.*

Fisk /fisk/, **James** (1834–72) U.S. financier. A stock market speculator, he and his partners caused Black Friday (1869) when they tried to gain a monopoly on gold.

fissi- *prefix.* **1.** cleft, separated ○ *fissipedal* **2.** biological fission ○ *fissparous* [From Latin *fissus*, the past participle of *findere* "to split." Ultimately from an Indo-European base that is also the ancestor of English *bite* and *boat*.]

fis·sile /físs'l/ *adj.* **1.** NUCLEAR PHYS = **fissionable** **2.** GEOL **ABLE TO BE SPLIT** used to describe a rock that can be split along a grain or a plane of cleavage, e.g., slate or schist [Mid-17thC. Formed from Latin *fiss-*, the past participle stem of *findere* (see FISSION).] —**fis·sil·i·ty** /fi síllətee/ *n.*

fis·sion /físh'n/ *n.* **1.** NUCLEAR PHYS **SPLITTING OF ATOMIC NUCLEUS RELEASING ENERGY** the spontaneous or induced splitting of an atomic nucleus into smaller nuclei, usually accompanied by a significant release of energy **2. BREAKING UP** the act or process of separating into parts **3.** BIOL **DIVISION OF AN ORGANISM** the division of a single-celled organism into two equal parts, each part growing into a complete organism [Early 17thC. From the Latin stem *fission-*, from *fiss-*, the past participle stem of *findere* "to split" (source of English *fissure*).]

fis·sion·a·ble /físh'nəb'l/ *adj.* able to undergo nuclear fission —**fis·sion·a·bil·i·ty** /físh'nə bíllətee/ *n.*

fis·sion bomb *n.* an atomic bomb (*technical*)

fis·sion-track dat·ing *n.* a method of determining the age of a mineral by observing the tracks made in it by fission products of the uranium atoms it contains

fis·sip·a·rous /fi síppərəss/ *adj.* BIOL used to describe an organism that reproduces by dividing into two equal parts, each of which grows into a complete organism —**fis·sip·a·rous·ly** *adv.*

fis·si·ped /físsə pèd/ *adj.* **fis·si·ped, fis·si·ped·al** ZOOL **WITH SEPARATED TOES** used to describe animals that have toes separated from each other, e.g., dogs and cats ■ *n.* **SEPARATE-TOED ANIMAL** an animal with separate toes. Suborder: Fissipedia. [Mid-17thC. From late Latin *fissiped-*, from, ultimately, Latin *findere* "to split" + *ped-*, *pes* "foot."]

fis·sure /físhər/ *n.* **1. CRACK** a long narrow crack or opening, especially in rock **2. PROCESS OF SPLITTING** the process of dividing along a line **3. SCHISM IN GROUP** a division in a group or party **4.** ANAT **SPLIT IN BODY PART** a natural or pathological division in a body part ■ *vti.* (**-sured, -sur·ing, -sures**) **SPLIT OR CAUSE TO SPLIT** to split something along fairly regular lines, or undergo this process [14thC. Directly or via French from Latin *fissura*, from the stem *fiss-* (see FISSION).]

fist /fist/ *n.* **1. CLENCHED HAND** a hand with the fingers closed in the palm **2. HAND** a hand (*informal*) **3.** = **fistful** **4.** PRINTING = **index** *n.* **6** ■ *v.* (**fist·ed, fist·ing, fists**) **1.** *vt.* **HIT SOMEBODY WITH THE FIST** to hit somebody or something with a fist **2.** *vt.* **HANDLE** to handle something roughly or carelessly (*informal*) **3.** *vti.* = **fistfuck** (*offensive taboo*) [Old English *fȳst*, from a prehistoric Germanic word of uncertain origin: probably ultimately from an Indo-European word meaning "five," which is also the ancestor of English *five*]

fist·fight /físt fìt/ *n.* a fight in which bare fists are used

fist·fuck /físt fùk/ (**-fucked, -fuck·ing, -fucks**) *vti.* to insert a fist into somebody's vagina or anus for sexual pleasure (*offensive taboo*)

fist·ful /físt fòol/ *n.* the amount that can be held within a fist

fist·ic /fístik/ *adj.* relating to boxing (*informal*)

fist·i·cuffs /fìsti kùfs/ *npl.* fighting using the fists (*archaic or humorous*) [Early 17thC. Origin uncertain: probably from *fisty* "with the fists" + CUFF "blow."]

fis·tu·la /físchələ/ (*plural* **-las** *or* **-lae** /-lee/) *n.* an abnormal opening or passage between two organs or between an organ and the skin, caused by disease, injury, or congenital malformation [14thC. Directly or via French from Latin *fistula* "pipe, flute" (source of English *fester*).]

fis·tu·lous /físchələss/, **fis·tu·lar** /físchələr/, **fis·tu·late** /físchələt/ *adj.* **1.** MED **WITH A FISTULA** having or resembling a fistula **2.** ANAT **TUBULAR** tubular **3.** ANAT **MADE UP OF TUBES** composed of or containing tubes

fit[1] /fit/ *v.* (**fit·ted** *or* **fit, fit·ting, fits**) **1.** *vti.* **BE THE RIGHT SIZE OR SHAPE** to be of a suitable size or shape for something or somebody ○ *See if this jacket fits.* **2.** *vti.* **BE APPROPRIATE** to be appropriate or suitable for something ○ *make the punishment fit the crime* **3.** *vti.* **BE COMPATIBLE** to agree or be in accordance with something ○ *no one fitting that description* **4.** *vt.* **TRY CLOTHING ON** to try clothing on somebody to determine if changes are necessary **5.** *vt.* **EQUIP SOMEBODY OR SOMETHING** to provide somebody or something with equipment of a particular kind ○ *fitted with extra security features* **6.** *vt.* **MAKE SOMETHING READY** to make somebody or something ready or suitable for a task, function, or purpose ○ *an education that will fit her for a career in business* **7.** *vt.* **INSTALL SOMETHING** to install something, or put something in place ■ *adj.* (**fit·ter, fit·test**) **1.** **APPROPRIATE** suitable, acceptable, or appropriate for a purpose ○ *dishes fit for everyday use* **2.** **WORTHY** worthy or deserving of something ○ *not fit to serve as an officer* **3.** **WELL IN HEALTH** in good health **4.** **STRONG AND HEALTHY** physically strong and healthy, especially because of taking regular exercise **5.** **APPEARING LIKELY TO DO SOMETHING** appearing likely to do something because of being in an extreme condition (*informal*) ○ *looked fit to burst in a shirt too small for him* ■ *n.* **1.** **WAY THAT SOMETHING FITS** the way in which something conforms to standards of proper length, tightness, and shape ○ *These shoes are a better fit than the other pair.* **2.** **RELATIONSHIP FOR BEST FUNCTION** a relationship between corresponding parts or related things that enables proper functioning ○ *check the replacement chassis for fit* **3.** MECH ENG **CLOSENESS OF SURFACES** the closeness of contact between adjacent surfaces in a mechanical assembly **4.** *Ireland* **STANZA** a verse in poetry (*formal*) [14thC. Origin uncertain: probably originally in the sense "to marshal troops," later "to be suitable."] ◇ **fit to be tied** very angry and exasperated (*informal*) ◇ **fit to kill** to an extreme degree that captures attention

fit in *v.* **1.** *vi.* **CONFORM WELL** to conform harmoniously to other members of a group or other things in a setting ○ *She's been able to fit in well at her new school.* **2.** *vt.* **FIND TIME FOR** to find a time or place for somebody or something that does not disturb other arrangements ○ *The dentist can fit you in at three.* ○ *I love the theater but can't fit it into my schedule.*

fit out *vt.* to equip or provide something or somebody with required items, e.g., supplies or clothes

fit[2] /fit/ *n.* **1.** **SUDDEN OUTBURST** a sudden occurrence of a physical activity or an emotional mood ○ *a fit of laughing* ○ *a coughing fit* **2.** **CONVULSIONS** sudden violent convulsions, e.g., in a child with a high fever or somebody experiencing a seizure [14thC. Origin uncertain: perhaps from Old English *fitt* "conflict." The meaning "sudden attack" evolved from "experience of hardship."] ◇ **by fits and starts** starting and stopping repeatedly ◇ **throw a fit** to show strong emotion, especially anger (*informal*)

fitch /fich/, **fitch·et** *n.* = **polecat** [15thC. From Middle Dutch *fisse*.]

Fitch /fich/, **John** (1743–98) U.S. inventor, who built the first successful steamboat (1787). His boats operated on the Delaware River (1787–90).

Fitch·burg /fích bùrg/ city in northern Massachusetts, south of the border with New Hampshire and northwest of Leominster. Population: 39,843 (1996).

fit·ful /fítfəl/ *adj.* starting and stopping irregularly ○ *a fitful sleep* —**fit·ful·ly** *adv.* —**fit·ful·ness** *n.*

fit·ly /fítlee/ *adv.* in an appropriate way or place (*archaic*)

fit·ness /fítnəss/ *n.* **1.** **BEING PHYSICALLY FIT** the state of being physically fit **2.** **SUITABILITY** suitability of somebody or something to a particular purpose **3.** GENETICS **ABILITY TO REPRODUCE SUCCESSFULLY** the ability of an individual to produce offspring that survive and reproduce

fit·ness cen·ter *n.* a place with facilities and equipment for people to maintain or improve their physical fitness

fit·ted /fíttəd/ *adj.* **1.** **MADE TO FIT** tailored to fit closely to the body **2.** *U.K.* **BUILT FOR A SPACE** built for and fixed into a designated space **3.** *U.K.* = **wall-to-wall**

fit·ted sheet *n.* a sheet with elastic at the corners that makes it fit snugly over a mattress

fit·ter /fíttər/ *n.* **1.** INDUST **SOMEBODY WHO MAINTAINS MACHINERY** somebody who maintains, repairs, or assembles mechanical equipment **2.** CLOTHES **SOMEBODY WHO ALTERS CLOTHES** somebody who alters clothes to make them fit

fit·ting /fítting/ *adj.* **SUITABLE** appropriate for the circumstances ○ *a fitting end to her career* ■ *n.* **1.** **TRYING ON OF CLOTHES** the trying on of a piece of clothing to see if it requires alteration **2.** **DETACHABLE PART** a detachable part, especially for a device or machine **3.** **FITTER'S WORK** the work performed by a fitter ■ **fit·tings** *npl.* **ASSOCIATED PARTS** decorations, furniture, and accessories that belong to a building, vehicle, or machine —**fit·ting·ly** *adv.* —**fit·ting·ness** *n.*

fit·ting room *n.* a room for trying on or fitting clothes in a store

AKG London

Ella Fitzgerald

Fitz·ger·ald /fits jérrəld/, **Ella** (1917–96) U.S. jazz singer. She was known for her scat singing and extensive song repertoire.

Library of Congress

F. Scott Fitzgerald

Fitz·ger·ald, F. Scott (1890–1940) U.S. writer. He penned novels and short stories that chronicled the mood and manners of the 1920s. Among his works is *The Great Gatsby* (1925). Full name **Francis Scott Key Fitzgerald**

five /fīv/ *n.* **1.** **NUMBER 5** the number 5 **2.** **GROUP OF FIVE** a group of five objects or people **3.** **SOMETHING WITH VALUE OF 5** something in a numbered series, e.g., a playing card, with a value of 5 ○ *the five of clubs* ○ *to throw a five* [Old English *fīf*. Ultimately from an Indo-European word meaning "five," which is also the ancestor of English *pentagon, punch* "beverage," and *Pentecost*.] —**five** *adj., pron.*

five-and-dime *n.* a variety store of a type, now obsolete, that sold housewares, toys, candy, small pets, and other assorted items at reasonable prices

five-and-ten, **five-and-ten-cent store** *n.* = **five-and-dime**

Five Civ·i·lized Na·tions, **Five Civ·i·lized Tribes** *npl.* five Native American tribes, the Choctaw, Cherokee, Chickasaw, Creek, and Seminole, who were briefly self-governing in the Indian Territory after being displaced from their land in the southeastern United States

five-fin·ger *n.* plant, e.g., cinquefoil, that has leaves or flowers with five segments

five-fin·ger dis·count *n.* an act of shoplifting (*slang*)

five·fold /fīv fòld/ *adj.* **1.** **TIMES FIVE** with or equal to five times as much or as many **2.** **WITH FIVE PARTS** composed of five parts or sections ■ *adv.* **BY FIVE TIMES AS MUCH** by five times as much or as many

five hun·dred *n.* euchre or rummy in which the winner is the first to reach 500 points

five o'clock shad·ow *n.* beard growth noticeable late in the day on a man who shaved in the morning

five of a kind *n.* a poker hand consisting of four cards of the same denomination plus a wild card

five·pen·ny /fīv pènnee/ *adj.* costing or worth five pence

five·pins /fīv pìnz/ *n.* a bowling game played in Canada in which five pins are used (*takes a singular verb*)

fiv·er /fīvər/ *n.* **1.** **FIVE-DOLLAR BILL** a banknote worth five dollars **2.** *U.K.* **FIVE-POUND BANKNOTE** in Britain, a banknote worth five pounds

five-spice pow·der *n.* a Chinese mixed spice consisting of star anise, anise or Szechuan pepper, cinnamon, fennel, and cloves

five-spot /fīv spòt/, **five·spot** *n.* a banknote worth five dollars

five-star *adj.* first-class, or offering the highest standards and quality

five-star gen·er·al *n.* a general of the highest rank, with an insignia of five stars

fix /fiks/ *v.* (**fixed, fix·ing, fix·es**) **1.** *vt.* **MEND OR CORRECT SOMETHING** to repair, mend, or correct something **2.** *vt.* **CURE SOMETHING** to cure or bandage a small wound (*babytalk*) **3.** *vt.* **PREPARE SOMETHING AS FOOD** to prepare something, especially a meal or a drink (*informal*) **4.** *vt.* **ARRANGE OR ORDER SOMETHING** to arrange something, or put something in order (*informal*) **5.** *vt.* **AGREE SOMETHING** to agree, arrange, or settle something, especially a time or a price **6.** *vt.* **INFLUENCE SOMETHING DISHONESTLY** to influence a person or outcome dishonestly (*informal*) ○ *The trial was fixed.* **7.** *vt.* **TAKE REVENGE ON SOMEBODY** to take revenge on or punish somebody (*informal*) **8.** *vt.* **ATTRIBUTE SOMETHING** to attribute something, especially blame ○ *to fix the blame on other people* **9.** *vt.* **DIRECT SOMETHING** to direct or concentrate the eyes, attention, or mind ○ *She fixed her eyes on the path ahead.* **10.** *vti.* **MAKE OR BECOME SECURE** to make something stable, firm, or secure, or become so **11.** *vt.* VET **STERILIZE AN ANIMAL** to spay or castrate an animal (*informal*) **12.** *vt.* **HOLD SOMEBODY'S ATTENTION** to hold or capture the attention or interest of somebody ○ *fixed us with a baleful smile* **13.** *vt.* **FASTEN SOMETHING** to fasten something in place ○ *She fixed the notice to the door with a thumbtack.* **14.** *vt.* BIOCHEM **CONVERT NITROGEN TO A STABLE FORM** to convert atmospheric nitrogen to a stable or biologically available form (*refers to soil bacteria*) **15.** *vt.* PHOTOGRAPHY, PAINTING **MAKE PERMANENT** to treat something such as a photographic film or plate with chemicals in order to make a permanent image **16.** *vti.* CHEM **MAKE OR BECOME STABLE** to make a chemical or compound stable and nonvolatile, or undergo this process **17.** *vt.* BIOL **PRESERVE SOMETHING FOR EXAMINATION** to prevent change and decay in a specimen by preserving it in a chemical solution, especially for study under the microscope **18.** *vi.* DRUGS **INJECT A DRUG** to inject an illegal drug (*slang*) ■ *n.* **1.** **PREDICAMENT** a predicament or difficult situation (*informal*) ○ *in a fix* **2.** **SUPERFICIAL SOLUTION** an immediate and often temporary solution (*informal*) ○ *a quick fix* **3.** **INFLUENCING DISHONESTLY** an instance of influencing an outcome or person dishonestly (*informal*) **4.** DRUGS **ILLEGAL DRUG INJECTION** an injection of an illegal drug (*slang*) **5.** **STIMULATING DOSE** a dose of or exposure to something pleasurable and stimulating (*humorous*) ○ *a chocolate fix* **6.** NAVIG **CALCULATION OF POSITION** a calculation of the position of an object using radar or other forms of observation **7.** **UNDERSTANDING** an understanding or identification of something (*informal*) ○ *Do you have a fix on what the problem is?* [15thC. Immediate origin uncertain: ultimately from Latin *fix-*, the past participle stem of *figere* "to fix."] —**fix·a·ble** *adj.* ◇ **be fixing to do something** to be on the verge of doing something (*regional*) ○ *They're fixing to get married.* ◇ **the fix is in** the case or other matter has already been dishonestly decided, e.g., by the use of bribes (*slang*)

fix on *vt.* to select something

fix up *vt.* **1.** ARRANGE A CONTACT FOR SOMEBODY to arrange a business or social contact, or a romantic or sexual partner, for somebody **2.** REPAIR SOMETHING to restore something to working order or proper order **3.** ARRANGE SOMETHING to arrange something, e.g., a meeting or a date

fix·ate /fík sàyt/ (**-at·ed, -at·ing, -ates**) *v.* **1.** *vti.* FOCUS ON SOMETHING to focus exclusively on something **2.** *vt.* OBSESS SOMEBODY to obsess or preoccupy somebody or something totally **3.** *vti.* PSYCHOL FORM A FIXATION to form or have a psychological fixation to a person or object **4.** *vti.* BECOME OR MAKE FIXED to make something stable or secure, or become so [Late 19thC. Formed from the Latin stem *fix-* (see FIX).]

fix·a·tion /fik sáysh'n/ *n.* **1.** OBSESSION an obsession or preoccupation **2.** PSYCHOL IMMATURE PSYCHOSEXUAL BEHAVIOR a theoretical abnormally strong libidinal attachment to a person or object, formed during early childhood, that results in neurotic or arrested psychosexual behavior in adulthood **3.** BIOCHEM CONVERSION OF NITROGEN the conversion by soil bacteria of atmospheric nitrogen to a stable and biologically available form ○ *nitrogen fixation* **4.** CHEM STABILIZATION OF CHEMICAL the process of stabilizing a chemical or compound **5.** BIOL PRESERVING FOR EXAMINATION the process of preserving a biological specimen with a chemical

fix·a·tive /fíksətiv/ *n.* **1.** LIQUID SPRAYED FOR PROTECTION a liquid sprayed onto a drawing, photograph, or other surface to protect it **2.** GLUE a substance used to hold something in place **3.** COSMETICS PERFUME ADDITIVE a substance added to a perfume to make it evaporate less rapidly **4.** BIOL CHEMICAL PRESERVATIVE a chemical solution that preserves a biological specimen for microscopic study **5.** TEXTILES FABRIC ADDITIVE a substance applied to dyed fabrics to make the dye colorfast ■ *adj.* TENDING TO FIX acting or tending to fix something

fixed /fikst/ *adj.* **1.** SECURE immovable or securely in position **2.** NOT SUBJECT TO CHANGE not subject to change in amount or time **3.** NOT CHANGING unchanging in expression **4.** AGREED ON arranged or agreed upon **5.** HELD IN MIND firmly or dogmatically held in the mind **6.** PROVIDED WITH SOMETHING in the position of having something at your disposal (*informal*) ○ *How are you fixed for money?* **7.** DISHONESTLY ARRANGED unfairly or illegally arranged (*slang*) **8.** CHEM CHEMICALLY STABLE combined in stable form ○ *fixed nitrogen* **9.** ZODIAC STABLE IN ZODIACAL TERMS used to describe Taurus, Leo, Scorpio, and Aquarius, signs of the zodiac associated with stability —**fix·ed·ly** /fíksədlee/ *adv.* —**fix·ed·ness** /-nəss/ *n.*

fixed as·set *n.* an asset of a business that is central to its operation and is not traded (*usually used in the plural*)

fixed cost *n.* a business expense that does not vary according to the amount of business (*usually used in the plural*)

fixed i·de·a *n.* = **idée fixe**

fixed oil *n.* a nonvolatile oil composed of fatty acids, usually of animal or vegetable origin

fixed pen·al·ty *n.* a fine for a specific amount given for a particular offense, especially a traffic violation

fixed point *n.* a temperature, e.g., boiling or freezing point, that has a fixed value under specific conditions and can be used to calibrate instruments

fixed-point *adj.* used to describe or relating to a mathematical notation system, e.g., the decimal system, in which the point separating whole numbers from fractional values is in a fixed position

fixed-wing *adj.* used to describe an aircraft that has stationary wings, especially as distinct from rotor blades

fix·er /fíksər/ *n.* **1.** SOMEBODY WHO ARRANGES SOMETHING DISHONEST somebody who arranges something, especially using dishonest or illegal means (*slang*) **2.** PHOTOGRAPHY CHEMICAL IN PHOTOGRAPHY a chemical that halts the development of a photographic image on film or paper **3.** SOMEBODY OR SOMETHING THAT FIXES a person who or object that fixes something

fix·ing /fíksing/ *npl.* **fix·ings 1.** COOK INGREDIENTS the ingredients required for a dish **2.** FOOD ACCOMPANIMENTS the typical accompaniments for a particular dish (*informal*)

fix·i·ty /fíksitee/ (*plural* **-ties**) *n.* **1.** STATE OF BEING FIXED the quality or state of being fixed and unchanging **2.** SOMETHING NOT CHANGING something that is unchanging (*formal*)

fix·ture /fíkschər/ *n.* **1.** OBJECT IN FIXED POSITION an object with a fixed position and function **2.** ESTABLISHED PERSON somebody considered to be permanently established in a place or position [Late 16thC. Origin uncertain: probably an alteration, on the model of MIXTURE, of *fixure*, from late Latin *fixura*, from Latin *fix-* (see FIX).]

fiz·gig /fízgig/ *n.* ANGLING = **fishgig** [Early 16thC. Origin uncertain: probably from FIZZ + *gig* "giddy girl"; "fishgig" sense probably ultimately from Spanish *fisga* "harpoon."]

fizz /fiz/ *vi.* (**fizzed, fizz·ing, fizz·es**) **1.** PRODUCE GAS BUBBLES to produce bubbles of gas **2.** HISS to make a hissing or continuous soft crackling sound ■ *n.* **1.** EFFERVESCENCE the sparkling quality of a drink caused by bubbles of gas **2.** HISSING SOUND a hissing or continuous soft crackling sound **3.** LIVELINESS a quality of liveliness or excitement ○ *All the fizz has gone out of the election campaign.* **4.** BEVERAGES SPARKLING DRINK a sparkling drink, especially champagne [Mid-17thC. An imitation of the sound.]

fiz·zle /fízz'l/ *vi.* (**-zled, -zling, -zles**) **1.** FAIL AFTER GOOD START to fail or peter out, especially after a good start **2.** MAKE HISSING SOUND to make a gentle hissing sound ■ *n.* **1.** FAILURE a fiasco or total failure (*informal*) **2.** HISSING SOUND a gentle hissing sound [Mid-16thC. Origin uncertain: probably from obsolete *fist* "to break wind" (source also of English *feist*), from prehistoric Germanic.]

fiz·zler /fízzlər/ *n.* **1.** FAILED FIRECRACKER a firecracker that sputters and hisses but does not explode (*informal*) **2.** FAILED EVENT an event that is not as lively or exciting as expected

fizz·y /fízzee/ (**-i·er, -i·est**) *adj.* producing or containing gas bubbles —**fizz·i·ly** *adv.* —**fizz·i·ness** *n.*

Fjord: Geiranger Fjord, Norway

fjord /fyawrd/, **fiord** *n.* a long narrow coastal inlet with steep sides, often formed by glacial action, especially along the west coast of Norway [Late 17thC. Via Norwegian from Old Norse *fjǫrðr*. Ultimately from an Indo-European word that is the ancestor of English *fare*, *firth*, and *ford*.]

Fkr *symbol.* Faeroese krona

FL *abbr.* **1.** Florida **2.** LANGUAGE foreign languages **3.** *U.K.* Flight Lieutenant

fl. *abbr.* **1.** floor **2.** MONEY florin **3.** floruit **4.** MUSIC flute

Fl. *abbr.* **1.** Flanders **2.** Flemish **3.** flanker

Fla. *abbr.* Florida

flab /flab/ *n.* excess or unwanted fat on somebody's body (*informal disapproving*) [Early 20thC. Back-formation from FLABBY.]

flab·ber·gast /flábbər gàst/ (**-gast·ed, -gast·ing, -gasts**) *vt.* to amaze or astonish somebody completely (*informal*) (*usually passive*) [Late 18thC. Origin uncertain: perhaps from FLABBY or FLAPPER + AGHAST.]

flab·by /flábbee/ (**-bi·er, -bi·est**) *adj.* **1.** HAVING EXCESS FAT having excess body fat or sagging flesh (*informal disapproving*) **2.** WEAK done without vitality or force (*informal*) [Late 17thC. Alteration of FLAPPY.] —**flab·bi·ly** *adv.* —**flab·bi·ness** *n.*

fla·bel·la plural of **flabellum**

fla·bel·late /flə béllət, flábbə làyt/, **fla·bel·li·form** /flə béllə fàwrm/ *adj.* shaped like an open handheld fan [Late 18thC. Formed from Latin *flabellum* (see FLABELLUM).]

fla·bel·lum /flə béllәm/ (*plural* **-la** /-béllə/) *n.* **1.** BIOL FAN-SHAPED BODY PART fan-shaped organ or body part **2.** CHR FAN USED IN ROMAN CATHOLIC CHURCH a fan with a long handle, used in the past in the Roman Catholic Church to keep away insects during the Eucharist service [Mid-19thC. From Latin *flabellum* "fan," from *flabrum* "gust," from *flare* "to blow" (source of English *flatulent*).]

flac·cid /fláksid, flássid/ *adj.* **1.** LIMP soft, limp, or lacking firmness **2.** LACKING VITALITY lacking energy, enthusiasm, or competence [Early 17thC. Directly or via French from Latin *flaccidus*, from *flaccus* "flabby."] —**flac·cid·i·ty** /flak síddətee, fla-/ *n.* —**flac·cid·ly** *adv.*

flack[1] /flak/ *n.* PRESS AGENT a press agent or publicist (*slang*) ■ *vti.* (**flacked, flack·ing, flacks**) BE PRESS AGENT to act as a press agent or publicity agent for somebody (*slang*) [Mid-20thC. Origin uncertain: possibly a variant of FLAK, from the supposed similarity between antiaircraft fire and the noisy babbling of publicists.] —**flack·er** *n.* —**flack·er·y** *n.*

flack[2] *n.* = **flak**

flac·on /flákən, flá kòn/ *n.* a small, often decorated, stoppered bottle used especially for perfume [Early 19thC. From French *fla(s)con* (see FLAGON).]

flag[1] /flag/ *n.* **1.** CLOTH FLOWN AS EMBLEM a piece of cloth, often rectangular and flown from a pole, carrying a distinctive design and used as an emblem or for signaling **2.** DECORATION a small ornament, emblem, or pin showing the colors and design of a flag **3.** POL NATIONAL IDENTITY SYMBOLIZED BY FLAG national or group identity symbolized by a flag **4.** MARKING DEVICE a marking device, e.g., a tab, attached to something to make it easier to identify or more conspicuous **5.** COMPUT COMPUTER PROGRAM MARKER an indicator generated by a computer program to indicate a certain condition, e.g., an error **6.** TRANSP MARKER SHOWING TAXI FOR HIRE formerly, a small marker on a taximeter, raised to show taxi's availablility for hire **7.** FOOTBALL PENALTY MARKER a colored cloth thrown to the ground by a football official to indicate illegal play **8.** MUSIC NOTE MARKER an angled line on the stem of a musical note, indicating its value **9.** NAVY = **flagship** *n.* 1 **10.** PRESS = **masthead** *n.* 1 **11.** ZOOL HAIR FRINGE BENEATH DOG'S TAIL a fringe of hair that grows on the lower part of the tail in some dog breeds, e.g., setters **12.** ZOOL DEER'S TAIL the tail of a deer ■ *vt.* (**flagged, flag·ging, flags**) **1.** STOP VEHICLE BY WAVING AT DRIVER to make a vehicle or its driver stop by making signs to the driver **2.** FOOTBALL INDICATE PENALTY to indicate a penalty by throwing down a flag **3.** MARK SOMETHING to mark something, e.g., a page or a place, in order to draw attention to it ○ *I've flagged the passages that need rewriting.* **4.** COMMUNICATION SEND INFORMATION BY FLAG to send information using a flag or flags **5.** CUT SOMEBODY OFF FROM DRINK to refuse to serve somebody more alcoholic beverages because of apparent drunkenness (*slang*) **6.** DECORATE SOMETHING WITH FLAGS to decorate something with flags **7.** HUNT ATTRACT ANIMAL'S ATTENTION to attract the attention or curiosity of wild game by waving something [Mid-16thC. Origin unknown. The English word is perhaps the source of the related forms found in all modern Germanic languages.] —**flag·ger** *n.*

WORD KEY: CULTURAL NOTE

Flag, a painting by Jasper Johns (1945). The first of many such variations that Johns created on this theme, it consists of a U.S. flag painted on canvas using encaustic. Its apparent banality infuriated many commentators; others responded positively to its playful ambiguity (is it a flag or a painting?) and saw it as Johns' reaction to the emotionalism of Abstract Expressionism.

flag[2] /flag/ (**flagged, flag·ging, flags**) *vi.* **1.** BECOME WEAK OR TIRED to become weak, tired, or less attentive **2.** HANG LIMPLY to hang down limply or droop [Mid-16thC. Origin uncertain: perhaps a variant of earlier *flakken*, *flakeren* "to flutter," both from a Scandinavian word.]

flag[3] /flag/ *n.* = **flagstone** *n.* 1 ■ *vt.* (**flagged, flag·ging, flags**) PAVE AREA WITH FLAGSTONES to pave a surface with flagstones [15thC. Origin uncertain: probably of Scandinavian origin.]

flag[4] /flag/ *n.* **1.** PLANTS IRIS PLANT a plant of the iris family, usually one with large flowers and leaves **2.** BOT LONG NARROW PLANT LEAF a long narrow leaf of a plant such as an iris or cattail [14thC. Origin uncertain: perhaps originally "flutterer," from Scandinavian.]

flag cap·tain *n.* the captain of the flagship of a fleet

Flag Day *n.* June 14, a holiday commemorating the official adoption of the design of the United States flag in 1777. It is marked by flying the flag in public places and by special activities in schools.

fla·gel·la plural of **flagellum**

flag·el·lant /flájjələnt/ *n.* **1.** RELIG **SELF-PUNISHING PENITENT** somebody who whips himself or herself as a form of penance **2.** PSYCHOL **SOMEBODY SEXUALLY STIMULATED BY WHIPPING** somebody who finds sexual gratification in whipping another or in being whipped [Late 16thC. From Latin *flagellant-*, present participle stem of *flagellare* "to whip," from *flagellum* (see FLAGELLUM).] —**flag·el·lant·ism** *n.*

fla·gel·lar /flə jéllər/ *adj.* relating to a flagellum

flag·el·late[1] (**-lat·ed, -lat·ing, -lates**) *vt.* /flájjə làyt/ to whip somebody, especially for sexual or religious purposes [Early 17thC. From Latin *flagellat-*, the past participle stem of *flagellare* "to whip," from *flagellum* (see FLAGELLUM).]

flag·el·late[2] /flájjələt, flájjə làyt, flə jéllət/ *adj.* **flag·el·late, flag·el·lat·ed** BIOL **1. RESEMBLING A LONG THREAD** similar to a long thin cellular appendage (**flagellum**) **2. WITH APPENDAGES RESEMBLING THREADS** used to describe an organism or cell that has long thin cellular appendages (**flagella**) ■ *n.* **MICROORGANISM WITH FLAGELLA** a microorganism with tiny cellular appendages (**flagella**). Some flagellates are pathogenic parasites that cause diseases such as giardiasis in humans.

flag·el·la·tion[1] /flàjjə láysh'n/ *n.* the act of whipping yourself or somebody else, especially for sexual or religious purposes

flag·el·la·tion[2] /flàjjə láysh'n/ *n.* the formation or arrangement of flagella on an organism

fla·gel·li·form /flə jéllə fàwrm/ *adj.* BIOL long, tapering, and very narrow [Early 19thC. Coined from FLAGELLUM + -FORM.]

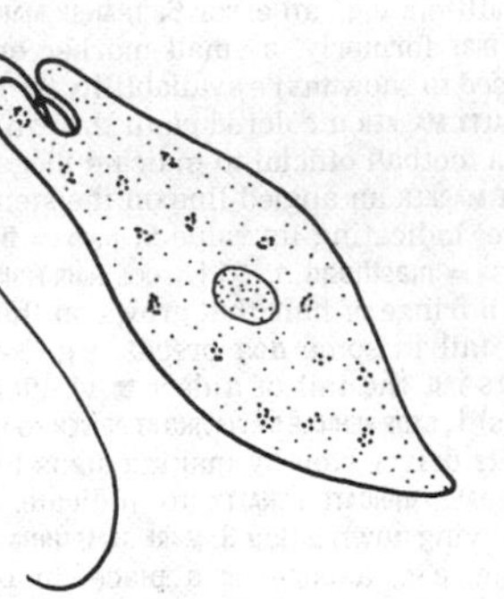

Flagellum

fla·gel·lum /flə jélləm/ (*plural* **fla·gel·la** /-jéllə/ *or* **fla·gel·lums**) *n.* **1.** BIOL **SLENDER CELLULAR APPENDAGE** a slender tapering narrow outgrowth of the cells of many microorganisms, e.g., protozoa, that is by itself or in groups, a means of locomotion **2.** INSECTS **ANTENNA PART** the very narrow terminal part of an insect's antenna [Early 19thC. From Latin *flagellum*, literally "little scourge," from *flagrum* "scourge" (probably the source of English *flail*).]

flag·eo·let[1] /flàjjə lét, flày-/ *n.* PLANTS a slender-podded variety of green bean that can be eaten either fresh or dried [Late 19thC. Via French from, ultimately, Latin *phaseolus* "bean."]

flag·eo·let[2] /flàjjə lét, flày-/ *n.* MUSIC a musical instrument of the 16th and 17th centuries similar to the flute [Mid-17thC. From French, literally "little flute," from Old French *flageol* "flute," of uncertain origin: probably ultimately from Latin *flare* "to blow."]

flag foot·ball *n.* a form of football in which play is stopped by the removal of a flag from the waist of the player with the ball, rather than by tackling

Flagg /flag/, **James Montgomery** (1877–1960) U.S. writer and illustrator. He created the Uncle Sam "I Want You" poster (1917) to recruit soldiers during World War I.

flagged /flagd/ *adj.* paved with flagstones

flag·ging[1] /flágging/ *adj.* **1. WEAKENING** decreasing in strength, power, or ability **2. HANGING LIMPLY** hanging down limply or drooping (*archaic*) —**flag·ging·ly** *adv.*

flag·ging[2] /flágging/ *n.* an area paved with flagstones

fla·gi·tious /flə jíshəss/ *adj.* (*formal*) **1. CRUEL OR WICKED** extremely cruel, wicked, or vicious **2. NOTORIOUS** notorious or infamous [14thC. From Latin *flagitiosus*, from *flagitium* "shameful crime," from *flagitare* "to demand vehemently."] —**fla·gi·tious·ly** *adv.* —**fla·gi·tious·ness** *n.*

flag·man /flágmən/ (*plural* **-men** /-mən/) *n.* somebody who carries a flag, usually to make signals

flag of con·ven·ience *n.* a flag of a country under which a ship is registered chosen for its favorable regulations, not for any real connection with the ship's owners or business

flag of·fi·cer *n.* in the Navy and Coast Guard, an officer above the rank of captain and, as an admiral, equivalent to general officer in the Army and Marines

flag of truce *n.* a white flag flown to indicate surrender, a request or offer of conference, or other peaceful intent

flag·on /flággən/ *n.* **1. CONTAINER FOR BEVERAGES** a container for beverages with a handle, narrow neck, spout, and sometimes a lid **2. LARGE BOTTLE FOR ALCOHOLIC DRINK** a large bottle with a short or narrow neck for an alcoholic drink **3. FLAGON'S CONTENTS** the amount that a flagon will hold [14thC. Via French from the late Latin *flascon-* "flask" (source of English *flask*).]

flag·pole /flág pōl/ *n.* a pole on which a flag is flown ◇ **run something up the flagpole** to put forward an idea or suggestion in order to gauge general reaction to it (*informal*)

flag rank *n.* the rank of admiral, above captain, in the Navy or Coast Guard

fla·grant /fláygrənt/ *adj.* **1. SCANDALOUS** very obvious and contrary to standards of conduct or morality ○ *a flagrant violation of the suspect's civil rights* **2. ON FIRE** on fire or blazing (*archaic*) [15thC. Directly or via French from Latin *flagrant-*, the present participle stem of *flagrare* "to burn" (source of English *conflagration*).] —**fla·grance** *n.* —**fla·gran·cy** *n.* —**fla·grant·ly** *adv.*

fla·gran·te /flə grántee/ ♦ **in flagrante delicto**

flag·ship /flág shìp/ *n.* **1.** NAVY **COMMANDING SHIP** the ship from which the admiral or unit commander controls the operation of a fleet **2.** SHIPPING **MAIN COMMERCIAL SHIP** the main ship in a commercial fleet **3. MOST IMPORTANT OF GROUP** the most important or prestigious among a group of similar and related things ○ *the flagship of the hotel spa chain*

flag·staff /flág stàf/ *n.* = **flagpole**

Flag·staff /flág stàf/ city in northern Arizona, northeast of Phoenix and southwest of the Painted Desert. Population: 55,094 (1996).

flag·stick /flág stìk/ *n.* GOLF the flag pole that marks the position of the hole on a putting green

flag·stone /flág stōn/ *n.* **1. PAVING STONE** a slab of stone or concrete used for making floors or paving **2.** GEOL **ROCK THAT SPLITS INTO SLABS** fine-textured rock that can be split into slabs suitable for use in paving [*Flag* from FLAG[3]]

flag stop *n.* a station or place where a bus or train stops only when signaled

flag·wav·ing *n.* an excessive and emotional display of patriotism —**flag·wav·er** *n.*

Fla·her·ty /flá ərtee/, **Robert Joseph** (1884–1951) U.S. documentary filmmaker. He is known for his ethnographic documentary about Inuit life, *Nanook of the North* (1920).

flail /flayl/ *v.* (**flailed, flail·ing, flails**) **1.** *vti.* **THRASH AROUND** to thrash or swing something around violently or uncontrollably, or move in this way **2.** *vt.* **HIT SOMETHING** to strike or hit something ■ *n.* **1.** AGRIC **MANUAL THRESHING IMPLEMENT** a manual threshing implement consisting of a wooden handle attached to a free-swinging wooden or metal bar **2.** ARMS **WEAPON SHAPED LIKE FLAIL** a weapon shaped like a threshing flail, used especially in the Middle Ages [Pre-12thC. Origin uncertain: probably from an assumed Old English word (influenced by Old French *flaiel*), from, ultimately, Latin *flagellum* "whip" (see FLAGELLUM).]

flair /flair/ *n.* **1. TALENT** a natural ability or aptitude **2. ELEGANCE** obvious elegance or stylishness [Late 19thC. From French *flair* "sense of smell," from Old French *flairer* "to smell," from late Latin *flagrare*, alteration of Latin *fragrare* "to emit an odor."]

WORD KEY: SYNONYMS

See Synonyms at ***talent.***

flak /flak/, **flack** *n.* **1.** ARMS **GROUND-BASED ANTIAIRCRAFT FIRE** antiaircraft fire directed from the ground **2. CRITICISM** strong adverse criticism (*informal*) [Mid-20thC. From German, an acronym from *Flieger* "airplane" + *Abwehr* "defense" + *Kanone* "canon."]

flake[1] /flayk/ *n.* **1. SMALL FLAT PIECE** a small flat piece or small part of a layer broken or detached from a larger object ○ *flakes of paint* **2. SMALL MANUFACTURED ITEM** a small thin flat object that is manufactured, sold, and used or consumed in quantity ○ *soap flakes* **3. SNOWFLAKE** a snowflake **4. ODD PERSON** somebody with unconventional and irrational behavior and ideas (*insult*) **5.** DRUGS **COCAINE** cocaine (*slang*) ■ *v.* (**flaked, flak·ing, flakes**) **1.** *vi.* **FORM INTO FLAKES AND FALL OFF** to form into flakes and fall or peel off **2.** *vt.* **BREAK SOMETHING INTO FLAKES** to break something into flakes, or break flakes from something ○ *flaked stones to fashion arrowheads* **3.** *vt.* **COVER SOMETHING WITH FLAKES** to cover or coat something with flakes [14thC. Origin uncertain; probably from Scandinavian.] —**flak·er** *n.*

flake out *vi.* (*slang*) **1. COLLAPSE FROM EXHAUSTION** to collapse or fall asleep because of exhaustion **2. LOSE REASON** to behave in an irrational way that prevents normal functioning

flake[2] /flayk/ *n.* a platform or frame for drying fish or other food [14thC. Origin uncertain: perhaps from Old Norse *flaki* "wicker shield."]

flake[3] /flayk/ *n.*, *vt.* (**flaked, flak·ing, flakes**) NAUT = **fake**[2] [Early 17thC. Related to FAKE.]

flake white *n.* a pigment made from flakes of white lead

flak jack·et *n.* a reinforced vest or jacket for protection against gunfire or shrapnel

flak·y /fláykee/ (**-i·er, -i·est**), **flak·ey** (**-i·er, -i·est**) *adj.* **1. UNCONVENTIONAL** unconventional or irrational (*informal*) **2. LIKE FLAKES** made of or similar to flakes **3. TENDING TO BREAK OFF IN FLAKES** forming or tending to break off in flakes —**flak·i·ly** *adv.* —**flak·i·ness** *n.*

flam /flam/ *n.* a drumbeat of two nearly simultaneous strokes [Late 18thC. Origin uncertain: probably an imitation of the sound.]

flam·bé /flaam báy/ *vt.* (**-béed, -bé·ing, -bés**) **POUR LIQUOR ON FOOD AND IGNITE** to pour liquor over food and light it in order to burn off the alcohol and impart the flavor of the liquor to the food ■ *adj.* **flam·bée SERVED IN IGNITED LIQUOR** served in liquor, usually brandy, that has been burned off or is still burning ○ *bananas flambée* [Late 19thC. From French, the past participle of *flamber* "to singe, pass through flame," ultimately from Latin *flamma* "flame."]

flam·beau /flám bō/ (*plural* **-beaux** *or* **-beaus**) *n.* **1. TORCH** a lighted torch made of wicks dipped in wax **2. CANDLESTICK** a large decorative candlestick **3.** *Carib* **TORCH LIT WITH KEROSENE** a torch made by stuffing cloth into a bottle or sometimes a bamboo joint containing kerosene [Mid-17thC. From French, "torch, flame," from *flambe* "flame," from, ultimately, Latin *flamma* "flame."]

flam·boy·ant /flam bóy ənt/ *adj.* **1. SHOWY** showy and dashing in a self-satisfied way **2. BRIGHTLY-COLORED** brightly-colored and striking **3. HIGHLY DECORATED** elaborate or richly decorated **4. AUDACIOUS** unrestrained by prevailing standards of propriety **5.** ARCHIT **OF FRENCH GOTHIC ARCHITECTURE** used to refer to the final stage of French Gothic architecture from the 14th to the 16th centuries that is noted for its fine detailing and pointed decoration ■ *n.* TREES = **royal poinciana** [Mid-19thC. From French, the present participle of *flamboyer* "to blaze," from *flambe* "flame," ultimately from Latin *flamma* "flame."] —**flam·boy·ance** *n.* —**flam·boy·ant·ly** *adv.*

flame /flaym/ *n.* **1. HOT GLOWING BODY OF BURNING GAS** a hot glowing body of burning gas, often carrying fine incandescent particles **2. STRONG FEELING** an intense feeling or emotion **3. LOVER** a sweetheart or lover (*informal*) ○ *an old flame* **4. REDDISH-ORANGE COLOR** a brilliant reddish-orange color ■ *adj.* **REDDISH-ORANGE COLOR** of a brilliant reddish-orange color ■ *v.* (**flamed, flam·ing, flames**) **1.** *vi.* **PRODUCE FLAME** to burn producing flame **2.** *vi.* **HAVE FIERY GLOW** to have or develop a fiery glow, especially suddenly ○ *Her cheeks flamed as she spoke.* **3.** *vti.* COMPUT **CRITICIZE SOMEBODY ELECTRONICALLY** to deluge somebody with offensive and disparaging e-mail **4.** *vi.* **FEEL STRONG EMOTION** to display or feel intense emotion **5.** *vt.* **IGNITE** to set fire to something **6.** *vt.* **MAKE SOMETHING BURN** to make something burn (*archaic*) ■ *n.* COMPUT **ANGRY E-MAIL MESSAGE** a rude, abusive, or threatening e-mail message or newsgroup posting [14thC. Via Anglo-Norman from French *flamme*, from Latin *flammula* "little flame," from *flamma* "flame."] —**flam·er** *n.* —**flamy** *adj.* ◇ **fan the flames** to make a tense or difficult situation worse ◇ **shoot somebody** *or* **something down in flames** to reject or refute an idea or suggestion emphatically

flame-arc lamp *n.* a lamp that uses an electric arc maintained between carbon electrodes that are infused with metallic salts to provide color to the flame

flame bait *n.* TECH an inflammatory statement intentionally posted in an online discussion group that is designed to elicit a strong response or start a flame war (*informal*)

flame car·bon *n.* a carbon electrode containing metallic salts that, with other similar carbon electrodes, has the effect of coloring the arc produced between the electrodes

flame cell *n.* a hollow excretory cell in certain invertebrates, e.g., flatworms, that has a tuft of projections (**cilia**) resembling hairs whose movement serves to force out waste products [*Flame* from the movement of the cilia, which resemble tongues of flame]

fla·men /fláymən/ (*plural* **fla·mens** *or* **flam·i·nes** /flámmə neez/) *n.* a priest in ancient Rome belonging to a group of 15, each of whom oversaw the rituals connected with a particular deity [14thC. From Latin.]

Barnaby's

Flamenco

fla·men·co /flə méngkō/ (*plural* **-cos**) *n.* **1.** DANCE **VIGOROUS SPANISH DANCE WITH HAND CLAPPING** a dance originating in Spain that features hand clapping and stamping of the feet **2.** MUSIC **MUSIC FOR SPANISH DANCE** the strongly rhythmic music that accompanies flamenco dancing [Late 19thC. Via Spanish, "Flemish person," from Middle Dutch *Vlaming* (see FLAMINGO).]

flame net·tle (*plural* **flame net·tle**) *n.* = **coleus**

flame·out /fláym owt/ *n.* the unintentional extinguishing of the flame of a jet engine in flight, e.g., through a failure of combustion or the fuel supply

flame·proof /fláym proof/ *adj.* **1. RESISTANT TO FIRE** resistant to catching fire (*often used of textiles and clothing*) **2.** ELEC ENG **NOT EXPLOSIVE** used to describe electrical apparatus that is designed so that an explosion of inflammable gas inside will not ignite inflammable gas outside **3.** COOK **FOR COOKING WITH DIRECT HEAT** used to describe containers that can be used when cooking on a stove top or under a grill ■ *vt.* (**-proofed, -proof·ing, -proofs**) **MAKE SOMETHING FLAME RESISTANT** to make something resistant to flames or combustion —**flame·proof·er** *n.*

flame-re·tard·ant *adj.* made or chemically treated to resist catching fire

flame test *n.* a test for the presence of various metals in a substance by noting the colors produced when a small amount is placed in a flame and vaporized

flame·throw·er *n.* a weapon that projects a stream of burning liquid

flame tree *n.* **1. TREE WITH REDDISH FLOWERS** a tropical tree that is cultivated for its bright orange, yellow, or red flowers. Royal poinciana is a flame tree. **2. FLOWERING AUSTRALIAN TREE** an Australian tree noted for its bright red flowers that bloom in spring when the tree is leafless. Latin name: *Brachychiton acerifolius.*

flame war *n.* COMPUT a period of repeated exchanges of abusive and insulting e-mail between individuals or groups

flamines *npl.* plural of **flamen** *n.*

flam·ing /fláyming/ *adj.* **1. PRODUCING FLAMES** burning and producing flames **2. INTENSE** very angry, intense, or passionate ○ *flaming indignation* **3. GLOWING** brightly glowing ○ *flaming cheeks* **4. VIVID IN COLOR** quite vivid in color ■ *n.* COMPUT **DELUGE OF CRITICAL E-MAIL** the directing of a large volume of abusive and insulting e-mail at somebody, often as part of a flame war

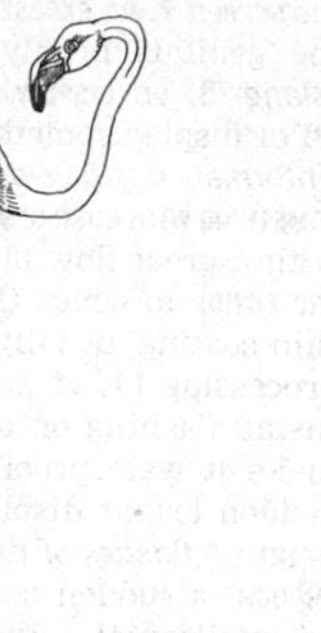

Flamingo

fla·min·go /flə míng gō/ *n.* (*plural* **-gos** *or* **-goes** *or* **-go**) **1.** BIRDS **LARGE PINK WADING BIRD** a large wading bird native to tropical brackish waters that has a long neck and legs, downward-curving bill, webbed feet, and pinkish-white feathers with black wing quills. Family: Phoenicopteridae. **2.** COLORS **DEEP PINK COLOR** a deep pink color tinged with orange ■ *adj.* COLORS **OF DEEP PINK COLOR** of a deep pink color tinged with orange [Mid-16thC. Via Portuguese from obsolete Spanish *flamengo*, of uncertain origin: perhaps from Dutch *Vlaming* "Flemish person" or ultimately from Latin *flamma* (see FLAME).]

WORD KEY: ORIGIN

Whether its ultimate source is Dutch or Latin, the motivation behind the bird's name is its bright appearance. The Latin derivation would make it the "flame"-colored bird; the Dutch derivation would depend on the reputation the people of Flanders had in the Middle Ages for bright flamboyant dress (whence the Spanish dance, the *flamenco*).

flam·ing sword *n.* a bromeliad, or subshrub, with yellow flowers and reddish bract pigmentation, native to French Guiana and cultivated elsewhere. Latin name: *Vriesea splendens.*

flam·ma·ble /flámməb'l/ *adj.* readily capable of catching fire —**flam·ma·bil·i·ty** /flàmmə bíllətee/ *n.*

flan /flan/ *n.* **1.** FOOD **CUSTARD DESSERT** a custard dessert topped with caramel syrup **2.** FOOD, COOK **OPEN FILLED PIE** an open, usually round, pie with a fruit or other filling **3.** METALL **METAL DISK FOR STAMPING AS COIN** a circular metal blank ready to be stamped as a coin [Mid-19thC. Via French from the medieval Latin stem *fladon-*, from a prehistoric Germanic base that is also the ancestor of English *flat*.]

Flan·ders /flándərz/ former region in northwestern Europe that was a powerful independent state between the 11th and 14th centuries. It is equivalent to the present-day provinces of Flanders in Belgium, Nord Department in France, and part of Zeeland Province in the Netherlands.

flâ·ne·rie /flaan rée, flaanə rée/ *n.* aimless idling or strolling (*literary*) [Late 19thC. From French, from *flâner* "to stroll, lounge around."]

flâ·neur /flaa núr/ *n.* somebody who is idling or loafing about (*literary*) [Mid-19thC. From French, from *flâner* (see FLANERIE).]

flange /flanj/ *n.* a projecting collar, rim, or rib on an object for fixing it to another object, holding it in place, or strengthening it. Flanges are often found on pipes and shafts. [Late 17thC. Origin uncertain: perhaps a variant of *flanch* "device at the side of an escutcheon." The current meaning evolved via "protruding rim" from "part that widens out."] —**flanged** *adj.*

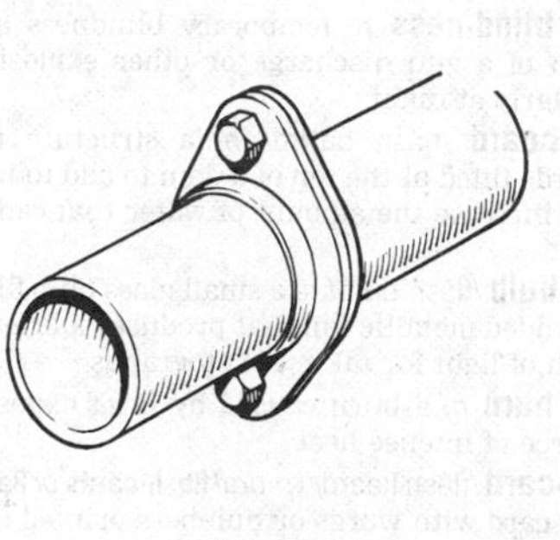

Flange

flanged rail *n.* an early form of rail with a raised edge (**flange**) on one side to stabilize wheels traveling on it. On modern trains the flange is on the wheel.

flank /flangk/ *n.* **1.** MIL **SIDE OF MILITARY FORMATION** the left or right side of a military formation **2.** ANAT **SIDE OF LOWER TORSO** either side of the body of a human or an animal between the last rib and the hip **3.** COOK **CUT OF MEAT FROM ANIMAL'S FLANK** a cut of meat, especially beef, from an animal's flank, that is typically tough and requires slow cooking in liquid **4. SIDE OF SOMETHING** the side of any object **5.** SPORTS **SIDE OF SPORTS FIELD** either of the sides of a sports field ○ *not used to playing on the left flank* ■ *vt.* (**flanked, flank·ing, flanks**) **BE BY SIDE OF** to be on or at the side of something or somebody ○ *He was flanked by secret service officers.* [Pre-12thC. From French *flanc*, of uncertain origin: probably from assumed Old Frankish *hlanca* "side," from a prehistoric Germanic base that is also the ancestor of English *flinch*.]

flan·ken /flaánkən/ *n.* a cut of meat taken from the short ribs of beef [Mid-20thC. Via Yiddish from German *Flanken*, plural of *Flank* "flank, side," ultimately from French *flanc* (see FLANK).]

flank·er /flángkər/ *n.* **1.** FOOTBALL = **split end** *n.* 1 **2.** FOOTBALL = **flankerback 3.** MIL **SOLDIER IN PROTECTIVE UNIT** one of the soldiers in a unit that protects the flank of a military column on the march

flank·er·back /flángkər bàk/ *n.* FOOTBALL an offensive back positioned outside the play formation

flan·nel /flánn'l/ *n.* **1. SOFT COTTON CLOTH** a soft cotton cloth with a nap on one side, used for warm clothing, sleepwear, and sheets **2. SOFT WOOLEN CLOTH** a soft closely woven woolen or wool-blend cloth used for clothing ■ *vt.* (**-neled, -nel·ing, -nels**) **WRAP SOMEBODY IN FLANNEL** to wrap or clothe somebody in flannel ■ **flan·nels** *npl.* **1. PANTS MADE OF FLANNEL** clothing, especially slacks, made from flannel **2. FLANNEL UNDERWEAR** woolen underwear of thick flannel [14thC. Origin uncertain: ultimately from either Welsh *gwlanen* "woolen article" (from *gwlân* "wool") or French *flaine*, a kind of coarse wool.] —**flan·nel·ly** *adj.*

flan·nel·board /flánn'l bàwrd/ *n.* a board covered with flannel to which pictures and cloth cutouts will stick that is used in primary education

flan·nel cake *n.* FOOD a pancake (*regional*)

flan·nel·ette /flànn'l ét/ *n.* a light cotton cloth with a soft brushed surface on one side

flan·nel·flow·er /flánn'l flòwr/ *n.* a plant that grows in eastern Australia and has white flowers covered with soft white hairs. Latin name: *Actinotus helianthi.*

flan·nel leaf *n.* = **mullein** [*Flannel* from its resemblance to the material]

flan·nel-mouthed *adj.* **1. GARBLED** garbled and indistinct **2. DECEPTIVE** speaking obsequiously and deceptively

flap /flap/ *v.* (**flapped, flap·ping, flaps**) **1.** *vti.* **MOVE WINGS UP AND DOWN** to move something up and down, especially wings or arms during or as if in flight, or to be moved up and down in this way **2.** *vi.* **FLY BY MOVING WINGS** to fly by moving the wings repeatedly **3.** *vti.* **MOVE OR SWAY REPEATEDLY** to cause something to move or sway in one direction and then another repeatedly and often noisily, or move in this way ○ *flags flapping in the breeze* **4.** *vt.* **HIT WITH BROAD OBJECT** to hit somebody or something with a broad flat object ○ *He flapped his hand on the table.* **5.** *vt.* **TOSS SOMETHING** to fling down or toss something (*informal*) ○ *flapped the report on the table* **6.** *vt.* PHON **MAKE AN "R" SOUND** to make an "r" sound by briefly striking the roof of the mouth with the tongue, as in "parrot" ■ *n.* **1. FLAT THIN PIECE USED AS COVER** a flat thin piece attached along one edge, usually used as a cover for an opening ○ *the flap of an envelope* **2.** PUBL **DUST JACKET PART** either of the two parts of a dust jacket that fold inside a book's cover and are usually printed with information about the book or author **3. ACT OR SOUND OF FLAPPING** an act of or the sound made by flapping ○ *The bird disappeared with a flap of its wings.* **4.** AIR **AIRCRAFT WING CONTROL SURFACE** a narrow movable surface attached to the rear edge of an aircraft wing that is used to create lift or drag **5.** COMMOTION a commotion or state of upset, especially a disordered argument (*informal*) ○ *Don't get into a flap about it.* **6.** SURG MASS OF TISSUE FOR GRAFTING a mass of tissue, used for surgical grafting, that remains partially attached and retains its blood supply **7.** BLOW FROM BROAD OBJECT a blow or slap from a broad object **8.** PHON "R" SOUND an "r" sound made by briefly striking the roof of the mouth with the tongue, as in "parrot" [14thC. Origin uncertain: the noun first meant "blow, slap," and so is probably imitative of the sound.]

flap·doo·dle /fláp do͞od'l/ *n.* silly talk or nonsense (*dated slang*) [Mid-19thC. Origin unknown: perhaps thought to suggest foolishness.]

flap·jack /fláp jàk/ *n.* **1.** = **pancake** *n.* 1 **2.** *U.K.* CHEWY CAKE MADE WITH OATS a cake made of oats, syrup, and butter and cut into squares before eating

flap·pa·ble /fláppəb'l/ *adj.* tending to get flustered or panicky (*informal*)

flap·per /fláppər/ *n.* **1.** YOUNG UNCONVENTIONAL WOMAN OF THE 1920S a young woman of the 1920s who disdained prior conventions of decorum and fashion. Flappers were associated with the Charleston dance, bobbed hair, heavy makeup, and drop-waisted very short dresses. **2.** YOUNG BIRD a bird that is learning to fly **3.** SOMETHING FLAPPING AROUND an object that flaps around **4.** BROAD FLAT OBJECT a broad flat object used for striking something [Late 16thC. "Young unconventional woman" of uncertain origin: either from *flapper* "young wild duck" (from FLAP), or dialectal *flap* "woman of loose character."]

flap·py /fláppee/ (**-pi·er, -pi·est**) *adj.* flapping around, or likely to flap around

flare /flair/ *v.* (**flared, flar·ing, flares**) **1.** *vti.* BURN SUDDENLY AND BRIGHTLY to burn, or cause something to burn, suddenly and brightly **2.** *vi.* START UP AGAIN to recur, worsen, or intensify suddenly **3.** *vi.* BECOME ANGRY to become suddenly angry **4.** *vti.* WIDEN OUT to widen out, or to cause something to widen out ○ *Her nostrils flared.* **5.** *vt.* SIGNAL SOMEBODY FOR HELP to signal somebody for help by means of a device used to produce a light signal **6.** *vt.* INDUST BURN OFF GAS to ignite and burn off unwanted waste gas in open air ■ *n.* **1.** SUDDEN BLAZE OF LIGHT a sudden blaze of light or fire, especially one used to signal distress or location or used for illumination ○ *the flare of naval signal lights* **2.** DEVICE FOR PRODUCING FLARE a device used to produce a light signal calling for help ○ *a distress flare* **3.** FLAME a sudden or unsteady flame ○ *the flare of distant oil wells* **4.** WIDENING SHAPE a shape that widens out ○ *a long skirt with a flare* **5.** FOOTBALL SHORT AND WIDE PASS in football, a pass to a back running laterally **6.** OPTICS, PHOTOGRAPHY UNWANTED LIGHT IN AN OPTICAL DEVICE unwanted light reaching a photographic image, especially when reflected from an internal lens **7.** OUTBURST OF EMOTION a sudden outburst, especially of a negative emotion ○ *a flare of anger* **8.** INDUST FLAME FOR BURNING OFF WASTE GAS a flame that burns off unwanted waste gas in the open air **9.** MED INFLAMMATION an area of inflammation on the skin ■ **flares** *npl. U.K.* PANTS WITH WIDE LEGS BELOW KNEE pants with legs that widen significantly below the knee, first popular in the late 1960s [Mid-16thC. Origin uncertain.]

flare·back /fláir bàk/ *n.* **1.** ARMS FLAME INSIDE GUN'S BREECH a flame inside a gun's breech caused by the ignition of gases remaining after the weapon has been fired **2.** REACTION DIRECTED BACK TOWARD ORIGIN a reaction or effect directed back toward a point of origin

flared /flaird/ *adj.* widening out

flare stack *n.* a large open-air burner used to dispose of excess flammable gas at an oil refinery, well, or platform

flare-up *n.* **1.** SUDDEN OUTBURST OF AGGRESSION a sudden occurrence of emotion or violence (*informal*) **2.** RECURRENCE OF SOMETHING a recurrence of something, especially a disease **3.** SUDDEN OCCURRENCE OF FIRE OR LIGHT a sudden occurrence or increase of fire or light

flar·ing /fláiring/ *adj.* **1.** BURNING DIMLY burning dimly or unsteadily **2.** SHOWY bright and showy **3.** BECOMING WIDER widening out —**flar·ing·ly** *adv.*

flash /flash/ *v.* (**flashed, flash·ing, flash·es**) **1.** *vti.* EMIT LIGHT SUDDENLY to cause light to appear suddenly or in brief bursts from something, or to appear in this way ○ *We could see the lights of police cars flashing in the distance.* **2.** *vti.* REFLECT LIGHT FROM ANOTHER SOURCE to reflect light suddenly or briefly, or make something such as a lamp reflect from a surface ○ *sunlight flashing on the water* **3.** *vti.* CATCH FIRE SUDDENLY to burst into flame suddenly, or cause something to burst into flame **4.** *vti.* COMMUNICATION SIGNAL TO SOMEBODY WITH LIGHTS to signal to somebody or communicate something by quickly turning lights on and off **5.** *vi.* MOVE QUICKLY to move or pass very quickly in a specified direction **6.** *vti.* APPEAR MOMENTARILY to appear briefly, or show something briefly ○ *flash a message onto the screen* **7.** *vi.* EXPOSE BODY INDECENTLY IN PUBLIC to expose the genitals briefly and intentionally in public (*slang*) **8.** *vt.* DISPLAY SOMETHING OSTENTATIOUSLY to show off or display something in order to impress people (*informal*) ○ *flashed her vulgar jewelry* **9.** *vt.* FILL SOMETHING WITH RUSH OF WATER to fill something suddenly with a great flow of water **10.** *vt.* COAT SOMETHING FOR PROTECTION to cover the surface of an object with a thin coating, usually for protection or as a stage in processing **11.** *vt.* BUILDING PROTECT ROOF FROM LEAKING to install flashing on a roof joint or window joint to make it waterproof ■ *n.* **1.** SUDDEN BURST OF LIGHT a sudden bright display of light, fire, or something bright ○ *flashes of lightning* **2.** SUDDEN BURST OF MOOD OR THOUGHT a sudden occurance of an emotional mood or intellectual activity ○ *a flash of inspiration* **3.** BRIEF MOMENT a brief moment or instant ○ *I'll be there in a flash.* **4.** LIGHT PATCH a patch of light or bright color on a dark background, e.g., on an animal's coat **5.** PHOTOGRAPHY BRIGHT LIGHTING USED IN PHOTOGRAPHY the brief illumination of a subject for photographic purposes **6.** PHOTOGRAPHY DEVICE USED TO LIGHT PHOTOGRAPHIC SUBJECT a device used in flash photography to produce a short, bright light (*informal*) **7.** FLASHLIGHT a flashlight (*informal*) **8.** RUSH OF WATER a sudden rush of water down a watercourse, or a device that produces this **9.** BROADCAST NEWS FLASH a sudden important news story requiring immediate broadcast (*informal*) **10.** GYN = **hot flash** (*informal*) **11.** DRUGS RUSH the sudden effects felt when taking a mind-altering recreational drug (*slang*) **12.** MIL BADGE ON UNIFORM OR VEHICLE a badge or insignia on a uniform or vehicle **13.** CLOTHES COLORED STRIP WORN ON SOCKS in Highland dress, a short strip of colored material folded over the garter and protruding below the folded-over top of the socks (*usually used in the plural*) **14.** LANGUAGE USED IN UNDERWORLD the language used by criminals, thieves, and their associates (*archaic slang*) ■ *adj. U.K.* INSINCERE insincere, false, or counterfeit ○ *an outpouring of flash sentiment* [13thC. Originally in the sense "to splash"; probably an imitation of the sound. Later senses probably evolved from the idea of light suddenly and briefly reflected from disturbed water.] ◇ **flash in the pan** a sudden brief success that is not, or not likely to be, repeated ◇ **in a flash 1.** very rapidly **2.** suddenly

flash back *vi.* **1.** PSYCHOL RECALL PAINFUL MEMORY to recall an intensely vivid memory of a traumatic experience **2.** CINEMA, LITERAT RETURN TO EARLIER EVENT to go back to a scene at an earlier point in a narrative, out of chronological order, to fill in information or explain something in the present

flash forward *vi.* to jump forward in time to a scene at a later point in a narrative, out of chronological order, usually for dramatic effect or irony

flash on *vt.* to remember or think of something suddenly (*informal*) ○ *I just flashed on my first day in school.*

flash·back /flásh bàk/ *n.* **1.** PSYCHOL PAINFUL MEMORY an intensely vivid memory of a traumatic experience that returns repeatedly **2.** CINEMA, LITERAT EARLIER EVENT OR SCENE a scene or event from the past that appears in a narrative out of chronological order, to fill in information or explain something in the present ○ *Much of the film's exposition is handled through flashbacks.* **3.** DRUGS DRUG AFTER-EFFECT the later experiencing of the effects of a hallucinogenic drug such as LSD long after discontinuing use of the drug

flash blind·ness *n.* temporary blindness after the flash of a gun discharge or other explosion, particularly at night

flash·board /flásh bàwrd/ *n.* a structure made of boards fitted at the top of a dam to add to its height and increase the amount of water that can be held back

flash·bulb /flásh bùlb/ *n.* a small glass bulb filled with shredded metallic foil that produces a brief intense flash of light for taking photographs

flash burn *n.* a burn caused by brief exposure to a source of intense heat

flash·card /flásh kaàrd/ (*plural* **flash·cards** *or* **flash cards**) *n.* a card with words or numbers printed on it that is briefly displayed as a learning device

flash·er /fláshər/ *n.* **1.** SOMEBODY WHO EXPOSES PRIVATE PARTS somebody who gains sexual pleasure from publicly exposing the genitals (*slang*) **2.** AUTOMOT FLASHING LIGHT a light that flashes as a signal, especially on a vehicle **3.** TECH DEVICE MAKING LIGHT FLASH a device that switches a light on and off automatically to make it flash

flash flood *n.* a sudden and often destructive surge of water down a narrow channel or sloping ground, usually caused by heavy rainfall

flash-for·ward *n.* a scene or event from the future that appears in a narrative out of chronological order, usually for dramatic effect or irony

flash·gun /flásh gùn/ *n.* a device that holds a flashtube or flashbulb and automatically discharges it as the attached camera's shutter opens

flash·ing /fláshing/ *n.* pieces of sheet metal attached around the joints and angles of a roof to protect against leakage

flash·light /flásh lìt/ *n.* **1.** PORTABLE LIGHT SOURCE a small hand-held lamp usually powered by batteries **2.** PHOTOGRAPHY BURST OF BRIGHT LIGHT FOR PHOTOGRAPHY a brief intense flash of light produced by a photographic lamp **3.** BRIGHT FLASHING LIGHT any bright light that flashes, e.g., a beacon

flash mem·o·ry *n.* a programmable read-only computer memory chip that can be erased and reprogrammed in blocks rather than one byte at a time

flash·o·ver /flásh òvər/ *n.* an unintended electric arc around or over the surface of an insulator

flash pho·tog·ra·phy *n.* photography that illuminates its subject with a brief flash of artificial light

flash pho·tol·y·sis (*plural* **flash pho·tol·y·ses**) *n.* a method of studying photochemical reactions in gases. The gas is exposed to very brief intense flashes of light and the results are analyzed with a spectroscope.

flash·point /flásh pòynt/ *n.* **1.** CHEM TEMPERATURE OF VAPOR IGNITION the lowest temperature at which a flammable liquid will give off enough vapor to ignite briefly when exposed to a flame **2.** CRITICAL STAGE the critical stage in some process, event, or situation at which action, change, or violence occurs **3.** TROUBLE SPOT a place where violence is likely to break out suddenly, usually as a result of social or political tension

flash·tube /flásh to͞ob/ *n.* a glass or quartz tube filled with xenon gas that emits a short intense burst of light for flash photography when electric current is passed through it

flash u·nit *n.* PHOTOGRAPHY **1.** FLASHTUBE AND POWER SOURCE a flashtube and its power supply in a single compact unit **2.** FLASHGUN WITH OR WITHOUT REFLECTOR a flashgun, or a unit comprising a flashgun and reflector

flash·y /fláshee/ (**-i·er, -i·est**) *adj.* **1.** OSTENTATIOUSLY STYLISH stylish and expensive-looking in an obvious or ostentatious way **2.** MOMENTARILY BRILLIANT showing momentary or superficial brilliance —**flash·i·ly** *adv.* —**flash·i·ness** *n.*

flask /flask/ *n.* **1.** SCI SMALL BOTTLE a small glass bottle, often with a long neck, of the type used in laboratory work **2.** HOUSEHOLD SMALL FLAT CONTAINER FOR ALCOHOL a small thin flat container with a narrow neck, carried in a pocket and usually used to hold liquor **3.** *Carib* HALF A BOTTLE OF RUM in Trinidad, half a bottle of rum (*informal*) **4.** ARMS = **powder horn 5.** METALL MOLD USED IN FOUNDRY a frame packed full of sand, used in a foundry to make a mold **6.** ENERGY CONTAINER FOR SPENT NUCLEAR FUEL a very strong container in which irradiated nuclear fuel is transported [14thC. Immediate origin uncertain: from medieval Latin *flasca*, ultimately, perhaps, from prehistoric Germanic.]

flat[1] /flat/ *adj.* (**flat·ter, flat·test**) **1.** LEVEL AND HORIZONTAL level and horizontal, without any slope ○ *The flat plains stretch for miles.* **2.** EVEN AND SMOOTH even and smooth, without any bumps or hollows ○ *back on the flat road* **3.** NOT CURVED not curved inward or outward ○ *a wok with a flat bottom* **4.** WITH LITTLE CURVATURE with relatively little depth or curvature ○ *a vase with flat sides* **5.** LYING HORIZONTAL in a horizontal position, parallel with or stretched out on the ground ○ *plants lying flat after the heavy rain* **6.** TOUCHING SOMETHING ELSE with whole extent touching another surface at all points ○ *Stand it flat against the wall.* **7.** BEVERAGES NO LONGER BUBBLY having lost effervescence ○ *flat champagne* **8.** NOT FULL OF AIR no longer full of air ○ *a flat tire* **9.** MUSIC **BELOW CORRECT PITCH** sounded or sounding a little lower than the intended pitch level ○ *Your E string is flat.* **10.** MUSIC **ONE HALF-STEP BELOW NATURAL** pitched one half-step below the specified note ○ *in the key of B flat minor* **11. LACKING EXCITEMENT** without any interest or excitement ○ *Some days life just seems flat.* **12.** COOK **FLAVORLESS** without flavor or seasoning ○ *This soup tastes flat.* **13. MONOTONOUS IN SOUND** with no variation in pitch or intonation ○ *expressed her displeasure in a flat voice* **14.** COMM **COMMERCIALLY INACTIVE** not commercially active ○ *The market is fairly flat at the moment.* **15.** FIN **NOT VARYING** not varying in amount or level ○ *They charge a flat fee of $50.* **16. EMPHATICALLY ABSOLUTE** categorical and without any qualification ○ *a flat denial of the charges* **17.** CLOTHES **LOW-HEELED** with low heels or no heels at all ○ *flat shoes* **18. NOT SHINY** not shiny or glossy ○ *a flat white paint* **19.** SAILING **TIGHT** stretched so as to be tight **20.** MED **INDICATING CESSATION OF PHYSIOLOGICAL ACTIVITY** showing no variation on a monitoring machine, and thereby indicating that physiological activity has stopped ○ *a flat EKG* **21.** PHON **RESEMBLING VOWEL SOUND IN "FAT"** used to describe the vowel "a" as it is pronounced in "fat" or "badge" ■ *adv.* (**flat·ter, flat·test**) **1.** MUSIC **BELOW PITCH** below the intended pitch ○ *She tends to sing flat.* **2. VERY** used to add emphasis (*informal*) ○ *flat broke* **3. EXACTLY** no more and no less ○ *He ran the mile in four minutes flat.* **4.** FIN **WITHOUT INTEREST** not accruing any interest ○ *The bonds were trading flat.* ■ *n.* **1. LEVEL SURFACE** a flat part or surface ○ *the flat of a knife blade* **2.** MUSIC **NOTE LOWERED BY HALF-STEP** a sign (♭) placed next to a note to show that it is to be lowered by a half-step, or a note that is lowered a half-step ○ *a key with four flats* **3.** GEOG **LARGE STRETCH OF LEVEL GROUND** a large level stretch of, e.g., mud exposed at low tide or of salt deposits (*usually used in the plural*) ○ *the great salt flats* **4.** TRANSP **DEFLATED TIRE** a tire that has become deflated (*informal*) **5.** GARDENING **SHALLOW BOX FOR SEEDLINGS** a shallow lidless box or frame for seedlings **6.** THEATER **MOVABLE SCENERY** theatrical scenery mounted on a movable wooden frame **7.** RAIL = **flatcar 8.** SHIPPING = **flatboat 9.** MAIL **BIG FLAT ENVELOPE** a large flat piece of mail ■ **flats** *npl.* CLOTHES **LOW-HEELED SHOES** shoes with low heels ■ *v.* (**flat·ted, flat·ting, flats**) **1.** *vti.* **FLATTEN** to make something flat or to become flat ○ *"in the winter the fur grew thick and flatted out along her sides"* (Henry David Thoreau, *Walden*; 1854) **2.** *vt.* MUSIC **MAKE NOTE FLAT** to lower a note a half step **3.** *vt.* MUSIC **SING OR PLAY SOMETHING FLAT** to sing or play a note below the intended pitch [14thC. From Old Norse *flatr.* Ultimately from an Indo-European word that is also the ancestor of English *flounder, flan,* and *plate.*] —**flat·ness** *n.*

flat[2] /flat/ *n. U.K.* = **apartment** [Early 19thC. Alteration, influenced by FLAT[1], of Scots *flet* "interior of a house," from Old English *flet(t)* "house," earlier "floor." Ultimately from the same Indo-European word as English *flat*[1].]

flat·bed /flát bèd/ *n.* **1.** = **flatbed trailer 2.** = **flatbed truck**

flat·bed press *n.* = **cylinder press**

flat·bed trail·er *n.* a trailer consisting of a completely open platform with no sides or railings

flat·bed truck *n.* a truck that has a completely open platform at the rear with no sides or railings

flat·boat /flát bòt/ *n.* a large boat with a flat bottom used for transporting goods on shallow waterways

flat·bread /flát brèd/ *n.* bread baked in round flat loaves and usually made with unleavened dough. Examples are pitta, nan, chapatis, and tortillas.

flat·car /flát kaar/ *n.* a railroad freight car that has no roof or sides

flat-chest·ed *adj.* having small breasts

flat-coat·ed re·triev·er *n.* a large dog with a thick, smooth, black or reddish-brown coat, belonging to a breed originally developed in England for retrieving game

flat·fish /flát fish/ (*plural* **-fish** *or* **-fish·es**) *n.* any fish with a flat body and both eyes on the upper side. Flounder, sole, and halibut are types of flatfish. Order: Pleuronectiformes.

flat·foot /flát fòot/ *n.* **1.** ANAT **FOOT PROBLEM** an abnormal condition of the feet in which the arches are so low that all of the sole makes contact with the ground. ◊ **splayfoot 2.** (*plural* **-foots** *or* **-feet**) **OFFENSIVE TERM** an offensive term for a police officer, typically one on foot patrol (*dated slang offensive*)

flat-foot·ed, flat·foot·ed *adj.* **1.** ANAT **HAVING FLAT FEET** used to describe somebody with flat feet **2. FIRMLY ON THE GROUND** with both feet on the ground **3. UNPREPARED** unable to react or respond quickly ○ *Her question caught me flat-footed.* ■ *adv.* **UNEQUIVOCALLY** without beating around the bush (*informal*) ○ *"a good many come out flatfooted and said it was scandalous"* (Mark Twain, *The Adventures of Huckleberry Finn*; 1884) —**flat-foot·ed·ly** *adv.* —**flat-foot·ed·ness** *n.*

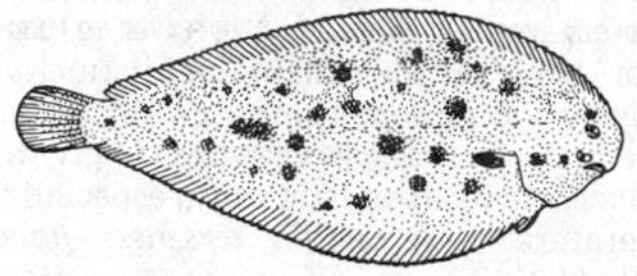

Flatfish

Flat·head[1] /flát hèd/ (*plural* **-head** *or* **-heads**) *n.* a member of a Native American people who originally lived in western Montana and northern Idaho

Flat·head[2] /flát hèd/ river in North America, rising in southeastern British Columbia, Canada, and flowing south into Montana, where it joins the Clark Fork River after passing through Flathead Lake. Length: 245 mi./394 km.

flat·head cat·fish /flát hèd/ *n.* a large catfish that has a yellowish body with brown markings. It is found in the streams of the Mississippi Valley and the southeastern United States. Latin name: *Pylodictis olivaris.*

flat·i·ron /flát ìrn/ *n.* an iron used to press clothes, especially one that has to be heated on a hearth or stove

flat·land /flát lànd/ *n.* an expanse of land that does not vary in height above sea level

flat·line /flát lìn/ (**-lined, -lin·ing, -lines**) *vi.* to show none of the electrical currents associated with heart activity on a cardiac monitor (*slang*) —**flat·lin·er** *n.*

flat·ling /fláttling/, **flat·lings** /-lingz/ *adv. U.K.* with the flat side of a sword (*archaic*)

flat·ly /fláttlee/ *adv.* **1. FIRMLY** firmly and without qualification ○ *They flatly rejected our offer.* **2. IN FLAT VOICE** in a voice that shows no emotion

flat·mate /flát màyt/ *n. U.K.* somebody with whom a person shares an apartment

flat out *adv.* (*informal*) **1. AS QUICKLY AS POSSIBLE** as fast and energetically as possible ○ *The factory is working flat out to finish the order.* **2. FAST** at top speed **3. BLUNTLY** in a blunt manner ○ *told me flat out he didn't trust me*

flat-out, flat·out *adj.* complete, utter, or absolute (*informal*) ○ *a flat-out lie*

flat race *n.* a horserace that is run over level ground, without fences to be jumped. ◊ **steeplechase** —**flat rac·ing** *n.*

flat sil·ver *n.* utensils used for eating, e.g., knives, forks, and spoons, made or plated with silver

flat·ten /flátt'n/ (**-tened, -ten·ing, -tens**) *v.* **1.** *vti.* **MAKE OR BECOME FLAT** to make something flat or flatter, or become flat or flatter **2.** *vr.* **STAND FLAT AGAINST SOMETHING** to press the body against a flat surface **3.** *vt.* **DEFEAT SOMEBODY** to defeat somebody convincingly (*informal*) **4.** *vt.* **CRUSH OR HUMILIATE SOMEBODY** to make somebody feel crushed or humiliated **5.** *vt. U.K.* MUSIC = **flat** —**flat·ten·er** *n.*

flatten out *v.* **1.** *vi.* **BECOME STABLE AND LOWER** to become lower and relatively stable ○ *Stock prices have flattened out over the year.* **2.** *vti.* **SPREAD OUT** to spread out, or spread something out, over an area

flat·ter[1] /fláttər/ (**-tered, -ter·ing, -ters**) *v.* **1.** *vt.* **COMPLIMENT SOMEBODY TO WIN FAVOR** to compliment somebody too much, often without sincerity, especially in order to gain an advantage **2.** *vt.* **APPEAL TO SOMEBODY'S VANITY** to please somebody by paying him or her particular attention, especially with a request to take some prominent role ○ *I was flattered to be asked to judge the competition.* **3.** *vt.* **MAKE SOMEBODY OR SOMETHING LOOK GOOD** to show somebody or something to advantage, or make somebody or something seem better looking than in reality ○ *a studio portrait that really flatters her* **4.** *vr.* **CONGRATULATE YOURSELF EXCESSIVELY** to feel satisfied with some aspect of yourself or with something you have done, especially when the perception is false ○ *He flatters himself on being a good judge of character.* [12thC. Origin unknown; perhaps a back-formation from FLATTERY.] —**flat·ter·er** *n.* —**flat·ter·ing** *adj.* —**flat·ter·ing·ly** *adv.*

flat·ter[2] /fláttər/ *n.* INDUST any tool used to make something flat, as used, e.g., by a blacksmith [From Old Norse *flatr* (see FLAT[1])]

flat·ter·y /fláttəree/ *n.* **1. PAYING OF COMPLIMENTS TO WIN FAVOR** an act or instance of complimenting somebody, often excessively or insincerely, especially in order to get something **2. COMPLIMENTS** complimentary remarks, especially when excessive or insincere [14thC. From Old French *flaterie*, from *flater* "to flatter." Probably ultimately from a prehistoric Germanic word that is also the ancestor of English *flat* "made smooth."]

flat·tish /fláttish/ *adj.* somewhat or relatively flat ○ *a flattish hairdo*

flat·top /flát tòp/ *n.* **1.** HAIR **FLAT HAIRCUT** a hairstyle in which the hair is brushed up and then cut short and flat across the top **2.** NAVY **AIRCRAFT CARRIER** an aircraft carrier (*informal*)

flat tun·ing *n.* the tuning of a musical instrument, or of a number of instruments playing together, such that the pitch of all the notes is lower than normal. This is sometimes done by early-music groups.

flat·u·lence /fláchələns/ *n.* **1.** MED **GAS IN DIGESTIVE SYSTEM** excessive gas in the stomach and intestines that causes discomfort **2. SENSE OF SELF-IMPORTANCE** an excessive sense of self-importance **3.** LANGUAGE **BOMBASTIC STYLE** pretentiousness or pomposity in speech or writing

flat·u·lent /fláchələnt/ *adj.* **1.** MED **CAUSING GAS IN DIGESTIVE SYSTEM** causing excessive gas to be created in the stomach and intestines **2.** MED **FULL OF DIGESTIVE GAS** having excessive gas in the digestive system **3. POMPOUS OR SELF-IMPORTANT** having or showing excessive self-importance [Late 16thC. Via French from modern Latin *flatulentus*, from Latin *flatus* "blowing, blast," from *flare* "to blow" (source of English *flare*).] —**flat·u·lent·ly** *adv.*

fla·tus /fláytəss/ (*plural* **-tus** *or* **-tus·es**) *n.* gas produced in the digestive system by bacterial fermentation and containing high amounts of hydrogen sulfide and methane, usually expelled from the body through the anus (*technical*) [Mid-17thC. From Latin (see FLATULENT).]

flat·ware /flát wàir/ *n.* **1. KNIVES, FORKS, AND SPOONS** knives, forks, and spoons used for eating **2. FLAT OR SHALLOW TABLEWARE** dishes used for eating that are flat or relatively shallow, e.g., plates and saucers, as opposed to deeper pieces such as cups and bowls (**hollowware**)

flat-wa·ter *adj.* done on a calm or slow-moving body of water

flat·ways *adv.* = **flatwise**

flat·weave /flát weev/ *adj.* woven without a pile ○ *flatweave carpet*

flat·wise /flát wìz/, **flat·ways** /-wàyz/ *adv.* with the flat side down or foremost

flat·work /flát wùrk/ *n.* large pieces of laundry such as sheets and tablecloths that are easier to iron in a mangle than by hand

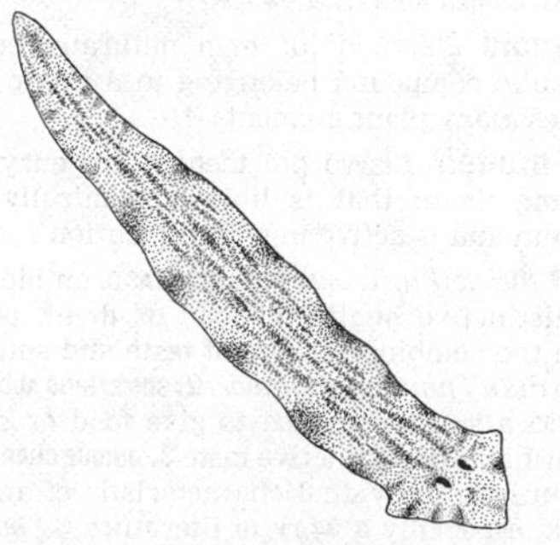

Flatworm

flat·worm /flát wùrm/ *n.* a worm with a soft, flattened body. Some flatworms, e.g., tapeworms, are parasites. Phylum: Platyhelminthes.

Flau·bert /flō báir/, **Gustave** (1821–80) French novelist. A dominant figure in the realist school, he achieved fame with his first published novel, *Madame Bovary* (1856). —**Flau·ber·tian** /flō bérsh'n, -bértee ən, flaw-/ *adj.*

flaunt /flawnt/ *v.* (**flaunt·ed, flaunt·ing, flaunts**) **1.** *vt.* SHOW SOMETHING OFF to display something ostentatiously ○ *She flaunts her wealth every chance she gets.* **2.** *vr.* PARADE YOURSELF to parade yourself without shame or modesty **3.** *vti.* WAVE OR MAKE SOMETHING WAVE to wave or flutter in the wind, or make something wave or flutter by moving it around (*dated*) ■ *n.* DISPLAY an ostentatious diplay [Mid-16thC. Origin unknown: perhaps a blend of FLOUT and VAUNT.] —**flaunt·er** *n.* —**flaunt·ing·ly** *adv.*

WORD KEY: USAGE

Flaunt or *flout* a rule? In terms of ignoring or showing gross contempt for a rule, for a convention, or for a law, only *flout* is the correct choice: *The motorist flouted the law when he double-parked.* When expressing the idea of vulgar or ostentatious display, the writer's only choice is ***flaunt***: *She flaunted her ill-gotten riches by purchasing a vulgar mansion and seven luxury cars.*

flaunt·y /fláwntee/ (**-i·er, -i·est**) *adj.* inclined to show off ○ *a flaunty sway to the hips* —**flaunt·i·ly** *adv.* —**flaunt·i·ness** *n.*

flau·ta /flów taa/ *n.* a tortilla rolled around a filling, usually beef or chicken, and fried [From Spanish, literally "flute," probably from Provençal *flaüt* (see FLUTE)]

flau·tist *n.* = **flutist**

flav- *prefix.* = **flavo-** (*used before vowels*)

fla·va·none /fláyvə nōn, flávvə-/ *n.* a colorless crystalline compound derived from flavone, or any plant substance derived from flavone. Formula: $C_{15}H_{12}O_2$. [Mid-20thC. Coined from FLAVO- + -ANE + -ONE.]

fla·vin /fláyvin/ *n.* a yellow pigment such as riboflavin that is soluble in water and occurs in organic tissues [Mid-19thC. Coined from Latin *flavus* "yellow" + -IN.]

fla·vine /fláy veen/ *n.* flavin (*dated*) [Mid-19thC. Coined from Latin *flavus* "yellow" + -INE.]

flavo- *prefix.* **1.** yellow ○ *flavin* **2.** flavin ○ *flavoprotein* [From Latin *flavus* "yellow." Ultimately from an Indo-European word denoting a bright color, which is also the ancestor of English *blue* and *bleach.*]

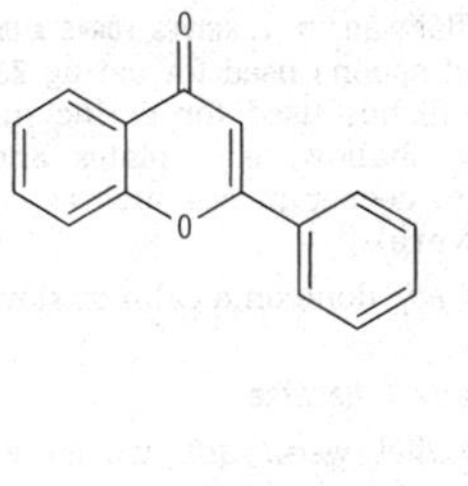

Flavone

fla·vone /fláy vōn/ *n.* a crystalline compound from which yellow pigments are derived, found on the leaves or in the stems and seed capsules of primroses and some other plants. Formula: $C_{15}H_{10}O_2$. [Late 19thC. Coined from FLAVO- + -ONE.]

fla·vo·noid /fláyvə nòyd/ *n.* a naturally occurring phenolic compound belonging to a group that includes many plant pigments

fla·vo·pro·tein /fláyvō prō teen/ *n.* an enzyme containing flavin that is linked chemically with a protein and is active in cell respiration

fla·vor /fláyvər/ *n.* **1.** CHARACTERISTIC TASTE an identifiable or distinctive quality of food or drink perceived with the combined senses of taste and smell ○ *The soup didn't have much flavor.* **2.** SOMETHING ADDING FLAVOR TO FOOD a substance used to give food or drink an identifiable or distinctive taste **3.** UNIQUE CHARACTERISTIC the unique individual characteristic of an artistic work, especially a work of literature ○ *"borrowing its flavor from the works of William Gibson and Austin sci-fi author Bruce Sterling"* (John Perry Barlow, *Crime and Puzzlement*; 1990) **4.** TYPE a type or kind of something (*slang*) ○ *"any flavor of mainframe you like"* (*The LOD/H Technical Journal, Issue 3*; 1988) **5.** PHYS PROPERTY OF ELEMENTARY PARTICLES a physical property that distinguishes types of quarks and some types of lepton **6.** ODOR OR FRAGRANCE a quality perceived with the sense of smell alone (*archaic*) ■ *vt.* (**-vored, -vor·ing, -vors**) **1.** GIVE FLAVOR TO FOOD to give food or drink an identifiable or distinctive taste, usually by adding something ○ *Flavor the stew with rosemary.* **2.** GIVE SOMETHING UNIQUENESS to give a unique characteristic to an artistic work, especially a work of literature ○ *A certain terseness flavors her prose.* [14thC. Alteration, influenced by savor, of Old French *flaor* "aroma" (the original sense in English), ultimately from a blend of Latin *flatus* "blowing" (see FLATULENT) and *foetor* "stench."] —**fla·vor·er** *n.*

fla·vor en·hanc·er *n.* a substance added to processed food or drink to improve or intensify its flavor

fla·vor·ful /fláyvərfəl/ *adj.* with a strong pleasant taste —**fla·vor·ful·ly** *adv.* —**fla·vor·ful·ness** *n.*

fla·vor·ing /fláyvəring/ *n.* a natural or artificial substance added to food or drink to give it an identifiable or distinctive taste

fla·vor·ist /fláyvərist/ *n.* somebody trained to isolate and blend chemicals in order to create artificially the taste and smell of a specific food

fla·vor·less /fláyvərləss/ *adj.* without an identifiable or distinctive taste

fla·vor·some /fláyvərsəm/ *adj.* = **flavorful**

fla·vor·y /fláyvəree/ *adj.* rich in flavor

fla·vour *n., vt.* U.K. = **flavor**

flaw[1] /flaw/ (**flawed, flaw·ing, flaws**) *n.* **1.** BLEMISH MAKING SOMETHING IMPERFECT a defect in an object that makes it imperfect or less valuable **2.** ABSTRACT IMPERFECTION an imperfection, shortcoming, or weakness in something abstract ○ *There's a flaw in your argument.* **3.** LAW INVALIDATING DEFECT IN DOCUMENT in a legal document, a defect that can make it invalid [14thC. Origin uncertain: perhaps from Old Norse *flaga* "stone slab," ultimately from prehistoric Germanic. The original meaning was "flake"; the sense "defect" probably originated in WHITLOW, literally "white fissure."]

WORD KEY: SYNONYMS

flaw, imperfection, fault, defect, failing, blemish

CORE MEANING: something that detracts from perfection

flaw used to describe something such as an unintended mark or crack that prevents something from being totally perfect and detracts from its value. It can also be used to describe a weakness in somebody's character or in a plan, theory, or system; **imperfection** a more formal word for "flaw"; **fault** used to describe something that prevents something or somebody from being perfect or from functioning correctly. It is usually used to talk about more serious problems than "flaw"; **defect** used to describe a fault in a machine, system, or plan, especially one that prevents it from functioning correctly; **failing** used to describe something that mars somebody or something in some way, often used to describe an unfortunate feature of somebody's personality or character; **blemish** used to describe a mark of some kind that detracts from something's appearance, often used of the complexion or skin. It can also be used to describe something that detracts from somebody's otherwise undamaged reputation or record.

flaw[2] /flaw/ *n.* **1.** METEOROL GUST OF WIND a brief gust of wind **2.** METEOROL SQUALL a short storm or spell of bad weather **3.** SUDDEN STRONG FEELING a sudden show of strong feeling (*archaic*) [Early 16thC. Probably from Middle Low German *vlāge*, or from Scandinavian. Ultimately from an Indo-European word meaning "to strike" that is also the ancestor of English *plague.*] —**flaw·y** *adj.*

flawed *adj.* imperfect or defective ○ *The interpretation is seriously flawed.*

flaw·less /fláwləss/ *adj.* without any blemish or imperfection ○ *a flawless performance* —**flaw·less·ly** *adv.* —**flaw·less·ness** *n.*

flax /flaks/ *n.* **1.** PLANTS PLANT YIELDING LINEN FIBER AND OIL a plant with blue flowers that is widely cultivated for its seeds, which produce linseed oil, and its stems, from which the fiber to make linen is obtained. Latin name: *Linum usitatissimum.* **2.** TEXTILES FIBER USED TO MAKE LINEN a fine light-colored textile fiber obtained from flax **3.** COLORS PALE YELLOW the pale yellow color of flax fiber [Old English *flæx.* Ultimately from an Indo-European word meaning "to braid" that was also the ancestor of English *plait, ply, complicate,* and *perplexed.*]

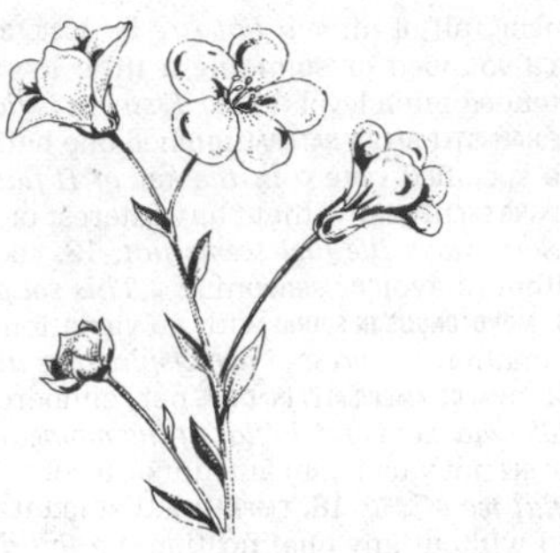

Flax

flax·en /fláksən/ *adj.* **1.** COLORS PALE GRAYISH-YELLOW having the pale grayish-yellow color of flax **2.** TEXTILES MADE FROM FLAX made from flax fibers

flax·y /fláksee/ (**-i·er, -i·est**) *adj.* resembling flax in appearance or texture

flay /flay/ (**flayed, flay·ing, flays**) *vt.* **1.** LASH OR FLOG to whip or beat a person or animal severely **2.** STRIP SKIN OFF to remove the skin or outer covering from somebody or something **3.** CRITICIZE HARSHLY to criticize somebody or something harshly and severely, and sometimes unfairly **4.** STRIP OF BELONGINGS to take all the money or valuables from somebody, especially by the use of deceit, intimidation, or similar means (*dated*) [Old English *flēan.* Ultimately from an Indo-European word meaning "to strike" that was also the ancestor of English *flaw*[2].] —**flay·er** *n.*

F lay·er *n.* GEOL the transition zone between the solid inner core of the Earth and its more fluid outer layer, at a depth of approximately 3,200 mi./5,100 km [*F* following the system of naming the three layers, beginning with *D*]

fld. *abbr.* field

fl. dr. *abbr.* fluid dram

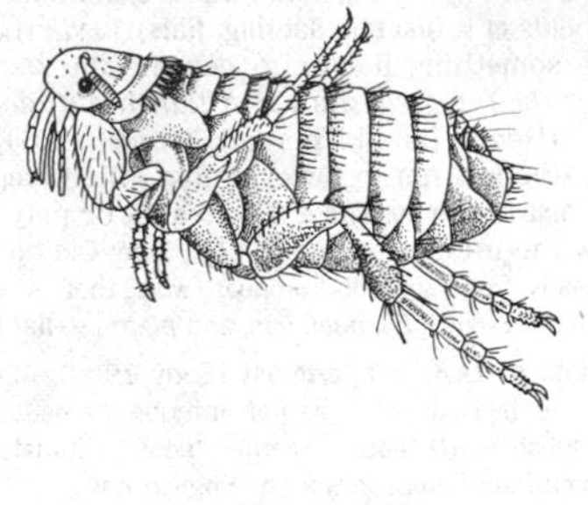

Flea (life size x50)

flea /flee/ *n.* **1.** INSECTS SMALL LEAPING BLOODSUCKING INSECT a small wingless insect with legs adapted for jumping that sucks blood and lives as a parasite on warm-blooded animals. Order: Siphonaptera. **2.** ZOOL ANIMAL RESEMBLING FLEA a small beetle or crustacean that resembles or jumps like a flea, e.g., a water flea, flea beetle, or sand flea [Old English *flēa(h).* Ultimately from an Indo-European word that was also the ancestor of English *puce.*]

flea·bag /flee bàg/ *n.* (*informal*) **1.** CHEAP SHABBY HOTEL a cheap shabby hotel or rooming house **2.** DIRTY OR FLEA-INFESTED CREATURE a dirty or scruffy living being, especially one that is infested with fleas

flea·bane /flee bàyn/ *n.* a wild plant with yellow flowers that was once believed to repel fleas. Cultivated varieties of fleabane have flowers of different colors. Genus: *Erigeron.*

flea bee·tle *n.* a very small beetle with large hind legs adapted for jumping. The beetle and its larvae are pests of vegetable crops. Subfamily: Halticinae.

flea·bite /flee bīt/ *n.* **1.** BITE OF FLEA the bite of a flea or the small red mark caused by this **2.** SMALL ANNOYANCE a small loss or petty annoyance (*informal*)

flea-bit·ten *adj.* **1.** COVERED WITH FLEAS OR FLEABITES covered with fleabites or infested with fleas **2.** CHEAP AND SHABBY cheap, shabby, or run-down (*informal*) **3.** ZOOL WITH PALE FLECKED COAT used to describe a horse that has a pale coat with reddish-brown flecks

flea col·lar *n.* a collar, usually for dogs or cats, containing a chemical that repels or kills fleas

flea-flick·er *n.* a football play in which the ball is quickly passed laterally from one player to another to confuse the defense

fleam /fleem/ *n.* **1.** WOODWORK **EDGE OF TOOTH ON SAW** a beveled cutting edge on a sawtooth **2.** SURG **KNIFE USED IN BLOODLETTING** a surgical knife formerly used to open a vein in bloodletting [15thC. Via Old French *flieme* from, ultimately, Greek *phlebotomon*, literally 'vein-cutter' (see PHLEBOTOMY), from *phlebos* "vein."]

flea mar·ket *n.* a market, usually outdoors, with individual stalls selling various kinds of merchandise, e.g., antiques, used household items, and cut-rate goods

flea·wort /flée wùrt, -wàwrt/ (*plural* **-wort** *or* **-worts**) *n.* = **psyllium** [Because the seeds look like fleas]

Flèche

flèche /flesh, flaysh/, **fleche** *n.* **1.** ARCHIT **SLENDER CHURCH SPIRE** a slender spire, especially one that emerges from the roof of a church at the point where the ridges intersect **2.** ARCHIT **BUTTRESS FEATURE** a joint at the top of a buttress, designed to add weight and assist in transferring load from roof to ground **3.** MIL **POINTED FORTIFICATION** a fortification with two faces that form a jutting angle [Early 18thC. From French, literally "arrow," from Old French *fleche* (see FLETCHER). Sense 2 of FLÈCHE, the earliest modern sense, dates from the early 18thC.]

flé·chette /flay shét, fle-/, **fle·chette** *n.* a small arrow or dart used in various kinds of missiles or projectiles intended to kill or injure people [Early 20thC. From French, literally "little arrow," from *flèche* (see FLÈCHE).]

fleck /flek/ *n.* **SMALL MARK** any one of a number of very small marks, streaks, or pieces scattered on a surface or throughout a block of something ○ *flecks of mica in granite* ■ *vt.* (**flecked, fleck·ing, flecks**) **STREAK OR SPOT** to mark something with small streaks or spots ○ *Sunlight flecked the path ahead.* [14thC. Origin uncertain.]

flec·tion *n.* = **flexion**

fled past participle, past tense of **flee**

fledge /flej/ (**fledged, fledg·ing, fledg·es**) *v.* **1.** *vt.* BIRDS **RAISE YOUNG BIRD** to raise a young bird until it can fly **2.** *vi.* BIRDS **GROW FLIGHT FEATHERS** to grow the wing and tail feathers necessary for flying **3.** *vt.* ARCHERY **EQUIP ARROW WITH FEATHERS** to put feathers on an arrow **4.** *vt.* **PROVIDE WITH FEATHERS** to provide or cover something with feathers or something similar [Mid-16thC. From the obsolete adjective *fledge* "fledged, ready to fly." Ultimately from a prehistoric Germanic word that is also the ancestor of English *fly.*]

fledg·ling /fléjjling/, **fledge·ling** *n.* **1.** BIRDS **YOUNG BIRD WITH NEW FLIGHT FEATHERS** a young bird that has recently developed the feathers necessary for flying **2. SOMEBODY INEXPERIENCED** a young or inexperienced person ■ *adj.* **INEXPERIENCED** inexperienced because still learning or just starting ○ *a fledgling business*

flee /flee/ (**fled** /fled/, **fled, flee·ing, flees**) *v.* **1.** *vti.* **RUN AWAY** to run away from something ○ *fled the burning building* **2.** *vi.* **DISAPPEAR QUICKLY** to pass or disappear quickly (*literary*) [Old English *flēon*. Ultimately from an Indo-European word also the ancestor of English *pneumonia.*] —**fle·er** *n.*

fleece /fleess/ *n.* **1.** ZOOL **WOOLLY COAT OF SHEEP** the coat of wool on a sheep or similar animal **2.** AGRIC **WOOL SHORN FROM SHEEP** the wool shorn at one time from a sheep or similar animal **3. SOFT COVERING** a soft woolly covering or mass ○ *rocks with a fleece of moss* **4.** TEXTILES **SOFT FABRIC WITH NAP OR PILE** a soft warm fabric with a brushed nap or woolly pile, especially one used to make or line outer garments **5.** CLOTHES **WARM JACKET** a jacket made from a soft warm fabric with a brushed nap ■ *vt.* (**fleeced, fleec·ing, fleec·es**) **1. SWINDLE OUT OF MONEY** to take too much money from somebody by cheating or overcharging (*informal*) ○ *They make their living by fleecing tourists.* **2.** AGRIC **SHEAR SHEEP** to shear wool from a sheep **3. COVER WITH SOMETHING RESEMBLING FLEECE** to cover something with something soft and woolly in texture or appearance (*literary*) ○ *Clouds fleeced the summer sky.* [Old English *flēos*. Probably ultimately from an Indo-European word that is also the ancestor of English *plume.*] —**fleec·er** *n.*

fleec·y /fléessee/ (**-i·er, -i·est**) *adj.* **1. MADE OF FLEECE** consisting of fleece or something similar **2. RESEMBLING FLEECE** soft and woolly in appearance or texture —**fleec·i·ly** *adv.* —**fleec·i·ness** *n.*

fleer /fleer/ *vi.* (**fleered, fleer·ing, fleers**) **LAUGH WITH CONTEMPT** to smile or laugh with contempt (*formal*) ■ *n.* **SCORNFUL LOOK OR REMARK** a taunting or derisive look, smile, or comment (*formal*) [14thC. Origin uncertain: probably from a Scandinavian language.] —**fleer·ing·ly** *adv.*

fleet[1] /fleet/ *n.* **1.** NAVY **GROUP OF NAVAL SHIPS** a number of warships functioning as a single unit under one command, or all the ships of a nation's navy **2.** COMM, TRANSP **VEHICLES OR CRAFT UNDER SINGLE OWNERSHIP** a number of road vehicles, boats, or aircraft owned, working, or managed as a unit, usually by a commercial enterprise ○ *The company has a large fleet of service vehicles.* [Old English *flēot* "ships," from *flēotan* "to float, swim." Ultimately from a prehistoric Germanic word that is the ancestor also of English *float* and probably of *fleet*[2].]

fleet[2] /fleet/ *adj.* (*literary*) **1. MOVING QUICKLY** moving quickly or nimbly **2. QUICKLY PASSING** passing or fading quickly ■ *v.* (**fleet·ed, fleet·ing, fleets**) (*literary*) **1.** *vi.* **MOVE QUICKLY** to move quickly or nimbly **2.** *vti.* **PASS QUICKLY** to pass or fade quickly, or cause something to pass or fade quickly [Early 16thC. Origin uncertain: probably from Old Norse *fljótr*, and ultimately from prehistoric Germanic (see FLEET[1]).] —**fleet·ly** *adv.* —**fleet·ness** *n.*

fleet ad·mi·ral, Fleet Ad·mi·ral *n.* an officer in the United States Navy of the highest rank, with an insignia of five stars

fleet·ing /fleéting/ *adj.* passing or fading quickly [Old English, from *flēotan* (see FLEET[1]). The original sense was "floating," later "flowing"; hence "flowing or gliding quickly away."] —**fleet·ing·ly** *adv.* —**fleet·ing·ness** *n.*

WORD KEY: SYNONYMS

See Synonyms at ***temporary.***

Fleet Street *n.* the British newspaper industry [Because most British national newspapers were formerly produced on *Fleet Street*, central London]

flei·shig /fláyshik, flī-/ *adj.* under Jewish dietary laws, relating to, containing, or used as meat or meat products. ◊ **milchig, parev** [Mid-20thC. From Yiddish *fleyshik*, from *fleysh* "meat." Utimately from a prehistoric Germanic word that is also the ancestor of English *flesh.*]

Flem. *abbr.* Flemish

Flem·ing /flémming/ *n.* **1. SOMEBODY FROM FLANDERS** somebody who lives in or was born or raised in Flanders **2. FLEMISH SPEAKER** a Belgian who speaks Flemish. ◊ **Walloon** [Old English *Flæming*. Directly and via Old Norse from Middle Dutch *Vlaminc.*]

Flem·ing /flémming/, **Sir Alexander** (1881–1955) British microbiologist. He shared a Nobel Prize in medicine in 1945 for his discovery of the world's first antibiotic, penicillin.

Flem·ing, Ian (1908–64) British writer. His fictional hero James Bond, secret agent 007, appeared in 12 novels and seven short stories, beginning with *Casino Royale* (1953).

Flem·ing, Sir Sandford (1827–1915) Scottish-born Canadian civil engineer and railway surveyor. He was instrumental in the adoption of standard time.

Flem·ish /flémmish/ *adj.* **OF FLANDERS** relating to or typical of Flanders, the Flemings, or their language or culture ■ *n.* LANG **BELGIAN LANGUAGE** one of the official languages of Belgium. It is from the West Germanic group of the Germanic branch of Indo-European and is very similar to Dutch. About five million people speak Flemish. ■ *npl.* PEOPLES **PEOPLE OF FLANDERS** the people of Flanders, or Flemish-speaking people [14thC. From Middle Dutch *Vlāmisch*, from *Vlāmland* "Flanders."]

Flem·ish bond *n.* a style of brickwork in which bricks laid with the end facing out (**headers**) alternate with those laid lengthwise (**stretchers**), horizontally and vertically

Flem·ish school *n.* art and artists of the 15th and 16th centuries in The Netherlands. Artists of the Flemish school, e.g., Van Eyck and Rogier van der Weyden, combined carefully observed subjects with complex religious iconography.

flense /flens/ (**flensed, flens·ing, flens·es**), **flench** /flench/ (**flenched, flench·ing, flench·es**) *vt.* to strip the skin or blubber from a whale or seal [Early 19thC. From Danish *flensa.*] —**flens·er** *n.*

flesh /flesh/ *n.* **1.** PHYSIOL **SOFT TISSUE OF BODY** the soft tissues, primarily muscle and fat, that cover the bones of people and other animals **2.** PHYSIOL **HUMAN SKIN AS OUTER SURFACE** the outer surface of the human body **3. UNWANTED WEIGHT** unwanted weight or fatty tissue (*informal*) ○ *could afford to lose some flesh* **4.** COOK **MEAT OF ANIMALS** the flesh of animals, including birds and fish, regarded as food **5.** COOK **MEAT EXCLUDING BIRDS AND FISH** the flesh of mammals, as opposed to birds or fish, regarded as food (*archaic*) **6.** FOOD, PLANTS **PULP OF FRUITS AND VEGETABLES** the soft pulpy edible parts of fruits and vegetables, as opposed to the skin, core, pit, and other parts that are not usually eaten **7.** = **flesh and blood** *n.* 1 **8. PEOPLE** people in general (*literary*) ○ *the way of all flesh* **9. PHYSICAL ASPECT OF HUMANITY** the physical body along with its needs and limitations, as opposed to the soul, mind, or spirit **10. SUBSTANCE** substance as distinct from form or style ○ *Actions give flesh to theory.* **11.** COLORS = **flesh-color** ■ *vt.* (**fleshed, flesh·ing, flesh·es**) **1.** HUNT **INSTRUCT ANIMAL BY FEEDING** to teach a dog or bird to hunt by feeding it the meat of a freshly killed animal **2. ACCUSTOM TO KILLING** to accustom somebody to bloodshed and the killing of other people (*literary*) **3. GET BLOOD ON WEAPON** to thrust a pointed weapon into somebody's flesh, especially when using it for the first time (*literary*) **4. CLEAN INSIDE OF ANIMAL SKIN** in tanning, to scrape away the soft tissue adhering to a hide [Old English *flǣsc* "soft tissue, meat"] ◇ **in the flesh** in person ◇ **press the flesh** to greet and shake the hands of many people in public, as a political or promotional exercise (*informal*)

flesh out *v.* **1.** *vt.* **AMPLIFY** to add substance and detail to something ○ *flesh out a business proposal* **2.** *vi.* **PUT ON WEIGHT** to put on weight or become overweight (*informal*)

flesh and blood *n.* **1. RELATIVES** people, or a person, related to somebody by birth **2.** = **flesh** *n.* 9 ■ *adj.* **flesh-and-blood** ARTS **REALISTICALLY REPRESENTING PEOPLE** representing life, people, and events in a way perceived as believable or realistic

flesh-col·or *n.* a pink color with tinges of yellow or gray, like that of a white person's skin —**flesh-col·ored** *adj.*

flesh·er /fléshər/ *n.* in tanning, a person who or device that removes any flesh adhering to the inside of an animal hide

flesh fly *n.* a fly whose larvae feed on the flesh of living or dead animals. Family: Sarcophagidae.

flesh·ings /fléshingz/ *npl.* **1.** THEATER, CLOTHES **FLESH-COLORED TIGHTS** flesh-colored tights formerly worn by actors **2. SCRAPED FLESH** flesh scraped from an animal's hide

flesh·ly /fléshlee/ (**-li·er, -li·est**) *adj.* **1. BODILY** relating to the human body ○ *the fleshly concerns of daily living* **2. RELATING TO PHYSICAL PLEASURE** enjoying or concerned with the pleasures of the body **3. NOT SPIRITUAL** not focused on spiritual matters **4. PLUMP** plump or fat (*archaic*) —**flesh·li·ness** *n.*

flesh·pot /flésh pòts/ *n.* a place known to provide sexual or sensual entertainment (*usually used in the plural*) ○ *Police keep an eye on the local fleshpots.* [Mid-16thC. Allusion to the Bible, *Exodus* 16:3, where the Israelites remember past feasting. Originally "cooking pot"; the underlying idea is of "physical or sensual gratification."]

flesh wound *n.* a wound that penetrates the flesh but does not damage bones or vital organs

flesh·y /fléshee/ (**-i·er, -i·est**) *adj.* **1. PLUMP** plump or fat **2. WITH MORE FLESH** with thicker or softer flesh than other parts of the body ○ *the fleshy part of the hand at the base of the thumb* **3. SOFT AND JUICY** with thick soft juicy pulp ○ *the fleshiest peaches of the season* —**flesh·i·ness** *n.*

fletch /flech/ (**fletched, fletch·ing, fletch·es**) *vt.* ARCHERY = **fledge** *v.* 3 [Mid-17thC. Alteration of FLEDGE, influenced by FLETCHER.]

fletch·er /fléchər/ *n.* somebody who makes arrows [13thC. From Old French *flech(i)er*, from *flèche* "arrow." Ultimately from a prehistoric Germanic word that is also the ancestor of English *fly, fledge*, and *flow*.]

fletch·ings /fléchingz/ *npl.* the feathered part of an arrow

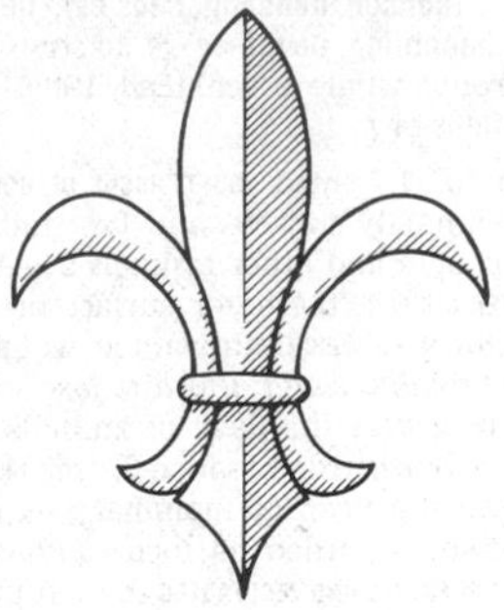

Fleur-de-lis

fleur-de-lis /flùr də lée/ (*plural* **fleurs-de-lis** /-léez/), **fleur-de-lys** (*plural* **fleurs-de-lys**) *n.* **1.** HERALDRY **HERALDIC DEVICE RESEMBLING LILY OR IRIS** a heraldic symbol or design in the form of three tapering petals tied by a surrounding band, formerly used by the kings of France **2.** PLANTS = **iris 3.** *Can* **FLAG OF QUEBEC** the flag of Quebec, which has four white fleurs-de-lis on a blue background [From Old French *flour de lys*, literally "flower of the lily"]

fleur·et /flur ét, flŏŏ rét/, **fleur·ette** *n.* a decorative motif in the form of a small flower [Early 19thC. From French, literally "little flower," from *fleur* "flower," from Old French *flour* (see FLOWER).]

flew past tense of **fly**[1]

flex /fleks/ *v.* (**flexed, flex·ing, flex·es**) **1.** *vt.* **BEND A BODY PART** to bend something, especially a joint of the body **2.** *vi.* **BEND** to bend or be able to be bent ○ *The board flexes as you step on it.* **3.** *vti.* **PRODUCE MUSCULAR CONTRACTION** to move or tense a muscle, or become tense or contracted ■ *n.* **BENDING ABILITY** bending or ability to bend [Early 16thC. From Latin *flex-* (see FLEXIBLE).]

flex·a·tone /fléksə tōn/ *n.* a musical percussion instrument consisting of a handle with a narrow metal sheet attached that is struck to produce a tunable sound

flex·i·bil·i·ty /flèksə bíllətee/ (*plural* **-ties**) *n.* **1. BEING ABLE TO BEND WITHOUT BREAKING** the ability to bend or be bent repeatedly without damage or injury **2. ABILITY TO ADAPT TO NEW SITUATION** the ability to change or be changed according to circumstances ○ *The proposed system lacks flexibility.* **3. BEING SUBJECT TO INFLUENCE** the capacity to be persuaded or influenced

flex·i·ble /fléksəb'l/ *adj.* **1. ABLE TO BEND WITHOUT BREAKING** able to bend or be bent repeatedly without damage or injury **2. ABLE TO ADAPT TO NEW SITUATION** able to change or be changed according to circumstances **3. SUBJECT TO INFLUENCE** able to be persuaded or influenced [15thC. Directly or via French from Latin *flexibilis*, from *flex-*, past participle stem of *flectere* "to bend" (source of English *deflect, reflect*, and *genuflect*).] —**flex·i·bly** *adv.* —**flex·i·ble·ness** *n.*

flex·i·ble time *n.* = **flextime**

flex·ile /fléksəl, flék sīl/ *adj.* = **flexible** *adj.* 1 [Mid-17thC. From Latin *flexilis*, from *flex-* (see FLEXIBLE).]

flex·ion /flékshən/, **flec·tion** *n.* **1. BENDING OF LIMB** the bending of a limb or joint **2. POSITION OF BENT PART** the position of a bent limb or joint **3. BENDING OF SOMETHING** the bending of something or its bent state **4.** GRAM **INFLECTION** an inflection (*archaic*) [Early 17thC. From the Latin stem *flexion-*, from *flex-* (see FLEXIBLE).] —**flex·ion·al** *adj.*

flex·i·time *n.* = **flextime**

flex·og·ra·phy /flek sóggrəfee/ *n.* a relief printing technique that uses a rotary press, a flexible plate, and a water-based ink [Mid-20thC. Coined from Latin *flexus* (see FLEXOR) + -GRAPHY.] —**flex·o·g·ra·pher** *n.* —**flex·o·graph·ic** /flèksə gráffik/ *adj.* —**flex·o·graph·i·cal·ly** *adv.*

flex·or /fléksər/ *n.* a muscle that bends a joint or limb when it is contracted [Early 17thC. From modern Latin, from Latin *flexus*, past participle of *flectere* (see FLEXIBLE).]

flex·time /fléks tīm/, **flex·i·time** /fléksi-/ *n.* a system that allows employees to set their own daily times of starting and finishing work, within certain limits [Late 20thC. Blend of FLEXIBLE and TIME.]

flex·u·ous /flékshoo əss/, **flex·u·ose** /-ōss/ *adj.* curving, winding, or turning (*formal*) [Early 17thC. From Latin *flexuosus*, from, ultimately, *flectere* (see FLEXIBLE).] —**flex·u·os·i·ty** /flèkshoo óssətee/ *n.* —**flex·u·ous·ly** /flékshoo əsslee/ *adv.*

flex·ur·al /flékshərəl/ *adj.* **1. BENDING** turning, curving, or bending **2. SITUATED IN BODILY CREASE** occurring at a crease or bend in part of the body, e.g., behind the knee

flex·ure /flékshər/ *n.* **1. BENDING** a bending or being flexed **2.** ANAT **BEND OR CURVE** a bend or curve, e.g., in a body part or organ [Late 16thC. From Latin *flexura*, from *flex-* (see FLEXIBLE).]

flg. *abbr.* **1.** flagging **2.** flooring **3.** following

flib·ber·ti·gib·bet /flìbbərti jíbbit/ *n.* a silly, irresponsible, or scatterbrained person, especially one who chatters or gossips (*dated offensive*) [15thC. Origin uncertain: probably an imitation of the sound of meaningless chatter.]

flic /flik/ *n.* a member of the French police (*slang*) [Late 19thC. From French, of unknown origin.]

flick[1] /flik/ *n.* **1. QUICK MOVEMENT** a quick jerking movement **2. QUICK BLOW** a sharp light blow made with a quick jerking movement, usually of the finger **3. SPLASH OF COLOR** a light splash or streak ○ *flicks of paint left on the floor* ■ *v.* (**flicked, flick·ing, flicks**) **1.** *vti.* **HIT WITH QUICK BLOW** to hit something sharply or lightly with the end of something, usually in a quick jerking movement ○ *He flicked me with his towel.* **2.** *vti.* **MOVE JERKILY** to move or make something move with a quick sharp jerk ○ *The cow's tail flicked back and forth.* **3.** *vt.* **MOVE WITH QUICK BLOW** to move, propel, or remove something with a sharp light blow or a quick movement of the finger or hand ○ *Would you flick that bug off me?* [15thC. An imitation of the sound of a light blow.]

flick through *vt.* to turn the pages of a book or magazine quickly ○ *flicked through a couple of magazines while I waited*

flick[2] /flik/ *n.* **FILM** a movie (*dated slang*) ■ **flicks** *npl.* **THE MOVIES** the movies in general (*dated informal*) [Early 20thC. Shortening of FLICKER[1]; from the flickering appearance of early films.]

flick[3] /flik/ *n. Wales, S England* animal fat found round kidneys and other offal (*informal*) [Late 16thC. Origin uncertain: probably a variant of FLITCH.]

flick·er[1] /flíkər/ *vi.* (**-ered, -er·ing, -ers**) **1. SHINE UNSTEADILY** to burn or shine unsteadily **2. FLUTTER OR MOVE JERKILY** to move with a fluttering or fast jerky motion **3. APPEAR BRIEFLY** to appear or exist only briefly ○ *A smile flickered across her face.* ■ *n.* **1. FLUCTUATING LIGHT** an unsteady or wavering light ○ *the flicker of candles in the dark* **2. QUICK MOVEMENT** a quick fluttering movement **3. TRANSIENT FEELING OR EXPRESSION** a brief feeling that quickly passes, or an indication of this on somebody's face ○ *A flicker of joy briefly lit her eyes.* [Old English *flicorian* "to flutter." The underlying sense is of wavering unsteady movement.] —**flick·er·ing·ly** *adv.*

flick·er[2] /flíkər/ *n.* a multi-colored North American woodpecker with wings that show yellow or red in flight, that lives in deciduous woods. Latin name: *Colaptes auratus.* [Early 19thC. Origin uncertain: probably an imitation of its call.]

flick·er·tail squir·rel /flíkər tàyl/, **flick·er·tail go·pher** *n.* **1. GROUND SQUIRREL** a ground squirrel (*regional*) **2.** = **Richardson's ground squirrel**

flick knife *n. U.K.* = **switchblade**

fli·er /flīr/, **fly·er** *n.* **1.** AIR **AIRCRAFT PILOT** the pilot of an aircraft **2.** AIR **AIRCRAFT PASSENGER** a passenger on an aircraft ○ *frequent fliers* **3.** PRESS **PRINTED SHEET WIDELY DISTRIBUTED** a short piece of printed matter, usually an advertisement, that is widely distributed **4.** BUILDING **STEP IN STRAIGHT STAIRCASE** a rectangular step in a straight flight of stairs **5. RISKY UNDERTAKING** a daring or risky financial undertaking (*informal*) **6.** SPORT, SWIMMING **FLYING START** a flying start (*informal*) [13thC. Originally in the general sense "something that flies."]

flies 3rd person present singular of **fly**[1]. plural of **fly**[2]

flight[1] /flīt/ *n.* **1. PROCESS OR ACT OF FLYING** the process or act of moving through the air or through space **2. AIR TRIP** a trip through air or space in a form of transport ○ *daily flights of a thousand miles or more* **3. SCHEDULED FLIGHT** a scheduled flight with a commercial airline, usually designated by letters and numbers ○ *flight TC546 to Vancouver* **4. ABILITY TO FLY** the ability to travel through the air with wings ○ *an experimental ultralight tested for flight* ○ *an ancient bird incapable of flight* **5.** BUILDING **SERIES OF STEPS BETWEEN FLOORS** a group of stairs that go from one level of a building to another ○ *We live three flights up.* **6. GROUP FLYING TOGETHER** a group of aircraft or birds flying together, sometimes in a set pattern **7.** AIR FORCE **GROUP OF MILITARY AIRCRAFT** a group of aircraft in the U.S. Air Force that forms a subdivision of a squadron **8. RAPID MOVEMENT** swift passage, progress, or motion, especially through the air **9. EXTRAORDINARY MENTAL FEAT** an act or the process of imagining extraordinary things ○ *flights of the imagination* **10. TAIL OF ARROW OR DART** the feathers on an arrow or dart ■ *v.* (**flight·ed, flight·ing, flights**) **1.** *vi.* **FLY TOGETHER** to fly or migrate together **2.** *vt.* **SHOOT FLYING BIRD** in hunting, to shoot a bird as it flies **3.** *vt.* **PUT TAIL ON ARROW OR DART** to put feathers on an arrow or dart **4.** *vt.* SPORTS **CAUSE TO FLOAT TOWARD TARGET** to make a ball or dart seem to float inexorably toward its target [Old English *flyht.* Ultimately from a prehistoric Germanic word that was also the ancestor of English *fly*[1].]

flight[2] /flīt/ *n.* the act of running away from something or somebody [12thC. Ultimately from a prehistoric Germanic word that was also the ancestor of English *flee.*]

flight ar·row *n.* a light arrow used for long-distance shooting

flight at·ten·dant *n.* somebody employed by an airline to attend to the needs, comfort, and safety of passengers during flights

flight bag *n.* a soft suitcase of a size that can be carried on an aircraft

flight deck *n.* **1.** NAVY **RUNWAY ON AIRCRAFT CARRIER** the upper deck of an aircraft carrier that is used as a runway **2.** AIR **PART OF AIRPLANE WITH THE CONTROLS** the compartment at the front of an airplane where the pilot, copilot, and flight engineer sit

flight en·gi·neer *n.* the crew member of an airplane who monitors the performance of its systems including the engines

flight en·ve·lope *n.* a set of limits to performance, such as speed, altitude, range, payload, and maneuverability, that exist in the design of an aircraft

flight feath·er *n.* any feather in a bird's wing or tail that is necessary for flight. These feathers are usually large and stiff.

flight·less /flítləss/ *adj.* used to describe birds that are incapable of flight. Ostriches, penguins, and kiwis are flightless.

flight lev·el *n.* the height at which a particular aircraft is allowed to fly at a particular time

flight lieu·ten·ant *n.* a junior commissioned rank in the Royal Air Force corresponding to the rank of U.S. Air Force captain, or the person holding this rank

flight line *n.* the area of an airfield, especially a military airfield, where airplanes are parked, serviced, and loaded or unloaded

flight of fan·cy *n.* an idea or thought that is very imaginative but completely impractical or even ridiculous

flight path *n.* the course taken by an aircraft, space vehicle, or projectile

flight pay *n.* pay in addition to the regular salary that the members of a U.S. military aircrew get when they take part in authorized flights

flight plan *n.* a record outlining the details of a proposed flight

flight re·cord·er *n.* an electronic instrument installed on an aircraft that records details of its performance in flight. The details recorded can be used to discover the cause of a crash.

flight sim·u·la·tor *n.* a computerized device that exactly reproduces the conditions that occur on the flight deck of an aircraft and that can be used to train pilots

flight suit *n.* a one-piece flame-retardant suit worn by military aircrews when flying

flight sur·geon *n.* a medical officer in the U.S. Air Force who practices aviation medicine and looks after the health of flight crews

flight-test (**flight-test·ed, flight-test·ing, flight-tests**) *vt.* to test the performance of an aircraft, spacecraft, missile, or component in flight —**flight test** *n.*

flight·wor·thy /flît wùrthee/ *adj.* in sufficiently good mechanical and structural condition to fly —**flight·wor·thi·ness** *n.*

flight·y /flîtee/ (**-i·er, -i·est**) *adj.* unreliable, capricious, and constantly changing opinions, especially in choice of sexual partners —**flight·i·ly** *adv.* —**flight·i·ness** *n.*

flim·flam /flím flàm/ *n.* (*slang*) **1. TRICK OR SWINDLE** a trick or attempt to cheat or swindle somebody **2. DECEPTIVE TALK** talk that confuses or deceives ■ *vt.* (**-flammed, -flam·ming, -flams**) **CHEAT OR TRICK** to swindle or cheat somebody (*slang*) [Mid-16thC. Origin uncertain.] —**flim·flam·mer** *n.* —**flim·flam·mer·y** *n.*

flim·sy /flímzee/ (**-si·er, -si·est**) *adj.* **1. FRAGILE** weak and easily broken **2. EASILY TORN** light, thin, and easily torn **3. UNCONVINCINGLY WEAK** unconvincing and difficult to believe ○ *The grounds for an appeal are flimsy at best.* [Early 18thC. Origin uncertain: probably formed from an alteration of FILM on the model of, e.g., CLUMSY.] —**flim·si·ly** *adv.* —**flim·si·ness** *n.*

WORD KEY: SYNONYMS

See Synonyms at ***fragile.***

flinch /flinch/ (**flinched, flinch·ing, flinch·es**) *vi.* **1. REACT PHYSICALLY TO PAIN OR FEAR** to make an involuntary small backward movement in response to pain or something frightening or shocking **2. AVOID CONFRONTING** to avoid thinking about something, confronting something, or doing something ○ *We will not flinch from danger.* [Mid-16thC. From Old French *flenchir* "to turn aside." Ultimately from a prehistoric Germanic word meaning "to bend," which is also the ancestor of English *link.*] —**flinch·er** *n.* —**flinch·ing·ly** *adv.*

WORD KEY: SYNONYMS

See Synonyms at ***recoil.***

flin·ders /flíndərz/ *npl.* tiny fragments of something [15thC. Origin uncertain: perhaps of Scandinavian origin.]

Flin·ders /flíndərz/, **Matthew** (1774–1814) British explorer. He was the first sailor to circumnavigate Tasmania (1798) and Australia (1802–03).

Flin·ders bar /flíndərz-/ *n.* a bar of soft iron mounted under a compass to compensate for local magnetism and prevent it affecting the reading of the compass [Named for Matthew FLINDERS]

Flin·ders Is·land island off the northeastern coast of Tasmania, Australia. Local industries include fishing, farming, and tourism. Population: 924 (1996). Area: 525 sq. mi./1,359 sq. km.

Flin·ders Range mountain chain in eastern South Australia. More than 310 mi./500 km long, its highest point is St. Mary's Peak, 3,825 ft./1,166 m.

fling /fling/ *v.* (**flung, flung** /flung/, **fling·ing, flings**) **1.** *vt.* **THROW VIOLENTLY** to throw something or somebody fast using a lot of force **2.** *vr.* **JUMP QUICKLY** to jump forcefully in a way that seems impressive or dramatic, or to jump on somebody or something in the same way ○ *She flung herself onto the chair and began to sob.* **3.** *vt.* **MOVE YOUR HEAD OR ARMS** to move your head or arms in a particular direction suddenly and dramatically **4.** *vr.* **WORK ENTHUSIASTICALLY AND ENERGETICALLY** to start doing something with great enthusiasm and energy ○ *You can depend on the fact that she will fling herself into every project she undertakes.* ■ *n.* (*informal*) **1. SHORT AFFAIR** a brief sexual relationship **2. TIME FOR PLEASURE** a period of carefree enjoyment, especially before a more serious or worried period [13thC. Of Scandinavian origin. Ultimately from an Indo-European word meaning "to strike," which is also the ancestor of English *complain, plague,* and *apoplexy.*] —**fling·er** *n.*

WORD KEY: SYNONYMS

See Synonyms at ***throw.***

fling off *vt.* to take off a piece of clothing quickly or to remove forcefully something that is covering you

flint /flint/ *n.* **1.** GEOL **VERY HARD QUARTZ THAT MAKES SPARKS** a very hard grayish-black fine-grained form of quartz that occurs widely as nodules and bands in chalk. It produces a spark when struck with steel and was used in prehistoric times to make tools. **2.** ARCHEOL **TOOL MADE OF FINE-GRAINED QUARTZ** a piece of fine-grained quartz shaped into a tool by prehistoric people **3. SPARK-MAKING ROCK** a piece of flint used to make a spark **4. PART OF CIGARETTE LIGHTER** the part of a cigarette lighter, consisting of a small iron alloy cylinder, that makes a spark ○ *a box of flints* [Old English. Ultimately from a prehistoric Germanic word meaning "to split," which is also the ancestor of English *split, splinter, splint,* and *splice.*]

flint corn *n.* a type of corn with kernels that contain hard starch. Popcorn is a type of flint corn. Latin name: *Zea mays.* ◊ **dent corn**

flint glass *n.* high-quality glass containing lead oxide that has a high index of refraction and is used to make lenses, cut glass, and costume jewelry

flint·head /flínt hèd/ *n.* = **wood stork** [Late 18thC. From its black head; originally used for "flint arrow-head."]

flint-heart·ed *adj.* pitilessly lacking in feeling, caring, and compassion (*literary*)

flint-knap·ping *n.* the activity, largely carried out by prehistoric people, of chipping and splitting flint to make tools —**flint-knapper** *n.*

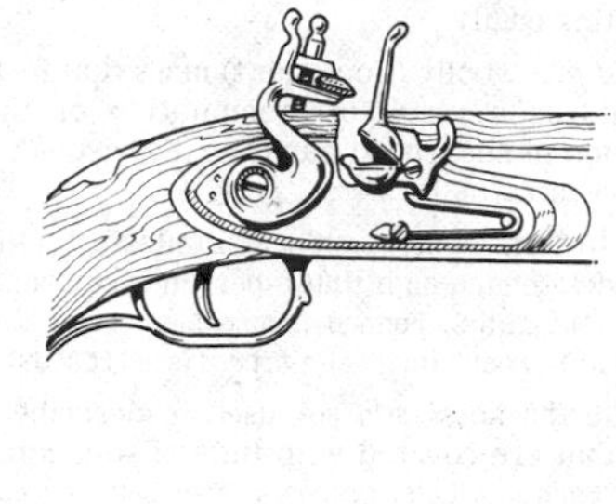

Flintlock

flint·lock /flínt lòk/ *n.* **1. TYPE OF FIREARM** a firearm with a firing mechanism (**gunlock**) where a flint embedded in the hammer ignites a gunpowder charge **2. EARLY FIRING MECHANISM** a firing mechanism (**gunlock**) that has a flint embedded in the hammer to produce the spark [Late 17thC]

flint·y /flíntee/ (**-i·er, -i·est**) *adj.* **1. STERN AND UNEMOTIONAL** hard, inflexible, and showing no emotion **2.** GEOL **CONTAINING FLINT** containing or related to flint —**flint·i·ly** *adv.* —**flint·i·ness** *n.*

flip /flip/ *v.* (**flipped, flip·ping, flips**) **1.** *vti.* **TURN SOMETHING OVER** to turn something over from one side to the other with a quick movement of the wrist, hand, or fingers **2.** *vt.* **MOVE WITH QUICK LIGHT MOTION** to move or flick something with a small sharp quick motion ○ *She flipped the light on and walked in.* **3.** *vt.* **TOSS CARELESSLY** to throw or toss something carelessly and lightly ○ *flip a pen across the table* **4.** *vti.* **TURN PAGES OF READING MATERIAL** to turn the pages of a magazine or book quickly ○ *flipping through a magazine* ○ *She was standing at her desk flipping the pages of her appointments book.* **5.** *vti.* **SPIN COIN** to flick the edge of a coin with your thumb so that it spins in the air, using the random nature of which side of the coin is uppermost when it lands to help make a decision **6.** *vi.* **GET SUDDENLY ANGRY** to become very angry or upset suddenly (*slang*) ○ *When I told her I wouldn't help her, she just flipped.* **7.** *vi.* **GET EXCITED AT SOMETHING NICE** to become excited over something that is pleasurable or attractive (*slang*) ■ *adj.* **FLIPPANT** showing a lack of seriousness that is considered inappropriate (*informal*) ○ *a flip remark* ■ *n.* **1. COIN'S SPIN** the spin of a coin or other object as it is tossed or thrown ○ *decided by the flip of a coin* **2.** GYMNASTICS **TURNING OF BODY** a turning of the body through 360 degrees by springing on the ground or in diving **3.** BEVERAGES **ALCOHOL AND EGG DRINK** an alcoholic drink containing beaten egg [Mid-16thC. Origin uncertain: probably an imitation of the sound.] ◇ **flip your lid** to react to something or somebody in the strongest, most emotionally uncontrolled manner possible (*slang*)

flip·book /flíp bo͝ok/ *n.* a small book containing a series of images of the same thing in different positions that create the illusion of movement when the pages are turned quickly

flip chart *n.* a visual aid consisting of a large pad of paper mounted on an easel, used to present information

flip-flop *n.* **1.** CLOTHES **BACKLESS SANDAL** a backless foam-rubber sandal with a V-shaped strap secured between the toes and at the sides of the foot (*informal*) **2. CHANGE OF MIND** a change of opinion, especially by a politician (*informal*) **3.** GYMNASTICS **BACKWARD FLIP** a backward flip of the body **4.** ELECTRON ENG **CIRCUIT WITH TWO STABLE STATES** an electronic circuit or mechanical device that has two stable states and can be switched between the two. Early computers used flipflops as their memory storage units.

flip·pant /flíppənt/ *adj.* showing a lack of seriousness that is thought inappropriate [Early 17thC. Formed from FLIP, on the model of heraldic adjectives such as RAMPANT.] —**flip·pan·cy** *n.* —**flip·pant·ly** *adv.*

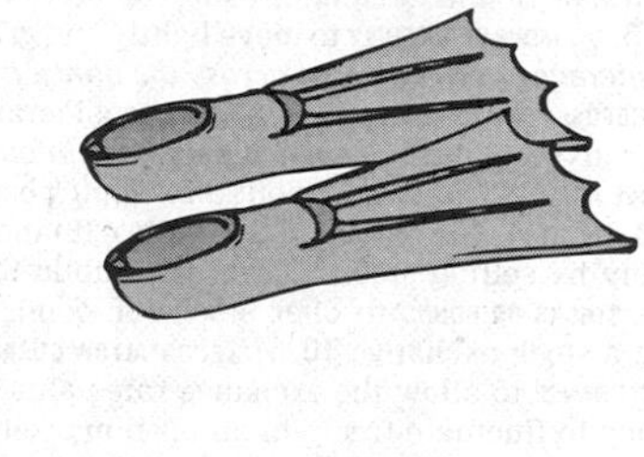

Flipper

flip·per /flíppər/ *n.* **1.** ZOOL **AQUATIC ANIMAL'S LIMB** a broad flat limb that an aquatic animal, such as a penguin, seal, or whale, uses for swimming **2.** SWIMMING **DIVER'S FOOTWEAR** a broad flat rubber extension worn on each of the feet to aid in swimming **3.** LEISURE **PINBALL FEATURE** a small button-operated bat in a pinball machine that is used to keep the ball in play

flip side *n.* **1. THE DISADVANTAGES** the disadvantages involved in doing something as opposed to the advantages that have previously been mentioned (*slang*) **2. LESS POPULAR SONG ON RECORD** the song on a single record that the record company thinks will be less popular with record buyers, or the side of the record with that song on it (*dated*)

flirt /flurt/ *v.* (**flirt·ed, flirt·ing, flirts**) **1.** *vi.* **BEHAVE IN PLAYFUL AND ALLURING WAY** to behave in a playfully alluring way **2.** *vt.* **FLICK SOMETHING** to flick or jerk something ■ *n.* **SOMEBODY BEHAVING IN A PLAYFULLY ALLURING WAY** somebody who behaves in a playfully alluring way [Mid-16thC. Origin uncertain.] —**flirt·er** *n.* —**flirt·ing·ly** *adv.*

flirt with *vt.* to consider an idea without doing anything serious about it or letting it have an effect ○ *flirted with the idea of going to college, but decided not to*

flir·ta·tion /flur táysh'n/ *n.* **1. PLAYFUL ROMANTIC INVOLVEMENT** a short playful interaction based on lighthearted feeling or behavior **2. PERIOD OF CASUAL INTEREST IN SOMETHING** a period of considering or participating in something in a superficial way ○ *a flirtation with vegetarianism*

flir·ta·tious /flur táyshəss/ *adj.* behaving playfully and in a way that gives the impression of sexual interest —**flir·ta·tious·ly** *n.* —**flir·ta·tious·ness** *adv.*

flirt·y /flúrtee/ (**-i·er, -i·est**) *adj.* **1.** = **flirtatious** (*informal*) **2. SUITABLE FOR A FLIRT** suitable for a flirtatious person or a person in a flirtatious mood —**flirt·i·ly** *adv.* —**flirt·i·ness** *n.*

flit /flit/ (**flit·ted, flit·ting, flits**) *vi.* **1. MOVE FROM PLACE TO PLACE** to move quickly from one place to another without stopping for long **2. BE BRIEFLY PRESENT** to be briefly present or visible [12thC. From Old Norse *flytja* "to carry about." Ultimately from a prehistoric Germanic base meaning "to float," which is also the ancestor of English *float* and *flutter.*] —**flit·ter** *n.*

flitch /flich/ *n.* **1.** FORESTRY **TIMBER CUT LENGTHWISE** a log cut lengthwise from a tree, ready for further processing at a mill **2.** FOOD **SIDE OF BACON** a side of bacon or one side of a pork carcass without the leg or shoulder [Old English *flicce.* Ultimately from a prehistoric Germanic word meaning "to tear," which is also the source of English *fleck, flay,* and *flesh.*]

flit·ter[1] /flíttər/ *vi.* (**-tered, -ter·ing, -ters**) **MOVE RESTLESSLY** to move around in a restless or nervous way ■ *n.* **QUICK MOVEMENT** a rapid, repetitive, or back-and-forth movement in something small [14thC. Formed from FLIT.]

flit·ter[2] /flíttər/ *n.* any one of various types of fritter or small cake (*regional*) [alteration of FRITTER]

WORD KEY: REGIONAL NOTE

In the Appalachian Highlands, *flitter* identifies a pancake or flapjack; especially in the Piedmont South, it signals a fritter cake, often containing fruit or meat, fried in deep fat; in the Highlands, it also designates a fritter of fried corn meal.

fliv·ver /flívvər/ *n.* a small, cheap, and usually old car (*archaic informal*) [Early 20thC. Origin unknown.]

float /flōt/ *v.* (**float·ed, float·ing, floats**) **1.** *vi.* REST ON SURFACE OF LIQUID to move or rest on the surface of a liquid without sinking **2.** *vt.* MOVE ON LIQUID to place something or make something move on the surface of a liquid **3.** *vi.* STAY UP IN AIR to move slowly and lightly through the air **4.** *vi.* BE HEARD OR SMELLED FAINTLY to carry across a distance, especially as a sound or smell ○ *The sound of laughter floated across the water.* **5.** *vi.* MOVE GRACEFULLY to move lightly and gracefully (*literary*) ○ *They floated across the dance floor.* **6.** *vt.* PROPOSE PLAN to propose a plan for consideration in order to see what response it receives (*informal*) **7.** *vi.* LIVE AIMLESSLY to live without a fixed purpose or plan **8.** *vt.* FIN SELL SHARES IN COMPANY to finance a company by selling stock in it to the public **9.** *vt.* FIN SELL STOCKS OR BONDS to offer stocks or bonds for sale on a stock exchange **10.** *vti.* ECON ALLOW CURRENCY VALUE TO CHANGE to allow the exchange rate value of a currency to fluctuate freely in an open market **11.** *vt.* AGRIC IRRIGATE LAND to flood or irrigate land ■ *n.* **1.** FLOATING OBJECT an object or device that floats or is used to keep another object buoyant **2.** VEHICLE IN PARADE a truck or other large vehicle that has been disguised with elaborate decorations, typically with a single theme, and then is driven as part of a parade **3.** ANGLING = **bobber 4.** BEVERAGES SOFT DRINK WITH ICE CREAM a soft drink with a scoop of ice cream floating in it **5.** BANKING PERIOD BETWEEN DEPOSIT AND WITHDRAWAL the period between the deposit of funds by a customer and the availability of the funds to the customer **6.** BUILDING A PLASTERER'S TROWEL a tool with a handle and flat rectangular blade for applying plaster to a wall **7.** MECH ENG BALL IN FLOW-REGULATING DEVICE the hollow ball that rests on the water level in a tank as part of the device (**ballcock**) that regulates the flow of water into the tank **8.** *U.K.* SWIMMING = **flutterboard 9.** SHIPPING PADDLE WHEEL BLADE a blade in a paddle wheel **10.** BIOL = **air bladder** [Old English *flotian*. Ultimately from a prehistoric Germanic base that is also the ancestor of English *fleet*[1].] —**float·a·bil·i·ty** /flōtə bíllətee/ *n.* —**float·a·ble** /flōtəb'l/ *adj.*

float around *vi.* to be the subject of frequent discussion or attention ○ *a rumor floating around about a pending engagement*

float cham·ber *n.* a chamber in a carburetor that has a floating valve to control the entry and level of gasoline

float·er /flṓtər/ *n.* **1.** SOMETHING FLOATING somebody or something that is floating **2.** HR CASUAL WORKER a casual worker who goes from job to job (*informal*) **3.** HR WORKER SHIFTING TO VARIOUS TASKS an employee who is switched from job to job as needed **4.** DEAD BODY a dead body found floating in the water (*slang*) **5.** POL ILLEGAL VOTER somebody who votes illegally in different polling stations using a false registration or the name of somebody who hasn't voted (*informal*) **6.** OPHTHALMOL SPOT INTERFERING WITH VISION a shadow of opaque debris in the vitreous humor of the eye seen as a moving dark spot, or as a group of them, by the person affected. Technical name **muscae volitantes**

float glass *n.* flat polished transparent glass made by solidifying molten glass as it floats on liquid of higher density, such as tin

float·ing /flṓting/ *adj.* **1.** NOT FIXED INTO POSITION not fixed but moving around **2.** MED OUT OF NORMAL POSITION not in the normal place in the body, having moved out of position ○ *a floating kidney* **3.** FIN FLUCTUATING IN MONETARY VALUE free to fluctuate in exchange rate value in relation to other currencies ○ *the floating euro* **4.** MECH ENG OPERATING SMOOTHLY operating smoothly and without vibration

float·ing dock *n.* **1.** SUBMERSIBLE DOCK a large structure that can be submerged to let a ship enter and then raised with the ship inside to be used as a dry dock **2.** MOVABLE SMALL DOCK a small dock supported by pilings on which it can move up and down with the flow and ebb of the tide or changing water level caused by other means

float·ing heart *n.* a perennial freshwater plant that has floating heart-shaped leaves. Genus: *Nymphoides.*

float·ing is·land *n.* a dessert consisting of custard on which are placed pieces of meringue or jelly that appear to float

float·ing-point *adj.* relating to the handling of large numbers, in a computer with limited memory, by moving the decimal point and calculating with each number expressed as a factor of 10

float·ing pol·i·cy *n.* a marine insurance policy that covers loss of or damage to goods being transported, regardless of the ship carrying them

float·ing rib *n.* a rib not attached to the breastbone. In humans the two lower ribs, the eleventh and twelfth, on each side are floating ribs.

float·ing vot·er *n. U.K.* = **swing voter**

float·plane /flṓt plàyn/ *n.* a seaplane that has one or more floats that enable it to land on water

float tank *n.* = **flotation tank**

float·y /flṓtee/ (**-i·er, -i·est**) *adj.* **1.** VERY LIGHT seeming to move slowly through the air **2.** ABLE TO FLOAT capable of floating easily

floc /flok/ *n.* a woolly (**flocculent**) mass that forms in a liquid as a result of precipitation or the aggregation of suspended particles [Early 20thC. Shortening of FLOCCULUS.]

floc·cil·la·tion /flòksi láysh'n/ *n.* aimless plucking at the bedclothes, a sign that a person is approaching death [Mid-19thC. Formed from modern Latin *floccillus* "little tuft of wool," from Latin *floccus* (see FLOCCUS).]

floc·cose /flό kòss/ *adj.* BOT used to describe plant parts that are covered with tufts of soft hair [Mid-18thC. From late Latin *floccosus*, from Latin *floccus* (see FLOCCUS).]

floc·cu·late /flόkyə làyt/ (**-lat·ed, -lat·ing, -lates**) *vti.* **1.** FORM MASSES to cause particles suspended in water to aggregate into clumps or masses that then sink or can be removed by filtering **2.** FORM FLUFFY MASSES to form or cause to form fluffy masses (*refers to clouds*) —**floc·cu·la·tion** /flòkyə láysh'n/ *n.*

floc·cule /flό kyool/ *n.* a small mass of wooly or cloudy particles [Mid-19thC. From modern Latin *flocculus* (see FLOCCULUS).]

floc·cu·lent /flόkyələnt/ *adj.* **1.** WITH FLUFFY APPEARANCE having a fluffy or wooly appearance **2.** WITH WOOLY MASSES used to describe the wooly mass of solids (**precipitate**) produced in a liquid by a chemical reaction [Early 19thC. Formed from Latin *floccus* (See FLOCCUS).] —**floc·cu·lence** *n.* —**floc·cu·len·cy** *n.* —**floc·cu·lent·ly** *adv.*

floc·cu·lus /flόkyələss/ (*plural* **-li** /-lī/) *n.* ASTRON a mass of gas that appears as either a dark or a bright spot on the surface of the Sun, often near to a sunspot [Late 18thC. From modern Latin, literally "small tuft of wool," from Latin *floccus* (see FLOCCUS).]

floc·cus /flόkəss/ (*plural* **-ci** /flό kī, -kee, flόk sī, -see/) *n.* BOT, ZOOL a tuft of wooly hair or a fluffy or downy covering [Mid-19thC. From Latin, "tuft of wool," of unknown origin.]

flock /flok/ *n.* **1.** GROUP OF BIRDS OR SHEEP a group of birds, sheep, or goats that travel, live, or feed together **2.** CROWD OF PEOPLE a large group of people of the same type **3.** CHR CONGREGATION the members of a church congregation under the leadership of a priest or pastor ■ *vi.* (**flocked, flock·ing, flocks**) GO IN LARGE NUMBERS TO SOMETHING to go to a place or event in large numbers [Old English *flocc*]

flock pa·per *n.* a type of wallpaper with a raised pattern [*Flock* "powdered wool" (with which this sort of paper was originally made), from Latin *floccus* (see FLOCCUS)]

floe /flō/ *n.* = **ice floe** [Early 19thC. Origin uncertain: probably from Norwegian *flo* "layer." Ultimately from an Indo-European base meaning "to be flat," which is also the ancestor of English *flake, flag, fluke,* and *plank.*]

flog /flog/ (**flogged, flog·ging, flogs**) *vt.* **1.** BEAT A PERSON OR ANIMAL VERY HARD to hit very hard using something such as a whip, strap, or stick **2.** PRESS PUBLICIZE AGGRESSIVELY to publicize or advertise something aggressively (*informal*) **3.** *U.K.* COMM SELL to sell something (*informal*) [Late 17thC. Origin uncertain: perhaps a shortening and alteration of Latin *flagellare* (see FLAGELLATE), originally in school slang.] —**flog·ger** *n.*

flo·ka·ti /flō kaátee/ (*plural* **-tis**) *n.* a handwoven woolen Greek rug with a shaggy pile [Mid-20thC. From modern Greek *phlokatē*, from, ultimately, Latin *floccus* (see FLOCCUS).]

flong /flawng/ *n.* a sheet of papier mache used to make a mold for the metal plate used to print a page of newspaper [Late 19thC. Anglicization of French *flan* "mold" (see FLAN).]

flood /flud/ *n.* **1.** WATER COVERING PREVIOUSLY DRY AREA a very large amount of water that has overflowed from a source such as a river or a broken pipe onto a previously dry area **2.** HUGE NUMBER a very large number of people or things ○ *a flood of complaints* **3.** HIGH TIDE the flowing in to land of water, associated with a rising tide **4.** = **floodlight** *n.* 1 ■ *v.* (**flood·ed, flood·ing, floods**) **1.** *vti.* COVER AREA WITH WATER to cover a previously dry area with large amounts of water, or to be covered with large amounts of water **2.** *vti.* OVERFLOW to undergo conditions in which water overflows banks or barriers **3.** *vi.* ARRIVE IN LARGE NUMBERS to arrive somewhere in very large numbers ○ *Messages of support are still flooding in.* **4.** *vt.* SEND LOTS OF CALLS OR LETTERS TO to send a very large number of calls, letters, or complaints to an organization (*usually used in the passive*) ○ *We have been flooded with offers of help.* **5.** *vi.* FEEL EMOTION SUDDENLY AND INTENSELY to feel a particular emotion, sensation, or memory suddenly and intensely **6.** *vt.* ECON FILL MARKET TO EXCESS to supply too much of a product to a market, pushing prices down and keeping them low **7.** *vti.* CARS SUPPLY TOO MUCH GAS TO CARBURETOR to send too much gas to a carburetor in a car engine, or be supplied with too much, so that the car fails to start **8.** *vti.* FILL WITH LIGHT to shine strongly so that a place becomes filled with a bright or glowing light (*literary*) **9.** *vi.* MED BLEED A LOT FROM THE WOMB to bleed profusely from the womb, e.g., after childbirth (*technical*) **10.** *vi.* GYN BLEED A LOT IN MENSTRUATION to bleed profusely during a menstrual period (*technical*) [Old English *flōd*. Ultimately from a prehistoric Germanic word that is also the ancestor of English *flow*.] —**flood·a·ble** *adj.* —**flood·er** *n.* ◇ **be in flood** to be very full of water, so that it overflows banks or barriers

flood out *vt.* to force somebody to leave a place or stop using something because flooding makes it impossible to stay or continue

Flood *n.* in the Bible (Genesis 7–8), a devastating flood covering the earth, a sign of God's anger at humanity's wickedness. The Flood was survived only by Noah, his family, and pairs of all the animal species who took refuge in the ship (**ark**) that Noah built at God's command.

flood·ed /flúddəd/ *adj.* **1.** UNDER WATER covered with water as a result of a river overflowing or a pipe bursting **2.** CARS FAILING TO SUSTAIN IGNITION failing to start after having been supplied with too much fuel

flood·gate /flúd gàyt/ *n.* a gate in a watercourse that is used to control the flow

flood·light /flúd lìt/ *n.* **1.** POWERFUL LAMP USED AT NIGHT a large powerful lamp that produces a strong broad beam of artificial light and is used to illuminate the outside of public buildings or sports events at night **2.** POWERFUL BEAM OF LIGHT a broad powerful beam of intense bright light produced artificially ■ *vti.* (**-light·ed** *or* **-lit, -light·ing, -lights**) LIGHT SOMETHING WITH FLOODLIGHTS to illuminate something with floodlights

flood·mark /flúd maàrk/ *n.* the highest level reached by a tide or flood water, or a mark that indicates this level

flood·plain /flúd plàyn/, **flood plain** *n.* an area of low-lying land across which a river flows that is covered with sediment as a result of frequent flooding

flood tide *n.* **1.** RISING TIDE the incoming tide or the period of time between low water and the following high water **2.** IRRESISTIBLE FORCE an irresistible or overwhelming force of feeling, such as strong public outrage or enthusiasm

flood·wall /flúd wàwl/ *n.* a wall built along the seashore or the bank of a river to prevent flooding of adjacent land

flood·wa·ter /flúd wàwtər, -wòttər/ *n.* the water of a flood that is carried over river and stream banks to inundate previously dry land

floo·ey /floo ee/ *adj.* in a disordered state or out of order (*dated slang*) [Early 20thC. Origin unknown.]

floor /flawr/ *n.* **1.** BUILDING **PART OF ROOM TO WALK ON** the flat horizontal part of a room on which people walk **2.** BUILDING **STORY** all the rooms on one level of a building ○ *an office on the fourth floor* **3.** GEOG **NATURAL GROUND LEVEL** the ground at the bottom of an ocean, lake, cave, valley or forest **4. LEVEL AREA** a flat open space for an activity or seating ○ *Are your seats in the stands or on the floor?* **5.** POL **PART OF LEGISLATURE WHERE MEMBERS SIT** the part of the building housing a legislative body where the members sit and where official debates and discussions take place ○ *the floor of the House* **6.** STOCK EXCH **PLACE WHERE SECURITIES ARE TRADED** the part of a stock exchange where securities, futures, or options contracts are traded **7.** MANUF **MANUFACTURING AREA OF FACTORY** the area of a factory where workers manufacture or assemble products ○ *the factory floor* **8.** COMM **PART OF STORE FOR MERCHANDISE DISPLAY** the part of a retail store where merchandise is displayed and sold **9.** DANCE **DANCE FLOOR** a dance floor (*informal*) **10. PEOPLE PRESENT AT MEETING** all the people present in the audience at a meeting as opposed to the main speakers ○ *I'll take questions from the floor later.* **11.** FIN **LOWEST LIMIT** a lower limit on an interest rate or the value of an asset ○ *The floating rate loan has a floor of 6%.* ■ *vt.* **(floored, floor·ing, floors) 1. ASTONISH** to leave somebody astonished and unable to react ○ *He was floored by the announcement of the changes.* **2.** BOXING **KNOCK DOWN** to knock somebody down with a punch **3.** CARS **PRESS ACCELERATOR DOWN HARD** to depress a motor vehicle's accelerator down as far as it will go in order to increase speed to the maximum (*slang*) [Old English *flōr*. Ultimately from an Indo-European word meaning "flat," which is also the ancestor of English *field, plain, plane,* and *palm.*] —**floor·er** *n.* ◇ **have the floor** to address a meeting or to have the right to address a meeting ◇ **take the floor 1.** to rise to speak to a group of people **2.** to begin to dance, e.g., in a ballroom or nightclub ◇ **take to the floor** to begin to dance, e.g., in a ballroom or nightclub ◇ **wipe** *or* **mop up the floor with somebody** to defeat somebody completely and decisively (*informal*)

floor·age /fláwrij/ *n.* the floor area of a building

floor·board /fláwr bàwrd/ *n.* **1.** BUILDING **WOODEN BOARD IN FLOOR** one of the strips of wood that are used to make a wood floor **2.** CARS **CAR FLOOR** the flat, lower part of a motor vehicle's interior where the accelerator, clutch, and brake pedals are found and where the driver and passengers put their feet

floor ex·er·cise *n.* an event in a gymnastics competition that consists of a series of tumbling exercises in a timed routine performed on a mat

floor hock·ey *n.* a version of hockey played using hockey sticks and a plastic puck or ball in a gymnasium. It is occasionally played with bladeless sticks and a rubber ring.

floor·ing /fláwring/ *n.* the materials from which a floor is made

floor lamp *n.* a tall lamp with a base that stands on the floor

floor lead·er *n.* a member of a legislative body chosen by fellow party members to organize their activities and strategy on the floor of the legislature

floor man·ag·er *n.* **1. SUPERVISOR IN STORE** an employee of a department store or large store who is in charge of one floor or department, supervising staff and dealing with customers' complaints **2. CONVENTION MANAGER** somebody who is in charge of the floor at a political convention, choosing speakers and controlling the debate

floor plan *n.* a plan of a room or floor of a building drawn to scale as if viewed from above

floor sam·ple *n.* a piece of merchandise that is sold at a reduced price because it has been used in store displays or as a demonstration model

floor·show /fláwr shṑ/ *n.* a series of shows featuring dancers, singers, comedians, or magicians at a nightclub [Early 20thC. Because it is presented on the floor.]

floor·walk·er /fláwr wàwkər/ *n.* = **floor manager** *n.* 1

floo·zy /flóozee/ (*plural* **-zies**) *n.* an insulting term for a woman who wears vulgar gaudy clothes and frequents disreputable places (*slang insult*) [Early 20thC. Origin uncertain.]

flop /flop/ *vi.* **(flopped, flop·ping, flops) 1. SIT OR LIE DOWN HEAVILY** to sit or lie down heavily by relaxing the muscles and letting the body fall **2. MOVE LIMPLY** to move limply or heavily **3. FAIL COMPLETELY** to be completely unsuccessful (*informal*) ■ *n.* **1. TOTAL FAILURE** a complete failure (*informal*) **2. HEAVY DULL SOUND** the sound made by something falling heavily [Early 17thC. Alteration of FLAP.] —**flop·per** *n.*

flop·house /flóp hòwss/ (*plural* **-houses** /-hòwzəz/) *n.* a cheap hotel or rooming house (*informal*) [Early 20thC. From FLOP "to lie down, sleep."]

flop·py /flóppee/ *adj.* **(-pi·er, -pi·est) HANGING LIMPLY** soft and tending to hang down limply or loosely ■ *n.* (*plural* **-pies**) COMPUT = **floppy disk** (*informal*) —**flop·pi·ly** *adv.* —**flop·pi·ness** *n.*

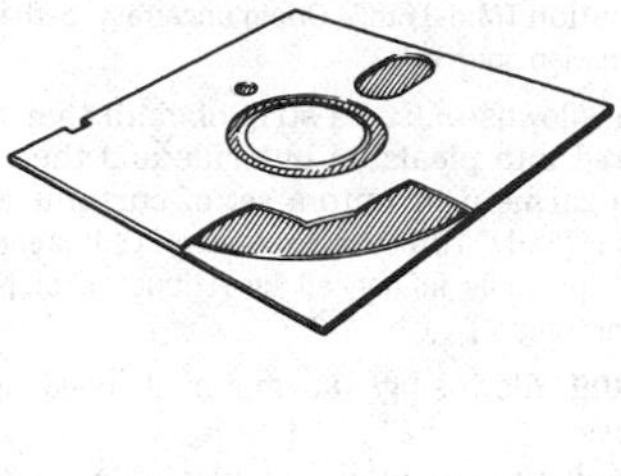

Floppy disk

flop·py disk /flóppi dìsk/ *n.* a small flexible magnetically coated disk on which data can be stored or retrieved by a computer, or the disk and the rigid protective plastic case in which it is contained [Late 20thC. From its flexibility, as opposed to a HARD DISK.]

flops /flops/, **FLOPS** *abbr.* floating-point operations per second (*used to indicate the speed of a computer*)

flop·ti·cal /flóptik'l/ *adj.* relating to or being a system for storing computer data on a disk that combines magnetic and optical technology [Late 20thC. Blend of FLOPPY and OPTICAL.]

flor., **fl.** *abbr.* floruit

flo·ra /fláwrə/ (*plural* **-ras** *or* **-rae** /-rèe/) *n.* **1.** BOT **PLANTS** plant life, especially all the plants found in a particular country, region, or time regarded as a group (*formal*) ○ *the flora of Australia.* ◊ **fauna 2.** BOT **DESCRIPTION OF PLANTS** a systematic set of descriptions of all the plants of a particular place or time **3.** MICROBIOL **BACTERIA THAT INHABIT BODY ORGANS** all the usually harmless bacteria inhabiting an area or part of the body, regarded as a group or population [Early 16thC. From Latin *Flora*, the Roman goddess of flowers, from *flor-*, the stem of *flos* "flower" (source of English *flower.*]

flo·ral /fláwrəl/ *adj.* **1.** PLANTS **CONSISTING OF FLOWERS** containing or made up of flowers **2. DECORATED WITH FLOWERS** ornamented or decorated with flowers or with representations of them **3.** BOT **RELATING TO FLOWERS** relating to or being a part of a flower [Mid-17thC. From Latin *Floralis* "pertaining to the goddess Flora" (the original English meaning), or formed from *flor-* (see FLORA).] —**flo·ral·ly** *adv.*

flo·ral en·ve·lope *n.* = **perianth**

Flo·ral /flàwrəl-/ **Park** town in Nassau County, Long Island, situated 1 mi./1.6 km east of New York City. Population: 15,947 (1990).

Flo·re·al /flàw rayáal/ *n.* CALENDAR the eighth month of the year in the French Revolutionary calendar, corresponding to April 21 to May 20 in the Gregorian calendar [Early 19thC. From French *Floréal*, from Latin *floreus* "flowery," from *flor-* (see FLORA).]

Flor·ence /fláwrənss/ **1.** capital of Firenze Province and Tuscany Region, central Italy. Situated on the Arno River, about 145 mi./233 km northwest of Rome, it is one of the world's leading artistic and cultural centers. Population: 397,434 (1992). Italian **Firenze 2.** city in northwestern Alabama on the northern bank of the Tennessee River, near Wilson Dam. Population: 38,999 (1996). **3.** city in northeastern South Carolina, northwest of Myrtle Beach and northeast of Columbia. Population: 30,168 (1996).

Flor·ence fen·nel *n.* = **fennel** *n.* 2 [Named for the city of FLORENCE, Italy]

Flor·en·tine /fláwrən tèen/ *adj.* **1.** PEOPLES **OF FLORENCE** relating to or typical of the Italian city of Florence, or its people or culture **2.** ARTS **TYPICAL OF ART OF RENAISSANCE FLORENCE** relating to or characteristic of the style of art or architecture that flourished in Florence during the Renaissance **3.** COOK **WITH SPINACH** cooked or served with spinach ○ *eggs Florentine* ■ *n.* PEOPLES **SOMEBODY FROM FLORENCE** somebody who lives in or was born or raised in the Italian city of Florence [13thC. From Latin *Florentinus*, from *Florentia* "Florence."]

Flor·en·tine stitch *n.* = **bargello stitch**

Flo·res /fláwrəss/ mountainous island in southeastern Indonesia, one of the Lesser Sunda Islands. The chief towns are Ende and Ruteng. Population: 272,750 (1989). Area: 5,480 sq. mi./14,200 sq. km.

flo·res·cence /flaw réssəns/ *n.* flowering (*formal*) [Late 18thC. From modern Latin *florescentia*, from Latin *florescent-*, the present participle stem of *florescere* (see FLOURISH).] —**flo·res·cent** *adj.*

flo·ret /fláwrət/ *n.* **1.** PLANTS **SMALL FLOWER** a small flower, especially one in a flowerhead consisting of many flowers **2.** COOK **PIECE OF CAULIFLOWER** a small part into which the edible flower head of cauliflower or broccoli can be separated [Late 17thC. Formed from Latin *flor-* (see FLORA).]

Flo·rey /fláwree/, **Sir Howard Walter, Baron Florey of Adelaide and Marston** (1898–1968) Australian scientist. He was the codeveloper of the world's first antibiotic, penicillin. He shared the Nobel Prize in medicine in 1945.

flo·ri·at·ed /fláwree àytəd/ *adj.* ARCHIT decorated with designs based on flowers and leaves [Mid-19thC. Formed from Latin *flor-* (see FLORA).]

flo·ri·bun·da /flàwrə búndə/ *n.* a hybrid type of cultivated rose that has small flowers growing in large sprays [Late 19thC. From modern Latin, feminine of *floribundus*, literally "flowering profusely," from Latin *flor-* (see FLORA).]

flor·i·cane /fláwri kàyn/ *n.* a plant stem that flowers and bears fruit in its second year, e.g., in raspberries [Coined from Latin *flor-* (see FLORA + CANE)]

flo·ri·cul·ture /fláwri kùlchər/ *n.* the growing of flowers as a crop [Early 19thC. Coined from Latin *flor-* (see FLORA) on the model of HORTICULTURE.] —**flo·ri·cul·tur·al** /flàwri kúlchərəl/ *adj.* —**flo·ri·cul·tur·al·ly** /-rəlee/ *adv.* —**flo·ri·cul·tur·ist** /fláwri kùlchərist, flàwri kúlchərist/ *n.*

flor·id /fláwrid/ *adj.* **1. OF RUDDY COMPLEXION** having an unhealthily glowing pink or red complexion **2. ORNATE IN WORDING AND STYLE** ornate and overly complicated in wording and general style **3. HEALTHY** in a state of good health (*archaic*) [Mid-17thC. Via French from Latin *floridus* "flowery," from *flor-* (see FLORA).] —**flo·rid·i·ty** /flə ríddətee/ *n.* —**flor·id·ly** /fláwridlee/ *adv.* —**flor·id·ness** /-nəss/ *n.*

Florida

Flor·i·da /fláwridə/ state in the southeastern United States bordered by Alabama, Georgia, the Atlantic Ocean, and the Gulf of Mexico. Capital: Tallahassee. Population: 14,653,945 (1997). Area: 59,928 sq. mi./155,213 sq. km. —**Flor·id·i·an** /flə ríddee ən/ *adj.*, *n.*

Flor·i·da ar·row·root *n.* = **coontie** *n.* 1 [Named for FLORIDA, where it was originally found]

Flor·i·da Keys chain of islands and reefs in southern Florida, extending southwestward in an arc from the southern end of Biscayne Bay into the Gulf of Mexico. The islands, which include Key Largo and Key West, are connected by bridges and causeways and are a popular vacation destination. Length: 225 mi./360 km.

flo·rif·er·ous /flaw ríffərəss/ *adj.* bearing or able to bear many flowers [Mid-17thC. Formed from Latin *florifer*, from *flor-* (see FLORA).] —**flo·rif·er·ous·ly** *adv.* —**flo·rif·er·ous·ness** *n.*

flo·ri·le·gi·um /flàwrə léejee əm/ (*plural* **-a** /-ə/) *n.* an anthology of literary extracts (*archaic*) [Early 17thC. From modern Latin, literally "a gathering of flowers," a translation of Greek *anthologion*.]

flor·in /fláwrin/ *n.* **1. OLD BRITISH COIN** a unit of currency used in Britian between 1849 and 1968, equivalent to two shillings **2. GOLD OR SILVER COIN** a gold or silver coin, especially a Dutch guilder **3. FLORENTINE COIN** a gold coin first minted in Florence in 1252, or any similar coin used elsewhere in Europe [14thC. Via Old French from, ultimately, Italian *fiore* "flower" (because the name was first used for a coin bearing the figure of a fleur-de-lis), from Latin *flor-* (see FLORA).]

flo·rist /fláwrist/ *n.* **1. SOMEBODY WHO SELLS FLOWERS** somebody who owns or works in a shop that sells flowers and ornamental plants **2. SHOP SELLING FLOWERS** a shop that sells flowers and other ornamental plants [Early 17thC. Formed from Latin *flor-* (see FLORA).]

flo·rist·ics /flaw rístiks/ *n.* a branch of botany dealing with the types, numbers, distribution, and relationships of plant species in a particular area or areas (*takes a singular verb*) [Late 19thC. Coined from FLORA + -ISTICS.]

-florous *suffix.* bearing flowers ○ *multiflorous* [Formed from Latin *flor-*, the stem of *flos* (see FLOWER)]

flo·ru·it /fláwryoo it/ *v.* used, especially abbreviated as "fl.", before the name or numeric designator of the period in the past when a specified person or movement was most active. (*literary formal*) [Mid-19thC. From Latin, literally "flourished."]

flo·ry /fláwree/ *adj.* HERALDRY containing a fleur-de-lis [14thC. Anglicization of Old French *floré*, from *flor* (see FLOWER).]

floss /flawss/ *vti.* (**flossed, floss·ing, floss·es**) DENT **CLEAN BETWEEN TEETH** to clean between individual teeth using dental floss ■ *n.* **1.** DENT = **dental floss 2.** TEXTILES **SILKWORM FIBERS** short or waste fibers prepared from the the outer surface of the cocoon of a silkworm **3.** PLANTS **PLANT FIBERS** the mass of fine silk fibers that covers the seeds of the ceiba tree or of a cotton plant **4.** SEW **EMBROIDERY THREAD** an embroidery thread made up of six strands loosely twisted together but which can be separated for fine work [Mid-18thC. Origin uncertain: possibly an alteration of French *floche* "down, velvet pile," from Latin *floccus* (see FLOCCUS).] —**floss·er** *n.*

floss·y /fláwssee/ (**-i·er, -i·est**) *adj.* **1. FLASHILY ORNATE** ornate or showy in a flashy, often almost vulgar way **2. OF OR LIKE FLOSS** consisting of or looking like floss —**floss·i·ly** *adv.* —**floss·i·ness** *n.*

flo·tage /flṓtij/ *n.* **1.** = **flotation** *n.* 3 **2.** = **flotsam** *n.* 1

flo·ta·tion /flō táysh'n/ *n.* **1. FLOATING** the act, process, or condition of floating **2. CAPABILITY OF FLOATING** the ability to float on a liquid or remain on top of a soft surface (*technical*) **3.** FIN **SELLING OF STOCK IN COMPANY** the financing of a company by selling stock in it or a new debt issue, or the offering of stock and bonds for sale on the stock exchange **4.** TRANSP **ADHERENCE OF TIRE TO SURFACE** the ability of a tire tread to adhere to and remain on top of a soft surface such as wet ground or snow **5.** CHEM **SEPARATION PROCESS** a process for separating materials, such as a mixture of minerals in an ore, according to their different abilities to float in a given liquid, such as water [Early 19thC. Formed from FLOAT.]

flo·ta·tion bags *npl.* large bags that inflate when a helicopter or spacecraft lands in the sea and keep it afloat and upright

flo·ta·tion de·vice *n.* a device to enable somebody to stay afloat in the sea, such as a life jacket or seat cushion, kept in an aircraft or vessel (*technical*)

flo·ta·tion tank *n.* a sealed tank filled with salt water and minerals that somebody can float in to relieve stress

flo·ta·tion ther·a·py *n.* a method of relieving stress that involves floating in salt water in a sealed tank while listening to music

flo·tel /flō tél/ *n.* a moored boat or an oil rig that provides lodging by workers on offshore oil rigs [Late 20thC. Contraction of *floating hotel*.]

flo·til·la /flō tíllə/ *n.* **1.** SAILING **FLEET OF VESSELS** a fleet of usually small vessels **2.** NAVY **U.S. NAVAL UNIT** a U.S. naval unit consisting of two squadrons of small warships **3. GROUP OF THINGS** a group of things operating or moving together [Early 18thC. From Spanish, literally "small fleet," from *flota* "fleet," which came via Old French *flote* from Old Norse *floti*.]

flot·sam /flótsəm/ *n.* **1.** SHIPPING **WRECKAGE FLOATING IN SEA** wreckage, debris, or refuse from a ship, found floating in the water. In maritime law flotsam is what is found floating after a ship has sunk and jetsam is what is thrown from a ship while it was in trouble. **2. MARGINALIZED PEOPLE** people who live on the margins of society, such as vagrants, the homeless, or the destitute (*offensive*) (*considered offensive in some contexts*) [Early 17thC. From Anglo-Norman *floteson*, from *floter* "to float," of prehistoric Germanic origin.] ◇ **flotsam and jetsam** discarded objects or odds and ends

flounce[1] /flowns/ *vi.* (**flounced, flounc·ing, flounc·es**) **MOVE WITH ANGRY SWAGGER** to move with exaggerated angry swaggering motions showing displeasure or indignance ■ *n.* **JERKY MOVEMENT** an exaggerated movement of the body that shows displeasure or indignation [Mid-16thC. Origin uncertain: perhaps from a Scandinavian source.]

flounce[2] /flowns/ *n.* SEW a strip of cloth that has been gathered into pleats on one side and then stitched onto a garment or onto a set of curtains as a decoration [Early 18thC. Alteration of Old French *fronce* "pleat" (probably influenced by FLOUNCE[1]), of prehistoric Germanic origin.]

flounc·ing /flównsing/ *n.* material used to make flounces

floun·der[1] /flówndər/ (**-dered, -der·ing, -ders**) *vi.* **1. MAKE UNCONTROLLED MOVEMENTS** to make clumsy uncontrolled movements while trying to regain balance or move forward **2. HESITATE IN CONFUSION** to act in a way that shows confusion or a lack of purpose **3. BE IN SERIOUS DIFFICULTY** to have serious problems and be close to failing [Late 16thC. Origin uncertain: possibly a blend of FOUNDER and BLUNDER.]

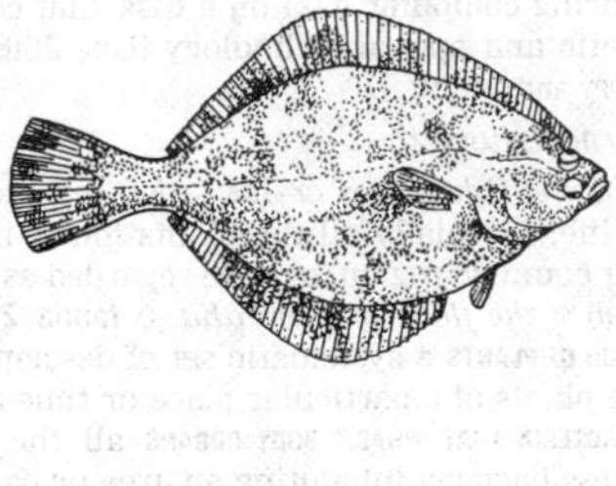

Flounder

floun·der[2] /flówndər/ (*plural* **-der** *or* **-ders**) *n.* **1. EDIBLE FLATFISH** a flatfish that lives at the bottom of shallow coastal waters and is an important food fish. Families: Pleuronectidae and Bothidae. **2. EDIBLE EUROPEAN FLATFISH** a European flatfish that has grayish-brown mottled skin with orange spots, is covered with prickly scales, and is edible. Latin name: *Platichthys flesus.* [15thC. Via Anglo-Norman *floundre* from a Scandinavian source related to Old Swedish *flundra*. Ultimately from an Indo-European word meaning "to be flat," the ancestor of English *flat, plate,* and *plant*.]

flour /flowr/ *n.* FOOD **1. FINELY GROUND CEREAL GRAINS** a powder made by grinding the edible parts of cereal grains and used to make bread, cakes, or pastry and to thicken sauces **2. GROUND FOODSTUFF** a finely ground powder made from any dried vegetable such as chickpea, banana, cassava, or potato ■ *vt.* (**floured, flour·ing, flours**) COOK **COVER WITH FLOUR** to cover or coat food, food preparation utensils, or a work surface with flour [13thC. Variant of FLOWER, in the sense "finest quality" (i.e. ground meal).]

flour·ish /flúrrish/ *v.* (**-ished, -ish·ing, -ish·es**) **1.** *vi.* **BE HEALTHY OR GROW WELL** to be strong and healthy or to grow well, especially because conditions are right **2.** *vi.* **DO WELL** to sustain continuous steady strong growth **3.** *vt.* **WAVE** to wave something in a dramatic way that draws attention to it ■ *n.* **1. HAND MOVEMENT** a dramatic body movement, such as a sweep of the hand, that attracts attention **2. LOOP OR CURL** an embellishment to something handwritten, such as a loop or curly line **3.** MUSIC **ORNAMENTAL TRUMPET CALL** a fanfare heralding the arrival of an important person **4.** MUSIC **SHORT PRELUDE OR POSTLUDE** a short, often improvised, passage at the beginning or end of a piece of music **5.** MUSIC **SHOWY MUSICAL INTERLUDE** brief, often showy, technical passage within a piece of music [13thC. From Old French *floriss-*, the stem of *florir* "to bloom," from, ultimately, Latin *florere*, from *flor-* (see FLORA).] —**flour·ish·er** *n.*

flour moth *n.* a gray moth with larvae that infest stored grain. Latin name: *Ephestia kuhniella.*

flour·y /flówree/ (**-i·er, -i·est**) *adj.* FOOD covered or coated with flour or tasting of flour

flout /flowt/ (**flout·ed, flout·ing, flouts**) *vt.* to show contempt for a law or convention by openly disobeying or defying it [Mid-16thC. Origin uncertain: perhaps from an earlier word meaning "to play the flute," as if in mockery.] —**flout·er** *n.* —**flout·ing·ly** *adv.*

WORD KEY: USAGE

See Usage note at ***flaunt***.

flow /flō/ *vi.* (**flowed, flow·ing, flows**) **1. MOVE FREELY FROM PLACE TO PLACE** to move or be moved freely from one place to another in large numbers or amounts in a steady unbroken stream ○ *measures to allow traffic to flow freely* **2.** PHYSIOL **CIRCULATE IN BODY** to move through the veins and arteries of the body (*refers especially to blood*) **3.** COMMUNICATION **BE SAID FLUENTLY** to be expressed uninhibitedly and eloquently ○ *The conversation began to flow.* **4. BE AVAILABLE IN QUANTITY** to be readily available and consumed in large amounts ○ *The lemonade flowed freely.* **5. BE EXPERIENCED INTENSELY** to be experienced very intensely, often in a way that is visible to other people ○ *A wave of love flowed across her face.* **6. EMANATE AS RESULT** to derive from something as a result or series of results (*literary*) ○ *The consequences that flowed from the decision were distressing.* **7. HANG LOOSELY** to fall or hang loosely and gracefully ○ *Her long hair flowed over her shoulders.* **8.** OCEANOG **MOVE TOWARD LAND** to move toward the land as the tide rises (*refers to the sea or tidal water*) **9.** GEOL **CHANGE SHAPE UNDER PRESSURE** to change shape gradually in response to pressure without the development of cracks or fissures ■ *n.* **1. MOVEMENT OF FLUID OR ELECTRICAL CHARGE** the movement of liquid, gas, or electrical charge **2. MASS OR QUANTITY FLOWING** a mass or quantity of material that is flowing or has flowed ○ *a giant lava flow pouring down into the valley* **3. MENSTRUAL FLOW** the flow or quantity of blood during menstruation **4. UNHINDERED STEADY MOVEMENT** the steady unbroken stream of people, goods, vehicles, money, or information from one place to another ○ *the unending flow of refugees* **5.** OCEANOG **TIDAL MOVEMENT TOWARD LAND** the movement of a rising tide toward the land **6.** COMMUNICATION **ELOQUENT EXPRESSION OF THOUGHTS** the continuous eloquent expression of thoughts or ideas in speech or writing **7.** PSYCHOL **EXPERIENCE OF HEIGHTENED AWARENESS** psychological and physical experience in which challenges presented are perfectly matched by the participants' skills, often resulting in heightened states of awareness, confidence, and performance [Old English *flōwan*. Ultimately from an Indo-European word that is also the ancestor of English *flood* and *pluvial*.] ◇ **go with the flow** to follow the lead of other people and react to their opinions or actions passively

flow·age /flṓwij/ *n.* **1. FLOWING** the act of flowing or overflowing **2. OVERFLOWING WATER** the water resulting from overflow **3.** CIV ENG **GRADUAL DEFORMATION** the gradual change in shape that occurs in certain solids, e.g., asphalt, that can flow without breaking when, e.g., heat is applied

flow chart, **flow·chart** *n.* a diagram that represents the sequence of operations in a process

flow-chart·ing *n.* the designing of a flow chart or charts

flow cy·tom·e·try *n.* a diagnostic test revealing the arrangement and amount of DNA in a cell, used to distinguish benign cells from malignant ones or to monitor the effect of anticancer treatment

flow di·a·gram *n.* = **flow chart**

flow·er /flówr/ *n.* **1. COLORED PART OF PLANT** a colored, sometimes scented, part of a plant that contains its reproductive organs. It consists of a leafy shoot with modified leaves, petals, and sepals surrounding male or female organs, stamens, and pistils. **2. STEM WITH FLOWER** a plant stem with one or more flowers that has been picked from the plant on which it grew **3. PLANT WITH FLOWERS** a small plant grown for the attractiveness of its flowers **4. BEST** the best part of or most perfect example of something ○ *the flower of the nation's youth* ■ **flow·ers** *npl.* CHEM **FINE CHEMICAL POWDER** a fine powder produced by sublimation or condensation ■ *vi.* (**-ered, -er·ing, -ers**) **1.** BOT **PRODUCE BLOOMS** to begin to produce blooms **2.**

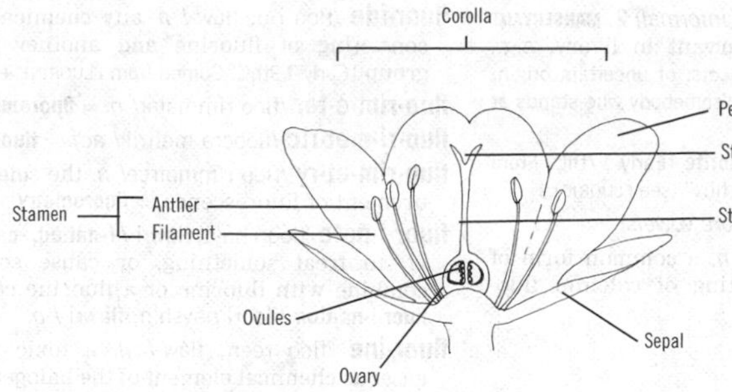

Flower: Cross section of a flower

DEVELOP TO MATURITY to develop and reach maturity [12thC. From Anglo-Norman *flur* and Old French *flour*, both from Latin *flor-* (see FLORA.]

flow·er·bed /flówr bèd/ *n.* a clearly delineated area of a garden or park planted with flowering plants

flow·er bug *n.* an insect that feeds on other small insects found in flowers. Family: Anthorcoridae.

flow·er child *n.* a young person in the 1960s-1970s who rejected materialism and war, especially the Vietnam War, and preached universal peace and love as the solution to the world's problems (*informal*) [From their custom of wearing or carrying flowers as a symbol of peace]

flow·ered /flówrd/ *adj.* **1.** ORNAMENTED WITH FLOWERS decorated with flowers or having a floral pattern **2.** WITH BLOOMS having flowers (*usually used in combination*) ○ *a large-flowered variety*

flow·er·er /flówrər/ *n.* a plant that flowers, usually at a particular time or in a particular manner ○ *a late flowerer*

flow·er·et /flówrət/ *n.* COOK = **floret** *n.* 2

flow·er girl *n.* a young girl who carries flowers in the procession preceding a bride at a wedding

flow·er head *n.* **1.** CLUSTER OF SMALL FLOWERS a cluster of small flowers on a single stem **2.** CLUSTER OF FLOWER BUDS a dense arrangement of flower buds, such as in cauliflower or broccoli

flow·er·ing /flówring/ *adj.* ABLE TO PRODUCE BLOOMS capable of producing noticeable flowers ■ *n.* PERIOD OF SUCCESS the moment in the development of an idea, style, or movement when it gains recognition and becomes successful

flow·er·ing dog·wood *n.* a spreading deciduous tree with green oval leaves that turn red or purple in the fall and small greenish flowers surrounded by four white or pink bracts resembling petals. Latin name: *Cornus florida.*

flow·er·ing ma·ple *n.* a tropical plant that has lobed leaves like the maple and brightly colored flowers. Genus: *Abutilon.*

flow·er·ing quince *n.* a spiny deciduous plant, native to Asia, that is grown for its attractive red or pink flowers and fragrant yellow fruit. Genus: *Chaenomeles.*

flow·er·ing rush *n.* a deciduous water plant similar to a rush that has narrow twisted leaves and is grown for its pink flowers. Latin name: *Butomus umbellatus.*

flow·er·ing win·ter·green *n.* = **fringed polygala**

flow·er-of-an-hour, **flow·er-of-the-hour** (*plural* **flow·ers-of-the-hour**) *n.* a European herbaceous annual plant that has oval serrated leaves and is grown for its trumpet-shaped creamy-white or pale yellow flowers. Latin name: *Hibiscus trionum.* [Because its petals are short-lived]

flow·er·peck·er *n.* a small songbird found in Australia and southeast Asia that has a long tongue and feeds on nectar, berries, and insects. Family: Dicaeidae.

flow·er peo·ple *npl.* young 1960s-1970s peace activists, the flower children, regarded as a group (*informal*)

flow·er·pot /flówr pòt/ *n.* a clay or plastic container in which plants are grown

flow·er pow·er *n.* the idea advocated by some young people in the 1960s and 1970s that universal peace and love should replace the materialism and militarism of Western society [From its adherents' custom of wearing flowers as a symbol of peace and love]

flow·er press·ing *n.* the process of preserving cut flowers by laying them on a flat surface and pressing them with a heavy object

flow·er·y /flówree/ (**-i·er, -i·est**) *adj.* **1.** LITERAT, COMMUNICATION POMPOUSLY LITERARY full of ornate, overly elaborate expressions **2.** ORNAMENTED WITH FLOWERS decorated or patterned with flowers **3.** LIKE FLOWERS relating to flowers —**flow·er·i·ness** *n.*

flow·me·ter /flów meetər/ *n.* an instrument for measuring the rate of flow of liquids or gases, especially in a pipe

flown past participle of **fly**[1]

flow sheet *n.* **1.** = **flow chart 2.** CHEM ENG DIAGRAM OF PIPEWORK a schematic diagram showing the equipment and connecting pipes that make up a process plant and sometimes showing flow rates and quantities of material

flow·stone /flṓ stòn/ *n.* a layered deposit of calcium carbonate (**calcite**) on rock where water has flowed or dripped, e.g., on the walls or floor of a cave. ◊ **dripstone**

fl oz, **fl. oz.** *abbr.* fluid ounce

FLQ *n.* a terrorist organization seeking the secession of Quebec from Canada. It was particularly active during the 1960s and 1970s. Full form **Front de Libération du Québec**

FLRA *abbr.* Federal Labor Relations Authority

FLSA *abbr.* Fair Labor Standards Act

flu /floo/ *n.* a viral illness producing a high temperature, sore throat, running nose, headache, dry cough, and muscle pain. The illness is widespread, especially during winter months, and can sometimes be fatal. [Mid-19thC. Shortening of INFLUENZA.]

flub /flub/ *vti.* (**flubbed, flub·bing, flubs**) MESS UP SOMETHING to blunder or make a mess of something (*slang*) ○ *He flubbed his lines and the audience boohed.* ■ *n.* (*slang*) **1.** BLUNDER OR GAFFE an embarrassing, clumsy mistake **2.** BLUNDERER somebody who makes embarrassing blunders [Early 20thC. Origin uncertain: probably thought to suggest clumsiness.] —**flub·ber** *n.*

fluc·lox·a·cil·lin /floo klòksə síllin/ *n.* a penicillin drug used to treat streptococcal infections in wounds or sometimes pneumonia. This form of penicillin is effective against bacteria resistant to earlier forms of the drug.

flu·con·a·zole /floo kónnə zōl/ *n.* a drug that is prescribed to combat and control fungi

fluc·tu·ate /flúkchoo àyt/ (**-at·ed, -at·ing, -ates**) *vi.* to change often from high to low levels or from one thing to another in an unpredictable way [Mid-17thC. From Latin *fluctuat-*, the past participle stem of *fluctuare*, from *fluctus*, the past participle of *fluere* "to flow" (see FLUENT).] —**fluc·tu·ant** *adj.*

fluc·tu·a·tion /flùkchoo áysh'n/ *n.* constant unpredictable change in the level, degree, or intensity of something

flue[1] /floo/ *n.* **1.** SMOKE OR HEAT OUTLET a shaft, tube, or pipe used as an outlet to carry smoke, gas, or heat from a chimney or furnace **2.** **flue, flue pipe** MUSIC TYPE OF ORGAN PIPE an organ pipe in which the sound is produced by passing air across a lipped opening **3.** MUSIC OPENING ON ORGAN PIPE the lipped opening on an organ pipe that initiates vibrations and sound when air passes across it [15thC. Origin unknown.]

flue[2] /floo/ (*plural* **flues** *or* **flews**) *n.* a type of fishing net, especially a dragnet [15thC. From Middle Dutch *vluwe* "fishing net."]

flue-cure (**flue-cures**) *vt.* to cure tobacco with radiant heat supplied through flues from a furnace —**flue-cured** *adj.*

flue gas *n.* the smoke in the uptake of a boiler fire that consists mainly of carbon dioxide, carbon monoxide, and nitrogen

flu·el·lin /floo éllin/, **flu·el·len** /-ən/ *n.* an annual wild plant related to the toadflax, foxglove, and snapdragon. Genus: *Kickxia.* [Mid-16thC. Alteration of Welsh *(llysiau) Llywelyn*, literally "Llewelyn's herbs," named after LLEWELYN AP GRUFFUDD or LLEWELYN AP IORWERTH.]

flu·en·cy /flóo ənsee/ *n.* **1.** ABILITY TO SPEAK LANGUAGE the ability to speak a language effortlessly and correctly **2.** EFFORTLESS CLEAR EXPRESSION the ability to express something effortlessly and clearly

flu·ent /flóo ənt/ *adj.* **1.** ABLE TO SPEAK WITH EASE able to speak a language effortlessly and correctly **2.** EFFORTLESSLY EXPRESSED spoken or expressed effortlessly and correctly **3.** SMOOTHLY FLOWING flowing in a smooth graceful way (*literary*) [Late 16thC. From Latin *fluent-*, the present participle stem of *fluere* "to flow."] —**flu·ent·ly** *adv.*

WORD KEY: ORIGIN

The Latin word *fluere*, from which ***fluent*** is derived, is also the source of English *affluent, effluent, flu, fluctuate, fluid, fluorides, flush, fluvial, flux, influence, mellifluous*, and *superfluous.*

flue stop *n.* an organ stop that controls a set of flue pipes

fluff /fluf/ *n.* **1.** LIGHT BALLS OF THREAD soft light balls of thread or fiber that collect together on material such as wool or cotton **2.** BIRDS, PLANTS DOWNY FUZZ the soft downy fuzz found on young birds or some seeds **3.** NONSENSE something that is of no importance or consequence (*slang*) ■ *vt.* (**fluffed, fluff·ing, fluffs**) **1.** SHAKE SO AS TO INSERT AIR to shake, pat, or brush something in order to get air into it **2.** DO BADLY to do something badly because of loss of concentration or forgetfulness (*informal*) **3.** BIRDS RAISE FEATHERS to raise the feathers in a way that makes the body appear bigger [Late 18thC. Origin uncertain.]

fluff·y /flúffee/ (**-i·er, -i·est**) *adj.* **1.** SOFT AND LIGHT consisting of something soft and light to the touch such as wool or feathers **2.** DOWNY OR FEATHERY covered in something soft and light to the touch such as down or feathers **3.** COOK SOFT AND LIGHT IN TEXTURE soft and light in texture because air has been beaten or whisked in —**fluff·i·ly** *adv.* —**fluff·i·ness** *n.*

flü·gel·horn /flóog'l hàwrn/, **flu·gel·horn** *n.* a brass instrument with valves, similar to a cornet but with a larger bell [Mid-19thC. From German *Flügelhorn*, literally "wing horn"; from its use to signal to beaters on the flanks in a shoot.] —**flü·gel·horn·ist** *n.*

flu·id /flóo id/ *n.* **1.** LIQUID anything liquid (*not used in technical contexts*) **2.** PHYS, CHEM LIQUID OR GAS a substance such as a liquid or gas whose molecules flow freely, so that it has no fixed shape and little resistance to outside stress ■ *adj.* **1.** PHYS FLOWING capable of flowing like a liquid or gas (*technical*) **2.** MOVING OR SMOOTHLY CARRIED OUT smooth and graceful in a way that seems relaxed ○ *a series of fluid arm movements* **3.** UNSTABLE likely to change ○ *The situation in the western sector is fluid.* [15thC. Via Old French from Latin *fluidus* "flowing," from *fluere* "to flow."] —**flu·id·al** *adj.* —**flu·id·al·ly** *adv.* —**flu·id·i·ty** /floo íddətee/ *n.* —**flu·id·ly** /-lee/ *adv.* —**flu·id·ness** /-nəss/ *n.*

flu·id clutch *n.* = **fluid drive**

flu·id dram *n.* a unit of liquid capacity in the apothecary system, equal to $\frac{1}{8}$ of a fluid ounce

flu·id drive *n.* a device for transmitting rotation between two shafts by means of the acceleration and deceleration of a hydraulic fluid by bladed turbines, used in automatic transmissions in motor vehicles

flu·id dy·nam·ics *n.* the scientific study of the forces acting on liquids and gases and the resulting movements of these fluids (*takes a singular verb*)

flu·id·ex·tract /flóo id ék stràkt/ *n.* a solution of a vegetable drug in alcohol with one milliliter of the solution having an equivalent activity of one gram of the powdered drug

flu·id·ic /floo íddik/ *adj.* **1.** OF FLUIDS relating to fluids **2.** OPERATED BY FLUIDICS relating to or operated by fluidics

flu·id·ics /floo íddiks/ *n.* the use of systems based on the movements and pressure of fluids to control operations, instruments, and industrial processes (*takes a singular verb*)

flu·id·ize /flóo i dìz/ (**-ized, -iz·ing, -iz·es**) *vt.* 1. **CAUSE TO BE FLUID** to make something fluid 2. **MAKE SOLID BEHAVE LIKE FLUID** to make a solid move as a fluid, e.g., by pulverizing it into fine powder and passing a gas through it to induce flow —**flu·id·i·za·tion** /flòo idi záysh'n/ *n.* —**flu·id·iz·er** /flóo i dìzər/ *n.*

flu·id·iz·ed bed *n.* a powder or other solid particulate material suspended in an upward flow of air or other gas. The material behaves like a fluid and is an effective way to transfer heat or moisture between a gas and a solid or to operate certain chemical reactions.

flu·id me·chan·ics *n.* the branch of mechanics that deals with the properties of gases and liquids and their application in practical engineering (*takes a singular verb*)

flu·id ounce *n.* 1. **U.S. UNIT OF LIQUID MEASUREMENT** a unit of volume measurement in the U.S. Customary system equal to $\frac{1}{16}$ of a U.S. pint or 29.57 ml 2. **U.K. UNIT OF LIQUID MEASUREMENT** a unit of liquid measurement in the British Imperial system equal to $\frac{1}{20}$ of an Imperial pint or 28.41 ml

fluke[1] /flook/ *n.* 1. **ACCIDENTAL SUCCESS** something surprising or unexpected that happens by accident (*informal*) 2. CUE GAMES **SHOT IN BILLIARDS** a successful shot in pool, billiards, or snooker that happens by accident ■ *vti.* (**fluked, fluk·ing, flukes**) CUE GAMES **POT BALL BY ACCIDENT** to make a successful shot by accident in pool, billiards, or pocket billiards [Mid-19thC. Origin unknown.]

fluke[2] /flook/ *n.* ZOOL 1. **PARASITIC FLATWORM** a parasitic flatworm that infests humans and animals, e.g., the liver fluke. Class: Trematoda. 2. = **flounder**[2] [Old English *flōc*. Ultimately from an Indo-European base meaning "to be flat," which is also the ancestor of English *flake*, *flag*, and *plank*.]

fluke[3] /flook/ *n.* 1. SHIPPING **PART OF ANCHOR** either of the triangular blades at the end of each arm of an anchor 2. ANGLING, ARCHERY **BARB ON HARPOON** a barb on the head of a harpoon or an arrow, or the barbed head itself 3. ZOOL **PART OF WHALE'S TAIL** either of the two horizontal lobes of the tail of a whale or other similar sea animal, used in propelling the animal through the water [Mid-16thC. Origin uncertain: perhaps from FLUKE[2], because of its shape.]

fluk·y /flóokee/ (**-i·er, -i·est**), **fluk·ey** (**-i·er, -i·est**) *adj.* accidentally and unexpectedly successful (*informal*) —**flukily** *adv.* —**fluk·i·ness** *n.*

flume /floom/ *n.* 1. GEOG **NARROW GORGE** a narrow gorge with a stream running through it 2. **ARTIFICIAL CHANNEL** an artificial water channel or chute used, e.g., to transport logs, for studying water and sediment movement, or as part of an amusement park ride 3. **ARTIFICIAL CHANNEL TO MEASURE RIVER'S FLOW** an artificial channel constructed in a river in order to measure water flow and movement of sediment 4. ENG **STRUCTURE FOR MEASURING WATER DISCHARGE** a structure in a river that is used to measure water discharge [12thC. Via Old French *flum* from Latin *flumen* "river," from *fluere* "to flow" (see FLUENT).]

flum·mer·y /flúmməree/ *n.* 1. **MEANINGLESS WORDS** meaningless words, statements, or language, especially when intended as flattery (*literary*) 2. FOOD **CREAM OR CUSTARD DESSERT** a cream, milk, or custard dessert set with gelatin and sometimes flavored with Madeira and lemon. It was originally made with liquid from boiled oatmeal set with gelatin or isinglass. [Early 17thC. Anglicization of Welsh *llymru*.]

flum·mox /flúmməks/ (**-moxed, -mox·ing, -mox·es**) *vt.* to leave somebody confused or perplexed and unable to react (*informal*) [Mid-19thC. Origin uncertain.]

flung past participle, past tense of **fling**

flunk /flungk/ (**flunked, flunk·ing, flunks**) *v.* (*informal*) 1. *vti.* **FAIL ACADEMICALLY** to fail an exam or subject 2. *vt.* **GIVE FAILING GRADE TO** to give a student a failing grade [Early 19thC. Origin unknown.] —**flunk·er** *n.*

flunk out *vi.* to be expelled from a school, college, or course because of failing grades (*informal*)

flun·key *n.* = **flunky**

flunk·out /flúngk òwt/ *n.* a student who fails in school or college and has to leave because of it (*disapproving*)

flun·ky /flúngkee/ (*plural* **-kies**), **flun·key** (*plural* **-keys**) *n.* 1. **SERVILE ASSISTANT** an assistant who carries out unimportant jobs for somebody and who behaves obsequiously to that person (*informal*) 2. **MANSERVANT IN LIVERY** a man who is a servant in livery, e.g., a footman [Mid-18thC. From Scots, of uncertain origin: perhaps an alteration of FLANKER "somebody who stands at your flank."] —**flun·ky·ism** *n.*

flu·or /flóo àwr, flóo ər/ *n.* = **fluorite** [Early 17thC. From modern Latin, "mineral used as a flux" (see FLUORIC).]

fluor- *prefix.* = **fluoro-** (*used before vowels*)

fluo·ra·pa·tite /flòo ráppə tìt/ *n.* a common form of the mineral apatite consisting of calcium fluorophosphate

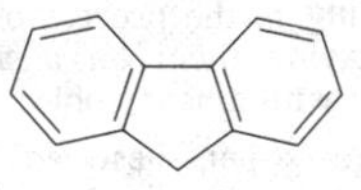

Fluorene

flu·o·rene /flóo reen, fláw-/ *n.* a white insoluble crystalline solid obtained from coal tar and used in making dyes. Formula: $C_{13}H_{10}$. [Late 19thC. Coined from FLUORO- (because the compound fluoresces + -ENE).]

fluo·resce /floo réss, flaw-/ (**-resced, -resc·ing, -resc·es**) *vi.* PHYS to exhibit or undergo the phenomenon of fluorescence [Late 19thC. Back-formation from FLUORESCENT.] —**fluo·resc·er** *n.*

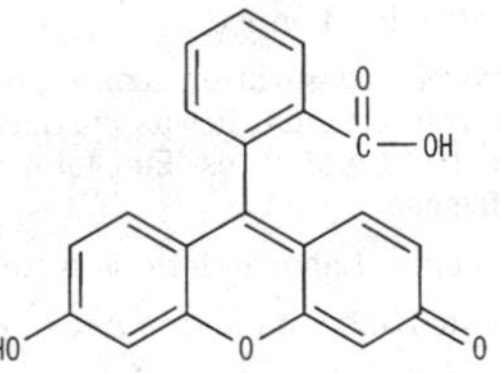

Fluorescein

fluo·res·ce·in /floo réssee in, flaw-/, **fluo·res·ce·ine** *n.* an orange-red crystalline compound that fluoresces green in blue light, used to detect defects in the cornea in the eye. Formula: $C_{20}H_{12}O_5$. [Late 19thC. Coined from FLUORESCE + -EIN.]

fluo·res·cence /floo réss'ns, flaw-/ *n.* 1. **EMISSION OF LIGHT** the emission of electromagnetic radiation, especially light, by an object exposed to radiation or bombarding particles 2. **LIGHT EMITTED** the radiation emitted as a result of fluorescence

fluo·res·cent /floo réss'nt, flaw-/ *adj.* 1. PHYS **CAPABLE OF FLUORESCING** exhibiting or able to undergo fluorescence ○ *a fluorescent dye* 2. **DAZZLING IN COLOR** very bright and dazzling in color ○ *fluorescent pink* [Mid-19thC. Coined from FLUORSPAR (because fluorspar has this property) + -ESCENT.]

fluo·res·cent lamp, **fluo·res·cent light** *n.* an electric lamp containing a low pressure vapor, usually mercury, in a glass tube. When an electric current is passed, ultraviolet radiation is produced and is converted into visible light by an internal coating on the tube.

fluo·res·cent tube *n.* the tube of a fluorescent lamp

fluo·ric /floo áwrik/ *adj.* relating to or produced from fluorine or fluorite [Late 18thC. From obsolete French *fluorique*, from modern Latin *fluor* "mineral used as a flux," from Latin, "flow," from *fluere* "to flow" (see FLUENT).]

fluor·i·date /flóori dàyt/ (**-dat·ed, -dat·ing, -dates**) *vt.* to treat water by adding small quantities of fluoride salts to the water supply in order to prevent tooth decay in a local population

fluor·i·da·tion /flòori dáysh'n/ *n.* the addition of small quantities of fluoride salts to the water supply as a public health measure to help prevent tooth decay

fluor·ide /flóo rìd, fláw-/ *n.* any chemical compound consisting of fluorine and another element or group [Early 19thC. Coined from FLUORINE + -IDE.]

fluo·rim·e·ter /floo rímmətər/ *n.* = **fluorometer**

fluo·ri·met·ric /flòorə méttrik/ *adj.* = **fluorometric**

fluo·rim·et·ry /floo rímmətree/ *n.* the scientific measurement of fluorescence. = **fluorometry**

fluor·i·nate /flóori nàyt, fláwri-/ (**-nat·ed, -nat·ing, -nates**) *vt.* to treat something, or cause something to combine with fluorine or a fluorine compound —**fluor·i·na·tion** /flòori náysh'n, flàwri-/ *n.*

fluor·ine /flóo reen, fláw-/ *n.* a toxic pale yellow gaseous chemical element of the halogen group that is the most reactive and oxidizing agent known and occurs principally in fluorite and cryolite. Symbol F [Early 19thC. Coined from modern Latin *fluor* (see FLUORIC) + -INE.]

fluor·ite /flóo rìt, fláw-/ *n.* a mineral form of calcium fluoride, occurring in veins with other minerals as well-formed crystals of various colors, including a banded purple variety, known as Blue John, used as a flux. Formula: CaF_2. [Mid-19thC. Coined from modern Latin *fluor* (see FLUORIC) + -ITE.]

fluoro- *prefix.* 1. fluorine ○ *fluoride* 2. fluorescence ○ *fluoroscope* [From FLUORINE and FLUOR]

fluor·o·car·bon /flòorō kaárbən, flàwrō-/ *n.* a chemically inert compound containing carbon and fluorine. Fluorocarbons are used as nonstick coatings, lubricants, refrigerants, and solvents.

fluor·o·chem·i·cal /flòorō kémmik'l, flàwrō-/ *n.* any chemical compound containing fluorine

fluor·o·chrome /flòorō krōm, flàwrō-/ *n.* a molecule or part of a molecule that exhibits fluorescence, used as a marker in biological specimens

fluo·rog·ra·phy /floo róggrəfee, flaw-/ *n.* = **photofluorography**

fluo·rom·e·ter /floo rómmətər, flaw-/ (*plural* **-rom·e·ters** *or* **-rim·e·ters**) *n.* an instrument used to detect and measure fluorescence —**fluo·ro·met·ric** /flòorō méttrik, flàwrō-/ *adj.* —**fluo·rom·e·try** /floo rómmətree, flaw-/ *n.*

fluor·o·scope /flóorə skōp, fláwrə-/ *n.* an instrument with which X-ray images of the body can be viewed directly on a screen —**fluor·o·scop·ic** /flòorō skóppik, flàwrō-/ *adj.* —**fluor·o·scop·i·cal·ly** *adv.*

fluo·ros·co·py /floo róskəpee, flaw-/ *n.* the examination of a person using a fluoroscope —**fluo·ros·co·pist** /floo róskəpist, flaw-/ *n.*

fluo·ro·sis /floo róssiss, flaw-/ *n.* a condition caused by excessive exposure to fluorine and marked by mottling of the teeth and damage to the bones —**fluo·rot·ic** /floo róttik, flaw-/ *adj.*

fluor·o·u·ra·cil /flòorō yóorəssìl, flàwrō-/ *n.* a chemical compound containing fluorine that is used as a treatment for certain forms of cancer. Formula: $C_4H_3FN_2O_2$.

flu·or·spar /flóor spaar, flóo ər-, fláwr-/ *n.* = **fluorite** [Late 18thC. From modern Latin *fluor*, "mineral used as a flux" (see FLUORIC) + SPAR.]

flu·phen·a·zine /floo fénnə zeen/ *n.* an antipsychotic drug used as a tranquilizer in the treatment of schizophrenia [Mid-20thC. Contraction of *fluorophenothiazine*, its chemical name.]

flur·ry /flúr ee, flúrree/ *n.* (*plural* **-ries**) 1. **BURST OF ACTIVITY** a short period when a lot of things happen 2. METEOROL **BURST OF SNOW** a short period of snowfall ■ *v.* (**-ried, -ry·ing, -ries**) 1. *vt.* **MAKE UNCERTAIN** to make somebody feel agitated and confused 2. *vi.* METEOROL **SNOW LIGHTLY** to snow lightly and intermittently ○ *It flurried for an hour or so, then it stopped.* [Late 17thC. Origin uncertain: probably a blend of obsolete *flurr* "to flutter" and HURRY.]

flush[1] /flush/ *v.* (**flushed, flush·ing, flush·es**) 1. *vti.* **TURN RED** to become or cause somebody to become red in the face or on the skin 2. *vti.* **HAVE ROSY COLOR** to glow or cause something to glow with a reddish color 3. *vti.* **MAKE WATER FLOW THROUGH TOILET** to clean a toilet by causing water to flow into the bowl, or undergo this process 4. *vt.* **DISPOSE OF IN TOILET** to put something into the toilet and flush it 5. *vt.* **CLEAN WITH WATER** to clean or clear something by liberally pouring water or another liquid into, on, or through it ■ *n.* 1. **SUDDEN FEELING** a sudden intense feeling 2. **BEGINNING OF GOOD TIME** the beginning of an exciting or pleasurable period 3. **SUDDEN RUSH OF THINGS** a sudden increased number of things 4. **REDDISHNESS** an appearance of reddish color **5. SURGE OF HEAT** a sudden surge of heat **6.** GARDENING **NEW GROWTH** a burst of new growth appearing rapidly on a plant [13thC. Origin uncertain: perhaps from FLUSH[3].] —**flush·er** *n.*

flush[2] /flush/ *adj.* **1. LEVEL** completely level so as to form an even surface **2. BESIDE OR AGAINST** directly next to or closely against something ○ *The chairs were flush against the wall.* **3. TEMPORARILY RICH** having plenty of money temporarily (*informal*) **4. ABUNDANT** abundant or overflowing ○ *a party flush with celebrities* **5.** PRINTING **WITH EVEN MARGIN** with an even margin on a printed page, without any indentations ■ *adv.* **1. COMPLETELY LEVEL** so as to be completely level and form an even surface without sticking out **2.** BOXING **DIRECTLY** directly or squarely ○ *was hit flush on the jaw* ■ *vt.* (**flushed, flush·ing, flush·es**) **FIT THINGS COMPLETELY LEVEL** to fit two things so that they are completely level and form an even surface [Mid-16thC. Origin uncertain: probably from FLUSH[1].] —**flush·ness** *n.*

flush[3] /flush/ *vt.* (**flushed, flush·ing, flush·es**) **DRIVE OUT OF HIDING** to force a person or animal out of hiding ■ *n.* HUNT **FRIGHTENED BIRDS** a bird or birds frightened out of hiding [13thC. Origin unknown.] —**flush·er** *n.*

flush[4] /flush/ *n.* in poker and other games, a hand consisting of cards all in the same suit [Early 16thC. Via obsolete French *flus* from, ultimately, Latin *fluxus* (see FLUX).]

flush·a·ble /flúshəb'l/ *adj.* that can be disposed of by flushing it down the toilet

flushed /flusht/ *adj.* **1. RED-FACED** red in the face **2. EXCITED** feeling excited or happy

flus·ter /flústər/ *vti.* (**-tered, -ter·ing, -ters**) **MAKE OR BECOME NERVOUS** to make somebody nervous or agitated, or become so ■ *n.* **CONFUSED STATE** a nervous or agitated state [Early 17thC. Origin uncertain.] —**flus·tered** *adj.*

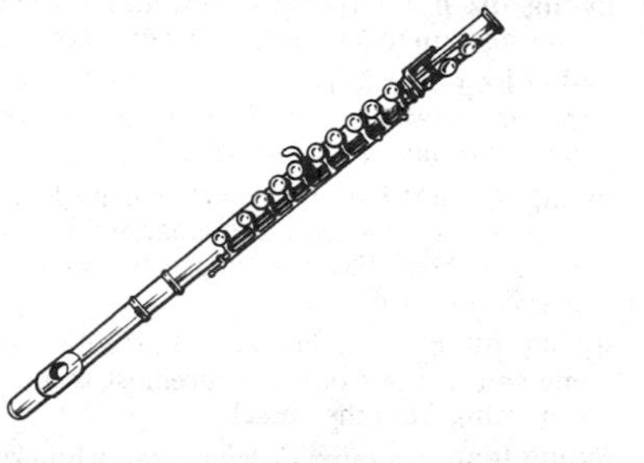

Flute

flute /floot/ *n.* **1.** MUSIC **WIND INSTRUMENT WITH HIGH SOUND** a woodwind instrument with a cylindrical metal body usually held out to the right of the player, who blows across a hole in the mouthpiece to generate a high-pitched sound. The flute family includes the piccolo, the alto flute, and the bass flute. **2.** MUSIC **REEDLESS INSTRUMENT** any wind instrument without a reed **3.** MUSIC **ORGAN STOP** an organ stop with a tone like a flute **4.** ARCHIT **GROOVE IN COLUMN** a groove running down an architectural column **5. DECORATIVE GROOVE** a decorative groove or pleat **6.** HOUSEHOLD, WINE **TALL GLASS FOR SPARKLING WINE** a tall narrow glass used for sparkling wines ■ *v.* (**flut·ed, flut·ing, flutes**) **1.** *vi.* **MAKE SOUND LIKE FLUTE** to whistle, sing, or speak in a way that suggests the sound of a flute **2.** *vt.* **MAKE FURROWS IN** to make rounded grooves in something [14thC. Via Old French *flaute* and Middle Dutch *flute* from Old Provençal *flaut*, of uncertain origin: possibly a blend of *flaujol* "flageolet" and *laut* "lute."]

flut·ed /flo͞otəd/ *adj.* **1. DECORATIVELY FURROWED** decorated with parallel grooves **2. SOUNDING LIKE FLUTE** similar in sound to a flute

flut·er /flo͞otər/ *n.* **1. FLUTING MAKER** somebody who makes fluting in something **2.** MUSIC **FLUTE-PLAYER** a flutist

flut·ing /flo͞oting/ *n.* **1. DECORATIVE FURROWS** decoration with parallel grooves **2. MAKING DECORATIVE FURROWS** the forming of decorative grooves **3. MAKING FLUTE SOUND** playing the flute, or making sounds like those of the flute

flut·ist /flo͞otist/, **flau·tist** /fláwtist, flów-/ *n.* somebody who plays the flute [Mid-19thC. From Italian *flautisto*, from *flauto* "flute," from Provençal *flaüt* (see FLUTE).]

flut·ter /flúttər/ *v.* (**-tered, -ter·ing, -ters**) **1.** *vi.* **WAVE GENTLY** to move gently but with quick changes in direction

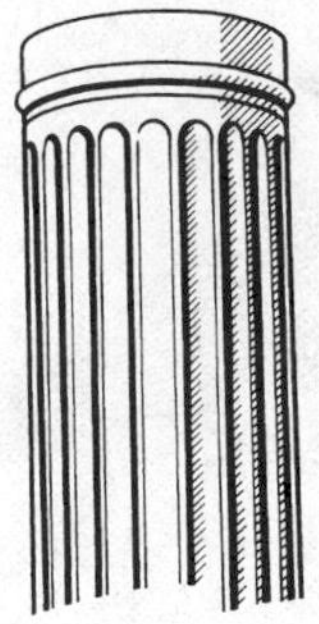

Fluting

or wavy motion **2.** *vti.* **MOVE SOMETHING LIGHT** to move something light or small in quick back-and-forth motions **3.** *vti.* **FLAP WINGS** to flap the wings rapidly **4.** *vi.* **FLY** to move by flapping the wings rapidly **5.** *vi.* **BEAT RAPIDLY** to beat rapidly, either as a disorder of the heart or because of nervousness or excitement **6.** *vi.* **QUIVER** to have a quivering feeling because of nervousness or excitement **7.** *vt.* **MAKE NERVOUS** to make somebody feel agitated or nervous (*usually used in the passive*) **8.** *vi.* **MOVE RESTLESSLY** to move around in a restless or nervous way ■ *n.* **1. QUICK MOVEMENT** a rapid, repetitive, or back-and-forth movement in something small **2. AGITATION** a state of nervous excitement or agitation **3.** MED **RAPID HEARTBEAT** a condition marked by rapid, but regular, heartbeat **4.** RECORDING **SOUND DISTORTION** a high frequency distortion in the pitch of recorded sound **5.** *U.K.* BETTING **SMALL BET** a small bet on something (*informal*) [Old English *floterian*. Ultimately from a prehistoric Germanic word that is also the ancestor of English *flit* and *fleet*.] —**flut·ter·er** *n.* —**flut·ter·ing·ly** *adv.* —**flut·ter·y** *adj.*

flut·ter·board /flúttər bàwrd/ *n.* a buoyant rectangular board that supports the arms and top of the body of a swimmer practicing leg strokes [Mid-20thC. From FLUTTER KICK + BOARD.]

flut·ter kick *n.* a swimming technique that consists of moving the legs rapidly up and down in short strokes

flut·ter tongu·ing *n.* a technique in wind-instrument playing in which a fluttering tone is produced by making a rolled "r" while blowing —**flut·ter-tongue** *vti.*

flut·y /flo͞otee/ (**-i·er, -i·est**) *adj.* high-pitched and clear, like a flute

flu·vi·al /flo͞ovee əl/ *adj.* produced by or found in a river or stream [14thC. From Latin *fluvialis*, from *fluvius* "river," from *fluere* "to flow" (see FLUENT).]

flu·vi·o·ma·rine /flo͞ovee ō mə reén/ *adj.* **1. OF RIVERS AND SEAS** relating to water and sediment deposits of rivers in a marine environment **2.** BIOL = **diadromous** [Mid-19thC. Coined from Latin *fluvius* "river" (see FLUVIAL) + MARINE.]

flux /fluks/ *n.* **1. CONSTANT CHANGE** constant change and instability **2. SOLDERING AID** a substance that promotes the fusion of two substances or surfaces, as in soldering or welding **3.** PHYS **RATE OF FLOW ACROSS AREA** the rate of flow of something, such as energy, particles, or fluid volume, across or onto a given area **4.** PHYS **STRENGTH OF FIELD IN PARTICULAR AREA** the strength of a field acting on a particular area, equal to the area size multiplied by the component of the field acting at right angles to the area **5.** MED **ABNORMAL BODILY DISCHARGE** an abnormal discharge or flow from the body, especially the bowels (*dated*) **6.** METALL **SMELTING AID** a substance added to molten ore that combines with impurities to form slag which can be extracted **7.** CERAMICS **GLAZE COMPONENT** a substance added to a ceramic glaze to make it flow more readily **8.** PHILOS **THEORY OF CHANGE** the notion that change is the fundamental nature of reality, as described by Heraclitus **9.** OCEANOG **QUANTITY OF MOVEMENT** the quantity of water or other material moved in a given direction during a given time period ■ *v.* (**fluxed, flux·ing, flux·es**) **1.** *vti.* **MAKE OR BECOME FLUID** to make something fluid, or become fluid **2.** *vt.* MECH ENG **APPLY FLUX TO** to apply flux to something, especially a joint being soldered **3.** *vi.* **FLOW ALONG OR OUT** to move in a steady current or stream (*archaic*) [14thC. Via Old French from Latin *fluxus*, the past participle of *fluere* "to flow" (see FLUENT).]

flux den·si·ty *n.* the amount of flux per unit area

flux·ion /flúkshən/ *n.* **1. FLOW OF SOMETHING** a flow or discharge of liquid **2.** MATH **DERIVATIVE OF FUNCTION** a derivative, representing the rate of change of a function in relation to an independent variable (*dated*) [Mid-16thC. Directly or via French from Latin *flux-*, the past participle stem of *fluere* (see FLUENT).] —**flux·ion·al** *adj.* —**flux·ion·al·ly** *adv.* —**flux·ion·ar·y** *adj.*

fly[1] /flī/ *v.* (**flew** /floo/, **flown** /flōn/, **fly·ing, flies**) **1.** *vi.* BIRDS, AIR **MOVE THROUGH AIR** to travel through the air using wings or an engine **2.** *vi.* AIR **TRAVEL IN AIRCRAFT** to travel in an aircraft **3.** *vt.* AIR **TAKE OR SEND BY AIR** to take or send things or passengers in an aircraft **4.** *vti.* AIR **BE PILOT** to pilot an aircraft or spacecraft **5.** *vt.* AIR **TRAVEL OVER AREA BY AIR** to travel over a particular area in an aircraft **6.** *vi.* AIR **TRAVEL WITH AIRLINE OR IN CLASS** to travel with a particular airline or in a particular class in an aircraft ○ *She always flies with the same airline.* **7.** *vti.* **FLOAT THROUGH AIR** to make something such as a kite move through the air, or move in this way **8.** *vti.* **DISPLAY FLAG ON POLE** to display a flag by attaching it to a pole, building, or mast, or be displayed in this way **9.** *vt.* SHIPPING **SHOW COUNTRY OF REGISTRATION** to display a flag that indicates the country of registration **10.** *vi.* **MOVE FREELY IN AIR** to move freely because of the speed of the air ○ *She ran down the street, her hair flying.* **11.** *vi.* **GO VERY FAST** to go somewhere or leave somewhere at top speed **12.** *vi.* **MOVE QUICKLY AND FORCEFULLY** to move with speed and explosive force **13.** *vi.* **PASS QUICKLY** to pass very fast ○ *The weekend had simply flown.* **14.** *vi.* **BE DISCUSSED INCREASINGLY** to be passed on or gossiped about by a swiftly increasing number of people ○ *Bad news flies.* **15.** *vi.* **BE QUICK TO DO SOMETHING** to rush to do something quickly **16.** *vi.* **BE ACCEPTABLE** to be acceptable, successful, or useful (*informal*) ○ *come up with a proposal that will fly* **17.** *vi.* **DISAPPEAR** to disappear or be used up quickly ○ *Money just flies out of her hands.* **18.** *vt.* THEATER **HANG ABOVE STAGE** to suspend lights or set components above a stage **19.** *vt.* HUNT **USE HUNTING HAWK** to cause a hawk to fly after prey **20. fly** (*past and past participle* **flied**) *vi.* BASEBALL **HIT FLY** to hit a fly ball ○ *She flied twice in the second inning.* ■ *n.* (*plural* **flies**) **1.** CLOTHES **FRONT OPENING OF PANTS** an opening at the front of a pair of pants with a fold of fabric that covers a zipper or row of buttons **2. ENTRANCE FLAP OF TENT** a flap at the entrance of a tent **3. OUTER ROOF OF TENT** a light tarpaulin secured over the top of a tent **4.** BASEBALL **BALL HIT HIGH** in baseball, a hit that goes high but usually not very far **5. WIDTH OF FLAG** the distance between the outer edge of a flag and the staff it is attached to **6. EDGE OF FLAG** the outer edge of a flag **7.** = **flywheel 8.** *U.K.* TRANSP **HORSE-DRAWN CARRIAGE** in former times, a carriage for hire, drawn by one horse ■ **flies** *npl.* THEATER **AREA ABOVE STAGE** the space above a stage in a theater, where lights, scenery, etc. are hung. [Old English *flēogan*. Ultimately from an Indo-European word that is also the ancestor of English *fly*[2], *flee*, *flight*, and *fledgling*.] —**fly·able** *adj.* ◇ **fly high** to enjoy a period of great success or happiness ◇ **let fly (at somebody) 1.** to speak angrily to somebody **2.** to throw something ◇ **on the fly 1.** while in a hurry ○ *caught me on the fly* **2.** while flying ○ *caught the ball on the fly* **3.** without preparation, in the present moment ○ *answered all their questions on the fly* ◇ **send somebody** *or* **something flying** to cause somebody or something to go through the air by force of impact

fly at *vt.* = **fly into**

fly in *vi.* to arrive by aircraft

fly into *vt.* **1. FEEL STRONGLY AND SUDDENLY** to suddenly start feeling and expressing a strong emotion ○ *fly into a rage* **2. ATTACK SOMEBODY PHYSICALLY OR VERBALLY** to attack somebody by rushing toward that person, hitting him or her or speaking angrily

fly out *vi.* **1.** AIR **GO BY PLANE** to travel by plane to a particular destination or from a particular airport **2.** BASEBALL **HAVE FLY CAUGHT** in baseball, to be put out when the ball you hit is caught by a fielder

fly[2] /flī/ (*plural* **flies**) *n.* **1.** INSECTS **SMALL TWO-WINGED INSECT** a two-winged insect. Many flies, e.g., houseflies, are pests. Order: Diptera. **2.** INSECTS **FLYING INSECT** any flying insect, e.g., a caddis fly or dragonfly (*usually used in combination*) **3.** ANGLING **FLY-FISHING LURE** a fishhook with feathers or other attachments to make it resemble a flying insect, used in fly-fishing [Old English *flēoge*. Ultimately from the same prehistoric Germanic base as FLY[1].] ◇ **a fly in the ointment** a problem that spoils a good situation ◇ **there are no flies on**

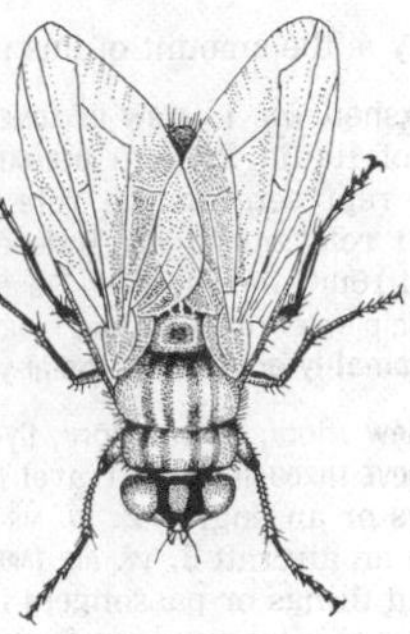

Fly (life size x10)

somebody used to say that somebody is not lacking in intelligence or understanding

fly[3] /flī/ *adj.* stylish and fashionable (*slang*) [Early 19thC. Origin unknown.]

fly[4] /flī/ (*plural* **flies**) *adj.* **1.** *U.K.* CRAFTY shrewd and clever, in a crafty way (*informal*) **2.** STYLISH attractive and stylish (*slang*)

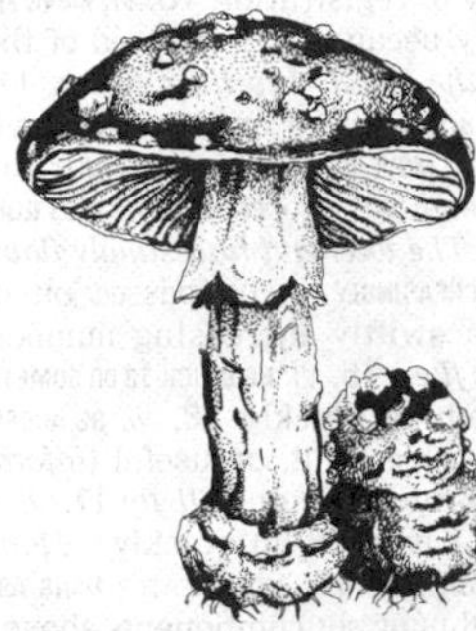

Fly agaric

fly ag·a·ric *n.* a poisonous mushroom with a bright red or orange cap and white spots. Latin name: *Amanita muscaria.* [From its former use as an insecticide]

fly ash *n.* fine particles of ash resulting from the combustion of a solid fuel

fly·a·way /flī ə wày/ *adj.* easily made airborne or affected by a breeze ○ *flyaway hair*

fly·back /flī bàk/ *n.* in a television tube, the rapid return of the electron beam in the direction opposite to scanning

fly ball *n.* BASEBALL = **fly**[1] *n.* 4

fly·blow /flī blō/ *n.* MAGGOT OR MAGGOTS the egg or larva of a blowfly or flesh fly, or an infestation with such eggs or larvae ■ *vt.* (**-blew** /flī blo͞o/, **-blown** /flī blōn/, **-blow·ing, -blows**) CONTAMINATE to contaminate something with something such as the eggs or larvae of a blowfly

fly·blown *adj.* **1.** WITH MAGGOTS containing maggots and therefore not fit to eat **2.** DIRTY dirty and in bad condition **3.** TAINTED contaminated with something undesirable

fly·boat /flī bōt/ *n.* a small fast boat [Late 16thC. By folk etymology from Dutch *vlieboot*, from *Vlie*, the name of a channel off the northern coast of The Netherlands.]

fly·boy /flī bòy/ *n.* a man who is a pilot in the Air Force (*informal*)

fly bridge *n.* = **flying bridge**

fly·by /flī bī/ *n.* a flight close to a particular position or object, usually by a space vehicle to a planet, usually for observation purposes

fly-by-night *adj.* **1.** UNSCRUPULOUS IN BUSINESS unscrupulous or not creditworthy in business or commerce **2.** EPHEMERAL not lasting long ■ *n.* **fly-by-night, fly-by-night·er 1.** ABSCONDING DEBTOR somebody who leaves without paying debts **2.** DUBIOUS OR SHAKY BUSINESS a business with financial problems or a bad reputation [From the tactic of sneaking away at night in order to avoid paying debts]

fly-by-wire *n.* an aircraft flight control system that has electronic rather than mechanical controls

Flycatcher

fly·catch·er /flī kàchər/ *n.* a songbird that has a slender bill and feeds on insects caught in flight. Families: Muscicapidae and Tyrannidae.

fly-drive *adj.* including a flight and a rental car at the destination

fly·er *n.* = **flier**

fly·fish *vi.* to fish using a rod, reel, and line and a fishhook lure meant to resemble a fly —**fly·fish·er** *n.* —**fly·fish·ing** *n.*

fly·fish·er·man (*plural* **-men**) *n.* somebody who fishes using a rod, reel, line, and fishhook lure meant to resemble a fly

fly front *n.* an opening at the front of a garment, with a fold of fabric that covers a zipper or row of buttons

fly gal·ler·y *n.* a hidden platform above a stage from where objects suspended from the flies are controlled

fly·ing /flī ing/ *adj.* **1.** AIR, BIRDS ABLE TO FLY capable of flight **2.** MOVING FAST moving very quickly **3.** PASSING QUICKLY happening or passing very quickly **4.** SAILING NOT HELD AT EDGE held at the corners only, not the edge (*refers to a sail*) ■ *n.* AIR AIR TRAVEL travel by aircraft, or the piloting of aircraft

WORD KEY: CULTURAL NOTE

The Flying Dutchman, an opera by German composer Richard Wagner (1843). The protagonist of this three-act composition is a Dutch seaman who, as a result of an act of blasphemy, has been condemned to roam the oceans until he is saved by the love of a woman. In Norway, he meets Senta, who commits a desperate act of faith that results in his redemption.

fly·ing boat *n.* a seaplane with a fuselage that acts like a boat's hull and provides buoyancy on water

fly·ing bomb *n.* any explosive robot plane, guided missile, or rocket bomb (*informal*)

fly·ing bridge *n.* an open deck of a boat or ship with a secondary set of navigational devices

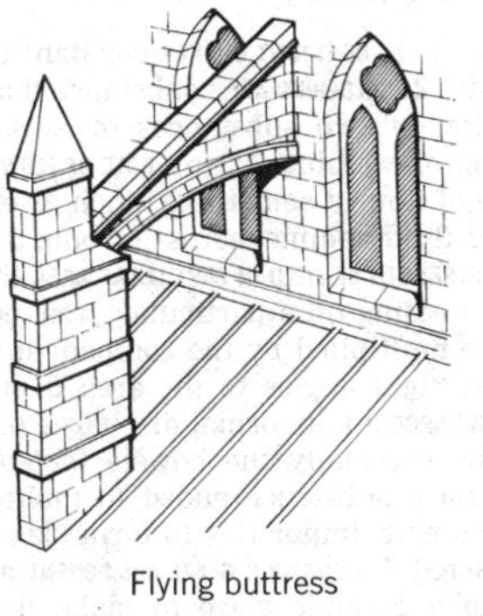

Flying buttress

fly·ing but·tress *n.* an exterior support for a wall (**buttress**) that sticks out from the wall and is typically arch-shaped, often used in Gothic cathedrals to withstand the outward thrust of the very high walls

fly·ing col·ors ◇ **with flying colors** very successfully

fly·ing drag·on *n.* = **flying lizard**

fly·ing field *n.* a small airfield from which aircraft, usually light aircraft, can operate

Flying fish

fly·ing fish *n.* a fish found in warm or tropical seas with fins that can be held out like wings, enabling it to glide short distances above the water. Family: Exocoetidae.

Flying fox

fly·ing fox *n.* a large Australasian fruit bat with a wingspan up to 5 ft./152 cm. Genus: *Pteropus.*

fly·ing frog *n.* an Asian frog that uses its webbed feet to glide between the trees in which it lives. Latin name: *Racophorus reinwardii.*

fly·ing gur·nard *n.* a tropical marine fish that resembles the gurnard but has large fins enabling it to glide short distances above the water. Family: Dactylopteridae.

fly·ing jib *n.* on a boat or ship with more than one sail at the front, the foremost triangular sail projecting from the vessel

fly·ing leap *n.* a jump or leap taken while running

fly·ing le·mur *n.* a mammal of Southeast Asia with a flap of skin between its front and back limbs that it uses to glide between the trees in which it lives. Family: Dermoptera.

fly·ing liz·ard *n.* a small tropical lizard with a flap of skin between its front and back limbs that it uses to glide through the air. Genus: *Draco.*

fly·ing ma·chine *n.* an aircraft, especially a very early one (*dated*)

fly·ing mare *n.* a wrestling maneuver in which the attacker grasps the opponent's arm and then turns to throw the opponent over the shoulder

fly·ing pha·lan·ger *n.* a small Australasian marsupial that uses a flap of skin between its front and back limbs to glide between trees. Family: Phalangeridae.

fly·ing sau·cer *n.* a disk-shaped flying object believed to be an extraterrestrial spacecraft

fly·ing squad *n.* a group of troops or police officers who can be quickly deployed

fly·ing squir·rel *n.* a nocturnal squirrel of northern Europe, North America, and Asia that uses a flap of skin between its front and back limbs to glide between trees. Family: Petauristinae.

fly·ing start *n.* a start of a race in which competitors cross the starting line at racing speed ◇ **off to a flying start, off to a running start** begun or beginning very successfully

fly·ing wedge *n.* a group of law-enforcement officers in a wedge-shaped formation who are thus able to move into crowds effectively

fly·ing wing *n.* in Canadian football, the 12th player, who has a variable position behind the scrimmage line

fly-kick *n.* in certain martial arts, a kick executed in mid-air with one leg straight and the other flexed at the knee and hip

fly·leaf /flī lèef/ (*plural* **-leaves** /-lèevz/) *n.* the first page in a hardbound book, which forms a continuous sheet with the page stuck inside the front cover [From FLY[1]]

fly·man /flīmən/ (*plural* **-men**) *n.* somebody whose job is to operate scene elements from the flies in a theater

fly net *n.* a net or sheet of netting used to keep flying insects out of or away from something

Errol Flynn: As the Earl of Essex in *The Private Lives of Elizabeth and Essex* (1939)

Flynn /flin /, **Errol** (1909–59) Australian-born U.S. actor. He played the swashbuckling hero in romantic costume dramas in films such as *Captain Blood* (1935) and *The Adventures of Robin Hood* (1938). Real name **Leslie Thomas Flynn**

fly or·chid *n.* a European orchid in which the lower part of the flower resembles an insect. Latin name: *Ophrys insectifera.*

fly·o·ver /flī ṑvər/ *n.* **1.** AIR **CEREMONIAL FLIGHT MADE BY AIRCRAFT** the flight of an aircraft or formation of aircraft over a place as a spectacle for people on the ground **2.** *U.K.* TRANSP = **overpass**

fly·pa·per /flī pàypər/ *n.* paper coated with a sticky and poisonous substance that attracts and kills flies

fly-past *n. U.K.* AIR = **flyover** *n.* 1 [Modeled on FLYOVER]

fly rod *n.* a long flexible fishing rod for use in fly-fishing

flysch /flish/, **Flysch** *n.* a thick deposit of sedimentary rock formed in marine environments by erosion of adjacent steep mountains [Early 19thC. From Swiss German.]

fly·sheet /flī shèet/ *n.* printed information or advertising on a sheet or pamphlet

fly sheet *n. U.K.* = **fly**[1] *n.* 3

fly·speck /flī spèk/ *n.* **1. FLY'S FECES** a tiny mark made by a fly's feces **2. TINY MARK** any tiny mark or stain ■ *vt.* (**-specked, -speck·ing, -specks**) **MARK WITH FLYSPECKS** to mark something with the tiny spots of flies' feces or similar stains (*usually used in the passive*)

fly swat·ter *n.* a tool used to strike and kill insects, consisting of a long flexible handle with a flat piece of plastic net attached

fly·trap /flī tràp/ *n.* **1.** PLANTS = **Venus flytrap 2. FLY-CATCHING DEVICE** a device for catching flies

fly-ty·ing *n.* the making of artificial flies that can be used to catch fish —**fly-ti·er** *n.*

fly·way /flī wày/ *n.* a route taken by migrating birds

fly·weight /flī wàyt/ *n.* a boxer of the lightest weight in professional competition, up to 112 lbs/51 kg

fly·wheel /flī wèel, -hwèel/ *n.* a heavy wheel or disk that helps to maintain a constant speed of rotation in a machine or to store energy

fm *abbr.* **1. fm.** fathom **2.** from

Fm *symbol.* fermium

FM *abbr.* **1.** (*plural* **FMs**) field manual **2.** AERON figure of merit **3. fm.** RADIO frequency modulation

F.M. *abbr.* field marshal

FMB *abbr.* Federal Maritime Board

FMCS *abbr.* Federal Mediation and Conciliation Service

Fmk, **FMk** *abbr.* Finnish markka

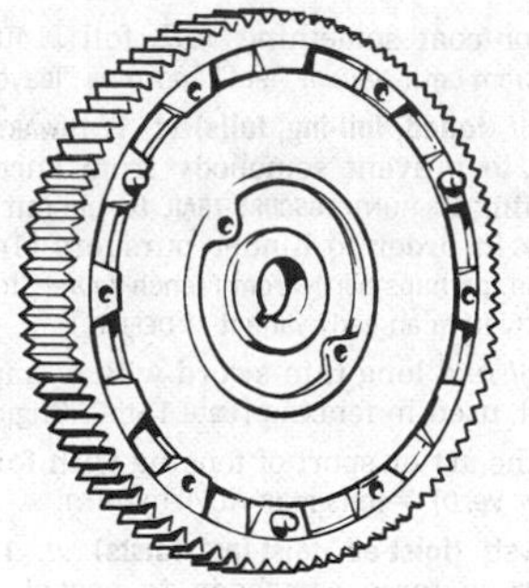
Flywheel

fml. *abbr.* formal

FMS *abbr.* **1.** AIR flight management system **2.** PSYCHOL false memory syndrome

FMVSS *abbr.* Federal Motor Vehicle Safety Standards

FN (*plural* **FNs**) *abbr.* foreign national

fn. *abbr.* footnote

fndr. *abbr.* founder

FNMA *abbr.* Federal National Mortgage Association

f-num·ber *n.* PHOTOGRAPHY the ratio of the focal length to the effective diameter of a camera lens. Symbol **f, f/** [*f* shortening of FOCAL]

FO, **F.O.** *abbr.* **1. FO, F.O.** field-grade officer **2.** field order **3.** finance officer **4. FO, F/O.** flight officer **5.** flying officer

fo. *abbr.* folio

F.O. *abbr.* field-grade officer

foal /fōl/ *n.* **YOUNG HORSE** an unweaned horse or related animal ■ *vti.* (**foaled, foal·ing, foals**) **GIVE BIRTH** to give birth to a foal [Old English *fola.* Ultimately from an Indo-European word meaning "small," also the ancestor of English *few, poor,* and *filly.*]

foam /fōm/ *n.* **1. MASS OF BUBBLES** a mass of bubbles of gas or air on the surface of a liquid **2. THICK FROTHY SUBSTANCE** a thick but light mixture that contains a lot of tiny bubbles ○ *Beat the egg whites into a foam.* **3. FIRE-EXTINGUISHING SUBSTANCE** a thick chemical froth used to extinguish flames **4. MATERIAL CONTAINING BUBBLES** rubber, plastic, or other material filled with many small bubbles of air to make it soft or light **5. FROTHY SALIVA** frothy saliva produced as a result of exertion or disease **6. SEA** the sea (*literary*) ■ *v.* (**foamed, foam·ing, foams**) **1.** *vi.* **PRODUCE BUBBLES** to produce a mass of bubbles **2.** *vi.* **PRODUCE FROTHY SALIVA** to produce foam from the mouth **3.** *vi.* **BE ANGRY** to express great anger (*informal*) **4.** *vi.* **TEEM** to be packed with people (*informal*) **5.** *vt.* **FILL WITH BUBBLES** to transform a material into foam by aerating it in liquid form and then solidifying it [Old English *fām.* Ultimately from an Indo-European word that is also the ancestor of English *spume* and *pumice.*] ◇ **foam at the mouth** to produce foam from the mouth as a result of exertion, illness, or anger

foamed slag *n.* slag from a blast furnace that is aerated while it is still molten, used as a building or insulation material

foam·flow·er /fōm flòwr/ *n.* a perennial woodland plant in eastern North America with clusters of small white flowers and indented leaves shaped like those of the maple. Latin name: *Tiarella cordifolia.*

foam rub·ber *n.* rubber that has been aerated to form a spongy material, used for mattresses, padding, and insulation

foam·y /fōmee/ (**-i·er, -i·est**) *adj.* covered with, full of, or consisting of foam —**foam·i·ly** *adv.* —**foam·i·ness** *n.*

fob /fob/ *n.* **1. CHAIN FOR POCKET WATCH** a chain or ribbon used to attach a pocket watch to a vest **2. ORNAMENT ON KEY RING** an ornament attached to a key ring **3. ORNAMENT ON CHAIN** a watch or ornament worn on the end of a chain or ribbon attached to clothing **4. POCKET FOR WATCH** a small pocket for a watch on a vest [Mid-17thC. Origin uncertain: perhaps from German dialect.]

fob off *vt.* **1. MISLEAD SO AS TO STALL QUESTIONING** to give false or inadequate information to somebody in order to stop further questions **2. GIVE SOMETHING INFERIOR TO** to provide somebody with something different from and inferior to what the person wanted **3. GIVE SOMETHING UNWANTED TO** to pass something unwanted to somebody else, using deceitful persuasion [Late 16thC. From obsolete FOB "to deceive," of uncertain origin: perhaps from German *foppen* "to deceive."]

f.o.b.[1], **F.O.B.** *abbr.* free on board

f.o.b.[2], **F.O.B., fob, FOB** *abbr.* COMM free on board

fob watch *n.* a round watch kept in a special pocket on a vest

f.o.c., F.O.C., foc, FOC *abbr.* COMM free of charge

fo·cac·cia *n.* a type of flat Italian bread, sprinkled with a topping before baking, and served hot or cold [Mid-20thC. From Italian, from assumed Vulgar Latin *focacia,* from, ultimately, Latin *focus* (see FOCUS). The underlying idea is of something baked in the hearth.]

fo·cal /fṓk'l/ *adj.* **1. PRINCIPAL** main and most important **2. RELATING TO FOCUSING IMAGE** relating to bringing an image into focus **3. AT OR FROM FOCAL POINT** located at, passing through, or measured from, a focal point —**fo·cal·ly** *adv.*

fo·cal dis·tance *n.* = **focal length**

fo·cal in·fec·tion *n.* a localized bacterial infection, often causing symptoms elsewhere in the body

fo·cal·ize /fṓk'l ìz/ (**-ized, -iz·ing, -iz·es**) *v.* **1.** *vti.* **FOCUS** to focus something or bring something into focus **2.** *vt.* **LOCALIZE SOMETHING** to limit something to a local area —**fo·cal·i·za·tion** /fṓk'li záysh'n/ *n.*

fo·cal length *n.* the distance from the center of a lens or the surface of a mirror to the point at which light passing through the lens or reflected from the mirror is focused. Symbol **f**

fo·cal-plane shut·ter *n.* a camera shutter positioned just in front of the film, as opposed to one built into the lens

fo·cal point *n.* **1. POINT WHERE RAYS FROM LENS CONVERGE** the point at which parallel rays meeting a lens, curved mirror, or other optical system converge or appear to diverge **2. CENTER OF ATTENTION** somebody or something receiving concentrated attention, or to which attention is drawn

fo·cal ra·tio *n.* = **f-number**

fo'c's'le *n.* = **forecastle**

fo·cus /fṓkəss/ *n.* **1. MAIN EMPHASIS** concentrated effort or attention on a particular thing ○ *The committee's focus must be on finding solutions to the problem.* **2. AREA OF CONCERN** an area of concern, responsibility, or investigation ○ *an inquiry with a narrow focus* **3. CONCENTRATED QUALITY** a concentrated and unified quality ○ *to bring focus to the problem* **4. SHARPNESS OF IMAGE** the quality of being sharply defined with clear edges and contrast **5. SEEING SHARPLY** the condition of seeing sharply and clearly **6.** (*plural* **-ci**) = **focal point 7.** (*plural* **-ci**) MED **DISEASE ORIGIN** the point from which a disease spreads, or where it localizes **8.** (*plural* **-ci**) GEOG, NUCLEAR PHYS **EARTHQUAKE ORIGIN** the point of origin within the earth of an earthquake or underground nuclear explosion **9.** (*plural* **-ci**) MATH **POINT ON CONE** a fixed point in a plane that in combination with a particular straight line specifies a conic section. For any point on the conic section the ratio of the distance from the focus to the nearest point on the line is constant. ■ *vti.* (**-cused** *or* **-cussed, -cus·ing** *or* **-cus·sing, -cus·es** *or* **-cus·ses**) **1. CONCENTRATE MAINLY ON SOMETHING** to give your main attention to one thing or one aspect of a thing **2. ADJUST VISION TO SEE CLEARLY** to adjust your vision so that you see clearly and sharply, or to become adjusted for clear vision **3. ADJUST LENS** to adjust a lens so that the image viewed is clear and sharp [Mid-17thC. From Latin *focus* "hearth, fireplace" (source also of English *foyer* and *fuel*), perhaps because it was the "center" of the home.] —**fo·cus·a·ble** *adj.* —**fo·cus·er** *n.*

fo·cused /fṓkəst/, **fo·cussed** *adj.* **1. CONCENTRATED** concentrated on a single thing **2. SINGLE-MINDED** single-minded and determined

fo·cus group *n.* a small group of representative people who are questioned about their opinions as part of political or market research

FOD *abbr.* TECH, TELECOM abbr for **fax-on-demand**

fod·der /fóddər/ *n.* **1. ANIMAL FOOD** hay, straw, and similar food for livestock **2. MATERIAL FOR STIMULATING RESPONSE** people, ideas, or images that are useful in stimulating a creative or critical response **3. EXPENDABLE PEOPLE OR THINGS** people or things regarded as the necessary but expendable ingredient that makes a system or scheme work (*usually used in combination*) ○ *case studies seized upon as thesis fodder* ■ *vt.* (**-dered, -der·ing, -ders**) **FEED LIVESTOCK** to give food to livestock [Old English *fōdor*. Ultimately from an Indo-European base meaning "to feed," which is also the ancestor of English *food, foster, repast,* and *companion.*] —**fod·der·er** *n.*

foe /fō/ *n.* an enemy or opponent of somebody or something (*literary*) [Old English *gefā*. Ultimately from an Indo-European base meaning "hostile," which is also the ancestor of English *fey, feud,* and *fickle.*]

FOE, **FoE** *abbr.* Fraternal Order of Eagles

foehn /fayn, fŏn/, **föhn** *n.* a warm dry wind blowing down the lee slope of a mountain range, originally and especially the Alps [Mid-19thC. Via German from, ultimately, Latin *favonius* "west wind," from *favere* "to favor, be well disposed toward."]

foe·tal *adj.* = **fetal**

foe·tid *adj.* = **fetid**

foe·tor *n.* = **fetor**

foe·tus *n.* = **fetus**

fog /fawg, fog/ *n.* **1. THICK MIST** condensed water vapor in the air at or near ground level **2. CLOUD OF SOMETHING** a cloud of something in the air, e.g., smoke, that reduces visibility **3. HAZY CONFUSION** a state of confusion or lack of clarity **4. OBSCURING AGENT** something that serves to obscure or conceal ○ *a fog of excuses* **5.** PHOTOGRAPHY **BLURRED AREA** an area on a photograph that is unclear or obscured by stray light **6.** CHEM **SUSPENDED PARTICLES** a cloud or suspension of liquid particles ■ *v.* (**fogged, fog·ging, fogs**) **1.** *vti.* **MAKE OR BECOME OBSCURED** to cause condensation to form on a transparent surface, or to become covered with condensation **2.** *vt.* **MAKE UNCLEAR** to make something unclear or confused **3.** *vti.* PHOTOGRAPHY **EXPOSE SOMETHING TO LIGHT** to contaminate film or a developing image with light, usually accidentally, or to undergo this process [Mid-16thC. Origin uncertain: perhaps of Scandinavian origin.] —**fogged** *adj.*

fog bank *n.* a mass of thick fog, especially at sea

fog·bound /fáwg bòwnd, fóg-/ *adj.* **1. STOPPED BY FOG** unable to move or operate because of visibility diminished by fog **2. SHROUDED IN FOG** enveloped in fog

fog·bow /fáwg bō, fóg-/ *n.* a faint arc of light seen in fog opposite the sun [Mid-19thC. Modeled on RAINBOW.]

fog·dog /fáwg dàwg, fóg dòg/ *n.* a bright white spot seen in breaking fog near the horizon [Mid-19thC. Modeled on SUN DOG.]

fo·gey /fṓgee/ *n.* = **fogy**

fog·gy /fáwgee, fóggee/ (**-gi·er, -gi·est**) *adj.* **1. CHARACTERIZED BY FOG** filled with or obscured by fog **2. VAGUE** very unclear or hazy ○ *We only had a foggy idea of the visitor's name.* **3. VISUALLY UNCLEAR** obscured or translucent because of a covering of condensation or something similar —**fog·gi·ly** *adv.* —**fog·gi·ness** *n.*

Fog·gy Bot·tom *n.* the U.S. Department of State in Washington, D.C. (*informal*) [Mid-20thC. Originally referring to the Potomac River in Washington, D.C., which often produces local fog, the name later becoming a humorous pun on the government's policies.]

fog·horn /fáwg hàwrn, fóg-/ *n.* a horn sounded on a ship or boat when fog reduces visibility, as a warning to other vessels

fog light *n.* a front or rear light on a car with a beam designed to penetrate fog

fo·gy /fṓgee/ (*plural* **-gies**), **fo·gey** *n.* an old-fashioned person who resists change or novelty [Late 18thC. From Scots, of uncertain origin.] —**fo·gy·ish** *adj.* —**fo·gy·ism** *n.*

föhn *n.* = **foehn**

FOIA *abbr.* Freedom of Information Act

foi·ble /fóyb'l/ *n.* **1. WEAKNESS OR QUIRK** an idiosyncrasy or small weakness (*usually used in the plural*) **2.** FENCING **BLADE PART** the weakest part of a sword blade from the middle to the point [Mid-17thC. Via obsolete French *foible* from Old French *feble* (see FEEBLE).]

foie gras *n.* goose liver swollen by force-feeding the bird on corn before slaughter. It is usually eaten in the form of pâté. [Early 19thC. From French, literally "fatted liver."]

foil[1] /foyl/ *n.* **1. METAL IN THIN SHEETS** metal in a thin flexible sheet **2. METAL COATING ON MIRROR** the thin reflective metal coating on the back of a mirror **3. GOOD CONTRAST** a useful or interesting contrast to something **4.** SHIPPING = **hydrofoil** *n.* 2 **5.** AIR = **airfoil 6.** ARCHIT **ARC IN GOTHIC WINDOW** an arc at the top of a Gothic window ■ *vt.* (**foiled, foil·ing, foils**) **COVER WITH FOIL** to cover or coat something with foil [14thC. Via Old French from Latin *folium* "leaf" and *folia* "leaves."]

foil[2] /foyl/ (**foiled, foil·ing, foils**) *vt.* **1. THWART SOMEBODY'S SUCCESS** to prevent somebody from succeeding in something **2.** HUNT **OBSCURE TRAIL** to obscure the trail of prey in order to hinder pursuers [14thC. Origin uncertain: perhaps partly from French *fouler* "to full cloth," and partly from an early variant of DEFILE.]

foil[3] /foyl/ *n.* a long thin sword with a small disc on the end, used in fencing [Late 16thC. Origin unknown.]

foils *n.* the art or sport of fencing with foils (*takes a singular verb*) —**foils·man** /fóylzmən/ *n.*

foist /foyst/ (**foist·ed, foist·ing, foists**) *vt.* **1. IMPOSE ON SOMEBODY** to force somebody to accept something undesirable **2. INSERT SURREPTITIOUSLY** to introduce or insert something surreptitiously **3. GIVE SOMEBODY SOMETHING INFERIOR** to give somebody something inferior on the pretence that it is genuine, valuable, or desirable [Mid-16thC. Origin uncertain: probably from Dutch dialect *vuisten* "to hold in one's hand" (as when hiding dice), from Middle Dutch *vuist* "fist."]

Fo·kine /faw kéen, fō-/, **Michel** (1880–1942) Russian-born U.S. dancer and choreographer. His work revitalized traditional classical ballet by introducing increased expression into the predominantly technical dance form. Born **Mikhail Mikhaylovich Fokine**

fol. *abbr.* **1.** folio **2.** followed **3. fol., ff.** following

fol·a·cin /fóllәsin/ *n.* = **folic acid** [Mid-20thC. Coined from FOLIC ACID + -IN.]

fo·late /fṓ làyt/ *n.* **1.** = **folic acid 2. FOLIC ACID DERIVATIVE** a salt or ester of folic acid [Mid-20thC. Coined from FOLIC ACID + -ATE.]

fold[1] /fōld/ *v.* (**fold·ed, fold·ing, folds**) **1.** *vt.* **BEND FLAT** to bend something thin and flat over on itself **2.** *vt.* **MAKE SMALLER BY FOLDING** to bend something over on itself more than once **3.** *vti.* **BEND TO MAKE COMPACT** to bend part of something so as to make it more streamlined or more compact ○ *a bicycle that folds to fit into the car* **4.** *vt.* **BEND LIMBS TOGETHER** to draw in the arms, legs, or hands toward the body or place them together with the joints bent **5.** *vt.* **BRING WINGS TOGETHER** to bring the wings together or next to the body **6.** *vt.* **COVER** to wrap or cover something ○ *folded the note inside a magazine* **7.** *vt.* **PUT ARMS AROUND** to put your arms around somebody **8.** *vi.* **GO OUT OF BUSINESS** to fail and stop operating as a business **9.** *vi.* **ACCEPT DEFEAT** to give in and accept defeat ○ *folded when he saw how many opposed him* **10.** *vi.* CARDS **GIVE UP HAND** in poker and other games, to stop playing your hand in the belief that it cannot win **11.** *vti.* GEOL **BEND ROCK** to cause a layer of rock to bend, or to undergo this process ■ *n.* **1. BENT PART** a part of something folded **2. CREASE** a line, crease, or raised part made when something has been folded **3. HANGING FOLDED PART** a part of something that hangs in a folded shape ○ *the folds of his cassock* **4. COIL** a single coil in a rope or a snake lying in coils **5.** GEOL **BEND IN ROCK** a bend formed in a rock layer in response to forces in the rock **6.** *U.K.* **SMALL VALLEY** a small valley in a hilly area [Old English *fealdan*. Ultimately from an Indo-European base meaning "to fold," which is also the ancestor of the *-ple* of English *triple, quadruple,* etc.] —**fold·a·ble** *adj.*

fold in *vt.* to add a food ingredient to a mixture carefully and lightly

fold up *v.* **1.** *vti.* **FOLD COMPLETELY** to fold something completely, or to become folded completely **2.** *vi.* **COLLAPSE** to collapse from laughter, pain, or strong emotion

fold[2] /fōld/ *n.* **1. GROUP WITH THINGS IN COMMON** a group to which something or somebody naturally belongs because of shared interests or traits **2. ENCLOSED AREA FOR SHEEP** an enclosed area where sheep or other livestock can be kept **3. ENCLOSED ANIMALS** sheep or other livestock in a fold **4. FLOCK** a flock of sheep ■ *vt.* (**fold·ed, fold·ing, folds**) **ENCLOSE LIVESTOCK** to enclose livestock safely [Old English *fald*, of unknown origin]

-fold *suffix.* **1.** divided into parts ○ *manifold* **2.** times ○ *tenfold* [Old English *-feald*; related to *fealdan* (see FOLD)]

fold·a·way /fṓldə wày/ *adj.* designed to be folded for compact storage

fold·boat /fṓld bōt/ *n.* a boat like a kayak consisting of a waterproof fabric that covers a collapsible frame [Early 20thC. Translation of German *Faltboot.*]

fold·er /fṓldər/ *n.* **1. FOLDED CARDBOARD TO HOLD PAPERS** a piece of cardboard folded to make a file in which papers can be held **2.** COMPUT **FILE CONTAINER** a conceptual container for computer files in some operating systems, corresponding to a directory or subdirectory **3. FOLDED PAMPHLET** a circular printed on folded paper

fol·de·rol /fóldə ràwl/, **fal·de·ral** /faáldə raàl/ *n.* **1.** silly nonsense (*dated*) **2. TRINKET** an attractive but valueless object or trinket [Early 19thC. From *fol de rol*, a nonsense refrain in songs.]

fold·ing /fṓlding/ *adj.* designed to be folded for compact storage

Folding door

fold·ing door *n.* a door consisting of hinged panels that fold against each other

fold·ing mon·ey *n.* money in the form of bills rather than coins (*informal*)

fold·ing press *n.* a wrestling maneuver in which the opponent is pressed into a fetal position and held down

fold·out /fṓld òwt/ *n.* **1.** = **gatefold 2. FURNITURE WITH FOLDING PART** a piece of furniture, or part of it, that unfolds and opens out of its stored position for use ■ *adj.* **DESIGNED TO FOLD** used to describe a piece of furniture, or part of it, that is designed to be unfolded and opened out for use

fold·up /fṓld up/ *adj.* **DESIGNED TO BE FOLDED** designed to be folded for compact storage ■ *n.* **END OF BUSINESS** a failure of a business ○ *foldups brought on by adverse economic conditions*

Fo·ley /fṓlee/, **Thomas** (*b.* 1929) U.S. politician. He served as a member of the U.S. House of Representatives from Washington state (1965–95) and was Speaker of the House (1989–95). Full name **Thomas Stephen Foley**

fo·ley art·ist (*plural* **fo·ley art·ists**) *n.* somebody who adds sound effects to a filmed or taped performance as part of the postproduction process [From the name of Jack *Foley*, the U.S. sound engineer who developed modern techniques of adding sound effects]

fo·li·a·ceous /fṓlee áyshəss/ *adj.* **1. OF OR RESEMBLING A LEAF** relating to or resembling a plant leaf or leaves **2. BEARING LEAVES** bearing leaves or similar structures [Mid-17thC. Formed from Latin *foliaceus*, from *folium* "leaf."]

fo·li·age /fṓlee ij, fṓlij/ *n.* **1. LEAVES** the leaves of a plant or tree **2. LEAFY DECORATION** decoration consisting of, or like, plant leaves **3.** ARCHIT **BUILDING ORNAMENTATION** architectural ornamentation based on leaves and stems [Mid-15thC. Alteration (influenced by Latin *folium*) of Old French *foillage*, from *foille* "leaf," from Latin *folium* "leaf."] —**fo·li·aged** *adj.*

fo·li·age plant *n.* GARDENING a plant cultivated for its good-looking leaves

fo·li·ar /fṓlee ər/ *adj.* relating to, producing, or being the leaves of a plant [Late 19thC. From modern Latin *foliaris*, from Latin *folium* "leaf."]

fo·li·ate *adj.* /fṓlee ət, fṓlee àyt/ **1. OF OR LIKE LEAVES** relating to or resembling leaves **2.** GEOL = **foliated** *adj.* 1 **3. LEAF-SHAPED** in the shape of a leaf ■ *v.* /fṓlee àyt/ (**-at·ed, -at·ing, -ates**) **1.** *vt.* **DECORATE WITH LEAVES** to decorate something with leaves or very thin layers **2.** *vt.* **MAKE METAL INTO FOIL** to form metal into a thin sheet or foil **3.** *vt.* PUBL **NUMBER A BOOK'S PAGES** to number the leaves of a book or manuscript **4.** *vi.* **DEVELOP FOLIAGE** to develop foliage **5.** *vti.* **LAYER** to separate something into very thin layers, or to undergo this process [Early 17thC. The adjective is from Latin *foliatus*, from *folium* "leaf"; the verb is formed directly from Latin *folium*.]

-foliate *suffix.* having leaves ○ *bifoliate* [From FOLIATE]

fo·li·at·ed /fṓlee àytəd/ *adj.* **1.** GEOL **LAYERED** formed in or composed of separable layers **2.** ARCHIT **DECORATED**

WITH LEAVES OR FOLIAGE decorated with stylized architectural leaves or foliage

fo·li·a·tion /fòlee áysh'n/ *n.* **1.** LEAF FORMATION the formation of leaves **2.** LEAF BEARING the state of being in leaf **3.** ARCHIT ORNAMENTATION architectural ornamentation consisting of stylized foliage **4.** ARCHIT GOTHIC WINDOW DECORATION architectural decoration consisting of carving between two arches (**cusps**) and arcs (**foils**) at the top of Gothic windows **5.** PUBL NUMBERING OF SHEETS the numbering of consecutive leaves in a book or manuscript **6.** GEOL ROCK TEXTURE a characteristic of metamorphosed rocks in which minerals are aligned in one direction so that the rock can readily be split into thin layers **7.** LEAF DECORATION decoration with a design based on leaves

fo·lic ac·id *n.* a vitamin of the B complex, found in green vegetables, fruit, and liver [*Folic* formed from Latin *folium* "leaf" , because the vitamin is found in leafy green vegetables]

fo·lie à deux (*plural* **fo·lies à deux**) *n.* a psychiatric disorder with symptoms common to two people who are very close. Often only one person actually has a disorder, the other choosing to share the symptoms or delusions of the first. [Late 19thC. From French, literally "dual delusion."]

fo·li·o /fólee ò/ *n.* (*plural* **-os**) **1.** LARGE BOOK OR MANUSCRIPT a book or manuscript in the largest size usual for books, about 12 × 15 in **2.** LARGE SHEET FOR BOOK a large sheet of paper that folds to give four pages **3.** PAGE NUMBERED ON FRONT a paper or parchment page that is numbered on the front but not the back **4.** PAGE NUMBER a page number (*technical*) **5.** LAW MEASUREMENT FOR LEGAL DOCUMENTS a unit for measuring the length of legal documents, usually 100 words in the U.S. and 72 or 90 in Britain **6.** ACCT LEDGER PAGE a page, or two facing pages, of a ledger ■ *vt.* (**-oed, -o·ing, -os**) NUMBER PAGES to number the pages in a book ■ *adj.* LARGE-FORMAT printed in folio size [Mid-15thC. From late Latin *folio*, literally "at the page," from Latin *folium* "leaf, page."]

fo·li·ose /fólee òss/ *adj.* used to describe the body (**thallus**) of a lichen or similar plant that is thin, flattened, and lobed like a leaf [Early 18thC. From Latin *foliosus*, from *folium* "leaf."]

folk /fòk/ *npl.* **1. folk, folks** PEOPLE IN GENERAL people, especially people of the same type (*both forms take a plural verb*) **2. folks** USED TO ADDRESS PEOPLE used to address a group of people informally (*informal*) ○ *Folks, we're ready to start now.* **3. folks** PARENTS OR RELATIVES parents or close family ■ *n.* MUSIC = **folk music** ■ *adj.* **1.** TRADITIONAL IN COMMUNITY traditional or passed down in a community or country **2.** RELATING TO IDEAS OF ORDINARY PEOPLE coming from the traditional beliefs or ideas of ordinary people [Old English *folc*. Ultimately from an Indo-European base meaning "to fill," which is also the ancestor of English *fill*, *full*, and possibly *plebeian*.]

folk art *n.* paintings and decorative objects made in a naive style

folk dance *n.* **1.** TRADITIONAL DANCE a dance that is traditional to a culture, community, or country **2.** MUSIC FOR TRADITIONAL DANCE a piece of music that accompanies a traditional folk dance

folk et·y·mol·o·gy *n.* **1.** REPLACEMENT OF UNKNOWN WORD the replacement of an unfamiliar word or form by a more familiar one. An example is the replacement of *girasole* with *Jerusalem* in *Jerusalem artichoke*. **2.** INCORRECT ORIGIN FOR WORD an idea about the origin of a word that is generally believed but is wrong

folk he·ro *n.* somebody who attains legendary status among the public

folk·ie /fókee/ *n.* (*informal*) **1.** FOLK SINGER a folk singer or musician **2.** FOLK MUSIC ENTHUSIAST a fan of folk music

folk·lore /fók làwr/ *n.* **1.** TRADITIONAL LOCAL STORIES traditional stories and explanations passed down in a community or country **2.** LOCAL LEGENDS stories and gossip that become traditional within a group of people **3.** ETHNOL STUDY OF TRADITIONS the study of traditional stories, music, and customs [Mid-19thC] —**folk·lor·ic** *adj.*

folk·lor·ist /fók làwrist/ *n.* somebody who studies the traditional stories, music, and customs of a particular culture or community, or these phenomena generally —**folk·lor·is·tic** /fòk law rístik/ *adj.*

folk mass *n.* a Christian mass in which folk music replaces some or all of the traditional music

folk med·i·cine *n.* medicine based on traditional customs and belief. It often uses herbal remedies and is usually practiced by healers not trained in conventional medicine.

folk mem·o·ry *n.* a memory kept alive by a community and passed from one generation to the next

folk mu·sic *n.* **1.** TRADITIONAL SONGS AND MUSIC traditional songs and music, passed from one generation to the next **2.** MODERN MUSIC IN TRADITIONAL STYLE modern music composed in imitation of traditional music

folk-rock *n.* popular music that combines the melodies of folk music with the rhythms of rock music

folk sing·er *n.* somebody who sings traditional or modern folk songs —**folk sing·ing** *n.*

folk song *n.* **1.** TRADITIONAL SONG a traditional song that has been passed down orally **2.** MODERN SONG LIKE TRADITIONAL a modern song composed in the style of traditional folk music. Modern folk songs are often performed by a solo singer.

folk·sy /fóksee/ (**-si·er, -si·est**) *adj.* **1.** IN STYLE OF FOLK TRADITIONS simple and unsophisticated in the tradition of folk crafts or folklore **2.** FRIENDLY friendly and informal **3.** AFFECTEDLY TRADITIONAL artificially or affectedly traditional and homey —**folk·si·ly** *adv.* —**folk·si·ness** *n.*

foll. *abbr.* **1. foll., fol.** followed **2. foll., fol., ff** following

fol·li·cle /fóllik'l/ *n.* **1.** ANAT SMALL SAC a small anatomical sac, cavity, or gland, involved in secretion or excretion **2.** BOT DRY SEED POD a dry case formed from a single fruit that splits along one side to release seeds [Early 15thC. From Latin *folliculus* "small sack," from *follis* "bellows." Ultimately from an Indo-European word meaning "to swell," which is also the ancestor of English *belly, billow*, and *bulge*.] —**fol·lic·u·lar** /fə líkyələr/ *adj.*

fol·li·cle-stim·u·lat·ing hor·mone *n.* a hormone that stimulates the growth of egg follicles in the ovaries and the making of sperm in the testes

fol·lic·u·li·tis /fə lìkyə lítəss/ *n.* inflammation of one or more follicles, especially of the hair, producing small boils

fol·lies /fólleez/ *n.* a somewhat old-fashioned theatrical revue with elaborate costumes, music, and dancing (*takes a singular or plural verb*)

fol·low /fóllō/ *v.* (**-lowed, -low·ing, -lows**) **1.** *vti.* COME AFTER SOMETHING/SOMEBODY to come after something or somebody in position, time, or sequence ○ *We had steak and salad followed by strawberries.* **2.** *vt.* ADD TO SOMETHING ALREADY DONE to add to something already done by doing something else, usually a related thing ○ *She followed her lecture with a demonstration.* **3.** *vti.* GO AFTER to go after or behind somebody or something, moving in the same direction, especially to find out where he, she, or it is going, or go to the same place ○ *The dog followed them home.* **4.** *vt.* KEEP UNDER SURVEILLANCE to have somebody's movements under constant surveillance ○ *We've had the suspect followed for the past week.* **5.** *vt.* WATCH CLOSELY to watch, observe, or pay close attention to somebody or something ○ *Her eyes followed me around the room.* **6.** *vt.* GO ALONG to go along something such as a road or path ○ *Follow the footpath to the edge of the forest.* **7.** *vt.* GO IN SAME DIRECTION AS to take the same course or go in the same direction as something else ○ *The road follows the river along the bottom of the valley.* **8.** *vt.* GO AS DIRECTED BY to go in the direction indicated by something such as a signpost **9.** *vt.* OBEY to act in accordance with something, especially with instructions or directions given by somebody else ○ *If you follow my instructions, nothing can go wrong.* **10.** *vt.* DEVELOP IN ACCORDANCE WITH to be or develop in accordance with something, usually already known about or established ○ *The behavior of such children usually follows the same pattern.* **11.** *vt.* BE INFLUENCED BY to be led, guided, or influenced by somebody or something ○ *They followed Plato in believing the material world to be essentially unreal.* **12.** *vti.* DO THE SAME AS to do the same as somebody or something, or take somebody or something as a model to be imitated ○ *She followed her father into medicine.* **13.** *vti.* UNDERSTAND SOMETHING to understand something such as an explanation or narrative ○ *He couldn't follow her explanation.* **14.** *vt.* ENGAGE IN ACTIVITY to engage in or practice something such as a career, occupation, or lifestyle ○ *I decided to follow a career in law.* **15.** *vt.* KEEP UP TO DATE WITH to keep yourself informed about or up to date with the progress of something you are interested in ○ *Are you following the television series about twins?* **16.** *vt.* BE ABOUT to be about somebody or something, especially to describe or depict what happens to somebody or something over a period of time ○ *The story follows a typical American family.* **17.** *vti.* RESULT FROM SOMETHING to happen after and as a result of something else ○ *Issue too many instructions and confusion invariably follows.* **18.** *vti.* BE LOGICAL RESULT to be a logical consequence of something ○ *That follows logically from their decision to cancel the project.* **19.** *vt.* READ WORDS OR MUSIC to read the words or music of something while listening to it ■ *n.* = **follow shot** [Old English *folgian, fylgan*] —**fol·low·a·ble** *adj.* ◇ **as follows** as listed or described next ◇ **follow your nose 1.** to go or continue straight ahead in the direction you are facing **2.** to act in accordance with your instincts or intuition ◇ **follow suit 1.** CARDS to play a card of the same suit as the previous player **2.** to do the same thing as somebody else

WORD KEY: SYNONYMS

follow, chase, pursue, tail, shadow, stalk, trail

CORE MEANING: to go after

follow a general word used to talk about one person going after another, for example by walking down the street behind him or her or driving along the same route. It can be used whether this is deliberate or happens by chance, and does not necessarily suggest that the person going after the other wants or intends to catch up; **chase** used to talk about one person following another and trying to reach or catch him or her. It usually suggests speed; **pursue** suggesting a determination and an ongoing effort to catch up with the person being followed; **tail** an informal word suggesting that somebody is following someone else secretly for purposes of surveillance; **shadow** similar to "tail," used especially to talk about the activities of spies and detectives; **stalk** used to talk about the stealthy following of an animal, often by a hunter in search of prey. It is now also used to talk about the obsessive following of somebody and the harassment of that person, especially when this constitutes a criminal offense; **trail** used to talk about following tracks or traces left by a person or animal, usually because the person or animal is no longer in sight.

follow on *vi.* to continue or resume a course of action, narrative, etc ○ *I'll follow on from where you left off.*

follow out *vt.* to carry something out in full, or to the end

follow through *vti.* **1.** FINISH DOING SOMETHING to take further action as a consequence or extension of a previous action, especially to continue something through to completion **2.** CONTINUE MOTION OF SWING OR THROW to continue the movement of the arm or leg past the point of contact or release after hitting, throwing, or kicking a ball or other object in a sport

follow up *vt.* **1.** ACT ON INFORMATION to act or make further investigations on the basis of information received ○ *Police are following up a new lead.* **2.** DO SOMETHING EXTRA to continue or add to something already done by doing some related thing ○ *I followed up my phone call with a letter of confirmation.*

fol·low·er /fóllō ər/ *n.* **1.** SOMEBODY LED BY ANOTHER somebody who is led, guided, or influenced by somebody, especially by a political or religious leader **2.** SUPPORTER a fan, supporter, or admirer of somebody or something, especially of a sports team **3.** MEMBER OF ENTOURAGE a servant, attendant, or subordinate, usually one of a number of people accompanying an important person **4.** IMITATOR somebody or something that copies or imitates something else

fol·low·er·ship /fóllō ər shìp/ *n.* **1.** BEING A FOLLOWER the fact of being a follower, supporter, or diciple of somebody or something **2.** = **following** *n.* 1 [Early 20thC]

fol·low·ing /fóllō ing/ *adj.* **1.** NEXT coming after in time or sequence **2.** ABOUT TO BE MENTIONED about to be mentioned or listed ○ *He has visited the following countries: Canada, France, and Australia.* **3.** MOVING THE SAME WAY blowing or flowing in the same direction as somebody or something, especially a boat or aircraft, is traveling ○ *a following wind* ■ *n.* **1.** GROUP OF FOLLOWERS a group of people who admire or support somebody or something over a period of time ○ *The band has a large following in this country.* **2.** SOMETHING TO BE SPECIFIED the people or things about to be mentioned or listed (*takes a plural verb*) ○ *You will need the following: a piece of wood, a saw, a hammer, and some nails.* ■ *prep.* AFTER after something, or after something and as a result of it ○ *Following the accident it was months before he felt safe in a car.*

fol·low-on *adj.* coming after as a continuation or consequence —**fol·low-on** *n.*

fol·low shot *n.* **1. fol·low shot, fol·low** TYPE OF SHOT IN BILLIARDS in billiards and similar games, a shot that makes the cue ball continue to move in the same direction as the target ball after striking it **2.** CINEMA SHOT MADE WITH MOVING CAMERA a camera shot in which the camera moves with the subject following along-side or behind

fol·low-the-lead·er *n.* a game in which the players, usually children, move along in a line, all copying the actions of the person at the front

fol·low-through *n.* **1.** CONTINUATION AND COMPLETION further action continuing or completing something previously done or begun ○ *Your follow-through on the project was less than satisfactory.* **2.** CONCLUDING PART OF STROKE the continuation of the movement of the arm or leg past the point of contact or release after hitting, throwing, or kicking a ball or other object in a sport

fol·low-up *n.* **1.** CONTINUATION further action or investigation or a subsequent event that results from and is intended to supplement something done before ○ *The conference was intended as a follow-up to the summit meeting in Vienna.* **2.** SOMETHING GIVING MORE INFORMATION a book, film, article, or report that continues a story or provides further information —**follow-up** *adj.*

fol·ly /fóllee/ (*plural* **-lies**) *n.* **1.** UNREASON thoughtlessness, recklessness, or thoughtless or reckless behavior ○ *She realized, too late, the folly of her course of action.* ○ *It would be folly to continue.* **2.** IRRATIONAL THING a thoughtless or reckless act or idea (*often used in the plural*) **3.** ARCHIT ECCENTRIC BUILDING a building of eccentric or overelaborate design, usually built for decorative rather than practical purposes **4.** MISGUIDED UNDERTAKING an undertaking that is excessively costly or extravagant, especially one that leads to financial loss or ruin [13thC. From Old French *folie*, from *fol* "foolish" (see FOOL).]

Fol·som /fólsəm/ *adj.* belonging to or typical of a prehistoric culture of the southern plains of North America that made leaf-shaped flint projectile points with a concave base [Early 20thC. Named for *Folsom*, a village in northeast New Mexico, where remains typical of the culture were found.]

fo·ment /fō mént/ (**-ment·ed, -ment·ing, -ments**) *vt.* to cause or stir up trouble or rebellion (*formal*) [14thC. From late Latin *fomentare*, from Latin *fomentum*, "warm soothing application," from *fovere*, "to warm, keep warm."] —**fo·men·ta·tion** /fōmən táysh'n, -men-/ *n.*

fo·mites /fō mìts/ *npl.* inanimate objects capable of carrying germs from an infected person to another person, e.g., clothes or bedding [Mid-19thC. From Latin, plural of *fomes* "kindling wood."]

fond[1] /fond/ *adj.* **1.** FEELING AFFECTION feeling love, affection, or a strong liking for somebody or something ○ *I've grown fond of this old house.* **2.** LIKING SOMETHING liking something, or finding enjoyment in doing it ○ *She's too fond of the sound of her own voice.* ○ *His dog is fond of chasing rabbits.* **3.** AFFECTIONATE showing or characterized by affection, love, or pleasant feelings ○ *fond memories of the time we spent there* **4.** OVERLY DOTING feeling or showing excessive affection, often to the point of being over-indulgent with somebody ○ *Her fond parents could deny her nothing.* **5.** OVEROPTIMISTIC unrealistic, though often dearly wished for ○ *fond hopes* **6.** UNCRITICALLY GULLIBLE gullible or easily led to believe something that is not true (*regional or archaic*) [14thC. Origin uncertain: probably from the past participle of obsolete *fonnen* "to be foolish," from *fonne* "fool," of unknown origin.] —**fond·ly** *adv.* —**fondness** *n.*

fond[2] /fond/ *n.* a background, especially of a piece of decorated lace [Mid-17thC. Via French from Latin *fundus* "bottom" (see FUND).]

Fon·da /fóndə/, **Henry** (1905–82) U.S. movie and stage actor. He is best known for films such as *The Grapes of Wrath* (1940) and *On Golden Pond* (1981), for which he won an Academy Award.

Fon·da, Jane (*b.* 1937) U.S. movie actor and political activist, The daughter of Henry Fonda, she won Academy Awards for *Klute* (1971) and *Coming Home* (1978). She also wrote and produced popular exercise books and videotapes.

Fon·da, Peter (*b.* 1939) U.S. movie actor and director. The son of Henry Fonda, he is best known for the biker film *Easy Rider* (1969).

fon·dant /fóndənt/ *n.* **1.** SUGAR PASTE a smooth paste made from boiled sugar syrup, often colored or flavored, used as a filling for chocolates or as a coating for cakes, nuts, or fruit **2.** SOFT CANDY a candy made from or filled with fondant [Late 19thC. From French, present participle of *fondre* (see FONDUE).]

Fond du Lac /foN dŏŏ lák/ industrial city in eastern Wisconsin, situated at the southern end of Lake Winnebago. Population: 37,757 (1990).

fon·dle /fónd'l/ (**-dled, -dling, -dles**) *v.* **1.** *vt.* STROKE LOVINGLY to stroke, handle, or touch something or somebody gently, in a loving or affectionate way ○ *idly fondling the cat's ears* **2.** TOUCH IN AN AGGRESSIVE WAY to touch or caress somebody in an aggressive or unwelcome way [Late 17thC. Back-formation from obsolete *fondling* "foolish person," from FOND[1].] —**fon·dler** *n.*

fon·due /fon dŏŏ, fon dyŏŏ/, **fon·du** *n.* any of various dishes eaten by dipping small pieces of food into the contents of a pot, usually melted cheese, hot oil, or a sauce, placed on the table [Late 19thC. From French, a form of the past participle of *fondre* "to melt," from Latin *fundere* (source of English *funnel, fusion,* and *confuse*).]

Fon·ga·fa·le /fòngə faalee/ capital of Tuvalu, located on Funafuti Atoll in the western Pacific Ocean. It is the country's only port of entry. Population: 3,839 (1996).

Fon·se·ca, Gulf of /fawn sáykə/ large inlet of the Pacific Ocean on the western coast of Central America, south of El Salvador, west of Honduras, and north of Nicaragua. Area: 750 sq. mi./1,940 sq. km.

font[1] /font/ *n.* **1.** RECEPTACLE FOR BAPTISMAL WATER a large container in a church for the water used in baptisms. A font is usually made of stone, sometimes ornately carved, and mounted on a stand. **2.** RECEPTACLE FOR HOLY WATER a container for holy water, usually found at the entrance to a Roman Catholic church **3.** HOLDER FOR LIQUID any holder for liquid, e.g., the part of an oil-burning lamp that contains the oil **4.** ABUNDANT SOURCE OF SOMETHING somebody or something seen as a source or inexhaustible supply of something (*literary*) **5.** FOUNTAIN a fountain, spring, or well (*literary*) [Pre-12thC. From the *font-* Latin stem of *fons* "spring."] —**font·al** *adj.*

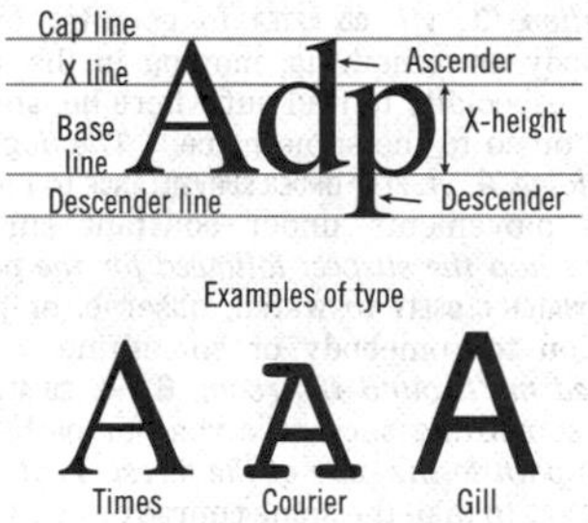

Font

font[2] /font/ *n.* a full set of printing type or of printed or screen characters of the same design and size [Late 16thC. From Old French *fonte* "casting," from *fondre* (see FONDUE).]

Fon·taine·bleau /fóntən blō, fàwN ten blṓ/ town in the Ile-de-France Region on the Seine River, about 40 mi./64 km southeast of Paris, France, the site of a magnificent 16th-century chateau. Population: 18,037 (1990).

Fon·tan·a /fon tánnə/ city in southern California, directly southeast of the San Gabriel Mountain and west of San Bernardino. Population: 104,124 (1996).

fon·ta·nelle /fòntə nélle/, **fon·ta·nel** *n.* a soft, membrane-covered space between bones at the front and the back of a young baby's skull [15thC. From Old French *fontenel*, literally "little spring," from *fontaine* (see FOUNTAIN); originally applied to an outlet for bodily secretions.]

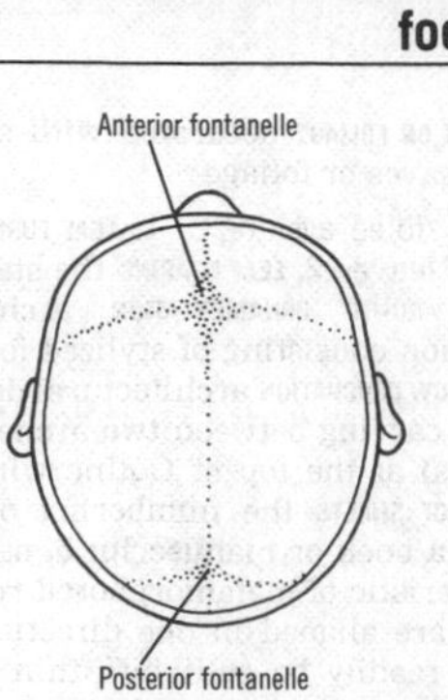

Fontanelle

Fon·tanne /fon tán/, **Lynn** (1887?–1983) British-born U.S. stage actress. She often worked with her husband Alfred Lunt on Broadway and in touring productions.

Dame Margot Fonteyn

Fon·teyn /fon táyn/, **Dame Margot** (1919–91) British ballet dancer She was known for her role as Aurora in *The Sleeping Beauty* and her partnership with Rudolf Nureyev during the 1960s and 1970s. Born **Margaret Hookham**

fon·ti·na /fon teénə/ *n.* a semihard mild Italian cheese made from cows' milk [Mid-20thC. From Italian dialect, of unknown origin.]

foo /foo / *n.* TECH a term used as a universal substitute for something real, especially when discussing technological ideas and problems (*slang*) ○ *I don't know what's wrong, maybe the computer has bad foo.* ○ *Can her foo be trusted with this software?*

food /food/ *n.* **1.** SOURCE OF NUTRIENTS FOR LIVING THINGS material that provides living things with the nutrients they need for energy and growth **2.** SOLID NOURISHMENT substances, or a particular substance, providing nourishment for people or animals, especially in solid as opposed to liquid form **3.** MENTAL OR SPIRITUAL STIMULUS something that sustains or stimulates the mind or soul ○ *food for thought* [Old English *fōda*. Ultimately from an Indo-European word that is also the ancestor of English *feed, fodder,* and *pastor*.] —**food·less** *adj.*

food ad·di·tive *n.* a natural or artificial substance that is added to food during processing to make it look or taste better or last longer

food chain *n.* a hierarchy of different living things, each of which feeds on the one below

food court *n.* the part of a shopping mall where snacks and light meals can be bought from a number of different outlets, often with a communal eating area

food fish *n.* any fish that people eat

food·ie /fŏŏdee/, **food·y** (*plural* **-ies**) *n.* somebody who takes an enthusiastic interest in cooking or eating good food (*informal*)

food poi·son·ing *n.* acute inflammation of the mucous membrane of the stomach and intestines caused by eating food contaminated with toxic substances or with microorganisms that generate toxins

food pro·ces·sor *n.* an electrical kitchen appliance consisting of a container in which food is cut, sliced, shredded, grated, blended, beaten, or liquidized automatically by a variety of removable revolving blades

food stamp *n.* a coupon that can be used to buy food, given by the government to needy people in the United States

food·stuff /fo͝od stùf/ *n.* something that can be eaten, especially one of the basic elements of the human diet (*usually used in the plural*)

food web *n.* the interlocking food chains within an ecological community

food·y *n.* = **foodie**

foo·fa·raw /fóofə ràw/ *n.* **1. SHOWY EXTRAVAGANCE** ornate or excessive ornamentation or finery **2. GREAT FUSS** a great fuss over something trivial [Mid-20thC. Origin uncertain: perhaps from Spanish *fanfarron* "braggart."]

fool /fool/ *n.* **1. UNINTELLIGENT OR THOUGHTLESS PERSON** somebody who lacks good sense or judgment ○ *Only a fool would invest in a scheme like this.* **2. RIDICULOUS PERSON** somebody who looks or is made to appear ridiculous, or who behaves in a ridiculous way ○ *I feel such a fool dressed like this.* **3. ENTHUSIAST** somebody who is particularly talented at, interested in, or fond of something specified ○ *an absolute fool for the finer things in life* **4. COURT ENTERTAINER** somebody employed in the past to amuse a monarch or noble, usually by telling jokes, singing comical songs, or performing tricks **5.** FOOD **CREAMY FRUIT DESSERT** a cold dessert made from puréed fruit mixed with cream or custard **6. OFFENSIVE TERM** an offensive term for somebody who has below average intelligence or a psychiatric disorder (*archaic offensive*) ■ *adj.* **UNINTELLIGENT AND NOT SENSIBLE** showing a lack of good sense or judgment (*informal*) ○ *That fool salesman said it would fit.* ■ *v.* (**fooled, fool·ing, fools**) **1.** *vt.* **TRICK** to trick or deceive somebody ○ *Don't be fooled by her promises.* **2.** *vi.* **SPEAK IN JEST** to say something jokingly or not seriously, or pretend, jokingly, that something false is true ○ *I was only fooling – of course you can come.* **3.** *vi.* **BEHAVE COMICALLY** to behave in a comical, playful, or silly way [13thC. Via Old French *fol* from Latin *follis* "bellows, windbag" (used by St. Augustine of Hippo in reference to a person).] ◇ **be nobody's fool** to be wise enough not to be easily deceived ◇ **make a fool (out) of somebody** to deceive or trick somebody, or make somebody look ridiculous

fool around *vi.* **1. BEHAVE IRRESPONSIBLY** to behave in a thoughtless or irresponsible way ○ *Don't fool around with those tools.* **2. CLOWN AROUND** to behave in a silly or comical way **3. WASTE TIME** to waste time by doing silly or unimportant things **4. HAVE CASUAL SEX** to participate in casual or illicit sexual relationships

fool away *vt.* to waste time or money in an aimless manner or on foolish things ○ *She fooled away her inheritance.*

fool with *vt.* to treat or handle somebody or something without due care or respect ○ *Who's been fooling with the TV?*

fool·er·y /fóoləree/ (*plural* **-ies**) *n.* (*dated*) **1. IRRESPONSIBLE BEHAVIOR** irresponsible or playful behavior **2. IRRESPONSIBLE ACT** an irresponsible or playful act

fool·har·dy /fóol haàrdee/ *adj.* showing boldness or courage but not wisdom or good sense —**fool·har·di·ly** *adv.* —**fool·har·di·ness** *n.*

fool·ish /fóolish/ *adj.* **1. NOT SENSIBLE** showing, or resulting from, a lack of good sense or judgment **2. SEEMING RIDICULOUS** feeling or appearing ridiculous ○ *Wipe that foolish grin off your face!* **3. EMBARRASSED** unsure about the appropriateness of one's actions or speech ○ *I've been foolish driving this enormous car.* **4. UNIMPORTANT** lacking importance or substance ○ *a foolish little worry* —**fool·ish·ly** *adv.* —**fool·ish·ness** *n.*

fool·proof /fóol proòf/ *adj.* **1. DESIGNED TO FUNCTION DESPITE HUMAN ERROR** designed to continue working properly in the face of any kind of human error, incompetence, or misuse **2. INFALLIBLE** so well thought out that failure is thought to be impossible

fools·cap /fóolz kàp/ *n.* **1. LARGE PAPER SIZE** a large size of paper, approximately 13.5 in. by 17 in., mostly used for writing and printing **2.** = **fool's cap** [Late 17thC. So called from the watermark of a fool's cap originally on this paper.]

fool's cap /fóolz kàp/, **fools·cap** *n.* **1. JESTER'S HAT** a brightly colored cap with points ending in bells or tassels, worn in the past by court jesters **2.** = **dunce cap**

fool's er·rand *n.* a task that is performed for no good reason or that fails to accomplish anything useful

fool's gold *n.* pyrite or any other iron or copper sulfide mineral that has a golden metallic luster

fool's mate *n.* the quickest checkmate in chess, achieved on the second move by the player with the black pieces

fool's par·a·dise *n.* a state of happiness that is temporary and insubstantial because it is based on illusions or unrealistic hopes ○ *living in a fool's paradise*

fool's-pars·ley *n.* a poisonous European weed, naturalized in North America, with white flowers and finely divided leaves that resemble parsley. Latin name: *Aethusa cynapium.*

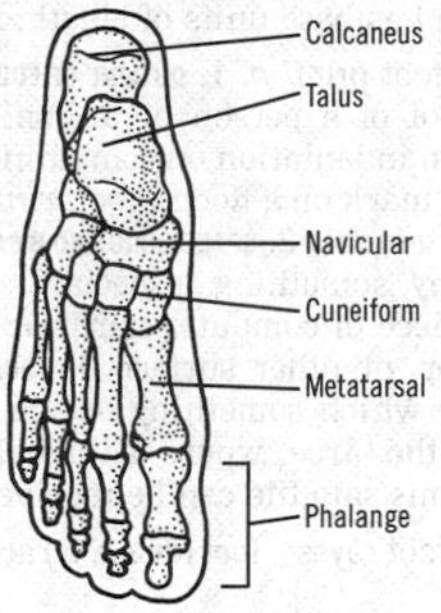

Foot: Bone structure of a human foot

foot /fo͝ot/ *n.* (*plural* **feet** /feet/) **1.** ANAT **PART AT END OF LEG** the part of the leg of a vertebrate below the ankle joint that supports the rest of the body and maintains balance when standing and walking ○ *The wave knocked me off my feet.* **2.** ZOOL **ORGAN OF ATTACHMENT** an organ or muscle surface that an invertebrate, such as a mollusk, uses to grip or move itself along **3.** MEASURE **UNIT OF LENGTH** a unit of length in the U.S. Customary and British Imperial systems equal to 12 inches/.3048. There are three feet in a yard. ○ *The aircraft is cruising at 30,000 feet* **4. LOWEST PART** the bottom or lowest part of something ○ *a note scribbled at the foot of the page* **5. PART OF SOCK** the part of a sock, stocking, or boot that is shaped to cover the foot **6. PART RESEMBLING FOOT** something that is shaped like or acts like a human or animal foot, e.g., a shaped part at the end of the leg of a chair **7.** BOT **LOWER PART OF PLANT** the lower part of the stem of a plant, or the base of the spore-producing body (**sporophyte**) of mosses and liverworts **8.** SEW **PART OF SEWING MACHINE** the part of a sewing machine, close to the needle, that is lowered onto the material to hold it in position. Most sewing machines have detachable and interchangeable feet for different functions. **9. WAY OF WALKING** a particular way of walking **10.** ARMY **SOLDIERS WHO FIGHT ON FOOT** soldiers who fight principally on foot, rather than on horses or in vehicles (*takes a plural verb*) ○ *an officer commanding a company of foot* **11.** POETRY **UNIT OF POETIC METER** a basic unit of rhythm in poetry, made up of a fixed combination of stressed and unstressed or long and short syllables ■ **foots** *npl.* **1.** FOOD TECH **SEDIMENT DEPOSITED IN LIQUID** the solid material that gradually falls to the bottom of various liquids, such as vegetable oil **2.** THEATER **FOOTLIGHTS** footlights (*informal*) ■ *vt.* (**foot·ed, foot·ing, foots**) **1. PAY FULL COST OF** to pay the full amount of something ○ *We had to foot the bill for the party.* **2. ADD UP FIGURES** to add up the figures in a column ○ *footed the columns of the budget* **3. MAKE FOOT OF SOCK** in knitting or sewing, to add the part that will cover the foot to a sock or stocking [Old English *fōt*] ◇ **drag your feet** to move or do something slowly and reluctantly on purpose (*informal*) ◇ **fall** *or* **land on your feet** to end up healthy or in a good position, especially after having been sick or in a difficult situation ◇ **find your feet 1.** to become accustomed to a new situation and able to cope with it **2.** to manage to stand up, especially after having fallen ◇ **a foot in the door** the first stage toward a goal, especially when this is difficult to achieve ◇ **foot it 1.** to walk rather than ride in a vehicle or on a horse ○ *We had to foot it all the way home.* **2.** to dance (*dated*) ◇ **get off on the wrong foot** to begin something badly, such as a new relationship or job ◇ **get on** *or* **to your feet 1.** to rise from a reclining or sitting position **2.** to return to a healthy or financially stable condition after a period of illness or financial difficulty ◇ **have somebody** *or* **something at your feet** to be the object of enormous admiration and devotion from somebody or something ◇ **have feet of clay** to have a weakness or flaw that is not obvious at first ◇ **have** *or* **keep both** *or* **your feet on the ground** to act and think sensibly and realistically ◇ **on foot** walking, as opposed to riding on horseback or in a vehicle ◇ **put your best foot forward** to try as hard as you can to impress or please somebody ◇ **put your feet up** to stop working and relax ◇ **put your foot down 1.** to be firm about something and make sure your wishes are obeyed or respected **2.** to make a motor vehicle travel faster by pressing the accelerator ◇ **put your foot in it, put your foot in your mouth** to make an embarrassing mistake, especially by being tactless (*informal*) ◇ **shoot yourself in the foot** to do something that unexpectedly turns out to be disadvantageous or harmful to your own interests ◇ **sweep somebody off his** *or* **her feet** to charm somebody completely or make somebody fall in love with you in a very short time

WORD KEY: ORIGIN

Foot The Indo-European ancestor of ***foot*** is also the ultimate source of English *antipodes, impede, octopus, pawn*, meaning "chess piece," *pedal, pedestal, pedestrian, pedigree, pioneer, podium, pajamas, quadruped, tripod*, and *vamp*, meaning "shoe part."

foot·age /fo͝otij/ *n.* **1.** CINEMA **FILMED SEQUENCE SHOWING EVENT** a shot or sequence of shots on film or videotape, usually of a particular scene or event, or the length of film or videotape that contains these shots ○ *They had some good footage of the president's visit to the island.* **2.** BUILDING **SIZE IN FEET** the size or amount of something measured in feet **3.** CINEMA **LENGTH OF PIECE OF FILM** the length of a piece of film in feet **4. PAYMENT BY SIZE** payment by the foot for work **5. AMOUNT PAID** the amount paid for work measured by the foot

foot-and-mouth dis·ease *n.* a highly contagious viral disease affecting animals with divided hooves, especially cattle, sheep, and pigs, in which the animal develops ulcers in the mouth and near the hooves

foot·ball /fo͝ot bàwl/ *n.* **1. GAME WITH OVAL BALL** a game in which two teams of 11 players score points by carrying an oval ball across their opponents' goal line or by kicking the ball through the opponents' goal posts **2.** *U.K.* = **soccer 3.** FOOTBALL **BALL GAME** any of various games in which two teams kick or carry a ball into a goal or over a line, such as rugby, Australian rules, or Gaelic football **4. BALL USED IN FOOTBALL** the large oval ball used in the game of football **5. PROBLEM PASSED AROUND** a point or problem that is used as an excuse for argument by opposing groups, without any real attempt at finding a solution **6. BRIEFCASE WITH NUCLEAR CODES** a nickname for the briefcase that holds the nuclear codes available to the President of the United States (*informal*) —**foot·ball·er** *n.*

foot·bath /fo͝ot bàth/ (*plural* **-baths** /fo͝ot bàths, -ba̱thz/) *n.* **1. CONTAINER FOR WASHING FEET** a bowl used when bathing the feet, or a shallow pool where people can disinfect their feet before entering a swimming pool **2. BATHING OF FEET** the action of bathing the feet

foot·board /fo͝ot bàwrd/ *n.* **1. BOARD AT BOTTOM OF BED** a vertical part across the bottom end of a bedstead **2. SUPPORT FOR FEET** a board or small platform used to support the feet in a vehicle

foot·boy /fo͝ot bòy/ *n.* a boy employed as a servant or page

foot brake *n.* a brake operated by pressing a pedal with the foot, especially in a motor vehicle

foot·bridge /fo͝ot brìj/ *n.* a narrow bridge suitable for people walking and not for vehicles

foot·cloth /fo͝ot klàwth/ *n.* a decorative cloth that is placed over the back of a horse and reaches the ground on both sides (*archaic*)

foot-drag·ger *n.* somebody who is slow or reluctant to do what is necessary (*informal*) —**foot-drag·ging** *n.*

foot·ed /fo͝otəd/ *adj.* having feet, a foot, or a walk of a specified kind, or a specified number of feet (*usually used in combination*) ○ *leaden-footed dancing*

foot·er /fo͝otər/ *n.* **1. TEXT AT BOTTOM OF PAGE** a piece of text, such as a title or date, below the main text on a page, especially one that is automatically inserted on each page by word-processing software **2. SOMEBODY OR SOMETHING MEASURED IN FEET** somebody or something of a specified height or length in feet (*usually used in combination*) ○ *Both of her sons were six-footers.* **3.** ARCHIT, BUILDING = **footing** *n.* 5

foot·fall /fo͝ot fàwl/ *n.* the sound made by somebody's foot striking the ground as he or she walks

foot fault *n.* a fault committed in tennis by a server whose foot touches any part of the baseline or court before the ball has been hit —**foot-fault** *vi.*

foot·gear /fo͝ot gèer/ *n.* coverings worn on the feet, especially shoes and boots

foot·hill /fo͝ot hìl/ *n.* a hill at the bottom of a higher mountain or mountain range and forming part of the approaches to it (*often used in the plural*)

foot·hold /fo͝ot hòld/ *n.* **1.** PLACE FOR CLIMBER'S FOOT a place or thing that will support the foot of a climber, especially a crack, hollow, or ledge in a rock face **2.** FIRM BASE FOR PROGRESS a secure starting position from which further advances can be made ○ *The company has gained a foothold in the multimedia industry.*

foot·ing /fo͝oting/ *n.* **1.** STABILITY OF FEET a stable secure position for or placement of the feet when standing or walking ○ *He missed his footing on the icy slope.* **2.** BASE FOR PROGRESS a foundation or basis for further advancement or development ○ *The project began on a firm financial footing.* **3.** STATUS OF SOMETHING the status or condition of something, often in relation to something else ○ *The government moved swiftly to place the armed forces on a war footing.* **4.** STATUS OF SOMEBODY the position or status of people in relation to one another ○ *I'm glad to be back on a friendly footing with her.* **5.** ARCHIT, BUILDING FOUNDATION the foundation or base of a structure, such as a wall or column **6.** CONDITION OF SURFACE the condition of a surface, such as that of a racetrack, for walking or running **7.** TOTAL the total of a column of figures

foo·tle /fo͞ot'l/ *vi.* (**-tled, -tling, -tles**) (*informal*) **1.** ACT AIMLESSLY to waste time doing unnecessary or unimportant things **2.** ACT OR TALK POINTLESSLY to talk nonsense or behave in a pointless way ■ *n.* NONSENSE silly nonsense [Late 19thC. Origin uncertain: perhaps from FOOTER.] —**foo·tler** *n.*

foot·less /fo͝otləss/ *adj.* **1.** WITHOUT FEET lacking a foot or feet **2.** LACKING SUBSTANCE lacking a firm foundation or basis ○ *footless speculation* **3.** LACKING SKILL lacking competence or ability ○ *a footless plan to set things right* —**foot·less·ly** *adv.* —**foot·less·ness** *n.*

foot·lights /fo͝ot lìts/ *npl.* **1.** LIGHTS ALONG FRONT OF STAGE a row of lights along the front of the stage in a theater, directed away from the audience and toward the performers **2.** THEATRICAL PROFESSION the theater as a profession

foo·tling /fo͞otling/ *adj.* (*informal*) **1.** UNIMPORTANT having no importance or serious usefulness **2.** LACKING SKILL lacking skill or competence [Late 19thC. Formed from FOOTLE.]

foot·lock·er /fo͝ot lòkər/ *n.* a strong case or box for personal belongings kept at the foot of somebody's bed, especially in a barracks or dormitory

foot·loose /fo͝ot lo͞oss/ *adj.* free to go anywhere and do anything because not limited by personal ties or responsibilities

foot·man /fo͝otmən/ (*plural* **-men**) *n.* **1.** LIVERIED SERVANT OF ARISTOCRACY a man employed as a servant, especially a servant in uniform in a mansion or palace **2.** HOUSEHOLD FIRESIDE STAND a low metal stand, usually with four legs, for utensils in a fireplace **3.** ARMY SOLDIER a soldier who fights on foot (*archaic*) **4.** WALKER somebody who travels by walking (*archaic*)

foot·mark /fo͝ot maark/ *n.* = **footprint** *n.* 1

foot·note /fo͝ot nòt/ *n.* **1.** INFORMATION AT FOOT OF PAGE a note at the bottom of a page, giving further information about something mentioned in the text above. A reference number or symbol is usually printed after the relevant word in the text and before the corresponding footnote. **2.** ADDITIONAL DETAIL an extra comment or information added to what has just been said ○ *As a footnote, let me say that I only found this out yesterday.* **3.** MINOR DETAIL a relatively unimportant part of a larger issue or event ○ *His career, considered glorious at the time, is now but a footnote in history.* ■ *vt.* (**-not·ed, -not·ing, -notes**) SUPPLY WITH FOOTNOTES to provide a text with footnotes, or to provide a footnote for a particular reference within the text

foot·pad[1] /fo͝ot pàd/ *n.* somebody who robs people who are traveling on foot (*archaic*) [Late 17thC. *Pad*, from obsolete *pad* "path, highway robbery, highwayman," from Dutch.]

foot·pad[2] /fo͝ot pàd/ *n.* a flat structure at the end of a leg of a spacecraft, designed to prevent the craft sinking into the surface it has landed on

foot pas·sen·ger *n.* a passenger on a car ferry who is not traveling with a motor vehicle

foot·path /fo͝ot pàth/ (*plural* **-paths** /fo͝ot pàthz, -pàths/) *n.* a narrow path for people on foot ○ *Please keep to the footpath.*

foot-pound *n.* a unit of work equal to the work done by lifting a mass of one pound vertically against gravity through a distance of one foot

foot-pound-sec·ond *adj.* relating or belonging to a system of measurements based on the foot, pound, and second as base units of length, mass, and time

foot·print /fo͝ot prìnt/ *n.* **1.** OUTLINE OF FOOT a mark made by the foot of a person or animal or a shoe, especially an indentation on something soft like snow or a dirty mark on a floor ○ *footprints in the ground below the window* **2.** SPACE OCCUPIED BY MACHINE the area covered by something, especially the amount of space a piece of computer hardware occupies on a desk, floor, or other surface **3.** BROADCAST RANGE the area over which something occurs or is effective, such as the area where a signal from a communications satellite can be received

foot·race /fo͝ot ràyss/, **foot race** *n.* a race run by people on foot

foot·rest /fo͝ot rèst/ *n.* a support for both feet when sitting down, e.g., beneath a desk, or for one foot while standing, e.g., a low rail at a bar

foot·rope /fo͝ot ròp/ *n.* **1.** ROPE AT LOWER EDGE OF SAIL a rope to which the lower edge of a sail is stitched **2.** ROPE FOR STANDING ON a rope fixed beneath a ship's yard for sailors to stand on as they furl a sail

foot rot /fo͝ot ròt/, **foot·rot** *n.* **1.** VET, AGRIC INFECTION OF SHEEP AND CATTLE a bacterial infection of sheep and cattle that causes inflammation of the hooves **2.** BOT PLANT DISEASE a fungal disease that causes the roots and base of a plant to rot

foot rule *n.* a strip of wood, metal, or plastic, used for measuring and drawing straight lines, that is one foot long or is marked in feet

foot·sie /fo͝otsee/ *n.* a form of flirtation in which people use their feet to touch the feet and legs of somebody else, especially done secretly while sitting at a table (*informal*) [Mid-20thC. A humorous formation from FOOT.] ◇ **play footsie 1.** to touch another person's foot or leg with your own, often secretly under a table, as a form of flirtation (*informal*) **2.** to collaborate with another person or organization, often in an underhand way (*informal*)

foot·slog /fo͝ot slòg/ (**-slogged, -slog·ging, -slogs**) *vi.* to march, tramp, or trudge on foot, especially over difficult ground, such as thick mud —**foot·slog·ger** *n.* —**foot·slog·ging** *n.*

foot sol·dier *n.* a soldier who fights principally on foot, not on horseback or in a vehicle

foot·sore /fo͝ot sàwr/ *adj.* with feet that are painful or tired, usually from too much walking —**foot·sore·ness** *n.*

foot·stall /fo͝ot stàwl/ *n.* **1.** BASE OF PILLAR the pedestal or base of a structure, especially a pillar or statue **2.** STIRRUP a stirrup on a sidesaddle

foot·step /fo͝ot stèp/ *n.* **1.** SOUND OF FEET the sound made when somebody's foot hits the ground in walking ○ *I heard footsteps on the stairs.* **2.** MOVEMENT OF FOOT the action of raising a foot and putting it down somewhere else while walking **3.** DISTANCE COVERED BY STEP the distance covered by a single step in walking **4.** MARK MADE BY FOOT a mark left by the sole of a foot or shoe **5.** STEP OR STAIR a single step or stair on which to put a foot while moving up or down ◇ **follow in somebody's footsteps** to take the same course in life or work as another person has done in the past

foot·stone /fo͝ot stòn/ *n.* a memorial stone at the foot of a grave

foot·stool /fo͝ot sto͞ol/ *n.* a low stool, often with a padded top, on which to rest the feet while sitting down

foot·wall /fo͝ot wàwl/ *n.* the rock layer that lies immediately beneath a vein of ore or other mineral deposit or a fault plane

foot·way /fo͝ot wày/ *n.* a narrow path or walk for people on foot, e.g., beside a road or railroad

foot·wear /fo͝ot wàir/ *n.* coverings worn on the feet, especially shoes, boots, sandals, or slippers, but often including socks or stockings

foot·well /fo͝ot wèl/ *n.* the hollow space below a motor vehicle's dashboard where people in the front seats can put their feet

foot·work /fo͝ot wùrk/ *n.* **1.** MOTION OF FEET the movement of somebody's feet in sports or dancing, especially when this is done with skill **2.** SKILLFUL MANEUVERING skillful or devious maneuvering in order to achieve or avoid something (*informal*) ○ *Their fancy footwork helped get them out of the problem.* **3.** WORK THAT INVOLVES WALKING work that involves a lot of moving around, especially on foot

foot·worn /fo͝ot wàwrn/ *adj.* **1.** WORN DOWN BY FEET worn down or made thin by being walked on by many people for a long time **2.** = **footsore**

foo·zle /fo͞oz'l/ *vti.* (**-zled, -zling, -zles**) BUNGLE SOMETHING to do something badly or clumsily, especially to bungle a shot in golf ■ *n.* SOMETHING DONE BADLY something done badly or clumsily, especially a bungled shot in golf [Mid-19thC. Origin uncertain: perhaps from German dialect *fuseln* "to do bad work."] —**foo·zler** *n.*

fop /fop/ *n.* a man who is so obsessed by fashion and vain about his own appearance that he becomes ridiculous [15thC. Origin uncertain.] —**fop·pish** *adj.* —**fop·pish·ly** *adv.* —**fop·pish·ness** *n.*

fop·per·y /fóppəree/ (*plural* **-ies**) *n.* any or all of the characteristics of a fop, such as his extravagant style of dress or affected manners

for[1] /fawr/; *unstressed* /fər/ CORE MEANING: a preposition indicating that something is directed at somebody, done to benefit somebody, or done on somebody's behalf ○ *Look – there's a letter for you.* ○ *I'd do anything for you.* ○ *The lawyer acted for some of the heirs.*

1. *prep.* AIMED AT intended to be received or used by, or aimed at somebody ○ *It's for you – it's a present.* ○ *advice for first-time buyers* **2.** *prep.* TO THE BENEFIT OF intending or intended to benefit somebody or something ○ *She would make any sacrifice for the cause.* **3.** *prep.* ON BEHALF OF on behalf of or instead of somebody or something ○ *Would you mind making my apologies for me?* **4.** *prep.* IN THE SERVICE OF in the service or employment of somebody or something ○ *She works for a large company.* **5.** *prep.* TOWARD in the direction of ○ *The following day, we headed for Paris.* **6.** *prep.* LASTING indicating how long something lasts, continues, or extends ○ *The interview only lasted for a few minutes.* ○ *There was fog for the next mile or so.* **7.** *prep.* BECAUSE OF indicating a reason why something happens or is done ○ *I did it for love.* **8.** *prep.* DESIGNED WITH A PURPOSE indicating the purpose of an object, action, or activity ○ *That towel is for drying your hands on.* **9.** *prep.* LINKS CONCEPTS used to link two concepts, one of which is the object of the other ○ *a cause for concern* ○ *a passion for opera* **10.** *prep.* IN EXCHANGE FOR at a cost of, or giving or receiving something in exchange ○ *I got this hat in the market for next to nothing* **11.** *prep.* INSTEAD OF instead of or in place of something, sometimes mistakenly ○ *You'll have to find a stand-in for him while he's away.* ○ *I took her for the boss.* **12.** *prep.* GIVEN WHAT IS USUAL with reference to the normal characteristics of something ○ *It's very warm for April.* **13.** *prep.* INDICATING OCCASION at, or planned to be at, a particular time, or on a particular occasion ○ *The meeting was scheduled for four o'clock.* ○ *Will you be home for Christmas?* **14.** *prep.* INDICATES COMPARISON indicating a comparison or equivalence between two things ○ *Pound for pound, the elephant's energy consumption is the lowest of all land animals.* **15.** *prep.* IN ORDER TO GET in order to get, achieve, have, keep, or become something ○ *Lee's hoping for promotion.* ○ *He was searching for a place to sit.* **16.** *prep.* DESPITE in spite of or notwithstanding something ○ *He enjoyed himself very much, for all his complaining.* **17.** *prep.* INDICATES RESPONSIBILITY indicating that somebody has the right or responsibility to do something ○ *I can't help you – it's for you to decide.* **18.** *prep.* HAVING THE SAME MEANING having the same meaning as another word or phrase ○ *The everyday term for rubella is German measles.* **19.** *prep.* INDICATES CROSS-REFERENCE indicating that information can be found elsewhere ○ *For further details, consult the owner's manual.* **20.** *adv., prep.* IN SUPPORT OF SOMETHING in favour of, or in support of something ○ (prep) *Who's for the motion and who's against?* ○ (adv) *Ten voted for, and eleven against.* **21.** *conj.* BECAUSE because, seeing that (*formal*) ○ *I left in haste, for I was already late for the appointment.* [Old English. Ultimately from an Indo-European word meaning "forward," which is also the ancestor of English *forth, hausfrau,* and *paramount.*]

for[2] *prefix.* **1.** away, down, falsely ○ *forfend* ○ *forswear* **2.** completely, extremely ○ *forgather* [Old English; related to *for* "before, in place of" (see FOR)]

FOR *abbr.* COMM free on rail

for. *abbr.* **1.** foreign **2.** forestry

for- *prefix.* **1.** FORMS NEGATIVE WORDS used to form words with a strong negative content, e.g., rejecting or prohibiting something ○ *forbid* ○ *forsake* **2.** FORMS INTENSE WORDS used to form words that suggest intensity or extremeness ○ *forlorn* [Old English]

fo·ra *npl.* plural of **forum**

for·age /fáwrij/ *n.* **1.** FOOD FOR ANIMALS food for animals, especially crops grown to feed horses, cattle, and other livestock **2.** SEARCH a search or the process of searching for something, especially a search for food and supplies or a search among a varied collection of things **3.** RAID BY SOLDIERS a raid carried out by soldiers, especially to seize food or supplies ■ *v.* (**-aged, -ag·ing, -ag·es**) **1.** *vi.* WANDER AROUND SEARCHING to go from place to place looking for food and supplies **2.** *vti.* RAID FOR FOOD to raid a place, especially for food or supplies **3.** *vi.* SEARCH FOR SOMETHING to search or try to find something ○ *He foraged around in the drawer and pulled out a faded photograph.* **4.** *vt.* FIND BY SEARCHING to obtain something, especially food, from a place by searching or rummaging ○ *She foraged a half-eaten cake from the trashcan.* **5.** *vt.* FEED ANIMALS to give fodder to horses, cattle, or other animals [14thC. From Old French *fourrage*, from *fuerre* "fodder, straw," from, ultimately, a prehistoric Germanic word that is also the ancestor of English *fodder*.]

for·age cap *n. U.K.* = **service cap**

for·ag·er *n.* a person or animal that forages for something, especially food

For·a·ker /fáwrəkər/ mountain of the Alaska Range in Denali National Park and Preserve, southern Alaska. Height: 17,400 ft./5,304 m.

for·am /fáwrəm/ *n.* a foraminifer [Early 20thC. Shortening.]

fo·ra·men /fə ráymən/ (*plural* **-ram·i·na** /fə rámmənə/ *or* **-ra·mens**) *n.* a natural opening or cavity in a human or animal body, usually one through which blood vessels and nerves pass through bone [Late 17thC. From Latin, from *forare* "to bore a hole."] —**fo·ram·i·nal** /fə rámmən'l/ *adj.* —**fo·ram·i·nous** /-nəss/ *adj.*

fo·ra·men mag·num /fə ràymən mágnəm/ *n.* the opening at the base of the skull through which the spinal cord passes to become the medulla oblongata of the brain [Late 19thC. From Latin, literally "large opening."]

fo·ra·men o·val·e /fə ràymən ō vállee, -váylee, -vaálee/ *n.* an opening in the wall between the two sides of the fetal heart that allows blood to pass from right to left. Sometimes it fails to close after birth and persists into adulthood. [Mid-19thC. From Latin, literally "oval opening."]

fo·ram·i·na plural of **foramen**

for·a·min·i·fer /fàwrə mínnəfər/ (*plural* **-fers**, *unmarked inflection* **-fera**) *n.* a large, mainly marine protozoan that has a shell perforated with many small holes through which temporary cytoplasmic protrusions (**pseudopodia**) project. The calcium-containing shells of foraminifera are the main component of chalk and certain limestone deposits. Order: Foraminfera. [Mid-19thC. From modern Latin *Foraminifera* (plural), order name, from Latin *foramen* (see FORAMEN) + *-fer* "bearing."] —**fo·ram·i·nif·er·al** /fə rámmə níffərəl/ *adj.* —**fo·ram·i·nif·er·ous** /-rəss/ *adj.*

for·as·much as /fàwrəz múch əz/ *conj.* since, or in view of the fact that (*formal*)

for·ay /fáw rày/ *n.* **1.** SUDDEN RAID a sudden attack or raid by a military force **2.** EXPLORATION OF SOMETHING UNFAMILIAR an attempt at some new occupation or activity ○ *the ex-player's first foray into management* **3.** BRIEF JOURNEY a short trip or visit to a place, usually for a particular purpose ■ *v.* (**-ayed, -ay·ing, -ays**) **1.** *vi.* MAKE INCURSION to make a sudden attack or raid **2.** *vt.* RAID to raid or loot a place [14thC. Back-formation from *forayer* "plunderer," from Old French *fourrier*, from *fuerre* (see FORAGE). The underlying idea is of a search for food.] —**for·ay·er** /fáw ràyr/ *n.*

forb /fawrb/ *n.* any broad-leaved herbaceous plant that is not a grass, especially one that grows in a prairie or meadow [Early 20thC. From Greek *phorbē* "food," from *pherbein* "to feed."]

for·bade, for·bad *vt.* past tense of **forbid**

for·bear[1] /fawr báir, fər-/ (**-bore** /fawr báwr, fər-/, **-borne** /fawr báwrn, fər-/, **-bear·ing, -bears**) *v.* **1.** *vi.* HOLD BACK FROM SOMETHING to not do or say something that you could do or say, especially when this shows self-control or consideration for the feelings of others (*formal*) ○ *I forbore to criticize their efforts, though criticism was well deserved.* **2.** *vti.* BE TOLERANT to tolerate something with patience or endurance (*formal*) ○ *patiently forbore their failures* **3.** *vt.* AVOID to give up or avoid something (*archaic*) ○ *I must forbear jealousy.* [Old English *forberan*, literally "to bear against"] —**for·bear·er** *n.* —**for·bear·ing** *adj.* —**for·bear·ing·ly** *adv.*

for·bear[2] /fáwr bàir/ *n.* = **forebear**

for·bear·ance /fawr báirəns, fər-/ *n.* **1.** PATIENCE patience, tolerance, or self-control, especially in not responding to provocation **2.** REFRAINING FROM DOING SOMETHING the fact of deliberately not doing or saying something when you could do or say it (*formal*) **3.** REFRAINING FROM LEGAL RIGHT the fact of not exercising a legal right, especially of not insisting on payment of a debt at the due date and giving the debtor more time to pay

for·bid /fər bíd, fàwr-/ (**-bade** /fər bád, fàwr-, fər báyd, -báyd/ *or* **-bad** /fər bád, fàwr-/, **-bid·den** /fər bídd'n, fàwr-/ *or* **-bid, -bid·ding, -bids**) *vt.* **1.** ORDER NOT TO DO SOMETHING to tell somebody, especially forcefully, not to do or have something ○ *I forbid you to mention his name.* **2.** NOT ALLOW to state authoritatively that something must not be done ○ *The rules of the game strictly forbid the use of a dictionary.* **3.** MAKE SOMETHING IMPOSSIBLE to make something impossible or prevent it from happening (*formal*) ○ *Discretion forbids me to mention any names.* [Old English *forbēodan*, literally "to command against"] —**for·bid·dance** /fər bídd'ns, fàwr-/ *n.* —**for·bid·der** /fər bíddər, fàwr-/ *n.* ◇ **God** *or* **heaven(s)** *or* **Lord forbid** used to express the hope that something will not happen or be done

for·bid·den /fər bídd'n, fàwr-/ *adj.* **1.** NOT PERMITTED not allowed by order of somebody or by law ○ *That's a forbidden subject in this company.* **2.** OUT OF BOUNDS to which entry is not allowed or allowed only to a certain person or group of people ○ *This part of the temple was forbidden to everybody except the high priest.* **3.** IMPROBABLE OR DISALLOWED LEVEL OR TRANSITION used to describe an energy level or transition in a quantum mechanical system that is either highly improbable or disobeys selection rules and is therefore not allowed

Forbidden City: Hall of Supreme Harmony

For·bid·den Cit·y *n.* a walled complex of buildings (1421–1911) in Beijing, China, that includes the former Imperial Palace. It was closed to ordinary citizens until 1912 and is now a museum.

for·bid·den fruit (*plural* **for·bid·den fruits** *or* **for·bid·den fruit**) *n.* something desired or pleasurable that somebody is not allowed to have or do, especially some form of sexual indulgence that is illegal or considered immoral [From the passage in the Bible (Genesis 2:17) that tells of the fruit, forbidden to Adam and Eve, of the tree of knowledge of good and evil]

for·bid·ding /fər bídding, fàwr-/ *adj.* **1.** HOSTILE presenting an appearance that seems hostile or stern ○ *The mountains looked distant and forbidding.* **2.** UNINVITING appearing to involve a great deal of unpleasantness or difficulty ○ *the forbidding prospect of further difficulties ahead* **3.** DANGEROUS OR THREATENING appearing to present a danger or threat ○ *a rocky and forbidding shore* —**for·bid·ding·ly** *adv.* —**for·bid·ding·ness** *n.*

for·bore past tense of **forbear**

for·borne past participle of **forbear**

force /fawrs/ *n.* **1.** POWER OR STRENGTH the power, strength, or energy that somebody or something possesses ○ *Trees were blown down by the force of the storm.* **2.** PHYSICAL POWER physical power, effort, or violence used against somebody or something that resists ○ *The use of force should be a last resort.* **3.** EFFECTIVENESS OR VALIDITY the condition of being effective, valid, or applicable ○ *The new regulations come into force next week.* **4.** NONPHYSICAL POWER power or strength that is intellectual or moral rather than physical ○ *swayed by the force of your argument* **5.** SOMEBODY OR SOMETHING WITH GREAT INFLUENCE somebody or something that has great power or influence, especially in a particular field ○ *She remained a force in local politics until her death.* **6.** MIL GROUP ORGANIZED TO FIGHT a body of military personnel, ships, or aircraft brought together to fight in a battle or a war ○ *A naval task force has been sent to the area.* **7.** POLICE OFFICERS a professional body of police officers ○ *He left the force in 1985.* **8.** PEOPLE WORKING TOGETHER a group of people who work together for a particular purpose **9.** PHYS INFLUENCE THAT MOVES SOMETHING a physical influence that tends to change the position of an object with mass, equal to the rate of change in momentum of the object. Symbol *F* **10.** METEOROL WIND STRENGTH the strength of the wind, especially as measured on the Beaufort scale, from 0 to 12 ○ *a force 9 gale* ■ **forc·es** *npl.* ORGANIZED MILITARY SERVICE the professional military organizations belonging to a particular country ○ *Were you in the forces?* ■ *vt.* (**forced, forc·ing, forc·es**) **1.** COMPEL to use superior strength, violence, or any kind of physical or mental power to make somebody or yourself do something against his, her, or your own will or inclination ○ *The weather forced us to turn back.* ○ *She forced herself to be polite to him.* **2.** MOVE WITH STRENGTH to use physical strength or violence to move something or somebody that puts up resistance ○ *If the key won't turn easily, don't force it.* ○ *She forced the dog back into the house.* **3.** CREATE BY STRENGTH to create something, such as a way through something, using physical strength or another kind of power ○ *They forced a path through the jungle.* **4.** OBTAIN BY PRESSURE to obtain something or make something happen by using physical or mental pressure ○ *She's been trying to force a confrontation all week.* **5.** BREAK OPEN to open something that is locked or jammed by using power or effort, often breaking or damaging it in the process ○ *This door has been forced.* **6.** STRAIN to produce or use something in a strained or unnatural way ○ *Just agree with whatever she says and try to force a smile.* **7.** GARDENING MAKE PLANT MATURE to cause a plant to flower or mature before its normal time **8.** RAPE to subject somebody to rape (*dated*) **9.** BASEBALL PUT RUNNER OUT to put out a runner in baseball on a force play **10.** BASEBALL CREATE A RUN to create a run in baseball by walking a batter when the bases are full **11.** CARDS, GAME MAKE PLAYER PLAY CERTAIN WAY to give a player in a game no choice but to play a particular card or make a particular bid or move [13thC. Via Old French from Latin *fortis* "strong" (source of English *fortress*, *effort*, and *fortitude*).] —**force·a·ble** *adj.* —**force·less** *adj.* —**forc·er** *n.* ◇ **in force** **1.** in a large or strong group **2.** effective or valid ◇ **join forces** to combine together or combine with somebody else for a joint effort

force down *vt.* **1.** SWALLOW WITH DIFFICULTY to eat or drink something very reluctantly, often because pressured to do so or to avoid offending somebody **2.** MAKE AIRCRAFT LAND to compel an aircraft to land, usually because of lack of fuel, damage, or bad weather

force on, force up·on *vt.* to make somebody or a group of people accept something unwillingly ○ *This method was forced upon us by head office.*

forced /fawrst/ *adj.* **1.** NOT NATURAL not natural or spontaneous, but produced by an act of will ○ *The courtiers greeted the king's witticism with forced laughter.* **2.** NECESSARY not done voluntarily but out of necessity **3.** COMPELLED done because somebody who has power requires it —**forc·ed·ly** /fáwrsədlee/ *adv.* —**forc·ed·ness** /-nəss/ *n.*

forced la·bor *n.* work that somebody is made to do against his or her will, often as a punishment or to repay a debt

forced land·ing *n.* an unscheduled landing that a pilot is compelled to make, usually because of an emergency

forced march *n.* a march made as quickly as possible and without the normal amounts of rest

force-feed (**force-fed, force-feed·ing, force-feeds**) *vt.* **1.** **COMPEL TO TAKE IN NOURISHMENT** to make people or animals swallow food, against their will, e.g., by putting it directly down their throat through a funnel or tube. Animals may be force-fed to fatten them up, and people who refuse to eat because of a protest or a psychiatric disorder may be force-fed to keep them alive. **2. FORCE TO LEARN** to make people study or learn things, often without fully understanding or appreciating them, that they might reject if given the choice

force field *n.* in science fiction, an invisible protective barrier around something

force·ful /fáwrsfəl/ *adj.* **1. POWERFUL** possessing or characterized by strength and power **2. IMPRESSIVE OR PERSUASIVE** tending to make a powerful impression on people or to persuade people ○ *a forceful argument for merging our businesses* —**force·ful·ly** *adv.* —**force·ful·ness** *n.*

force-land (**force-land·ed, force-land·ing, force-lands**) *vti.* to land an aircraft before it gets to its destination because of an emergency ○ *The pilot had to force-land in a field.*

force ma·jeure /fàwrs maa zhúr/ *n.* **1.** LAW **EVENT THAT MAKES SOMEBODY DO SOMETHING** an unexpected event that crucially affects somebody's ability to do something and can be put forward in law as an excuse for not having carried out the terms of an agreement (*formal*) **2. SUPERIOR POWER** a force that is superior in power or impossible to resist [Late 19thC. From French, literally "superior force."]

force-march (**force-marched, force-march·ing, force-march·es**) *vti.* to make soldiers or prisoners march somewhere in the shortest possible time and without the normal amounts of rest ○ *The infantry escaped by force-marching back to the river crossing.* ○ *The captured personnel were force-marched north.*

force·meat /fáwrs meet/ *n.* finely chopped meat, fish, or vegetables mixed with spices or other ingredients and used as a stuffing or garnish [Late 17thC. *Force*, variant of FARCE.]

force of hab·it *n.* the ability of a pattern of behavior that has become habitual to reassert itself automatically even in situations where it is no longer appropriate ○ *Even after she retired, she woke at six every morning by force of habit.*

force-out *n.* in baseball, an act of putting a base runner out by a force play

force play *n.* a baseball play in which a runner, forced to run to the next base because the batter hits the ball, is put out by a fielder at that base

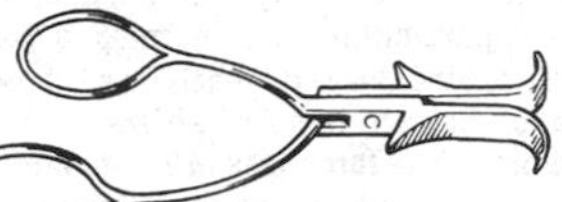

Forceps

for·ceps /fáwrsəps, fáwr sèps/ (*plural* **-ceps**) *npl.* **1.** SURG **SURGICAL INSTRUMENT** a specialized surgical instrument resembling tongs or tweezers, used for grasping or moving tissues or organs or for applying materials such as gauze pads during operations **2.** BIOL **BODY PART SIMILAR TO PINCER** a body part that is shaped or works like pincers, such as the grasping parts of some insects [Mid-16thC. From Latin, "pincers," of uncertain origin: perhaps from assumed *formiceps*, from *formus* "warm" + *capere* "to take."]

force pump *n.* a pump that uses pressure to move a liquid

forc·i·ble /fáwrsəb'l/ *adj.* **1. USING STRENGTH** using physical power against somebody or something that resists ○ *the forcible removal of the lock* **2. PERSUASIVE** powerful or tending to persuade people ○ *It was a forcible reminder that we must be on our guard.* —**forc·i·bil·i·ty** /fàwrsə bíllətee/ *n.* —**forc·i·ble·ness** /fáwrsəb'lnəss/ *n.* —**forc·i·bly** /-blee/ *adv.*

ford /fawrd/ *n.* **CROSSING PLACE THROUGH SHALLOW WATER** a shallow part of a river or stream where people, animals, or vehicles can cross it ■ *vt.* (**ford·ed, ford·ing, fords**) **CROSS IN SHALLOW WATER** to walk, ride, or drive across a river or stream at a place where the water is shallow [Old English, from a prehistoric Germanic word that is also the ancestor of English *fjord*] —**ford·a·ble** *adj.*

Gerald R. Ford

Ford /fawrd/, **Gerald R.** (*b.* 1913) U.S. statesman and 38th president of the United States. He was the only president (1974–77) elected neither president nor vice president, having attained those posts following the resignations of Richard Nixon and Spiro Agnew, respectively. Full name **Gerald Rudolph Ford**

Ford, Glenn (*b.* 1916) Canadian-born U.S. movie actor. His movies include *The Big Heat* (1953) and *Blackboard Jungle* (1955). Real name **Gwyllyn Samuel Newton**

Ford, Harrison (*b.* 1942) U.S. movie actor. He is best known for his roles as Han Solo in the *Star Wars* trilogy (1977–83) and as Indiana Jones in the *Raiders of the Lost Ark* trilogy (1981–89).

Henry Ford

Ford, Henry (1863–1947) U.S. industrialist, best known for his pioneering achievements in the automobile industry. In 1903 he founded a major motor company, introducing assembly-line production on a massive scale.

Ford, John (1895–1973) U.S. movie director. Winner of six Academy Awards, he is best known for his work on classic Westerns, including *Stagecoach* (1939). Real name **John Martin Feeney**

fore /fawr/ *n.* **FRONT** the front of something, or something at the front (*literary*) ■ *adj.* **AT FRONT OF SHIP OR AIRCRAFT** having a position at or near the front of something, especially a ship, an aircraft, or an animal ■ *adv.* **TOWARD THE FRONT** at or toward the front, especially of a ship or aircraft ■ *interj.* GOLF **WARNING ABOUT GOLF BALL** shouted to warn people that you are hitting a golf ball in their direction [Old English, "before, previously"] ◇ **to the fore** to a position of prominence or importance

fore- *prefix.* **1.** before, earlier ○ *forejudge* **2.** front, in front ○ *forebrain* [Old English, from *fore* (see FORE)]

fore-and-aft *adj.* parallel to or running along the length of something, especially a ship

fore-and-af·ter *n.* a ship with a fore-and-aft rig ["After," from AFT + -ER]

fore-and-aft rig *n.* an arrangement of a ship's sails such that, when set, they are parallel to the length of the vessel

fore-and-aft sail *n.* a quadrilateral sail that extends behind the mast rather than across the boat. The upper edge is supported by a pole (**gaff**) attached to the mast.

fore·arm[1] /fáwr aarm/ *n.* the part of the human arm between the elbow and the wrist, or the corresponding part of an animal's foreleg

fore·arm[2] /fawr áarm/ (**-armed, -arm·ing, -arms**) *vt.* to prepare or arm somebody in advance

fore·arm smash *n.* a blow struck with the forearm in wrestling

fore·bear /fáwr bàir/, **for·bear** *n.* ancestor, especially one who died a long time ago (*often used in the plural*) [15thC. From FORE- + *bear*, variant of obsolete *beer* "someone who is," from BE.]

fore·bode /fawr bṓd/ (**-bod·ed, -bod·ing, -bodes**) *vti.* (*formal*) **1. PORTEND OR PREDICT** to be or give an advance warning of something that may happen, especially something undesirable ○ *The gathering clouds foreboded a terrible storm.* **2. HAVE PREMONITION** to have a feeling that something bad is going to happen before it does —**fore·bod·er** *n.*

fore·bod·ing /fawr bṓding/ *n.* **1. PREMONITION** a feeling that something bad is going to happen **2. BAD OMEN** a sign or warning that something bad is going to happen ■ *adj.* **OMINOUS** indicating, warning, or suggesting that something undesirable is likely to happen —**fore·bod·ing·ly** *adv.* —**fore·bod·ing·ness** *n.*

fore·cad·die /fáwr kàddee/ *n.* a caddie on a golf course who watches from the fairway to see where the balls land

fore·cast /fáwr kàst/ *vt.* (**-cast·ed, -cast** *or* **-cast·ed, -cast·ing, -casts**) **1. SUGGEST WHAT WILL HAPPEN** to predict or work out something that is likely to happen, e.g., the weather conditions for the days ahead **2. BE EARLY SIGN OF SOMETHING** to be an advance indication of something that is likely or certain to happen ■ *n.* **1. WEATHER PREDICTION** a prediction of weather conditions for the near future, usually broadcast on television or radio or printed in a newspaper ○ *Have you heard the forecast for tomorrow?* **2. PREDICTION OF FUTURE DEVELOPMENTS** an estimation or calculation of what is likely to happen in the future, especially in business or finance [15thC. Originally "to contrive in advance."] —**fore·cast·a·ble** *adj.* —**fore·cast·er** *n.*

fore·cas·tle /fṓks'l, fáwr kàss'l/, **fo'c's'le** /fṓks'l/ *n.* **1. FRONT PART OF SHIP** the space at the front end of a ship below the maindeck, traditionally where the crew's quarters were located **2. RAISED DECK AT BOW** a raised section of deck at the bow of a ship

fore-check (**fore-checked, fore-check·ing, fore-checks**) *vi.* to check a player of an opposing ice hockey team in the opposition's defensive zone —**fore-check·er** *n.*

fore·close /fawr klṓz/ (**-closed, -clos·ing, -clos·es**) *v.* **1.** *vti.* LAW, FIN **END A MORTGAGE** to take away a mortgagee's right to redeem a mortgage, usually because payments have not been made ○ *The bank foreclosed on the property.* **2.** *vt.* **SHUT OUT** to bar or exclude somebody or something (*formal*) **3.** *vt.* **SETTLE BEFOREHAND** to settle or resolve something in advance (*formal*) **4.** *vt.* **PREVENT** to prevent or hinder something (*formal*) **5.** *vt.* **HOLD EXCLUSIVELY** to have an exclusive right or claim to something (*formal*) [13thC. From Old French *forclos*, past participle of *forclore*, ultimately from Latin *foris* "outside" + *claudere* "to close" (see CLOSE "to shut").] —**fore·clos·a·ble** *adj.*

fore·clo·sure /fawr klṓzhər/ *n.* a legal process by which a mortgagee's right to redeem a mortgage is taken away, usually because of failing to make payments

fore·course /fáwr kàwrs/ *n.* a foresail, especially the lowest of a ship's foresails

fore·court /fáwr kàwrt/ *n.* **1. SPACE IN FRONT OF BUILDING** an open area at the front of a building, especially one in front of a service station, hotel, or railroad station **2.** SPORTS **FRONT SECTION OF COURT** the part of the court nearest the net or front wall in games such as tennis, badminton, and handball

fore·deck /fáwr dèk/ *n.* the part of a ship's deck between the bridge and the forecastle

fore·doom /fawr dóom/ (**-doomed, -doom·ing, -dooms**) *vt.* to condemn something or somebody in advance to failure or destruction (*literary*) (*usually passive*)

fore-edge *n.* the outer edge of a printed page

fore·fa·ther /fáwr faathər/ (*plural* **-thers** *literary*) *n.* (*often used in the plural*) **1. MALE ANCESTOR** a male ancestor, usually one who died long ago (*literary*) ○ *in the proud tradition of our forefathers* **2. PRECURSOR** a member of an earlier generation from whom traditions, values, or ideas have been inherited

fore·fend /fawr fénd/ (**-fend·ed, -fend·ing, -fends**) *vt.* = **forfend** (*literary*)

fore·fin·ger /fáwr fing gər/ *n.* ANAT = **index finger**

fore·foot /fáwr fo͝ot/ (*plural* **-feet** /-feet/) *n.* **1.** ZOOL **ANIMAL'S FRONT FOOT** either of the front feet of a four-legged animal **2.** NAUT **FRONT OF KEEL** the front end of a ship's keel

fore·front /fáwr frùnt/ *n.* **1. LEADING POSITION** the most prominent, important, active, or responsible position in something **2. FOREMOST PART** the part at or nearest the front of something

fore·gath·er (**-ered, -er·ing, -ers**) *vi.* = **forgather**

fore·go[1] /fawr gṓ/ (**-went** /-wént/, **-gone** /-gón/, **-go·ing, -goes**) *vti.* to go or come before something in position, time, or sequence (*formal*) [Old English *foregan*] —**fore·go·er** *n.*

fore·go[2] *vt.* = **forgo**

fore·go·ing /fawr gṓ ing, fáwr gō ing/ *adj.* **PREVIOUSLY MENTIONED** going or coming before something, especially in speech or writing ■ *n.* **PRECEDING ITEM** in speech or writing, the thing that has just been mentioned ○ *As is evident from the foregoing, much remains to be done.*

fore·gone *adj.* **1. DONE ALREADY** previously completed or determined **2. PAST** previous or former (*archaic*)

fore·gone con·clu·sion *n.* something that will inevitably happen as a result of something else

fore·ground /fáwr grównd/ *n.* **1. PART THAT APPEARS NEAREST** the part of a picture or scene that appears nearest the viewer **2.** = **forefront** *n.* 1 ■ *adj.* COMPUT **CURRENTLY RECEIVING COMMANDS** currently receiving commands, usually through the keyboard, at the same time as one or more other programs or tasks are operating independently ○ *foreground processing* ■ *vt.* (**-ground·ed, -ground·ing, -grounds**) **HIGHLIGHT** to put something in an important position and so draw attention to it

fore·gut /fáwr gùt/ *n.* the front end of the embryonic gut in animals. In vertebrates it develops into the pharynx, esophagus, stomach, and top part of the intestines.

fore·hand /fáwr hànd/ *n.* **1.** SPORTS **STROKE IN RACKET GAMES** in racket games, a basic stroke played with the palm of the racket hand facing forward **2.** EQU **FRONT PART OF HORSE** the part of a horse in front of the rider and saddle ■ *adj.* SPORTS **PLAYED AS FOREHAND** in racket games, played with the palm of the racket hand facing forward, or relating to a stroke played in this way ■ *adv.* **WITH FOREHAND STROKE** in racket games, with a forehand stroke or action ■ *vt.* (**-hand·ed, -hand·ing, -hands**) SPORTS **PLAY WITH FOREHAND STROKE** in racket games, to hit the ball with a forehand stroke

fore·hand·ed /fawr hándəd/ *adj., adv.* = **forehand** ■ *adj.* (*literary*) **1. PRUDENT** prudent about saving money **2. WELL-TO-DO** financially well-off —**fore·hand·ed·ly** *adv.* —**fore·hand·ed·ness** *n.*

fore·head /fáwrəd, fáwr hèd/ *n.* the part of the face above the eyebrows, below the hairline and between the temples [Old English *foreheafod*, literally "front head," from *heafod*, an earlier form of HEAD]

fore·hoof /fáwr ho͝of/ (*plural* **-hooves** /-ho͝ovz/ *or* **-hoofs**) *n.* the hoof of either of the two front legs of a four-legged animal (**quadruped**)

for·eign /fáwrən/ *adj.* **1. OF ANOTHER COUNTRY** relating to, from, or located in a country or countries other than your own ○ *She speaks three foreign languages.* **2. DEALING WITH ANOTHER COUNTRY** dealing with or involved with a country or countries other than your own ○ *foreign policy* **3. COMING FROM OUTSIDE** introduced from outside into a place where it does not belong, often in the human body ○ *a foreign body in her eye* **4. UNCHARACTERISTIC** not usually associated with a particular person or thing ○ *Such outbursts are quite foreign to her nature.* **5. IRRELEVANT** not related or relevant (*formal*) ○ *observations that are foreign to the matter in hand* **6.** LAW **BEYOND JURISDICTION** being beyond the jurisdiction of a particular area or country [13thC. Via Old French *forein* from, ultimately, Latin *foras* "out of doors, abroad," from *fores* "door" (source of English *forest*).] —**for·eign·ly** *adv.* —**for·eign·ness** *n.*

for·eign bill *n.* a bill of exchange that is issued in one country but payable in another

for·eign cor·re·spon·dent *n.* a journalist who sends news reports from other countries for broadcast or publication in his or her own country

for·eign draft *n.* = **foreign bill**

for·eign·er /fáwrənər/ *n.* **1. SOMEBODY FROM ANOTHER COUNTRY** somebody who was born in or comes from a country other than your own **2. OUTSIDER** somebody who does not feel or is not considered to be part of a particular group

for·eign ex·change *n.* **1. DEALINGS IN FOREIGN MONEY** the conversion of one currency into another or the buying and selling of different currencies **2. FOREIGN MONEY** the currencies of countries other than your own, or international currencies generally

for·eign·ism /fáwrə nìzzəm/ *n.* something that is characteristically foreign, especially a custom or idiom (*formal*)

for·eign le·gion *n.* a section of an army consisting of foreign volunteers, especially that of the French army

for·eign min·is·ter *n.* in many countries a minister in a government who is responsible for relations with other countries

for·eign min·is·try *n.* in many countries, the department of government responsible for relations with other countries

for·eign mis·sion *n.* **1.** POL **DIPLOMATIC PERSONNEL** diplomatic personnel sent to represent their country abroad **2.** CHR **MISSIONARIES** missionaries who try to convert the inhabitants of another country to Christianity or another religion

for·eign of·fice *n.* in the United Kingdom and some other countries, the department of the government that is responsible for relations with other countries

for·eign sec·re·tar·y *n.* the cabinet minister in the United Kingdom government responsible for relations with other countries

for·eign ser·vice *n.* a country's diplomatic and consular staff

fore·judge /fawr júj/ (**-judged, -judg·ing, -judg·es**) *vti.* to judge a matter before knowing all the facts or evidence (*formal*) —**fore·judg·ment** *n.*

fore·know /fawr nṓ/ (**-knew** /fawr no͞o/, **-known** /fawr nṓn/, **-know·ing, -knows**) *vt.* to have knowledge or awareness that something is going to happen, either from information that has been acquired, or by paranormal means (*formal*) —**fore·know·a·ble** *adj.* —**fore·know·ing·ly** *adv.*

fore·knowl·edge /fawr nóllij/ *n.* knowledge or awareness that something is going to happen, either from information that has been acquired, or by paranormal means (*formal*)

fore·la·dy /fáwr làydee/ (*plural* **-dies**) *n.* = **forewoman** *n.* 1

fore·land /fáwrlənd/ *n.* **1.** GEOG **HEADLAND** a stretch of land that juts out into the sea or an estuary **2.** GEOG **LAND IN FRONT** land described in relation to what lies behind it, especially a plain in front of mountains **3. ROCK IN FRONT OF MOUNTAINS** a stable undeformed mass of rock that juts out in front of a mountain belt

fore·leg /fáwr lèg/ *n.* either of the two front legs of a four-legged animal (**quadruped**)

fore·limb /fáwr lìm/ *n.* either of the two front limbs of a four-limbed vertebrate, e.g., a flipper, arm, wing, or fin

fore·lock[1] /fáwr lòk/ *n.* **1. LOCK OF HAIR ON FOREHEAD** a lock of hair that grows or falls over the forehead **2.** ZOOL **FRONT OF HORSE'S MANE** the part of a horse's mane that falls forward between its ears

fore·lock[2] /fáwr lòk/ *n.* a pin or wedge inserted through the end of a bolt to stop it being removed

fore·man /fáwrmən/ (*plural* **-men**) *n.* **1. MAN IN CHARGE OF OTHER WORKERS** a man who is in charge of a group of other workers, e.g., on a construction site or in a factory **2.** LAW **LEADER OF JURY** somebody chosen by the other members of a jury to be their leader [13thC. Because he is the most important man.] —**fore·man·ship** *n.*

Fore·man /fáwrmən/, **George** (*b.* 1949) U.S. professional boxer. Winner of the world heavyweight championship title (1973–74), he made a comeback to regain the title in 1994 at the age of 45.

fore·mast /fáwr màst/; *nautical usage* /fáwrməst/ *n.* the mast nearest the front or bow of a vessel with two or more masts

fore·milk /fáwr mìlk/ *n.* the relatively low-fat milk with a high sugar content that is produced by a woman's breast at the beginning of a breast feed

fore·most /fáwr mōst/ *adj.* **1. CHIEF** most important or notable **2. FURTHEST FORWARD** nearest to the front ○ *the foremost section of the aircraft* ■ *adv.* **1. IN FIRST POSITION** most importantly, or in the most important position ○ *a partner who will put your interests foremost* **2. TO THE FRONT** at or toward the front [Old English *formest*, from *forma* "first" + -EST, but later understood as if from FORE and -MOST]

fore·moth·er /fáwr mùthər/ *n.* a woman ancestor, usually one who died long ago

fore·name /fáwr nàym/ *n.* = **first name**

fore·named /fáwr nàymd/ *adj.* previously named or mentioned (*formal*)

fore·noon /fáwr no͞on, fawr no͞on/ *n.* the period of time between dawn and noon or immediately before noon

fo·ren·sic /fə rénsik, -rénzik/ *adj.* **1. CRIME-SOLVING** relating to the application of science to decide questions arising from crime or litigation ○ *forensic evidence* **2. OF DEBATING** relating to debate and formal argumentation ○ *forensic oratory* [Mid-17thC. From Latin *forensis* "of legal proceedings," originally "of the forum (as a place of discussion)," from *forum* (see FORUM).] —**fo·ren·si·cal·i·ty** /fə rènsi kállətee, -rènzi-/ *n.* —**fo·ren·si·cal·ly** /-kəlee/ *adv.*

fo·ren·sic med·i·cine *n.* the branch of medicine that has a specifically legal purpose, e.g., establishing the cause of a death

fo·ren·sics /fə rénsiks, -rénziks/ *npl.* the practice or study of formal debate (*takes a singular or plural verb*)

fore·or·dain /fàwr awr dáyn/ (**-dained, -dain·ing, -dains**) *vt.* to arrange or determine an event in advance of its happening (*formal*) —**fore·or·dain·ment** *n.* —**fore·or·di·na·tion** /fàwr awrd'n áysh'n/ *n.*

fore·part /fáwr pàart/ *n.* **1. FRONT PART** the front part of something or the part of something in front **2. EARLY PART** the first or early part of a given period of time

fore·paw /fáwr pàw/ *n.* either of the two front feet of a land mammal that does not have hooves

fore·peak /fáwr peek/ *n.* the interior part of a vessel nearest the bow

fore·per·son /fáwr pùrs'n/ (*plural* **-per·sons** *or* **-peo·ple** /-peep'l/) *n.* **1. WORKER IN CHARGE OF OTHERS** a skilled worker who is in charge of a group of other workers, e.g., on a building site or in a factory **2.** LAW **JURY LEADER** somebody chosen by the other members of a jury to be their leader

fore plane *n.* a plane used in carpentry or joinery for preliminary smoothing, intermediate in size between a jack plane and a jointer plane

fore·play /fáwr plày/ *n.* mutual sexual stimulation that takes place before intercourse

fore·quar·ter /fáwr kwàwrtər/ *n.* **CARCASS PORTION** half of the front half of a pork, lamb, or beef carcass ■ **fore·quar·ters** *npl.* **FRONT PART OF ANIMAL** the front legs, shoulders, and adjoining parts of a horse or similar animal

fore·reach /fawr reech/ (**-reached, -reach·ing, -reach·es**) *v.* **1.** *vti.* **SAIL AHEAD** to gain on or pass another sailing vessel, especially when sailing into the wind **2.** *vi.* **MOVE ON WATER WITHOUT POWER** to continue moving in a ship after the sails have been taken down or the engine switched off

fore·run /fawr rún/ (**-ran** /-rán/, **-run, -run·ning, -runs**) *vt.* **1. HERALD** to serve as an indication of or anticipate something that is to happen (*formal*) **2. GO BEFORE** to go before something (*archaic*) **3. PREVENT** to prevent or forestall something (*archaic*)

fore·run·ner /fáwr rùnnər/ *n.* **1. PREDECESSOR** an earlier person or thing that had a role or function similar to somebody or something coming later ○ *the forerunner of the modern food processor* **2. SOMEBODY OR SOMETHING SHOWING FUTURE** somebody or something that brings news of or is an indication of what is to happen ○ *a forerunner of unsettled weather* **3. ONE AHEAD OF OTHERS** somebody or something that goes ahead of others, e.g., a skier who skis down a course just before the beginning of a race

fore·said /fáwr sèd/ *adj.* aforesaid (*archaic*)

fore·sail /fáwr sàyl/; *nautical usage* /fáwrs'l/ *n.* **1. MAIN SQUARE SAIL** the main square sail on the front mast of a square-rigged vessel **2. MAIN TRIANGULAR SAIL** the main or lowest triangular sail on a fore-and-aft-rigged vessel

fore·see /fawr sée/ (**-saw** /-sáw/, **-seen** /-seén/, **-see·ing, -sees**) *vti.* to know or expect that something is going to happen before it does ○ *He couldn't have foreseen the consequences of his scheme.* [Old English *foresēon*, literally "to see before"] —**fore·see·a·ble** *adj.* —**fore·se·er** *n.*

fore·shad·ow /fawr sháddō/ (**-owed, -ow·ing, -ows**) *vt.* to indicate or suggest something, usually something unpleasant, that is going to happen —**fore·shad·ow·er** *n.*

fore·shank /fáwr shàngk/ *n.* **1. TOP PART OF ANIMAL'S FRONT LEG** the upper part of either of the two front legs of a four-legged animal **2. CUT OF MEAT** a cut of meat taken from the foreshank of a lamb or sheep

fore·sheet /fáwr sheet/ *n.* **ROPE FOR FORESAIL** a rope used to keep a corner of a foresail in place ■ **fore·sheets** *npl.* **PART OF BOAT** the part of an open boat that lies forward of the structural member used as the foremost rower's seat

fore·shock /fáwr shòk/ *n.* a slight tremor or minor earthquake, often one of many and usually preceding a larger earthquake or volcanic eruption

fore·shore /fáwr shàwr/ *n.* **1. SHORE BETWEEN HIGH AND LOW WATERMARKS** the part of a shore that lies between the highest and lowest watermarks **2. DRY SHORE** the part of a shore between the high watermark and cultivated or economically exploited land

fore·short·en /fawr sháwrt'n/ (**-ened, -en·ing, -ens**) *vt.* **1. ABRIDGE** to make a text shorter (*formal*) **2. DRAWING SHOW SOMETHING SHORTER THAN IT IS** in drawing, to make something appear shorter than it actually is in order to create a three-dimensional effect on the basis of the laws of perspective

fore·show /fawr shṓ/ (**-showed, -shown** /-shṓn/, **-show·ing, -shows**) *vt.* to indicate something that is going to happen (*archaic*)

fore·sight /fáwr sìt/ *n.* **1. ABILITY TO THINK AHEAD** the ability to envision possible future problems or obstacles **2. PREMONITION** an act or instance of knowing something beforehand **3. LOOKING FORWARD** the act of looking forward **4. READING TAKEN IN SURVEYING** in surveying, an observation or measurement made looking forward **5. ARMS FRONT GUNSIGHT** the front sight on a gun —**fore·sight·ed** *adj.*

fore·skin /fáwr skìn/ *n.* a fold of skin that covers the end of the penis

for·est /fáwrəst/ *n.* **1. LARGE DENSE GROWTH OF TREES** a large area of land covered in trees and other plants growing close together, or the trees growing on it **2. WOODLAND FOR HUNTING** especially in former times, an area of woodland owned by a monarch and set aside for hunting **3. LARGE NUMBER OF UPRIGHT OBJECTS** a collection of often tall upright objects, densely packed and so resembling a forest of trees ○ *a forest of microphones* ■ *vt.* (**-est·ed, -est·ing, -ests**) **CREATE FOREST ON LAND** to plant an area with a large number of trees [13thC. Via Old French from late Latin *forestis (silva)*, literally "outside (woods)," from *foris* "out of doors" (see FOREIGN).] —**for·est·al** *adj.* —**for·est·ed** *adj.* —**fo·res·tial** /fə réschəl/ *adj.*

fore·stall /fawr stáwl/ (**-stalled, -stall·ing, -stalls**) *vt.* **1. PREVENT OR HINDER** to prevent or hinder somebody from doing something or something from happening by acting in advance **2. ANTICIPATE** to think of or do something beforehand (*archaic*) **3. COMM HINDER SALE OF** to stop or slow down sales of a product at a one-off event or market by buying that product in large quantities beforehand [14thC. From Old English *foresteall* "ambush," literally "position in front," from *steall* "standing position."] —**fore·stall·er** *n.* —**fore·stall·ment** *n.*

for·es·ta·tion /fàwrə stáysh'n/ *n.* the planting or incidence of trees over a large area

fore·stay /fáwr stày/ *n.* a rope or cable (**stay**) extending from the head of the foremast to the deck of a ship and used for supporting the mast

for·est·er /fáwrəstər/ *n.* **1. MANAGER OF FOREST** somebody engaged in forest management and conservation **2. FOREST DWELLER** a person or animal living in a forest (*archaic*) **3. INSECTS WOODLAND MOTH** a woodland moth that flies by day. Family: Zyglaenidae.

for·est floor *n.* the layer of organic matter on the ground in a forest

for·est green *adj.* of a dark green color, like the foliage on a pine tree ○ *forest-green uniforms* —**for·est green** *n.*

For·est Hills /fàwrəst-/ residential area in the borough of Queens, New York City, at the western end of Long Island. The U.S. Open tennis championship was held there until 1978.

for·est·land /fáwrəst lànd/ *n.* a piece of land covered with trees or set aside for the cultivation of trees

for·est o·ri·ole *n.* = **oriole**

for·est rang·er *n.* = **ranger** *n.* 1

for·est·ry /fáwrəstree/ *n.* **1. PLANTING AND GROWING TREES** the science or skill of planting and growing trees or managing forests **2. FOREST MANAGEMENT** the management of forests for profitable ends such as timber production **3. COMMERCIAL FORESTLAND** forestland, especially that planted and commercially managed rather than growing naturally

fore·taste *n.* /fáwr tàyst/ **SAMPLE OF FUTURE** a sample or indication of what is to come ■ *vt.* /fawr táyst, fáwr tàyst/ (**-tast·ed, -tast·ing, -tastes**) **HAVE FORETASTE OF** to have a sample or indication of what is to come

fore·tell /fawr tél/ (**-told** /fawr tṓld/, **-tell·ing, -tells**) *vt.* to predict what is going to happen, especially by means of supposed magic or supernatural powers (*literary*) —**fore·tell·er** *n.*

fore·thought /fáwr thàwt/ *n.* careful thought in order to be prepared for the future —**fore·thought·ful** *adj.* —**fore·thought·ful·ly** *adv.* —**fore·thought·ful·ness** *n.*

fore·time /fáwr tìm/ *n.* time before the present (*archaic*)

fore·to·ken *n.* /fáwr tòkən/ **WARNING SIGN** a warning sign of what is to come (*literary*) ■ *vt.* /fawr tṓkən/ (**-kened, -ken·ing, -kens**) **WARN OF** to be or give a warning sign of what is to come (*literary*)

fore·told past participle, past tense of **foretell**

fore·top /fáwr tòp/; *nautical usage* /fáwtəp/ *n.* a platform at the top of a ship's foremast

fore·top·gal·lant /fàwr top gállənt/; *nautical usage* /fàwtəp gállənt/ *adj.* relating to the section of a mast directly above the foremast

fore·top·mast /fawr tóp màst/; *nautical usage* /fàwr tópməst/ *n.* the mast above the platform at the top of a ship's foremast

fore·top·sail /fawr tóp sàyl/; *nautical usage* /fawr tóps'l/ *n.* a sail attached to the mast above the platform at the top of a ship's foremast

for·ev·er /faw révvər, fə-/ *adv.* **1. FOR ALL TIME** for all future time **2. FOR VERY LONG TIME** for a very long time, or what seems to be a very long time (*informal*) ○ *If we wait for him, we'll be here forever.* **3. CONSTANTLY** regularly or constantly, and often annoyingly (*informal*) **4. AT ALL TIMES** at all times or on every occasion (*literary*) ○ *From that moment on, she was forever careful.* [13thC. From *for ever*, not used as one word until the late 17thC.]

for·ev·er·more /faw rèvvər máwr, fə-/ *adv.* from now on and for all time (*literary*)

fore·warn /fawr wáwrn/ (**-warned, -warn·ing, -warns**) *vt.* to warn somebody about something that is going to happen (*often passive*) —**fore·warn·er** *n.* —**fore·warn·ing·ly** *adv.*

fore·wing /fáwr wìng/ *n.* either of the pair of front wings on a four-winged insect

fore·wom·an /fáwr wŏŏmmən/ (*plural* **-en** /-wìmmin/) *n.* **1. WOMAN IN CHARGE OF OTHER WORKERS** a woman who is in charge of a group of workers, e.g., on a construction site or in a factory **2. LAW WOMAN JURY LEADER** a woman chosen by the other members of a jury to be their leader

fore·word /fáwr wùrd, fáwrwərd/ *n.* an introductory note, essay, or chapter in a book, often written by somebody other than the author

fore·yard /fáwr yaàrd/ *n.* the lowest spar for supporting a sail on a foremast

for·feit /fáwrfət/ *n.* **1. GIVING SOMETHING UP** the act or an instance of giving something up or being deprived of something as a punishment **2. PENALTY FOR WRONGDOING** something that is taken away as a punishment or has to be given up to make up for a mistake or wrongdoing **3. LAW PENALTY FOR BREAKING LAW** something that is taken away as a penalty for breaking a law or contract **4. LEISURE PENALTY IN GAME** an object that a player must give up or a task that a player must perform as a penalty in a game ■ *adj.* **TAKEN AWAY AS PUNISHMENT** taken away or given up as a punishment for a mistake or wrongdoing ■ *vt.* (**-feit·ed, -feit·ing, -feits**) **1. LOSE** to lose something or have something taken away as punishment for a mistake or wrongdoing ○ *forfeit the right to your inheritance* **2. GIVE UP** to give something up willingly in order to pursue or obtain something else ○ *forfeited her inheritance and married outside her parents' faith* **3. LAW TAKE AWAY AS PENALTY** to take something away as a penalty for breaking a law or contract [13thC. From Old French *forfet*, past participle of *forfaire* "to commit a crime," literally "to do beyond," from *fors* "beyond," from Latin *foris* (see FOREIGN).] —**for·feit·a·ble** *adj.* —**for·feit·er** *n.*

for·feits *n.* LEISURE a game in which a player must give something up or perform a task each time he or she commits a fault or loses a round (*takes a singular verb*)

for·fei·ture /fáwrfə chŏŏr, fáwrfəchər/ *n.* LAW **1. SOMETHING FORFEITED** something that has been taken away or has had to be given up as a penalty for breaking a law or contract **2. GIVING SOMETHING UP** the act of forfeiting something

for·fend /fawr fénd/ (**-fend·ed, -fend·ing, -fends**), **fore·fend** (**-fend·ed, -fend·ing, -fends**) *v.* (*archaic*) **1.** *vti.* **PREVENT SOMETHING HAPPENING** to protect or secure against something happening ○ *Heaven forfend that I should end up like that!* **2.** *vt.* **FORBID** to forbid or prohibit something [14thC. Literally "to fend before," formed from FEND.]

for·gath·er /fawr gáthər/ (**-ered, -er·ing, -ers**), **fore·gath·er** (**-ered, -er·ing, -ers**) *vi.* (*formal*) **1. ASSEMBLE AS GROUP** to come together as a group **2. MEET BY CHANCE** to meet, usually by chance **3. ASSOCIATE WITH** to spend time socially with somebody [15thC. By folk etymology (by association with GATHER) from Dutch *vorgaderen* "to meet, assemble."]

for·gave past tense of **forgive**

forge[1] /fawrj/ *n.* **1. METAL WORKSHOP** a workshop where metal is heated and shaped into objects by hammering **2. FURNACE FOR HEATING METAL** a furnace used to heat metal to a very high temperature **3. MACHINE FOR HAMMERING METAL** a machine with two tool faces that are brought together to hammer pieces of metal into specific shapes ■ *v.* (**forged, forg·ing, forg·es**) **1.** *vti.* **MAKE ILLEGAL COPY OF SOMETHING** to make or produce an illegal copy of something so that it looks genuine, usually for financial gain **2.** *vt.* **ESTABLISH WITH EFFORT** to establish and strive to develop something with great effort ○ *forge a durable relationship with the community* **3.** *vt.* **SHAPE METAL** to shape or form metal by heating and hammering it [13thC. From French *forger* "to make," from Latin *fabricare* (source of English *fabricate*).] —**forge·a·bil·i·ty** /fàwrjə bíllətee/ *n.* —**forge·a·ble** /fáwrjəb'l/ *adj.*

forge[2] /fawrj/ (**forged, forg·ing, forg·es**) *vi.* **1. MOVE FORWARD** to move forward with a sudden increase of speed ○ *forging past the runner on the inside* **2. MAKE PROGRESS** to move slowly and steadily ○ *"We were forging through a narrow passage, rock-lined, and tube-like."* (Edgar Rice Burroughs, *The Gods of Mars*; 1913) [Mid-18thC. Origin uncertain: perhaps an alteration of FORCE.]

forge ahead *vi.* to move forward rapidly or steadily and persistently

forg·er /fáwrjər/ *n.* somebody who makes or produces illegal copies, e.g., of documents or signatures, usually for financial gain

for·ger·y /fáwrjəree/ (*plural* **-ies**) *n.* **1. COPYING SOMETHING ILLEGALLY** the act of making or producing an illegal copy of something so that it looks genuine, usually for financial gain **2. ILLEGAL COPY** an illegal copy of something, e.g., a document or painting, that has been made to look genuine

for·get /fər gét/ (**-got** /-gót/, **-got·ten** /-gótt'n/, **-get·ting, -gets**) *v.* **1.** *vti.* **NOT REMEMBER** to fail or be unable to remember something ○ *I'll never forget my first day in school.* **2.** *vt.* **LEAVE BEHIND** to leave something behind accidentally ○ *I've forgotten my keys.* **3.** *vti.* **NEGLECT SOMEBODY OR SOMETHING** to fail to give due attention to somebody or something ○ *Don't just disappear and forget about us all.* **4.** *vt.* **STOP WORRYING** to stop thinking or worrying about somebody or something ○ *I'd just forget about it if I were you.* **5.** *vti.* **NOT**

MENTION to fail to mention somebody or something **6.** *vr.* **LOSE CONTROL OF** to lose control of your manners, emotions, or behavior ○ *Oh dear, I'm forgetting myself! Let me take your coat.* [Old English *forgietan*, literally "to miss your hold on," from a prehistoric Germanic word that is also the ancestor of English *get*] —**for·get·ter** *n.* ◇ **forget it 1.** used to let somebody know that something is not really very important and so not worth worrying about (*informal*) **2.** used to tell somebody that you are definitely not going to do something that has been suggested, proposed, or asked of you (*informal*)

WORD KEY: SYNONYMS

See Synonyms at ***neglect.***

for·get·ful /fər gétfəl/ *adj.* **1. ABSENT-MINDED** tending to forget things **2. NEGLECTFUL** not giving due attention to somebody or something (*formal*) ○ *forgetful of his contractual obligations* **3. CAUSING FORGETFULNESS** causing somebody to forget something (*archaic literary*) —**for·get·ful·ly** *adv.* —**for·get·ful·ness** *n.*

Forget-me-not

for·get-me-not *n.* a small herbaceous plant of the borage family that has small delicate pale blue flowers. Genus: *Myosotis.* [A translation of Old French *ne m'oubliez mie*, because the flower was worn by lovers]

for·get·ta·ble /fər géttəb'l/ *adj.* not easily remembered or not worthy of being remembered

for·give /fər gív/ (**-gave** /fər gáyv/, **-giv·en** /fər gívvən/, **-giv·ing, -gives**) *v.* **1.** *vti.* **STOP BEING ANGRY ABOUT SOMETHING** to stop being angry about or resenting somebody or somebody's behavior **2.** *vt.* **PARDON** to excuse somebody for a mistake, misunderstanding, wrongdoing, or an inappropriateness **3.** *vt.* **CANCEL OBLIGATION** to cancel an obligation, such as a debt [Old English *forgiefan*, literally "to abstain from giving." The underlying idea is of giving up resentment or a claim.] —**for·giv·a·ble** *adj.* —**for·giv·a·bly** *adv.* —**for·giv·er** *n.*

for·give·ness /fər gívnəss/ *n.* **1. ACT OF PARDONING SOMEBODY** the act of pardoning somebody for a mistake or wrongdoing **2. FORGIVING QUALITY** the tendency to forgive offenses readily and easily ○ *She had little forgiveness in her nature.* [Old English *forgiefenes*, formed from the past participle of *forgiefan* (see FORGIVE). Etymologically "forgiven-ness."]

for·giv·ing /fər gívving/ *adj.* **1. INCLINED TO FORGIVE** willing to forgive, especially in most circumstances **2. ALLOWING FOR DEGREE OF IMPERFECTION** allowing for or coping well with a degree of imprecision, lack of skill, or other imperfection ○ *You'll have to improve your technique or get a more forgiving fishing rod.* —**for·giv·ing·ly** *adv.* —**for·giv·ing·ness** *n.*

for·go /fawr gṓ/ (**-went** /fawr wént/, **-gone** /fawr gón/, **-going, -goes**), **fore·go** (**-went, -gone, -going, -goes**) *vt.* to do without something, especially voluntarily ○ *forgo the comforts of home while traveling* [Old English *forgan*, literally "to go away from, pass by"]

for·got past tense of **forget**

for·got·ten past participle of **forget**

for·got·ten man (*plural* **fore·got·ten men**) *n.* **1. FORMER PROMINENT FIGURE** a once prominent man no longer in the news or the public's awareness **2. WAGE EARNER** during the Great Depression, an average worker considered by some to be deprived and ignored by the federal government

Fo·ril·lon Na·tion·al Park /fawri yàwN-/ national park and wildlife sanctuary on the Gaspe Peninsula, Quebec, Canada, in the gulf of St. Lawrence. Area: 93 sq. mi./240 sq. km.

for in·stance *n.* an example of something (*informal*) ○ *Give me a for instance.*

fo·rint /fáwrint/ *n.* **1.** see table at **currency 2. FORINT COIN** a coin worth one forint [Mid-20thC. From Hungarian, from Italian *fiorino* "florin" (see FLORIN).]

fork /fawrk/ *n.* **1. UTENSIL FOR EATING** a small, usually metal utensil with a handle and two, three, or four prongs, used for picking up food for eating or turning food in cooking **2. GARDEN OR AGRICULTURAL TOOL** a garden or agricultural tool with a handle and usually three or four prongs. It is used for digging, lifting, and turning over. **3. DIVIDING POINT IN ROAD OR RIVER** the point where a road or river divides into two or more parts **4. BRANCH OF ROAD OR RIVER** one of the branches that a road or river divides into **5.** TECH **PART OF MACHINE** a part of a machine or device that has prongs or is fork-shaped **6.** CHESS **CHESS POSITION** a chess position in which two pieces are under attack from one of the opponent's pieces, usually the knight **7.** METEOROL **FLASH OF LIGHTNING** a branch or flash of forked lightning ■ *v.* (**forked, fork·ing, forks**) **1.** *vti.* **MOVE WITH FORK** to carry, pick up, dig, or turn something over using a fork **2.** *vi.* **DIVIDE INTO TWO** to split into two or more branches (*refers to roads and rivers*) **3.** *vi.* **GO ALONG FORK** to take one of the branches that a road or river has divided into **4.** *vt.* **CAUSE TO BRANCH** to make something into a shape that branches in two **5.** *vt.* CHESS **MOVE PIECE IN CHESS** to position a piece so that it is threatening two of the opponent's pieces at the same time [Old English *forca*, via prehistoric Germanic from Latin *furca* "pitchfork" (source of English *bifurcate*] — **fork·er** *n.* —**fork·ful** /fáwrk fo͝ol/ *n.*

fork over, fork out, fork up *vti.* to pay the money required for something or spend a lot of money, often grudgingly (*informal*)

fork·ball /fáwrk bàwl/ *n.* in baseball, a pitch in which the ball is held between the spread index and middle finger. It usually dips sharply before reaching the batter. —**fork·ball·er** *n.*

forked /fawrkt/ *adj.* divided into two or more branches —**fork·ed·ly** *adv.* —**forked·ness** *n.*

forked light·ning *n. U.K.* = **chain lightning**

forked tongue *n.* a tongue that speaks lies or words that are insincere or misleading (*literary or humorous*)

fork·lift /fáwrk lìft/ *n.* **1. LIFTING DEVICE** a lifting device with two long rigid steel bars that can be raised and lowered, used especially to move pallets loaded with boxes or other goods **2.** = **forklift truck** ■ *vt.* (**-lift·ed, -lift·ing, -lifts**) **LIFT HEAVY GOODS** to lift or move heavy loads using a forklift

Forklift truck

fork·lift truck *n.* a small motor-driven vehicle equipped with a forklift, used especially in factories for moving goods on pallets

for·lorn /fər láwrn, fawr-/ *adj.* **1. LONELY AND MISERABLE** lonely and miserable, as though deserted or abandoned **2. DESOLATE** deserted or abandoned and showing signs of neglect **3. HOPELESS** desperate and doomed to failure (*literary*) **4. DEPRIVED** deprived of something (*archaic literary*) ○ *"My only strength and stay: forlorn of thee, Whither shall I betake me, where subsist?"* (John Milton, *Paradise Lost*; 1667) [Old English *forloren*, originally the past participle of *forlēosan*, literally "to lose completely"] —**for·lorn·ly** *adv.* — **for·lorn·ness** *n.*

for·lorn hope *n.* **1. FUTILE HOPE** a desperate or futile hope **2. DESPERATE UNDERTAKING** a desperate or doomed undertaking **3.** MIL **SOLDIERS ON DESPERATE MISSION** a group of soldiers sent on a very dangerous if not hopeless mission [By folk etymology from Dutch *forloren hoop*, literally "lost troop"]

form /fawrm/ *n.* **1. BASIC STRUCTURE** the nature, structure, or essence of a thing, considered apart from its content, color, texture, or composition **2. MANIFESTATION** the particular way that something is or appears to be ○ *bonuses in the form of extra days off or cash payments* **3. VARIETY OF SOMETHING** a type or kind of something that has various different types or kinds ○ *Friction is a form of energy.* **4. SHAPE OF SOMETHING** the shape or appearance of a thing that makes it identifiable ○ *a constellation in the form of a diamond* **5. INDISTINCT SHAPE** a shape like a person or other living thing that cannot be clearly made out ○ *a shadowy form in the distance* **6. DOCUMENT** a document, usually with blank spaces for answers or information to be supplied ○ *fill out the form* **7. CONDITION OF SOMEBODY OR SOMETHING** the condition of an organization, team, performer, athlete, or animal, with regard to fitness, health, and ability to perform well ○ *a violinist at the top of her form.* **8.** SPORTS **TRACK RECORD** the previous record of a horse, athlete, or team **9.** ARTS **OUTLINE STRUCTURE** the structure, design, or arrangement of a work of art or piece of writing, as opposed to its content **10.** ARTS **MODE OF EXPRESSION** a fixed mode of literary or musical expression ○ *a strict adherence to sonata form* **11. MOLD OR FRAME** a mold, frame, or model within which or around which something can be shaped ○ *concrete forms* **12.** BIOL **SUBDIVISION OF VARIETY** a subdivision of a classification of organisms, usually indicating a minor difference among members, e.g., in color **13. BEHAVIOR** behavior or manners with reference to propriety ○ *It's considered bad form to cheat at games.* **14. FORMULA** a fixed set of words or procedures, e.g., in a religious ceremony or a legal document **15.** CLOTHES **HUMAN SHAPE** a model of a human body or torso, used for fitting or displaying clothes **16.** FURNITURE **BENCH** a long low wooden seat or bench with no back rest **17.** PRINTING **PRINTING TEMPLATE** a body of typographic elements assembled in a chase in preparation for printing **18.** ZOOL **HARE'S LAIR** the lair or nest in which a hare lives **19.** LING **WORD IN RELATION TO ITS ROOT** a word considered in relation to its root or the word it is derived from **20.** LING **LOOK OR SOUND OF WORD** the way a word is written or how it sounds, as opposed to its meaning **21.** *U.K.* EDUC **BRITISH SCHOOL GRADE** British school grade ■ *v.* (**formed, form·ing, forms**) **1.** *vti.* **GIVE SHAPE TO SOMETHING** to give a shape or arrangement to something, or take shape ○ *A circle of onlookers formed around the injured man.* **2.** *vti.* **START TO EXIST** to cause something to develop or exist, or begin to develop or exist, especially as part of a natural process ○ *Crystals began to form at the bottom of the jar.* **3.** *vt.* **MAKE** to make or construct something, often by arranging or combining component parts ○ *The plural is formed by adding an "s."* **4.** *vt.* **CONCEIVE OF** to develop an opinion, impression, or idea in the mind ○ *not enough information to form an opinion* **5.** *vt.* **CAUSE TO DEVELOP** to influence somebody strongly through teaching, discipline, or example, and cause a particular personal development ○ *an early life in the country that formed his quiet nature* **6.** *vt.* **CREATE** to acquire or establish and develop something intangible, such as a habit or relationship ○ *form an alliance with other family members* **7.** *vt.* **SERVE AS** to constitute or be a basic element or characteristic of something ○ *a mountain range forming a natural boundary between the two countries* **8.** *vt.* **SET UP** to establish something, e.g., a structure ○ *form a fan club* [13thC. Via French *forme* from Latin *forma* "mold, shape, beauty" (source of English *formal*, *formula* and *uniform*).] —**form·a·ble** *adj.* ◇ **take form** to become visible, distinct, or discernible ○ *A plan started to take form in his mind.* ◇ **true to form** as could be expected judging from somebody's past behavior ○ *True to form, she was exactly twenty minutes late.*

-form *suffix.* having a particular form ○ *fibriform* [From Latin *forma* "form"]

for·mal /fáwrm'l/ *adj.* **1. CONVENTIONALLY CORRECT** characterized by or organized in accordance with conventions governing ceremony, behavior, or dress ○ *He's terribly formal* **2. OFFICIAL** done or carried out in accordance with established or prescribed rules ○ *We made a formal protest.* **3. METHODICAL** done in an organized and precise manner ○ *We don't have the skills in this lab to do formal research in artificial intelligence.* **4. NOT FAMILIAR IN STYLE** used in serious, official, or public communication but not appropriate in everyday contexts ○ *a formal word* **5.** CLOTHES **ELEGANT TO WEAR** suitable to wear for an important occasion, e.g., a tuxedo for men and a long dress or gown for women ○ *formal dress required* **6.** EDUC **ACQUIRED IN SCHOOL OR COLLEGE** undertaken or acquired by study in an educational institution, e.g., a school, college, or university ○ *no formal training as a journalist* **7. ORDERED** arranged or laid out in a regular, ordered, or symmetrical way ○ *a formal garden* **8. OF FORM OF SOMETHING** relating to the form of something **9. OFFICIALLY CONSTITUTED** officially constituted or organized as opposed to spontaneously developed ○ *a formal organization* **10.** LOGIC, MATH **SYMBOLIC** relating to or using symbols and abstract structures rather than natural language **11.** PHILOS **OF ESSENCE RATHER THAN CONTENT** relating to the structure or essence of something rather than its content ■ *n.* **1. IMPORTANT OCCASION** an important social or ceremonial occasion **2. CLOTHES** an outfit of clothing for an important social occasion, especially a woman's full-length dress ○ *a new formal for the prom* [14thC. From Latin *formalis*, from *forma* (see FORM).] —**for·mal·ly** *adv.* —**for·mal·ness** *n.*

for·mal·de·hyde /fawr máldə hīd/ *n.* a colorless gas with a distinctive smell that is used in making resins and fertilizers and that, when dissolved in water, gives a solution in which organic specimens are preserved. Formula: HCHO. [Late 19thC. Coined from FORMIC + ALDEHYDE.]

for·ma·lin /fáwrməlin/ *n.* a solution of formaldehyde in water, used as a disinfectant and for preserving organic specimens [Late 19thC. Coined from FORMALDEHYDE + -IN.]

for·mal·ism /fáwrm'l ìzzəm/ *n.* **1.** RELIG, ARTS **EMPHASIS ON OUTWARD APPEARANCE** a strong or excessive emphasis on outward appearance or form instead of content or meaning **2.** PHILOS, MATH **THEORY OF SYMBOLS** the view that mathematical symbols are meaningless, though mathematical concepts and structures can be valuable **3.** THEATER **STYLIZATION** stylization and emphasis on symbolism in theatrical productions —**for·mal·ist** *n.* —**for·mal·is·tic** /fàwrm'l ístik/ *adj.* —**for·mal·is·ti·cal·ly** /-kəlee/ *adv.*

for·mal·i·ty /fawr mállətee/ (*plural* **-ties**) *n.* **1. FORMALNESS** the quality or condition of being formal, or the degree to which something is formal ○ *dress to suit the formality of the occasion* **2. OFFICIAL PROCEDURE** an official procedure that must be followed as part of a longer procedure or event (*often used in the plural*) ○ *several formalities to complete at customs* **3. NECESSARY BUT INSIGNIFICANT PROCEDURE** a procedure that must be followed because it is a rule or custom, but has little significance or effect in itself ○ *just a formality* **4. ATTENTION TO PROPRIETY** strict or excessive attention to propriety or ceremony

for·mal·ize /fáwrm'l īz/ (**-ized, -iz·ing, -iz·es**) *v.* **1.** *vt.* **MAKE OFFICIAL** to make something official or valid, often by deciding on the details and then signing a document **2.** *vt.* **GIVE SHAPE TO** to give a particular shape or form to something **3.** *vti.* **MAKE SOMETHING FORMAL** to make something formal or more formal ○ *a formalized version of his earlier account* —**for·mal·iz·a·ble** *adj.* —**for·mal·i·za·tion** /fàwrm'li záysh'n/ *n.* —**for·mal·iz·er** /fáwrm'l īzər/ *n.*

for·mal log·ic *n.* PHILOS the branch of logic concerned with the formal methods of deducing conclusions from propositions

for·mal meth·ods *npl.* methods of specifying and evaluating computer systems that draw on techniques from mathematics and logic

for·mal·wear /fáwrm'l wàir/ *n.* clothes suitable for an important occasion, e.g., a tuxedo for men and a long dress or gown for women

for·mant /fáwrmənt/ *n.* a frequency range where vowel sounds are at their most distinctive and characteristic pitch [Early 20thC. Via German from Latin *formant-*, present participle stem of *formare*, from *forma* (see FORM).]

for·mat /fáwr màt/ *n.* **1. STRUCTURE** the way in which something is presented, organized, or arranged ○ *change the format of the conference to accommodate more speakers* **2.** PUBL **LAYOUT** the layout and presentation of a publication, including its size, and the type of paper and type used ○ *a small-format reference work* **3.** COMPUT **DATA ORGANIZATION** the structure or organization of digital data for storing, printing, or displaying ○ *files in ASCII format* ■ *vt.* (**-mat·ted, -mat·ting, -mats**) **1. ARRANGE LAYOUT OF** to arrange the layout or organization of something **2.** COMPUT **ORGANIZE DISK FOR DATA STORAGE** to organize a disk in such a way that data can be stored on it [Mid-19thC. Via French and German from Latin *formatus (liber)* "(book) shaped (in a special way)," from *formare* (see FORMANT).]

for·mate /fáwr màyt/ *n.* any salt or ester of formic acid [Early 19thC. Coined from FORMIC + -ATE.]

for·ma·tion /fawr máysh'n/ *n.* **1. DEVELOPMENT** the process by which something develops or takes a particular shape ○ *a strong influence on the formation of her character* **2. CREATION** the process of creating something or coming into existence ○ *the formation of a bipartisan legislative committee* **3. SHAPE OF SOMETHING** the shape or structure that something develops into ○ *interesting cloud formations* **4. FORMAL PATTERN** the pattern into which a number of people or things is arranged ○ *Twelve planes flew past in formation.* **5.** GEOL **ROCK UNIT** a unit of rock consisting of a succession of strata or an igneous intrusion —**for·ma·tion·al** *adj.*

form·a·tive /fáwrmətiv/ *adj.* **1. INFLUENTIAL** important and influential, particularly in the shaping or development of character ○ *during their formative years* **2.** LING **USED TO FORM WORDS** relating to or used in the formation of derived words or inflected forms of words ■ *n.* LING **WORD-FORMING ELEMENT** an element such as a suffix or prefix used in the formation of derived words or inflected forms of words —**form·a·tive·ly** *adv.*

form·a·tive as·sess·ment *n.* EDUC the assessment at regular intervals of a student's progress with accompanying feedback in order to help to improve the student's performance

form class *n.* **1.** LING **PART OF SPEECH** a part of speech **2. SET OF WORDS** a group of words with one or more grammatical characteristics in common

form crit·i·cism *n.* **1.** LITERAT **LITERARY CRITICISM** textual criticism that examines the literary conventions used in order to discover the origin and history of a text or its creators **2.** BIBLE **BIBLE SCHOLARSHIP** a method of analyzing the Bible to determine the presumed original oral form of the written text by removing known historical conventions that emerged at a later period —**form crit·ic** *n.* —**form crit·i·cal** *adj.*

forme /fawrm/ *n. U.K.* PRINTING = **form** n. 17 [15thC. Variant of FORM.]

for·mer[1] /fáwrmər/ *adj.* **1. PREVIOUS** occurring at or existing in an earlier time or period ○ *met her on a former occasion* **2. HAVING BEEN SOMETHING** having had the name or status specified during an earlier period ○ *the former Soviet Union* **3. FIRST OF TWO** being the first of two things or people mentioned **4. PRECEDING** earlier or near the beginning of a text or list ○ *a conclusion inconsistent with the argument in the former part of the paper* ■ *n.* **THE FIRST OF TWO** the first of two things or people mentioned ○ *Smith and Brown are both married, the former three years ago and the latter eighteen months ago* [12thC. Literally "more first," formed from Old English *forma* "first," literally "most before," from a prehistoric Germanic word that is also the ancestor of English *fore*.]

for·mer[2] /fáwrmər/ *n.* **1. SHAPER OF SOMETHING** somebody or something that forms, creates, or shapes something **2.** *U.K.* **SCHOOL STUDENT** a member of a British school grade (*always used in combination*) ○ *a sixth former* **3.** ELEC ENG **SHAPING TOOL** a tool used for giving the correct shape to an electrical coil or winding

for·mer·ly /fáwrmərlee/ *adv.* during or at an earlier period, but no longer

for·mes·tane *n.* a drug used to treat certain breast cancers that works by blocking the formation of the estrogen needed for the growth of the tumor

form·fit·ting /fáwrm fìtting/ *adj.* fitting tightly around the contours of the body ○ *formfitting sportswear*

form ge·nus *n.* an artificial taxonomic category based on similarities that may be superficial. Imperfect fungi and fragmented plant fossils are grouped in form genera.

for·mic /fáwrmik/ *adj.* **1.** ZOOL **OF ANTS** relating to ants **2.** CHEM **OF FORMIC ACID** relating to or containing formic acid [Late 18thC. Formed from Latin *formica* "ant."]

For·mi·ca /fawr mīkə/ *tdmk.* a trademark for a strong plastic laminate sheeting that is durable and easy to clean, and is often used to cover work surfaces, e.g., in kitchens

for·mic ac·id *n.* a colorless corrosive liquid that occurs naturally in ants and some plants. It is commonly used in the paper and textile industries and in the manufacture of insecticides and refrigerants. Formula: HCOOH.

for·mi·car·y /fáwrmi kèrree/ (*plural* **-ies**), **for·mi·car·i·um** /fàwrmi káiree əm/ (*plural* **-a** /-ə/) *n.* an ant hill, including its subterranean passages (*technical*) [Early 19thC. From medieval Latin *formicarium*, from Latin *formica* "ant."]

for·mi·ca·tion /fàwrmi káysh'n/ *n.* a neurologically based hallucination in which somebody feels as if insects are crawling on his or her skin. It is found in some cases of chemical toxicity and among drug and alcohol abusers. [Early 18thC. From the Latin stem *formication-*, from *formicare* "to crawl like an ant," from *formica* "ant."]

for·mi·da·ble /fáwrmədəb'l, fər míddəb'l, fàwr míddəb'l/ *adj.* **1. DIFFICULT TO DEAL WITH** difficult to deal with or overcome ○ *a formidable task* **2. AWE-INSPIRING** inspiring respect or wonder because of size, strength, or ability ○ *a formidable display of skill* **3. FRIGHTENING** causing fear, dread, or alarm [14thC. Directly or via French from Latin *formidabilis*, from *formidare* "to fear," from *formido* "terror."] —**for·mi·da·bil·i·ty** /fàwrmədə bíllətee, fər míddə bíllətee, fàwr míddə bíllətee/ *n.* —**for·mi·da·ble·ness** /fáwrmədəbəlnəss, fər míddəbəlnəss, fàwr míddəbəlnəss/ *n.* —**for·mi·da·bly** /-blee/ *adv.*

form·less /fáwrmləss/ *adj.* **1. SHAPELESS** lacking a clear shape or structure ○ *a formless figure in the mist* **2. DISORGANIZED** lacking apparent organization or structure **3. NOT MATERIAL** existing without a physical form ○ *formless beings* —**form·less·ly** *adv.* —**form·less·ness** *n.*

form let·ter *n.* a printed letter that is sent out to a large number of people, e.g., one dealing with a frequently arising complaint, or one used in advertising

for·mu·la /fáwrmyələ/ (*plural* **-las** *or* **-lae** /fáwrmyə lèe/) *n.* **1. PLAN OR METHOD** a plan for or method of doing something ○ *draw up a peace formula between two countries* **2. METHOD OF DOING SOMETHING** a prescribed and more or less invariable way of doing something to achieve a particular end **3. ESTABLISHED FORM OF WORDS** an established and recognized form of words, e.g., in a ceremony or legal document **4.** CHEM **SET OF SYMBOLS REPRESENTING CHEMICAL COMPOSITION** a representation of the chemical composition of a chemical compound using symbols to represent the types of atom involved **5.** MATH, PHYS **RULE EXPRESSED IN SYMBOLS** a rule or principle represented in symbols, numbers, or letters, often in the form of an equation ○ *a formula for calculating the distance between planets* **6. for·mu·la, For·mu·la** MOTOR SPORTS **CATEGORY OF RACING CAR** a category of racing car according to technical specifications such as engine capacity, size, and weight, used as a basis for professional competition (*usually used in combination*) ○ *formula one racing* **7.** FOOD **MILK FOR BABIES** a preparation used as an alternative to human breast milk and intended to provide all the nutrients an infant requires [Early 17thC. From Latin, literally "little form," from *forma* (see FORM).]

for·mu·la·ic /fàwrmyə láy ik/ *adj.* **1. EXPRESSED AS FORMULA** having the nature of or expressed in terms of a formula **2. UNORIGINAL** unoriginal and reliant on previous models or ideas ○ *His writing is stilted and formulaic.* —**for·mu·la·i·cal·ly** /fàwrmyə láy ikəlee/ *adv.*

for·mu·la·rize /fáwrmyələ rīz/ (**-rized, -riz·ing, -riz·es**) *vt.* = **formulate** *v.* 5 —**for·mu·la·ri·za·tion** /fàwrmyələri záysh'n/ *n.* —**for·mu·la·riz·er** /fáwrmyələ rīzər/ *n.*

for·mu·lar·y /fáwrmyə lèrree/ *n.* (*plural* **-ies**) **1.** PHARM **PHARMACEUTICAL REFERENCE BOOK** a reference book containing a list of pharmaceutical products with details of their use, preparation, properties, and formulas **2.** RELIG **RELIGIOUS WRITINGS** a book or collection of writings or procedures, especially ones connected with a Church **3. FIXED FORMULA** a fixed formula for doing something or dealing with something (*archaic or technical*) ■ *adj.* **OF FORMULA** relating to or having the nature of a formula

for·mu·late /fáwrmyə làyt/ (**-lat·ed, -lat·ing, -lates**) *vt.* **1. DEVISE** to draw something up carefully and in detail ○ *formulated his plan* **2. EXPRESS** to express or communicate something carefully or in specific words ○ *formulate an opinion* **3.** CHEM **PREPARE** to mix or prepare something according to a specific formula **4.** CHEM **DEVELOP FORMULA FOR** to develop a formula for the preparation of something **5.** MATH, PHYS **EXPRESS IN FORMULA** to express something by means of a formula —**for·mu·la·tion** /fàwrmyə láysh'n/ *n.* — **for·mu·la·tor** /fáwrmyə làytər/ *n.*

for·mu·la weight *n.* = **molecular weight**

for·mu·lism /fáwrmyə lìzzəm/ *n.* a belief in or reliance on formulas, especially inadequate or obsolete ones —**for·mu·list** *n., adj.* —**for·mu·lis·tic** /fàwrmyə lístik/ *adj.*

for·mu·lize /fáwrmyə lìz/ (**-lized, -liz·ing, -liz·es**) *vt.* = **formulate** *v.* 5 —**for·mu·li·za·tion** /fàwrmyəli záysh'n/ *n.*

form word *n.* = **function word**

form·work /fáwrm wùrk/ *n.* a structure generally made of timber in which liquid concrete is placed, compacted, and allowed to harden

for·myl /fáwr mìl/ *n.* a chemical group containing carbon, hydrogen, and oxygen. Formula: HCO. [Mid-19thC. Coined from FORMIC + -YL.]

for·ni·cate[1] /fáwrni kàyt/ (**-cat·ed, -cat·ing, -cates**) *vi.* to have sexual intercourse outside marriage [Mid-16thC. Ultimately from ecclesiastical Latin *fornicari*, from the Latin stem *fornic-* "arch" (see FORNIX), later "brothel" because prostitutes in Rome solicited under building arches.] —**for·ni·ca·tor** *n.*

for·ni·cate[2] /fáwrnikət, fáwrni kàyt/, **for·ni·cat·ed** /fáwrni kàytəd/ *adj.* with an arched, vaulted, or bending form [Early 19thC. From Latin *fornicatus*, from the stem *fornic-* (see FORNIX).]

for·ni·ca·tion /fàwrni káysh'n/ *n.* **1. COMMIT FORNICATION** to commit fornication **2.** LAW **CONSENTING SEX INVOLVING SOMEBODY UNMARRIED** sexual intercourse between two consenting adults, who are not married **3.** BIBLE **SEXUAL BEHAVIOR CONSIDERED IMMORAL** in the Bible, sexual intercourse between a man and woman who are not married, or any form of sexual behavior considered to be immoral

for·nix /fáwrniks/ (*plural* **-ni·ces** /fáwrni seèz/) *n.* ANAT a structure or fold in the shape of an arch, especially either of two bands of white fibers that meet at the base of the brain [Late 17thC. From Latin (stem *fornic-*), "arch, vault," of uncertain origin: probably from *furnus* "oven with an arched shape" (source of English *furnace*).]

for-prof·it *adj.* established or designed to make a profit

For·rest /fáwrəst, fawr-/, **Edwin** (1806–72) U.S. stage actor, known for his powerful tragedy acting. He encouraged drama writing in the United States by offering prize money for plays.

For·rest, Nathan Bedford (1821–77) U.S. general. He was one of the Confederacy's most daring cavalry commanders during the Civil War.

For·res·tal /fáwrəstəl, -stàwl/, **James Vincent** (1892–1949) U.S. public official. He was U.S. secretary of the navy (1944–47) and the first secretary of defense (1947–49).

for·sake /fər sáyk, fawr-/ (**-sook** /fər so͝ok, fawr-/, **-sak·en** /fər sáykəb, fawr-/, **-sak·ing, -sakes**) *vt.* **1. ABANDON** to withdraw companionship, protection, or support from somebody **2. GIVE UP** to give up, renounce, or sacrifice something that gives pleasure [Old English *forsacan*, literally "to abstain from disputing," later "to give up," hence "to abandon," from *sacan* "to dispute"] —**for·sak·en** *adj.* —**for·sak·en·ly** *adv.* —**for·sak·en·ness** *n.* —**for·sak·er** *n.*

for·sooth /fər so͞oth, fawr-/ *adv.* in truth (*archaic*) [Old English *forsoð*, literally "for the truth"]

for·spent /fawr spént/ *adj.* exhausted or tired out (*archaic*) [Late 16thC. From the past participle of Old English *forspendan* "to spend completely, exhaust."]

For·ster /fáwrstər/, **E. M.** (1879–1970) British novelist. He was the author of *A Room with a View* (1908), *Howards End* (1910), and *A Passage to India* (1924). Full name **Edward Morgan Forster**

for·ster·ite /fáwrstə rìt/ *n.* a magnesium silicate mineral of the olivine group [Early 19thC. Named for the German naturalist J.R. *Forster* (1729–98).]

for·swear /fawr swáir/ (**-swore** /-swáwr/, **-sworn** /-swáwrn/, **-swear·ing, -swears**) *v.* (*archaic or literary*) **1.** *vt.* **REJECT STRONGLY** to vow to stop doing, having, or using something ○ *forswear political violence* **2.** *vt.* **DENY** to deny something under oath or completely ○ *foreswore all knowledge of the crime* **3.** *vi.* **PERJURE YOURSELF** to be guilty of giving false evidence under oath [Old English *forswerian*, literally "to renounce by swearing"]

for·syth·i·a /fər síthee ə, fàwr-/ *n.* a shrub grown for its small bell-shaped bright yellow flowers that come out in early spring before the leaves. Genus: *Forsythia*. [Mid-19thC. Named in honor of the Scottish horticulturalist William *Forsyth* (1737–1804).]

fort /fawrt/ *n.* **1. FORTIFIED POSITION** a building or group of buildings with strong defenses, usually strategically located and guarded by troops **2. MILITARY COMPOUND** a permanent military post consisting of several buildings ○ *Fort Bragg* [15thC. Directly or via French from Italian *forte* "strong (place)," from Latin *fortis* "strong."] ◇ **hold the fort** to take charge of something in the absence of the person usually responsible

WORD KEY: ORIGIN

The Latin word *fortis* from which ***fort*** is derived is also the source of English *forte, fortitude, fortress*, and *pianoforte*.

fort. *abbr.* fortification

For·ta·le·za /fàwrtə láyzə/ port and capital city of Ceará State, northeastern Brazil, situated at the mouth of the Paeju River on the Atlantic Ocean. Population: 1,967,365 (1996).

for·ta·lice /fáwrtəliss/ *n.* a small fort or part of the fortifications of a larger fort (*archaic*) [15thC. From medieval Latin *fortalitia*, from Latin *fortis* "strong."]

For·tas /fáwrtəss/, **Abe** (1910–82) U.S. jurist. He was forced to resign from the U.S. Supreme Court (1965–69) for financial improprieties. Full name **Abraham Fortas**

Fort Bragg /-brág/ military reservation in Cumberland County, central North Carolina, approximately 10 mi./16 km northwest of Fayetteville

Fort Col·lins /-kóllinz/ city and county seat of Larimer County, northern Colorado, 46 mi./64 km northeast of Boulder. Population: 87,758 (1990).

Fort Dodge /-dój/ city in north central Iowa, on the eastern bank of the Des Moines River, northwest of Des Moines. Population: 24,755 (1996).

for·te[1] /fawrt, fáwr tày/ *n.* **1. STRONG POINT** something that somebody is particularly good at ○ *Cooking is not really my forte.* **2.** FENCING **STRONG PART OF SWORD** the strongest section of a sword's blade, between the middle and the hilt [Mid-17thC. Via French *fort* "strong" from Latin *fortis*; later influenced by FORTE[2].]

for·te[2] /fáwr tày, fáwrtee/ *adv.* **LOUDLY** to be played or sung loudly (*used as a musical direction*) Symbol **f** ■ *n.* **LOUD NOTE OR PASSAGE** a note or passage of music played or sung, or to be played or sung, loudly [Early 18thC. Via Italian, "strong, loud," from Latin *fortis*.] — **for·te** *adj.*

for·te·pi·an·o /fàwr tay pyánnō, -pyaánō/ (*plural* **-os**) *n.* an early form of the piano, especially the piano of the 18th century [Mid-18thC. From Italian, from *forte* "loud" + *piano* "soft."]

for·te·pi·an·o *adv.* starting loud and then becoming suddenly soft (*used as a musical direction*) Symbol **fp** —**for·te·pi·a·no** *adj.*

forth /fawrth/ *adv.* **1. ONWARD** forward in time, place, degree, or order (*formal*) ○ *from this day forth* **2. INTO VIEW** out into view (*formal*) ○ *brought forth the prisoner* **3. ABROAD** away from a particular place, e.g., a country or region (*archaic*) ■ *prep.* **AWAY FROM** out of or away from (*archaic*) [Old English *forð*. Ultimately from an Indo-European word that is also the ancestor of English *fore*.] ◇ **and so forth** used to indicate that there are more things of the kind just mentioned, without having to name them ○ *bottles, cans, jars, and so forth*

forth·com·ing /fawrth kúmming, fáwrth kùmming/ *adj.* **1. FUTURE** about to appear or happen ○ *plans for the forthcoming celebration* **2. READY WHEN WANTED** available when required or requested ○ *We were assured that the money would be forthcoming.* **3. INFORMATIVE** willing to talk or give information ○ *not very forthcoming about his personal life*

forth·right /fáwrth rìt/ *adj.* **1. OUTSPOKEN** direct in speech or manner and very honest **2. SIMPLE** plain and simple in style ■ *adv.* **1. OUTSPOKENLY** in a direct and very honest way **2. IMMEDIATELY** at once (*archaic*) [Old English, from FORTH + RIGHT in the sense "directly"] —**forth·right·ly** *adv.* —**forth·right·ness** *n.*

forth·with /fawrth wíth/ *adv.* without delay (*formal*) [13thC. From *forth with* "along with."]

for·ti·eth /fáwrtee əth/ *n.* **1. ONE OF 40 PARTS OF SOMETHING** one of 40 equal parts of something **2. 40TH BIRTHDAY** somebody's 40th birthday —**for·ti·eth** *adj., adv.*

for·ti·fi·ca·tion /fàwrtəfi káysh'n/ *n.* **1. STRUCTURE FOR DEFENSE** a structure or structures, e.g., a wall, ditch, or rampart, built in order to strengthen a place's defenses (*often used in the plural*) **2. BUILDING OF DEFENSES** the art or practice of strengthening or creating defenses, e.g., by building walls or digging ditches **3. PLACE THAT CAN BE DEFENDED** a position or place that can be defended

for·ti·fied wine *n.* a drink such as sherry, port, or marsala, that is made from wine to which a strong alcohol, such as grape brandy, has been added. Fortified wines are usually drunk as aperitifs, digestifs, or liqueurs.

for·ti·fy /fáwrtə fì/ (**-fied, -fy·ing, -fies**) *vt.* **1. MAKE PLACE SAFER** to make a place less susceptible to attack by building or creating defensive structures such as walls, ditches, or ramparts **2. MAKE STRUCTURE STRONGER** to strengthen or reinforce the structure of something ○ *fortify a seawall* **3. ADD INGREDIENTS TO FOOD OR DRINK** to add further ingredients to food or drink in order to improve its flavor or add nutrients (*usually passive*) ○ *breakfast cereal fortified with vitamins* **4. STRENGTHEN OR ENCOURAGE** to give somebody physical, mental, or moral strength or encouragement **5. MAKE MORE POWERFUL** to make something more powerful or persuasive ○ *fortify an argument* [15thC. From French *fortifier*, from late Latin *fortificare*, literally "to make strong," from Latin *fortis* "strong."] —**for·ti·fi·a·ble** *adj.* — **for·ti·fi·er** *n.* —**for·ti·fy·ing·ly** *adv.*

for·tis /fáwrtiss/ *adj.* **PRONOUNCED FORCEFULLY** denoting a consonant, e.g., "p" or "t," that is produced with great muscular tension and pressure of breath ■ *n.* (*plural* **-tes** /-teèz/) **FORCEFULLY PRONOUNCED CONSONANT** a fortis consonant, such as "p" or "t" [Early 20thC. From Latin, "strong."]

for·tis·si·mo /fawr tíssəmō/ *adv.* **VERY LOUDLY** extremely loudly (*used as a musical direction*) Symbol **ff** ■ *n.* (*plural* **-mos** *or* **-mi** /fawr tíssə meè/) **FORTISSIMO PIECE OF MUSIC** a passage of music, or an individual note or chord, played fortissimo [Early 18thC. From Italian, "loudest," from *forte* "loud, strong" (see FORTE[2]).] — **for·tis·si·mo** *adj.*

for·ti·tude /fáwrtə to͞od/ *n.* strength and endurance in a difficult or painful situation [14thC. Via French from Latin *fortitudo* "strength, courage," from *fortis* "strong."] — **for·ti·tu·di·nous** /fàwrtə to͞odeenəss/ *adj.*

Fort Knox /-nóks/ a military reservation in northern Hardin County, central Kentucky. It has been the location of the U.S. Gold Depository since 1936. Area: 33,000 acres/13,350 hectares.

Fort Lau·der·dale /-láwdər dàyl/ city and county seat of Broward County, southeastern Florida, situated on the Atlantic Ocean 25 mi./40 km north of Miami. Population: 162,842 (1994).

Fort Lee /-leè/ borough in Bergen County, northeastern New Jersey, situated on the Palisades along the Hudson River 10 mi./16 km northeast of Jersey City. Population: 31,997 (1990).

Fort Mc·Mur·ray /-mək múr ee/ town on the Athabaska River in northeastern Alberta, western Canada. Population: 34,706 (1991).

Fort Meade /-meèd/ city in Polk County, central Florida, 25 mi./40 km south of Lakeland. Population: 4,976 (1990).

Fort My·ers /-mìrz/ city and county seat of Lee County, southwestern Florida, situated south of Charlotte Harbor. Population: 45,206 (1990).

fort·night /fáwrt nìt/ *n.* *U.K.* a period of 14 days [Old English *feowertine niht* "fourteen nights"]

fort·night·ly /fáwrt nìtlee/ *adj., adv.* **EVERY TWO WEEKS** occurring once every 14 days ■ *n.* (*plural* **-lies**) **PUBLICATION APPEARING EVERY OTHER WEEK** a publication that appears once every two weeks

Fort Pierce /-peèrss/ city and county seat of St. Lucie County, eastern Florida, 30 mi./48 km northeast of Lake Okeechobee. Population: 36,830 (1990).

For·tral /fáwrtrəl/ *tdmk.* a trademark for a narcotic pain reliever used for severe injury, cancer, or chronic pain

FOR·TRAN /fáwr tràn/ *n.* the earliest high-level computer programming language [Mid-20thC. Contraction of FORMULA + TRANSLATION.]

for·tress /fáwrtrəss/ *n.* **1. MILITARY INSTALLATION** a fortified place with a long-term military presence, often including a town **2. SOMETHING IMPOSSIBLE TO GET INTO** something that is impenetrable or acts as protection [14thC. From Old French *forteresse* "strong place," from, ultimately, Latin *fortis* "strong."]

Fort Saint John /-saynt jón/ town on the Peace River in northeastern British Columbia, Canada. Population: 15,021 (1996).

Fort Sas·katch·e·wan town in Alberta, Canada, 18 mi./29 km northeast of Edmonton. Population: 12,078 (1991).

Fort Smith /-smíth/ city at the confluence of the Arkansas and Poteau rivers in western Arkansas on the border with Oklahoma. It is the second largest city in the state. Population: 75,776 (1996).

Fort Stan·wix Nat·ion·al Mon·u·ment /-stànwiks-/ national monument on the site of a reconstructed 18th-century fort in Rome, New York. Area: 16 acres/6 hectares.

Fort Sum·ter Na·tion·al Mon·u·ment /-sùmtər-/ national monument on the site of a historic fort situated on the southern side of the entrance to Charleston Harbor, South Carolina. It was the site of the first battle of the Civil War in 1861.

Fort Thom·as /-tómməss/ city in northern Kentucky, north of Independence and southeast of Covington, a southern suburb of Cincinnati, Ohio. Population: 15,300 (1996).

for·tu·i·tous /fawr to͞o itəss/ *adj.* **1. ACCIDENTAL OR UNPLANNED** happening by chance **2. HAPPENING BY LUCKY CHANCE** happening as a result of a lucky accident **3. LUCKY** bringing or indicating good fortune [Mid-17thC. From Latin *fortuitus*, from, ultimately, *fors* "chance, luck."] —**for·tu·i·tous·ly** *adv.* —**for·tu·i·tous·ness** *n.*

for·tu·i·ty /fawr to͞o itee/ (*plural* **-ties**) *n.* **1. CHANCE OCCURRENCE** something that happens by chance or accident **2. LUCKY CHANCE** lucky chance or accident

for·tu·nate /fáwrchənət/ *adj.* **1. LUCKY** enjoying good luck **2. RESULTING FROM LUCK** happening as a result of good luck **3. BRINGING LUCK** bringing good luck [14thC. From Latin *fortunatus*, from *fortuna* "Fate, luck."] —**for·tu·nate·ness** *n.*

WORD KEY: SYNONYMS

See Synonyms at ***lucky***.

for·tu·nate·ly /fáwrchənətlee/ *adv.* **1. LUCKILY** by lucky chance **2. HAPPILY** used to show that the speaker or writer is happy to be able to report something ○ *Fortunately, we've been given more time to finish the job.*

for·tune /fáwrchən/ *n.* **1. GREAT WEALTH OR PROPERTY** a large amount of financial wealth or material possessions **2. LARGE SUM OF MONEY** an extremely large amount of money **3. for·tune, For·tune FATE** chance, or the personification of chance, regarded as affecting human activities **4. LUCK** luck, especially good luck **5. DESTINY** an individual's destiny ■ **for·tunes** *npl.* **LIFE'S UPS AND DOWNS** chance happenings throughout life that may turn out well or badly [13thC. Via French from Latin *fortuna* "Fate, luck" (especially good luck).]

for·tune cook·ie *n.* a Chinese cookie folded and baked around a piece of paper on which a saying or a prediction of somebody's fortune is written. Fortune cookies are served in Chinese restaurants.

for·tune hunt·er *n.* somebody who wants to become rich quickly and easily, especially by making a deliberate attempt to marry a wealthy partner —**for·tune hunt·ing** *n.* —**for·tune-hunt·ing** *adj.*

for·tune-tell·er *n.* somebody who makes predictions about somebody's future by such methods as reading palms, looking into a crystal ball, using tarot cards, or examining tea leaves —**for·tune-tell·ing** *n., adj.*

Fort Wal·ton Beach /-wàwlt'n be͞ech/ city on the Gulf of Mexico in Oskaloosa County, northwestern Florida, east of Pensacola. Population: 24,471 (1990).

Fort Wayne /-wáyn/ city in northeastern Indiana, southeast of Elkhart. The St. Joseph, St. Marys, and Maumee rivers run through the city. Population: 184,783 (1996).

for·ty /fáwrtee/ *n.* (*plural* **-ties**) **1. NUMBER 40** the number 40 **2. GROUP OF 40** a group of forty objects or people **3.** TENNIS **TENNIS POINT** in a game of tennis, the score awarded to a player with a score of thirty on winning a further point ■ **for·ties** *npl.* **1. NUMBERS 40 TO 49** the numbers 40 to 49, e.g., as a range of temperature ○ *in the low forties* **2. 1940 TO 1949** the years 1940 to 1949 **3. PERIOD FROM AGE 40 TO 49** the period of somebody's life from the age of 40 to 49 [Old English *feowertig*, literally "four tens," from *feower* "four"] —**for·ty** *adj., pron.*

for·ty-five *n.* **1. .45-CALIBER PISTOL** a pistol with a .45 caliber. **2. SMALL PHONOGRAPH RECORD** a record smaller than an LP that is played at 45 revolutions per minute

for·ty·ish /fáwrtee ish/ *adj.* **1. APPROXIMATELY 40** approximately 40 in number **2. AROUND AGE 40** around the age of 40

for·ty-nin·er *n.* a prospector in the gold rush of 1849 in California

for·ty-ninth par·al·lel *n. Can* the border between the United States and Canada, that runs at 49° latitude along most of its length

for·ty·some·thing /fáwrti sùmthing/ *n.* **SOMEBODY IN FORTIES** somebody between 40 and 49 years of age (*informal*) ■ *adj.* **BETWEEN 40 AND 49** between 40 and 49 years of age

for·ty winks *n.* a short sleep (*informal; takes a singular or plural verb*)

fo·rum /fáwrəm/ (*plural* **fo·rums** *or* **fora** /-rə/) *n.* **1. PLACE TO EXPRESS YOURSELF** a medium, e.g., a magazine or newspaper, in which the public may debate an issue or express opinions **2. MEETING FOR DISCUSSION** a meeting to discuss matters of general interest **3.** HIST **PUBLIC SQUARE IN ROMAN CITIES** a public square or marketplace in ancient Roman cities where business was conducted and the law courts were situated **4.** LAW **LAW COURT** a law court or tribunal **5.** COMPUT **INTERNET DISCUSSION GROUP** an Internet discussion group for participants with common interests [15thC. From Latin, literally "outdoor place," denoting an enclosed space around a house, later a marketplace. Ultimately from an Indo-European word that was the ancestor of English *door* and *foreign*.]

for·ward /fáwrwərd/ CORE MEANING: to or toward a front position or direction ○ (adv) *Conover pushed his cup forward, but Jonny ignored it.* ○ (adj) *Most of the energy in gasoline makes engines hot; less than half gets converted to forward motion.*

1. *adv.* **AHEAD** to or toward what is ahead in space or time ○ (adv) *He sprang forward and embraced his grandmother.* **2.** *adv.* **PROGRESSING** towards a goal ○ *The company has taken a step forward in employee safety.* **3.** *adv.* **INDICATES IMPROVEMENT** indicates that something progresses or improves ○ *The EU is moving forward on monetary union.* **4.** *adv.* NAUT **TO FRONT OF VESSEL** toward the front of a boat or ship ○ *I was ordered forward to swab the deck.* **5.** *adv.* **TOWARDS THE FRONT** toward the front of something such as an aircraft or a building ○ *I'd like to be seated further forward.* **6.** *adv.* **TO PUBLIC ATTENTION** from obscurity into public view ○ *The unknown actor came forward and accepted the lead role.* **7.** *adj.* **AHEAD** directed towards what is ahead in space and time ○ *The magnetic field exerts a forward force on charged particles* **8.** *adj.* **RELATING TO THE FUTURE** directed towards a future goal ○ *forward planning* **9.** *adj.* NAUT **AT FRONT OF VESSEL** situated at or near the front of a boat or ship ○ *the forward deck* **10.** *adj.* **AT THE FRONT** situated at or near the front of something such as an aircraft or a building ○ *The forward seats are the most popular.* **11.** *adj.* **UNRESTRAINED IN BEHAVIOR** behaving boldly in defiance of moral or social restraints ○ *I'm not sure I approve of her behavior – she's very forward.* **12.** *n.* SPORTS **ATTACKING PLAYER** one of several players in some team sports, e.g., basketball, hockey, or soccer, who are the principal offensive players **13.** *vt.* **for·ward** (*past participle* **-ward·ed,** *present participle* **-ward·ing,** *3rd person present singular* **-wards**) **REDIRECT MAIL** to send on mail from the address to which it was originally sent ○ *She was anxious to know if any letters might have come that had not been forwarded to her.* **14.** *vt.* **ADVANCE OR PROMOTE** to assist the progress of something ○ *I will do anything you like if it means we can forward your cause.* [Old English *forweard*, literally "in the direction of the front," from *fore* (see FORE)]

for·ward bi·as *n.* a bias applied to an electronic circuit, e.g., a semiconductor device, in the direction that produces the larger current

for·ward·er /fáwrwərdər/ *n.* an individual or company whose business is the collection, shipment, and delivery of goods

for·ward·ing /fáwrwərding/ *n.* the collection, shipment, and delivery of goods

for·ward·ing ad·dress *n.* a new address to which mail is to be redirected

for·ward-look·ing *adj.* planning for or looking ahead to the future

for·ward·ly /fáwrwərdlee/ *adv.* in a bold manner, defying moral or social restraints

for·ward·ness /fáwrwərdnəss/ *n.* bold behavior in defiance of moral or social restraints

for·ward pass *n.* FOOTBALL in football, a pass thrown from a position behind the line of scrimmage in the direction of the opposing team's goal

Fos·bur·y flop /fŏzbəri-/ *n.* a technique used in the high jump in which the contestant clears the bar with the back of the shoulders followed by the arched body [Mid-20thC. Named for the U.S. athlete Richard (Dick) *Fosbury* (born 1947), who developed the technique.]

fos·car·net *n.* a drug used to treat a type of herpes virus that is often associated with AIDS

fos·sa[1] /fóssə/ (*plural* **-sae** /fó se͞e/) *n.* a hollow, pit, or groove in a part of the body, e.g., a bone [Mid-17thC. From Latin, literally "ditch" (see FOSSE).]

fos·sa[2] /fóssə/ (*plural* **-sas** *or* **-sa**) *n.* a slender reddish-brown carnivorous mammal from Madagascar that resembles a cat, has sharp retractile claws, and feeds on small animals, birds, and insects. Species: *Cryptoprocta ferox.* [Mid-19thC. From Malagasy *fosa*.]

fosse /fawss/ *n.* a wide ditch, usually filled with water and used for defense [Pre-12thC. Via French from Latin *fossa*, from *fodere* "to dig" (source of English *fossil*).]

Fos·se /fáwssee/, **Bob** (1927–87) U.S. dancer, choreographer, and director. He won his first Tony Awards for his imaginative dance sequences in the Broadway musicals *Pajama Game* (1953) and *Damn Yankees* (1955), and he directed the Academy Award-winning films *Cabaret* (1972) and *All That Jazz* (1980). Full name **Robert Louis Fosse**

Barnaby's

Fossil: Trilobite

fos·sil /fóss'l/ *n.* **1. PRESERVED REMAINS OF ANIMAL OR PLANT** the remains of an animal or plant preserved from an earlier era inside a rock or other geological deposit, often as an impression or in a petrified state **2. SOMEBODY WHO WILL NOT CHANGE** somebody who is hopelessly out of date or unwilling to accept change (*informal insult*) **3. SOMETHING OUTDATED** something that has outlived its usefulness, e.g., a discredited theory **4.** LING **OLD WORD NOW USED SPECIFICALLY** a word or part of a word that was once used generally but now survives only in a few contexts, such as *couth* in *uncouth* [Mid-16thC. Via French *fossile* from Latin *fossilis* "dug up," from *fodere* "to dig." Originally denoting a fossilized fish that was believed to have lived underground.]

fos·sil fu·el *n.* any carbon-containing fuel, e.g., coal, peat, petroleum, and natural gas, derived from the decomposed remains of prehistoric plants and animals

fos·sil·if·er·ous /fòssə líffərəss/ *adj.* having fossils within it (*refers to rocks or other geological deposits*)

fos·sil·ize /fóss'l īz/ (**-ized, -iz·ing, -iz·es**) *vti.* **1. MAKE OR BECOME FOSSIL** to convert something into a fossil, to preserve something as a fossil, or to become a fossil **2. BE UNABLE TO CHANGE** to become outdated, fixed, or unchanging, or to make somebody or something incapable of change —**fos·sil·iz·a·ble** *adj.* —**fos·sil·i·za·tion** /fòss'li záysh'n/ *n.* —**fos·sil·ized** /fóss'l īzd/ *adj.*

fos·sil wa·ter *n.* water in underground strata that has accumulated over millions of years and is therefore not a renewable resource, unlike other ground water

fos·so·ri·al /fo sáwree əl/ *adj.* used to describe animals that have large forelimbs or other adaptations for digging and burrowing, or to describe the parts of the body used for this purpose [Mid-19thC. Formed from medieval Latin *fossorius*, from Latin *fossor* "digger," from *fodere* (see FOSSIL).]

fos·ter /fáwstər, fóstər/ *vt.* **(-tered, -ter·ing, -ters) 1. NURTURE A CHILD** to provide a child with care and upbringing **2. DEVELOP** to encourage the development of something **3. KEEP ALIVE FEELING OR THOUGHT** to keep a feeling or thought alive ■ *adj.* **PROVIDING OR RECEIVING PARENTAL CARE** giving or receiving a home and parental care and upbringing, usually on a short-term basis, although unrelated by blood or adoption. Foster care is provided for children whose natural parents are dead, absent, or unfit or unable to look after them. [Old English *fostrian* "to nourish," later "to raise a child," from *foster* "food." Ultimately from a prehistoric Germanic word that was also the ancestor of English *food* and *forage*.] —**fos·ter·er** *n.*

Fos·ter /fóstər/, **Jodie** (*b.* 1962) U.S. movie actor and director. She won the Academy Award for best actress for her roles in *The Accused* (1988) and *The Silence of the Lambs* (1991). Real name **Alicia Christian Foster**

Andrew Ward

Sir Norman Foster

Fos·ter, Sir Norman (*b.* 1935) British architect. His designs such as the terminal building (1991) for Stansted Airport, Essex, England, combine elegant forms with complex engineering and technologically advanced materials. Full name **Sir Norman Robert Foster**

Fos·ter, Stephen Collins (1826–64) U.S. songwriter. His songs include "My Old Kentucky Home" (1853) and "Beautiful Dreamer" (1864).

fos·ter·age /fáwstərij, fóstərij/ *n.* **1. CARING FOR ANOTHER'S CHILD** the act of looking after or bringing up a child who is not one's own, often on a short-term basis and in exchange for payment by a local authority **2. BEING A FOSTER CHILD** the process of being looked after or brought up in a home by parents who are not one's own **3. ENCOURAGING DEVELOPMENT** the process of encouraging the development of something beneficial

Fos·ter Cit·y /fáwstər-, fóstər-/ city in California on the San Mateo Peninsula, a southeastern suburb of San Francisco. Population: 29,698 (1996).

FOT, f.o.t. *abbr.* free on truck

Fou·cault /foo kṓ/, **Michel** (1926–84) French philosopher. He showed how ideas of truth about human nature change in the course of history. His chief works were *Madness and Civilization* (1960), *The Order of Things* (1966), and *Discipline and Punish* (1975).

Fou·cault pen·du·lum *n.* a heavy free-swinging pendulum suspended by a long thin wire, whose plane of motion appears to change as the earth rotates [Mid-19thC. Named for the French physicist Jean-Bernard Léon *Foucault* (1819–68), who first used such a pendulum to demonstrate the rotation of the earth.]

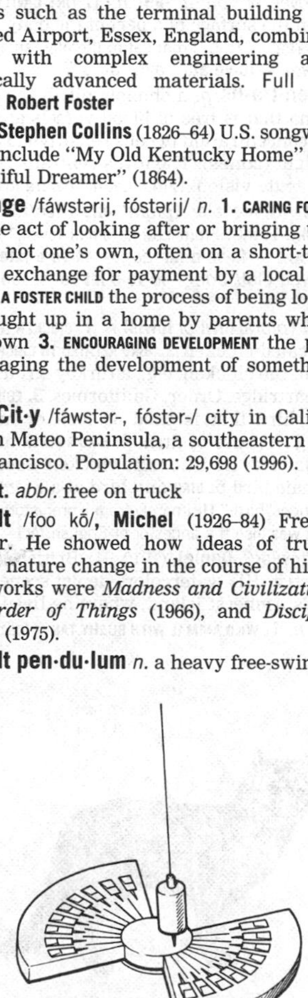

Foucault pendulum

fouet·té /fwe táy, foo ə táy/ *n.* a ballet step in which the dancer stands on one foot and moves the other leg quickly out and in again, often while doing a pirouette [Mid-19thC. From French, past participle of *fouetter* "to whip."]

fought past tense, past participle of **fight**

foul /fowl/ *adj.* **1. DISGUSTING** disgusting to the senses **2. FILLED WITH DIRT** clogged with dirt or so obstructed as to be unusable **3. DIRTY** covered in dirt **4. CONTAMINATED** contaminated by impurities **5. UNPLEASANT** extremely unpleasant or disagreeable in nature (*informal*) **6. VULGAR** obscene or otherwise offensive in expression or behavior **7.** SPORTS **ILLEGAL IN SPORT** contrary to the rules of a sport **8. OUTSIDE FOUL LINES** outside the foul lines in baseball **9. DISHONEST** behaving in an unfair and unacceptable way **10. INCLEMENT** stormy or wet and unpleasant for outdoor activities (*refers to weather*) **11. ROTTEN** decaying and rotten **12. EVIL** spiritually or morally vicious **13. ENSNARLED** entangled with something and unable to move **14. UNENJOYABLE** extremely low in quality ■ *n.* **1.** SPORTS **ILLEGAL ACTION IN SPORT** an illegal action against an opposing player or an action that breaks the rules of a sport **2. FOUL BALL** a foul ball in baseball **3.** NAUT **ENTANGLEMENT PREVENTING MOVEMENT** in sailing, an entanglement or collision that prevents movement ■ *v.* **(fouled, foul·ing, fouls) 1.** *vti.* SPORTS **ACT ILLEGALLY IN SPORT** to act illegally against an opposing player or to violate a rule of a sport **2.** *vti.* **HIT BALL FROM FAIR TERRITORY** in baseball, to hit a ball outside a foul line **3.** *vti.* **ENSNARL AND PREVENT MOVEMENT** to entangle or catch something so that it cannot move, or become entangled or caught and unable to move **4.** *vti.* **OBSTRUCT OR BECOME OBSTRUCTED** to clog or block something, or to become clogged or blocked **5.** *vt.* **MAKE DIRTY** to make something dirty, especially by defecation **6.** *vt.* **BRING DISGRACE ON** to bring disgrace to a person or to somebody's reputation [Old English *ful* "filthy, decaying." Ultimately from a prehistoric Germanic word that was also the ancestor of English *defile* and *filth*.] —**foul·er** *n.* —**foul·ly** *adv.* —**foul·ness** *n.*

foul out *vi.* to be forced to leave a game after committing more than the permitted number of fouls

foul up *vti.* **1. HANDLE SOMETHING POORLY** to do something badly or incompetently, or to be bungled or mismanaged (*informal*) **2. OBSTRUCT OR BECOME OBSTRUCTED** to choke, clog, or entangle something, or to become choked, clogged, or entangled

fou·lard /foo laárd/ *n.* **1. SOFT PATTERNED CLOTH** a soft silk or rayon fabric, usually patterned **2. ARTICLE MADE OF SOFT PATTERNED FABRIC** something made of foulard, especially a scarf or handkerchief [Mid-19thC. From French, of unknown origin.]

foul ball *n.* in baseball, a ball that is hit so as to land outside a foul line

foul line *n.* **1.** BASEBALL **LINE SHOWING FAIR OR FOUL BALL** either of the lines extending from home plate through first and third bases to the end of the playing field. A ball hit inside the lines is a fair ball. **2.** BASKETBALL **LINE FOR FREE THROWS** either of two lines on a court from which players get unobstructed chances to make a basket after they have been fouled **3. DESIGNATED LIMIT OF PLAY** in some sports, a boundary beyond which a ball or player is not permitted, e.g., the line in bowling where the player must stop before releasing the ball

foul-mouthed *adj.* using obscene or otherwise offensive language, especially habitually

foul play *n.* **1. UNFAIRNESS** unfair action or behavior **2. CRIME** treachery or criminal violence **3.** SPORTS **ACTION AGAINST RULES** action that is contrary to the rules of a sport

foul shot *n.* = **free throw**

foul tip *n.* in baseball, a pitched ball that glances off a bat and is deflected into foul territory, usually back toward the catcher

foul-up *n.* a blunder or the confusion or failure that results from error (*informal*)

found[1] /fownd/ **(found·ed, found·ing, founds)** *vt.* **1. SET UP INSTITUTION** to establish and organize something for the future, e.g., an institution or business **2. PROVIDE WITH BASIS** to support something, e.g., a conclusion, with evidence or reasoning [13thC. Via French *fonder* from Latin *fundare*, from *fundus* "bottom, base" (source of English *fund, fundamental*, and *profound*).]

found[2] /fownd/ **(found·ed, found·ing, founds)** *vt.* **1. CAST METAL OR GLASS** to cast something, especially metal or glass, by melting it and pouring it into a mold **2. CAST FROM MOLD** to produce objects, e.g., machine parts, by melting metal or glass and pouring it into molds [14thC. Via French *fondre* "to dissolve and blend" (the original sense in English) from Latin *fundere* "to pour or melt" (source of English *fuse, diffuse*, and *confound*).]

found[3] past tense, past participle of **find**

foun·da·tion /fown dáysh'n/ *n.* **1. SUPPORT FOR A BUILDING** a part of a building, usually below the ground, that transfers and distributes the weight of the building onto the ground (*often used in the plural*) **2. SUPPORT FOR IDEA** the basis of something, e.g., a theory or an idea **3.** COSMETICS **BASE LAYER OF MAKEUP** a type of cosmetic in liquid, cream, or cake form, usually colored, that is applied as a base for makeup **4. ESTABLISHING OF INSTITUTION OR ORGANIZATION** the setting up of an institution or organization **5. CHARITABLE OR EDUCATIONAL ORGANIZATION** an institution, e.g., a school, research establishment, charitable trust, or hospital, that has been formally set up with an endowment fund **6. FUND SUPPORTING INSTITUTION** an endowment fund that supports an institution **7.** = **foundation garment 8. BASE FABRIC FOR PATCHWORK** a type of fabric to which other pieces of fabric are sewn, e.g., in log-cabin patchwork or appliqué —**foun·da·tion·al** *adj.* —**foun·da·tion·al·ly** *adv.*

foun·da·tion gar·ment *n.* a piece of women's underwear intended to control and shape the figure, e.g., a corset

foun·da·tion stone *n.* **1. STONE BEGINNING CONSTRUCTION** a stone laid during a ceremony to mark the start of construction of a building or institution **2. BASIS FOR SOMETHING** the basis on which something is founded

foun·da·tion stop *n.* an organ stop with a strong fundamental tone

found·er[1] /fówndər/ *n.* a person who establishes an institution, business, or organization

foun·der[2] *v.* **(-dered, -der·ing, -ders) 1.** *vti.* **SINK OR CAUSE TO SINK** to become filled with water and sink, or to make something sink **2.** *vi.* **BREAK DOWN** to collapse and fail ○ *Negotiations foundered on a single issue.* **3.** *vi.* **CRUMPLE** to give way and fall to the ground **4.** *vi.* **BE BOGGED DOWN** to become stuck in soft ground or snow **5.** *vi.* **STUMBLE** to stumble or injure a leg **6.** *vti.* **MAKE OR BECOME ILL BY OVERFEEDING** to make livestock ill by overfeeding or to become ill by overfeeding ■ *n.* VET = **laminitis** [14thC. From Old French *fondrer* "to send or sink to the bottom, fall in ruins," from, ultimately, Latin *fundus* "bottom" (source of English *found*[1]).]

found·ing fa·ther *n.* somebody who creates an important institution, movement, or organization

Found·ing Fa·ther *n.* one of the members of the convention that drafted the U.S. Constitution

found·ling /fówndling/ *n.* an abandoned baby of unknown parentage (*dated*) [13thC. Formed from the past participle of FIND, possibly influenced by Dutch *vondeling*.]

found ob·ject *n.* ARTS = **objet trouvé**

found·ry /fówndree/ (*plural* **-ries**) *n.* **1. WORKPLACE FOR CASTING METAL OR GLASS** a building equipped for the casting of metal or glass **2. MAKING CASTINGS** the skill or practice of casting metal or glass

fount[1] /fownt/ *n.* (*literary*) **1. SOURCE** a source of something **2. FOUNTAIN** a fountain or spring of water [16thC. Shortening of FOUNTAIN.]

fount[2] *n. U.K.* = **font**[2]

foun·tain /fównt'n/ *n.* **1. ORNAMENTAL WATER FEATURE** an

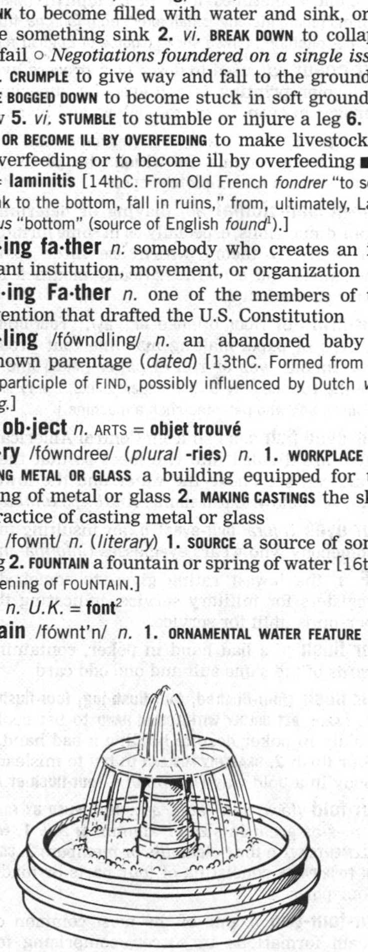

Fountain

ornamental structure featuring a jet or jets of water, often emerging from a statue into a pool **2. NATURAL SPRING** a natural source of water **3. DRINKING FOUNTAIN** a small jet of drinking water, especially one in a public place that can be activated by a button or handle **4. SPRAY OF LIQUID** a jet of water or some other liquid **5. SPRAY OF SUBSTANCE** a sudden discharge of something into the air, e.g., sparks, lava, or steam **6. SOURCE** the source of something abstract **7. RESERVOIR OF LIQUID** a reservoir of liquid for use as needed, e.g., in an oil lamp or for printing ink [14thC. Via French *fontaine* from Latin *fontanus* "of a spring," from *fons* "spring" (also the original sense in English).]

foun·tain·head /fównt'n hèd/ *n.* **1. SOURCE OF STREAM** a spring that is the source of a stream **2. PRIMARY SOURCE** the primary source of something abstract

foun·tain pen *n.* a pen with a pointed metal tip (**nib**) that is supplied with ink from a refillable reservoir in the body of the pen or from an inserted cartridge

Foun·tain Val·ley /fównt'n-/ city on the Santa Ana River, southwestern California, a southeastern suburb of Los Angeles. Population: 55,790 (1996).

four /fawr/ *n.* **1. NUMBER 4** the number 4 **2. SOMETHING WITH VALUE OF 4** something in a numbered series, e.g., a playing card, with a value of 4 ○ *the four of spades* ○ *throw a four* **3. GROUP OF FOUR** a group of four objects or people ○ *a four for bridge* **4.** ROWING **FOUR-OARED RACING BOAT** a light narrow racing boat with four oars **5.** ROWING **FOUR-MEMBER ROWING CREW** a rowing crew with four members **6.** BOWLING **BOWLING TEAM** a team of four lawn bowling players ■ **fours** *npl.* ROWING **BOAT RACES** races for boats with a crew of four [Old English *fēower.* Ultimately from an Indo-European word that was also the ancestor of English *square, quadrant, trapezium,* and *tetra-.*] —**four** *adj., pron.*

four-bag·ger *n.* BASEBALL a home run (*informal*)

four-by-four *n.* four-wheel-drive motor vehicle

four-by-two *n. U.K.* = **two-by-four**

four·chette /foor shét/ *n.* a small band that joins the folds of skin at the back of the opening to the vagina, sometimes torn in childbirth [Mid-18thC. From French, literally "small fork," from *fourche,* from Latin *furca* "pitchfork, forked stick" (source of English *fork*).]

four-col·or *adj.* used to describe a process by which full-color printing is achieved by superimposing images in cyan, magenta, yellow, and black

four-cy·cle *adj.* used to describe an internal combustion engine in which the piston makes four strokes to complete a cycle

four-di·men·sion·al *adj.* having or determined by four dimensions, especially as in some formulations of relativity theory which use three spatial dimensions and a mathematically modified form of time as the fourth

four·drin·i·er /foor drínnee ər, -àyl/, **Four·drin·i·er** *n.* a type of paper-making machine that produces a continuous web or roll of paper [Mid-19thC. Named for the 19th-century British papermakers, Henry and Sealy *Fourdrinier,* who patented such a machine.]

four-eyed fish *n.* a fish from Central America whose eyes are divided into two lobes so that the upper part can see above the water and the lower part can see below. Latin name: *Anableps anableps.*

four-eyes (*plural* **four-eyes**) *n.* an insulting term for somebody who wears eyeglasses (*informal insult*)

4-F *n.* the lowest rating given to somebody who registers for military service, indicating that the person is unfit for service

four flush *n.* a bad hand in poker, containing four cards of the same suit and one odd card

four-flush (**four-flushed, four-flush·ing, four-flush·es**) *vi.* **1.** CARDS **BET BOLDLY WITH LOSING HAND** to bet coolly and boldly in poker despite holding a bad hand, e.g., a four flush **2. BRAZENLY MISLEAD** to try to mislead somebody in a bold way (*informal*) —**four-flush·er** *n.*

four·fold /fáwr fòld/ *adj., adv.* **MULTIPLIED BY FOUR** four times as great in size or amount ■ *adj.* **1. WITH FOUR ELEMENTS** with four elements or members **2. CONSISTING OF FOUR PARTS** consisting of four parts or made up of four parts

four-four-two *n.* one of the most common outfield team formations in soccer, comprising four defenders, four midfielders, and two attackers

4GL *abbr.* COMPUT fourth-generation language

4-H, Four-H *n.* a national youth organization sponsored by the Department of Agriculture in rural areas, with programs for young people in home economics, agriculture, community service, and personal development [Because the aim is to improve the head, heart, hands and health] —**4-H'er** *n.*

four-hand·ed *adj.* **1.** GAME **HAVING FOUR PLAYERS** played by four people (*refers to a game, especially a card game*) **2.** MUSIC **FOR TWO PIANO PLAYERS** composed or arranged for two people to play at the piano

Four Hun·dred *n.* the wealthiest or most exclusive group of people in a community [Said to be the number of people that would fill the ballroom of Mrs. William Astor, 19th-century American socialite.]

Fou·rier /fóoree ày/, **Charles** (1772–1837) French social scientist. His *Theory of Four Movements and of General Destinies* (1808) advocated a socialist reorganization of society. Full name **François Marie Charles Fourier**

Fou·ri·er a·nal·y·sis *n.* the analysis of a periodic function using the terms of a Fourier series as an approximation [Early 20thC. Named for J. B. J. *Fourier* (see FOURIER SERIES).]

Fou·ri·er se·ries *n.* an infinite trigonometric series of terms consisting of constants multiplied by sines or cosines, used in the approximation of periodic functions [Late 19thC. Named for the French mathematician Jean Baptiste Joseph *Fourier* (1768–1830), who devised the series.]

four-in-hand *n.* **1. FOUR-HORSE CARRIAGE** a carriage drawn by four horses with one driver **2. FOUR HORSES DRAWING CARRIAGE** a team of four horses drawing a carriage **3. WAY OF TYING NECKTIE** a necktie tied in a slipknot at the collar with the ends left hanging

four-leaf clo·ver *n.* a clover leaf divided into four leaflets instead of the usual three, believed to bring good luck to the person who finds it

four-let·ter word *n.* any short English word relating to sex or excretion that is often used as a swearword and is generally regarded as offensive or taboo [From the fact that the most common words of this kind consist of four letters]

four-o'clock (*plural* **four-o'clock** *or* **four-o'clocks**) *n.* a tropical American plant with tubular red, white, or yellow flowers that open in the late afternoon. Latin name: *Mirabilis jalapa.*

401(k) (*plural* **401(k)s** *or* **401(k)'s**) *n.* a retirement plan for employed people that allows them to invest part of their income without paying any tax until the money is withdrawn after retirement

four·pen·ny nail /fáwrpənee-, fáwr pènnee-/ *n.* a nail 1.5 in./3.8 cm long [From the medieval price, fourpenny per hundred]

Four-poster

four-post·er, four-post·er bed *n.* a bed with a tall post at each corner, from which a canopy and drapes are sometimes hung

four·ra·gère /fóorə zháir/ *n.* a braided cord awarded as a military decoration to a unit or individual, and usually worn on the left shoulder of a uniform [Early 20thC. From French, from *fourrage* (see FORAGE).]

four·score /fawr skáwr/ *adj.* the number 80 or a quantity of 80 (*archaic*) ○ *fourscore years and ten* [13thC]

four·some /fáwrsəm/ *n.* **1. GROUP OF 4 PEOPLE** a group of four people, usually taking part in some activity together **2.** GOLF **GOLF GAME WITH PARTNERS** a game of golf between two pairs of players, especially when each pair has one ball that the partners hit alternately

four·square /fawr skwáir/ *adv., adj.* showing certainty and determination [14thC. The main modern meanings all derive from the original sense "having four equal sides," and hence, "stable and firm."]

four-stroke *adj. U.K.* = **four-cycle**

four·teen /fawr téen/ *n.* **1. NUMBER 14** the number 14 **2. SOMETHING WITH VALUE OF 14** something in a numbered series with a value of 14 **3. GROUP OF 14** a group of 14 objects or people —**four·teen** *adj., pron.*

four·teenth /fawr téenth/ *n.* **1. ONE OF 14 PARTS OF SOMETHING** one of 14 equal parts of something **2. 14 IN A SERIES** the ordinal number assigned to item number 14 in a series —**four·teenth** *adj.*

fourth /fawrth/ *n.* **1. ONE OF 4 PARTS OF SOMETHING** one of four equal parts of something **2.** MUSIC **INTERVAL OF 4 NOTES** in a standard musical scale, the interval between one note and another that lies three notes above or below it. In the scale of C major, C and F form a fourth. **3.** MUSIC **NOTE A 4TH AWAY FROM ANOTHER** in a standard musical scale, a note that is a fourth away from another note —**fourth** *adj., adv.*

fourth di·men·sion *n.* time in relativity theory modified mathematically and used in combination with the usual three spatial dimensions to specify the location in space and time of events —**fourth-di·men·sion·al** *adj.*

fourth es·tate, Fourth Es·tate *n.* journalists, the press, or the media in general [Originally, any significant power other than the three estates (the Lords Spiritual, the Lords Temporal, and the House of Commons); Edmund BURKE supposedly first applied it to the press]

fourth-generation language *n.* an advanced computer programming language that is more like human language than are the standard high-level programming languages

fourth·ly *adv.* used to introduce the fourth point in an argument or discussion

Fourth World *n.* the poorest or least developed countries in the Third World

4WD *abbr.* four-wheel drive

four-wheel drive *n.* a system of transmitting power from the drive shaft to all four wheels of a motor vehicle in order to provide better traction under difficult conditions

fo·ve·a /fóvee ə/ (*plural* **-ae**) *n.* **1. TINY CAVITY** a small hollow in the surface of a part of the body **2.** = **fovea centralis** [Late 17thC. From Latin, literally "small pit."] —**fo·ve·al** *adj.* —**fo·ve·ate** /-àyt, -ət/ *adj.*

fo·ve·a cen·tra·lis *n.* a shallow pit in the center of the retina that is free of blood vessels and has the highest concentration of cells sensitive to color and bright light (**cones**). The fovea centralis is the area of most acute vision. [From Latin, "centra foveal"]

fo·ve·o·la /fō vée ələ/ (*plural* **-lae** /-lèe/) *n.* a small fovea [Mid-19thC. From Latin, "small fovea," from *fovea* (see FOVEA).] —**fo·ve·o·lar** *adj.* —**fo·ve·o·late** /fóvee ə làyt, fō vée ələt/ *adj.* —**fo·ve·o·lat·ed** /fóvee ə làytəd/ *adj.*

fowl /fowl/ (*plural* **fowl** *or* **fowls**) *n.* **1. CHICKEN** a common domesticated chicken **2. BIRD RELATED TO CHICKEN** a bird related to the chicken, e.g., a turkey, grouse, pheasant, or partridge. Order: Galliformes. **3. EDIBLE OR GAME BIRD** any bird that is used as food or hunted for sport, e.g., a goose or duck **4. BIRD'S FLESH** the flesh of an edible bird, traditionally chicken, especially an old or male bird **5. BIRD** any bird at all (*archaic*) [Old English *fugol* "bird." Ultimately from a prehistoric Germanic word that was also the ancestor of English *fly.*]

Fow·ler /fówlər/, **Daniel** (1810–94) British-born Canadian artist. His watercolors depict scenes of Lake Ontario's Amherst Island, where he lived.

fox /foks/ *n.* **1. WILD ANIMAL WITH BUSHY TAIL** a carnivorous

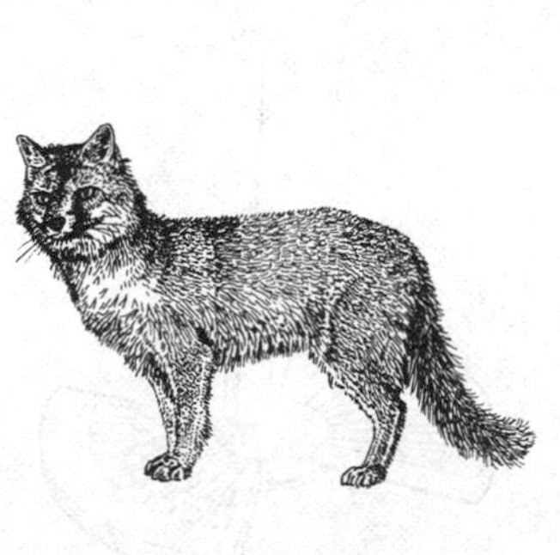

Fox

mammal of the dog family that has a pointed muzzle, large ears, a long bushy tail, and usually reddish-brown or gray fur. Foxes are found throughout most of the world and hunt alone, mainly at night, relying on cunning and an acute sense of hearing and smell. Genus: *Vulpes*. **2.** FOX FUR the fur of the fox **3.** TRICKSTER a sly and cunning person (*informal*) **4.** GOOD-LOOKING PERSON a good-looking young person (*informal*) ■ *vt.* **(foxed, fox·ing, fox·es) 1.** DECEIVE OR OUTWIT to deceive or outwit somebody by means of sly trickery **2.** BAFFLE to confuse or baffle somebody (*often passive*) [Old English. Ultimately from an Indo-European word probably meaning "tail."]

Fox[1] /foks/ *n.* **1.** PEOPLES MEMBER OF NATIVE N AMERICAN PEOPLE a member of a Native North American people that lived in Michigan, Wisconsin, Illinois, and Iowa, and whose members now live mainly in Oklahoma and Iowa. Following U.S. attempts under a spurious treaty to move the Fox from their lands in Illinois, they joined with the Sauk in the Black Hawk War of 1832. **2.** LANG ALGONQUIAN LANGUAGE a language spoken in parts of Iowa and Oklahoma. It is one of the Algonquian group of the Algonquian-Wakashan family of North American languages. About 2,000 people speak Fox. ■ *adj.* RELATING TO FOX relating or belonging to the Fox people, or their language or culture

Fox[2] /foks/ river of eastern Wisconsin, rising in Columbia County and flowing southwestward before emptying into Lake Michigan at Green Bay. Length: 175 mi./282 km.

Fox, Michael J. (*b.* 1961) Canadian-born U.S. television and movie actor. He starred in the television show series *Family Ties* and the movie trilogy *Back to the Future* (1985–90).

Foxe Ba·sin /fóks-/ bay in Nunavut, northeastern Canada, surrounded by Baffin Island, Melville Peninsula, and Hudson Bay. Depth: 295 ft./90 m.

foxed /fokst/ *adj.* stained with yellowish-brown spots from having been kept in damp conditions (*refers to books or paper*)

fox·fire /fóks fìr/ *n.* a luminescent glow produced by some fungi when in contact with rotting wood

Foxglove

fox·glove /fóks glùv/ (*plural* **-glove** *or* **-gloves**) *n.* a tall plant that has numerous thimble-shaped purple or white flowers and is the source of the drug digitalis. Latin name: *Digitalis purpurea.*

fox grape *n.* a wild grape of the eastern United States that has purplish fruits and is the source of many cultivated grape varieties. Latin name: *Vitis labrusca.*

fox·hole /fóks hōl/ *n.* a small hole dug in the ground to protect a sniper or other soldier from enemy fire

fox·hound /fóks hòwnd/ *n.* a small short-haired dog that has great speed and stamina, belonging to either of two breeds that are used to hunt foxes

fox hunt·er *n.* **1.** HUNTER OF FOXES somebody who regularly hunts foxes for sport **2.** FOXHUNTING HORSE a horse used for foxhunting

fox·hunt·ing *n.* a sport in which mounted hunters pursue a fox through open countryside with a pack of foxhounds

fox·tail /fóks tàyl/, **fox·tail grass** *n.* a grass with soft cylindrical spikes resembling the tail of a fox. Genera: *Alopecurus Setaria* and *Hordeum.*

fox ter·ri·er *n.* a small wire-haired or smooth-haired dog belonging to a breed that has a white coat with dark markings

fox·trot /fóks tròt/ *n.* **1.** DANCE BALLROOM DANCE a ballroom dance that alternates longer slower walking steps and shorter quicker running steps to music with four, or sometimes two, beats to the bar **2.** MUSIC MUSIC FOR FOXTROT a piece of music for dancing the foxtrot **3.** EQU A HORSE'S SLOW TROTTING PACE a slowish pace for a horse, between a trot and a walk, in which it takes short steps in a broken rhythm ■ *vi.* **(-trot·ted, -trot·ting, -trots)** DANCE THE FOX TROT to dance the fox trot [Early 20th C. From the short steps of the fox; in the dance sense perhaps reinforced by the name of Harry *Fox*, a vaudeville performer.]

Fox·trot *n.* a code word for the letter "F," used in international radio communications

fox·y /fóksee/ **(-i·er, -i·est)** *adj.* **1.** LIKE A FOX like a fox, especially in appearance or through having a strong pungent smell **2.** COLORS REDDISH-BROWN of a reddish-brown color, like the fur of the fox **3.** CRAFTY clever in a cunning or deceitful way **4.** ALLURING sensually alluring (*informal*) **5.** WINE SHARP OR MUSKY having the rather sharp, pungent, or musky flavor of fox grapes **6.** PAPER = **foxed**

foy·er /fóy ər, fwaá yày/ *n.* **1.** PUBLIC LOBBY the lobby in a public building such as a hotel or theater **2.** ENTRANCE HALL the entrance hall or vestibule in a private house [Mid-19thC. Via French from medieval Latin *focarius*, from Latin *focus* "fireplace, hearth" (see FOCUS).]

FPC *abbr.* **1.** Federal Power Commission **2.** fish protein concentrate

fpm *abbr.* feet per minute

FPO *abbr.* fleet post office

fps *abbr.* **1.** MEASURE feet per second **2. fps, f.p.s.** MEASURE foot-pound-second **3.** PHOTOGRAPHY frames per second

fps u·nits, **fps sys·tem of u·nits** *n.* a system of units based on the foot, second, and pound mass that is now almost wholly superseded by SI units

Fr *symbol.* francium

fr. *abbr.* from

Fr. *abbr.* **1.** Father **2.** France **3.** French **4.** Friday **5.** Friar **6.** Frau

f.r. *abbr.* on the right-hand page

Fra /fraa/, **fra** *n.* used as a title for an Italian monk or friar, the equivalent of the English title "Brother" [Late 19thC. From Italian, shortening of *frate* "brother, friar," from Latin *frater* (source of English *fraternal*).]

fra·cas /fráykəss, frákəss/ (*plural* **-cas**) *n.* a noisy quarrel or fight [Early 18thC. From French, "crash, roar," from, ultimately, Italian *fracassare* "to cause an uproar."]

frac·tal /frákt'l/ *n.* REPEATING GEOMETRIC PATTERN an irregular or fragmented geometric shape that can be repeatedly subdivided into parts, each of which is a smaller copy of the whole. Fractals are used in computer modelling of natural structures that do not have simple geometric shapes, e.g., clouds, mountainous landscapes, and coastlines. ■ *adj.* OF FRACTALS involving or relating to fractals [Late 20thC. From French, coined by the mathematician Benoît Mandelbrot from Latin *fract-*, the past participle stem of *frangere* (see FRACTION).]

frac·tion /frákshən/ *n.* **1.** MATH NUMBER THAT IS NOT A WHOLE a number that is not a whole number, such as $\frac{1}{2}$ **(vulgar fraction)** or 0.5 **(decimal fraction)**, formed by dividing one quantity into another **2.** SMALL AMOUNT a small part, amount, or proportion of something ○ *a fraction of the cost* **3.** PART a part or element of a larger whole or group **4.** CHR BREAKING OF BREAD BY PRIEST during Holy Communion in the Roman Catholic tradition, the breaking off of a piece of bread by the priest who places it in the chalice **5.** CHEM SEPARATED COMPONENT an individual component or portion of a mixture, separated by differences in chemical or physical properties [14thC. Via Old French from the late Latin stem *fraction-*, from Latin *fract-*, past participle stem of *frangere* "to break." Ultimately from an Indo-European base that is also the ancestor of English *break*.] ◇ **a fraction** by or over a very small amount or distance

WORD KEY: ORIGIN

The Latin *frangere*, from which ***fraction*** is derived is also the source of English *fracture, fragile, fragment, frail*, and *saxifrage*.

frac·tion·al /frákshən'l/ *adj.* **1.** MATH OF FRACTIONS involving or relating to fractions **2.** SLIGHT very small or slight ○ *a fractional increase in temperature* **3.** CHEM RELATING TO COMPONENT SEPARATION relating to the process of separating individual components from a mixture on the basis of the chemical or physical properties that make them different from other components

frac·tion·al dis·til·la·tion *n.* the process of separating components that have different boiling points from a volatile liquid, by first heating the liquid and then condensing and collecting the components as they vaporize

frac·tion·al·ize /frákshən'l ìz/ **(-ized, -iz·ing, -izes)** *vt.* to divide something into parts or sections — **frac·tion·al·i·za·tion** *n.*

frac·tion·al·ly /frákshən'lee/ *adv.* very slightly, or to a very slight degree

frac·tion·ate /frákshə nàyt/ **(-at·ed, -at·ing, -ates)** *v.* **1.** *vti.* DIVIDE OR BREAK INTO PARTS to divide or break, or to divide or break something, into parts (*formal*) **2.** *vt.* CHEM SEPARATE MIXTURE INTO ITS COMPONENTS to separate a mixture into its components, e.g., by crystallization or distillation —**frac·tion·a·tion** /fràkshə náysh'n/ *n.* —**frac·tion·a·tor** /frákshə nàytər/ *n.*

frac·tious /frákshəss/ *adj.* irritable and likely to complain or misbehave [Late 17thC. Formed from FRACTION, originally perhaps in the sense "disposed to break up relationships."] —**frac·tious·ly** *adv.* —**frac·tious·ness** *n.*

frac·ture /frákchər/ *n.* **1.** BREAK OF BONE a break in a bone **2.** ACT OF BREAKING SOMETHING the act of breaking something, especially a bone **3.** BREAK OR CRACK a break, split, or crack in an object or a material **4.** SPLIT IN SYSTEM OR ORGANIZATION a split or division in something such as a system, organization, or agreement ○ *the fractures that are already starting to appear in the peace treaty* **5.** GEOL ROCK BREAK a break in a rock or mineral, across which there is a separation ■ *vti.* **(-tured, -tur·ing, -tures) 1.** BREAK to break or crack something, especially a particular bone or a bone in a particular part of the body **2.** CAUSE OR UNDERGO DAMAGE to cause damage or disruption to something or destroy it, or to be damaged, disrupted, or destroyed [Mid-16thC. Directly or via French from Latin *fractura*, from, ultimately, *frangere* "to break" (see FRACTION).] —**frac·tur·a·ble** *adj.*

frae /fray/ *prep. Scotland* from [13thC. Variant of FRO.]

frag /frag/ *n.* GRENADE a fragmentation grenade (*slang*) ■ *vt.* **(fragged, frag·ging, frags)** KILL SOMEBODY WITH EXPLOSIVE to kill or wound a soldier on your own side with a fragmentation grenade or other explosive device (*slang*) [Mid-20thC. Shortening of FRAGMENTATION.] —**frag·ger** *n.* —**frag·ging** *n.*

frag·ile /frájjəl/ *adj.* **1.** EASILY BROKEN easy to break, damage, or harm, usually because delicate or brittle ○ *The models were too fragile to be used as toys.* **2.** EASILY DESTROYED not strong, sound, or secure and unlikely to withstand any severe stresses and strains that may be put on it ○ *a fragile peace* **3.** PHYSICALLY WEAK in a weak or delicate bodily state, usually as a result of illness ○ *Her mother's in rather fragile health and doesn't get out much.* [15thC. Directly or via French from Latin *fragilis* (source also of English *frail*), from, ultimately, the same base as *frangere* "to break" (see FRACTION).] —**frag·ile·ly** *adv.* —**fra·gil·i·ty** /frə jíllətee/ *n.*

WORD KEY: SYNONYMS

fragile, delicate, frail, flimsy, frangible, friable

CORE MEANING: easily broken or damaged

fragile used to describe things that do not have a strong structure or are not made of robust materials, and are therefore easily broken or damaged; **delicate** similar to "fragile," used especially to talk about things that are beautiful or remarkable because of their fragility; **frail** used especially in written English to talk about something easily broken or damaged. It is also used to talk about people who are so physically weak that they seem very vulnerable to injury; **flimsy** used showing disapproval to describe something that is easily broken, torn, or damaged because it is badly or cheaply made. It can also be used to describe clothing that is light and insubstantial; **frangible** a formal or technical word meaning brittle or easily broken; **friable** a formal or technical word meaning likely or easy to crumble.

frag·ile-X syn·drome *n.* a genetic condition caused by an abnormal X chromosome with an apparently almost detached part near the end of the long arm, that causes learning difficulties in boys and men

frag·ment *n.* /frágmənt/ **1.** BROKEN PIECE a piece, usually a small piece, broken off something or left when something is shattered **2.** INCOMPLETE PIECE an incomplete or isolated piece of something ○ *I noted* *down fragments of the conversation.* ■ *vti.* /frag mént/ **(-ment·ed, -ment·ing, -ments) 1. BREAK INTO SMALL PIECES** to break, or break something, into small pieces ○ *The metal is designed to fragment on impact.* **2. BREAK UP** to lose, or to cause something to lose, a sense of unity or cohesion, with the result that something splits into isolated and often conflicting elements ○ *Society is starting to fragment.* [Mid-16thC. Directly or via French from Latin *fragmentum*, from, ultimately, the same base as produced *frangere* "to break" (see FRACTION).]

frag·men·tal /frag mént'l/ *adj.* **1.** = **fragmentary 2.** GEOL **MADE UP OF ROCK FRAGMENTS** used to describe rocks that are made up of fragments of preexisting rocks

frag·men·tar·y /frágmən tèrree/ *adj.* consisting of the physical fragments of something, or of small disconnected items that are usually insufficient to form a whole or serve a satisfactory purpose —**frag·men·tar·i·ly** /fràgmən térrilee/ *adv.*

frag·men·ta·tion /fràgmən táysh'n/ *n.* **1. BREAKING UP OF SOMETHING** the process of shattering or breaking up into fragments **2. LOSS OF UNITY AND COHESION** the loss of unity and cohesion and the breakup of something into isolated and often conflicting elements ○ *The result, inevitably, would be social fragmentation.* **3. SHATTERING OF EXPLOSIVE DEVICE** the scattering of the shattered parts of a grenade or other explosive device **4.** COMPUT **BREAKING UP OF DATA PACKET** a process in which packets of computer data are broken up into smaller pieces for more efficient storage and transmission. The danger inherent in this process is that the relationship between the pieces may be lost.

frag·men·ta·tion bomb *n.* a bomb or shell with a thick casing that is designed to shatter on detonation into many destructive fragments in order to cause maximum damage or injury

frag·men·ta·tion gre·nade *n.* a grenade with a thick casing that is designed to shatter on detonation into many destructive fragments, causing maximum damage or injury

frag·ment·ed /frag méntəd/ *adj.* made up of disconnected parts or elements and lacking overall coherence

frag·men·tize /frágmən tīz/ **(-tized, -tiz·ing, -tiz·es)** *vti.* = **fragment**

fra·grance /fráygrəns/ *n.* **1. NICE ODOR** a pleasant smell **2. SWEETNESS OF SMELL** the characteristic of being sweet-smelling **3. PERFUME** something such as a perfume or cologne, which has a distinctive smell ○ *a great new fragrance for men*

WORD KEY: SYNONYMS

See Synonyms at ***smell.***

fra·grance strip *n.* a sealed strip of card or paper included with something such as a magazine advertisement and impregnated with a fragrance that is released when the cover is peeled off

fra·gran·cy /fráygrənsee/ *n.* = **fragrance** *n.* 2

fra·grant /fráygrənt/ *adj.* having a pleasant or sweet smell [15thC. Directly or via French from Latin *fragrant-*, the present participle stem of *fragrare* "to emit a (good or bad) odor."] —**fra·grant·ly** *adv.*

fraid·y-cat *n.* somebody who is scared or who lacks courage (*informal*) (*usually used by or to children*) [*Fraidy* formed from a shortening of AFRAID. *Cat* perhaps from that animal's generally skittish nature.]

frail /frayl/ **(frail·er, frail·est)** *adj.* **1. WEAK** in a weakened state or in bad health **2. EASY TO BREAK OR DAMAGE** made of weak or delicate materials and easy, or apparently easy, to break or damage **3. INSUBSTANTIAL** lacking any substantial foundation in fact or reality and unlikely to be realized or be successful ○ *frail hopes of success* **4. MORALLY WEAK** easily tempted and led into sin or wrongdoing [14thC. Via Old French *fraile* from Latin *fragilis* (see FRAGILE).] —**frail·ly** *adv.*

WORD KEY: SYNONYMS

See Synonyms at ***fragile*** and ***weak.***

frail·ty /fráyltee/ (*plural* **-ties**) *n.* **1. WEAKNESS** physical weakness or weakness of materials and construction **2. MORAL WEAKNESS** inherent moral weakness in humanity or in an individual leading to difficulty in resisting temptation or avoiding wrongdoing **3. CHARACTER FLAW** a character flaw arising out of moral weakness (*often used in the plural*) ○ *ordinary human frailties*

fraise /frayz/ *n.* a cone-shaped grooved drill bit used for enlarging a previously drilled hole [Early 17thC. From French, literally "abdominal lining of a calf"; from the numerous folds of this lining.]

Frak·tur /frak to͝or/, **frak·tur** *n.* a thick ornate style of printed letter, the standard typeface for all printing in German until around the middle of the 20th century. It was used in the calligraphy and artwork of the Pennsylvania Dutch. [Late 19thC. Via German from, ultimately, Latin *fractura* (see FRACTURE). The underlying sense is that the elaborate shape of the letters seems to break up the words.]

Fra Mauro /fraa máwrō/ *n.* an eroded crater on the Moon north of Mare Nubium, approximately 59 mi./95 km in diameter. Apollo 14 landed close to Fra Mauro in 1971.

fram·be·sia /fram beézhə/ *n.* MED = **yaws** [Early 19thC. From modern Latin, coined from French *framboise* "raspberry"; from the shape and color of the sores produced by the disease.]

frame /fraym/ *n.* **1. SUPPORTING STRUCTURE** an underlying or supporting structure that consists of solid parts such as beams or struts with spaces between them and that has something built around or on top of it ○ *a bike with a steel frame* **2. SURROUNDING STRUCTURE** a structure that surrounds or encloses a particular space ○ *a picture frame* ○ *a door frame* **3. frame, frames** OPHTHALMOL **LENS-HOLDING PART OF EYEGLASSES** the part of a pair of eyeglasses that holds the lenses and fits around the wearer's face **4.** CRAFT **HOLLOW SHAPE FOR NEEDLECRAFTS AND PAINTING** an open structure across which a piece of material can be stretched to be painted or embroidered, or across which threads can be stretched for weaving **5. CONTEXT** the general background or context against or within which something takes place ○ *the story's historical frame* **6. HUMAN BODY** a person's body, especially with reference to its size and shape ○ *He eased his enormous frame into the chair.* **7.** CINEMA, PHOTOGRAPHY **SINGLE PICTURE ON STRIP OF FILM** any one of the individual pictures that make up a strip of movie film, or a single exposure on a strip of photographic negative or slide images **8.** CINEMA, TV **VISIBLE PART OF FILMED ACTION** in film, video, or TV, the particular area of action that is captured by the camera and forms the rectangular image that appears on the screen ○ *characters moving out of the frame to the left* **9.** PHOTOGRAPHY **IMAGE BORDER** the border or set of borders of a projected image **10.** PUBL **SINGLE PICTURE IN COMIC STRIP** any one of the individual pictures that make up a comic strip **11.** GARDENING = **cold frame 12.** BOWLING **ROUND OF BOWLING** one of the 10 rounds in a bowling game **13.** *U.K.* CUE GAMES = **rack 14.** TELECOM, COMPUT **SINGLE CYCLE OF PULSES** a single cycle of pulses in a string of repeated pulses **15.** = **frame-up** *n.* 1 (*slang*) ■ *vt.* **(framed, fram·ing, frames) 1. MOUNT IN A FRAME** to mount a picture in a frame **2. FORM SURROUNDING FRAMEWORK FOR** to form a surrounding border or a framework, especially a decorative or contrasting one, around something (*often passive*) ○ *a delicate face framed by abundant black hair* **3. CONSTRUCT IDEA OR STATEMENT** to construct or compose something that is to be written or spoken ○ *She framed her words carefully.* **4. EXPRESS IN PARTICULAR WAY** to express something in a particular type of language ○ *framed the argument in legal language* **5. MOUTH WORDS** to mouth words silently **6. CAUSE TO APPEAR GUILTY** to make an innocent person appear guilty, e.g., by forging incriminating evidence (*slang*) **7. ARRANGE RESULT IN ADVANCE** to use dishonest or illegal methods to arrange the result of a contest in advance, e.g., by paying a player to lose deliberately (*slang*) ■ *adj.* CONSTR, ARCHIT **WITH WOODEN FRAMEWORK** constructed on a framework of wooden beams, then covered with boards or shingles ○ *a white frame house with black shutters* [Old English *framian* "to make progress, be helpful," hence "to prepare, shape." Formed from *fram* "forward" (related to modern English *from*). The noun developed from the verb, originally in the sense "structure."] —**frame·a·ble** *adj.*

Frame /fraym/, **Janet** (*b.* 1924) New Zealand writer. Her novels, short stories, and autobiographical works include *To the Is-land* (1983) and *An Angel at My Table* (1984). Real name **Janet Paterson Frame Clutha**

frame of mind *n.* a person's psychological state, attitude, or mood at a particular time

frame of ref·er·ence *n.* **1. STANDARDS USED FOR JUDGING OR DECIDING** the set of norms, values, or ideas that affect the way somebody interacts with others, either in everyday life or in particular situations **2.** GEOM **SET OF GEOMETRIC AXES** a set of geometric axes used to determine the location of a point in space

Janet Frame

fram·er /fráymər/ *n.* **1. PERSON FITTING FRAMES FOR PICTURES** a person who makes and fits frames for pictures **2. fram·er, Fram·er WRITER OF U.S. CONSTITUTION** any one of the delegates who drew up the Constitution of the United States

frame sto·ry *n.* a narrative that provides the framework within which a number of different stories, which may or may not be connected, can be told. An example of a frame story is the pilgrims' ride to Canterbury, which provides the starting point for Chaucer's *Canterbury Tales.*

frame-up *n.* (*slang*) **1. PLOT MAKING SOMEBODY INNOCENT APPEAR GUILTY** a conspiracy to make an innocent person appear guilty, e.g., by forging incriminating evidence **2. DISHONEST PREARRANGING OF CONTEST RESULT** a situation in which the result of a contest is dishonestly or illegally arranged in advance

frame·work /fráym wùrk/ *n.* **1. SYSTEM OF INTERCONNECTING BARS** a structure of connected horizontal and vertical bars with spaces between them, especially one that forms the skeleton of another structure **2. UNDERLYING SET OF IDEAS** a set of ideas, principles, agreements, or rules that provides the basis or the outline for something that is more fully developed at a later stage ○ *The purpose of this meeting is to provide a framework for the discussions at next week's conference.* **3. CONTEXT** the general background or context to a particular action or event ○ *within the framework of Jewish religious tradition* **4.** CRAFT **ARTICLES WOVEN OR EMBROIDERED ON FRAME** articles produced by weaving or embroidering cloth on a frame

fram·ing /fráyming/ *n.* **1. WAY SOMETHING IS FRAMED** the way that something is framed **2.** CINEMA **ADJUSTMENT OF FILM PROJECTOR SETTINGS** adjustment of the settings on a film projector so that the image is in the correct position on the screen **3.** CINEMA **COMPOSITION OF FILM SCENE** the composition of a scene within the visual field of the camera for shooting in a film

Fra·ming·ham /fráyming hàm/ town in eastern Massachusetts, a western suburb of Boston. Population: 64,536 (1996).

franc /frangk/ *n.* **1.** see table at **currency 2. FRANC COIN** a coin worth a franc. Symbol **F** [14thC. From French, of uncertain origin: probably from the Latin phrase *Francorum rex* "King of the Franks," imprinted on a type of gold coin first minted in 1360.]

France

France /franss/ republic and the largest country in western Europe. Its present constitution was established in 1958 with the proclamation of the Fifth Republic. Language: French. Currency: franc. Capital: Paris. Population: 58,609,285 (1997). Area:

210,026 sq. mi./543,965 sq. km. Official name **French Republic**

France, Anatole (1844–1924) French writer. He produced a large body of writings, including novels, drama, verse, critical and philosophical essays, and historical works. He won the Nobel Prize in literature in 1921. Pseudonym of **Jacques Anatole Francois Thibault**

fran·chise /frán chīz/ *n.* **1. RIGHT TO VOTE** the right to vote, especially to elect representatives to a national legislature or a parliament **2. PRIVILEGE GRANTED BY AUTHORITY** a right or privilege, or an exemption from a duty or obligation, granted by a government or other authority **3.** COMM **LICENSE TO SELL COMPANY'S PRODUCTS** an agreement or license to sell a company's products exclusively in a particular area, or to operate a business that carries that company's name **4.** COMM **AREA OF COMMERCIAL OPERATION** the area in which somebody has a commercial franchise **5.** SPORTS **PROFESSIONAL TEAM** a professional sports team that is a member of an organized league **6. fran·chise, fran·chise play·er** SPORTS **VALUABLE PLAYER** a player who is valuable and important to the team ■ *vt.* **(-chised, -chis·ing, -chis·es) GRANT TRADING FRANCHISE TO** to grant a commercial franchise to a person or small company [14thC. From French, formed from *franc* "free" (see FRANK).] —**fran·chise·ment** /frán chīzmənt, fránchizmənt/ *n.*

fran·chis·ee /fràn chī zée/ *n.* a person or small company granted a license to sell a company's products or operate under a company's name exclusively within a stated area

fran·chis·er /frán chīzər/, **fran·chi·sor** *n.* a company that grants somebody an exclusive license to sell its products or operate under its name in a stated area

Fran·cis I /fránsiss/, **King of France** (1494–1547) French monarch. His reign (1515–47) was dominated by conflict with Charles V, Holy Roman Emperor.

Fran·cis·can /fran sískən/ *n.* **MEMBER OF RELIGIOUS ORDER** a member of an order of friars and nuns, founded by St. Francis of Assisi, that now has three separate branches and is largely devoted to missionary and charitable work. ■ *adj.* **RELATING TO ST. FRANCIS OR FRANCISCANS** relating to St. Francis of Assisi, or to the religious order he founded. [Late 16thC. Via French *franciscain* from modern Latin *Franciscanus*, from *Franciscus* "Francis."]

Fran·cis of Sales /frànsiss əv saál/, **St.** (1567–1622) French churchman and writer. A leader of the Counter-Reformation, he became bishop of Geneva (1602).

fran·ci·um /fránsee əm/ *n.* an unstable radioactive chemical element of the alkali-metal group, found in uranium ore and made artificially from actinium and thorium. Symbol **Fr** [Mid-20thC. Named after *France*, home of the element's discoverer.]

fran·ci·za·tion /frànsissi záysh'n/ *n. Can* the process of establishing French as the language of the workplace or establishing French-language schools in places previously without them

fran·cize /frán sīz/ **(-cized, -ciz·ing, -cizes)** *vt. Can* to enable a group in Canada to use French, or ensure that they are doing so [Late 20thC. From French *franciser*, from *français* "French."]

AKG London

Francisco Franco

Fran·co /frángkō/, **Francisco** (1892–1975) Spanish general and authoritarian leader. He defeated the Republican army during the Spanish Civil War (1936–39) and established a dictatorship in Spain in 1939, ruling until his death in 1975.

Franco- *prefix.* France, French ○ *Francophile* [From late Latin *Francus* "Frank," of Germanic origin]

Fran·co·ni·an /frang kōnee ən/ *n.* **GROUP OF MEDIEVAL GERMAN DIALECTS** a group of medieval dialects of German that were spoken in an area stretching from present-day Bavaria and Alsace, and up the Rhine valley ■ *adj.* **OF FRANCONIAN** relating to the Franconian group of dialects

Fran·co·phile /frángkə fīl/, **Fran·co·phil** /frángkə fil/ *n.* **PERSON WHO LIKES FRANCE** a person who likes France, the French people, and the French way of life ■ *adj.* **LIKING FRANCE AND FRENCH** liking or admiring France, the French, or the French way of life

Fran·co·phobe /frángkə fōb/ *n.* a person who dislikes France and the French people —**Fran·co·pho·bi·a** /frànkə fōbee ə/ *n.*

Fran·co·pho·bic /-fōbik/ *adj.* having an intense dislike of France, French people, or the French way of life

Fran·co·phone /frángkə fōn/ *n.* **SPEAKER OF FRENCH** a person who speaks French, especially as his or her native language ■ *adj.* **1. FRENCH-SPEAKING** having French as his or her native or main language **2. OF FRENCH-SPEAKING AREA** relating to a place where French is used as the main language, the official language, or a lingua franca ○ *Francophone Africa* —**Fran·co·phon·ic** /frànkə fónnik/ *adj.*

fran·gi·ble /fránjəb'l/ *adj.* capable of being broken or damaged [15thC. Directly or via Old French from medieval Latin *frangibilis*, from *frangere* "to break" (see FRACTION).] —**fran·gi·bil·i·ty** /frànjə bíllətee/ *n.*

WORD KEY: SYNONYMS

See Synonyms at ***fragile.***

fran·gi·pane /fránjə pàyn/ *n.* an almond-flavored cream or custard used in pastries, cakes, and other sweet foods [Mid-19thC. From French, "frangipani"; from the bitter almonds used in making the perfume frangipani.]

Frangipani

fran·gi·pan·i /frànjə pánnee, -paánee/ (*plural* **-is**) *n.* **1.** TREES **TREE WITH PERFUMED FLOWERS** a tropical American deciduous tree with white, yellow, or pink flowers that have an extremely strong sweet perfume. Genus: *Plumeria.* **2. PERFUME** perfume made from the flowers of the frangipani tree, or in imitation of their scent **3.** COOK = **frangipane** [Mid-19thC. Named for Muzio *Frangipani*, an Italian marquis of the 16thC, who created a perfume for scenting gloves.]

Fran·glais /frong gláy, fróng glày/, **fran·glais** *n.* **MIXTURE OF FRENCH AND ENGLISH** an informal form of French that includes a liberal sprinkling of English loanwords and phrases. For French traditionalists, it is a pejorative term, the concept seen as tangible evidence of the extent to which American and British cultural imperialism has permeated French and French-Canadian life. ■ *adj.* **OF FRANGLAIS** relating to Franglais [Mid-20thC. From French, blend of *français* "French" and *anglais* "English."]

frank[1] /frangk/ *adj.* **1. EXPRESSING TRUE OPINION** open, honest, and sometimes forceful in expressing true feelings and opinions **2. OPEN AND BLUNT** allowing people's true feelings and opinions to be openly and often bluntly stated **3. PLEASINGLY HONEST** having or showing an appealingly open and honest nature ○ *a frank manner that won her many friends* **4. UNDISGUISED** openly expressed, and so not concealed or disguised ○ *regarded him with frank loathing* ■ *vt.* **(franked, frank·ing, franks)** MAIL **1. PRINT MARK OVER STAMP** to print an official mark over the stamp on a letter or package to show that payment has been formally accepted **2. PRINT MARK TO SHOW POSTAGE PAID** to print a mark on a piece of mail, instead of using a postage stamp, to show that postage has been paid or that there is no postage charge ■ *n.* MAIL **1. OFFICIAL MARK ON PIECE OF MAIL** an official mark printed on a piece of mail to show that postage has been paid or that postage is free of charge **2. RIGHT TO FREE MAIL DELIVERY** the right to have mailed items delivered free of charge [14thC. Via French, "free, generous, candid" from medieval Latin *francus* "Frank, free" (see FRANK); from the granting of full political freedom in Gaul only to the Franks.] —**frank·ness** *n.*

frank[2] /frangk/ *n.* a frankfurter (*informal*) [Mid-20thC. Shortening.]

Frank *n.* a member of any of several Germanic peoples who originally lived along the Rhine valley, and spread westward during the decline of the Roman Empire in the 4th century A.D. They conquered vast areas of western Europe, taking over Gaul and becoming the dominant people in an area covering much of present-day western Germany. [Old English *Franca.* Later reinforced by French *Franc* and medieval Latin *Francus* (source of English *franc* and *frank*[1]), from the same prehistoric Germanic ancestor.]

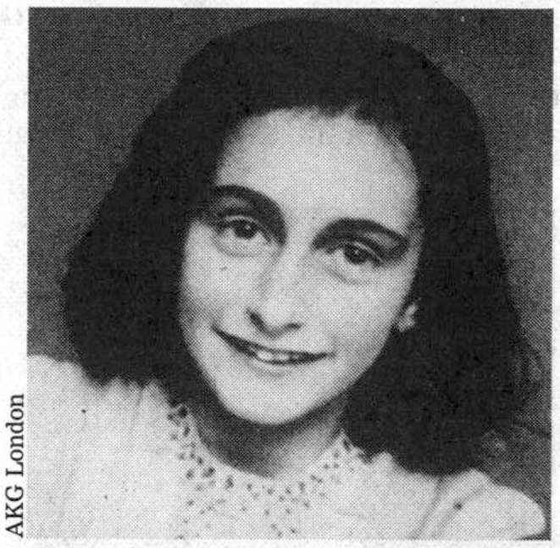

AKG London

Anne Frank

Frank /frangk/, **Anne** (1929–45) German-born Dutch writer. She kept a diary during her years in hiding during the German occupation of the Netherlands (1942–44). She and her family were captured in 1944, and she died in a concentration camp.

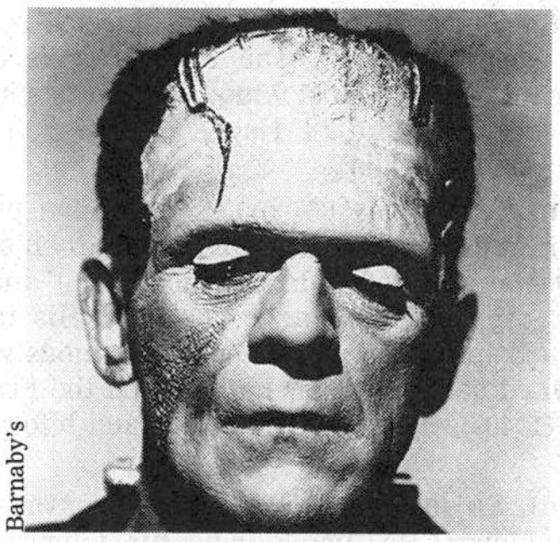

Barnaby's

Frankenstein

Frank·en·stein /frángk/ *n.* **1. CREATOR OF DESTRUCTIVE THING** somebody who creates something that causes widespread ruin or destruction, or that brings about the creator's own downfall **2. Frank·en·stein, Frank·en·stein's mon·ster OUT-OF-CONTROL INVENTION** a creation or invention that may get beyond its maker's control and cause problems **3. MONSTER** a monster in the shape of a very large coarse-featured person, often with features such as bolts in the neck and a shambling walk [Early 19thC. From the title of Mary Shelley's 1818 novel in which the hero creates a living man.]

Frank·en·thal·er /frángkən thàwlər, -thòllər/, **Helen** (*b.* 1928) U.S. artist. She is known for her abstract expressionism and innovative techniques for applying color to canvas.

Frank·fort /fránkfərt/ **1.** city in central Indiana, southeast of Lafayette and northwest of Indianapolis. Population: 15,231 (1996). **2.** capital of Kentucky, in the north central part of the state on the Kentucky River, northwest of Lexington and east of Louisville. Population: 26,695 (1996).

Frank·furt /frángkfərt, -fōort/, **Frank·furt am Main** /-aam mīn/ city in the state of Hessen, west central Germany. Situated on the Main River, it is a major commercial and financial center. Population: 656,200 (1994).

frank·furt·er /frángkfərtər/, **frank·furt** *n.* a thin-skinned sausage, originally from Germany, that is made of finely minced smoked pork or beef and is often grilled, fried, or boiled [Late 19thC. From German *Frankfurter Wurst*, a smoked sausage first produced at Frankfurt am Main.]

Frank·furt·er /frángkfərtər/, **Felix** (1882–1965) Austrian-born U.S. jurist. An associate justice of the U.S. Supreme Court (1939–62), he advocated judicial restraint.

frank·in·cense /frángkən sèns/ *n.* an aromatic gum or resin, often burned as an incense, especially in religious ceremonies, and also used in perfumes. It is obtained from an African tree. Latin name: *Boswellia sacra.* [14thC. From Old French *franc encens*, literally "superior-quality incense."]

Frank·ish /frángkish/ *n.* EXTINCT GERMANIC LANGUAGE an extinct ancient language spoken by the Franks, one of the West Germanic group of the Germanic branch of Indo-European languages. The French vocabulary shows a huge Frankish influence. ■ *adj.* **1.** OF FRANKS relating to or typical of the Franks, or their culture or language **2.** OF FRANKISH LANGUAGE relating to the Frankish language

Frank·lin /frángklən/ city in Williamson County on the Harpeth River, central Tennessee. Population: 20,098 (1990).

Aretha Franklin

Frank·lin, Aretha (*b.* 1942) U.S. soul singer. Known as "The Queen of Soul," she began her recording career in 1960. Her most famous recordings include "Respect" (1967)and "I Never" (1967). Full name **Aretha Louise Franklin**

Frank·lin, Benjamin (1706–90) U.S. statesman, printer, author, and scientist. He helped draft, then signed, the Declaration of Independence (1776) and was a U.S. diplomat to France (1776–85). His famous autobiography was published posthumously. Also renowned as a scientist, he invented the Franklin stove (1740s), lightning rod (1752), and bifocal lens (1760).

Frank·lin, Sir John (1786–1847) British naval officer and explorer. He died during his fourth Arctic expedition, in which the Northwest Passage was discovered (1845).

Frank·lin, William (1731–1813) American colonial administrator. The illegitimate son of Benjamin Franklin, he was a Loyalist governor of New Jersey (1763–76) during the Revolution. After 1782 he lived in England.

frank·lin·ite /frángkli nìt/ *n.* a black weakly magnetic mineral of the spinel group, consisting of an oxide of iron, manganese, and zinc. Formula: $ZnFe_2O_4$. [Early 19thC. Named for *Franklin*, New Jersey, where it is found.]

Frank·lin Square residential town in Nassau County, southeastern Long Island, New York. Population: 28,205 (1990).

Frank·lin stove *n.* a cast-iron heating stove with doors, whose interior is like an open fireplace [Late 18thC. Named for Benjamin FRANKLIN, who invented it.]

Frank·lin Strait body of water in Nunavut territory, north central Canada, between Prince of Wales Island and Boothia Peninsula

frank·ly /frángklee/ *adv.* **1.** HONESTLY in an honest and sincere, and often in a blunt and forthright way, without trying to hide true feelings or opinions ○ *a number of personal questions that he answered remarkably frankly* **2.** INTRODUCING HONEST OPINION used to indicate that you are expressing an honest personal opinion, often a negative one ○ *Most of what she said was, frankly, a pack of lies.*

fran·tic /frántik/ *adj.* **1.** OUT OF CONTROL EMOTIONALLY in a state in which it is impossible to keep feelings or behavior under control, usually through fear, worry, or frustration **2.** EXCITED, HURRIED, AND CONFUSED characterized by great haste and excitement and a lot of usually disorganized activity [Early 16thC. Via French *frénétique* from Latin *phreneticus* (see FRENETIC).] —**fran·ti·cal·ly** /frántikəlee/ *adv.*

Franz Jo·sef Land /frànts jṓzəf-, fraànts yṓssəf-/ archipelago of about 100 small ice-covered islands in the Arctic Ocean, northwestern Russia, including Alexandra Land, George Land, Wilczek Land, and Graham Bell Island. Area: 8,000 sq. mi./20,700 sq. km.

frap /frap/ (**frapped, frap·ping, fraps**) *vt.* to tie something down, or tie things together, with ropes [Mid-16thC. From Old French *fraper* "to hit."]

frappe /frapp/ = **frappé** *n.* 3

frap·pé /fra páy/ *adj.* BEVERAGES CHILLED chilled, or poured over crushed ice ○ *a café frappé* ■ *n.* **1.** BEVERAGES ICED ALCOHOLIC DRINK an alcoholic drink, especially a liqueur, served poured over crushed ice **2.** FOOD COLD DESSERT a dish consisting of fruit-flavored water ice, served before a meal or as a dessert **3.** *New England* BEVERAGES MILK SHAKE a milk shake [Mid-19thC. From French, the past participle of *frapper* "to hit, chill."]

Fra·ser /fráyzər/ river in south central British Columbia, Canada. It rises in the Rocky Mountains and empties into the Strait of Georgia, near Vancouver. Length: 850 mi./1,370 km.

Fra·ser, Simon (1776–1862) Canadian fur trader and explorer. He founded settlements in British Columbia (1805–08) and explored the Fraser River.

Fra·ser Is·land island off the coast of southern Queensland, Australia. It is the largest sand island in the world. Area: 642 sq. mi./1,662 sq. km.

frass /frass/ *n.* insect excrement or debris left behind by an insect or insect larva [Mid-19thC. From German, formed from *fressen* "to eat, devour."]

frat /frat/ *n.* a fraternity at a college or university (*informal*) [Late 19thC. Shortening.]

fra·ter·nal /frə túrn'l/ *adj.* **1.** OF BROTHERS existing between brothers, or felt by one brother for another **2.** SHOWING FRIENDSHIP AND MUTUAL SUPPORT showing friendship and mutual support between people or groups that share the same interests or aims ○ *fraternal greetings* **3.** OF FRATERNITIES relating to or organized as a fraternity **4.** EMBRYOL FROM TWO SEPARATE OVA used to describe twins that have developed from two separate ova, rather than a single ovum [15thC. From medieval Latin *fraternalis*, from, ultimately, Latin *frater* "brother." Ultimately from the same Indo-European word as English *brother*.] —**fra·ter·nal·ism** *n.* —**fra·ter·nal·ly** *adv.*

fra·ter·ni·ty /frə túrnətee/ (*plural* **-ties**) *n.* **1.** SOCIETY FOR COLLEGE MEN a social society for men who are students at a college or university, with a name consisting of individually pronounced Greek letters. ◊ **sorority** **2.** PEOPLE WITH SOMETHING IN COMMON a group of people with something in common, e.g., being in the same job or sharing the same pastime ○ *the banking fraternity* **3.** BROTHERLY LOVE brotherly love, or feelings of friendship and mutual support between people ○ *liberty, equality, and fraternity* **4.** SOCIETY FORMED FOR COMMON PURPOSE a group or society formed by people who share the same interests [14thC. Via French *fraternité* from Latin *fraternitas*, from, ultimately, *frater* (see FRATERNAL).]

frat·er·nize /fráttər nìz/ (**-nized, -niz·ing, -niz·es**) *v.* **1.** *vi.* SPEND TIME WITH PEOPLE to spend time with other people socially, especially people with whom you should not be friendly ○ *fraternizing with the enemy* **2.** *vti.* MIL HAVE SEXUAL RELATIONSHIPS AGAINST REGULATIONS to enter into a sexual relationship with a person of a different rank against military regulations [Early 17thC. Via French *fraterniser* from medieval Latin *fraternizare*, from, ultimately, Latin *frater* (see FRATERNAL).] —**frat·er·ni·za·tion** /fràttərni záysh'n/ *n.* —**frat·er·niz·er** /fráttər nìzər/ *n.*

frat·ri·cide /fráttri sìd/ *n.* **1.** KILLING A BROTHER the crime in which somebody kills his or her own brother **2.** KILLER OF BROTHER somebody who kills his or her own brother [15thC. Via French from Latin *fratricida* "brother-killer."] —**frat·ri·cid·al** /fràttri sìd'l/ *adj.*

fraud /frawd/ *n.* **1.** CRIME OF CHEATING PEOPLE the crime of obtaining money or some other benefit by deliberate deception **2.** SOMEBODY WHO DECEIVES BY PRETENDING somebody who deliberately deceives people by imitation or impersonation **3.** SOMETHING INTENDED TO DECEIVE something that is intended to deceive people ○ *a story that was subsequently exposed as a fraud* [14thC. Via Old French *fraude* from the Latin stem *fraud-* "cheating, fraud."]

fraud·u·lent /fráwjələnt/ *adj.* not honest, true, or fair, and intended to deceive people —**fraud·u·lence** *n.* —**fraud·u·lent·ly** *adv.*

fraught /frawt/ *adj.* **1.** FULL OF full of or accompanied by problems, dangers, or difficulties ○ *an evening fraught with embarrassment* **2.** TENSE AND ANXIOUS full of, or expressing, nervous tension and anxiety ○ *looking fraught and close to tears* [14thC. From the past participle of obsolete English *fraught* "to load with cargo," from Middle Dutch or Middle Low German *vrachten*.]

Fraun·ho·fer lines /frówn hṑfər-/ *npl.* narrow dark lines in the sun's spectrum, caused mainly by absorption in the cooler outer layers of the sun's atmosphere [Mid-19thC. Named for the German scientist, Joseph von *Fraunhofer* (1787–1826).]

frax·i·nel·la /fràksə néllə/ *n.* PLANTS = **gas plant** [Mid-17thC. From modern Latin, literally "small ash tree," from Latin *fraxinus* "ash"; from the shape of the leaves.]

fray[1] /fray/ *vti.* (**frayed, fray·ing, frays**) **1.** WEAR AWAY AND HANG IN THREADS to wear away the edge or surface of cloth or rope by friction, or to be worn away, causing threads to hang loose ○ *The jacket had frayed at the cuffs.* **2.** BECOME STRAINED OR STRAIN to become strained, causing irritability or anger, or to cause somebody's nerves, temper, or patience to become strained ○ *Soon tempers would start to fray.* ■ *n.* WORN PART WITH LOOSE THREADS a worn area on cloth or rope, with loose threads showing [15thC. Via French *frayer* from Latin *fricare* "to rub" (see FRICTION).]

fray[2] /fray/ *n.* **1.** ARGUMENT OR FIGHT an argument, quarrel, or fight ○ *Local newspapers were not slow to join the fray.* **2.** LIVELY ACTIVITY OR SITUATION an exciting, energetic, or stressful activity or situation ○ *back into the fray* [14thC. Shortening of AFFRAY.]

fra·zil /fráyz'l, frázz'l/ *n.* ice that forms as small plates drifting in rapidly flowing water where it is too turbulent for pack ice to form [Late 19thC. From Canadian French *frasil*.]

fraz·zle /frázz'l/ *n.* **1.** EXHAUSTED STATE a state of complete emotional and physical exhaustion **2.** FRAYED STATE a frayed or tattered condition ○ *drying her hair reduced it to a frazzle* ■ *v.* (**-zled, -zling, -zles**) **1.** *vt.* EXHAUST to tire somebody out emotionally and physically **2.** *vi.* BE FRAYED to fray or become worn ○ *a perm that frazzled under the drier* [Early 19thC. Origin uncertain: probably a blend of FRAY[1] and FRIZZLE[1] or obsolete *fazle* "to ravel."]

fraz·zled /frázz'ld/ *adj.* **1.** EXHAUSTED AND CONFUSED OR IRRITABLE exhausted and in a very confused or irritable state (*informal*) **2.** FRAYED frayed and in a generally worn, tangled, or otherwise unsatisfactory state

FRB *abbr.* Federal Reserve Board

FRCPC *abbr.* Fellow of the Royal College of Physicians, Canada

FRCSC *abbr.* Fellow of the Royal College of Surgeons, Canada

freak[1] /freek/ *n.* **1.** STRIKINGLY UNUSUAL PERSON, ANIMAL, PLANT a person, animal, or plant that is strikingly unusual, and appears to be unique or occurs very rarely (*offensive in some contexts*) **2.** UNUSUAL OCCURRENCE a highly unusual or unlikely occurrence, often brought about by a unique or very rare combination of circumstances **3.** SOMEBODY UNCONVENTIONAL somebody who behaves unusually or has unusual tastes or habits (*informal insult*) **4.** FANATIC somebody who is fanatical about something (*informal*) ○ *a club for fitness freaks* **5.** DRUG USER an addict or user of a particular drug (*slang*) **6.** HIPPIE a hippie (*dated slang*) **7.** IMPULSE something somebody suddenly does or decides for no real reason ■ *adj.* HIGHLY UNUSUAL OR UNLIKELY highly unusual or unlikely, and often brought about by a unique or very rare combination of circumstances ■ *vti.* (**freaked, freak·ing, freaks**) (*slang*) **1.** BECOME OR MAKE OVEREMOTIONAL to become, or make somebody, very nervous, upset, or angry ○ *She'll freak when she hears what she missed by not going with us.* **2.** DRUGS BEHAVE STRANGELY ON DRUGS to experience, or cause somebody to experience, wild or irrational behavior, sometimes accompanied by hallucinations or feelings of paranoia, often as a result of taking drugs [Mid-16thC. Origin uncertain:

perhaps originally a dialect word, from Old English *frician* "to dance."]

freak[2] /freek/ (**freaked, freak·ing, freaks**) *vt.* to streak or spot something with color (*literary*) [Mid-17thC. Origin uncertain: perhaps an alteration of obsolete *freck* "to dapple" (probably a shortening of FRECKLE), by association with STREAK.]

freak·ing /fréeking/ *adj.* used euphemistically in place of *frigging* or *fucking* to indicate the intensity of the user's feelings toward somebody or something (*slang offensive*) [Late 20thC. Formed from FREAK[1].]

freak·ish /fréekish/ *adj.* **1. VERY UNUSUAL** extremely, disconcertingly, or ridiculously unusual (*offensive in some contexts*) ○ *a freakish accident* **2. SUDDENLY VARIABLE** tending to change suddenly and unpredictably ○ *freakish weather* —**freak·ish·ly** *adv.*

freak-out /fréek owt/, **freak·out** *n.* (*slang*) **1. EMOTIONAL OUTBURST** an outburst of emotion or wild behavior **2. DRUG-INDUCED ATTACK OF PARANOIA** a drug-induced bout of hallucination or paranoia, especially a frightening one

freak·y /fréekee/ (**-i·er, -i·est**) *adj.* unusual, strange, or bizarre (*slang*) —**freak·i·ly** *adv.* —**freak·i·ness** *n.*

Fréch·ette /fray shét/, **Louis Honoré** (1839–1908) French-Canadian poet and politician. He is known for the epic cycle of historical poems, *Story of a People* (1887).

freck·le /frék'l/ *n.* **BROWN SKIN SPOT** a harmless small brownish patch on somebody's skin, usually one of a cluster, that becomes larger and deeper in color when the skin is exposed to the sun. Freckles are caused by the presence of larger melanin-containing cells in the basal layer of the skin. ■ *vti.* (**-led, -ling, -les**) **MARK WITH FRECKLES** to become marked with, or mark something with, freckles [15thC. Alteration of obsolete *frecken* "freckle," from Old Norse *freknur* "freckles."] —**freck·ly** *adj.*

Fred·die Mac *n.* the Federal Home Loan Mortgage Corporation, a private corporation sponsored by the U.S. government that supplies funds for mortgages, or a publicly traded security backed by it

Fred·er·ick /fréddrik/ city in north central Maryland, west of the Monocacy River. It is a trade and shipping center in an agricultural region. Population: 46,227 (1996).

Fred·er·ick II, King of Prussia (1712–86). Under his political and military leadership (1740–86), Prussia doubled in size and became a major European power. He gathered a circle of writers and musicians about him at his palace of Sans Souci. Known as **Frederick the Great**

Fred·er·ic·ton /fréddriktən/ capital of New Brunswick Province, eastern Canada, situated in the south central part of the province, on the St. John River. Population: 46,500 (1996).

free /free/ *adj.* (**fre·er, fre·est**) **1. NOT REGULATED** not controlled, restricted, or regulated by any external thing ○ *You are free to choose.* **2. NOT A PRISONER** not, or no longer, physically bound or restrained, e.g., as a prisoner or in slavery ○ *Once outside the prison walls he would be a free man.* **3. NOT RESTRICTED IN RIGHTS** not subject to censorship or control by a ruler, government, or other authority, and enjoying civil liberties ○ *It's a free country.* **4. SELF-RULING** not ruled by a foreign country or power **5. DISREGARDING TRADITIONAL LIMITATIONS** performed or written without being subjected to traditional conventions or restraints ○ *free verse* **6. NOT AFFECTED BY SOMETHING STATED** not subject to or affected by something specified, especially something undesirable ○ *drinking water that is free of contamination* ○ *free of charge* **7. NOT CONTAINING SOMETHING** not containing something specified (*often used in combination*) ○ *a salt-free diet* **8. COSTING NOTHING** requiring no money to be paid ○ *Win a free meal for two.* **9. NOT BUSY** not busy or working, or during which somebody is not busy or working ○ *She'll be free in a moment.* **10. NOT BEING USED** not being used, or not already reserved or taken by somebody else ○ *no free seats left* **11. NOT ATTACHED** not tied or attached to something ○ *grabbed the free end of the rope* **12. NOT BLOCKED** not blocked or obstructed by anything ○ *allowing the free flow of electricity* **13. NOT PHYSICALLY RESTRICTED** not restricted by something such as tight clothing, stiffness, or lack of space ○ *a layer of dirt interfering with the free movement of the mechanism* **14. GIVING SOMETHING READILY** giving or expending something generously, or too readily ○ *They're very free with their advice.* **15. NOT EXACT** not following the original version of something word for word or very precisely ○ *a free translation* **16. OPEN AND HONEST** spontaneous, open, and without awkwardness or reserve in speaking to or dealing with other people ○ *an appealingly free manner* **17.** CHEM **NOT CHEMICALLY COMBINED** not chemically combined with another substance **18.** PHYS **NOT ATTACHED TO LARGER BODY** not permanently attached to a larger body such as an atom or molecule, and thus having a relatively wide range of movement **19.** NAUT **FAVORABLE** favorable to sailing ○ *a free wind* **20.** LING **ABLE TO BE USED ALONE** used to describe a unit of meaning (**morpheme**) that can be used on its own as a word, rather than needing to be part of another word. ◊ **bound**[4] ■ *adv.* **WITHOUT COST** without paying any money ○ *They let you in free if you show your student card.* ■ *vt.* (**freed, free·ing, frees**) **1. RELEASE FROM CAPTIVITY** to release somebody from physical bonds or restrictions, captivity, or slavery ○ *The defendants were freed after having been found not guilty.* **2. RID OF SOMETHING** to remove a restriction, a burden, or an unwanted or undesirable thing from somebody or something ○ *freed from the cares of high public office* **3. MAKE AVAILABLE OR ENABLE** to make somebody or something available for use or able to do something ○ *This should free you to do more of your own research.* **4. UNCLOG SOMETHING OBSTRUCTED** to clear something of an obstruction [Old English *freo*. Ultimately from an Indo-European word meaning "dear, beloved," which is also the ancestor of English *friend*.] —**free·ness** *n.* ◇ **for free** without paying ◇ **make free with somebody** to behave in too familiar and informal a way toward somebody ◇ **make free with something** to use something in an over-familiar or over-indulgent way, without showing respect or restraint

WORD KEY: USAGE

See Usage essay at ***gift***.

free up *vt.* **1. MAKE AVAILABLE** to make available for use something that is currently occupied, otherwise employed, or subject to a restriction ○ *I need to free up some space on my hard disk.* **2. LOOSEN OR UNJAM** to enable something that is tightly fastened, jammed, or blocked to move freely (*informal*)

free a·gent *n.* **1. SOMEBODY ABLE TO ACT FREELY** somebody who is not responsible to or for anyone else and can do as he or she pleases **2. UNATTACHED PROFESSIONAL PLAYER** a professional athlete who is in a position to sign a contract to play for any team

free a·long·side ship *adj., adv.* COMM with the cost of delivery to the dockside included, but not the cost of loading onto a ship

free as·so·ci·a·tion *n.* **1. SPONTANEOUS EXPRESSION OF THOUGHTS** the spontaneous and uncensored expression of thoughts or ideas, allowing each one to lead to or suggest the next **2.** PSYCHOANAL **TECHNIQUE FOR EXPLORING THE UNCONSCIOUS** in psychoanalysis, a technique for exploring a patient's unconscious by stimulating the spontaneous and uncensored expression of thoughts or feelings through the use of stimuli such as key words —**free-as·so·ci·ate** *vi.*

free·base /frée bàyss/ *n.* **CONCENTRATED COCAINE** cocaine that has been concentrated using water and a volatile liquid such as ether ■ *v.* (**-based, -based, -bas·ing**) **1.** *vt.* **PREPARE COCAINE FOR SMOKING** to prepare cocaine for smoking by heating it with water and a volatile liquid such as ether to concentrate it **2.** *vti.* **SMOKE COCAINE** to smoke freebased cocaine (*slang*) [From the idea that the concentrated cocaine base of the original mixture is "freed" in the process of treatment with ether]

free·bie /fréebee/ *n.* something given or obtained free of charge, especially a promotional gift (*informal*)

free·board /frée bàwrd/ *n.* the distance between the deck of a ship and the level of the water

free·boot /frée bòot/ (**-boot·ed, -boot·ing, -boots**) *vi.* to live off things stolen or plundered [Late 16thC. Back-formation from FREEBOOTER.]

free·boot·er /frée bòotər/ *n.* somebody who lives by plundering others, especially a pirate [Late 16thC. From Dutch *vrijbuiter*, literally "somebody who takes booty freely" (source also of English *filibuster*).]

free·born /frée bàwrn/ *adj.* **1. BORN AS FREE CITIZEN** born as a free citizen, rather than in slavery or serfdom **2. RELATING TO FREE CITIZENS** relating to or intended for people who are freeborn

free climb·ing *n.* mountain or rock climbing without aids such as spikes and ladders, though usually with ropes and other safety equipment

freed·man /fréedmən, -màn/ (*plural* **-men** /-mən, -mèn/) *n.* a man who has been freed from slavery

free·dom /fréedəm/ *n.* **1. ABILITY TO ACT FREELY** a state in which somebody is able to act and live as he or she chooses, without being subject to any, or to any undue, restraints and restrictions ○ *live in freedom* **2. RELEASE FROM CAPTIVITY OR SLAVERY** release or rescue from being physically bound, or from being confined, enslaved, captured, or imprisoned ○ *hostages enjoying their first taste of freedom for months* **3. COUNTRY'S RIGHT TO SELF-RULE** a country's right to rule itself, without interference from or domination by another country or power **4. RIGHT TO ACT OR SPEAK FREELY** the right to speak or act without restriction, interference, or fear ○ *were given the freedom to take photographs and interview workers* **5. ABSENCE OF SOMETHING UNPLEASANT** the state of being unaffected by, or not subject to, something unpleasant or unwanted ○ *Freedom from want or fear is one of society's four principal freedoms.* **6. EASE OF MOVEMENT** the ability to move easily without being limited by something such as tight clothing or lack of space ○ *Releasing the catch allows complete freedom of movement in all directions.* **7. RIGHT TO TREAT PLACE AS OWN** the right to use or occupy a place and treat it as your own ○ *Off-season, we had the freedom of the whole house and the beach.* **8. HONORARY CITIZENSHIP** citizenship of a town or city, together with special privileges, formally awarded to somebody as an honor **9. FRANKNESS** openness and friendliness in speech or behavior **10. EXCESSIVE CONFIDENCE OR FAMILIARITY** overconfidence, overfamiliarity, or a lack of proper restraint or decorum **11.** PHILOS **FREE WILL** the ability to exercise free will and make choices independently of any external determining force

free·dom fight·er *n.* somebody who participates in an armed revolution against a government or political system regarded as unjust

free·dom march *n.* an organized march by people campaigning for civil rights, e.g., any of the marches that took place in the United States in the 1960s aimed at ending racial segregation —**free·dom march·er** *n.*

free·dom rid·er *n.* a civil rights activist who, during the early 1960s, joined one of the interracial groups riding buses through parts of the southern United States to protest against racial segregation — **free·dom ride** *n.*

freed·wom·an /fréed wòommən/ (*plural* **-en** /-wìmmin/) *n.* a woman who has been freed from slavery

free e·lec·tron *n.* an electron that is not bonded to an atom or molecule and so is free to move under external electric or magnetic fields

free en·er·gy *n.* a measure of the useful work resulting from a chemical or physical change. The determination of the change in free energy for a chemical reaction is a measure of the likelihood of that reaction to form products or the capacity of a system to do work. Symbol *G*

free en·ter·prise *n.* the doctrine or practice of giving companies the freedom to trade and make a profit without government control

free fall, free-fall *n.* **1. DESCENT WITH UNOPENED PARACHUTE** a descent through the air with an unopened parachute as the first part of a parachute jump **2. RAPID DECLINE** a sudden, rapid, and uncontrollable decline or descent in a particular system ○ *The news sent the stock market into a free fall.* **3.** PHYS **UNRESTRICTED MOVEMENT IN GRAVITATIONAL FIELD** an ideal state in which the only force to which something is subjected is the earth's gravitational attraction. A craft in space, e.g., is subject only to a diminished gravitational force and is not restricted by buoyancy or air resistance, producing near weightlessness.

free-fall (**free-fell, free-fall·en, free-fall·ing, free-falls**) *vi.* **1. DESCEND WITH UNOPENED PARACHUTE** to descend toward the ground with an unopened parachute during the first part of a parachute jump **2. DROP SUDDENLY** to undergo a sudden sharp drop in value, popularity, or credibility

free-fire zone *n.* an area in a zone of conflict where troops may fire on targets at will without requesting permission from a higher command

free flight *n.* the movement of a rocket or missile through the air after its engine has stopped

free-float·ing *adj.* not committed or dedicated to one

particular thing, especially a political party or cause

free-float·ing anx·i·e·ty *n.* PSYCHOANAL a state of anxiety that is not associated with any specific event or external condition

free-for-all *n.* a disorganized argument, contest, or fight, usually with everybody present joining in (*informal*)

free form *n.* **1.** IRREGULARLY SHAPED SCULPTURE a shape, especially a piece of sculpture, that is asymmetrical and irregular though usually with a flowing outline **2.** LING SELF-CONTAINED LINGUISTIC UNIT a unit of meaning (**morpheme**) that can be used on its own as a word, rather than needing to be part of another word

free·form /freé fàwrm/ *adj.* **1.** WITH FLOWING SHAPES OR OUTLINES unconventional in shape or design, especially flowing and curving as opposed to regular or geometrical **2.** ORIGINAL, NOT STANDARD spontaneously or individually created, rather than being produced in accordance with accepted or prescribed standards

free hand *n.* complete freedom to take action or make decisions

free·hand /freé hànd/ *adj., adv.* done by hand and without using drawing instruments such as rulers or compasses

free·hold /freé hōld/ *n.* **1.** LEGAL OWNERSHIP OF PROPERTY legal ownership of a property giving the owner unconditional rights, including the right to grant leases and take out mortgages **2.** FREEHOLD PROPERTY a property that has freehold status

free·hold·er /freé hōldər/ *n.* a property owner who has a freehold

free jazz *n.* a style of jazz, developed in the 1960s, that has no set harmonies or melodic patterns

free kick *n.* in soccer, a kick of a stationary ball for an infringement by opponents, who must stand at least 10 yards from where the kick is made. A goal can be scored by a player making a direct free kick, whereas an indirect free kick requires that the ball touch another player before entering the goal.

free·lance /freé lànss/ *n.* **1. free·lance, free·lanc·er** SOMEBODY WORKING FOR DIFFERENT COMPANIES a self-employed person working, or available to work, for a number of employers, rather than being committed to one, and usually hired for a limited period **2.** MAVERICK somebody, especially a politician, who is not committed to any group and takes action or forms alliances independently **3. free·lance, free lance** HIST MEDIEVAL MERCENARY a mercenary soldier in medieval Europe ■ *adj.* WORKING AS A FREELANCE working or earning a living as a freelance ■ *adv.* AS A FREELANCE independently, as a freelance ○ *worked freelance as a journalist* ■ *vi.* **(-lanced, -lanc·ing, -lanc·es)** WORK AS A FREELANCE to work independently as a freelance [Early 19thC. From the idea of a medieval knight with a lance offering his services to whoever was willing to pay.]

free-liv·ing *adj.* BIOL able to live or move independently, rather than being parasitic, symbiotic, or sessile ○ *free-living organisms*

free·load /freé lōd/ **(-load·ed, -load·ing, -loads)** *vi.* to live shamelessly on somebody else's generosity or hospitality, never sharing costs or responsibilities (*informal*) [Mid-20thC. Back-formation from FREELOADER.] —**free·load·ing** *n.*

freeloader /freé lōdər/ *n.* somebody who lives on somebody else's generosity or hospitality without sharing costs or responsibilities (*informal*) [Mid-20thC. Originally U.S. truckers' slang for somebody who had goods carried along with somebody else's cargo at no charge.]

free love *n.* sexual relationships without marriage or any commitment to a single partner, especially as practiced by the 19th- and early-20th-century avant garde and in the 1960s

free lunch *n.* something given free and with nothing expected in return (*informal*) [From the expression "There's no such thing as a free lunch," implying that recompense is always eventually exacted for an apparent act of selfless generosity]

free·ly /freélee/ *adv.* **1.** WITHOUT RESTRICTIONS without restrictions, controls, or limits ○ *able to move freely from country to country* **2.** IN LARGE AMOUNTS in large or generous quantities ○ *Conversation flowed freely all night.* **3.** OPENLY honestly and openly ○ *felt able to speak freely about his ordeal for the first time* **4.** WITHOUT TIGHTNESS OR STIFFNESS without being restricted by something such as tight clothing, stiffness, or lack of space ○ *clothes that allowed him to move more freely* **5.** USED TO EMPHASIZE HONESTY used to persuade others that somebody is being open and honest by accepting criticism ○ *I freely admit that mistakes were made.*

free·man /freéman/ (*plural* **-men**) *n.* **1.** MAN NOT ENSLAVED a man who is not enslaved or not in serfdom **2.** MAN GIVEN FREEDOM OF A PLACE a man who has been formally given citizenship of a place, together with various special privileges, as an honor ○ *a freeman of the city*

Free·man /freé man/, **Morgan** (*b.* 1937) U.S. stage, television, and movie actor, best known for his critically acclaimed character roles. Among his moviecredits are *Driving Miss Daisy* (1989) and *The Shawshank Redemption* (1994).

free mar·ket *n.* an economic system in which businesses operate without government control in matters such as pricing and wage levels —**free-mar·ket** *adj.* —**free-mar·ket·eer** *n.*

free·mar·tin /freé maart'n/ *n.* a sterile female twin born with a male calf [Late 17thC. Origin uncertain: perhaps from FREE + Irish *mart* "cow."]

Free·ma·son /freé mayss'n/ *n.* a member of a worldwide society of men, the Free and Accepted Masons, that is known particularly for its charitable work and for its secret rites

Free·ma·son·ry /freé mayss'nree/ *n.* **1.** PRACTICES OF FREEMASONS the institutions, beliefs, and practices of the Freemasons **2. Free·ma·son·ry, free·ma·son·ry** INSTINCTIVE UNDERSTANDING AND COMRADESHIP an instinctive understanding and comradeship among people with something in common

free·net /freé nèt/ *n.* an online computer information network or service that charges low or no access fees, and is often run by volunteers as a public service

free on board *adj., adv.* with the cost of delivery to a port and loading onto a ship included

free on rail *adj., adv.* with the cost of delivery to a railroad station and loading onto a train included

free port *n.* **1.** PORT OPEN TO ALL SHIPPING a port open to commercial ships from all countries on equal terms **2.** DUTY-FREE ZONE a zone, connected to a port or airport, that allows the duty-free import of goods that are to be reexported

Free·port /freé pawrt/ **1.** city in northern Illinois, east of Dubuque and west of Rockford. Population: 26,173 (1996). **2.** town and tourist center situated on the southwestern coast of Grand Bahama Island, the Bahamas. Population: 26,574 (1990). **3.** village in southeastern New York, on the southern coast of Long Island. Population: 40,164 (1996).

free rad·i·cal *n.* a highly reactive atom or group of atoms with an unpaired electron

free-range *adj.* **1.** NOT CAGED free to move about and feed at will, rather than being confined in a battery or pen ○ *free-range chickens* **2.** FROM FREE-RANGE ANIMALS produced by free-range poultry or livestock ○ *free-range eggs*

free rein *n.* complete freedom to make decisions and take action without consulting anyone else

free ride *n.* something obtained at no cost or with no effort

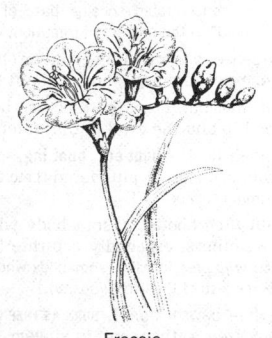

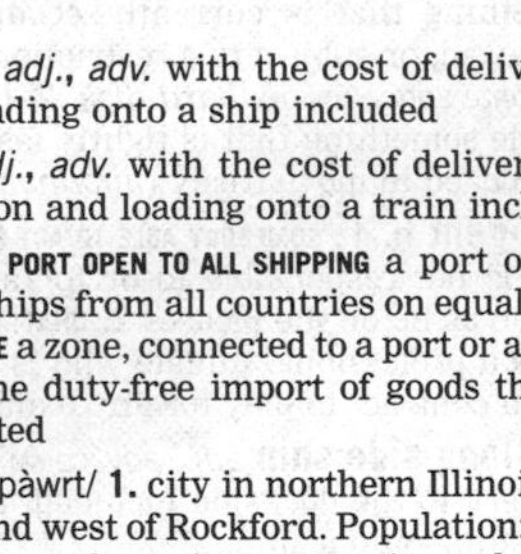

Freesia

free·sia /freézhə, -zee ə/ *n.* a plant native to southern Africa, popular for its clusters of fragrant flowers in a variety of bright colors. Genus: *Freesia.* [Late 19thC. Named for Friedrich H. T. *Freese*, German physician.]

free size *adj.* CLOTHES made in one size only, a size large enough to fit most people ○ *All the T-shirts are free size.*

free skat·ing *n.* competitive ice skating in which the skater makes up his or her own program from a list of approved moves

free soil *n.* those states in the United States in which slavery was prohibited before the Civil War. ◊ **Free State**

free-soil *adj.* HIST that prohibited slavery or opposed its extension to other states in the time before the Civil War (*refers to states in the United States*)

free space *n.* a region in which there is no matter and no gravitational or electromagnetic fields

free speech *n.* the right to express any opinion publicly

free spir·it *n.* somebody who lives the way he or she wants to, regardless of what convention dictates or what others expect

free-spo·ken *adj.* expressing opinions frankly, without worrying about embarrassing or offending others

free·stand·ing /free stánding/ *adj.* **1.** NOT ATTACHED TO A SUPPORT standing alone, and not attached to a wall, floor, or other structure for support **2.** INDEPENDENT existing or operating as an independent unit or entity ○ *a freestanding hospital not associated with the nearby university medical school* **3.** GRAM GRAMMATICALLY INDEPENDENT grammatically independent and able to function as a main clause

Free State *n.* **1.** NONSLAVE STATE OF PRE-CIVIL-WAR UNITED STATES any one of the U.S. states that prohibited slavery before the Civil War. ◊ **free soil 2.** *S Africa* S AFRICAN PROVINCE a province of South Africa, in the center of the country, north of the Orange River. Former name **Orange Free State 3.** *U.K.* HIST IRISH FREE STATE the Irish Free State

free·stone /freé stōn/ *n.* **1.** BUILDING STONE THAT CUTS WITHOUT BREAKING a variety of masonry stone that has a uniform texture and can be chiseled without breaking or splitting, e.g., limestone or fine sandstone **2.** FOOD FRUIT PIT a pit to which the flesh of a fruit does not cling, or any fruit that has such a pit

free·style /freé stīl/ *adj.* **1.** SPORTS WITH FREE CHOICE OF STYLE in which each competitor may use a style of his or her own choosing (*refers to a sporting event*) **2.** SWIMMING USING FRONT CRAWL in which the competitors use the fastest swimming stroke, the front crawl stroke (*refers to a swimming contest*) **3.** WRESTLING NO-HOLDS-BARRED in which all legal holds and tactics are allowed (*refers to a wrestling style*) ■ *n.* SPORTS FREESTYLE CONTEST a freestyle race or event —**free·styl·er** *n.*

free-swim·ming *adj.* able to swim about freely, as opposed to living attached to something or in one position ○ *free-swimming larvae*

free-swing·ing *adj.* bold and blunt in speech, style, or approach (*informal*)

free·think·er /free thíngkər/ *n.* somebody who refuses to accept established views or teachings, especially on religion, and forms opinions as a result of independent inquiry —**free·think·ing** *adj., n.*

free thought *n.* thinking that does not recognize the authority of, and is unrestricted by, established views or teachings, especially in religious matters

free throw *n.* in basketball, an opportunitity to shoot at the basket unhindered by the opposing players, awarded to a player who has been fouled

free-throw line *n.* = **foul line** *n.* 2

Free·town /freé tòwn/ capital, largest city, and chief port of Sierra Leone, on the western coast of Africa. Founded in 1787 as a settlement for freed slaves, it became the capital when Sierra Leone gained independence in 1961. Population: 470,000 (1994).

free trade *n.* international trade that is not subject to protective regulations or tariffs intended to restrict foreign imports —**free-trad·er** *n.*

free verse *n.* verse without a fixed metrical pattern, usually having unrhymed lines of varying length

free·ware /freé wàir/ *n.* any computer program or application that is available at no cost to the user

free·way /freé wày/ *n.* **1.** = **expressway 2.** TOLL-FREE ROAD a highway that can be used without paying a toll

free-weight *n.* a weight such as a dumbbell or barbell that is used for lifting exercises and is not attached to any other piece of apparatus

free·wheel /free weel, -hweel/ *vi.* (**-wheeled, -wheel·ing, -wheels**) 1. TRAVEL WITHOUT USING POWER to continue moving on a bicycle or in a vehicle without using power to drive the wheels ○ *Once you get to the top, you can freewheel all the way down the other side.* 2. LIVE IN CAREFREE WAY to live or act without conventional constraints, purpose, or regard for responsibilities ■ *n.* 1. DEVICE ON BICYCLE a mechanism in the hub of the rear wheel of a bicycle that enables the rear wheel to continue to rotate when the rider stops pedaling 2. AUTOMOT DEVICE IN MOTOR VEHICLE TRANSMISSION a mechanism in the transmission of a motor vehicle that disengages the drive shaft and allows it to rotate freely when revolving at a higher speed than the engine shaft

free·wheel·ing /free weeling, -hweel-/ *adj.* 1. TRAVELING WITHOUT POWER continuing to move without the use of power 2. CAREFREE without conventional constraints, purpose, or regard for responsibilities ○ *led a free-wheeling life of travel and adventure* 3. UNSTRUCTURED not restricted by rules, formal structure, or established procedures ○ *a freewheeling discussion that touched on many topics* 4. TRANSP WITH A FREEWHEEL relating to, having, or using a freewheel mechanism on a bicycle or vehicle

free will *n.* the ability to act or make choices as a free and autonomous being and not solely as a result of compulsion or predestination ◇ **of your own free will** without being forced by somebody or something else

free-will /free wìl/ *adj.* done willingly rather than by compulsion

free world *n.* the countries of the world with democratic governments and capitalistic or moderately socialistic economic systems, as opposed to those with totalitarian or Communist governments or economic systems

freeze /freez/ *v.* (**froze** /frōz/, **fro·zen** /frṓz'n/, **freez·ing, freez·es**) 1. *vti.* CHEM TURN LIQUID TO SOLID THROUGH COLD to be changed, or cause liquid to change, into a solid by the loss of heat, especially to change water into ice ○ *Salt water freezes at a lower temperature than fresh water.* 2. *vti.* COVER OR BECOME COVERED WITH ICE to become covered, or cause the surface of something to be covered, with ice ○ *The lake froze for only the second time in living memory.* 3. *vti.* BLOCK OR BECOME BLOCKED WITH ICE to become blocked, or cause something to become blocked, with ice ○ *Do you think it's cold enough to freeze the pipes in the attic?* 4. *vti.* BECOME HARD to harden, or cause something to harden, through the effects of cold or frost ○ *We couldn't play because the ground was frozen solid.* 5. *vti.* STICK TO SOMETHING BECAUSE OF COLD to become, or cause something to become, fixed or stuck to something else as a result of cold ○ *The wipers were frozen to the windshield.* 6. *vt.* PRESERVE WITH EXTREME COLD to preserve something, especially food, by subjecting it to and storing it at a temperature well below freezing point ○ *Store airtight up to two weeks or freeze.* 7. *vti.* FEEL VERY COLD to feel, or cause somebody to feel, extremely cold ○ *They left us to freeze outside, while they went into the house.* 8. *vti.* BE HARMED OR KILLED BY COLD to be harmed or killed, or harm or kill somebody or something, with cold or frost 9. *vi.* DROP TO FREEZING POINT to be at or fall to a temperature at or below freezing point ○ *The forecast says it's likely to freeze again tonight.* 10. *vti.* STOP MOVING to stop, or cause somebody to stop and remain still, e.g., as a result of fear or surprise or as part of a game ○ *A loose floorboard creaked in the hallway; Jenny froze.* 11. *vi.* COME TO A STANDSTILL THROUGH SHOCK to become unable to act, react, or speak in a normal way, usually through fear or shock ○ *I was OK in rehearsals, but in front of an audience, I simply froze.* 12. *vt.* TREAT ICILY to discourage or intimidate somebody by behaving in an unfriendly or hostile way ○ *She froze him with an icy glare.* 13. *vt.* HALT SOMETHING BEFORE COMPLETION to halt or limit the development or production of something ○ *The talks remain frozen at the procedural stage.* 14. *vt.* KEEP AT PRESENT LEVEL to fix something such as prices, rents, or wages at a particular level, usually by government action to prevent an increase ○ *Interest rates were frozen at their 1996 level.* 15. *vt.* KEEP ASSET FROM DISAPPEARING to prevent a financial asset from being sold or liquidated ○ *They froze her bank account* 16. *vt.* PROHIBIT to stop the manufacture, sale, or use of something 17. *vi.* BECOME UNFRIENDLY to become suddenly unfriendly and uncommunicative ○ *When I asked him about campaign contributions, he simply froze, and I couldn't get anything out of him for the rest of the interview.* 18. *vt.* MED ANESTHETIZE BODY PART to anesthetize part of somebody's body with a local anesthetic (*informal*) 19. *vt.* CINEMA, VIDEO STOP FILM AT PARTICULAR FRAME to stop a moving film at a particular frame and show that frame as a still image 20. *vt.* CAPTURE INSTANT OF MOVEMENT to produce a still photographic image of somebody or something in movement or action ○ *He pressed the Pause button, freezing her delighted expression.* 21. *vt.* SPORTS KEEP POSSESSION OF PUCK OR BALL in sports, to keep possession of the puck or ball and prevent the other team from attempting to score ■ *n.* 1. METEOROL VERY COLD WEATHER a period when the temperature drops and stays below freezing point especially for a long time 2. RESTRICTION ON SOMETHING a restrictive measure that prevents something such as prices, wages, or production from rising above a particular level ○ *a temporary freeze on imports* ■ *vi.* (**froze** /frōz/, **fro·zen** /frṓz'n/, **freez·ing, freez·es**) to stop responding (*refers to computers*) ○ *The screen freezes whenever I attempt to save a document.* [Old English *frēosan.* Ultimately from an Indo-European word meaning "to freeze, burn," which was also the ancestor of English *frost* and *prurient.*]

freeze out *vt.* to exclude somebody from participation in something by cold or unfriendly treatment ○ *We feel we are being frozen out of the negotiations.*

freeze-dry *vt.* to preserve something, especially food, by first freezing it, then placing it in a vacuum to remove moisture before returning it to room temperature. The low processing temperature and absence of liquid water help to retain color, flavor, and texture. —**freeze-dried** *adj.* —**freeze-dry·ing** *n.*

freeze-etch·ing *n.* SCI the preparation of a specimen for examination by an electron microscope by freezing and fracturing it so that its internal structure can be seen and a replica made of it —**freeze-etch** *vt.* —**freeze-etched** *adj.*

freeze-frame *n.* a single frame of a film or video recording viewed as a static image

freeze-out *n.* an excluding of somebody from participation by cold or unfriendly treatment

freez·er /freezər/ *n.* a storage cabinet, compartment, or room, where food or other perishable goods can be frozen and preserved at a very low temperature

freez·er burn *n.* the pale dry spots that form when moisture evaporates from frozen food that is inadequately wrapped

freez·ing /freezing/ *adj.* VERY COLD extremely cold ■ *n.* FREEZING POINT the freezing point of water

freez·ing point *n.* the temperature at which a liquid solidifies, e.g., the temperature at which water turns to ice

free zone *n.* an area at a port or in a city where goods may be received or stored without payment of customs duties

F re·gion *n.* the highest part of the ionosphere that reflects high frequency radio waves. It is divided into two layers, the F_1 that extends upward from 112 mi./180 km and is present only during the day, and the F_2 extending upward from 186 mi./300km.

freight /frayt/ *n.* 1. GOODS FOR TRANSPORTATION goods or cargo carried by a commercial means of transportation 2. COMMON CLASS OF TRANSPORTATION the ordinary method or class of commercial transportation for goods, slower and cheaper than express 3. CHARGE FOR CARRYING GOODS a charge paid for the transportation of goods 4. = **freight train** 5. BURDEN a load or burden (*literary*) ■ *vt.* (**freight·ed, freight·ing, freights**) 1. TRANSPORT GOODS to send or transport goods or cargo by commercial carrier 2. LOAD TRANSPORT WITH CARGO to load a ship, train, aircraft, or vehicle with goods or cargo to be transported 3. FILL OR BURDEN to load something said or done with something such as significance or emotion, or to burden somebody or something with a feeling or emotion (*literary*) (*usually passive*) [15thC. From Middle Low German or Middle Dutch *vrecht*, a variant of *vracht* (source of English *fraught*).]

freight·age /fráytij/ *n.* 1. TRANSPORTATION CHARGE a charge paid for the transportation of goods or cargo 2. COMMERCIAL CARRIAGE OF GOODS the commercial transportation of goods or cargo 3. GOODS CARRIED the goods that are carried by a particular ship or vehicle

freight car *n.* a railroad car that carries freight, usually one that is enclosed

freight·er /fráytər/ *n.* 1. FREIGHT CARRIER a ship or aircraft designed to carry freight 2. SHIPPER OR CHARTERER somebody who is responsible for sending, forwarding, or receiving freight, or who charters a ship to carry freight

freight train *n.* a railroad train that carries only freight

Frei Ru·iz-Ta·gle /fràу roo eèss taá glay /, **Eduardo** (*b.* 1942) Chilean government leader. He became president in 1994 and attempted to curb military power by constitutional reform.

frem·i·tus /frémmitəss/ (*plural* **-tus**) *n.* a vibration or tremor, resulting from a physical action such as speaking or coughing, felt by hand and used to assess whether the chest is affected by disease [Early 19thC. From Latin, literally "roaring," from *fremere* "to roar."]

Fre·mont /freemont / city on San Fransisco Bay in western California, southeast of San Francisco. Population: 187,800 (1996).

Fré·mont /free mònt/, **John Charles** (1813–90) U.S. army officer, explorer, and politician. He charted and mapped much of the Far West, including most of the Oregon Trail (1842).

fre·na plural of **frenum**

French /french/ *n.* LANG LANGUAGE OF FRANCE the official language of France and many countries worldwide. It belongs to the Romance group of Indo-European languages that developed from Latin. French is spoken by about 70 million native speakers, with about a further 220 million people using it as a second language. ■ *npl.* PEOPLES FRENCH PEOPLE the people of France collectively ■ *adj.* 1. OF FRANCE relating to or typical of France, or its people or culture 2. OF FRENCH LANGUAGE belonging or relating to the French language [Old English *frencisc.* Ultimately from a prehistoric Germanic word that was also the ancestor of English *Frank.*]

WORD KEY: CULTURAL NOTE

The French Connection, a movie by William Friedkin (1971). Set in New York, it depicts the attempts of an uncompromising policeman, Popeye Doyle, to break up an international drug ring originating in Marseille, France. It is memorable for Gene Hackman's intense performance and a dramatic chase along elevated railway tracks. "*French Connection*-style drug enforcement operations" and other such expressions soon came to be used regularly in the United States as a result of the movie's fame.

French /french/, **Daniel Chester** (1850–1931) U.S. sculptor. The most popular U.S. sculptor of his day, he is known for the *Minute Man* in Concord, Massachusetts (1875) and his monumental sculpture of Abraham Lincoln (1919) in the Lincoln Memorial, Washington, D.C.

French bean *n. U.K.* = **string bean**

French bread *n.* white bread in the form of a long slim cylindrical loaf with a crisp crust and soft inside

French Cam·e·roons former region in west central Africa, administered by France from 1919 to 1960, and now part of Cameroon

French Can·a·da *n.* the parts of Canada where French is spoken

French-Ca·na·di·an *n.* 1. **French-Ca·na·di·an, French Ca·na·di·an** PEOPLES FRENCH-SPEAKING CANADIAN somebody who was born in or who lives in any of the French-speaking parts of Canada 2. LANG CANADIAN FORM OF FRENCH the form of the French language spoken in Canada ■ *adj.* CONCERNING FRENCH-SPEAKING CANADA OR CANADIAN FRENCH relating to the French-speaking part of Canada or to the form of French spoken there

French chalk *n.* a soft white variety of talc used by tailors to make marks on cloth and by dry cleaners to remove grease stains from clothes

French Cre·ole *n.* somebody of European and African descent whose ancestors were French immigrants to Trinidad

French cuff *n.* a wide cuff, usually for a shirtsleeve, that is designed to be folded back upon itself and fastened with a cufflink

French curve *n.* ARCHIT, TECH a thin piece of plastic or other material with curved edges and a number of curved shapes cut out of it, designed to help designers and engineers draw curves

French door *n.* = **French window** (*usually used in the plural*)

French dress·ing *n.* **1.** MIXTURE OF OIL, VINEGAR, AND SEASONING a salad dressing made of oil and vinegar with seasoning, whisked or shaken until emulsified or mixed **2.** MIXTURE OF MAYONNAISE AND TOMATO a creamy salad dressing, usually made commercially, consisting of mayonnaise with tomato flavoring

French For·eign Le·gion *n.* = **Foreign Legion**

French fries *npl.* thin strips of potato fried in deep fat

French harp *n.* a reed harmonica (*regional*)

WORD KEY: REGIONAL NOTE

The incidence of this term is highest in the West Midlands, from Kentucky to Texas, including Missouri, Arkansas, Louisiana, and Mississippi. In the Gulf States, ***French harp*** helps delimit the South Midland territory, as far east as Tennessee, Georgia, and Alabama.

French heel *n.* a curved heel of medium height for women's shoes

French horn

French horn *n.* a brass musical instrument consisting of a long looped pipe ending in a wide round bell, with additional straight or curved pipes and valves attached to it within the loop

French·i·fy /frénchə fī/ (**-fied, -fy·ing, -fies**), **french·i·fy** (**-fied, -fy·ing, -fies**) *vt.* to give a French appearance or character to something or somebody — **French·i·fi·ca·tion** /frènchəfi káysh'n/ *n.*

French kiss *n.* a kiss in which one partner's tongue is inserted in the other partner's mouth

French knot *n.* an ornamental embroidery stitch made by looping the thread three or four times around the needle before inserting the needle in the fabric

French leave *n.* a quick departure or absence, without explanation or permission [From a supposed French custom of leaving a party without saying goodbye to the host or hostess. The French equivalent, however, *filer à l'anglaise*, translates as "to leave in the English way."]

French·man /frénchmən/ (*plural* **-men**) *n.* a man who was born in or is a citizen of France

French mar·i·gold *n.* a flower, originally from Central America, that is widely cultivated in gardens for its flower heads of yellowish-orange and red petals. Latin name: *Tagetes patula.*

French pol·ish *n.* shellac dissolved in alcohol, used as a varnish for wood

French-pol·ish *vt.* to varnish something with French polish

French press pot *n.* a coffee pot fitted with a plunger that is used to push the floating coffee grounds to the bottom of the pot when the coffee is ready to drink

French pro·vin·cial *n.* a contemporary style of architecture or furnishings based on those of the French provinces in the 17th and 18th centuries

French Re·pub·li·can Cal·en·dar, **French Rev·o·lu·tion·ar·y Cal·en·dar** *n.* the calendar adopted by the French during and briefly after the French Revolution. It had 12 months of 30 days, each made up of three ten-day weeks. The months were given names Vendémiaire, Brumaire, Frimaire, Nivôse, Pluviôse, Ventôse, Germinal, Floréal, Prairial, Messidor, Thermidor, and Fructidor, alluding to nature and seasonal weather.

French seam *n.* a seam stitched twice, completely enclosing the raw or cut edges of the fabric

French toast *n.* sliced bread dipped in egg beaten with milk and lightly fried or grilled. It is typically eaten with maple syrup.

French West Af·ri·ca former French colonial territory in western Africa between 1895 and 1958. It consisted of the present countries of Benin, Burkina Faso, Côte d'Ivoire, Guinea, Mali, Mauritania, Niger, and Senegal.

French win·dow *n.* either of a pair of doors in an outside wall made of glass panels and opening in the middle (*usually used in the plural*)

French·wom·an /frénch wŏŏmmən/ (*plural* **-en** /frénch wìmmin/) *n.* a woman who was born in or is a citizen of France

Fre·neau /fri nṓ/, **Philip Morin** (1752–1832) U.S. journalist and poet. He is known for his patriotic verse, written during and after the Revolution.

fre·net·ic /frə néttik/ *adj.* characterized by feverish activity, confusion, and hurry ○ *frenetic activity* [14thC. Via French *frénétique* from, ultimately, Greek *phrenitis* "delirium," literally "brain disease," from *phrēn* "mind."] —**fre·net·i·cal·ly** *adv.* —**fre·net·i·cism** /frə nétti sìzzəm/ *n.*

fren·u·lum /frénnyələm/ (*plural* **-la** /-lə/) *n.* **1.** BRISTLE ON HIND WING OF MOTHS a small stiff bristle on the hind wing of moths that keeps the forewings and hind wings together during flight **2.** ANAT SMALL MEMBRANE a small fold of skin or membrane that limits the movement of an organ, typically smaller than a frenum [Early 18thC. From modern Latin, literally "small frenum," from Latin *frenum* (see FRENUM).]

fre·num /freénəm/ (*plural* **-nums** *or* **-na** /-nə/) *n.* a small fold of skin or membrane that limits the movement of an organ, especially the band of tissue connecting the tongue to the floor of the mouth [Mid-18thC. From Latin *frenum* "bridle," from *frendere* "to grind."]

fren·zied /frénzeed/ *adj.* characterized by uncontrolled activity, agitation, or emotion such as excitement or rage

fren·zy /frénzee/ *n.* **1.** OUT-OF-CONTROL BEHAVIOR a state of uncontrolled activity, agitation, or emotion such as excitement or rage **2.** BURST OF ACTIVITY a burst of energetic activity **3.** MENTAL ILLNESS a temporary period of symptoms of a psychiatric disorder (*often considered offensive*) [14thC. Via Old French *frenesie* from, ultimately, Greek *phrenitis* (see FRENETIC).]

Fre·on /freé òn/ *tdmk.* a trademark for any of a number of chemical compounds containing fluorine, and often chlorine or bromine, used, e.g., as solvents, as aerosol propellants, and in refrigeration

freq. *abbr.* **1.** frequency **2.** GRAM frequentative **3.** frequently

fre·quen·cy /freékwənssee/ (*plural* **-cies**) *n.* **1.** **frequency, frequence** FREQUENT OCCURRENCE the fact of happening often or regularly at short intervals ○ *quite good friends, judging by the frequency of his visits* **2.** RATE OF OCCURRENCE the number of times that something happens during a particular period of time ○ *We're trying to establish the frequency of his visits. Did he come once a month?* **3.** BROADCAST BROADCASTING WAVELENGTH a wavelength on which a radio or television signal is broadcast and to which a receiving set can be tuned **4.** PHYS RATE OF RECURRENCE the number of times that something such as an oscillation, a waveform, or a cycle is repeated within a particular length of time, usually one second. Symbol ν **5.** STATS NUMBER OF OCCURRENCES OF STATISTICAL RESULT the number of times a particular result occurs in a statistical survey (**absolute frequency**), or the ratio of that number to the total results obtained in the survey (**relative frequency**) **6.** MED ➧ **urinary frequency**

fre·quen·cy dis·tri·bu·tion *n.* a way of classifying statistical data that allows comparisons of the results in each category

fre·quen·cy mod·u·la·tion *n.* a method of radio transmission in which the frequency of the wave carrying the signal is varied in accordance with the particularities of the sound being broadcast

fre·quent *adj.* /freékwənt/ **1.** OCCURRING OFTEN happening often or regularly at short intervals ○ *Her frequent appearances on television suggested she was moving up the party hierarchy.* **2.** HABITUAL belonging to the class specified on a regular basis ○ *a frequent visitor to the museum* ■ *vt.* /fri kwént, freékwənt/ (**-quent·ed, -quent·ing, -quents**) GO OFTEN TO PLACE to go to or be in a place often [15thC. Via French *fréquent* from Latin *frequent-*, the stem of *frequens* "crowded, numerous."] —**fre·quen·ta·tion** /freèkwən táysh'n/ *n.* —**fre·quent·er** /fri kwéntər, freékwəntər/ *n.* —**fre·quent·ness** /freékwəntnəss/ *n.*

fre·quen·ta·tive /fri kwéntətiv/ *adj.* LING EXPRESSING REPETITION OF ACTION that expresses repeated action (*refers to a verb, verb form, or affix*) ■ *n.* FREQUENTATIVE WORD a frequentative verb, verb form, or affix

fre·quent·ly /freékwəntlee/ *adv.* on many occasions with little time between them ○ *They change their address so frequently, it's difficult to know where to send the letter.*

Fresco: Detail of 16th-century wall painting at Sigirya, Sri Lanka

fres·co /fréskō/ *n.* (*plural* **-coes** *or* **-cos**) **1.** PAINTING DONE ON FRESH PLASTER a painting on a wall or ceiling made by brushing watercolors onto fresh damp plaster, or onto partly dry plaster **2.** TECHNIQUE OF PAINTING ON FRESH PLASTER the technique or method of painting on fresh plaster ■ *vt.* (**-coed, -co·ing, -coes**) PAINT WALL OR CEILING WITH FRESCO to paint a fresco on a wall or ceiling [Late 16thC. From Italian, "fresh" (referring to plaster). Ultimately of prehistoric Germanic origin.] —**fres·co·er** *n.* —**fres·co·ist** *n.*

fresh /fresh/ *adj.* **1.** NOT OLD OR STALE recently harvested or made and showing no sign of staleness or decay ○ *Peas fresh from the pod.* **2.** NOT PRESERVED, PROCESSED, OR MATURED that has not been preserved, aged, or processed, e.g., by canning or freezing ○ *You can't get fresh peas here, only canned or frozen.* **3.** ADDITIONAL OR AS REPLACEMENT additional to or replacing something that existed, was used before, or is past its best ○ *I took out the old ink cartridge and put in a fresh one.* **4.** NEW OR GOOD AS NEW new or clean and showing no signs of previous use ○ *The hotel provides fresh towels.* **5.** NOT AFFECTED BY TIME PASSING not changed, diminished, or spoiled by the passage of time ○ *Write it down while it's still fresh in your memory.* **6.** PURE AND WHOLESOME natural, pure, and wholesome, especially in smell ○ *the fresh smell of clean linen* **7.** EXCITINGLY DIFFERENT excitingly or refreshingly different from what somebody is used to or what has been done previously ○ *fresh ideas.* **8.** NOT TIRED alert and full of energy ○ *I'd better get this done while my mind is still fresh.* **9.** NOT SALT not salty (*refers to water*) **10.** BLOWING STRONGLY blowing quite strongly (*refers to a breeze or wind*) ◊ **fresh breeze, fresh gale** **11.** COOL cool or colder than usual **12.** BRIGHT pleasantly bright, light, and pure or clear **13.** YOUTHFUL young and healthy-looking **14.** MAKING UNWANTED SEXUAL ADVANCES making inappropriate sexual overtures to somebody (*informal*) **15.** OVERFAMILIAR bold and overfamiliar toward somebody, especially toward somebody considered a superior (*informal*) ○ *Don't you get fresh with me, young man.* **16.** RECENTLY ARRIVED having recently come from a place, activity, or production ○ *Fresh from his trip to the Antarctic, Sir Ronald is in the studio to tell us about his experiences.* **17.** WITHOUT EXPERIENCE lacking experience **18.** AGRIC HAVING RECENTLY CALVED having recently calved and able to give milk ■ *adv.* RECENTLY very recently ■ *n.* COOL PERIOD the cool early part of the day [Partly Old English *fersc* "pure, not salty," and partly from Old French *freis* "new, recent," both ultimately of the same prehistoric Germanic origin] —**fresh·ness** *n.*

WORD KEY: SYNONYMS

See Synonyms at ***new.***

fresh breeze *n.* a force-five wind on the Beaufort Scale, blowing at between 19 and 24 mph/30 and 38 km/h

fresh·en /frésh'n/ (**-ened, -en·ing, -ens**) *v.* **1.** *vti.* **MAKE OR BECOME FRESH** to make something fresh or fresher or to become fresh or fresher **2.** *vi.* **INCREASE IN STRENGTH** to blow more strongly (*refers to wind*) ○ *wind force three, freshening from the south-west* **3.** *vt.* **REFILL A DRINK** to refill somebody's glass or drink **4.** *vi.* **CALVE AND LACTATE** to calve and begin to produce milk

freshen up *v.* **1.** *vi.* **WASH AND IMPROVE APPEARANCE** to become and feel clean and neat by washing or changing clothes **2.** *vt.* = **freshen** *v.* 3

fresh·en·er /frésh'nər/ *n.* a substance, or a device releasing a substance, designed to remove or cover odors, e.g., in a carpet or room

fresh·er /fréshər/ *n. U.K.* = **freshman** (*informal*) [Late 19thC. Formed from a shortening of FRESHMAN.]

fresh·et /fréshət/ *n.* **1. SUDDEN FLOOD** a small sudden flood or rise in the level of a river, caused by heavy rainfall or a rapid thaw, especially after a period of dry weather **2. STREAM OF FRESH WATER** a stream of fresh water emptying into a body of salt water [Late 16thC. Origin uncertain: probably from Old French *freschete*, from *freis* (see FRESH).]

fresh gale *n.* a force-eight wind on the Beaufort Scale, blowing at between 39 and 46 mph/62 and 74 km/h

fresh·ly /fréshlee/ *adv.* done recently

fresh·man /fréshmən/ (*plural* **-men**) *n.* **1. FIRST-YEAR STUDENT** a student in the first year of high school or college **2. BEGINNER** somebody who is new in a particular job or position or is a beginner at something

fresh·wa·ter /frésh wàwtər, -wòttər/ *adj.* **1.** GEOG **NOT MARINE** relating to, consisting of, or living in fresh water **2.** SAILING **INLAND** used on or accustomed to only inland waters, not the sea **3. PROVINCIAL** located inland and considered provincial and unsophisticated (*informal*)

fresh·wa·ter Yan·kee *n. Carib* an offensive term for somebody who returns to the Caribbean after a visit abroad, usually to the United States, behaving and speaking like somebody from the place visited (*slang offensive*)

Fres·nel lens /frə nél-/ *n.* a thin lens of short focal length with a surface comprised of concentric rings, each having a curvature corresponding to a similar ring of a plain convex lens [Mid-19thC. Named for the French physicist, Augustin-Jean FRESNEL who invented it.]

Fres·no /fréznō/ city and county seat of Fresno County, central California, 155 mi./249 km south-east of San Francisco. Population: 386,551 (1994).

fret[1] /fret/ *v.* (**fret·ted, fret·ting, frets**) **1.** *vti.* **WORRY OR MAKE SOMEBODY WORRY** to be or to cause somebody to be worried, irritated, or agitated about something **2.** *vti.* **WEAR AWAY** to wear away or corrode the surface of something or to become worn away or corroded **3.** *vt.* **MAKE BY CONSTANT RUBBING** to create a hole or groove in something by constant wear or rubbing **4.** *vti.* **FLOW IN RIPPLES OR SMALL WAVES** to flow, or to cause water to flow, with a constant busy rippling motion or with small choppy waves (*literary*) ○ *"I love the brooks that down their channels fret"* (Wordsworth, *Ode on Intimations of Immortality*; 1807) ■ *n.* **HOLE MADE BY FRETTING** a hole, groove, or mark made by constant wear or rubbing [Old English *fretan* "to devour." Ultimately from a prehistoric Germanic word meaning "to eat up," formed from the ancestor of English *eat* and *etch*.]

fret[2] /fret/ *n.* MUSIC a small ridge across the fingerboard of a stringed instrument such as a guitar or sitar, indicating the position in which to place the fingers to produce a particular note [Early 16thC. Origin unknown.] —**fret·less** *adj.* —**fret·ted** *adj.*

fret[3] /fret/ *n.* **ORNAMENT OR BORDER WITH GEOMETRICAL PATTERN** a pattern of repeated geometrical figures, usually consisting of straight lines, used as an ornament or in an ornamental border ■ *vt.* (**fret·ted, fret·ting, frets**) **DECORATE WITH A FRET** to decorate something with a fret or with fretwork [14thC. From Old French *frete* "trellis," of unknown origin.]

fret·ful /frétfəl/ *adj.* easily worried, irritated, or agitated by something —**fret·ful·ly** *adv.* —**fret·ful·ness** *n.*

fretman (*plural* **fretmen**) *n.* MUSIC a musician who plays guitar, especially in jazz or pop music (*slang*)

fret·saw /frét sàw/ *n.* a saw with a thin narrow fine-toothed blade usually mounted across a U-shaped frame and used for cutting curved shapes in wood [Mid-19thC. From FRET[3].]

fret·work /frét wùrk/ *n.* **1. ORNAMENTAL WOODWORK WITH OPEN PATTERN** ornamental woodwork made by cutting many holes in a piece of wood with a fretsaw to create an intricate pattern of wood and spaces **2. FRET PATTERNS** decorative designs consisting of frets [Early 17thC. From FRET[3].]

AKG London

Sigmund Freud

Freud /froyd/, **Sigmund** (1856–1939) Austrian physician and founder of psychoanalysis. He developed many theories central to psychoanalysis, the psychology of human sexuality, and dream interpretation. His works include *The Interpretation of Dreams* (1899) and *Totem and Taboo* (1913).

Freu·di·an /fróydee ən/ *adj.* **1. RELATING TO FREUD** relating to Sigmund Freud, his writings, or his psychoanalytical theories and methods **2. CONCERNING ROLE OF SEXUALITY IN BEHAVIOR** demonstrating or understandable in terms of Freud's theories, especially with regard to sexuality and its role in human relations ■ *n.* **FOLLOWER OF FREUD** somebody who follows Freud or is influenced by Freud's theories or methods of psychoanalysis —**Freu·di·an·ism** *n.*

Freu·di·an slip *n.* an accidental mistake, usually the use of the wrong word in a sentence, that is thought to betray somebody's subconscious preoccupations

F.R.G., FRG *abbr.* Federal Republic of Germany

Fri. *abbr.* Friday

fri·a·ble /frí əb'l/ *adj.* easily reduced to tiny particles ○ *sand incorporated to make the soil more friable* [Mid-16thC. Directly or via French from Latin *friabilis*, from *friare* "to crumble."] —**fri·a·bil·i·ty** /frì ə bíllətee/ *n.* —**fri·a·ble·ness** *n.*

WORD KEY: SYNONYMS

See Synonyms at ***fragile.***

fri·ar /frír/ *n.* a man belonging to any of several Roman Catholic religious orders [13thC. Via French *frère* from Latin *frater* "brother" (see FRATERNAL).] —**fri·ar·ly** *adj.*

fri·ar's lan·tern *n.* BIOL = **ignis fatuus**

fri·ar·y /fríree/ (*plural* **-ies**) *n.* a community of friars or the buildings in which they live

frib·ble /fríbb'l/ *vti.* (**-bled, -bling, -bles**) **WASTE SOMETHING** to waste or fritter something away (*archaic*) ■ *n.* **SOMEBODY IDLE** somebody who is idle or frivolous (*archaic*) [Early 17thC. Originally in the sense "to stammer, mumble," an imitation of the sound.]

fric·as·see /fríkə sée, fríkə sèe/ *n.* (*plural* **-sees**) **MEAT STEWED IN WHITE SAUCE** fish or meat such as chicken or veal cooked in white stock, or a wine and stock mixture, that is thickened with cream ■ *vt.* (**-seed, -see·ing, -sees**) **COOK AS FRICASSEE** to cook fish or meat as a fricassee [Mid-16thC. From French *fricassée*, the feminine past participle of *fricasser* "to cut up and cook in sauce," possibly a blend of *frire* "to fry" and *casser* "to break."]

fric·a·tive /fríkətiv/ *adj.* PHON **MADE BY BREATH FRICTION** made by forcing the breath through a narrow opening ■ *n.* **FRICATIVE CONSONANT** a fricative consonant, e.g., "f" or "z" [Mid-19thC. From modern Latin *fricativus*, from Latin *fricare* (see FRICTION).]

Frick /frik/, **Henry Clay** (1849–1919) U.S. industrialist and philanthropist. He amassed a fortune in the steel industry and bequeathed his Manhattan town-house, with its notable collection of paintings, to the city of New York.

fric·tion /fríkshən/ *n.* **1. RUBBING** the rubbing of two objects against each other when one or both are moving **2.** PHYS **RESISTANCE ENCOUNTERED BY MOVING OBJECT** the resistance encountered by an object moving relative to another object with which it is in contact **3.** MED **DELIBERATE RUBBING** deliberate rubbing of a body part as a way of stimulating blood circulation, warming, or relieving pain **4. DISAGREEMENT** disagreement or conflict, stopping short of violence, between individuals, groups, or nations with differing aims or views [Mid-16thC. Via French from the Latin stem *friction-*, from *fricare* "to rub" (source of English *dentifrice* and *fray*).] —**fric·tion·al** *adj.*

fric·tion clutch *n.* a clutch in a vehicle or machine that transmits power through surface friction between two plates covered with a layer of a fibrous material, e.g., asbestos

fric·tion match *n.* a match that lights when rubbed against an abrasive surface

fric·tion tape *n.* waterproof adhesive tape made of cloth or plastic and used to insulate electrical conductors

Fri·day /frí dày, -dee/ *n.* the fifth day of the week, coming after Thursday and before Saturday [Old English *Frīgedæg* "day of the goddess Frigg," whose name comes ultimately from a prehistoric Germanic verb meaning "to love" that was also the ancestor of English *friend* and *free*]

Fri·days *adv.* **1.** every Friday **2. EACH FRIDAY** on every Friday

fridge /frij/ *n.* a refrigerator [Early 20thC. Shortening.]

fried /frīd/ *adj.* **1. COOKED BY FRYING** having been cooked by frying **2. INTOXICATED** incapacitated by alcohol or drugs (*informal*) **3. EXHAUSTED** incoherent from fatigue (*slang*)

Popperfoto

Betty Friedan

Frie·dan /free dán/, **Betty** (*b.* 1921) U.S. feminist leader, author, and founder in 1966 of the National Organization for Women (NOW). Her landmark book *The Feminine Mystique* (1963) challenged the idealization of women's traditional roles. Born **Betty Naomi Goldstein**

Fried·man /freédmən/, **Milton** (*b.* 1912) U.S. economist and Nobel laureate (1976). He is considered a leading protagonist of the theory that a free market, rather than government intervention, can best produce a balanced rate of economic growth.

friend /frend/ *n.* **1. SOMEBODY EMOTIONALLY CLOSE TO ANOTHER** somebody who has a close personal relationship of mutual affection and trust with another ○ *I know her, in fact she's a friend of mine.* **2. ACQUAINTANCE** somebody who has a casual relationship with another, e.g., a business acquaintance ○ *I've got a friend at the office who might be able to help out.* **3. ALLY** somebody who is not an enemy ○ *You can say what you like about the principal; you're among friends here.* **4. ADVOCATE OF A CAUSE** somebody who defends or supports a cause, group, or principle ○ *She's no friend of tax-and-spend policies.* **5. PATRON OF INSTITUTION OR ORGANIZATION** somebody who supports a charity or institution by donating time or money ○ *a friend of the New York City Ballet* [Old English *frēond*. Ultimately from the present participle of a prehistoric Germanic verb meaning "to love" that was also the ancestor of English *free, affray,* and *Friday.*] ◇ **fair-weather friend** somebody whose friendship with another is conditional upon the other's good fortune ◇ **friends (with)** a friend of or on friendly terms with somebody ◇ **make friends (with)** to begin a friendship or get on friendly terms with somebody

Friend *n.* a member of the Religious Society of Friends, called Quakers

friend·less /fréndləss/ *adj.* without a friend —**friend·less·ness** *n.*

friend·ly /fréndlee/ *adj.* (**-li·er, -li·est**) **1. AFFECTIONATE AND TRUSTING** characteristic of or suitable to a relationship between friends ○ *She's been friendly to* *us since we moved in.* **2.** HELPFUL tending to be beneficial or favorable toward somebody or something ○ *They're on quite friendly terms with one another, but I wouldn't say they were close.* **3.** ON THE SAME SIDE not antagonistic toward or in conflict with another ○ *All the aircraft we saw were friendly.* **4.** PLEASANT AND WELCOMING with a pleasant welcoming atmosphere **5.** NOT FIERCELY COMPETITIVE not played or undertaken in a fiercely competitive mood **6.** EASY TO USE safe or easy to use or operate or easy to understand (*usually used in combination*) ○ *made of child-friendly materials* ■ *adv.* (**-li·er, -li·est**) LIKE A FRIEND in a manner that befits friends ■ *n.* (*plural* **-lies**) **1.** *U.K.* SPORTS GAME NOT FORMING PART OF COMPETITION a game that is played mainly for practice or entertainment and not as a scheduled event in a competition or league ○ *a series of friendlies* **2.** SOMEBODY WHO BEHAVES LIKE A FRIEND somebody who is amicable and shows no enmity (*informal*) —**friend·li·ly** *adv.* —**friend·li·ness** *n.* ◇ **friendly with** being a friend of or on friendly terms with somebody

friend·ly fire *n.* gunfire or artillery fire coming from your own or your allies' forces, not the enemy, and sometimes causing accidental death or injury

Friend·ly Is·lands /fréndlee-/ = **Tonga**

friend of the court (*plural* **friends of the court**) *n.* = **amicus curiae**

friend·ship /frénd shìp/ *n.* **1.** RELATIONSHIP BETWEEN FRIENDS a relationship between two or more people who are friends ○ *a friendship that has lasted more than 40 years* **2.** MUTUALLY FRIENDLY FEELINGS the mutual feelings of trust and affection and the behavior that typify relationships between friends ○ *Any feeling of friendship toward him had long since disappeared.* **3.** FRIENDLY RELATIONS a relationship between individuals, organizations, or countries that is characterized by mutual assistance, approval, and support ○ *Anglo-American friendship*

Friends of the Earth *n.* an international organization that lobbies and campaigns on environmental matters (*takes a singular or plural verb*)

fri·er *n.* = **fryer**

fries *npl.* = **French fries**

Frie·sian /freézh'n/ *n.* *U.K.* = **Holstein** ■ *n., adj.* = **Frisian** [Early 20thC. Variant of FRISIAN.]

Fries·land /freézlənd/ coastal province in northern Netherlands, that includes four of the West Frisian Islands. Population: 609,579 (1995). Area: 1,295 sq. mi./3,353 sq. km.

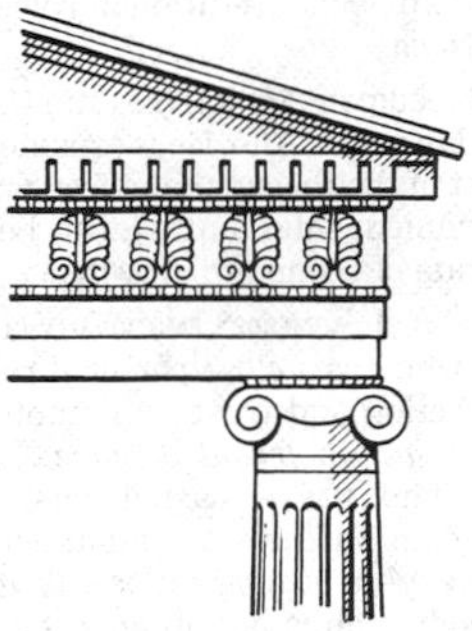

Frieze

frieze[1] /freez/ *n.* **1.** DECORATIVE BAND ALONG WALL a band of decoration running along the wall of a room, usually just below the ceiling **2.** HORIZONTAL BAND ON CLASSICAL BUILDING a horizontal band forming part of the entablature of a classical building, situated between the architrave and the cornice, and often decorated with sculpted ornaments or figures [Mid-16thC. Via French *frise* from, ultimately, Latin *Phrygium (opus)* "Phrygian (work)" (the Phrygians being famous for their craftmanship).]

frieze[2] /freez/ *n.* **1.** COARSE SHAGGY WOOLEN CLOTH coarse woolen cloth with a long shaggy nap **2.** LONG SHAGGY CARPET PILE a carpet pile with a long shaggy nap [15thC. Via French *frise* from medieval Latin *frisia*, literally "Frisian (cloth)."]

frig /frig/ (**frigged, frig·ging, frigs**) *vti.* (*taboo*) **1.** TABOO WORD MEANING TO HAVE SEX a taboo term that means to have sexual intercourse with somebody **2.** *U.K.* TABOO WORD MEANING TO MASTURBATE a taboo term that means to masturbate, or to masturbate somebody [Late 16thC. Origin uncertain: perhaps via Old French *friquer* "to rub" from Latin *fricare* (see FRICTION).]

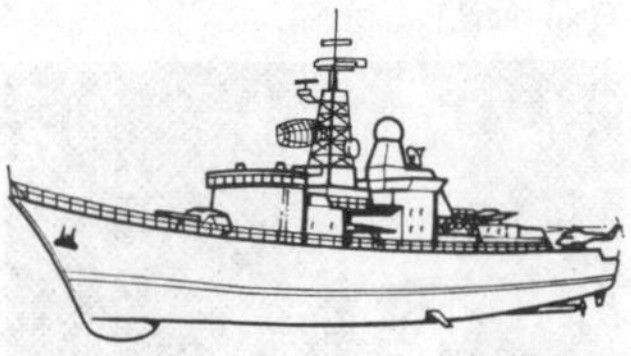

Frigate

frig·ate /fríggət/ *n.* **1.** MEDIUM-SIZED WARSHIP a U.S. warship of medium size, larger than a destroyer but smaller than a cruiser, and used mainly for escort duty **2.** *U.K.* WARSHIP BETWEEN CORVETTE AND DESTROYER a British warship next in size below a destroyer and with a similar armament and function **3.** SAILING SHIP EQUIPPED FOR WAR a fast square-rigged fighting ship in the 18th and early 19th centuries, next in size below a ship of the line [Late 16thC. Via French *frégate* from Italian *fregata*, of unknown origin. The word originally denoted a light, fast rowboat or sailboat.]

frig·ate bird *n.* a large tropical seabird with large powerful wings, dark-colored plumage, a forked tail, and a down-turned beak. Latin name: *Family Fregatidae.* [Said to be so named because of its swift flight]

frig·ging /frígging/ *adj., adv.* used as a swearword or to add emphasis (*taboo offensive*)

fright /frīt/ *n.* **1.** SUDDEN FEAR a sudden intense feeling of being threatened or in danger **2.** EXPERIENCE OF BEING AFRAID an experience of fright **3.** SOMETHING VERY UNPLEASANT LOOKING somebody or something that looks grotesque, ludicrous, or extremely unattractive (*informal*) ○ *My hair's a fright this morning.* [Old English *fryhto*]

fright·en /frít'n/ (**-ened, -en·ing, -ens**) *v.* **1.** *vti.* MAKE OR BECOME AFRAID to make somebody feel fear or to be made to feel fear **2.** *vt.* SCARE INTO LEAVING to force or drive somebody or something away through fear [Mid-17thC. Formed from FRIGHT.] —**fright·en·er** *n.*

fright·ened /frít'nd/ *adj.* feeling afraid or alarmed

fright·en·ing /frítning/ *adj.* causing fear or alarm —**fright·en·ing·ly** *adv.*

fright·ful /frítfəl/ *adj.* **1.** VERY SERIOUS used to indicate the seriousness or severity of something ○ *now faced the frightful prospect of losing their farm* **2.** FOUL extremely bad or unpleasant ○ *a frightful odor* **3.** VERY GREAT used to indicate that somebody or something is an extreme example of something specified ○ *a frightful liar* ○ *The speaker turned out to be a frightful bore.* **4.** TERRIFYING capable of causing fear, shock, or dread ○ *looked down from a frightful height* —**fright·ful·ness** *n.*

fright·ful·ly /frítfəlee/ *adv.* extremely or excessively

fright wig *n.* a wig that is intended to be amusing, with long hair sticking out in all directions

frig·id /fríjjid/ *adj.* **1.** SEXUALLY UNRESPONSIVE unable or unwilling to respond sexually, to enjoy sexual intercourse, or to have orgasm during intercourse **2.** LACKING EMOTIONAL WARMTH without or behaving without warmth, friendliness, or enthusiasm **3.** VERY COLD with a very cold temperature ○ *I was kept waiting in a frigid little room.* [15thC. From Latin *frigidus*, from *frigus* "cold" (source of English *refrigerate*).] —**fri·gid·i·ty** /fri jíddətee/ *n.* —**frig·id·ly** *adv.* —**frig·id·ness** *n.*

Frig·id Zone *n.* either of two areas of the Earth's surface, one lying between the Arctic Circle and the North Pole, the other lying between the Antarctic Circle and the South Pole

frig·o·rif·ic /frìggə ríffik/ *adj.* producing extreme cold (*archaic*) [Mid-17thC. From Latin *frigorificus*, from *frigus* (see FRIGID).]

fri·jo·le /fri hṓlee/, **fri·jol** /fri hṓl, freé hṑl/ (*unmarked inflection* **-jo·les** /free hṓleez, freé hṑleez/) *n.* in the cooking of Mexico and the southwestern United States, a bean such as the pinto, kidney, or black bean [Late 16thC. Via Spanish, Catalan *fesol*, and Latin *phaseolus* from, ultimately, Greek *phasēlos* "legume," of unknown origin.]

WORD KEY: REGIONAL NOTE

This name marks the Mexican American territory of South and West Texas, New Mexico, Arizona, and Southern California. ***Frijoles*** are sometimes called *Mexican beans*.

frill /fril/ *n.* **1.** DECORATIVE BAND WITH MANY FOLDS a strip of material gathered into many tight folds and sewn along one edge, and usually attached as a decoration to something **2.** COOK PAPER BAND WITH FRINGED EDGE a paper band with one edge cut into a decorative fringe, placed on bone ends as decoration and to allow the meat to be picked up by the bone end **3.** ZOOL RUFF OF FEATHERS, FUR, OR SKIN a ring of fur or feathers or a fold of skin around the neck of a bird or animal that looks like a decorative frill **4.** UNNECESSARY ADDITION an addition to something that is unnecessary, though it may enhance its appearance, interest, or value (*usually used in the plural*) ○ *I just want a basic, simple, no-frills stereo.* ■ *vt.* (**frilled, frill·ing, frills**) **1.** MAKE INTO FRILL to make a strip of fabric or paper into a frill **2.** ADD FRILL TO to decorate something with a frill [Late 16thC. Origin uncertain: perhaps from Flemish *frul*.] —**frilled** *adj.* —**frill·y** *adj.*

frilled liz·ard *n.* a large Australian lizard, with a broad membrane of skin around its neck that it can spread out like a ruff. Latin name: *Chlamydosaurus kingii.*

Friml /frímm'l/, **Rudolf** (1879–1972) Czech-born U.S. composer. He wrote operettas, such as *Rose Marie* (1923), and songs, including "Indian Love Call." Full name **Charles Rudolf Friml**

fringe /frinj/ *n.* **1.** DECORATIVE EDGING OF STRANDS a decorative border of short parallel strands or raveled threads held closely together at one end by stitching or a band of fabric and hanging loosely at the other end **2.** ANY BORDER OR EDGING something that serves as or resembles a border **3.** OUTER LIMIT the outer edge or something considered to be on the outer edge and not central to an activity, interest, or issue (*often used in the plural*) ○ *outposts on the fringes of civilization* **4.** LESS IMPORTANT AREA an area of action that is far away from the center of activity or interest in a particular field (*usually used in the plural*) ○ *on the fringes of political life* **5.** GOLF AREA BORDERING PUTTING GREEN the area surrounding a putting green on a golf course where the grass is allowed to grow slightly longer than it is on the green itself **6.** *U.K.* HAIR HANGING OVER FOREHEAD a border of hair cut to fall over the forehead. = **bangs** **7.** POL FACTION WITHIN A GROUP members of a group or organization such as a political party who hold views not representative of the group and usually more extreme than those of the group **8.** OPTICS BAND PRODUCED BY DIFFRACTION OF LIGHT a light, dark, or colored band of light produced by diffraction or interference **9.** = **fringe benefit** (*informal*) ■ *adj.* **1.** OUTLYING situated on the edge or away from the center of something **2.** LITERAT, THEATER MINOR playing a minor role in a play or story **3.** UNCONVENTIONAL not part of the established or conventional mainstream of something such as the movie industry, theater, or medicine **4.** NOT IN MAIN PART not in the main part of something such as a conference or organization, especially if putting forward or discussing radical or unconventional ideas ■ *vt.* (**fringed, fring·ing, fring·es**) **1.** FORM FRINGE ROUND to form a fringe or border around something ○ *A thin mustache and beard fringed his lips.* **2.** DECORATE WITH FRINGE to decorate something with a fringe [14thC. Via Old French from, ultimately, Latin *fimbriae* "threads," of unknown origin.] —**fringed** *adj.* —**fring·y** *adj.*

fringe ar·e·a *n.* BROADCAST an area at or just beyond the edge of a radio or television transmitter's range where signals are likely to be weak or distorted

fringe ben·e·fit *n.* **1.** ADDITIONAL EMPLOYEE BENEFIT an additional benefit provided to an employee, e.g., a company car or health insurance **2.** ADDITIONAL ADVANTAGE any additional or incidental advantage derived from a particular activity

fringed gen·tian *n.* a North American plant with blue bell-shaped flowers and fringed petals. Latin name: *Gentianopsis crinita.*

fringed or·chis *n.* an orchid with a fringed lip. Different species have yellow, white, purple, or greenish flowers. Genus: *Habenaria.*

fringed po·lyg·a·la *n.* a plant, growing mainly in eastern North America, that has fringed reddish-purple flowers. Latin name: *Polygala paucifolia.*

fringe tree *n.* either of two ornamental small trees, one native to the eastern United States and the other to China, that have hanging clusters of white flowers with narrow petals. Genus: *Chionanthus.*

fring·ing reef *n.* a coral reef that borders or is directly attached to the shore of an island or a continent

frip·per·y /fríppəree/ (*plural* **-ies**) *n.* **1.** ARTICLE OF ADORNMENT WORN FOR SHOW a showy article of clothing or an adornment worn for display or effect **2.** OSTENTATION pretentious display or showiness **3.** SOMETHING TRIFLING something of little value or importance [Mid-16thC. Via French *friperie* from, ultimately, Old French *frepe* "rag, old clothes," of uncertain origin.]

Fris. *abbr.* Frisian

Fris·bee /frízbee/ *tdmk.* a trademark for a plastic disk thrown from person to person in a game

fri·sé /free záy/ *n.* a fabric with long nap, usually of uncut loops, used for upholstery and rugs [Late 19thC. From French, from the past participle of *friser* (see FRIZZ[1]).]

Fri·sian /frízh'n, freézh'n/, **Frie·sian** *n.* **1.** LANG GERMANIC LANGUAGE a language spoken in parts of the Netherlands and Germany. It belongs to the West Germanic group of the Germanic branch of Indo-European languages. **2.** PEOPLES SOMEBODY FROM FRIESLAND OR FRISIAN ISLANDS somebody who was born in or is a citizen of Friesland or the Frisian Islands [Late 16thC. Formed from Latin *Frisii* "the Frisians," from Old Frisian *Frīsa.*] —**Fri·sian** *adj.*

Fri·sian Is·lands ISLANDS group of islands in the North Sea off the coasts of the Netherlands, northwestern Germany, and southwestern Denmark. They include the Dutch West Frisian Islands, the German East Frisian Islands, and the North Frisian Islands, divided between Germany and Denmark.

frisk /frisk/ *v.* (**frisked, frisk·ing, frisks**) **1.** *vi.* LEAP OR DANCE AROUND PLAYFULLY to leap, skip, or dance around in a carefree way **2.** *vt.* SEARCH QUICKLY to search somebody with a quick pass of the hands over clothes and into pockets ■ *n.* **1.** PLAYFUL LEAP a playful leap, skip, or dance **2.** QUICK SEARCH a quick search of somebody's clothes and pockets [Early 16thC. From Old French *frisque* "lively," of uncertain origin: probably from prehistoric Germanic.] —**frisk·er** *n.* —**frisk·ing** *n.*

fris·ket /frískət/ *n.* a thin frame that keeps a sheet of paper in position and masks any portions not to be printed while the sheet is being printed on a hand-operated press [Late 17thC. From French *frisquette*, from Old French *frisque* (see FRISK).]

frisk·y /fréskee/ (**-i·er, -i·est**) *adj.* behaving or tending to behave in a lively, playful way —**frisk·i·ly** *adv.* —**frisk·i·ness** *n.*

fris·son /fri sáwN/ *n.* a brief intense reaction, usually a feeling of excitement, recognition, or terror, accompanied by a physical shudder or thrill [Late 18thC. Via French, literally "shiver," from, ultimately, an assumed Vulgar Latin stem *friction-*, from Latin *frigere* "to be cold."]

frit /frit/ *n.* CERAMICS **1.** BASIC MATERIALS FOR GLASS OR GLAZE the basic materials from which glass, pottery glazes, or enamels are made, when they are in a partially bonded state at the beginning of the manufacturing process **2.** GROUND FLUX a flux that is stabilized by melting it with silica and regrinding it into a fine powder ■ *vt.* (**frit·ted, frit·ting, frits**) MAKE INTO FRIT to fuse or partially fuse materials in order to make frit [Mid-17thC. From Italian *fritta*, the feminine past participle of *friggere* "to fry," from Latin *frigere* (source of English *fry*[1]).]

frit fly *n.* a small black fly whose larvae are destructive to cereal crops. Latin name: *Oscinella frit.* [From Latin *frit*, "speck on an ear of grain"]

frit·il·lar·y /frítt'l èrree/ (*plural* **-ies**) *n.* **1.** PLANTS FLOWER WITH SPOTTED PETALS a plant of the lily family with long narrow leaves and one or two bell-shaped flowers whose petals are marked with a spotted or checkered pattern. Genus: *Fritillaria.* **2.** ZOOL SPOTTED BUTTERFLY a brownish butterfly with black spots or narrow bands on its wings and usually silver spots on the underside of its hind wings. Family: Nymphalidae. [Mid-17thC. From modern Latin *Fritillaria*, genus name, from Latin *fritillus* "dice box"; probably because the flower of some varieties resembles a small checkered box.]

frit·ta·ta /fri taátə, fri taátə/ *n.* a firm thick Italian omelet that may contain any of a variety of chopped ingredients, including meat or vegetables [Mid-20thC. From Italian, from *fritto*, the past participle of *friggere* (see FRIT).]

frit·ter[1] /fríttər/ *n.* a cake formed by frying a small amount of a soft batter and often containing chopped fruit, vegetables, or meat [14thC. From French *friture*, from, ultimately, Latin *frict-*, the past participle stem of *frigere* "to fry" (source of English *fry*[1]).]

frit·ter[2] /fríttər/ (**-tered, -ter·ing, -ters**) *vt.* to break, cut, or tear something into small pieces or shreds [Early 18thC. From obsolete *fritters* "fragments, scraps," of unknown origin.]

fritter away *vt.* to waste something by expending it in small quantities over a period of time on things that are not worthwhile

frit·to mis·to /frìttō místō/ (*plural* **frit·to mis·tos** *or* **frit·ti mis·ti** /frìtti místee/) *n.* an Italian dish consisting of a mixture of bite-sized pieces of various foods such as seafood, meat, or vegetables, and sometimes sweet things such as cake, deep-fried in light batter [From Italian, literally "mixed fry"]

fritz /frits/*n.* [Early 20thC. Origin unknown.] ◇ **on the fritz** out of order or not working properly (*informal*)

Fri·u·li·an /free óolee ən/, **Fri·u·lan** /free óolən/ *n.* **1.** LANG DIALECT SPOKEN IN NORTHERN ITALY a dialect of Rhaetian spoken in northwestern parts of Italy. ◊ **Ladin, Romansch 2.** PEOPLES SOMEBODY FROM FRIULI OR SPEAKING FRIULIAN somebody who was born in or is a citizen of Friuli or a speaker of the Friulian dialect —**Friu·lian** *adj.*

friv·ol /frívvəl/ (**-oled, -ol·ing, -ols**) *v.* **1.** *vi.* BEHAVE FRIVOLOUSLY to behave or spend time in a frivolous way **2.** *vt.* WASTE FOOLISHLY to spend or waste something such as time or money foolishly or frivolously [Mid-19thC. Back-formation from FRIVOLOUS.] —**friv·ol·er** *n.*

fri·vol·i·ty /fri vóllətee/ (*plural* **-ties**) *n.* **1.** FRIVOLOUS BEHAVIOR silly and trivial behavior or activities **2.** SOMETHING FRIVOLOUS a frivolous action or thing **3.** TRIVIALITY the state of being trivial and unimportant [Late 18thC. Via French *frivolité* from, ultimately, Latin *frivolus* (see FRIVOLOUS).]

friv·o·lous /frívvələss/ *adj.* **1.** NOT WORTH TAKING SERIOUSLY lacking in intellectual substance and not worth serious consideration **2.** SILLY silly and trivial [15thC. Formed from Latin *frivolus* "silly, unimportant," of uncertain origin.] —**friv·o·lous·ly** *adv.* —**friv·o·lous·ness** *n.*

frizz[1] /friz/ *vti.* (**frizzed, frizz·ing, frizz·es**) FORM INTO TIGHT CURLS to form or to cause the hair to form a mass of tight curls or tufts ■ *n.* FRIZZED HAIR a mass of tightly curled or tufted hair [Late 16thC. From French *friser* "to curl," of uncertain origin: perhaps formed from *fris-*, the stem of *frire* (see FRY[1]).]

frizz[2] /friz/ (**frizzed, frizz·ing, frizz·es**) *vti.* to sizzle while frying or cooking or to fry or cook something so that it sizzles [Mid-19thC. Shortening of FRIZZLE[1].]

friz·zle[1] /frízz'l/ (**-zled, -zling, -zles**) *vti.* **1.** BURN OR SHRIVEL to burn or shrivel, or to cause to burn or shrivel, especially while cooking **2.** FRY AND SIZZLE to sizzle while frying or cooking or to fry and cook something so that it sizzles [Mid-18thC. Origin uncertain: probably a blend of FRY and FIZZLE or SIZZLE.]

friz·zle[2] /frízz'l/ *vti.* (**-zled, -zling, -zles**) FRIZZ to frizz hair or to become frizzed ■ *n.* CURL a short tight curl [Mid-16thC. Origin uncertain: possibly formed from FRIZZ[1].]

friz·zy /frízzee/ (**-zi·er, -zi·est**), **frizz·ly** (**friz·zli·er, friz·zli·est**) *adj.* forming or styled in tight curls —**friz·zi·ly** *adv.* —**friz·zi·ness** *n.* —**friz·zli·ness** *n.*

Frl. *abbr.* Fräulein

frm *abbr.* from

fro[1] /frō/ *adv.* ◆ **to and fro** [13thC. From Old Norse *frá* "from." Ultimately from a prehistoric Germanic word that was also the ancestor of English *from.*]

fro[2] /frō/ *n.* an Afro hairstyle (*informal*) [Mid-20thC. Shortening.]

frock /frok/ *n.* **1.** DRESS a woman's or girl's dress (*dated*) **2.** LOOSE OUTER GARMENT a loose baggy outer garment with sleeves that covers the top half of the body to below the waist, traditionally worn by artists and farm workers **3.** CHR MONK'S GOWN the loose full-length gown with wide sleeves worn by the monks, friars, or clerics of some religious orders **4.** CLOTHES, HIST 18TH-CENTURY MAN'S COAT an informal coat with narrow skirts and collar worn by men in the 18th century ■ *vt.* (**frocked, frock·ing, frocks**) CHR INDUCT AS MEMBER OF CLERGY to invest somebody as a member of the clergy [14thC. From French *froc*, ultimately of prehistoric Germanic origin.]

Frock coat

frock coat *n.* in the 19th century, a man's knee-length coat for formal day wear

froe /frō/, **frow** *n.* a cutting tool with one end of its blade fastened at right angles to a short handle, used to split wood along the grain to make shingles or barrel staves [Late 16thC. Origin uncertain: possibly from FROWARD, in the sense "turned away."]

Froe·bel·i·an /fray beelee ən, frō-/ *adj.* relating to Friedrich Wilhelm August Froebel, the German educator who established the first kindergarten, or to the system of education through kindergartens (**the Froebel system**) that he advocated

Frog

frog[1] /frawg, frog/ *n.* **1.** AMPHIB SMALL WEB-FOOTED WATER ANIMAL a small tailless amphibious animal with smooth moist skin, webbed feet, and long back legs used for jumping. Family: Ranidae. **2.** CRAFT SUPPORT FOR FLOWERS IN ARRANGEMENT an object, usually with spikes or perforations, used to support the stems of flowers when making a flower arrangement **3.** MUSIC NUT ON BOW a nut used to secure and tighten the strings of a violin bow and hold them away from the bow stick [Old English *frogga*] ◇ **have a frog in the** *or* **your throat** to be hoarse and unable to speak clearly

frog[2] /frawg, frog/ *n.* a decorative fastening for the front of a garment, consisting of a loop of braid or cord and a button, knot, or toggle that fits into the loop [Early 18thC. Origin unknown.] —**frogged** *adj.*

frog[3] /frawg, frog/ *n.* a tough flexible pad in the middle of the sole of a horse's hoof [Early 17thC. Origin uncertain: possibly an alteration (influenced by FROG[1]) of Italian *forchetta* or French *fourchette* of the same meaning, both literally "little fork."]

frog[4] /frawg, frog/ *n.* a steel plate used to guide the wheels of a train over a place where two rails cross one another [Mid-19thC. Origin uncertain: possibly from FROG[1], because the shape of the rails resembles a frog's legs.]

Frog /frawg, frog/, **frog** *n.* an offensive term for a French person (*slang offensive*) [Late 18thC. From the supposed prominence of frog's legs in the French diet.]

frog·bit /fráwg bìt, fróg-/ *n. U.K.* = **frog's bit** [Late 16thC. *Bit* in the obsolete sense "something bitten, food."]

frog·eye /fráwg ī, fróg-/ *n.* a fungal disease of plants that causes rounded spots to appear on the leaves

frog·fish /fráwg fish, fróg-/ (*plural* **-fish** *or* **-fish·es**) *n.* a fish living at the bottom of the sea that has a globe-shaped warty or prickly body and fins adapted for catching its prey. Family: Antennariidae.

frog·hop·per /fráwg hòppər, frόg-/ *n.* = **spittlebug** [Early 18thC. Because of their shape and because they leap.]

frog kick *n.* a kick used especially in swimming the breaststroke, in which the legs are first simultaneously bent, then straightened, to push the swimmer along

frog·man /fráwgmən, frόg-/ (*plural* **-men**) *n.* an underwater swimmer equipped with breathing apparatus, a wetsuit, flippers, and other underwater gear, especially somebody engaged in military, police, or rescue work

frog·march /fráwg maàrch, frόg-/ (**-marched, -march·ing, -march·es**) *vt.* to force somebody to walk with arms pinned behind the back

frog's-bit *n.* PLANTS a floating plant that grows in stagnant water and has heart-shaped leaves and white flowers. Latin name: *Hydrocharis morsus-ranae.*

frog spit *n.* **1.** **MASS OF AQUATIC PLANTS** a foamy green mass of small aquatic plants or algae floating on the surface of a pond **2.** INSECTS = **cuckoo spit** [From its resemblance to spittle]

frol·ic /fróllik/ *vi.* (**-icked, -ick·ing, -ics**) **PLAY LIGHTHEARTEDLY** to frisk around, behave, or play in a carefree, uninhibited way ○ *children frolicking at the beach* ■ *n.* **1.** **SOMETHING LIVELY AND CAREFREE** a lively carefree game, action, or amusement **2.** **CAREFREE PLAY** lively carefree play or behavior ○ *"As a result, Anne had the golden summer of her life as far as freedom and frolic went."* (Lucy Maud Montgomery, *Anne of Green Gables*; 1908) [Early 16thC. From Dutch *vrolijk* "glad, joyous," from *vro* "happy."] —**frol·ick·er** *n.*

frol·ic·some /fróllikəm/ *adj.* frisky and full of fun and high spirits

from /frum, from/; *unstressed* /frəm/ CORE MEANING: a preposition used to indicate the source or beginning of something, in terms of location, situation, or time ○ *The condition can manifest itself anytime from adolescence onward.* ○ *Most funding comes from government and private grants and loans.* ○ *highlights from her latest novel* ○ *You can connect to our computer network from home.*
prep. **1.** **RANGE** used to indicate a range, either of time, amount, or things ○ *We are open from 2 to 4.30* ○ *They sell everything, from washing machines to magazines.* **2.** **DISTANCE** used to indicate the distance between two things or places ○ *The nearest town is not far from here.* **3.** **USING** indicating the materials or substances used in order to make something ○ *built from native pine* **4.** **CAUSE** used to indicate the cause of or reason for something ○ *low morale resulting from staff cuts* **5.** **RESTRAINT** used to indicate that an action does not happen or should not happen ○ *prevented from seeing her* [Old English. Ultimately from an Indo-European word meaning "forward, toward" that was also the ancestor of English *forth, before, primary,* and *private.*]

Fromm /from/, **Erich** (1900–80) German-born U.S. psychoanalyst. He emphasized the link between human personalities and socioeconomic patterns. His books include *Escape from Freedom* (1941) and *The Sane Society* (1955).

frond /frond/ *n.* **1.** **LARGE DIVIDED LEAF** a large leaf divided into many thin sections that is found on many flowerless plants, especially ferns and palms **2.** **SEAWEED RESEMBLING FERN LEAVES** any growth that resembles the leaf of a fern or palm tree, especially a growth of seaweed that resembles leaves [Late 18thC. From Latin *frond-*, the stem of *frons* "leaf," of unknown origin.] —**frond·ed** *adj.*

front /frunt/ *n.* **1.** **PART OR SURFACE FACING FORWARD** the part or surface that faces forward, is intended to be seen first, has the main entrance, or is facing the direction of motion or the direction people face ○ *You can only see the front of the house from here.* **2.** **FORWARD AREA, SECTION, OR POSITION** the area, section, or position just ahead of, close to, or at the forward part of something ○ *You sit in the front and I'll ride in the back.* **3.** **FRONT DOOR OR YARD** the front door or the area beyond it ○ *I'll go out the front, and you go out the back.* **4.** **BEGINNING OR FIRST PAGES** the beginning or first pages of a book or magazine **5.** **FAÇADE OF BUILDING** a façade of a building, especially the one that faces the street, or a part of it ○ *bring the car around to the front* **6.** **SIDE OF PROPERTY ADJOINING SOMETHING** the side of a property that borders something else, e.g., a street, lake, or river **7.** **FORWARD DIRECTION** the direction straight ahead ○ *face the front* **8.** **POSITION AHEAD OF**

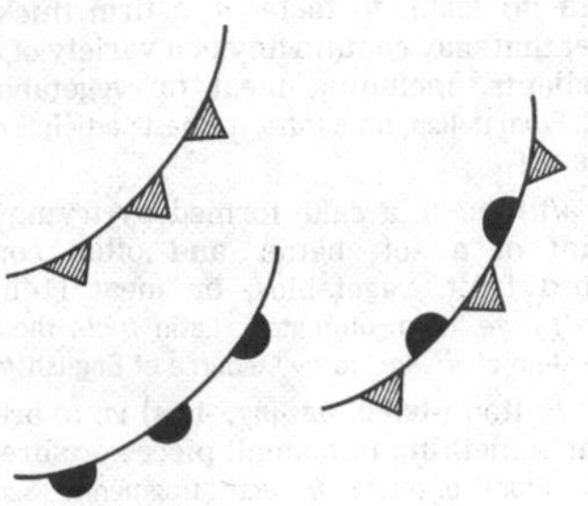

Front: Meteorological symbols indicating warm and cold weather fronts

SOMEBODY a place or position approximately ahead of somebody ○ *Just up to our front was a clump of trees.* **9.** **LEADING POSITION** a prominent or leading position in any field of activity ○ *companies at the front of genetic research* **10.** **NOTICEABLE POSITION** a conspicuous position ○ *a disturbing aspect that came to the front* **11.** **ASPECT OF SOMETHING** a way of viewing a situation ○ *Things looked desperate on all fronts.* **12.** *U.K.* **SEASIDE PROMENADE** a street, area of land, or promenade running along beside the beach or shore at a seaside or lakeside resort **13.** MIL **BATTLE ZONE** an area where armies are facing one another or where fighting between armies is taking place ○ *soldiers returning from the front* **14.** MIL **SPACE DEFENDED BY ARMY UNIT** the width of territory occupied or defended by an army or a military unit facing an enemy ○ *Each section was defending a front of some two miles.* **15.** MIL **DIRECTION IN WHICH TROOPS ARE FACING** the direction in which troops are facing when formed in line **16.** **AREA OF ACTIVITY** a stated area of activity or operations ○ *There have been a lot of changes on the domestic front since we last got together.* **17.** METEOROL **INTERFACE BETWEEN DIFFERING AIR MASSES** a line along which one mass of air meets another that is different in temperature or density **18.** POL **GROUP WITH COMMON PURPOSES** a group of people or organizations with a common purpose, especially a broad political coalition ○ *a national liberation front* **19.** CLOTHES **FRONT PART OF GARMENT** the part of a garment, or the clothing, that covers the front part of the body, especially the chest ○ *You've got gravy all down your front.* **20.** CLOTHES **DETACHABLE SHIRT FRONT** a detachable shirt front, especially part of a man's formal dress shirt **21.** **DELIBERATELY ASSUMED BEHAVIOR** a manner or type of behavior adopted by somebody in order to deal with a situation or disguise the person's true feelings ○ *put on a brave front* **22.** **COVER FOR ILLEGAL ACTIVITIES** an apparently respectable person, organization, or business acting as a cover for illegal or secret activities **23.** **FIGUREHEAD** a nominal leader or head who has no real authority **24.** *U.K.* **IMPERTINENCE** cheek or cockiness ○ *That took a bit of front!* **25.** **FACE** the face or forehead (*archaic*) ■ *adj.* **1.** **AT OR NEAR THE FRONT** situated at, on, or near the front of something, or placed further forward than others **2.** LING **PRODUCED WITH TONGUE FORWARD IN MOUTH** produced with the back of the tongue close to the forward part of the roof of the mouth ■ *v.* (**front·ed, front·ing, fronts**) **1.** *vti.* **FACE SOMETHING** to have a front that faces towards something ○ *a hotel fronting the ocean* **2.** *vt.* **GIVE FRONT COVERING OR APPEARANCE TO** to give something a front or visible surface of a particular kind ○ *The building is fronted with red brick.* **3.** *vi.* **ACT AS RESPECTABLE COVER FOR** to act as a respectable cover for something secret or illegal or for somebody doing something secret or illegal **4.** *vt.* **PROVIDE SOMETHING BEFORE PAYMENT** to provide something such as money, or to provide a service in advance of payment (*informal*) ○ *If you can front me the money, I'll rent some movies for the weekend.* **5.** *vt.* **BE THE HEAD OF** to be the head, leader, or spokesperson of a group or organization such as a band ○ *a group fronted by a young lawyer from Chicago* **6.** *vt.* **HOST A SHOW** to act as the emcee or host of a television or radio program **7.** *vt.* **CONFRONT** to confront somebody or something (*archaic*) [13thC. Via French from Latin *front-*, the stem of *frons* "forehead, front," of unknown origin.] ◇ **in front 1.** leading or ahead of somebody or something else **2.** close to or in the front of something or farther forward than somebody else **3.** in the lead in a race or competition ○ *Polls show the current mayor far in front as the election nears.* ◇ **in front of 1.** ahead of somebody or in the direction in which somebody is facing **2.** close to the front of something **3.** in the presence, sight, or hearing of somebody ◇ **out front 1.** THEATER in front of the curtain or in the auditorium, as opposed to on the stage **2.** at or to the front of a building ○ *I'll go out front and talk to them.* ◇ **up front 1.** close to the front of something, or further forward than others **2.** in advance, e.g., before any work is done or any goods are delivered **3.** direct and honest (*informal*) ○ *He was very up front about having no money.*

WORD KEY: CULTURAL NOTE

All Quiet on the Western Front, a novel by German writer Erich Maria Remarque (1929). This classic anti war novel, which was based on the author's own experiences as an 18-year-old soldier in the German army during World War I, is a grimly realistic account of trench warfare. It was made into a movie by Lewis Milestone in 1930.

front. *abbr.* frontispiece

front·age /frúntij/ *n.* **1.** **FRONT OF BUILDING** the front side of a building or piece of property **2.** **LAND BETWEEN BUILDING AND STREET** the land between a building and a street or road **3.** **LENGTH OF FRONT** the length of the front of a building or piece of land next to a street, river, or lake **4.** **PIECE OF LAND ADJOINING SOMETHING** a piece of land situated next to a street, river, or lake **5.** **EXPOSURE** the direction in which a building faces or its exposure

front·age road *n.* = **service road**

fron·tal[1] /frúnt'l/ *adj.* **1.** **AT OR IN THE FRONT** situated at or in the front of something **2.** **SHOWING THE FRONT OF SOMETHING** showing or depicting the front of somebody or of something, especially the full view of a naked body **3.** MIL **TOWARD ENEMY FRONT** directed against an enemy's front, usually across open ground ○ *a frontal attack* **4.** **DIRECT AND FORCEFUL** direct, forceful, and intended to be overwhelming **5.** ANAT **RELATING TO FOREHEAD** relating to the forehead or the front part of the skull **6.** METEOROL **RELATING TO WEATHER FRONTS** involving or relating to weather fronts —**fron·tal·ly** *adv.*

fron·tal[2] /frúnt'l/ *n.* **1.** **ALTAR CLOTH** a cloth covering for the front of an altar **2.** **FAÇADE OF BUILDING** the façade of a building or tomb [14thC. Via Old French *frontel* "ornament for the forehead" from Latin *frontale*, from *front-*(see FRONT).]

fron·tal bone *n.* the bone forming the front part of the skull that shapes the forehead and part of the eye sockets and nasal cavity

fron·tal lobe *n.* the front part of each hemisphere of the brain

fron·tal lo·bot·o·my *n.* a prefrontal lobotomy (*dated*)

front bench *n.* in a parliament, the bench on each side nearest the floor of the House, reserved for government ministers on one side and their opposition-party counterparts on the other

front burn·er *n.* a position of importance or priority (*informal*) ○ *a plan which seems to be no longer on the front burner* [From the part of a hob which is used for rapid cooking]

front·court /frúnt kàwrt/, **front court** *n.* **1.** **TARGET HALF OF BASKETBALL COURT** in basketball, the half of a court containing the basket in which a team attempts to score **2.** **FRONT-PLAYING BASKETBALL PLAYERS** the forwards and center of a basketball team

front door *n.* **1.** **CHIEF ENTRANCE** the main entrance to a house or other building, closed by a door **2.** **CHIEF MEANS** the usual and unsuspicious way of achieving a position

front end *n.* **1.** COMPUT **USER INTERFACE** the user interface of a computer system **2.** = **front-end processor**

front-end *adj.* **1.** CARS **OF FRONT OF MOTOR VEHICLE** relating to or located on or in the forward part of a motor vehicle ○ *sustained front-end damage when running into a huge pothole* **2.** FIN **OF START OF PROCESS** relating to the start of a process or project, especially a commercial or financial one ○ *heavy front-end costs* **3.** COMPUT **OF USER INTERFACE** relating to the user interface of a computer system

front-end load *n.* an amount, making up a large part of the initial payments, paid by an investor in a mutual fund or other long-term investment, intended to cover commissions and other expenses

front-end load·er *n.* an excavating machine with a hydraulically operated shovel on the front

front-end pro·ces·sor *n.* a computer used to receive data and carry out preliminary processing on it before passing it on to another computer for further processing

fron·ten·is /frun ténniss, frón tènniss/ *n.* a Latin American form of tennis played in a court with three walls [Late 20thC. From American Spanish, a blend of *frontón* "jai-alai court" and *tenis* "tennis."]

fron·tier /frun teér/ *n.* **1. INTERNATIONAL BORDER** a border between two countries, or the land immediately adjacent to this ○ *cross the frontier into Spain* **2. EDGE OF SETTLEMENT** the part of a country with expanding settlement that is being opened up by hunters, herders, and other pioneers in advance of full urban settlement **3. LIMIT OF KNOWLEDGE** the furthest limit of knowledge in a particular field ○ *pushing back the frontiers of science* [14thC. From Anglo-Norman *frounter*, French *frontière* "front part (of an army)," from *front* "forehead" (see FRONT). The original English sense was "front side, forepart."]

fron·tiers·man /frun teérzmən/ (*plural* **-men**) *n.* a man living in a frontier area, especially an area newly opened up for settlement

fron·tiers·wom·an /frun teérz wòomən/ (*plural* **-en** /frun teérz wìmmin/) *n.* a woman living in a frontier area, especially an area newly opened up for settlement

fron·tis·piece /frúntiss peess/ *n.* **1.** PUBL **BOOK ILLUSTRATION** an illustration at the beginning of a book, usually facing the title page **2.** ARCHIT **BUILDING FAÇADE** the principal façade of a building, treated as a separate element **3.** ARCHIT **PEDIMENT** a pediment, usually ornamental, above a window or door [Late 16thC. By folk etymology from French *frontispice* (by association with PIECE), from late Latin *frontispicium* "façade" (literally "viewing the forehead"), from, ultimately, Latin *frons* "forehead" + *specere* "to look at."]

front·let /frúntlət/ *n.* **1.** HIST **DECORATIVE BAND** a decorative band worn on the forehead **2.** ZOOL **ANIMAL'S FOREHEAD** an animal's forehead, especially when, as in certain birds, it has a different color from the rest of the head **3.** CHR **ALTAR-CLOTH BORDER** a decorated border on the frontal of an altar [15thC. From Old French *frontelet* "little forehead band," from *frontel* (see FRONTAL[2]).]

front line /frúnt lìn/, **frontline** *n.* **1.** MIL **FORWARD LINE** the forward line of a battle, position, or formation **2. ADVANCED POSITION** the most advanced, important, or conspicuous position in any situation **3.** BASKETBALL = **frontcourt** *n.* **2** ■ *adj.* **1. frontline, front-line AT LIMITS OF ATTAINMENT** that is the most advanced or important of its kind ○ *a frontline technological development* **2. frontline, front-line BORDERING A TROUBLE SPOT** relating to countries that border another country in which an armed conflict is taking place **3.** SPORTS **REGULAR** belonging among or relating to regular members of a team ○ *a frontline pitcher*

front-load *vt.* to assign the bulk of the costs of something, e.g., a mutual fund investment, to an early stage

front man *n.* (*informal*) **1. FIGUREHEAD** somebody who is presented as being in charge of an organization or activity while the real authority is, for reasons of illegality or secrecy, kept hidden **2.** MUSIC **LEAD SINGER** the lead singer of a band or other musical group

front mat·ter *n.* the material that appears in a book before the main text, e.g., the title page, the cataloguing-in-publication data, the table of contents, and the preface

front mon·ey *n.* payment made in advance for services or goods

front of·fice *n.* the management or executives of an organization who decide on policy

fron·to·gen·e·sis /frùn tō jénnəssis/ *n.* the formation or development of a weather front [Mid-20thC. Coined from FRONT + -GENESIS.]

fron·tol·y·sis /frun tólləssis/ *n.* the weakening or disappearance of a weather front [Mid-20thC. Coined from FRONT + -LYSIS.]

fron·ton /frón tòn/ *n.* a court used for the game of jai alai [Late 19thC. From Spanish "gable, wall of a frontón," from *fronte* "forehead," from the Latin stem *front-* (see FRONT).]

front-page *adj.* **NEWSWORTHY** important or interesting enough to appear on the front page of a newspaper ■ *vt.* (**front-paged, front-pag·ing, front-pag·es**) **PRINT ON FRONT PAGE** to print something on the front page of a newspaper

front room *n.* a living room in the front of a house

front·run·ner /frúnt rùnnər/, **front-runner** *n.* somebody in a leading position in a race or contest (*informal*) ○ *the new frontrunner in the senatorial race*

front·ward /frúntwərd/, **front·wards** /frúntwərdz/ *adv.* toward or in the direction of the front —**frontwards** *adv.*

front-wheel drive *n.* a system of powering motor vehicles that uses the engine to drive the front wheels only

frosh /frawsh/ (*plural* **frosh**) *n.* a freshman (*informal*) [Early 20thC. Shortening and alteration of FRESHMAN, perhaps influenced by German *Frosch* "frog," (dialect) "grammar-school pupil."]

frost /frawst/ *n.* **1. FROZEN WATER** crystals of frozen water deposited on a cold surface **2. FREEZING TEMPERATURE** an outdoor temperature below freezing point, resulting in the deposit of ice crystals ○ *had a hard frost as late as May* **3. CHILLY MANNER** a coldness of manner **4. FREEZING** the act or process of freezing **5. FAILURE OR FLOP** something, e.g., an artistic performance or a new book, that meets with an unenthusiastic reception (*informal*) ○ *The opening night was a true frost.* ■ *v.* (**frost·ed, frost·ing, frosts**) **1.** *vti.* METEOROL **COVER WITH FROST** to cover something with frost, especially hoarfrost, or become covered with frost **2.** *vt.* **MAKE OPAQUE** to make something, especially glass or a window, unable to be seen through by giving its surface a rough or fine-grained texture **3.** *vt.* FOOD **PUT FROSTING ON** to cover a cake or other pastry with icing or frosting ○ *a frosted sponge cake* **4.** *vt.* HAIR **TINT HAIR STRANDS** to change the color of isolated strands of hair by pulling the strands through a rubber or plastic cap with holes in it and then dyeing or peroxiding the hair **5.** *vt.* AGRIC, GARDENING **KILL BY FREEZING** to damage or kill crops or garden plants by frost [Old English *forst, frost*, from a prehistoric Germanic base that also produced English *freeze*]

frost up *vi.* to become covered in frost or ice, especially in a way that hinders a function ○ *The freezer has frosted up so much that the door won't close.*

Library of Congress

Robert Frost

Frost /frawst/, **Robert** (1874–1963) U.S. poet, best known for his spare poems about New England life, including "Stopping by Woods on a Snowy Evening" and "The Road Not Taken." The unofficial poet laureate of the United States, he won the Pulitzer Prize four times (1924, 1931, 1937, and 1943). Full name **Robert Lee Frost**

frost·bite /fráwst bìt/ *n.* **INJURY BY FREEZING** damage to body extremities caused by prolonged exposure to freezing conditions, characterized by numbness, tissue death, and gangrene ■ *vt.* (**-bit, -bit·ten, -bit·ing, -bites**) **INJURE BY FREEZING** to damage something by prolonged exposure to freezing conditions (*usually passive*) ■ *adj.* SPORTS **OF WINTER SPORTS** relating to or involving sports pursued in extremely cold winter weather e.g., racing small boats or riding on frozen lakes on windsurfers equipped with blades ○ *a frostbite derby on the frozen lake*

frost-free *adj.* used to describe an appliance such as a refrigerator or freezer that does not need to be defrosted

frost heave, **frost heav·ing** *n.* the cracking of the surface of a road or piece of ground by the freezing and upward expansion of subsurface water, or a damaged surface resulting from this

frost·ing /fráwsting/ *n.* **1. SOFT ICING** a variety of soft icing for cakes made by whisking egg whites and sugar over hot water or incorporating hot syrup into whisked egg whites **2. RICH ICING** icing that is typically thick and rich from the addition of milk, eggs, butter, or cream **3. ROUGH SURFACE** a roughened or dull surface produced on something, especially glass or metal

frost line *n.* **1.** GEOG **DEPTH LIMIT OF FROST** the point below the surface of the ground beyond which frost will not penetrate **2.** METEOROL **LINE ON MAP SHOWING FROST** a line on a map joining places subject to the same number of frosts a year or to the same degree of frost

frost weath·er·ing *n.* the shattering of rock caused by the freezing of water in surface cracks and hollows, and in the pore spaces

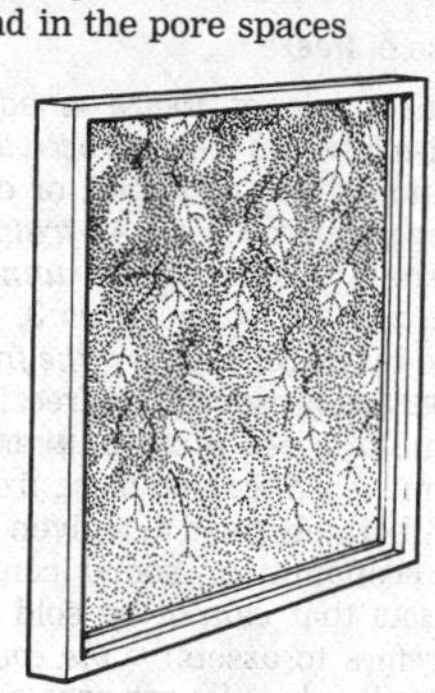

Frostwork

frost·work /fráwst wùrk/ *n.* **1.** ARTS **PATTERNS MADE BY FROST** the patterns made by frost on various surfaces, especially windows, that often resemble tracery or the fronds of ferns **2. IMITATION OF FROST PATTERNS** decoration on metal or glass imitating the patterns made naturally by frost

frost·y /fráwstee/ (**-i·er, -i·est**) *adj.* **1. VERY COLD** cold enough for the formation of frost **2. COVERED IN FROST** covered in frost, especially hoarfrost **3. COLD IN MANNER** cold and unwelcoming in manner **4. WHITE LIKE FROST** looking like hoarfrost, especially in whiteness ○ *a shock of matted frosty hair* —**frost·i·ly** *adv.* —**frost·i·ness** *n.*

froth /frawth/ *n.* **1. FOAM** a mass of bubbles in or on the surface of a liquid **2. FOAMY SALIVA** a foamy mixture of saliva and air bubbles produced at the mouth in some diseases or by exhaustion **3. TRIVIA** anything seen as being insubstantial or trivial ○ *The conversation at the party was mostly froth and posturing.* ■ *v.* (**frothed, froth·ing, froths**) **1.** *vt.* **CAUSE TO FOAM** to make something produce foam, or cover something with foam **2.** *vi.* **CREATE FOAM** to produce foam or emerge as foam ○ *froth at the mouth* [14thC. From Old Norse *froða* or *frauð*.]

froth flo·ta·tion *n.* = **flotation** *n.* **5**

froth·y /fráwthee/ (**-i·er, -i·est**) *adj.* **1. FULL OF FOAM** characterized by, covered in, or producing foam **2. TRIVIAL** with no serious content or purpose ○ *a frothy sitcom* —**froth·i·ly** *adv.* —**froth·i·ness** *n.*

frot·tage /fraw taázh/ *n.* **1.** ARTS **RUBBING IN ART** an art technique in which a rubbing is taken of a surface to create a design **2.** PSYCHOL **SEXUAL RUBBING** the obtaining of sexual pleasure by rubbing the clothed body against that of others, usually strangers in crowded places [Mid-20thC. From French, "rubbing, friction," from *frotter* "to rub," of unknown origin.]

frou·frou /froó froo/ *n.* **1. RUSTLING OF SILK** the sound made by the rustling of silk, especially women's dresses **2. FANCY TRIMMINGS** fancy trimmings or elaborate decoration, especially on women's clothes [Late 19thC. From French, an imitation of the sound.]

fro·ward /frṓ ərd/ *adj.* stubbornly disobedient or contrary (*formal*) ○ *always a froward child* [Old English *frāward* "in a direction leading away from," formed from Old Norse *frá* "from" (see FRO) + -WARD] —**fro·ward·ly** *adv.* —**fro·ward·ness** *n.*

frown /frown/ *v.* (**frowned, frown·ing, frowns**) **1.** *vi.* **MAKE DISPLEASED EXPRESSION** to show a facial expression of displeasure or concentration by wrinkling the brow **2.** *vt.* **EXPRESS BY FROWNING** to communicate something by frowning ■ *n.* **DISPLEASED EXPRESSION** a facial expression of displeasure or concentration made by wrinkling the brow [14thC. From Old French *froignier* "to frown, snort," from *froigne* "scowl."] —**frown·er** *n.* —**frown·ing·ly** *adv.*

frown on, frown up·on *vt.* to dislike or disapprove of something

WORD KEY: SYNONYMS

See Synonyms at ***disapprove.***

frowst·y /frówstee/ (**-i·er, -i·est**) *adj. U.K.* = **frowzy** *adj.* 2 [Mid-19thC. Originally a dialect word, of uncertain origin: perhaps an alteration of FROWZY.] —**frowst·i·ness** *n.*

frowz·y /frówzee/ (**-i·er, -i·est**), **frows·y** (**-i·er, -i·est**) *adj.* **1. MESSY** messy or shabby in personal appearance or manner of dress ○ *a frowzy loafer* **2. STUFFY** unpleasant to be in because of mustiness, staleness, or a bad smell. = **frowsty** [Late 17thC. Origin unknown.] —**frowz·i·ness** *n.*

froze past tense of **freeze**

fro·zen past participle of **freeze** ■ *adj.* **1. WITH ICE** covered by or made into ice ○ *a frozen lake* **2. AFFECTED BY ICE** made inoperable, damaged, or obstructed by ice or freezing temperatures ○ *All trains are delayed because of frozen signals.* ○ *no running water in the house because of frozen pipes* **3. EXTREMELY COLD** characterized by extreme cold ○ *the frozen north* **4. PRESERVED BY FREEZING** preserved by freezing for eating at a later time ○ *frozen pizza* **5. IMMOBILE** immobile or unable to move ○ *She stood there, frozen in terror.* **6.** FIN **FIXED** deliberately fixed at a given level to avoid undesirable economic or social consequences **7.** FIN **NOT TO BE SOLD** that cannot be sold or otherwise liquidated (refers to assets) ○ *the country's frozen assets* —**fro·zen·ly** *adv.* —**fro·zen·ness** *n.*

fro·zen shoul·der *n. U.K.* a condition in which a shoulder joint becomes stiff and painful, especially after having been kept in one position for a time

F.R.S. *abbr.* Fellow of the Royal Society

frt. *abbr.* freight

fruc·tan /frúktən/ *n.* a natural polymer, composed of units of fructose arranged in a chain, that is an important source of stored energy for some plants [Mid-20thC. Coined from FRUCTOSE + -AN.]

Fruc·ti·dor /frùkti dáwr/ *n.* the 12th month of the year in the French Revolutionary calendar, corresponding to August 18 to September 16 in the Gregorian calendar [Late 18thC. From French, formed from Latin *fructus* "fruit"(see FRUIT) + Greek *dōron* "gift"; from its being the time when fruit is ripe for gathering.]

fruc·tif·er·ous /fruk tíffərəss, frŏŏk-/ *adj.* used to describe a tree or other plant that bears fruit [Mid-17thC. Formed from Latin *fructifer* "fruit-bearing," from *fructus* "fruit" (see FRUIT).]

fruc·ti·fi·ca·tion /frùktəfi káysh'n, frŏŏk-/ *n.* **1. PRODUCTION OF FRUIT** the production of fruit or fruits by a tree or other plant **2. FRUIT OF SEED-BEARING PLANT** the fruit produced by a seed-bearing plant **3. SEED-BEARING PART** a seed-bearing or spore-bearing part of a plant, alga, or fungus

fruc·ti·fy /frúktə fī, frŏŏk-/ (**-fied, -fy·ing, -fies**) *vti.* to become, or cause to become, productive or fruitful [14thC. Via French *fructifier* from Latin *fructificare*, from *fructus* "fruit" (see FRUIT).]

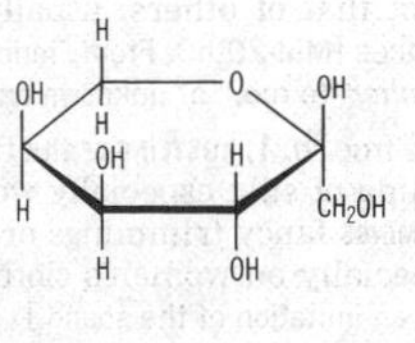

Fructose

fruc·tose /frúk tōz, -tōss, frŏŏk-, -/ *n.* a sugar found in certain fruits and honey. Formula: $C_6H_{12}O_6$. [Mid-19thC. Coined from Latin *fructus* "fruit" (see FRUIT) + -OSE.]

fruc·tu·ous /frúkchoo əss, frŏŏkchoo əss/ *adj.* productive of much fruit, or full of fruit (*literary*) [14thC. Directly or via Old French from Latin *fructuosus*, from *fructus* "fruit" (see FRUIT).]

fru·gal /frŏŏg'l/ *adj.* **1. THRIFTY** characterized by thriftiness and avoidance of waste **2. MEAGER** involving very little expense [Early 16thC. Directly or via French from Latin *frugalis*, from *frugi* "economical, useful," from *frug*, the stem of *frux* "fruit, value."] —**fru·gal·i·ty** /froo gállətee/ *n.* —**fru·gal·ly** /frŏŏgəlee/ *adv.* —**fru·gal·ness** /-nəss/ *n.*

fru·gi·vore /frŏŏjə vàwr/ *n.* an animal that eats mainly fruit [Mid-20thC. Coined from the Latin stem *frug-* "fruit" + *-vore* "eating" (via French from Latin *-vorus*; see -VOROUS).]

fru·giv·o·rous /froo jívvərəss/ *adj.* used to describe an animal that eats mainly fruit [Early 18thC. Coined from the Latin stem *frug-* "fruit" (source of English *frugal*) + -VOROUS.]

fruit /froot/ *n.* **1. EDIBLE PART OF PLANT** an edible part of a plant, usually fleshy and containing seeds **2. OVARY OF PLANT** the ripened seed-bearing ovary of a plant. It is usually considered to be sweet and fleshy, as in plums, but may be dry, as in poppies, or be a simple edible supporting structure, as in strawberries. **3. PRODUCE** the produce of any plant grown or harvested by humans ○ *the fruits of the field* **4. PRODUCT OF SOMETHING** the product or consequence of something done ○ *We are now seeing the fruits of our efforts.* **5. OFFSPRING** the offspring of humans or animals (*dated*) **6. SPORE-PRODUCING PART** a spore-producing part of a plant **7. OFFENSIVE TERM** an offensive term for a gay man (*offensive insult*) **8.** WINE **FRUITY TASTE** a fruity taste in wine ○ *a big red with lots of fruit* ■ *vti.* (**fruit·ed, fruit·ing, fruits**) **PRODUCE FRUIT** to bear fruit, or cause a plant or tree to bear fruit ○ *This variety fruits in August.* [12thC. Via French from Latin *fructus* "enjoyment, produce, fruit," from the past participle of *frui* "to enjoy, have the use of").] ◇ **bear fruit** to be successful in the end, typically after planning and effort have been expended

fruit·age /frŏŏtij/ *n.* **1. FRUIT PRODUCTION** the production of fruit, the condition of a plant or tree when bearing fruit, or the time when this happens **2. FRUITS** fruits as a group **3. RESULT OR EFFECT** the results or cumulative set of effects deriving from a usually long-term process (*formal*)

frui·tar·i·an /froo táiree ən/ *n.* somebody who follows a rare vegetarian diet consisting only of fruit, including nuts, seeds, and any other form of plant fruit [Late 19thC. Modeled on VEGETARIAN.]

fruit bat *n.* a large bat found in Europe, Asia, and Africa. Most fruit bats eat fruit but others eat pollen or nectar. Suborder: Megachiroptera.

fruit·cake /froot kàyk/ *n.* **1.** FOOD **CAKE WITH DRIED FRUIT IN IT** a dense cake containing dried fruit such as raisins, currants, and sultanas. Rich fruitcakes with a high proportion of fruit have a long shelf life, as the high sugar content acts as a preservative. **2. SOMEBODY IRRATIONAL** somebody considered to be irrational or out of touch with reality (*informal insult*)

fruit cock·tail *n.* a mixture of small or diced fruits such as pears, peaches, and pineapple, typically sold canned in syrup

fruit drop *n.* the falling from the tree of fruit that is not fully ripe

fruit fly *n.* **1. PLANT-EATING FLY** a small insect that eats plant tissue. Order: Trypetidae. **2. FRUIT-EATING FLY** a small insect that eats decaying fruit. Genus: *Drosophila.*

fruit·ful /frŏŏtfəl/ *adj.* **1. BEARING MUCH FRUIT** bearing fruit, especially in abundance **2. PROLIFIC** producing many offspring ○ *a fruitful marriage* **3. CAUSING FERTILITY** causing or promoting fertility or productivity ○ *fruitful soil* **4. CREATIVE** highly productive or creative **5. SUCCESSFUL OR BENEFICIAL** producing useful results or benefits —**fruit·ful·ly** *adv.* —**fruit·ful·ness** *n.*

fruit·ing bod·y (*plural* **fruit·ing bod·ies**) *n.* a part of certain fungi from which spores are released

fru·i·tion /froo ísh'n/ *n.* **1. COMPLETION** a state or point in which something has come to maturity or had a desired outcome ○ *Our plans have come to fruition.* **2. ENJOYMENT OF INTENDED OUTCOME** the enjoyment of a desired outcome when it happens **3.** BOT **PLANT'S FRUIT PRODUCTION** the production of fruit by a tree or other plant [15thC. Via French from the late Latin stem *fruition-*, from, ultimately, Latin *frui* "to enjoy" (see FRUIT).]

fruit·less /frŏŏtləss/ *adj.* **1. UNSUCCESSFUL** producing nothing or nothing worthwhile ○ *a fruitless discussion* **2. NOT BEARING FRUIT** producing no fruit —**fruit·less·ly** *adv.* —**fruit·less·ness** *n.*

fruit·let /frŏŏtlət/ *n.* **1. SMALL FRUIT** a fruit of smaller than normal size **2. PART OF MULTIPLE FRUIT** any of the parts that make up a multiple fruit

fruit ma·chine *n. U.K.* = **slot machine**

fruit sal·ad *n.* **1. SALAD WITH FRUIT** a dish of various pieces of fresh or canned fruit, often served with lettuce and dressing **2. MILITARY DECORATIONS** the rows of small narrow colorful campaign, service, and combat decorations worn by U.S. military personnel on the left chest area of their uniforms (*slang*)

fruit sug·ar *n.* = **fructose**

fruit tree *n.* a tree that produces edible fruit and is cultivated for that reason

fruit·wood /frŏŏt wŏŏd/ *n.* the wood of a fruit tree, especially when used in cabinetmaking

fruit·y /frŏŏtee/ (**-i·er, -i·est**) *adj.* **1. OF FRUIT** relating to, resembling, or reminiscent of fruit **2. RICH IN TONE** rich and resonant in voice tone **3. EXCESSIVELY SENTIMENTAL** excessively sentimental in behavior or content (*informal*) ○ **4. OFFENSIVE TERM** an offensive term meaning regarded by the speaker as excessively or inappropriately effeminate (*slang offensive*) —**fruit·i·ly** *adv.* —**fruit·i·ness** *n.*

fru·men·ta·ceous /frŏŏmən táyshəss/ *adj.* made from, containing, or like wheat or any similar grain [Mid-17thC. Formed from late Latin *frumentaceus*, from *frumentum* "corn, grain" (see FRUMENTY).]

fru·men·ty /frŏŏməntee/, **fur·mi·ty** /fúrmətee/ *n.* a dish made from wheat cooked to a porridge, usually with milk added and sweetened and flavored with spices [14thC. From Old French *frumentee, fourmentee*, from *frument, fourment* "grain," from Latin *frumentum*, perhaps from *frui* "to enjoy" (see FRUIT).]

frump /frump/ *n.* (*informal insult*) **1. INSULT TO WOMAN'S APPEARANCE** term used to insult a woman considered by the speaker not to be good looking or to dress well **2. DULL PERSON** a drab, dull, or old-fashioned person [Mid-16thC. Origin uncertain: probably a shortening of earlier *frumple* "wrinkle," from, ultimately, Middle Dutch *verrompelen* "to rumple completely." The original English meaning was "sneering speech."]

frump·y /frúmpee/ (**-i·er, -i·est**), **frump·ish** /-pish/ *adj.* unattractive, drab, or dowdy —**frump·i·ly** *adv.* —**frump·i·ness** *n.*

fru·se·mide /frússə mīd/ *n. U.K.* = **furosemide** [Mid-20thC. Coined from *fru-* (alteration of the first syllable of *furyl* "chemical derived from furan") + *-sem-* (of unknown origin) + -IDE.]

frus·trate /frú stràyt/ *vt.* (**-trat·ed, -trat·ing, -trates**) **1. THWART** to prevent somebody or something from succeeding something or from coming to fruition ○ *All attempts to put to sea were frustrated by high winds.* **2. DISCOURAGE** to make somebody feel discouraged, exasperated, or weary ■ *adj.* **THWARTED** thwarted or blocked (*archaic*) ○ *All their schemes for their new house were frustrate* [15thC. From Latin *frustrari* "to deceive, frustrate, render useless," from *frustra* "in vain, without effect."] —**frus·trat·er** *n.* —**frus·trat·ing** *adj.* —**frus·trat·ingly** *adv.*

frus·trat·ed /frú stràytəd/ *adj.* feeling unfulfilled or unsatisfied

frus·tra·tion /fru stráysh'n/ *n.* **1. FRUSTRATING OF SOMEBODY OR SOMETHING** an act or instance of causing somebody or something to be dissatisfied or unfulfilled **2. SOMETHING THAT THWARTS** something that blocks, thwarts, and upsets somebody all at the same time ○ *His lack of ambition was a frustration to his father.* **3. DISSATISFACTION** a feeling of disappointment, exasperation, or weariness caused by aims being thwarted or desires unsatisfied

frus·tule /frús chōōl/ *n.* the hard cell wall of a microscopic organism (**diatom**) [Mid-19thC. From Latin *frustulum* "small piece," from *frustum* "bit (cut off), piece (of a whole)."]

frus·tum /frústəm/ *n.* the part of a solid between its base and a plane that cuts it parallel to the base [Mid-17thC. From Latin "bit (cut off), piece (of a whole)" (source of English *frustule*).]

fru·tes·cent /froo téss'nt/ *adj.* looking or growing like a shrub [Early 18thC. Coined from Latin *frutex* "shrub" + -ESCENT.] —**fru·tes·cence** *n.*

fru·ti·cose /frŏŏti kōss/ *adj.* = **frutescent** [Mid-17thC. From Latin *fruticosus*, from *frutic-*, the stem of *frutex* "shrub."]

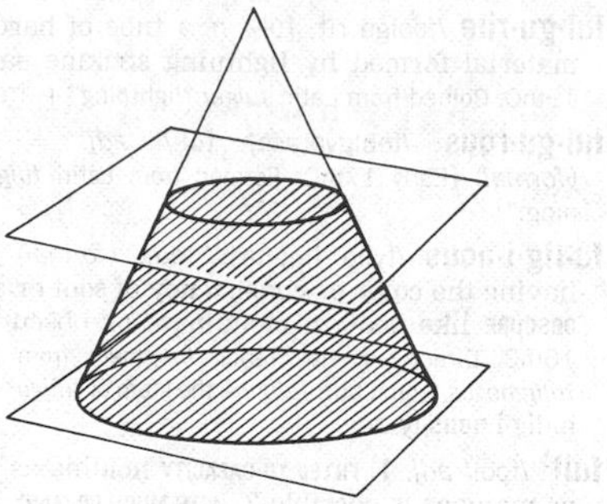

Frustum

Fuchsia

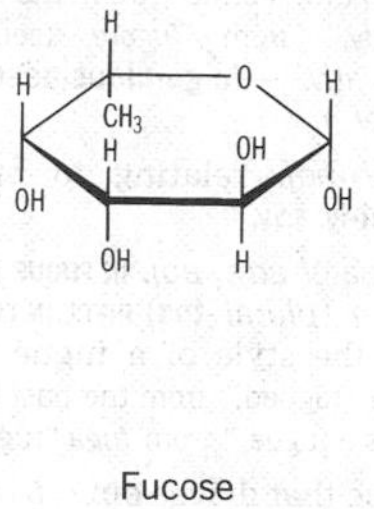

Fucose

frwy., **frwy** *abbr.* freeway

fry[1] /frī/ *v.* (**fried, fry·ing, fries**) **1.** *vti.* COOK QUICKLY IN FAT to cook something in fat over high heat, or be cooked in this way **2.** *vi.* BECOME HOT OR OVERHEATED to become extremely hot as a result of the surrounding environment or temperature (*informal*) ○ *We'll fry in this heat!* **3.** *vt.* BURN OUT to burn out an electrical component or circuit by passing too much power through it (*slang*) ○ *Turn it down before you fry the speakers.* **4.** *vti.* EXECUTE OR BE EXECUTED to execute somebody or be executed in an electric chair (*slang*) (*offensive in some contexts*) ■ *n.* (*plural* **fries**) **1.** FRIED DISH a fried dish, sometimes of various items mixed together ○ *a mixed fry of various kinds of shellfish, served with a light salad* **2.** OCCASION WITH FRIED FOOD a social occasion at which the food is fried ○ *a fish fry on the beach* [13thC. Via French *frire* from Latin *frigere* "to roast, fry" (source of English *fritter*[1]).]

fry[2] /frī/ *npl.* **1.** YOUNG FISHES the young of various fish **2.** YOUNG ANIMALS the young of various animals that breed or hatch in large numbers **3.** CHILDREN small offspring of human parents (*humorous*) [13thC. Origin uncertain: probably from Anglo-Norman *frei*, Old French *frai* "spawn," from *froier* "to rub, spawn," from Latin *fricare* "to rub" (source of English *friction*).]

Frye /frī/, **Northrop** (1912–91) Canadian literary critic. He is best known as a proponent of archetypal criticism. His most important work is his *Anatomy of Criticism* (1957). Full name **Herman Northrop Frye**

fry·er /frīər/, **fri·er** *n.* **1.** VESSEL FOR FRYING a vessel in which food is fried (*usually used in combination*) **2.** CHICKEN a young chicken suitable for frying

fry·ing pan *n.* a shallow metal pan with a long handle, used for frying food ◇ **out of the frying pan (and) into the fire** from one difficult or dangerous situation to an even worse one

FS *abbr.* **1.** Foreign Service **2.** Forest Service

FSH *abbr.* follicle-stimulating hormone

FSLIC *abbr.* Federal Savings and Loan Insurance Corporation

f-stop *n.* any of the settings for a lens aperture that correspond with an f-number

ft., **ft** *abbr.* **1.** foot *or* feet **2.** fortification

FTC *abbr.* Federal Trade Commission

fth. *abbr.* fathom

ft-lb *abbr.* foot-pound

FTP *n.* STANDARD PROCEDURE FOR TRANSFERRING FILES a set of rules or standard procedure that allows a user on one computer to transfer files to and from another computer over a network, e.g., the Internet. Full form **file-transfer protocol** ■ *vt.* (**FTPed, FT·Ping, FTPs**) TRANSFER USING FTP to transfer data using FTP

FTSE 100 In·dex an average of the London stock exchange prices of the stocks of the 100 largest British companies, published daily. Full form **Financial Times Stock Exchange 100 Index**

fuch·sia /fyo͝oshə/ *n.* **1.** PLANTS FLOWERING PLANT a plant or shrub widely grown for its drooping purplish, reddish, or white flowers. Genus: *Fuchsia.* **2.** COLORS DEEP PINK COLOR a brilliant deep pink color tinged with purple ■ *adj.* COLORS OF DEEP PINK COLOR of a brilliant deep pink color tinged with purple [Late 18thC. From modern Latin, genus name, named for Leonhard *Fuchs* (1501–66), a German botanist.]

fuch·sin /fyo͝oksin/, **fuch·sine** /fyo͝ok seen, fyo͝oksin/ *n.* a dark-green crystalline solid that when dissolved in water makes a bluish-red solution. It is used to dye textiles, to stain bacteria, and as a disinfectant. Formula: $C_{20}H_{19}N_3.HCl$. [Mid-19thC. Either from French *fuchsine*, or formed from its source, German *Fuchs* "fox" (a translation of French *Renard*, name of the company that first produced the dye).]

fu·ci plural of **fucus**

fuck /fuk/ *v.* (**fucked, fuck·ing, fucks**) (*taboo offensive*) **1.** *vti.* OFFENSIVE TERM an offensive term meaning to have sexual intercourse, or have sexual intercourse with a specified person **2.** *vt.* OFFENSIVE TERM an offensive term used like a command, often followed by you, it, or another word to express anger, contempt, or rejection **3.** *vt.* OFFENSIVE TERM an offensive term meaning to ruin, botch, or destroy something **4.** *vt.* OFFENSIVE TERM an offensive term meaning to treat somebody unjustly or harshly ■ *n.* (*taboo offensive*) **1.** OFFENSIVE TERM an offensive term meaning an act of sexual intercourse **2.** OFFENSIVE TERM an offensive term meaning somebody considered as a sexual partner of a specified quality **3.** OFFENSIVE TERM an offensive term meaning a person, usually of a specified nature **4.** OFFENSIVE TERM an offensive term meaning something of little or no value ■ *interj.* OFFENSIVE TERM an offensive term used without a following word to express anger, disgust, fear, or surprise (*taboo offensive*) [Early 16thC. Origin uncertain: perhaps from a Scandinavian source, in which case the underlying sense might be "to beat, bang."]

fuck around *vt.* (*taboo offensive*) **1.** OFFENSIVE TERM an offensive term meaning to behave stupidly or carelessly **2.** OFFENSIVE TERM an offensive term meaning to treat somebody in a careless, insincere, or inconsiderate way

fuck off *vi.* (*taboo offensive*) **1.** OFFENSIVE TERM an offensive term used as a command dismissing somebody in an angry or contemptuous way **2.** OFFENSIVE TERM an offensive term meaning to go away **3.** OFFENSIVE TERM an offensive term meaning to pass time idly

fuck over *vt.* an offensive term meaning to treat people unjustly or take advantage of them (*taboo offensive*)

fuck up *v.* (*taboo offensive*) **1.** *vt.* OFFENSIVE TERM an offensive term meaning to damage or botch something **2.** *vt.* OFFENSIVE TERM an offensive term meaning to make somebody confused or inflict emotional or mental damage on somebody **3.** *vi.* OFFENSIVE TERM an offensive term meaning to make a bad mistake or bungle something

fuck with *vt.* an offensive term meaning to treat somebody in a careless or disrespectful way (*taboo offensive*)

fuck·er /fúkər/ *n.* **1.** OFFENSIVE TERM a highly offensive term expressing extreme dislike for the person so addressed (*taboo insult*) **2.** OFFENSIVE TERM an offensive term meaning any unnamed person, an obscene equivalent of guy or fellow (*taboo offensive*) **3.** OFFENSIVE TERM an offensive term meaning somebody, especially a man, who has sexual intercourse (*taboo offensive*)

fuck·face /fúk fàyss/ *n.* a highly offensive term for a despicable person (*taboo insult*)

fuck·ing /fúking/ *adj.* an offensive term used to intensify or emphasize a word or statement (*taboo offensive*)

fuck-up /fúk ùp/ *n.* (*taboo offensive*) **1.** OFFENSIVE TERM an offensive term meaning a bad mistake or something bungled **2.** OFFENSIVE TERM an offensive term meaning an incompetent or bungling person

fu·coid /fyo͝o kòyd/, **fu·coi·dal** /fyoo kóyd'l/ *adj.* relating to, typical of, or resembling the seaweed fucus

fu·cose /fyo͝o kòss/ *n.* a sugar found in glycosides and polysaccharides associated with certain blood groups [Early 20thC. Coined from FUCUS + -OSE; from its presence in brown algae.]

fu·co·xan·thin /fyo͝o kō zánthin/ *n.* a brown carotenoid pigment found in some algae [Late 19thC. Coined from FUCUS + XANTHO- + IN; from its presence in brown algae.]

fu·cus /fyo͝okəss/ (*plural* **-ci** /fyo͝o sī/ *or* **-cus·es**) *n.* a greenish-brown seaweed. Genus: *Fucus.* [Early 17thC. Via modern Latin, genus name, from Latin, "rock lichen, red or purple color," from Greek *phukos* "seaweed."]

fud·dle /fúdd'l/ *v.* (**-dled, -dling, -dles**) **1.** *vt.* CONFUSE AS IF WITH DRINK to make a person or mental faculty confused, often through intoxication **2.** *vi.* DRINK TOO MUCH to drink too much alcohol regularly (*archaic*) ■ *n.* FUDDLED STATE a state of confusion or drunkenness [Late 16thC. Origin uncertain: perhaps related to Low German *fuddeln* "to work carelessly as if drunk."]

fud·dy-dud·dy (*plural* **fud·dy-dud·dies**) *n.* an old-fashioned or dull person, especially one past middle age (*informal*) (*offensive in some contexts*) ○ *This is for kids, not fuddy-duddies like us.* [Early 20thC. Origin uncertain: perhaps an alteration of FUSSY + DAD.]

fudge /fuj/ *n.* **1.** CONFECTION a type of soft candy made by boiling milk and sugar and then beating the liquid until it crystallizes and becomes slightly grainy in texture. Many flavorings and other ingredients can be added. **2.** NONSENSE nonsensical talk (*informal*) ■ *vti.* (**fudged, fudg·ing, fudg·es**) ALTER TO DECEIVE to fiddle with or otherwise alter something in order to deceive or remain noncommittal (*informal*) ○ *fudged the figures to make the bottom line look better* [Early 17thC. Origin uncertain: perhaps an alteration of earlier *fadge* "to make fit, adjust"; the underlying meaning of the confectionery sense is perhaps "botched toffee."]

Fu·e·gi·an /fyoo éejee ən, fwáy-/ *adj.* OF TIERRA DEL FUEGO relating to or typical of Tierra del Fuego, or its people or culture ■ *n.* S AMERICAN FROM TIERRA DEL FUEGO a Native South American who was born on or lives on any of the islands of Tierra del Fuego

fu·el /fyo͝o əl/ *n.* **1.** SOURCE OF ENERGY something that is burned to provide power or heat **2.** SOURCE OF NUCLEAR ENERGY the fissionable material used to create power in a nuclear generator **3.** SOURCE OF STIMULATION something that stimulates or maintains something else, especially an emotion ○ *Her refusal to answer questions added fuel to his curiosity.* ■ *v.* (**-eled, -el·ing, -els**) **1.** *vt.* SUPPLY WITH FUEL to supply something with material to burn for power or heat **2.** *vt.* STIMULATE to stimulate or maintain something, especially an emotion **3.** *vi.* OBTAIN FUEL to take on supplies of fuel for running a vehicle [12thC. Via Anglo-Norman *fuaille*, Old French *fouaille* from assumed Vulgar Latin *focalia*, literally "(things) for the fire," from Latin *focus* "fireplace, hearth" (see FOCUS).] —**fu·el·er** *n.*

fu·el cell *n.* a device that generates electricity by converting the chemical energy of a fuel and an oxidant to electric energy

fu·el ef·fi·cien·cy *n.* the ability to make the best use of the fuel being used —**fu·el-ef·fi·cient** *adj.*

fu·el in·jec·tion *n.* a system for running an internal-combustion engine without using a carburetor, forcing vaporized fuel under pressure directly into the combustion chamber —**fu·el-in·ject·ed** *adj.*

fu·el oil *n.* a product of liquid petroleum, burned chiefly to power ships and locomotives and to provide domestic heating

fu·el rod *n.* a metal tube containing nuclear fuel that is used in some types of nuclear reactor

Fu·en·tes /foo én tàyss, fwén-/, **Carlos** (*b.* 1928) Mexican writer. He is known for his metaphysical novel *The Death of Artemio Cruz* (1962).

fug /fug/ *n.* a stale or airless atmosphere [Late 19thC. Origin uncertain: probably an alteration of FOG.]

fu·ga·cious /fyoo gáyshəss/ *adj.* **1.** BRIEF fleeting or passing away quickly (*formal*) **2.** BOT **QUICKLY WITHERING** lasting only briefly before withering or dropping [Early 17thC. Formed from the Latin stem *fugac-* "fleeing swiftly," from *fugere* (see FUGITIVE).] —**fu·ga·cious·ly** *adv.* —**fu·ga·cious·ness** *n.* —**fu·gac·i·ty** /fyoo gássətee/ *n.*

fu·gal /fyóog'l/ *adj.* relating to or resembling a fugue —**fu·gal·ly** *adv.*

fu·ga·to /foo gaátō/ *adv., adj.* **IN FUGUE STYLE** in the style of a fugue ■ *n.* (*plural* **-tos**) **PIECE IN FUGUE STYLE** a piece of music in the style of a fugue [Mid-19thC. From Italian, literally "fugued," from the past participle of *fugare* "to compose as a fugue," from *fuga* "fugue" (see FUGUE).]

-fuge *suffix.* one that drives out ○ *febrifuge* [Via French from, ultimately, Latin *fugere* "to flee" (see FUGITIVE) and *fugare* "to drive out" (from *fuga* "flight")]

fu·gi·tive /fyóojətiv/ *n.* **1.** **SOMEBODY WHO RUNS AWAY** somebody who is running away, e.g., from justice, enemies, or brutal treatment **2.** **SOMETHING ELUSIVE** an elusive or ephemeral thing ■ *adj.* **1.** **RUNNING AWAY FROM SOMETHING** fleeing, especially fleeing arrest or punishment **2.** **BRIEF** lasting only briefly ○ *the fugitive hours* **3.** **ITINERANT** moving around from place to place **4.** **DIFFICULT TO UNDERSTAND** difficult to understand or retain ○ *the fugitive nature of higher mathematics* **5.** **WRITTEN FOR PARTICULAR OCCASION** written or composed for a particular occasion or on a subject of only passing interest ○ *a collection of essays, letters, and fugitive pieces* [14thC. Directly or via French from Latin *fugitivus*, from *fugit=*, the past participle stem of *fugere* "to flee" (source of English *fugacious, refuge*, and *refugee*).] —**fu·gi·tive·ly** *adv.* —**fu·gi·tive·ness** *n.*

fu·gle /fyóog'l/ (**-gled, -gling, -gles**) *vi.* to act as or like a fugleman in training or leading others [Mid-19thC. Back-formation from FUGLEMAN.]

fu·gle·man /fyóog'l màn, -mən/ (*plural* **-men** /-mèn, -mən/) *n.* **1.** MIL **SOLDIER TRAINING OTHERS** a soldier formerly used to teach drill movements by performing them in front of trainees **2.** **LEADER** somebody acting as a leader or example to others [Early 19thC. Alteration of German *Flügelmann*, literally "wing man, man on the flank."]

fu·gu /foó goo/ *n.* any of several poisonous fish related to the puffers that are eaten, especially in Japan, after the poisonous parts are removed [Mid- 20thC. From Japanese.]

fugue /fyoog/ *n.* **1.** MUSIC **MUSICAL FORM** a musical form in which a theme is first stated, then repeated and varied with accompanying contrapuntal lines **2.** **fugue, fugue state** PSYCHIAT **SELECTIVE MEMORY LOSS** a disordered state of mind, in which somebody typically wanders from home and experiences a loss of memory relating only to the previous, rejected, environment [Late 16thC. Directly or via French from Italian *fuga*, from Latin, "flight."]

Barnaby's

Mount Fuji

Fu·ji, Mount /foójee/, **Fu·ji·ya·ma** /foóji yaámə, -yaá maá/ the highest mountain in Japan, on central Honshu Island, southwest of Tokyo. A dormant volcano in the shape of an almost perfect cone, it is considered to be sacred by many Japanese people. Height: 12,387 ft./3,776 m.

Fu·jian /foo jyaán/, **Fu·kien** /-kyén/ province of southeastern China, on the coast opposite the island of Taiwan. Capital: Fuzhou. Population: 31,830,000 (1994). Area: 46,720 sq. mi./121,000 sq. km.

Fu·ji·mo·ri /foóji máwree/, **Alberto** (*b.* 1938) Peruvian political leader. He became president of Peru in 1990 and is the first person of Japanese descent to lead a Latin American country.

Fu·ji·sa·wa /foóji saáwə, -saá waá/ city southwest of Yokohama in Kanagawa Prefecture, southeastern Honshu, Japan. Population: 350,370 (1990).

Fu·ji·ya·ma /foóji yaámè/ = **Fuji [Mount]**

Fu·kien = **Fujian**

Fu·ku·i /foo koó ee/ capital city of Fukui Prefecture, west central Honshu, Japan. Population: 252,743 (1990).

Fu·ku·o·ka /foókoo ṓkə, -ṓ kaá/ port and capital of Fukuoka Prefecture on northern Kyushu, southwestern Japan. Kyushu University was founded here in 1911. Population: 1,237,062 (1990).

Fu·ku·shi·ma /foókoo sheémə, -sheé maá/ capital city of Fukushima Prefecture, on the Abukuma River in north central Honshu, Japan. Population: 280,958 (1990).

Fu·ku·ya·ma /foókoo yaámə, -yaá maá/ city on the Inland Sea in Hiroshima Prefecture, Honshu Island, Japan. Population: 365,612 (1990).

-ful *suffix.* **1.** full of ○ *hateful* **2.** having the nature of ○ *rightful* **3.** tending to ○ *forgetful* **4.** an amount that fills ○ *capful* **5.** full to ○ *brimful* [Old English, from *full* (see FULL)]

Fu·la /foólə/ (*plural* **-la** *or* **-las**), **Fu·lah** (*plural* **-lah** *or* **-lahs**) *n.* **1.** PEOPLES **MEMBER OF AFRICAN NOMADIC PEOPLE** a member of an ethnically diverse nomadic people living in various parts of western and central Africa **2.** = **Fulani** *n.* 1 [Late 18thC. From Fulani *pulo* "person."]

Fu·la·ni /foó laánee, foo laánee/ (*plural* **-ni** *or* **-nis**) *n.* **1.** LANG **W AFRICAN LANGUAGE** a language spoken over a large area of West Africa, especially in Nigeria, Guinea-Bissau, Burkina-Faso, Gambia, Benin, Guinea, and Senegal. It is one of the Niger-Congo family of African languages. About 15 million people speak Fulani. **2.** PEOPLES = **Fula** *n.* 1 [Mid-19thC. From Hausa.]

Ful·bright /foól brìt/, **J. William** (1905–95) U.S. educator and politician. As a U.S. Democratic senator from Arkansas (1945–74) and chair of the influential Senate Foreign Relations Committee (1959–74), he was a leading critic of the Vietnam War. He sponsored the Fulbright Act (1946), which enacted a major U.S. program of international educational exchanges. Full name **James William Fulbright**

ful·crum /foólkrəm, fúlkrəm/ (*plural* **-crums** *or* **-cra** /-krə/) *n.* **1.** **PIVOT** the point or support about which a lever turns **2.** **PROP** something that supports something else revolving about it or depending on it ○ *The fulcrum of the building plan is the major retail tenant.* **3.** ZOOL **SUPPORT IN ANIMAL** part of an animal that acts as a hinge or support, especially scales on the fins of some fish [Late 17thC. From Latin, "post or foot of a couch, bedpost," formed from the base of *fulcire* "to prop up, support."]

ful·fill /foól fíl/ (**-filled, -fill·ing, -fills**), **ful·fil** (**-filled, -fill·ing, -fils**) *v.* **1.** *vt.* **ACHIEVE SOMETHING DESIRED** to do what is necessary to bring about or achieve something expected, desired, or promised ○ *went on to fulfill her early promise of greatness* **2.** *vt.* **CARRY OUT** to do what is necessary to carry out a request or command ○ *The instructions have been fulfilled to the letter.* **3.** *vt.* **SATISFY REQUIREMENT** to be good enough or of the type necessary to meet a standard or requirement **4.** *vt.* **COMPLETE** to do what is necessary to complete or bring something to an end **5.** *vt.* **SUPPLY AMOUNT OF ORDER** to supply the full amount of something ordered **6.** *vr.* **REALIZE AMBITIONS** to feel satisfied with what you are doing, or realize your expectations or ambitions [Old English *fullfyllan* "to fill up, make full," from earlier forms of FULL + FILL] —**ful·fill·er** *n.* —**ful·fill·ment** *n.*

ful·fill·ing *adj.* giving satisfaction to somebody as an activity or goal in life ○ *a fulfilling job opportunity*

ful·gent /foóljənt, fúl-/ *adj.* shining or gleaming brilliantly (*literary*) [15thC. From Latin *fulgere* "to flash, shine" (source of English *effulgent* and *refulgent*).] —**ful·gen·cy** *n.* —**ful·gent·ly** *adv.*

ful·gu·rant /foólgərənt, fúl-/ *adj.* flashing with or like lightning (*formal*) [Mid-17thC. From Latin *fulgurant-*, the present participle stem of *fulgurare* (see FULGURATE).]

ful·gu·rate /foólgə ràyt, fúl-/ (**-rat·ed, -rat·ing, -rates**) *v.* **1.** *vi.* **FLASH** to flash with or like lightning (*formal*) **2.** *vt.* MED **DESTROY BY ELECTRICITY** to destroy unwanted tissue, such as warts, using a high-frequency electric current [Mid-17thC. From Latin *fulgurat-*, the past participle stem of *fulgurare* "to lighten, flash," from, ultimately, *fulgere* (see FULGENT).] —**ful·gu·ra·tion** /foólgə ráysh'n, fùlgə-/ *n.*

ful·gu·rite /foólgə rìt, fúl-/ *n.* a tube of hard, glassy material formed by lightning striking sand [Mid-19thC. Coined from Latin *fulgur* "lightning" + -ITE.]

ful·gu·rous /foólgyərəss, fúl-/ *adj.* = **fulgurant** (*formal*) [Early 17thC. Formed from Latin *fulgur* "lightning."]

fu·lig·i·nous /fyoo líjjənəss/ *adj.* (*formal*) **1.** **SOOTY** having the color or consistency of soot or smoke **2.** **OBSCURE** like soot in cloudiness or obscurity [Late 16thC. Directly or via French *fuligineux* from late Latin *fuliginosus*, from Latin *fuligin-*, the stem of *fuligo* "soot."] —**fu·lig·i·nous·ly** *adv.*

full[1] /foól/ *adj.* **1.** **FILLED TO CAPACITY** holding as much or as many as is possible **2.** **WITH MUCH OR MANY** having a large amount or number of something ○ *full of mischief* **3.** **GREATEST IN EXTENT** being at the highest degree or largest extent ○ *at full speed* ○ *I like my coffee full strength.* **4.** **COMPLETE WITH NOTHING MISSING** with nothing or nobody left out or missing, or with no part uncompleted or used ○ *the full complement of staff* **5.** **COMPLETELY DEVELOPED** at the end or peak of development ○ *roses in full bloom* **6.** **COMPLETELY SO** having reached or fulfilled all requirements for a position, rank, or description ○ *a full colonel* **7.** **HAVING EATEN ENOUGH** satisfied by an amount eaten or drunk **8.** **BUSY WITH ACTIVITY** filled with activity or achievement ○ *live a full life* **9.** **PLUMP** fleshy and with a rounded shape **10.** **WITH SAME PARENTS** sharing both natural parents ○ *my full brother* **11.** **CHARGED WITH EMOTION** affected by strong deep emotion ○ *We left the place with full hearts and shining eyes.* **12.** **PREOCCUPIED** deeply preoccupied with a large filled agenda, or with some fact or idea to the extent of being unable to think or talk about anything else ○ *She's always full of her troubles.* **13.** **SONOROUS** with depth or power, e.g., of sound **14.** WINE **RICHLY FLAVORED** with a rich strong flavor and substantial quality **15.** CLOTHES **WITH MUCH FABRIC** made with a lot of fabric and not close-fitting **16.** BASEBALL **WITH THREE RUNNERS** in baseball, with a runner at first, second, and third base ○ *bases are full* ■ *adv.* **1.** **COMPLETELY** to the greatest or complete extent ○ *turn full around* **2.** **DIRECTLY OR EXACTLY** in a precise or exact position ○ *He took a punch full on the mouth.* **3.** **VERY** to a high degree ○ *What happened next we know full well.* ■ *n.* **FULLEST STATE** the greatest extent or highest degree ○ *We enjoyed ourselves to the full.* ■ *v.* (**fulled, full·ing, fulls**) **1.** *vt.* SEW **SEW GATHERS AND TUCKS** to make a garment full by sewing gathers or tucks in it **2.** *vi.* **BECOME FULL** to wax and become full (*refers to the moon*) [Old English. From a prehistoric Germanic word that is also the ancestor of English *fill*; ultimately from an Indo-European base that is also the ancestor of English *complete*.] ◇ **be full of yourself** to be very conceited and arrogant ◇ **in full** to the complete amount or extent, omitting nothing ○ *The opera has never been performed in full.*

full[2] /foól/ (**fulled, full·ing, fulls**) *vti.* TEXTILES to make cloth bulkier by dampening and beating it, or become bulkier by being dampened and beaten [14thC. Origin uncertain: probably a back-formation from *fuller*[1], perhaps influenced by French *fouler* "to press."]

full·back /foól bàk/ *n.* a player in a defensive position in sports such as football, or field hockey

full-blood·ed *adj.* **1.** **THOROUGHBRED** of unmixed breed **2.** **VIGOROUS** healthily vigorous, or forceful —**full-blood·ed·ly** *adv.* —**full-blood·ed·ness** *n.*

full-blown *adj.* **1.** **COMPLETE** in its most complete, extreme, strongest, or developed form ○ *full-blown malaria* **2.** **FULLY IN BLOOM** blooming and fully open

full board *n.* = **American plan**

full-bod·ied *adj.* **1.** WINE **RICHLY FLAVORED** with a rich strong flavor and substantial quality **2.** **RICHLY SOUNDING** rich in tone and strong in volume

full-bot·tomed *adj.* long and full at the back (*refers to a wig*)

full cir·cle *adv.* back to the starting point, usually after passing through various stages

full count *n.* in baseball, the situation in which the batter has three balls and two strikes

full-court press *n.* **1.** **WIDESPREAD PRESSURE** in basketball, the practice of putting pressure on opposing players in all parts of the court as opposed to merely defending the backcourt **2.** **MAJOR EFFORT** any major effort involving several people (*informal*) ○ *The DA wants a full-court press on this case.*

full dress *n.* clothes suitable or prescribed for a ceremony or formal occasion (*hyphenated when used before a noun*)

full-dress *adj.* of considerable importance and often complete or exhaustive ○ *a full-dress investigation*

full·er[1] /fŏŏllər/ *n.* TEXTILES somebody who makes cloth bulkier by dampening and beating it [Pre-12thC. Formed from Latin *fullo*, of unknown origin.]

full·er[2] /fŏŏllər/ *n.* METALL a hammer used by a blacksmith for forging grooves and spreading hot iron [Early 19thC. Origin uncertain: perhaps from FULL[1] in the sense "to make full."]

Ful·ler /fŏŏllər/, **Buckminster** (1895–1983) U.S. engineer, designer, architect, and writer. He is noted for his innovative use of technology to deal with global problems facing humanity in the second half of the 20th century. Full name **Richard Buckminster Fuller**

Ful·ler, Margaret (1810–50) U.S. writer and critic. She was the founding editor of the transcendentalist journal *The Dial* (1840–42) and author of the classic feminist work *Women in the Nineteenth Century* (1845). Full name **Sarah Margaret Fuller**

Ful·ler, Melville W. (1833–1910) U.S. politician and jurist. He was chief justice of the U.S. Supreme Court (1888–1910). Full name **Melville Weston Fuller**

ful·ler·ene /fŏŏllə rēen/ *n.* a form of carbon comprising up to 500 carbon atoms arranged in a sphere or tube. Fullerenes are very heat resistant and have unique electrical properties, with potential uses in electronics and as lubricants. [Late 20thC. Shortening.]

ful·ler's earth *n.* an absorbent clay used in fulling cloth and in filtering liquids

ful·ler's tea·sel *n.* a plant of Europe and Asia with prickly flower heads, formerly used to raise the nap on cloth. Latin name: *Dipsacus sativus.*

Ful·ler·ton /fŏŏllərt'n/ city in Orange County, southwestern California, 17 mi./27 km northeast of Long Beach. Population: 116,863 (1994).

full-faced *adj.* with the whole of the face visible, facing the viewer ○ *a full face portrait*

full-fash·ioned *adj.* shaped to fit the lines of the body ○ *full-fashioned stockings*

full-fledged *adj.* **1.** BIRDS **WITH ADULT FEATHERS** having grown adult feathers and so being able to fly **2. COMPLETELY DEVELOPED** at a point of complete development or maturity ○ *a full-fledged microelectronics industry* **3. FULLY QUALIFIED** with full status or rank ○ *a full-fledged helicopter pilot*

full-fron·tal *adj.* **1. EXPOSING GENITALS** showing the whole front of the body including the genitals **2. UNRESTRAINED** whole-hearted and uninhibited (*informal*) ○ *She made a full-frontal attack on her opponents.*

full house *n.* a poker hand containing three cards of the same value and a pair of a different value

full-length *adj.* **1. FALLING TO ANKLES** extending to the ankles or floor (*refers to a garment, e.g. a coat or skirt*) **2. SHOWING WHOLE BODY** showing the whole length of the body (refers to a portrait mirror, or the like) (*refers to a portrait mirror, or the like*) **3. NOT SHORTENED** consisting of the whole or usual amount or duration of something

full mon·ty *n.* everything that is needed or appropriate or makes up a full set or the whole of something (*slang*) [*Monty* of uncertain origin: perhaps a shortening of *Montague*, from *Montague Burton*, name of a British firm of gentleman's outfitters, with reference to a full suit of clothes]

full moon *n.* **1. MOON APPEARING AS COMPLETE CIRCLE** the phase of the Moon when its surface as seen from the Earth is fully illuminated by the Sun **2. TIME OF FULL MOON** the period of time during which the Moon appears fully illuminated as a circle [Origin uncertain]

full-mouthed *adj.* **1.** VET **WITH ALL TEETH** having the complete set of adult teeth **2. LOUD** said loudly or vigorously

full nel·son *n.* a wrestling hold in which one wrestler puts both arms beneath an opponent's arms from behind and then exerts pressure by clasping the hands at the back of the opponent's neck

full·ness /fŏŏlnəss/ *n.* the quality or condition of being full or complete ○ *the fullness of her explanation*

full-rigged *adj.* having at least three square-rigged masts

full-scale *adj.* **1. LIFE-SIZE** having exactly the same dimensions and proportions as the original **2. TOTAL** done with total commitment of effort and resources ○ *a full-scale manhunt*

full-ser·vice *adj.* providing a complete range of services ○ *a full-service gas station*

full-size, full-sized *adj.* **1. OF USUAL SIZE** being the normal size for its kind **2. OF STANDARD SIZE FOR BED** measuring 54 by 75 in./137 by 190 cm or suitable as linen for this size of bed

full stop *n.* **1.** *U.K.* GRAM = **period 2. COMPLETE STOP** a complete halt or an end ○ *This delay has brought production to a full stop.*

full time *adj., adv.* **full-time, full time FOR THE WHOLE USUAL TIME** during all of the time considered standard or appropriate for the activity in question ■ *n.* **END OF MATCH** the end of a match in soccer and other sports —**full-tim·er** *n.*

full-wave rec·ti·fi·er *n.* a circuit used in the design of electronic equipment such as radios, computers, and televisions that operates on both the positive and negative cycles of an alternating current

ful·ly /fŏŏllee/ *adv.* **1. COMPLETELY** to the greatest extent possible or required ○ *The flight is fully booked.* **2. FOR WHAT IS SPECIFIED** to the full extent of the time, quantity, or number specified ○ *We waited fully 40 minutes.*

ful·ly-fledged *adj.* U.K. = **full-fledged**

ful·mar /fŏŏlmər, -maar/ *n.* a heavy short-tailed seabird living in polar regions. Genus: *Fulmarus.* [Late 17thC. Originally a Hebridean Norn dialect word, from Old Norse *fúll* "foul" (from the bird's habit of regurgitating its stomach's contents when disturbed) + *már* "gull."]

ful·mi·nant /fŏŏlmənənt, fúl-/ *adj.* **1. EXPLODING** exploding violently **2.** MED **SUDDEN AND SEVERE** coming on suddenly and with severe symptoms of short duration [Early 17thC. Directly or via French from, ultimately, Latin *fulminare.*]

ful·mi·nate /fŏŏlmə nàyt, fúl-/ *vti.* (**-nat·ed, -nat·ing, -nates**) **1. SPEAK SCATHINGLY** to express forceful criticism ○ *an article fulminating against the arms trade* **2. EXPLODE** to detonate or explode violently, or cause something to detonate or explode violently ■ *n.* CHEM **EXPLOSIVE SALT OR ESTER** any explosive salt or ester of fulminic acid, especially fulminate of mercury [15thC. From Latin *fulminare* "to lighten, strike with lightning," from *fulmen* "lightning."] —**ful·mi·na·tion** /fŏŏlmə náysh'n, fùl-/ *n.* —**ful·mi·na·tor** /fŏŏlmə nàytər, fúl-/ *n.* —**ful·mi·na·to·ry** /fŏŏlmənə tàwree, fúl-/ *adj.*

ful·mi·nate of mer·cu·ry *n.* the mercury salt of fulminic acid, often used in explosives and detonators. Formula: $HgC_2N_2O_2$.

ful·mi·nat·ing /fŏŏlmə nàyting, fúl-/ *adj.* **1. EXPLOSIVE** able or likely to explode or detonate **2.** MED = **fulminant** *adj.* 2

ful·min·ic ac·id /fŏŏl mìnnik-, ful-/ *n.* an unstable compound that smells of bitter almonds. It is used in the manufacture of explosives. Formula: HONC. [Formed from the Latin stem *fulmin-* the stem of *fulmen* "lightning that strikes" (see FULMINATE)]

ful·some /fŏŏlsəm/ *adj.* **1. EXCESSIVELY COMPLIMENTARY** effusive or fawning to the point of being offensive ○ *embarrassed by their fulsome praise* **2. LAVISH** great in amount or intensity [13thC. From FULL + -SOME.] —**ful·some·ly** *adv.* —**ful·some·ness** *n.*

Ful·ton /fŏŏlt'n/ city in Oswego County, central New York, 24 mi./39 km north of Syracuse. Population: 12,929 (1990).

Ful·ton, Robert (1765–1815) U.S. inventor and engineer. He built the first efficient steamboat, the *"Clermont"* (1807), thus inaugurating a new era of power-driven navigation.

ful·vous /fŏŏlvəss/ *adj.* of an orange-brown color (*literary*) [Mid-17thC. Formed from Latin *fulvus* "reddish-yellow."]

Fu Man·chu mus·tache /foo mán chōo-, fōo man chōo-/ *n.* a mustache with long drooping ends [Named for *Fu Manchu*, a character with such a moustache in the novels of Sax Rohmer, pen name of British writer Arthur Sarsfield Ward (1886–1959)]

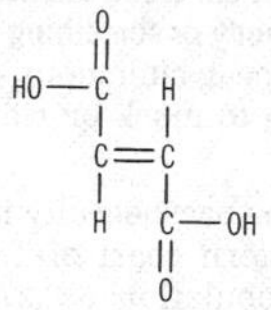

Fumaric acid

fu·mar·ic ac·id /fyoo mèrrik-/ *n.* a colorless crystalline solid that occurs naturally in certain plants and molds and is synthesized from benzene. It is used in making resins. Formula: $C_4H_4O_4$. [Formed from modern Latin *Fumaria*, genus name or fumitory, from late Latin, "fumitory," from Latin *fumus* "smoke"]

fu·ma·role /fyŏŏmə rōl/ *n.* a vent in a volcanic area from which steam and hot gases such as sulfur dioxide are emitted [Early 19thC. Via Italian *fumaruolo* from late Latin *fumariolum* "vent, smoke-hole," from, ultimately, Latin *fumus* "smoke."] —**fu·ma·rol·ic** /fyŏŏmə róllik/ *adj.*

fu·ma·to·ry /fyŏŏmə tàwree/ (*plural* **-ries**) *adj.* relating to, involving, or typical of fumigation or smoking [Mid-19thC. From assumed Latin *fumatorius*, from *fumare.*]

fum·ble /fúmb'l/ *v.* (**-bled, -bling, -bles**) **1.** *vti.* **GROPE CLUMSILY** to grope clumsily in searching for something ○ *He fumbled in his pockets for his keys.* **2.** *vi.* **HESITATE** to act clumsily, hesitantly, or unsuccessfully ○ *She fumbled through the introductions.* **3.** *vt.* **BUNGLE** to do something clumsily or inefficiently ○ *This is your last chance, so don't fumble it.* **4.** *vti.* SPORTS **DROP OR MISHANDLE BALL** in sports, to drop or fail to catch a ball ■ *n.* **1. FUMBLED ACTION** an act or instance of fumbling **2.** SPORTS **FUMBLED BALL** a ball in sports that is dropped or mishandled [Mid-16thC. Origin uncertain: possibly from a Scandinavian source.] —**fum·bler** *n.* —**fum·blingl·y** *adv.*

fume /fyoom/ *v.* (**fumed, fum·ing, fumes**) **1.** *vi.* **BE ANGRY** to feel great anger, especially anger that is not fully expressed **2.** *vi.* **EMIT GAS** to emit gas, smoke, or vapor, or be emitted in this form **3.** *vt.* **FUMIGATE** to treat something with a gas, smoke, or other fumigant ■ *n.* **1. SMOKE** smoke, gas, or vapor, especially when unpleasant or harmful (*often used in the plural*) ○ *a chemical that emits noxious fumes when exposed to air* **2. ACRID SMELL** an acrid or nauseating smell (*often used in the plural*) **3. FIT OF ANGER** a state of great anger [14thC. Via Old French *fum* from Latin *fumus* "smoke" (source of English *perfume*).] —**fum·ing·ly** *adv.* —**fum·y** *adj.*

fu·met /fyŏŏmət/ *n.* a strongly-flavored stock obtained from cooking fish, meat, or vegetables [Early 18thC. From French, from *fumer* "to smoke," ultimately from Latin *fumus* (see FUME).]

fu·mi·gant /fyŏŏmigənt/ *n.* a substance that gives off fumes, especially one used as a disinfectant or to kill pests [Late 19thC. From Latin *fumigare* (see FUMIGATE).]

fu·mi·gate /fyŏŏmi gàyt/ (**-gat·ed, -gat·ing, -gates**) *vti.* to treat something with fumes, especially to disinfect it or to kill pests [Mid-16thC. From *fumigare* "to smoke," from *fumus* "smoke."] —**fu·mi·ga·tion** /fyŏŏmi gáysh'n/ *n.* —**fu·mi·ga·tor** /fyŏŏmi gàytər/ *n.*

fum·ing sul·fu·ric ac·id *n.* a very concentrated solution of sulfuric acid that gives off fumes

fun /fun/ *n.* **1. AMUSEMENT** a time or feeling of enjoyment or amusement ○ *Just for fun, we wore silly hats.* **2. SOMETHING AMUSING** something such as an activity that provides enjoyment or amusement ○ *Skiing is fun for the whole family.* **3. MOCKERY** playful joking, often at the expense of another ○ *What's said in fun can still hurt.* ■ *adj.* **1. AMUSING** providing enjoyment or amusement (*informal*) ○ *We'll have a fun time tonight.* **2. CHEAP AND FLAMBOYANT** flamboyant in style and often made of cheap synthetic materials, designed to be used or worn for fun ○ *fun jewelry* ■ *vi.* (**funned, fun·ning, funs**) **BEHAVE PLAYFULLY** to behave in a playful or joking way (*informal*) ○ *Don't pay any attention to him; he's just funning.* [Late 17thC. From earlier English *fon* "fool," the probable source of *fond.*]

◇ **fun and games 1.** activity, difficulty, or trouble (*informal*) (*used ironically*) ○ *A broken sprinkler in the stockroom overnight gave us some fun and games in the morning.* **2.** carefree amusement (*informal*) ◇ **make fun of somebody** *or* **something** to make somebody or something appear ridiculous ◇ **poke fun at somebody** *or* **something** to mock or ridicule somebody or something

Fu·na·ba·shi /fo͞onə bâashee/ city in Chiba Prefecture on the northeastern coast of Tokyo Bay, Honshu Island, Japan. Population: 533,270 (1990).

fu·nam·bu·list /fyoo námbyəlist/ *n.* an acrobat who walks while balancing on a suspended rope [Late 18thC. Formed from French *funambule* or its source, Latin *funambulus*, from *funis* "rope" + *ambulare* "to walk" (source of English *amble*).] —**fu·nam·bu·lism** *n.* —**fu·nam·bu·late** /-làyt/ *vi.*

func·tion /fúngkshən/ *n.* **1. PURPOSE** an action or use for which something is suited or designed ○ *a watch with an alarm function* **2. ROLE** an activity or role assigned to somebody or something **3. EVENT** a social gathering or ceremony, especially a formal or official occasion ○ *a black-tie function* **4.** MATH **VARIABLE QUANTITY DETERMINED BY OTHERS' VALUES** a variable quantity whose value depends upon the varying values of other quantities **5. DEPENDENT FACTOR** a quality or characteristic that depends upon and varies with another ○ *Success is a function of determination and ability.* **6.** MATH **CORRESPONDENCE BETWEEN MEMBERS OF DIFFERENT SETS** a relationship between two mathematical sets, in which each member of one set corresponds uniquely to a member of the other set. Symbol **f 7.** COMPUT **SINGLE COMPUTER OPERATION** a named and stored basic operation of a computer yielding a single result when invoked **8.** COMPUT **COMPUTER PROGRAM'S MAIN PURPOSE** the purpose of a computer program or piece of computer equipment, e.g., database management or printing **9.** LING **ROLE OF WORD OR PHRASE** a grammatical role performed by a word or phrase in a particular construction ○ *Noun phrases can fulfill many functions.* ■ *vi.* **(-tioned, -tion·ing, -tions) 1. SERVE PURPOSE** to serve a particular purpose or perform a particular role ○ *hats functioning both as fashion statements and as protection against the sun* **2. BE IN WORKING ORDER** to operate normally, fulfilling a purpose or role ○ *When the heart ceases to function, the patient is clinically dead.* [Mid-16thC. From the Latin stem *function-*, from *funct-*, the past participle stem of *fungi* "to perform" (source of English *defunct*).] —**func·tion·less** *adj.*

func·tion·al /fúngksh-/ *adj.* **1. PRACTICAL** having a practical application or serving a useful purpose ○ *designs that are functional yet fun* **2. OPERATIONAL** in good working order or working at the moment ○ *The elevator will not be functional for several hours.* **3.** MED **HAVING NO ORGANIC CAUSE** without apparent organic or structural cause ○ *a functional disorder* **4.** LING **RELATING TO LANGUAGE AS COMMUNICATION** relating to the function of language as a communicating tool, rather than to its form ○ *functional linguistics* — **func·tion·al·i·ty** /fùngkshə-/ *n.* —**func·tion·al·ly** *adv.*

func·tion·al group *n.* a group of atoms that reacts as a single unit and determines the properties and structure of a particular class of compounds, e.g., a hydroxyl group in alcohols

func·tion·al il·lit·er·ate *n.* somebody whose reading and writing abilities are inadequately developed to meet everyday needs —**func·tion·al·ly il·lit·er·ate** *adj.*

func·tion·al·ism /fúngkshə-/ *n.* **1. BELIEF IN FUNCTION OVER FORM** belief that the intended function of something should determine its design, construction, and choice of materials, or a 20th-century design movement based on this **2.** PHILOSOPHY **PHILOSOPHY EMPHASIZING THE PRACTICAL** any philosophy or system that gives practical and utilitarian concerns priority over esthetic concerns **3.** SOC SCI **ASSESSMENT OF SOCIAL INSTITUTIONS BY ROLE** the analysis and explanation of social institutions according to the function they perform in society, e.g., the family seen as an institution for social stability and cohesion — **func·tion·al·ist** *n., adj.* —**func·tion·al·is·tic** *adj.*

func·tion·al lit·er·a·cy *n.* the level of skill in reading and writing that an individual needs to cope with everyday adult life

func·tion·al shift *n.* a change in the grammatical function of a word, e.g., from noun to verb, as happens when the noun wallpaper is used as the verb to wallpaper

func·tion·ar·y /fúngksh-/ (*plural* **-ies**) *n.* somebody who performs official duties, especially somebody whose duties are regarded as trivial

func·tion key *n.* a button on a computer keyboard or terminal that instructs the computer to perform a specific task. The same key may be programmed to perform different tasks in different programs.

func·tion word *n.* a word that has little meaning of its own but serves a particular syntactic or semantic function in a phrase or sentence, e.g., conjunctions such as and and but

func·tor /fúngktər/ *n.* **1. SOMETHING PERFORMING FUNCTION** somebody or something that performs a function (*formal*) **2.** LING = **function word** [Mid-20thC. Formed from FUNCTION, on the model of such words as *factor.*]

fund /fund/ *n.* **1. SUPPLY** a source or stock of something **2. RESERVE OF MONEY** a sum of money saved or invested for a particular purpose ○ *We've started an education fund for our children.* **3. ORGANIZATION ADMINISTERING RESERVE OF MONEY** an organization that manages a sum of money for a particular purpose ○ *a mutual fund* ■ **funds** *npl.* **1. MONEY** money, especially money that is available to spend ○ *I'm a bit short of funds at the moment.* **2. U.K. GOVERNMENT SECURITIES** British government securities that finance the national debt and pay a fixed rate of interest ■ *vt.* **(fund·ed, fund·ing, funds) 1. PROVIDE MONEY FOR** to provide money needed to finance a project or keep it running (*often passive*) ○ *environmental projects funded by local government* **2. PROVIDE MONEY TO PAY DEBT** to provide a sum of money to pay off a debt or its interest **3. MAKE DEBT LONG-TERM** to convert a short-term debt into a long-term debt with a fixed rate of interest **4. PUT IN RESERVE** to store something up for future use ○ *a notebook in which snippets of overheard conversations are funded* [Mid-17thC. From Latin *fundus* "bottom" (source of English *found*[1]). The word was first borrowed in the Latin senses "bottom, basis"; the modern meanings developed from the sense "source of supply."]

fun·da·ment /fúndəmənt/ *n.* **1.** ANAT **BUTTOCKS** the buttocks or the anus (*archaic or humorous*) **2.** GEOG **NATURAL LANDFORM** a natural land surface that has not been altered by people **3. FOUNDING PRINCIPLE** an underlying principle or theory on which something is founded (*formal*) (*often used in the plural*) [13thC. Via Old French *fondement* from, ultimately, Latin *fundus* "bottom."]

fun·da·men·tal /fùndə mént'l/ *adj.* **1. BASIC** relating to or affecting the underlying principles or structure of something ○ *We need to make fundamental changes in our business.* **2. CENTRAL** serving as an essential part of something ○ *Free speech is one of the fundamental rights guaranteed by the constitution.* **3.** MUSIC **OF A CHORD'S LOWEST NOTE** relating to the lowest note of a chord in root position, the note that gives the chord its basic harmony **4.** PHYS **OF LOWEST FREQUENCY** relating to or produced by the lowest frequency component in a complex vibration ■ *n.* **1. BASIC PRINCIPLE OR ELEMENT** a basic and necessary component of something, especially an underlying rule or principle (*often used in the plural*) ○ *The class teaches the fundamentals of karate.* **2.** MUSIC **PRINCIPAL TONE** the principal tone in a chord, from which other harmonics are generated **3.** PHYS **LOWEST FREQUENCY** the lowest frequency in a vibration or periodic wave

fun·da·men·tal in·ter·ac·tion *n.* PHYS = **interaction** *n.* 3

fun·da·men·tal·ism /fùndə mént'l ìzzəm/ *n.* **1. MOVEMENT ADVOCATING RETURN TO TRADITIONAL PRINCIPLES** a religious or political movement based on a literal interpretation of and strict adherence to doctrine, especially as a return to former principles **2. SUPPORT FOR LITERAL EXPLANATION** the belief that religious or political doctrine should be implemented literally, not interpreted or adapted —**fun·da·men·tal·ist** *n., adj.* — **fun·da·men·tal·ist·ic** /fùndə ment'l ístik/ *adj.*

fun·da·men·tal law *n.* the founding rules and principles or constitution on which a government is based, as distinct from its legislative acts

fun·da·men·tal·ly /fùndə mént'lee/ *adv.* in a way that relates to or affects something at its most basic level ○ *Your argument is fundamentally flawed.*

fun·da·men·tal par·ti·cle *n.* = **elementary particle**

-funded *suffix.* with money provided by a particular institution or person ○ *a number of government-funded schemes*

fun·di plural of **fundus**

fund·ing /fúnding/ *n.* financial support

fund·rais·er /fúnd ràyzər/ *n.* **1. SOMEBODY WHO RAISES MONEY** somebody who solicits money for a nonprofit or political organization, especially somebody whose job is to organize campaigns to raise money **2. MONEY-RAISING ACTIVITY** an activity or event that is intended to generate money to support a non-profit or political organization

fund·rais·ing /fúnd ràyzing/ *n.* the organized activity of soliciting and collecting funds for a non-profit or political organization

fun·dus /fúndəss/ (*plural* **-di** /fún dī/) *n.* the part of a hollow organ farthest from its opening, e.g., the part of the eye's retina opposite the pupil [Mid-18thC. From Latin, "bottom."] —**fun·dic** /fúndik/ *adj.*

Fun·dy, Bay of /fúndee/ inlet of the Atlantic Ocean off Canada, separating New Brunswick and Nova Scotia, Canada. Its rapid tides are among the highest in the world, reaching 60 ft./18 m. Depth: 650 ft./200 m. Length: 94 mi./150 km.

Fun·dy Na·tion·al Park national park and wildlife reserve along the Bay of Fundy, southwestern New Brunswick, Canada. Area: 80 sq. mi./206 sq. km.

fu·ner·al /fyo͞onərəl/ *n.* **1. CEREMONY FOR SOMEBODY WHO HAS DIED** a rite held to mark the burial or cremation of a corpse, especially a ceremony held immediately before burial or cremation **2. END** an end to something's existence ○ *We have witnessed the funeral of the amateur game.* **3. FUNERAL PROCESSION** a procession of mourners following a body to its place of burial or cremation **4. FUNERAL SERMON OR MEMORIAL SERVICE** a sermon or eulogy delivered at a funeral ceremony or a memorial service held some time after the death (*regional*) [14thC. Via Old French *funerailles* "funeral rites" from medieval Latin *funeralia*, from late Latin *funeralis* "of death rituals," from Latin *funer-*, the stem of *funus* "death ritual."] ◇ **be somebody's funeral** to be somebody else's problem or worry (*informal*) ○ *If he wants to work extra hours, that's his funeral.*

fu·ner·al di·rec·tor *n.* somebody, especially the proprietor of a funeral home, whose job is to manage funerals and often also to prepare corpses for burial or cremation

fu·ner·al home, fu·ner·al par·lor *n.* a business establishment where corpses are prepared for burial or cremation and where a funeral service may also be held and the body viewed by mourners

fu·ner·ar·y /fyo͞onə rèrree/ *adj.* relating to or suitable for a burial or funeral ○ *a funerary urn* [Late 17thC. From late Latin *funerarius*, from Latin *funer-*, the stem of *funus* "funeral."]

fu·ne·re·al /fyə neéree əl/ *adj.* **1. OF OR LIKE A FUNERAL** relating to or suitable for a funeral **2. GLOOMY** very slow, solemn, mournful, or dismal [Early 18thC. Formed from Latin *funereus*, from *funer-*, the stem of *funus* "funeral."] —**fu·ne·re·al·ly** *adv.*

fun·fest /fún fèst/ *n.* a party, especially one at which amusing activities are organized (*informal*)

fun·gal /fúng g'l/, **fun·gous** *adj.* **1. OF OR LIKE FUNGUS** in the form of a fungus or similar to a fungus in appearance or texture **2. FROM A FUNGUS** caused by a fungus ○ *a fungal infection*

fun·gi *plural of* **fungus**

fun·gi·ble /fúnjəb'l/ *adj.* **1. SUBSTITUTABLE** capable of being interchanged **2. TRADABLE UNDER A CONTRACT** used to described commodities that can be traded or substituted for an equal amount of a like commodity, usually to satisfy a contract ■ *n.* **SOMETHING TRADED OR SUBSTITUTED** a commodity that is fungible (*often used in the plural*) [Late 17thC. From medieval Latin *fungibilis*, from Latin *fungi* "to perform" (see FUNCTION).] —**fun·gi·bil·i·ty** /fùnjə bíllətee/ *n.*

fun·gi·cide /fúnjə sīd, fúng gə-/ *n.* a substance used to destroy or inhibit the growth of fungi —**fun·gi·cid·al** /fùnjə sīd'l, fùng gə-/ *adj.* —**fun·gi·cid·al·ly** /fùnjə sīd'lee, fùng gə-/ *adv.*

fun·gi·form /fúnjə fàwrm, fúng gə-/ *adj.* shaped like a mushroom

fun·gi·stat /fúnjə stàt, fúng gə-/ *n.* a substance that inhibits the growth of fungi without killing them — **fun·gi·stat·ic** /fùnjə státtik, fùng gə-/ *adj.*

fun·go /fúng gō/ (*plural* **-goes**) *n.* BASEBALL **1. BASEBALL SHOT** in baseball, an act of hitting the ball high into the air, usually to give fielders catching practice **2.** = **fungo bat** [Mid-19thC. Origin unknown.]

fun·go bat *n.* BASEBALL a lightweight bat used in baseball practice to hit fungoes

fun·goid /fúng gòyd/ *adj.* **OF OR LIKE FUNGUS** resembling, characteristic of, or caused by a fungus ○ *a fungoid growth* ■ *n.* **FUNGUS** a fungus, or a growth resembling a fungus

fun·gous *adj.* = **fungal**

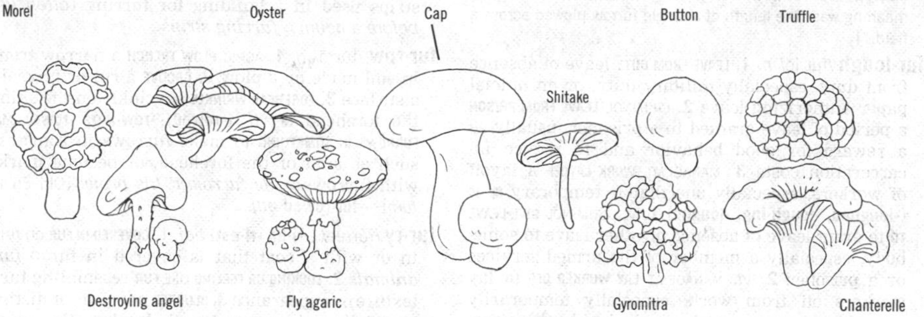

Fungus: Varieties of mushroom

fun·gus /fúng gəss/ (*plural* **-gi** /fún jī, fúng gī/ *or* **-gus·es**) *n.* a single-celled or multicellular organism without chlorophyll that reproduces by spores and lives by absorbing nutrients from organic matter. Fungi comprise the mildews, molds, mushrooms, rusts, smuts, and yeasts. [Early 16thC. From Latin, of unknown origin.]

fun house *n.* a building at an amusement park that customers walk or ride through, encountering objects and devices designed to amuse or startle

fu·ni·cle /fyóonik'l/ *n.* = **funiculus** [Mid-17thC. An anglicization of Latin *funiculus* (see FUNICULUS).]

fu·nic·u·lar /fyoo níkyələr/ *adj.* **1. OF ROPE'S TENSION** relating to a rope, especially its tension **2.** MECH ENG **ROPE-OPERATED** operated by a rope or cable, especially one wound or pulled by a machine **3.** ANAT, BOT **OF A FUNICULUS** relating to a funiculus ■ *n.* RAIL **CABLE-OPERATED RAILWAY** a funicular railway or railway car [Mid-17thC. Formed from FUNICULUS.]

Funicular railway

fu·nic·u·lar rail·way *n.* a railway used on short steep inclines in which cars that counterbalance each other run on parallel tracks linked to a cable

fu·nic·u·lus /fyoo níkyələss/ (*plural* **-li** /-lī/) *n.* **1.** ANAT **CORD-SHAPED BODY PART** a cord-shaped part of the body such as the umbilical cord or a bundle of nerve fibers in the spinal cord **2.** BOT **OVULE STALK** a stalk of a plant ovule that connects it or a seed to the placenta [Mid-17thC. From Latin, literally "little rope," from *funis* "rope."]

funk[1] /fungk/ *n.* **1.** MUSIC **MUSICAL STYLE** a type of popular music that derives from jazz, blues, and soul and is characterized by a heavy rhythmic bass and backbeat **2.** MUSIC **EARTHY MUSICAL QUALITY** a rhythmic earthy quality in music (*slang*) **3. LACK OF WORLDLINESS** lack of sophistication, especially the kind of simplicity or naivety thought by some to be typical of rural or provincial areas (*slang*) [Mid-20thC. Back-formation from FUNKY[1].]

funk[2] /fungk/ (**funked, funk·ing, funks**) *n.* a state of melancholy or hopeless sadness (*informal*) ○ *He's been in a funk since the divorce.* [Mid-18thC. Origin unknown.] ◇ **be in a blue funk** to be in a melancholy state (*dated informal*)

funk[3] /fungk/ *n.* a strong unpleasant odor (*slang*) ○ *get the funk out of my clothes* [Early 17thC. Origin uncertain: possibly via dialectal French *funquer* "to smoke" from, ultimately, Latin *fumigare* (see FUMIGATE).]

funk·y[1] /fúngkee/ (**-i·er, -i·est**) *adj.* **1.** MUSIC **SYNCOPATED AND RHYTHMIC** with the beat and the syncopated rhythmic bass typical of funk music (*slang*) **2. UNWORLDLY** simple or unsophisticated in style (*slang*) **3.** FASHION **HIP** unconventional and individualistic in behavior or style (*slang*) ○ *a return to the funky styles of the 1970s* **4. TASTELESS** lacking style or good taste (*dated slang*) ○ *These clothes are too funky to wear to a banquet.* **5. STYLISH AND NEW** unconventionally stylish and new (*informal*) ○ *The sleek lines of the computer make it both fun and funky.* [Mid-20thC. Formed from FUNK[3].] —**funk·i·ly** *adv.* —**funk·i·ness** *n.*

funk·y[2] /fúngkee/ (**-i·er, -i·est**) *adj.* having a strong unpleasant odor (*slang*) [Late 18thC. Formed from FUNK[3].] —**funk·i·ness** *n.*

fun·nel /fúnn'l/ *n.* **1. UTENSIL USED IN POURING LIQUIDS** a cone-shaped utensil with a large opening at the top and a small opening or tube at the bottom, used to guide liquids and other substances into containers **2. CHIMNEY** a vertical pipe from which smoke and exhaust gases escape, especially one on a steamship or steam engine ■ *v.* (**-neled, -nel·ing, -nels**) **1.** *vti.* **MOVE INTO NARROW SPACE** to move or direct something into and through a narrow space ○ *an efficient system for funneling crowds through the turnstiles* **2.** *vt.* **CONCENTRATE RESOURCES SOMEWHERE** to direct or channel all of something from one place or use to another ○ *Funds were funneled away from other projects.* **3.** *vt.* **MAKE FUNNEL-SHAPED** to form something into the shape of a funnel [15thC. Via Provençal *fonilh* from, ultimately, Latin *infundibulum*, from *infundere* "to pour in," from *fundere* "to pour" (source of English *found*, *fuse*, and *confuse*).]

fun·nel cloud *n.* a funnel-shaped cloud that projects from the base of a thundercloud and often develops into a tornado

fun·nel·form /fúnn'l fàwrm/ *adj.* used to describe a flower or other plant part that is shaped like a funnel or cone

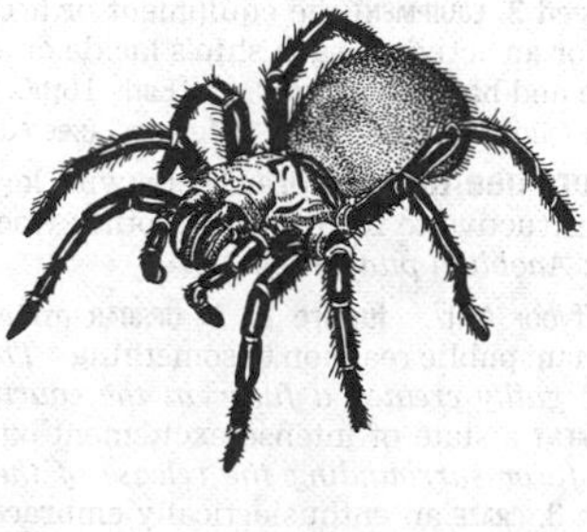

Funnel-web spider

fun·nel-web spi·der, **fun·nel-web** *n.* a large black highly venomous spider that is native to Australia and makes funnel-shaped webs. Family: Dipluridae.

fun·ni·ly /fúnnilee/ *adv.* **1. INTRODUCING COMMENT ON SOMETHING STRANGE** used to introduce a comment on something considered strange or odd ○ *Funnily enough, nobody seemed to notice.* **2. STRANGELY** in a way that seems strange or odd ○ *She has been acting funnily ever since the operation.* **3. COMICALLY** in an amusing or humorous way

fun·ny /fúnnee/ *adj.* (**-ni·er, -ni·est**) **1. COMICAL** causing amusement, especially enough to provoke laughter **2. STRANGE** odd or perplexing ○ *That's funny, I can't find my keys.* **3. UNCONVENTIONAL** out of the ordinary in a quaint or comical way ○ *a funny old aunt who talks to plants* **4. UNWELL** slightly ill, e.g. nauseated or faint (*informal*) **5. TRICKY** sly, deceitful, or dishonest (*informal*) ○ *Don't try anything funny, or I'll call the police .* ■ *n.* (*plural* **-nies**) **JOKE** an amusing remark or joke (*informal*) ■ **fun·nies** *npl.* **NEWSPAPER COMIC STRIPS** the section of a newspaper containing the comic strips [Mid-18thC. Formed from FUN.] —**fun·ni·ness** *n.*

WORD KEY: SYNONYMS

funny, comic, comical, droll, facetious, humorous, waggish, witty, hilarious, side-splitting

CORE MEANING: causing or intended to cause amusement

funny a general word used to describe something that causes amusement or laughter, whether intentionally or not; **comic** used in the same way as "funny," especially to describe books, poems, or plays; **comical** suggesting that somebody or something is funny to the extent of being absurd, especially if this is unintentional; **droll** used to describe something that is funny because it is whimsical or odd. It is also used to suggest humor that is rather dry in tone; **facetious** used showing disapproval to suggest that an attempt at humor is ill-timed, inappropriate or silly; **humorous** giving rise to amusement, smiles, or laughter, but with the suggestion that this is more genial, sympathetic, or light-hearted than is necessarily the case with "funny"; **waggish** suggesting humor with overtones of playfulness; **witty** suggesting quick and clever, inventive verbal humor; **hilarious** used to describe something that is very funny indeed; **side-splitting** used to describe something that is very funny indeed, especially when it causes a great deal of uncontrollable laughter.

fun·ny bone *n.* **1. ELBOW POINT** the point at the outside of the elbow where a nerve is so close to the longer arm bone that a blow often causes a tingling sensation (*informal*) **2. SENSE OF HUMOR** somebody's perception of what is amusing [From the tingling feeling when the nerve is hit, probably also with some punning reference to HUMERUS "arm bone" and HUMOROUS]

fun·ny book *n.* a comic book (*dated informal*)

fun·ny busi·ness *n.* dealings or goings-on that involve trickery, deceit, or dishonesty (*informal*)

fun·ny farm *n.* an offensive term, once considered humorous, referring to a psychiatric hospital (*slang offensive*)

fun·ny·man /fúnni màn/ (*plural* **-men** /fúnni mèn/) *n.* a man who is a comedian, clown, or humorist

fun·ny mon·ey *n.* (*informal*) **1.** CRIMINOL **COUNTERFEIT MONEY** counterfeit or forged currency **2.** CRIMINOL **ILLICITLY GAINED MONEY** money obtained from a legally or morally suspect source **3.** FIN **CURRENCY WITH LITTLE VALUE** currency, especially an unfamiliar one, with an inflated value

fun·ny pa·per *n.* a section of a newspaper that contains the comic strips (*often used in the plural*)

fun park *n.* an area with amusement facilities, especially water slides and rides

fun run *n.* a noncompetitive run over a moderately long course, organized to promote health and fitness or to raise money for charity

fun·ster /fúnstər/ *n.* somebody who enjoys telling or playing jokes or who simply likes to have fun (*informal*)

fur /fur/ *n.* **1.** ZOOL **MAMMAL'S COAT** the soft dense coat of hair on a hairy mammal **2.** ZOOL **ANIMAL HAIR** hairs from an animal's coat **3.** INDUST **DRESSED PELT** a dressed pelt from an animal such as a mink or seal that includes the animal's soft coat of hair and is used for garments and decoration **4.** CLOTHES **FUR COAT** a garment made from fur pelts, especially a coat, jacket, or stole **5. SOMETHING HAIRY** something with a fuzzy or hairy texture or appearance **6.** MED **COATING ON THE TONGUE** a whitish coating of dead cells on the tongue that sometimes accompanies an illness (*informal*) **7.** HERALDRY **PELT ON COAT OF ARMS** a representation of an animal skin on a coat of arms [14thC. From Old French *forrer* "to line" (the original sense in English), from *forre* "lining." The noun came from the verb. Ultimately from a prehistoric Germanic word meaning "protector, feeder" (ancestor also of English *fodder*).] —**fur·less** *adj.* —**furred** *adj.* ◇ **make the fur fly** to cause trouble or a disturbance (*informal*)

Fur /fur/ *n.* a language spoken in parts of Chad and in western Sudan. It belongs to the Nilo-Saharan family of African languages. Fur is spoken by about 400,000 people. —**Fur** *adj.*

fur. *abbr.* furlong

fu·ran /fyŏŏr àn, fyoor án/ *n.* a colorless flammable liquid. It is used as a solvent and in the manufacture of polymers, especially. Formula: C_4H_4O. [Late 19thC. Contraction of FURFURAN.]

fu·ra·nose /fyŏŏrə nōz/ *n.* a sugar with a chemical structure that contains a ring of four carbon atoms and one oxygen atom

fur·bear·er /fúr bàirər/ *n.* an animal with fur, especially fur with a high commercial value such as that of a fox or mink —**fur·bear·ing** *adj.*

fur·be·low /fúrbə lō/ *n.* **1.** FASHION **RUFFLE** a gathered or pleated piece of material, especially as an ornament on a woman's garment ○ *Her dress was decorated with furbelows.* **2. FLAMBOYANT BEHAVIOR** a showy or pretentious way of behaving (*literary*) (*often used in the plural*) ■ *vt.* (**-lowed, -low·ing, -lows**) FASHION **DECORATE SOMETHING WITH RUFFLE** to add a furbelow to a garment for ornamentation [Late 17thC. Origin uncertain: possibly an alteration of French dialect *farbella* or Provençal *farbello* "fringe," from Italian *faldella*, literally "small fold," from *falda* "fold."]

fur·bish /fúrbish/ (**-bished, -bish·ing, -bish·es**) *vt.* **1. POLISH** to brighten something by polishing **2. REFURBISH** to refurbish something (*literary*) [14thC. From the Old French verb stem *fourbiss-*, which was ultimately of prehistoric Germanic origin.] —**fur·bish·er** *n.*

fur·cate /fúr kàyt/ *vi.* (**-cat·ed, -cat·ing, -cates**) **TO FORK** to divide into two separate strands or branches ■ *adj.* **FORKED** divided into separate strands or branches ○ *furcate leaves* [Early 19thC. From late Latin *furcatus* "forked," from Latin *furca* "fork" (source of English *fork*).] —**fur·cate·ly** *adv.* —**fur·ca·tion** *n.*

fur·cu·la /fúrkyələ/ (*plural* **-lae** /fúrkyə lèe/) *n.* the wishbone of a bird (*technical*) [Mid-19thC. From Latin, literally "small fork," from *furca* "fork."] —**fur·cu·lar** *adj.*

fur·fur /fúr fùr/ (*plural* **-fur·es**) *n.* DERMAT a tiny piece of scaly or flaky skin, e.g., a particle of dandruff (*technical*) [From Latin, "bran, scales"]

fur·fu·ra·ceous /fùrfə ráyshəss, fùrfyə-/ *adj.* **1.** DERMAT **SCALY** covered with or resembling particles of dandruff **2.** BOT **LIKE BRAN** relating to or resembling bran

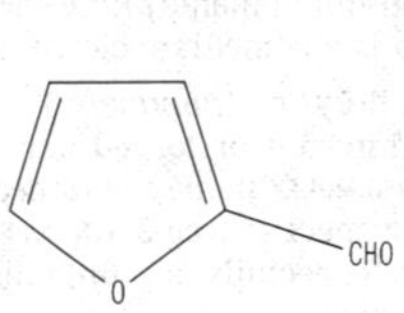

Furfural

fur·fu·ral /fúrfərəl, fúrfyə-/ *n.* a colorless liquid with a distinctive smell. It occurs widely in plants and is used in making plastics, in oil refining, and in agriculture. Formula: $C_5H_4O_2$.

fur·fu·ran /fúrfə ràn, fúrfyə-/ *n.* = **furan**

Fu·ries /fyŏŏreez/, **fu·ries** *npl.* in Greek mythology, three terrifying snake-haired winged goddesses who mercilessly punished wrongdoing, especially when committed within families. There were three Furies, named Alecto, Megaera, and Tisiphone. They were transformed in later mythology into the more benign Eumenides. (*See also* EUMENIDES.)

fu·ri·o·so /fyŏŏri ṓsō/ *adv.* to be played with vigor and passion (*used as a musical direction*) [Mid-17thC. Via Italian from Latin *furiosus* (see FURIOUS).] —**fu·ri·o·so** *adj.*

fu·ri·ous /fyŏŏree əss/ *adj.* **1. INFURIATED** extremely or violently angry ○ *I was furious with him for spreading such lies.* **2. VERY ENERGETIC** involving a great deal of energy, violence, or speed ○ *the pianist's furious assault on the keys* [14thC. Via Old French *furieus* from Latin *furiosus*, from *furia* "rage" (see FURY).] —**fu·ri·ous·ly** *adv.* —**fu·ri·ous·ness** *n.*

furl /furl/ *vti.* (**furled, furl·ing, furls**) **ROLL OR BECOME ROLLED UP** to roll up and secure something made of fabric, e.g., an umbrella, a flag, or a sail, or be rolled up and secured ■ *n.* **FURLED SECTION** a rolled-up section of something such as a flag or sail [Late 16thC. From French *ferler*, from *ferm* "firm, firmly" (see FIRM[1]) + *lier* "to tie" (source of English *liable*).]

fur·long /fúr làwng/ *n.* a measure of distance equal to 220 yards (approximately 201 meters), now used mainly on racetracks [Old English *furlang*, from *furh* "furrow" (see FURROW) + *lang* "long" (see LONG). The original meaning was "the length of a single furrow plowed across a field."]

fur·lough /fúr lō/ *n.* **1. LEAVE FROM DUTY** leave of absence from duty, especially military duty, or an official paper authorizing leave **2.** CRIMINOL **LEAVE FROM PRISON** a period of leave granted to a prisoner, usually as a reward for good behavior and to reduce incarceration costs **3.** MANAGEMT **WORK LAYOFF** a layoff of workers, especially one that is temporary ■ *v.* (**-loughed, -lough·ing, -loughs**) **1.** *vt.* CRIMINOL **GIVE LEAVE TO** to grant leave of absence or other leave to somebody, especially a member of the armed services or a prisoner **2.** *vt.* MANAGEMT **LAY WORKER OFF** to lay workers off from work, especially temporarily ○ *Sixty workers were furloughed after the Christmas rush.* **3.** *vi.* **GO SOMEWHERE ON LEAVE** to spend a leave in a particular place ○ *We furloughed for a week in a beach house.* [Early 17thC. From Dutch *verlo* "leave." Ultimately from a prehistoric Germanic word that is also the ancestor of English *leave*.]

fur·mi·ty /fúrmətee/ *n.* = **frumenty**

furn. *abbr.* furnished

fur·nace /fúrnəss/ *n.* **1.** TECH **ENCLOSURE PRODUCING GREAT HEAT** an enclosure in which heat is produced by burning fuel, e.g., to warm a building or smelt metal ○ *an oil furnace* **2. SOMEWHERE HOT** an intensely hot place (*informal*) ○ *This kitchen is a furnace!* [13thC. Via Old French *fornais* from Latin *fornax*. Ultimately from an Indo-European base meaning "to warm, heat" that is also the ancestor of English *burn*, *brandy*, and *brimstone*.]

fur·nish /fúrnish/ (**-nished, -nish·ing, -nish·es**) *vt.* **1. PUT FURNITURE IN A PLACE** to provide and install furniture and other fittings, e.g., carpets and drapes, in a place ○ *The lobby is furnished in an Art Deco style.* **2. SUPPLY** to supply something or to provide somebody with something (*formal*) ○ *Could you furnish us with the names and addresses of your clients?* [15thC. From Old French *furniss-*, the stem of *furnir* (source also of English *veneer*). Ultimately from a prehistoric Germanic base denoting "furtherance, advance" that is also the ancestor of English *from*.] —**fur·nish·er** *n.*

fur·nish·ings /fúrnishingz/ *npl.* **1. FURNITURE** articles of furniture and other useful or decorative items for a room, such as carpets and drapes **2.** FASHION **CLOTHES** clothes and clothing accessories, e.g., belts and scarves

fur·ni·ture /fúrnichər/ *n.* **1. TABLES AND CHAIRS** the movable items such as chairs, desks, or cabinets in an area such as a room or patio **2.** PRINTING **TYPE SEPARATORS** strips of wood, metal, or plastic that are placed between type in order to make spaces and hold the type in place in the frame (**chase**) in which they are arranged **3. EQUIPMENT** the equipment or accessories used for an activity, e.g. a ship's tackle or a horse's saddle and harnesses (*archaic*) [Early 16thC. From Old French *fourniture*, from *furnir* "to furnish" (see FURNISH).]

fur·ni·ture bee·tle *n.* a borer beetle with larvae that are destructive to furniture and other wood. Latin name: *Anobium punctatum*.

fu·ror /fyŏŏr àwr/, **fu·rore** *n.* **1. UPROAR** an angry or indignant public reaction to something ○ *The verdict of not guilty created a furor in the courtroom.* **2. EXCITEMENT** a state of intense excitement or activity ○ *the furor surrounding the release of their latest album* **3. CRAZE** an enthusiastically embraced fad **4. ANGRY OUTBURST** a violent outburst of anger (*archaic*) [15thC. From Latin, from *furere* "to rage."]

fu·ro·se·mide /fyoo rṓssə mīd/ *n.* a drug that induces urination, used especially to treat edema [Mid-20thC]

fur·ri·er /fúrree ər/ *n.* **1. FUR DEALER** somebody who buys and sells furs **2. MAKER OR SELLER OF FUR GARMENTS** a person or establishment that makes or sells clothes and accessories of animal fur [14thC. Alteration (on the model of CLOTHIER) of earlier *furrer*, from Old French *forreor*, from *forrer* "to line with fur" (see FUR).]

fur·ri·er·y /fúrree əree/ *n.* **1.** CLOTHES **FUR GARMENTS** fur accessories and articles of clothing considered collectively **2.** BUSINESS **FURRIER'S BUSINESS** the business or craft of a furrier

fur·ring /fúrring/ *n.* **1.** CLOTHES **FUR PART OF CLOTHING** fur trim or lining for a garment **2. WHITE COVERING** a whitish coating, e.g., on the tongue of somebody who is sick **3.** CONSTR **MAKING A SURFACE OF STRIPS** the placing of strips of wood, metal, or brick across the studs or joists in a building to create a firm and level foundation for plaster, plasterboard, flooring, or another surface **4.** INDUST **STRIPS USED UNDER SURFACE** strips used in a building for furring (*often used before a noun*) ○ *furring strips*

fur·row /fúrrō/ *n.* **1.** AGRIC **PLOW TRENCH** a narrow trench in soil made by a plow **2. GROOVE** a rut or groove in a surface **3. FOREHEAD WRINKLE** a wrinkle on the skin of the forehead ■ *vti.* (**-rowed, -row·ing, -rows**) **MAKE FURROWS IN SOMETHING** to make furrows in something such as land or the forehead, or become marked with furrows ○ *He furrowed his brow.* [Old English *furh*] —**fur·rowed** *adj.*

fur·ry /fúree/ (**-ri·er, -ri·est**) *adj.* **1. COVERED IN FUR** covered in or with a coat that is covered in fur ○ *furry animals* **2. LOOKING OR FEELING LIKE FUR** resembling fur in texture or appearance **3. BLURRED** not clear or distinct, especially not seen or heard clearly ○ *the last few words of a pretty furry radio message* **4.** MED **COVERED IN WHITISH COATING** covered with a whitish coating of dead cells (*refers to the tongue or the inside of the mouth*)

fur seal *n.* a seal with a double coat of fur, including a dense soft underfur that is highly valued for making garments. Many fur seal populations have been severely decreased by commercial hunting. Genera: *Arctocephalus* and *Callorhinus*.

Fur Seal Is·lands /fur sèel-/ = **Pribilof Islands**

Fürth /fōŏrt/ city in the state of Bavaria, southern Germany, situated just northwest of Nuremburg. Population: 108,000 (1993).

fur·ther /fúrthər/ *adj.* **ADDITIONAL** that is more than or adds to the quantity or extent of something ○ *until further notice* ○ *Do you have anything further to add?* ■ *adv.* **1. TO GREATER DISTANCE** to or at a point that is more distant in place or time ○ *further into the future.* ◊ **farther 2. TO GREATER EXTENT** to a greater degree or extent ○ *Let's not pursue the matter any further.* ◊ **farther 3. IN ADDITION** used to introduce an additional statement or point ○ *She said further that she would not accept any excuses.* ■ *vt.* (**-thered, -ther·ing, -thers**) **ADVANCE** to help or give a boost to the progress of something ○ *All this media attention will further our cause.* [Old English *furðor*, *furður* "more forward." Ultimately from a prehistoric Germanic base that is also the ancestor of English *forth*.] —**fur·ther·er** *n.* —**fur·ther·most** /-mōst/ *adj.* ◇ **further to** following on from something that has been written or discussed ○ *Further to our phone conversation, I would like to confirm the order.*

fur·ther·ance /fúrthərəns/ *n.* the aiding or advancing of the progress of something ○ *In furtherance of our campaign, we ask that everyone make a contribution.*

fur·ther·more /fúrthər màwr, fùrthər máwr/ *adv.* used to introduce an additional statement or point ○ *She claimed furthermore that he did not own the business but only worked there.*

fur·thest /fúrthəst/ *adj.* **MOST DISTANT** more distant in place or time than anything else ○ *In our solar system, Pluto is the furthest planet from the sun.* ◊ **farthest** ■ *adv.* ◊ **farthest 1. TO GREATEST DISTANCE** to or at a more distant point in space or time than anything else ○ *Whoever gets the furthest wins the prize.* **2. TO GREATEST EXTENT** to a greater degree or extent than anything else ○ *The dollar has fallen furthest against the pound in the last year.*

fur·tive /fúrtiv/ *adj.* **1. SECRETIVE** done in a way that is intended to escape notice ○ *conspirators exchanging furtive glances* **2. SHIFTY** with the appearance, or giving the impression, of somebody who has something to hide [Early 17thC. Via Old French *furtif* from Latin *furtivus* "hidden, stolen," from *furtum* "theft," from *fur* "thief" (source of English *ferret*). Ultimately from an Indo-European word meaning "to carry."] —**fur·tive·ly** *adv.* —**fur·tive·ness** *n.*

WORD KEY: SYNONYMS

See Synonyms at ***secret***.

fu·run·cle /fyŏŏ rùngk'l/ *n.* a boil on the skin (*technical*) [Late 17thC. From Latin *furunculus*, literally "small thief," hence "knob on a vine" (because it "steals" the sap), from *fur* (see FURTIVE).] —**fu·run·cu·lar** /fyə rúngkyələr/ *adj.*

fu·run·cu·lo·sis /fyə rùngkyə lṓssiss/ *n.* **1.** DERMAT **SKIN DISORDER WITH MULTIPLE BOILS** a condition in which large areas of the skin are covered in persistent boils **2.** BIOL **FISH DISEASE** a virulent bacterial disease that affects salmon and trout and can be devastating in densely populated waters, e.g., in fish farms

fu·ry /fyŏoree/ (*plural* **-ries**) *n.* **1. RAGE** violent anger ○ *She could not contain her fury any longer.* **2. BURST OF ANGER** a state or outburst of violent anger ○ *He stormed off in a fury.* **3. WILD FORCE** a state of excited or frenetic activity ○ *debris scattered in the wake of the tornado's fury* **4. fu·ry, Fu·ry** ➧ **Furies 5. OFFENSIVE TERM FOR ANGRY WOMAN** an offensive term for a woman who is considered by the speaker to be malevolent and spiteful (*offensive*) [14thC. Via Old French *furie* from Latin *furia*, from *furere* "to rage."] ◇ **like fury** with great speed or energy

WORD KEY: SYNONYMS

See Synonyms at ***anger.***

WORD KEY: CULTURAL NOTE

The Sound and the Fury, a novel by William Faulkner (1929). Set in the South, it recounts the financial and moral decline of a wealthy family. The story, which centers on the daughter Caddy, is told in four parts, three of which are narrated by family members, one of them a mentally challenged son, Benjy.

fu·sain /fyoo záyn, fyŏo zàyn/ *n.* **1.** DRAWING **CHARCOAL STICK** a fine stick of charcoal for drawing, made from wood from the spindle tree **2.** DRAWING **CHARCOAL DRAWING** a drawing or sketch done with fusain charcoal **3.** MINERALS **GRAY COAL** dark gray bituminous carbon found in some kinds of coal [Late 19thC. Via French, "spindle tree, charcoal made from its wood" from, ultimately, Latin *fusus* "spindle."]

fus·cous /fúskəss/ *adj.* of a dark brown color tinged with gray [Mid-17thC. Formed from Latin *fuscus* "dusky." Ultimately from an Indo-European word that is also the ancestor of English *dusk*.]

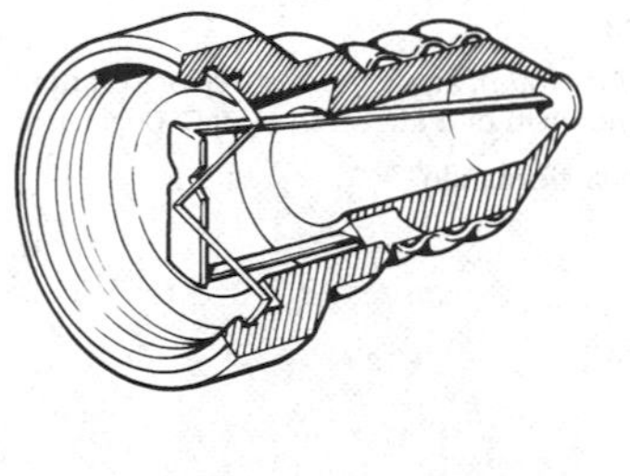

Fuse

fuse[1] /fyooz/ *n.* ELEC ENG **ELECTRICAL CIRCUIT BREAKER** an electrical safety device containing a piece of a metal that melts if the current running through it exceeds a certain level, thereby breaking the circuit ■ *vti.* **(fused, fus·ing, fus·es) 1. COMBINE** to unite or blend things, or become united or blended into a whole ○ *sensations and ideas fusing intimately together* **2. LIQUEFY** to melt something such as metal or plastic, or become melted at a very high temperature [Late 16thC. From Latin *fus-*, the past participle stem of *fundere* "to melt, pour" (source of English *foundry* and *fusion*).] ◇ **blow a fuse 1.** ELEC ENG to overload an electric circuit causing the fuse to melt, thereby breaking the circuit **2.** to fly into a temper (*informal*) ○ *She'll blow a fuse when you tell her.*

fuse[2] /fyooz/, **fuze** *n.* **1. EXPLOSIVE LEAD** a cord or trail of a combustible substance that is ignited at one end to carry a flame to an explosive device farther away **2. DETONATOR** a mechanical or electrical detonator that triggers an exploding device such as a bomb or grenade ■ *vt.* **(fused, fus·ing, fus·es; fuzed, fuz·ing, fuz·es) EQUIP DEVICE WITH DETONATOR** to equip an exploding device such as a bomb or grenade with a mechanical or electrical detonator [Mid-17thC. Via Italian *fuso* "spindle" from Latin *fusus* (source of English *fuselage*). So called because early bomb fuses were spindle-shaped hollow tubes filled with gunpowder.]

fused /fyoozd/ *adj.* fitted with a fuse for safety purposes (*refers to an electrical appliance*)

fused quartz, fused sil·i·ca *n.* = **quartz glass**

fu·see /fyoo zée/, **fu·zee** *n.* **1. FLARE** a red flare used as a warning device on railroads or roads **2. WINDPROOF MATCH** a large-headed match that is not easily extinguished in the wind **3.** MECH ENG **CLOCK PULLEY** a conical pulley with a spiral groove, used in clock and watch mechanisms **4.** ARMS **EXPLOSIVES FUSE** a combustible fuse leading to an explosive device [Late 16thC. Via French *fusée* "spindle, fuse, flare" from, ultimately, Latin *fusus* "spindle" (source also of English *fuse*[2]).]

fu·se·lage /fyŏossə laàzh, fyŏozə-/ *n.* an airplane's body, containing the cockpit, passenger seating, and cargo hold but excluding the wings [Early 20thC. From French, from, ultimately, Latin *fusus* "spindle" (source of English *fuse*[2]). The underlying meaning is "spindle-shaped."]

fu·sel oil /fyŏoz'l-/ *n.* an oily liquid mixture that occurs in insufficiently distilled alcoholic liquors. It is used as a solvent and in chemical manufacturing. [Mid-19thC. *Fusel* from German, "bad liquor."]

Fu·shun /fŏo shŏon/ city and industrial center in Liaoning Province, northeastern China. Population: 1,202,388 (1991).

fu·si·ble /fyŏozəb'l/ *adj.* easily melted or liquefied (*refers to metals and other materials*) ○ *fusible alloys* —**fu·si·bil·i·ty** /fyŏozə bíllətee/ *n.*

fu·si·form /fyŏozə fàwrm/ *adj.* tapering at both ends, like a spindle ○ *fusiform bacteria* [Mid-18thC. Formed from Latin *fusus* "spindle."]

fu·sil /fyŏoz'l/ *n.* a lightweight musket with a flintlock firing mechanism [Late 16thC. From French, "steel in a flintlock, musket," from, ultimately, late Latin *focus* "fire."]

fu·sile /fyŏo zīl, -sīl/, **fu·sil** /fyŏoz'l/ *adj.* (*archaic*) **1. MADE BY CASTING** made by melting or casting metal **2. MELTABLE** easily melted or liquefied **3. MADE LIQUID** in a molten state [14thC. From Latin *fusilis* "melted," from the stem *fus-* (see FUSE[1]).]

fu·sil·ier /fyŏozə léer/, **fu·sil·eer** *n.* **1. SOLDIER WITH MUSKET** in former times, a soldier armed with a lightweight musket **(fusil) 2. BRITISH SOLDIER IN SOME REGIMENTS** a soldier in any of several British army regiments that were formerly armed with lightweight muskets **(fusils)** [Late 17thC. From French, formed from *fusil* "musket" (see FUSIL).]

fu·sil·lade /fyŏossə laàd, fyŏossə làyd, -, fyŏozə-/ *n.* **1.** ARMS **BLAST OF GUNFIRE** a firing of several guns at once or in quick succession **2. ONSLAUGHT** a sustained attack or barrage, e.g., of missiles or words ■ *vt.* **(-lad·ed, -lad·ing, -lades) FIRE AT ENEMY** to subject an enemy to a sustained burst of gunfire [Early 19thC. From French, formed from *fusiller* "to shoot," from *fusil* "musket" (see FUSIL).]

fu·sil·li /fyoo zíllee/ *npl.* pasta in the form of short spiral shapes [Late 20thC. From Italian, literally "little spindles," from, ultimately, Latin *fusus* "spindle."]

fu·sion /fyŏozh'n/ *n.* **1. HEATING AND LIQUEFYING SOMETHING** the molten state of a substance, or the change it undergoes to become molten **2. BLENDING OF THINGS** the merging or blending of two or more things, e.g., materials or ideas ○ *a fusion of vegetarianism and pacifism* **3.** PHYS = **nuclear fusion 4.** MUSIC **COMBINATION OF MUSICAL STYLES** the blending or resulting blend of musical styles or elements from more than one tradition, e.g., jazz and rock [Mid-16thC. Directly or via French from the Latin stem *fusion-*, from *fundere* "to melt" (see FUSE[1]).]

fu·sion bomb *n.* a nuclear bomb, especially a hydrogen bomb, whose explosion is caused by the energy released by a nuclear fusion reaction

fu·sion·ism /fyŏozh'n ìzzəm/ *n.* the formation of political coalitions, support for their formation, or belief in their effectiveness —**fu·sion·ist** *n., adj.*

fuss /fus/ *n.* **1. COMMOTION** needlessly or excessively busy or excited activity **2. NEEDLESS WORRY** excessive concern over details or trivial matters **3. PROTEST** a complaint or protestation, often over something insignificant ○ *The kids made a fuss about going to bed early.* **4. ARGUMENT** a noisy disagreement or dispute ○ *There'll be a fuss if he gets home late again.* **5. DISPLAY OF AFFECTION OR CONCERN** an excited or abundant display of affection or affectionate concern ○ *irritated by the fuss they make over her little brother* ■ *v.* **(fussed, fuss·ing, fuss·es) 1.** *vi.* **WORRY TOO MUCH** to be too concerned about details or trivial matters **2.** *vi.* **FIDDLE WITH SOMETHING** to keep moving or touching something busily, nervously, or aimlessly ○ *He fussed with the dials, hoping he'd look like he knew what he was doing.* **3.** *vt.* **DISTURB SOMEBODY** to bother somebody with annoyingly trivial matters [Early 18thC. Origin unknown.] —**fuss·er** *n.*

fuss·budg·et /fúss bùjjət/ *n.* somebody who typically worries about trivial things (*informal*) [Early 20thC. From BUDGET "bundle."]

fuss·pot /fúss pòt/ *n.* = **fussbudget** (*informal*)

fuss·y /fússee/ (**-i·er, -i·est**) *adj.* **1. CONCERNED WITH MINOR THINGS** tending to worry over details or trivial things **2. CHOOSY** very dogmatic about likes and dislikes ○ *a very fussy eater* **3. EASILY UPSET** frequently or easily irritated **4. ELABORATE** made or decorated with excessive detail ○ *a dress with a fussy lace collar* **5. DEMANDING AND DETAILED** requiring or accomplished with care and attention to details ○ *I'd better open that window for you — the lock is a bit fussy.*

WORD KEY: SYNONYMS

See Synonyms at ***careful.***

fus·tian /fúschən/ *adj.* **BOMBASTIC** written or spoken with pretentiousness or pomposity ■ *n.* **1.** TEXTILES **COTTON-LINEN CLOTH** a coarse sturdy cloth of a cotton-linen blend **2.** TEXTILES **COTTON FABRIC WITH NAP** any durable fabric with a raised nap made mainly from cotton, e.g., corduroy or moleskin **3. BOMBAST** pompous or pretentious speech or writing [13thC. Via Old French from medieval Latin *fustaneum*, perhaps from Latin *fustis* "wooden club," translation of Greek *xulina (lina)* "linen from wood." The underlying idea is "heavy, used as padding."]

fus·tic /fústik/ *n.* **1.** TREES **DYE-YIELDING TREE** a tropical American tree that belongs to the mulberry family. Its wood yields a yellow dye. Latin name: *Chlorophora tinctoria.* **2.** INDUST **WOOD YIELDING YELLOW DYE** the wood of the fustic tree **3.** INDUST **YELLOW DYE** a yellow dye obtained from the wood of the fustic tree **4.** TREES **TREE OF EUROPE YIELDING DYE** a European sumac tree whose wood is a source of yellow dye. Latin name: *Cotinus coggyria.* [15thC. Via Old French *fustoc* from Arabic *fustuḳ*, from Greek *pistakē* "pistachio tree."]

fus·ti·gate /fústi gàyt/ (**-gat·ed, -gat·ing, -gates**) *vt.* **1. CLUB** to beat somebody with a club (*archaic*) **2. CHASTISE** to criticize somebody or something severely (*literary*) [Mid-17thC. From late Latin *fustigare*, from Latin *fustis* "club" (see FUSTY) + *agere* "to do" (source of English *act*).] —**fus·ti·ga·tion** /fùsti gáysh'n/ *n.*

fus·ty /fústee/ (**-ti·er, -ti·est**) *adj.* **1. STALE-SMELLING** smelling of damp, dust, mildew, or age **2. OUTDATED** old-fashioned and conservative in style, appearance, habits, or attitudes (*disapproving*) ○ *transform a rather fusty image* [Late 15thC. Formed from obsolete *fust* "wine cask," which came via Old French from Latin *fustis* "wood, club." The underlying meaning is "having the musty smell of old wood."] —**fus·ti·ly** *adv.* —**fus·ti·ness** *n.*

fut. *abbr.* **1.** future **2.** FIN futures

fu·thark /fŏo thaàrk/, **fu·thorc** /-thàwrk/, **fu·thork** *n.* the common runic alphabet of 24 letters, used in northwestern Europe from the 3rd to 17th centuries [Mid-19thC. From the first six letters: *f, u,* þ, *a* or *o, r,* and *k*.]

fu·tile /fyŏot'l/ *adj.* **1. IN VAIN** with no practical effect or useful result **2. FRIVOLOUS** lacking serious value, substance, or a sense of responsibility [Mid-16thC. From Latin *futilis* "leaky, worthless." Ultimately from an Indo-European base meaning "to pour," which is also the ancestor of English *fuse*[1] and *gush*.] —**fu·tile·ly** *adv.* —**fu·tile·ness** *n.*

fu·til·i·tar·i·an /fyoo tìllə térree ən/ *n.* **BELIEVER IN FUTILITY OF HUMAN EFFORT** somebody who believes that human efforts are wasted and futile ■ *adj.* **BELIEVING IN HUMAN FUTILITY** holding or expressing the belief that all human effort is futile [Early 19thC. Formed from FUTILITY, on the model of UTILITARIAN.] —**fu·til·i·tar·i·an·ism** *n.*

fu·til·i·ty /fyoo tíllətee/ (*plural* **-ties**) *n.* **1. POINTLESSNESS** lack of usefulness or effectiveness **2. POINTLESS ACTION** an action that has no use, purpose, or effect **3. FRIVOLITY** lack of importance, seriousness, or sensibleness

fu·ton /fŏo tòn/ *n.* **1. JAPANESE-STYLE MATTRESS** a firm Japanese-style cotton-covered mattress used as a seat or bed, either on the floor or on a wooden frame **2. FUTON WITH WOODEN FRAME** a futon together with the wooden frame it sits on, especially a frame designed to convert from a sofa to a bed [Late 19thC. From Japanese.]

fut·tock /fúttək/ *n.* any of the curved middle timbers that form the frame of a traditional wooden boat or ship [13thC. Origin uncertain: possibly an alteration of assumed *fothok*, literally "foot-hook."]

fut·tock plate *n.* any of the circular metal plates fitted to the tops of a ship's shorter masts. Ropes or rods supporting a taller mast are secured to them.

fut·tock shroud *n.* a rope or rod stretching from the top of a taller mast to the top of a lower mast, to support the taller mast

fu·ture /fyoóchər/ *n.* **1.** TIME TO COME time that has yet to come ○ *saving money for the future* **2.** HAPPENINGS TO COME events that have not yet happened ○ *The future will be shaped by our advancing technology.* **3.** FUTURE CONDITION an expected or projected state ○ *Her future is bleak.* **4.** GRAM TENSE REFERRING TO THINGS TO COME the tense or form of a verb used to refer to events that are going to happen or have not yet happened ■ **fu·tures** *npl.* **1.** FIN COMMODITIES TRADED FOR LATER DELIVERY goods or stocks sold for future delivery, or the contracts for them **2.** COMPENSATION TO COME something to be given later as compensation (*informal*) ○ *He was willing to make the concession with the expectation that some futures would be forthcoming.* ■ *adj.* **1.** YET TO OCCUR expected to be or happen at a time still to come ○ *my future sister-in-law* **2.** GRAM OF OR IN TENSE EXPRESSING FUTURE in or relating to the form of a verb that expresses actions or states that are going to happen or have not yet happened [14thC. Via Old French from Latin *futurus* "going to be." Ultimately from an Indo-European verb meaning "to grow, become, be," which is also the ancestor of English *be* and *build*.]

fu·ture·less /fyoóchərləss/ *adj.* seeming to have no chance of developing or being successful ○ *poured money into futureless schemes* —**fu·ture·less·ness** *n.*

fu·ture per·fect *n.* the form of a verb expressing a completed action in the future, as "will have finished" does in the sentence "They will have finished by tomorrow"

fu·ture shock *n.* difficulty in and stress from coping with rapid changes in society, especially with technological changes [From the title of a book by Alvin Toffler (b. 1928)]

fu·ture tense *n.* = **future** *n.* **4**

fu·tur·ism /fyoóchə rìzzəm/ *n.* **1. fu·tur·ism, Fu·tur·ism** ARTS ARTISTIC MOVEMENT VALUING TECHNOLOGY'S BEAUTY an early 20th-century artistic movement that attempted to express the dynamic nature of the modern age using technology as its subject **2.** BELIEF IN NEED TO LOOK FORWARD belief in the need to look to the future rather than reflect on the past, coupled with an optimism that personal and social fulfillment lies in the future [Early 20thC. Modeled on Italian *futurismo* and French *futurisme*.] —**fu·tur·ist** *n., adj.*

fu·tur·is·tic /fyoóchə rístik/ *adj.* **1.** AHEAD OF THE TIMES suggesting some future time in its design or technology, or using designs and technology thought likely to become popular or commonplace in the future **2.** SHOWING FUTURE LIFE depicting life in some future time —**fu·tur·is·ti·cal·ly** *adv.*

fu·tu·ri·ty /fyoo toórətee, -choórətee/ (*plural* **-ties**) *n.* **1.** FUTURE the future as a concept or state ○ *a grammatical construction expressing futurity* **2.** FUTURE EVENT an event that is going to happen or has not happened yet (*formal*) **3.** = **futurity race**

fu·tu·ri·ty race *n.* a horse race in which horses are entered well in advance, often before they are born. The race is usually run when the horses are two years old.

fu·tur·ol·o·gy /fyoóchə róllәjee/ *n.* the study and forecasting of the future, with predictions based on the likely outcomes of current trends —**fu·tur·o·log·i·cal** /fyoóchərə lójjik'l/ *adj.* —**fu·tu·rol·o·gist** /-rólləjist/ *n.*

futz /futs/ (**futzed, futz·ing, futz·es**) *vi.* to spend time frivolously, lazily, or aimlessly (*informal*) ○ *spends hours futzing with that computer* [Early 20thC. Origin uncertain: probably an alteration of Yiddish *arumfartzen* "to fool around."]

Fu·xin /fóo shín/ city in Liaoning Province, northeastern China, west of Shenyang. Population: 635,473 (1990).

fuze *n., vt.* = **fuse**[2]

fu·zee *n.* = **fusee**

Fu·zhou /fóo jṓ/ city and capital of Fujian Province, southeastern China, near the mouth of the Min River, northeast of Taiwan. Population: 874,809 (1990).

fuzz[1] /fuz/ *n.* FLUFF a mass of short fine hairs or fibers ■ *vti.* (**fuzzed, fuzz·ing, fuzz·es**) **1.** COVER SOMETHING WITH FUZZ to become covered or cover something with fuzz ○ *sweaters that fuzz after the first wash* **2.** BLUR OR BECOME BLURRED to make something, e.g., an image or explanation, blurred or unclear, or become blurred or unclear ○ *All this talk has fuzzed my brain.* [Late 16thC. Origin uncertain: probably from Dutch or Low German.]

fuzz[2] /fuz/ *n.* the police (*slang offensive*) [Early 20thC. Origin unknown.]

fuzz·box /fúz bòks/ *n.* an electrical device that distorts the sound that passes through it, especially a pedal-operated device wired to an electric guitar

fuzz·y /fúzzee/ (**-i·er, -i·est**) *adj.* **1.** COVERED WITH FUZZ covered with a mass of short fine hairs or fibers **2.** CONSISTING OF FUZZ in the form of a mass of short fine hairs or fibers **3.** FRIZZY growing in a very tight curly mass (*refers to hair*) **4.** BLURRED not sharp enough to be seen or heard clearly ○ *a fuzzy picture* **5.** INCOHERENT not clearly thought out or set out ○ *The initial plan was fairly fuzzy.* [Early 17thC. Origin uncertain: possibly from Low German *fussig* "spongy." The earliest meaning in English was "spongy, not firm."] —**fuzz·i·ly** *adv.* —**fuzz·i·ness** *n.*

fuzz·y·head·ed *adj.* not thinking clearly, or not expressing thoughts or ideas clearly (*informal*) ○ *a fuzzyheaded notion* —**fuzz·y·head·ed·ness** *n.*

fuzz·y log·ic *n.* logic that allows for imprecise or ambiguous answers to questions. It forms the basis of the kind of computer programming designed to allow computers to mimic human intelligence.

f.v. *abbr.* folio verso [Latin, "on the reverse (i.e. left-hand) page"]

FWD *abbr.* **1.** four-wheel drive **2.** front-wheel drive

fwd. *abbr.* forward

FWIW *abbr.* for what it's worth (*used in e-mail messages*)

fwy. *abbr.* freeway

FX *abbr.* **1.** FIN foreign exchange **2.** CINEMA (special) effects [Late 20thC. Representing a pronunciation of EFFECTS.]

FY *abbr.* fiscal year

-fy *suffix.* to make, cause to become ○ *gasify* ○ *ladify* [Via Old French *-fier* from, ultimately, Latin *facere* "to do, make" (see FACT)]

FYI *abbr.* for your information

fyke /fīk/ *n.* a bag-shaped fishing net, held open by hoops [Mid-19thC. Via Dutch *fuik* from Middle Dutch *fuke*.]

fyl·fot /fíl fòt/ *n.* an old decorative or religious symbol in the form of a swastika [15thC. Origin unknown.]

fz. *abbr.* sforzando

Gg

g^1 /jee/ (*plural* **g's**), **G** (*plural* **G's** *or* **Gs**) *n.* **1. 7TH LETTER OF ENGLISH ALPHABET** the seventh letter of the modern English alphabet **2. SPEECH SOUND CORRESPONDING TO LETTER "G"** the speech sound that corresponds to the letter "G" **3. LETTER "G" WRITTEN** a written representation of the letter "G"

g^2 *symbol.* PHYS acceleration of free fall as a result of gravity

g^3 *abbr.* MEASURE gram

G^1 (*plural* **G's** *or* **Gs**) *n.* **1.** CINEMA **GENERAL-AUDIENCE MOVIE RATING** a movie rating meaning that a movie or video is suitable for anyone to watch **2.** MONEY **$1,000** one thousand dollars (*slang*) **3.** MUSIC **5TH NOTE OF SCALE IN C** the fifth note of a scale in C major **4.** MUSIC **SOMETHING THAT PRODUCES A G** a string, key, or pipe tuned to produce the note G **5.** MUSIC **SCALE BEGINNING ON G** a scale or key that starts on the note G **6.** MUSIC **WRITTEN SYMBOL OF G** a graphic representation of the tone of G

G^2 *symbol.* **1.** ELEC conductance **2.** PHYS gauss **3.** PHYS gravitational constant **4.** BIOCHEM guanine

G^3 *abbr.* **1.** MEASURE giga- **2.** EDU good (*used as a grade*)

g. *abbr.* **1.** gauge **2.** GRAM gender **3.** GRAM genitive **4.** MONEY guilder **5.** MONEY guinea

G. *abbr.* **1.** Gulf (*used in place names*) **2.** MONEY guilder **3.** MONEY guinea

G8 *n.* the group of the eight most industrialized nations in the world, comprising Canada, France, Germany, Italy, Japan, Russia, the United Kingdom, and the United States. Representatives from these countries meet regularly to discuss and draw up global economic policies. Full form **Group of Eight** [*G*, a shortening of GROUP]

Ga *symbol.* gallium

GA *abbr.* **1.** general agent **2.** General Assembly (of the United Nations) **3.** Georgia

ga. *abbr.* gauge

Ga. *abbr.* Georgia

G.A. *abbr.* **1.** General Assembly (of the UN) **2.** SHIPPING, INSUR general average

GAAP *abbr.* generally accepted accounting principles

gab /gab/ *vi.* (**gabbed, gab·bing, gabs**) **CHAT IDLY** to talk at length about trivial matters (*informal*) ○ *We just sat there gabbing all afternoon.* ■ *n.* **CHITCHAT** light conversation about nothing in particular (*informal*) [Early 18thC. Origin uncertain, possibly shortening of GABBLE.] —**gab·ber** *n.*

GABA *abbr.* gamma-aminobutyric acid

gab·ar·dine /gábbər deen/ *n.* **1.** TEXTILES **SMOOTH TWILL FABRIC** a smooth durable cotton, wool, or synthetic fabric woven with a pattern of parallel diagonal ridges (**twill**) ○ *a gabardine jacket* **2.** CLOTHES **GABARDINE GARMENT** a garment made of gabardine **3.** CLOTHES = **gaberdine** *n.* 1 [Early 20thC. Alteration of GABERDINE.]

gab·ble /gább'l/ *v.* (**-bled, -bling, -bles**) **1.** *vti.* **SPEAK UNINTELLIGIBLY** to speak or say something rapidly and incoherently **2.** *vi.* BIRDS **MAKE THROATY GOOSE SOUND** to make the high throaty sounds that geese and some other birds make ■ *n.* **1. FAST UNINTELLIGIBLE TALK** rapid incoherent talking **2.** BIRDS **SOUND GEESE MAKE** the high throaty sounds that geese and some other birds make [Late 16thC. Origin uncertain, possibly from Middle Dutch *gabbelen*, an imitation of the sound.] —**gab·bler** *n.*

gab·bro /gá brō/ *n.* a dark coarse-grained basic igneous rock containing calcium-rich plagioclase feldspar and pyroxene [Mid-19thC. Via Italian dialect from, possibly, Latin *glaber* "smooth, bald."] —**gab·bro·ic** /ga brṓ ik/ *adj.*

gab·by /gábbee/ (**-bi·er, -bi·est**) *adj.* talking or inclined to talk to an excessive, irritating degree (*informal*)

ga·belle /gə bél/ *n.* **1.** HIST **SALT TAX** a French tax on salt imposed until 1790 **2. TAX IN ANOTHER COUNTRY** any tax, especially a tax imposed in a foreign country (*literary*) [15thC. Via Old French *gabel* from, ultimately, Arabic *ḳabāla* "tax, duty."]

gab·er·dine /gábbər deen/ *n.* **1.** CLOTHES **MEDIEVAL GARMENT** a long loose coat or smock made of coarse cloth, worn by men, especially Jewish men, during the Middle Ages **2.** TEXTILES = **gabardine** *n.* 1 **3.** CLOTHES = **gabardine** *n.* 2 [Early 16thC. Via Old French *gauvardine* from, ultimately, perhaps, Middle High German *wallevart* "pilgrimage," from *wallōn* "to wander" + *vart* "journey." The underlying meaning is thus "pilgrim's garb."]

gab·fest /gáb fèst/ *n.* (*informal*) **1. MEETING FOR CHAT** an informal gathering where idle chat or gossip is exchanged **2. LONG CONVERSATION** a long informal chat or discussion ○ *The student's simple question started a gabfest among the pundits.*

ga·bi·on /gáybee ən/ *n.* **1.** MIL **ROCK-FILLED BASKET AS FORTIFICATION** a wickerwork basket filled with rocks, used as a temporary fortification **2.** CIV ENG **STONE-FILLED DRUM IN WATERWAY CONSTRUCTION** a cylindrical metal container filled with earth and stones, used in the construction and rerouting of waterways and in flood control [Mid-16thC. Via French from Italian *gabbione*, literally "large cage," from *gabbia* "cage," from Latin *cavea* (source of English *cage*).]

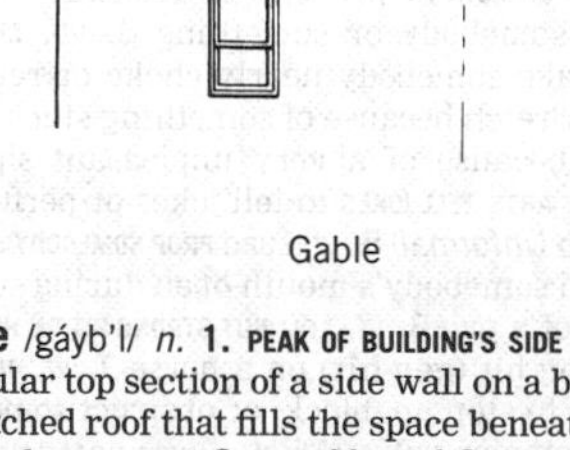

Gable

ga·ble /gáyb'l/ *n.* **1. PEAK OF BUILDING'S SIDE WALL** the triangular top section of a side wall on a building with a pitched roof that fills the space beneath where the roof slopes meet **2.** = **gable end 3. TRIANGULAR BUILDING DECORATION** a triangular structure, e.g., a canopy over a door or window, added to a building for decoration [14thC. Directly or via Old French from Old Norse *gafl*. Possibly, ultimately, from an Indo-European word meaning "head," the underlying idea being "something at the top."] —**ga·bled** *adj.*

WORD KEY: CULTURAL NOTE

Anne of Green Gables, a children's story by Canadian writer Lucy Maud Montgomery (1908). Set on Prince Edward Island in Canada, it is the story of a vivacious 11-year-old orphan, Anne Shirley, who is sent to live with farmers Matthew and Marilla Cuthbert. Having expected a boy, the Cuthberts cannot hide their disappointment, but Anne's courage, spirit, and vivid imagination soon win them over.

Clark Gable

Ga·ble /gáyb'l/, **Clark** (1901 60) U.S. movie actor. He won an Academy Award for his performance in the romantic comedy *It Happened One Night* (1934), but he is best known for his role as Rhett Butler in *Gone With the Wind* (1939). Full name **William Clark Gable**

ga·ble end *n.* a side wall that comes to a peak where the slopes of a pitched roof meet

ga·ble roof *n.* a roof with two slopes and a gable at each end

Ga·bo /gaábō/, **Naum** (1890–1977) Russian-born U.S. sculptor, one of the founders of the constructivist school. His work drew on cubism, and he experimented with kinetic art. Real name **Neemia Pevsner**

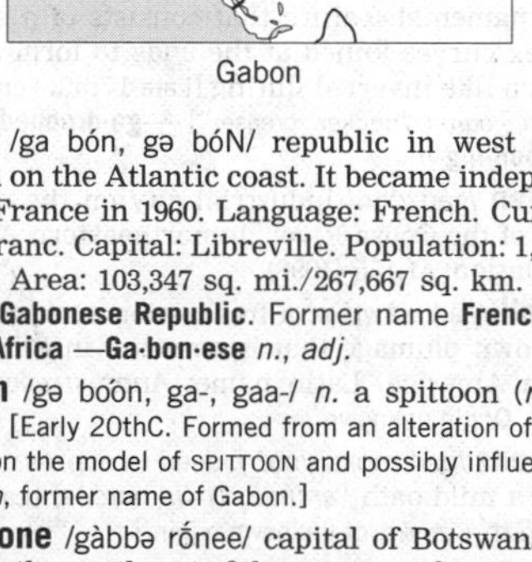

Gabon

Ga·bon /ga bón, gə bóN/ republic in west central Africa on the Atlantic coast. It became independent from France in 1960. Language: French. Currency: CFA franc. Capital: Libreville. Population: 1,190,159 (1997). Area: 103,347 sq. mi./267,667 sq. km. Official name **Gabonese Republic**. Former name **French Equatorial Africa** —**Ga·bon·ese** *n., adj.*

ga·boon /gə boón, ga-, gaa-/ *n.* a spittoon (*regional dated*) [Early 20thC. Formed from an alteration of *gob* "to spit," on the model of SPITTOON and possibly influenced by *Gaboon*, former name of Gabon.]

Ga·bo·rone /gàbbə rṓnee/ capital of Botswana, situated in the southeast of the country, about 12 mi./19 km from the border with South Africa. Population: 133,791 (1991).

gad[1] /gad/ *vi.* (**gad·ded, gad·ding, gads**) **BE OUT HAVING FUN** to go around having fun in a carefree and aimless manner (*dated*) ○ *gadding about* ■ *n.* **WANDERING** carefree or aimless wandering (*dated*) [15thC. Origin uncertain: probably a back-formation from obsolete *gadling* "wanderer," from Old English *gædeling* "companion," ultimately from a prehistoric Germanic word that is also the ancestor of English *gather*.] —**gad·der** *n.*

gad[2] /gad/ *n.* **1.** MINING **HEAVY TOOL USED IN MINING** a heavy steel or iron wedge with a pointed or chisel-shaped edge used in mining to break coal, rock, or ore from the rock face **2.** AGRIC **CATTLE PROD** a sharp pointed tool used to drive cattle ■ *vt.* (**gad·ded, gad·ding, gads**) MINING **SEPARATE MINERALS FROM ROCK** to break up coal or ore using a gad [13thC. From a prehistoric Germanic word meaning "pointed stick" that is also the ancestor of English *yard* ("three feet").]

gad·a·bout /gáddə bòwt/ *n.* somebody who goes about looking for pleasure in an aimless and restless way (*dated informal*)

gad·a·rene /gáddə rèen/ *adj.* rushing headlong en masse (*literary*) [Early 19thC. Via Latin from Greek *Gadarēnos* "inhabitant of Gadara," the town that was the site of the herd of swine's headlong rush into the sea in Matthew 8:28 in the Bible.]

Gad·da·fi = **Muammar al- Qaddafi**

Gad·dis /gáddiss/, **William** (*b.* 1922) U.S. writer. He is known for darkly humorous novels such as *The Recognitions* (1955) and *Carpenter's Gothic* (1985).

gad·fly /gád flī/ (*plural* **-flies**) *n.* **1.** INSECTS **FLY THAT BITES LIVESTOCK** a fly that irritates livestock by biting them and sucking their blood. Horseflies are a type of gadfly. Family: Tabanidae. **2. SOMEBODY ANNOYING** somebody who persistently irritates or torments another person (*dated*) [*Gad* from GAD[2]]

gadg·et /gájjət/ *n.* **1. INGENIOUS DEVICE** a small device that performs or aids a simple task **2. TRIVIAL DEVICE** a small object or device that appears useful but is often unnecessary or superfluous [Late 19thC. Origin unknown. Said to have started as a sailors' slang term for some unspecified tool.] —**gadg·et·y** *adj.*

gadg·e·teer /gàjjə tèer/ *n.* somebody who invents or enjoys using gadgets

gadg·et·ry /gájjətree/ *n.* gadgets collectively, especially when perceived as impressively complicated

Gad·hel·ic /gə déllik/ *n.* LANG = **Goidelic** [Early 16thC. Via medieval Latin *gathelicus*, from *Gathelus*, from Irish *Gaedheal*, plural of *Gaedhil*, which evolved from Old Irish *Goídel* (see GAEL).]

ga·did /gáddid, gáydid/, **ga·doid** /gá dòyd/ *n.* **FISH OF COD FAMILY** a sea fish of the family that includes cod, haddock, and hake. Family: Gadidae. ■ *adj.* **OF COD FAMILY** belonging to the family of sea fish that includes cod, haddock, and hake [Mid-19thC. Formed from modern Latin *gadus* "cod," from Greek *gados*.]

gad·o·lin·ite /gádd'lə nīt/ *n.* a black or brown silicate of beryllium, iron, and yttrium that occurs in pegmatite [Early 19thC. Named for Johan *Gadolin* (1760–1852), Finnish mineralogist.]

gad·o·lin·i·um /gàdd'l ínnee əm/ *n.* a rare silvery-white metallic chemical element that is used to improve the characteristics of alloys at high temperatures. Because it is a strong neutron absorber, gadolinium is used in control rods in nuclear reactors and in nuclear fuels to slow the chain reaction. Symbol **Gd** [Late 19thC. Formed from GADOLINITE.]

ga·droon /gə dróon/ (*plural* **ga·droons** *or* **go·droons**) *n.* an ornamental feature that consists of a series of convex curves joined at the ends to form a raised pattern like inverted fluting [Late 17thC. Formed from French *godron* "pucker, crease."] —**ga·drooned** *adj.* —**ga·droon·ing** *n.*

Gads·den /gádzdən/ industrial city on the northern bank of the Coosa River, in northeastern Alabama. Population: 41,155 (1996).

gad·wall /gád wàwl/ *n.* a freshwater duck with gray or brown plumage that is common in Europe and North America. Latin name: *Anas strepera*. [Mid-17thC. Origin unknown.]

gad·zooks /gad zóoks/ *interj.* used to express surprise or as a mild oath (*archaic or humorous*) [Late 17thC. From GAD + *zooks*, of unknown origin.]

Gael /gayl/ *n.* **1. SOMEBODY WHO SPEAKS GAELIC** somebody from Scotland, Ireland, or the Isle of Man who speaks Gaelic **2. SCOTTISH HIGHLANDER** somebody from the Scottish Highlands [Mid-18thC. From Scots Gaelic *Gael* and *Gàidheal*, from Old Irish *Goídel* plural of Gáidl.]

Gael·ic /gáylik/ *n.* LANG **CELTIC LANGUAGE OF BRITISH ISLES** any of the Celtic languages used in parts of Ireland, Scotland, and the Isle of Man ■ *adj.* **1. OF GAELIC** belonging to or using any of the Celtic languages of Ireland, Scotland, or the Isle of Man **2. OF GAELIC-SPEAKING PEOPLE** relating to or typical of Gaelic-speaking people or their culture

gaff[1] /gaf/ *n.* **1.** ANGLING **HOOKED FISH POLE** a pole with a large hook on the end that is used to hold and land a large fish **2.** SAILING **POLE AT TOP OF SAIL** a pole attached to a mast and used to support the upper edge of a fore-and-aft sail **3.** GAMBLING **METAL SPUR ON FIGHTING COCK** a metal spur that is fixed to the leg of a fighting cock **4.** UTIL **HOOK FOR SOMEBODY MAINTAINING OVERHEAD LINE** a climbing hook used by somebody erecting or repairing a telephone or power line **5. GIMMICK USED IN A HOAX** a gimmick or trick, often used in a hoax or attempt at fraud ■ *vt.* (**gaffed, gaf·fing, gaffs**) **1.** ANGLING **CATCH FISH WITH HOOKED POLE** to catch and hold a fish with a gaff **2. ARM WITH A GAFF** to provide or arm something, e.g., a fighting cock, with a gaff **3. CHEAT OR SWINDLE** to cheat or swindle somebody (*slang*) [14thC. From Old French *gaffe* "boat hook" (see GAFFE).]

gaff[2] /gaf/ *n. U.K.* worthless nonsense (*informal*) [Early 19thC. Origin unknown.] ◇ **blow the gaff** *U.K.* to reveal a secret (*slang*)

gaffe /gaf/, **gaff** *n.* a clumsy social mistake or breach of etiquette, e.g., an insensitive remark [Early 20thC. From French, originally "boat hook," from Old French, from Old Provençal *gaf*, of uncertain origin: perhaps from prehistoric Germanic.]

gaf·fer /gáffər/ *n.* **1.** CINEMA **CHIEF LIGHTING ELECTRICIAN ON MOVIE SET** the chief electrician in charge of lighting on a movie or television set (*informal*) **2.** *U.K.* **MAN** man of advanced years, especially a man from the country (*informal*) **3.** *U.K.* **BOSS** the boss, owner, or supervisor of a workplace (*informal*) **4.** *U.K.* **HUSBAND** somebody's husband (*regional*) [Late 16thC. Origin uncertain: probably a contraction of GODFATHER, with "ga-" by association with GRANDFATHER.]

gaff-rig *n.* a sailing vessel rigged with fore-and-aft sails supported by a gaff —**gaff-rigged** *adj.*

gaff·sail /gáf sàyl/; (*nautical*) /gáfs'l/ *n. U.K.* = **fore-and-aft sail**

gaff-top·sail *n.* a small, usually triangular sail set above a gaff

gag /gag/ *n.* **1. SOMETHING PUT OVER MOUTH** something, such as a piece of cloth that is forcibly put over or into somebody's mouth to prevent the person from speaking or crying out **2. RESTRAINT OF SPEECH** a restraint on free speech ○ *put a gag on a newspaper* **3.** ARTS **COMIC WORDS OR ACTION** a comic story, action, or incident told or performed by an actor or comedian **4. TRICK** a trick, hoax, or practical joke (*informal*) **5.** SURG **MOUTH PROP** a device that is placed in a patient's mouth to keep it open during surgical work on the mouth or throat **6. CHOKING** an instance or the action of choking or retching (*informal*) ■ *v.* (**gagged, gag·ging, gags**) **1.** *vt.* **PUT SOMETHING OVER SOMEBODY'S MOUTH** to put something over or into somebody's mouth to prevent the person from speaking or crying out **2.** *vt.* **RESTRAIN SPEECH** to prevent or restrain the free speech of somebody or something **3.** *vti.* **CHOKE OR RETCH** to make somebody nearly choke or retch, or to choke or retch because of something stuck in the throat or because of a very unpleasant sight or smell **4.** *vi.* ARTS **TELL JOKES** to tell jokes or perform as a comedian (*informal*) **5.** *vt.* SURG **PROP SOMEBODY'S MOUTH OPEN** to hold somebody's mouth open during surgery by means of a gag **6.** *vt.* EQU **PUT STRONG BIT ON HORSE** to put a strong bit (**gag-bit**) on a horse **7.** *vt.* **OBSTRUCT PIPE OR VALVE** to stop up, block, or obstruct something such as a pipe or valve [15thC. Origin uncertain: probably an imitation of the sound of choking.]

ga·ga /gáa gàa/ *adj.* **1. OFFENSIVE TERM MEANING IRRATIONAL** an offensive term that deliberately insults somebody's mental abilities, epecially those of a senior citizen (*informal offensive*) **2. VERY ENTHUSIASTIC** completely infatuated or very enthusiastic (*informal*) ○ *totally gaga over his girlfriend* [Early 20thC. From French, an imitation of the sound of mumbling.]

ga·ga·ku /gaa gáa koo/ *n.* an ancient form of Japanese classical music used at the imperial court and on ceremonial occasions [Early 20thC. From Japanese, from *ga* "elegance" + *gaku* "court music."]

AKG London

Yuri Gagarin

Ga·ga·rin /gə gáarən/, **Yuri** (1934–68) Soviet cosmonaut. He became the first person to be launched into space when he orbited the earth in *Vostok I* on April 12, 1961. Full name **Yuri Alekseyevich Gagarin**

Ga·gauz /gə gáwz/ (*plural* **-gauz** /-zèe/ *or* **-gau·zi**) *n.* **1.** LANG **TURKIC LANGUAGE** a Turkic language spoken in an area to the north of the Black Sea, especially in southern parts of Moldova, Ukraine, and Romania. About 150,000 people speak Gagauz. **2. Ga·gauz** (*plural* **-gauz** *or* **-gau·zi**), **Ga·gau·zi·an** PEOPLES **MEMBER OF TURKIC PEOPLE** a member of a Turkic people who live in the southwestern region of Moldova —**Ga·gauz** *adj.*

gag-bit *n.* a strong bit sometimes used to help control an unruly horse

gage[1] /gayj/ *n.* (*archaic*) **1. PLEDGE** something that is given or left as security until a debt is paid or an obligation is fulfilled **2. TOKEN OF CHALLENGE** a glove or other object that is thrown down or offered as a challenge to fight **3. CHALLENGE** a challenge to fight ■ *vt.* (**gaged, gag·ing, gag·es**) (*archaic*) **1. OFFER SOMETHING AS PLEDGE** to offer something as security against a debt or other obligation **2.** BETTING **OFFER AS STAKE IN BET** to offer something as a stake in a bet [13thC. From Old French, ultimately from a prehistoric Germanic word that is also the ancestor of English *wed*.]

gage[2] *n., vt.* = **gauge**

Gage /gayj/, **Thomas** (1721–87) British-born general and colonial administrator. He commanded British forces in North America (1763–72), and his actions as governor of Massachusetts colony (1774–76) helped precipitate the Revolution.

gag·er /gáyjər/ *n.* = **gauger**

gag·ger /gággər/ *n.* a piece of metal used to wedge the core of a casting mold in position

gag·gle /gágg'l/ *n.* **1.** BIRDS **GROUP OF GEESE** a flock of geese **2. GROUP OF PEOPLE** a group of people, especially a noisy or disorderly group ○ *a gaggle of children* [14thC. Origin uncertain: perhaps literally "to cry like a goose repeatedly," an imitation of the sound.]

gag·man /gág màn/ (*plural* **-men** /-mèn/) *n.* somebody who writes or tells jokes (*informal*) [Early 20thC. "Gag" from GAG.]

gag or·der *n.* a court order that forbids any public commentary or media reporting on a case that is currently being heard in court

gag rule *n.* a rule in a legislative body that limits or prevents discussion or debate on a particular issue

gag·ster /gágstər/ *n.* (*informal*) **1.** ARTS **COMEDIAN** somebody who writes or tells jokes **2. PRANKSTER** somebody who plays tricks or practical jokes

gahn·ite /gáa nīt/ *n.* a dark green mineral consisting of zinc aluminum oxide [Early 19thC. Named for J. G. *Gahn* (1745–1818), Swedish chemist.]

GAI *abbr.* guaranteed annual income

gai·e·ty /gáy ətee/ (*plural* **-ties**), **gay·e·ty** (*plural* **-ties**) *n.* **1. JOYFULNESS** a lighthearted and lively feeling or way of behaving **2. SPIRITED ACTIVITY** joyful and lively activity or festivity **3. BRIGHT OR FANCY APPEARANCE** the showiness or bright colorful appearance of something such as clothing (*dated*) [Mid-17thC. From Old French *gaieté*, from *gai* (see GAY).]

gai·jin /gī jin/ (*plural* **-jin**) *n.* a foreigner in Japan or among Japanese [Mid-20thC. From Japanese, contraction of *gaikoku-jin*, literally "somebody from a foreign country."]

gai·ly /gáylee/, **gay·ly** *adv.* **1. JOYFULLY OR LIGHTHEARTEDLY** in a happy, cheerful, or carefree manner **2. IN BRIGHT COLORS** brightly or colorfully (*dated*)

gain[1] /gayn/ *v.* **(gained, gain·ing, gains) 1.** *vt.* **ACQUIRE SOMETHING EARNED** to obtain something through effort, skill, or merit ○ *gain recognition as an actor* **2.** *vt.* **WIN SOMETHING BY COMPETING** to win something in competition or conflict ○ *gained second place in the dash* **3.** *vt.* **EARN SOMETHING** to earn or obtain something by work ○ *gain a living* **4.** *vi.* **PROFIT** derive advantage from something ○ *No one stands to gain from the deal.* **5.** *vti.* **BECOME GREATER** to grow or increase, or acquire more of something ○ *She was steadily gaining in confidence.* **6.** *vt.* **MAKE ARISE** to cause something to arise or become operative ○ *gain his confidence* **7.** *vt.* **ESTABLISH RELATIONSHIP** to begin to have or establish a particular relationship with somebody ○ *gain a mentor and a friend* **8.** *vi.* **GET BETTER** to improve or become better in some respect ○ *gaining in proficiency* **9.** *vi.* **GET CLOSER OR FARTHER AWAY** to come closer to somebody or something pursued, or increase the distance from a pursuer ○ *They are behind but they're gaining on us.* **10.** *vti.* **INCREASE IN OR BY SOMETHING** to come to have more of something, or increase by a specified amount ○ *The dollar had gained two points* **11.** *vti.* TIME **RUN AHEAD OF CORRECT TIME** to run fast so as to record a time ahead, or a specified amount of time ahead, of the correct one ○ *My watch gains at least 10 minutes every day.* **12.** *vt.* **REACH** to arrive at a place that it was intended or hoped to reach (*literary*) ○ *once we had finally gained the shore* **13.** *vi.* **ADD WEIGHT** to put on weight ○ *I gain if I don't exercise regularly* ■ *n.* **1. ACHIEVEMENT** an advantage or improvement that has been earned or acquired through effort ○ *despite the political gains of recent years* **2. AMOUNT INCREASED** an increase or profit of a specified amount ○ *a small weight gain* **3. BENEFIT** financial profit or personal advantage **4.** ELEC ENG **MEASURE OF INCREASE IN SIGNAL STRENGTH** a ratio of the output power to the input power of an amplifier that is more than one and indicates an increase in signal strength **5.** ELEC ENG = **antenna gain** ■ **gains** *npl.* **EARNINGS AND ACQUISITIONS** something acquired, earned, or won, especially money [15thC. Via Old French from a prehistoric Germanic word meaning "to graze, hunt."] —**gain·a·ble** *adj.*

WORD KEY: SYNONYMS

See Synonyms at ***get***.

gain[2] /gayn/ *n.* **NOTCH TO FIT SOMETHING INTO** a notch or groove cut into a board so that another part can be fitted into it ■ *vt.* **(gained, gain·ing, gains) 1. CUT NOTCH IN SOMETHING** to cut a notch or groove into a board so that another part can be fitted into it **2. FIT PART IN NOTCH** to fit a part into a gain or connect parts using a gain [Mid-19thC. Origin unknown.]

gain·er /gáynər/ *n.* **1. SOMEBODY GAINING** somebody who or something that gains **2.** STOCK EXCH **RISING STOCK** a stock that increases in value during a trading period **3.** SWIMMING **DIVE WITH BACK SOMERSAULT** a dive in which the diver jumps forward does a back somersault in the air, and enters the water feet first, facing away from the board

Gaines·ville /gáynzvil/ **1.** city and county seat of Alachua County, northern Florida, 65 mi./105 km southwest of Jacksonville. Population: 84,770 (1990). **2.** city and county seat of Hall County, north central Georgia, 50 mi./80 km northeast of Atlanta. Population: 17,885 (1990).

gain·ful /gáynfəl/ *adj.* bringing profit or advantage —**gain·ful·ly** *adv.* —**gain·ful·ness** *n.*

gain·say /gayn sáy, gáyn sày/ (**-said, -said** /-sáyd, -sèd/, **-say·ing, -says** /gayn sáyz, gáyn sàyz, gayn séz/) *vt.* (*formal*) **1. DENY SOMETHING** to say that something is false **2. CONTRADICT SOMEBODY OR SOMETHING** to deny the truth of something or of what somebody says ○ *I won't gainsay you .* [14thC. Coined from *gain-*, from Old English *gegn* "against" (source of English *again*), + SAY.] —**gain·say·er** *n.*

'gainst /gaynst/, **gainst** *prep.* against (*literary*) [Late 16thC. Shortening.]

Gaird·ner, Lake /gáirdnər/ dry salt lake in south central South Australia, about 240 mi./385 km northwest of Adelaide. Area: 1,840 sq. mi./4,766 sq. km.

gait /gayt/ *n.* **1. MANNER OF WALKING** a way of walking, running, or moving along on foot ○ *his familiar unsteady gait* **2.** RIDING **PATTERN OF HORSE'S STEPS** any one of the four paces of a horse, walk, trot, canter, and gallop, each having a specific pattern of leg movements **3. SPEED OF PROGRESS** the speed at which something moves or progresses ○ *Work proceeded at a steady gait.* [15thC. Variant of GATE "way, street."]

-gaited *suffix.* with a particular way of walking ○ *slow-gaited*

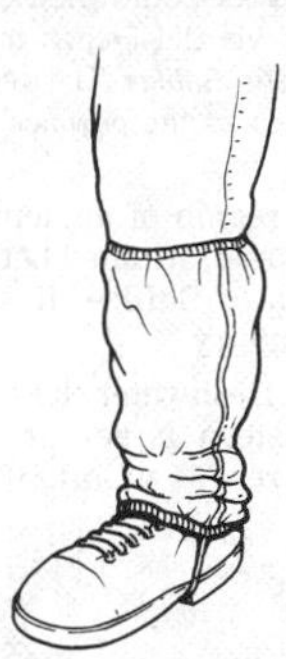

Gaiter

gai·ter /gáytər/ *n.* (*usually used in the plural*) **1. LEG COVERING** a strip of fabric, leather, or lightweight waterproof material covering the leg from the instep to either the ankle or the knee. Modern gaiters are usually made of waterproof fabric and worn by climbers, walkers, or skiers. **2. ELASTICATED SHOE** an ankle-high shoe with elastic at the sides and no laces **3. OVERSHOE WITH CLOTH UPPER** an overshoe with a fabric top [Early 18thC. Via French from a prehistoric Germanic base meaning "twist," later, "ankle."] —**gaitered** *adj.*

Gai·thers·burg /gáythərz burg/ city in central Maryland, northwest of Rockville and Washington, D.C. Population: 45,361 (1996).

gal[1] /gal/ *n.* a girl or woman (*informal*) (*sometimes considered offensive*) [Late 18thC. Reproducing a certain pronunciation of GIRL.]

gal[2] /gal/ *n.* a unit of acceleration in the centimeter-gram-second system equal to 1 cm per second per second. It is primarily used in gravitational field and geodetic measurements. [Early 20thC. Shortening of GALILEO.]

gal. *abbr.* gallon

Gal. *abbr.* BIBLE Galatians

ga·la /gáylə, gáalə/ *n.* **1. PARTY** a special festive occasion that typically includes food and entertainment **2.** *U.K.* **SPORTING COMPETITION** a sporting event, especially a swimming contest with a variety of different races and competitions [Early 17thC. Via Old French *gale* "merrymaking" from, ultimately, Arabic *khil'a* "fine garment given as a present," hence "festive attire," "festive occasion."]

galact- *prefix.* = **galacto-**

ga·lac·ta·gogue /gə láktə gòg/ *adj.* BIOL **INDUCING MILK FLOW** causing the production and secretion of milk ■ *n.* MED **MILK STIMULATOR** an agent that stimulates the production and flow of breast milk [Coined from GALACT- + Greek *agōgos* "leading," from *agein* "to lead"]

ga·lac·tic /gə láktik/ *adj.* **1. RELATING TO GALAXY** relating or belonging to a galaxy, especially the Milky Way **2. HUGE** of immense or enormous size or quantity (*informal*) [Mid-19thC. Formed from *galakt-*, the stem of *gala* "milk" (see GALAXY).] —**ga·lac·ti·cal·ly** *adv.*

ga·lac·tic e·qua·tor, ga·lac·tic cir·cle *n.* the imaginary circle on the sky formed by extending the plane which passes through the center of the Galaxy. It is inclined at approximately 62° to the celestial equator.

ga·lac·to·poi·e·sis /gə làktō póyəssiss/ *n.* the production of milk by the cells of the glandular structure of the breast

ga·lac·to·poi·et·ic /gə làktə poy éttik/ *adj.* **OF MILK PRODUCTION BY BODY** relating to or stimulating milk production in the mammary glands ■ *n.* **AGENT STIMULATING MILK FLOW** a substance that stimulates the secretion of milk

ga·lac·tor·rhe·a /gə làktə rée ə/ *n.* excessive milk flow during lactation, or spontaneous milk flow in the absence of childbirth and nursing

ga·lac·tor·rhoe·a *n.* *U.K.* = **galactorrhea**

gal·ac·tos·am·ine /gə làk tóssə meen, gàllək-/ *n.* a crystalline amino acid derived from the sugar, galactose, and found in cartilage and bacterial cell walls. Formula: $C_6H_{13}O_5N$.

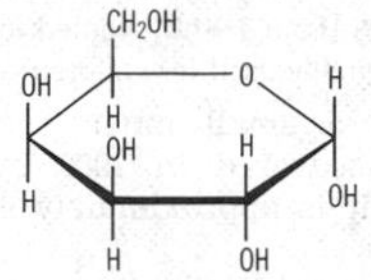

Galactose

ga·lac·tose /gə lák tòss, -tōz/ *n.* a white crystalline sugar found in certain plant gums and mucilages and one of the principal constituents of lactose, which is the main sugar of milk. Formula: $C_6H_{12}O_6$.

ga·lac·to·se·mi·a /gə làk tō séemee ə/ *n.* a genetic disorder causing the absence of an enzyme necessary for the breakdown of galactose in milk to glucose

ga·lac·to·si·dase /gə làktə sí dàyss, -dàyz/ *n.* an enzyme involved in the breakdown of a galactoside

ga·lac·to·side /gə láktə sìd/ *n.* a sugar derivative **(glycoside)** that is formed by the chemical combination of galactose with a non-sugar

ga·la·go /gə láy gō/ (*plural* **-gos**) *n.* = **bush baby** [Mid-19thC. From modern Latin, genus name.]

ga·lah /gə láa/ *n.* an Australian cockatoo with a gray back and wings, a pink breast and head, and a pale pink crest. It is the most common parrot in Australia. Latin name: *Eulophus roseicapillus.* [Mid-19thC. From an Aboriginal language.]

Gal·a·had /gállə hàd/ *n.* **1. KNIGHT OF THE ROUND TABLE** the purest knight of the Round Table in Arthurian legend, who succeeded in his quest for the Holy Grail **2. SOMEBODY WHO ACTS NOBLY** a man considered to be chivalrous, noble, or pure in actions or attitudes

ga·lan·gal /gə láng g'l/ *n.* **1.** PLANTS **PLANT OF GINGER FAMILY** a plant of the ginger family grown in eastern Asia for its pungent underground stem. Latin name: *Alpinia officinarum.* **2.** FOOD **SPICE RESEMBLING GINGER** the underground stem of a galangal plant, sold fresh, or dried and ground, and used in cookery and medicine **3.** PLANTS = **galingale** [Pre-12thC. Via Old French *galingal* from Arabic *kalanjān*, of uncertain origin: perhaps from Chinese *gāoliángjiāng*, from *gāoliáng*, district in Guangdong Province + *jiāng* "ginger."]

gal·an·tine /gállən téen/ *n.* a dish of boned and cooked white meat, poultry, or fish, usually stuffed, that is molded into shape and served cold in its own jelly or coated with aspic [14thC. Via Old French from medieval Latin *galatina.*]

ga·lan·ty show /gə lánti-/ *n.* a play performed by manipulating paper figures and casting their shadows on a screen ["Galanty" of uncertain origin: perhaps from Italian *galanti*, plural of *galante*]

Ga·la·pa·gos gi·ant tor·toise /gə láapə gòss-, -gəss-/, **Ga·la·pa·gos tor·toise** *n.* a giant tortoise that is native to the Galápagos Islands. It grows up to 4 ft./1.2 m long and weighs up to 500 lb./225 kg. Latin name: *Geochelone elephantopus.*

Galápagos Islands

Ga·lá·pa·gos Is·lands /gə láppəgəss-/ group of islands in the Pacific Ocean approximately 650 mi./1,050 km west of Ecuador. They are known for harboring unique species of wildlife, especially the giant tortoise. Area: 3,029 sq. mi./7,844 sq. km.

gal·a·te·a /gàllə teé ə/ *n.* a strong cotton fabric with a twill weave that is often striped and is used to make clothes [Late 19thC. Named for HMS *Galatea*; the fabric was originally used for children's sailor suits.]

Ga·la·te·a *n.* a small inner natural satellite of Neptune, discovered in 1989 by the spacecraft Voyager 2. It is approximately 95 mi./150 km in diameter.

Ga·la·tians /gə láysh'nz/ *n.* a book of the Bible believed to be a letter from St. Paul to the people of Galatia. (*takes a singular verb*) [Early 17thC. Formed from *Galatia*, an ancient country of central Asia Minor.]

gal·a·vant *vi.* = **gallivant**

ga·lax /gáy làks/ *n.* an evergreen plant of the southeastern United States with glossy leaves and white berries. Genus: *Galax.*

gal·ax·y /gálləksee/ (*plural* **-ies**) *n.* **1.** ASSEMBLY OF STARS, GAS, AND DUST a group of billions of stars and their planets, gas, and dust that extends over many thousands of light-years and forms a unit within the universe. Held together by gravitational forces, most of the estimated 50 billion galaxies are shaped as spirals and ellipses, with the remainder being asymmetric. **2.** DISTINGUISHED ASSEMBLY a gathering of famous, brilliant, or distinguished people or things [14thC. Via Old French from, ultimately, Greek *galaxias (kuklos)*, literally "milky (circle)," from *galakt-*, the stem of *gala* "milk."]

Gal·ax·y /gálləksee/ *n.* = **Milky Way**

gal·ba·num /gálbənəm/ *n.* a yellowish to green or brown aromatic bitter gum resin derived from several related Asian plants and used in incense or medicinally as a counterirritant. Genus: *Ferula.* [12thC. Via Latin from Greek *khalbanē*, from Semitic.]

gale /gayl/ *n.* **1.** WIND OF FORCE 8 OR 9 an extremely strong wind that measures 8 or 9 on the Beaufort scale and has a speed of between 39 mi./63 km and 54 mi./87 km per hour **2.** STRONG WIND a very strong wind **3.** BREEZE a light breeze (*archaic*) [Mid-16thC. Origin uncertain: perhaps from Norwegian *galen* "bad" (referring to wind).]

ga·le·a /gáylee ə/ (*plural* **-ae** /-ee/) *n.* a part or organ shaped like a helmet, e.g., the upper petal of some flowers or one of the mouthparts of an insect [Mid-19thC. From Latin, "helmet."] —**ga·le·ate** /gáylee àyt/ *adj.*

ga·le·na /gə leénə/ *n.* a lustrous blue-gray crystalline mineral that consists mainly of lead sulfide and is the main source of lead. Galena crystals were once used as rectifiers in crystal radio sets. [Late 17thC. From Latin, "lead at a certain stage of smelting."]

ga·len·i·cal /gə leénik'l/ *n.* NATURAL DRUG any medicinal preparation that is made from plant or animal tissue, especially vegetable matter, rather than being created synthetically ■ *adj.* NOT SYNTHETIC made from plant or animal tissue rather than synthesized [Mid-17thC. Formed from GALEN, because he prescribed such remedies.]

ga·len·ite /gə leé nīt/ *n.* = **galena**

ga·lè·re /gə láir/ *n.* **1.** GROUP OF PEOPLE WITH COMMON FEATURE a group of people with a particular attribute or interest, especially something undesirable, in common **2.** UNPLEASANT SITUATION an unpleasant predicament [Mid-18thC. Via French, "galley," from Catalan *galera*, from Middle Greek *galea*.]

Gales·burg /gáylz burg/ city in northwestern Illinois, south of Moline and northwest of Peoria. Population: 33,162 (1996).

Ga·li·bi /gə leébee/ (*plural* **-bi** *or* **-bis**) *n.* **1.** PEOPLES MEMBER OF NATIVE S AMERICAN PEOPLE a member of an indigenous South American people who live in French Guiana **2.** LANG CARIB LANGUAGE a language spoken in French Guiana, one of the Carib group of American languages. Galibi is spoken by fewer than a thousand people. [Late 19thC. From Carib, literally "strong man."] —**Ga·li·bi** *adj.*

Gal·i·le·an[1] /gàllə leé ən/, **Gal·i·lae·an** *n.* **1.** PEOPLES SOMEBODY FROM GALILEE somebody who lives or was born or raised in Galilee **2.** CHR CHRISTIAN a Christian (*archaic*) **3.** CHR JESUS CHRIST Jesus Christ (*archaic or literary*) ■ *adj.* RELATING TO GALILEE relating to or typical of Galilee, or its people or culture [Mid-16thC. Formed from Latin *Galilea* "GALILEE."]

Gal·i·le·an[2] /gàllə leé ən/ *adj.* relating to the Italian scientist Galileo, his theories, or his inventions

gal·i·lee /gállə lee/ *n.* a small porch or chapel found at the western end of some medieval churches or cathedrals [15thC. Via Old French from medieval Latin *galilea*, named for Latin *Galilea* "GALILEE," said to be from the position of Galilee as the province most distant from Jerusalem.]

Gal·i·lee /gálli lee/ region of ancient Palestine, now part of northern Israel, situated between the Jordan River and the Sea of Galilee. It was the scene of Jesus Christ's ministry.

Gal·i·lee, Sea of freshwater lake on the Jordan River in northeastern Israel. It is 686 ft./209 m below sea level. Area: 64 sq. mi./166 sq. km.

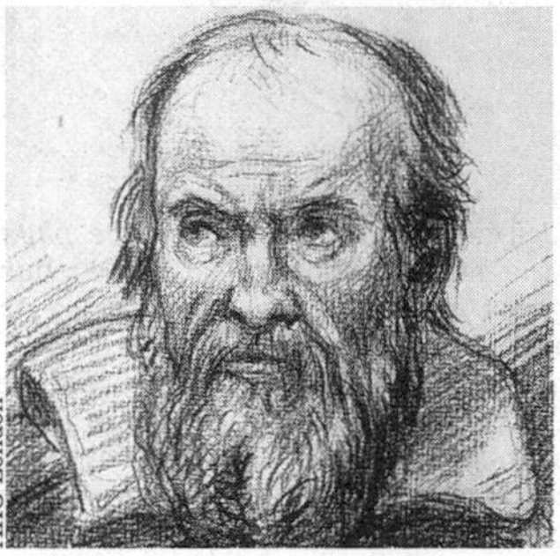

Galileo: Portrait drawing by Guido Reni

Ga·li·le·o /gàlli láy ō/ (1564–1642) Italian physicist and astronomer. One of the founders of Europe's scientific revolution, his main contributions include the application of the telescope to astronomy and the discovery of the laws of falling bodies and the motions of projectiles. Born **Galileo Galilei**

gal·in·gale /gállin gàyl/ *n.* a plant of the sedge family with reddish flowers growing in a cluster directly from the stem and aromatic roots that were used medicinally in the past. Latin name: *Cyperus longus.* [See GALANGAL]

gal·i·ot /gállee ət, -òt/, **gal·li·ot** *n.* **1.** LIGHT FAST GALLEY a light fast ship propelled by sails and oars that was used in the past in the Mediterranean **2.** SINGLE-MASTED SHIP a light shallow single-masted Dutch merchant ship used in the past [15thC. Via Old French (literally "little galley") from, ultimately, medieval Latin *galea* "galley."]

gal·i·pot /gálli pòt/ *n.* crude turpentine in resin form that is obtained from several species of pine found in southern Europe [Late 18thC. Via French from Provençal *garapot* "pine resin."]

gall[1] /gawl/ *n.* **1.** AUDACITY impudent boldness ○ *And then he had the gall to tell us to leave!* **2.** BITTER FEELING OR EXPERIENCE a feeling of bitterness or resentment (*literary*) ○ *Her betrayal turned his love to gall.* **3.** PHYSIOL BILE bile (*archaic*) [12thC. From Old Norse *gall* "bile," from a prehistoric Germanic word meaning "yellow."]

gall[2] /gawl/ *n.* **1.** VET SORE CAUSED BY RUBBING a sore on the skin of an animal that is caused by friction **2.** CAUSE OF ANGER something that angers or irritates somebody (*dated*) **3.** ANGER a feeling of annoyance or anger (*dated*) ■ *vt.* (**galled, gall·ing, galls**) **1.** ANGER SOMEBODY to make somebody extremely angry **2.** VET CAUSE FRICTION SORE ON to cause a sore on the skin by rubbing [14thC. From Middle Low German *galle* "sore," of uncertain origin: perhaps originally "astringent substance."]

gall[3] /gawl/ *n.* a swelling on a tree or plant caused by insects, fungi, bacteria, or external damage [14thC. Via Old French from Latin *galla* "oak gall."]

gall. *abbr.* gallon

Gal·la /gállə/ *n., adj.* LANG, PEOPLES = **Oromo** [Late 19thC. Origin uncertain: perhaps from Arabic *galīz* "rough."]

gal·la·mine /gállə meen/ *n.* a short-acting but powerful muscle relaxant used by anesthetists during the induction of general anesthesia [Late 19thC. From *gallic* (from GALLIUM) + AMINE.]

gal·lant *adj.* /gə lánt, gə laánt/ **1.** COURTEOUS courteous and thoughtful, especially toward women **2.** BRAVE brave, spirited, and honorable (*literary*) **3.** MAJESTIC grand and majestic (*archaic*) **4.** STYLISH stylish or showy in dress (*archaic*) ■ *n.* /gə lánt, gə laánt, gállənt/ **1.** MAN COURTEOUS TO WOMEN a man who is courteous and thoughtful in his behavior toward women (*dated*) **2.** MALE LOVER a man who is a woman's lover (*archaic*) **3.** DANDY a fashionable young man (*archaic*) **4.** BRAVE MAN a brave and honorable man (*archaic*) ■ *vti.* /gə lánt, gə laánt/ (**-lant·ed, -lant·ing, -lants**) WOO to court a woman (*archaic*) [14thC. From Old French, the present participle of *galer* "to make merry."] —**gal·lant·ly** *adv.*

Gal·lant /gə lánt/, **Mavis** (*b.* 1922) Canadian writer. She is known for her incisively written short stories, collected in volumes such as *Home Truths* (1981). Born **Mavis Young**

gal·lant·ry /gálləntree/ (*plural* **-ries**) *n.* **1.** COURAGE bravery, especially in war or in a situation of great danger **2.** COURTESY courteous and thoughtful behavior, especially toward women **3.** SOMETHING GALLANT SAID OR DONE a courageous or chivalrous action or remark (*dated*)

Gal·la·tin /gállətin/ river that rises in northwestern Wyoming and flows northward into Montana, where it joins the Jefferson and Madison rivers to form the Missouri River. Length: 125 mi./201 km.

Gal·la·tin /gállətin/, **Albert** (1761–1849) Swiss-born U.S. statesman. As secretary of the treasury (1801–14) he reduced the public debt and oversaw the Louisiana Purchase (1803). Full name **Abraham Alfonse Albert Gallatin**

Gal·lau·det /gàllə dét/, **Thomas** (1787–1851) U.S. educator. He founded the first free school for hearing-impaired people in the United States, in Hartford, Connecticut (1817). Full name **Thomas Hopkins Gallaudet**

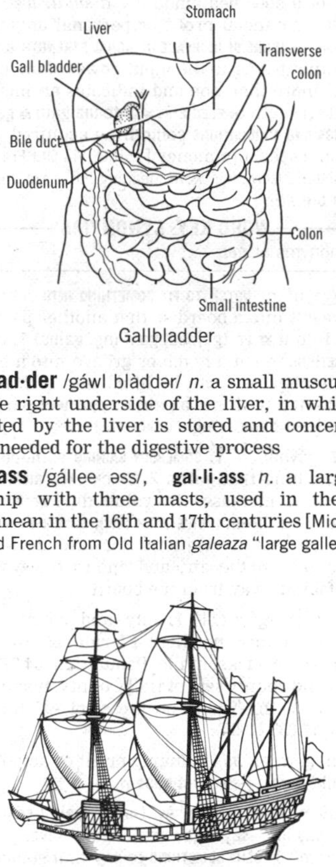

Gallbladder

gall·blad·der /gáwl blàddər/ *n.* a small muscular sac on the right underside of the liver, in which bile secreted by the liver is stored and concentrated until needed for the digestive process

gal·le·ass /gállee əss/, **gal·li·ass** *n.* a large fast warship with three masts, used in the Mediterranean in the 16th and 17th centuries [Mid-16thC. Via Old French from Old Italian *galeaza* "large galley."]

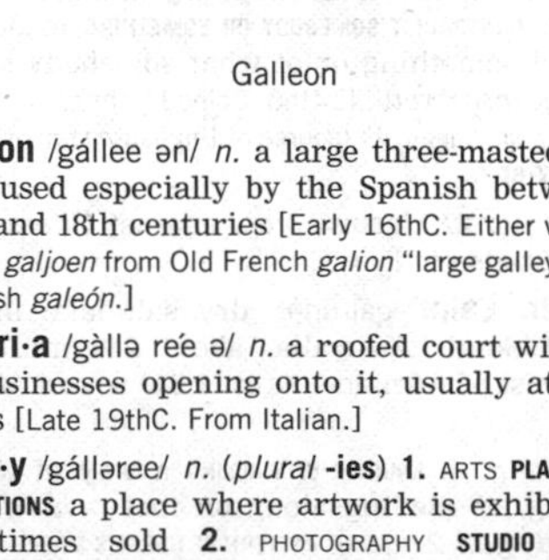
Galleon

gal·le·on /gállee ən/ *n.* a large three-masted sailing ship used especially by the Spanish between the 15th and 18th centuries [Early 16thC. Either via Middle Dutch *galjoen* from Old French *galion* "large galley," or from Spanish *galeón*.]

gal·le·ri·a /gàllə reé ə/ *n.* a roofed court with shops or businesses opening onto it, usually at several levels [Late 19thC. From Italian.]

gal·ler·y /gálləree/ *n.* (*plural* **-ies**) **1.** ARTS PLACE FOR ART EXHIBITIONS a place where artwork is exhibited and sometimes sold **2.** PHOTOGRAPHY STUDIO a photographer's studio **3.** ARCHIT COVERED WALKWAY a long covered passageway that is open on one or both sides **4.** ARCHIT ENCLOSED WALKWAY a corridor, hall, or other enclosed passageway inside a building **5.** ARCHIT **LONG NARROW ROOM** a long narrow space or room used for a particular purpose **6.** ARCHIT **BALCONY** a balcony or passage running along the wall of a large building **7.** *Southern U.S.* ARCHIT **VERANDA** an open-roofed porch or veranda that runs along the side of a house **8.** *Carib* ARCHIT **PORCH AT FRONT OF HOUSE** a porch at the front of a house **9. UNDERGROUND TUNNEL OR PASSAGE** an underground tunnel or passage, especially one made by an animal or one that is part of a mine or a military site **10.** THEATER **PART OF THEATER** a seating area projecting from the back and sides out over the main floor of a theater or auditorium, especially the highest section of this area containing the cheapest seats **11.** THEATER **SEATS IN THE GALLERY** the seats located in the gallery of a theater or auditorium **12.** THEATER **AUDIENCE IN CHEAPEST SEATS** the people who sit in the gallery of a theater **13. UNDISCRIMINATING GENERAL PUBLIC** the general public, viewed as having no discrimination or sophistication (*offensive*) **14.** THEATER **STAGE RIG** a narrow platform above a stage from which technicians can adjust lights, move props, or operate machinery **15.** SPORTS **SPECTATORS AT A COMPETITION** a group of spectators, especially at a tennis or golf match **16. ASSORTED COLLECTION** a varied collection of people or things ○ *a gallery of famous names* **17.** NAUT **SHIP'S BALCONY** a platform or balcony at the rear of a ship **18.** FURNITURE **DECORATIVE RAIL** a decorative metal or wooden rail on a table top, shelf, or tray ■ *vi. Carib* **SHOW OFF OR BOAST** to show off or flaunt possessions or status (*informal*) [15thC. Via Old French *galerie* "portico" from, ultimately, medieval Latin *galeria*, of uncertain origin: perhaps an alteration of *galilea* (see GALILEE).] —**gal·ler·ied** *adj.* ◇ **play to the gallery** to do or say something that will appeal to those regarded as less educated, discriminating, or sophisticated

gal·ler·y for·est *n.* a strip of forest that grows along a river in an area where there are no other trees

gal·ley /gállee/ (*plural* **-leys**) *n.* **1.** SHIPPING **LARGE SHIP USING OARS OR SAILS** a large ship propelled by oars or sails or both, that was used in ancient and medieval times, especially in the Mediterranean **2.** SHIPPING **ROW BOAT** a long boat propelled by oars, especially in England **3.** TRANSP **BOAT, TRAIN, OR AIRCRAFT KITCHEN** a kitchen on a boat, ship, train, or aircraft **4.** PRINTING **PRINT TRAY** a long metal tray used for holding type that is ready for printing **5.** PRINTING = **galley proof** [13thC. Via Old French and medieval Latin from medieval Greek *galea*, of unknown origin.]

gal·ley proof *n.* PRINTING a first test copy of printed material, usually not divided into pages, on which corrections are marked

gal·ley slave *n.* **1.** HIST **ENSLAVED OARSMAN** one of a team of criminals or enslaved men forced in the past to row a galley **2. DRUDGE** somebody who is given menial tasks to do (*dated humorous*)

gal·ley-west *adv.* into a state of disorder, confusion, or destruction (*archaic slang*) ○ *"Then she grabbed up the basket and slammed it across the house and knocked the cat galley-west"* (Mark Twain, *The Adventures of Huckleberry Finn*; 1884) [Late 19thC. Alteration of *Colly-west* "awry," from *Collyweston*, a village in Northamptonshire, England.]

gall·fly /gáwl flī/ (*plural* **-flies**) *n.* an insect such as the gall midge or gall wasp that causes swellings (**galls**) on plants when it deposits its eggs on them [*Gall* from GALL[3]]

gal·liard /gállyərd/ *n.* **1.** DANCE **SPIRITED DANCE** a lively dance popular in England, France, Spain, and Italy in the 16th and 17th centuries **2. MUSIC FOR GALLIARD** the music for a galliard, written in triple time, part of the baroque dance suite ■ *adj.* **LIVELY** lively or spirited (*archaic*) [14thC. From Old French, of uncertain origin: perhaps from a Celtic word.]

gal·li·ass /gállee əss/ *n.* SHIPPING = **galleass**

Gal·lic /gállik/ *adj.* **1. FRENCH** relating to or typical of France, or its people or culture **2. GAULISH** relating or belonging to ancient Gaul or the Gauls [Late 17thC. Formed from Latin *Gallia* "Gaul."]

gal·lic ac·id /gàllik-/ *n.* a colorless crystalline solid that occurs in plants and is obtained from tannin. It is used as a tanning agent, in making inks and paper, and in photography. Formula: $C_7H_6O_5$. [*Gallic*, formed from Latin *galla* "oakgall" (because the acid is made from the oakgall and other vegetable products)]

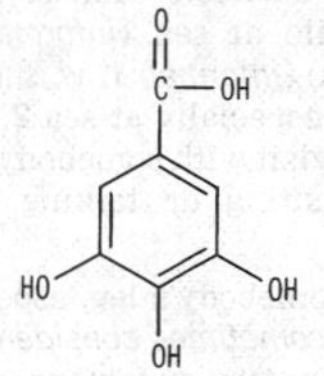

Gallic acid

Gal·li·can /gállikən/ *n.* **SUPPORTER OF GALLICANISM** a supporter of Gallicanism in the Roman Catholic Church ■ *adj.* **1. RELATING TO GALLICANISM** relating to or advocating Gallicanism **2.** = **Gallic**

Gal·li·can·ism /gállikə nìzzəm/ *n.* CHR a French movement in favor of giving the Roman Catholic Church in individual countries more autonomy and reducing the authority of the pope

Gal·li·cism /gálli sìzzəm/ *n.* **1. EXPRESSION BORROWED FROM FRENCH** a word or phrase of French origin used in another language **2. FRENCH CHARACTERISTIC** a characteristic of the French

Gal·li·cize /gálli sīz/ (**-cized, -ciz·ing, -ciz·es**) *vti.* to become French or like something French, or make something, e.g., a word, custom, or characteristic French —**Gal·li·ci·za·tion** /gàllissi záysh'n/ *n.*

gal·li·gas·kins /gàlli gáskinz/ *npl.* CLOTHES **1. BREECHES OR STOCKINGS** loose-fitting breeches or stockings that were worn by men in the 16th and 17th centuries **2. LOOSE TROUSERS** very loose-fitting trousers **3.** *U.K.* **LEATHER LEGGINGS** leather leggings worn in the 19th century [Late 16thC. Origin uncertain: perhaps an alteration of French *garguesques*, which is, ultimately, from Latin *Graecus* "Greek."]

gal·li·mau·fry /gàlli máwfree/ (*plural* **-fries**) *n.* a jumble of various things or people (*dated*) [Mid-16thC. From French *galimafrée*, of unknown origin.]

gall·ing /gáwlling/ *adj.* with the effect of frustrating and annoying somebody —**gall·ing·ly** *adv.*

gal·li·nip·per /gállə nìppər/ *n.* a large mosquito or biting fly (*regional humorous*) [Late 17thC. Of uncertain origin; partly influenced by NIPPER.]

gal·li·nule /gállə noōl/ *n.* an aquatic bird of swampy regions that both wades and swims and typically has dark plumage and a yellow-tipped red bill with a red shield above it. Family: Rallidae. [Late 18thC. From modern Latin *gallinula* "little hen."]

gal·li·ot *n.* = **galiot**

Gal·lip·o·li /gə líppəlee/ peninsula in European Turkey, extending into the Dardanelles, and including an important seaport of the same name. It has historically been of great strategic importance to Istanbul. The peninsula was the site of a major World War I campaign in 1915, when Allied troops including many from Australia and New Zealand, failed to take control of the Dardanelles.

gal·li·pot /gállə pòt/ *n.* a small pot used by pharmacists as a container for medications. In the past these were earthenware, but modern gallipots are made of foil, stainless steel, or polypropylene. [15thC. Origin uncertain: probably coined from GALLEY + POT, with the idea that such pots were brought in galleys from the Mediterranean.]

gal·li·um /gállee əm/ *n.* a rare metallic chemical element, blue-gray when solid and silver when liquid, that is found in coal and ores. Symbol **Ga** [Late 19thC. Formed from Latin *Gallia* "France."]

gal·li·um ar·se·nide *n.* a dark-gray crystalline solid containing gallium and arsenic. It is used in making semiconductors, solar cells, and lasers. Formula: GaAs.

gal·li·vant /gállə vànt/ (**-vant·ed, -vant·ing, -vants**), **gal·a·vant** (**-vant·ed, -vant·ing, -vants**) *vi.* (*informal*) **1. TRAVEL AROUND FOR PLEASURE** to travel around with no purpose except enjoyment **2. PLAY AROUND AMOROUSLY** to play romantically with others [Early 19thC. Origin uncertain; perhaps an alteration of GALLANT.]

gal·li·wasp /gállə wàwsp/ *n.* a lizard with a long body that is related to the slowworm and is found in marshes of Central America and the West Indies. Family: Anguidae. [Late 17thC. Origin unknown.]

gall midge *n.* a small fly resembling a mosquito whose larvae cause swellings (**galls**) on plants. Family: Cecidomyiidae.

gall mite *n.* a mite that causes swellings (**galls**) on the fruits, leaves, or buds of plants. Family: Phytoptidae.

gall·nut /gáwl nùt/ *n.* a small round swelling (**gall**) on a plant

gal·lo·glass /gállō glàss/, **gal·low·glass** *n.* a medieval mercenary soldier or armed servant of a Celtic chieftain, especially in Ireland [15thC. From Irish *gallóglach*, literally "young foreign servant, warrior."]

gal·lon /gállən/ *n.* **1.** **U.S. UNIT OF VOLUME** a unit of capacity in the U.S. Customary system equal to eight U.S. pints (approximately 3.79 liters) **2.** *U.K.* **BRITISH UNIT OF VOLUME** a unit of capacity in the British Imperial system equal to eight British Imperial pints (approximately 4.55 liters) ■ *adj.* **HOLDING A GALLON** with a capacity of one gallon ○ *a gallon jar* [13thC. Via Old French from medieval Latin *galleta* "jug," of uncertain origin: perhaps from Celtic.]

gal·lon·age /gállənij/ *n.* **1. CAPACITY IN GALLONS** a capacity or amount measured in gallons **2. RATE OF LIQUID TRANSFER** the rate at which a liquid is used, pumped, or transmitted, measured in gallons per second, minute, or hour

gal·loon /gə loōn/ *n.* a narrow band of embroidery, lace, braid, or silver or gold thread, used as a trimming on clothes or upholstery [Early 17thC. From French *galon*, from *galonner* "to trim with braid," of unknown origin.] —**gal·looned** *adj.*

gal·loot *n.* = **galoot**

gal·lop /gálləp/ *n.* **1. FASTEST PACE OF HORSE** the fastest pace of a horse, in which all four feet are off the ground at the same time **2. FAST PACE OF FOUR-LEGGED ANIMAL** a fast movement similar to a horse's gallop made by any four-legged animal **3. FAST RIDE ON HORSE** a ride on a horse at a gallop ■ *v.* (**-loped, -lop·ing, -lops**) **1.** *vti.* **RIDE HORSE FAST** to ride a horse at a gallop **2.** *vt.* **MOVE SOMETHING QUICKLY** to move or transport something at a gallop or at a very fast pace **3.** *vi.* **DO SOMETHING VERY FAST** to do something in a great hurry ○ *gallop through lunch* [Early 16thC. From Old French *galoper*, a variant of *waloper*, of prehistoric Germanic origin.] —**gal·lop·er** *n.*

gal·lo·pade /gàllə payd, -paad, gàllə paád/ *n.* DANCE, MUSIC = **galop** [Mid-18thC. From French *galopade*, from *galoper* (see GALLOP).]

gal·lop·ing /gálləping/ *adj.* **1. FAST-DEVELOPING** proceeding or developing at a very fast rate ○ *galloping pneumonia* **2. LIKE GALLOP** relating to or resembling a gallop, in speed or rhythm

Gal·lo-Ro·mance, **Gal·lo-Ro·man** *n.* a group of dialects spoken in France between the seventh and the tenth centuries A.D. It constitutes an intermediate developmental stage between the end of Vulgar Latin and the appearance of Old French. —**Gal·lo-Ro·mance** *adj.*

gal·low·glass *n.* HIST = **galloglass**

gal·lows /gállōz/ (*plural* **-lows**) *n.* **1. FRAME FOR HANGING CRIMINALS** a wooden frame, usually made of two upright posts and a crossbeam with a noose attached, used to execute people by hanging **2. STRUCTURE RESEMBLING GALLOWS** a structure that resembles a gallows, e.g., one used to suspend slaughtered animals **3. EXECUTION BY HANGING** death by hanging as capital punishment for a criminal offense [13thC. Via Old Norse *gálgi* from a prehistoric Germanic word meaning "pole." The use of the plural form developed because the structure has two upright posts.]

gal·lows bird *n.* somebody who deserves to be hanged (*archaic informal*)

gal·lows hu·mor *n.* macabre humor that finds irony or comedy in serious matters such as death

gal·lows tree *n.* = **gallows** *n.* 1

gall·stone /gáwl stōn/ *n.* a small hard mass that forms in the gallbladder, sometimes as a result of infection or blockage

Gal·lup /gálləp/ city in northwestern New Mexico, near the Arizona border. It is located in a coal and uranium mining region, and is an important Navajo and Zuñi trading center. Population: 20,591 (1996).

Gal·lup, George (1901–84) U.S. public opinion analyst and statistician. A pioneer in the use of statistical methods for determining public opinion on social, economic, and political issues, he is best known for founding the Gallup Poll (1935). Full name **George Horace Gallup**

Gal·lup Poll *n.* a survey in which a sample of people taken as a representative cross section of society are asked their opinions on a given subject [Mid-20thC. Named for George H. GALLUP.]

gal·lus·es /gálləssəz/ *npl. U.S., Scotland* suspenders for trousers [Mid-19thC. Plural of *gallus*, alteration of GALLOWS; from the two supports.]

gall wasp *n.* a wasp that lays its eggs in plant tissue, causing swellings (**galls**). Family: Cynipidae.

ga·loot /gə lo͞ot/, **gal·loot** *n.* somebody who is clumsy or thoughtless (*archaic slang insult*) [Early 19thC. Origin unknown.]

gal·op /gálləp/ *n.* **1.** DANCE **LIVELY DANCE** a lively dance that was popular in the 19th century **2.** MUSIC **MUSIC FOR DANCE** the music for a galop, in double time [Mid-19thC. From French.]

ga·lore /gə láwr/ *adj.* in large quantities or numbers ○ *There'll be food galore at the party.* [Early 17thC. From Irish *go leor*, literally "to sufficiency."]

ga·losh·es /gə lóshəz/ *npl.* a pair of waterproof shoes, often made of rubber, worn over other shoes as protection against rain or snow [14thC. Via Old French *galoche* "little sandal" from Latin *gallicula*, from *gallica (solea)* "sandal (from Gaul)."]

Galt /gawlt/, **Sir Alexander Tilloch** (1817–93) British-born Canadian statesman. He was a Liberal legislator and cabinet minister who helped negotiate U.S. access to Canadian fisheries.

ga·lumph /gə lúmf/ (**-lumphed, -lumph·ing, -lumphs**) *vi.* (*informal*) **1. MOVE BOISTEROUSLY OR CLUMSILY** to walk or run in a boisterous or clumsy way **2. MOVE EXULTANTLY** to stride or march in a prancing triumphant way [Late 19thC. Blend of GALLOP and TRIUMPH, coined by Lewis Carroll in *Through the Looking Glass* (1872).]

ga·luth /gaa lo͞ot, -lo͞oth/ *n.* the Jewish Diaspora [Late 20thC. From Hebrew *gālūth*, literally "exile."]

galv. *abbr.* **1.** galvanic **2.** galvanized

gal·van·ic /gal vánnik/ *adj.* **1.** ELEC ENG **RELATING TO CHEMICALLY PRODUCED DIRECT CURRENT** relating to or involving the direct-current electricity that is chemically generated between dissimilar metals, e.g., in a battery **2. LIKE ELECTRIC SHOCK** sudden, startling, or convulsive, like an electric shock or its effects [Late 18thC. (See GALVANISM).] —**gal·van·i·cal·ly** *adv.*

gal·van·ic skin re·sponse *n.* a change in the electrical conductivity of the skin caused by sweating and increased blood flow and linked to a strong emotion such as fear. Lie detector tests use this change as a way of measuring whether somebody is telling the truth.

gal·va·nism /gálvə nìzzəm/ *n.* **1.** ELEC ENG **PRODUCTION OF ELECTRICITY BY CHEMICAL REACTION** the production of direct-current electricity from a chemical reaction, e.g., between dissimilar metals in a battery **2.** MED **ELECTRICITY AS MEDICAL THERAPY** the application of electricity to the human body to stimulate nerves and muscles as part of a medical treatment [Late 18thC. From French, named for Luigi GALVANI whose research led to the discovery that electricity can result from chemical action.]

gal·va·nize /gálvə nìz/ (**-nized, -niz·ing, -niz·es**) *vt.* **1. STIMULATE TO ACT** to stimulate somebody or something into great activity **2.** ELEC ENG **COAT METAL WITH ZINC** to coat a metal, usually iron or steel, with zinc to prevent corrosion **3.** MED **STIMULATE ELECTRICALLY** to stimulate the nerves or muscles of somebody's body using an electric current [Early 19thC. From French (see GALVANISM).] —**gal·va·ni·za·tion** /gàlvəni záysh'n/ *n.* —**gal·va·niz·er** /gálvə nìzər/ *n.*

gal·va·nom·e·ter /gàlvə nómmətər/ *n.* an instrument used to detect or measure the strength and direction of small electric currents by means of a coil in a magnetic field that moves a pointer or light —**gal·va·no·met·ric** /gàlvənə méttrik/ *adj.* —**gal·va·nom·e·try** /gàlvə nómmətree/ *n.*

Gal·way /gáwl way/ seaport on Galway Bay and capital of Galway County, on the western coast of the Republic of Ireland. Population: 50,853 (1991).

Gal·way Bay inlet of the Atlantic Ocean on the western coast of Ireland

gam[1] /gam/ *n.* **1.** ZOOL **MIGRATING WHALES** a group of migrating whales **2.** SHIPPING **SOCIAL VISIT BETWEEN WHALERS** a social visit between whalers or other sailors, especially while at sea (*informal*) ■ *v.* (**gammed, gam·ming, gams**) (*informal*) **1.** *vi.* SHIPPING **MEET AT SEA** to meet socially, especially at sea **2.** *vt.* **TO VIST OR SPEND TIME CHATTING** to visit with somebody socially or spend some time visiting or talking [Mid-19thC. Origin unknown.]

gam[2] /gam/ *n.* somebody's leg, especially a woman's (*dated slang*) (*sometimes considered offensive*) [Late 18thC. Origin uncertain: probably an alteration of *gamb*, a heraldic term for a device on a shield, resembling an animal's leg.]

ga·ma grass /gámmə-/ *n.* a tall coarse grass that is grown in North America for fodder. Latin name: *Tripsacum dactyloides.* [Mid-19thC. *Gama* of uncertain origin: perhaps an alteration of GRAMA.]

ga·may /gá mày/ *n.* a red grape used in making wine, especially Beaujolais [Mid-19thC. Named for *Gamay*, the village in Burgundy, eastern France, where this grape is a native variety.]

gam·ba /gámbə/ *n.* MUSIC = **viola da gamba**

gambade *n.* = **gambado**[2] [Early 16thC. From French, of uncertain origin: possibly from Italian *gambata*, from *gamba* "leg," or via late Latin *gamba* "horse's leg," from Greek *kampē* "bend."]

gam·ba·do[1] /gam báy dō, -báa-/ (*plural* **-does** *or* **-dos**) *n.* **1. LEATHER FOOT PROTECTOR** either of a pair of protective leather holders for a rider's feet attached to a horse's saddle **2. LEG COVERING** either of a pair of rider's leggings [Mid-17thC. Formed from Italian *gamba* "leg" + *-ado*.]

gam·ba·do[2] /gam báy dō, -báa-/ (*plural* **-does** *or* **-dos**), **gam·bade** /gam báyd, -báad/ *n.* **1.** DRESSAGE **LOW JUMP BY HORSE** in dressage, a low leap in which the horse has all four feet off the ground **2. LEAP** a leap or caper **3. PRANK** a prank or escapade [Early 19thC. From Spanish *gambada*, from *gamba* "leg."]

Gam·bi·a /gámbee ə/ river in western Africa that rises in Guinea, flows westward through the Gambia, and empties into the Atlantic Ocean near Banjul. Length: 700 mi./1,100 km.

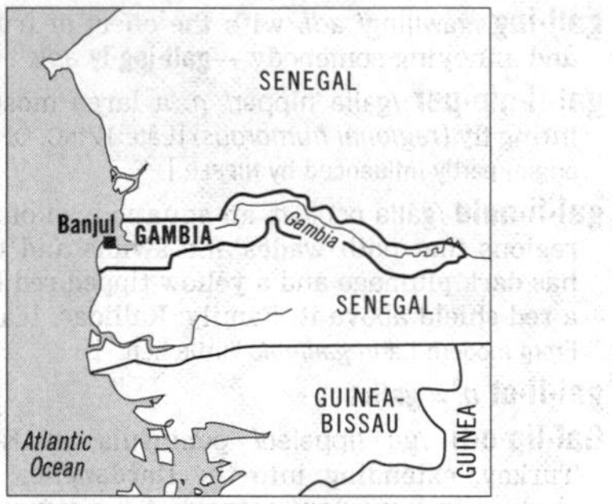

The Gambia

Gam·bi·a, The republic on the western coast of Africa, bordered on the north, east, and south by Senegal. Language: English. Currency: dalasi. Capital: Banjul. Population: 1,248,085 (1997). Area: 4,361 sq. mi./11,295 sq. km. —**Gam·bi·an** *n., adj.*

gam·bier /gám beer/, **gam·bir, gam·beer** *n.* a resinous astringent substance obtained from the leaves of a tropical Asian woody vine and used medicinally as an astringent or tonic and also in tanning and dyeing. Latin name: *Uncaria gambir.* [Early 19thC. From Malay *gambir*, the name of the plant.]

gam·bit /gámbit/ *n.* **1. STRATAGEM** a maneuver or stratagem used to secure an advantage **2. CONVERSATIONAL OPENER** a remark used to open a conversation **3.** CHESS **OPENING MOVE IN CHESS** in chess, an opening move in which a player sacrifices a pawn or other minor piece in order to gain a strategic advantage [Mid-17thC. From Italian *gambetto* "act of tripping someone up (in wrestling)" (modeled on French *gambit*), from *gamba* "leg."]

gam·ble /gámb'l/ *v.* (**-bled, -bling, -bles**) **1.** *vi.* **PLAY GAMES OF CHANCE** to play games such as poker or roulette that involve risking money, or bet on horse races or other events, in the hope of winning money **2.** *vt.* **BET MONEY** to bet a sum of money on the outcome of an event or competition **3.** *vi.* **TAKE A CHANCE ON SOMETHING** to take a risk in the hope and expectation of a desired result ○ *gambling on nice weather* **4.** *vi.* **ENDANGER SOMETHING** to behave in a way that risks harming somebody or something ○ *gambled with the success of the show* **5.** *vt.* **PUT SOMETHING DANGEROUSLY AT RISK** to lose or risk losing something, especially money, by betting or doing something dangerous or rash ○ *She gambled her inheritance away.* ■ *n.* **1. BET** a bet made in the hope of winning money **2. SOMETHING DONE THAT IS RISKY** an action whose outcome is uncertain and very possibly undesirable [Early 18thC. Coined from GAME + *-le*, literally "to keep on playing."] —**gam·bler** *n.*

gam·bling /gámbling/ *n.* playing games of chance or betting in the hope of winning money

gam·boge /gam bṓj/ *n.* **1. RESIN** a resin obtained from an Asian tree that is the main constituent of a yellow pigment **2. PIGMENT** a yellow pigment made from gamboge resin **3.** COLORS **YELLOW COLOR** a strong yellow color [Mid-17thC. Coined from modern Latin *gambaugium*, from *Cambodia*, CAMBODIA, where the tree is native.]

gam·bol /gámb'l/ *vi.* (**-boled** *or* **-bolled, -bol·ing** *or* **-bol·ling, -bols**) **LEAP PLAYFULLY** to leap or skip about playfully ■ *n.* **PLAYFUL LEAPING** an instance of leaping about playfully [Mid-16thC. Alteration of GAMBADE.]

gam·brel /gámbrəl/ *n.* **1.** ZOOL **JOINT ABOVE HORSE'S FOOT** the joint of a leg of an animal, especially a horse, that corresponds to the human ankle **2. BUTCHER'S FRAME** a frame in the shape of a horse's hind leg used by butchers for hanging animal carcasses **3.** ARCHIT = **gambrel roof** [Mid-16thC. From Old Northern French *gamberel*, from *gambier* "forked stick," from *gambe*, a variant of *jambe* "leg."]

gam·brel roof *n.* ARCHIT **1. ROOF WITH TWO SLOPES** a roof that has two slopes on each side, the lower slope being steeper than the upper **2.** *U.K.* **ROOF WITH SLOPING ENDS AND SIDES** a roof with sloping ends and sides and a small gable at both ends

game[1] /gaym/ *n.* **1. SOMETHING PLAYED FOR FUN** an activity that people participate in, together or on their own, for fun ○ *It's only a game!* **2. COMPETITIVE ACTIVITY WITH RULES** a sporting or other activity in which players compete against one another by following a fixed set of rules ○ *How many people do you need to play this game?* **3. COMPETITION** a particular occasion when a competitive game is played ○ *Saturday's game has been cancelled.* **4.** SPORTS **PART OF COMPETITION** in sports such as tennis, a specific subsection of play that goes toward making up a set or match **5. ASPECT OF GAME** a particular aspect of a competition ○ *They lost because their offensive game was terrible.* **6. STYLE OF PLAYING** the style or level of skill with which somebody plays a particular sport ○ *raise your game* **7. NUMBER NEEDED TO WIN** the total number of points needed to win a contest **8. RULES GOVERNING SPORT** the rules governing a particular competition or sport **9. EQUIPMENT** an item or set of items such as a board, dice, counters, a deck of cards, or a piece of computer software that is needed to play a particular game ○ *"Did you bring any games with you?" – "Yes, we brought Scrabble."* **10. ACTIVITY RESEMBLING GAME** any activity that resembles a game, e.g., one that involves intense interest and competitiveness and is carried out by its own specific and often unspoken rules **11. STRATAGEM OR TACTIC** a way of behaving that is aimed at manipulating people or trying to deceive them ○ *So that's your game?* **12. ILLEGAL ACTIVITY OR RACKET** a strategy, activity, or behavior that is questionable, and often illegal (*informal*) **13. OCCUPATION** a business or occupation (*informal*) ○ *the advertising game* **14. SOMETHING NOT TAKEN SERIOUSLY** an activity or situation that somebody does not treat seriously ○ *Life's a game as far as he's concerned.* **15.** HUNT **ANIMALS FOR HUNTING** wild animals, birds, or fish that are hunted for sport **16.** FOOD **MEAT OF HUNTED ANIMALS** the meat of wild animals, birds, or fish that have been killed for sport **17. RIDICULE OR THE OBJECT OF IT** the act of ridiculing somebody for fun, or the target of ridicule, criticism or trickery ○ *She's easy game for a trickster like him.* **18.** MATH **MATHEMATICAL MODEL OF CONTEST** a mathematical model describing a contest played under specified rules in which each participant has only partial control ■ **games** *npl.* **EVENT WITH MANY SPORTING CONTESTS** an event that consists of many different sporting activities and usually lasts for several days ■ *adj.* **1. READY AND WILLING** ready and willing to do something, especially something new or unusual **2. BRAVE** brave in spirit or character ■ *vi.* (**gamed, gam·ing, games**) **GAMBLE** to play games of chance for money [Old English, from a prehistoric Germanic compound meaning "people participating together"] —**game·ly** *adv.* —**game·ness** *n.* ◇ **ahead of the game** anticipating and reacting more promptly than others to new developments ◇ **give the game away, give away the game** to reveal a secret, usually without intending to ◇ **play the game** to follow the rules of a given situation, even if they are unspoken ◇ **the game's up** the plan or trick has failed or been discovered (*informal*) ◇ **the only game in town** the only possibility

game² /gaym/ *adj.* an offensive term meaning injured or with impaired mobility, formerly applied to limbs ○ *a game left foot* [Late 18thC. Origin uncertain, perhaps from Old French *gambi* "crooked."]

game ball *n.* the ball from a winning game given to one of the players or coaches in recognition of a contribution to the victory

game bird *n.* a bird such as a pheasant or grouse that is hunted for sport

Game·boy /gáym bòy/ *tdmk.* a trademark for a handheld video-game machine with a very small monochrome LCD screen, graphics capability, and an extensive selection of games

game·cock /gáym kòk/ *n.* a rooster that has been bred and trained for fighting

game fish *n.* **1.** FISH CAUGHT FOR SPORT any fish, particularly any sea fish, that is caught for sport, especially one favored for its fighting ability. Sharks are popular game fish. **2.** FISH RESERVED FOR ANGLERS ONLY a fish that is reserved by law or other regulation for anglers and that cannot be caught and sold commercially —**game fish·ing** *n.*

game fowl *n.* a domestic fowl bred and trained for fighting

game·keep·er /gáym keepər/ *n.* somebody employed to look after birds or animals hunted for sport, e.g., on an estate or game preserve —**game·keep·ing** *n.*

gam·e·lan /gámmə làn/ *n.* an Indonesian orchestra that consists mainly of percussion instruments such as chimes, gongs, and wooden xylophones [Early 19thC. From Javanese.]

game law *n.* a law that controls the catching and killing of fish, birds, or other animals for sport, e.g., one that specifies the extent of a hunting or shooting season

game of chance *n.* a game, usually played for money, in which the outcome depends to some degree on chance, e.g., on the throw of dice

game of skill *n.* a game such as chess or bridge, in which the outcome depends entirely or principally on the skill of the players

game plan *n.* **1.** SPORTS STRATEGY TO WIN COMPETITION the strategy that a team or player devises beforehand to use during a game **2.** STRATEGY TO ACHIEVE OBJECTIVE a strategy that somebody devises to achieve a particular goal

game point *n.* **1.** SITUATION WITH POTENTIAL TO WIN in games such as tennis and badminton, a situation in which one player or side has only to win the next point to win the game **2.** WINNING POINT the point that will decide the final outcome of a game

game re·serve, game pre·serve *n.* a large area of land where birds or animals are kept in protected conditions in the wild, either for conservation purposes or to be hunted for sport

game room *n.* a room in a house or public building that is set aside and equipped for games such as pool or table tennis

game show *n.* a television program in which people compete for money or prizes

games·man·ship /gáymzmən shìp/ *n.* **1.** STRATEGIC BEHAVIOR the use of tactics or stratagems to gain an advantage in business, politics, or life ○ *political gamesmanship* **2.** PLAY OF QUESTIONABLE FAIRNESS the use of unconventional but not strictly illegal tactics to gain an advantage in a competitive game —**games·man** *n.*

game·some /gáymsəm/ *adj.* eager to play or have fun (*archaic*) —**game·some·ly** *adv.* —**game·some·ness** *n.*

game·ster /gáymstər/ *n.* somebody who plays gambling games (*archaic*)

gamet- *prefix.* = **gameto-**

gam·e·tan·gi·um /gàmmə tánjee əm/ (*plural* **-a** /-ə/) *n.* BOT the part of a plant, especially an organ or cell in algae and fungi, where gametes are produced [Late 19thC. Coined from modern Latin *gameta* (see GAMETE) + Greek *aggeion* "vessel" + -IUM.] —**gam·e·tan·gi·al** *adj.*

gam·ete /gá meet/ *n.* GENETICS a specialized male or female cell with half the normal number of chromosomes that unites with another cell of the opposite sex in the process of sexual reproduction. Ova and spermatozoa are gametes that unite to produce a cell (**zygote**) that may develop into an embryo. [Late 19thC. From modern Latin, ultimately from Greek *gamos* "marriage."] —**ga·met·ic** /gə méttik/ *adj.* —**ga·met·i·cal·ly** /-kəlee/ *adv.*

game the·o·ry *n.* a mathematical theory primarily concerned with determining an optimal strategy for situations in which there is competition or conflict, such as in business activities or military operations —**game the·o·retic** *adj.*

gameto-, gamet- *prefix.* relating to a gamete [From GAMETE]

ga·me·to·cyte /gə meetə sìt/ *n.* **1.** GENETICS CELL PRODUCING MALE OR FEMALE CELLS a cell that divides to produce two specialized male or female cells (**gametes**) **2.** MICROBIOL MALARIA ORGANISM the malaria organism in the stage in its life cycle during which it reproduces in the blood of a mosquito

ga·me·to·gen·e·sis /gə meetə jénnəssis/ *n.* GENETICS the production of gametes from gametocytes by cell division (**meiosis**) —**ga·me·to·gen·ic** *adj.* —**gam·e·tog·e·nous** /gàmmə tójjənəss/ *adj.*

ga·me·to·phore /gə meetə fàwr/ *n.* an upright branch in plants such as mosses that bears the reproductive organs —**ga·me·to·phor·ic** /gə meetə fáwrik/ *adj.*

ga·me·to·phyte /gə meetə fìt/ *n.* the phase in the life cycle of a plant in which sex organs and gametes are produced —**ga·me·to·phyt·ic** /gə meetə fíttik/ *adj.*

game war·den *n.* a civil servant whose responsibility includes the welfare of fish, birds, and other animals in a state or national forest

gam·ey *adj.* = **gamy**

gam·in /gámmin/ *n.* a young child, usually a boy, often homeless, who roams the streets (*archaic*) [Mid-19thC. From French, of uncertain origin: perhaps from French dialect *gamer* "to steal."]

ga·mine /gá meen/ *n.* **1.** BOYISH GIRL a girl or young woman who is boyish in appearance **2.** GIRL STREET URCHIN a young girl, often homeless, who roams the streets ■ *adj.* APPEALINGLY BOYISH charmingly boyish in appearance [Late 19thC. From French, feminine of *gamin* (see GAMIN).]

gam·ing /gáyming/ *n.* GAMBLING playing games such as poker or roulette for money ■ *adj.* RELATING TO GAMBLING relating to or involving gambling games

gam·ma /gámmə/ *n.* **1.** 3RD LETTER OF GREEK ALPHABET the third letter of the Greek alphabet, represented in the English alphabet as "g." See table at **alphabet** **2.** THIRD ITEM the third item in a classification system or in a series of things **3.** PHYS UNIT OF MASS a unit of mass equal to 10^{-6} gram **4.** PHOTOGRAPHY MEASURE OF CONTRAST OF IMAGE a measure of the degree of contrast in a developed photograph or a television picture **5.** CHEM THIRD IN POSITION IN CARBON CHAIN the third position in a carbon chain or ring, starting from a particular group or atom. Symbol γ ■ *adj.* CHEM THIRD NEAREST TO DESIGNATED ATOM used to describe the third nearest atom to a designated atom or group of atoms in an organic molecule [15thC. Via Latin from Greek.]

gam·ma-a·mi·no bu·ty·ric a·cid *n.* an amino acid that inhibits the transmission of nerve impulses

gam·ma cam·er·a *n.* an instrument used in medicine to produce images of internal organs after the injection of a radioactive drug into the body, where the drug releases gamma rays

gam·ma·di·on /gə máydee òn, -ən/ *n.* a pattern consisting of four capital Greek gammas, especially when joined at the center to form a swastika [Mid-19thC. From late Greek, from *gamma* (see GAMMA).]

gam·ma glob·u·lin *n.* a protein component of blood serum that contains the antibodies, the body's main defense against infection. It is also produced commercially from human plasma and used in the treatment and prevention of diseases such as measles, hepatitis, and poliomyelitis.

gam·ma ra·di·a·tion *n.* electromagnetic waves of higher frequency and shorter wavelength than X-rays that is emitted by some radioactive isotopes or in some nuclear reactions

gam·ma ray *n.* a high-energy photon emitted after nuclear reactions or spontaneously from the nucleus of a radioactive atom that lowers the energy level of the nucleus. Gamma rays do not carry any electric charge or mass and share the high-frequency end of the electromagnetic spectrum with X-rays, which have similar properties.

gam·mon¹ /gámmən/ *n.* **1.** BACON the lower part of a side of bacon, cooked whole or cut into slices **2.** HAM cured or smoked ham [15thC. From Old Northern French *gambon* "ham," from *gambe* "leg."]

gam·mon² /gámmən/ *n.* WIN AT BACKGAMMON a win in backgammon when the losing player has not succeeded in removing any pieces from the board ■ *vt.* (**-moned, -mon·ing, -mons**) BEAT SOMEBODY AT BACKGAMMON to beat somebody in backgammon before the person has managed to remove any pieces from the board [Mid-18thC. Formed from Middle English *gamen*, earlier form of GAME.]

gam·mon³ /gámmən/ *n.* *U.K.* NONSENSE false or meaningless talk that is intended to deceive somebody (*dated informal*) ■ *vti.* (**-moned, -mon·ing, -mons**) *U.K.* DECEIVE SOMEBODY to trick or deceive somebody, especially by talking nonsense (*dated informal*) [Early 18thC. Origin uncertain: perhaps from GAMMON².]

gam·mon⁴ /gámmən/ (**-moned, -mon·ing, -mons**) *vt.* to fasten a bowsprit to the front of a ship [Late 17thC. From GAMMON¹, probably with reference to the tying up of a ham.]

gamo- *prefix.* **1.** joined together ○ *gamophyllous* **2.** sexual ○ *gamogenesis* [From Greek *gamos* "marriage"]

gam·o·gen·e·sis /gàmmō jénnəssis/ *n.* sexual reproduction (*technical*) —**gam·o·ge·net·ic** /gàmmō jə néttik/ *adj.* —**gam·o·ge·net·i·cal·ly** /-néttikəlee/ *adv.*

gam·o·sep·al·ous /gàmmə séppələss/ *adj.* used to describe plants with sepals that are joined or partially joined together

gamp /gamp/ *n.* *U.K.* an umbrella, especially a large old one (*archaic informal*) [Mid-19thC. Named for Sarah *Gamp*, a character in the Charles Dickens novel *Martin Chuzzlewit*, who carries an umbrella.]

gam·ut /gámmət/ *n.* **1.** FULL RANGE the entire range of something **2.** COMPLETE RANGE OF MUSICAL NOTES the whole series of recognized musical notes, from lowest to highest **3.** LOWEST MEDIEVAL MUSICAL NOTE the lowest note of medieval musical theory, two Gs below middle C **4.** MEDIEVAL MUSICAL SCALE SYSTEM the medieval scale system based around a repeated series of six notes (**hexachord**) [15thC. Contraction of medieval Latin *gamma ut*, from Greek *gamma*, the letter representing the musical note one below the top note in the medieval scale, + *ut*, the lowest note.]

gam·y /gáymee/ (**-i·er, -i·est**), **gam·ey** (**-i·er, -i·est**) *adj.* **1.** FOOD TASTING OF OR LIKE GAME having a strong flavor like that of a wild bird or animal that is hunted for food **2.** RANK-SMELLING having a strong bad smell **3.** LEWD sexually suggestive or obscene —**gam·i·ly** *adv.* —**gam·i·ness** *n.*

-gamy *suffix.* **1.** marriage ○ *polygamy* **2.** reproductive union ○ *syngamy* **3.** reproductive organs, method of fertilization ○ *karyogamy* [Formed from Greek *gamos* "marriage"] —**-gamic** *suffix.* —**-gamous** *suffix.*

Ga·na·pa·ti /gaanə pátee/ *n.* EASTERN RELIG = **Ganesha**

Gan·da /gándə/ *n.* a language spoken in parts of Uganda that is a member of the Bantu group of the Benue-Congo branch of the Niger-Congo family of African languages. About four million people speak Ganda. [Mid-20thC. From Bantu.] —**Gan·da** *adj.*

gan·der /gándər/ *n.* **1.** MALE GOOSE an adult male goose **2.** SOMEBODY SILLY somebody who is silly **3.** LOOK a look or glance at somebody or something (*informal*) [Old English *gandra*. Ultimately from an Indo-European word meaning "goose" that is also the ancestor of English *goose*, *gannet*, and *gunsel*.]

Gan·der /gándər/ town on Canada's Island of Newfoundland that is home to the region's air traffic control center. Population: 10,364 (1996).

Gan·dhi /gaandee/, **Indira** (1917–84) Indian national leader. The daughter of Jawaharlal Nehru, she was twice prime minister of India (1966–77, 1980–84) and was assassinated by members of her Sikh bodyguard. Born **Indira Priyadarshini Nehru**

Gan·dhi, Mohandas Karamchand (1869–1948) Indian national leader. His campaign of nonviolent civil resistance to British rule led to India's in-

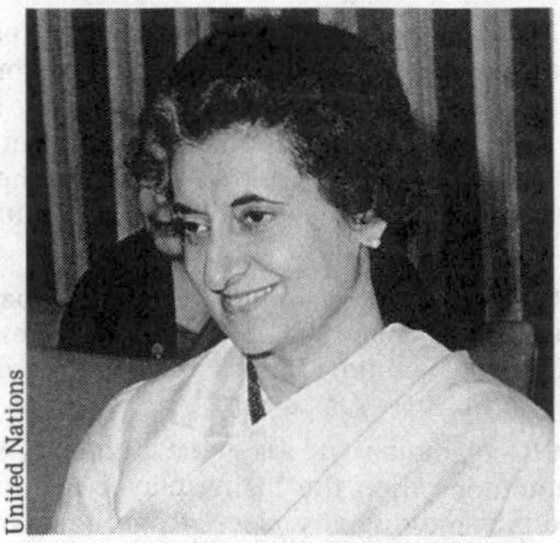

Indira Gandhi

Mohandas Karamchand Gandhi

dependence (1947). He was assassinated by a Hindu extremist. Known as **Mahatma "Great Soul" Gandhi**

gan·dy danc·er /gándee-/ *n.* a laborer in a railroad section gang who lays or maintains tracks (*slang*) [Origin unknown]

ga·nef /gánəf/, **ga·nev** /gánəv/, **ga·nof** /gónnəf/, **go·nif, gonof** *n.* a thief, cheater, or somebody who is unscrupulous (*informal insult*) [Early 20thC. Via Yiddish from Hebrew *gannāḇ*.]

Ga·ne·sha /gə néeshə/, **Ga·ne·sa, Ga·nesh** /gə néesh/ *n.* in Hinduism, the god of wisdom and problem-solving who is the son of Shiva and Parvat and is represented as a pot-bellied man with an elephant's head

ga·nev *n.* = **ganef**

gang[1] /gang/ *n.* **1. GROUP OF TROUBLEMAKING YOUNG PEOPLE** a group of young people who spend time together for social reasons and may engage in delinquent behavior **2. GROUP OF CRIMINALS** a group of people who work together for some criminal or antisocial purpose **3. GROUP OF WORKERS** a group of people working together, especially a group of laborers **4. PEOPLE WHO ENJOY EACH OTHER'S COMPANY** a group of people with similar interests who like to spend time together **5. SET OF TOOLS** a set of tools or devices arranged to be used or operated together ■ *v.* **(ganged, gang·ing, gangs) 1.** *vt.* **PUT OBJECTS IN GROUP** to group similar objects in a set **2.** *vi.* **FORM GROUP** to form, act, or move in a gang ○ *The kids ganged together to clean the park.* **3.** *vt.* **ATTACK IN GANG** to attack somebody as a group **4.** *vt.* ELECTRON ENG **COMBINE SWITCHES** to combine several switches or devices on a single shaft so as to switch multiple connections at one time [12thC. From Old Norse *gangr* "journey." Ultimately from a prehistoric Germanic word meaning "to go." The underlying idea is of a group of people going about together.]

gang up *vi.* **1. JOIN TOGETHER FOR ATTACK** to join together to attack a person or group **2. ACT TOGETHER** to join together to exert pressure or accomplish something

gang[2] /gang/ *n.* = **gangue**

Gan·ga /gúng gə/ *n. S Asia* the Ganges River

gang·bang /gáng bàng/ *n.* (*slang*) (*considered offensive by some people*) **1. SERIAL INTERCOURSE WITH ONE PERSON** sexual intercourse between one consenting person and several others in succession **2. GANG RAPE** a multiple rape by a gang of people ■ *v.* (*slang*) (*considered offensive by some people*) **1.** *vti.* **HAVE MULTIPLE INTERCOURSE WITH ONE PERSON** to participate in an occasion where several people in succession have intercourse with the same person **2.** *vti.* **GANG-RAPE** to gang-rape somebody **3.** *vi.* **BE MEMBER OF VIOLENT GANG** to participate in the activities of a criminal or violent gang —**gang·bang·er** *n.*

gang·bus·ter /gáng bùstər/ *n.* **POLICE OFFICER COMBATING CRIMINAL GANGS** a law-enforcement officer charged with breaking up criminal gangs (*dated slang*) ■ *adj.* = **gangbusters** (*slang*)

gang·bus·ters, gang·bus·ter *adj.* unusually successful or effective (*slang*) ○ *It's a gangbusters promotion that brings the customers in.*

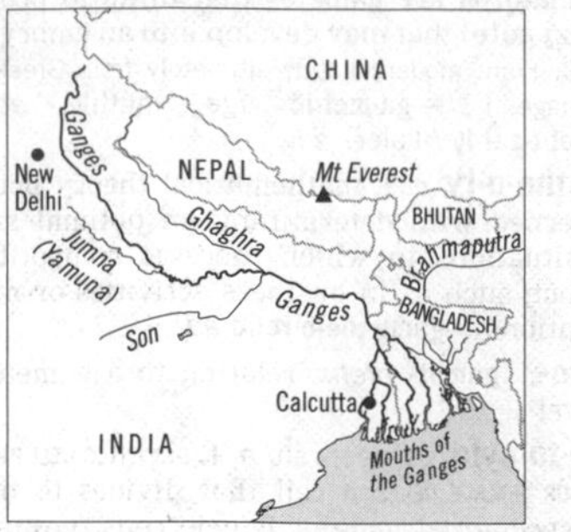

Ganges

Gan·ges /gánj eez/ river in northern India, regarded as sacred by Hindus. It rises in the Indian Himalayas, flows southeastward through Bangladesh, and empties into the Bay of Bengal, forming one of the world's largest deltas. Length: 1,560 mi./2,511 km.

gang·land /gáng lànd, -lənd/ *n.* the world of organized crime —**gang·land** *adj.*

gan·gling /gáng gling/, **gan·gly** /gáng glee/ **(-gli·er, -gli·est)** *adj.* tall and thin, with a loose awkward gait [Early 19thC. Origin uncertain: perhaps formed from GANG[2].]

gan·gli·on /gáng glee ən/ (*plural* **-a** /-ə/ *or* **-ons**) *n.* **1.** ANAT **CLUSTER OF NERVE CELLS** a structure that contains a dense cluster of nerve cells **2.** MED **SWELLING ON JOINT OR TENDON** a harmless swelling similar to a cyst that forms on a joint or tendon [Late 17thC. From Greek *gagglion* "tumor, nerve bundle."] —**gan·gli·al** *adj.* —**gan·gli·on·at·ed** /gáng glee ə nàytəd/ *adj.* —**gan·gli·on·ic** /gàng glee ónnik/ *adj.*

gan·gly *adj.* = **gangling** [Late 19thC. Alteration of GANGLING.]

gang·plank /gáng plàngk/ *n.* a movable structure such as a bridge or plank used when boarding or disembarking from a ship [Mid-19thC. Literally "plank for going" (see GANG[1]).]

gang rape *n.* a rape of one person by several people in succession —**gang-rape** *vti.*

gan·grene /gáng green, gang gréen/ *n.* **DEATH OF TISSUE** local death and decay of soft tissues of the body as a result of lack of blood to the area. It has various causes, including extreme heat or cold, obstruction of blood vessels by disease or a blood clot, or a neurological disorder. ■ *vti.* **(-grened, -gren·ing, -grenes) GET GANGRENE** to affect body tissue with gangrene, or become affected, with gangrene [Mid-16thC. Via French from, ultimately, Greek *gaggraina*.] —**gan·gre·nous** /gáng grənəss/ *adj.*

gang·sta rap /gángstə-/ *n.* a type of rap music in which the lyrics tend to deal with gangs and killings [*Gangsta*, alteration of GANGSTER]

gang·ster /gángstər/ *n.* a member of an organized gang of criminals, especially a racketeer —**gang·ster·ish** *adj.* —**gang·ster·ism** *n.*

gangue /gang/, **gang** *n.* worthless rock or other matter occurring in a vein or deposit within or alongside a valuable mineral. ◊ **matrix** [Early 19thC. Via French from German *Gang* "way, lode."]

gang·way /gáng wày/ *n.* **1. NARROW WALKWAY** a narrow passageway, especially a temporary walkway **2. ENTRANCE IN SHIP'S SIDE** an opening in the side of a ship through which it is boarded by means of a gangplank **3.** = **gangplank** ■ *interj.* **MAKE WAY** used to indicate to people in a crowd that they should make way because somebody is coming through [Late 17thC. Literally "way for going" (see GANG[1]).]

gan·is·ter /gánnistər/ *n.* a hard silica-containing hard that can endure high temperatures and is used to line furnaces [Early 19thC. Origin unknown.]

gan·ja /gaánjə, gán-/ *n.* a potent form of marijuana used for smoking [Early 19thC. From Hindi *gājā*.]

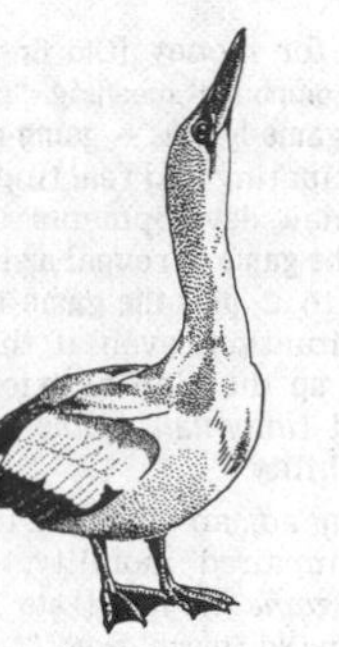
Gannet

gan·net /gánnət/ *n.* a large fish-eating seabird, typically white with black-tipped wings, that lives in offshore colonies in oceanic regions. Genus: *Morus.* [Old English *ganot.* Ultimately from an Indo-European word meaning "goose" (see GANDER).]

Gan·nett Peak /gànnit-/ mountain in the Central Rocky Mountains, western Wyoming. It forms part of the Wind River Range and is the highest peak in the State. Height: 13,804 ft./4,207 m.

gan·nis·ter *n.* = **ganister**

ga·nof *n.* = **ganef**

gan·oid /gá noyd/ *adj.* **BONY AND DIAMOND-SHAPED** used to describe a type of scale found on gars and other primitive fish, consisting of dentine-covered bone with a thick outer layer of a substance **(ganoine)** similar to enamel ■ *n.* **FISH WITH GANOID SCALES** a primitive fish that has ganoid scales [Mid-19thC. Via French from, ultimately, Greek *ganos* "brightness." From its shiny surface.]

gan·sey /gánzee/ (*plural* **-seys**) *n. U.K.* CLOTHES a heavy sweater, especially one worn by a fisherman (*regional*) [Late 19thC. Alteration of GUERNSEY.]

Gan·su /gàn sóo/ province of northern China dominated by semiarid plateaus and basins. It is a major agricultural region, producing wheat, millet, kaoliang, and soybeans. Industry has also developed there from the 1950s. Capital: Lanzhou. Population: 23,780,000 (1994). Area: 175,300 sq. mi./454,000 sq. km.

gant·let[1] /gáwntlət, gaánt-/ *n.* **TYPE OF RAILROAD TRACK** a section of railroad track where two parallel lines are arranged so that one rail of each line is between the rails of the other line ■ *vt.* **(-let·ed, -let·ing, -lets) CONVERGE LINES IN GANTLET** to construct or merge two railroad tracks to form a gantlet [Variant of GAUNTLET[2] "type of punishment involving men standing in two parallel lines"]

gant·let[2] /gáwntlət, gaántlət/ *n.* MIL = **gauntlet**[2] *n.*

gant·line /gánt līn/ *n.* a rope run through a pulley on a mast and used to hoist people or things [Mid-18thC. Origin uncertain: perhaps an alteration of *girtline*, from a variant of GIRTH.]

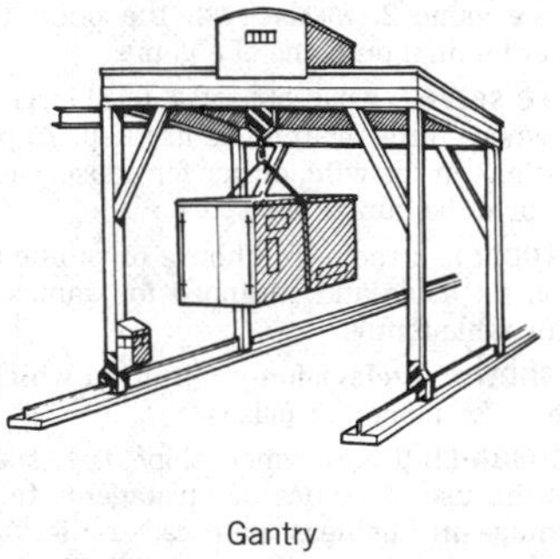
Gantry

gan·try /gántree/ (*plural* **-tries**) *n.* **1.** RAIL **SUPPORT FRAMEWORK FOR RAILROAD SIGNALS** a frame spanning railroad tracks and used to display signals **2.** ENG **SUPPORT FRAMEWORK FOR MACHINERY** a spanning framework used to support machinery, e.g., the platform that supports a crane or the structure used to erect and service rockets [Late 16thC. Origin uncertain: perhaps an alteration of Old Northern French *gantier* "trellis" (via Latin *cantherius* from, ultimately, Greek *kanthēlia* "carrying-baskets"), or from *gawn* "bucket" (alteration of GALLON) + TREE.]

Gan·y·mede /gánnə meèd/ *n.* **1.** MYTHOL **CUPBEARER OF GREEK GODS** in Greek mythology, a beautiful young Trojan prince whom Zeus carried off to Mount Olympus to be cupbearer to the gods. In later times he symbolized homosexual love, or the spirit's ascent to heaven. **2.** ASTRON **MOON OF JUPITER** the largest of Jupiter's moons

GAO *abbr.* General Accounting Office

Gao Ke·gong /gòw kə góng/ (1248–1310?) Chinese artist. He is noted for his paintings of the mountain landscapes of southern China.

gaol *n., vt. U.K.* = **jail** [13thC. From Old Northern French *gaiole*, a variant of Old French *jaiole* (see JAIL).]

WORD KEY: CULTURAL NOTE

The Ballad of Reading Gaol, a poem by English writer Oscar Wilde (1898). Wilde's last work, written while he was incarcerated for "homosexual activities," it is the story of the trial and execution of murderer Charles Thomas Wooldridge, a fellow inmate at the jail. It deals with the harshness of prison conditions and the idea of forgiveness.

gap /gap/ *n.* **1.** **BREAK IN STRUCTURE** a break or opening in a structure or arrangement, e.g., a fence or military defense line **2.** **SOMETHING MISSING** an area where there is a complete or partial absence of something, such as data ○ *gaps in his employment record* **3.** **INTERVAL OF TIME** an interval of time during which some action or event stops occurring ○ *a gap of three years* **4.** **DISPARITY** a significant difference between two things, attitudes, or perceptions ○ *the gap between rich and poor* **5.** **PROBLEM CAUSED BY DISPARITY** a problem caused by a difference between things, attitudes, or perceptions ○ *technology gap* ○ *generation gap* **6.** GEOG **OPENING BETWEEN MOUNTAINS** a ravine or pass in a mountain range **7.** ELEC ENG = **spark gap** ■ *v.* **(gapped, gap·ping, gaps) 1.** *vti.* **PRODUCE OR DEVELOP GAP** to create a gap or opening in a barrier, or become open or separated by a gap **2.** *vt.* ELEC ENG **ADJUST SPARK PLUG GAP** to adjust the gap between the electrodes of a spark plug [14thC. From Old Norse, "chasm."] —**gap·py** *adj.*

gape /gayp/ *vi.* **(gaped, gap·ing, gapes) 1.** **STARE WITH MOUTH OPEN** to stare in open-mouthed surprise or wonder **2.** **OPEN THE MOUTH** to open the mouth wide **3.** **OPEN A GAP** to open or split apart with a gap ■ *n.* **1.** **OPEN-MOUTHED STARE** a stare of wonder or surprise in which the mouth is wide open **2.** **OPENING OF MOUTH** an opening of the mouth wide, e.g., when surprised **3.** **YAWN** an opening of the mouth to yawn **4.** ZOOL **WIDTH OF OPEN MOUTH** the width of the open mouth of an animal **5.** **BIG GAP** a wide opening in something [13thC. From Old Norse *gapa* "to open the mouth."]

WORD KEY: SYNONYMS

See Synonyms at ***gaze***.

gap·ing /gáyping/ *adj.* wide open and deep —**gap·ing·ly** *adv.*

gap-toothed *adj.* with wide spaces between the teeth

gar /gaar/ (*plural* **gar** *or* **gars**) *n.* **1.** **AMERICAN FRESHWATER FISH** a large primitive freshwater fish found in North and Central America that has a heavy armor of bony scales and a long toothy jaw. Family: Lepisosteidae. **2.** **FISH SIMILAR TO GAR** a fish such as a needlefish that is similar in appearance to or related to a gar, such as a needlefish [Mid-18thC. Shortening of GARFISH.]

GAR, G.A.R. *abbr.* Grand Army of the Republic

ga·rage /gə raázh, -raáj/ *n.* **1.** **BUILDING FOR MOTOR VEHICLES** a building for parking or storing one or more motor vehicles **2.** **ESTABLISHMENT REPAIRING MOTOR VEHICLES** an establishment that repairs and often sells motor vehicles, and that sometimes sells oil, diesel, and gasoline ■ *vt.* **(-raged, -rag·ing, -rag·es)** **PUT VEHICLE IN GARAGE** to park or store a motor vehicle in a garage [Early 20thC. From French, formed from *garer* "to shelter." Ultimately from a prehistoric Germanic word meaning "to protect" (see GARRET).]

ga·rage sale *n. U.S., ANZ* a sale of used or unwanted household items that is held in the garage or driveway of the seller's home

ga·ram ma·sa·la /gaa raàm mə saálə/ *n.* a mixture of spices used in Indian cooking to impart a hot pungent flavor to a dish [Mid-20thC. From Hindi *garam masālā*, literally "hot spices."]

Gar·a·mond /gérrə mònd, gaa raa móN/, **Gar·a·mond type** *n.* a Roman typeface often used in books [Mid-19thC. Named for the French type founder Claude *Garamond* (1499–1561).]

garb /gaarb/ *n.* **1.** CLOTHES **TYPICAL OUTFIT** a particular type of clothing, especially the uniform or typical outfit worn by a profession **2.** **APPEARANCE** the outward appearance that somebody or something has ○ *The garb of compromise concealed their war plans.* ■ *vt.* **(garbed, garb·ing, garbs) 1.** **DRESS SOMEBODY** to clothe somebody or yourself in a particular type of clothing **2.** **COVER SOMETHING WITH SOMETHING ELSE** to cover or disguise something as something else ○ *garbed his philanthropic activities in anonymity* [Late 16thC. Via obsolete French *garbe* "elegance" from Italian *garbo*. Ultimately from a prehistoric Germanic word meaning "to make ready" that is also the ancestor of English *gear*.]

gar·bage /gaárbij/ *n.* **1.** **DISCARDED WASTE OR USELESS MATERIAL** discarded food waste, or any other unwanted or useless material **2.** **NONSENSE** talk or writing that is worthless nonsense or lies **3.** **SOMEBODY OR SOMETHING WORTHLESS** somebody who or something that is considered totally worthless **4.** COMPUT **WORTHLESS DATA** inaccurate, useless, or meaningless data in a computer [15thC. From Anglo-Norman, of unknown origin.] —**gar·bag·y** *adj.*

gar·bage can *n.* any container for waste matter, especially one for food waste or one that is kept outside for collection by a waste-disposal service. = **dustbin**

gar·bage dis·pos·al *n.* an electrical device, installed beneath a kitchen sink, that grinds up food so that it can go into the waste pipe

gar·bage man *n.* somebody employed to haul away trash

gar·ban·zo /gaar baán zō/ (*plural* **-zos**), **gar·ban·zo bean** *n.* = **chickpea** [Mid-18thC. From Spanish.]

gar·ble /gaárb'l/ *vt.* **(-bled, -bling, -bles) 1.** **JUMBLE MEANING OF SOMETHING** to confuse something unintentionally or through ignorance and thereby give the wrong impression **2.** COMMUNICATION **SCRAMBLE TRANSMISSION OF SOMETHING** to cause the corruption of a transmitted message or signal ○ *The announcement was completely garbled.* ■ *n.* COMMUNICATION **CONFUSING MESSAGE** a confused or jumbled message, piece of information, or signal, or the confusing or jumbling of information [15thC. Via Italian *garbellare* "to sift" and Arabic *ġarbala* from, ultimately, late Latin *cribellum* "small sieve," from Latin *cribrum* "sieve."] —**gar·bled** *adj.*

Gar·bo /gaárbō/, **Greta** (1905–90) Swedish-born U.S. movie actor, noted for her beauty and reticence. Her movies include *Anna Christie* (1930), *Grand Hotel* (1932), *Camille* (1937), and *Ninotchka* (1939). After her retirement in 1941, she lived as a recluse. Born **Greta Gustaffson**

gar·board /gaár bàwrd/ *n.* the continuous band of planking on a ship's hull next to its keel [Early 17thC. From obsolete Dutch *gaarboord*, of uncertain origin: perhaps from *garen* "to gather" + *boord* "board."]

gar·bol·o·gy /gaar bóllәjee/ *n.* the study of a cultural group by an examination of what it discards —**gar·bol·o·gist** *n.*

Gar·cí·a /gaar seé ə/, **Carlos Poléstico** (1896–1971) Filipino statesman. He was vice president of the Philippines (1953–57) before serving as president (1957–61).

Gar·cí·a Már·quez /gaar seé ə maár kess/, **Gabriel** (*b.* 1928) Colombian writer. Among his works is *One Hundred Years of Solitude* (1967), a classic example of magic realism. He won a Nobel Prize in literature in 1982.

Gar·cí·a Rob·les /gaar seé ə rṓbləss/, **Alfonso** (1911–91) Mexican statesman. He helped draft the international Nuclear Nonproliferation Treaty (1968), and shared the Nobel Peace Prize (1982) for his long campaign against nuclear weapons.

gar·çon /gaar sṓN, -sáwN/ *n.* a waiter in a French restaurant or café [Early 17thC. From French.]

gar·da /gaárdə/ (*plural* **-daí** /-dee/) *n.* a police officer in the Republic of Ireland and a member of the Garda [See GARDA]

Gar·da /gaárdə/ *n.* the police force of the Republic of Ireland [Early 20thC. From Irish, shortening of *Garda Síochána*, literally "civic guard."]

Gar·da, Lake /gaárdə/ the largest lake in Italy and a major resort region. It is situated in northern Italy, between Brescia and Verona. Area: 143 sq. mi./370 sq. km.

gar·daí plural of **garda**

gar·den /gaárd'n/ *n.* **1.** **PLANTED AREA OF GROUND** a plot of ground where plants such as fruits, vegetables, and flowers are grown **2.** **PARK** a park or recreational area for the public, generally planted with flowers, shrubs, and trees (*often used in the plural*) **3.** **FARMING REGION** a fertile, well-cultivated region **4.** **OUTDOOR EATING AND DRINKING ESTABLISHMENT** an eating or drinking establishment that serves its patrons outdoors **5.** *U.K.* = **yard** ■ *adj.* **1.** **RELATING TO GARDENS** produced in, frequenting, or used in a garden **2.** *U.K.* = **garden-variety** ■ *vi.* **(-dened, -den·ing, -dens)** **LOOK AFTER GARDEN** to plan or tend a garden [14thC. Via Old Northern French *gardin* from Vulgar Latin *(hortus) gardinus* "enclosed (garden)." Ultimately from a prehistoric Germanic word that is also the ancestor of English *yard*.] ◇ **lead** *or* **take somebody up** *or* **down the garden path** to mislead or deceive somebody, often gradually over a period of time

WORD KEY: CULTURAL NOTE

The Secret Garden, a children's story by English writer Frances Hodgson Burnett (1911). It is the tale of a lonely orphan, Mary Lennox, who is sent to live with her uncle Archibald, a widower whose wife died as a result of a fall from a tree in her beloved garden. In restoring the garden, Mary finds happiness and helps the family recover from its misfortune.

Gar·de·na /gaar deénə/ city and suburb of Los Angeles, situated in Los Angeles County, southwestern California. Population: 49,847 (1990).

gar·den a·part·ment *n.* **1.** **APARTMENT WITH GARDEN ACCESS** an apartment on the ground floor or in the basement of a building with access to a lawn or garden **2.** **APARTMENT BUILDING WITH GARDEN** an apartment building that has a garden or lawn

gar·den cen·ter *n.* a retail establishment that sells plants and gardening equipment

gar·den cit·y *n.* a planned residential community with landscaped gardens and parks

Gar·den Cit·y /gaárd'n síttee/ **1.** city near Detroit in Wayne County, southeastern Michigan. Population: 31,846 (1990). **2.** city in southeastern New York, on Long Island, east of Queens. It is the site of Adelphi University. Population: 21,721 (1996).

gar·den·er /gaárd'nər/ *n.* somebody who tends a garden or lawn, either as a profession or a hobby

gar·den flat *n. U.K.* = **garden apartment**

Gar·den Grove /-grṓv/ city in Orange County, southwestern California, south of Anaheim. Population: 147,958 (1994).

gar·de·nia /gaar deénee ə/ *n.* **1.** **EVERGREEN TREE BEARING WHITE FLOWERS** an evergreen tree or shrub native to warm regions of Africa and Asia and widely cultivated for its shiny leaves and fragrant white flowers. Genus: *Gardenia*. **2.** **GARDENIA FLOWER** the flower of a gardenia tree or shrub [Mid-18thC. From modern Latin, genus name. Named for the Scottish-American naturalist Alexander *Garden* (1730–91).]

gar·den par·ty *n.* a party held in a garden or yard

gar·den-va·ri·e·ty *adj.* common or ordinary

Gar·di·ners Is·land /gaárdnərz-/, **Gar·di·ner's Is·land** island off the eastern tip of Long Island, New York, in Gardiners Bay. In 1639 it became the first English settlement in the present-day state of New York. Area: 3,300 acres/1,335 hectares.

Gard·ner /gaárdnər/, **Erle Stanley** (1889–1970) U.S. writer. A practicing attorney for twenty years, he is best known for his fictional sleuth Perry Mason, who appeared in over 80 of his detective novels.

Gar·field /gaár feeld/ city in Bergen County, northeastern New Jersey, situated on the Passaic River, southeast of Paterson. Population: 26,727 (1990).

Gar·field, James A. (1831–81) U.S. statesman and 20th president of the United States. A Republican member of the U.S. House of Representatives (1863–80), he was president for only four months before he was assassinated. Full name **James Abram Garfield**

gar·fish /gaár fish/ (*plural* **-fish·es** *or* **-fish**) *n.* = **gar**

gar·gan·tu·an /gaar gánchoo ən/ *adj.* tremendously large in amount, number, or size [Late 16thC. Formed from *Gargantua*, the name of the giant hero of *Gargantua* by Rabelais.]

gar·gle /gaárg'l/ *v.* **(-gled, -gling, -gles) 1.** *vti.* **CLEANSE MOUTH AND THROAT** to rinse or disinfect the mouth and throat by holding liquid in the back of the mouth

James A. Garfield

and stirring it up with air breathed out from the lungs **2.** *vi.* **MAKE GUTTURAL SOUND** to make a sound like that made when rinsing the mouth with liquid ■ *n.* **1. MOUTHWASH** a liquid used to rinse the mouth **2. GUTTURAL SOUND** a sound like that made when rinsing the mouth with liquid [Early 16thC. From French *gargouiller,* from Old French *gargouille* "throat" (source of English *gargoyle*), from Latin *gurgulio* "gullet" (source of English *gurgle*).]

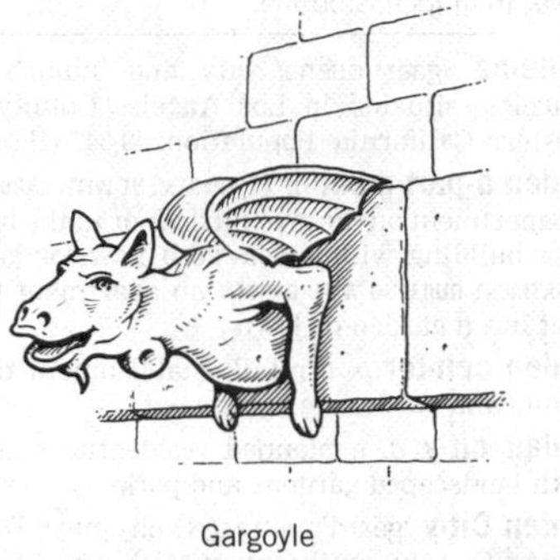

Gargoyle

gar·goyle /gaár gòyl/ *n.* **1. GROTESQUE DRAINAGE SPOUT ON BUILDING** a spout in the form of a grotesque animal or human figure that projects from the gutter of a building and is designed to cast rainwater clear of the building **2. STATUE OF GROTESQUE FIGURE** a grotesque carved figure **3. SOMEBODY LIKE CARVED FIGURE** somebody who is said to resemble a carved gargoyle (*insult*) [15thC. From Old French *gargouille* (see GARGLE), because the water seems to come out of its throat.]

gar·i·bal·di /gèrrə báwldee/ *n.* a woman's loose-fitting blouse that imitates the red shirt worn by Giuseppe Garibaldi [Mid-19thC. Named for GARIBALDI.]

Gar·i·bal·di /gàrrə báwldee/, **Giuseppe** (1807–82) French-born Italian patriot. He played a leading role in the unification of Italy (1859–61), defeating the rulers of Sicily and Naples at the head of his army, the so-called "Red Shirts."

gar·ish /gérrish/ *adj.* **1. GAUDY** crudely showy ○ *a garish outfit* **2. OVERLY ORNAMENTED** excessively ornate or elaborate ○ *a garish balcony and staircase* **3. DRESSED TOO BRIGHTLY** wearing clothing or makeup that is extemely brightly colored **4. TOO BRIGHT** excessively bright ○ *a hideous garish yellow* [Mid-16thC. Origin unknown.] —**gar·ish·ly** *adv.* —**gar·ish·ness** *n.*

gar·land /gaárlənd/ *n.* **1. FLOWER WREATH** a wreath of intertwined flowers or leaves worn as ornament or as a sign of honor **2. HANGING FLOWER DECORATION** a festoon of flowers or paper hung as decoration **3. LITERAT ANTHOLOGY** a collection of short pieces of literature ■ *vt.* **(-land·ed, -land·ing, -lands) DECORATE WITH GARLAND** to decorate or adorn somebody or something with garlands [14thC. From Old French *garlande,* of unknown origin.]

Gar·land /gaárlənd/, **Hamlin** (1860–1940) U.S. writer. A writer of harshly realistic social novels, he is remembered for his autobiographical *Son of the Middle Border* (1917), and the Pulitzer Prize-winning *Daughter of the Middle Border* (1921). Full name **Hannibal Hamlin Garland**

Gar·land, Judy (1922–69) U.S. movie actor and singer. She starred in films including *The Wizard of Oz* (1939), *Meet Me in St. Louis* (1944), and *A Star is Born* (1955), and from the 1950s performed primarily as a singer. Born **Frances Gumm**

Garlic

gar·lic /gaárlik/ (*plural* **-lic** *or* **-lics**) *n.* **1. PLANTS STRONG-TASTING PLANT USED IN COOKING** a plant grown for its strongly flavored bulbs that are used in cooking and medicine. Latin name: *Allium sativum.* **2. COOK CLOVE OF GARLIC** a bulb or clove of garlic with a pungent odor and flavor that is commonly used in cooking **3. PLANTS PLANT SIMILAR TO GARLIC** any plant related to or resembling true garlic [Old English *gārlēac.* From Old English *gār* "spear" + an earlier form of LEEK. From its spearlike leaves.] —**gar·lick·y** *adj.*

gar·lic bread *n.* bread seasoned with butter and garlic and baked or toasted

gar·lic press *n.* a small kitchen tool, usually metal or plastic, that minces a clove of garlic by squeezing it through small holes

gar·lic salt *n.* a preparation of salt and powdered garlic used as a food seasoning

gar·ment /gaármənt/ *n.* **CLOTHING ITEM** a piece of clothing ■ *vt.* **(-ment·ed, -ment·ing, -ments) DRESS SOMEBODY** to put clothing on somebody (*literary*) (*often passive*) [14thC. From French *garnement,* literally "equipment," from *garnir* (see GARNISH).]

gar·ment bag *n.* a piece of soft-sided luggage specifically shaped for carrying dresses, suits, or other clothing on hangers

Gar·neau /gaar nṓ/, **François Xavier** (1809–66) Canadian historian. Considered the first historian of French Canada, he wrote the *History of Canada* (1845–48).

gar·ner /gaárnər/ *vt.* **(-nered, -ner·ing, -ners) 1. GATHER IN SOMETHING** to gather something into storage or into a granary **2. WIN OR GAIN SOMETHING** to earn or acquire something by effort **3. GATHER INFORMATION** to collect or accumulate something such as information or facts ■ *n.* **GRANARY** a storage place for grain (*archaic*) [12thC. Via Anglo-Norman *gerner* "storehouse" from, ultimately, Latin *granarium* (see GRANARY).]

gar·net /gaárnət/ *n.* **1. RED SEMIPRECIOUS STONE** a crystalline silicate mineral common in metamorphic and some igneous rocks, whose color varies according to its composition. Some deep red garnets are used as semiprecious gemstones. **2. COLORS DARK RED COLOR** a dark red color ■ *adj.* **COLORS DARK RED IN COLOR** of a dark red color [13thC. Origin uncertain: probably via Middle Dutch *garnate* from Old French *grenat* "dark red," from *pome grenate* "pomegranate," because of its color.]

gar·net·if·er·ous /gaàrnə tíffərəss/ *adj.* used to describe minerals that contain garnets

gar·ni·er·ite /gaárnee ə rīt/ *n.* a soft green mineral that consists of nickel-rich serpentine, a form of hydrated nickel magnesium silicate, and is an important source of nickel [Late 19thC. Named for the French geologist Jules *Garnier* (1839?–1904), who discovered it.]

gar·nish /gaárnish/ *vt.* **(-nished, -nish·ing, -nish·es) 1. ENHANCE FOOD OR DRINK** to add something as an accompaniment to food or drink that enhances its flavor or appearance **2. EMBELLISH SOMETHING** to decorate something with an ornament **3. LAW = garnishee** *v.* 1, **garnishee** *v.* 2 ■ *n.* **1. ENHANCEMENT FOR FOOD OR DRINK** something added as an accompaniment to food or drink to enhance its flavor or appearance **2. SOMETHING DECORATIVE** an ornament or decoration for something [14thC. From French *garniss-,* the stem of *garnir* "to equip, adorn, warn," of prehistoric Germanic origin.] —**gar·nish·ing** *n.*

gar·nish·ee /gaàrni shée/ *vt.* **(-eed, -ee·ing, -ees) 1. CONFISCATE DEBTOR'S MONEY** to take the money or property of a debtor by legal authority **2. SUMMONS DEBTOR** to serve somebody with a legal summons concerning the taking of wages or property to satisfy a debt ■ *n.* **SUMMONSED DEBTOR** somebody who is served with a legal summons concerning the taking of wages or property to satisfy a debt

gar·nish·ment /gaárnishmənt/ *n.* **1. LAW SUMMONS FOR DEBTOR** a legal summons or warning concerning the taking of property or wages of a debtor to satisfy a debt **2. DECORATION** an ornamentation or embellishment on or of something

gar·ni·ture /gaárnichər, -chòor/ *n.* something that decorates or embellishes something [15thC. From French, formed from *garnir* (see GARNISH).]

gar·pike /gaár pīk/ (*plural* **-pikes** *or* **-pike**) *n.* = **gar** *n.* 1

gar·ret /gérrət/ *n.* a room at the top of a house, immediately below the roof [15thC. From Old French *garite* "watchtower," from *garir* "to defend." Ultimately from a prehistoric Germanic word meaning "to protect" that also produced English *warn.*]

gar·ri·son /gérriss'n/ *n.* **1. STATIONED TROOPS** a body of troops stationed at a military post **2. PLACE FOR STATIONING TROOPS** a military post where troops are stationed ■ *vt.* **(-soned, -son·ing, -sons) 1. SUPPLY PLACE WITH TROOPS** to provide a fort or town with a military post and troops **2. STATION TROOPS AT PLACE** to station troops at a military post [13thC. From Old French, "fortification," formed from *garir* (see GARRET).]

Gar·ri·son /gárriss'n/, **William Lloyd** (1805–79) U.S. abolitionist and reformer. The founding editor of the abolitionist journal *The Liberator* (1831–65), he was an uncompromising and eloquent opponent of slavery. He later campaigned for the rights of women and Native Americans.

garrison cap *n.* MIL = **overseas cap**

gar·ri·son house *n.* a style of house common in New England in which the second floor projects over the first floor at the front [From its resemblance to early forts]

gar·rote /gə rót, -rṓt/, **gar·rotte** *n.* **1. METHOD OF EXECUTION BY STRANGULATION** a method of execution in which an iron band is tightened around the neck of the condemned person until death occurs **2. METAL BAND USED TO EXECUTE SOMEBODY** a band of metal placed around the neck in order to execute somebody by strangulation **3. WEAPON FOR STRANGULATION** a weapon consisting of a wire or cord with handles at either end, used in strangulation ■ *vt.* **(-rot·ed, -rot·ing, -rotes; -rot·ted, -rot·ting, -rottes) STRANGLE SOMEBODY** to execute or kill somebody by strangling with a garrotte [Early 17thC. From Spanish *garrote* "cudgel, stick for tightening a cord," perhaps of Celtic origin.]

gar·ru·li·ty /gə roólətee/ *n.* excessive or pointless talkativeness

gar·ru·lous /gérrələss/ *adj.* **1. TALKING TOO MUCH** excessively or pointlessly talkative **2. WORDY** using many or too many words [Early 17thC. Formed from Latin *garrulus,* from *garrire* "to chatter."] —**gar·ru·lous·ly** *adv.* —**gar·ru·lous·ness** *n.*

WORD KEY: SYNONYMS

See Synonyms at ***talkative.***

Gar·son /gaárss'n/, **Greer** (1908?–96) Irish-born U.S. actor, known for her matriarchal movie roles in the 1940s and 1950s. She won an Academy Award for *Mrs. Miniver* (1942).

gar·ter /gaártər/ *n.* **1. RETAINING BAND** an elastic band used to hold up a stocking, sock, or shirt sleeve **2. CLIP FOR STOCKINGS** a clip device, attached to a band, girdle, or belt, that fastens to the top of socks or stockings to hold them up ■ *vt.* **(-tered, -ter·ing, -ters) SUPPORT BY GARTER** to hold up a stocking, sock, or sleeve with a garter [14thC. From Old French *gartier,* from *garet* "bend of the knee," of Celtic origin.]

gar·ter belt *n.* a woman's undergarment in the form of a belt to which two or more garters are attached to hold up stockings

gar·ter snake *n.* a small nonpoisonous snake of North and Central America whose back is typically marked with yellow or red stripes running the length of the body. If disturbed, it may emit a pungent odor. Genus: *Thamnophis.*

garth /gaarth/ *n.* a small courtyard or enclosed space [14thC. From Old Norse *gar-r.*]

Popperfoto
Marcus Garvey

Gar·vey /gaárvee/, **Marcus** (1887–1940) Jamaican-born U.S. civil rights advocate. He founded the Universal Negro Improvement Association (1914) and created a "Back to Africa" movement in the United States. Full name **Marcus Moziah Garvey**

Gar·y /gárree/ steel-producing city in northwestern Indiana, on the southern shore of Lake Michigan, west of Portage. Population: 110,975 (1996).

Gar·y, Elbert Henry (1846–1927) U.S. business executive. He led the United States Steel Corporation (1903–27). Gary, Indiana, is named for him.

gas /gass/ *n.* (*plural* **gas·es** *or* **gas·ses**) **1.** CHEM **SUBSTANCE SUCH AS AIR** a substance such as air that is neither a solid nor a liquid at ordinary temperatures and that has the ability to expand indefinitely **2.** UTIL, GEOL **FOSSIL FUEL** a combustible gaseous substance such as natural gas or propane, used as a fuel **3.** AUTOMOT **GASOLINE** gasoline for internal-combustion engines **4.** AUTOMOT **CAR ACCELERATOR** the pedal used for accelerating a motor vehicle (*informal*) ○ *step on the gas* **5.** MIL, CRIMINOL **GAS FOR POISONING OR ASPHYXIATING** a gaseous mixture used as a poison, irritant, or asphyxiating agent **6.** PHARM **ANESTHETIC** a gaseous substance used as an anesthetic **7.** PHYSIOL **FLATULENCE** gaseous product of digestion (*informal*) **8.** MINING **METHANE AND AIR** the highly explosive product of methane combined with air **9. SOMEBODY OR SOMETHING ENTERTAINING** somebody or something such as an experience that is very thrilling or entertaining (*slang*) **10. NONSENSE** meaningless empty talk (*slang*) ■ *v.* **(gassed, gas·sing, gas·es** *or* **gas·ses) 1.** *vt.* **TO HARM SOMEBODY WITH GAS** to attack, injure, or kill a person or animal with a poisonous, irritating, or asphyxiating gas **2.** *vi.* **RELEASE GAS** to give off gas or a gas **3.** *vi.* **TALK IDLY** to talk too much, especially about unimportant matters (*informal*) [Mid-17thC. From Dutch, coined by the Flemish chemist J. B. van Helmont (1577–1644), based on Greek *khaos* "empty space" (source of English *chaos*).] —**gas·sing** *n.*

gas up *vti.* to fill the fuel tank of a motor vehicle with gasoline

gas·bag /gáss bàg/ *n.* somebody who talks too much, especially about unimportant matters (*informal*)

gas burn·er *n.* the nozzle or opening from which gas issues and burns, e.g., on a stove

gas cham·ber *n.* a room in which people are killed by means of poisonous gas (*technical*) = **gas oven**

gas chro·mat·o·graph *n.* a device used in gas chromatography for separating the volatile constituents of a substance

gas chro·ma·tog·ra·phy *n.* a method of separating the volatile constituents of a substance by means of gas, for the purpose of analysis

gas·con /gáskən/ *n.* somebody who is very boastful [Late 18thC. From the legendary boastfulness of the people of Gascony.]

Gas·con *n.* **1.** PEOPLES **SOMEBODY FROM GASCONY** somebody who lives in or was born or raised in Gascony, formerly a province in southwestern France **2.** LANGUAGE **FRENCH DIALECT** a dialect of French spoken in Gascony [14thC. Via French from, ultimately, Latin *Vasco* (source of English *Basque*).] —**Gas·con** *adj.*

gas con·stant *n.* the constant in an equation that describes the relation of the pressure and volume of a gas to its absolute temperature. It equals 8.314 joules per kelvin. Symbol **R**

gas-cooled re·ac·tor *n.* a nuclear reactor that uses carbon dioxide or helium as a coolant

Gas·coyne /gásk oyn/ river in northern Western Australia, that rises between the Collier and Robinson ranges and empties into the Indian Ocean at Shark Bay. Length: 472 mi./760 km.

gas-dis·charge tube *n.* a tube containing gas from which light is emitted when an electric current is passed through the gas atoms and excites them

gas·e·ous /gássee əss, gásh-/ *adj.* **1. RESEMBLING GAS** neither solid nor liquid and with a tendency to expand infinitely **2. VERBOSE** having or using too many words, especially in a meaningless way (*informal*) **3. CONTAINING GAS** full of gas, or containing a gas such as carbon dioxide [Late 18thC. Formed from GAS, on the model of AQUEOUS.] —**gas·e·ous·ness** *n.*

gas fit·ter *n.* a worker who fits and repairs gas pipes, fittings, and appliances

gas gan·grene *n.* a form of gangrene, caused by aerobic clostridia bacteria, in which gas forms in injured body tissue

gas-guz·zler *n.* a motor vehicle that burns comparatively large amounts of fuel (*informal*)

gash /gash/ *n.* **DEEP CUT** a long deep narrow slash or cut ■ *vt.* **(gashed, gash·ing, gash·es) MAKE CUT IN** to make a long deep narrow slash or cut in flesh or a surface [Mid-16thC. Alteration of Old Northern French *garser* "to cut," via late Latin *charaxare* "to sharpen" from Greek *kharassein* (source of English *character*).]

gas·hold·er /gáss hōldər/ *n.* a very large tank used to store gas that is used as combustible fuel

gas·house /gáss howss/ (*plural* **-houses**) *n.* = **gasworks**

gas·i·form /gássə fawrm/ *adj.* = **gaseous** *adj.* 1

gas·i·fy /gássə fī/ **(-fied, -fy·ing, -fies)** *vti.* to convert a solid or liquid into a gas, or become a gas — **gas·i·fi·ca·tion** /gàssəfi káysh'n/ *n.*

gas jet *n.* **1.** = **gas burner 2. GAS FLAME** a flame of burning gas

gas·ket /gáskət/ *n.* **1.** TECH **RUBBER SEAL** a piece of material such as rubber, used to render a joint impermeable to gas or liquid **2.** SAILING **ROPE FOR SAIL** a light line for securing a furled sail [Early 17thC. Origin uncertain: perhaps an alteration of French *garcette* "thin cord," literally "little girl," (perhaps in allusion to a girl's pigtail).] ◇ **blow a gasket** to explode in anger or rage (*informal*)

gas·kin /gáskin/ *n.* ZOOL **PART OF HORSE'S REAR LEG** the part of the back leg of a four-legged hoofed animal, especially a horse, that is equivalent to the lower thigh in humans ■ **gas·kins** *npl.* CLOTHES **GALLIGASKINS** galligaskins (*archaic*) [Late 16thC. Origin uncertain: perhaps a shortening of GALLIGASKINS, or an alteration of GASCON.]

gas·light /gás līt/ *n.* **1. ILLUMINATION FROM BURNING GAS** light produced by burning coal gas or natural gas **2. LAMP FUELED BY GAS** a lamp or fixture that produces light by burning gas

gas-liq·uid chro·ma·tog·ra·phy *n.* = **gas chromatography**

gas·lit /gáslit/ *adj.* illuminated by light from lamps or fixtures that burn gas

gas·man /gáss màn/ (*plural* **-men** /-mèn/) *n.* a worker who checks gas meters in order to note the amount of gas used in a specific period

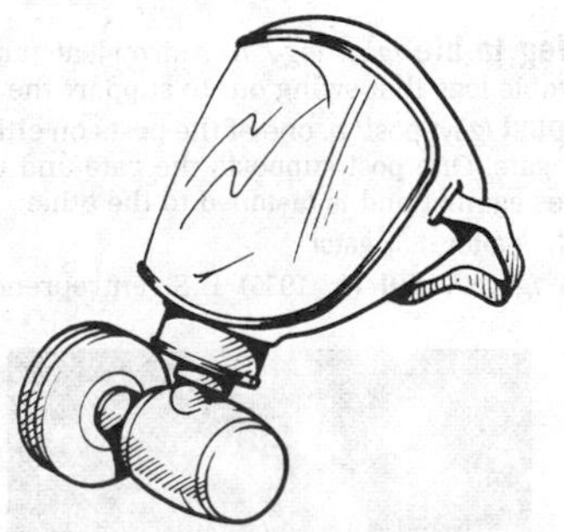
Gas mask

gas mask *n.* a mask provided with a filter and worn to protect the wearer's face and lungs from harmful gases

gas me·ter *n.* a device installed inside or outside a residential or commercial building to measure the amount of gas consumed in a specific period

gas·o·hol /gássə hàwl/ *n.* a fuel used in motor vehicles that consists of 90 percent gasoline blended with 10 percent alcohol. The alcohol is produced by the fermentation of an agricultural product high in sugar, e.g., corn. [Late 20thC. A blend of GASOLINE and ALCOHOL.]

gas·o·line /gássə leèn, gàssə leén/ *n.* a volatile flammable liquid made from petroleum and used as fuel in internal-combustion engines [Mid-19thC. Coined from GAS + -OL + -INE.]

gas·om·e·ter /ga sómmətər/ *n.* **1. GAS-MEASURING APPARATUS** an apparatus for measuring and storing gas in a laboratory **2.** = **gasholder**

gasp /gasp/ *n.* **1. SUDDEN BREATH** a sudden short audible intake of breath, e.g., in surprise or pain **2. DIFFICULT BREATHING** a laborious effort to breathe ■ *v.* **(gasped, gasp·ing, gasps) 1.** *vi.* **LABOR TO BREATHE** to breathe with difficulty **2.** *vi.* **BREATHE IN SHARPLY** draw in breath loudly and spasmodically **3.** *vt.* **SAY SOMETHING WITH GASP** to say something with a sudden intake of breath [14thC. From Old Norse *geispa* "to yawn."] ◇ **the last gasp** somebody's final attempt or action, or the final phase of something

Gas·pé /ga spáy/ city in southeastern Quebec Province, Canada, near Forillon National Park. Population: 16,517 (1996).

Gas·pé Pen·in·su·la peninsula in southeastern Quebec Province, Canada, bounded by the St. Lawrence River, Chaleur Bay, and New Brunswick. Area: 11,390 sq. mi./29,500 sq. km.

gasp·er /gáspər/ *n. U.K.* a cigarette, especially a cheap one (*dated slang*)

gas·per·gou /gàspər goó/ (*plural* **-gous** *or* **-gou**) *n. Southern U.S.* ZOOL the freshwater drum, native to North and Central America [Early 9thC. From Louisiana French *casseburgau*.]

gas plant *n.* a Eurasian perennial plant of the rue family with white flowers and strong-smelling leaves that give off a flammable gas. Latin name: *Dictamnus albus.*

gas·ser /gássər/ *n.* **1.** UTIL **GAS WELL** a well that produces natural gas **2. FUN THING** something, such as a joke, that is very thrilling or entertaining (*slang*)

gas sta·tion *n.* a place at which drivers can buy fuel, oil, and other motoring supplies, and sometimes also have car repairs done. ◊ **service station**

gas·sy /gássee/ **(-si·er, -si·est)** *adj.* **1. FULL OF GAS** full of or containing gas such as carbon dioxide **2. LIKE GAS** resembling gas **3. VERBOSE** having or using too many words, especially in a meaningless way (*informal*) — **gas·si·ly** *adv.* —**gas·si·ness** *n.*

gas·tight /gás tīt/ *adj.* preventing any gas from passing through

gastr- *prefix.* = **gastro**

gas·trec·to·my /gas tréktəmee/ (*plural* **-mies**) *n.* surgical removal of all or part of the stomach. It is usually performed in the treatment of stomach cancer or severe stomach ulcers.

gas·tric /gástrik/ *adj.* relating to, involving, or near the stomach [Mid-17thC. From modern Latin *gastricus*, from Greek *gastēr* "stomach." Ultimately from an Indo-European word meaning "to devour" that is also the ancestor of English *gangrene* and *cress*.]

gas·tric juice *n.* the acidic digestive fluid secreted by glands in the stomach

gas·tric ul·cer *n.* an erosion in the stomach wall caused by gastric acid, digestive enzymes, and other factors that may include bacterial infection

gas·trin /gástrin/ *n.* a hormone produced in the stomach and duodenum that increases the production of gastric acid

gas·tri·tis /gass trítəss/ *n.* inflammation of the mucous membrane that lines the stomach. It may be acute or chronic, and it is often associated with excessive intake of alcohol.

gastro- *prefix.* stomach, belly ○ *gastrectomy* [From Greek *gastr-*, the stem of *gastēr* "belly" (see GASTRIC)]

gas·troc·ne·mi·us /gàs trok neémee əss, -trək-/ (*plural* **-i** /-mee ī, -mee ī/) *n.* the largest muscle in the calf of the leg, extending from the thigh bone to the Achilles tendon. When it contracts it causes the foot to point downward. [Late 17thC. Via modern Latin from Greek *gastroknēmia* "calf of the leg," literally "stomach of the leg" (from its bulging form).]

gas·tro·en·ter·i·tis /gàstrō entə rítəss/ *n.* inflammation of the stomach and the intestines, usually as a result of bacterial or viral infection.

The symptoms include vomiting and diarrhea, and the illness typically lasts three to five days.

gas·tro·en·ter·ol·o·gy /gàstrō entə róllәjee/ *n.* the branch of medicine concerned with the study and treatment of diseases of the stomach and intestines and their associated organs —**gas·tro·en·ter·o·log·ic** /gàstrō entərə lójjik/ *adj.* —**gas·tro·en·ter·ol·o·gist** /-entə róllәjist/ *n.*

gas·tro·in·tes·ti·nal /gàstrō in téstən'l/ *adj.* relating to the stomach and intestines

gas·tro·lith /gástrə lìth/ *n.* **1.** ZOOL **STONE SWALLOWED TO AID DIGESTION** a stone swallowed by an animal such as a bird or dinosaur, as an aid to the digestion of food **2.** MED **STONE FORMED IN STOMACH** a stone that has formed in the stomach

gas·tro·nome /gástrə nōm/, **gas·tron·o·mist** /gas trónnəmist/ *n.* a connoisseur of good food [Early 19thC. From French, back-formation from *gastronomie* (see GASTRONOMY).]

gas·tron·o·my /gas trónnəmee/ (*plural* **-mies**) *n.* **1.** **GOURMET EATING** the art and appreciation of preparing and eating good food **2.** **PARTICULAR CUISINE** a particular style of cooking or dining, e.g., one that is typical of a country or region [Early 19thC. Via French *gastronomie* from Greek *gastronomia*, an alteration of *gastrologia*, literally "study of the stomach."] —**gas·tro·nom·ic** /gàstrə nómmik/ *adj.* —**gas·tro·nom·i·cal·ly** /-nómmiklee/ *adv.*

gas·tro·plas·ty /gástrə plàstee/ (*plural* **-ties**) *n.* a surgical operation to repair a malformation of the stomach

gas·tro·pod /gástrə pòd/ *n.* a mollusk that has a head with eyes, a single shell, and a large flattened foot. Limpets, snails, and slugs are types of gastropod. Class: Gastropoda. [Early 19thC. From modern Latin *Gastropoda*, class name, literally "stomach-foot."] —**gas·tro·pod** *adj.* —**gas·trop·o·dan** /gas tróppəd'n/ *adj.* —**gas·trop·o·dous** /-dəss/ *adj.*

gas·tro·scope /gástrə skōp/ *n.* an instrument passed through the mouth and used to examine the stomach, consisting of a flexible tube that contains optical fibers coupled to an eyepiece and light source —**gas·tro·scop·ic** /gàstrə skóppik/ *adj.* —**gas·tros·co·py** /gas tróskəpee/ *n.*

gas·tros·to·my /gas tróstəmee/ (*plural* **-mies**) *n.* a surgical operation in which an opening is made through the wall of the stomach and is joined to an opening in the adjacent abdominal wall. It is performed to allow food and liquids to be placed directly into the stomach via a tube when the esophagus is affected by disease or recovering from surgery.

gas·trot·o·my /gas tróttəmee/ (*plural* **-mies**) *n.* a surgical incision into the stomach, for examination of the cavity or to remove a foreign object

gas·tro·vas·cu·lar /gàstrō váskyələr/ *adj.* used to describe a part of the body involved in both digestion and circulation, e.g., the central body cavity of certain jellyfish

gas·tru·la /gástrələ/ (*plural* **-las** *or* **-lae** /-lee/) *n.* the stage in embryonic development after the blastula during which the embryo develops two layers [Late 19thC. From modern Latin, literally "little stomach," formed from Greek *gastēr* "stomach" (see GASTRIC).] —**gas·tru·lar** *adj.*

gas·tru·la·tion /gàstrə láysh'n/ *n.* the process of cell movements by which a developing embryo forms distinct layers that later grow into particular organs —**gas·tru·late** /gástrə làyt/ *vi.*

gas tur·bine *n.* an internal-combustion engine in which a turbine is turned by hot gases consisting of compressed air and the products of the fuel's combustion

gas·works /gás wùrks/ *n.* a factory where gas for heating and illuminating is produced, especially from coal (*takes a singular or plural verb*)

gat[1] /gat/ *n.* a passage or channel of water that extends inland from a shore [Late 16thC. Origin uncertain: probably from Old Norse *gat* "hole."]

gat[2] /gat/ *n.* a handgun (*dated slang*) [Early 20thC. Shortening of GATLING GUN.]

gat[3] past tense of **get** (*archaic*)

gate /gayt/ *n.* **1.** **HINGED BARRIER ACROSS GAP** a movable barrier, usually on hinges, that closes a gap in a fence or wall **2.** **OPENING IN WALL** an opening in a wall or fence **3.** **OPENING IN DEFENSIVE STRUCTURE** an opening in a castle or city wall or other defensive structure **4.** **POINT OF ACCESS** a means of access or entrance **5.** **BARRIER AT TOLLBOOTH** a movable barrier restricting access, e.g., at a tollbooth **6.** **STARTING GATE** a starting gate (*informal*) **7.** TRANSP **ARRIVAL OR DEPARTURE POINT FOR PASSENGERS** the area at a railroad or bus station or an airport where passengers arrive and depart **8.** **BARRIER FOR FLUID** a sliding barrier, valve, or other mechanism for regulating the passage of a fluid **9.** **SPECTATORS ADMITTED TO EVENT** the total number of persons who pay for admission to an entertainment or sports event **10.** **TOTAL MONEY FROM TICKETS** the total amount of money paid for tickets of admission to an entertainment or sports event **11.** SKIING **PATH BETWEEN POLES IN SLALOM** the space between two markers through which a skier passes in a slalom race **12.** COMPUT **LOGIC CIRCUIT** a logical device in a computer, with one output channel and one or more input channels, that emits a signal only when certain input conditions are met **13.** ELECTRON ENG **REGULATING SWITCH** an electronic switch that regulates the flow of current or the passage of a signal in a circuit **14.** ROWING **HINGED FASTENING FOR OAR** a fastening with a hinge that serves to keep an oar in its oarlock **15.** *N England, Scotland* **WAY** a path or road **16.** *N England, Scotland* **HABIT** a habitual method or style of doing something ■ *vt.* (**gat·ed, gat·ing, gates**) **1.** **CONTROL USING GATE** to control or regulate somebody or something with a gate **2.** **PUT GATE IN SOMETHING** to install a gate in something, e.g., in a fence [Old English *geat*. Partly from, and influenced by, Old Norse *gata* "path" (source also of English *gait*). Ultimately from a prehistoric Germanic word meaning "opening in a wall."]

ga·teau /ga tṓ, gaa-/ (*plural* **-teaux** *or* **-teaus**), **gâ·teau** (*plural* **-teaux** /-tṓ/) *n.* **1.** **RICH CAKE** a rich cake, usually consisting of several layers held together with a cream filling **2.** **BAKED FOOD** food baked and served in a form resembling a cake [Mid-19thC. From French, "cake."]

gate·crash·er /gáyt kràshər/ *n.* somebody who attends a party, entertainment, or sports event without an invitation or ticket —**gate·crash** /gáyt kràsh/ *vti.*

gate·fold /gáyt fòld/ *n.* a page in a publication that is larger than the other pages and is folded to fit

gate·house /gáyt hòwss/ (*plural* **-hous·es** /-hòwzəz/) *n.* a building or house above or beside a gate

gate·keep·er /gáyt keepər/ *n.* **1.** **GUARD AT GATE** a supervisor or guard who tends a gate **2.** **ACCESS CONTROLLER** an individual or group that controls access to somebody or something

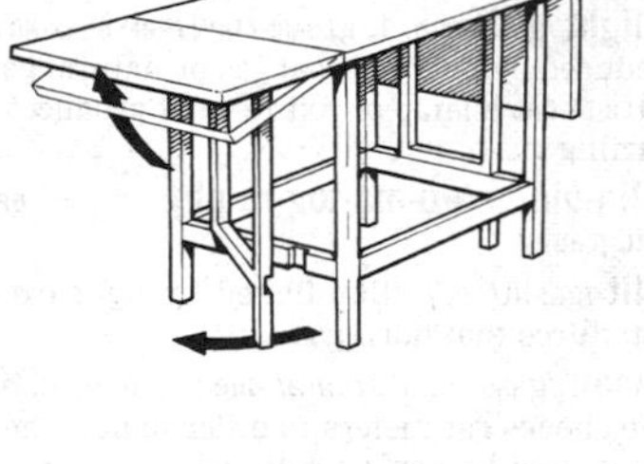

Gateleg table

gate·leg ta·ble /gàyt leg-/ *n.* a drop-leaf table with movable legs that swing out to support the leaves

gate·post /gáyt pōst/ *n.* one of the posts on either side of a gate. One post supports the gate and the gate closes against and is fastened to the other.

ga·ter, **'ga·ter** *n.* = **gator**

Gates /gayts/, **Bill** (*b.* 1955) U.S. entrepreneur. He cofounded Microsoft Corporation to develop the DOS operating system, and developed a major international telecommunications corporation. He wrote *The Road Ahead* (1995) about his vision of society and technology. Full name **William Henry Gates III**

Popperfoto

Bill Gates

Gates, Horatio (1728?–1806) British-born U.S. army officer. A general in the Continental Army, he was credited with the American victory at Saratoga in 1777.

Gates of the Arc·tic Na·tion·al Park and Pre·serve national park consisting mainly of tundra in northern Alaska, north of the Arctic Circle. Area: 11,756 sq. mi./30,448 sq. km.

gate·way /gáyt wày/ *n.* **1.** **OPENING FITTED WITH GATE** an opening that may be closed by a gate **2.** **ACCESS POINT** a means of entrance or access to somebody or something **3.** COMPUT **COMPUTER-NETWORK CONNECTION** software or hardware that links two computer networks

gate·way drug *n.* a drug that does not cause physical dependence but may lead to the use of addictive drugs

gath·er /gáthər/ *v.* (**-ered, -er·ing, -ers**) **1.** *vti.* **FORM INTO GROUP** to bring people or things together, or come together, to form a group **2.** *vt.* **HARVEST SOMETHING** to pick or harvest a crop **3.** *vt.* **COLLECT IDEAS OR DATA** to compile something such as information or ideas from various sources **4.** *vt.* **ATTRACT FOLLOWING** to attract a group of people as supporters, followers, or an audience ○ *The street players have gathered quite a crowd.* **5.** *vti.* **ACCUMULATE SOMETHING** to accumulate a gradually increasing mass or quantity of something, or to be accumulated gradually ○ *clouds gathered on the horizon* **6.** *vt.* **DRAW ON SOMETHING** to summon up energies, courage, or strength from within **7.** *vt.* **SURMISE SOMETHING** to conclude something from intuition or observation **8.** *vt.* **BRING CLOSE** to draw somebody or something close **9.** *vt.* **LIFT SOMEBODY OR SOMETHING UP** to pick or scoop somebody or something up **10.** *vti.* **WRINKLE BROW** to draw the brow into wrinkles, or be drawn into wrinkles **11.** *vt.* SEW **PULL FABRIC TOGETHER** to draw fabric together in a series of folds along a line of stitching **12.** *vt.* PRINTING **PUT PAGES IN ORDER** to assemble the printed sections of a book in the correct order for binding **13.** *vt.* CRAFT **PREPARE MOLTEN GLASS FOR BLOWING** to collect molten glass at the end of a tube for blowing and shaping **14.** *vi.* MED **FORM PUS-FILLED HEAD** to form and fill with pus ■ *n.* **1.** SEW **FOLD IN FABRIC** one in a series of folds in fabric **2.** CRAFT **MOLTEN GLASS BALL** a ball of molten glass collected on a tube for blowing and shaping [Old English *gaderian*. Ultimately from an Indo-European word meaning "to bring together" that is also the ancestor of English *together* and *good*.] —**gath·er·er** *n.*

WORD KEY: SYNONYMS

See Synonyms at ***collect***.

gath·er·ing /gáthəring/ *n.* **1.** **ASSEMBLY** a meeting or crowd of people **2.** **CLUSTER OF THINGS** a collection of objects **3.** **COLLECTING OF SOMETHING** the collecting of people or objects into a group **4.** MED **BOIL** a pus-filled swelling **5.** SEW **FOLDS IN CLOTH** a series of folds in fabric

Gat·ling gun /gáttling-/ *n.* an early machine gun with multiple barrels firing in rotation [Mid-19thC. Named for the U.S. inventor Richard Jordan *Gatling* (1818–1903), who developed it.]

ga·tor /gáytər/, **'ga·tor, ga·ter, 'ga·ter** *n.* an alligator (*informal*) [Mid-19thC. Shortening.]

GATT /gat/, **Gatt** *abbr.* HIST General Agreement on Tariffs and Trade

Ga·tún, Lake /ga tóon láyk/ artificial lake on the Chagres River in Panama, an important part of the Panama Canal system. Area: 166 sq. mi./430 sq. km.

Gat·wick /gáttwik/ London's second largest international airport, located to the south of the city on the border between the counties of Surrey and Sussex, England. It is on the site of an old racecourse.

gauche /gōsh/ *adj.* lacking grace or tact in social situations [Mid-18thC. From French, literally "left-handed."] —**gauche·ly** *adv.* —**gauche·ness** *n.*

gau·che·rie /gōshə rée/ *n.* **1.** **SOCIAL AWKWARDNESS** a lack of grace or tact in social situations **2.** **SOCIALLY AWKWARD ACT** an act that is graceless or tactless [Late 18thC. From French, formed from *gauche* (see GAUCHE).]

gau·cho /gów chō/ *n.* (*plural* **-chos**) **S AMERICAN COWBOY** a cowboy of the South American pampas or prairie

■ **gau·chos, gau·cho pants** *npl.* CLOTHES **TYPE OF CULOTTES** women's culottes adapted from the wide-bottomed mid-calf leather pants worn by South American cowboys and first popular in the late 1960s [Early 19thC. From American Spanish, of uncertain origin: probably from Araucanian *kaučū*.]

gaud /gawd/ *n.* a showy trinket or ornament [14thC. Origin uncertain: perhaps via Old French *gaudir* "to rejoice" from Latin *gaudere* (source of English *joy* and *rejoice*).]

gaud·er·y /gáwdəree/ (*plural* **-ies**) *n.* showy and ostentatious clothing or jewelry, or its display

gaud·y[1] /gáwdee/ (**-i·er, -i·est**) *adj.* brightly colored or showily decorated to an unpleasant or vulgar degree [15thC. From GAUD.] —**gaud·i·ly** *adv.* —**gaud·i·ness** *n.*

gaud·y[2] /gáwdee/ (*plural* **-ies**) *n. U.K.* an annual celebration or dinner held at certain universities and university colleges [Mid-16thC. From Latin *gaudium* "joy" (source of English *joy*), from *gaudere* "to rejoice."]

gauge /gayj/, **gage** *vt.* (**gauged, gaug·ing, gaug·es; gaged, gag·ing, gag·es**) **1. CALCULATE** to determine the amount, quantity, size, or extent of something ○ *It's quite difficult to gauge the distance accurately.* **2. EVALUATE** to form a judgment of something uncertain or variable, especially somebody's behavior, feelings, or abilities ○ *Try to gauge his mood before raising the proposal.* **3. ENSURE CONFORMITY TO STANDARD** to ensure that something conforms to a standard of measurement ■ *n.* **1. MEASUREMENT** a standard measurement or scale of measurement **2. MEASURING DEVICE** a device or instrument for measuring an amount or quantity or for testing accuracy **3. CRITERION** a standard or system of measurement for assessing somebody or something ○ *a gauge of the applicant's ability* **4.** RAIL **DISTANCE BETWEEN RAILS** the distance between the two rails of a railroad track **5.** AUTOMOT **DISTANCE BETWEEN WHEELS** the distance between two wheels on an axle of a vehicle **6. THICKNESS OF WIRE** the diameter of something, especially of wire or a needle **7. THICKNESS OF SHEET METAL** the thickness of a thin material such as sheet metal or plastic film **8.** NAUT **RELATIVE POSITION** the position of a ship in relation to another vessel and the wind **9.** TEXTILES **FINENESS OF A KNIT** the fineness of knitted fabric expressed in terms of the number of loops for each unit of width **10.** CONSTR **ADDED PROPORTION OF PLASTER OF PARIS** the proportion of plaster of Paris that is added to mortar to speed up the setting of the mixture [14thC. From Old Northern French, a variant of French *jauge*, of uncertain origin: probably ultimately from a prehistoric Germanic word.] —**gauge·a·ble** *adj.*

gaug·er /gáyjər/, **gag·er** *n.* **1.** *U.K.* **CUSTOMS OFFICER INSPECTING BULK GOODS** a customs officer whose job is to inspect bulk goods on which duty is supposed to be paid **2. SOMETHING FOR GAUGING** a person who or instrument that gauges something

Gau·guin /gō gáN/, **Paul** (1848–1903) French painter. One of the most influential postimpressionist painters, he is known for his use of flat fields of deep color. After 1891 he lived mostly in Polynesia, the inspiration of many for his most powerful works. Full name **Eugène Henri Paul Gauguin**

Gau·ha·ti /gow háatee/ industrial city and port on the Brahmaputra River in Assam State, northeastern India. Population: 584,342 (1991).

Gaul /gawl/ *n.* **1.** HIST **ANCIENT FRANCE** in ancient times, a region of western Europe that covered roughly what is now France, Belgium, and neighboring parts of Italy, the Netherlands, and Germany. It was invaded and conquered by the Romans first before 100 B.C. and then again in the Gallic Wars (58–51 B.C.) under Julius Caesar. **2.** HIST, PEOPLES **SOMEBODY FROM GAUL** somebody who was born in or lived in ancient Gaul **3.** PEOPLES **FRENCH PERSON** somebody who is French [15thC. From Latin *Gallus*, of uncertain origin: probably from Celtic.]

Gaul·ish /gáwlish/ *n.* **EXTINCT CELTIC LANGUAGE** an extinct language spoken in Gaul before the Roman conquest and belonging to the Celtic branch of the Indo-European languages ■ *adj.* **OF GAUL OR GAULISH** relating to or typical of ancient Gaul, or its people, language, or culture

Gaull·ism /gáw lìzzəm/ *n.* **1. BELIEFS OF CHARLES DE GAULLE** the nationalist and conservative principles and policies of General Charles de Gaulle, leader of France after World War II, and his followers **2. FRENCH POLITICAL MOVEMENT** the political movement founded on the principles of Charles de Gaulle —**Gaull·ist** *n., adj.*

gaunt /gawnt/ *adj.* **1. THIN** extremely thin and bony in appearance **2. STARK** stark in outline or appearance [15thC. Origin unknown.] —**gaunt·ly** *adv.* —**gaunt·ness** *n.*

gaunt·let[1] /gáwntlət/, **gant·let** *n.* a glove with a long wide cuff that covers part of the forearm, usually made of fabric, leather, or, in the past, metal, when worn as part of armor [15thC. From French *gantelet* "little glove," ultimately from a prehistoric Germanic word.] ◇ **throw down the gauntlet** to issue a challenge

gaunt·let[2] /gáwntlət/, **gant·let** *n.* a punishment formerly used in the military in which somebody was forced to run between two lines of men armed with weapons who beat him as he passed [Mid-17thC. Alteration, influenced by GAUNTLET[1], of *gantlop*, from Swedish *gatlopp* "passageway."] ◇ **run the gauntlet, run the gantlet** to have to endure attack or criticism from all sides

gaur /gowr/ *n.* a large wild ox with a dark coat that lives in the mountains of southeastern Asia. Latin name: *Bos gaurus.* [Early 19thC. From Sanskrit *gaura*; ultimately from an Indo-European word that is also the ancestor of English *cow*.]

Gause's prin·ci·ple /gòwzəz-/, **Gause prin·ci·ple** *n.* ECOL = **competitive exclusion** [Named for the Russian biologist G. F. *Gause* (born 1910) , who established the principle.]

gauss /gowss/ (*plural* **gauss** *or* **gauss·es**) *n.* the centimeter-gram-second unit of magnetic flux density, equivalent to 10^{-4} tesla. Symbol **G** [Late 19thC. Named for the German mathematician Karl Friedrich *Gauss* (1777–1855), who applied mathematical principles to magnetism.]

Gauss·i·an /gówssee ən/ *adj.* with the characteristics or shape of a normal curve or normal statistical distribution [Late 19thC. Named for K. F. *Gauss* (see GAUSS).]

Gau·teng /khow téng/ province created in 1994 in northern South Africa, containing Johannesburg, the province's capital, Soweto, and Pretoria. Population: 7,048,300 (1995). Area: 7,260 sq. mi./18,810 sq. km.

gauze /gawz/ *n.* **1.** TEXTILES **FINELY WOVEN FABRIC** a thin loosely woven cloth, usually cotton or silk, that is almost transparent and is used for curtains and clothes **2.** MED **SURGICAL DRESSING** a dressing made of loosely woven material such as cotton that is applied in many layers to wounds **3.** INDUST **WIRE MESH** a thin mesh made of wire or other material **4. HAZE** a fine haze or mist [Mid-16thC. From French *gaze*, of uncertain origin: perhaps named for the town of *Gaza* in Palestine, where fine fabrics were made, or perhaps ultimately from Arabic *qazz* "raw silk."] —**gauz·i·ly** /gáwzee/ *adv.* —**gauz·y** *adj.*

ga·vage /gə vaázh/ *n.* the feeding of an animal or a person through a tube passed into the stomach [Late 19thC. From French, formed from *gaver* "to stuff down the throat."]

gave past tense of **give**

gav·el /gávvəl/ *n.* **SMALL HAMMER** a small hammer used by a judge, chair of a meeting, or auctioneer to draw people's attention or to mark the conclusion of a transaction ■ *vti.* (**-eled, -el·ing, -els**) **USE GAVEL** to use a gavel to bring an end to something or to stop discussion [Early 19thC. Origin unknown.]

gav·el-to-gav·el *adj.* extending from the beginning to the end of a political meeting or similar event (*informal*)

ga·vi·al /gáyvee əl/ *n.* a large reptile resembling a crocodile that has a very long narrow snout, feeds on fish and frogs, and is native to India, Borneo, and Sumatra. Latin name: *Gavialis gangeticus.* [Early 19thC. Via French (possibly as a scribal error) from Hindi *ghaṛiyāl* GHARIAL.]

ga·votte /gə vót/ *n.* **1.** DANCE **FRENCH COUNTRY DANCE** a French country dance popular in the 18th century and similar to the minuet but slightly faster in pace **2.** MUSIC **MUSIC FOR GAVOTTE** a piece of music for the gavotte, written in 4/4 time [Late 19thC. Via French from, ultimately, Provençal *Gavot* "an inhabitant of the Alps."]

Ga·wain /gə wáyn/ *n.* in Arthurian legend, a knight who was the enemy of Sir Lancelot and who fought a mysterious green knight

Gawd /gawd/, **gawd** *interj., n.* God (*slang*) (*used to suggest irony or rustic pronunciation in oaths*)

gawk /gawk/ *vi.* (**gawked, gawk·ing, gawks**) **STARE** to stare stupidly (*informal*) ■ *n.* **CLUMSY PERSON** somebody who is awkward or clumsy (*dated insult*) [Late 17thC. Origin uncertain: perhaps from, ultimately, Old Norse *gá* "to heed."]

WORD KEY: SYNONYMS

See Synonyms at ***gaze***.

gawk·y /gáwkee/ (**-i·er, -i·est**) *adj.* awkward and clumsy, often because of being tall and not well coordinated (*informal*) —**gawk·i·ly** *adv.* —**gaw·ki·ness** *n.*

gay /gay/ *adj.* **1. HOMOSEXUAL** homosexual in sexual orientation **2. MERRY** full of light-heartedness and merriment (*dated*) **3. BRIGHT IN COLOR** brightly colored (*dated*) **4. CAREFREE** having or showing a carefree spirit (*dated*) **5. DEBAUCHED** leading a debauched or dissolute life (*dated*) ■ *n.* **SOMEBODY HOMOSEXUAL** a homosexual, especially a male homosexual [13thC. From Old French *gai* "happy," of uncertain origin: probably from Frankish.] —**gay·ness** *n.*

ga·yal /gə yaál/ (*plural* **-yal** *or* **-yals**) *n.* a wild or semidomesticated ox of India and Myanmar (Burma) with a dark coat and white leg markings. Latin name: *Bos frontalis.* [Late 18thC. From Bengali.]

Marvin Gaye

Gaye /gay/, **Marvin** (1939–84) U.S. singer and songwriter. He was one of the most successful soul singers from the 1960s and had an international bestselling hit with "I Heard It Through the Grapevine" (1968).

gay·e·ty *n.* = **gaiety**

gay·ly *adv.* = **gaily**

gay pride *n.* a movement in the gay community that encourages gays to be open about their homosexuality and to be proud of being gay (*informal*)

gaz. *abbr.* **1.** gazette **2.** gazetteer

Ga·za /gaázə/ seaport and principal city of the Gaza Strip, on the Mediterranean coast. An important city in biblical times, it has both historic and current political significance. Population: 293,000 (1990).

ga·zar /gə zaár/ *n.* a stiff loosely woven kind of silk [Mid-20thC. Origin uncertain: perhaps from, ultimately, Arabic *qazz* "raw silk."]

Ga·za Strip region on the eastern Mediterranean coast bordered on the south by Egypt and on the east and north by Israel. Administered by Egypt from 1949 and Israel from 1967, it became an autonomous zone under the control of the Palestinian National Authority in 1994. The city of Gaza is the region's administrative center. Population: 731,296 (1994). Area: 139 sq. mi./360 sq. km.

gaze /gayz/ *vi.* (**gazed, gaz·ing, gaz·es**) **LOOK FIXEDLY** to look for a long time with a fixed stare ○ *He gazed longingly at the yacht.* ■ *n.* **STEADY LOOK** a long steady look or stare [14thC. Origin uncertain: perhaps from a Scandinavian language.] —**gaz·er** *n.*

WORD KEY: SYNONYMS

gaze, stare, gape, gawk, gawp, ogle, rubberneck

CORE MEANING: to look at somebody or something steadily or at length

gaze to look at somebody or something steadily and for a long time, especially with great attention, admiration, or fascination; **stare** to look at somebody or something fixedly and intently, often with wide-open eyes, in amazement, fear, or admiration. It can also be used to mean to look fixedly at somebody or something in a rude way or in a way that makes the person being looked at feel uncomfortable; **gape** to look at somebody or something in amazement or wonder, usually with an open mouth; **gawk** an informal word meaning to look at somebody or something fixedly and often rather rudely, especially with a stupid expression; **gawp** an informal word used in British English with the same meaning as "gawk"; **ogle** to look steadily at somebody in a lecherous, suggestive way; **rubberneck** an informal word, usually used showing disapproval, meaning to look fixedly at somebody or something with great curiosity.

---

ga·ze·bo /gə zeébō/ (*plural* **-bos** *or* **-boes** /-bōz/) *n.* a small, usually open-sided and slightly elevated building, situated in a spot that commands a pleasant view [Mid-18thC. Origin uncertain: perhaps from GAZE on the model of Latin future tenses in *-ebo*, intended to mean "I shall gaze."]

gaze·hound /gáyz hòwnd/ *n.* a dog e.g., a greyhound or Afghan hound that hunts by sight rather than by smell

Gazelle

ga·zelle /gə zél/ (*plural* **-zelles** *or* **-zelle**) *n.* a small graceful swift antelope, native to the arid plains of Africa and Asia, that has long ringed horns and black face markings. Genera: *Gazella* and *Procapra.* [Early 17thC. From Old French *gazel*, of uncertain origin: probably via Spanish from Arabic *ghazāl*.]

ga·zette /gə zét/ *n.* **1.** NEWSPAPER a newspaper, especially the official paper of an organization ○ *the Medical Union Gazette* **2.** *U.K.* PUBLICATION WITH OFFICIAL NEWS an official publication in which government appointments, public notices, lists of bankruptcies, and other items appear ■ *vt.* (**-zet·ted, -zet·ting, -zettes**) *U.K.* PUBLISH IN GAZETTE to publish or announce something or name somebody in a gazette (*often passive*) [Early 17thC. Directly or via French from Italian *gazzetta*, from Venetian dialect *gazeta de la novità* "a pennyworth of news."]

gaz·et·teer /gàzzə teér/ *n.* **1.** GEOGRAPHICAL REFERENCE BOOK a dictionary or index of places, usually with descriptive or statistical information **2.** JOURNALIST a journalist (*archaic*)

gaz·pa·cho /gə spaáchō, gəz paáchō/ (*plural* **-chos** /-chōz/) *n.* a chilled Mexican or Spanish soup based on stock or tomato juice and containing chopped raw vegetables and seasoning [Early 19thC. From Spanish.]

G.B. *abbr.* **1.** PHYS gilbert **2.** Great Britain

Gbyte *abbr.* COMPUT gigabyte

GCA *abbr.* AIR ground-controlled approach

G.C.D. *abbr.* greatest common divisor

G.C.F., **g.c.f.** *abbr.* MATH greatest common factor

G clef *n.* = **treble clef**

Gd *symbol.* gadolinium

GD *abbr.* HOUSEHOLD garbage disposal

gd. *abbr.* good

G·dansk /gə dánsk/ city, seaport, and shipbuilding center in northern Poland. It is situated at the mouth of the Vistula River, on the Baltic Sea. Population: 462,800 (1995). German **Danzig**

g'day /gə dáy/ *interj.* *Australian* hello or good day (*informal*) [Contraction]

GDP *abbr.* gross domestic product

GDR, **G.D.R.** *abbr.* German Democratic Republic

gds. *abbr.* goods

Ge *symbol.* germanium

ge- *prefix.* = **geo-** (*used before vowels*)

ge·an·ti·cline /jee ánti klīn/ *n.* a large region of rock raised up from the earth's surface [Late 19thC. Coined from Greek *gē* "earth" + ANTICLINE.] —**ge·an·ti·cli·nal** /jee ànti klīn'l/ *adj.*

gear /geer/ *n.* **1.** ENG DEVICE TO TRANSMIT MOTION a mechanism that transmits motion from one part to another part for performing a specific function ○ *steering gear* **2.** ENG PART THAT TRANSMITS MOTION a toothed mechanical part, e.g., a wheel or cylinder that engages with a similar toothed part to transmit motion from one rotating body to another **3.** ENG FIXED TRANSMISSION SETTING one of several fixed transmission settings in a vehicle that determine power or direction **4.** LEVEL OF EFFICIENCY the particular speed or efficiency with which somebody works (*informal*) ○ *I feel as if I'm still in first gear.* **5.** AUTOMOT ENGAGED STATE the state of a vehicle when one of its gears is engaged ○ *The car won't start when it's in gear* **6.** MACHINERY a piece or system of machinery with a particular function **7.** EQUIPMENT the equipment that is needed for a specific activity (*informal*) ○ *hiking gear* **8.** FASHION CLOTHES clothes and accessories of a particular kind (*informal*) ○ *You've got to have the right gear* **9.** NAUT SAILING EQUIPMENT the equipment, rigging, and other objects that belong to a particular boat or sailor **10.** RIDING HARNESS a horse's harness ■ *vt.* (**geared, gear·ing, gears**) **1.** ENG PUT GEARS IN SOMETHING to equip something with gears **2.** AUTOMOT ENGAGE GEAR to put a vehicle into gear [13thC. From Old Norse *gervi* "to make ready."]

gear to/toward *vt.* to adapt or adjust something so that it fits in or works effectively with something else (*usually passive*) ○ *We've tried to gear ourselves to the younger market.*

gear up *vti.* to prepare somebody or take action in preparation for something or to do something (*usually passive or continuous*) ○ *We're all geared up for the next round of talks.*

gear·box /geér bòks/ *n.* **1.** CASING AROUND GEARS the protective casing surrounding a set of gears **2.** = **transmission**

gear·ing /geéring/ *n.* **1.** SET OF GEARS a set of mechanical gears, or the power that it provides ○ *complaints about the gearing on the older model* **2.** PROVIDING SOMETHING WITH GEARS the process or act of providing a system with gears **3.** *U.K.* FIN = **leverage**

gear lev·er *n. U.K.* = **gearshift**

gear·shift /geér shìft/ *n.* a lever or mechanism in a car or other vehicle or machine that is used to shift or engage gears

gear train *n.* a collection of gears used to transmit power

gear·wheel /geér hweèl/ *n.* = **gear** *n.* 2

Gecko

geck·o /gékō/ (*plural* **-os** *or* **-oes** /-ōz/) *n.* a small tropical or subtropical nocturnal insect-eating lizard with hooked ridges on the pads of its feet that permit it to climb smooth vertical surfaces. Family: Gekkonidae. [Late 18thC. From Malay dialect *geko(k)*.]

ge·dank·en·ex·per·i·ment /gə daángkən ik spèrrimənt/ *n.* a test of a hypothesis that can be performed only in the mind [Mid-20thC. From German.]

gee *n.* MONEY = **G** (*informal*)

geek /geek/ *n.* **1.** SOMEBODY AWKWARD somebody who is considered unattractive and socially awkward (*insult*) **2.** ARTS OUTRAGEOUS CARNIVAL PERFORMER a carnival performer whose act consists of outrageous feats such as biting the heads off live animals **3.** COMPUT OBSESSIVE COMPUTER USER somebody who enjoys or takes pride in using computers or other technology, often to what others consider an excessive degree (*informal disapproving*) [Late 19thC. Origin uncertain: perhaps from, ultimately, Low German *gek* "fool."] —**geek·y** *adj.*

geese plural of **goose**

gee whiz *interj.* = **gee**

gee-whiz *adj.* causing or characterized by wonderment (*informal*) ○ *a gee-whiz new electronic gadget*

Geez /gee éz, gay-/, **Ge'ez** *n.* an ancient language formerly spoken in Ethiopia and still the liturgical language in the Ethiopian Christian Church [Late 18thC. From Ethiopic.]

gee·zer /geézər/ *n.* an offensive term for a man past middle age (*informal offensive*) [Late 19thC. Representing a dialect pronunciation of guiser (from GUISE), literally "somebody in disguise," later used to denote an odd-looking person.]

ge·fil·te fish /gə fíltə-/ *n.* a Jewish dish consisting of finely chopped fish mixed with crumbs, eggs, and seasoning and served as balls or cakes. Gefilte fish was originally finely chopped or minced fish stuffed in a fish's body cavity before boiling or poaching. [Late 19thC. From Yiddish, "stuffed fish."]

ge·gen·schein /gáygən shīn/ *n.* a faint elliptical glow in the night sky opposite the setting sun, caused by the reflection of sunlight by dust in space [Late 19thC. From German, literally "opposite glow."]

Geh·rig /gérrig/, **Lou** (1903–41) U.S. baseball player. A star first baseman for the Yankees (1923–39), he played in 2,130 consecutive games, retiring with a lifetime batting average of .340. Full name **Henry Louis Gehrig**. Known as **the Iron Horse**

Gei·ger count·er /gígər-/ *n.* an instrument used to detect and measure the intensity of ionizing radiation, e.g., particles from a radioactive substance [Early 20thC. Named for the German physicist Hans Geiger (1882–1945), its inventor.]

gei·sha /gáyshə, geé-/ (*plural* **-sha** *or* **-shas**), **gei·sha girl** *n.* **1.** JAPANESE HOSTESS a Japanese woman educated to accompany men as a hostess, with skills such as dancing, conversation, and music **2.** JAPANESE PROSTITUTE a Japanese prostitute [Late 19thC. From Japanese *geisha* "entertainer."]

gel /jel/ *n.* **1.** CHEM SEMISOLID a semisolid mixture of small particles of a solid in a liquid (**colloid**) **2.** THEATER LIGHT FILTER a sheet of colored acetate used in theater, television, and film lighting to create different lighting effects **3.** HAIR HAIR STYLING CREAM a substance with the consistency of jelly that is used for styling hair ■ *vi.* (**gelled, gel·ling, gels**) **1.** BECOME GEL to become semisolid, having been in a liquid state **2.** TAKE FORM to take on a definite form (*informal*) ○ *The idea didn't begin to gel until I'd gotten home.* **3.** GET ALONG to get along well together (*informal*) [Late 19thC. Shortening of GELATIN.] —**gel·a·ble** *adj.*

ge·la·da /jéllədə, jə laádə/ (*plural* **-das** *or* **-da**), **ge·la·da ba·boon** *n.* a large baboon with brown hair and a bare red patch on its chest, native to northeastern Africa. Latin name: *Theropithecus gelada.* [Mid-19thC. From Amharic *č,ällada*.]

gel·ate /jé làyt/ (**-at·ed, -at·ing, -ates**) *vi.* to become or form a gel [Early 20thC. Back-formation from GELATION.]

ge·la·ti plural of **gelato**

gel·a·tin /jéllət'n/, **gel·a·tine** *n.* **1.** SEMISOLID PROTEIN a transparent protein material made from boiling animal hides, bone, and cartilage that forms a firm gel when mixed with water. It is used in foods, medicine, glue, and photography. **2.** SUBSTANCE WITH CONSISTENCY OF JELLY a substance, e.g., agar, that resembles gelatin **3.** FOOD JELLYLIKE FOOD a sweet food made of flavored gelatin **4.** THEATER = **gel** *n.* 2 [Early 19thC. Via French *gélatine* from Italian *gelatina* from, ultimately, Latin *gelata* "frozen."]

gel·a·tin dy·na·mite *n.* = **gelignite**

ge·lat·i·nize /jə látt'n ìz, jéllət-/ (**-nized, -niz·ing, -niz·es**) *v.* **1.** *vti.* CHANGE TO THE CONSISTENCY OF GELATIN to make something gelatinous, or become gelatinous **2.** *vt.* PHOTOGRAPHY COAT SOMETHING WITH GELATIN to coat a photographic medium with gelatin —**ge·lat·i·ni·za·tion** /jə làtt'ni záysh'n/ *n.* —**ge·lat·i·niz·er** *n.*

ge·lat·i·nous /jə látt'nəss/ *adj.* **1.** SEMISOLID having a semisolid form resembling gelatin **2.** RELATING TO GELATIN relating to or containing gelatin —**ge·lat·i·nous·ly** *adv.* —**ge·lat·i·nous·ness** *n.*

ge·la·tion[1] /jə láysh'n/ *n.* the solidification of a liquid by freezing [Mid-19thC. From the Latin stem *gelation-*, from *gelare* "to freeze."]

ge·la·tion[2] /jə láysh'n/ *n.* the process of becoming a gel [Early 20thC. From GEL.]

ge·la·to /jə laátō/ (*plural* **-ti** /-tee/ *or* **-tos**) *n.* an Italian ice cream made from milk, gelatin, sugar, and fruit [Early 20thC. From Italian, literally "frozen," from, ultimately, Latin *gelare* "to freeze."]

geld[1] /geld/ (**geld·ed** *or* **gelt, geld·ed** *or* **gelt** /gelt/, **geld·ing, gelds**) *vt.* **1.** VET **CASTRATE ANIMAL** to castrate an animal, especially a horse **2. REMOVE SOMEBODY'S STRENGTH** to take away the strength or virility of somebody or something [13thC. From Old Norse *gelda*, from *geldr* "barren."]

geld[2] /geld/ *n.* a land tax paid by landholders to the crown in late Anglo-Saxon and Norman times [15thC. Via medieval Latin *geldum* from Old English *gield* "payment." Ultimately from a prehistoric Germanic word that is also the ancestor of English *yield*.]

geld·ing /gélding/ *n.* a castrated horse or other animal [14thC. From GELD[1].]

Gel·dof /géld awf/, **Bob** (*b.* 1954) Irish musician and philanthropist. He was the leader of the rock group the Boomtown Rats (1975–86), founded the charity Band Aid for famine relief (1984), and received an honorary knighthood (1986). Full name **Robert Frederick Xenon Geldof**

gel·id /jéllid/ *adj.* exceedingly cold (*literary*) [Early 17thC. From Latin *gelidus*, from *gelu* "frost, intense cold" (source of English *jelly*).] —**ge·lid·i·ty** *n.* —**gel·id·ly** /jə líddətee/ *adv.*

gel·ig·nite /jéllig nīt/ *n.* dynamite consisting of gelled nitroglycerin, potassium nitrate, and wood pulp or guncotton. It is often used under water. [Late 19thC. Coined from GELATIN + Latin *ignis* "fire."]

UPI/Corbis-Bettmann

Martha Gellhorn

Gell·horn /géll hàwrn/, **Martha** (1908–98) U.S. journalist and novelist. She became a war correspondent in 1937 and reported on the Spanish Civil War (1936–39) and World War II. Her novels include *Stricken Field* (1940) and *Liana* (1948).

Gell-Mann /gèl mán/, **Murray** (*b.* 1929) U.S. physicist. He proposed the existence of quarks and won the Nobel Prize in physics (1969).

gelt[1] *n.* money (*slang*) [Early 16thC. From German *Geld* and Yiddish *gelt*, both ultimately from a prehistoric Germanic word that is also the ancestor of English *geld*[2] and *yield*.]

gelt[2] past participle, past tense of **geld**

gem /jem/ *n.* **1. JEWEL** a precious stone that has been cut and polished for use as jewelry or decoration **2. SOMEBODY OR SOMETHING EXCELLENT** somebody or something considered to be valuable, useful, or beautiful (*informal*) ○ *Our babysitter is such a gem!* ■ *vt.* (**gemmed, gem·ming, gems**) **DECORATE SOMETHING WITH GEMS** to decorate something with gems or with something resembling gems (*literary*) (*usually passive*) [Pre-12thC. From Latin *gemma* "bud, jewel."]

GEM *abbr.* ground-effect machine

Ge·ma·ra /gə maárə/ *n.* JUDAISM the second part of the Talmud, forming a set of commentaries on the first part of the Talmud, the Mishnah [Early 17thC. From Aramaic *gĕmārā* "completion."] —**gemaric** *adj.* —**Ge·ma·rist** *n.*

gem·i·nate *adj.* /jémminət, -nàyt/ **gem·i·nate, gem·i·nat·ed IN PAIRS** growing or arranged in pairs ○ *a geminate leaf* ■ *vti.* /jémmi nàyt/ (**-nat·ed, -nat·ing, -nates**) **DOUBLE** to make something paired, or become paired or doubled [Late 16thC. From Latin *geminat-*, the past partiple stem of *geminare*, from *geminus* "twin."] —**gem·i·na·tion** /jèmmi náysh'n/ *n.*

Gem·i·ni /jémmə nī, -nèe/ *n.* **1.** ASTRON **THE TWINS CONSTELLATION** a constellation in the northern hemisphere, also known as the Twins or Castor and Pollux, after its two brightest stars **2.** ZODIAC **THIRD ZODIAC SIGN** in astrology, the third sign of the zodiac, falling between Taurus and Cancer, roughly between the dates May 21 and June 20 ■ *n., v.* **Gem·i·ni, Gem·i·ni·an** ZODIAC **SOMEBODY BORN UNDER GEMINI** somebody whose birthday falls between May 21 and June 20 [Pre-12thC. From Latin, plural of *geminus* "twin."] —**Gem·i·ni** *adj.*

gem·ma /jémmə/ (*plural* **-mae** /-mee/) *n.* an asexual bud-shaped structure that can detach from the parent plant and form a new individual. Liverworts and mosses produce gemmae. [Late 18thC. From Latin, literally "bud, jewel."] —**gem·ma·ceous** /je máyshəss/ *adj.*

gem·mate /jé màyt/ *adj.* **REPRODUCING BY GEMMAE** forming gemmae or reproducing by means of gemmae ■ *vi.* (**-mat·ed, -mat·ing, -mates**) **REPRODUCE BY GEMMAE** to form gemmae or reproduce by means of gemmae [Early 17thC. From Latin *gemmat-*, the past participle stem of *gemmare* "to produce buds," from *gemma* "bud, jewel."] —**gem·ma·tion** /je máysh'n/ *n.*

gem·mif·er·ous /je míffərəss/ *adj.* **1.** GEOL **PRODUCING GEMS** producing precious stones **2.** BIOL **WITH GEMMAE** bearing gemmae

gem·mip·a·rous /je míppərəss/ *adj.* = gemmate *adj.* —**gem·mip·a·rous·ly** *adv.*

gem·mu·la·tion /jèmmyə láysh'n/ *n.* production of gemmules, or reproduction by means of gemmules

gem·mule /jémmyool/ *n.* **1.** BIOL **REPRODUCTIVE BUD** a reproductive structure produced by asexual reproduction in freshwater and marine sponges **2.** GENETICS **DARWINIAN HEREDITARY PARTICLE** in Darwin's theory of pangenesis, the particle that contains the hereditary information necessary to reproduce offspring with similar traits

gem·ol·o·gy /je móllәjee/, **gem·mol·o·gy** *n.* the study of gems and gemstones —**gem·o·log·i·cal** /jèmmə lójjik'l/ *adj.* —**gem·ol·o·gist** /je móllәjist/ *n.*

ge·mot /gə mṓt/, **ge·mote** *n.* an assembly for judicial or legislative purposes in pre-Norman England [Old English *gemōt*. Formed from *mōt* (see MOOT).]

gems·bok /gémz bòk/ (*plural* **-boks** *or* **-bok**) *n.* a large antelope with long straight horns and broad black markings on its head and upper legs, found in southwestern and eastern Africa. Latin name: *Oryx gazella*. [Late 18thC. Via Afrikaans from Dutch, literally "wild antelope buck."]

gem·stone /jém stṓn/ *n.* a mineral or stone suitable for use in jewelry after cutting and polishing

ge·müt·lich /gə mṓotlik, -mǘtlikh/ *adj.* warm and friendly (*literary*) [Mid-19thC. From German, formed from *Gemüt* "heart, spirit."]

ge·müt·lich·keit /gə mṓotlik kīt, -mǘtlikh-/ *n.* warmth and friendliness (*literary*) [Mid-19thC. From German *Gemütlichkeit*, from *gemütlich* "GEMUTLICH."]

gen. *abbr.* **1.** gender **2.** general **3.** GRAM genitive **4.** genus

Gen. *abbr.* **1.** General **2.** BIBLE Genesis

-gen *suffix.* **1.** one that produces ○ *hallucinogen* **2.** one that is produced ○ *cultigen* [Via French *-gène* from Greek *-genēs* "born." Ultimately from an Indo-European base meaning "to beget," which is also the ancestor of English *kin*, *generic*, and *gene*.] —**-genic** *suffix.* —**-genous** *suffix.* —**-geny** *suffix.*

gen·darme /zhón daarm/ *n.* a police officer in France and French-speaking countries. In France gendarmes are part of the armed forces, their responsibility being that of general law enforcement. [Mid-16thC. From French, a singular formed from *gens d'armes*, literally "men of arms."]

gen·dar·me·rie /zhon daármaree/ *n.* **1. GENDARMES COLLECTIVELY** gendarmes considered as a body **2. FRENCH POLICE STATION** in France and French-speaking countries, a police station or police barracks [Mid-16thC. From French, formed from *gendarme* "GENDARME."]

gen·der /jéndər/ *n.* **1. SOMEBODY'S SEX** the sex of a person or organism, or of a whole category of people or organisms (*often used euphemistically to avoid the word "sex"*) **2.** LING **CATEGORIZATION OF NOUNS** the classification of nouns and pronouns in certain languages according to the forms taken by adjectives, modifiers, and other grammatical items associated syntactically with them **3.** LING **CATEGORY OF NOUN** any one of the categories, e.g., masculine, feminine, neuter, or common into which nouns and pronouns are divided in languages that have gender [14thC. Via Old French *gendre* from, ultimately, Latin *gener-*, the stem of *genus* "birth, kind" (source of English *genus*).]

WORD KEY: USAGE

gender or **sex**? Traditionally, ***gender*** has referred to grammatical classifications in languages that have masculine, feminine, and neuter nouns; and ***sex*** has referred to the biological classifications to which gender is analogous. For some time, however, anthropologists have used ***gender*** to distinguish cultural categories from biological ones (*Gender roles are indistinct among the young of this society; the two sexes play together frequently*). Cultural and biological categories are interrelated, of course, and thus at times it can be difficult to decide which word is more appropriate. ***Sex*** is for the most part to be preferred, except where the word may be ambiguous (*When you're looking at résumés, does sex matter to you?*) and in idiomatic expressions such as *gender gap* ("difference between the sexes") and *gender-bending* ("the blurring of distinctions between the sexes").

gen·der bend·er *n.* **1. OFFENSIVE TERM** an offensive term for somebody who dresses or acts in a way that is intended to blur the traditional distinctions between men and women (*slang offensive*) **2.** COMPUT **ALTERING DEVICE** a device that converts a male plug or connector to female, or vice versa —**gen·der ben·ding** *n.*

gen·dered /jéndərd/ *adj.* relating to or appropriate to one gender rather than the other ○ *gendered clothing*

gen·der gap *n.* a noticeable difference in behavior or attitudes between men and women or boys and girls

gen·der-neu·tral *adj.* avoiding references to masculinity and femininity and their cultural associations

gene /jeen/ *n.* the basic unit capable of transmitting characteristics from one generation to the next. It consists of a specific sequence of DNA or RNA that occupies a fixed position (**locus**) on a chromosome. [Early 20thC. Via German *Gen* from Greek *genos* "birth, race."]

WORD KEY: ORIGIN

The Indo-European ancestor of ***gene*** is also the ultimate source of English *gender, genealogy, generate, generous, genesis, genie, genital, genius, genocide, gingerly, gonorrhea, indigenous, ingenuous, jaunty, kin, kind, nation,* and *nature*.

-gene *suffix.* = **-gen**

ge·ne·al·o·gy /jèenee óllәjee/ (*plural* **-gies**) *n.* **1. STUDY OF THE HISTORY OF FAMILIES** the study of the history of families and the line of descent from their ancestors **2. FAMILY HISTORY** a pedigree or line of descent that can be traced directly from an ancestor or earlier form, especially that of an individual or family **3. FAMILY TREE** a chart or table that shows the line of descent from an ancestor or earlier form, especially that of an individual or family [14thC. Via French *généalogie* from, ultimately, Greek *genealogia*, from *genea* "race, generation."] —**ge·ne·a·log·i·cal** /jèenee ə lójjik'l/ *adj.* —**ge·ne·a·log·i·cal·ly** *adv.* —**ge·ne·al·o·gist** *n.*

gene am·pli·fi·ca·tion *n.* the production of many copies of a section of DNA, naturally or by technological means

gene flow *n.* the natural transfer of genes from one population into the genetic makeup of another population through hybridization and interbreeding

gene fre·quen·cy *n.* the ratio of a specific variation of a gene (**allele**) to the total number of variations in a particular population

gene gun *n.* a device that inserts DNA directly into cells

gene pool *n.* **1. ALL GENES OF POPULATION** the total of all genes carried by all individuals in an interbreeding population **2. ALL GENES OF SPECIES** the total of all genes existing among all individuals of a species

gene probe *n.* a fragment of DNA or RNA that is labeled with a radioactive isotope and used to identify or isolate a gene

gen·er·a plural of **genus**

gen·er·a·ble /jénnərəb'l/ *adj.* capable of being generated [15thC. From Latin *generabilis*, from *generare* (see GENERATE).]

gen·er·al /jénnərəl/ *adj.* **1.** OVERALL relating to or including all or nearly all of the members of a category or group, or all or nearly all parts of a whole ○ *a general increase in demand* **2.** USUAL applying or happening in most cases ○ *as a general rule* **3.** WIDESPREAD shared or participated in by many ○ *a general sense that something ought to be done* **4.** MISCELLANEOUS having a varied content or wide scope ○ *a general store* **5.** NOT SPECIALIZED not specialized, or lacking specialized knowledge ○ *a book that was intended for the general reader* **6.** NOT SPECIFIC not specific, detailed, or clearly defined ○ *She spoke in the most general terms.* **7.** HIGH-RANKING with overall authority or of superior rank ○ *a general manager* ■ *n.* **1.** (*plural* **gen·er·als** *or* **Gen·er·als**) MIL HIGH MILITARY RANK a military rank above a lieutenant general, or an officer who holds this rank **2.** MIL = **general officer 3.** MED GENERAL ANESTHETIC a general anesthetic (*informal*) **4.** GENERAL HOSPITAL a general hospital (*informal*) **5.** PRINCIPLE a general principle or fact (*archaic*) (*usually plural*) **6.** THE PUBLIC the public as a whole (*archaic*) [12thC. Via French from Latin *generalis* "of the whole class," from, ultimately, *genus* "race, kind" (source of English *genus*).] —**gen·er·al·ness** *n.* ◇ **in general 1.** as a whole **2.** in most cases or circumstances

WORD KEY: CULTURAL NOTE

The General, a movie by director Buster Keaton (1926). Regarded as one of the greatest silent comedies, it is set during the Civil War and based on a historical incident: the hijack of a Confederate train by Union soldiers. Keaton plays railroad man Johnnie Gray, whose attempts to recapture the train involve superb visual gags, gripping drama, and brilliantly timed stunts.

gen·er·al ad·mis·sion *n.* the price for a seat in an unreserved area at a spectator event

gen·er·al an·es·thet·ic *n.* an anesthetic that produces loss of sensation in the whole body together with unconsciousness

gen·er·al as·sem·bly, **Gen·er·al As·sem·bly** *n.* **1.** POL STATE LEGISLATURE any of various U.S. state legislatures **2.** HIGHEST CHURCH LEGISLATIVE BODY the highest governing body of various Presbyterian churches, or the meeting of such a body

Gen·er·al As·sem·bly *n.* RELIG the assembly of the United Nations

gen·er·al av·er·age *n.* liability for loss or damage to an insured ship or its cargo that is shared among all those with an interest in the venture

Gen·er·al Court *n.* **1.** POL STATE LEGISLATIVE BODY a state legislative body in Massachusetts or New Hampshire **2.** HISTORY NEW ENGLAND COURT a legislative body in colonial New England

gen·er·al·cy /jénnərəlsee, jénnrəlsee/ *n.* **1.** OFFICE OF GENERAL the office of general, or the period during which this office is held **2.** GENERALS generals considered collectively

gen·er·al de·liv·er·y *n.* **1.** MAIL GENERAL ADDRESS a service of the post office that holds mail for people without an address or post office box **2.** MAIL DIRECTION an address on an item of mail indicating that it should be held at a post office until collection by the addressee

gen·er·al e·lec·tion *n.* an election in which the citizens of a country or state vote to elect representatives of most or all constituencies to a legislative body

Gen·er·al Head·quar·ters *n.* MIL full form of **GHQ**

gen·er·al hos·pi·tal *n.* a hospital that does not specialize in any one particular kind of medicine

gen·er·al·is·si·mo /jènnərə líssəmō/ (*plural* **-mos**) *n.* in some countries, the supreme commander of a combined military force consisting of the air force, navy, and army [Early 17thC. From Italian, literally "great general," from, ultimately, Latin *generalis* (see GENERAL).]

gen·er·al·ist /jénnərəlist/ *n.* somebody who has knowledge, skills, or interests in a variety of fields but no specialist knowledge in any one field

gen·er·al·i·ty /jènnə rállətee/ (*plural* **-ties**) *n.* **1.** STATE OF BEING GENERAL the quality or state of being general **2.** GENERAL STATEMENT a statement or remark that concerns the main aspects of something rather than the details **3.** GENERAL PRINCIPLE a statement or principle that is true or applies in most cases **4.** UNIMPORTANT REMARK a remark about something that is not important in itself but is useful to open or keep up a conversation **5.** MAJORITY the majority (*archaic*)

gen·er·al·i·za·tion /jènnərəli záysh'n/ *n.* **1.** GENERAL STATEMENT a statement or conclusion that is derived from and applies equally to a number of cases ○ *not enough data to permit a generalization* **2.** SWEEPING STATEMENT a statement presented as a general truth but based on limited or incomplete evidence **3.** MAKING OF GENERALIZATIONS the making of general or sweeping statements **4.** LOGIC INFERENCE FROM INSTANCE the application of the rules of inference that go from an instance to a universal or to an existential statement **5.** PSYCHOL USE OF LEARNED RESPONSE the act of responding to a new stimulus in a similar way as to a conditioned stimulus

gen·er·al·ize /jénnərə līz/ (**-ized, -iz·ing, -iz·es**) *v.* **1.** *vti.* EXPRESS SOMETHING GENERAL to express something general on the basis of particulars **2.** *vi.* MAKE SWEEPING STATEMENT to state a supposed general truth about something on the basis of limited or incomplete evidence **3.** *vti.* GIVE WIDER USE TO to use something or be used in a wider or different range of circumstances **4.** *vt.* MAKE GENERALLY KNOWN to bring something into general use or to general knowledge (*usually passive*) **5.** *vi.* MED SPREAD to spread to other parts of the body **6.** *vti.* LOGIC MAKE INFERENCE to infer a general conclusion from particulars, or a universal statement from an instance —**gen·er·al·iz·a·ble** *adj.*

gen·er·al·ly /jénnərəlee/ *adv.* **1.** USUALLY in most cases or circumstances **2.** AS A WHOLE as a whole or without exception ○ *not meant for the public generally* **3.** VAGUELY without being specific, detailed, or clearly defined ○ *spoke generally about his life* **4.** WIDESPREAD so as to be widespread

gen·er·al meet·ing *n.* a meeting to which all members of a group or organization are invited

gen·er·al ob·li·ga·tion *adj.* supported by all the resources and revenue-raising powers of a municipality or other issuer of a bond

gen·er·al of·fi·cer *n.* an officer of the army, navy, or air force who ranks above a colonel

Gen·er·al of the Air Force *n.* the highest officer rank in the Air Force, above that of general

Gen·er·al of the Ar·mies *n.* the highest officer rank in the Army

Gen·er·al of the Ar·my *n.* the next to highest officer rank in the Army, above that of general, below that of General of the Armies

gen·er·al prac·tice *n.* the work of a doctor who treats patients' general medical problems, referring them to hospitals for more specialized care (*dated*)

gen·er·al prac·ti·tion·er *n.* a doctor who treats patients' general medical problems, either at an office or, sometimes, at patients' homes (*dated*)

gen·er·al pur·pose *adj.* useful for a wide variety of purposes

gen·er·al rel·a·tiv·i·ty *n.* PHYS = **relativity** *n.* **2**

gen·er·al·ship /jénnərəl shìp/ *n.* **1.** MIL MILITARY COMMAND the art or practice of exercising military leadership in a war **2.** MIL GENERAL'S RANK the rank or period of tenure of a general **3.** LEADERSHIP skillful leadership or management of people or an organization

gen·er·al staff *n.* a group of military officers whose job is to assist senior officers in the planning and coordination of military operations

gen·er·al store *n.* a store that sells a wide variety of goods such as groceries and household supplies, most often found in small communities where there are no department stores or supermarkets

gen·er·al the·o·ry of rel·a·tiv·i·ty *n.* = **relativity** *n.* **2**

gen·er·ate /jénnə ràyt/ (**-at·ed, -at·ing, -ates**) *vt.* **1.** CREATE to bring something into existence or effect ○ *measures to generate more income* **2.** ENERGY PRODUCE ENERGY to produce or originate a form of energy through a chemical or physical process **3.** MATH, LING PRODUCE SET to produce a set or sequence by the application of defined rules or the performance of defined operations **4.** GEOM PRODUCE FORM to create a curve with a moving point or a surface with a moving curve [Early 16thC. From Latin *generat-*, the past participle stem of *generare* "to beget," from, ultimately, *genus* "race, birth."]

gen·er·a·tion /jènnə ráysh'n/ *n.* **1.** GROUP OF CONTEMPORARIES all of the people who were born at approximately the same time, considered as a group, and especially when considered as having shared interests and attitudes ○ *a generation that grew up with rationing* **2.** STAGE IN DESCENT a single stage in the descent of a family or a group of people or animals or plants, or the individuals belonging to the same stage ○ *three generations down the line* **3.** TIME TAKEN TO PRODUCE NEW GENERATION the period of time that it takes for people, animals or plants to grow up and produce their own offspring, in humans held to be between 30 and 35 years ○ *after three generations of war and conflict* **4.** SPECIFIC GENERATION a specified numbered stage in the sequence of generations born or living in a country into which a family came as immigrants (*usually used in combination*) ○ *first-generation immigrants* **5.** TECH NEW TYPE a particular stage in the development of a product or technology, especially one marking a significant advance ○ *one of the new generation of computers* **6.** BIOL PHASE IN LIFE CYCLE one of the successive phases that make up the life cycle of certain organisms ○ *the gametophyte generation* **7.** ENERGY PRODUCTION OF POWER the production of electricity, heat, or some other form of energy **8.** BIOL PRODUCTION OF YOUNG the act or process of bringing offspring into being **9.** MATH, GEOM GENERATING OF GROUP OR SHAPE the act or process of generating a set, sequence, curve, or surface **10.** PHYS NUCLEI IN CHAIN REACTION in a chain reaction, a group of nuclei that come from a previous group —**gen·er·a·tion·al** *adj.*

gen·er·a·tion gap *n.* the difference in attitudes, behavior, and interests between people of different generations, especially between parents and their children

gen·er·a·tion X, **Gen·er·a·tion X** *n.* the generation of people born roughly during the years 1965 to 1980 in Western countries, especially the United States, often regarded as disillusioned, cynical, or apathetic [From the novel by Douglas Coupland, *Generation X: Tales for an Accelerated Culture*] —**gen·er·a·tion X·er** *n.*

gen·er·a·tion Y, **Gen·er·a·tion Y** *n.* the generation of people born approximately in or after 1980 in Western countries, especially the United States (*informal*) [From GENERATION X]

gen·er·a·tive /jénnə ràytiv, -rətiv/ *adj.* **1.** BIOL RELATING TO REPRODUCTION relating to the production of young **2.** WITH PRODUCTIVE CAPABILITY involving the ability to produce or originate something ○ *generative linguistic theory* —**gen·er·a·tive·ly** *adv.* —**gen·er·a·tive·ness** *n.*

gen·er·a·tive cell *n.* BIOL = **gamete**

gen·er·a·tive gram·mar *n.* the rules from which all the grammatical sentences, and only the grammatical sentences, of a language can be generated

gen·er·a·tor /jénnə ràytər/ *n.* **1.** ELEC ENG DEVICE FOR PRODUCING ELECTRICITY a machine or device that is used to convert mechanical energy, e.g., that provided by the combustion of fuel, into electricity **2.** CHEM DEVICE FOR PRODUCING GAS a device in which a gas is formed **3.** ORIGINATOR somebody or something responsible for generating something such as an idea, plan, or strategy

gen·er·a·trix /jènnə ráytriks/ (*plural* **-tri·ces** /-tri sēez, jènnərə trī́-/) *n.* an element such as a point or line that is used in the production of a geometric figure such as a curve or surface

ge·ner·ic /jə nérrik/ *adj.* **1.** APPLYING GENERALLY applying to any member of a group or class ○ *a generic weakness in the design* **2.** SUITABLE FOR A BROAD RANGE usable or suitable in a variety of contexts ○ *generic software that can run on a variety of machines* **3.** BIOL OF A GENUS relating to or characteristic of a genus **4.** PHARM WITH GENERAL NAME used to describe a pharmaceutical product that does not have a brand name or trademark ■ *n.* PHARM = **generic drug** [Late 17thC. Via French *générique* from, ultimately, Latin *genus* "race, kind."] —**ge·ner·i·cal·ly** *adv.*

ge·ner·ic drug *n.* a drug sold or dispensed under a name that is not protected by a trademark. Examples are ibuprofen and acetaminophen.

gen·er·os·i·ty /jènnə róssətee/ (*plural* **-ties**) *n.* **1.** KINDNESS willingness to give money, help, or time freely **2.** NOBILITY nobility of character **3.** SUBSTANTIAL SIZE pleasingly large size or quantity ○ *He ate everything, despite the generosity of the portions.* **4.** GENEROUS ACT a generous, kind, or noble act [15thC. From Latin *generositas*, from *generosus* (see GENEROUS).]

gen·er·ous /jénnərəss/ *adj.* **1.** KIND having or showing a willingness to give money, help, or time freely ○ *a very generous offer* **2.** NOBLE having or showing nobility of character ○ *a generous gesture of forgiveness* **3.** SUBSTANTIAL pleasingly large in size or quantity ○ *a generous slice of cake* **4.** WINE FULL-FLAVORED used to describe wine that is rich and full-flavored [Late 16thC. Via French *généreux* from Latin *generosus* "of noble birth," from, ultimately, *genus* "race, birth."] —**gen·er·ous·ly** *adv.* —**gen·er·ous·ness** *n.*

WORD KEY: SYNONYMS

generous, magnanimous, munificent, bountiful, liberal

CORE MEANING: giving readily to others

generous used of somebody to suggest a warm-hearted desire to give and to help others. It is also used of something given, when the thing or amount given is considerably more than might have been anticipated; **magnanimous** a formal word suggesting more a general generosity of mind and spirit than a desire to give generously to an individual. It is sometimes used to suggest paternalism or a tendency to patronize or condescend; **munificent** more formal than "magnanimous" and used both of somebody giving and something given, to indicate generosity on a very grand scale, often indicating great wealth on the part of the giver; **bountiful** a formal and literary word, not commonly used in modern English. It describes somebody who is exceptionally generous, particularly to less fortunate people; **liberal** used to describe somebody who is exceptionally generous. It can be used of something given to indicate that it is substantial and freely given.

Gen·e·see /jènnə sée/ river in the northeastern United States, rising in Pennsylvania and flowing northward past Rochester, New York, before emptying into Lake Ontario. Length: 144 mi./232 km.

gene se·quence *n.* the order of nucleotides in a gene

gene se·quenc·ing, ge·net·ic se·quenc·ing *n.* the process of determining the individual arrangement of nucleotides that compose a given gene, used especially in studying genetic changes in a virus

gen·e·sis /jénnisiss/ (*plural* **-ses** /-sèez/) *n.* the time or circumstances of something's coming into being ○ *the genesis of this new project* [Early 17thC. From GENESIS.]

Gen·e·sis *n.* the first book of the Bible, in which the story of the creation of the world is told [Pre-12thC. Via Latin from Greek.]

-genesis *suffix.* production, origin ○ *sporogenesis* [Via Latin from Greek, "birth" (see GENESIS)]

genesplic·ing *n.* a technique in which segments of DNA or RNA, often from different organisms, are combined, in order to be introduced into an organism

gen·et[1] /jénnit/ *n.* **1.** ZOOL SMALL CARNIVORE a small carnivorous mammal related to the civet that inhabits wooded regions of southern Europe and Africa and has a ringed tail, spotted sides, and retractable claws. Genus: *Genetta.* **2.** GENET FUR the fur of the genet [14thC. From Old French *genette*, of uncertain origin: probably from Arabic *jarnait.*]

gen·et[2] *n.* = **jennet**

Ge·net /zhə náy/, **Jean** (1910–86) French writer. He is best known for existentialist dramas such as *The Maid* (1947) and *The Balcony* (1957).

gene ther·a·py *n.* the treatment of a genetic disease through the insertion of normal or genetically altered genes into cells in order to replace or make up for the nonfunctional or missing genes

ge·net·ic /jə néttik/, **ge·net·i·cal** /-tik'l/ *adj.* involving, resulting from, or relating to genes or genetics [Mid-19thC. From GENESIS, modeled on words such as *antithesis, antithetic.*] —**ge·net·i·cal·ly** *adv.*

ge·net·i·cal·ly mod·i·fied *adj.* used to describe an organism that has received genetic material from another, resulting in a permanent change in one or more of its characteristics

ge·net·i·cal·ly mod·i·fied or·gan·ism *n.* a plant, animal, or microorganism produced by genetic engineering (*usually plural*) Abbr of **G.M.O.**

ge·net·ic code *n.* the specific order of the nucleotide sequences in DNA or RNA that form the basis of heredity through their role in protein synthesis

ge·net·ic coun·sel·ing *n.* counseling that concerns the risks, treatments, and management of inherited genetic disorders for people with some likelihood of being affected by them, either personally or as parents —**ge·net·ic coun·sel·or** *n.*

ge·net·ic drift *n.* the random changes that occur in the gene frequency of small populations, resulting in the loss or preservation of certain genes over the generations

ge·net·ic en·gi·neer·ing *n.* the alteration and recombination of genetic material by technological means, with applications in treating disease, enhancing desired plant and animal characteristics, and manufacturing biological products such as insulin —**ge·net·ic en·gi·neer** *n.*

ge·net·ic fin·ger·print *n.* a DNA sequence taken from a section of a gene that is known to be highly variable, used as an accurate means of identifying an individual

ge·net·ic fin·ger·print·ing *n.* the analysis and use of DNA patterns from body tissues such as blood, saliva, or semen in order to establish somebody's identity

ge·net·i·cist /jə néttəssist/ *n.* somebody who studies or is an expert in genetics

ge·net·ic map *n.* a graphic representation of the specific arrangement of genes on a chromosome

ge·net·ic map·ping *n.* the technique or process of identifying genes on a chromosome

ge·net·ic mark·er *n.* a known, usually dominant, gene that is used to identify specific genes, chromosomes, and traits known to be associated with that gene

ge·net·ic probe *n.* a fragment of DNA marked by a chemical or radioactive substance that will bind to a given gene, used as a tag in order to identify that gene

ge·net·ics /jə néttiks/ *n.* **1.** STUDY OF HEREDITY a branch of biology dealing with heredity and genetic variations (*takes a singular verb*) **2.** ORGANISM'S GENETIC MAKEUP the genetic makeup of an organism or group of organisms (*takes a singular or plural verb*)

gene trans·fer *n.* the insertion of genetic material from one organism into another in a laboratory procedure, to produce a specific effect, e.g., resistance to disease

ge·net·rix /jénnətriks/ (*plural* **-ri·ces** /-trī seez/) *n.* ANTHROP a biological mother (*technical*) ◊ **genitor** [15thC. Via Old French *genetris* or directly from Latin *genetrix*, from *gignere* "to beget."]

ge·ne·va /jə néevər/ *n.* = **genever**

Ge·ne·va /jə néevə/ city in western Switzerland, capital of Geneva Canton, situated at the western end of Lake Geneva. It is the headquarters of many international organizations, including the International Red Cross and The World Health Organization. Population: 174,363 (1994). French **Genève**

Ge·ne·va, Lake the largest lake in central Europe. It straddles the border between Switzerland and the Haut-Savoie Department in southeastern France. Area: 225 sq. mi./583 sq. km.

Ge·ne·van /jə néevən/ *n.* PEOPLES SOMEBODY FROM GENEVA somebody who lives in or who was born or raised in Geneva, Switzerland ■ *adj.* **1.** PEOPLES OF GENEVA relating to or typical of the city of Geneva, Switzerland or its inhabitants or culture **2. Ge·ne·van, Gen·e·vese** RELIG OF CALVINISM relating to the teachings of Protestant reformer John Calvin or to Calvinism

Gen·e·vese /jènnə véez, jènnə véess/ *npl.* PEOPLE OF GENEVA the people of Geneva, Switzerland ■ *adj.* = **Genevan**

Gen·ghis Khan /jèng giss kaán/ (1167?–1227) Mongol conqueror. His conquests extended the Mongolian empire throughout Asia from the Pacific to the Black Sea. Real name **Temujin**

gen·ial /jéenyəl/ *adj.* **1.** KIND having a kind and good-natured disposition or manner **2.** MILD pleasantly mild and warm so as to be conducive to life and growth ○ *a genial climate* [Mid-16thC. From Latin *genialis* "nuptial," from *genius* (see GENIUS).] —**ge·ni·al·i·ty** /jèenee állətee/ *n.* —**gen·ial·ly** /jéenyəlee/ *adv.* —**gen·ial·ness** /-nəss/ *n.*

gen·ic /jéenik, jénnik/ *adj.* relating to or produced by a gene or genes —**gen·i·cal·ly** *adv.*

ge·nic·u·late /jə níkyələt/ *adj.* **1.** BENT LIKE A KNEE bent at an angle like a knee ○ *geniculate antennae* **2.** WITH JOINT THAT BENDS with a joint or joints that can be bent like a knee [Early 17thC. From Latin *geniculatus* "knotted," from, ultimately, *genu* "knee."] —**ge·nic·u·late·ly** *adv.* —**ge·nic·u·la·tion** /jə nikyə láysh'n/ *n.*

ge·nie /jéenee/ *n.* a magical spirit in Arabian folklore that has supernatural powers and will obey the commands of the person who summons it. ◊ **jinni** [Mid-17thC. Via French *génie* from Latin *genius* (see GENIUS).]

ge·ni·i plural of **genius**

gen·i·pap /jénnə pàp/ *n.* **1.** TREES TROPICAL EVERGREEN TREE a tropical American evergreen tree of the madder family that has an edible fruit. Latin name: *Genipa americana.* **2.** FOOD FRUIT OF THE GENIPAP the edible reddish-brown fruit of the genipap tree, resembling an orange and used in preserves and drinks [Early 17thC. Via Portuguese *jenipapo* from Tupi *ianipaba.*]

gen·i·tal /jénnit'l/ *adj.* relating to the external sexual organs or to reproduction [14thC. Directly or via French from Latin *genitalis*, from, ultimately, *gignere* "to beget."] —**gen·i·tal·ly** *adv.*

gen·i·tal her·pes *n.* a sexually transmitted disease caused by the herpes simplex virus and affecting the genital and anal regions with painful blisters

gen·i·tals /jénnit'lz/, **gen·i·ta·li·a** /jènni táylee ə/ *npl.* the reproductive organs, especially the external sex organs

gen·i·tal warts *npl.* warts of the genital and anal areas caused by a sexually transmitted virus

gen·i·tive /jénnitiv/ *n.* **1.** POSSESSIVE GRAMMATICAL CASE a grammatical case in some languages that affects nouns, pronouns, and adjectives and that usually indicates possession **2.** INSTANCE OF GENITIVE a word, phrase, or form in the genitive ■ *adj.* OF THE GENITIVE belonging or relating to the genitive [14thC. Directly or via French *génitif* from Latin *genitivus*, from ultimately, *gignere* "to beget."]

gen·i·tor /jénnitər/ *n.* ANTHROP a natural or biological father (*technical*) ◊ **genetrix** [15thC. Directly or via French *géniteur* from Latin *genitor*, from, ultimately, *gignere* "to beget."]

gen·i·to·u·ri·nar·y /jènnitō yo͝orə nèrree/ *adj.* relating to or affecting the genital and urinary organs

gen·i·ture /jénni cho͝or, jénnichər/ *n.* somebody's birth (*literary or archaic*) [Mid-16thC. Directly or via French from Latin *genitura*, from *gignere* "to beget."]

gen·ius /jéenyəss, jéenee əss/ *n.* **1.** SOMEBODY WITH OUTSTANDING TALENT somebody with exceptional ability, especially somebody whose intellectual or creative achievements gain worldwide recognition **2.** OUTSTANDING TALENT exceptional talent of a particular kind **3.** SOMEBODY WITH PARTICULAR SKILL somebody who has a particular skill ○ *a genius with computers* **4.** (*plural* **ge·ni·i**) QUALITY a special quality that characterizes a place, period, or people **5.** (*plural* **ge·ni·i**) GUARDIAN SPIRIT in Roman mythology, a guardian spirit of a person, place, or institution **6.** (*plural* **ge·ni·i**) DEMON a demon or supernatural being **7.** INFLUENCE a strong influence, or somebody who exerts a strong influence ○ *an evil genius* [14thC. From Latin, "guardian spirit," from *gignere* "to beget."]

WORD KEY: SYNONYMS

See Synonyms at ***talent.***

ge·ni·us lo·ci /jèenee əss lṓ sī/ *n.* **1.** CHARACTERISTIC ATMOSPHERE OF A PLACE the atmosphere that characterizes a place **2.** GUARDIAN OF A PLACE the guardian spirit of a place [From Latin, literally "spirit of the place"]

gen·o·a /jénnō ə/, **gen·o·a jib** *n.* a particularly large triangular front sail on a sailboat, especially a racing yacht [Mid-20thC. Named for GENOA.]

Gen·o·a /jénnō ə/, **Gen·o·va** /-və/ seaport and industrial city on the Gulf of Genoa, northwestern Italy, the capital of Genoa Province, Liguria Region. Population: 659,754 (1993). —**Gen·o·ese** /jènnō éez/ *n., adj.*

gen·o·cide /jénnə sīd/ *n.* the systematic killing of all the people from a national, ethnic, or religious group, or an attempt to do this [Mid-20thC. Coined from Greek *genos* "race" + -CIDE.] —**gen·o·cid·al** /jènnə sīd'l/ *adj.* —**gen·o·cid·al·ly** /-sīdlee/ *adv.*

ge·nome /jée nōm/ *n.* the full complement of genetic information that an individual organism inherits from its parents, including DNA located in chromosomes and DNA outside cell nuclei, in mitochondria and chloroplasts [Mid-20thC. Coined from Greek *genos* "offspring, race" + CHROMOSOME.] —**ge·nom·ic** /ji nómmik/ *adj.*

ge·nom·ics /ji nómmiks, -nṓmmiks/ *n.* the study of the relationships between gene structure and biological function in organisms (*takes a singular verb*)

gen·o·type /jénnə tīp/ *n.* **1.** GENETIC MAKEUP the genetic makeup of an organism, as opposed to its physical characteristics (**phenotype**) **2.** GENETIC GROUP a group of organisms that share a similar genetic makeup [Early 20thC. From German *Genotypus*, from Greek *genos* "offspring, race" + Latin *typus* (see TYPE).] —**gen·o·typ·ic** /jènnə típpik/ *adj.* —**gen·o·typ·i·cal·ly** /-típpikəlee/ *adv.*

-genous *suffix.* a suffix that forms adjectives from nouns ending in -gen and -geny

gen·re /zhaánrə, -Nrə/ *n.* **1.** CATEGORY OF ARTISTIC WORKS one of the categories that artistic works of all kinds can be divided into on the basis of form, style, or subject matter. For example, detective novels are a genre of fiction. **2.** PAINTING PAINTINGS OF HOUSEHOLD SCENES a type of painting depicting household scenes [Early 19thC. Via French, "type," from, ultimately, Latin *genus* (see GENDER).]

WORD KEY: SYNONYMS

See Synonyms at ***type***.

gen·ro /gèn rṓ/ (*plural* **-ro**) *n.* **1.** JAPANESE EMPEROR'S ADVISERS in Japan in the 19th and early-20th centuries, a group of elder statesmen who advised the emperor (*takes a singular or plural verb*) **2.** MEMBER OF THE GENRO a member of the genro advising the Japanese emperor [Late 19thC. From Japanese, literally "first elders."]

gens /jenz/ (*plural* **gen·tes** /jénteez/) *n.* **1.** ROMAN CLAN in ancient Rome, a group of aristocratic families with the same name, descended from a common ancestor on the male side **2.** ANTHROP CLAN a clan, especially one that traces its descent on the male side (*dated*) [Mid-19thC. From Latin, "race, clan."]

gent /jent/ *n.* a humorous, sometimes ironic, term for "gentleman" (*informal*) ◊ **gents**

gen·ta·mi·cin /jèntə mísś'n/ *n.* an antibiotic used to treat many infections and usually administered by injection. It can cause serious side effects. [Mid-20thC. From *genta-*, of uncertain origin, perhaps from GENTIAN VIOLET, + an alteration of -MYCIN.]

gen·teel /jen teél/ *adj.* **1.** WELL-MANNERED having or displaying refinement and good manners, especially manners that suggest, or are thought typical of, an upper-class background **2.** PRETENTIOUS overdoing the refinement, delicacy of behavior, or snobbishness thought typical of the upper classes in order to create an impression of higher social status **3.** RELATING TO THE UPPER CLASSES relating to the upper classes (*dated*) [Late 16thC. From French *gentil* (see GENTLE).] —**gen·teel·ly** *adv.* —**gen·teel·ness** *n.*

gen·teel·ism /jen teé lìzzəm/ *n.* a word or phrase used in place of another one considered vulgar

gen·tes plural of **gens**

gen·tian /jénshən/ *n.* **1.** SHOWY FLOWERING PLANT a plant with bright blue, yellow, white, or red trumpet-shaped flowers that belongs to either of two genera, one alpine and arctic, the other temperate. Genera: *Gentiana* and *Gentianella*. **2.** ROOT OF THE GENTIAN the dried roots and rhizome of a yellow-flowered gentian, used as a digestive stimulant in herbal medicine [14thC. From Latin *gentiana*, named for *Gentius*, the 2ndC B.C. king of Illyria.]

gen·tian blue *adj.* of a purplish-blue color —**gen·tian blue** *n.*

gen·tian vi·o·let *n.* a green dye derived from rosaniline that forms a violet solution in water and is used as a biological stain. It was formerly used in antiseptic lotions.

gen·tile /jén tīl/ *n.* **1.** NON-JEW somebody who is not Jewish **2.** SOMEBODY CHRISTIAN somebody who is Christian, as distinguished from somebody who is Jewish **3.** NON-MORMON in the Church of Latter Day Saints, somebody who is not Mormon **4.** HEATHEN somebody who does not believe in God (*disapproving*) ■ *adj.* **1.** NOT JEWISH not belonging to the Jewish people or faith **2.** CHRISTIAN Christian, as distinguished from Jewish **3.** GRAM DENOTING PLACE OR PEOPLE used to describe a noun such as "Welsh" or "Texan" that gives the name of a place or a people [14thC. From Latin *gentilis*, literally "of the same clan" (see GENTLE). The meaning "non-Jewish" evolved from its use in translations of biblical Hebrew *goy* "(non-Jewish) nation."]

gen·til·i·ty /jen tíllətee/ *n.* **1.** REFINEMENT courteous and well-mannered behavior, especially when it suggests an upper-class background **2.** UPPER-CLASS STATUS the status or way of life of somebody from the upper classes **3.** PRETENTIOUSNESS exaggeratedly refined, delicate, or snobbish behavior, affected in order to create an impression of higher social status **4.** MEMBERS OF THE UPPER CLASS people from the upper classes [From French *gentilité*, from *gentil* (see GENTLE)]

gen·tle /jént'l/ *adj.* (**-tler, -tlest**) **1.** KIND having a mild and kind nature or manner **2.** MILD OR MODERATE being moderate in force or degree so that the effects are not severe ○ *a gentle reprimand* **3.** USING LITTLE FORCE using little force or violence ○ *a gentle tap on the shoulder* **4.** NOT STEEP not very steep ○ *a gentle slope* **5.** CHIVALROUS having a gracious and honorable manner (*archaic*) **6.** UPPER-CLASS relating to or having a high social status or class ■ *vt.* (**-tled, -tling, -tles**) **1.** SOOTHE SOMEBODY to cause somebody to become less agitated by means of words or actions (*literary*) **2.** TAME AN ANIMAL to calm an animal and make it domesticated (*formal*) **3.** RAISE TO THE NOBILITY to raise somebody to the nobility (*archaic*) ■ *n.* SOMEBODY FROM UPPER CLASS somebody of high social class (*archaic*) [Pre-12thC. Via French *gentil* "well-born" from Latin *gentilis*, literally "of the same clan," from *gens* (see GENS). The underlying sense is of befitting a well-bred person.] —**gen·tle·ness** *n.*

gen·tle breeze *n.* a wind with a speed of between 8 and 12 mi./13 and 19 km per hour

gen·tle·folk /jént'l fōk/, **gen·tle·folks** *npl.* upper class people (*archaic*) ◊ **gentlepeople**

gen·tle·man /jént'lmən/ (*plural* **-men** /-mən/) *n.* **1.** POLITE AND CULTURED MAN a cultured man who behaves with courtesy and thoughtfulness **2.** MAN used as a polite term to refer to a man, regardless of social position or behaviour ○ *Good morning, ladies and gentlemen.* **3.** UPPER-CLASS MAN a man from a high social class, especially a man with an independent income **4.** HIST MAN WITH A COAT OF ARMS in English history, a man who was not strictly of noble birth but was entitled to a coat of arms. He ranked above a yeoman in the social order. —**gen·tle·man·li·ness** *n.* —**gen·tle·man·ly** *adj.*

gen·tle·man-at-arms *n.* a member of a troop of forty men who act as a ceremonial guard for the British sovereign on state occasions

gen·tle·man farm·er *n.* **1.** FARMER WITH INDEPENDENT MEANS a farmer with an independent source of income who farms for pleasure rather than for money **2.** FARM OWNER a man who owns a farm but employs a manager and staff to work it

gen·tle·man's a·gree·ment, gen·tle·men's a·gree·ment *n.* an agreement based on trust, not written down, and not enforceable by law

gen·tle·man's gen·tle·man *n.* the manservant of an upper-class man (*dated*)

gen·tle·wom·an /jént'l wòomən/ (*plural* **-en** /jént'l wìmmin/) *n.* **1.** POLITE AND CULTURED WOMAN a polite and cultured woman who behaves with courtesy and thoughtfulness **2.** UPPER-CLASS WOMAN a woman from a high social class, especially a woman with an independent income **3.** HIST LADY'S PERSONAL ATTENDANT a woman acting as a personal attendant to a lady of high social rank

gen·tly /jéntlee/ *adv.* **1.** SOFTLY softly, using little pressure ○ *touched him gently on the shoulder* **2.** MILDLY mildly or moderately ○ *gently falling rain* **3.** NOT STEEPLY not steeply or sharply ○ *land rising gently to the foothills*

gen·tri·fi·ca·tion /jèntrəfi káysh'n/ *n.* the process of transforming an unprosperous neighborhood of buildings needing repair into a more prosperous one, e.g., through investment in remodeling buildings or houses

gen·tri·fy /jéntrə fī/ (**-fied, -fy·ing, -fies**) *vt.* to transform a run-down or aging neighborhood into a more prosperous one, e.g., through investment in remodeling buildings or houses

gen·try /jéntree/ *n.* **1.** THE UPPER CLASSES the group of people who make up the upper social classes **2.** ENGLISH SOCIAL CLASS the English social class that ranks just below the aristocracy and consists of families who are not of noble birth but are entitled to have a coat of arms **3.** PEOPLE people of a particular kind [14thC. From Old French *genterie* "nobility," from *gentil* (see GENTLE).]

gents /jents/ *n. U.K.* = **men's room**

gen·u·flect /jénnyə flèkt/ (**-flect·ed, -flect·ing, -flects**) *vi.* **1.** KNEEL to bend the right knee to the floor and rise again as a gesture of religious respect, particularly in a Roman Catholic or Anglican church **2.** SHOW EXCESSIVE RESPECT to show undeserved or unnecessarily deferential respect for somebody or something [Mid-19thC. From ecclesiastical Latin *genuflectere*, literally "to bend the knee," from *genu* "knee" + *flectere* "to bend."] —**gen·u·flec·tion** /jènnyə fléksh'n/ *n.*

gen·u·ine /jénnyoo in/ *adj.* **1.** REAL, NOT ARTIFICIAL having the qualities or value claimed ○ *a genuine Cézanne* **2.** SINCERELY FELT not affected or pretended ○ *a look of genuine surprise* **3.** CANDID honest and open in relationships with others ○ *a very genuine person* **4.** OF UNMIXED BREEDING being of unmixed breeding ○ *of genuine stock* [Late 16thC. From Latin *genuinus*, of uncertain origin: perhaps an alteration of *ingenuus* "native."] —**gen·u·ine·ly** *adv.* —**gen·u·ine·ness** *n.*

ge·nus /jeénəss/ (*plural* **gen·e·ra** /jénnərə/) *n.* **1.** SET OF CLOSELY RELATED SPECIES a category in the taxonomic classification of related organisms, comprising one or more species. Similar genera are grouped into families. **2.** LOGIC BROADER TERM FOR SOMETHING the more general class or kind in which something is included, e.g., the species "dog" is included in the genus "animal" **3.** GROUP a class or group of any kind [Mid-16thC. From Latin, "birth, race, kind" (source of English *general*).]

geo- *prefix.* **1.** earth, soil ○ *geomagnetic* ○ *geophyte* **2.** geography, global ○ *geostrategy* [From Greek *gē* "earth" (source of English *geode* and *apogee*)]

ge·o·bot·a·ny /jeè ō bótt'nee/ *n.* = **phytogeography** —**ge·o·bo·tan·i·cal** /jeè ō bə tánnik'l/ *adj.* —**ge·o·bot·a·nist** /-bótt'nist/ *n.*

ge·o·cen·tric /jeè ō séntrik/ *adj.* **1.** HAVING EARTH AT ITS CENTER used to describe the solar system when it is regarded as having the Earth as its center **2.** CONSIDERED FROM EARTH'S CENTER measured from, or considered as if viewed from, the center of the Earth **3.** WITH EARTH AS THE CENTER OF FOCUS having the Earth and its inhabitants as the center of a theory or belief —**ge·o·cen·tri·cal·ly** *adv.*

ge·o·chem·is·try /jeè ō kémmistree/ *n.* the study of the chemical composition of the earth's solid matter, as well as the solid matter of other planets, meteors, and asteroids —**ge·o·chem·i·cal** *adj.* —**ge·o·chem·i·cal·ly** *adv.* —**ge·o·chem·ist** *n.*

ge·o·chro·nol·o·gy /jeè ō krə nóllәjee/ *n.* the study of the ages and relative ages of geologic events and rock formations —**ge·o·chron·o·log·i·cal** /jeè ō kronnə lójjik'l/ *adj.* —**ge·o·chron·o·log·i·cal·ly** *adv.* —**ge·o·chro·nol·o·gist** /-krə nólləjist/ *n.*

ge·o·chro·nom·e·try /jeè ō krə nómmətree/ *n.* the measurement of the age of a rock, mineral, or sequence of rocks, or of an event such as a volcanic eruption —**ge·o·chron·o·met·ric** /jeè ō kronnə méttrik/ *adj.*

ge·o·co·ro·na /jeè ō kə rṓnə/ *n.* the outermost region of the Earth's atmosphere reaching to approximately 15 Earth radii in height and consisting mainly of hydrogen

ge·ode /jeé ōd/ *n.* **1.** HOLLOW ROCK WITH CRYSTALS a roughly spherical rock mass containing a cavity lined or filled with crystals that have grown unimpeded and so are frequently perfectly formed **2.** CAVITY IN HOLLOW ROCK the crystal-lined cavity within a geode [Late 17thC. Via Latin *geodes* from Greek *geōdēs* "earthy," from *gē* "earth."]

ge·o·des·ic /jeè ə déssik/ *adj.* **1.** GEOM RELATING TO THE GEOMETRY OF CURVES relating to the geometry of curved surfaces **2.** GEOL = **geodetic** ■ *n.* GEOM SHORTEST LINE the shortest line between two points on a curved or flat surface

ge·o·des·ic dome *n.* a dome that has many flat straight-sided faces formed by a framework of bars that intersect to form equilateral triangles or polygons

ge·o·des·ic line *n.* = **geodesic** *n.*

ge·od·e·sy /jee óddəsee/ *n.* the branch of science that deals with the precise measurement of the size and shape of the Earth, the mapping of points on its surface, and the study of its gravitational field [Late 16thC. Via modern Latin from Greek *geōdaisia*, from *daiein* "to divide."] —**ge·od·e·sist** *n.*

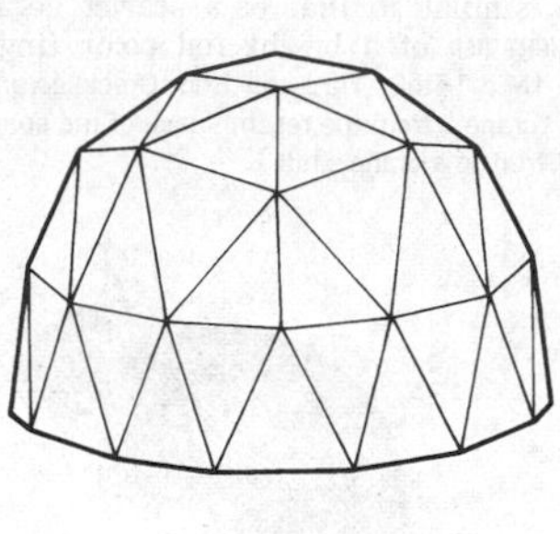

Geodesic dome

ge·o·det·ic /jeè ə déttik/, **ge·o·det·i·cal** /-déttik'l/ *adj.* relating to the precise measurement of the Earth's surface or of points on its surface [Late 17thC. From Greek *geōdaitēs* "land surveyor," from *daiein* "to divide."] —**ge·o·det·i·cal·ly** *adv.*

ge·o·det·ic sur·vey *n.* a survey of a very large area of land, with the curvature of the Earth's surface taken into account

geo·duck /goó i dùk/, **gwe·duc** *n.* a very large edible clam found on the northwestern Pacific coast of North America. Latin name: *Panope generosa.* [Late 19thC. From a Salishan language.]

ge·o·ec·o·nom·ics /jeè ō ekə nómmiks, -eekə-/ *n.* the study of how the economies of the world's nations relate to and affect one another (*takes a singular verb*) —**ge·o·ec·o·nom·ic** *adj.* —**ge·o·ec·o·nom·i·cal·ly** *adv.* —**ge·o·e·con·o·mist** /jeè ō i kónnəmist/ *n.*

geog. *abbr.* **1.** geographic **2.** geographical **3.** geography

ge·og·ra·pher /jee óggrəfər/ *n.* somebody who studies geography or is an expert in geography [Mid-16thC. Via late Latin from Greek *geōgraphos,* literally "writer about the Earth."]

ge·o·graph·ic /jeè ə gráffik/, **ge·o·graph·i·cal** *adj.* relating to geography in general, or to the geography of a specific region [Mid-16thC. Via French *géographique* or late Latin *geographicus* from Greek *geōgraphikos,* from *geōgraphos* (see GEOGRAPHER).] —**ge·o·graph·i·cal·ly** *adv.*

ge·o·graph·ic mile *n.* = **nautical mile**

ge·og·ra·phy /jee óggrəfee/ (*plural* **-phies**) *n.* **1. STUDY OF EARTH'S PHYSICAL FEATURES** the study of all the physical features of the Earth's surface, including its climate and the distribution of plant, animal, and human life **2. PHYSICAL FEATURES** the physical features of a place or region, e.g., mountains and rivers **3. BOOK ON GEOGRAPHY** a book on geography **4. LAYOUT OF A PLACE** the arrangement of the different parts of a building, city, or other place **5. ARRANGEMENT** the way that something is arranged and the relationships between its different elements ○ *the geography of the criminal mind* [15thC. Via Latin *geographia* from Greek *geōgraphia,* literally "writing about the Earth."]

ge·o·hy·drol·o·gy /jeè ō hī drólləjee/ *n.* = **hydrogeology** —**ge·o·hy·dro·log·ic** /jeè ō hīdrə lójjik/ *adj.* —**ge·o·hy·drol·o·gist** /-hī drólləjist/ *n.*

ge·oid /jeè òyd/ *n.* **1. EARTH'S SHAPE** the slightly flattened sphere that is the shape of the Earth, used in calculating the precise measurements of points on the earth's surface. ◊ **geodesy 2. HYPOTHETICAL SURFACE OF EARTH** a hypothetical surface of the Earth that would exist if a cross section were taken at sea level. It is perpendicular to the force of gravity at every point. [Late 19thC. From Greek *geoeidēs* "earthlike," from *gē* "Earth."] —**ge·oi·dal** *adj.*

geol. *abbr.* **1.** geologic **2.** geological **3.** geology

ge·o·log·ic time *n.* the period of time that extends from the beginning of the world to the present day

ge·ol·o·gize /jee óllə jīz/ (**-gized, -giz·ing, -giz·es**) *vti.* to study geology in general, or the geology of a specific place

ge·ol·o·gy /jee óllәjee/ *n.* **1. STUDY OF ROCKS AND MINERALS** the study of the structure of the earth or another planet, in particular its rocks, soil, and minerals, and its history and origins **2. STRUCTURE OF AN AREA** the rocks, minerals, and physical structure of a particular area **3. BOOK ON GEOLOGY** a book on geology [Mid-18thC. From modern Latin *geologia,* literally "description of the Earth."] —**ge·o·log·ic** /jeè ə lójjik/ *adj.* —**ge·o·log·i·cal** /-lójjik'l/ *adj.* —**ge·ol·o·gically** /-klee/ *adv.* —**ge·ol·o·gist** /jee óllәjist/ *n.*

geom. *abbr.* **1.** geometric **2.** geometrical **3.** geometry

ge·o·mag·net·ic pole *n.* = **magnetic pole** *n.* 2

ge·o·mag·net·ic storm *n.* = **magnetic storm**

ge·o·mag·ne·tism /jeè ō mágnə tìzzəm/ *n.* **1. EARTH'S MAGNETISM** the magnetic properties of the Earth **2. STUDY OF EARTH'S MAGNETISM** the study of the magnetic properties of the Earth —**ge·o·mag·ne·tic** /jeè ō mag néttik/ *adj.* —**ge·o·mag·net·i·cal·ly** /-néttikəlee/ *adv.*

ge·o·man·cy /jeè ə mànsee/ *n.* the art or practice of making predictions based on patterns made by a handful of earth thrown on the ground or by lines connecting randomly placed dots [14thC. Via medieval Latin from Greek *geōmanteia,* literally "divination from the Earth," from *manteia* "divination."] —**ge·o·man·cer** *n.* —**ge·o·man·tic** /jeè ə mántik/ *adj.*

ge·om·e·ter /jee ómmətər/ *n.* somebody who studies, or is an expert in, geometry [15thC. Via late Latin from Greek *geōmetrēs,* literally "land measurer," from, ultimately, *gē* "Earth" + *metrēs* "measurer."]

ge·o·met·ric /jeè ə méttrik/, **ge·o·met·ri·cal** *adj.* **1. RELATING TO GEOMETRY** conforming to the laws and methods of geometry **2. USING SIMPLE LINES** using straight lines and simple shapes, e.g., circles or squares **3. INCREASING FAST** increasing or decreasing very rapidly ○ *geometric growth* [Mid-17thC. Via French *géométrique* from, ultimately, Greek *geōmetrikos,* from *geōmetrēs* (see GEOMETER).] —**ge·o·met·ri·cal·ly** *adv.*

Ge·o·met·ric /jeè ə méttrik/ *adj.* relating to a period of ancient Greek culture, between 900 and 700 B.C., noted for its decorative use of simple lines and shapes, especially on pottery

ge·o·met·ric mean *n.* the average of a set of *n* values, described mathematically as the *nth* root of their product

ge·o·met·ric pro·gres·sion *n.* a series of numbers in which each number is separated by a numerical step. In the series 1, 4, 16, 64, the numerical step is 4.

ge·o·met·rics /jeè ə méttriks/ *npl.* straight lines and simple shapes, e.g., circles or squares, used in design and decoration

ge·o·met·ric se·ries *n.* a series of numbers (**geometric progression**) separated by a constant numerical step expressed as a sum, e.g., 1+4+16+64

ge·om·e·trid /jee ómmətrid/ *n.* a moth with a slender body and broad wings and larvae that crawl with a characteristic looping movement. Family: Geometridae. [Late 19thC. From modern Latin *Geometridae,* genus name, literally "land measurers" (see GEOMETRY). So called because the caterpillar moves as though measuring the ground.] —**ge·om·e·trid** *adj.*

ge·om·e·trize /jee ómmə trīz/ (**-trized, -triz·ing, -triz·es**) *v.* **1.** *vt.* **REPRESENT IN GEOMETRIC FORM** to represent something in geometric form **2.** *vti.* **APPLY RULES OF GEOMETRY** to apply the principles of geometry to something —**ge·om·e·tri·za·tion** /jee òmmətri záysh'n/ *n.*

ge·om·e·try /jee ómmətree/ *n.* **1. MATHEMATICS OF SHAPES** the branch of mathematics that is concerned with the properties and relationships of points, lines, angles, curves, surfaces, and solids **2. KIND OF GEOMETRY** any subclass of geometry, e.g., a set of distinct theories or its application to a particular type of problem or object **3. BOOK ON GEOMETRY** a book on geometry **4. ARRANGEMENT OF SOMETHING** the way the different parts of something fit together in relation to each other [14thC. Via French *géométrie* from, ultimately, Greek *geōmetria,* literally "measuring of the Earth," from *gē* "Earth" + *metron* "measure."]

ge·o·mor·phic /jeè ə máwrfik/ *adj.* relating to the surface features of the Earth or another planet

ge·o·mor·phol·o·gy /jeè ə mawr fólləjee/ *n.* the branch of geology that examines the formation and structure of the features of the surface of the Earth or another planet's surface —**ge·o·mor·pho·log·ic** /jeè ə mawrfə lójjik/ *adj.* —**ge·o·mor·pho·log·i·cal·ly** /-kəlee/ *adv.* —**ge·o·mor·phol·o·gist** /-mawr fólləjist/ *n.* —**ge·o·mor·pho·log·i·cal** *adj.*

ge·oph·a·gy /jee óffəjee/ *n.* the eating of soil, clay, or chalk

ge·o·phone /jeè ə fōn/ *n.* an electronic instrument that picks up vibrations in the Earth

ge·o·phys·ics /jeè ə fízziks/ *n.* the branch of earth science that deals with the physics and physical processes of the Earth, especially using noninvasive techniques, e.g., acoustic surveys of the structure of rocks —**ge·o·phys·i·cal** *adj.* —**ge·o·phys·i·cal·ly** *adv.* —**ge·o·phys·i·cist** /jeè ə fízzəssist/ *n.*

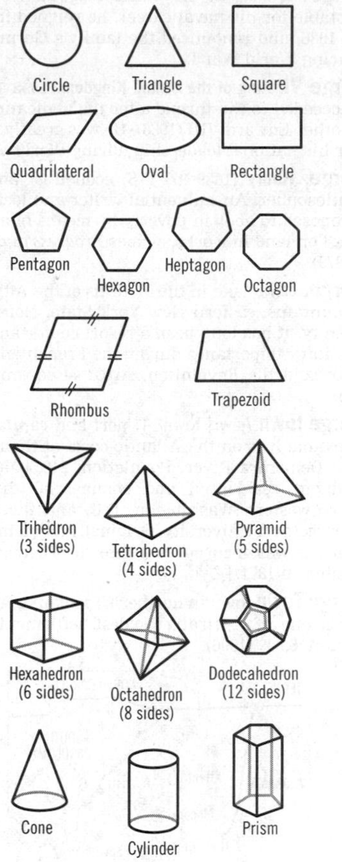

Geometry: Shapes and solids

ge·o·phyte /jeè ə fīt/ *n.* a perennial plant that propagates from organs that are below ground, e.g., bulbs, tubers, or rhizomes

ge·o·pol·i·tics /jeè ō póllitiks/ *n.* (*takes a singular verb*) **1. INFLUENCES OF GEOGRAPHY ON POLITICS** the relationships that exist between a country's politics and its geography and population distribution, or the influences that geography and population distribution have on political relations between countries **2. STUDY OF GEOPOLITICS** the study of geopolitics [Early 20thC. Blend of GEOGRAPHY and POLITICS.] —**ge·o·po·lit·i·cal** /jeè ō pəlíttik'l/ *adj.* —**ge·o·po·lit·i·cal·ly** /-pə líttikəlee/ *adv.* —**ge·o·pol·i·ti·cian** /jeè ō pollə tísh'n/ *n.*

ge·o·pon·ics /jeè ə pónniks/ *n.* the scientific study of agriculture (*takes a singular verb*) —**ge·o·pon·ic** *adj.*

Geor·die /jáwrdee/ *n.* **1.** *U.K.* **SOMEBODY FROM TYNESIDE** somebody who was born on or lives on Tyneside in northeastern England, especially somebody who speaks the local dialect of English **2. DIALECT SPOKEN IN TYNESIDE** the dialect of English spoken in Tyneside in northeastern England [Mid-19thC. From the local pronunciation of *Georgie,* diminutive of the name *George.*] —**Geor·die** *adj.*

George I /jawrj/, **King of Great Britain and Ireland** (1660–1727) German-born British monarch. The great-grandson of James I, he was the first of Britain's Hanoverian kings (1714–27).

George II, King of Great Britain and Ireland (1683–1760) German-born British monarch. As king (1727–60), he was a field commander in the War of the Austrian Succession (1740–48).

George III, King of the United Kingdom (1738–1820). He was the first British-born Hanoverian king. His reign (1760–1820) was marked by the American Revolution. In later years, he was increasingly affected by a psychiatric disorder that led finally to the establishment of a regency (1811) under his son, later George IV.

George IV, King of the United Kingdom (1762–1830). Notorious for his extravagant habits, he was regent for George III (1811–20) and king (1820–30).

George V, King of the United Kingdom (1865–1936). Notable for his naval career, he reigned from 1910 to 1936, and renounced the family's German titles during World War I.

George VI, King of the United Kingdom (1895–1952). He succeeded to the throne after the abdication of his brother Edward VIII (1936). He was greatly admired for his national leadership during World War II.

George, Henry (1839–97) U.S. economist and social philosopher. An influential writer and lecturer, he proposed to abolish poverty by means of a "single-tax" on land in works such as *Progress and Poverty* (1879).

George, Lake lake in the foothills of the Adirondack Mountains, eastern New York State. Noted for its beauty, it has long been a resort center and was of military importance during the French and Indian War and the Revolution. Area: 44 sq. mi./114 sq. km.

George·town /jáwrj town/ **1.** port and capital city of Guyana. It is on the Atlantic coast at the mouth of the Demerara River. Population: 248,500 (1992). **2.** affluent residential and commercial district of northwestern Washington, D.C. and the home of Georgetown University. Originally a Potomac River port, it was incorporated into the District of Columbia in 1871.

George Town town in northern Tasmania, Australia. It is one of Australia's oldest settlements. Population: 6,929 (1996).

Georgia

Geor·gia /jáwrjə/ **1.** U.S. state bordered by South Carolina, the Atlantic Ocean, Florida, Alabama, North Carolina, and Tennessee. Capital: Atlanta. Population: 7,486,242 (1997). Area: 58,977 sq. mi./152,750 sq. km. **2.** republic on the eastern coast of the Black Sea bordered on the north by Russia and on the south by Turkey, Armenia, and Azerbaijan. The country is dominated by the Greater Caucasus to the north and the Lesser Caucasus to the south. Language: Georgian. Currency: lari. Capital: Tbilisi. Population: 5,160,042 (1997). Area: 26,900 sq. mi./69,700 sq. km. Official name **Republic of Georgia**

Geor·gian[1] /jáwrjən/ *adj.* **1.** HIST **OF 1714 TO 1830 IN BRITAIN** relating to the time of Kings George I, II, III, and IV of Great Britain and Ireland, who reigned consecutively from 1714 to 1830 **2.** ARCHIT **OF 18THC ARCHITECTURAL STYLE** built in or imitating a style of architecture or furniture that flourished in Great Britain and the United States in the 18th and early 19th centuries **3.** LITERAT **RELATING TO 20THC LITERARY MOVEMENT** relating to a movement in early 20th-century poetry that favored traditional styles ■ *n.* LITERAT **GEORGIAN WRITER** a writer whose works belong to the Georgian literary movement

Geor·gian[2] *n.* **1.** LANG **OFFICIAL LANGUAGE OF GEORGIA** the official language of the Republic of Georgia. It belongs to the Kartvelian family of languages. **2.** **SOMEBODY FROM U.S. STATE OF GEORGIA** somebody who was born in or lives in the state of Georgia in the United States **3.** PEOPLES **SOMEBODY FROM GEORGIA** somebody who was born or lives in or is a citizen of the Republic of Georgia [15thC. Formed from *Georgia*, a region in the Caucasus and a state of the United States.] —**Geor·gian** *adj.*

Geor·gian Bay /jàwrjən báy/ northeastern arm of Lake Huron, in southeastern Ontario, Canada. Area: 5,800 sq. mi./15,000 sq. km.

Geor·gian Bay Is·lands Na·tion·al Park national park incorporating fifty-nine islands on the eastern side of Georgian Bay in southeastern Ontario, Canada. Area: 10 sq. mi./25 sq. km.

geor·gic /jáwrjik/ *adj.* **RURAL** relating to or depicting rural life (*literary*) ■ *n.* POETRY **POEM ABOUT RURAL LIFE** a poem about rural life ■ *adj.* AGRIC **OF AGRICULTURE** relating to agriculture [Early 16thC. Via Latin from Greek *geōrgikos*, from *geōrgos* "farmer," from *gē* "Earth."]

ge·o·sci·ence /jèe ō sí əns/ *n.* a science such as geology or geophysics that deals with the Earth —**ge·o·sci·en·tist** *n.*

ge·o·sphere /jée ō sfeer/ *n.* the solid matter of the earth, as distinct from the seas, plants, animals, and surrounding atmosphere —**ge·o·spher·ic** /jèe ō sfírrik, -sférrik/ *adj.*

ge·o·sta·tion·ar·y /jèe ō stáysh'n èrree/ *adj.* used to describe the orbit of satellite that circles the earth above the equator at a speed matching the earth's rotation, thus appearing to remain stationary, or the satellite itself. Most communications satellites are in geostationary orbit.

ge·o·strat·e·gy /jèe ō stráttəjee/ (*plural* **-gies**) *n.* **1.** **STRATEGY IN RELATION TO GEOPOLITICS** the study of strategy in relation to the geopolitical situation of a country or region **2.** **POLICY BASED ON GEOPOLITICS** the policy of a nation based on a combination of geographical and political factors —**ge·o·stra·te·gic** /-strə téejik/ *adj.* —**ge·o·strat·e·gist** /-stráttəjist/ *n.*

ge·o·stroph·ic /jèe ə stróffik/ *adj.* arising from the rotation of the Earth —**ge·o·stroph·i·cal·ly** *adv.*

ge·o·syn·chro·nous /jèe ō síng krənəss/ *adj.* = **geostationary**

ge·o·syn·cline /jèe ō síng klīn/ *n.* a long broad depression in the Earth's crust where it has sunk over time as it has accumulated a thick layer of sedimentary deposits —**ge·o·syn·cli·nal** /jèe ō sing klín'l/ *adj.*

ge·o·tax·is /jèe ō tákssiss/ *n.* movement by an organism or cell in response to the force of gravity —**ge·o·tac·tic** *adj.* —**ge·o·tac·ti·cal·ly** *adv.*

ge·o·tec·ton·ic /jèe ō tek tónnik/ *adj.* relating to the large-scale structure of the Earth's crust —**ge·o·tec·ton·i·cal·ly** *adv.*

ge·o·ther·mic /-mik/, **ge·o·ther·mal** /jèe ō thúrm'l/ *adj.* relating to or produced by the heat in the interior of the Earth —**ge·o·ther·mal·ly** *adv.*

ge·ot·ro·pism /jee óttrə pìzzəm/ *n.* plant growth or movement in response to gravity. Upward growth of plant parts, against gravity, is called negative geotropism, and downward growth of roots, positive geotropism. —**ge·o·tro·pic** /jèe ə tróppik/ *adj.* —**ge·o·tro·pi·cal·ly** *adv.*

ger. *abbr.* gerund

Ger. *abbr.* **1.** German **2.** Germany

ge·rah /géerə/ *n.* an ancient Hebrew coin worth one twentieth of a shekel [Mid-16thC. From Hebrew *gērāh*.]

ge·ra·ni·ol /jə ráynee àwl/ *n.* a pale yellow or colorless alcohol that is found in many essential oils. It smells like geraniums and is used in making perfumes and flavorings. Formula: $C_{10}H_{18}O$. [Late 19thC. Coined from GERANIUM + -OL.]

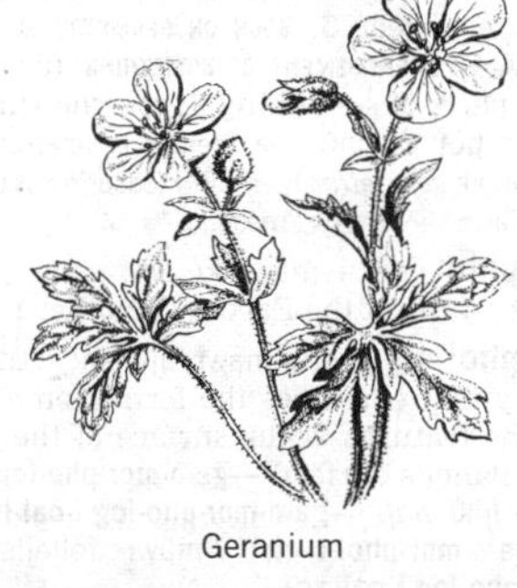
Geranium

ge·ra·ni·um /jə ráynee əm/ *n.* **1.** PLANTS **PLANT WITH BRIGHTLY COLORED FLOWERS** a popular garden plant with large rounded leaves and bright red, pink, or white flowers on tall stalks. Genus: *Pelargonium.* (*not used technically*) **2.** PLANTS **PLANT WITH SAUCER-SHAPED FLOWERS** a plant with divided leaves and pink, blue, white, or red saucer-shaped flowers. Cranesbill and herb Robert are types of geranium. Genus: *Geranium.* **3.** COLORS **BRIGHT RED COLOR** a bright red color tinged with orange, similar to that of a scarlet geranium ■ *adj.* **BRIGHT RED** of a bright red color tinged with orange [Mid-16thC. Via Latin from Greek *geranion*, from *geranos* "crane," from the resemblance of the spur on some species' fruit to a crane's bill.]

Gerbil

ger·bil /júrb'l/ *n.* a small rodent resembling a mouse with long back legs that is native to hot dry parts of Africa and Asia. Some species are popular as pets. Subfamily: Gerbillinae. [Mid-19thC. Via French *gerbille* from modern Latin *gerbillus*, diminutive of *gerboa* (see JERBOA).]

ge·rent /jérrənt/ *n.* a ruler or leader (*literary*) [Late 16thC. From, ultimately, Latin *gerere* "to carry on."]

ge·re·nuk /gérrə nòok, gə rénnək/ (*plural* **-nuks** *or* **-nuk**) *n.* a slender East African antelope, the male of which has long horns that curve backward. Latin name: *Litocranius walleri.* [Late 19thC. From Somali.]

ger·fal·con *n.* BIRDS = **gyrfalcon**

ger·i·at·ric /jèrree áttrik/ *adj.* **1.** MED **RELATING TO SENIOR CITIZENS** relating to the diagnosis, treatment, and prevention of illness in senior citizens **2.** **OFFENSIVE TERM REFERRING TO AGE** an offensive term meaning very old, especially when somebody is considered too old to be useful or taken seriously (*offensive*) ■ *n.* MED **SENIOR CITIZEN** a senior citizen, in a medical context (*technical*) [Early 20thC. Coined from Greek *gēras* "old age" + -IATRIC on the model of PEDIATRIC.]

ger·i·a·tri·cian /jèrree ə trísh'n/ *n.* a doctor who specializes in medical care for senior citizens

ger·i·at·rics /jèrree áttriks/ *n.* the branch of medicine that deals with the illnesses and medical care of senior citizens (*takes a singular verb*) ◊ **gerontology**

ger·i·at·rist /jèrree áttrist/ *n.* = **geriatrician**

Ge·rin-La·joie /zhay ràN lə zhwàa/, **Antoine** (1824–82) Canadian writer. He wrote poems, novels, and plays, and founded two magazines.

germ /jurm/ *n.* **1.** BIOL **MICROORGANISM** a microorganism, especially one that can cause disease **2.** BIOL **CELL** the smallest element in an organism, e.g., a spore or a fertilized egg, that is capable of growing into a complete adult or part **3.** **BEGINNING** the first sign of something that will develop ○ *the germ of an idea* [Mid-15thC. Via French *germe* from Latin *germen* "seed, sprout," from *gignere* "to beget."]

ger·man /júrmən/ *adj.* having the same parents, or closely related ○ *brothers-german* [Via French *germain* from Latin *germanus* "having the same parents," from *germen* (see GERM)]

Ger·man *n.* **1.** PEOPLES **SOMEBODY FROM GERMANY** somebody who was born or raised in Germany, or who has German citizenship **2.** LANG **OFFICIAL LANGUAGE OF GERMANY** the official language of Germany, Austria, and Liechtenstein and one of the official languages of Switzerland. It belongs to the Germanic branch of Indo-European languages and is spoken in many parts of the world by about 100 million native speakers, with approximately a further 100 million using it as a second language. **3.** **SOMEBODY WHO SPEAKS GERMAN** somebody whose first language is German ■ *adj.* **1.** **RELATING TO GERMANY** relating to or typical of Germany, or its people or culture **2.** **RELATING TO GERMAN** relating to the German language [14thC. From Latin *Germanus*, applied to a group of related peoples of northern and central Europe.]

Ger·man cock·roach *n.* a small brown cockroach that is a common pest throughout the world. Latin name: *Blattella germanica.*

ger·man·der /jər mándər/ (*plural* **-ders** *or* **-der**) *n.* a flowering plant that has small pink, white, or pale purple flowers with a small upper lip. Genus: *Te-*

ucrium. [15thC. Via medieval Latin *germandr(e)a* from, ultimately, Greek *khamaidrus,* literally "ground oak."]

ger·mane /jər máyn/ *adj.* suitably related to something, especially something being discussed (*formal*) [Early 17thC. Variant of GERMAN.] —**ger·mane·ly** *adv.* —**ger·mane·ness** *n.*

Ger·man·ic /jər mánnik/ *n.* **EUROPEAN LANGUAGE GROUP** a group of languages spoken across northwestern Europe that forms a branch of Indo-European and is conventionally divided into the three subgroups West, North, and East Germanic. About 500 million people use one of the languages classified as Germanic as their first language. ■ *adj.* **1. OF GERMANIC** relating to the group of languages classified as Germanic **2. OF GERMANY** of Germany, or its people or culture [Mid-17thC. From Latin *Germanicus,* from *Germanus* (see GERMAN).]

Ger·man·ism /júrmə nìzzəm/ *n.* **1. GERMAN WORD** a word or phrase borrowed or adapted from the German language **2. GERMAN QUALITY** a custom or trait regarded as typically German **3. LIKING FOR GERMANY** fondness for Germany and all things German

Ger·man·ist /júrmənist/ *n.* a student of or specialist in German language, literature, and culture

ger·ma·ni·um /jər máynee əm/ *n.* a brittle gray crystalline chemical element that is a metalloid used as a semiconductor and in alloys. Symbol **Ge** [Late 19thC. Coined from Latin *Germanus* "German" by Clemens Winkler, the German chemist who discovered it (see GERMAN).]

ger·man·ize /júrmə nīz/ (**-ized, -iz·ing, -izes**) *vti.* to adopt German styles, tastes, institutions, or customs, or introduce them into something —**ger·man·i·za·tion** /jùrməni záysh'n/ *n.*

Ger·man mea·sles *n.* = **rubella**

Ger·man·o·phile /jər mánnə fīl/ *n.* an admirer of Germany and the Germans

Ger·man·o·phobe /jər mánnə fōb/ *n.* somebody who dislikes Germany and the Germans

Ger·man shep·herd *n.* a large working dog with medium-length hair, pointed ears, and a muscular build, belonging to a breed of German origin that is often used as a guard dog or police dog

Ger·man sil·ver *n.* = **nickel silver**

Ger·man·town /júrmən town/ town near Philadelphia, Pennsylvania, that was the site of an unsuccessful attack on the British camp by Washington's troops in the Revolution in 1777

Germany

Ger·ma·ny /júrmənee/ federal republic in central Europe. Divided into East and West Germany following World War II, it became a unified country again in 1990. Language: German. Currency: deutsche mark. Capital: Berlin. Population: 82,071,765 (1997). Area: 137,823 sq. mi./356,959 sq. km. Official name **Federal Republic of Germany**

germ cell *n.* BIOL = **germ** *n.* 2

ger·mi·cide /júrmə sīd/ *n.* a preparation that kills germs —**ger·mi·ci·dal** /júrmə sīd'l/ *adj.*

ger·mi·nal /júrmən'l/ *adj.* **1. OF REPRODUCTIVE CELLS** relating to reproductive cells **2. OF THE EARLY STAGES** relating to or belonging to the earliest stage in the development of something (*formal*) [Early 19thC. From Latin *germen* (see GERM).] —**ger·mi·nal·ly** *adv.*

Ger·mi·nal *n.* the seventh month of the year in the French Revolutionary calendar, corresponding to March 22 to April 20 in the Gregorian calendar [Early 19thC. Via French from Latin *germen* (see GERM).]

ger·mi·nal ves·i·cle *n.* the enlarged nucleus of an egg before it develops into an ovum

ger·mi·nate /júrmə nàyt/ (**-nat·ed, -nat·ing, -nates**) *v.* **1.** *vti.* **START GROWING FROM SEED** to start to grow from a seed or spore into a new individual **2.** *vi.* **DEVELOP** to be created and start to develop [Late 16thC. From Latin *germinare,* from *germen* (see GERM).] —**ger·mi·na·tion** /jùrmə náysh'n/ *n.* —**ger·mi·na·tive** /júrmə nàytiv/ *adj.* —**ger·mi·na·tor** /júrmə nàytər/ *n.*

germ lay·er *n.* any of the three distinct layers of cells formed during an embryo's early stages of development (**gastrulation**)

germ line *n.* a group of cells in a developing embryo from which reproductive cells (**gametes**) develop, regarded as the line of descent from one generation to another

germ plasm /-plàzzəm/ *n.* the hereditary material that is transmitted from one generation to another

germ the·o·ry *n.* **1. THEORY THAT GERMS CAUSE INFECTIONS** the theory that all infectious and contagious diseases are caused by microorganisms **2. THEORY OF BIOLOGICAL DEVELOPMENT** the theory that organisms develop from previous generations through the growth of germ cells

germ tube *n.* a hollow tube that grows from a germinating spore

germ war·fare *n.* = **biological warfare**

germ·y /júrmee/ (**-i·er, -i·est**) *adj.* full of harmful microorganisms (*informal*) —**germ·i·ness** *n.*

ger·o·don·tics /jèrrə dóntiks/ *n.* the branch of dentistry focusing on the needs of senior citizens (*takes a singular verb*) [Late 20thC. Coined from Greek *gēras* "old age" + ODONTO- + -ICS.] —**ger·o·don·tic** *adj.*

Geronimo

Ge·ron·i·mo /jə rónnəmō/ (1829–1909) U.S. Chiricahua Apache leader. He was a legendary warrior who led his people in raids on settlers and U.S. troops before being captured in 1886. Born **Goyathlay**

geront-, geronto- *prefix.* aging, old age ○ *gerontology* [Via French from, ultimately, Greek *geront-,* the stem of *gerōn* "old man"; related to *gēras* "old age" (source of English *geriatrics*)]

ger·on·toc·ra·cy /jèrrən tókrəssee/ (*plural* **-cies**) *n.* **1. GOVERNMENT BY ELDERS** a system of government in which the elders are chosen as rulers **2. GOVERNING ELDERS** a group of elders who make up a government —**ge·ron·to·crat** /jə róntə kràt/ *n.* —**ge·ron·to·crat·ic** /-kráttik/ *adj.*

ger·on·tol·o·gy /jèrrən tóllәjee/ *n.* the scientific study of aging and its effects. ◊ **geriatrics** —**ge·ron·to·log·ic** /jə ròntə lójjik/ *adj.* —**ge·ron·to·log·i·cal** *adj.* —**ger·on·tol·o·gist** /jèrrən tólləjist/ *n.*

Ger·ry /gérree/, **Elbridge** (1744–1814) U.S. statesman and vice president of the United States. He signed the Declaration of Independence and the Articles of Confederation, and as governor of Massachusetts (1810–12) reorganized electoral districts in a process that came to be called "gerrymandering."

ger·ry·man·der /jérri màndər/ *vti.* (**-dered, -der·ing, -ders**) **TRY TO GET EXTRA VOTES UNFAIRLY** to manipulate an electoral area, usually by altering its boundaries, in order to gain an unfair political advantage in an election ■ *n.* **1. ACT OF GERRYMANDERING** an unfair manipulation of an electoral area for political advantage **2. MANIPULATED ELECTORAL AREA** an electoral area manipulated in such a way as to give one political party an unfair advantage in an election [Early 19thC. A blend of Elbridge GERRY and SALAMANDER, from the shape of an electoral district he created to favor his own party.]

George Gershwin

Gersh·win /gúrshwin/, **George** (1898–1937) U.S. composer. Jazz, classical, and popular influences combined in his outstandingly inventive works, many of which became American classics. He wrote *Rhapsody in Blue* (1924), the opera *Porgy and Bess* (1935), and, with his brother Ira Gershwin, songs including "Someone to Watch Over Me." Born **Jacob Gershvin**

Gersh·win, Ira (1896–1983) U.S. lyricist and dramatist. A collaborator with his brother George Gershwin and other leading composers, he wrote lyrics for 20 Broadway musicals, and shared a Pulitzer Prize for *Of Thee I Sing* (1931). Born **Israel Gershvin**

ger·und /jérrənd/ *n.* **1. NOUN FROM A VERB** a noun formed from a verb, describing an action, state, or process. In English, it is formed from the verb's *-ing* form, as "smoking" is in the phrase "No smoking." **2. LATIN NOUN** a Latin noun ending in "-ndum," formed from a verb and describing an action, state, or process [Early 16thC. From late Latin *gerundium,* from, ultimately, Latin *gerere* "to carry on."] —**ge·run·di·al** /jə rúndee əl/ *adj.*

ge·run·dive /jə rúndiv/ *n.* a Latin adjective ending in "-ndus," formed from a verb and meaning "that must or ought to be done" [15thC. From late Latin *gerundivus modus* "gerundive mood," from *gerundium* (see GERUND).] —**ge·run·di·val** /jèrrən dīv'l/ *adj.*

Ge·sell /gi zél/, **Arnold** (1880–1961) U.S. psychologist. He pioneered research into child development using movie cameras and one-way mirrors. Full name **Arnold Lucius Gesell**

Ges·ner /géssnər/, **Abraham** (1797–1864) Canadian inventor and geologist. He is known as the founder of the modern petroleum industry because of his patents for distilling bituminous material.

ges·so /jéssō/ (*plural* **-soes**) *n.* **1. PLASTER USED IN ART** a mixture of plaster and glue or size, used in sculpture and as a background for paintings **2. PIECE OF ART USING GESSO** a painting done on gesso, or a sculpture done in gesso [Late 16thC. Via Italian from Latin *gypsum* (see GYPSUM).] —**ges·soed** *adj.*

gest /jest/, **geste** *n.* (*archaic*) **1. ADVENTURE** a heroic exploit or adventure **2. TALE OF ADVENTURE** a story or romance, especially one written in verse [12thC. Via Old French from Latin *gesta* "actions," from *gerere* "to carry, act."]

ge·stalt /gə shtaált/ (*plural* **-stalts** *or* **-stalt·en** /-shtaált'n/), **Ge·stalt** *n.* a set of elements such as a person's thoughts and experiences considered as a whole and regarded as amounting to more than the sum of its parts [Early 20thC. From German, "shape."] —**ge·stalt·ist** *n.*

Ge·stalt psy·chol·o·gy, ge·stalt psy·chol·o·gy *n.* a branch of psychology that treats behavior and perception as an integrated whole and not simply the sum of individual stimuli and responses

Ge·stalt ther·a·py, ge·stalt ther·a·py *n.* a form of psychotherapy in which emphasis is placed on feelings and on the influence on personality development of unresolved personal issues from the past

Ge·sta·po /gə staá pō, -shtaá-/ *n.* the secret state police under the Nazi regime in Germany, noted for its brutality [Mid-20thC. A German acronym, formed from *Geheime Staatspolizei* "Secret State Police."]

ges·tate /jés tàyt/ (**-tat·ed, -tat·ing, -tates**) *vti.* **1.** MED **CARRY OFFSPRING IN THE WOMB** to carry offspring in the womb, or develop as offspring in the womb **2. DEVELOP IDEAS IN THE MIND** to develop in the mind, or allow an idea or plan to develop in the mind [Mid-19thC. From Latin *gestare* (see GESTATION).]

ges·ta·tion /je stáysh'n/ *n.* **1.** MED **CARRYING OF OFFSPRING IN THE WOMB** the process of carrying offspring in the womb during pregnancy **2.** MED **PERIOD OF DEVELOPMENT OF THE FETUS** the period of development of the offspring during pregnancy **3. DEVELOPMENT** the development of an idea or plan in the mind, or the time it takes to develop [Mid-16thC. From the Latin stem *gestation-*, from *gestare* "to carry in the womb," from *gerere* "to carry."] —**ges·ta·tion·al** *adj.* —**ges·ta·to·ry** /jéstə tàwree/ *adj.*

geste /jest/ *n.* = **gest**

ges·tic·u·late /je stíkyə làyt/ (**-lat·ed, -lat·ing, -lates**) *vti.* to move the arms or hands when speaking, or express something with movements of the arms or hands [Early 17thC. From Latin *gesticulari*, from, ultimately, *gestus* "action, gesture," from *gerere* "to carry, act."] —**ges·tic·u·la·tive** *adj.* —**ges·tic·u·la·tor** *n.* —**ges·tic·u·la·to·ry** /je stíkyələ tàwree/ *adj.*

ges·tic·u·la·tion /je stìkyə láysh'n/ *n.* movement with the hands or arms, usually accompanying speech [15thC. From the Latin stem *gesticulation-*, from *gesticulari* (see GESTICULATE).]

ges·ture /jéschər/ *n.* **1. BODY MOVEMENT** a movement made with a part of the body in order to express meaning or emotion, or to communicate an instruction **2. ACTION COMMUNICATING SOMETHING** an action intended to communicate feelings or intentions **3. USE OF GESTURES** the use of body movements to communicate ■ *vti.* (**-tured, -tur·ing, -tures**) **MAKE A BODY MOVEMENT** to make a movement with a part of the body in order to express meaning or emotion, or to communicate an instruction [15thC. From medieval Latin *gestura* "deportment," from Latin *gerere* "to carry, act" (source of English *digest* and *suggest*).] —**ges·tur·al** *adj.* —**ges·tur·al·ly** *adv.*

WORD KEY: ORIGIN

The Latin word *gerere* from which ***gesture*** is derived is also the source of English *congest, digest, gestation, gesticulate, ingest, jest, jester,* and *suggest.*

ge·sund·heit /gə zǒont hìt/ *interj.* used as an expression of good health to somebody who has just sneezed [Early 20thC. From German, literally "health."]

get[1] /get/ (**got, got** /got/ *or* **got·ten** /gótt'n/, **get·ting, gets**) CORE MEANING: a verb indicating that somebody obtains, receives, earns, or is given something. It is often used instead of more formal terms such as "obtain" or "acquire." ○ *When you drop your child off at school, you want to know that he or she is getting a good education.* ○ *Where will they get the money to buy the land?*

1. *vi.* **BECOME** to become, or begin to have a particular quality ○ *When I get nervous, I get scared.* **2.** *vt.* **CAUSE SOMETHING TO BE DONE** to cause something to happen or be done ○ *I must get the car cleaned.* **3.** *vt.* **BRING SOMETHING** to fetch or bring something ○ *I'm going back to my apartment to get my watch.* ○ *I'll get your coat for you.* **4.** *vt.* **CATCH AN ILLNESS** to be affected by an illness or medical condition ○ *He got chicken-pox last year.* **5.** *vi.* **BE IN A PARTICULAR STATE** to enter or leave a particular state or condition ○ *Get ready to leave in five minutes.* **6.** *vi.* **MOVE SOMEWHERE** to succeed in moving somewhere, or arrive somewhere ○ *It was already midnight when we got home.* **7.** *vt.* **BEGIN SOMETHING** to begin doing something (*informal*) ○ *Let's get going – we have to be there by eight.* **8.** *v.* **FORMS PASSIVES** used instead of "be" as an auxiliary verb to form passives ○ *If you play with matches you will get burned.* **9.** *vt.* **ARREST SOMEBODY** to arrest or capture somebody (*informal*) ○ *They got him just as he was running out of the bank.* **10.** *vt.* **MANAGE SOMETHING** to manage or contrive something (*informal*) ○ *How did they get to be so successful?* **11.** *vt.* **PREPARE FOOD** to prepare a meal ○ *I'll get dinner tonight.* **12.** *vt.* **PERSUADE SOMEBODY** to persuade somebody to do something ○ *Colleagues had tried to get her to take a vacation.* **13.** *vt.* **UNDERSTAND SOMETHING** to hear or understand something, e.g., a joke or somebody's point (*informal*) ○ *What's that? I didn't get what you said.* **14.** *vt.* **USE A FORM OF TRANSPORTATION** to take a particular form of transportation ○ *I don't want to drive – I'd rather get a plane.* **15.** *vt.* **OBTAIN A RESULT** to obtain a result, e.g. by experiment or calculation ○ *What's the answer? I get nine.* **16.** *vt.* **RECEIVE A SIGNAL** to receive a broadcast signal, e.g. a radio or television broadcast ○ *I can't get Channel 5 with that antenna.* **17.** *vt.* **IRRITATE SOMEBODY** to annoy or irritate somebody (*informal*) ○ *That high whining noise really gets me.* **18.** *vt.* **HAVE THE TIME** to have the time or opportunity to do something ○ *I'll fix it as soon as I get the time.* **19.** *vt.* **HAVE AN IDEA** to have or receive an idea, impression, feeling, or benefit ○ *You've got the wrong impression – I'm not like that at all.* ○ *I get a lot of pleasure from his stories.* **20.** *vt.* **MANAGE TO SEE SOMETHING** to succeed in seeing something ○ *get a close-up look* **21.** *vt.* **HIT SOMEBODY** to hit somebody (*informal*) ○ *The blow got him in the face.* **22.** *vt.* **HAVE REVENGE ON SOMEBODY** to have revenge on somebody, especially by killing the person (*informal*) ○ *The heroes get Dracula in the end.* **23.** *vi.* **GAIN ACCESS TO SOMEBODY** to gain access to somebody with intent to bribe him or her (*informal*) ○ *I thought he was incorruptible, but they finally got to him.* **24.** *vi.* **TO LEAVE** to leave (*informal*) (*often used in commands*) ○ *Now get!* **25.** *vt.* **CONCEIVE SOMEBODY** to beget or conceive somebody (*archaic*) [13thC. Via Old Norse *geta* from, ultimately, an Indo-European base meaning "to seize," which is also the ancestor of English *guess.*] —**get·a·ble** *adj.* ◇ **get with it** become fashionable and responsive to new styles and ideas (*informal*)

WORD KEY: USAGE

got or **gotten**? The past participles ***got*** and ***gotten*** convey slightly different ideas. *They have gotten an apartment in Boston* means they have recently taken the apartment, whereas *they have got an apartment in Boston* simply indicates that they have it. (There are those who would argue, with reason, that in a sentence like this one ***got*** is redundant, and that *have* alone would do the job.) In informal usage, *have got* can also be followed by an infinitive to denote obligation (*I've got to go to the party* means "I must"), whereas *have gotten* with an infinitive denotes opportunity (*I've gotten to go to the party* means "I've been given the chance to attend").

WORD KEY: SYNONYMS

get, acquire, obtain, gain, procure, secure

CORE MEANING: to come into possession of something

get a general word, meaning to become the owner of something or to succeed in finding and possessing it, that can be substituted for any of the other words in this group; **acquire** a more formal word than ***get***, sometimes used to suggest that getting something took a lot of time or effort; **obtain** a more formal word than ***get***, sometimes used to emphasize the active seeking out of or striving to get something; **gain** used to suggest greater effort than *obtain* and possibly that merit or expertise was involved in getting something, and is often used to emphasize that the thing gained is advantageous or profitable; **procure** used to emphasize a great degree of effort that has gone into coming into possession of something; **secure** used to suggest that something was difficult to get but that the ownership of it is now certain.

get about *vi.* **1. MOVE AROUND** to be able to move with a medical condition **2.** = **get around** *v.* **1**

get across *vti.* to make something understood or to communicate clearly ○ *I don't seem to be getting across to you.*

get after *vt.* to keep telling somebody to do something in an annoying way (*informal*) ○ *You'll have to get after him if you want it finished by the weekend.*

get ahead *vi.* to become successful, especially when compared to others ○ *He's a good worker, but he hasn't got what it takes to get ahead in this line of business.*

get along *vi.* **1. BE FRIENDLY WITH SOMEBODY** to be on good terms with somebody socially **2. MANAGE** to make progress in a situation ○ *How's he getting along in the new job?* **3. LEAVE** to leave a place (*often used in commands*)

get around *v.* **1.** *vi.* **HAVE A SOCIAL LIFE** to be socially active and aware of what is happening ○ *I have the feeling you don't get around much.* **2.** *vi.* **BECOME KNOWN** to become widely known ○ *If news of this gets around, I may have to leave town* **3.** *vt.* **EVADE SOMETHING** to manage to operate in spite of a regulation, prohibition, or difficulty ○ *There must be some way of getting around the regulations.* **4.** *vi.* **SAY OR DO SOMETHING AT LAST** finally to say or do something after delay, hesitation, or being involved with other things ○ *I wondered when you'd get around to telling me that.*

get at *vt.* **1. REACH SOMEBODY OR SOMETHING** to succeed in reaching, finding, or making contact with somebody or something ○ *I'm determined to get at the truth if it takes all night.* **2. MEAN SOMETHING** to imply, suggest, or be trying to say something ○ *What exactly are you getting at?* **3. CRITICIZE SOMEBODY REPEATEDLY** to criticize somebody continually and unreasonably ○ *You're always getting at me, and I'm sick of it.* **4. FIND SOMETHING OUT** to discover or find out something ○ *We were determined to get at the source of the rumors.*

get away *vi.* **1. ESCAPE** to escape from somebody or something ○ *They caught one man, but the rest got away.* **2. LEAVE A PLACE** to succeed in leaving or spending time away from a place ○ *We hope to get away for a few days next month.*

get away with *vt.* to manage to do something without being blamed or penalized, or without experiencing some other bad result that should have been expected ○ *You could get away with a phone call, but it would be better to write.*

get back *vi.* **1. RETURN TO SOMETHING** to return to a place, topic, or activity ○ *Let's get back to what Steve was saying earlier.* **2. REPLY TO SOMEBODY** to give somebody an answer or continue a discussion, especially by letter, e-mail, or telephone ○ *Leave it with me, and I'll get back to you as soon as possible.* ◇ **get back at** to take your revenge on somebody

get by *v.* **1.** *vi.* **JUST MANAGE TO KEEP GOING** to manage to survive or just make ends meet ○ *It's hard to get by on $100 a week.* **2.** *vi.* **SUCCEED WITH MINIMAL EFFORT** to get through something by doing as little work as possible **3.** *vt.* **CLOSELY PASS SOMEBODY OR SOMETHING** to pass or move behind somebody or something closely ○ *We got by that parked truck with only an inch to spare.* **4.** *vt.* **PASS INSPECTION** to pass somebody's inspection or receive somebody's approval, with the implication that this should not have happened ○ *How on earth did those errors get by the proofreader?*

get down *v.* **1.** *vt.* **DEMORALIZE SOMEBODY** to make somebody demoralized or discouraged ○ *This job is beginning to get me down.* **2.** *vt.* **WRITE SOMETHING** to write something down, especially immediately **3.** *vt.* **SWALLOW SOMETHING** to swallow something, especially unwillingly or with difficulty ○ *The medicine smelled so bad I just couldn't get it down.* **4.** *vi.* **HAVE FUN** to relax and enjoy yourself in an unrestrained way (*informal*) ○ *It's time to get down and party.*

get down to *vt.* to start concentrating seriously on something or getting something done

get in *v.* **1.** *vi.* **TO ARRIVE** to arrive somewhere, especially home ○ *When does your plane get in?* **2.** *vi.* **BE CHOSEN** to succeed in being admitted to a group or organization, e.g., by election or interview ○ *You know if they get in they'll change some of the old laws.* **3.** *vti.* **GET INVOLVED WITH SOMEBODY OR SOMETHING** to become involved, or let somebody become involved, with a group or in an activity ○ *She got in with the golf club crowd.* **4.** *vt.* **MANAGE TO DO SOMETHING** to succeed in finding or making an opportunity to do something ○ *I don't think we can get four interviews in before lunch.*

get into *vt.* **1. START TO BE IN A BAD SITUATION** to begin to experience difficulties, or make somebody experience difficulties ○ *You'll get into all kinds of trouble if you do that.* **2. GET INVOLVED OR INTERESTED IN SOMETHING** to become involved or absorbed in something ○ *She's starting to get into programming.*

get off *v.* **1.** *vi.* **LEAVE** to leave a place or position ○ *We have to get off at the crack of dawn tomorrow.* **2.** *vti.* **BE ABLE TO LEAVE WORK** to be allowed to leave work, especially at the end of the working day ○ *What time do you get off this afternoon?* **3.** *vt.* **SEND A COMMUNICATION OR PACKAGE** to send a written communication or package ○ *I need to get these letters off tonight.* **4.** *vi.* **HAVE A LUCKY ESCAPE** to experience only minor consequences of a mistake, misguided action, or accident ○ *Considering what might have happened, I think you got off very lightly.* **5.** *vti.* **GAIN AN ACQUITTAL** to be acquitted in a court of law, or successfully defend somebody in a court of law (*informal*) ○ *A good lawyer could get him off with no trouble.* **6.** *vi.* **BE SO BOLD** to be bold enough to say or do something (*informal*) (*usually disapproving*) ○ *Where does he get off thinking he can speak to me that way?* **7.** *vi.* **BE AROUSED OR EXCITED** to experience excitement, physical arousal, or the effects of a drug (*slang*) **8.** *vi.* **HAVE ORGASM** to have an orgasm (*slang*) (*vulgar*)

get on *vi.* **1. DEAL WITH A SITUATION** to deal with a situation and make reasonable progress of a particular kind ○ *How's Ben getting on in school?* **2.** *U.K.* **BE FRIENDLY** to have a reasonably friendly social relationship with somebody ○ *She gets on well with the neighbours.* **3. KEEP GOING** to continue doing something **4. BECOME OLDER** to become more advanced in years ○ *She's getting on, you know; you can't expect her to do everything she used to.*

get out *v.* **1.** *vti.* **LEAVE OR MAKE SOMEBODY LEAVE** to leave a place or situation, or enable somebody to leave one **2.** *vi.* **BECOME KNOWN** to become widely known, especially contrary to somebody's wishes ○ *If this* *ever gets out, I'll be so embarrassed!* **3.** *vt.* **PRODUCE OR PUBLISH SOMETHING** to produce or publish something, especially a newspaper or magazine **4. MAKE SOUND** to make a sound or say something (*informal*) ○ *too choked up to get anything out* ■ *interj.* **EXPRESSING DISBELIEF** used as an expression of disbelief (*informal*) ○ *Get out! You actually said that?*

get out of *vt.* to avoid doing or having to experience something, or enable somebody to avoid something ○ *He got out of paying for the meal.*

get over *vt.* **1. RECOVER FROM SOMETHING** to recover from an illness or bad experience ○ *He's upset, but he'll get over it.* **2. DEAL WITH A DIFFICULTY** to overcome or cope with a difficulty ○ *Once she'd gotten over her lack of confidence, she enjoyed the meeting.* **3. MAKE PEOPLE UNDERSTAND OR ACCEPT SOMETHING** to succeed in making something clear or persuasive ○ *He's very good at getting his ideas over to an audience.* **4. GET SOMETHING FINISHED** to finish dealing with something boring, annoying, or unpleasant ○ *I just want to get the whole thing over with as soon as possible.*

get round *vt. U.K.* = **get around** *v.* 3 ○ *There must be some way of getting round the regulations*

get through *v.* **1.** *vt.* **SURVIVE DIFFICULT TIME** to endure to the end of a difficult time or situation ○ *How I got through those weeks I just don't know.* **2.** *vt.* **FINISH** to finish something ○ *Did you ever get through that novel?* **3.** *vt.* **USE OR SPEND SOMETHING** to use, eat, or spend something, especially a large amount in a short time ○ *We seem to be getting through the copier paper at an alarming rate.* **4.** *vti.* **MAKE SOMEBODY UNDERSTAND** to make somebody understand something that is being communicated ○ *How can I get it through to you that this is our only hope?* **5.** *vi.* **SUCCEED IN CONTACTING SOMEBODY** to contact somebody, especially by telephone ○ *I finally got through to her.*

get to *vt.* **1. START DEALING WITH SOMETHING** to start dealing with something ○ *Leave it with me; I'll get to it later today.* **2. START DOING SOMETHING** to start to do something ○ *If they get to arguing, we'll never stop them.* **3. EVOKE EMOTIONS** to have an emotional impact on somebody ○ *Goodbyes always get to me.* **4. ANNOY SOMEBODY** to start to annoy somebody ○ *His whining was beginning to get to me.*

get together *v.* **1.** *vi.* **MEET** to meet for social or business purposes ○ *The project team needs to get together once a week or so.* **2.** *vi.* **FORM AN ALLIANCE** to form an alliance or relationship ○ *They may be getting together to corner the market.* **3.** *vi.* **REACH AGREEMENT** to reach agreement with somebody ○ *get together on the major issues* **4.** *vt.* **GATHER SOMETHING** to bring together or accumulate something, especially money ○ *They managed to get together enough capital to open a business.* **5.** *vt.* **GET SOMETHING ORGANIZED** to organize your personal affairs or focus your approach to an activity (*informal*) ○ *took some time off to get her life together* ○ *better get it together before his boss loses patience*

get up *v.* **1.** *vti.* **GET OUT OF BED** to get out of bed, or make somebody get out of bed **2.** *vti.* **CLIMB** to ascend or climb something **3.** *vi.* **STAND UP** to rise to your feet from a seated position **4.** *vt.* **ROUSE ENERGY** to rouse your energy, strength, courage, or similar qualities ○ *I'm trying to get up the enthusiasm to go back to work.* **5.** *vt.* **ORGANIZE SOMETHING** to organize something by persuading other people to take part ○ *She got up a collection to help homeless people.* **6.** *vt.* **DRESS SOMEBODY** to dress somebody in a particular way (*informal*) ○ *She was got up as Cleopatra.* **7.** *vi.* **GET STRONGER** to become stronger or more turbulent (*refers to wind or the sea*)

get up to *vt.* to do something bad or annoying (*informal*) ○ *I have no idea what they've been getting up to while we've been away.*

get[2] /get/ *n.* **1.** *Scotland, N England* **BRAT** an unpleasant child (*often used as an insult, implying illegitimacy*) **2. MALE ANIMAL'S OFFSPRING** the progeny sired by an animal, especially a racehorse **3.** RACKET GAMES **DIFFICULT TENNIS RETURN** in tennis and some other racket games, a shot that makes a difficult return

ge·ta /gé taá/ (*plural* **-ta** *or* **-tas**) *n.* a Japanese shoe with a wooden sole [Late 19thC. From Japanese.]

get·a·way /géttə wày/ *n.* **1. ACT OF LEAVING** an act of leaving a place, especially a quick exit made by somebody who has just committed a crime **2. START OF MOVEMENT** an act of starting to move, e.g., in a race **3. SHORT VACATION** a short vacation or break ○ *a weekend getaway* **4. PLACE TO ESCAPE TO** a place remote from everyday life to use for a vacation ○ *It's only a rough cabin that we use as a getaway.*

get-go, **get·go** *n.* the very beginning of something (*informal*) ○ *I knew from the get-go this thing wasn't going to work.*

Geth·sem·a·ne, Garden of /geth sémmənee/ in a book of the Bible, the olive grove just outside Jerusalem where Jesus Christ was betrayed after the Last Supper (Matthew 26: 36)

get·ter /géttər/ *n.* a substance added to absorb the unwanted product of a chemical process, e.g., the excess gas in a light bulb

get-to·geth·er *n.* a meeting or social gathering (*informal*)

get-tough *adj.* taking a firm and decisive approach to social or political problems

Get·ty /géttee/, **J. Paul** (1892–1976) U.S. oil executive. He became a multimillionaire at the head of his own oil company, and he founded the J. Paul Getty Museum in Malibu, to display his collection of art. Full name **Jean Paul Getty**

get·up /gét ùp/, **get-up** *n.* the costume or clothes that somebody is wearing (*informal*)

get-up-and-go *n.* energy and enthusiasm (*informal*)

get-well *adj.* expressing the hope that somebody will soon recover from an illness ○ *a get-well card*

geul·lah /gə oǒ laá/ *n.* a Jewish prayer of thanks to God for the deliverance of the Jews from Egypt

GeV *abbr.* giga-electron volt

ge·valt /gə váalt/, **ge·vald** *interj.* an expression of alarm, shock, or dismay

gew·gaw /gyoǒ gàw/ *n.* a showy but inexpensive object, especially an ornament [12thC. Origin uncertain: perhaps a doubled form of Old French *gogue* "joke" (source of English *agog*).]

Ge·würz·tra·mi·ner /gə vùrts trámmìnər/ *n.* **1. WHITE GRAPE** a white grape used in winemaking, grown especially in Alsace and in Germany **2. WHITE WINE** a medium-dry, slightly spicy, white wine made from the Gewürztraminer grape [Mid-20thC. From German, from *Gewürz* "spice" + *Traminer*, name of a type of grape, from *Termeno*, a village in northern Italy where it was originally identified.]

Barnaby's

Geyser: Rotorua, New Zealand

gey·ser /gízər/ *n.* GEOG a spring that throws a jet of hot water or steam into the air at regular or irregular intervals [Late 18thC. Named for *Geysir*, a hot spring in Iceland, from Old Norse *geysa* "to gush."]

gey·ser·ite /gízə rìt/ *n.* a gray or white mineral deposited by geysers and hot springs. It looks like opal and, like opal, is a form of hydrated silica.

GFE *abbr.* government-furnished equipment

G-force *n.* the force of gravity [Mid-20thC. *G* a shortening of *gravity*.]

GGPA *abbr.* graduate grade point average

GH *abbr.* **1.** Ghana (*international vehicle registration*) **2.** growth hormone

Gha·na /gáanə/ republic on the northern coast of the Gulf of Guinea in western Africa, bordered by Burkino Faso, Togo, and Côte d'Ivoire. It became independent from Britain in 1957. Language: English. Currency: cedi. Capital: Accra. Population: 18,100,703 (1997). Area: 92,100 sq. mi./238,537 sq. km. Former name **Gold Coast** (until 1957) —**Gha·na·ian** *n., adj.*

gha·ri·al /gérree əl/ *n.* = **gavial** [Early 19thC. From Hindi *ghariyāl*.]

ghar·ry /gérree/ (*plural* **-ries**) *n.* *S Asia* a horse-drawn carriage in the Indian subcontinent, especially one for hire [Early 19thC. From Hindi *gārī*.]

Ghana

ghast·ly /gástlee/ *adj.* (**-li·er, -li·est**) **1. HORRIFYING** horrifying, shocking, or very upsetting ○ *She had a ghastly experience with the last dentist she went to.* **2. TERRIBLE** very bad or unpleasant ○ *There's a ghastly smell coming from somewhere in this room.* **3. NOT WELL** very unwell (*informal*) ○ *If I drink too much, I always wake up feeling ghastly in the morning.* **4. VERY PALE** very pale or white, reminiscent of a ghost or a corpse (*literary*) ■ *adv.* **EXTREMELY** used to emphasize paleness or whiteness ○ *"Her eyes grew large, her face ghastly pale."* (Charlotte Gilman, *Herland*; 1915) [14thC. Formed from obsolete *gast* "to frighten." The *gh-* spelling was first used in the late 16thC, under the influence of GHOST.] —**ghast·li·ness** *n.*

ghat /gaat/ *n.* in the Indian subcontinent, a place on a river bank with steps down to the water, especially one where people bathe as a sacred rite or one near which the dead are cremated [Early 17thC. From Hindi *ghāṭ*.]

Ghats /gaats, gawts, guts/ ♦ **Eastern Ghats, Western Ghats**

Gha·za·li /gə zaálee/, **al-** (1058–1111) Islamic theologian and philosopher. His *Revival of the Religious Sciences* is a classic work of Islam. Full name **Abu Hamid Muhammad ibn Muhammad al-Tusi al- Ghazali**

gha·zi /gaázee/ *n.* a warrior who has fought for Islam against non-Muslims [Mid-18thC. From Arabic *al-ġāzī*, active participle of *ġazā* "to invade."]

GHB *abbr.* gamma hydroxybutyrate

ghee /gee/, **ghi** *n.* clarified butter, especially as used in Indian cooking. Traditionally a mark of generous hospitality, ghee is also used in Hindu religious observances. [Mid-17thC. Via Hindi *ghī* from Sanskrit *ghṛtam*, of uncertain origin: perhaps formed from *gharati* "to sprinkle."]

Ghent /gent/ capital of East Flanders Province, northwestern Belgium. One of Belgium's oldest cities, it is situated about 35 mi./56 km northwest of Brussels. Population: 226,464 (1996).

gher·kin /gúrkin/ *n.* **1.** FOOD **SMALL CUCUMBER** a small cucumber used for pickling **2.** FOOD **PRICKLY FRUIT** a prickly hard-skinned fruit from a West Indian climbing plant, used for pickling when it is unripe. Also called **gooseberry gourd 3.** PLANTS **TROPICAL CLIMBING PLANT** a West Indian climbing plant of the cucumber family that produces gherkins. Latin name: *Cucumis anguria.* [Early 17thC. From assumed obsolete Dutch *gurkkijn*, literally "small cucumber," from *gurk* "cucumber," of uncertain origin: perhaps from, ultimately, late Greek *aggourion* "watermelon."]

ghet·to /géttō/ (*plural* **-tos** *or* **-toes**) *n.* **1. MINORITY'S AREA OF A CITY** an area of a city lived in by a minority group, especially a run-down and densely populated area lived in by a group that experiences discrimination **2. JEWISH QUARTER** in former times, an area in European towns in which the Jewish population was required to live **3. ENVIRONMENT OF ISOLATION** an environment where a group of people live or work in isolation, whether by choice or circumstance [Early 17thC. From Italian, of uncertain origin: possibly an alteration of *getto* "foundry," after the site of a 16thC Venetian ghetto.]

ghet·to blast·er *n.* a large radio and cassette or CD player with a built-in speaker at each end, carried by a handle at the top (*informal*) (*often considered offensive*) [From its popularity among inner-city youth]

ghet·to·ize /géttō ìz/ (**-ized, -iz·ing, -iz·es**) *vt.* **1. SEGREGATE A MINORITY GROUP** to restrict a minority group to a specific area of a city **2. LIMIT OPPORTUNITIES** to limit the opportunities of a group of people (*sometimes*

Ghetto blaster

considered offensive) —**ghet·to·i·za·tion** /gèttō i záysh'n/ *n.*

ghi *n.* COOK = **ghee**

ghil·lie *n.* CLOTHES = **gillie**

ghost /gōst/ *n.* **1.** **SUPPOSED SPIRIT REMAINING AFTER DEATH** the spirit of somebody who has died, supposed to appear as a shadowy form or to cause sounds, the movement of objects, or a frightening atmosphere in a place **2.** **TRACE** a faint, weak, or greatly reduced appearance, trace, or possibility of something ○ *The ghost of a smile hovered around her lips.* **3.** **WEAK VERSION** a weakened or watered-down version of somebody or something **4.** **SECONDARY IMAGE** a faint duplicate image of something seen on a screen or through a telescope, and caused by the reception of a double signal or by a mechanical defect **5.** **NON-EXISTENT PERSON OR THING** somebody who or something that seems to exist but does not, e.g., a name entered on a list by mistake **6.** **ABSENTEE REPORTED TO BE PRESENT** somebody who is absent from school or work but who is recorded as being present **7.** = **ghostwriter** **8.** RELIG **SOUL** somebody's soul or spirit (*archaic*) ■ *v.* (**ghost·ed, ghost·ing, ghosts**) **1.** *vt.* = **ghostwrite** **2.** **GLIDE** to glide silently like a ghost [Old English *gāst*. The *gh-* spelling appeared in the 15thC, probably under the influence of Middle Dutch *gheest*.] —**ghost·y** *adj.* ◇ **give up the ghost** **1.** to die (*literary*) **2.** to stop working or functioning for good (*informal*)

ghost·bust·er /gṓst bùstər/ *n.* somebody who is supposed to be able to drive away ghosts, poltergeists, and other apparitions from the places they haunt (*informal*)

ghost crab *n.* a white burrowing crab that inhabits sandy shorelines in many parts of the world. Genus: *Ocypoda.* [From its pale appearance]

ghost dance *n.* **1.** **NATIVE AMERICAN DANCE** a religious dance of western Native Americans, performed with the spirits of all the Native Americans murdered by the European immigrants **2.** **ghost dance, Ghost Dance** **NATIVE AMERICAN RELIGIOUS MOVEMENT** a religious movement, widely spread among Plains Native American peoples in North America in the late 19th century, that promised the revival of traditional Native American culture

ghost·ing /gṓsting/ *n.* the appearance of faint duplicate images on a screen or monitor, or through a telescope

ghost·ly /gṓstlee/ (**-li·er, -li·est**) *adj.* **1.** **LIKE A GHOST** like a ghost in being insubstantial, pale, or apparently not of this world **2.** **REMINISCENT OF GHOSTS** having an atmosphere or quality that suggests ghosts or the presence of ghosts ○ *the ghostly music that opens the symphony* **3.** RELIG **OF THE SOUL** spiritual, or connected with the soul (*archaic*) —**ghost·li·ness** *n.*

ghost site *n.* a Web site that is obselete and no longer updated but that is still available for viewing

ghost sto·ry *n.* a story about a ghost or ghosts, or a haunted place or person, intended to make the reader or hearer feel frightened or uneasy

ghost town *n.* **1.** **DESERTED TOWN** a town with no inhabitants, or very few, especially one that was formerly a busy prosperous place, e.g., an abandoned mining town **2.** **DESERTED PLACE** a formerly or normally inhabited place that is deserted (*informal*) ○ *The business district is a ghost town on weekends.*

ghost word *n.* LING a word created through a mistake that may be copied afterward into other texts and eventually enter a language

ghost·write /gṓst rīt/ (**-wrote, -writ·ten, -writ·ing, -writes**) *vti.* to write something as a ghostwriter

ghost·writ·er /gṓst rītər/ *n.* somebody who writes something for or with another person on the understanding that the other person will receive sole credit as the author

ghoul /gool/ *n.* **1.** **SOMEBODY MORBIDLY INTERESTED IN REPULSIVE THINGS** somebody who has a morbid fascination with death, disaster, or repulsive things in general **2.** MYTHOL **EVIL SPIRIT** an evil and terrifying spirit **3.** ISLAM **BODY-SNATCHING DEMON** an evil demon in Islamic folklore that eats freshly buried bodies, and often abducts children or attacks unwary travelers [Late 18thC. From Arabic *ḡūl*.]

ghoul·ish /gṓolish/ *adj.* **1.** **MORBID** showing an unpleasant or unhealthy fascination with death and destruction **2.** **HIDEOUS** terrifyingly hideous or cruel —**ghoul·ish·ly** *adv.* —**ghoul·ish·ness** *n.*

GHQ *n.* the headquarters of an organization, especially a military headquarters commanded by a general. Full form **General Headquarters**

GHz *abbr.* gigahertz

gi[1] *abbr.* MEASURE gill

gi[2] /gee/, **gie** *n.* a uniform worn for karate or judo

GI[1] /gee ī/ *n.* **U.S. SOLDIER** a soldier in the United States armed forces ■ *adj.* **1.** **FOR SOLDIERS** provided or issued by the armed forces for the use of its members ○ *a GI hat* **2.** **FOR VETERANS** for veterans of the armed forces ○ *GI benefits* [Mid-20thC. Shortening of *government issue*, a reinterpretation of *GI* "galvanized iron" written on various items of U.S. Army equipment (e.g. *GI can* "galvanized iron trash can").]

GI[2], **g.i.** *abbr.* **1.** galvanized iron **2.** gastrointestinal

gi·ant /jīənt/ *n.* **1.** MYTHOL **VERY TALL OR LARGE CREATURE** in fairytales and legends, a being who is usually similar to a human in shape but is much taller, larger, and stronger **2.** MYTHOL **MYTHOLOGICAL CREATURE** in Greek mythology, a being of immense size and strength who fought against Zeus and the other gods of Mount Olympus **3.** **SOMETHING LARGER THAN THE NORM** a person, animal, plant, or organization that is much larger than the norm **4.** **SOMEBODY EXTRAORDINARILY ACCOMPLISHED** somebody whose talents or achievements are particularly outstanding ○ *one of the giants of the silent-movie era* **5.** MINING = **monitor** *n.* 10 **6.** ASTRON = **giant star** ■ *adj.* **1.** **VERY BIG** taller, larger, or more powerful than the norm ○ *a giant tidal wave* **2.** **LARGER THAN USUAL** greater than the usual number or amount ○ *giant savings* [13thC. Via Old French *geant* from, ultimately, Greek *gigas* (source of English *giga-*).]

gi·ant ant·eat·er *n.* a large bushy-tailed anteater, now rare, of the pampas regions of South America. Latin name: *Myrmecophaga tridactyla.*

gi·ant clam *n.* an extremely large clam of the Pacific and Indian oceans, weighing as much as 500 lbs/230kg. Latin name: *Tridacna gigas.*

gi·ant·ism /jīənt ìzzəm/ *n.* MED = **gigantism**

gi·ant pan·da *n.* = **panda** *n.* 1

gi·ant plan·et *n.* any of the four largest planets in the solar system, Jupiter, Saturn, Uranus, and Neptune

Gi·ant's Cause·way /jī ənts káwz way/ headland on the northern coast of Northern Ireland, consisting of thousands of polygonal columns of basalt, thought to be ancient lava formations

gi·ant se·quoi·a, **gi·ant red·wood** *n.* a very tall coniferous evergreen tree of California that can reach a height of 260 ft./80 m and can measure 100 ft./30 m around the base. Latin name: *Sequoiadendron giganteum.*

gi·ant star *n.* a low-density star with a diameter up to 100 times greater than that of the Sun

giaour /jowr/ *n.* a non-Muslim, especially a Christian (*archaic insult*) [Mid-16thC. Via Turkish *gâvur* from, ultimately, Arabic *kāfir* "unbeliever."]

gi·ar·di·a /jee áardee ə, jaárdee ə/ *n.* **1.** MICROBIOL **PARASITIC ORGANISM** a single-celled protozoan, some forms of which live as parasites in the gut of humans and other vertebrates, causing an infection (**giardiasis**). Genus: *Giardia.* **2.** MED = **giardiasis** [Early 20thC. From modern Latin, genus name, named for A. *Giard* (1846–1908), the French biologist who discovered it.]

gi·ar·di·a·sis /jèe aar dī əssiss, jee ər-, jaar-/ *n.* infection of the gut by a water-borne microscopic portozoan giardia. It is usually caused by drinking contaminated water and results in severe diarrhea and vomiting.

gib /gib/ *n.* **METAL WEDGE** something such as a wedge, pin, bolt, or plate that is made of metal and holds another piece of metal or a machine part in place ■ *vt.* (**gibbed, gib·bing, gibs**) **SECURE SOMETHING WITH GIB** to hold something in place with a gib [Late 18thC. Origin unknown.]

gib·ber /jíbbər/ *vi.* (**-bered, -ber·ing, -bers**) **BE INCOHERENT** to make sounds or speak words unintelligibly ○ *Stop gibbering and tell me what's wrong.* ■ *n.* **GIBBERING SPEECH** rapid incoherent or unintelligible speech [Early 17thC. Supposedly imitative of the sound.]

gib·ber·el·lic ac·id /jibbə rèllik-/ *n.* a plant growth hormone involved in stem elongation. Formula: $C_{19}H_{22}O_6$.

gib·ber·el·lin /jibbə réllin/ *n.* a hormone that occurs in fungi and plants that stimulates cell elongation and the growth of stems and leaves [Mid-20thC. Formed from modern Latin *Gibbera*, genus of fungi, from Latin *gibbus* "hump."]

gib·ber·ish /jíbbərish/ *n.* spoken or written language perceived as incomprehensible, and probably not worth comprehending [Early 16thC. Origin uncertain: probably formed from GIBBER on the model of SPANISH, POLISH, etc.]

gib·bet /jíbbit/ *n.* **1.** **HANGING POST** an upright post with a beam projecting horizontally from its top, from which the bodies of executed criminals were hung on public display **2.** = **gallows** ■ *vt.* (**-bet·ed, -bet·ing, -bets**) **1.** **HANG SOMEBODY** to execute somebody by hanging (*archaic*) **2.** **DISPLAY SOMEBODY'S BODY AFTER EXECUTION** to display the body of a criminal on a gibbet after execution **3.** **ATTACK SOMEBODY'S REPUTATION** to expose somebody to ridicule or contempt, especially in popular publications (*archaic*) [12thC. From Old French *gibet* "staff, gallows," literally "small staff," from *gibe* "staff," of uncertain origin: possibly from prehistoric Germanic.]

Gibbon

gib·bon /gíbbən/ *n.* a small tree-dwelling ape of Southeast Asia with a slender body and long arms that allow it to swing rapidly and agilely from branch to branch. Genus: *Hylobates.* [Late 18thC. From French, of unknown origin.]

gib·bous /gíbbəss/ *adj.* **1.** ASTRON **MORE THAN HALF ILLUMINATED** used to describe the moon or a planet before and after it is full, when it has more than half its disk illuminated **2.** BIOL **BULGING** bulging outward, or swollen [14thC. From late Latin *gibbosus* "hunchbacked," from Latin *gibbus* "hump."] —**gib·bos·i·ty** *n.* —**gib·bous·ly** *adv.* —**gib·bous·ness** *n.*

Gibbs /gibz/, **J. Willard** (1839–1903) U.S. mathematical physicist. He laid the foundation for the science of physical chemistry in *On the Equilibrium of Heterogeneous Substances* (1876–78). Full name **Josiah Willard Gibbs**

gibb·site /gíb zīt/ *n.* a gray-white mineral that is a hydrated aluminum oxide, found in deposits of laterite and bauxite. It is used as a source of aluminum. [Early 19thC. Named for George *Gibbs* (1776–1833), the U.S. mineralogist who discovered it.]

gibe /jīb/, **jibe** *n.* **MOCKING REMARK** a comment that is intended to hurt or provoke somebody or to show derision or contempt ■ *vti.* (**gibed, gib·ing, gibes; jibed, jib·ing, jibes**) **MAKE INSULTING REMARKS** to make deliberately provocative or mocking remarks about somebody or something [Mid-16thC. Origin uncertain: perhaps from Old French *giber* "to handle roughly."] —**gib·ing·ly** *adv.*

gib·lets /jíbbləts/ *n.* the liver, heart, gizzard, and neck of a bird that has been prepared for cooking. Giblets are often boiled to make stock for gravy. [14thC. From Old French *gibelet* "game stew," of uncertain origin: perhaps formed from *gibier* "game."]

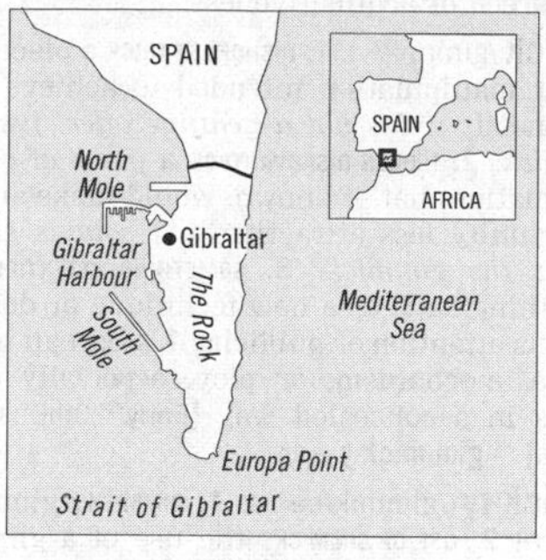

Gibraltar

Gib·ral·tar /ji bráwltər/ **1.** British dependency on a narrow promontory that is the southernmost point of the Iberian Peninsula. It occupies a strategic position at the western entrance to the Mediterranean Sea. Population: 27,170 (1995). Area: 2.3 sq. mi./5.8 sq. km. **2.** city in Wayne County, southeastern Michigan, approximately 12 mi./19 km south of Detroit. Population: 4,297 (1990). —**Gi·bral·tar·ian** /jì brawl táiree ən/ *n., adj.*

Gib·ral·tar, Rock of limestone and shale ridge at the southern tip of the Iberian Peninsula, overlooking the Strait of Gibraltar. Height: 1,396 ft./426 m.

Gib·ral·tar, Strait of channel connecting the Mediterranean Sea to the Atlantic Ocean and separating North Africa from the Rock of Gibraltar. Length: approximately 40 mi./65 km.

Gib·son /gíbss'n/, **Althea** (*b.* 1927) U.S. tennis player and golfer. She won Wimbledon and the U.S. Open tennis championships in 1957 and 1958, and became a professional golfer in 1963.

Gib·son, Charles Dana (1867–1944) U.S. illustrator. He is known for his sketches of the "Gibson girl," an idealized fashionable young woman of the late 1890s and early 1900s.

Gib·son, Mel (*b.* 1956) U.S.-born Australian actor. Best known for his action roles in *Mad Max* (1979) and the *Lethal Weapon* series (1987–98), he also directed and starred in the Academy Award-winning *Braveheart* (1995). Real name **Columcille Gerard Gibson**

Gib·son Des·ert desert in central Western Australia, consisting mainly of sand ridges and plains. Area: 60,200 sq. mi./156,000 sq. km.

Gib·son girl *n.* an idealized fashionable young woman of the late 1890s and early 1900s, as depicted in drawings of illustrator Charles Dana Gibson. Gibson's wife, Irene Langhorne, inspired the drawings, which show clothes with a high neck, full sleeves, and a narrow waist.

gid /gid/ *n.* a disease affecting primarily sheep that makes them walk and stand unsteadily. It is caused by an infestation of the brain by the larva of a tapeworm. [Early 17thC. Back-formation from GIDDY.]

gid·dap /gi dáp, -dúp/ *interj.* = **giddyup**

gid·dy /gíddee/ (**-di·er, -di·est**) *adj.* **1.** DIZZY feeling unsteady and as if about to fall down **2.** CAUSING DIZZINESS causing dizziness or a feeling of unsteadiness **3.** NOT SENSIBLE not level-headed and sensible, and liable to act impulsively or behave foolishly (*dated*) [Old English *gidig* "severely mentally challenged." Ultimately from a prehistoric Germanic base that is also the ancestor of English *God*.] —**gid·di·ly** *adv.* —**gid·di·ness** *n.*

gid·dy·up /gìddi úp/ *interj.* used to make horses go faster [Early 20thC. Alteration of GET UP.]

gie *n.* = **GI**[2]

Giel·gud /géel gŏŏd/, **Sir John** (*b.* 1904) English actor. He was one of the leading Shakespearian interpreters of his generation. Full name **Sir Arthur John Gielgud**

GIF *abbr.* graphic interchange format

gift /gift/ *n.* **1.** SOMETHING GIVEN TO SOMEBODY something that is given to somebody, usually to give pleasure or to show gratitude ○ *a birthday gift* **2.** SPECIAL TALENT a talent or skill that somebody appears to have been born with ○ *a gift for making people feel at ease* **3.** SOMETHING EASILY GAINED something that is obtained or achieved easily, thus allowing an advantage (*informal*) ○ *The final goal was a gift from the Uruguay defense.* **4.** ACT OF GIVING the act of giving something to somebody ○ *her gift of $500,000 to build a new school* ■ *vt.* (**gift·ed, gift·ing, gifts**) GIVE SOMETHING to give or concede something to somebody as a gift [13thC. From Old Norse *gipt*. Ultimately from a prehistoric Germanic base that is also the ancestor of English *give*.]

WORD KEY: USAGE

Marketers are fond of the expression ***free gift***, if the frequency with which they use it is any indication. But because any ***gift*** worthy of its name is free, the result of using the two words together is both illogical and exaggerated. The phrase ***free gift*** should be avoided.

WORD KEY: SYNONYMS

See Synonyms at ***talent***.

GIFT /gift/ *n.* a method designed to aid conception in which eggs are removed from a woman's ovary, mixed with sperm, and placed in one of her fallopian tubes. Full form **gamete intrafallopian transfer**

gift cer·tif·i·cate *n.* a slip of paper issued by a store that can be exchanged for goods worth its purchase price, usually bought as a gift

gift·ed /gíftəd/ *adj.* **1.** TALENTED having great natural talent or intelligence **2.** SHOWING TALENT showing that somebody has great natural talent ○ *a gifted performance* **3.** EDUC EXCEPTIONAL requiring special education because of exceptional talent or intelligence ○ *a gifted student* —**gift·ed·ly** *adv.* —**gift·ed·ness** *n.*

WORD KEY: SYNONYMS

See Synonyms at ***intelligent***.

gift of gab *n.* a natural ability to talk fluently, eloquently, or persuasively (*informal*)

gift of tongues *n.* a form of speech produced in a state of religious ecstasy or trance, usually unintelligible and thought by some to manifest the influence of the Holy Spirit. ◊ **speaking in tongues**

gift to·ken, **gift vouch·er** *n. U.K.* = **gift certificate**

gift·ware /gíft wàir/ *n.* goods such as china and crystal that are marketed to be bought as gifts for other people

gift·wrap /gíft ràp/ *n.* DECORATED WRAPPING PAPER specially decorated paper used to wrap gifts ■ *vt.* (**-wrapped, -wrap·ping, -wraps**) WRAP SOMETHING IN GIFTWRAP to wrap something in specially decorated paper

gig[1] /gig/ *n.* **1.** ONE-HORSE CARRIAGE a light open two-wheeled carriage pulled by a single horse. It was a popular form of private transportation in 19th-century Europe and the United States. **2.** ROWBOAT a small light rowboat carried on board a sailing ship **3.** RACING BOAT a light rowboat used for racing [Late 18thC. Origin uncertain: perhaps from obsolete *gig* "rotary machine for raising nap on fabric, whirling thing" (now only in WHIRLIGIG).]

gig[2] /gig/ *n.* (*informal*) **1.** MUSICAL PERFORMANCE a performance by a musician or group of musicians at a place where they are booked to play but do not regularly perform **2.** TEMPORARY JOB a temporary or short-term job ■ *vi.* (**gigged, gig·ging, gigs**) PLAY A GIG to give a musical performance to an audience in exchange for payment (*informal*) [Early 20thC. Origin unknown.]

gig[3] /gig/ *n.* **1.** PRONGED SPEAR a spear with a prong on one end used to catch fish or frogs **2.** ARRANGEMENT OF HOOKS USED FOR FISHING a system of barbless hooks that is dragged through schools of fish in order to catch them ■ *vti.* (**gigged, gig·ging, gigs**) FISH WITH A GIG to catch fish using a gig [Early 18thC. Abbreviation of FISHGIG.]

gig[4] /gig/ *n.* MIL DEMERIT a military demerit (*slang*) ■ *vt.* (**gigged, gig·ging, gigs**) MIL ISSUE SOLDIER WITH A DEMERIT to give a soldier a demerit (*slang*) [Mid-20thC. Origin unknown.]

gig[5] *n.* a gigabyte (*informal*)

giga- *prefix.* **1.** a billion (10^9) ○ *gigaton* **2.** a binary billion ○ *gigabyte* [From Greek *gigas* (see GIANT)]

gig·a·bit /gíggə bìt/ *n.* a unit of capacity of a computer local area network, equal to one megabyte of computer information, or 1,073,741,824 bits

gi·ga·byte /gíggə bìt/ *n.* a unit of computer data or storage space equivalent to 1024 megabytes

gig·a·cy·cle /gíggə sìk'l/ *n.* a unit of electric oscillation equal to one billion cycles

gig·a·flop /gíggə flòp/ *n.* a unit of measure of computer processing speed equal to one billion floating-point operations per second [Late 20thC. Coined from GIGA- + an acronym formed from *floating-point operations per second*.]

gig·a·hertz /gíggə hùrts/ (*plural* **-hertz**) *n.* a unit of frequency equal to one billion hertz, or cycles, per second

gi·gan·tesque /jì gan tésk, -gən-/ *adj.* as big as, or big enough for, a giant (*literary*)

gi·gan·tic /jì gántik/ *adj.* **1.** VERY BIG very large, tall, or bulky **2.** GREAT very great ○ *Clearing the site is a gigantic task in itself.* [Early 17thC. Formed from the Latin stem *gigant-* "giant," from Greek *gigas* (source of English *giant*).] —**gi·gan·ti·cal·ly** *adv.*

gi·gan·tism /jì gán tìzzəm, jí gàn-/ *n.* excessive growth due to over-production of growth hormone by the pituitary gland before the end of adolescence

gig·a·ton /gíggə tùn/ *n.* a unit of explosive force equal to one billion tons of TNT

gig·a·watt /gíggə waat/ *n.* a unit of electric power equal to one billion watts. Symbol **GW**

gig·gle /gígg'l/ *vti.* (**-gled, -gling, -gles**) LAUGH LIGHTLY to laugh audibly but not loudly, sometimes without meaning to, in a way that is typical of children ■ *n.* NERVOUS LAUGH a quiet laugh that is often nervous or half-suppressed ■ **gig·gles** *npl.* FIT OF LAUGHTER an uncontrollable and recurring urge to laugh (*informal*) [Early 16thC. Imitative of the sound.] —**gig·gler** *n.* —**gig·gling** *adj.* —**gig·gly** *adj.*

GIGO /gí gō/ *n.* COMPUT the principle in computer technology that a program or process is only as good as the ideas and data put into it. Full form **garbage in, garbage out**

gig·o·lo /jíggə lō/ (*plural* **-los**) *n.* **1.** PAID MAN COMPANION a man who receives payments or gifts from a woman in exchange for being her sexual or social partner **2.** PROFESSIONAL DANCING PARTNER a man whose job is to be a dancing partner or escort for a woman [Early 20thC. From French, formed as the masculine of *gigole* "professional woman dance partner."]

gig·ot /jíggət, zhi gṓ/ *n.* a leg of lamb or mutton [Early 16thC. From French, literally "small leg," formed from French dialect *gigue* "leg," from *giguer* "to hop."]

gig·ot sleeve *n.* a sleeve that is close-fitting on the lower arm and full and loose on the upper arm [From its shape]

Gila monster

Gi·la mon·ster /heélə-/ *n.* a large brightly colored venomous lizard that lives in the desert areas of the southwestern United States and Mexico and feeds on eggs and small mammals. Latin name: *Heloderma suspectum*. [Late 19thC. Named for the GILA RIVER where the lizards are found.]

Gi·la Riv·er /heélə-, geélə-/ river that rises in southwestern New Mexico and flows westward, crossing Arizona to join the Colorado River near Yuma. It is an important source of irrigation water. Length: 630 mi./1,014 km.

gil·bert /gílbərt/ *n.* a unit of magnetomotive force in the centimeter-gram-second system, equal to 0.7958 ampere-turns in the SI system [Late 19thC. Named for William *Gilbert* (1544–1603), English physician and scientist.]

Gil·bert /gílbərt/ town in Maricopa County, central

Arizona, part of the greater Phoenix metropolitan area. Population: 64,326 (1996).

Gil·bert, Cass (1858–1934) U.S. architect. He designed the 60-storey Gothic Revival Woolworth Building in New York City (1909–13) and the U.S. Supreme Court Building, Washington, D.C. (1924–35).

Gil·bert, Sir Humphrey (1539?–83) English navigator. The half-brother of Sir Walter Raleigh, he claimed Newfoundland for England in 1583 and founded the first English colony in North America, near present-day St. John's.

Gil·bert and El·lice Is·lands /gìlbərt ənd élliss-/ former British colony situated in the western Pacific Ocean. The group consisted of the Gilbert Islands, now part of Kiribati, and the Ellice Islands, now Tuvalu. Area: 283 sq. mi./733 sq. km.

gild /gild/ (**gild·ed, gild·ing, gilds**) *vt.* **1.** COVER SOMETHING WITH GOLD to cover something with a thin layer of gold leaf or of a substance that looks like gold **2.** COLOR SOMETHING GOLD to give a golden color or tinge to something (*literary*) [Old English *gyldan*. Ultimately from a prehistoric Germanic base that is also the ancestor of English *gold*.] —**gild·er** *n.*

gild·ed /gíldəd/ *adj.* **1.** ARTS = **gilt**[1] *adj.* **2.** WEALTHY wealthy and privileged ○ *gilded youth*

gild·ing /gílding/ *n.* **1.** COVERING SOMETHING WITH GOLD the process of applying a thin layer of gold leaf, or something that looks like gold, to a surface **2.** GILT the thin layer of gold or a substance that looks like gold on a gilded surface

Gil·e·ad, Mount /-gíllee ad/ mountain in northwestern Jordan that also gives its name to an area east of the Jordan River, the Dead Sea, and the Sea of Galilee. Height: 3,597 ft./1,096 m.

gill[1] /gil/ *n.* **1.** BREATHING ORGAN OF FISH the organ that fish and some other aquatic animals use to breathe, consisting of a membrane containing many blood vessels through which oxygen passes. They are internal in most fish and external in tadpoles and some mollusks. **2.** SPORE-PRODUCING ORGAN OF MUSHROOM any of the thin radiating plates on the underside of the cap of a mushroom or other fungus where its spores are produced [14thC. From Old Norse.] —**gilled** *adj.* ◇ **green around the gills, white around the gills** appearing nauseated (*informal*) ◇ **to the gills** to the fullest possible extent

gill[2] /jil/ *n.* a unit of liquid measure equal to a quarter of a pint (118 ml in the U.S. and 142 ml in Britain. [The U.K. pint is 1.201 times the volume of a U.S. pint]. [14thC. Via Old French *gille* from, ultimately, late Latin *gillo* "water pot."]

gill[3] /gil/, **ghyll** *n. U.K.* a ravine with tree-covered sides (*regional*) [14thC. From Old Norse *gil*.]

gill[4] /jil/, **jill** *n.* a young woman (*archaic*) (*sometimes considered offensive*) [15thC. Shortening of the female given name *Gillian* from, ultimately, Latin *Juliana*, from *Julius*, name of a Roman gens.]

gill arch /gíll-/ *n.* the bony or cartilaginous arch supporting the filaments that make up the gill of a fish

Gilles de la Tour·ette syn·drome /zhéel də laa Too̅ rét-/ *n.* MED full form of **Tourette's syndrome**

Gil·les·pie /gi léspee/, **Dizzy** (1917–93) U.S. jazz musician. A trumpeter with both large and small bands, he was a leading exponent of bebop and pioneered Afro-Cuban jazz in the United States. Full name **John Birks Gillespie**

Gil·lette /ji lét/, **William** (1855–1937) U.S. actor and playwright. A successful adapter of works for the stage, he was best known for his dramatic version of *Sherlock Holmes* (1899). Full name **William Hooker Gillette**

gill fun·gus /gíll-/ *n.* a fungus that produces its spores from gills underneath a cap

gil·lie /gíllee/, **ghil·lie** *n.* a low-cut tongueless shoe that laces across the foot and sometimes up the ankle [Late 17thC. From Gaelic *gille*.]

gill net /gíl-/ *n.* a net that is suspended vertically in the water like a curtain in order to catch fish by their gills —**gill·net·ter** *n.*

gill slit /gíl-/ *n.* one of the openings on either side of the head of a fish or amphibian that contain its gills

gil·ly·flow·er /jílli flòwr/ *n.* **1.** SWEET-SCENTED FLOWER a scented flower, such as a stock or wallflower (*archaic*) **2.** CLOVE-SCENTED PINK a clove-scented pink or carnation [14thC. By folk etymology (by association with FLOWER) from French *girofle*, via medieval Latin *caryophyllum* "clove" (its original English meaning) from Greek *karuophullon*, literally "nut leaf."]

Gil·roy /gíl roy/ city in Santa Clara County, western California, 30 mi./48 km southeast of San Jose. Population: 31,487 (1990).

Gil·son·ite /gílsə nìt/ *tdmk.* a trademark for a pure bitumen, used in manufacturing waterproof coatings

gilt[1] /gilt/ *n.* **1.** ARTS THIN LAYER OF GOLD a thin layer of gold, or a substance that looks like gold, applied to a surface **2.** FIN GOVERNMENT BOND a bond issued by the government in Britain, (*often used in the plural*) ■ *adj.* COVERED WITH GILT covered with a thin layer of gold, or a substance that looks like gold [15thC. From the past participle of GILD.]

gilt[2] /gilt/ *n.* a young female pig, especially one that has not yet had a litter [14thC. From Old Norse *gyltr*.]

gilt-edged *adj.* **1.** FIN VERY SAFE FINANCIALLY very safe as an investment **2.** ARTS WITH A GOLD EDGE having a gilded edge

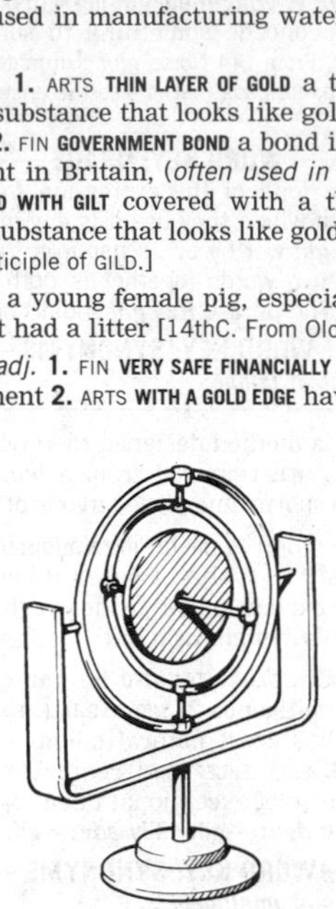

Gimbal

gim·bal /gímb'l, jím-/ *n.* **1.** NAVIG RING FOR HOLDING A COMPASS STEADY a pivoted ring mounted at right angles to one or two others to ensure that something such as a ship's compass always remains horizontal **2.** MECH ENG CONNECTION OF THE REVOLVING PARTS OF A MACHINE an interconnection that allows one part of a mechanism such as a clock's works to revolve independently of another revolving part that contains it ■ *vt.* (**-baled, -bal·ing, -bals**) PUT ON GIMBALS to support something on gimbals [Late 16thC. Variant of GIMMAL.]

gim·crack /jím kràk/ *adj.* SHOWY BUT SHODDILY MADE showy or superficially appealing, but badly made and worthless ■ *n.* SOMETHING SUPERFICIALLY APPEALING BUT SHODDY something that is showy but cheap and badly made [14thC. Origin unknown.] —**gim·crack·er·y** *n.*

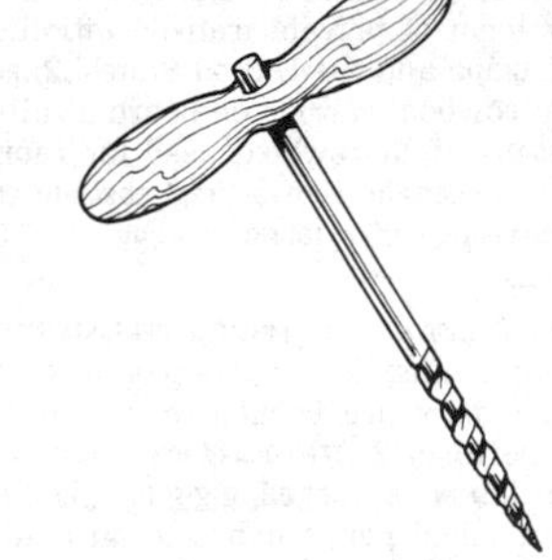

Gimlet

gim·let /gímmlət/ *n.* **1.** JOINERY TOOL FOR BORING HOLES IN WOOD a small tool for boring holes in wood consisting of a slim metal rod with a sharp corkscrew end, fitted in a handle at a right angle **2.** BEVERAGES COCKTAIL WITH LIME JUICE a cocktail made of vodka or gin with lime juice ■ *vt.* (**-let·ed, -let·ing, -lets**) BORE INTO SOMETHING to pierce or penetrate something ■ *adj.* PIERCING seeming to penetrate or pierce somebody or something ○ *"to meet anew the gimlet glances"* (Thomas Hardy, *Jude the Obscure*; 1895) [14thC. From Old French *guimbelet*, literally "small auger," from *guimble* "auger," of prehistoric Germanic origin.]

gim·let-eyed *adj.* having eyes that seem to pierce and penetrate or to notice everything

gim·mal /gímm'l, jímm'l/ *n.* = **gimbal** [Late 16thC. Alteration of obsolete *gemel* "double ring," via Old French from Latin *gemellus*, literally "little twin," from *geminus* "twin."]

gim·me /gímmee/ *contr.* GIVE ME give me (*nonstandard*) ■ *n.* (*informal*) **1. gimme, gim·mie** SOMETHING EASILY GOTTEN something easily gained or accomplished **2.** GOLF SHORT PUTT TAKEN AS SUCCESSFUL a short putt that is considered successful without actually executing it **3.** GREED greed or acquisitiveness

gim·mick /gímmik/ *n.* **1.** DISHONEST TRICK a piece of trickery or manipulation intended to achieve a result dishonestly ○ *It's not a genuine offer, just a sales gimmick.* **2.** HIDDEN DISADVANTAGE a piece of concealed information that, if known, would make an offer or opportunity less attractive ○ *It sounds great, but what's the gimmick?* **3.** SOMETHING ATTENTION-GRABBING something such as a new technique or device that attracts attention or publicity **4.** GADGET an ingenious device, mechanism, or ploy, especially one that works in a concealed way [Early 20thC. Origin unknown.] —**gim·mick·y** *adj.*

gim·mick·ry /gímmikree/ *n.* **1.** GIMMICKS gimmicks in general **2.** USE OF GIMMICKS the use of a gimmick or gimmicks to deceive or attract attention

gimp[1] /gimp/, **guimpe** *n.* a silk or cotton trimming that has a wire or cord running through it [Mid-17thC. From Dutch, of unknown origin.]

gimp[2] /gimp/ *n.* **1.** DIFFICULTY IN WALKING difficulty in walking, caused by injury, or stiffness (*informal*) **2.** OFFENSIVE TERM FOR PHYSICALLY CHALLENGED a highly offensive term for a physically challenged person, especially somebody who has difficulty walking or who uses a wheelchair (*slang offensive*) **3.** CLUMSY PERSON somebody who is clumsy or ineffectual (*slang insult*) (*often considered offensive*) ■ *vi.* (**gimped, gimp·ing, gimps**) WALK WITH DIFFICULTY walk with difficulty (*informal*) [Early 20thC. Origin uncertain: perhaps an alteration of GAMMY.] —**gimp·y** *adj.*

gin[1] /jin/ *n.* **1.** BEVERAGES COLORLESS ALCOHOLIC DRINK a strong colorless alcoholic drink distilled from grain and flavored with juniper berries **2.** CARDS GIN RUMMY gin rummy (*informal*) [Early 18thC. Shortening of GENEVER.]

gin[2] /jin/ *n.* **1.** HIST = **cotton gin 2.** HOIST a simple hoist operated by hand **3.** HUNT TRAP a snare or trap, usually one consisting of a noose made of wire for catching small animals ■ *vt.* (**ginned, gin·ning, gins**) **1.** HUNT CATCH SOMETHING IN GIN to trap an animal with a gin **2.** CLEAN RAW COTTON to separate cotton from its seeds with a gin [13thC. Shortening of Old French *engin* "engine." The underlying idea is of a clever device.]

gin up *vt.* to concoct or invent something, or exaggerate its importance (*regional informal*) ○ *a story ginned up by the public relations people*

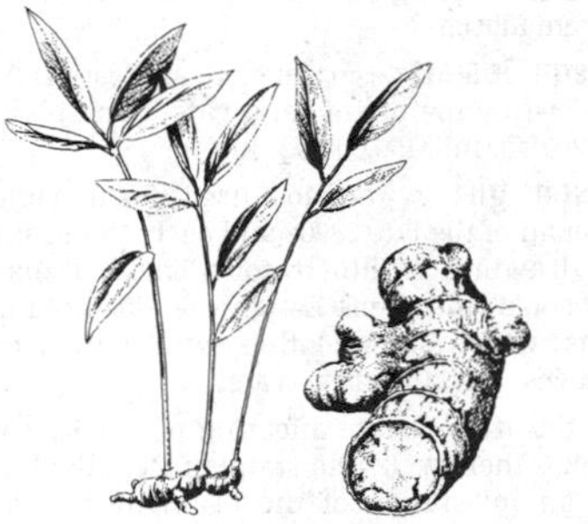

Ginger

gin·ger /jínjər/ *n.* **1.** PLANTS PLANT a widely cultivated Asian plant with an edible underground stem (**rhizome**). Latin name: *Zingiber officinale.* **2.** FOOD HOT-TASTING SPICE the hot-tasting edible underground stem (**rhizome**) of the ginger plant, used fresh in Asian cooking and as a spice in powdered form **3.** COLORS ORANGE- OR BROWNISH-YELLOW COLOR a yellow color with an orange or brownish tinge **4.** VIGOR OR PEP excitement, liveliness, or animation (*informal*) ■ *adj.* **1.** FLAVORED WITH GINGER flavored with fresh or powdered ginger **2.** HAVING GINGER COLOR of an orange- or brownish-yellow color ■ *vt.* (**-gered, -ger·ing, -gers**) **1.** COOK ADD GINGER TO SOMETHING to add ginger as a spice to something **2.** ADD EXCITEMENT TO SOMETHING to enliven or add excitement to something (*informal*) [Pre-12thC. From Old English *gingifer* and Old French *gingi(m)bre*, via Latin and Greek from Pali *singivera*.] —**gin·ger·y** *adj.*

WORD KEY: ORIGIN

The source of the Pali word from which ***ginger*** derives was a Sanskrit compound meaning literally "horn-body" – a reference to the shape of the edible ginger root. By the time it had passed through Greek *ziggiberis* into Latin, it had become *zinziberi*. In post-classical times this developed to *gingiber* or *gingiver*, which Old English borrowed as *gingifer*. English acquired the word again in the 13th century from Old French, and this combined with the descendant of the Old English form to produce Middle English *gingivere*, from which modern English "ginger" is derived.

gin·ger ale *n.* an effervescent nonalcoholic drink, flavored with ginger

gin·ger beer *n.* a nonalcoholic beverage sometimes carbonated strongly flavored with fermented ginger

gin·ger·bread /jínjər brèd/ *n.* **1. GINGER-FLAVORED CAKE** a moist dark cake made with molasses and flavored with ginger **2. GINGER-FLAVORED COOKIE** a ginger-flavored cookie, often cut into the stylized shape of a person, animal, or Christmas tree **3.** ARCHIT **ELABORATE DECORATION** showy and elaborate decoration, especially on the outside of a building (*often used before a noun*) ○ *a Victorian gingerbread style of cottage* [13thC. By folk etymology (by association with BREAD) from Old French *gingembrat* "preserved ginger" from, ultimately, medieval Latin *gingiber* "ginger."]

gin·ger·bread man *n.* a cookie in the stylized shape of a person, made from gingerbread and often decorated

gin·ger group *n. U.K., Can* a group, often within a party or association, whose aim is to stimulate debate and press for more radical or decisive action on something

gin·ger·ly /jínjərlee/ *adv.* **VERY CAUTIOUSLY** in a very cautious, wary, or tentative way ○ *He gingerly unscrewed the radiator cap.* ■ *adj.* **VERY CAUTIOUS** very cautious, wary, or tentative ○ *Not for her the gingerly approach – she came right out with the question.* [Early 16thC. Origin uncertain: perhaps formed from Old French *gensor* "pretty."] —**gin·ger·li·ness** *n.*

gin·ger·root /jínjər ròot/ *n.* fresh ginger in the form of whole rhizomes

ging·ham /gíngəm/ *n.* a light plain-weave fabric with checks, stripes, or plaids in white and colored cotton (*often used before a noun*) ○ *a gingham dress* [Early 17thC. Via Dutch *gingang* from Malay *genggang* "striped."]

gin·gi·va /jin jívə, jínjəvə/ (*plural* **-vae** /-vee/) *n.* gum around the roots of the teeth (*technical*) [Late 19thC. From Latin.]

gin·gi·val /jin jív'l/ *adj.* relating to or affecting the gums (*technical*)

gin·gi·vec·to·my /jìnjə véktəmee/ (*plural* **-mies**) *n.* a surgical operation to remove tissue from the gums

gin·gi·vi·tis /jìnji vítiss/ *n.* inflammation of the gums around the roots of the teeth

ging·ko *n.* = **ginkgo**

gin·gly·mus /jíng gləməss/ (*plural* **-mi** /-mì/) *n.* ANAT a hinge joint of the human body (*technical*)

Gin·grich /gíng rich/, **Newt** (*b.* 1943) U.S. political leader. A Georgia Republican, he sat in the U.S. House of Representatives for 20 years, and was Speaker of the House (1995–98). Full name **Newton Leroy Gingrich**

gink /gingk/ *n.* somebody, especially a man, who is considered strange, unintelligent, or clumsy (*informal insult*) [Early 20thC. Origin unknown.]

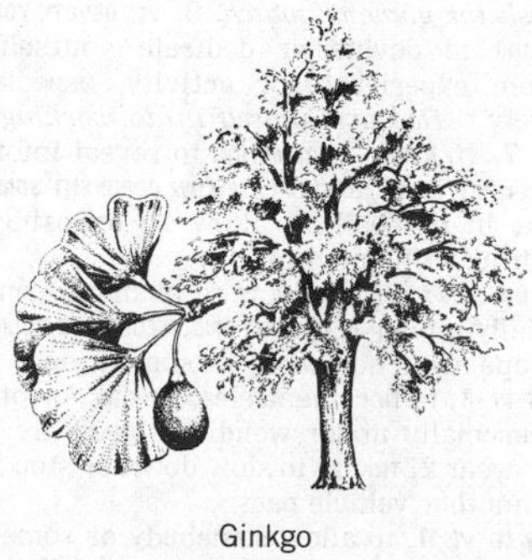

Ginkgo

gink·go /gíng kō/ (*plural* **-goes**), **ging·ko** (*plural* **-koes**) *n.* a tall deciduous tree with small fan-shaped leaves and edible seeds. Native to China and widely cultivated elsewhere, it is the only remaining member of a primitive order of trees. Latin name: *Ginkgo biloba*. [Late 18thC. Via Japanese *ginkyō* from Chinese *yínxìng* "silver apricot."]

gink·go bi·lo·ba *n.* a herbal preparation made from the pulverized leaves of the ginkgo tree and used to treat a variety of disorders [From the Modern Latin genus name]

gin mill *n.* a low-class bar or saloon (*dated slang*)

Ginnie Mae /jìnni máy/ *n.* the Government National Mortgage Association, a U.S. government agency that provides liquidity to the mortgage market [Late 20thC]

gin rum·my *n.* a card game similar to rummy in which two players collect sets and sequences of cards. A hand can be won if cards totalling ten or fewer points are uncombined. [From GIN[1]; a pun on RUMMY, as if it were formed from RUM the alcoholic drink]

Gins·berg /gínzbərg/, **Allen** (1926–97) U.S. poet. His *Howl* (1956) launched the Beat movement.

Gins·burg /gínzbərg/, **Ruth Bader** (*b.* 1933) U.S. Supreme Court justice. A legal activist on behalf of women's rights, she was appointed to the U.S. Supreme Court in 1993.

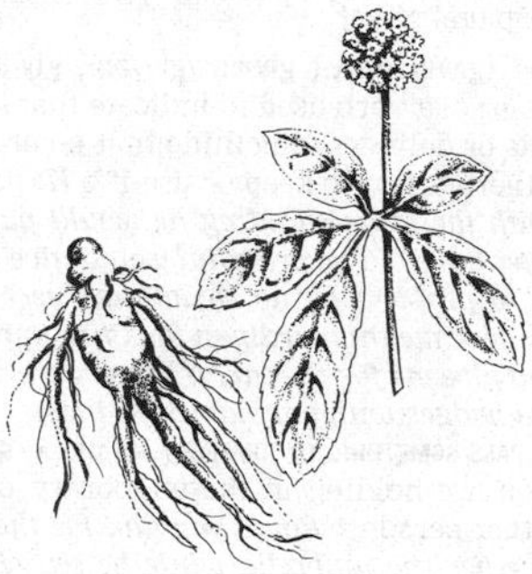

Ginseng

gin·seng /jín sèng/ (*plural* **-sengs** *or* **-seng**) *n.* **1. TONIC MEDICINE** a forked aromatic root used in traditional Chinese medicine. Ginseng is now widely used as a tonic, and is credited with stimulative and restorative powers. **2. MEDICINAL PLANT** a plant that produces the ginseng root, found in Asia and in North America. Genus: *Panax*. [Mid-17thC. From Chinese *rénshēn*, from *rén* "man" + *shēn* a type of herb. Perhaps from the shape of the root.]

gin·zo /gín zō/ *n.* an offensive term used to refer to somebody of Italian ancestry (*dated insult*) [Mid-20thC. Origin uncertain: perhaps formed from GUINEA in its offensive use denoting a Spanish or Italian immigrant.]

Giot·to /jáwtō, jee óttō/ (1266?–1337) Italian painter. One of the first European painters to portray human forms naturalistically, he exerted a profound influence on artists of the Renaissance. Full name **Giotto di Bondone**

gip *vt., n.* = **gyp**

gip·po /jíppō/ (*plural* **gippos**) *n. U.K.* an offensive term for a Romany person (*regional offensive*)

Gip·sy *n., adj.* = **Gypsy**

Giraffe

gi·raffe /jə ráf/ (*plural* **-raffes** *or* **-raffe**) *n.* an African ruminant mammal with an extremely long neck, long legs, and a yellowish coat mottled with brown patches that lives in open grassland. The giraffe is the tallest living animal. Latin name: *Giraffa camelopardalis*. [Late 16thC. Via French *girafe* or Italian *giraffa*, both from Arabic *zarāfa*.]

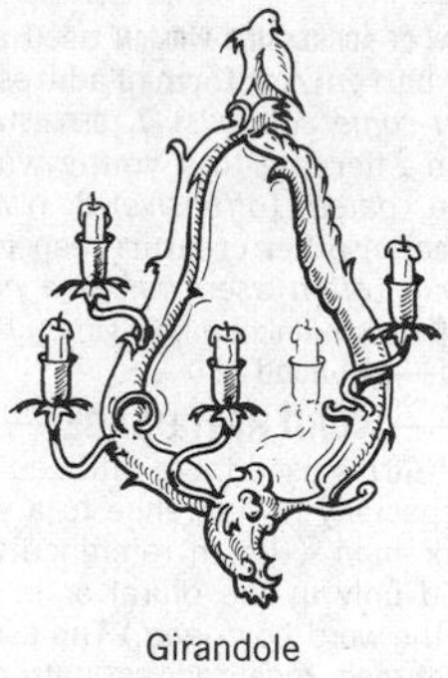

Girandole

gir·an·dole /jírrəndōl/, **gir·an·do·la** /ji rándələ/ *n.* **1. WALL-MOUNTED CANDLEHOLDER** a wall-mounted branched candleholder that often incorporates a mirror between the candlestick branches **2. STARBURST JEWELRY** an earring or pendant with a large central stone surrounded by several smaller ones **3. ROTATING FIREWORK** an elaborate rotating firework **4. WATER JET** a revolving water jet [Mid-17thC. Via French from Italian *girandola* from, ultimately, late Latin *gyrare* "to gyrate."]

Gi·rard /jə raárd/, **Stephen** (1750–1831) French-born U.S. banker. He was a principal stockholder in both the First and Second Banks of the United States, and largely financed the U.S. government during the War of 1812.

gir·a·sol /jírrə sàwl/ (*plural* **-sols**), **gir·o·sol** *n.* **1.** MINERALS = **fire opal 2. gir·a·sol, gir·a·sole** PLANTS = **Jerusalem artichoke** [Late 16thC. From Italian *girasole* "sunflower," from *girare* "to turn" + *sole* "sun."]

gird /gurd/ (**gird·ed** *or* **girt** /gurt/, **gird·ed** *or* **girt, gird·ing, girds**) *v.* **1.** *vr.* **GET READY** to prepare yourself for conflict or vigorous activity **2.** *vt.* **PUT BELT AROUND SOMEBODY** to put a girdle or belt around yourself or another person (*literary*) **3.** *vt.* **FASTEN SOMETHING ON** to secure something to yourself with a belt, straps, or a girdle (*literary*) **4.** *vt.* **SURROUND SOMETHING** to surround or encompass something (*literary*) ○ *a castle girded with a moat* **5.** *vt.* **INVEST SOMEBODY** to provide somebody with or dress somebody in something that is a sign of rank or honor (*literary*) [Old English *gyrdan*. Ultimately from a prehistoric Germanic base that is also the ancestor of English *girth*.]

gird·er /gúrdər/ *n.* a large strong beam, often of steel, forming a main spanning and supporting element in a framework [Early 17thC. Formed from GIRD. Originally applied to a wooden beam in a floor; from the idea that it "girds" or supports the joists.]

gir·dle /gúrd'l/ *n.* **1.** CLOTHES **WOMAN'S FOUNDATION GARMENT** a woman's elasticized foundation garment or corset extending from the waist to the thigh **2.** ACCESSORIES **NARROW BELT** a cord worn around the waist to hold in a large loose-fitting garment such as a kaftan or a monk's habit **3. SOMETHING THAT SURROUNDS** anything that surrounds or encircles something (*literary*) **4.** ANAT **RING OF BONE** a ring-shaped structure of bone, especially the pelvic girdle and pectoral girdle that support the upper and lower limbs **5. PART OF CUT GEMSTONE** the outer edge of a gem, by which it is held in its setting **6.** FORESTRY **RING AROUND TREE TRUNK** a ring around a tree trunk made by removing the bark and a layer of the underlying cellular tissue (**cambium**) in order to kill the tree ■ *vt.* (**-dled, -dling, -dles**) **1. SURROUND SOMETHING** to surround or encircle something (*literary*) **2. CUT RING OF BARK FROM TREE** to remove a ring of bark and a layer of the underlying cellular tissue (**cambium**) from around a tree trunk in order to kill the tree [Old English *gyrdel*, of prehistoric Germanic origin]

gird·ler /gúrdlər/ *n.* an insect that makes a groove around a branch or twig in which to lay its eggs, thereby killing the branch

gir·i /gírree/ *n.* a social obligation or debt (*informal*) [From Japanese]

girl /gurl/ *n.* **1. FEMALE CHILD** a human female from birth until the age at which she is considered an adult **2. YOUNG WOMAN** a young woman (*often considered offensive*) **3. ANY WOMAN** a woman of any age, especially one who is a friend, a contemporary, or younger than the speaker (*informal*) (*often considered offensive*) ○ *a night out with the girls* **4. DAUGHTER** somebody's daughter, especially when a child (*informal*) **5. GIRLFRIEND** a man's or boy's girlfriend **6.** WAY OF ADDRESSING WOMAN used as a friendly, intimate, or patronizing form of address to a woman (*offensive in some contexts*) **7.** OFFENSIVE TERM an offensive term referring to a young woman servant or employee (*dated*) (*offensive*) **8.** FEMALE CREATURE a female animal or other creature, especially a young one (*informal*) (*often used before a noun*) ○ *a girl kitten* [13thC. Origin unknown. Originally denoting a child of either sex.] —**girl·hood** *n.*

WORD KEY: USAGE

girl or **woman**? ***Girl*** is used more often as an alternative for ***woman***, especially in reference to a young woman, than *boy* is for *man*. (*Boy* in reference to an adult is normally found only in the plural or in meanings associated with the word *boyfriend*.) The use of ***girl*** for an adult is sometimes regarded as patronizing or disrespectful, especially when it comes from a man.

girl Fri·day *n.* a young woman whose job is to be somebody's personal assistant and to do general office work (*sometimes considered offensive*) [Modeled on "Man Friday," the hero's all-around helper in *Robinson Crusoe* (1719) by the English writer Daniel Defoe]

girl·friend /gúrl frènd/ *n.* **1.** WOMAN OR GIRL SWEETHEART OR LOVER a girl or woman with whom somebody has a romantic or sexual relationship **2.** WOMAN FRIEND a woman who is the friend of another woman

girl·ie /gúrlee/ *adj.* SHOWING NUDE WOMEN showing or involving naked or scantily dressed women (*often considered offensive*) ■ *n.* **1.** OFFENSIVE TERM an offensive term of address when used by a man to a woman (*offensive*) **2.** LITTLE GIRL a little girl (*dated informal*) ■ *adj.* (*comparative* **girlier**, *superlative* **girliest**) = **girly**

girl·ish /gúrlish/ *adj.* **1.** OF GIRLS typical or characteristic of girls **2.** IMMATURE more suitable for a girl than for an adult woman —**girl·ish·ly** *adv.* —**girl·ish·ness** *n.*

Girl Scout *n.* a member of the Girl Scouts, an organization that aims to enable girls to socialize and learn skills in a wholesome environment

girl·y /gúrlee/ (**-i·er, -i·est** *or* **-i·est**) *adj.* extremely or deliberately feminine ○ *a girly lace collar*

girn /gurn/ (**girned, girn·ing, girns**), **gurn** (**gurned, gurn·ing, gurns**) *vi. Scotland, N England* **1.** COMPLAIN to complain, whine, or grumble **2.** GRIMACE to make a bad-tempered or discontented face [14thC. Alteration of GRIN by changing the central sounds around. Originally meaning "to snarl," the present senses became current in the 18thC.]

gi·ro /jí rō/ (**-roed, -ro·ing, -ros,** *plural* **-ros**) *n.* **1.** BANK TRANSFER SYSTEM in European countries and Great Britain, a system that enables money to be transferred quickly and cheaply between accounts or between the financial institutions of a country **2.** *U.K.* BENEFIT CHECK a check, cashable at a post office in European countries, for the payment of a government benefit such as unemployment (*informal*) [Late 19thC. Via German from Italian, "circulation (of money)."]

gi·ron *n.* = **gyron**

gir·o·sol *n.* = **girasol**

girt[1] past tense, past participle of **gird**

girt[2] /gurt/ (**girt·ed, girt·ing, girts**) *vt.* **1.** ENCIRCLE SOMETHING to encircle or surround something (*literary*) **2.** MEASURE AMOUNT AROUND BODY to measure a particular amount around the body (*archaic*)

girth /gurth/ *n.* **1.** DISTANCE AROUND the distance around something thick and cylindrical, e.g., a tree trunk or somebody's waist ○ *a man of ample girth* **2.** RIDING SADDLE BAND a broad band fastened around the belly of a horse to keep a saddle in place ■ *vt.* (**girthed, girth·ing, girths**) **1.** SADDLE A HORSE to put or fasten a girth on a horse **2.** SURROUND SOMETHING to surround or encircle something (*literary*) [14thC. From Old Norse *gjörð* "girdle."]

gi·sarme /gi záarm, ji-/ *n.* a medieval foot soldier's weapon that had a long shaft and a head with an ax blade on one side and a sharp point on the other [13thC. From Old French *guisarme*, of uncertain origin: probably from prehistoric Germanic.]

Gish /gish/, **Dorothy** (1898–1968) U.S. actor. The sister of Lillian Gish, she was a star of silent movies and later of the stage. Born **Dorothy de Guiche**

Gish, Lillian (1893?–1993) U.S. actor. Perhaps the greatest of all silent-movie actresses, she continued a long career on both stage and screen, appearing on film for the last time in 1987. Born **Lillian de Guiche**

gis·mo *n.* = **gizmo**

gist /jist/ *n.* **1.** MAIN POINT the essential point or meaning of something **2.** GROUNDS FOR LEGAL ACTION the essential grounds for a legal action [Early 18thC. From the Old French phrase *cest action gist* "this action lies," from the idea of the "basis" of a legal action, third person singular of *gesir* "to lie."]

git[1] /git/ *n. U.K.* an annoying, troublesome, unpleasant, or thoughtless person (*informal insult*) [Mid-20thC. Variant of GET[2].]

git[2] /git/ (**got·ten, got·ten** /gótt'n/, **git·ting, gits**) *vti.* to get (*regional nonstandard*)

gite /zheet/ *n.* a house, cottage, or apartment in France offering fairly simple accommodations, that can be rented for a vacation [Late 18thC. From French *gîte* "stopping place."]

git-go *n.* = **get-go**

git·tern /gíttərn/ *n.* a medieval stringed instrument that was a forerunner of the guitar [14thC. Via Old French *guiterne* from, ultimately, Latin *cithara* "CITHARA."]

git·tin *n.* plural of **get**[2]

git·tin *n.* plural of **get**[2]

give /giv/ (**gave** /gayv/, **giv·en** /gívvən/, **giv·ing, gives**) CORE MEANING: a verb used to indicate that somebody presents or delivers something that he or she owns to another person to keep or use it ○ *He gave Brian $800 with the understanding he would pay the rest at a later date.* ○ *The program would give education grants to people who do community service.* ○ *My mother gave me this cardigan for Christmas.* ○ *What will you give me for the car?* ○ *When we arrived they gave us badges with our names on them.*

1. *vt.* PASS SOMETHING TO SOMEBODY to place something that you are holding in the temporary possession of another person ○ *Could you give me the phone?* ○ *He gave her the umbrella while he searched in his pockets for some loose change.* **2.** *vt.* GRANT SOMETHING TO SOMEBODY to allow somebody to have something such as power or a right ○ *Opponents of the bill claimed it gave too much power to the mine owners.* **3.** *vt.* COMMUNICATE SOMETHING to impart or convey something such as information, advice, or opinions **4.** *vt.* CONVEY SOMETHING to cause somebody to have an idea or impression ○ *Whatever gave you that idea?* **5.** *vt.* IMPART SOMETHING to make somebody experience a particular physical or emotional feeling ○ *She said the steady paycheck gave her a sense of security.* **6.** *vt.* PERFORM SOMETHING to carry out or perform something in public ○ *Not one of these actors gave a performance that was worthy of the prize.* **7.** *vt.* MAKE OR DO SOMETHING used with nouns referring to physical actions to indicate that the action is being made or done ○ *She gave Paul a quick, accusing glance.* **8.** *vt.* PROVIDE SERVICE to perform an action or service for somebody ○ *He gave her a foot massage to relax her.* ○ *The guide gave us a tour of the ruins.* **9.** *vt.* DEVOTE SOMETHING to devote something such as time or effort, or sacrifice something for somebody ○ *He gave his whole life to helping children in need.* **10.** *vt.* ORGANIZE SOMETHING to spend time organizing a social event ○ *They gave her a great send off when she retired last year.* **11.** *vt.* CAUSE SOMEBODY TO BELIEVE SOMETHING to lead somebody to have a particular understanding about something ○ *I was given to understand that they would be coming to us for one weekend.* **12.** *vt.* VALUE SOMETHING to estimate something at a particular amount or value ○ *What do you give him for his chances of getting her back?* **13.** *vi.* YIELD to collapse or break under pressure ○ *The wheel gave under the heavy load.* ○ *When people are under constant pressure from work and home, something has to give.* **14.** *vt.* CONCEDE SOMETHING to yield to somebody, or admit that somebody has an advantage or a particular characteristic or ability **15.** *vt.* TOAST SOMEBODY to propose a toast to somebody ○ *I give you the bride and groom!* **16.** *n.* RESILIENCE the ability or tendency to yield under pressure [Old English *giefan*. Ultimately from an Indo-European base meaning "to give," which is also the ancestor of English *habit*.] ◇ **give it up for somebody** *or* **something** to applaud somebody or something enthusiastically (*slang*) ◇ **give me** I'd rather do or have (*informal*) ○ *Give me a quiet evening with a book any time.* ◇ **give or take** used to indicate that a figure given is fairly accurate, within the stated range ○ *worth about half a million, give or take a few thousand dollars*

WORD KEY: SYNONYMS

give, present, confer, bestow, donate, grant

CORE MEANING: to hand over something to somebody

give a general word used to talk about the handing over of something to somebody else, often without compensation; **present** used especially to talk about giving something in a formal or ceremonial way; **confer** a fairly formal word used to talk about giving somebody an honor, privilege, or award, often at a formal ceremony; **bestow** a formal word used, like "confer," to talk about giving somebody an honor, privilege, or award. It can also be used to talk about giving a gift and is often used to suggest that this is an act of great generosity, or to suggest condescension on the part of the giver; **donate** used to talk about giving a contribution to some kind of good cause. It is used specifically in a medical context to talk about the giving of blood for blood transfusions or of organs for purposes of transplant; **grant** used to talk about giving something abstract such as permission or approval, especially at the discretion of a person in authority. It can also be used to talk about giving concrete gifts such as money.

give away *vt.* **1.** GIVE SOMETHING AS A PRESENT to give or offer something without charging for it **2.** DISCLOSE BY MISTAKE to reveal information or a secret, often without meaning to **3.** BETRAY to betray somebody by providing information **4.** PRESENT BRIDE TO HUSBAND AT WEDDING to accompany a bride to her future husband's side and formally present her to him just before the words of the wedding ceremony are spoken **5.** SPORTS LET OPPONENT SCORE POINT to allow an opponent to get an advantage, especially inadvertently, through poor or illegal play

give back *vt.* to return something, especially to its rightful or original owner

give in *vi.* **1.** LOSE to admit defeat **2.** BREAK to collapse or break under pressure **3.** ACCEPT CONDITIONS to accept demands or conditions

give of *vr.* to devote or dedicate your time or energy to something

give off *vt.* to send out or emit something

give on to *vt. U.K.* to overlook or lead to something ○ *The patio doors give on to a small paved area.*

give out *v.* **1.** *vt.* HAND OVER to hand over or distribute something **2.** *vt.* MAKE SOMETHING KNOWN to declare something or make something known, especially publicly ○ *She gave out the exam grades in reverse order.* **3.** *vt.* EMIT to send out or emit something **4.** *vi.* BE USED UP to run out or be finished ○ *My courage gave out, and I couldn't face her after all.* **5.** *vi.* STOP WORKING to fail, or stop working

give over *vt.* to hand somebody or something over to somebody or something else

give over to *v.* **1.** *vt.* RESERVE SOMETHING FOR A PURPOSE to dedicate or assign something to a particular purpose or use ○ *This area will be given over to a children's playground.* **2.** *vr.* ABANDON YOURSELF TO SOMETHING to abandon yourself to an emotion or experience (*literary*) ○ *She gave herself over to despair.*

give up *v.* **1.** *vi.* SURRENDER to surrender or admit defeat **2.** *vt.* HAND OVER SOMEBODY OR SOMETHING to hand over, part with, or abandon somebody or something ○ *We gave up all hope of finding any survivors.* **3.** *vt.* LOSE HOPE FOR GOOD OUTCOME to stop hoping for a good outcome with regard to somebody or something ○ *Where have you been? We'd given you up as lost.* **4.** *vt.* STOP USING OR DOING SOMETHING to stop or renounce using or doing something ○ *give up chocolate for a week* **5.** *vt.* STOP TRYING to abandon a pursuit that has a goal ○ *Darkness fell, but they didn't give up trying to finish the game or match.* **6.** *vt.* DEVOTE YOURSELF TO SOMETHING to devote or dedicate yourself to an emotion, experience, or activity, especially exclusively ○ *He gave himself up to working for the cause.* **7.** *vt.* REVEAL INFORMATION to reveal information or a secret **8.** *vt.* BASEBALL ALLOW OPPONENT SOMETHING IN BASEBALL in baseball, to allow an opposing player something while pitching

give up on *vt.* **1.** ABANDON PLAN to abandon something, especially a plan **2.** DESPAIR OF SOMEBODY OR SOMETHING to lose hope about somebody or something

give way *vi.* **1.** to become useless, break, or otherwise fail, especially under weight or pressure or from age or wear **2.** TRANSP to slow down or stop in order to let another vehicle pass

give way to *vt.* **1.** to allow somebody or something to have priority or to take precedence **2.** to be replaced or superseded by somebody or something ○ *The rain gave way to patchy sunshine.* **3.** to allow something, especially an emotion, to be expressed

give-and-take *n.* (*informal*) **1. COOPERATION AND COMPROMISE** mutual cooperation and understanding between people or groups, often involving concessions on all sides **2. MUTUALLY BENEFICIAL EXCHANGE OF IDEAS** a useful exchange of ideas or information in which everyone involved benefits

give·a·way /gívvə wày/ *n.* **1. SOMETHING THAT REVEALS** something that serves to reveal, betray, or expose something ○ *Her accent's a dead giveaway.* **2. GIFT** something that is offered free of charge or at very little cost, often as a publicity gimmick or incentive to buy (*informal*) **3. GAME SHOW** a radio or TV game show that offers contestants the chance to win prizes, especially cash prizes (*informal*) ■ *adj.* (*informal*) **1. VERY INEXPENSIVE** extremely low in price **2. FREE** free of charge ○ *a giveaway sample of a new shampoo*

give·back /gív bàk/ *n.* **1. CONCESSION BY EMPLOYEES** a concession over wages or other gesture of goodwill made by employees, often in return for later benefits from the employer or management **2. SOMETHING RETURNED** something that is or has been returned (*informal*)

giv·en /gívvən/ past participle of **give** ■ *adj.* **1. PARTICULAR** relating to a specific person, thing, or concept **2. ARRANGED EARLIER** previously arranged or specified **3. VALIDATED** validated or executed on the date mentioned (*formal*) ○ *this last will and testament given by my hand this 13th day of February 1898* ■ *prep.* **1. GRANTED** assuming that somebody has the opportunity or ability to do or have something ○ *Given time, I'm sure we can find a solution.* **2. IN VIEW OF** taking into consideration ○ *given the uncertainty of the situation* ■ *n.* **ACCEPTED FACT** a fact or event that is accepted as true or definite at the outset and that affects following or subsequent reasoning ◇ **be given to** to be inclined to something or likely to do or be something

giv·en name *n.* the name or names that somebody is given at birth or baptism in addition to the family name

giv·er /gívvər/ *n.* somebody who gives something (*often used in combination*)

Gi·za /geézə/ city in northern Egypt on the western bank of the Nile River, southwest of Cairo. It is the site of the Sphinx and Egypt's three most famous pyramids. Population: 2,144,000 (1992).

giz·mo /gíz mō/ (*plural* **-mos**), **gis·mo** (*plural* **-mos**) *n.* a gadget, especially a mechanical or electrical device considered to be more complicated than necessary (*informal*) ○ *a new video recorder with all the latest gizmos* [Mid-20thC. Origin unknown.]

giz·zard /gízzərd/ *n.* **1.** BIRDS **PART OF BIRD'S DIGESTIVE TRACT** a thick-walled muscular sac in the alimentary tract of birds, situated immediately behind the first chamber of the stomach, where food is broken down by muscular action. The food is also ground against small stones ingested for that purpose. **2.** ZOOL **DIGESTIVE STRUCTURE** a structure in invertebrates and fish, where digestion takes place **3.** ANAT **STOMACH** the stomach or alimentary canal generally (*informal*) [14thC. Via Old French *giser* from, ultimately, Latin *gigeria* "cooked poultry entrails."]

Gk. *abbr.* Greek

gla·bel·la /glə béllə/ (*plural* **-lae** /-lee/) *n.* the part of the human forehead that lies just above the nose and between the eyebrows. It is one of the crucial points used in measuring and classifying skull types in physical anthropology and craniometry. [Early 19thC. Via modern Latin from, ultimately, Latin *glaber* (see GLABROUS).] —**gla·bel·lar** *adj.*

gla·brate /gláy bràyt, -brət/ *adj.* **1.** = **glabrous** *adj.* **2. ALMOST HAIRLESS** almost completely smooth and hairless [Mid-19thC. Formed from Latin *glabrare* "to make bald," from *glaber* (see GLABROUS).]

gla·bres·cent /glay bréss'nt/ *adj.* becoming hairless over time

gla·brous /gláybrəss/ *adj.* smooth and lacking hairs or bristles ○ *glabrous leaves* [Mid-17thC. Formed from Latin *glaber* "bald."] —**gla·brous·ness** *n.*

gla·cé /gla sáy/ *adj.* **1. GLAZED WITH SUGAR SOLUTION** coated with a sugar solution that results in a glazed finish ○ *glacé cherries* **2. MADE FROM POWDERED SUGAR AND LIQUID** made by mixing powdered sugar and a liquid, usually water **3. SMOOTHLY GLOSSY** having a smooth glossy finish [Mid-19thC. From French, the past participle of *glacer* "to glaze," from *glace* (see GLACIER).]

Glace Bay /glàyss-/ town on the Atlantic coast in Cape Breton County, northeastern Nova Scotia, Canada, situated on the Atlantic Ocean 12 mi./19 km east of Sydney. Population: 19,501 (1991).

gla·cial /gláysh'l/ *adj.* **1. RELATING TO GLACIER** relating to or caused by a glacier or glaciers ○ *glacial movements and deposits* **2. CONTAINING EXPANSES OF ICE** characterized by the presence of ice masses **3.** GEOL **ICE-AGE** used to describe any geological time when a large part of the earth was covered in ice **4. FRIGID** icily cold ○ *a glacial wind* **5. COLDLY HOSTILE** unfriendly or hostile ○ *a glacial look* **6. DETACHED** characterized by detachment and an absence of emotion ○ *glacial determination* **7. SLOW** moving or advancing extremely slowly ○ *the glacial pace of the negotiations* ■ *n.* **gla·cial, Gla·cial** = **glacial period** [Mid-17thC. Via Old French from Latin *glacialis* "icy," from *glacies* (see GLACIER).] —**gla·cial·ly** *adv.*

gla·cial a·ce·tic ac·id *n.* acetic acid that is 99.8% or more pure [Because it forms crystals that resemble ice]

gla·cial pe·ri·od, **gla·cial ep·och** *n.* any period of geological time when most of the earth was covered in ice

gla·ci·ate /gláyshee àyt/ (**-at·ed, -at·ing, -ates**) *v.* **1.** *vti.* **ICE OVER** to cover something, or become covered, with a glacier **2.** *vt.* **AFFECT BY GLACIER** to affect something by the action of a glacier, especially by erosion [Early 17thC. From Latin *glaciare* "to freeze," from *glacies* (see GLACIER).] —**gla·ci·a·tion** /glàyshee áysh'n/ *n.*

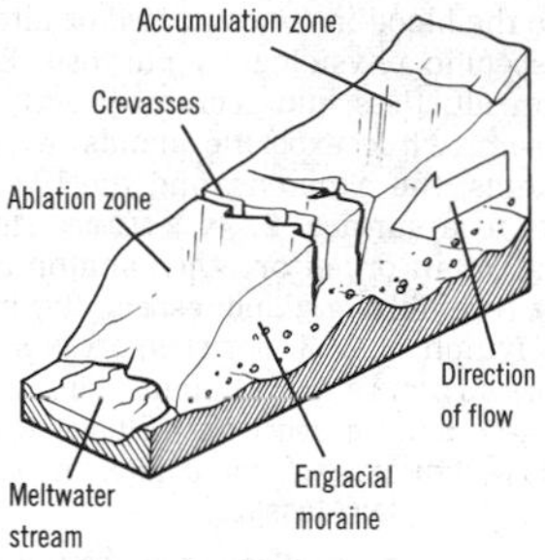

Glacier: Composition of a glacier

gla·cier /gláyshər/ *n.* a large body of continuously accumulating ice and compacted snow, formed in mountain valleys or at the Poles, that deforms under its own weight and slowly moves [Mid-18thC. From French, formed from *glace* "ice," from, ultimately, Latin *glacies*.] —**gla·ciered** *adj.*

Gla·cier Bay Na·tion·al Park and Pre·serve /glàyssee ər bay, glàssi-/ national park in southeastern Alaska, established as a national monument in 1925 and a national park in 1980. It is noted for its glaciers and wide variety of plant and animal life. Area: 3,283,168 acres/1,328,651 hectares.

gla·cier meal *n.* = **rock flour**

gla·cier milk *n.* water cloudy with particles of rock that flows from a melting glacier

Gla·cier Na·tion·al Park 1. mountainous park with about 50 glaciers and over 200 lakes in northwestern Montana, established in 1910. Area: 1,584 sq. mi./4,102 sq. km. **2.** national park in the Selkirk and Purcell mountains in southeastern British Columbia, Canada, established in 1886. Area: 521 sq. mi./1,349 sq. km.

gla·ci·ol·o·gist /glàyshee óllәjist/ *n.* somebody who studies the formation, movement, and effects of glaciers

gla·ci·ol·o·gy /glàyshee óllәjee/ *n.* the branch of scientific study concerned with the formation, movement, and effects of glaciers and ice in general — **gla·ci·o·log·ic** /glàyshee ə lójjik/ *adj.* —**gla·ci·o·log·i·cal** /-lójjik'l/ *adj.*

gla·cis /gla seé, glássee, gláyssiss/ (*plural* **-cis**) *n.* **1. GENTLE INCLINE** a slope, especially one that is not very long or steep **2. DEFENSIVE SLOPE** a slope in front of a fortification designed to make it easier to fire on attacking forces **3. NEUTRAL TERRITORY** a stretch of neutral ground between two opposing or warring forces **4.** = **glacis plate** [Late 17thC. From French, formed from Old French *glacier* (see GLANCE).]

gla·cis plate *n.* the armored plate at the front of a military tank [From its slant]

Glack·ens /glákənz/, **William** (1870–1938) U.S. artist. Known for his impressionist paintings, he was a member of the group called The Eight. Full name **William James Glackens**

glad[1] /glad/ *adj.* (**glad·der, glad·dest**) **1. DELIGHTED** happy and pleased ○ *I'm so glad you came.* **2. CHEERFULLY WILLING** willing or ready to do something ○ *always glad to help* **3. GRATEFUL** appreciative of or grateful for something ○ *glad of the chance to relax* **4. PLEASING** giving pleasure, delight, or happiness ○ *on this glad occasion* **5. BRIGHT** bright and cheerful (*literary*) ○ *this glad June day* ■ *vti.* (**glad·ded, glad·ding, glads**) **GLADDEN** to gladden somebody (*archaic*) [Old English *glæd*. Ultimately from a prehistoric Germanic word. Originally in the meaning "bright, shining."] —**glad·ness** *n.*

glad[2] /glad/ *n.* PLANTS a gladiolus (*informal*) [Early 20thC. Shortening.]

glad·den /gládd'n/ (**-dened, -den·ing, -dens**) *vti.* to feel or cause somebody to feel cheerful and hopeful ○ *It gladdens my heart to hear that.*

glade /glayd/ *n.* **1. CLEARING IN FOREST** an area in a wood or forest without trees or bushes **2. EVERGLADE** an everglade [Early 16thC. Origin uncertain.] —**glad·y** *adj.*

glad hand *n.* **1. WARM BUT INSINCERE HANDSHAKE** a hand extended in welcome or greeting, especially one offered insincerely or for motives of self-advancement **2. CONVIVIAL HELLO** a friendly welcome

glad-hand (**glad-hand·ed, glad-hand·ing, glad-hands**) *vti.* to offer somebody a friendly greeting or handshake, often insincerely or for motives of self-advancement —**glad-hand·er** *n.*

glad·i·ate /gláddee àyt, -ət/ *adj.* shaped like a sword ○ *the gladiate leaves of an iris* [Late 18thC. Formed from Latin *gladius* (see GLADIATOR).]

glad·i·a·tor /gláddee àytər/ *n.* **1. FIGHTER IN ROMAN ARENA** a professional fighter in ancient Rome who fought another combatant or a wild animal in public entertainments set in an arena. Often gladiators were criminals or enslaved men who were equipped variously with nets, nooses, swords, or other weapons. **2. AVID SUPPORTER OR CAMPAIGNER** somebody who vigorously fights for or against a cause or actively campaigns for or against something **3. BOXER** a professional boxer (*informal*) [Mid-16thC. From Latin, formed from *gladius* "sword."] —**glad·i·a·to·ri·al** /glàddee ə táwree əl/ *adj.*

glad·i·o·lus /gladee ólәss/ (*plural* **-lus** *or* **-li** /-lī/ *or* **-lus·es**), **glad·i·o·la** /glàddi ólə/ (*plural* **-las** *or* **-la**) *n.* **1.** PLANTS **TALL FLOWERING GARDEN PLANT** a tropical and southern African plant with long sword-shaped leaves and large funnel-shaped flowers growing in tall spikes that is widely grown as a garden flower. Genus: *Gladiolus*. **2.** ANAT **CENTER OF BREASTBONE** the large central part of the breastbone (**sternum**) [16thC. From Latin, literally "little sword," from *gladius* (see GLADIATOR).]

glad·ly /gláddlee/ *adv.* **1. WITH GREAT WILLINGNESS** more than willingly ○ *I'll gladly help.* **2. HAPPILY** in a pleased, cheerful, or happy way

glad rags *npl.* somebody's best clothes, reserved for special occasions (*informal*)

glad·some /gládsəm/ *adj.* feeling, showing, or bringing happiness (*literary*) ○ *gladsome tidings* — **glad·some·ly** *adv.* —**glad·some·ness** *n.*

Glad·stone /glád stōn/ *n.* **1. PASSENGER VEHICLE PULLED BY HORSES** a small four-wheeled horse-drawn carriage with a collapsible roof **2.** = **Gladstone bag** [Mid-19thC (see GLADSTONE BAG)]

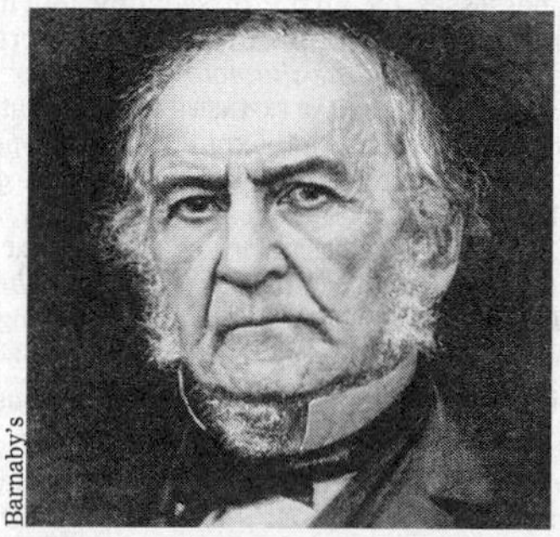

W. E. Gladstone

Glad·stone /glád stōn/, **W. E.** (1809–98) British statesman. The leader of the Liberal Party after 1867, he was four times prime minister between 1868 and 1894. He introduced national education in Britain (1870). Full name **William Ewart Gladstone**

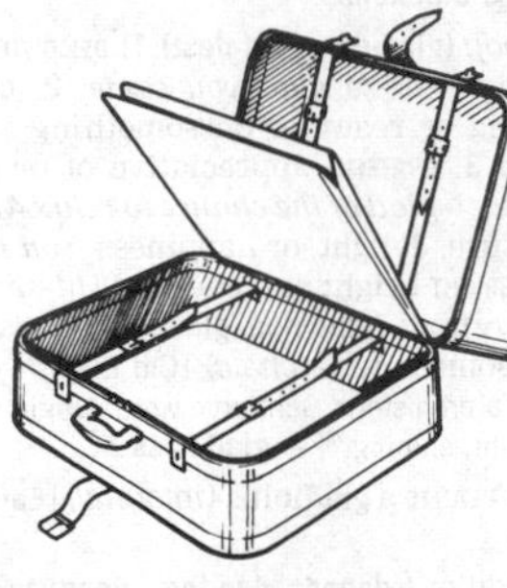

Gladstone bag

Glad·stone bag *n.* a small suitcase or portmanteau consisting of a rigid frame on which two compartments of the same size are hinged together [Late 19thC. Named for William Ewart GLADSTONE, who was noted for the unusual amount of traveling he undertook in the course of his public life.]

Glag·o·lit·ic /glàggə líttik/ *adj.* **1.** LANG **OF OR IN SLAVONIC ALPHABET** belonging or relating to or written in the ancient Slavonic alphabet that was replaced by the Cyrillic alphabet and survives only in certain Roman Catholic liturgical books **2.** CHR **OF CROATIAN CATHOLIC COMMUNITY** belonging or relating to a Roman Catholic community of southwestern Croatia, whose liturgical books continue to be written in the Glagolitic alphabet [Early 19thC. Via modern Latin *glagoliticus* and Serbo-Croatian *glagŏljica* from, ultimately, Old Church Slavonic *glagolŭ* "word."]

glair /glair/, **glaire** *n.* **1. EGG WHITE** a sizing, glazing, or adhesive substance made from egg white and used especially in bookbinding **2. SUBSTANCE SIMILAR TO EGG-WHITE SIZING** a substance that resembles glair in appearance or function ■ *vt.* **(glaired, glair·ing, glairs; glaired, glair·ing, glaires) PUT GLAIR ON SOMETHING** to apply glair to something [14thC. Via French from, ultimately, Latin *clarus* "clear."]

glam /glam/ *adj.* **EXTREMELY GLAMOROUS** glamorous, especially in an overstated or ironic way (*slang*) ○ *a really glam dress* ■ *n.* **EXTREME GLAMOUR** glamour, especially when it is overstated or ironic (*slang*) ■ *vt.* **(glammed, glam·ming, glams) glam, glam up GLAMORIZE EXCESSIVELY** to make somebody or something glamorous, especially in an overstated or camp way (*slang*) [Mid-20thC. Shortening.]

glam·or·ize /glámmə rīz/ (**-ized, -iz·ing, -iz·es**), **glam·our·ize** (**-ized, -iz·ing, -iz·es**) *vt.* **1. MAKE GLAMOROUS** to make somebody or something glamorous **2. ROMANTICIZE** to make something seem more interesting, romantic, or glamorous than it really is —**glam·or·i·za·tion** /glàmmərì záysh'n/ *n.* —**glam·or·iz·er** /-rīzər/ *n.*

glam·or·ous /glámmərəss/, **glam·our·ous** *adj.* **1. ARTIFICIALLY GOOD LOOKING** dressed or made up to be good looking, especially in a high-fashion manner ○ *glamorous models strutting down the runway* **2. EXCITING AND DESIRABLE** desirable, especially in an exciting, stylish, or opulent way ○ *a glamorous lifestyle* —**glam·or·ous·ly** *adv.* —**glam·or·ous·ness** *n.*

glam·our /glámmər/, **glam·or** *n.* **1. EXCITING ALLURE** an irresistible alluring quality that somebody or something possesses by virtue of seeming much more exciting, romantic, or fashionable than ordinary people or things ○ *the glamour of a career in the movies* **2. HIGH-FASHION AND EXPENSIVE GOOD LOOKS** striking physical good looks or sexual impact, especially when it is enhanced with highly fashionable clothes or makeup **3. SPELL** a magical spell or charm (*archaic*) ■ *adj.* **HAVING STYLISH GOOD LOOKS OR DESIRABLE EXCITEMENT** characterized by glamour ○ *a glamour job in advertising* [Early 18thC. Originally a Scottish English alteration of GRAMMAR, meaning "enchantment, spell."]

glam·our·ous *adj.* = **glamorous** *adj.* 2, **glamorous** *adj.* 1

glance /glans/ *v.* **(glanced, glanc·ing, glanc·es) 1.** *vi.* **LOOK QUICKLY** to look at something quickly, especially for only a second or two ○ *He glanced in our direction.* **2.** *vi.* **MAKE A CURSORY EXAMINATION** to look over or through something without really studying it **3.** *vi.* **TOUCH ON BRIEFLY** to make a brief or passing allusion to something ○ *an introductory course that merely glances at the wider historical issues* **4.** *vi.* **GLINT OR SHINE** to reflect or shine, especially intermittently or for only a short time ○ *green feathers glancing in the sunlight* **5.** *vt.* **STRIKE AT ANGLE** to strike something briefly or lightly at an angle ○ *The stone glanced his shoulder.* ■ *n.* **1. QUICK LOOK** a quick look at somebody or something ○ *a glance in our direction* **2. PASSING MENTION** a brief mention of something ○ *The book takes only a brief glance at contemporary music.* **3. CURSORY EXAMINATION** a cursory quick examination of something ○ *I haven't even had a glance at the report yet.* **4. OBLIQUE STRIKE** an act or instance of something striking another thing briefly or lightly at an angle **5. GLINT OF LIGHT** a sudden or quick flash or gleam of light ○ *glances of sunlight through the trees* [15thC. Alteration (influenced by *glent* "to shine") of earlier glace, from Old French *glacier* "to slide" (see GLACIER.] ◇ **at a glance** immediately and without having to make a close study ◇ **at first glance** initially or on first examination

glance off *vt.* to come into quick light contact with something and then deflect at an angle ○ *The stone glanced off the windshield.*

glanc·ing /glánsing/ *adj.* **1. STRIKING OBLIQUELY** coming into contact with another object and then deflecting at an angle ○ *a glancing blow* **2. FLICKERING OR FLASHING** giving off light in a flickering or flashing manner **3. TEMPORARY** lasting only a short time —**glanc·ing·ly** *adv.*

gland[1] /gland/ *n.* **1.** ANAT **SECRETING CELL MASS** a mass of cells or an organ that removes substances from the bloodstream and excretes them, or secretes them back into the blood in concentrated or altered form with a specific physiological purpose. Endocrine glands are ductless and secrete directly into the glands are ductless and secrete directly into the bloodstream, while exocrine glands, e.g., the salivary glands, the pancreas, and the liver, secrete via ducts to a surface. **2.** ANAT **ORGANIC STRUCTURE RESEMBLING GLAND** an organ or other anatomical structure that resembles a gland, especially, in popular usage, a lymph node **3.** BOT **PLANT ORGAN** a secreting organ or structure of a plant, e.g., a nectary gland [Late 17thC. Via French from, ultimately, Latin *glandula*, literally "little acorn," "tonsil" (from its shape), from *glans* "acorn."] —**gland·less** *adj.*

gland[2] /gland/ *n.* a metal sleeve put around a rotating shaft or rod to prevent leakage, e.g., around a shaft emerging from a ship's hull [Early 19thC. Origin uncertain: probably from, ultimately, Old Norse *glam* "noise."]

glan·ders /glándərz/ *n.* an infectious, often fatal disease of horses, characterized by ulcers of the skin, lungs, or upper respiratory tract and heavy discharge of mucus from the nose. It is caused by a bacterium *Pseudomonas mallei.* (*takes a singular verb*) [15thC. Via Old French *glandres* "swelling of the glands" from, ultimately, Latin *glandula* (see GLAND[1]).] —**glan·dered** *adj.* —**glan·der·ous** *adj.*

glan·des plural of **glans**

glan·du·lar /glánjələr/, **glan·du·lous** /glánjələss/ *adj.* **1.** ANAT **RELATING TO GLANDS** relating to, functioning as, or affecting a gland or glands **2.** MED **RESULTING FROM GLAND DYSFUNCTION** used to describe a condition caused by a malfunctioning gland or glands **3. HAVING GLAND** characterized by the presence of a gland or glands **4. BODILY** natural to the body, especially hormonally or sexually (*informal*) [Mid-18thC. Via French *glandulaire* from, ultimately, Latin *glandula* (see GLAND[1]).]

glan·dule /glán dool/ *n.* a small gland or a part resembling a small gland [14thC. Directly or via French from Latin *glandula* (see GLAND[1]).]

glan·du·lous *adj.* ANAT = **glandular** *adj.* 1 [14thC. From Latin *glandulosus*, from *glandula* (see GLAND[1]).] —**glan·du·lous·ly** *adv.*

glans /glanz/ (*plural* **glan·des** /glándeez/) *n.* **1. glans, glans pe·nis TIP OF PENIS** the rounded tip of a penis **2. glans, glans cli·tor·i·dis TIP OF CLITORIS** the erectile tissue at the tip of a clitoris [Mid-17thC. From Latin, "acorn." From its shape.]

glare[1] /glair/ *vi.* **(glared, glar·ing, glares) 1. STARE STONILY** to stare intently and angrily **2. LOOK ANGRILY** to express or signal anger, disapproval, contempt, or another negative emotion by giving a steady stare **3. BE UNPLEASANTLY BRIGHT** to shine brightly and intensely, often dazzlingly **4. STAND OUT OBTRUSIVELY** to be very conspicuous, blatant, or obtrusive ○ *Mistakes glared from every page of the report.* ■ *n.* **1. ANGRY LOOK** a prolonged stare, usually expressing anger, disapproval, contempt, or another negative emotion **2. EXCESSIVE BRIGHTNESS** dazzling or uncomfortable brightness ○ *a screen on the monitor to reduce glare* **3. MEDIA SPOTLIGHT** excessive attention from the media **4. GAUDY ORNAMENTATION** gaudy coloration or decoration [13thC. From Middle Low German *glaren* "to gleam."]

glare[2] /glair/ *n.* = **black ice** ■ *adj.* **SLIPPERY** having a smooth and slippery surface [Mid-16thC. Origin uncertain: perhaps from GLARE[1].]

glare ice *n.* = **black ice** [From GLARE[2]]

glar·ing /gláiring/ *adj.* **1. OBVIOUS** very obvious, or easily seen or detected ○ *a report full of glaring mistakes* **2. ANGRY** expressing anger, disapproval, contempt, or another negative emotion ○ *a glaring look of sheer contempt* **3. UNPLEASANTLY BRIGHT** intensely or dazzlingly bright **4. GARISH** gaudy or brash, especially in a tasteless way ○ *painted in glaring oranges and greens* —**glar·ing·ly** *adv.* —**glar·ing·ness** *n.*

glar·y /gláiree/ (**-i·er, -i·est**) *adj.* **1. STARING** staring steadily and often angrily ○ *glary eyes* **2. EXCESSIVELY BRIGHT** dazzlingly or uncomfortably bright ○ *a glary computer screen*

Glas·gow /glaázgō, glàzgō, glaáss-, glàss-/ **1.** city on the Clyde River, southwestern Scotland. An industrial and commercial center, it has a cathedral and three universities. Population: 616,430 (1996). **2.** city in southern Kentucky, northeast of Barren River Lake, east of Bowling Green and near Mammoth Cave National Park. Population: 13,739 (1996).

Glas·gow /gláskō/, **Ellen** (1873–1945) U.S. writer. Her novels critically examined the problems of the South. She won a Pulitzer Prize for *In This Our Life* (1941). Full name **Ellen Anderson Gholson Glasgow**

glas·nost /glaáz nōst, -nòst/ *n.* a policy that commits a government or organization to greater accountability, openness, discussion, and freer disclosure of information than previously, especially that of Mikhail Gorbachev in the former Soviet Union. ◊ **perestroika** [Late 20thC. From Russian, literally "publicness."]

glass /glass/ *n.* **1. TRANSPARENT SOLID SUBSTANCE** a hard, usually transparent, substance that shatters easily and is used for making such objects as windows, bottles, and lenses. It is made by melting sand in combination with other oxides such as lime or soda without crystallizing them. **2. UNCRYSTALLIZED SUBSTANCE RESEMBLING GLASS** a solid substance similar to glass formed by melting and cooling without crystallizing **3. GLASS CONTAINER** a container without a handle made from glass, for drinking from **4.** MEASURE **AMOUNT IN GLASS** the amount a drinking glass holds **5.** HOUSEHOLD = **glassware 6.** GARDENING **PROTECTING COVER** a glass cover, greenhouse, or other insulating material used to protect germinating plants ○ *Keep the seedlings under glass for the first four weeks.* **7.** = **looking glass 8. BAROMETER** a barometer (*dated*) **9.** = **magnifying glass 10.** = **volcanic glass 11.** = **fiberglass** ■ *adj.* **OF GLASS** made from or fit with glass ■ *vt.* **(glassed, glass·ing, glass·es) 1. COVER WITH GLASS** to cover or fit something with glass ○ *glassed the porch* **2. INSERT INTO A GLASS CONTAINER** to put something into a glass container or one made of a material resembling glass ○ *glassed the specimens in formalin* [Old English *glæs.* Ultimately from a prehistoric Germanic word that is also the ancestor of English *glare* and German *Glas* "glass."]

Philip Glass

Glass /glass/, **Philip** (*b.* 1937) U.S. composer. He is known for his minimalist compositions, including the opera *Einstein on the Beach* (1976).

glass blow·ing *n.* the forming or shaping of a glass object by blowing air through a tube into a mass of semimolten glass —**glass blow·er** *n.*

glass ceil·ing *n.* an unofficial but real impediment to somebody's advancement into upper-level management positions because of discrimination based on the person's gender, age, race, ethnicity, or sexual preference [From the idea that it is an invisible barrier]

glass chin *n.* = **glass jaw**

glass cloth *n.* a polishing cloth with fine particles of glass in it

glass cut·ter *n.* **1. IMPLEMENT FOR CUTTING GLASS** a tool used to cut glass or to etch designs into glass **2. SOMEBODY WHO CUTS GLASS** somebody whose job is to cut glass or to make cut glass

glassed-in *adj.* made using glass panes ○ *a glassed-in Florida room*

glass eel *n.* a larval form of the American or European eel with a flattened transparent body, found in the Atlantic Ocean

glass·es /glássəz/ *npl.* **1. OUTER EYEWEAR** a pair of sight-correcting or protective lenses set in frames that fit over the ears and sit on the bridge of the nose **2. BINOCULARS** a pair of binoculars

glass eye *n.* an artificial eye made from glass, or material similar to glass, so as to resemble a natural eye

glass·fish /gláss fish/ (*plural* **glass·fish** *or* **glassfishes**) *n.* **1. TROPICAL FISH POPULAR FOR AQUARIUMS** a small transparent tropical fish found along the coasts and rivers of Africa and the Indian and western Pacific oceans that is commonly kept as an aquarium fish. Genus: *Chanda.* **2. PACIFIC FOOD FISH** a slender, almost transparent, food fish belonging to one of 14 species found in the northwestern Pacific Ocean. Family: Salangidae.

glass·ful /glássfŏŏl/ *n.* = **glass** *n.* 4

glass har·mon·i·ca *n.* a set of drinking glasses or glass bowls, filled to graduated levels with water, that produce sounds of different pitches when their rims are rubbed with a moist finger. It was popular as a musical instrument in the 18th century when various mechanical versions also existed, including one designed by Benjamin Franklin.

glass·house /gláss hòws/ (*plural* **-hous·es** /-hòwzəz/) *n.* **1. MEDIA PROMINENCE** a public position that brings somebody a high level of media attention and scrutiny **2.** = **glassworks 3.** *U.K.* = **greenhouse**

glass·ine /gla sēen/ *n.* a transparent paper treated with a glaze to make it greaseproof and resistant to the passage of air, and used for book jackets and food packaging

glass jaw *n.* in boxing, a jaw that is highly vulnerable to an opponent's punches (*informal*) [From the idea that it is easily broken]

glass·mak·er /gláss màykər/ *n.* somebody whose job is to make glass —**glass·mak·ing** *n.*

glass snake *n.* a limbless lizard, or one with vestigial limbs, of Europe, Asia, and North America that can, as a defense mechanism, snap off its tail to confuse predators. Genus: *Ophisaurus.* [From its brittle tail]

glass·ware /gláss wàir/ *n.* objects made of glass considered as a group

glass wool *n.* fine-spun glass fibers formed into a woolly mass and used for insulation, as air filters, or in the manufacture of fiberglass

glass·work /gláss wùrk/ *n.* **1. FITTING OF GLASS** the technique or result of cutting and fitting glass, especially glass panes for windows and doors **2. MAKING OF GLASS** the production or manufacture of glass or glass objects **3.** = **glassware** —**glass·work·er** *n.*

glass·works /gláss wùrks/ (*plural* **-works**) *n.* a factory for the manufacture of glass or glass objects

glass·wort /gláss wùrt, -wàwrt/ (*plural* **-wort** *or* **-worts**) *n.* a plant with fleshy stems and small leaves that grows in salt marshes and was formerly a source of the soda used in making glass. Genus: *Salicornia.*

glass·y /glássee/ (**-i·er, -i·est**) *adj.* **1. SMOOTH AND SLIPPERY** having a highly smooth, slippery, often reflective, surface **2. LIKE GLASS** resembling glass in being smooth, reflective, or transparent **3. BLANKLY EXPRESSIONLESS** lacking expression or animation ○ *a blank glassy look* —**glass·i·ly** *adv.* —**glass·i·ness** *n.*

glass·y-eyed *adj.* having a blank staring expression

Glas·we·gian /glass wéejən, glaz-/ *n.* somebody who lives in or was born or raised in Glasgow, Scotland [Early 19thC. Formed from GLASGOW, on the model of NORWEGIAN.] —**Glas·we·gian** *adj.*

Glau·ber's salt /glówbərz-, gláw-/, **Glau·ber salt** /glówbər-, gláw-/ *n.* a colorless crystalline sodium sulfate. It is used in solar energy systems, in making dyes, glass, and paper, and as a laxative. [Mid-18thC. Named for the German chemist Johann Rudolf *[Glauber]* (1604–68), who first produced it.]

glau·co·ma /glaw kṓmə/ *n.* eye disorder marked by abnormally high pressure within the eyeball that leads to damage of the optic disk and, if not treated, causes impaired vision and sometimes blindness [Mid-17thC. Directly or via Latin from Greek *glaukōma,* from *glaukos* (see GLAUCOUS).] —**glau·co·ma·tous** *adj.*

glau·co·nite /gláwkə nìt/ *n.* a clayey green mineral consisting of a silicate of iron, potassium, and aluminum, and used as a fertilizer [Mid-19thC. Via German *Glaukonit* from Greek *glaukos* (see GLAUCOUS).] —**glau·co·nit·ic** /glàwkə níttik/ *adj.*

glau·cous /gláwkəss/ *adj.* **1. COVERED IN GRAYISH POWDER** covered in a grayish, whitish, or bluish waxy or powdery substance that rubs off easily, e.g., the bloom on grapes **2.** COLORS **GRAYISH-GREEN OR BLUE** having a dull grayish-green or blue color [Late 17thC. Formed from Latin *glaucus* "blue-gray, green," which came from Greek *glaukos.*]

glau·cous gull *n.* a large gull with a white head and tail and a light gray back and wings that is found in northern regions. Genus: Larus hyperboreus.

glaze /glayz/ *v.* (**glazed, glaz·ing, glaz·es**) **1.** *vt.* CERAMICS **COVER WITH FINISH LIKE GLASS** to put a clear or colored coating on a ceramic object and fire it in a kiln, in order to fix the coloration, make it watertight, or give it a shiny appearance **2.** *vt.* COOK **COAT WITH MILK OR EGG** to brush food with milk, egg, or sugar before baking in order to produce a shiny brown finish **3.** *vt.* PAINTING **COAT OIL PAINTING** to give something, especially an oil painting, a transparent or semitransparent coating in order to enhance or slightly alter the color tones **4.** *vt.* COVERINGS **GIVE PROTECTIVE COVERING TO MATERIAL** to place a protective or decorative coating on something, especially a natural material such as leather, cotton, or paper **5.** *vti.* **MAKE OR BECOME GLASSY IN APPEARANCE** to become, or cause the eyes to become, unfocused and expressionless as a result of loss of interest, distraction, or tiredness **6.** *vt.* METEOROL **COVER WITH ICE** to put a thin layer of ice on something **7.** *vt.* CONSTR **FIT SOMETHING WITH GLASS** to fit glass into or over something, especially a window, door, or picture ■ *n.* **1.** CERAMICS **COVERING RESEMBLING GLASS** a shiny, smooth, transparent, or colored glassy coating on a ceramic object, produced by firing the treated object in a kiln, or the substance or process employed to achieve this **2.** COOK **COATING FOR FOOD** a shiny brown finish on food or the substance used for achieving this effect **3.** PAINTING **COATING FOR OIL PAINTING** a transparent or semitransparent coating on something, especially an oil painting, used to enhance or slightly alter the color tones, or the substance used to achieve this effect **4.** COVERINGS **PROTECTIVE COVERING ON MATERIAL** a protective or decorative coating on something, especially a natural material such as leather, cotton, or paper, or the substance used for making this kind of coating **5.** METEOROL **LAYER OF ICE** a thin coating of ice formed when rain or moisture in the air comes into contact with a surface that is cold enough to cause it to freeze [14thC. Formed from GLASS, on the model of GRAZE from GRASS.] —**glaz·er** *n.*

glaze over *vi.* to become unfocused and expressionless as a result of loss of interest, distraction, or tiredness (*refers to eyes*) ○ *Her eyes glazed over as the sedative began to take effect.*

glaze ice, glazed frost *n. U.K.* = **glaze** *n.* 5

gla·zier /gláyzhər/ *n.* somebody whose job is to install glass, especially in windows and doors

glaz·ing /gláyzing/ *n.* **1. HARD SHINY COATING** the glaze coating on an object **2. COVERING OF SOMETHING WITH GLAZE** an act or the process of putting a glaze on something **3. GLASS FOR WINDOW** glass in general, especially the type of glass used in doors or windows or glass that has been installed in windows or doors **4. INSTALLATION OF GLASS** an act or the process of installing glass

GLC *abbr.* gas-liquid chromatography

GLCM *abbr.* ground-launched cruise missile

gleam /gleem/ *vi.* (**gleamed, gleam·ing, gleams**) **1. SHINE BRIGHTLY** to shine brightly and continuously **2. FLASH FOR SHORT TIME** to flash, flicker, or appear briefly or indistinctly ■ *n.* **1. BRIGHT SHINE** a steady bright shine **2. FLASH OF LIGHT** a beam of light, especially one that is reflected, dim, or coming from an indistinct source **3. BRIEF SHOW OF SOMETHING** a slight or momentary indication of something ○ *a gleam of intelligence* [Old English *glǣm.* Ultimately from a prehistoric Germanic word that is also the ancestor of English *glimmer* and *glimpse.*] —**gleam·er** *n.* ◇ **a gleam in somebody's eye** something at the very earliest stage of planning or development

gleam·ing /gléeming/ *adj.* shining, especially with health, cleanliness, or newness ○ *gleaming black hair* —**gleam·ing·ly** *adv.*

glean /gleen/ (**gleaned, glean·ing, gleans**) *v.* **1.** *vt.* **ACCUMULATE SOMETHING** to obtain information in small amounts over a period of time **2.** *vti.* AGRIC **GATHER AFTER HARVEST** to go over a field or area that has just been harvested and gather by hand any usable parts of the crop that remain [14thC. Via Old French *glener* from late Latin *glennare,* of Celtic origin.] —**glean·er** *n.*

glean·ings /gléeningz/ *npl.* **1. THINGS COLLECTED** objects or ideas that have been gathered or amassed over a period of time, especially when they form a collection or comprehensive whole **2.** AGRIC **HARVEST LEFTOVERS** the usable parts of a crop that are left behind in a harvested field or area and can be gathered in by hand

gle·ba /gléebə/ (*plural* **-bae** /glée bee/) *n.* the mass of tissue in which spores are formed in the fruiting bodies of certain fungi such as truffles and puffballs [Mid-19thC. From Latin (see GLEBE).]

glebe /gleeb/ *n.* **1. ARABLE LAND** land or soil, especially when considered as a source of abundant natural produce (*literary*) **2.** *U.K.* **BRITISH CHURCH LAND** in Great Britain, a piece of land belonging to a church and lent temporarily to a member of the clergy to provide additional income [14thC. From Latin *gleba* "clod."]

glee /glee/ *n.* **1. GREAT DELIGHT** joyful or animated delight **2. GLOATINGLY JUBILANT FEELING** jubilant, often smug pleasure, especially as a result of somebody else's bad luck or failure **3.** MUSIC **SONG FOR UNACCOMPANIED VOICES** a part song for three or more unaccompanied voices, usually men's, of a type that first became popular in England in the 18th century [Old English *glēo.* Ultimately from a prehistoric Germanic word meaning "merriment."]

glee club *n.* a group of people who get together to sing, especially short part songs

glee·ful /gléef'l/ *adj.* **1. JOYFULLY HAPPY** very happy or joyful **2. GLOATINGLY JUBILANT** jubilant and smugly pleased, especially as a result of somebody else's bad luck or failure —**glee·ful·ly** *adv.* —**glee·ful·ness** *n.*

gleet /gleet/ *n.* **1. INFLAMMATION OF URETHRA** inflammation of the urethra, accompanied by a discharge of pus and mucus, and characteristic of a late stage in the development of gonorrhea **2. DISCHARGE OF PUS** a discharge of pus and mucus in a late stage of gonorrhea [14thC. Via Old French *glette* "slime" from Latin *glittus* "sticky."]

glei *n.* = **gley**

Gleich·schal·tung /glīk shaal tung/ *n.* the forced standardization and complete suppression of all opposition in the political, social, and economic life and institutions of a country by an oppressive government or regime [Mid-20thC. From German.]

glen /glen/ *n.* a long narrow valley [15thC. From Scottish Gaelic *gleann.*]

Glen Cove /glèn kṓv/ city on the northern shore of Long Island, southeastern New York. Population: 21,746 (1996).

Glen·dale /glén dayl/ **1.** city in Los Angeles County, southwestern California, just north of Los Angeles. Population: 178,481 (1994). **2.** city in central Arizona, a western suburb of Phoenix. Population: 182,219 (1996).

Glen·dale Heights village in northeastern Illinois, north of Wheaton, a western suburb of Chicago. Population: 30,321 (1996).

Glen·do·ra /glen dáwrə/ city in Los Angeles County,

southwestern California, 17 mi./27 km northeast of Los Angeles. Population: 47,828 (1990).

Glen·ea·gles /glen éeg'lz/ picturesque valley in Perth and Kinross, Scotland, the site of a well-known golf course

Glen El·lyn /glèn éllin/ village in northeastern Illinois, a western suburb of Chicago. Population: 25,759 (1996).

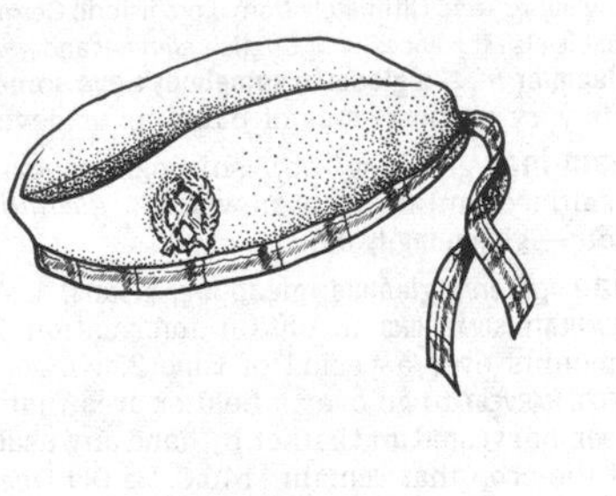

Glengarry

glen·gar·ry /glen gérree/ (*plural* **-ries**) *n.* a small brimless hat with a crown creased from front to back and usually a pair of ribbons hanging from the back. It forms part of the uniform of certain Scottish regiments and is sometimes worn as part of Scottish highland dress. [Mid-19thC. Named for *Glengarry*, a valley in northern Scotland, where it originated.]

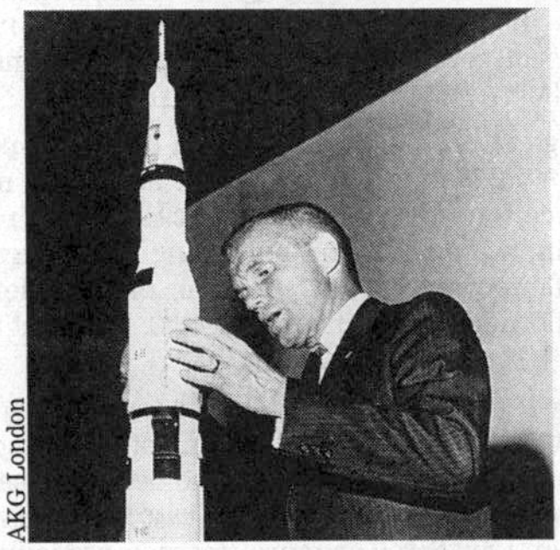

John Glenn

Glenn /glen/, **John** (*b.* 1921) U.S. astronaut and senator. He was the first U.S. astronaut to orbit the earth (1962), and the oldest astronaut ever to go into space (1998). He was first elected a Democratic U.S. senator from Ohio in 1975. Full name **John Herschel Glenn, Jr.**

gle·noid /glé nòyd, glee-/ *adj.* **1. SHAPED LIKE SMALL CUP** shaped like a small shallow cup or socket **2.** ANAT **OF SHOULDER SOCKET** relating to the cup-shaped socket in the shoulder that holds the head of the humerus [Early 18thC. Via French *glénoïde* from, ultimately, Greek *glēnē* "eyeball, socket."]

Glens Falls /glènz-/ city in Warren County, eastern New York, situated at a waterfall on the Hudson River, 38 mi./61 km northeast of Amsterdam. Population: 15,023 (1990).

Glen·view /glen vyoó, glén vyoo/ village on the Chicago River in northeastern Illinois, northwest of Skokie, a northern suburb of Chicago. Population: 39,159 (1996).

gley /glay/, **glei** *n.* a sticky bluish-gray clay soil or soil layer that forms in heavily waterlogged areas [Early 20thC. From Ukrainian *glei*.]

gli·a /glī́ ə, glée ə/ *n.* = **neuroglia** [Late 19thC. From Greek (see GLIADIN).] —**gli·al** *adj.*

gli·a·din /glī́ əd'n/, **gli·a·dine** /-deen/ *n.* any of several simple cereal proteins, e.g., those from wheat or rye [Mid-19thC. Via French from Greek *glia* "glue," from Greek *gloios* "glutinous substance."]

glib /glib/ *adj.* **1. SLICK** fluent in a superficial or insincere way ○ *a glib talker* **2. SUPERFICIAL** shallow and lacking thought or preparation ○ *a glib generalization* **3. CASUAL AND RELAXED** easy, unconcerned, and informal in attitude ○ *a glib smile* [Late 16thC. Origin uncertain: perhaps from, ultimately, Middle Low German *glibberich* "slippery, smooth," of unknown origin.] —**glib·ly** *adv.* —**glib·ness** *n.*

glide /glīd/ *v.* (**glid·ed, glid·ing, glides**) **1.** *vti.* **MOVE SMOOTHLY** to move, or cause something to move, in a smooth, effortless, and often graceful way ○ *seals gliding through the water* **2.** *vi.* **CHANGE STATE SMOOTHLY** to pass smoothly, slowly, or gradually into a specified state ○ *gliding in and out of consciousness* **3.** *vti.* AIR **LAND WITHOUT USING ENGINE** to bring an aircraft in to land without using the engine, or come into land in this way **4.** *vi.* MUSIC **USE PORTAMENTO** to slide from one note to another in music **5.** *vi.* PHON **MAKE INTERMEDIATE SPEECH SOUND** to produce an intrusive speech sound when moving from one point of articulation to the next ■ *n.* **1.** DANCE **SMOOTH MOVEMENT** a smooth, effortless, and often graceful movement **2.** DANCE **SMOOTH FLOWING DANCE** a dance characterized by smooth flowing movement **3.** DANCE **DANCE STEP** a dance step characterized by smooth flowing movement **4.** AIR **LANDING WITHOUT USING ENGINE** a controlled aircraft descent using no engine power **5.** GEOG **SLOW-MOVING CALM WATER** a stretch of calm, slowly flowing water in a river or large stream **6.** MUSIC = **portamento 7.** MUSIC **EXTENSION FOR TROMBONE** a piece of metal tubing used to extend the length of a trombone so that lower notes can be produced **8.** PHON **INTERMEDIATE SPEECH SOUND** an intrusive speech sound produced when a speaker is moving from one point of articulation to the next, e.g., the /w/ sound in the middle of "going" **9.** PHON = **semivowel 10.** CRYSTALS = **slip 11.** FURNITURE **METAL DISK ON FURNITURE LEG BOTTOM** a metal or plastic disk affixed to the bottom of the leg of a piece of furniture, to facilitate moving it across the floor **12.** FURNITURE **METAL TRACK FOR DRAWER** a metal track along which a drawer can be slid in or out easily [Old English *glīdan*. Ultimately from a prehistoric Germanic word that is also the ancestor of English *glissade* and *glitch*.]

glide path *n.* the prescribed descent of an aircraft coming in to land that is shown to the pilot by means of a radio beam and acts as an aid to navigation

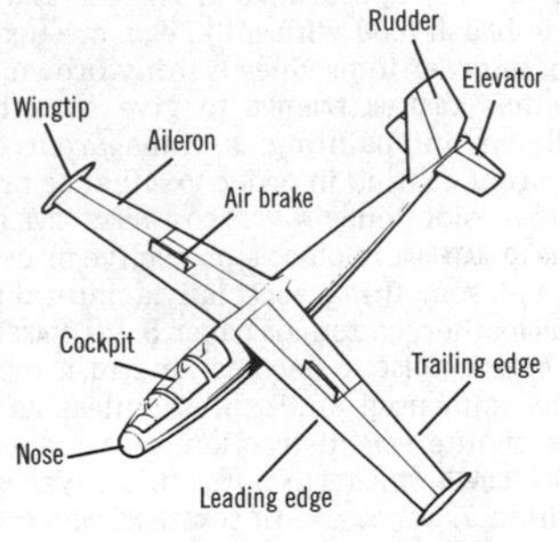

Glider

glid·er /glī́dər/ *n.* **1.** AIR **AIRCRAFT WITH NO ENGINE** an engineless aircraft that flies by riding air currents. It becomes airborne by being towed up by an airplane or by being catapulted into the air from the ground. ◊ **sailplane 2. PORCH SWING** a porch swing hung from an upright framework instead of from the ceiling

glide slope *n.* AIR = **glide path** *n.*

glim /glim/ *n.* (*archaic slang*) **1. LIGHT SOURCE** something such as a candle or lamp that is a source of light **2. LIGHT FROM CANDLE** light given off by a candle, lamp, or other light source [Late 17thC. Origin uncertain: perhaps a shortening of GLIMMER.]

glim·mer /glímmər/ *vi.* (**-mered, -mer·ing, -mers**) **1. EMIT DIM GLOW** to emit a faint or intermittent light **2. BE PRESENT TO SMALL EXTENT** to be present faintly or in only a small amount ○ *Hope still glimmered in their hearts.* ■ *n.* **1. FAINT FLASHING LIGHT** a faint or intermittent glowing light ○ *a glimmer of campfires in the distance* **2. SMALL AMOUNT OF SOMETHING** a faint sign or small amount of something ○ *a glimmer of interest* [15thC. Origin uncertain: probably from the ancestor of Swedish *glimra* "to glimmer."]

glim·mer·ing /glímməring/ *n.* = **glimmer** *n.* **2** ■ *adj.* **EMITTING DIM GLOW** emitting a faint or intermittent light

glimpse /glimps/ *n.* **1. BRIEF LOOK** a quick or incomplete look or sighting of somebody or something **2. SMALL INDICATION** a small, brief, or indistinct indication or appearance of something ■ *v.* (**glimpsed, glimps·ing, glimps·es**) **1.** *vt.* **CATCH BRIEF SIGHT OF** to see somebody or something briefly or incompletely **2.** *vi.* **TAKE BRIEF LOOK** to have a quick or incomplete look at or through something **3.** *vi.* **EMIT FAINT LIGHT** to give off a faint or intermittent light (*archaic*) [14thC. Ultimately from a prehistoric Germanic word that is also the ancestor of English *gleam* and *glimpse*.]

glint /glint/ *vi.* (**glint·ed, glint·ing, glints**) **FLASH BRIEFLY** to gleam or flash, especially brightly or momentarily ○ *Anger glinted in her eyes.* ■ *n.* **1. BRIEF FLASH** a slight or momentary gleam or flash ○ *a glint of daylight through the curtains* **2. SLIGHT INDICATION** a slight sign or indication of something ○ *a glint of humor in his eyes* **3. SHININESS OR GLOSSINESS** a shiny or glossy appearance [15thC. Origin uncertain: probably an alteration of earlier *glent* "to gleam," of Scandinavian origin.]

gli·o·ma /glī ómə/ (*plural* **-mas** *or* **-ma·ta** /-ómətə/) *n.* a tumor composed of connective tissue (**neuroglial tissue**) of the nervous system and affecting the brain or spinal cord [Late 19thC. Formed from Greek *glia* (see GLIADIN).] —**gli·o·ma·tous** *adj.*

glis·sade /gli saád/ *n.* **1.** BALLET **GLIDING BALLET STEP** a gliding ballet step in which one foot slides forward, backward, or to one side **2. ACT OF SLIDING ON SNOW** a controlled slide down a snowy slope made without skis by somebody in a standing or crouching position ■ *vi.* (**-sad·ed, -sad·ing, -sades**) **1.** BALLET **MAKE GLIDING BALLET STEP** to perform a glissade in ballet **2. TO SLIDE ON SNOW** to slide down a snowy slope in a controlled manner without skis in a standing or crouching position [Mid-19thC. From French, formed from Old French *glisser* "to slide," from, ultimately, Old Dutch *glissen*.] —**glis·sad·er** *n.*

glis·san·do /gli sán dō/ (*plural* **-di** /-dee/ *or* **-dos**) *n.* **1. SLIDING MOVEMENT ON KEYBOARD OR HARP** an act of sliding a finger or thumb up or down a keyboard or harp strings from one note to another **2. SLIDING MOVEMENT ON VIOLIN OR TROMBONE** an act of sliding a finger along a string instrument's fingerboard or slowly moving a trombone's slide in and out to create a smooth change in pitch between two notes [Late 19thC. Via Italian from, ultimately, Old French *glisser* (see GLISSADE).]

glis·ten /glíss'n/ *vi.* (**-tened, -ten·ing, -tens**) **1. BE SHINY AND WET-LOOKING** to shine brightly, or reflect light from a wet surface ○ *leaves glistening after the rain* **2. HAVE SHEEN** to have a glossy sheen (*refers to hair or an animal's pelt*) ■ *n.* **BRIGHT SHINE** a bright shine or reflection of light from a wet surface [Old English *glisnian*. Ultimately from a prehistoric Germanic word.]

glis·ter /glístər/ (**-tered, -ter·ing, -ters**) *vi.* to glitter brightly (*archaic*) [14thC. Origin uncertain: probably from Middle Low German *glistern*.]

glitch /glich/ *n.* **1. SMALL PROBLEM** a minor hitch or technical problem ○ *glitches in the software* **2.** ELEC ENG **UNWANTED ELECTRONIC SIGNAL** a sudden unwanted electronic signal such as results from a power surge or a temporary irregular supply of power [Mid-20thC. Origin uncertain: probably via Yiddish *glitsh* "slip" from, ultimately, Old High German *glītan* "to glide."] —**glitch·y** *adj.*

glit·ter /glíttər/ *vi.* (**-tered, -ter·ing, -ters**) **1. SPARKLE** to sparkle or shimmer brightly ○ *an evening gown glittering with sequins* **2. SHINE WITH EMOTION** to look bright or expressive with an emotion such as anger or love (*refers to eyes*) **3. BE VIVACIOUS** to exhibit liveliness and charm ○ *a radiant personality who glittered at every event she attended* **4. BE DAZZLING** to be characterized by the presence of somebody or something glamorous ○ *The event glittered with Hollywood stars.* ■ *n.* **1. SPARKLY DECORATION** small pieces of reflective material, e.g., sequins **2. SPARKLING LIGHT** bright sparkling light **3. GLAMOUR** dazzling glamour ○ *the glitter of a command performance at the opera* **4.** *Can* = **glaze** *n.* **5** [14thC. From Old Norse *glitra*.] —**glit·ter·ing·ly** *adj.* —**glit·ter·y** *adj.*

glit·te·ra·ti /glìttə raátee/ *npl.* famous, rich, or fashionable people thought of as a group, especially those who are frequently photographed by the press [Mid-20thC. Humorous blend of GLITTER and LITERATI.]

glitz /glits/ *n.* **1. GLAMOUR** glamour, especially that associated with show business or celebrities **2. FLASHY SHOW OF WEALTH** extravagant and often tasteless display, especially of wealth [Late 20thC. Back-formation from GLITZY.]

glitz·y /glítsee/ (**-i·er, -i·est**) *adj.* **1. GLAMOROUS** glamorous, especially in relation to show business or celebrities **2. SHOWY** extravagant and often tasteless, especially in the display of wealth [Mid-20thC. Origin uncertain: probably formed from German *glitzern* "to glitter."] —**glitz·i·ness** *n.*

gloam·ing /glṓming/ *n.* the period of fading light after sunset but before dark (*literary*) [Old English *glōmung*, from *glōm* "twilight." Ultimately from a prehistoric Germanic word.]

gloat /glōt/ *vi.* (**gloat·ed, gloat·ing, gloats**) BE SMUGLY HAPPY to feel or express smug self-satisfaction about something such as an achievement, a possession, or somebody else's misfortune ■ *n.* ACT OF FEELING SMUGLY HAPPY the act or an instance of feeling or expressing smug self-satisfaction about something [Late 16thC. Origin uncertain.] —**gloat·er** *n.* —**gloat·ing·ly** *adv.*

glob /glob/ *n.* an amount of something soft or semiliquid (*informal*) [14thC. Origin uncertain: perhaps from Latin *globus* (see GLOBE).] —**glob·by** *adj.*

glob·al /glṓb'l/ *adj.* **1.** WORLDWIDE relating to or happening throughout the whole world **2.** OVERALL taking all the different aspects of a situation into account **3.** COMPUT RELATING TO WHOLE OF SYSTEM covering or affecting the whole of a computer system, program, or file **4.** SPHERICAL shaped like a globe or sphere —**glob·al·ly** *adv.*

glob·al·ism /glṓb'l ìzzəm/ *n.* the belief that political policies should take worldwide issues into account before focusing on national or state concerns, or the advocacy of this belief —**glob·al·ist** *n.*

glob·al·i·za·tion /glṓb'li záysh'n/ *n.* **1.** GLOBAL ADOPTION OF SOCIAL INSTITUTIONS the process by which social institutions become adopted on a global scale **2.** OPERATION AT INTERNATIONAL LEVEL the process by which a business or company becomes international or starts operating at an international level

glob·al·ize /glṓb'l īz/ (**-ized, -iz·ing, -iz·es**) *vti.* **1.** MAKE SOMETHING BECOME ADOPTED GLOBALLY to become, or cause something, especially social institutions, to become adopted on a global scale **2.** BECOME OR MAKE SOMETHING BECOME INTERNATIONAL to become, or cause something, especially a business or company, to become international or start operating at the international level —**glob·al·iz·er** *n.*

glob·al vil·lage *n.* the whole world considered as a single community served by electronic media and information technology

glob·al warm·ing *n.* an increase in the world's temperatures, believed to be caused in part by the greenhouse effect and depletion of the ozone layer

globe /glōb/ *n.* **1.** MAP OF EARTH ON SPHERE a hollow sphere representing the Earth and illustrated with the continents, seas, and islands, especially one showing and labeling the countries **2.** EARTH the planet Earth **3.** HOLLOW SPHERICAL OBJECT a rounded hollow object, especially one made of glass, e.g., a cover for a lamp, or a goldfish bowl **4.** PART OF MONARCH'S REGALIA a hollow sphere, usually made of gold or another precious metal, that forms part of a monarch's regalia and symbolizes the power or sovereignty of the ruler ■ *vti.* (**globed, glob·ing, globes**) MAKE INTO OR BECOME GLOBE to form, or cause something to form, a globe [Mid-16thC. Directly or via Old French from Latin *globus* "ball, sphere."]

globe am·a·ranth *n.* an ornamental garden plant with colorful whorls of leaves and flower heads made up of several distinct blossoms. Latin name: *Gomphrena globosa.*

globe ar·ti·choke *n.* = **artichoke**

globe·fish /glṓb fish/ (*plural* **-fish** *or* **-fish·es**) *n.* **1.** = **puffer 2.** = **porcupine fish** [From the puffer's shape when inflated]

globe·flow·er /glṓb flòwr/ *n.* a poisonous plant with ball-shaped flowers consisting of large white, pale-yellow, or orange sepals that almost entirely enclose the smaller petals. Genus: *Trollius.*

globe this·tle *n.* a plant native to Asia and the Mediterranean with jagged-edged leaves and large white or bluish ball-shaped flowers. Genus: *Echinops.*

globe·trot /glṓb tròt/ (**-trot·ted, -trot·ting, -trots**) *vi.* to travel frequently and to a great variety of distant destinations [Back-formation from GLOBETROTTER]

globe·trot·ter /glṓb tròttər/ *n.* somebody who travels frequently and to a great variety of distant destinations

glo·big·er·i·na /glō bìjjə rī́nə/ (*plural* **-nas** *or* **-nae** /glō bìjjə rī́ nee, -rée nee/) *n.* a marine protozoan with a spiny rounded spiral shell. Genus: *Globigerina.* [Mid-19thC. From modern Latin, genus name, from Latin *globus* "GLOBE" + *gerere* "to carry," because it carries around its globe-shaped shell.] —**glo·big·er·i·nal** *adj.*

glo·big·er·i·na ooze *n.* a deposit on the ocean floor that consists of globingerina shells and is found almost worldwide

glo·bin /glṓbin/ *n.* a colorless protein component of the oxygen-carrying pigments myoglobin and hemoglobin [Late 19thC. Shortening of HEMOGLOBIN.]

glo·boid /glṓ bòyd/ *adj.* BALL-SHAPED shaped like a ball ■ *n.* BALL-SHAPED PART a ball-shaped part, especially one found in plant granules

glo·bose /glṓ bōss/, **glo·bous** *adj.* = **globoid** [15thC. From Latin *globosus*, from *globus* (see GLOBE).] —**glo·bose·ly** *adv.* —**glo·bos·i·ty** /glō bóssitee/ *n.*

glob·u·lar /glóbbyələr/ *adj.* **1.** SPHERICAL having the shape of a ball or globule **2.** HAVING GLOBULES containing or consisting of globules [Mid-17thC. Formed from Latin *globolus* (see GLOBULE).] —**glob·u·lar·i·ty** /glòbbyə lérratee/ *n.* —**glob·u·lar·ly** /glóbbyələrlee/ *adv.*

glob·u·lar clus·ter *n.* an approximately spherical cluster of densely-packed stars, located within a spherical halo around the Milky Way galaxy

glob·ule /glóbbyool/ *n.* a small ball-shaped object, especially one that is liquid or semiliquid [Mid-17thC. Via French from Latin *globulus*, literally "little globe," from *globus* "GLOBE."]

glob·u·lif·er·ous /glòbbyə líffərəss/ *adj.* composed of, containing, or producing globules

glob·u·lin /glóbbyəlin/ *n.* a simple protein belonging to a class that is found in plant and animal tissue. Globulins are soluble in weak salt solutions and form a mass when heated.

glo·chid·i·um /glō kíddee əm/ (*plural* **-a** /-kíddee ə/) *n.* **1. glo·chid·i·um, glo·chid** BARBED HAIR OR BRISTLE a barbed hair or bristle that grows on plants such as the prickly pear or among the spores on ferns **2.** MUSSEL LARVA the parasitic larva of certain mussels that has hooks or suckers that it uses to attach itself to the fins or gills of fish. Family: Unionidae. [Late 19thC. Via modern Latin from, ultimately, Greek *glōkhis* "arrowhead."] —**glo·chid·i·al** *adj.* —**glo·chid·i·ate** /glō kíddee ət/ *adj.*

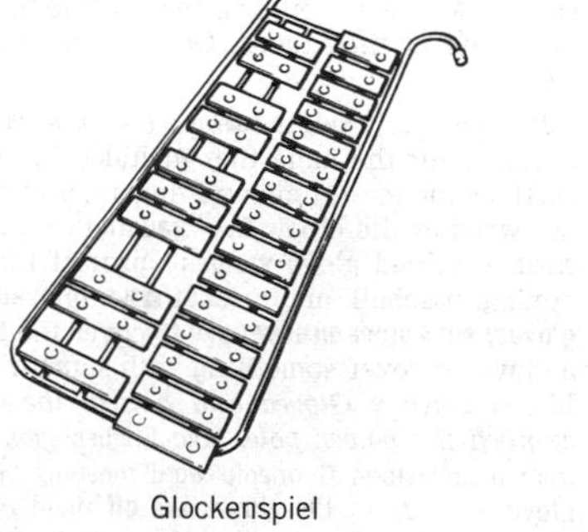

Glockenspiel

glock·en·spiel /glókən spee̍l, -shpee̍l/ *n.* a percussion instrument consisting of a set of tuned metallic bars, played by striking the individual bars with small light hammers [Early 19thC. From German, literally "bell-play."]

glogg /glog/ *n.* a hot punch consisting of brandy, red wine, and sherry, and flavored with sugar, spices, fruit pieces, and blanched almonds. It was originally served in Scandinavia at Christmas. [Early 20thC. From Swedish *glögg*.]

glom /glom/ (**glommed, glom·ming, gloms**) *vi.* (*slang*) **1.** GRAB SOMETHING to grab or seize hold of something ○ *businesspeople who glom any idea that has been floated by a management guru* **2.** BEGIN TO UNDERSTAND to begin to understand or realize ○ *Kids soon glom onto what's considered to be cool.* [Early 20thC. Origin uncertain: probably a variant of Scottish English *glaum* "to snatch at," of unknown origin.]

glom·er·ate /glómmərət, -ràyt/ *adj.* **1.** MADE INTO COMPACT BALL formed into a tight ball or cluster **2.** WOUND INTO TIGHT BALL tightly wound together, like a ball of string [Late 18thC. From Latin *glomerare* "to make into a ball," from *glomus* "ball of thread."]

glom·er·ule /glómmə ro͝ol/ *n.* **1.** HEAD OF FLOWER a flat-topped flower head formed by a compact cluster of short-stalked flowers **2.** SPORE CLUSTER a cluster of spores formed into a ball shape [Late 18thC. Via French from modern Latin *glomerulus* (see GLOMERULUS).] —**glo·mer·u·late** /glo mérrələt, glə-/ *adj.*

glo·mer·ul·o·ne·phri·tis /glo mèrrəlōnə frítəss, glə-/ *n.* an inflammatory disease affecting the clusters of capillaries (**glomeruli**) in the cortex of a kidney

glo·mer·u·lus /glo mérryələss, glə-/ (*plural* **-li** /-lī/) *n.* **1.** CLUSTER OF NERVES OR BLOOD VESSELS a tightly packed cluster of blood vessels, nerve fibers, or other cells **2.** ROUND STRUCTURE IN KIDNEY a round cluster of interconnected capillaries found in the cortex of a kidney, that remove body waste to be excreted as urine [Mid-19thC. Via modern Latin, literally "little ball," from Latin *glomus* "ball of thread."]

gloom /gloom/ *n.* **1.** MURKY DARKNESS a state of darkness or partial darkness, especially one where shadows or poor visibility create a cheerless or dispiriting atmosphere **2.** DESPONDENCY a feeling or atmosphere of despair, despondency, or misery ■ *v.* (**gloomed, gloom·ing, glooms**) **1.** *vi.* BE DESPONDENT to feel or look despondent or miserable **2.** *vti.* MAKE OR BECOME DARK to become, or cause something to become, dark [13thC. Origin unknown.] ◇ **gloom and doom** a feeling or expression of despondency and a belief that disaster is about to strike

gloom·y /glo͞omee/ (**-i·er, -i·est**) *adj.* **1.** MURKILY DARK dark in a way that creates a cheerless or dispiriting atmosphere **2.** SAD sad and hopeless in offering little prospect that things will improve **3.** DESPONDENT feeling sad and without hope, often with a morbid or uninterested outlook on life —**gloom·i·ly** *adv.* —**gloom·i·ness** *n.*

gloop /gloop/ *n. U.K.* = **goop** (*informal*) [Late 20thC. An imitation of the sound it makes when poured or handled.]

glop /glop/ *n.* (*informal*) **1.** SOFT MASS a soft lump or mixture of something, especially unappetizing food ○ *a glop of cold, greasy mashed potatoes* **2.** SOMETHING WORTHLESS something such as a piece of music or writing that is considered to be overly sentimental or of little value [Early 20thC. (As GLOOP).] —**glop·py** *adj.*

Glo·ri·a /gláwree ə/ *n.* **1.** CHRISTIAN RELIGIOUS WORDS a hymn or set of words in Latin that begins with the word "Gloria" and is used in the Christian liturgy to praise God **2.** MUSICAL SETTING OF GLORIA the words of the Gloria set to music [15thC. From Latin, "glory."]

Glo·ri·a in Ex·cel·sis *n.* **1.** CHRISTIAN RELIGIOUS WORDS a hymn or set of words in Latin that begins with the words "Gloria in Excelsis" and is used in the Christian liturgy to praise God **2.** MUSICAL SETTING OF GLORIA IN EXCELSIS the words of Gloria in Excelsis set to music [From Latin, literally "Glory in the High Places"]

Glo·ri·a Pa·tri *n.* **1.** CHRISTIAN RELIGIOUS WORDS a short hymn or set of words in Latin that begins with the words "Gloria Patri" and is used in the Christian liturgy to praise God **2.** MUSICAL SETTING OF GLORIA PATRI the words of Gloria Patri set to music [From Latin, literally "Glory to the Father"]

glo·ri·fied /gláwrə fīd/ *adj.* described in much more grandiose or fanciful terms than are warranted ○ *They call it an antique auction, but it's really just a glorified garage sale.*

glo·ri·fy /gláwrə fī/ (**-fied, -fy·ing, -fies**) *vt.* **1.** MAKE APPEAR SUPERIOR to cause something to seem more pleasant, important, or desirable than is actually the case **2.** EXTOL to praise somebody or something highly **3.** RELIG PRAISE DEITY to worship or offer praise to a deity —**glo·ri·fi·ca·tion** /glàwrəfi káysh'n/ *n.* —**glo·ri·fi·er** /gláwrə fīr/ *n.*

glo·ri·ole /gláwree àwl/ *n.* a halo around somebody's head [Mid-19thC. Via French from Latin *gloriola*, literally "little glory," from *gloria* (see GLORY).]

glo·ri·o·sa /glàwri ṓssə/ (*plural* **-ri·o·sas** *or* **-riosa**) *n.* a tropical climbing plant of the lily family that has large brightly colored, yellow, orange, or red flowers, and is popular as a greenhouse plant. Genus: *Gloriosa.* [Via its modern Latin genus name, from Latin *gloriosus* (see GLORIOUS)]

glo·ri·ous /gláwree əss/ *adj.* **1.** EXCEPTIONALLY LOVELY beautiful in a way that inspires wonder or joy ○ *glorious summer weather* **2.** OUTSTANDING so good or distinguished as to merit praise and lasting fame ○ *a glorious career* **3.** ENJOYABLE highly enjoyable [14thC. Via Anglo-Norman and Old French *glorios* from Latin *gloriosus*, from *gloria* "glory."] —**glo·ri·ous·ly** *adv.* —**glo·ri·ous·ness** *n.*

Glo·ri·ous Rev·o·lu·tion *n.* in England, the overthrow of King James II in 1688 that established the power of Parliament over the monarch

glo·ry /gláwree/ *n.* (*plural* **-ries**) **1. EXALTATION** the fame, admiration, and honor that is given to somebody who does something important **2. ACHIEVEMENT OR DISTINCTION** something that brings or confers admiration, praise, honor, or fame **3. PRAISE OF DEITY** praise and thanksgiving offered as an act of worship to a deity ○ *Glory to God in the highest.* **4. AWESOME SPLENDOR** majesty or splendor **5. ASTOUNDING BEAUTY** beauty that inspires feelings of wonder or joy ○ *the glory of a bright spring morning* **6. HEAVEN** the idealized beauty and bliss of heaven **7.** ARTS, CHR **HALO** a halo around somebody's head ■ *interj.* **EXPRESSING SURPRISE** used to express great surprise, shock, dismay, or pleasure (*dated*) [13thC. Via Anglo-Norman and Old French *glorie* from Latin *gloria*.] ◇ **glory be** used to express great surprise, shock, dismay, or pleasure (*dated*) ◇ **go to glory** to die (*dated*) ◇ **in your glory** in a state of great happiness, satisfaction, or triumph

glory in *vt.* to derive great pride, pleasure, amusement, or satisfaction from something

glo·ry-of-the-snow (*plural* **glo·ry-of-the-snow** *or* **glo·ry-of-the-snows**) *n.* a small bulbous plant of the lily family, native to the eastern Mediterranean and western Asia but now cultivated in many regions for its early blue flowers. Latin name: *Chionodoxa luciliae.*

gloss[1] /glawss, gloss/ *n.* **1. SHININESS** a shiny quality, especially on a smooth surface **2. DECEPTIVE AND SUPERFICIAL ATTRACTIVENESS** an attractive appearance that often conceals something unattractive or inferior **3.** = **gloss paint** ■ *vt.* (**glossed, gloss·ing, gloss·es**) **MAKE SHINY** to apply a coating or gloss to a surface to make it shine [Mid-16thC. Origin uncertain.]

gloss over *vt.* to leave out negative information on purpose, or address a subject superficially to make it appear more attractive or acceptable

gloss[2] /glawss, gloss/ *n.* **1. EXPLANATORY WORD OR PHRASE** a short definition, explanation, or translation of a word or phrase possibly unfamiliar to the reader, often located in a page margin or collected in an appendix or glossary **2. INTERPRETATION** an interpretation or explanation of something ○ *Her account provides an interesting gloss on the theme of widowhood.* ■ *vt.* (**glossed, gloss·ing, gloss·es**) **1. EXPLAIN WORD OR PHRASE** to give a short definition, explanation, or translation of a word or phrase that may be unfamiliar to the reader **2. INSERT EXPLANATIONS IN A TEXT** to add or enter the necessary glosses in a manuscript or piece of writing **3. GIVE DELIBERATELY MISLEADING EXPLANATION OF SOMETHING** to interpret or explain something in a deliberately misleading or negative way [Mid-16thC. Via Old French *glose* from, ultimately, medieval Latin *glossa* "obscure word," from Greek *glōssa*, "tongue, language" (source of English *epiglottis* and *polyglot*).]

gloss. *abbr.* glossary

glos·sa /gláwssə, glossə/ (*plural* **-sae** /-ssee/ *or* **-sas**) *n.* **1.** ANAT **TONGUE** a tongue (*technical*) **2.** INSECTS **INSECT'S MOUTH STRUCTURE** a structure resembling a tongue in the mouth of an insect [Late 19thC. Via modern Latin from Greek *glōssa* (see GLOSS[2]).] —**glos·sal** *adj.*

glos·sa·ry /gláwssəree, glóssəree/ (*plural* **-ries**) *n.* an alphabetical collection of specialist terms and their meanings, usually in the form of an appendix to a book [14thC. From Latin *glossarium*, from *glossa* (see GLOSS[2]).] —**glos·sar·i·al** /glaw sáiree əl, glo sáiree əl/ *adj.* —**glos·sar·i·al·ly** /-əlee/ *adv.* —**glos·sa·rist** /gláwssərist, glóssərist/ *n.*

glos·sec·to·my /glaw séktəmee, glo-/ (*plural* **-mies**) *n.* partial or total surgical removal of the tongue

glos·seme /gláw seem, gló-/ *n.* the smallest meaningful unit of a language [Early 20thC. From Greek *glōssema* "word requiring explanation," from *glōssa* (see GLOSS[2]).]

glos·si·tis /glaw sítiss, glo-/ *n.* inflammation of the tongue [Early 19thC. Formed from Greek *glōssa* (see GLOSS[2]).] —**glos·sit·ic** /glaw síttik, glo síttik/ *adj.*

glos·sog·ra·phy /glaw sóggrəfee, glo-/ *n.* the writing of glosses, glossaries, or commentaries as part of a text (*formal*) [Early 17thC. Coined from Greek *glōssa* (see GLOSS[2]) + -GRAPHY.] —**glos·sog·ra·pher** *n.*

glos·so·la·li·a /glàwssō láylee ə, glòssō-/ *n.* **1.** RELIG = **speaking in tongues 2.** PSYCHOL **NONSENSE SPEECH** nonsensical or invented speech, especially resulting from a trance or schizophrenia [Late 19thC. Coined from Greek *glōssa* (see GLOSS[2]) + -LALIA.]

glos·so·pha·ryn·ge·al /glàwssō fə rínj'l, -fèrrin jée əl, glòssō-/ *adj.* relating to the tongue and pharynx [Early 19thC. Coined from Greek *glōssa* (see GLOSS[2]) + PHARYNGEAL.]

glos·so·pha·ryn·ge·al nerve *n.* either of the ninth pair of cranial nerves, which activate the muscles of the tongue, pharynx, and parotid gland

gloss paint *n.* a paint that gives a smooth shiny durable surface, used especially as a final coat on wood

gloss·y /gláwssee, glóssee/ *adj.* (**-i·er, -i·est**) **1. SHINY AND SMOOTH** having a smooth shiny surface or texture ○ *a glossy coat is the sign of a healthy animal* **2. SUPERFICIALLY STYLISH** creating a superficial impression of wealth, beauty, or fashionable elegance (*informal*) ○ *a glossy lifestyle that conceals years of financial struggle* ■ *n.* (*plural* **-ies**) PHOTOGRAPHY **PHOTO WITH A SHINY FINISH** a photograph printed on shiny smooth paper ○ *Please provide an 8 x 10 glossy.* —**gloss·i·ly** *adv.* —**gloss·i·ness** *n.*

gloss·y mag·a·zine *n. U.K.* = **slick** *n.* 2

glot·tal /glótt'l/ *adj.* **1.** ANAT **OF THE GLOTTIS** relating to the glottis **2.** PHON **USING THE GLOTTIS IN SPEECH** used to describe a speech sound that is produced by wholly or partially closing the glottis

glot·tal stop *n.* a consonantal speech sound created by closing and then opening the glottis before a vowel, which produces a sudden audible release of air as in "uh oh!" between "uh" and "oh." In some languages such as Arabic glottal stops are part of the standard consonant system.

glot·tis /glóttiss/ (*plural* **-tis·es** *or* **-ti·des** /glótti dèez/) *n.* **1. OPENING BETWEEN THE VOCAL CORDS** the elongated opening between the vocal cords at the upper part of a vertebrate's windpipe (**larynx**). The glottis is open during breathing but is closed by the epiglottis during swallowing. **2. VOICE BOX** all of the anatomy of the larynx that is involved in producing the voice in a human or vertebrate animal [Late 16thC. Via modern Latin from, ultimately, Greek *glōtta*, a variant of *glōssa* (see GLOSS[2]).]

Glouces·ter /glóstər/ resort city and port in northeastern Massachusetts, on the southeastern side of Cape Ann, on the Atlantic Ocean. Population: 29,267 (1996).

glove /gluv/ *n.* **1. SHAPED COVERING FOR THE HAND** a shaped covering for the hand that includes five separated sections for the thumb and fingers, and extends to the wrist or the elbow **2.** = **gauntlet**[1] *n.* **3. PROTECTIVE GLOVE** a padded glove worn to protect the hand in boxing, baseball, and cricket ■ *vt.* (**gloved, glov·ing, gloves**) **PUT A GLOVE ON SOMETHING** to cover the hand with a glove, or cover something with something that is like a glove ○ *Gloved and hatted, the electrician climbed the power pole.* [Old English *glōf*. Ultimately from a prehistoric Germanic word meaning "hand."] —**glove·less** *adj.* ◇ **the gloves are off** used to indicate that a course of action is about to be pursued in a ruthless and uncompromisingly aggressive way ○ *The gloves are off in the political debate.*

glove box *n.* **1.** = **glove compartment 2. BOX FOR HANDLING TOXIC MATERIALS** a sealed container that allows radioactive or toxic substances to be handled safely using a pair of gloves attached to openings in its sides

glove com·part·ment *n.* a small enclosed storage space in the dashboard of a vehicle

glove pup·pet *n. U.K.* = **hand puppet**

Glov·er /glúvvər/, **Danny** (*b.* 1947) U.S. actor. He played a variety of leading roles in movies including *The Color Purple* (1985) and the *Lethal Weapon* series (1987–98).

glow /glō/ *n.* **1. LIGHT FROM SOMETHING HOT** a light produced by something that has been heated to a high temperature but is not in flames ○ *the glow of the embers in the grate* **2. SOFT STEADY LIGHT** a soft steady light, especially one without heat or flames ○ *the glow of the neon lights* **3. SOFT WARM REFLECTED LIGHT** a soft warm reflected light ○ *the golden glow of the tapestries on the far wall* **4. ROSINESS OF COMPLEXION** a brightness or redness in somebody's complexion, e.g., because of exercise or good health ○ *the healthy glow that exercise gives you* **5. REDNESS OF EMBARRASSMENT** a redness of the face or complexion, especially one caused by embarrassment ○ *face suffused with a glow of shame* **6. HAPPY FEELING** a sense of happiness or wellbeing ○ *a warm glow of satisfaction* ■ *vi.* (**glowed, glow·ing, glows**) **1. EMIT LIGHT AND HEAT** to emit light as a result of being extremely hot ○ *The embers of the fire still glowed in the grate.* **2. EMIT A SOFT STEADY LIGHT** to emit a soft steady light without heat or flames ○ *the neon signs glowing red and blue* **3. REFLECT LIGHT SOFTLY** to emit a soft warm reflected light ○ *the walls glowing orange and gold in the afternoon sun* **4. SHINE WITH HEALTH OR HAPPINESS** to show the bright eyes and smooth skin that are a sign of good health, contentment, or high spirits. = **"flesh-colored" bandage, i.e., pink 5. BE FLUSHED WITH EMBARRASSMENT** to have a blood rush to the face, especially because of embarrassment **6. FEEL WARM AND CONTENTED** to feel a pleasant warm sensation owing to happiness, satisfaction, or love ○ *The winning team glowed with pride.* [Old English *glōwan*. Ultimately from a prehistoric Germanic word that is probably also the ancestor of English *glower*.]

glow·er /glówr/ *vi.* (**-ered, -er·ing, -ers**) **GLARE SILENTLY** to stare or look at somebody or something with sullen anger or strong resentment ■ *n.* **ANGRY LOOK** a sullen or resentful stare or look [15thC. Origin uncertain: perhaps from a Scandinavian word that had the same prehistoric Germanic ancestor as English *glow*.] —**glow·er·ing·ly** *adv.*

glow·ing /glṓ ing/ *adj.* **1. SHINING SOFTLY AND STEADILY** emitting a soft steady light **2. REDDISH-GOLD** rich, strong, or bright in color, especially when reddish or gold ○ *the glowing colors of autumn* **3. FULL OF PRAISE** praising somebody or something in very warm appreciative terms ○ *glowing reports of their daughter's performance in medical school* **4. ROSY** red or rosy as a result of excitement, wellbeing, or good health —**glow·ing·ly** *adv.*

glow plug *n.* a plug attached to a diesel engine that makes it easier to start in cold weather by warming it up

glow·worm /glṓ wùrm/ *n.* a larva of some types of firefly, or a beetle of a closely related family, that emits greenish light from organs in its abdomen. Families: Lampyridae and Phengodidae.

glox·in·i·a /glok sínnee ə/ *n.* a tropical American plant popular as a house plant for its large colorful bell-shaped flowers. Genus: *Sinningia.* [Early 19thC. Named for the 18thC German botanist Benjamin P. *Gloxin*, who first described it.]

gloze /glōz/ (**glozed, gloz·ing, gloz·es**) *v.* **1.** *vt.* **GLOSS OVER SOMETHING** to attempt to underplay or minimize something unpleasant or embarrassing ○ *tried to gloze over the scandalous story* **2.** *vti.* **USE FLATTERY** to use flattery on somebody (*archaic*) [13thC. Via French *glose* from, ultimately, Latin *glossa* (see GLOSS[2]).]

gluc- *prefix.* = **gluco-** (*used before vowels*)

glu·ca·gon /glóokə gòn/ *n.* a hormone produced by the pancreas that raises the blood sugar level by promoting the conversion of glycogen to glucose in the liver [Early 20thC. Coined from GLUCO- + Greek *agōn*, the present participle of *agein* "to lead."]

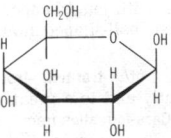

gluco- *prefix.* glucose ○ *glucocorticoid* [From GLUCOSE]

glu·co·cor·ti·coid /gloo kō káwrti kòyd/ *n.* a steroid hormone (**corticoid**) that controls the metabolism of carbohydrates, proteins, and fats. Glucocorticoids have anti-inflammatory properties useful in treating rheumatoid arthritis.

glu·co·ne·o·gen·e·sis /gloo kō nee ə jénnəssiss/ *n.* the production of glucose by the liver from substances other than carbohydrates, e.g., proteins and fats —**glu·co·ne·o·ge·net·ic** /gloo kō nee əjə néttik/ *adj.*

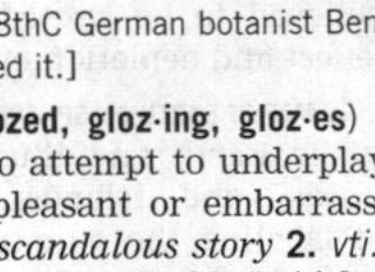

Glucose

glu·cose /glóo kòss/ *n.* **1.** BIOCHEM **SUGAR ENERGY SOURCE** a simple sugar produced in plants by photosynthesis and in animals by the conversion of carbohydrates, proteins, and fats. The commonest form, dextrose, is used by all living organisms. Formula: $C_6H_{12}O_6$. **2.** FOOD **SYRUPY MIXTURE** a syrup containing dextrose, maltose, dextrin, and water that is obtained from starch and used in food manufacture and in alcoholic fermentation [Mid-19thC. Via French from Greek *gleukos* "sweet wine."] —**glu·co·sic** /gloo kóssik/ *adj.*

glu·co·si·dase /gloo kṓssi dàyss, -dàyz/ *n.* an enzyme such as maltase that hydrolyzes glucosides

glu·co·side /glóokə sīd/ *n.* a glycoside with glucose as the sugar component, which it yields upon reacting chemically with water —**glu·co·si·dal** /glóokə sīd'l/ *adj.* —**glu·co·sid·ic** /-síddik/ *adj.* —**glu·co·sid·i·cal·ly** /-kəlee/ *adv.*

glu·co·su·ri·a /gloo kō shóoree ə, -sóoree ə/ *n.* = **glycosuria** —**glu·co·su·ric** *adj.*

glu·curonic ac·id an acid derived from glucose, important in human metabolism for its ability to combine with certain toxic substances, rendering them harmless. Formula: $OC_6H_9O_6$. [Early 20thC. Coined from GLUCO- on the model of GLYCURONIC.]

glue /gloo/ *n.* **1. ANIMAL-BASED ADHESIVE** an adhesive substance obtained by boiling animal parts such as bones, hides, horns, and hooves **2. ADHESIVE** a natural or synthetic substance used as an adhesive **3. SOMETHING THAT UNITES PEOPLE** a unifying factor or influence ○ *Mutual love and understanding is the glue that holds this family together.* ■ *vt.* (**glued, glu·ing, glues**) **1. STICK THINGS TOGETHER** to stick things together or reconstitute something using an adhesive substance ○ *It took hours to glue the vase back together.* **2. KEEP SOMEBODY STILL** to cause somebody to remain still because of concentrating on something with full attention (*informal*) (*often passive*) ○ *You've been glued to that computer all day!* [13thC. Via French *glu* from, ultimately, Latin *gluten* (source of English *agglutinate* and *gluten*).] —**glu·ey** *adj.* —**glu·i·ly** *adv.* —**glu·i·ness** *n.*

glue-sniff·ing *n.* the practice of inhaling the fumes from glues and volatile solvents in order to become intoxicated —**glue-sniff·er** *n.*

glum /glum/ (**glum·mer, glum·mest**) *adj.* quietly melancholic or miserable [Mid-16thC. From an earlier verb meaning "to look sullen," which evolved from GLOOM.] —**glum·ly** *adv.* —**glum·ness** *n.*

glume /gloom/ *n.* BOT either of a pair of dry leaves at the base of the spikelet in an ear of grass [Late 18thC. From Latin *gluma* "husk."] —**glu·ma·ceous** /gloo máyshəss/ *adj.*

glu·on /glóo òn/ *n.* a theoretical elementary particle without mass, thought to be involved in binding the subatomic particles (**quarks**) together [Late 20thC. Formed from GLUE.]

glut /glut/ *n.* **OVERSUPPLY** a larger supply of something than is needed, especially of a crop or product ○ *There is usually a glut of fresh vegetables in August.* ■ *vt.* (**glut·ted, glut·ting, gluts**) **1. OVERSUPPLY SOMETHING** to supply a market with an excess of something, especially a product, leading to a fall in price ○ *Cheaper products from abroad glutted the market, lowering profits.* **2. GIVE SOMEBODY ENOUGH OR TOO MUCH** to feed or supply somebody with enough or more than enough of something [14thC. Origin uncertain: probably via Old French *gloutir* "to swallow" from Latin *gluttire* (see GLUTTON).]

glu·ta·mate /glóotə màyt/ *n.* a salt or ester of glutamic acid, especially its sodium salt (**monosodium glutamate**)

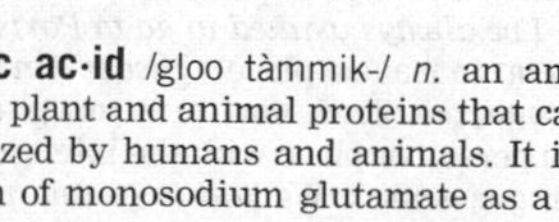

Glutamic acid

glu·tam·ic ac·id /gloo tàmmik-/ *n.* an amino acid found in plant and animal proteins that can also be synthesized by humans and animals. It is used in the form of monosodium glutamate as a flavoring in food. Formula: $C_5H_9NO_4$. [*Glutamic* from GLUTEN + AMINE + -IC]

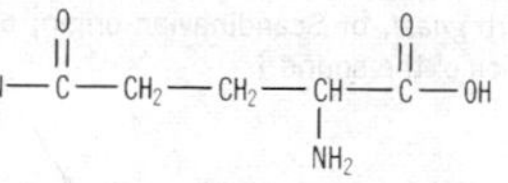

Glutamine

glu·ta·mine /glóotə meen/ *n.* an amino acid found in proteins that can also be synthesized by humans and animals. It is used in medicines and in biochemical research. Formula: $C_5H_{10}N_2O_3$. [Late 19thC. Blend of GLUTAMIC ACID and AMINE.]

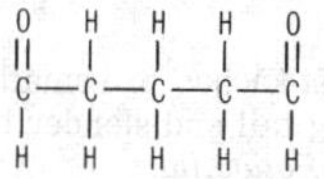

Glutaraldehyde

glu·tar·al·de·hyde /glòotə ráldə hīd/ *n.* an oily water-soluble liquid used as a disinfectant, a tanning agent, and a biological fixative. Formula: $C_5H_8O_2$. [Mid-19thC. Blend of *glutaric* (formed from GLUTEN) + ALDEHYDE.]

glu·tath·i·one /glòotə thī ōn/ *n.* a chemical compound (**peptide**) found in plant and animal tissues that consists of glutamic acid, cysteine, and glycine. It is important in biological oxidation-reduction reactions and the activation of some enzymes. Formula: $C_{10}H_{17}N_3O_6S$. [Early 20thC. Coined from *glutamic* + THIO- + -ONE.]

glu·te·i plural of **gluteus**

glu·ten /glóot'n/ *n.* a protein combination found in some cereals, especially wheat. It makes dough elastic, and enables it to rise by trapping gas. People who haveceliac disease are allergic to gluten and must avoid it in their diets. [Late 16thC. Via French from Latin (see GLUE).]

glu·te·us /glóotee əss/ (*plural* **-i** /-ī/) *n.* any of the three large buttock muscles that move the thigh in humans, especially the gluteus maximus. The other two muscles are the gluteus medius and the gluteus minimus. [Late 17thC. From modern Latin, formed from Greek *gloutos* "buttock."] —**glu·te·al** *adj.*

glu·te·us max·i·mus /-máksiməss/ (*plural* **glu·te·i max·i·mi** /-máksi mī/) *n.* the outermost of the three large gluteus muscles that form each buttock in humans [*Maximus* from Latin, "largest"]

glu·ti·nous /glóot'nəss/ *adj.* having a sticky consistency ○ *glutinous rice*

glut·ton /glútt'n/ *n.* **1. GREEDY PERSON** somebody who eats and drinks to excess **2.** ZOOL = **wolverine** [13thC. Via Old French *gluton* from, ultimately, Latin *gluttire* "to swallow," from *gula* "throat" (source of English *gullet*).] —**glut·ton·ous** *adj.* —**glut·ton·ous·ly** *adv.* ◇ **a glutton for punishment** somebody who deliberately takes on, and appears to need or enjoy, difficulty, discomfort, or stress

glut·ton·y /glútt'nee/ *n.* the act or practice of eating and drinking to excess. Gluttony is one of the seven deadly sins in Christian tradition.

glyc- *prefix.* = **glyco-**

glyc·er·ide /glíssə rīd/ *n.* an ester formed by the combination of glycerol with an acid. The occur widely in animal and vegetable fats and oils. [Mid-19thC. Formed from GLYCERIN.]

glyc·er·in /glíssərin/, **glyc·er·ine** *n.* a thick, sweet, odorless, colorless or pale yellow liquid obtained from fats and oils as a byproduct of soap manufacture. Used as a solvent, antifreeze, plasticizer, drug medium, and sweetener, and in the manufacture of soaps, cosmetics, inks, lubricants, and dynamite. Formula: $C_3H_8O_3$. [Mid-19thC. From French, formed from Greek *glukeros*, an alteration of *glukus* (see GLYCO-).]

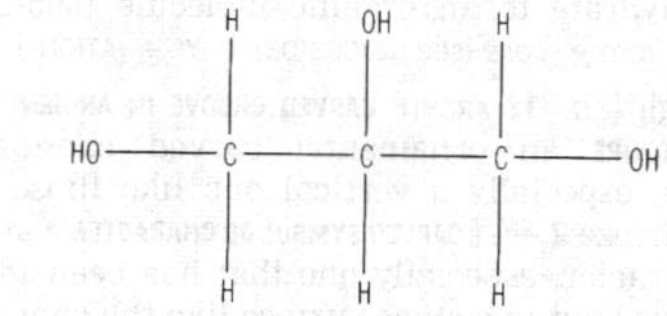

Glycerol

glyc·er·ol /glíssə ràwl/ *n.* glycerin (*technical*) [Late 19thC. Formed from GLYCERIN.]

glyc·er·yl /glíssəril/ *n.* a chemical group derived from glycerol by removing or replacing hydroxide, especially a trivalent group CH_2CHCH_2 [Mid-19thC. Coined from GLYCERIN + -YL.]

glyc·er·yl tri·ni·trate *n.* = **nitroglycerin**

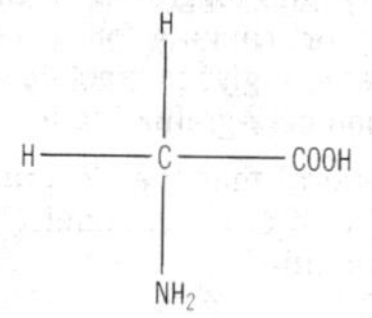

Glycine

gly·cine /glī seen/ *n.* a sweet crystalline amino acid that is found in most proteins and can also be synthesized by humans and animals. It acts as a neurotransmitter. Formula: $C_2H_5NO_2$. [Mid-19thC. Formed from Greek *glukus* (see GLYCO-).]

glyco-, **glyc-** *prefix.* **1.** sugar ○ *glycosuria* **2.** glycogen ○ *glycolysis* [From Greek *glukus* "sweet" (source of English *licorice*). Ultimately from an Indo-European base that is also the ancestor of *glucose* and *dulcet*.]

gly·co·gen /glīkəjən/ *n.* a white compound (**polysaccharide**) stored in the liver and muscles of humans and animals and easily converted to glucose as a source of energy. Formula: $(C_6H_{10}O_5)_n$. —**gly·co·gen·ic** /glīkə jénnik/ *adj.*

gly·co·gen·e·sis /glīkə jénnəssiss/ *n.* the formation or conversion of glycogen in the body —**gly·co·ge·net·ic** /glīkəjə néttik/ *adj.*

gly·co·gen·ol·y·sis /glīkəjə nóllississ/ *n.* the breakdown of glycogen, especially to glucose, in the bodies of humans and animals —**gly·co·gen·o·lyt·ic** /glīkəjenn'l íttik/ *adj.*

gly·col /glī kol/ *n.* = **ethylene glycol** [Mid-19thC. Formed from GLYCERIN.] —**gly·col·ic** *adj.*

gly·col·ic ac·id /glī kòllik-/ *n.* a colorless crystalline compound found in unripe grapes, sugar cane, and sugar beet. Used in tanning and the manufacture of pesticides, pharmaceuticals, adhesives, and plasticizers. Formula: $C_2H_4O_3$.

gly·co·lip·id /glīkə líppid/ *n.* a lipid that contains a carbohydrate group, especially glucose or galactose

gly·col·y·sis /glī kóllississ/ *n.* the breakdown of a compound such as glycogen or glucose by enzymes, producing pyruvic or lactic acid and releasing energy for use in the body. This metabolic process takes place in nearly all living cells. —**gly·co·lyt·ic** /glīkə líttik/ *adj.*

gly·co·pro·tein /glīkə prṓ teen/ *n.* a complex protein in which the nonprotein part is a carbohydrate

gly·co·side /glīkə sīd/ *n.* a sugar derivative that breaks down into a sugar and a nonsugar compound (**aglycone**). Some glycosides such as digitoxin are used medicinally. [Mid-20thC. Formed from *glycose*, a variant of GLUCOSE.] —**gly·co·sid·ic** /glīkə síddik/ *adj.*

gly·co·su·ri·a /glī kō shóoree ə, -sóo-/ *n.* the presence of sugar in the urine, usually a sign of diabetes [Mid-19thC. Coined from *glycose* (see GLYCOSIDE) + -URIA.] —**gly·co·su·ric** *adj.*

gly·co·sy·la·tion /glīkō sī láysh'n/ *n.* the addition of a carbohydrate to an organic molecule [Mid-20thC. Coined from *glycose* (see GLYCOSIDE) + -YL + -ATION.]

glyph /glif/ *n.* **1.** ARCHIT **CARVED GROOVE IN ANCIENT GREEK ARCHITECTURE** an ornamental carved channel or groove, especially a vertical one like those on a Doric frieze **2.** HIST **CARVED SYMBOL OR CHARACTER** a symbol or character, especially one that has been incised or carved out in a stone surface like the characters of the ancient Mayan writing system **3. MODERN SYMBOLIC CHARACTER** a nonverbal symbol such as one used on a road sign **4.** COMPUT **CHARACTER IN FONT** the symbol or symbols that form a single character in a font [Late 18thC. Via French *glyphe* from Greek *gluphē* "carving," from *gluphein* "to carve."] —**glyph·ic** *adj.*

glyp·tic /glíptik/ *adj.* relating to the art of engraving or carving, especially on precious stones [Early 19thC. Directly or via French *glyptique* from Greek *gluptikos*, from *gluptēs* "carver," from *gluphein* (see GLYPH).]

glyp·tics /glíptiks/ *n.* = **glyptography** (*takes a singular verb*)

glyp·to·graph /glíptə gràf/ *n.* an engraving or carving on a precious stone [Late 18thC. Coined from Greek *gluptos* "carved" + -GRAPH.]

glyp·tog·ra·phy /glip tóggrəfee/ *n.* the art or process of engraving or carving on precious stones —**glyp·tog·ra·pher** *n.* —**glyp·to·graph·ic** /gliptə gráffik/ *adj.* —**glyp·to·graph·i·cal** /-gráffik'l/ *adj.*

GM *abbr.* **1.** general manager **2.** grand master **3.** MIL guided missile **4.** GENETICS genetic manipulation **5.** genetically modified

gm. *abbr.* gram

G-man (*plural* **G-men**) *n.* an agent of the Federal Bureau of Investigation (*archaic slang*) [G from GOVERNMENT]

GMAT *abbr.* **1.** Graduate Management Admissions Test **2.** Greenwich Mean Astronomical Time

GMO *n., abbr.* genetically modified organism

GMP *abbr.* BIOL guanosine monophosphate

GMT *abbr.* Greenwich Mean Time

GMW *abbr.* gram-molecular weight

gn. *abbr.* guinea

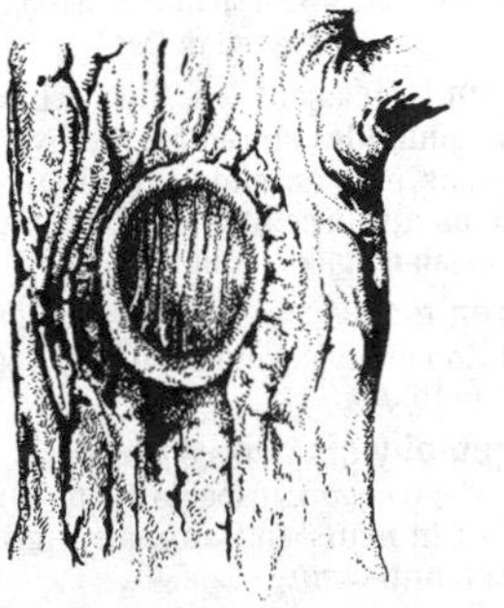

Gnarl

gnarl[1] /naarl/ (**gnarled, gnarl·ing, gnarls**) *n.* a hard lump, knot, or swelling on a tree trunk or branch [Early 19thC. Back-formation from GNARLED.]

gnarl[2] /naarl/ *vi.* to snarl or growl (*archaic*) [Late 16thC. Formed from *gnar* "to snarl, growl," an imitation of the sound.]

gnarled /naarld/ *adj.* **1. KNOTTED AND TWISTED** twisted and full of knots ○ *an ancient gnarled tree* **2. TWISTED, MISSHAPEN, OR WEATHERBEATEN** twisted, misshapen, or weatherbeaten because of age, hard work, or illness ○ *gnarled hands* [Early 17thC. Alteration of *knurled*.]

gnarl·y /naárlee/ (**-i·er, -i·est**) *adj.* (*slang*) **1. HIGHLY DANGEROUS** extremely difficult, risky, and challenging ○ *gnarly surf off Santa Monica beach* **2. EXCELLENT** extraordinarily good or pleasurable ○ *bought a gnarly skateboard* [From GNARL[2]]

gnash /nash/ (**gnashed, gnash·ing, gnash·es**) *vti.* to grind your teeth together, especially in pain, anger, or frustration [15thC. Origin uncertain: perhaps from an earlier verb *gnast*, of Scandinavian origin, or, alternatively, an imitation of the sound.]

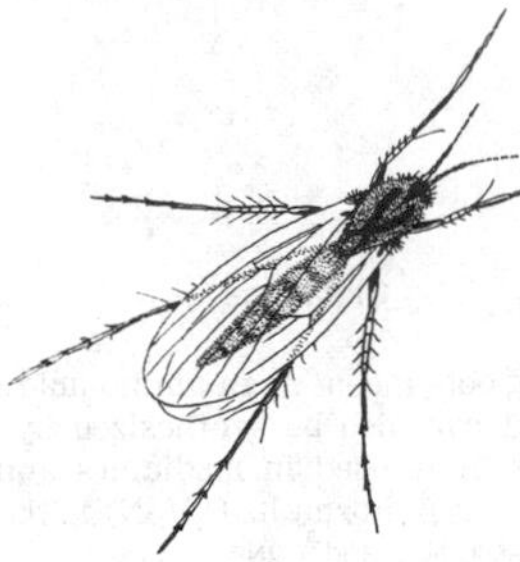

Gnat

gnat /nat/ *n.* a small two-winged biting fly such as a black fly or a midge [Old English *gnætt*. Ultimately from an Indo-European word that is also the ancestor of English *gnaw*.]

gnat·catch·er /nát kàchər/ *n.* a small American songbird with a long tail and slender bill that feeds on insects. Genus: *Polioptila*.

gnath·ic /náthik/, **gna·thal** /náth'l/ *adj.* relating to the jaw [Late 19thC. Formed from Greek *gnathos* "jaw."]

gna·thi·on /náythee on/ *n.* the lowest point on the midline of the lower jaw [Late 19thC. From Greek *gnathos* (see GNATHIC).]

gna·thite /náy thīt, ná-/ *n.* a mouthpart similar to a jaw that is used for grasping or chewing by insects, lobsters, and other arthropods [Late 19thC. From Greek *gnathos* (see GNATHIC).]

gna·thos·tome /náythə stōm, náth-/ *n.* a vertebrate that has a mouth with jaws, as do all vertebrates except agnathans such as lampreys and hagfish are gnathostomes. Superclass: Gnathostomata. [Early 20thC. Coined from Greek *gnathos* (see GNATHIC) + *stoma* "mouth."]

-gnathous *suffix.* having a particular kind of jaw ○ *prognathous* [Formed from Greek *gnathos* "jaw." Ultimately from an Indo-European base meaning "jaw," which is also the ancestor of English *chin*.]

gnaw /naw/ (**gnawed, gnaw·ing, gnaws**) *v.* **1.** *vti.* **CHEW AT SOMETHING** to chew or bite on something persistently, often reducing it gradually to a particular state ○ *a terrier gnawing away at a huge bone* **2.** *vt.* **MAKE SOMETHING BY CHEWING** to make something by grinding with the teeth and chewing ○ *The hamster escaped by gnawing a hole in its cage.* **3.** *vt.* **ERODE** to wear something away often until it reaches a particular shape or size ○ *The wind and waves had gnawed the rocks into fantastic shapes.* **4.** *vi.* **CAUSE SOMEBODY WORRY** to cause somebody constant anxiety or distress ○ *That question still gnaws at me after all these years.* **5.** *vi.* **GRADUALLY REDUCE SOMETHING'S POWER** to reduce the effectiveness or influence of something bit by bit ○ *a profound sense of unease that gnaws at our sense of wellbeing* [Old English *gnagen*. Ultimately from a prehistoric Germanic word thought to suggest the action.] —**gnaw·a·ble** *adj.* —**gnaw·er** *n.*

gnaw·ing /náw ing/ *adj.* persistent and troubling or uncomfortable ○ *gnawing doubts* —**gnaw·ing·ly** *adv.*

gneiss /nīss/ *n.* a coarse-grained high-grade metamorphic rock formed at high pressures and temperatures, in which light and dark mineral constituents are segregated into visible bands [Mid-18thC. From German, of uncertain origin: probably an alteration of Old High German *gneisto* "spark," from its luster.] —**gneiss·ic** *adj.* —**gneiss·ose** *adj.*

gnoc·chi /nókee, nyókee/ *npl.* in Italian or Italian-style cookery, dumplings made of potato, semolina, or flour, usually boiled and served with soup or a sauce [Late 19thC. From Italian, of uncertain origin: perhaps an alteration of *nocchio* "knot in wood."]

gnome[1] /nōm/ *n.* **1.** MYTHOL **TINY SUPERNATURAL BEING** according to old folk tales, one of a race of small beings usually portrayed as hunchbacked men with long white beards who live in the earth guarding treasure **2. STATUE OF GNOME** a small figure or statue representing a gnome, used as an ornament **3. OFFENSIVE TERM** an offensive term deliberately insulting somebody thought of as small and, often, ugly (*insult*) [Mid-17thC. Via French from modern Latin *gnomus*, which was coined by PARACELSUS.] —**gnome·like** *adj.* —**gnom·ish** *adj.* ◇ **the gnomes of Zurich** international bankers and financiers, especially those based in Switzerland (*humorous*)

gnome[2] /nōm/ *n.* a short saying or proverb that expresses a general idea or principle [Late 16thC. Via Greek *gnōmē* "opinion, judgment" from, ultimately, *gignōskein* "to know."]

gno·mic /nṓmik/ *adj.* **1. EPIGRAMMATIC** resembling or containing proverbs or other short pithy sayings that express basic truths ○ *his gnomic utterances were widely quoted by financial journalists* **2. CRYPTIC** opaque or difficult to understand —**gnom·i·cal·ly** *adv.*

gno·mon /nṓ mòn, nṓmən/ *n.* **1.** TIME **ARM OF SUNDIAL** the arm of a sundial, used to show the time of day by the position of its shadow **2.** GEOM **PART OF A PARALLELOGRAM** the part of a parallelogram that is left when a smaller similar parallelogram has been taken from its corner [Mid-16thC. Directly or via French or Latin from Greek *gnōmōn* "indicator," from *gignōskein* (see GNOME[2]).] —**gno·mon·ic** /nō mónnik/ *adj.* —**gno·mon·i·cal·ly** /-kəlee/ *adv.*

gno·sis /nṓssiss/ *n.* knowledge of spiritual truths reputedly possessed by the ancient Gnostics, who believed them to be essential to salvation [Late 16thC. From Greek *gnōsis* "investigation, knowledge," from *gignōskein* (see GNOME[2]).]

gnos·tic /nóstik/ *adj.* relating to knowledge, especially knowledge of spiritual truths [Mid-17thC. See GNOSTIC.]

Gnos·tic *n.* **BELIEVER IN GNOSTICISM** somebody who believes in Gnosticism ■ *adj.* **OF GNOSTICISM** relating to Gnosticism [Late 16thC. Via ecclesiastical Latin and Greek *gnōstikos* from, ultimately, *gignōskein* (see GNOME[2]).]

Gnos·ti·cism /nósti sìzzəm/ *n.* a pre-Christian and early Christian religious movement teaching that salvation comes by learning esoteric spiritual truths that free humanity from the material world, believed in this movement to be evil

gno·to·bi·ot·ics /nṓtō bī óttiks/ *n.* the scientific study of organisms living either in a germ-free or a controlled environment, as when a known contaminant has been introduced [Mid-20thC. Coined from Greek *gnōtos* "known" + BIOTIC.] —**gno·to·bi·ot·ic** *adj.* —**gno·to·bi·ot·i·cal·ly** *adv.*

GNP *abbr.* gross national product

Gnu

gnu /noo/ (*plural* **gnu** *or* **gnus**) *n.* a large African antelope with a head resembling that of an ox, short mane, beard, downward curving horns, and tufted tail. Latin name: *Connochaetes gnou* and *Connochaetes taurinus*. [Late 18thC. Origin uncertain: probably via Dutch *gnoe* from Khoisan.]

go[1] /gō/ (**went** /went/, **gone** /gawn, gon/, **going, goes** /gōz/, *plural* **gos**) CORE MEANING: a basic intransitive verb of motion expressing movement from an unspecified point of departure or from a place that is already known or assumed ○ *Have you any idea where he went?* ○ *She never went anywhere without her spectacles.* ○ *Johnny went back inside for another coffee.* ○ *I've always wanted to go to Paris.*

1. *vi.* **DEPART** to leave a place ○ *Please don't go.* ○ *He's going tomorrow.* **2.** *vi.* **MOVE TO DO SOMETHING** to move toward a person or place with the intention of doing something specific ○ *We had to go and pick up our* young son who was playing at a friend's house. ○ *After the wedding they went to live in Spain.* **3.** *vi.* **PROCEED TO AN ACTIVITY** to leave a place and proceed toward an activity, often a recreational activity ○ *They go for a jog every morning.* **4.** *vi.* **ATTEND** to attend a place regularly ○ *She went to Rutgers University at night to earn her teaching degree.* **5.** *vi.* **TAKE PART IN** to take part in a television or radio program ○ *The President went on television to defend his government's decision.* **6.** *vi.* **LEAD TO** to lead to, or begin or end at, a particular place (*refers to a route or travel service*) ○ *Take the road that goes into the city center.* ○ *The new bus service will go from New York to Buffalo.* **7.** *vi.* **ELAPSE** to elapse or pass (*refers to time*) ○ *As time went on, he pursued lesser jobs.* **8.** *vi.* **BE ALLOTTED TO** to be allotted to a particular recipient or used for a particular purpose (*refers to money or other resources*) ○ *The house will go to his surviving children.* ○ *Much of her income went on household bills.* **9.** *vi.* **BE GIVEN TO** to be given to somebody as a quality or attribute ○ *The credit should go to the one who tries hardest.* **10.** *vi.* **BE DISCARDED** to be eliminated, given up, or got rid of ○ *This old sweater has just got to go!* ○ *Thousands of jobs will have to go, they say, if the company is to prosper.* **11.** *vi.* **BE SPENT** to be spent or used up ○ *By the end of the evening all the food had gone.* **12.** *vi.* **LEAVE A JOB** to leave a job or organization ○ *He was costing the company thousands and had to go.* **13.** *vi.* **BLEND IN** to be suited in a place, or blend or harmonize with other things ○ *They wanted to find a carpet that would go with the existing decor.* ○ *Those pants just don't go.* **14.** *vi.* **FIT IN** to fit in a place because of being the right shape or size ○ *I tried to push the package through the mailbox but it wouldn't go.* **15.** *vi.* **BELONG** to have somewhere as a usual or proper place ○ *The towels go in the cupboard in the bathroom.* **16.** *vi.* **BE PUT** to be put into something as one of the parts that form it ○ *all the elements that go into making a successful musical* **17.** *vi.* **FUNCTION** to function or operate ○ *Can you get my car going again?* ○ *Without capital to make it go, our business plan was merely hopes written out on paper.* **18.** *vi.* **FAIL** to get weaker and begin to fail or give way ○ *My eyesight is starting to go* **19.** *vi.* **BREAK DOWN** to stop working properly and start to break down ○ *I think the battery may be going* **20.** *vi.* **DIE** to die (*used euphemistically*) ○ *I'm afraid she has gone.* **21.** *vi.* **BECOME** to change so as to come to be in a particular state or condition ○ *Their pet's behavior went out of control.* **22.** *vi.* **BE DRESSED OR EQUIPPED AS SPECIFIED** to be in a particular state with regard to dress or equipment ○ *They went barefoot on the beach.* **23.** *vi.* **PROCEED** to proceed or happen in a particular way ○ *How did it go at work today?* ○ *We were trying to figure out what really went wrong.* ○ *The intruder went unchallenged.* **24.** *vi.* **MAKE A NOISE AS A SIGNAL** to make a noise such as a ring or a knock to attract attention ○ *She had just closed the front door when the phone went.* **25.** *vi.* **MAKE A NOISE** to make a particular noise ○ *The horn went beep.* ○ *Cows go "moo."* **26.** *vi.* **REACH A PARTICULAR POINT** to proceed to or reach a particular position or level ○ *"The freedom she experienced, the indulgence with which she was treated, went beyond her expectations."* (Thomas Hardy, *The Mayor of Casterbridge*; 1886) **27.** *vi.* **SERVE TO DO SOMETHING** to be of such a nature or quality as to do something ○ *It just goes to show how careful you have to be* **28.** *vi.* **COMPARE** to compare with other people or things of the same kind ○ *As vacations abroad go, it was probably the best we've ever had.* **29.** *vi.* **SOUND** to proceed in terms of sound or words (*refers to a piece of music or writing*) ○ *How does that tune go again?* **30.** *vi.* **ACCOMPANY** to occur with or be present at the same time as something else ○ *It's not necessarily the case that intelligence and common sense go together.* **31.** *vi.* **CIRCULATE** to circulate as information around a place or among people ○ *It soon went around the whole village that she had inherited a fortune.* **32.** *vi.* **HAVE RECOURSE TO** to turn to a procedure as a result of unresolved problems ○ *They couldn't agree, so they went to arbitration.* **33.** *vi.* **BE THE AUTHORITY** to be necessarily accepted as what will be the case in a given situation ○ *Whatever she says goes in our home* **34.** *vi.* **ENDURE** to continue surviving or succeeding in a difficult situation ○ *Human beings can go for much longer without food than without water.* **35.** *vt.* **BET IN CARDS** to bet or bid in a card game ○ *I go three clubs.* **36.** *vt.* **SAY** to say something quoted (*nonstandard*) ○ *So she goes, "If you want it done then do it yourself."* **37.** *vi.* **EXPRESSING FUTURE ACTION** used to express future action or intent (*used in progressive tenses*) ○ *What are we going to do?* **38.** *n.* **ATTEMPT AT SOMETHING** an attempt or chance to do something ○ *She passed the exam on the second go.* **39.** *n.* **MOVE OR TURN TAKEN** a move or turn in a game ○ *It's your go.* **40.** *n.* **ENERGY** energy and vibrancy (*informal*) ○ *I've had so much more go since changing my diet.* **41.** *adj.* **FUNCTIONING** ready and operating properly (*informal*) ○ *All systems are go.* [Old English *gān*. Ultimately from an Indo-European word that is also the ancestor of German *gehen* "to go."] ◇ **anything goes** used to indicate that anything is to be tolerated or accepted as the norm ○ *In this place almost anything goes!* ◇ **on the go** very active and busy ○ *a two-career couple, always on the go* ◇ **have a go (at something)** to make an attempt at something (*informal*) ○ *He said that he had never skied before but he was willing to have a go at it.* ◇ **make a go of something** to make a success of something ○ *They couldn't make a go of the relationship.* ◇ **here we go (again)!** used to express displeasure or resignation that something, usually something bad, that has happened before is now happening again ○ *Here we go again! This old car simply won't start.* ◇ **there you go** used to express general encouragement or approval to somebody else (*informal*) ◇ **there you go again** used to complain that somebody has done something bad or wrong yet again ○ *There you go again, misinterpreting and twisting what I'm saying* ◇ **to go** to be taken home rather than consumed on the premises ○ *one pizza to go*

go about *v.* **1.** *vt.* **DEAL WITH SOMETHING** to deal with a problem, assignment, or task **2.** *vti.* **BE WIDELY KNOWN OR CURRENT** to be experienced or known by a lot of people, often in a particular place ○ *wild rumors going about Washington* **3.** *vi.* SAILING **CHANGE TACK** to change tack in a sailing boat

go after *vt.* to make a deliberate effort to get or find something seen as desirable or advantageous ○ *I decided to go after a teaching job I saw in the paper.*

go ahead *vi.* to start or continue with something, especially after a period of uncertainty or delay ○ *We decided to go ahead and start our meal without her.*

go along *vi.* **1.** **ACCOMPANY SOMEBODY** to accompany somebody on a trip ○ *I decided to go along just to keep her company.* **2.** **FOLLOW ANOTHER'S LEAD** to follow the lead of somebody else ○ *When she suggested that they study Chinese before the trip, he went right along.* **3.** **DEVELOP IN SPECIFIED MANNER** to develop or progress in a manner specified, especially favorably (*informal*) ○ *Things were going along reasonably well until she lost her job again.*

go along with *vt.* to accept something or obey somebody, especially reluctantly or to the surprise of others ○ *You can't go along with it – it's breaking the law.*

go around *v.* **1.** *vi.* **SPEND TIME WITH SOMEBODY** to spend a lot of time with a particular person or as a member of a particular group (*informal*) ○ *We went around together all the time.* **2.** *vi.* **TRAVEL FROM PLACE TO PLACE** to travel from one place to another ○ *We tend to go around by taxi.* **3.** *vti.* **BE WIDELY KNOWN OR SHARED** to be experienced or shared by a lot of people ○ *a flu virus that's going around at work* **4.** *vti.* **BE ENOUGH FOR EVERYONE** to be able to be distributed to everyone ○ *There aren't enough pens to go around, so you'll have to share.* ◇ **what goes around comes around** used to say that whatever happens now will have an effect in the future (*informal*)

go at *vt.* to attempt something enthusiastically or energetically ○ *He went at the snow shoveling as if it were a race.*

go away *vi.* **1.** **TAKE A VACATION** to leave the place where you live, especially in order to take a vacation (*informal*) ○ *Are you going away this summer?* **2.** **GET OUT OF HERE** used to tell somebody to get away from you and leave the place where you are because he or she is annoying you ○ *Go away! I'm busy.* ○ *I just had to tell him to go away, and so he went.*

go back *vi.* to originate from a particular date, period, or time ○ *a tradition that goes back to the time of George Washington*

go back on *vt.* to change your mind about something you have agreed or promised to do ○ *You can't go back on what we originally agreed – a deal's a deal.*

go by *v.* **1.** *vi.* **PASS IN TIME** to move onward in terms of time ○ *As the years go by he gets more and more mellow* **2.** *vt.* **REGARD SOMETHING AS TRUE** to treat advice or information as reliable or true **3.** *vt.* **USE PARTICULAR SOURCE OF INFORMATION** to use a particular way of doing something or finding something out ○ *All we had to go by was a soggy map.* **4.** *vi.* **MAKE A BRIEF VISIT** to pay a brief, often unannounced or informal, visit to somebody ○ *I'll go by your mother and give her the books.*

go down *vi.* **1.** **GO BELOW HORIZON** to sink below the horizon ○ *The sun had already gone down by the time we got back.* **2.** **SINK BENEATH SOMETHING** to sink beneath the surface of a body of water ○ *An oil tanker went down off the coast of Alaska.* **3.** **CRASH** to fall from the air and crash ○ *The kite went down in the treetops.* **4.** **SUFFER DISGRACE** to be disgraced or ruined (*informal*) ○ *If he goes down, he'll take the whole department with him.* **5.** **BE REMEMBERED** to be remembered in a specified way ○ *She will surely go down as one of the greatest athletes of all time.* **6.** **BE RECEIVED** to be received in a particular way ○ *an idea that didn't go down at all well with the stockholders* **7.** **BE EATABLE OR DRINKABLE** to be able to be eaten or drunk, especially easily or enjoyably (*informal*) ○ *With sick children, soup tends to go down more easily than solid foods.* **8.** COMPUT **MALFUNCTION** to break down or stop working ○ *Since the airline's computers have gone down, we can't get flight information yet.* **9.** **TAKE PLACE** to happen or be happening (*slang*) ○ *Hey, what's going down?* ○ *When the robbery went down, the cops rushed to the scene.* **10.** *U.K.* UNIV **LEAVE UNIVERSITY AT THE END OF TERM** to leave college or a university at the end of term or the end of the academic year **11.** BRIDGE **FAIL TO ACHIEVE BRIDGE TRICKS** in the game of bridge, to fail to attain the number of tricks that has been contracted for

go down on *vt.* to perform oral sex on somebody (*slang taboo*)

go for *vt.* **1.** **TRY TO OBTAIN SOMETHING YOU WANT** to make an effort to obtain something because it is suitable for you or important to you (*informal*) ○ *I really think you should go for that sales job.* **2.** **LIKE SOMETHING OR SOMEBODY A LOT** to prefer, like, or be interested in a particular thing or person (*informal*) ○ *I don't really go for science fiction.* **3.** **CHOOSE SOMETHING** to choose one particular thing rather than another (*informal*) ○ *I think I'll go for the chocolate cheesecake – how about you?* **4.** **ATTACK SOMEBODY** to attack somebody physically or verbally **5.** **COMMAND A PRICE** to be worth or sold for a particular amount ○ *In the end the house went for far less than its market value.* **6.** **BE RELEVANT TO SOMEBODY** to apply or be relevant to somebody ○ *She needs to be more careful in her work – and that goes for you, too!* ◇ **go for it** not to stop or relax until you aggressively reach your goal (*slang*) ○ *The coach told the team just before the last game to get out there and go for it.* ◇ **have something going for you** to be in a situation where something is useful or helpful to you to a particular extent (*informal*) ○ *She has a lot going for her in the tennis championship, given her season's record.*

go in *vi.* **1.** **BE OBSCURED BY CLOUD COVER** to become hidden by clouds ○ *Once the sun went in, it got really cold sitting in the ski lift.* **2.** **BEGIN AN ATTACK** to launch an attack or begin another maneuver ○ *After the police went in, things rapidly got out of hand.*

go in for *vt.* **1.** **ENJOY DOING SOMETHING** to enjoy a particular activity ○ *I don't really go in for team sports myself.* **2.** SPORTS **SUBSTITUTE FOR ANOTHER PLAYER** to substitute for another player on a team such as an injured or ejected teammate ○ *Number 8 went in for the injured first-string quarterback.*

go into *vt.* **1.** **ENTER SPACE** to enter a place or building ○ *Let's go into the house – it's freezing out here.* **2.** **BEGIN A CAREER** to begin a job or career in a particular area of activity ○ *She went into advertising and made lots of money.* **3.** **LOOK INTO SOMETHING** to examine or look into something in detail and with thoroughness **4.** **BE A FACTOR OF A NUMBER** to be a factor of a particular number or amount ○ *15 won't go into 125.* **5.** **BE SPENT ON SOMETHING** to be used or spent for a particular purpose ○ *Millions have gone into finding a cure.*

go in with *vt.* to begin participating in a project or venture with other people ○ *I went in with four friends to start a restaurant.*

go off *vi.* **1.** **DETONATE** to explode or be fired **2.** **BEGIN SOUNDING OR VIBRATING** to start to ring, sound, or vibrate ○ *The smoke alarm goes off whenever we make toast.* **3.** **BE CARRIED OUT** to be carried out or conducted in a particular manner ○ *I think the conference went off as well as could be expected.* **4.** **DEPART** to set out, or set out for a particular place ○ *There were endless TV images of soldiers going off to war.*

go on *v.* **1.** *vi.* **CONTINUE RIGHT ALONG** to continue to happen ○ *The dispute went on for another nine months before it was resolved.* **2.** *vi.* **OCCUR** to happen or take place ○ *I asked him what was going on.* **3.** *vti.* **MAKE A PUBLIC ENTRANCE** to make an entrance on a stage or other public place ○ *She went on every night to rapturous applause.* **4.** *vi.* **TALK TOO MUCH** to talk too much and much too long ○ *She's always going on about her yacht.* **5.** *vi.* **CONTINUE SPEAKING** to continue speaking, especially after a pause ○ *She then went on about the latest international incident.* **6.** *vi.* **DO SOMETHING AFTERWARD** to do something after the time or period you are referring to ○ *She finished fourth, but went on to win the championship the following year.* **7.** *vt.* **USE AS RELIABLE INFORMATION** to use something as reliable information ○ *The police have very little to go on at this stage.* **8.** *vi.* **USED TO EXPRESS ENCOURAGEMENT** used to encourage somebody to do something, usually something the person is reluctant or afraid to try (*informal*) ○ *Go on, you'll have a great time skiing down that hill!* **9.** *vt.* **APPROXIMATE SOMETHING** to be close to a particular age, time, or number (*used in progressive tenses*) ○ *He must be going on 50.*

go out *vi.* **1.** **SOCIALIZE** to socialize and enjoy yourself away from home ○ *She loves going out, but he prefers to stay at home.* **2.** **FLOW OUTWARD FROM SHORE** to flow away from the shoreline ○ *the tide had gone out* **3.** **GO OUT OF STYLE** to stop being fashionable ○ *Muttonchop whiskers went out in the late 1800s.* **4.** **DATE SOMEBODY** to date somebody, or date each other ○ *They've been going out for six months.* ■ **BE EXTINGUISHED** to stop burning or functioning ○ *the fire has gone out*

go out to *vt.* to be offered or extended to a person or group ○ *Our thoughts go out tonight to the friends and relatives of the victims.*

go over *v.* **1.** *vi.* **CHANGE ALLEGIANCE** to change allegiance and start supporting somebody or something else ○ *In a surprise move, the Senator went over to the Republicans.* **2.** *vt.* **EXAMINE SOMETHING CAREFULLY** to examine or check something carefully ○ *The police went over the car looking for fingerprints.* **3.** *vt.* **REHEARSE AND MEMORIZE** to practice or repeat something in order to learn it ○ *The actors were all busy going over their lines.* **4.** *vi.* **BE RECEIVED** to be received in a particular way ○ *The campaign platform went over well with the convention delegates.*

go through *v.* **1.** *vt.* **UNDERGO UNPLEASANTNESS OF SOME KIND** to undergo hardship or difficulties, usually in stages and over a period of time ○ *They're going through a series of business setbacks.* **2.** *vt.* **EXAMINE THOROUGHLY AND PHYSICALLY** to examine or inspect something very carefully ○ *The police went through his luggage but found nothing suspicious.* **3.** *vi.* **GAIN OFFICIAL APPROVAL** to be accepted or approved officially, after having gone through channels or set procedural stages **4.** *vt.* **CONSUME IN QUANTITY** to use, eat, or spend something, especially a large amount in a short time ○ *They go through hundreds of dollars of groceries a week.*

go under *vi.* **1.** **SINK IN WATER** to sink below the surface of the water ○ *I managed to grab him as he went under for the third time.* **2.** **FAIL** to close down, or be unable to keep going **3.** **LOSE CONSCIOUSNESS** to lose consciousness, especially after being given an anesthetic ○ *They began the operation as soon as she'd gone under.*

go up *vi.* **1.** **BE BUILT** to be constructed ○ *A new supermarket went up where the theater used to be.* **2.** **BE DISPLAYED** to be put on display ○ *A notice has gone up saying how we can be contacted.* **3.** **DETONATE OR IGNITE** to explode or burst into flames ○ *The whole place went up in a matter of seconds.* **4.** *U.K.* UNIV **GO TO A UNIVERSITY** to go to or return to a university at the beginning of a term or academic year

go with *vt.* **1.** **DATE SOMEBODY** to spend time romantically and socially with somebody (*informal*) ○ *Anna's been going with Alex for a month now.* **2.** **BE PART OF SOMETHING** to be a normal or usual part of something ○ *The long hours go with the job.* **3.** **ADOPT OR FOLLOW AN IDEA** to adopt or follow a particular approach or point of view ○ *Just go with the plan as it stands for the time being and we'll see what happens.*

go without *vt.* to be deprived financially, or be deprived of a particular thing ○ *You'll have to go without breakfast if you want to catch the early train.* ○ *Sometimes the poor family just had to go without.*

go² /gō/ *n.* a Japanese board game played with black and white stones on a surface marked with 19 lines intersecting each other to create 367 crossing points. The object of the game is to capture the larger part of the board and the opponent's stones. [Late 19thC. From Japanese.]

GO *abbr.* MIL general order

go·a /gō ə/ *n.* a Tibetan gazelle with a brownish-gray coat, the male of which has backward curving horns. Latin name: *Procapra picticaudata.* [Mid-19thC. From Tibetan *dgoba.*]

Go·a /gō ə/ state on the western coast of India. Formerly a Portuguese territory, it was incorporated into India in 1961 and became a separate Indian state in 1987. Capital: Panaji. Population: 1,235,000 (1994). Area: 1,472 sq. mi./3,813 sq. km.

goad /gōd/ *vt.* (**goad·ed, goad·ing, goads**) **1.** **DRIVE SOMEBODY TO DO SOMETHING** to provoke or incite somebody into action (*often passive*) **2.** **PROD WITH A STICK** to prod an animal with a long pointed stick ■ *n.* **1.** **POINTED ANIMAL PROD** a long pointed stick used for prodding cattle and other animals **2.** **STIMULUS** something used to motivate somebody or stir somebody into action [Old English *gād.* Ultimately from a prehistoric Germanic word that also produced Old English *gār* "spear" (source of English *garlic*).]

WORD KEY: SYNONYMS

See Synonyms at ***motive***.

go-a·head *n.* permission or approval to proceed with something (*informal*) ○ *Once we get the go-ahead from the bank, we can get things moving.*

goal /gōl/ *n.* **1.** SPORTS **TARGET AREA** the space or opening into which a ball or puck must go to score points in a game such as football or hockey, usually a pair of posts with a crossbar and often a net ○ *The kick landed just to the left of the goal.* **2.** SPORTS **SCORE** the score gained by getting the ball or puck into the goal ○ *leading by three goals to two* **3.** SPORTS **SUCCESSFUL SHOT** a successful attempt at hitting, kicking, throwing, or passing a ball or hitting a puck into or over a goal ○ *one of the greatest goals of all time* **4.** **AIM** something that somebody wants to achieve ○ *One of my goals for this year is to learn Spanish.* **5.** **RACE'S END** the end of a race ○ *The runners are still several minutes from the goal.* [14thC. Origin unknown.]

goal-di·rect·ed *adj.* strongly motivated and highly organized in achieving tasks that are specified in advance

goal·ie /gōlee/ *n.* a goalkeeper

goal·keep·er /gōl keepər/ *n.* in games such as soccer and fieldhockey, a defensive player positioned in or near a goal whose main task is to keep the ball or puck from crossing the goal line into the goal

goal kick *n.* **1.** SOCCER **FREE KICK BY THE DEFENDER NEAR THE GOAL** a free kick taken from the six-yard-line by a defensive player when the ball has been driven out of play over the end line (**goal line**) by an opposing player **2.** RUGBY **ATTACKER'S FREE KICK TO CONVERT A TRY** in rugby, a free kick by a member of the attacking team, aimed at clearing the defenders' crossbar and designed to convert a five-point try into a seven-point score

goal·less /gōləss/ *adj.* having no goals to aim for in life or work

goal line *n.* in games such as football and field hockey, the line where goalposts are positioned and over which the ball must pass or be carried to make a score. A touchdown can be scored anywhere along the line; in other circumstances the ball may also have to pass between the posts.

goal·mouth /gōl mowth/ (*plural* **-mouths** /-mouthz/) *n.* in games such as soccer and hockey, the area directly in front of the goal

goal-o·ri·ent·ed *adj.* = **goal-directed**

goal·post /gōl pōst/ *n.* either of two posts, usually supporting a crossbar between them, that together mark the boundary of the goal in games such as football and field hockey ◇ **move the goalposts** *U.K.* to change the rules or conditions after a project has started or a course of action has been embarked on ○ *We'll never finish the software if Marketing keeps moving the goalposts.*

goal·tend·er /gōl tendər/ *n.* = **goalkeeper**

goal·tend·ing /gōl tènding/ *n.* **1.** **GUARDING THE GOAL** the act of trying to keep a puck or ball from entering a goal, especially in hockey **2.** **ILLEGAL INTERFERENCE WITH A BASKETBALL IN PLAY** in basketball, illegal interference with a ball that is in its downward arc toward the basket or that is in or on the rim of the basket

Goanna

goan·na /gō ánnə/ *n.* a large Australian monitor lizard of which there are several varieties. Genus: *Varanus.* [Mid-19thC. Alteration of IGUANA.]

go-a·round *n.* (*informal*) **1.** **ONE INSTANCE** an instance of something ○ *The question was settled during the first go-around of talks.* **2.** **CIRCLING OF SOMETHING** the act or occurrence of going around something ○ *The plane made one more go-around of the airport and landed.* **3.** **VOCAL ARGUMENT** an argument, often a loud one ○ *A noisy go-around in the foyer was heard by all in the restaurant.*

Goat: Mountain goat

goat /gōt/ (*plural* **goats** *or* **goat**) *n.* **1.** ZOOL **HORNED MAMMAL RELATED TO SHEEP** an agile ruminant mammal that is related to sheep and has backward curving horns, straight hair, and a short tail. Domestic goats are raised for their wool, meat, and milk. Genus: *Capra.* **2.** **LECHER** a lecherous man (*insult*) **3.** = **scapegoat** [Old English *gāt.* Ultimately from an Indo-European word that also produced German *Geiø* "goat." Originally in the meaning "she-goat," it came to denote both sexes by the 14thC.] — **goat·ish** *adj.* ◇ **get somebody's goat** to annoy or irritate somebody (*informal*) ○ *Their constant carping over trivia really gets my goat.*

Goat *n.* ZODIAC = **Capricorn**

goat cheese, goat's cheese *n.* cheese made from goat's milk

Goatee: Actor Tom Hanks wearing a goatee

goat·ee /gō tée/ *n.* a short pointed beard on the chin but not the cheeks [From its resemblance to a goat's beard]

goat·fish /gōt fish/ (*plural* **-fish** *or* **-fish·es**) *n.* a distinctively colored fish with two thin flexible appendages (**barbels**) beneath the mouth that are probably used as feelers. It lives near the sea bed in warm seas. Family: Mullidae. [From the barbels beneath its mouth]

goat·herd /gṓt hùrd/ *n.* somebody who looks after goats

goat moth *n.* a large pale-gray European moth with wood-boring larvae that give off an odor like that of goats. Latin name: *Cossus cossus.*

goats·beard /gṓts bèerd/ *n.* **1.** FLOWER LIKE A DANDELION a Eurasian plant, now also growing in the United States, that has woolly stems and large yellow flowers like those of the dandelion. Latin name: *Tragopogon pratensis.* **2.** PLANT WITH WHITE FLOWERS an eastern North American plant that has long spikes of small white flowers. Latin name: *Aruncus dioicus.* [From the down on the seeds]

goat's cheese *n.* = **goat cheese**

goat·skin /gṓt skìn/ *n.* **1.** SKIN OF A GOAT the skin or hide of a goat **2.** INDUST, CLOTHES LEATHER leather made from the skin of a goat **3.** LEATHER WINE FLASK a wine container made from the skin of a goat

goat's milk *n.* milk from a goat, used for drinking and for making cheese

goat's rue *n.* a North American legume plant with pink and yellow flowers, used for feeding livestock. Latin name: *Teprosia virginiana.*

goat·suck·er /gṓt sùkər/ *n.* BIRDS = **nightjar** [From the belief that it sucked milk from goats]

gob[1] /gob/ *n.* **1.** CLOT a lump of a soft or wet substance (*slang*) ○ *a huge gob of whipped cream* **2.** MASSIVE AMOUNT a large quantity or amount (*slang humorous*) (*often used in the plural*) ○ *She wears gobs of makeup.* ○ *They made a gob of dough on that land deal.* [14thC. From Old French *gobe* "mouthful," from *gober* "to swallow," of uncertain origin.]

gob[2] /gob/ *n. U.K.* the human mouth (*slang disapproving*) [Mid-16thC. Origin uncertain: perhaps from Scottish, Irish, and Gaelic.]

gob[3] /gob/ *n.* a sailor in the U.S. Navy (*dated slang*) [Early 20thC. Origin uncertain: perhaps a shortening of earlier *gobby* "coast guard."]

gob·bet /góbbət/ *n.* **1.** QUANTITY OF LIQUID a quantity of liquid, often in a sticky blotch ○ *Gobbets of grease covered the top of the stove.* **2.** EXCERPT an extract from a text, especially one chosen for translation or comment in an examination [13thC. From Old French *gobet* "a small gob," from *gobe* (see GOB[1]).]

gob·ble[1] /góbb'l/ (**-bled, -bling, -bles**) *vt.* **1.** EAT QUICKLY AND GREEDILY to eat something quickly and greedily ○ *He gobbled up all the pizza.* **2.** USE SOMETHING UP to use something up quickly or in large amounts (*informal humorous*) ○ *watching the pay phone gobble her money* [Early 17thC. Origin uncertain: probably formed from GOB[1].]

gob·ble[2] /góbb'l/ *vi.* (**-bled, -bling, -bles**) MAKE THE SOUND OF A TURKEY to make the characteristic gurgling sound of a male turkey, or a sound resembling this ■ *n., interj.* TURKEY SOUND the gurgling sound made by a male turkey [Late 17thC. An imitation of the sound.]

gob·ble·dy·gook /góbb'ldi go͝ok/, **gob·ble·de·gook** *n.* language that is difficult or impossible to understand, especially either nonsense or long-winded technical jargon (*informal disapproving*) ○ *This manual is full of gobbledygook.* [Mid-20thC. An imitation of the sound made by a male turkey.]

gob·bler /góbblər/ *n.* a male turkey (*informal*)

Go·be·lin /gṓbəlin/ *n.* a tapestry produced by the Gobelin factory in Paris, characterized by vivid pictorial scenes

go-be·tween *n.* somebody who communicates or mediates between two groups or two individuals during a negotiation, transaction, or secret operation ○ *used as a go-between to ease communication between the enemy generals prior to surrender*

Go·bi De·sert /gṑbee-/ desert in northern China and southern Mongolia, the coldest and one of the largest deserts in the world. Area: 500,000 sq. mi./1,300,000 sq. km.

gob·let /góbblət/ *n.* **1.** PIECE OF STEMWARE a drinking vessel with a stem and base, especially one of metal or glass **2.** LARGE CUP a large bowl-shaped cup used for drinking in former times (*archaic*) [14thC. From Old French *gobelet* "small cup," from *gobel* "cup."]

gob·let cell *n.* a cell shaped like a goblet that secretes mucus. Goblet cells are found in the intestines and respiratory system of mammals and the epidermis of fish.

gob·lin /góbblin/ *n.* in folk tales, a creature resembling a small man of unpleasant appearance, usually evil or mischievous [14thC. Origin uncertain: probably via Anglo-Norman from medieval Latin *gobelinus*, the name of a spirit that supposedly haunted the French town of Évreux in the 12thC.]

go·bo /gṓ bṑ/ (*plural* **go·bos** *or* **gob·oes**) *n.* **1.** MICROPHONE SHIELD a shield that is placed around a microphone to keep out unwanted sounds **2.** LENS SHIELD a black screen placed around the lens of a camera or video camera to keep out unwanted light [Mid-20thC. Origin unknown.]

gob·smacked /gób smàkt/, **gob·struck** /gób strùk/ *adj. U.K.* extremely surprised or shocked (*slang*)

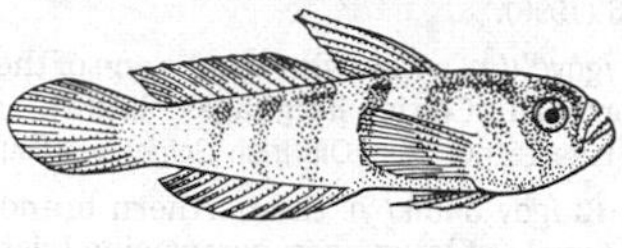

Goby

go·by /gṓbee/ (*plural* **-bies** *or* **-by**) *n.* a small elongated spiny-finned freshwater or marine fish whose pelvic fins form a sucker. Gobies are usually found in burrows or crevices. Family: Gobiidae. [Mid-18thC. Via Latin *gobius* from Greek *kōbios*, the name of a small fish.]

go-cart *n.* **1.** CHILD'S CAR WITH AN ENGINE a light open-framed car large enough for a child or young teenager to sit in, containing a small engine and used for racing **2.** MOTOR SPORTS = **kart**

god /god/ *n.* **1.** SUPERNATURAL BEING one of a group of supernatural male beings in some religions, each of which is worshiped as the personification or controller of some aspect of the universe ○ *Thor, the Norse god of thunder.* ◊ **goddess** *n.* 1 **2.** FIGURE OR IMAGE a representation of a god, used as an object of worship ○ *the little bronze god standing in a niche above the altar.* ◊ **goddess** *n.* 2 **3.** SOMETHING THAT DOMINATES SOMEBODY'S LIFE something that is so important that it takes over somebody's life (*informal*) ○ *worshiping the false god of fame* **4.** MUSIC SOMEBODY ADMIRED AND IMITATED a man who is widely admired or imitated (*informal*) ○ *He was one of the rock music gods of the early Seventies.* ◊ **goddess** *n.* 3 ■ **gods** *npl.* FATE the entire group of supernatural beings viewed as deciding human fate [Old English. Ultimately from an Indo-European word, meaning "that which is invoked," which is also the ancestor of German *Gott* "god."]

God *n.* **1.** RELIG SUPREME BEING the being believed in monotheistic religions such as Judaism, Islam, and Christianityto be the all-powerful all-knowing creator of the universe, worshiped as the only god **2.** CHR THE TRINITY one supreme being worshiped by Christians in the form of three persons, Father, Son, and Holy Ghost ■ *interj.* EXPRESSION OF STRONG FEELING used to express or emphasize feelings such as anger, helplessness, and frustration (*sometimes considered offensive*)

Go·da·va·ri /gō daávəree/ river in western India that is sacred to Hindus. It rises in the Western Ghats and empties into the Bay of Bengal. Length: 900 mi./1,448.

god-aw·ful, **God-aw·ful** *adj.* extremely bad or unpleasant (*slang*) (*sometimes considered offensive*) ○ *a god-awful racket*

god·child /gód chīld/ (*plural* **-chil·dren** /-chìldrən/) *n.* somebody whose spiritual upbringing is made the responsibility of a godmother or a godfather, or both. This arrangement is usually declared at the person's baptism or christening.

god·damn /gód dàm/ *adj., adv.* **god·damn, god·dam, god·damned** EXPRESSION OF STRONG FEELING used to emphasize a word or idea, or to express anger, frustration, or some other strong emotion (*slang*) (*sometimes considered offensive*) ■ *interj.* EXPRESSION OF STRONG EMOTION used to express anger, frustration, or some other strong emotion (*slang offensive*)

God·dard /góddərd/, **Robert** (1882–1945) U.S. physicist. His innovations in rocket design included the development of liquid-fuel rockets (1926), instrument-carrying rockets (1929), and the first rocket to exceed the speed of sound (1935). Full name **Robert Hutchings Goddard**

god·daugh·ter /gód dàwtər/ *n.* a girl or woman who is somebody's godchild

god·dess /góddəss/ *n.* **1.** SUPERNATURAL BEING one of the group of supernatural female beings in some religions, worshiped as the personification or controller of some aspect of the universe. ◊ **god** *n.* 1 **2.** FIGURE OR IMAGE a representation of a goddess, used as an object of worship ○ *the statue of the goddess, standing in the temple's first niche.* ◊ **god 3.** SOMEBODY ADMIRED AND IMITATED a woman who is widely admired or imitated, especially for her beauty (*informal*) ○ *a screen goddess.* ◊ **god** *n.* 2

Gö·del /gṓd'l/, **Kurt** (1906–78) Austrian-born U.S. mathematician. He is noted for his theories about the completeness of logic and the consistencies of arithmetic. Full name **Kurt Friedrich Gödel**

Go·dey /gṓdee/, **Louis Antoine** (1804–78) U.S. publisher. He published *Godey's Lady's Book* (1830–77), the leading U.S. women's magazine of its time.

god·fa·ther /gód faathər/ *n.* **1.** MAN GODPARENT a man who is somebody's godparent **2.** ORGANIZED-CRIME BOSS a man who heads an illegal organized-crime organization, especially a Mafia leader (*informal*) **3.** PATRON OR FOUNDER a man who provides inspiration or support, especially financial help, for a person or cause (*informal*) ○ *the godfather of the joint venture*

WORD KEY: CULTURAL NOTE

The Godfather, a movie by Francis Ford Coppola (1972). Based on the novel by Mario Puzo (1969), it describes the attempts of the Sicilian Corleone family to maintain its control of the New York Mafia when a group of renegade families set up a drug-smuggling ring. It and its two sequels, *The Godfather Part II* (1974) and *The Godfather Part III* (1990), brought new meaning to terms such as "godfather" and "consigliere."

God-fear·ing *adj.* devout or deeply religious

god·for·sak·en /gódfər sàykən, gòdfər sáykən/ *adj.* depressing, deserted, or empty ○ *The soldiers couldn't wait to get out of that godforsaken desert.*

God-giv·en *adj.* existing or applying as part of the natural order of the universe rather than arranged by humanity

god·head /gód hèd/ *n.* the nature or essence of being divine (*formal*)

God·head *n.* the Christian God, especially when considered as the Holy Trinity (*formal*)

god·hood /gód ho͝od/ *n.* = **godhead** (*formal*)

god·less /góddləss/ *adj.* **1.** WITHOUT GOD OR A GOD not believing in or worshiping God, or any god (*disapproving*) **2.** WICKED of an evil or immoral character or nature (*formal disapproving*) —**god·less·ly** *adv.* —**god·less·ness** *n.*

god·like /gód līk/ *adj.* fit for God or a god, or having the qualities of a god or of God, e.g., superhuman power, beauty, or imagination

god·ly /góddlee/ (**-li·er, -li·est**) *adj.* **1.** DEVOUT devoted to or worshiping God (*formal*) **2.** DIVINE fit for God or a god, or having godlike qualities —**god·li·ness** *n.*

god·moth·er /gód mùthər/ *n.* a woman who is somebody's godparent

go·down /gṓ dòwn/ *n.* a warehouse, especially in India and Malaysia [Late 16thC. Via Portuguese *gudao* from Tamil *kitanku* and Kannada *gadangu* "store."]

god·par·ent /gód pèrrənt/ *n.* somebody who is named as a sponsor when a child is baptized. Godparents often maintain close, almost familial relationships with a godchild.

God's A·cre /gòdz áykər/ *n.* any churchyard or cemetery (*literary*) [From the German *Gottesacker*]

God's coun·try *n.* a nation or piece of land that is dearly loved

god·send /gód sènd/ *n.* **1.** UNEXPECTED GOOD something good that happens unexpectedly **2.** SOMETHING OR SOMEBODY VERY USEFUL something received that proves extremely useful, or somebody who arrives and gives much-needed help [Early 19thC. From *God's send* "something sent by God": *send* from SEND[1] (noun) in the obsolete sense "thing sent."]

god's eye *n.* a small object displaying the form of a circle within a rectangle, used as a decoration and symbol of good fortune. A god's eye is usually made with colored yarns or thread wound around a framework of sticks.

God's gift *n.* an extremely admirable, valued, or talented person (*often used ironically*) ○ *He thought he was God's gift to the movie industry.*

god·son /gód sùn/ *n.* a man or boy who is somebody's godchild

God·speed /gód spéed/ *interj.* used to wish somebody a safe trip or successful endeavor (*dated*) [15thC. From *God speed you* "may God speed you."]

God·win Aus·ten, Mount /-góddwin óstin/ = **K2**

god·wit /gód wìt/ *n.* a large wading bird, found worldwide, that has a long slightly upturned bill and long legs and is related to curlews and sandpipers. Genus: *Limosa*. [Mid-16thC. Origin unknown.]

Goeb·bels /gőbbl'z/, **Joseph** (1897–1945) German Nazi politician. He was Adolf Hitler's minister of propaganda (1933–45). Full name **Paul Joseph Goebbels**

go·er /gő ər/ *n.* **1. REGULAR ATTENDER** somebody who attends performances or other events on a regular basis (*usually used in combination*) ○ *festival-goer* **2. FAST MOVER** a spirited or fast-moving person or animal (*informal*)

Goe·thals /gőthʼlz/, **George Washington** (1858–1928) U.S. engineer and army officer. He was chief engineer of the Panama Canal (1907–14).

Johann Wolfgang von Goethe: Portrait (1826) by Heinrich Christoph Kolbe

Goe·the /gőtə/, **Johann Wolfgang von** (1749–1832) German writer and scientist. A seminal figure of European literature, he was a prolific writer of poems, novels, plays, criticism, and letters. His masterwork is the dramatic poem *Faust* (1808–32). He was also author of *The Sorrows of Young Werther* (novel, 1774).

goe·thite /gő thìt, gő thìt/ *n.* an earthy, rust-colored hydrated iron oxide mineral formed by the alteration of iron minerals [Early 19thC. Named for J. W. von *Goethe* (1749–1832), German writer.]

go·fer /gőfər/ *n.* somebody who runs errands, especially somebody employed to do this and other low-level, basic tasks (*informal*) [Mid-20thC. From a reduced pronunciation of *go for*.]

gof·fer /góffər/, **gauf·fer** *vt.* (**-fered, -fer·ing, -fers**) **1. HAIR CRIMP HAIR** to make hair wavy or crimped using a heated iron or similar device **2. PRESS FRILLS INTO FABRIC** to press pleats into fabric to produce an ornamental frill using a heated iron or similar implement ■ *n.* **GOFFERING TOOL** a tool used for goffering frills [Late 16thC. From French *gaufrer* "mark with a decorative tool," from *gaufre* "honeycomb," from, ultimately, Middle Low German *wafel*.]

go-get·ter *n.* somebody who is enterprising and aggressive (*informal*)

gog·gle /gógg'l/ *v.* (**-gled, -gling, -gles**) **1.** *vi.* **STARE WIDE-EYED** to stare with eyes wide open, usually in astonishment **2.** *vti.* **ROLL THE EYES** to roll the eyes about, or roll about in the eyesocket ■ *adj.* **BULGING** bulging from the eyesocket ○ *goggle eyes* ■ *n.* **WIDE-EYED STARE** a staring or leering at somebody with eyes wide [14thC. Origin uncertain: probably literally "to move back and forth repeatedly," formed from assumed *gog* "to move back and forth," an imitation of the movement.] —**gog·gly** *adj.*

gog·gle-eyed *adj.* with staring eyes

gog·gles /gógg'lz/ *npl.* protective eyeglasses, usually made of plastic or glass and fitting tight to the face

go-go *adj.* **1. ENERGETIC** characterized by energy and forcefulness **2. FIN SPECULATIVE** bringing or expected to bring quick or high returns on any investment ○ *These go-go stocks carry risk and are not for the timid investor.* **3. DISCO** relating to or seen in discotheques or music clubs (*dated*) ■ *n.* **MUSIC TYPE OF MUSIC** type of U.S. popular music from the 1980s, an amalgamation of disco, funk, and Latin sounds [Doubling of GO, probably referring to French *à gogo* "galore"]

go-go danc·er *n.* an energetic and usually scantily dressed dancer providing entertainment in a nightclub (*dated*)

Goi·a·ni·a /goy áanee ə, go yánnyə/ capital city of Goiania state in south central Brazil. Population: 972,766 (1996).

Goi·â·ni·a /goy áanee ə, go yánnyə/ capital city of Goiás State in south central Brazil. Population: 972,766 (1996).

Goi·del /góyd'l/ *n.* a Celt who speaks one of the branch of northern Celtic languages known as Goidelic [Late 19thC. From Old Irish *Goídel* (see GAEL).]

Goi·del·ic /goy déllik/ *n.* the northern branch of the Celtic family of languages, comprising Irish Gaelic, Scottish Gaelic, and Manx —**Goi·del·ic** *adj.*

go·ing /gőing/ *n.* **1. ACT OF LEAVING** an act of leaving somewhere **2. CONDITIONS FOR PROGRESS** conditions for making progress of any kind ○ *The going gets tough when you reach the rocky terrain.* **3. CONDITIONS UNDER FOOT** the state of the ground as it affects ease and speed of movement, especially for horses in a race ○ *The going is good.* ■ *adj.* **1. SUCCESSFUL** currently operating successfully **2. ACCEPTED AS STANDARD** currently accepted as standard or valid ○ *the going rate for platinum* **3. EXISTING** currently in existence or available ○ *the best going*

go·ing-o·ver (*plural* **go·ings-o·ver**) *n.* (*informal*) **1. THOROUGH EXAMINATION** a thorough examination or check ○ *They gave the results a thorough going-over before making their report.* **2. OVERHAUL** an action by which something is thoroughly improved or restored to a previous condition such as an act of cleaning, polishing, or dusting something ○ *The house got a complete going-over before the arrival of the in-laws.* **3. SCOLDING OR BEATING** a verbal scolding or physical beating

go·ings-on *npl.* events or activities, especially of a noteworthy or suspicious nature (*informal*)

goi·ter /góytər/ *n.* enlargement of the thyroid gland appearing as a swelling of the front of the neck. Iodine deficiency is one of several causes. [Early 17thC. From French, from, ultimately, Latin *guttur* "throat."] —**goi·trous** *adj.*

goi·tre /góytər/ *n.* U.K. = **goiter**

go-kart, **go-cart** *n.* = **go-cart** *n.* 1

Go·lan Heights /gő laan-/ disputed upland region on the border between Israel and Syria, northeast of the Sea of Galilee. Administered by Syria until 1967, it was first occupied and then, in 1981, annexed by Israel. Highest peak: 7,294 ft./2,224. Area: 485 sq. mi./1,250 ft.

gold /gőld/ *n.* **1. MINERALS SOFT YELLOW METALLIC ELEMENT** a soft heavy yellow metal that is highly valued and widely used to make jewelry, often in alloy form. The most ductile and malleable metal, it is corrosion-resistant and is found in underground veins and alluvial deposits. Symbol **Au 2. COLORS DEEP RICH YELLOW HUE** a deep rich yellow color that resembles that of the metal gold **3. THINGS MADE OF GOLD** things made of gold, e.g., coins or pieces of jewelry **4. WEALTH** much money or wealth **5. SPORTS GOLD MEDAL** a gold medal (*informal*) **6. ARCHERY BULL'S EYE** the bull's eye of a target, which is usually gilt ■ *adj.* **1. OF OR LIKE GOLD** made of, covered with, or looking like gold, often as a symbol of high quality or achievement **2. OF RICH DEEP YELLOW HUE** of a deep rich yellow color **3. INDICATIVE OF TOP RECORDING SALES** used to describe a golden replica of a recording that has achieved exceptionally high sales, the replica being presented to the recording artist or artists. Sales of an album must exceed 500,000 copies, or 250,000 in the U.K., and those of a single, one million, or 500,000 in the U.K. [Old English. Ultimately from an Indo-European word that is also the ancestor of English *yellow* and *gild*.]

Gold·berg /gőldbərg/, **Arthur J.** (1908–90) U.S. statesman and Supreme Court justice. He sat on the U.S. Supreme Court (1962–65), and was U.S. delegate to the United Nations (1965–68).

Gold·berg, Rube (1883–1970) U.S. cartoonist. He is known for his comic diagrams of complex contraptions that performed ridiculously simple actions. Full name **Reuben Lucius Goldberg**

Popperfoto

Whoopi Goldberg

Gold·berg, Whoopi (*b.* 1949) U.S. actor. Her movies include *The Color Purple* (1985) and an Academy Award-winning performance in *Ghost* (1990). Real name **Caryn Johnson**

gold brick *n.* **1. SOMETHING ONLY SUPERFICIALLY VALUABLE** a brick or other thing that appears to be made of gold but is not actually valuable **2. LAZY PERSON** a loafer or shirker (*informal*) [From the gold rush era, when cheaters sold fake gold bricks, or sold real gold bricks but later replaced them with fake ones]

gold·brick /gőld brìk/ (**-bricked, -brick·ing, -bricks**) *vi.* to avoid work by making excuses (*informal*) —**gold·brick·er** *n.*

gold bug *n.* a supporter of a single gold standard (*dated informal*)

gold cer·tif·i·cate *n.* a security representing ownership of a quantity of gold, with the actual bullion held in a designated repository

gold coast, **Gold Coast** *n.* **1. EXCLUSIVE RESIDENTIAL AREA** the most exclusive residential area of a place **2. EXCLUSIVE OFFICE SPACE** the floor or area in an office building where the top management of a company has its offices (*slang*)

Gold Coast /gőld kōst/ **1.** city on the Pacific coast, southeastern Queensland, Australia. It straddles the border between Queensland and New South Wales. Population: 311,932 (1996). **2.** former name for **Ghana** (1874–1957)

Goldcrest

gold·crest /gőld krèst/ *n.* a small, very active, olive-green songbird with a yellow and black crown, common in Europe. Latin name: *Regulus regulus.*

gold dig·ger *n.* **1. SOMEBODY WHO COURTS SOMEBODY FOR MONEY** somebody, who pursues personal relationships in order to obtain wealth (*insult*) **2. GOLD MINER** a miner looking for gold deposits —**gold-dig·ging** *n.*

gold disk *n.* **1.** *U.K.* MUSIC = **gold record 2.** COMPUT **MASTER DISK FOR CD** the master disk from which a CD-ROM is made

gold dust *n.* *U.K.* = **alyssum**

gold·en /gőld'n/ *adj.* **1. COLORED LIKE GOLD** with the deep rich yellow color or sheen of gold ○ *golden hair* **2. MADE OF GOLD** made largely or wholly of gold ○ *a golden crown* **3. EXCELLENT** especially good ○ *a golden opportunity* **4. IDYLLIC** when there is general or individual success, happiness, or prosperity ○ *the golden years of their lives* 5. **FAVORED** very popular or successful, or likely to become so ○ *the golden boys and girls of the downhill ski circuit* 6. **50TH** that is fiftieth in a series ○ *golden jubilee* —**gold·en·ly** *adv.* —**gold·en·ness** *n.*

Gold·en /gṓld'n/ city at the foothills of the Rocky Mountains in Jefferson County, north central Colorado, 10 mi./16 km west of Denver. Population: 13,116 (1990).

gold·en age *n.* 1. **PERIOD OF EXCELLENCE** a period of great prosperity or achievement, especially in the arts 2. **EARLIEST AND BEST AGE** the first age of the world in classical mythology, characterized by idyllic happiness and innocence

gold·en ag·er *n.* somebody over retirement age

gold·en Al·ex·an·ders (*plural* **gold·en Al·ex·an·ders**) *n.* a perennial North American plant of the carrot family that has small yellow flowers and is found in woods and meadows. Latin name: *Zizia aurea.* (*takes a singular or plural verb*) [*Alexanders* of uncertain origin: probably from medieval Latin (*petroselinum*) *Alexandrinum* "horse parsley," named for]

gold·en an·ni·ver·sa·ry *n.* a fiftieth anniversary, e.g., of a wedding, or its celebration

gold·en as·ter *n.* a North American plant with yellow flowers resembling those of daisies. Genus: *Chrysopsis.*

Gold·en Bay bay on the northern coast of the South Island, New Zealand. It extends 25 mi./40 km from Farewell Spit in the west to Separation Point in the east.

gold·en brown *n.* a yellowish brown color —**gold·en-brown** *adj.*

gold·en-brown al·ga *n.* a freshwater or marine alga that is yellow to golden-brown in color. Division: *Chrysophyta.* (*often used in the plural*)

gold·en calf *n.* an unworthy object that is esteemed or worshiped, especially money [From the golden calf made by Aaron and worshiped by the Israelites (Exodus 32)]

gold·en club *n.* an eastern North American aquatic plant that has a yellow club-shaped floral spike and small blue-green berries. Latin name: *Orontium aquaticum.*

Gold·en De·li·cious *n.* a variety of eating apples with greenish or yellowish skin and a soft sweet flesh

gold·en ea·gle *n.* a large dark-brown eagle that has golden-brown feathers on its head and neck. It is found in mountainous areas of the northern hemisphere. Latin name: *Aquila chrysaetos.*

gol·den·eye /gṓld'n ī/ *n.* 1. **BLACK-AND-WHITE DUCK** a black-and-white diving duck with yellow eyes. There are two species, both found in northern regions. Latin name: *Bucephala clangula* and *Bucephala islandica.* 2. **INSECT WITH YELLOW EYES** an insect with yellow eyes and delicate lacy wings. Family: Chrysopidae.

Gold·en Fleece *n.* in Greek mythology, the fleece of the winged ram Chrysomallus, kept in a sacred grove by King Aeëtes, from where it was stolen by Jason

Barnaby's

Golden Gate Bridge

Gol·den Gate Bridge long suspension bridge across the entrance to San Fransisco Bay, California. It was opened in 1937 and links San Fransisco with Marin County.

gold·en glow *n.* a tall plant grown for its attractive multiple yellow flower heads. Latin name: *Rudbeckia laciniata.*

gold·en ham·ster *n.* a small mammal with tan fur, a short tail, and large cheek pouches for storing food that is often kept as a pet or used as a laboratory animal. The widespread domestic population came from a single female and 12 young caught in Syria in 1930. Latin name: *Mesocricetus auratus.*

gold·en hand·cuffs *npl.* generous benefits promised to an employee on joining a company to discourage him or her from leaving to work elsewhere (*informal*)

gold·en hand·shake *n.* a large sum of money given to an employee to compensate for the loss of a job or compulsory early retirement (*informal*)

Gold·en Horde *n.* the Mongol army that invaded and dominated large parts of eastern Europe in the 13th century

Gold·en Horse·shoe *n. Can* the prosperous region of southern Ontario running around the western end of Lake Ontario from St. Catharine's in the west to Oshawa in the east and including Toronto and Hamilton.

gold·en li·on tam·a·rin *n.* a small monkey with brilliant golden fur and mane, found in the coastal forests of Brazil. Although its survival is endangered, a 1996 zoo breeding program successfully reintroduced it into its natural habitat. Latin name: *Leontopithecus rosalia.*

gold·en mean *n.* 1. **MODERATION** the middle course that avoids extremes in either direction 2. ARTS = **golden section**

gold·en nem·a·tode *n.* a small worm that can infest potato fields, causing severe damage to crops and loss of productive farm land. Latin name: *Heterodera rostochiensis.*

gold·en old·ie *n.* a song that was popular in the past and has remained popular or become popular again (*informal*)

gold·en o·ri·ole *n.* a songbird found in warmer European and Asian climates, the male of which has bright yellow plumage with a black tail and wings, while the female is yellowish-green. Latin name: *Oriolus oriolus.*

gold·en par·a·chute *n.* an employment agreement that gives generous benefits to a senior executive who is forced to leave a company (*informal*)

gold·en pheas·ant *n.* a brightly colored long-tailed pheasant native to the mountainous regions of China and Tibet and often seen in aviaries elsewhere. Latin name: *Chrysolophus pictus.*

gold·en plov·er *n.* a northern European shorebird with brown and black plumage and gold spots on its head and back. It migrates seasonally as far as the Mediterranean coast. Latin name: *Pluvialis apricaria.*

gold·en re·triev·er *n.* a medium-sized dog of a breed with soft cream to golden hair. Its companionable nature makes it a popular family pet.

gold·en·rod /gṓld'n ròd/ (*plural* **-rods** *or* **-rod**) *n.* a tall-stemmed, late summer-blooming plant with clusters of small yellow flowers. It is widespread in Europe and North America. Genus: *Solidago.*

gold·en rule *n.* 1. **ESSENTIAL RULE** any basic rule that must be followed 2. **RULE OF CONDUCT** the rule of conduct that advises people to treat others in the same manner as they wish to be treated themselves 3. MATH = **rule of three**

gold·en·seal /gṓld'n sēel/ *n.* a small perennial woodland plant of the buttercup family that has small greenish flowers and is native to eastern North America. Its thick yellow rootstock is used in herbal medicine for its healing and antiseptic properties. Latin name: *Hydrastis canadensis.*

gold·en sec·tion *n.* ARTS the proportion arising from the division of a straight line into two, so that the ratio of the whole line to the larger part is exactly the same as the ratio of the larger part to the smaller part. It is considered to be the most aesthetically pleasing proportion.

gold·en shin·er *n.* a common freshwater fish of the minnow family, native to eastern North America, that has a deep body and a golden color. Latin name: *Notemigonus crysoleucas.*

gold·en tri·an·gle *n.* the part of Southeast Asia where Laos, Thailand, and Myanmar (formerly Burma) meet and where much opium is grown

gold·field /gṓld fēeld/ *n.* an area with gold mines

gold-filled *adj.* made of metal covered with a layer of gold

gold·finch /gṓld finch/ *n.* a small finch with yellow and black markings, found in North America, Europe, and Asia. Genus: *Carduelis.*

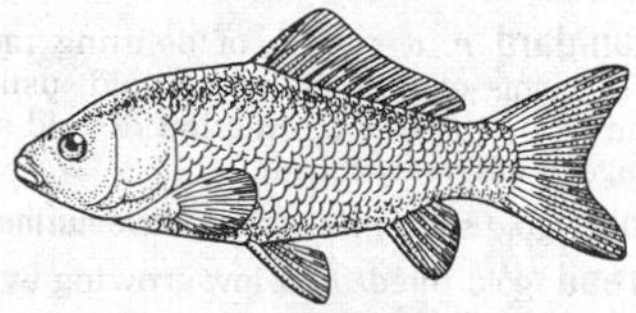

Goldfish

gold·fish /gṓld fish/ (*plural* **-fish** *or* **-fish·es**) *n.* a small orange-red freshwater fish native to eastern Asia but commonly kept in aquariums, ponds, and tanks. It is related to the carps and minnows. Latin name: *Carassius auratus.*

gold·fish bowl *n.* 1. *U.K.* **BOWL FOR GOLDFISH** a clear glass or plastic bowl in which to raise and keep goldfish 2. **PLACE WITHOUT PRIVACY** a situation or place that is always open to public view or scrutiny

gold leaf *n.* gold that is beaten out into very thin sheets and used for gilding and lettering

UPI/Corbis-Bettmann

Emma Goldman

Gold·man /gṓldmən/, **Emma** (1869–1940) Russian-born U.S. anarchist. A fiery writer and lecturer, she was imprisoned and deported (1919) for her radical political activities in the United States, and wrote the autobiographical *Living my Life* (1931).

gold med·al *n.* a medal that is made of gold or something representing gold, given as a first prize for excellence or winning a competition —**gold med·al·ist** *n.*

gold mine *n.* a rich source of something valuable, especially easily obtained wealth ○ *Some of the smaller shops are little gold mines.*

gold plate *n.* 1. **ITEMS MADE OF GOLD** bowls, goblets, and other utensils made of gold 2. **THIN LAYER OF GOLD** a thin coating of gold on another metal, usually produced by electroplating

gold-plat·ed *adj.* having a thin coating of gold, usually produced by electroplating —**gold-plate** *vt.*

gold record *n.* MUSIC a golden replica of a recording that has achieved exceptionally high sales. Sales of an album must exceed 500,000, and those of a single one million.

gold re·serve *n.* a fund of gold in coins or bullion held by a central bank and regarded as providing a foundation for a paper currency and security for borrowing

gold rush *n.* 1. **RUSH TO A NEW GOLDFIELD** a sudden wave of migration to new territory because gold has been discovered there. One of the most famous gold rushes was to the Klondike in Yukon, Canada, from 1896. 2. **RUSH FOR NEW WEALTH** a sudden rush to make money from a new source or by a new means

WORD KEY: CULTURAL NOTE

The Gold Rush, a movie by director and actor Charles Chaplin (1925). Set during the California gold rush of

1849, it places Chaplin's gentle and sensitive Tramp character in the materialistic, amoral environment of a mining town to great comic effect. In one famous scene, Chaplin is reduced to eating his shoes, but eventually he strikes it rich and returns home a wealthy man.

---

gold·smith /gṓld smith/ *n.* somebody who makes articles out of gold or deals in them

gold·smith bee·tle *n.* a beetle of the scarab family that has a metallic gold color. Latin name: *Cotalpa lanigera.*

gold stan·dard *n.* a system of defining monetary units in terms of their value in gold, usually accompanied by the free circulation of gold and free exchange of currency into it

gold·stone /gṓld stōn/ *n.* MINERALS = **aventurine**

gold·thread /gṓld thrèd/ *n.* a low-growing evergreen plant that is common in mossy woods or swamps in North America and Europe. The yellow rootstock has provided a popular traditional remedy for inflammation. Genus: *Coptis.*

Gold·wa·ter /gṓld wawtər/, **Barry M.** (1909–98) U.S. politician. He was a conservative Republican U.S. senator from Arizona (1953–65, 1969–87). He was defeated by Lyndon B. Johnson for the presidency (1964). Full name **Barry Morris Goldwater**

Gold·wyn /gṓldwin/, **Samuel** (1882–1974) Russian-born U.S. movie producer. He was one of Hollywood's most influential producers. His movies include *Stella Dallas* (1937), *The Best Years of Our Lives* (1946), and *Porgy and Bess* (1959). Real name **Schmuel Gelbfisz**

go·lem /gṓləm/ *n.* in Jewish legend, a creature made of clay and brought to life by magical incantations. The most famous was the golem made by the Maharal, Rabbi Loew, in the 16th century to defend the Jews of Prague from a pogrom. [Late 19thC. From Yiddish *goylem*, from Hebrew *golem* "shape, mass."]

golf /gawlf/ *n.* GAME WITH BALL AND CLUBS an outdoor game in which an array of specially designed clubs with long shafts are used to hit a small ball from a prescribed starting point into a hole. The object of the game is to complete the course in as few strokes as possible. ■ *vi.* (**golfed, golf·ing, golfs**) PLAY GOLF to play the game of golf [15thC. Origin uncertain: perhaps from Dutch *kolf* "club."]

Golf *n.* a code word for the letter "G," used in international radio communications

golf ball *n.* a small hard ball used for playing golf

golf cart *n.* a motorized vehicle used to drive around on a golf course during play

golf club *n.* **1.** STICK FOR HITTING GOLF BALLS a specially designed club with a long shaft and a metal or wooden head, used in golf to strike the ball **2.** GOLFERS' ASSOCIATION an association of people who play golf, usually on the same course **3.** PREMISES OF GOLFERS' ASSOCIATION the premises or facilities used by a golf club

golf course *n.* an area of land designed for playing the game of golf

golf·er *n.* somebody who plays the game of golf

golf·ing /gáwlfing/ *n.* the activity of playing golf (*often used before a noun*) ○ *a golfing umbrella*

golf links *npl.* = **golf course**

golf wid·ow *n.* a woman whose husband or partner spends many hours playing golf (*informal*)

Gol·gi ap·pa·ra·tus, **Gol·gi bod·y, Gol·gi com·plex** /gáwljee-/ *n.* a membranous structure in the cytoplasm of cells consisting of layers of flattened sacs. It functions in the processing and transporting of proteins. [Early 20thC. Named for Camillo *Golgi* (1844–1926), Italian histologist.]

Gol·go·tha[2] /gólgəthə/ site outside the city of Jerusalem where Jesus Christ was crucified, according to the Bible. Hebrew for **Calvary**

gol·iard /gṓlyərd, gṓl yaárd/ *n.* in 12th- and 13th-century Western Europe, a wandering scholar who was noted for writing bawdy and satirical Latin verses, and for buffoonery and riotous living [Late 15thC. From Old French, "glutton," via Latin *gula* from Sanskrit *gir-ami.*]

go·li·ath /gə lī́ əth/, **Go·li·ath** *n.* a gigantic or overpowering opponent or competitor ○ *a corporation regarded as the goliath of the oil industry* [Late 16thC. The name of the giant killed by David in the Bible (1 Samuel 17).]

Go·li·ath *n.* in the Bible, a giant Philistine who was slain by David using a sling and a stone

Go·li·ath bee·tle *n.* a very large tropical African scarab beetle that can measure up to 6 in./15 cm in length and has bold black, white, and brown markings. Latin name: *Goliathus giganteus.*

Go·li·ath frog *n.* a very large frog of central Africa that can measure up to 12 in./30 cm. Latin name: *Rana goliath.*

gol·li·wog /gólli wòg/, **gol·li·wogg** *n.* an offensively grotesque cloth doll with a black face and hair and brightly colored clothes. Now rarely made, the dolls are offensive to Black people, as is the term itself. (*offensive*) [Late 19thC. Named for a fictional character in books by U.S. writer and illustrator Florence Upton (1873–1922).]

gol·ly /góllee/ *interj.* used to express surprise, amazement, or anxiety, or for emphasis (*dated informal*) ○ *Golly, we're in real trouble now!* [Late 18thC. Alteration of GOD.]

go·ma·sio /gō maássee ō/, **gho·ma·sio** *n.* a seasoning mixture made of ground sesame seeds and salt, used especially in Japanese cooking

gom·broon /góm bròon/ *n.* pottery made in Iran and elsewhere in imitation of white Chinese porcelain [Late 17thC. Named for *Gombroon*, a port in Iran, now called Bandar Abbas.]

Go·mor·rah /gə máwrə/ *n.* a place or society marked by evil, depravity, and promiscuousness (*disapproving*) [Early 20thC. Named for an ancient biblical city destroyed by God because of its wickedness,(Genesis 19).]

Gom·pers /gómpərz/, **Samuel** (1850–1924) British-born U.S. labor leader. As the first president of the American Federation of Labor (AFL) (1886–95, 1896–1924), he was the dominant figure in the U.S. labor movement.

gon- *prefix.* = **gono-** (*used before vowels*)

-gon *suffix.* a figure having a particular number of angles ○ *undecagon* ○ *polygon* [Via Greek *-gōnon* from, ultimately, *gōnia* "angle, corner." Ultimately from an Indo-European word meaning "knee, bend," which is also the ancestor of English *knee* and *genuflect.*]

go·nad /gṓ nàd/ *n.* an organ that produces reproductive cells (**gametes**), e.g., a testis or an ovary [Late 19thC. From modern Latin *gonad*, stem of *gonas*, from Greek *gonos* "seed, generation."] —**go·nad·al** /gō nád'l/ *adj.* —**go·nad·ic** /gō náddik/ *adj.*

go·nad·o·troph·ic *adj.* = **gonadotropic**

go·nad·o·tro·phin *n.* = **gonadotropin**

go·nad·o·trop·ic /gō nàddə tróffik, gònədō-/, **go·nad·o·troph·ic** /-tróppik/ *adj.* stimulating or acting on the gonads [Mid-20thC. Coined from GONAD + -TROPIC or TROPHIC.]

go·nad·o·tro·pin /gō nàddə trṓpin, gónnədə-/, **go·nad·o·tro·phin** /-trṓfin/ *n.* a hormone secreted by the pituitary gland, and in some mammals by the placenta during pregnancy, that influences gonadal activity, including the onset of sexual maturity and regulation of reproductive activity [Mid-20thC. Coined from GONAD + -TROPIN or TROPHIN.]

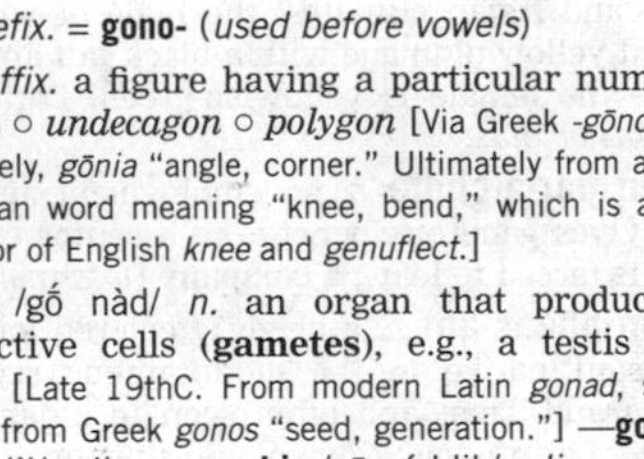

Gondola

gon·do·la /gónd'lə, gən dṓlə/ *n.* **1.** VENETIAN CANAL BOAT a narrow flat-bottomed boat, used on the canals of Venice, that has a curved prow and stern and is moved along with a long pole **2.** CABLE CAR a car or cabin suspended from cables, especially one attached to a ski lift **3.** AIR CAR BELOW A BALLOON a basket or cabin suspended from a balloon or airship, for carrying people or equipment **4.** FLAT-BOTTOMED RIVERBOAT a large, flat-bottomed riverboat **5.** RAIL = **gondola car** **6.** WIDE-MOUTHED CONTAINER a wide-mouthed vase or bowl, usually broader than it is high [Mid-16thC. Via Venetian Italian from Rhaeto-Romance *gondolà* "to roll, rock."]

gon·do·la car *n.* a long, open, low-sided rail car

gon·do·lier /gònd'l éer, gónd'l èer/ *n.* somebody who propels a gondola through the water, especially on the canals of Venice

Gond·wa·na·land /gon dwaánə land/ ancient landmass, consisting of the southern part of the supercontinent of Pangaea. Comprised of South America, Africa, peninsular India, Australia, and Antarctica, it began to break up approximately 200 million years ago. ◊ **Laurasia, Pangaea**

gone past participle of **go** ■ *adj.* **1.** ABSENT absent after leaving somewhere ○ *She has been gone for hours.* **2.** IRRECOVERABLE beyond hope of recovery ○ *All hopes for a truce are gone.* **3.** USED UP having been completely used up ○ *If the milk is all gone, we'll drink our coffee black.* **4.** PREGNANT having been pregnant for a particular number of months ○ *She's eight months gone.* **5.** DEAD no longer living (*informal*) **6.** UNEASY giving a sensation of giddiness or mild nausea **7.** INFATUATED affected by a strong feeling of attraction toward somebody (*informal*) ○ *He's gone on your sister.* **8.** EXHILARATED excited or exhilarated, e.g., while listening to music (*slang*)

gon·er /gónnər/ *n.* somebody or something beyond hope of recovery, especially somebody who is dead or about to die (*slang*) [Mid-19thC. Coined from GONE + -ER.]

gon·fa·lon /gónfə lòn/ *n.* a banner suspended from a crossbar, often with an edge cut like streamers, used especially as the standard of some medieval Italian republics or carried in church processions [Late 16thC. Via Italian *gonfalone* from Frankish, ultimately from prehistoric Germanic words meaning "war" and "banner."]

gon·fa·lon·ier /gònfələ néer/ *n.* **1.** GONFALON CARRIER somebody who carries a gonfalon **2.** MEDIEVAL ITALIAN MAGISTRATE the chief magistrate of some medieval Italian republics, who carried the republic's gonfalon

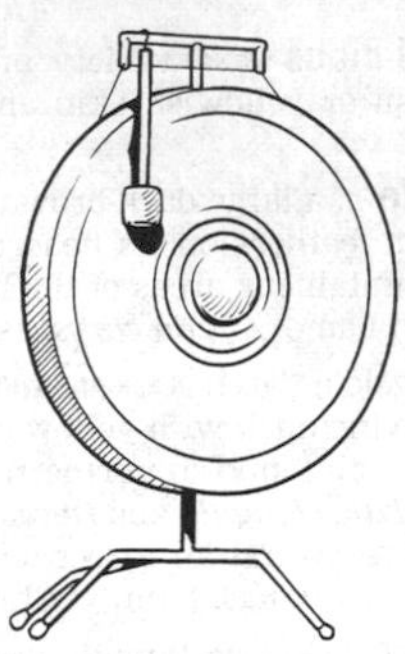

Gong

gong /gawng/ *n.* **1.** RESONANT BRONZE PLATE a circular bronze plate that makes a resonant sound when struck with a mallet, used especially as an orchestral percussion instrument or to summon people to meals **2.** WARNING BELL a round metal bell that is struck by a mechanically operated hammer, used especially as an alarm ■ *v.* (**gonged, gong·ing, gongs**) **1.** *vi.* SOUND LIKE A GONG to sound resonantly like a gong **2.** *vt.* SUMMON to summon somebody with a gong [Early 17thC. From Malay, an imitation of the sound of striking a gong.]

Gon·gor·ism /gáwng gə rìzzəm/ *n.* a style in Spanish literature characterized by ornate devices, classical allusions, and deliberate obscurity [Early 19thC. Named for the Spanish poet *Góngora* y Argote (1561–1627).] —**Gon·gor·is·tic** *adj.*

go·nid·i·um /gō nídee əm/ (*plural* **-a** /-ə/) *n.* **1.** ALGAL REPRODUCTIVE CELL an asexual reproductive cell in some algae, e.g., a zoospore **2.** ALGAL CELL IN LICHEN a chlorophyll-containing algal cell in the body (**thallus**) of a lichen [Mid-19thC. From modern Latin, from Greek *gonos* "offspring."] —**go·nid·i·al** *adj.*

go·nif *n.* = **ganef**

go·ni·om·e·ter /gōnee ómmətər/ *n.* **1.** INSTRUMENT FOR MEASURING ANGLES an instrument for measuring angles, especially those between crystal faces **2.** RADIO SIGNAL DIRECTION FINDER a device for establishing the bearing of an incoming radio signal [Mid-18thC. From French *goniomètre*, from Greek *gonia* "angle" + METER.] —**go·ni·o·met·ric** /gònee ə méttrik/ *adj.* —**go·ni·o·met·ri·cal** /-méttrik'l/ *adj.* —**go·ni·om·e·try** /gònee ómmətree/ *n.*

go·ni·on /gónee àn/ *n.* the point on either side of the lower jaw where it turns upward [Late 19thC. From French, from Greek *gonia* "angle."]

go·ni·ot·o·my /gònee óttəmee/ (*plural* **-mies**) *n.* an operation to treat glaucoma by cutting into the narrow angle between the back of the cornea and the root of the iris to allow drainage of aqueous humor

gonk /gawngk/ (**gonked, gonking, gonks**) *vti.* COMPUT to lie about something or embellish the truth, especially in an online conversation in a chat room (*slang*) ○ *Are you gonking me?* [Mid-20thC. An invented word.] —**gonk** *n.*

gon·na /gónnə/ *contr.* going to (*nonstandard*) [Early 20thC. Alteration.]

gono-[1] *prefix.* sexual, generative, semen, or seed [From Greek *gonos* or *gonē* "generation, offspring, seed"]

gono-[2] *prefix.* sex, seed, reproduction ○ *gonophore* [From Greek *gonos* "offspring, procreation." Ultimately from an Indo-European base meaning "to beget," which is also the ancestor of English *kin, genus,* and *germ.*]

gon·o·coc·cus /gònnə kókəss/ (*plural* **-ci** /-kók sī, -kó kī/) *n.* a spherical bacterium that causes gonorrhea. Latin name: *Neisseria gonorrhoeae.* [Late 19thC. From GONORRHOEA + COCCUS.] —**gon·o·coc·cal** *adj.* —**gon·o·coc·cic** *adj.*

gon·of *n.* = **ganef**

go-no-go *adj.* requiring or involving a definitive decision either to proceed with a course of action or to abandon it

gon·o·pore /gónnə pàwr/ *n.* an external reproductive pore in some insects and worms through which reproductive cells are secreted

gon·or·rhe·a /gònnə reé ə/, **gon·or·rhoe·a** *n.* a sexually transmitted disease that causes inflammation of the genital mucous membrane, burning pain when urinating, and a discharge. It is caused by a gonococcus bacterium. [16thC. Via modern Latin from Greek *gonorrhoia*, literally "flowing of semen," from *gonos* "semen."] —**gon·or·rhe·al** *adj.*

-gony[1] *suffix.* generation or reproduction [From Greek *-gonia* "generation, production"]

-gony[2] *suffix.* **1.** origin ○ *cosmogony* **2.** method of reproduction ○ *schizogony* [Formed from Greek *gonos* "offspring, procreation" (see GONO-)]

Gon·za·les /gən zaáləss/, **Pancho** (1928–95) U.S. tennis player. He dominated men's tennis in the 1950s, and in 1969 played the longest ever match at Wimbledon, defeating Charlie Pasarell after 112 games. Full name **Richard Alonzo Gonzales**

gon·zo /gón zō/ *adj.* (*slang*) **1.** IDIOSYNCRATICALLY SUBJECTIVE characterized by subjective interpretation and exaggeration ○ *Gonzo journalism is unlike the work of the impartial observer.* **2.** UNCONVENTIONAL unusual or strange [Late 20thC. Origin uncertain: perhaps from Italian, "foolish," or Spanish *ganso* "goose, fool."]

goo /goo/ *n.* (*informal*) **1.** SOMETHING STICKY any sticky substance, typically something unpleasant **2.** EXCESS EMOTION cloying emotionalism [Early 20thC. Origin uncertain: perhaps an abbreviation of BURGOO.]

goo·ber /goóbər/, **goo·ber pea** *n.* *Southern U.S.* a peanut [Mid-19thC. From Angolese *nguba*, Kikongo, and other West African languages.]

good /gŏŏd/ (**bet·ter** /béttər/, **best** /best/) CORE MEANING: an adjective indicating that something is approved of or desirable ○ *It's a good idea to change your password now and again.* ○ *It's good to talk.*

1. *adj.* OF HIGH QUALITY of a high quality or standard, either on an absolute scale or in relation to another or others ○ *The meal wasn't good.* ○ *He'll make a very good doctor.* ○ *I smashed one of my good plates.* **2.** *adj.* SUITABLE having the appropriate qualities to be something or to fit a particular purpose ○ *Futons make good chairs as well as beds.* ○ *The bicycle is good for short trips.* **3.** *adj.* SKILLED possessing the necessary skill or talent to do something ○ *I'm not a very good driver.* ○ *She's good at science.* **4.** *adj.* VIRTUOUS having or showing an upright and virtuous character ○ *You're a good man, Joe.* **5.** *adj.* KIND having or showing a kind and generous disposition ○ *She was always very good to me.* **6.** *adj.* AFFORDING PLEASURE affording pleasure or comfort ○ *He's a man who insists on the finer things in life: good food, good books, and the theater.* **7.** *adj.* UNDAMAGED having undergone no deterioration or damage ○ *I smelled the meat and found it was still good.* **8.** *adj.* AMPLE sufficiently large, or providing more than enough of something ○ *Between them they have a good income.* **9.** *adj.* HONORABLE worthy of honor or high esteem ○ *They come from a good family.* **10.** *adj.* VALID acceptable as true or genuine and sufficient for the purpose ○ *There had better be a good explanation for this mess.* ○ *Don't travel unless your insurance is good.* **11.** *adj.* HELPFUL helping somebody to organize thoughts or make decisions ○ *She gave me some good advice.* **12.** *adj.* PLEASANT pleasant to look at ○ *Don't let her good looks distract you from her intelligence.* **13.** *adj.* BENEFICIAL beneficial to health or wellbeing ○ *Eating lots of fruit is good for you.* **14.** *adj.* FAVORABLE suitable and likely to produce the right results or conditions ○ *a good time to take a vacation* **15.** *adj.* THOROUGH that goes to the fullest extent of the action ○ *Take a good look around.* **16.** *adj.* FIN FINANCIALLY ADVANTAGEOUS financially or commercially advantageous or reliable ○ *I made a few good investments last year.* **17.** *adj.* GENUINE that is what it appears to be ○ *a good dollar bill* **18.** *adj.* OBEDIENT well behaved and obedient ○ *The children are always good when we take them out.* **19.** *adj.* WELL-MANNERED socially correct ○ *very good behavior* **20.** *adj.* ABLE TO DO MORE remaining in operation or effect, or able to continue doing something ○ *The car will be good for another 6,000 miles.* **21.** *adj.* FIN ABLE TO PAY able to pay or contribute something, or to allow a sum to be drawn ○ *He's good for at least a thousand dollars.* **22.** *adj.* FIN THAT WILL BE PAID that the debtor is expected to honor in full ○ *a good debt* **23.** *adj.* PRODUCING A RESULT able to produce a particular result ○ *John is always good for a laugh.* **24.** *adj.* SIZABLE considerable in extent or size ○ *a good selection of books on computers* **25.** *adj.* FULLY at least a particular time or length ○ *It's a good 30 years since we met.* **26.** *adj.* RACKET GAMES WITHIN BOUNDS inside the required area for the shot to be allowed ○ *The umpire said that the ball was good.* **27.** *adj.* USED IN EXCLAMATIONS used in exclamations of surprise, dismay, or other strong feelings (*informal*) ○ *Good heavens! I've won first prize!* **28.** *interj.* USED TO EXPRESS SATISFACTION used to express satisfaction or pleasure in something that has just been said, or to confirm it ○ *"They've just arrived.""Good."* **29.** *n.* BENEFICIAL EFFECT something resulting in a beneficial effect or state ○ *the common good* ○ *What good will complaining do?* **30.** *n.* = **goodness** *n.* 1 **31.** *n.* POSITIVE PART the positive part or aspect of something ○ *You have to take the good with the bad in this agreement.* **32.** *n.* SOMETHING WORTH HAVING something worth having or achieving ○ *Let's work for the future good of the nation.* [Old English *god*, from a prehistoric Germanic word meaning "to unite," which is also the ancestor of English *gather*] ◇ **be (all) to the good** to be to somebody's benefit ◇ **be up to no good** to be in the process of doing or planning something wrong or illegal (*informal*) ◇ **for good** permanently from the time in question ○ *They've gone for good.* ◇ **give as good as you get** to contend as effectively as your opponent ○ *Her tennis opponent is tough, but she can give as good as she gets.* ◇ **good and** completely and entirely (*informal*) ○ *I'll get up in the morning when I'm good and ready, and not before.* ◇ **make good** to become successful, often after an unpromising start ○ *Though he didn't do very well at school, he made good as a businessman.* ◇ **make something good 1.** to perform something successfully ○ *We must make good our attempt to win the trophy.* **2.** to carry out something intended or promised ○ *She made good her promise to repay the money on time.* **3.** to compensate for something, especially for damage or loss ○ *They made good the damage they had accidentally caused.* **4.** to demonstrate the truth or correctness of something ○ *If you cannot make good these charges, the defendant will not stand trial.* ◇ **throw good money after bad** to put more money, better used elsewhere, into a bad investment ○ *If you have the car repaired again, you'll just throw good money after bad.* ◇ **to the good** richer by a particular amount of money ○ *By the end of the day, we were 50 dollars to the good.*

good af·ter·noon *interj.* used when people meet or part, or begin or end a telephone conversation, during the afternoon

Good Book *n.* the Christian Bible

good·bye /gŏŏd bī/, **good-bye** *interj.* FAREWELL used when people part or end a telephone conversation ○ *With the hurricane approaching, it's goodbye to our vacation at the beach.* ■ *n.* ACT OF LEAVING an act of making a farewell ○ *It's time to say our goodbyes and catch the plane.* [Late 16thC. From *God be with you.*]

good cause *n.* **1.** CHARITY something or somebody deserving help, especially a charity **2.** LEGAL REASON a sufficient legal standard or reason

good eve·ning *interj.* used to convey good wishes when people meet or part, or begin or end a telephone conversation, during the evening

good faith *n.* honesty of intention ○ *an effort to fulfill the contract in good faith.*

good-for-noth·ing *n.* LAZY PERSON somebody who is perceived as lazy and irresponsible (*insult*) ■ *adj.* LAZY lazy and irresponsible

Good Fri·day *n.* the Christian holy day observed on the Friday before Easter, commemorating the death of Jesus Christ on the Cross (**Crucifixion**) [*Good* in the sense of "holy"]

Good Fri·day plant *n.* = **moschatel**

good guy *n.* somebody who is good or law-abiding, especially in a Western, crime novel, or movie (*informal*)

good·heart·ed /gŏŏd haártəd/ *adj.* having or showing a kind and generous nature —**good·heart·ed·ly** *adv.* —**good·heart·ed·ness** *n.*

Good Hope, Cape of ➧ **Cape of Good Hope**

good-hu·mored *adj.* disposed to be cheerful and friendly, or reflecting such an attitude —**good-hu·mored·ly** *adv.*

good·ie *n.* = **goody**

good·ish /gŏŏddish/ *adj.* **1.** RATHER GOOD moderately good in quality **2.** RATHER LARGE moderately large in quantity or extent ○ *a goodish helping*

good life *n.* a life of carefree comfort and luxury ○ *a retired ambassador living the good life in Palm Springs*

good-look·ing *adj.* having a pleasant personal, especially facial, appearance —**good-look·er** *n.*

WORD KEY: SYNONYMS

good-looking, attractive, beautiful, handsome, lovely, pretty

CORE MEANING: having a pleasing facial appearance

good-looking used of either men or women to indicate pleasing looks; **attractive** used in a similar way to *good-looking*. It is also used to describe people who are not conventionally good-looking but who are still very appealing, especially to members of the opposite sex; **beautiful** most often used to describe women or girls whose appearance is very pleasing, especially in a way that is generally considered ideal or perfect; **handsome** used to talk about men whose appearance is very pleasing, especially men who have strong, rugged-looking features. It can also be used to describe women who have strong, imposing features; **lovely** most often used to talk about women who are very pleasing to look at but possibly not beautiful; **pretty** used to talk about women and especially girls who are very attractive, usually in a way that is not conventionally beautiful.

good looks *npl.* a pleasant personal appearance, especially facial appearance

good·ly /gŏŏdlee/ (**-li·er, -li·est**) *adj.* **1.** SOMEWHAT LARGE moderately large in quantity or extent **2.** ATTRACTIVE having a fine appearance (*archaic*) **3.** PLEASANT of a pleasing quality (*archaic*) ○ *the goodly fellowship of the prophets* —**good·li·ness** *n.*

good·man /gŏŏdmən/ (*plural* **-men** /-mən/) *n.* the man in charge of a household or family, especially a married man (*archaic*)

Good·man /gŏŏdmən/, **Benny** (1909–86) U.S. jazz musician. A virtuoso clarinetist, he popularized swing music during the 1930s and 1940s leading his own band. Full name **Benjamin David Goodman**. Known as **the King of Swing**

good morn·ing *interj.* used to convey good wishes when people meet or part, or begin or end a telephone conversation, during the morning

good name *n.* somebody's reputation for honesty and integrity

good na·ture *n.* a pleasant and obliging disposition

good-na·tured *adj.* having or showing a pleasant and obliging disposition —**good-na·tured·ly** *adv.* —**good-na·tured·ness** *n.*

good·ness /gŏŏdnəss/ *n.* 1. GOOD QUALITY the quality of being good 2. VIRTUOUSNESS personal virtue or kindness 3. GOOD PART the nutrition or other benefit to be derived from something ○ *Vegetables lose a lot of their goodness if you overcook them.* ■ *interj.* USED TO EXPRESS SURPRISE used to express surprise or amazement, or for emphasis ○ *For goodness sake, stop that!* ◇ **goodness knows** used to indicate bafflement or lack of knowledge about something ○ *Goodness knows what they're doing out there at midnight.*

good night *interj.* used to convey good wishes when people part or end a telephone conversation at night, especially at bedtime

good of·fic·es *npl.* help or support, especially help in resolving a dispute

good old boy, good ol' boy, good ole boy *n.* stereotype of a man who is part of a peer group and conforms to the behavior characteristic of the group, especially applied to a white man in parts of the rural southern United States. The good old boy is often perceived as a caricature of the relaxed, convivial, conservative Southern white man. (*sometimes often offensive*)

goods /gŏŏdz/ *npl.* 1. MERCHANDISE articles for sale or use, often those produced for later consumption, as opposed to services (*takes a singular or plural verb*) 2. PORTABLE PROPERTY portable personal property 3. *U.K.* MERCHANDISE MOVED BY RAIL merchandise that is transported, especially by rail, as opposed to passengers (*often used before a noun*) ○ *a goods train* 4. COMMERCIAL FABRICS commercial textile fabrics (*takes a singular or plural verb*) 5. SOMETHING PROMISED something promised or expected (*informal*) ○ *You can rely on her to come up with the goods.* 6. INCRIMINATING EVIDENCE information or evidence that will incriminate somebody (*slang*)

Good Sa·mar·i·tan *n.* somebody who voluntarily helps others who are in trouble [From the parable of the Good Samaritan (Luke 10:30–37), who helps a man beaten by robbers]

good-sized *adj.* rather large in size ○ *The recipe called for a good-sized piece of chocolate.*

good-tem·pered *adj.* having or showing a placid disposition —**good-tem·pered·ly** *adv.* —**good-tem·pered·ness** *n.*

good turn *n.* a friendly act that helps or benefits somebody else ○ *One good turn deserves another.*

good·wife /gŏŏd wīf/ (*plural* **-wives** /-wīvz/) *n.* the woman in charge of a household or family, especially a married woman (*archaic*)

good·will /gŏŏd wíl, gŏŏd wil/ *n.* 1. FRIENDLY DISPOSITION friendly disposition toward somebody or something (*often used before a noun*) ○ *a goodwill gesture* 2. WILLINGNESS cheerful willingness to do something 3. ACCT NONTANGIBLE VALUE OF BUSINESS the value of a business over and above its tangible assets 4. CHARITY SHOP a shop that sells donated goods in order to raise money for charity

good word *n.* 1. FAVORABLE COMMENT a comment recommending somebody or made in favor or defense of somebody ○ *He promised to put in a good word for me.* 2. WANTED INFORMATION the information or answer to a question that somebody would wish to have (*informal*) ○ *What's the good word? Will the plane take off?*

good·y /gŏŏddee/, **good·ie** *n.* (*plural* **-ies**) SOMETHING SWEET TO EAT something desirable, especially something sweet to eat (*often used in the plural*) ■ *interj.* USED TO INDICATE DELIGHT used to express great pleasure (*informal*) ○ *Oh goody, ice cream!* [Coined from GOOD + -Y]

Good·year /gŏŏd yeer/, **Charles** (1800–60) U.S. inventor. He discovered the vulcanization process for rubber (1839).

good·y-good·y *n.* (*plural* **good·y-good·ies**) = **goody two-shoes** ■ *adj.* SMUGLY VIRTUOUS irritatingly well-behaved or smugly virtuous (*informal*) [Mid-19thC. Reduplication of GOODY.]

good·y two-shoes (*plural* **good·y two-shoes**) *n.* somebody smugly well-behaved, irritatingly virtuous, or sanctimonious (*informal*) [Mid-20thC. From the name of a character in a children's book perhaps by Oliver Goldsmith.]

goo·ey /gōō ee/ (**-i·er, -i·est**) *adj.* 1. STICKY sticky and soft ○ *gooey chocolate frosting* 2. SENTIMENTAL cloyingly sentimental (*informal*) ○ *a gooey romantic novel*

goof /gōōf/ *n.* (*informal*) 1. MISTAKE a mistake or blunder ○ *A colossal goof caused the whole computer system to crash.* 2. UNINTELLIGENT PERSON an unintelligent or incompetent person (*insult*) ■ *v.* (**goofed, goof·ing, goofs**) (*informal*) 1. *vi.* MAKE MISTAKE to make a thoughtless or unintelligent mistake 2. *vt.* BOTCH to spoil something through incompetence or lack of intelligence [Early 20thC. Origin uncertain: probably from dialect *goff* "simpleton."]

goof around *vi.* to behave in a playful or silly way (*informal*) ○ *Once the pressure of exams was off, the students just goofed around.*

goof off *v.* to waste time instead of working (*informal*) ○ *The crew goofed off when the boss left early.*

goof·ball /gōōf bàwl/ *n.* 1. UNINTELLIGENT PERSON a silly or unintelligent person (*insult*) 2. DRUG PILL a barbiturate or other drug in the form of a pill (*slang*)

goof-off (*plural* **goof-offs**) *n.* somebody who does not work industriously (*insult*)

goof·proof /gōōf prōōf/ *adj.* = **foolproof** (*informal*)

goof·y /gōōfee/ (**-i·er, -i·est**) *adj.* silly or unintelligent (*informal insult*) —**goof·i·ly** *adv.* —**goof·i·ness** *n.*

goo·gol /gōōg'l, gōō gàwl/ *n.* the number equal to the numeral 1 followed by 100 zeros, or 10^{100} [Mid-20thC. Invented word.]

goo·gol·plex /gōōg'l plèks, gōō gawl plèks/ *n.* the number equal to the numeral 1 followed by 10^{100} zeros [Mid-20thC. From GOOGOL + Latin *plexus* "intricate, braided."]

goo-goo *adj.* expressing affection or sentimental attachment (*informal*) ○ *goo-goo eyes* [Early 20thC. Origin uncertain: perhaps from GOGGLE.]

gook[1] /gook/ *n.* a highly offensive term for an Asian person or somebody of Asian descent (*slang offensive*) [Mid-20thC. Origin unknown.]

gook[2] /gook/ *n.* = **guck** [Early 20thC. Origin unknown.]

goom·bah /gōōm baa/ *n.* a close friend or associate, especially an older person acting as somebody's mentor (*slang*) [Mid-20thC. Origin uncertain: probably from Italian dialect, an alteration of Italian *compàre* "godfather, accomplice, friend."]

goon /gōōn/ *n.* 1. THUG a professional gangster whose work is beating up or terrorizing people 2. CLUMSY PERSON somebody who is clumsy or uncouth (*insult*) [Mid-19thC. Origin uncertain: perhaps from *goon(e)y*, variant of *gony* "simpleton"; or from Alice the Goon, a character invented by the U.S. cartoonist, E. C. Segar (1894–1938).]

goo·ney /gōōnee/ (*plural* **-neys**), **goo·ny** (*plural* **-nies**), **goo·ney bird, goo·ny bird** *n.* an albatross, especially the black-footed albatross. Latin name: *Diomedea nigripes.* [Late 16thC. Origin unknown.]

goop /gōōp/ *n.* a semiliquid sticky or messy substance (*informal*) [Early 20thC. Variant of GOOF.] —**goop·y** *adj.*

goos·an·der /goo sándər/ *n.* U.K. = **common merganser** [Early 17thC. Probably ultimately from GOOSE + Old Norse *andar-*, stem of *ond* "duck."]

Goose

goose /gooss/ *n.* (*plural* **geese** /geess/) 1. LONG-NECKED WATER BIRD a large waterfowl with a long neck and webbed feet, noted for its seasonal migrations and distinctive honking sound. Geese resemble swans but have shorter necks. Subfamily: Anserinae. 2. FEMALE GOOSE a female goose. ◊ **gander** 3. FOOD FLESH OF THE GOOSE the flesh of the goose, cooked and eaten as food 4. SILLY PERSON somebody who is silly 5. TAILOR'S IRON an iron with a long curved handle, used by tailors for pressing and smoothing cloth 6. PROD IN THE BUTTOCKS a poke between or pinch on the buttocks (*slang*) ■ *vt.* (**goosed, goos·ing, goos·es**) (*slang*) 1. PROD SOMEBODY IN THE BUTTOCKS to poke or pinch somebody on the buttocks 2. SPUR SOMEBODY TO ACTION to spur somebody on to action [Old English *gōs*. Ultimately from an Indo-European word.] ◇ **kill the goose that laid the golden egg** to destroy something that is or has been a regular, dependable source of profit or benefit

goose bar·na·cle *n.* a barnacle that has a flattened shell, feathery appendages, and a fleshy stalk that it uses to attach itself to surfaces, especially floating wood. Genus: *Lepas.*

Gooseberry

goose·ber·ry /gŏŏss bèrree/ (*plural* **-ries**) *n.* 1. SPINY FRUIT BUSH a spiny fruit bush, native to Europe and Asia, that produces green or sometimes red edible berries. Latin name: *Ribes uva-crispa.* 2. FRUIT OF GOOSEBERRY the acid-tasting fruit of a gooseberry plant, usually eaten cooked and sweetened (*often used before a noun*) ○ *gooseberry pie* 3. PLANT WITH BERRIES LIKE GOOSEBERRIES a plant bearing berries similar to gooseberries, such as the currant [Mid-16thC. *Goose* of uncertain origin: perhaps from GOOSE, or by folk etymology from French *groseille* "redcurrant."]

goose·ber·ry gourd *n.* = **gherkin** *n.* 2

goose bumps *npl.* temporary pimples on the skin brought on by cold or fear or by sudden excitement, and caused by the contraction of connective tissues (**papillae**) at the base of hairs

Goose Creek /gooss kreek/ city in southeastern South Carolina, directly northwest of Charleston and southeast of Columbia. Population: 25,943 (1996).

goose egg *n.* a zero, especially one or a set of them indicating no score in a game or contest (*slang*)

goose·fish /gooss fish/ (*plural* **-fish** *or* **-fish·es**) *n.* = **monkfish** [Early 19thC. From GOOSE + FISH.]

goose·flesh /gooss flèsh/ *n.* = **goose bumps** *npl.*

goose·foot /gooss fŏŏt/ *n.* a weed with small greenish flowers and berries, and leaves that resemble a goose's foot. Genus: *Chenopodium.*

goose·grass /gooss gràss/ *n.* BOT 1. = **cleavers** 2. = **yard grass**

goose·neck /gooss nèk/ *n.* something curved like a goose's neck or U-shaped such as a pipe joint or a flexible neck on a lamp (*often used before a noun*) ○ *a gooseneck lamp*

goose·neck bar·na·cle *n.* = **goose barnacle**

goose pim·ples *npl.* = **goose bumps**

goose step *n.* a military marching step performed with straight legs swung high in a forward movement —**goose-step** *vi.*

goos·y /goossee/ (**-i·er, -i·est**), **goos·ey** (**-i·er, -i·est**) *adj.* 1. RESEMBLING A GOOSE similar to a goose 2. HAVING GOOSE BUMPS affected by goose bumps, or the nervousness or fear that can cause them (*informal*) 3. SILLY behaving in a silly or scatterbrained way

GOP *abbr.* Grand Old Party

go·pher /gōfər/ *n.* 1. BURROWING RODENT a small short-tailed rodent of North and Central America that has fur-lined cheek pouches and short legs. It digs sizable burrows. Family: Geomyidae. 2. = **ground squirrel** 3. COMPUT SYSTEM PROVIDING INTERNET LINKS an Internet system that organizes files into menus containing links to text files, graphic images, databases, and additional menus (*often used before a noun*) ○ *a gopher site* 4. *Southern U.S.* TORTOISE a large burrowing tortoise. Genus: *Gopherus.* [Late 18thC. Origin uncertain: perhaps from Canadian French *gaufre* "honeycomb," referring to the burrows made by the animals.

For computing sense, alteration of GOFER, from the idea that it tunnels from place to place.]

go·pher ball *n.* in baseball, a pitched ball that is hit for a home run (*informal*)

go·pher snake *n.* = **bull snake**

go·pher tor·toise *n.* a burrowing tortoise found in the southeastern United States. Genus: *Gopherus.*

go·pher·wood /gṓfər wŏŏd/ *n.* in the Bible, the wood from which Noah's ark was made, or the tree from which it came [Early 17thC. *Gopher* from Hebrew *gōpher.*]

gor·al /gṓrəl/ *n.* a small short-horned antelope found in the rugged country of the Himalayas and adjacent Southeast Asia. Genus: *Nemorhaedus.* [Mid-19thC. From a Himalayan language.]

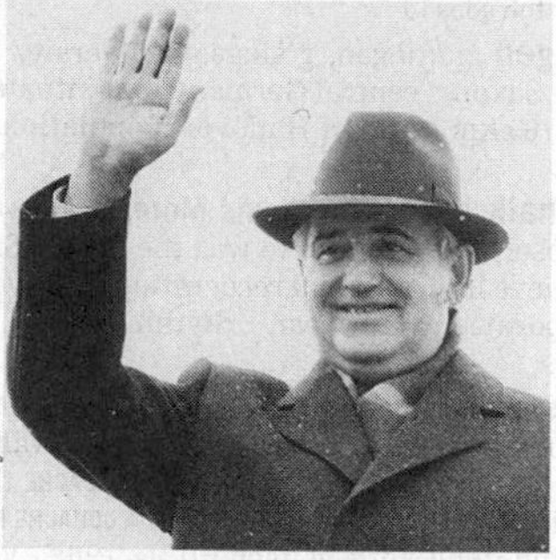

Mikhail Gorbachev

Gor·ba·chev /gáwrbə chàwf/, **Mikhail** (*b.* 1931) Soviet statesman. As general secretary of the Soviet Communist Party (1985–91) and president (1988–91), he initiated democratic reforms that precipitated the disintegration of the Soviet Union and the end of the Cold War. He won the Nobel Peace Prize in 1990. Full name **Mikhail Sergeyevich Gorbachev**

Gor·di·an knot /gàwrdee ən-/ *n.* a problem for which it is very difficult to find a solution [Late 16thC. From the knot of *Gordius*, king of Gordium, that was to be loosened only by the future ruler of Asia: Alexander the Great sliced through it.]

Nadine Gordimer

Gor·di·mer /gáwrdəmər/, **Nadine** (*b.* 1923) South African novelist. Her works examined the tensions of apartheid in South Africa. She won the Nobel Prize in literature in 1991.

Gor·don /gáwrd'n/, **Charles William** (1860–1937) Canadian missionary and novelist. He ministered to the workers in the mines and forests of northwestern Canada and wrote, among other novels, *Black Rock* (1888). Pseudonym **Ralph Connor**

Gor·don set·ter *n.* a gun dog with a long black-and-tan coat, belonging to a breed developed in Scotland [Mid-19thC. Named for Alexander *Gordon*, 4th Duke of Gordon (1743–1827), who promoted the breed.]

gore[1] /gawr/ (**gored, gor·ing, gores**) *vt.* to pierce the flesh of a person or animal with horns or tusks [14thC. Origin uncertain: perhaps a variant of *gore* "spear," from Old English *gār* (source of English *garlic*).]

gore[2] /gawr/ *n.* thick coagulating blood, especially blood shed as a result of violence [Old English *gor* "dirt, dung," from prehistoric Germanic. The meaning "blood" first appeared in the mid-16thC.]

gore[3] /gawr/ *n.* a triangular piece of cloth used, e.g., in making a loose skirt [Old English *gāra*, of uncertain origin] —**gored** *adj.*

Gore /gawr/, **Al** (*b.* 1948) U.S. statesman and vice president of the United States. A Democrat from Tennessee, he was a U.S. representative (1977–85) and senator (1985–93) before becoming Bill Clinton's vice president (1993). Full name **Albert Arnold Gore, Jr.**

Go·ren /gáw ràyn/, **Charles** (1901–91) U.S. bridge player. He invented point-count bidding and wrote a popular newspaper column and many books about contract bridge. Full name **Charles Henry Goren**. Known as **Mr. Bridge**

Gor·gas /gáwrgəss/, **William Crawford** (1854–1920) U.S. physician and army officer. He rid Havana (1898) and the Panama Canal Zone (1904–10) of yellow-fever-carrying mosquitoes, and was the army surgeon general during World War I.

gorge /gawrj/ *n.* **1. NARROW VALLEY** a deep narrow, usually rocky valley **2. CONTENTS OF STOMACH** the contents of the stomach, especially when they are perceived as rising in the throat out of disgust or anger **3.** MIL **ENTRANCE TO OUTWORK** a narrow entrance at the rear of an outwork in a fortification **4. OBSTRUCTION IN PASSAGE** a mass of something obstructing a passage, especially a mass of ice obstructing a river **5. GREEDY EATING** an act of eating greedily and to excess **6. HAWK'S CROP** the crop of a hawk ■ *v.* (**gorged, gorg·ing, gorg·es**) **1.** *vti.* **EAT GREEDILY** to eat something greedily and to excess ○ *They gorged on chocolates.* ○ *They sat at the counter gorging meat and potatoes.* **2.** *vt.* **EAT** to devour something greedily ○ *They sat at the counter gorging meat and potatoes.* **3.** *vt.* = **engorge** *v.* 1 [14thC. From French, "throat," from Latin *gurge* "abyss, whirlpool."] —**gorg·er** *n.*

gor·geous /gáwrjəss/ *adj.* **1. BEAUTIFUL** outstandingly beautiful or richly colored ○ *dressed in gorgeous silks* **2. PLEASING** very pleasant (*informal*) ○ *a gorgeous spring morning* [15thC. From Old French *gorgias* "stylish, elegant," of uncertain origin: perhaps formed from *gorge* "throat" (see GORGE), because the neck can be adorned with stylish things.] —**gor·geous·ly** *adv.* —**gor·geous·ness** *n.*

Gor·ges, Sir Ferdinando (1566?–1647) English soldier and colonizer. He founded two companies (1606–19 and 1620–35) for colonizing lands in present-day Maine.

gor·get /gáwrjət/ *n.* **1.** MIL **ARMOR FOR THROAT** a crescent-shaped piece of armor for protecting the throat **2.** CLOTHES **PART OF NUN'S HEADDRESS** the part of a nun's headdress that covers the neck and shoulders **3.** ACCESSORIES **NECKLACE** a circular or crescent-shaped ornament worn around the neck **4.** ZOOL **COLORED BAND ON THROAT** a band or patch of distinctive color on the throat of a bird or other animal [15thC. From Old French *gorgete*, from *gorge* "throat" (see GORGE).]

Gor·gon /gáwrgən/ *n.* **1.** MYTHOL **GREEK MONSTER** in Greek mythology, a monstrous woman with snakes for hair, who turned those who looked at her into stone **2. gor·gon, Gor·gon TERRIFYING WOMAN** a woman regarded as very frightening or ugly (*insult*) [14thC. From Latin *Gorgon-*, stem of *Gorgo*, from Greek *Gorgō*, from *gorgos* "terrible."]

gor·go·ni·an /gawr gṓnee ən/ *n.* a coral with a flexible horny branched skeleton. Family: Gorgonacea. [Mid-19thC. Formed from modern Latin *Gorgonia*, genus name, ultimately from Latin *Gorgon-* (see GORGON), referring to its power to turn to stone.] —**gor·go·ni·an** *adj.*

Gor·go·ni·an *adj.* relating to or resembling a mythological female monster called a Gorgon

gor·gon·ize /gáwrgə nīz/ (**-ized, -iz·ing, -iz·es**) *vt.* to petrify or mesmerize somebody (*literary*)

Gor·gon·zo·la /gàwrgən zṓlə/, **gor·gon·zo·la** *n.* a moist Italian blue cheese with a strong flavor [Late 19thC. Named for *Gorgonzola*, the Milanese village where the cheese was first made.]

Gor·ham /gáwrəm/ city in southwestern Maine, north of Saco and west of Portland. Population: 12,906 (1996).

go·ril·la /gə rílə/ *n.* **1.** ZOOL **LARGEST APE** the largest ape, native to central Africa, with a relatively short but very powerful body and coarse dark hair. Latin name: *Gorilla gorilla.* **2. THUG** a large or brutal person, especially a hired thug (*informal*) [Mid-19thC. Via modern Latin from Greek *gorillas*, from, ultimately, an assumed African word meaning "wild or hairy man."]

Gor·ki /gáwrkee/ former name for **Nizhni Novgorod**

Gor·ky /gáwrkee/, **Arshile** (1904–48) Armenian-born U.S. painter. His work helped introduce European surrealism into American art and influenced the abstract expressionists. Real name **Vosdanig Manoog Adoian**

Gorilla

gor·mand·ize /gáwrmən dīz/ (**-ized, -iz·ing, -iz·es**) *vti.* to eat food gluttonously [Mid-16thC. Ultimately from French *gourmandise* "gluttony," from *gourmand* (see GOURMAND).] —**gor·mand·iz·er** *n.*

gorm·less /gáwrmləss/ *adj. U.K.* lacking intelligence, common sense, or initiative (*informal*) [Mid-19thC. Variant of *gaumless*, literally "lacking understanding," from *gaum* "understanding, heed," from Old Norse *gaumr* "heed."]

go-round *n.* = **go-around** (*informal*)

gorp /gawrp/ *n.* a snack mixture used especially by hikers and campers, often made of nuts, seeds, dried fruits, and chocolate chips [Mid-20thC. Origin unknown.]

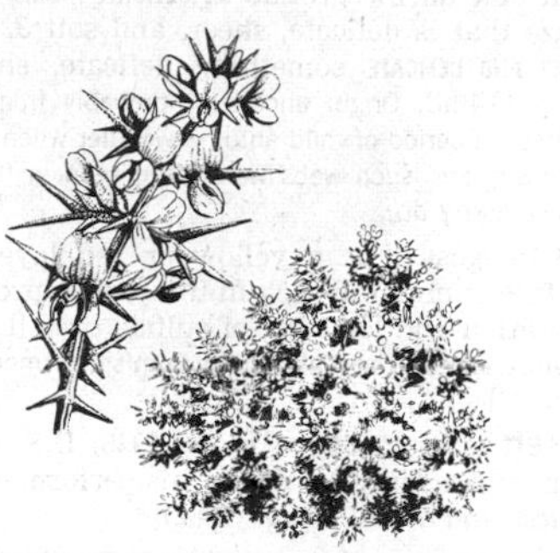
Gorse

gorse /gawrs/ (*plural* **gors·es** *or* **gorse**) *n.* a shrub with fragrant yellow flowers, thick green spines, and black pods. Genus: *Ulex.* [Old English *gors.* Ultimately from an Indo-European word meaning "to be prickly or rough."]

go·ry /gáwree/ (**-ri·er, -ri·est**) *adj.* **1. BLOODY** covered with blood or gore **2. ATTENDED BY BLOODSHED** involving much bloodshed **3. HORRIBLE** arousing horror or terror ○ *the gory details* —**gor·i·ly** *adv.* —**gor·i·ness** *n.*

Gos·ford /góssfərd/ coastal city in eastern New South Wales, Australia, situated 53 mi./85 km north of Sydney. Population: 144,840 (1996).

gosh /gosh/ *interj.* used to express surprise, amazement, or pleasure (*informal*) [Mid-18thC. Substitution for GOD.]

Goshawk

gos·hawk /góss hàwk/ *n.* a large fierce hawk with broad rounded wings and a long tail, found in Europe and North America. Latin name: *Accipiter gentilis.* [12thC. From Old English *goshafoc*, from *gos* + *hafoc*, earlier forms of GOOSE and HAWK.]

Go·shen /góshʹn/ city in northern Indiana, on the Elkhart River, northwest of Fort Wayne and southeast of Elkhart. Population: 24,930 (1996).

gos·ling /gózzling/ *n.* a young goose [15thC. From Old Norse *gæslingr*, from *gas* "goose."]

go-slow *n. U.K.* = **slowdown**

gos·pel /góspəl/ *n.* **1.** SET OF BELIEFS a set of beliefs held strongly by a group or person **2.** ABSOLUTE TRUTH something believed to be absolutely and unquestionably true **3.** = **gospel music**

Gos·pel *n.* **1.** TEACHINGS OF JESUS CHRIST the teachings of Jesus Christ and the story of his life **2.** BOOK OF BIBLE any of one the biblical books Matthew, Mark, Luke, or John **3.** BIBLE EXTRACT an extract from one of the Gospels read as part of a Christian religious service [Old English *gōdspel*, literally "good news," from *gōd* "good" + *spel* "tidings" (see SPELL), ultimately a translation of Greek *euaggelion*]

gos·pel·er /góspələr/, **gos·pel·ler** *n.* **1.** GOSPEL READER somebody who reads the Gospel in a Christian religious service **2.** PREACHER OF THE GOSPEL somebody who preaches the Gospel (*disapproving*)

gos·pel mu·sic *n.* highly emotional evangelical vocal music that originated among African American Christians in the southern United States and was a strong influence in the development of soul music

gos·pel side *n.* in a Christian church, the left side of the altar as faced by the congregation. ◊ **epistle side**

gos·pel truth *n.* = **gospel** *n.* 2

gos·sa·mer /góssəmər/ *n.* **1.** FINE COBWEBS a fine film of cobwebs, often seen floating in the air or covered with dew on the ground **2.** DELICATE FABRIC fabric or gauze that is delicate, sheer, and soft **3.** SOMETHING SHEER AND DELICATE something delicate, sheer, and filmy [14thC. Origin uncertain: probably from GOOSE + SUMMER, a period of mild autumn weather when goose was in season and such webs were often seen in the air.] —**gos·sa·mer·y** *adj.*

gos·san /góss'n/ *n.* a yellow or red layer on the surface of minerals rich in iron oxide, produced by alteration and leaching of sulfide ores [Late 18thC. Origin uncertain: probably from Cornish, formed from *gōs* "blood."]

Gos·sett /góssət/, **Louis, Jr.** (*b.* 1936) U.S. actor. He won an Academy Award for his performance in *An Officer and a Gentleman* (1982).

gos·sip /góssip/ *n.* **1.** CONVERSATION ABOUT PERSONAL MATTERS conversation about personal or intimate rumors or facts, especially when malicious **2.** CASUAL CONVERSATION informal and chatty conversation or writing about recent and often personal events **3.** HABITUAL TALKER somebody given to spreading personal or intimate information about other people ■ *vi.* (**-siped, -sip·ing, -sips**) SPREAD RUMORS to tell people rumors or personal or intimate facts about other people, especially maliciously [Old English *godsibb* "godparent," later "close friend," from *god* "god" + *sibb* "relative" (source of *sibling*). The underlying meaning is "chat with a close friend."] —**gos·sip·er** *n.* —**gos·sip·ry** *n.* —**gos·sip·y** *adj.*

gos·sip col·umn *n.* a regular feature in a magazine or newspaper where rumors and personal or intimate facts about celebrities are exposed —**gos·sip col·um·nist** *n.*

gos·sip·mong·er /góssip mùng gər, -mòng-/ *n.* somebody who is a gossip

gos·sy·pol /góssə pàwl/ *n.* a substance extracted from cotton seeds that has been shown to inhibit the production of sperm and has been studied for possible use as a contraceptive. Formula: $C_{30}H_{30}O_8$. [Late 19thC. Formed from modern Latin *Gossypium*, genus name of the cotton plant, from Latin *gossypion* "cotton tree."]

got past participle, past tense of **get**

Gö·ta Ca·nal /yùrtə-, yṓtə-/ waterway in southwestern Sweden, linking Gothenburg on the western coast with Stockholm on the Baltic coast. Length: 347 mi./558 km.

got·cha /góchə/ *interj.* used to indicate that somebody has been successfully tricked or caught out in some way, or to indicate comprehension of something (*informal*) [Mid-20thC. From a pronunciation of *I got you.*]

goth /goth/ *n.* **1.** SOMEBODY BARBARIC somebody who is uncivilized or barbaric **2. goth, Goth** MUSIC MUSICAL STYLE a style of popular music that combines elements of heavy metal with punk **3. goth, Goth** FASHION FASHION OF DARK CLOTHES AND MAKE-UP a style of fashion popular among men and women in the 1980s, characterized by black clothes, heavy silver jewelry, black eye makeup and lipstick, and often pale face make-up **4. goth, Goth** SOMEBODY FOLLOWING GOTHIC MUSIC AND FASHION somebody who follows gothic music and fashion

Goth *n.* a member of an ancient Germanic people who settled south of the Baltic and from the 3rd to the 5th century founded kingdoms in many parts of the Roman Empire [Old English *gotan* "Goths." From late Latin *Gothi*, of prehistoric Germanic origin.]

Goth. *abbr.* Gothic

Goth·am /góthəm/ *n.* a nickname for New York City

Goth·en·burg /góth'n burg/, **Göt·e·borg** /yṓtə báwree/ seaport and industrial city on the Göta River estuary in southwestern Sweden. It is the second largest city and principal port of Sweden. Population: 449,189 (1995).

goth·ic /góthik/ *adj.* UNCIVILIZED barbarous or uncivilized ■ *n.* **1.** MUSIC, FASHION = **goth** *n.* 2, **goth** *n.* 3 **2.** PRINTING SIMPLE TYPEFACE a simple sans serif typeface with strokes of uniform width **3.** PRINTING HEAVY ANGULAR TYPEFACE a heavy bold angular early typeface —**goth·i·cal·ly** *adv.* —**goth·ic·ness** *n.*

WORD KEY: CULTURAL NOTE

American Gothic, a painting by artist Grant Wood (1930). It portrays an elderly, rather dour farming couple standing in front of a gothic-style farmhouse. Initially criticized as a cruel caricature of country folk, it is now one of the best-known and most popular of all American paintings. A generic term, *American gothic*, came to mean very hard-working, conservative, and rigidly self-disciplined. It is one of the relatively few such terms whose meaning derives not merely from the title of a painting but from the visual representation in the painting.

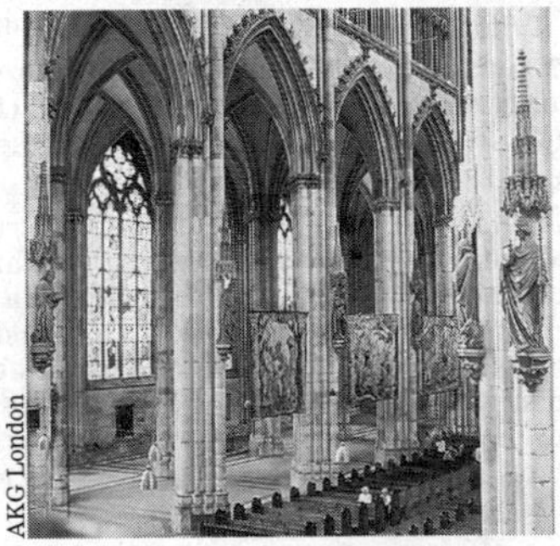

Gothic: Interior of Cologne Cathedral, Germany (begun 1248)

Goth·ic *adj.* **1.** ARCHIT OF MEDIEVAL ARCHITECTURAL STYLE belonging to a style of architecture used in Western Europe from the 12th to the 15th century, and characterized by pointed arches, flying buttresses, and high curved ceilings **2.** ARTS OF MEDIEVAL ARTISTIC STYLE belonging to a style of music, painting, or sculpture practiced in parts of Europe from the 12th to the 15th century **3.** HIST OF MIDDLE AGES relating to the Middle Ages **4. Goth·ic, goth·ic** LITERAT OF EERIE FICTION STYLE belonging to a genre of fiction characterized by gloom and darkness, often with a grotesque or supernatural plot unfolding in an eerie or lonely location such as a ruined castle **5.** PEOPLES OF THE GOTHS relating to or typical of the Goths, or their language or culture ■ *n.* LANG EXTINCT LANGUAGE OF ANCIENT GOTHS an extinct language formerly spoken by the ancient Goths in parts of Scandinavia and around the Baltic Sea. It is one of the East Germanic group of the Germanic branch of Indo-European. —**Goth·i·cal·ly** *adv.* —**Goth·ic·ness** *n.*

Goth·ic arch *n.* a pointed arch, as found in Gothic churches

goth·i·cism /góthi sìzzəm/ *n.* crudeness of style or manner, or an example of crudeness

Goth·i·cism *n.* use of the Gothic style of architecture, art, or literature —**Goth·i·cist** *n.*

Goth·i·cize /góthi sīz/ (**-cized, -ciz·ing, -ciz·es**) *vt.* to make something Gothic in style —**Goth·i·ciz·er** *n.*

Goth·ic Re·viv·al *n.* a style of architecture based on a reintroduction of the Gothic style, popular in the 18th and 19th centuries

Got·land /góttlənd/, **Gott·land** island and county of Sweden, situated in the Baltic Sea about 50 mi./80 km from the mainland. Capital: Visby. Population: 58,120 (1995). Area: 1,212 sq. mi./3,140 sq. km.

got·ta /góttə/ *vi.* used as a written representation of "got to," reflecting popular pronunciation (*informal*) [Early 20thC. From a pronunciation of *got to.*]

got·ten past participle of **get**

WORD KEY: USAGE

See Usage note at ***got***.

göt·ter·däm·mer·ung /gòttər dámmə ròong/, **Göt·ter·däm·mer·ung** *n.* **1.** MYTHOL DESTRUCTION OF GERMAN GODS in Germanic mythology, the destruction of the gods after battle with the forces of doom **2.** VIOLENT END OF REGIME the overthrow or violent ending of a regime or institution [Early 20thC. From German, "twilight of the gods."]

Göt·tin·gen /gúrtingən, gṓtingən/ university town in Lower Saxony, central Germany. It is situated about 55 mi./89 km south of Hanover. Population: 127,900 (1994).

Gott·schalk /góch àwk/, **Louis Moreau** (1829–69) U.S. composer and pianist. He was the first U.S. pianist to achieve international recognition. His own works incorporated Caribbean rhythms and melodic styles.

gouache /gwaash, goo áash/ *n.* **1.** PAINTING TECHNIQUE a method of painting in which opaque watercolors are mixed with gum **2.** PAINT USED IN GOUACHE the paint used in the gouache technique **3.** A GOUACHE PAINTING a painting done with gouache [Late 19thC. Via French from Italian *guazzo*, "puddle," of uncertain origin; probably via Latin *aquatio* from, ultimately, *aqua* "water" (see AQUA).]

Gou·da[1] /góodə/ *n.* a mild Dutch cheese, typically sold in a flattened sphere covered in wax [Mid-19thC. Named for GOUDA, where it is made.]

Gou·da[2] /gówdə, góodə/ city in South Holland Province, western Netherlands. Famous for its cheese, it is situated about 13 mi./21 km northeast of Rotterdam. Population: 69,916 (1994).

Gou·dy /gówdee/, **Frederic William** (1865–1947) U.S. typographer. He created over 100 different typefaces and wrote a number of books, including *A Half Century of Type Design and Typography* (1946).

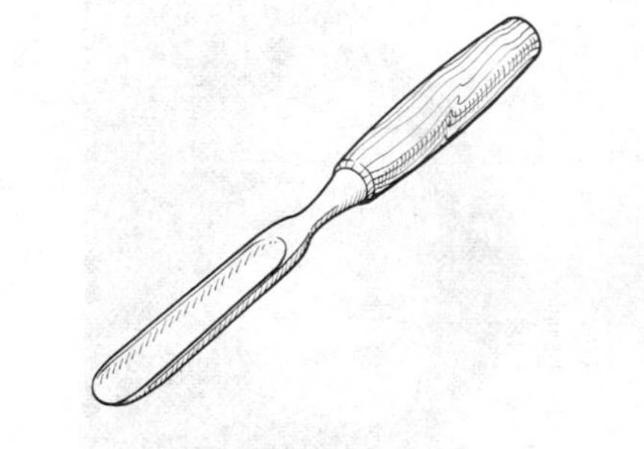
Gouge

gouge /gowj/ *vti.* (**gouged, goug·ing, goug·es**) **1.** CARVE OUT HOLE to cut or scoop a hole or groove in something, usually using a sharp tool **2.** FORM ROUGHLY BY CUTTING to form something by roughly cutting it out of surrounding material **3.** OVERCHARGE SOMEBODY to cheat somebody or act dishonestly by demanding an unreasonably high price for services or goods (*informal*) **4.** INJURE SOMEBODY'S EYE to attack somebody's eye with the thumb ■ *n.* **1.** WOODWORK CHISEL WITH CONCAVE BLADE a chisel with a concave blade used for cutting grooves and holes in wood **2.** SMALL HOLE a mark, groove, or hole, usually made with a pointed tool **3.** ACT OF OVERCHARGING an instance of paying too much or being charged exorbitantly for goods or services (*informal*) **4.** GEOL ROCK FRAGMENTS clay material produced by the grinding together of rock surfaces in a fault or within a mineral vein [Late 15thC. Via French from late Latin *gubia*, variant of *gulbia*, of Celtic origin.] —**goug·er** *n.*

gou·lash /góo laash, -làsh/ *n.* **1.** COOK HUNGARIAN STEW a stew of Hungarian origin, made with beef, veal, lamb, or pork and seasoned with paprika **2.** MIXTURE an eclectic and uncoordinated mixture of something **3.** BRIDGE DEALING OF CARDS a way of dealing cards that have already been arranged in a specific order, without shuffling them first [Mid-19thC. From Hungarian *gulyás*, a shortening of *gulyás hús* "herdsman's meat."]

Gould /goold/, **Morton** (1913–96) U.S. composer and conductor. He used folk and jazz themes in works such as *Fall River Legend* (1948) and the Pulitzer Prize-winning *String Music* (1994).

Gould, Stephen Jay (*b.* 1941) U.S. paleontologist. He helped to originate the "punctuated equilibrium" theory of evolution, and reached a popular audience with his *Natural History* magazine column (1974-).

gou·ra·mi /goo ráamee/ (*plural* **-mi** *or* **-mis**) *n.* a freshwater fish of Southeast Asia, many species of which are capable of breathing air and are often kept in aquariums. Family: Anabantidae. [Late 19thC. Via Malay *gurami* "freshwater carp" from Javanese *graméh.*]

Gourd

gourd /gawrd/ *n.* **1. HARD-SKINNED FRUIT** a hard-skinned fleshy fruit produced by several different plants related to cucumbers and marrows, eaten when ripe or dried and used as decoration, bowls, or cups **2. GOURD-PRODUCING PLANT** a plant that produces gourds [14thC. Via Anglo-Norman *gurde* from, ultimately, Latin *cucurbita* (source also of English *courgette* and *zucchini*).]

gourde /goord/ *n.* **1. HAITIAN CURRENCY UNIT** the basic unit of currency in Haiti. See table at **currency 2. BILL WORTH A GOURDE** a bill worth one gourde [Mid-19thC. Via Haitian Creole from French *gourd* "dull, heavy," from Latin *gurdus* "dolt," later "dull, blunt."]

gour·mand /góor maand, góormənd/ *n.* somebody who loves food and often eats excessively or greedily [15thC. From French, "glutton," of uncertain origin.]

gour·man·dise /góormən deez/ *n.* an appreciation of good food and drink [Mid-16thC. From French, formed from *gourmand* "glutton."]

gour·met /goor máy, góor mày/ *n.* FOOD **FOOD EXPERT** somebody who has an expert knowledge and an enjoyment of good food and drink ■ *adj.* COOK **OF SPECIAL FOOD** relating to or preparing high-quality food that is sophisticated, expensive, rare, or meticulously prepared [Early 19thC. From French, an alteration (influenced by *gourmand* "GOURMAND") of Middle French *groumet* "servant, vintner's assistant," from English *groom.*]

gout /gowt/ *n.* **1. DISEASE CAUSING SWOLLEN JOINTS** a metabolic disorder mainly affecting men in which excess uric acid is produced and deposited in the joints, causing painful swelling, especially in the toes and feet **2. BLOB** a large blob or clot of something, usually of blood [13thC. Via Old French *goute* from Latin *gutta*, literally "drop of liquid"; so called from the idea that gout was caused by drops of a morbid fluid in the blood.]

gout·weed /gówt weed/ *n.* a plant with clusters of small white flowers that is found in Europe and North America and causes problems as a weed in gardens. Latin name: *Aegopodium podagraria.* [From its use in treating gout]

gout·y /gówtee/ (**-i·er, -i·est**) *adj.* **1. WITH GOUT** resulting from or causing gout **2. AFFECTED BY GOUT** affected by or tending to contract gout —**gout·i·ness** *n.*

gov. /guv/ *abbr.* **1.** government **2.** governor

gov·ern /gúvvərn/ (**-erned, -ern·ing, -erns**) *v.* **1.** *vti.* POL **HAVE POLITICAL AUTHORITY** to be responsible officially for directing the affairs, policies, and economy of a state, country, or organization **2.** *vt.* **CONTROL SOMETHING** to control, regulate, or direct something **3.** *vt.* **RESTRAIN SOMETHING** to control something by restraint **4.** *vt.* **HAVE INFLUENCE OVER** to have or exercise an influence over something **5.** *vt.* MECH ENG **CONTROL SPEED OF** to maintain the speed of an engine or keep it from going above a specific level by controlling the fuel or steam supply **6.** *vt.* LAW **BE LAW FOR** to be the defining rule for something **7.** *vt.* GRAM **DETERMINE FORM OF WORD** to dictate the inflection, mood, or case of another word [13thC. Via Old French *governer* and Latin *gubernare* from Greek *kubernan* "to steer" (source of English *cybernetics*), of unknown origin.] —**gov·ern·a·ble** *adj.*

gov·er·nance /gúvvərnəns/ *n.* **1. MANNER OF GOVERNMENT** the system or manner of government **2. STATE OF GOVERNING A PLACE** the act or state of governing a place **3. AUTHORITY** control or authority (*formal*)

gov·ern·ess /gúvvərnəss/ *n.* especially in former times, a woman employed to teach children in their own homes, and sometimes also to care for the children [15thC. From Old French *governeresse*, feminine of *governeour* "governor."]

gov·ern·ment /gúvvərnmənt/ *n.* **1.** POL **POLITICAL AUTHORITY** a group of people who have the power to make and enforce laws for a country or area **2.** POL **STYLE OF GOVERNMENT** a type of political system **3.** POL **THE STATE VIEWED AS RULER** the state and its administration viewed as the ruling political power **4.** POL **BRANCH OF GOVERNMENT** a branch or agency of a government, taken as the whole (*informal*) **5. CONTROL OF SOMETHING** the management or control of something **6.** EDUC **POLITICAL SCIENCE** political science as a subject of study **7.** GRAM **DETERMINATION OF INFLECTION** the determination of the inflection, mood, or case of a word by another word ■ *adj.* **OF GOVERNMENT** relating to or provided by a government, usually a national government —**gov·ern·ment·al** /gùvvərn mént'l/ *adj.* —**gov·ern·ment·al·ly** *adv.*

gov·ern·ment·al·ize /gùvvərn mént'l ìz/ (**-ized, -iz·ing, -iz·es**) *vt.* to put a sphere of activity under the power of the government

gov·ern·ment·ese /gùvvərnmən teez, -teess/ *n.* language that is full of difficult jargon, thought to be typical of language used by government, e.g., in regulations and laws

Gov·ern·ment House *n. Can* in Canada, the official residence of the governor general or, in some provinces, the lieutenant governor

gov·er·nor /gúvvərnər/ *n.* **1.** POL **U.S. STATE EXECUTIVE** the popularly elected executive of state government in U.S. states **2.** POL **GOVERNING OFFICIAL** an appointed or elected official who governs a state, colony, or province for a specified term **3. GOVERNING BODY MEMBER** a member of a governing body of an institution **4.** MECH ENG **REGULATING DEVICE** a device for regulating the speed of an engine **5. AUTHORITY FIGURE** an authority figure such as an employer or boss (*informal*) **6.** *U.K.* CRIMINOL = **warden**

gov·er·nor·ship /gúvvərnər shìp/ *n.* the position, duties, or term of office of a governor

Gov·er·nors Is·land /gúvvərnərz-/ island in New York Bay, just south of the tip of Manhattan Island, that was used as a military post until the 19th century. Area: 175 acres/70 hectares.

govt. *abbr.* government

Gow·er Pen·in·su·la /gòw ər-/ rocky peninsula on the coast of Swansea district, southen Wales. Length: 15 mi./24 km.

gown /gown/ *n.* CLOTHES **1. ELEGANT OR FORMAL DRESS** a woman's full-length elegant or formal dress for special occasions **2. LONG ROBE** a long robe, often dark in color, worn on official occasions by people such as judges, professors, and university graduates **3. LOOSE OUTER GARMENT** a loose cloak or robe such as that worn by surgeons that is worn to protect clothes ■ *vt.* (**gowned, gown·ing, gowns**) **DRESS IN GOWN** to dress somebody in a loose robe [14thC. Via Old French *goune* from late Latin *gunna* "fur or leather garment," of unknown origin.]

gowns·man /gównzmən/ (*plural* **-men** /-mən/) *n.* a man, e.g., an academic who wears a gown for professional reasons

Go·ya /góy ə/, **Francisco de** (1746–1828) Spanish painter. One of the greatest Spanish masters, he was known for his naturalistic tapestry designs, portraits, and several series of satirical etchings, including *The Caprices* (1797–99). Full name **Francisco José de Goya y Lucientes**

GP *abbr.* **1.** MUSIC general pause **2.** MED general practice **3.** MED general practitioner **4.** SPORTS Grand Prix

Gp. *abbr.* STOCK EXCH group

GPA *abbr. U.S., Aus* grade point average

g.p.d., **G.P.D.** *abbr.* gallons per day

g.p.h., **G.P.H.** *abbr.* gallons per hour

Francisco Goya: Self-portrait

g.p.m., **G.P.M.** *abbr.* gallons per minute

GPO *abbr.* Government Printing Office

g.p.s., **G.P.S.** *abbr.* gallons per second ■ *n.* NAVIG **SATELLITE NAVIGATION SYSTEM** a worldwide navigation system that uses information received from orbiting satellites. Full form **Global Positioning System**

WORD KEY: USAGE

See Usage note at ***ATM.***

GPU *n.* the Soviet secret police, from 1922 to 1923. Full form **Gosudarstvennoe politicheskoe upravlenie** [From Russian, "State Political Directorate"]

GQ *abbr.* General Quarters

gr. *abbr.* **1.** grade **2.** grain **3.** gram **4.** gross

Gr. *abbr.* **1.** Greece **2.** Greek

Graaf·i·an fol·li·cle /graafee ən-, gràffee ən-/ *n.* a small fluid-filled sac (**vesicle**) containing a maturing ovum. Graafian follicles are found in the ovaries of mammals. ◊ **ovisac** [Mid-19thC. Named for the Dutch anatomist Regnier de *Graaf* (1641–73), who discovered the vesicles.]

grab /grab/ *v.* (**grabbed, grab·bing, grabs**) **1.** *vt.* **GRASP SOMETHING** to grasp something quickly, suddenly, or forcefully ○ *Grab a pen and sit down.* **2.** *vti.* **TRY TO GRASP** to try to grasp something that is hard to reach or in short supply ○ *Stop grabbing or I won't give you any.* **3.** *vt.* **SEIZE SOMETHING** to take something violently or dishonestly ○ *grab the money and run* **4.** *vt.* **HAVE EMOTIONAL IMPACT ON SOMEBODY** to appeal to, attract, impress, or affect somebody emotionally (*informal*) ○ *The movie didn't really grab me.* **5.** *vt.* **HURRIEDLY GET SOMETHING** to obtain something quickly and without difficulty (*informal*) ○ *I'll just grab a bite to eat.* **6.** *vi.* **TAKE HOLD SUDDENLY** to take hold suddenly or intermittently ○ *The brakes grabbed and the car went into a skid.* ■ *n.* **1. GRABBING** the act of grabbing something ○ *He made a grab at my arm.* **2. SOMETHING GRABBED** something that is grabbed **3. DEVICE FOR GRABBING** an apparatus or device used for grasping hold of something **4. GRABBING ABILITY** the ability or capacity to hold something fast [Late 16thC. Origin uncertain: probably from Middle Dutch or Middle Low German *grabben.* Ultimately from a prehistoric base that is also the ancestor of English *grasp.*] —**grab·ba·ble** *adj.* —**grab·ber** *n.* ◇ **up for grabs** available for the first comer to take or use (*informal*)

WORD KEY: SYNONYMS

See Synonyms at ***catch.***

grab bag *n.* **1. BOX OF OBJECTS** a box full of sealed bags containing unknown objects that can be purchased for a fixed price or are the prize of a party game **2. MISCELLANEOUS COLLECTION** something composed of miscellaneous or mismatched components (*informal*)

grab bar *n.* a bar attached to a wall to provide a grip, e.g., near a bath tub or next to a toilet for people who have difficulty in standing up

grab·ble /grább'l/ (**-bled, -bling, -bles**) *vi.* **1. GROPE AROUND** to scratch or search around with the hands **2. SPRAWL** to tumble or fall to the ground on all fours [Late 16thC. Origin uncertain: probably from Dutch *grabbelen*, from *grabben.*] —**grab·bler** *n.*

grab·by /grábbee/ (**-bi·er, -bi·est**) *adj.* **1. GRASPING** pushy and grasping (*informal insult*) **2. ADHERING** capable of holding fast or adhering (*informal*) **3. DRAWING ATTENTION** drawing people's attention (*informal*) ○ *a grabby headline* **4. OVERTLY SEXUAL** prone to making overt sexual advances (*informal disapproving*) —**grab·bi·ness** *n.*

gra·ben /graàbən/ *n.* a broad valley, especially a rift valley [Late 19thC. From German *Graben*, literally "ditch."]

Gra·ble /gráyb'l/, **Betty** (1916–73) U.S. actor, dancer, and singer. She was a star of musical films in the 1940s. Full name **Elizabeth Ruth Grable**

grace /grayss/ *n.* **1.** ELEGANCE elegance, beauty, and smoothness of form or movement **2.** POLITENESS dignified, polite, and decent behavior ○ *She fended off queries with her usual grace.* **3.** GENEROSITY OF SPIRIT a capacity to tolerate, accommodate, or forgive people **4.** CHR PRAYER AT MEALTIMES a short prayer of thanks to God said before, or sometimes after, a meal **5.** FIN = **grace period 6.** PLEASING a pleasing and admirable quality or characteristic (*usually plural*) **7.** CHR GIFT OF GOD TO HUMANKIND in Christianity, the infinite love, mercy, favor, and goodwill shown to humankind by God **8.** CHR FREEDOM FROM SIN in Christianity, the condition of being free of sin, e.g., through repentance to God **9.** MUSIC = **grace note** ■ *vt.* **(graced, grac·ing, grac·es) 1.** CONTRIBUTE PLEASINGLY to make a pleasing contribution to an event, often by attending it (*often used ironically*) ○ *So good of you to grace us with your presence.* **2.** ADD ELEGANCE to add elegance, beauty, or charm to something **3.** MUSIC ORNAMENT to add ornamental or decorative notes to a piece of music [12thC. Via Old French from Latin *gratia* (source of English *gracious*), from *gratus* "pleasing" (see GRATEFUL).] ◇ **fall from grace** to lose a favored or privileged position ◇ **with (a) bad grace** in a rude bad-tempered way ◇ **with (a) good grace** in a polite and willing way

Grace /grayss/ *n.* used as a title when addressing a duke, duchess, or archbishop

grace cup *n.* a cup of wine or liquor passed around at the end of a meal for a final toast

grace·ful /gráyssfəl/ *adj.* **1.** ELEGANT AND BEAUTIFUL showing elegance, beauty, and smoothness of form or movement **2.** POISED AND DIGNIFIED marked by poise, dignity, and politeness —**grace·ful·ly** *adv.* —**grace·ful·ness** *n.*

grace·less /gráyssləss/ *adj.* **1.** WITHOUT ELEGANCE lacking elegance in form or movement **2.** LACKING DIGNITY bad-mannered and undignified —**grace·less·ly** *adv.* —**grace·less·ness** *n.*

grace note *n.* a note added to a piece of music as an embellishment, usually played quickly before a principal note and written smaller than a normal note on the page

grace pe·ri·od *n.* the extra time allowed before having to pay a debt or complete a transaction

Grac·es /gráyssəz/ *n.* in Greek mythology, three sister goddesses, Aglaia, Euphrosyne, and Thalia, who have the power to grant charm, happiness, and beauty

grac·ile /gráss'l/ *adj.* gracefully slender and slight (*literary*) [Early 17thC. From Latin *gracilis*, of unknown origin.] —**grac·ile·ness** *n.* —**gra·cil·i·ty** /grə síllətee/ *n.*

gra·cious /gráyshəss/ *adj.* **1.** KIND AND POLITE full of tact, kindness, and politeness ○ *a gracious refusal* **2.** CONDESCENDINGLY POLITE condescendingly indulgent and generous to perceived inferiors **3.** ELEGANT AND COMFORTABLE luxurious and elegant ○ *gracious living* **4.** CHR HAVING DIVINE GRACE displaying divine grace, mercy, or compassion ■ *interj.* EXPRESSING SURPRISE used to express surprise, dismay, or indignation [13thC. Via Old French from Latin *gratiosus* "agreeable," from *gratia* "grace" (see GRACE).] —**gra·cious·ly** *adv.* —**gra·cious·ness** *n.*

grack·le /grák'l/ *n.* **1.** N AMERICAN BLACKBIRD a noisy North American blackbird with metallic black plumage and a long keel-shaped tail. Genus: *Quiscalus.* **2.** STARLING a European and Asian starling with mostly black plumage. Genus: *Gracula.* [Late 18thC. Via modern Latin *Gracula*, genus name, from Latin *graculus* "jackdaw." Ultimately from an Indo-European word meaning "to croak," which is also the ancestor of English *crow* and *crane*.]

grad /grad/ *n.* a graduate (*informal*) [Shortening]

grad. *abbr.* **1.** gradient **2.** EDUC graduated

grad·a·ble /gráydəb'l/ *adj.* **1.** ABLE TO BE GRADED capable of being graded **2.** GRAM ALLOWING VARIATION OF DEGREE capable of having a comparative and superlative form —**grad·a·bil·i·ty** /gràydə bíllətee/ *n.*

gra·date /gráy dàyt/ **(-dat·ed, -dat·ing, -dates)** *v.* **1.** *vti.* CHANGE IMPERCEPTIBLY to pass imperceptibly from one shade or degree of intensity to another, or cause something to do this **2.** *vt.* ARRANGE IN DEGREES to arrange something in steps, grades, or ranks [Mid-18thC. Back-formation from GRADATION.]

gra·da·tion /gray dáysh'n/ *n.* **1.** SERIES OF DEGREES a series of gradual and progressive degrees, steps, or stages **2.** SINGLE DEGREE a degree, step, or stage in a gradual progression **3.** DISCRETE ARRANGEMENT the arrangement of something according to size, rank, or quality **4.** COLOR CHANGE the gradual and progressive change from one color or tone to another **5.** PHON VOWEL CHANGE a change in the length or quality of a vowel within a word, signifying a change in function such as tense or number **6.** GEOG LEVELING OF LAND the process of leveling land by erosion or deposition of sediment [Late 16thC. Directly or via French from the Latin stem *gradation-*, literally "making steps," from *gradus* (see GRADE).] —**gra·da·tion·al** *adj.* —**gra·da·tion·al·ly** *adv.*

grade /grayd/ *n.* **1.** EDUC YEAR IN SCHOOL a class or year in a school, especially in the U.S. and Canadian school systems ○ *She'll be in the tenth grade this year.* **2.** EDUC MARK FOR QUALITY OF WORK a mark or rating given for work in school or college, usually using the descending scale of A, B, C, D, and F **3.** LEVEL IN A SCALE OF PROGRESSION a level, step, or stage in a scale of progression, quality, or size (*often used in combination*) ○ *low-grade gasoline* **4.** MARK SHOWING A LEVEL a mark to indicate a level, step, or stage in a process **5.** RANK a rank or class, e.g., in the military **6.** PEOPLE IN RANK a group of people of the same rank **7.** FOOD FOOD CLASSIFICATION a category indicating the relative quality of food as determined by the U.S. Department of Agriculture ○ *grade A eggs* **8.** GRADIENT a gradient or slope, especially on a road or railroad **9.** BUILDING GROUND LEVEL the level at which the ground meets a building ○ *below-grade wiring* **10.** AGRIC MIXED OFFSPRING an animal with one purebred parent and one of unknown breeding **11.** PHON VOWEL FORM a form of vowel morpheme when a vowel varies owing to gradation ■ *vt.* **(grad·ed, grad·ing, grades) 1.** ARRANGE BY DEGREES to arrange or classify things or people according to rank, quality, or level **2.** ASSIGN A GRADE to assign a mark or rating, e.g., to a student's work **3.** TRANSP MAKE A ROAD LEVEL to level a road or railroad by adjusting its gradients **4.** AGRIC IMPROVE A BREED to improve a breed by crossing with a purebred animal [Early 16thC. Via French from Latin *gradus* "step, stage" (source also of English *degree*). Ultimately from an Indo-European base meaning "to walk," which is the ancestor of *progress* and *transgress*).] ◇ **make the grade** to meet the required standard

WORD KEY: ORIGIN

The Latin word *gradus* from which ***grade*** is derived, and its related verb *gradi* "to walk, go," are also the sources of English *aggression, congress, degrade, degree, digress, gradient, gradual, ingredient, progress, retrograde,* and *transgress.*

grade cross·ing *n.* a place where the road crosses the railroad or two rail lines cross at the same level

grad·ed sed·i·ment *n.* a sediment deposited on land or the seabed in which there is an upward gradation of the grains from coarse to fine

grade in·fla·tion *n.* the assignment of higher than deserved grades to students' work in order to compensate for diminishing expectations and falling educational standards (*disapproving*)

grade point av·er·age *n. U.S., Can, Aus* the average of a student's grades over a fixed period, calculated by assigning a value of 4 to A, 3 to B, 2 to C, 1 to D, and 0 to F

grad·er /gráydər/ *n.* **1.** SOMEBODY WHO OR SOMETHING THAT GRADES a person who or machine that grades something **2.** EDUC STUDENT a student in a particular grade in school ○ *first graders* **3.** CONSTR EARTH LEVELER a machine with a wide blade that levels ground, used in road construction

grade school *n.* an elementary or primary school —**grade-school·er** *n.*

grade sep·a·ra·tion *n.* a crossing of roads or railroads requiring an overpass or underpass

gra·di·ent /gráydee ənt/ *n.* **1.** SLOPE an upward or downward slope, e.g., in a road or railroad **2.** STEEPNESS the rate at which the steepness of a slope increases **3.** PHYS MEASURE OF CHANGE a measure of change in a physical quantity such as temperature or pressure over a specified distance **4.** BIOL RATE OF GROWTH any of a series of changes in the rate of growth or metabolism of an organism, cell, or organ **5.** MATH SLOPE ON A CURVE the slope of a line or a tangent at any point on a curve ■ *adj.* SLOPING sloping evenly and uniformly [Mid-17thC. Partly via Latin *gradient-*, the present participle stem of *gradi* "to walk," (from *gradus* "step"; see GRADE), and partly formed from GRADE on the model of "quotient."]

gra·di·ent post *n.* a small post with arms to represent gradients that is used beside a railroad line to indicate where the gradient changes

gra·din /gráyd'n/, **gra·dine** /gráy deen, grə deen/ *n.* **1.** STEP NEAR AN ALTAR a raised step above or behind an altar **2.** STEP ON A SLOPE one of a set of steps arranged on a slope [Mid-19thC. Via French from Italian *gradino*, literally "small step," from *grado* "step," from Latin *gradus* (see GRADE).]

grad·u·al /grájjoo əl/ *adj.* **1.** HAPPENING SLOWLY proceeding or developing slowly by steps or degrees ○ *a gradual improvement* **2.** CHANGING SLOWLY changing slowly ○ *a gradual incline* ■ *n.* CHR **1.** SUNG VERSES in some Christian services, a set of scriptural verses sung after the epistle at Communion **2.** RELIGIOUS MUSIC BOOK a book of music for the sung parts of the Communion Service [15thC. From medieval Latin *gradualis*, from Latin *gradus* "step" (see GRADE).] —**grad·u·al·ness** *n.*

grad·u·al·ism /grájjoo ə lìzzəm/ *n.* **1.** GRADUAL CHANGE the principle, theory, or policy of allowing change, especially political change, to take place gradually rather than suddenly or drastically **2.** GEOL THEORY OF ROCK CHANGE the theory that change in rocks and fossils happens by a gradual historical process —**grad·u·al·ist** *n., adj.* —**grad·u·al·is·tic** /gràjjoo ə lístik/ *adj.*

grad·u·al·ly /grájjoo əlee/ *adv.* in a way that proceeds or develops slowly by steps or degrees

grad·u·ate *n.* /grájjoo ət/ **1.** EDUC SOMEBODY WHO HAS COMPLETED A COURSE OF STUDIES somebody who has obtained a diploma or degree after completing a course of study, e.g., from high school or college **2.** EDUC HOLDER OF A DEGREE somebody who has obtained a bachelor's degree from a college, university, or other higher education institution **3.** SCI CONTAINER WITH MARKINGS a container such as a flask or tube with graduated markings that is used for measuring liquids ■ *v.* /grájjoo àyt/ **(-at·ed, -at·ing, -ates) 1.** *vi.* EDUC FINISH SCHOOL OR COLLEGE to receive a diploma or degree after completing a course of study in a school, college, or university ○ *We both graduated from high school in 1996.* **2.** *vt.* EDUC GIVE A CERTIFICATE to give a diploma or degree to a student completing a course of study **3.** *vi.* MOVE UP to move upward from one level or activity to another ○ *I've graduated from skiing to snowboarding.* **4.** *vt.* MARK WITH DEGREES OR LEVELS to mark something with units of measurement **5.** *vt.* SORT BY DIFFERENCES to sort something into groups according to quality, size, or type ■ *adj.* /grájjoo ət/ EDUC PAST BACHELOR'S DEGREE relating to education for students who have acquired a bachelor's degree —**grad·u·a·tor** *n.*

grad·u·at·ed /grájjoo àytəd/ *adj.* **1.** IN STAGES divided into regular steps or stages **2.** MEASURE MARKED WITH LINES marked with lines to enable measurement **3.** FIN BASED ON INCOME used to describe or relating to a system of taxation under which those with the greatest income or assets pay the highest percentage of tax

grad·u·ate school *n.* a university or university division for advanced students who have obtained a bachelor's degree

grad·u·a·tion /gràjjoo áysh'n/ *n.* **1.** EDUC COMPLETION OF STUDIES the completion of a course of academic study ○ *the number of credits required for graduation* **2.** EDUC DEGREE CEREMONY a ceremony in which degrees or diplomas are awarded to students who have successfully completed their studies ○ *attended her grandson's graduation* **3.** MEASURE MARK ON AN INSTRUMENT a unit of measurement or division marked on an instrument **4.** MEASURE DIVIDING PROCESS the process of marking or dividing something according to quantity or quality

Graec·ism *n.* U.K. = **Grecism**

Grae·cize *vt.* U.K. = **Grecize**

Graec·o-Ro·man *adj.* U.K. = **Greco-Roman**

Graf /graaf/, **Steffi** (*b.* 1969) German tennis player. She turned professional at age 13, and went on to become only the fifth player to win the tennis Grand Slam (1988). She won five singles titles at Wimbledon.

graf·fi·ti /grə feetee/ *n.* drawings or writing that is scratched, painted, or sprayed on walls or other surfaces in public places (*takes a singular or plural verb*) [Mid-19thC. From Italian, plural of *graffito* (see GRAFFITO).]

graf·fi·tist /grə féetist/ *n.* somebody who makes graffiti

graf·fi·to /grə fée tō/ (*plural* **-ti** /-tee/) *n.* **1. WRITTEN MARK ON WALL** an instance of graffiti scratched, painted, or sprayed on a surface (*formal*) **2.** ARCHEOL **ANCIENT INSCRIPTION** an ancient drawing or inscription on a wall or rock surface [Mid-19thC. From Italian, literally "scribbling," via *graffio* "scratching" from, ultimately, Latin *graphium* "stylus," from Greek *grapheion*, from *graphein* "to write" (see GRAPHIC).]

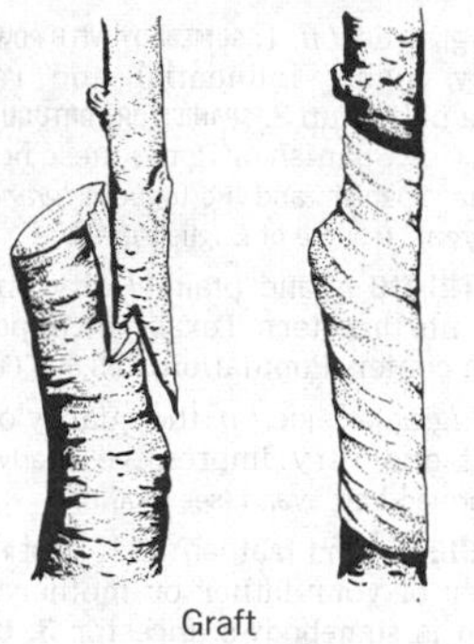

Graft

graft[1] /graft/ *n.* **1.** SURG **TRANSPLANTED TISSUE** a piece of living tissue or an organ that is transplanted to a part of a patient's body, either from a donor or another part of the patient's body. Grafts are used to replace damaged or diseased tissue or organs. **2.** BOT **PLANT TISSUE JOINED TO ANOTHER PLANT** a piece of living tissue from the shoot of a plant that is joined to the stem and root system of another plant, resulting in the growth of a single plant **3.** SURG, BOT **GRAFT LOCATION** the place where tissue is implanted by means of a graft **4.** BOT **GRAFTED PLANT** a plant that is the product of a graft **5. JOINING PROCESS** the process of joining one thing to another ■ *vt.* (**graft·ed, graft·ing, grafts**) **1.** SURG **TRANSPLANT TISSUE** to transplant a piece of living tissue or an organ to a part of a patient's body. The tissue or organ may be either from a donor or from another part of the patient's body. **2.** BOT **UNITE PLANT TISSUE** to join a piece of tissue from a part of one plant to the stem and root system of another plant to produce desirable characteristics such as vigor or resistance to disease in the new plant **3. JOIN DISSIMILAR THINGS** to join two things that do not share a natural relationship or affinity for each other [15thC. Via Old French *grafe* "pencil" (from a perceived similarity with the shoot of a plant), from late Latin *graphium* "writing implement, stylus" (see GRAFFITO).] —**graft·er** *n.*

graft[2] /graft/ *n.* **1. CHEATING BY A CORRUPT INDIVIDUAL** the use of dishonest or illegal means to gain money or property by somebody in a position of power or in elected office **2. MONEY OBTAINED CORRUPTLY** something obtained illegally by taking advantage of high position or office ■ *vti.* (**graft·ed, graft·ing, grafts**) **GET BY DECEIT** to obtain money or property by deceit (*informal*) [Mid-19thC. Origin uncertain: perhaps from GRAFT[1], the underlying idea being "digging."] —**graft·er** *n.*

Gra·ham /gráy əm/, **Billy** (*b.* 1918) U.S. evangelist. A charismatic preacher, he held large-scale evangelistic rallies throughout the United States and Europe after 1949. Full name **William Franklin Graham**

Gra·ham, Katharine (*b.* 1917) U.S. newspaper executive. She was publisher of the *Washington Post* (1969–79). Born **Katharine Meyer**

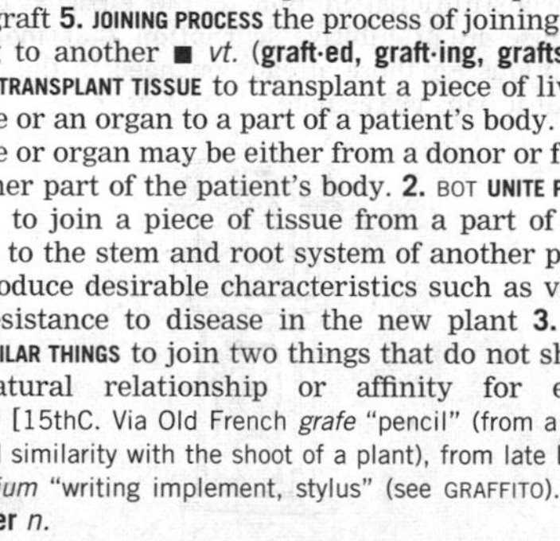

Popperfoto

Katharine Graham

AKG London

Martha Graham: Performing in *Judith* (1957)

Gra·ham, Martha (1893–1991) U.S. dancer, choreographer, and teacher. The most influential figure in modern dance, she created a dance language using flexible movements intended to express emotional power.

gra·ham crack·er /gráyəm/ *n.* a flat dry sweetened cracker, light brown in color and made from graham flour

gra·ham flour *n.* unbolted whole-wheat flour [Named for Dr. Sylvester *Graham* (1794–1851), a North American dietary reformer.]

grail /grayl/ *n.* something that is eagerly sought after

Grail *n.* CHR according to medieval legend, the cup said to be used by Jesus Christ at the Last Supper, and by Joseph of Arimathea to collect his blood and sweat at the Crucifixion. It was sought after by medieval knights. [14thC. Via Old French *grael* from medieval Latin *gradalis* "dish," of uncertain origin.]

grain /grayn/ *n.* **1.** AGRIC **CEREALS** cereal crops **2.** BOT **SMALL SEED** a small hard seed or fruit **3. TINY SINGLE PIECE** a tiny individual piece of something, e.g., sand or salt **4. SMALL AMOUNT** a tiny amount of something ○ *He doesn't have one grain of common sense!* **5. PATTERN IN MATERIAL, ESPECIALLY WOOD** the arrangement, direction, or pattern of the fibers in wood, leather, stone, or paper, typically aligned along a single axis ○ *When painting, follow the grain of the wood.* **6.** MEASURE **UNIT OF WEIGHT** the smallest unit of weight in the avoirdupois (1/7000 pound) and apothecaries' systems (1/5760 pound), equal to approximately 0.065 grams **7.** PHOTOGRAPHY **PHOTOGRAPHIC PARTICLE** any of the small particles in a photographic emulsion that form an image, limiting the extent of possible enlargement **8.** TEXTILES **DIRECTION OF THREADS** the line of the threads in a fabric **9.** INDUST **SIDE OF LEATHER** the side of leather from which hair has been removed **10. BASIC QUALITY** the basic quality or characteristic of something or somebody ○ *firmly set in the grain* **11.** CHEM **SMALL CRYSTAL** a small crystal, especially one forming part of a crystalline solid **12.** SPACE TECH **PROPELLANT FOR ROCKET** a mass of solid propellant for a rocket or missile **13.** CHEM **DYE** red or purple dye made from cochineal insects (*archaic*) ■ *v.* (**grained, grain·ing, grains**) **1.** *vti.* **GRANULATE** to break down into small particles or grains, or make something break down into small particles **2.** *vt.* **MIMIC PATTERN OF WOOD** to paint or stain a material with a pattern similar to wood or leather **3.** *vt.* CRAFT **TREAT LEATHER** to soften or raise the pattern of leather **4.** *vt.* INDUST **REMOVE HAIR** to remove the hair from leather **5.** *vt.* **GIVE A GRAINY APPEARANCE** to give something a rough or granular appearance **6.** *vt.* AGRIC **FEED GRAIN** to feed grain to an animal [13thC. Via Old French from Latin *granum* "seed." Ultimately from an Indo-European word that is also the ancestor of *corn* and *kernel*.] —**grain·er** *n.* ◇ **go against the grain** be contrary to somebody's natural inclinations, wishes, or feelings

WORD KEY: ORIGIN

The Latin word *granum* from which ***grain*** is derived is also the source of English *filigree, garner, granary, grange, granite, gravy, grenade, ingrained,* and *pomegranate.*

grain al·co·hol *n.* alcohol made from a fermented cereal

grained /graynd/ *adj.* having grain of a particular type

grain el·e·va·tor *n.* = **elevator** *n.* 2

Grain·ger /gráynjər/, **Percy** (1882–1961) Australian-born U.S. pianist and composer. His 400 compositions, many based on folk music, include *Green Bushes* (1921) and *Shepherds Hey* (1922). Born **George Percy Grainger**. Full name **Percy Aldridge Grainger**

grains of par·a·dise *npl.* the peppery brown seeds of a West African plant, formerly used in veterinary medicine and for adding piquancy to mulled wine and other drinks *Aframomum melegueta*

grain sor·ghum *n.* a variety of sorghum that is grown for grain or forage

grain wee·vil *n.* a small beetle that feeds on and damages cereal grains. Latin name: *Calendra granaria.*

grain·y /gráynee/ (**-i·er, -i·est**) *adj.* **1.** PHOTOGRAPHY **NOT CLEAR** unclear and poorly defined because of a large grain size or overenlargement **2. RESEMBLING GRAINS** resembling or composed of grains **3. NOT SMOOTH** having a granular rather than a smooth texture **4. LIKE WOOD GRAIN** resembling the grain of wood, leather, stone, or paper —**grain·i·ness** *n.*

gram[1] /gram/ *n.* a metric unit of mass, equal to 0.001 kg or equivalent to approximately 0.035 oz. Symbol **g** [Late 18thC. Via French *gramme* and late Latin *gramma* from Greek *gramma* "small weight."]

gram[2] /gram/ *n.* any of various edible beans, e.g., the chickpea, lentil, or mung bean, used as food [Early 18thC. Via obsolete Portuguese *gram* from Latin *granum* (see GRAIN).]

gram. *abbr.* **1.** grammar **2.** GRAM grammatical

-gram *suffix.* **1.** something written, drawn, or recorded ○ ***trigram*** ○ ***oscillogram*** **2.** a message delivered by a third party ○ ***radiogram*** ○ ***kissagram*** [From Greek *gramma*; related to *graphein* "to write" (see GRAPHIC)]

gra·ma /grámə/, **gram·ma, gra·ma grass, gram·ma grass** *n.* a pasture grass that grows in western North America and South America. Genus: *Bouteloua.* [Mid-19thC. Via American Spanish from, ultimately, Latin *gramen* "grass" (see GRAMINEOUS).]

gram·a·rye /grámmaree/, **gram·a·ry** *n.* magic and enchantment (*archaic*) [14thC. From Anglo-Norman *gramarie* "Latin grammar," a variant of Old French *gramaire* (see GRAMMAR).]

gram at·om *n.* a quantity of a chemical element whose mass in grams is the same as its atomic weight

gram cal·o·rie *n.* = **calorie** *n.* 1

gram e·quiv·a·lent *n.* a quantity of a substance whose mass in grams is the same as its chemical equivalent weight

gra·mer·cy /grə múrsee/ *interj.* (*archaic*) **1. EXPRESSION OF THANKS** used as an expression of thanks **2. EXPRESSION OF WONDER** used as an expression of surprise or wonder [14thC. From Old French *grant merci*, literally "(God give you) great reward."]

gram·i·ci·din /gràmmi síd'n/, **gram·i·ci·din D** *n.* an antibiotic too toxic for internal use but widely sold as an ingredient of various ointments, creams, and eye and ear drops [Mid-20thC. Coined from GRAM-POSITIVE + -CIDE + -IN.]

gra·min·e·ous /grə mínnee əss/, **gram·i·na·ceous** /gràmmə náyshəss/ *adj.* **1. IN GRASS FAMILY** belonging to the grass family **2. GRASSY** resembling grass (*technical*) [Mid-17thC. Via Latin *gramineus* from *gramin-*, the stem of *gramen* "grass, fodder." Ultimately from an Indo-European word meaning "to devour," ancestor also of English *cress, gastric,* and *gangrene*.] —**gra·min·e·ous·ness** *n.*

gram·i·niv·o·rous /gràmmi nívvərəss/ *adj.* that feeds on grass (*technical*) [Mid-18thC. Coined from Latin *gramin-*, the stem of *gramen* "grass" (see GRAMINEOUS) + -VOROUS.]

gram·ma /grámmə/ *n.* BOT = **grama**

gram·mar /grámmər/ *n.* **1. RULES FOR LANGUAGE** the system of rules by which words are formed and put together to make sentences **2. PARTICULAR SET OF LANGUAGE RULES** the rules for speaking or writing a particular language, or a particular analysis of the rules of language ○ *Spanish grammar* ○ *case grammar* **3. QUALITY OF LANGUAGE** the spoken or written form of language somebody uses, as related to accepted standards of correctness **4. GRAMMAR BOOK** a book dealing with the grammar of a language **5. ANALYTICAL SYSTEM** a systematic treatment of the elementary principles of a subject and their interrelationships [14thC. Via

Old French *gramaire* and Latin *grammatica* from, ultimately, Greek *grammatikos*, "relating to letters," from *grammat-*, the stem of *gramma* "written character, letter" (see -GRAM).]

gram·mar·ian /grə máiree ən/ *n.* **1.** GRAMMAR EXPERT somebody who is very skilled in grammar **2.** WRITER ON GRAMMAR a writer on grammar, especially one who espouses prescriptive rules

gram·mar school *n.* an elementary school

gram·mat·i·cal /grə máttik'l/ *adj.* **1.** IN GRAMMAR in or relating to the rules of grammar **2.** CORRECT IN TERMS OF GRAMMAR conforming to the accepted rules of grammar [Early 16thC. Via late Latin *grammaticalis* from, ultimately, Greek *grammatikos* (see GRAMMAR).] —**gram·mat·i·cal·i·ty** /grə màtti kállətee/ *n.* —**gram·mat·i·cal·ly** /grə máttikəlee/ *adv.* —**gram·mat·i·cal·ness** /-ikəlnəss/ *n.*

gram·ma·tol·o·gy /gràmmə tóllәjee/ *n.* the study of writing systems [Mid-20thC. Coined from Greek *grammat-*, the stem of *gramma* "written letter" + -LOGY.] —**gram·ma·to·log·ic** /gràmmətə lójjik/ *adj.* —**gram·ma·to·log·i·cal** /-lójjik'l/ *adj.* —**gram·ma·tol·o·gist** /gràmmə tóllәjist/ *n.*

gram mol·e·cule *n.* a quantity of a molecular chemical compound whose mass in grams is the same as its molecular weight —**gram-mo·lec·u·lar** *adj.*

gram·my /grámmee/ (*plural* **-mies**) *n.* a grandmother (*informal*) (*usually used by or to children*) [Shortening]

Gram·my *tdmk.* a service mark for an award given annually for achievement in the recorded music industry

Gram-neg·a·tive, **gram-neg·a·tive** *adj.* used to describe bacteria that lose the color of a gentian violet stain, used in Gram's method of classifying bacteria

gram·o·phone /grámmə fōn/ *n.* a record player (*dated*) [Late 19thC. Alteration of PHONOGRAM.]

gram·pa /grámpə/ *n.* a grandfather (*informal; usually used by or to children*) [Contraction of GRANDPAPA]

Gram·pi·an Moun·tains /gràmpee ən-/ mountain range in central Scotland that forms a natural division between the Highlands and Lowlands. The highest peak is Ben Nevis, 4,406 ft./1,343 m.

Gram-pos·i·tive, **gram-pos·i·tive** *adj.* used to describe bacteria that retain the color of a gentian violet stain, according to Gram's method of classifying bacteria

gramps /grámps/ *n.* a grandfather (*informal; usually used by or to children*) [From a contraction of GRANDPAPA]

gram·pus /grámpəss/ (*plural* **-pus** *or* **-pus·es**) *n.* a large gray dolphin with a blunt snout, short flippers, and a tall dark gray fin. It is widely distributed throughout warm seas. Latin name: *Grampus griseus.* [Early 16thC. Alteration of Old French *graspeis*, from medieval Latin *crassus piscis*, literally "fat fish."]

Gram's meth·od, **Gram's stain** *n.* a technique used to classify bacteria according to their ability to lose or retain the color of a gentian violet stain, applied within the framework of an established test procedure. The retention or loss of stain indicates a particular cell-wall structure and distinguishes two types of bacteria. [Late 19thC. Named for the Danish physician H. C. J. *Gram* (1853–1938), who developed it.]

gran /gran/ *n.* a grandmother (*informal; usually used by or to children*) [Mid-19thC. Shortening.]

gra·na plural of **granum**

Gra·na·da /grə naadə/ city and capital of Granada Province in the autonomous region of Andalusia, southern Spain. It is the site of the Alhambra, a Moorish palace and citadel. Population: 272,738 (1995).

gran·a·dil·la /grànnə díllə, -dee yə/ *n.* **1.** PLANTS PASSION FRUIT PLANT a tropical passionflower with edible egg-shaped fruit. Latin name: *Passiflora quadrangularis.* **2.** FOOD FRUIT OF THE GRANADILLA the fruit that grows on the granadilla [Early 17thC. From Spanish, literally "little pomegranate," formed from *granada* "pomegranate."]

gran·a·ry /gránəree, gráy-/ (*plural* **-ries**) *n.* **1.** GRAIN WAREHOUSE a warehouse or storeroom for grain **2.** GRAIN-GROWING REGION a region where grain is abundant [Late 16thC. From Latin *granarium*, from *granum* (see GRAIN).]

Gran Cha·co /gran chákō/ thinly populated region in south central South America, extending from southern Bolivia through Paraguay to northern Argentina. Area: 250,000 sq. mi./647,500 sq. km.

grand /grand/ *adj.* **1.** OUTSTANDING outstanding and impressive in appearance, extent, or style ○ *making a grand entrance* **2.** IMPRESSIVE impressive, ambitious, and far-reaching ○ *a grand plan* **3.** WORTHY OF RESPECT worthy of great respect by virtue of exceptional ability or high rank ○ *among the grandest orchestras of our time* **4.** WONDERFUL wonderful, enjoyable, and memorable ○ *We had a grand time.* **5.** PRINCIPAL main or principal ○ *And now we move into the Grand Banqueting Hall* ■ *n.* (*informal*) **1.** MONEY 1,000 DOLLARS a thousand dollars ○ *made ten grand on the deal* **2.** MUSIC = **grand piano** [Early 16thC. Via Old French from Latin *grandis* "full grown," of unknown origin.] —**grand·ly** *adv.* —**grand·ness** *n.*

grand- *prefix.* one generation further removed ○ *grandniece* [From GRAND]

gran·dad *n.* = **granddad**

gran·dad·dy *n.* = **granddaddy**

gran·dam /grán dàm, -dəm/, **gran·dame** /grán dàym, grándəm/ *n.* a grandmother or woman who is no longer young (*archaic*) [13thC. From Anglo-French *graund dame* "grandmother," literally "great lady."]

grand·aunt /grànd ánt/ *n.* = **great-aunt**

grand·ba·by /gránd bàybee/ *n.* a grandchild who is still a baby

Grand Ba·ha·ma /grànd bə haamə/ island of the western Bahamas in the Atlantic Ocean off the eastern coast of Florida. Population: 40,898 (1990). Area: 430 sq. mi./1,114 sq. km.

Grand Banks /-bángks/ shallow section of the Atlantic Ocean, off southeastern Newfoundland, Canada that is an important fishing region. Area: 109,000 sq. mi./282,500 sq. km.

Grand Ca·nal main thoroughfare of Venice, Italy. There are almost 200 palaces on the banks of the canal. Length: 2 mi./3 km.

Grand Canyon

Grand Can·yon /-kánnyən/ spectacular natural gorge carved by the Colorado River in northwestern Arizona. Its width varies from 5 to 18 mi./8 to 29 km, and its depth can exceed 1 mi./1.6 km. Length: 227 mi./443 km.

Grand Can·yon Na·tion·al Park national park in northern Arizona, established in 1919. Its primary feature is the Grand Canyon of the Colorado River. Area: 1,904 sq. mi./4,930 sq. km.

grand·child /gránd chīld/ (*plural* **-chil·dren** /-childrən/) *n.* a child of your son or daughter

Grand Cou·lee Dam /-kooli-/ dam in Washington State on the Columbia River, 90 mi./145 km west of Spokane. Completed in 1942, it is the world's largest concrete structure and a major source of hydroelectric power. Height: 550 ft./168 m.

grand·dad /grán dàd/, **gran·dad** *n.* (*informal*) **1.** GRANDFATHER a grandfather **2.** TERM FOR MAN PAST MIDDLE AGE used as a slightly disrespectful name for a man of advanced years (*is sometimes considered offensive*)

grand·dad·dy /grán dàddee/ (*plural* **-dies**), **gran·dad·dy** (*plural* **-dies**) *n.* **1.** GRANDFATHER a grandfather (*informal*) **2.** FIRST ONE something considered the oldest, first, or most important of its time

grand·daugh·ter /grán dàwtər/ *n.* a daughter of your son or daughter

grand duch·ess *n.* **1.** GRAND DUKE'S SPOUSE the wife or widow of a grand duke **2.** HIGH NOBLEWOMAN a woman who holds a rank just below that of a queen **3.** RUSSIAN PRINCESS in tsarist Russia, a daughter of a tsar, or a daughter of a tsar's descendants

grand duch·y *n.* a country, territory, or estate that has a grand duke or a grand duchess as its ruler

grand duke *n.* **1.** HIGH-RANKING NOBLEMAN a nobleman who holds a rank just below that of a king **2.** RUSSIAN NOBLE in tsarist Russia, a brother, son, uncle, or nephew of a tsar

grande dame /grάnd dàm, graand daam/ *n.* a socially important, dignified, and usually older woman [From French, "great lady"]

Grande Dix·ence Dam /grand dìksənss-/ concrete dam on the Dixence River, southwestern Switzerland. Completed in 1962, it is one of the world's highest dams. Height: 932 ft./284 m.

gran·dee /gran dee/ *n.* **1.** SOMEBODY WITH POWER TO PERSUADE somebody highly influential and respected, especially a politician **2.** SPANISH OR PORTUGUESE NOBLEMAN a high-ranking Spanish or Portuguese nobleman [Late 16thC. Via Spanish and Portuguese *grande* from Latin *grandis* "great" (source of English *grand*).]

Grande Prai·rie /grand práiree/ city on the Trinity River in northeastern Texas, on important manufacturing center. Population: 108,908 (1994).

gran·deur /gránjər, -joor/ *n.* the quality of being great or grand and very impressive [Early 16thC. From French, formed from *grand* (see GRAND).]

grand·fa·ther /gránd faathər/ *n.* **1.** FATHER OF YOUR PARENT the father of your father or mother **2.** ANCESTOR a man who is somebody's ancestor **3.** USED TO ADDRESS MAN used as a name for a man considered to be advanced in years (*dated informal*) ■ *vt.* (**-thered, -ther·ing, -thers**) EXEMPT to exempt somebody from something by means of a grandfather clause —**grandfa·ther·ly** *adj.*

grand·fa·ther clause *n.* **1.** HIST VOTING RIGHTS CLAUSE a clause in some U.S. Southern states' constitutions that waived electoral literacy requirements for descendants of those allowed to vote before 1867, in effect enabling illiterate white people to vote while excluding illiterate Black people. It was declared unconstitutional in 1915. **2.** LAW EXEMPTING CLAUSE a clause in prohibitive legislation that makes exceptions for those already engaged in the activity that it bans or regulates

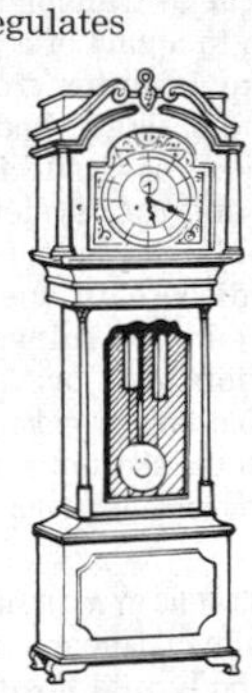
Grandfather clock

grand·fa·ther clock *n.* a large clock in a tall case that stands on the floor. = **longcase clock**

grand fi·nal *n.* the last round in a series of contests, competitions, or sports matches

grand fi·nal·e *n.* the closing spectacular scene or section of a performance or other show

Grand Forks /-fáwrks/ city on the Red River, in eastern North Dakota, north of Fargo. Population: 50,675 (1996).

Grand Gui·gnol /graaN gi nyáwl/ *n.* THEATER a sensational drama, often structured in short scenes with violent or horrific subject matter, that aims to horrify its audience [Early 20thC. From *Le Grand Guignol*, the name of a theater in Paris that specialized in short sensational dramas.] —**grand gui·gnol** *adj.*

gran·dil·o·quence /gran díllәkwəns/ *n.* a pompous or lofty manner of speaking or writing [Late 16thC. Formed from Latin *grandiloquus* "speaking grandly," from *grandis* "great" + *loqui* "to speak."] —**gran·dil·o·quent** *adj.* —**gran·dil·o·quent·ly** *adv.*

gran·di·ose /grándee ōss/ *adj.* **1.** PRETENTIOUS AND POMPOUS pretentious, pompous, and imposing **2.** MAGNIFICENT impressive and magnificent **3.** OVERLY COMPLEX too complicated and unrealistic ○ *a grandiose plan* [Mid-19thC. Via French from Italian *grandioso* "imposing," from *grande* "great," from Latin *grandis.*] —**gran·di·ose·ly**

adv. —**gran·di·ose·ness** *n.* —**gran·di·os·i·ty** /gràndee óssətee/ *n.*

gran·di·o·so /gràndi óssō/ *adj., adv.* in a grand or imposing style (*used as a musical direction*) [Late 19thC. From Italian, "grandly."]

Grand Junc·tion /-júngksh'n/ city in Mesa County, western Colorado, where the Gunnison and Colorado rivers meet. Population: 29,034 (1990).

grand ju·ry *n.* in U.S. and Canadian law, a panel of 12 to 23 jurors called to decide whether there are grounds for a criminal prosecution in a case —**grand ju·ror** *n.*

grand·kid /grán kìd/ *n.* a grandchild (*informal*)

grand lar·ce·ny *n.* a robbery or theft of money or property with a value over the amount specified by law to constitute petit larceny

grand·ma /grán maà/ *n.* a name for a grandmother (*informal*) [Late 18thC. Shortening.]

grand mal /gràn maál/ *n.* a serious form of epilepsy in which there is loss of consciousness and severe convulsions. ◊ **petit mal** [From French, literally "great illness"]

Grand Ma·nan Is·land /-mə nán-/ island at the entrance to the Bay of Fundy in southwestern New Brunswick, southeastern Canada. Area: 53 sq. mi./137 sq. km.

grand mas·ter, **grand·mas·ter** *n.* **1.** CHESS **TOP CHESS PLAYER** a champion chess player who plays at an international level **2. SOMEBODY OUTSTANDING** somebody who is at the highest level of ability or achievement in a particular field **3. GROUP HEAD** a head of a brotherhood of knights, or of a fraternal organization such as the Masons

grand·moth·er /grán mu̇thər/ *n.* **1. PARENT'S MOTHER** the mother of your father or mother **2. ANCESTOR** a woman who is somebody's ancestor **3. USED TO ADDRESS WOMAN** used to address a woman of advanced years (*dated informal*) (*sometimes considered offensive*) —**grand·moth·er·ly** *adj.*

grand·moth·er clock *n.* a clock in a tall case that stands on the floor, smaller than a grandfather clock

grand·neph·ew /gràn néffyoo/ *n.* a son of somebody's nephew or niece

grand·niece /grán neéss/ *n.* a daughter of your nephew or niece

grand old man *n.* a man usually past middle age who is respected for his contribution to some field of activity such as politics, music, or sports ○ *the grand old man of American jazz*

grand op·er·a *n.* an opera on a serious dramatic theme in which all the words are sung and there is no spoken dialogue

grand·pa /grán paà, grám paà/ *n.* (*informal*) **1. GRANDFATHER** a name for a grandfather **2. MAN PAST MIDDLE AGE** a slightly disrespectful name for man of advanced years (*sometimes considered offensive*)

grand·par·ent /grán pàirənt/ *n.* the mother or father of your mother or father —**grand·pa·ren·tal** /grànpə rént'l/ *adj.* —**grand·par·ent·hood** /gránd pàirənt hòod/ *n.*

Grand piano

grand pi·an·o *n.* a large piano in which the strings are fixed horizontally behind the keyboard in a long harp-shaped frame

Grand Pré /gron práy, graaN-/ village in central Nova Scotia, Canada, on Minas Basin, the site of Grand Pré National Historic Park

Grand Prix /gròn preé, gròN preé/ (*plural* **Grand Prix** *or* **Grands Prix** /gròn preé, gròN preé/) *n.* **1. IMPORTANT CAR RACE** any one of a number of important international annual races for racing cars, held to decide the world automobile-racing championship **2. IMPORTANT SPORTS COMPETITION** any one of various competitions in a variety of sports that have the same importance and prestige as a Grand Prix in automobile racing [From French, literally "big prize"]

grand·sire /gránd sìr/ *n.* **1. GRANDFATHER** a grandfather (*archaic*) **2. ANCESTOR** a man who is somebody's ancestor (*archaic or literary*) (*often used in the plural*) **3. MAN PAST MIDDLE AGE** a man of advanced years (*archaic*)

grand slam *n.* **1.** SPORTS **WINNING OF ALL MAJOR COMPETITIONS** in some sports, e.g., tennis and golf, the winning of all of a specified group of major competitions by one player or team in one year **2.** SPORTS **MAJOR COMPETITION** any one of a specified group of major competitions in a particular sport **3.** BASEBALL **4 RUNS** in baseball, a home run made when the bases are loaded **4.** CARDS **WINNING OF ALL TRICKS** in bridge and similar card games, the winning of all 13 tricks in a game by one player or pair of players, or a contract to do so

grand·son /grán sùn/ *n.* a son of your son or daughter

grand·stand /gránd stànd/ *n.* **1. STRUCTURE FOR SPECTATORS' SEATS** an open building or platform, usually with a roof, containing rows of seats for spectators at a sports stadium or racetrack **2. SPECTATORS IN A GRANDSTAND** the spectators sitting in a grandstand ■ *adj.* **UNOBSTRUCTED** clear, close, and unobstructed ○ *We had a grandstand view of the proceedings.* ■ *vi.* (**-stand·ed, -stand·ing, -stands**) **SEEK ATTENTION OR ADMIRATION** to show off in order to impress people, especially spectators —**grand·stand·er** *n.*

grand·stand play *n.* an action or play, e.g., in sports, that is made more elaborate than necessary in order to gain attention or applause

Grand Te·ton Na·tion·al Park /-teét'n-/ national park south of Yellowstone in northwestern Wyoming, established in 1929. The highest peak is Grand Teton, 13,771 ft./4,197 m. Area: 309,994 acres/125,450 hectares.

grand to·tal *n.* a final and complete total of all amounts to be added

grand tour *n.* **1. TOUR OF SEVERAL PLACES** a trip or tour that takes in visits to several places, or a visit that allows a complete inspection of all parts of one place **2. TOUR OF EUROPEAN CITIES** in the past, a tour of the main European cities and cultural centers undertaken by young upper-class Englishmen as a way of completing their education

grand·un·cle /gránd ùngk'l/ *n.* = **great-uncle**

grange /graynj/ *n.* **1.** *U.K.* **LARGE FARMHOUSE** a large farmhouse or country house with other buildings such as stables or barns attached to it **2. GRANARY OR BARN** a large farm building used for storing grain or hay (*archaic*) [13thC. Via French from medieval Latin *granica villa*, literally "grain house" (the original sense in English), from Latin *granum* (see GRAIN).]

Grange *n.* **1. FARMERS' ORGANIZATION** the Patrons of Husbandry, an association of U.S. farmers founded in 1867 for their mutual support **2. BRANCH OF THE GRANGE** a local branch of the Grange —**Grang·er** *n.*

Grange /graynj/, **Red** (1903–91) U.S. football player. Playing mostly for the Chicago Bears during a 10-year career, he was an early popularizer of the professional game, and later became a sports announcer. Real name **Harold Edward Grange**

grang·er /gráynjər/ *n.* a farmer

grani- *prefix.* grain, seed ○ *granivorous* [From Latin *granum* (see GRAIN)]

gran·i·ta /grə neétə/ *n.* a type of sweetened flavored water ice with a grainy texture, sometimes served as a refresher between courses rather than as a dessert [Mid-19thC. From Italian, the feminine form of *granito* (see GRANITE).]

gran·ite /gránnit/ *n.* **1.** MINERALS **COARSE-GRAINED IGNEOUS ROCK** a coarse-grained igneous rock made up of feldspar, mica, and at least 20 percent quartz. It is used extensively in building. **2. TOUGHNESS** determination or toughness of character **3.** SPORTS **STONE USED IN CURLING** the rounded stone used in the sport of curling [Mid-17thC. Via Italian *granito*, literally "grainy," from, ultimately, Latin *granum* (see GRAIN).] —**gra·nit·ic** /grə níttik, grə-/ *adj.* —**gran·it·oid** /gránni tòyd/ *adj.*

Gran·ite City /grànnit-/ city in southwestern Illinois, on the Mississippi River near St. Louis. Population: 31,449 (1996).

Gran·ite Peak /grànnit peék/ mountain in the Northern Rockies of southern Montana, the highest peak in the state. Height: 12,799 ft./3,901 m.

gran·ite·ware /gránnit wàir/ *n.* **1. SPECKLED POTTERY** a type of earthenware with a speckled glaze that gives it the appearance of granite **2. SPECKLED IRON DISHES** iron articles, e.g., pots and bowls, coated with a glaze that gives a finish with the appearance of granite

gra·niv·o·rous /grə nívvərəss/ *adj.* ZOOL that eats seeds

gran·ny /gránnee/ (*plural* **-nies**), **gran·nie** *n.* **1. GRANDMOTHER** a grandmother (*informal*) **2. WOMAN OF ADVANCED YEARS** a slightly disrespectful name for a woman of advanced years **3. FUSSY PERSON** an annoyingly fastidious or fussy person (*insult*) **4.** *Southern U.S.* **MIDWIFE** a nurse or midwife **5.** = **granny knot** [Mid-17thC. Shortening of *grannam*, a common pronunciation of GRANDAM.]

gran·ny dress *n.* a type of long dress in a style considered to have been worn by earlier generations of women that was popular in the late 1960s and early 1970s

gran·ny dump·ing *n.* the abandonment of a senior citizen who is in deteriorating mental or physical health by a family member or members in a public place (*disapproving*)

gran·ny flat *n.* *U.K.* = **mother-in-law apartment**

gran·ny gear *n.* the lowest gear on a bicycle that makes it possible to pedal up steep inclines (*informal*)

gran·ny glass·es *npl.* eyeglasses consisting of small lenses set in gold or steel frames

gran·ny knot *n.* a square knot incorrectly tied and therefore likely to come apart

Gran·ny Smith *n.* a type of eating apple with green skin and crisp white flesh [Late 19thC. From the nickname of Maria Ann *Smith* (1801 70), who first grew the apple in her garden in Sydney, Australia.]

gran·ny specs *npl.* = **granny glasses** (*informal*)

grano- *prefix.* granite ○ *granolith* [Via German from, ultimately, Italian *granito* (see GRANITE)]

gran·o·di·or·ite /grànnō dí ə rìt/ *n.* a coarse-grained igneous rock containing plagioclase and orthoclase, whose composition is intermediate between granite and diorite —**gran·o·di·or·it·ic** /grànnō dì ə ríttik/ *adj.*

gra·no·la /grə nṓlə/ *n.* a breakfast cereal consisting of rolled oats mixed with other ingredients such as brown sugar, dried fruit, nuts, honey, and sesame seeds [Early 20thC. Originally a trade name.]

gran·o·lith /gránnə lìth/ *n.* a paving material made from cement and granite chips —**gran·o·lith·ic** /grànnə líthik/ *adj.*

gran·o·phyre /gránnə fìr/ *n.* a medium-grained light-colored igneous rock consisting mainly of crystals of feldspar and quartz that have crystallized together [Late 19thC. From German *Granophyr*, from *Granit* "granite" + *Porphyr* "porphyry."] —**gran·o·phyr·ic** /grànnə feérik/ *adj.*

Gran Pa·ra·di·so /gram pàrrə deézō/ mountain in the Western Alps, northern Italy, situated within the Gran Paradiso National Park. Height: 13,323 ft./4,061 m.

grant /grant/ *vt.* (**grant·ed, grant·ing, grants**) **1. COMPLY WITH A REQUEST** to carry out or comply with a request for something **2. ALLOW SOMETHING AS A FAVOR OR PRIVILEGE** to give somebody something or allow somebody to have something, especially as a favor or privilege ○ *She refused to grant any interviews.* **3. AGREE THE TRUTH OF SOMETHING** to acknowledge that what somebody else has said, or what a person thinks somebody else is thinking, is true **4.** LAW **TRANSFER SOMETHING LEGALLY** to transfer property or rights in a legal transaction ■ *n.* **1. MONEY GIVEN FOR A PURPOSE** a sum of money given by the government or some other organization to fund such things as education or research **2. GIFT** anything that is given to somebody as a favor or privilege, or the giving of it ○ *a land grant* **3.** LAW **LEGAL TRANSACTION** something transferred from one person to another in a legal transaction, or the transaction itself **4.** LAW **TRANSFER DOCUMENT** a legal document recording a transaction in which something is transferred from one person to another **5. AREA OF LAND** a land division in New Hampshire, Maine, or Vermont [13thC. From Old French *granter,* a variant of *creanter* "to guarantee," via assumed Vulgar Latin *credentare* from, ultimately, Latin *credere* (see CREDIBLE).] —**grant·a·ble** *adj.* —**grant·er** *n.* ◇ **take somebody for granted** to fail to realize or appreciate the value of somebody ◇ **take something for granted 1.** to assume that something is true without checking **2.** to fail to appreciate or realize the value of something

WORD KEY: SYNONYMS

See Synonyms at ***give.***

Grant /grant/, **Cary** (1904–86) British-born U.S. movie actor. He was a sophisticated leading man in movies including *The Philadelphia Story* (1940) and *North by Northwest* (1959). Real name **Alexander Archibald Leach**

Grant, Cuthbert (1793–1854) Canadian fur trader. He led the Metis attack on the Hudson's Bay Company's settlers at Seven Oaks (1816), the site of present-day Winnipeg.

Ulysses S. Grant

Grant, Ulysses S. (1822–85) U.S. statesman and 18th President of the United States. As the Union army's greatest general, he led his troops to victory in the Civil War. His Republican administration (1869–77) is regarded as one of the most corrupt in U.S. history. Full name **Hiram Ulysses Simpson Grant**

grant·ed /grántəd/ *adv., conj.* used when acknowledging the truth of something somebody has said or is thinking

grant·ee /gran tée/ *n.* somebody to whom something is transferred in a legal transaction

Granth /graanth, granth/ *n.* one of the sacred scriptures of Sikhism [Late 18thC. Via Hindi from Sanskrit *granthaḥ* "book," literally "binding."]

grant-in-aid (*plural* **grants-in-aid**) *n.* a sum of money given as funding by a federal government to a state or local government, or by federal or local government to a department or institution

gran·tor /grántər, grán tàwr/ *n.* somebody from whom something is transferred in a legal transaction

grants·man /grántsmən/ (*plural* **-men** /-mən/) *n.* somebody who is skilled in obtaining grants, particularly for research —**grants·man·ship** *n.*

gran·u·lar /grànnyələr/ *adj.* **1. MADE UP OF GRAINS** consisting of small grains or particles **2. WITH TEXTURE OF GRANULES** appearing to consist of or be covered in small grains or particles **3. DIVISIBLE** made up of conveniently small and independent parts ○ *a granular interface* [Late 18thC. Formed from late Latin *granulum* (see GRANULE).] —**gran·u·lar·i·ty** /grànnyə lérratee/ *n.* —**gran·u·lar·ly** /grànnyələrlee/ *adv.*

gran·u·late /grànnyə làyt/ (**-lat·ed, -lat·ing, -lates**) *v.* **1.** *vti.* **MAKE INTO SMALL PARTICLES** to form or cause something to form into small grains or particles **2.** *vti.* **BECOME OR MAKE GRAINY IN TEXTURE** to become rough and grainy in texture or appearance, or give something a rough and grainy texture or appearance **3.** *vi.* MED **FORM HEALING WOUND TISSUE** to form the type of tissue that grows over healing wounds (**granulation tissue**) [Mid-17thC. Formed from late Latin *granulum* (see GRANULE).] —**gran·u·la·tive** *adj.* —**gran·u·la·tor** *n.*

gran·u·lat·ed sug·ar *n.* white sugar in the form of a coarse powder with large particles

gran·u·la·tion /grànnyə láysh'n/ *n.* **1. MAKING OF SMALL PARTICLES** the formation of small grains or particles **2. GRAINY TEXTURE** a grainy texture or appearance **3. SMALL LUMP** any one of the individual small lumps that, together, give something a rough grainy texture or appearance **4.** MED **FORMATION OF TISSUE OVER HEALING WOUND** the formation of the type of tissue that grows over healing wounds (**granulation tissue**) or the tissue itself **5.** ASTRON **CELLULAR APPEARANCE OF SUN'S SURFACE** the cellular appearance of the Sun's disk when seen at high magnification [Early 17thC. Formed from late Latin *granulum* (see GRANULE).]

gran·u·la·tion tis·sue *n.* connective tissue in the form of small grainy particles along with masses of tiny blood vessels that forms over healing wounds

gran·ule /grán yool/ *n.* **1. SMALL PARTICLE** a small grain or particle **2.** GEOL **SMALL ROCK FRAGMENT** a mineral or rock particle that is the size of a small grain **3.** ASTRON **TEMPORARY BRIGHT REGION ON SUN'S SURFACE** a temporary bright region on the Sun's surface, typically having an approximate diameter of 320 mi./1,000 km [Mid-17thC. From late Latin *granulum,* literally "small seed," from Latin *granum* (see GRAIN).]

gran·u·lite /grànnyə lìt/ *n.* a coarse-grained metamorphic rock in which the minerals are of roughly equal size —**gran·u·lit·ic** /grànnyə líttik/ *adj.*

gran·u·lo·cyte /grànnyə lō sìt/ *n.* a white blood cell that contains many granular particles in its cytoplasm —**gran·u·lo·cyt·ic** /grànnyə lō síttik/ *adj.*

gran·u·lo·ma /grànnyə lṓmə/ (*plural* **-mas** *or* **-ma·ta** /-lṓmətə/) *n.* a small mass of granulation tissue caused by chronic infection —**gran·u·lo·ma·tous** *adj.*

gran·u·lose /grànnyə lòss/ *adj.* **1. MADE UP OF SMALL PARTICLES** consisting of small grains or particles **2. WITH THE TEXTURE OF GRANULES** appearing to consist of or be covered in small grains or particles

gran·u·lo·sis /grànnyə lṓssiss/ *n.* a virus disease affecting insect larvae in which the infected cells contain tiny granular particles

gra·num /gráynəm/ (*plural* **-na** /gráynə/) *n.* a stack of thin layers in a chloroplast in which the green pigment chlorophyll is contained [Late 19thC. Via German from Latin, "seed" (see GRAIN).]

Grape

grape /grayp/ *n.* **1. FRUIT OF THE GRAPE VINE** an edible green or purple berry with sweet juicy flesh that grows in bunches on a vine. It may be eaten fresh or used to make wine or grape juice. Raisins, sultanas, and currants are dried grapes. **2. BERRY-PRODUCING PLANT** a woody vine that produces grapes. Genus: *Vitis.* **3. PLANT WITH FRUIT RESEMBLING GRAPES** a plant that produces fruit resembling grapes in some way ○ *Oregon grape* **4.** BEVERAGES **WINE** the drink wine (*humorous*) **5.** ARMS = **grapeshot 6.** COLORS **DARK PURPLE COLOR** a dark purple color ■ *adj.* COLORS **DARK PURPLE IN COLOR** of a dark purple color [13thC. From Old French, "bunch of grapes," ultimately from a prehistoric Germanic word meaning "hook" (as used to harvest grapes), which was also the ancestor of English *cramp, crimp,* and *grapnel.*]

WORD KEY: CULTURAL NOTE

The Grapes of Wrath, a novel by writer John Steinbeck (1939). A sympathetic portrayal of the plight of the rural poor during the Depression and an attack on capitalism it tells of the tribulations suffered by the Joad family when they leave drought-stricken Oklahoma in search of work. It was made into a film by John Huston in 1940.

grape fern *n.* any one of various ferns with fronds that bear clusters of spore capsules similar to grapes. Genus: *Botrychium.*

grape·fruit /gráyp froot/ (*plural* **-fruits** *or* **-fruit**) *n.* **1. LARGE YELLOW OR PINKISH CITRUS FRUIT** a large round yellow or pinkish citrus fruit with very tart juicy edible flesh **2. CITRUS TREE** an evergreen tree, related to oranges and lemons, that has dense dark green foliage, large white flowers, and produces grapefruit. Latin name: *Citrus paradisi.* [Early 19thC. Probably so called because the fruit grows in bunches, like grapes.]

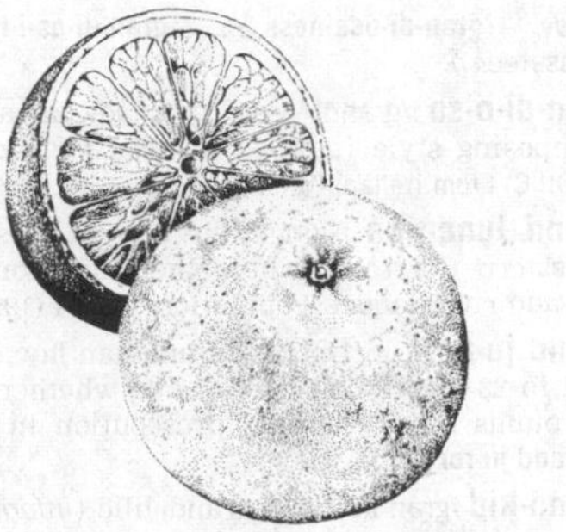

Grapefruit

grape hy·a·cinth *n.* a perennial plant belonging to the lily family with dense clusters of cup-shaped, usually blue, flowers. Genus: *Muscari.*

grape i·vy *n.* a South American evergreen climbing plant commonly kept as a house plant. Latin name: *Rhoicissus rhomboidea.*

grape·shot /gráyp shòt/ *n.* a number of small iron balls fired simultaneously from a cannon in order to kill enemy soldiers [From the resemblance of the bunches of shot to a cluster of grapes]

grape sug·ar *n.* a fruit sugar obtained from grapes

grape·vine /gráyp vìn/ *n.* **1.** = **grape** *n.* 2 **2. PATH ALONG WHICH INFORMATION SPREADS** the path of communication along which news, gossip, or rumor passes unofficially from person to person within a group, organization, or community (*informal*) ○ *I heard through the office grapevine that she was leaving.*

grap·ey /gráypee/ (**-i·er, -i·est**), **grap·y** (**-i·er, -i·est**) *adj.* looking or tasting like a grape or grapes —**grap·i·ness** *n.*

graph[1] /graf/ *n.* **DIAGRAM SHOWING VARYING QUANTITIES** a diagram used to indicate relationships between two or more variable quantities. The quantities are measured along two axes, usually at right angles. A graph may consist, e.g., of a line joining points plotted between coordinates, a series of parallel bars or boxes, or a circle divided into wedges. ■ *vt.* (**graphed, graph·ing, graphs**) **PUT DATA ON A GRAPH** to represent data by means of a graph, or add data to a graph [Late 19thC. Shortening of *graphic formula.*]

graph[2] /graf/ *n.* a symbol, letter, or combination of letters used in writing to represent the smallest discrete unit of speech [Mid-20thC. From Greek *graphē* (see GRAPHIC).]

graph- *prefix.* = **grapho-** (*used before vowels*)

-graph *suffix.* **1.** something written or drawn ○ *digraph* ○ *zincograph* **2.** an instrument for writing, drawing, or recording ○ *pantograph* ○ *seismograph* [Via French from, ultimately, Greek *graphein* "to write" (see GRAPHIC)]

graph·eme /grá feem/ *n.* any of a set of written symbols, letters, or combinations of letters that represent the same sound, e.g., f in "fat," ph in "photo," and gh in "tough" —**gra·phe·mic** /gra féemik/ *adj.* —**gra·phe·mi·cal·ly** *adv.*

gra·phe·mics /gra féemiks/ *n.* = **graphology** *n.* 2 (*takes a singular verb*)

-grapher *suffix.* one who writes, draws, or records ○ *calligrapher* ○ *cinematographer* [Formed from late Latin *-graphus,* via Greek *-graphos* from *graphein* "to write" (see GRAPHIC)]

graph·ic /gráffik/ *adj.* **1. VIVIDLY DETAILED** including a number of vivid descriptive details, especially exciting or unpleasant ones ○ *her graphic description of the accident* **2. SHOWN IN WRITING** representing something such as a sound by means of letters or other written symbols. "Moo," "woof," and "meow" are graphic representations of the sounds made by cows, dogs, and cats respectively. **3. SHOWN IN PICTURES** representing something in the form of pictures or images **4.** MATH **RELATING TO GRAPHS** given in the form of a graph or diagram, or relating to graphs or diagrams **5. OF GRAPHIC ARTS** relating to the graphic arts **6. OF GRAPHICS** relating to graphics **7.** GEOL **CONTAINING CRYSTALS LIKE LETTERS** containing crystal structures that resemble letters ■ *n.* (*often used in the plural*) **1.** COMPUT **PICTURE PRODUCED BY COMPUTER** a picture, design, or visual display of data produced by a computer program **2.** PUBL **BOOK ILLUSTRATION** an illustration or diagram in a book or magazine **3.** CINEMA, TV **DISPLAYED TEXT OR DRAWING IN MOVIE** any part of a movie that consists of illustration and text, e.g., titles, credits, or drawings [Mid-18thC. Via Latin from, ultimately, Greek *graphein* "to write." Ultimately from an Indo-European word meaning "to scratch," which is also the ancestor of English *carve*.] —**graph·i·cal·ly** *adv.* —**graph·ic·ness** *n.*

graph·i·ca·cy /gráffikəssee/ *n.* the ability to use and understand such things as symbols, diagrams, plans, and maps [Mid-20thC. Formed from GRAPHIC, on the model of *literacy*.]

graph·i·cal /gráffik'l/ *adj.* MATH = **graphic** *adj.* 4

graph·i·cal us·er in·ter·face *n.* a user interface on a computer that relies on icons, menus, and a mouse rather than typing in commands

graph·ic arts *npl.* any of the artistic processes such as drawing, calligraphy, engraving, and printmaking that are based on the use of lines rather than color —**graph·ic art·ist** *n.*

graph·ic de·sign *n.* the art of integrating text, typography, and illustrations in the production of books and magazines —**graph·ic de·sign·er** *n.*

graph·ic e·qual·iz·er *n.* a device, e.g., on a radio or CD player, that allows adjustments to be made to the strength of sounds of different frequencies. The variable levels of the sounds are often displayed electronically in graphical format.

graph·ic nov·el *n.* a fictional story for adults published in the form of a comic book

graph·ics /gráffiks/ *n.* (*takes a singular verb*) **1. DIAGRAMS AND ILLUSTRATIONS** the presentation of information in the form of diagrams and illustrations as opposed to words and numbers **2.** COMPUT **DISPLAY OF COMPUTER DATA AS SYMBOLS** the art and science of storing, manipulating, and displaying computer data in the form of pictures, diagrams, graphs, or symbols **3.** ARCHIT, ENG **MATHEMATICAL DRAWING** the science of drawing something in accordance with mathematical principles, e.g., in architecture and engineering ■ *npl.* ARTS = **graphic arts**

graph·ics tab·let *n.* a device consisting of an electronic pen and an electronically sensitive surface, used to enter pictures or designs into a computer by drawing them

graph·ite /grá fīt/ *n.* a soft, dark gray or black form of carbon that occurs naturally as a mineral and is also produced industrially. It conducts electricity. Graphite is used in batteries, lubricants, polishes, electric motors, nuclear reactors, and carbon fibers, and, mixed with clay, is the lead of pencils. [Late 18thC. From German *Graphit*, from Greek *graphein* "to write" (see GRAPHIC).] —**gra·phit·ic** /gra fíttik/ *adj.*

graph·i·tize /gráffi tīz/ (**-tized, -tiz·ing, -tiz·es**) *vt.* **1. MAKE INTO GRAPHITE** to convert something into graphite **2. COVER OR COMBINE WITH GRAPHITE** to coat something with graphite, or mix graphite into it —**graph·i·tiz·a·ble** *adj.* —**graph·i·ti·za·tion** /gràffiti záysh'n/ *n.*

gra·phol·o·gy /gra fólləjee/ *n.* **1. STUDY OF HANDWRITING** the study of handwriting, especially in order to make an assessment of an individual's personality from characteristic patterns or features of his or her writing **2.** LING **LINGUISTIC STUDY OF WRITING** the study of writing systems and their relationship to the sound systems of languages —**graph·o·log·i·cal** /gràffə lójjik'l/ *adj.* —**gra·phol·o·gist** /gra fólləjist/ *n.*

graph pa·per *n.* paper on which a series of usually equally or logarithmically spaced vertical and horizontal intersecting lines has been imprinted to facilitate the drawing of graphs and diagrams

-graphy *suffix.* **1.** a method of writing or making an image by means of a particular process or technique ○ *chirography* ○ *radiography* **2.** writing about or study of a particular subject ○ *biography* ○ *ethnography* [Via Latin *-graphia* from, ultimately, Greek *graphein* "to write" (see GRAPHIC)]

grap·nel /grápnəl/ *n.* **1. DEVICE WITH HOOKS** a device consisting of an iron shaft with several hooks at one end and a rope at the other by which it can be thrown to attach itself to something **2.** NAUT **ANCHOR FOR A SMALL BOAT** an anchor with three or more arms, especially one for anchoring a small boat [14thC. Via Anglo-Norman from Old French *grapon*, from *grape* "hook" (see GRAPE).]

grap·pa /graápə/ (*plural* **-pas** *or* **-pa**) *n.* an Italian brandy that is distilled from what remains of grapes after they have been pressed for winemaking [Late

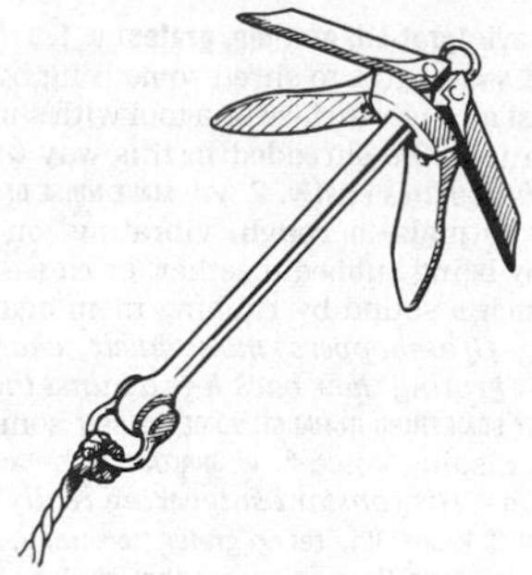

Grapnel

19thC. From Italian, literally "grape stalk, brandy." Ultimately from a prehistoric Germanic word that is also the ancestor of English *grape*.]

Grap·pel·li /grə péllee/, **Stephane** (1908–97) French musician, known for his playing of the violin in the jazz style.

Stephane Grappelli

grap·ple /grápp'l/ *v.* (**-pled, -pling, -ples**) **1.** *vi.* **SEIZE AND STRUGGLE WITH SOMEBODY** to grab hold of somebody and struggle with him or her in a hand-to-hand fight **2.** *vi.* **STRUGGLE TO DEAL WITH SOMETHING** to struggle with something that is difficult to deal with, e.g., a problem that is difficult to solve or a concept or theory that is difficult to grasp **3.** *vt.* **GRAB SOMEBODY** to grab hold of somebody **4.** *vt.* **HOLD SOMETHING WITH A HOOKED DEVICE** to hook or hold something with a grapnel or other hooked device ■ *n.* **1.** = **grapnel** *n.* 1 **2. STRUGGLE** a close struggle **3.** WRESTLING **GRIP OR HOLD** in wrestling, a grip or hold on an opponent [14thC. From Old French *grapil*, literally "small hook," from *grape* "hook" (see GRAPE).]

grap·pler /grápplər/ *n.* a wrestler (*informal*)

grap·pling /grápplìng/ *n.* = **grapnel** *n.* 1

grap·pling i·ron, grap·pling hook *n.* = **grapnel**

grap·to·lite /gráptə līt/ *n.* any one of various small floating sea animals that lived in colonies that existed between about 550 million and 325 million years ago and are now found as fossils. Graptolite fossils are often used to date rocks. Orders: Graptoloidea and Dendroidea. [Mid-19thC. Coined from Greek *graptos* (the past participle of *graphein* "to write"; see GRAPHIC) + -LITH. So called because their fossils leave marks like pencil marks on the surrounding rocks.]

grap·y *adj.* = **grapey**

GRAS *abbr.* generally recognized as safe (*used on food labels to show that the ingredients are not harmful to human beings*)

grasp /grasp/ *v.* (**grasped, grasp·ing, grasps**) **1.** *vt.* **TAKE HOLD OF SOMETHING** to take hold of somebody or something firmly, especially with the hand or hands **2.** *vi.* **TRY TO TAKE HOLD OF SOMETHING** to attempt to take hold of somebody or something, especially with the hand or hands ○ *he grasped at the rope* **3.** *vt.* **HOLD SOMETHING** to hold something, especially in the hand or hands **4.** *vt.* **TAKE AN OPPORTUNITY** to take the opportunity to do something when it arises **5.** *vi.* **TRY TO TAKE OPPORTUNITY** to attempt to take the opportunity to do something when it arises **6.** *vt.* **UNDERSTAND SOMETHING** to manage to understand something ○ *I just can't grasp what you're getting at.* ■ *n.* **1. HAND GRIP** a hold or grip, especially in the hand or hands **2. UNDERSTANDING** somebody's understanding of something, or his or her ability to understand something ○ *a poor grasp of the facts* **3. ABILITY TO ACHIEVE SOMETHING** ability to achieve or get something ○ *Success was within her grasp.* **4. CONTROL** power or control ○ *in the tyrant's grasp* [14thC. Origin uncertain; ultimately from a prehistoric Germanic word that is also the ancestor of English *grab*.] —**grasp·a·ble** *adj.*

WORD KEY: SYNONYMS

See Synonyms at ***catch***.

grasp·er /gráspər/ *n.* **1. GREEDY PERSON** somebody who is greedy for money **2. SOMEBODY WHO GRASPS** somebody who grasps something

grasp·ing /grásping/ *adj.* greedy for money —**grasp·ing·ly** *adv.* —**grasp·ing·ness** *n.*

Grass: Annual meadow grass

grass /grass/ *n.* **1.** (*plural* **grass·es** *or* **grass**) **GREEN PLANT THAT FORMS LAWNS** a low green narrow-leaved plant that grows in fields and gardens, is eaten by animals such as cows and sheep, and is used to make lawns and playing fields **2. GRASS-COVERED AREA** an area of grass, e.g., a lawn or pasture ○ *Keep off the grass.* **3. HOLLOW-STEMMED GREEN PLANT** a plant with hollow jointed stems and long narrow, usually green leaves and tiny flowers arranged in spikes. Grasses include important food plants such as wheat, oats, barley, rice, rye, corn, millet, and sorghum as well as sugar cane and bamboo. Family: Gramineae. **4. PLANT RESEMBLING GRASS** a green plant such as cleavers or knotgrass not related to the true grasses **5. MARIJUANA** the drug marijuana (*slang*) **6.** *U.K.* **INFORMER** somebody who informs on somebody else, especially to the police (*slang*) ■ *v.* (**grassed, grass·ing, grass·es**) **1.** *vti.* **COVER OR BECOME COVERED WITH GRASS** to become covered with grass, or to cause ground to become covered with grass **2.** *vt.* **FEED AN ANIMAL ON GRASS** to put an animal into a pasture to feed on grass **3.** *vi.* *U.K.* **BE INFORMER** to inform on somebody, especially to the police (*slang*) [Old English *græs*. Ultimately from an Indo-European word that is also the ancestor of English *green* and *grow*.] ◇ **not let the grass grow under your feet** to act without delay or wasting time

WORD KEY: CULTURAL NOTE

Leaves of Grass, a collection of verse by poet Walt Whitman (1855–92). Whitman constantly revised and expanded this collection to create a work that celebrates all aspects of human life from politics to the natural world and from procreation to mortality. Both its subject matter and its self-consciously modern style, based on long, loosely rhymed lines, were highly influential.

Günter Grass

Grass /graass/, **Günter** (*b.* 1927) German writer and political activist. His novels such as *The Tin Drum* (1963) combine fantasy and symbolism with the theme of the materialism of modern life. He has also campaigned for the Social Democratic Party in Germany.

grass box *n. U.K.* = **grass catcher**

grass carp *n.* a plant-eating fish, originally from Russia and China, used for keeping waterweeds under control. Latin name: *Ctenopharyngodon idella.*

grass catch·er *n.* the container attached to a lawnmower that catches the grass cuttings

grass cloth *n.* cloth made from loosely woven plant fibers

grass court *n.* a grass-covered tennis court

grass-green *adj.* of the same color as green grass —**grass green** *n.*

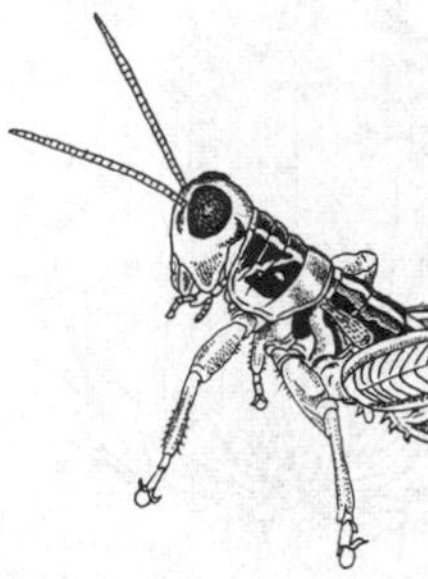

Grasshopper

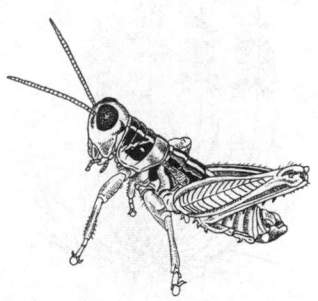

grass·hop·per /gráss hòppər/ *n.* **1.** INSECTS **JUMPING INSECT** a slender plant-eating flying and jumping insect that produces a buzzing or whirring sound by rubbing its back legs against its forewings. Order: Orthoptera. **2.** BEVERAGES **CREAMY COCKTAIL** a cocktail consisting of crème de menthe, crème de cacao, and cream **3.** AIR **RECONNAISSANCE AIRCRAFT** a light, unarmed military airplane used for reconnaissance [14thC. Formed from earlier *grasshop*, from Old English *gærshoppa*.]

grass·land /gráss lànd/ *n.* **1.** **GRASS-COVERED LAND** land on which grass or low green plants are the main vegetation **2.** **PASTURE LAND** land kept for pasture or for the production of forage crops

Grass·lands Na·tion·al Park /gràsslandz-/ national park in southwestern Saskatchewan, Canada, on the border with the United States. It is a conservation area for grasses, animals, and birds. Area: 350 sq. mi./907 sq. km.

grass moth *n.* a small straw-colored night-flying moth that spends the daytime clinging to grass stems. Family: Pyralidae.

grass-of-Par·nas·sus *n.* a white-flowered plant of the saxifrage family found in marshes and on wet moorland. Latin name: *Parnassia palustris.*

grass·roots /gráss ròots, -ròots/ *npl.* **1.** **ORDINARY PEOPLE** the ordinary people in a community or the ordinary members of an organization, as opposed to the leadership **2.** **BASIS OF SOMETHING** the origin, basis, fundamental aim, or basic meaning of something ○ *the grassroots of socialism* **3.** **RURAL AREAS** agricultural or rural areas **4.** **RURAL PEOPLE** the people living in rural areas —**grass·roots** *adj.*

grass snake *n.* a nonpoisonous dark green snake found in Europe, North Africa, and Asia. It is the most common snake in Europe. Genus: *Natrix.*

grass tree *n.* an eastern Australian tree that has a thick unbranching trunk with a tuft of leaves like grass at the top. Genus: *Xanthorrhoea.*

grass wid·ow *n.* a woman whose husband is frequently away from home or who has divorced or completely deserted her [Originally denoting a discarded mistress, thought of as having made love in a field]

grass wid·ow·er *n.* a man whose wife is frequently away from home or who has divorced or completely deserted him

grass·y /grássee/ (**-i·er, -i·est**) *adj.* **1.** **GRASS-COVERED** covered with grass **2.** **LIKE GRASS** looking, tasting, or feeling like grass

grate[1] /grayt/ *n.* **1.** **BARS IN FRONT OF FIRE** a framework of metal bars used to keep solid fuel such as coal or wood within a fireplace, stove, or furnace **2.** **FIREPLACE** a fireplace, stove, or furnace **3.** **BARS OVER OPENING** a framework of bars covering and blocking an opening **4.** MINING **SIEVE FOR GRADING ORE** an iron plate with holes in it for grading crushed ore [14thC. Via Old French from, ultimately, Latin *cratis* "wickerwork" (see CRATE).]

grate[2] /grayt/ (**grat·ed, grat·ing, grates**) *v.* **1.** *vti.* **MAKE INTO OR BECOME SMALL PIECES** to shred something by rubbing it against a rough surface or a tool with sharp-edged holes in it, or be shredded in this way ○ *Choose a cheese that grates easily.* **2.** *vti.* **MAKE NOISE OF RUBBING OR VIBRATING** to make a rough, vibrating, or creaking sound by being rubbed together, or cause things to make such a sound by rubbing them against each other ○ *Grasshoppers make their characteristic sound by grating their back legs against their wings.* **3.** *vt.* **SAY SOMETHING IN HARSH VOICE** to say something in a harsh rasping voice **4.** *vi.* **IRRITATE** to be a source of irritation ○ *His constant sniggering really grates on me.* [14thC. From Old French *grater* "to scrape," ultimately from a prehistoric Germanic word that is also the ancestor of English *scratch*.] —**grat·ed** *adj.*

grate·ful /gráytfəl/ *adj.* **1.** **FEELING THANKS** having the desire or reason to thank somebody ○ *I'm very grateful to you for your help.* **2.** **COMFORTING** giving pleasure or comfort (*archaic or literary*) [Mid-16thC. Formed from earlier *grate* "pleasing, thankful," from Latin *gratus* (source also of English *grace*, *disgrace*, and *gratitude*).] —**grate·ful·ly** *adv.* —**grate·ful·ness** *n.*

grat·er /gráytər/ *n.* **1.** **DEVICE WITH SHARP-EDGED HOLES** a device with many sharp-edged holes against which something such as cheese can be rubbed to reduce it to shreds or fine particles **2.** **SOMEBODY WHO GRATES** a person who grates something

grat·i·cule /grátti kyòol/ *n. U.K.* = **reticle** [Late 19thC. Via French from, ultimately, Latin *craticula*, literally "small grid," from *cratis* (see CRATE).]

grat·i·fi·ca·tion /gràttəfi káysh'n/ *n.* **1.** **SATISFACTION** pleasure or satisfaction **2.** **ACT OF PLEASING OR SATISFYING** the act of giving somebody pleasure or satisfaction **3.** **SOMETHING SATISFYING** something that gives pleasure or satisfaction **4.** **TIP** a gratuity (*archaic*)

grat·i·fy /gráttə fì/ (**-fied, -fy·ing, -fies**) *vt.* **1.** **PLEASE** to make somebody feel pleased or satisfied (*often passive*) **2.** **FULFILL A DESIRE** to satisfy a desire [15thC. Directly or via French *gratifier* from Latin *gratificari*, from *gratus* "agreeable" (see GRATEFUL).] —**grat·i·fi·er** *n.* —**grat·i·fy·ing** *adj.* —**grat·i·fy·ing·ly** *adv.*

gra·tin /grátt'n, graát'n, gra táN/ (*plural* **-tins** *or* **-tin**) *n.* **1.** **TOPPING OF BREADCRUMB OR MELTED CHEESE** a crust of browned breadcrumbs or melted grated cheese on top of food. ◊ **au gratin 2.** **DISH WITH BREADCRUMB OR CHEESE CRUST** a cooked dish with a breadcrumb or melted cheese crust [Mid-17thC. From French, formed from Old French *grater* (see GRATE[2]).]

grat·i·nee /gràtt'n áy, graàt-/ *adj.* cooked or served with browned breadcrumbs or melted grated cheese on top. ◊ **au gratin** [Early 20thC. From French *gratinée*, the feminine past participle of *gratiner* "to cook au gratin."]

grat·ing[1] /gráyting/ *n.* **1.** **METAL GRILLE** a framework of metal bars covering an opening **2.** = **diffraction grating**

grat·ing[2] /gráyting/ *adj.* **1.** **ROUGH** unpleasantly rough, harsh, or vibrating **2.** **IRRITATING** causing irritation or annoying ■ **grat·ings** *npl.* **SMALL GRATED PIECES** shreds or fine particles produced by grating something —**grat·ing·ly** *adv.*

grat·is /gráttiss, graát-, gráyt-/ *adj., adv.* received or given without cost or payment [15thC. From Latin, literally "out of kindness," formed from *gratia* (see GRACE).]

grat·i·tude /grátti tòod/ *n.* a feeling of being thankful to somebody for doing something ○ *I'd like to find some way of expressing my gratitude to her for all she did.* [15thC. Directly or via French from Latin *gratitudo*, from *gratus* (see GRATEFUL).]

gra·tu·i·tous /grə tòo itəss/ *adj.* **1.** **UNNECESSARY** unnecessary and unjustifiable ○ *gratuitous remarks* **2.** **FREE** received or given without payment or obligation **3.** LAW **WITHOUT RETURN BENEFIT** not requiring any benefit or compensation in return [Mid-17thC. Via French from Latin *gratuitus* "freely given," from *gratus* (see GRATEFUL).] —**gra·tu·i·tous·ly** *adv.* —**gra·tu·i·tous·ness** *n.*

gra·tu·i·ty /grə tòo itee/ (*plural* **-ties**) *n.* a small gift, usually of money, given to somebody such as a waiter as thanks for service given [15thC. Via French *gratuité* from medieval Latin *gratuitas* "gift," from Latin *gratus* (see GRATEFUL). The word originally denoted the gift of God's grace.]

grat·u·la·to·ry /gráchələ tàwree/ *adj.* expressing congratulations (*formal*)

Grau /grow/, **Shirley Ann** (*b.* 1929) U.S. writer. Her fiction portrays Southern life, and includes the Pulitzer Prize-winning *The Keepers of the House* (1964).

grau·pel /grówp'l/ *n.* small soft white ice particles that fall as hail or snow [Late 19thC. From German, literally "small hulled grain," ultimately from a Slavic word.]

Grau San Mar·tín /gròw san maar teén/, **Ramón** (1887–1969) Cuban statesman. He was twice president of Cuba (1933–34 and 1944–48).

grav /grav/ *n.* a unit of acceleration that corresponds to the standard acceleration of free fall. Symbol **g** [Shortening of GRAVITY]

gra·va·men /grə váymən/ (*plural* **-va·mens** *or* **-vam·i·na** /-vámmənə/) *n.* **1.** **SUBSTANCE OF ACCUSATION** the most serious part of an accusation or charge made against an accused person **2.** **GRIEVANCE** a grievance against somebody (*formal*) [Early 17thC. Via medieval Latin "grievance," literally "obligation," from, ultimately, Latin *gravare* "to weigh upon," from *gravis* "heavy" (see GRAVE[2]).]

grave[1] /grayv/ *n.* **1.** **BURIAL PLACE OF DEAD BODY** a hole dug in the ground for a dead person's body, or the place where a dead person's body is buried **2.** **LAST RESTING PLACE** any final resting place ○ *the sunken ship's watery grave* **3.** **DEATH** the end of life ○ *health care from the cradle to the grave* **4.** **END OF SOMETHING** the end or destruction of something ○ *the grave of his ambition* [Old English *græf*. Ultimately from an Indo-European word meaning "to scratch, dig" that is also the ancestor of English *groove*, *grub*, and *engrave*.] —**grave·less** *adj.* ◇ **turn over in his** *or* **her grave** used to emphasize how displeased or upset somebody who is dead would be if he or she knew what was happening

grave[2] /grayv/ (**grav·er, grav·est**) *adj.* **1.** **SERIOUS IN MANNER** solemn and serious in manner **2.** **HAVING SERIOUS EFFECT** very important and with serious consequences, and therefore needing to be thought about carefully **3.** **WITH POSSIBLE HARM OR DANGER** causing, involving, or arising from a threat of danger or harm or other bad consequences ○ *Things are looking pretty grave here as the air raid sirens wail.* [15thC. Via French from Latin *gravis* "heavy" (source also of English *gravity* and *grief*). Ultimately from an Indo-European base that is also the ancestor of English *baryon*, *brute*, and *guru*.] —**grave·ly** *adv.* —**grave·ness** *n.*

grave[3] /grayv, graav/ *n.* **MARK INDICATING PRONUNCIATION** a mark used to indicate pronunciation in some languages, consisting of a little line sloping downward to the right above a letter, as in ò and è. ◊ **acute, circumflex** ■ *adj.* **WITH A GRAVE ACCENT** having or being a grave ○ *e grave* [Early 17thC. From French, "heavy" (see GRAVE[2]).]

grave[4] /grayv/ (**graved, graved** *or* **grav·en** /gráyv'n/, **grav·ing, graves**) *vt.* **1.** **FIX SOMETHING IN MIND** to fix something firmly in the mind (*literary*) ○ *graved it in her mind* **2.** **ENGRAVE SOMETHING** to carve or engrave something (*archaic*) [Old English *grafan* "to dig, carve." The underlying meaning is "to engrave on the mind."]

grave[5] /grayv/ (**graved, grav·ing, graves**) *vt.* to clean the bottom of a wooden ship and coat it with pitch [15thC. Origin uncertain: probably from French dialect *grave* "sand, shore," from Old French (see GRAVEL), because the work was done while the ship was hauled up on a beach.]

gra·ve[6] /graa vày/ *adv.* to be played seriously or solemnly (*used as a musical direction*) [Late 16thC. Via Italian from Latin *gravis* "heavy" (see GRAVE[2]).] —**gra·ve** *adj.*

grave ac·cent *n.* = **grave**[3]

grave·clothes /gráyv klōthz, -klōz/ *npl.* the clothes or other wrappings that a dead body is buried in

grave·dig·ger /gráyv diggər/ *n.* somebody employed to dig graves

grav·el /grávv'l/ *n.* **1.** **SMALL STONES** small stones used for paths or for making concrete **2.** GEOL **ROCK FRAGMENTS** a deposit or stratum of loose fragmentary sedimentary material **3.** MED **SMALL PARTICLES IN KIDNEY OR BLADDER** hard particles in the kidney or bladder that are much smaller than kidney stones and can pass through the urinary tract without causing a blockage, although they may cause severe pain ■ *vt.* (**-eled, -el·ing, -els**) **1.** **COVER SOMETHING WITH GRAVEL** to cover a surface with gravel **2.** **BEWILDER SOMEBODY** to puzzle or confuse somebody **3.** **ANNOY** to annoy or irritate somebody (*informal*) [13thC. From Old French *gravel*, from *grave* "pebbles, shore," of Celtic origin.]

grav·el-blind *adj.* almost totally sightless (*literary*) (*considered offensive in most contexts*) [Modeled on SAND-BLIND]

grav·el·ly /grávvəlee/ *adj.* **1.** GRATING sounding rough or harsh ○ *a gravelly voice* **2.** LIKE GRAVEL like or covered with gravel **3.** WITH GRAVEL made or manufactured with gravel

grav·en /gráyv'n/ past participle of **grave**[4]

grav·en im·age *n.* a carving representing a god (*literary*)

grav·er /gráyvər/ *n.* a tool used for carving or engraving

grave rob·ber *n.* somebody who steals things from graves or tombs, usually either valuable artifacts or corpses for dissection

Graves /graav/ *n.* a white or red wine from the district of Graves in southwestern France

Graves /grayvz/, **Robert** (1895–1985) British poet and novelist. A classical scholar, he was also a prolific writer of poetry and fiction. His works include *Goodbye to All That* (1929), *I, Claudius* (1934), and *The White Goddess* (1947). Full name **Robert Ranke Graves**

Graves' dis·ease /gráyvz-/ *n.* an inflammatory disorder of the thyroid gland commonly associated with protrusion of the eyes [Mid-19thC. Named for the Irish physician Robert J. *Graves* (1796–1853), who was one of the first to describe the condition.]

grave·side /gráyv sīd/ *n.* the area surrounding a grave (*often used before a noun*) ○ *a graveside service*

grave·site /gráyv sīt/ *n.* the place where somebody's grave is

grave·stone /gráyv stōn/ *n.* an ornamental piece of stone put at the head of a grave, on which are written the name, birth date, and death date of the person buried there. ◊ **headstone**

grave·yard /gráyv yaard/ *n.* **1.** AREA WHERE PEOPLE ARE BURIED a piece of ground, sometimes beside a church, set aside for people to be buried in **2.** DUMPING PLACE a place where old, unwanted, useless objects, especially old cars, are left

grave·yard po·et·ry *n.* sad reflective poems about death, often set in graveyards and typically by 18th century English writers —**grave·yard po·et** *n.*

grave·yard shift *n.* a shift of work running through the early hours of the morning, especially one running from midnight till eight o'clock the following morning, or the workers on such a shift

grav·id /grávvid/ *adj.* carrying young or eggs (*technical*) [Late 16thC. From Latin *gravidus*, from *gravis* "heavy" (see GRAVE[2]).] —**gra·vid·i·ty** /grə víddətee/ *n.* —**grav·id·ly** *adv.* —**grav·id·ness** *n.*

grav·i·da /grávvədə/ (*plural* **-das** *or* **-dae** /-dee/) *n.* a pregnant woman (*technical*) ◊ **multigravida, primigravida** [Mid-20thC. From Latin, the feminine form of *gravidus* (see GRAVID).]

gra·vim·e·ter /grə vímmətər, grávvə meetər/ *n.* **1.** DEVICE FOR MEASURING GRAVITATION an instrument for measuring variations in the strength of the Earth's gravitational field from one place to another **2.** DEVICE FOR MEASURING SPECIFIC GRAVITY an instrument used to measure the relative density of a substance [Late 18thC. From French *gravimètre*, from Latin *gravis* (see GRAVE[2]).]

grav·i·met·ric /gràvvə méttrik/ *adj.* **1.** RELATING TO MEASUREMENT OF WEIGHT relating to or using the measurement of weight **2.** MEASURING GRAVITATIONAL VARIATIONS relating to the measurement of variations in the strength of the Earth's gravitational field from one place to another **3.** OF CHEMICAL ANALYSIS AND WEIGHT relating to chemical analysis involving the measurement of the weights of substances used in and produced by a chemical reaction. ◊ **volumetric** —**grav·i·met·ri·cal** *adj.* —**grav·i·met·ri·cal·ly** *adv.*

gra·vim·e·try /grə vímmətree/ *n.* **1.** MEASUREMENT OF WEIGHT the measurement of density or weight **2.** MEASUREMENT OF GRAVITATIONAL DIFFERENCES the measurement of variations in the strength of the Earth's gravitational field from one place to another [Mid-19thC. Formed from GRAVIMETER.]

grav·ing dock *n.* = **dry dock** [From GRAVE[5]]

grav·i·tas /grávvi taass/ *n.* a serious and solemn attitude or way of behaving (*formal*) [Early 20thC. From Latin (see GRAVITY).]

grav·i·tate /grávvi tàyt/ (**-tat·ed, -tat·ing, -tates**) *v.* **1.** *vi.* MOVE STEADILY TOWARD SOMETHING to move gradually and steadily to or toward somebody or something as if drawn by some force or attraction ○ *guests slowly gravitating to the kitchen* **2.** *vti.* PHYS MOVE BECAUSE OF GRAVITY to move or cause something to move under the influence of the force of gravity [Mid-17thC. From modern Latin *gravitat-*, the stem of *gravitare*, from Latin *gravitas* (see GRAVITY).] —**grav·i·tat·er** *n.* —**grav·i·ta·tive** *adj.*

grav·i·ta·tion /gràvvi táysh'n/ *n.* **1.** MOVING IN DIRECTION OF SOMETHING a gradual and steady movement to or toward somebody or something as if drawn by some force or attraction **2.** PHYS FORCE THAT ATTRACTS THINGS the mutual force of attraction between all particles or bodies that have mass —**grav·i·ta·tion·al** *adj.* —**grav·i·ta·tion·al·ly** *adv.*

grav·i·ta·tion·al field *n.* the region of space around an object that has mass, within which another object that has mass experiences the force of attraction

grav·i·ta·tion·al wave *n.* a hypothetical wave, predicted by relativity theory, that travels at the speed of light and propagates a gravitational field

grav·i·ton /grávvi tòn/ *n.* a hypothetical particle with zero charge and rest mass that is considered to be the quantum particle of gravitational interaction [Mid-20thC. Formed from GRAVITATION.]

grav·i·ty /grávvitee/ *n.* **1.** ASTRON GRAVITATIONAL FORCE OF EARTH the attraction due to gravitation that the Earth or another celestial body exerts on an object on or near its surface **2.** PHYS = **gravitation** *n.* 2 **3.** SERIOUSNESS OR SIGNIFICANCE the serious nature of something because, e.g., of the worrying or significant consequences it has or could have **4.** SERIOUS BEHAVIOR solemnity and seriousness in somebody's attitude or behavior **5.** HEAVINESS the quality of being heavy **6.** HEAVINESS the heaviness of something (*formal*) [15thC. Via French *gravité* from Latin *gravitas* "heaviness," from *gravis* (see GRAVE[2]).]

WORD KEY: CULTURAL NOTE

Gravity's Rainbow, a novel by writer Thomas Pynchon (1973). Set in Europe during World War II, it describes the attempts of various interest groups to exploit the extrasensory powers of U.S. soldier Tyrone Slothrop, whose sexual encounters reliably predict the impact sites of German V2 rockets. It is noted for its extraordinary erudition, broad range of styles, and complex characterization.

grav·i·ty feed *n.* a mechanism or process for supplying something such as fuel to a boiler or materials to a manufacturing process by their downward movement under the influence of gravity —**grav·i·ty-fed** *adj.*

grav·lax /graav laaks/ *n.* a Scandinavian dish consisting of thin slices of dried salmon marinated in sugar, salt, pepper, and herbs, especially dill, and usually served as an appetizer [Mid-20thC. From Swedish or Norwegian *gravlaks*, literally "buried salmon" (because originally the fish was marinated in a hole in the ground).]

gra·vure /grə vyoor/ *n.* **1.** = **intaglio** *n.* 4 **2.** PLATE OR PRINT a plate used in or a print produced by intaglio printing **3.** = **photogravure** [Late 19thC. From French, formed from *graver* "to engrave." Ultimately from a prehistoric Germanic word that was also the ancestor of English *grave*[4] and *engrave*.]

gra·vy /gráyvee/ (*plural* **-vies**) *n.* the juices produced by meat while it is being roasted, fried, or broiled, or a sauce made with these juices or another liquid and poured over cooked meat and vegetables [14thC. From Old French *grave*, of uncertain origin; perhaps a misreading of *grane* "stew, sauce," probably ultimately from Latin *granum* (see GRAIN).]

gra·vy boat *n.* a small pitcher, usually long and narrow, in which gravy and other sauces are served

gra·vy train *n.* a way of getting a large amount of money or other benefits for very little effort (*informal*) ○ *scrambling to get on the gravy train*

gray[1] /gray/ *adj.* (**gray·er, gray·est**) **1.** OF THE COLOR OF ASH having the color of ash or lead **2.** DISMAL dismal or gloomy **3.** DULL dull and colorless ■ *n.* **1.** COLOR OF ASH the color of ash or lead **2.** PIGMENT MADE FROM BLACK AND WHITE a pigment or dye that is formed from a combination of black and white and is or is near to the color of ash or lead **3.** GRAY CLOTHING fabric or clothing that is gray in color **4. gray, Gray** CONFEDERATE SOLDIER a soldier of the Confederacy in the Civil War. ◊ **blue** *n.* 5 **5.** CONFEDERATE ARMY the Confederate army in the Civil War, because of its gray uniforms. ◊ **blue** *n.* 6 **6.** SOMETHING GRAY a gray object ■ *vi.* (**grayed, gray·ing, grays**) TURN GRAY to turn the color gray ○ *His hair is graying.* [Old English *gr_æg*, ultimately from a prehistoric Germanic base that is also the ancestor of English *grizzle*; in the sense "soldier," from the colour of their uniforms] —**grey·ness** *n.*

gray[2] /gray/ *n.* the derived SI unit for the absorbed dose of ionizing radiation, equal to an absorption of 1 joule per kilogram. Symbol **Gy** [Late 20thC. Named for the English radiobiologist L. H. *Gray* (1905–65).]

Gray /gray/, **Asa** (1810–88) U.S. botanist. He replaced the Linnaean taxonomic system with a new method of classification and wrote the classic *Manual of Botany of the Northern United States* (1848), known as "Gray's Manual."

Gray, Elisha (1835–1901) U.S. inventor. An inventor of telegraphic equipment, he filed his intent to patent the telephone two hours after Alexander Graham Bell (1876).

gray ar·e·a *n.* **1.** UNCLEAR SITUATION a situation, subject, or category of something that is unclear or hard to define or classify **2.** SOMETHING THAT CANNOT BE CLASSIFIED a part of something that does not belong to any specific category but contains features of more than one

gray·back /gráy bàk/ *n.* **1.** CREATURE WITH GRAY BACK an animal, bird, fish, or insect with a gray back **2.** CONFEDERATE SOLDIER a soldier of the Confederacy in the Civil War

gray·bar land /gráy baar-/ *n.* the state of waiting for the gray bar graphic device on a computer screen slowly to fill up as a time-consuming computer process nears completion (*informal*)

gray·beard /gráy beerd/ *n.* **1.** MAN OF ADVANCED YEARS a man of advanced years (*dated*) **2.** CONTAINER FOR ALCOHOL an earthenware container for alcohol —**gray·beard·ed** *adj.*

gray em·i·nence *n.* = **éminence grise**

gray fox *n.* a fox with a gray and red coat that is found in woodlands throughout the United States and Central America. Latin name: *Urocyon cinereoargenteus.*

gray·hen /gráy hèn/ (*plural* **-hens** *or* **-hen**) *n.* a female black grouse

gray·ish /gráy ish/ *adj.* slightly or somewhat gray in color

gray jay *n.* a North American bird of the crow family that is gray in color with black markings on the head. It inhabits coniferous forests, especially spruce forests. Latin name: *Perisoreus canadensis.*

gray·lag /gráy làg/, **gray·lag goose** *n.* a common Eurasian wild goose that is a light brownish gray in color with a large orange or pink bill. It is the ancestor of the domestic farm goose. Latin name: *Anser anser.* [Early 18thC. From GREY + dialect *lag* "goose," of unknown origin.]

gray·ling /gráyling/ (*plural* **-lings** *or* **-ling**) *n.* **1.** ZOOL FISH RESEMBLING TROUT a northern freshwater fish that resembles the trout, with silvery scales and a large dorsal fin. It is valued as a game and food fish. Genus: *Thymallus.* **2.** INSECTS EUROPEAN BUTTERFLY a common gray European butterfly. Latin name: *Eumenis semele.*

gray·mail /gráy màyl/ *n.* a maneuver used by the defense in a spy trial whereby the government is threatened with the revelation of national secrets unless the case against the defendant is dropped. ◊ **blackmail, greenmail** [Late 20thC. Modeled on BLACKMAIL.]

gray mar·ket *n.* **1.** STOCK EXCH TRADING IN SHARES BEFORE ISSUE trading in new shares before they have been officially issued on the stock exchange **2.** COMM SECRET TRADING IN GOODS clandestine but legal trading in goods either at excessively high prices or at prices well below the manufacturer's recommended price. ◊ **black market**

gray mat·ter *n.* **1.** INTELLIGENCE intelligence or brains (*informal*) **2.** BROWNISH-GRAY TISSUE WITHIN BRAIN brownish-gray nerve tissue consisting mainly of nerve cell bodies within the brain and spinal cord. ◊ **white matter**

gray mul·let *n.* = **mullet**

gray plov·er *n.* = **black-bellied plover**

gray seal *n.* a large earless seal of the North Atlantic with mottled gray markings that breeds on rocky shores. Latin name: *Halichoerus grypus.*

gray squir·rel *n.* a large tree squirrel of North America, Great Britain, Ireland, and South Africa that has gray fur with a reddish tinge in the legs and head. Latin name: *Sciurus carolinensis.* ◊ **red squirrel**

gray·wacke /gráy wàk, -wàkə/ *n.* a conglomerate rock composed of well-rounded pebbles cemented by a sandy infill [Late 18thC. From German *Grauwacke* "gray sandstone."]

gray wag·tail *n.* a small songbird, found in Europe, Asia, and Africa, with a gray back and head, yellow underside, and a long tail that it wags to keep its balance. Latin name: *Motacilla cinerea.*

gray·weth·er /gráy wethər/ *n.* GEOL = **sarsen**

gray whale *n.* a large baleen whale of coastal waters of the North Pacific that has no dorsal fin but a line of bumps along part of its back. Latin name: *Eschrichtius gibbosus.*

gray wolf *n.* a large intelligent highly social wild dog of North America, Europe, and Asia, varying in color from white in the north of its range to black in the south. Latin name: *Canis lupus.*

graze[1] /grayz/ **(grazed, graz·ing, graz·es)** *v.* **1.** *vti.* EAT GRASS IN FIELDS to eat grass and other green plants in fields, or eat the grass and plants of a particular field or fields **2.** *vt.* ALLOW ANIMALS TO EAT GRASS to allow animals such as cows and sheep to eat grass in fields **3.** *vt.* USE LAND FOR FEEDING ANIMALS to allow animals such as cows and sheep to eat the grass and green plants of a particular field or fields ○ *We usually graze those two fields over there.* **4.** *vi.* EAT SNACKS to eat snacks throughout the day instead of regular meals, especially while working (*slang*) **5.** *vi.* EAT FOOD IN SUPERMARKET to eat food from the shelves of a supermarket while shopping without subsequently paying for it at the checkout (*slang*) **6.** *vi.* SAMPLE DIFFERENT FOODS to eat small portions of several different appetizers or entrees instead of a complete meal (*slang*) **7.** *vi.* CHANGE TV CHANNELS to switch television channels frequently without watching much of any one program (*slang*) **8.** *vi.* KEEP STOPPING AND STARTING to perform an activity in a desultory manner, e.g., by picking up and putting down magazines without reading much of any one (*slang*) [Old English *grasian*, from *græs* (see GRASS)] —**graze·a·ble** *adj.* —**graz·er** *n.* ◇ **put somebody out to graze** to cause somebody to retire

graze[2] /grayz/ *v.* **(grazed, graz·ing, graz·es) 1.** *vti.* TOUCH SOMETHING LIGHTLY to touch against the surface of something lightly in passing **2.** *vt.* BREAK THE SKIN SLIGHTLY to damage the surface of the skin of a part of the body slightly when it is rubbed against something rough and hard ■ *n.* **1.** SLIGHT BREAK IN SKIN slight and shallow damage to the skin caused by rubbing against something rough and hard **2.** TOUCH OF SOMETHING the act of rubbing something or touching it lightly ○ *the graze of a bullet* [Late 16thC. Origin uncertain; perhaps from GRAZE[1], with the idea of cropping grass very short.]

graz·ing /gráyzing/ *n.* **1.** EATING SNACKS eating snacks throughout the day instead of regular meals, especially while working (*slang*) **2.** EATING FOOD IN SUPERMARKET eating food from the shelves of a supermarket while shopping without subsequently paying for it at the checkout counter (*slang*) **3.** EATING DIFFERENT APPETIZERS eating small portions of several different appetizers or entrees, especially instead of a complete meal (*slang*) **4.** CHANGING TV CHANNELS switching television channels frequently without watching much of any one program (*slang*) **5.** FREQUENTLY STOPPING AND STARTING performing an activity in a desultory manner, e.g., by picking up and putting down magazines without reading much of any one (*slang*) **6.** FOOD FOR COWS AND SHEEP grass and green plants for animals such as cows and sheep to eat **7.** LAND WITH GRASS land with grass suitable for animals such as cows and sheep to feed on

gra·zi·o·so /graàtsi óssō/ *adv.* in a graceful way (*used as a musical direction*) [Early 19thC. From Italian.] —**gra·zi·o·so** *adj.*

GRE *abbr.* graduate record examination

grease *n.* /greess/ **1.** ANIMAL FAT thick soft animal fat, e.g., from cooked meat **2.** THICK LUBRICANT a thick oily substance, especially one used to make machinery run smoothly **3.** OIL FOR HAIR an oily substance used as a cosmetic for the hair **4.** BRIBERY bribes or bribery (*slang*) **5.** AGRIC OILY WOOL untreated wool from sheep that still contains its natural oils, or the natural oils in this wool ■ *vt.* /greess, greez/ **(greased, greas·ing, greas·es) 1.** PUT GREASE ON SOMETHING to put grease on something, e.g., in order to make it move smoothly or to stop something else from sticking to it **2.** MAKE SOMETHING EASIER OR QUICKER to make something such as progress or promotion easier or quicker (*informal*) ○ *His father's money certainly greased his path to the boardroom.* [13thC. Via Anglo-Norman *grece*, from, ultimately, Latin *crassus* "fat, thick" (source of English *crass*).] ◇ **grease somebody's palm** *or* **hand** to bribe somebody to do something (*informal*)

grease·ball /greéss bàwl/ *n.* **1.** SOMEBODY WITH GREASY HAIR somebody who has greasy hair, especially somebody who rides a motorcycle and wears a leather jacket (*slang insult*) **2.** OFFENSIVE TERM a highly offensive term for somebody of Mediterranean or Latin American, especially Mexican, origin (*slang offensive*)

grease gun *n.* **1.** ENG DEVICE FOR GREASING SOMETHING a hand-held device for forcing grease into machinery to lubricate it **2.** ARMS SUBMACHINE GUN a submachine gun (*dated slang*)

grease mon·key *n.* an offensive term for a mechanic, especially one who works on motor vehicles or aircraft (*slang offensive*)

grease·paint /greéss pàynt/ *n.* a thick, greasy, or waxy form of colored makeup used by actors

grease pen·cil *n.* a pencil containing a core of a waxy colored substance that can write on glossy surfaces

grease·proof /greéss proof/ *adj.* not allowing oil or grease to soak into it or pass through it

grease·proof pa·per *n. U.K.* = **waxed paper**

greas·er /greéssər, greézər/ *n.* **1.** = **greaseball 2.** LONG-HAIRED MOTORCYCLIST a usually young, long-haired, leather-jacketed motorcyclist, especially a member of a motorcycle gang (*slang insult*) **3.** MECHANIC OR ENGINEER somebody whose job involves greasing machinery, especially a mechanic who works on motor vehicles (*slang*)

grease·wood /greéss wòod/ *n.* **1.** SPINY N AMERICAN SHRUB a spiny shrub that grows in desert areas of western North America and yields an oil that is used as a fuel. Latin name: *Sarcobatus vermiculatus.* **2.** SHRUB RELATED TO GREASEWOOD a shrub that is similar to or related to the greasewood, e.g., the creosote bush

greas·y /greéssee, greézee/ (**-i·er, -i·est**) *adj.* **1.** THICK WITH GREASE covered with or containing grease, often a lot of grease or too much of it **2.** SMARMY unpleasantly and insincerely flattering, friendly, or groveling **3.** MADE OF GREASE consisting of grease or something with the consistency of grease **4.** HAVING EXCESSIVE NATURAL OILS producing or containing a lot of natural oils **5.** PRODUCED BY GREASE caused by grease or something with the consistency of grease **6.** SLIPPERY difficult to move, walk, or drive on because of wetness or iciness —**greas·i·ly** *adv.* —**greas·i·ness** *n.*

greas·y spoon *n.* a small, cheap, and often dirty café, especially one that serves fried food (*informal*)

great /grayt/ *adj.* **1.** EXCEPTIONALLY TALENTED with exceptional talents, or having made remarkable achievements ○ *He was a great humanitarian as well as a talented artist.* **2.** IMPORTANT very significant or important ○ *a truly great novel* **3.** POWERFUL powerful and influential ○ *in this great nation* **4.** VERY GOOD very good or pleasing (*informal*) **5.** MUCH extreme or more than usual ○ *It gives me great pleasure to introduce our speaker tonight.* **6.** IMPRESSIVELY LARGE very large and impressive **7.** LARGE IN NUMBER large in number or with many parts ○ *a great crowd of well-wishers* **8.** BEING A GOOD EXAMPLE OF SOMETHING doing something often, enjoying something very much, or being a very good example of something **9.** GOOD AT SOMETHING able to do something very well, or very skillful with something (*informal*) ○ *great at spelling* **10.** BIGGER THAN OTHERS larger or more important than others of the same kind **11.** USEFUL very useful or suitable for a particular task (*informal*) ○ *This cast-iron pan is great for making pancakes.* **12.** USED FOR EMPHASIS used to emphasize how much of a quality somebody or something has (*informal*) ○ *Their new house is a great big place out in the country.* **13.** LASTING A LONG TIME lasting a long time, or covering a long distance ○ *We endured a great delay.* **14.** PREGNANT pregnant (*archaic*) ○ *She was great with child.* ■ *n.* **1.** SOMEBODY GREAT somebody whose fame or influence has proved to be long-lasting ○ *one of the all-time greats of blues music* **2.** MUSIC PART OF PIPE ORGAN the principal division of a pipe organ ■ *adv.* VERY WELL very well (*informal*) ○ *That's it; you're doing great.* ○ *Steve and I get along just great.* [Old English *grēat* "thick, coarse." Ultimately from a prehistoric Germanic word that is also the ancestor of English *grit, groat,* and *grout.*] —**great·ly** *adv.* —**great·ness** *n.*

WORD KEY: CULTURAL NOTE

The Great Gatsby, a novel by U.S. writer F. Scott Fitzgerald (1925). Set on Long Island, New York, it is the story of enigmatic businessman Jay Gatsby, a symbol of the American obsession with wealth and status, whose attempts to revive a relationship with an old girlfriend lead to his downfall. It was made into movies by Elliott Nugent in 1949 and by Jack Clayton in 1974. Terms such as *Gatsbyesque*, obsessed with social status and the acquisition of great riches, derive directly from the book title and the character.

great- *prefix.* **1.** BEING A PARENT OF GRANDPARENT being a parent of somebody's grandparent **2.** BEING GRANDCHILD'S CHILD being a child of one of somebody's grandchildren

great ape *n.* any of the larger apes such as the gorilla, chimpanzee, or orangutan

Great At·trac·tor *n.* a large aggregation of galaxies, approximately 150 to 350 million light years away, whose gravitational pull might account for the unexpected motions of many galaxies including our own

great auk *n.* a large flightless sea bird that was native to northern Atlantic coasts until it was hunted to extinction in the middle of the 19th century. Latin name: *Pinguinus impennis.*

great-aunt *n.* an aunt of somebody's father or mother

Great Aus·tra·lian Bight /gràyt o stráylee ən bīt/ wide inlet of the Indian Ocean off the southern coast of Australia. It stretches 685 mi./1,100 km from Cape Pasley in Western Australia to Cape Carnot in South Australia.

Great Bar·ri·er Reef /-bàrree ər reef/ chain of coral reefs in the Coral Sea, located off the coast of Queensland, Australia. The largest deposit of coral in the world, the reef extends for 1,250 mi./2,010 km. Area: 134,600 sq. mi./348,600 sq. km.

Great Ba·sin /-báyss'n/ area of inland drainage covering most of Nevada and parts of Utah, Oregon, Idaho, and California. Area: 210,000 sq. mi./543,900 sq. km.

Great Ba·sin Na·tion·al Park national park established in 1986 in eastern Nevada, noted for its limestone formations. Area: 120 sq. mi./312 sq. km.

Great Bear *n.* = **Ursa Major**

Great Bear Lake /-bàir-/ freshwater lake in Canada's Northwest Territories, lying astride the Arctic Circle. It is the world's eighth largest lake. Area: 12,028 sq. mi./31,153 sq. km. Depth: 1,345 ft./410 m.

Great Bend /-bénd/ city in central Kansas, on the northern bank of the Arkansas River, northeast of Dodge City. It is located on the old Santa Fe Trail. Population: 14,718 (1996).

great black-backed gull *n.* a large sea bird with a white head and body and black wings that is native to the shores of the North Atlantic. Latin name: *Larus marinus.*

great blue her·on *n.* a large long-legged long-necked North American heron with grayish-blue plumage. Latin name: *Ardea herodias.*

Great Brit·ain the largest island of the British Isles in northwestern Europe. It includes England, Scotland, and Wales. ➧ **United Kingdom**

great cir·cle *n.* a circle on the surface of a sphere such as the Earth that has a radius equal to the radius of the sphere, and whose center is also the sphere's center. ◊ **small circle**

great·coat /gráyt kōt/ *n.* a long thick heavy overcoat worn especially by soldiers

great crest·ed grebe *n.* a large diving waterfowl of Europe, Africa, Asia, and Australia with no tail and a ruff on its head that is expanded during courtship rituals. Latin name: *Podiceps cristatus.*

Great Dane

Great Dane *n.* a very large dog with long legs, a square head and deep muzzle, and short hair, belonging to a breed originating in Germany [Because it was developed in Germany, whose inhabitants were formerly called Danes]

Great De·pres·sion *n.* a drastic decline in the world economy resulting in mass unemployment and widespread poverty that lasted from 1929 until 1939

Great Dis·mal Swamp /-dízm'l swómp/ low-lying marshland in southeastern Virginia and northeastern North Carolina that is densely forested in parts and rich in wildlife. George Washington once owned most of the area. Area: 750 sq. mi./1,940 sq. km.

great di·vide *n.* **1.** MAJOR DEMARCATION a major demarcation between two contrasting things, especially life and death **2.** LINE BETWEEN LIFE AND DEATH the boundary between life and death

Great Di·vide *n.* = **Continental Divide**

Great Di·vid·ing Range /gràyt di vī́ding ráynj/ system of mountain ranges and plateaus in Queensland, New South Wales, and Victoria, extending along the eastern border of Australia. The highest point is Mount Kosciusko, 7,310 ft./2,228 m.

great·er cel·an·dine *n.* = **celandine.** ◊ **lesser celandine**

Great·er Sun·da Is·lands /gràytər súndə-/ ➧ **Sunda Islands**

great·er yel·low·legs *n.* a large North American wading bird of the sandpiper family that has a gray body and long yellow legs. Latin name: *Tringa melanoleuca.* ◊ **lesser yellowlegs**

great·est com·mon di·vi·sor, great·est com·mon fac·tor *n.* the highest number that can be exactly divided into each member of a set of numbers. The highest common factor of 12, 60, and 84 is 12.

great-grand·child *n.* a son or daughter of your grandchild

great·heart·ed /gràyt haártəd/ *adj.* **1.** LARGE-SPIRITED with a generous and forgiving nature **2.** UNDAUNTED not easily frightened or dispirited —**great·heart·ed·ly** *adv.*

Great In·di·an Des·ert /-índee ən-/ = **Thar Desert**

Great Ka·roo /-kə rōō/ ➧ **Karoo**

Great Lakes

Great Lakes group of five freshwater lakes in north central North America, interconnected by natural and artificial channels. The largest group of lakes in the world, they are Lakes Superior, Michigan, Huron, Erie, and Ontario. Area: 94,251 sq. mi./244,108 sq. km.

great lau·rel *n.* = **rosebay rhododendron**

Great Leap For·ward *n.* the attempt by the People's Republic of China in 1958 to 1960 to modernize agriculture by labor-intensive methods

great north·ern div·er *n.* BIRDS = **common loon**

great or·gan *n.* the main keyboard of an organ, and the pipes and mechanism relating to it. ◊ **choir organ**

Great Plains /-pláynz/ vast high plateau region in central North America that stretches from northeastern Canada to southern Texas between the Canadian Shield and Central Lowlands on the east and the Rocky Mountains on the west

Great Pow·er *n.* a nation that has a far-reaching political, social, economic, and usually military influence internationally (*hyphenated when used before a noun*)

Great Re·bel·lion *n.* the Royalists' name for the English Civil War

Great Rift Val·ley /-rìft-/ depression extending more than 3,000 mi./4,830 km from the valley of the Jordan River in Syria to Mozambique, forming the most extensive rift in the earth's surface. The area is marked by a chain of seas and lakes and a series of volcanoes.

Great Rus·sian *n.* **1.** LANG RUSSIAN LANGUAGE the Russian language (*dated*) **2.** PEOPLES RUSSIAN a member of the main Russian-speaking ethnic group in Russia ■ *adj.* OF THE RUSSIAN PEOPLE relating to or belonging to the Great Russian people

Great Salt Lake /-sàwlt láyk/ shallow body of salt water in northwestern Utah, near Salt Lake City. It is the largest salt lake in North America. Area: 1,700 sq. mi./4,403 km.

Great San·dy Des·ert /-sàndi-/ desert in northwestern Australia that contains large areas of sand dunes and salt marshes and some grassland. Area: 150,000 sq. mi./310,000 sq. km.

Great Schism *n.* **1.** TIME OF TWO POPES the period between 1378 and 1415 when there were rival popes, one reigning in Rome and the other in Avignon **2.** HISTORICAL SEPARATION OF CHURCHES the separation of the Roman Catholic and Eastern Orthodox churches in 1054, as a result of theological disagreement

Great Seal *n.* in the United States, the seal kept in the charge of the Secretary of State and used in sealing important state papers

great sku·a *n.* a large brown predatory seabird of the North Atlantic that feeds on fish, eggs, and other adult birds. Latin name: *Catharacta skua.*

Great Slave Lake /-slàyv láyk/ freshwater lake in the Northwest Territories, northwestern Canada. It is the deepest lake in North America. Depth: 2,015 ft./614 m. Area: 11,031 sq. mi./28,570 sq. km.

Great Smok·y Moun·tains Na·tion·al Park /-smòki-/ national park in the southeastern United States, in western North Carolina and eastern Tennessee. Established in 1930, it contains some of the highest peaks in eastern North America. Area: 813 sq. mi./2,106 sq. km.

Great St. Ber·nard Pass /gràyt s'nt búrnərd páss, grayt sàN bər naárd-/ mountain pass in western Europe, on the border between Valais, central Switzerland, and Aosta Province, Piedmont, northern Italy. Founded in the 11th century, it is named for the hospice founded at its summit by the French monk St. Bernard. Height: 8,090 ft./2,468 m.

Great Trek *n.* a mass movement between 1836 and 1844 of Boer cattlemen in South Africa from the Cape to the north, that eventually resulted in the establishment of the Transvaal and the Orange Free State

great-un·cle *n.* an uncle of your father or mother

Great Vic·to·ri·a Des·ert /-vík táwree ə-/ desert in the states of Western Australia and South Australia, consisting of sand dunes, salt lakes, and low scrubland. Area: 250,000 sq. mi./650,000 sq. km.

Great Wall *n.* **1.** ASTRON IMMENSE GALACTIC SUPERCLUSTER a huge expanse of thousands of galaxies arranged in a supercluster that forms the largest system of astronomical objects observed in the universe **2.** = **Great Wall of China**

Barnaby's

Great Wall of China

Great Wall of Chi·na *n.* a vast Chinese defensive fortification begun in the 3rd century B.C. and running along the northern border of the country for 1,500 mi./2,400 km

Great War *n.* = **World War I**

great white shark *n.* a large shark of warm and tropical waters that is gray-brown with white underparts. It preys on large fish, marine mammals, and carrion, and has a reputation for eating human beings. Latin name: *Carcharodon carcharias.*

Great White Way *n.* the historic entertainment district in Manhattan stretching along Broadway north of Times Square and distinguished by its many brightly-lit signs and marquees

great year *n.* a period of about 25,800 years, representing a complete cycle of the precession of the equinoxes

greave /greev/ *n.* a piece of armor worn from the ankle to the knee (*usually used in the plural*) [14thC. From Old French *greve* "calf, shin."]

Grebe

grebe /greeb/ (*plural* **grebes** *or* **grebe**) *n.* a freshwater diving bird with lobed toes that is a strong swimmer. Family: Podicipedidae. [Mid-18thC. From French *grèbe.*]

Grec- *prefix.* = **Greco-** (*used before vowels*)

Gre·cian /gréesh'n/ *adj.* **1.** IN ANCIENT GREEK STYLE relating to or typical of the ancient Greek style of architecture or sculpture **2.** = **Greek** *adj.* **1** ■ *n.* **1.** HELLENIST a Hellenist (*dated*) **2.** = **Greek** *n.* **1** —**Gre·cian·ize** *vt.*

Gre·cism /grée sìzzəm/ *n.* **1.** GREEK IDIOM an idiom of the Greek language used in another language, often for stylistic effect **2.** GREEK STYLE AND SPIRIT Greek style, spirit, or characteristics as related to Greek culture, arts, architecture, and philosophy

Gre·cize /grée sīz/ (**-cized, -ciz·ing, -ciz·es**) *vt.* to make something Greek or Hellenic in style or form so that it becomes characteristic of the culture, civilization, or language of the ancient Greeks. U.K. = **Graecize**

Gre·co /grékō/, **El** (1541–1614) Greek-born Spanish painter. His works combine the baroque style with exaggerated mannerism, and are characterized by lambent lighting and elongated figures. Real name **Domenikos Theotokopoulos**

Greco- *prefix.* Greece, Greek ○ *Greco-Roman* [From Latin *Graecus* (see GREEK)]

Gre·co-Ro·man, Grae·co-Ro·man *adj.* **1.** ANCIENT GREEK AND ROMAN relating to, or typical of, both ancient Greece and ancient Rome or the influence of their civilizations **2.** WRESTLING RELATING TO A WRESTLING HOLD used to describe a style of wrestling allowing no hold below the waist and no use of the legs to obtain a fall

Greece

Greece /greess/ country in southeastern Europe, on the southernmost part of the Balkan Peninsula and numerous islands in the Aegean, Ionian, and Mediterranean seas. Language: Greek. Currency: drachma. Capital: Athens. Population: 10,493,000 (1996). Area: 50,949 sq. mi./131,957 sq. km. Official name **Hellenic Republic**

greed /greed/ *n.* an overwhelming desire to have more of something such as money than is actually needed [Late 16thC. Back-formation from GREEDY.]

greed·y /greédee/ (**-i·er, -i·est**) *adj.* **1.** EATING TOO MUCH eating to excess, or wanting to do so **2.** STRONGLY DESIRING MORE THAN REQUIRED having an overwhelming desire to have more of something such as money than is actually needed [Old English *grædig.* Ultimately from a prehistoric Germanic base meaning "hunger, greed."] —**greed·i·ly** *adv.* —**greed·i·ness** *n.*

gree·gree *n.* = **grigri**

Greek /greek/ *n.* **1.** SOMEBODY FROM GREECE somebody who was born in or raised in Greece, or who has Greek citizenship **2.** LANGUAGE OF GREECE the official language of Greece and part of Cyprus, spoken by about 12 million people. ◊ **Ancient Greek, Demotic, Katharevousa, Late Greek, modern Greek 3.** FRATERNITY OR SORORITY MEMBER a member of a college or university fraternity or sorority whose name consists of Greek letters ■ *adj.* **1.** OF GREECE OR GREEKS relating to or typical of Greece, or its people or culture **2.** LANG OF THE GREEK LANGUAGE relating to the Greek language **3.** CHR OF GREEK ORTHODOX CHURCH relating to or belonging to the Greek Orthodox Church [Old English *grecas.* Ultimately from Latin *Graecus,* from Greek *Graikos,* the prehistoric name for the Hellenic people.] ◇ **beware of Greeks bearing gifts** be careful of possible treachery from somebody who appears to be kind ◇ **go Greek** to pledge and then join a college fraternity or sorority (*informal*) ○ *About 40% of the student body is expected to go Greek after rush.* ◇ **it's (all) Greek to me** used to say that you cannot understand something

Greek Cath·o·lic *n.* **1.** MEMBER OF EASTERN ORTHODOX CHURCH a member of the Eastern Orthodox Church **2.** MEMBER OF UNIAT GREEK CHURCH a member of the Uniat Greek Church

Greek Church *n.* = **Greek Orthodox Church**

Greek cross *n.* a cross consisting of four arms of the same length

Greek key *n.* an ornate pattern for a cornice or border consisting of lines that change direction at right angles to form a continuous band

Greek Or·tho·dox Church *n.* **1.** NATIONAL CHURCH OF GREECE the national church of Greece, an independent section of the Eastern Orthodox Church **2.** = **Orthodox Church**

Greek sal·ad *n.* a salad of tomatoes, lettuce, cucumber, olives, oregano, and feta cheese

Gree·ley /greélee/ city in northern Colorado, founded as a farm cooperative and temperance colony in 1870. Population: 60,536 (1990).

Gree·ley, Horace (1811–72) U.S. politician and journalist. He was founding editor of the *New York Tribune* (1841–72), and used the newspaper and lectures to promote his liberal political views. He popularized the phrase, "Go West, young man."

Gree·ly /greélee/, **Adolphus Washington** (1844–1935) U.S. explorer and army officer. He led an expedition to the Arctic (1881–84) and established a meteorological base on Ellesmere Island.

green /green/ *adj.* **1.** GRASS-COLORED of a color in the spectrum between yellow and blue, like the color of grass **2.** HAVING EDIBLE GREEN LEAVES consisting of or containing green leaves of vegetables ○ *a green salad* **3.** GRASSY OR LEAFY consisting of or containing grass, plants, or foliage **4. green, Green** POL ADVOCATING PROTECTION OF THE ENVIRONMENT supporting or promoting the protection of the environment **5.** ENVIRON MADE WITH LITTLE ENVIRONMENTAL HARM produced in an environmentally and ecologically friendly way, e.g., by using renewable resources **6.** FOOD NOT RIPE unripe or not mature ○ *green bananas* **7.** UNSEASONED newly cut and still unseasoned (*refers to leather*) ○ *green wood* **8.** UNTANNED not yet tanned (*refers to leather*) **9.** METALL UNFIRED not yet fired **10.** JEALOUS envious or jealous **11.** SICKLY-LOOKING pale and sickly-looking, especially as a result of nausea **12.** INNOCENT naive and lacking in experience, especially because of being new to something **13.** NEW young, new, recent, or fresh ■ *n.* **1.** THE COLOR OF GRASS a primary color between yellow and blue in the spectrum, like the color of grass **2.** GREEN COLORING a green pigment or dye **3.** GREEN CLOTH green fabric or clothing **4.** SOMETHING GREEN a green object **5.** GRASSY AREA an area of ground that is covered with grass, especially a public or communal area **6.** SPORTS GRASSY AREA FOR LAWN BOWLING an area of grass that is maintained for lawn bowling and similar games **7.** GOLF GRASSY AREA SURROUNDING A GOLF HOLE the closely mowed area at the end of a fairway on a golf course on which the hole for the ball is located **8.** *U.K.* = **greens** *npl.* 2 **9. green, Green** ADVOCATE OF PROTECTION OF ENVIRONMENT somebody who supports or promotes the protection of the environment, especially a member of a political party concerned with environmental issues **10.** MONEY cash or paper money (*slang*) ■ *vti.* (**greened, green·ing, greens**) **1.** BECOME OR MAKE GREEN to become green, or make something green **2.** BECOME AN ENVIRONMENTAL ADVOCATE to become, or make somebody become, aware of environmental issues [Old English *grene.* Ultimately from a prehistoric Germanic base that is also the ancestor of English *grass* and *grow.*] —**green·ish** *adj.* —**green·ly** *adv.* ◇ **go green** to become actively interested in environmental issues and support environmental causes

green al·ga *n.* an alga found mostly in fresh water. Division: *Chlorophyta.*

green·back /greén bàk/ *n.* a U.S. bank note of any denomination (*slang*)

Green·back Par·ty *n.* a political party formed after the Civil War that was against reducing the amount of paper money in circulation and in favor of the use of fiat money

Green Bay city in Brown County, northeastern Wisconsin, on the southern shores of Lake Michigan. Population: 102,708 (1994).

green bean *n.* a type of bean such as string beans that is eaten complete with its pod

green·belt *n.* **1.** UNDEVELOPED LAND AROUND A CITY a strip of undeveloped land around a city that contains parks, farms, or vacant land **2.** IRRIGATED LAND BORDERING A DESERT an irrigated area of land on the edge of a desert, designed to prevent any further encroachment by the desert

Green·belt /greén belt/ city in west central Maryland, northeast of Washington, D.C., developed in the 1930s to house government employees. Population: 21,840 (1996).

Green Be·ret *n.* (*informal*) **1.** SPECIAL FORCES MEMBER a U.S. Special Forces soldier **2.** COMMANDO a British commando [From the regulation green beret worn by members]

green·bot·tle /greén bòtt'l/, **green·bot·tle fly** *n.* a fly that is metallic green in color and lays its eggs in rotting vegetation or flesh. Genus: *Lucilia.*

green card *n.* in the United States, an identity card and work permit issued to nationals of other countries —**green-card·er** *n.*

green Christ·mas *n. Can* a Christmas without snow

green drag·on *n.* a tuberous North American plant that has divided leaves and small green flowers arranged along a stalk enclosed in a tight green sheath. Latin name: *Arisaema dracontium.*

Greene /green/, **Graham** (1904–91) British writer. His major novels, including *Brighton Rock* (1938) and *The Power and the Glory* (1940), incorporate themes of spiritual and moral struggle. Full name **Henry Graham Greene**

Graham Greene

Greene, Nathanael (1742–86) U.S. revolutionary soldier. He commanded revolutionary armies in New Jersey and South Carolina.

green earth *n.* PAINTING = **terre verte**

green·er·y /greénəree/ *n.* **1.** GREEN PLANTS growing green foliage and plants **2.** *U.K.* = **evergreens**

green-eyed mon·ster *n.* jealousy or envy personified

Green·field /greén feeld/ town in northern Massachusetts, on the western bank of the Connecticut River, north of Northampton. Population: 18,580 (1996).

green·finch /greén finch/ (*plural* **-finch·es** *or* **-finch**) *n.* a European green-gray and yellow finch. Latin name: *Carduelis chloris.*

green fin·gers *npl. U.K.* = **green thumb** —**green-fin·gered** *adj.*

green·fly /greén flī/ (*plural* **-flies** *or* **-fly**) *n.* a green winged aphid that is a pest of garden plants, houseplants, and crops

green·gage /greén gàyj/ *n.* **1.** KIND OF PLUM TREE a variety of plum tree that has roundish sweet green fruits. Latin name: *Prunus domestica italica.* **2.** PLUM FRUIT the fruit of the greengage tree [Early 18thC. *Gage* from the name of Sir William *Gage,* who introduced it to England.]

green·gro·cer /greén grṑssər/ *n. U.K.* somebody who sells fresh fruit and vegetables. ◊ **grocer**

green·head /greén hèd/ *n.* a male mallard duck

green·heart /greén haart/ (*plural* **-hearts** *or* **-heart**) *n.* **1.** TROPICAL AMERICAN TREE an evergreen tropical American tree of the laurel family with dark greenish wood. Latin name: *Ocotea rodiaei.* **2.** TREE RESEMBLING THE GREENHEART any of a number of trees similar to the true greenheart. ◊ **African greenheart 3.** GREENHEART TREE WOOD the wood of any of the greenheart trees

green·horn /greén hàwrn/ *n.* somebody who is naïve and unsophisticated

WORD KEY: SYNONYMS

See Synonyms at ***beginner.***

green·house /greén hòwss/ (*plural* **-hous·es** /-howzizz/) *n.* **1.** HOTHOUSE a glass or transparent plastic structure, often on a metal or wooden frame, in which plants that need heat, light, and protection from the elements are grown **2.** SEE-THROUGH DOME ON AIRCRAFT a transparent plastic dome or cover for part of an aircraft (*informal*)

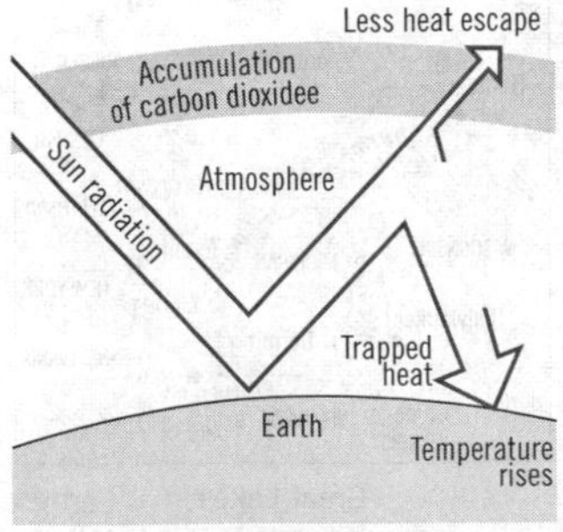

Greenhouse effect

green·house ef·fect *n.* warming of the Earth's surface as a result of atmospheric pollution by gases. It is now feared that the warming effects are being undesirably increased, causing climate changes and melting polar icecaps.

green·house gas *n.* a gas such as carbon dioxide, ozone, or water vapor that contributes to the warming of the Earth's atmosphere by reflecting radiation from the Earth's surface

green keep·er *n. U.K.* = **greenskeeper**

Greenland

Green·land /greénlənd/ island situated between the North Atlantic and Arctic oceans. The largest island in the world, it is a self-governing part of Denmark. Capital: Nuuk. Population: 58,000 (1996). Area: 840,000 sq. mi./2,175,600 sq. km. —**Green·land·er** /greén ləndər/ *n.*

Green·land·ic /green lándik/ *n.* **INUIT DIALECT** a dialect of Inuit spoken in Greenland by about 60,000 people ■ *adj.* **1. OF GREENLAND DIALECT** relating to the dialect Greenlandic **2. OF GREENLAND** relating to or typical of Greenland or its people or culture

Green·land right whale *n.* ZOOL = **bowhead**

Green·land Sea section of the Atlantic Ocean off the coast of northeastern Greenland that is covered by pack ice for most of the year

green light *n.* **1. SIGNAL TO PROCEED** a light that is green in color and is used as a signal at intersections for vehicles or pedestrians to proceed **2. PERMISSION TO BEGIN** permission to start work on something, especially a project or plan

green·light /greén lìt/ (**-light·ed, -light·ing, -lights**) *vt.* to give approval or permission for something to proceed (*informal*) ○ *Are they going to get the green light for the project?* [From the traffic signal of green meaning to proceed]

green·ling /greénling/ (*plural* **-lings** *or* **-ling**) *n.* a fish of coastal waters in the northern Pacific Ocean with large pectoral fins, a large head, and a skin flap over each eye. Family: Hexagrammidae.

green·mail /greén màyl/ *n.* **BUSINESS PRESSURE BY THREAT OF TAKEOVER** the purchase of enough of a company's stock to threaten it with takeover, thereby forcing the company to buy back the stock at a higher price to avoid the takeover. ◊ **blackmail, graymail** ■ *vt.* (**-mailed, -mail·ing, -mails**) **GREENMAIL SOMEBODY** to subject a company to greenmail [Late 20thC. From GREEN "money" + BLACKMAIL.] —**green·mail·er** *n.*

green ma·nure *n.* a growing crop that is plowed directly back into the soil to act as a fertilizer

green·mar·ket *n.* = **farmers' market**

green mon·key *n.* a small olive green African monkey that lives in large troops in woodlands or on the edge of savannah grasslands. Latin name: *Cercophithecus aethiops.*

green mon·key dis·ease *n.* MED = **Marburg disease**

Green Moun·tains mountain range in the Appalachian system, extending from Canada into western Massachusetts. The highest point is Mount Mansfield, 4,393 ft./1,339 m.

green·ock·ite /greénə kìt/ *n.* a yellowish crystalline mineral consisting of cadmium sulfide [Mid-18thC. Named for Charles Murray Cathcart, Lord *Greenock*.]

Gree·nough /greénō/, **Horatio** (1805–52) U.S. sculptor. He worked in Italy from 1828 to 1851, and is known for his neoclassical statue of George Washington (1832–40) at the Smithsonian Institution in Washington, D.C.

green pa·per *n.* in the United Kingdom or Canada, a document that contains the government's policy proposals that are to be discussed in Parliament. ◊ **white paper**

Green Par·ty *n.* a British political party formed in 1985 whose primary policy is the protection of the environment

Green·peace /greén peèss/ *n.* an international organization that advocates the protection of the environment and takes nonviolent action to achieve its goals

green pep·per *n.* an unripe sweet pepper eaten raw or cooked. Latin name: *Capsicum annuum.* ◊ **red pepper, bell pepper**

green plov·er *n.* BIRDS = **lapwing**

green rev·o·lu·tion *n.* the introduction of modern farming techniques and higher yielding, more pest-resistant varieties of crops in order to significantly increase crop production

green·room /greén ròom, -ròom/ *n.* a room in a studio, theater, or concert hall where performers may relax before or after a performance or appearance

greens /greenz/ *npl.* **1. VEGETABLES WITH GREEN LEAVES AND STEMS** vegetables with green leaves and stems, e.g., cabbage and spinach **2. DECORATIVE GREENERY** green foliage used for decoration **3. GREEN-COLORED CLOTHING** green clothing, e.g., Army uniforms or operating room scrubs (*informal*)

green·sand /greén sànd/ *n.* sandstone flecked with the dark green clay mineral glauconite

Greens·bor·o /greénz bùrə, -bùrō/ city in northern North Carolina, the site of the University of North Carolina. Population: 196,167 (1994).

green·shank /greén shàngk/ (*plural* **-shanks** *or* **-shank**) *n.* a large sandpiper of Europe and Asia with long greenish legs. Latin name: *Tringa nebularia.*

green·sick·ness /greén sìknəss/ *n.* = **chlorosis** *n.* 2 —**green·sick** *adj.*

greens·keep·er /greénz keèpər/ *n.* somebody employed to maintain a golf course or bowling green

green snake *n.* a North American snake that is yellow-green in color and feeds on insects, especially grasshoppers. Genus: *Opheodryas.*

green·stick frac·ture /greén stìk-/ *n.* a bone fracture usually occurring in children, in which one side of the bone is broken and the other side is bent [*Greenstick* from GREEN "immature" + STICK because it resembles a stick]

green·stone /greén stòn/ *n.* GEOL **1. GREEN IGNEOUS ROCK** a green igneous rock containing the minerals feldspar and hornblende **2. ROCK SIMILAR TO JADE** a rock that includes material similar to jade and was used in antiquity to fabricate decorative objects such as ceremonial axes

green·strip /greén strìp/ *n.* a firebreak on open grassland, planted with vegetation that does not burn easily

green·sward /greén swàwrd/ *n.* a grass-covered piece of ground, or an area of turf (*archaic or literary*)

green·tail·ing /greén tàyling/ *n.* environmentally responsible retailing that involves the sale of products with the least impact on the environment or that increases the ecological awareness of the consumer (*informal*) [Coined from GREEN + *tailing* from retail]

green tea *n.* tea made from leaves that have been dried but not fermented, and that is pale green in color. ◊ **black tea**

green thumb *n.* a natural ability to make plants grow well

green tur·tle *n.* a large marine turtle of warm waters, sometimes killed for food. It comes to land only to bask, sleep, and lay eggs. Latin name: *Chelonia mydas.* [From its green shell]

Green·ville /greénvil/ industrial city on the Reedy River in northwestern South Carolina, on the Piedmont Plateau. Population: 57,064 (1996).

green vit·ri·ol *n.* = **ferrous sulfate**

green·way /greén wày/ *n.* a stretch of undeveloped land close to an urban area that is kept for recreational use

Green·wich /grénnich, -ij/ **1.** borough of London, England, on the southern bank of the Thames River. It is the site of the prime meridian, which passes through the Royal Greenwich Observatory. Population: 211,410 (1995). **2.** fashionable residential community and resort town in southwestern Connecticut, on Long Island Sound near the border with New York State. Population: 58,441 (1990).

Green·wich Mean Time /grìnnij-/, **Green·wich Time** *n.* the time in a zone that includes the 0° meridian of Greenwich, London, England, used internationally as the main standard from which the time in other zones is calculated

Green·wich Vil·lage /grènnich-, grìnnich-/ *n.* a residential area in lower Manhattan, once popular with bohemians, artists, and writers and now a tourist attraction

green·wood /greén wòod/ *n.* a forest or woods in the summer when the leaves are green. It is the traditional location for stories about outlaws such as Robin Hood. (*archaic*)

Green·wood /greénwòod/ city and county seat of Greenwood County in western South Carolina, northwest of Columbia. Population: 20,807 (1990).

green wood·peck·er *n.* a large European woodpecker with green feathers and a red crown, often found feeding on the ground. Latin name: *Picus viridis.*

Germaine Greer

Greer /greer/, **Germaine** (*b.* 1939) Australian writer and feminist. She launched her career as a passionate advocate of women's empowerment with her first book, *The Female Eunuch* (1970).

greet /greet/ (**greet·ed, greet·ing, greets**) *vt.* **1. WELCOME SOMEBODY** to welcome somebody in a cordial and usually conventional way **2. ADDRESS SOMEBODY COURTEOUSLY** to address somebody in a polite and usually conventional way on meeting **3. ADDRESS SOMEBODY IN A LETTER** to address a person or group at the start of a letter using a set formula **4. REPLY TO SOMETHING** to receive or respond to something in a particular way ○ *the news was greeted with dismay* **5. BECOME NOTICEABLE** to become perceptible to somebody, especially by way of the senses such as vision, hearing, or smell ○ *The smell of a cake baking greeted them.* [Old English *grētan.* Ultimately from a prehistoric West Germanic word meaning "to resound."]

greet·er /greéter, -ər/ *n.* somebody employed to greet customers in a restaurant or similar business

greet·ing /greéting/ *n.* **1. FRIENDLY GESTURE** a cordial and often conventional gesture or expression used when welcoming, meeting, or addressing somebody **2. WELCOMING SOMEBODY** an act of welcoming or addressing somebody with a greeting ■ *npl.* **MESSAGE** a friendly message or good wishes [Old English *grēting*]

greet·ing card *n.* a folded piece of heavy paper with an image or design and a message to somebody to mark a special occasion

greet·ings card *n.* U.K. = **greeting card**

greg·a·rine /gréggə reèn/ *n.* **PARASITIC PROTOZOAN** a protozoan that lives as a parasite in the digestive tracts of some insects, arthropods, annelids, and other invertebrates. Order: Gregarinida. ■ *adj* .**greg·a·rine, greg·a·rin·i·an OF GREGARINE PROTOZOANS** relating to or belonging to the order that comprises the gregarines [Mid-19thC. Formed from modern Latin *Gregarina*, genus name, from Latin *gregarius* (see GREGARIOUS).]

gre·gar·i·ous /grə gáiree əss/ *adj.* **1. FRIENDLY** very friendly and sociable **2.** ZOOL **LIVING COMMUNALLY** used to describe organisms that live in groups **3.** PLANTS **GROWING TOGETHER** used to describe plants that grow in clusters [Mid-17thC. Formed from Latin *gregarius*, from *grex* "flock."] —**gre·gar·i·ous·ly** *adv.* —**gre·gar·i·ous·ness** *n.*

WORD KEY: ORIGIN

The Latin word *grex* from which ***gregarious*** is derived is also the source of English *aggregate, congregation,* and *egregious.*

Gre·go·ri·an cal·en·dar /gri gáwree ən/ *n.* the calendar introduced in 1582 by Pope Gregory XIII that is still in use and is a modification of the previous Roman calendar. ◊ **Julian calendar, Hegira calendar**

Gre·go·rian chant *n.* a liturgical chant of the Roman Catholic Church that is sung without accompaniment [From its supposedly having been introduced by Pope *Gregory* I]

Gre·go·ri·an tel·e·scope *n.* an astronomical telescope that has a concave primary mirror with a central hole through which light is reflected from a smaller secondary concave mirror [Mid-18thC. Named for the Scottish mathematician J. *Gregory* (1638–75) who invented it.]

grei·sen /grī́z'n/ *n.* a granite-derived rock consisting of mica and quartz [Late 19thC. From German, probably formed from *greis* "gray with age."]

grem·lin /grémmlin/ *n.* a tiny imaginary mischievous creature that is blamed for faults in tools, machinery, and electronic equipment (*informal*) [Early 20thC. Origin uncertain: probably modeled on GOBLIN, first used by air force personnel in World War II.]

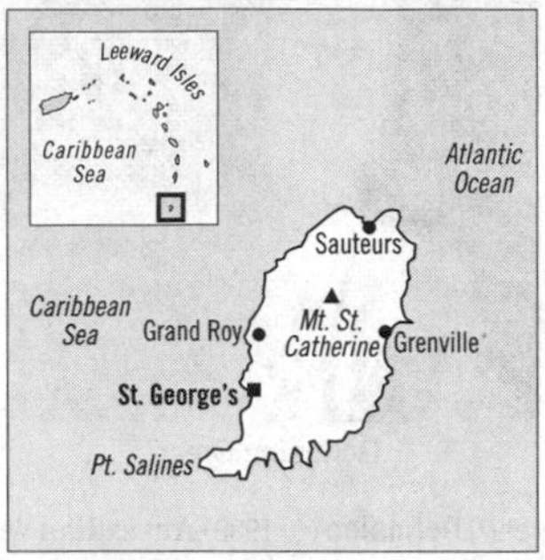

Grenada

Gre·na·da /gri náydə/ independent state in the southeastern Caribbean Sea, comprising the island of Grenada and some of the southern Grenadines. Language: English. Currency: East Caribbean dollar. Capital: St. George's. Population: 95,535 (1997). Area: 133 sq. mi./344 sq. km. —**Gre·na·di·an** /grə náydee ən/ *n., adj.*

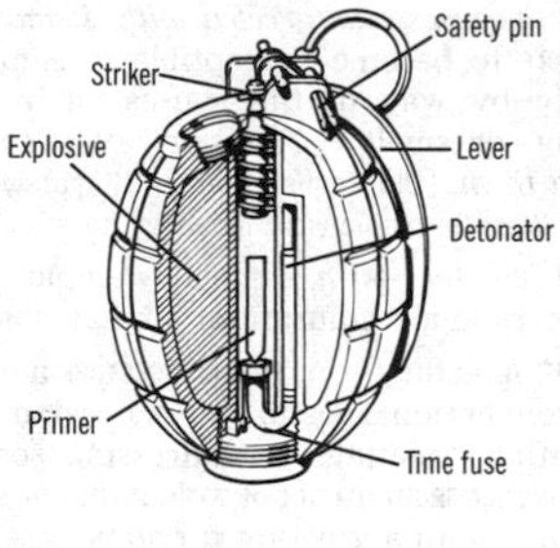

Grenade

gre·nade /grə náyd/ *n.* **1.** HAND-THROWN BOMB a small bomb that is thrown by hand or shot from a rifle or other weapon **2.** SEALED GLASS PROJECTILE a sealed glass projectile that breaks on impact, releasing tear gas or chemicals to put out fires [Mid-16thC. From French, an alteration of *grenate* "pomegranate" (influenced by Spanish *granada*), from *pome grenate.* The powder capsules in a grenade were thought to resemble the seeds in the fruit.]

gren·a·dier /grènnə deér/ (*plural* **-diers** *or* **-dier**) *n.* **1.** GRENADE-CARRYING SOLDIER formerly, a soldier armed with grenades **2.** TALL STRONG SOLDIER formerly, a soldier assigned to a special company of a regiment on the basis of exceptional height and ability **3.** ZOOL BOTTOM-DWELLING FISH a bottom-dwelling marine fish with a tapering body and no tail fin. Family: Macrouridae. **4.** BIRDS EAST AFRICAN FINCH an East African finch with purple patches, a red beak, and a tapering tail. Latin name: *Uraeginthus ianthinogaster.* **5.** BIRDS AFRICAN WEAVERBIRD an African weaverbird with a black head and bright red plumage on its crown and back. Latin name: *Euplectes orix.* [Late 17thC. Formed from GRENADE.]

Gren·a·dier, Gren·a·dier guard *n.* a British soldier belonging to the first regiment of the Guards Division, the troops of the Royal Household

gren·a·dine[1] /grènnə deén, grénnə deèn/ *n.* **1.** POMEGRANATE SYRUP a syrup made from pomegranates, used especially in cocktails **2.** RED-ORANGE a reddish-orange color ■ *adj.* RED-ORANGE of a reddish-orange color [Late 19thC. From French (*sirop de*) *grenadine*, from *grenade* (see GRENADE).]

gren·a·dine[2] /grènnə deén, grénnə deèn/ *n.* a dress fabric of silk or wool woven like gauze [Mid-19thC. From French, "silk having a texture like grain," from, ultimately, *grain* (see GRAIN).]

Gre·no·ble /gri nṓb'l, grə nóbb'l/ industrial city and capital of Isère Department, in the Rhône-Alpes Region, southeastern France. Population: 150,758 (1990).

Gresh·am's law /gréshəmz-/, **Gresh·am's the·o·rem** *n.* the theory that bad money drives good money out of circulation because a currency of lower intrinsic value will be used while one of higher intrinsic value will be hoarded [Mid-19thC. Named for Sir Thomas *Gresham* (1519?-79), the founder of the Royal Exchange in London, England, sub-financial advisor to Queen Elizabeth I.]

Gret·na /grétnə/ city in the southeastern corner of Louisiana, across the Mississippi River from New Orleans. Population: 16,862 (1996).

Gret·zky /grétskee/, **Wayne** (*b.* 1961) Canadian ice hockey player. He led the Edmonton Oilers to four Stanley Cup championships. He was named the NHL's most valuable player nine times and became the league's all-time leading scorer. Known as **the Great One**

grew past tense of **grow**

grey *adj., n., vti.* = **gray**

Grey /gray/, **Albert Henry George, 4th Earl** (1851–1917) British colonial administrator. He was governor-general of Canada (1904–11).

Grey, Lady Jane, Queen of England (1537–54). The great-granddaughter of Henry VII, she was named as the successor of Edward VI in 1553. She ruled for only nine days before being forced to abdicate, and was executed for treason.

Grey, Zane (1872–1939) U.S. writer. His dozens of popular "dime novels", including *Riders of the Purple Sage* (1912), helped define the Western as a literary genre. Full name **Pearl Zane Grey**

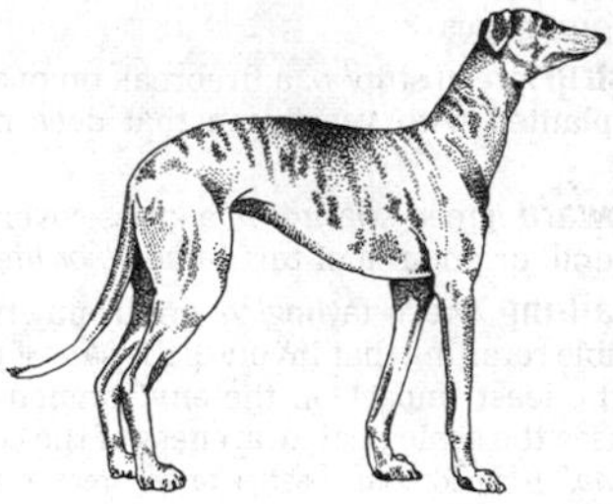

Greyhound

grey·hound /gráy hòwnd/ *n.* a tall slim fast-running dog with a smooth coat, narrow head, and long legs, widely used for racing [Old English *grīghund. Grey-* ultimately from a prehistoric Germanic base that is also the ancestor of Old Norse *grey* "bitch."]

grey·mail /gráy mayl/ *n.* U.K. = **graymail**

Grey·mouth /gráymәth/ town on the western coast of the South Island, New Zealand. A former gold-mining town, it is now the commercial center of a mining and industrial region. Population: 10,191 (1996).

grib·ble /gríbb'l/ *n.* a small marine crustacean of the woodlouse family that burrows into submerged wooden structures. Genus: *Limnoria.* [Late 18thC. Origin uncertain.]

grid /grid/ *n.* **1.** MAPS REFERENCE LINES ON A MAP a network of evenly spaced horizontal and vertical lines on a map, used as a basis for finding specific points **2.** ADJACENT SQUARES a network of squares formed by horizontal and vertical lines **3.** GRATING MADE OF BARS a set of parallel or crisscrossing bars that form a grating **4.** UTIL NETWORK a network of cables, lines, or pipes for distributing electricity, gas, or water ○ *the Northeast power grid* **5.** ELECTRON ENG CONTROL ELECTRODE the part of a vacuum tube that controls the flow of current between the other electrodes, usually constructed as a metal screen or coil **6.** MOTOR SPORTS = **starting grid 7.** FOOTBALL = **gridiron** *n.* 3 [Mid-19thC. Shortening of GRIDIRON.] —**grid·ded** *adj.*

grid bi·as *n.* a fixed voltage applied between the control electrode and the cathode in a vacuum tube

grid·der /gríddər/ *n.* a football player (*informal*) [Early 20thC. Formed from GRID.]

grid·dle /grídd'l/ *n.* HEATED COOKING SURFACE a heavy flat metal plate heated and used for cooking food ■ *vt.* (**-dled, -dling, -dles**) COOK SOMETHING ON A GRIDDLE to cook something on a flat hot surface [Pre-12thC. From Old French *gredil* "gridiron," from, ultimately, Latin *cratis* "crate."]

grid·i·ron /gríd ìrn/ *n.* **1.** = **grill**[1] *n.* 2 **2.** GRATING a structure consisting of parallel bars **3.** FOOTBALL FOOTBALL FIELD a field marked with parallel white lines, on which football is played **4.** FOOTBALL FOOTBALL the game of football (*informal*) **5.** THEATER STRUCTURE ABOVE A THEATER STAGE a structure of beams or bars above a theater stage from which lighting and scenery are suspended [13thC. Alteration of GRIDDLE, by association with IRON.]

grid·lock /gríd lòk/ *n.* **1.** TRAFFIC JAM a traffic jam in which congestion at one or two intersections affects a wide area so that traffic is unable to move in any direction **2.** DEADLOCK a situation in which no progress can be made —**grid·locked** *adj.*

grid ref·er·ence *n.* a reference, usually using numbers or letters, that specifies a position on a map or chart by referring to the superimposed grid

grief /greef/ *n.* **1.** INTENSE SORROW great sadness, especially as a result of a death **2.** CAUSE OF INTENSE SORROW the cause of intense, deep, and profound sorrow, especially a specific event or situation **3.** TROUBLE annoyance or trouble (*informal*) [Pre-12thC. Via Anglo-Norman *gref* from Old French *grief* "grieved," from *grever* (see GRIEVE).] ◇ **come to grief** to suffer misfortune or ruin ◇ **good grief!** used to express surprise, exasperation, or dismay (*dated informal*)

grief-strick·en *adj.* deeply affected by sadness

Edvard Grieg

Grieg /greeg/, **Edvard** (1843–1907) Norwegian composer. His work was permeated by the melodies and harmonies of Norwegian folk music. He was a noted composer of songs, and wrote the music to Henrik Ibsen's *Peer Gynt* (1875). Full name **Edvard Hagerup Grieg**

griev·ance /gréevənss/ *n.* **1.** SOMETHING THOUGHT REASON ENOUGH TO COMPLAIN a cause for complaint or resentment that may or may not be well-founded **2.** RESENTMENT bitterness or anger at having received unfair treatment **3.** FORMAL OBJECTION a formal complaint made on the basis of something that somebody feels is unfair

griev·ance com·mit·tee *n.* a committee in the workplace formed by management and employees to resolve workers' grievances

grieve /greev/ (**grieved, griev·ing, grieves**) *v.* **1.** *vti.* EXPERIENCE INTENSE SORROW to experience great sadness, e.g., at a death **2.** *vt.* MAKE SAD to cause great sadness to somebody [Pre-12thC. Via Old French *grever* "to burden" from Latin *gravare,* from *gravis* "heavy, grave" (source of English *gravity*).] —**griev·er** *n.*

griev·ous /gréevəss/ *adj.* **1.** VERY SERIOUS extremely serious or significant **2.** SEVERE very bad or severe —**griev·ous·ly** *adv.* —**griev·ous·ness** *n.*

Griffin

grif·fin /gríffin/, **grif·fon, gryph·on** *n.* a mythical monster with the head and wings of an eagle and the body and tail of a lion [13thC. Via Old French *grifoun* from Latin *gryphus*, from Greek *grups*.]

Grif·fin /gríffin/ city and county seat of Spalding County, central Georgia, situated 42 mi./68 km southeast of Atlanta. Population: 21,347 (1990).

Grif·fith /gríffith/, **D. W.** (1875–1948) U.S. movie director. He originated many now-standard cinematic techniques, including the close-up, fade-out, and flashback. Notable films include *The Birth of a Nation* (1915) and *Intolerance* (1916). Full name **David Lewelyn Wark Griffith**

Grif·fith, Melanie (*b.* 1957) U.S. movie actor. She made her mark in such films as *Something Wild* (1986) and *Working Girl* (1988).

Grif·fith Joy·ner /grìffith jóynər/, **Florence** (1959–98) U.S. athlete. A sprinter, she was an Olympic gold and silver medallist who was also known for her eye-catching running clothes. Born **Delorez Florence Griffith**. Known as **Flojo**

grif·fon /gríffən/ *n.* **1. SMALL DOG** a small dog like a terrier belonging to a breed with wiry hair and a short muzzle **2.** MYTHOL = **griffin** [Late 18thC. Via French from Old French *grifoun* (see GRIFFIN).]

grif·fon vul·ture *n.* a large light-colored vulture with dark wing and tail feathers, found in southern Europe, North Africa, and the Middle East. Genus: *Gyps*.

grift /grift/ *n.* (*informal*) **1. FRAUD** a swindle or confidence game **2. PROCEEDS FROM FRAUD** money made from a swindle or confidence game ■ *vti.* **(grift·ed, grift·ing, grifts) SWINDLE SOMEBODY** to carry out a swindle or obtain something by swindling (*informal*) [Early 20th. Origin uncertain: probably an alteration of *graft*.] —**grift·er** *n.*

gri·gri /gree gree/ (*plural* **-gris** /gree gree/), **gree·gree** (*plural* **-grees**), **gris-gris** (*plural* **gris-gris**) *n.* an African talisman or fetish [Late 18thC. Via American Spanish from Caribbean *grugru* "palm."]

grill[1] /gril/ *v.* **(grilled, grill·ing, grills) 1.** *vti.* **COOK OVER DIRECT HEAT** to cook food or be cooked by direct heat **2.** *vt.* **INTERROGATE** to interrogate or cross-examine somebody in a persistent manner (*informal*) **3.** *vti.* **SUBJECT TO GREAT HEAT** to subject somebody or something or be subjected to great heat, especially from the sun **4.** *vt.* **MARK SOMETHING USING GRIDIRON** to mark a gridiron pattern on something ■ *n.* **1.** *U.K.* = **broiler 2. PLATE FOR GRILLING** flat plate made of parallel metal bars used for grilling **3.** INDUST **GRIDIRON PATTERN** a pattern made on a surface by a grill or gridiron **4.** FOOD **FOOD COOKED ON GRILL** a dish or portion of food cooked on a grill **5.** COOK **RESTAURANT SERVING GRILLED FOOD** an establishment that serves food cooked on a grill [Mid-17thC. From French *griller*, from *grille* (see GRILLE).] —**grill·er** *n.*

WORD KEY: SYNONYMS

See Synonyms at ***question***.

grill[2] *n.* = **grille**

gril·lage /grillij/ *n.* a framework of beams and crossbeams built as a foundation for a building on soft ground

grille /gril/, **grill** *n.* **1.** BUILDING **CRISSCROSSED BARS** a pattern or lattice of bars, especially in front of a window **2.** AUTOMOT **PART OF COOLING SYSTEM** a metal grating that allows cooling air into the radiator of a vehicle's engine **3.** TENNIS **COURT TENNIS WALL OPENING** in court tennis, the opening in one corner of an end wall of the court [Mid-17thC. Via French from Old French *graille*, from, ultimately, Latin *cratis* "grating, hurdle."] —**grilled** *adj.*

grill·room /gríl ròom, gríl ro͞om/ *n.* = **grill**[1] *n.* 5

grill·work /gríl wùrk/ *n.* = **grille** *n.* 1

grilse /grils/ (*plural* **grils·es** *or* **grilse**) *n.* a salmon the first time it returns from the sea [15thC. Origin unknown.]

grim /grim/ **(grim·mer, grim·mest)** *adj.* **1. DEPRESSING** depressingly gloomy ○ *a grim economic forecast* **2. FORBIDDING** forbidding and unattractive in appearance ○ *a grim mining town of Great Depression times* **3. STERNLY SERIOUS** stern in a frightening and unnerving way ○ *a grim, set look on his face* **4. UNPLEASANT** extremely unpleasant, distressing, or sinister ○ *a grim accident scene* **5. IRONIC** disquietingly ironic ○ *a grim reminder of humankind's penchant for folly* [Old English. Ultimately from a prehistoric Germanic word that is also the ancestor of English *grumble* and Spanish *grima* "fright" (source of English *grimace*).] —**grim·ly** *adv.* —**grim·ness** *n.*

grim·ace /grímməss, gri máyss/ *n.* **EXPRESSION ON FACE** contorted twisting of the face that expresses disgust or pain ■ *vi.* **(-aced, -ac·ing, -ac·es) MAKE A GRIMACE** to twist the face in a grimace [Mid-17thC. Via French *grimache* from Spanish *grimazo* "caricature," from *grima* (see GRIM).] —**grim·ac·er** *n.* —**gri·mac·ing·ly** *adv.*

Grim·al·di /gri máwldee/ *n.* ASTRON a very large, dark-floored enclosure near the western edge of the moon, approximately 135 mi./220 km in diameter

gri·mal·kin /gri máwlkin, -málkin/ *n.* an old female cat [Late 16thC. From GRAY + obsolete *malkin* "cat" (from a pet form of the female names *Maud* or *Matilda*).]

grime /grīm/ *n.* **ACCUMULATED DIRT** dirt or soot, usually accumulated in a black layer or ingrained into a surface ■ *vt.* **(grimed, grim·ing, grimes) COVER WITH GRIME** to coat something with dirt or soot [13thC. From Middle Low German *greme*.]

Grim·ké /grímkee/, **Angelina Emily** (1805–79) U.S. abolitionist and reformer. She was a leading abolitionist and women's rights campaigner whose works include the antislavery tract *Appeal to the Christian Women of the South* (1836). Sarah Moore Grimké was her sister.

Grim·ké, Sarah Moore (1792–1873) U.S. abolitionist and reformer. The sister of Angelina Emily Grimké, she lectured and wrote in support of women's rights and the abolition of slavery.

Grimm /grim/, **Jakob** (1785–1863) German philologist and folklorist. He was the founder of comparative linguistics, and formulated Grimm's Law. In collaboration with his brother, Wilhelm Karl Grimm (1786–1859), he collected old German folk tales and published them in collections now known as *Grimm's Fairy Tales* (1812–22). Full name **Jakob Ludwig Karl Grimm**

Grim Reap·er *n.* a personification of death, shown as a cloaked man or skeleton holding a scythe

grim·y /grímee/ **(-i·er, -i·est)** *adj.* heavily soiled, usually with dirt or soot —**grim·i·ly** *adv.* —**grim·i·ness** *n.*

WORD KEY: SYNONYMS

See Synonyms at ***dirty***.

grin /grin/ *vi.* **(grinned, grin·ning, grins) SMILE BROADLY** to smile broadly, usually showing the teeth ■ *n.* **BROAD SMILE** a broad smile that usually shows the teeth [Old English *grennian* "to bare your teeth." Ultimately from an Indo-European base meaning "to be open," ancestor also of English *groan*. The underlying idea is "opening the mouth."] —**grin·ner** *n.* ◇ **grin and bear it** to tolerate something unpleasant without complaining (*informal*)

grinch /grinch/ *n.* somebody grouchy and contrary who spoils the fun of others (*informal*) [Late 20thC. From the character in the children's story *How the Grinch Stole Christmas* by Dr. Seuss (1957), pseudonym of Theodor Seuss Geisel.]

grind /grīnd/ *v.* **(ground, grind·ing, grinds) 1.** *vti.* **PULVERIZE SOMETHING** to crush something into very small pieces by rubbing it between two hard surfaces, or to be crushed in this way **2.** *vti.* **MAKE A RASPING NOISE** to rub two surfaces together with a grating noise or make a grating noise by rubbing things together ○ *He ground the gears every time he shifted.* **3.** *vt.* **PUSH DOWN WITH TWISTING MOTION** to push something down firmly or crush something on a surface with a twisting or rotating motion ○ *ground the cigarette out on the pavement* **4.** *vt.* **CHOP INTO TINY PIECES** to chop food, especially meat, into tiny pieces, using a mechanical device **5.** *vt.* **SMOOTH OR SHARPEN SOMETHING** to make something smooth or sharp by rubbing it against an abrasive surface **6.** *vi.* **MOVE NOISILY** to move with a grating noise **7.** *vt.* **TURN A HANDLE TO RUN SOMETHING** to operate something such as a barrel organ by turning its handle **8.** *vi.* **LABOR AT SOMETHING** to study or work hard, especially too hard (*informal*) **9.** *vi.* **DANCE EROTICALLY** to dance erotically with a circling of the hips (*informal*) ■ *n.* **1. SOMETHING BORING AND REPETITIVE** something that is routine, dull, and tedious (*informal*) **2. GRINDING** an act of grinding **3. GRINDING NOISE** a grating noise like that of something grinding **4. TEXTURE** the texture of something that is ground **5. HARD WORKER** somebody who works or studies too hard (*informal*) **6. EROTIC DANCE MOVEMENT** an erotic circling and thrusting of the hips in dancing (*informal*) [Old English *grindan*]

grind down *vt.* to weaken somebody gradually by persistent oppression

grind on *vi.* to continue in an unrelenting way

grind out *vt.* **1. DO SOMETHING ROTE** to perform or produce something mechanically as a result of boredom or excessive familiarity with the process **2. SAY WITH ROUGH VOICE** to say something with a rough or grating voice **3. PUT SOMETHING OUT BY CRUSHING** to extinguish something by crushing it on a surface with a twisting motion

grind·er /grīndər/ *n.* **1. SOMEBODY OR SOMETHING THAT GRINDS** somebody or something that grinds something ○ *a coffee grinder* **2. TOOTH** a molar tooth **3.** *New England* **LARGE SANDWICH** a sandwich with a filling of meat or seafood, chopped raw vegetables, cheese, and dressing, served on a long roll [Old English *grindere*. Originally, "somebody who grinds anything in a mill."]

grind·ing /grīnding/ *adj.* **1. OPPRESSIVE** oppressive and relentless ○ *grinding poverty* **2. GRATINGLY NOISY** characterized by a grating sound —**grind·ing·ly** *adv.*

grind·stone /grīnd stōn/ *n.* **1. STONE WHEEL FOR SHARPENING** an abrasive wheel that sharpens or polishes something **2. STONE FOR SHARPENING** any stone used for sharpening or polishing something **3.** = **millstone** ◇ **keep** *or* **put your nose to the grindstone** to keep working hard without taking a break

grin·go /gríng gō/ (*plural* **-gos**) *n.* an offensive term used in Spain and Latin America to refer to an English-speaking foreigner (*slang insult*) [Mid-19thC. From Spanish, "foreigner."]

grin·nie *n.* (*regional*) **1. CHIPMUNK** a chipmunk **2. GROUND SQUIRREL** a ground squirrel [Of unknown origin]

gri·ot /gree ō, gree ót/ *n.* a member of a caste of professional oral historians in the Mali Empire [Early 19thC. From French.]

grip /grip/ *n.* **1. GRASPING OR HOLDING ACTION** an act of taking or keeping a firm hold of something **2. MANNER OF HOLDING** the way that somebody holds something ○ *a firm grip* **3. GRASP** a grasp or hold of something **4.** = **handgrip** *n.* 2 **5.** = **handgrip** *n.* 3 **6. HOLDING DEVICE** any device for holding something firmly **7. ABILITY NOT TO SLIP** the ability of something to adhere to a surface without slipping **8. CONTROL** power over somebody or something ○ *The dictator had millions of lives in his grip.* **9. COMPREHENSION** a proper understanding of something **10. SMALL SUITCASE** a bag or small holdall **11.** CINEMA, TV **MEMBER OF FILM CREW** a stagehand on a movie or television set who moves equipment **12.** THEATER **STAGEHAND** somebody who moves sets and props in a theater ■ *v.* **(gripped, grip·ping, grips) 1.** *vt.* **GRASP SOMETHING FIRMLY** to take or keep a firm hold of something **2.** *vti.* **STICK TO SOMETHING** to adhere to a surface without slipping **3.** *vt.* **TAKE CHARGE OF SOMEBODY OR SOMETHING** to take control of somebody or something ○ *I was gripped by a sudden, awful realization* **4.** *vt.* **CAPTURE INTEREST** to capture somebody's interest, imagination, or attention ○ *a performance that gripped the audience* [Partly from Old English *gripe* "grasp" and partly from Old English *gripa* "handful," both ultimately from the same prehistoric Germanic base] —**grip·per** *n.* ◇ **come to grips with something** to begin to understand and deal with something ◇ **lose your grip** to stop being as effective or as much in control as formerly

WORD KEY: SYNONYMS

See Synonyms at ***catch***.

gripe /grīp/ *v.* **(griped, grip·ing, gripes) 1.** *vi.* **GRUMBLE CONSTANTLY** to complain continually and irritatingly (*informal*) **2.** *vti.* **EXPERIENCE OR CAUSE STOMACH PAINS** to experience or cause somebody to suffer severe stomach pains (*informal*) **3.** *vt.* ANNOY SOMEBODY to irritate somebody intensely (*slang*) ○ *It really gripes me when you do something selfish like that.* ■ *n.* MINOR COMPLAINT a minor but irritating grievance (*informal*) [Old English *grīpan* "to seize." Ultimately from a prehistoric Germanic base that was also the ancestor of English *grip* and *grope.* The sense "to complain" probably evolved from "to cause stomach pain."] —**grip·er** *n.*

WORD KEY: SYNONYMS

See Synonyms at ***complain.***

grip·ing /grīping/ *adj.* sudden, sharp, and intense (*refers to stomach pain*) —**grip·ing·ly** *adv.*

grip·man /grípmən, -màn/ (*plural* **-men** /grípmən, -mèn/) *n.* a cable car operator who starts or stops the car by releasing or engaging a gripping device on the moving cable

grippe /grip/, **grip** *n.* influenza (*archaic*) [Late 18thC. From French, literally "seizure."] —**grip·py** *adj.*

grip·ping /grípping/ *adj.* holding the interest and attention completely

Gris /greess/, **Juan** (1887–1927) Spanish-born French artist. After 1906 he lived in Paris, where he was much influenced by cubism. In addition to paintings and collages, he designed sets for Diaghilev's ballets. Real name **José Vittoriano González**

Grisaille: *David and Goliath* by Andrea Mantegna

gri·saille /gri zī, gri záyl/ *n.* **1.** PAINTING TECHNIQUE a method of painting that uses shades of gray **2.** WORK IN GRISAILLE STYLE a work of art produced by the grisaille method [Mid-19thC. From French, from *gris* "gray."]

gris·e·o·ful·vin /grìzzee ō fóolvin/ *n.* an antibiotic used to treat external fungal infections, obtained from a fungus *Penicillium griseofulvum* [Mid-20thC. Coined from modern Latin *griseofulvum*, species name (from medieval Latin *griseus* "gray" + Latin *fulvus* "reddish-yellow") + -IN.]

gri·sette /gri zét/ *n.* formerly, a young working-class French woman [Early 18thC. From French, from *gris* "gray."]

gris-gris *n.* = **grigri**

Grish·am /gríshəm/, **John** (*b.* 1955) U.S. writer. His bestselling legal thrillers include *The Firm* (1991).

gris·ly /grízzlee/ (**-li·er, -li·est**) *adj.* gruesomely unpleasant or creating a sense of horror [12thC. Ultimately from a prehistoric West Germanic base denoting "terror," which was also the ancestor of Old English *āgrīsan* "to terrify."] —**gris·li·ness** *n.*

gri·son /grīss'n, gríz-/ (*plural* **-sons** *or* **-son**) *n.* a South American weasel that has striking gray, white, and black markings, and is sometimes used to hunt chinchillas. There are two species. Latin name: *Galictis vittata* and *Galictis cuja.* [Late 18thC. From French, from *gris* "gray."]

grist /grist/ *n.* **1.** GRAIN GROUND INTO FLOUR grain that is ground into flour **2.** GRAIN PRODUCED AT ONE GRINDING the quantity of grain that is ground in one batch [Old English. Ultimately from a prehistoric Germanic base that was also the ancestor of English *grind.*] ◇ **grist for the mill, grist for somebody's mill** a potential source of advantage or profit to somebody

gris·tle /gríss'l/ *n.* tough cartilage, especially in meat prepared for eating [Old English, of unknown origin]

gris·tly /grísslee/ (**-tli·er, -tli·est**) *adj.* consisting of, containing, or resembling gristle —**gris·tli·ness** *n.*

grist·mill /gríst mìl/ *n.* a mill where grain or corn is ground

grit /grit/ *n.* **1.** SAND OR STONE GRAINS small pieces of sand or stone **2.** TEXTURE OF GRAINS the texture of stone used for grinding **3.** PARTICLE SIZE a measure of the size of particles ○ *coarse grit* **4.** FIRMNESS OF CHARACTER determination or strength of character ■ *vt.* (**grit·ted, grit·ting, grits**) **1.** CLENCH TEETH to clench the teeth, especially when under stress **2.** *U.K.* COVER WITH GRIT to cover something with grit, especially an icy road [Old English *grēot.* Ultimately from a prehistoric Germanic base that is also the ancestor of English *groats* "husked grain."]

grits /grits/ *npl.* **1.** COARSELY GROUND CORN coarsely ground hulled corn that is boiled and eaten hot with butter, especially at breakfast in the southern United States (*takes a singular or plural verb*) **2.** GRAIN WITH HUSKS REMOVED grain that has had its husks removed or been coarsely ground [Late 16thC. Plural of obsolete *grit* "chaff," from Old English *grytta* "coarse meal."]

grit·ty /gríttee/ (**-ti·er, -ti·est**) *adj.* **1.** RESOLUTE courageous, resolute, or persistent **2.** REALISTIC having a stark realism **3.** LIKE OR WITH GRIT resembling, containing, or covered with grit —**grit·ti·ly** *adv.* —**grit·ti·ness** *n.*

griz·zle /grízz'l/ *vti.* (**-zled, -zling, -zles**) BECOME OR MAKE GRAY to make something gray, or become gray ■ *n.* **1.** GRAY a gray color **2.** GRAY HAIR hair that is gray or streaked with gray **3.** GRAY WIG a gray-colored wig [14thC. From Old French *grisel*, from *gris* "gray."]

griz·zled /grízz'ld/ *adj.* **1.** STREAKED WITH GRAY streaked with gray, especially with gray hair **2.** GRAY-HAIRED having hair that is gray or streaked with gray

griz·zly bear /grízzlee/, **griz·zly** *n.* a variety of brown bear found in northwestern North America that has brown fur tipped with white. Latin name: *Ursus arctos horribilis.*

groan /grōn/ *n.* **1.** MOURNFUL SOUND a long low cry expressing pain or misery **2.** LOUD CREAKING SOUND a loud creaking sound of something affected by pressure ○ *the ship's timbers groaned and creaked* **3.** GRIEVANCE an aggrieved complaint (*informal*) ■ *v.* (**groaned, groan·ing, groans**) **1.** *vi.* MOAN to utter a moan **2.** *vt.* EXPRESS WITH GROAN to express something by means of a groan **3.** *vi.* MAKE A LOUD CREAKING SOUND to make a loud creaking sound as a result of pressure **4.** *vi.* COMPLAIN to complain in an aggrieved way (*informal*) [Old English *grānian.* Ultimately from an Indo-European base meaning "to be open," which is also the ancestor of English *grin*, the underlying idea being "open-mouthed."] —**groan·er** *n.* —**groan·ing·ly** *adv.*

groats /grōts/ *npl.* grain, especially oats, that has been crushed or has had the husks removed (*takes a singular or plural verb*) [14thC. From Old English *grotan*; related to *grit.*]

gro·cer /grṓssər/ *n.* somebody who owns or runs a store selling food and other household goods [13thC. Via Old French *grossier* from medieval Latin *grossarius* "wholesale dealer," from *grossus* "large" (source of English *gross*).]

gro·cer·y /grṓssəree/ *n.* (*plural* **-ies**) **1.** = **grocery store** **2.** GROCER'S TRADE the trade or profession of a grocer ■ **gro·cer·ies** *npl.* FOOD SOLD IN GROCERY STORE goods, especially food, sold in a grocery store

gro·cer·y store *n.* a store that sells food and other household goods

gro·dy /grṓdee/ (**-di·er, -di·est**) *adj.* disgusting or extremely unpleasant (*slang*) [Mid-20thC. Formed by alteration from GROTESQUE.]

Groen·ing /grṓning/, **Matt** (*b.* 1954) U.S. cartoonist. He created the comic strips "Life in Hell" (1980) and television's animated cartoon family "The Simpsons" (1987).

Gro·fé /grṓ fày/, **Ferde** (1892–1972) U.S. composer and arranger. A pianist and orchestrator for Paul Whiteman's orchestra, he wrote the atmospheric *Grand Canyon Suite* (1931). Full name **Ferdinand Rudolph von Grofé**

grog /grog/ *n.* a mixture of alcohol, especially rum, and water, now often served hot with sugar and lemon juice [Mid-18thC. Shortening of *Old Grogram*, the nickname of Admiral Edward Vernon (from the grogram cloak he wore), who introduced the practice of watering down rum served to sailors.]

grog·gy /gróggee/ (**-gi·er, -gi·est**) *adj.* feeling weak or dizzy, especially because of illness, or overindulgence —**grog·gi·ly** *adv.* —**grog·gi·ness** *n.*

grog·ram /gróggrəm, grṓgrəm/ *n.* a stiff fabric of silk and wool or mohair. ◊ **grosgrain** [Mid-16thC. From French *gros grain* "coarse grain."]

Groin

groin /groyn/ *n.* **1.** AREA BETWEEN THIGHS AND ABDOMEN the area between the tops of the thighs and the abdomen **2.** GENITALS the genitals, especially the testicles **3.** CONSTRUCTION PROTECTING BEACH FROM EROSION a narrow wooden or concrete construction that extends from a shore into the sea to protect a beach from erosion **4.** ARCHIT EDGE BETWEEN VAULTS a curved line forming the edge between two intersecting vaults [14thC. Origin uncertain: possibly from Old English *grynde* "depression, hole," the underlying idea being "depression between the thighs."]

grok /grok/ (**grok·ked, grok·king, groks**) *vt.* to understand something completely by intuition (*slang*) ○ *Do you grok that?* [Mid-20thC. Coined by Robert HEINLEIN in the novel *Stranger in a Strange Land*, 1961.]

grom·met /grómmət, grúmmət/, **grum·met** /grúm-/ *n.* **1.** PROTECTIVE EYELET a protective eyelet in a material that prevents tearing either of the material or of a rope passed through it **2.** REINFORCEMENT AROUND EYELET a small ring of metal or plastic that reinforces an eyelet **3.** SAILING RING TO FASTEN A SAIL a ring used to fasten the edge of a sail to its stay [Early 17thC. From obsolete French *gromette* "curb of a bridle," from *gourmer* "to curb."]

grom·well /grómmwəl, gróm wèl/ *n.* a hairy flowering plant of the borage family that produces hard smooth white seeds. Genus: *Lithospermum.* [13thC. Anglicization of Old French *gromil*, of uncertain origin: perhaps from a variant of *graine* "grain" + *mil* "millet," from Latin *milium.*]

groom /groom, grŏom/ *n.* **1.** = **bridegroom** **2.** EQU SOMEBODY WHO CARES FOR HORSES somebody whose job is to look after horses by cleaning them and their stables **3.** OFFICER IN ROYAL HOUSEHOLD any of various officers in a royal household ■ *v.* (**groomed, groom·ing, grooms**) **1.** *vt.* CARE FOR AN ANIMAL'S APPEARANCE to clean and brush or comb an animal **2.** *vti.* ZOOL CLEAN ITS BODY to clean the fur, skin, or feathers of another animal or of itself, often with the tongue (*refers to an animal, especially a dog or cat*) **3.** *vt.* CARE FOR YOUR PERSONAL APPEARANCE to keep somebody else's or your own personal appearance neat **4.** *vt.* TRAIN to train and prepare somebody for a particular position **5.** *vt.* SKIING MAKE A PATH IN SNOW to clear a path or track in snow by compacting the snow [12thC. Origin uncertain: possibly from assumed Old English *groma* "boy, male servant," related to *grow.*] —**groom·er** *n.*

grooms·man /grŏomzmən, grŏom-/ (*plural* **-men** /-mən/) *n.* a man who is an attendant to a bridegroom

Groote Ey·landt /groot áy lant/ island in the Gulf of Carpentaria, off the northeastern coast of the Northern Territory of Australia. Population: 14,209 (1996). Area: 882 sq. mi./2,285 sq. km.

groove /groov/ *n.* **1.** NARROW PASSAGE a narrow channel or path in a surface **2.** TRACK CUT IN A RECORD a spiral track cut into a vinyl record along which the needle of the record player passes **3.** REGULARLY FOLLOWED PROCEDURE a routine into which somebody has settled (*informal*) **4.** ACTIVITY FITTED TO SOMEBODY an activity or situation suited to somebody's talents or tastes (*slang*) **5.** MUSIC MUSICAL BEAT a strong beat or rhythm in music (*slang*) ■ *v.* (**grooved, groov·ing, grooves**) **1.** *vt.* MAKE A GROOVE to cut a groove in a surface **2.** *vti.* MUSIC PLAY MUSIC RHYTHMICALLY to play jazz or dance music with a strong beat (*slang*) [14thC. From Dutch *groeve.* Ultimately from the same prehistoric Germanic base as English *grave*[1].] —**groov·er** *n.* ◇ **in the groove** **1.** functioning perfectly and with great ease (*slang*) **2.** MUSIC playing or performing in a highly accomplished manner (*dated slang*) **3.** up-to-date and in fashion (*dated slang*)

groov·y /gro͞ovee/ (**-i·er, -i·est**) *adj.* used, often as an exclamation, to describe somebody or something that is fashionable, excellent, or pleasing (*dated slang*) [Mid-20thC. From the phrase *in the groove*, originally referring to the grooves on a vinyl record.] —**groov·i·ly** *adv.* —**groov·i·ness** *n.*

grope /grōp/ *v.* (**groped, grop·ing, gropes**) **1.** *vi.* **SEARCH BY FEELING** to search for something blindly or uncertainly by feeling with the hands **2.** *vi.* **BE WITHOUT GUIDANCE** to strive blindly or uncertainly for something ○ *groping for inspiration* **3.** *vt.* **EXPLORE UNCERTAINLY** to feel your way forward slowly and hesitantly, e.g., in the dark ○ *They groped their way back out of the tunnel.* **4.** *vt.* **FONDLE SOMEBODY** to caress or touch somebody's body for sexual pleasure, often roughly, awkwardly, or without the person's consent (*slang*) ■ *n.* **1. ACT OF GROPING** an act or instance of groping **2. A FONDLE** a rough or unsolicited caress or touch for sexual pleasure (*slang*) [Old English *grāpian* "to grasp at." Ultimately from the same prehistoric Germanic base as English *grip* and *gripe*.] —**grop·er** *n.*

Walter Gropius

Gro·pi·us /grṓpee əss/, **Walter** (1883–1969) German-born U.S. architect and educator. A pioneer of the international style, he directed the Bauhaus design school in Weimar, Germany (1919–28). As head of Harvard University's architecture department (1938–52) he trained a generation of U.S. architects in the modernist idiom. Full name **Walter Adolph Gropius**

gros·beak /grṓss beek/ *n.* a finch found in Europe and North America with a large beak that it uses to crush seeds. Some classifications also include the cardinals. Family: Fringillidae and Emberizidae. [Late 17thC. From French *grosbec*, literally "large-beak."]

gro·schen /grṓsh'n/ (*plural* **-schen**) *n.* **1.** a minor unit of currency in Austria, one hundred of which are worth a schilling. See table at **currency 2. COIN WORTH ONE GROSCHEN** a coin worth one groschen **3. COIN WORTH TEN PFENNIGS** a coin in Germany worth 10 pfennigs (*informal*) **4. OLD GERMAN COIN** a silver coin issued in various regions of Germany from the 13th century [Early 17thC. Via German from, ultimately, medieval Latin *(denarius) grossus* "thick (penny)."]

gros·grain /grṓ gràyn/ *n.* a heavy corded silk or rayon fabric used mainly for trimmings and ribbons. ◊ **grogram** [Mid-19thC. From French, literally "coarse grain," which is also the source of English *grogram*.]

Gros Morne Na·tion·al Park /grṑ máwrn/ national park that is situated on the western coast of Newfoundland, Canada. It contains lakes and part of the Long Range Mountains. Area: 697 sq. mi./1,805 sq. km.

gros point /grṓ pòynt/ *n.* = **raised point** [From French *gros point (de Venise)*, literally "large stitch (from Venice," applied to a type of lace first manufactured in Venice]

gross /grōss/ *adj., adv.* **WITHOUT DEDUCTIONS** before any usual deductions such as tax or expenses have been made ■ *adj.* **1. VULGAR** vulgar or coarse **2. OBVIOUSLY WRONG** flagrantly wrong or unmitigated ○ *a gross breach of the rules* **3. DISGUSTING** disgusting or highly unpleasant (*slang*) ○ *The coffee in here is totally gross.* **4. WITHOUT GOOD TASTE OR APPRECIATION** not sensitive to, or not able to appreciate, the finer things in life **5. EXTREMELY OVERWEIGHT** overweight to an unhealthy or repellent degree (*informal*) **6. LUXURIANT** growing thickly or densely ■ *n.* **1.** (*plural* **gross**) **MEASURE TWELVE DOZEN** a quantity of 144 or twelve dozen **2. SUM BEFORE DEDUCTIONS** a total, especially a total amount of money before usual deductions are made ■ *vt.* (**grossed, gross·ing, gross·es**) **EARN MONEY** to earn or make an amount of money as profit before usual deductions are made ○ *This games arcade grosses more in a week than I make in a year.* [14thC. Via French from late Latin *grossus* "bulky, coarse" (source of English *engross* and *grocer*).] —**gross·ly** *adv.* —**gross·ness** *n.*

WORD KEY: SYNONYMS

See Synonyms at ***vulgar***.

gross out *vt.* to be disgusting or repellent to somebody (*slang*) ○ *language that really grossed me out*

Gross /grōss/, **Chaim** (1904–91) Austrian-born U.S. sculptor. He is noted for his flowing expressionist figures sculpted from wood and, later, stone and clay.

gross a·nat·o·my *n.* a branch of anatomy dealing with body parts that are visible to the naked eye

gross do·mes·tic prod·uct *n.* the total value of all goods and services produced within a country in a year, minus net income from investments in other countries

gross na·tion·al prod·uct *n.* the total value of all goods and services produced within a country in a year, including net income from investments in other countries

gross-out *n.* something considered disgusting or repellent (*slang*)

gross prof·it *n.* the difference between sales revenue and the cost of goods sold

gros·su·la·rite /gróssyələ rìt/, **gros·su·lar** /gróssyələr/ *n.* a yellow, green, or brown garnet found in chalky rock. The green variety often used as a gemstone. [Early 19thC. Via German from modern Latin *grossularia* "gooseberry" (because of the gem's color), from French *groseille* (a possible source of English *gooseberry*).]

Grosve·nor /grṓvnər/, **Gilbert** (1875–1966) Turkish-born U.S. editor and geographer. He edited *National Geographic Magazine* (1903–54). As president of the National Geographic Society (1920–54), he developed it into a major research organization. Full name **Gilbert Hovey Grosvenor**

grosz /grawsh/ (*plural* **gro·szy** /grawshee/ *or* **grosze**) *n.* **1.** a minor unit of Polish currency, one hundred of which are worth one zloty. See table at **currency 2. COIN WORTH ONE GROSZ** a coin worth one grosz [Mid-20thC. Via Polish *grosz* and Czech *groš* from medieval Latin *(denarius) grossus* (see GROSCHEN).]

Grosz /grōss/, **George** (1893–1959) German-born U.S. artist. He is known for his satirical caricatures of Berlin life during the 1920s and 1930s. Born **Georg Grosz**

grot /grot/ *n.* a grotto (*literary*) [Early 16thC. Via French *grotte* from Italian *grotta* (see GROTTO).]

gro·tesque /grō tésk, grə-/ *adj.* **1. DISTORTED** misshapen, especially in a strange or disturbing way ○ *The flames cast grotesque shadows on the wall.* **2. INCONGRUOUS** seeming strange or ludicrous through being out of place or unexpected **3.** ARTS **BLENDING REALISTIC AND FANTASTIC** relating to or typical of a style of art that mixes the realistic and the fantastic ■ *n.* **1.** ARTS **ART MIXING REALISTIC AND FANTASTIC** a style of art, especially in 16th-century Europe, in which representations of real and fantastic figures are mixed **2.** ARTS **GROTESQUE ARTISTIC PIECE** a piece of art in the grotesque style **3. SOMETHING GROTESQUE** somebody or something considered to be grotesque [Mid-16thC. Via French *crotesque* from Italian *grottesca* "like a grotto," from *grotta* "grotto," referring to the fanciful wall paintings found in excavated Roman ruins (see GROTTO).] —**gro·tesque·ly** *adv.* —**gro·tesque·ness** *n.*

gro·tes·que·rie /grō téskəree, grə-/, **gro·tes·que·ry** (*plural* **-ries**) *n.* **1. GROTESQUE QUALITY** the grotesque quality of something **2. SOMETHING STRANGE OR FANTASTIC** something grotesque, especially a piece of art in the grotesque style

Grot·on /grṓt'n/ town in southeastern Connecticut, situated on Long Island Sound opposite New London. Population: 45,144 (1990).

grot·to /gróttō/ (*plural* **-toes** *or* **-tos**) *n.* **1. CAVE** a cave, especially one with interesting natural features **2. IMITATION CAVE** an imitation cave, especially as an ornamental shelter in a formal garden [Early 17thC. Via Italian *grotta* from, ultimately, Latin *crypta* (see CRYPT).]

grot·ty /gróttee/ (**-ti·er, -ti·est**) *adj. U.K.* **1. DIRTY OR SHABBY** distastefully dirty, shabby, or in poor condition (*informal*) **2. GENERALLY UNPLEASANT** generally unpleasant or despicable (*informal*) **3.** dirty (*regional*) [Mid-20thC. Formed from GROTESQUE.] —**grot·ti·ly** *adv.* —**grot·ti·ness** *n.*

grouch /growch/ *vi.* (**grouched, grouch·ing, grouch·es**) **COMPLAIN** to complain or grumble (*informal*) ■ *n.* (*informal*) **1. COMPLAINT** an instance of complaining **2. COMPLAINER** somebody who is habitually bad-tempered or complaining **3. BAD MOOD** a mood characterized by complaining or sulking ○ *a day-long grouch* [Late 19thC. Variant of earlier *grutch*, of uncertain origin: possibly from Old French *groucher* (see GRUDGE).] —**grouch·i·ly** *adv.* —**grouch·i·ness** *n.* —**grouch·y** *adj.*

ground[1] /grownd/ *n.* **1. LAND SURFACE** the surface of the land **2. EARTH** the earth or soil **3. LAND FOR A PURPOSE** an area of land used for a particular purpose (*often used in the plural*) ○ *burial ground* **4. BATTLE AREA** the land held or fought over in battle ○ *The partisans retreated, yielding ground to the government troops.* **5. SUBJECT** an area of knowledge or debate ○ *Most of the ground had been covered in an earlier lecture.* **6. FOUNDATION** a reason or basis (*often used in the plural*) ○ *There are grounds for believing his story.* **7.** PAINTING **PAINTING SURFACE** an underlying surface or prepared area that paint is applied to **8. BACKGROUND** a background, e.g., the background of a painting or the background color of a flag **9.** PAINTING **FIRST COAT OF PAINT** a first coat of paint applied to a surface being decorated **10. SEA BOTTOM** the bottom of the sea, a river, or a lake **11.** MUSIC = **ground bass 12.** ELEC ENG **CONDUCTING BODY** a large conducting body, especially the earth, or a connection with this, considered as being at zero potential ■ **grounds** *npl.* **1. SURROUNDING LAND** the land surrounding and belonging to a building (*sometimes singular*) **2.** BEVERAGES **DREGS** the sediment or dregs of a drink, especially coffee ■ *adj.* **ON THE GROUND** happening, living, or operating on the ground ○ *ground crews* ■ *v.* (**ground·ed, ground·ing, grounds**) **1.** *vt.* **GIVE SOMEBODY FOUNDATION** to teach somebody the basics about something ○ *He had been well grounded in the techniques.* **2.** *vt.* **SUPPORT SOMETHING** to base ideas, arguments, or beliefs on something ○ *Her beliefs are grounded on an unshakable faith.* **3.** *vt.* ELEC ENG **CONNECT WITH THE GROUND** to connect a circuit or appliance with the ground **4.** *vt.* AIR **STOP A PILOT OR PLANE FROM FLYING** to prevent or forbid an aircraft or aviator from flying ○ *Bad weather grounded all outgoing flights.* **5.** *vt.* **FORBID TO GO OUT** to restrict somebody to a place, especially a child to his or her home, as a punishment (*informal*) ○ *My dad grounded me for a week.* **6.** *vti.* SAILING **RUN VESSEL AGROUND** to become stranded in a vessel or cause a vessel to become stranded by running aground ○ *The ferry grounded on a reef.* **7.** *vi.* **LAND ON THE GROUND** to land on the ground or hit the ground **8.** *vt.* **PUT SOMETHING ON THE GROUND** to put something on the ground ○ *ground your rifles* **9.** *vt.* **FIX** to fix something on or in something else as a foundation ○ *The fence posts are grounded in concrete.* **10.** *vt.* FOOTBALL **THROW A BALL TO THE GROUND** to throw the ball against the rules to the ground to avoid being tackled **11.** *vti.* BASEBALL **HIT A BALL TO THE GROUND** to strike a ball so that it hits or rolls along the ground **12.** *vt.* PAINTING **PREPARE A PAINTING SURFACE** to apply a preparatory coat to a surface that is to be painted [Old English *grund*] ◇ **break fresh** *or* **new ground** to do or discover something new ◇ **get (something) off the ground** to get something started or operating ◇ **hit the ground running** to begin to deal with a new situation with great energy and without delay, generally because of good prior preparation (*informal*) ◇ **hold** *or* **stand your ground** to stick resolutely to decisions, attitudes, or principles in the face of pressure to abandon them ◇ **run somebody** *or* **something to ground** to find somebody or something finally, after a long and determined search ◇ **suit somebody down to the ground** to be perfectly suited to or suitable for somebody ◇ **the moral high ground** a position of moral superiority in relation to other people

ground out *vi.* to be put out in baseball after hitting a ground ball that is fielded and thrown to first base

ground[2] /grownd/ past participle, past tense of **grind**

ground ball *n.* in baseball, a ball that bounces on the ground or rolls along it after being hit

ground bass *n.* a short bass part continually repeated as the basis for a changing melody

ground bee·tle *n.* = **carabid**

ground·break·er /grównd bràykər/ *n.* somebody or something that invents, discovers, or develops something new

ground·break·ing /grównd bràyking/ *adj.* new and pioneering or innovative [Early 20thC. From the expression *break ground* "turn the first spade of earth for a new building."]

ground·burst /grównd bùrst/ *n.* an explosion of a bomb or warhead on the ground rather than in the air

ground cher·ry *n.* **1. FRUIT WITH A PAPERY HUSK** a small round cherrylike fruit that has a papery husk **2. PLANT WITH EDIBLE BERRIES** a plant found mainly in North America on which ground cherries grow. Genus: *Physalis.*

ground cloth *n.* **1. WATERPROOF SHEET AS TENT FLOOR** a sheet of waterproof material placed on the ground to protect a sleeping bag or the floor of a tent from ground dampness **2.** SPORTS **WATERPROOF COVER PROTECTING SPORTS FIELD** a sheet of waterproof material spread over a playing surface to protect it against rain

ground con·trol *n.* the staff and equipment on the ground that monitor or guide the flight of an aircraft or spacecraft (*takes a singular or plural verb*)

ground cov·er *n.* plants that grow densely and close to the ground, especially growing wild in a forest or deliberately planted in a garden to prevent weeds or soil erosion

ground crew *n.* people working in aviation, especially technicians or mechanics, who do not normally work in the air

ground·ed /grówndəd/ *adj.* having a secure feeling of being in touch with reality and personal feelings

ground-ef·fect ma·chine *n.* = **hovercraft**

ground el·der *n. U.K.* BOT = **goutweed**

ground·er /grówndər/ *n.* = **ground ball**

ground fish *n.* any fish that inhabits the bottom of a body of water, especially a marine fish such as a cod or flounder

ground floor *n.* the floor of a building that is level with or nearest to street level ◇ **in on the ground floor** involved in something, especially a business venture, at the earliest stage

ground fog *n.* fog lying at or near ground level

ground frost *n.* a temperature below freezing as registered on a thermometer at or near the ground

ground glass *n.* **1. ROUGHENED GLASS** glass with a roughened nontransparent surface produced by abrading or etching **2. GLASS PARTICLES** glass that has been ground into fine particles, used as an abrasive

ground hem·lock *n.* a low-growing yew tree found in northeast North America. Latin name: *Taxus canadensis.*

ground·hog /grównd hàwg/ *n.* ZOOL = **woodchuck**

Ground·hog Day *n.* February 2, when groundhogs emerge from hibernation to test the weather. In sunshine, they supposedly sense a late spring and return to their burrows. The day is celebrated annually in Punxsutawney, Pennsylvania.

ground·ing /grównding/ *n.* training in or knowledge of the basics of something ○ *had a good grounding in math*

ground i·vy *n.* an invasive evergreen ivy native to Europe and Asia and naturalized in North America. It has scalloped leaves and small purple-blue flowers. Latin name: *Glechoma hederacea.*

ground·keep·er /grównd keepər/ *n.* = **groundskeeper**

ground·less /grówndləss/ *adj.* not based on evidence or reason and not justified or true —**ground·less·ly** *adv.* —**ground·less·ness** *n.*

ground·ling /grówndling/ *n.* **1.** BIOL **ANIMAL OR PLANT NEAR THE GROUND** an animal or plant that lives on or near the ground, or at the bottom of a river, lake, or the sea **2.** THEATER **STANDING SPECTATOR** a member of an Elizabethan theater audience standing in front of the stage in the cheapest part of the theater (*archaic*) **3. UNCULTURED PERSON** somebody disdained for having little or no appreciation of culture ○ *a movie pitched firmly at the groundlings* **4.** AIR **AVIATION WORKER ON GROUND** a member of the ground crew at an airport or airforce base (*slang*)

ground loop *n.* a sharp involuntary turn made by an aircraft that is taxiing, taking off, or landing, caused by unbalanced drag

ground·mass /grówndmass/ (*plural* **-mass·es**) *n.* in some kinds of rock, the fine-grained base rock in which larger crystals are embedded

ground mer·i·stem *n.* tissue in the stems and roots of plants consisting of actively dividing cells that become new tissue

ground·nut /grównd nùt/ *n.* **1.** (*plural* **-nuts** *or* **-nut**) **N AMERICAN CLIMBING PLANT** a North American climbing vine with fragrant brownish flowers and edible tubers. Latin name: *Apios americana.* **2. EDIBLE TUBER OF GROUNDNUT PLANT** the edible tuber of a groundnut plant **3. PLANT WITH EDIBLE TUBERS** a plant that produces underground pods or tubers containing edible nuts **4.** FOOD = **peanut**

ground·out /grównd òwt/ *n.* in baseball, a play in which a batter is put out after hitting a ground ball that is fielded and thrown to first base

ground pea *n. Southern U.S.* a peanut

ground pine *n.* **1. PLANT WITH PINE SMELL** a variety of bugle plant, native to Europe and North Africa, that has two-lipped yellow flowers with red spots. The flowers smell of pine if crushed. Latin name: *Ajuga chamaepitys.* **2. N AMERICAN MOSS** a North American moss with spore-producing tissues grouped in cones. Genus: *Lycopodium.*

ground plan *n.* **1.** ARCHIT **PLAN OF FLOOR OF BUILDING** a scale drawing of a floor of a building, especially the ground floor **2. FIRST PLAN** a preliminary plan or general outline of something ○ *a ground plan for corporate expansion*

ground plum *n.* a flowering plant native to central and western regions of the United States, with edible green fruits that resemble plums. Genus: *Astragalus.*

ground rule *n.* (*often used in the plural*) **1. FUNDAMENTAL RULE** a basic rule of procedure ○ *Let's establish a few ground rules before we go any further.* **2.** SPORTS **SPECIFIC RULE** a rule that applies to the conduct of a game or race on a particular court, field, or course

ground·sel /grówndsʼl, grówn-/ *n.* a yellow-flowered plant native to Europe and Asia, generally regarded as a weed. Genus: *Senecio.* [Old English *grundeswylige*, an alteration of *gundeswilgie*, literally "pus-swallower," because of its use in poultices]

ground·sheet /grównd sheet/ *n.* = **ground cloth**

ground·sill /grównd sìl/ *n.* the joist that is nearest the ground in a timber structure

grounds·keep·er /grówndz keepər/ *n.* somebody who maintains a playing field or the grounds of a property —**grounds·keep·ing** *n.*

ground sloth *n.* an extinct ground-dwelling sloth that lived in North, Central, and South America, and is believed to be the ancestor of modern tree sloths. Family: Megalonychoidea.

grounds·man /grówndzmən/ (*plural* **-men**) *n. U.K.* = **groundskeeper**

ground speed *n.* the speed of a flying aircraft measured in relation to the ground it is traveling over and used for calculating flight times

ground squir·rel *n.* **1. BURROWING SQUIRREL** a ground-dwelling burrowing rodent related to the tree squirrels and found in North America, Europe, Africa, and Asia. Family: Sciuridae. **2. CHIPMUNK** a chipmunk (*regional*)

ground state *n.* PHYS the state of lowest energy for a particle, atom, molecule, or system

ground·stroke /grównd stròk/ *n.* in tennis, a shot played from any part of the court after the ball has bounced

ground sub·stance *n.* the solid, semi-solid, or liquid material that exists between the cells in connective tissue, cartilage, or bone

ground·swell /grównd swèl/ *n.* **1. DEEP WAVES** a deep wide up-and-down movement of the sea, often caused by a far-off storm or an earthquake **2. RISING FEELING** a strong growth of feeling or opinion that is evident but not always attributable to a specific source ○ *a groundswell of public opinion against the new measures*

ground wa·ter *n.* water held underground in soil or permeable rock, often feeding springs and wells

ground wave *n.* a radio wave transmitted directly from a transmitter to a receiver, without reflection from the ionosphere

ground·work /grównd wùrk/ *n.* basic preparatory tasks that form a foundation for something else

ground ze·ro *n.* the point on the surface of land or water that is precisely the site of detonation of a nuclear weapon, or the point immediately above or below it

group /groop/ *n.* **1. SET OF PEOPLE OR THINGS** a number of people or things considered together or regarded as belonging together **2. PEOPLE WITH SOMETHING IN COMMON** a number of people sharing something in common such as an interest, belief, or political aim ○ *an unemployed workers' group* **3.** MUSIC **BAND OF MUSICIANS** a small number of musicians, especially in pop music, who play together as a unit **4.** COMM **COMPANIES UNDER COMMON CONTROL** a number of companies all controlled by a single company or common owner **5.** ARTS **SET OF FIGURES IN ARTISTIC WORK** a number of figures forming a distinct unit in a painting, sculpture, or other artistic composition **6.** MIL **SET OF TWO OR MORE BATTALIONS** a military formation made up of two or more battalions and a headquarters **7.** AIR FORCE **AIR FORMATION BETWEEN SQUADRON AND WING** an air force formation made up of two or more squadrons, but smaller than a wing **8.** CHEM **COLLECTION OF ATOMS** a collection of atoms that form an electrochemical unit such as the hydroxy group **9.** CHEM **COLLECTION OF SIMILAR ELEMENTS** a set of chemical elements classified according to the vertical column they occupy in the periodic table. There are 18 such groups, and elements in the same group have similar properties. ○ *the alkaline earth group of elements* **10.** GEOL **SET OF ROCK FORMATIONS** a collection of rock formations that date from the same geological era and are considered as a stratigraphic unit **11.** MATH **MATHEMATICAL SET UNDER AN OPERATION** a set of mathematical entities that are related by a particular operation. For example, consecutive numbers are a group under addition but not under multiplication. (*often used before a noun*) ■ *vti.* (**grouped, group·ing, groups**) **FORM GROUP** to come together as a unit, or to bring people or things together to form a unit ○ *spectators grouped in ones and twos on the sidelines* ■ *adj.* **OF GROUPS** relating to groups or forming a group ○ *group tours* [Late 17thC. Via French *groupe* from Italian *gruppo*, "group, knot." Ultimately from a prehistoric Germanic word.] —**group·a·ble** *adj.*

group cap·tain, Group Cap·tain *n. U.K.* AIR FORCE an officer in the Royal Air Force senior to a wing commander and junior to an air commodore

group dy·nam·ics *n.* the interpersonal processes, conscious and unconscious, that take place in the course of interactions among a group of people (*takes a singular verb*)

grou·per /grōōpər/ (*plural* **-pers** *or* **-per**) *n.* **1. LARGE WIDE-MOUTHED FISH** a heavy-bodied large-jawed food fish that lives in tropical and temperate seas. Family: Serranidae. **2. ROCKFISH** a rockfish of Southern California. Family: Scorpaenidae. (*regional*) [Early 17thC. From Portuguese *garupa*.]

group·ie /grōōpee/ *n.* (*informal*) **1. ADORING FAN** an enthusiastic fan of a pop group, especially a teenager seeking a sexual relationship with the object of her adulation **2. ENTHUSIASTIC FAN** any enthusiastic fan or supporter

group·ing /grōōping/ *n.* a set of people or things gathered into a group

Group of Eight full form of **G8**

group prac·tice *n.* a medical, dental, or veterinary practice operated by several doctors, dentists, or vets working together

group the·o·ry *n.* the study of the formation and properties of mathematical groups. It has applications in the study of the symmetry of molecules and crystal shapes.

group ther·a·py *n.* the treatment of psychological problems by placing patients in groups and, under the guidance of a trained therapist, encouraging them to discuss their problems with each other —**group ther·a·pist** *n.*

group·think /grōōp thingk/ *n.* conformity in thought and behavior among the members of a group, especially an unthinking acceptance of majority opinions

group·ware /grōōp wàir/ *n.* software designed to be shared collaboratively by a number of users on a network. It may offer such features as e-mail, scheduling capabilities, and file distribution.

Grouse

grouse[1] /growss/ (*plural* **grouse**) *n.* BIRDS a large game bird that nests on the ground on moors and in forests. Most species are reddish brown in color with feathered feet and legs. Family: Tetraonidae. [Early 16thC. Origin uncertain: perhaps from Latin *gruta*, name of a game bird, or *grus* "crane," or from Welsh *grugiar* "heath hen."]

WORD KEY: SYNONYMS

See Synonyms at ***complain.***

grouse[2] /growss/ *vi.* (**groused, grous·ing, grous·es**) **COMPLAIN** to complain in a grumbling, often self-serving way (*informal*) ■ *n.* **GRUMBLE** a grumbling complaint (*informal*) [Early 19thC. Origin uncertain: perhaps from Old French *grouchier* "to grumble" (see GRUDGE).] —**grous·er** *n.*

grout /growt/ *n.* **1. MORTAR FOR FILLING GAPS** thin mortar used to fill gaps, especially between tiles **2. PLASTER** fine plaster used to finish ceilings and walls ■ **grouts** *npl. U.K.* **DREGS** the sediment that lies at the bottom of a liquid ■ *vt.* (**grout·ed, grout·ing, grouts**) **APPLY GROUT TO** to use grout to fill gaps, especially between tiles, or to finish a ceiling or wall [Old English *grūt*. Ultimately from a prehistoric Germanic word that is also the ancestor of English *grit* and *groats*.] —**grout·er** *n.*

grove /grōv/ *n.* **1. GROUP OF TREES** a small group of trees ○ *a grove of maples* **2.** AGRIC **ORCHARD** an area where many trees are commercially grown, e.g., for their fruit [Old English *grāf*, of unknown origin]

Grove /grōv/, **Frederick Philip** (1871–1948) Russian-born Canadian writer. He is known for novels about life on the Canadian prairies such as *Our Daily Bread* (1928).

Grove, Lefty (1900–75) U.S. baseball player. One of the best left-handed pitchers in the game, he played for the Philadelphia Athletics and the Boston Red Sox. Real name **Robert Moses Grove**

grov·el /gróvv'l, grúvv'l/ (**-eled, -el·ing, -els**) *vi.* **1. BEHAVE SERVILELY** to act in a servile way, showing exaggerated and false respect in order to apologize to somebody or out of fear ○ *I've already apologized but now he wants me to grovel.* **2. CRAWL** to crawl or lie face down on the ground in humility or fear **3. WALLOW** to indulge in something unworthy (*literary*) [Late 19thC. From obsolete *groof* "face downward," from, ultimately, Old Norse *á grúfu*, from *grúfa* "proneness," of unknown origin.] —**grov·el·er** *n.* —**grov·el·ing·ly** *adv.*

grow /grō/ (**grew** /groo/, **grown** /grōn/, **grow·ing, grows**) *v.* **1.** *vi.* **GET BIGGER** to become larger in size through natural development **2.** *vi.* **BECOME LARGER** to expand or become larger in any way ○ *The number of members will grow rapidly.* **3.** *vi.* **INCREASE** to increase in degree ○ *Excitement is growing.* **4.** *vi.* **BE ABLE TO DEVELOP NATURALLY** to be capable of developing naturally and remaining in a naturally healthy state ○ *Flowers won't grow in this soil.* **5.** *vi.* **BE PRODUCT OF SOMETHING** to develop from something else ○ *Hatred grew out of mutual ignorance.* **6.** *vi.* **BECOME** to move from one condition to another, especially gradually ○ *The night grew cold.* **7.** *vt.* **CAUSE TO GROW** to make something, especially plants, grow and develop ○ *We grow tomatoes in the greenhouse.* **8.** *vt.* **DEVELOP NATURALLY** to produce something as part of a natural process, or allow it to be produced ○ *He thought he might grow a mustache.* **9.** *vt.* **EXPAND** to develop, expand, and stimulate something, especially a business, a line of business, or an economic market ○ *She was brought in to grow the firm's market share.* [Old English *grōwan*. Ultimately from an Indo-European word that is also the ancestor of English *green* and *grass*.] —**grow·er** *n.*

WORD KEY: USAGE

Object of the verb: Metaphorical uses of *grow* as a transitive verb are widely disliked: *grow the economy* and *grow a stock portfolio*, for example, strike many as uncouth, even wrong. There are no grounds for objecting to literal physical senses of the transitive verb: *grow a beard, grow corn.* Nor are there grounds for objecting to metaphorical uses of the intransitive verb: *The economy grew rapidly.*

grow into *vt.* to develop in size, maturity, or capability to suit something

grow on *vt.* **1. GRADUALLY BECOME PLEASING TO** to become gradually more acceptable or pleasing to somebody **2. BECOME APPARENT TO** to become gradually more apparent or powerful to somebody

grow out of *vt.* to become too mature or too big in size for something

grow up *vi.* **1. BECOME ADULT** to develop into an adult **2. BEHAVE MORE MATURELY** to behave in a more mature and sensible way **3. COME INTO EXISTENCE** to come into existence and develop ○ *A town had grown up at the junction of the two rivers.*

grow·ing pains *npl.* **1. ADOLESCENT PAIN** pains in the limbs that adolescents are sometimes affected by, thought to be caused by rapid bodily growth **2. EARLY PROBLEMS** problems associated with the early stages of something such as a developing project

grow·ing point *n.* the area in a plant where the cells are actively dividing to produce new tissue in the stems and roots

grow·ing sea·son *n.* the time of year during which annual plants, especially farm crops, develop to maturity. It may be defined according to mean air temperature or the absence of frost.

growl /growl/ *v.* (**growled, growl·ing, growls**) **1.** *vti.* **MAKE HOSTILE SOUND** to make, or communicate something by means of, a low nonverbal sound in the throat that expresses hostility **2.** *vti.* **SPEAK IN HOSTILE WAY** to speak, or say something, in a deep voice that expresses impatience or hostility ○ *He was growling at the children.* **3.** *vi.* **MAKE RUMBLING NOISE** to make a low rumbling noise ■ *n.* **1. ANIMAL'S HOSTILE NOISE** the low throaty noise made by a hostile animal, especially a dog **2. HOSTILE UTTERANCE** something said in a hostile throaty voice [Mid-17thC. Origin uncertain: probably from Old French *grouler*, of prehistoric Germanic origin; ultimately an imitation of the sound.] —**growl·ing** *adj.* —**growl·ing·ly** *adv.* —**growl·y** *adj.*

growl·er /grówlər/ *n.* **1.** *Can* **SMALL ICEBERG** a small iceberg with very little showing above water **2. BEER CONTAINER** a container for beer such as a pitcher, brought by a customer (*informal*) **3. GROWLING PERSON OR ANIMAL** a person or animal that growls

grow light *n.* a fluorescent lamp giving out light similar to sunlight and used to grow plants indoors

grown past participle of **grow** ■ *adj.* **HAVING MATURED** having developed and matured

grown-up *adj.* **1. FULLY MATURE** fully developed and mature **2. FOR ADULTS** relating to or for adults ■ *n.* (*plural* **grown-ups**) **ADULT** an adult person (*usually used by or to children*) ○ *Ask a grown-up to put it in the oven for you.*

growth /grōth/ *n.* **1. GROWING PROCESS** the process of becoming larger and more mature through natural development ○ *A child needs protein for healthy growth.* **2. INCREASE** an increase in numbers, size, power, or intensity **3. SOMETHING THAT GROWS** something that grows or has grown ○ *three days' growth of beard on his chin* **4.** MED **ABNORMAL TISSUE** an abnormal formation of tissue such as a tumor growing in or in an organ ■ *adj.* **EXPANDING** in the process of expanding or developing, especially rapidly ○ *growth industries*

growth fac·tor *n.* a substance produced by cells that stimulates them to multiply. When produced in excessive amounts, a growth factor may be associated with abnormal growth such as that seen in cancer.

growth fund *n.* a mutual fund offering long-term appreciation of capital invested, rather than a high income

growth hor·mone *n.* a hormone, made and stored in the pituitary gland in the brain, that stimulates protein synthesis and the growth of the long bones of the limbs

growth reg·u·la·tor *n.* a natural or synthetic preparation that promotes or inhibits plant growth

growth ring *n.* a sheath of cells forming concentric rings in the cross-section of a woody stem or trunk, and representing the result of the yearly growth spurt that begins in the spring. The age of a tree can be determined by counting its growth rings.

growth sub·stance *n.* a chemical produced by a plant that regulates its growth and development, and is usually made in the shoot tip and transported to other regions

groyne *n.* = **groin** [Late 16thC. From obsolete *groin* "pig's snout," which came via Old French from Latin *grunnire* "to grunt" (see GRUNION).]

Groz·ny /gróznee/, **Groz·nyy** city at the foot of the Caucasus Mountains in southeastern Europe. It is the capital of the Russian republic of Chechnya. Population: 388,000 (1992).

GRP *abbr.* glass-reinforced plastic

grub /grub/ *v.* (**grubbed, grub·bing, grubs**) **1.** *vt.* **DIG UP** to dig or pull something out of the ground, especially without proper tools ○ *grubbing potatoes in rock-hard soil* **2.** *vt.* **CLEAR GROUND** to remove roots and stumps from an area of ground **3.** *vi.* **SEARCH ON GROUND** to search on or in the ground for something **4.** *vi.* **SEARCH LABORIOUSLY** to search for something laboriously, usually by moving things and looking under things ○ *grubbing around in the archives for evidence* **5.** *vi.* **TOIL** to work hard, especially at something dull or arduous **6.** *vt.* **SCROUNGE SOMETHING** to obtain something by scrounging or begging (*slang*) ○ *grub a couple of bucks* ■ *n.* **1.** INSECTS **LARVA** the wormlike larva of various insects, especially beetles **2. FOOD** food, especially a meal (*informal*) [14thC. From assumed Old English *grybban*. Ultimately from an Indo-European word meaning "to scratch, dig" that was also the ancestor of English *grave*[1], *groove*, and *engrave*. In the sense "food," perhaps from the eating of larvae by birds.] —**grub·ber** *n.*

grub·by /grúbbee/ (**-bi·er, -bi·est**) *adj.* **1. DIRTY** dirty or slovenly **2. HAVING GRUBS** infested with grubs **3. CONTEMPTIBLE** disliked or despised, especially for being sordid or dishonorable ○ *articles in his grubby little newssheet* —**grub·bi·ly** *adv.* —**grub·bi·ness** *n.*

WORD KEY: SYNONYMS

See Synonyms at ***dirty.***

grub·stake /grúb stàyk/ *n.* **1.** MINING **MONEY ADVANCED TO PROSPECTOR** supplies or money given to a prospector in return for a share in any profits **2.** COMM **ADVANCE FOR STARTING UP BUSINESS** money or materials given to somebody starting a business in return for a share in any profits ■ *vt.* (**-staked, -stak·ing, -stakes**) **ADVANCE MONEY TO** to give money or supplies to somebody in business in return for a share of any profits [Mid-19thC. From GRUB "food" + STAKE[2].] —**grub·stak·er** *n.*

Grub Street *n.* the world of literary hack work and those who work at it [Named for a former street in London, England, once well known for its population of hack writers]

grudge /gruj/ *n.* **RESENTMENT** a feeling of resentment or ill will, especially one lasting for a long time ■ *vt.* (**grudged, grudg·ing, grudg·es**) **1. GIVE RELUCTANTLY** to allow or give something reluctantly ○ *I grudge the price of the air fare.* **2. ENVY** to be envious or resentful of somebody for something [14thC. From Old French *grouchier* "to grumble" (possible source of English *grouch* and *grouse*[2]). Probably ultimately of prehistoric Germanic origin.] —**grudg·er** *n.*

grudge match *n.* SPORTS a match between players or teams who have a long-standing animosity between them or who have a particular score to settle

grudg·ing /grújjing/ *adj.* done or given reluctantly, or doing or giving something reluctantly —**grudg·ing·ly** *adv.*

gru·el /gróo əl, gróol/ *n.* **1. THIN PORRIDGE** a thin porridge made by boiling meal, especially oatmeal, in water **2.** *U.K.* **SEVERE PUNISHMENT** severe punishment or harsh treatment (*archaic*) [14thC. From Old French, ultimately of prehistoric Germanic origin.]

gru·el·ing /gróo əling, gróol-/ *adj.* extremely arduous or exhausting [Mid-19thC. From GRUEL in the obsolete verb sense "to punish," from the idea of giving gruel as a punishment.] —**gru·el·ing·ly** *adv.*

grue·some /gróossəm/ *adj.* involving or depicting death or injury in a disturbing or sickening way [Late 16thC. Formed from obsolete *grue* "to shudder," of Scandinavian origin.] —**grue·some·ly** *adv.* —**grue·some·ness** *n.*

gruff /gruf/ *adj.* **1.** SURLY abrupt, angry, or impatient in manner or speech **2.** HARSH-SOUNDING harsh-sounding or throaty ○ *a gruff voice* [15thC. From Flemish or Dutch *grof*, "rough, harsh."] —**gruff·ly** *adv.* —**gruff·ness** *n.*

grum·ble /grúmb'l/ *v.* (**-bled, -bling, -bles**) **1.** *vi.* EXPRESS DISSATISFACTION to complain or mutter in a discontented way **2.** *vt.* SAY AS COMPLAINT to say something as a complaint ○ *Some entrants grumbled that there wasn't enough time.* **3.** *vi.* MAKE RUMBLING NOISES to make rumbling or growling noises ○ *thunder grumbling in the distance* ■ *n.* **1.** COMPLAINT a complaint or expression of discontent **2.** RUMBLING NOISE a rumbling or growling noise [Late 16thC. Origin uncertain: probably from Middle Dutch *grommelen* "to mumble, grunt." Ultimately from the same prehistoric Germanic base as English *grim* and *grimace*.] —**grum·bler** *n.* —**grum·bly** *adj.*

WORD KEY: SYNONYMS

See Synonyms at ***complain.***

grum·bling /grúmbling/ *n.* COMPLAINT a muted complaint or protest ○ *grumblings of discontent* ■ *adj.* TENDING TO COMPLAIN with a tendency to complain —**grum·bling·ly** *adv.*

grum·met *n.* = **grommet**

grump /grump/ *n.* SOMEBODY IN A BAD MOOD somebody who is bad-tempered or sullen (*informal*) ■ **grumps** *npl.* BAD-TEMPERED MOOD a bad-tempered or sullen mood (*informal*) ○ *a fit of the grumps* ■ *vi.* (**grumped, grump·ing, grumps**) COMPLAIN to complain or be sullen (*informal*) [Early 18thC. An imitation of the sound of someone expressing displeasure.]

grump·y /grúmpee/ (**-i·er, -i·est**) *adj.* bad-tempered or sullen —**grump·i·ly** *adv.* —**grump·i·ness** *n.*

Grun·dy·ism /grúndee ìzzəm/ *n.* a prudish narrow-minded attitude toward other people (*disapproving*) [Mid-19thC. From the name of "Mrs. Grundy," a character in Thomas Moreton's play *Speed the Plough* 1798, who was noted for her prudish attitude.]

grunge /grunj/ *n.* **1.** FILTH filth or garbage (*informal*) **2.** MUSIC KIND OF ROCK MUSIC a variety of rock music that emerged in the 1980s in the United States and owes much to punk and heavy metal (*often used before a noun*) ○ *grunge rock* **3.** FASHION UNKEMPT FASHION STYLE a style of dress, popularized by fans of grunge music, typified by secondhand clothes worn in layers, heavy footwear, unkempt hair, and an overall scruffy appearance ○ *designer grunge* **4.** SOMEBODY OBJECTIONABLE somebody who is regarded as undesirable, especially somebody who is or looks dirty (*slang insult*) [Mid-20thC. Back-formation from GRUNGY.]

grun·gy /grúnjee/ (**-gi·er, -gi·est**) *adj.* **1.** DIRTY OR INFERIOR dirty, shabby, inferior, or otherwise undesirable (*informal*) **2.** MUSIC, FASHION OF GRUNGE MUSIC OR FASHIONS relating to or typical of grunge music or grunge fashions [Mid-20thC. Origin uncertain: perhaps a blend of GRUBBY and DINGY.]

grun·ion /grúnnyən/ *n.* a small fish, native to the coastal waters of California and Mexico, that spawns on beaches. Latin name: *Leuresthes tenuis.* [Early 20thC. Origin uncertain: probably from Spanish *gruñón*, literally "grunter," from, ultimately, Latin *grunnire* "to grunt." Ultimately from an Indo-European word that is the ancestor of English *grunt* and *grudge*.]

grunt¹ /grunt/ *v.* (**grunt·ed, grunt·ing, grunts**) **1.** *vi.* MAKE NOISE OF OR LIKE A PIG to make the half-nasal, half-throaty noise that a pig makes **2.** *vti.* SAY SOMETHING IN THROATY BURST to make a deep sound in the throat as an annoyed, half-hearted, or inattentive response to what somebody has said, or to indicate or say something in this way ○ *He grunted in acknowledgment of my greeting.* ■ *n.* **1.** NOISE OF OR LIKE PIG a half-throaty, half-nasal noise that a pig makes, or a speech sound that resembles it **2.** ZOOL MARINE FISH a bony tropical marine fish that grunts when taken out of the water. Some species have patterns of bright colors. Family: Pomadasyidae. **3.** SOMEBODY DOING MENIAL TASKS somebody who does routine unexciting work (*slang*) [Old English *grunettan.* Ultimately from an Indo-European word that is also the ancestor of English *grudge* and *grunion*.] —**grunt·er** *n.*

grunt² *n.* MIL an infantryman in the United States Army or Marine Corps, especially one serving in Vietnam [Mid-20thC. From earlier *grunt* "unskilled assistant, dogsbody," alteration of *ground*, from *ground man* "low-ranking railway worker."]

grun·tled /grúnt'ld/ *adj.* pleased or happy (*informal humorous*) [Early 20thC. Back-formation from DISGRUNTLED.]

Gru·yère /groo yáir/ *n.* a hard cheese with occasional holes in it, originally made in Switzerland, that has a mild nutty slightly sweet flavor. It is often used in cooking, e.g., in fondues. [Early 19thC. Named for *Gruyère*, the town in Switzerland where it was first produced.]

gryph·on *n.* MYTHOL = **griffin**

GS *abbr.* **1.** General Secretary **2.** MIL general staff **3.** ground speed

GSA *abbr.* Girl Scouts of America

GSC *abbr.* MIL general staff corps

GSL *abbr.* guaranteed student loan

GSO *abbr.* MIL General Staff Officer

G-spot *n.* a highly sensitive small area in the vagina that, when stimulated, gives extreme sexual pleasure (*informal*) [Late 20thC. Shortening of *Gräfenberg spot*, named for Ernst *Gräfenberg* 1881–1957, the German gynecologist who first identified this spot.]

GSR *abbr.* galvanic skin response

Gstaad /gə staát/ alpine ski resort in Bern Canton, western Switzerland. Population: 2,500 (1980).

G-string *n.* a piece of material covering only the pubic area, supported by a narrow cord between the buttocks and around the waist. It is worn, e.g., by striptease dancers. [Late 19thC. Origin uncertain.]

G-suit *n.* a close-fitting garment worn by pilots and astronauts that counters the blackout effects of high acceleration by applying pressure to the legs and lower body, thereby reducing blood supply loss to the head [Mid-20th C. Shortening of *gravity-suit.*]

GT *abbr.* Gran Turismo (*used as part of the name of a fast car*) [Italian, "grand touring"]

gt. *abbr.* **1.** gilt **2.** PHARM drop (*on prescriptions*) [Latin, *gutta*]

G.T.C. *abbr.* COMM good till canceled

gtd. *abbr.* guaranteed

GTP *abbr.* BIOCHEM guanosine triphosphate

GTS *abbr.* gas turbine ship

GTT *abbr.* MED glucose tolerance test

gtt. *abbr.* PHARM drops (*on prescriptions*) [Latin, *guttae*]

GU, g.u. *abbr.* **1.** genitourinary **2.** GEOG Guam

gua·ca·mo·le /gwaákə mólee/ *n.* avocado mashed or puréed with tomato and lightly spiced with chili, and served as a dip or in salads [Early 20thC. Via American Spanish from Nahuatl *ahuacamolli*, literally "avocado paste."]

gua·cha·ro /gwaáchə rò/ (*plural* **-ros**) *n.* = **oilbird** [Early 19thC. Via American Spanish *guácharo* from, ultimately, Quechua *wáhcha* "orphan."]

Gua·da·la·ja·ra /gwaàd'lə haárə/ city in west central Mexico, capital of Jalisco State, and the country's second largest city. Founded in 1530, it is a holiday resort and commercial center. Population: 1,628,617 (1990).

Gua·dal·ca·nal /gwòdd'lkə nál/ mountainous island in the southwestern Pacific Ocean. It is the largest island of the Solomon Islands. In World War II, heavy fighting took place there between the United States and Japanese forces. Area: 2,060 sq. mi./5,336 sq. km.

Gua·da·lupe /gwaàdə loópe/ **1.** river in southeastern Texas that rises north of Austin and empties into the Gulf of Mexico south of Houston. Length: 250 mi./402 km. **2.** island off the Baja California coast of Mexico in the Pacific Ocean. Area: 80 sq. mi./207 sq. km. **3.** city near Monterrey in Nuevo León State, northeastern Mexico. Population: 534,782 (1990).

Gua·da·lupe Moun·tains mountain range of the Rocky Mountains that runs from New Mexico to Texas. The highest peak is Guadalupe Peak, 8,749/2,667 m.

Gua·da·lupe Moun·tains Na·tion·al Park national park in southwestern Texas that was established in 1972 and is noted for its limestone formations and unusual wildlife. The highest point is Guadalupe Peak, 8,749 ft./2,667 m. Area: 86,416 acres/34,971 hectares.

Gua·de·loupe /gwàdə loóp/ an overseas department of France consisting of a group of islands in the eastern Caribbean. Capital: Basse-Terre. Population: 418,000 (1993). Area: 687 sq. mi./1,780 sq. km.

guai·ac /gwí ak, -ək/ *n.* = **guaiacum** *n.* 3

guai·a·col /gwí ə kàwl/ *n.* a yellowish oily liquid extracted from guaiacum resin or wood creosote and used medicinally as an expectorant, antiseptic, and local anesthetic. Formula: $C_7H_8O_2$. [Mid-19thC. Coined from GUAIACUM + -OL.]

guai·a·cum /gwí əkəm/ *n.* **1.** TREES TROPICAL AMERICAN TREE a tropical American evergreen tree with small leaves that grow in clusters. One species yields the resin that contains guaiacol. Genus: *Guaiacum.* ◊ **lignum vitae** **2.** INDUST GUAIACUM WOOD the hard dense oily wood of the guaiacum tree **3.** PHARM GUAIACUM RESIN the brownish green resin of the guaiacum tree, used in medicine and in making varnishes [Mid-16thC. Via modern Latin, genus name, from American Spanish *guayacán*, from Taino.]

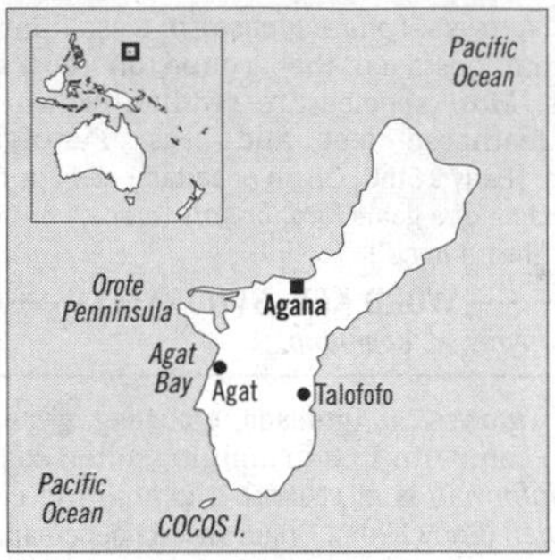

Guam

Guam /gwaam/ island and tourist resort in the northwestern Pacific Ocean. An unincorporated territory of the United States, it is the largest of the Marianas Islands. Capital: Agana. Population: 156,974 (1996). Area: 209 sq. mi./541 sq. km. —**Gua·ma·ni·an** /gwaa máynee ən/ *n., adj.*

guan /gwaan/ *n.* a large tree-dwelling fruit-eating bird found in Central and South America. Family: Cracidae. [Late 17thC. Via American Spanish from Miskito *kwamu*.]

gua·na·co /gwə naá kō/ (*plural* **-cos**) *n.* a South American animal that looks like, and is related to, the domesticated llama and alpaca. It lives in the arid regions of the Andes mountains. Latin name: *Lama guanaco.* [Early 17thC. Via Spanish from Quechua *huanacu*.]

gua·neth·i·dine /gwaa néthə deen/ *n.* a drug used in its sulfate form in the treatment of high blood pressure. Formula: $C_{10}H_{22}N_4$. [Mid-20thC. Blend of GUANIDINE and ETHYL.]

Guang·dong /gwaáng dóong/ province of southern China, on the South China Sea. Capital: Guangzhou. Population: 66,890,000 (1994). Area: 76,100 sq. mi./197,100 sq. km.

Guang·zhou /gwaáng jō/ capital of Guangdong Province and the chief port in southeastern China. It lies about 80 mi./129 km northwest of Hong Kong. A major international trade fair is held there twice yearly. Population: 3,560,000 (1993).

gua·ni·dine /gwaáni deen/ *n.* a strongly alkaline substance found in urine as a product of protein metabolism and also found in plant tissues. It is used in the manufacture of plastics and resins. Formula: CH_5N_3. [Mid-19thC. Coined from GUANO + -IDE + -INE¹.]

gua·nine /gwaá neen/ *n.* a component of nucleic acids that pairs with cytosine to carry hereditary information in DNA and RNA in cells. Chemically, it is a purine derivative. Formula: $C_5H_5N_5O$. Symbol **G** [Mid-19thC. Coined from GUANO + -INE¹.]

gua·no /gwaá nō/ *n.* **1.** ANIMAL DROPPINGS accumulated droppings of birds, bats, and seals, occurring where large established colonies of these animal are situated **2.** AGRIC GUANO FERTILIZER fertilizer consisting of dried bird or bat droppings, and rich in nutrients, including urates, oxalates, and phosphates, or a synthetic fertilizer with properties similar to those of natural guano [Early 17thC. Via American Spanish from Quechua *huanu* "dung."]

gua·no·sine /gwaánə seen, -sin/ *n.* a nitrogen-containing compound formed from guanine and the sugar ribose. Formula: $C_{10}H_{13}N_5O_5$. [Early 20thC. Coined from GUANINE + RIBOSE + -INE¹.]

gua·no·sine mon·o·phos·phate *n.* a constituent of the nucleic acids DNA and RNA that plays a part in various metabolic reactions and is composed of guanosine linked to a phosphate group

gua·no·sine tri·phos·phate *n.* a constituent of the nucleic acids DNA and RNA that participates in various metabolic reactions, including the formation of proteins, and consists of guanosine linked to three phosphate groups

Guan·tá·na·mo Bay /gwan taánəmō-/ sheltered inlet of the Caribbean Sea, southeastern Cuba. It is the site of a major U.S. naval base. Area: 30 sq. mi./78 sq. km.

Guan·xiu /gwaán syoó/ (832–912) Chinese artist. He is noted for his paintings of Buddhist monks with exaggerated and grotesque features.

gua·nyl·ic ac·id /gwaa nìllik-/ *n.* = **guanosine monophosphate** [Late 19thC. *Guanylic* coined from GUANOSINE + -YL + -IC.]

Gua·po·ré /gwàppō ráy, gwàppə-/ river in central South America that rises in western Brazil and flows northwest along the Brazil-Bolivia border before joining the Mamoré River. Length: 950 mi./1,530 km.

guar /gwaar/ *n.* **1.** PLANTS **INDIAN FODDER PLANT** a plant originally from India but widely cultivated in arid conditions as fodder and for its seeds, which are used to make a gum with numerous commercial applications. Latin name: *Cyamopsis tetragonolobus.* **2.** INDUST = **guar gum** [Late 19thC. From Hindi *guār.*]

gua·ra·ni /gwaarə neé/ (*plural* **-nies** *or* **-nis**) *n.* **1. CURRENCY UNIT OF PARAGUAY** the standard unit of currency of Paraguay, made up of 100 centimos. See table at **currency 2. COIN WORTH ONE GUARANI** a coin worth one guarani

Gua·ra·ni /gwaarə neé/ (*plural* **-ni** *or* **-nis**) *n.* **1. MEMBER OF NATIVE SOUTH AMERICAN PEOPLE** a member of a Native South American people who live in parts of Paraguay, Uruguay, Bolivia, and Brazil, and belong to the Tupi-Guaranian group of peoples **2. LANGUAGE OF PARAGUAY** an official language of Paraguay, also spoken in other parts of central South America. It is one of the Tupi-Guarani branch of the Andean-Equatorial family of Native South American languages. About three million people speak Guarani. [Mid-20thC. Via Spanish *Guaraní* from *Guarini,* the name of a Native South American people of Paraguay.] —**Gua·ra·ni** *adj.*

guar·an·tee /gèrrən teé/ *n.* **1. ASSURANCE** something that assures a particular outcome ○ *There's no guarantee that the plan will work.* **2.** COMM **PROMISE OF QUALITY** a formal promise that a product will be repaired free of charge if it breaks or fails within a stated period, or that substandard work will be redone ○ *a five-year guarantee.* **3. guar·an·tee** LAW **PROMISE TO BE RESPONSIBLE FOR ANOTHER** a formal promise by one person to take responsibility for the debts or obligations of another person if that person fails to meet them **4.** LAW **SOMEBODY RECEIVING FORMAL ASSURANCE** a person or company given an assurance that somebody's debts or obligations will be dealt with **5.** COMM **CERTIFICATE STATING PROMISE OF QUALITY** a document setting out a promise of quality made by a manufacturer or the provider of a service **6.** = **guarantor** ■ *vt.* (**-teed, -tee·ing, -tees**) **1. ASSURE** to promise something or make something certain ○ *We can't guarantee availability of seats on tomorrow's flight.* **2.** COMM **PROMISE QUALITY OF GOODS OR SERVICES** to give a formal, usually printed promise that a product will be repaired free of charge if it fails within a specified period, or that substandard work will be redone **3.** LAW **TO ACCEPT RESPONSIBILITY FOR SOMEBODY** to promise to fulfill another person's debts or obligations if that person fails to meet them [Late 17thC. Alteration (on the model of GUARANTY) of earlier *garant,* from Old French (see GUARANTY).]

guar·an·teed in·vest·ment cer·tif·i·cate *n. Can* an investment that provides a guaranteed rate of interest over a certain term, usually one to five years

guar·an·tor /gèrrən táwr, gérrəntər/ *n.* somebody who gives a guarantee, especially a formal promise to be responsible for somebody else's debts or obligations [Mid-19thC. Formed from GUARANTEE.]

WORD KEY: SYNONYMS

See Synonyms at ***backer.***

guar·an·ty /gérrəntee/ *n.* (*plural* **-ties**) **1.** LAW = **guarantee** *n.* 3 **2. SECURITY** something used as security for a formal promise **3. PLEDGING** the giving of something as security for a promise **4.** = **guarantor** ■ *vt.* (**-tied, -ty·ing, -ties**) LAW = **guarantee** *v.* 3 [Early 16thC. Via Anglo-Norman *guarantie* from Old French *garantir* "to warrant," from *garant* "warrant" (see WARRANT.]

guard /gaard/ *vt.* (**guard·ed, guard·ing, guards**) **1. PROTECT** to protect somebody or something against danger or loss **2. PREVENT ESCAPE OF** to watch over and prevent the escape of somebody held captive ○ *Two MPs were guarding the prisoner.* **3. CONTROL PASSAGE THROUGH PLACE** to watch over and control passage through an entrance or across a boundary ○ *All of the mountain passes are guarded by troops.* **4.** BASKETBALL **HAMPER OPPONENT** in basketball, to prevent an opponent from scoring or playing effectively **5. CONTROL** to control or restrain something such as speech or behavior ○ *guard your tongue* **6. PUT PROTECTIVE COVER ON** to equip a machine or device with a protective cover **7. ESCORT** to escort somebody (*archaic*) ■ *n.* **1. ACT OF GUARDING** an act of guarding somebody or something or the responsibility of guarding somebody or something **2. PROTECTOR** a person or group that protects, watches over, restrains, or controls somebody or something ○ *The prisoner broke away from his guards.* **3. DEFENSE** a defensive posture or state of mind ○ *Her guard was up.* **4. CEREMONIAL ESCORT** a usually mounted or motorized group forming a ceremonial escort **5. BODY PROTECTION** a piece of tough material worn to protect a part of the body from injury **6.** *U.K.* RAIL = **conductor 7.** BASKETBALL **DEFENSIVE POSITION IN BASKETBALL** either of the two players in basketball who regularly defend the backcourt and initiate offensive plays **8.** FOOTBALL **LINEMAN** either of two offensive linemen on either side of the center **9. guard, Guard** MIL **SOLDIER** in the British army and other armies, a soldier who belongs to any regiment originally formed to provide protection for the sovereign **10. WAY TO PROTECT SOMEBODY OR SOMETHING** any means of protection ○ *The snow fence serves as a guard against drifts.* **11. PROTECTIVE DEVICE** a device or part intended to protect the user against injury ○ *a guard on a lathe* **12.** *Ireland* **GARDAI** a member of the Garda (*informal*) [15thC. From French *garde* (noun) and *garder* (verb), both ultimately from a prehistoric Germanic base that is also the ancestor of English *ward, warden,* and *wary.*] ◇ **stand guard** to keep a watch or defensive posture ◇ **off (your) guard** having relaxed the usual precautions against attack ◇ **on (your) guard** prepared against attack

WORD KEY: SYNONYMS

See Synonyms at ***safeguard.***

guard against *vt.* to be wary of something or take precautions against it

guar·dant /gaárd'nt/, **gar·dant** *adj.* having the face turned toward the observer (*refers to an animal on a coat of arms*) ○ *a lion guardant* [Late 16thC. From French *gardant,* the present participle of *garder* (see GUARD).]

guard cell *n.* either of two specialized cells bordering pores in the epidermis of leaves that move to control the size of the aperture in response to changes in water levels. The guard cells and pore are called the stoma, and are situated on the underside, and sometimes the top side, of leaves and on young shoots.

guard dog *n.* a dog used for guarding property or people

guard·ed /gaárdəd/ *adj.* wary, cautious, or noncommittal —**guard·ed·ly** *adv.* —**guard·ed·ness** *n.*

WORD KEY: SYNONYMS

See Synonyms at ***cautious.***

guard hair *n.* the long coarse outer hair on mammals that forms a protective layer over the softer underfur

guard·house /gaárd hóws/ (*plural* **-houses** /-hówzəz/) *n.* a building used to house soldiers acting as guards and as a place for detaining military prisoners

Guar·di /gwaárdee/, **Francesco** (1712–93) Italian painter. He painted romantic landscapes of his native city, Venice, which are characterized by lively line and color and a mood of fantasy

guard·i·an /gaárdee ən/ *n.* **1. PROTECTOR** a person who watches over or protects somebody or something, or an organization with a protecting role **2.** LAW **LEGALLY RESPONSIBLE INDIVIDUAL** somebody who is legally appointed to look after the affairs of another, especially those of a minor **3.** CHR **SUPERIOR IN FRANCISCAN HIERARCHY** a superior in a Franciscan monastery ■ *adj.* **PROTECTING** acting as somebody's protector [15thC. From Anglo-Norman *gardein,* from, ultimately, Old French *garder* (see GUARD).] —**guard·i·an·ship** *n.*

guard·i·an an·gel *n.* **1. PERSONAL ANGEL** an angel believed to look after a particular individual **2. PROTECTOR** somebody seen as the special protector of somebody's interests (*informal*)

Guard·i·an An·gel *n.* a member of a vigilante group that patrols the streets of a city as a volunteer crime prevention squad. New York was the birthplace of the first such group.

Guard·mem·ber /gaárd membər/ *n.* somebody who serves in the National Guard

guard of hon·or *n.* a body of troops acting as a formal escort for somebody important during a ceremony

guard·rail /gaárd ràyl/ *n.* **1. SAFETY RAIL** a rail acting as a safety barrier at the side of a freeway, highway, road, or ship's deck **2.** RAIL **EXTRA RAIL GIVING TRAIN STABILITY** an additional rail laid close inside the main running rail on tight curves and at a junction to help a train's wheels stay on the track

guard ring *n.* a ring worn to stop another ring from slipping off the finger

guard·room /gaárd ròom, -ròom/ *n.* a room used by soldiers acting as guards and as a place for detaining military prisoners

guards·man /gaárdzmən/ (*plural* **-men** /-mən/) *n.* **1.** MIL **MEMBER OF NATIONAL GUARD** a member of the National Guard **2.** *U.K.* **SOLDIER IN GUARDS REGIMENT** a soldier who belongs to any of several regiments of the British army originally formed to provide protection for the sovereign

guar gum /gwaár-/ *n.* gum extracted from the seeds of the guar plant, added to processed food as a thickener and stabilizer and also used in paper manufacture

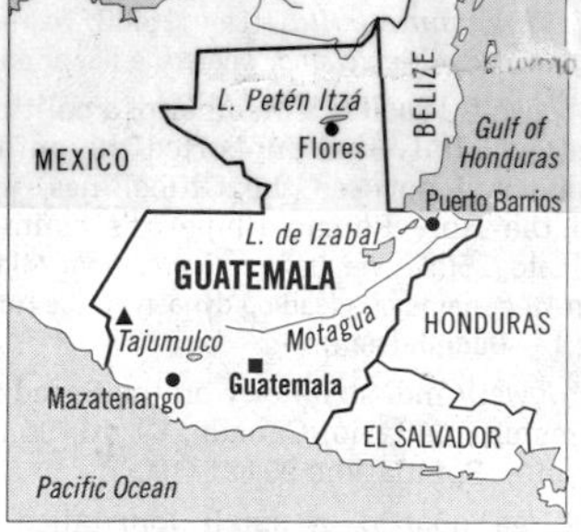

Guatemala

Gua·te·ma·la /gwaàtə maálə/ the third largest country in central America, bordered on the north and east by Belize, Mexico, and the Gulf of Honduras and on the south and west by Honduras and El Salvador. About two-thirds of the total land area of Guatemala is mountainous. Language: Spanish. Currency: quetzal. Capital: Guatemala City. Population: 11,685,695 (1997). Area: 42,042 sq. mi./108,889 sq. km. Official name **Republic of Guatemala** —**Gua·te·ma·lan** /gwaàtə maálən/ *adj., n.*

Gua·te·ma·la Cit·y capital city of Guatemala, located in the south central part of the country. It is the largest city in Central America and the nation's economic center. It was the capital of the United Provinces of Central America between 1823 and 1834. Population: 1,167,495 (1994).

gua·va /gwaávə/ (*plural* **-vas**) *n.* **1.** FOOD **TROPICAL FRUIT** the large pear-shaped edible fruit of a tropical American tree that has red or yellow-green skin and cream or pink flesh, and is eaten raw and often made into jelly **2.** TREES **TROPICAL TREE BEARING GUAVAS** a small tropical American tree related to the myrtle, that has guavas as fruit. Genus: *Psidium.* [Mid-16thC. Alteration of Spanish *guayaba,* of Caribbean Native American origin.]

gua·ya·be·ra /gwaàyə bérrə/ *n.* a light short-sleeved sports shirt, usually worn outside the trousers [From American Spanish, formed from *guayaba* "guava"]

gua·yu·le /gwaa yóolee/ *n.* **1. SHRUB THAT PROVIDES RUBBER** a bushy shrub found in the southwestern United States and Mexico whose sap is a source of rubber.

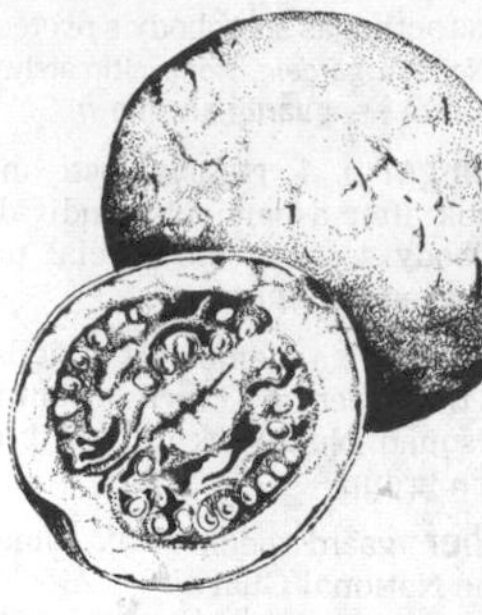

Guava

Latin name: *Parthenium argentatum.* **2.** RUBBER rubber made from the sap of the guayule shrub [Early 20thC. Via American Spanish from Nahuatl *cuauhuli*, literally "gum tree."]

gu·ber·na·to·ri·al /gòobərnə táwree əl/ *adj.* relating to, involving, belonging to, or typical of a governor [Mid-18thC. Formed from Latin *gubernator* "governor," from *gubernare* (see GOVERN).]

guck /guk/ *n.* any slimy, oily, gooey, or otherwise unpleasant substance (*informal*) [Mid-20thC. Origin uncertain: perhaps a blend of GOO and MUCK.]

gudg·eon[1] /gújjən/ *n.* a small European freshwater fish that belongs to the minnow family and is often used as bait. Latin name: *Gobio gobio.* [14thC. Via Old French *goujon* from, ultimately, Latin *gobius* (see GOBY).]

gudg·eon[2] /gújjən/ *n.* a socket that a pin fits into, e.g., the pin of a hinge or the pivoting bolt of a ship's rudder [15thC. From Old French *goujon*, literally "little gouge," from late Latin *gubia* (see GOUGE).]

gudg·eon pin *n. U.K.* = **wrist pin**

guel·der rose /géldər-/ *n.* a deciduous bushy Eurasian shrub with lacy clusters of white flowers that are followed by bunches of rounded red fruit. Latin name: *Viburnum opulus.* [Late 16thC. Named for the Dutch province of *Gelderland*, where the flower originated.]

Guelph[1] /gwelf/, **Guelf** *n.* a member of a political party in medieval Italy that supported the authority of the pope and opposed the Ghibellines, who supported the Holy Roman Emperor's claim to rule Italy [Late 16thC. Via Italian *Guelfo* from Middle High German *Welf*, name of a leading dynasty of the Holy Roman Empire.] —**Guelph·ism** *n.*

Guelph[2] /gwelf/ industrial city on the Speed River in southeastern Ontario, Canada, 60 mi./96 km west of Toronto. Population: 95,821 (1996).

gue·non /gə nón/ *n.* a small long-tailed African monkey that lives in trees. Genus: *Cercopithecus.* [Mid-19thC. From French, of uncertain origin.]

guer·don /gúrd'n/ *n.* REWARD a reward or recompense (*literary*) ■ *vt.* (**-doned, -don·ing, -dons**) GIVE REWARD TO to give somebody a reward or recompense (*literary*) [14thC. Via Old French from medieval Latin *widerdonum* "repayment," a partial translation of Old High German *widarlōn*, literally "giving back."]

guer·e·za /gə rézzə/ (*plural* **-zas**) *n.* a large long-haired monkey that lives in the forests of East and Central Africa. Latin name: *Colobus abyssinicus.* [Mid-19thC. Origin uncertain.]

gue·ri·don /gérri dòn, gèrri dáwN/ *n.* a small, round, ornate table or stand with a central pedestal [Mid-19thC. From French *Guéridon*, a person's name.]

gue·ril·la *n.* = **guerrilla**

guern·sey /gúrnzee/ (*plural* **-seys**) *n.* AGRIC a light-brown and white dairy cow that produces rich milk, belonging to a breed originating on the island of Guernsey

Guern·sey /gúrnzee/ island in the English Channel, the second largest of the Channel Islands. Dairy farming, tourism, and banking are the main trades. Capital: St. Peter Port. Population: 58,867 (1991). Area: 25 sq. mi./64 sq. km.

guer·ril·la /gə ríllə/, **gue·ril·la** *n.* a member of an irregular paramilitary unit, usually with some political objective such as the overthrow of a government. Guerrillas usually operate in small groups to harass and carry out sabotage. ○ *guerrilla warfare* [Early 19thC. From Spanish, "raiding party, skirmish," from *guerra* "war." Ultimately from a prehistoric Germanic word that is also the ancestor of English *war.*]

guer·ril·la the·a·ter *n.* = **street theater**

guess /gess/ *v.* (**guessed, guess·ing, guess·es**) **1.** *vt.* PREDICT to form an opinion about something without enough evidence to make a definite judgment ○ *She guessed the playing card he'd turn up.* **2.** *vt.* CONCLUDE CORRECTLY to arrive at a correct answer or to conjecture about something ○ *I guessed it would be you.* **3.** *vt.* SUPPOSE to think or suppose something ○ *I guess I'll have the steak.* **4.** *vi.* FORM OPINION to form an opinion without knowing for sure **5.** *vi.* FIND CORRECT ANSWER to be correct in your thinking about what might be the case ■ *n.* **1.** OPINION an opinion or answer arrived at by guessing ○ *My guess is she'll head for home.* **2.** ACT OF GUESSING an act or the process of guessing ○ *Take another guess.* [13thC. Of Scandinavian origin; ultimately from a prehistoric Germanic word meaning "to try to get."] —**guess·a·ble** *adj.* —**guess·er** *n.*
◇ **anybody's** *or* **anyone's guess** something that cannot be reliably predicted (*informal*)

guess·ti·mate *n.* /géstimət/ ESTIMATE BASED ON CONJECTURE an estimate based largely on incomplete information or evidence (*informal*) ■ *vti.* /gésti màyt/ (**-mat·ed, -mat·ing, -mates**) MAKE CONJECTURE ABOUT to make an estimate of something based largely on incomplete evidence or information (*informal*) [Mid-20thC. A blend of GUESS and ESTIMATE.]

guess·work /géss wùrk/ *n.* the process of making guesses, or the conclusions arrived at by guessing

guest /gest/ *n.* **1.** RECIPIENT OF HOSPITALITY somebody who receives hospitality at the home of somebody else **2.** SOMEBODY ENTERTAINED AT ANOTHER'S EXPENSE somebody who receives entertainment such as a meal or attendance at a social event that is paid for by somebody else ○ *Club members are allowed to sign two people in as guests.* **3.** CUSTOMER somebody who pays to use the facilities of a hotel, restaurant, or other establishment **4.** SOMEBODY ASKED TO JOIN OTHERS somebody who is invited by an organization or institution to receive hospitality ○ *We have a distinguished guest at the meeting tonight.* **5.** BROADCAST SOMEBODY MAKING SPECIAL APPEARANCE somebody who appears on a radio or television program who does not appear on it regularly ○ *our special guest for tonight's show* **6.** ZOOL ANIMAL USING ANOTHER'S NEST a creature, especially an insect, that shares the shelter of another or lives alongside the other as a parasite ■ *v.* (**guest·ed, guest·ing, guests**) **1.** *vi.* BROADCAST MAKE SPECIAL APPEARANCE to appear as a guest on a radio or television program ○ *the trend for big-time movie stars to guest on sitcoms* **2.** *vt.* ENTERTAIN SOMEBODY to entertain or play host to somebody ■ *adj.* **1.** APPEARING AS GUEST appearing or invited as a guest **2.** FOR GUESTS for guests to use [13thC. From Old Norse *gestr.* Ultimately from an Indo-European word meaning "stranger" that is also the ancestor of English *host, hostile,* and *xenophobia.*] ◇ **be my guest** used to tell people that they are welcome to do as they please (*informal*)

Guest /gest/, **Edgar A.** (1881–1959) British-born U.S. poet. His popular verses were collected in anthologies such as *A Heap o' Livin'* (1916). Full name **Edgar Albert Guest**

guest book *n.* a book or register that visitors or guests sign, e.g., at a bed-and-breakfast

guest·house /gést hòws/ (*plural* **-hous·es** /-hòwzəz/) *n.* **1.** HOUSE FOR VISITORS a small house used to accommodate visitors to a main house **2.** *U.K.* SMALL HOTEL a small hotel or private home that offers accommodations to paying guests

guest night *n.* an evening during which nonmembers are welcome to participate in the activities of a club or society

guest of hon·or *n.* somebody invited to attend a gathering or event who is seen as highly important or the most important of the invited guests

guest·room /gést ròom, -ròom/, **guest room** *n.* a bedroom for visitors who stay for a short time

guest star *n.* a well-known performer who makes a single or occasional appearance in a television or radio program

guest-star *vti.* to appear as a guest star, or feature somebody as a guest star

guest work·er *n.* a foreign national allowed to come and work, but not take up permanent residence, in a European country

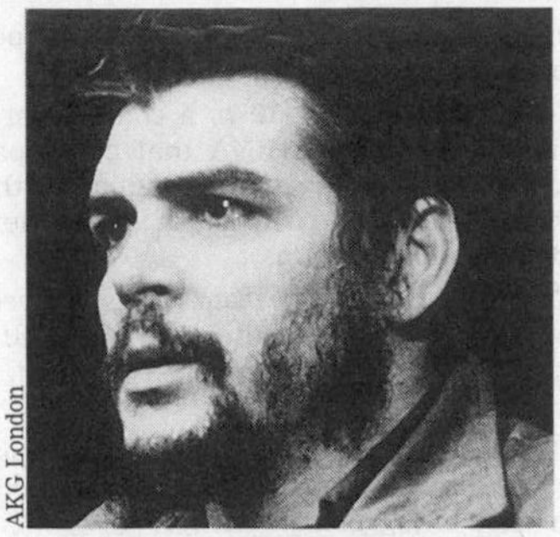

AKG London

Che Guevara

Gue·va·ra /gə vaárə/, **Che** (1928–67) Argentine-born South American revolutionary leader. A radical political theorist and guerrilla fighter, he played a significant part in Fidel Castro's revolution (1956–59) and early administration in Cuba. He was executed while planning an uprising in Bolivia. Real name **Ernesto Guevara de la Serna**

guff /guf/ *n.* nonsense or empty talk (*informal*) [Early 19thC. Thought to suggest a whiff of bad smelling air.]

guf·faw /gə fáw/ *vi.* (**-fawed, -faw·ing, -faws**) LAUGH LOUDLY to laugh loudly and raucously ■ *n.* RAUCOUS LAUGH a loud and raucous laugh [Early 18thC. An imitation of the sound.]

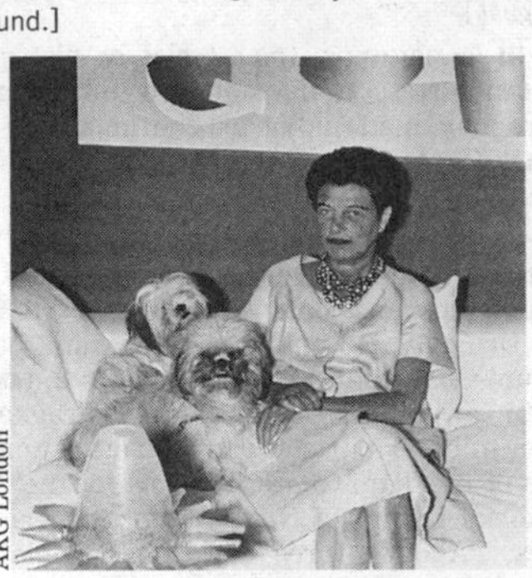

AKG London

Peggy Guggenheim

Gug·gen·heim /góoggən hīm/ **1. Meyer** (1828–1905) Swiss-born U.S. financier and industrialist. With his seven sons, he established large mining and metal-processing companies. **2. Peggy** (1898–1979) U.S. art collector and philanthropist. She helped to promote the careers of such avant-garde artists as Max Ernst and Jackson Pollock and was one of the earliest collectors of surrealist and abstract art.

GUI /gōo ee/ *abbr.* COMPUT graphical user interface

guid·ance /gīd'ns/ *n.* **1.** LEADERSHIP leadership or direction **2.** ADVICE advice or counseling, especially counseling given to students on academic matters ○ *the school's guidance counselor* **3.** SYSTEMS THAT CONTROL FLIGHT the systems and devices that control the flight of an aircraft, missile, or spacecraft ○ *onboard guidance*

guide /gīd/ *v.* (**guid·ed, guid·ing, guides**) **1.** *vti.* SHOW SOMEBODY THE WAY to lead somebody in the right direction **2.** *vt.* STEER to steer a vehicle or animal **3.** *vt.* HELP SOMEBODY LEARN SOMETHING to teach somebody or oversee training in something ○ *A tutor guided me through the intricacies of calculus.* **4.** *vt.* RUN ORGANIZATION to control the affairs of an organization or body **5.** *vt.* ADVISE OR INFLUENCE to advise or counsel somebody, or influence the way somebody behaves or acts ○ *Be guided by your conscience.* ■ *n.* **1.** SOMEBODY WHO SHOWS THE WAY somebody who leads others in the right direction **2.** SOMEBODY WHO LEADS TOURISTS somebody who supervises a tour **3.** INFLUENCE ON DECISION somebody who or something that strongly affects the decisions and behavior of another ○ *Her grandmother's wisdom was her guide throughout life.* **4.** GUIDEBOOK a guidebook to a place. = **guidebook** **5.** SOURCE OF INFORMATION a publication or a section of a magazine or newspaper giving information on a subject ○ *a movie guide* **6.** CONTROLLING DEVICE a device that controls the movement or operation of a machine **7.** MIL SOLDIER CONTROLLING MARCH a soldier stationed at the side of a column of marching soldiers to control alignment and lead the way [14thC. From Old French *guider*, ultimately of prehistoric Germanic origin.] —**guid·a·ble** *adj.*

WORD KEY: SYNONYMS

guide, conduct, direct, lead, steer

CORE MEANING: to show somebody the way to somewhere

guide used to talk about a situation where somebody shows somebody else or a group of people the way somewhere, or gives a tour of a particular place. It is used especially when the person showing the way has personal knowledge of the place and is able to supply detailed information; **conduct** used when the person showing the way has some kind of authority or specialized knowledge, for example, the guide in a museum; **direct** used to talk about one person showing another the way somewhere, usually without going there with that person; **lead** used to suggest that the person showing the way is out in front of the person or people being shown the way, and often implying that he or she is in charge or control; **steer** used in a similar way to "guide," especially to talk about showing somebody to a particular place or location; **usher** used specifically to talk about showing somebody to a seat in a place such as a church, theater, or restaurant.

guide·book /gīd bŏŏk/ *n.* a book containing information for tourists about a country, area, city, or institution

guid·ed mis·sile *n.* a self-propelled missile that can be steered in flight by remote control or by an onboard homing device

guide dog *n.* a dog trained to lead a sightless person

guide fos·sil *n.* = **index fossil**

guide·line /gīd līn/ *n.* **1.** OFFICIAL ADVICE an official recommendation indicating how something should be done or what sort of action should be taken in a particular circumstance **2.** LINE MARKING CORRECT POSITION a line that shows a correct position, route, or alignment, e.g. a fine line printed as an aid to lining up text or illustrations on a page

guide·post /gīd pōst/ *n.* **1.** DIRECTION SIGN a direction sign at a roadside **2.** GUIDELINE something that serves as an example or is recommended as a rule to live by

guide rope *n.* a rope attached to an object or to another rope or cable and used to maneuver it into position or to steady a load

guide·way /gīd wày/ *n.* a groove or channel that controls the direction in which a moving object travels

guide word *n.* a word printed at the top of a page in a dictionary or other reference book, usually the first or last entry for that page

guid·ing light *n.* somebody who or something that serves as a guide, example, or inspiration

gui·don /gí dòn, gīd'n/ *n.* a regimental flag or pennant, or the soldier who carries it [Mid-16thC. Via French from Italian *guidone*, from *guida* "guide."]

guild /gild/, **gild** *n.* **1.** ASSOCIATION OF PEOPLE WITH SIMILAR INTERESTS a club, society, or other organization of people with common interests or goals **2.** MEDIEVAL TRADE ASSOCIATION an association of merchants or craftspeople in medieval Europe, formed to give help and advice to its members and to make regulations and set standards for a particular trade **3.** GROUP OF ORGANISMS a group of organisms that use the same environmental resources in a similar way [14thC. Origin uncertain: probably from Middle Low German and Middle Dutch *gilde*, of the same prehistoric Germanic origin as German Geld "money." Probably named from the members' subscriptions.] —**guild·ship** *n.*

guil·der /gíldər/ *n.* **1.** CURRENCY UNIT OF NETHERLANDS the standard unit of currency of the Netherlands, made up of 100 cents. See table at **currency 2.** GUILDER COIN a coin worth one guilder **3.** OLD COIN a gold or silver coin formerly used as a unit of currency in Germany, Austria, or the Netherlands [15thC. Alteration of Dutch *gulden*, literally "golden."]

guild·hall /gíld hàwl/ *n.* the meeting place of a modern or medieval guild

guilds·man /gíldzmən/ (*plural* **-men** /-mən/) *n.* a man who is member of a guild

guild so·cial·ism *n.* a socialist movement in Great Britain in the early 20th century, advocating state ownership of industry but with each branch managed by guilds of workers —**guild so·cial·ist** *n.*

guilds·wo·man (*plural* **-men**) *n.* a woman who is a member of a member of a guild

guile /gīl/ *n.* a cunning, deceitful, and treacherous quality or type of behavior, or particular skill and cleverness in tricking or deceiving people [13thC. Via Old French from Old Norse.] —**guile·ful** *adj.* —**guile·ful·ly** *adv.* —**guile·ful·ness** *n.*

guile·less /gīl ləss/ *adj.* having or showing no deceit or expectation of being deceived —**guile·less·ly** *adv.* —**guile·less·ness** *n.*

WORD KEY: SYNONYMS

See Synonyms at ***naive***.

Guil·ford /gílfərd/ town in southern Connecticut, situated on Long Island Sound east of New Haven. Population: 19,848 (1990).

guil·le·mot /gíllə mòt/ *n.* a black-and-white or grayish narrow-billed diving sea bird of the auk family, found in northern Atlantic and northern Pacific waters. Genera: *Uria* and *Cepphus.* [Late 17thC. From French, literally "little William," perhaps from the custom of using male names such as *Robin* for birds.]

guil·loche /gi lṓsh, gi yṓsh/ *n.* ARCHIT an ornamental border formed by two or more interlaced bands around a series of interlocking circles [19thC. From French, of uncertain origin: possibly the personal name *Guillaume* "William."]

guil·lo·tine /gíllə teen/ *n.* **1.** MACHINE FOR BEHEADING PEOPLE a machine for executing people by beheading, consisting of a vertical wooden frame with grooves for a heavy sliding blade to be dropped from a height onto a person's neck. It became famous for its use during the French Revolution. **2.** EXECUTION BY GUILLOTINE execution by means of the guillotine **3.** INSTRUMENT FOR CUTTING METAL OR PAPER a cutting instrument, especially one for cutting sheet metal or paper, consisting of a platform with a blade attached to one side that is pulled down like a lever **4.** *U.K.* TIME LIMIT ON LEGISLATIVE DEBATE a limit on the time available for debate on a piece of legislation, designed to speed up parliamentary proceedings and prevent opponents of the legislation from obstructing its progress ■ *vt.* (**-tined, -tin·ing, -tines**) **1.** BEHEAD SOMEBODY to execute somebody using a guillotine **2.** CUT METAL OR PAPER WITH MACHINE to cut something such as paper or sheet metal using a guillotine **3.** *U.K.* LIMIT LEGISLATIVE DEBATE to set a time limit on the discussion of a piece of legislation [Late 18thC. Named for the French physician Joseph-Ignace *Guillotin* (1738–1814), who suggested its use as a more humane means of beheading in 1789.]

guilt /gilt/ *n.* **1.** AWARENESS OF WRONGDOING an awareness of having done wrong or committed a crime, accompanied by feelings of shame and regret ○ *feelings of guilt* **2.** FACT OF WRONGDOING the fact of having committed a crime or done wrong ○ *an admission of guilt* **3.** RESPONSIBILITY FOR WRONGDOING the responsibility for committing a crime or doing wrong ○ *Some of the guilt must attach to the parents.* **4.** LAW LEGAL CULPABILITY the responsibility, as determined by a court or other legal authority, for committing an offense that carries a legal penalty [Old English *gylt*, of unknown origin]

guilt·less /gíltləss/ *adj.* not responsible for a crime or wrongdoing, or not deserving blame or criticism —**guilt·less·ly** *adv.* —**guilt·less·ness** *n.*

guilt trip *n.* an exaggerated feeling or display of shame and regret, usually lasting for a considerable time (*slang*)

guilt·y /gíltee/ (**-i·er, -i·est**) *adj.* **1.** RESPONSIBLE FOR WRONGDOING responsible for a crime, wrong action, or error and deserving punishment, blame, or criticism ○ *He was guilty of a serious error of judgment.* **2.** LAW OFFICIALLY FOUND RESPONSIBLE FOR CRIME found and declared responsible for committing an offense by a court or other legal authority **3.** ASHAMED OF WRONGDOING aware of having done wrong or committed a crime and regretful and ashamed about it ○ *I still feel guilty about having forgotten your birthday.* **4.** SHOWING GUILT indicating or suggesting that somebody feels guilt, has done wrong, or has something to hide ○ *a guilty look on his face* **5.** CAUSING GUILT causing or likely to cause emotions of shame and regret ○ *a guilty secret* —**guilt·i·ly** *adv.* —**guilt·i·ness** *n.*

guilt·y con·science *n.* a feeling of having done wrong, especially something that is hidden from others or denied

guimpe /gamp, gimp/ *n.* **1.** SHORT BLOUSE a short blouse designed to be worn under a jumper or pinafore **2.** PART OF NUN'S HABIT a starched cloth that covers the neck and shoulders and is worn by some nuns as part of their habit **3.** = **gimp**[1] *n.* [Mid-19thC. From French, from Old French *guimple* "wimple."]

Guin. *abbr.* Guinea

guin·ea[1] /gínnee/ *n.* **1.** OLD UNIT OF BRITISH CURRENCY a gold coin worth 21 shillings (£1.05p) that was a British unit of currency between 1663 and 1813 **2.** AMOUNT EQUIVALENT TO £1.05 an amount equivalent to £1.05 or 21 shillings, the value of a guinea [Mid-16thC. Because they were first made for trade with the African country of *Guinea* and made from Guinean gold.]

guin·ea[2] /gínnee/ *n.* a highly offensive term referring to an Italian person or a person of Italian descent (*slang offensive*) [Late 19thC. Origin uncertain: possibly an alteration of the personal name "Gianni."]

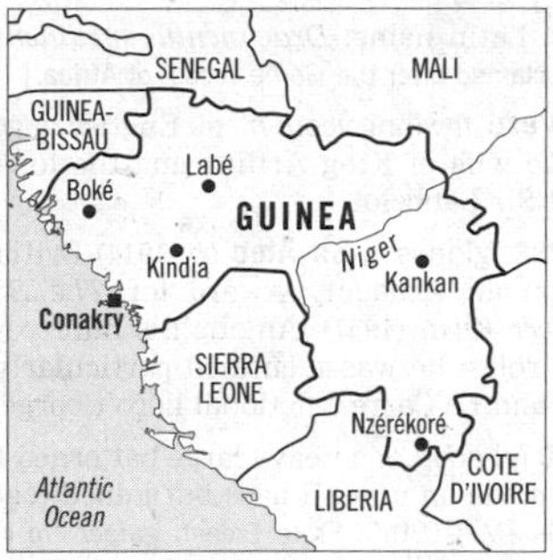

Guinea

Guin·ea /gínnee/ republic on the Atlantic coast in western Africa, between Guinea-Bissau and Sierra Leone. It became independent from France in 1958. Language: French. Currency: Guinean franc. Capital: Conakry. Population: 7,405,375 (1997). Area: 94,926 sq. mi./245,857 sq. km. Official name **Republic of Guinea** —**Guin·e·an** *adj., n.*

Guinea-Bissau

Guin·ea-Bis·sau /gìnni bi sów/ republic on the Atlantic coast in western Africa, between Senegal and Guinea. It became independent from Portugal in 1974. Language: Portuguese. Currency: Guinea-Bissau peso. Capital: Bissau. Population: 1,096,000 (1996). Area: 13,948 sq. mi./36,125 sq. km. Official name **Republic of Guinea-Bissau**

guin·ea fowl *n.* a plump short-tailed bird with a bare head and neck, typically black with white speckles, and related to the pheasant. It is native to Africa, but bred worldwide for food. Subfamily: Numidinae. [18thC. Named for the GUINEA coast of Africa.]

guin·ea grass *n.* a tall grass, native to Africa but grown in Central and South America and parts of the United States as animal fodder. Latin name: *Panicum maximum.* [Mid-18thC. See GUINEA FOWL.]

guin·ea hen *n.* a female guinea fowl

guin·ea pig *n.* **1.** RODENT KEPT AS PET a plump short-eared furry domesticated rodent, native to South America, that is larger than a hamster, widely kept as a pet, and used as a subject in scientific experiments. Latin name: *Cavia porcellus.* **2.** SOMEBODY OR SOMETHING EXPERIMENTED ON somebody or something used as the subject of an experiment, or used for any kind of test or trial [17thC. Named for GUINEA in Africa, probably from confusion with *Guiana* in South America.]

guin·ea worm *n.* a long thin worm, found in Africa and Asia, that lives as a parasite under the skin of people and animals and can grow to several feet in

Guinea pig

length. Latin name: *Dracunculus medinensis.* [Late 17thC. Named after the *Guinea* coast of Africa.]

Guin·e·vere /gwínni veer/ *n.* in English legend, she was the wife of King Arthur and the lover of the knight Sir Lancelot

Guin·ness /gínnəss/, **Sir Alec** (*b.* 1914) British actor. He won an Academy Award for *The Bridge on the River Kwai* (1957). Among his numerous other movie roles, he was identified particularly closely with John Le Carré's fictional hero George Smiley.

gui·pure /gi pŏor/ *n.* a heavy large-patterned lace that is not made on a mesh base but joined together by threads [Mid-19thC. From French *guiper* "to cover with cloth or yarn," from, ultimately, a prehistoric Germanic word meaning "to wind around."]

gui·ro /gwee rō/ (*plural* **-ros**) *n.* a musical instrument, popular throughout Central and South America, made from a gourd with grooves cut into its surface that creates a rasping sound when a stick is scraped across it [Late 19thC. From Spanish, literally "gourd."]

guise /gīz/ *n.* **1.** DECEPTIVE OUTWARD APPEARANCE a false outward appearance ○ *hiding her treacherous intentions under the guise of friendship* **2.** FORM OR APPEARANCE a shape or form, especially a changed one, in which something presents itself or is presented ○ *old ideas in a new guise* **3.** COSTUME a style of dress or personal appearance [14thC. Via French from, ultimately, a prehistoric Germanic word that is also the ancestor of English *wise* "manner," the original sense in English.]

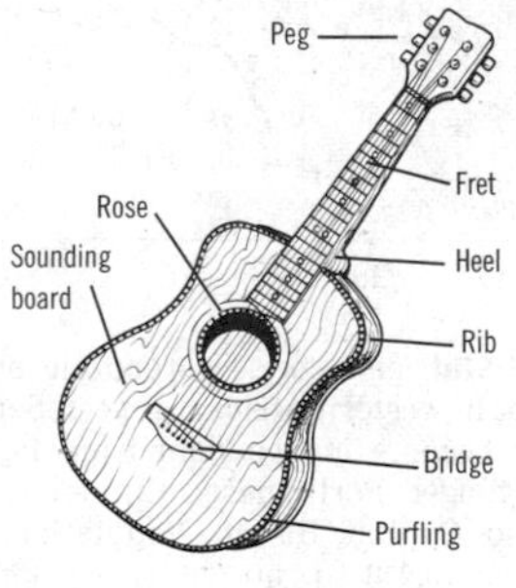

Guitar

gui·tar /gi taar/ *n.* a musical instrument with a long neck, a flat body shaped like a figure eight, and usually six strings that are plucked or strummed [Early 17thC. Via Spanish *guitarra* from Greek *kithara* "cithara," an ancient musical instrument (source also of English *zither*).] —**gui·tar·ist** *n.*

gui·tar·fish /gi taar fìsh/ (*plural* **-fish·es** *or* **-fish**) *n.* a ray found in tropical and subtropical seas, with large curving pectoral fins that give its body a guitar shape when seen from above. Family: Rhinobatidae.

Gu·ja·rat /gŏojjə raat/ state in western India, bordered in the northwest by Pakistan and in the south and southwest by the Arabian Sea. Capital: Gandhinagar. Population: 44,235,000 (1994). Area: 75,685 sq. mi./196,024 sq. km.

Gu·ja·ra·ti /gŏojə raatee/ (*plural* **-ti**), **Gu·je·ra·ti** (*plural* **-ti**) *n.* **1.** INDIAN LANGUAGE a language spoken in the Indian states of Gujarat and Maharashtra and in southern parts of Pakistan. It belongs to the Indic group of the Indo-Iranian branch of Indo-European. Gujarati is spoken by about 35 million people. **2.** MEMBER OF INDIAN PEOPLE a member of a people living mainly in the Indian state of Gujarat [Early 19thC. From Hindi.] —**Gu·ja·ra·ti** *adj.*

gul /gool, gŏol/ *n.* a large octagonal motif used in the patterns on oriental rugs and resembling a rose with straight-sided petals [Early 20thC. From Persian, "rose" (source also of English *julep*.]

gu·lag /gŏo laag/ *n.* **1.** POLITICAL PRISON IN FORMER USSR a prison or labor camp in the former Soviet Union, to which opponents of the government were sent **2.** PRISON CAMP NETWORK IN FORMER USSR the network of political prisons and labor camps in the former Soviet Union **3.** FORMER SOVIET DEPARTMENT ADMINISTERING PRISONS the department of the former Soviet security service that was responsible for running the network of political prisons **4.** PRISON FOR DISSENTERS any place that dissenters are sent to, or the isolating or imprisoning of dissenters [Mid-20thC. From Russian, an acronym of *Glavnoe upravlenie ispravitelno-trudovykh lagerei* "Chief Administration for Corrective Labor Camps."]

gulch /gulch/ *n.* a small rocky ravine, especially one with a fast-flowing stream running through it (*often used in placenames*) [Mid-19thC. Origin uncertain: perhaps from obsolete *gulch* "to gush."]

gul·den /gŏoldən/ (*plural* **-dens** *or* **-den**) *n.* = **guilder** [Late 19thC. From German and Dutch (source of English *guilder*), "golden."]

gules /gyoolz/ *n.* the color red on a coat of arms [14thC. From Old French *go(u)les* "red fur neckpiece," a plural use of *go(u)le* (see GULLET).]

gulf /gulf/ *n.* **1.** INLET OF SEA a large inlet of a sea similar to a bay but often longer and more enclosed by land (*often used in placenames*) ○ *the Gulf of Mexico* **2.** WIDE HOLE a deep wide hole in the ground **3.** VAST DIFFERENCE a great difference, e.g., in points of view, regarded as dividing or separating people or groups [14thC. Via French *golfe* from, ultimately, Greek *kolfos*, originally "bosom," hence "bag, trough between waves, abyss."]

Gulf /gulf/ county on the northwestern coast of Florida. Population: 11,504 (1990). Area: 565 sq. mi./1,463 sq. km.

Gulf·port /gúlf pawrt/ **1.** city in Pinellas County, west central Florida, a suburb of St. Petersburg. Population: 11,727 (1990). **2.** city and port in Harrison County, southeastern Mississippi, situated on the Gulf of Mexico. Population: 40,775 (1990).

Gulf States *n.* **1.** OIL-PRODUCING COUNTRIES BORDERING PERSIAN GULF the countries that border the Persian Gulf, considered as an economic or geopolitical unit, especially as oil producers. The Gulf States include Iran, Iraq, Kuwait, Saudi Arabia, Bahrain, Qatar, the United Arab Emirates, and Oman. **2.** U.S. STATES BORDERING GULF OF MEXICO the states of the southern United States that border the Gulf of Mexico, including Florida, Alabama, Mississippi, Louisiana, and Texas

Gulf Stream /gúlf streem/ warm current of the Atlantic Ocean, originating in the Gulf of Mexico and flowing northeastward along the coast of North America toward Newfoundland

gulf·weed /gúlf weed/ *n.* a brown seaweed that forms thick floating masses in tropical Atlantic waters. Genus: *Sargassum.*

Gull

gull[1] /gul/ *n.* a fairly large web-footed white-and-gray sea bird with a yellow beak. Gulls are the commonest birds in coastal North America and Europe. Genus: *Larus.* [15thC. From Celtic.] —**gull·er·y** *n.*

gull[2] /gul/ *vt.* (**gulled, gull·ing, gulls**) DECEIVE to trick or deceive somebody (*often passive*) ■ *n.* A DUPE somebody who is easily deceived [Mid-16thC. Origin unknown.]

Gul·lah /gúllə/ (*plural* **-lahs** *or* **-lah**) *n.* **1.** AFRICAN AMERICANS OF SE U.S. COAST a member of a people of African descent who live along the coasts of South Carolina, Georgia, and northern Florida, and on the neighboring Sea Islands **2.** CREOLE LANGUAGE OF GULLAH PEOPLE the creole language of the Gullah people. It is a form of English that has been influenced by several West African languages in its vocabulary, pronunciation, and grammatical structure. About 300,000 people speak Gullah. [Mid-18thC. Origin uncertain: perhaps an alteration of *[Angola]* or from *[Gola]*, a people of Sierra Leone and Liberia.] —**Gul·lah** *adj.*

gul·let /gúllət/ *n.* **1.** THROAT the esophagus or throat **2.** INDENTATION IN A PROTOZOAN a groove or indentation in the protoplasm of certain protozoans that has a function in the intake of food [14thC. From Old French *goulet*, literally "little throat," from *go(u)le* "throat," from Latin *gula* (source also of English *glutton*).]

gul·li·ble /gúlləb'l/ *adj.* tending to trust and believe people, and therefore easily tricked or deceived [Early 19thC. Formed from GULL[2].] —**gul·li·bil·i·ty** /gùllə bíllətee/ *n.* —**gul·li·bly** /gúlləblee/ *adv.*

gull·wing /gúl wìng/ *adj.* UPWARD-OPENING hinged at the top and opening upward (*refers to a type of car door*) ■ *n.* UPWARD-SLANTING AIRCRAFT WING an aircraft wing in which the section attached to the fuselage slants upward and the outer section is horizontal, or an aircraft with such a wing

gul·ly /gúllee/ *n.* (*plural* **-lies**) **1.** SMALL VALLEY a channel or small valley, especially one carved out by persistent heavy rainfall **2.** NARROW MOUNTAIN PASSAGE a narrow passage between two rocky slopes on a mountain **3.** CHANNEL MADE FOR WATER a gutter, open drain, or other artificial channel for water, especially one at a roadside ■ *vti.* (**-lied, -ly·ing, -lies**) CUT OUT CHANNELS to wear away channels in land or soil, or be worn into channels, by heavy rainfall [Mid-17thC. From French *goulet* (see GULLET).]

gul·ly·wash·er /gúlli wòshər, -wàwshər/ *n.* a heavy rain or its runoffs (*informal*)

gu·los·i·ty /gyoo lóssətee/ *n.* gluttony or greed (*archaic*) [15thC. From late Latin *gulositas* from, ultimately, Latin *gula* "throat, appetite."]

gulp /gulp/ *v.* (**gulped, gulp·ing, gulps**) **1.** *vt.* SWALLOW FAST to swallow something greedily, hurriedly, or frantically, taking in large amounts at a time ○ *She gulped down her coffee and grabbed her coat.* **2.** *vi.* GASP to gasp or choke **3.** *vi.* MAKE SWALLOWING MOTION to make a swallowing movement with the throat, especially because of being frightened or nervous ○ *He gulped and looked around nervously for the exit.* **4.** *vi.* MAKE SWALLOWING SOUND to make a loud swallowing sound with the throat, especially because of drinking too fast ■ *n.* **1.** SWALLOWING MOTION OR SOUND a swallowing movement or noise made with the throat **2.** AMOUNT SWALLOWED a quantity of something, especially drink, consumed in one large swallow [15thC. Origin uncertain: probably from Middle Dutch *gulpen* "to swallow, guzzle."] —**gulp·er** *n.* —**gulp·ing·ly** *adv.*

gulp back *vt.* to attempt to stifle tears or sobs

gum[1] /gum/ *n.* **1.** BOT STICKY PLANT SUBSTANCE THAT HARDENS a sticky substance found inside some plants, especially trees, that hardens when it is exposed to air and dissolves when put in water **2.** BOT ANY STICKY PLANT SUBSTANCE any sticky substance found inside plants, e.g., resins **3.** SOMETHING STICKY any sticky substance or deposit **4.** INDUST ADHESIVE glue made from or containing a sticky plant substance, or any soft synthetic glue used for sticking paper or other lightweight materials **5.** PLANTS TREE PRODUCING GUM any of numerous trees that produce gum. Genera: *Eucalyptus* and *Liquidambar* and *Nyssa.* **6.** CHEWING GUM chewing gum (*informal*) ■ *vt.* (**gummed, gum·ming, gums**) STICK SOMETHING TO SOMETHING ELSE to stick something to something else, with or without gum or glue [14thC. Via Old French *gomme*, from, ultimately, Greek *kommi*, from Egyptian *kemai*.]

gum up *vt.* to block or immobilize something with a sticky substance that prevents parts from moving ○ *eyes all gummed up* ◇ **gum up the works** to bring everything to a halt, usually by being obstructive or incompetent (*informal*)

gum[2] /gum/ *n.* **FLESH AROUND TEETH** the firm flesh that surrounds the roots of the teeth (*often used in the plural*) ■ *vt.* **EAT WITHOUT TEETH** to be without teeth and chew food with the gums (*informal*) [Old English *goma*, of uncertain origin]

gum ac·croi·des *n.* = **acaroid gum**

gum am·mo·ni·ac *n.* = **ammoniac**

gum a·ra·bic *n.* a sticky substance taken from some acacia trees and used as an ingredient in adhesives, confectionery, and medicines [Because the trees that produce it grow in the Middle East and near Arabia]

gum·ball /gúm bàwl/ *n.* a ball of chewing gum coated with a thin candy shell, bought from a machine

gum·bo /gúm bō/ (*plural* **-bos**) *n.* **1.** FOOD **THICK STEW WITH OKRA** a stew of fish, poultry, or meat that has been thickened with okra **2.** PLANTS = **okra** *n.* 2, **okra** *n.* 1 **3. STICKY SOIL** silty soil that turns very sticky and muddy when it becomes wet, and is found throughout the central United States **4. MIXTURE** a mixture or hodgepodge (*informal*) ○ *The band played a gumbo of Cajun, zydeco, and jazz music.* [Early 19thC. From Louisiana French *gombo*, of African, probably Bantu origin.]

Gum·bo *n.* a French patois that incorporates aspects of African languages and is spoken in parts of Louisiana and the French West Indies —**Gum·bo** *adj.*

gum·boil /gúm bòyl/ *n.* an abscess on the gum, especially near the root of a decayed tooth

gum·bo-lim·bo *n.* a deciduous tree with small white flowers that is found in Florida, Central America, and the West Indies and produces the reddish aromatic resin elemi, used in varnishes and ointments. Latin name: *Bursera simaruba.* [Mid-19thC. "-limbo" of uncertain origin: perhaps an alteration of ELEMI "resin," or perhaps from a Bantu language.]

gum boot *n.* a waterproof boot made of rubber or plastic, especially one coming to just below the knee

gum·drop /gúm dròp/ *n.* a chewy fruit-flavored candy coated with sugar

gum·ma /gúmmə/ (*plural* **-ma·ta** /gúmmətə/ *or* **-mas**) *n.* a rubbery tumor that can occur in the tertiary stage of syphilis [Early 18thC. From modern Latin, from, ultimately, Greek *kommi* (see GUM[1]).] —**gum·ma·tous** *adj.*

gum·mite /gú mīt/ *n.* a brownish-yellow to orange mixture of naturally occurring hydrated oxides of uranium, thorium, and lead [Mid-19thC. Coined from GUM[1] (because of its appearance) + -ITE.]

gum·mo·sis /gə mṓssiss/ *n.* the production of too much gum by a tree, especially a fruit tree, as a result of infection, a wound, or adverse weather [Late 19thC. Coined from GUM[1] + -OSIS.]

gum·mous /gúmməss/ *adj.* **1. RESEMBLING GUM** sticky like the gum from a tree **2. HAVING GUM** containing gum

gum·my[1] /gúmmee/ (**-mi·er, -mi·est**) *adj.* **1. STICKY LIKE GUM** like gum, especially in being sticky or thick and slow-flowing **2. STUCK OR BLOCKED WITH GUM** covered, clogged, or stuck together with a sticky substance of some kind —**gum·mi·ness** *n.*

gum·my[2] /gúmmee/ (**-mi·er, -mi·est**) *adj.* with only the gums showing, but no teeth, usually because the person concerned has no teeth —**gum·mi·ly** *adv.*

gump /gump/ *vi.* **MUDDLE THROUGH** to muddle through difficult situations thanks to a series of lucky chances [Late 20thC. From the 1994 movie *Forrest Gump*.]

WORD KEY: CULTURAL NOTE

Forrest Gump, a movie by Robert Zameckis (1994). It is the sentimental tale of a mentally challenged boy who grows up to become a sports star, war hero, and successful entrepreneur thanks to his uncomplicated worldview, traditional moral values, and uncanny ability to be in the right place at the right time. The movie's special effects seamlessly incorporated Gump into real footage of historical events.

gum plant *n.* a yellow-flowered North American plant with sticky flowerheads or leaves. Genus: *Grindelia.*

gump·tion /gúmpshən/ *n.* (*informal*) **1. COURAGE TO ACT** the courage to take what action is needed ○ *He wouldn't have the gumption to say so, even if he disagreed.* **2. COMMON SENSE** practical common sense and presence of mind ○ *Luckily, he had the gumption to call the police.* [Early 18thC. Originally Scots, of uncertain origin: perhaps formed from obsolete *gome* "attention, heed," of Scandinavian origin.]

gum res·in *n.* a naturally occurring mixture of gum and resin taken from some plants and trees, e.g., the yellow pigment gamboge

gum·shoe /gúm sho͝o/ *n.* a detective, especially a private investigator (*informal*) [Early 20thC. Originally in the sense "galosh"; the modern meaning arose from the idea of moving with stealth, as if wearing gumshoes.]

gum tree *n.* any of numerous trees that produce gum. Genera: *Eucalyptus* and *Liquidambar* and *Nyssa.*

gum tur·pen·tine *n.* = **turpentine**

gum·wood /gúm wo͝od/ *n.* wood from any gum tree, especially a eucalyptus tree

gun /gun/ *n.* **1. WEAPON THAT FIRES BULLETS** a weapon, from a small handheld pistol to a large piece of artillery, with a metal tube through which bullets or missiles are fired by an explosive charge **2. DEVICE THAT FIRES SOMETHING** any tool or instrument that forces something out under pressure **3. SHOT FROM GUN** a shot fired from a gun, e.g., as a military salute or a signal for a race to begin, or the sound of the shot ○ *Wait for the gun.* **4. SOMEBODY WITH GUN** somebody who is armed with a gun (*informal*) ○ *the fastest gun in the West* **5. GAS PEDAL** a vehicle's gas pedal (*informal*) ○ *Give it the gun.* **6. HUNTER** a member of a party of hunters armed with shotguns ■ *vt.* (**gunned, gun·ning, guns**) **PRESS THROTTLE** to rev up an engine (*informal*) [14thC. Origin uncertain: probably from a pet form of the Scandinavian female name *Gunnhildr* (itself from *gunnr* "battle" + *hildr* "war"), from the custom of giving women's names to weapons.] ◇ **go great guns** to be working, operating, or doing something at great speed or very effectively and successfully ◇ **jump the gun 1.** to start a race before the starting gun goes off **2.** to act prematurely ◇ **stick to your guns** to refuse to change your plans or opinions even though under attack ◇ **with (both) guns blazing** in a determined aggressive way

gun down *vt.* to shoot and kill or severely injure somebody (*informal*)

gun for *vt.* (*informal*) **1. INTEND TO HARM** to set out to attack or criticize somebody, or bring about somebody's downfall **2. INTEND TO GET** to plan or intend to get something for yourself ○ *She's gunning for a position in the Paris office.*

gun·boat /gún bōt/ *n.* a small fast ship with large guns mounted on it, used, e.g., by the Coast Guard

gun·boat di·plo·ma·cy *n.* negotiations between nations that involve threats to use military force

gun car·riage *n.* a platform with wheels on which a large military gun is mounted and transported, or on which a coffin is laid during state funerals

gun con·trol *n.* legal measures to control, license, review, put conditions on or restrict the ownership of firearms by members of the public

gun·cot·ton /gùn kótt'n/ *n.* = **nitrocellulose**

gun deck *n.* a deck of an old-fashioned sailing warship, below the main deck, where the cannons were situated

gun dog *n.* **1. HUNTER'S OR GAMEKEEPER'S DOG** a dog trained to find game and to bring back any game shot by a hunter or gamekeeper **2. DOG OF HUNTING BREED** a dog of a breed such as a pointer that is traditionally regarded as suitable for training as a hunter's or gamekeeper's dog

gun·fight /gún fīt/ *n.* a fight between two or more people armed with handguns, especially in the days of the Wild West —**gun·fight·er** *n.*

gun·fire /gún fīr/ *n.* shots fired from a gun or guns, or the sound of shots

gun·flint /gún flint/ *n.* a small piece of flint that ignites the gunpowder in an old-fashioned flintlock gun

gunge /gunj/ *n. U.K.* an unpleasantly sticky, slimy, or messy semi-liquid substance (*informal*) [Mid-20thC. Origin uncertain: perhaps thought to suggest stickiness, or perhaps a blend of GOO and SPONGE.] —**gungy** *adj.*

gung ho *adj.* (*informal*) (*hyphenated when used before a noun*) **1. VERY ENTHUSIASTIC** extremely or excessively enthusiastic or eager **2. WANTING TO FIGHT** eager to fight, especially in a military conflict [Mid-20thC. From Mandarin Chinese *hónghé*, literally "work together" (a motto of the U.S. marines in Asia in World War II), a shortening of *gōngyèhézuòshè* "Chinese Industrial Cooperative Society."]

gun·ite /gú nīt/ *n.* a concrete building material that is sprayed from a high-pressure gun onto a mold, or over reinforced concrete or steel in light construction [Early 20thC. Coined from GUN + -ITE, originally as a trademark.]

gunk /gunk/ *n.* a greasy messy near-solid mass (*informal*) [Mid-20thC. Originally the trademark of a degreasing solvent, probably thought to suggest lumpy grease.] —**gunk·y** *adj.*

gun lap *n.* in track, the last lap of a race, sometimes signaled by the firing of a gun, more often by the ringing of a bell, as the lead runner begins it

gun lob·by *n.* lobbyist groups who argue for the right of ordinary members of the public to buy and own guns, and who resist legislative attempts to put conditions on the ownership and availability of firearms and ammunition

gun·lock /gún lòk/ *n.* the mechanism by which the gunpowder charge was exploded in early types of gun, such as flintlock, matchlock, or wheel lock

gun·man /gúnmən/ (*plural* **-men** /-mən/) *n.* **1. MAN WITH GUN** a man armed with a gun, especially a criminal or an assassin **2. SKILLFUL SHOOTER** a man skilled in firing guns

gun·met·al /gún mètt'l/ *n.* **1. GRAY BRONZE FOR CANNONS** a dark gray bronze formerly used to make cannons **2. ANY DARK GRAY METAL** any of various dark gray alloys formerly widely used to make household and industrial items and especially children's toys **3. gun·met·al, gun·met·al gray** COLORS **DARK GRAY COLOR** a dark gray color with a tinge of blue —**gun·met·al-gray** *adj.*

Gunn ef·fect /gún-/ *n.* in a semiconductor, the microwave oscillation produced by a steady electric field that is larger than the normal threshold value [Mid-20thC. Named for J.B. *Gunn*, (1928-), an Egyptian-born British physicist.]

gun·nel[1] *n.* = **gunwale**

gun·nel[2] /gúnn'l/ (*plural* **-nels** *or* **-nel**) *n.* a small fish that is similar to an eel and is found in coastal areas of the Atlantic and Pacific oceans. Family: Pholidae. [Late 17thC. Origin unknown.]

gun·ner /gúnnər/ *n.* **1. SOLDIER WHO FIRES LARGE GUN** a soldier who operates a large gun **2. NCO WITH GUN-RELATED RESPONSIBILITIES** a warrant officer in the United States Marines or the British navy who is responsible for training gun operators and running the ammunition stores **3. ARTILLERY SOLDIER** a soldier in an artillery regiment, especially a private

gun·ner·a /gúnnərə/ (*plural* **-as**) *n.* a tropical plant with huge leaves that resemble the leaves of a palm, especially a gigantic South American variety. Genus: *Gunnera.* [Late 18thC. From modern Latin, genus name, named for the Norwegian botanist J.E. *Gunnerus*, (1718–73).]

gun·ner·y /gúnnəree/ *n.* **1. SCIENCE OF GUNS AND THEIR USE** the knowledge and techniques involved in the effective use of guns or in their design and construction **2. USE OF GUNS** the use of guns, especially of large guns in battle

gun·ner·y ser·geant *n.* a noncommissioned officer in the U.S. Marines, equivalent to an Army sergeant first class

gun·ny /gúnnee/ (*plural* **-nies**) *n.* **1. COARSE CLOTH** coarse jute or hemp cloth, commonly used for making sacks **2.** = **gunnysack** [Early 18thC. From Hindi *gonī*.]

gun·ny·sack /gúnni sàk/ *n.* a sack made from coarse jute or hemp

gun·play /gún plày/ *n.* the shooting of guns, especially by armed criminals

gun·point /gún pòynt/ *n.* the muzzle of a firearm ◇ **at gunpoint** under the threat of being shot and killed if orders are not obeyed

gun·pow·der /gún pòwdər/ *n.* an explosive mixture of potassium nitrate, charcoal, and sulfur, formerly used as the charge in firearms, and still used in fireworks and other explosives, e.g., in quarry blasting

Gunpowder Plot *n.* a conspiracy by a group of Roman Catholics, including Guy Fawkes, to blow up the British parliament in 1605

gun·pow·der tea *n.* a kind of Chinese green tea with individual leaves rolled into small pellets

gun·room /gún ro͞om, -ro͝om/ *n.* **1. ROOM FOR GUNS** a room in a house where guns are kept, especially shotguns **2. NAVY OFFICERS' QUARTERS** the quarters of midshipmen and junior officers on a ship in the British navy

gun·run·ning /gún rùnning/ *n.* the smuggling of illegal arms into a country, usually in order to supply terrorist or insurrectionist organizations —**gun·run·ner** *n.*

gun·sel /gúns'l/ *n.* (*slang*) **1. ARMED THUG** a thug or criminal, especially one who carries a gun **2. YOUNG**

HOMOSEXUAL SUPPORTED BY A MAN a homosexual young man who is living with and supported by an older man [Early 20thC. Via Yiddish *gendzel* from German *Gänslein* "gosling."]

gun·ship /gún shìp/ *n.* a military aircraft, usually a helicopter, that is fitted with guns for intrinsic use against ground targets

gun·shot /gún shòt/ *n.* **1.** GUN'S NOISE the sound of a gun being fired **2.** BULLETS FIRED bullets or shot fired from a gun **3.** GUN'S RANGE the maximum distance that a bullet fired from a gun can travel

gun-shy *adj.* **1.** TIMID extremely cautious, timid, or wary of taking risks **2.** SCARED OF GUNS afraid of guns or the noise they make when fired

gun·sling·er /gún slìngər/ *n.* an armed fighter or criminal, especially in the frontier days of the Wild West (*informal*) —**gun·sling·ing** *n.*

gun·smith /gún smìth/ *n.* somebody who makes and repairs firearms, or sells them in a store

gun·stock /gún stòk/ *n.* the shaped wooden or metal handle of a rifle that is pressed against the shoulder when the rifle is being fired

gun·wale /gúnn'l/ *n.* the top edge of a ship's sides that forms a ledge around the whole ship above the deck (*often used in the plural*) [15thC. From GUN + *wale* "strip, stripe" (from Old English *walu*); because it was used in the past to support guns.]

Guo Xi /gwŏ shée/ (*fl.* 1060–75) Chinese artist. He is noted for his large landscape murals and scrolls.

gup·py /gúppee/ (*plural* **-pies**) *n.* a small freshwater fish with a brightly colored tail, native to the West Indies and South America, that is popular in aquariums and produces live young, rather than eggs. Latin name: *Poecilia reticulata.* [Early 20thC. Named for the Reverend R. J. Lechmere *Guppy* (1836–1916), who sent the first specimen from Trinidad to the British Museum.]

Gup·ta /gŏŏptə/ *n.* an Indian dynasty of the 3rd to 6th centuries that established a loose empire in much of the subcontinent [Late 19thC. Named for *Chandragupta*, the dynasty's founder.]

Gur /goor/ *n.* a group of around about 70 languages, including Mossi, Dagomba, and Mamprusi, spoken in western parts of Central Africa. It is a branch of the Niger-Congo family of African languages. About 10 million people speak one of the languages classified as being in the Gur group. —**Gur** *adj.*

gur·dwa·ra /goor dwaárə/ *n.* a Sikh temple or other place of worship where Sikh scriptures are kept [Early 20thC. From Punjabi *gurduārā.*]

gur·gi·ta·tion /gùrji táysh'n/ *n.* the swirling or surging movement of liquid flowing fast (*literary*) [Mid-16thC. From late Latin *gurgitare* "to engulf," from Latin *gurges* "whirlpool."]

gur·gle /gúrg'l/ *v.* (**-gled, -gling, -gles**) **1.** *vi.* MAKE BUBBLING NOISE to make the deep bubbling noise that liquid makes when it is poured from a bottle **2.** *vti.* MAKE BUBBLING WATER SOUND to make a bubbling sound in the throat, or to say something with a bubbling sound ■ *n.* GURGLING SOUND the sound or act of gurgling [Mid-16thC. Via assumed Vulgar Latin *gurguliare* from Latin *gurgulio* "gullet" (source of English *gorge* and *regurgitate*).] —**gur·gling·ly** *adv.*

Gur·kha /gúrkə/ (*plural* **-kha** *or* **-khas**) *n.* **1.** MEMBER OF HINDU PEOPLE a member of a Hindu people living mainly in Nepal, with small communities in Bhutan **2.** GURKHA IN ARMY a Gurkha serving in the British or Indian army [Early 19thC. From Nepalese *Gurkha*, a place name.] —**Gur·kha** *adj.*

gur·nard /gúrnərd/ (*plural* **-nards** *or* **-nard**) *n.* **1.** FISH WITH SPINY FINS a widely distributed spiny-finned marine fish with an armored head and sets of pectoral fins modified for crawling on the sea bottom. Family: Triglidae. **2.** = **flying gurnard** [14thC. From Old French *gornart*, from, ultimately, Latin *grunnire* "to grunt," from the sound it makes when caught.]

gur·ney /gúrnee/ (*plural* **-neys**) *n.* a wheeled stretcher for transporting hospital patients [Late 19thC. Origin uncertain: perhaps named for J.T. *Gurney* of Boston who patented a new cab design in 1883. Originally used for a type of cab.]

gu·ru /gŏŏ roo/ (*plural* **-rus**) *n.* **1.** HINDU OR SIKH RELIGIOUS TEACHER in Hinduism and Sikhism, a religious leader or teacher **2.** LEADER OF RELIGIOUS GROUP a spiritual leader of or intellectual guide for a religious group or movement especially one being described as non-mainstream **3.** SOMEBODY INFLUENTIAL somebody who is prominent and influential in a specific field and sets a trend or starts a movement ○ *a meeting of the world's software gurus* **4.** INDIVIDUAL'S REVERED TEACHER AND COUNSELOR a teacher or counselor in spiritual or intellectual matters who is especially revered and followed by an individual [Early 17thC. From Sanskrit, "elder, teacher."]

Gu·ru Na·nak Ja·nan·ti /gŏŏroo naánək jə naántee/ *n.* INDIAN RELIG an annual Hindu festival held on the anniversary of the birthday of Guru Nanak

gu·sano /gŏŏ saánó, -zaá-/ *n.* a Cuban, usually living in exile, who is opposed to the regime of Fidel Castro

gush /gush/ *vti.* (**gushed, gush·ing, gush·es**) **1.** FLOW OUT FAST to flow out, or to send a liquid out, rapidly and in large quantities **2.** SPEAK, BEHAVE, OR SAY EFFUSIVELY to speak or behave in an extremely or exaggeratedly enthusiastic, affectionate, or sentimental way ○ *"Your children are simply delightful!", she gushed.* ■ *n.* **1.** FLOW OF LIQUID a fast or copious flow of liquid from somewhere **2.** EMOTIONAL OUTBURST an outburst of overenthusiastic or overemotional speech or behavior [14thC. Origin uncertain: probably an imitation of the sound of liquid gushing.] —**gush·ing** *adj.* —**gush·ing·ly** *adv.*

gush·er /gúshər/ *n.* **1.** FREE-FLOWING OIL WELL an oil well from which oil flows freely and in large amounts, without having to be pumped **2.** EFFUSIVE PERSON somebody who tends to speak or behave in an exaggeratedly emotional or enthusiastic way

gush·y /gúshee/ (**-i·er, -i·est**) *adj.* characterized by overenthusiastic or overemotional speech or behavior —**gush·i·ly** *adv.* —**gush·i·ness** *n.*

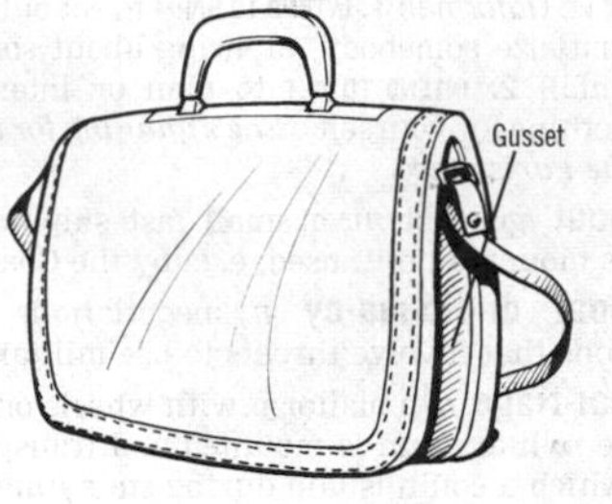

Gusset

gus·set /gússət/ *n.* **1.** INSET PIECE OF FABRIC a piece of fabric, usually triangular in shape, inserted in a garment where added strength or freedom of movement is needed **2.** FLAT PLATE REINFORCING A JOINT a flat, often triangular plate, usually of steel or plywood, used to connect and reinforce a joint where several members meet at different angles, e.g., in a pitched roof **3.** CHAIN MAIL AT AN ARMOR JOINT a section of chain mail protecting the unarmored joints of a suit of armor ■ *vt.* (**-set·ed, -set·ing, -sets**) FIT SOMETHING WITH A GUSSET to fit a garment, a wooden joint, or a suit of armor with a gusset [14thC. From French *gousset*, literally "little pod," from *gousse* "pod, shell," of unknown origin.]

gus·sy up /gússee-/ (**gus·sied up, gus·sy·ing up, gus·sies up**) *vt.* to dress somebody in fancy clothes, or decorate something elaborately (*informal*) (*often passive*) ○ *all gussied up in a frilly dress* ○ *The city was gussied up for the visit of the mayor.* [Mid-20thC. *Gussy* of uncertain origin: perhaps from Australian slang *gussie* "an effeminate man," a pet form of the male first name *Augustus*.]

gust /gust/ *n.* **1.** BURST OF WIND a sudden violent rush of wind **2.** EMOTIONAL OUTBURST an outburst of emotion such as anger ■ *vi.* (**gust·ed, gust·ing, gusts**) BLOW IN BURSTS to blow, or be blown by the wind, in sudden violent bursts [Late 16thC. From Old Norse *gustr*, from *gjósa* "to gush."]

gus·ta·tion /gu stáysh'n/ *n.* the action of tasting, or the sense or faculty of taste (*formal*) [Late 16thC. Directly or via French from the Latin stem *gustation-*, from *gustare* "to taste."]

gus·ta·to·ry /gústə tàwree/, **gus·ta·to·ri·al** /gùstə táwree əl/ *adj.* relating to the sense of taste or to the action or experience of tasting something (*formal*) [Late 17thC. Formed from Latin *gustare* (see GUSTATION).] —**gus·ta·to·ri·ly** *adv.*

Gu·stav·o A. Ma·der·o /gŏŏ staávō aa mə dérrō/ city in south central Mexico, near Mexico City. The Treaty of Guadalupe Hidalgo ending the Mexican War was signed here in 1848. Population: 1,268,068 (1990). Former name **Guadalupe Hidalgo**

gus·to /gústō/ *n.* lively enthusiasm or enjoyment [Early 17thC. Via Italian from Latin *gustus* "taste."]

gust·y /gústee/ (**-i·er, -i·est**) *adj.* blowing or arising in gusts, or characterized by gusts ○ *a gusty day*

gut /gut/ *n.* **1.** ALIMENTARY CANAL the whole of the alimentary canal in people and animals, from the mouth to the anus, or the lower part of it, (**the intestine**), from the stomach to the anus **2.** = **catgut** **3.** FISHING CORD cord made of fibrous material taken from silkworms, used to make fishing lines **4.** PLACE WHERE INSTINCTS ARE FELT somebody's deepest instinctively felt emotions or responses, as distinct from rational or logical responses (*often used in the plural*) ○ *a gut reaction* **5.** ABDOMEN somebody's belly, especially if it is noticeably large (*slang disapproving*) ○ *I've got to work off this gut.* ■ **guts** *npl.* **1.** INTESTINES the insides of a person or animal, especially the intestines **2.** INNER OR CENTRAL PARTS the inner or central parts of something such as the working parts of a machine or the basic principles that a theory is based on **3.** STRENGTH OF CHARACTER courage or boldness (*slang*) ■ *vt.* (**gut·ted, gut·ting, guts**) **1.** REMOVE AN ANIMAL'S INSIDES to remove the insides of a dead animal **2.** DESTROY A BUILDING'S INTERIOR to destroy the internal parts of a building, leaving only the outer walls standing ○ *The factory was completely gutted in the fire.* **3.** EMPTY to remove all the internal fixtures and furnishings from a room or building **4.** TAKE EXTRACTS FROM A TEXT to select extracts from a piece of writing for use elsewhere **5.** MAKE SOMETHING INEFFECTIVE to make something powerless or ineffective, especially by removing essential parts or features from it [Old English *guttas.* Ultimately from an Indo-European word meaning "to pour," which was also the ancestor of English *funnel.* The underlying meaning is "tube through which something flows."] ◇ **bust a gut** to struggle or work exceptionally hard to get something done (*slang*) ◇ **hate somebody's guts** to dislike somebody very much (*slang*)

GUT /gut/ *abbr.* PHYS Grand Unified Theory

gut·buck·et /gút bùkət/ *n.* **1.** HOMEMADE BASS a homemade instrument played like a double bass, made by fixing a stick to an upturned basin and stretching a string along its length **2.** KIND OF JAZZ a simple but highly emotional style of jazz or blues [Early 20thC. Originally a bucket used for carrying beer, or for catching the slops from a barrel, later used for the instrument made from the bucket.]

gut course *n.* a college or university course that is very easy to pass (*informal*)

Johannes Gutenberg: 15th-century engraving showing Gutenberg (left foreground) printing the Gutenberg Bible (1456?)

Gu·ten·berg /gŏŏt'n bùrg/, **Johannes** (1400?–68) German printer. He is credited with the invention of moveable type, which he used in his Mainz printing press to print the 42-line Bible, known as the Gutenberg Bible. Full name **Johannes Gensfleisch Gutenberg**

Guth·rie /gúthree/, **Sir Tyrone** (1900–71) British stage director. He was closely identified with the Old Vic-Sadler's Wells Company, London, in the 1940s and 1950s, and founded the Tyrone Guthrie Theater in Minneapolis in 1963. Full name **Sir William Tyrone Guthrie**

Guth·rie, Woody (1912–67) U.S. folk singer and composer. Many of his hundreds of songs protested the social injustice of the Depression. He wrote "This Land Is Your Land" (1940). Full name **Woodrow Wilson Guthrie**

Guth·run *n.* MYTHOL = **Gudrun**

gut is·sue *n.* a political issue that causes an emotional response rather than a strictly rational one

gut job *n.* the restoration or repair of a building that includes the removal and rebuilding of the interior (*informal*)

gut·less /gútləss/ *adj.* lacking in courage and determination —**gut·less·ness** *n.*

WORD KEY: SYNONYMS

See Synonyms at ***cowardly.***

gut re·ha·bil·i·ta·tion, gut ren·o·va·tion *n.* = **gut job** (*informal*)

guts·y /gútsee/ (**-i·er, -i·est**) *adj.* (*informal*) **1. COURAGEOUS** showing courage, boldness and determination **2. DONE WITH EMOTION** done or performed with a great deal of vigor, passion, or emotion —**guts·i·ly** *adv.* —**guts·i·ness** *n.*

gut·ta /gúttə/ (*plural* **-tae** /gú tee/) *n.* **1. ORNAMENT CARVED ON A DORIC ENTABLATURE** one of a series of ornaments shaped like drops that are attached to the underside of a Doric entablature **2. DROP OF MEDICINE** a drop of medicine (*dated*) (*formerly used in the instructions on prescriptions to indicate the dose to be taken*) [14thC. From Latin, "drop."]

gut·ta-per·cha /gùttə púrchə/ *n.* **1. PLIABLE SUBSTANCE MADE FROM LATEX** a soft pliable substance made from the latex taken from a Malaysian tree, used in golf balls, for waterproofing substances, and as insulation for electrical wires **2. TREE FROM WHICH GUTTA-PERCHA COMES** a tree from which gutta-percha is taken. Genera: *Palaquium* and *Payena.* [Mid-19thC. Alteration (by influence of Latin *gutta* "drop") of Malay *getah perca*, literally "gum strips of cloth," because it resembles cloth.]

gut·tate /gú tàyt/, **gut·tat·ed** /-tàytəd/ *adj.* BIOL having or resembling drops or spots [Early 19thC. From Latin *guttatus*, from *gutta* (see GUTTA).]

gut·ta·tion /gu táysh'n/ *n.* the oozing out of water droplets from the uninjured surface of a plant leaf

gut·ter /gúttər/ *n.* **1. RAINWATER CHANNEL ON A ROAD** a channel at the edge of a road that carries water into a drain **2. RAINWATER CHANNEL ON A ROOF** a metal or plastic channel on a roof for carrying away rainwater **3. POOR OR DEGRADED STATE** an impoverished and degraded existence or way of life ○ *She dragged me out of the gutter and made me respect myself.* **4.** BOWLING **CHANNEL ON BOWLING LANE** the channel on either side of a bowling lane **5.** PRINTING **INNER MARGINS OF BOOK** the blank space formed by the inner margins of two facing pages of a book **6.** STAMPS **SPACE BETWEEN STAMPS ON SHEET** the space between the printed design of one stamp and the next one on the sheet, where the perforations lie ■ *v.* (**-tered, -ter·ing, -ters**) **1.** *vi.* **MELT QUICKLY** to burn down more quickly than usual because the melting wax has formed a channel on one side (*refers to a candle*) **2.** *vi.* **FLICKER** to flicker when on the point of being extinguished **3.** *vt.* **FORM CHANNELS IN** to wear away channels in the surface of something **4.** *vi.* **TRICKLE** to run in a narrow stream or trickle ■ *adj.* **OF THE WORST KIND** of the most vulgar, corrupt, or morally degraded kind (*disapproving*) ○ *the gutter press* [13thC. From Anglo-Norman *gotere*, from, ultimately, Latin *gutta* "drop" (source of English *gout*). The underlying sense is of something along which "drops" of water run.]

gutter out *vi.* **1. STOP BURNING** to go out after flickering for a while **2. COME TO A GRADUAL FINISH** to come to an end finally, after gradually declining

gut·ter ball *n.* in bowling, a ball that, when bowled, rolls into the gutter and does not knock over any pins

gut·ter·snipe /gúttər snìp/ *n.* (*insult*) **1. POOR DIRTY CHILD** a child who wears dirty ragged clothes, has rough manners, and lives in the streets **2. SOMEBODY FROM LOWER CLASS** somebody with a rough or vulgar manner, especially somebody with a lower-class background [Mid-19thC. The modern sense evolved from "the common snipe" (a bird that likes wet muddy conditions) via "street cleaner."] —**gut·ter·snip·ish** *adj.*

gut·tur·al /gúttərəl/ *adj.* **1. GRUFF-SOUNDING** characterized by harsh and grating speech sounds made in the throat or toward the back of the mouth **2.** PHON = velar *adj.* 1 ■ *n.* **GUTTURAL SPEECH SOUND** a speech sound produced in the throat or at the back of the mouth [Late 16thC. Directly or via French from medieval Latin *gutturalis*, from Latin *guttur* "throat."] —**gut·tur·al·ism** *n.* —**gut·tur·al·i·ty** /gùttə rállətee/ *n.* —**gut·tur·al·ly** *adv.* —**gut·tur·al·ness** *n.*

gut·tur·al·ize /gúttərə lìz/ (**-ized, -iz·ing, -iz·es**) *v.* **1.** *vt.* **SAY IN GUTTURAL WAY** to pronounce a speech sound in the throat or toward the back of the mouth **2.** *vti.* **SPEAK OR SAY HARSHLY** to speak or say something in a harsh rasping way —**gut·tur·al·i·za·tion** /gùttərəli záysh'n/ *n.*

gut-wrench·ing *adj.* having a very powerful effect on the feelings, especially in stirring up pity or sympathy

guy[1] /gì/ (**guyed, guy·ing, guys**) *n.* (*informal*) **1. MAN** a man **2. PERSON** somebody of either sex, especially one of a group of people

WORD KEY: USAGE

Informal uses: ***Guy*** in reference to a person is not standard English. In informal usage the word has two contrary meanings. It is used to mean "man," often in contexts relating to the two sexes: *Guys like her because she's smart.* And, almost always in the plural, it can mean people of either sex: *You guys are my best friends.*

guy[2] /gì/ *n.* = **guywire** ■ *vt.* (**guyed, guy·ing, guys**) **SUPPORT WITH GUYWIRES** to support or anchor something using ropes, cables, or chains [14thC. Origin uncertain: probably from a Low German word that is, perhaps, also the source of Dutch *gei* and German *Geitau* "brail" (a type of rope).]

Guy. *abbr.* Guyana

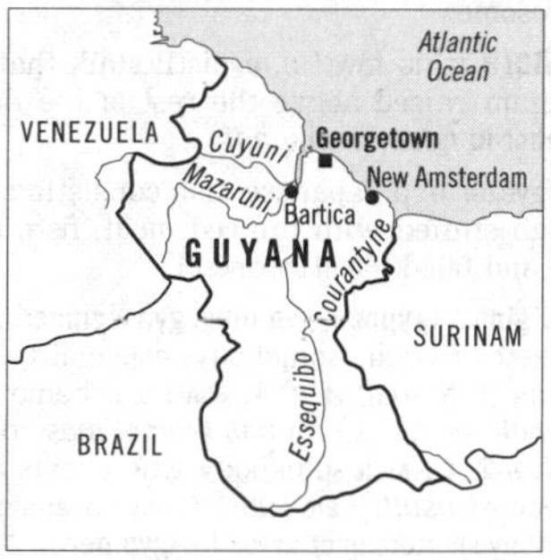

Guyana

Guy·a·na /gee ánnə, gee áanə/ republic on the North Atlantic coast of South America bordered on the northwest by Venezuela, on the southwest by Brazil and on the east by Surinam. Formerly a British colony, it gained independence in 1966. Language: English. Currency: Guyana dollar. Capital: Georgetown. Population: 711,759 (1997). Area: 83,000 sq. mi./215,000 sq. km. Official name **Cooperative Republic of Guyana** —**Guy·a·nese** *adj., n.*

Guy Fawkes Night /gì fáwks- / *n.* = **Bonfire Night** [Named for *Guy Fawkes* (1570–1606), one of the conspirators who tried to blow up Parliament (see GUNPOWDER PLOT)]

guy·line *n.* = **guywire**

guy·ot /gee ṓ/ *n.* a flat-topped underwater mountain, commonly found in the Pacific Ocean and considered to be an extinct volcano [Mid-20thC. Named for Arnold Henri *Guyot*, (1807–84), a Swiss-born U.S. geologist and geographer.]

guy·rope /gì rṑp/ *n.* U.K. = **guywire**

guy·wire /gì wìr/, **guy·line** /gì lìn/ *n.* a wire or chain tightened to hold something in position, e.g., any of the wires that hold up a telephone pole

Guz·mán Blan·co /gooss maan blaangkō/, **Antonio** (1829–99) Venezuelan statesman. As president of Venezuela (1870–77, 1879–84, 1886–88), he promoted public education and foreign investment.

guz·zle /gúzz'l/ (**-zled, -zling, -zles**) *vti.* to drink something greedily, or consume something rapidly and in large quantities (*informal*) [Late 16thC. Origin uncertain: perhaps from Old French *gosillier* "to chatter, vomit," from, ultimately, late Latin *geusiae* "cheeks."] —**guz·zler** *n.*

GVW *abbr.* gross vehicular weight

GW *symbol.* gigawatt

gwe·duc /góo ee dùk/ *n.* ZOOL = **geoduck**

Gwin·nett /gwə nét/, **Button** (1735?–77) British-born American patriot. A member of the Continental Congress, he was one of the signers of the Declaration of Independence.

GWRBI *abbr.* BASEBALL game winning run batted in

Gy *symbol.* NUCLEAR PHYS gray

gybe *vti., n.* NAUT = **jibe**[1]

gym /jim/ *n.* **1. GYMNASIUM** a gymnasium (*informal*) **2. PHYSICAL EDUCATION** physical education, especially as a school subject (*informal*) **3. CHILD'S CLIMBING STRUCTURE** a sturdy metal or hard plastic frame designed for children's outdoor play and exercise (*often used in combination*) [Late 19thC. Shortening.]

gym·kha·na /jim káanə/ *n.* **1. SPORTING CONTEST** a sporting event or contest **2. ATHLETICS MEETING OR FACILITY** a place where a sporting event or contest is held (*dated*) [Mid-19thC. Alteration (by influence of words such as GYMNAST) of Urdu *gendkānah*, literally "ball house." Originally used for a public sports facility.]

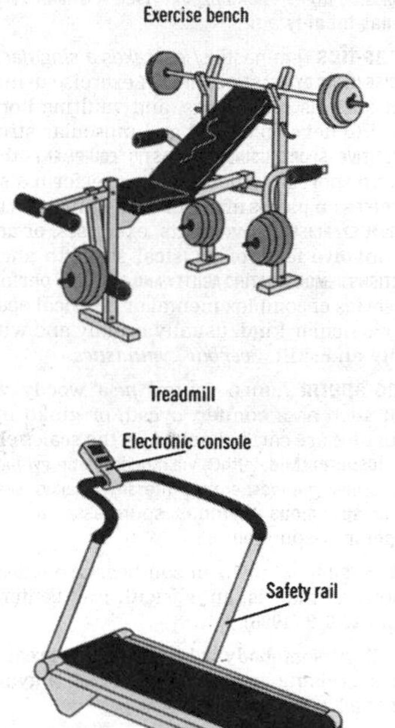

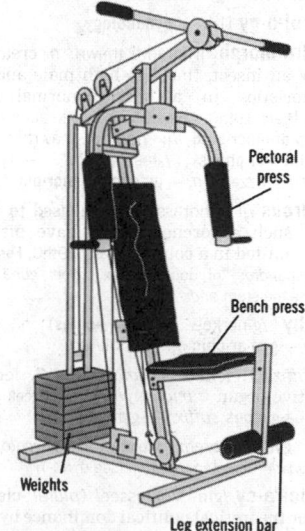

Gymnasium: Typical equipment used in a gymnasium

gym·na·si·um /jim náyzee əm/ (*plural* **-ums** *or* **-a** /-zee ə/) *n.* **1. LARGE EXERCISE ROOM** a large room equipped for physical exercise or training of various kinds, e.g., in a school or a private club **2. EUROPEAN ACADEMIC SECONDARY SCHOOL** in Europe, principally Germany and ə/) *n.* **1.** LARGE EXERCISE ROOM a large room equipped for physical exercise or training of various kinds, e.g., in a school or a private club **2.** EUROPEAN ACADEMIC SECONDARY SCHOOL in Europe, principally Germany and other German-speaking countries, a secondary school where the emphasis is on academic subjects rather than on technical training [Late 16thC. Via Latin, "school," from, ultimately, Greek *gumnazein* "to exercise naked" (a custom in ancient times), hence "to train," from *gumnos* "naked."]

gym·nast /jím nàst, jímnəst/ *n.* somebody who is good at gymnastics, especially somebody involved in gymnastics as a competitive sport [Late 16thC. Directly or via French from Greek *gumnastēs* "trainer of athletes," from *gumnazein* (see GYMNASIUM).]

gym·nas·tic /jim nástik/ *adj.* **1.** INVOLVING GYMNASTICS relating to or involving gymnastics ○ *gymnastic equipment* **2.** INVOLVING ATHLETICISM involving or demonstrating athleticism and agility ○ *a gymnastic dancing style* [Late 16thC. Via Latin from Greek *gumnastikos*, from *gumnazein* (see GYMNASIUM).] —**gym·nas·ti·cal·ly** *adv.*

gym·nas·tics /jim nástiks/ *n.* (*takes a singular verb*) **1.** EXERCISE USING GYMNASTIC EQUIPMENT exercise using equipment such as bars, rings, and vaulting horses, designed to develop agility and muscular strength **2.** COMPETITIVE SPORT USING GYMNASTIC EQUIPMENT the competitive sport in which athletes perform a series of exercises on pieces of gymnastic equipment ■ *npl.* **1.** PHYSICAL EXERCISES movements, exercises, or activities that involve feats of physical strength and agility **2.** ACTIONS DEMONSTRATING AGILITY AND SKILL the performance of a series of complex mental or physical operations of a particular kind, usually rapidly and with great agility and skill ○ *verbal gymnastics*

gym·no·sperm /jímnə spùrm/ *n.* a woody vascular plant such as a conifer, cycad, or ginko in which the ovules are carried naked on the scales of a cone. ◊ **angiosperm** [Mid-19thC. Via modern Latin *gymnospermus* from Greek *gumnospermos*, literally "naked seed."] —**gym·no·sper·mous** /jìmnə spúrməss/ *adj.* —**gym·no·sper·my** /-spùrmee/ *n.*

Gym·pie /gímpee/ town in southeastern Queensland, Australia, that is an agricultural center. Population: 10,813 (1996).

gym rat *n.* somebody who spends a great deal of time exercising or playing a sport at a gymnasium (*informal*)

gyn. *abbr.* **1.** gynecological **2.** gynecologist **3.** gynecology

gyn- *prefix.* = **gyno-** (*used before vowels*)

gynaeco- *prefix.* U.K. = **gyneco-**

gynaecol. U.K. = **gynecol.**

gy·nae·col·o·gy U.K. = **gynecology**

gy·nan·dro·morph /ji nándrə màwrf/ *n.* creature, especially an insect, that has both male and female characteristics in a way abnormal for its species [Late 19thC. Coined from GYNANDROUS + MORPH.] —**gy·nan·dro·mor·phic** /ji nàndrə máwrfik/ *adj.* —**gy·nan·dro·mor·phous** /-fəss/ *adj.* —**gy·nan·dro·mor·phism** /-fìzzəm/ *n.* —**gy·nan·dro·mor·phy** /-fee/ *n.*

gy·nan·drous /ji nándrəss/ *adj.* BOT used to describe flowers such as orchards that have pistils and stamens united in a column [Early 19thC. Formed from Greek *gunandros* "of doubtful sex," from *gunē* "woman, female" + the stem *andr-* "man."]

gyn·ar·chy /gínərkee/ (*plural* **-chies**) *n.* = **gynecocracy** —**gyn·ar·chic** /gī naárkik/ *adj.*

-gyne *suffix.* **1.** female ○ *androgyne* **2.** female reproductive organ ○ *trichogyne* [From Greek *gunē* (see GYNO-)] —**-gynous** *suffix.* —**-gyny** *suffix.*

gynec-, **gyneco-** *prefix.* woman ○ *gynecology* [From Greek *gunaik-*, the stem of *gunē* (see GYNO-)]

gyn·e·coc·ra·cy /gìnə kókrəssee/ (*plural* **-cies**) *n.* an actual or theoretical political dominance by women, or a political system that gives supremacy to women

gy·ne·coid /gínə kòyd/ *adj.* physically resembling or typical of a woman ○ *a gynecoid pelvis*

gynecol. *abbr.* **1.** gynecological **2.** gynecologist **3.** gynecology

gy·ne·co·log·i·cal /gìnəkə lójjik'l/, **gy·ne·co·log·ic** /-lójjik/ *adj.* relating to women's health, especially to diseases of the reproductive organs

gy·ne·col·o·gy /gìnə kóllәjee/ *n.* the branch of medicine that deals with women's health, especially with the health of women's reproductive organs —**gy·ne·col·o·gist** *n.*

gy·ne·co·mas·ti·a /gìnə kō mástee ə/ *n.* enlarged breasts on a man caused by hormonal imbalance or hormone therapy [Mid-19thC. Coined from GYNECO- + Greek *mastos* "breast."]

gyn·e·cop·a·thy /gìnə kóppəthee/ (*plural* **-thies**) *n.* any disease that only affects women

gy·ne·pho·bi·a /gìnə fṓbee ə/ *n.* an irrational and pathological fear of women

gyno- *prefix.* **1.** female reproductive organ ○ *gynophore* **2.** woman ○ *gynocracy* [From Greek *gunē* "woman." Ultimately from the Indo-European word for "woman," which is also the ancestor of English *queen* and *banshee*.]

gy·noc·ra·cy /gī nókrəssee/ (*plural* **-cies**) *n.* = **gynecocracy**

gyn·o·di·oe·cious /gìnō dī éeshəss/ *adj.* used to describe a plant species that has bisexual flowers on some plants and single-sex flowers on others —**gy·no·di·oe·cism** /-ée sìzzəm/ *n.*

gy·noe·ci·um /gī néeshee əm, -shəm/ (*plural* **-a** /-shə/) *n.* the carpels of a plant considered together [Mid-19thC. From an alteration (influenced by Greek *oikos* "house") of modern Latin *gynaeceum* "women's apartments," from the neuter of Greek *gunaikeios* "of women," from *gunē* "woman."]

gyn·o·gen·e·sis /gìnə jénnəssiss/ *n.* the development of an embryo without fusion of the egg and sperm nuclei, so that the embryo has only maternal chromosomes

gyn·o·phore /gínə fàwr/ *n.* a pistil stalk that has its gynoecium raised above the rest of the flower —**gyn·o·phor·ic** /gìnə fáwrik/ *adj.*

gyo·za /gyṓzə/ *n.* a Japanese dish consisting of cases of dough stuffed with minced meat, fish, or vegetables, and fried [From Japanese]

gyp /jip/, **gip** *vt.* (**gypped, gyp·ping, gyps; gipped, gip·ping, gips**) CHEAT to cheat somebody, especially by overcharging (*informal*) ■ *n.* **1.** SCAM a scheme to trick or swindle people (*informal*) (*sometimes considered offensive*) **2.** CHEATER somebody who cheats or swindles people (*insult*) [Late 19thC. Origin uncertain: perhaps a derogatory shortening of GYPSY.] —**gyp·per** *n.*

gyp·sif·er·ous /jip síffərəss/ *adj.* containing gypsum

gyp·soph·i·la /jip sóffilə/ *n.* a plant of the carnation family native to the Mediterranean, with delicate tiny white or pink flowers on long branching stalks. It is popular in bouquets. Genus: *Gypsophila.* [Late 18thC. From modern Latin, genus name, literally "chalk-loving," from Greek *gupsos* "chalk," because it grows in chalky soil.]

gyp·sum /jípsəm/ *n.* **1.** WHITE MINERAL a naturally occurring colorless or white mineral, hydrated calcium sulfate, that is used to make cement, plaster of Paris, chalk, and agricultural fertilizers. Formula: $CaSO_4.2H_2O$. **2.** PLASTERBOARD plasterboard (*informal*) [14thC. Via Latin from Greek *gupsos* "chalk, gypsum."]

gyp·sum board *n.* = **plasterboard**

gyp·sy /jípsee/ (*plural* **-sies**) *n.* somebody who has a nomadic or unconventional lifestyle

Gyp·sy /jípsee/ (*plural* **-sies**), **Gip·sy** (*plural* **-sies**) *n.* an offensive term for a member of the Romany people (*offensive*) [Mid-16thC. Shortening of EGYPTIAN, because Gypsies were once thought to have come from Egypt.] —**Gyp·sy** *adj.*

gyp·sy cab *n.* a taxi that has a license to pick up only passengers who call by telephone, not passengers who hail it in the street

gyp·sy moth *n.* a European tussock moth, common in North America since the 19th century, where its hairy caterpillar has become a serious pest of trees. The caterpillar is grayish with bright red and blue spots and stiff hairs. Latin name: *Lymantria dispar.*

gy·ral /jírəl/ *adj.* moving in a path that is spiral or circular —**gy·ral·ly** *adv.*

gy·rate /jī ràyt/ *vi.* (**-rat·ed, -rat·ing, -rates**) MOVE IN CIRCLE OR SPIRAL to move with a circular or spiral motion, especially around a fixed central point ■ *adj.* BIOL GROWING IN A SPIRAL growing in a winding spiral or coil [Early 19thC. From late Latin *girat-*, the past participle stem of *gyrare*, "to revolve," from Latin *gyrus* "circle" (see GYRUS).] —**gy·ra·tor** *n.*

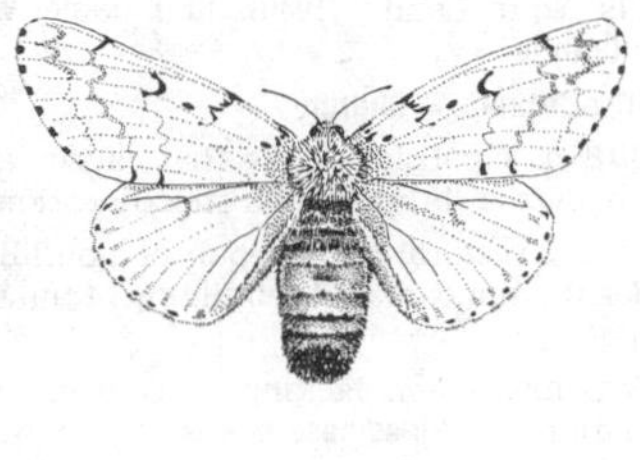

Gypsy moth

gy·ra·tion /jī ráysh'n/ *n.* **1.** CIRCULAR MOVEMENT movement in a circle around a fixed center ○ *the gyration of the rotor* **2.** SOMETHING GYRATE a spiral or coil-shaped thing or part

gy·ra·to·ry /jírə tàwree/ *adj.* moving in a spiral or circle or involving movement in a circle or spiral

gyre /jīr/ *n.* a circle or spiral (*literary*) [Mid-16thC. From Latin *gyrus* "circle" (see GYRUS).]

gy·rene /jī réen, -réen/ *n.* a soldier in the U.S. Marine Corps (*slang*) [Mid-20thC. Origin uncertain: perhaps a blend of GI and MARINE.]

gyr·fal·con /júr fàlkən/ *n.* a large powerful falcon of cold northern regions, varying in color from white to dark brown. Latin name: *Falco rusticolus.* [14thC. By folk etymology (by association with Latin *gyrare* "to revolve") from Old French *gerfaucon*; *ger-* of uncertain origin: perhaps from Old High German *gir* "vulture."]

gy·ro /jī rṑ/; (*sandwich*) /jī rō, jée-/ (*plural* **-ros**) *n.* minced lamb that has been cooked on a spit in a molded block, then sliced thin and served in pita bread with onion and tomato [Late 20thC. From modern Greek *guros*, literally "turning."]

gyro- *prefix.* **1.** spinning or rotating in a circle ○ *gyrostatics* **2.** gyroscope, gyroscopic ○ *gyrostabilizer* [From Greek *guros* "ring, circle"]

gy·ro·com·pass /jī rō kùmpəss, -kòmpəss/ *n.* a navigational compass fitted with a gyroscope instead of a magnet

gy·ro·mag·net·ic /jì rō màg néttik/ *adj.* relating to or caused by the magnetism produced by the spinning motion of a charged particle ○ *gyromagnetic effect*

gy·ro·mag·net·ic ra·tio *n.* PHYS the ratio of the magnetic moment to the angular momentum of a system

gy·ron /jírən, -ròn/, **gi·ron** *n.* in heraldry, a triangular form made by two blinds drawn from the edge of an escutcheon to meet at the fesse-point and occupying half of the quarter [Late 16thC. From French, literally "gusset"; ultimately from a prehistoric Germanic word that is also the source of English *gore*[2].]

gy·ro·plane /jírə plàyn/ *n.* an aircraft fitted with an unpowered rotor for producing lift. ◊ **autogiro**

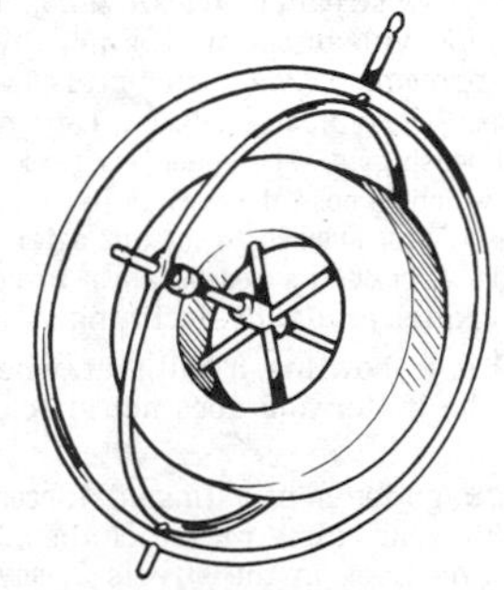

Gyroscope

gy·ro·scope /jírə skṑp/ *n.* a device consisting of a rotating heavy metal wheel pivoted inside a circular frame. The wheel's rotation enables it to retain its original orientation in space when the frame turns. Gyroscopes are used in compasses and other navigational aids, and in stabilizing mechanisms on ships and aircraft. —**gy·ro·scop·ic** /jīrə skóppik/ *adj.* —**gy·ro·scop·i·cal·ly** /-kəlee/ *adv.*

gy·ro·sta·bi·liz·er /jī rō stàbb'l īzər/ *n.* a stabilizing system that uses gyroscopes to compensate and reduce the rolling or pitching motion of a ship or aircraft

gy·ro·stat /jī rō stàt/ *n.* a type of gyroscope or gyrostabilizer in which the rotating wheel is pivoted within a rigid case [Late 19thC. Coined from GYRO- + Greek *statos* "standing."]

gy·ro·stat·ics /jī rō státtiks/ *n.* the science that deals with rotating bodies (*takes a singular verb*) —**gy·ro·stat·ic** *adj.* —**gy·ro·stat·i·cal·ly** *adv.*

gy·rus /jīrəss/ (*plural* **-ri** /-rī/) *n.* any of the rounded ridges on the outer layer of the brain [Mid-19thC. Via Latin, literally "circle," from Greek *guros* "ring, circle" (source of English *gyro-*).]

GySgt *abbr.* gunnery sergeant

Gyum·ri /gyoómree/ city in northwestern Armenia, the country's second most populated urban area. Population: 123,000 (1990). Former name **Leninakhan**

gyve /jīv/ *n.* **LEG SHACKLE** a shackle or fetter, usually for the leg (*archaic*) (*usually used in plural*) ■ *vt.* (**gyved, gyv·ing, gyves**) **SHACKLE** to shackle or fetter somebody, especially by the leg (*archaic*) [13thC. Origin unknown.]

Hh

h[1] (*plural* **h's**), **H** (*plural* **H's** *or* **Hs**) *n.* **1. 8TH LETTER OF ENGLISH ALPHABET** the eighth letter of the modern English alphabet **2. SPEECH SOUND CORRESPONDING TO THE LETTER "H"** the speech sound that corresponds to the letter "H" **3. LETTER "H" WRITTEN** a written representation of the letter "H"

h[2] *symbol.* **1.** Planck's constant **2.** hecto-

H *symbol.* **1.** ELECTRON ENG henry **2.** CHEM hydrogen **3.** PHYS enthalpy **4.** Hamiltonian **5.** magnetic field strength

h. *abbr.* **1. h., H.** harbor **2. h., H.** hard **3. h., H.** hardness **4. h., H.** height **5. h., H.** high **6. h., h** hit **7.** hospital **8.** horizontal **9.** MUSIC horn **10.** hundred **11.** husband

H. *abbr.* hospital

ha[1] /haa/, **hah** *interj.* **1. EXPRESSING VARIOUS EMOTIONS** used to express surprise, triumph, scorn, or happiness, depending on the way the speaker says it **2. REPRESENTING LAUGHTER** a word repeated to represent in writing the sound of laughter [13thC. An imitation of the sound.]

ha[2] *symbol.* hectare

ha[3] *abbr.* **1.** ARMS high angle **2.** hoc anno **3.** ASTRON hour angle

Ha. *abbr.* **1.** Haiti **2.** Haitian **3.** Hawaii **4.** Hawaiian

HAA *abbr.* heavy anti-aircraft

Hab. *abbr.* Habakkuk

Ha·bak·kuk /hábbə ko͝ok, hə bákək/, **Hab·a·cuc** *n.* **1. BIBLICAL HEBREW PRIEST** in the Bible, a Hebrew priest who lived in the seventh century B.C. **2. BOOK OF THE BIBLE** one of the prophetic books of the Bible. See table at **Bible**

ha·ba·ne·ra /haabə nérrə/ *n.* **1. SLOW DANCE** a slow dance in two-four time, originally from Cuba **2.** MUSIC **DANCE MUSIC FOR HABANERA** a piece of music for the habanera, which has a characteristic dotted rhythm **3. A HOT CHILI PEPPER** a hot chili pepper, originally from Cuba [Late 19thC. From Spanish *habanera*, "Havana."]

hab. corp. *abbr.* LAW habeas corpus

hab·da·lah /haavdə laá, haav dáwlə/, **hav·da·lah** *n.* a Jewish ceremony that marks the end of the Sabbath or another holy day, or a prayer said during the ceremony [Mid-18thC. From Hebrew *habdālāh* "separation, division."]

ha·be·as cor·pus *n.* a writ issued in order to bring somebody who has been detained into court, usually for a decision on whether the detention is lawful [From Latin, literally "you may have the body"]

Ha·ber-Bosch proc·ess /háybər báwsh-, -bósh-/ *n.* CHEM = **Haber process** [Named for the German chemists Fritz *Haber* (1869–1934) and Karl *Bosch* (1874–1940)]

hab·er·dash·er /hábbər dàshər/ *n.* **1. DEALER IN MEN'S CLOTHING** somebody who owns or works in a store that sells men's clothing and accessories **2.** *U.K.* **DEALER IN SEWING ARTICLES** somebody who deals in small articles used in sewing, e.g., thread, ribbons, and buttons [14thC. Probably from Anglo-Norman *hapertas* "small items of merchandise," of unknown origin.]

hab·er·dash·er·y /hábbər dàsharee/ (*plural* **-ies**) *n.* **1. GOODS SOLD BY A HABERDASHER** the items sold by a haberdasher **2. STORE SELLING HABERDASHERY** a store that sells haberdashery

hab·er·geon /hábbərjən, hə búrjən/ *n.* a sleeveless chain mail jacket worn under armor [14thC. From French *haubergeon*, from Old French *hauberc*, literally "a little hauberk" (see HAUBERK).]

Ha·ber proc·ess *n.* a commercial process for catalytically producing ammonia from atmospheric nitrogen and hydrogen at high temperature and pressure [See HABER-BOSCH PROCESS]

hab·ile /hább'l/ *adj.* able to do something with ease (*literary*) [Late 15thC. Via French from Latin *habilis* "able, easy to hold" (source of English *able*), from *habere* "to have, hold."]

ha·bil·i·ment /hə bílləmənt/ *n.* **GARMENT OR GARMENTS** clothing, or an item of clothing (*formal*) (*usually used in the plural*) ■ **ha·bil·i·ments** *npl.* **1. SPECIALIZED EQUIPMENT** the equipment and gear needed for a task or activity **2. SPECIAL CLOTHES** items of clothing associated with somebody's work or position, or an occasion [Early 17thC. From Old French *habillement*, from *habiller* "to fit out," from *habile* (see HABILE). The sense "clothing" developed in French, probably by association with "habit."]

ha·bil·i·tate /hə bíllə tàyt/ (**-tat·ed, -tat·ing, -tates**) *v.* **1.** *vi.* **PREPARE FOR POSITION** to qualify for employment or an office (*formal*) **2.** *vt.* **CLOTHE** to clothe somebody in a particular way (*literary*) **3.** *vt.* **EQUIP A MINING OPERATION** to provide a mine with the equipment and money needed for operation [Early 17thC. From medieval Latin *habilitare*, from Latin *habilitas* "ability," from *habilis* (see HABILE).] —**ha·bil·i·ta·tion** /hə bìllə táysh'n/ *n.* —**ha·bil·i·ta·tor** /hə bíllə tàytər/ *n.*

hab·it /hábbit/ *n.* **1. SOMETHING DONE ALL THE TIME** an action or behavior pattern that is regular, repetitive, and often unconscious ○ *I really need to get into the habit of writing down what I spend.* ○ *He has a really annoying habit of finishing your sentences for you.* **2. ADDICTION** an addiction to a drug (*slang*) **3.** RELIG **CLOTHING OF RELIGIOUS ORDER** a long loose gown, usually black, brown, gray, or white, traditionally worn by nuns and monks **4.** CLOTHES = **riding habit 5.** BOT, ZOOL **GROWTH PATTERN** the characteristic appearance, behavior, or growth pattern of a plant or animal **6. SHAPE OF A CRYSTAL** the characteristic growth pattern or shape of a crystal **7. ATTITUDE** somebody's attitude or general disposition ■ *vt.* (**-it·ed, -it·ing, -its**) **CLOTHE SOMEBODY SPECIALLY** to dress somebody in clothing distinctive to a particular position or office (*literary*) [12thC. Via Old French *abit* from Latin *habitus* from, ultimately, *habere* "to have, wear."]

WORD KEY: SYNONYMS

habit, custom, tradition, practice, routine, wont

CORE MEANING: established pattern of behavior

habit something that is done on such a regular basis that it becomes normal to act in this way and can be difficult to stop. It can be used to suggest that something is done compulsively; **custom** something that somebody regularly does at a particular time or on a particular occasion. It is also used to describe something that is an established action or pattern of behavior for a particular community or group of people; **tradition** an established action or pattern of behavior in a particular community or group of people, especially one that has existed for a long time and is considered an important part of a particular culture or way of life; **practice** an established way of doing something, especially a way that has developed through experience and knowledge; **routine** a sequence of actions that is regularly followed on a day-to-day basis, sometimes with the suggestion that this is monotonous and tedious; **wont** a formal or literary word used to describe something that somebody does regularly or habitually.

WORD KEY: ORIGIN

The Latin word *habere* from which ***habit*** is derived was used reflexively to mean "to be," and so its past participle *habitus* came to be used as a noun for "how you are," that is, your "state" or "condition." Subsequently this developed along the lines of both "outward condition or appearance," hence "clothing," and "inner condition, quality, nature, character," and later came to mean "usual way of behaving." (The notion of adapting a verb meaning "to have" to express "how you are, how you comport yourself" is duplicated in English "behave").

hab·it·a·ble /hábbitəb'l/ *adj.* considered fit to be lived in ○ *A lot of structural work will be needed before the house is habitable.* [14thC. Via Old French from Latin *habitabilis*, from *habitare* "to possess, inhabit" (see HABITAT).] —**hab·it·a·bil·i·ty** /hàbbitə bíllətee/ *n.* —**hab·it·a·ble·ness** /hábbitəb'lnəss/ *n.* —**hab·it·a·bly** /-blee/ *adv.*

hab·i·tant /hábbit'nt/ *n.* **1. N AMERICAN FARMER OF FRENCH ORIGIN** a farmer of French descent living in Canada or the United States **2. INHABITANT** somebody living in a place [15thC. From French, from the present participle of Old French *habiter* "to dwell," from Latin *habitare* (see HABITAT).]

hab·i·tat /hábbi tàt/ *n.* **1. HOME ENVIRONMENT** the natural conditions and environment, e.g., forest, desert, or wetlands, in which a plant or animal lives **2. TYPICAL LOCATION** the place in which a person or group is usually found **3. ARTIFICIALLY CREATED ENVIRONMENT** a sealed controlled environment in which people can live, e.g., to do research on the sea floor [Late 18thC. 3rd person present singular form of Latin *habitare* "to possess, inhabit," literally "to keep having" (source also of English *inhabit*), from *habere* "to have."]

hab·i·ta·tion /hàbbi táysh'n/ *n.* **1. OCCUPANCY** the occupancy of a place by people or animals **2. LIVING PLACE** a place in which to live ○ *The squirrels found a new habitation in a hollow tree.* **3. DWELLINGS** a group of dwellings and their inhabitants ○ *There is little evidence remaining of the ancient habitation.* [14thC. Via Old French from, ultimately Latin *habitare* (see HABITAT).] —**hab·i·ta·tion·al** *adj.*

hab·it-form·ing *adj.* capable of causing a physiological or psychological need in somebody

ha·bit·u·al /hə bíchoo əl/ *adj.* **1. REGULAR** done regularly and frequently **2. PERSISTING IN SOME BEHAVIOR** continuing in some practice as a result of an ingrained tendency **3. CHARACTERISTIC** typical of somebody's character or behavior ○ *She tackled the problem with her habitual single-mindedness.* —**ha·bit·u·al·ly** *adv.* —**ha·bit·u·al·ness** *n.*

WORD KEY: SYNONYMS

See Synonyms at ***usual***.

ha·bit·u·ate /hə bíchoo àyt/ (**-at·ed, -at·ing, -ates**) *v.* **1.** *vt.* **MAKE SOMEBODY USED TO SOMETHING** to accustom a person or animal to something through prolonged and regular exposure (*formal*) ○ *People living in cities become habituated to crowds.* **2.** *vti.* PSYCHOL **LEARN OR TEACH SOMEBODY TO IGNORE SOMETHING** to learn or teach a person or animal not to respond to a stimulus that is frequently repeated **3.** *vi.* **BECOME ACCUSTOMED TO** to become dependent on or less affected by a medical or illegal drug through frequent use [16thC. From late Latin *habituare* "to bring into a state," from Latin *habitus* (see HABIT).]

ha·bit·u·a·tion /hə bìchoo áysh'n/ *n.* **1. GETTING USED TO SOMETHING** the act of becoming accustomed to something through prolonged and frequent exposure (*formal*) **2.** PSYCHOL **DECREASED RESPONSE TO REPEATED STIMULUS** a basic form of learning in which an organism's response to a repeated stimulus decreases in strength **3. DRUG TOLERANCE OR DEPENDENCY** tolerance to or dependence on a medical or illegal drug, through frequent and prolonged use

hab·i·tude /hábbi tòod/ *n.* a tendency to act in a particular way (*literary*) —**hab·i·tu·di·nal** /hàbbi tòod'nəl/ *adj.*

ha·bit·u·é /hə bíchoo ày, hə bìchoo áy/ (*plural* **-bi·tu·és**) *n.* somebody who visits a place regularly [Early 19thC. From French, from the past participle of *habituer,* from late Latin *habituare* (see HABITUATE).]

hab·i·tus /hábbitəss/ (*plural* **-tus**) *n.* the general appearance, posture, or physical state of a patient, especially with regard to susceptibility to disease [Late 19thC. From Latin (see HABIT).]

ha·boob /hə bóob/ *n.* a violent sandstorm or dust storm that sweeps across the deserts of northern Africa and Arabia and the plains of India [Late 19thC. From Arabic *habub* "violent storm."]

Habs·burg *n.* HIST = **Hapsburg**

ha·bu /haá bòo/ (*plural* **-bus**) *n.* a large poisonous snake native to Okinawa and neighboring Pacific islands. Latin name: *Trimeresurus flavoviridis.* [Late 19thC. From Japanese.]

há·ček /há chèk/ *n.* a mark ˇ placed over a letter in some Slavic and other languages to indicate a change in pronunciation. In Czech, e.g., if placed over the letter "c" it changes the sound to "ch." [Mid-20thC. From Czech, literally "small hook," formed from *hak* "hook."]

ha·cen·da·do /haà sen daádō/ (*plural* **-dos**), **ha·ci·en·da·do** /haàssee en daádō/ (*plural* **-dos**) *n.* an owner or operator of a hacienda [Mid-19thC. From Spanish, from *hacienda* "HACIENDA."]

ha·chure /ha shóor, háshər/ *n.* **SHORT LINE SHOWING A SLOPE** any of the short parallel lines used for shading on a map to indicate the direction and steepness of a slope ■ *vt.* (**-chured, -chur·ing, -chures**) **SHADE** to shade a map with hachure lines to show the direction and steepness of slopes [Mid-19thC. From French, formed from *hacher* "to mark with hatches" (see HATCH[3]).]

ha·ci·en·da /haàssee éndə, hàssee-/ *n.* **1. LARGE ESTATE** a large estate, farm, or ranch in Spain or Spanish-speaking parts of America **2. HOUSE ON A LARGE ESTATE** the main residence on a hacienda [Mid-18thC. Via Spanish, "domestic work, large estate," from Latin *facienda* "things needing to be done," from *facere* "to do" (see FACT).]

ha·ci·en·da·do *n.* = **hacendado**

Ha·ci·en·da Heights /haàssee éndə híts/ unincorporated area of Los Angeles County, southwestern California. Population: 52,354 (1990).

hack[1] /hak/ *v.* (**hacked, hack·ing, hacks**) **1.** *vti.* **CUT USING REPEATED BLOWS** to cut or chop something by striking it with short repeated blows using a sharp tool such as a knife or an ax **2.** *vt.* **CLEAR A WAY** to open a path by cutting through an obstruction ○ *I had to hack my way through the bureaucracy to get the job done.* **3.** *vt.* **CHOP OFF OR INTO PARTS** to cut, shape, or divide something roughly or carelessly (*informal*) ○ *He's hacked a whole chunk off that article I wrote for the magazine.* **4.** *vi.* COMPUT **GET INTO A COMPUTER SYSTEM** to explore and manipulate the workings of a computer or other technological device or system, either for the purpose of understanding how it works or to gain unauthorized access **5.** *vt.* **COPE WITH SOMETHING** to succeed at or endure something (*informal*) ○ *I wonder if he can hack it.* **6.** *vi.* **MAKE A COUGHING NOISE** to cough persistently in short dry bursts with a rasping noise **7.** *vt.* **KICK SOCCER PLAYER'S SHINS** to commit a foul by kicking the shins of an opposing player in soccer **8.** *vt.* BASKETBALL **HIT A BASKETBALL PLAYER'S ARM** to commit a foul in basketball by striking another player on the arm ■ *n.* **1. QUICK CHOP** a short violent blow with a sharp tool **2. COUGHING NOISE** a short dry cough **3. CUT MADE BY HACKING SOMETHING** a rough cut made by a quick blow with a sharp tool, e.g., a notch in a tree made with an ax **4. TOOL FOR HACKING** a tool, e.g., a pickax, used for chopping something or breaking up hard ground **5. WOUND FROM A KICK** a wound from being kicked **6. DISABLING KICK IN SOCCER** a kick on the shins in soccer, meant to disable a player temporarily **7.** COMPUT **SUCCESSFUL EFFORT** an extremely good, often very time-consuming, work effort that produces exactly what is needed (*informal*) [Old English *haccian* "to cut in pieces." Ultimately from a prehistoric West Germanic word.]

hack[2] /hak/ *n.* **1.** POL **LOYAL PARTY WORKER** a political party member who serves the party unquestioningly (*disapproving*) **2. TAXICAB** a taxicab (*informal*) **3.** = **hackie** (*informal*) **4. DRUDGE** somebody who does dull and tedious work **5. HIRED WRITER** a writer paid to produce routine often down-market writing, e.g., for newspapers or movies (*disapproving*) **6. CAR OR CARRIAGE FOR HIRE** an automobile or a carriage for hire **7. OLD HORSE** a horse that is in bad condition through age or overwork **8. HORSE FOR HIRE** a horse that is hired out **9. HORSE FOR RIDING** a horse for riding or driving ■ *adj.* **TRITE** lacking quality and originality ○ *The movie had a really hack plot.* ■ *v.* (**hacked, hack·ing, hacks**) **1.** *vi.* **DRIVE A TAXICAB** to drive a taxicab (*informal*) **2.** *vi.* EQU **GO HORSEBACK RIDING** to ride a horse for exercise at a normal pace **3.** *vt.* **MAKE SOMETHING HACKNEYED** to make an expression or phrase trite through overuse [Early 18thC. Shortening of HACKNEY.]

hack·a·more /hákə màwr/ *n.* a bridle without a bit but with an adjustable band by which a rider can exert pressure on a horse's nose, used especially to break young horses [Mid-19thC. By folk etymology (by association with HACK[2]) from Spanish *jaquima,* from, ultimately, Arabic *šaqīmah* "restraint, bit."]

WORD KEY: REGIONAL NOTE

Hackamore had currency in the western states before the Civil War. Not limited to the Mexican-American settlements, this ranching term spread from Texas and New Mexico to Oregon, but is virtually unknown east of Texas.

hack·ber·ry /hák bèrree/ (*plural* **-ries**) *n.* a North American tree of the elm family that has soft yellowish wood, small flowers, and small round or egg-shaped dark-red edible fruit. Latin name: *Celtis occidentalis.* [Mid-18thC. Variant of *hagberry* "bird cherry"; *hag* of Scandinavian origin.]

hack·but /hák bùt/ *n.* = **harquebus** [15thC. From French *haquebut(e),* alteration of *haquebusche,* from Middle Dutch *hakebus,* literally "hook-gun," from *hake(n)* "hook" + *bus(se)* "gun," from the hook cast on the gun as a fixture.] —**hack·but·eer** /hàkbə teér/ *n.* —**hack·but·ter** /hák bùttər/ *n.*

Hack·en·sack /hákən sàk/ city in northeastern New Jersey, originally settled by the Dutch and now a suburb of New York City. Population: 37,049 (1990).

hack·er /hákər/ *n.* **1.** COMPUT **SOMEBODY ACCESSING ANOTHER'S COMPUTER** somebody who uses computer expertise to gain unauthorized access to a computer system belonging to another, either to learn about the system or to examine its data **2.** COMPUT **COMPUTER ENTHUSIAST** somebody who is very interested or skilled in computer technology and programming **3.** SPORTS **AMATEUR PLAYER** somebody who enjoys a sport but is not very good at it **4. SOMEBODY WHO CHOPS** somebody who cuts or chops something

hack·ie /hákee/ *n.* a taxicab driver (*informal*)

hack·le[1] /hák'l/ *n.* **1.** BIRDS **BIRD'S NECK FEATHER** any of the long slender feathers on the neck or lower back of a male bird, especially a fowl **2.** ANGLING **FEATHERS USED IN A FISHING FLY** a tuft of feathers from the neck of a bird used in making an artificial fly for fishing **3.** ANGLING **FISHING FLY MADE FROM FEATHERS** an artificial fly for fishing made from the neck feathers of a bird **4.** TEXTILES **FLAX COMB** a steel comb with long teeth used to comb out flax, hemp, or jute fibers ■ **hack·les** *npl.* **HAIRS ON AN ANIMAL'S NECK** the hairs on the back of the neck and along the spine of an animal, especially a dog or cat, that stand on end when it is threatened or angry ■ *vt.* (**-led, -ling, -les**) **1.** ANGLING **PUT FEATHERS ON A FISHING FLY** to trim an artificial fly with the neck feathers from a bird **2.** TEXTILES **COMB FLAX BEFORE SPINNING** to comb out flax, hemp, or jute fibers using a hackle [15thC. Variant of earlier *heckle,* probably from an Old English word meaning literally "little hook," from the prehistoric Germanic ancestor of English *hook.*] —**hack·ler** *n.* ◇ **make somebody's hackles rise** to produce anger or hostility in somebody

hack·le[2] /hák'l/ (**-led, -ling, -les**) *vti.* to mangle something by cutting it roughly [Late 16thC. From HACK[1].]

hack·ly /háklee/ (**-li·er, -li·est**) *adj.* having a rough jagged surface

hack·man /hák mən/ (*plural* **-men** /-mən/) *n.* a man who drives a taxicab

Hack·man /hákmən/, **Gene** (*b.* 1930) U.S. movie actor. He won Academy Awards for *The French Connection* (1971) and *Unforgiven* (1992).

hack·ma·tack /hákmə tàk/ *n.* TREES **1.** = **tamarack 2.** = **balsam poplar** [Late 18thC. From Algonquian *akemantek* "snowshoe wood."]

hack·ney /háknee/ *n.* **1. VEHICLE FOR HIRE** an automobile or carriage for hire **2. HORSE FOR RIDING** a horse for riding or driving ■ *adj.* **TRITE** ordinary and boring [13thC. Origin uncertain: probably named for *Hackney,* area of northeastern London where horses were formerly grazed.] —**hack·ney·ism** *n.*

hack·neyed /hákneed/ *adj.* made commonplace and stale by overuse ○ *the same old hackneyed sales talk*

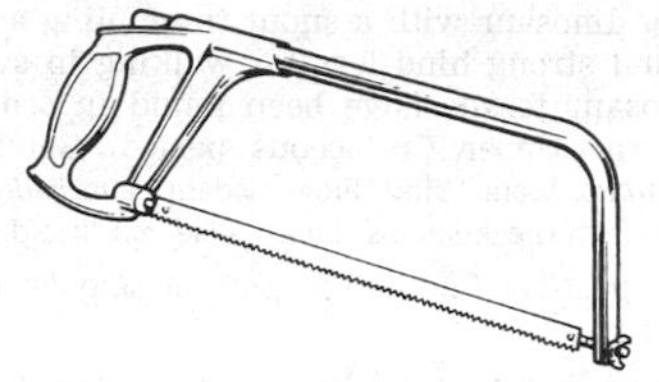

Hacksaw

hack·saw /hák sàw/ *n.* **SAW FOR CUTTING METAL** a handsaw with a small-toothed steel blade stretched taut across a frame, used for cutting metal ■ *vt.* (**-sawed, -sawn** *or* **-sawed, -saw·ing, -saws**) **CUT SOMETHING WITH A HACKSAW** to cut something using a hacksaw

hack·work /hák wùrk/ *n.* ordinary literary, artistic, or professional work that somebody is hired to do (*disapproving*)

had past tense, past participle of **have**

had·dock /háddək/ (*plural* **-dock** *or* **-docks**) *n.* a North Atlantic fish that is related to but smaller than the cod. It is a popular food fish. Latin name: *Melanogrammus aeglefinus.* [14thC. Via Anglo-Norman *hadoc* from Old French *(h)adot,* whose origin is unknown.]

hade /hayd/ *n.* GEOL **ANGLE OF A FAULT PLANE** the angle between the vertical plane and a plane containing a vein, fault, or lode ■ *vi.* (**had·ed, had·ing, hades**) **SLOPE FROM THE VERTICAL** to be at an angle with the vertical [Late 17thC. Origin uncertain; perhaps from a dialect form of HEAD.]

Ha·des /háy deez/ *n.* **1. ha·des, Ha·des HELL** hell (*informal*) **2. GREEK UNDERWORLD** in Greek mythology, the underworld kingdom inhabited by the souls of the dead **3. GREEK GOD OF THE UNDERWORLD** in Greek mythology, the god of the underworld and husband of Persephone. Roman equivalent **Pluto** [Late 16thC. From Greek *Haidēs* god of the dead; ultimate origin unknown.] —**Had·e·an** /hay deé ən/ *adj.*

Ha·dhra·maut /haàdrə máwt/, **Ha·dra·maut** coastal region in the southern Arabian peninsula, shared between Yemen and Oman. The ancient civilization that flourished there is called "Hazarmaveth" in the Bible. Area: 60,000 sq. mi./155,400 sq. km.

Ha·dith /hə deéth/, **ha·dith** *n.* the collected traditions, teachings, and stories of the prophet Muhammad, accepted as a source of Islamic doctrine and law second only to the Koran [Early 18thC. From Arabic *ḥadīṯ* "tradition."]

hadj *n.* = **hajj**

hadj·i *n.* = **hajji**

had·n't /hád'nt/ *contr.* had not

Had·ra·maut = **Hadhramaut**

Ha·dri·an /háydree ən/, **Emperor of Rome** (76–138). As emperor (117–38) he ended Rome's policy of territorial expansion.

Ha·dri·an's Wall /háydree ənz wáwl/ *n.* a fortified wall built across northern England in the early 2nd century A.D. as a defense against invasion by the Picts. It was built on the orders of Roman emperor Hadrian and marked the northern boundary of the Roman Empire.

had·ron /háddrən, hád ròn/ *n.* an elementary particle that is subject to the strong interaction [Mid-20thC. Coined from Greek *hadros* "bulky" + -ON.] —**had·ron·ic** /had rónnik, hə-/ *adj.*

Barnaby's
Hadrian's Wall

had·ro·saur /háddrə sàwr/ *n.* an amphibious plant-eating dinosaur with a snout resembling a duck's bill and strong hind legs for walking in swamps. Hadrosaur fossils have been found in sediments from the Upper Cretaceous period. Genus: *Anatosaurus.* [Late 19thC. From modern Latin *hadrosaurus*, formed from Greek *hadros* "bulky" + *sauros* "lizard."]

hadst /hadst/ *vt.* 2nd person present singular of **have** (*archaic*)

haec·ce·i·ty /hek sée ətee/ *n.* PHILOS the essential property that makes an individual uniquely that individual [Mid-17thC. From medieval Latin *heicceitas*, formed from Latin *haec*, feminine singular form of *hic* "this."]

Haeck·el /hék'l/, **Ernst** (1834–1919) German zoologist and evolutionist. He was an early advocate of Charles Darwin, and is chiefly remembered for producing genealogical trees of species development. Full name **Ernst Heinrich Philipp August Haeckel**

Haeck·el's law /hék'lz-/ *n.* the theory proposing as a law that an embryo in each stage of development resembles an organism that its species descended from [Late 19thC. Named for Ernst Heinrich HAECKEL.]

haem /heem/ *n.* BIOCHEM *U.K.* = **heme**

haema- *prefix.* = **hema-**

haemat- *prefix.* = **hemat-**

haemato- *prefix.* = **hemato-**

-haemia *suffix.* = **-hemia**

haemo- *prefix.* = **hemo-**

ha·fiz /haáfiz/ *n.* the title used to address somebody who has committed the Koran to memory [Mid-17thC. Via Persian from Arabic *ḥāfiẓ* "guardian."]

haf·ni·um /háfnee əm/ *n.* a bright silvery metallic chemical element found in zirconium ores. It is used to absorb neutrons in nuclear reactor rods and in the manufacture of tungsten filaments. Symbol **Hf** [Early 20thC. From modern Latin, formed from *Hafnia*, the Latin name for Copenhagen, Denmark, where the element was discovered.]

haft /haft/ *n.* HANDLE the handle of a knife, ax, or other weapon or tool (*literary*) ■ *vt.* (**haft·ed, haft·ing, hafts**) PROVIDE WITH HANDLE to fit a weapon or tool with a handle (*literary*) [Old English *hæft(e)*. From a prehistoric Germanic base that also produced English *heave*.] —**haft·er** *n.*

haf·ta·rah /hàftə raá/ (*plural* **-rahs** *or* **-roth** /-rōth/ *or* **-rot** /-rōt/), **haf·to·rah** (*plural* **-rahs** *or* **-roth** *or* **-rot**), **haph·ta·rah** (*plural* **-rahs** *or* **-roth** *or* **-rot**) *n.* a reading from the Prophets following each lesson from the Torah in synagogue services on the Sabbath [Early 18thC. From Hebrew *haphṭārāh* "conclusion."]

hag /hag/ *n.* **1.** OFFENSIVE TERM an offensive term that deliberately insults a woman's appearance, temperament, and age **2.** WITCH a witch, especially one late in life **3.** ZOOL = **hagfish 4.** A WOMAN DEMON a demon in the shape of a woman (*archaic*) [14thC, but rare before the 16thC. Origin uncertain: perhaps shortening of Old English *hægtesse* "witch," from a prehistoric Germanic word that also produced German *Hexe* "witch."] —**hag·gish** *adj.*

Hag. *abbr.* BIBLE Haggai

Ha·gar /háy gaar, háygər/ *n.* in the Bible, an Egyptian servant of Sarah who bore Sarah's husband, Abraham, a son named Ishmael (Genesis 16, 21:1–21) [From Hebrew *Haghar*]

Ha·gen /háygən/, **Walter** (1892–1969) U.S. golfer. He won the U.S. Open (1914 and 1919) and the British Open (1922, 1924, and 1928–29). Full name **Walter Charles Hagen**

Ha·gers·town /háygərz town/ industrial city in northwestern Maryland, near the Potomac River, founded in 1762. Population: 34,633 (1996).

hag·fish /hág fish/ (*plural* **-fish** *or* **-fish·es**) *n.* a primitive jawless marine fish with an elongated body and a sucking mouth that it uses for feeding off other fishes. Family: Myxinidae.

Hag·ga·dah /ha gaádə/ (*plural* **-dahs** *or* **-doth** /ha gaádōt/), **Hag·ga·da** (*plural* **-das** *or* **-doth**) *n.* **1.** BOOK CONTAINING THE PASSOVER SERVICE the service for the ritual meal (**Seder**) celebrated by Jews at Passover, or the book containing this service. It includes the story of the Exodus from Egypt. **2.** RABBINIC LITERATURE ON BIBLICAL STORIES those sections of the Talmud and other rabbinic literature that deal with biblical narrative and stories and legends on biblical themes rather than with religious law and regulations **3.** STORY OF ISRAELITES' EXODUS FROM EGYPT the account of the Exodus of the Israelites from Egypt that is central to the Jewish Passover ritual [Mid-19thC. From Hebrew *haggādāh* "tale," formed from *higgīḏ* "to tell."] —**hag·gad·ic** /ha gáddik/ *adj.*

Hag·ga·i /há gī, hággee ī/ *n.* **1.** HEBREW PROPHET in the Bible, a Hebrew prophet who urged the Israelites to rebuild their temple in Jerusalem in prophecies believed to have been made in 520 B.C. **2.** BOOK OF THE BIBLE a book of the Bible that tells the story of the rebuilding of the Israelites' temple after their return to Jerusalem from exile in Babylon and records Haggai's prophecies. See table at **Bible** [From Hebrew]

hag·gard /hággərd/ *adj.* **1.** TIRED-LOOKING AND THIN IN THE FACE showing signs of tiredness, anxiety, or hunger on the face, e.g., dark rings around the eyes **2.** UNRULY wild and unruly in appearance **3.** UNMANAGEABLE used in falconry to describe a hawk that has reached maturity before being captured and is therefore wild and unmanageable ■ *n.* HAWK a captured wild adult hawk [Late 16thC. From French *hagard* "untamed" (used of hawks), perhaps ultimately from a prehistoric Germanic word meaning "hedge"; the underlying meaning would be "like a wild hawk of the woods."] —**hag·gard·ly** *adv.* —**hag·gard·ness** *n.*

hag·gis /hággiss/ (*plural* **-gis·es**) *n.* a Scottish dish made from the chopped heart, lungs, and liver of lamb or beef mixed with suet, oats, onions, herbs, and spices and packed into a round sausage skin and usually boiled. Haggis is traditionally cooked in a cleaned sheep's stomach, but artificial casings are now frequently used. [15thC. Origin uncertain.]

WORD KEY: ORIGIN

One possible source of ***haggis*** is Middle English *haggen*, meaning "to chop," a northern variant of HACK[1]. From this view, its name would refer to its chopped-up contents. An alternative possibility is Old French *agace*, meaning "magpie." This is supported by a parallel semantic development of English "pie," which originally meant "magpie" but was apparently applied to a "pastry case with a filling" from the notion that the collection of edible odds and ends in a pie resembles the collection of trinkets assembled by the acquisitive magpie. The miscellaneous assortment of sheep's entrails and other ingredients in a haggis therefore would represent the magpie's hoard.

hag·gle /hágg'l/ *v.* (**-gled, -gling** *or* **-gled, -gles**) **1.** *vi.* TRY TO SETTLE ON A PRICE to argue over something, e.g., a price or contract, in order to reach an agreement **2.** *vti.* CUT ROUGHLY to cut something roughly (*regional*) ■ *n.* ARGUMENT LEADING TO AGREEMENT an argument over something in an attempt to reach an agreement [Late 16thC. Literally "to keep chopping," from Middle English *haggen* "to chop," a variant of HACK[1]. The modern meaning may have developed via the idea of "chopping away" at a price.] —**hag·gler** *n.*

hagio- *prefix.* saints, holy ○ *hagiolatry* ○ *hagioscope* [From Greek *hagios* "holy"]

hag·i·oc·ra·cy /hàggee ókrəssee, hàyjee-/ (*plural* **-cies**) *n.* **1.** GOVERNMENT BY HOLY PEOPLE government by saints, prophets, or other holy people **2.** PLACE GOVERNED BY HOLY PEOPLE a state or community governed by holy people

Hag·i·og·ra·pha /hàggee óggrəfə, hàyjee-/ *n.* the last of the three main parts into which the Hebrew Bible is divided. See table at **Bible** [Late 16thC. Via late Latin from Greek *hagios* "holy" + *grapha* "writings."]

hag·i·og·raph·er /hàggee óggrəfər, hàyjee-/, **hag·i·og·raph·ist** /hàggee óggrəfist, hàyjee-/ *n.* **1.** BIOGRAPHER OF SAINTS somebody who writes biographies of the saints **2.** REVERENTIAL BIOGRAPHER somebody who writes biographies that treat their subjects with undue reverence **3.** WRITER OF PART OF THE HEBREW BIBLE any of the writers of the Hagiographa

hag·i·og·ra·phy /hàggee óggrəfee, hàyjee-/ (*plural* **-phies**) *n.* **1.** BIOGRAPHY OF SAINT biography of a saint or the saints **2.** BIOGRAPHY REVERING ITS SUBJECT biography that treats its subject with undue reverence —**hag·i·o·graph·ic** /hàggee ə gráffik, hàyjee-/ *adj.*

hag·i·ol·a·try /hàggee óllətree, hàyjee-/ *n.* the worship or idolizing of saints

hag·i·ol·o·gy /hàggee óllәjee, hàyjee-/ (*plural* **-gies**) *n.* **1.** WRITINGS ABOUT SAINTS literature about the lives of the saints **2.** BIOGRAPHY OF A SAINT a biography of a saint, or a collection of such biographies **3.** LIST OF SAINTS an authoritative list of saints **4.** COLLECTION OF SACRED WRITINGS a collection or history of sacred writings —**hag·i·o·log·ic** /hàggee ə lójjik, hàyjee-/ *adj.* —**hag·i·ol·o·gist** /hàggee óllәjist, hàyjee-/ *n.*

hag·i·o·scope /hággee ə skōp, háyjee-/ *n.* a narrow opening in an interior wall of a church that allows members of the congregation seated at the sides to see the altar —**hag·i·o·scop·ic** /hàggee ə skóppik, hàyjee-/ *adj.*

hag·rid·den *adj.* plagued by fear or mental anguish (*literary*)

Hague, The /thə háyg/ city in the western Netherlands, seat of the Dutch government and capital of South Holland Province. Population: 444,661 (1993).

hah *interj.* = **ha**

ha-ha[1], **haw-haw** *interj.* **1.** REPRESENTATION OF LAUGHTER used in writing to indicate the sound of somebody laughing **2.** USED TO MOCK SOMEBODY used to tease or ridicule somebody (*informal*) ○ *"Where is it?" "Ha-ha, wouldn't you like to know?"* [Old English. An imitation of the sound.]

ha-ha[2], **haw-haw** *n.* a deep ditch or steep change in level, sometimes supported by a wall, that marks the boundary of a large garden but is not visible from within it [Early 18thC. From French; presumably from a cry of surprise when finding one.]

hah·ni·um /haánee əm/ *n.* dubnium or hassium (*dated*) Symbol **Hn** [Late 20thC. Named for Otto *Hahn* (1879–1968), German chemist.]

Hai·da /hídə/ (*plural* **-da** *or* **-das**) *n.* **1.** PEOPLES MEMBER OF A NATIVE AMERICAN PEOPLE a member of a Native North American people living along the coast of British Columbia in Canada, the adjoining Alaskan coast, and the islands lying off these areas. The Haida are particularly noted for their intricately carved dugout canoes and miniature totems. **2.** LANG HAIDA LANGUAGE the language of the Haida, now spoken by very few people [Early 20thC. From Haida, "people."] —**Hai·da** *adj.* —**Hai·dan** *adj.*

Hai·da Gwai'i /hìdə gwí/ *n.* the traditional territory of the Haida, including the Queen Charlotte Islands off the Pacific coast of Canada

Hai·fa /hífə/ city and chief seaport of Israel, situated in the northern part of the country. Population: 252,300 (1996).

haik /hīk, hayk/, **haick** *n.* a loose-fitting garment made from a rectangle of cloth, usually white, that is wrapped around the head and body. It is worn by men and women in North Africa. [Early 18thC. From Arabic *hā'ik*.]

Hai·kou /hī kóo/ capital of Hainan Province in China, on the northern side of the island of Hainan. Population: 280,153 (1990).

hai·ku /hí koo/ (*plural* **-ku**) *n.* a form of Japanese poetry with 17 syllables in three unrhymed lines of five, seven, and five syllables, often describing nature or a season [Late 19thC. From Japanese, shortening of *haikai no ku*, literally "not serious verse."]

hail[1] /hayl/ *n.* **1.** PELLETS OF ICE small balls of ice and hardened snow that fall like rain **2.** POURING DOWN OF SOMETHING HARMFUL a barrage of something, e.g., missiles or insults ■ *vi.* (**hailed, hail·ing, hails**) RAIN ICE PELLETS to rain small balls of ice or hardened snow [Old English *hagol, hægl*. Ultimately from an Indo-European word that also produced Greek *kakhlēx* "pebble."]

hail[2] /hayl/ *vt.* (**hailed, hail·ing, hails**) **1.** GREET to welcome or greet somebody upon meeting ○ *We hailed each other like long-lost buddies.* **2.** ACCLAIM to praise or approve a person, action, or accomplishment with enthusiasm ○ *The press hailed her as a child prodigy.* **3. SHOUT OR SIGNAL FOR ATTENTION** to attract the attention of somebody or something, e.g., a taxicab or ship, by calling or signaling ■ *n.* **1. GREETING** an expression of greeting or acclamation **2. SHOUT OR SIGNAL** a shout or signal to attract attention ■ *interj.* **EXCLAMATION OF GREETING** used to greet, welcome, or acclaim somebody (*archaic or literary*) [12thC. Variant of HALE[1], originally used as an interjection for wishing somebody good health.] —**hail·er** *n.* ◇ **within hail** near enough to hear a shout or see a signal (*dated*)

hail from *vt.* to live in or come from a particular place, especially as a birthplace or place of origin ○ *Her husband hails from Seattle.*

hail-fel·low-well-met, hail-fel·low *adj.* **EXCESSIVELY FRIENDLY** very friendly, especially in a way that presumes an intimacy that does not exist ■ *n.* **VERY FRIENDLY PERSON** an exuberantly friendly person (*old*) [From the greeting *Hail, fellow! Well met!*]

Hail Mar·y (*plural* **Hail Mar·ys**) *n.* **1.** CHR **PRAYER INVOKING VIRGIN MARY'S INTERCESSION** a Roman Catholic prayer to the Virgin Mary based on Gabriel's and Elizabeth's greetings to her as recorded in the Gospel of Luke in the Bible. Churchgoers are often required to repeat the prayer as penance. **2.** FOOTBALL **LAST-MINUTE PASS** a long high pass into the end zone in football, in an effort to score a touchdown before time runs out in the half or game (*slang*) **3. LAST-DITCH EFFORT OR PLAN** a proposition, plan, request, or effort that is made as a last resort or final recourse (*informal*) [Translation of medieval Latin *Ave, Maria,* the opening words of the prayer]

hail·stone /háyl stōn/ *n.* a pellet of ice and hardened snow that falls like rain

hail·storm /háyl stàwrm/ *n.* a storm that includes a downpour of hail

haim·ish /háymish/, **heim·ish** *adj.* having qualities associated with home, e.g., warmth and informality (*informal*) ○ *The inn was very haimish and comfortable.* [Mid-20thC. From Yiddish *heymish* "homelike," from Middle High German *heimisch,* literally "of the home."]

Hai·nan /hī naán/ province in southeastern China comprising the island of Hainan in the South China Sea. Capital: Haikou. Population: 7,110,000 (1994). Area: 13,240 sq. mi./34,300 sq. km.

haint /haynt/ *n. Southern U.S.* a ghost or other phenomenon believed to be supernatural

Hai·phong /hī fóng/ city and seaport in northern Vietnam, on the Red River delta. Population: 1,447,523 (1989).

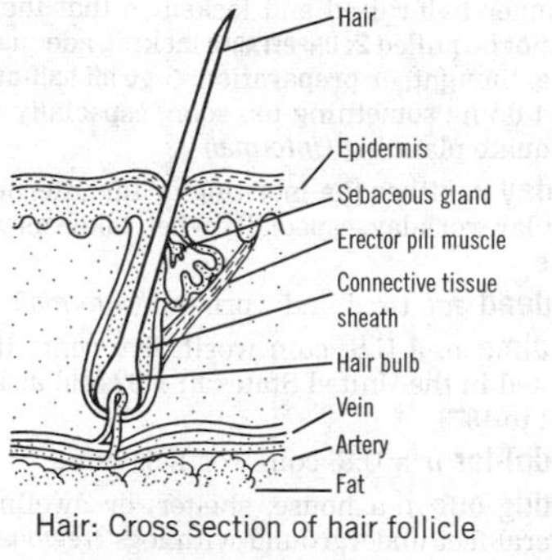

Hair: Cross section of hair follicle

hair /hair/ *n.* **1. STRANDS GROWING ON THE HEAD OR BODY** the mass of fine flexible protein strands that grow from follicles on the skin of a person or animal, especially those on somebody's head **2. SINGLE STRAND** any of the fine strands that grow on the skin of a person or animal ○ *The rug was covered with dog hairs.* **3.** BOT **GROWTH ON A PLANT RESEMBLING HAIR** a thin flexible growth on a plant resembling a human or animal hair **4.** TEXTILES **FABRIC** fabric made from animal hair **5. TINY AMOUNT** a tiny amount or degree [Old English *hær.* Ultimately from a prehistoric Germanic word that also produced German *Haar.* There is no general Indo-European word for "hair."] —**hair·less** *adj.* ◇ **be tearing your hair out** to be very irritated or frustrated ◇ **not turn a hair** to remain completely calm ◇ **split hairs** to argue about or give undue significance to fine distinctions and details ◇ **the hair of the dog (that bit you)** an alcoholic drink taken as a supposed cure for a hangover

hair·ball /háir bàwl/ *n.* a ball of hair that accumulates in the stomach of some animals, e.g., cats and cows, when they clean themselves. It often causes indigestion and retching.

hair·breadth /háir brèdth/ *n.* = **hairsbreadth** ■ *adj.* **VERY NARROW** exceedingly narrow

hair·brush /háir brùsh/ *n.* a brush for smoothing and styling hair

hair cell *n.* a sensory cell with fine projections resembling hairs, especially one in the inner ear that transmits information on sound or movement to the brain

hair·cloth /háir klàwth/ *n.* a thick coarse fabric made from horse's or camel's hair, used in upholstery

hair·cut /háir kùt/ *n.* **1. CUTTING OF SOMEBODY'S HAIR** a session in which somebody's hair is cut **2. WAY SOMEBODY'S HAIR IS CUT** the shape or style in which somebody's hair is cut ○ *How do you like my new haircut?* —**hair·cut·ter** *n.* —**hair·cut·ting** *n., adj.*

hair·do /háir doo/ (*plural* **-dos**) *n.* the way in which somebody's hair has been cut or styled (*informal*)

hair·dress·er /háir drèssər/ *n.* **1. SOMEBODY WHOSE WORK IS STYLING HAIR** somebody who cuts, styles, colors, or curls hair as a profession **2. HAIRDRESSER'S PLACE OF BUSINESS** a shop or salon where a hairdresser works

hair·dress·ing /háir drèssing/ *n.* **1. CARE OF THE HAIR** the cutting, styling, coloring, or curling of hair **2. HAIRDRESSER'S PROFESSION** the occupation of a hairdresser **3. HAIR CARE PRODUCT** a preparation, e.g., an oil or gel, used to style or care for the hair

hair dry·er *n.* a device that uses heated air for drying hair, either handheld or in the shape of a dome that fits over the head

haired /háird/ *adj.* having hair of a particular length, color, type, or style (*used in combination*) ○ *long-haired*

hair fol·li·cle *n.* a small tubular pit in the outer layer of skin (**epidermis**) enclosing the base of a growing hair

hair·grip /háir grìp/ *n. U.K.* = **bobby pin**

hair·line /háir līn/ *n.* **1. WHERE HAIR BEGINS ON HEAD** the line across the top of the forehead behind which the hair grows **2. THIN LINE** a very narrow line that is barely visible **3.** PRINTING **THIN STROKE** a very thin line on a typeface, or a typeface containing thin lines **4.** TEXTILES **FABRIC WITH FINE STRIPES** a textile pattern of very thin stripes, usually one thread wide, or a fabric with such stripes

hair·net /háir nèt/ *n.* a circular piece of fine netting with an elastic edge, worn to hold the hair in place, especially in bed

hair·piece /háir peess/ *n.* a wig, toupee, or other piece of false hair, worn to conceal hair loss or to add bulk or length to somebody's natural hair

hair·pin /háir pìn/ *n.* **1. BENT WIRE FOR HOLDING HAIR** a U-shaped piece of metal wire used to hold the hair in place **2. SOMETHING WITH A SHARP BEND** something with a U-shape resembling a hairpin, especially a sharp bend in a road **3.** MUSIC **SYMBOL FOR CRESCENDO OR DIMINUENDO** a long V-shaped mark used in written music to indicate an increase or decrease in loudness (*informal*)

hair-rais·ing *adj.* causing intense fear or excitement ○ *Landing on that makeshift runway was the most hair-raising experience of my life.* —**hair-rais·er** *n.* —**hair-rais·ing·ly** *adv.*

hairs·breadth /háirz brèdth/, **hair's-breadth** *n.* a very small margin or distance

hair shirt *n.* **1. HAIRCLOTH SHIRT** a shirt made from a harsh scratchy haircloth that was once worn next to the skin by religious people as a form of self-imposed punishment **2. PERSONAL PUNISHMENT** a self-imposed punishment in the form of private suffering

hair space *n.* the thinnest space used to separate words and letters in typesetting

hair·split·ting /háir splìtting/ *n.* **ARGUING OVER DETAILS** overattention to unimportant details and fine distinctions, especially in an argument ○ *Whether it was five after or ten after is just hairsplitting: you kept me waiting for over an hour.* ■ *adj.* **CONCERNED TOO MUCH WITH DETAILS** giving undue significance to fine distinctions and details [From the phrase *split hairs* "to make too fine distinctions"] —**hair·split·ter** *n.*

hair spray *n.* a substance sprayed onto the hair to hold it in place

hair·spring /háir spring/ *n.* a very fine coiled spring that controls the movement of the balance wheel in a watch or clock

hair·streak /háir streek/ *n.* a brown or grayish tropical American butterfly with delicate streaks on the underside of its wings and fine tails resembling hairs on its hind wings. Subfamily: Theclinae.

hair stroke *n.* a very fine line in writing or printing

hair·style /háir stīl/ *n.* the way in which somebody's hair is cut and arranged ○ *How do you like my new hairstyle?* —**hair·styl·ing** *n.* —**hair·styl·ist** *n.*

hair trig·ger *n.* **1. SENSITIVE TRIGGER** a gun trigger that needs very little pressure to activate it **2. QUICK RESPONSE** a response or mechanism that reacts to the slightest provocation or impulse (*hyphenated before a noun*) [From the thin spring that it activates]

hair·weav·ing /háir weeving/ *n.* the interweaving of a hairpiece with somebody's own hair, often done to disguise hair loss —**hair·weave** *vt.* —**hair·weav·er** *n.*

hair·worm /háir wùrm/ *n.* **1. PARASITIC NEMATODE** a nematode worm that lives as a parasite in the digestive tracts of domestic animals. Genus: *Trichostrongylus.* **2. PARASITE OF ARTHROPODS** a long slender aquatic worm whose larva lives as a parasite on arthropods. Phylum: Nematomorpha.

hair·y /háiree/ (**-i·er, -i·est**) *adj.* **1. COVERED WITH HAIR** covered with hair or filaments resembling hair **2. MADE OF HAIR** made of hair, or similar in texture to something made of hair **3. FRIGHTENING** filled with dangers or difficulties (*informal*) —**hair·i·ness** *n.*

hair·y vetch *n.* a type of vetch with hairy stems and purplish flowers that is native to Europe and Asia. It is widely grown for ground cover and forage. Latin name: *Vicia villosa.*

hair·y wood·peck·er *n.* a common North American woodpecker with black and white markings that, except for its long bill and larger size, looks like the downy woodpecker

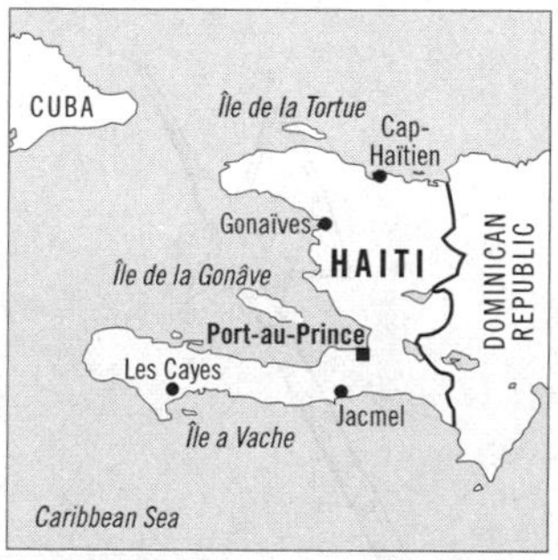

Haiti

Hai·ti /háytee/ republic occupying the western third of the island of Hispaniola in the northern Caribbean. Language: French, Haitian Creole. Currency: gourde. Capital: Port-au-Prince. Population: 6,732,000 (1996). Area: 10,714 sq. mi./27,750 sq. km. Official name **Republic of Haiti**

Hai·tian /háysh'n/ *n.* **1.** PEOPLES **SOMEBODY FROM HAITI** somebody who was born or raised in Haiti, or who has Haitian citizenship **2.** LANG = **Haitian Creole** —**Hai·tian** *adj.*

Hai·tian Cre·ole *n.* the French-based creole spoken on the island of Haiti. It has about four million speakers. —**Hai·tian Cre·ole** *adj.*

haj *n.* = **hajj**

haj·i *n.* = **hajji**

hajj /haj/ (*plural* **ha·j·jes**), **hadj** (*plural* **had·jes**), **haj** (*plural* **ha·jes**) *n.* the pilgrimage to Mecca, Saudi Arabia, that is a principal religious obligation of adult Muslims [Late 17thC. From Arabic, "pilgrimage."]

Haj·jaj /ha jaáj, kha jaáj/ *n.* the governor of the eastern provinces of India during the Arab Umayyad dynasty, the first time the Indian subcontinent was occupied by a Muslim force

haj·ji /haájee/ (*plural* **-jis**), **hadj·i** (*plural* **had·jis**), **haj·i** (*plural* **-is**) *n.* a Muslim who has made the pilgrimage to Mecca (*also used as a title*) [Early 17thC. Directly or via Turkish from Persian *ḥājī* "pilgrim," formed from Arabic *ḥajj* "pilgrimage."]

hake /hayk/ (*plural* **hake** *or* **hakes**) *n.* a marine fish similar to the cod, with two dorsal fins and an elongated body. It is a valuable food fish. Genus: *Merluccius.* [15thC. Origin uncertain: perhaps shortening of assumed *hakefish*, from dialectal *hake* "hook," from Old Norse *haki*, from the shape of its lower jaw.]

ha·kim[1] /haá ke̍em, hə ke̍em/, **ha·keem** *n.* a Muslim doctor who uses traditional remedies [From Arabic *ḥakīm* "wise man"]

ha·kim[2] /haákim/ *n.* a Muslim judge, ruler, or administrator [Early 17thC. From Arabic *ḥākim* "ruler."]

Ha·ko·da·te /haákō daát ay/ seaport on Tsugaru Strait in southern Hokkaido, Japan. Population: 307,249 (1990).

ha·ku /haá ko͝o/ *n. Hawaii* a crown made of fresh flowers

hal- *prefix.* = **halo-** (*used before vowels*)

Ha·la·cha /haá laa khaá, haa laákhə/, **Ha·la·kha, Ha·la·khah** *n.* the body of Jewish law beginning with the Pentateuch and developed by the rabbis [Mid-19thC. From Hebrew *hă lāḵāh* "law."]

ha·lal /hə laál/ *adj.* **SUITABLE FOR MUSLIMS** used to describe meat from animals that have been slaughtered in the ritual way prescribed by Islamic law, or relating to such meat ■ *n.* **HALAL MEAT** halal meat ■ *vt.* (**-lalled, -lal·ling, -lals**) **SLAUGHTER ANIMALS IN THE ISLAMIC WAY** to slaughter animals for meat in the ritual way prescribed by Islamic law [Mid-19thC. From Arabic *ḥalāl* "lawful."]

ha·la·la /hə laálə/ (*plural* **-la** *or* **-las**) *n.* **1. MINOR UNIT OF SAUDI ARABIAN CURRENCY** a minor unit of currency in Saudi Arabia, one hundred of which are worth one rial. See table at **currency 2. COIN WORTH ONE HALALA** a coin worth one halala [Mid-20thC. From Arabic.]

ha·la·tion /hə láysh'n/ *n.* **1. FUZZY GLOW IN A PHOTOGRAPH** a blurred bright patch around a light source on a photographic image. It is caused by light being reflected off the film base and back onto the light-sensitive layer. **2. HALO AROUND A BRIGHT TELEVISION IMAGE** a patch or ring of glowing light around a bright object on a television screen [Mid-19thC. Coined from HALO + -ATION.]

Halberd

hal·berd /hálbərd, háwlbərd/, **hal·bert** /-bərt/ *n.* an ax blade and pick with a spearhead on top, mounted on a long handle and used as a weapon in the 15th and 16th centuries [15thC. Via French from, ultimately, Middle High German *helmbarde*, from *helm* "handle" + *barde* "hatchet."] —**hal·ber·dier** /hàlbər de̍er, hàwl-/ *n.*

hal·cy·on /hálsee ən/ *adj.* **TRANQUIL** tranquil and free from disturbance or care (*literary*) ■ *n.* **1.** MYTHOL **MYTHOLOGICAL BIRD THAT CALMED THE SEA** in Greek mythology, a bird resembling the kingfisher, believed to have had the power to calm the waves at the time of the winter solstice when it nested at sea **2. KINGFISHER** a kingfisher [14thC. Via Latin from Greek *(h)alkuōn* "mythical bird," of unknown origin.]

hal·cy·on days *npl.* **1. TRANQUIL HAPPY TIME** a time of happiness and tranquility (*literary*) **2. CALM DAYS AT WINTER'S START** two weeks of calm weather during the winter solstice

hale[1] /hayl/ (**hal·er, hal·est**) *adj.* in robust good health [Old English *hāl* "whole, healthy" (also the source of modern English *whole*), later reinforced by Old Norse *heill*] —**hale·ness** *n.*

hale[2] /hayl/ (**haled, hal·ing, hales**) *vt.* **1. MAKE SOMEBODY GO SOMEWHERE** to compel somebody to go somewhere, especially to court **2. HAUL SOMEBODY OR SOMETHING** to pull or drag somebody or something with great effort (*archaic*) [13thC. Via Old French *haler* from Old Norse *hala.*] —**hal·er** *n.*

Hale /hayl/, **Edward Everett** (1822–1909) U.S. clergyman and writer. A noted abolitionist, he was a prolific and influential writer. His works include "The Man Without a Country" (1863).

Hale, George Ellery (1868–1938) U.S. astronomer. He established the Yerkes Observatory, Wisconsin (1895) and Mount Wilson Observatory, California (1904) and designed the reflecting telescope for Mount Palomar, near San Diego (1948).

Hale, Nathan (1755–76) American revolutionary hero. He was captured by the British as a spy and hanged.

Ha·le·a·ka·la Na·tion·al Park /haálee aak aa laá-, haálee aakə laá-/ park on the island of Maui, Hawaii, established in 1916. Its main feature is the large crater of an inactive volcano. Area: 28,099 acres/11,371 hectares.

ha·ler /haálər/ (*plural* **hal·ers** *or* **ha·le·ru** /-lə ro͞o/) *n.* **1. MINOR UNIT OF CZECH CURRENCY** a minor unit of currency of the Czech Republic, one hundred of which are worth one koruna. See table at **currency 2. COIN WORTH A HALER** a coin worth a haler [Mid-20thC. Via Czech from Middle High German *haller* "silver coin," named for *Hall*, a Swabian town where they were minted.]

Ha·ley /háylee/, **Alex** (1921–92) U.S. writer. He is best known for his autobiographical novel *Roots* (1976). Full name **Alexander Murray Palmer Haley**

Ha·ley, Bill (1927–81) U.S. musician. He drew on his background in country and western and rhythm and blues in recording some of the first rock-and-roll hits, including "Rock Around the Clock" (1955), with Bill Haley and the Comets, the band he formed in 1952. Full name **William John Haley**

half /haf/ *n.* (*plural* **halves** /havz/), *adj.*, *adj.*, *pron.* **ONE OF TWO EQUAL PARTS** either of two equal or nearly equal parts into which a whole can be divided ○ *Arrange the apricot halves, skin uppermost, in a gratin dish.* ○ *The recession began in the second half of 1990.* ○ (adj) *You don't have to pay for the first half hour.* ○ (adj) *I'll pay half the bill.* ○ (pron) *I invited twenty, but only half showed up.* ■ *n.* (*plural* **halves** /havz/) **1.** SPORTS **TIME BETWEEN PERIODS** the break between two playing periods in a game ○ *The score was tied at the half.* **2.** SPORTS **HALFBACK** a halfback in any sport **3.** *U.K.* EDUC = **semester 4.** *U.K.* **HALF FARE** a fare costing more or less half the ordinary amount, e.g., for a child or senior citizen, on public transport ○ *Two and two halves please.* **5.** MONEY a half-dollar ■ *adj.*, *adv.* **1. PARTIAL** to some extent but not complete or completely ○ (adj) *She gave me a half-smile* ○ (adv) *She was half laughing, half crying* **2. EQUALLY** in equal parts ○ (adj) *We each have half ownership in the building.* ○ (adv) *He's half French, half Spanish.* [Old English *healf*. Ultimately from a prehistoric Germanic word that also produced German *halb*. The original meaning was "side."] ◇ **by half** to a too great extent ○ *I don't trust him – he is too friendly by half.* ◇ **go halves (with somebody)** to share something equally with somebody ○ *If we go halves on the gas the trip shouldn't be too expensive.* ◇ **not do things by halves** to do things thoroughly and often on a large scale ◇ **not half 1.** not at all ○ *Mmm! This cake's not half bad!* **2.** much less than half ○ *She's not half as busy as you are.* ○ *This isn't half the fun I thought it would be.* **3.** *U.K.* used as an understatement to indicate enthusiasm (*informal*) ○ *Just look at them – his new girlfriend can't half dance!*

WORD KEY: USAGE

Singular or plural? The noun ***half*** is singular, but the word is treated as plural when it is followed by a plural noun (with or without *of*) or when it refers back to a plural: *Half the people are late. The other half of them aren't coming at all. At least half are behaving inexcusably.* With many singular nouns, ***half*** can be used in the form *half a share, half of a share*, or *a half share.*

half-and-half *n.* (*plural* **half-and-halfs**) **1. DAIRY PRODUCT FOR COFFEE** a mixture of cream and milk in equal parts, used in coffee and tea **2. TWO THINGS MIXED EQUALLY** a mixture of two things in equal parts ■ *adj.* **WITH HALF OF EACH** containing half each of two things ■ *adv.* **IN HALF** in two equal portions

half-assed *adj.* (*slang offensive*) **1. OFFENSIVE TERM** badly organized or carried out **2. WEAK** lacking forcefulness or effectiveness

half·back /háf bàk/ *n.* **1. FOOTBALL PLAYER BEHIND THE FRONT LINE** in football, the player who is positioned next to the fullback and behind the front line at the start of play **2. SOCCER MIDFIELDER** a midfielder in soccer **3. PLAYER FORWARD OF THE LAST DEFENSIVE LINE** any player in a team sport who is positioned just in front of the last defensive line **4. POSITION OF A HALFBACK** the position of somebody playing as a halfback

half-baked *adj.* **1. POORLY PLANNED** not well thought out and likely to fail (*informal*) **2. UNINTELLIGENT** lacking the ability to act with reason and common sense (*informal*) ○ *That's about what you'd expect from a department run by a bunch of half-baked idealists.* **3. UNDERCOOKED** not baked enough

half·beak /háf be̍ek/ *n.* a small fish with a short upper jaw and long lower jaw, found in warm seas, lakes, and rivers. Family: Hemiramphidae.

half bind·ing *n.* a type of bookbinding in which the back and sometimes the corners of a book are bound in one material and the sides in another

half blood *n.* **1. HALF BROTHER OR HALF SISTER** somebody who is related to somebody else by having one parent in common **2. half blood, half-blood RELATIONSHIP SHARING ONE PARENT** the relationship between two people who have one parent in common **3. OFFENSIVE TERM** an offensive term referring to somebody of racially mixed parentage, especially Native American and Caucasian (*offensive*)

half-blood·ed *adj.* **1. WITH ONE PARENT IN COMMON** with only one parent in common **2. OFFENSIVE TERM** an offensive term meaning with racially different parents (*offensive*) **3.** ZOOL = **half-bred**

half boot *n.* a boot that reaches anywhere from the top of the ankle to mid-calf

half-bound *adj.* used to describe a book that is bound on the back and sometimes the corners in one material and on the sides in another

half-bred *adj.* ZOOL used to describe a domestic animal that has only one parent of a known pedigree

half-breed *n.* **1. OFFENSIVE TERM** an offensive term referring to a person of mixed racial parentage, especially Native American and Caucasian (*offensive*) **2.** ZOOL **OFFSPRING OF ONLY ONE PUREBRED PARENT** a domestic animal with only one parent of known pedigree **3.** ZOOL, BOT **HYBRID ANIMAL OR PLANT** an animal or plant that is a hybrid product of two distinct types

half broth·er *n.* a son of one of your parents by a different partner

half-caste *n.* an offensive term referring to somebody of mixed racial parentage (*offensive*) —**half-caste** *adj.*

half cock *n.* a position on a single-action firearm in which the hammer is half-raised and locked so that the trigger cannot be pulled

half-cocked *adj.* **1. WITH THE TRIGGER IN LOCKED POSITION** used to describe a single-action firearm with the hammer half-raised and locked so that the trigger cannot be pulled **2. UNPREPARED** lacking adequate planning, thought, or preparation ◇ **go off half-cocked** to start doing something too soon, especially without adequate planning (*informal*)

half-day *n.* either the morning or the afternoon of a regular workday, especially when taken as vacation time

half-dead *adj.* tired and worn-out (*informal*)

half dime *n.* a U.S. coin worth five cents that was minted in the United States in 1792 and again from 1794 to 1873

half-dol·lar *n.* a U.S. coin worth 50 cents

half-dug·out *n.* a house, shelter, or dwelling built several feet underground with logs (*regional*)

WORD KEY: REGIONAL NOTE

Once common as far north as Montana, the term ***half-dugout*** today marks Oklahoma speech.

half ea·gle *n.* a U.S. coin worth five dollars that was minted between 1795 and 1916 and again in 1929

half gain·er *n.* a type of dive in which the diver jumps from the board facing forward and then does a half backward somersault to enter the water headfirst, facing the board

half-hard·y *adj.* used to describe a plant that can survive outdoors in mild frosts

half-heart·ed *adj.* with little enthusiasm and no real interest in the result —**half-heart·ed·ly** *adv.* —**half-heart·ed·ness** *n.*

half hitch *n.* a knot made by looping a piece of rope around an object then passing the end of the rope around itself and through the loop

half-hour *n.* **1.** **30 MINUTES** a period of thirty minutes ○ *I'll be gone for about a half-hour.* **2.** **POINT IN TIME HALFWAY BETWEEN HOURS** the point in time thirty minutes after the start of an hour ○ *Isn't that clock supposed to chime on the half-hour?* —**half-hour·ly** *adv., adj.*

half-inch *n.* a measurement of length equal to half an inch or roughly 13 mm

half-length *adj.* **1.** PAINTING **SHOWN ABOVE THE WAIST** used to describe a portrait depicting the subject from the waist up but including the hands **2.** CLOTHES **REACHING TO THE KNEE** coming down to the knee rather than the ankles ■ *n.* **PORTRAIT FROM WAIST UP** a portrait depicting the subject from the waist up but including the hands

half-life (*plural* **half-lives**) *n.* **1.** PHYS **TIME TAKEN TO LOSE HALF OF RADIOACTIVITY** the time a radioactive substance takes to lose half its radioactivity through decay. Symbol $T_{\frac{1}{2}}$ **2.** PHYSIOL **TIME TAKEN TO LOSE HALF OF DRUG** the time it takes for half a given amount of a substance such as a drug to be removed from living tissue through natural biological activity

half-light *n.* the soft dim light seen at dawn and dusk

half-line, **half line** *n.* MATH = **ray**[1] *n.* **4**

half-mar·a·thon *n.* a race on foot covering 13 mi. 352 yd./21.243 km

half-mast *n.* **FLAG POSITION AS A TRIBUTE TO SOMEBODY** the position, roughly halfway down a flagpole, to which a flag is lowered as a sign of respect when an important person dies ■ *vt.* (**half-mast·ed, half-mast·ing, half-masts**) **LOWER A FLAG AS A TRIBUTE** to position a flag roughly halfway down a flagpole as a mark of respect when an important person dies

half meas·ure *n.* an inadequate or ineffectual action

half-moon *n.* **1.** **MOON SEEN AS A SEMICIRCLE** the moon when only half its face is illuminated during the first or last quarter **2.** **SOMETHING SEMICIRCULAR** anything with the shape of a semicircle or crescent **3.** **AREA OF THE FINGERNAIL** a pale semicircle at the base of the fingernail

half nel·son *n.* a hold in which a wrestler passes an arm under the opponent's arm from behind to the back of the neck and then levers the opponent's arm backward [From the fact that only one arm is held, not both, as in a full nelson]

half note *n.* a note that has the time value of one half of a whole note

half·pen·ny /háypnee, háypənee/ *n.* (*plural* **-ny** *or* **-nies**) a former British coin worth half an old or new penny, finally withdrawn in 1985

half-pint *n.* **1.** **HALF A PINT** half of a pint **2.** **SHORT PERSON** a small or unimposing person (*informal insult*)

half·pipe *n.* SPORTS a large frozen snow structure in the shape of the bottom half of a pipe, built for freestyle snowboarding

half-price *n.* **HALF REGULAR PRICE** half the regular price ■ *adj., adv.* **FOR HALF THE PRICE** at half the regular price

half rhyme *n.* an imperfect rhyme where there is a similarity in the sounds but not the identity of stressed vowels that is found in full rhymes

half-run·ner *n.* *Southern U.S.* a rambling white bean

WORD KEY: REGIONAL NOTE

The term ***half-runner*** is used in the South Midland and Southern regions, being most common in West Virginia, Kentucky, and Tennessee. Sometimes called *half-white runner, white half-runner,* and *half-runner bean,* the legume takes its name from its growing closer to the ground than higher-rising running beans.

half shell *n.* one half of the shell of a bivalve mollusk, often served containing the soft edible part of the animal, eaten raw as an appetizer ○ *Do you like oysters on the half shell?*

half sis·ter *n.* a daughter of one of your parents by a different partner

half-size *n.* **1.** **SIZE FOR SHORT-WAISTED LARGER WOMEN** any clothing size that is designed for a short-waisted full-figured woman **2.** **SIZE IN BETWEEN** a size that is halfway between two whole-numbered sizes ○ *Do you have half-sizes in this style?*

half-slip *n.* a woman's undergarment that hangs from the waist and is worn as a lining for a skirt or dress

half sole *n.* a sole on a shoe that covers the wide part at the front of the base

half-sole (**half-soled, half-sol·ing, half-soles**) *vt.* to put a new half sole on a shoe or boot

half-staff *n.* = **half-mast**

half step *n.* **1.** MUSIC = **semitone** **2.** **MARCH STEP** a marching step that is 15 in./38 cm long in quick time and 18 in./46 cm long in double time

half tide *n.* the time during which the tide is halfway between its high and low levels

Half-timbered

half-tim·bered, **half-tim·ber** *adj.* built with a visible frame of wooden beams as well as plaster, stone, or brick. Many Tudor buildings in England were half-timbered. —**half-tim·ber·ing** *n.*

half·time /háf tìm/ *n.* a short break between the halves of a game during which players rest

half ti·tle *n.* the title of a book printed on the right-hand page before the main title page

half·tone /háf tòn/ *n.* **1.** **INTERMEDIATE SHADE** a shade or tone halfway between light and dark **2.** PRINTING **PROCESS FOR REPRODUCING SHADING IN PRINT** a photoengraving process by which shading is produced by photographing an image through a screen, then etching a plate so that the shading is reproduced as dots

half tone *n.* MUSIC = **semitone**

half-track *n.* a military vehicle with wheels on the front axles and Caterpillar™ treads on the axles that supply motive power

half-truth *n.* a statement that includes only some of the relevant facts or information and so is intended or likely to be misleading

half vol·ley *n.* **STROKE IN BALL OR RACKET GAMES** a stroke or shot that makes contact with the ball immediately after it has bounced ■ *vti.* **half-vol·ley** (**half-vol·leyed, half-vol·ley·ing, half-vol·leys**) **STRIKE A BALL IMMEDIATELY AFTER BOUNCE** to strike a ball immediately after it has bounced

half·way /hàf wáy, háf wày/ *adv., adj.* **1.** **MIDWAY BETWEEN** at or to the middle point between two things in space or time ○ *reach the halfway point* **2.** **ONLY PART WAY** to only some extent, degree, or distance

half·way house *n.* **1.** **REHABILITATION CENTER** a residence or center designed to ease people back into society after their release from an institution, e.g., prison or a psychiatric hospital **2.** **STOPPING PLACE** a resting place for travelers halfway through a long journey **3.** **HALFWAY TO THE END OF SOMETHING** the halfway point in progress toward a goal

half·wit /háf wìt/ *n.* an offensive term for somebody who behaves in a thoughtless or unintelligent way (*informal insult*) —**half-wit·ted** *adj.* —**half-wit·ted·ly** *adv.* —**half-wit·ted·ness** *n.*

Hal·i·bur·ton /hálli bùrt'n/, **Thomas Chandler** (1796–1865) Canadian jurist and writer. He created the Yankee peddler and philosopher Sam Slick (1835–55).

hal·i·but /hálləbət/ (*plural* **-buts** *or* **-but**) *n.* a large edible flatfish of the northern Atlantic and Pacific oceans. Genus: *Hippoglossus.* [15thC. From an earlier form of HOLY + dialect *butt* "flatfish" (from Middle Low German or Middle Dutch), perhaps because it was eaten on holy days.]

Ha·li·car·nas·sus /hàli kaar nássəss/ ancient city in the southwestern part of present-day Turkey. It was the site of the Mausoleum, the tomb of King Mausolus, which was one of the Seven Wonders of the World.

hal·ide /há lìd, háy-/ *n.* a binary compound of a halogen with a more electropositive element [Late 19thC. Coined from HALOGEN + -IDE.]

Hal·i·fax /hálli fàks/ Atlantic seaport and capital of Nova Scotia Province, Canada. Population: 332,518 (1996).

hal·i·plank·ton /hàlli plángktən/ *n.* plankton found in the sea

hal·ite /há lìt, háy-/ *n.* a colorless or white mineral found on dried-up lake beds in the form of cubic crystals. It is mined for use as table salt and to make chlorine. Formula: NaCl. [Mid-19thC. Coined from Greek *hals* "salt" + -ITE.]

hal·i·to·sis /hàlli tóssiss/ *n.* = **bad breath** [Late 19thC. Coined from Latin *halitus* "breath" + -OSIS.]

hall /hawl/ *n.* **1.** **CORRIDOR** a connecting passage or corridor with doors leading to other rooms **2.** **ENTRANCE ROOM** an entrance room in a house, apartment, or building, with doors leading to other rooms **3.** **BUILDING WITH A LARGE PUBLIC ROOM** a building with a large room used for public events or activities such as meetings, entertainment, and exhibitions **4.** **LARGE ROOM** a large room in a building such as a school, university, or castle, used for such purposes as dining or receptions **5.** **LARGE HOUSE** the main house on a large estate **6.** **CAMPUS BUILDING** a building at a university, college, or school used as a dormitory or for classrooms **7.** **DINING ROOM** a large dining room in a university, college, or school [Old English. Ultimately from a prehistoric Germanic base meaning "to cover, conceal," the underlying meaning being "roofed space."]

Hall /hawl/, **Lyman** (1724–90) U.S. patriot, statesman, and physician. He signed the Declaration of Independence (1776) and served as governor of Georgia (1783).

hal·lah *n.* JUDAISM = **challah**

Hal·lan·dale /hállən dàyl/ city in southeastern Florida on the Atlantic Ocean, north of Miami. Population: 30,996 (1990).

Hal·leck /hállik/, **Henry Wager** (1815–72) U.S. army officer. He served as general in chief (1862–64) and chief of staff (1864–65) of the Union army during the Civil War.

Hal·lel /haa láyl, haá làyl/, **hal·lel** *n.* Psalms 113 through 118, recited during the Jewish morning service at festivals as an expression of joy [Early 18thC. From Hebrew, "praise."]

hal·le·lu·jah /hàllə lóoyə/, **hal·le·lu·iah, al·le·lu·ia** /àllə lóoyə/ *interj.* **1.** **USED TO EXPRESS PRAISE TO GOD** used to express praise or thanks to God **2.** **USED TO EXPRESS RELIEF** used to express relief, welcome, or gratitude ○ *Hallelujah! The old car finally started on the fifth try.* ■ *n.* **1.** **CRY OF "HALLELUJAH!"** a thankful cry of "hallelujah!" **2.** **HYMN OF PRAISE** a song or piece of religious music expressing praise to God [Old English, via Latin from, ultimately, Hebrew *hallĕlūyāh*, literally "praise ye the Lord"]

hal·liard *n.* = **halyard**

Hallmark

hall·mark /háwl maark/ *n.* **1.** **MARK OF QUALITY** a mark showing that something is of high quality **2.** **DISTINGUISHING MARK** a feature of something that distinguishes it from others ○ *Discreet service is the hallmark of a fine restaurant.* **3.** **OFFICIAL MARK ON PRECIOUS METAL** in Great Britain, a mark stamped on articles made of gold, silver, or platinum to show that the metal used meets the proper standards of purity ■ *vt.* (**-marked, -mark·ing, -marks**) **STAMP WITH A MARK OF QUALITY** to stamp an article made of gold, silver, or platinum to show that the metal used meets the proper standards of purity [Early 18thC. Named for *Goldsmiths' Hall* in London, where the Goldsmiths' Company assayed and stamped gold and silver articles.]

hal·loa *interj., n., vti.* = **halloo**

hall of fame *n.* a museum where portraits, memorabilia, or belongings of people who have excelled in a particular sphere of activity, such as baseball, are displayed ○ *the Baseball Hall of Fame* ○ *the Football and Basketball Halls of Fame*

hall of res·i·dence *n. U.K.* = **dormitory**

hal·loo /hə lóo/, **hal·loa** /hə lṓ/ *interj.* **1.** CALL TO ATTRACT ATTENTION used to try to attract somebody's attention **2.** CALL TO URGE ON HUNTING DOGS used to spur on dogs in a hunt ■ *n.* (*plural* **-loos**; *plural* **-loas**) CRY OF "HALLOO!" a cry of "halloo!" used to attract attention or spur on dogs ■ *v.* (**-looed, -loo·ing, -loos; -loaed, -loa·ing, -loas**) **1.** *vi.* CALL OUT "HALLOO!" to utter a call of "halloo!" **2.** *vt.* SPUR ON WITH HALLOOS to spur hunting dogs on by shouting halloos **3.** *vt.* SHOUT SOMETHING to shout out something to somebody ○ *hallooed a warning from the shore* [Late 17thC. Alteration of earlier *holla*, from French *holà*.]

hal·low /hállō/ (**-lowed, -low·ing, -lows**) *vt.* **1.** MAKE HOLY to make somebody or something holy **2.** RESPECT GREATLY to have great respect or reverence for somebody or something [Old English *hālgian*. Ultimately from an Indo-European base that is also the ancestor of English *holy, whole,* and *health.*] —**hal·low·er** *n.*

hal·lowed /hállōd/ *adj.* **1.** SANCTIFIED holy or kept for religious use ○ *buried in hallowed ground* **2.** RESPECTED regarded with great respect or reverence ○ *the hallowed pages of our country's history* —**hal·lowed·ness** *n.*

Hal·low·een /hàllə wéen/, **Hal·low·e'en** *n.* the night of October 31, the eve of All Saints' Day, originally celebrated by Celtic peoples but now popular in the United States, Canada, and the United Kingdom. Traditionally, children dress up as witches or ghosts and go from door to door asking for candy and threatening to play tricks if refused. [Late 18thC. Shortening of *All Hallow Even*, from ALLHALLOWMAS + EVEN.]

Hal·low·mas /hállōməss, hállō màss/ *n.* = **All Saints' Day** (*archaic*) [14thC. Shortening of ALLHALLOWMAS.]

halls of i·vy *npl.* institutions or an institution of higher learning, especially those regarded as especially prestigious ○ *After four years in the halls of ivy, she had to adjust to life with a 9 to 5 job.* [From the traditional ivy-covered buildings at universities]

hall stand *n. U.K.* = **hall tree**

Hall·statt /háwl stàt, haál shtaàt/, **Hall·stat·ti·an** /hàwl státtee ən, haàl-/ *adj.* relating to or typical of a European culture of the late Bronze Age and early Iron Age [Mid-19thC. Named for the town of *Hallstatt* in Austria, where a large burial site of the period was found.]

hall tree *n.* a piece of furniture, usually kept in the hall of a house, on which people can hang their coats, hats, and umbrellas

hal·lu·ces plural of **hallux**

hal·lu·ci·nate /hə lóoss'n àyt/ (**-nat·ed, -nat·ing, -nates**) *vti.* to imagine seeing, hearing, or otherwise sensing people, things, or events that are not present or actually occurring at the time [Early 19thC. From Latin *hallucinari* "to dream, be distracted."] —**hal·lu·ci·na·tor** *n.* —**hal·lu·ci·na·tive** *adj.*

hal·lu·ci·na·tion /hə lòoss'n áysh'n/ *n.* **1.** FALSE SENSE PERCEPTION the perception of somebody or something that is not really there, often as a symptom of a psychiatric disorder or as a response to certain drugs **2.** SOMETHING IMAGINED something that somebody imagines seeing, hearing, or otherwise sensing when it is not present or actually occurring at the time (*often used in the plural*) —**hal·lu·ci·na·tion·al** *adj.*

hal·lu·ci·na·to·ry /hə lóossʼnə tàwree/ *adj.* **1.** RELATING TO FALSE SENSE PERCEPTION relating to or involving the belief that something is being seen, heard, or otherwise sensed when it is not present or actually occurring **2.** CAUSING FALSE SENSE PERCEPTION causing somebody to believe that he or she is seeing, hearing, or otherwise sensing things that are not present or actually occurring at the time

hal·lu·cin·o·gen /hə lóossʼnəjən/ *n.* a substance, especially a drug, that causes hallucinations, e.g., LSD —**hal·lu·cin·o·gen·ic** /hə lòossʼnə jénnik/ *adj.*

hal·lu·ci·no·sis /hə lòoss'n óssiss/ *n.* a psychiatric disorder that involves hallucinations

hal·lux /hálləks/ (*plural* **-lu·ces** /hállyə seez, hállə-/) *n.* the big toe on the human foot, or the first digit on the hind foot of some mammals, birds, reptiles, and amphibians (*technical*) [Mid-19thC. Via modern Latin from Latin *hallus.*]

hal·lux val·gus *n.* an abnormal bending of the big toe in which its tip points toward the little toe and its base sticks out on the inner edge of the foot [*Valgus* from Latin "bowlegged"]

hall·way /háwl wày/ *n.* = **hall** *n.* 2

hal·ma /hálmə/ *n.* a board game similar to Chinese checkers [Late 19thC. From Greek, "leap." Ultimately from an Indo-European word that is also the ancestor of English *salient* and *assail.*]

ha·lo /háylō/ *n.* (*plural* **-loes** *or* **-los**) **1.** CIRCLE OF LIGHT AROUND A SAINT'S HEAD a ring or circle of light around the head of a saint in a religious painting **2.** IMAGINED AURA OF GLORY an aura of glory imagined to surround somebody or something famous or revered **3.** SOMETHING RESEMBLING A RING OF LIGHT something that resembles or suggests a ring of light **4.** ASTRON LIGHT CIRCLE AROUND MOON OR SUN a circle of light around the Moon or Sun, caused by light refracting from ice crystals in the atmosphere **5.** ASTRON BODY OF STARS a thinly populated spherical region of stars and other luminous objects surrounding a galaxy ■ *vt.* (**-loed, -lo·ing, -los**) SURROUND WITH HALO to surround somebody or something with a halo [Mid-16thC. Via medieval Latin from, ultimately, Greek *halos* "disk around the Sun or Moon."]

halo- *prefix.* **1.** salt ○ *halobiont* **2.** halogen ○ *halocarbon* [Via French from, ultimately, Greek *hals.* Ultimately from the Indo-European word for "salt," which is also the ancestor of English *salt* and *saline.*]

hal·o·bi·ont /hàllō bī́ ònt/ *n.* an organism that lives in a salty environment, especially the sea —**hal·o·bi·on·tic** /hàllō bī óntik/ *adj.*

hal·o·car·bon /hállə kaárbən/ *n.* a compound, e.g., fluorocarbon, containing carbon and a halogen

hal·o·cline /hállə klīn/ *n.* a vertical gradient in the saltiness of the ocean

ha·lo ef·fect *n.* the tendency to judge somebody as being totally good because one aspect of his or her character is good [From the halos of angels]

hal·o·gen /hállәjən/ *n.* ELECTRONEGATIVE CHEMICAL ELEMENT any of the five electronegative diatomic elements, fluorine, chlorine, iodine, bromine, or astatine ■ *adj.* USING HALOGEN used to describe lamps or other light sources containing a filament heated by a halogen ○ *a halogen uplighter* [Mid-19thC. So called because the elements readily form salts when combined with metals.]

hal·o·ge·nate /hálləjə nàyt, hə lójjə-/ (**-nat·ed, -nat·ing, -nates**) *vt.* to treat something or combine it with a halogen —**hal·o·ge·na·tion** /hàlləjə náysh'n, hə lòjjə-/ *n.*

ha·lon /háy lòn/ *n.* a stable halocarbon used to put out fires

hal·o·per·i·dol /hàllō pérri dàwl/ *n.* a drug used as a tranquilizer, especially in the treatment of schizophrenia, mania, organic psychoses, delirium tremens, and behavioral disorders in children. Formula: $C_{21}H_{23}ClFNO_2$. [Mid-20thC. Coined from HALO- + PIPERIDINE + -OL.]

hal·o·phile /hállə fīl/ *n.* a plant that thrives in salty soil —**hal·o·phil·ic** /hàllə fíllik/ *adj.*

hal·o·phyte /hállə fīt/ *n.* a plant capable of growing in salty soil —**hal·o·phyt·ic** /hàllə fíttik/ *adj.* —**ha·lo·phyt·ism** /hállō fī tìzzəm/ *n.*

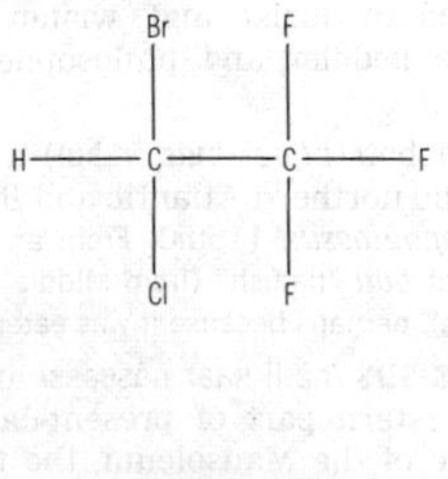

Halothane

hal·o·thane /hállə thàyn/ *n.* a colorless liquid used as an inhaled anesthetic. Formula: $C_2HBrClF_3$. [Mid-20thC. Coined from HALO- + ETHANE.]

ha·lou·mi (*plural* **-mis**) *n.* a salty white Greek cheese with a tough rubbery texture that is usually grilled until a crust has formed on both sides and eaten hot

Hal·sey /háwlzee/, **William F.** (1884–1959) U.S. admiral. In 1944 he commanded the U.S. Third Fleet in the battle for the Philippines. Full name **William Frederick Halsey**

halt[1] /hawlt/ *n.* TEMPORARY STOP an end or temporary stop ○ *The sudden rain brought the game to a halt.* ■ *interj.* COMMAND USED TO MAKE SOMEBODY STOP used to command somebody to stop ○ *Halt! Identify yourself!* ■ *vti.* (**halt·ed, halt·ing, halts**) STOP to stop, or make somebody or something stop [Late 16thC. From German *halten* "to stop, hold."]

halt[2] /hawlt/ *vi.* (**halt·ed, halt·ing, halts**) **1.** ACT HESITANTLY to act or behave without certainty or confidence **2.** BE DEFECTIVE to have defects or inconsistencies in logical development or in poetic rhythm **3.** OFFENSIVE TERM an offensive term meaning to have mild, moderate, or severe difficulty in walking (*archaic offensive*) ■ *npl.* OFFENSIVE TERM an offensive term referring to people who have difficulty in walking (*offensive*) ■ *adj.* OFFENSIVE TERM an offensive term meaning walking with difficulty (*archaic offensive*) [Old English *healtian* "to walk with a limp"]

hal·ter[1] /háwltər/ *n.* **1.** ROPE OR LEATHER DEVICE FOR A HORSE an arrangement of ropes or leather straps put over the head of an animal, especially a horse, and used to lead it **2.** BACKLESS GARMENT a woman's garment, worn between the shoulders and waist, that fastens or passes behind the neck and leaves the arms, shoulders, and back bare ○ *wore shorts and a halter on hot summer days* **3.** ROPE FOR HANGING SOMEBODY a rope with a noose, used to hang somebody **4.** HANGING death by hanging ○ *destined for the halter* ■ *vt.* (**-tered, -ter·ing, -ters**) **1.** PUT A HALTER ON to put a halter on an animal **2.** HANG SOMEBODY to execute somebody by hanging [From Old English *hælftre.* Ultimately from a prehistoric Germanic word meaning "to hold on to," which is also the ancestor of English *helm* and *halberd.*]

hal·ter[2] /háwltər/ *n.* = **haltere**

hal·tere /háwl teer/ (*plural* **-ter·es**), **hal·ter** (*plural* **-ter·es**) *n.* either of a pair of projecting parts in insects of the fly family that are rudimentary hind wings and are used to maintain balance in flight [Mid-16thC. From Greek. Formed from *hallesthai* "to jump." The word originally denoted weights athletes held in their hands to gain extra impetus in jumping.]

hal·ter-top *n.* CLOTHES = **halter**[1] *n.* 3

halt·ing /háwlting/ *adj.* **1.** CONTAINING FREQUENT STOPS hesitant or done with frequent irregular pauses ○ *halting speech* **2.** OFFENSIVE TERM an offensive term meaning having difficulty in walking (*archaic offensive*) —**halt·ing·ly** *adv.* —**halt·ing·ness** *n.*

ha·lutz *n.* = **chalutz**

hal·vah /haál vaá, haál vaà/, **hal·va** *n.* a confection, originally from the Middle East, made from crushed sesame seeds and honey with various flavorings such as chocolate or nuts [Mid-17thC. Via Turkish from, ultimately, Arabic *ḥalwā.*]

halve /hav/ (**halved, halv·ing, halves**) *v.* **1.** *vt.* DIVIDE IN TWO to divide something into two equal parts **2.** *vt.* SPLIT EQUALLY to divide something equally between two people **3.** *vti.* REDUCE BY HALF to reduce something by half, or be reduced by half **4.** *vt.* GOLF SCORE EVENLY AT to draw at a hole or match by playing the same number of strokes as an opponent [14thC. Formed from HALF.]

halves plural of **half**

hal·yard /hállyərd/, **hal·liard** *n.* a rope used to raise or lower something, e.g., a sail or flag [14thC. Alteration of earlier *halier*, from *halen* "to pull," from Old French *haler* (see HAUL).]

ham[1] /ham/ *n.* **1.** MEAT FROM A HOG'S THIGH meat cut from the thigh of the hind leg of a hog after curing by salting or smoking ○ *a slice of ham* ○ *a ham sandwich* **2.** HOG'S THIGH the thigh of the hind leg of a hog **3.** BACK OF THE LEG the back of somebody's leg from the knee up to and including the buttock **4.** HOLLOW AREA BEHIND THE KNEE a hollow area behind somebody's knee [Old English *hamm* "back of the knee." The meaning developed from "back of the knee" to "back of the thigh" to "thigh."]

ham[2] /ham/ *n.* SOMEBODY WHO OVERACTS somebody, especially an actor, who performs in an exaggerated showy style ■ *vti.* (**hammed, ham·ming, hams**) OVERACT to behave, overact, or perform a role in an exaggerated showy style [Late 19thC. Origin uncertain: possibly a shortening of *ham-fatter* "amateurish actor," which might derive from blackface minstrels' practice of cleaning their faces with ham fat after the show.]

ham³ /ham/ *n.* a licensed amateur radio operator [Early 20thC. Origin uncertain: perhaps a shortening of AMATEUR.]

Ham in the Bible, he was the second son of Noah and was formerly considered to be the ancestor of the Hamite people (Genesis 10:1)

Ha·ma /haám aa/, **Ha·māh** ancient city in west central Syria, 75 mi./121 km southwest of Aleppo. Population: 254,000 (1992).

ham·a·dry·ad /hàmmə drí əd/ *n.* **1.** MYTHOL **WOOD NYMPH** in Greek and Roman mythology, a minor deity who lives in a tree and dies when the tree dies **2.** ZOOL = **king cobra** [14thC. Via Latin from the Greek stem *Hamadruad-*, from *hama* "together" + *Druas* (see DRYAD).]

ham·a·dry·as ba·boon /hàmmə drí əss-/ *n.* a baboon native to northeastern Africa and Arabia that was sacred to the ancient Egyptians. The adult male has a long silvery mane. Latin name: *Papio hamadryas.* [Late 19thC. Via modern Latin from Latin *Hamadryas* (see HAMADRYAD).]

ha·mal /hə maál/, **ham·mal** *n.* somebody who works as a porter or servant in a Muslim country [Mid-18thC. From Arabic *ḥammāl*, formed from *ḥamala* "to carry."]

Ha·ma·ma·tsu /hàmmə mát soo/ coastal manufacturing city in southern Honshu, Japan. Population: 534,624 (1990).

ha·man·tasch /haámən taàsh/ (*plural* **-tasch·en** /-taàshən/) *n.* a triangular pastry filled with spiced dried fruit or poppy seeds and eaten during the Jewish feast of Purim [From Yiddish, from *Haman*, the persecutor of the Jews in the Book of Esther (in the Bible) + *tasch*, from German *Tasche* "bag, pocket"]

ha·mar·ti·a /haa maártee ə/ *n.* LITERAT a defect in the character of the hero of a tragedy that brings about his or her downfall [Late 18thC. From Greek *hamartia* "error, sin," from *hamartanein* "to miss the mark, make a mistake."]

ha·mate /háy màyt/ *adj.* **HAVING A HOOK SHAPE** shaped like a hook ■ *n.* **HOOKED BONE IN THE WRIST** a hook-shaped bone in the wrist [Early 18thC. From Latin *hamatus*, from *hamus* "hook."]

ham·burg /hám burg/, **ham·burg steak** *n.* = **hamburger** (*regional*) [Late 19thC. Shortening of HAMBURGER.]

WORD KEY: REGIONAL NOTE

The term ***hamburg*** is used in New England and the North Central States, as far west as Michigan. The Northern usage contrasts with the general-currency terms *hamburger* and *hamburger steak* used elsewhere in the United States. And in the North, especially among the young, the ***hamburg*** forms yield to the primary American terms.

Ham·burg /hám burg/ city and major seaport in north central Germany, situated on the Elbe and Alster rivers. Population: 1,703,800 (1994).

ham·burg·er /hám bùrgər/ *n.* **1.** **GROUND BEEF** ground beef **2.** **PATTY OF GROUND MEAT** a flat patty of ground meat, usually beef, that is broiled, grilled, or fried and usually served in a bun **3.** **GROUND-BEEF SANDWICH** a sandwich containing a flat patty of broiled, grilled, or fried ground beef or other meat in a bun, usually with other ingredients such as lettuce and condiments [Late 19thC. Formed from *Hamburg steak*, named for HAMBURG, Germany.]

ham·burg·er steak *n.* = **hamburger** *n.* 2, **hamburger** *n.* 3

Ham·den /hámdən/ *n.* town in southern Connecticut near New Haven, first settled in 1664. Population: 52,434 (1990).

hame /haym/ *n.* either of a pair of metal or wooden bars curved to fit over the neck of a draft animal and to which the traces are attached [14thC. From Middle Dutch.]

Ham·er·sley Range /hàmmərzlee-/ range of mountains in northwestern Western Australia, containing large iron ore deposits

ha·metz *n.* JUDAISM = **chametz**

ham-fist·ed *adj.* = **ham-handed** (*informal*) —**ham-fist·ed·ly** *adv.* —**ham-fist·ed·ness** *n.*

ham-hand·ed *adj.* **1.** **CLUMSY** clumsy with the hands (*informal*) **2.** **HAVING BIG HANDS** having hands that are very large —**ham-hand·ed·ly** *adv.* —**ham-hand·ed·ness** *n.*

Ham·il·ton /hámm'ltən/ industrial town in central Scotland, near Glasgow. Population: 49,991 (1991).

Ham·il·ton, Alexander (1757–1804) U.S. lawyer and statesman. He was the principal author of *The Federalist* (1787–88) and the first secretary of the U.S. Treasury (1789–95).

Ham·il·ton, Sir William Rowan (1805–65) Irish mathematician. He introduced the method of quaternions into algebra and helped to discover the wave theory of light.

Ham·il·to·ni·an func·tion /hàmm'l tōnee ən-/ *n.* a mathematical function used to describe the dynamics of a system, e.g., particles in motion, that uses momentum and spatial coordinates. Symbol *H* [Mid-19thC. Named for the Irish mathematician Sir William Rowan HAMILTON.] —**Ham·il·to·ni·an·ism** *n.*

Ham·il·ton Is·land island and tourist destination, situated 719 mi./1,160 km north of Brisbane off the eastern coast of Queensland, Australia

Ham·ite /há mīt/ *n.* a member of a group of peoples who live in various parts of North Africa [Mid-19thC. Named for HAM.]

Ha·mit·ic /ha míttik/ *n.* **GROUP OF AFRICAN LANGUAGES** a group of languages spoken in parts of northeastern Africa that is sometimes regarded as a branch of the Afro-Asiatic family of African languages. About six million people speak a Hamitic language. ■ *adj.* **1.** **OF THE HAMITES** relating to or typical of the Hamites, their culture, or their language **2.** **OF OR IN HAMITIC** relating to the Hamitic group of languages

Ham·i·to-Se·mit·ic *n., adj.* = **Afro-Asiatic** (*no longer used technically*)

ham·let /hámmlət/ *n.* **1.** **SMALL VILLAGE** a small village or group of houses **2.** ANTHROP **GROUP OF HOMESTEADS** a group of homesteads or households [14thC. Via Old French *hamelet* "small village" from, ultimately, *ham* "village." Ultimately from a prehistoric West Germanic word that is also the ancestor of English *home*.]

Ham·lin /hámlin/, **Hannibal** (1809–91) U.S. statesman and vice president of the United States. A Democrat from Maine, his long congressional career (1843–81) was interrupted by a term as Abraham Lincoln's vice president (1861–65).

ham·mal *n.* = **hamal**

Ham·mar·skjöld /hámmər shòld/, **Dag** (1905–61) Swedish diplomat. He was known as a skillful mediator as secretary general of the United Nations (1953–61), and won a Nobel Peace Prize posthumously in 1961.

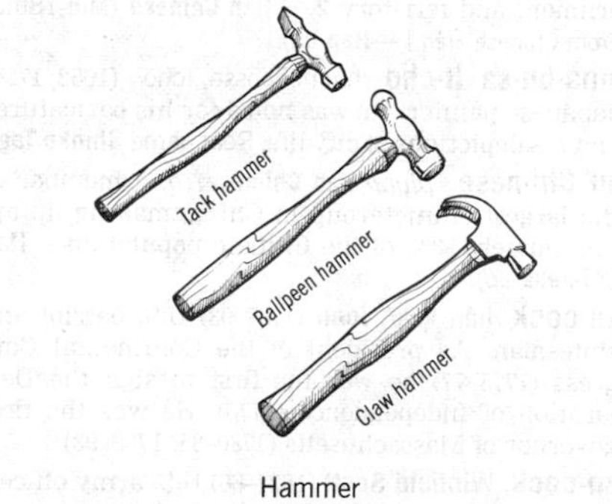

Hammer

ham·mer /hámmər/ *n.* **1.** **POUNDING TOOL** a hand tool consisting of a shaft with a metal head at right angles to it, used mainly for driving in nails and beating metal **2.** **MECHANICAL STRIKING TOOL** a powered mechanical striking tool used, e.g., in forging metal ○ *a steam hammer* **3.** **STRIKING PART** a part that strikes another in various devices, e.g., in a piano or striking clock **4.** ARMS **PART OF GUN** the part of the firing mechanism of a gun that delivers the impact that detonates the cartridge **5.** SPORTS **OBJECT FOR THROWING IN A SPORTS EVENT** a heavy metal ball attached to a handle of flexible wire, thrown in an athletics field event **6.** SPORTS = **hammer throw** **7.** **AUCTIONEER'S GAVEL** a gavel used by an auctioneer **8.** ANAT = **malleus** ■ *v.* (**-mered, -mer·ing, -mers**) **1.** *vti.* **POUND SOMETHING IN** to force something such as a nail into something else by pounding it with a hammer **2.** *vt.* **BEAT INTO SHAPE** to beat something with a hammer, especially to shape it ○ *hammering tin into bowls* **3.** *vt.* **CAUSE SOMETHING TO BE REMEMBERED** to cause something to be remembered, realized, or understood by repeating it forcefully and frequently ○ *They had caution hammered into them by the driving instructor.* **4.** *vti.* **HIT SOMETHING HARD AND REPEATEDLY** to hit or strike something hard and repeatedly ○ *hammering at the door* **5.** *vi.* **PRODUCE A RHYTHMICAL MOVEMENT OR BEAT** to produce fast, powerful, rhythmical movements or beats **6.** *vt.* **DAMAGE SOMETHING SEVERELY** to inflict serious damage on something **7.** *vt.* **GIVE SOMEBODY A BEATING** to beat or batter somebody severely (*informal*) **8.** *vt.* **DEFEAT SOMEBODY BY LARGE MARGIN** to inflict a convincing defeat on somebody, especially an opponent in a competitive sport (*informal*) ○ *Our team got hammered in last week's game.* **9.** *vt.* **CRITICIZE SOMEBODY OR SOMETHING HEAVILY** to subject somebody or something to severe criticism (*informal*) ○ *The critics really hammered his last play.* [Old English *hamor*. From a prehistoric Germanic word meaning "stone, stone tool" that is also the ancestor of English *heaven*.] —**ham·mer·er** *n.* ◇ **go** *or* **come under the hammer** to be up for auction or sale ◇ **go at it hammer and tongs 1.** to do something with maximum energy and force **2.** to fight or argue violently

hammer away at *vt.* to work hard, determinedly, and steadily at something ○ *hammering away at the new novel*

hammer out *vt.* **1.** **SHAPE WITH A HAMMER** to shape or reshape metal with a hammer **2.** **AGREE ON OR ESTABLISH** to agree on or establish something after prolonged discussion or argument ○ *hammer out a revised contract* **3.** **PLAY MUSIC ENERGETICALLY** to play a piece of music on a piano energetically and forcefully ○ *She can really hammer out a tune.*

Ham·mer /hámmər/, **Armand** (1898–1990) U.S. industrialist, art collector, and philanthropist. He established trade links with the Soviet Union in the 1920s and increased his personal fortune as the chair and CEO of Occidental Petroleum (1956–89). He made major philanthropic gifts to art and educational institutions.

Hammer and sickle

ham·mer and sick·le *n.* a symbol of Communism representing industrial and agricultural workers, used on the flag of the former Soviet Union

ham·mer dul·ci·mer *n.* a large dulcimer played with light hammers and supported by a stand

ham·mer·head /hámmər hèd/ (*plural* **-heads** *or* **-head**) *n.* **1.** **TROPICAL AFRICAN WADING BIRD** a large brown wading bird of tropical African wetlands, ponds, and lakes that has a prominent crest on the back of its head. Latin name: *Scopus umbretta.* **2.** = **hammerhead shark** **3.** **AFRICAN FRUIT BAT** a fruit bat native to Africa, the male of which has an enlarged square head and a muzzle shaped like the head of hammer. Latin name: *Hypsignathus monstrosus.*

ham·mer·head·ed /hámmər hèddəd/ *adj.* having a head shaped like a hammer

ham·mer·head shark *n.* a shark with a head that has a lateral extension on each side with an eye at the end. Genus: *Sphyrna.*

ham·mer·kop /hámmər kòp/ (*plural* **-kops** *or* **-kop**) *n.* = **hammerhead** *n.* 1 [Mid-19thC. From Afrikaans *hamerkop*, literally "hammerhead."]

ham·mer·lock /hámmər lòk/ *n.* a wrestling hold in which an opponent's arm is twisted upward behind the back [Possibly because the position of the wrestler's arms resembles the head of a claw hammer]

Ham·mer·stein /hámmər stīn/, **Oscar** (1846?–1919) German-born U.S. impresario. He founded New York City's Harlem Opera House (1880) and Manhattan Opera House (1906).

Hammerhead shark

Ham·mer·stein, Oscar II (1895–1960) U.S. librettist. He collaborated with Richard Rodgers on some of the classics of the musical stage, including the Pulitzer Prize-winning *Oklahoma!* (1943) and *South Pacific* (1949).

ham·mer throw *n.* a field event in which competing athletes try to throw a heavy metal ball attached to a handle of flexible wire as far as they can

ham·mer·toe /hámmər tō/ *n.* **1. TOE CONDITION** an abnormal condition of a toe in which the joint between the two small bones of the toe is permanently bent downward in a claw shape **2. TOE IN AN ABNORMAL CONDITION** a toe affected by hammertoe

Ham·mett /hámmit/, **Dashiell** (1894–1961) U.S. writer. He helped to establish and define the detective genre with *The Maltese Falcon* (1930) and *The Thin Man* (1932). Full name **Samuel Dashiell Hammett**

ham·mock[1] /hámmək/ *n.* a hanging bed made of canvas or netting and suspended at both ends by ropes tied between two supports [Mid-16thC. Via Spanish *hamaca* from Taino.]

ham·mock[2] /hámmək/ *n.* in the southern United States, an area of forested land that rises above a marsh (*regional*) [Mid-16thC. Original form of HUMMOCK.]

Ham·mond /hámmənd/ **1.** industrial city in northwestern Indiana on Lake Michigan, near Chicago. Population: 80,081 (1996). **2.** city in southeastern Louisiana, east of Baton Rouge. Population: 16,689 (1996).

Ham·mu·ra·bic code /hàmmə raábik-/ *n.* the first known code of law, written down in the 18th century B.C. by Hammurabi, king of Babylonia

ham·my /hámmee/ (**-mi·er, -mi·est**) *adj.* performing something such as a role in an exaggerated showy style (*informal*) —**ham·mi·ly** *adv.* —**ham·mi·ness** *n.*

ham·per[1] /hámpər/ *vt.* (**-pered, -per·ing, -pers**) **IMPEDE** to prevent the free movement or action of somebody or something ■ *n.* **SHIP'S EQUIPMENT** equipment on board a ship that is essential but likely to get in the way [14thC. Origin unknown.] —**ham·per·er** *n.*

WORD KEY: SYNONYMS

See Synonyms at ***hinder.***

ham·per[2] /hámpər/ *n.* **1. LARGE FOOD BASKET** a large basket with a cover that is used for carrying food, especially for picnics **2. LARGE BASKET FOR LAUNDRY** a large basket with a cover that is used for holding soiled laundry [14thC. Via Anglo-Norman *hanaper* "basket for holding goblets" from Old French *hanap* "goblet," of Germanic origin.]

Hamp·shire /hámpshər/ (*plural* **-shires** *or* **-shire**) *n.* **1. BLACK-AND-WHITE PIG** a black-and-white pig of a breed developed in the United States from stock imported from Hampshire, England **2. HORNLESS BLACK-FACED SHEEP** a large English sheep of a breed with a black face and no horns [Mid-17thC. Named for the English county where the breed originated.]

Hamp·shire Down *n.* = **Hampshire** *n.* 2

Hamp·ton /hámptən/ city and port in southeastern Virginia, situated on the Hampton Roads opposite Norfolk. It is the home of Langley Air Force Base and Hampton University. Population: 139,628 (1994).

Hamp·ton, Wade (1818–1902) U.S. army officer. He led the Confederate cavalry (1864–65) during the Civil War and later served as U.S. senator for South Carolina (1879–91).

Hamp·ton Court royal palace by the Thames River in southwestern London, mainly dating from the Tudor period

Hamster

ham·ster /hámstər/ *n.* **1.** ZOOL **SMALL RODENT WITH CHEEK POUCHES** a small Eurasian rodent with a short tail and large cheek pouches for storing food. Golden hamsters are often kept as pets. Family: Muridae. **2.** COMPUT **MOUSE DEVICE WITH NO CORD** a cordless mouse device for a computer that operates through an infrared connection [Early 17thC. Via German from Old High German *hamustro*, possibly of Slavic origin.]

ham·string /hám strìng/ *n.* **1.** ANAT **LEG TENDON** either of the two prominent common tendons of the three ham muscles behind the knee **2.** ANAT = **hamstring muscle 3.** ZOOL **TENDON IN AN ANIMAL'S LEG** a large tendon at the back of the hock of an animal's hind leg ■ *vt.* (**-strung, -strung** /hám strùng/, **-string·ing, -strings**) **1. CUT THE HAMSTRING** to cut the hamstring of a person or animal causing inability to use the leg normally (*often considered offensive*) **2. THWART** to make somebody or something powerless or ineffective ○ *hamstrung by lack of funds*

ham·string mus·cle *n.* any of three muscles at the back of the thigh that control certain leg movements, e.g., flexing the knee

ham·strung past tense, past participle of **hamstring**

ham·u·lus /hámmyələss/ (*plural* **-li** /-lī/) *n.* a hook-shaped part at the end of a bone [Early 18thC. From Latin, "small hook," from *hamus* "hook."] —**ham·u·lar** *adj.* —**ham·u·late** *adj.* —**ham·u·lose** *adj.* —**ham·u·lous** *adj.*

ham·za /hámzə, haám zaa/, **ham·zah** *n.* the sign ʾ used in Arabic script to represent a glottal stop [Early 19thC. From Arabic.]

Han /han/ (*plural* **Han** *or* **Hans**) *n.* **1. ANCIENT CHINESE DYNASTY** a member of a Chinese dynasty that ruled from 206 B.C. to A.D. 220 and was responsible for systematizing Chinese bureaucracy, promoting Confucianism, and consolidating Chinese government and territory **2.** = **Han Chinese** [Mid-18thC. From Chinese *Hàn*.] —**Han** *adj.*

Ha·na·bu·sa It·cho /hànnəbōōssə íchō/ (1652–1724) Japanese painter. He was noted for his caricatures and his depictions of city life. Real name **Shinko Tage**

Han Chi·nese (*plural* **Han Chi·nese**) *n.* a member of the largest ethnic group in China, making up approximately 93% of the Chinese population —**Han Chi·nese** *adj.*

Han·cock /hán kòk/, **John** (1737–93) U.S. patriot and statesman. As president of the Continental Congress (1775–77) he was the first to sign the Declaration of Independence (1776). He was the first governor of Massachusetts (1780–85, 1789–93).

Han·cock, Winfield Scott (1824–86) U.S. army officer. A Union commander during the Civil War, he was noted for rallying his troops at the Battle of Gettysburg (1863).

hand /hand/ *n.* **1. END OF THE HUMAN ARM** the part of the human arm below the wrist, consisting of a thumb, four fingers, and a palm and capable of holding and manipulating things **2. ANIMAL PART CORRESPONDING TO THE HUMAN HAND** the part of an animal's limb that corresponds to a human hand in shape or function **3. POINTER ON A CLOCK** a pointer on a clock, watch, dial, or gauge **4. PLAYER'S CARDS** the cards dealt to a player in a card game ○ *a losing hand* **5. ROUND IN A CARD GAME** a round in a card game **6. CARD PLAYER** in cards, somebody who plays a particular card game **7. INFLUENCE** the influence or directing action of somebody or something **8. PART IN DOING SOMETHING** a share in the performance of an action ○ *Who else had a hand in this?* **9. HELP** help to do something ○ *Give me a hand moving this table.* **10. OFFER OF AGREEMENT** a sign of agreement or acceptance, especially of an offer of marriage ○ *Here's my hand on it.* **11. SIDE** side or direction ○ *surrounded by enemies at every hand.* **12. CLAP** a round of applause ○ *a big hand for our next contestant* **13.** TEXTILES **FEEL OF A FABRIC** the feel of a textile, used to determine its quality **14. POSSESSION OR POWER** the possession, power, responsibility, or care of somebody ○ *Your future is in your own hands.* **15. DEGREE OF CLOSENESS TO A SOURCE** a degree of closeness to actual involvement in something being talked about ○ *I heard about it third hand.* **16. SAILOR** a member of the crew of a vessel ○ *Attention, all hands!* **17. SOMEBODY DOING OR MAKING SOMETHING** somebody who does or makes something, especially with a particular level of competence or experience ○ *I'm not much of a hand at hanging wallpaper.* ○ *an old hand at whitewater kayaking* **18. WORKER** a worker, especially one doing manual or farm work ○ *a ranch hand* **19. HANDWRITING** somebody's handwriting ○ *an admirably clear hand* **20. SKILL** ability or skill ○ *She has a good hand for gardening.* **21. APPROACH OR METHOD** a distinctive way of doing something ○ *the bungling hand of an amateur* **22. MEASURE OF A HORSE'S HEIGHT** a measure of the height of a horse, equal to 4 in./10.2 cm **23.** PRINTING = **index** *n.* 6 **24. BUNCH** a bunch of something, especially bananas **25. CUT OF PORK** a cut of pork from the front leg of the animal ■ *v.* (**hand·ed, hand·ing, hands**) **1.** *vt.* **PASS BY HAND** to pass something to somebody by hand ○ *She handed me a glass.* **2.** *vt.* **LEAD BY THE HAND** to help or lead somebody by the hand ○ *She handed her aunt into the taxi.* **3.** *vti.* **FURL** to furl a sail [Old English, of prehistoric German origin] —**hand·less** *adj.* ◇ **at hand 1.** nearby **2.** about to happen ◇ **be hand in glove (with somebody)** to cooperate with somebody, usually for some secret or illegal purpose ◇ **change hands** to pass to a different owner ◇ **force somebody's hand** to pressure somebody to do something against his or her will or earlier than planned ◇ **hand in hand 1.** in close cooperation **2.** inseparably closely **3.** holding hands ◇ **(from) hand to mouth** with barely enough to live on for your daily needs ◇ **hold somebody's hand** to provide reassurance, guidance, and support to somebody ◇ **in hand 1.** under control **2.** remaining or unused ◇ **not turn a hand (to do something)** make no attempt to help somebody ◇ **off somebody's hands** no longer somebody's responsibility or problem ◇ **on hand** near and available ◇ **on the one hand... on the other hand** used to present two conflicting aspects of a situation ○ *On the one hand we have plenty of time, but on the other hand our resources are limited.* ◇ **out of hand** immediately and without consideration or explanation ◇ **take somebody** *or* **something in hand** to begin to bring somebody *or* something under control ◇ **the upper hand** the advantage in a given situation ◇ **try your hand at something** to make an attempt at something, usually for the first time ◇ **turn your hand to something** to do something for the first time and be competent at it

WORD KEY: REGIONAL NOTE

Referring to a farm worker, the term ***hand*** has highest currency in the South Midland territory, from Kentucky to Texas, and the Lower South. The terms *cowhand, farm hand,* and *field hand* respectively mark Western, Northern, and Southern dialects. The general-currency word is *hired man*, which recurs throughout the country, but is most common in the North.

hand down *vt.* **1. BEQUEATH** to pass something on to a later generation or time **2. PASS CLOTHES ON** to pass clothes on from an older to a younger child **3. PRONOUNCE A VERDICT OR SENTENCE** to decide on a verdict or sentence and announce it in court

hand in *vt.* **1. SUBMIT SOMETHING** to give or submit something to somebody ○ *She handed in her resignation.* **2. SURRENDER SOMETHING** to return or surrender something, especially something lost or illegal

hand off *vt.* **1.** FOOTBALL **GIVE THE BALL TO ANOTHER PLAYER** in football, to hand the ball to a teammate during play ○ *The quarterback handed off the ball to the running back.* **2. RELINQUISH CONTROL** to pass control of something to another party ○ *We've handed off the disks to the printer.*

hand on *vt.* to pass something to the next person or generation

hand out *vt.* **1. DISTRIBUTE** to distribute or give something by hand **2. AWARD** to administer or award something

hand over *v.* **1.** *vt.* **SURRENDER SOMEBODY OR SOMETHING** to surrender somebody, or give something away to somebody else ○ *Hand over the money and nobody gets hurt.* **2.** *vti.* BROADCAST **TRANSFER A COMMENTARY** to transfer control of a commentary during a broadcast to somebody else ○ *Now we'll hand you over to our reporter at the scene.*

hand up *vt.* to deliver an indictment, especially from a grand jury to a court for further action [Because the judge's bench is higher than the jury box]

Hand /hand/, **Learned** (1872–1961) U.S. jurist. His 3,000 opinions, issued during the course of a 52-year career in district and appeals courts, were important contributions to U.S. jurisprudence. Full name **Billings Learned Hand**

hand ax *n.* **1. SHORT-HANDLED AX** an ax with a short handle, for use with one hand **2. PREHISTORIC STONE TOOL** a chipped stone tool rounded at one end and pointed at the other, used for a variety of purposes during the Lower and Middle Paleolithic periods

hand axe *n.* U.K. = **hand ax**

hand·bag /hánd bàg/ *n.* **1. WOMAN'S SMALL BAG** a small bag, with or without a strap or handle, used by women to carry personal items such as keys, money, and cosmetics **2. TRAVELING BAG** a small light traveling bag that is easily carried by hand

hand·ball /hánd bàwl/ *n.* **1. BALL GAME PLAYED AGAINST A WALL** a game for two or four people in which players hit a small hard ball against a wall with their hands **2. BALL USED IN HANDBALL** the small hard rubber or synthetic ball used in the game of handball **3. GOAL-SCORING BALL GAME** a team game similar to basketball in which players dribble the ball and pass it, and goals are scored by hitting the ball into the goal with the hand —**hand·ball·er** *n.*

hand·bar·row /hánd bèrrō/ *n.* a flat rectangular board for transporting loads that has a pair of handles at either end and is carried by two people

hand·bas·ket /hánd bàskət/ *n.* a small basket carried by hand ◇ **go to hell in a handbasket** to deteriorate quickly and utterly

hand·bell /hánd bèl/ *n.* a small bell held in the hand to be rung, often one of a tuned set used to play a musical piece or to practice change ringing

hand·bill /hánd bìl/ *n.* a small sheet of paper with a notice or advertisement printed on it, distributed by hand

hand·blown /hánd blōn/ *adj.* used to describe glassware blown using a hand-held tube ○ *a handblown vase*

hand·book /hánd bo͝ok/ *n.* **1. REFERENCE BOOK** a reference book, especially one small enough to be carried in the hand, giving concise information on a particular subject ○ *Where's my handbook of English–French expressions?* **2. SHORT TRAVEL GUIDE** a concise guide designed to help travelers and tourists find their way around a region, city, or other geographic location **3. BOOKMAKER'S RECORD** a notebook in which a bookmaker records bets, or a place where bets are taken **4.** *U.K.* = **manual** [Early 19thC. A translation of German *Handbuch*, which in turn was translated from medieval Latin *manualis liber* "manual."]

hand brake *n.* **1. HANDLEBAR BRAKES** either of two manual brakes on the handlebars of a bicycle or motorcycle, used to slow or stop the vehicle **2.** *U.K.* = **emergency brake**

hand·breadth /hánd brèdth/, **hand's-breadth** *n.* the width of a hand, used as an approximate measure of length

h & c *abbr.* hot and cold (water)

hand·car /hánd kaàr/ *n.* a small, open, four-wheeled railroad vehicle propelled by a manual pumping mechanism or a small motor

hand·cart /hánd kaàrt/ *n.* a small cart with two or four wheels, pulled or pushed by hand

hand·clap /hánd klàp/ *n.* a clapping of the hands, done to gain attention, applaud, or keep a rhythm. ◊ **slow handclap**

hand·clasp *n.* = **handshake**

hand·craft /hánd kràft/ *n.* = **handicraft** *n.* 3 ■ *vt.* **(-craft·ed, -craft·ing, -crafts) MAKE BY HANDICRAFT** to make something using manual skill

hand·cuff /hánd kùf/ *npl.* **hand·cuffs DEVICE FOR RESTRAINING THE HANDS** a pair of strong usually metal rings joined by a chain or bar, placed as a restraint around somebody's wrists and locked ■ *vt.* **(-cuffed, -cuff·ing, -cuffs) 1. PUT IN HANDCUFFS** to restrain somebody by using handcuffs **2. MAKE INEFFECTIVE** to make somebody or something ineffective ○ *handcuffed by bureaucratic regulations*

hand·ed·ness /hándədnəss/ *n.* **1. USE OF A FAVORITE HAND** the tendency to prefer the use of one hand over the other **2.** CHEM **PROPERTY OF BEING ASYMMETRIC** the property of some objects whereby they cannot be superimposed on their mirror images

George Frederick Handel

Han·del /hánd'l/, **George Frederick** (1685–1759) German-born British composer. He is best known for his oratorio *Messiah* (1742) and the orchestral suites *Music for the Royal Fireworks* (1749) and *Water Music* (1717).

hand-feed **(hand-feed·ing, hand-feeds)** *vt.* **1. GIVE FOOD TO SOMEBODY BY HAND** to feed a person or an animal by hand **2. FEED A MACHINE BY HAND** to feed material into a machine by hand rather than by means of an automatic or machine feed

hand·ful /hánd fo͝ol/ *n.* **1. AMOUNT CONTAINED BY THE HAND** an amount that can be held in the hand **2. SMALL AMOUNT OR NUMBER** a small amount or number of people or things ○ *Only a handful of students turned up for the lecture.* **3. SOMEBODY OR SOMETHING DIFFICULT** a somebody or something that is difficult to cope with or control (*informal*) ○ *Together those two are a real handful!*

WORD KEY: CULTURAL NOTE

A Handful of Dust, a novel by English writer Evelyn Waugh (1934). One of Waugh's early satires, it tells the story of Tony Last, a haughty country gent whose wife leaves him for a young socialite. His response is to set off on an ill-advised expedition to South America, where he ends up the captive of an eccentric local with a penchant for Dickens.

hand glass *n.* **1. MAGNIFYING GLASS** a magnifying glass with a handle for holding in the hand **2. HAND MIRROR** a small mirror for holding in the hand (*dated*)

hand gre·nade *n.* a small bomb designed to be thrown by hand and detonated by a time fuse

hand·grip /hánd grìp/ *n.* **1.** = **grip** *n.* 2 **2. HANDLE** a handle or the part of something that can be held with the hand ○ *My motorcycle needs a new handgrip.* **3. COVERING FOR A HANDLE** a piece of material that covers a handle and makes it easier to keep hold of **4. TRAVELING BAG** a small light traveling bag that is easily carried by hand ■ **hand·grips** *npl.* **HAND-TO-HAND FIGHTING** fighting carried out hand-to-hand

hand·gun /hánd gùn/ *n.* a gun that can be held and fired in one hand

hand·held /hánd hèld/, **hand-held** *adj.* **1. HELD IN THE HAND** made to be operated while held in the hand **2.** CINEMA, TV **SHOT WITH A PORTABLE CAMERA** filmed with a camera that is carried by the operator rather than mounted on a support ○ *black-and-white handheld footage*

hand·hold /hánd hòld/ *n.* **1. SOMETHING TO HOLD ON TO** something for somebody climbing to grasp for support, e.g., a projecting piece of rock or a fissure in a cliff face **2. GRIP** a firm grip with the hand or hands

hand·hold·ing /hánd hòlding/ *n.* the giving of reassurance and guidance to somebody

hand·i·cap /hándee kàp/ *n.* **1. HINDRANCE** something that hinders or is a disadvantage to somebody or something **2.** SPORTS **BALANCED CONTEST** a contest in which individual competitors are given an advantage or disadvantage in an attempt to give every contestant an equal chance ○ *a handicap race* **3.** SPORTS **ADDED ADVANTAGE OR DISADVANTAGE** an advantage or disadvantage given to a competitor in a handicap **4.** GOLF **GOLFER'S COMPENSATION IN STROKES** a compensation in strokes given to a golfer on the basis of skill in past performances **5. PHYSICAL OR MENTAL CHALLENGE** a particular way in which somebody is physically or mentally challenged (*often considered offensive*) ■ *vt.* **(-capped, -cap·ping, -caps) 1. HINDER** to hinder or be a disadvantage to somebody or something **2. GIVE SPORTS HANDICAPS** to give an advantage or disadvantage to a competitor in a contest **3. ASSESS CHANCES** to assess the chances of competitors in a contest [Mid-17thC. From *hand in cap* "betting game in which contestants place their hands in a hat with their wagers."]

WORD KEY: ORIGIN

In the original game of ***handicap***, one contestant put up an item of personal property against something belonging to the other contestant, offering to exchange the one for the other. An umpire adjudicated on the difference in value between the two articles. The contestants then placed their hands in a hat, along with some forfeit money, and the way in which they withdrew their hands – full or empty – signified whether they accepted the adjudication. If they both either accepted or rejected it, the umpire got the forfeit money; if they disagreed, the one who accepted it got the money. The application to horseracing arose in the 18th century from the notion of an umpire adjudicating on the weight disadvantage to be given to a particular horse.

hand·i·capped /hándee kàpt/ *adj.* **PHYSICALLY OR MENTALLY CHALLENGED** physically or mentally challenged (*often considered offensive*) ■ *npl.* **OFFENSIVE TERM** an offensive term for people who are physically challenged (*offensive*)

hand·i·cap·per /hándee kàppər/ *n.* **1. SOMEBODY WHO ASSIGNS SPORTS HANDICAPS** somebody who assigns handicaps to competitors in a contest **2. SOMEBODY WHO PREDICTS THE WINNER OF A HORSE RACE** somebody who tries to forecast the outcome of a horse race, especially one who provides published advice to people betting

hand·i·craft /hándee kràft/ *n.* **1. CRAFT** a craft or occupation in which manual skill is needed, e.g., weaving **2. OBJECT MADE BY HAND** something made using manual skill **3. MANUAL SKILL** skill in making things with the hands [13thC. An alteration of HANDCRAFT, modeled on HANDIWORK.] —**hand·i·craft·er** *n.*

hand·i·ly /hándilee/ *adv.* **1. CONVENIENTLY** in a convenient way ○ *handily close to the train station* **2. SKILLFULLY** in a skillful way **3. EASILY** in an easy way ○ *She took the second set handily.*

hand·i·work /hándee wùrk/ *n.* **1. SOMEBODY'S ACTION** action taken by somebody, or the result of somebody's action ○ *The broken window was the handiwork of local vandals.* **2. WORK DONE BY HAND** work done or produced by hand **3. SKILL WITH WHICH SOMETHING IS DONE** the skill with which something is done, especially manual skill [From Old English *handgeweorc*, from *hand* "hand" + *geweorc*, literally "body of work," from *weorc* (see WORK)]

hand-jam *n.* CLIMBING an act of wedging the hand into a rock crack to aid in climbing

hand·ker·chief /hángkərchif, -chēef/ (*plural* **-chiefs** *or* **-chieves** /-chivz, -chēevz/) *n.* **1. CLOTH FOR WIPING THE NOSE** a square of cloth or absorbent paper used mainly to wipe areas of the face, especially the nose **2. SCARF** a large, often brightly colored square of cloth used as a clothing accessory or to cover the hair

hand-knit *vti.* to knit something by hand, not on a machine

han·dle /hánd'l/ *n.* **1. PART FOR HOLDING OR OPERATING SOMETHING** a part of a thing by which it is held, moved, or operated **2. NAME** somebody's name (*slang*) ○ *What's your handle?* **3. MEANS** an opportunity, pretext, or means of doing something **4.** *U.K.* TEXTILES = **hand** *n.* 13 **5.** GAMBLING **TOTAL AMOUNT BET** the total sum of money bet on a race, series of races, or other event ■ *v.* **(-dled, -dling, -dles) 1.** *vt.* **TOUCH** to touch, pick up, or move something with the hands ○ *Don't handle the merchandise.* **2.** *vt.* **OPERATE** to operate or make use of something with the hands **3.** *vt.* **TAKE CHARGE OF** to take care of or be responsible for something ○ *Who handles the import side of the business?* **4.** *vt.* **DEAL WITH** to manage or control somebody or something ○ *She's good at handling difficult customers.* **5.** *vt.* **BE MANAGER OF** to manage or supervise somebody ○ *He handles a string of professional boxers.* **6.** *vt.* **BE ABOUT SOMETHING** to discuss or deal with a subject ○ *The novel handles the theme of unrequited love in an original way.* **7.** *vt.* **TRADE IN** to deal in particular goods **8.** *vi.* **RESPOND TO CONTROL** to respond to control or use, often in a particular way ○ *The little yacht handled like a dream.* [Old English. The noun is *handle* and the verb *handlian*, both of which were formed from *hand* "hand."] —**han·dle·a·bil·i·ty** /hànd'lə bíllətee/ *n.* —**han·dle·a·ble** /hánd'ləb'l/ *adj.* — **han·dle·less** /hánd'l ləss/ *adj.* ◇ **fly off the handle** to lose your temper, especially without justification (*informal*) ◇ **get a handle on something** to understand a situation fully or be able to control it fully ○ *It's a difficult problem to get a handle on.*

AKG London

Handlebar mustache: William II, Emperor of Germany and King of Prussia (photographed in 1898)

han·dle·bar mus·tache *n.* a thick broad mustache that curls up at the ends like handlebars

han·dle·bars /hánd'l baárz/ *npl.* a bar with handles at each end, used to steer a vehicle such as a bicycle or motorcycle

hand lens *n.* = **hand glass** *n.* **1**

han·dler /hándlər/ *n.* **1.** ANIMAL TRAINER somebody who trains or manages animals that perform in movies, television programs, or judged shows **2.** SOMEBODY USING A TRAINED DOG somebody who uses a specially trained dog, e.g., in the police or armed forces **3.** BOXER'S TRAINER a boxer's trainer or second **4.** MANAGER somebody who manages the career of somebody or the running of something **5.** SOMEBODY WORKING WITH SOMETHING somebody who works or deals with a particular thing ○ *a baggage handler for an airline*

han·dling /hándling/ *n.* **1.** WAY SOMEBODY HANDLES SOMETHING the way in which somebody handles or deals with something ○ *The report criticized his handling of the affair.* **2.** TREATMENT the way in which a subject is treated or dealt with in a written work or other work of art **3.** COMM TRANSPORT AND PACKAGING the transportation and packaging of goods ○ *The cost includes a charge for handling.* **4.** *U.K.* = **fencing**

hand·made /hand máyd, hánd màyd/ *adj.* made by hand, not by machine ○ *handmade furniture*

hand·maid /hánd màyd/, **hand·maid·en** /-màyd'n/ *n.* **1.** WOMAN SERVANT a woman or girl servant (*archaic*) **2.** SOMETHING HELPFUL something that provides help or support in a subsidiary role (*literary*) ○ *Hard work and focus are the handmaids of genius.* [The underlying meaning is "somebody who is at hand when needed"]

hand-me-down *n.* **1.** USED GARMENT an item of clothing, usually outgrown, passed down from a family member or friend to another **2.** SOMETHING PREVIOUSLY DISCARDED something taken up or used by a person or group that has been used before and discarded

hand·off *n.* **1.** FOOTBALL GIVING OF THE BALL TO ANOTHER in football, a handing of the ball to another teammate during play **2.** FOOTBALL BALL IN A HANDOFF the ball played in a handoff **3.** RELINQUISHMENT OF CONTROL the passage of control over something from one party to another ○ *The handoff of flight 796 occurred at exactly midnight, and the receiving tower confirmed it.*

hand or·gan *n.* a mechanical musical instrument with a bellows, played by turning a crank

hand·out /hánd òwt/ *n.* **1.** CHARITABLE GIFT something such as money or food given as charity to somebody in need **2.** DOCUMENT DISTRIBUTED TO A GROUP a document, such as a press release, an advertisement, or material accompanying a meeting or lecture that is distributed to a group

hand·o·ver /hánd ȍvər/ *n.* **1.** SURRENDERING a surrendering of somebody, or a giving away of something to somebody else ○ *the handover of power to the civilian authorities* **2.** BROADCAST TRANSFER OF COMMENTARY a transfer of the control of the commentary during a broadcast to somebody else

hand·pick /hánd pìk/ (**-picked, -pick·ing, -picks**) *vt.* **1.** CHOOSE SOMEBODY OR SOMETHING CAREFULLY to choose somebody or something carefully and personally, e.g., members of a team **2.** PICK OR HARVEST BY HAND to pick or harvest something by hand, not by machine

hand press /hánd prèss/, **hand·press** *n.* a printing press operated by hand

hand·print /hánd prìnt/ *n.* a mark or impression made by the palm of the hand and fingers

hand pup·pet *n.* a puppet that fits over the hand like a glove and is operated by the user's thumb and fingers

hand·rail /hánd ràyl/ *n.* a rail to hold with the hand for support, e.g., at the side of stairs or a ramp

hand·saw /hánd sàw/ *n.* a saw for use with one hand

hand's-breadth *n.* = **handbreadth**

hands down *adv.* **1.** EASILY without encountering any problems, obstacles, or opposition **2.** UNQUESTIONABLY without any doubt whatsoever ○ *they won hands down*

hands-down *adj.* **1.** UNQUESTIONABLE accepted without any question **2.** VERY EASY having no trouble doing something [From horseracing, when a jockey wins by such a wide margin that he can relax his grip on the reins]

hand·set /hánd sèt/ *n.* the part of a telephone that is held in the hand and contains the parts used for speaking into and listening to

hand·shake /hánd shàyk/ *n.* **1.** GRIP WITH THE HAND a gesture of gripping and shaking another person's hand, used as a greeting or farewell and to seal an agreement **2.** COMPUT EXCHANGE OF SIGNALS an exchange of signals between a computer and another computer or external device indicating that a link is established and communication is possible

hand·shak·ing /hánd shàyking/ *n.* the exchanging of signals between a computer and another computer or external device indicating that a link is established and communication is possible

hands-off *adj.* not wanting or needing to interfere in or control something ○ *The boss has a hands-off policy with respect to the day-to-day running of the business.*

hand·some /hánssəm/ *adj.* **1.** GOOD-LOOKING with good-looking facial features or a pleasing general appearance **2.** GENEROUS amounting to a higher sum than expected **3.** IMPRESSIVE well-made or skillfully executed [Mid-16thC. The underlying meaning is "handy, skilled."] —**hand·some·ness** *n.*

WORD KEY: SYNONYMS

See Synonyms at ***good-looking***.

hand·some·ly /hánssəmlee/ *adv.* **1.** GENEROUSLY in an amount that is more than expected **2.** IMPRESSIVELY in a way that requires great skill or agility **3.** OF GREAT SIZE OR EXTENT in a way that is very large in extent or size

hands-on *adj.* **1.** USING SOMETHING involving the actual use of something ○ *Learning computer skills is a hands-on process.* **2.** INVOLVING PHYSICAL TOUCHING involving physical touching of something ○ *The children's science museum has many hands-on exhibits.* **3.** PERSONALLY INVOLVED giving personal attention to or taking personal control of somebody or something ○ *She's very much a hands-on manager.*

hand·spike /hánd spìk/ *n.* a metal bar used as a lever [Early 16thC. Alteration of Dutch *handspaak*, from *hand* "hand" + *spaak* "spoke."]

hand·spring /hánd sprìng/ *n.* a gymnastic movement in which somebody flips the body forward or backward and lands briefly on the hands before continuing the flip so as to land on the feet again

hand·stand /hánd stànd/ *n.* an act of balancing the body on the hands with the legs straight up in the air

hand-to-hand *adj.* taking place at close quarters and involving bodily contact —**hand to hand** *adv.*

hand-to-mouth *adj.* POOR having barely enough money or food for daily needs ■ *adv.* IN POVERTY with only just enough money or food for daily needs [From the idea that everything somebody earns goes to meet the immediate need for food]

hand truck *n.* an upright vehicle with two wheels and a shallow platform, used to carry heavy loads to be moved by hand

hand·work /hánd wùrk/ *n.* work done by hand, not by a machine —**hand·work·er** *n.*

hand·wo·ven /hánd wȍvən/ *adj.* **1.** WOVEN BY HAND LOOM woven on a hand-operated loom, not a mechanical one **2.** WOVEN BY HAND woven using the hands

hand·wring·ing /hánd rìnging/ *n.* **1.** DEMONSTRATION OF CONCERN the demonstration or expression of concern about something, often without any constructive action being taken **2.** NERVOUS CLASPING OF THE HANDS the repeated clasping and squeezing of the hands together as a result of anxiety or grief

hand·write /hánd rìt/ (**-wrote** /-rȍt/, **-writ·ten** /-rìtt'n/, **-writ·ing, -writes**) *vt.* to use a writing implement such as a pen or pencil to put words on paper

hand·writ·ing /hánd rìting/ *n.* **1.** WRITING DONE BY HAND writing done by hand using a pen or pencil **2.** MANNER OF WRITING somebody's individual way of writing by hand ○ *I recognized my father's handwriting on the envelope.* [Early 16thC. Translation of Latin *manuscriptum.*] ◇ **handwriting on the wall** something that predicts a future disaster or decline in somebody's fortunes ○ *She saw the handwriting on the wall and resigned before they could fire her.*

hand·wrought /hand ráwt, hánd ràwt/ *adj.* shaped by hand, especially by hammering

hand·y /hándee/ (**-i·er, -i·est**) *adj.* **1.** CONVENIENT located in a convenient place, especially nearby and easy to reach **2.** USEFUL useful or easy to use **3.** SKILLFUL skillful at doing a number of different things — **hand·i·ness** *n.*

Han·dy /hándee/, **W. C.** (1873–1958) U.S. composer. He was known for blues compositions including "St. Louis Blues" (1914), and brought blues to a wide audience. Full name **William Christopher Handy**

hand·y·man /hándee màn/ (*plural* **-men** /-mən/) *n.* **1.** SOMEBODY WHO DOES SMALL JOBS somebody who earns money by doing a variety of small jobs **2.** SOMEBODY SKILLFUL somebody who has the experience and skill to perform a variety of small jobs

Han·ford /hánfərd/ city in central California, 30 mi./49 km south of Fresno. Population: 30,897 (1990).

hang /hang/ *v.* (**hung, hung** /hung/, **hang·ing, hangs**) **1.** *vti.* SUSPEND to suspend or fasten something so that it is held up from above and not supported from below **2.** *vt.* PUT ON HINGES to put something such as a door on hinges so that it can move freely **3.** (*past and past participle* **hanged**) *vti.* KILL SOMEBODY WITH ROPE to kill somebody or yourself by fastening a rope around the neck and removing any other support for the body, or die in this way, especially as a form of legal execution **4.** *vt.* DECORATE WITH SOMETHING to decorate or furnish a place or object with something ○ *hang the Christmas tree with lights and decorations* **5.** *vt.* PUT UP WALLPAPER to attach wallpaper to walls **6.** *vti.* DISPLAY A PAINTING to put pictures or paintings on display, or be put on display **7.** *vt.* PUT UP ARTWORK to put paintings or other artwork on walls for exhibit **8.** *vt.* LET DROOP to let something, especially the head, droop ○ *They should hang their heads in shame.* **9.** *vt.* SUSPEND A GUTTED ANIMAL to suspend meat or a recently killed game animal until the flesh begins to decompose slightly and becomes more tender and highly flavored **10.** *vt.* LAW PREVENT A JURY FROM DECIDING to prevent a jury from reaching a verdict **11.** *vti.* BASEBALL PITCH A BALL THAT FAILS TO BREAK in baseball, to pitch the ball in such a way that it fails to break, or be pitched in this way **12.** (*past and past participle* **hanged**) *vt.* EXCLAMATION INDICATING ANNOYANCE used as a euphemism for damn (*dated informal*) ○ *Hang it all!* ○ *I'll be hanged if I'll let them get away with this!* **13.** *vt.* MAKE A TURN to make a particular turn, especially when driving a car (*informal*) ○ *Hang a right at the next street.* **14.** *vi.* BE UNRESOLVED to be unresolved or in doubt ○ *His academic future hangs in the balance.* **15.** *vti.* FOLD OR DROOP to fold or bend something over or across something, or be folded or bent over or across something **16.** *vi.* DRAPE to drape from a point of suspension in a particular way ○ *The jacket hung badly on her.* **17.** *vi.* ELAPSE SLOWLY to pass by or elapse slowly ○ *Time hung heavily when she was away.* **18.** *vi.* COMPUT ALLOW NO INPUT OR OUTPUT to refuse additional input and be unable to generate output until rebooted (*refers to a computer*) **19.** *vi.* = **hang out** (*slang*) ■ *n.* **1.** WAY OF HANGING SOMETHING the way that something hangs **2.** SLOPE a downward slope **3.** EXHIBITION OF ARTWORK an exhibition of artwork, especially paintings [Old English *hangian* (intransitive), from a prehistoric West Germanic base] ◇ **get the hang of something** to learn a skill or activity thoroughly ◇ **not give** *or* **care a hang**

(for *or* **about somebody** *or* **something)** to be completely unconcerned or indifferent about somebody or something (*dated informal*)

hang around *vi.* **1.** WASTE TIME to loiter or waste time ○ *She doesn't like her kids hanging around in the mall all day Saturday.* **2.** ASSOCIATE REGULARLY to spend time regularly with somebody ○ *He hangs around with the drama crowd.*

hang back *vi.* to show reluctance to do something

hang in *vt.* to endure or persevere in doing something (*informal*) ○ *She hung in as long as she could.*

hang on *v.* **1.** *vi.* HOLD ON TIGHTLY to hold on tightly to something **2.** *vi.* KEEP GOING to persist in an endeavor in spite of obstacles or difficulties **3.** *vt.* DEPEND ON SOMETHING to depend on something **4.** *vt.* CLING to cling to somebody in a possessive or dependent way **5.** *vi.* WAIT to wait or show patience for a short time **6.** *vt.* LISTEN CLOSELY TO to listen attentively to what somebody says

hang onto *vt.* = **hang on** *v.* **1**, **hang on** *v.* **5**

hang out *v.* **1.** *vt.* SUSPEND OUTSIDE to put something outside, e.g., on a line, pole, or balcony, so that it will dry or so that it can be seen **2.** *vi.* BE AROUND SOMEWHERE to be regularly present somewhere (*informal*) **3.** *vi.* SPEND TIME SOMEWHERE to spend time somewhere in a casual or relaxed way (*informal*) ○ *Do you want to hang out at the mall?* **4.** *vi.* ASSOCIATE to spend time regularly with somebody (*informal*)

hang over *vt.* to be imminent or threatening for, or be unwelcomely associated with, somebody or something

hang together *vi.* to be consistent or cohesive

hang up *v.* **1.** *vt.* SUSPEND to put something on a peg, hook, nail, or hanger **2.** *vti.* REPLACE A PHONE IN ITS CRADLE to end a telephone call by returning the receiver to its original position, often abruptly **3.** *vti.* CAUSE DELAY to cause or be caused delay

hang upon *vt.* = **hang on** *v.* **4**, **hang on** *v.* **6**

han·gar /hángər/ *n.* a large building in which aircraft are kept or repaired [Late 17thC. Via French, "shed," from Old French *hangard*, possibly from medieval Latin *angarium* "shed for shoeing horses," or of prehistoric Germanic origin.]

hang·dog /háng dòg/ *adj.* having an expression that indicates guilt or sadness [Late 17thC. Originally referring to somebody who deserved to be hanged like a dog.]

hang·er /hángər/ *n.* **1.** NAIL OR HOOK FOR HANGING SOMETHING a support from which something can be hung, e.g., a nail or hook **2.** FRAME FOR HANGING A GARMENT a triangular frame of metal, wood, or plastic over which clothes can be draped for storage or display **3.** SOMEBODY WHO HANGS SOMETHING somebody who hangs or suspends something **4.** SHORT SWORD a short sword worn on a belt

hang·er-on (*plural* **hang·ers-on**) *n.* somebody who latches on to a richer or more prominent person or group in the hope of personal gain

Hang glider

hang glid·er *n.* an aircraft without an engine that consists of a rigid frame in the shape of a wing, with the pilot usually suspended in a harness below the wing. Hang gliders can be launched by foot, with the pilot running down a slope, or by being towed by a truck, winch, or ultralight aircraft. —**hang glid·ing** *n.*

hang·ing /hánging/ *n.* **1.** METHOD OF KILLING the act of killing somebody by putting the neck in a noose and removing the support, especially as a form of legal execution **2.** FABRIC HUNG ON A WALL a drapery, tapestry, or decorative fabric hung on a wall (*often used in the plural*) ■ *adj.* **1.** PUNISHABLE BY DEATH punishable by death, or seen as deserving the death penalty ○ *a hanging offense* **2.** SEVERE OR UNMERCIFUL tending to impose severe punishments, especially the death penalty ○ *a hanging judge* **3.** AT THE TOP OF A SLOPE positioned at the top of a steep slope or height

hang·ing in·den·ta·tion *n.* an indenting of all the lines of a paragraph of text except the first

hang·ing wall *n.* the rocks that hang over a seam of coal or other mineral vein

hang·man /hángmən, háng màn/ (*plural* **-men** /-mən, -mèn/) *n.* **1.** EXECUTIONER an official who carries out the death penalty of hanging **2.** GAMES LETTER GAME a game in which one player has to guess a word, letter by letter, while the other player draws a sketch of a hanged person. To win, the player has to guess the word before the drawing is complete.

hang·nail /háng nàyl/ *n.* a small piece of skin partly detached from the side or base of a fingernail [Late 17thC. By folk etymology from *agnail* "corn on the foot," from Old English *angnægl*, from *ang-*, from a prehistoric Germanic word meaning "tight," + NAIL.]

hang·o·ver /háng ōvər/ *n.* **1.** ILLNESS AFTER DRINKING the symptoms of headache, nausea, thirst, and sickness that result from drinking too much alcohol **2.** ASPECT ROOTED IN THE PAST something that remains from an earlier time

Hang Seng in·dex /hàng séng-/ *n.* an index based on the relative prices of selected stocks on the Hong Kong Stock Exchange

hang·tag /háng tàg/ *n.* a small paper, plastic, or fabric slip attached to an item being sold and giving information about it

hang time *n.* **1.** TIME A KICKED BALL IS IN THE AIR the amount of time a ball remains in the air after being kicked, or an athlete remains in the air after leaping **2.** MIL TIME MISSILE IS AIRBORNE the time that a missile, especially a nuclear missile, is airborne between its launch and its landing

Han·gul /haáng go͝ol, háng-/, **han·gul** *n.* the alphabet used for Korean writing [Mid-20thC. From Korean *han kul*, literally "Korea alphabet."]

hang-up *n.* **1.** CONTINUING ANXIETY ABOUT SOMETHING a psychological or emotional problem or fixation about something (*informal*) **2.** CAUSE OF PROBLEMS a persistent impediment or source of delay ○ *Bureaucratic inefficiency was the main hang-up.*

Hang·zhou /hàng jṓ/ seaport and capital city of Zhejiang Province in southeastern China. Population: 1,340,000 (1991).

Han Jiang /haán jyaáng/, **Han** river of central China, a tributary of the the Yangtze River and major trade artery. Length: 952 mi./1,532 km.

hank /hangk/ *n.* **1.** LOOSE BALL OF SOMETHING a piece of something such as hair, rope, or wool that has been wrapped around itself to form a loose ball **2.** SAILING ATTACHMENT FOR A SAIL a ring-shaped fitting that can be opened to secure the leading edge of a sail **3.** MEASURE LENGTH OF SOMETHING a length of yarn when reeled. A hank of cotton is 840 yd./767 m. [14thC. From Old Norse *hönk*, from a prehistoric Germanic word that is also the ancestor of English *hook*.]

han·ker /hángkər/ (**-kered, -ker·ing, -kers**) *vi.* to want something very badly and persistently ○ *hankering after something I can't have* [Early 17thC. Origin uncertain: possibly from Dutch dialect *hankeren*.] —**hank·er·er** *n.*

han·kie /hángkee/, **han·ky** (*plural* **-kies**) *n.* a handkerchief (*informal*) [Late 19thC. Shortening.]

Hanks /hangks/, **Tom** (*b.* 1956) U.S. actor, who won Academy Awards for *Philadelphia* (1993) and *Forrest Gump* (1994).

han·ky-pan·ky /hàngkee pángkee/ *n.* **1.** SUSPICIOUS ACTIVITY illicit or suspicious behavior **2.** FRIVOLOUS SEXUAL BEHAVIOUR frivolous and slightly indecent sexual activity [Mid-19thC. An alteration, via the form *hokey-pokey*, of HOCUS POCUS, the earliest uses of the word being for "juggling, conjuring."]

Han·na /hánnə/, **Mark** (1837–1904) U.S. entrepreneur and statesman. He took U.S. presidential campaigns to new levels of sophistication and expense in masterminding the election of William McKinley (1896). Full name **Marcus Alonzo Hanna**

Han·ni·bal /hánnəb'l/ (247–183 B.C.) Carthaginian general. At the beginning of the Second Punic War (218–202 B.C.), he marched across the Alps to northern Italy with elephants and a 40,000-strong army. It was one of the most famous military exploits in history. He was less successful in a subsequent African campaign against Scipio, and died in exile.

Han·ni·bal city and port in eastern Missouri, on the Mississippi River. It was the boyhood home of Mark Twain. Population: 18,004 (1990).

Ha·noi /ha nóy/ capital city of Vietnam, located in the north of the country. Population: 2,154,900 (1993).

Han·o·ver[1] /hánnōvər/ city in northwestern Germany, situated on the Leine River. Population: 517,476 (1992).

Han·o·ver[2] /hánnōvər/ *n.* the royal house of Great Britain from 1714, when the elector of Hanover ascended the British throne as George I, until 1901, when Queen Victoria died

Han·o·ve·ri·an /hànnə vérree ən/ *adj.* **1.** OF HOUSE OF HANOVER relating to or characteristic of the British rulers from 1714 to 1901 **2.** OF HANOVER relating to or typical of Hanover, Germany, or of its inhabitants or culture ■ *n.* HANOVERIAN MONARCH a supporter or monarch of the British Hanoverian line

Han·o·ver Park village in northeastern Illinois, a western suburb of Chicago. Population: 35,599 (1996).

Han·sa /hánsə, haánzə/, **Han·se** /hans, haánzə/ *n.* **1.** = **Hanseatic League 2.** FEE FOR HANSA MAMBERSHIP the fee paid by a new member of the Hansa [12thC. From Old High German, "troop, company."]

Han·sard /hánsərd/ *n.* the official published reports of proceedings in the British or Canadian Parliaments or of similar legislative bodies in the British Commonwealth [Late 19thC. Named for the British printer Luke *Hansard* (1752–1828), who first published it.]

Han·se *n.* = **Hansa**

Han·se·at·ic /hànsee áttik/ *adj.* relating to the Hanseatic League or one of the towns in it [Early 17thC. From medieval Latin *Hanseaticus*, from *Hansa* (see HANSA).]

Han·se·at·ic League *n.* an organized network of towns in northern Europe from the 15th to the 16th centuries that protected each other and promoted trade with each other

han·sel *n.* = **handsel**

Han·sen's dis·ease /hàns'nz-/ *n.* = **leprosy** [Early 20thC. Named for the Norwegian physician Gerhard *Hansen* (1841–1921), who described it.]

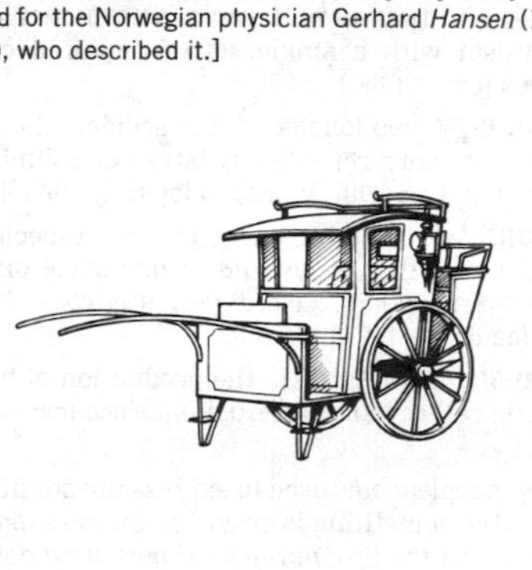
Hansom

han·som /hánsəm/, **han·som cab** *n.* a covered two-wheeled vehicle drawn by one horse and carrying two passengers inside while the driver sits outside on a raised seat at the rear [Mid-19thC. Named for the British architect Joseph Aloysius *Hansom* (1803–82), who patented an improved design of cab in 1834.]

han·ta·vi·rus /hántə vìrəss/ *n.* a virus belonging to a group that affects small rodents and can be passed to humans by inhalation or ingestion of their secretions or excreta. Symptoms include fever, headache, nausea, and vomiting.

Ha·nuk·kah /hánnəkə, haán-, khaán-/, **Ha·nu·kah, Cha·nu·kah, Cha·nuk·kah** *n.* an eight-day Jewish festival beginning on the 25th day of Kislev in December and commemorating the rededication to Judaism of the Temple in Jerusalem. The temple was rededicated in 165 B.C. after a period during which it had been used for the worship of Greek gods under Antiochus Epiphanes. [Late 19thC. From Hebrew *hanukkah* "consecration."]

Han·u·man /húno͝o maàn, haáno͞o-/ *n.* **1. Han·u·man, han·u·man** SACRED MONKEY a slender long-tailed langur monkey of southern Asia, considered sacred in India. Latin name: *Presbytis entellus.* **2.** INDIAN RELIG MONKEY CHIEF in Hinduism, a leader of monkeys who assists Rama [Early 19thC. From Sanskrit, literally "large-jawed."]

hao /how/ (*plural* **hao**) *n.* **1. SUBUNIT OF VIETNAMESE CURRENCY** a minor currency unit of Vietnam, ten of which are worth one dong. **2. COIN WORTH A HAO** a coin worth one hao [Mid-20thC. From Vietnamese.]

hao·le /hówlee/ *n.* somebody, especially a white person, who lives in Hawaii but is not a Polynesian [Mid-19thC. From Hawaiian.] —**hao·le** *adj.*

hap[1] /hap/ *n.* **HAPPENING** a happening or occurrence (*archaic*) ■ *vi.* (**happed, hap·ping, haps**) **HAPPEN** to happen or occur (*archaic*) [13thC. From Old Norse *happ.*]

hap[2] /hap/ *n. Scotland* **COVERING** something used to cover a person or bed, e.g., a cloak or comforter ■ *vt.* (**happed, hap·ping, haps**) *Scotland, U.S.* **WEAR WARM CLOTHES** to wrap up in warm clothes (*regional*) [13thC. Origin uncertain: perhaps from Scandinavian.]

ha·pax le·go·me·non /hà paks lə gómmə nòn, -gómmənən/ (*plural* **ha·pax le·go·me·na** /-gómmənə/) *n.* a word of which there is only one recorded use [Mid-17thC. From Greek, "said only once."]

ha'pen·ny /háyp'nee/ (*plural* **-nies**) *n. U.K.* = **half-penny** [Mid-16thC. Contraction.]

hap·haz·ard /hap házzərd/ *adj.* happening or done in a way that has not been planned [Late 16thC. From HAP[1] + HAZARD, literally "hazard of chance."] —**hap·haz·ard·ly** *adv.* —**hap·haz·ard·ness** *n.*

haph·ta·rah *n.* JUDAISM = **haftarah**

hapl- *prefix.* = **haplo-** (*used before vowels*)

hap·less /hápləss/ *adj.* unlucky or unfortunate —**hap·less·ly** *adv.* —**hap·less·ness** *n.*

hap·lite /há plìt/ *n.* = **aplite** —**hap·lit·ic** /ha plíttik/ *adj.*

haplo- *prefix.* **1.** single ○ *haplology* **2.** haploid ○ *haplont* [From Greek *haplous.* Ultimately from an Indo-European word that is also the ancestor of English *simple.*]

hap·log·ra·phy /hap lóggrəfee/ *n.* the accidental omission of a letter or syllable that should be repeated, e.g., "mispell" for "misspell" [Late 19thC]

hap·loid /háp lòyd/ *adj.* **hap·loid, hap·loid·ic WITH UNPAIRED CHROMOSOMES** having a single set of unpaired chromosomes ■ *n.* **ORGANISM WITH UNPAIRED CHROMOSOMES** a cell or organism with a single set of unpaired chromosomes [Early 20thC]

hap·lol·o·gy /hap lólləjee/ *n.* the accidental omission of one or more repeated syllables or sounds when speaking [Late 19thC] —**hap·lo·log·ic** /hàplə lójjik/ *adj.*

hap·lont /há plònt/ *n.* an organism, especially an algal plant, that is haploid at one stage of its life cycle [Early 20thC. Coined from HAPLOID + -ONT.] —**hap·lon·tic** /ha pláwntik/ *adj.*

hap·lo·sis /ha plóssiss/ *n.* the production of haploids during cell division (**meiosis**) [Coined from HAPLOID + -OSIS]

hap·ly /hápplee/ *adv.* used to express the possibility or hope that something is or will be the case (*archaic*) ○ *"I will kiss thy lips; haply some poison yet doth hang on them"* (William Shakespeare, *Romeo and Juliet*; 1594)

hap·pen /hápp'n/ (**-pened, -pen·ing, -pens**) *v.* **1.** *vi.* **OCCUR** to take place ○ *How did it happen?* **2.** *vt.* **DO SOMETHING BY CHANCE** to do something by chance and without a previous plan ○ *If you happen to see him, give him these keys.* **3.** *vi.* **AFFECT SOMEBODY** to affect somebody or something, especially in an unpleasant way ○ *If anything happens to me, you'll regret it.* **4.** *vi.* **OCCUR BY CHANCE** to occur or exist by chance [14thC. Formed from HAP[1].]

happen along, hap·pen by *vi.* to appear or pass by chance or unexpectedly (*informal*)

happen on *vt.* to discover or encounter something or somebody by chance

happen upon *vt.* = **happen on**

hap·pen·chance /hápp'n chàns/ *n.* = **happenstance** [Mid-20thC. Alteration of HAPPENSTANCE.]

hap·pen·ing /háppəning/ *n.* **1. OCCURRENCE** something that occurs **2. ARTISTIC PERFORMANCE** an improvised or informal performance or demonstration, often dramatic in form and using audience participation (*informal*) ■ *adj.* **FASHIONABLE** at the forefront of what is fashionable and exciting (*informal*)

hap·pen·stance /háppən stàns/ *n.* a chance occurrence or event [Late 19thC. Blend of HAPPENING and CIRCUMSTANCE.]

hap·pi coat /háppee-/ *n.* an open Japanese jacket that has wide loose sleeves and is usually tied with a sash, or a fashion garment resembling this [Late 19thC. *Happi* from Japanese.]

hap·pi·ly /háppilee/ *adv.* **1. FORTUNATELY** used to indicate that something that could have been difficult or disastrous is luckily the reverse ○ *Happily, no one was hurt.* **2. WILLINGLY** with willingness ○ *I'd happily contribute.* **3. IN A HAPPY WAY** in a pleased, contented, or joyful way

hap·py /háppee/ (**-pi·er, -pi·est**) *adj.* **1. FEELING PLEASURE** feeling or showing pleasure, contentment, or joy ○ *happy smiling faces* **2. CAUSING PLEASURE** causing or characterized by pleasure, contentment, or joy ○ *a happy childhood* **3. SATISFIED** feeling satisfied that something is right or has been done right ○ *Are you happy with your performance?* **4. WILLING** willing to do something ○ *I'd be only too happy to help.* **5. FORTUNATE** resulting in something pleasant or welcome ○ *a happy coincidence* **6. TIPSY** slightly drunk (*informal*) **7. USED IN GREETINGS** used in formulae to express a hope that somebody will enjoy a special day or holiday ○ *Happy birthday!* **8. TOO READY TO USE SOMETHING** inclined to use a particular thing too readily or be too enthusiastic about a particular thing (*used in combination*) ○ *trigger-happy* [14thC. Formed from HAP[1].] —**hap·pi·ness** *n.*

WORD KEY: SYNONYMS

See Synonyms at ***lucky***.

hap·py e·vent *n. U.K.* the birth of a baby (*informal*)

hap·py-go-luck·y *adj.* tending not to worry about the future

hap·py hard·core *n.* uplifting hardcore music, often achieving its emotional effect by the use of piano riffs over straightforward rhythms

hap·py hour *n.* a period of time, usually in the late afternoon or early evening, during which a bar serves alcoholic drinks at reduced prices

hap·py hunt·ing ground *n.* **1. HUNTING AND FEASTING PARADISE** among some Native North American peoples, a place of peace and abundance to which people go after death **2. PLACE WITH ABUNDANT SUPPLY** a place that provides plenty of something desired

hap·py me·di·um *n.* a satisfying compromise

Haps·burg /háps bùrg, haáps bòorg/, **Habs·burg** *n.* a member of a German royal family, prominent between the 13th and 20th centuries in Europe, that included rulers of the Holy Roman Empire, Spain, and Austria-Hungary

hap·ten /háp tèn/, **hap·tene** /háp tèen/ *n.* an antigen that can stimulate production of antibodies only in combination with a specific protein [Early 20thC. Formed from Greek *haptein* "to fasten."]

hap·tic /háptik/ *adj.* relating to the sense of touch [Late 19thC. From Greek *haptikos,* from *haptesthai* "to grasp, touch," from *haptein* "to fasten."]

hap·to·glo·bin /hàptə glóbin/ *n.* any of several plasma proteins that combine with free hemoglobin in the bloodstream [Mid-20thC. Coined from Greek *haptein* "to fasten" + GLOBIN.]

hap·to·trop·ism /hàp tóttrə pìzzəm/ *n.* BIOL = **thigmotropism** [Late 19thC. Coined from Greek *haptein* "to fasten" + -TROPISM.]

ha·ra-ki·ri /hèrrə kéeree/ *n.* a traditional form of suicide, sometimes ritually performed as a point of honor in Japan, involving disembowelment with a sword [Mid-19thC. From Japanese, literally "belly-cutting."]

ha·rangue /hə ráng/ *vti.* (**-rangued, -rangu·ing, -rangues**) **ADDRESS SOMEBODY LOUDLY AND FORCEFULLY** to criticize or question somebody or try to persuade somebody to do something in a forceful angry way ■ *n.* **FORCEFUL CRITICISM OR PERSUASION** a loud, forceful, and angry speech criticizing somebody or trying to persuade somebody to do something [15thC. Via French from medieval Latin *harenga* of uncertain origin: possibly ultimately from prehistoric Germanic.] —**ha·rangu·er** *n.*

Ha·ra·re /hə raáree/ capital city of Zimbabwe, located in the northeastern part of the country. Population: 1,184,169 (1992).

ha·rass /hérrəss, hə ráss/ (**-rassed, -rass·ing, -rass·es**) *vt.* **1. KEEP BOTHERING OR ATTACKING SOMEBODY** to persistently annoy, attack, or bother somebody **2. EXHAUST AN ENEMY WITH REPEATED ATTACKS** to exhaust an enemy by repeatedly attacking [Early 17thC. From French *harasser,* from *harer* "to set a dog on (by crying "hare")," ultimately of uncertain origin: perhaps from Old High German *haren.*] —**ha·rass·er** *n.* —**ha·rass·ment** *n.*

WORD KEY: USAGE

See Usage note at ***embarrass.***

Har·bin /haár bèen, bín/ capital city of Heilongjiang Province in northeastern China. Population: 2,830,000 (1991).

har·bin·ger /haárbinjər/ *n.* **SOMEBODY OR SOMETHING THAT ANNOUNCES SOMETHING** somebody or something that foreshadows or anticipates a future event ■ *vt.* (**-gered, -ger·ing, -gers**) **HERALD SOMETHING** to herald or foreshadow somebody or something [12thC. From Old French *herberger,* from *herbergier* "to provide shelter for an army," ultimately from prehistoric Germanic words meaning "army" and "protect."]

har·bor /haárbər/ *n.* **1. PORT** part of a body of water near a coast in which ships can anchor safely (*often used in placenames*) **2. PLACE OF REFUGE** any place that is safe and sheltered ■ *v.* (**-bored, -bor·ing, -bors**) **1.** *vt.* **KEEP SOMETHING IN MIND** to continue to think privately about an emotion or thought for a long time ○ *had harbored a secret fear of the dark since childhood* **2.** *vt.* **SHELTER SOMEBODY** to provide somebody with shelter or sanctuary **3.** *vti.* NAUT **KEEP A SHIP IN HARBOR** to take shelter in a harbor, or shelter a ship in a harbor [Old English *herebeorg* "lodging," literally "army shelter," ultimately from a prehistoric Germanic word that is also the ancestor of English *harbinger*] —**har·bor·er** *n.* —**har·bor·less** *adj.*

har·bor·age /haárbərij/ *n.* = **harbor** *n.* **1**, **harbor** *n.* **2**

har·bor mas·ter *n.* an official who supervises and administers the general activities of a port or harbor

har·bor seal *n.* a small seal that is grayish black with paler spots and lives on the northern coasts of North America, Europe, and Asia. Latin name: *Phoca vitulina.*

har·bour *n., vti., vti.* U.K. = **harbor**

hard /haard/ *adj.* **1. NOT EASILY BENT** firm, stiff, or rigid and not easily cut, pierced, or bent ○ *a hard mattress* **2. DIFFICULT OR AWKWARD** difficult or awkward to do or achieve ○ *a hard decision* **3. INVOLVING EFFORT** involving a great deal of labor or effort ○ *a hard climb* **4. PERFORMING ENERGETICALLY** acting or producing something with energy or industriousness ○ *a hard worker* **5. MIGHTY** using a lot of force or violence **6. DEMANDING AND STRICT** making inflexible and heavy demands ○ *a hard taskmaster* **7. PROBLEMATIC** difficult and full of problems ○ *a hard life* **8. UNSYMPATHETIC** showing little or no sympathy, compassion, or gentleness ○ *She's as hard as nails.* **9. RESENTFUL** marked by resentment or bitterness ○ *no hard feelings* **10. REAL OR TRUE** demonstrably real, true, or certain ○ *cold, hard facts* **11. DIFFICULT TO UNDERSTAND** difficult to understand or explain **12.** POL **RADICAL** politically radical or extreme ○ *the hard left* **13. SEVERE** marked by weather conditions such as extreme cold or severe storms ○ *a hard winter* **14. VISUALLY HARSH** harsh and glaring to the sight **15. TOUGHENED** rough or leathery, and unyielding ○ *hard skin* **16.** CHEM **CONTAINING MINERAL SALTS** containing mineral salts and preventing soap from lathering well **17. PENETRATING** seeming to penetrate and discover intentions or thoughts ○ *a hard stare* **18. FIRM OR CRISP IN TEXTURE** having a crisp, firm, or stale crust or texture **19. ERECT** stiff and erect (*informal*) **20.** PHYS **READILY ABLE TO PENETRATE SUBSTANCES** used to describe radiation, especially high frequency X-rays, that has a high energy and is thus readily able to penetrate substances including metals, or relating to this ○ *hard vacuum* **21.** FIN **STRONG AND STABLE** stable in value and in demand by currency traders **22.** FIN **IN CASH** in the form of coins and paper money rather than, e.g., checks **23.** BEVERAGES **HIGH IN ALCOHOL** having a high alcoholic content, especially alcohol produced by distillation **24.** DRUGS **ADDICTIVE AND DANGEROUS TO HEALTH** highly addictive and particularly dangerous to the health **25.** PHON **PRONOUNCED LIKE "K" OR "G"** used to describe the consonants "c" and "g" when they are pronounced with a "k" sound, as in "come," and a "g" sound, as in "go." ◊ **soft** ■ *adv.* **1. FORCEFULLY** with a lot of force ○ *hit the ball hard* **2. INTENSELY** to an extreme degree ○ *pulled the truck over hard* **3. ENERGETICALLY** with vigor and energy or industriousness ○ *worked hard* **4. WITH CONCENTRATION** with great mental concentration **5. WITH DIFFICULTY** with effort and great difficulty **6. COMPACTLY** into a solid or compact state ○ *set hard* **7. PAINFULLY**

in a way that causes anguish or hardship ○ *hit hard by the recession* **8.** SLOWLY slowly and with difficulty ○ *hatred that dies hard* [Old English *heard.* Ultimately meaning "resistant to pressure," from an Indo-European word meaning "strength," which is also the ancestor of English *democracy.*] ◇ **be hard on somebody 1.** to treat somebody severely **2.** to be unfortunate for somebody ◇ **be hard put to do something** to find it difficult to do something ◇ **hard by** close by

WORD KEY: SYNONYMS

hard, difficult, strenuous, tough, arduous, laborious

CORE MEANING: requiring effort or exertion

hard a general word used to describe something that requires effort or exertion to do or achieve; **difficult** similar in meaning to *hard,* but suggesting more complexity and a need for skill or patience; **strenuous** used to describe something that requires a great deal of physical effort and stamina; **tough** used to describe something that is extremely difficult or strenuous; **arduous** a fairly formal word used to describe something that requires great energy, effort, and often physical exertion to do or achieve; **laborious** a fairly formal word, emphasizing the need for physical effort and great exertion in order to do something, and also suggesting tedium.

WORD KEY: CULTURAL NOTE

Hard Times, a novel by English writer Charles Dickens (1854) was the story of the loveless upbringing of Tom and Louisa Gradgrind to contrast the soullessness of utilitarianism, as personified by their father Thomas Gradgrind, with the natural warmth and generosity of the human spirit, symbolized by their adopted sister Sissy Jupe, a member of a traveling circus.

hard-and-fast *adj.* unable to be changed or adapted [Originally a nautical phrase referring to a ship run aground]

hard-ass *n.* somebody who is perceived as inflexible and uncompromising (*slang offensive*) —**hard-assed** *adj.*

hard·back /haárd bàk/ *n.* a book with a rigid cover

hard·ball /haárd bàwl/ *n.* **1.** = **baseball 2.** RUTHLESS BEHAVIOR tough or ruthless behavior, especially in politics or business (*informal*) ○ *These guys play hardball.*

hard·bit·ten *adj.* tough and experienced

hard·board /haárd bàwrd/ *n.* thin stiff sheets of compressed sawdust and wood chips, often used in constructing walls

hard-boil (**hard-boiled, hard-boil·ing, hard-boils**) *vt.* to boil an egg until both the white and the yolk are firm

hard-boiled *adj.* **1.** COOKED UNTIL FIRM used to describe an egg boiled until the yolk and white are firm **2.** UNSENTIMENTAL tough, realistic, and unsentimental (*informal*)

hard·bound /haárd bòwnd/ *adj.* bound as a book in a stiff cover

hard ci·der *n.* apple juice that has an alcoholic content

hard coal *n.* = **anthracite**

hard cop·y *n.* data from a computer that is printed out, usually on paper, rather than read from the screen

hard core *n.* **1.** COMMITTED NUCLEUS OF A GROUP the most committed, faithful, and active members of a group or organization **2.** MUSIC TYPE OF FAST ROCK MUSIC a type of dance music notable for its repetitive rhythmic synthesized sounds and fast tempo **3.** *U.K.* TRANSP FOUNDATION FOR ROADS OR PAVING stones and other rubble used to form a foundation under roads or paving

hard-core *adj.* **1.** UNCOMPROMISING uncompromising and committed **2.** SHOWING EXPLICIT SEX depicting sexual acts in an explicit way

hard·cov·er /haárd kuvər/ *n.* = **hardback**

hard disk, hard drive *n.* a rigid disk inside a computer that is magnetized to hold a large quantity of computer data and programs

hard-edge *adj.* used to describe a U.S. style of abstract painting that arose in the 1960s and is marked by sharply outlined colored forms

hard·en /haárd'n/ (**-ened, -en·ing, -ens**) *v.* **1.** *vti.* BECOME OR MAKE HARD to become hard, firm, or solid, or make something become hard, firm, or solid ○ *The glue hardened overnight.* **2.** *vti.* MAKE OR BECOME LESS SYMPATHETIC to become or make somebody become more tough, callous, or unfeeling **3.** *vti.* MAKE OR BECOME MORE DETERMINED to become or make somebody become more determined and resolute **4.** *vti.* MAKE OR BECOME STRONGER to become or make somebody or something become stronger or more resistant **5.** *vi.* COMM STABILIZE to become stable after fluctuation ○ *Prices are hardening.*

harden off *vti.* to accustom a plant grown indoors to outdoor conditions by gradually exposing it to cold, wind, or sunlight before planting it out, or become accustomed to outdoor conditions in this way

hard·en·er /haárd'nər/ *n.* an ingredient or element that makes something hard, e.g., a substance added to paint to make it more durable

hard·en·ing of the ar·ter·ies *n.* loss of elasticity in the walls of the arteries, formerly believed to be a major cause of heart disease (*no longer used technically*)

hard-fist·ed *adj.* not generous with money

hard goods *npl.* COMM = **durables**

hard·hack /haárd hàk/ (*plural* **-hacks** *or* **-hack**) *n.* a North American shrub that belongs to the rose family and has short downy leaves and tapering clusters of small pink or white flowers. Latin name: *Spiraea tomentosa.* [Mid-19thC. Origin uncertain: perhaps literally "hard to hack," from HARD + HACK.]

hard·hand·ed /haárd hàndəd/ *adj.* showing little or no sympathy or pity —**hard·hand·ed·ness** *n.*

hard·hat /haárd hàt/ *n.* **1.** PROTECTIVE HELMET a helmet made of metal or plastic worn for protection by workers in a factory or on a construction site **2.** WORKER a construction worker (*informal*) **3.** CONSERVATIVE a politically very conservative patriot (*informal*)

hard·head /haárd hèd/ *n.* somebody who is strictly logical and unsentimental

hard·head·ed /haárd héddəd/ *adj.* **1.** REALISTIC behaving in a shrewd, tough, and logical way that is not influenced by emotions **2.** STUBBORN determined not to give in —**hard·head** *n.* —**hard·head·ed·ly** *adv.* —**hard·head·ed·ness** *n.*

hard·heart·ed /haárd haártəd/ *adj.* showing no sympathy for other people's feelings —**hard·heart·ed·ly** *adv.* —**hard·heart·ed·ness** *n.*

hard-hit·ting *adj.* direct and uncompromising ○ *a hard-hitting documentary*

har·di·hood /haárdi hòod/ *n.* **1.** RESOLUTENESS the quality of being tough and able to withstand difficulty or hard work **2.** AUDACITY bold audacity

Library of Congress

Warren G. Harding

Har·ding /haárding/, **Warren G.** (1865–1923) U.S. statesman and 29th President of the United States. A conservative Republican from Ohio elected on the promise of a "return to normalcy" after World War I, he presided (1921–23) over a federal administration distinguished primarily by its flagrant corruption. Full name **Warren Gamaliel Harding**

hard la·bor *n.* a sentence of compulsory work imposed in addition to a term of imprisonment

hard land·ing *n.* **1.** AIR UNCONTROLLED LANDING an uncontrolled landing by an aircraft or spacecraft that results in its being damaged or destroyed **2.** ECON ECONOMIC DOWNTURN AFTER SUCCESS a downward trend in economic activity after a period of expansion

hard·line /haárd lìn/ *adj.* inflexible and uncompromising —**hard·lin·er** *n.*

hard·ly /haárdlee/ CORE MEANING: an adverb with negative meaning, used to indicate that something is true or exists to a very minimal extent ○ *She lived so privately, hardly anyone even spoke to her.* ○ *Though we hardly knew him, we could sense his good humour.* ○ *I looked out of the window; it was hardly raining.*

adv. **1.** NOT indicates that something is almost entirely untrue or impossible ○ *We are hardly going to give up with success in view.* ○ *It's hardly likely that I would tell you.* **2.** ONLY WITH DIFFICULTY only with great awkwardness, difficulty, or embarrassment ○ *I was so shocked I could hardly speak.* **3.** SELDOM indicates that something seldom occurs (*used with a negative such as "without"*) ○ *Hardly a day passes without acclaim for this exciting new invention.* **4.** AS SOON AS indicates that one event follows quickly after another ○ *Hardly had I rung the bell when the bolt was shot back.* **5.** USED TO DISAGREE used to indicate surprise, disagreement or annoyance ○ *"I thought you were going at about sixty miles an hour.""Well, hardly. Maybe forty."* [13thC. Coined from HARD + -LY. Originally "vigorously, with energy," hence "not easily," hence "almost not."]

WORD KEY: USAGE

Grammar: ***Hardly,*** like *barely* and *scarcely,* has a negative force, rendering unnecessary the use of another negative in the clause or sentence: *I can [not: can't] hardly see you.* Note that *when* and not *than* is used in any continuation of the sentence: *Hardly [or barely or scarcely] had I begun to speak when [not than] she interrupted me.* (After *no sooner,* however, *than* is correct.) ***Hardly*** is limited to these special uses; the routine adverb from the adjective *hard* is *hard*: *They are all working hard to get ready for their exams.*

hard man *n.* a man who is perceived as vicious and ruthless, probably with criminal tendencies

hard ma·ple *n.* = **sugar maple**

hard mouth *n.* a horse's mouth that is insensitive to pressure from the bit, or a horse's ability to resist this pressure

hard·mouthed /haárd mòwthd, -mòwtht/ *adj.* used to describe a horse that fails to respond when the rider pulls on the bit in the horse's mouth

hard·ness /haárdnəss/ *n.* **1.** FIRMNESS, SOLIDITY, AND COMPACTNESS the state or quality of being firm, solid, and compact **2.** UNYIELDING TOUGHNESS the state or quality of being tough and unyielding **3.** CHEM WATER QUALITY the degree to which water contains mineral salts **4.** METALL, MEASURE DEGREE TO WHICH A METAL IS HARD the degree to which a metal may be scratched, abraded, indented, or machined, measured according to any of several scales

hard-nosed *adj.* tough, realistic, and unsentimental (*informal*)

hard-of-hear·ing *adj.* unable to hear as much as others do (*often considered offensive*)

hard-on *n.* an erect penis (*slang taboo*)

hard pal·ate *n.* the bony front portion of the roof of the mouth

hard·pan /haárd pàn/ *n.* a layer of hard matter, especially clay, that lies under soft soil and that plant roots cannot penetrate

hard-pressed *adj.* **1.** WITHOUT SUFFICIENT RESOURCES under a lot of pressure and without sufficient resources **2.** HAVING DIFFICULTY finding something very difficult

hard rock *n.* a form of rock music that has simple lyrics and a strong insistent beat, and that is usually very loud

hard·rock /haárd ràwk/ *adj. Can* relating to the extraction of minerals from igneous and metamorphic rocks by blasting or drilling

hard rub·ber *n.* rubber treated with sulfur to make it hard and stiff

hard sauce *n.* butter creamed with sugar and often flavored with brandy or whiskey, usually served with plum pudding

hard sci·ence *n.* any science in which data can be precisely quantified and theories tested. Physics, chemistry, geology, and astronomy are hard sciences.

hard·scrab·ble /haárd skràbb'l/ *adj.* not yielding or earning a return for hard effort (*informal*)

hard sell *n.* a direct, aggressive, and insistent way of selling or advertising. ◊ **soft sell**

hard-set *adj.* firmly or rigidly in place

hard-shell, hard-shelled *adj.* rigid and uncompromising in attitude

hard-shell clam *n.* = **quahog**

hard-shell crab *n.* a crab that has not recently shed its shell and as a result has a shell that is particularly tough

hard·ship /haárd shìp/ *n.* **1. DIFFICULTIES** difficulty or suffering caused by a lack of something, especially money **2. CAUSE OF HARDSHIP** something that causes hardship

hard·stand /haárd stànd/ *n.* a hard surface on which aircraft or heavy motor vehicles may be parked

hard stuff *n.* something that is intoxicating, addictive, and potentially very dangerous to the health (*informal*)

hard·tack /haárd tàk/ *n.* a hard thin unsalted bread or biscuit formerly eaten aboard ships and as military rations

hard-times to·ken *n.* any of several U.S. copper tokens, issued between 1834 and 1841, that carried an advertising or political message and served as currency during coin shortages

hard up *adj.* short of money (*informal*)

hard·ware /haárd wàir/ *n.* **1. TOOLS AND IMPLEMENTS** tools and implements that are typically made of metal, e.g., hinges, screws, and hammers **2.** MIL **MILITARY WEAPONS** heavy military weapons and equipment **3.** COMPUT **COMPUTER EQUIPMENT AND PERIPHERALS** the equipment and devices that make up a computer system as opposed to the programs that are used on it **4.** ARMS **GUN** a gun or guns (*informal*)

hard wheat *n.* a kind of wheat with hard kernels and a high gluten content that is used to make the flour for bread

hard·wire /haárd wír/ (**-wired, -wir·ing, -wires**) *vt.* to build a function into a computer with hardware rather than programming

hard·wood /haárd wòòd/ *n.* **WOOD LIKE OAK** wood from a broad-leaved tree, e.g., oak, ash, or birch, as opposed to from a conifer ■ *adj.* **TREE PRODUCING HARDWOOD** a tree that produces hardwood

hard-work·ing *adj.* tending to work industriously

har·dy /haárdee/ (**-di·er, -di·est**) *adj.* **1. ROBUST** sufficiently robust to withstand fatigue, hardship, or adverse physical conditions **2.** PLANTS **NOT SENSITIVE TO COLD** used to describe plants that are able to live outdoors during the winter ○ *a hardy shrub* **3. COURAGEOUS** courageous and daring [13thC. From French *hardi*, from *hardir* "to become bold," from a prehistoric Germanic word that is also the ancestor of English *hard*.] — **har·di·ly** *adv.* —**har·di·ness** *n.*

Har·dy /haárdee/, **Oliver** (1892–1957) U.S. actor. He appeared with Stan Laurel in a series of classic movies in the 1920s and 1930s.

Har·dy, Thomas (1840–1928) British novelist and poet. He wrote brooding novels of the British West Country including *The Mayor of Casterbridge* (1886), and from the 1890s devoted himself to poetry.

Har·dy-Wein·berg law /haárdi wín burg-/, **Har·dy-Wein·berg dis·tri·bu·tion** *n.* a principle of genetics stating that gene frequencies remain constant from one generation to the next if mating is random and there are no outside influences such as mutation and immigration [Mid-20thC. Named for the British mathematician G. H. *Hardy* (1877–1947) and the German physician Wilhelm *Weinberg* (1862–1937), who each formulated the law independently in 1908.]

Hare

hare /hair/ (*plural* **hare** *or* **hares**) *n.* a fast-running animal that resembles a rabbit but is larger, has longer ears and legs, and does not burrow. Genus: *Lepus.* [Old English *hara*, from a prehistoric Germanic word of uncertain origin: probably ultimately from an Indo-European word meaning "gray," from its color]

hare and hounds, hare and hounds race *n.* an outdoor game in which one group of players, the hounds, follow a trail of scattered scraps of paper left by another group of players, the hares. The hares attempt to reach a designated point before the hounds catch them.

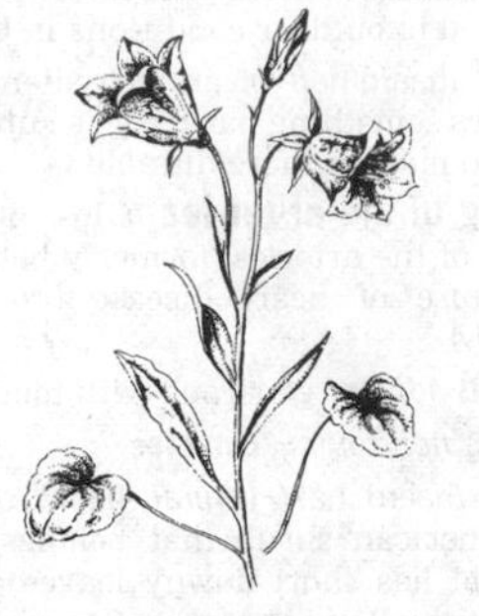

Harebell

hare·bell /háir bèl/ *n.* a low-growing plant found in northern temperate regions that has narrow leaves and blue bell-shaped flowers. Latin name: *Campanula rotundiflora.* [Perhaps because the plant grows in places frequented by hares]

hare·brained /háir brāynd/ *adj.* impractical and likely to fail (*insult*)

Ha·re Krish·na /haáree-/ *n.* **1. HINDU RELIGIOUS GROUP** a religious group that bases its practice on worship of the god Krishna **2. MEMBER OF HARE KRISHNA** somebody who is a member of Hare Krishna [Late 20thC. From Sanskrit, "O Lord Krishna," a chant used by devotees.]

hare·lip /háir lìp/ *n.* an offensive term for a facial deformity, now rare, in which somebody born with the upper lip in two parts has had the separation incompletely rectified by surgery. It is often associated with a cleft palate. (*offensive*) —**hare·lipped** *adj.*

har·em /háirəm/ *n.* **1. WOMEN'S PART OF A HOUSE** the separate private quarters reserved for wives and concubines in a Muslim home **2. GROUP OF WOMEN** the wives and concubines who live in a harem **3.** ZOOL **GROUP OF ANIMALS** a group of female animals of the same species associated for breeding purposes with one male **4. WOMEN FOLLOWERS** any group of women admirers or followers (*humorous*) (*sometimes considered offensive*) [Mid-17thC. Via Turkish from, ultimately, Arabic *ḥaram* "prohibited (place), women's quarters."]

har·em pants *npl.* women's pants made of soft thin cloth and having wide legs that are gathered at the ankle

hare's-foot (*plural* **hare's-foot** *or* **hare's-foots**), **hare's-foot clo·ver** *n.* a clover that grows on sandy soil and has white or pink flowers almost hidden by its calyx. Latin name: *Trefolium arvense.* [From the soft hair around the flowers, giving the plant the appearance of a hare's foot]

hares·tail /háirz tàyl/ *n.* a variety of cotton grass that grows on moors and has a single flower head [From the similarity of the plant to a hare's tail]

hare·wood /háir wòòd/ *n.* the greenish-colored wood of the sycamore maple, used in making furniture [Late 17thC. *Hare* by folk etymology from German dialect *Ehre*, from, ultimately, Latin *acer* "maple, sycamore."]

har·i·cot /hérri kō, -kòt/ *n.* **1. WHITE BEAN** a small white oval dried bean, cooked and eaten as a vegetable **2. PLANT PRODUCING EDIBLE SEEDS** a bean plant whose seeds are dried and stored as haricots. Latin name: *Phaseolus vulgaris.* [Mid-17thC. From French, of uncertain origin: probably from Nahuatl *ayacotli*.]

Har·i·jan /hérri jàn/ *n.* a member of a class of people in India whose touch was formerly considered to defile a Hindu of a higher caste [Mid-20thC. From Sanskrit, literally "God's people," an appellation introduced by M. K. Gandhi.]

ha·ris·sa /hə rízzə/ *n.* a hot spicy oily paste used as an ingredient in North African and Middle Eastern cooking or served as an accompaniment for dishes, especially for couscous

hark /haark/ (**harked, hark·ing, harks**) *vi.* to listen to something or somebody (*literary or humorous*) [12thC. Origin uncertain: probably from assumed Old English *heorcnian*, from a prehistoric Germanic word that is also the ancestor of English *hearken* and *hear*.]

hark back *vi.* **1. REVERT TO SOMETHING** to think or speak again about something from the past **2. BE SIMILAR TO A PAST THING** to be similar in some respects to something in the past

har·ken *vi.* = **hearken**

Hark·ness /haárknəss/, **Edward Stephen** (1874–1940) U.S. philanthropist, who gave funds to U.S. and European educational and medical institutions.

Har·lan /haárlən/, **John Marshall** (1833–1911) U.S. Supreme Court justice. He was a Kentucky politician before his appointment to the Supreme Court (1877–1911).

Har·lan, John Marshall (1899–1971) U.S. Supreme Court justice. The grandson of John Marshall Harlan, he held government positions before his tenure on the Supreme Court (1955–71).

Har·lem /haárləm/ district of New York City, on Manhattan Island, originally named Nieuw Haarlem by Dutch settlers in 1658

Har·lem Globe·trot·ters *npl.* a U.S. basketball team that tours widely to play exhibition matches during which the team displays skilled comic maneuvers

har·le·quin /haárləkwin, haárləkin/ *n.* **CLOWN** a clown or buffoon ■ *adj.* **HAVING MULTICOLORED SHAPES** varied in color and having a pattern of irregular shapes [Late 16thC. Via obsolete French from *Hellequin*, legendary leader of night-raiding demon horsemen.]

Har·le·quin *n.* **Har·le·quin, har·le·quin** a comic dramatic character featured in the Italian commedia dell'arte and the English harlequinade, usually shown wearing multicolored diamond-patterned tights and a black mask

har·le·quin·ade /haárləkwə náyd, haárləkə-/ *n.* **1. ENTERTAINMENT FEATURING A HARLEQUIN** a pantomime, play, or other performance featuring a harlequin as a character **2. CLOWNISH BEHAVIOR** the action of clowning around or acting in a silly way

har·le·quin bug *n.* a black bug of North and Central America that has black and red markings and feeds on cabbages and similar plants. Latin name: *Murgantia histrionica.*

har·le·quin duck *n.* a small duck native to North America, Iceland, and eastern Siberia that dives for its food and has blue and red plumage with black and white markings. Latin name: *Histrionicus histrionicus.*

har·lot /haárlət/ *n.* a prostitute (*archaic or literary*) [13thC. From Old French, "vagabond, rogue, beggar," of unknown origin.]

Har·low /haárlō/, **Jean** (1911–37) U.S. actor. Her platinum-blond hair and frankly sexual screen presence characterized her movies, including *Dinner at Eight* (1933). Real name **Harlean Carpenter**

harm /haarm/ *n.* **DAMAGE OR INJURY** physical or mental damage or injury ■ *vt.* (**harmed, harm·ing, harms**) **INJURE SOMEBODY OR SOMETHING** to injure or damage somebody or something physically, mentally, or morally [Old English *hearm*, from a prehistoric Germanic word meaning "harm, grief"]

WORD KEY: SYNONYMS

harm, damage, hurt, injure, wound

CORE MEANING: to weaken or impair something or somebody

harm a general term meaning to cause physical, emotional, or mental impairment or deterioration of health in living things. It can also refer to weakening or impairing something such as a system; **damage** a slightly narrower term meaning to weaken or spoil objects or plants, not usually used with reference to people or animals. It can also refer to weakening or impairing something abstract such as a chance or somebody's reputation; **hurt** a general word meaning to cause pain and physical damage to people and animals. It can also mean upsetting or offending somebody; **injure** to cause physical damage to a person or animal, usually serious enough to cause at least a temporary loss of function or use. Like *damage*, it can also apply to abstract things such as somebody's reputation or pride; **wound** a narrower term than *hurt* meaning to cause physical damage to somebody, especially as a result of the use of a weapon, a violent incident, or a serious accident. It can also refer to upsetting or offending somebody.

har·mat·tan /haármə taán, haar mátt'n/ *n.* an extremely dry dusty wind from the Sahara that blows toward the western coast of Africa, especially between November and March [Late 17thC. From Twi *haramata,* of uncertain origin: possibly from Arabic *ḥaram* "evil or prohibited (thing)" (source of *harem*).]

harm·ful /haármfəl/ *adj.* causing damage or injury ○ *The plant is harmful to humans.* —**harm·ful·ly** *adv.* —**harm·ful·ness** *n.*

harm·less /haármləss/ *adj.* **1. UNOBJECTIONABLE** not likely to cause offense or upset ○ *Don't worry; he's harmless enough.* **2. NOT DANGEROUS** not likely to cause damage or injury —**harm·less·ly** *adv.* —**harm·less·ness** *n.*

har·mon·ic /haar mónnik/ *adj.* **1. PRODUCED BY HARMONY** relating to, produced, or marked by harmony **2. RELATING TO INTEGRAL MULTIPLE OF FREQUENCY** used to describe a frequency that is an integral multiple of a fundamental frequency ■ *n.* **1. MULTIPLE OF A FUNDAMENTAL FREQUENCY** a single oscillation having a frequency that is an integral multiple of a fundamental frequency, e.g. 220 Hz and 330 Hz are both harmonics of 110 Hz **2. OVERTONE ON A STRINGED INSTRUMENT** an overtone produced on an instrument, e.g., by lightly touching a vibrating string at a point where the string to either side will continue to vibrate [Late 16thC. Via Latin *harmonicus* from Greek *harmonika* "theory of music," from *harmonia* (see HARMONY).]

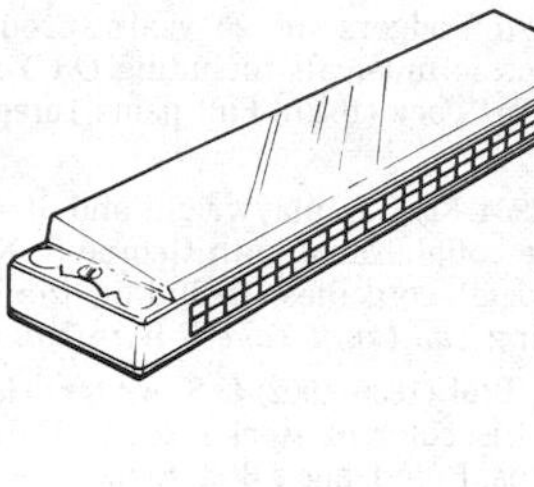

Harmonica

har·mon·i·ca /haar mónnikə/ *n.* a musical instrument consisting of a small narrow metal case containing a set of metal reeds that are made to sound by exhaling or inhaling air past them. ◊ **glass harmonica** [Mid-18thC. Via Italian *armonica* from Latin *harmonicus* HARMONIC.]

har·mon·ic a·nal·y·sis *n.* MATH the representation of a periodic function by a series of sines and cosines, especially by a Fourier series

har·mon·ic dis·tor·tion *n.* the unwanted presence of distorted frequencies at the output of an electronic device, e.g., the output of an audio amplifier

har·mon·ic mean *n.* the reciprocal of the arithmetic mean of the reciprocals of a finite set of numbers

har·mon·ic mo·tion *n.* a periodic vibration, e.g., of a violin string or pendulum, that has a single frequency or an even multiple of one or is symmetric about a point of equilibrium

har·mon·ic pro·gres·sion *n.* any sequence of numbers whose reciprocals form an arithmetic progression, e.g., 1/2, 1/5, 1/8, 1/11

har·mon·ics *n.* the branch of science that deals with the physical properties of musical sound (*takes a singular verb*)

har·mon·ic se·ries *n.* any infinite series of numbers constructed by adding the numbers in a harmonic progression to one another, e.g., 1/2+1/5+1/8+ 1/11

har·mo·ni·ous /haar mṓnee əss/ *adj.* **1. RELATING TO HARMONY** relating to or sounding in harmony **2. BLENDING PLEASANTLY** having a pleasing combination of parts or colors **3. SHOWING ACCORD** characterized by friendly agreement or accord —**har·mo·ni·ous·ly** *adv.* —**har·mo·ni·ous·ness** *n.*

har·mo·nist /haármənist/ *n.* **1. MAKER OF HARMONY** somebody who creates musical harmony well **2. SOMEBODY STUDYING PARALLEL TEXTS** somebody who researches and tries to find similarities in parallel texts, especially the four Gospels —**har·mo·nis·tic** /haármə nístik/ *adj.* —**har·mo·nis·ti·cal·ly** /-kəlee/ *adv.*

har·mo·ni·um /haar mṓnee əm/ *n.* a type of organ in which a pair of bellows operated by the player's feet blow air into the reeds to produce sound [Mid-19thC. Via French from either Latin *harmonia* "harmony" or Greek *harmonios* "harmonious."]

har·mo·nize /haármə nīz/ (**-nized, -niz·ing, -niz·es**) *v.* **1.** *vti.* **BLEND PLEASINGLY** to blend pleasingly, be in a pleasant combination, or make things combine pleasantly **2.** *vt.* **MAKE SYSTEMS SIMILAR** to make rules, regulations, or systems similar or in accord with each other **3.** *vt.* **ADD HARMONY TO A MELODY** to provide a harmony for a melody **4.** *vi.* **PLAY IN HARMONY** to sing or play musical instruments together in harmony —**har·mo·niz·a·ble** /haármə nīzəb'l/ *adj.* —**har·mo·ni·za·tion** /haàrməni záysh'n/ *n.* —**har·mo·niz·er** /haármə nīzər/ *n.*

har·mo·ny /haármənee/ (*plural* **-nies**) *n.* **1. PLEASING COMBINATION OF SOUNDS** a pleasing combination of musical sounds **2. NOTES SUNG OR PLAYED TOGETHER** any combination of notes that are sung or played at the same time. Changing harmony is one of the most characteristic features of Western music, providing momentum and richness to the melody. **3. STUDY OF CHORDS IN MUSIC** the study of the way in which musical chords are constructed and function in relation to one another **4. HAPPY AGREEMENT** a situation in which there is agreement **5. PLEASANTNESS IN THE ARRANGEMENT OF PARTS** a pleasing effect produced by an arrangement of things, parts, or colors **6. STUDY OF TEXTS** a study or collation of the similarities in parallel texts, particularly the four Gospels **7. PARALLEL TEXT** a book or manuscript in which several versions of the same text, often a biblical text, are laid out in parallel columns ○ *a Gospel harmony* [14thC. Via French *harmonie* from Greek *harmonia* "agreement, concord," from *harmozein* "to fit together."]

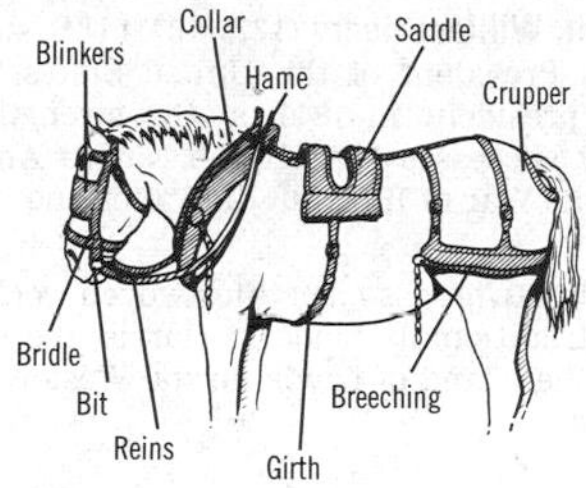

Harness

har·ness /haárnəss/ *n.* **1. LEATHER STRAPS FOR AN ANIMAL** a set of straps fixed together and fitted to an animal such as a horse so that it can be attached to a cart or carriage for pulling **2. STRAPS FITTED TO A PERSON** an arrangement of straps fitted to somebody to fasten the person to something or to keep the person in position **3. ARMOR** the armor worn by a soldier, or by a mounted soldier and the soldier's horse (*archaic*) ■ *vt.* (**-nessed, -ness·ing, -ness·es**) **1. FIT AN ANIMAL WITH A HARNESS** to put a harness on an animal **2. GET CONTROL OF AND USE SOMETHING** to gain control of something and use it for some purpose **3. FIT SOMEBODY WITH ARMOR** to equip somebody with armor (*archaic*) [13thC. Via Old French *harneis* from assumed Old Norse *hernest* "provisions for an army," from *herr* "army."] —**har·ness·er** *n.* ◇ **in harness 1.** doing your usual work **2.** working together cooperatively with a person or group

har·ness hitch *n.* a knot with one loop and no free ends, used in tying harnesses

har·ness horse *n.* a horse that is used to pull a vehicle or for racing

har·ness race *n.* a horse race in which trotters or pacers pull small carriages around a course wearing special harnesses to ensure that they move as required by rule

Har·ney Peak /haárni-/ mountain in the Black Hills, southwestern South Dakota, and the highest point in the state. Height: 7,242 ft./2,207 m.

harp /haarp/ *n.* **1. TRIANGULAR STRINGED INSTRUMENT** a triangular-shaped instrument that has a curved neck and strings stretched between the neck and the body, at an angle to the sound box. The modern orchestral harp is large and played by a seated player. **2. HARMONICA** a reed harmonica (*informal*) ■ *vi.* (**harped, harp·ing, harps**) **PLAY THE HARP** to play the harp [Old English *hearpe,* from prehistoric Germanic] —**harp·er** *n.* —**harp·ist** *n.*

harp on *vti.* to repeat or stress something in a way that becomes tiresome

Harp

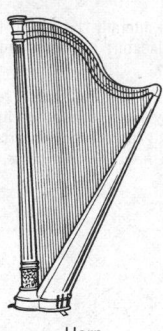

Har·pers Fer·ry /haárpərz férree/ historic town and tourist resort in eastern West Virginia, situated at the confluence of the Potomac and Shenandoah rivers. Population: 308 (1990).

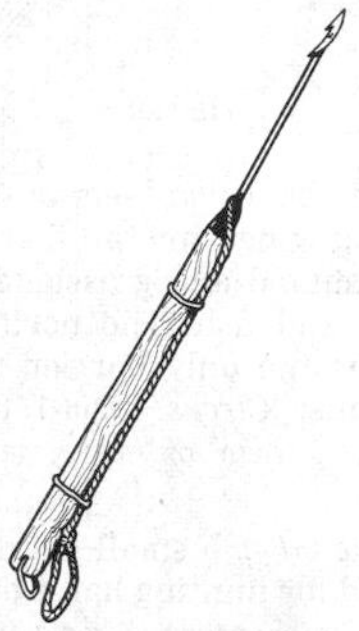

Harpoon

har·poon /haar pṓon/ *n.* **WEAPON SIMILAR TO SPEAR** a long pointed piece of metal that is attached to a cord and thrown or fired from a gun in order to capture whales or other large sea animals ■ *vt.* (**-pooned, -poon·ing, -poons**) **CATCH SOMETHING USING HARPOON** to catch a whale or other large sea animal using a harpoon [Early 17thC. From Old French *harpon* "clamp," from *harpe* "dog's claw, clamp" from, ultimately, Greek *harpē* "sickle."] —**har·poon·eer** /haàr poo néer/ *n.* —**har·poon·er** /haar pṓonər/ *n.*

harp seal *n.* a brownish-gray earless seal that is whitish when very young and lives in coastal regions and on ice floes of the North Atlantic Ocean. It was formerly hunted for its fur but is now protected from large-scale commercial hunting. Latin name: *Pagophilus groenlandicus.* [*Harp* from the shape of the seal's markings]

harp·si·chord /haárpsi kàwrd/ *n.* a keyboard instrument resembling a piano and having horizontal strings plucked by leather or quill points connected to the keys. It was superseded by the piano in the 19th century. [Early 17thC. From French *harpechorde,* from Latin *harpa* "harp" + *chorda* "string."] —**harp·si·chord·ist** *n.*

Har·pur /haárpər/, **Charles** (1813–68) Australian poet and playwright. Considered by many to be Australia's first major poet, he wrote *The Bushranger* (1853).

har·py /haárpee/ (*plural* **-pies**) *n.* an offensive term for a woman that deliberately insults her attitude toward others in the pursuit of personal goals (*insult*) [From HARPY]

Har·py /haárpee/ (*plural* **-pies**) *n.* in Greek mythology, a monster that was half woman half bird of prey. The Harpies were thought to live on the Strophades Islands and carry out acts of vengeance on behalf of the gods. [14thC. Directly or via French from Latin *harpyia,* from Greek *harpuiai* (plural) "snatchers," from *harpazein* "to seize."]

har·py ea·gle *n.* a huge eagle with a black back, white underparts, and a gray head with a double crest, native to lowland forests from southern Mexico to northern Argentina. It feeds on monkeys, sloths, opossums, and snakes. Latin name: *Harpia harpyja.*

har·que·bus /haárkəbəss, haárkwə-/, **ar·que·bus** /aár-/ *n.* an early type of portable gun supported on a tripod by a hook, or on a forked post [Mid-16thC. Via French *(h)arquebuse* from, ultimately, Middle Dutch *hakebus,* Middle High German *hake(n)bühse,* or Middle Low

German *hakebusse*, literally "hook-gun" (because supported by a hook); see HACKBUT.] —**har·que·bus·ier** /haàrkəbə seér, haàrkwə-/ *n.*

har·ri·dan /hérrid'n/ *n.* an offensive term for a woman that deliberately insults her age and temperament (*offensive*) [Late 17thC. Origin uncertain: perhaps an alteration of French *haridelle* "old horse, gaunt woman," of unknown origin.]

Harrier

har·ri·er[1] /hérree ər/ (*plural* **-ers** *or* **-er**) *n.* a slender hawk with long wings and tail that hunts by flying low over marshland and grassland to catch mice, snakes, frogs, and fish. The northern harrier or marsh hawk is the only harrier native to North America. Genus: *Circus.* [Mid-16thC. Formed from *harrow* "to rob," variant of HARRY; later influenced by HARRIER[3].]

har·ri·er[2] /hérree ər/ *n.* a small hound, resembling a foxhound, used for hunting hares or rabbits [15thC. Origin uncertain: perhaps formed from HARE (later influenced by HARRIER[3]) on the model of French *lévrier* "greyhound," literally "dog for hunting hares."]

har·ri·er[3] /hérree ər/ *n.* somebody who harries somebody with repeated verbal or physical attacks, or somebody who raids or pillages a place

Har·ri·man /hárrimən/, **Edward H.** (1848–1909) U.S. financier and railroad executive. He reorganized the Union Pacific Railroad (1895). He was renowned for his ruthlessness in pursuing his extensive business interests. Full name **Edward Henry Harriman**

Har·ris /hárriss/, **Frank** (1856–1931) British journalist and writer. He gained notoriety for his scandalous semifictional autobiography, *My Life and Loves* (1923–27). Full name **Frank James Thomas Harris**

Har·ris, Joel Chandler (1848–1908) U.S. writer. He published several collections of folksy Southern tales narrated by the fictional Uncle Remus.

Har·ris, Lawren (1885–1970) Canadian artist. A founder member of the Group of Seven, he is noted for his Arctic landscapes such as *Icebergs* (1930). Full name **Lawren Stewart Harris**

Har·ris, Townsend (1804–78) U.S. diplomat. As U.S. consul to Japan (1856–60), he negotiated a treaty that greatly increased Japan's international trade.

Har·ris·burg /hárrəss bùrg/ city and capital of Pennsylvania, located in the southern part of the state. Population: 52,376 (1990).

Har·ri·son /hárriss'n/ **1.** town in northeastern New Jersey, on the Passaic River opposite Newark. Population: 23,308 (1990). **2.** village in southeastern New York. It is a northeastern suburb of New York City. Population: 23,658 (1996).

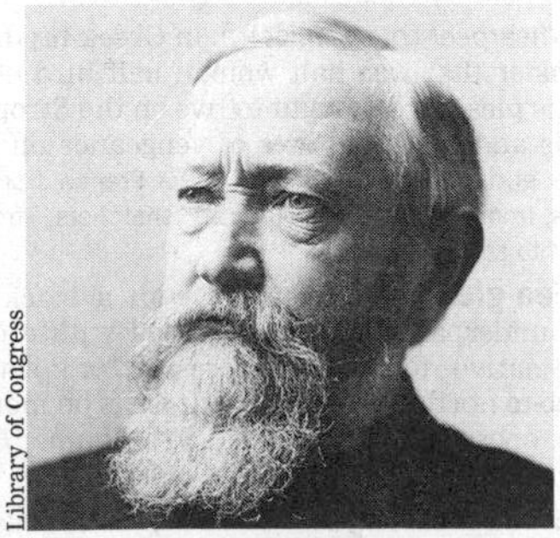

Library of Congress

Benjamin Harrison

Har·ri·son /hárriss'n/, **Benjamin** (1726?–91) American patriot. A longtime member of the Virginia House of Burgesses (1749–75), he presided over the Continental Congress (1774–77) and signed the Declaration of Independence (1776). He was governor of Virginia (1781–84).

Har·ri·son, Benjamin (1833–1901) U.S. statesman and 23rd President of the United States. The grandson of William Henry Harrison, he was a Republican senator (1881–87) before his election as president. His administration (1889–93) enacted protectionist tariffs and other pro-business legislation.

Har·ri·son, George (*b.* 1943) British musician. The lead guitarist with The Beatles, he later turned to solo music projects and movie production.

Har·ri·son, Sir Rex (1908–90) British actor. He starred in comedies including *Blithe Spirit* (1945) and *My Fair Lady* (1964), for which he won an Academy Award. Full name **Sir Reginald Carey Harrison**

U.S. Military History Institute

William Henry Harrison

Har·ri·son, William Henry (1773–1841) U.S. statesman and 9th President of the United States. He was elected president in 1840 on the strength of his military successes against the Native Americans and in the War of 1812, but died after one month in office.

Har·ris tweed /hérriss-/ *n.* a thick woven woolen cloth that is traditionally made in Harris, the southern part of the island of Lewis, in the Western Isles of Scotland

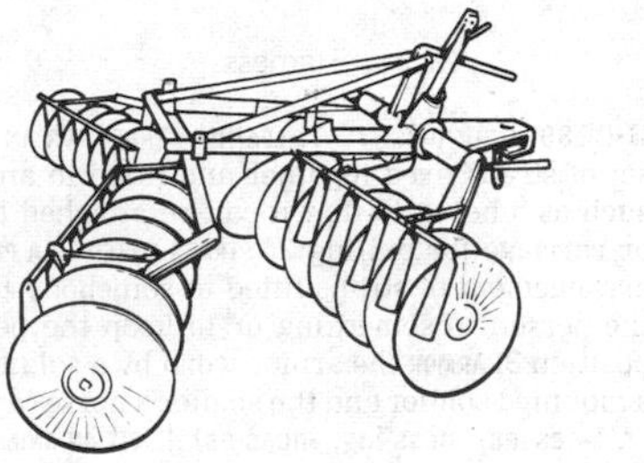

Harrow

har·row[1] /hárrō/ *n.* FARM MACHINE FOR BREAKING UP SOIL a piece of farm equipment with sharp teeth or disks that is used to break up soil and clods of dirt and to even up a plowed field ■ *vti.* (**-rowed, -row·ing, -rows**) BREAK UP LAND to break up land by pulling a harrow over it, or be broken up with a harrow [12thC. From Old Norse *herfi.*] —**har·row·er** *n.*

har·row[2] *vt.* = **harry** (*archaic*)

har·row·ing /hérrō ing/ *adj.* evoking feelings of fear, horror, or disgust ○ *harrowing scenes of hurricane devastation*

Har·row School /hèrrō-/ *n.* a private school for boys in northwestern London, England. It was founded in 1571.

har·rumph /hə rúmf/ (**-rumphed, -rumph·ing, -rumphs**) *vti.* **1.** CLEAR THE THROAT to clear the throat, or make a noise that resembles the sound of clearing the throat **2.** MUTTER CRITICAL REMARKS to make comments of criticism and displeasure, often muttering so that listeners are aware of the tone but cannot hear the exact words [Mid-20thC. An imitation of the sound.]

har·ry /hérree/ (**-ried, -ry·ing, -ries**), **har·row** *archaic* /hérrō/ (**-rowed, -row·ing, -rows**) *vt.* **1.** CAUSE DISTRESS BY REPEATED ATTACKS to cause somebody mental, emotional, or physical distress by repeated verbal or physical attacks ○ *The crows have harried the cat so badly that it no longer goes outside.* **2.** RAID OR PILLAGE to raid or pillage an area, or a town or village, especially during a war [Old English *hergian* "to ravage (literally as an army does)," from a prehistoric Germanic word meaning "army," which is also the ancestor of English *harangue* and *herald*]

harsh /haàrsh/ *adj.* **1.** DIFFICULT TO ENDURE difficult to live in or endure because very uncomfortable or inhospitable ○ *a harsh winter* ○ *harsh prison conditions* **2.** SEVERELY CRITICAL severely scrutinizing, critical, and rigid in manner **3.** PUNITIVE extremely exacting to the point of being punitive ○ *Harsh penalties will be imposed.* **4.** JARRING jarring or unpleasant to the senses [14thC. Origin uncertain: perhaps from Scandinavian.] —**harsh·ly** *adv.* —**harsh·ness** *n.*

Har·sha /haàrshə/ *n.* a descendant of the Guptas in India, who created a loose empire in northern India between A.D. 616 and 654

harsh·en /haàrsh'n/ (**-ened, -en·ing, -ens**) *vti.* to make or become harsh or harsher

hars·let *n.* = **haslet**

hart /haart/ (*plural* **harts** *or* **hart**) *n.* a male deer, especially a male red deer over five years of age [Old English *heor(o)t.* Ultimately from an Indo-European word meaning "horn, head," which is also the ancestor of English *carrot, rhinoceros,* and *reindeer.*]

Hart /haart/, **John** (1711?–79) American patriot. He signed the Declaration of Independence (1776) as a New Jersey delegate to the Continental Congress.

Hart, Lorenz (1895–1943) U.S. lyricist. He collaborated with Richard Rodgers for 20 years, producing a string of classic musicals including *On Your Toes* (1936) and *Pal Joey* (1940). Full name **Lorenz Milton Hart**

Hart, Moss (1904–61) U.S. playwright and director. In the 1930s he collaborated with George S. Kaufman on witty social comedies, including the Pulitzer Prize-winning *You Can't Take It With You* (1936).

Harte /haart/, **Bret** (1836–1902) U.S. writer. He is best known for his colorful stories set in California's mining towns. Born **Francis Brett Harte**

Hartebeest

har·te·beest /haàrtə beést, haàrt-/ (*plural* **-beests** *or* **-beest**) *n.* a large social antelope of African sub-Saharan grasslands that is fawn to dark brown in color, with high shoulders, a sloping back, and a long head with large ringed horns. Genus: *Alcelaphus.* [Late 18thC. From obsolete Afrikaans, "deer, hart," literally "hart-beast."]

Hart·ford /haàrtfərd/ city and capital of Connecticut, situated on the Connecticut River 36 mi./58 km northeast of New Haven. Population: 124,195 (1994).

Hart·ley /haàrtlee/, **Marsden** (1877–1943) U.S. painter. Strongly influenced by contemporary European artists, he developed a bold personal style exemplified in works such as *Evening Storm, Schoodic, Maine* (1942). Full name **Edmund Marsden Hartley**

hart's-tongue (*plural* **hart's-tongues** *or* **hart's-tongue**) *n.* a Eurasian evergreen fern that has narrow undivided fronds bearing rows of spore-producing organs. Latin name: *Phyllitis scolopendrium.* [Translation of medieval Latin *lingua cervi* (from the shape of its fronds)]

har·um-scar·um /hàirəm skáirəm/ *adj.* exhibiting reckless disorganized abandon ○ *Her outfit looks harum-scarum, but it's a planned effect.* [Late 17thC. Origin uncertain: probably a rhyming alteration of HARE (verb) + SCARE.] —**har·um-scar·um** *adv.*

Ha·run ar-Ra·shid /ha ro͝on al ra sheéd/ (766–809) Abbasid caliph of Baghdad. His splendid court, a center of Islamic culture, is the one depicted in the *Arabian Nights.*

ha·rus·pex /hə rú spèks, hérrə-/ (*plural* **-pi·ces** /hə rúspi seèz/), **a·rus·pex** /ə rú-, érrə-/ (*plural* **-pi·ces** /ə rúspi seèz/) *n.* in ancient Rome, a priest who attempted to foretell the future, especially by examining the entrails of animals [15thC. From Latin, of uncertain origin: perhaps literally "somebody who looks at entrails."]

Har·vard sys·tem /haárvərd-/ *n.* a bibliographic reference system in academic publishing, in which the author and date are given in the text, and the full reference is supplied in a general list of references

Har·vard U·ni·ver·si·ty /haárvərd yoónəvérsitee/ the oldest university in the United States, founded in 1636 in Massachusetts

har·vest /haárvəst/ *n.* **1. QUANTITY OF CROP** the quantity of a crop that is gathered or ripens during a particular season ○ *a record harvest of wheat for Midwestern grain farmers* **2. CROP THAT IS GATHERED OR RIPENS** the crop that is gathered or ripens during a particular season ○ *A few days of rain can destroy an entire harvest of strawberries.* **3. SEASON IN WHICH CROPS ARE GATHERED** the season during which crop plants mature and crops are gathered **4. CONSEQUENCES OF PREVIOUS ACTION** the results of past or prior actions or behavior **5.** MED **REMOVAL OF ORGAN FOR TRANSPLANTATION** the removal of an organ, fluid, or tissue for transplantation, testing, or research ■ *v.* (**-vest·ed, -vest·ing, -vests**) **1.** *vti.* **GATHER CROP** to gather a crop for use or sale **2.** *vt.* **GATHER NONPLANT ITEMS** to collect or gather something other than a plant crop, e.g., fish raised commercially in a hatchery **3.** *vt.* **REAP RESULTS** to reap the results of past or prior actions or behavior, whether good or bad **4.** *vt.* MED **REMOVE ORGAN FOR TRANSPLANTATION** to remove an organ, fluid, or tissue for transplantation, testing, or research [Old English *hærfest* "autumn" ("time for gathering crops"). Ultimately from an Indo-European word meaning "to gather," which is also the ancestor of English *carpet* and *scarce.*] —**har·vest·a·bil·i·ty** /haárvəstə bíllətee/ *n.* —**har·vest·a·ble** /haárvəstəb'l/ *adj.*

har·vest·er /haárvəstər/ *n.* **1. MACHINE THAT GATHERS CROPS** a machine that gathers crops from the fields, especially a combine harvester **2. SOMEBODY WHO GATHERS CROPS** somebody who gathers crops, especially by hand

har·vest fly *n.* a cicada, native to the United States, that sings loudly near the end of the summer. Genus: *Tibicen.*

har·vest home *n.* the gathering of the harvest, especially its safe completion

har·vest·man /haárvəstmən/ (*plural* **-men** /-mən/) *n.* **1.** INSECTS = **daddy longlegs** *n.* 1 **2.** AGRIC **AGRICULTURAL WORKER** an agricultural worker, especially, before agriculture became mechanized, one who left home to find work at harvest time

har·vest mite *n.* = **chigger** [*Harvest* from its being common at harvest time]

har·vest moon *n.* the full moon nearest to the autumnal equinox. It rises for several nights at nearly the same time at points successively further north on the eastern horizon.

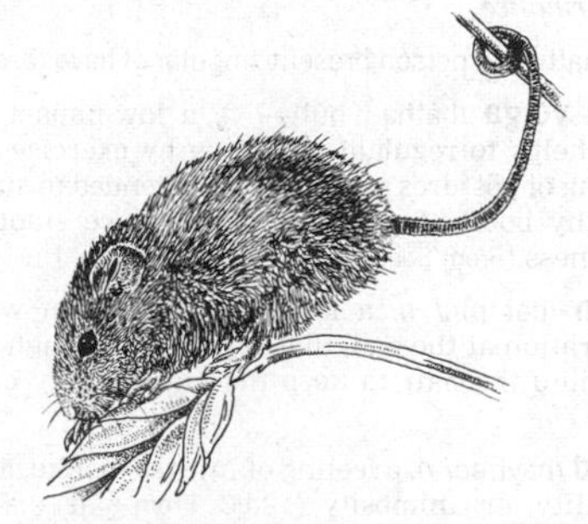

Harvest mouse

har·vest mouse *n.* a small reddish-brown Eurasian mouse that often lives in fields of corn and other grain. Latin name: *Micromys minutus.*

Har·vey /haárvee/ **1.** city in northeastern Illinois, an industrial center near Chicago. Population: 29,097 (1996). **2.** city in Jefferson County, Louisiana. Population: 21,222 (1990).

Har·wich /hárrij, -ich/ town and summer resort in southeastern Massachusetts, on south central Cape Cod. Population: 11,328 (1996).

Harz Moun·tains /haárts-/ mountain range in central Germany, between the Elbe and Weser rivers south of Brunswick. The highest peak is Brocken. Height: 3,743 ft./1,141 m.

has 3rd person present singular of **have**

has-been *n.* somebody who was popular or important in the past but is now largely forgotten (*informal*) ○ *It's hard to be a hero one day and a has-been the next.*

Has·brouck Heights /házbrook-/ borough in northeastern New Jersey, southeast of Paterson. Population: 11,488 (1990).

Ha·se·ga·wa To·ha·ku /haássə gaáwə to haá koo/ (1539–1610) Japanese artist. He was noted for his ink screen paintings, which often featured monkeys, and founded his own school of painting.

ha·sen·pfef·fer /haáz'n fèffər, haáss'n-/ *n.* marinated rabbit, highly seasoned and served as a hot stew [Late 19thC. From German, literally "hare's pepper," from a form of *Hase* "hare" + *Pfeffer* "pepper."]

hash[1] /hash/ *n.* **1.** COOK **FRIED DISH OF POTATOES AND MEAT** a dish made of cooked potatoes or other vegetables, usually combined with chopped-up pieces of cooked meat, and reheated, usually by frying until golden brown ○ *corned-beef hash.* ◊ **hash browns 2.** *U.K.* = **pound sign** ■ *vt.* (**hashed, hash·ing, hash·es**) COMPUT **APPLY ALGORITHM TO A STRING** to apply an algorithm to a character string, especially in order to find an address of a record [Late 16thC. From French *hacher* "to hack, cut into small pieces," from *hache* "ax" (see HATCHET).] ◇ **make a hash of something** to do something very badly (*informal*) ○ *I made a real hash of the exam – I couldn't answer any questions.* ◇ **settle somebody's hash** to assert yourself over somebody, especially somebody hostile or troublesome (*informal*)

hash out, hash over *vt.* to have a long, drawn-out, and usually involved discussion of a matter or a problem ○ *They hashed out their differences with an arbitrator.*

hash[2] /hash/ *n.* hashish (*slang*) [Mid-20thC. Shortening.]

hash browns *npl.* cooked potatoes that are chopped up, sometimes with onions, and fried until golden brown. Occasionally, hash browns are formed into small cakes or patties.

Ha·Shem /haa shém/ *n.* in Judaism, a substitute word used when referring to God in contexts other than prayers or scriptural readings, because the name for God is too holy for such use [From Hebrew, literally "the name"]

hash house *n.* a restaurant that serves cheap food (*informal*)

hash·ish /há sheèsh, há shìsh, haa sheèsh/, **hash·eesh** /há sheèsh, haa sheèsh/ *n.* a purified resin, prepared from the flowering tops of the female cannabis plant, that is smoked or chewed for its narcotic and intoxicating properties and is widely illegal [Late 16thC. From Arabic *ḥašīš*, literally "dry herb, powdered hemp" (source of English *assassin*).]

hash mark *n.* MIL **LONGEVITY STRIPE ON UNIFORM** a stripe sewn on U.S. Army uniforms, one for every two years of active duty ■ FOOTBALL **LINE FOR FOOTBALL POSITION** a line indicating how close to a sideline a football may be at the start of a play

hash sling·er *n.* a cook in a cheap restaurant (*slang*)

Ha·sid /khaássid, haá-/ (*plural* **-si·dim** /-seédim/), **Has·sid** (*plural* **-si·dim**), **Chas·sid** (*plural* **-si·dim**), **Cha·sid** (*plural* **-si·dim**) *n.* a member of a Jewish movement of popular mysticism founded in Eastern Europe in the 18th century. It emphasized the individual's emotional relationship with God, and is now represented by a number of different religious groups. [Early 19thC. From Hebrew *ḥāsîd*, literally "pious."] —**Ha·si·dic** /khaa síddik, haa-/ *adj.* —**Ha·si·dism** /khaa sí dìzzəm, haa-/ *n.*

Ha·ska·lah /hàskə laá/, **Ha·ska·la** *n.* the Jewish enlightenment movement, originating in 18th-century Germany under the influence of Moses Mendelssohn. It aimed to integrate Jews into Western European society, e.g., by the use of German, not Yiddish, and by emphasizing secular intellectualism rather than religious learning. [From Hebrew *haśkālāh* "enlightenment"]

has·let /hásslət, házzlət/, **hars·let** /haárslət/ *n.* internal organs such as the heart and liver, usually of a hog, used as food [14thC. From Old French *hastelet*, literally "small piece of meat roasted on a spit," from *haste* "spit," of uncertain origin.]

has·n't /házz'nt/ *contr.* has not

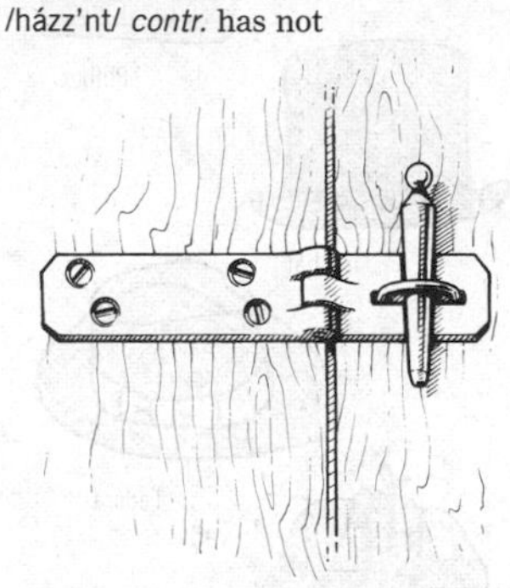

Hasp

hasp /hasp/ *n.* **HINGED METAL FASTENING** a hinged metal fastening that fits over a staple and is secured by a pin, bolt, or padlock ■ *vt.* (**hasped, hasp·ing, hasps**) **CLOSE SOMETHING WITH A HASP** to close something, especially a door or window, with a hasp [Old English *hæpse* "fastening" (*hæpsian*, verb), from prehistoric Germanic]

Has·sam /hássəm/, **Childe** (1859–1935) U.S. artist. His impressionist paintings are distinctive for the brilliant coloring of their street scenes and landscapes. Full name **Frederick Childe Hassam**

Has·sid *n.* = **Hasid**

has·sium /hássee əm/ *n.* an extremely rare, unstable chemical element produced in high-energy atomic collisions. Symbol **Hs** [Late 20thC. From modern Latin, from Latin *Hassias* "Hesse," German state where it was discovered.]

has·sle /háss'l/ *n.* **DIFFICULTY, TROUBLE, OR AGGRAVATION** a source or the experience of aggravation or annoying difficulty (*informal*) ○ *It's just not worth the hassle.* ■ *vt.* (**-sled, -sling, -sles**) **KEEP BOTHERING OR ANNOYING SOMEBODY** to bother or annoy somebody, especially by continually asking that person to do something (*informal*) ○ *Stop hassling me about washing the car.* [Late 19thC. Origin uncertain: perhaps a blend of HAGGLE and TUSSLE. Originally a dialect verb meaning "to hack at."]

has·sock /hássək/ *n.* **1.** FURNITURE **PADDED STOOL** a piece of furniture that is round or square, and padded, with an upholstered cover, used as a seat or footrest **2. CUSHION ON WHICH TO KNEEL** a thick firm cushion used for kneeling on, especially in church **3. GRASS CLUMP** a thick clump of grass [Old English *hassuc* "clump of grass," of unknown origin]

hast /hast/ *vt.* 2nd person present singular of **have** (*archaic*)

has·tate /hás tàyt/ *adj.* having a pointed tip and two outward-pointing basal lobes at right angles (*refers to leaves*) ○ *hastate leaves* [Late 18thC. From Latin *hastatus* "armed with a spear," from *hasta* "spear" (possible source of English *haslet*).]

haste /hayst/ *n.* **GREAT SPEED** great speed, especially in situations where time is limited (*formal*) ○ *Act in haste, repent at leisure.* ■ *vti.* (**hast·ed, hast·ing, hastes**) **HURRY** to hasten (*archaic literary*) [13thC. Via Old French from a prehistoric Germanic word.]

has·ten /háyss'n/ (**-tened, -ten·ing, -tens**) *v.* **1.** *vt.* **SPEED SOMETHING UP** to make something happen more quickly ○ *A vacation would hasten his recovery.* **2.** *vi.* **GO SOMEWHERE QUICKLY** to go somewhere quickly or without delay **3.** *vi.* **DO SOMETHING IMMEDIATELY** to do or say something without delay, often in order to correct what might otherwise be a misleading impression ○ *"But she's perfectly right," he hastened to add.*

hast·y /háystee/ (**-i·er, -i·est**) *adj.* done, taking place, or acting in a hurry because of impetuosity or lack of time ○ *a hasty marriage* —**hast·i·ly** *adv.* —**hast·i·ness** *n.*

hast·y pud·ding *n.* mush made from crushed cereal grains and milk. It is usually made with cornmeal and sweetened with brown sugar or maple syrup. [*Hasty* of uncertain origin: perhaps because the pudding can be made speedily]

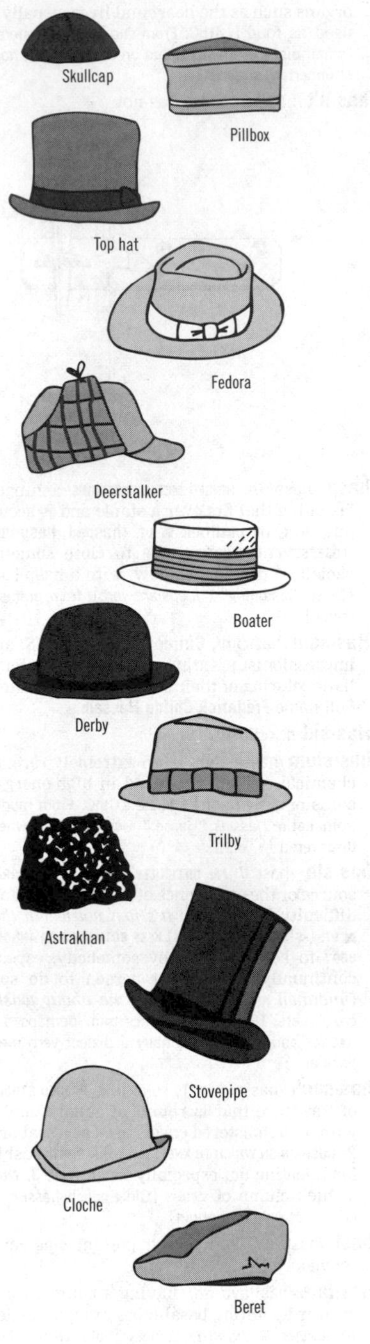

Hat

hat /hat/ *n.* **1. HEAD COVERING** a covering for the head, worn for protection from the weather or as a fashion accessory **2. AREA OF RESPONSIBILITY** used for a single area of interest, knowledge, or responsibility in an individual with many interests and responsibilities ○ *She put on her accountant's hat and gave the committee some suggestions for maximizing profits.* [Old English *hæt(t)* "hat, head covering," via a prehistoric Germanic word meaning "hood, cowl" from an Indo-European base meaning "to cover," which is also the ancestor of English *hood*] —**hat·ted** *adj.* ◇ **hang up your hat 1.** to retire from work ○ *When this project's finished he's going to hang up his hat and retire to the country.* **2.** to settle down to a calmer, more stable lifestyle following an extended period of stress or activity ○ *Children of military personnel move so frequently that they'd like to find just one place in which to hang up their hats.* ◇ **hat in hand** asking or begging for something such as assistance or money ○ *He had to go hat in hand to the courthouse, asking for legal relief in the matter.* ◇ **hats off to somebody** a way of saying that somebody has gained your respect or admiration ◇ **keep something under your hat** to keep something secret ◇ **pass the hat around** to collect contributions for somebody or something ◇ **pull something out of your hat** to do, accomplish, make, or get something as if by a magic trick when the resources appear to be unavailable (*informal*) ◇ **take your hat off to somebody** to acknowledge admiration or respect for somebody ◇ **talk through your hat** to talk nonsense ◇ **throw your hat into the ring** to volunteer to take part in a particular contest

hat·band /hát bànd/ *n.* a thin strip of leather, cloth, ribbon, or other material that is attached to and wound around a hat just above the brim

hat·box /hát bòks/ *n.* a large hard box with a removable or liftable lid, used for storing, carrying, and protecting a hat or hats

hatch[1] /hach/ *n.* **1. TYPE OF DOOR** a door cut into the floor or ceiling of something, especially on a boat or an aircraft. It is lifted to provide access to the area below or above it. A hatch may also provide access to an attic or cellar in a building. **2. SMALL HOLE BETWEEN TWO ROOMS** a small connecting hole in a wall between two rooms, or the small doors that cover this hole ○ *an escape hatch* **3.** CARS = **hatchback** [Old English *hæcc* "lower half of a door, wicket." From a prehistoric Germanic base of unknown origin that is also the ancestor of Dutch *hek* "gate."]

hatch[2] /hach/ *v.* (**hatched, hatch·ing, hatch·es**) **1.** *vi.* **COME OUT OF EGG** to emerge from an egg **2.** *vt.* **CAUSE YOUNG TO EMERGE FROM EGG** to cause a young organism, e.g., a chick, fish, or insect, to emerge from its egg ○ *Birds hatch their chicks by sitting on the nests.* **3.** *vt.* **SECRETLY DEVISE A PLOT** to secretly devise a plot, plan, or scheme, usually an illicit or illegal one, or one that is ill-advised in some way **4.** *vi.* **BREAK OPEN FOR RELEASE OF YOUNG** to break open so that the young inside may be released ■ *n.* **YOUNG ORGANISMS NEWLY HATCHED** a group of young organisms, e.g., chicks, fish, or insects, that have just recently emerged from eggs [15thC. Origin uncertain.]

hatch[3] /hach/ (**hatched, hatch·ing, hatch·es**) *vti.* in graphic art, to mark or cover something with parallel crossed lines to show shading, or be marked in this way [15thC. From French *hacher* "to chop," from *hache* "ax" (see HATCHET).] —**hatch·ing** *n.*

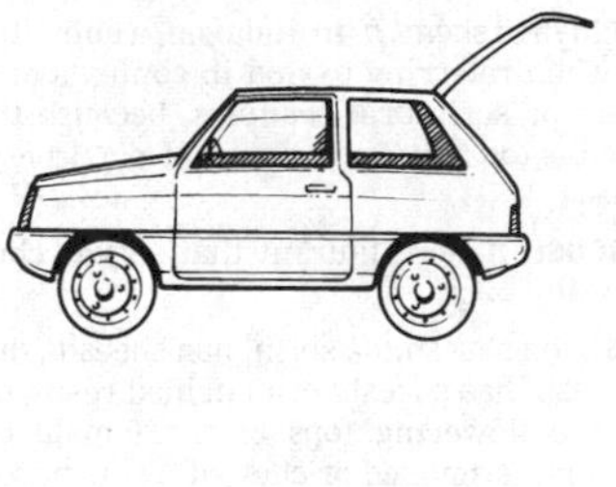
Hatchback

hatch·back /hách bàk/ *n.* a type of car with a door at the back that is hinged from the roof to allow easy access to storage space behind the rear seats. The storage space usually has a removable shelf between the top of the seats and the rear window, which hides what is being kept below. ○ *a five-door hatchback*

hat·check /hát chèk/ *n.* a room where hats, coats, and other outerwear are checked with an attendant for safekeeping, e.g., in a bar or restaurant

hatch·er·y /háchəree/ (*plural* **-ies**) *n.* a place where fish or poultry eggs are hatched commercially under artificial conditions ○ *a fish hatchery*

hatch·et /háchət/ *n.* a small ax that can be used with one hand ○ *wield a hatchet* [14thC. From French *hachette*, literally "small ax," from *hache* "ax" (source of English *hash*[1]), from medieval Latin *hapia*, from prehistoric Germanic.] ◇ **bury the hatchet** to make peace with somebody after a disagreement ◇ **do a hatchet job on somebody** *or* **something** criticize somebody or something unfairly, especially in print (*informal*) ○ *The reviewer did a hatchet job on the author of the novel.*

hatch·et face *n.* an unpleasantly long thin face with sharp or gaunt features —**hatch·et-faced** *adj.*

Hatchet

hatch·et man *n.* **1. HIRED KILLER** somebody who is hired to murder another person (*slang*) **2. SOMEBODY HIRED TO MAKE CUTS** somebody who is hired to do something unpopular or unscrupulous, especially to make cuts in staff or funding (*informal*)

hatch·ling /háchling/ *n.* a bird, fish, insect, or other organism that has just hatched from an egg

hatch·ment /háchmənt/ *n.* a diamond-shaped panel bearing the coat of arms of somebody who has died [Early 16thC. Origin uncertain: probably from obsolete French *hachement*, alteration of Old French *acesmement* "adornment," from *acesmer* "to adorn," of unknown origin.]

hatch·way /hách wày/ *n.* = **hatch**[1] *n.* 2

hate /hayt/ *v.* (**hat·ed, hat·ing, hates**) **1.** *vt.* **DISLIKE SOMEBODY OR SOMETHING INTENSELY** to dislike somebody or something intensely, often in a way that evokes feelings of anger, hostility, or animosity **2.** *vti.* **HAVE STRONG DISTASTE FOR** to have strong distaste or aversion for something, somebody, or something that has to be done ○ *I hate this show; it's so boring.* ○ *They hate cleaning the horse stall every day.* ○ *I hate to say it, but I know we're going to lose.* ■ *n.* **1. FEELING OF INTENSE DISLIKE OR ANGER** a feeling of intense dislike, anger, hostility, or animosity ○ *You could see the hate in his eyes.* **2. SOMETHING HATED** something that is hated [Old English *hete* (noun) and *hatian* (verb). Ultimately from an Indo-European word perhaps meaning "strong feeling," which is also the ancestor of English *heinous.*] —**hate·a·ble** *adj.* —**hat·ed** *adj.* —**hat·er** *n.*

WORD KEY: SYNONYMS

See Synonyms at ***dislike***.

hate crime *n.* a crime that is motivated by hate, prejudice, or intolerance of somebody's race, religion, ethnicity, or sexual orientation

hate·ful /háytfəl/ *adj.* **1. SPITEFULLY MALEVOLENT** characterized by malevolence or spite **2. EVOKING FEELINGS OF HATRED** eliciting feelings or reactions of hatred, detestation, or abhorrence —**hate·ful·ly** *adv.* —**hate·ful·ness** *n.*

hate mail *n.* mail that expresses the sender's anger about something, usually toward the recipient, in a threatening or offensive way

hat·ful /hát fo͝ol/ *n.* a large quantity or number of something ○ *received a hatful of compliments on the performance*

hath /hath/ 3rd person present singular of **have** (*archaic*)

ha·tha yo·ga /háthə-, hŭttə-/ *n.* a low-impact yoga that helps to regulate breathing by exercises consisting of postures and stretches intended to sustain healthy bodily functioning and induce emotional calmness [From Sanskrit, literally "force yoga"]

hat·pin /hát pìn/ *n.* a long thin pin, often with a decoration at the end, that is pushed through a hat and into the hair to keep the hat securely on the head

ha·tred /háytrəd/ *n.* a feeling of intense dislike, anger, hostility, or animosity [12thC. From HATE + a suffix formed from Old English *ræden* "state, condition" (found also in English *kindred*).]

WORD KEY: SYNONYMS

See Synonyms at ***dislike***.

Hat·shep·sut /hàt shép so͞ot/, **Queen of Egypt** (1520?–1483? B.C.). She crowned herself pharoah in 1503 B.C. after years of ruling jointly with her husband, Thutmose II, and his son, Thutmose III.

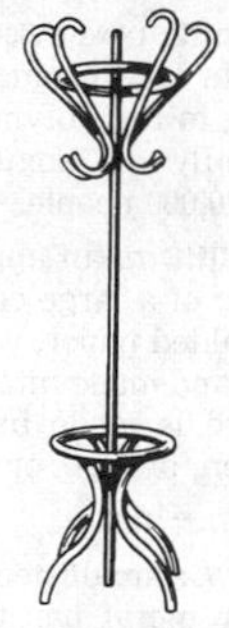

Hat stand

hat stand *n.* a tall freestanding piece of furniture consisting of a base with a pole embedded in it with hooks around the top on which hats, coats, and umbrellas can be hung

hat·ter /háttər/ *n.* somebody who makes and sells hats

Hat·ter·as, Cape /-háttərəss/ headland projecting into the Atlantic Ocean in eastern North Carolina renowned for treacherous weather conditions

hat tree *n.* = **hat stand**

hat trick *n.* a series of three wins or successes, especially three goals scored by the same player in a game of ice hockey or soccer [Origin uncertain: probably from the former cricketing practice of awarding a hat to a bowler who took three wickets with three consecutive balls]

hau·berk /háwbərk/ *n.* a long, often sleeveless, tunic made of chain mail. It was originally intended as protection just for the neck and shoulders but it developed into a longer tunic in the 12th and 13th centuries. [13thC. Via Old French *hau(s)berc* from a prehistoric Germanic word meaning literally "neck-protector," the first element of which is also the ancestor of English *hawse*.]

haugh /haw, hawkh/ *n. Scotland* a low-lying stretch of land in a river valley, often unproductive because of frequent flooding [Origin uncertain: probably from Old English *healh* "corner, nook, small hollow in a slope"]

haugh·ty /háwtee/ (**-ti·er, -ti·est**) *adj.* behaving in a superior, condescending, or arrogant way ○ *She always took a haughty tone* [Mid-16thC. Formed from archaic *haught*, from French *haut(e)* "high."] —**haugh·ti·ly** *adv.* —**haugh·ti·ness** *n.*

haul /hawl/ *v.* (**hauled, haul·ing, hauls**) **1.** *vt.* **MOVE SOMETHING WITH EFFORT** to transport something that is heavy and bulky from one place to another **2.** *vt.* **PULL OR DRAG SOMETHING** to pull or drag something with continuous and laborious movements **3.** *vt.* SAILING **CHANGE COURSE** to change a vessel's course so as to sail closer to the wind **4.** *vi.* NAUT **BLOW CLOSER TO BOW** to blow from a direction that is closer to a vessel's bow **5.** *vt.* SHIPPING **HOIST INTO DRY DOCK** to hoist a vessel from the water into a dry dock, e.g., to make repairs ■ *n.* **1. STOLEN ITEMS** goods that have been stolen, or the value of these stolen goods **2.** TRANSP **DISTANCE SOMETHING IS TRANSPORTED** a distance over which something is transported or pulled, or which somebody travels with difficulty ○ *a long haul* **3.** FISHING **SINGLE CATCH OF FISH** the amount of fish caught in a single catch **4. CONFISCATED CONTRABAND** illegal goods that are confiscated by the authorities [13thC. Variant of HALE.] ◇ **haul somebody over the coals** *U.K.* = **rake somebody over the coals**

WORD KEY: SYNONYMS

See Synonyms at ***pull***.

haul off *vi.* **1. GET READY TO STRIKE SOMEBODY** to pull back the arm in preparation for striking somebody (*informal*) ○ *If you do that again, I'll haul off and sock you.* **2.** NAUT **MANEUVER VESSEL TO AVOID SOMETHING** to maneuver a vessel in order to avoid something

haul up *vt.* to force somebody to appear before a court or some other disciplinary body for judgment

haul·age /háwlij/ *n.* **1. TRANSPORTING GOODS** the business or process of transporting goods, usually by road or rail **2. COST OF TRANSPORTING GOODS** the cost of transporting goods, or the rate charged for transporting goods

haul·er /háwlər/ *n.* a person or company whose business is transporting goods, especially by road

haul·ier /háwlyər, -lee ər/ *n. U.K.* = **hauler**

haulm /hawm/, **halm** *n. U.K.* the stems or stalks of grain, beans, peas, potatoes, or grasses, especially after harvesting and used for thatching or litter [Old English *h(e)alm*. Ultimately from an Indo-European word that is also the ancestor of English *culm* and *calamus*.]

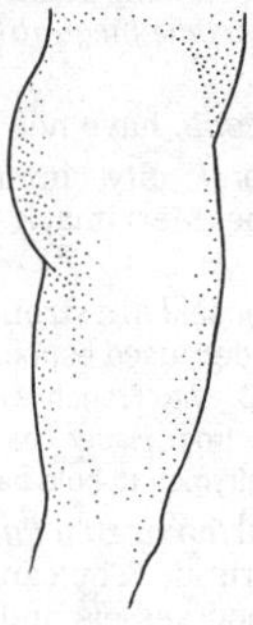

Haunch

haunch /hawnch/ *n.* **1. HIP, BUTTOCK, AND UPPER THIGH** the part of the body comprising the hip, buttock, and upper thigh ○ *She sat back on her haunches.* **2.** FOOD, ZOOL **ANIMAL LEG** one of the back legs of a four-legged animal, either when it is alive, or as a cut of meat **3.** ARCHIT **UPPER PART OF ARCH** the upper curving part of either side of an arch [12thC. Via French *hanche* from prehistoric Germanic.]

haunt /hawnt/ *vt.* (**haunt·ed, haunt·ing, haunts**) **1.** PARANORMAL **APPEAR TO SOMEBODY AS A GHOST** to frequent a place or appear to somebody in the form of a ghost or other supposed supernatural being **2. DISCOMFIT SOMEBODY BY UNPLEASANT REMINDERS** to cause somebody unease, worry, or regret by continual presence or recurrence in his or her life ○ *haunted by doubt* **3. VISIT SOMEWHERE CONTINUALLY** to go often to a place ■ *n.* **1. PLACE SOMEBODY OFTEN VISITS** a place that somebody likes and often visits **2.** PARANORMAL **GHOST** a supposed supernatural being or a manifestation of one, especially one associated with a particular place [12thC. Via French *hanter* "to frequent a place" (literally "as a home") from, ultimately, a prehistoric Germanic word that is also the ancestor of English *home*.] —**haunt·er** *n.*

haunt·ed /háwntəd/ *adj.* **1.** PARANORMAL **FREQUENTED BY A GHOST** inhabited by or visited regularly by a ghost or other supposed supernatural being **2. STRANGELY TERRIFIED IN APPEARANCE** looking strangely frightened or worried

haunt·ing /háwnting/ *adj.* evoking strong emotion, especially a sense of sadness, that persists for a long time ○ *a tender, haunting melody* —**haunt·ing·ly** *adv.*

Hau·ra·ki Gulf /how ràki/ bay on the northeastern coast of North Island, New Zealand. The city of Auckland is located on its southwestern shore. Area: 884 sq. mi./2290 sq. km.

Hau·sa /hówssə, -zə/ (*plural* **-sa** *or* **-sas**) *n.* **1.** PEOPLES **MEMBER OF W AFRICAN PEOPLE** a member of a people living mainly in northern Nigeria and southern Niger **2.** LANG **LANGUAGE OF EASTERN W AFRICA** a language widely spoken in Nigeria, Niger, and other parts of eastern West Africa. It is one of the Chadic branch of the Afro-Asiatic family of languages. Hausa is spoken by about 25 million native speakers, with approximately a further 40 million people using it as a second language. **3. SPIRITUAL TRADITION OF NIGERIA** the tradition combining elements of Islam and of local religious beliefs associated with the Hausa, after the collapse of the Songhay Empire, [Early 19thC. From Hausa.] —**Hau·sa** *adj.*

haus·frau /hówss fròw/ (*plural* **-fraus**) *n.* a traditional housewife, conventionally believed to be interested mostly in her home and family (*disapproving*) (*offensive in some contexts*) ○ *She wanted a career, not a life as a hausfrau.* [Late 18thC. From German, from *Haus* "house" and *Frau* "wife, woman."]

haus·tel·lum /haw stélləm/ (*plural* **-la** /-lə/) *n.* the tip of the proboscis, or elongated mouthpart, that is adapted for sucking food in many insects, e.g., flies [Early 19thC. From modern Latin, literally "small scoop," from Latin *haustrum* "scoop," from, ultimately, *haurire* "to draw up" (source of English *exhaust*).]

haus·to·ri·um /haw stáwree əm/ (*plural* **-a** /-ə/) *n.* a food-absorbing structure of a parasitic plant or fungus. It penetrates host tissues and obtains food and water from a host plant. [Late 19thC. Formed from Latin *haustor* "water-drawer, drinker," from, ultimately, *haurire* "to draw up" (see HAUSTELLUM).]

haut·boy /ṓ bòy, hṓ-/ (*plural* **-boys**), **haut·bois** (*plural* **-bois**) *n.* **1.** MUSIC **OBOE** an oboe (*archaic*) **2. TYPE OF STRAWBERRY** a strawberry, native to central Europe and Asia, with large fruit. Latin name: *Fragaria moschata*. [Mid-16thC. From French *hautbois* "oboe" (source of English *oboe*), from *haut* "high" (from its high pitch) + *bois* "wood," from Germanic.]

haute cou·ture /ṓt koo tóor/ *n.* exclusive and expensive clothing made for an individual customer by a fashion designer, or the industry that produces such clothing [Early 20thC. From French, literally "high dressmaking."]

haute cui·sine /ṓt kwi zéen/ *n.* classic high-quality French cooking (*hyphenated when used before a noun*) [Early 20thC. From French, literally "high cooking."]

haute é·cole /ṓt ay káwl/ *n.* the skill and art of expert horsemanship [Mid-19thC. From French, literally "high school."]

hau·teur /hō túr, haw-/ *n.* a haughty manner, feeling, or quality (*formal*) [Early 17thC. From French, from *haute* "high," feminine of *haut*, from, ultimately, Latin *altus* (source of English *altitude* and *haughty*).]

haut monde /ṓ máwNd/ *n.* the highest stratum of society, international or domestic, and those in it [Mid-19thC. From French, literally "high world."]

Ha·van·a[1] /hə vánnə, -vaánə/ capital, port, and largest city of Cuba, on the northwestern coast of the country. Population: 2,241,000 (1995). —**Ha·van·an** *adj.*, *n.*

Ha·van·a[2], **Ha·van·a ci·gar** *n.* a high-quality cigar made in Cuba

Ha·var·ti /hə vaártee/ *n.* a moist pale semihard cheese with lots of tiny holes and a slightly rubbery texture, made in Denmark. It has a mild buttery flavor. [Mid-20thC. Named for *Havarti*, the farm of Hanne Nielsen, the 19th-century Danish cheese maker who popularized it.]

Ha·va·su·pai /haávə sóo pī/ (*plural* **-pai**) *n.* **1.** PEOPLES **NATIVE AMERICAN FROM ARIZONA** a member of a Native American people living in Arizona, southeast of the Grand Canyon **2.** LANG **LANGUAGE OF THE HAVASUPAI** the language of the Havasupai, belonging to the Yuman family of languages [Late 19thC. From Yuma, literally "blue or green water people."] —**Ha·va·su·pai** *adj.*

hav·da·lah *n.* = **habdalah**

have (*stressed*) /hav/; (*unstressed*) /həv, əv/ (**had, had** (*stressed*) /had/; (*unstressed*) /həd, əd/, **hav·ing, has** (*stressed*) /haz/; (*unstressed*) /həz, əz/) CORE MEANING: a verb indicating that somebody possesses something, either materially or as a characteristic or attribute ○ *She has a small cottage in the country.* ○ *He has beautiful eyes.*

1. *vt.* **OWN SOMETHING** to be the owner or possessor of something ○ *I don't have a lot of money.* **2.** *vt.* **POSSESS A CHARACTERISTIC** to be the possessor of a quality or characteristic ○ *She had long blond hair.* **3.** *v.* **FORMS PERFECT TENSES** used to form the following tenses or aspects: the present perfect, the past perfect, the future perfect, and the continuous forms of these (*used before the past participle of a verb or at the beginning of a question, or with "got" to indicate possession*) ○ *I have finished my dinner, thank you.* ○ *Have you finished yet?* ○ *I have got a new car.* **4.** *v.* **EXPRESSES COMPULSION** expresses compulsion, obligation, or necessity ○ *We have to do the economic analysis.* **5.** *v.* **EXPRESSES CERTAINTY** expresses conviction or certainty ○ *There just has to be a solution to the problem.* **6.** *vt.* **RECEIVE** to receive or obtain something ○ *I had a Christmas card from him.* **7.** *vt.* **EAT SOMETHING** to eat or drink something ○ *We have breakfast at eight.* **8.** *vt.* **THINK OF SOMETHING** to think of something, or hold something in the mind ○ *Listen! I have a good idea.* **9.** *vt.* **EXPERIENCE SOMETHING** to experience or undergo something ○ *He went to the carnival to have a good time.* ○ *I had a shock.* **10.** *vt.* **BE AFFECTED BY** to be affected by something, especially something of a medical nature ○ *I've had the flu for the last week.* **11.** *vt.* **ENGAGE IN SOMETHING** to engage or participate in something ○ *We had a long talk about cars.* **12.** *vt.* **ARRANGE SOMETHING** to organize or arrange something ○ *We had a party last week.* **13.** *vt.* **ARRANGE FOR SOMETHING TO BE DONE** to arrange for somebody to do something for you or on your behalf ○ *I've just had my hair cut.* **14.** *vt.* **TOLERATE SOMETHING** to tolerate or put up with something (*usually used in negative statements*) ○ *I won't have such behavior any longer!* **15.** *vt.* **RECEIVE SOMEBODY** to receive somebody as a guest ○ *We had Mother to stay over Christmas.* **16.** *vt.* **BRING A CHILD INTO EXISTENCE** to be the parent of a child, or conceive, carry, or give birth to a child ○ *She's had three children and now she's having another one.* **17.** *vt.* **PUT SOMEBODY OR SOMETHING SOMEWHERE** to put or place somebody or something in a particular place ○ *I'll have you two in the front row, please.* ○ *I'll have the desk over there.* **18.** *vt.* **UNDERGO SOMETHING** to be the victim of an unpleasant action or experience ○ *I had my car stolen.* **19.** *vt.* **MAKE SOMETHING HAPPEN** to direct or cause somebody to do something, or cause something to happen ○ *If you see him tomorrow, have him call me.* **20.** *vt.* **CHEAT SOMEBODY** to cheat or outwit somebody (*usually passive*) ○ *I think you'll find that you've been had in this deal.* **21.** *npl.* **haves PRIVILEGED PEOPLE** people who are rich and privileged, especially compared with those who are not [Old English *habban.* Ultimately from an Indo-European word meaning "to grasp," which is also the ancestor of English *capable* and *heave.*] ◇ **has** *or* **had it** declares or asserts, or declared or asserted ○ *Rumor has it that they are planning to get engaged.* ◇ **have done with something** to finish with something ○ *Let's put everything else in this box and have done with it.* ◇ **have had it 1.** to have no prospect of success ○ *We've had it now.* **2.** to be too worn out, damaged, or exhausted to function properly (*informal*) ○ *I'm afraid this printer has just about had it.* ○ *I've had it – you go on, I'm turning back.* ◇ **have had it with** to have lost patience with somebody or something ○ *I've had it with delays.* ◇ **have it coming** to be about to receive punishment or retribution, or deserve it ○ *He has it coming to him.* ◇ **have it in for somebody** to hold hard feelings against somebody and intend to do that person harm ○ *She has it in for him, and you can expect that she will seek revenge soon.* ◇ **have it out (with somebody)** to engage in a spirited, aggressive argument over an issue with somebody ○ *OK, let's have it out now and get this settled once and for all.* ◇ **have to do with 1.** to be relevant to ○ *Does your question have anything to do with the topic under discussion?* **2.** to have a friendship or relationship with ○ *She will have nothing to do with him anymore.* ◇ **have what it takes** to have the necessary skills, personality, or attitude to be successful at something ○ *He doesn't really have what it takes to be a professional actor.* ◇ **let somebody have it** to deliver an attack on somebody ○ *He refused to change his behavior, and in the end I let him have it.* ◇ **never had it so good** to have not possessed so many benefits before ○ *Look at these sales figures – we've never had it so good!* ◇ **not having any** refusing to take part or become involved in something ○ *They tried to involve him in the conspiracy, but it soon became clear that he wasn't having any.*

WORD KEY: USAGE

See Usage note at ***do.***

have at *vt.* attack somebody (*informal*) ◇ **have at it** to set about something with vigor ○ *Let's have at it – this project has to be done in June.*

have on *vti.* to have an article of clothing on your body

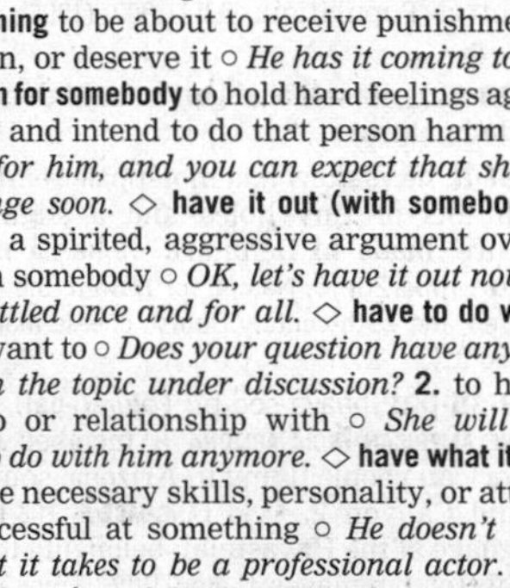

Havelock

have·lock /hάv lòk, hάvvlәk/ *n.* a light-colored cover for a soldier's cap, with a flap extending over the back of the neck to protect the head and neck from the sun [Mid-19thC. Named for Sir Henry *Havelock* (1795–1857), a British major-general who served in India; he introduced it as part of his troops' uniform.]

ha·ven /háyv'n/ *n.* **1. SHELTERED PLACE** a place sought for rest, shelter, or protection ○ *a haven for wildlife* **2.** NAUT **ANCHORAGE** a harbor or port facility where ships and boats come in and tie up (*literary*) [Pre-12thC. From Old Norse *höfn,* literally "place that holds (ships)."]

have-nots *npl.* people who are not rich or privileged, especially compared with those who are ○ *a country with the highest income inequality between the haves and have-nots*

have·n't /hάvv'nt/ *contr.* have not

Hav·er·hill /háyvәril/ city in northeastern Massachusetts on the Merrimack River. Population: 53,952 (1996).

hav·er·sack /hάvvәr sàk/ *n.* a strong bag carried on the back or the shoulder, used especially by travelers or hikers [Mid-18thC. Via French *havresac* from obsolete German *Habersack,* from *Haber* "oats" + *Sack* "bag"; originally used by cavalrymen to hold oats for their horses.]

Ha·ver·sian ca·nal /hә vùrzh'n-/ *n.* a tiny longitudinal channel in bone tissue. The canals form a network that contains blood vessels and nerve fibers. [Mid-19thC. Named for Clopton *Havers* (1650?-1702), the English physician and anatomist who discovered them.]

Ha·ver·sian sys·tem *n.* a Haversian canal along with the concentric layers of compact bone surrounding it

hav·er·sine /hάvvәr sīn/ *n.* in mathematics, half the value of the versed sine [Late 19thC. Contraction of *half versed sine.*]

hav·oc /hάvvәk/ *n.* **1. DEVASTATION** widespread damage, destruction, or devastation ○ *the havoc wreaked by the storm* **2. CHAOS** a condition or situation of disruptive chaos [15thC. From Anglo-Norman *(crier) havok* "(to cry) havoc," signal to an army to seize plunder, alteration of Old French *havo(t)* "pillage," of uncertain origin: probably from prehistoric Germanic.]

Ha·vre de Grace /hàvvәr dә grάss/ city in northeastern Maryland, on Chesapeake Bay at the mouth of the Susquehanna River. Population: 10,092 (1996).

haw^{1} /haw/ *n.* **1.** = **hawthorn 2. FRUIT OF HAWTHORN** the round or oval fruit of the hawthorn, usually red or yellow and containing seeds [Old English *haga,* of uncertain origin: perhaps the same word as Old English *haga* "hedge"]

haw^{2} /haw/ *n.* **UTTERANCE SHOWING HESITATION** a sound that people make when they are hesitating to speak ■ *vi.* **(hawed, haw·ing, haws) MAKE HESITATING SOUND** to make a sound indicative of hesitation while speaking [Mid-17thC. An imitation of the sound.]

haw^{3} /haw/ *interj.* used to command an animal or a team of animals to turn left [Late 17thC. Origin unknown.]

haw^{4} /haw/ *n.* = **nictitating membrane** [Early 16thC. Origin unknown.]

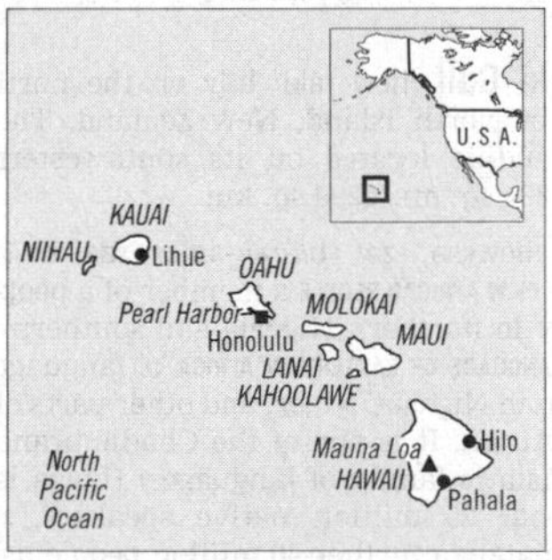

Hawaii

Ha·wai·i /hә wī ee/ state of the United States in the northern Pacific Ocean, consisting of eight main islands and over 100 others. Capital: Honolulu. Population: 1,183,723 (1997). Area: 6,459 sq. mi./16,729 sq. km. ■ the largest island in the state of Hawaii. Population: 120,317 (1990). Area: 4,028 sq. mi./10,443 sq. km.

Ha·wai·i-A·leu·tian Stan·dard Time *n.* the standard time in the time zone centered on longitude 150° W, which includes an area of the Pacific Ocean that includes Hawaii and the western Aleutian Islands. It is ten hours earlier than Universal Coordinated Time.

Ha·wai·ian /hә wάa yәn/ *n.* **1.** PEOPLES **SOMEBODY FROM HAWAII** somebody who was born in or raised in the state of Hawaii, especially somebody of Melanesian or Tahitian descent **2.** LANG **LANGUAGE SPOKEN IN HAWAII** a language spoken in Hawaii and other neighboring islands, belonging to the Polynesian branch of the Austronesian family of languages. Hawaiian is spoken by about 70,000 people. —**Ha·wai·ian** *adj.*

Ha·wai·ian ap·pli·qué *n.* an appliqué developed in Hawaii, consisting of a large central motif, from a design cut from folded paper, which is applied to a foundation fabric and made into a quilt. Traditional Hawaiian appliqué is made in two solid colours, typically red, green, orange, or blue on white.

Ha·wai·ian goose *n.* = **nene**

Ha·wai·ian gui·tar *n.* a small steel-strung guitar with a sliding glass or metal bar that fits across the strings in order to change the pitch of the whole instrument. It is usually played horizontally on a stand, and the strings are plucked with a thimble.

Ha·wai·ian shirt *n.* a short-sleeved shirt with brightly colored designs, often featuring Hawaiian motifs, printed on it

Ha·wai·i Stan·dard Time, Ha·wai·i Time *n.* = **Hawaii-Aleutian Standard Time**

Ha·wai·i Vol·ca·noes Na·tion·al Park national park on the island of Hawaii, Hawaii, established in 1916. Its features include the active volcanoes of Mauna Loa and Kilauea. Area: 209,695 acres/84,861 hectares.

Hawfinch

haw·finch /háw finch/ (*plural* **-finch·es** *or* **-finch**) *n.* a Eurasian bird that has a thick conical silvery beak, brown plumage, black and white wings, and a white-tipped tail. Latin name: *Coccothraustes coccothraustes.* [*Haw* from HAW^{1}]

haw-haw *n.* = **ha-ha**^{1}, **ha-ha**^{2}

Haw·ick /háw ik/ historic town in the Scottish Borders district on the Teviot River. Population: 15,812 (1991).

hawk^{1} /hawk/ *n.* **1.** BIRDS **BIRD OF PREY** a diurnal bird of prey, typically having broad wings, a short hooked bill, strong talons, and a long tail. Subfamilies: Accipitridae and Buteoninae. **2.** BIRDS **SMALL BIRD OF PREY** any one of various small birds of prey, including the falcons but not the larger birds such as the eagle. Order: Falconiformes. **3.** POL, MIL **SOMEBODY FAVORING FORCE** somebody who favors the use of military force in implementing foreign policy rather than diplomatic solutions. ◊ **dove 4. AGGRESSIVE COMPETITOR** a fiercely competitive, aggressive, predatory, or combative person ○ *a marketing hawk who wanted to put the competition out of business* **5. RUTHLESS SWINDLER** a ruthless con man or other swindler who preys on unsuspecting victims ■ *v.* **(hawked, hawk·ing, hawks) 1.** *vi.* HUNT **HUNT WITH HAWKS** to hunt for prey on the wing, or hunt for prey using hawks and similar birds of prey **2.** *vti.* BIRDS **ATTACK ON THE WING** to pursue or attack while flying in a way similar to that of a hawk ○ *tiny birds hawking insects in the morning sky* [Old English *h(e)afoc.* Ultimately from an Indo-European word meaning "to grasp" (see HAVE).] —**hawk·er** *n.* —**hawk·ing** *n.*

hawk^{2} /hawk/ **(hawked, hawk·ing, hawks)** *vti.* to engage in selling merchandise on the street or from door to door [14thC. Origin uncertain: probably a back-formation from *hawker,* probably from Middle Low German *höker,* from *höken* "to peddle."] —**hawk·er** *n.*

hawk^{3} /hawk/ *v.* **(hawked, hawk·ing, hawks) 1.** *vi.* **CLEAR THE THROAT** to clear the throat noisily of phlegm **2.** *vt.* **COUGH UP PHLEGM** to clear the throat and noisily cough up phlegm ■ *n.* **ATTEMPT AT CLEARING THROAT** a noisy attempt to clear the throat of phlegm [Late 16thC. Origin uncertain: probably an imitation of the sound.]

hawk[4] /hawk/ *n.* a metal square with a wooden handle underneath, used by a plasterer to hold wet plaster or mortar before applying it to a surface [15thC. Origin uncertain: perhaps the same word as HAWK[1].]

hawk·bill *n.* = **hawksbill**

hawk·bit /háwk bìt/ (*plural* **-bits** *or* **-bit**) *n.* a perennial plant found in grasslands that has yellow flowers and lobed leaves. There are three varieties. Genus: *Leontodon.* [Early 18thC. Blend of HAWKWEED and DEVIL'S BIT.]

Hawke Bay /hàwk báy/ bay on the eastern coast of North Island, New Zealand. It extends from Mahia Peninsula in the north to Cape Kidnappers in the south.

Hawke's Bay /hàwks báy/ administrative region of New Zealand, located in eastern North Island and bordering Hawke Bay. Population: 144,292 (1996). Area: 8,177 sq. mi./21,178 sq. km.

Hawkes·bury /háwksbəree/ river in eastern New South Wales, Australia, which rises in the Great Dividing Range. Length: 300 mi./480 km.

Hawk·eye /háwk ì/ *n.* somebody who was born in or who lives in the state of Iowa (*informal*) [Early 19thC. From Iowa's popular name "the Hawkeye State."]

hawk-eyed *adj.* quick to see things that are not obvious, often as a result of having very keen eyesight ○ *The hawk-eyed appraiser spotted a tiny chip in the antique teapot.*

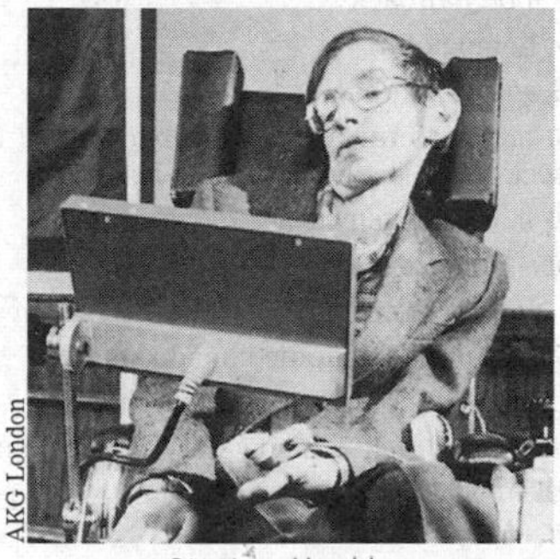
AKG London
Stephen Hawking

Hawk·ing /háwking/, **Stephen** (*b.* 1942) British physicist and mathematician. His research focused on space-time and unified field theory. His lectures, films, and books, including his best-selling *A Brief History of Time* (1988), made difficult concepts in physics accessible to the public. Full name **Stephen William Hawking**

Haw·kins /háwkinz/, **Coleman** (1904–69) U.S. musician. His technique and improvisational skills laid the foundations for the tenor saxophone in bebop jazz. His best known album is *Body and Soul* (1939).

hawk·ish /háwkish/ *adj.* favoring the use of military force in implementing foreign policy rather than diplomatic solutions ○ *The senator was hawkish on Iraq.* ◊ **dovish**

Hawk moth

hawk moth *n.* a moth with a thick body and long narrow wings that enable it to hover over flowers and feed on their nectar. Family: Sphingidae.

hawk owl *n.* an owl with a long slender tail and brownish speckled plumage that resembles a hawk when in flight. It is found in North America and northern Eurasia. Latin name: *Surnia ulula.*

Hawks /hawks/, **Howard** (1896–1977) U.S. movie director. During his 45-year career, he directed many Hollywood classics, including *Bringing Up Baby*

Hawk owl

(1938) and *The Big Sleep* (1946). Full name **Howard Winchester Hawks**

hawk's beard (*plural* **hawk's beards** *or* **hawk's beard**) *n.* a plant with small yellow flowers resembling those of the dandelion. Genus: *Crepis.*

hawks·bill /háwks bìl/ (*plural* **-bills** *or* **-bill**), **hawks·bill tur·tle, hawk·bill** /háwk bìl/ (*plural* **-bills** *or* **-bill**) *n.* a tropical sea turtle, reaching 2 ft./61 cm in length and now classified as endangered, that has a yellowish-brown shell of overlapping plates once valued as a source of tortoiseshell. Latin name: *Eretmochelys imbricata.* [From the shape of its mouth, likened to a hawk's beak]

hawk's-eye *n.* a semiprecious gemstone that is a dark blue variety of the mineral crocidolite

Hawkweed

hawk·weed /háwk wèed/ (*plural* **-weed** *or* **-weeds**) *n.* a composite plant that is typically hairy and has yellow or orange rayed flowers. Genus: *Hieracium.* [Translation of Latin *hieracium*, from Greek *ierakion*, from *ierax* "hawk".]

Hawn /hawn/, **Goldie** (*b.* 1945) U.S. actor and producer. She achieved fame on television's *Rowan and Martin's Laugh-In* (1968–70) and went on to a movie career. She won an Academy Award for *Cactus Flower* (1969).

Haworthia

ha·wor·thi·a /haw wúrthee ə, -thee ə/ (*plural* **-as** *or* **-a**) *n.* a succulent herb, native to South Africa, with densely overlapping, often warty leaves, clustered in rosettes. Genus: *Haworthia.* [Named for Adrian Hardy *Haworth* (1768–1833), who wrote extensively on succulent plants]

hawse /hawz/ *n.* **1. LOCATION OF SHIP'S HAWSEHOLES** the area of a ship in which the hawseholes are to be found **2. = hawsehole 3. SPACE BETWEEN BOW AND ANCHOR** the space between the bow and the anchors of a ship lying at anchor **4. ANCHOR DEPLOYMENT** the way in which a ship's anchor lines are deployed, starboard and port, when both are deployed together at the same time ■ *vi.* (**hawsed, haws·ing, haws·es**) **PITCH VIOLENTLY WHEN AT ANCHOR** to pitch violently when lying at anchor [Origin uncertain: either 13thC, from Old Norse *hals*, or from Old English *h(e)als*, both "neck, ship's prow." Ultimately from an Indo-European word meaning "to revolve."]

hawse·hole /hawz hòl/ *n.* an opening in the bow of a ship through which a large heavy line is passed for towing or mooring the ship

hawse·pipe /háwz pìp/ *n.* a pipe on each side of a ship's bow for use in deploying and weighing anchor, with the anchor lines running through each pipe

haw·ser /háwzər/ *n.* a large heavy cable that is used when mooring or towing a ship [13thC. From Anglo-Norman *haucer*, from Old French *haucier* "to hoist," literally "to make high," ultimately from Latin *altus* "high" (see ALTITUDE).]

haw·ser-laid *adj.* used to describe rope composed of three strands, each of which has been made by being twisted in a left-handed direction. The three strands are then twisted together in a right-handed direction.

haw·thorn /háw thàwrn/ *n.* a thorny tree or shrub of the rose family that has clusters of white or pink flowers and small reddish fruits. Genus: *Crataegus.*

Haw·thorne /háwth awrn/ industrial and residential city in southwestern California, situated 5 mi./8 km south of the city of Los Angeles. Population: 71,349 (1990).

Library of Congress
Nathaniel Hawthorne

Haw·thorne /háw thawrn/, **Nathaniel** (1804–64) U.S. writer. His novels and short stories frequently deal with Puritan sin and atonement, and include *The Scarlet Letter* (1850). Born **Nathaniel Hathorne**

Haw·thorne ef·fect /háw thàwrn-/ *n.* social research findings attributable to the attention of researchers to the subjects of their research rather than to factors significant to the research topic. An example would be when variables of both a positive and a negative nature produce the same effect. [Mid-20thC. Named for the *Hawthorne* plant of the Western Electric Company in Cicero (Chicago, Illinois), where it was first observed.]

hay /hay/ *n.* **1. CUT AND DRIED GRASS** grass or other plants that are cut, dried, and then often used as fodder **2. MINUSCULE AMOUNT OF MONEY** a very small amount of money (*slang*) (*almost always used in negative statements*) ○ *He made five thousand bucks out of the deal, and that isn't hay.* ■ *v.* (**hayed, hay·ing, hays**) **1.** *vi.* **CUT, BALE, AND STORE HAY** to mow hay and bale or roll it, and then store it ○ *He's been haying all day.* **2.** *vt.* **FEED WITH HAY** to feed animals with hay [Old English *hēg*, literally "something that can be cut down." Ultimately from an Indo-European word meaning "to hew, strike," which is also the ancestor of English *haggle, hew,* and *hoe.*] ◇ **a roll in the hay** an instance of having sex with somebody (*slang*) ◇ **hit the hay** to go to bed (*informal*) ◇ **make hay while the sun shines** to take advantage of all opportunities when they present themselves (*informal*)

Hay /hay/, **John** (1838–1905) U.S. diplomat and writer. He was Abraham Lincoln's private secretary (1861–65), and wrote a monumental 10-volume biography of him (1890). Full name **John Milton Hay**

hay·cock /háy kòk/ *n. U.K.* a cone-shaped pile of hay that is left in a field until it is dry enough to be stored

Hay·den /háyd'n/, **Melissa** (*b.* 1928) Canadian ballet dancer. She danced with the New York City Ballet from 1950 and appeared in the movie *Limelight* (1952). Real name **Mildred Herman**

Hay di·et /háy/ *n.* a way of eating in which protein and carbohydrate foods are not eaten at the same time, claimed to be helpful for digestive complaints and weight loss [Mid-20thC. Named for William Howard *Hay* (1866–1940), who devised it.]

Haydn /hī́d'n/, **Joseph** (1732–1809) Austrian composer. His hundreds of symphonies, concertos, string quartets, and operas helped define the classical style, and include the popular oratorio *The Creation* (1798). Full name **Franz Joseph Haydn**

Hayes /hayz/, **Helen** (1900–93) U.S. actor. One of the most distinguished stage performers of the century, she was closely identified with the title role in *Victoria Regina* (1935). She won Academy Awards for *The Sin of Madelon Claudet* (1931) and *Airport* (1970). Born **Helen Hayes Brown**

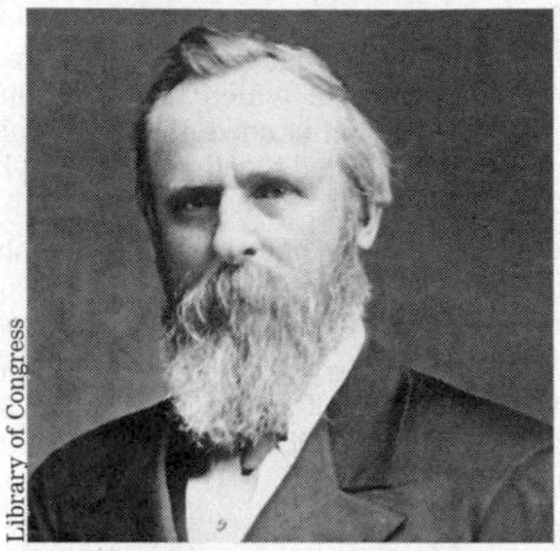

Rutherford B. Hayes

Hayes, Rutherford B. (1822–93) U.S. statesman and 19th President of the United States. A Republican, he reformed the civil service and withdrew the last federal troops from the Reconstruction South during his presidential term (1877–81). Full name **Rutherford Birchard Hayes**

hay fe·ver *n.* an allergic reaction to pollen that irritates the upper respiratory tract and the eyes, resulting in symptoms including a runny and itchy nose, itchy and watering eyes, and sneezing. Technical name **pollinosis**

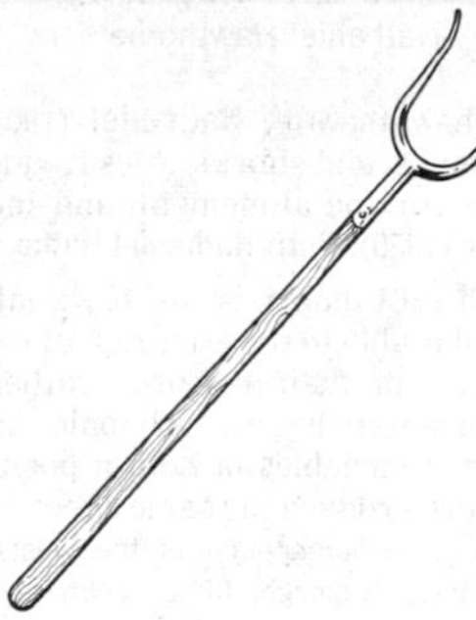

Hayfork

hay·fork /háy fàwrk/ *n.* **1.** = **pitchfork 2.** HAY-MOVING MACHINE a machine-operated fork for moving hay

hay·lage /háylij/ *n.* silage made from partially dried grass [Mid-20thC. Blend of HAY and SILAGE.]

hay·loft /háy lòft/ *n.* a loft for storing hay over a stable or a barn

hay·mak·er /háy màykər/ *n.* **1.** BOXING **POWERFUL SWINGING PUNCH** a powerful swinging punch, especially in a boxing match (*slang*) **2.** AGRIC **MACHINE PROCESSING HAY** a machine for breaking down stems of hay to improve the drying process **3.** AGRIC **WORKER PROCESSING HAY** an agricultural worker whose job it is to cut, turn, toss, spread, or carry hay after it has been mown

hay·mow /háy mŏ/ *n.* **1.** = **hayloft 2. QUANTITY OF HAY STORED IN BARN** a quantity of hay stored in a barn or loft

hay·rack /háy ràk/ *n.* **1. RACK HOLDING FEED** a rack that holds hay and from which livestock feed **2. RACK ON WAGON** a rack attached to a wagon to increase its capacity for carrying hay **3. WAGON WITH HAYRACK** a wagon equipped with a hayrack

hay·rick /háy rìk/ *n.* = **haystack**

hay·ride /háy rīd/ *n.* a ride taken for pleasure by a group of people in a wagon or other vehicle that is full of hay or straw

Hays /hayz/ city in central Kansas, west of Salina and northwest of Great Bend. Population: 17,991 (1996).

hay·seed /háy sèed/ *n.* **1. OFFENSIVE TERM** an offensive term that deliberately insults somebody's rural residence or background and his or her intelligence and level of sophistication (*slang insult*) **2. GRASS SEED FROM HAY** grass seed that is shaken out of hay **3. PIECES OF GRASS** pieces of grass or straw that fall from hay

hay·stack /háy stàk/ *n.* a large pile of hay, especially one that is built in the open and covered with thatch for winter storage

Hay·ward /háywərd/ city in northwestern California, on San Francisco Bay. Population: 115,590 (1994).

Hay·ward, Susan (1918–75) U.S. actor. She won an Academy Award for *I Want to Live!* (1958). Real name **Edythe Marrener**

hay·wire /háy wīr/ *adj.* (*informal*) **1. FUNCTIONING ERRATICALLY** functioning erratically, or not functioning at all ○ *A powerful magnet can make the television set go haywire.* **2. BEHAVING ODDLY** behaving unpredictably or extravagantly [From the springy nature of wire used to tie up bundles of hay, and sometimes for makeshift repairs]

Hay·wood /háy wŏŏd/, **William Dudley** (1869–1928) U.S. labor leader. He cofounded the radical Industrial Workers of the World (1905) and advocated the violent overthrow of capitalism. Known as **Big Bill**

Hay·worth /háywərth/, **Rita** (1918–87) U.S. actor. A dancer from her childhood, she appeared in movies including *Gilda* (1946). Real name **Margarita Carmen Cansino**

haz·ard /házzərd/ *n.* **1. POTENTIAL DANGER** something that is potentially very dangerous **2.** ENG **DANGEROUS OUTCOME** a dangerous or otherwise unwanted outcome, especially one resulting from the failure of an engineered system **3.** GOLF **OBSTACLE ON GOLF COURSE** a natural or constructed obstacle on a golf course, e.g., a sand trap or a lake **4.** GAMBLING **DICE GAME** a dice game resembling craps **5.** CUE GAMES **SCORING STROKE IN BILLIARDS** a scoring stroke in billiards, made when a ball is pocketed, either a ball other than the striker's (**winning hazard**) or the striker's cue ball itself (**losing hazard**) **6.** TENNIS **RECEIVER'S SIDE IN COURT TENNIS** in court tennis, the receiver's side of the court ■ *vt.* (**-ard·ed, -ard·ing, -ards**) **1. SUGGEST TENTATIVELY** to offer a tentative explanation of something ○ *Would anyone like to hazard a guess as to what this could possibly mean?* **2. RISK LOSS OF SOMETHING** to chance or risk something, especially in order to gain something else [13thC. Via Old French *hasard* "game of chance played with dice" from, ultimately, Arabic *az-zahr*, literally "the die" or "the chance."]

haz·ard light *n.* either of a pair of car lights, usually the blinkers, that flash on and off to warn other drivers of potential danger

haz·ard·ous /házzərdəss/ *adj.* potentially very dangerous to living beings or the environment — **haz·ard·ous·ly** *adv.* —**haz·ard·ous·ness** *n.*

haz·ard·ous waste *n.* a by-product of manufacturing processes or nuclear processing that is toxic and presents a potential threat to people and the environment

haz·ard pay *n.* extra money given to employees because of the dangerous nature of their work

haz·ard warn·ing light *n.* = **hazard light**

haze[1] /hayz/ *n.* **1. PARTICLES IN THE ATMOSPHERE** mist, cloud, or smoke suspended in the atmosphere and obscuring or obstructing the view **2. VAGUE OBSCURING FACTOR** something that is vague and serves to obscure something **3. DISORIENTED MENTAL OR PHYSICAL STATE** a mental or physical state or condition when feelings and perceptions are vague, disorienting, or obscured ■ *vi.* (**hazed, haz·ing, haz·es**) **BECOME SATURATED WITH PARTICLES** to become filled with suspended atmospheric particulate matter such as pollution ○ *It's going to be hot and muggy and in the afternoon it will begin to haze over.* [Early 18thC. Origin uncertain: probably a back-formation from HAZY.]

haze[2] /hayz/ (**hazed, haz·ing, haz·es**) *vti.* to persecute or torture somebody in a subordinate position, e.g., a fraternity pledge or a first-year military academy cadet. Hazing may be illegal, and many institutions have prohibited it. [Late 17thC. Origin uncertain: perhaps from obsolete French *haser* "to tease, annoy," ultimately of unknown origin. First attested in English as a dialect verb meaning "to frighten, scold."] —**haz·er** *n.* — **haz·ing** *n.*

ha·zel /háyz'l/ *n.* (*plural* **-zels** *or* **-zel**) **1.** TREES **SMALL TREE WITH EDIBLE NUTS** a shrub or small tree of the birch family that has edible brown nuts. Genus: *Corylus.* **2.** INDUST **WOOD OF HAZEL** the wood of the hazel tree **3.** FOOD = **hazelnut 4.** COLORS **LIGHT BROWN COLOR** a light-brown color with a tinge of green or gold, like a ripe hazelnut ○ *hazel eyes* ■ *adj.* COLORS **HAZEL-COLORED** of the color hazel [Old English *hæsel*. Ultimately from an Indo-European word.]

ha·zel·nut /háyz'l nùt/ *n.* an edible nut from a hazel tree

Ha·zel·wood /háyz'lwŏŏd/ **1.** village in eastern Missouri, northwest of the city of St. Louis. Population: 15,324 (1990). **2.** city in northwestern Oregon, a suburb of Portland. Population: 11,480 (1998).

Haz·litt /házlit/, **William** (1778–1830) British essayist. He is regarded as one of the most brilliant English prose stylists. His collections of essays include *Table Talk* (1821–22) and *The Spirit of the Age* (1825).

HAZ·MAT /ház màt/ *abbr.* hazardous material

haz·y /háyzee/ (**-i·er, -i·est**) *adj.* **1. VISUALLY OBSCURED** unclear, especially because partially obscured or obstructed by mist, cloud, or smoke **2. IMPRECISE** not specific or clearly remembered ○ *I have a hazy recollection of having met her.* **3. NOT KNOWLEDGEABLE** showing a lack of understanding or knowledge [Early 17thC. Origin unknown. Originally in the sense "foggy."] — **haz·i·ly** *adv.* —**haz·i·ness** *n.*

hb, **hb.** *abbr.* halfback

Hb *abbr.* hemoglobin

HB, **H/B** *abbr.* hatchback

H-beam *n.* a structural steel member shaped like an H in section. It is similar to an I-beam.

H-bomb *n.* = **hydrogen bomb**

H.C. *abbr.* House of Commons

H.C.F., **h.c.f., hcf** *abbr.* highest common factor

HCG *abbr.* human chorionic gonadotrophin

HCI *abbr.* human-computer interaction

HD *abbr.* **1.** hard disk **2.** heavy-duty **3.** high density **4.** hard drive

hd. *abbr.* **1.** hand **2.** head

hdbk. *abbr.* handbook

hdkf. *abbr.* handkerchief

HDL *abbr.* high-density lipoprotein

hdqrs. *abbr.* headquarters

HDTV *abbr.* high-definition television

hdwe. *abbr.* hardware

he[1] (*stressed*) /hee/; (*unstressed*) /hee, ee/ *pron.* **MALE NOT REFERRED TO BY NAME** used to refer to a male person or animal who has been previously mentioned or whose identitiy is known (*used as the subject of a verb*) ■ *n.* **MALE ANIMAL OR BOY** a male animal or boy, especially used of a new baby ○ *Is your pup a he or a she?* [Old English *he*. Ultimately from an Indo-European word meaning "this (here)," which is also the ancestor of English *hence, here,* and *her.*]

he[2] /hay/ *n.* the fifth letter of the Hebrew alphabet, represented in the English alphabet as "h." See table at **alphabet** [Mid-17thC. From Hebrew *hē'*.]

He *symbol.* helium

H.E. *abbr.* **1.** His Eminence **2.** His Excellency

head /hed/ *n.* **1.** ANAT **TOP PART OF BODY** the topmost part of a vertebrate body, where the brain, eyes, nose, ears, mouth, and jaws are situated **2.** ZOOL **MOST FORWARD SECTION OF BODY** the section of the body of an invertebrate that is forward of all other segments **3. CENTER OF INTELLECT** the center of a human being's faculties of intellect, emotion, and reasoning ○ *a good head for figures* **4.** ARTS **REPRESENTATION OF HUMAN HEAD** an artistic, photographic, or televised representation or image of a human being's face, hair, eyes, mouth, nose, and ears **5. LEADER OF OTHERS** somebody who is in charge of, has responsibility for, and supervises others ○ *All department heads attended the meeting.* **6. CRISIS POINT** a critical juncture in a series of events, at which time some action must be taken, however painful ○ *The looming deadline for a budget brought matters to a head.* **7. MORE IMPORTANT END** the more important end of something ○ *Our guest sat at the head of the table.* **8. TOP OF LONG THIN OBJECT** the wider, often flattened, top of a long thin object ○ *He hit the nail on the head.* **9. HIGHEST PART** the highest or uppermost part of something ○ *the head of the valley* **10.** BEVERAGES **FROTH**

ON BEER the froth that forms on the top of beer when it is poured into a glass **11.** (*plural* **head**) COUNTABLE UNIT a single unit in a number of people or animals, especially when they are being counted ○ *500 head of cattle* **12.** MEASURE OF DISTANCE the height or length of a head, used as a measure of distance between two individuals, especially racehorses at the winning post ○ *The favorite won by a head.* **13.** BOT FLOWER OR VEGETABLE the top part of a plant where a flower or a cluster of leaves grows **14.** MED TOP OF PIMPLE OR BOIL the visible pus-filled center of a pimple or boil **15.** DRUGS DRUG USER somebody who habitually uses drugs (*slang*) **16.** COINS OBVERSE OF COIN the side of a coin that shows a leader's head or other main design **17.** NAUT SHIP'S TOILET a lavatory on a ship (*slang*) **18.** ENG = **cylinder head** **19.** PRINTING TITLE a heading, either like a newspaper headline or before a section in a text **20.** GEOG SOURCE OF RIVER the source of a river or stream **21.** MECH ENG DEVICE FOR HOLDING CUTTING TOOLS a part of a boring or turning machine, e.g., a lathe, that holds cutting tools to the work in progress **22.** TRANSP TERMINAL the destination point of a transport route **23.** GEOG PROMONTORY a headland that juts out into the sea or other stretch of water (*often used in placenames*) **24.** MUSIC PART OF DRUM the stretched membrane of a drum or tambourine **25.** MED HEADACHE a headache (*informal*) ○ *I've got a terrible head.* **26.** ORAL SEX an act of performing oral sex on somebody (*slang taboo*) **27.** COMMUNICATION SECTION IN SPEECH OR TEXT one of the main sections or topics of a written or spoken discourse **28.** PHYS PRESSURE OF LIQUID the pressure at the lower of two points in a column of liquid resulting from the difference in height **29.** ELEC ENG ELECTROMAGNETIC RECORDING DEVICE the part of a machine such as a tape recorder that uses, e.g., magnetic tape to record, read, or erase sounds, images, or data (*often used in the plural*) **30.** PHYS PRESSURE the pressure exerted by a liquid or gas ○ *a head of steam* **31.** MINING PART OF COAL MINE a passage where coal is mined underground **32.** PHYS REQUIRED HEIGHT OF LIQUID SURFACE the height that the surface of a liquid has to be above a specified level to produce a stated pressure at the specified level **33.** *Carib* STATE OF MIND somebody's specified state of mind at a given time, especially as perceived by others ○ *Wha' head you pushing?* ■ *v.* (**head·ed, head·ing, heads**) **1.** *vi.* GO IN CERTAIN DIRECTION to move or go in a specified direction or to a specified position ○ *He headed toward the station.* **2.** *vt.* CONTROL OTHERS OR ORGANIZATION to be in the first position of authority and exercise control over people or an organization **3.** *vt.* SOCCER HIT WITH HEAD to use the head to hit a soccer ball ○ *He headed the ball into the goal.* **4.** *vt.* CAUSE TO GO SOMEWHERE to make something move in a specified direction or to a certain place ○ *The pilot headed the plane in a northeasterly course.* **5.** *vt.* PRINTING BE OR GIVE A HEADING to act as or supply a heading on a written page ○ *Let's head the letter with our logo.* **6.** *vt.* BE AT FRONT OF GROUP to be at the front or the top of something ○ *The mayor headed the procession as it entered the town.* [Old English *hēafod*. Ultimately from an Indo-European word that is also the ancestor of English *captain, cattle, chapter,* and *chief.*] ◇ **above somebody's head** too difficult for somebody to understand ◇ **be head and shoulders above somebody** to be notably superior to somebody ◇ **be off your head** to be mentally disturbed ◇ **give somebody his** *or* **her head** to relax control or supervision of somebody ◇ **go off your head** to become completely irrational (*informal*) ◇ **go to somebody's head 1.** to make somebody conceited or overconfident **2.** to make somebody dizzy or lightheaded ○ *The champagne went right to my head.* ◇ **head over heels 1.** completely ○ *They fell head over heels in love.* **2.** in a headfirst rolling movement ◇ **keep your head** to remain calm or unexcited ◇ **let somebody have his** *or* **her head** = **give somebody his** *or* **her head** ◇ **lose your head** to panic or lose self-control ◇ **over somebody's head** = **above somebody's head**

head off *v.* **1.** *vt.* INTERCEPT to stop a person or animal from proceeding in a particular direction by placing yourself between the person or animal and the goal sought ○ *Let's try to head the rustlers off at the pass.* ○ *We took a shortcut to head her off before she reached the station.* **2.** *vt.* FORESTALL to try in advance to prevent something from taking place, or to prevent somebody from doing something, that might prove difficult or unpleasant ○ *We need to head off any attempt to have the matter raised again in committee.* **3.** *vi.* GO to go, or leave a place and go, in a particular direction ○ *The others headed off down the hill while we stayed to enjoy the view a little longer.*

Head /hed/, **Edmund Walker, 8th Baronet** (1805–68) British-born Canadian administrator, who served as Lieutenant Governor of New Brunswick (1848–54), Governor-General of British North America (1854–61), and Governor of the Hudson's Bay Company (1863–68).

head·ache /héd àyk/ *n.* **1.** MED PAIN IN THE HEAD a pain in the head caused, e.g., by dilation of cerebral arteries or muscle tightness **2.** SOURCE OF WORRY something that causes worry or difficulty (*informal*) —**head·ach·y** *adj.*

head bag /héd bàg/, **head·bag** *n.* **1.** BAG COVERING HEAD a bag that is placed over the head in order to prevent somebody from being identified ○ *the suspect wore a head bag when leaving the court* **2.** AUTOMOT AIRBAG TO PROTECT HEAD an automobile airbag that is designed to protect the head in the event of a collision

head·band /héd bànd/ *n.* a band of material that is worn around the head across the forehead, especially to keep hair off the face

head·bang /héd bàng/ (**-banged, -bang·ing, -bangs**) *vi.* to dance to heavy metal music by moving the head violently backward and forward to the beat of the music (*slang*)

head·bang·er /héd bàngər/ *n.* somebody whose favorite music is heavy metal (*slang*)

head·board /héd bàwrd/ *n.* an upright board, often padded or covered in fabric, used to form the head of a bed

head·butt *vt.* (**head-butt·ed, head-butt·ing, head-butts**) HIT SOMEBODY WITH HEAD to hit somebody a deliberate hard blow with the forehead or the top of the head ■ *n.* BLOW WITH THE HEAD a deliberate blow with the forehead or the top of the head

head·case /héd kàyss/ *n.* an offensive term that deliberately shows contempt for or ridicules somebody's mental condition (*slang insult*)

head·cheese /héd chèez/ (*plural* **-chees·es** *or* **-cheese**) *n.* a mixture of chopped cooked meat, mainly from the head and feet of a hog, that is pressed into the form of a loaf or sausage and eaten cold [*Cheese* from the ingredients being pressed together as in cheese-making]

WORD KEY: REGIONAL NOTE

The general currency word ***headcheese*** prevails in all parts of the country except in the South Midland and Southern regions. In the South Midland, usual terms include *press meat, pressed meat, souse, souse meat, hog souse,* and *pressed souse meat.* The *souse* forms prevail across all of the South, as well, except in the coastal regions. There, the terms *hoghead cheese* and *hog's head cheese* are mainly used.

head cold *n.* a viral infection of the nose, throat, and bronchial tubes, characterized by coughing, sneezing, headaches, and nasal congestion

head count *n.* the process of counting the people in a group one by one, or the number arrived at by this process ○ *After a head count, we found there were 265 people in the hall.*

head·dress /héd drèss/ *n.* a decorative covering worn on the head, usually as a sign of rank, for ceremonial purposes, or as personal display

head·ed /héddəd/ *adj.* **1.** WITH A HEADING with a heading, e.g., a letterhead, title, or similar inscription **2.** WITH A PARTICULAR HEAD with a specified kind of head or heads (*usually used in combination*) **3.** WITH HAIR OF PARTICULAR KIND with a specified color or type of hair (*usually used in combination*) **4.** WITH A PARTICULAR TEMPERAMENT with a specified temperament, characteristic, or ability (*usually used in combination*)

head·er /héddər/ *n.* **1.** SOCCER SHOT OR PASS WITH HEAD a deliberate use of the head to play, pass, or shoot the ball in soccer ○ *He scored with a flying header.* **2.** HEADLONG FALL a headlong plunge or fall **3.** PRINTING HEADING FOR PAGE a heading for each page of a word-processed or faxed document, usually automatically inserted and consisting of text or a page number **4.** COMPUT PLACE FOR INFORMATION ABOUT MESSAGE a place at the top of a piece of electronic mail where the sender can state what a message is about and where it is being sent from and to **5.** CONSTR CROSSWISE BRICK IN WALL a brick or stone positioned crosswise in a wall and level with its outer surface **6.** MECH ENG, CARS PIPE CONNECTING OTHER PIPES a pipe that links other pipes to direct the flow of fluid to a system, especially an exhaust system **7.** ENG = **header tank** **8.** INDUST MAKER, FITTER, OR REMOVER OF TOPS a person who, or a machine that, makes, fits, or removes the tops of something

head·er tank /héddər/ *n.* a raised tank that ensures a constant pressure or supply of fluid to a system, especially water to a central heating system

head·fast /héd fàst/ *n.* a mooring rope at the bow of a ship

head·first /hed fúrst/ *adv., adj.* WITH THE HEAD LEADING in a movement or position where the head is in front of the rest of the body and is the first thing that reaches, enters, or strikes something ○ *He insisted on going down the slide headfirst.* ○ *taking a headfirst dive into the pool* ■ *adv.* RASHLY AND THOUGHTLESSLY abruptly and without taking time to think about or prepare for something ○ *They rush into things headfirst and think about the consequences afterwards.*

head·fore·most /hed fáwrmōst/ *adv., adj.* = **headfirst**

head·ful /héd fo͝ol/ *n.* **1.** LARGE AMOUNT a large amount of something that has been learned, thought, or imagined (*informal*) ○ *a headful of facts* **2.** MASS OF HAIR a thick mass of hair ○ *a headful of curls*

head gate *n.* **1.** UPSTREAM GATE OF LOCK the gate that controls the flow of water into the upstream end of a canal lock **2.** = **floodgate**

head·gear /héd gèer/ *n.* **1.** CLOTHES SOMETHING COVERING THE HEAD something worn on the head, especially a hat ○ *wearing some pretty impressive headgear* **2.** MINING HOISTING MECHANISM AT MINESHAFT an apparatus at the top of a mineshaft for lifting things out of and lowering them into a mine **3.** RIDING PART OF HARNESS the part of a harness that fits over a horse's head

head·hunt /héd hùnt/ (**-hunt·ed, -hunt·ing, -hunts**) *v.* **1.** *vt.* BUSINESS, HR RECRUIT SOMEBODY FROM ANOTHER COMPANY to recruit, or attempt to recruit, an executive or highly valued employee from one company to fill a similar position in another enterprise ○ *The agency headhunted her to work for an investment bank.* **2.** *vi.* HR ENGAGE IN EMPLOYEE RECRUITING to engage in the profession of employee recruitment ○ *an agency that headhunts for engineers only* **3.** *vi.* ANTHROP COLLECT HEADS to seek, collect, and preserve the heads of enemies as trophies or ceremonial objects

head·hunt·er /héd hùntər/ *n.* **1.** BUSINESS, HR RECRUITER somebody whose job is to seek personnel for a company **2.** ANTHROP SOMEBODY WHO COLLECTS HEADS a member of a people practicing headhunting

head·hunt·ing /héd hùnting/ *n.* **1.** BUSINESS, HR RECRUITMENT OF EMPLOYEES the business of recruiting people who already hold positions in companies or who are unemployed to fill positions in other enterprises **2.** ANTHROP HEAD-COLLECTING the practice among some peoples of cutting off the heads of enemies killed in battle and preserving them as trophies or ceremonial objects

head·ing /hédding/ *n.* **1.** TITLE something that forms the head, top, edge, or front of something, especially as a title for a paragraph, section, chapter, or page ○ *The chapter headings are to be set in 24-point bold.* **2.** CATEGORY OF SUBJECT MATTER any of the divisions into which the subject matter of a document, discourse, or discussion is divided ○ *That information definitely comes under the heading of matters not to be aired in public.* **3.** NAVIG COURSE the direction in which a ship or aircraft is traveling, often given as a compass bearing ○ *If we continue on our present heading we should sight land in one hour.* **4.** MINING MINE TUNNEL a horizontal tunnel in a mine, or the end of such a tunnel

head·lamp /héd lamp/ *n.* = **headlight**

head·land /héddlənd, héd lànd/ *n.* **1.** GEOG PROMONTORY a narrow piece of land jutting out into water, usually with steep, high cliffs **2.** AGRIC UNPLOWED STRIP a strip of land left unplowed at the edge of a field

head·less /héddləss/ *adj.* **1.** WITHOUT HEAD without a head on the body **2.** WITHOUT LEADER having no leader, guide, or director —**head·less·ness** *n.*

head·light /héd lìt/ *n.* a powerful light attached to the front of a motor vehicle or a locomotive, or the beam of light cast by it ○ *He was driving without headlights.*

head·line /héd lìn/ *n.* **1.** PRESS TITLE OF NEWSPAPER ARTICLE a caption printed at the top of a page or article in a newspaper, usually in large heavy letters and often summarizing the content that follows it ○ *an article with the headline "Sharp Fall in Stock Prices"*

2. PRINTING **LINE AT TOP OF PAGE** a line printed at the top of a page of a book or document giving the page number and sometimes other information such as the title or the author's name ■ **head·lines** *npl.* PRESS, BROADCAST **MAIN NEWS ITEMS** the most important items of news covered by a newspaper or a news broadcast ○ *Her name has seldom been out of the headlines since she announced her intention to sue.* ○ *We bring you the headlines every hour on the hour.* ■ *vt.* **(-lined, -lin·ing, -lines) 1.** PRESS **PROVIDE PROMINENT HEADING** to give a prominent title or caption to something ○ *They headlined the story POPSTAR ENTERS HOSPITAL.* **2. PUBLICIZE AS STAR** to present somebody as the leading attraction of a show **3.** ARTS **APPEAR AS STAR** to appear as the leading attraction of a show

head·lin·er /héd lìnər/ *n.* a performer who is advertized as a leading attraction in a show

head-load *vt. S Africa* to transport something by carrying it on the head

head·lock /héd lòk/ *n.* a hold in which a wrestler tightly grips an arm around an opponent's head

head·long /hèd láwng/ *adv., adj.* **1. WITH HEAD FOREMOST** with the head in front of the rest of the body, especially in a rapid uncontrolled movement **2. MOVING FAST AND OUT OF CONTROL** moving or traveling in a fast uncontrolled way **3. WITH TOO MUCH HASTE** acting, happening, or done in an impetuous way with little or no thought for the consequences ○ *She had thrown herself headlong into an even worse situation.* ■ *adj.* **VERY STEEP** very steep (*archaic*) [14thC. By folk etymology from earlier *headling,* by association with *-long* "foremost," in, for example, SIDELONG.]

head louse *n.* a louse that lives on a human head among the hair, feeding by sucking blood and gluing its eggs to the hair shafts near the skin surface. Latin name: *Pediculus humanus capitis.*

head·man /héd màn/ (*plural* **-men** /-mèn/) *n.* **1. CHIEF** the leader of a community or village in some small-scale societies **2. LEADER** a leader or overseer

head·mas·ter /hed màstər/ *n.* a man who is in charge of a private school

head·mis·tress /héd mìstriss/ *n.* a woman who is in charge of a private school

head mon·ey *n.* **1. BOUNTY** a reward paid for the capture or killing of a fugitive or outlaw **2. POLL TAX** a tax on individuals (*archaic*)

head·most /héd mōst/ *adj.* forward to the greatest extent

head·note /héd nōt/ *n.* a brief note at the top of a chapter or a page that summarizes what follows, especially points of law or a legal decision

head of pro·gram·ming *n. U.K.* = **program director**

head of state *n.* the chief representative of a country or state, who may or may not also be the head of government

head-on *adv., adj.* **WITH FRONT FACING FORWARD** with the front facing toward something ○ *We were sailing head-on into the teeth of the gale.* ○ *a head-on collision* ■ *adv.* **WITHOUT EVASION OR COMPROMISE** making no attempt to avoid the dangers or difficulties involved in something ○ *addressed the controversy head-on* ■ *adj.* **UNCOMPROMISING** involving direct, fundamental, and uncompromising opposition ○ *He tried to avoid a head-on clash with his business partner.*

head o·ver heels *adv.* rolling or turning so that the feet are in the air and the head below them so as to land on the back or the feet [From earlier *heels over head*] ◇ **head over heels in love** completely and rapturously in love

head·phones /héd fōnz/ *npl.* a pair of listening devices joined by a band across the top of the head and worn in or over the ears

head·piece /héd pēess/ *n.* **1.** PRINTING **DESIGN AT TOP OF PAGE** an ornamental design printed at the beginning of a text **2.** CLOTHES **HEAD PROTECTOR** a covering for the head, especially a protective one **3.** EQU **BRIDLE PART** the part of a horse's bridle that fits around the head

head pin *n.* = **kingpin** *n.* 3

head·quar·ter /héd kwàwrtər/ **(-tered, -ter·ing, -ters)** *v.* (*informal*) **1.** *vt.* **PROVIDE WITH BASE** to provide somebody with a center of operations ○ *They headquartered their office in a former barracks.* **2.** *vi.* **BE BASED** to set up a headquarters ○ *She headquartered in Paris.*

head·quar·ters /héd kwàwrtərz/ *npl.* (*takes a singular or plural verb*) **1.** BUSINESS **MAIN OFFICE** the administrative center from which the affairs of an organization are directed **2.** MIL **COMMANDER'S OPERATIONAL BASE** a military commander's central office, from which operations are controlled and orders issued ○ *Napoleon's headquarters were in a disused windmill.* ○ *Headquarters is on the radio; they want to know our precise position.*

head·race /héd ràyss/ *n.* a channel conveying water to a water wheel or turbine

head·rail /héd ràyl/ *n.* **1.** CUE GAMES **STARTING END OF BILLIARD TABLE** the end of the table from which a game of billiards is started, nearest the balk line **2.** SAILING **RAILING ON SAILING SHIP** a railing on a sailing vessel extending from the rear of the bow to the back of the figurehead

head·reach /héd rēech/ *n.* **DISTANCE MADE TO WINDWARD** the distance that a sailboat makes to windward when tacking ■ *vt.* **(-reached, -reach·ing, -reach·es) OUTDISTANCE OTHER BOAT** to make a better distance than another boat when tacking

head reg·is·ter *n.* the higher register or falsetto of men's and boys' singing voices in which tone production is concentrated in the head and assisted by sympathetic vibration of the nasal and skull cavities

head·rest /héd rèst/ *n.* an often padded support for the head, usually on the back of a seat, especially in a motor vehicle

head re·straint *n.* an adjustable headrest fitted to the back of a seat of a motor vehicle, designed to prevent neck injuries in an accident

head rhyme *n.* = **alliteration**

head·room /héd ro͝om, -ro͞om/ *n.* the space or clearance overhead, e.g., in a room, doorway, the interior of a motor vehicle, or the underside of a bridge ○ *There's plenty of headroom in this car, even in the back seat.*

head·sail /héd sàyl/ *n.* a sail attached on or set forward of the foremast

head·scarf /héd skaarf/ (*plural* **-scarves** /-skaarvz/) *n.* a woman's scarf in the form of a square of fabric, often tied around the neck

head sea *n.* waves or a current running in a direction opposite to the course of a ship

head·set /héd sèt/ *n.* a pair of earphones, often with a small mouthpiece attached to enable two-way communication

head·shak·ing /héd shàyking/ *n.* a series of side-to-side movements of the head, communicating or suggesting something such as disagreement, doubt, or refusal ○ *I noticed a lot of headshaking in the audience as you made that claim.*

head·ship /héd shìp/ *n.* **1. POSITION OF LEADER** somebody's position or authority as a leader **2.** *U.K.* EDUC **POST OF PRINCIPAL** a position as the principal of a school

head shop *n.* a shop that specializes in selling articles associated with the use of drugs such as hashish and marijuana (*slang*)

head·shot /héd shòt/ *n.* **1.** PHOTOGRAPHY, CINEMA **PHOTO OF HEAD** a photograph or cinematic shot of a head, especially a person's head **2.** ARMS **GUNSHOT TO HEAD** a gunshot aimed to hit the head of a person or animal

head·shrink·er /héd shrìngkər/ *n.* a psychiatrist (*dated informal insult*)

heads·man /hédzmən/ (*plural* **-men** /-mən/) *n.* a public executioner who beheaded prisoners condemned to death

head·stall /héd stàwl/ *n.* = **headpiece** *n.* 3 [*Stall* "stable" in the earlier sense of "position, place"]

head·stand /héd stànd/ *n.* a position in gymnastics or yoga in which the body is balanced upside down on the head, usually using the hands for support

head start *n.* an advantage in a competition or endeavor ○ *A good education gives you a head start when it comes to getting a job.*

head·stock /héd stòk/ *n.* an assembly or part of a machine, especially in a lathe, that holds and supports a revolving part

head·stone /héd stōn/ *n.* **1. GRAVESTONE** a slab of stone placed at the head of a grave as a memorial to the person or people buried there **2. head·stone, head stone** ARCHIT = **keystone**

head·stream /héd strēem/ *n.* a stream that is the source, or one of the sources, of a river

head·strong /héd stràwng/ *adj.* self-willed and determined not to follow orders or advice — **head·strong·ly** *adv.* —**head·strong·ness** *n.*

heads up *interj.* a command to watch out, especially for danger from overhead, e.g., a falling object or a ball coming through the air

heads-up *n.* **1. WARNING** an early warning to somebody that something, typically something undesirable, is soon to happen ○ *gave the law firm a heads-up on the impending subpoena* **2. SOMETHING REQUIRING ATTENTION** something that requires alert attention ■ *adj.* **ALERT AND RESOURCEFUL** showing quick resourcefulness and alertness in doing or observing something

heads-up dis·play *n.* a display of instrument data projected onto a screen at eye level so that a pilot or driver does not have to look down to see it

head teach·er *n. U.K.* somebody who is in charge of the teaching staff of a school and who oversees its day-to-day running

head-to-head *adv., adj.* **WITH A DIRECT ENCOUNTER** in or involving direct contact or confrontation ■ *adv.* **WITH HEADS ADJACENT** placed or arranged with heads adjacent ○ *We put the beds head-to-head.* ■ *n.* **DIRECT ENCOUNTER** a direct and immediate encounter

head trip *n.* (*dated slang*) **1. MENTALLY STIMULATING EXPERIENCE** an experience that stimulates or excites somebody mentally **2. SOMETHING DONE FOR PERSONAL GRATIFICATION** something done or a way of behaving that is intended mainly for personal gratification

head-up dis·play *n. U.K.* = **heads-up display**

head voice *n.* MUSIC = **head register**

head·wait·er /héd wàytər/ *n.* the person in charge of a group of servers at a restaurant. The headwaiter is often also responsible for taking reservations and seating customers. ○ *She has been head waiter at the club for five years.*

head wall *n.* a cliff forming one end of a valley

head·wa·ters /héd wàwtərz/ *npl.* the streams that make up the beginnings of a river

head·way /héd wày/ *n.* **1. PROGRESS** progress toward achieving something ○ *We're unable to make much headway with the project.* **2. FORWARD MOVEMENT** movement or rate of progress forward **3.** = **headroom** **4.** TRANSP **DIFFERENCE IN TIME OR DISTANCE** the interval or distance between two vehicles, trains, or ships traveling in the same direction along the same route ◇ **make headway** to make progress in doing something or going somewhere

head·wind /héd wìnd/ *n.* a wind blowing against the direction of travel

head·word /héd wùrd/ *n.* a word or phrase that forms a heading at the start of a text and is usually printed in distinctive type, especially a main entry word in a dictionary

head·work /héd wùrk/ *n.* **1. MENTAL EFFORT** mental activity or effort **2.** ARCHIT **ARCHITECTURAL DECORATION** decoration on the keystone of an arch

head·y /héddee/ **(-i·er, -i·est)** *adj.* **1. EXHILARATING** causing or involving a feeling of energy, confidence, and elation **2. INTOXICATING** causing a feeling of lightheadedness or intoxication **3. IMPETUOUS** impulsive and rash in behavior —**head·i·ly** *adv.* —**head·i·ness** *n.*

heal /heel/ **(healed, heal·ing, heals)** *v.* **1.** *vt.* **CURE FROM AILMENT** to make a person or injury healthy and whole **2.** *vi.* **REPAIR NATURALLY** to be repaired and restored naturally, e.g., by the formation of scar tissue ○ *The broken bone seems to be healing up quite nicely.* **3.** *vt.* **SETTLE OR RECTIFY** to repair or rectify something that causes discord and animosity ○ *Unless she can heal the rift within her party, she stands little chance in the election.* **4.** *vti.* **EMOTIONALLY RECOVER** to get rid of a wrong, evil, or painful affliction ○ *After losing his job, he's taken a while to heal.* [Old English *hǣlan.* Ultimately from a prehistoric Germanic base that is also the ancestor of English *health* and *whole.*] —**heal·a·ble** *adj.*

heal-all *n.* = **selfheal**

heal·er /hēelər/ *n.* somebody who cures or treats illnesses or injuries, often using spiritual rather than scientific methods

heal·ing /hēeling/ *n.* **PROCESS OF CURING OR BECOMING WELL** the process of curing somebody or something, or of becoming well ○ *spiritual healing* ■ *adj.* **CURATIVE** with the effect of curing or improving something ○ *the healing process*

health /helth/ *n.* **1.** MED **PRESENCE OR ABSENCE OF WELL-BEING** the general condition of the body or mind, especially in terms of the presence or absence of illnesses, injuries, or impairments **2. OVERALL CONDITION OF SOMETHING** the general condition of something in terms of soundness, vitality, and proper functioning ○ *There is concern about the financial health of the company.* **3. DRINKING TOAST** a toast drunk to wish for somebody's well-being and prosperity ○ *He drank a health to all his guests.* ■ *adj.* **1.** MED **DEVOTED TO GENERAL WELL-BEING** with the function of maintaining physical and mental well-being among the general public and the administration of medical and related services **2. GOOD FOR PEOPLE** promoting physical and mental well-being [Old English *hǣlþ*. Ultimately from a prehistoric Germanic base that is also the ancestor of English *heal* and *whole*, the underlying idea being of "wholeness."]

health camp *n. NZ* a camp for children who need health care, usually located on the coast

health care *n.* the provision of medical and related services aimed at maintaining good health in individuals or the public, especially through the prevention and treatment of disease

health·care /hélth kàir/ *adj.* concerned with or involved in providing physical and mental services, preventive medicine, and treatment to individuals or the public

health·care as·sis·tant *n. U.K.* = **nurses' aide**

health cen·ter *n.* a place, operated by a school or university, that houses a medical practice and other healthcare services for students

health farm *n. U.K.* = **health spa**

health food *n.* food that is considered to be more beneficial to health than ordinary food, especially products that are organically grown or without chemical additives

health·ful /hélthfəl/ *adj.* beneficial to physical or mental health —**health·ful·ly** *adv.* —**health·ful·ness** *n.*

WORD KEY: USAGE

See Usage note at ***healthy.***

health in·sur·ance *n.* insurance to cover the costs or losses incurred if an insured person falls ill

health main·te·nance or·gan·i·za·tion *n.* full form of **HMO**

health spa *n.* a commercial establishment similar to a hotel, usually rural, that offers ways of improving health and fitness, such as a controlled diet, exercise, and massage

health·y /hélthee/ (**-i·er, -i·est**) *adj.* **1. IN GOOD CONDITION** in good physical or mental condition **2. BENEFICIAL TO HEALTH** helping to maintain or bring about good health ○ *a healthy diet* ○ *This is not a very healthy place to live.* **3. SUGGESTIVE OF GOOD HEALTH** showing that somebody is in good health **4. MORALLY OR PSYCHOLOGICALLY SOUND** showing or encouraging moral or psychological soundness **5. FUNCTIONING WELL** in a prosperous and efficient condition ○ *My bank balance isn't looking very healthy at the moment.* **6. CONSIDERABLE** large, usually satisfyingly large, in size or quantity (*informal*) ○ *a healthy dose of contrition* —**health·i·ly** *adv.* —**health·i·ness** *n.*

WORD KEY: USAGE

healthy or **healthful**? It is sometimes argued that ***healthy*** should be used only to describe a living being that is in good health, and that ***healthful*** is the word for such things as habits or foods that promote good health. There is nothing wrong with observing this distinction, but there is also nothing wrong with using ***healthy*** as a synonym for ***healthful***, as reputable writers have been doing for centuries. Indeed, this usage received federal sanction in 1995, when the U.S. Department of Agriculture and the Food and Drug Administration issued regulations governing the ways ***healthy*** may be used on labels to describe food products.

heap /heep/ *n.* **1. ROUNDED PILE** a large number of things lying on top of one another, or a large quantity of material, forming a roughly rounded shape ○ *They'd left all their dirty clothes in a heap on the floor.* **2. LARGE AMOUNT** a large quantity or amount (*informal*) ○ *I've got a heap of things to see to before I can go home.* **3. SOMETHING OLD OR BATTERED** something that is old, dilapidated, or messy, especially an old building or car (*slang*) ○ *You'll never get to California in this old heap.* ■ *vt.* (**heaped, heap·ing, heaps**) **1. PUT IN A PILE** to collect or arrange something into a loose pile ○ *heaping the stuff all together in the middle of the yard* **2. PILE UP** to load or put a lot of something into a shallow container, forming a roughly rounded mound **3. GIVE IN ABUNDANCE** to give or supply something in large quantities or amounts ○ *They heaped scorn on my suggestion.* [Old English *hēap*. Ultimately from a prehistoric Germanic base that is also the ancestor of Dutch *hoop* "hope," the underlying idea being of something forlorn.]

heap up *v.* **1.** *vti.* **FORM INTO HEAP** to accumulate something, or be gathered, into a roughly rounded mound **2.** *vt.* **COLLECT** to collect or acquire something in large amounts

heaped /heept/ *adj. U.K.* = **heaping**

heap·ing /héeping/ *adj.* in sufficient quantity to rise above the rim of the spoon in a small heap

heaps /heeps/ *adv. U.K.* very much or greatly (*informal*) ○ *I feel heaps better since I went to the doctor.*

hear /heer/ (**heard, heard** /hurd/, **hear·ing, hears**) *v.* **1.** *vti.* **PERCEIVE SOUNDS** to perceive or be able to perceive sound **2.** *vti.* **GET TO KNOW SOMETHING** to be informed of something, especially by being told about it **3.** *vt.* **LISTEN TO SOMETHING** to listen to somebody or something ○ *I'm sure I've heard him on the radio.* **4.** *vti.* **UNDERSTAND** to understand fully by listening attentively ○ *Did you hear what I just said?* ○ *I won't stand for it, do you hear?* **5.** *vt.* LAW **PRESIDE OVER SOMETHING** to consider something officially as a judge, commissioner, or member of a jury ○ *the judge who heard the case* **6.** *vt.* CHR **ATTEND MASS** to attend Mass in a Roman Catholic church ○ *The congregation heard Mass at ten o'clock.* [Old English *hīeran*. Ultimately from a prehistoric Germanic word (source also of German *hören*) of uncertain origin.] —**hear·a·ble** *adj.* —**hear·er** *n.* ◇ **hear, hear!** used as an exclamation to show great approval

hear from *vt.* to receive a communication, e.g., a letter or telephone call, from a person, place, or organization

hear of *vt.* to consider something as a possibility ○ *She wouldn't hear of their paying their own way.*

hear out *vt.* to continue listening until somebody or something has finished

hear·ing /héering/ *n.* **1. AWARENESS OF SOUND** the perception of sound, made possible by vibratory changes in air pressure on the ear drums ○ *My hearing's going, so you'll have to speak louder.* **2. EARSHOT** the range within which something can be heard ○ *She moved out of hearing and I lost the end of the sentence.* **3. CHANCE TO BE HEARD** an opportunity to be heard, especially a chance to state an opinion or fact ○ *All I want is for my views to get a fair hearing.* **4.** LAW **TRIAL** the trial of a case in a court of law **5.** LAW **PRELIMINARY EXAMINATION OF ACCUSED** a preliminary judicial examination of an accused person to decide whether the case should proceed to trial **6.** LAW **SESSION TO HEAR EVIDENCE** a session of an investigative or legislative body at which witnesses are heard ◇ **hard of hearing** unable to hear well

hear·ing aid *n.* a small amplifying device to enable somebody to hear better, usually worn in or behind the ear

hear·ing dog *n.* a dog trained to help a hearing-impaired person by indicating that it has heard a certain sound, e.g. , the ringing of a telephone or doorbell

hear·ing-im·paired *adj.* with a reduced or deficient ability to hear

hear·ing loss *n.* a measurable reduction of the ability to hear or distinguish sounds, especially of a specific frequency

hear·ken /haárkən/ (**-kened, -ken·ing, -kens**), **har·ken** (**-kened, -ken·ing, -kens**) *vi.* to listen and pay attention (*archaic*) [Old English *he(o)rcnian* (from an earlier form of HARK), by folk etymology from association with HEAR] —**hear·ken·er** *n.*

Hearn /hurn/, **Lafcadio** (1850–1904) Greek-born U.S. writer and teacher. A translator and journalist, he moved to Japan in 1890, became a Japanese citizen, and wrote a stream of books that introduced Japanese culture and literature to the West. Full name **Patricio Lafcadio Tessima Carlos Hearn.** Japanese name **Yakumo Koizumi**

Hearne, Samuel (1745–92) British explorer. Working for the Hudson's Bay Company, he was the first European to travel overland to the North American coast on the Arctic Ocean (1770–72).

hear·say /héer sày/ *n.* **SECOND-HAND INFORMATION** information that is heard from other people ■ *adj.* **HEARD SECOND-HAND** being or containing information heard from other people [Mid-16thC. Translation of Old French *par ouïr dire*, literally "by hear say."]

hear·say ev·i·dence *n.* evidence consisting of testimony about other people that is not based on direct or personal knowledge. Hearsay evidence is not usually admissible in a court of law.

hearse /hurs/ *n.* a vehicle in which a decedent is carried to a funeral and in which a decedent is transported to a funeral home immediately after death [13thC. Originally "toothed frame for holding candles over coffins," via French *herse* from, ultimately, Latin *hirpex* "rake, harrow," of uncertain origin: probably from Oscan *hirpus* "wolf," from the teeth.]

WORD KEY: ORIGIN

Agricultural harrows in the Middle Ages were typically toothed triangular frames, so the word for a harrow came to be applied in French to a triangular toothed frame for holding candles, as used in a church, and particularly as placed over a coffin at funeral services. This was the meaning of ***hearse*** when English acquired it, and it only gradually developed via "canopy placed over a coffin" and "coffin, bier" to the modern sense "funeral vehicle" (first recorded in the mid-17thC).

Hearst /hurst/, **William Randolph** (1863–1951) U.S. publisher and politician. He built up a vast national newspaper and media empire, and after 1927 lived in seclusion at his California castle, San Simeon. Orson Welles's *Citizen Kane* (1941) is based on his career.

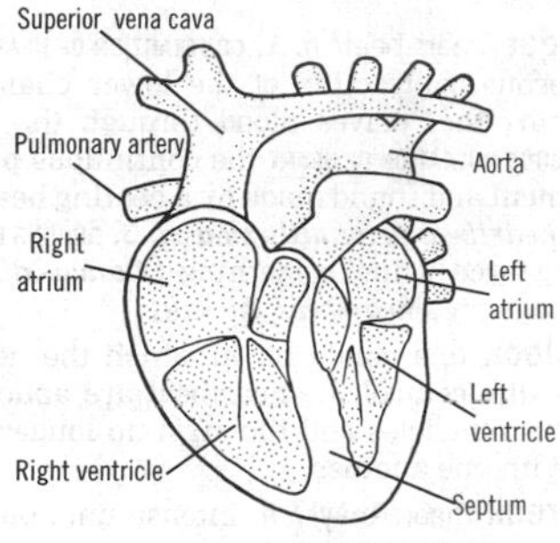

Heart: Human heart

heart /haart/ *n.* **1.** PHYSIOL **BLOOD-PUMPING ORGAN** a hollow muscular organ that pumps blood around the body, in humans situated in the center of the chest with its apex directed to the left **2.** ANAT **POSITION OF CHEST ABOVE HEART** the area on the front of the human body that corresponds roughly to the position of the heart **3. BASIS OF EMOTIONAL LIFE** the human heart, considered as the source and center of emotional life, where the deepest and sincerest feelings are located and an individual is most vulnerable to pain **4. CHARACTER** somebody's essential character ○ *He's an abrupt-sounding cuss, but he's got a very good heart.* **5. COMPASSION** the ability to feel humane and altruistic feelings ○ *If she had any heart she would forgive him.* **6. AFFECTION** affection, love, or warm admiration ○ *The chorus's singing won the hearts of the audience.* **7. SPIRIT** the capacity for courage and determination ○ *The team played with a lot of heart.* ○ *They put their whole hearts into making a go of the business.* **8. DISPOSITION** a mood, mental state, or frame of mind **9. ESSENTIAL PART OF SOMETHING** the distinctive, significant, and characteristic center of something ○ *the heart of rural America* **10.** PLANTS **PART OF VEGETABLE AROUND CORE** the often tasty or succulent compact central part of a vegetable, e.g., a lettuce or cabbage, where the leaves curl in tightly ○ *artichoke hearts* **11.** FOOD **ANIMAL HEART USED AS FOOD** the heart of an animal that is cleaned and trimmed, then roasted, stewed, or braised as food **12. SYMBOLIC DEPICTION OF HEART** a simplified and conventionalized picture of a heart as a rounded, roughly triangular shape, often used to signify love **13.** CARDS **PLAYING CARD** any one of a suit of cards marked with a symbolic depiction of one or more hearts. ◊ **hearts 14. BELOVED PERSON** somebody who is dearly loved ○ *Come to me, dear heart.* [Old English *heorte*. Related to German *Herz*.] ◇ **at heart** in essence or reality, and despite contrary appearances ◇ **break somebody's heart** to cause somebody intense unhappiness and suffering ◇ **do somebody's heart good** to make somebody feel happy or satisfied ◇ **eat your heart out 1.** to brood about something that makes you feel unhappy (*informal*) **2.** to be consumed with envy ◇ **from the bottom of your heart** with the utmost sincerity ◇ **have somebody's welfare** *or* **interests at heart** to have somebody's well-being or interests in mind ◇ **heart and soul** completely, or with the greatest devotion ◇ **in your heart of hearts** in your deepest inner feelings ◇ **learn** *or* **know something by heart** to memorize or have memorized something ◇ **lose heart** to become discouraged ◇ **not have the heart to do something** to be unable to bring yourself to do something that is liable to hurt somebody else ◇ **set your heart on something, have your heart set on something** to have something as your ambition or greatest wish ◇ **take heart** to become encouraged and more confident ◇ **take something to heart 1.** to take something seriously **2.** to be upset by something ◇ **wear your heart on your sleeve** to reveal your feelings openly ◇ **with all your heart** completely or very willingly

WORD KEY: ORIGIN

The Indo-European ancestor of ***heart*** is also the ultimate source of English *cardiac, concord, cordial, courage, quarry,* and *record.*

heart·ache /haárt àyk/ *n.* a powerful feeling of sorrow, anguish, or regret

heart at·tack *n.* **1.** MED **DAMAGE TO HEART** a sudden, serious, painful, and sometimes fatal interruption of the heart's normal functioning, especially due to a blockage in the coronary artery **2. SUDDEN SHOCK** a sudden severe shock (*informal*) ○ *I had a heart attack when I looked in the drawer and saw that the money was gone.*

heart·beat /haárt bèet/ *n.* **1. CONTRACTION OF HEART MUSCLE** a vigorous contraction of the lower chambers of the heart that drives blood through the body **2. CONTINUOUS PULSATION OF HEART** the continuous pulsating movement and sound made by a beating heart ○ *Her rapid heartbeat gradually slowed.* **3. DRIVING FORCE** the driving force behind something ○ *Caucus discussion was the party's heartbeat, he said.*

heart block *n.* a condition in which the nerve impulses that control the heartbeat are abnormal so that the ventricles and the atria no longer beat in time with one another

heart·break /haárt bràyk/ *n.* intense unhappiness or grief

heart·break·er *n.* somebody who or something that makes people very unhappy, especially somebody with whom many people fall in love and are subsequently hurt

heart·break·ing /haárt bràyking/ *adj.* causing intense sadness or distress —**heart·break·ing·ly** *adv.*

heart·bro·ken /haárt brōkən/ *adj.* feeling intensely unhappy or disappointed because of something that has happened ○ *The children were heartbroken when we had to cancel the trip.* —**heart·bro·ken·ly** *adv.* —**heart·bro·ken·ness** *n.*

heart·burn /haárt bùrn/ *n.* an uncomfortable burning sensation in the lower chest, usually caused by stomach acid flowing back into the lower end of the esophagus [Formed from HEART in the obsolete sense "stomach"]

heart cher·ry *n.* a variety of sweet cherries that is heart-shaped and soft-fleshed

heart dis·ease *n.* an abnormal condition of the heart or the blood vessels supplying it that impairs cardiac functioning

heart·en /haárt'n/ (**-ened, -en·ing, -ens**) *vt.* to make somebody feel more cheerful and hopeful [Formed from HEART in the obsolete sense "to encourage"]

heart·en·ing /haárt'ning/ *adj.* giving somebody optimism or encouragement

heart fail·ure *n.* **1. END OF HEARTBEAT** cessation of the normal functioning of the heart, leading to death ○ *He died from heart failure at 92, while gardening.* **2. HEART INSUFFICIENCY** a condition in which the heart cannot pump blood in sufficient volume to meet the needs of the body, causing breathlessness, enlargement of the liver, swollen ankles, and other symptoms

heart·felt /haárt fèlt/ *adj.* arising from strong and sincere emotion

hearth /haarth/ *n.* **1. FLOOR OF FIREPLACE** the floor of a fireplace, especially when it extends into the room **2. HOME AND FAMILY LIFE** the fireplace of a home, thought of as a symbol of the home and the life of the family who live in it **3.** METALL **PART OF FOUNDRY FURNACE** the lowest part of a foundry furnace where molten metal collects or ore is smelted [Old English *heorþ*. Ultimately from a prehistoric Germanic word, (which also produced German *herd*), of uncertain origin.]

hearth rug *n.* a rug for the floor in front of a fireplace

hearth·side /haárth sīd/ *n.* = **fireside**

hearth·stone /haárth stōn/ *n.* **1. STONE FORMING HEARTH** a large stone used to form the hearth in a fireplace **2. CLEANSING STONE FOR HEARTHS** a soft variety of stone or a compound of pipe clay and stone used to clean and whiten fireplaces and doorsteps

heart·i·ly /haártilee/ *adv.* **1. ENTHUSIASTICALLY** in a sincere and enthusiastic way **2. GOOD-NATUREDLY** in a loud, vigorous, good-natured way **3. COMPLETELY** in a full and complete way **4. HUNGRILY** with a good appetite

heart·land /haárt lànd/ *n.* a central area of a country or region, or an area of it that has special economic, political, military, or sentimental significance

heart·leaf /haárt leef/ *n.* = **wild ginger** [From the heart-shaped leaves]

heart·less /haártləss/ *adj.* having or showing no pity or kindness —**heart·less·ly** *adv.* —**heart·less·ness** *n.*

heart-lung ma·chine *n.* a machine that is used to take over the functions of the heart and lungs in pumping and oxygenating the blood, chiefly during heart surgery

heart mas·sage *n.* = **cardiac massage**

heart mur·mur *n.* an unusual sound coming from the heart that can be detected by a stethoscope and may indicate the presence of a heart defect

heart of palm *n.* the terminal bud of the cabbage palm, cooked and served as a vegetable or in salads

heart rate *n.* the number of heartbeats occurring within a specified length of time

heart·rend·ing /haárt rènding/ *adj.* causing intense sadness or distress, especially in sympathy with somebody else's unhappiness or hardship —**heart·rend·ing·ly** *adv.*

hearts /haarts/ *n.* **1. SUIT OF CARDS** a suit of cards marked with red heart symbols (*takes a singular or plural verb*) **2. CARD GAME** a card game in which players try to avoid winning cards of the suit hearts or the queen of spades, or else to win all of these (*takes a singular verb*)

heart-search·ing /haárt sùrching/ *n.* a thorough and often painful examination of your own conscience, feelings, or motives

hearts·ease /haárts èez/ (*plural* **-eas·es** *or* **-ease**) *n.* a pansy, especially the wild pansy. Latin name: *Viola tricolor.*

heart·sick /haárt sìk/ *adj.* deeply disappointed or sad ○ *I'm heartsick when I think of how things ought to have been.* —**heart·sick·ness** *n.*

heart·sore /haárt sàwr/ *adj.* extremely sad or regretful (*archaic or literary*)

heart·strings *npl.* somebody's feelings, especially tender emotions [*String* in the obsolete sense "tendon," from the earlier belief that tendons brace the heart]

heart·throb /haárt thròb/ *n.* somebody who is thought to be extraordinarily attractive, especially a young movie star or singer (*dated informal*)

heart-to-heart *adj.* **VERY FRANK AND INTIMATE** frank and intimate, often about personal matters ■ *n.* **FRANK TALK** a frank, intimate conversation

heart ur·chin *n.* a variety of sea urchins with a heart-shaped body. Genus: *Echinocardium.*

heart·warm·ing /haárt wàwrming/ *adj.* inspiring warm or kindly feelings, usually by showing life and human nature in a positive and reassuring light

heart·wood /haárt wŏŏd/ *n.* the wood at the center of a tree trunk or branch that is older, darker, and harder than the wood surrounding it

heart·worm /haárt wùrm/ (*plural* **-worms** *or* **-worm**) *n.* **1.** ZOOL **PARASITIC WORM** a parasitic filarial worm that lives in the heart and associated blood vessels of members of the dog family, and occasionally in cats and seals **2.** VET **HEART INFECTION IN DOGS** an infection of the heart in members of the dog family, and occasionally in cats and seals, that is caused by parasitic worms

heart·y /haártee/ (**-i·er, -i·est**) *adj.* **1. SINCERE AND ENTHUSIASTIC** sincere and expressed in a cheerful, enthusiastic way **2. LOUD AND ENTHUSIASTIC** done in an unrestrainedly loud, vigorous, but usually good-humored way **3. HEALTHY** showing physical health, strength, and vigor **4. STRONGLY FELT** sincerely and strongly felt **5. SUBSTANTIAL AND NOURISHING** substantial, or giving great satisfaction and nourishment ○ *I need a hearty breakfast to get my day started.* **6.** *U.K.* **OVERLOUD AND OVERENTHUSIASTIC** annoyingly or boorishly loud or boisterous, and usually overenthusiastic about sports or outdoor activities (*informal*) —**heart·i·ness** *n.*

heat /heet/ *n.* **1. ENERGY PERCEIVED AS TEMPERATURE** a form of transferred energy that arises from the random motion of molecules and is felt as temperature, especially as warmth or hotness. Heat is transmitted by conduction, convection, or radiation. ○ *There was virtually no heat coming from the fire.* Symbol **Q 2. DEGREE OF HOTNESS** the perceptible degree of hotness ○ *The heat in that kitchen is absolutely unbearable.* ○ *At what heat do I cook this?* **3. SOURCE OF HIGHER TEMPERATURE** a source of warmth, e.g., to cook something or to keep a building warm ○ *The heat turns off automatically when the room reaches a certain temperature.* **4. INTENSE EMOTION** emotional intensity, especially in the form of anger or excitement ○ *I replied with some heat that my conscience was perfectly clear.* ○ *in the heat of the moment* **5. TIME OF MOST ACTIVITY AND EXCITEMENT** the period or phase of something at which activity and excitement is at its most intense ○ *During the heat of the campaign, many rash promises were made.* **6.** FOOD **SPICY HOTNESS FELT IN MOUTH** the hot or burning sensation produced in the mouth by certain spicy foods **7.** ZOOL **SEXUALLY RECEPTIVE STAGE** a time during a female mammal's reproductive cycle when she is fertile and ready to mate **8.** SPORTS, GAME **PRELIMINARY ROUND** one of several preliminary rounds before a race or contest, especially one in which competitors are eliminated, or one that determines the main event's starting order **9. MENTAL PRESSURE** psychological pressure on a person or group, especially to produce or achieve something (*informal*) ○ *We're beginning to feel the heat as the deadline gets closer and closer.* **10. CRITICISM** harsh criticism or reproach (*slang*) ○ *What's your problem? Can't you take the heat?* **11.** CRIMINOL **INTENSE POLICE ACTIVITY** intensive police activity carried out in order to catch criminal suspects (*slang*) **12.** CRIMINOL **POLICE** the police (*slang*) ■ *vti.* (**heat·ed, heat·ing, heats**) **RAISE TEMPERATURE** to become or make something warm or hot [Old English *hǣtu*. Ultimately from a prehistoric Germanic word that was formed from a word meaning "hot" (the ancestor of English *hot*).] —**heat·less** *adj.* ◇ **turn on** *or* **up the heat (on somebody)** to apply increased pressure on somebody (*slang*)

heat up *vti.* **1. MAKE OR BECOME HOTTER** to make something hotter, or become hotter **2. MAKE OR BECOME MORE INTENSE** to become or make something more intense, exciting, or excited

heat bar·ri·er *n.* = **thermal barrier**

heat ca·pac·i·ty *n.* the quantity of heat required to raise the temperature of one mole or gram of a substance by one degree Celsius. Symbol *C*

heat death *n.* a condition of a closed system in which energy is uniformly distributed throughout it, with none available for use. The universe might ultimately suffer heat death if the universe is a closed system.

heat·ed /heétəd/ *adj.* **1. MADE WARM** made warm by artificially generated heat **2. INTENSE OR ANGRY** showing emotional intensity or anger —**heat·ed·ness** *n.*

heat·ed·ly /heétədlee/ *adv.* with anger or emotional intensity

heat en·gine *n.* a machine that transforms heat into mechanical power, e.g., a steam or gasoline engine

heat·er /heétər/ *n.* **1. HEATING DEVICE** a device that uses fuel to produce heat in order to make something else warm or hot, especially a device to heat the air in a room or vehicle **2. HEATING ELEMENT IN VACUUM TUBE** an element in a vacuum tube that carries the current for heating a cathode **3. HANDGUN** a revolver or other handgun (*dated slang*)

heat ex·chang·er *n.* a device, e.g., a car radiator, that transfers heat from one medium to another, usually by conduction through a solid barrier

heat ex·haus·tion *n.* a condition of physical weakness or collapse often accompanied by nausea, muscle cramps, and dizziness, that is caused by exposure to intense heat

heath /heeth/ *n.* **1.** GEOG **GRASSY AND SHRUBBY UNCULTIVATED LAND** a tract of uncultivated, open land with infertile, often sandy soil covered with rough grasses and small shrubs or heather **2.** PLANTS **LOW EVERGREEN SHRUB** a plant of a family that includes heather and some other low-growing evergreen shrubs with small bell-shaped flowers, commonly found on heaths. Genera: *Erica* and *Calluna*. **3.** INSECTS **BROWN BUTTERFLY** a butterfly with coppery-brown wings. Genus: *Coenonympha*. [Old English *hǣþ*. Ultimately from a prehistoric Germanic base meaning "unplowed land," which is also the ancestor of German and Dutch *heide*, and English *heathen*.]

heath·cock /he͞eth kòk/ *n.* the male of the black grouse (*archaic*)

hea·then /he͞ethən/ *n.* **1.** **OFFENSIVE TERM** an offensive term that deliberately insults somebody who does not acknowledge the God of the Bible, Torah, or Koran **2.** **OFFENSIVE TERM** an offensive term that deliberately insults somebody's nonbelief in religion, way of life, or degree of knowledge [Old English *hǣþen*. Ultimately from a prehistoric Germanic word meaning "inhabiting heaths," hence "uncivilized," from a word meaning "heath" (source also of English *heath*).] —**heathen** *adj.* —**heathenish** *adj.* —**heathenishly** *adv.* —**heathenishness** *n.* —**heathenize** *vti.*

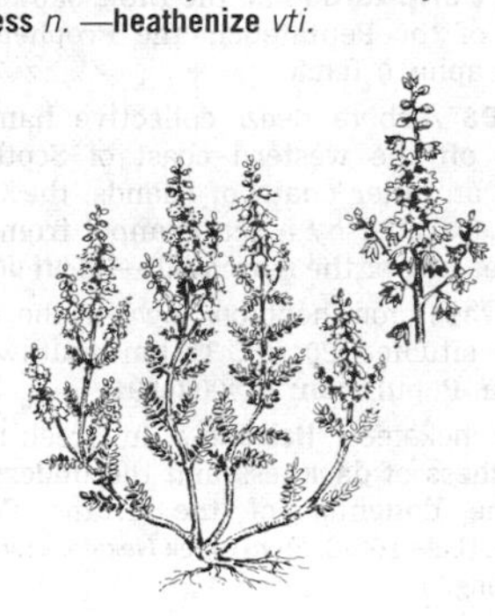

Heather

heath·er /héthər/ *n.* **1.** PLANTS **SMALL-FLOWERED SHRUB** a low shrubby evergreen plant with spiky leaves and small bell-shaped purple, pink, or white flowers, that grows in clusters on heaths and mountainsides in Europe and Asia. Latin name: *Calluna vulgaris*. **2.** COLORS **PURPLE COLOR** a purple color tinged with pink and blue ■ *adj.* COLORS **OF PURPLE COLOR** of a purple color tinged with pink and blue [14thC. By folk etymology from earlier Scottish and northern English *hadder* or *hathir*, by association with HEATH (on which it grows), of unknown origin.] —**heath·er·y** *adj.*

heath·er grass *n.* a European perennial grass with flat hairless leaves. Latin name: *Sieglingia decumbens*. [Because it grows in the same places as heather]

heath grass *n.* = **heather grass**

heath hen *n.* **1.** *U.K.* **FEMALE BLACK GROUSE** the female of the black grouse **2.** **EXTINCT GROUSE** an extinct grouse native to New England and related to the prairie chicken. Latin name: *Typanuchus cupido cupido*.

Heath Rob·in·son /heeth ráwbənsʼn/ *adj. U.K.* = **Rube Goldberg** (*humorous*) [Early 20thC. Named for W. *Heath Robinson* (1872–1944), a British humorous artist whose illustrations featured humorously overcomplex devices.]

Heath·row Air·port /he͞eth rō-/ the largest and busiest airport serving London, England, situated on the western outskirts of the capital

heat·ing /he͞eting/ *n.* **1.** **PROCESS OF WARMING SOMETHING** the operation of warming something, e.g., food, a room, or the interior of a building **2.** **EQUIPMENT THAT CREATES HEAT** the equipment that produces heat to warm something, e.g., a central heating system ○ *The heating doesn't come on again until six o'clock in the evening.*

heat·ing el·e·ment *n.* an insulated or covered wire whose high resistance to an electrical current causes its temperature to rise, providing heat to surrounding materials, e.g., an electric blanket

heat·ing pad *n.* a fabric-covered pad that encloses an electric heating element and is used to apply heat to various parts of the body

heat is·land *n.* an urban area where the air temperature is consistently higher than in the surrounding region because of the generation and retention of heat created by human activity and human-made structures

heat light·ning *n.* lightning seen near the horizon, especially on hot evenings, without the sound of thunder. It is thought to be a reflection of lightning on clouds. The thunder accompanying the lightning is too distant to be heard.

heat of com·bus·tion *n.* the amount of heat produced when one mole of a substance is burned in oxygen

heat pros·tra·tion *n.* = **heat exhaustion**

heat pump *n.* a mechanical or chemical device used to heat and air-condition buildings

heat rash *n.* = **prickly heat**

heat-seal *vt.* to make packaging material, usually a thin clear plastic film, airtight around something by applying heat and pressure

heat·seek·er *n.* a customer who always purchases the latest version of most recent update of an existing product (*slang*)

heat-seek·ing *adj.* able to detect and follow infrared radiation from heat ○ *The aircraft was brought down by a heat-seeking missile.*

heat shield *n.* a coating or structure designed to protect against the effects of very high temperatures, especially the coating that protects spacecraft during re-entry into the Earth's atmosphere

heat sink *n.* a device, often a metal plate, that conducts and dissipates unwanted heat generated by an electronic component or power supply

heat·stroke /héet strōk/ *n.* a condition caused by prolonged exposure to high temperatures, in which people experience high fever, headaches, hot dry skin, physical exhaustion, and sometimes physical collapse and coma

heat-treat *vt.* **1.** METALL **TEMPER METAL BY HEATING AND COOLING** to bring metal to the desired hardness by alternately heating and cooling it **2.** MED **TREAT MUSCULAR PAINS BY HEAT** to use heat, e.g., generated by massage, as a means of treating rheumatism or muscular injuries —**heat treat·ment** *n.*

heat wave *n.* a period of unusually hot weather

heave /heev/ *v.* (**heaved, heav·ing, heaves**) **1.** *vt.* **MOVE USING MUCH EFFORT** to pull, push, lift, or throw something heavy by exerting great physical effort, especially in a concentrated or concerted burst ○ *We picked up the sack between us and heaved it into the truck.* **2.** *vi.* **EXERT PHYSICAL EFFORT IN RHYTHMIC BURST** to exert great physical effort, especially in concentrated or concerted rhythmic bursts, when pulling on a rope or attempting to move something heavy ○ *All together now, heave!* ○ *We heaved and heaved, but the car remained firmly stuck in the mud.* **3.** *vt.* **DIRECT BY TOSSING SOMETHING** to throw something fairly heavy in a particular direction, often in a casual way (*informal*) ○ *Heave the empty boxes into that corner.* **4.** *vi.* **RISE AND FALL RHYTHMICALLY** to rise and fall in a rhythmic or spasmodic way ○ *After the footraces his chest was heaving, and he was covered in sweat.* **5.** *vi.* **MAKE A SUDDEN INVOLUNTARY MOVEMENT** to move suddenly in a violent involuntary motion, often associated with feelings of nausea ○ *The sight made my stomach heave.* **6.** *vti.* **VOMIT** to vomit something up, or try to vomit (*informal*) **7.** *vt.* **LABORIOUSLY UTTER SOMETHING** to utter a sound, especially a sigh, with a long outflow of breath or with effort and pain ○ *We can heave a sigh of relief now that the waiting is over.* **8.** (*past* **hove**) *vti.* NAUT **MOVE A SHIP** to move or make a ship move in a particular direction **9.** (*past* **hove**) *vi.* **APPEAR** to become visible, like a ship appearing over the horizon ○ *An enemy ship hove into sight.* ○ *Gradually, the end of summer hove into sight.* **10.** *vt.* GEOL **DISPLACE HORIZONTALLY** to displace rock strata or a mineral lode in a horizontal direction, usually by the intersection of other strata or another lode ■ *n.* **1.** **EFFORTFUL BURST** a burst of physical effort to pull on something or move something heavy ○ *We gave one final heave and the tree began to topple over.* **2.** **THROW** an act of throwing something fairly heavy, or the distance something is thrown **3.** **UP-AND-DOWN MOVEMENT** a rhythmical or spasmodic movement that rises and falls ○ *the heave of a heavy ocean swell* **4.** GEOL **HORIZONTAL DISPLACEMENT** rock strata or a lode that is displaced horizontally **5.** **ACT OF VOMITING** an act of or attempt at vomiting (*informal*) ■ **heaves** *npl.* **VOMITING ATTACK** an attack of vomiting or retching (*slang*) [Old English *hebban* "to lift." Ultimately from a prehistoric Germanic word (source also of German *heben*).] —**heav·er** *n.*

WORD KEY: SYNONYMS

See Synonyms at *throw*.

heave down *vt.* to turn a boat over for cleaning

heave to *vti.* to bring a ship to a stop ○ *We have to about a cable's length from her stern.*

heave-ho *interj.* NAUT **COMMAND TO PULL** used to command or encourage sailors to pull together on a rope ■ *n.* **DISMISSAL OR REJECTION** dismissal from something, or rejection by somebody (*informal*) ○ *He's just been given the heave-ho from his job.*

heav·en /hévvʼn/ *n.* **1.** **Heaven, heaven** RELIG **PERFECT DWELLING PLACE AFTER DEATH** a place or condition of supreme happiness and peace where good people are believed to go after death, and, especially in Christianity, the dwelling place of God and the angels **2.** **BLISSFUL EXPERIENCE** an experience of blissful happiness ○ *It's heaven not to have get up early in the morning.* ○ *This place would be heaven, if it weren't for the people who live here.* **3.** **SKY OVERARCHING EARTH** the sky by day or at night as seen from Earth (*often used in the plural*) ○ *After weeks of drought the heavens opened up.* **4.** **Heaven, heaven** CHR **POWER OF GOD** in Christian belief, the power of God to direct events on earth ○ *Heaven protect us!* ○ *a gift from heaven* ■ *interj.* **heav·en, heav·ens** **EXPRESSING ASTONISHMENT** used to express great surprise, annoyance, or gratitude (*informal*) ○ *Good heavens, is that the time?* [Old English *heofon*, of uncertain origin] ◇ **for heaven's sake** used to express annoyance or exasperation ◇ **heaven knows** used to emphasize the truth of what somebody is saying ○ *Heaven knows, I warned you about that already.* ◇ **heaven (only) knows** used to emphasize the fact that somebody is unable even to make a reasonable guess at something unknown or mysterious ○ *Heaven only knows what he's done with my keys.* ◇ **move heaven and earth** to do everything possible to make something happen

heav·en·ly /hévvʼnlee/ (**-li·er, -li·est**) *adj.* **1.** CHR **OF GOD AND HEAVEN** belonging to the heaven and God of Christian belief ○ *A heavenly voice spoke to him out of the clouds.* **2.** **LOVELY** supremely delightful, delicious, or beautiful (*informal*) ○ *The chocolate mousse was heavenly.* ○ *a sweet little cottage with the most heavenly view* **3.** **IN THE SKY** in the sky or space as seen from Earth —**heav·en·li·ness** *n.*

heav·en·ly bod·y *n.* ASTRON = **celestial body**

heav·en-sent *adj.* happening or arriving at just the right time to help or benefit somebody greatly

heav·en·ward /hévvʼnwərd/, **heav·en·wards** /hévvʼnwərdz/ *adv., adj.* moving or directed upward toward the sky or heaven ○ *He rolled his eyes heavenward, shrugged his shoulders, and said "That's the way the cookie crumbles!"*

heaves /heevz/ *n.* a chronic lung disorder in horses marked by difficulty in breathing and believed to be caused by dust, molds, or other air pollutants. The heaves resembles asthma in human beings. (*informal*) (*takes a singular or plural verb*)

heav·i·er-than-air *adj.* unable to float in air because it weighs more than the air it displaces, and thus only able to fly under power using aerodynamic lift

heav·i·ly /hévvilee/ *adv.* **1.** **WITH GREAT WEIGHT** with a great weight **2.** **LABORIOUSLY** in a slow, clumsy, or laborious way **3.** **SEVERELY** in a severe, onerous, or comprehensive way **4.** **IN LARGE NUMBERS** in large numbers or quantities **5.** **SADLY** in a sad and resigned way ○ *"It was my fault," he replied heavily.* **6.** **SERIOUSLY** in a serious or enthusiastic way (*informal*) ○ *I didn't know you were heavily into astrology.*

Heav·i·side lay·er /hévvi sīd-/ *n.* = **E layer** [Early 20thC. Named for Oliver HEAVISIDE, its discoverer.]

heav·y /hévvee/ *adj.* (**-i·er, -i·est**) **1.** **WEIGHING A LOT** weighing a relatively large amount and thus difficult to lift, carry, or move ○ *Daddy can't carry you any more, you're too heavy.* ○ *We put heavy stones on the corners of the rug to stop it from blowing away.* **2.** **PRESENT IN LARGE AMOUNTS** occurring or produced in large amounts or in greater amounts than normal **3.** **FULL, THICK, OR DENSE** involving or using a larger amount of material or having a thicker, denser texture than usual **4.** **ABUNDANTLY USING SOMETHING** using or consuming something a great deal **5.** **NEEDING STRENGTH** needing much strength and effort ○ *heavy* *road work* **6.** **DEMANDING** difficult to fulfill or cope with, and often burdensome or oppressive **7.** **BUSY** filled with a large or larger than normal amount of activity, business, or commitments **8.** **POWERFUL** struck or striking with a great deal of weight or force **9.** **BROAD AND DARK** thick and dark-colored, or made with thick dark lines **10.** **EXPLICIT** intended to give emphasis to something and to make the meaning or intention obvious **11.** **UNSUBTLE** lacking subtlety or delicacy ○ *heavy sarcasm* **12.** **FLESHY** large and solidly fleshy ○ *a huge, heavy body* **13.** **CLUMSY** typical of somebody who is large and who moves slowly and deliberately or clumsily **14.** **SOUNDING LOUD AND DULL** loud and dull in sound, as if produced by something large hitting or falling onto something **15.** INDUST **EXTENSIVELY PRODUCING OR REFINING SOMETHING** involved in large-scale industrial processes requiring large premises and a lot of equipment **16.** **RUGGED AND STRONG** specially adapted for rough work or for carrying large loads ○ *heavy excavating equipment* **17.** MIL **LARGE-CALIBER** firing large-caliber ammunition **18.** MIL, NAVY **WITH LARGE WEAPONS** carrying more or larger guns and armaments than is standard ○ *building a new heavy cruiser* **19.** **SAD** sad, or likely to make somebody feel sad **20.** **SERIOUS AND REQUIRING CONCENTRATION** requiring concentrated attention to be understood or appreciated ○ *a heavy novel* **21.** **TURGID** difficult and requiring effort rather than being pleasurable ○ *I'm trying to finish reading the novel, but it's heavy going.* **22.** **STRICT** strict or severe in behavior **23.** **VIOLENT** using or prepared to use violence (*informal*) **24.** **POWERFUL AND LINGERING** strong and lingering in smell ○ *a heavy odor of leeks* **25.** NAUT **ROUGH** with large waves causing difficulties for boats **26.** METEOROL **DARK AND OVERCAST** dark in color and threatening rain or snow **27.** METEOROL **SULTRY AND THREATENING** sultry and overcast, as if threatening a storm or thunder **28.** FOOD **HARD TO DIGEST** large in quantity and difficult to digest **29.** MUSIC **WITH POWERFUL BEAT** used to describe rock music with a powerful, insistent beat **30.** **SERIOUS AND OPPRESSIVE** significant, oppressively serious, or emotionally demanding (*slang*) ○ *I had a heavy scene with my girlfriend tonight.* **31.** CHEM **WITH HIGH ATOMIC WEIGHT** with a higher than normal atomic weight **32.** PHYS **WITH HIGH SPECIFIC GRAVITY** with a higher than normal specific gravity ■ *n.* (*plural* **-ies**) **1.** ARTS **VILLAIN** a villain in a play, movie, or other dramatic performance ○ *He played the heavy in a couple of westerns.* **2.** **SOMEBODY WHO IS VIOLENT** somebody hired to persuade people, by threats or violence, to do something (*slang*) (*often used in the plural*) ○ *He sent in a bunch of heavies to do his dirty work.* **3.** **IMPORTANT PERSON** somebody who is important or influential (*informal*) **4.** SPORTS **HEAVYWEIGHT** a heavyweight, e.g., a heavyweight boxer (*informal*) ■ *adv.* **HEAVILY** in a heavy way [Old English *hefig.* Ultimately from a prehistoric Germanic word meaning "weighty" (ancestor also of Dutch *hevig*), from, ultimately, a word meaning "to lift" (source also of English *heave*).] —**heav·i·ness** *n.*

heav·y breath·er *n.* **1.** **NUISANCE CALLER** somebody who makes anonymous nuisance calls, breathing loudly into the telephone in a way that is intended to suggest sexual excitement or a physical threat **2.** **NOISY BREATHER** somebody who breathes noisily or with difficulty, usually because of a medical condition —**heav·y breath·ing** *n.*

heav·y chain *n.* either of the larger polypeptide chains in an antibody. ◊ **light chain**

heav·y cream *n.* cream with a high fat content that can be whipped to make it thicker

heav·y-dut·y *adj.* **1.** **TOUGH AND DURABLE** designed for hard wear or use in rough conditions **2.** *U.K.* **SERIOUS** more serious, substantial, or intensive than usual (*informal*) ○ *a heavy-duty meeting*

heav·y-foot·ed /-fòotəd/ *adj.* slow, lumbering, or clumsy in walking

heav·y-hand·ed /hèvvi hándəd/ *adj.* **1.** **PHYSICALLY OR SOCIALLY CLUMSY** lacking skill or delicacy in handling objects or dealing with people **2.** **HARSH AND OPPRESSIVE** relying on force or intimidation to exercise authority —**heav·y-hand·ed·ly** *adv.* —**heav·y-hand·ed·ness** *n.*

heav·y-heart·ed *adj.* feeling or showing sadness (*literary*) —**heav·y-heart·ed·ly** *adv.* —**heav·y-heart·ed·ness** *n.*

heav·y hit·ter *n.* **1.** **POWERFUL PERSON** somebody with power or influence (*slang*) **2.** BASEBALL **POWERFUL BATTER** a batter of great strength, capable of hitting long balls and home runs [Probably from the idea of a boxer who relies on powerful slugging rather than skill]

heav·y hy·dro·gen *n.* an isotope of hydrogen with a mass number greater than 1, especially deuterium

heav·y-lad·en *adj.* carrying a heavy burden, e.g., of sorrow or guilt (*literary*)

heav·y lift·ing *n.* **1.** **STRENUOUS LIFTING** the lifting of heavy objects **2.** **SUSTAINED EFFORT** serious or sustained effort in a demanding task ○ *Who's going to do the heavy lifting on this project?* **3.** **WORK REQUIRING MENTAL OR PHYSICAL EFFORT** work that requires labor- or brain-intensive activity (*slang*) ○ *wanted a position involving no heavy lifting*

heav·y met·al *n.* **1.** MUSIC **TYPE OF ROCK MUSIC** a style of loud rock music with a very strong beat (*hyphenated when used before a noun*) **2.** METALL **METAL WITH HIGH RELATIVE DENSITY** a metal, often toxic to organisms, that has a relative density of 5.0 or higher, e.g., lead, mercury, copper, and cadmium

heav·y oil *n.* a mixture of hydrocarbons distilled from coal tar that is heavier than water

heav·y par·ti·cle *n.* = **baryon**

heav·y-set /hèvvi sét/ *adj.* with a compact and powerful-looking build

heav·y spar *n.* a mineral form of barium sulfate. Formula: $BaSO_4$.

heav·y wa·ter *n.* technical name **deuterium oxide**

heav·y-wa·ter re·ac·tor *n.* a nuclear reactor in which heavy water is used as a moderator

heav·y·weight /hévvi wàyt/ *n.* **1.** BOXING **BOXER IN HIGHEST WEIGHT CATEGORY** a boxer of the heaviest weight class. Professional heavyweight boxers must weigh more than 175 lbs./79.5 kg. **2.** SPORTS **CONTESTANT IN HEAVIEST WEIGHT CLASS** a contestant in the heaviest weight class of a sport **3.** **HEAVY PERSON OR THING** somebody or something whose weight is considerably above the average **4.** **SOMEBODY OR SOMETHING POWERFUL OR INFLUENTIAL** a person or organization with considerable power or influence, usually in a specified area (*slang*)

Heb. *abbr.* **1.** Hebrew **2.** BIBLE Hebrews

heb·do·mad /hébdə màd/ *n.* (*formal*) **1.** **GROUP OF SEVEN** a group of seven people or things **2.** **WEEK** a period of seven days [Mid-16thC. Via late Latin from the Greek stem *hebdomad-* "the number seven, a period of seven days," from *hepta* "seven" (source of English *heptagon*).]

heb·dom·a·dal /heb dómməd'l/ *adj.* occuring on a weekly basis (*formal*)

he·be /héebee/ *n.* a flowering evergreen shrub with drooping spikes of blue, mauve, or white flowers and overlapping leaves resembling scales. Genus: *Hebe.* [Mid-20thC. Named for HEBE.]

He·be *n.* in Greek mythology, the goddess of youth and the daughter of Zeus and Hera. She married Hercules. [Early 17thC. From Greek *Hēbē*, literally "youthful prime."]

He·bei /hő báy/ province in northern China. Its territories include the economic heartland of ancient Chinese civilization. Capital: Shijiazhuang. Population: 63,880,000 (1994). Area: 72,600 sq. mi./188,000 sq. km.

heb·e·tate /hébbə tàyt/ (**-tat·ed, -tat·ing, -tates**) *adj.* used to describe a plant part that has a blunt or soft point [Late 16thC. From Latin *hebetat-*, the past participle stem of *hebetare*, from the stem *hebet-* "blunt, dull," of unknown origin.]

he·be·tic /hə béttik/ *adj.* occurring at or concerning puberty (*formal*) [From Greek *hēbētikos*, from, ultimately, *hēbē* "youth," from *Hēbē* "HEBE"]

heb·e·tude /hébbə tòod/ *n.* mental lethargy (*literary*) [Early 17thC. From late Latin *hebetudo*, from the Latin stem *hebet-* "dull," of unknown origin.]

Hebr. *abbr.* **1.** Hebrew **2.** BIBLE Hebrews

He·bra·ic /hi bráy ik/, **He·bra·i·cal** /-ik'l/ *adj.* relating to the Hebrews or their language or culture [14thC. Via late Latin from Greek *Hebraikos*, from *Hebraios* (see HEBREW).] —**He·bra·i·cal·ly** *adv.*

He·bra·ism /hée bray ìzzəm/, **He·bra·i·cism** *n.* a characteristic feature of the Hebrew language, especially one borrowed by another language, or something frequently found among the Hebrew people or their culture [Late 16thC. Via French or modern Latin from late Greek *Hebraismos*, from *Hebraios* (see HEBREW).]

He·bra·ist /hée bràyist/ *n.* a scholar who specializes in the study of Hebrew —**He·bra·is·ti·cal·ly** /hée bray ístikəlee/ *adv.*

He·bra·ize /hée bray ìz/ (**-ized, -iz·ing, -iz·es**) *v.* **1.** *vt.* **MAKE RESEMBLE HEBREW** to give a language or culture Hebrew characteristics **2.** *vi.* **BECOME LIKE HEBREW** to adopt Hebrew idioms or customs [Mid-17thC. From late Greek *Hebraizein*, from *Hebraios* (see HEBREW).] —**He·bra·i·za·tion** /hée bray i záysh'n/ *n.* —**He·bra·iz·er** /hée bray ìzər/ *n.*

He·brew /hée broo/ *n.* **1.** LANG **ONE OF OFFICIAL LANGUAGES OF ISRAEL** one of the official languages of Israel, also spoken in the United States and parts of Europe. It is one of the Canaanitic subgroup of the Semitic group of the Afro-Asian family of African languages. Hebrew is spoken by about five million people. **2.** PEOPLES, HIST = **Israelite** ■ *adj.* LANG, HIST = **Hebraic** [13thC. Via Old French *ebreu* from, ultimately, late Greek *Hebraios*, from Aramaic *ibrāy*, a rendering of Hebrew *ibrī* "Israelite," literally "somebody from the other side (of the Euphrates river)."]

He·brew cal·en·dar *n.* = **Jewish calendar**

He·brews /hée brooz/ *n.* in the Bible, an epistle that is thought to have been written toward the end of the first century A.D. (*takes a singular verb*) See table at **Bible**

He·brew Scrip·tures *npl.* the Bible of Judaism, consisting of the Pentateuch, the Prophets, and the Hagiographa. ◊ **Torah**

Heb·ri·des /hébbrə deez/ collective name for the islands off the western coast of Scotland, comprising an outer chain of islands, the Outer Hebrides, separated by a sea channel from the Inner Hebrides nearer the mainland —**He·bri·de·an** *adj., n.*

He·bron /héeb ron, hébbron/ town in the West Bank region, situated 20 mi./32 km southwest of Jerusalem. Population: 70,400 (1994).

Hec·a·te /hékatee/, **Hek·a·te** *n.* in Greek mythology, the goddess of darkness and the underworld. She was the daughter of the Titans Perses and Asteria. [Late 16thC. From Greek *Hekatē*, a form of *hekatos* "far-darting."]

hec·a·tomb /hékə tòm/ *n.* **1.** **ANCIENT GREEK OR ROMAN SACRIFICE** a public sacrifice and feast in ancient Greece or Rome, originally involving the slaughter of 100 oxen **2.** **GREAT SACRIFICE** any large-scale sacrifice (*literary*) [Late 16thC. Via Latin from Greek *hekatombē*, from *hekaton* "hundred" + *bous* "ox."]

Hecht /hekt/, **Ben** (1894–1964) U.S. writer. The author of fiction, plays, and screenplays, he is best remembered for his collaborations with Charles MacArthur on the plays *The Front Page* (1928) and *Twentieth Century* (1933).

heck /hek/ *interj.* **EXPRESSING IRRITATION OR EMPHASIS** used as a mild way of expressing annoyance or frustration, or emphasizing a statement (*informal*) ○ *Oh heck, I suppose that means we can't go.* ■ *n.* **EXCLAMATION** sometimes used as a less offensive alternative for the word "hell" (*informal*) ○ *What the heck is going on?* [Late 19thC. Euphemistic alteration of HELL.] ◇ **a heck of a, one heck of a** used to indicate that something is particularly large, intense, or impressive (*informal*) ○ *There's still a heck of a lot to do before closing time.*

heck·el·phone /hék'l fōn/ *n.* a bass musical instrument of the oboe family, in pitch between the English horn and the bassoon [Early 20thC. From German *Heckelphon*, named for the German instrument maker Wilhelm *Heckel* (1856–1909), its inventor. Modeled on SAXOPHONE.]

heck·le /hék'l/ *v.* (**-led, -ling, -les**) **1.** *vti.* **INTERRUPT SOMEBODY WITH SHOUTING** to shout remarks, insults, or questions in order to disconcert somebody who is making a speech or giving a performance ○ *A very angry crowd of voters heckled the candidate for mayor.* **2.** *vt.* **DRESS FLAX OR HEMP** to comb flax or hemp ■ *n.* **COMB FOR FLAX OR HEMP** a comb used for dressing flax or hemp [14thC. Variant of HACKLE. The underlying idea of the interrupting sense is "scratching, irritating."]

heck·ler /héklər/ *n.* somebody who deliberately interrupts a speaker or performer by shouting

hect- *prefix.* = **hecto-** (*used before vowels*)

hec·tare /hék tàar/ *n.* a metric unit of area equal to 100 ares or 10,000 sq. m (2.471 acres) [Early 19thC. From French, from Greek *hekaton* "hundred" + French *are* "unit of area," from Latin *area* "open space" (source of English *area*).]

hec·tic /héktik/ *adj.* **1.** CONSTANTLY BUSY AND HURRIED characterized by continual activity and haste, the lack of any time to rest or relax, and a sense of things barely under control ○ *Things have been pretty hectic at work this week.* **2.** MED FEVERISH symptomatic of or involving a recurrent afternoon fever, especially one accompanying tuberculosis ○ *hectic fever* ○ *a hectic flush* [14thC. Via Old French *etique* from, ultimately, Greek *hektikos* "habitual, consumptive," from, ultimately, Greek *ekhein* "to have."]

hecto- *prefix.* one hundred ○ *hectogram* [Via French from Greek *hekaton.* Ultimately from the Indo-European word for "hundred," which is also the ancestor of English *hundred* and *centum.*]

hec·to·cot·y·lus /hèktō kótt'ləss/ (*plural* **-li** /-lī/) *n.* a tentacle with which male octopuses and related mollusks transfer sperm to the female during mating [Mid-19thC. From modern Latin, genus name (given in the mistaken belief that the tentacles were separate organisms), from French *hecto-* "HECTO-" + Greek *kotulē* "cup, something hollow."]

hec·to·gram /héktə gràm/ *n.* a metric unit of mass equal to 100 grams [Late 18thC. From French *hectogramme,* from *hecto-* "HECTO-" + -GRAM.]

hec·to·li·ter /héktə lēetər/ *n.* a metric unit of capacity equal to 100 liters [Early 19thC. From French, from *hecto-* "HECTO-" + LITER.]

hec·to·me·ter /héktə mēetər/ *n.* a metric unit of length equal to 100 meters [Early 19thC. From French *hectomètre,* from *hecto-* "HECTO-" + METER.]

hec·tor /héktər/ *vti.* (**-tored, -tor·ing, -tors**) SPEAK IN INTIMIDATING WAY to speak to somebody in a loud, threatening, or domineering tone intended to intimidate ■ *n.* BULLY a bully (*archaic or literary*) [Mid-17thC. From HECTOR. The name became associated with a London gang.]

Hec·tor *n.* in Greek mythology, the main Trojan hero in the Trojan War and the son of King Priam and Queen Hecuba. He was killed by Achilles. [14thC. Via Latin from Greek *Hektōr,* literally "holding fast," ultimately from *ekhein* "to hold."]

Hec·u·ba /hékyəbə/ *n.* in Greek mythology, the queen of Troy and wife of King Priam. She had 16 children, including Cassandra, Hector, and Paris. [Via Latin from Greek *Hekabē*]

he'd /heed/ *contr.* **1.** HE HAD he had **2.** HE WOULD he would

hed·dle /hédd'l/ *n.* one of the sets of vertical cords or wires in the frame on a loom that guides the warp threads [Early 16thC. Origin uncertain: perhaps from Old English *hefeld,* related to English *heave.*]

hedge /hej/ *n.* **1.** ROW OF SHRUBS a close-set row of bushes, usually with their branches intermingled, forming a barrier or boundary in a garden, lawn, or field **2.** FIN PROTECTIVE METHOD a means of protection against something, especially a means of guarding against financial loss ○ *a hedge against inflation* **3.** EVASIVE STATEMENT an evasive or noncommittal statement ■ *v.* (**hedged, hedg·ing, hedg·es**) **1.** *vt.* PUT BUSHES AROUND SOMETHING to put a row of intermingled shrubs around an area of ground **2.** *vi.* WORK ON HEDGES to work at repairing, trimming, or planting a hedge **3.** *vt.* RESTRICT SOMETHING to restrict the scope or applicability of something by means of something else, e.g., a set of regulations, conditions, or qualifications ○ *It was a promise, but hedged in with so many ifs and buts that I wouldn't rely on it.* **4.** *vi.* BE EVASIVE to avoid answering a question directly or definitely ○ *She could have given a straight answer, but instead she hedged.* **5.** *vi.* FIN TRY TO OFFSET POSSIBLE LOSSES to take measures to offset any possible loss on a financial transaction, especially by investing in counterbalancing securities as a guard against price fluctuations [Old English *hegg.* Ultimately from a prehistoric Germanic word meaning "to grasp."] —**hedg·y** *adj.*

hedge·ap·ple /héj àpp'l/, **hedge·ball** *n.* the inedible fruit of the Osage orange (*regional*)

WORD KEY: REGIONAL NOTE

Hedgeapple is a West Midland designation for the fruit of the Osage orange, most common in Ohio, Indiana, Illinois, Kentucky, and Tennessee. *Hedgeball* is used in Illinois, Kentucky, and Kansas.

hedge fund *n.* an investment company that is organized as a limited partnership and uses high-risk techniques in the hope of making large profits

Hedgehog

hedge·hog /héj hòg/ *n.* **1.** ZOOL SMALL SPINY ANIMAL any of various small mammals of Europe, Africa, and Asia that have a small pointed head and a round body with stiff spines on the back. Hedgehogs eat insects, eggs, and mice, frogs, and other small animals, and can roll into a ball when attacked to protect themselves by means of their spines. Family: Erinaceidae. **2.** MIL DEFENSE AGAINST LANDING CRAFT an underwater obstacle designed to keep landing craft from reaching a beach by ripping holes in the hulls

hedge·hog cac·tus *n.* any of various low-growing round or cylindrical cacti of Mexico and the southwestern United States, with white, yellow, red, or purple bell-shaped flowers. Genus: *Echinocereus.*

hedge·hop /héj hòp/ (**-hopped, -hop·ping, -hops**) *vi.* to fly very low above the ground, often so low that the aircraft must ascend to avoid obstacles on the ground —**hedge·hop·per** *n.*

hedge·row /héj rō/ *n.* a row of bushes or small trees forming a hedge, especially around a field or along a rural road or path

hedge-school *n.* in 17th- and 18th-century Ireland, an unofficial school for Catholic children designed to evade legal restrictions on their education, often held out of doors

hedge spar·row *n.* = **dunnock**

he·don·ic /hi dónnik/ *adj.* **1.** OF PLEASURE concerned with pleasure **2.** HEDONISTIC characteristic of or relating to hedonism or hedonists [Mid-17thC. From Greek *hēdonikos,* from *hēdonē,* "pleasure."]

he·don·ism /hēed'n ìzzəm/ *n.* **1.** SEEKING OF PLEASURE a devotion, especially a self-indulgent one, to pleasure and happiness as a way of life **2.** PHILOS PHILOSOPHY OF PLEASURE a philosophical doctrine that holds that pleasure is the highest good or the source of moral values [Mid-19thC. From Greek *hēdonē* "pleasure."] —**he·don·ist** *n.* —**he·don·is·tic** /hēed'n ístik/ *adj.* —**he·don·is·ti·cal·ly** *adv.*

-hedron *suffix.* a figure or crystal having a particular number or kind of surfaces ○ *pentahedron* [Via modern Latin from, ultimately, Greek *hedra* "face" (see CATHEDRAL)] —**-hedral** *suffix.*

hee·bie-jee·bies /hēebi jēebeez/ *npl.* uncomfortable nervous or anxious feelings (*slang*) ○ *There's something about the way he speaks that gives me the heebie-jeebies.* [Early 20thC. Coined by the U.S. cartoonist Billy DeBeck (1890–1942) in his comic strip *Barney Google.*]

heed /heed/ *vti.* (**heed·ed, heed·ing, heeds**) PAY ATTENTION TO ADVICE to give serious attention to a warning or advice and take it into account when acting ■ *n.* SERIOUS ATTENTION serious attention paid to somebody or to something such as a warning, piece of advice, or request [Old English *hēdan,* ultimately from a prehistoric Germanic word] —**heed·er** *n.*

heed·ful /hēedfəl/ *adj.* paying attention to somebody or to something such as a warning, piece of advice, or danger —**heed·ful·ly** *adv.* —**heed·ful·ness** *n.*

heed·less /hēedləss/ *adj.* not paying attention to somebody or to something such as a warning, piece of advice, or danger —**heed·less·ly** *adv.* —**heed·less·ness** *n.*

hee·haw /hēe hàw/ *n.* **1.** DONKEY'S BRAY the natural sound made by a donkey **2.** NOISY LAUGH an unrefined noisy laugh (*informal*) ■ *vi.* (**-hawed, -haw·ing, -haws**) **1.** BRAY LIKE DONKEY to make a natural heehaw **2.** LAUGH NOISILY to laugh in an unrefined noisy way [Early 19thC. An imitation of the sound.]

heel[1] /heel/ *n.* **1.** PHYSIOL BACK PART OF FOOT the back part of a person's foot immediately below the ankle, or the same part of an animal's foot or paw **2.** CLOTHES BACK OF SHOE OR SOCK the part of a sock, stocking, shoe, or boot that covers the back part of somebody's foot **3.** CLOTHES BACK OF SHOE SOLE the back, usually thicker, portion of the sole of a shoe or other footwear that raises the foot off the ground ○ *I'll need to get new heels on these boots.* **4.** CLOTHES PART OF GLOVE the part of a glove that covers the part of the palm located next to the wrist **5.** FOOD BREAD CRUST a crusty end of a loaf of bread **6.** OFFENSIVE TERM an offensive term, especially for a man, that deliberately insults somebody's behavior (*informal insult*) **7.** GOLF PART OF GOLF CLUB the part of the head of a golf club where the shaft is attached **8.** PHYSIOL THICKER PART OF PALM the thicker part of the palm of the hand, located next to the wrist **9.** MUSIC END OF VIOLIN BOW the end of a violin bow that is held while playing the violin **10.** FOOD CHEESE RIND the hard rind from a wedge of cheese **11.** GARDENING PIECE ATTACHED TO CUTTING a small piece of a plant stem or tuber left attached to a cutting to promote the growth of new roots **12.** SAILING BOTTOM OF MAST the bottom end of a ship's or boat's mast **13.** NAUT STERN the stern end of a ship's keel ■ **heels** *npl.* CLOTHES HIGH HEELS high-heeled shoes ■ *v.* (**heeled, heel·ing, heels**) **1.** *vt.* FIT OR REPAIR SHOE'S HEEL to fit, replace, or repair the heel of a shoe or boot **2.** *vi.* FOLLOW BY SOMEBODY'S HEELS to follow closely at somebody's heels when commanded (*refers to dogs*) **3.** *vt.* EQU DIG HEELS INTO MOUNT to hit or prod an animal being ridden with the heel **4.** *vi.* DANCING MOVE HEELS IN DANCE to move the heels in time with music, or touch the ground with the heels when dancing **5.** *vt.* GOLF MISHIT GOLF BALL to mishit a golf ball with the heel of a club [Old English *hēla.* Ultimately from a prehistoric Germanic word that is also the ancestor of English *hough.*] —**heel·less** *adj.* ◇ **cool your heels** to wait or be kept waiting for a long time (*informal*) ◇ **dig in your heels** to hold stubbornly to a position or attitude ◇ **(hard) on the heels of somebody** *or* **something 1.** close behind somebody or something **2.** soon after somebody or something ◇ **take to your heels** to run off ◇ **to heel 1.** directly behind the person with whom a dog is walking **2.** under control or discipline ◇ **turn on your heel** to turn around suddenly

heel[2] /heel/ *vti.* (**heeled, heel·ing, heels**) LEAN TO ONE SIDE to lean over to one side so far as to be in danger of falling, or cause something such as a ship to lean in this way ○ *The ship heeled in the wind.* ■ *n.* SIDEWAYS LEAN a leaning to one side, or the degree to which something such as a ship is leaning [Late 16thC. Alteration of Middle English *helden* (taken to be a past participle), from Old English *hieldan* "to lean or bend."]

heel-and-toe *adj.* SPORT CONSTITUTING WALKING NOT RUNNING used to describe walking or racing that requires the heel of one foot to touch the ground before the toe of the other is lifted from the ground ■ *vi.* (**heel-and-toed, heel-and-toe·ing, heel-and-toes**) MOTOR SPORTS PRESS BRAKE AND ACCELERATOR to operate the brake and accelerator pedals at the same time with one foot, usually to keep the engine revolutions high when shifting to a lower gear while racing

heel bone *n.* the quadrangular bone that forms the heel of the foot. Technical name **calcaneus**

heeled /heeld/ *adj.* with a heel or heels, often of a specified type (*often used in combination*) ○ *a high-heeled shoe*

heel·er /hēelər/ *n.* **1.** SOMEBODY OR SOMETHING THAT HEELS SHOES a person or machine that fits, replaces, or repairs the heels of shoes or boots ○ *the quickest heeler in the shoe factory* **2.** = **ward heeler** (*informal*)

heel in /heel ín/ (**heeled in, heel·ing in, heels in**) *vt.* to place a bare-root plant at a sharp angle in a holding bed and cover the roots with soil until it can be planted properly [Old English *helian* "to conceal"; ultimately from a prehistoric Germanic word that is also the ancestor of English *hell.* Originally spelt *hele;* the current spelling arose by association with HEEL[1].]

heel·piece /hēel pēess/ *n.* the part of a sock, stocking, shoe, or boot that fits around the heel of the foot

heel·post /hēel pōst/ *n.* a post to which the hinges of a gate or door are attached

heel·tap /hēel tàp/ *n.* **1.** DRINK LEFT IN GLASS a small quantity of an alcoholic drink remaining at the bottom of a glass after the rest has been swallowed **2.** LAYER OF MATERIAL IN SHOE HEEL a layer of leather or other material in the heel of a shoe or boot

He·fei /hŏ fáy/ capital city of Anhui Province, west of Nanjing, eastern China. Population: 1,000,000 (1991).

Hef·ner /héfnər/, **Hugh** (*b.* 1926) U.S. publisher. He founded *Playboy* in 1953, and through the magazine a string of related nightclubs. His own much publicized hedonistic lifestyle epitomized the sexual revolution of the 1960s and 1970s. Full name **Hugh Marston Hefner**

heft /heft/ *vt.* (**heft·ed, heft·ing, hefts**) *U.S.* **1.** LIFT SOMETHING to lift up something heavy, especially with a burst of effort ○ *He hefted the load onto his back and slowly started up the mountain.* **2.** ESTIMATE WEIGHT OF SOMETHING to lift something in order to estimate its weight ■ *n. U.S.* GREAT WEIGHT substantial heaviness or bulk [15thC. Originally as the noun. Of uncertain origin; probably from HEAVE, modeled on pairs of words such as *cleave, cleft.*] —**heft·er** *n.*

heft·y /héftee/ (**-i·er, -i·est**) *adj.* **1.** POWERFULLY BUILT big and strong in physique **2.** HEAVY large and heavy to lift **3.** EXPENSIVE involving a large sum of money **4.** FORCEFUL delivered with or characterized by great force and power **5.** STRENUOUS requiring a lot of effort to do **6.** LARGER THAN USUAL much larger than is usual or required —**heft·i·ly** *adv.* —**heft·i·ness** *n.*

he·ga·ri /hə gérree, héggəree/ *n.* any of various originally Sudanese varieties of sorghum grown for grain [Early 20thC. From Arabic (Sudanese) dialect *hegiri.*]

He·gel·i·an·ism /hə gáylee ə nìzzəm/ *n.* the philosophy of G.W.F. Hegel, which proposes a unified solution to all philosophical problems through development of a reasoning process that ultimately interprets reality by way of the dialectic method

he·gem·o·ny /hə jémmənee, héjjə mōnee/ *n.* control or dominating influence by one person or group over others, especially by one political group over society or one nation over others (*formal*) [Mid-16thC. From Greek *hēgemonia* "leadership," ultimately from *hēgisthai* "to lead."] —**heg·e·mon·ic** /hèjjə mónnik/ *adj.* —**he·gem·o·nism** /hə jémmə nìzzəm/ *n.* —**he·gem·o·nist** /hə jémmənist/ *n.*

he·gi·ra /hə jīrə, héjjərə/, **he·ji·ra** *n.* a flight or withdrawal from somewhere, especially to escape from danger [Late 16thC. Via medieval Latin from Arabic *hijra*, literally "the leaving of home and friends."]

He·gi·ra, **He·ji·ra** *n.* **1.** MUHAMMAD'S WITHDRAWAL FROM MECCA the withdrawal of the Prophet Muhammad from Mecca to Medina to escape persecution **2.** MUSLIM ERA the Muslim era, dated from the first day of the lunar year in which Muhammad's withdrawal to Medina took place. This was July 16, A.D. 622 in the Gregorian calendar.

Hei·an /háyən/ *adj.* characteristic of or relating to Japan from A.D. 794–1185, when Confucianism and other Chinese influences were at their height [Late 19thC. From Japanese *Heian-kyo*, now Kyoto, former capital of Japan.]

Hei·del·berg /hīd'l burg/ university city in Baden-Württemberg, southwestern Germany, situated on the Neckar River. Population: 139,392 (1992).

Hei·del·berg man /hīd'l bùrg-/ *n.* an extinct early human of the Pleistocene epoch that is known mainly from a fossilized jawbone [Early 20thC. Named for the city of HEIDELBERG in southwestern Germany, near where a jawbone from Heidelberg man was found.]

Hei·den /hīd'n/, **Eric** (*b.* 1958) U.S. ice skater. He was world speed-skating champion (1977–79) and won five gold medals in the 1980 Olympics. Full name **Eric Arthur Heiden**

heif·er /héffər/ *n.* a young cow, especially one that has never had a calf [Old English *heahfore*, of unknown origin]

Hei·fetz /hīfits/, **Jascha** (1901–87) Lithuanian-born U.S. violinist. Noted for his technical mastery, he was considered one of the greatest classical violinists of his time.

heigh-ho *interj.* **1.** EXPRESSING DISAPPOINTMENT used to express boredom, disappointment, or weary resignation ○ *Heigh-ho. Here we go again.* **2.** EXPRESSING ENCOURAGEMENT used to express happiness or encouragement

height /hīt/ *n.* **1.** LENGTH UPWARD the distance between somebody or something's lowest point and highest point ○ *a steep cliff about 200 feet in height* **2.** DISTANCE ABOVE SOMETHING the distance that somebody or something is above the ground, sea, or another reference point **3.** NOTICEABLE TALLNESS the condition of being noticeably high or tall compared to others ○ *His height makes him stand out in a crowd.* **4.** HIGHEST POINT the top or highest point of something ○ *When you reach the height, you'll get a wonderful view.* **5.** HIGH POSITION a high place or position, especially one where somebody can see a view or how high up he or she is (*often used in the plural*) **6.** HIGHEST LEVEL the time of greatest intensity, activity, importance, or success ○ *She was at the height of her powers.* **7.** HIGH LEVEL a high level of intensity or severity (*often used in the plural*) ○ *Their arrogance is reaching new heights.* **8.** EXTREME the most extreme example of something ○ *It was the height of folly to have gone there on your own.* ■ **heights** *npl.* HILLS OR MOUNTAINS an area of hilly or mountainous terrain, especially one that is noticeably elevated above the surrounding region (*often used in place names*) [Old English *hēhþu* "the highest part." Ultimately from a prehistoric Germanic word that is also the ancestor of English *high.*]

WORD KEY: CULTURAL NOTE

Wuthering Heights, a novel by English writer Emily Brontë (1847). Brontë's only novel, it is the story of a foundling, Heathcliff, whose mistreatment at the hands of his adoptive family leads him to seek revenge later in life. The novel is noted for its evocative descriptions of the Yorkshire moors, its complex morality, and its intensity of feeling.

height·en /hīt'n/ (**-ened, -en·ing, -ens**) *vti.* **1.** MAKE OR BECOME GREATER to make something such as a feeling or emotion greater or more intense, or become greater or more intense ○ *His attempts to reassure them served only to heighten their fears.* **2.** MAKE OR BECOME HIGHER to make something higher, or become higher ○ *As protection, they heightened the city walls by a further three feet.* **3.** APPEAR BRIGHTER OR MAKE SOMETHING BRIGHTER to make something such as a color appear brighter or stronger, or appear to become brighter or stronger ○ *The sunlight heightened the flush on her cheeks.* —**height·ened** *adj.* —**height·en·er** *n.*

height of land *n. Can* a ridge of high land that is a watershed

Hei·long·jiang /hày lŏng jyáang/ province in the Manchurian region of northeastern China, bordering Russia. Capital: Harbin. Population: 36,720,000 (1994). Area: 179,000 sq. mi./463,600 sq. km.

Heim·dall /háym daal/, **Heim·dal, Heim·dallr** /háym daalər/ *n.* in Norse mythology, a giant warrior who was the god of light and dawn [From Old Norse *Heimdallr*, from *heimr* "home, world" + *dallr*, of uncertain origin: perhaps related to Old English *deall* "bold"]

Heim·lich ma·neu·ver /hímlik-/ *n.* a emergency method for treating choking that uses an upward thrust immediately below the breastbone to expel food or another blockage from the windpipe [Late 20thC. Named for the American surgeon Henry J. *Heimlich* (born 1920), who devised it.]

hei·nie /hīnee/ *n.* the human buttocks (*slang*) [Mid-20thC. Alteration of HINDER.]

Hein·lein /hín līn/, **Robert** (1907–88) U.S. writer. His many works of science fiction, known for their technological sophistication, include *Stranger in a Strange Land* (1961). Full name **Robert Anson Heinlein**

hei·nous /háynəss/ *adj.* shockingly evil or wicked [14thC. From Old French *haineus*, from *hair* "to hate," ultimately from a prehistoric Germanic word that is also the ancestor of English *hate.*] —**hei·nous·ly** *adv.* —**hei·nous·ness** *n.*

heir /air/ *n.* **1.** LEGAL INHERITOR OF SOMETHING somebody who receives or who has by law the right to receive the property, position, or title of another when that person dies **2.** RECIPIENT OF TRADITION somebody who or something that inherits something such as a tradition, problem, or characteristic from a predecessor ○ *Our generation is the unfortunate heir to decades of pollution.* [14thC. Via Old French *(h)eir* from, ultimately, Latin *heres.*] —**heir·less** *adj.* —**heir·ship** *n.*

heir ap·par·ent (*plural* **heirs ap·par·ent**) *n.* **1.** UNDOUBTED LEGAL HEIR an heir whose entitlement to receive an inheritance cannot be altered by the birth of another heir **2.** EXPECTED SUCCESSOR somebody who is expected to inherit another's position, status, or influence

heir at law (*plural* **heirs at law**) *n.* the heir of somebody's property under the law if that person dies without a valid will

heir·ess /áirəss/ *n.* a woman or girl who receives or has by law the right to receive the property, position, or title of another when that person dies

heir·loom /áir lo͞om/ *n.* **1.** SOMETHING HANDED DOWN something that has been in the possession of a family for a long time and has been passed on from one generation to the next **2.** LAW SOMETHING INHERITED BY LAW an item of personal property that is attached to the estate that the legal heir will inherit [LOOM^2, in an obsolete sense "tool, utensil"]

heir pre·sump·tive (*plural* **heirs pre·sump·tive**) *n.* an heir whose entitlement to an inheritance will cease if another heir is born whose entitlement is greater

Hei·sen·berg un·cer·tain·ty prin·ci·ple /hīz'n burg un súrt'nti prinsəp'l/ *n.* = **uncertainty principle** [Named for the German physicist Werner HEISENBERG (1901–76), who deduced it]

heist /hīst/ *n.* THEFT a theft or robbery, especially of money or valuables, usually involving the use of weapons (*slang*) ■ *vt.* (**heist·ed, heist·ing, heists**) STEAL SOMETHING to steal or rob something, especially money or valuables, usually while carrying weapons (*slang*) [Mid-19thC. Representing a local American pronunciation of HOIST.] —**heist·er** *n.*

He·jaz /he jáz/ province of western Saudi Arabia, bordering the Red Sea. Area: 134,600 sq. mi./348,600 sq. km.

he·ji·ra, **He·ji·ra** *n.* = **hegira, Hegira**

Hek·a·te *n.* = **Hecate**

Hek·la /héklə/ active volcano in southwestern Iceland. Height: 4,892 ft./1,491 m.

Hel /hel/, **Hel·a** *n.* **1.** NORSE GODDESS OF THE DEAD in Norse mythology, the daughter of Loki, and the goddess of the dead and the underworld **2.** NORSE UNDERWORLD in Norse mythology, the underworld of the dead [From Old Norse, related to English *hell*]

He·La cell /héllə-/, **He·La cell** *n.* a cell from a strain of human cervical cancer cells that is used in medical and biological research [Mid-20thC. Acronym formed from the name of *Henrietta Lacks*, the patient from whom the original cells were taken.]

held past tense, past participle of **hold**

hel·den·te·nor /hèld'ntə náwr/, **Hel·den·te·nor** *n.* a tenor or tenor voice with a robust dramatic quality that is suited especially for heroic roles in the operas of Richard Wagner [Early 20thC. From German, literally "hero tenor."]

Hel·en /héllən/, **Hel·en of Troy** *n.* in Greek mythology, the daughter of Zeus and Leda and the most beautiful woman in Greece. Her husband was Menelaus, the king of Sparta. Her abduction by Paris sparked the Trojan War.

Hel·e·na /héllənə/ city and capital of Montana, located in the western part of the state. Population: 24,569 (1990).

He·le·ne /hə leénee/ *n.* a very small natural satellite of Saturn, discovered in 1980. It is irregular in shape, with a maximum dimension of 22 mi./36 km and occupies an intermediate orbit.

he·le·ni·um /hə leénee əm/ (*plural* **-ums** *or* **-um**) *n.* a plant of the daisy family that is native to North and South America and has yellow or dark reddish flowers, or in cultivated varieties sometimes bicolored flowers. Genus: *Helenium.* [Early 17thC. Via modern Latin from Greek *helenion*, perhaps named for HELEN OF TROY.]

He·lens·vale /héllənz vayl/ town in southeastern Queensland, Australia, a residential, tourist, and cattle grazing center. Population: 13,823 (1996).

hel·i /héllee/ (*plural* **-is**) *n.* a rotary-wing aircraft (*informal*) [Shortening of HELICOPTER]

heli- *prefix.* helicopter ○ *helipad* [From HELICOPTER]

he·li·a·cal /hə lī ək'l/ *adj.* used to describe the rising or setting of a star that occurs at the same time as the rising or setting of the sun, because of their near conjunction [Mid-16thC. Via late Latin *heliacus* from, ultimately, Greek *hēlios* "sun."] —**he·li·a·cal·ly** *adv.*

he·li·an·the·mum /heelee ánthəməm/ *n.* any of various evergreen perennials native to the United States, Europe, and Asia Minor with white, yellow, pink, or orange flowers. Genus: *Helianthemum.* [Early 19thC. From modern Latin, formed from Greek *hēlios* "sun" + *anthemon* "flower" (because the flower turns to follow the path of the sun).]

he·li·an·thus /hēelee ánthəss/ (*plural* **-thus·es** *or* **-thus**) *n.* a tall perennial plant related to the sunflower with yellow flowers resembling those of the daisy. Some cultivated varieties have double flowers. Genus: *Helianthus.* [Late 18thC. From modern Latin, formed from Greek *hēlios* "sun" + *anthos* "flower" (because the flower turns to follow the path of the sun).]

hel·i·borne /héllə bàwrn/ *adj.* transported by helicopter

helic- *prefix.* = **helico-** (*used before vowels*)

hel·i·cal /héllik'l, hée-/ *adj.* in the shape of a helix or spiral [Late 16thC. From Latin *helix* (see HELIX).] —**hel·i·cal·ly** *adv.*

hel·i·cal gear *n.* a gear whose teeth are formed to curve along a spiral path on the surface of the gear on an axis oblique to the axis of the gear itself

hel·i·ces plural of **helix**

he·li·chry·sum /hèllə kríssəm/ (*plural* **-sums** *or* **-sum**) *n.* an annual or perennial plant of the daisy family grown especially for its variously colored flowers that retain their color when dried. Genus: *Helichrysum.* [Mid-16thC. From Latin, literally "golden spiral."]

helico- *prefix.* helix, spiral ○ *helicograph* [From Greek *helik-*, the stem of *helix* (see HELIX)]

he·li·co·graph /héllikə gràf, hée-/ *n.* an instrument for drawing spiral curves on a flat surface

hel·i·coid /hélli kòyd, hééli-/ *adj.* BIOL **SPIRAL** shaped or coiled like a spiral (*technical*) ○ *a helicoid shell* ■ *n.* GEOM **SPIRAL SURFACE** a spiral geometric surface that resembles a thread on a screw [Late 17thC. From Greek *helicoidēs*, from *helix* "HELIX."] —**he·li·coid·al** /-kóyd'l/ *adj.* —**he·li·coid·al·ly** *adv.*

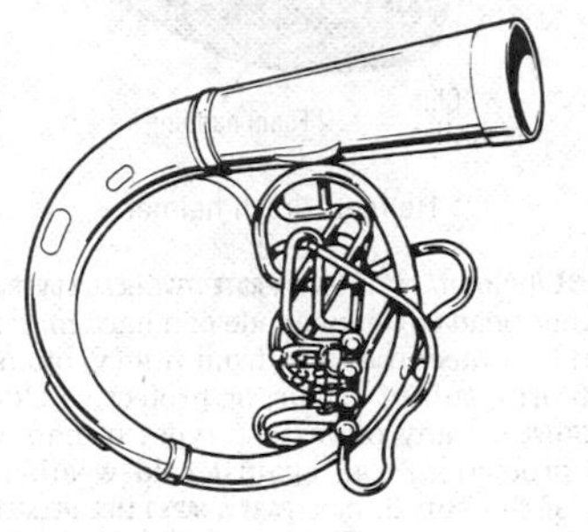

Helicon

hel·i·con /hélli kòn, -kən/ *n.* a large bass tuba that encircles the player's body, used in marching bands [Late 19thC. From *Helicon*; influenced by HELIX (because of the shape).]

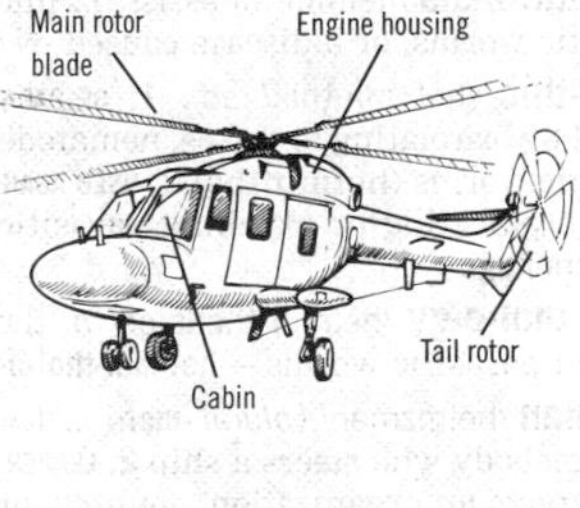

Helicopter

hel·i·cop·ter /hélli kòptər/ *n.* **AIRCRAFT WITH ROTORS** an aircraft without wings that moves by means of large blades (**rotors**) that spin around above it. It can fly vertically and horizontally and can hover. ■ *vti.* (**-tered, -ter·ing, -ters**) **FLY IN HELICOPTER** to travel or transport somebody or something in a helicopter ○ *The survivors were helicoptered to a hospital.* [Late 19thC. From French *hélicoptère*, from Greek *helix* "spiral" + *pteron* "wing."]

hel·i·cop·ter gun·ship *n.* a large heavily armed helicopter used to protect troops on the ground

hel·i·cul·ture /hélli kùlchər, hééli-/ *n.* the science or the profession of raising snails for food [From modern Latin *Helix*, a genus of spiral-shelled mollusks (from Greek *helix* "HELIX") + CULTURE] —**hel·i·cul·tur·al** /hèlli kúlchərəl, hééli kúlchərəl/ *adj.* —**he·li·cul·tur·al·ist** *n.*

hel·i·deck /héllə dèk/ *n.* a deck on something such as a ship or offshore oil platform that is used as a landing site for helicopters

helio- *prefix.* sun ○ *heliostat* [From Greek *hēlios* (source of English *helium*). Ultimately from the Indo-European word for "sun," which is also the ancestor of *sun* and *solar.*]

he·li·o·cen·tric /hēelee ə séntrik/, **he·li·o·cen·tri·cal** /-séntrik'l/ *adj.* **1. WITH THE SUN CENTRAL** with the sun at the center ○ *a heliocentric orbit* **2. FROM CENTER OF SUN** measured from or considered as if viewed from the center of the sun —**he·li·o·cen·tri·cal·ly** /-séntrikəlee/ *adv.* —**he·li·o·cen·tric·i·ty** /-sen tríssətee/ *n.*

he·li·o·dor /hēelee ə dàwr/ *n.* a clear yellow variety of beryl found in southwestern Africa, used as a gemstone [Early 20thC. Coined from HELIO- + Greek *dōron* "gift."]

he·li·o·graph /hēelee ə gràf/ *n.* **1.** COMMUNICATION **SIGNALING APPARATUS** an apparatus that is used to send messages in Morse code by flashes of reflected sunlight **2.** ASTRON **PHOTOGRAPHING APPARATUS** an apparatus used to photograph the sun —**he·li·og·raph·er** /hēelee óggrəfər/ *n.* —**he·li·o·graph·ic** /hēelee ə gráffik/ *adj.*

he·li·o·la·try /hēelee óllətree/ *n.* worship of the sun —**he·li·o·lat·er** *n.* —**he·li·o·la·trous** *adj.*

he·li·o·li·thic /hēelee ə líthik/ *adj.* used to describe a culture or society characterized by worship of the sun and the construction of monuments or temples using huge stones (**megaliths**)

he·li·om·e·ter /hēelee ómmətər/ *n.* a refracting telescope with a divided objective that is used to measure small angular distances between celestial objects or points on the moon —**he·li·o·met·ric** /hēelee ə méttrik/ *adj.* —**he·li·o·met·ri·cal** /-méttrik'l/ *adj.* —**he·li·o·met·ri·cal·ly** *adv.* —**he·li·om·e·try** /hēelee ómmətree/ *n.*

he·li·o·phyte /hēelee ə fīt/ *n.* a plant that can survive and grow in direct sunlight or that grows best in direct sunlight

He·li·op·o·lis /hēelee óppəliss/ city of ancient Egypt, northeast of present-day Cairo in the Nile delta. The great temple there was the center of sun worship, and reached the height of its influence in the 13th century B.C.

He·li·os /hēelee òss/ *n.* in Greek mythology, the god of the sun. The son of Hyperion and Thea, he drove his golden chariot across the sky from east to west each day. Roman equivalent **Sol**

he·li·o·seis·mol·o·gy /hēelee ō sīz mólləjee/ *n.* the scientific study of the sound waves in the sun's atmosphere

he·li·o·sphere /hēelee ə sfeer/ *n.* a spherical region around the sun, approximately 100 astronomical units in radius, outside which interstellar space begins

he·li·o·stat /hēelee ə stàt/ *n.* an instrument with an automatically rotated mirror that reflects the sun's light in a constant direction, used to measure the sun's radiation [Mid-18thC. From modern Latin *heliostata* or French *héliostat*, both formed from Greek *hēlios* "sun" + *statos* "standing."] —**he·li·o·stat·ic** /hēelee ə státtik/ *adj.*

he·li·o·tax·is /hēelee ə táksiss/ *n.* movement toward or away from sunlight in an organism that is able to move about freely —**he·lio·tac·tic** *adj.*

he·li·o·ther·a·py /hēelee ə thérrəpee/ *n.* treatment of illness by exposure to direct sunlight

he·lio·trope /hēelee ə trōp/ *n.* (*plural* **-tropes** *or* **-trope**) **1.** PLANTS **PLANT WITH PURPLE FLOWERS** any of various hairy herbs or shrubs of the borage family, especially a South American species cultivated for its small, very fragrant purple flowers. Genus: *Heliotropium.* **2.** PLANTS **FLOWER THAT TURNS TOWARD SUN** any of a number of plants with flowers that turn toward the sun **3.** COLORS **BLUISH COLOR** a bluish purple color **4.** MINERALS = **bloodstone 5.** CIV ENG **SURVEY INSTRUMENT** an instrument used in geodesic surveying to reflect the sun's rays over long distances ■ *adj.* COLORS **OF BLUISH COLOR** of a bluish purple color [Pre-12thC. Via Latin *heliotropium* from Greek *heliotropion*, literally "sun turning."]

he·li·ot·ro·pism /hēelee óttrə pìzzəm/ *n.* growth toward sunlight by a plant. ◊ **phototropism** —**he·li·o·trop·ic** /hēelee ə tróppik/ *adj.* —**he·li·o·trop·i·cal** *adj.* —**he·li·o·trop·i·cal·ly** *adv.*

he·li·o·zo·an /hēelee ə zṓ ən/ *n.* a free-living, usually freshwater, protozoan that has a spherical shell and radiating projections (**pseudopodia**). Class: Heliozoa. [Late 19thC. From modern Latin *Heliozoa*, class name, from Greek *hēlios* "sun" + *zōion* "animal."] —**he·li·o·zo·ic** *adj.*

hel·i·pad /héllə pàd/ *n.* an area where helicopters take off and land

hel·i·port /héllə pàwrt/ *n.* an airport designed for helicopters

hel·i·ski·ing /hélli skèe ing/ *n.* skiing in which skiers are taken to a usually remote ski slope by helicopter

hel·i·stop /héllə stòp/ *n.* a place where helicopters can take off and land, usually without the support facilities found at a heliport

he·li·um /hēelee əm/ *n.* a nonflammable inert gas that is colorless and odorless. Symbol **He** [Late 19thC. From Greek *hēlios* "sun" (because its existence was deduced from its emission line in the solar spectrum).]

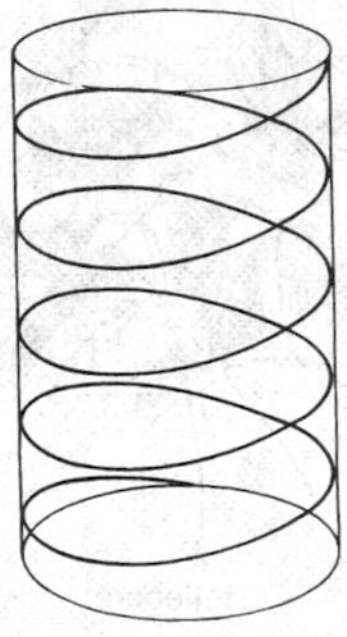

Helix

he·lix /hēeliks/ (*plural* **he·lix·es** *or* **hel·i·ces** /hélli seez, hēelə-/) *n.* **1. SPIRAL OR COIL** something in the form of a spiral or coil, e.g., a corkscrew or a coiled spring **2.** GEOM **SPIRAL CURVE** a mathematical curve that lies on a cylinder or cone and makes a constant angle with the straight lines lying in the cylinder or cone **3.** ANAT **RIM OF EAR** the rim of the external ear [Mid-16thC. Via Latin from Greek.]

hell /hel/ *n.* **1. hell, Hell PLACE OF PUNISHMENT AFTER DEATH** according to many religions, the place where the souls of people who are damned suffer eternal punishment after death **2. hell, Hell DEVILISH POWER** according to some religions, Satan or the powers of evil that live in hell **3. UNDERWORLD** according to some religions, the place where the spirits of all people go after death **4. SUFFERING OR ITS CAUSE** a state or place of extreme pain or misery, or something or somebody that causes extreme pain or misery ○ *I tell you, migraine is just hell.* ○ *The January sales are absolute hell.* ○ *She went through hell until she heard they were safe.* ■ *interj.* **EXPRESSING ANNOYANCE** used to express annoyance or surprise or for emphasis (*sometimes considered offensive*) ○ *Hell! I've lost the key.* ○ *Oh, hell. The store is closed.* ○ *Hell, no. I don't want that.* ■ *vi.* (**helled, hell·ing, hells**) **BEHAVE WILDLY** to live or behave recklessly or riotously (*slang*) ○ *sailors helling around port while on leave* [Old English *hel(l)*. Ultimately from an Indo-European word meaning "to conceal," which is also the ancestor of English *conceal, occult, eucalyptus,* and *apocalypse.*] ◇ **a hell of a, one hell of a** used as an intensifier (*informal*) ◇ **come hell or high water** whatever difficulties there may be ◇ **from hell** of the worst sort imaginable (*informal*) ○ *The bus ride in the blizzard was a trip from hell.* ◇ **give somebody hell 1.** to scold somebody severely (*informal*) **2.** to cause somebody trouble or pain (*informal*) ◇ **hell to pay** serious trouble or punishment that is sure to result from something (*informal*) ◇ **(just) for the hell of it** just for amusement or excitement (*informal*) ◇ **like hell 1.** very fast or very intensely (*informal*) **2.** used to emphasize disagreement or denial (*informal*) ◇ **play** *or* **raise hell with something** to cause harm, disruption, or damage to something (*informal*) ◇ **raise hell 1.** to object to something strongly and loudly (*informal*) **2.** to celebrate or party wildly (*informal*) ◇ **the hell 1.** used to emphasize annoyance (*informal*) **2.** used to emphasize disagreement or denial (*informal*)

he'll /heel/ *contr.* **1. HE WILL** he will **2. HE SHALL** he shall

hel·la·cious /he láyshəss/ *adj.* **1. EXTREMELY BAD** extremely bad, unpleasant, or unbearable (*informal*) **2. EXTREMELY LARGE** extremely large (*slang*) [Mid-20thC. From HELL, perhaps modeled on *bodacious.*]

Hel·lad·ic /he láddik/ *adj.* associated with or characteristic of the Bronze Age civilization that flourished in Greece from 3000 to 1100 B.C. [Early 19thC. From Greek *Helladikos,* from *Hellas* "Greece."]

Hel·las /hélləss/ *n.* **1. GREECE** the ancient name for Greece **2.** ASTRON **PLAIN ON MARS** an extensive plain on the surface of Mars in the southern hemisphere, approximately 1100 mi./1800 km across

hell·bend·er /hél bèndər/ *n.* a large, dark gray salamander found in rivers in eastern and central parts of the United States. Latin name: *Cryptobranchus alleganiensis.*

hell-bent *adj.* absolutely determined to do something, regardless of the consequences

hell-bent-for-leath·er *adv., adj.* = **hell-for-leather** (*informal*)

Hellebore

hel·le·bore /héllə bàwr/ (*plural* **-bores** *or* **-bore**) *n.* **1. EARLY-FLOWERING PLANT** an early-flowering, often poisonous perennial plant, native to Europe and Asia, that has large divided leaves and drooping white, pink, dark purple, or sometimes green flowers. The Christmas rose is a hellebore. Genus: *Helleborus.* **2. GREENISH-FLOWERED PLANT** any of various poisonous plants of North America with greenish flowers. Genus: *Veratrum.* [Pre-12thC. Via Old French *ellebre* from, ultimately, Greek *helleboros.*]

Hel·len /héllən/ *n.* in Greek mythology, a king of Thessaly and ancestor of the ancient Hellenic peoples

Hel·lene /hé leen/, **Hel·le·ni·an** /he léenee ən/ *n.* (*formal*) **1. ANCIENT GREEK** an ancient Greek **2. SOMEBODY FROM MODERN GREECE** somebody who was born or raised in modern Greece [Mid-17thC. From Greek *Hellēn* "a Greek."]

Hel·len·ic /he lénnik/ *adj.* PEOPLES **OF ANCIENT GREECE** relating to or typical of ancient Greece, or its people, languages, or culture ■ *n.* LANG **GROUP OF GREEK LANGUAGES** the branch of Indo-European consisting of the ancient and modern forms of Greek [Mid-17thC. From Greek *Hellēnikos,* from *Hellēn* (see HELLENE).] —**Hel·len·i·cal·ly** *adv.*

Hel·le·nism /héllə nìzzəm/ *n.* **1. ANCIENT GREEK CULTURE** the culture and civilization of ancient Greece, especially in the period after Alexander the Great when it spread to other parts of the Mediterranean and Middle East and North Africa **2. ADMIRATION FOR ANCIENT GREEK CULTURE** the enthusiasm for or adoption of ancient Greek culture or customs **3. GREEK CHARACTERISTIC** a Greek custom or idiom **4. GREEK NATIONAL CHARACTER** the national character of the Greeks [Early 17thC. From Greek *Hellēnismos* (see HELLENIZE).]

Hel·le·nist /héllənist/ *n.* **1. GREEK EXPERT** somebody who is a specialist in the study of Greek language, literature, culture, or history, or somebody who has a great enthusiasm for things Greek **2.** HIST **ADOPTER OF GREEK WAYS** somebody, especially a Jew, who adopted Greek customs, language, and culture during the 4th to 1st centuries B.C. [Early 17thC. From Greek *Hellēnistēs* (see HELLENIZE).]

Hel·le·nis·tic /hèllə nístik/ *adj.* **1. OF ANCIENT GREEK CIVILIZATION** characteristic of or concerned with ancient Greek civilization from the late 4th to 1st centuries B.C. **2. OF GREEKS** characteristic of or associated with the Greeks **3. PREFERRING GREEK CULTURE** enthusiastic for or adopting ancient Greek culture or customs ○ *the Hellenistic Jews of Alexandria* —**Hel·len·is·ti·cal·ly** *adv.*

Hel·le·nize /héllə nìz/ (**-nized, -niz·ing, -niz·es**) *vti.* to adopt the language and culture of the ancient Greeks, or make something such as a culture more like that of the ancient Greeks [Early 17thC. From Greek *Hellēnizein* "to speak Greek, to make Greek," from *Hellēn* (see HELLENE).] —**Hel·le·ni·za·tion** /hèlləni záysh'n/ *n.* —**Hel·le·niz·er** /héllə nìzər/ *n.*

hel·ler[1] /héllər/ (*plural* **-ler**) *n.* **1. OLD GERMAN OR AUSTRIAN COIN** any of several obsolete German or Austrian coins **2.** = **haler** [Late 16thC. From German, ultimately named for the town of *Schwäbisch Hall* in Germany, where it was first minted.]

hell·er[2] /héllər/ *n.* = **hellion** (*informal*) [Formed from HELL]

Hel·ler /héllər/, **Joseph** (*b.* 1923) U.S. writer. He is best known for his antiwar novel *Catch-22* (1961).

hel·ler·i /héllə rì/ (*plural* **-is**) *n.* a brightly colored freshwater aquarium fish that is a hybrid of a swordtail and platy [Mid-20thC. Named after C. *Heller,* tropical fish collector.]

hell·fire /hél fìr/ *n.* **FIERY PUNISHMENT IN HELL** punishment in hell, often described as eternal torment in the flames of hell's fires ■ *adj.* **EMPHASIZING PUNISHMENT IN HELL** detailing the punishment sinners can expect in hell in a vigorous and emotional way

hell-for-leath·er *adv., adj.* extremely quickly and often recklessly (*informal*)

hell·gram·mite /hélgrə mìt/ *n.* the large aquatic carnivorous larva of the North American dobsonfly, often used as fish bait [Mid-19thC. Origin unknown.]

hell·hole /hél hōl/ *n.* a terrifying, unbearable, or evil place

hell·hound /hél hòwnd/ *n.* **1. FIEND** a fiend or fiendish, wicked person **2.** MYTHOL **HOUND GUARDING HELL** a hound said to guard the gates of hell, especially in Greek mythology

hel·lion /héllyən/ *n.* a troublesome or rowdy person, especially a child (*informal*) [Mid-19thC. Origin uncertain; probably an alteration, influenced by HELL, of Scots and northern English dialect *hallion* "idler."]

hell·ish /héllish/ *adj.* **1. VILE** so wicked or cruel that it seems characteristic of the devil **2. OF HELL** like, from, or typical of hell **3. DREADFUL** extremely unpleasant or difficult (*informal*) ○ *The exam was absolutely hellish.* —**hell·ish·ly** *adv.* —**hell·ish·ness** *n.*

Lillian Hellman

Hell·man /hélmən/, **Lillian** (1905–84) U.S. playwright. She was known for her powerful moral dramas such as *Watch on the Rhine* (1941) and *Toys in the Attic* (1960). Full name **Lillian Florence Hellman**

hel·lo /hə lṓ, he lṓ/ *interj., n.* (*plural* **-los**) **1. WORD USED AS GREETING** a word used to greet somebody you meet, to answer a telephone call, or to begin a radio or television program ○ *Hello. Pleased to meet you.* ○ *Hello, and welcome to the show.* ○ *After we had all said our hellos, we settled down to eat.* **2. WORD TO ATTRACT ATTENTION** a word used to attract attention ○ *Hello! Is anyone there ?* **3. WORD EXPRESSING SURPRISE** a word used to express surprise ○ *Hello! What's that doing here?* ■ *interj.* **USED TO ADD IRONIC EMPHASIS** used to add ironic, sarcastic, or sometimes angry emphasis (*slang*) ○ *He's like, hello? who do you think you are?* ○ *I'm living my own life now, hello? Please mind your own business.* [Late 19thC. Origin uncertain; probably ultimately from French *holá,* literally "stop there!", used to attract attention.]

hell-rais·er *n.* somebody whose idea of having a good time involves behaving in ways that other people consider drunken, rowdy, and disruptive

Hells Can·yon /hèlz-/ gorge of Snake River on the Idaho-Oregon border, and the deepest canyon in the United States. Depth: 7,900 ft./2,400 m. Length: 40 mi./64 km.

hell·uv·a /hélləvə/ *adj.* used as an intensifier (*informal*) ○ *a helluva party* [Early 20thC. Representing "hell of a."]

hell week *n.* the week when college fraternity or sorority pledges are subjected to hazing before their initiation

helm[1] /helm/ *n.* **1.** NAUT **SHIP'S STEERING APPARATUS** the apparatus used to steer a ship, especially the wheel or handle (**tiller**) by which the rudder is turned **2. POSITION OF CONTROL** a position of leadership or control within an organization, country, or endeavor ○ *The failing company needed a new chief at its helm.* ■ *vt.* (**helmed, helm·ing, helms**) **1.** NAUT **STEER SHIP** to be at the helm of a ship steering it **2. DIRECT SOMETHING** to be at the head of an organization, country, or endeavor directing it [Old English *helma,* from a prehistoric Germanic word meaning "handle" that is also the ancestor of English *halter* and *helve*] —**helm·less** *adj.*

helm[2] /helm/ *n.* **HELMET** an ancient or medieval helmet (*archaic or literary*) ■ *vt.* (**helmed, helm·ing, helms**) **PROVIDE SOMEBODY WITH HELMET** to provide a soldier or knight with a helmet (*archaic or literary*) [Old English. Ultimately from a prehistoric Germanic word meaning "to conceal or cover," which is also the ancestor of English *hell* and *helmet.*]

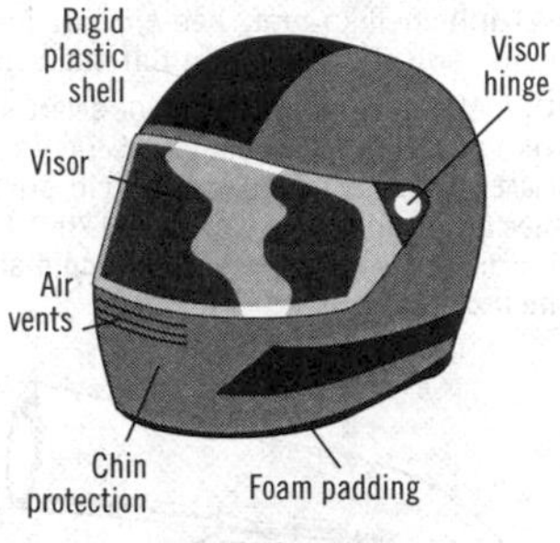

Helmet: Crash helmet

hel·met /hélmət/ *n.* **1. HARD PROTECTIVE HEAD COVERING** a hat or other head covering made of a hard material and worn to protect the head from injury, often part of a uniform, suit of armor, or protective clothing **2. PROTECTIVE HAT** any of various types of hats worn to give protection, e.g., against cold weather or the heat of the sun **3.** BIOL **PART SHAPED LIKE HELMET** a part of an organism, e.g., a flower's sepal or corolla, resembling a helmet [15thC. From Old French, diminutive of *helme* "helmet." Ultimately from the same prehistoric Germanic word as English *helm.*] —**hel·met·ed** *adj.*

hel·minth /hélminth/ *n.* any of various parasitic worms, e.g., a fluke, nematode, or tapeworm [Mid-19thC. From Greek *helminth-*"intestinal worm."] —**hel·min·thoid** /hel mín thòyd, hélmin-/ *adj.*

hel·min·thi·a·sis /hèlmin thí əssiss/ *n.* infestation by parasitic worms, or a disease caused by this

hel·min·thic /hel mínthik/ *adj.* **1. OF PARASITIC WORMS** caused by or relating to flukes, nematodes, or other parasitic worms (**helminths**) **2. USED AGAINST PARASITIC WORMS** eradicating or expelling parasitic worms ■ *n.* = **vermifuge**

hel·min·thol·o·gy /hèlmin thóllәjee/ *n.* the scientific study of parasitic worms —**hel·min·thol·o·gist** *n.*

helms·man /hélmzmən/ (*plural* **-men**) *n.* **1.** NAUT **STEERSMAN** somebody who steers a ship **2. LEADER** somebody who directs an organization, country, or endeavor ○ *the country's helmsman in the crisis* —**helms·man·ship** *n.*

hel·o /héllō/ (*plural* **-os**) *n.* (*informal*) **1. HELICOPTER** a rotary-winged aircraft **2. HELIPORT** an airport designed for helicopters [Mid-20thC. Shortening and alteration.]

hel·ot /héllət/ *n.* a serf or enslaved person [Late 16thC. Via Latin *Helotes* from Greek *Heilōtes,* said to be named for *Helos,* a town in Laconia whose inhabitants were enslaved.] —**hel·ot·age** *n.*

Hel·ot *n.* in ancient Sparta, a member of a class of serfs claimed as property by the state but assigned to individual Spartans to work on their land [Late 16thC. (See HELOT).]

hel·ot·ism /héllə tìzzəm/ *n.* **1.** POL **SOCIOPOLITICAL SYSTEM** a political or social system in which one group, class, or nation is systematically oppressed by another **2.** BIOL **ANIMAL SYMBIOSIS** a type of symbiosis found especially among ants, in which one species acts as workers for another, dominant species

help /help/ *v.* (**helped, help·ing, helps**) **1.** *vti.* ASSIST SOMEBODY WITH ACTIVITY to make it easier for somebody to do something, or possible for somebody to do something that one person cannot do alone, by providing assistance of some sort ○ *Let me help you with those packages.* ○ *Can you help me solve this problem?* **2.** *vti.* ADVISE to provide somebody with advice, directions, or other information ○ *I wonder if you could help me? I'm trying to find Belmont Road.* **3.** *vti.* BE USEFUL to make something easier or more likely ○ *It would help if you didn't keep shaking the ladder.* ○ *Would a business degree help me get a better job?* **4.** *vti.* MAKE THINGS BETTER to bring about an improvement in something unpleasant, unbearable, or unfortunate ○ *I took two pills, but they didn't help my headache.* ○ *You look ridiculous in that dress, and the hat doesn't help.* **5.** *vti.* PROVIDE FOR SOMEBODY'S NEEDS to provide somebody with something that he or she needs, especially money **6.** *vti.* ADVANCE SOMETHING to promote the advancement or improvement of something ○ *Opening a new sports center won't end teenage crime, but it might help.* **7.** *vt.* WAIT ON SOMEBODY to wait on somebody in a store, restaurant, or other establishment ○ *Can I help you, sir?* **8.** *vt.* SERVE FOOD to give somebody or yourself a serving of food ○ *He helped himself to some cake.* **9.** *vt.* KEEP SOMEBODY FROM DOING SOMETHING to keep somebody or yourself from doing something (*usually used in negative statements*) ○ *We couldn't help overhearing your conversation.* ○ *I didn't want to laugh, but I couldn't help myself.* **10.** *vt.* PREVENT SOMETHING to prevent something from happening (*usually used in negative statements*) ○ *The child couldn't have helped the accident.* ■ *n.* **1.** ASSISTANCE something that is done for or given to somebody in order to make something easier, possible, or better ○ *I could do with some help in the kitchen.* **2.** SOMEBODY OR SOMETHING THAT ASSISTS somebody who or something that provides aid or assistance to somebody else ○ *The headaches are pretty bad, but the new medicine is a help.* **3.** WAY OUT OF SOMETHING a way of avoiding doing something or of undoing something (*often used in negative statements*) ○ *a situation for which there was no help* **4.** SERVANT OR LABORER a person or persons who are paid to help, especially servants or farmhands (*often considered offensive*) ○ *He treated all the employees like help, and they resented it.* ■ *interj.* CALL FOR ASSISTANCE used to call for assistance when somebody is in danger or difficulty [Old English *helpan*, ultimately from a prehistoric Germanic word] —**help·er** *n.* ◇ **help yourself** take something for your own use, usually without permission

WORD KEY: USAGE

can't help but Traditionally, speakers and writers had a choice between, for example, *can't help doing* and *can't [or cannot] but do.* The latter is now very uncommon. *Can't help but do* is often seen, but it is a redundant, improper mixture of the two forms, and should be avoided in favor of *can't help doing.*

help out *vti.* to give somebody some help, e.g., by doing some work or giving money

help·er T cell, help·er cell *n.* a white blood cell that is part of the body's immune response, recognizing foreign antigens and stimulating the production of cells to control them

help·ful /hélpfəl/ *adj.* providing or willing to provide assistance, information, or other aid ○ *You might find this book helpful.* —**help·ful·ly** *adv.* —**help·ful·ness** *n.*

help·ing /hélping/ *n.* an amount of food served to somebody at one time

help·ing hand *n.* something done to assist somebody else

help·less /hélpləss/ *adj.* **1.** NEEDING HELP unable to manage without help **2.** DEFENSELESS unprotected and unable to provide an adequate defense against an attack **3.** UNABLE TO ACT EFFECTIVELY unable to do anything to protect somebody or prevent something happening ○ *He was helpless to stop the assault.* **4.** UNRESTRAINED unable to exert control or restraint ○ *His jokes had us absolutely helpless.* —**help·less·ly** *adv.* —**help·less·ness** *n.*

help·line /hélp līn/ *n.* a telephone service that provides advice or information to people who call in with problems or questions

help·mate /hélp màyt/ *n.* a helpful companion or partner, especially a spouse

help·meet /hélp mēet/ *n.* a helpmate, especially a wife (*archaic*) (*sometimes considered offensive*) [Late 17thC. From MEET[2] "suitable," from the biblical phrase "an help meet for him" (Genesis 2:18, 20).]

Hel·sing·borg /hélssing bawrg/ city and seaport in Malmöhus province, southern Sweden, on the Öresund, opposite Denmark. Population: 111,853 (1993).

Hel·sing·ør /hèlseng úr, hélseng ŏr/ town and seaport in eastern Denmark on the island of Zealand, the setting of William Shakespeare's play *Hamlet.* Population: 43,302 (1992).

Hel·sin·ki /hel síngkee/ capital city and chief seaport of Finland, situated on the Gulf of Finland in the south of the country. Population: 497,542 (1991).

hel·ter·skel·ter /hèltər skéltər/ *adv., adj.* **1.** HURRIEDLY OR HURRIED with hurry and confusion ○ *The prairie dogs rushed helter-skelter down their burrows.* **2.** HAPHAZARDLY OR HAPHAZARD without order or organization ○ *The winds had knocked the huge trees helter-skelter all over the park.* ■ *n.* CONFUSED STATE a hurried or disorganized situation or state ○ *the helter-skelter in the junk shop* [Late 16thC. A playful formation thought to suggest hurried action, perhaps formed on Middle English *skelten* "to come, go."]

helve /helv/ *n.* the handle of a tool such as an ax, pick, or hammer [Old English *helfe.* Ultimately from a prehistoric Germanic word that is also the ancestor of English *halter* and, probably, *helm*[1].]

Hel·ve·tian /hel vēesh'n/ *n.* **1.** SOMEBODY FROM SWITZERLAND somebody who was born in or is a citizen of Switzerland **2.** HIST MEMBER OF HELVETII a member of the ancient Celtic people the Helvetii ■ *adj.* **1.** SWISS relating to or typical of Switzerland **2.** HIST OF HELVETII relating to or typical of the Helvetii [Mid-16thC. From Latin *Helvetia* "Switzerland," from *Helvetius* "of or with the Helvetii."]

Hel·ve·tic /hel véttik/ *adj.* **1.** SWISS relating to or typical of Switzerland **2.** CHR OF SWISS PROTESTANTISM following or relating to the religious teachings of Ulrich Zwingli and other Swiss Protestant reformers ■ *n.* PEOPLES SOMEBODY FROM SWITZERLAND somebody who was born in or raised in Switzerland, or who has Swiss citizenship [Early 18thC. (See HELVETIAN).]

Hel·ve·ti·i /hel vēeshi ī/ *npl.* a Celtic people who originally came from southern Germany and migrated to Helvetia where they settled during the second century B.C. [Late 19thC. From Latin.]

hem[1] /hem/ *n.* **1.** FOLDED FABRIC EDGE a neat nonfraying edge on something made of cloth, e.g., at the bottom of a skirt or dress, made by folding the fabric over and stitching it down **2.** = **hemline** *n.* 1 ■ *v.* (**hemmed, hem·ming, hems**) **1.** *vti.* MAKE HEM ON SOMETHING to fold over and stitch down fabric to make a hem on something ○ *hem curtains* **2.** *vt.* ENCLOSE SOMEBODY OR SOMETHING to surround and enclose somebody or something ○ *The small yard was hemmed about by a tall hedge.* [Old English, related to Old Frisian *hemme* "enclosed land"]

hem in *vt.* to confine and restrict somebody or something

hem[2] /hem/ *interj., n.* NOISE MADE IN THROAT a word used to represent the sound made by somebody clearing his or her throat or coughing quietly in order to attract attention, warn somebody else, or hide embarrassment or uncertainty ■ *vi.* (**hemmed, hem·ming, hems**) HESITATE IN SPEECH to make the sound "hem" or otherwise hesitate in speech [15thC. An imitation of the sound.] ◇ **hem and haw** to hestitate while speaking or deciding about something

hem- *prefix.* = **hemo-** (*used before vowels*)

hem- *prefix.* = **hemo-**

he·mag·glu·ti·nate /hēemə glōot'n àyt/ (**-nat·ed, -nat·ing, -nates**) *vti.* to cause red blood cells to clump together, or become clumped together —**he·mag·glu·tin·a·tion** /hēemə gloot'n áysh'n/ *n.*

he·mag·glu·ti·nin /hēemə glōot'nin/ *n.* an agent such as a virus or an antibody that causes red blood cells to clump together

he·mal /hēem'l/ *adj.* **1.** OF BLOOD found in or associated with the blood or blood vessels **2.** ASSOCIATED WITH HEART'S POSITION located on or associated with the side of the body where the heart and major arteries and veins are found [Mid-19thC. From Greek *haima* "blood."]

he-man /hēe man/ (*plural* **he-men** /hēe mən/) *n.* a strong, muscular man (*informal*)

he·man·gi·o·ma /hi mànjee ṓmə/ (*plural* **-mata** *or* **-mas** /-ṓmətə/) *n.* a benign tumor or birthmark consisting of a dense, often raised cluster of blood vessels in the skin

he·ma·pher·e·sis *n.* MED = **apheresis**

hemat- *prefix.* = **hemato-** (*used before vowels*)

he·ma·te·in /hēemmə tēe in, hēemə tēen/ *n.* a chemical compound consisting of reddish-brown crystals, used to stain samples for microscope study. Formula: $C_{16}H_{12}O_6$.

he·mat·ic /hi máttik/ (*plural* **he·mat·ics** *or* **hae·mat·ics**) *adj.* relating to or acting on blood

he·ma·tin /hēemətin/ *n.* a bluish- to brownish-black compound derived from the decomposition of hemoglobin. Formula: $C_{34}H_{33}N_4O_5Fe$.

he·ma·tin·ic /hēemə tínnik/ (*plural* **he·ma·tin·ics** *or* **hae·ma·tin·ics**) *adj.* used to describe a drug or other agent that causes an increase in the amount of hemoglobin in the blood

he·ma·tite /hēemə tīt/ (*plural* **he·ma·tites** *or* **hae·ma·tites**) *n.* a mineral that is an important iron ore and occurs as black, brown, or red crystals or in a massive uncrystallized form, often in very large deposits. Formula: Fe_2O_3. [15thC. Via Latin *hematites* and Greek, "blood-like stone."] —**he·ma·tit·ic** /hēemə títtik/ *adj.*

hemato- *prefix.* blood ○ *hematoblast* [From Greek *haimat-*, the stem of *haima*]

he·ma·to·blast /hēemətə blàst, hi máttə blàst/ (*plural* **he·ma·to·blasts** *or* **hae·ma·to·blasts**) *n.* an immature blood cell, especially a red blood cell

he·mat·o·crit /hi máttəkrit/ *n.* **1.** PERCENTAGE OF BLOOD THAT IS CELLS the percentage of a blood sample that consists of red blood cells, measured after the blood has been centrifuged and the cells compacted **2.** CENTRIFUGE THAT COMPACTS RED BLOOD CELLS a centrifuge used to compact the red blood cells in a blood sample in order to determine the percentage of the blood that consists of cells [Late 19thC. Coined from HEMATO- + Greek *kritēs* "judge" (see CRITIC).]

he·ma·to·gen·e·sis /hēemətō jénnəsiss, hi màttə-/ *n.* = **hematopoiesis** —**he·ma·to·gen·ic** *adj.*

he·ma·tog·e·nous /hēemə tójjənəss/ *adj.* **1.** MAKING BLOOD producing blood **2.** OF BLOOD originating in or derived from blood **3.** SPREAD BY BLOOD spread by means of blood

he·ma·tol·o·gy /hēemə tóllәjee/ *n.* the branch of medicine devoted to the study of blood, blood-producing tissues, and diseases of the blood —**he·ma·to·log·ic** /hēemətə lójjik/ *adj.* —**he·ma·to·log·i·cal·ly** /-lójjikəlee/ *adv.* —**he·ma·tol·o·gist** /hēemə tólləjist/ *n.*

he·ma·to·ma /hēemə tṓmə/ (*plural* **-mas** *or* **-ma·ta** /-tṓmətə/) *n.* a semisolid mass of blood in the tissues, caused by injury, disease, or a clotting disorder

he·ma·to·pha·gous /hēemə tóffəgəss/ *adj.* feeding on blood [Mid-19thC. Coined from HEMAT- + Greek *phagein* "to eat."]

he·ma·to·poi·e·sis /hēemətō poy ēessiss, hi màttə poy ēessiss/, **he·mo·poi·e·sis** /hēemə poy ēessiss/ *n.* the formation of red blood cells in the blood-forming tissues of the body [Mid-19thC. Coined from HEMAT- + *poiēsis* "making."] —**he·ma·to·poi·et·ic** /hēemətō poy éttik/ *adj.*

he·ma·tox·y·lin /hēemə tóksəlin/ *n.* a chemical compound in the form of yellow or red crystals, derived from logwood and used as a pigment in inks, dyes, and stains. Formula: $C_{16}H_{14}O_6 \cdot 3H_2O$. [Mid-19thC. Formed from modern Latin *Haematoxylum*, genus name of logwood, from the Greek stem *haimat-* "blood" + *xulon* "wood."]

he·ma·to·zo·on /hēemətō zō òn, hi màttə-/ (*plural* **-a** /-zṓ ə/) *n.* a parasitic protozoan or other microorganism that lives in blood —**he·ma·to·zo·al** *adj.*

he·ma·tu·ri·a /hēemə tōoree ə/ *n.* the presence of blood in the urine, as a result of injury to or disease of the kidneys, ureters, bladder, or urethra. ◊ **hemoglobinuria** [Early 19thC. Coined from HEMAT- + Latin *urina* "urine."] —**he·ma·tu·ric** *adj.*

heme /heem/ *n.* the deep red, nonprotein portion of hemoglobin that contains iron [Early 20thC. Back-formation from HEMOGLOBIN.]

hem·er·a·lo·pi·a /hèmmərə lṓpee ə/ *n.* impaired vision in daylight (*technical*) [Early 18thC. Via modern

Latin from Greek *hēmeralōps*, literally "day-blind eye."] —**hem·er·a·lop·ic** /hèmmərə lóppik/ *adj.*

hem·er·o·cal·lis /hèmmə rō kálləss/ *n.* = **day lily** [Mid-17thC. From Greek *hēmerokallis* "lily that flowers for a day," from *hēmera* "day" + *kallos* "beauty."]

Hem·et /hémmət/ city in southeastern California, situated southeast of San Bernadino. Population: 36,094 (1990).

hemi- *prefix.* half, partial ○ *hemihydrate* ○ *hemimetabolous* [From Greek *hēmi-*. Ultimately from an Indo-European word that is also the ancestor of English *semi-* and *sand-blind*.]

-hemia[1] *suffix.* = **-emia**

-hemia[2] *suffix.* = **-hemia**

he·mic *adj.* relating to blood [Mid-19thC. From Greek *haima* "blood."]

hem·i·cel·lu·lose /hèmmi séllyə lōss, -lōz/ *n.* any of a group of polysaccharides found in plants, especially in the cell wall [So called because it is less complex than cellulose]

hem·i·chor·date /hèmmi káwr dàyt, hèmmi káwrdət/ *n.* a marine animal resembling a worm that has a rudimentary cartilaginous skeleton (**notochord**) and numerous gill slits. Phylum: Hemichordata. [Late 19thC. From modern Latin *Hemichordata*, phylum name, from Greek *hemi-* "HEMI-" + Latin *chorda* "CORD."] —**hem·i·chor·date** *adj.*

hem·i·cy·cle /hémmi sìk'l/ *n.* a structure or arrangement that has a semicircular shape (*formal*) [15thC. Via French and Latin from Greek *hēmikuklion* "semicircle."] —**hem·i·cy·clic** /hèmmi síklik, -síklik/ *adj.*

hem·i·dem·i·sem·i·qua·ver /hèmmi demmi semmi kwáyvər/ *n. U.K.* MUSIC = **sixty-fourth note**

hem·i·he·dral /hèmmi heédrəl/ *adj.* used to describe crystals that have only half the number of faces needed for complete symmetry [Mid-19thC. Coined from HEMI- + *-hedral* from -HEDRON.]

hem·i·hy·drate /hèmmi hí dràyt/ *n.* a hydrate, e.g., plaster of Paris, that consists of two parts compound to one part water

hem·i·me·tab·o·lous /hèmmi mə tábbələss/, **hem·i·met·a·bol·ic** /hèmmi mettə bóllik/ *adj.* used to describe winged insects that lack complete metamorphosis, as do grasshoppers, whose increasingly larger nymphs approach adult form without going through a pupal stage

hem·i·mor·phic /hèmmi máwrfik/ *adj.* used to describe crystals that do not have a horizontal axis of symmetry, so that the top and bottom of the crystal display different forms [Mid-19thC. Coined from HEMI- + Greek *morphē* "form."]

Ernest Hemingway

Hem·ing·way /hémming wày/, **Ernest** (1899–1961) U.S. writer. He wrote fiction including *A Farewell to Arms* (1929) and *For Whom the Bell Tolls* (1940) in a distinctive terse style that complemented his own macho image and made him one of the century's leading novelists. He won the Nobel Prize in literature in 1954. Full name **Ernest Miller Hemingway**

hem·i·o·la /hèmmee ólə/ *n.* a rhythmic alternation of two notes in place of three, or three notes in place of two [14thC. Via medieval Latin *hemiolia* from Greek *hēmiolia* "in the ratio of one and a half to one," from *holos* "whole."]

hem·i·ple·gia /hèmmi pleéjə/ *n.* total or partial inability to move, experienced on one side of the body, and caused by brain disease or injury. ◊ **paraplegia, quadriplegia** [Early 17thC. Via modern Latin from Greek *hēmiplēgia*, from *plēgē* (see -PLEGIA).] —**hem·i·ple·gic** *adj., n.*

hem·i·pode /hémmi pōd/, **hem·i·pod** /hémmi pòd/ *n.* a small round-bodied ground-dwelling bird of the grasslands of Africa, Australasia, and southern Europe and Asia. Family: Turnicidae. [Mid-19thC. From modern Latin HEMI- + Greek *podos* "foot."]

he·mip·ter·an /hə míptərən/ *n.* INSECT BELONGING TO BUG ORDER any insect that has mouthparts adapted for piercing and sucking and two pairs of wings, belonging to an order that includes stinkbugs, bedbugs, and other true bugs. Order: Hemiptera. ■ *adj.* = **hemipterous** [Late 19thC. Formed from modern Latin *Hemiptera*, order name, literally "with half a wing," from Greek *pteron* "wing"; from the partly hardened forewings of bugs.]

he·mip·ter·ous /hə míptərəss/ *adj.* relating to or belonging to an order of insects that have mouthparts adapted for piercing and sucking [Early 19thC. From modern Latin *Hemiptera* (see HEMIPTEROUS).]

hem·i·sphere /hémmi sfeer/ *n.* **1.** HALF OF THE EARTH a half of the Earth, especially a half north or south of the equator or west or east of the prime meridian **2.** HALF OF SPHERE a half of a sphere or of anything spherical in shape **3.** ANAT = **cerebral hemisphere 4.** ASTRON HALF OF CELESTIAL SPHERE either half of the celestial sphere north or south of the celestial equator [14thC. Via French or Latin from Greek *hēmisphairion*, from *sphaira* "SPHERE."] —**hem·i·spher·ic** /hèmmi sfeer ik, -sférrik/ *adj.* —**hem·i·spher·i·cal·ly** *adv.*

hem·i·stich /hémmi stìk/ *n.* half of a line of poetry, usually separated from the rest by a caesura [Late 16thC. Via late Latin *hemistichium* from Greek *hēimstikhion*, from *stikhos* "STICH."]

hem·i·zy·gous /hèmmi zígəss/ *adj.* having only one of a specified pair of genes, as, e.g., do the unpaired X chromosomes of male mammals

hem·line /hém lìn/ *n.* **1.** CLOTHES' BOTTOM EDGE the bottom edge of a skirt, dress, or coat **2.** HEIGHT OF HEM the height of the hem of an item of women's clothing, especially the typical height of hems on fashionable women's clothing during a certain period ○ *Hemlines are up again.*

Hemlock

hem·lock /hém lòk/ (*plural* **-locks** *or* **-lock**) *n.* **1.** = **poison hemlock 2.** POISONOUS PLANT a very poisonous herb of the carrot family that has small white flowers and finely cut leaves, especially poison hemlock. Genus: *Conium.* **3.** POISON a poison obtained from the fruit of the poison hemlock plant. Hemlock was used in ancient Greece to execute people. Socrates was forced to drink hemlock when he was condemned to death. **4.** EVERGREEN TREE an evergreen tree of the pine family that has small cones and short blunt needles. Genus: *Tsuga.* ◊ **western hemlock 5.** HEMLOCK WOOD the wood of the hemlock tree [Old English *hymlic(e)*, *hemlic*, of unknown origin]

hem·lock fir, **hem·lock spruce** *n.* = **hemlock** *n.* 3

hem·mer /hémmər/ *n.* **1.** SEWER OF HEMS somebody who hems clothes or other items **2.** DEVICE FOR SEWING HEMS a sewing machine attachment for sewing hems

hemo- *prefix.* blood ○ *hemolysis* [From Greek *haima*, of unknown origin]

he·mo·chro·ma·to·sis /heèmə krōmə tóssiss/ *n.* a genetic disorder in which there is excess accumulation of iron in the body leading to damage of many organs, especially the liver and pancreas [Late 19thC. Coined from HEMO- + Greek *khroma* "color."]

he·mo·coel /heèmə seel/ (*plural* **he·mo·coels** *or* **hae·mo·coels**) *n.* a body cavity in spiders, crustaceans, and other arthropods through which the blood or hemolymph circulates [Mid-19thC. Coined from HEMO- + Greek *koilos* "hollow."]

he·mo·cy·a·nin /heèmō sí ənin/ *n.* a bluish pigment found in the blood or hemolymph of certain arthropods and mollusks that functions like hemoglobin, transporting oxygen to tissues [Late 19thC. Coined from HEMO- + Greek *kuan(e)os* "dark blue" + -IN.]

he·mo·cyte /heèmə sìt/ (*plural* **he·mo·cytes** *or* **hae·mo·cytes**) *n.* blood cell (*technical*) [Early 20thC. Coined from HEMO- + Greek *kutos* "receptacle."]

he·mo·di·al·y·sis /heèmō dī állississ/ *n.* dialysis of the blood (*technical*)

he·mo·flag·el·late /heèmō flájjə làyt, -lət, -flə jéllət/ (*plural* **he·mo·flag·el·lates** *or* **hae·mo·flag·el·lates**) *n.* a flagellate protozoan that lives as a parasite in blood

he·mo·glo·bin /heèmō glṓbin/ *n.* an iron-containing protein in red blood cells that combines reversibly with oxygen and transports it from the lungs to body tissues

he·mo·glo·bi·nu·ri·a /heèmō glōbə nooree ə/ *n.* the presence in the urine of hemoglobin that has been freed from red blood cells. ◊ **hematuria** —**he·mo·glo·bi·nu·ric** *adj.*

he·mo·lymph /heèmə lìmf/ *n.* a fluid in certain invertebrates that functions like the blood in vertebrates [Late 19thC. Coined from HEMO- + Latin *lympha* "clear liquid."] —**he·mo·lym·phat·ic** /heèmə lim fáttik/ *adj.*

he·mo·ly·sin /heèmə líssin, hi móllissin/ (*plural* **he·mo·ly·sins** *or* **hae·mo·ly·sins**) *n.* a bacterial toxin, antibody, or other agent that destroys red blood cells, releasing free hemoglobin

he·mol·y·sis /hi móllississ, heèmə líssiss/ *n.* the destruction of red blood cells and the release of the hemoglobin they contain —**he·mo·lyt·ic** /heèmə líttik/ *adj.*

he·mo·lyt·ic a·ne·mi·a *n.* anemia that results from the destruction of red blood cells and may be caused by bacteria, genetic disorders, or toxic chemicals

he·mo·lyze /heèmə lìz/ (**-lyzed, -lyz·ing, -lyz·es**) *vti.* to destroy red blood cells and release hemoglobin, or undergo destruction and release hemoglobin [Early 20thC. HEMO- + -LYZE.]

Hé·mon /ay maàn/, **Louis** (1880–1913) French writer. He went to Canada in 1911, and is best known for his novel of French-Canadian pioneer life, *Maria Chapdelaine* (1914).

he·mo·phil·i·a /heèmə féllee ə, -feélyə/ *n.* a disorder linked to a recessive gene on the X-chromosome and occurring almost exclusively in men and boys, in which the blood clots much more slowly than normally, resulting in extensive bleeding from even minor injuries [Late 19thC. Coined from HEMO- + Greek *philia* "friendship," formed from Greek *philos* "dear."]

he·mo·phil·i·ac /heèmə féllee àk, -feélee àk/ (*plural* **he·mo·phil·i·acs** *or* **hae·mo·phil·i·acs**) *n.* somebody who has hemophilia

he·mo·phil·ic /heèmə féllik/ *adj.* **1.** OF HEMOPHILIA relating to, resembling, or affected with hemophilia **2.** MICROBIOL PREFERRING BLOOD used to describe bacteria that are adapted to thrive in blood or a medium rich in blood

he·mo·poi·e·sis *n.* = **hematopoiesis**

he·mop·ty·sis /hi móptississ/ *n.* the coughing up of blood or mucus containing blood (*technical*) [Mid-17thC. Coined from HEMO- + Greek *ptysis* "act of spitting."]

hem·or·rhage /hémmərij/ *n.* (*plural* **hem·or·rhag·es** *or* **haem·or·rhages**) **1.** MED EXCESSIVE BLEEDING the loss of blood from a ruptured blood vessel, either internally or externally **2.** UNCONTROLLED LOSS a large uncontrolled loss of something valuable ○ *a hemorrhage of cash that threatened the firm* ■ *v.* (**hem·or·rhaged** *or* **haem·or·rhaged, haem·or·rhaged, hem·or·rhag·ing** *or* **haem·or·rhag·ing, hem·or·rhag·es** *or* **haem·or·rhages**) **1.** *vi.* MED BLEED HEAVILY to bleed profusely and uncontrollably **2.** *vti.* LOSE SOMETHING VALUABLE to experience a sudden, uncontrolled, and massive loss of something valuable ○ *The failed business had been hemorrhaging money for months.* [15thC. Via Old French or Medieval Latin *emorosagia*, from Greek *haimorrhagia*, from *haima* "blood"+ *rhēgnunai*, "break, burst."] —**hem·or·rhag·ic** /hèmmə rájjik/ *adj.*

hem·or·rhag·ic fe·ver *n.* a viral infection such as dengue or Ebola that results in fever, chills, and profuse internal bleeding from the capillaries

hem·or·rhoid·ec·to·my /hèmmə roy déktəmee/ (*plural* **hem·or·rhoid·ec·to·mies** *or* **haem·or·rhoid·ec·to·mies**) *n.* a surgical procedure to remove hemorrhoids

hem·or·rhoids /hémmə ròydz/ *npl.* painful varicose veins in the canal of the anus —**hem·or·rhoid·al** /hèmmə róyd'l/ *adj.*

hem·o·sid·er·in /hèmmō síddərin/ *n.* a protein that stores iron

he·mo·sta·sis /heémə stáyssiss, hi móstəssiss/, **he·mo·sta·sia** /heémə stáyzhə/ *n.* **1. STOPPING OF BLEEDING** the stopping of bleeding or hemorrhaging in an organ or body part **2. STOPPING OF BLOOD FLOW** the stopping of the blood flow through an organ or body part

he·mo·stat /heémə stàt/ (*plural* **he·mo·stats** *or* **hae·mo·stats**) *n.* **1.** SURG **SURGICAL CLAMP** a surgical instrument that stops bleeding by clamping a blood vessel **2.** CHEM **CHEMICAL ANTIBLEEDING AGENT** a chemical agent that stops bleeding

he·mo·stat·ic /heémə státtik/ *adj.* **STOPPING BLOOD FLOW** stopping or slowing down the flow of blood ■ *n.* (*plural* **-ics** *or* **-ics**) **HEMOSTATIC AGENT** an agent that stops or slows down the flow of blood

hemp /hemp/ *n.* **1.** PLANTS **PLANT WITH TOUGH FIBERS** a plant native to Asia, widely grown for the tough fibers obtained from its stems and as the source of marijuana or cannabis **2.** TEXTILES **TOUGH FIBER FROM HEMP PLANT** the tough fiber from the stems of the hemp plant, used in making canvas, rope, paper, and cloth **3.** TEXTILES **TOUGH FIBER FROM PLANTS** any of several types of strong fibers obtained from plant stems and used like hemp **4.** DRUGS **NARCOTIC DRUG FROM HEMP PLANT** any of several narcotic drugs made from various parts of the hemp plant, smoked, chewed, eaten, or drunk to produce a mildly euphoric reaction and illegal in many countries. ◊ **bhang, cannabis, ganja, hashish, marijuana** [Old English *henep*. Ultimately from an Indo-European word that is also the ancestor of Greek *kannabis* (source of English *cannabis* and *canvas*).] —**hemp·en** *adj.*

hemp ag·ri·mo·ny *n.* a tall Eurasian or North African plant with clusters of red, pink, or purple composite flowers and leaves like those of the hemp plant. Latin name: *Eupatorium cannabinum.*

hemp net·tle *n.* **1. FLOWERING PLANT** a bristly Eurasian plant resembling the nettle, with red, pink, purple, or white two-lipped flowers and serrated leaves, now naturalized in the United States. Latin name: *Galeopsis tetrahit.* **2. BRISTLY PLANT** any one of several Eurasian bristly plants that resemble the nettle. Genus: *Galeopsis.*

Hemp·stead /hémpstid, -sted/ village on western Long Island, southeastern New York, a residential suburb of New York City. Population: 46,609 (1996).

hem·stitch /hém stìch/ *n.* **1. STITCH USED FOR HEMMING** a small overcast stitch used to secure a hem **2. DECORATIVE STITCH** a decorative stitch used to ornament the edge of a piece of material, in which, after horizontal threads are removed, vertical threads are gathered in small regular bunches ■ *vti.* (**-stitched, -stitch·ing, -stitch·es**) **EDGE SOMETHING WITH HEMSTITCH** to hem or decorate an edge of material using hemstitch —**hem·stitch·er** *n.*

hen /hen/ *n.* **1.** AGRIC **CHICKEN** an adult female chicken **2.** BIRDS **FEMALE BIRD** any adult female bird **3.** MARINE BIOL **FEMALE AQUATIC ANIMAL** the female of some aquatic animals, e.g., the octopus, crab, and lobster **4. OFFENSIVE TERM** an offensive term that deliberately insults a woman's personality, activity, and age (*offensive dated*) [Old English *henn*. Ultimately from an Indo-European word with the basic meaning "to sing" that is also the ancestor of Latin *cantare* (source of English *canticle* and *chant*).] —**hen·nish** *adj.* —**hen·nish·ly** *adv.* —**hen·nish·ness** *n.*

He·nan /hŏ naán/ densely populated province in eastern China, including important sites of early Chinese civilization. Capital: Zhengzhou. Population: 90,270,000 (1994). Area: 64,500 sq. mi./167,000 sq. km.

hen-and-chick·ens (*plural* **hen-and-chick·ens** *or* **hens-and-chick·ens**) *n.* any one of several plants, especially the houseleek, producing new plants as offsets that grow at the end of horizontal shoots or runners from the main plant [From the resemblance to young chicks surrounding the mother hen]

hen·bane /hén bàyn/ *n.* a poisonous Eurasian plant of the nightshade family with hairy, sticky leaves, a strong unpleasant smell, and greenish-yellow flowers. It is a source of the drugs hyoscyamine and scopolamine. Latin name: *Hyoscyamus niger.*

hen·bit /hén bìt/ *n.* a plant of the mint family with small white or reddish-purple lipped flowers. It was originally native to Europe and Asia, but is now naturalized in the United States. Latin name: *Lamium amplexicaule.* [*Bit* in the obsolete sense "morsel of food"]

hence /henss/ *adv.* **1. BECAUSE OF THIS** from this cause, or for this reason (*formal*) ○ *I lent him money before, and he never paid it back; hence my reluctance to lend him more.* ○ *Her grandfather was Polish, hence her interest in Polish culture* **2. LATER THAN NOW** later than the present time (*formal*) ○ *I'm sure the company will be in a much better financial position a year hence.* **3. AWAY FROM HERE** away from this place (*archaic*) ○ *Get you hence.* [13thC. Formed from Old English *heonan* "hence" + the adverb suffix *-s* (as in "backwards," "besides"). Ultimately from an Indo-European demonstrative pronoun meaning "this" that is also the ancestor of English *he*.]

hence·forth /hénss fàwrth/, **hence·for·ward** /henss fáwrwərd/ *adv.* from this time forward (*formal*)

hench·man /hénchmən/ (*plural* **-men**) *n.* **1. SUPPORTER OF SOMEONE DUBIOUS** a supporter or associate of somebody in a dubious cause, e.g., a member of a criminal's entourage, or somebody whose status comes from supporting a politician (*disapproving*) **2. LOYAL FOLLOWER** a loyal supporter or follower, especially of somebody who holds a high office or position **3. PAGE OR SQUIRE** a page or squire to somebody of high rank (*archaic*) [14thC. *Hench* from Old English *hengest* "stallion."]

hen·coop /-kòop/ *n.* a cage, hutch, or small building where hens or other domestic birds are kept

hendeca- *prefix.* forming words that signify eleven of something such as sides, facets, or units [From Greek *hendeka* "eleven"]

hen·dec·a·syl·la·ble /hen dèkə sílləb'l/ *n.* a line of verse that consists of 11 syllables —**hen·dec·a·syl·lab·ic** /hen dèkəsi lábbik/ *adj.*

Hen·der·son /héndərss'n/ city in northwestern Kentucky on the Ohio River, on the border with Indiana. Population: 26,456 (1996).

hen·di·a·dys /hen dí ədiss/ *n.* a literary device expressing an idea by means of two words linked by "and," instead of by a grammatically more complex form such as an adverb qualifying an adjective. Everyday examples of hendiadys are the expressions "nice and soft," rather than "nicely soft," and "good and tight." [Late 16thC. From medieval Latin, coined from Greek *hen dia duoin* "one through two."]

Jimi Hendrix

Hen·drix /héndriks/, **Jimi** (1942–70) U.S. musician. A virtuoso blues-rock guitarist, he was known for songs like "Wild Thing" and albums including *Are You Experienced?* (1967). His charismatic stage performance was captured in the movie *Woodstock* (1970). Full name **James Marshall Hendrix**

hen·e·quen /hénnikwin/, **hen·e·quin** *n.* **1.** PLANTS **MEXICAN PLANT** a tropical American plant that has large thick fibrous leaves shaped like swords and is found chiefly in the Yucatan peninsula of Mexico. Latin name: *Agave fourcroydes.* **2.** TEXTILES **FIBER OBTAINED FROM HENEQUEN PLANT** the reddish fiber obtained from the leaves of the henequen plant, used in making rope, twine, and coarse fabric. ◊ **sisal** [Early 17thC. Via Spanish from perhaps, ultimately, Arawakan.]

hen har·ri·er *n. U.K.* = **northern harrier**

hen·house /hén hòwss/ (*plural* **-hous·es** /-zəz/) *n.* a shelter or small shed where hens or other domestic birds are housed

Hen·le's loop /hènleez-/ *n.* ANAT = **loop of Henle**

hen·na /hénnə/ *n.* **1.** PLANTS **SHRUB** a shrub of the loosestrife family that grows in Asia and North Africa and has fragrant white or reddish flowers and leaves that are used to make a dye. Latin name: *Lawsonia inermis.* **2.** MANUF **RED DYE** a strong red dyestuff made from the leaves of the henna plant, used primarily as a hair dye. Henna is also used to stain the skin or nails, in cosmetics, and in coloring fabric. **3.** COLORS **REDDISH-BROWN COLOR** a rich reddish-brown color ■ *adj.* COLORS **OF REDDISH-BROWN COLOR** of a rich reddish-brown color ■ *vt.* (**-naed, -na·ing, -nas**) COLORS **COLOR SOMETHING WITH HENNA** to dye or color something with henna [Early 17thC. From Arabic *ḥinnā'*.]

Hen·ne·pin /hénnəpin/, **Louis** (1626–1705?) Flemish-born American missionary and explorer. A missionary among the Iroquois people, he explored the upper Mississippi River. Real name **Johannes Hennepin**

Hen·ning /hénning/, **Doug** (*b.* 1947) Canadian magician and perfomer on television and in movies and the Broadway musicals *The Magic Show* (1974) and *Merlin* (1983).

hen·o·the·ism /hénnə thee ìzzəm/ *n.* the worship of one god, e.g., as the special god of a social group or occupation, while acknowledging or believing in the existence of other gods [Mid-19thC. Coined from the Greek stem *heno-* "one" + *theos* "god" + -ISM.] —**hen·o·the·ist** *n.* —**hen·o·the·is·tic** /hènnə thee ístik/ *adj.*

hen·peck /hén pèk/ (**-pecked, -peck·ing, -pecks**) *vt.* an offensive term meaning to annoy or torment a husband or partner through continual nagging and faultfinding (*offensive*) [Back-formation from *henpecked*, from the hens' practice of plucking the rooster]

Hen·ri /hénree/, **Robert** (1865–1929) U.S. artist. He was the guiding force behind the Eight, the so-called Ashcan school of realistic painting formed in 1908.

hen·ry /hénree/ (*plural* **-ries**) *n.* the SI unit of electrical inductance, equal to an electrical potential of one volt induced in a closed circuit by a current varying uniformly by one ampere per second. Symbol **H** [Late 19thC. Named for Joseph HENRY.]

Hen·ry I, King of the English (1068–1135). He was the youngest son of William the Conqueror. His reign (1100–35) is notable for his conquest of Normandy (1106) and consolidation of his English and French realms.

Hen·ry II, King of the English (1133–89) French-born English monarch. The first Plantagenet English king (1154–89), he imposed a strong central administration and judicial reform and annexed Ireland (1171–72). His knights murdered Thomas à Becket (1170) after a long dispute over the power of the church.

Hen·ry III, King of England (1207–72). The son of King John, he began his long reign (1216–72) at the age of nine. He seized arbitrary power in 1232 and spent 35 years struggling against the barons, who in 1266 finally reinstated the rights granted them by the Magna Carta (1215).

Hen·ry IV, King of England (1367–1413). The son of John of Gaunt, he was the first Lancastrian English king. His reign (1399–1413) was marked by bitter hostilities with France, Wales, and Scotland. Born **Henry Bolingbroke**

Hen·ry V, King of England (1387–1422). He was the son of Henry IV. During his reign (1413–22) he invaded France and won a famous victory, against resounding odds, at the Battle of Agincourt (1415).

Hen·ry VI, King of Germany and Holy Roman Emperor (1165–97). As German king (1169–97), he conquered and annexed Sicily (1194).

Hen·ry VI, King of England (1421–71). The son of Henry V, he lost all of England's French possessions except Calais during his reign (1422–61, 1470–71). His ineffectual leadership at home sparked the Wars of the Roses (1455–85).

Hen·ry VII, King of England (1457–1509). He ended the Wars of the Roses by defeating Richard III at Bosworth (1485), and founded the Tudor dynasty. His reign (1485–1509) was noted for national unity and efficient government administration. Born **Henry Tudor**

Hen·ry VIII, King of England and Ireland (1491–1547). He succeeded his father, Henry VII. During his reign (1509–47), he broke with the Catholic Church (1534) and assumed control over the Church of England. He is notorious for his six marriages and execution of two of his wives.

Hen·ry, Alexander (1739–1824) Canadian fur trader. He wrote of his experiences in *Travels and Adventures in Canada and the Indian Territories* (1809).

Hen·ry, Joseph (1797–1878) U.S. physicist. He discovered electromagnetism independent of Michael Faraday, and developed the first electric motor (1829), telegraph (1831), and electric relay (1835). He was the Smithsonian Institution's first secretary and director (1846–77).

Hen·ry, O. (1862–1910) U.S. writer. His short stories relied heavily on coincidence and surprise endings. Pseudonym of **William Sydney Porter**

Hen·ry, Patrick (1736–99) American orator and revolutionary. He is famous for his revolutionary declaration to the Virginia assembly in 1775, "Give me liberty or give me death." He was Virginia's first governor (1776–79, 1784–86).

Hen·ry the Lion, Duke of Saxony and Duke of Bavaria (1129?–95). He expanded his territories to the east of Saxony and challenged the power of the Holy Roman Empire, but lost his duchies in 1180 to Frederick I.

Hen·son /hénss'n/, **Jim** (1936–90) U.S. puppeteer. He invented the Muppets, which appeared on the television programs *Sesame Street* and *The Muppet Show* (1976–81). Full name **James Maury Henson**

Hen·son, Matthew (1866–1955) U.S. explorer. As Robert Peary's assistant, he participated in seven polar expeditions, including the one credited with the discovery of the North Pole (1909). Full name **Matthew Alexander Henson**

hent /hent/ (**hent·ed, hent·ing, hents**) *vt.* to take hold of somebody or something (*archaic*) [Old English *hentan*. Ultimately from a prehistoric Germanic word.]

hep /hep/ (**hep·per, hep·pest**) *adj.* hip (*dated slang*)

hep·a·rin /héppərin/ *n.* a polysaccharide present in living tissue, especially the lungs and liver, that functions naturally as an anticoagulant and is used medicinally to treat thrombosis [Early 20thC. Coined from obsolete *hepar* "sulfur compound" (which came via late Latin from Greek *hēpar* "liver") + -IN.] —**hep·a·rin·oid** /héppəri nòyd/ *adj.*

hepat- *prefix.* = **hepato-** (*used before vowels*)

hep·a·tec·to·my /hèppə téktəmee/ (*plural* **-mies**) *n.* surgical removal of all or part of the liver

he·pat·ic /hi páttik/ *adj.* **1.** ANAT, MED **OF THE LIVER** relating to or affecting the liver **2.** COLORS **LIVER-COLORED** of a deep brownish-red color like that of liver **3.** BOT **OF OR LIKE LIVERWORT FAMILY** relating to, belonging to, or resembling the members of the liverwort family of flowerless green plants ■ *n.* **1.** PHARM **DRUG FOR TREATING LIVER DISEASE** any of several drugs that combat diseases of the liver **2.** PLANTS = **liverwort** [14thC. Via Latin from Greek *hēpatikos*, from the stem *hēpat-* "liver."]

he·pat·i·ca /hi páttikə/ *n.* any of a group of woodland plants of northern temperate regions, related to the buttercup, that have three-lobed leaves and white, lilac, or purple flowers. Genus: *Hepatica.* [15thC. Via medieval Latin from Greek *hēpatikos* (see HEPATIC); from the shape of the leaves.]

hep·a·ti·tis /hèppə títiss/ *n.* inflammation of the liver, causing fever, jaundice, abdominal pain, and weakness

hep·a·ti·tis A *n.* a relatively mild form of hepatitis that is caused by a virus and transmitted through contaminated food and water. ◊ **hepatitis B**

hep·a·ti·tis B *n.* a sometimes chronic or fatal form of hepatitis that is caused by a virus and transmitted through contact with infected blood, blood products, and bodily fluids. ◊ **hepatitis A**

hepato- *prefix.* liver ○ *hepatotoxic* [From Greek *hēpat-*, the stem of *hēpar*. Ultimately from the Indo-European word for "liver" that is also the ancestor of English *gizzard*.]

hep·a·to·cel·lu·lar /hèppətō séllyələr, hi pàttə-/ *adj.* relating to liver cells

hep·a·to·cyte /héppətə-, hi páttə sìt/ *n.* a cell of the liver

hep·a·tog·e·nous /hèppə tójjənəss/ *adj.* originating in the liver

hep·a·to·ma /hèppə tṓmə/ (*plural* **-mas** *or* **-ma·ta** /-tṓmətə/) *n.* a tumor of the liver

hep·a·to·meg·a·ly /hèppətō méggəlee, hi pàttə-/ *n.* enlargement of the liver

hep·a·to·tox·ic /hèppətō tóksik, hi pàttə-/ *adj.* a condition in which the liver is damaged

hep·a·to·tox·ic·i·ty /hèppətō tok síssətee, hi pàttə-/ (*plural* **-ties**) *n.* **1. DAMAGE TO THE LIVER** a condition in which the liver is damaged **2. ABILITY TO DAMAGE THE LIVER** the capacity or tendency of something to damage the liver

hep·a·to·tox·in /hèppətō tóksin, hi pàttə-/ *n.* a substance that causes damage to the liver

Audrey Hepburn

Hep·burn /hép bùrn/, **Audrey** (1929–93) Belgian-born U.S. actor. She starred in numerous movies, including *Funny Face* (1957) and *Breakfast at Tiffany's* (1961). During her last years she was a roving ambassador for UNICEF. Real name **Edda van Heemstra Hepburn-Ruston**

Katharine Hepburn

Hep·burn, Katharine (*b.* 1907?) U.S. actor. She was known for her roles as strong-willed heroines, and won Academy Awards for *Morning Glory* (1933), *Guess Who's Coming to Dinner* (1967), *The Lion in Winter* (1968), and *On Golden Pond* (1981). Full name **Katharine Houghton Hepburn**

hep·cat /hép kàt/ *n.* somebody who is considered to be cool, especially a jazz fan in the 1940s (*dated slang*)

He·phaes·tus /hi féstəss/, **He·phais·tos** *n.* in Greek mythology, the son of Hera and Zeus and the god of fire and fire-based arts such as metalwork. Roman equivalent **Vulcan**

Hep·ple·white /hépp'l wìt, -hwìt/ *adj.* **IN 18THC FURNITURE STYLE** in or relating to the style of the 18th-century English cabinetmaker George Hepplewhite. Pieces typically have graceful curving lines and delicate inlays, often featuring floral or ribbon designs. Open chairbacks, heart- or shield-shaped, are a feature of the style. ■ *n.* **FURNITURE IN 18THC STYLE** furniture or a piece of furniture made by or in the style of Hepplewhite

Barnaby's

Hepplewhite: 18th-century elbow chair decorated with the Prince of Wales's feathers

hept- *prefix.* = **hepta-** (*used before vowels*)

hepta- *prefix.* seven ○ *heptahedron* [From Greek *hepta.* Ultimately from the Indo-European word for "seven" that is also the ancestor of English *seven* and *septet.*]

hep·ta·chlor /héptə klàwr/ *n.* a pesticide containing chlorine

hep·tad /hép tàd/ *n.* set or series of seven [Mid-17thC. From the Greek stem *heptad-* "the number seven," from *hepta* "seven."]

hep·ta·gon /héptə gòn/ *n.* a two-dimensional shape with seven angles and seven sides [Late 16thC. Via French *heptagone* or medieval Latin *heptagonum* from, ultimately, Greek *heptagōnos* "having seven angles."] —**hep·tag·o·nal** /hep tággən'l/ *adj.*

hep·ta·he·dron /hèptə héedrən/ (*plural* **-drons** *or* **-dra** /-héedrə/) *n.* a solid figure with seven plane faces —**hep·ta·he·dral** *adj.*

hep·tam·er·ous /hep támmərəss/ *adj.* used to describe plant parts, e.g., petals or sepals, that grow or are arranged in groups of seven

hep·tam·e·ter /hep támmətər/ *n.* a line of poetry or verse composed of seven metric feet [Late 19thC. Via late Latin from Greek *heptametron*, from *hepta* "seven" + *metron* "meter'."] —**hep·ta·met·ri·cal** /hèptə méttrik'l/ *adj.*

hep·tane /hép tàyn/ *n.* an isomeric form of an organic chemical obtained from petroleum, especially a colorless flammable liquid alkane hydrocarbon used as a solvent and anesthetic and to determine octane ratings. Formula: C_7H_{16}.

hep·tarch /hép taàrk/ *n.* one of the seven rulers in a heptarchy

hep·tar·chy /hép taàrkee/ (*plural* **-chies**) *n.* **1. GOVERNMENT BY SEVEN RULERS** government by seven rulers or leaders **2. STATE WITH SEVEN RULERS** a state governed by seven rulers or one divided into seven parts, each ruled by a different head —**hep·tar·chic** /hep taàrkik/ *adj.* —**hep·tar·chic·al** *adj.*

Hep·tar·chy *n.* the association consisting of the seven English kingdoms of Kent, Sussex, Wessex, Essex, Northumbria, East Anglia, and Mercia during the period from the 5th to the 9th centuries A.D.

hep·ta·stich /héptə stìk/ *n.* a seven-line stanza or poem

Hep·ta·teuch /héptə tòok, -tyòok/ *n.* the first seven books of the Bible, comprising Genesis, Exodus, Leviticus, Numbers, Deuteronomy, Joshua, and Judges. ◊ **Hexateuch, Pentateuch** [Late 17thC. Via late Latin from Greek *heptateukhos*, from *hepta* "seven" + *teukhos* "book."]

hep·tath·lon /hep táth lòn, -lən/ *n.* an athletic competition, often for women, in which each contestant must compete in seven events, which are typically the javelin, hurdles, high jump, long jump, shot put, sprint, and 800-meter race. ◊ **pentathlon, decathlon** [Late 20thC. Coined from HEPTA- + Greek *athlon* "contest."] —**hep·tath·lete** /hep táth leèt/ *n.*

hep·tose /hép tōss, -tōz/ *n.* any of a group of carbohydrates that are simple sugars (**monosaccharides**) with seven carbon atoms per molecule

Hep·worth /hépwərth/, **Dame Barbara** (1903–75) British sculptor. Many of her works, e.g., the Dag Hammarskjöld Memorial (1964) at the U.N. headquarters in New York, are massive abstract shapes in stone or wood, pierced by holes. Full name **Dame Jocelyn Barbara Hepworth**

her /hur/; *unstressed form* /hər, ər/ *pron., adj.* **1. WOMAN OR GIRL NOT REFERRED TO BY NAME** used to refer to a woman, girl, or female animal who has been previously mentioned or whose identity is known (*used as the object of a verb or preposition*) ○ (det) *Tell her I'll be there in ten minutes.* ○ (det) *We left the report with her.* ○ (det) *What is her name?* ○ (pron) *He handed her the car keys.* ○ (pron) *I know it's her.* **2. COUNTRY** used to refer to a country or nation when it has been mentioned or its identity is known (*formal*) ○ (adj) *Britain's dealings with her EU partners have*

Dame Barbara Hepworth: Working on the plaster model for the bronze sculpture *Rock (Porthcurno)*

often been complex. **3.** **MACHINE** used to refer to a car, machine, or ship ○ (pron) *Fill her up, will you?* ○ (adj) *Sea water washed across her decks.* [Old English *hire* Ultimately from an Indo-European demonstrative pronoun meaning "this" that is also the ancestor of English *he* and *hence*]

her. *abbr.* **1.** heraldic **2.** heraldry

He·ra /héerə, hérrə/, **He·re** /héeree, hérree/ *n.* in Greek mythology, the wife of Zeus and goddess of marriage. She was often portrayed as jealous and resentful of infidelity. Roman equivalent **Juno**

Her·a·cles /hérrə kleez/, **Her·a·kles** *n.* in Greek mythology, the son of Zeus and a mortal woman, Alcmene. He was noted for his courage and great strength and was required to perform 12 near-impossible labors. Roman equivalent **Hercules** — **Her·a·cle·an** /hèrrə klée ən/ *adj.*

Her·a·clid /hérrəklid/ (*plural* **-cli·dae** /-klīdee/) *n.* in Greek mythology and ancient Greek history, somebody who was descended, or claimed descent from, the hero Heracles —**Her·a·clid·an** /hèrrə klīd'n/ *adj.*

Her·a·cli·tus /hérrə klītəss/ (*fl.* 500? B.C.) Greek philosopher. He was an early metaphysician. Only fragments remain of his major work, *On Nature.* — **He·ra·cli·te·an** /hèrrə klītee ən/ *adj.*

Her·a·kles *n.* = **Heracles**

Her·ak·li·on /he ráaklee on/ seaport and the largest city on the Greek island of Crete. Population: 117,167 (1991). Greek **Iráklion**

her·ald /hérrəld/ *n.* **1.** **BRINGER OF NEWS** somebody who brings or announces important news **2.** **SIGN OF WHAT WILL HAPPEN** somebody or something that is a forerunner of something or gives an indication of something that is going to happen (*literary*) ○ *The robin is the herald of spring.* **3.** **OFFICIAL MESSENGER** an official messenger and representative of a king or leader in former times **4.** **HERALDIC OFFICIAL** in England, an official who is concerned with heraldry **5.** **OFFICIAL AT MEDIEVAL TOURNAMENTS** somebody who performed official duties at medieval tournaments and jousting contests ■ *vt.* (**-ald·ed, -ald·ing, -alds**) **1.** **SIGNAL SOMETHING** to give or be a sign that something is going to happen **2.** **WELCOME SOMEBODY OR SOMETHING** to welcome or announce somebody or something with enthusiasm [14thC. Via Old French *herault* from a prehistoric Germanic compound meaning "commander of the army," whose elements are also the ancestors of English *harangue, harbor,* and *wield.*]

he·ral·dic /hə ráldik/ *adj.* belonging or relating to heraldry or heralds —**he·ral·di·cal·ly** *adv.*

her·ald moth *n.* a nocturnal hibernating moth of northern Europe marked by mottled brown forewings and dull gray hind wings. Latin name: *Scoliopteryx libatrix.*

her·ald·ry /hérrəldree/ (*plural* **-ries**) *n.* **1.** **STUDY OF COATS OF ARMS** the profession or study of the devising and granting of coats of arms and of determining who is entitled to bear them **2.** **COATS OF ARMS** coats of arms and the symbols and conventions connected with them **3.** **POMP** pomp and ceremony

He·rat /he rát/ city in northwestern Afghanistan, situated on the Hari River. Population: 177,300 (1988).

herb /urb, hurb/ *n.* **1.** **CULINARY AND MEDICINAL PLANT** a low-growing aromatic plant used fresh or dried for seasoning in cooking, for its medicinal properties, or in perfumes. Sage and rosemary are herbs. (*often used before a noun*) **2.** **BOT** **PLANT WITHOUT WOODY STEMS** a seed-producing flowering plant that does not

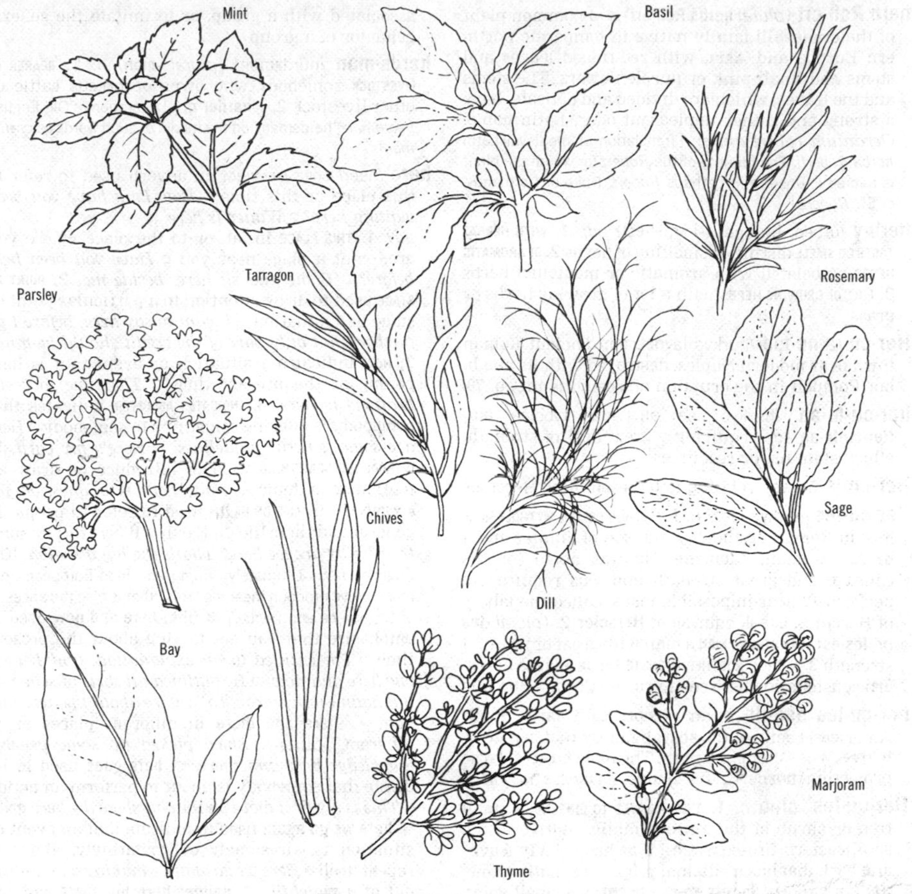

Herb

produce woody stems and that forms new stems and leaves each season **3.** **DRUGS** **MARIJUANA** marijuana (*slang*) [13thC. Via Old French *erbe* from Latin *herba* "grass, herb."]

her·ba·ceous /hur báyshəss, ur-/ *adj.* **1.** **WITHOUT WOODY STEMS** used to describe plants or plant parts that are fleshy and wither after each growing season, as opposed to plants such as trees that grow woody stems and are persistent **2.** **RESEMBLING LEAVES** similar to leaves in color and general appearance **3.** **OF AROMATIC PLANTS** relating to aromatic herbs such as sage, dill, or thyme [Mid-17thC. From Latin *herbaceus,* from *herba* "grass, herb."] —**her·ba·ceous·ly** *adv.*

her·ba·ceous bor·der *n.* a flower bed that is mainly planted with perennial plants rather than with annuals

herb·age /úrbij, húrbij/ *n.* **1.** **HERBACEOUS PLANTS** herbaceous plants, especially their leafy or succulent and edible parts **2.** **VEGETATION GROWING IN FIELDS** grass and other vegetation growing in fields, pasture land, and meadows [14thC. Via Old French *erbage* from medieval Latin *herbagium,* from Latin *herba* "grass, herb."]

herb·al /úrb'l, húrb'l/ *adj.* **OF AROMATIC HERBS** characteristic of, consisting of, or made with aromatic herbs ■ *n.* **BOOK LISTING HERBS** a book that lists individual herbs and describes their particular properties and possible uses [Early 16thC. From medieval Latin *herbalis,* from Latin *herba* "grass, herb."]

herb·al·ist /úrbəlist, húr-/ *n.* **1.** **SOMEBODY KNOWLEDGEABLE ABOUT HERBS** somebody who grows, collects, sells, or dispenses aromatic herbs, especially those considered to have medicinal properties **2.** **BOTANIST** a botanist, especially one concerned with the classification of plants (*archaic*)

herb·al med·i·cine *n.* **1.** **TREATMENT WITH HERBS** a system of medical treatment based on the properties of medicinal herbs **2.** **MEDICINE FROM HERBS** a medication made from an herb or herbs

her·bar·i·um /hur báiree əm, ur b-/ (*plural* **-ums** *or* **-a** /-báiree ə/) *n.* **1.** **COLLECTION OF DRIED PLANTS** a collection of dried plants, especially one in which the plants have been mounted, systematically classified, and labeled for use in scientific studies **2.** **HOME OF DRIED PLANT COLLECTION** a building, room, or other place where an herbarium is kept [Late 18thC. From late Latin, formed from Latin *herbarius* "herbalist," from *herba* "grass, herb."] —**her·ba·ri·al** *adj.*

herb ben·net /-bénnət/ *n.* a common wild plant of Europe, Asia, and North Africa that has small yellow flowers, long hairy stems, and hooked seeds. Its sweet-smelling roots were formerly used medicinally and thought to give protection against the devil. Latin name: *Geum urbanum.*

herb doc·tor *n.* somebody who is an expert on the properties of aromatic herbs, especially somebody who makes and dispenses herbal preparations, remedies, and medicines

herbed /urbd, hurbd/ *adj.* flavored with herbs

Her·bert /húrbərt/, **Victor** (1859–1924) Irish-born U.S. composer. He wrote more than 40 operettas including *Babes in Toyland* (1903) and *Naughty Marietta* (1910).

her·bi·cide /húrbə sīd, úrbə-/ *n.* a chemical preparation designed to kill plants, especially weeds, or to inhibit their growth —**her·bi·cid·al** /hùrbi sīd'l, ùrbi-/ *adj.* —**her·bi·ci·dal·ly** /-sīdəlee/ *adv.*

her·bi·vore /húrbi vàwr, úrbi-/ *n.* an animal that feeds only or mainly on grass and other plants [Mid-19thC. From French, or back-formation from HERBIVOROUS.]

her·biv·o·rous /hur bívvərəss, ur b-/ *adj.* eating only or mainly grass or other plants, or relating to the eating of such plants [Mid-17thC. From modern Latin *herbivorus,* literally "eating grass," from Latin *herba* "grass, herb."]

herb of grace *n. U.K.* rue (*archaic*) [From the formal identity between the plant name RUE and RUE "regret, repentance," a different word]

herb Par·is (*plural* **herbs Par·is**) *n.* a tall woodland plant that grows throughout Europe, characterized by a whorl of four leaves and a single greenish-yellow flower similar to an eight-pointed star. The flower is made up of four sepals and four petals, and the fruit is a single black berry. Latin name: *Paris quadrifolia.* [Partial translation of medieval Latin *herba paris,* literally "herb of a pair," probably because the configuration of its leaves resembles a true lover's knot]

herb Rob·ert (*plural* **herbs Rob·ert**) *n.* a common plant of the cranesbill family native to temperate northern Europe and Asia, with red-tinged leaves and stems and small pink or purple flowers. The stems and the leaves, which are divided and delicate, have a strong and rather unpleasant odor. Latin name: *Geranium robertianum.* [Translation of medieval Latin *herba Roberti.* The identity of the *Robert* for whom the plant is named is uncertain, perhaps *Robert,* Duke of Normandy, or St. *Robert.*]

herb·y /úrbee, húrbee/ (**-i·er, -i·est**) *adj.* **1. WITH HERBAL TASTE OR SMELL** tasting or smelling of herbs **2. OF AROMATIC HERBS** associated with aromatic or medicinal herbs **3. FULL OF GROWING HERBS** with a lot of growing herbs or grass

Her·cu·la·ne·um /hùrkyə láynee əm/ ancient Roman town near modern Naples, destroyed with its neighbor Pompeii in the eruption of Vesuvius in A.D. 79

her·cu·le·an /hùrkyə lée ən, hur kyóolee ən/, **Her·cu·le·an** *adj.* requiring a great deal of strength, effort, stamina, or resources

Her·cu·le·an *adj.* relating to or resembling Hercules

Her·cu·les /húrkyə lèez/ *n.* **1.** MYTHOL **ROMAN MYTHOLOGICAL HERO** in Roman mythology, the son of Jupiter and a mortal woman, Alcmene. He was noted for his courage and great strength and was required to perform 12 near-impossible tasks, called the labors of Hercules. Greek equivalent **Heracles 2.** (*plural* **-les** *or* **-les·es**) **VERY STRONG MAN** a man with great or unusual strength **3.** ASTRON **NORTHERN CONSTELLATION** a large northern constellation between Lyra and Corona Borealis

her·cu·les bee·tle *n.* an exceptionally large South American beetle of the scarab family that can grow to over 6 in./15 cm in length. The male has two large projecting horns. Latin name: *Dynastes hercules.*

Her·cu·les' club *n.* **1. TREE RELATED TO GINSENG** a small tree or shrub of the ginseng family, native to the southeastern United States, that has prickly leaves and bark that has medicinal properties. Latin name: *Aralia spinosa.* **2. TREE RELATED TO CITRUS** a small spiny tree or shrub related to the citrus family and native to the southern United States, with bark and berries that have medicinal properties. Latin name: *Zanthoxylum clava-herculis.*

Her·cy·ni·an /hur sínnee ən/ *adj.* relating to the period during the late Paleozoic era when some of the major European mountain ranges were being formed [Late 16thC. Formed from Latin *Hercynia (silva),* from Greek *Herkunios drumos,* the name given to a forested mountain region situated between the Carpathian Mountains and the Rhine River.]

herd[1] /hurd/ *n.* **1.** AGRIC **LARGE GROUP OF DOMESTIC ANIMALS** a large number of domestic animals, especially cattle, often of the same breed, that are kept, driven, or reared together **2.** ZOOL **LARGE GROUP OF WILD ANIMALS** a large number of wild animals of the same kind that live, feed, and travel as a group **3. LARGE GROUP OF PEOPLE** a large group of people, often with a common interest, purpose, or bond ○ *herds of eager shoppers* **4. ORDINARY PEOPLE ACTING AS GROUP** ordinary people, considered as acting or thinking as a group and lacking the ability to think as individuals (*disapproving*) ○ *She was never one to follow the herd.* ■ *v.* (**herd·ed, herd·ing, herds**) **1.** *vt.* AGRIC **CONTROL GROUP OF ANIMALS** to drive, keep, or look after domestic animals as a group **2.** *vt.* **MOVE OR COLLECT A GROUP** to move people or animals somewhere as a group, or collect them into a group ○ *We were herded onto buses.* **3.** *vi.* **FORM OR MOVE IN A GROUP** to gather together or go somewhere as a group [Old English *heord.* Ultimately from an Indo-European word meaning "row, group" that is also the ancestor of German *Herde.*] ◇ **ride herd on somebody** to supervise somebody strictly

herd[2] /hurd/ *n.* somebody who looks after domestic animals (*archaic*) (*usually used in combination*) ◊ **cowherd, goatherd, shepherd** [Old English *hirdi.* Ultimately from the same prehistoric Germanic word that produced HERD[1] "group of animals."]

herd·book /húrd bòok/ *n.* a book that gives details of the pedigrees of domestic animals, especially cattle or hogs

herd·er /húrdər/ *n.* **1. SOMEBODY WHO TENDS DOMESTIC ANIMALS** somebody who tends or drives domestic animals in groups, especially on open pasture or land **2.** = **herdsman** *n.* 1

herd in·stinct *n.* the innate desire to belong to or be associated with a group, or to imitate the general behavior of a group

herds·man /húrdzmən/ (*plural* **-men**) *n.* **1. REARER OF LIVESTOCK** somebody who owns or breeds cattle or other livestock **2.** = **herder** *n.* 1 [Alteration of Old English *heordman* "herdsman" on the model of such words as *craftsman*]

here /heer/ CORE MEANING: an adverb used to refer to this place or this time ○ *How long have you been waiting here?* ○ *Winter is here.*

adv. **1. THIS PLACE** in, at, or to the place where you are, or at a place near you ○ *Have you been here before?* ○ *Come and sit here, beside me.* **2. POINT OR STAGE** used to draw attention to a particular point or stage in a situation ○ *I want to say here, before I go further, that only part of the credit should be mine.* **3. NOW** indicates a situation or event that is happening at the present time ○ *The time for celebrations is here.* **4. INDICATES AN OFFER** indicates that somebody is offering something to somebody ○ *Here are some general guidelines.* ○ *Here's my card.* **5. INTRODUCES SOMETHING** used to introduce or draw attention to a topic ○ *Now, here is a question for everybody.* **6. LIFE ON EARTH** used to refer to people in general and their life on Earth ○ *Where did we come from? Why are we here? That's the big question.* [Old English *hēr.* Ultimately from an Indo-European demonstrative pronoun meaning "this" that is also the ancestor of English *he* and *hence.*] ◇ **(the) here and now** used to emphasize that you are talking about the present time ○ *I'm entitled to an explanation, and I want one here and now.* ○ *He outlined all sorts of schemes, but hadn't much practical advice about the here and now.* ◇ **here and there** in different places or at different points ○ *She'd picked up some general knowledge here and there.* ◇ **here goes** used to indicate that somebody is about to perform an action ○ *This is my first move on the chessboard – here goes!* ◇ **here we go again** used to indicate that an event or situation is, tiresomely or irritatingly, about to repeat itself ○ *Here we go again – making a mountain out of a molehill.* ◇ **neither here nor there** not important or relevant ○ *Why she wants this is neither here nor there, but we have to decide how we're going to reply.*

here·a·bout /héerə bòwt/, **here·a·bouts** *adv.* near here, or in this neighborhood or area

here·af·ter /heer áftər/ *adv.* (*formal*) **1. AFTER THE PRESENT TIME** from now on or at a time in the future ○ *He believes this to be a universal law of nature; and we may hope hereafter to see the law proved true.* ○ *No one of us knows what may happen hereafter.* **2. IN ANY FOLLOWING PART** in any following part of an article or document ○ *Here is established a Commerce Technology Advisory Board (hereafter in this section referred to as the "Advisory Board").* ■ *adv., n.* **LIFE AFTER DEATH** the life that is thought by some to exist after death (*formal*) ○ (adv) *Mercy and forgiveness will be ours hereafter.* ○ (n) *Your deeds will be judged in the hereafter.*

here·by /heer bí/ *adv.* by means of this declaration, document, or ruling (*formal*) ○ *I hereby renounce all claim to the estate.*

he·red·it·a·ble /hə rédditəb'l/ *adj.* capable of being inherited [15thC. From obsolete French *héréditable* or medieval Latin *hereditabilis,* both from ecclesiastical Latin *hereditare* "to inherit" (see HEREDITAMENT).] — **he·red·it·a·bil·i·ty** /hə rèdditə bíllətee/ *n.*

her·e·dit·a·ment /hèrrə dídtəmənt/ *n.* a piece of property that can be inherited [15thC. From medieval Latin *hereditamentum,* from ecclesiastical Latin *hereditare* "to inherit," from the Latin stem *hered-* "heir."]

he·red·i·tar·i·an /hə rèddi táiree ən/ *n.* somebody who believes that inherited characteristics play a more important part in forming people's characters and determining human behavior than do environmental and social factors. ◊ **environmentalist** — **he·red·i·tar·i·an** *adj.* —**he·red·i·tar·i·an·ism** *n.*

he·red·i·tar·y /hə réddi tèrree/ *adj.* **1.** GENETICS **PASSED ON GENETICALLY** passed genetically, or capable of being passed genetically, from one generation to the next **2. HANDED DOWN THROUGH GENERATIONS** handed down, or legally capable of being handed down, through generations by inheritance **3. HAVING INHERITED STATUS** holding a right, function, or property by right of inheritance **4. TRADITIONALLY HELD** possessed by or characteristic of both ancestors and descendants although not physically transmitted ○ *the family's hereditary fondness for city life* **5. RELATING TO INHERITANCE** relating to inheritance or heredity **6.** MATH, LOGIC **SHARING A RELATIONSHIP OR PROPERTY** sharing or transmitting a particular relationship or property [15thC. From Latin *hereditarius,* from *hereditas* "inheritance" (see HEREDITY).] —**he·red·i·tar·i·ly** /hə rèddi táirilee/ *adv.* — **he·red·i·tar·i·ness** /-táireenəss/ *n.*

he·red·i·ty /hə réddətee/ (*plural* **-ties**) *n.* GENETICS **1. PASSING ON OF GENETIC FACTORS** the passing on of genetic factors such as the color of hair or eyes from one generation to the next, resulting in similarities between members of one family or strain **2. SET OF INHERITED CHARACTERISTICS** the complete set of inherited characteristics of an organism [Mid-16thC. Directly or via French from Latin *hereditas* "inheritance," from the stem *hered-* "heir."]

Here·ford /hérrifərd, hurfərd/ *n.* a hardy cow that has a distinctive red coat with white markings, belonging to a breed originating in England and bred for beef [Early 19thC. Named for *Hereford* the English county where the animal was first bred.]

here·in /heer ín/ *adv.* (*formal*) **1. IN THIS DOCUMENT** in this document, article, or proceeding ○ *Disclaimer: The views represented herein do not necessarily represent the views of the moderators.* **2. IN THIS RESPECT** introduces a clause in which somebody states an opinion about the nature or cause of something or goes on to give further detail ○ *People are not always conscious of the effect their behavior is having on others, and herein lies the main problem.*

here·in·af·ter /héerin áftər/ *adv.* later in this document, article, or proceeding (*formal*) ○ *the Federal Reserve Board (hereinafter referred to as FRB)*

here·in·be·fore /héerinbi fáwr/ *adv.* earlier in this document, article, or proceeding (*formal*)

here·in·to /heer ín tóo/ *adv.* into this matter, situation, or place (*formal*)

he·rem *n.* JUDAISM = **cherem**

here·of /heer úv, -óv/ *adv.* of or concerning this (*formal*)

here·on /heer ón/ *adv.* following immediately after this (*archaic*)

He·re·ro /hə ráirō, hérrə rō/ (*plural* **-ro** *or* **-ros**) *n.* **1.** PEOPLES **MEMBER OF AFRICAN PEOPLE** a member of a largely cattle-rearing people living mainly in Namibia and Botswana **2.** LANG **LANGUAGE OF HERERO PEOPLE** a Bantu language spoken by the Herero people. It belongs to the Benue-Congo group of the Niger-Congo family of African languages, and is spoken by about 25,000 people. [Mid-19thC. From Bantu.] —**He·re·ro** *adj.*

he·re·si·arch /hə réezee àark, hérrəssee-/ *n.* somebody who leads or instigates a heretical religious group or movement [Mid-16thC. Via ecclesiastical Latin from ecclesiastical Greek *hairesiarkhēs,* from Greek *hairesis* "choice, group" (see HERESY) + *-arkhēs* "ruler" (see -ARCH).]

her·e·sy /hérrəssee/ (*plural* **-sies**) *n.* **1.** RELIG **UNORTHODOX RELIGIOUS OPINION** an opinion or belief that contradicts established religious teaching, especially one that is officially condemned by a religious authority **2.** RELIG **HOLDING OF UNORTHODOX RELIGIOUS BELIEF** the holding of, or adherence to, an opinion or belief that contradicts established religious teaching, especially one that is officially condemned by religious authorities ○ *guilty of heresy* **3. UNORTHODOX OPINION** an opinion or belief that does not coincide with established or traditional theory, especially in philosophy, science, or politics **4. HOLDING OF UNORTHODOX OPINION** the holding of an unorthodox opinion that is in conflict with established or traditional theory [12thC. Via Old French from, ultimately, Greek *hairesis* "choice, sect," from *haireisthai* "to choose." The underlying idea is of somebody's choice of a way of thinking.]

her·e·tic /hérrətik/ *n.* **1.** RELIG **SOMEBODY WHO HOLDS UNORTHODOX RELIGIOUS BELIEF** somebody who holds or adheres to an opinion or belief that contradicts established religious teaching, especially one that is officially condemned by religious authorities **2. SOMEBODY WITH UNCONVENTIONAL BELIEFS** somebody whose opinions, beliefs, or theories in any field are considered by others in that field to be extremely unconventional or unorthodox [14thC. Via Old French from, ultimately, Greek *hairetikos* "able to choose," from *haireisthai* (see HERESY).]

he·ret·i·cal /hə réttik'l/ *adj.* **1.** RELIG **SERIOUSLY UNORTHODOX IN RELIGIOUS VIEWS** at variance with established religious teaching in such a way or to such an extent as to attract official condemnation **2. NOT FOLLOWING ESTABLISHED VIEWS** going against established or traditional theories, especially in philosophy, science, or politics —**he·ret·i·cal·ly** /-kəlee/ *adv.* — **he·ret·i·cal·ness** /-k'lnəss/ *n.*

here·to /heer to͞o/ *adv.* to this document, proceeding, or matter (*formal*)

here·to·fore /heértə fáwr/ *adv.* up until this time (*formal*) ○ *He had more liberty now than he had known heretofore.*

here·un·der /heer úndər/ *adv.* (*formal*) **1.** AFTER THIS after this introduction, heading, or sentence **2.** BY THE TERMS OF THIS by the terms of this instruction, agreement, or ruling

here·un·to /heer ún to͞o/ *adv.* to this document, proceeding, or matter (*formal*)

here·up·on /heérə pón/ *adv.* **1.** AT THIS immediately after or in response to this ○ *Hereupon the entire delegation left.* **2.** ON THIS MATTER on this point, subject, or matter (*formal*) ○ *retired to deliberate before pronouncing hereupon*

here·with /heer wíth, -wíth/ *adv.* **1.** WITH THIS COMMUNICATION with this letter or other written, typed, or printed message ○ *Herewith the documents you requested.* **2.** BY THIS STATEMENT by this statement, ruling, or document (*formal*) ○ *I herewith pronounce sentence of banishment.*

He·rez /hə réz/, **He·riz** /hə ríz/ *n.* a Persian rug of high quality that is woven with a pattern of flowers or trees [Named for *Heris,* an Iranian town]

her·i·ot /hérree ət/ *n.* in feudal England, a tribute or gift, often a prized animal or a treasured possession, given by a tenant's or villein's family to his lord at the tenant's death [Old English *heregeatwa,* literally "army trappings." In origin, the word referred to the return of weapons.]

her·i·ta·ble /hérritəb'l/ *adj.* **1.** ABLE TO BE INHERITED able to be passed on to an heir by the laws of inheritance **2.** ABLE TO INHERIT having the legal right or qualification to inherit something [14thC. From French, formed from *hériter* "to inherit," from ecclesiastical Latin *hereditare* (see HEREDITAMENT).] —**her·i·ta·bil·i·ty** /hèrritə bíllətee/ *n.* —**her·i·ta·bly** /hérritəblee/ *adv.*

her·i·tage /hérritij/ *n.* **1.** SOMETHING SOMEBODY IS BORN TO the status, conditions, or character acquired by being born into a particular family or social class ○ *the responsibilities that were his heritage* **2.** RICHES OF PAST a country's or area's history and historical buildings and sites that are considered to be of interest and value to present generations (*often used before a noun*) ○ *the town's heritage trail* **3.** SOMETHING PASSING FROM GENERATION TO GENERATION something such as a way of life or traditional culture that passes from one generation to the next in a social group ○ *The celebration of Passover is part of the Jewish heritage.* **4.** LEGAL INHERITANCE property or land that is or can be passed on to an heir [13thC. From Old French, formed from *hériter* (see HERITABLE).]

her·i·tage in·dus·try *n.* a branch of the the tourism industry responsible for preserving the art and artefacts of a place

her·i·tor /hérritər/ *n.* an inheritor of property by law (*archaic or technical*) [15thC. Via Anglo-Norman from French *héritier,* from *hériter* (see HERITABLE).]

her·i·tress /hérritrəss/ *n.* a woman or girl who is inheritor of property by law (*archaic or technical*)

He·riz *n.* TEXTILES = **Herez**

Her·ki·mer /húrkimər/, **Nicholas** (1728–77) American soldier. Defending the Mohawk Valley in New York during the Revolution, his troops weakened British forces at the Battle of Oriskany (1777).

herk·y-jerk·y /hùrki júrkee/ *adj.* moving in an irregular or spasmodic way (*informal*) [Late 20thC. Rhyming expansion of JERKY.]

herl /hurl/ *n.* **1.** FEATHER BARB the barb or barbs of a feather used for trimming an artificial fishing fly **2.** FISHING FLY a fishing fly trimmed with a barb or barbs of a feather [Origin uncertain: probably from Middle Low German *herle* "fiber of hemp or flax"]

herm /hurm/, **her·ma** /húrmə/ (*plural* **-mae** /-mee/ *or* **-mai** /-mī/) *n.* a square pillar topped with a bust, usually of the god Hermes, used as a marker in ancient Greece and Rome, and as an ornament in classical architecture [Late 16thC. Via Latin from Greek *Hermēs* HERMES.]

her·maph·ro·dite /hər máffrə dīt/ *n.* **1.** BIOL ORGANISM HAVING BOTH SEXES a plant or animal having with both male and female reproductive organs and secondary sexual characteristics **2.** PHYSIOL PERSON HAVING BOTH SEXES somebody who has both male and female elements of genital structure and both male and female secondary sexual characteristics **3.** SOMEBODY OR SOMETHING COMBINING CONTRADICTORY ELEMENTS somebody or something that combines two very different elements or qualities, or seems to belong to two different classifications at once ■ *adj.* WITH HERMAPHRODITE'S CHARACTERISTICS having the characteristics of a hermaphrodite [15thC. Via Latin from Greek *Hermaphroditos* HERMAPHRODITUS.] —**her·maph·ro·dism** *n.* — **her·maph·ro·dit·ic** /hər máffrə dī tízzəm/ *adj.* —**her·maph·ro·dit·i·cal** /hər màffrə díttik/ *adj.* —**her·maph·ro·dit·i·cal·ly** /-díttik'l/ *adv.* —**her·maph·ro·dit·ism** /-díttikəlee/ *n.*

her·maph·ro·dite brig *n.* a two-masted sailing vessel with a square-rigged foremast and a square-rigged topsail above a schooner rig on the mainmast

Her·maph·ro·di·tus /hər màffrə dītəss/ *n.* in Greek mythology, the son of Hermes and Aphrodite, whose body was merged with the body of the nymph Salmacis to become half male and half female

her·me·neu·tic /hùrmə no͞otik/, **her·me·neu·ti·cal** /-no͞otik'l/ *adj.* **1.** OF INTERPRETATION OF TEXTS relating to or consisting in the interpretation of texts, especially the books of the Bible **2.** SERVING TO EXPLAIN serving to interpret or explain something (*formal*) [Late 17thC. From Greek *hermēneutikos* "of interpreting," from *hermēneuein* "to interpret," from *hermēneus* "interpreter."] — **her·me·neu·ti·cal·ly** *adv.* —**her·me·neu·tist** *n.*

her·me·neu·tics /hùrmə no͞otiks/ *n.* (*takes a singular verb*) **1.** SCIENCE OF INTERPRETING TEXTS the science and methodology of interpreting texts, especially the books of the Bible **2.** THEOLOGY OF RELIGIOUS CONCEPTS the branch of theology that is concerned with explaining or interpreting religious concepts, theories, and principles

Her·mes /húr meez/ *n.* in Greek mythology, the messenger of the gods and a son of Zeus. He was the patron of athletes, thieves, and trade, and was usually depicted with wings on his cap and sandals. Roman equivalent **Mercury**

Her·mes Tris·me·gis·tus /-trismə jístəss, -trizmə-/ *n.* a name given to the Egyptian god Thoth by Greek Neoplatonists, who regarded him as a teacher of religion, magic, and alchemy

her·met·ic /hər méttik/, **her·met·i·cal** /-méttik'l/ *adj.* **1.** AIRTIGHT so tightly or perfectly fitting as to exclude the passage of air **2.** PROTECTED FROM OUTSIDE INFLUENCE protected from or preventing any outside interference or influence ○ *lead a solitary, hermetic existence* **3.** HARD TO UNDERSTAND obscure and difficult for outsiders to understand **4. her·met·ic, Her·met·ic** INVOLVING ALCHEMY OR MAGIC associated with alchemy or magic [Mid-17thC. From modern Latin *hermeticus,* from HERMES TRISMEGISTUS. The meaning "airtight" comes from a magic seal supposedly invented by Hermes Trismegistus.] —**her·met·i·cal·ly** *adv.*

her·mit /húrmit/ *n.* **1.** SOMEBODY WHO CHOOSES TO LIVE ALONE somebody who chooses to live alone and to have little or no contact with other people **2.** CHR, HIST EARLY CHRISTIAN LIVING APART FROM SOCIETY somebody who, in early Christian times, chose to reject material things and to live apart from the rest of society, especially in order to be completely devoted to God **3.** FOOD SOFT SPICY COOKIE a soft cookie containing molasses, raisins, nuts, and various spices [12thC. Via Old French *hermite* or medieval Latin *heremita* from Greek *erēmitēs,* from *erēmia* "desert," from *erēmos* "solitary."] —**her·mit·ic** /hur míttik/ *adj.* —**her·mit·i·cal** /-míttik'l/ *adj.* —**her·mit·i·cal·ly** /-míttikəlee/ *adv.*

her·mit·age /húrmitij/ *n.* **1.** PLACE WHERE HERMIT LIVES a building or shelter where a hermit lives, or where a group of people live an isolated religious life **2.** ISOLATED PLACE a place of isolation or solitude where somebody can live apart from society [13thC. From Old French, from *hermite* "hermit" (see HERMIT).]

Her·mit·age *n.* a museum in St. Petersburg, Russia, that contains one of the world's major collections of paintings. The nucleus of its collection was the art collection of Catherine the Great.

her·mit crab *n.* a soft-bodied crab that takes over an empty mollusk shell, usually a whelk shell, and carries it around on its back for protection and to retire into. It starts off with a small shell that, as it grows, is discarded for increasingly larger ones, so that it may change shells several times during its lifespan. Order: Decapoda.

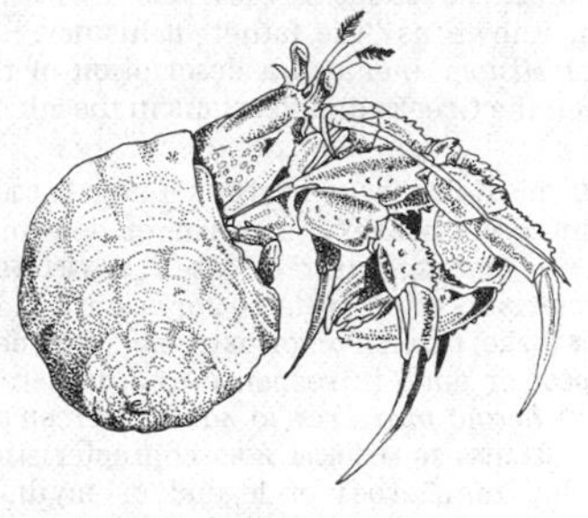

Hermit crab

her·mit thrush *n.* a brownish North American songbird with a speckled breast, reddish tail, and a distinctive spiraling song reminiscent of the sound of a flute. Latin name: *Catharus guttatus.*

Her·mon, Mount /-húrmən/ the highest peak in the Anti-Lebanon Mountains, on the Syria-Lebanon border. It has many associations with ancient Palestine. Height: 9,232 ft./2,814 m.

Her·mo·sa Beach /hur mṓssə-/ city and coastal resort in southwestern California, southwest of the city of Los Angeles. Population: 18,219 (1990).

hern /hurn/ *n.* a heron (*archaic or literary*) [14thC. Variant of HERON.]

her·ni·a /húrnee ə/ (*plural* **-as** *or* **-ae** /-ee/) *n.* a condition in which part of an internal organ projects abnormally through the wall of the cavity that contains it, especially the projection of the intestine from the abdominal cavity. It may be present at birth, especially in the region of the navel, or caused by muscular strain or injury, or result from a congenital weakness in the cavity wall. ◊ **hiatal hernia** [14thC. From Latin. Ultimately from an Indo-European word meaning "gut" that is also the ancestor of English *yarn* and Greek *khorion* "afterbirth" (source of English *chorion*).] —**her·ni·al** *adj.*

her·ni·ate /húrnee àyt/ (**-at·ed, -at·ing, -ates**) *vi.* to project through an abnormal opening in the wall of a body cavity, or through a normal or potential opening that has become abnormally enlarged (*refers to an organ or body part*) —**her·ni·at·ed** *adj.* — **her·ni·a·tion** /hùrnee áysh'n/ *n.*

her·ni·or·rha·phy /hùrnee áwrəfee/ (*plural* **-phies**) *n.* the surgical repair of an abnormal opening in the wall of a body cavity

he·ro /heérō/ (*plural* **-roes**) *n.* **1.** MYTHOL LEGENDARY MAN WITH SUPERHUMAN POWERS in classical mythology, a man, especially the son of a god and a mortal, who is famous for possessing some extraordinary gift, e.g., superhuman strength ○ *the Greek heroes* **2.** REMARKABLY BRAVE PERSON somebody who commits an act of remarkable bravery or who has shown great courage, strength of character, or another admirable quality ○ *a war hero* **3.** SOMEBODY ADMIRED somebody who is admired and looked up to for outstanding qualities or achievements ○ *heroes of the war against poverty.* ◊ **superhero 4.** LITERAT, CINEMA MAIN CHARACTER IN FICTIONAL PLOT the principal man or boy character in a movie, novel, or play, especially one who plays a vital role in plot development or around whom the plot is structured ○ *"Whether I shall turn out to be the hero of my own life, or whether that station will be held by anybody else, these pages must show."* (Charles Dickens, *David Copperfield*; 1849–50) ◊ **antihero 5.** FOOD LONG SANDWICH a sandwich made from a long roll or loaf of bread, typically with a filling of meat and cheese with lettuce and tomato [Mid-16thC. Via Latin from Greek *hērōs* "hero, warrior." Possibly related to Latin *servare* "to protect" (see SERVE).]

He·ro /heérō/ *n.* in Greek mythology, a priestess of Aphrodite whose lover Leander swam the Hellespont to visit her every night, and who drowned herself after he drowned in the strait

Her·od (the Great) /hèrrəd-/, **King of Judea** (73–4 B.C.). Born in Palestine and supported by the Romans, he ruled Judea (37 B.C.-4 B.C.) over a period of relative prosperity. He is remembered in Jewish and Christian tradition as a tyrant, and according to the Bible, ordered the massacre of every male baby in Jerusalem (Matthew 2:16).

He·rod·o·tus /hə róddətəss/ (484?–425? BC) Greek historian. Known as "the father of history," his anecdotal *History* includes a description of the war between the Greeks and Persians in the 5th century B.C.

he·ro·ic /hi rṓ ik/, **he·ro·i·cal** /-ik'l/ *adj.* **1. COURAGEOUS** showing great bravery, courage, or determination ○ *a heroic fight against a disease* **2. SUITABLE FOR A HERO** characteristic of or suitable for a hero **3. LARGE OR EXTREME** large, extensive, or extreme, often daunting in aspect or done in response to a desperate situation ○ *heroic measures to save a person's life* **4.** MYTHOL **RELATING TO MYTHICAL HERO** characteristic of or involving the heroes of legend or mythology **5.** POETRY **IN OR OF HEROIC VERSE** written in or characteristic of heroic verse. ◊ **mock-heroic 6.** SCULPTURE **LARGER THAN LIFE-SIZE** used to describe a piece of sculpture that is larger than life-size. ◊ **colossal** —**he·ro·i·cal·ly** *adv.* —**he·ro·i·cal·ness** *n.* —**he·ro·ic·ness** *n.*

he·ro·ic age *n.* a time in a culture's mythology when heroes were believed to exist, especially the time in ancient Greek legend up to and including the return from Troy

he·ro·i·cal *adj.* = **heroic**

he·ro·ic cou·plet *n.* two lines of verse in iambic pentameters that rhyme, usually part of a series of rhyming pairs

he·ro·ic dra·ma *n.* a type of play popular during the Restoration period, especially one written by John Dryden, generally involving a warrior hero who must find a way to resolve a dilemma. This often involves finding a way of preserving both his honor and his love for a woman.

he·ro·ic me·ter *n.* = **heroic verse**

he·ro·ic quat·rain *n.* a four-line unit of verse in which each line consists of five iambic feet and either alternate or adjacent lines rhyme

he·ro·ics /hi rṓ iks/ *npl.* **1. OVERDRAMATIC BEHAVIOR OR TALK** rash, inappropriate, or extravagantly courageous behavior or talk ○ *There is no room for heroics on this expedition.* **2.** = **heroic verse**

he·ro·ic stan·za *n.* four lines of verse in which the first and third lines and the second and fourth lines rhyme

he·ro·ic ten·or *n.* = **heldentenor**

he·ro·ic verse *n.* a verse form used in epic poetry or other narrative poetry on heroic subjects, especially the ancient Greek and Latin hexameter, the iambic pentameter, or the alexandrine

her·o·in /hérrō in/ *n.* a white powder derived from morphine that is a highly addictive narcotic drug. It is prohibited for medical use in most countries. (*often used before a noun*) [Late 19thC. From German. Coined from Greek *hērōs* "hero, warrior" (see HERO), reputedly because of the delusions of heroism that affect those who use it.]

her·o·ine /hérrō in/ *n.* **1. REMARKABLY BRAVE WOMAN** a woman who commits an act of remarkable bravery or who has shown great courage, strength of character, or another admirable quality **2. ADMIRED WOMAN** a woman who is admired or looked up to for her qualities or achievements ○ *heroines of the women's suffrage movement* **3.** LITERAT, CINEMA **MAIN WOMAN CHARACTER IN FICTIONAL PLOT** the principal woman or girl character in a movie, novel, or play, especially one who plays a vital role in plot development or around whom the plot is structured

her·o·ism /hérrō ìzzəm/ *n.* remarkable physical or moral courage

her·on /hérrən/ *n.* any of several long-legged wading birds with long necks and tapered beaks that live in a range of freshwater habitats and feed mainly on fish, frogs, and small mammals. They have rather unkempt drooping feathers, and many species have crested heads. Family: Ardeidae. [14thC. Via Old French from a prehistoric Germanic word that is also the ancestor of Swedish *häger* "heron."]

Heron

her·on·ry /hérrənree/ (*plural* **-ries**) *n.* an area where herons nest and raise their young

he·ro wor·ship *n.* **1. GREAT ADMIRATION FOR SOMEBODY** great admiration for somebody, especially if it borders on the excessive **2.** MYTHOL **WORSHIPING OF HEROES** the ancient Greek or Roman practice of worshiping a mythological hero or heroes

he·ro-wor·ship *vt.* to admire somebody, often to the extent of obsession —**hero-wor·ship·er** *n.*

herp. *abbr.* herpetology

her·pes /húrpeez/ *n.* a viral infection causing small painful blisters and inflammation, most commonly at the junction of skin and mucous membrane in the mouth or nose or in the genitals [14thC. Via Latin from, ultimately, Greek *herpein* "to creep." Ultimately from an Indo-European word meaning "to creep" that is also the ancestor of English *serpent*.]

her·pes sim·plex /-sím plèks/ *n.* either of two viral diseases marked by clusters of small watery blisters, one affecting the area of the mouth and lips and the other the genitals [From modern Latin, literally "simple herpes"]

her·pes·vi·rus /húrpeez vīrəss/ *n.* any of various related DNA-containing animal viruses that replicate in cell nuclei and cause such diseases as chickenpox, herpes, and shingles

her·pes zos·ter /-zóstər/ *n.* shingles (*technical*) [From modern Latin; *zoster* via Latin from Greek, "girdle"]

herpet. *abbr.* herpetology

her·pet·ic /hər péttik/ *adj.* relating to, affected by, or indicative of herpes

her·pet·ol *abbr.* herpetology

her·pe·tol·o·gy /hùrpə tólləjee/ *n.* the scientific study of reptiles and amphibians [Early 19thC. Coined from Greek *herpeton* "creeping thing, reptile," from *herpein* "to creep" (see HERPES) + -O- + -LOGY.] —**her·pe·to·log·ic** /hùrpətə lójjik/ *adj.* —**her·pe·to·log·i·cal** /-lójjik'l/ *adj.* —**her·pe·to·log·i·cal·ly** /-lójjikəlee/ *adv.* —**her·pe·tol·o·gist** /hùrpə tólləjist/ *n.*

Herr /hair, hur/ (*plural* **Her·ren** /hérrən/) *n.* the German equivalent of "Mister", used as a title before a surname or profession [Mid-17thC. From German.]

Her·ren·volk /hérrən fòk, -fàwlk/ *n.* in Nazi ideology the Germans as a master race (*often considered offensive*) [Mid-20thC. From German, literally "master people."]

her·ring /hérring/ (*plural* **-rings** *or* **-ring**) *n.* **1. FISH OF N ATLANTIC** a small edible fish with silvery scales that lives in large shoals in the North Atlantic and is commercially very important to the area's fishing industry. Latin name: *Clupea harengus*. ◊ **red herring 2. FISH RELATED TO HERRING** any fish related to and resembling the herring. Family: Clupeidae. [Old English *hāring*, of prehistoric West Germanic origin]

her·ring·bone /hérring bṑn/ *n.* **1. PATTERN OF INTERLOCKING V SHAPES** a regular geometric pattern made by placing two contrasting rows of slanting lines or blocks together so that they form rows of Vs, zigzags, or chevrons. The technique is used in bricklaying, textiles, parquet flooring, weaving, and embroidery. **2.** TEXTILES **FABRIC WITH HERRINGBONE PATTERN** fabric woven in a herringbone pattern (*often used before a noun*) ○ *a herringbone jacket* **3.** SKIING **METHOD FOR ASCENDING ON SKIS** a method for climbing a slope by standing sideways to it, with skis pointing out at an angle, and moving them upward one step after the other ■ *v.* (**-boned, -bon·ing, -bones**) **1.** *vti.* **DECORATE SOMETHING WITH HERRINGBONE** to decorate or make something such as cloth with a herringbone pattern **2.** *vi.* SKIING **GO UP SLOPE ON SKIS** to ascend a slope on skis using the herringbone method

her·ring·bone bond *n.* a type of decorative bricklaying in which the bricks are placed at an angle to one another to form a herringbone pattern

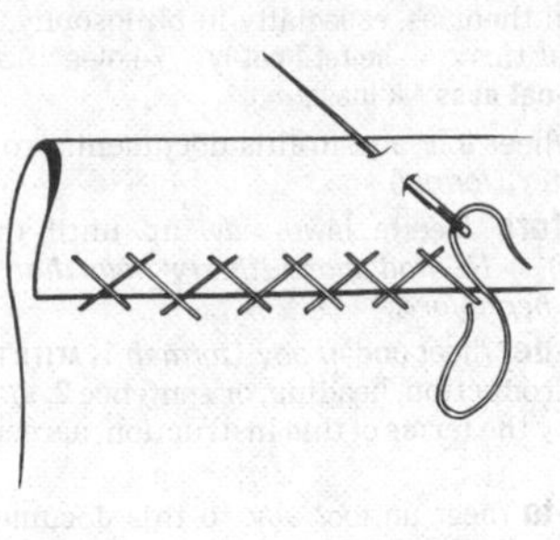

Herringbone stitch

her·ring·bone stitch *n.* an embroidery stitch made with overlapping cross stitches that form a zigzag line, often used as a border stitch or hemming stitch

her·ring gull *n.* a common gull that is widespread throughout the northern hemisphere, with a body that is mainly white, a gray back, and gray wings with black tips. Latin name: *Larus argentatus*.

Her·ri·ot /hérree ət/, **Édouard** (1872–1957) French statesman. He served as premier of France (1924–25, 1926, 1932) and was imprisoned (1942–45) for resisting the Vichy government during World War II.

hers /hurz/ *pron.* **1. SOMETHING BELONGING TO HER** indicates that something belongs or relates to a woman, girl, or female animal who has been previously mentioned or whose identity is known ○ *She drew my face to hers and kissed me.* ○ *I knew an uncle of hers.* **2. BELONGING TO A COUNTRY** belonging to or associated with a country or nation when its identity is known (*formal*) **3. BELONGING TO A MACHINE** belonging to or associated with a car, machine, or ship [14thC. Formed from HER + -'S.]

her·self /hər sélf/ CORE MEANING: the form of "her" used in reflexive and emphatic contexts ○ *She did it herself.*

pron. **1. REFERRING TO FEMALE SUBJECT OF VERB** used to refer to the same woman, girl, or female animal as the subject of the verb ○ *She put her hand on the rail to support herself.* ○ *She decided to treat herself.* **2. USED FOR EMPHASIS** used to emphasize or clarify which woman, girl, or female animal is being referred to, often introducing a note of surprise or awe ○ *I received a letter from the author herself.* **3. ALONE OR WITHOUT HELP** used to show that a woman, girl or female animal is alone or unaided ○ *sitting by herself in the garden* ○ *wrote the song herself* **4. COUNTRY** used to refer to a nation or country whose identity is known (*formal*) ○ *Britain is causing problems for herself with this policy.* **5. MACHINE** used to refer to a car, machine, or ship **6. NORMAL SELF** her normal self in terms of personality, health, or behavior ○ *She's not herself today – I don't know what's the matter with her.*

Her·sey /húrssee, húrzee/, **John** (1914–93) U.S. writer and journalist. His most famous work is his documentary fiction of nuclear war, *Hiroshima* (1946). Full name **John Richard Hersey**

Her·shey /húrshee/ town in central Pennsylvania, center of confectionery manufacture. Population: 11,860 (1990).

her·sto·ry /húrstəree/ (*plural* **-ries**) *n.* **1. HISTORY FROM WOMEN'S PERSPECTIVE** history as it affects women or looked at from the point of view of women, especially in contrast to conventional treatment of history, seen in feminist terms as having favored men **2. LIFE EXPERIENCES OF WOMAN OR WOMEN** the study or recording of the life experiences, achievements, or expectations of a particular woman or group of women [Late 20thC. Formed on the model of HISTORY as if *his-* were the masculine possessive pronoun.]

hertz /hurts/ (*plural* **hertz**) *n.* the SI unit of frequency equal to one cycle per second. Symbol **Hz** [Late 19thC. Named for Heinrich HERTZ.]

Hertz /hurts/, **Heinrich** (1857–94) German physicist. He was the first to produce electromagnetic waves under laboratory conditions, leading to the development of the telegraph and radio. The unit of frequency, hertz, is named for him. Full name **Heinrich Rudolf Hertz**

Hertz·i·an wave /húrtsee ən-, háirtsee ən-/ *n.* a radio wave (*archaic*) [See HERTZ]

Hert·zog /húrts og/, **J. B. M.** (1866–1942) South African politician. He founded the Nationalist Party (1914). As South African prime minister (1924–39), he secured the rights of Dutch-descended Afrikaners in South Africa while pursuing a policy of racial segregation. Full name **James Barry Munnik Hertzog**

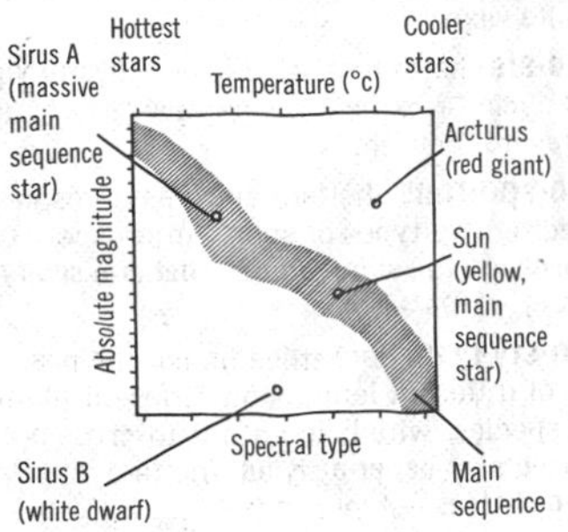

Hertzsprung-Russell diagram

Hertzsprung-Rus·sell di·a·gram *n.* a graph that plots the brightness of stars against their spectral type or color

Her·vey Bay /haárvi-, húrvee-/ town located on a bay of the same name in southern Queensland, Australia. Population: 32,054 (1996).

Herz·berg /húrts bùrg/, **Gerhard** (*b.* 1904) German-born Canadian physicist. He won the Nobel Prize in chemistry in 1971 for his work in molecular spectroscopy.

Her·ze·go·vi·na /hùrtsə gō véenə/ ➧ **Bosnia and Herzegovina**

he's /heez/ *contr.* **1. HE IS** he is ○ *He's not the man I saw.* **2. HE HAS** he has ○ *He's finished his lunch.*

he-said-she-said *adj.* involving conflicting accounts of events from the parties in a dispute

Hesh·van /héshvən, khésh vaan, khéshvən/, **Hesh·wan** *n.* CALENDAR, JUDAISM = **Cheshvan**

He·si·on·e /hi sī́ anee/ *n.* in Greek mythology, a princess whom Hercules rescued from a sea monster

hes·i·tant /hézzit'nt/ *adj.* hesitating or reluctant to do or say something because of indecision or lack of confidence —**hes·i·tance** *n.* —**hes·i·tan·cy** *n.* —**hes·i·tant·ly** *adv.*

WORD KEY: SYNONYMS

See Synonyms at ***unwilling***.

hes·i·tate /hézzi tàyt/ (**-tat·ed, -tat·ing, -tates**) *vi.* **1. BE SLOW TO ACT** to be slow in doing something, or pause while doing or saying something, often because of uncertainty or doubt **2. NOT BE EAGER TO DO SOMETHING** to be reluctant to do or say something ○ *If you're puzzled by anything, don't hesitate to ask.* [Early 17thC. From Latin *haesitat-*, the past participle stem of *haesitare* "to stick fast," from *haerere* "to stick" (source of English *adhere* and *cohere*).] —**hes·i·tat·er** *n.* —**hes·i·tat·ing·ly** *adv.* —**hes·i·ta·tive** *adj.*

WORD KEY: SYNONYMS

hesitate, pause, falter, stumble, waver, vacillate

CORE MEANING: to show uncertainty or indecision

hesitate to take or cause a short break in an activity, as a result of uncertainty or reluctance to continue; **pause** to cause an interruption in an activity that is already under way. It can be used to describe an interruption that is intentional, for example, to allow somebody time to do something. It can also be used to describe an interruption that is due to hesitation or uncertainty; **falter** used to describe a series of short stoppages and a failure to run smoothly, for example, because of nervousness, fear, awkwardness, or incompetence; **stumble** meaning the same as "falter," used especially to talk about hesitation and noticeable awkwardness in saying something; **waver** to hesitate or be undecided about a course of action, sometimes after the course of action has begun; **vacillate** used to describe a process of indecision and hesitation that involves veering between extremes.

hes·i·ta·tion /hèzzi táysh'n/ *n.* **1. ACT OF HESITATING** the act of hesitating or pausing **2. RELUCTANCE** the state of being reluctant or undecided

Hes·pe·ri·a /he spéeree ə/ city in southeastern California, north of San Bernardino. Population: 50,418 (1990).

Hes·pe·ri·an /he spéeree ən/ *adj.* **1. WESTERN** belonging to or connected with the west (*literary*) **2. OF HESPERIDES** relating to the Hesperides [Late 15thC. Via Latin from Greek *hesperios* "western," from *hesperos* "western, evening" (see HESPERIDES).]

Hes·per·i·des /he spérri deez/ *npl.* **1. MYTHOLOGICAL GREEK NYMPHS** in Greek mythology, the daughters of Atlas and Hesperus and the guards of a tree bearing golden apples from which Hercules was required to gather fruit as one of his twelve labors **2. ISLANDS OF GREEK MYTHOLOGY** in Greek mythology, islands far to the west in which a tree with golden apples grew [Late 16thC. From Greek, the plural of *hesperis* "western," from *hesperos* "western, evening." Ultimately from an Indo-European base that also produced English *west* and *vespers*.] —**Hes·per·id·e·an** /hèspə ríddee ən/ *adj.*

hes·per·i·din /he spérridin, -d'n/ *n.* a white or colorless crystalline glycoside obtained from citrus fruits and used medicinally to treat capillary disease [Mid-19thC. Coined from the Greek stem *hesperid-* "western" (see HESPERIDES) + -IN.]

hes·per·id·i·um /hèspə ríddee əm/ *n.* a fruit, e.g., a citrus fruit, made up of a thick leathery rind and soft segmented pulp [Mid-19thC. Coined from HESPERIDES, with reference to the golden apples, + -IUM.]

Hes·per·us /héspərəss/ *n.* the planet Venus, especially just after sunset when it shines brightly (*literary*) [From Latin, from Greek *hesperos* "western, evening"]

Hess /hess/, **Rudolf** (1894–1987) German Nazi deputy leader. Adolf Hitler's private secretary and deputy in the 1920s and 1930s, he was captured as a prisoner of war in Scotland (1941), convicted of war crimes at Nuremberg (1945–46), and imprisoned for life in Spandau Prison, West Berlin. Full name **Walter Richard Rudolf Hess**

Hes·se /hess, héssə/ state and historic duchy in west central Germany. Largely an agricultural region, it is drained by the Rhine and Main rivers in the west and, in the northeast, by the Weser River.

Hes·se, Hermann (1877–1962) German novelist and poet. His spiritually probing novels include *Siddhartha* (1922) and *Steppenwolf* (1927). He was awarded the Nobel Prize for literature in 1946.

hes·sian /hésh'n/ *n. U.K.* a coarse strong fabric made from jute or hemp and used for making bags and in upholstery. It was also formerly used as a backing for linoleum. [Late 19thC. Named for the German state of *Hesse*, where the fabric originated. Compare the origins of DENIM, JERSEY, and WORSTED.]

Hes·sian *n.* **1.** PEOPLES **SOMEBODY FROM HESSE** somebody who lives in or was born or raised in the central German state of Hesse **2.** MIL **GERMAN MERCENARY SOLDIER** a German mercenary soldier, especially one from the kingdom of Hesse, who fought for the British army during the American Revolution or the Napoleonic Wars **3.** MIL **MERCENARY** any mercenary soldier ■ *adj.* **OF HESSE** relating to or typical of Hesse, or its people or culture

Hes·sian boot *n.* a men's knee-high boot with a tasseled top, first worn by Hessian soldiers and fashionable at the beginning of the 19th century

Hes·sian fly *n.* a small fly of the gall fly family that lays its eggs on the stems of grain plants, where the larvae bore into the stems and weaken them. It causes severe damage to crops, especially wheat, barley, and rye. Latin name: *Mayetiola destructor*. [From having been inadvertently brought to North America by Hessian troops]

hes·site /hé sīt/ *n.* a gray metallic mineral composed of silver telluride [Mid-19thC. Named for the Russian chemist G. H. *Hess* (1802–50).]

hes·so·nite /héssə nīt/ *n.* = **essonite**

hest /hest/ *n.* somebody's order, command, or pressing request (*archaic*) [Old English *hǣs*. Possibly from an Indo-European word meaning "to set in motion" that is also the ancestor of Latin *citare* "to urge" (see CITE).]

Hes·ti·a /héstee ə/ *n.* in Greek mythology, the goddess of the hearth. Roman equivalent **Vesta**

Hes·ton /hést'n/, **Charlton** (*b.* 1923) U.S. actor. He specialized in heroic roles that capitalized on his rugged good looks and powerful physique, and won an Academy Award for *Ben-Hur* (1959). In his later years he made frequent public appearances on behalf of conservative political causes. Real name **John Charlton Carter**

Hes·y·chast /héssi kàst/ *n.* a member of a school of meditative devotion developed by monks of the Greek Orthodox Church on Mount Athos —**Hes·y·chas·tic** /hèssi kástik/ *adj.*

he·tae·ra /hə téerə/ (*plural* **-rae** /-r ee/ *or* **-ras**), **he·tai·ra** /-tī́rə/ (*plural* **-rai** /hi tī́ rī/ *or* **-ras**) *n.* one of a special class of women who were used by the men of ancient Greece as prostitutes, and who were valued as intelligent, witty, educated, and highly cultured companions [Early 19thC. From Greek, the feminine form of *hetairos* "companion." Ultimately from an Indo-European word that is also the ancestor of English *idiot* and *sodality*.] —**he·tae·ric** *adj.*

he·tae·rism /hi téer ìzzəm/, **he·tai·rism** /-tī́-/ *n.* **1. LIFE AS OR WITH CONCUBINE** the social condition or institution of concubinage **2. CUSTOM OF SHARING SEXUAL PARTNERS** the practice in some societies of sharing spouses or sexual partners —**he·tae·rist** *n.* —**he·tae·ris·tic** /hèttə rístik/ *adj.*

heter- *prefix.* = **hetero-** (*used before vowels*)

het·er·o /héttərō/ *n.* (*plural* **-os**) **HETEROSEXUAL PERSON** somebody who is heterosexual (*informal*) ■ *adj.* **HETEROSEXUAL** heterosexual (*informal*) [Mid-20thC. Shortening.]

hetero- *prefix.* **1.** different, other ○ *heterochromatic* **2.** containing atoms of different kinds ○ *heterocyclic* [From Greek *heteros* "other." Ultimately from an Indo-European word meaning "one of two."]

het·er·o·at·om /héttərō àttəm/ *n.* a noncarbon atom in a heterocyclic compound

het·er·o·cer·cal /hèttərō súrk'l/ *adj.* used to describe a fish's tail in which the vertebral column bends upward and extends into the upper and larger lobe of the tail fin, as in some sharks [Mid-19thC. Coined from HETERO- + Greek *kerkos* "tail."]

het·er·o·chro·mat·ic /-krō máttik/ *adj.* containing many different colors —**het·er·o·chro·ma·tism** /hèttərō krṓmə tìzzəm/ *n.*

het·er·o·chro·ma·tin /hèttərō krṓmətin/ *n.* chromatic material that contains few genes but stains readily with basic dyes and appears as nodules between chromosomes. ◊ **euchromatin**

het·er·o·chro·mo·some /hèttərō krṓmə sṑm/ *n.* a chromosome consisting mainly of heterochromatin, especially a sex chromosome

het·er·o·chro·mous /hèttərə krṓməss/ *adj.* used to describe plant parts that exhibit different colors

het·er·o·clite /héttərə klīt/, **het·er·o·clit·ic** /hèttərō klíttik/ *adj.* **OF UNUSUAL FORMATION** used to describe a word that is formed in an unusual or irregular way ■ *n.* **IRREGULARLY FORMED WORD** a word that is formed in an unusual or irregular way [Late 15thC. Via late Latin from Greek *heteroklitos*, from *heteros* "the other one of two" + *klīnein* "to lean" (source of English *climax*).]

het·er·o·cy·clic /hèttərō sī́klik, -síklik/ *adj.* used to describe or relating to a ring system composed of atoms in which at least one is not a carbon atom

het·er·o·dact·y·lous /hèttərō dákt'ləss/, **het·er·o·dact·yl** /-dákt'l/ *adj.* used to describe the feet of certain birds, e.g., the trogons, in which the first and second toes point backward and the third and fourth toes point forward. ◊ **zygodactyl**

het·er·o·dont /héttərə dònt/ *adj.* used to describe a mammal that has teeth of different types, e.g., incisors, canines, premolars, and molars

het·er·o·dox /héttərə dòks/ *adj.* at variance with established or accepted beliefs or theories, especially in the field of religion (*formal*) [Early 17thC. Via late Latin from Greek *heterodoxos*, from *heteros* "the other one of two" + *doxa* "opinion" (source of English *doxology*).]

het·er·o·dox·y /héttərə dòksee/ (*plural* **-ies**) *n.* (*formal*) **1. DISAGREEMENT WITH ESTABLISHED OPINIONS** the condition of being at variance with established or accepted beliefs or theories, especially in the field of religion **2. UNORTHODOX OPINION** an opinion, belief, or theory that is at variance with established or accepted ones

het·er·o·dyne /héttərə dīn/ *vt.* (**-dyned, -dyn·ing, -dynes**) **COMBINE RADIO-FREQUENCY WAVES** to combine a received radio-frequency wave with a wave of a different frequency to produce frequencies equal to the sum of and the difference between the original two signals ■ *adj.* **INVOLVING COMBINED RADIO WAVES** consisting of, produced by, or operated by heterodyning signals

het·er·oe·cious /hèttə réeshəss/ *adj.* used to describe a parasite such as a tapeworm that lives in two or more hosts in the course of its life cycle [Late 19thC. Coined from HETERO- + Greek *oikia* "house."] —**het·er·oe·cism** /hèttə rée sìzzəm/ *n.*

het·er·o·gam·ete /hèttərō gá meet, hèttərōgə méet/ *n.* **1. EITHER OF UNITING REPRODUCTIVE CELLS** either of two reproductive cells (**gametes**) that differ in size, structure, and function, and that unite in the process of reproduction, e.g., the small sperm and large ova in humans **2. SEX-DETERMINING REPRODUCTIVE CELL** a reproductive cell produced by the sex that carries the chromosomes that determine the sex of the offspring

het·er·o·ga·met·ic /hèttərōgə méttik/ *adj.* **1. PRODUCING TWO DIFFERENT REPRODUCTIVE CELLS** used to describe the sex that produces reproductive cells (**gametes**) of two different types, one type producing males and the other females **2. OF HETEROGAMETES** relating to heterogametes

het·er·og·a·my /hèttə róggəmee/ *n.* **1.** BIOL **UNION OF DISSIMILAR REPRODUCTIVE CELLS** in sexual reproduction, the union of two types of sex cell (**heterogamete**) that are dissimilar in size, structure, and function **2.** BIOL **ALTERNATING OF FORMS OF REPRODUCTION** the alternation of sexual and asexual reproduction in certain species, e.g., aphids, in which every second generation is produced from the female with no need for a male **3.** BOT **HAVING DIFFERENT FLOWERS ON ONE PLANT** the production on the same plant of two kinds of flower, one bearing both male and female organs and the other bearing only female organs or being asexual —**het·er·o·gam·ic** /hèttərō gámmik/ *adj.* —**het·er·og·a·mous** /hèttə róggəməss/ *adj.*

het·er·o·ge·ne·i·ty /hèttə rō jə née itee/ *n.* **1. DIVERSITY** the diverse nature of something **2.** CHEM **HETEROGENEOUS STATE** the state of being chemically heterogeneous

het·er·o·ge·ne·ous /hèttərō jéenee əss/, **het·er·og·e·nous** /hèttə rójjənəss/ *adj.* **1. CONSISTING OF DISSIMILAR PARTS** consisting of parts or individual elements that are unrelated or unlike each other **2. UNRELATED** not related or similar **3.** CHEM **WITH TWO OR MORE PHASES** used to describe a chemical substance that has two or more phases [Early 17thC. Formed from medieval Latin *heterogeneus*, from Greek *heterogenēs*, literally "other kind," from *heteros* "other" + *genos* "kind."] —**het·er·o·ge·ne·ous·ly** *adv.* —**het·er·o·ge·ne·ous·ness** *n.*

het·er·o·gen·e·sis /hèttərō jénnəssiss/ *n.* the appearance of a mutation in a population

het·er·o·ge·net·ic /hèttərō jə néttik/ *adj.* **1. OF HETEROGENESIS** relating to heterogenesis **2.** BIOL **FROM DISPARATE ANCESTORS** derived from ancestors not closely related **3. MUTATING** reproducing by heterogenesis —**het·er·o·ge·net·i·cal·ly** *adv.*

het·er·o·gen·ic /hèttərō jénnik/ *adj.* used to describe a reproductive cell (**gamete**), individual, or population that has more than one variant (**allele**) of a particular gene

het·er·og·e·nous /hèttə rójjənəss/ *adj.* **1.** = **heterogeneous 2.** MED **NOT FROM THE SAME BODY** originating outside the body, from another individual or species [Late 17thC. Variant of HETEROGENEOUS.] —**het·er·og·e·ny** *n.*

het·er·og·o·ny /hèttə róggənee/ *n.* a life cycle involving alternating parasitic and free-living generations —**het·er·og·o·nous** *adj.* —**het·er·og·o·nous·ly** *adv.*

het·er·o·graft /héttərō gràft/ *n.* a graft of living tissue from one animal to another of a different species

het·er·og·ra·phy /hèttə róggrəfee/ (*plural* **-phies**) *n.* **1. DIFFERENT LETTERS FOR SAME SOUND** the use of different letters or groups of letters to represent the same sound or sounds **2. WRITING SYSTEM WITH HETEROGRAPHY** a writing system that uses different combinations of letters to represent the same sound or sounds [Late 18thC. Coined from HETERO- + -GRAPHY on the model of ORTHOGRAPHY.] —**het·er·o·graph·ic** /hèttərō gráffik/ *adj.*

het·er·o·kar·y·on /hèttərō kérree òn/ (*plural* **-a** /-ree ə/) *n.* a cell that has two or more genetically different nuclei

het·er·o·kar·y·o·sis /hèttərō kerree ṓssiss/ *n.* the presence in a cell of two or more nuclei of different genetic origin. Heterokaryosis occurs naturally in certain fungi when cells fuse but their nuclei do not, and can be induced artificially to study the interaction of cellular components of different species. —**het·er·o·kar·y·ot·ic** /hèttərō kerree óttik/ *adj.*

het·er·ol·o·gous /hèttə rólləgəss/ *adj.* **1.** MED **FROM DIFFERENT SPECIES** derived or taken from a different species **2.** IMMUNOL **NOT CORRESPONDING** used to describe an antigen and an antibody that do not correspond to each other **3.** BIOL **IN ABNORMAL LOCATION** not normally found in the particular part of the body in which it has been found **4.** BIOL **DIFFERING IN STRUCTURE AND ORIGIN** used to describe organisms or parts that differ from each other in structure or origin [Mid-19thC. Coined from HETERO- + Greek *logos* "relation, ratio."] —**het·er·ol·o·gous·ly** *adv.*

het·er·ol·y·sis /hèttə rólləsiss/ *n.* **1.** CHEM **FORMATION OF OPPOSITELY CHARGED PARTICLES** the breaking of a chemical bond in a compound, producing particles or ions of opposite charge, e.g., the formation of sodium and chloride ions in a salt solution **2.** BIOL **CELL DESTRUCTION** the destruction of cells or proteins of one species by the action of enzymes or lysins from another, e.g., when the blood of one species causes the red blood cells of another species to rupture —**het·er·o·lyt·ic** /hèttərō líttik/ *adj.*

het·er·om·er·ous /hèttə rómmərəss/ *adj.* **1.** BIOL **WITH DIFFERENT PARTS** with parts of different types **2.** BOT **WITH DIFFERENT NUMBERS OF PARTS** with flowers that do not have the same number of petals in each case, or with other parts that are made up of different numbers of elements

het·er·o·mor·phic /hèttərō máwrfik/, **het·er·o·mor·phous** /-fəss/ *adj.* **1.** BIOL **TAKING DIFFERENT FORMS DURING LIFE CYCLE** taking different forms at different stages of its life cycle **2.** GENETICS **OF DIFFERENT SIZE OR SHAPE** differing in size or shape, as the X and Y sex chromosomes do **3.** BIOL, PATHOL **ABNORMAL** differing in shape, size, or structure from the normal form of an organism **4.** PATHOL **INVOLVING ABNORMAL FORM** characterized by an abnormal form or forms —**het·er·o·mor·phism** *n.* —**het·er·o·mor·phy** /-màwrfee/ *n.*

het·er·on·o·mous /hèttə rónnəməss/ *adj.* **1.** POL **UNDER OTHER LAWS** subject to other laws or rules or to laws and rules imposed by other people or institutions **2.** BIOL **GROWING OR DEVELOPING DIFFERENTLY** used to describe parts of an organism that have different modes of development, growth, and different functions [Early 19thC. Coined from HETERO- + Greek *nomos* "law."] —**het·er·on·o·mous·ly** *adv.* —**het·er·on·o·my** *n.*

het·er·o·nym /héttərənim/ *n.* either of two or more words that are spelled the same, but differ in meaning and often in pronunciation, e.g., "bow" (a ribbon) and "bow" (of a ship) [Late 19thC. Coined from HETERO- + *-nym*.] —**het·er·on·y·mous** /hèttə rónniməss/ *adj.* —**het·er·on·y·my** /-imee/ *n.*

het·er·o·ou·si·an /hèttərō óossee ən, -ówssee ən/, **het·er·ou·si·an** /hèttə róossee ən, -rówssee ən/ *n.* in Christian theology, somebody who believes that God the Father and God the Son are not formed of the same substance [Late 17thC. Formed from Greek *heter(o)ousios*, literally "other substance," from *heteros* "other" + *ousia* "substance."] —**het·er·o·ou·si·an** *adj.*

het·er·o·phyl·lous /hèttərō fílləss/ *adj.* used to describe plants such as the sassafras tree that have different shapes of leaves on the same plant —**het·er·o·phyl·ly** /héttərō fillee/ *n.*

het·er·o·plas·ty /héttərō plàstee/ (*plural* **-ties**) *n.* **1. GRAFTING FROM SOMEBODY OR SOMETHING ELSE** a surgical procedure to graft or transplant tissues or organs from one person or animal to another **2.** = **heterograft** —**het·er·o·plas·tic** /hèttərō plástik/ *adj.*

het·er·o·ploid /héttərō plòyd/ *adj.* **WITH ABNORMAL CHROMOSOME NUMBER** with a number of chromosomes that is, unusually, not an exact multiple of the basic chromosome number for that species ■ *n.* **HETEROPLOID CELL** a heteroploid cell or organism

het·er·o·po·lar /hèttərō pṓlər/ *adj.* CHEM = **polar** —**het·er·o·po·lar·i·ty** /hèttərō pō lérrətee, -pə-/ *n.*

het·er·op·ter·an /hèttə róptərən/ *n.* an insect, e.g., a bedbug or another true bug, with mouthparts adapted for piercing and sucking, and partially hardened forewings with membranous tips. Order: Heteroptera. [Mid-19thC. Coined from HETERO- + Greek *pteron* "wing."] —**het·er·op·ter·an** *adj.*

het·er·o·sex·ism /hèttərō sék sìzzəm/ *n.* discrimination against gays and lesbians by heterosexuals —**het·er·o·sex·ist** *n.*, *adj.*

het·er·o·sex·u·al /hèttərō sékshoo əl/ *n.* **SOMEBODY SEXUALLY DESIRING OPPOSITE SEX** somebody who sexually desires members of the opposite sex ■ *adj.* **1. DESIRING OPPOSITE SEX** sexually desiring members of the opposite sex **2. INVOLVING BOTH SEXES** relating to sexual desire or sexual relations between people of opposite sexes —**het·er·o·sex·u·al·ly** *adv.*

het·er·o·sex·u·al·i·ty /hèttərō sekshoo állətee/ *n.* sexual desire or sexual relations between people of opposite sexes

het·er·o·sis /hèttə rṓssiss/ *n.* BIOL = **hybrid vigor** [Mid-19thC. From Greek *heterōsis*, literally "making different," from *heteros* "different."]

het·er·o·spo·rous /hèttərō spáwrəss, -róspərəss/ *adj.* producing two types of spore, microspores and megaspores, on the same plant —**het·er·o·spo·ry** /héttərō spàwree, -róspəree/ *n.*

het·er·o·sty·ly /héttərō stìlee/ *n.* BOT the possession of styles of different lengths on different plants of the same species, which is an aid to cross-pollination by insects —**het·er·o·styled** /héttərō stīld/ *adj.* —**het·er·o·sty·lous** /-stīləss/ *adj.*

het·er·o·tro·phic /hèttərō tróffik/ *adj.* obtaining nourishment by digesting plant or animal matter, as animals do, as opposed to photosynthesizing food, as plants do —**het·er·o·troph** /héttərə tròf/ *n.* —**het·er·ot·ro·phy** /hèttə róttrəfee/ *n.*

het·er·o·trop·i·a /hèttərō trṓpee ə/ *n.* an abnormal alignment of the eyes

het·er·o·typ·ic /hèttərō típpik/, **het·er·o·typ·i·cal** /-típpik'l/ *adj.* **1. ABNORMAL** differing from the standard or normal type in an organism **2.** GENETICS **OF TYPE OF CELL DIVISION** relating to a form of division of the nucleus of a cell in which the nucleii produced contain half the chromosomes of the parent cell

het·er·ou·sian *n.*, *adj.* = **heteroousian**

het·er·o·zy·gote /hèttərō zígət/ *n.* an animal or plant possessing two forms of a particular gene encoding some inheritable characteristic, which may therefore produce offspring differing from their parents and each other in that characteristic [Early 20thC. Coined from HETERO- + ZYGOTE.]

het·er·o·zy·gous /hèttərō zígəss/ *adj.* used to describe a cell or organism that has two or more different versions (**alleles**) of at least one of its genes. The offspring of such an organism may thus differ with regard to the characteristics determined by the gene or genes involved, depending on which version of the gene they inherit. —**het·er·o·zy·gote** /hèttərō zígət/ *n.*

heth /het, heth, khet, kheth/ *n.* the eighth letter of the Hebrew alphabet, represented in the English alphabet as "h." See table at **alphabet** [Early 19thC. From Hebrew *ḥēth*.]

het·man /hétmən/ (*plural* **-mans**) *n.* = **ataman** [Mid-18thC. Via Polish, of uncertain origin: probably from German *Hauptmann* "headman, captain."]

het up *adj.* extremely excited as a result of anticipation, anger, or anxiety (*regional*) [*Het* originally the past participle of HEAT]

heu·che·ra /hyóokərə/ *n.* a plant native to North America but grown elsewhere that has sprays of small, usually red, flowers and low-growing heart-shaped leaves. Genus: *Heuchera*. [Late 19thC. From modern Latin, named for the German botanist J. H. *Heucher* (1677–1747).]

heu·land·ite /hyóolən dìt/ *n.* a mineral of the zeolite family, consisting of a hydrated silicate of calcium, sodium, and aluminum, occurring in rock cavities as long white, yellow, red, or brown crystals [Early 19thC. Formed from the name of the English mineralogist H. *Heuland* (1777–1856).]

heu·ris·tic /hyoo rístik/ *adj.* **1.** EDUC **ENCOURAGING DISCOVERY OF SOLUTIONS** relating to or using a method of teaching that encourages learners to discover solutions for themselves **2.** PHILOS, SCI **INVOLVING TRIAL AND ERROR** using or arrived at by a process of trial and error rather than set rules **3.** COMPUT **ABLE TO CHANGE** used to describe a computer program that can modify itself in response to the user, e.g., a program for checking spelling ■ *n.* LOGIC **PROCEDURE FOR GETTING SOLUTION** a helpful procedure for arriving at a solution but not necessarily a proof [Early 19thC. Alteration of Greek *heuriskein* "to find" (source of English *eureka*).] —**heu·ris·ti·cal·ly** *adv.*

heu·ris·tics /hyoo rístiks/ *n.* a method of solving a problem for which no formula exists, based on informal methods or experience, and employing a form of trial and error (**iteration**) (*takes a singular verb*)

he·ve·a /héevee ə/ *n.* a tree native to the Amazon jungle, whose bark contains a milky sap that provides rubber. The best known species is the rubber tree, widely planted throughout the tropics as a source of natural rubber. Genus: *Hevea.* [Late 19thC. Via modern Latin from Quechua *hyeve.*]

hew /hyoo/ (**hewed, hewn** /hyoon/ *or* **hewed, hew·ing, hews**) *v.* **1.** *vti.* CUT DOWN OR UP to cut, break, or destroy something, especially wood or stone, with a cutting implement, especially an ax **2.** *vt.* MAKE BY CUTTING OR CARVING to form or create something by cutting wood or stone ○ *hewed a path through the forest* **3.** *vt.* SEVER FROM SOMETHING ELSE to cut something off from a larger block or mass [Old English *hēawen,* of prehistoric Germanic origin] —**hew·er** *n.*

hew to *vt.* to conform closely to something, e.g., a code or procedure (*formal*)

Hewes /hyooz/, **Joseph** (1730–79) American patriot. He signed the Declaration of Independence (1776) as a North Carolina delegate to the Continental Congress.

hex /heks/ *n.* **1.** CURSE a curse or evil spell **2.** BRINGER OF BAD LUCK somebody believed to bring bad luck or misfortune ■ *vt.* (**hexed, hex·ing, hex·es**) **1.** CURSE OR BEWITCH to put a curse or spell on somebody or something **2.** HAVE BAD EFFECT ON to appear to have a bad effect on something, as if it were cursed or bewitched ○ *A string of accidents hexed their first attempt to climb the mountain.* [Mid-19thC. Via Pennsylvanian Dutch from German *Hexe* "witch."] —**hex·er** *n.*

hex. *abbr.* **1.** hexagon **2.** hexagonal

hex- *prefix.* = **hexa-** (*used before vowels*)

hexa- *prefix.* six ○ *hexapod* [From Greek *hex.* Ultimately from the Indo-European word for "six" that is also the ancestor of English *six* and *sextet.*]

hex·a·chlo·ro·phene /hèksə kláwrə féen/ *n.* a white odorless organic compound that has antiseptic properties and is used as an antibacterial agent in soaps and toothpaste and as an antiseptic in deodorants. Formula: $(C_6HCl_3OH)_2CH_2$. [Late 20thC. Coined from HEXA- + CHLORO- + Greek *phaino-* "shining."]

hex·a·chord /héksə kàwrd/ *n.* a series of six adjacent diatonic notes forming the basis of medieval and classical Greek music theory. There were three variants, the so-called natural, hard, and soft hexachords, which approximate to the modern C major, G major, and F major scales respectively.

hex·a·dec·i·mal /hèksə déssim'l/ *adj.* COMPUT BASED ON NUMBER 16 used to describe a number system based on the number 16, in which the letters A to F are used as digits in addition to the digits 0 to 9. It is used especially to represent binary code in computers. ■ *n.* **1.** NUMBER WITH BASE 16 a number expressed using the base 16 rather than, e.g., the usual base 10 **2.** NOTATION FOR NUMBERS WITH BASE 16 the notation used to represent numbers with a base 16

hex·a·gon /héksə gòn/ *n.* a two-dimensional figure that has six sides [Late 16thC. Via late Latin *hexagonum* from, ultimately, Greek *hexagōnos* "six-cornered," from *hexa-* "six."]

hex·ag·o·nal /hèk sággən'l/ *adj.* **1.** GEOM SIX-SIDED with six straight sides and six angles **2.** GEOM CONTAINING OR BASED ON HEXAGON containing a hexagon, or having a hexagon as a base **3.** CRYSTALS HAVING A SIX-SIDED CROSS SECTION belonging to one of the seven crystal systems, the members of which are six-sided in cross section, are elongated perpendicular to that cross section, and have sixfold symmetry around the long axis —**hex·ag·o·nal·ly** *adv.*

hex·a·gram /héksə gràm/ *n.* **1.** GEOM SIX-POINTED GEOMETRIC FIGURE a six-pointed star-shaped figure formed by extending the sides of a regular hexagon until they meet at six points **2.** EASTERN RELIG PATTERN OF SIX LINES any of the 64 possible combinations of six broken or unbroken lines, used in divination, especially in the *I Ching*

hex·a·hy·drate /hèksə hī dràyt/ *n.* a crystalline compound, each molecule of which contains six loosely bound water molecules (**water of crystallization**) from which the water escapes when the compound is heated, leaving the compound unchanged

hex·am·er·ous /hek sámmərəss/, **hex·am·er·al** /-rəl/ *adj.* with parts, especially petals or stamens, arranged in sets of six —**hex·am·er·ism** *n.*

hex·am·e·ter /hek sámmətər/ *n.* a line of verse that has six metrical feet, usually all in the same or a related meter. The classical Greek and Latin epic poems, the *Iliad, Odyssey,* and *Aeneid,* are composed in dactylic hexameters. [14thC. Via Latin from Greek *hexametros* "of six measures," from *hexa-* "six" + *metron* "measure."] —**hex·a·met·ric** /hèksə méttrik/ *adj.*

hex·ane /hék sàyn/ *n.* a volatile hydrocarbon found in petroleum that is a major ingredient of gasoline and is commonly used as a solvent. Formula: C_6H_{14}.

Hex·a·pla /héksəplə/ *n.* an ancient version of the Hebrew Scriptures, compiled by the early Christian theologian, Origen, that contains six parallel versions of the text [Early 17thC. From *(ta) hexapla,* its Greek title, the neuter plural of *hexaplous* "sixfold," from *hexa-* "six."]

hex·a·po·dy /hek sáppədee/ (*plural* **-dies**) *n.* a line of poetry consisting of six feet [Mid-19thC. Coined from HEXA- + -POD on the model of words such as TETRAPODY.] —**hex·a·po·dic** /hèksə póddik/ *adj.*

hex·a·stich /héksə stìk/, **hex·a·sti·chon** /hek sásti kòn/ (*plural* **-cha** /-kə/) *n.* a unit of verse, e.g., a stanza or a short poem, that contains six lines [Late 16thC. Via modern Latin *hexastichon* from Greek, "of six rows," from *hexa-* "six" + *stichos* "row."]

hex·a·style /héksə stīl/ *adj.* ARCHIT WITH SIX COLUMNS with six architectural columns, or in the form of six columns ■ *n.* ARCHIT CONSTRUCTION WITH SIX COLUMNS a building, or a portico or other part, that has six columns

Hex·a·teuch /héksə tòok/ *n.* the first six books of the Bible, comprising Genesis, Exodus, Leviticus, Numbers, Deutoronomy, and Joshua. ◊ **Heptateuch, Pentateuch** [Late 19thC. Coined from HEXA- + Greek *teuchos* "book," on the model of *Pentateuch.*]

hex·a·va·lent /hèksə váylənt/ *adj.* with a chemical valence of six

hex·cen·tric /hèksə séntrik/ *n.* a six-sided metal chock used in rock climbing

hex·o·san /héksō sàn/ *n.* a complex carbohydrate (**polysaccharide**) found in the cell walls of plants that breaks down to form a hexose. Formula: $C_6H_{10}O_5$.

hex·ose /hék sōss/ *n.* a simple sugar, e.g., glucose, that contains six carbon atoms per molecule

hex sign *n.* any one of various stylized signs incorporating a circle and other elements that were formerly painted on barns to ward off evil or bad luck [See HEX]

hex·yl /héksəl/ *n.* an organic group or radical derived from hexane and containing six carbon atoms. Formula: C_6H_{13}.

hey /hay/ *interj.* **1.** DEMANDING ATTENTION used to get somebody's attention (*informal*) **2.** EXPRESSING VARIOUS EMOTIONS used to express amazement, delight, disappointment, or irritation **3.** GREETING used as a greeting (*informal*) [12thC. Natural exclamation.]

hey·day /háy dày/ *n.* the time of somebody's or something's greatest success, popularity, or power [Late 16thC. By folk etymology from earlier *heyda* "hurrah" (by association with DAY), of uncertain origin: probably an extension of HEY, modeled partly on Low German *heida.*]

Hey·er·dahl /háy ər daal, hī-/, **Thor** (*b.* 1914) Norwegian anthropologist. He successfully crossed the Pacific in the balsa raft *Kon-Tiki* (1947) in an attempt to prove that Native South Americans could have migrated to Polynesia.

Hey·ward /háywərd/, **Thomas Jr.** (1746–1809) American patriot. He signed the Declaration of Independence (1776) as a South Carolina delegate to the Continental Congress.

Hez·e·ki·ah /hèzzi kī ə/ (*fl.* 715 B.C.) Judean king. An important religious reformer, he ruled Judah from 715 B.C. to 687 B.C.

hf *abbr.* RADIO high frequency

Hf *symbol.* hafnium

HF *abbr.* **1.** hard firm (*used to indicate hardness of lead on pencils*) **2.** RADIO high frequency

hf. *abbr.* MEASURE half

hg[1] *symbol.* MEASURE hectogram

hg[2] *abbr.* BIOCHEM hemoglobin

HG, H.G. *abbr.* LANG High German

hgb. *abbr.* hemoglobin

HGH *abbr.* human growth hormone

hgt. *abbr.* height

hgwy. *abbr.* highway

H.H. *abbr.* **1.** Her Highness **2.** His Highness **3.** LAW Her Honor **4.** LAW His Honor **5.** RELIG His Holiness

hhd *abbr.* hogshead

HH.D. *abbr.* Doctor of Humanities [Latin, *Humanitatum Doctor*]

H-Hour *n.* the appointed time for a military event, e.g., a planned attack, to take place [*H* abbreviation of "hour"]

HHS *abbr.* (Department of) Health and Human Services

hi /hī/ *interj.* used as an informal greeting (*informal*) [12thC. Natural exclamation.]

HI *abbr.* **1.** MAIL Hawaii **2.** MED hearing-impaired **3.** METEOROL humidity index

H.I. *abbr.* GEOG Hawaiian Islands

Hi·a·le·ah /hī ə lée ə/ city in southeastern Florida, 5 mi./8 km north and west of Miami. Population: 194,120 (1994).

hi·a·tal /hī áyt'l/ *adj.* relating to an opening, gap, or aperture in an organ of the body

hi·a·tal her·ni·a *n.* a hernia in which the part of the stomach around the esophagus entrance is forced up into the chest cavity through the normal opening in the diaphragm for the esophagus. Hiatal hernia is associated with heartburn and can usually be corrected by surgery.

hi·a·tus /hī áytəss/ (*plural* **-tus·es** *or* **-tus**) *n.* **1.** UNEXPECTED GAP a break in something where there should be continuity **2.** ANAT OPENING an opening or aperture in an organ, e.g., the opening in the diaphragm for the esophagus **3.** LING SEPARATION BETWEEN CONSECUTIVE VOWELS a break in pronunciation between two vowels that are next to each other in consecutive syllables without an intervening consonant, as in "re-examine" **4.** PRINTING OMISSION a gap where something is missing, especially in manuscripts [Mid-16thC. From Latin, "gaping, opening," from *hiare* "to gape," from, ultimately, an Indo-European word that is also the ancestor of English *yawn.*]

hi·a·tus her·ni·a *n.* = **hiatal hernia**

Hi·a·wa·tha /hī ə wáwthə/ (*fl.* 1550) Native North American leader. He was instrumental in uniting the Iroquois League of Five Nations in about 1550. Known only through Iroquois legend, he is nevertheless believed by historians to have been a real person. Born **Heowenta**

hi·ba·chi /hi báatchee/ (*plural* **-chis**) *n.* a portable barbecue of Japanese design, with a base for the fire with vents under it, and one or more adjustable cooking racks [Mid-19thC. From Japanese, literally "fire bowl."]

hi·ba·ku·sha (*plural* **-sha** *or* **-shas**) *n.* somebody who survived the atomic bombing of Hiroshima or Nagasaki in 1945 [Mid-20thC. From Japanese, literally "somebody who suffers an explosion."]

hi·ber·nac·u·lum /hībər nákyələm/ (*plural* **-la** /-lə/) *n.* **1.** ZOOL HIBERNATION PLACE the winter den of a hibernating animal or insect **2.** BOT BUD COVER the covering of a plant bud that protects it during its dormant phase [Late 17thC. From Latin, from *hibernare* (see HIBERNATE).]

hi·ber·nal /hī búrn'l/ *adj.* relating to winter as one of the six divisions of the year used to describe ecological communities [Early 17thC. From late Latin *hibernalis,* from *hibernus* "wintry."]

hi·ber·nate /hībər nàyt/ (**-nat·ed, -nat·ing, -nates**) *vi.* **1.** BIOL PASS WINTER ASLEEP to be in a sleeplike dormant state over the winter while living off reserves of body fat, with a decrease in body temperature and pulse rate and slower metabolism. Animals that hibernate include bears, bats, and many amphibians. **2.** BECOME LESS ACTIVE to become less active, especially by staying at home rather than going out to socialize (*informal humorous*) [Early 19thC. From Latin *hibernare,* from *hiberna* "winter quarters," a noun use of a form of *hibernus* "wintry."] —**hi·ber·na·tion** /hībər náysh'n/ *n.* —**hi·ber·na·tor** *n.*

Hi·ber·ni·a /hī búrnee ə/ *n.* Ireland (*archaic or literary*) [From Latin, "Ireland," alteration of *Iverna*, which came via Greek *I(w)ernē* from Celtic]

Hi·ber·ni·an /hī búrnee ən/ *n.* PEOPLES **SOMEBODY FROM HIBERNIA** somebody who was born in or was a citizen of Hibernia ■ *adj.* **IRISH** relating to or typical of Ireland (*archaic or literary*) —**Hi·ber·ni·an** *n.*

Hi·ber·ni·cism /hī búrni sìzzəm/, **Hi·ber·ni·an·ism** /-ə nìzzəm/ *n.* = **Irishism**

Hiberno- *prefix.* Irish [Formed from medieval Latin *Hibernus* "Irish," from Latin *Hibernia* "HIBERNIA"]

Hi·ber·no-Eng·lish *n.* the variety of English spoken in Ireland with features from Irish Gaelic, including intonation and some Gaelic words and phrases —**Hi·ber·no-Eng·lish** *adj.*

Hibiscus

hi·bis·cus /hī bískəss, hi-/ *n.* a shrub or small tree of the mallow family that has large brightly-colored flowers with prominent stamen tubes. It is pollinated by birds. Genus: *Hibiscus.* [Early 18thC. Via Latin from Greek *hibiskos*, "marshmallow," perhaps of Celtic origin.]

hic /hik/ *interj.* used to represent the sound of a hiccup [Late 19thC. An imitation of the sound.]

hic·cup /hí kùp, híkəp/, **hic·cough** *n.* **1.** MED **CONVULSIVE GASP** an abrupt involuntary contraction of the diaphragm that causes an intake of breath and closes the sound-producing folds at the top of the windpipe (**vocal cords**), resulting in a convulsive gasp **2. GULPING SOUND** the gulping sound that accompanies a hiccup, or a sound like this **3. HITCH IN ARRANGEMENTS** a temporary setback to somebody's plans or arrangements (*informal*) ■ **hic·cups, hic·coughs** *npl.* **GULPING INTAKES OF BREATH** an attack of repeated involuntary spasms of the diaphragm, resulting in periodic noisy gulps of breath ■ *v.* (**-cuped** *or* **-cupped, -cup·ing** *or* **-cup·ping, -cups; -coughed, -cough·ing, -coughs**) **1.** *vi.* **PRODUCE HICCUP** to have a spasm of the diaphragm resulting in a hiccup **2.** *vi.* **MAKE HICCUP NOISES** to make the sound of, or a sound like, a hiccup **3.** *vt.* **TALK WHILE HICCUPPING** to say something while hiccupping [Late 16thC. An imitation of the sound.]

hic ja·cet /hìk jáyssət/ an inscription often found on gravestones, meaning "here lies" [From Latin]

hick /hik/ *n.* **BUMPKIN** an unsophisticated and uncultured rural or small-town person (*informal insult*) ■ *adj.* **RURAL, RUSTIC, AND UNSOPHISTICATED** remote from big cities and lacking in sophistication (*informal insult*) [Mid-16thC. From *Hick*, an old nickname for "Richard."]

hick·ey /híkee/ (*plural* **-eys** *or* **-ies**) *n.* **1.** = **doohickey** (*informal*) **2. MARK ON SKIN** a mark on the skin caused by kissing, biting, or sucking and associated with physical intimacy (*informal*) **3. PIMPLE** a pimple (*informal*) **4.** PRINTING **PRINTING ERROR** a printing error or imperfection **5.** MECH ENG **PIPE-BENDING TOOL** a device for bending pipes **6.** MECH ENG **THREADED FITTING** a threaded fitting for joining two parts [Early 20thC. Origin unknown.]

Hick·ok /hík ok/, **Wild Bill** (1837–76) U.S. law enforcer, gunfighter, and scout. He was a Union spy and scout during the Civil War and later a Kansas marshal known for his marksmanship. His touring Buffalo Bill's Wild West Show (1872–73) was a popular attraction. Real name **James Butler Hickok**

hick·o·ry /híkəree/ (*plural* **-ries**) *n.* **1.** TREES **N AMERICAN NUT TREE** a deciduous North American tree of the walnut family with compound leaves and nuts that are edible in some species. Genus: *Carya.* **2.** INDUST **HICKORY WOOD** the hard light-colored wood of a hickory tree, used in tool handles and agricultural implements **3. HICKORY STICK** a walking stick or switch

U.S. Signal Corps

Wild Bill Hickok

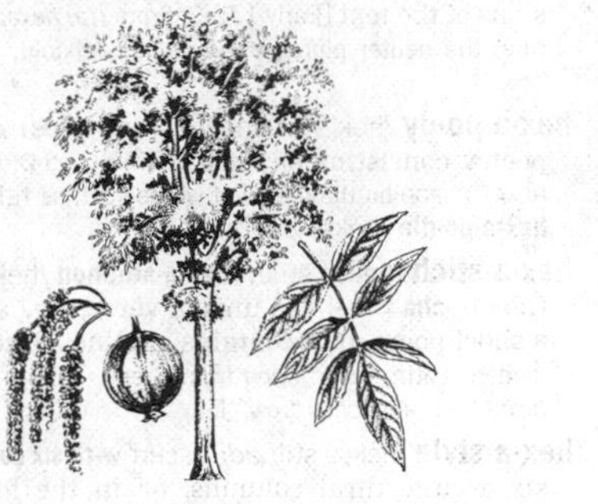

Hickory

made of hickory wood [Late 17thC. From Algonquian, a shortening of *pockerchicory, pohickery*, a type of walnut.]

Hick·o·ry /híkəree/ city in central North Carolina, west of Statesville. Population: 28,301 (1990).

Hicks·ville /híksvil/ unincorporated village in southeastern New York, on Long Island, a residential and industrial center. Population: 40,174 (1990).

hid past tense, past participle of **hide**[1]

hi·dal·go /hi dálgō/ (*plural* **-gos**) *n.* a man belonging to the lowest rank of Spanish nobility [Late 16thC. From Spanish, a contraction of *hijo de algo*, literally "son of something."]

Hi·dal·go /hi dálgō/ state in east central Mexico. Capital: Pachuca. Population: 2,100,000 (1995). Area: 8,103 sq. mi./20,987 sq. km.

Hi·dat·sa /hi daátsə/ (*plural* **-sa** *or* **-sas**) *n.* **1.** PEOPLES **MEMBER OF NATIVE AMERICAN PEOPLE** a member of a Native American people now living along the Missouri valley in South Dakota **2.** LANG **HIDATSA LANGUAGE** the Siouan language of the Hidatsa people. It belongs to the Siouan group of Hokan Siouan family of Native American languages. [Late 19thC. From Hidatsa *hiratsa*, literally "willow wood lodge."] —**Hi·dat·sa** *adj.*

hid·den past participle of **hide**[1] —**hid·den·ness** *n.*

hid·den a·gen·da *n.* a plan, motive, or aim underlying somebody's actions that is kept secret from others

hid·den·ite /hídd'n ìt/ *n.* a rare green variety of the mineral spodumene, used as a gemstone. It is an aluminum lithium silicate found in hydrothermal deposits. [Late 19thC. Formed from the name of U.S. mineralogist W. E. *Hidden*, who discovered it.]

hid·den tax *n.* = **indirect tax**

hide[1] /hīd/ *v.* (**hid, hid·den** /hídd'n/ *or* **hid** /hid/, **hid·ing, hides**) **1.** *vti.* **MOVE OUT OF SIGHT** to conceal yourself, or something or somebody else, from view **2.** *vt.* **KEEP SECRET** to prevent something from becoming known **3.** *vt.* **BLOCK VIEW OF** to obscure something by passing, or passing something, in front of it, or by being temporarily or permanently in front of it ○ *The clouds hid the sun for a while* **4.** *vt.* **TURN AWAY** to turn away or cover the face or eyes with the hands, e.g., so that the expression cannot be seen or in order to avoid seeing something ■ *n. U.K.* HUNT, LEISURE = **blind** *n.* 5 [Old English *hȳdan*. Ultimately from a prehistoric West Germanic word that is also the ancestor of English *hoard, huddle*, and *hut.*]

hide out *vi.* to be in, or go into, hiding

hide[2] /hīd/ *n.* **1. ANIMAL SKIN** the skin of some larger animals, e.g., deer, cow, or buffalo (*often used in combination*) **2. HUMAN SKIN** a person's skin (*informal*) ○ *"A vengeance on your crafty wither'd hide!"* (William Shakespeare, *The Taming of the Shrew*; 1593) [Old English *hȳd*. Ultimately from an Indo-European word that is also the ancestor of *hide*[1] and of Latin *cutis* (source of English *cuticle*) , the underlying idea being "covering."] ◇ **neither hide nor hair of somebody** *or* **something** no trace of somebody or something ◇ **tan somebody's hide** to beat or whip somebody (*informal*)

hide[3] /hīd/ *n.* in Old English law, a measure of land equal to 120 acres [Old English *hīd*, "measure of land for supporting a family," of prehistoric Germanic origin]

hide-and-seek, **hide-and-go-seek** *n.* a children's game in which one player lets the others hide, and then tries to find them

hide·a·way /hídə wày/ *n.* a secluded place of retreat or concealment

hide·bound /híd bòwnd/ *adj.* **1. NARROW-MINDED AND CONSERVATIVE** unwilling to consider new ideas or new ways of doing things (*disapproving*) **2.** AGRIC **WITH DRY, STIFF SKIN** with skin that is dry, stiff, and closely attached to the flesh, as a result of poor feeding ○ *hidebound cattle*

hid·e·ous /híddee əss/ *adj.* **1. HORRIBLE TO SEE** extremely unpleasant or horrible to see **2. HORRIBLE TO HEAR** frighteningly horrible to hear ○ *a hideous shriek* **3. MORALLY REPULSIVE** morally repulsive or disgusting **4. CAUSING SUFFERING** causing a great deal of suffering [14thC. From Anglo-Norman *hidous* and Old French *hidos*, from *hi(s)de* "fear."] —**hid·e·ous·ness** *n.*

WORD KEY: SYNONYMS

See Synonyms at ***unattractive***.

hid·e·ous·ly /híddee əsslee/ *adv.* **1. FRIGHTENINGLY OR REVOLTINGLY** in an extremely unpleasant, frightening, or revolting way **2. EXTREMELY** to a frightening or revolting extent

hide·out /híd òwt/ *n.* a place where somebody is hiding, especially somebody wanted by the police

hid·ey-hole, **hid·y-hole** *n.* a place of concealment for somebody or something (*informal*) [*Hidey* a variant of HIDING]

hid·ing[1] /híding/ *n.* a place where somebody is hiding or can hide, or the state of being hidden [From HIDE[1]]

hid·ing[2] /híding/ *n.* the punishment of being beaten (*informal*) [From HIDE[2]]

hi·dro·sis /hī-/ *n.* **1. SWEAT PRODUCTION** the production or excretion of sweat (*technical*) **2. DISEASE OF SWEAT GLANDS** a skin disease that affects the sweat glands [Mid-19thC. From Greek, from *hidrōs* "sweat."] —**hi·drot·ic** /hī-/ *adj.*

hid·y-hole *n.* = **hidey-hole**

hie /hī/ (**hied, hie·ing** *or* **hy·ing, hies**) *vi.* to go somewhere in a hurry (*archaic*) [Old English, of unknown origin]

hi·e·mal /hī əməl/ *adj.* relating to or occurring in winter (*formal*) [Mid-16thC. From Latin *hiemalis*, from *hiems* "winter."]

hier- *prefix.* = **hiero-** (*used before vowels*)

hi·er·arch /hī raàrk, hī ə raàrk/ *n.* somebody of high rank in a hierarchy, especially a priestly hierarchy [15thC. Via medieval Latin *hierarcha* from Greek *hierarkhēs*, literally "ruling sacred person," from *hieros* "sacred" + *arkhēs* "ruling."]

hi·er·ar·chi·cal /hī raárkik'l, hī ə-/, **hi·er·ar·chic** /hī raárkik, hī ə-/ *adj.* **1. RIGIDLY GRADED IN ORDER** relating to or arranged in a formally ranked order **2.** RELIG **ADMINISTERED BY RANKED CLERGY** administered by a hierarchy composed of members of the clergy —**hi·er·ar·chi·cal·ly** *adv.*

hi·er·ar·chize /hī raar kìz, hī ə raar kìz/ (**-chized, -chiz·ing, -chiz·es**) *vt.* to arrange something, e.g., an organization, in graduated ranks —**hi·er·ar·chi·za·tion** /hī raarki záysh'n, hī ə raarki záysh'n/ *n.*

hi·er·ar·chy /hī raàrkee, hī ə raàrkee/ (*plural* **-chies**) *n.* **1. FORMALLY RANKED GROUP** an organization or group whose members are arranged in ranks, e.g., in ranks of power and seniority **2. FORMAL GRADING OF A GROUP** categorization of members of a group according to the importance of each **3.** BIOL **ANIMAL GROUP ORGANIZATION** a form of social organization in animals in which different members of a group possess different levels of status, affecting their feeding and mating behavior **4.** RELIG **RANKED GROUP OF CLERGY** a body of clergy organized into ranks **5.** BIOL **SUBSET WITHIN A RANKED SYSTEM** a subset within a classification system, e.g., that for plants or animals **6. CONTROLLING GROUP IN FORMAL ORGANIZATION** those who are in charge of a formally organized group, especially the priests in control of the Roman Catholic Church or a local part of it

hi·er·at·ic /hī ráttik, hī ə ráttik/, **hi·er·at·i·cal** /-ráttik'l/ *adj.* **1.** RELIG **OF PRIESTS** relating to priests **2.** LING **OF ANCIENT WRITING SYSTEM** relating to a cursive version of ancient Egyptian hieroglyphics **3.** ARTS **IN STYLIZED FORM** fixed, formal, and stylized in a traditional way, e.g., as ancient Egyptian art is ■ *n.* LING **ANCIENT WRITING SYSTEM** a cursive version of ancient Egyptian hieroglyphics [Mid-17thC. Via Latin *hieraticus* from Greek *hieratikos* "priestly," from *hiereus*, literally "sacred person," from *hieros* "sacred."] —**hi·er·at·i·cal·ly** *adv.*

hiero- *prefix.* holy, sacred ○ *hierocracy* [From Greek *hieros.* Ultimately from an Indo-European word denoting strong feeling that is also the ancestor of English *irate, iron,* and *estrus.*]

hi·er·oc·ra·cy /hī rókrəssee, hī ə-/ (*plural* **-cies**) *n.* **1.** **CLERICAL GOVERNMENT** government by clergy **2.** **RULING CLERGY** a body of clergy that rules a place or country —**hi·er·o·crat·ic** /hīrə kráttik, hī ərə-/ *adj.*

hi·er·o·dule /hírə dōōl, hī ərə-/ *n.* in ancient Greece, an enslaved person kept in or associated with a temple, especially a prostitute [Mid-19thC. Via late Latin *hierodulus* from Greek *hierodoulos* "temple slave," from *hieron*, literally "sacred place," from *hieros* "sacred" + *doulos* "slave."] —**hi·er·o·du·lic** /hīrə dōōlik, hī ərə dōōlik/ *adj.*

Hieroglyph: Detail of wall painting in the tomb of Inherkha, Thebes, Egypt (1279–1212 B.C.)

hi·er·o·glyph /hírə glìf, hī ərə-/ *n.* a symbol or picture used in a writing system to denote an object, concept, sound, or sequence of sounds, originally and especially in the writing system of ancient Egypt [Late 16thC. Back-formation from HIEROGLYPHIC.]

hi·er·o·glyph·ic /hīrə glíffik, hī ərə-/ *adj.* **1.** **hi·er·o·glyph·ic, hi·er·o·glyph·i·cal** **IN HIEROGLYPHS** relating to or written in hieroglyphs **2.** **HARD TO READ** difficult to read (*informal*) ■ *n.* = **hieroglyph** [Late 16thC. Directly or via French *hiéroglyphique*, from Late Latin *hieroglyphicus* from Greek *hierogluphikos*, literally "sacred carving," from *hieros* "sacred" + *gluphē* "carving," because hieroglyphs were associated with priests.] —**hi·er·o·glyph·i·cal·ly** *adv.*

hi·er·o·glyph·ics /hīrə glíffiks, hī ərə-/ *n.* **PICTURE WRITING SYSTEM** a writing system that uses symbols or pictures to denote objects, concepts, or sounds, originally and especially in the writing system of ancient Egypt (*takes a singular verb*) ■ *npl.* **SOMETHING HARD TO DECIPHER** writing that is difficult to decipher, or other indecipherable symbols (*informal*) (*takes a plural verb*)

hi·er·o·gram /hírə gràm, hī ərə-/ *n.* a symbol with religious significance

Hi·er·o·nym·i·an /hīrə nímmee ən, hī ərə-/, **Hi·er·o·nym·ic** /hīrə nímmik, hī ərə-/ *adj.* relating to St. Jerome. [Mid-17thC. Formed from Latin *Hieronymus* "JEROME."]

hi·er·o·phant /hírə fànt, hī ərə-, hī érrə-/ *n.* **1.** **EXPLAINER OF MYSTERIES** somebody who interprets and expounds the meaning of obscure and mysterious matters, especially sacred doctrines or mysteries **2.** **INTERPRETER OF EVENTS** somebody who explains or comments on everyday matters (*formal*) **3.** **ANCIENT GREEK PRIEST** a priest who revealed the mysteries at the annual festival of Eleusis in ancient Greece [Late 17thC. Via late Latin *hierophanta* from Greek *hierophantēs*, literally "sacred person who reveals something" from *hieros* "sacred" + *phen-*, the stem of *phainein* "to reveal."] —**hi·er·o·phan·tic** /hīrə fántik, hī ərə-, hī èrrə-/ *adj.* —**hi·er·o·phan·ti·cal·ly** *adv.*

hi·fa·lu·tin *adj.* = **highfalutin**

hi-fi /hī fī/ (*plural* **hi-fis**) *n.* **1.** **HIGH-QUALITY AUDIO EQUIPMENT** a set of high-quality equipment for reproducing and usually recording sound, which may include a CD player, tape deck, turntable, tuner, amplifier, and speakers (*dated*) **2.** = **high fidelity** [Mid-20thC. Shortening of HIGH FIDELITY.]

Hig·gin·son /hígginss'n/, **Thomas Wentworth** (1823–1911) U.S. writer and reformer. He led the first Black regiment in the U.S. army and wrote about his experience in *Army Life in a Black Regiment* (1870). He also championed women's rights and edited Emily Dickinson's poetry. Full name **Thomas Wentworth Storrow Higginson**

hig·gle /hígg'l/ *vi.* to haggle (*archaic*) [Mid-17thC. Variant of HAGGLE.] —**hig·gler** *n.*

hig·gle·dy-pig·gle·dy /hìgg'ldi pígg'ldee/ *adj.* **DISORGANIZED** disorganized and messy ■ *adv.* **MESSILY** in a disorganized, messy state ○ *"Jasper had already unpacked her young lady's things and laid them higgledy-piggledy in the spacious wardrobe."* (L. T. Meade, *A Very Naughty Girl*; 1907) [Late 16thC. Origin uncertain: probably from the idea of pigs being messy, or being huddled together when herded.]

high /hī/ *adj.* **1.** **OF GREAT HEIGHT** extending a long way from bottom to top, especially when viewed from the bottom **2.** **ABOVE SOMEBODY OR SOMETHING** situated in a position above the onlooker or above somebody or something else referred to ○ *The window was too high for him to see in.* **3.** **IN HEIGHT ABOVE SOMETHING** above or stretching upward from a known base level such as sea or ground level ○ *ten feet high* **4.** **ABOVE AVERAGE** greater than the normal or average, e.g., in quantity, number, quality, intensity, or cost, or well above a smaller or lower level or amount ○ *a high cost of living* **5.** MUSIC **RAISED IN PITCH** raised in pitch toward the upper end of a range of sound ○ *can hit the high notes* **6.** METEOROL **BLOWING STRONGLY** blowing with a great deal of force ○ *a high wind* **7.** **ADVANCED** advanced in development or complexity ○ *high finance* **8.** **BETTER** superior in quality, character, or morals ○ *sets a high example* **9.** **WITH ELEVATED RANK** important in status or rank ○ *a high official* **10.** **VERY FAVORABLE** considering somebody or something to be particularly good ○ *held in high esteem* **11.** **AT A PEAK** at the busiest or most important stage ○ *high summer* **12.** **HAPPY** animated and cheerful ○ *in high spirits* **13.** **OVEREXCITED** overexcited or overly stimulated **14.** DRUGS **INTOXICATED** under the influence of alcohol or drugs (*slang*) **15.** GEOG **FAR FROM EQUATOR** at a considerable distance either north or south of the equator ○ *high latitude* **16.** PHON **WITH TONGUE RAISED IN MOUTH** formed with the back of the tongue close, or relatively close, to the roof of the mouth ○ *high vowel sounds* **17.** MECH ENG **PRODUCING TOP SPEEDS** resulting in a relatively large number of revolutions of the driven part as compared with the driving part in a transmission gear, and giving the top speed of travel or rotation ■ *adv.* **WAY UP** at, in, or into a high position ○ *The balloon rose high in the sky.* ■ *n.* **1.** **TOP PLACE** a high level or position ○ *an all-time high* **2.** METEOROL = **anticyclone** **3.** METEOROL **TOP TEMPERATURE** the highest temperature reached or expected to be reached in a particular period ○ *Today's high will be in the nineties.* **4.** **ELATED STATE** a state of euphoria (*informal*) **5.** **INTOXICATED STATE** a state of intoxication by drugs or alcohol **6.** EDUC **HIGH SCHOOL** a particular high school (*informal*) ○ *She goes to Valley High.* **7.** MECH ENG **HIGH GEAR** the top gear of a vehicle, allowing the greatest speed (*informal*) [Old English *hēah*. Ultimately from a prehistoric Germanic word that is also the ancestor of German *hoch* and Dutch *hoog*.] ◇ **high and dry 1.** stranded and abandoned, and perhaps helpless **2.** beyond the reach of water ◇ **high and mighty** arrogant and self-important ◇ **run high** to be at a level of great intensity

WORD KEY: CULTURAL NOTE

High Noon, a film by director Fred Zinnemann (1952). In this classic Western, lawman Will Kane (Gary Cooper) valiantly awaits and then confronts a killer seeking revenge for his recent incarceration. Shot in real time, the film's suspense is heightened by close-ups of Kane's anxious expressions and of clocks ticking steadily toward the moment of truth.

high·ball /hī bàwl/ *n.* **1.** BEVERAGES **LIQUOR WITH WATER OR CARBONATED DRINK** a drink consisting of liquor mixed with ice and water or a carbonated drink, usually served in a tall glass **2.** RAIL **RAILROAD SIGNAL** a railroad signal indicating that the way ahead is clear and that a train may go ahead at full speed ■ *vti.* (**-balled, -ball·ing, -balls**) TRANSP **GO AT HIGH SPEED** to travel, or drive a vehicle, at high speed (*slang*) [From the earlier sense "a type of poker played with balls and a tall glass receptacle"]

high beam *n.* the setting of a vehicle's headlights that sheds light far in front of the vehicle

high·bind·er /hī bìndər/ *n.* **1.** POL **CORRUPT POLITICIAN** a corrupt politician (*informal dated*) **2.** CRIMINOL **GANGSTER** a thug or gangster (*informal dated*) **3.** CRIMINOL **CHINESE GANGSTER IN U.S.** a member of a Chinese secret society of blackmailers and murderers operating in U.S. cities and victimizing especially gamblers and prostitutes (*dated*) [Early 19thC. From *Highbinders*, the name of a New York gang of the time, probably an alteration of *hellbender*.]

high blood pres·sure *n.* abnormally high arterial blood pressure. It encompasses abnormal elevation of either systolic pressure, the peak blood pressure with each beat, or diastolic pressure, the running pressure between heart beats, or both.

high·born /hī bàwrn/ *adj.* born into an aristocratic or wealthy family (*literary*)

high·boy /hī bòy/ *n.* a tall chest of drawers, sometimes in two sections

high·bred /hī brèd/ *adj.* **1.** AGRIC **FROM GOOD STOCK** born of or descended from superior breeding stock **2.** **REFINED** showing or having refined manners (*archaic*)

high·brow /hī bròw/ *adj.* **INTELLECTUAL** dealing with serious subjects, especially cultural subjects, in an intellectual way ○ *"conceits which would be only highbrow wisecracks in inferior writing have fused into a form that can only be called inevitable, the way it should be"* (Northrop Frye, *The Bush Garden*; 1972) ■ *n.* **INTELLECTUAL PERSON** somebody with highbrow interests or tastes [From the idea that a high forehead signifies greater brain power] —**high·brow·ism** *n.*

high·bush blue·ber·ry /hī bōōsh-/ *n.* a shrub of eastern North America that is cultivated for the commercial production of blueberries. Latin name: *Vaccinium corymbosum.* [From HIGH + BUSH]

high·bush cran·ber·ry *n.* = **cranberry bush**

high·chair /hī chàir/ *n.* a small chair with long legs and often a detachable tray, for older babies and toddlers to use at mealtimes

High Church *n.* a section of the Episcopal Church that stresses the essential unity of Episcopal Christianity with Roman Catholicism and Orthodoxy, holds traditional views about the sacraments, and favors ritual and ceremony

high-class *adj.* **1.** **FOR THE RICH** appealing to the rich or sophisticated, and therefore usually expensive **2.** **SOPHISTICATED** showing or having the kind of sophistication associated with wealth

high com·e·dy *n.* comedy with humor depending on witty dialogue and a clever plot rather than slapstick

high com·mand *n.* **1.** **SENIOR OFFICERS** the senior officers in a country's armed forces, who jointly make decisions on strategy and tactics **2.** **MILITARY HEADQUARTERS** the main headquarters of a military force

High Com·mis·sion *n.* the embassy of one country of the British Commonwealth of Nations in another Commonwealth country

high com·mis·sion·er *n.* **1.** **HEAD OF INTERNATIONAL COMMISSION** the person leading an international commission **2.** **AMBASSADOR** the chief representative of a country of the British Commonwealth of Nations in another Commonwealth country

high-con·cept *adj.* used to describe a movie that contains features likely to attract a large audience, e.g., big stars, fast action, and glamour

high-count *adj.* TEXTILES having a large number of threads per square inch

high coun·try *n.* lands that are in a mountainous region, but not so high as to have no pastoral or agricultural use (*hyphenated when used before a noun*)

high court *n.* a principal or supreme court, especially the Supreme Court of the United States

high-def·i·ni·tion tel·e·vi·sion *n.* a television system with twice the scanning capacity of normal television systems, allowing for far greater definition and less flickering

high-den·si·ty lip·o·pro·tein *n.* a complex composed of fat and protein molecules that is responsible for transporting cholesterol away from the arteries. High levels of high-density lipoproteins are associated with a decreased risk of heart disease.

high-end *adj.* sophisticated and discerning, or likely to appeal to sophisticated and discerning people

high-en·er·gy *adj.* **1.** CHEM **RELEASING A LOT OF ENERGY** used to describe chemical reactions that take place with the release of substantial amounts of energy **2.** FOOD **PROVIDING ENERGY EASILY** used, especially in marketing, to describe foods that can be broken down by the body to provide a ready supply of energy, e.g., glucose drinks or high-sugar items such as honey

high-en·er·gy phys·ics *n.* = **particle physics**

high·er crit·i·cism *n.* the establishment of the sources of biblical texts, using the techniques of textual criticism —**high·er crit·ic** *n.*

high·er ed·u·ca·tion *n.* education generally begun after high school, usually carried out at a university or college, and usually involving study for a degree or diploma

high·er law *n.* a moral law or ethical principle that is believed to be of greater validity than civil law

high·er learn·ing *n.* education or study at college or university level (*formal or literary*)

high·er math·e·mat·ics *n.* mathematics at an abstract and sophisticated level, including number theory and topology (*takes a singular verb*)

high·er-up *n.* somebody in a position of authority or at a higher level in a hierarchy (*informal*)

high·est com·mon fac·tor *n. U.K.* = **greatest common divisor**

high ex·plo·sive *n.* a liquid or solid substance that undergoes explosive decomposition **(detonation)** without burning to produce a large release of energy. High explosives are used for rock blasting and have military applications.

high·fa·lu·tin /hī fə lo͞ot'n/, **hi·fa·lu·tin, highfaluting** /hī fə lo͞oting/ *adj.* affecting a grand style in an unconvincing way (*informal*) [Mid-19thC. Origin of *falutin* uncertain: perhaps from *fluting*, the present participle of FLUTE.]

high fash·ion *n.* = **haute couture**

high fi·del·i·ty *n.* extremely high-quality sound reproduction with minimal distortion, achieved with electronic equipment (*hyphenated when used before a noun*)

high-five *n.* an informal greeting or gesture of elation or victory in which somebody slaps a raised palm against the raised palm of somebody else (*slang*) —**high-five** *vti.*

high-fli·er, **high-fly·er** *n.* somebody who enjoys great success, especially professional success, or who seems destined for great achievement

high-flown *adj.* giving an unconvincing appearance of being elegant, refined, or exalted ○ *"a warning against high-flown pretensions"* (Henry James, *Roderick Hudson*; 1876)

high-fly·er *n.* = **high-flier**

high fre·quen·cy *n.* a radio frequency in the range 3–30 MHz or of wavelength 10–100 meters (*hyphenated when used before a noun*)

high gear *n.* **1. HIGHEST GEAR OF SYSTEM** the highest gear of a transmission system, giving the greatest speed of travel **2. FAST PACE** a very quick pace or rate of development

High Ger·man *n.* the form of German spoken originally in the southern part of the country that gave rise to a literary and cultured form of the language that has become standard German —**High-Ger·man** *adj.*

high-grade *adj.* of a high quality, especially because of purity or concentration of contents

high ground *n.* **1. RAISED AREA** an area of land higher than its surroundings **2. SUPERIORITY** a position of superiority or advantage over others

high-hand·ed *adj.* overbearing and inconsiderate of other people's views or feelings —**high-hand·ed·ly** *adv.* —**high-hand·ed·ness** *n.*

high-hat *adj.* **SNOBBISH** snobbish and arrogant (*archaic informal*) ■ *n.* **SNOB** a snob (*archaic informal*) ■ *vti.* **(high-hat·ted, high-hat·ting, high-hats) BEHAVE SNOBBISHLY** to treat somebody in a haughty, disdainful way (*dated*)

high-hat cym·bals *npl.* a pair of cymbals on a stand, with the upper one made to rise and fall against the lower one by the drummer's foot

high heels *n.* women's shoes with tall slender heels that raise the back of the foot off the ground

High Hol·i·days, **High Ho·ly Days** *npl.* the Jewish festivals of Rosh Hashana and Yom Kippur, along with the days in between

high horse *n.* an attitude of arrogance and haughty disregard for others (*informal*) ○ *is on her high horse this morning* ○ *told him to get off his high horse*

high hur·dles *n.* a track event for men, in which the athletes cover a distance of 110 m outdoors, jumping over hurdles 42 in./107 cm high (*takes a singular or plural verb*)

high·jack *v.* = **hijack**

high jinks /hī jìngks/, **hijinks** *n.* good-humored boisterousness, frequently including mischievousness and pranks (*informal*) (*takes a singular or plural verb*)

high jump *n.* a track-and-field event in which the athletes run forward to gain momentum, and then jump over a horizontal pole. The pole is raised higher in each successive round until all competitors have failed to get over it. —**high jump·er** *n.* —**high jump·ing** *n.*

high·land /hīlənd/ *n.* **HILLY LAND** hilly ground, higher than its surroundings ■ **high·lands** *npl.* **HILLY AREA** an area or region that is largely hilly or mountainous. ◊ **Highlands** ■ *adj.* **RELATING TO HIGHLANDS** relating to or coming from highlands

High·land /hīlənd/ city in northwestern Indiana, south of Lake Michigan, part of the suburban area of Chicago. Population: 23,569 (1996).

high·land·er /hīləndər/ *n.* somebody who was born in or lives in a highland area

High·land fling *n.* an energetic Scottish solo dance originally danced by men in Highland dress, but now also by women and children

High·land Park city in northeastern Illinois, on Lake Michigan, a northern suburb of Chicago. Population: 30,998 (1996).

High·lands /hīləndz/ mountainous area of mainland Scotland, north and west of a line from Dumbarton in the west to Stonehaven in the east

high-lev·el *adj.* involving participation by people at a high level in their organization or country, e.g., politicians, civil servants, or corporate directors

high-lev·el lan·guage *n.* a computer programming language that has syntax and grammar crudely approximating a natural language, e.g., English, and requires translation to a low-level language that a computer can recognize. The pioneering high-level languages, FORTRAN, COBOL, and ALGOL, have largely been supplanted by BASIC, FORTH, PASCAL, and C, especially for educational and personal-computer applications.

high-lev·el waste *n.* radioactive waste material retaining sufficient activity that it needs to be continuously cooled

high life *n.* the luxurious lifestyle of fashionable society (*often used ironically*) —**high lif·er** *n.*

high·life /hī līf/ *n.* a style of music that blends West African elements with American jazz forms and is popular in West Africa

high·light /hī līt/ *n.* **1. BEST PART** the most memorable, important, or exciting part of an experience or event **2. REPRESENTATIVE PART** an exemplary extract from a larger work that, along with others, is meant to represent it ○ *gave us highlights of the President's speech* **3.** PAINTING, PHOTOGRAPHY **CONTRASTING PALE AREA** an area in a very light tone in a painting or photograph that provides contrast, illumination, or the appearance of illumination **4.** PHOTOGRAPHY **REFLECTION** the reflection of a light source in a picture, e.g., the reflection of a studio light in shiny hair or the reflection of light in somebody's eye ■ **high·lights** *npl.* HAIR **LIGHT STREAKS IN HAIR** strands of hair that are deliberately made lighter than the rest of the hair ■ *vt.* **(-light·ed, -light·ing, -lights) 1. EMPHASIZE** to draw attention to something, or make something particularly prominent or noticeable ○ *The report highlights the problems of inner-city areas.* **2. MARK WITH HIGHLIGHTER** to mark something, e.g., parts of a text, with a highlighter pen **3.** HAIR **PUT STREAKS IN** to put highlights in somebody's hair **4.** PAINTING **ADD LIGHT AREAS IN** to add highlights to parts of a picture to provide contrast, illumination, or the appearance of illumination

high·light·er /hī lītər/ *n.* **1. MARKER PEN** a broad-tipped felt pen, often with transparent, brightly colored ink, for marking important passages of text **2.** COSMETICS **FACE COSMETIC** a cosmetic for the face that is used to emphasize features such as the eyes or cheekbones

high-low *n.* **1.** CARDS **VARIANT OF POKER** a variety of poker in which both high and low hands win **2.** BRIDGE **SIGNAL IN BRIDGE** a signal to a bridge partner to lead a particular suit

high·ly /hīlee/ *adv.* **1. EXTREMELY** very much ○ *highly likely to succeed* **2. FAVORABLY** very favorably ○ *highly regarded* **3. IN HIGH PLACE** in a high position or rank ○ *highly placed officials who denied the story* **4. GREATLY** to a great extent or in many ways ○ *highly improbable*

high·ly-strung *adj. U.K.* = **high-strung**

High Mass *n.* an elaborate Roman Catholic Mass in which a choir sings much of the service. It is usually celebrated by more than one priest.

high-mind·ed *adj.* having or showing high moral principles —**high-mind·ed·ly** *adv.* —**high-mind·ed·ness** *n.*

high·most /hī mōst/ *adj.* highest (*literary*)

high-muck-a-muck /hī mùkə múk/, **high-muck·et·y-muck** /-mùkəti-/ *n.* somebody in a position of importance and authority who behaves in an overbearing way (*informal*) [Mid-19thC. Origin uncertain: probably by folk etymology from Chinook Jargon *hiyu muckamuck*, literally "ten portions of choice whalemeat," by association with HIGH.]

High·ness /hīnəss/ *n.* a title and style of address for members of a royal family other than a sovereign

high noon *n.* **1. NOON EXACTLY** the exact moment of noon **2. PEAK OF ACHIEVEMENT** the high point or most creative part of somebody's career or achievements **3. high noon, High Noon CRUCIAL TIME** a time of confronting a serious problem or making a hard decision

high-oc·tane *adj.* **1.** ENERGY **WITH HIGH OCTANE CONTENT** used to describe fuel that has a high octane content **2. DYNAMIC** showing or demanding a high degree of commitment and effort in a drive for success (*informal*)

high-pitched *adj.* **1. AT TOP OF SOUND RANGE** toward the upper end of the range of audible sound **2.** BUILDING **WITH STEEP SLOPE** having a very steep slope **3. EMOTIONAL** extremely emotional and intense

high plac·es *npl.* positions of power, authority, or influence

High Point /hī póynt/ city in central North Carolina, a major furniture-manufacturing center. Population: 69,496 (1990).

high-pow·ered, **high-pow·er** *adj.* **1.** BUSINESS **DYNAMIC** possessing great energy and impressive ability, especially as displayed in a professional environment ○ *a high-powered sales pitch* **2. INFLUENTIAL** having a lot of power or influence **3.** OPTICS **GREATLY ENLARGING** giving a high magnification **4.** TECH **VERY POWERFUL** operating much more powerfully, or able to handle material of greater complexity and more quickly, than others of the same type **5.** ENG **NEEDING OR MAKING LOTS OF POWER** requiring or producing a lot of power

high-pres·sure *adj.* **1.** TECH **OPERATING AT GREATER THAN NORMAL PRESSURE** using, or designed to withstand, forces exerted by liquid or gas at pressures higher than normal atmospheric pressure **2. STRESSFUL** causing stress, e.g. from deadlines or excessive demands ○ *She's at her best in high-pressure situations.* **3. PERSISTENT** aggressively persistent in seeking to bring about a result

high priest *n.* **1. MAIN PROPONENT** the leading figure propounding a doctrine or ideology **2.** JUDAISM **JEWISH CHIEF PRIEST** a chief priest, especially the head of the priestly caste at the time of the Temple in Jerusalem **3.** CHR **MORMON PRIEST** a man who is a priest in the Church of the Latter Day Saints, belonging to the order of Melchizedek —**high priest·hood** *n.*

high priest·ess *n.* **1.** RELIG **WOMAN RELIGIOUS LEADER** a woman who leads a religion, or a religious group **2. MAIN PROPONENT** the leading woman propounding a doctrine or ideology

high pro·file *n.* a prominent position or presence in the public eye

high-pro·file *adj.* in or intended to be in the public eye, e.g., to attract attention, support, or business

high re·lief *n.* a version of relief sculpture in which the carving projects from the background to more than half its natural depth

High Re·nais·sance *n.* the period in European art between about 1490 and 1520, when the work of Leonardo da Vinci, Michelangelo, Raphael, and other great artists reached the highest point of Renaissance perfection

high-rent *adj.* expensive or pricey (*informal*)

high res·o·lu·tion *n.* the use in a video display or printed image of a large number of dots or lines to portray an image in great detail

high-rise *adj.* **1.** ARCHIT **MULTISTORY** consisting of several storys, but usually fewer than for a skyscraper **2.** TRANSP **WITH HIGH HANDLEBARS** used to describe a child's bicycle that has small wheels, very high handlebars, and a long narrow seat ■ *n.* **1.** ARCHIT **TALL BUILDING** a multistory building **2.** TRANSP **HIGH-RISE BICYCLE** a child's high-rise bicycle

high·road /hī̍ rōd/, **high road** *n.* **1. DIRECT ROUTE** the easiest or most direct way to somewhere **2.** *U.K.* TRANSP **MAIN ROAD** a main road, usually in a town or village

high roll·er *n.* (*slang*) **1.** FIN **BIG SPENDER** a person or organization that spends money freely and extravagantly **2.** LEISURE **GAMBLER** a gambler who plays for high stakes —**high-roll·ing** *adj.*

high school *n.* a school that includes grades 9 or 10 through 12 —**high school·er** *n.*

high seas *npl.* the open ocean, not under any nation's jurisdiction

high sea·son *n.* = **peak season**

high sign *n.* a secret signal, often prearranged, given as a warning or to convey information

high so·ci·e·ty *n.* the fashionable wealthy people in society as a group

high-sound·ing *adj.* grandiose and pretentious but unlikely to come to anything

high-spir·it·ed *adj.* lively and full of fun or mischief —**high-spir·it·ed·ly** *adv.* —**high-spir·it·ed·ness** *n.*

high-stick·ing *n.* in ice hockey, the offense of holding the hockey stick higher than is allowed by the rules

high street *n. U.K.* in the United Kingdom, a principal street where the main stores are located

high-strung *adj.* tense, nervous, or easily upset by nature

high style *n.* the most up-to-date and stylish fashion, especially in clothing (*hyphenated when used before a noun*)

high ta·ble *n. U.K.* in the United Kingdom, a table in a large dining hall in some schools and university colleges at which the staff, principal teachers, or fellows sit

high·tail /hī̍ tàyl/ (**-tailed, -tail·ing, -tails**) *vti.* to rush away from a place (*slang*) [With reference to the erect tail of a fleeing animal]

high tea *n. U.K.* in the United Kingdom, a meal served in the late afternoon or early evening, consisting of a cooked dish, usually hot, with bread and butter, cakes, and tea

high tech, **hi-tech** *n.* **1.** TECH **ADVANCED TECHNOLOGY** advanced technology and state-of-the-art techniques, especially in electronic engineering **2.** DESIGN **PLAIN AND SIMPLE DESIGN** a style of architecture and interior design that makes use of metal, glass, and plastic in a simple utilitarian way —**high-tech** *adj.*

high tech·nol·o·gy *n.* **1.** = **high tech** *n.* 1 **2. MODERN INDUSTRY** the computing and telecommunications industries, collectively

high-ten·sion *adj.* ELEC designed for or operating at high voltage

high-test *adj.* ENERGY = **high octane**

high tide *n.* **1.** GEOG **HIGHEST POINT OF TIDE** the tide at its highest level **2.** NAUT **MOMENT OF HIGHEST TIDE** the time when the tide reaches its highest level **3. PEAK OF SOMETHING** the culmination or high point of something

high-toned *adj.* culturally, morally, or socially superior (*dated*)

high-tops *npl.* sneakers or athletic shoes such as those worn by basketball players that cover the foot up to the ankle

high trea·son *n.* treason against somebody's own country

high-volt·age *adj.* ELEC involving a voltage higher than 650 volts

high wa·ter *n.* GEOG, NAUT **1.** = **high tide** *n.* 1, **high tide** *n.* 2 **2. HIGHEST WATER LEVEL** the highest level reached by any stretch of water, e.g., during a flood (*hyphenated when used before a noun*) **3. TIME OF HIGHEST WATER** the time when the water level of a river or other stretch of water is at its highest

high-wa·ter mark *n.* **1.** GEOG, NAUT **HIGHEST WATER LEVEL** the highest level reached by any natural stretch of water, principally by the sea at high tide, but also, e.g., a river during a flood **2.** GEOG, NAUT **MARK SHOWING HIGHEST LEVEL** a mark drawn to indicate the highest level reached by any natural stretch of water **3. PEAK OF SOMETHING** a high point in an enterprise ○ *Winning the book award was the high-water mark in her career.*

high·way /hī̍ wày/ *n.* **1.** TRANSP **MAIN ROAD** a principal road, especially one that connects towns or cities and is part of a numbered system (*often used before a noun*) **2. DIRECT WAY** a direct route or course ○ *the highway to fame*

high·way·man /hī̍ wàymən/ (*plural* **-men**) *n.* formerly, somebody who forced people traveling by road to stop, usually at gunpoint, and robbed them

high·way pa·trol *n.* the law enforcement agency that patrols the public highways in some states of the United States

high·way rob·ber·y *n.* **1. OVERCHARGING** the charging of inflated prices for goods or services (*informal*) **2. THEFT FROM A TRAVELER** a robbery, usually of a traveler, committed on or near a public road

high wire *n.* a tightrope stretched high above the ground on which circus performers balance and perform acrobatics

high-wire *adj.* holding the possibility of great risk, e.g., to life or reputation

hi·jack /hī̍ jàk/, **high·jack** *vt.* (**-jacked, -jack·ing, -jacks**) **1. SEIZE AIRCRAFT, SHIP, OR TRAIN** to take control of a public transport vehicle, e.g., a passenger aircraft, while in transit, taking the people on board hostage, and diverting it to another destination **2. STOP A VEHICLE TO ROB IT** to seize a motor vehicle, e.g., an armored car carrying money, in order to rob it of its contents **3. STEAL SOMETHING FROM A SEIZED VEHICLE** to steal merchandise, money, or any other items from a hijacked motor vehicle **4. STEAL IDEA** to take somebody else's idea and use it, especially to the exclusion or detriment of the person from whom it was taken (*informal*) ■ *n.* = **hijacking** [Early 20thC. Origin uncertain.] —**hi·jack·er** *n.*

hi·jack·ing /hī̍ jàking/ *n.* the forcible seizure of a public transport vehicle, e.g., a passenger aircraft, while in transit, taking those on board hostage, and compelling diversion of the vehicle to another destination

hi·ji·ki /he jéekee/ (*plural* **-kis** *or* **-ki**), **hi·zi·ki** (*plural* **-kis** *or* **-ki**) *n.* a Japanese seaweed that is sold shredded and dried. When soaked and cooked it has a light, slightly sweet flavor. [Late 20thC. From Japanese.]

hi·jinks *npl.* = **highjinks**

hike /hīk/ *v.* (**hiked, hik·ing, hikes**) **1.** *vti.* **TAKE A LONG WALK** to go for a long walk in the countryside, usually for pleasure **2.** *vti.* MIL **GO ON A TRAINING MARCH** to march in a training exercise **3.** *vt.* **RAISE AMOUNT OF SOMETHING** to increase taxes, prices, or the level or quantity of something suddenly and by a large amount ○ *rumors that the Fed plans to hike interest rates* **4.** *vt.* **PULL SOMETHING UPWARD** to pull or raise something with a sudden strong movement **5.** *vt.* = **snap** *v.* 12 ■ *n.* **1. PLEASURABLE LONG WALK** a long walk, usually in the country for pleasure **2.** MIL **MILITARY MARCH** a long military march, usually as a training exercise **3. SUDDEN LARGE INCREASE IN SOMETHING** a sudden large increase in prices, taxes, or the level or quantity of something ○ *an unexpected hike in interest rates* **4.** = **snap** *n.* 9 [Early 19thC. Origin uncertain: perhaps an alteration of HITCH.] ◇ **take a hike** to leave abruptly, or, more often, used to tell somebody who is unwelcome to leave (*slang*)

hike out *vi.* SAILING to lean backwards over the side of a sailboat to counterbalance the wind in the sails and keep the boat flat in the water

hike up *vti.* to move up or become moved up from the proper position ○ *Her coat had hiked up at the back.*

hik·er /hī̍kər/ *n.* somebody who takes long walks in the country, usually for pleasure

hi·la·hi·la *adj. Hawaii* bashful, shy, or ashamed [From Hawaiian]

Hi·lar·i·on /hi lárree ən/, **St.** (290?–371) Palestinian monk. He was educated in Alexandria, Egypt, where he converted to Christianity. On his return to Palestine, he lived as a hermit in marshes near Gaza.

hi·lar·i·ous /hi láiree əss/ *adj.* causing great amusement [Early 19thC. Formed from Latin *hilaris* "cheerful," from Greek *hilaros*.] —**hi·lar·i·ous·ly** *adv.* —**hi·lar·i·ous·ness** *n.*

WORD KEY: SYNONYMS

See Synonyms at ***funny***.

hi·lar·i·ty /hi lérrətee/ *n.* amusement or merry laughter [15thC. Via French *hilarité* from Latin *hilaritas*, from *hilaris* (see HILARIOUS).]

hill /hil/ *n.* **1. HIGH LAND** an area of land, usually rounded in shape, that is higher than the surrounding land but not as high as a mountain ○ *the hills surrounding Colorado Springs* **2. GRADIENT IN ROAD** a slope or gradient in a road ○ *You'll need to shift down into second gear for this hill.* **3. PILE OF EARTH** a pile of something such as earth **4. GROUP OF PLANTS OR SEEDS** plants or seeds arranged in a cluster rather than planted in rows ○ *a hill of squash* ■ *vt.* (**hilled, hill·ing, hills**) **MAKE EARTH INTO PILE** to pile up earth, especially around the base of plants [Old English *hyll*. Ultimately from an Indo-European word meaning "to be prominent" that is also the ancestor of English *column, culminate*, and *excellent*.] —**hill·er** *n.* ◇ **over the hill** at an age considered too advanced in years for something or supposedly past the prime of life

Hill *n.* Capitol Hill (*informal*) ○ *has worked on the Hill for two years*

Hill /hil/, **Ambrose** (1825–65) U.S. army officer. A Confederate corps commander, he initiated the battle of Gettysburg (1863) and died when his troops were defeated at the Siege of Petersburg (1865). Full name **Ambrose Powell Hill**

Hill, James Jerome (1838–1916) Canadian-born U.S. entrepreneur and financier. He managed and controlled the Great Northern Railway Company (1890–1912).

Hil·la·ry /híllaree/, **Sir Edmund** (*b.* 1919) New Zealand mountaineer and explorer. On May 29, 1953, he and Tenzing Norgay became the first climbers to reach the summit of Mount Everest. Full name **Sir Edmund Perceval Hillary**

hill·bil·ly /híl billee/ (*plural* **-lies**) *n.* a term used by people from the country to describe themselves with pride, but used by others as an insult to mean somebody ignorant and unsophisticated (*informal*) (*offensive in some contexts*) [Early 20thC. *Billy* pet-form of the name *William*.]

hill·bil·ly mu·sic *n.* a variety of country music, especially the music of the Appalachian Mountains, that features fiddles, banjos, guitars, or hammer dulcimers

hill climb *n.* a competition in which automobile or motorcycle drivers compete to set the fastest time in reaching the top of a steep slope

hill·crest /híl krèst/ *n.* the summit or the highest ridge of a hill

Hil·lel (the El·der) /hil el-/ (70? B.C.–A.D. 10?) Jewish rabbi and teacher. He founded a liberal school of scriptural interpretation that influenced later Jewish religious leaders.

Hill·man /hílmən/, **Sidney** (1887–1946) Lithuanian-born U.S. labor leader. A skilled negotiator, he was president of the Amalgamated Clothing Workers of America (1914–46).

hill my·na, **hill my·nah** *n.* a black bird belonging to the starling family and native to southern Asia, often kept as a cage bird because of its ability to mimic human words. Latin name: *Gracula religiosa*.

hill·ock /híllək/ *n.* a small hill or mound —**hill·ocked** *adj.* —**hill·ock·y** *adj.*

Hills·bor·ough /hĭlzbərə, -bərō/ town in northern North Carolina, a site of Patriot resistance before and during the Revolution. Population: 4,263 (1990).

hill·side /hĭl sīd/ *n.* the slope or side of a hill

Hill·side /hĭl sīd/ town in northeastern New Jersey, north of Elizabeth. Population: 21,044 (1990).

hill·top /hĭl tòp/ *n.* the summit of a hill

hill·y /hĭllee/ (**-i·er, -i·est**) *adj.* **1.** WITH MANY HILLS having many hills ○ *hilly countryside* **2.** WITH STEEP SLOPE having a steep incline

Hi·lo /héelō/ city and county seat of the island of Hawaii, situated on the eastern coast of the island. Population: 37,808 (1990).

hilt /hilt/ *n.* the handle of a sword, knife, or dagger [Old English *hilt(e)*. Ultimately from a prehistoric Germanic word that is perhaps also the ancestor of English *helve.*] ◇ **(up) to the hilt** to the maximum

Hil·ton Head /hĭltən héd/ ◊ **Sea Islands**

hi·lum /hī́ləm/ (*plural* **-la** /hī́lə/) *n.* **1.** BOT SCAR ON SEED a scar on the seed of a plant indicating where it was attached to the ovule **2.** ANAT OPENING FOR VESSELS AND NERVES an opening through which blood vessels and nerves enter and leave an organ [Mid-17thC. From Latin, "trifle." The current meanings evolved from the belief that the Latin word originally meant "something that adheres to a bean."]

him /him/; *unstressed* /im/ *pron.* used to refer to a man, boy, or male animal who has been previously mentioned or whose identity is known (*used as the object of a verb or preposition*) ○ *She handed him the phone without a word.* ○ *John closed the door behind him.*

Himalaya

Him·a·la·ya /hìmmə láy ə/, **Him·a·la·yas** /-əz/ mountain system in Asia, forming the northern boundary of the Indian subcontinent. Its highest peak, and the highest mountain in the world, is Mount Everest, 29,028 ft./8,848 m. Length: 1,500 mi./2,414 km. —**Him·a·la·yan** /hìmmə láy ən/ *adj.*

Him·a·la·yan cat *n.* a long-haired cat with the markings of a Siamese cat, bred by crossing a Persian cat with a Siamese cat

Hi·ma·lia /hi maályə/ *n.* a small natural satellite of Jupiter, discovered in 1904. It is approximately 112 mi./180km in diameter. [Late 20thC. Origin uncertain: probably via Greek *himalis*, a name for DEMETER, the goddess of agriculture, fertility, and marriage, from, ultimately, *himalios* "abundant."]

hi·mat·i·on /hi máttee òn, -ən/ *n.* a loose outer garment worn by men and women in ancient Greece, consisting of a large rectangular piece of cloth draped over one shoulder and under the opposite arm [Mid-19thC. From Greek, literally "small garment," formed from *hima* "garment," from *hennunai* "to clothe."]

him/her /hìm ər húr/ *pron.* him or her, used to avoid the sexist use of "him" in reference to somebody whose sex is unknown

Himm·ler /hímmlər/, **Heinrich** (1900–45) German Nazi politician. The head of the Nazi police forces (1936–45), he committed suicide rather than face trial for his part in the Holocaust.

him·self /him sélf/; *unstressed* /im sélf/ CORE MEANING: the form of "him" used in reflexive and emphatic contexts ○ *After a final struggle with himself, he handed the papers over.* ○ *If he himself doesn't know what he's doing, I don't see how I can help her.* ○ *He did it himself.*

pron. **1.** REFERRING TO MALE SUBJECT OF VERB used to refer to the same man, boy, or male animal as the subject of the verb ○ *He decided to treat himself.* ○ *his sense of pride in himself* **2.** USED FOR EMPHASIS used to emphasize or clarify which man, boy, or male animal is being referred to, often introducing a note of surprise or awe ○ *a visit from the Prince himself* **3.** ALONE OR WITHOUT HELP used to show that a man, boy, or male animal is alone or unaided ○ *sitting by himself in a corner* ○ *tied his shoelaces himself* **4.** NORMAL SELF his normal self in terms of personality, health, or behavior ○ *not feeling himself* **5.** *Scotland, Ireland* IMPORTANT MALE PERSON an important, or often self-important, man or boy (*informal*) (*often used ironically*) ○ *Himself is wanting a word.*

Him·yar·ite /hímmyə rīt/ *n.* (*plural* **-ites** *or* **-ite**) MEMBER OF ANCIENT ARABIAN PEOPLE a member of an ancient people who lived in southern parts of the Arabian Peninsula ■ *adj.* RELATING TO HIMYARITES relating to or typical of the Himyarites or their culture [Mid-19thC. Formed from *Himyar*, the name of a legendary king of Yemen.] —**Him·yar·ite** *adj.*

Him·yar·it·ic /hìmmyə ríttik/ *n.* an extinct language spoken by the ancient Himyarites in southwestern Arabia. It belongs to the Semitic branch of the Afro-Asiatic family of African languages. —**Him·yar·it·ic** *adj.*

Hi·na·ya·na /heenə yaánə/ *n.* the form of Buddhism, mainly found in Sri Lanka and Southeast Asia, characterized by adherence to the early Pali scriptures and the nontheistic pursuit of purification through Nirvana [Mid-19thC. From Sanskrit, literally "lesser vehicle." From its fewer followers when compared with MAHAYANA Buddhism.] —**Hi·na·ya·nist** *n.* —**Hi·na·ya·nis·tic** /heenə yaa nístik/ *adj.*

Hinch·in·brook Is·land /hìnchinbrŏŏk-/ island off the northeastern coast of Australia, near the town of Caldwell in northern Queensland. Area: 152 sq. mi./394 sq. km.

Hincks /hingks/, **Sir Francis** (1807–85) Irish-born Canadian colonial administrator. He advocated a bicultural nation and cofounded the Reform Party in 1841.

hind[1] /hīnd/ *adj.* at or forming the back part of an animal ○ *the hind legs of a donkey* [13thC. Origin uncertain: probably a shortening of Old English *behindan* "BEHIND."]

hind[2] /hīnd/ *n.* **1.** FEMALE DEER a female red deer **2.** SPOTTED MARINE FISH a spotted marine fish that is a type of grouper, found in the Atlantic Ocean. Genus: *Epinephelus.* [Old English. Ultimately from an Indo-European word meaning "hornless" that is also the ancestor of English *scant.*]

Hind. *abbr.* **1.** Hindi **2.** Hindu **3.** Hindustan **4.** Hindustani

hind·brain /hīnd brayn/ *n.* the rearmost part of the brain in a vertebrate embryo, which develops into the cerebellum, pons, and medulla oblongata

Hin·den·burg /híndən bùrg/, **Paul von** (1847–1934) Prussian-born German statesman. A general in World War I, he became second president of the German Republic in 1925, and appointed Hitler chancellor in 1933.

Hin·den·burg line /híndən bùrg-/ *n.* a strong defensive line of fortifications built by the German Army near the border with France and Belgium in 1916–17 and breached by an Allied offensive in 1918 [Early 20thC. Named for Paul von HINDENBURG, who devised the plan.]

hin·der[1] /híndər/ *vti.* (**hin·dered, hin·der·ing, hin·ders**) GET IN THE WAY OF to delay or obstruct the development or progress of somebody or something ○ *A heavy snowfall has hindered rescuers' attempts to reach the stranded climbers.* ■ *n.* SPORTS INTERFERENCE WITH BALL in squash and handball, an opponent's accidental interference, preventing fair and unobstructed return of the ball [Old English *hindrian*. Ultimately from a prehistoric Germanic word that is also the ancestor of English *behind*. The underlying idea is of keeping something or somebody behind.] —**hin·der·er** *n.*

WORD KEY: SYNONYMS

hinder, block, hamper, hold back, impede, obstruct

CORE MEANING: to put difficulties in the way of progress

hinder to delay or slow down the progress of something, either accidentally or by deliberate interference; **block** to cause a complete stoppage of progress; **hamper** to create or cause restraints or obstacles that may make action or progress extremely difficult; **hold back** an expression used to describe the prevention or restriction of the advance of somebody or something; **impede** a fairly formal word used to describe the prevention of progress, usually to a greater extent than is suggested by "hinder" or "hamper"; **obstruct** used to suggest a serious delay in action or progress to a much greater extent than "hinder," and often, like "block," a complete stoppage.

hind·er[2] /hīndər/ *adj. U.K.* at or toward the rear of something ○ *at the hinder end of the conference* [Old English. Origin uncertain: perhaps a shortening of Old English *hinderweard* "backward."]

Hin·di /híndee/ *n.* an official language of India that developed from a literary form of Hindustani and is widely used as a lingua franca in many parts of the world. Of the Midland subgroup of the Indic group of the Indo-Iranian branch of Indo-European, Hindi is spoken by about 200 million native speakers, and by about 700 million people as a second language. [Early 19thC. From Urdu *hindī*, from *Hind* "India."] —**Hin·di** *adj.*

hind·most /hīnd mōst/ *adj.* farthest back or last (*dated*)

hind·quar·ter /hīnd kwàwrtər/ *n.* BACK PART OF CARCASS either of the two back quarters of a carcass of beef, lamb, veal, or mutton consisting of one leg and one or two ribs ■ **hind·quar·ters** *npl.* REAR OF FOUR-LEGGED ANIMAL the hind legs and adjoining parts of a four-legged animal

hin·drance /híndrəns/ *n.* **1.** SOMETHING IN THE WAY somebody or something that prevents or makes it difficult for somebody to do something **2.** OBSTRUCTION OF PROGRESS the act of obstructing progress

hind·sight /hīnd sīt/ *n.* the ability or opportunity to understand and judge an event or experience after it has occurred ○ *easy to say with the benefit of hindsight*

Hin·du /híndoo/ *n.* **1.** FOLLOWER OF HINDUISM somebody who practices the religion of Hinduism **2.** SOMEBODY FROM HINDUSTAN somebody who was born in or raised in the Indian region of Hindustan ■ *adj.* **1.** OF HINDUISM relating to or following Hinduism **2.** OF HINDUS OR THEIR CULTURE relating to or typical of Hindus or their culture **3.** RELATING TO INDIA OR ITS PEOPLE relating to or found in India, especially Hindustan, or its people or culture [Mid-17thC. Via Urdu from Persian *Hindū*, from *Hind* "India."]

Hin·du·ism /híndoo ìzzəm/ *n.* the religion of India and the oldest of the worldwide religions, characterized by a belief in reincarnation and the essential unity of forms and theories. Hinduism has a large pantheon of gods and goddesses, and traditionally had a caste system.

Hin·du Kush /híndoo kŏŏsh, hin dŏŏ-/ mountain system in central Asia mainly in Afghanistan but extending into Jammu and Kashmir. The highest peak is Tirich Mir, 25,230 ft./7,690 m. Length: 500 mi./800 km.

Hin·du·stan /híndoo staán/ *n.* a loosely defined term that usually refers to the northern Hindi-speaking region of India, stretching from the Himalayas southward to the Deccan and from Assam in the east to Punjab in the west. The term is sometimes used to indicate the Ganges Plain, or sometimes the whole of India or the Indian subcontinent.

Hin·du·sta·ni /híndoo stánee/ *n.* GROUP OF INDIAN LANGUAGES a group of Indian languages and dialects that includes all forms of both Urdu and Hindi ■ *adj.* **1.** RELATING TO HINDUSTAN relating to Hindustan or its language, people, or culture **2.** LANGUAGE OF HINDUSTANI relating to the group of languages and dialects that includes all forms of both Urdu and Hindi [Early 17thC. Via Urdu from Persian *Hindūstānī*, literally "of the Indian country."]

Hine /hīn/, **Lewis** (1874–1940) U.S. photographer. His works show a concern for social justice, frequently depicting subjects such as child laborers in sweatshops and mines. Full name **Lewis Wickes Hine**

Hines /hīnz/, **Earl** (1905–83) U.S. musician. A jazz pianist, he formed his own band (1928) and collaborated with Charlie Parker, Dizzie Gillespie, and Louis Armstrong. Full name **Earl Kenneth Hines**. Known as **Fatha Hines**

Hines, Gregory (*b.* 1946) U.S. dancer and actor. A skilled tap dancer, he is known for his appearances in the musicals *Sophisticated Ladies* (1981) and *Jelly's Last Jam* (1992).

Hines·ville /hínzvil/ city in southeastern Georgia. Population: 21,603 (1990).

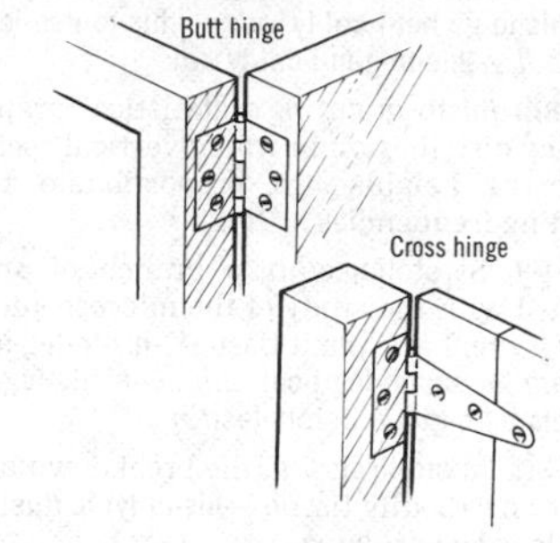

Hinge

hinge /hinj/ (**hinged, hing·ing, hing·es**) *n.* **1. JOINT THAT FASTENS DOOR TO FRAME** a movable joint of metal or plastic used to fasten two things, e.g., a box and its lid, together and allow one of them to pivot ○ *The hinges on the door need oiling.* **2.** ZOOL **LIGAMENT FOR PIVOTING** a part in animals that operates like a hinge, as does the ligament that opens and closes the two halves of a clam or other bivalve mollusk **3.** ANAT = **hinge joint 4. SOMETHING VITAL TO OUTCOME** something on which a subsequent action or an outcome depends **5. STICKY PAPER STRIP** a thin gummed paper strip that is folded in half to affix postage stamps to the pages of an album [13thC. Origin uncertain: probably from a prehistoric Germanic word that is also the ancestor of English *hang*.] —**hinge·less** *adj.*

hinge on *vt.* to depend completely on something ○ *The success of the plan hinges on your full cooperation.*

hinge joint *n.* a joint, e.g., a knee or elbow joint, that allows movement in only one plane. Technical name **ginglymus**

Hing·ham /híngəm/ coastal town in eastern Massachusetts southeast of Boston, first settled about 1633. Population: 20,265 (1996).

hin·ny /hínnee/ (*plural* **-nies**) *n.* the offspring of a stallion and a female donkey [Early 17thC. Via Latin *hinnus* from Greek *(g)innos*.]

Hins·dale /hínz dayl/ village in northeast Illinois, northeast of Downers Grove, a western suburb of Chicago. Population: 16,353 (1996).

hint /hint/ *vi.* (**hint·ed, hint·ing, hints**) **SUGGEST SOMETHING INDIRECTLY** to convey an idea or information in a roundabout way ○ *The President hinted that he might not seek a second term.* ■ *n.* **1. INDIRECT SUGGESTION** an idea or information conveyed in a roundabout way ○ *Our daughter has been dropping hints that she'd like a guitar for her birthday.* **2. PIECE OF ADVICE** a useful piece of advice, or a practical suggestion ○ *The book had lots of useful hints on how to grow vegetables.* **3. VERY SMALL AMOUNT** an amount or trace of something that is so small that it can only just be noticed ○ *The walls need a hint of yellow.* [Early 17thC. Origin uncertain: probably an alteration of obsolete *hent* "grasp." Originally meaning "opportunity," the underlying idea is of something that may be seized.] —**hint·ing·ly** *adv.* ◇ **take the hint** to understand what is being implied or suggested and to act accordingly

hin·ter·land /híntər lànd/ *n.* **1. REMOTE COUNTRY REGION** a region that is remote from cities or their cultural influence **2. LAND ADJACENT TO WATER** the land that lies next to coastline or a river [Late 19thC. From German, from *hinter* "behind" + *Land* "land."]

hip¹ /hip/ *n.* **1. SIDE OF BODY BELOW WAIST** the region on either side of the body between the waist and the thigh **2.** = **hip joint 3.** ARCHIT **ROOF ANGLE** the angle formed where two adjacent sides of a sloping roof meet [Old English *hype*. Ultimately from a prehistoric Germanic word that is also the ancestor of German *Hüfte* "hip."]

hip² /hip/ (**hip·per, hip·pest**) *adj.* aware of and influenced by the latest fashions in clothes, music, or ideas (*slang*) ○ *He is one hip dude.* [Early 20thC. Alteration of earlier HEP, of uncertain origin: perhaps from Wolof *hepi* "to be aware."] —**hip·ly** *adv.* —**hip·ness** *n.* ◇ **be hip to something** to be aware of something that is going on (*informal*)

hip³ /hip/ *n.* = **rose hip** [Old English *hēope*. Ultimately from an Indo-European word meaning "thorn."]

HIP *abbr.* health insurance plan

hip·bone /híp bōn/ *n.* either of the two large bones forming the sides of the pelvis and made up of the ilium, ischium, and pubis, fused together in adults. Technical name **innominate bone**

hip boot *n.* a boot reaching to the hip, usually worn by people who fish

hip flask *n.* a small flat metal flask, usually containing an alcoholic beverage, that can be carried in a pocket (*dated*)

hip hip hoo·ray *interj.* used as a cheer to express joy or approval of somebody or something [*Hip* of unknown origin]

hip-hop *n.* a form of popular culture that started in the United States in the 1980s in African American inner-city areas. Its elements include rap music, graffiti art, and breakdancing. [From HIP²]

hip-hug·gers *npl.* pants that end at the hips instead of the waist

hip joint *n.* the joint formed between the head of the thigh bone and the hipbone

hip·pe·as·trum /hìppee ástrəm/ *n.* a plant belonging to the daffodil family and native to Central and South America, often grown for its huge red or pink funnel-shaped flowers. Genus: *Hippeastrum.* ◊ **amaryllis** [Early 19thC. From modern Latin, formed from Greek *hippeus* "horseman" + *astron* "star."]

hipped¹ /hipt/ *adj.* having hips, especially of a particular kind (*usually used in combination*) ○ *narrow-hipped*

hipped² /hipt/ *adj.* preoccupied or obsessed with something ○ *She's just hipped on clothes.* [Early 20thC. Formed from HIP².]

hipped roof *n.* = **hip roof**

hip·pie /híppee/, **hip·py** (*plural* **-pies**) *n.* a young person, especially in the 1960s, who rejected accepted social and political values and proclaimed a belief in universal peace and love. Hippies often dressed unconventionally, lived communally, and used psychedelic drugs. (*informal*) [Mid-20thC. Formed from HIP².] —**hip·pie·dom** *n.* —**hip·pie·hood** *n.* —**hip·pie·ness** *n.*

hip·po /híppō/ (*plural* **-pos**) *n.* a hippopotamus (*informal*) [Late 19thC. Shortening.]

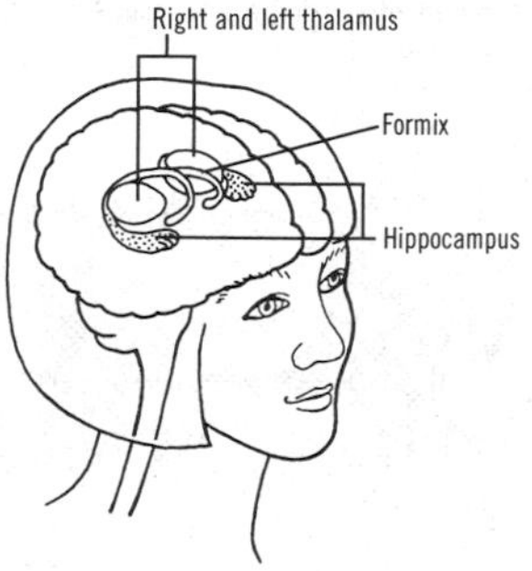

Hippocampus

hip·po·cam·pus /hìppə kámpəss/ (*plural* **-pi** /-pī/) *n.* **1.** MYTHOL **SEA CREATURE IN MYTHS** a mythological sea creature with the head and forelegs of a horse and the tail of a fish **2.** ANAT **AREA OF BRAIN ASSOCIATED WITH MEMORY** either of two curved ridges of tissue in the brain, located in the floor of the cavity (**ventricle**) within each of the cerebral hemispheres and concerned with basic drives, emotions, and short-term memory. Together with the hypothalamus, the hippocampi and their connections form part of the limbic system. [Late 16thC. Via Latin from Greek *hippokampos*, from *hippos* (see HIPPO-) + *kampos* "sea monster."] —**hip·po·cam·pal** *adj.*

hip·po·cras /híppə kràss/ *n.* a medieval drink of spiced wine sweetened with honey [14thC. Via Old French *hypocras* from medieval Latin *(vinum) Hippocraticum*, literally "(wine of) Hippocrates." Named for HIPPOCRATES, because he supposedly invented the filter used for straining the wine.]

Hip·poc·ra·tes /hi pókrə teez/ (460?–377? BC) Greek physician. Known as the father of medicine, he gave his name to the Hippocratic Oath. —**Hip·po·crat·ic** /hìppə kráttik/ *adj.*

Hip·po·crat·ic oath *n.* an oath taken by newly graduated physicians to observe the ethical standards of their profession, specifically to seek to preserve life [Because Hippocrates was the supposed author of such an oath]

hip·po·drome /híppə drōm/ *n.* **1. STADIUM USED FOR HORSE-RACING** an open-air stadium in ancient Greece or Rome with an oval track that was used for horse or chariot racing **2. ARENA FOR HORSES** an arena for equestrian events [Late 16thC. Via French and Latin from Greek *hippodromos*, from *hippos* (see HIPPO-) + *dromos* "racecourse."]

hip·po·griff /híppə grìf/ *n.* a monster from Greek mythology with the body of a horse and the head, wings, and claws of a griffin [Mid-17thC. Via French *hippogriffe* from Italian *ippogrifo*, from Greek *hippos* (see HIPPO-) + Italian *grifo* "GRIFFIN."]

Hip·pol·y·ta /hi páwlətə/ *n.* in Greek mythology, a queen of the Amazons. The daughter of Ares, the god of war, she was killed by Hercules when, as one of his labors, he took her girdle.

Hippopotamus

hip·po·pot·a·mus /hìppə póttəməss/ (*plural* **-mus·es** *or* **-mi** /-mī/) *n.* a large amphibious mammal of the rivers of eastern equatorial Africa that has a large head with a wide mouth, short legs, and a thick gray skin. Latin name: ***Hippopotamus amphibius***. [Mid-16thC. Via Latin from Greek *hippopotamos*, from *hippos* "horse" + *potamos* "river."]

hip·py¹ /híppee/ (**-pi·er, -pi·est**) *adj.* having wide hips

hip·py² /híppee/ *n.* = **hippie**

hip roof *n.* a roof with sloping ends as well as sides

hip shoot·er *n.* somebody who thinks and moves quickly, often making rash decisions (*slang*) ○ *The auto company CEO is very able, but he's a hip shooter who has made some avoidable mistakes.* [(See HIP-SHOOTING)]

hip-shoot·ing *adj.* **HASTY** too quick to take action or make decisions (*slang*) ■ *n.* **HASTINESS** taking action or making decisions hastily (*slang*) [The underlying idea is of shooting without taking formal aim]

hip·ster /hípstər/ *n.* somebody who is up-to-date with the latest fashions in music, clothes, and social attitudes, especially somebody who is interested in modern jazz (*dated slang*) [Formed from HIP² + -STER]

hip·ster·ism /hípstər ìzzəm/ *n.* the quality of being hip (*dated slang*)

hip·sters /hípstərz/ *npl. U.K.* = **hip-huggers** [Formed frm HIP¹ + -STER]

hi·ra·ga·na /heèrə gaánə/ *n.* a cursive set of symbols used by the Japanese primarily for inflections. ◊ **kana, katakana** [Early 19thC. From Japanese, literally "plain syllabary."]

hire /hīr/ *v.* (**hired, hir·ing, hires**) **1.** *vti.* **GIVE SOMEBODY WORK** to employ somebody to work for you, or pay somebody to do a job for you **2.** *vt.* **PAY FOR THE USE OF SOMETHING** to rent something from somebody for a period of time ○ *hired the Women's Club for the wedding reception* ■ *n.* **1. ACT OF HIRING SOMETHING OR SOMEBODY** the activity of renting something to somebody or of making the services of somebody available to another for pay **2. EMPLOYEE** somebody who is employed [Old English *hȳr*. Ultimately from a prehistoric Germanic word that is also the ancestor of German *Heuer* "sailor's wages."] —**hir·a·ble** *adj.*

hire on *vti.* to obtain work, or provide work for somebody ○ *He hired on as an oil rig wildcatter.*

hire out *vt.* to rent something to somebody, or make the services of somebody available to another for pay

hired gun *n.* (*slang*) **1. PROFESSIONAL KILLER** a professional killer **2. PROBLEM SOLVER** an expert brought in to solve a particularly complex or intractable problem ○ *The* *law firm brought in a hired gun from New York to handle the cross-examination of the prosecution's genetics expert*.

hired hand *n.* a paid employee, usually on a farm or ranch

hire·ling /hīrling/ *n.* somebody who works only for money, especially somebody who will do menial or unpleasant tasks (*disapproving*)

hire pur·chase *n. U.K.* = **installment plan**

hi-res /hī réz/ *adj.* high-resolution and therefore showing a lot of detail (*informal*) ○ *a hi-res graphic* [Shortening]

Hi·ri Mo·tu /heèri mṓ toò/ *n.* a pidginized form of Motu that has now acquired the status of one of the official languages of Papua New Guinea. Hiri Motu is spoken by about 150,000 people. —**Hi·ri Mo·tu** *adj.*

hir·ing hall *n.* a union-operated employment agency where registered applicants are given jobs on a seniority basis or by rotation

Hi·ro·hi·to /heèrō heétō/, **Emperor of Japan** (1901–89). His reign (1926–89) was the longest in Japanese history. He renounced the belief that Japanese rulers are divine at the end of World War II (1945) and oversaw the transition to a constitutional monarchy.

Hi·ro·shi·ma /hi róshimə, hìrrə sheémə/ city in southwestern Honshu, Japan, devastated by the first atomic bomb to be used in war, August 1945. Population: 1,085,705 (1990).

hir·sute /húr soòt, heér-, hər soót/ *adj.* **1.** PHYSIOL **WITH A LOT OF HAIR** having a large amount of hair ○ *a hirsute young man* **2.** BOT **COVERED WITH STIFF HAIRS** used to describe a plant or plant part covered with long stiff hairs ○ *a hirsute leaf* [Early 17thC. From Latin *hirsutus* "shaggy."] —**hir·sute·ness** *n.*

hir·sut·ism /húr soo tìzzəm, heér-, hər soó tìzzəm/ *n.* an abnormal growth of hair, e.g., on a woman's face or body

hir·u·din /heérəd'n, hi roód'n/ *n.* a substance produced by the salivary glands of leeches that prevents blood from clotting [Early 20thC. Formed from Latin *hirudo* "leech."]

his (*stressed*) /hiz/; (*unstressed*) /iz/ *adj., pron.* indicates something belonging or relating to a man, boy, or male animal who has been previously mentioned or whose identity is known ○ *He stood at the sink washing his hands.* ○ *The fault was all his.* ○ *I went to school with a cousin of his.*

His·an /hì sán/ city and capital of Shaanxi province, central China, situated on the southern bank of the Wei approximately 80 mi./130 km above its junction with the Huang

his/her /hìz ər húr/ *pron.* his or her, used to avoid the sexist use of "his" in reference to somebody whose sex is unknown

His·pan·ic /hi spánnik/ *n.* = **Hispanic American** ■ *adj.* **1. OF SPAIN AND SPANISH PEOPLE** relating to or typical of Spain, or its people or culture **2. OF SPANISH-SPEAKING PEOPLE** relating to or typical of Spanish-speaking people or their culture **3. OF PEOPLE OF SPANISH DESCENT** relating to or typical of people descended from Spanish or Latin American people or their culture [Late 16thC. From Latin *Hispanicus*, from *Hispania* "Spain."]

His·pan·ic A·mer·i·can *n.* somebody who was born in or is a citizen of the United States and who is of Spanish or Latin American descent —**His·pan·ic-A·mer·i·can** *adj.*

His·pan·i·cism /hi spánni sìzzəm/ *n.* a Spanish word, expression, or other linguistic feature that has been adopted into another language

His·pan·i·cist /hi spánnissist/ *n.* a scholar of the languages and cultures of Spain and Spanish-speaking countries

His·pan·i·cize /hi spánni sìz/ (**-cized, -ciz·ing, -ciz·es**) *vt.* to make somebody or something Spanish in character, style, or culture —**His·pan·i·ci·za·tion** /hi spànnəssi záysh'n/ *n.*

His·pan·ism /híspənìzəm/ *n.* = **Hispanicism** [Mid-20thC. Formed from Latin *Hispania* "Spain."]

His·pa·nist /híspənist/ *n.* = **Hispanicist**

His·pa·no /hi spánnō, hi spaánō/ (*plural* **-nos**) *n.* **1. DESCENDANT OF SPANIARDS** somebody of Spanish descent who lives in the southwestern United States. Many Hispanos are descended from people who lived in the region before its annexation by the United States. **2.** = **Hispanic** *adj.* 1 [Mid-20thC. Shortening of HISPANO AMERICAN.]

His·pa·no A·mer·i·can /hi spànnō ə mérrəkən, hi spaànō-, hìspənō-/ *n.* = **Hispanic American** —**His·pa·no-A·mer·i·can** *adj.*

his·pid /híspid/ *adj.* rough, especially covered with stiff hairs or bristles ○ *a hispid leaf* [Mid-17thC. From Latin *hispidus.*] —**his·pid·i·ty** /his píddətee/ *n.*

hiss /hiss/ *v.* (**hissed, hiss·ing, hiss·es**) **1.** *vi.* **MAKE "S" SOUND** to make a sound like a loud continuous "s" ○ *the sound of car tires hissing over a wet road* **2.** *vti.* **SHOW NEGATIVE OPINION OF SOMETHING** to show disapproval or dislike of somebody or something, e.g., a performance, by making a hissing sound **3.** *vti.* **WHISPER LOUDLY** to whisper loudly and angrily ○ *"Stop biting your nails," she hissed.* ■ *n.* **1. SOUND LIKE "S"** a sound like a loud continuous "s" ○ *the hiss of escaping air* **2. SOUND EXPRESSING DISAPPROVAL** a hissing sound used to express disapproval or dislike of something or somebody [14thC. An imitation of the sound.] —**hiss·er** *n.*

Hiss /hiss/, **Alger** (*b.* 1904) U.S. lawyer and government official. A former senior State Department official, he was accused by Whittaker Chambers (1948) of spying for the Soviet Union, and imprisoned for perjury despite his protestations of innocence.

his·self /hiss sélf/; *unstressed* /iss sélf/ *pron.* = **himself** (*nonstandard*)

his·sy fit /híssee-/ *n. Southern U.S.* a temper tantrum [*Hissy* of uncertain origin: perhaps a shortening and alteration of HYSTERICAL]

hist. *abbr.* **1.** histology **2.** historic **3.** historical **4.** history

hist- *prefix.* = **histo-** (*used before vowels*)

his·tam·i·nase /hi stámmi nàyss, hístəmi-, -nàyz/ *n.* an enzyme found in the digestive system that inactivates histamine and certain diamines

his·ta·mine /hístə meèn/ *n.* an amine compound released by cells of the body's immune system in allergic reactions that causes irritation, contraction of smooth muscle, stimulation of gastric secretions, and dilation of blood vessels. Formula: $C_5H_9N_3$. [Early 20thC. A blend of HISTIDINE and AMINE.] —**his·ta·min·ic** /hìstə mínnik/ *adj.*

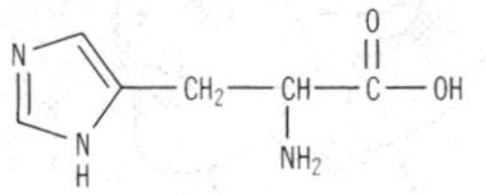

Histidine

his·ti·dine /hísti deèn/ *n.* an essential amino acid involved in the growth and repair of tissues and important as the iron-binding site for hemoglobin. Formula: $C_6H_9N_3O_2$.

his·ti·o·cyte /hístee ə sīt/ *n.* a large immobile scavenging cell (**macrophage**) found in connective tissue —**his·ti·o·cyt·ic** /hìstee ə síttik/ *adj.*

histo- *prefix.* living tissue ○ *histochemistry* [From Greek *histos* "web"; related to *histanai* "to set up" (see APOSTASY)]

his·to·chem·is·try /hìstō kémmistree/ *n.* the biochemistry of cells and tissues —**his·to·chem·i·cal** *adj.* —**his·to·chem·i·cal·ly** *adv.*

his·to·com·pat·i·bil·i·ty /hìstō kəm pattə bíllətee/ *n.* the degree of similarity between certain antigens (**histocompatibility antigens**) that determines the degree of success of a tissue graft or blood transfusion —**his·to·com·pat·i·ble** /hìstō kəm páttəb'l/ *adj.*

his·to·com·pat·i·bil·i·ty an·ti·gen *n.* an antigen occurring on the surface of tissue cells that is used in self-identification and determines the acceptance of a tissue graft or blood transfusion

his·to·di·al·y·sis /hìstō dī álləssəs/ *n.* = **histolysis**

his·to·gen·e·sis /hìstō jénnəssiss/ *n.* the formation and development of tissues and organs from undifferentiated cells —**his·to·ge·net·ic** /hìstōjə néttik/ *adj.* —**his·to·ge·net·i·cal·ly** *adv.* —**his·to·gen·ic** /hìstə jénnik/ *adj.* —**his·to·gen·i·cal·ly** *adv.*

his·to·gram /hístə gràm/ *n.* a statistical graph of a frequency distribution in which vertical rectangles of different heights are proportionate to corresponding frequencies

his·tol·o·gy /hi stóllәjee/ *n.* a branch of anatomy concerned with the study of the microscopic structures of animal and plant tissue —**his·to·log·ic** /hìstə lójjik/ *adj.* —**his·to·log·i·cal** *adj.* —**his·to·log·i·cal·ly** *adv.* —**his·tol·o·gist** /hi stólləjəst/ *n.*

his·tol·y·sis /hi stóllississ/ *n.* the breakdown and disintegration of bodily tissue —**his·to·lyt·ic** /hìstə líttik/ *adj.* —**his·to·lyt·i·cal·ly** *adv.*

his·tone /heé stōn/ *n.* a protein whose molecules organize and pack the DNA in chromosomes into the greatly condensed form (**chromatin**) it normally adopts. There are five types, together constituting about half the mass of chromosomes. [Late 19thC. From German *Histon*, of uncertain origin: perhaps from Greek *histanai* or from *histos* (see HISTO-).]

his·to·pa·thol·o·gy /hìstōpə thóllәjee/ *n.* a branch of pathology concerned with the study of the microscopic changes in diseased tissues —**his·to·path·o·log·ic** /hìstō pathə lójjik/ *adj.* —**his·to·path·o·log·i·cal** *adj.* —**his·to·path·o·log·i·cal·ly** *adv.* —**his·to·pa·thol·o·gist** /hìstō pə thólləjist/ *n.*

his·to·phys·i·ol·o·gy /hìstō fizee ólləjee/ *n.* a branch of physiology concerned with the structure and function of tissues —**his·to·phys·i·o·log·ic** /hìstō fizee ə lójjik/ *adj.* —**his·to·phys·i·o·log·i·cal** *adj.*

his·to·plas·mo·sis /h-stō plaz mōssiss/ *n.* a severe disease of the lungs with symptoms resembling flu, caused by the fungus *Histoplasma capsulatum* [Early 20thC. Formed from modern Latin *Histoplasma*, genus name.]

his·to·ri·an /hi stáwree ən/ *n.* **1. STUDENT AND SCHOLAR OF HISTORY** somebody who is knowledgeable in history and who may write about or teach it **2. RECORDER OF EVENTS** somebody who writes an account of historical events [15thC. From French *historien*, from Latin *historia*, on the model of *logicien* "logician" (see HISTORY).]

his·to·ri·at·ed /hi stáwree àytəd/ *adj.* used to describe decorative initials in books or maps and plans that are illustrated with symbolic flowers and animals or symbols in the form of flowers or animals [Late 19thC. Directly or via French from medieval Latin *historiare* "to adorn (with historical scenes), relate," from Latin *historia* (see HISTORY).]

his·tor·ic /hi stáwrik/ *adj.* **1. SIGNIFICANT IN HISTORY** important in or affecting the course of history ○ *a historic decision affecting world peace* **2.** = **historical** *adj.* 1

his·tor·i·cal /hi stáwrik'l/ *adj.* **1. EXISTING OR HAPPENING IN THE PAST** existing, happening, or relating to the past ○ *an important historical personage* **2. USED IN THE PAST** worn or used by people in the past ○ *historical uniforms of the 18th century* **3. SUPPORTED BY FACTS FROM HISTORY** based on or describing people who lived in the past or events that happened in the past ○ *historical fiction* ○ *a historical movie* **4. RELATING TO STUDY OF HISTORY** relating to or involving the study of history **5. RELATING TO THE EVOLUTION OF PHENOMENA** relating to the gradual change and development of phenomena, e.g., languages or societies ○ *historical sociology* —**his·tor·i·cal·ness** *n.*

his·tor·i·cal ge·ol·o·gy *n.* a branch of geology that deals with the geological history of the earth

his·tor·i·cal lin·guis·tics *n.* the study of language as it changes and develops through time

his·tor·i·cal·ly /hi stáwriklee/ *adv.* **1. REGARDING HISTORY** according to or with reference to history or its course ○ *The law will prove to be historically significant.* **2. MANY TIMES BEFORE** used to indicate that something has happened often in the past ○ *Historically, a rise in interest rates slows the rate of inflation.*

his·tor·i·cal ma·te·ri·al·ism *n.* the part of Marx's theory of dialectical materialism that maintains that the development of social thought and institutions is based on material economic forces

his·tor·i·cal nov·el *n.* a novel set in the past that includes real events and people from that period

his·tor·i·cal pres·ent *n.* the present tense used to narrate actions that happened in the past to make them seem more vivid

his·tor·i·cism /hi stáwrə sìzzəm/ *n.* **1. THEORY THAT NATURAL LAWS GOVERN HISTORY** the belief that natural laws beyond human control determine historical events **2. BELIEF IN UNIQUENESS OF HISTORICAL PERIODS** the theory that each period of history has its own unique beliefs and values and can only be understood in its historical context —**his·tor·i·cist** *n.*

his·to·ric·i·ty /hìstə rissítee/ *n.* the state or fact of being historically authentic

his·tor·i·cize /hi stáwrə sīz/ (**-cized, -ciz·ing, -ciz·es**) *vt.* to give something the appearance of historical truth —**his·tor·i·ci·za·tion** /hi stàwrəssi záysh'n/ *n.*

his·to·ri·og·ra·phy /hi stàwree óggrəfee/ *n.* **1. METHODS OF HISTORICAL RESEARCH** the principles, theories, or methods of historical research or writing **2. THE WRITING OF HISTORY** the writing of history based on scholarly disciplines such as the analysis and evaluation of source materials **3. AVAILABLE DATA ON HISTORICAL TOPIC** the existing findings and interpretations relating to a particular historical topic **4. HISTORICAL LITERATURE** a body of historical literature [Mid-16thC. Via medieval Latin from Greek *historiographia*, from *historia* (see HISTORY) + *graphia* "writing."] —**his·to·ri·o·graph·ic** /hi stàwree ə gráffik/ *n.* —**his·to·ri·o·graph·i·cal** *adj.* —**his·to·ri·o·graph·i·cal·ly** *adv.*

his·to·ry /hístəree/ (*plural* **-ries**) *n.* **1. WHAT HAS HAPPENED IN THE PAST** the past events of a period in time or in the life or development of a people, an institution, or a place **2. STUDY OF THE PAST** the branch of knowledge that records and analyzes past events **3. RECORD OF EVENTS** a chronological account of past events of a period or in the life or development of a people, an institution, or a place ○ *a history of Byzantium* **4. PERSONAL BACKGROUND** the events and experiences of an individual's past ○ *We don't know very much about her personal history.* **5.** SCI **SYSTEMATIC RECORD OF NATURAL PHENOMENA** an account of related natural phenomena based on observation and investigation ○ *a history of volcanoes* **6. INTERESTING PAST** an interesting or colorful past ○ *The car has something of a history attached to it.* **7. SOMETHING NO LONGER IMPORTANT** something that belongs to the past and is no longer important ○ *The scandal is history, as far as I'm concerned.* **8. SOMEBODY NO LONGER IMPORTANT** somebody who has suffered total loss of power, high position, or importance (*slang*) ○ *If he's found guilty of bribery, he's history as far as the Senate is concerned.* **9.** LITERAT **HISTORICAL PLAY** a play that deals with historical events **10.** LITERAT **LIFE STORY** a narrative that deals with the events of a fictional character's life (*archaic*) [15thC. Via Latin from Greek *historia* "history, knowledge, narrative" (source of English *story*), from *histōr* "learned man."] ◇ **be ancient history** to be something that happened a long time ago, or perhaps only recently in the past, and is no longer important or relevant

his·tri·on·ic /hìstree ónnik/, **his·tri·on·i·cal** /-ónnik'l/ *adj.* **1. OVERDRAMATIC** overdramatic in reaction or behavior ○ *Paul gave a histrionic sigh and slumped in his chair.* **2.** THEATER **RELATING TO ACTING** relating to acting or actors (*formal*) [Mid-17thC. From late Latin *histrionicus*, from the Latin stem *histrion-* "actor."] —**his·tri·on·i·cal·ly** *adv.*

his·tri·on·ics /hìstree ónniks/ *n.* **OVERDONE EMOTION** exaggerated emotional behavior done for show or to get a reaction from somebody (*takes a singular or plural verb*) ○ *Let's hope there won't be any histrionics when you tell them.* ■ *npl.* THEATER **DRAMATIC PERFORMANCES** performances of dramatic works (*formal*) (*takes a plural verb*)

hit /hit/ *v.* (**hit, hit·ting, hits**) **1.** *vti.* **STRIKE SOMEBODY OR SOMETHING DELIBERATELY** to strike somebody or something deliberately with the hand or something held in it ○ *He hit me on the jaw.* **2.** *vti.* **COME INTO CONTACT** to come into violent contact with something ○ *His van skidded and hit a parked car.* **3.** *vt.* SPORTS **MAKE BALL MOVE** to make something such as a ball move by striking it with a bat or racket ○ *She kept hitting the ball over the fence into the next yard.* **4.** *vt.* **STRIKE BUTTON OR KEY** to press or push a button or part of a machine (*informal*) ○ *Hit the accelerator.* **5.** *vt.* BASEBALL **MAKE BASE HIT** to make a base hit ○ *hit a double* **6.** *vi.* BASEBALL **BAT** to be at bat **7.** *vt.* **STRIKE TARGET** to reach an intended target with a ball or missile **8.** *vt.* **REACH A PLACE** to reach a particular place (*slang*) ○ *You'll hit a toll-free road about five miles farther on.* **9.** *vt.* **ARRIVE AT SPECIFIED LEVEL** to reach a particular level on a scale ○ *Unemployment has hit the two million mark.* **10.** *vi.* **HAPPEN** to take place, usually with undesirable or adverse effects (*informal*) ○ *The storm hit before we could get home.* **11.** *vt.* **PRODUCE SOMETHING ACCURATELY** to render or represent something accurately ○ *hit a high C* **12.** *vti.* **COME TO MIND** to realize or become conscious of something ○ *It suddenly hit him that he was unlikely to see her again.* **13.** *vt.* **AFFECT SOMEBODY OR SOMETHING BADLY** to have an adverse effect on somebody or something ○ *The rise in interest rates is going to hit exporters hard.* **14.** *vt.* **GIVE SOMEBODY INFORMATION** to tell somebody something that may be of interest (*slang*) ○ *"I've got a great idea. Want to hear it?" "OK, hit me. I'm listening."* **15.** *vt.* **CONFORM TO SOMETHING** to conform to or agree with something ○ *Your comments hit a sympathetic chord.* **16.** *vt.* CRIMINOL **EMPLOY SOMEBODY TO KILL SOMEBODY** to murder somebody, especially by employing a professional killer (*slang*) **17.** *vt.* **GIVE SOMEBODY SOMETHING** to give somebody something, e.g., a drink or a card in the game of twenty-one (*slang*) **18.** *vi.* MIL **ATTACK** to launch an attack on something or somebody ○ *The troops hit before daylight.* **19.** *vt.* SPORTS **MAKE A SCORE WITH BALL** to score points in a sport by striking a ball well or delivering it successfully to a target ○ *She hit the first goal in the second minute of the game.* **20.** *vi.* CARS **IGNITE AND START** to ignite the fuel and air mixture in the cylinders (*refers to internal combustion engines*) ○ *The engine finally hit and we could leave.* = **base hit 21.** *vt.* **VIEW WEB PAGE** to visit or view a particular Web page (*informal*) ■ *n.* **1.** BASEBALL = **base hit 2. SUCCESS** somebody who or something that is popular and successful ○ *That rock band had a big hit with its last CD.* ○ *The clown was a hit with the kids.* **3. SOMETHING THAT HITS TARGET** a ball or missile that successfully strikes the target ○ *We've taken a couple of hits, but nothing serious.* **4. HARD BLOW** a hard blow delivered with the hand or something held in it ○ *That was some hit.* **5. COLLISION** a violent impact between things **6.** COMPUT **ACCESSING OF DATABASE OR INTERNET FILE** an instance of a user retrieving an item from a database or contacting a file, e.g., a home page, through the Internet ○ *Her home page has received 3,000 hits since she opened it last month.* **7. SOMETHING GIVEN** a single item given or taken, e.g., a drink or a card at the game of twenty-one (*slang*) **8.** DRUGS **EFFECT OF DRUG** a sense of a drug's effect (*slang*) **9.** CRIMINOL **PROFESSIONAL KILLING** a murder, especially one committed by a professional killer (*slang*) [Pre-12thC. From Old Norse *hitta* "to find." Originally used in the Old Norse sense (which survives in HIT ON), the underlying idea of its current meaning is "to reach."] —**hit·ta·ble** *adj.* ◇ **hit it off** to get on very well with somebody (*informal*)

hit back *vi.* to retaliate against somebody or something for an attack

hit on *vt.* **1. APPROACH SEXUALLY** to make sexual advances to somebody (*slang*) **2. ASK FAVOR** to ask somebody a favor (*slang*) **3. hit on, hit up·on FIND AN ANSWER** to think of a solution to a problem ○ *She then hit on the idea of painting the inside of the box black.*

hit up *vt.* to ask somebody for something (*slang*) ○ *How come you're suddenly hitting me up for cab fare?*

Hi·ta·chi /hi táchee/ coastal industrial city in eastern Honshu, Japan. Population: 202,141 (1990).

hit-and-miss *adj.* **1. WITH VARIABLE SUCCESS** sometimes successful and sometimes not ○ *He ran a hit-and-miss travel agency, never making much money.* **2.** *U.K.* = **hit-or-miss**

hit-and-run *adj.* **1. NOT STOPPING AFTER AN ACCIDENT** used to describe or relating to a road accident in which the driver who has hit another person or motor vehicle leaves the scene without stopping ○ *a hit-and-run driver* **2. FAST AND WITHOUT WARNING** relying on surprise and speed to overcome an enemy ○ *Three fighter planes launched a hit-and-run attack at dawn.* **3.** BASEBALL **SWINGING AT BASEBALL TO PROTECT RUNNER** used to describe a baseball play in which a base runner starts for the next base as the pitcher throws the ball, which the batter must swing at to protect the runner from being thrown out ■ *n.* **HIT-AND-RUN ACCIDENT** a hit-and-run road accident

hitch /hich/ *v.* (**hitched, hitch·ing, hitch·es**) **1.** *vti.* TRANSP **HITCHHIKE** to hitchhike a ride (*informal*) **2.** *vt.* **JOIN SOMETHING POWERED TO SOMETHING ELSE** to connect two things so that one can move the other, e.g., a horse to a wagon or a trailer to a car **3.** *vt.* **FASTEN SOMETHING TO STOP IT** to fasten or tie something temporarily to keep it from moving away ○ *Hitch the boat to the dock before the current catches it.* **4.** *vi.* **MOVE IN JERKY WAY** to move in an awkward jerky way ■ *n.* **1. OBSTACLE** an obstacle in the way of progress ○ *There's been a slight technical hitch.* **2. MEANS OF CONNECTING TWO THINGS** a device used to connect two things, e.g., a ball on a vehicle for connecting a trailer **3.** MIL **TIME IN THE MILITARY** a period of time spent in military service **4.** TRANSP **FREE RIDE** a ride solicited by means of hitchhiking (*informal*) **5. KNOT THAT UNTIES EASILY** a knot that can be easily untied, used for temporarily securing a line to something **6. TUG** a sudden pull on something **7. WAY OF WALKING** an awkward jerky manner of walking [14thC. Origin unknown.] —**hitch·er** *n.*

hitch up *v.* **1.** *vi.* **JOIN** get together with somebody else, especially in partnership or marriage (*informal*) **2.** *vt.* **PULL UP CLOTHING** to pull up an article of clothing

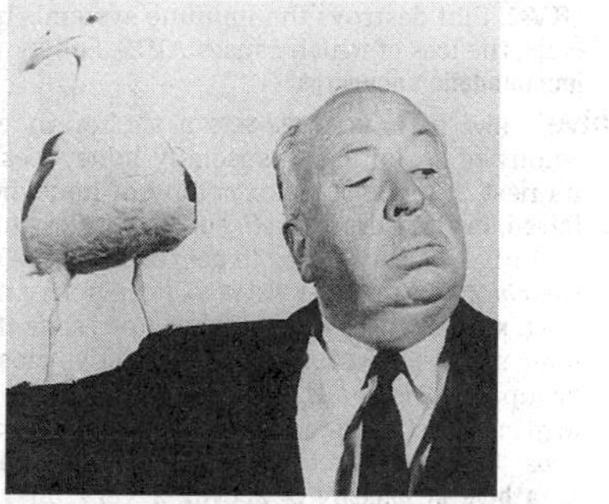

Sir Alfred Hitchcock

Hitch·cock /hích kok/, **Sir Alfred** (1899–1980) British movie director. A prolific director and master of suspense, his movies include *The Thirty-Nine Steps* (1935), *Rebecca* (1940), and *Psycho* (1960). Full name **Sir Alfred Joseph Hitchcock**

hitched /hicht/ *adj.* married (*informal*) ○ *They're getting hitched in a couple of weeks.*

hitch·hike /hích hīk/ (**-hiked, -hik·ing, -hikes**) *vti.* to get a ride from a passing vehicle, usually by standing at the side of the road and holding out the hand with the thumb raised —**hitch·hik·er** *n.*

hitch·ing post *n.* a post or rail used to tie the reins of a horse to

hi-tech /hī ték/ *n., adj.* = **high tech, high-tech**

hith·er /hít̲hər/ *adv.* **HERE** to this place (*archaic*) ○ *Come hither, child.* ■ *adj.* **ON NEAR SIDE** on the near side of something (*archaic*) [Old English *hider*. Ultimately from an Indo-European word meaning "here, this."]

hith·er·most /hít̲hər mòst/ *adj.* nearest this direction (*archaic*)

hith·er·to /hìt̲hər tóo, hít̲hər tòo/ *adv.* up to the present time or the time in question (*formal*)

hith·er·ward /hít̲hərwərd/ *adv.* in this direction (*archaic*)

hit in (*unmarked inflection* **hits in**) *n.* in field hockey, a hit from the sideline awarded to the opposition when the team in possession of the ball fails to keep it on the pitch

Hit·ler /hítlər/, **Adolf** (1889–1945) Austrian-born German Nazi leader. He cofounded the Nazi party in Germany (1919) and became chancellor in 1933. His invasion of Poland in 1939 led to the outbreak of World War II. He implemented anti-Semitic policies that led to the Holocaust.

Hit·ler·ism /hítlə rìzzəm/ *n.* the extreme nationalistic ideology and fascistic policies developed by the Nazi Party under Adolf Hitler —**Hit·ler·ist** *n.* —**Hit·ler·ite** *adj.*

hit list *n.* (*slang*) **1. LIST OF PROBLEMS NEEDING ELIMINATING** a list of things or people considered problems to be eliminated in the near future **2.** CRIMINOL **LIST OF POSSIBLE MURDER VICTIMS** a list of potential murder victims

hit man *n.* = **hired gun** (*slang*)

hit-or-miss *adj.* done in a careless haphazard way ○ *The survey was hit-or-miss, so we cannot trust the results.*

hit out (*plural* **hit outs** *or* **hits out**) *n.* in field hockey, a hit taken from the 16-yard line that is awarded to the defence when the attacking team hit the ball over the goal line without scoring a goal

hit pa·rade *n.* a list of the best-selling pop records in the previous week (*dated*)

hit squad *n.* (*slang*) **1. HIRED KILLERS** a team of hired assassins or other killers **2. HIRED PROBLEM SOLVERS** a team of experts sent in to solve serious problems

Hit·tite /hí tīt/ *n.* **1.** PEOPLES **MEMBER OF ANCIENT ANATOLIAN PEOPLE** a member of an ancient people of Anatolia whose empire flourished in parts of western Asia during the second millennium B.C. **2.** LANG **EXTINCT ANATOLIAN LANGUAGE** an extinct language spoken in Anatolia, parts of Syria, and the surrounding areas during the second millennium B.C. Linguists agree that it is an Indo-European language, but, despite evidence from ample cuneiform inscriptions, there is no consensus over which branch of Indo-European it belongs to. [Mid-16thC. Formed from Hebrew *Ḥittīm*, from Hittite *Hatti*.] —**Hit·tite** *adj.*

HIV *n.* either of two strains of a retrovirus, HIV-1 or HIV-2, that destroys the immune system's helper T cells, the loss of which causes AIDS. Full form **human immunodeficiency virus**

hive[1] /hīv/ *n.* **1. HOME FOR BEES** a shelter in which a colony of social bees, especially honeybees, builds its nest **2. COLONY OF BEES** a colony of honeybees ■ *v.* (**hived, hiv·ing, hives**) **1.** *vti.* **PUT BEES INTO HIVE** to gather in a hive, or cause bees to gather in a hive ○ *hive a swarm* **2.** *vt.* **KEEP HONEY IN HIVE** to store honey in a hive **3.** *vt.* **KEEP SOMETHING TO USE LATER** to store something for later use **4.** *vi.* **LIVE CLOSELY TOGETHER** to live closely in a group [Old English *hȳf*. Ultimately from an Indo-European word meaning "round container," which also produced Latin *cupa* "barrel" (source of English *coop*).] —**hive·less** *adj.*
◇ **a hive of industry** *or* **activity** a very busy, active place

hive off *vt.* to separate something from the whole or from a larger group, e.g., to divert work to a subsidiary company or to split a branch of knowledge into specialties

hive[2] /hīv/ *n.* a lesion due to urticaria [Back-formation from HIVES]

hives /hīvz/ *n.* MED = **urticaria** [Early 16thC. Originally a Scottish dialect word, of unknown origin.]

HIV-neg·a·tive *adj.* having taken a test that revealed no antibodies to HIV in the bloodstream

HIV-pos·i·tive *adj.* shown by a test for antibodies to HIV in the bloodstream to be infected with the HIV virus

hi·zi·ki *n.* = **hijiki**

hiz·zon·er /hi zónnər/ *n.* used jokingly to refer to a man who is a mayor (*slang*) [Early 20thC. Alteration of *his honor*.]

HJ *abbr.* hic jacet (*on gravestones*) [Latin, "here lies"]

HK *abbr.* Hong Kong (*international vehicle registration*)

HKJ *abbr.* (Hashemite Kingdom of) Jordan (*international vehicle registration*)

hl *symbol.* hectoliter

H.L. *abbr.* House of Lords

HLA *n.* the major antigen compatibility complex in humans that is genetically determined and is involved in cell self-identification and histocompatibility. Full form **human lymphocyte antigen**

HLL *abbr.* high-level language

hm *abbr.* hectometer

H.M. *abbr.* **1.** headmaster **2.** headmistress **3.** MUSIC heavy metal

HMAS, H.M.A.S. *abbr. U.K.* **1.** Her Majesty's Australian ship **2.** His Majesty's Australian ship

HMCS, H.M.C.S. *abbr. U.K.* **1.** Her Majesty's Canadian Ship **2.** His Majesty's Canadian Ship

HMF, H.M.F. *abbr.* **1.** Her Majesty's Forces **2.** His Majesty's Forces

HMI *abbr.* human-machine interface

HMO *n.* a form of health insurance that combines a range of coverage, usually on a group basis in order to alleviate medical costs. Full form **health maintenance organization**

Hmong /máwng, hə máwng/ (*plural* **Hmongs** *or* **Hmong**) *n.* **1.** PEOPLES **MEMBER OF PEOPLE OF S CHINA** a member of a people living in southern parts of China and northern parts of Laos, Thailand, and Vietnam, where they tend to inhabit the more remote, mountainous areas of these regions **2.** LANG **LANGUAGE SPOKEN IN S CHINA** a language spoken in parts of southern China and by scattered communities in Laos, Thailand, Vietnam, and the United States. Hmong forms one main branch of the Miao-Yao language family. Over five million people speak Hmong. —**Hmong** *adj.*

HMS, H.M.S. *abbr.* **1.** Her Majesty's Ship **2.** His Majesty's Ship

Hn symbol **Hn**

HN *abbr.* head nurse

ho[1] /hō/ (*plural* **hos** *or* **hoes**) *n.* **1. PROSTITUTE** a prostitute (*slang*) **2. OFFENSIVE TERM** an offensive term for a woman (*slang offensive*) [Late 20thC. Pronunciation of WHORE.]

ho[2] /hō/ *interj.* **1. EXPRESSING VARIOUS EMOTIONS** used to express surprise, triumph, admiration or derision, depending on the way the speaker says it **2. CALL FOR ATTENTION** used to attract somebody's attention **3. USED TO POINT OUT SOMETHING** used to draw somebody's attention to something (*used in combinations*) ○ *Land ho!*

Ho *symbol.* holmium

HO, H.O. *abbr.* head office

ho. *abbr.* house

Ho. *abbr.* BIBLE Hosea

h.o. *abbr.* COMM hold over

hoac·tzin *n.* = **hoatzin**

hoa·gie /hṓgee/ *n. Northeast U.S.* a large sandwich made from a long roll split lengthwise and filled with layers of meat, cheese, and a variety of vegetables, including tomatoes, lettuce, and onions [Mid-20thC. Alteration of *hoggy*.]

hoar /hawr/ *adj.* white or grayish white in color, usually as a result of age or frost (*literary*) [Old English *hār*. Ultimately from an Indo-European word meaning "shine," which also produced English *hue* and German *heiter* "merry."]

hoard /hawrd/ *vti.* (**hoard·ed, hoard·ing, hoards**) **STORE A SUPPLY OF SOMETHING** to collect and store, often secretly, a large quantity of something such as food or money for use in the future ■ *n.* **SECRET STORE** a store of something such as food or money that has been hidden for use in the future [Old English *hord*. Ultimately from an Indo-European word that is also the ancestor of English *hide* and *obscure*.]

WORD KEY: SYNONYMS

See Synonyms at ***collect***.

hoar frost *n.* the white frost that forms on grass or leaves in the morning when the dew freezes

hoarse /hawrss/ (**hoars·er, hoars·est**) *adj.* **1. SOUNDING ROUGH** sounding rough and grating **2. WITH HARSHLY GRATING VOICE** having a rough, harsh, grating voice [Old English *hās*, of prehistoric Germanic origin] —**hoarse·ly** *adv.* —**hoarse·ness** *n.*

hoars·en /háwrss'n/ (**-ened, -en·ing, -ens**) *vti.* to become hoarse, or make the voice hoarse

hoar·y /háwree/ (**-i·er, -i·est**) *adj.* **1. OVERUSED** old and stale from overuse ○ *Do we have to hear those hoary knock-knock jokes again?* **2. WHITE WITH AGE** used to describe hair that has become white or gray with age **3.** BIOL **COVERED WITH PALE HAIRS** covered with gray or white hairs ○ *a plant with hoary leaves* —**hoar·i·ly** *adv.* —**hoar·i·ness** *n.*

hoar·y mar·mot *n.* a marmot found in the mountains of northwestern North America, with a grayish coat and a shrill cry. Latin name: *Marmota caligata.*

hoat·zin /waát seén/, **hoac·tzin** /waák seén, waákt seén/ *n.* a South American bird with brownish plumage, a very small crested head, and a specialized digestive system for leaves. Young birds have a clawlike digit on each wing, used for climbing and swimming. Latin name: *Opisthocomus hoazin.* [Mid-17thC. Via American Spanish from Nahuatl *uatzin*, of uncertain origin: probably an imitation of the sound made by the bird.]

hoax /hōks/ *n.* **DECEPTION** an act intended to trick people into believing something is real that is not ■ *vt.* (**hoaxed, hoax·ing, hoax·es**) **DECEIVE PEOPLE** to trick people into believing something is real that is not [Late 18thC. Origin uncertain: probably an alteration of HOCUS.] —**hoax·er** *n.*

hob[1] /hob/ *n.* a small shelf or rack level with the top of the grate of a fireplace on which to set pans to keep them warm [Late 17thC. Alteration of earlier *hub*, of unknown origin.]

hob[2] /hob/ *n.* a hobgoblin or elf (*archaic*) [15thC. Formed from the name *Robert* or *Robin*.]

Ho·ban /hṓbən/, **James** (1762?–1831) Irish-born U.S. architect. He designed and supervised the construction of the White House (1792–99 and 1815–29) and the U.S. Capitol in Washington, D.C.

Ho·bart /hṓ baart/ **1.** capital city of the island state of Tasmania in Australia, located on the Derwent River. Population: 126,118 (1996). **2.** city in northwestern Indiana, southeast of Gary. Population: 24,463 (1996).

Hobbes /hobz/, **Thomas** (1588–1679) English philosopher and political theorist. In *Leviathan* (1651) he advocated absolute monarchy as the only means of controlling clashing human interests and desires and guaranteeing their rights of self-preservation and happiness. —**Hobbes·i·an** *adj., n.* —**Hobb·ism** *n.* —**Hobb·ist** *adj., n.*

hob·bit /hóbbit/ *n.* a member of an imaginary kind of good-natured little people who have brown furry legs and live underground. Hobbits are the creation of writer J. R. R. Tolkien, whose most famous hobbit is Bilbo Baggins, the hero of *The Hobbit.* [Mid-20thC. Coined by J. R. R. Tolkien.]

hob·ble /hóbb'l/ *v.* (**-bled, -bling, -bles**) **1.** *vt.* **RESTRICT SOMEBODY'S ACTIONS** to put restrictions on somebody or something to slow or prevent progress **2.** *vi.* **LIMP ALONG** to walk haltingly and unsteadily, taking short steps **3.** *vt.* **LIMIT HORSE'S MOVEMENT** to tie the legs of a horse loosely together with a rope or strap to prevent it from moving away ■ *n.* **1. ROPE OR STRAP** something such as a loop of rope or a strap used to tie the legs of a horse **2. UNSTEADY WALK** a halting unsteady walk [13thC. Origin uncertain: probably from Low German.]

hob·ble·bush /hóbb'l bo͝osh/ *n.* a deciduous bush of eastern North America with clusters of white flowers, rounded leaves, and red berries. Latin name: *Viburnum alnifolium.* [Mid-19thC. From the fact that it obstructs the way with its branches.]

hob·ble·de·hoy /hóbb'ldi hòy/ *n.* a clumsy or rude young man (*archaic*) [Mid-16thC. Origin unknown.]

hob·ble skirt *n.* a long skirt designed to be full at the hips but narrow at the ankles, first popular between 1910 and 1914

Hobbs city in southeastern New Mexico, on the Texas border, northeast of Carlsbad. Population: 27,986 (1996).

hob·by /hóbbee/ (*plural* **-bies**) *n.* **1. ENJOYABLE ACTIVITY** an activity engaged in for pleasure and relaxation during spare time **2.** BIRDS **SMALL GRAY FALCON** a small gray falcon with chestnut legs that breeds in Europe and Asia and winters in Africa. Its speed and deftness make it popular as a hunting bird. Latin name: *Falco subbuteo.* [13thC. Origin uncertain: probably from *Hobin*, a variant of the name *Robin*. Originally a nickname for a horse, the word in its main current meaning is a shortening of HOBBYHORSE.]

hob·by·horse /hóbbi hàwrss/ *n.* **1.** = **rocking horse 2. TOY HORSE FROM A STICK** a toy consisting of a long stick with the shape of a horse's head at one end **3. HORSE FIGURE USED IN FOLK DANCES** a representation of a horse that a Morris dancer or mummer wears around the waist so that it appears that the horse is being ridden **4. FAVORITE TOPIC** a favorite subject about which somebody will talk given the slightest opportunity

hob·gob·lin /hób gòbblin/ *n.* **1.** = **goblin 2. SOMETHING TROUBLING** a source of fear or worry [*Hob* from HOB[2]]

hob·nail /hób nàyl/ *n.* a short nail with a broad head that is used to protect the soles of boots ○ *the sound of hobnails on stone barracks stairs*

hob·nob /hób nòb/ (**-nobbed, -nob·bing, -nobs**) *vi.* to socialize in a familiar manner with somebody, especially somebody considered to be of a higher social class (*disapproving*) [Mid-18thC. Origin uncertain: probably from obsolete *hob or nob*, literally "have or not have." Originally in the meaning "to drink together" (perhaps from the notion of buying alternate rounds).]

ho·bo /hṓ bṑ/ (*plural* **-boes**) *n.* somebody who is poor and homeless, especially somebody who traveled around the United States looking for work in the 1920s and 1930s by hiding on freight trains [Late 19thC. Origin unknown.]

Ho·bo·ken /hṓbōkən/ city in northeastern New Jersey, on the Hudson River opposite New York City. Population: 33,397 (1990).

Hob·son's choice /hòbsənz-/ *n.* a choice between what is offered and nothing at all [Mid-17thC. Named for the English liveryman Thomas *Hobson* (1554–1631), who would let his customers take only the horse nearest the door.]

Ho Chi Minh /hṑ chee mín/ (1890–1969) Vietnamese statesman. A founder member of the Communist Party (1918), he led Vietnamese resistance to French colonial rule (1941–54) and was prime minister (1954–55) and president (1945–69) of North Vietnam. Real name **Nguyen Tat Thanh**

Ho Chi Minh Cit·y the largest city of Vietnam, located in the south of the country. Population: 4,22,300 (1993). Former name **Saigon**

hock[1] /hok/ *n.* **1.** ZOOL **ANIMAL'S LOWER LEG JOINT** the joint in the hind leg of a four-legged animal such as a horse or cow, corresponding to the human ankle **2.** BIRDS **FOWL'S ANKLE** the ankle joint in the leg of a fowl **3.** FOOD **LEG OF MEAT** a cut of cured meat, especially ham, taken from the lower joint of the leg immediately above the foot. It contains a comparatively small amount of meat but has a good flavor and jelly properties and is often used in stocks and soups. [16thC. Shortening of obsolete *hockshin*, from Old English *hōhsinu*, literally "heel-sinew," from *hōh* "heel" (related to English *heel*).]

hock[2] /hok/ *n.* German white wine, especially from the Rhineland and strictly from Hochheim in the Rheingau [Early 17thC. Shortening of obsolete English *hockamore*, an Anglicization of German *Hochheimer*, from *Hochheim*, a German town that is a center of wine production.]

hock[3] /hok/ **(hocked, hock·ing, hocks)** *vt.* to deposit something as security against money borrowed, with the risk of losing it if the money is not paid back by a certain time (*slang*) [Mid-19thC. From Dutch *hok* "prison," hence "debt."] ◇ **in hock 1.** left as security against money borrowed (*slang*) ○ *With so many things in hock, the shelves were quite bare.* **2.** in debt (*informal*) ○ *in hock to finance an expensive car*

hock·ey /hókee/ *n.* **1.** **TEAM SPORT PLAYED ON ICE** a game played on ice between two teams of six players. The aim is to hit a small hard rubber disk into the opposing goal using the curved end of a long wooden stick. **2.** *U.K.* = **field hockey 3.** = **street hockey** [Early 16thC. Origin uncertain.]

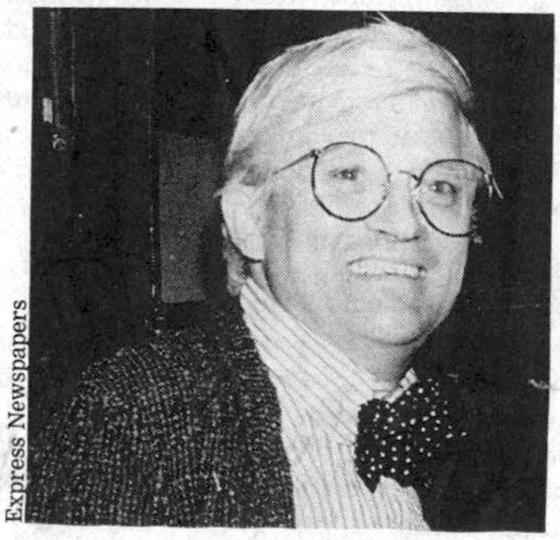

Express Newspapers

David Hockney

Hock·ney /hóknee/, **David** (*b.* 1937) British painter. He was closely associated with the Pop Art movement. His fascination with water inspired "swimming pool" paintings such as *A Bigger Splash* (1967).

hock·shop /hók shòp/, **hock shop** *n.* a pawnshop (*slang*)

ho·cus /hṓkəss/ (**-cused, -cus·ing, -cus·es**) *vt.* (*archaic*) **1.** **DECEIVE** to deceive or trick somebody **2.** **DOPE SOMEBODY** to drug somebody or an animal by deception **3.** **ADD DRUG TO ALCOHOLIC DRINK** secretly to add a drug to an alcoholic drink [Late 17thC. Shortening of HOCUS-POCUS.]

ho·cus-po·cus /hṑkəss pṓkəss/ *n.* **1.** **CONJURER'S INCANTATION** a phrase or chant used by a magician or conjurer during a performance **2.** **MAGIC TRICK** a trick performed by a magician or conjurer **3.** **TRICKERY** a hoax or trickery ○ *The negotiations were ruined by the parties' hocus-pocus.* **4.** **CONJURER** a juggler or magician (*dated*) ■ *vti.* **(ho·cus-po·cused, ho·cus-po·cus·ing, ho·cus-po·cus·es) DECEIVE** to deceive or trick somebody ○ *It was something to see a rookie player hocus-pocus an old pro.* [Formed from pseudo-Latin *hax pax max Deus adimax*, used by conjurers to impress audiences. Originally in the meaning of "conjurer, trickster."]

hod /hod/ *n.* **1.** **TROUGH ON A POLE** a V-shaped tray on the end of a long pole, usually carried on the shoulder. It is used to carry bricks, mortar, and other building materials. **2.** = **coal scuttle** [Late 16thC. Originally a dialect word meaning "pannier, basket," from Old French *hotte*, of prehistoric Germanic origin.]

hod car·ri·er *n.* somebody hired to carry bricks and mortar in a hod

Ho·dei·da /hō dáydə/ seaport in western Yemen, situated on the Red Sea. Population: 292,392 (1986).

hodge·podge /hój pòj/ *n.* a mixture of several unrelated things [14thC. Variant of HOTCHPOTCH.]

Hodg·kin /hójkin/, **Alan** (*b.* 1914) British physiologist. He shared the Nobel Prize in physiology or medicine (1963) for his research into the chemical processes of nerve impulses. Full name **Alan Lloyd Hodgkin**

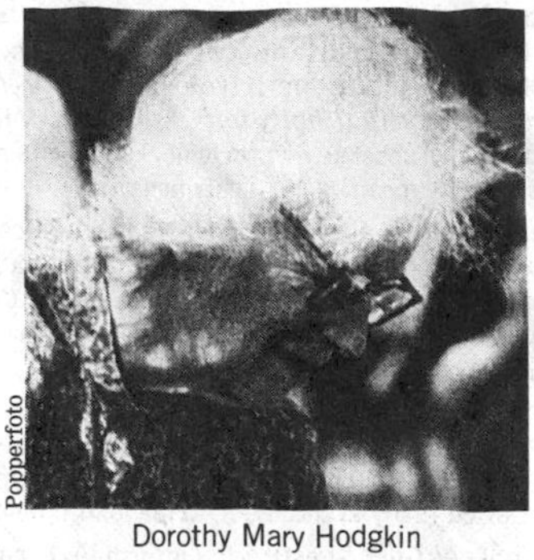

Popperfoto

Dorothy Mary Hodgkin

Hodg·kin, Dorothy Mary (1910–94) Egyptian-born British chemist. She was awarded the Nobel Prize in chemistry (1964) for work on X rays, molecular science, and penicillin. Born **Dorothy Mary Crowfoot**

Hodg·kin, Thomas (1798–1866) British pathologist. He was the first person to detect the glandular disease of the lymph tissue later named Hodgkin's disease.

Hodg·kins /hójkinz/, **Frances Mary** (1869–1947) New Zealand painter. Noted for her watercolor still lifes and landscapes, she spent most of her working life in Europe.

Hodg·kin's dis·ease /hòjkinz-/ *n.* a malignant form of lymphoma marked by progressive enlargement of the lymph nodes and spleen and sometimes of the liver [Mid-19thC. Named for Thomas HODGKIN.]

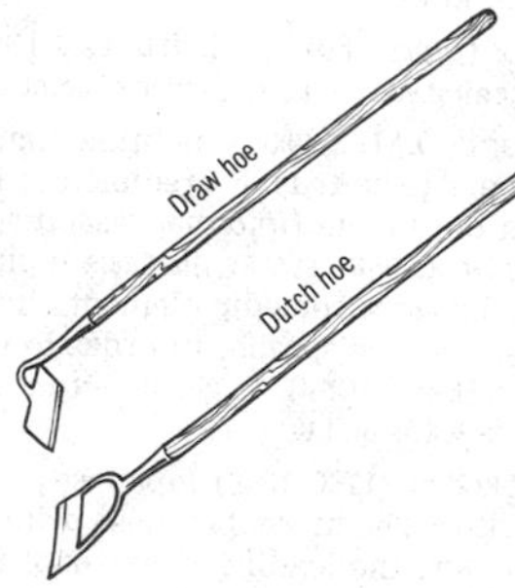

Hoe

hoe /hō/ *n.* **WEEDING TOOL** a garden implement used for weeding or turning over soil. It consists of a long pole with a small flat metal blade set into one end at a right angle to the pole. ■ *vti.* **(hoed, hoe·ing, hoes) DIG USING HOE** to dig or weed using a hoe [14thC. Via Old French *houe* from assumed Frankish, "to cut," from a prehistoric Germanic word meaning "to cut down," which is also the ancestor of English *haggle*.] —**ho·er** *n.*

Hoe /hō/, **Richard M.** (1812–86) U.S. inventor. He revolutionized the daily newspaper industry from 1847 with his new printing presses. Full name **Richard March Hoe**

hoe·cake /hṓ kàyk/ *n.* *Southern U.S.* a bread made with cornmeal, originally baked in a fireplace on the blade of a hoe [*Hoe* because it was originally baked on the blade of a hoe]

hoe·down /hṓ dòwn/ *n.* *Southern U.S., Can* **1.** **COUNTRY DANCE** a noisy lively dance, especially a square dance, or a party that includes square dancing **2.** MUSIC **DANCE MUSIC** music used at or intended for use at a hoedown [From the idea of stopping work]

Ho·fei /hṑ fáy/ = **Hefei**

Hof·fa /hóffə/, **Jimmy** (1913–75?) U.S. labor leader. He was president of the International Brotherhood of Teamsters (1957–71) and disappeared in 1975, presumed murdered. Full name **James Riddle Hoffa**

Hoff·man /hóffmən/, **Dustin** (*b.* 1937) U.S. actor. He starred in *The Graduate* (1967), and won Academy Awards for *Kramer vs. Kramer* (1979) and *Rain Man* (1988). Full name **Dustin Lee Hoffman**

Hoff·man Es·tates /hòfmən-/ village in northeastern Illinois, a residential suburb of Chicago. Population: 48,708 (1996).

Hof·mann /hóffmən/, **Hans** (1880–1966) German-born U.S. painter. He opened the Hans Hofmann School of Fine Art in New York. He was a pioneer of improvisatory abstract painting.

Hof·stadt·er /hóf stàttər/, **Robert** (1915–90) U.S. physicist. He was joint winner of the Nobel Prize in physics (1961) for his research into the structure of atom nuclei.

hog /hog/ *n.* **1.** ZOOL **PIG** a full-grown domestic pig, especially a castrated male pig **2.** **MEMBER OF THE PIG FAMILY** any of various mammals of the pig family, including both domesticated and wild species, e.g., the wild boar. Family: Suidae. **3.** **OFFENSIVE TERM** an offensive term that deliberately insults somebody's appetite, consideration for others, tidiness, or cleanliness (*informal offensive*) **4. hog, hogg** *ANZ, U.K.* **YOUNG SHEEP** a young sheep that is older than a lamb and that has not yet been sheared (*regional*) **5.** NAUT **SHIP'S BROOM** a broom used to clean the bottom of a ship while it is in the water **6.** **LARGE MOTORCYCLE** a large powerful motorcycle or any large car or truck that consumes a large amount of gas (*slang*) ■ *v.* **(hogged, hog·ging, hogs) 1.** *vt.* **TAKE AN EXCESS OF SOMETHING** to take more of something or keep something for longer than is fair or polite (*informal*) ○ *He's been hogging the fast lane for the past two miles.* **2.** *vt.* **ARCH THE BACK** to arch the back upward **3.** *vt.* EQU **TRIM A HORSE'S MANE** to trim the mane of a horse very short, causing it to stand up like the bristles of a hog's back **4.** *vti.* NAUT **WARP** to cause the keel or plank of a ship to curve upward in the middle, or curve in this way **5.** *vt.* NAUT **SCRUB WITH A BROOM** to clean a ship's bottom with a broom while the ship is in the water [Pre-12thC. Origin uncertain: perhaps ultimately from Celtic. The word probably originally applied in English to the age of a pig or sheep.] —**hog·like** *adj.* ◇ **go the whole hog, go whole hog** to do something wholeheartedly or completely and without restraint (*slang*) ◇ **live high off** *or* **on the hog** to have a luxurious standard of living (*slang*)

ho·gan /hṓgən/ *n.* a traditional Navajo dwelling made of logs and mud, with a roof of earth [Late 19thC. From Navajo.]

Ho·gan /hṓgən/, **Ben** (1912–97) U.S. golfer. He won over 60 major golfing tournaments including four U.S. Open championships (1948, 1950, 1951, 1953). Full name **William Benjamin Hogan**

Ho·gan, Paul (*b.* 1940) Australian actor. Originally a television performer, he starred in the movie *Crocodile Dundee* (1986) and cowrote and produced *Crocodile Dundee II* (1988).

hog·back /hóg bàk/ *n.* **1.** GEOG **LOW NARROW RIDGE** a steep and narrow low ridge produced by the erosion of the softer surrounding rock strata **2.** **ARCHED BACK** an arched back, similar to a hog's back (*slang*)

hog badg·er *n.* a nocturnal badger native to Southeast Asia that has an elongated snout with which it roots for insects and grubs. Latin name: *Arctonyx collaris*. [*Hog* from its cloven hooves]

hog chol·er·a *n.* a very infectious often fatal viral disease of hogs marked by fever, weakness, lesions, loss of appetite, and diarrhea

hog·fish /hóg fìsh/ (*plural* **-fish** *or* **-fish·es**) *n.* **1.** **FISH OF CORAL REEFS** a fish in the wrasse family found on tropical coral reefs and often brightly colored, especially one with the first three spines of its dorsal fin thickened and elongated. Latin name: *Lachnolaimus maximus*. **2.** = **pigfish** [*Hog* from the grunting sound it makes]

hogg *n.* *ANZ, U.K.* = **hog** *n.* 4 (*regional*)

hog·get /hóggit/ *n.* *ANZ, U.K., U.S.* = **hog** *n.* 4 (*regional*)

hog·gish /hóggish/ *adj.* **1.** **GREEDY OR SLOVENLY** greedy, selfish, or slovenly **2.** **FILTHY** filthy dirty —**hog·gish·ly** *adv.* —**hog·gish·ness** *n.*

hog heav·en *n.* a state of complete contentment or satiation (*slang*)

Hog·ma·nay /hógmə này, hògmə náy/, **hog·ma·nay** *n.* *Scotland* New Year's Eve as celebrated in Scotland and in parts of northern England [Early 17thC. Origin uncertain: probably from Norman dialect *hoguinané*, said when exchanging New Year's gifts, from Old French *aguillanneuf*, a contraction of *accueillis l'an neuf* "welcome the new year."]

hog·nosed skunk /hòg nōzd-/ *n.* a large skunk of Central and South America that has a broad white stripe down its back and a snout resembling a hog's with which it roots for insects and grubs. Latin name: *Conepatus mesoleucas*.

hog·nose snake /hòg nōz-/, **hog·nosed snake** /-nōzd-/ *n.* a nonvenomous North American snake with a stout body and an upturned snout resembling a hog's that is used for burrowing. Genus: *Heterodon*. [Hognose from its upturned snout]

hog·nut /hóg nut/ *n.* = **pignut**

hog pea·nut *n.* a North American vine of the legume family that has clusters of white or pinkish flowers and edible, fleshy, single-seeded pods that ripen on or beneath the ground. Latin name: *Amphicarpaea bracteata*.

hog's back /hògz bák/ *n.* = **hogback**

hogs·head /hógz hèd/ *n.* **1.** LIQUID MEASURE a unit of capacity for liquids or dry goods, used especially for alcohol, having various values but typically 63 U.S. gallons or 54 British imperial gallons **2.** LARGE CASK a large cask or barrel, especially one having a capacity of one hogshead [14thC. Literally "head of a hog" (the reason for the name is unknown).]

hog-tie *vt.* **1.** TRUSS to tie the legs of an animal or the feet and hands of a person together **2.** IMPEDE to hamper somebody in his or her actions, or impede the progress of something (*informal*) ○ *Without that evidence, I'm hog-tied.*

hog·wash /hóg wòsh/ *n.* **1.** NONSENSE worthless stuff or nonsense (*informal*) ○ *What a pile of hogwash* **2.** PIGSWILL leftovers of food that are given to hogs to eat

Hogweed

hog·weed /hóg wèed/ *n.* any of several coarse weeds such as sow thistle and knotweed

hog-wild *adj.* excited or enthusiastic to the point of losing any inhibitions (*slang*) ○ *That man's gone hog-wild ever since he inherited some money.*

Hoh·hot /hō hŏt/ capital city of Inner Mongolia, an autonomous region in northeastern China. Population: 652,534 (1990).

ho hum /hō húm/ *interj.* used to express boredom, disappointment, or resignation (*informal*) [Thought to suggest a yawn]

ho-hum *adj.* **1.** DULL boring or lacking in originality (*informal*) ○ *All in all it was a pretty ho-hum affair.* **2.** INDIFFERENT indifferent or lacking enthusiasm (*slang*) ○ *He had a very ho-hum attitude toward my project.*

hoick /hoyk/ (**hoicked, hoick·ing, hoicks**) *vti.* to pull or lift something or somebody violently or suddenly (*informal*) [Late 19thC. Origin uncertain: perhaps a variant of HIKE "to pull up."]

hoicks /hoyks/ *n.* a shout in hunting, used to urge hounds to move along faster [Early 17thC. Origin unknown.]

hoi pol·loi /hòy pə lóy/ *n.* ordinary people as opposed to the wealthy, well-educated, and cultivated elite [From Greek, literally "the many"]

hoi·sin sauce /hoy sín-, hóyssin-/ *n.* a dark sweet and spicy sauce of thick consistency made from fermented soy beans and used to flavor Chinese dishes and as a condiment [*Hoisin* from Chinese (Cantonese), literally "delicacy of the sea"]

hoist /hoyst/ *vt.* (**hoist·ed, hoist·ing, hoists**) LIFT UP to raise or lift somebody or something up, especially using a mechanical device such as a winch ■ *n.* **1.** DEVICE FOR LIFTING a mechanical device or apparatus such as a winch or elevator designed for lifting people or heavy objects **2.** LIFTING UP an act of hoisting somebody or something **3.** SHIPPING SIGNAL a message or signal conveyed from ship to ship by flags hoisted up the mast **4.** MEASURE OF A SAIL the height of a sail or flag [16thC. Alteration of *hoise*, itself an alteration of obsolete *heise*, of uncertain origin: probably from Dutch *hijsen* or Low German *hissen* "to raise."] —**hoist·er** *n.*

WORD KEY: SYNONYMS

See Synonyms at *raise*.

hoi·ty-toi·ty /hòyti tóytee/ *adj.* **1.** SELF-IMPORTANT arrogant and self-important (*informal disapproving*) **2.** FRIVOLOUS silly, giddy, or frivolous ○ *We were confronted by giggling, hoity-toity nonsense.* [Alteration and repetition of obsolete *hoit* "to romp," of uncertain origin. Originally in the meaning of "flighty behavior."]

Ho·kan /hṓkən/ *n.* a group of Native American languages of the southwestern United States, including Chumash, Yuman, and other languages and linguistic groups [Early 20thC. Formed from Hokan *hok* "two."] —**Ho·kan** *adj.*

hoke /hōk/ (**hoked, hok·ing, hokes**) *vt.* to introduce highly melodramatic or broadly comic elements into a story, play, or speech, in order to captivate an audience [Early 20thC. Back-formation from HOKUM.]

hok·ey /hṓkee/ (**-i·er, -i·est**) *adj.* (*informal*) **1.** CONTRIVED obviously contrived or clearly not genuine **2.** CORNY corny, sentimental, or melodramatic [Mid-20thC. Formed from HOKE or HOKUM.] —**hok·ey·ness** *n.* —**hok·i·ly** *adv.*

hok·ey cok·ey /hōki kṓkee/ *n.* U.K. = **hokey-pokey** *n.* 1 [Origin uncertain: perhaps by repetition and alteration from HOKEY]

hok·ey-poke·y /hōki pṓkee/ (*plural* **hok·ey-po·keys**) *n.* **1.** = **hocus-pocus** *n.* 3 **2.** CHILDREN'S DANCE a dance done especially by children in which a circle of people sing out the instructions for movements that they perform at the same time [In the sense of "trickery," an alteration of HOCUS-POCUS; other sense of unknown origin]

Hok·kai·do /ho kídō/ the second largest island of Japan, situated north of the main island of Honshu. Population: 5,643,647 (1990). Area: 32,247 sq. mi./83,520 sq. km.

hok·ku /hṓkoo/ (*plural* **-ku**) *n.* = **haiku** [Late 19thC. From Japanese, "opening verse (of a sequence of comic verses)."]

ho·kum /hṓkəm/ *n.* **1.** BUNK something that on the surface appears to be true or credible but is in fact meaningless or untrue (*informal disapproving*) ○ *a load of hokum* **2.** UNNECESSARY THEATRICS highly melodramatic or broadly comedic elements introduced into a story, play, or speech, in order to captivate an audience [Early 20thC. Origin uncertain: perhaps a blend of HOCUS-POCUS and BUNKUM.]

Ho·ku·sai /hṓkŏŏ sí/ (1760–1849) Japanese painter and book illustrator. The finest Japanese printmaker of his time, he was the leading member of the "Ukiyo-e" school. His best known work is *Views of Mount Fuji* (1835). Full name **Katsushika Hokusai**

hol- *prefix.* = **holo-** (*used before vowels*)

ho·lan·dric /hō lándrik, ho-/ *adj.* used to describe genetic traits carried on the Y chromosome and therefore carried and inherited only by males [Mid-20thC. Coined from HOLO- + ANDRO- + -IC.]

Hol·arc·tic /hō laárktik, -laártik, ho-/ *adj.* found in or typical of the regions of North America and Eurasia combined, which share many faunal characteristics

hold[1] /hōld/ *v.* (**held** /held/, **held, hold·ing, holds**) **1.** *vt.* GRASP SOMETHING to take something firmly and retain it in the hand or arms **2.** *vt.* LIFT AND KEEP IN POSITION to carry, lift, or support temporarily an object or part of the body in a particular position ○ *Hold the rope a bit higher.* **3.** *vt.* FIX to keep something fixed in a particular position ○ *The picture is held in place by two large hooks.* **4.** *vt.* EMBRACE to bring or have somebody within an embrace or supported by the arms **5.** *vt.* CONTAIN to be the place where something is or can be kept ○ *a basket to hold all your sewing equipment* **6.** *vt.* KEEP IN CUSTODY to keep somebody in a particular place or condition, especially in custody **7.** *vt.* DELAY to cause delay to somebody ○ *What held you so long?* **8.** *vt.* RETAIN to retain or reserve something for later use or collection by somebody else ○ *Ask if they can hold the tickets for us at the box office.* **9.** *vt.* REFRAIN to refrain from doing or saying something ○ *The captain told his soldiers to hold their fire.* **10.** *vt.* STOP LEAVING to stop something leaving or happening at the appointed time, usually for a particular purpose ○ *The conductor held the train so that we could board.* **11.** *vt.* MIL KEEP BY FORCE to keep possession of something by force, especially while under attack ○ *The insurgents held the town for some time before retreating.* **12.** *vt.* HAVE CERTAIN CAPACITY to contain or be able to contain a particular number or amount ○ *This cup holds eight ounces.* **13.** *vt.* BE ABLE TO CONSUME to consume something, especially alcohol, without ill effect **14.** *vt.* ARRANGE to arrange, take part in, or observe an actvity or event ○ *They hold a party every Friday night.* **15.** *vt.* POSSESS to have the right to something as a possession or achievement ○ *The author holds the copyright to this book.* **16.** *vt.* HAVE PARTICULAR POSITION to fulfill the duties of a particular title, office, or position ○ *She has held the position of vice president since 1994.* **17.** *vti.* KEEP PROMISE to keep a promise, or make sure that somebody keeps a promise or is true to a stated intention ○ *The prosecutor held to his promise to bring them to justice.* **18.** *vt.* BELIEVE OR FEEL to have a particular belief, opinion, or feeling ○ *As Jefferson expressed it in the Declaration of Independence, "We hold these truths to be self-evident."* **19.** *vt.* REGARD to regard somebody or something in a particular way ○ *She holds her professor in very high esteem.* **20.** *vt.* HAVE A PARTICULAR BEARING to keep or carry the body or a part of it in a particular attitude or position ○ *The old general holds himself stiffly.* **21.** *vt.* ENGROSS to engage or captivate somebody or somebody's attention ○ *She held their attention with the dramatic tale of her rescue.* **22.** *vt.* KEEP SOMEBODY GOING to be enough to satisfy or sustain somebody ○ *Such a huge breakfast will hold us all day.* **23.** *vt.* LAW DECIDE LEGALLY to decide or lay down something legally or authoritatively ○ *The appeals court held that the lower court acted properly.* **24.** *vt.* LAW BAIL to bind somebody to or in bail ○ *The court will hold the prisoner for $50,000.* **25.** *vt.* MUSIC SUSTAIN to keep singing or playing a note or a chord without stopping ○ *The trumpeter held the note for at least a full minute.* **26.** *vi.* PERSIST to continue in a particular state or course ○ *I can't believe this run of bad luck will hold.* ○ *The snow still holds on the mountains.* **27.** *vi.* REMAIN FIRM to remain fast or firm and not break or give way ○ *The levee held throughout the flooding.* ○ *I don't think the rope is going to hold for much longer.* **28.** *vi.* STAND FIRM to maintain a position against attack or opposition ○ *Their defensive line held, despite heavy losses.* **29.** *vi.* REMAIN VALID to remain in force or continue to be valid ○ *Many old sayings still hold true.* **30.** *vi.* STAY FINE continue to be fine and, e.g., not rain, snow, or become cold (*refers to the weather*) ○ *We're going to a picnic on Saturday so I hope the weather holds.* **31.** *vt.* LEASE PROPERTY to maintain the right to use property by some kind of tenure, e.g., a lease or easement ○ *They held the farm under a very long lease.* **32.** *vti.* COMMUNICATION WAIT ON TELEPHONE to wait during a telephone call and not break the connection, usually so that the person being called can speak to somebody else or transfer the call ○ *Hold, please, while I try to connect you?* ○ *Hold the line please.* ■ *n.* **1.** GRASP ON SOMETHING the act or position of grasping or keeping possession of something ○ *a firm hold on the child's arm* ○ *no hold on reality* **2.** WRESTLING WRESTLING TECHNIQUE a position or manner of grasping an opponent in wrestling **3.** SOMETHING GIVING SUPPORT something that may be grasped or used as a support ○ *There were few holds on the sheer rock face.* **4.** SOMETHING THAT RESTRAINS a structure or receptacle used for keeping something in check, e.g., a lock on a canal **5.** CONTROL OVER SOMEBODY a controlling power or influence ○ *a firm hold on the public's imagination* **6.** DELAYING SOMETHING an act of delaying or restraining something, or an order to effect this ○ *Because of excessive traffic, there was a hold put on the plane's takeoff.* ○ *Put a hold on their dinner order.* **7.** MUSIC MUSIC NOTATION a symbol appearing above or below a note or rest, signaling that it can be prolonged beyond its prescribed time **8.** PRISON a prison cell or place of confinement **9.** STRONGHOLD a fortified place in a castle or other structure (*dated*) [Old English *haldan*, *healdan*, from a prehistoric Germanic word meaning "to guard, watch," which is also the ancestor of English *behold* and *halt*] ◇ **get hold of somebody** *or* **something** to succeed in finding somebody or obtaining something ◇ **hold good** to apply, or be true or valid ◇ **hold it** used to tell somebody to stop or wait ◇ **hold something**

against somebody to resent something that somebody has done and to bear a grudge because of it ◇ **on hold 1.** COMMUNICATION waiting to be connected or reconnected to somebody during a telephone call **2.** into or in a state of suspension or postponement ◇ **no holds barred** with no restrictions on what is allowed or included

hold back *v.* **1.** *vti.* **RESTRAIN** to keep back or restrain somebody from doing something ○ *His shyness holds him back from making friends.* **2.** *vt.* **KEEP BACK** to withhold something or retain something within your own control ○ *accused of holding back vital information* ○ *holding back tears*

WORD KEY: SYNONYMS

See Synonyms at ***hinder***.

hold down *vt.* to do enough in a job or position to keep it (*informal*) ○ *She is holding down two jobs.*

hold forth *vi.* to speak at length and sometimes tediously on a particular subject (*formal*) ○ *holding forth for hours about their flashy new car*

hold in *vt.* **1. KEEP IN CHECK** to keep back or in check ○ *It was nearly impossible to hold in the hounds until the hunt began.* **2. RESTRAIN EMOTIONS** to suppress something such as an emotion or feeling ○ *They held in their emotions throughout the crisis.*

hold off *v.* **1.** *vti.* **REFRAIN** to refrain from doing something ○ *We decided to hold off until after the election.* ○ *It might be wise to hold off making any decisions until after the results come out.* **2.** *vt.* **RESIST** to keep somebody or something away, or prevent somebody from approaching too close ○ *A handful of soldiers held off several enemy attacks.* **3.** *vi.* **NOT HAPPEN** to not produce bad weather conditions after threatening to do so ○ *The rain held off, and the barbecue went ahead as planned.*

hold on *vi.* **1. WAIT** to wait, especially for a short while ○ *Hold on, and let's see if we can figure out this problem.* **2. PERSIST** to continue on a course of action or direction, or maintain something such as a set of principles or a particular state of mind ○ *He held on until he knew all was lost.* ○ *The scientist held on to her theory and finally proved it correct.*

hold out *v.* **1.** *vt.* **EXTEND** to stretch out or extend a part of the body, or offer something to somebody in doing this ○ *She held out her hand.* **2.** *vi.* **LAST** to keep up or continue to be in supply ○ *The water supply will hold out only until tomorrow night.* **3.** *vi.* **ENDURE** to continue to resist and not give in to something ○ *We managed to hold out for three days against the enemy.* **4.** *vi.* **WITHHOLD** to keep back something such as information which is wanted, expected, or needed ○ *It was pretty clear that she was holding out on the interviewer.* **5.** *vi.* **RESIST** to refuse to settle something or accept something until all demands or conditions are met ○ *holding out for a 6% pay raise*

hold over *v.* **1.** *vt.* **DEFER** to postpone action on or consideration of something until a later date **2.** *vi.* MUSIC **HOLD NOTE TO NEXT BAR** to hold a note from one bar of music to the next **3.** *vt.* **NOT LET SOMEBODY FORGET SOMETHING** to blackmail somebody with information, or not let somebody forget something embarrassing or shameful in order to have power over him or her (*informal*) ○ *You're not going to keep holding that over me, are you?*

hold together *vti.* to remain united, or cause a group of people to remain united, often despite problems or disagreements ○ *He held the family together single-handed.* ○ *It was nothing more than a desire to earn money that held them together.*

hold up *v.* **1.** *vt.* **CAUSE DELAY** to cause somebody or something to be late or take longer than intended ○ *Minor disagreements hold up any negotiation.* ○ *I was held up in traffic.* **2.** *vt.* CRIMINOL **ROB** to rob a person or place using violence or threats, usually at gunpoint **3.** *vt.* **PRESENT** to show or display somebody or something for a specific reason ○ *The firefighter was held up as a good example of bravery.* **4.** *vi.* **ENDURE** to continue to function or survive ○ *How's the bike holding up?* ○ *You've been holding up well under the strain.* **5.** *vi.* **REMAIN SAME** to remain or be maintained at a particular level or in a particular state ○ *Prices have not held up well in this recession.* **6.** *vi.* **STAND UP TO SCRUTINY** to remain persuasive or convincing even after closer examination ○ *I don't think these ideas will hold up.* **7.** *vi.* BRIDGE **NOT PLAY HIGH CARD** to delay playing a high card in order to prevent a suit from being established

hold with *vt.* to approve or agree with something ○ *She doesn't hold with that kind of thinking.*

hold[2] /hōld/ *n.* the area below the deck of a ship or the area inside an aircraft in which cargo is carried [Late 16thC. Alteration of HOLE, influenced by HOLD[1].]

hold·all /hṓld àwl/ *n.* **1.** = **carryall 2. MEDLEY** a group of various unrelated objects or ideas ○ *The essay was a disorganized holdall of the writer's frustrations.*

hold·back /hṓld bàk/ *n.* **1. SOMETHING THAT HINDERS** something that prevents somebody from doing or achieving something or that prevents an event or plan from going ahead **2. DEVICE ON A WAGON OR CARRIAGE** a device on the shaft of a wagon or carriage that attaches to the horse's harness, allowing the horse to hold back or back up the vehicle **3. SOMETHING HELD BACK** something withheld, usually wages or money

hold but·ton *n.* a button on a telephone that allows somebody to put a caller on hold

hold-down *n.* a restraint or limitation of price increases or pay raises

Hol·den /hṓld'n/, **William** (1918–81) U.S. actor. He was a popular clean-cut hero in many 1940s and 1950s Hollywood movies such as *Sunset Boulevard* (1950) and *Bridge on the River Kwai* (1957).

hold·er /hṓldər/ *n.* **1. CONTAINER** something designed to hold another thing (*often used in combination*) ○ *a candle holder* ○ *pot holders* **2. OWNER** somebody who owns, occupies, or is in possession of something, e.g., property or a title ○ *the current holder of the world title* **3.** FIN **SOMEBODY WITH A PROMISE OF PAYMENT** somebody in possession of and legally entitled to receive payment on or negotiate a note, bill, or check

hold·fast /hṓld fàst/ *n.* **1. CLAMP** a device such as a clamp or grip designed to hold something securely **2.** BOT **PLANT'S MEANS OF ATTACHING ITSELF** an organ at the base of a seaweed, aquatic plant, or fungus that attaches the organism to a surface **3. FIRM GRASP** the action or fact of holding something fast or firmly

hold·ing /hṓlding/ *n.* **1. LEASED LAND** a piece of land that is leased from somebody else, especially when used for agricultural purposes **2. PROPERTY** legally owned property of any kind, but especially stocks or bonds (*often used in the plural*) **3.** SPORTS **ILLEGAL USE OF THE ARMS** use of the arms to hold or obstruct an opponent when such use is not allowed in the rules of a game, e.g., in basketball or football **4.** PSYCHOL **SENSE OF SECURITY** the ability of a therapist or parent to make a client or child feel contained and secure during times of growth or change

hold·ing com·pa·ny *n.* a company that has a controlling interest in one or more other companies through ownership of stocks or bonds

hold·ing op·er·a·tion *n.* a procedure or operation designed to maintain the present situation as it is

hold·ing pat·tern *n.* **1. AIR WAITING PATH OF PLANE** a usually circular course taken by an aircraft while awaiting permission to land **2. LIMBO** a state of suspended action or progress ○ *He's in a holding pattern until he knows whether he's been given the scholarship.*

hold·out /hṓld òwt/ *n.* **1. REFUSAL TO AGREE** a refusal to agree or compromise in order to obtain better terms in any kind of settlement ○ *The holdout lasted three weeks.* **2. SOMEBODY WHO HOLDS OUT** an individual or group that refuses to submit to or comply with a situation, trend, or order ○ *a small group of holdouts who refuse to leave the building*

hold·o·ver /hṓld ṑvər/ *n.* **1. RETAINED OFFICIAL** somebody who continues to hold an office after its term has expired ○ *The Attorney General is a holdover from the last administration.* **2.** EDUC **REPEATING STUDENT** a student who repeats a course or grade ○ *Five of my students are inattentive holdovers.* **3.** TREES **LONE TREE** a tree left standing after others surrounding it have been felled ○ *The trees that dot the meadow are holdovers from a stand of maples.* **4.** ARTS **SOMETHING OR SOMEBODY GIVEN EXTENDED RUN** a performer or a presentation such as a play or series of concerts that continues beyond the term originally agreed

hold·up /hṓld ùp/ *n.* **1.** CRIMINOL **ROBBERY** an act of robbing a person or place using violence or threats, usually at gunpoint **2. DELAY** an act of causing somebody or something to be late or take longer than planned ○ *Travel was slowed by holdups on the interstate.* **3.** BRIDGE **WITHHOLDING OF CARD** the holding back of a card rather than playing it to take a trick early in the play of a hand

WORD KEY: SYNONYMS

See Synonyms at ***theft***.

hole /hōl/ *n.* **1. CAVITY** a hollow space in a solid object or area ○ *The hole had filled with water.* **2. APERTURE** a gap or opening in or through something ○ *a hole in my socks* **3. BURROW** a hollowed-out area in the ground where an animal such as a rabbit or mouse lives ○ *a rabbit hole* **4. UNPLEASANT PLACE TO BE** a dark or dirty place, especially a place where somebody lives (*informal*) **5. FLAW** a fault or flaw in something such as logic, an argument, or a position ○ *But there are so many holes in her theory.* **6. AWKWARD SITUATION** an awkward or embarrassing situation (*informal*) **7. PRISONER'S CELL** a prison cell or dungeon, or solitary confinement (*informal*) **8.** ELECTRON ENG **MOBILE SPACE IN SEMICONDUCTOR** a space normally occupied by an electron in the lattice structure of a semiconductor material that is mobile and can act as a carrier of a positive charge **9.** GOLF **TARGET IN GOLF** a small round cavity or cup on a golf course into which the ball is hit **10.** GOLF **AREA OF GOLF COURSE** a part of a golf course that consists of a tee, a fairway, and a green with a hole and is a basic element in scoring. A golf course usually has18 holes. **11.** GEOG **COVE** a small bay or harbor on the coast ■ *v.* (**holed, hol·ing, holes**) **1.** *vti.* **PERFORATE** to make a hole or holes in something ○ *This new device holes a ream of paper perfectly.* **2.** *vt.* GOLF **PUT IN A HOLE** to hit or drive a ball into one of the holes of a golf course **3.** *vi.* **GO INTO A HOLE** to go or climb into a hole [Old English *hol* "hollow," ultimately of uncertain origin: probably from an Indo-European word meaning "to hide" (ancestor of English *conceal*)] ◇ **make a hole in something** to use up a large part of something (*slang*) ○ *The monthly rent makes a considerable hole in my salary.* ◇ **pick holes in something** to find fault with something, often over minor imperfections

hole out *vi.* to hit a golf ball into a hole

hole up *vi.* **1. HIDE AWAY** to hide away somewhere (*slang*) **2. SHELTER** to go into a hole, cave, or other similar place to shelter or hibernate

hole in one (*plural* **holes in one**) *n.* a shot in golf that enters the hole directly from the tee

hole-in-the-wall (*plural* **holes-in-the-wall**) *n.* a small unpretentious out-of-the-way place such as a little restaurant or other business (*informal*) ○ *It's only a little hole-in-the-wall, but they serve great food.*

hol·ey /hṓlee/ *adj.* having or full of holes

Ho·li /hṓlee/ *n.* the Hindu festival of spring that honors the time when Krishna paid amorous attention to young women tending cows. As part of the celebrations people spray colored water over each other. [Late 17thC. From Hindi *holī*.]

hol·i·day /hóllidày/ *n.* **1. DAY OF LEISURE** a day taken off or set aside for leisure and enjoyment, when somebody is exempt from work or normal activity **2.** *U.K., ANZ* = **vacation 3. LEGAL DAY OFF** a day set aside by law or statute as exempt from regular labor or business activities, usually to celebrate or commemorate something that happened on or near that date. In the United States, public holidays include Memorial Day and Labor Day. **4. HOLY DAY** the day or days of a religious festival ■ *vi.* (**-dayed, -day·ing, -days**) *U.K.* = **vacation** *v.* [Old English *hāligdæg*, literally "holy day," a day set aside as a religious festival, and hence when no work was done]

Hol·i·day /hóllə dày/, **Billie** (1915–59) U.S. jazz singer. Known for her emotionally charged renditions of popular songs, she collaborated with Count Basie and Artie Shaw. Her autobiography *Lady Sings the Blues* (1956) was later made into a movie. Real name **Eleanora Fagan McKay Holiday**. Known as **Lady Day**

hol·i·day·mak·er /hólliday màykər/ *n. U.K., ANZ* = **vacationer**

ho·li·er-than-thou *adj.* **SELF-RIGHTEOUS** aggressively or offensively pompous or self-righteous (*informal*) ○ *Her holier-than-thou attitude puts people off.* ■ *n.* **SELF-RIGHTEOUS PERSON OR ORGANIZATION** an aggressively or offensively pompous or self-righteous person or organization (*informal*) ○ *The chairman is regarded as one of the bigger holier-than-thous.*

ho·li·ness /hṓlinəss/ *n.* the state or quality of being holy

Ho·li·ness /hṓleenəss/ *n.* a title used in addressing or referring to the Pope

ho·lism /hṓ lìzzəm/ *n.* **1.** PHILOS **PHILOSOPHICAL THEORY** the view that a whole system of beliefs must be analyzed rather than simply its individual components **2.**

MED **THEORY OF HEALTH** the theory of the importance of taking all of somebody's physical, mental, and social conditions, not just physical symptoms, into account in the treatment of illness [Early 20thC. Coined from Greek *holos* "whole" + -ISM.] —**ho·list** *n.*

ho·lis·tic /hō lístik/ *adj.* including or involving all of something, especially all of somebody's physical, mental, and social conditions, not just physical symptoms, in the treatment of illness —**ho·lis·ti·cal·ly** *adv.*

hol·land /hólland/ *n.* a type of strong smooth linen fabric used especially for upholstery [14thC. Named for HOLLAND, where it was originally produced.]

Hol·land /hólland/ = **Netherlands**

hol·lan·daise sauce /hóllan dàyz-/, **hol·lan·daise** *n.* a rich creamy piquant sauce made from butter, egg yolks, and vinegar or lemon juice. It is served with many different foods. [*Hollandaise* from French, the feminine of *Hollandais* "Dutch"]

Hol·lan·der /hóllandar/ *n.* somebody born, raised, or living in the Netherlands (*dated*)

Hol·lands /hóllandz/ *n.* genever, or Dutch gin (*archaic*) [Late 18thC. Formed from obsolete Dutch *Hollandsch genever* "Dutch gin."]

hol·ler[1] /hóllar/ *vti.* (**-lered, -ler·ing, -lers**) **YELL** to call out or shout something (*informal*) ○ *If you need me, just holler!* ■ *n.* (*informal*) **1. LOUD CRY** a loud cry or shout **2. WORK SONG** a type of work song originally sung by enslaved and laboring Black American people [Late 17thC. Origin uncertain: probably ultimately from both Old French *halloer* "to pursue with shouting," an imitation of the sound, and French *holà* "stop!", from *ho* "ho" + *là* "there."]

hol·ler[2] /hóllar/ *n.* small valley or hollow (*regional*) [Variant of HOLLOW]

Hol·li·day/hólla dày/, **Judy** (1922–65) U.S. actor. She is known for her roles in the stage and screen versions of *Born Yesterday* (1946, 1950) and *Bells are Ringing* (1956, 1960).

Hol·lins /hóllinz/ unincorporated settlement in Roanoke County, central Virginia, situated just north of the city of Roanoke

Hol·lis·ton /hóllistan/ town in eastern Massachusetts, south of Framingham and southwest of Boston. Population: 13,381 (1996).

hol·low /hóllō/ *adj.* **1. NOT SOLID** having empty space inside ○ *The tree trunk was hollow inside.* **2. CONCAVE** sunk deep into the surface of something **3. NOT FULL-TONED** resonating or echoing as if in an empty space ○ *It gave a huge, hollow, booming sound.* **4. INSINCERE** not sincere, genuine, or significant ○ *He gave a hollow laugh.* **5. HUNGRY** having the feeling of an empty stomach ■ *n.* **1. CAVITY** a hollow or concave place or area, as in a tree trunk or somebody's back ○ *The child held the chick in the hollow of his hand.* **2. VALLEY** a sunken or low-lying area of the earth's surface ■ *v.* (**-lowed, -low·ing, -lows**) **1.** *vt.* **MAKE A CAVITY IN SOMETHING** to form something by removing contents to leave a concave area or cavity ○ *to hollow a canoe from a log* **2.** *vti.* **MAKE OR BECOME HOLLOWED** to make something hollow or become hollow ○ *hollow out a pumpkin* ○ *eyes hollowed from lack of sleep* ■ *adv.* **HOLLOWLY** in a hollow way ○ *Their voices rang hollow in the emptied streets.* [Old English *holh* "hollow place, hole, cave," of uncertain origin: probably from a prehistoric Germanic word that is also the ancestor of English *hole*] —**hol·low·ly** *adv.* —**hol·low·ness** *n.*

WORD KEY: SYNONYMS

See Synonyms at ***vain***.

WORD KEY: CULTURAL NOTE

The Hollow Men, a poem by U.S.-born British writer T. S. Eliot (1925). One of Eliot's most pessimistic works, it depicts a barren, ghostly land peopled by soulless beings. Its imagery and concern with the sterility of modern civilization link it to "The Waste Land," but in "The Hollow Men" the message, conveyed in short lines and repetitive phrases, is more direct and bereft of any hope of redemption. The oft-quoted words "This is the way the world ends/ Not with a bang but a whimper" come from this poem.

hol·low·ware /hóllō wàir/ *n.* articles of tableware and kitchenware such as pots, bowls, cups, vases, and pitchers that are hollow, as opposed to items such as plates and saucers

Holly

hol·ly /hóllee/ (*plural* **-lies**) *n.* **1. EVERGREEN SHRUB WITH RED BERRIES** an evergreen tree or shrub with glossy, prickly leaves and bright red berries. Genus: *Ilex.* **2. DECORATIVE FOLIAGE** the leaves and berries of holly used especially as a Christmas decoration [12thC. Shortening of Old English *hole(g)n*, from prehistoric Germanic.]

Hol·ly /hóllee/, **Buddy** (1938–59) U.S. musician. His band, the Crickets, was one of the earliest rock-and-roll groups, and helped establish the standard lineup of two guitars, bass, and drums. His hit songs included "That'll Be the Day" and "Peggy Sue" (both 1957). Real name **Charles Hardin Holley**

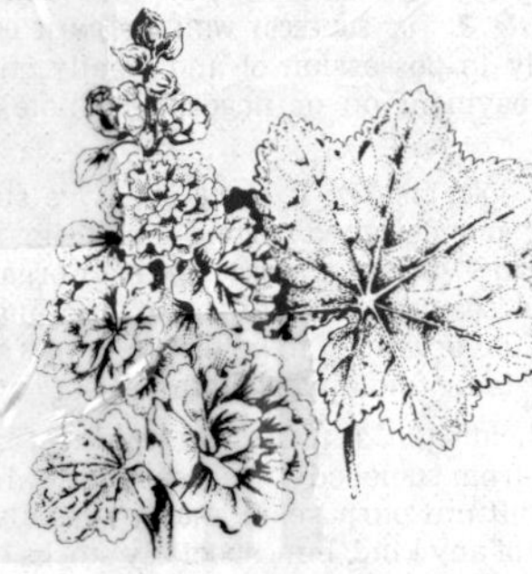

Hollyhock

hol·ly·hock /hólli hòk/ *n.* a plant of the mallow family that has very tall hairy stems and is often grown for its spikes of variously colored flowers. Latin name: *Alcea rosea.* [13thC. From an alteration of HOLY (perhaps from its being connected with a saint) + obsolete *hock* "mallow," of unknown origin.]

hol·ly oak *n.* = **holm oak** [Because its foliage resembles holly]

Hol·ly·wood[1] /hólliwòod/ *n.* the U.S. movie industry as a whole

Hol·ly·wood[2] /hólliwòod/ district of Los Angeles, California, a center of the U.S. movie and television industry ■ city in southeastern Florida on the Atlantic Ocean north of Miami. Population: 124,992 (1994).

holm[1] /hōm, hōlm/, **holme** *n.* **1. FLAT LAND BY RIVER** low-lying flat land next to a river or stream **2. SMALL ISLAND** a small island in a river, lake, estuary, or near the coastal mainland [Old English, from Old Norse *holmr* "islet in a bay, meadow." Ultimately from an Indo-European base meaning "to be prominent" (ancestor of English *hill*).]

holm[2] /hōm/ *n.* **1.** = **holm oak 2. HOLLY** a holly plant (*regional*) [14thC. Alteration of obsolete *hollin*, from Old English *hole(g)n*, an earlier form of HOLLY.]

holme *n.* = **holm**[1]

Holmes /hōmz/, **Oliver Wendell** (1809–94) U.S. physician and writer. He is best known for his essays collected in volumes including *The Autocrat of the Breakfast-Table* (1858). His poems "Old Ironsides" and "Chambered Nautilus" are considered classics of American literature.

Holmes, Oliver Wendell, Jr. (1841–1935) U.S. jurist. Known for his liberal interpretations of the U.S. Constitution, he was associate justice of the U.S. Supreme Court (1902–32). Known as **the Great Dissenter**

hol·mic /hṓlmik/ *adj.* resembling or containing the metallic element holmium

hol·mi·um /hṓlmee am/ *n.* a silvery-white malleable metallic chemical element of the rare-earth group often found with yttrium in gadolinite and monazite. Symbol **Ho** [Late 19thC. Coined from *Holmia* (a Latinized form of "Stockholm," the capital city of Sweden), + -IUM.]

holm oak *n.* a broad-leaved evergreen tree native to southern Europe but grown widely elsewhere for ornament. Latin name: *Quercus ilex.* [From HOLM[2] because its foliage resembles holly]

holo- *prefix.* whole, complete ○ *hologynic* [From Greek *holos* "whole, entire." Ultimately from an Indo-European word that is also the ancestor of English *solid, safe,* and *catholic.*]

hol·o·caust /hólla kàwst, hṓla-/ *n.* **1. COMPLETE DESTRUCTION BY FIRE** complete consumption by fire, especially of a large number of human beings or animals **2. TOTAL DESTRUCTION** wholesale or mass destruction of any kind **3. BURNT OFFERING** a sacrifice that is totally consumed by fire [13thC. Via Old French *holocauste* from, ultimately, Greek *holokaustos*, literally "burned whole," from, ultimately, *kaiein* "to burn."] —**ho·lo·caus·tal** /hòlla káwst'l, hṓla-/ *adj.* —**ho·lo·caus·tic** /hòlla káwstik, hṓla-/ *adj.*

WORD KEY: ORIGIN

Holocaust was originally used in English for a "burnt offering," a "sacrifice completely consumed by fire" (Mark 12:33, "more than all whole burnt offerings and sacrifices," in the King James Version of the Bible, was translated by William Tyndale in 1526 as "a greater thing than all holocausts and sacrifices"). John Milton is the first English writer recorded as using it in the wider sense "complete destruction by fire," in the late 17th century, and in the succeeding centuries several precedents were set for its modern application to "nuclear destruction" and "mass murder" – Bishop Ken, for instance, wrote in 1711 "Should general Flame this World consume ... An Holocaust for Fontal Sin," and Leitch Ritchie in 1833 refers to Louis VII making "a holocaust of thirteen hundred persons in a church." The specific application to the mass murder of the Jews by the Nazis during World War II was introduced by historians during the 1950s, probably as an equivalent to Hebrew *ḥurban* and *shoah* "catastrophe" (used in the same sense).

Hol·o·caust *n.* the systematic extermination of millions of European Jews, Romany people, Slavs, intellectuals, and political dissidents by the Nazis and their allies during World War II. In popular usage, especially in the United States, Holocaust refers particularly to the extermination of European Jews. ○ *Holocaust survivors*

Hol·o·cene /hólla seèn, hṓla-/ *n.* the most recent epoch of the Quaternary period, extending to the present day [Late 19thC. From French from an earlier form of HOLO- + Greek *kainos* "new, recent."] —**Hol·o·cene** *adj.*

hol·o·crine /hóllakrin, -krīn, hṓla-/ *adj.* relating to a gland such as a sebaceous gland whose secretions are derived from the substance of the gland itself

hol·o·en·zyme /hòllō én zīm, hṓlō-/ *n.* an active enzyme comprising a protein and coenzyme

hol·o·gram /hólla gràm, hṓla-/ *n.* **1. THREE-DIMENSIONAL PHOTOGRAPHIC IMAGE** a three-dimensional image of an object that is a photographic record of light interference patterns produced using a photographic plate and light from a laser **2. HOLOGRAM IMAGE** the image produced by a hologram

hol·o·graph /hólla gràf, hṓla-/ *n.* **1. ORIGINAL MANUSCRIPT** a manuscript or other document entirely handwritten by its author. This term is used especially in reference to the value of manuscripts and letters, and to unwitnessed wills. **2.** = **hologram** *n.* **1**, **hologram** *n.* **2** ■ *adj.* **IN THE HANDWRITING OF THE AUTHOR** used to describe a manuscript or other document wholly written in the handwriting of its author [Early 17thC. Via late Latin *holographus* from Greek *holographos*, literally "written whole."]

ho·log·raph·y /hō lóggrafee/ *n.* a method of recording and showing a three-dimensional image of an object using a photographic plate and light from a laser —**hol·o·graph·ic** /hòlla gráffik, hṓla-/ *adj.* —**ho·lo·graph·i·cal·ly** /-gráffikalee/ *adv.*

hol·o·gyn·ic /hòlla jínnik, -gínik, hòla-/ *adj.* used to describe genetic traits that are inherited and passed on only by females [Coined from HOLO- + Greek *gunē* "woman" (see GYNO-) + -IC]

hol·o·he·dral /hòlla heédral, hòla-/ *adj.* used to describe crystals having all the faces required for complete symmetry

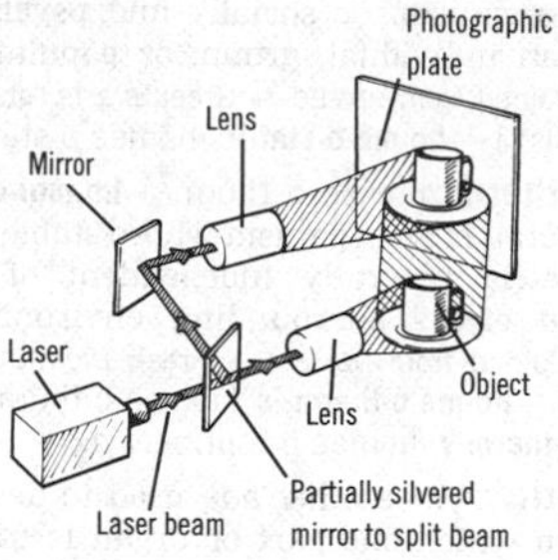

Holography

hol·o·me·tab·o·lism /hòllə mə tábbə lìzzəm, hōlə-/ *n.* the condition of developing by metamorphosing from a distinct larval into a distinct adult stage —**hol·o·me·tab·o·lous** *adj.*

hol·o·mor·phic /hòllə máwrfik, hōlə-/ *adj.* = **holohedral** —**hol·o·mor·phism** *n.*

hol·o·phras·tic /hòllə frástik, hòlə-/ *adj.* containing the idea of a sentence or phrase in one word, e.g., "goodbye" [Mid-19thC. Coined from HOLO- + Greek *phrastikos*, from *phrazein* "to tell."]

hol·o·phyte /hóllə fìt, hólə-/ *n.* an organism that synthesizes complex organic molecules by photosynthesis

hol·o·phyt·ic /hòllə fíttik, hòlə-/ *adj.* able to synthesize complex organic molecules by photosynthesis. ◊ **holozoic**

hol·o·plank·ton /hòllə plángktən, hòlə-/ *n.* organisms that remain free-swimming plankton throughout their life cycle

hol·o·thu·ri·an /hòllə thóoree ən, hòlə-/ *n.* a marine invertebrate animal (**echinoderm**) of the class that includes the sea cucumber. Holothurians have a mouth surrounded by tentacles at one end, an anus at the other, and a body that contains calcitic material but is not rigid. Class: Holothuroidea. [Mid-19thC. Formed from modern Latin *Holothuria*, genus name, from Latin *holothurion*, a marine creature.] —**hol·o·thu·ri·an** *adj.*

hol·o·type /hóllə tìp, hólə-/ *n.* the individual organism used in naming and describing a new species and usually preserved afterwards —**hol·o·typ·ic** /hòllə típpik, hòlə-/ *adj.*

hol·o·zo·ic /hòllə zó ik, hòlə-/ *adj.* obtaining nutrition from other organisms or organic matter, as most animals do. ◊ **holophytic**

holp /hōlp/ past tense of **help** (*archaic*)

hol·pen /hólpən/ past participle of **help** (*archaic*)

Hol·stein /hól stìn, -stèen/, **Hol·stein-Frie·sian** *n.* a large black-and-white dairy cow belonging to a breed known for its abundant milk production [Mid-19thC. Named for the region, formerly of the Netherlands, now of northern Germany, from which it originates.]

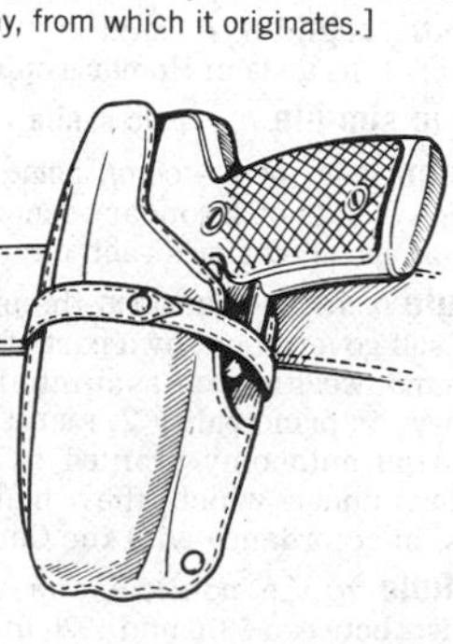
Holster

hol·ster /hólstər/ *n.* GUN HOLDER a holder for a pistol, usually worn on the hip or shoulder ■ *vt.* (**-stered, -ster·ing, -sters**) PUT GUN IN HOLDER to put a pistol in a holster [Mid-17thC. Origin uncertain: probably from Dutch, from, ultimately, an Indo-European word meaning "to cover" (ancestor of English *conceal*).] —**hol·stered** *adj.*

holt /hōlt/ *n.* 1. WOODED AREA a wood or copse (*archaic*) 2. *U.K.* WOODED HILL a wooded hill (*regional*) [Old English, of prehistoric Germanic origin]

ho·lus-bo·lus /hòləss bóləss/ *adv.* all at once or all together (*dated informal*) [Mid-19thC. Origin uncertain: possibly pseudo-Latin for "whole bolus," or humorously representing Greek *holos bōlos* "the whole lump" (see BOLUS).]

ho·ly /hólee/ *adj.* (**-li·er, -li·est**) 1. SACRED relating to, belonging to, or coming from a divine being or power ○ *holy relics* 2. SAINTLY devoted to the service of God, a god, or a goddess 3. PURE morally and spiritually perfect and of a devoutly religious character ○ *a holy man* 4. CONSECRATED dedicated or set apart for religious purposes ○ *holy water* ○ *Native American holy ground* 5. AWE-INSPIRING of a unique character, evoking reverence ○ *Gettysburg is a holy place for many people of the United States.* ■ *n.* (*plural* **-lies**) 1. HOLY THING something sanctified or venerated 2. HOLY PERSON a devoutly religious, saintly person ■ *interj.* USED IN EXPRESSIONS OF SURPRISE used in various expressions to show surprise (*informal*) ○ *Holy cow!* ○ *Holy smoke!* [Old English *hālig*, from a prehistoric Germanic word that is the ancestor of English *whole*, the underlying idea being "unimpaired"] —**ho·li·ly** *adv.*

Ho·ly Al·li·ance *n.* an alliance among Russia, Prussia, and Austria in 1815 advocating government according to Christian principles

Ho·ly Ark *n.* = **ark** *n.* 4

Ho·ly Cit·y *n.* 1. RELIG JERUSALEM Jerusalem as a city of great religious significance 2. CHR HEAVEN heaven in Christian tradition

Ho·ly Com·mu·nion *n.* CHR = **Communion**

Ho·ly Cross *n.* in Christianity, the cross that Jesus Christ died on

ho·ly day *n.* a day set aside for the celebration of a religious festival

ho·ly day of ob·li·ga·tion *n.* a Roman Catholic festival on which Catholics are required to attend mass and abstain from certain types of work

Ho·ly Fam·i·ly *n.* in Christianity, the young Jesus Christ, his mother Mary, and Mary's husband Joseph, especially as represented in art

Ho·ly Fa·ther *n.* in the Roman Catholic Church, the Pope

Ho·ly Ghost *n.* = **Holy Spirit**

Ho·ly Grail *n.* = **Grail**

Ho·ly In·no·cents' Day *n.* in the Christian church, December 28, the day that commemorates the order given by Herod to massacre all baby boys in Bethlehem

Ho·ly Is·land = **Lindisfarne** ■ = **Holyhead Island**

Ho·ly Joe *n.* (*dated slang*) 1. ARMED FORCES CHAPLAIN a chaplain in the armed forces 2. CLERGYMAN a clergyman 3. SOMEBODY SANCTIMONIOUS a sanctimonious or self-righteous person

Ho·ly Of·fice *n.* 1. COMMITTEE OF CARDINALS a permanent committee of the Roman Catholic College of Cardinals that deals with doctrine and morals. It was established in 1542, and was also called the Inquisition. In 1965 its title was changed to Congregation for the Doctrine of the Faith. 2. HIST = **Inquisition**

ho·ly of ho·lies *n.* 1. INNER SANCTUM FOR ARK the inner chamber inside the Sanctuary in the Jewish Temple in Jerusalem, where the Ark of the Covenant was kept 2. SACRED PLACE any place considered to be especially sacred

Hol·yoke /hól yōk, hólee ōk/ manufacturing city in southwestern Massachusetts, on the Connecticut River. Population: 41,461 (1996).

ho·ly or·ders *npl.* 1. RITE OF ORDINATION the rite or sacrament of ordination as a Christian minister or priest 2. MINISTER'S OR PRIEST'S RANK the rank or position of a Christian minister or priest 3. ROMAN CATHOLIC OR ANGLICAN RANKS in the Roman Catholic Church, the ranks of priest, deacon, and subdeacon, or in the Anglican Church, the ranks of bishop, priest, and deacon

Ho·ly Roll·er *n.* an offensive term for a member of a Christian group that worships in what is perceived to be an ecstatic or frenzied way, with shouting, bodily movements, and trances (*slang offensive*) [From the movement of the body during worship]

Ho·ly Ro·man Em·pire *n.* an empire in Germany and northern Italy (800–1806). Initially a revival of the Western Roman Empire, it became confined to Germany and the emperor's authority was negligible after 1254. From 1438 the imperial crown, although elective, was held almost continously by the Hapsburg family. ◊ **Roman Empire**

Ho·ly Sat·ur·day *n.* in Christianity, the Saturday preceding Easter Sunday

Ho·ly Scrip·ture *n.* the Christian Bible, or a particular part of it that is being cited or referred to

Ho·ly See *n.* 1. PAPACY in the Roman Catholic Church, the see of the Pope as Bishop of Rome 2. PAPAL COURT in the Roman Catholic Church, the government departments, jurisdiction, and authority of the Vatican

Ho·ly Sep·ul·chre *n.* in Christianity, the tomb in which the body of Jesus Christ was laid after the Crucifixion

Ho·ly Spir·it *n.* in Christianity, the third person of the Trinity, understood as the spiritual force of God

ho·ly·stone /hóli stòn/ *n.* DECK SCOURER a piece of soft sandstone used for scouring the decks of ships ■ *vt.* (**-stoned, -ston·ing, -stones**) CLEAN WITH HOLYSTONE to scour the deck of a ship with a holystone [*Holy* perhaps because it is used while kneeling]

Ho·ly Syn·od *n.* the governing body of any of the Eastern Orthodox Christian churches

ho·ly ter·ror *n.* somebody who is especially difficult or frightening to deal with (*informal*) ○ *That child is a holy terror.*

Ho·ly Thurs·day *n.* 1. ASCENSION DAY in the Anglican Church, Ascension Day, the 40th day after Easter 2. MAUNDY THURSDAY in the Roman Catholic Church, Maundy Thursday, the Thursday before Easter commemorating the Last Supper and the day before Jesus Christ was crucified

ho·ly·tide /hóli tìd/ *n.* a period having particular religious significance (*archaic*) [12thC. *Tide* from TIDE in the obsolete sense of "period of time."]

Ho·ly Trin·i·ty *n.* CHR = **Trinity**

ho·ly war *n.* a war undertaken in the name of a particular religion

ho·ly wa·ter *n.* water that has been blessed by a priest and is used in a church for blessings, baptisms, and other holy rituals

Ho·ly Week *n.* in the Christian calendar, the final week of Lent, beginning on Palm Sunday and including Ash Wednesday, Maundy Thursday, Good Friday, and Holy Saturday

Ho·ly Writ *n.* sacred Christian writings, especially the Bible

Ho·ly Year *n.* in the Roman Catholic Church, a period of remission from sin declared by the Pope with certain conditions attached, usually at 25 year intervals

hom- *prefix.* = **homo-** (*used before vowels*)

hom·age /hómmij, ómmij/ *n.* 1. DEFERENCE a show of reverence and respect toward somebody 2. HIST VASSAL'S RESPECT DUE TO LORD allegiance or a formal public acknowledgment of allegiance on the part of a vassal toward a feudal lord [13thC. From Old French, of uncertain origin: probably from *homme* "man," from the allegiance of one person to another.]

hom·bre /óm bray, ómbree/ *n.* (*informal*) 1. MAN a man 2. HE-MAN a macho or very strong, tough, and masculine man [Mid-19thC. Via Spanish from Latin *homo* "human being" (source of English *homicide*).]

hom·burg /hóm bùrg/ *n.* a man's felt hat with an upturned brim and a lengthwise crease in the crown [Late 19thC. Named for the town in western Germany where it was first worn.]

home /hōm/ *n.* 1. RESIDENCE the place where a person, family, or household lives 2. FAMILY GROUP a family or any other group that lives together ○ *Theirs was a happy home, full of love.* 3. BIRTHPLACE where somebody was born or raised or feels he or she belongs ○ *Home is New York.* 4. NATIVE HABITAT the place where something is most common or indigenous, or where something had its origins 5. SAFE PLACE a place where a person or animal can find refuge and safety or live in security 6. PLACE OF ASSISTANCE an establishment where somebody who is in need of care, rest, or medical attention can stay or find help ○ *My grandmother moved into a home.* 7. GRAVE the place where somebody is imagined to dwell after death (*literary*) 8. SPORTS GOAL the place or point that must be hit in order to score in many games, or that must be reached in order to be safe from attack 9. BASEBALL = **home plate** ■ *adj.* 1. DOMESTIC related in some way to somebody's own home or country **2.** OF A HOUSEHOLD for or belonging to or produced in a dwelling or household ○ *He loved his wife's home cooking.* **3.** NATIVE happening in or coming from somebody's native territory or permanent base, especially a sports team's own ground ○ *The home team usually has the advantage in a game.* **4.** EFFECTIVE to the point, or central to achieving a goal ○ *She won the argument with that home thrust.* **5.** PRINCIPAL belonging or relating to the headquarters of a business or enterprise ○ *She was promoted to the company's home office.* **6.** BASEBALL INVOLVING THE SCORING BASE at or near the scoring base or plate ○ *Jim made a home play and the game was over.* ■ *adv.* **1.** AT OR TO SOMEBODY'S HOME at or to the house, household, or country where somebody lives ○ *He desperately wanted to get home.* **2.** EFFECTIVELY to the point or desired goal ○ *Her criticisms of his behavior hit home.* **3.** TO THE CENTER to the center or heart of something, or as far as possible into a desired position ○ *In one stroke, she drove the nail home.* ■ *v.* **(homed, hom·ing, homes) 1.** *vi.* GO HOME to go back to the house, household, or country where somebody lives **2.** *vi.* RETURN HOME to return home, especially to fly home accurately (*refers to animals and birds*) **3.** *vi.* DWELL to have a home and live in it (*dated*) **4.** *vt.* TAKE OR SEND HOME to take or send something home (*dated*) **5.** *vt.* PROVIDE WITH A HOME to give a home to somebody or something (*dated*) [Old Englsh *hām*, from, ultimately, a prehistoric Germanic word meaning "home," which is also the ancestor of English *hamlet* and *hangar*] —**home·like** *adj.* ◇ **at home 1.** staying or working in the home **2.** ready to receive visitors **3.** at ease or in a familiar and friendly place **4.** having knowledge of or familiarity with a subject or activity ◇ **home free** with something successfully completed

WORD KEY: USAGE

See Usage note at ***hone***.

WORD KEY: USAGE

home or **house**? Many consider ***home*** an affectation when used anywhere that ***house*** would be appropriate (*Home for Sale*). ***Home*** is nonetheless useful to express the idea of dwelling places of various sorts, including apartments and condominiums, hogans and huts, and other dwellings that are not accurately described as houses. ***House***, in many contexts, suggests a single-family dwelling. For example, if *The tornado destroyed 17 homes* is meant to convey that 17 residential structures were demolished, the word should have been ***houses***. *Most homes in town lost electricity*, however, no doubt refers to households of all descriptions, so here ***homes*** is the better choice.

WORD KEY: CULTURAL NOTE

Home Alone, a movie by Chris Columbus (1990). A comedy set in Chicago at Christmas time, it portrays the adventures of a young boy, Kevin (Macauley Culkin), who is inadvertently left at home by his family when they go on vacation in Europe. Delighting in his new-found independence, the boy manages not only to take care of himself but also to outwit a pair of hapless burglars. In U.S. popular culture, *Home Alone* soon came to mean not only children left alone by negligent traveling parents but also the parents themselves, as this headline indicates: "'Home Alone' Parents Indicted by States on 64 Criminal Counts" *Washington Post* (February 10, 1993).

home in *vi.* **1.** PROCEED TOWARDS TARGET to locate and proceed straight toward a target **2.** DIRECT ATTENTION TO SOMETHING to direct all attention or energy toward something ○ *She instinctively homed in on the weakest aspects of the production.*

home bank·ing *n.* an electronic banking system that allows a customer to carry out transactions at home

home base *n.* **1.** BASEBALL = **home plate 2.** = **headquarters**

home·bod·y /hṓm bòdee/ (*plural* **-ies**) *n.* somebody who likes to stay at home (*informal*) ○ *Greg likes to go out on Friday nights, but I'm a real homebody.*

home·bound /hṓm bòwnd/ *adj.* confined to the home, usually because of illness, age, or inability to travel ○ *The state provides funds for the homebound.*

home·boy /hṓm bòy/ *n.* a man or boy from somebody's home town, state, or neighborhood, especially somebody who shares that person's own culture and customs (*slang*)

home·bred /hòm bréd/ *adj.* **1.** BRED AT HOME bred or raised at home **2.** UNSOPHISTICATED without worldly experience

home·brew /hṓm bròo/ *n.* an alcoholic beverage, especially beer, that has been brewed at home for personal consumption —**home·brewed** *adj.*

home·build·er /hṓm bìldər/ *n.* somebody who builds or designs houses —**home·build·ing** *n.*

home·buy·er /hṓm bìr/ *n.* somebody who is buying or interested in buying a house or apartment

home·com·ing /hṓm kùmming/ *n.* **1.** RETURN HOME the arrival home of somebody who has been away ○ *a party to celebrate his homecoming* **2.** RETURN TO OLD SCHOOL the annual return to somebody's old school or college, usually at a prescribed time of year, for celebrations with other alumni

Home Coun·ties the counties nearest to London, England, usually taken to include Kent, Surrey, Essex, Buckinghamshire, Berkshire, Hertfordshire, and East and West Sussex. Middlesex, formerly included, is now part of London.

home ec·o·nom·ics *n.* the science or study of food, diet, cookery, sewing, childcare, and other subjects related to the running of a home, as taught in schools

home fries *npl.* boiled sliced potatoes fried in butter or oil, sometimes with onions and seasonings

home front *n.* the civilian effort and activity at home in support of a war waged overseas ○ *Back on the home front, factories worked around the clock to provide everything from bandages to ammunition.*

home·girl /hṓm gùrl/ *n.* a girl or woman from somebody's home town, state, or neighborhood, especially one who shares that person's own culture and customs (*slang*)

home·grown /hṓm grṑwn/ *adj.* **1.** GROWN IN SOMEBODY'S OWN GARDEN grown in somebody's own garden or on somebody's own land **2.** LOCALLY PRODUCED produced by or coming from the area or region in question ○ *homegrown talent*

home·land /hṓm lànd/ *n.* **1.** NATIVE COUNTRY the country where somebody was born or where somebody lives and feels that he or she belongs **2.** HIST SELF-GOVERNING TERRITORY FOR BLACK PEOPLE any of the partially self-governing regions of South Africa created and set aside for the Black population under the former policy of racial apartheid

home·less /hṓmləss/ *adj.* WITH NO HOME without a home of any kind ■ *npl.* PEOPLE WITH NO HOME people without a home of any kind —**home·less·ness** *n.*

home·ly /hṓmlee/ (**-li·er, -li·est**) *adj.* **1.** NOT GOOD-LOOKING plain or less than pleasing in appearance ○ *a homely face* **2.** COZY simple, comfortable, and unpretentious, as if it were somebody's home or part of one **3.** UNPRETENTIOUS IN MANNER having a simple, unpretentious, and warm-hearted manner —**home·li·ness** *n.*

WORD KEY: SYNONYMS

See Synonyms at ***unattractive***.

home·made /hṓm màyd/ *adj.* **1.** MADE AT HOME made at home using traditional methods rather than by a manufacturer ○ *Have you tried some of my homemade marmalade?* **2.** MAKESHIFT roughly or crudely constructed to perform a specific function or purpose, usually by an individual in his or her home

home·mak·er /hṓm màykər/ *n.* somebody who stays at home to manage the household affairs and often the child-rearing

homeo- *prefix.* similar, alike ○ *homeotherm* [From Greek *homoios* "similar," from *homos* "same" (see HOMO-)]

Home Of·fice *n.* in the United Kingdom, the department of the government that is responsible for domestic and internal affairs

ho·me·op·a·thy /hṑmee óppəthee/ *n.* a complementary disease treatment system in which a patient is given minute doses of natural drugs that in larger doses would produce symptoms of the disease itself. The system was created by Dr. Samuel Hahnemann (1755–1843) on the assumption that like can be cured by like. —**ho·me·o·path** /hṓmee ə pàth/ *n.* —**ho·me·o·path·ic** /hṓmee ə páthik/ *adj.* —**ho·me·o·path·i·cal·ly** /-páthiklee/ *adv.* —**ho·me·op·a·thist** /hṑmee óppəthist/ *n.*

ho·me·o·sta·sis /hṑmee ō stáyssiss/ *n.* a state of equilibrium, or a tendency to reach equilibrium. Such equilibrium may be reached or maintained metabolically through biochemical reactions within a cell or organism, or socially and psychologically within an individual, group, or population. [Early 20thC. Coined from HOMEO- + Greek *stasis* "standing still" (see STASIS).] —**ho·me·o·stat·ic** /hṑmee ō státtik/ *adj.*

ho·me·o·therm /hṓmee ə thùrm/, **ho·moi·o·therm** /hō móyə thùrm/ *n.* an organism whose stable body temperature is generally independent of the temperature of its surrounding environment [Late 19thC. Coined from HOMEO- + Greek *thermē* "heat" (see THERM).] —**ho·me·o·therm·ic** /hṑmee ō thúrmik/ *adj.* —**ho·me·o·therm·y** /hṓmee ō thùrmee/ *n.*

ho·me·o·tic /hṑmee óttik/ *adj.* used to describe mutation in which one part or organ is transformed into another part associated with a different segment of the organism. It was originally discovered in the fruit fly. [Late 19thC. Via Greek *homoiotikos* "becoming like" from, ultimately *homóios* "like" (see HOMEO-).]

home page *n.* **1.** WEB SITE OPENING PAGE the opening page of an Internet Web site **2.** PERSONAL SITE ON INTERNET somebody's personal Web site on the Internet, often containing personal data, photographs, or contact information

home plate *n.* a flat slab marking the area over which a pitcher must throw the ball for a strike and on which a base runner must land in order to score

home port *n.* the place of registry or regular base of a ship

home-port **(home-port·ed, home-port·ing, home-ports)** *vt.* to base a vessel at a particular port

hom·er /hṓmər/ *n.* **1.** BASEBALL HOME RUN a home run in baseball (*informal*) **2.** ELECTRON ENG HOMING DEVICE a device that provides signals for guiding missiles, ships, or aircraft to their destinations **3.** ZOOL HOMING PIGEON a homing pigeon (*informal*) ■ *vi.* **(-ered, -er·ing, -ers)** BASEBALL MAKE HOME RUN to score a home run in baseball (*slang*) ○ *He homered in the last seconds of the third inning.*

Ho·mer /hṓmər/ (*fl.* 8th century B.C.) Greek poet. He is credited as the author of the great epics, the *Iliad* and the *Odyssey*.

Ho·mer city in southern Alaska on the southeastern shore of Cook Inlet. Population: 4,608 (1996).

Ho·mer, Winslow (1836–1910) U.S. artist. He is best known for his use of light and color in his watercolor seascapes and landscapes such as *Gulf Stream* (1899).

home range *n.* the specific geographic area to which an animal generally restricts its activities

Ho·mer·ic /hō mérrik/ *adj.* **1.** OF HOMER relating to or belonging to Homer, his work, or his times ○ *"Thus vain and false are the mere human surmises and doubts which clash with Homeric writ!"* (Alexander William Kinglake, *Eothen*; 1844) **2.** OF HOMER'S GREEK relating to the early form of ancient Greek used in Homer's poetry **3.** HEROIC characteristic or worthy of a hero (*literary*) [Early 17thC. Via Latin from Greek *Homērikos*, from *Homēros* HOMER.] —**Ho·mer·i·cal·ly** *adv.*

Ho·mer·ic laugh·ter *n.* loud continuous laughter, like that of the gods in Homer's epic poems (*literary*)

Ho·mer·ic sim·i·le *n.* = **epic simile**

home·room /hṓm ròom, -rŏŏm/, **home room** *n.* the room to which a class of secondary-school students must report at specified times each day

home rule *n.* **1.** SELF-GOVERNMENT the principle or practice of self-government by a part of a larger country or commonwealth such as a municipality, colony, territory, or principality **2.** PARTIAL AUTONOMY OF CITIES the partial autonomy granted to cities and some counties, under which they manage their own affairs, in accordance with the Constitution

Home Rule *n.* the political aim of the Irish nationalists between 1870 and 1920 in their struggle to secure self-government for Ireland

home run *n.* in baseball, a hit that allows a player to make a circuit of all four bases and score a run, usually by hitting the ball out of the playing area

home·school /hṓm skŏŏl/ *vti.* **(-schooled, -school·ing, -schools)** TEACH OR BE TAUGHT AT HOME to teach children at home, or be taught at home rather than in the public school system ○ *She's homeschooling her boys from K through 12.* ■ *n.* SCHOOL RUN AT HOME a school run typically by parents in the home for their children, using an approved curriculum

home·school·er /hṓm skòolər/ *n.* **1. CHILD EDUCATED AT HOME** a child who is undergoing or has undergone private education, typically by the parents, at home rather than in the public schools **2. PARENT EDUCATOR** a parent who educates his or her child or children at home rather than in the public school system

home·school·ing /hṓm skòoling/ *n.* the philosophy, curriculum, practice, or result of educating children at home, using typically an approved study plan ○ *The product of homeschooling, she later became a nurse.*

home shop·ping *n.* shopping done electronically from home either through an on-line retail service or a television shopping channel

home·sick /hṓm sìk/ *adj.* feeling sadness and longing to be at home with family and friends when away from them —**home·sick·ness** *n.*

home·site /hṓm sīt/ *n.* a plot of land on which a new home can be or is constructed

home·spun /hṓm spùn/ *adj.* **1. PLAIN AND SIMPLE** simple and unpretentious **2.** CRAFT **MADE BY HAND AT HOME** spun or woven by hand at home **3.** CLOTHES, HOUSEHOLD **MADE OF HOMESPUN FABRIC** made of fabric woven or spun by hand at home ■ *n.* TEXTILES **1. ROUGH CLOTH** a coarse plain, usually woolen or linen, cloth woven from homespun thread **2. ROUGH CLOTH WOVEN ON POWER LOOM** a cloth similar to homespun, but woven on an automatic or electric loom

home stand *n.* a series of games played on a team's home field, especially in baseball

home·stay /hṓm stày/ *n.* a visit to somebody's home in a foreign country, often a stay by an exchange student in a family's home (*informal*)

home·stead /hṓm sted/ *n.* **1. HOUSE, OUTBUILDINGS, AND LAND** a house, especially a farmhouse, with its dependent buildings and land, considered as a whole **2.** LAW **RESIDENCE EXEMPT FROM FORCED SALE** a house, adjoining land, and buildings declared as the owner's fixed residence and therefore exempt from seizure and forced sale for the recovery of debts **3.** HIST **LAND CLAIMED BY SETTLER** a piece of land occupied by a settler or squatter under the terms of the U.S. Homestead Act or the Canadian Dominion Lands Act ■ *vi.* (**-stead·ed, -stead·ing, -steads**) **CLAIM AND WORK FARMLAND** to settle and farm land, especially under the terms of the Homestead Act

Home·stead /hṓm sted/ city in southeastern Florida, southwest of Miami. Population: 26,866 (1990).

Home·stead Act *n.* **1. ACT GRANTING LAND TO SETTLERS** an act passed by Congress in 1862, promising ownership of 160 acres of public land to a citizen who lived on the land and cultivated it for five years **2. CANADIAN ACT GRANTING LAND TO SETTLERS** the Dominion Lands Act, passed by the Canadian Parliament in 1872, and modeled after the U.S. Homestead Act of 1862

home·stead·er /hṓm stèddər/ *n.* **1. OWNER OF HOMESTEAD** somebody who owns and manages a homestead **2. SETTLER GRANTED GOVERNMENT LAND** somebody who settles and farms land under the terms of either the U.S. Homestead Act or the Canadian Dominion Lands Act

home·stead law *n.* any one of several laws granting privileges to homesteaders such as exemption from having their property sold to recover debts

home stretch *n.* **1. LAST SECTION OF RACECOURSE** the part of a racecourse between the last turn and the finish line **2. LAST STAGE OF UNDERTAKING** the last part of a trip, task, or operation

home-style *adj.* **PREPARED OR SERVED AS AT HOME** made or presented as it would be in somebody's home ○ *served a home-style meal in the inn* ■ *adv.* **AS AT HOME** in a way that is like the way something is prepared or served at home ○ *served the meal home-style even though the inn was huge*

home teach·er *n. U.K.* = **visiting teacher**

home·town /hṓm tòwn/, **home town** *n.* the town or city where somebody was born or raised

home truth *n.* an unpleasant but true basic fact about somebody's character or behavior

home·ward /hṓmwərd/ *adv.* **TOWARD HOME** in the direction of home ○ *homeward bound* ■ *adj.* **GOING HOME** going home, or in the direction of home

Home·wood /hṓmwòod/ **1.** village in northeastern Illinois, a southern suburb of Chicago. Population: 19,279 (1996). **2.** city in northern Alabama, a south-eastern suburb of Birmingham. Population: 23,156 (1996).

home·work /hṓm wùrk/ *n.* **1.** EDUC **SCHOOLWORK DONE AT HOME** schoolwork that students do after school at home or outside of class **2. PRELIMINARY OR PREPARATORY WORK** facts that are found out about a particular subject, especially in preparation for writing or talking about it (*informal*) **3. PAID WORK DONE AT HOME** work done at home for money, especially piecework ◇ **do your homework** to do all the necessary research and preparation for something in a thorough manner

hom·ey[1] /hṓmee/ (**-i·er, -i·est**), **hom·y** (**-i·er, -i·est**) *adj.* feeling as comfortable and familiar as somebody's own home ○ *a homey little hotel* —**hom·ey·ness** *n.*

hom·ey[2] /hṓmee/ *n.* = **homeboy, homegirl** (*slang*) [Late 20thC. Shortening and alteration.]

hom·i·cid·al /hòmmi sīd'l/ *adj.* capable of or intending to kill another human being unlawfully — **hom·i·cid·al·ly** *adv.*

hom·i·cide /hómmi sīd/ *n.* **1. KILLING OF SOMEBODY** the act or an instance of unlawfully killing another human being **2. SOMEBODY WHO HAS COMMITTED HOMICIDE** somebody who has killed another human being unlawfully [13thC. Via French from Latin *homicidium* and Latin *homicida*, both from *homo* "human being" (see HOMINOID) + *caedere* "to kill" (see -CIDE).]

Hom·i·cide *n.* the part of a police department, including its personnel, that investigates unlawful killings (*informal*) (*takes a singular or plural verb*)

hom·i·let·ic /hòmmə léttik/, **hom·i·let·i·cal** /-léttik'l/ *adj.* **1. RELATING TO HOMILETICS** relating to the art of writing and preaching sermons **2. RELATING TO HOMILIES** relating to, or in the style of, a sermon or homily [Mid-17thC. Via late Latin from, ultimately, Greek *homilein* "to associate with, converse," from *homilos* "crowd" (see HOMILY).] —**hom·i·let·i·cal·ly** *adv.*

hom·i·let·ics /hòmmə léttiks/ *n.* the art of writing and preaching sermons (*takes a singular verb*)

hom·i·ly /hómmәlee/ (*plural* **-lies**) *n.* **1. MORAL OR RELIGIOUS LECTURE** a sermon or other piece of writing on a moral or religious topic **2. MORALIZING SPEECH** a speech or other piece of writing with a moralizing theme **3. SHORT SAYING** a short inspirational saying ○ *a calendar that gives a little homily for each day* [14thC. Via Old French *omilie* from, ultimately, Greek *homilia* "sermon," from *homilos* "crowd." Ultimately from an Indo-European word meaning "together" that is also the ancestor of English *same*.] —**hom·i·list** *n.*

hom·ing /hṓming/ *adj.* **1.** ZOOL **RELATING TO ABILITY TO RETURN HOME** relating to or possessing the ability to find the way home after traveling a long distance **2.** AEROSP **ABLE TO GUIDE ITSELF TO TARGET** used to describe a missile or aircraft that has equipment that enables it to guide itself to its target

hom·ing guid·ance *n.* a system that enables a missile or aircraft to guide itself to its target

hom·ing pi·geon *n.* a pigeon, used in racing and carrying messages, that is trained to return to its roost

hom·i·nid /hómmənid/ *n.* **MEMBER OF A PRIMATE FAMILY INCLUDING HUMANS** a primate belonging to a family of which the modern human being is the only species still in existence. Family: Hominidae. ■ *adj.* **OF HOMINIDS** relating to the hominids [Late 19thC. Via modern Latin *Hominidae*, family name, from, ultimately, Latin *homo* "human being" (see HOMINOID).]

hom·i·ni·za·tion /hòmməni záysh'n/ *n.* the theorized evolutionary development of human characteristics that set hominids apart from other primates [Mid-20thC. Via French from Latin *homin-*, the stem of *homo* "human being" (see HOMINOID).]

hom·i·noid /hómmə nòyd/ *adj.* **1. SIMILAR TO HUMAN** resembling a human being **2. OF HUMAN BEINGS AND APES** belonging or relating to the superfamily that includes human beings and apes. Superfamily: Hominoidea. [Early 20thC. Formed from Latin *homin-*, the stem of *homo* "human being," literally "earthling." Ultimately from an Indo-European word meaning "earth," also the ancestor of English *human* and *humble*.]

hom·i·ny /hómmənee/ (*plural* **-nies**) *n.* puffed and dried hulled whole kernels of corn that are eaten boiled, especially in the Southwestern dish known as "posole" [Early 17thC. Contraction of Virginia Algonquian *uskatahomen*.]

hom·i·ny grits *npl.* FOOD grits (*dated*)

hom·mos *n.* = **hummus**

ho·mo /hṓ mṑ/ (*plural* **-mos**) *n.* an offensive term referring to a man who is gay (*dated slang offensive*) [Early 20thC. Shortening.]

homo- *prefix.* alike, same ○ ***homograph*** [From Greek *homos*. Ultimately from an Indo-European word meaning "one," which is also the ancestor of English *same, some, similar*, and *hetero-*.]

ho·mo·cen·tric /hṑmə séntrik/ *adj.* used to describe circles and spheres that have the same center

ho·mo·cer·cal /hṑmə súrk'l, hòmmə-/ *adj.* used to describe a fish that has a tail with two symmetrical lobes that extend beyond the end of the vertebral column, or a tail of this kind

ho·mo·chro·mat·ic /hṑmə krō máttik/ *adj.* = **monochromatic** *adj.* **1**

ho·mo·chro·mous /hṑmə krṓməss, hòmmə-/ *adj.* being of just one color [Mid-19thC. Coined from HOMO- + Greek *khrōma* "color."]

ho·mo·cy·clic /hṑmə sīklik, -síklik, hòmə-/ *adj.* used to describe a chemical compound in which molecules take the form of a ring in which all the atoms are the same

ho·mo·dont /hṓmə dònt/ *adj.* used to describe vertebrates that have teeth that are all similar in shape and not of different shapes as in most nonmammalian vertebrates [Late 19thC. Coined from HOMO- + the Greek stem *odont-* "tooth."]

Ho·mo e·rec·tus /hṑmō i réktəss/ *n.* an extinct ancestor of the modern human being (**Homo sapiens**) living approximately 1.5 million years ago and known by fossils to have had an upright stature, a smallish brain, and a low forehead [From modern Latin, literally "upright man"]

ho·mo·e·rot·ic /hṑmō i róttik/ *adj.* relating to or characterized by homosexual eroticism

ho·mo·e·rot·i·cism /hṑmō i rótti sìzzəm/, **ho·mo·er·o·tism** /hṑmō é rrə tìzzəm/ *n.* eroticism that is focused on or inspired by people of the same sex

ho·mo·ga·met·ic /hṑmō gə méttik/ *adj.* producing gametes that have the same type of sex chromosome

ho·mog·a·my /hō móggəmee, ho-/ *n.* the condition of a flower in which male and female organs mature at the same time

ho·mog·e·nate /hō mójjə nàyt, hə mój-/ *n.* a substance produced by homogenizing

ho·mo·ge·ne·i·ty /hṑmə jə née ətee, hòmmə-/ *n.* **1. QUALITY OF BEING THE SAME** the quality of being of the same or a similar nature **2. QUALITY OF BEING UNIFORM** the quality of having a uniform appearance or composition [Early 17thC. From medieval Latin *homogeneitas*, from *homogeneus* (see HOMOGENEOUS).]

ho·mo·ge·ne·ous /hṑmə jéenee əss, hòmmə-/ *adj.* **1. OF SAME KIND** having the same kind of constituent elements, or being similar in nature **2. HAVING UNIFORM COMPOSITION** having a uniform composition or structure [Mid-17thC. Formed from medieval Latin *homogeneus*, from Greek *homogenēs*, literally "of the same kind."] —**ho·mo·ge·ne·ous·ly** *adv.* —**ho·mo·ge·ne·ous·ness** *n.*

ho·mog·e·nize /hə mójjə nīz, hō-/ (**-nized, -niz·ing, -niz·es**) *v.* **1.** *vt.* **GIVE MILK OR CREAM EVEN CONSISTENCY** to emulsify the fat particles in milk or cream so as to give it an even consistency and prevent cream from separating from the rest of the milk **2.** *vti.* **BECOME OR MAKE HOMOGENEOUS** to become or cause something to become homogeneous [Late 19thC. Formed from HOMOGENEOUS.] —**ho·mog·e·ni·za·tion** /hə mòjjəni záysh'n, hō-/ *n.* —**ho·mog·e·niz·er** /hə mójjə nīzər, hō-/ *n.*

ho·mog·e·nous /hə mójjənəss, hō mójjənəss/ *adj.* = **homogeneous** —**ho·mog·e·nous·ly** *adv.*

ho·mog·e·ny /hə mójjənee, hō-/ *n.* a similarity in individuals, organs, or parts caused by a common ancestry [Late 19thC. Coined from HOMO- + -GENY.]

ho·mo·graft /hómmə gràft, hṓmə-/ *n.* a graft of tissue from one organism to another of the same species. ◊ **allograft**

hom·o·graph /hómmə gràf, hṓmə-/ *n.* a word that is spelled in the same way as one or more other words but is different in meaning, e.g., the verb "project" and the noun "project." ◊ **homophone, homonym** — **hom·o·graph·ic** /hòmmə gráffik, hṑmə-/ *adj.*

Ho·mo hab·i·lis /hṑmō hábbiliss/ *n.* an extinct ancestor of the modern human being (**Homo sapiens**) living approximately 1.5 million years ago and characterized by its ability to make and use tools [From modern Latin, literally "skillful man"]

homoio- *prefix.* = **homeo-**

ho·moi·o·therm *n.* = **homeotherm**

Ho·moi·ou·si·an /hō moy óossee ən, -óozee-/ *n.* **CHRISTIAN BELIEVING JESUS CHRIST IS NOT GOD** a Christian who believes that Jesus Christ is of a similar, but not identical, substance to God. ◊ **Homoousian** ■ *adj.* **OF DOCTRINE OF HOMOIOUSIANS** relating to the doctrine of the Homoiousians. ◊ **Homoousian** [Late 17thC. Formed from Greek *homoiousios* "of similar substance," from *homoios* "similar" + *ousia* "substance."] —**Ho·moi·ou·si·an·ism** *n.*

hom·o·log *n.* = **homologue**

ho·mol·o·gate /hə móllə gàyt, hō-/ (**-gat·ed, -gat·ing, -gates**) *v.* **1.** *vti.* LAW **CONFIRM SOMETHING** to confirm or sanction the validity of something **2.** *vt.* CARS **OFFICIALLY RECOGNIZE CAR MODEL OR COMPONENT** to give official recognition to a prototype car or car component, thus allowing it to be used in a race [Early 16thC. Via medieval Latin *homologare* "to agree," from, ultimately, Greek *homologos* "agreeing" (see HOMOLOGOUS).]

ho·mo·log·i·cal /hòmə lójjik'l, hòmmə-/ *adj.* = **homologous** —**ho·mo·log·i·cal·ly** *adv.*

ho·mol·o·gize /hə móllə jìz, hō-/ (**-gized, -giz·ing, -giz·es**) *vt.* to make something have a similar or related structure, position, function, or value to something else —**ho·mol·o·giz·er** *n.*

ho·mol·o·gous /hə mólləgəss, hō-/ *adj.* **1. SIMILAR** sharing a similar or related structure, position, function, or value **2.** BIOL **HAVING SAME ORIGIN BUT DIFFERENT FUNCTION** sharing the same origin but having a different function, as do, e.g., the wing of a bird and the fin of a fish **3.** CHEM **OF RELATED CHEMICAL COMPOUNDS** relating to a series of organic chemical compounds such as a methylene group, each of which differs from the preceding by the addition of a constant component **4.** MED **HAVING IDENTICAL TISSUE** produced from identical tissue [Mid-17thC. Via medieval Latin from Greek *homologos* "agreeing," literally "speaking the same," from *homos* "same" and *legein* "to speak."]

hom·o·lo·graph·ic /hòməlo gráffik/ *adj.* MAPS = **equal-area** [Mid-19thC. Alteration (under the influence of *homo-*) of *homalographic*, from Greek *homalos* "even, level" + -GRAPHIC.]

hom·o·logue /hómmə làwg, hṓmə-/, **hom·o·log** *n.* **1.** BIOL **HOMOLOGOUS PART OR ORGAN** a part or organ that has the same evolutionary origin as another but differs in function, e.g., a bird's wing in relation to the fin of a fish **2.** CHEM **HOMOLOGOUS COMPOUND** a homologous chemical compound [Mid-19thC. Via French from, ultimately, Greek *homologos* "agreeing" (see HOMOLOGOUS).]

ho·mol·o·gy /hə móllajee, hō-/ *n.* **1.** BIOL **LIKENESSES BETWEEN ANIMALS** similar characteristics in two animals that are a product of descent from a common ancestor rather than a product of a similar environment **2.** CHEM **SIMILARITY BETWEEN COMPOUNDS** the correspondence between chemical compounds in a homologous series [Early 17thC. Via late Latin from Greek *homologia* "agreement," from *homologos* (see HOMOLOGOUS.]

ho·mol·o·sine pro·jec·tion /hō mòllə sīn-/ *n.* a map of the earth's surface that distorts the oceans in order to represent the continents with a minimum of distortion [Coined from HOMOLOGRAPHIC + SINE, because it is a homolographic projection based on sinusoidal curves]

ho·mol·y·sis /hō mólləssiss/ *n.* the breakdown of a molecule into neutral atoms or radicals — **ho·mo·lyt·ic** /hṓmə líttik, hòmmə-/ *adj.*

hom·o·nym /hómmənim/ *n.* **1. WORD WITH SAME SPELLING OR SOUND** a word that is spelled or pronounced in the same way as one or more other words but has a different meaning. "Fleet" (group of vehicles) and "fleet" (swift), "plane" and "plain," and the verb "sow" (plant seeds) and the noun "sow" (female swine) are homonyms of three types. ◊ **homograph, homophone 2. SOMEBODY WITH SAME NAME** somebody with the same name as somebody else **3.** BIOL **DUPLICATE TAXONOMIC NAME** a taxonomic name that is the same as one already designating a different species or genus and cannot therefore be used [Late 17thC. Via Latin *homonymum* from, ultimately, Greek *homōnumos* (see HOMONYMOUS).] —**hom·o·nym·ic** /hòmmə nímmik/ *adj.* —**hom·o·nym·i·ty** /-nímmatee/ *n.* —**ho·mon·y·my** /hə mónnimee/ *n.*

ho·mon·y·mous /hə mónnimass/ *adj.* **1. OF HOMONYMS** relating to homonyms or in the form of a homonym ○ *The words "peace" and "piece" are homonymous.* **2. HAVING SAME NAME** having the same name as somebody or something else [Early 17thC. Via Latin from, ultimately, Greek *homōnumos*, literally "having the same name," from *onuma* "name" (see ONOMASTIC).] —**ho·mon·y·mous·ly** *adv.*

Ho·mo·ou·si·an /hòmō óossee ən, -óozee-/ *n.* **CHRISTIAN BELIEVING JESUS CHRIST IS GOD** a Christian who believes that Jesus Christ is of the same substance as God, in accordance with the Council of Nicaea's definition of the Trinity. ◊ **Homoiousian** ■ *adj.* **OF DOCTRINE OF HOMOOUSIANS** relating to the doctrine of the Homoousians. ◊ **Homoiousian** [Mid-16thC. Formed from Greek *homoousios* "of the same substance," from *homos* "same" + *ousia* "substance."] —**Ho·mo·ou·si·an·ism** *n.*

ho·mo·phile /hṓmə fīl/ *adj.* **1. ADVOCATING GAY AND LESBIAN RIGHTS** supporting the rights of gay and lesbian people and appreciating their culture **2. GAY OR LESBIAN** relating to or being gay or lesbian ■ *n.* **SOMEBODY GAY OR LESBIAN** a gay man or lesbian woman, or a supporter of gay and lesbian rights

ho·mo·pho·bi·a /hṓmə fṓbee ə/ *n.* an irrational hatred, disapproval, or fear of homosexuality, gay and lesbian people, and their culture [Mid-20thC. Coined from HOMOSEXUAL + -PHOBIA.]

ho·mo·pho·bic /hṓmə fṓbik/ *adj.* showing an irrational hatred, disapproval, or fear of homosexuality, gay and lesbian people, and their culture

hom·o·phone /hómmə fōn, hṓmə-/ *n.* **1. WORD WITH SAME PRONUNCIATION** a word that is pronounced in the same way as one or more other words but is different in meaning and sometimes spelling, as are "hair" and "hare." ◊ **homograph, homonym 2. LETTER WITH SAME SOUND** a letter or diphthong that has the same sound as one or more other letters or diphthongs [Early 17thC. From Greek *homophōnos* "having the same sound."]

hom·o·phon·ic /hòmmə fónnik, hṓmə-/ *adj.* **1.** LING **SOUNDING THE SAME** sharing the same sound **2.** MUSIC **RELATING TO HOMOPHONY** relating to part music in which the parts move together in simple harmonization — **ho·mo·phon·i·cal·ly** *adv.*

ho·moph·o·ny /hō móffənee, hə-/ *n.* **1.** LING **IDENTICAL PRONUNCIATION OF WORDS** the quality of having the same pronunciation as one or more other words with a different origin and meaning **2.** MUSIC **HOMOPHONIC MUSIC** music of a largely chordal style in which there is no independence of voice parts, but rather a simple harmonization of a melody [Mid-18thC. From Greek *homophōnia* "unison," from *homophōnos* (see HOMOPHONE).]

ho·mo·plas·tic /hṓmə plástik, hòmmə-/ *adj.* used to describe a tissue graft that is obtained from a member of the same species as the recipient — **ho·mo·plas·ti·cal·ly** *adv.*

ho·mo·po·lar /hṓmə pṓlər, hòmmə-/ *adj.* having uniform polarity —**ho·mo·po·lar·i·ty** /hṓmə pō lérrətee, hòmmə-/ *n.*

ho·mop·ter·an /hō móptərən/ *n.* **INSECT SUCKING PLANT JUICES THROUGH MOUTHPARTS** any insect that has the ability to suck plant juices through its mouthparts, e.g., the cicada, scale insect, or aphid. Order: Homoptera. ■ *adj.* **OF HOMOPTERANS** being or relating to a homopteran [Mid-19thC. From modern Latin *Homoptera*, order name, from Greek *homos* "same" and *pteron* "wing." So called because their wings have a uniform texture.]

Ho·mo sa·pi·ens /hṓmō sáypee ənz, -ènz/ *n.* the species of modern human beings, the only extant species of the family that also included other species named Homo. Family: Hominidae. [From modern Latin, literally "wise man"]

ho·mo·sce·das·tic /hṓmōsə dástik, hṓmōskə-/ *adj.* characterized by equal statistical variances [Early 20thC. Coined from HOMO- + Greek *skedastos* "able to be scattered," from *skedannunai* "to scatter." Ultimately from an Indo-European base that also produced English *scatter* and *shingle*.] —**ho·mo·sce·das·tic·i·ty** /hṓmō sə das tíssətee, -skə-/ *n.*

ho·mo·sex·u·al /hṓmə sékshoo əl, hṓmō-/ *n.* **SOMEBODY ATTRACTED TO SAME SEX** somebody who is sexually attracted to members of his or her own sex ■ *adj.* **1. ATTRACTED TO SAME SEX** sexually attracted to members of the same sex **2. OF HOMOSEXUALITY** relating to sexual attraction or activity among members of the same sex

ho·mo·sex·u·al·i·ty /hṓmə sekshoo állətee, hṓmō-/ *n.* sexual attraction to, and sexual relations with, members of the same sex

ho·mo·spo·rous /hṓmō spáwrəss, hòmmō-, ho móspərəss/ *adj.* producing asexual spores of only one type

ho·mo·tax·is /hṓmō táksiss, hòmmō-/ *n.* a similarity of composition, arrangement, or fossil content among rock strata of different ages or locations — **ho·mo·tax·i·al** *adj.* —**ho·mo·tax·i·al·ly** *adv.* —**ho·mo·tax·ic** *adj.*

ho·mo·thal·lic /hṓmō thállik, hòmō-/ *adj.* used to describe a plant that has both male and female reproductive organs on one thallus and is therefore able to fertilize itself —**ho·mo·thal·lism** *n.*

ho·mo·zy·gote /hṓmō zī gōt, hòmmō-/ *n.* an organism that has two identical genes at the same place on two corresponding chromosomes —**ho·mo·zy·got·ic** /hṓmō zī góttik, hòmmō-/ *adj.*

ho·mo·zy·gous /hṓmō zígəss, hòmmō-/ *adj.* having two identical genes at the corresponding loci of homologous chromosomes —**ho·mo·zy·gous·ly** *adv.*

Homs /homz/ historic city in western Syria, situated on the Orontes River. Population: 518,000 (1992).

ho·mun·cu·lus /hō múngkyələss/ (*plural* **-li** /-lī/), **ho·mun·cule** /hō múng kyool/ *n.* **1. VERY SMALL HUMAN BEING** a diminutive human being without any deformity of physiology **2. MINIATURE PERSON INSIDE EGG OR SPERM** in early biological theory, the fully formed human being that was thought to exist inside an egg or spermatozoon [Mid-17thC. From Latin *homunculus*, literally "little person," from *homo* (see HOMINOID).] — **ho·mun·cu·lar** *adj.*

hom·y *adj.* = **homey**²

hon /hun/ *n.* = **honey** *n.* 3 (*informal*) [Early 20thC. Shortening.]

hon. *abbr.* **1.** honorary **2.** honorable

Hon. *abbr.* Honorable

ho·nan /hṓ naán/ *n.* a rough-woven raw silk fabric, originally from China [Early 20thC. Named for *Honan*, a province of northern China where the fabric was originally manufactured.]

hon·cho /hón chō/ *n.* (*plural* **-chos**) **SOMEBODY IN CHARGE** somebody who is in charge of a project or situation, or of other people, or who behaves in a self-important way (*slang*) ○ *Who's the head honcho around here?* ■ *vt.* (**-choed, -cho·ing, -chos**) **BE IN CHARGE OF SOMETHING** to manage or organize people or events (*slang*) ○ *He's the one who honchoed their election campaign.* [Mid-20thC. From Japanese *hanchō* "group leader." The term was adopted by U.S. soldiers during the Korean War.]

Hond. *abbr.* Honduras

Hon·da /hóndə/, **Soichiro** (1906–92) Japanese engineer and business executive. He founded the Honda Motor Company to manufacture motorcycles (1948) and cars (1963).

Honduras

Hon·du·ras /hon dyóorəss/ republic in Central America, with coastlines on the Caribbean Sea and the Pacific Ocean. Language: Spanish. Currency: lempira. Capital: Tegucigalpa. Population: 5,666,000 (1996). Area: 43,277 sq. mi./112,088 sq. km. Official name **Republic of Honduras** —**Hon·du·ran** /hon dóorən/ *adj., n.*

Hon·du·ras, Gulf of inlet of the Caribbean Sea, situated between southern Belize, eastern Guatemala, and northern Honduras

hone¹ /hōn/ *vt.* (**honed, hon·ing, hones**) **1. IMPROVE SOMETHING WITH REFINEMENTS** to bring something to a state of increased intensity, excellence, or completion, especially over a period of time **2. SHARPEN BLADE ON WHETSTONE** to sharpen a blade on a fine whetstone ■ *n.* **1. WHETSTONE** a fine-grained sedimentary rock used as a whetstone for sharpening razors and other cutting tools. Emery and silicon carbide products are now largely used instead. **2.** **MACHINE TOOL** a tool with a rotating abrasive head, used to bore holes [Old English *hān* "whetstone." Ultimately from an Indo-European word meaning "to sharpen," which may also be the ancestor of English *cone*.] —**hon·er** *n.*

WORD KEY: USAGE

hone in and **home in** It is hard to imagine any context in which ***hone in*** could be correct. ***Hone*** is a transitive verb that means "sharpen" (*hone a blade*) or, in a metaphorical extension of that idea, "perfect, refine" (*hone his ideas before speaking out*). It is the verb ***home***, generally intransitive, whose meanings include "be guided toward, move toward," that makes sense with the particle *in*: as in *home in on his enemy's weaknesses*.

hone[2] /hōn/ (**honed, hon·ing, hones**) *vi.* (*regional*) **1.** **WANT VERY MUCH** to long for somebody or something **2.** **COMPLAIN CONTINUOUSLY** to complain about somebody or something, especially in a whining manner [Early 17thC. From Old French *hognier* "to grumble," of uncertain origin.]

hon·est /ónnəst/ *adj.* **1.** **MORALLY UPRIGHT** never cheating, lying, or breaking the law **2.** **TRUTHFUL OR TRUE** expressing or embodying the truth **3.** **IMPARTIAL** presenting information in an impartial way **4.** **REASONABLE IN A PARTICULAR SITUATION** reasonable and acceptable, given the circumstances ○ *an honest mistake* **5.** **UNPRETENTIOUS** having simple manners and no pretensions ○ *honest country folk* **6.** **RESPECTABLE** respectable and virtuous (*dated*) [13thC. Via Old French from Latin *honestus* "honorable," from *honos* "honor" (source of English *honor*).] —**hon·est·ness** *n.* ◇ **honest to God** *or* **goodness 1.** used to express surprise or shock **2.** used to emphasize the truth of a statement

hon·est bro·ker *n.* a person, country, or organization that mediates in disputes [Translation of German *ehrlicher Makler*, a phrase describing the German statesman Otto von Bismarck (1815–98)]

hon·est·ly /ónnəstlee/ *adv.* **1.** **FAIRLY OR JUSTLY** in a way that is fair, just, truthful, and morally upright **2.** **GENUINELY** really and truly ○ *Can you honestly say that you care?* ■ *interj.* **USED TO EXPRESS SURPRISE** used to express surprise, annoyance, or disapproval

hon·est-to-God, hon·est-to-good·ness *adj.* completely real or authentic (*informal*) ○ *You made a real, honest-to-God mess of that.*

hon·es·ty /ónnəstee/ (*plural* **-ties**) *n.* **1.** **MORAL UPRIGHTNESS** the quality, condition, or characteristic of being fair, just, truthful, and morally upright **2.** **TRUTHFULNESS** truthfulness, candor, or sincerity ○ *In all honesty, I really didn't know.* **3.** PLANTS **PLANT WITH FLAT PAPERY SEED PODS** a hardy European plant with purplish or white flowers and flat silvery seed pods that are often used for indoor decoration. Latin name: *Lunaria annua*.

hone·wort /hṓn wùrt, -wàwrt/ *n.* **1.** **N AMERICAN FLOWERING PLANT** a perennial plant native to eastern North America that has clusters of small white flowers and compound leaves. Latin name: *Cryptoaenia canadensis*. **2.** **EUROPEAN FLOWERING PLANT** a European plant that has clusters of small white flowers. Latin name: *Trinia glauca*. [Mid-17thC. *Hone*, of unknown origin.]

hon·ey /húnnee/ *n.* **1.** FOOD **SWEET STICKY SUBSTANCE MADE BY BEES** a sweet sticky golden-brown fluid produced by bees from the nectar of flowers, used especially in cooking, spread on bread, or added to tea **2.** **SWEET SUBSTANCE MADE BY OTHER INSECTS** a sweet sticky substance produced from nectar by insects other than bees **3.** **AFFECTIONATE TERM OF ADDRESS** a term of affection or endearment used to address somebody (*informal*) **4.** **SOMEBODY VERY NICE** somebody who is considered to be very nice or sweet (*informal*) **5.** **SOMETHING EXTREMELY GOOD** an object, situation, or idea that is exceptionally good (*informal*) ○ *That's a honey of a motorboat!* **6.** COLORS **YELLOWISH-BROWN COLOR** a yellowish-brown color, like that of honey ■ *adj.* COLORS **OF YELLOWISH-BROWN COLOR** yellowish brown in color, like honey ■ *vt.* (**-eyed** *or* **-ied, -ey·ing, -eys**) **TALK FLATTERINGLY TO SOMEBODY** to talk to somebody in an affectionate and flattering way, especially insincerely and for selfish reasons (*informal*) [Old English *hunig*, of prehistoric Germanic origin]

hon·ey badg·er *n.* = **ratel** [From its fondness for honey]

hon·ey bear *n.* = **kinkajou** [From its practice of sucking honey from the nests of bees]

hon·ey·bee /húnni bee/ *n.* a honey-producing bee that lives in organized groups and has been domesticated for its honey and beeswax since ancient times. Latin name: *Apis mellifera*.

hon·ey·bun /húnni bun/, **hon·ey·bunch** /húnni bùnch/ *n.* = **honey** *n.* 3 (*informal*)

hon·ey·buz·zard *n.* a bird of prey that is native to Europe and feeds on honey from bees' nests. Latin name: *Perno apivorus*.

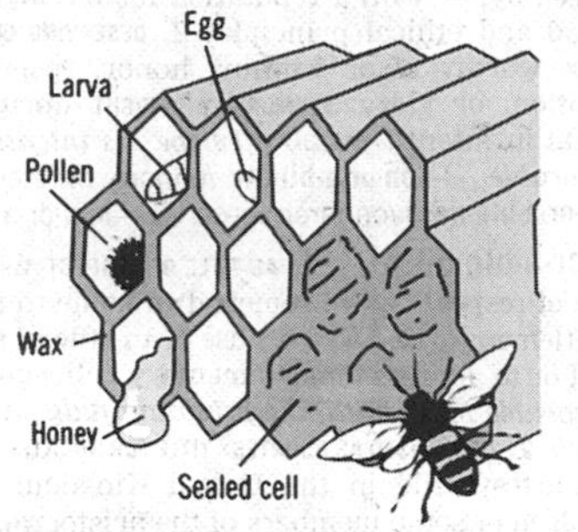

Honeycomb

hon·ey·comb /húnni kōm/ *n.* **1.** **STRUCTURE OF SIX-SIDED CELLS** a collection of hexagonal cells constructed of wax by bees inside a hive or nest in which honey is stored, eggs are laid, and larvae develop **2.** FOOD **CELLS CONTAINING HONEY EATEN AS FOOD** a structure made up of waxy hexagonal cells containing honey that is extracted from a bees' hive or nest and eaten by animals and humans **3.** **SOMETHING RESEMBLING HONEYCOMB** an object resembling a honeycomb in pattern or structure, especially by consisting of a network of hexagons **4.** TEXTILES **HONEYCOMB-PATTERNED FABRIC** a soft fabric woven in a pattern of ridges and hollows similar to those in a honeycomb, usually used for towels and bedspreads ■ *vt.* (**-combed, -comb·ing, -combs**) **1.** **FILL SOMETHING WITH HOLES** to fill a wall, cliff, or structure with many cavities **2.** **INFILTRATE SOMETHING THOROUGHLY** to infiltrate a place or organization thoroughly ○ *an intelligence agency honeycombed by double agents* [Possibly so called because the arrangement of the plates hanging from the roof of a hive resembles a comb with its teeth] —**hon·ey·combed** *adj.*

hon·ey·comb moth *n.* = **wax moth**

hon·ey·creep·er /húnni kreepər/ *n.* **1.** **SMALL TROPICAL AMERICAN BIRD** a small tropical American bird that has brightly-colored plumage and a long slender beak for sucking nectar from flowers. Family: Coerebidae. **2.** **SMALL HAWAIIAN BIRD** a Hawaiian bird that resembles the honeycreeper of tropical America. Family: Drepanididae.

hon·ey·dew /húnni dōō/ *n.* **1.** INSECTS **SWEET SUBSTANCE PRODUCED BY APHIDS** a sweet sticky substance deposited on leaves by aphids and certain other insects as a by-product of the juices they suck from plants **2.** BOT **SWEET SUBSTANCE EXUDED BY PLANTS** a sweet sticky substance produced by the leaves of some plants **3.** FOOD = **honeydew melon** [From the belief that the substance was distilled from the air like dew] —**hon·ey·dewed** *adj.*

hon·ey·dew mel·on *n.* a melon with sweet green flesh and a smooth greenish-white rind. Latin name: *Cucumis melo*.

hon·ey·eat·er /húnnee eetər/ *n.* a slender bird, found from Australia to Hawaii, that has a long beak and a long brush-tipped tongue for extracting nectar from flowers. Family: Meliphagidae.

hon·eyed /húnneed/, **hon·ied** *adj.* **1.** **INGRATIATING** intended to flatter or soothe **2.** **PLEASANT-SOUNDING** sweet and pleasant to hear **3.** **SWEETENED WITH HONEY** containing or sweetened with honey —**hon·eyed·ly** *adv.*

hon·ey fun·gus *n.* a mushroom that has a golden or brown cap and is edible when cooked. It grows in small tight clusters at the base of trees, and is possibly the most serious fungal parasite affecting coniferous trees. Latin name: *Armillaria mellea*. [From its color]

hon·ey guide *n.* **1.** BIRDS **SMALL TROPICAL BIRD FEEDING ON BEESWAX** a small bird of tropical African and Asian forests that feeds on the wax and larvae remaining after people or animals have removed the honey from bees' nests. Family: Indicatoridae. **2.** BOT **MARKINGS ON FLOWER** dots or lines on the perianth of a flower that guide insects toward the nectar. They are sometimes only visible to the human eye in ultraviolet photographs.

hon·ey lo·cust *n.* a thorny tree native to eastern North America with compound leaves and long pods containing a sweet pulp. Genus: *Gleditsia*.

hon·ey mes·quite *n.* a species of mesquite tree found in the southwestern United States, with an edible, nutritious pod. Latin name: *Prosopis juliflora*. [So called because of the sweet-tasting pulp of its edible pods]

hon·ey·moon /húnni mōōn/ *n.* **1.** **VACATION FOR NEWLY-MARRIED COUPLE** a period of time spent alone together, especially away, by a newly-married couple, usually immediately following the wedding or reception **2.** **PERIOD OF GOOD FEELING** a short period of harmony or goodwill at the beginning of a relationship, especially in politics or business ■ *vi.* (**-mooned, -moon·ing, -moons**) **GO ON HONEYMOON** to go on vacation just after getting married [Originally in the sense "waning affection," from the idea that although married love is at first as sweet as honey, it soon wanes like the moon] —**hon·ey·moon·er** *n.*

hon·ey mouse *n.* a small Australian marsupial with a very long snout adapted for feeding on pollen and honey, a long tail, and light brown fur with dark stripes. Latin name: *Tarsipes spenserae*.

hon·ey plant *n.* a plant that provides bees with nectar

hon·ey·suck·er /húnni sukər/ *n.* = **honey mouse**

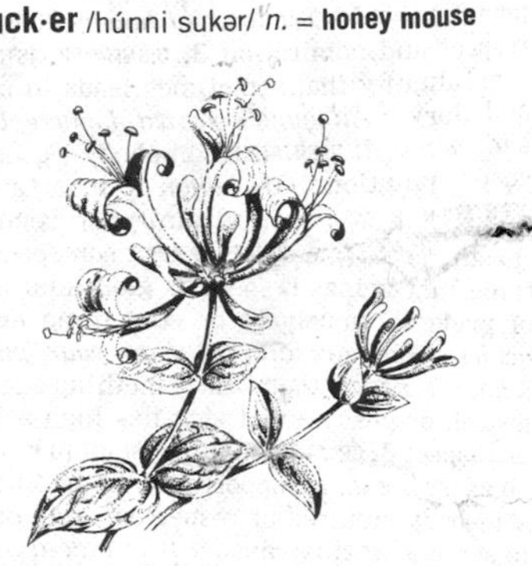
Honeysuckle

hon·ey·suck·le /húnni sùk'l/ *n.* **1.** **CLIMBING SHRUB WITH FRAGRANT FLOWERS** a climbing shrub that has twining stems and fragrant tubular flowers with spreading twin-petal lobes. Genus: *Lonicera*. **2.** **AUSTRALIAN PLANT** an Australian plant with flowers that grow in spike-shaped clusters. Genus: *Banksia*. **3.** *Ireland* **FUCHSIA** a fuchsia plant [Old English *hunigsūce*, from HONEY + SUCK. So called from the belief that bees extract honey from it.]

hon·ey·suck·le or·na·ment *n.* = **anthemion**

hon·ey-sweet *adj.* sounding or appearing sweet and attractive

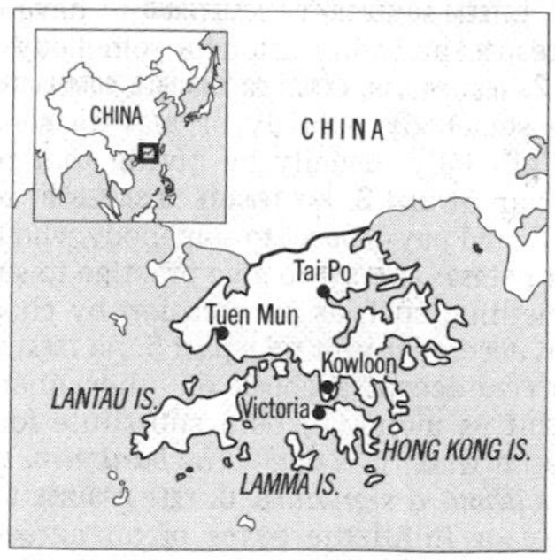

Hong Kong

Hong Kong /hóng kòng/ seaport and major commercial center on the southeastern coast of China. A former British colony, it is now a Chinese Special Administrative Region. Population: 6,189,800 (1995). Area: 415 sq. mi./1,076 sq. km.

hon·ied *adj.* = **honeyed**

honk /hongk/ *n.* **1.** **SOUND OF CAR HORN** the sound made by a car horn **2.** **CRY OF GOOSE** the raucous sound made by a goose **3.** **SOUND RESEMBLING GOOSE OR CAR HORN** any sound, e.g., a laugh or a blowing of the nose, that resembles the sound made by a goose or a car horn ■ *v.* (**honked, honk·ing, honks**) **1.** *vti.* **SOUND CAR HORN** to cause a car horn to make a honk **2.** *vi.* **PRODUCE HONK**

to let out or give out a honk [Mid-19thC. An imitation of the sound.]

honk·er /hóngkər/ *n.* 1. SOMEBODY OR SOMETHING THAT HONKS a person, animal, or object, e.g., a goose or a car horn, that makes a honking sound 2. LARGE NOSE a nose, especially a large one (*informal*) 3. *Can* CANADA GOOSE a Canada goose (*informal*)

hon·ky /hóngkee/ (*plural* **-kies**), **hon·kie** (*plural* **-kies**), **hon·key** (*plural* **-keys**) *n.* an offensive term for a Caucasian (*slang offensive*) [Mid-20thC. Origin uncertain: possibly from Wolof (an African language) *honq* "pink," perhaps also influenced by HUNKY.]

hon·ky-tonk /-tòngk/ *n.* 1. CHEAP NIGHTCLUB a cheap, noisy, and often disreputable bar or nightclub (*slang*) 2. RAGTIME PIANO-PLAYING a style of ragtime with a heavy beat, usually played on an upright piano with a tinny sound 3. COUNTRY MUSIC a style of country music associated with honky-tonks ○ *honky-tonk blues* ■ *vi.* (**hon·ky-tonked, hon·ky-tonk·ing, hon·ky-tonks**) VISIT HONKY-TONKS to frequent cheap noisy bars and nightclubs [Late 19thC. Origin unknown.]

Hon·o·lu·lu /hònnə lóo loo/ urban area and capital of Hawaii, located on Oahu Island, Hawaii. Population: 365,272 (1990).

hon·or /ónnər/ *n.* 1. PERSONAL INTEGRITY strong moral character or strength, and adherence to ethical principles ○ *It's a matter of honor.* 2. RESPECT great respect and admiration 3. DIGNITY OR DISTINCTION personal dignity that sometimes leads to recognition and glory ○ *Although defeated, he accepted the loss with honor* 4. REPUTATION somebody's good name or good reputation ○ *My honor is at stake.* 5. WOMAN'S REPUTATION a woman's virginity or reputation for chastity (*dated*) 6. SOURCE OF PRIDE somebody or something that brings respect or glory and is a source of pride to somebody or something else ○ *Your achievements are an honor to your parents and school.* 7. MARK OF DISTINCTION something such as a gift, award, or gesture that signifies high achievement or respect 8. GREAT PRIVILEGE a special privilege that is cherished, e.g., an opportunity to be introduced to somebody admired or respected or an opportunity to serve a worthy cause ○ *It is indeed an honor to have you here today.* 9. MEN'S CODE OF INTEGRITY a code of integrity in some societies, e.g., in feudal Europe and medieval Japan, that men upheld by force of arms 10. DIGNITY OF HIGH POSITION a certain high degree of dignity with which high positions, e.g., the Presidency, are regarded by those elected to them and by the people they serve ○ *actions detrimental to the honor of his office* 11. GOLF RIGHT TO TEE OFF FIRST the right to drive off first from the tee in golf ■ *npl.* 1. **hon·ors, Hon·ors** EDUC ACADEMIC DISTINCTION official recognition of academic excellence given to students by colleges and universities at graduation 2. **honors** BRIDGE FOUR OR FIVE HIGHEST CARDS four or five of the highest cards, especially the ace, king, queen, jack, and ten of the trump suit ■ *vt.* (**-ored, -or·ing, -ors**) 1. ESTEEM SOMEBODY OR SOMETHING to have or show great respect and admiration for somebody or something 2. DISTINGUISH, EXALT, OR ENNOBLE SOMEBODY to recognize somebody publicly or elevate somebody's status officially, usually by giving that person a title or an award 3. PAY TRIBUTE TO SOMEBODY to praise publicly and pay respect to somebody who has died 4. DIGNIFY PERSON OR EVENT to give prestige to somebody or something such as an occasion by choosing to appear, accompany, or take part 5. FIN TREAT SOMETHING AS MONEY to accept a check or other financial instrument as money or as a substitute for money and pay it when it is due ○ *The bank won't honor a check without a signature.* 6. KEEP PROMISE to keep a promise or fulfill the terms of an agreement or contract 7. DANCE BOW TO DANCING PARTNER to bow to another dancer in square dancing [12thC. Via Old French from Latin *honor-*, the stem of *honos* (source also of English *honest*), of unknown origin.] —**hon·or·er** *n.* — **hon·or·less** *adj.* ◇ **do somebody the honor of doing something** to make somebody feel proud and pleased by agreeing to do something for that person (*formal*) ○ *Will you do me the honor of dancing the last waltz with me?* ◇ **do the honors** to act as host or hostess by doing something for a group of guests, e.g., pouring wine, carving meat, or cutting a cake (*informal*) ◇ **honor bound** obligated by a promise or ethical principles to do something ◇ **in honor of somebody** *or* **something** in recognition of or for the glorification of somebody or something ○ *I'd like to propose a toast in honor of the bride and groom.* ◇ **on your honor** 1. staking your reputation on something ○ *On my honor, I will tell the truth, the whole truth, and nothing but the truth.* 2. being trusted to act in a particular way ○ *You are on your honor to behave well while I am gone.*

Hon·or *n.* used as a form of address to dignitaries such as judges and mayors ○ *Your Honor, may we approach the bench?*

hon·or·a·ble /ónnərəb'l/ *adj.* 1. HAVING PERSONAL INTEGRITY guided by, or with a reputation for having, strong moral and ethical principles 2. DESERVING OR GAINING HONOR worthy of or winning honor, respect, recognition, or glory 3. MORALLY UPRIGHT upright and moral in intent (*formal*) ○ *I hope his intentions are honorable.* —**hon·or·a·bil·i·ty** /ònnərə bíllətee/ *n.* — **hon·or·a·ble·ness** /ónnərəb'lnəss/ *n.* —**hon·or·a·bly** *adv.*

Hon·or·a·ble *adj.* 1. USED AS TITLE OF RESPECT used as a title of respect before somebody's name to indicate entitlement to respect because of an official position held or to address a parliamentary colleague ○ *The Honorable Mr. Smith, the presiding judge, is on the bench.* 2. *U.K.* USED AS COURTESY TITLE FOR NOBILITY used as a courtesy title in the United Kingdom for the children of some members of the aristocracy

hon·or·a·ble dis·charge *n.* an official separation from the armed forces, signifying that all duties have been honorably fulfilled

hon·or·a·ble men·tion *n.* an official or public commendation, usually granted to somebody who has done well in a competition but not actually won an award

hon·o·rar·i·um /ònnə ráiree əm/ (*plural* **-ums** *or* **-a** /-ə/) *n.* an amount of money paid to somebody, especially a professional or famous person, for providing a service such as addressing a conference [Mid-17thC. Via Latin, "gift made on being admitted to a post of honor," from, ultimately, *honor* "HONOR."]

WORD KEY: SYNONYMS

See Synonyms at *wage*.

hon·or·ar·y /ónnə rèrree/ *adj.* 1. AWARDED AS HONOR given, elected, or awarded for outstanding service or distinguished achievements, rather than for the completion of formal educational or legal requirements 2. SYMBOLIZING HONOR CONFERRED representing the bestowal of an honor or distinction on somebody 3. UNPAID holding an office awarded as an honor and receiving no payment for services provided in that office 4. NOT LEGALLY ENFORCEABLE dependent on somebody's sense of honor and honesty for fulfillment, rather than on a legal agreement

hon·or·ee /ònnə rée/ *n.* somebody who is receiving an award or being distinguished in some way, e.g., at a ceremony

hon·or guard *n.* a group of soldiers, sailors, air force personnel, or Marines who perform a ceremonial duty, e.g., attending a casket at a military funeral or raising and lowering a flag

hon·or·if·ic /ònnə ríffik/ *adj.* CONFERRING OR SHOWING HONOR given as a mark of distinction, or reflecting esteem and respect ■ *n.* 1. TITLE OF RESPECT a title of respect, e.g., "The Honorable," used in speech or writing before the full name or the surname of a social or governmental superior 2. GRAM GRAMMATICAL FORM ACKNOWLEDGING INFERIORITY OF SPEAKER a phrase or word, e.g., a pronoun or a verb inflection, that is used to show respect to somebody of a highter status

hon·or·is cau·sa /o nàwriss kówssə, -ków zaa/ *adv.* as a mark of honor (*formal*) ○ *a doctorate in humane letters conferred honoris causa* [From Latin, "for the sake of honor"]

hon·or roll *n.* a list of secondary-school students, e.g., in high school, who have excellent grades or a high grade point average ○ *Seven seniors made the honor roll first semester.*

hon·or so·ci·e·ty *n.* a club, usually in high school, of students who have excellent grades or a high grade point average

hon·ors of war *npl.* 1. PRIVILEGES ACCORDED TO DEFEATED ENEMY certain privileges that are accorded members of a defeated army 2. RESPECT TO DEAD SOLDIER marks of respect paid by troops at the burial of another soldier

hon·or sys·tem *n.* a system under which people are relied on to be honest without direct supervision

hon·our *n., vt.* U.K. = **honor**

Hon·ours List *n.* a list of individuals who have been or are to be awarded honors such as a peerage or membership in a chivalric order by the British monarch

Hon·shu /hón shoo/ the largest and most populous island of Japan. Area: 89,166 sq. mi./230,940 sq. km. Population: 99,254,194 (1990).

hoo /hoo/ (*plural* **hoos**) *n.* the hooting sound made by an owl [15thC. An imitation of the sound.]

hooch[1] /hooch/, **hootch** *n.* (*slang*) 1. CHEAP OR ILLEGAL ALCOHOL hard liquor, especially when very cheap or illegally obtained or distilled 2. MARIJUANA marijuana [Late 19thC. Shortening of *hoochinoo*, from *Hoochinoo*, a Tlingit village in Alaska where illegal liquor was made, from Tlingit *xutsnu:wú*, literally "brown bear's fort."]

hooch[2] /hooch/, **hootch** *n.* a semipermanent structure such as a hut used as a quarters for troops in Southeast Asia (*dated slang*) [Mid-20thC. Origin uncertain: possibly from Japanese *uchi* "dwelling," influenced by English *hut*.]

hood[1] /hŏŏd/ *n.* 1. LOOSE COVERING FOR HEAD a covering for the head that is usually attached to the neck of a coat 2. COVER FOR DEVICE a cover for an appliance or machine, or a device such as a camera lens 3. AUTOMOT ENGINE COVER the hinged cover over the engine of a car or other vehicle ○ *Let's check under the hood to see what's wrong.* 4. PART OF ACADEMIC ROBE an ornamental piece of cloth, often trimmed with fur or luxurious fabric, that hangs from the shoulders of an academic or ecclesiastical robe to indicate the status of the wearer 5. FOLDING ROOF the folding roof of a vehicle such as a carriage or convertible car 6. COVER FOR CHIMNEY a fixed or revolving cover attached to the top of a chimney to prevent downdrafts 7. HEAD COVERING FOR FALCON a bag placed over the head of a falcon to keep it calm when it is not hunting 8. ZOOL GROWTH OR MARKING ON ANIMAL'S HEAD a crest, marking, or other conspicuous part on the head of an animal ■ *vt.* (**hood·ed, hood·ing, hoods**) COVER SOMETHING WITH HOOD to cover the head of a person, animal, or bird with a hood [Old English *hōd*. Ultimately from an Indo-European base meaning "to cover," which is also the ancestor of English *hat* and *heed*.] —**hood·less** *adj.* — **hood·like** *adj.*

hood[2] /hŏŏd/ *n.* a hoodlum (*slang*) [Late 19thC. Shortening.]

hood[3] /hŏŏd/ *n.* a neighborhood (*slang*) [Late 20thC. Shortening.]

-hood *suffix.* 1. quality, state, condition ○ *knighthood* 2. a group of people ○ *brotherhood* [Old English *-hād* (related to German *-heit*)]

hood·ed /hŏŏdəd/ *adj.* 1. COVERED BY A HOOD covered by or having a hood 2. PARTLY HIDDEN partly concealed or covered ○ *dark, hooded eyes* 3. ZOOL HAVING CREST having a crest, markings, or a specialized structure on the head —**hood·ed·ness** *n.*

hood·ed crow *n.* a crow of Europe and Asia with a black head, tail, and wings, and a gray body. It is a subspecies of the carrion crow. Latin name: *Corvus corone cornix.*

hood·ed seal *n.* a large gray-spotted seal of the North Atlantic and Arctic oceans. The mature male has an inflatable sac near its nose that it uses in fighting. Latin name: *Cystophora cristata.*

Hood·less /hŏŏdləss/, **Adelaide** (1857–1910) Canadian educational reformer. She campaigned for improved education for women and founded the first Women's Institute in Canada (1897). Born **Adelaide Hunter**

hood·lum /hŏŏdləm, hŏŏd-/ *n.* 1. GANGSTER a criminal or gangster, especially one prone to violence 2. YOUNG VANDAL OR CRIMINAL a young person who is violent or prone to committing crimes [Late 19thC. Origin uncertain: perhaps from a word related to German dialect *hudelum* "disorderly" or *huddelumpe* "rags, careless person."] —**hood·lum·ish** *adj.* —**hood·lum·ism** *n.*

hood·mold *n.* = **dripstone**

hoo·doo /hŏŏ dŏŏ/ *n.* (*plural* **-doos**) 1. = **voodoo** 2. BAD LUCK bad luck or misfortune 3. BRINGER OF BAD LUCK somebody or something believed to bring bad luck 4. ODDLY-SHAPED ROCK COLUMN in the western United States and Canada, a column of rock that has been weathered into a strange shape ■ *vt.* (**-dooed, -doo·ing, -doos**) JINX SOMEBODY OR SOMETHING to appear to bring bad luck or misfortune to somebody or something [Late 19thC. Origin uncertain: possibly an alteration of VOODOO.] —**hoo·doo·ism** *n.*

hood·wink /ho͝od wìngk/ (**-winked, -wink·ing, -winks**) *vt.* **1. TRICK SOMEBODY** to deceive or dupe somebody, especially by trickery **2. BLINDFOLD SOMEBODY** to put a blindfold on somebody (*archaic*) **3. CONCEAL SOMETHING** to conceal or hide something (*archaic*) —**hood·wink·er** *n.*

hoo·ey /hoó ee/ *n.* empty or nonsensical talk or ideas (*informal*) [Early 20thC. Origin unknown.]

hoof /ho͝of, hoof/ *n.* (*plural* **hooves** /ho͝ovz, hoovz/ *or* **hoofs**) **1. ANIMAL'S FOOT OF HORNY MATERIAL** the foot of a horse, deer, cow, or similar animal, covered with horny material **2. HORNY COVERING OF FOOT** the horny material covering the feet of animals such as horses, deer, and cattle **3. ANIMAL WITH HOOVES** an animal such as a horse, deer, or cow that has hooves **4. HUMAN FOOT** the foot of a human being (*slang humorous*) ■ *vt.* (**hoofed, hoof·ing, hoofs**) **1. TRAVEL DISTANCE ON FOOT** to walk a specified distance (*slang*) **2. KICK SOMEBODY OR SOMETHING** to kick or trample a person or animal [Old English *hōf*. Ultimately from an Indo-European word.] —**hoof·less** *adj.* ◇ **hoof it 1.** to walk (*slang*) **2.** to dance (*slang*) ◇ **hoof it up** to dance (*slang*) ◇ **on the hoof 1.** alive and not yet butchered **2.** without sufficient thought or attention (*informal*)

hoof-and-mouth dis·ease *n.* = **foot-and-mouth disease**

hoofed /ho͝oft, hooft/, **hooved** *adj.* having hooves, or having hooves of a particular size and type

hoof·er /ho͝ofər, hoófər/ *n.* a professional dancer, especially a tap dancer (*slang*)

hoof·print /ho͝of print, hoóf-/ *n.* an imprint of an animal's hoof

hoo-hah /hoó haá/, **hoo-ha** *n.* a loud noisy aggressive public fuss, controversy, or disturbance (*slang*) [Mid-20thC. Origin uncertain: probably from Yiddish *hu-ha*, ultimately an imitation of the sound.]

hook /ho͝ok/ *n.* **1. BENT PIECE OF METAL** a bent or curved piece of metal or other material, used to attach, suspend, fasten, or lift another object **2. SOMETHING RESEMBLING HOOK** something resembling a curved piece of metal, especially a plant or animal part **3.** ANGLING = **fishhook 4.** AGRIC = **sickle** *n.* 1 **5. TRAP OR SNARE** a stratagem for trapping or snaring somebody **6. SOMETHING THAT ATTRACTS** a means of attracting or interesting somebody, especially a potential customer (*informal*) **7.** BOXING **SHORT SWINGING BLOW** in boxing, a short blow to an opponent delivered with a swing and a bent arm **8.** GOLF **GOLF SHOT CURVING SHARPLY** a golf shot that swerves sharply from right to left in the case of a right-handed player **9.** BASEBALL = **curve ball 10.** BASKETBALL = **hook shot 11. CREST OF BREAKING WAVE** the crest of a wave that is about to break **12.** HOCKEY **ACT OF RESTRAINING ICE HOCKEY PLAYER** the act of using an ice hockey stick to prevent another player from moving freely **13. PART OF LETTER** in writing or printing, a short curve of a letter that extends above or below the line ○ *the hook of the "g"* **14.** MUSIC **CATCHY REFRAIN** a pleasing and easily remembered refrain in a pop song ■ *v.* (**hooked, hook·ing, hooks**) **1.** *vti.* **FASTEN WITH HOOK** to fasten by means of hooks or hooks and eyes **2.** *vt.* **ATTACH ONE THING TO ANOTHER** to attach one thing to another by means of a specially designed mechanical device ○ *hook the trailer to the car* **3.** *vti.* **BEND LIKE HOOK** to curve or cause something to curve in the shape of a hook ○ *The road hooks sharply to the left.* **4.** *vt.* **ENSNARE SOMETHING** to catch or ensnare something using a hook **5.** *vt.* **CATCH SOMEBODY'S ATTENTION** to attract and hold somebody's interest or attention **6.** *vt.* DRUGS **MAKE SOMEBODY ADDICTED** to cause somebody to become addicted or dependent on something, especially a drug (*slang*) **7.** *vt.* BOXING **HIT SOMEBODY WITH CURVING BLOW** in boxing, to deliver a sharp curving blow to an opponent, using a curved or bent arm **8.** *vt.* GOLF **STRIKE SWERVING BALL IN GOLF** in golf, to strike the ball so that it swerves sharply from right to left in the case of a right-handed player **9.** *vt.* BASEBALL **THROW CURVED BALL IN BASEBALL** in baseball, to pitch the ball with a curve **10.** *vt.* BASKETBALL **SHOOT BALL IN BASKETBALL** in basketball, to shoot the ball by sweeping the hand upward and farther away from the basket while moving sideways toward the basket **11.** *vt.* HOCKEY **RESTRAIN PLAYER WITH ICE HOCKEY STICK** to use an ice hockey stick to prevent another player from moving freely **12.** *vi.* **BE PROSTITUTE** to work as a prostitute (*slang*) **13.** *vt.* **GORE SOMEBODY OR SOMETHING** to gore a person or animal with the horns or tusks **14.** *vt.* AGRIC **CUT SOMETHING WITH SICKLE** to cut grass or similar plants with a sickle **15.** *vt.* CRAFT **MAKE RUG** to make a rug by pulling pieces of wool through holes in stiff canvas using a special hook **16.** *vt.* **STEAL SOMETHING** to seize and steal something (*slang*) [Old English *hōc*. Ultimately from an Indo-European word meaning "hook, tooth," which is also the ancestor of English *hack* and *heckle*.] —**hook·less** *adj.* ◇ **by hook or by crook** by some means or other ◇ **get the hook** to be removed unceremoniously from a place or position (*slang*) ◇ **hook, line, and sinker** to a complete and total degree (*informal*) ◇ **off the hook 1.** free of a difficult situation (*informal*) **2.** with the receiver off its cradle so that no telephone calls can be received ◇ **on the hook** caught in a difficult situation (*informal*)

hook up *v.* (*informal*) **1.** *vt.* **CONNECT ELECTRONIC DEVICES** to set up or connect electronic or electric devices ○ *Is the microphone hooked up?* **2.** *vti.* **GET TOGETHER** to meet and become associated, or cause somebody to meet and become associated with somebody else

hook·ah /ho͝okə, hoókə/ *n.* an Asian pipe for smoking tobacco or marijuana, consisting of a flexible tube with a mouthpiece attached to a container of water through which smoke is drawn and cooled [Mid-18thC. Via Urdu from Arabic *ḥukka* "jar."]

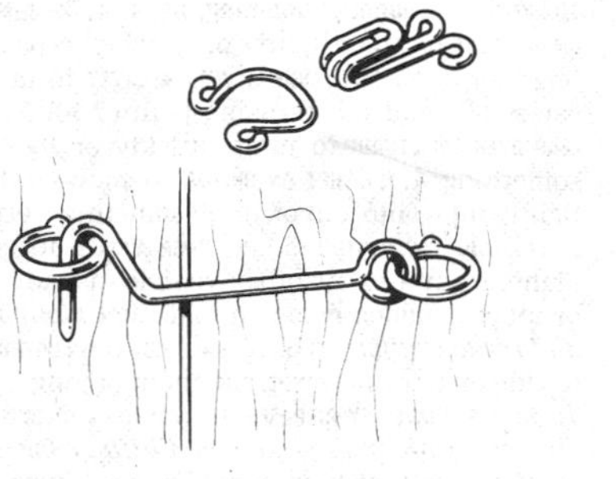

Hook and eye: Clothes fastener (top) and latch (bottom)

hook and eye (*plural* **hooks and eyes**) *n.* **1. CLOTHES FASTENER** a fastening for clothes consisting of a small hook inserted into a metal or thread loop **2. LATCH** a latch for a gate or door consisting of a metal hook inserted into a metal loop

hook-and-lad·der truck *n.* a fire engine equipped with extension ladders and hooked poles

hook·check *n.* HOCKEY = **hook** *n.* 12

hooked /ho͝okt/ *adj.* **1.** DRUGS **ADDICTED** addicted to a drug (*slang*) **2. OBSESSED WITH SOMEBODY OR SOMETHING** in love with or compulsively attracted to somebody, or obsessed with something (*slang*) **3. SHAPED LIKE HOOK** bent or shaped like a hook **4. HAVING HOOK AT END** ending in a hook **5.** CRAFT **MADE USING YARN HOOK** made by hooking yarn through canvas

hook·er[1] /ho͝okər/ *n.* a prostitute (*informal*) [Mid-19thC. Origin uncertain: possibly from an earlier meaning "sneak thief."]

hook·er[2] /ho͝okər/ *n.* a drink of hard liquor, typically a big one (*slang*) [Mid-19thC. Origin unknown.]

hook·er[3] /ho͝okər/ *n.* a person, animal, or object that catches something by hooking it

hook·er[4] /ho͝okər/ *n.* **1. FISHING BOAT** a commercial fishing vessel that uses hooks and line instead of nets **2. CARGO BOAT** a large cargo boat with several sails, formerly used off the western coast of Ireland and now used as a pleasure craft **3 SHABBY BOAT** an old, shabby, or ungraceful boat [Mid-17thC. From Dutch *hoeker*, a shortening of Middle Dutch *hoeckboot* "fishing boat," from *hoec* "fishhook."]

Hook·er /ho͝okər/, **Joseph** (1814–79) U.S. general. Known as an aggressive leader, he was put in command of the Army of the Potomac (1863). Known as **Fighting Joe**

hook·ey *n.* = **hooky**

hook·nose /ho͝ok nōz/ *n.* a nose with a noticeable curve at the end, like an eagle's beak —**hook·nosed** *adj.*

Hook of Hol·land 1. cape on the North Sea coast of South Holland province, southwestern Netherlands. Dutch **Hoek van Holland 2.** seaport on the Hook of Holland, situated approximately 6 mi./10 km northwest of Rotterdam

hook shot *n.* a shot that is made by sweeping the hand upward and farther away from the basket while moving sideways toward the basket

hook·tip /ho͝ok tìp/ *n.* a moth that has forewings ending in a hooked point. Genus: *Daepana.*

hook·up /ho͝ok ùp/ *n.* **1.** ELECTRON ENG **ELECTRONIC SYSTEM** a number of items of electronic equipment designed to operate together (*informal*) **2.** UTIL **LINK BETWEEN SOURCE AND USER** a connection allowing a user access to a utility such as electricity, gas, or water ○ *a gas hookup* **3. RELATIONSHIP** an alliance between people, groups, or things, especially an unlikely one (*informal*) ○ *a bizarre hookup between political enemies over an issue* **4.** ANGLING **CATCH IN OFFSHORE FISHING** in offshore big game fishing, an act of catching a fish on the end of the line

hook·worm /ho͝ok wùrm/ *n.* **1. PARASITIC WORM** a bloodsucking, disease-causing nematode worm that bores through the skin, attaching itself to the intestinal walls with its hooked mouthparts. Family: Ancylostomatidae. **2.** = **ancylostomiasis**

hook·worm dis·ease *n.* = **ancylostomiasis**

hook·y /ho͝okee/, **hook·ey** *n.* absence, especially from school, without permission (*informal*) [Mid-19thC. Origin uncertain: perhaps from HOOK in the meaning "to run away."] ◇ **play hooky** to be absent without permission, especially from school (*informal*)

hoo·li·gan /hoóligən/ *n.* a young person who is violent or prone to committing crimes (*informal*) [Late 19thC. Origin uncertain: possibly from *Hooligan*, surname of a fictional rowdy Irish family in a music-hall song, and name of a comic Irish character in a cartoon.]

hoo·li·gan·ism /hoóligə nìzzəm/ *n.* acts of vandalism and violence in public places, committed especially by youths

hoop /hoop, ho͝op/ *n.* **1. RING HOLDING BARREL TOGETHER** the metal or wooden ring used to hold the staves of a barrel in place **2. RING JUMPED THROUGH IN CIRCUS** a large light ring, often with paper stretched over it, through which trained animals or performers jump **3.** ACCESSORIES **SUPPORT FOR PETTICOAT OR SKIRT** a lightweight cane, wire, or whalebone ring, or a structure made of several such rings, used, especially formerly, to stiffen a woman's skirt or petticoat **4.** CLOTHES **WIDE STIFF PETTICOAT OR SKIRT** a petticoat or skirt stiffened by cane, wire, or whalebone rings **5.** SEW **BAND FOR KEEPING EMBROIDERY FABRIC TAUT** either of a pair of wooden or metal bands used to keep fabric taut when it is being embroidered **6. EARRING** an earring formed from a continuous ring of metal **7. CIRCULAR PART OF FINGER RING** the part of a ring that the finger fits through **8.** BASKETBALL **METAL RING HOLDING NET IN BASKETBALL** in basketball, the metal ring from which an open-bottomed net is suspended, through which the ball is thrown in order to score points **9.** BASKETBALL **BASKETBALL GAME** the game of basketball (*slang*) **10.** SPORTS **CROQUET WICKET** in croquet, a metal arch through which the ball is driven ■ *vt.* (**hooped, hoop·ing, hoops**) **PUT HOOP AROUND SOMETHING** to surround something with a hoop or band [Old English *hōp*, of prehistoric West Germanic origin] ◇ **jump through hoops (for somebody), go through hoops (for somebody)** to go to extreme lengths to gain favor with somebody or to carry out somebody's wishes (*informal*)

hoop·er /hoópər, ho͝opər/ *n.* somebody who makes or repairs barrels

hoop·la /hoóp laà, ho͝op laà/ *n.* **1. LOUD CELEBRATION** noisy excited commotion or joyous celebrating (*slang*) **2. GREAT PUBLIC UPROAR** a great amount of public fuss, commotion, or uproar with attendant publicity or media interest (*slang*) **3. MISLEADING TALK** intentionally misleading talk or propaganda (*informal*) [Late 19thC. Origin uncertain: perhaps from French *houp-là* "upsy-daisy!"]

hoo·poe /hoó pō, -poo/ (*plural* **-poes** *or* **-poe**) *n.* a Eurasian bird with a pinkish-brown head and back, a very prominent crest, a downward-curving bill, and a loud cry. Latin name: *Upupa epops.* [Mid-17thC. Alteration of earlier *hoop*, via Old French *huppe* from, ultimately, Latin *upupa*, an imitation of the bird's cry.]

hoop pine *n.* an Australian timber tree with rough bark. Latin name: *Araucaria cunninghamii.*

hoop skirt *n.* a long full skirt held out in the shape of a bell by a series of connected hoops, fashionable in the 18th and early 19th centuries

hoop snake *n.* any harmless North American snake such as the mud snake that was once believed to be

Hoopoe

Library of Congress

Herbert Hoover

able to take its tail in its mouth and roll along like a hoop

hoop·ster /hóopstər/ *n.* a basketball player (*informal*)

hoo·ray /hōō ráy/, **hoo·rah, hur·ray** *interj.* **USED AS SHOUT OF JOY** used as a shout of happy excitement, victory, or jubilation ■ *n.* **SHOUT OF JOY** a shout of happy excitement, victory, or jubilation [Late 17thC. Alteration of HURRAH.]

hoose·gow /hóoss gòw/ *n.* a jail (*slang*) [Early 20thC. From Mexican Spanish *jusgado*, from Spanish *juzgado*, "courtroom," from the past participle of *juzgar* "to judge," from Latin *judicare* (see JUDGE).]

Hoo·sier /hóozhər/ *n.* somebody who was born or who lives in the state of Indiana (*slang*) [Early 19thC. Origin uncertain: perhaps from an English dialect word meaning "something large of its kind."]

hoot /hoot/ *n.* **1. OWL'S CRY** the long cry, including a sound like "hoo," of some owls **2. SOUND LIKE OWL'S CRY** a sound similar to an owl's cry, e.g., the sound made by a train whistle or car horn **3. LAUGHING SOUND** a shout, especially of laughter, derision, or scorn **4. SOMEBODY OR SOMETHING HILARIOUS** a highly amusing person, object, or situation (*slang*) ■ *v.* (**hoot·ed, hoot·ing, hoots**) **1.** *vi.* **EMIT HOOT** to emit or produce a hoot **2.** *vi.* **MAKE LAUGHING SOUND** to utter a sound of laughter, derision, or scorn **3.** *vt.* **DRIVE PERFORMER OFF STAGE** to drive a public performer or speaker off a stage by jeering **4.** *vt.* **EXPRESS FEELING WITH JEERS** to express a feeling such as contempt, derision, or scorn by jeering [12thC. Origin uncertain: perhaps an imitation of the sound.] ◇ **not care** *or* **give a hoot** not care at all

hootch[1] *n.* = **hooch**[1]

hootch[2] *n.* = **hooch**[2]

hootch·y-kootch·y /hóochi kóochee/ (*plural* **hootch·y-kootch·ies**) *n.* a sensual belly dance (*dated slang*) [Late 19thC. Origin unknown.]

hoot·en·an·ny /hóot'n ànnee/ (*plural* **-nies**) *n.* (*informal*) **1. PERFORMANCE BY FOLK SINGERS** an informal or impromptu performance by folk singers, in which the audience often participates **2. UNNAMED OBJECT** an object or gadget for which the name is not known [Early 20thC. Origin unknown.]

hoot·er /hóotər/ *n.* **SOMEBODY OR SOMETHING THAT HOOTS** a person, animal, or object that hoots, especially a horn ■ **hoot·ers** *npl.* **OFFENSIVE TERM** an offensive term for a woman's large breasts, especially when large (*slang offensive*)

hoot owl *n.* an owl that has a hooting call

hooved *adj.* = **hoofed**

Hoo·ver[1] /hóovər/ *tdmk.* a trademark for a vacuum cleaner

Hoo·ver[2] /hóovər/ city in northern Alabama, a suburb of Birmingham. Population: 55,464 (1996).

Hoo·ver, Herbert (1874–1964) U.S. statesman and 31st president of the United States. A Republican president (1929–33), he opposed government assistance during the Great Depression. This made him unpopular, and he was defeated after one term by Franklin D. Roosevelt. Full name **Herbert Clarke Hoover**

Hoo·ver, J. Edgar (1895–1972) U.S. lawyer. During his remarkably long and powerful directorship of the FBI (1924–72), he targeted gangsters in the 1930s, Communists in the 1940s and 1950s, and liberals and opponents of the Vietnam War in the 1960s. Full name **John Edgar Hoover**

Hoo·ver Dam /hóovər dám/ dam on the Colorado River, on the Arizona-Nevada border, completed in 1936. Height: 726 ft./221 m.

Hoo·ver·ville /hóovər vìl/ *n.* a camp erected on the outskirts of a city during the Great Depression of the 1930s to house the poor and homeless, named after the then-president, Herbert Hoover

hooves plural of **hoof**

hop[1] /hop/ *v.* (**hopped, hop·ping, hops**) **1.** *vi.* **JUMP LIGHTLY ON ONE FOOT** to jump lightly or quickly, especially on one foot **2.** *vi.* **JUMP LIGHTLY WITH ALL FEET** to move in a series of small jumps using both or all feet **3.** *vti.* **LEAP OVER SOMETHING** to jump quickly or lightly over something **4.** *vi.* **GET ON OR OFF** to move quickly or lightly into, onto, out of, or off something, especially a vehicle (*informal*) **5.** *vt.* **JUMP ABOARD** to get on a plane, train, bus, or other vehicle, usually quickly or after a sudden decision to do so (*informal*) ○ *hop a plane to California* **6.** *vt.* RAIL **RIDE TRAIN WITHOUT TICKET** to ride on a train secretly without paying (*informal*) **7.** *vi.* AIR **TRAVEL BY AIRPLANE** to make a short trip by airplane (*informal*) ○ *hop to Chicago for the convention* ■ *n.* **1. SMALL QUICK JUMP** a small jump on one, both, or all feet **2.** AIR **FLIGHT** a flight or leg of a flight in an airplane (*informal*) ○ *a short hop from New York to Chicago* **3.** TRANSP **JOURNEY** a usually short journey (*informal*) ○ *a weekend hop to the mountains* **4.** LEISURE **DANCE** a social occasion at which people dance together, usually to popular music (*dated informal*) **5.** SPORTS **BOUNCE** a bounce or rebound of a ball ○ *caught the grounder on its second hop* **6. FREE RIDE** a free ride in a vehicle [Old English *hoppian* "to leap, limp," from a prehistoric Germanic base that is also the ancestor of English *hip*[1]. The sense "to jump on one foot" dates from the early 18thC.]

hop[2] /hop/ *n.* **1.** PLANTS **CLIMBING VINE** a climbing vine of the mulberry family that has lobed leaves and green female flowers arranged in spikes that look like pine cones. Latin name: *Humulus lupulus*. **2.** DRUGS **DRUG** a narcotic drug such as opium (*dated slang*) ■ **hops** *npl.* BEVERAGES **DRIED HOP FLOWERS** the dried flowers of the hop plant, used in brewing to add a distinctive bitter taste to beer [15thC. From Middle Low German or Middle Dutch *hoppe*.]

hop up *vt.* (*slang*) **1. INTOXICATE WITH DRUGS** to make somebody excited, or intoxicated, especially with drugs (*often passive*) **2.** AUTOMOT = **soup up**

hop, skip, and jump *n.* a short distance ○ *It's just a hop, skip, and jump to the station.*

hop, step, and jump *n.* SPORT = **triple jump**

HOP *abbr.* high oxygen pressure

hop clo·ver *n.* a plant of northern temperate grasslands that is related to peas, beans, and clover and has yellow flowers that resemble hops. Latin name: *Trifolium campestre.*

hope /hōp/ *vi.* (**hoped, hop·ing, hopes**) **WANT OR EXPECT SOMETHING** to have a wish to get or do something or for something to happen or be true, especially something that seems possible or likely ■ *n.* **1. CONFIDENT DESIRE** a feeling that something desirable is likely to happen ○ *The research offers hope to sufferers.* **2. LIKELIHOOD OF SUCCESS** a chance that something desirable will happen or be possible ○ *There's not much hope that things will improve.* **3. WISH OR DESIRE** something that somebody wants to have or do or wants to happen or be true ○ *My hope is that she will change her mind.* **4. SOURCE OF SUCCESS OR RELIEF** somebody or something that seems likely to bring success or relief ○ *We have to do this, it's our only hope.* **5. TRUST** a feeling of trust (*archaic*) [Old English *hopian* "to hope" and *hopa* "hope," of uncertain origin: probably from Low German] —**hop·er** *n.*

Hope /hōp/, **Bob** (*b.* 1903) British-born U.S. comedian. He is best known for his "Road" pictures with Bing Crosby and Dorothy Lamour (1940–52) including *Road to Singapore* (1940) and *Road to Bali* (1953). Real name **Leslie Townes Hope**

HOPE /hōp/ *n., abbr.* Health Opportunity for People Everywhere

hope chest *n.* **1. HOUSEHOLD ITEMS COLLECTED BEFORE MARRIAGE** a collection of household items such as linens, silver, and clothing that a young woman traditionally accumulates in anticipation of marriage **2. CHEST FOR STORING HOUSEHOLD ITEMS** a chest used to store household items traditionally accumulated by a young woman before marriage

hope·ful /hṓpfəl/ *adj.* **1. HAVING HOPE** feeling fairly sure that something that is wanted will happen **2. GIVING HOPE** making somebody feel confident that something desirable will happen ○ *It looks hopeful that she'll be able to dance again.* **3. SHOWING HOPE** showing a desire for something ■ *n.* **SOMEBODY DESIRING SUCCESS** somebody who wants to achieve something, especially somebody who hopes to be successful in acting, music, sport, politics, or some other endeavor —**hope·ful·ness** *n.*

hope·ful·ly /hṓpfəlee/ *adv.* **1. IN HOPEFUL WAY** in a way that shows somebody's hope of having or receiving something **2. IT IS HOPED** used to indicate that somebody hopes something will happen or will be the case

WORD KEY: USAGE

Sentence adverb: Many adverbs that express a wish or comment, for example, *clearly, obviously,* and *thankfully,* are routinely used to qualify a whole sentence: *They clearly haven't understood the issue; Obviously, there is a problem; Thankfully, they didn't arrive too late.* Many people object when ***hopefully*** is used in this way — in, for example, *Hopefully, someone can resolve this* — typically on the grounds that there is no one present in the sentence who is meant to be doing the hoping. This argument would tell against a number of the well-established sentence adverbs as well. For example, in *They clearly haven't understood the issue,* "they" are not finding anything clear. The grounds on which to object to the sentence-adverbial ***hopefully*** may be illogical, therefore, but many well-educated, well-spoken people revile it regardless. A recommendation often made is to replace the word with *it is to be hoped.* That, however, strikes many people as stilted and even worse than ***hopefully***. Frequently the best choice is *let's hope.*

Ho·peh /hō páy/ = **Hebei**

hope·less /hṓpləss/ *adj.* **1. WITH NO HOPE OF SUCCESS** unable to succeed or improve, or be resolved, helped, or cured **2. DESPAIRING** feeling no hope, or showing that somebody has no hope **3. VERY BAD** showing a complete lack of ability, competence, or efficiency —**hope·less·ness** *n.*

hope·less·ly /hṓpləslee/ *adv.* **1. IN WAY SHOWING LACK OF HOPE** in a way that shows somebody has no hope of success, relief, or of getting what he or she wants **2. VERY BADLY** actually or supposedly to too great a degree to be improved or of use

Hope·well[1] /hṓp wel/ *adj.* relating to an early Native North American culture of the Ohio and Illinois river valleys from A.D. 300 to A.D. 500, known especially for large-scale earthworks such as burial mounds [Late 19thC. Named for Cloud *Hopewell*, owner of a farm in Ohio where remains were first identified.]

Hope·well[2] /hṓp wel/ city in eastern Virginia, used as a base by Ulysses S. Grant during the Civil War. Population: 23,101 (1990). Area: 7 sq. mi./18 sq. km.

hop·head /hóp hèd/ *n.* somebody addicted to a narcotic drug such as heroin (*slang*)

hop horn·beam *n.* a tree of the birch family found in the eastern United States that has fruit clusters resembling hops. Latin name: *Ostrya virginiana.*

Ho·pi /hṓpee/ (*plural* **-pi** *or* **-pis**) *n.* **1.** PEOPLES **MEMBER OF NATIVE AMERICAN PEOPLE** a member of a Native American people of northeastern Arizona **2.** LANG **NATIVE AMERICAN LANGUAGE** a language spoken in northeastern Arizona that is one of the Shoshonean group of the Uto-Aztecan branch of the Aztec-Tanoan family of Native American languages. Hopi is spoken by about 5,000 people. [Late 19thC. From Hopi, literally "peaceable."] —**Ho·pi** *adj.*

Hop·kins /hópkinz/, **Sir Anthony** (*b.* 1937) Welsh actor. His movies include *Silence of the Lambs* (1991), *Remains of the Day* (1993), and *Shadowlands* (1993).

Hop·kins, Harry Lloyd (1890–1946) U.S. administrator and presidential aide. He headed the Works Progress Administration (1935–38), working closely with Franklin D. Roosevelt.

Hop·kins, Stephen (1707–85) U.S. patriot. One of the signers of the Declaration of Independence (1776), he served as governor of Rhode Island (1755–67).

Hop·kin·son /hópkinss'n/, **Francis** (1737–91) U.S. writer and composer. He wrote satires, e.g., *The Battle of the Kegs* (1778) attacking British rule, composed the first American opera, and signed the Declaration of Independence.

Hop·kins·ville /hópkinzvil/ city in southwestern Kentucky, a manufacturing and tobacco marketing center. Population: 28,317 (1996).

hop·lite /hó plìt/ *n.* a heavily armed foot soldier in ancient Greece [Early 18thC. From Greek *hoplitēs*, from *hoplon* "weapon," from *hepein* "to care for, work at."] —**hop·lit·ic** /hop líttik/ *adj.*

ho·plol·o·gy /hop lóllәjee/ *n.* the study of weapons and armor [Late 19thC. Coined from Greek *hoplon* "weapon" (see HOPLITE) + -LOGY.] —**ho·plol·o·gist** *n.*

hop-o'-my-thumb /hòppә mә thúm, -mī-/ *n.* an offensive term for somebody who is extremely small (*offensive*) [From a 16th-century instruction *hop on my thumb*, directed at somebody so small that he or she might fancifully be thought able to do so]

hop·per[1] /hóppәr/ *n.* **1.** TECH **FUNNEL-SHAPED DISPENSER** a large funnel-shaped container for storing and dispensing grain, fuel, or other materials **2.** RAIL, FREIGHT **VEHICLE THAT DISCHARGES LOAD THROUGH FLOOR** a wagon or railroad car with sloping floors designed to carry dry bulk goods such as grain or cement that are discharged through an opening in the bottom **3. SOMEBODY OR SOMETHING THAT HOPS** somebody who or something that hops **4.** INSECTS **JUMPING INSECT** a jumping insect such as a leafhopper, treehopper, froghopper, or planthopper. Order: Homoptera.

hop·per[2] /hóppәr/ *n.* a machine used to harvest hops

UPI/Corbis-Bettmann

Edward Hopper

Hop·per /hóppәr/, **Edward** (1882–1967) U.S. artist. His work, e.g., *Nighthawks* (1942) is known for its stark realism.

hop-pick·er *n.* a person or machine that harvests hops

hop·ping /hópping/ *adj.* **BUSY** very active or busy (*informal*) ■ *n.* **GOING FROM PLACE TO PLACE** going from one place of a specified kind to another of the same kind (*usually used in combination*) ○ *job-hopping*

hop·ping John, **hop·pin' John** *n.* a dish of black-eyed peas, spices, and bacon or salt pork, traditionally served with rice and cooked greens on New Year's Day in the South for good luck

hop·ping mad *adj.* extremely angry (*informal*) [*Hopping* from the bodily movements often accompanying extreme anger]

hop·ple *vt., n.* = **hobble** *v.* 3, **hobble** *n.* 1 [Late 16thC. Origin uncertain: probably from Low German.] —**hop·pler** *n.*

hop·py /hóppee/ (**-pi·er, -pi·est**) *adj.* with a strong taste of hops

hop·sack /hóp sàk/ *n.* **1. FABRIC FOR CLOTHING** a coarsely woven cotton or woolen fabric used to make clothes **2. FABRIC FOR SACKS** a coarse fabric of hemp or jute, used to make sacks or bags

Barnaby's

Hopscotch

hop·scotch /hóp skòch/ *n.* a children's game in which players hop along squares marked in a pattern on the ground to pick up a small object thrown into one of the squares [Early 19thC. *Scotch* from SCOTCH in the sense "scratched line." The game was formerly called *scotch-hoppers* and *hop-scot*.]

hop tre·foil *n. U.K.* = **hop clover**

hor. *abbr.* **1.** horizon **2.** horizontal **3.** horology

ho·ra /háwrә/, **ho·rah** *n.* **1.** DANCE **CIRCLE DANCE** a traditional dance of Israel and Romania, performed in a circle **2.** MUSIC **MUSIC FOR HORA** the traditional music to which the hora is danced [Late 19thC. From Romanian *horă* and Hebrew *hōrāh*.]

Hor·ace /háwrәss/ (65–8 B.C.) Roman poet. The son of a slave, he was educated in Rome and Athens, and became the preeminent lyric poet of his time. His most famous works are *Odes* (23 B.C.) and *Epistles* (20? B.C.). Full name **Quintus Horatius Flaccus**

Ho·rae /háw rèe/ *n.* in ancient Greece, the goddesses of the seasons and the order of nature

ho·rah *n.* = **hora**

ho·ral /háwrәl/ *adj.* hourly (*formal*) [Early 18thC. From late Latin *horalis*, from Latin *hora* (see HOUR).]

ho·ra·ry /háwrәree/ *adj.* (*formal*) **1. RELATING TO HOUR** relating to an hour or hours **2. HOURLY** hourly [Early 17thC. From medieval Latin *horarius*, from Latin *hora* (see HOUR).]

Ho·ra·tian /hә ráysh'n/ *adj.* written by or in the style of the ancient Roman poet Horace ○ *Alexander Pope's Horatian odes.* [Early 17thC. From Latin *Horatianus*, from Quintus *Horatius* Flaccus, Latin name of HORACE.]

Ho·ra·tian ode *n.* an ode that has several stanzas, each of which has the same rhythmic pattern

horde /hawrd/ *n.* **1. THRONG** a large group of people (*often used in the plural*) **2.** ANTHROP **NOMADIC GROUP** a group of nomads, especially of a people who live by hunting and foraging for food (**hunter-gatherers**) **3.** ZOOL **SWARM OR PACK** a large group of insects or other animals moving in a mass ■ *vi.* (**hord·ed, hord·ing, hordes**) **1. FORM OR LIVE IN CROWD** to gather together, move, or live in a large crowd or mass **2.** ANTHROP **LIVE IN GROUP** to live together in a nomadic group [Mid-16thC. Directly and via French and German from Polish *horda*, from, ultimately, Turkish *ordu* "camp, army" (source of English *Urdu*).]

hore·hound /háwr hòwnd/ *n.* **1.** PLANTS **MINT PLANT EASING COUGHS** a bitter perennial mint of Europe and Asia that has downy leaves, square stems, and small white flowers whose juice was used as a flavoring and is used in cough remedies. Latin name: *Marrubium vulgare.* **2. SOMETHING PREPARED FROM HOREHOUND** an extract of the horehound plant, or something flavored with it, e.g., cough drops [Old English *hāre hūne*, from *hār* "HOAR" + *hūne* "horehound," of unknown origin]

ho·ri·zon /hә rīz'n/ *n.* **1. PLACE WHERE EARTH MEETS SKY** the line in the furthest distance where the land or sea seems to meet the sky **2.** ASTRON **CIRCLE ON APPARENT SPHERE OF SKY** a circle formed on the celestial sphere by a plane tangent to a point on the earth's surface **3.** ASTRON **CIRCLE ON CELESTIAL SPHERE** a circle formed on the celestial sphere by a plane through the center of the earth and parallel to the tangent of a point on the earth's surface **4.** GEOG **DISTINCT LAYER OF SOIL** a layer of soil having characteristics that distinguish it from other layers **5.** ARCHEOL **GEOLOGICAL LAYER** a distinct layer of rock or geological deposit within a stratum that can be dated, e.g., by its fossil content ■ **ho·ri·zons** *npl.* **RANGE OF EXPERIENCE** the range or limits

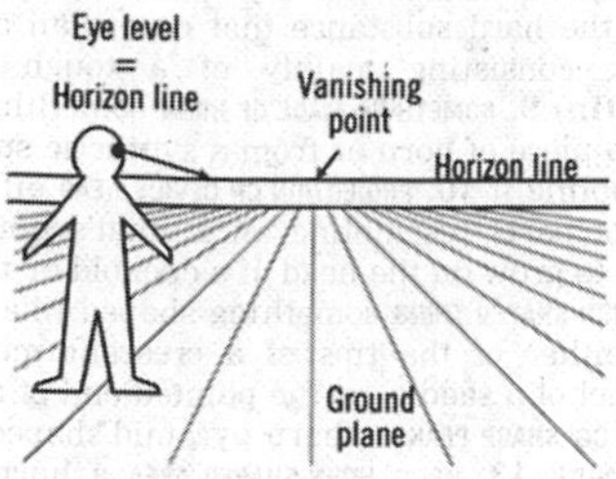

Horizon

of somebody's interests, knowledge, or experience [14thC. Via Old French *orizon(te)* from, ultimately, Greek *horizōn (kuklos)*, literally "limiting (circle)," present participle of *horizein* "to limit," from *horos* "limit."] —**ho·ri·zon·al** *adj.*

hor·i·zon·tal /hàwri zónt'l/ *adj.* **1. LEVEL** parallel to the horizon **2. MEASURED IN HORIZONTAL PLANE** measured or operating in a plane parallel to the horizon **3. LYING DOWN** lying down or in a reclining position (*informal*) **4.** BUSINESS **BEING OR HAVING SAME STATUS** being at or having the same level within a group of people ○ *a horizontal promotion* **5.** BUSINESS **APPLIED TO ALL** applied equally to all members, parts, or aspects of something ○ *a horizontal bonus* **6. OF HORIZON** relating to the horizon ■ *n.* **SOMETHING HORIZONTAL** a horizontal line, surface, or position [Mid-16thC. From French, or modern Latin *horizontalis*, from the late Latin stem *horizont-* of *horizon* "horizon," from Greek *horizōn* (see HORIZON).] —**hor·i·zon·tal·i·ty** /hàwri zon tállәtee/ *n.* —**hor·i·zon·tal·ness** *n.* —**hor·i·zon·tal·ly** *adv.*

hor·i·zon·tal bar *n.* **1. RAISED METAL BAR** a metal bar fixed in a horizontal position and used for gymnastic exercises **2. GYMNASTICS EVENT** a competitive gymnastics event involving feats of skill and strength on the horizontal bar

hor·i·zon·tal mo·bil·i·ty *n.* a change in social situation that does not involve a change in social status

hor·i·zon·tal un·ion *n.* HR = **craft union**

hor·mo·go·ni·um /hàwrmә gṓnee әm/ (*plural* **-a** /-ә/) *n.* a section of a filament of blue-green algae that detaches and reproduces by cell division [Late 19thC. From modern Latin, from Greek *hormos* "chain" + *gonos* "generation, seed" (see GONAD).]

hor·mone /háwr mōn/ *n.* **1.** BIOCHEM **REGULATING CHEMICAL IN BODY** a chemical substance produced in the body's endocrine glands or certain other cells that exerts a regulatory or stimulatory effect, e.g., in metabolism **2.** PLANTS **REGULATING CHEMICAL IN PLANTS** a nonnutrient substance synthesized by plants that regulates growth and development **3.** INSECTS **REGULATING CHEMICAL IN INSECTS** a substance produced in the body of an insect that regulates various aspects of growth and development such as the change from larva to adult **4.** CHEM **SYNTHETIC REGULATING CHEMICAL** a synthetic chemical that acts like a hormone [Early 20thC. Formed from Greek *hormōn*, present participle of *horman* "to set in motion," from *hormē* "assault."] —**hor·mon·al** /hawr mṓn'l/ *adj.* —**hor·mon·al·ly** *adv.*

hor·mone re·place·ment ther·a·py *n. U.K.* = **estrogen-replacement therapy**

Hor·muz, Strait of /hawr móoz, háwr mooz/ narrow waterway between Iran and the Arabian Peninsula, linking the Persian Gulf with the Arabian Sea. Formerly **Ormuz**

horn /hawrn/ *n.* **1.** CARS, EMERGENCIES **NOISE-MAKING WARNING DEVICE** a device, e.g., in a car, that produces a loud noise as a warning or signal (*often used in combination*) **2.** ZOOL **PROJECTION ON ANIMAL'S HEAD** one of a permanent pair of pointed projections on the head of certain mammals, e.g., the cow, sheep, or antelope, made of a sheath of hardened protein over bone **3.** ZOOL **PROJECTION FROM NOSE OF RHINOCEROS** a solid outgrowth of keratin and fused hair from the nasal bone of a rhinoceros **4.** ZOOL **PROJECTION RESEMBLING HORN** any of various hard, pointed, or horn-shaped projections on animals, birds, reptiles, fish, or insects **5.** MUSIC **BRASS MUSICAL INSTRUMENT** a wind instrument usually made of brass and consisting of a long tube with a flared end that produces a sound when the player's lips vibrate together into the mouthpiece **6.** MUSIC **JAZZ INSTRUMENT** any wind instrument played in a jazz band (*informal*) **7.** MUSIC **SIMPLE WIND INSTRUMENT** a simple or early type of musical instrument made from an animal's horn **8.** INDUST **HARD SUBSTANCE OF HORNS** the hard substance that covers an animal's horns, consisting mainly of a tough protein (**keratin**) **9. SOMETHING MADE OF HORN** something made with a piece of horn or from a synthetic substance resembling it **10. PROJECTION ON DEVIL'S HEAD** either of a pair of parts resembling an animal's horns supposed to grow on the head of a cuckold or the devil **11. HORN-SHAPED THING** something shaped like a horn, e.g., either of the tips of a crescent moon, the pommel of a saddle, or the pointed end of an anvil **12.** GEOG **SHARP PEAK** a sharp pyramid-shaped mountain peak **13.** GEOG **HORN-SHAPED AREA** a horn-shaped body of water or land **14.** UTIL **TELEPHONE** a telephone (*slang*) ■ *vt.* (**horned, horn·ing, horns**) **1. PROVIDE WITH HORNS** to give something a horn or horns **2. ATTACK WITH HORNS** to butt or gore somebody with the horns **3.** *Carib, U.S.* **HAVE SEX WITH SOMEBODY ELSE'S PARTNER** to make a cuckold of somebody by having a sexual relationship with the spouse or partner (*informal*) [Old English. Ultimately from an Indo-European base meaning "horn, head."] ◇ **pull in your horns 1.** to spend or invest less money than usual or before **2.** to adopt a less active or less assertive position ◇ **on the horns of a dilemma** faced with making a decision between two things or two courses of action, each of which is problematic or unattractive

WORD KEY: ORIGIN

The Indo-European ancestor of ***horn*** is also the ultimate source of English *carrot, corn, cornea, corner, cornet, cranium, ginger, hart, hornet, keratin, rhinoceros,* and *triceratops.*

horn in *vi.* to intrude, interfere, or get involved in something without invitation (*informal*)

Horn, Cape /kayp háwrn/ cape at the southern tip of South America, on an island now belonging to Chile. It was notorious for shipwrecks in the age of sailing ships.

horn·beam /háwrn be͞em/ *n.* **1.** TREES **TREE WITH SMOOTH BARK** a tree that has smooth grayish bark and hard white wood. Genus: *Carpinus.* **2.** INDUST **WOOD OF HORNBEAM** the hard white wood of the hornbeam tree

horn·bill /háwrn bìl/ *n.* a noisy tropical bird that has a very large curved bill with a horny protuberance. Hornbills are often found in large groups. Family: Bucerotidae.

horn·blende /háwrn blènd/ *n.* a variety of a silicate mineral (**amphibole**) ranging in color from dark green to black and containing aluminum, calcium, iron, magnesium, and sodium [Late 18thC. From German, literally "horn blende."] —**horn·blend·ic** /hawrn bléndik/ *adj.*

horn·book /háwrn bo͝ok/ *n.* **1. TEXT PROTECTED BY HORN** a page of text formerly made for the teaching of reading, usually printed with the alphabet, letter combinations, and a religious passage, and covered with a thin layer of horn **2.** EDUC **BEGINNERS' TEXTBOOK** a book containing elementary teaching material for those learning a particular subject or skill

Horne /hawrn/, **Marilyn** (*b.* 1934) U.S. mezzo-soprano. She is known for her roles in operas by Rossini, Berg, and Stravinsky.

horned /hawrnd/ *adj.* having a horn or horns, or one or more projections that resemble horns

horned liz·ard *n.* a small insect-eating lizard of the desert regions of the southwestern United States and Mexico that has a flattened body, a short tail, and spikes like horns on its head. Genus: *Phrynosoma.*

horned owl *n.* a large owl that has prominent ear tufts resembling horns. Latin name: *Bubo virginianus.*

horned pout *n.* = **hornpout**

horned toad *n.* = **horned lizard**

horned vi·per *n.* a poisonous snake of the desert regions of the Near East and Africa that has spines on its head that look like horns. Latin name: *Cerastes cornutus.*

hor·net /háwrnət/ *n.* a large social stinging wasp that builds large group nests underground or hanging from a tree. Family: Vespidae. [Old English *hyrnet(u).* Ultimately from an Indo-European word that is also the ancestor of English *horn.*]

hor·net's nest *n.* a highly controversial issue or situation that is likely to lead to confrontation, opposition, or argument

Hor·ney /háwrnee/, **Karen** (1885–1952) German-born U.S. psychoanalyst. She advanced and developed Freudian theory in books such as *New Ways in Psychoanalysis* (1939).

horn·fels /háwrn fèlz/ (*plural* **-fels**) *n.* a fine-grained metamorphic rock composed of silicate minerals and formed through the action of heat and pressure on shale [Mid-19thC. From German, literally "horn rock."]

horn fly *n.* a small bloodsucking black fly that is a pest of cattle. Latin name: *Haematobia irritans.* [*Horn* from its sucking blood from the base of the horns of cattle]

horn·ing /háwrning/ *n. Northeast U.S.* = **shivaree**

hor·nist /háwrnist/ *n.* a musician who plays a horn

horn-mad *adj.* extremely angry or enraged (*archaic*) [The word originally described the rage of horned beasts]

horn of plen·ty *n.* **1.** = **cornucopia 2.** FUNGI **HORN-SHAPED EDIBLE FUNGUS** a funnel-shaped, black and brown edible fungus found in deciduous woodland in fall. Latin name: *Craterellus cornucopioides.*

horn·pipe /háwrn pīp/ *n.* **1.** DANCE **SAILORS' DANCE** a lively British dance traditionally performed by sailors **2.** MUSIC **MUSIC ACCOMPANYING HORNPIPE** the music for a hornpipe, or an orchestral piece based on this **3.** MUSIC **REED INSTRUMENT** a musical instrument with a single reed and a mouthpiece made of horn, traditionally used to play the music for a hornpipe

horn·pout /háwrn pòwt/ *n.* a small North American fish with a large head and eight barbels. Latin name: *Ictalurus nebulosus.*

horn-rims, horn-rimmed glasses *npl.* glasses with frames made from dark-colored horn or a synthetic substance made to resemble this —**horn-rimmed** *adj.*

Horns·by /háwrnzbee/, **Rogers** (1896–1963) U.S. baseball player and manager. Considered one of the best batters of all time, he was inducted into the Baseball Hall of Fame (1942).

horn·stone /háwrn stōn/ *n.* = **hornfels** [Early 18thC. Translation of German *Hornstein,* literally "horn stone."]

horn·swog·gle /háwrn swògg'l/ (**-gled, -gling, -gles**) *vt.* to cheat, trick, or deceive somebody (*informal*) [Early 19thC. Origin unknown.]

horn·tail /háwrn tàyl/ *n.* an insect that resembles a wasp and whose larvae burrow in wood. The female has a specialized egg-laying organ (**ovipositor**) used to lay eggs in wood. Family: Siricidae.

horn·worm /háwrn wùrm/ *n.* the caterpillar of certain hawkmoths, with a projection on its tail that resembles a horn. Hornworms are often destructive agricultural pests.

horn·wort /háwrn wùrt, -wàwrt/ *n.* a rootless aquatic plant that grows in branching submerged masses and has finely dissected leaves and tiny flowers. Genus: *Ceratophylum.* [Modeled on Greek *keratophullon,* literally "horn leaf"; from the appearance of its branching stem]

horn·y /háwrnee/ (**-i·er, -i·est**) *adj.* **1. AS TOUGH AS HORN** hard or rough like horn **2. OF OR LIKE HORN** made of or resembling horn **3. FEELING SEXY** sexually excited, or easily aroused sexually (*slang*) **4. WITH HORNS** having a horn or horns —**horn·i·ly** *adv.* —**horn·i·ness** *n.*

horol. *abbr.* **1.** horological **2.** horology

hor·o·loge /háwrə lòj/ *n.* any device used to tell the time, e.g., a clock or sundial (*formal*) [13thC. Via Old French *or(i)loge* from, ultimately, Greek *hōrologion,* literally "little time-telling (instrument)," ultimately from *hōra* "time, hour" (source of English *hour*).]

ho·rol·o·gist /haw róllәjist/, **ho·rol·o·ger** /haw róllәjәr/ *n.* **1.** TIME **STUDIER OF TIME** somebody who studies the science of measuring time **2.** CRAFT **CLOCKMAKER** somebody skilled in making clocks and watches

Hor·o·lo·gi·um /hàwrə lṓjee əm, hàwrə lṓjəm/ *n.* a faint constellation of the southern hemisphere situated between Hydrus and Eridanus

ho·rol·o·gy /haw róllәjee/ *n.* **1.** TIME **TIME MEASUREMENT** the study or science of measuring time **2.** CRAFT **CLOCKMAKING** the art or skill of making clocks, watches, and other devices for telling the time [15thC. Coined from Greek *hōra* "time, hour" (source of English *hour*) + -LOGY.] —**hor·o·log·ic** /hàwrə lójjik/ *adj.* —**hor·o·log·i·cal** *adj.* —**hor·o·log·i·cal·ly** /-lójjikəlee/ *adv.*

hor·o·scope /háwrə skōp/ *n.* **1. DIAGRAM OF PLANETARY RELATIONSHIP** the relative position of the stars or planets at a particular moment, especially somebody's time of birth, or a diagram showing this **2. ASTROLOGICAL FORECAST** an astrologer's description of an individual's personality and future based on the position of the planets in relation to the sign of the zodiac under which the person was born [Pre-12thC. Via Latin *horoscopus* from Greek *hōroskopos,* literally "time observer," from *hōra* "time, hour" (source of English *hour*), referring to the time of birth.] —**hor·o·scop·ic** /hàwrə skóppik/ *adj.*

ho·ros·co·py /hə róskəpee/ *n.* the making and interpretation of horoscopes

Ho·ro·witz /háwrə wits/, **Vladimir** (1904–89) Russian-born U.S. pianist. He was known for his brilliant virtuosity. His interpretations of works by Liszt and Rachmaninoff achieved popular and critical acclaim.

hor·ren·dous /hə réndəss, haw-/ *adj.* **1. DREADFUL** sufficiently unpleasant, frightening, or shocking as to provoke horror **2. VERY LARGE** very large, great, or high, often unreasonably or excessively so (*informal*) ○ *horrendous prices* [Mid-17thC. Formed from Latin *horrendus* "to be shuddered at," a form of *horrere* (see HORRIBLE).]

hor·ren·dous·ly /hə réndəsslee, haw-/ *adv.* to a very great, and often unreasonable or excessive, degree

hor·rent /háwrənt/ *adj.* standing on end like bristles (*archaic*) ○ *"With bright imblazonrie, and horrent arms"* (John Milton, *Paradise Lost;* 1667) [Mid-17thC. From Latin *horrent-,* the present participle stem of *horrere* (see HORRIBLE).]

hor·ri·ble /háwrəb'l/ *adj.* **1. VERY UNPLEASANT** very bad, very unpleasant, or caused by anxiety or fear about something bad ○ *a horrible smell* **2. CAUSING HORROR** sufficiently frightening, distressing, or shocking as to provoke horror ○ *a horrible crime* **3. NASTY** unkind, rude, or ill-behaved (*informal*) [13thC. Via Old French *(h)orrible* from Latin *horribilis,* from *horrere* "to bristle, shudder with fear at" (source of English *horror* and *ordure*).] —**hor·ri·ble·ness** *n.*

hor·ri·bly /háwrəblee/ *adv.* **1. IN UNPLEASANT WAY** in an unpleasant, disagreeable, distressing, or shocking way **2. VERY** to a great or excessive extent ○ *horribly late*

hor·rid /háwrid/ *adj.* **1. NASTY** callously unkind or nasty (*informal*) ○ *a horrid thing to say* **2. CAUSING DISGUST** provoking disgust or extreme displeasure ○ *a horrid taste* **3. CAUSING HORROR** dreadful, shocking, or frightening enough to cause horror ○ *a horrid accident* **4. BRISTLY** rough, shaggy, or bristly (*archaic*) [Late 16thC. From Latin *horridus* "bristly, rough, horrid," from *horrere* (see HORRIBLE).] —**hor·rid·ly** *adv.* —**hor·rid·ness** *n.*

hor·rif·ic /haw ríffik/ *adj.* frightening or disturbing enough to cause horror [Mid-17thC. Directly or via French *horrifique* from Latin *horrificus,* from *horrere* (see HORRIBLE).] —**hor·rif·i·cal·ly** *adv.*

hor·ri·fy /háwrə fī/ (**-fied, -fy·ing, -fies**) *vt.* **1. CAUSE SOMEBODY TO FEEL HORROR** to make somebody feel horror, disgust, or fright **2. DISMAY SOMEBODY** to make somebody shocked or dismayed [Late 18thC. From Latin *horrificare,* literally "to cause horror," from, ultimately, *horrere* (see HORRIBLE).] —**hor·ri·fi·ca·tion** /hàwrəfi káysh'n/ *n.* —**hor·ri·fied** /háwrə fīd/ *adj.* —**hor·ri·fy·ing** /-ing/ *adj.* —**hor·ri·fy·ing·ly** /-inglee/ *adv.*

hor·rip·i·la·tion /haw rìppi láysh'n/ *n.* the standing on end of somebody's hair, e.g., because of fear or cold [Mid-17thC. From the late Latin stem *horripilation-,* from, ultimately, Latin *horripilare* "to become hairy," from *horrere* "to stand on end" (see HORRIBLE) + *pilus* "hair."]

hor·ror /háwrər/ *n.* **1. INTENSE FEAR OR SHOCK** a very strong, painful feeling of fear, shock, or disgust **2. INTENSE DISLIKE OR DISMAY** a feeling of distress or distaste **3. SOMETHING CAUSING HORROR** something, or an aspect of something, that causes a feeling of great fear or disgust ○ *the horrors of war* **4. SOMETHING UNPLEASANT** a very unpleasant or unattractive thing (*informal*) ○ *The new building is an absolute horror.* ■ **hor·rors** *npl.* (*informal*) **1. FEELING OF TERROR** a feeling of intense fear, anxiety, or hopelessness **2.** = **delirium tremens** ■ *adj.* CINEMA, LITERAT **GROTESQUE AND TERRIFYING** used to describe a genre of motion picture or literature intended to thrill viewers or readers by provoking fear or revulsion through the portrayal of grotesque, violent, or supernatural events. ◊ **horror story** [14thC. Directly or via Old French *(h)orrour* from Latin *horror*, from *horrere* (see HORRIBLE).]

hor·ror sto·ry *n.* **1.** LITERAT **FRIGHTENING FICTIONAL TALE** a story that is intended to frighten people, usually by describing gruesome or supernatural events **2.** **REPORT OF HORRIFYING EXPERIENCE** a true account of something very unpleasant or shocking

hor·ror-struck, hor·ror-strick·en *adj.* suddenly shocked, frightened, or dismayed

hors con·cours /awr kawN ko͝or/ *adj.* in the capacity or manner of somebody who is not competing [From French, literally "out of the competition"]

hors de com·bat /àwr də kawN baá/ *adj.* out of action and often in a seriously wounded condition [From French, literally "out of the fight"]

hors d'oeuvre /awr dúrv/ (*plural* **hors d'oeuvre** *or* **hors d'oeuvres**) *n.* a small portion of food served cold or hot before a meal to stimulate the appetite [From French, literally "outside the work"]

horse /hawrss/ *n.* **1.** ZOOL **ANIMAL THAT NEIGHS** a large four-legged animal with a mane, tail, hooves, and a long head. Horses are kept as domestic animals for riding, pulling vehicles, and carrying loads. Latin name: *Equus caballus.* **2.** ZOOL **STALLION OR GELDING** an adult male horse **3.** ZOOL **ANIMAL OF THE HORSE FAMILY** an animal, e.g., a donkey or zebra, that belongs to the family including the horse. Family: Equidae. **4.** GYMNASTICS = **vaulting horse** **5.** **FRAME OR SUPPORT** a type of frame or support, especially one mounted on four legs **6.** ARMY **MOUNTED SOLDIERS** soldiers riding horses (*takes a singular verb*) **7.** GEOL **ROCK MASS IN AN ORE VEIN** a mass of rock located in an ore vein **8.** DRUGS **HEROIN** heroin (*dated slang*) **9.** AUTOMOT **HORSEPOWER** horsepower (*informal*) (*usually used in the plural*) ■ **hors·es** *npl.* **HORSERACING** horseracing, especially as a gambling activity (*informal*) ■ *v.* (**horsed, hors·ing, hors·es**) **1.** *vt.* **GIVE SOMEBODY A HORSE** to provide somebody with a horse **2.** *vti.* RIDING **PUT OR GET ON A HORSE** to put a rider on a horse's back, or mount a horse **3.** *vi.* ZOOL **BE IN HEAT** to be ready to mate with a male horse (*refers to a mare*) [Old English *hors*, from a prehistoric Germanic word of uncertain origin] ◇ **get on your high horse** to adopt an arrogant attitude ◇ **beat a dead horse** to pursue a topic or course of action that is likely to be totally unproductive ◇ **from the horse's mouth** from a well-informed and reliable source ◇ **look a gift horse in the mouth** to criticize something that has been given to you

horse around *vi.* to play or fool around in a boisterous manner

horse-and-bug·gy *adj.* **1.** **FROM BEFORE THE AUTOMOBILE** belonging or relating to the era before the invention of the automobile **2.** **OLD-FASHIONED** adhering to things, fashions, or ideas that are old-fashioned and out of date [From the obsolescence of this means of transportation]

horse·back /háwrss bàk/ *adj., adv.* on a horse's back ◇ **on horseback** sitting on or riding a horse

horse bean *n.* = **broad bean** [From its use as fodder for horses]

horse·car /háwrss kaàr/ *n.* a vehicle, such as a truck or railroad car, used to transport horses

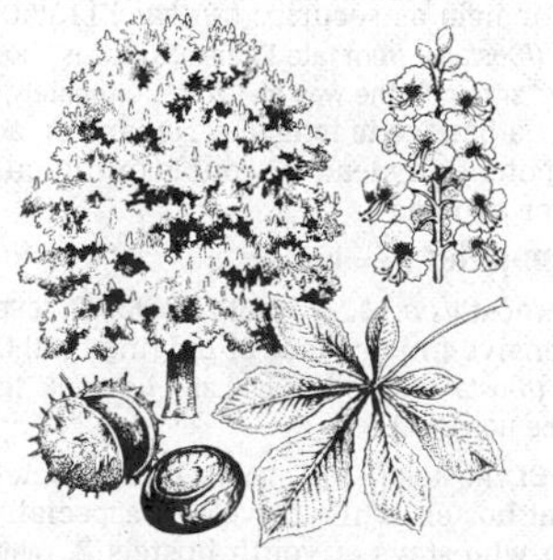

Horse chestnut

horse chest·nut *n.* **1.** TREES **TREE WITH LARGE SHINY BROWN SEEDS** a large tree of Europe and Asia that has five-lobed leaves, conical clusters of flowers, and shiny brown seeds that resemble nuts. Latin name: *Aesculus hippocastanum.* **2.** **A FRUIT OF HORSE CHESTNUT TREE** the shiny brown inedible fruit of the horse chestnut tree. ◊ **conker** **3.** INDUST **HORSE CHESTNUT WOOD** the soft wood of the horse chestnut tree [Translation of obsolete modern Latin *Castanea equina*; *equina* "horse" perhaps because the leaf stalk bears the image of a horse's hock and foot with shoe and nails]

horse·feath·ers /háwrss fèthərz/ *n., interj.* nonsense (*humorous slang*) (*takes a singular verb*) [Early 20thC. Alteration of HORSESHIT.]

horse·flesh /háwrss flèsh/ *n.* **1.** EQU **HORSES OR HORSE** horses collectively **2.** FOOD **MEAT FROM A HORSE** the flesh of a horse, especially when sold or eaten as meat

horse·fly /háwrss flì/ (*plural* **-flies**) *n.* a large two-winged fly, the female of which sucks the blood of horses and other mammals. Genus: *Tabanus.*

horse gen·tian *n.* a North American plant of the honeysuckle family with purplish-brown flowers and orange fruit. Genus: *Triosteum.* [See HORSELEECH]

horse·hair /háwrss hàir/ *n.* **1.** INDUST **LONG HAIR FROM A HORSE** hair from a horse's mane and tail, used to upholster furniture, and to make cloth **2.** TEXTILES **HORSEHAIR CLOTH** fabric woven from the hair of a horse's mane and tail

horse·hair worm *n.* = **hairworm** [*Horsehair* from its form, likened to a hair of a horse]

Horse·head neb·u·la /háwrss hed-/ *n.* a dark nebula in the constellation Orion, shaped like a horse's head

horse·hide /háwrss hìd/ *n.* **1.** **SKIN OF A HORSE** the tough thick skin of a horse, or leather made from a horse's skin **2.** BASEBALL **BASEBALL** the ball used in the game of baseball (*informal*)

horse lat·i·tudes *npl.* either of two regions at sea near the latitudes 30° S and 30° N marked by high atmospheric pressure and light variable winds or calms [Late 18thC. Origin uncertain.]

horse·laugh /háwrss làf/ *n.* a loud, coarse, and often scornful laugh

horse·leech /háwrss leèch/ *n.* a large freshwater leech. Genus: *Haemopis.* [*Horse* in animal and plant names usually denotes "large size" or "coarseness," the horse typifying a large creature]

horse·less car·riage *n.* an automobile, at a time when horse-drawn vehicles were still the usual form of transport (*archaic*)

horse mack·er·el *n.* a swift torpedo-shaped fish found in the Atlantic Ocean, the Mediterranean Sea, and the Black Sea. Latin name: *Trachurus trachurus.* [See HORSELEECH]

horse·man /háwrssmən/ (*plural* **-men** /-mən/) *n.* **1.** **RIDER OF HORSES** a man who rides or is riding a horse, especially a man who does so with skill **2.** **HORSE OWNER** a man who owns or breeds horses

horse·man·ship /háwrssmən shìp/ *n.* skill in riding horses

horse·mint /háwrss mìnt/ *n.* **1.** **N AMERICAN MINT** a coarse North American mint that has showy yellow flowers with purple spots. Latin name: *Monarda punctata.* **2.** **EURASIAN WILD MINT** a hairy wild mint of Europe and Asia that has elongated clusters of small pinkish-purple flowers. Latin name: *Mentha longifolia.* [See HORSELEECH]

horse net·tle *n.* a coarse prickly North American weed of the nightshade family with white or blue flowers and yellow berries. Latin name: *Solanum carolinese.* [See HORSELEECH]

horse o·pe·ra *n.* a Western movie (*informal*) [*Horse* from the ubiquity in such works of horses; *opera* from the use of dramatic music and themes]

horse pis·tol *n.* a large pistol formerly used by horsemen and carried in a holster

horse·play /háwrss plày/ *n.* rough, boisterous, playful behavior

horse·play·er /háwrss plàyr/ *n.* somebody who frequently bets on horse races

horse·pow·er /háwrss pòwr/ *n.* a unit of power equal in the United States to 745.7 watts and in the United Kingdom to 550 foot-pounds per second [*Horse* from one such unit being supposedly equivalent to the work rate of a horse]

horse·race *n.* a race between horses ridden by jockeys on a flat circuit or over obstacles

horseracing *n.* a sport in which horses ridden by jockeys race against each other, usually with spectators and others betting on the result

Horseradish

horse·rad·ish /háwrss ràddish/ *n.* **1.** PLANTS **PLANT WITH PUNGENT ROOTS** a tall coarse plant that has white flowers and thick white pungent roots. Latin name: *Amoracia lapathifolia.* **2.** FOOD **HORSERADISH ROOT AS FOOD** the long slim pungent root of the horseradish plant used in cooking, especially peeled and grated to make a hot, sharp-tasting sauce often served with beef [See HORSELEECH]

hors·e's ass *n.* an offensive term for a person who is disliked or objectionable because of being mean, conceited, unintelligent, or obnoxious (*offensive insult*)

horse sense *n.* common sense (*informal*)

horse·shit /háwrss shìt/ *n.* **1.** **OFFENSIVE TERM** an offensive term for nonsense (*slang offensive*) **2.** **OFFENSIVE TERM** an offensive term for the excrement of a horse (*offensive*)

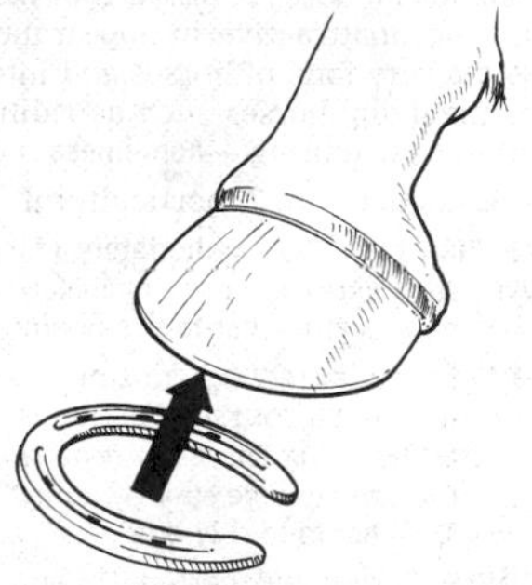

Horseshoe

horse·shoe /háwrss shoō/ *n.* **1.** EQU **PROTECTION FOR A HORSE'S HOOF** a flat U-shaped piece of iron nailed to the bottom of a horse's hoof to protect it against hard surfaces. Horseshoes are regarded as symbols of good luck. **2.** **GOOD-LUCK TOKEN** a representation of a horseshoe regarded as a symbol of good luck **3.** **HORSESHOE-SHAPED THING** something that has the curved shape of a horseshoe ○ "*... every known superstition in the world is gathered into the horseshoe of the Carpathians ...*" (Bram Stoker, *Dracula*; 1897) ■ *vt.* (**-shoed, -shoe·ing, -shoes**) EQU **SHOE A HORSE** to fit a horse with horseshoes —**horse·sho·er** *n.*

horse·shoe arch *n.* an arch that narrows slightly below the upper rounded part. Horseshoe arches are characteristic of the Islamic architecture of southern Spain and North Africa.

horse·shoe bat *n.* a bat that has a horseshoe-shaped appendage that surrounds the nostrils. Horseshoe bats are found in Europe, but most abundantly in the tropics and subtropics. Family: Rhinolophidae.

horse·shoe crab *n.* a large marine arthropod of eastern North America and Asia that has a stiff pointed tail and rounded brown body resembling a horseshoe. Class: Merostomata.

Horse·shoe Falls /hàwrss shoo-/ crescent-shaped Canadian section of the Niagara Falls on the U.S.-Canadian border. Height: 161 ft./49 m.

horse·shoes *n.* LEISURE a game in which players throw horseshoes at a post and score points based on how close they land to the post (*takes a singular verb*)

horse show *n.* a sporting event in which horses and usually riders are judged on their skills in a variety of competitions such as riding or jumping

horse·tail /háwrss tàyl/ *n.* **1.** PLANTS **NONFLOWERING PLANT** a nonflowering plant that has a hollow jointed stem, tiny thin leaves, and spore-producing cones produced at the top of the stems. Genus: *Equisetum.* **2.** HIST **TURKISH EMBLEM OF RANK** a former emblem of rank of Turkish pashas in the Ottoman Empire

horse-trad·ing *n.* negotiation that involves hard bargaining and mutual compromise, shrewdness, and sometimes unscrupulous tactics such as secret or unofficial deals —**horse-trade** *vi.* —**horse-trad·er** *n.*

horse·weed /háwrss wèed/ *n.* a North American fleabane that has thin hairy leaves and clusters of small greenish or white flowers. Latin name: *Erigeron canadensis.* [Late 18thC. See HORSELEECH.]

horse·whip /háwrss wìp, -hwìp/ *n.* **1. WHIP FOR A HORSE** a whip formerly used to keep a horse under control, e.g., when being driven, and usually made of a long strip of leather attached to a short handle **2.** *Carib* ZOOL **W INDIAN SNAKE** a long thin snake common in the forests of Trinidad and frequently found in bushes near homes ■ *vt.* **(-whipped, -whip·ping, -whips) BEAT SEVERELY** to flog a person or animal with a horsewhip or with something similar, usually as a punishment —**horse·whip·per** *n.*

horse·wom·an /háwrss wòomman/ (*plural* **-en** /-wìmmin/) *n.* **1. WOMAN RIDER OF HORSES** a woman who rides or is riding a horse, especially one who does so with skill **2. WOMAN HORSE OWNER** a woman who owns or breeds horses

hors·ey /háwrsee/ *adj.* = **horsy**

horst /hawrst/ *n.* an elevated block of the Earth's crust forced upward between faults [Late 19thC. From German, "heap, mass."]

hors·y /háwrssee/ **(-i·er, -i·est), hors·ey (-i·er, -i·est)** *adj.* **1. RELATING TO HORSES** belonging to, relating to, or characteristic of a horse **2. LOOKING LIKE A HORSE** heavy, awkward, and unattractive in appearance **3. INTERESTED IN HORSES** very fond of horses and interested in activities involving horses such as riding, racing, showjumping, or hunting —**hors·i·ness** *n.*

hort. *abbr.* **1.** horticulture **2.** horticultural

hor·ta·tive /háwrtətiv/ *adj.* = **hortatory** (*formal*) [Early 17thC. Via Latin *hortativus* from, ultimately, *hortari* "to exhort" (see HORTATORY).] —**hor·ta·tive·ly** *adv.*

hor·ta·to·ry /háwrtə tàwree/ *adj.* urging, encouraging, or strongly advising a course of action to somebody (*formal*) [Late 16thC. Via late Latin *hortatorius* from, ultimately, Latin *hortari* "to urge strongly, exhort" (source of English *exhort*).] —**hor·ta·to·ri·ly** *adv.*

hor·ti·cul·ture /háwrti kùlchər/ *n.* **1.** BOT, GARDENING **CULTIVATION OF GARDENS** the science, skill, or occupation of cultivating plants, especially flowers, fruit, and vegetables, in gardens or greenhouses **2.** ANTHROP **SIMPLE AGRICULTURE WITHOUT MANY TOOLS** a simple form of agriculture based on working small plots of land without using draft animals, plows, or irrigation [Late 17thC. Formed from Latin *hortus* "garden" (source of English *orchard*). Ultimately from an Indo-European word meaning "to enclose," which is also the ancestor of English *yard* and *garden*.] —**hor·ti·cul·tur·al** /hàwrti kúlchərəl/ *adj.* —**hor·ti·cul·tur·al·ly** /-kúlchərəlee/ *adv.* —**hor·ti·cul·tur·ist** /-kúlchərist/ *n.*

Ho·rus /háwrəss/ *n.* in Egyptian mythology, the god of the sun, the sky, and goodness, usually depicted as having a falcon's head. Horus was the son of Isis and Osiris.

Hos. *abbr.* Hosea

ho·san·na /hō zánnə/, **ho·san·nah** *n., interj.* a cry of praise to God [Pre-12thC. Via late Latin from Greek *hōsanna*, from Rabbinic Hebrew *hōšaʿnā*, shortening of Hebrew *hōšīʿā-nnā* "save, (we) pray" (Psalm 118:25).]

Ho·say /hō sáy/, **Ho·sein** /hō sáyn/ *n.* an Islamic religious festival held on the tenth day of the month of Moharram celebrating the martyrdom of Imam Hosein. In Port of Spain, Trinidad, floats depicting religious sites and figures are paraded through the streets and thrown into the sea as a symbol of the vanity of worldly things.

hose /hōz/ *n.* **FLEXIBLE TUBE** a flexible tube or pipe, often made of rubber or plastic, through which fluids such as water or gasoline can flow ■ *npl.* **1.** CLOTHES **LEG COVERING** a skintight leg covering such as stockings or socks (*takes a plural verb*) **2.** CLOTHES, HIST **TIGHT-FITTING TROUSERS** a garment formerly worn by men, fitting closely to the legs and attaching to a doublet ■ *vt.* **(hosed, hos·ing, hos·es) 1. DIRECT WATER ON SOMEBODY OR SOMETHING** to spray, soak, wash, or rinse something or somebody with water from a hose **2. TRICK SOMEBODY** to deceive or trick somebody (*slang*) **3. DEGRADE A COMPUTER'S PERFORMANCE** to make a computer system nonfunctional or greatly degrade the performance of a system (*slang*) [Old English *hosa* "leg covering, husk" (hence "flexible tube"). Ultimately from an Indo-European word meaning "to cover," which is also the ancestor of English *hut, scum,* and *sky.*]

Ho·se·a /hō záy ə/ *n.* in the Bible, a short prophetic book. See table at **Bible**

Ho·sein *n.* = **Hosay**

ho·sel /hṓz'l/ *n.* the socket in the head of a golf club where the shaft is attached [Late 19thC. Formed from HOSE + the suffix *-el* "small" (from Latin *-ellus*).]

hos·er /hṓzər/ *n. Can* an unintelligent vulgar person, especially a man whose main interests are hockey and drinking beer (*slang insult*)

ho·sier /hṓzhər/ *n.* somebody who makes or sells hosiery (*archaic*)

ho·sier·y /hṓzhəree/ *n.* socks, stockings, pantyhose, and tights, considered collectively

hosp. *abbr.* hospital

hos·pice /hóspiss/ *n.* **1.** MED, SOC WELFARE **NURSING HOME FOR THE DYING** a usually small residential institution for terminally ill patients where treatment focuses on the patient's wellbeing rather than a cure and includes drugs for pain management and often spiritual counseling **2.** MED **HOME CARE FOR THE DYING** a program of hospice care for the terminally ill that includes home visits by professionals such as nurses and clergy to provide for the person's physical and emotional needs **3.** HIST **REFUGE FOR TRAVELERS AND DESTITUTE** in former times, a place where pilgrims, travelers, and the homeless or destitute were offered lodging, usually by a religious order [Early 19thC. Via French from Latin *hospitium* "guesthouse, hospitality," from the stem *hospit-* of *hospes* "host, guest" (source of English *host*[1]).]

hos·pi·ta·ble /ho spíttəb'l, hóspitəb'l/ *adj.* **1. TREATING VISITORS WELL** friendly, welcoming, and generous to guests or strangers ○ *That's very hospitable of you.* **2. AGREEABLE** pleasant, agreeable, and providing what somebody needs to live comfortably ○ *a hospitable climate* [Late 16thC. From French, from obsolete *hospiter* "to receive a guest," from, ultimately, the Latin stem *hospit-* of *hospes* (see HOST[1]).] —**hos·pi·ta·ble·ness** *n.* —**hos·pi·ta·bly** *adv.*

hos·pi·tal /hóspit'l/ *n.* **1.** MED **BUILDING FOR MEDICAL CARE** an institution where people receive medical, surgical, or psychiatric treatment and nursing care **2. PLACE OF REPAIR** a place where something is repaired **3.** SOC WELFARE **CHARITABLE HOME OR SCHOOL** a charitable institution providing shelter, care, or education for orphaned children, senior citizens, or the homeless or destitute (*archaic*) [13thC. Via Old French, "hostel," from medieval Latin *hospitale* "guesthouse, inn," from the Latin stem *hospit-* of *hospes* (see HOST[1]).]

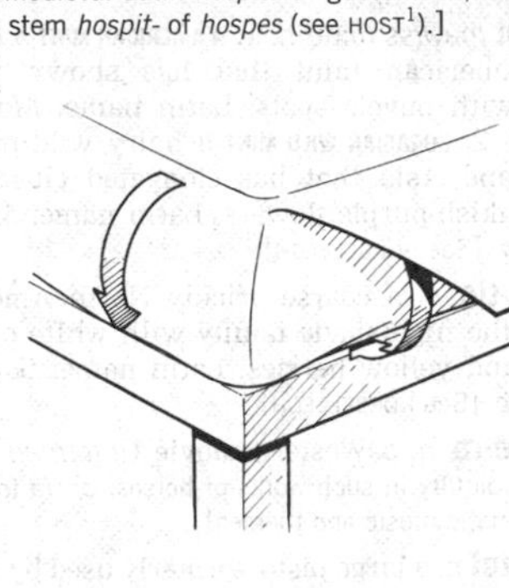

Hospital corner

hos·pi·tal cor·ner *n.* either of the corners at the foot of a bed in which the sheets and blankets are tucked under the mattress in neat triangular folds [*Hospital* from its use in hospitals]

Hos·pi·tal·er /hóspitlər/, **Hos·pi·tal·ler** *n.* **1.** RELIG, HIST **MEMBER OF A CRUSADING ORDER** a member of a military religious order, the Knights of the Hospital of St John, founded in the late 11th century by European crusaders to care for sick pilgrims in Jerusalem **2. RELIGIOUS OR CHARITABLE CAREGIVER** a member of a religious order or charitable institution involved in the care of the sick, especially in the hospital [14thC. Via Old French *hospitalier* from medieval Latin *hospitalarius*, from *hospitale* "guesthouse, inn" (see HOSPITAL).]

hos·pi·tal·i·ty /hòspi tálləteе/ *n.* a friendly welcome and kind or generous treatment offered to guests or strangers

hos·pi·tal·i·ty suite *n.* a room or suite of rooms where invited guests or clients of a company, delegates to a conference, or other official visitors are welcomed and usually provided with free refreshments

hos·pi·tal·ize /hóspit'l ìz/ **(-ized, -iz·ing, -iz·es)** *vt.* to admit somebody to the hospital for treatment, diagnosis, or observation, usually as an inpatient —**hos·pi·tal·i·za·tion** /hòspit'li záysh'n/ *n.*

Hos·pi·tal·ler *n.* = **Hospitaler**

hos·po·dar /hóspə daar/ *n.* a prince or governor of Moldavia or Wallachia during the time of Ottoman rule [Late 16thC. Via Romanian from Ukrainian.]

host[1] /hōst/ *n.* **1. SOMEBODY ENTERTAINING GUESTS** somebody who invites, welcomes, and entertains guests, often providing them with food and drink **2.** BROADCAST **SOMEBODY INTRODUCING GUESTS ON A SHOW** somebody who presents and interviews guests on a radio or television program **3. PLACE WHERE AN EVENT IS HELD** a place or organization that provides the space and facilities for a special event, e.g., an international sporting competition **4.** BIOL **ORGANISM INFECTED BY A PARASITE** a human, animal, plant, or other organism in or on which another organism, especially a parasite, lives **5.** MED **GRAFT OR TRANSPLANT RECIPIENT** the recipient of a transplanted or grafted embryo, tissue, or organ **6. LANDLORD OF AN INN** somebody who owns or runs a bed and breakfast, guest house, or hotel **7. RESTAURANT GREETER** somebody employed in a restaurant to greet and seat customers **8. host, host com·pu·ter** COMPUT **MAIN COMPUTER IN A NETWORK** in a computer network, the main computer that controls certain functions or files ■ *vt.* **(host·ed, host·ing, hosts) 1. ACCOMMODATE AN EVENT** to provide the space and facilities for a special event, e.g., an international sporting competition **2.** BROADCAST **INTRODUCE GUESTS ON A SHOW** to act as the host of a television or radio program **3. ENTERTAIN GUESTS** to be the host of a social or official gathering [13thC. Via Old French *(h)oste* "host, guest" from the Latin stem *hospit-* of *hospes* (source of English *hospital* and *hotel*), of uncertain origin: probably from *hostis* "stranger, enemy."]

host[2] /hōst/ *n.* **1. LARGE GROUP** a very large number of people or things **2.** MIL **ARMY** an army (*archaic*) [14thC. Via Old French from Latin *hostis* "stranger, enemy" (in medieval Latin, "army") (source of English *hostile*).]

Host, host *n.* the bread or wafer consecrated and eaten during the Christian ceremony of Communion [14thC. Via Old French *(h)oiste* from Latin *hostia* "sacrificial animal, victim."]

hos·ta /hṓstə, hóstə/ *n.* = **plantain lily** [Early 19thC. From modern Latin (genus name), named for Nicolaus T. *Host* (1761–1834), an Austrian botanist.]

hos·tage /hóstij/ *n.* **1. CAPTIVE HELD FOR RANSOM** somebody held prisoner by a person or group, e.g., a criminal or a terrorist organization, until certain demands are met or money is handed over **2. SOMEBODY MANIPULATED BY ANOTHER** a person or group of people whose freedom of action is restricted or controlled by a more powerful organization by implied threats or other means **3. SECURITY OR PLEDGE** a person or thing given or held as security (*archaic*) [13thC. From Old French *(h)ostage*, from late Latin *obsidiatus* "hostageship," literally "sitting in the way of," from, ultimately, *sedere* "to sit."] ◇ **a hostage to fortune** a remark or action that could potentially lead to trouble or difficulty and so is better avoided

host com·put·er *n.* = **host**[1] *n.* 8

hos·tel /hóst'l/ *n.* **1.** = **youth hostel 2. CHEAP INN** an inexpensive inn or place of lodging [13thC. From Old French *(h)ostel*, from medieval Latin *hospitale* "guesthouse, inn" (see HOSPITAL).]

hos·tel·er /hóstələr/ *n.* **1. HOSTEL LODGER** somebody who stays at hostels while traveling, especially a young person who stays at youth hostels **2. LANDLORD OF INN** somebody who owns or runs an inn or a cheap hotel (*archaic*)

hos·tel·ing /hóstəling/ *n.* staying at hostels, especially youth hostels, while traveling around for pleasure

hos·tel·ler *n.* U.K. = **hosteler**

hos·tel·ling *n.* U.K. = **hosteling**

hos·tel·ry /háwstəlree/ (*plural* **-ries**) *n.* a hotel, pub, or inn (*archaic*)

host·ess /hṓstəss/ *n.* **1.** WOMAN ENTERTAINING GUESTS a woman who invites, welcomes, and entertains guests, often providing them with food and drink **2.** BROADCAST WOMAN INTRODUCING GUESTS ON SHOW a woman who presents a television or radio program in which invited guests take part, e.g., a talk show or game show **3.** PAID DANCE PARTNER a woman who is paid to be a man's dancing partner at a nightclub or dance hall **4.** WOMAN GREETER IN A RESTAURANT a woman who is employed in a restaurant to greet and seat customers **5.** TRANSP WOMAN ATTENDANT FOR PASSENGERS a woman who is employed to provide for the safety and comfort of passengers on an aircraft, ship, train, or bus ■ *vti.* (-essed, -ess·ing, -ess·es) ACT AS HOSTESS to act as the hostess to an event, or perform the duties of a hostess [12thC. From Old French *(h)ostesse*, from *(h)oste* "host" (see HOST[1]).]

hos·tile /hóst'l/ *adj.* **1.** VERY UNFRIENDLY showing or feeling hatred, enmity, antagonism, or anger toward somebody **2.** AGAINST strongly opposed to somebody or something ○ *hostile to the idea* **3.** MIL RELATING TO AN ENEMY relating to, characteristic of, or belonging to an enemy, especially in warfare ○ *hostile fire* **4.** ADVERSE not favorable to life, health, development, or success ○ *a hostile environment* **5.** COMM AGAINST A MANAGEMENT'S WILL opposed by the owner or management of a corporation ○ *a hostile takeover* ■ *n.* **1.** MIL ENEMY an enemy in warfare **2.** HOSTILE PERSON somebody who is antagonistic or opposed to somebody or something [Late 16thC. Directly or via French from Latin *hostilis*, from *hostis* "enemy, stranger" (source of English *host*[2]).] —**hos·tile·ly** *adv.*

hos·tile wit·ness *n.* LAW a witness called by an opposing party who gives evidence against that party

hos·til·i·ty /ho stíllətee/ *n.* (*plural* -ties) **1.** INTENSE AGGRESSION OR ANGER a feeling or attitude of hatred, enmity, antagonism, or anger toward somebody **2.** STRONG OPPOSITION strong opposition to somebody or something **3.** HOSTILE ACT an aggressive act against somebody ■ **hos·til·i·ties** *npl.* MIL ATTACKS open acts of warfare

hos·tler /hósslər, óssIər/, **os·tler** *n.* **1.** ENGINEER somebody employed to service a large vehicle or machine, e.g., a locomotive or crane **2.** HORSE MINDER a person employed to look after horses at an inn (*archaic*)

hot /hot/ *adj.* (**hot·ter, hot·test**) **1.** VERY WARM at a high, relatively high, or very high temperature ○ *the hottest day of the year* **2.** TOO WARM FOR COMFORT feeling warmer than normal or desirable **3.** FOOD VERY SPICY OR PEPPERY spicy or peppery enough to cause a burning sensation in the mouth or throat **4.** CAUSING CONTROVERSY causing much discussion, disagreement, or controversy ○ *a hot topic* **5.** UNPLEASANT OR DANGEROUS unpleasant or uncomfortable because of antagonism, trouble, or danger (*informal*) ○ *It got too hot for him to handle.* **6.** QUICKLY ANGERED easily provoked or aroused ○ *a hot temper* **7.** INTENSE OR VIOLENT felt, done, or expressed with forceful, intense energy ○ *hot competition* **8.** COLORS INTENSE very bright and vivid ○ *hot pink* **9.** CLOSE following somebody or something very closely ○ *hot on the trail* **10.** REQUIRING ATTENTION requiring immediate attention and offering potential success or good fortune ○ *a hot tip* **11.** CURRENT OR TOPICAL very recent or new and therefore of interest or importance ○ *hot off the press* **12.** EXCITING new, fresh, and exciting (*informal*) ○ *a hot new talent* **13.** SUCCESSFUL very popular or successful (*informal*) ○ *one of the hottest items in the range* **14.** KNOWLEDGEABLE having or showing particular skill or knowledge (*informal*) ○ *not very hot at math* **15.** LUCKY very lucky, e.g., in gambling (*informal*) **16.** WISE very good, wise, or sensible (*informal*) ○ *That idea's not so hot.* **17.** WELL well or good (*informal*) ○ *I don't feel too hot.* **18.** ANGRY angry or agitated about something (*informal*) ○ *Watch out, the captain is hot!* **19.** KEEN enthusiastically eager (*informal*) ○ *She's really hot on jazz.* **20.** PHYSICALLY ATTRACTED physically attracted or aroused (*slang*) ○ *She's hot for you.* **21.** PHYSICALLY ATTRACTIVE physically attractive or exciting (*slang*) **22.** STOLEN obtained illegally, especially by stealing (*slang*) ○ *hot jewels* **23.** ON THE RUN wanted by the police (*slang*) ○ *a hot suspect* **24.** EAGER full of activity, energy, enthusiasm, or excitement ○ *I'm really hot to get started.* **25.** MUSIC INVENTIVE AND EXCITING with strong rhythms or exciting improvisation (*informal*) **26.** CARS POWERFUL very fast and powerful (*slang*) **27.** ELEC LIVE electrically charged ○ *a hot wire* **28.** *U.K.* STRICT very strict about something (*informal*) ○ *He's hot on getting the paperwork right.* **29.** NUCLEAR PHYS RADIOACTIVE dangerously radioactive **30.** BIOL INFECTIOUS OR LETHAL extremely infectious or lethal, or containing infectious viruses **31.** PHYS IN AN ELEVATED ENERGY STATE in an elevated energy state, usually caused by nuclear processes ○ *a hot atom* **32.** NEAR THE ANSWER OR A MISSING OBJECT very close to something to be found or discovered in a hunting or guessing game (*informal*) ○ *You're getting hotter.* **33.** ABSURD funny, absurd, or unbelievable (*slang*) ■ **hots** *npl.* DESIRE strong physical desire (*informal*) ■ *adv.* INTENSELY in an eager, intense, or angry way ○ *They argued hot and long.* [Old English *hāt*, from a prehistoric Germanic word that is also the ancestor of English *heat*] —**hot·ness** *n.* ◇ **blow** *or* **run hot and cold** to keep changing your mind, e.g., by being enthusiastic about something then unenthusiastic ◇ **hot to trot** eager and willing (*slang*)

hot air *n.* impressive or boastful talk about achievements or intentions that has no substance (*informal*)

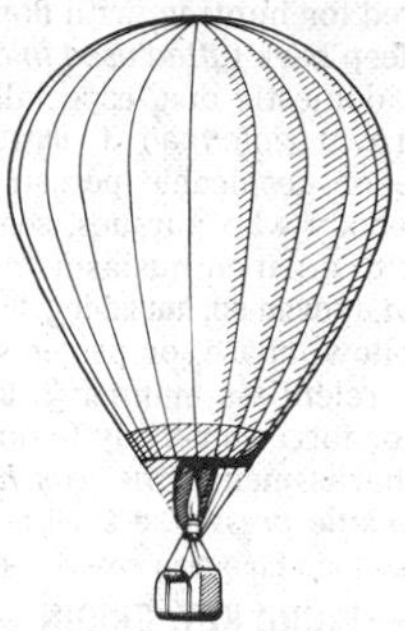

Hot-air balloon

hot-air bal·loon *n.* a lighter-than-air craft in which a compartment for pilot and passengers is suspended from a large nylon balloon that holds heated air or helium

hot·bed /hót bèd/ *n.* **1.** CENTER OF ACTIVITY an environment where something flourishes or happens frequently, especially something undesirable ○ *a hotbed of corruption.* **2.** GARDENING HEATED GLASS-COVERED SOIL BED a planting bed covered with glass and heated with electricity or by the action of fermenting manure to aid in quick germination of seeds and growth of plants

hot-blood·ed *adj.* easily angered, excited, or physically aroused —**hot-blood·ed·ness** *n.*

hot but·ton *n.* something that is known or likely to provoke a strong response, especially among voters or consumers ◇ **press somebody's hot button** to provoke a strong immediate reaction, usually a predictable one

hot-but·ton *adj.* arousing strong feelings (*slang*)

hotch·pot /hóch pòt/ *n.* in law, the gathering together of property belonging to different people in order to divide it equally [14thC. Ultimately from Old French *hochepot* "hotchpotch," from *hocher* "to shake" (see HOTCH) + *pot* "pot" (from assumed Vulgar Latin *pottus*, source of English *pot*).]

hotch·potch /hóch pòch/ *n.* = **hodgepodge** [Late 16thC. Rhyming alteration of HOTCHPOT.]

hot comb *n.* a comb that can be heated, usually electrically, and used to style or straighten the hair

hot-comb *vt.* to style or straighten the hair using a hot comb

hot cor·ner *n.* in baseball, the fielding position of third base

hot cross bun *n.* a sweet bun containing yeast, spices, and dried fruit and marked with a cross on the top, traditionally eaten hot on Good Friday

hot-desk·ing *n.* BUSINESS the practice of sharing the same work desk among several employees at different times in the work day —**hot-desk** *vi.*

hot dog *n.* **1.** WIENER IN A BUN a type of long wiener typically served hot on a bread roll with toppings such as mustard, ketchup, or relish **2.** = **frankfurter** *n.* **3.** PERFORMER OF STUNTS somebody who performs difficult, dangerous, or acrobatic stunts in skiing, surfing, and similar sports (*slang*) ■ *interj.* EXPRESSION OF ENTHUSIASTIC PLEASURE used to express strong approval, delight, or surprise (*informal*)

hot-dog (**hot-dog·ged, hot-dog·ging, hot-dogs**) *vi.* to perform difficult, dangerous, or acrobatic stunts in a showy or impressive manner in skiing, surfing, and similar sports (*slang*) —**hot-dog·ger** *n.* —**hot-dog·ging** *n.*

ho·tel /hō tél/ *n.* **1.** PLACE FOR AN OVERNIGHT STAY a building or commercial establishment where people pay for lodging, and where meals and other facilities such as conference rooms are often available **2.** *Aus* PUB an establishment that sells alcoholic beverages **3.** *S Asia* RESTAURANT a restaurant **4.** COMMUNICATION CODE WORD FOR LETTER "H" a code word for the letter "H," used in international radio communications [Mid-17thC. Via French *hôtel* from Old French *hostel* "lodging, hostel," from medieval Latin *hospitale* (see HOSPITAL).]

ho·te·lier /àw tel yáy, hō téllyər/ *n.* somebody who owns or runs a hotel [Early 20thC. Via French *hôtelier* from Old French *hostelier* "hosteler," from, ultimately, medieval Latin *hospitale* (see HOSPITAL).]

ho·tel·ing *n.* BUSINESS the practice of providing temporary desk space for an employee [From the idea that a hotel is a temporary place to stay]

hot flash *n.* a sudden hot feeling, sometimes accompanied by sweating and redness of the face, experienced by some women during menopause and caused by an endocrine imbalance

hot·foot /hót fòot/ *adv.* QUICKLY as quickly as possible ■ *n.* LIGHTING OF A MATCH IN SOMEBODY'S SHOE a practical joke in which a match is put between the sole and upper of somebody's shoe, without the person's knowledge, and then lit ◇ **hotfoot it** to go with great haste and eagerness, usually on foot (*informal*)

hot-gos·pel·er *n.* somebody who preaches religion or spreads propaganda in a very forceful or enthusiastic manner (*informal*) (*offensive in some contexts*)

hot·head /hót hèd/ *n.* somebody who acts hastily without thinking or who is too easily angered or excited

hot·head·ed /hot héddəd/ *adj.* too easily angered or excited and usually acting impetuously —**hot·head·ed·ly** *adv.* —**hot·head·ed·ness** *n.*

hot·house /hót hòwss/ *n.* (*plural* -**hous·es** /-hòwzəz/) **1.** GARDENING HEATED GREENHOUSE a heated building, usually with glass walls and roof, in which tropical or delicate plants can grow at a stable warm temperature **2.** CENTER OF ACTIVITY a place where a particular thing flourishes and develops, usually in an intensive way ○ *a hothouse of technological innovation* ■ *adj.* SENSITIVE sensitive and delicate (*informal*) ○ *hothouse views on political strategy*

hot·hous·ing /hót hòwzing/ *n.* a program of providing children with intensive education

hot·line /hót līn/ *n.* **1.** COMMUNICATIONS LINK BETWEEN LEADERS a telephone connection or similar link that allows direct communication between heads of government or other important people, especially in an emergency ○ *The Chief of Staff has a hotline to the President.* **2.** DIRECT TELEPHONE LINK TO A SERVICE a telephone number that enables members of the public to make direct contact with a special service offering information, advice, or help, usually on a serious or urgent matter

hot·ly /hóttlee/ *adv.* **1.** ANGRILY in an angry way **2.** FIERCELY in an intense and committed way ○ *hotly contested*

hot-melt *n.* a fast-drying adhesive applied in a molten state

hot met·al *n.* **1.** METAL PRINTING TYPE printing type cast from molten metal in a crucible beside the printing machine **2.** METHOD OF PRINTING printing using hot metal type

hot mon·ey *n.* funds transferred from one form of currency to another in order to take advantage of better exchange rates

hot pants *npl.* **1.** CLOTHES TIGHT SHORTS very brief close-fitting shorts for women, first fashionable in the early 1970s **2.** PHYSICAL DESIRE very strong physical desire (*slang*)

hot pep·per *n.* **1.** PLANTS PUNGENT PEPPER PLANT a pungent variety of the pepper plant. Latin name: *Capsicum frutescens.* **2.** FOOD PUNGENT FRUIT OF HOT PEPPER PLANT the hot-tasting fruit of the hot pepper plant, used in cooking, especially Mexican, Southwestern U.S., Indian, or Chinese cooking

hot plate *n.* **1.** HEATED COOKING SURFACE a flat heated surface, usually iron and part of a stove, on which food can be cooked **2.** DEVICE FOR KEEPING FOOD WARM a portable device with a flat heated surface on which cooked food can be heated or kept warm

hot pot *n.* a small heated pot of boiling water or broth used to cook pieces of food at the table, especially in Asian cooking

hot po·ta·to *n.* a sensitive or controversial issue that is awkward or difficult to deal with

hot press *n.* a machine used to apply heat and pressure to a material such as paper or cloth —**hot-press** *vt.*

hot rod *n.* a car that has been modified to make it go very fast (*slang*)

hot-rod (**hot-rod·ded, hot-rod·ding, hot-rods**) *v.* (*slang*) **1.** *vt.* **INCREASE A CAR'S POWER** to modify a car or its engine to make it very fast or powerful **2.** *vi.* **DRIVE** to drive a hot rod

hot-rod·der *n.* somebody who drives a hot rod (*slang*)

hot seat *n.* the electric chair (*slang*) ◇ **in the hot seat** facing or liable to face criticism or difficult questioning ○ *in the hot seat after the latest round of allegations*

hot shoe *n.* a camera accessory used to connect the camera and an electric flash

hot·shot /hót shòt/ *n.* **1. SELF-ASSURED EXPERT** a successful, important, or highly skilled person, especially one who is showily confident (*informal*) **2.** FREIGHT, RAIL **FAST TRAIN** a very fast freight train

hot spot *n.* **1.** MIL **PLACE OF POTENTIAL UNREST** an area where fighting or trouble is likely to break out **2.** LEISURE **CENTER OF ENTERTAINMENT** a place that is a center of entertainment and social activity, e.g., a popular nightclub (*informal*) **3.** ENG **SMALL AREA OF INTENSE HEAT** a small area of something, e.g. , an engine, that is at a much higher temperature than the rest **4.** GEOG **AREA OF GEOTHERMAL ACTIVITY** a part of the Earth's surface subject to greater than usual geothermal activity

hot spring *n.* a spring of water heated by geothermal energy. ◊ **geyser**

Hot Springs /hòt spríngz/ city in central Arkansas in the eastern Ouachita Mountains, on the Ouachita River. Population: 36,255 (1996).

Hot Springs Na·tion·al Park national park in west central Arkansas, established in 1921, with 47 thermal springs that have an average temperature over 60°C/140°F. Area: 5,543 acres/2,243 hectares.

hot·spur /hót spùr/ *n.* a rash or impetuous person [From *Hotspur,* the nickname of Henry Percy (1364–1403), English rebel]

hot stuff *n.* (*informal*) **1. VERY GOOD PERSON OR THING** somebody who or something that is particularly impressive, attractive, exciting, or important **2. ATTRACTIVE PERSON** a physically attractive person

Hot·ten·tot /hótt'n tòt/ (*plural* **-tot** *or* **-tots**) *n.* (*dated offensive*) **1.** PEOPLES **KHOIKHOI** a former name of the Khoikhoi people **2.** LANG **KHOIKHOI LANGUAGE** the language of the Khoikhoi people [Late 17thC. Ultimately from Dutch, of uncertain origin: probably originally a formula in a Nama song used by Dutch sailors to refer to the people themselves.]

Hot·ten·tot fig *n.* a low-growing succulent plant that has purplish or yellowish flowers resembling daisies, and edible fruit. It is native to South Africa, but is now grown in many frost-free places. Latin name: *Carpobrotus edulis.*

hot tick·et *n.* somebody who or something that is very popular at a particular time

hot·tish /hóttish/ *adj.* fairly but not excessively hot

hot tod·dy *n.* = **toddy**

hot tub *n.* a large round bathtub filled with hot water for one or more people to relax, bathe, or socialize in

hot war *n.* armed conflict between groups or nations, as opposed to political hostility. ◊ **cold war**

hot wa·ter *n.* a situation of trouble or difficulty, usually resulting from doing something wrong (*informal*)

hot-wa·ter bot·tle *n.* a container, usually made of rubber, filled with hot water and used to warm part of the body

hot-wire (**hot-wired, hot-wir·ing, hot-wires**) *vt.* to start a car by bringing the ignition wires into contact (*informal*)

Hou·dan /hŏŏ dàn/ *n.* a breed of domestic fowl that has black and white plumage and a characteristic full crest [Late 19thC. Named for *Houdan,* village in the French department of Seine-et-Oise, where the breed originated.]

Hou·di·ni /hŏŏ deénee/, **Harry** (1874–1926) Hungarian-born U.S. magician. President of the Society of American Magicians, he was a master escapologist and specialized in escaping from various locked containers. Real name **Ehrich Weiss**

hou high /hóo-/ *n. Hong Kong* a state of intoxication or excitement, e.g., from a drug (*slang*)

hou inch *n. Hong Kong* somebody who is aloof or arrogant (*slang insult*)

Hou·ma /hṓmə/ city in southeastern Louisiana, southeast of Baton Rouge and southwest of New Orleans. It is on the Intracoastal Waterway. Population: 30,148 (1996).

hound /hownd/ *n.* **1.** ZOOL **DOG BRED FOR HUNTING** a dog originally bred for hunting, with floppy ears, short hair, and a deep bark (*often used in combination*) **2.** ZOOL **DOG** any domestic dog, especially one viewed with disapproval (*informal*) **3. UNPLEASANT PERSON** a contemptible or despicable person (*dated*) **4. ENTHUSIAST** somebody who pursues, seeks, or collects something with great enthusiasm or determination (*informal*) ■ *vt.* (**hound·ed, hound·ing, hounds**) **1. PURSUE DOGGEDLY** to follow, chase, or pester somebody in a persistent or relentless manner **2. URGE OR NAG SOMEBODY** to urge or force somebody to do something by nagging or harassment ○ *he was hounded out of office by a hostile press* [Old English *hund* "dog." Ultimately from an Indo-European base.] —**hound·er** *n.*

WORD KEY: ORIGIN

The Indo-European word that is the ancestor of ***hound*** is also the ultimate source of English *canary, canine, chenille, corgi, cynic, dachshund,* and *kennel.*

hound·fish /hównd fish/ (*plural* **-fish** *or* **-fish·es**) *n.* a small shark or dogfish

hounds /howndz/ *npl.* the part of a ship's masthead that supports the topmast and the rigging [15thC. By folk etymology from *hune* "wooden projection below a masthead," of uncertain origin: probably from Old Norse *húnn* "knob at the top of a masthead."]

hound's-tongue *n.* a coarse plant of the borage family, native to Europe and Asia, that has small reddish-purple flowers and spiny clinging fruit. Latin name: *Cynoglossum.* [Translation of Latin *cynoglossus* "dog-tongued," from the shape and texture of its leaves, likened to the tongue of a dog]

hound·stooth check /hówndz tōōth-/, **hound's-tooth check** *n.* a fabric design of small jagged checks

hour /owr/ *n.* **1. 60 MINUTES** 3,600 seconds, or one of 24 equal parts of a day **2. 60-MINUTE INTERVAL SHOWN ON A TIMEPIECE** one of the intervals of sixty minutes shown on a clock or watch ○ *There's a bus at 20 past the hour.* **3. TIME OF DAY** time of day, with emphasis on the general portion of day or night being referred to ○ *at this unearthly hour* **4. REGULAR TIME FOR SOMETHING** a time at which something usually takes place or is done ○ *my lunch hour* **5. SIGNIFICANT PERIOD** a period during which something particularly significant happens ○ *Enjoy your hour of glory while it lasts.* **6. TIME OF SUCCESS** a time when somebody is powerful, successful, or famous ○ *This is your hour, so seize the opportunity!* **7. TIME OF DEATH** the time when somebody is going to die ○ *As he started falling, he thought his hour had surely come.* **8. WORK DONE IN 60 MINUTES** the amount of work done in a period of sixty minutes ○ *I have a couple of hours left to do in the yard.* **9. DISTANCE TRAVELED IN 60 MINUTES** the distance that can be traveled in sixty minutes ○ *My office is only an hour away.* **10.** MEASURE, NAVIG **MEASURE OF LONGITUDE** a measure of longitude equal to 15 degrees or one twenty-fourth of a great circle **11. SINGLE SESSION** one meeting of a class or course of therapeutic treatment, usually 50 or 55 minutes ○ *I missed my hour with the therapist last week.* **12.** = **credit hour** [12thC. Via Old French *houre* from Latin *hora,* from Greek *hōra* "time period, season." Ultimately from an Indo-European word meaning "season," which is also the ancestor of English *year.*] ◇ **at any hour** at any time, day or night ◇ **of the hour** enjoying the highest degree of relevance, importance, or popularity at the current moment or particular time ○ *She is clearly the woman of the hour.*

hour an·gle *n.* ASTRON the angle, measured positively westward, between the plane containing the observer and the Earth's poles and the plane containing a particular celestial body and the Earth's poles

hour cir·cle *n.* ASTRON a great circle passing through the poles of the celestial sphere and intersecting the celestial equator at right angles, containing a point on the celestial sphere such as a star

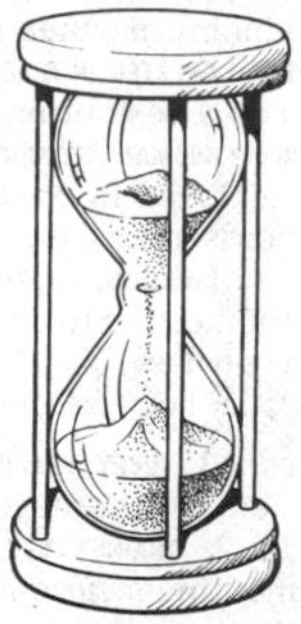

Hourglass

hour·glass /ówr glàss/ *n.* a time-measurement device consisting of two transparent bulbs connected by a narrow tube and containing an amount of sand that takes a specified time to flow between the bulbs after inversion

hour·glass fig·ure *n.* a woman's body shape, curving out above and below a narrow waist like the shape of an hourglass

hour hand *n.* the shorter, wider hand of a nondigital clock or watch, which indicates the hour

hou·ri /hŏŏree/ *n.* **1.** ISLAM **YOUNG WOMAN IN PARADISE** in Islamic belief, one of the beautiful young women who attend Muslim men in paradise **2. LOVELY WOMAN** an attractive woman (*dated*) (*sometimes considered offensive*) [Mid-18thC. Via French from, ultimately, Arabic *ḥawrā'* "woman with dark eyes."]

hour·ly /ówrlee/ *adj.* **1. EACH HOUR** happening at sixty-minute intervals ○ *hourly news* **2. OCCURRING A LOT** happening frequently or continually ○ *hourly changes* **3. CALCULATED BY THE HOUR** calculated as a particular amount for each hour worked ○ *hourly wages* **4. PAID BY THE HOUR** working for pay that is calculated as a particular amount for each hour worked ■ *adv.* **1. ONCE AN HOUR** happening once during an hour ○ *The news is broadcast hourly.* **2. SOON** at any time shortly from now ○ *Her arrival is expected hourly.* **3. OFTEN** frequently or continually ○ *The situation is changing hourly.* **4. BY THE HOUR** with a particular amount being paid for each hour worked ■ *n.* (*plural* **-lies**) **WORKER PAID BY THE HOURS WORKED** an employee paid by the number of hours worked ○ *The factory is hiring more hourlies.*

hours /owrz/ *npl.* **1. LONG TIME** a long but unspecified amount of time (*informal*) **2. TIMES FOR DOING PARTICULAR THINGS** the times of day between which particular things are done ○ *during school hours* **3. TIME IN A 24-HOUR CLOCK** the time of day, when using a 24-hour clock ○ *The flight leaves at 1300 hours.* **4. CANONICAL HOURS** the canonical hours taken as a whole

Hou·sa·ton·ic /hŏŏssə tónnik/ river in northwestern Massachusetts and Connecticut, rising in the Berkshire Hills. Length: 150 mi./240 km.

house *n.* /howss/ **1. DWELLING** a building made for people to live in, especially one built for a single set of occupants **2. OCCUPANTS OF A HOUSE** all of the people who are in a house at one time, particularly the people who usually live there **3. COMMUNITY DWELLING** a building in which a community of people lives ○ *a sorority house* **4. BUILDING FOR ANIMALS** a building where animals are kept, especially in a zoo ○ *the monkey house* **5. PLACE WHERE PEOPLE PAY TO EAT** a place where members of the public pay for food, drink, or entertainment, e.g., a restaurant or club ○ *the specialty of the house* **6.** THEATER **THEATER** a theater, or the audience at a theater ○ *The dancers performed to an appreciative house.* **7.** BUSINESS **BUSINESS OPERATION** a company or a corporation creating or selling a particular product ○ *a publishing house* **8. GAMBLING CASINO** a gambling casino or the people who manage it ○ *The odds always favor the house.* **9. COLLEGE OR UNIVERSITY RESIDENCE HALL** a residential college or a residence hall within a university **10. house, House** POL **LEGISLATIVE GROUP** a legislative group in a government or the place where it meets **11. FAMILY LINE** a family line, including ancestors and descendants, especially a royal family **12.** BROTHEL a brothel (*dated*) **13.** ZODIAC DIVISION OF THE ZODIAC one of the 12 divisions of the zodiac in astrology **14.** ZODIAC ZODIAC SIGN WHERE A PLANET LIES the sign of the zodiac in which a planet is found at a specific time **15.** SPORTS CURLING TARGET an area of concentric circles at either end of an ice rink marked out for curling, with the target in its center ■ *vt.* /howz/ (**housed, hous·ing, hous·es**) **1.** GIVE SOMEWHERE TO LIVE to provide somebody with a place to live **2.** CONTAIN to contain, keep, or store something **3.** NAUT PUT AWAY SAFELY to put something away safely, e.g., oars or an anchor [Old English *hūs*, of prehistoric Germanic origin] ◇ **on the house** given free by somebody who would normally be paid ◇ **bring the house down** to provoke a great deal of laughter or applause ◇ **like a house on fire** very quickly, successfully, or strongly ○ *They got along like a house on fire.* ◇ **play house** to take part in a children's game of pretending to be a family, with children playing the roles of both adults and children (*informal*) ◇ **put your house in order** to organize your life properly

WORD KEY: USAGE

See Usage note at ***home.***

house ar·rest *n.* a form of legal confinement in which people who have been arrested are not allowed to leave their own homes

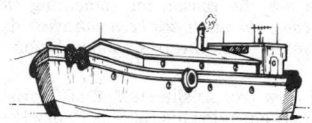

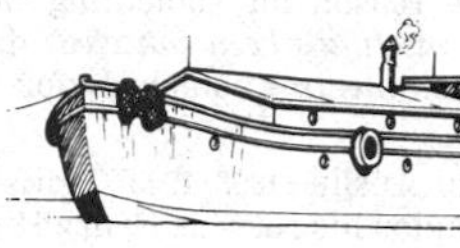

Houseboat

house·boat /hówss bṓt/ *n.* a boat, especially a flat-bottomed river boat or barge, that is permanently moored and used as a house

house·bound /hówss bòwnd/ *adj.* = **homebound**

house·boy /hówss bòy/ *n.* a term, often considered offensive, referring to a man employed to perform various household tasks

house brand *n.* a product made by or for a specific retailer and often sold under that retailer's name

house·break /hówss bràyk/ *vt.* (**-broke, -bro·ken, -break·ing, -breaks**) **1.** TEACH AN ANIMAL TO EXCRETE OUTDOORS to teach an animal to excrete outdoors or in a place. Also called **housetrain 2.** MAKE SOMEBODY BEHAVE to teach acceptable behavior to somebody (*informal humorous*) ○ *Do you think we will ever housebreak those kids?* ■ *n.* = **break-in**

house call *n.* a visit made by a doctor or other professional to a patient or client at home

house cat *n.* a cat that lives with people as a pet

house·clean·ing /hówss klèening/ *n.* **1.** MAKING A HOUSE CLEAN the performance of a range of tasks to make a house clean, e.g., dusting, mopping, vacuuming, and washing windows **2.** MAKING A BUSINESS MORE EFFICIENT the process of getting rid of unwanted employees, policies, or other aspects of a business in order to improve the quality of a product or to increase profits (*informal*)

house·coat /hówss kṓt/ *n.* a woman's outer garment, often loose and comfortable, worn at home

house crick·et *n.* a dark brown cricket found throughout North America and Europe where it can become a nuisance indoors. Latin name: *Acheta domesticus.*

house de·tec·tive *n.* somebody employed by a business, e.g., a hotel or department store, to patrol the premises and guard against theft or other unlawful behavior

house doc·tor *n.* a physician on duty in a hotel or other business organization

house·dress /hówss drèss/ *n.* a loose comfortable dress worn around the house

house·fa·ther /hówss faàthər/ *n.* a man who is responsible for a group of young people living in a dormitory or an institution such as a hostel. ◊ **houseparent**

house finch *n.* a small common finch native to the western United States and Mexico, now also found in the eastern United States. Males have a red forehead, throat, breast, and rump. Latin name: *Carpodacus mexicanus.*

house·fly /hówss flī/ (*plural* **-flies**) *n.* a common fly that lives in and around human dwellings in most parts of the world and is responsible for spreading numerous diseases. Latin name: *Musca domestica.*

house·guest *n.* somebody who stays in somebody else's home as a guest

house·hold /hówss hṑld/ *n.* PEOPLE WHO LIVE TOGETHER the people who live together in a single home ■ *adj.* **1.** BELONGING TO A HOUSEHOLD relating to, belonging to, or used in a household **2.** FAMILIAR TO ALL very widely known ○ *Thanks to the media, their personal problems are household knowledge.*

house·hold arts *npl.* all the skills useful or essential in running a house, e.g., cooking, cleaning, and child care. ◊ **home economics**

house·hold·er /hówss hṑldər/ *n.* **1.** HOUSE OWNER OR RENTER somebody who owns or rents a house, either alone or as the head of a family **2.** HEAD OF FAMILY the head of a household

house·hold gods *npl.* the deities believed to protect the home and its inhabitants, especially in the religion of ancient Rome. ♦ **lares and penates**

house·hold goods *npl.* = **housewares**

house·hold name *n.* somebody or something that most people know about

house·hold word *n.* a popular saying, the name of a famous person, or an event that is very well known

house·hus·band /hówss hùzbənd/ *n.* a man who does not go out to work but stays at home to manage a household [Mid-20thC. Modeled on HOUSEWIFE.]

house·keep·er /hówss keèpər/ *n.* **1.** SOMEBODY RUNNING A HOUSEHOLD somebody who performs the work of taking care of a house and the people who live there **2.** SOMEBODY RUNNING SOMEBODY ELSE'S HOUSE somebody employed to perform or manage the work of taking care of somebody else's house and the people who live there **3.** MANAGER OF CLEANING PERSONNEL somebody employed by a hotel, hospital, or other establishment to manage the people who clean and do other housekeeping tasks

house·keep·ing /hówss keèping/ *n.* **1.** HOUSEHOLD MAINTENANCE the maintenance of a household, or the range of tasks involved in this **2.** COMMERCIAL CLEANING DEPARTMENT a work unit in a hotel or other such establishment tasked with cleaning rooms, changing linens, and related jobs **3.** MANAGEMENT OF PROPERTY AND EQUIPMENT the management and upkeep of equipment and property for a business or other organization **4.** COMPUT MAINTENANCE OF COMPUTER SYSTEM the performance of routine tasks needed to keep a computer system working efficiently, e.g., deletion of unwanted files

House Lead·er *n.* *Can* a member of the Canadian government who initiates and supervises business in the legislature

house·leek /hówss leèk/ *n.* any one of various European flowering succulent plants that have rosettes of leaves at the base of the stems. Genus: *Sempervivum.* [So called because it was formerly planted on walls and roofs, in the belief that it protected the house from lightning]

house·lights /hówss līts/ *npl.* the lights inside a theater or auditorium that illuminate the area where the audience sits

house·maid /hówss mày d/ *n.* a woman employed to do housework (*dated*)

house·maid's knee *n.* a swelling of the fluid-filled sac in front of the kneecap, caused by kneeling too much

house·man /hówssmən/ (*plural* **-men** /-mən/) *n.* a man whose job is to perform routine tasks of cleaning and maintenance in a house or hotel

house man·ag·er *n.* THEATER the person in charge of managing the ushers and the area in a theater where the audience sits

house mar·tin *n.* a small swallow, native to Europe, China, and Africa that has blue-black feathers, a white rump, and a forked tail. Latin name: *Delichon urbica.* [From its habit of nesting under the eaves of houses]

house·mas·ter /hówss màstər/ *n.* a man who is in charge of the students living together in a dormitory or residence hall at certain prep schools and colleges or universities

house·mate /hówss màyt/ *n.* somebody who shares a house with one or more other people who are not relatives

house·moth·er /hówss mùthər/ *n.* a woman who is responsible for a group of young people living in an institution such as a college residence hall or a sorority house. ◊ **houseparent**

house mouse *n.* a gray or brownish-gray mouse that is common worldwide and is a household pest. Latin name: *Mus musculus.*

house mu·sic *n.* a style of dance music first developed by adding electronic beats to disco records, and later characterized by the addition of repetitive vocals, extracts from other recordings, or synthesized sounds [Origin uncertain: probably named for the *Warehouse*, a nightclub in Chicago, where this style of music originated]

house of as·sem·bly *n.* the lawmaking body or lower house of the legislature in some countries of the Commonwealth of Nations

House of As·sem·bly *n.* the provincial legislative body in Nova Scotia and Newfoundland

House of Bur·gess·es *n.* the lower house of the colonial legislature in Virginia

house of cards *n.* something that is unstable and likely to fall down, like a structure built of playing cards

House of Com·mons *n.* the lower house of Parliament in the United Kingdom and Canada

house of cor·rec·tion *n.* an institution where people convicted of minor offenses are imprisoned

House of Del·e·gates *n.* the lower house in the legislatures of Maryland, Virginia, and West Virginia

house officer *n.* *U.K.* = **intern** *n.* 1

house of God *n.* = **house of worship**

house of ill re·pute, house of ill fame *n.* a brothel (*dated*)

House of Lords *n.* the nonelected upper house of Parliament in the United Kingdom, made up of hereditary peers, life peers, and certain bishops

House of Rep·re·sen·ta·tives *n.* the lower house of Congress and of most state legislatures in the United States

house of wor·ship, house of God *n.* a church, temple, synagogue, or other building used for religious services

house or·gan *n.* a magazine published by a business or other organization for its employees or customers, containing information about the company, its products, and its employees

house·paint·er /hówss pàyntər/ *n.* somebody who paints houses for a living

house·par·ent /hówss pèrrənt/ *n.* one of a married couple who is responsible for a group of young people living in an institution such as a dormitory or hostel. ◊ **housefather, housemother**

house par·ty *n.* **1.** PARTY AT SOMEBODY'S HOME a party at somebody's home or at a residence, e.g., a fraternity or sorority house, at which the guests stay overnight or for several days **2.** GUESTS AT A HOUSE PARTY the group of guests attending a house party

house phy·si·cian *n.* **1.** RESIDENT OR INTERN a medical doctor, especially a resident or an intern in a hospital, who cares for patients under the supervision of the regular medical staff **2.** = **house doctor**

house·plant /hówss plànt/ *n.* a decorative plant grown indoors, especially one that would die if planted outdoors in a cold climate

house-poor *adj.* financially encumbered because of having purchased property, especially a house for which mortgage payments must be made and on which expensive repairs and maintenance must be done

house-proud *adj.* taking pride in the appearance of

your home and its state of cleanliness or repair, sometimes in an excessive or fussy way

house-rais·ing *n.* a gathering of friends and neighbors, especially in a rural community, to help somebody build a house

house rule *n.* a rule, usually not one of the regular rules in a game, that is observed in a casino or among a group of friends

house seat *n.* a seat in a theater reserved for friends of members of the cast or producers and other special guests

house-sit *vti.* to live in temporarily and take care of somebody else's house and property while that person is away

house sit·ter *n.* somebody who lives in and takes care of a house while its usual occupants are away [Modeled on BABY-SITTER]

Houses of Parliament, London, designed by Sir Charles Barry (1840–60)

Houses of Par·lia·ment *npl.* the building in which the House of Commons and the House of Lords of the United Kingdom meet and work

house spar·row *n.* a small hardy brown and gray bird with a black throat, originally European and Asian but now common in many areas of the world. Latin name: *Passer domesticus.* [From its habit of living in or near human settlements]

house-to-house *adj.* going or done from one house to the next ○ *a house-to-house search*

house·top /hówss tòp/ *n.* the very top or roof of a house

house trail·er *n.* a trailer used as a dwelling or an office and containing facilities such as a bathroom, bedroom, and kitchen (*dated*)

house·train /hówss tràyn/ (**-trained, -train·ing, -trains**) *vt.* = **housebreak** *v.* 1 —**house·trained** *adj.*

House Un-A·mer·i·can Ac·tiv·i·ties Com·mit·tee *n.* a former Congressional committee created in 1938 to investigate possibly subversive activities. Renamed the House Internal Security Committee in 1969, it was abolished in 1975.

house·wares /hówss wàirz/ *npl.* things that people use in a house, especially kitchen utensils and small electrical appliances

house·warm·ing /hówss wàwrming/, **house·warm·ing par·ty** *n.* a party that somebody gives to celebrate moving into a new house

house·wife /hówss wīf/ (*plural* **-wives** /-wīvz/) *n.* a woman who does not go out to work but stays at home to manage a household (*dated*)

house·wife·ly /hówss wīflee/ *adj.* relating to, belonging to, done by, or thought appropriate for a housewife

house·work /hówss wùrk/ *n.* tasks such as dusting, vacuuming, washing clothes, and cooking that are regularly done in a house

hous·ing[1] /hówzing/ *n.* **1. ACCOMMODATION** houses and other buildings where people live, considered collectively ○ *Decent housing is often hard to find.* **2. PROVISION OF ACCOMODATION** the provision of places to live ○ *Housing of the homeless is our first priority.* **3.** ENG **MACHINE'S PROTECTIVE STRUCTURE** a frame or structure that protects part of a machine ○ *a wheel housing* **4.** WOODWORK **PLACE WHERE A PIECE FITS** a slot, groove, or hole in one piece of wood into which another piece is inserted **5. NICHE FOR A STATUE** a small recess or hollow in which a statue can be placed **6.** SHIPPING **BELOW-DECK PART OF A MAST** the portion of a mast that is below the deck

hous·ing[2] /hówzing/ *n.* **1. COVERING FOR A HORSE'S BACK** a piece of cloth that covers the back of a horse, used for protection or decoration **2. HORSE TRAPPINGS** the ornamental trappings for a horse (*often used in the plural*) [Mid-17thC. Formed from Old French *houce*, from medieval Latin *hultia* "protective covering," ultimately of prehistoric Germanic origin.]

hous·ing de·vel·op·ment *n.* an area of houses or apartment buildings, usually built at the same time to a similar design and managed by the same person or company

hous·ing pro·ject *n.* a group of houses or apartment buildings built with public money for low-income families

Hou·ston /hyoóst'n/ city in Texas, the fourth largest city in the United States. Population: 1,630,553 (1990).

Hous·ton, Sam (1793–1863) U.S. frontiersman and politician. He served as president of the Republic of Texas (1836–38 and 1841–44) and was one of the state's first senators after its admission to the Union (1845). Full name **Samuel Houston**

hous·to·nia /hyoo stṓnee ə, yoo-/ *n.* a small North American flowering plant of the mallow family such as the common bluet. Genus: *Houstonia.* [Early 19thC. Via modern Latin, genus name, from the name of the Scottish botanist William *Houston* (died 1733).]

hout·ing /hówting/ (*plural* **-ings** *or* **-ing**) *n.* an edible European fish of the whitefish family that lives in salt water but produces its young in fresh water. Latin name: *Coregonus oxyrhynchus.* [Late 19thC. Via Dutch from Middle Dutch *houtic*, of uncertain origin.]

Houy·hn·hnm /hwínnəm/ *n.* a wise being looking like a horse in *Gulliver's Travels* by Jonathan Swift [Early 18thC. Coined as an imitation of the sound of a horse's neigh.]

HOV *abbr.* high-occupancy vehicle

hove /hōv/ past participle of **heave** *v.* 8. past tense of **heave** *v.* 9 (*literary*)

hov·el /húvv'l/ *n.* a small, dirty, or poorly built house [14thC. Origin uncertain: perhaps from Low German.]

hov·er /húvvər/ *vi.* (**-ered, -er·ing, -ers**) **1. FLOAT IN THE AIR** to float in the air without moving very far from the same spot **2. BE FLYING IN ONE SPOT** to stay in the air in the same position by rapidly beating the wings (*refers to birds*) **3. WAIT NEAR SOMEBODY OR SOMETHING** to wait near a person or place, usually in a nervous, inquisitive, or expectant way **4. BE UNDECIDED** to be unable to decide between alternatives **5. BE IN AN UNSTABLE CONDITION** to be in a condition that is neither one of two alternatives nor the other ○ *He hovered between life and death.* **6. STAY AROUND THE SAME LEVEL** to stay near a particular point, changing only slightly ○ *Inflation has been hovering at the same level for several months.* ■ *n.* **ACT OF HOVERING** an act or the condition of floating in the air without moving very far from the same spot [14thC. Formed from obsolete *hove* "to linger," of unknown origin.] —**hov·er·er** *n.* —**hov·er·ing·ly** *adv.*

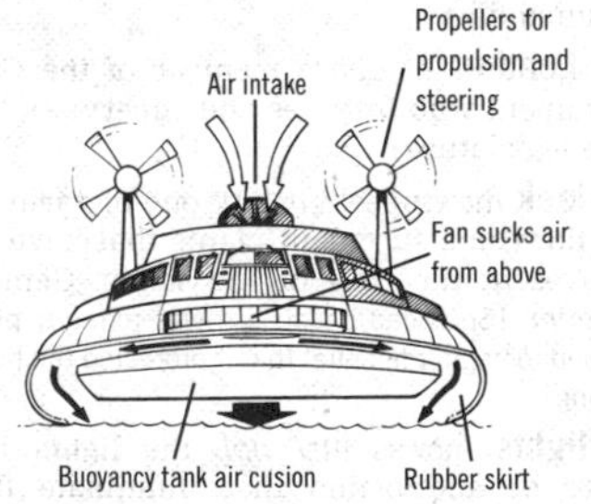

Hovercraft

hov·er·craft /húvvər kràft/ (*plural* **-crafts** *or* **-craft**) *n.* a vehicle that can travel over land and water supported by a cushion of air that it creates by blowing air downward

hov·er·port /húvvər pàwrt/ *n.* a place where hovercrafts load and unload [Mid-20thC. Coined from HOVERCRAFT + AIRPORT.]

how /how/ CORE MEANING: an adverb used when asking questions about manner, quantity, degree, or quality ○ *How did the trouble start?* ○ *How much did you pay?* ○ *How wide is that table?*

1. *adv.* **IN WHAT WAY** used to ask or report questions or to introduce statements about the manner in which something happens or is done ○ *How do I open the window here?* ○ *I don't know how you manage to sew so neatly.* **2.** *adv.* **TO WHAT EXTENT** used to ask or report questions or to introduce statements about the quantity or degree of something ○ *How high is the roof?* ○ *Tell me honestly how serious the situation is.* **3.** *adv.* **WHAT IS SOMETHING LIKE** used to ask or report questions or to introduce statements about the quality or success of something ○ *How was the movie?* **4.** *adv.* **USED IN EXCLAMATIONS** used in exclamations to emphasize a word or statement ○ *How beautiful she was!* **5.** *adv.* **IN WHATEVER WAY** used to indicate that it does not matter in what way somebody does something ○ *Fix it how you want – just as long as it gets fixed.* **6.** *conj.* **THAT** used to mention a fact or event ○ *Do you remember how we were ridiculed and derided?* [Old English *hū*. Ultimately from an Indo-European base that is also the ancestor of English *what, when, where, why,* and *who*.] ◇ **and how** used to show strong agreement with or to emphasize something that has just been said (*informal*) ◇ **how about 1.** used to make a suggestion (*informal*) ○ *How about some lunch?* **2.** used to change the subject of conversation (*informal*) ○ *That's enough of my ideas. How about your own policies?* ◇ **how are you?, how are you doing?** used to ask about somebody's health, or simply as a greeting when you meet somebody, especially somebody already known ◇ **how come?** used to ask the reason for something (*informal*) ○ *How come the meeting's been canceled?* ◇ **how do you do?** used when meeting somebody for the first time

How·ard /hów ərd/, **Leslie** (1893–1943) British actor. He is best known for his roles as Henry Higgins in *Pygmalion* (1938) and Ashley Wilkes in *Gone With the Wind* (1939). Real name **Leslie Howard Steiner**

How·ard, Trevor (1916–88) British actor. An accomplished stage and screen performer, his movies include *Brief Encounter* (1945) and *Mutiny on the Bounty* (1962). Full name **Trevor Wallace Howard**

how·be·it /how beé it/ *adv.* **HOWEVER** however or nevertheless (*formal*) ■ *conj.* **THOUGH** although (*archaic*) [14thC. Formed from HOW + BE + IT, meaning literally "however it may be."]

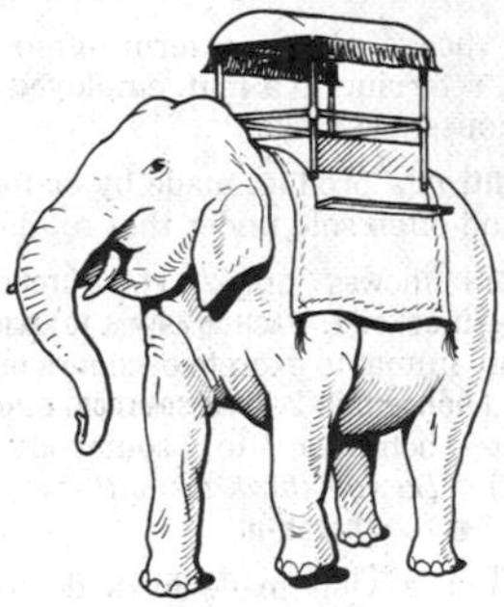
Howdah

how·dah /hówdə/ *n.* a large seat for several people, often with a canopy, that rests on the back of an elephant [Late 18thC. Via Urdu *haudah* from Arabic *hawdaj* "litter carried by a camel."]

how-do-you-do *n.* **1. GREETING** a greeting or welcome ○ *got to business as soon as the how-do-you-dos were finished* **2. BOTHERSOME SITUATION** a difficult or unsatisfactory situation (*informal*) ○ *a fine how-do-you-do* [From the greeting *how do you do?*]

how·dy /hówdee/ *interj.* **HELLO** used as a greeting (*informal*) ■ *n.* (*plural* **-dies**) **WELCOMING GREETING** a greeting or welcome (*informal*) ○ *"Give your granddad a big howdy!"* [Early 19thC. Shortening of *how d'ye*, a variant of *how do you do?*]

Howe /how/, **Elias** (1819–67) U.S. inventor. He developed and patented the first sewing machine (1846).

Howe, Gordie (*b.* 1928) Canadian ice hockey player. He played for the Detroit Red Wings (1946–71), the Houston Aeros (1973–77), and the Hartford Whalers (1977–80). Full name **Gordon Howe**

Howe, Joseph (1804–73) Canadian journalist and statesman. He served as prime minister of Nova

Scotia (1860–63) and president of the council in the first Canadian government (1869–73).

Howe, Julia Ward (1819–1910) U.S. writer and reformer. She wrote the poem "The Battle Hymn of the Republic" (1862) and was the first woman to be elected to the American Academy of Arts and Letters (1908).

how·e'er /how áir/ *contr.* however (*literary*) [Contraction of HOWEVER]

How·ells /hów əlz/, **William Dean** (1837–1920) U.S. writer and critic. He is best known for his novel *The Rise of Silas Lapham* (1885).

how·ev·er /how évvər/ CORE MEANING: an adverb introducing some form of contrast ○ *I'm not sure how effective the campaign has been. I do however think that it has been distinctively different.*
adv. **1.** TO WHATEVER DEGREE used to indicate that no matter what happens, a situation remains the same ○ *However objective it may believe itself to be, it is still only an opinion.* **2.** IN WHATEVER WAY used to indicate that it does not matter in what way somebody does something ○ *Peel and prepare the potatoes however you like.* **3.** HOW used as an emphatic form of "how" ○ *What a surprise to see you! However did you find us?*

how·it·zer /hówitsər/ *n.* a cannon with a bore diameter greater than 30 mm and a maximum elevation of 60 degrees that fires projectiles in a curved trajectory. Self-propelled or towed, it also has a muzzle velocity lower than that of a gun. [Late 17thC. Via Dutch *houwitser* from, ultimately, Czech *haufnice* "catapult," from *hauf* "heap" (of stones), of prehistoric Germanic origin.]

howl /howl/ *v.* **(howled, howl·ing, howls) 1.** *vi.* MAKE A WAVERING SOUND to make a long wavering or whining sound ○ *a coyote howling* **2.** *vi.* CRY OUT to cry out in pain, anger, or distress **3.** *vi.* ROAR WITH LAUGHTER to laugh loudly and unrestrainedly (*slang*) **4.** *vi.* CAROUSE to go on a spree (*slang*) ○ *out howling all night* **5.** *vt.* CALL OUT to call something out in a long wavering way ■ *n.* **1.** LONG MOANING CRY a long sad wavering cry **2.** LOUD CRY a cry of pain, anger, or distress **3.** DRAWN-OUT WAVERING SOUND a long high loud wavering noise ○ *the howl of the wind* **4.** SOMETHING OR SOMEBODY HILARIOUS an extremely funny person or thing (*slang*) [13thC. Origin uncertain: probably ultimately an imitation of the sound, and possibly related to English *owl*.]

howl down *vt.* to prevent somebody or something from being heard by making loud cries of protest or mockery

howl·er /hówlər/ *n.* **1.** LAUGHABLE MISTAKE a mistake that is so bad that it is funny (*slang*) **2.** SOMEBODY OR SOMETHING THAT HOWLS somebody who or something that makes a howling noise **3.** ZOOL = **howler monkey**

howl·er mon·key *n.* any one of various tropical mainly leaf-eating monkeys of Central and South America that live in trees and have a very loud booming call. Genus: *Alouatta.*

howl·ing /hówling/ *adj.* **1.** LOUD AND WAVERING making a loud high wavering noise ○ *a howling gale* **2.** DISMALLY DESOLATE dismal, or empty of human beings (*literary*) ○ *alone in the howling desert* **3.** VERY GREAT extreme or great in degree (*informal*) ○ *Our presentation was a howling success!* ■ *n.* NOISE a succession of long high wavering noises, e.g., animal cries or the sound of a strong wind ○ *the howling of the wind* —**howl·ing·ly** *adv.*

Howl·in' Wolf /hówlən wŏolf/ (1910–76) U.S. musician. He was an electric blues singer who profoundly influenced rock'n'roll during its early years. His most famous song was "Smokestack Lightnin" (1956). Real name **Chester Arthur Burnett**

how·so·ev·er /hòwssō évər/ *adv.* however (*formal* or *archaic*)

how-to *adj.* SHOWING HOW SOMETHING IS DONE giving practical information and instructions on the way to do something (*informal*) ○ *another how-to guide on home decorating* ■ *n.* (*plural* **how-tos**) BOOK GIVING PRACTICAL INFORMATION a book, manual, or experience that gives practical information and detailed instructions (*informal*) ○ *Before you tinker with your car, read a how-to first.*

hoy·a /hóyə/ *n.* an Asian and Australian evergreen climbing plant or shrub that is related to milkweed and has waxy white flowers. Genus: *Hoya.* [Mid-19thC. From modern Latin, genus name, from the name of the English gardener Thomas *Hoy* (died 1821).]

hoy·den /hóyd'n/ *n.* an offensive term that deliberately insults a girl's self-control and thoughtfulness (*dated offensive*) [Late 17thC. Origin uncertain: probably from Dutch *heiden* "lout, heathen."]

hp *abbr.* horsepower

HP *abbr.* **1.** BOT hardy perennial **2.** high pressure

h.p. *abbr.* high pressure

HPF *abbr.* highest possible frequency

HQ, H.Q., h.q. *abbr.* headquarters

HR *abbr.* homeroom

hr., hr *abbr.* hour

h.r. *abbr.* BASEBALL home run

H.R. *abbr.* House of Representatives

H.R.E. *abbr.* **1.** Holy Roman Emperor **2.** Holy Roman Empire

H. Rept. *abbr.* POL House Report

H. Res. *abbr.* POL House Resolution

H.R.H. *abbr.* **1.** Her Royal Highness **2.** His Royal Highness

hrs., hrs *abbr.* hours

HRT *abbr.* hormone replacement therapy

Hs *symbol.* hassium

HS, H.S. *abbr.* High School

HSGT *abbr.* high-speed ground transit

H.S.H. *abbr.* **1.** Her Serene Highness **2.** His Serene Highness

Hsi·en Nien /syèn nyén/ *n.* = **Chinese New Year**

HST, H.S.T. *abbr.* hypersonic transport

ht *abbr.* **1.** heat **2.** height

HT *abbr.* **1.** halftime **2.** ELEC ENG high tension **3.** high tide

HTH *abbr.* hope this helps

HTLV *abbr.* human T-cell lymphotropic virus

HTLV-I *n.* a virus associated with cancers of the lymphatic system. Full form **human T-cell lymphotropic virus I**

HTLV-II *n.* a virus associated with leukemia. Full form **human T-cell lymphotropic virus II**

HTML *n., abbr.* hypertext markup language

Hts. *abbr.* GEOG Heights

HTTP *abbr.* hypertext transfer protocol

HUAC *abbr.* House Un-American Activities Committee

hua·ca /wa͡akə/ *n.* any one of the sacred spirits and powers whom Native South American peoples of the Andes believe to live in caves, rocks, and other natural formations [Early 17thC. From Spanish *huaca guaca* from Quechua *waca,* "god of the house."]

Huai·nan /hwī na͡an/ industrial city in Anhui Province, eastern China, the center of a large coalmining area. Population: 1,200,000 (1991).

Huang He /hwa͡ang hée, -háy/ China's second longest river, flowing through the north central part of the country. Length: 2,900 mi./4,667 km.

hua·ra·che /wə ra͡a chee/ *n.* a sandal originally worn in Mexico, with the upper part made of woven leather straps [Late 19thC. Via Mexican Spanish from, probably, Japanese *warachi* "straw sandal."]

hub /hub/ *n.* **1.** CENTRAL PART the central part of a wheel or a similar device that rotates, e.g., a propeller **2.** CENTER OF ACTIVITY a place that is a center of activity or interest **3. hub, hub airport** AIR CENTRAL AIRPORT IN A NETWORK a central airport that passengers can fly to from smaller local airports in order to catch an international or long-distance flight [Early 16thC. Origin uncertain; probably an alteration of HOB; the underlying meaning is perhaps "lump, mass."]

Hub /hub/ *n.* the city of Boston, Massachusetts (*informal*) [So called because most of its main roads lead into the central city like the spokes of a wheel]

hub·ba-hub·ba /hùbbə húbbə/ *interj.* used to express approval, enthusiasm, or pleasure (*dated slang*) [Mid-20thC. Origin uncertain.]

Hub·bard squash /húbbərd-/, **hub·bard squash** *n.* = **winter squash** (*regional*) [Mid-19thC. From the name *Hubbard.*]

Hub·ble /húbb'l/, **Edwin** (1889–1953) U.S. astronomer. Through his study of galaxies he proved the universe to be larger than had previously been thought, and still expanding. The Hubble Space Telescope is named for him. Full name **Edwin Powell Hubble**

hub·ble-bub·ble /hùbb'l-/ *n.* **1.** = **hookah 2.** = **hubbub** [Early 17thC. Alteration of BUBBLE.]

Hub·ble con·stant /húbb'l-/, **Hub·ble's con·stant** *n.* the ratio that expresses the rate of the universe's expansion, equal to the speed at which galaxies appear to be moving away from the Earth divided by their distance [Mid-20thC. Named for the U.S. astronomer Edwin P. HUBBLE, who discovered the relationship.]

Hub·ble's law *n.* the law holding that the speed at which distant galaxies are moving away from the Earth is proportional to their distance from the observer [Mid-20thC. See HUBBLE CONSTANT.]

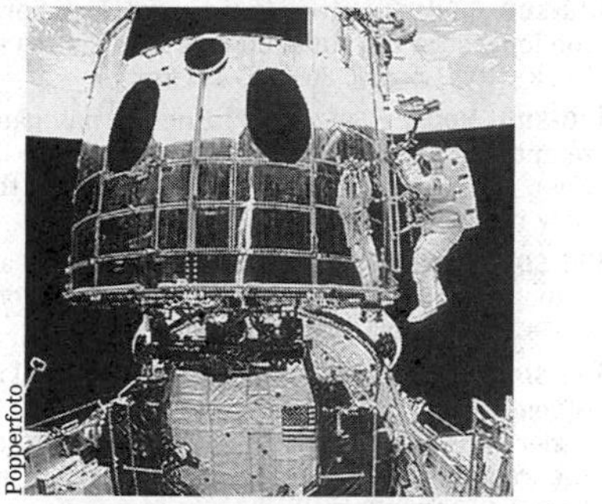

Hubble Telescope: A space shuttle astronaut repairs the Hubble Telescope

Hub·ble Tel·e·scope, Hub·ble Space Tel·e·scope *n.* a telescope mounted on a satellite that orbits the Earth, used to observe distant parts of the universe and photograph them. It was launched in 1990. [Late 20thC. Named in honor of Edwin P. HUBBLE.]

hub·bub /hú bùb/ *n.* **1.** CONFUSION OF VOICES a confused din, especially a number of voices speaking at once **2.** EXCITED FUSS a fuss or period of excitement [Mid-16thC. Origin uncertain: probably from Celtic.]

hub·by /húbbee/ (*plural* **-bies**) *n.* a husband (*informal*) [Late 17thC. Alteration of HUSBAND.]

hub·cap /húb kàp/ *n.* a round cover that protects the outside of the central part of a vehicle's wheel

Hu·bei /ho͝o báy/ province in central China comprising both mountainous territory and the lake-studded plain of the Yangtse River. Capital: Wuhan. Population: 57,190,000 (1994). Area: 72,394 sq. mi./187,500 sq. km.

hu·bris /hyo͞obriss/ *n.* **1.** PRIDE excessive pride or arrogance **2.** EXCESSIVE AMBITION the excessive pride and ambition that usually leads to the downfall of a hero in classical tragedy [Late 19thC. From Greek.] —**hu·bris·tic** /hyoo brístik/ *adj.* —**hu·bris·tic·al·ly** /-brístiklee/ *adv.*

huck·a·back /húkə bàk/, **huck** /huk/ *n.* a coarse absorbent type of cotton or linen fabric used mainly for towels [Late 17thC. Origin unknown.]

huck·le·ber·ry /húk'l bèrree/ (*plural* **-ries**) *n.* **1.** PLANT LIKE A BLUEBERRY a North American shrub that is related to the blueberry and bears edible fruit. Genus: *Gaylussacia.* **2.** FRUIT the edible, dark blue fruit of the huckleberry [Late 16thC. Origin uncertain: probably an alteration of *hurtleberry* "whortleberry."]

huck·ster /húkstər/ *n.* **1.** AGGRESSIVE SALESPERSON somebody who uses aggressive methods to sell or promote something **2.** RETAILER somebody who sells small articles, especially a street peddler **3.** COPYWRITER somebody who writes advertising copy, especially for the broadcast media (*informal*) ■ *v.* **(-stered, -ster·ing, -sters) 1.** *vt.* PEDDLE MERCHANDISE to sell or peddle something **2.** *vti.* SELL AGGRESSIVELY to use aggressive methods to sell or promote something [12thC. Origin uncertain: perhaps from Middle Dutch *hokester,* from *hoeken* "to peddle."]

HUD *abbr.* **1.** heads-up display **2.** (Department of) Housing and Urban Development

hud·dle /húdd'l/ *n.* **1.** TIGHT GROUP a group of people or things gathered closely together **2.** FOOTBALL GATHERING OF FOOTBALL PLAYERS a group of football players gathered behind the line of scrimmage to hear what the next play will be **3.** BRIEF TALK a quick private talk or gathering (*informal*) ■ *v.* **(-dled, -dling, -dles) 1.** *vti.* GATHER TIGHTLY TOGETHER to gather together in a tightly packed group, or make people or things do this ○ *The small crowd of spectators huddled together for warmth.* **2.** *vi.* CROUCH to draw your arms and legs tightly into your body, or move in close to something, often for shelter or comfort ○ *He huddled in a doorway to get out of the rain.* **3.** *vi.* FOOTBALL **GATHER TO PLAN PLAY** in football, to gather together behind the line of scrimmage in order to plan the next play **4.** *vi.* **TALK PRIVATELY** to gather privately to confer, make plans, or gossip (*informal*) [Late 16thC. Origin uncertain: perhaps from Low German *hudeln* "to crowd together," ultimately from an Indo-European base meaning "to cover, conceal."]

Hu·di·bras·tic /hyo͝odi brástik/, **hu·di·bras·tic** *adj.* mock-heroic, especially written in the style or meter used by Samuel Butler in his poem *Hudibras*

Hud·son /húdss'n/ river in eastern New York, and the longest in the state, flowing into the sea at New York City. Length: 306 mi./492 km.

Hud·son, Henry (1565?–1611?) English navigator. Attempting to find a northeastern passage to the Far East, he traveled the river, bay, and strait that are now named for him.

Hud·son, Rock (1925–85) U.S. actor. He was a handsome romantic lead in movies such as *Pillow Talk* (1959). Real name **Roy Harold Scherer, Jr.**

Hud·son Bay /hùdss'n-/ almost landlocked inland sea of east central Canada, rich in wildlife. Native Americans and Inuit are the chief inhabitants of the region. Area: 280,000 sq. mi./730,000 sq. km. Depth: 846 ft./258 m.

Hud·son's Bay blan·ket *n. Can* a wool blanket, usually cream-colored with distinctive red, black, yellow, and indigo stripes. First introduced as a trade item in the 18th century, it is still made today. [Late 19thC. So called because it was originally traded by the *Hudson's Bay* Company.]

Hud·son's Bay Com·pa·ny *n.* a fur-trading company chartered in England in 1670 to trade in North America and later much involved in fur trading, exploring, and claiming territory for the British crown [Late 17thC. So called because its original charter was to trade in the areas of North America adjacent to Hudson Bay.]

Hud·son Strait body of water in northeastern Canada connecting Hudson Bay with the Atlantic Ocean and separating Baffin Island from northern Quebec. Depth: 2,890 ft./880 m. Length: 450 mi./720 km.

hue /hyoo/ *n.* **1. COLOR** a color ○ *flowers of every hue* **2. SHADE OF COLOR** a specific shade of a particular color ○ *a pleasing hue of green* **3.** COLORS **PROPERTY OF A COLOR** a property of a color that enables it to be perceived, e.g., as red or green and that is determined by its dominant wavelength **4. TYPE** a type or kind in a particular range ○ *All hues of political opinion should be represented in the discussions.* **5. ASPECT** an aspect, or the way that something looks ○ *This puts a completely different hue on the matter.* [Old English *hē(o)w*, of prehistoric Germanic origin]

Hue /hway/ historic city in central Vietnam on the Huong River, near the South China Sea. The Nguyen royal capital from 1802 to 1945, it was heavily damaged during the Vietnam War. Population: 260,489 (1989).

hue and cry *n.* **1. UPROAR** a great uproar or commotion about something **2. PURSUIT** in the past, a pursuit of somebody accused of a crime, with the pursuers calling on bystanders to join in the chase [From Anglo-Norman *hu e cri*, literally "outcry and cry." *Hu* "outcry" is from Old French *huer* "to shout," an imitation of the sound of hunting or battle cries.]

-hued *suffix.* of a particular color or number of colors ○ *the many-hued rainbow* ○ *a rose-hued sunset*

Huer·ta /wértə/, **Victoriano** (1854–1916) Mexican revolutionary and politician. He became provisional president of Mexico (1913), but resigned and fled amid rebellions (1914).

hue·vos ran·che·ros /wàyvōs ran chérrōs/ *npl.* a Mexican dish of fried or poached eggs covered with chili or tomato sauce and cheese, often served on a corn tortilla and accompanied by refried beans and sour cream [From American Spanish, "ranch-style eggs"]

huff /huf/ *n.* **FIT OF ANGER** a brief mood of anger or resentment at something somebody has done ■ *v.* **(huffed, huff·ing, huffs) 1.** *vti.* **ANGER SOMEBODY OR GET ANGRY** to anger or offend somebody, or become angry or offended **2.** *vi.* **BLOW OR PANT** to blow, pant, or breathe laboriously [Late 16thC. An imitation of the sound of blowing.] ◇ **huff and puff 1.** to blow or pant, or do this while moving with great difficulty **2.** to make noisy but empty threats, or raise objections without any intention of taking action

huff·y /húffee/ (**-i·er, -i·est**) *adj.* **1. TOUCHY** easily offended or put into a huff **2. IRRITATED** annoyed or irritated about something **3. ARROGANT** haughtily arrogant and condescending —**huff·i·ly** *adv.* —**huff·i·ness** *n.*

hug /hug/ *v.* **(hugged, hug·ging, hugs) 1.** *vti.* **EMBRACE AFFECTIONATELY** to put your arms around somebody's body and hold the person tight to show affection or pleasure **2.** *vt.* **PUT YOUR ARMS AROUND** to clasp your arms around a part of your own body ○ *hugging her knees to her chest* **3.** *vr.* **PUT YOUR ARMS AROUND YOURSELF** to put your arms around your own body, especially to keep warm **4.** *vr.* **CONGRATULATE YOURSELF** to congratulate yourself or show great delight **5.** *vt.* **KEEP CLOSE** to remain in close linear proximity to something while moving in a forward direction ○ *The sailboat hugged the coastline.* ■ *n.* **AFFECTIONATE EMBRACE** an affectionate embrace [Mid-16thC. Origin uncertain: probably from a Scandinavian source.] —**hug·ga·ble** *adj.* —**hug·ger** *n.*

huge /hyooj/ (**hug·er, hug·est**) *adj.* **1. ENORMOUS** very big in size or amount **2. LARGE IN SCOPE** very large in scope or scale ○ *huge talent* **3. SIGNIFICANTLY SUCCESSFUL** very important or successful (*informal*) ○ *This band is going to be huge.* [12thC. Shortening of Old French *ahuge*, of unknown origin.] —**huge·ness** *n.*

huge·ly /hyo͝ojlee/ *adv.* to a great degree ○ *hugely successful*

hug·ger·mug·ger /húggər mùggər/ *n.* **1. MUDDLED MESS** a disorderly mess or muddle **2. SECRECY** secretive behavior or concealment ■ *adj.* **1. DISORDERED** confused or jumbled **2. SECRETIVE** clandestine or secret ■ *v.* **(-gered, -ger·ing, -gers) 1.** *vt.* **CONCEAL** to keep something secret **2.** *vi.* **ACT SECRETIVELY** to behave in a secretive manner [Early 16thC. Origin uncertain.] —**hug·ger·mug·ger** *adv.*

Hughes /hyooz/, **Charles** (1862–1947) U.S. jurist and statesman. He served as secretary of state (1921–25) and chief justice of the U.S. Supreme Court (1930–41). Full name **Charles Evans Hughes**

Hughes, Howard (1905–76) U.S. industrialist. He became one of the richest people in the United States by expanding his family manufacturing business into a huge corporate conglomerate. A record-setting pilot during the 1930s, he was notorious for his reclusiveness and eccentricity in his later years. Full name **Howard Robard Hughes**

Library of Congress

Langston Hughes

Hughes, Langston (1902–67) U.S. writer. A leader of the Harlem Renaissance, he incorporated the rhythms of jazz into his poems and stories about Black urban life. Full name **James Mercer Langston Hughes**

Hughes, Ted (1930–98) British poet. He was poet laureate (1984–98) and married the poet Sylvia Plath in 1956. His works include *Lupercal* (1960) and *Wodwo* (1967). Full name **Edward James Hughes**

Hu·go /hyo͞ogō/, **Victor** (1802–85) French poet, novelist, and dramatist. A leading writer of the 19th century, he wrote *The Hunchback of Notre Dame* (1831) and *Les misérables* (1862). Full name **Victor Marie Hugo**

Hu·gue·not /hyo͞ogə nòt/ *n.* **FRENCH PROTESTANT** a French Protestant, especially in the 16th and 17th centuries ■ *adj.* **OF THE FRENCH PROTESTANT CHURCH** relating to, belonging to, or typical of the French Protestant Church [Mid-16thC. From French, an alteration (based on the name of Besançon *Hugues*, leader of a Swiss political movement) of obsolete *eiguenot*, from, ultimately, Swiss German *Eidgenosse* "confederate," literally "oath-companion."] —**Hu·gue·not·ism** *n.*

huh /hu/ *interj.* **1. EXPRESSION OF SURPRISE OR DISDAIN** used to show surprise, inquiry, disdain, or lack of interest **2. INVITATION TO AGREE** used after giving an opinion to invite comment, especially agreement ○ *Great shot, huh?* [Early 17thC. A natural exclamation.]

hui·a /ho͞oyə/ (*plural* **-a**) *n.* a New Zealand bird, now thought to be extinct, with tail feathers that were much prized by Maoris. Latin name: *Heteralocha acutirostris.* [Mid-19thC. From Hawaiian; an imitation of the sound of its whistle.]

hui·sa·che /wee saá chee/ *n.* a thorny shrub with fragrant clusters of deep yellow flowers, found in the southern United States and Mexico. Latin name: *Acacia farnesiana.* [Mid-19thC. Via Mexican Spanish from Nahuatl *huixachi*, literally "many-thorn(ed) shrub."]

hu·la /ho͞olə/ *n.* **POLYNESIAN DANCE** a Polynesian or Hawaiian dance, often accompanied by drumming and chanting, in which the performers move their hips back and forth and make miming gestures with their hands ■ *vi.* **(-laed, -la·ing, -las) PERFORM A HULA** to dance a hula [Early 19thC. From Hawaiian.]

Hu·la-Hoop *tdmk.* a trademark for a plastic ring that is placed around the waist and kept twirling by rhythmically moving the hips

hulk /hulk/ *n.* **1. SOMEBODY BIG** somebody who is big, powerful, and often clumsy **2. EMPTY HULL** the empty hull of a ship that has been wrecked or is too old to be sailed **3. UNWIELDY SHIP** a heavy ship that is difficult to steer **4. SHELL OF A STRUCTURE** the shell of any old, abandoned, or burned-out structure or vehicle ■ *vi.* **(hulked, hulk·ing, hulks) 1. APPEAR AS A LARGE OBJECT** to appear as a large looming object ○ *Suddenly, a huge truck hulked up on the horizon.* **2. MOVE CLUMSILY** to move in a clumsy or awkward way [Pre-12thC. Origin uncertain: probably via Anglo-Latin *hulcus* from Greek *holkas* "merchant barge, ship that is towed," from *helkein* "to pull."]

hulk·ing /húlking/, **hulk·y** /húlkee/ (**-i·er, -i·est**) *adj.* large, bulky, and often clumsy

hull /hul/ *n.* **1. BODY OF SHIP** the body of a ship, excluding other parts, e.g., the masts and engines **2. BODY OF A VEHICLE** the main body of a large vehicle such as a tank or airplane **3.** AEROSP **ROCKET CASING** the external casing of a rocket, missile, or spaceship **4. OUTER COVERING** the outer covering of a seed or fruit **5. CALYX ON A STRAWBERRY** the calyx on a strawberry that stays attached to the fruit when it is picked but is not eaten ■ *vt.* **(hulled, hull·ing, hulls) 1. REMOVE THE OUTER RIND FROM FRUIT** to remove the outer rind or shell from a fruit or vegetable **2. TAKE OFF A STRAWBERRY CALYX** to remove the calyx from a strawberry [Old English *hulu*. Ultimately from an Indo-European base meaning "to cover, conceal," which is also the ancestor of English *helmet*, *hole*, and *hell*.]

Hull /hul/ city in southwestern Québec, Canada, situated on the Ottawa River opposite Ottawa. Population: 60,707 (1991).

Hull, Cordell (1871–1955) U.S. statesman. He was secretary of state from 1933 to 1944 and was awarded the Nobel Peace Prize in 1945.

hul·la·ba·loo /hùlləbə lo͞o/, **hul·la·bal·loo** *n.* noisy excitement or fuss [Mid-18thC. Alteration of earlier *hollo-ballo*, from *holla*, an early variant of HELLO.]

hul·lo *interj.*, *n. U.K.* = **hello**

hum /hum/ *v.* **(hummed, hum·ming, hums) 1.** *vti.* **SING WITH THE LIPS CLOSED** to sing with lips closed and without words, or sing something in this way **2.** *vi.* **MAKE A DRONING SOUND** to make a steady prolonged droning sound ○ *bees humming* **3.** *vi.* **GIVE OFF A LOW STEADY SOUND** to be filled with a low, continuous, indistinct noise ○ *a room that hummed with strange electronic equipment* **4.** *vi.* **BE EXTREMELY BUSY** to be very busy or active (*informal*) ○ *This place is really humming.* ■ *n.* **DRONING NOISE** a steady droning sound ■ *interj.* **EXPRESSION OF DISPLEASURE OR INDECISION** a low sound made to express displeasure, doubt, surprise, or indecision [14thC. An imitation of the sound.]

hu·man /hyo͞omən/ *adj.* **1. OF PEOPLE** relating to, involving, or typical of human beings ○ *human nature* ○ *human frailty* **2. MADE UP OF PEOPLE** composed of people ○ *the human race* ○ *a human chain of protestors* **3. COMPASSIONATELY KIND** showing kindness, compassion, or approachability **4. IMPERFECT** having the imperfections and weaknesses of a human being rather than a machine or divine being ○ *Remember he's only human, so don't expect too much.* ■ *n.* **PERSON**

a human being [14thC. Via French *humain* from Latin *humanus*.] —**hu·man·ness** *n.*

WORD KEY: CULTURAL NOTE

The Human Comedy, a collection of novels and stories by French writer Honoré de Balzac (published 1833–50). By linking his novels and stories through the use of common themes and characters, Balzac planned an oeuvre that would portray the human species in all stages of its development and aspects of its behavior. At the time of his death, the collection included a hundred novels and stories and about fifty incomplete works.

hu·man be·ing *n.* **1. MEMBER OF THE HUMAN SPECIES** a member of the species to which men and women belong. Latin name: *Homo sapiens*. **2. PERSON** a person, viewed especially as having imperfections and weaknesses ○ *I'm a human being, not a machine.*

hu·mane /hyoo máyn/ *adj.* **1. COMPASSIONATE** showing the better aspects of the human character, especially kindness and compassion **2. INVOLVING MINIMAL PAIN** without inflicting any more pain than is necessary **3. WITH AN EMPHASIS ON LIBERAL VALUES** with an emphasis on respect for other people's views [15thC. Variant of HUMAN.] —**hu·mane·ly** *adv.* —**hu·mane·ness** *n.*

hu·man e·col·o·gy *n.* a branch of sociology that studies the relationships between human beings and their natural and social environments

hu·man en·gi·neer·ing *n.* = **ergonomics**

hu·mane so·ci·e·ty *n.* any one of various organizations that promote compassionate treatment of animals

hu·man e·thol·o·gy *n.* the study of human behavior, especially aggressive and submissive behavior in social contexts

hu·man fac·tors en·gi·neer·ing *n.* = **ergonomics**

hu·man im·mun·o·de·fi·cien·cy vi·rus *n.* full form of **HIV**

hu·man in·ter·est *n.* an element in something, especially a news report, that is about somebody's personal life or feelings and is expected to appeal to the public's sympathy or curiosity —**hu·man-in·ter·est** *adj.*

hu·man·ism /hyóomə nìzzəm/ *n.* **1. BELIEF IN A HUMAN-BASED MORALITY** a system of thought that is based on the values, characteristics, and behavior that are believed to be best in human beings, rather than on any supernatural authority **2. CONCERN FOR PEOPLE** a concern with the needs, wellbeing, and interests of people **3. hu·man·ism, Hu·man·ism RENAISSANCE CULTURAL MOVEMENT** the secular cultural and intellectual movement of the Renaissance that spread throughout Europe as a result of the rediscovery of the arts and philosophy of the ancient Greeks and Romans —**hu·man·ist** /hyóomənist/ *n., adj.* —**hu·man·ist·ic** /hyóomə nístik/ *adj.* —**hu·man·is·ti·cal·ly** /hyóomə nístikəlee/ *adv.*

hu·man·i·tar·i·an /hoo mànni táiree ən/ *adj.* **1. CARING** committed to improving the lives of other people ○ *a humanitarian organization* **2. HUMAN** involving and affecting human beings, especially in a harmful way (*informal*) ○ *a humanitarian disaster* ■ *n.* **1. CARING PERSON** somebody who is committed to improving the lives of other people **2. SOMEBODY BELIEVING IN HUMANITARIANISM** somebody who believes in a philosophical theory of humanitarianism [Mid-19thC. Formed from HUMAN, on the model of UNITARIAN and EGALITARIAN.]

hu·man·i·tar·i·an·ism /hoo mànni táiree ənìzzəm/ *n.* a commitment to improving the lives of other people —**hu·man·i·tar·i·an·ist** *n.*

hu·man·i·ties /hyoo mánniteez/, **Hu·man·i·ties** *npl.* **1. LIBERAL ARTS** the liberal arts as subjects of study, as opposed to the sciences **2. CLASSICAL STUDIES** the study of the language and literature of the ancient Greeks and Romans

hu·man·i·ty /hyoo mánnitee/ *n.* **1. HUMAN RACE** the human race considered as a whole **2. QUALITIES OF A HUMAN BEING** the qualities or characteristics considered as a whole to be typical of human beings **3. KINDNESS** kindness or compassion for others

hu·man·ize /hyóomə nìz/ (**-ized, -iz·ing, -iz·es**) *vti.* **1. MAKE OR BECOME HUMAN** to make something human or like humans, or become human or like humans **2. MAKE OR BECOME HUMANE** to make or become humane in character, characteristics, or nature —**hu·man·i·za·tion** /hyóomənì záysh'n/ *n.* —**hu·man·iz·er** /hyóomə nìzər/ *n.*

hu·man·kind /-kìnd/ *n.* all human beings considered as a whole ○ *"Human kind cannot bear very much reality."* (T. S. Eliot, *Four Quartets, Burnt Norton*; 1935)

hu·man·ly /hyóomənlee/ *adv.* **1. IN A WAY TYPICAL OF HUMANS** in a way generally considered to be typical of humans **2. WITHIN THE LIMITS OF HUMAN ABILITY** within the limits of human ability and knowledge ○ *They did all that was humanly possible to save him.* **3. ACCORDING TO HUMAN EXPERIENCE** as far as human knowledge or experience can judge

hu·man-made /hyóomən màyd/ *adj.* made by human beings and not occurring naturally. = **manmade**

hu·man na·ture *n.* the typical character that all human beings share, often seen as being imperfect

hu·man pap·il·lo·ma vi·rus *n.* a virus that causes warts in the genital area of humans

hu·man re·sourc·es *n.* **EMPLOYEE RECRUITMENT AND MANAGEMENT** the field of business concerned with recruiting and managing employees (*takes a singular verb*) ○ *a career in human resources* ■ *npl.* **PERSONNEL** all the people who work in a business or organization, considered as a whole (*takes a plural verb*)

hu·man rights *npl.* the rights that are considered by most societies to belong automatically to everyone, e.g., the rights to freedom, justice, and equality (*sometimes singular*)

hum·ble /húmb'l/ *adj.* (**-bler, -blest**) **1. MODEST** modest and unassuming in attitude and behavior **2. RESPECTFUL** feeling or showing respect and deference toward other people **3. LOWLY** relatively low in rank and without pretensions ○ *of humble origins* ■ *vt.* (**-bled, -bling, -bles**) **1. MAKE SOMEBODY FEEL LESS IMPORTANT** to make somebody feel less proud or convinced of his or her own importance **2. DEGRADE** to lower somebody in rank or importance [13thC. Via Old French *(h)umble* from Latin *humilis* "lowly" (source of English *humiliate*), from *humus* "earth"; the underlying idea is "close to the ground."] —**hum·ble·ness** *n.* —**hum·bly** *adv.*

hum·ble·bee /húmb'l bèe/ *n.* = **bumblebee** [15thC. Origin uncertain: probably an alteration of Middle Low German *hummelbē*, literally "humming bee," from *hummel* "hum, buzz" + *bē* "bee."]

hum·bled /húmb'ld/ *adj.* made to feel less important, proud, or confident

hum·ble pie *n.* a pie made in the past using the entrails of a newly killed animal, especially a deer (*archaic*) [Mid-17thC. Alteration (modeled on HUMBLE) of earlier *umble pie*, from *umbles* "edible animal entrails," via French dialect *nombles* from, ultimately, Latin *lumbulus* "small loin."] ◇ **eat humble pie** to apologize or admit you have been wrong, especially in a way that makes you feel humiliated

hum·bling /húmbling/ *adj.* making somebody lose confidence, self-importance, or pride —**hum·bling·ly** *adv.*

Hum·boldt Cur·rent /húm bòlt-/ *n.* a cold current of the South Pacific Ocean that flows north along the coastline of South America [Named for the German scientist Baron Friedrich von *Humboldt* (1769–1859), who explored the coasts of Central and South America in the early 19thC]

hum·bug /húm bùg/ *n.* **1. NONSENSE** something that is silly or makes no sense **2. DECEPTION** something that is meant to deceive or cheat people **3. FRAUD** somebody who deceives others by taking on a false identity or pretending to have a certain background or skills ■ *vti.* (**-bugged, -bug·ging, -bugs**) **DECEIVE** to take part in a deception, or deceive somebody ■ *interj.* **NONSENSE!** used to express the opinion that something is nonsense or deception (*archaic*) [Mid-18thC. Origin unknown.]

hum·ding·er /hùmdíngər/ *n.* an exceptional or outstanding person or thing (*slang*) [Early 20thC. Origin uncertain: probably from HUM in the sense of an approving murmur + *dinger* "superlative thing" (formed from DING in the sense "to beat, excel").]

hum·drum /húm drùm/ *adj.* dull because of being too familiar and lacking variety [Mid-16thC. Origin uncertain: probably an expressive alteration of HUM.]

Hume /hyoom/, **Basil, Cardinal** (*b.* 1923) British Roman Catholic cardinal. He became Archbishop of Westminster in 1976, the first Benedictine monk to hold this office. Full name **George Basil Hume**

Hume, David (1711–76) Scottish philosopher and historian. His major works were *A Treatise of Human Nature* (1739–40) and *An Enquiry Concerning Human Understanding* (1748).

hu·mec·tant /hyoo méktənt/ *n.* **ABSORBENT SUBSTANCE** a substance such as a skin lotion that absorbs or helps retain moisture ■ *adj.* **MOISTURE-ABSORBING** capable of absorbing or retaining moisture [Early 19thC. Formed from Latin *(h)umectare* "to moisten," from *(h)umectus* "moist," from *(h)umere* "to be moist" (see HUMID).]

hu·mer·al /hyóomərəl/ *adj.* relating to, involving, or located in the humerus of the upper arm or forelimb ○ *a humeral injury*

hu·mer·al veil *n.* a silk shawl covering the shoulders and hands, worn by a Roman Catholic priest while holding sacred vessels

hu·mer·us /hyóomərəss/ (*plural* **-i** /-rì/) *n.* the long bone of the human upper arm or in a forelimb in other animals [14thC. From Latin, "upper arm." Ultimately from an Indo-European word meaning "shoulder."]

hu·mic /hyóomik/ *adj.* relating to, involving, containing, or typical of humus [Mid-19thC. Formed from HUMUS.]

hu·mid /hyóomid/ *adj.* with a relatively high level of moisture in the air [14thC. From Latin *(h)umidus*, from *(h)umere* "to be moist." Ultimately from an Indo-European word meaning "wet," which is also the ancestor of English *wake, humor*, and *hygro-*.] —**hu·mid·ly** *adv.* —**hu·mid·ness** *n.*

WORD KEY: SYNONYMS

See Synonyms at ***wet***.

hu·mi·dex /hyóomi dèks/ *n. Can* an index of the level of discomfort likely to be experienced as a result of the combined effects of humidity and heat [Late 20thC. Contraction of *humidity index*.]

hu·mid·i·fi·er /hyoo míddi fìr/ *n.* a device or machine that keeps the air moist inside an enclosed space

hu·mid·i·fy /hyoo míddi fì/ (**-fied, -fy·ing, -fies**) *vt.* to make something, especially the air, more moist or damp —**hu·mid·i·fi·ca·tion** /hyoo mìddifi káysh'n/ *n.*

hu·mid·i·stat /hyoo míddi stàt/ *n.* an instrument that measures or controls the relative humidity of air [Early 20thC. Formed from HUMIDITY, on the model of THERMOSTAT.]

hu·mid·i·ty /hyoo míddətee/ *n.* **1. ATMOSPHERIC MOISTURE** the amount of moisture in the air **2. HIGH MOISTURE LEVEL** the condition of having a high amount of moisture in the air **3.** = **relative humidity**

hu·mi·dor /hyóomi dàwr/ *n.* a container, often a box or jar, in which tobacco products, especially cigars, can be stored to prevent them from drying out [Early 20thC. Formed from HUMID, on the model of CUSPIDOR.]

hu·mi·fy /hyóomi fì/ (**-fied, -fy·ing, -fies**) *vti.* to turn a substance into humus, or turn into humus

hu·mil·i·ate /hyoo míllee àyt/ (**-at·ed, -at·ing, -ates**) *vt.* to damage somebody's dignity or pride, especially publicly [Mid-16thC. From late Latin *humiliare*, from Latin *humilis* (see HUMBLE).] —**hu·mil·i·at·ing** *adj.* —**hu·mil·i·at·ing·ly** *adv.* —**hu·mil·i·a·tor** *n.*

hu·mil·i·a·tion /hyoo mìllee áysh'n/ *n.* **1. LOSS OF DIGNITY** the feeling or condition of being lessened in dignity or pride **2. LESSENING OF SOMEBODY'S DIGNITY** the act of damaging somebody's dignity or pride **3. SOMETHING THAT HUMILIATES** something that damages somebody's pride or dignity

hu·mil·i·ty /hyoo míllitee/ *n.* the quality of being modest or respectful [13thC. Via French *humilité* from Latin *humilitas*, from *humilis* (see HUMBLE).]

hum·ma·ble /húmməb'l/ *adj.* memorable and melodious enough to make people want to hum it (*informal*)

hum·ming·bird /húmming bùrd/ *n.* a small brightly colored bird of North, Central, and South America that can beat its wings rapidly, making a humming sound and allowing it to hover. Family: Trochilidae.

hum·ming·bird moth *n.* = **hawk moth** [From its flight, likened to that of a hummingbird]

hum·mock /húmmək/ *n.* **1. SMALL HILL** a small hill or mound **2.** = **hammock**[2] **3. ICE RIDGE** a ridge of ice in an ice field [Mid-16thC. Origin unknown. Originally a nautical term for a coastal hillock.] —**hum·mock·y** *adj.*

Hummingbird

hum·mus /ho͝oməss, hŭmməss/, **hu·mus, hom·mos** *n.* a Middle Eastern dip made with mashed chickpeas, tahini, oil, lemon juice, and garlic, combined into a thick paste [Mid-20thC. From Arabic *ḥummuṣ* "chickpea."]

hu·mon·gous /hyoo múngəss/, **hu·mun·gous** *adj.* extremely large in size or amount (*informal*) [Mid-20thC. Origin uncertain: perhaps a blend of HUGE and MONSTROUS.] —**hu·mon·gous·ly** *adv.*

hu·mor /hyóomər/ *n.* **1. FUNNY QUALITY** the quality or content of something, e.g., a story, performance, or joke, that elicits amusement and laughter **2. ABILITY TO SEE SOMETHING AS FUNNY** the ability to see that something is funny, or the enjoyment of things that are funny ○ *He has no sense of humor.* **3. FUNNY THINGS AS A GENRE** writings and other material created to make people laugh **4. SOMEBODY'S USUAL TEMPERAMENT** somebody's character or usual attitude ○ *a writer of melancholy humor* **5. MOOD** a temporary mood or state of mind **6.** HIST **BODY FLUID** according to medieval science and medicine, any of the four main fluids of the human body, blood, yellow bile, black bile, or lymph, that determined a person's mood and temperament (*archaic*) ■ *vt.* (**-mored, -mor·ing, -mors**) **1. DO WHAT SOMEBODY WANTS** to do what somebody wants in order to keep him or her happy **2. COMPLY** to act in accordance with something [14thC. Via Anglo-Norman from Latin *humor* "body fluid," from *humere* "to be wet" (see HUMID).]

hu·mor·al /hyóomərəl/ *adj.* relating to, involving, or typical of body fluids, especially blood serum

hu·mored /hyóomərd/ *adj.* with a particular character or frame of mind (*usually used in combination*) ○ *good-humored*

hu·mor·esque /hyòomə résk/ *n.* a light or whimsical piece of music, especially in 19th century music [Late 19thC. Alteration of German *Humoreske*, from *Humor* "humor," from English.]

hu·mor·ist /hyóomərist/ *n.* **1. FUNNY PERSON** somebody known to be amusing and to have a quick wit **2. COMIC WRITER** somebody who writes or performs comic material

hu·mor·less /hyóomərləss/ *adj.* **1. WITHOUT A SENSE OF HUMOR** lacking a sense of humor **2. NOT FUNNY** having no amusing aspect —**hu·mor·less·ly** *adv.* —**hu·mor·less·ness** *n.*

hu·mor·ous /hyóomərəss/ *adj.* **1. FUNNY** amusing, or intended to make people laugh **2. WITTY** witty, or able to make people laugh —**hu·mor·ous·ly** *adv.* —**hu·mor·ous·ness** *n.*

WORD KEY: SYNONYMS

See Synonyms at ***funny***.

hu·mour *n.*, *vt.* U.K. = **humor**

hump /hump/ *n.* **1. BUMP ON AN ANIMAL'S BACK** a rounded protuberance on the back of some animals, e.g., camels and some cattle **2. CURVE OF THE BACK** a pronounced convex curvature of somebody's upper spine resulting from injury or disease, a congenital abnormality, or an accumulation of fat **3. BUMP IN THE SURFACE OF SOMETHING** a rounded protruding mass such as a mound of earth ■ *v.* (**humped, hump·ing, humps**) **1.** *vt.* **MOVE SOMETHING WITH EFFORT** to carry something heavy with difficulty (*informal*) **2.** *vti.* **HAVE SEX** to have sexual intercourse with somebody (*slang offensive*) **3.** *vt.* **MAKE SOMETHING INTO A HUMP** to form something into a hump [Mid-17thC. Origin uncertain: probably from or related to Dutch *homp* or Low German *humpe*.] ◇ **over the hump** past the worst or most difficult part of something

hump·back /húmp bàk/ *n.* **1.** = **hunchback 2.** ZOOL = **humpback whale 3.** ZOOL = **pink salmon**

hump·back salm·on *n.* = **pink salmon** [*Humpback* because the male develops a humped back during the breeding season]

Humpback whale

hump·back whale, hump·back *n.* a large dark gray or black whale, up to 50 ft./15.2 m long, with a humped back and long white flippers, that feeds by sieving plankton and fish through baleen plates. Humpback whales communicate with one another using distinctive complex sounds that can travel over considerable distances. Latin name: *Megaptera novaeangliae*.

humph /humf/ *interj.* used to express annoyance, doubt, or dissatisfaction [Mid-16thC. A natural exclamation.]

Hum·phrey /húmfree/, **Hubert H.** (1911–78) U.S. statesman. He served as Democratic vice president (1965–69), and ran for the presidency in 1968. Full name **Hubert Horatio Humphrey, Jr.**

Hum·phreys Peak /hùmfriz-/ mountain in northern Arizona in the San Francisco Mountains, and the highest point in the state. Height: 12,633 ft./3,851 m.

hump·y /húmpee/ (**-i·er, -i·est**) *adj.* having or full of humps —**hump·i·ness** *n.*

hu·mun·gous *adj.* = **humongous**

hu·mus[1] /hyóoməss/ *n.* a dark brown organic component of soil that is derived from decomposed plant and animal remains and animal excrement. Humus improves the water-retaining properties of soil, making it more fertile and workable. [Late 18thC. From Latin, "soil."]

hu·mus[2] *n.* FOOD = **hummus**

Hum·vee /húmvee/, **hum·vee** *n.* a military vehicle for transporting troops and supplies that combines the features of a light truck and a jeep [Late 20thC. From *HMMWV*, abbreviation of *High Mobility Multipurpose Wheeled Vehicle*.]

Hun /hun/ *n.* **1. MEMBER OF AN EARLY ASIAN NOMADIC PEOPLE** a member of a nomadic people, probably originating in northern central Asia, who invaded China in the 3rd century B.C. and then spread westward to Asia and Europe. During the 4th century A.D., under their leader, Attila, they overran much of the Roman Empire. **2. BARBARICALLY CRUEL PERSON** a barbaric destructive person **3.** HIST **OFFENSIVE TERM** an offensive term used to refer to a German person or the German people, especially by the Allies during World Wars I and II (*dated slang offensive*) [Old English *Hūne*, via a prehistoric Germanic word from late Latin *Hunni*, from, ultimately, Sogdian *xwn*]

Hu·nan /hòo na̋an/ province in central China, and an important agricultural and mineral producing region. Capital: Changsha. Population: 63,550,000 (1994). Area: 81,270 sq. mi./210,500 sq. km.

hunch /hunch/ *n.* **1. FEELING** an intuitive feeling about something **2. STOOP** a curved posture of the body with the head down and shoulders forward **3.** MED = **hump** *n.* 2 **4. PIECE** a large lump or slice of something (*archaic*) ■ *v.* (**hunched, hunch·ing, hunch·es**) **1.** *vti.* **BEND UPPER BODY FORWARD** to bend the head down and the shoulders forward, e.g., because of bad posture, illness, or the cold ○ *a typist hunching over the keyboard* ○ *hunched her shoulders against the wind* **2.** *vt.* **PUSH OR SHOVE SOMEBODY** to push or jostle somebody **3.** *vi.* **PUSH SELF FORWARD** to lunge or push yourself forward in a clumsy manner [15thC. Origin unknown.]

hunch·back /húnch bàk/ *n.* **1. HUMPED BACK** a back that shows a pronounced curvature of the spine **2. SOMEBODY WITH HUMP ON BACK** somebody who has a hump on his or her back —**hunch·backed** *adj.*

WORD KEY: CULTURAL NOTE

The Hunchback of Notre Dame, a novel by French writer Victor Hugo (1831). In this richly evocative medieval tragedy, Quasimodo, the hunchbacked bell-ringer at the Cathedral of Notre Dame in Paris, falls in love with a beautiful girl, Esmerelda. When corrupt priest Claude Frollo's harassment of Esmerelda results in her being executed for sorcery, Quasimodo murders Frollo by pushing him off the bell tower.

hun·dred /húndrəd/ *n.* **1. NUMBER 100** the number 100 **2. GROUP OF 100** a group of a hundred objects or people **3. LARGE NUMBER** an unspecified large number (*usually used in the plural*) ○ *attended by hundreds* **4. NUMBER THIRD FROM DECIMAL POINT** the number that is three places to the left of the decimal point in an Arabic numeral **5. POSITION THIRD FROM DECIMAL POINT** the position that is three places to the left of the decimal point in an Arabic numeral **6.** MONEY **$100 NOTE** a bill worth a hundred dollars **7.** HIST **COUNTY SUBDIVISION** a historical subdivision of English, Irish, and some North American counties ■ **hun·dreds** *npl.* **1. NUMBERS 100 TO 999** the numbers 100 to 999 **2. YEARS OF A CENTURY** the years of a particular century, regarded as those beginning with a particular number ○ *the seventeen hundreds* [Old English. Ultimately from an Indo-European word that is related to Latin *centum* (source of English *cent* and *century*).]

hun·dredth /húndrədth/ *n.* one of 100 equal parts of something

hun·dred·weight /húndrəd wàyt/ *n.* **1. WEIGHT OF 100 LB., USED IN U.S.** a unit of mass in the U.S. customary system equal to 100 lb. (45.36 kgs) **2. WEIGHT OF 112 LB., USED IN U.K.** a unit of mass in the British imperial system equal to 112 lb. (50.80 kg) [Early 16thC. The exact weight has varied from time to time; it was probably originally 100 pounds.]

Hun·dred Years' War *n.* a series of wars fought between England and France from 1337 to 1453 that resulted in the final expulsion of England from all French territories except Calais

hung[1] past participle, past tense of **hang**

hung[2] *adj.* **1. WITHOUT CONSENSUS** unable to form a required consensus to make decisions or reach a verdict ○ *a hung jury* ○ *a hung parliament* **2. OFFENSIVE TERM** an offensive term meaning having male sexual organs of a particular size (*offensive slang*)

Hung. *abbr.* **1.** Hungarian **2.** Hungary

Hun·gar·i·an /hung gáiree ən/ *n.* **1.** PEOPLES **SOMEBODY FROM HUNGARY** somebody who was born or raised in Hungary, or who is a Hungarian citizen **2.** LANG **OFFICIAL LANGUAGE OF HUNGARY** the official language of Hungary, also spoken in parts of neighboring countries, belonging to one of the Ugric subgroups of the Finno-Ugric branch of the Uralic family of languages. It is spoken by about 14 million people. —**Hungarian** *adj.*

Hun·gar·i·an gou·lash *n.* = **goulash**

Hungary

Hun·ga·ry /húng gəree/ republic in central Europe, first united as a country around A.D.1000. Language: Hungarian. Currency: forint. Capital: Budapest. Population: 10,225,000 (1995). Area: 35,919 sq. mi./93,030 sq. km. Official name **Republic of Hungary**

hun·ger /húng gər/ *n.* **1. NEED TO EAT** the need or desire for food **2. CRAVING** a great need or desire for something ○ *a hunger for knowledge* **3. STARVATION** lack of food leading to sickness or death ○ *children dying of hunger* ■ *vi.* (**-gered, -ger·ing, -gers**) **CRAVE** to feel a very strong need or desire for something [Old English *hungur,* from prehistoric Germanic]

hun·ger strike *n.* a refusal to eat over a period of time as a form of protest, especially by a prisoner —**hun·ger strik·er** *n.*

hung-o·ver /hung ṓvər/, **hung o·ver, hungo·ver** *adj.* suffering from the aftereffects of drinking too much alcohol or using drugs

hun·gry /húng gree/ (**-gri·er, -gri·est**) *adj.* **1. WANTING TO EAT** wanting or needing food **2. AVID** wanting or desiring something very much ○ *hungry for new experiences* **3. AMBITIOUS** having great ambition or a powerful desire to win (*informal*) ○ *They won because they were hungrier than we were.* **4. CAUSING HUNGER** using up a lot of energy and making somebody feel hungry ○ *hungry work* [Old English *hungrig,* related to *hungur* (see HUNGER)] —**hun·gri·ly** *adv.* —**hun·gri·ness** *n.* ◇ **go hungry** to go without food

hung up *adj.* (*informal*) **1. OBSESSED** obsessed with somebody or something ○ *He's completely hung up on her.* **2. WORRIED** in a state of worry or anxiety over something ○ *hung up over minor details* **3. DELAYED** held up or otherwise delayed ○ *hung up in rush hour traffic*

hunk /hungk/ *n.* **1. CHUNK** a large piece of something such as bread or cheese that is cut or torn off a larger portion **2. MALE WITH A GOOD PHYSIQUE** used to describe a man who is well-built and very physically impressive (*informal*) [Early 19thC. Origin uncertain: perhaps from Flemish *hunke* "piece of food."]

hun·ker /húngkər/ (**-kered, -ker·ing, -kers**) *vi.* to squat down close to the ground [Early 18thC. Origin uncertain.]

hunker down *vi.* **1. SETTLE INTO SERIOUS WORK** to apply yourself seriously to something ○ *time to hunker down and start studying* **2. HOLD STUBBORNLY TO AN OPINION** to hold your ground and refuse to change your mind (*informal*)

hun·kers /húngkərz/ *npl.* the hips, buttocks, and upper thighs of humans or animals (*dated informal*) [Mid-18thC. Origin uncertain: probably from HUNKER in the sense of "thing with which you hunker."]

Hunk·pa·pa /húngk paàpə/ (*plural* **-pa** *or* **-pas**) *n.* a member of a Native American people who originally lived in the border regions between Montana and North and South Dakota. The Hunkpapa now live in an area that straddles the border between North and South Dakota. [Literally "at the end of the circle," referring to the position of the Hunkpapa in the great camping circle of the Teton] —**Hunk·pa·pa** *adj.*

hunk·y /húngkee/ (**-i·er, -i·est**) *adj.* masculine, well-built, and very physically attractive (*informal*)

Hun·ky *n.* an offensive term for a laborer or other worker of eastern European origins (*dated slang offensive*) [Early 20thC. Origin uncertain: probably formed from HUNGARIAN.]

hun·ky-do·ry /hùngkee dáwree/ *adj.* absolutely fine or satisfactory (*informal*) [Origin uncertain: probably an alteration of *hunky* "all right," from obsolete *hunk* "place where a game player is safe from capture," from Dutch *honk* "home"]

Hun·nish /húnnish/ *adj.* **1. RELATING TO HUNS** typical of or relating to the Huns **2. Hun·nish, hun·nish DESTRUCTIVELY CRUEL** destructive and barbarous

hunt /hunt/ *v.* (**hunt·ed, hunt·ing, hunts**) **1.** *vt.* **SEEK PREY** to pursue an animal with the intention of capturing or killing it for sport or food ○ *Cats hunt mice and small birds.* **2.** *vt.* **SEEK OUT** to search for and try to capture somebody **3.** *vi.* **SEARCH** to search persistently for something difficult to find ○ *hunting for his missing keys* **4.** *vt.* **HOUND SOMEBODY** to seek out and harass or persecute somebody **5.** *vi.* **CHASE ANIMALS WITH HOUNDS** to engage in a sport involving the pursuit of an animal, usually a fox, on horseback and with the aid of hounds **6.** *vt.* **HUNT IN A PARTICULAR PLACE** to search a particular area for animals to capture or kill for sport or food **7.** *vi.* ENG **OSCILLATE AROUND POSITION** to oscillate around a fixed point ■ *n.* **1. ACT OF SEARCHING** the act of looking for somebody or something carefully, thoroughly, and persistently **2. SEEKING OF PREY** a pursuit of animals to capture or kill them for sport or food ○ *a deer hunt* **3. ORGANIZED GROUP OF HUNTERS** a group of people engaged in hunting as a sport ○ *She joined the local hunt.* [Old English *huntian,* from prehistoric Germanic] ◇ **hunt high and low for somebody** *or* **something** to search extremely thoroughly for somebody or something ◇ **that dog won't hunt** *Southern U.S.* that person or thing will not perform up to expectations or perform the job as required (*informal*)

Hunt /hunt/, **Richard Morris** (1827–95) U.S. architect. He is known for his addition to the Louvre in Paris (1854–55) and the Great Hall (1895–1902) of the Metropolitan Museum of Art in New York.

hunt-and-peck *n.* a slow and inefficient typing technique used by untrained typists in which each key is laboriously searched for before being struck (*informal*)

hunt·ed /húntəd/ *adj.* startled and panic-stricken, as if being pursued or hunted ○ *a hunted look*

hunt·er /húntər/ *n.* **1. PREDATOR** a person or animal that hunts birds or animals for food or sport **2. HORSE** a powerful fast horse that is bred for and used in hunting **3. DOG** a dog that is specially bred for and used in hunting **4. SEEKER** somebody who seeks out somebody or something specific, especially as an occupation or hobby **5. WATCH** a watch with a hinged metal cover to protect the watch face

WORD KEY: CULTURAL NOTE

The Heart is a Lonely Hunter, a novel by writer Carson McCullers (1940). A work about isolation, alienation, and the search for love, it is the story of four lonely individuals, all of whom find themselves drawn to a local boy who is unable to hear or speak. The novel's central irony is that the boy is even more isolated than they are, his loneliness eventually leading him to suicide.

hunt·er-gath·er·er *n.* a member of a society in which people live by hunting and gathering only, with no crops or livestock being raised for food

hunt·er green *adj.* a dark green color

hunt·er-kill·er *adj.* used to describe a naval force consisting of an antisubmarine warfare carrier and its associated elements

hunt·er's moon *n.* the first full moon directly following the harvest moon

hunt·ing /húnting/ *n.* **1. KILLING OF ANIMALS FOR SPORT** the sport or practice of pursuing and killing or capturing wild animals **2. SEEKING OUT** the process of searching carefully for something, usually over a period of time ○ *job hunting*

hunt·ing and gath·er·ing *n.* seeking game and edible plants for subsistence, as practiced by pre-agricultural and nomadic people, rather than raising livestock and crops for food

hunt·ing ground *n.* **1. AREA FOR HUNTING** a place where hunting takes place or that is suitable for hunting **2. SOURCE OF SOMETHING** a source of useful or desired objects or information ○ *The town is a great hunting ground for antiques.*

hunt·ing knife *n.* a broad knife used for killing or gutting game

hunt·ing spi·der *n.* = **wolf spider**

Hunt·ing·ton /húntingtən/ **1.** town on the northern shore of Long Island, southeastern New York. Population: 191,474 (1990). **2.** city and river port in West Virginia on the Ohio River, near the Kentucky border. Population: 53,941 (1996).

Hunt·ing·ton Beach coastal city in southern California, 14 mi./23 km southeast of Long Beach, that was formerly an oil-producing center. Population: 189,220 (1994).

Hunt·ing·ton Park city in southwestern California, near Los Angeles. Population: 56,065 (1990).

Hunt·ing·ton's cho·re·a *n.* a hereditary disorder of the nervous system that manifests as jerky involuntary movements in early middle age, with behavioral changes and progressive dementia [Late 19thC. Named for the American neurologist George *Huntington* (1851–1916), who first described it.]

Hunt·ing·ton Sta·tion town in southeastern New York, on the northern shore of Long Island. Population: 28, 247 (1990).

hunt·ing watch *n.* = **hunter** *n.* **5**

hunt·ress /húntrəss/ *n.* a woman or goddess who hunts

hunts·man /húntsmən/ (*plural* **-men**) *n.* **1. HUNT OFFICIAL** an official who is in charge of the hounds belonging to a hunt **2. HUNTING MAN** a man who hunts, either for a living or for a pastime

hunts·man's-cup *n.* = **pitcher plant**

Hunts·ville /húnts vìl/ city in northern Alabama, a major center of aerospace research and manufacture. Population: 170,424 (1996).

Hu·on pine /hyoō ən-/ *n.* a large coniferous tree that grows in South America, Australia, and Southeast Asia and is used for timber. Latin name: *Dacrydium franklinii.* [Early 19thC. Named for the *Huon* River in southern Tasmania, where it was first found.]

hup /hup/ *interj.* used when marching to mark time or when lifting or raising something (*informal*) [Mid-20thC. Origin uncertain: perhaps an alteration of *hep,* used when marching to mark time, of unknown origin.]

hup·pah /khoōpə, khoō paá/ (*plural* **hup·pahs** *or* **hup·pot** *or* **hu·pot**), **chup·pah** /khoō pŏt, khoō pŏt/ (*plural* **chup·pahs** *or* **chup·pot** *or* **chu·pot**) *n.* **1. JEWISH WEDDING CANOPY** a canopy under which a Jewish wedding ceremony is performed **2. JEWISH WEDDING** a Jewish wedding ceremony [Late 19thC. From Hebrew *ḥuppāh* "cover, canopy."]

hur·dle /húrd'l/ *n.* **1.** SPORTS **FRAME FOR RUNNER TO JUMP** one of a number of light barriers over which runners have to jump in some track-and-field events **2.** SPORTS **RACE OVER BARRIERS** a track-and-field event in which runners have to race to clear a series of light barriers **3. DIFFICULTY OR OBSTACLE** a difficulty or obstacle that has to be overcome **4.** HORSERACING **FENCE USED IN HORSE RACE** a fence of intertwined branches or wattle that horses race over, or a race over fences of this type ■ *v.* (**-dled, -dling, -dles**) **1.** *vi.* SPORTS **RACE OVER HURDLES** to run in a track-and-field event in which hurdles must be jumped **2.** *vt.* SPORTS **CLEAR RACING BARRIER** to clear a barrier in a race **3.** *vt.* **OVERCOME A DIFFICULTY** to overcome an obstacle or difficulty [Old English *hyrdel.* Ultimately from an Indo-European word meaning "to turn" that is also the ancestor of English *grate*[1] and *grille.*] —**hur·dler** *n.*

Hurdy-gurdy

hur·dy-gur·dy /hùrdi gúrdee, húrdi gùrdee/ (*plural* **hur·dy-gur·dies**) *n.* **1. BARREL ORGAN** a mechanical musical instrument such as a barrel organ that is played by turning a handle **2. MEDIEVAL MUSICAL INSTRUMENT** a medieval string instrument played by turning a wheel with one hand and depressing keys on a keyboard with the other. Sound was produced by adding violin-bow rosin to the outer edge of the wheel, which made the strings vibrate when it was turned against them. [Mid-18thC. An imitation of the sound.]

hurl /hurl/ *v.* (**hurled, hurl·ing, hurls**) **1.** *vt.* **FLING SOMETHING** to throw something with great force **2.** *vt.* **YELL SOMETHING** to utter something with great violence or vehemence ○ *hurling abuse* **3.** *vti.* BASEBALL **PITCH** to pitch a baseball **4.** *vi.* **VOMIT** to vomit, especially with considerable force (*slang*) ■ *n.* **STRONG THROW** a forceful throw, or the act of throwing something with great force [12thC. Origin uncertain: probably suggests the action.] —**hurl·er** *n.*

WORD KEY: SYNONYMS

See Synonyms at ***throw.***

hurl·ey /húrlee-/ *n.* a long wooden stick with a curved end used in the game of hurling

hurl·ing /húrling/ *n.* an Irish field sport resembling hockey and lacrosse that is played with broad sticks and a leather ball that is passed from player to player through the air

hur·ly-bur·ly /hùrlee búrlee, húrlee bùrlee/ *n.* noisy and bustling activity [Alteration of *hurling and burling,* a playful formation ultimately based on HURL]

Hur·ok /hyoōr ŏk/, **Sol** (1888–1974) Russian-born U.S. impresario. He brought entertainers from around the world to the United States. Full name **Solomon Hurok**

Hu·ron[1] /hyŏŏr on/ (*plural* **-ron** *or* **-rons**) *n.* a member of a confederacy of four Native American peoples who originally lived around the Great Lakes but today live in Quebec, Ontario, and Oklahoma. During the 17th century, the Huron population was greatly reduced by continual warring with the Iroquois and the arrival of smallpox and other European diseases. [Mid-17thC. From French, literally "boar," from Old French *hure* "bristling hair."] —**Hu·ron** *adj.*

Hu·ron[2] /hyŏŏr on/ city in eastern South Dakota, east of Pierre and northwest of Sioux Falls. Population: 12,428 (1996).

Hu·ron, Lake second largest of the Great Lakes, lying between the state of Michigan, United States, and the province of Ontario, Canada. Area: 23,000 sq. mi./59,600 sq. km. Depth: 751 ft./229 m.

hur·rah /hŏŏ raá, hə raá/ (**-rahed, -rah·ing, -rahs**) *interj.* = **hooray** [Late 17thC. Alteration of archaic *huzza* (see HUZZAH).] ◇ **(the) last hurrah** a final experience in the limelight, brush with fame, or spree (*informal*)

hur·ray /hŏŏ ráy, hə-/ *interj., vi.* = **hooray**

Hur·ri·an /hŏŏree ən/ *n.* **1.** PEOPLES **MEMBER OF ANCIENT SYRIAN PEOPLE** a member of an ancient people who lived in Syria and Mesopotamia around 1500 B.C. **2.** LANG **LANGUAGE OF HURRIAN** the language of the Hurrians. Its affinities are unknown. [Early 20thC. Formed from Hittite and Assyrian *Harri* and *Hurri*.] —**Hur·ri·an** *adj.*

hur·ri·cane /húrri kàyn/ *n.* **1.** METEOROL **SEVERE STORM** a severe tropical storm with torrential rain and winds above 74 mi./119 km per hour. Hurricanes originate in areas of low pressure in equatorial regions of the Atlantic or Caribbean, then strengthen, traveling northwest, north, or northeast. **2.** METEOROL **HIGH WIND** a wind with speeds above 74 mi./119 km per hour and a force of 12 or above on the Beaufort scale **3. FAST FORCEFUL THING** somebody or something resembling a violent storm in force, speed, or effect [Mid-16thC. Via Spanish *huracán* from Taino *hurakán* "god of the storm."]

hur·ri·cane deck *n.* a deck on a ship with a cover from the sun

hur·ri·cane lamp *n.* an oil or kerosene lamp with a glass cover to prevent the wick from being extinguished in wind or rain

hur·ried /húrreed/ *adj.* done, made, or performed too quickly because of a real or perceived lack of time —**hur·ried·ly** *adv.* —**hur·ried·ness** *n.*

hur·ry /húrree/ *v.* (**-ried, -ry·ing, -ries**) **1.** *vi.* **RUSH** to move or do something with great or excessive speed because of a real or perceived lack of time **2.** *vt.* **SPEED UP** to make or encourage somebody or something to act with greater speed ■ *n.* **1. HASTE** a state in which somebody is doing something or moving at a great or excessive speed ○ *We were in such a hurry we left the tickets behind.* **2. URGENCY** the need to do something quickly ○ *What's the hurry?* [Early 17thC. Origin uncertain; perhaps suggests the action.] —**hur·ri·er** *n.*

hur·ry-scur·ry *n.* an undue rush to do something [Mid-18thC. Repetition of HURRY.]

Hurst /hurst/, **Fannie** (1889–1968) U.S. writer. A prolific and popular writer, she is best known for her novels *Back Street* (1931) and *Imitation of Life* (1933). Born **Fannie Danielson**

hurt /hurt/ *v.* (**hurt, hurt·ing, hurts**) **1.** *vt.* **INJURE SOMEBODY OR SOMETHING** to cause physical pain in somebody or in yourself or part of the body ○ *hurt his back when he fell down* **2.** *vti.* **EXPERIENCE PAIN** to experience physical pain, or cause somebody to experience physical pain ○ *Ouch! That hurts!* **3.** *vti.* **UPSET** to feel emotional pain, or make somebody feel emotional pain ○ *hurt by his unkind remarks* **4.** *vti.* **IMPAIR** to have a negative effect on something ○ *This could hurt her chances of reelection.* **5.** *vi.* **EXPERIENCE DIFFICULTIES** to undergo or experience difficulties or setbacks, e.g., in business or financial affairs (*informal*) ○ *too much competition, so the business is really hurting* ■ *n.* **1. PAIN** emotional or mental pain or suffering ○ *after all the hurt he's caused* **2. INJURY** an injury or wound, whether emotional or physical ○ *old hurts* ■ *adj.* **1. INJURED** injured or in physical pain **2. UPSET** feeling or showing emotional pain or suffering [12thC. From Old French *hurter* "to ram, collide," probably ultimately from prehistoric Germanic.] —**hurt·er** *n.* ◇ **in a world of hurt** in a condition of great physical, emotional, or financial distress (*informal*)

WORD KEY: SYNONYMS

See Synonyms at *harm.*

hurt·ful /húrtfəl/ *adj.* causing emotional pain or suffering —**hurt·ful·ly** *adv.* —**hurt·ful·ness** *n.*

hur·tle /húrt'l/ (**-tled, -tling, -tles**) *vi.* to move or travel at very high speed [13thC. Formed from HURT.]

hus·band /húzbənd/ *n.* **WOMAN'S SPOUSE** the man to whom a woman is married ■ *vt.* (**-band·ed, -band·ing, -bands**) **BE THRIFTY WITH SOMETHING** to use and manage something economically, e.g., resources or money [Pre-12thC. From Old Norse *húsbóndi* "man in charge of the house, farmer," from *hús* "house" + *bóndi* "dweller," present participle of *búa* "to dwell."] —**hus·ban·dage** *n.* —**hus·ban·der** *n.*

hus·band·man /húzbəndmən/ (*plural* **-men**) *n.* a farmer (*archaic*)

hus·band·ry /húzbəndree/ *n.* **1. FARMING** the science, skill, or art of farming **2. FRUGAL MANAGEMENT** the frugal and sensible management of resources

hush /hush/ *vti.* (**hushed, hush·ing, hush·es**) **MAKE SOMEBODY BE QUIET** to become silent, or make somebody become quiet or silent ■ *interj.* **BE QUIET** used as a request or demand for silence ■ *n.* **SILENCE** a stillness or silence, especially after a period of noise or in expectation of something [Mid-16thC. Origin uncertain; probably a back-formation from archaic *husht* "silent," earlier "hush!", a natural exclamation.]

hush up *v.* **1.** *vt.* **KEEP SECRET** to prevent something, especially something dishonorable or discreditable, from becoming publicly known (*informal*) **2.** *vi.* **REQUEST SILENCE** to ask or tell somebody to become silent or quieter

hush-hush *adj.* secret or confidential (*informal*)

hush mon·ey *n.* money paid as a bribe not to disclose information (*informal*)

hush pup·py *n.* a small deep-fried ball of cornmeal dough, originally a strictly Southern form of bread

husk /husk/ *n.* **1.** BOT **OUTER PLANT COVERING** the outer membranous covering of some fruits, nuts, and grains **2. USELESS OUTER SHELL** an empty outer shell or covering that no longer serves any useful purpose [14thC. Origin uncertain: perhaps from Low German *hūske* "little house, cover."] —**husk·er** *n.*

hus·kie *n.* = **husky**

husk·ing bee /húsking-/ *n.* a gathering of people, usually farm families, for the purpose of husking corn

husk to·ma·to *n.* = **ground cherry**

husk·y[1] /húskee/ (**-i·er, -i·est**) *adj.* **1. BURLY AND COMPACT IN PHYSIQUE** with a solid, burly, strong, and compact physique ○ *a husky boy* **2. THROATY** hoarse and dry, either naturally or as a result of illness or emotion ○ *a husky voice* **3. RELATING TO HUSKS** containing or resembling husks [Mid-16thC. Formed from HUSK.] —**husk·i·ly** *adv.* —**husk·i·ness** *n.*

hus·ky[2] /húskee/ (*plural* **-kies**), **hus·kie** *n.* a large long-haired dog with a curled tail and pricked ears, originally bred in Arctic regions and trained to pull sleds [Mid-19thC. Origin uncertain: probably a shortening and alteration of ESKIMO, the original name being *Eskimo dog*.]

Huss /huss/, **John** (1372?–1415) Bohemian religious reformer. He was burnt at the stake for supporting the teachings of the English reformer, Wycliffe. His execution led to the outbreak of the Hussite Wars (1419–34).

hus·sar /hə zaár, hŏŏ-/ *n.* **1. HUNGARIAN CAVALRY MEMBER** a member of the Hungarian cavalry in the 15th century **2. EUROPEAN CAVALRY SOLDIER** a soldier in any European light cavalry unit in the 18th and 19th centuries that adopted an ornate uniform similar to that of the Hungarian cavalry in the 15th century [Mid-16thC. Via Hungarian *huszár* "light horseman" from, ultimately, Italian *corsaro* "corsair."]

Hus·sein I /hŏŏ sáyn/, **King of Jordan** (1935–99). Throughout his reign (1952–99), he was a moderating influence in Middle East politics.

Hus·sein, Saddam (*b.* 1937) Iraqi president. As leader of the Baath party, he became president in 1979. Two years after the end of the Iran-Iraq War (1980–88), his invasion of Kuwait led to the Persian Gulf War.

Huss·ite /hú sīt, hŏŏ-/ *n.* a follower of the teachings of the Bohemian nationalist and religious reformer John Huss (1372?-1415) —**Huss·it·ism** /hússi tìzzəm, hŏŏssi-/ *n.*

hus·sy /hússee/ (*plural* **-sies**) *n.* **1. OFFENSIVE TERM** an offensive term that deliberately insults a woman's manner or behavior (*insult*) **2. OFFENSIVE TERM** an offensive term for a young woman that deliberately insults her tact and self-restraint [Mid-16thC. Contraction of HOUSEWIFE (the original sense).]

hust·ings /hústingz/ *npl.* **1. ELECTIONEERING CIRCUIT** the rounds of political activities, e.g., speech-making and the organization of public rallies, that take place before an election **2. ELECTION PLATFORM FORMERLY USED IN BRITAIN** in Great Britain before 1872, a platform from which parliamentary candidates were nominated and addressed electors (*archaic*) [Pre-12thC. From Old Norse *húsþing* "council held by a king and his immediate followers," from *hús* "house" + *þing* "meeting."]

hus·tle /húss'l/ *v.* (**-tled, -tling, -tles**) **1.** *vi.* **HURRY** to go somewhere or do something fast or hurriedly (*informal*) ○ *We'd better hustle, or we'll be late.* **2.** *vti.* CRIMINOL **ENGAGE IN SMALL-TIME ILLEGAL DEALS** to engage in small-time crimes, e.g., petty theft or prostitution (*slang*) **3.** *vt.* **SELL SOMETHING AGGRESSIVELY** to sell something aggressively, e.g., drinks in a bar **4.** *vti.* CRIMINOL **SOLICIT CUSTOMERS IN SHADY DEALS** to solicit customers in shady or illegal deals, e.g., as a prostitute (*slang*) **5.** *vt.* **PROPEL** to convey somebody roughly or hurriedly from a place ○ *hustled her into a waiting car* **6.** *vt.* **DEAL WITH SOMETHING FAST** to deal with something hurriedly ○ *Let's hustle this project along.* **7.** *vi.* **PLAY SPORT AGGRESSIVELY** to play a sport with great aggressiveness, intensity, and concentration ■ *n.* **1.** CRIMINOL **RACKET OR SWINDLE** an act or scheme involving deceit, swindling, fraud, or petty theft (*slang*) **2. NOISY ACTIVITY** lively, noisy, continual activity ○ *enjoyed the hustle of the big city* **3. INITIATIVE** personal aggressive initiative, e.g., in advancing your career (*slang*) [Late 17thC. From Dutch *hutselen* "to shake or toss," literally "to shake repeatedly," ultimately from *hotsen* "to shake."]

hus·tler /hússlər/ *n.* **1.** CRIMINOL **PETTY CRIMINAL** a small-time operator who engages in illegal activities, e.g., petty theft or illegal gambling (*informal*) **2.** CRIMINOL **PROSTITUTE** a prostitute, especially a streetwalker or one who solicits in bars (*slang*) **3. AGGRESSIVE PERSON** a person who works aggressively and consistently, especially to advance his or her career (*informal*)

Hus·ton /hyŏŏstən/, **John** (1906–87) U.S. movie director and actor. The son of Walter Huston, he directed *Maltese Falcon* (1941), *The African Queen* (1952), and won two Academy Awards for *The Treasure of the Sierra Madre* (1948).

Hus·ton, Walter (1884–1950) Canadian-born U.S. actor. He won an Academy Award for *The Treasure of the Sierra Madre* (1948).

hut[1] /hut/ *n.* **ONE-ROOM BUILDING** a small single-story building, often made of wood, that is used as a simple house or shelter, or for storage, temporary accommodation, or leisure activities ○ *a fishing hut* ■ *vt.* (**hut·ted, hut·ting, huts**) **PROVIDE WITH HUTS** to provide huts for a place, especially for accommodation [Mid-16thC. Via French *hutte* from High German *hütte*, of uncertain origin.]

hut[2] /hut/ *interj.* used to mark time while marching (*informal*) [Mid-20thC. Origin uncertain: probably an alteration of *hep*, of unknown origin.]

hutch /huch/ *n.* **1. CAGE** a small shelter, usually constructed from wire and wood, for keeping small animals such as rabbits **2.** HOUSEHOLD **CHINA CABINET** a cupboard with drawers and usually open shelves on top, often used for storing and displaying dishes and kitchen utensils [12thC. Via French *huche* from medieval Latin *hutica*, of unknown origin.]

Hutch·ins /húchinz/, **Robert Maynard** (1899–1977) U.S. educator. He was a reforming president and chancellor of the University of Chicago (1929–51), where he introduced, most notably, the Great Books program.

Hutch·in·son /húchinss'n/ city in central Kansas on the Arkansas River. Population: 39,015 (1996).

Hutch·in·son, Anne (1591–1643) English-born U.S. colonial religious reformer. She was banished from Massachusetts for preaching her liberal religious doctrine that was opposed to the Puritans. Born **Anne Marbury**

Hutch·in·son-Gil·ford syn·drome /-gílfərd-/ *n.* MED = **progeria** [Named for the British physicians Sir Jonathan

Hutchinson (1828–1913) and Hastings *Gilford* (1861–1941)]

hut·ment /hútmənt/ *n.* a group of huts forming a military encampment

Hut·ter·ite /hóttə rìt/ *n.* a member of an Anabaptist religious group that immigrated from Moravia mainly to Alberta and Manitoba in Canada but also to areas of the northwestern United States where they formed farming communities [Late 19thC. Named for Jacob *Hutter* (d. 1536), Moravian Anabaptist leader.]

Hutt Val·ley /hùt-/ urbanized region in the south of the North Island, New Zealand, near the city of Wellington

Hu·tu /hóo too/ (*plural* **-tu** *or* **-tus**) *n.* **1.** PEOPLES **MEMBER OF A RWANDAN AND BURUNDIAN PEOPLE** a member of a people who make up the majority of the population of Rwanda and Burundi **2.** LANG **LANGUAGE OF RWANDA AND BURUNDI** a language spoken in Rwanda and Burundi that is one of the Bantu group of the Niger-Congo family of African languages. Hutu is spoken by about 14 million people. [Mid-20thC. From a Bantu language.] —**Hu·tu** *adj.*

hutz·pah *n.* = **chutzpah**

Hux·ley /húkslee/, **Aldous** (1894–1963) British novelist and essayist. His novels include *Point Counter Point* (1928), *Brave New World* (1932), and *Eyeless in Gaza* (1936). Full name **Aldous Leonard Huxley**

Hux·ley, Sir Julian (1887–1975) British biologist. He was the first director general of UNESCO (1947–48) and the author of *Essays of a Biologist* (1923). Full name **Sir Julian Sorrell Huxley**

Hux·ley, T. H. (1825–95) British biologist. A supporter of Darwin, he wrote *Zoological Evidences as to Man's Place in Nature* (1863) and *Collected Essays* (1893–94). Full name **Thomas Henry Huxley**

Huy·gens' eye·piece /hígənz-/ *n.* an eyepiece consisting of two planoconvex lenses with their flat sides toward the eye, fitted mainly on optical instruments that are used for observation rather than measurement [Mid-19thC. Named for the Dutch physicist and astronomer Christiaan *Huygens* (1629–95), who invented it.]

Huy·gens' prin·ci·ple *n.* PHYS the proposition that every point on a wavefront acts as a source of secondary waves of light and that the wavefront at a later time is the envelope of these secondary waves [See HUYGEN'S EYEPIECE]

huz·zah /hə zaá/ (**-zahed, -zah·ing, -zahs**) *n.* = **hooray** (*archaic*) [Late 16thC. Variant of *huzza*, of uncertain origin: perhaps a sailor's work-chant when hauling on ropes; or related to German *Hussa*, a hunting cry.]

H.V. *abbr.* **1.** high velocity **2.** high voltage

HVAC *abbr.* heating, ventilating, and air conditioning

hvy. *abbr.* heavy

HW *abbr.* **1.** hazardous waste **2.** high water **3.** hot water

H·wan·ge Na·tion·al Park /hwàng gay-/ the largest national park in Zimbabwe, established in 1929. Area: 5,657 sq. mi./14,651 sq. km.

HWM *abbr.* high-water mark

hwy *abbr.* highway

Hyacinth

hy·a·cinth /hí əsinth/ *n.* a plant of the lily family, native to the northeastern Mediterranean, cultivated widely for its spikes of highly fragrant pink, white, or blue flowers. Latin name: *Hyacinthus orientalis.* [Mid-16thC. Via French and Latin from Greek *huakinthos* "plant sprung from the blood of HYACINTHUS," also "blue stone" (source of English *jacinth*).] —**hy·a·cin·thine** /hì ə sínthin, hì ə-/ *adj.*

hy·a·cinth bean *n.* a deciduous woody-stemmed leguminous climbing plant with attractive pink or white flowers. Latin name: *Dolichos lablab.*

Hy·a·cin·thus /hì ə sínthəss/ *n.* a young boy in Greek mythology who was loved and accidentally killed by the god Apollo, who made a flower grow on the spot where the boy died

Hy·a·des /hí ə deez/ *n.* a cluster of over 200 stars in the constellation Taurus. Its five brightest members form a V-shaped group that is visible to the naked eye.

hy·ae·na *n.* = **hyena**

hyal- *prefix.* = **hyalo-** (*used before vowels*)

hy·a·lin /hí əlin/ *n.* a clear glassy material found in hyaline cartilage or formed as a product of some skin diseases

hy·a·line /hí əlin, -lìn/ *adj.* clear, translucent, and containing no fibers or granular material

hy·a·line car·ti·lage *n.* the most common type of cartilage, consisting of a bluish-white elastic material containing fine collagen fibers that provides flexibility and support at the joints. Hyaline cartilage is found at the ends of the long bones and in the nose and the larynx, and forms most of the fetal skeleton.

hy·a·line mem·brane dis·ease *n.* = **respiratory distress syndrome**

hy·a·lite /hí ə lìt/ *n.* a clear colorless variety of the semiprecious gemstone opal

hy·a·li·tis /hì ə lítiss/ *n.* inflammation of the transparent jelly (**vitreous humor**) that fills the chamber of the eye behind the lens

hyalo- *prefix.* glass, glassy ○ *hyaloplasm* [From Greek *hualos* "glass," of unknown origin]

hy·a·loid /hí ə lòyd/ *adj.* clear and glassy in appearance

hy·a·loid mem·brane *n.* a transparent insubstantial membrane surrounding the transparent jelly (**vitreous humor**) of the eye and separating it from the retina

hy·al·u·ron·ic ac·id /hìə loo ronnik-/ *n.* a viscous slippery complex sugar that lubricates joints and helps maintain the shape of the eyeballs. It is present in connective tissue, and also plays a role in the healing of wounds. [*Hyaluronic* from HYALOID (because the substance was first isolated in the vitreous humor) + *uronic* "connected with urine"]

hy·a·lu·ron·i·dase /hì əloo rónni dàyss, -dàyz/ *n.* an enzyme that breaks down hyaluronic acid, increasing the permeability of connective tissues

Hy·an·nis /hì ánniss, hee ánniss/ resort village and commercial center in southeastern Massachusetts, on the southern coast of Cape Cod. Population: 14,120 (1990).

Hy·atts·ville /hí əts vìl/ city in west central Maryland, a northeastern suburb of Washington, D.C. Population: 14,674 (1996).

hy·brid /híbrid/ *n.* **1.** BOT **PLANT RESULTING FROM CROSSING** a plant produced from a cross between two plants with different genetic constituents. Hybrids from crosses between crop varieties are often stronger and produce better yields than the original stock. **2.** ZOOL **ANIMAL RESULTING FROM CROSS-SPECIES MATING** an animal that results from the mating of parents from two distinct species or subspecies **3. COMPOUND** something made up of a mixture of different elements **4.** LING **WORD DERIVED FROM TWO LANGUAGES** a word that has derived from two different languages, e.g., "appendicitis," in which "appendic" is from Latin and "itis" is from Greek **5.** AUTOMOT **USING TWO FUELS** a vehicle with an engine that runs on electricity and gasoline, which it can alternate between ■ *adj.* **1.** BIOL **CROSS-BRED** bred from two distinct species or subspecies **2. CONTAINING MIXED ELEMENTS** made up of different elements or components ○ *a hybrid literary form* **3.** ELECTRON ENG **UNUSUAL AS AN ELECTRONIC CIRCUIT** used to describe an electronic circuit that consists of two or more components not ordinarily combined with one another, e.g., a circuit that has integrated circuitry, transistors, and vacuum tubes **4.** ELECTRON ENG **WITH MULTIPLE INTEGRATED CIRCUITRY** used to describe an electronic circuit containing more than one integrated circuit, all of which are attached to the same ceramic substrate [Early 17thC. From Latin *hybrida*, of uncertain origin: probably from Greek *hubrida* "mongrel."] —**hy·brid·ism** *n.* —**hy·brid·ist** *n.* —**hy·brid·i·ty** /hī bríddətee/ *n.*

hy·brid an·ti·bod·y *n.* an artificial antibody synthesized to attach to two different antigens

hy·brid com·put·er *n.* a computer employing both analog and digital techniques

hy·brid·ize /híbri dìz/ (**-ized, -iz·ing, -iz·es**) *vti.* to generate a new form of plant or animal, either by human intervention or naturally, by combining the genes of two different species or subspecies —**hy·brid·iz·a·ble** *adj.* —**hy·brid·i·za·tion** /hìbridi záysh'n/ *n.* —**hy·brid·iz·er** /híbri dìzər/ *n.*

hy·brid·o·ma /hìbri dómə/ *n.* a hybrid cell produced by the fusion of a tumor cell with a normal antibody-producing cell, which then proliferates and yields large amounts of a monoclonal antibody

hy·brid rock *n.* rock formed when molten magma incorporates solid material from the rock through which it flows, yielding a mixture of rock types

hy·brid vig·or *n.* the increased growth, disease resistance, and fertility seen in hybrid species. Mules, the offspring of mares and donkeys, are stronger and longer-lived than the parent animals.

hyd. *abbr.* hydraulics

hy·da·thode /hídə thòd/ *n.* a pore in the outer layer of a leaf that secretes water when the rate of transpiration is low, e.g., in humid conditions [Late 19thC. From Greek *hudat-*, stem of *hudōr* "water," + *hodos* "way."]

hy·da·tid /hídətid/, **hy·da·tid cyst** *n.* a cyst formed in human tissue that contains the larvae of a tapeworm [Late 17thC. Via modern Latin from Greek *hudatis* "drop of water, watery vesicle," from *hudat-*, stem of *hudōr* "water."]

hy·da·tid dis·ease *n.* a condition resulting from the presence of hydatid cysts in the liver, lungs, or brain, which can cause malignancies, blindness, epilepsy, and fever

Hy·der·a·bad /hídərə bad/, **Hy·der·ā·bād** **1.** former state in central India, now divided between the states of Andhra Pradesh, Karnataka, and Maharashtra **2.** city and capital of Andhra Pradesh, India, founded in 1589, situated on the Musi River. Population: 3,145,939 (1991). **3.** city in Sind Province, southeastern Pakistan, situated on the Indus River. Population: 795,000 (1981).

hyd·no·car·pate /hìdnə kaár pàyt/ *n.* a salt of hydnocarpic acid

hyd·no·carp·ic ac·id /hìdnə kaárpik-/ *n.* a fatty acid containing a carbon ring in its structure, occurring as gylcerides in chaulmoogra oil. Formula: $C_{16}H_{28}O_2$. [*Hydnocarpic* from *hydnocarpus*, plant yielding an oil containing this acid, ultimately from Greek *hudnon* "truffle" + *karpos* "fruit," from the fruit's appearance]

hydr- *prefix.* = **hydro-** (*used before vowels*)

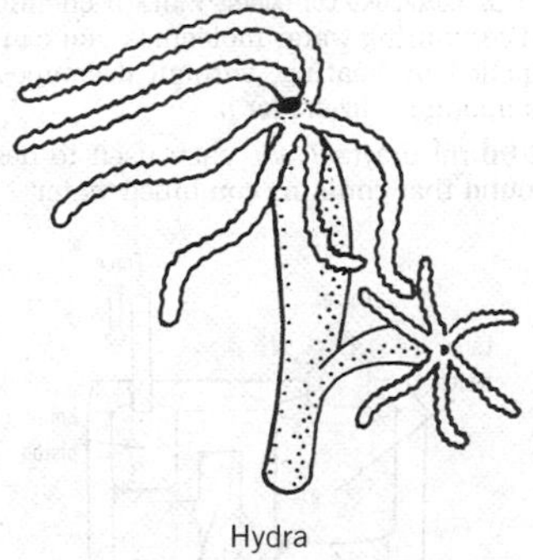

Hydra

hy·dra /hídrə/ (*plural* **-dras** *or* **-drae** /-dree/) *n.* a freshwater polyp with a cylindrical body at one end and a mouth surrounded by tentacles at the other. Genus: *Hydra.* [Late 18thC. Via modern Latin, genus name, from, ultimately, Greek *hudra* "water snake."]

Hy·dra *n.* **1.** ASTRON **LARGEST CONSTELLATION** the largest constellation, between Leo in the northern hemisphere and Centaurus in the southern hemisphere **2.** MYTHOL **MANY-HEADED MONSTER** a monster in Greek mythology that had nine heads and was killed by Hercules. When one head was cut off, another grew instantly in its place.

hy·drac·id /hì drássid/ *n.* an acid in which the hydrogen atoms are bound to an atom other than oxygen, e.g., hydrochloric acid

hy·dra·gogue /hī́drə gòg/ *n.* a laxative that acts osmotically by drawing water into the intestinal canal from the blood, thereby softening the contents. Epsom salts was once the principal hydragogue but has now been superseded by complex sugars such as lactulose that work in the same way. [Mid-17thC. Via late Latin *hydragogus* from Greek *hudragōgos* "conveying water," from the stem *hudr-* "water."]

hy·dra-head·ed *adj.* with many heads or parts like heads

hy·dral·a·zine /hī drállə zeen/ *n.* a drug that lowers blood pressure, usually given with drugs that cause increased urine output [Mid-20thC. Coined from HYDRO + PHTHALIC ACID + AZINE.]

hy·dran·gea /hī dráynjə/ *n.* an erect or climbing evergreen or deciduous shrub, native to Asia, that has large clusters of white, pink, or blue flowers in a variety of shapes. Genus: *Hydrangea.* [Mid-18thC. From modern Latin, genus name, literally "water pot"; from its cup-shaped seed pod.]

hy·drant /hī́drənt/ *n.* an upright pipe, usually in a street, connected to a water main with a valve to which a hose can be attached, e.g., by the fire department [Early 19thC. Formed from HYDRO-.]

hy·dranth /hī́ drànth/ *n.* the sedentary form in the life cycle of a cnidarian such as a sea anemone or a hydra [Late 19thC. From HYDRA + Greek *anthos* "flower."]

hy·drarch /hī́ draark/ *adj.* used to describe the development of a sequence of ecological stages that begins in a freshwater habitat such as a pond [Early 20thC. Coined from HYDRO- + Greek *arkhē* "beginning."]

hy·dra·rgy·rum /hī draarjərəm/ *n.* CHEM ELEM mercury (*archaic*) [Mid-16thC. Via modern Latin from, ultimately, Greek *hydrarguros*, from the stem *hudr-* "water" + *arguros* "silver."]

hy·drase /hī́ dràyss, -dràyz/ *n.* an enzyme that catalyzes the addition or removal of water

hy·dras·tine /hī drá steen, hī drástin/ *n.* a poisonous white substance extracted from the thick yellow roots of the goldenseal plant, once used medicinally to stop hemorrhaging, shrink the uterus, and reduce inflammation of mucous membranes. Formula: $C_{21}H_{21}NO_6$. [Mid-19thC. Formed from *hydrastis*, plant genus name, formed from HYDRO- + *astis*, of unknown origin.]

hy·dras·ti·nine /hī drásti neen, hī drástinin/ *n.* an organic compound forming colorless crystals, soluble in water and resembling hydrastine in its medicinal properties. Formula: $C_{11}H_{13}NO_3$.

hy·drate /hī́ dràyt/ *vt.* (**-drat·ed, -drat·ing, -drates**) **1.** GIVE WATER TO to provide water for somebody or something in order to reestablish or maintain a correct fluid balance **2.** CHEM ADD WATER TO to add water to a chemical compound so that different crystals are formed ■ *n.* CHEM COMPOUND CONTAINING WATER a chemical compound containing water molecules that can usually be expelled by heating, without decomposition of the compound —**hy·dra·tor** *n.*

hy·drat·ed /hī́ dràytəd/ *adj.* CHEM used to describe a compound that contains combined water

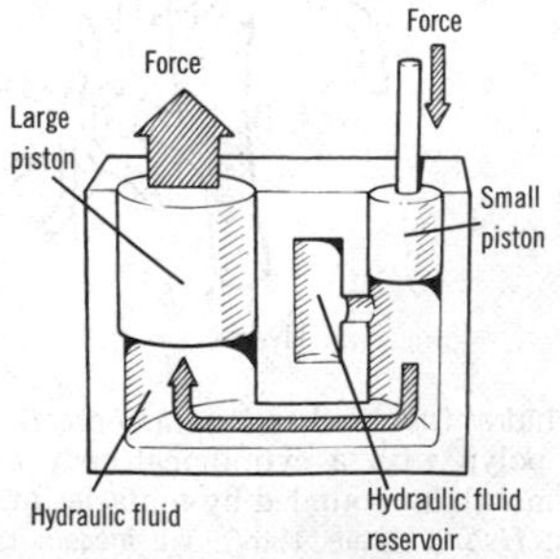

Hydraulic: Cross section of hydraulic mechanism

hy·drau·lic /hī dróllik/ *adj.* relating to or operated by a device in which pressure applied to a piston is transmitted by a fluid to a larger piston, giving rise to a larger force [Early 17thC. Via Latin *hydraulicus* from Greek *hudraulikos*, from *hudōr* "water" + *aulos* "pipe."] —**hy·drau·li·cal·ly** *adv.*

hy·drau·lic brake *n.* a brake in which force applied to a pedal is transmitted to the brake pads by an enclosed liquid, usually a glycol mixture

hy·drau·lic cou·pling *n.* an arrangement in which two pistons of different sizes are connected by an enclosed fluid that can transmit pressure from one piston to the other

hy·drau·lic press *n.* a device in which a relatively small force applied to a piston results in movement of a larger piston to which it is hydraulically coupled by an enclosed liquid. A hydraulic press is often the key part of machinery that forces materials to flow plastically into a preformed shape.

hy·drau·lic ram *n.* **1.** HYDRAULIC-PRESS PISTON the larger working piston of a hydraulic press **2.** RESERVOIR WATER-LEVEL CONTROLLING DEVICE a device that uses the kinetic energy of a flow of water to raise water to a reservoir that is higher than the water source itself

hy·drau·lics /hī drólliks/ *n.* the study of water or other fluids at rest or in motion, especially with respect to engineering applications (*takes a singular verb*)

hy·dra·zide /hī́drə zīd/ *n.* a compound formed when one of the hydrogen atoms in hydrazine is replaced by a radical containing the CO moiety [Late 19thC. Coined from HYDR- + AZO- + -IDE.]

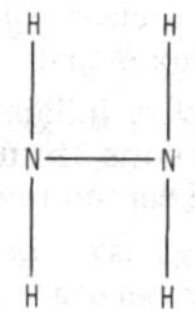

Hydrazine

hy·dra·zine /hī́drə zeen/ *n.* a highly reactive colorless liquid or white crystalline solid made from sodium hypochlorite and ammonia, used in rocket fuel. Formula: $H_2N.NH_2$. [Late 19thC. Coined from HYDR- + AZO- + -INE.]

hy·dra·zo·ic ac·id /hīdrə zō ik-/ *n.* a colorless liquid that is highly toxic and explosive in the presence of oxygen. Formula: HN_3. [*Hydrazoic* coined from HYDR- + AZO- + -IC]

hy·dric /hī́drik/ *adj.* **1.** WITH MUCH WATER containing or using considerable amounts of water **2.** ECOL VERY WET used to describe or relating to an environment that is extremely wet

hy·dride /hī́ drīd/ *n.* a chemical compound formed between hydrogen and a more electropositive atom, e.g., sodium hydride, or via a covalent bond, e.g., boron hydride. Hydrides can also be formed with transition metals such as platinum and palladium.

hy·dril·la /hī drílla/ (*plural* **-las** *or* **-la**) *n.* a plant that grows underwater in large masses and oxygenates the water. Introduced into the southern United States, it has proliferated to such an extent that in some places it chokes fish and blocks water traffic. Genus: *Hydrilla.* [Early 19thC. From modern Latin, genus name, literally "little hydra," from Latin *hydra* (see HYDRA).]

hy·dri·od·ic ac·id /hīdree òddik-/ *n.* a colorless or pale yellow strong acid formed when hydrogen iodide gas dissolves in water [*Hydriodic* coined from HYDR- + IODINE + -IC]

hy·dro /hī́drō/ (*plural* **-dros**) *n.* **1.** HYDROELECTRIC POWER PLANT a power plant that generates electricity using water pressure **2.** HYDROELECTRIC POWER power generated using water pressure **3.** *Can* ELECTRIC POWER electricity from an electric utility ○ *the hydro bill* [Early 20thC. Shortening of HYDROELECTRIC.]

hydro- *prefix.* **1.** water, liquid, moisture ○ *hydrobiology* **2.** hydrogen ○ *hydrocarbon* [From Greek *hudr-*, the stem of *hudōr* "water." Ultimately from the Indo-European word for "water," which is also the ancestor of English *water, undulate, otter,* and *vodka.*]

hy·dro·a·cous·tics /hīdrō ə kóostiks/ *n.* the branch of acoustics that studies how sound travels in water (*takes a singular verb*)

hy·dro·bi·ol·o·gy /hīdrō bī óllәjee/ *n.* the branch of biology that studies aquatic animals and plants — **hy·dro·bi·o·log·i·cal** /hīdrō bī ə lójjik'l/ *adj.* —**hy·dro·bi·ol·o·gist** /hīdrō bī óllәjist/ *n.*

hy·dro·bro·mic ac·id /hīdrə brōmik-/ *n.* a colorless or pale yellow strong acid formed when hydrogen bromide gas is dissolved in water

hy·dro·car·bon /hīdrə kaarbən/ *n.* an organic chemical compound containing only hydrogen and carbon atoms, arranged in rows, rings, or both, and connected by single, double, or triple bonds. Hydrocarbons constitute a very large group including alkanes, alkenes, and alkynes. —**hy·dro·car·bo·na·ceous** /-kaarbə náyshəss/ *adj.* —**hy·dro·car·bon·ic** /-kaar bónnik/ *adj.* —**hy·dro·car·bon·ous** /-kaarbənəss/ *adj.*

hy·dro·cele /hīdrə seel/ *n.* an abnormal accumulation of watery liquid in a body cavity, especially in the sac around the testes. It is a painless condition that can be treated surgically by drainage of the fluid.

hy·dro·cel·lu·lose /hīdrə séllyə lōss/ *n.* a gelatinous substance formed when cellulose is mixed with water, acids, or alkalis, e.g., in the manufacture of paper or rayon

hy·dro·ceph·a·lus /hīdrō séffələss/, **hy·dro·ceph·a·ly** /-séffəlee/ *n.* an abnormal increase of cerebrospinal fluid around the brain, resulting in infants in an enlargement of the head because the bones of the skull are still unfused. The fluid is blocked by a congenital condition or a disease, and can be drained into the abdominal cavity. [Late 17thC. Via modern Latin from, ultimately, Greek *hudōr* "water" + *kephalē* "head."] —**hy·dro·ce·phal·ic** /hīdrō sə fállik/ *adj.* —**hy·dro·ceph·a·loid** /-séffə lòyd/ *adj.* —**hy·dro·ceph·a·lous** /-séffələss/ *adj.*

hy·dro·chlo·ric ac·id /hīdrə kláwrik-/ *n.* a strong colorless acid formed when hydrogen chloride gas dissociates in water, used in industrial and laboratory processes. Hydrochloric acid is also produced in the stomach, where it initiates the digestion of proteins.

hy·dro·chlo·ride /hīdrə kláw rīd/ *n.* a salt formed when hydrochloric acid reacts with an organic base, e.g., aniline

hy·dro·chlo·ro·thi·a·zide /hīdrə kláwrə thī́ ə zīd/ *n.* a drug used in the treatment of fluid retention and high blood pressure

hy·dro·col·loid /hīdrə kó lòyd/ *n.* a substance that forms a gel when mixed with water — **hy·dro·col·loid·al** /hīdrəkə lóyd'l/ *adj.*

hy·dro·cor·al /hīdrə káwrəl/ *n.* a marine multicellular organism that lives in colonies and builds calcareous skeletons within which the animals live. Order: Milleporina and Stylasterina.

hy·dro·cor·ti·sone /hīdrə káwrti sōn, -zōn/ *n.* **1.** PHYSIOL HORMONE ASSOCIATED WITH INFLAMMATION a steroid hormone secreted by the adrenal glands in response to tissue damage causing inflammation. It is important in the stress reaction and in regulating blood sugar and fat deposition. **2.** PHARM HYDROCORTISONE DRUG a synthetic form of hydrocortisone used as a drug to treat inflammatory and allergic conditions and adrenal failure

hy·dro·crack·ing /hīdrō kràking/ *n.* an industrial process in which the action of hydrogen under high pressure fragments long-chain hydrocarbons to produce more volatile compounds, e.g., gasoline and kerosene

hy·dro·cy·an·ic ac·id /hīdrō sī ànnik-/ *n.* a colorless weak acid that smells of almonds, formed when hydrogen cyanide is dissolved in water

hy·dro·dy·nam·ic /hīdrō dī námmik/, **hy·dro·dy·nam·i·cal** /-námmik'l/ *adj.* **1.** OF LIQUIDS' MECHANICAL PROPERTIES relating to the mechanical properties of liquids **2.** MOVED BY LIQUID operated by a moving liquid —**hy·dro·dy·nam·i·cal·ly** *adv.*

hy·dro·dy·nam·ics /hīdrō dī námmiks/ *n.* the area of fluid dynamics that is concerned with the study of liquids (*takes a singular verb*) —**hy·dro·dy·nam·i·cist** /hīdrō dī námmissist/ *n.*

hy·dro·e·lec·tric /hīdrō i léktrik/ *adj.* **1.** GENERATED BY WATER POWER generated by converting the pressure of falling or running water to electricity by means of a turbine coupled to a generator **2.** OF HYDROELECTRIC POWER GENERATION relating to the generation of electricity by means of water pressure — **hy·dro·e·lec·tri·cal·ly** *adv.*

hy·dro·fluor·ic ac·id /hĭdrō fláwrrik-, hĭdrō flàwrik-/ *n.* an extremely poisonous corrosive colorless liquid formed by solution of hydrogen fluoride in water. It is used to etch glass, treat metal surfaces, and clean masonry.

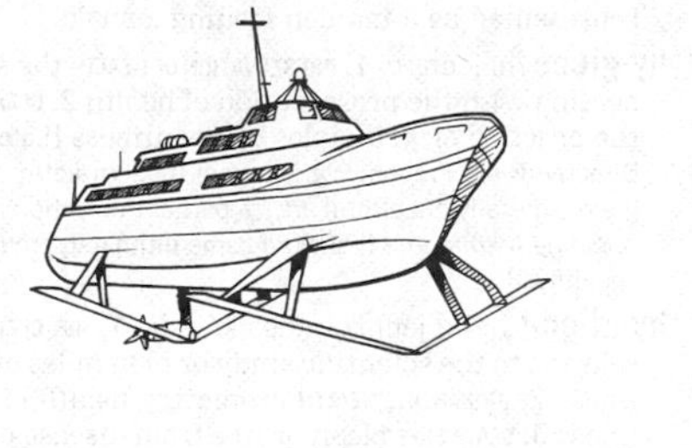

Hydrofoil

hy·dro·foil /hĭdrə fòyl/ *n.* **1.** HIGH-SPEED BOAT a boat with wing-shaped blades attached to struts under the hull that lift the boat out of the water as speed increases **2.** WING-SHAPED BLADE ON HYDROFOIL a wing-shaped blade that lifts a hydrofoil out of the water

hy·dro·form·ing /hĭdrə fàwrming/ *n.* **1.** CHEM ENG CONVERSION OF HYDROCARBONS a high-temperature process in which hydrogen, with other catalysts, causes certain hydrocarbons to break down, lose hydrogen, and rearrange themselves into aromatic or cyclic forms. It is used in the petroleum industry to impart better antiknock properties to gasoline. **2.** METALL METAL SHAPING PROCESS a process in which sheet metal is shaped by a punch forced against a flexible shaped block resting on a fluid-filled bag

hy·dro·gel /hĭdrə jèl/ *n.* a thick fluid like a jelly, formed by the addition of a substance to water

hy·dro·gen /hĭdrəjən/ *n.* a highly reactive colorless gas, the lightest chemical element and the most abundant in the universe, occurring mainly in water and in most organic compounds. Hydrogen is widely used in many industrial processes, especially in the production of ammonia and in the reduction of metal ores to metals. Symbol **H** [Late 18thC. From French *hydrogène*, from Greek *hudōr* "water" + French *-gène* (see -GEN).] —**hy·drog·e·nous** /hī drójjənəss/ *adj.*

hy·drog·e·nase /hī drójjə nàyss, -nàyz/ *n.* an enzyme that catalyzes reduction reactions by hydrogen

hy·dro·gen·ate /hī drójjə nàyt/ (**-at·ed, -at·ing, -ates**) *vt.* to add hydrogen to a compound in a chemical reaction —**hy·dro·gen·a·tion** /hī dròjjə náysh'n/ *n.* —**hy·dro·gen·a·tor** /hī drójjə nàytər/ *n.*

hy·dro·gen bomb *n.* an explosive weapon of mass destruction in which huge amounts of energy are released by the fusion of hydrogen nuclei

hy·dro·gen bond *n.* an electrostatic interaction between molecules of compounds in which hydrogen atoms are bound to electronegative atoms, e.g., oxygen and nitrogen. The attraction between water molecules due to hydrogen bonds accounts for the relatively high boiling point of water.

hy·dro·gen bro·mide *n.* a colorless gas usually made by combination of hydrogen and bromine in the presence of a catalyst such as platinum. It forms hydrobromic acid in water solution. Formula: HBr.

hy·dro·gen car·bon·ate *n.* a salt of carbonic acid in which one hydrogen atom has been replaced, usually by a metal

hy·dro·gen chlo·ride *n.* a colorless fuming corrosive gas made by heating sodium chloride with sulfuric acid or by a combination of hydrogen and chlorine at high temperatures. Hydrogen chloride, which forms hydrochloric acid in water, is used in the manufacture of PVC. Formula: HCl.

hy·dro·gen cy·a·nide *n.* an extremely poisonous colorless liquid or gas with a characteristic smell of almonds that is formed by the reaction between an acid and a metal cyanide. Formula: HCN.

hy·dro·gen em·brit·tle·ment *n.* a process in which a metal is weakened by incorporation of hydrogen in or below its surface, e.g., during plating or etching

hy·dro·gen fluor·ide *n.* a colorless corrosive liquid formed by the action of sulfuric acid on a metal fluoride. Hydrofluoric acid is formed when it dissolves in water. Formula: HF.

hy·dro·gen i·o·dide *n.* a colorless gas formed by direct reaction of hydrogen and iodine in the presence of a catalyst, usually platinum. Formula: HI.

hy·dro·gen i·on *n.* a positively charged ion of hydrogen that is formed by the removal of an electron from a hydrogen atom and is present in solutions of acids in water. The degree to which a compound produces hydrogen ions in solution is measured on the pH scale, 1 being highly acidic, 7 being neutral, and 14 being highly alkaline.

hy·dro·ge·nize /hī drójjə nīz, hĭdrəjə nīz/ (**-nized, -niz·ing, -niz·es**) *vt.* = **hydrogenate** —**hy·dro·ge·ni·za·tion** /hī dròjjəni záysh'n, hĭdrəjəni-/ *n.*

hy·dro·gen·ol·y·sis /hĭdrəjə nóllississ/ *n.* the breaking of a bond in a molecule of an organic compound by the action of hydrogen, accompanied by the addition of a hydrogen atom to each of the fragments

hy·drog·e·nous /hī drójjənəss/ *adj.* containing hydrogen

hy·dro·gen per·ox·ide *n.* a colorless viscous unstable liquid that readily decomposes in water and oxygen. A strong oxidizing agent, it is used as a bleach, as a mild antiseptic, and as a component in rocket fuel. Formula: H_2O_2.

hy·dro·gen sul·fate *n.* a salt containing the ion HSO_4^-, formed when one hydrogen atom is removed from sulfuric acid by reaction with a metal, metal salt, or organic group

hy·dro·gen sul·fide *n.* a colorless flammable poisonous gas with a characteristic smell of rotten eggs that is formed by the action of a mineral acid such as hydrochloric acid on a metal sulfide. North Sea gas contains hydrogen sulfide, and so do volcanic emissions. Formula: H_2S.

hy·dro·gen sul·fite *n.* a salt containing the ion HSO_3^-

hy·dro·gen tar·trate *n.* a salt or ester of tartaric acid, e.g., potassium hydrogen tartrate, that forms deposits in wine vats

hy·dro·ge·ol·ogy /hĭdrō jee óllәjee/ *n.* a branch of geology that studies the movement of subsurface water through rocks, either as underground streams or percolating through porous rocks. Hydrogeology also considers the effect of moving water on rocks, including their erosion. —**hy·dro·ge·o·log·ic** /hĭdrō jee ə lójjik/ *adj.* —**hy·dro·ge·o·log·i·cal** *adj.* —**hy·dro·ge·ol·o·gist** /hĭdrō jee óllәjist/ *n.*

hy·dro·graph /hĭdrə gràf/ *n.* a graph showing the change over time in the amount of water flowing down a river

hy·drog·ra·phy /hī dróggrəfee/ *n.* the scientific study of seas, lakes, and rivers, especially the charting of tides and changes in coastal bathymetry or the measurement and recording of river flow —**hy·drog·ra·pher** /hī dróggrəfər/ *n.* —**hy·dro·graph·ic** /hĭdrə gráffik/ *adj.* —**hy·dro·graph·i·cal·ly** *adv.*

hy·droid /hī dròyd/ *n.* **1.** MARINE INVERTEBRATE ANIMAL a marine invertebrate animal with an internal body cavity that lives in colonies, forming growths like tufts. Order: Hydroida. **2.** POLYP an asexual polyp that is part of the life cycle of hydrozoans [Mid-19thC. Formed from HYDRA.]

hy·dro·ki·net·ic /hĭdrōki néttik, -kī-/, **hy·dro·ki·net·i·cal** /-néttik'l/ *adj.* **1.** OF HYDROKINETICS relating to or involving hydrokinetics **2.** OF FLUID IN MOTION relating to, involving, or typical of fluids in motion

hy·dro·ki·net·ics /hĭdrōki néttiks, -kī-/ *n.* the branch of physics concerned with the scientific study of the properties and behavior of fluids in motion (*takes a singular verb*)

hy·dro·lase /hĭdrə làyss, -làyz/ *n.* an enzyme that controls hydrolysis, e.g., an esterase [Early 20thC. Formed from HYDROLYSIS.]

hy·dro·log·ic cy·cle /hĭdrə lójjik-/, **hy·dro·log·i·cal cy·cle** /hĭdrə lòjjik'l-/ *n.* the water cycle (*technical*)

hy·drol·o·gy /hī drólləjee/ *n.* the scientific study of the properties, distribution, use, and circulation of the water of the earth and the atmosphere in all of its forms —**hy·drol·o·gist** *n.*

hy·drol·y·sate /hī dróllə sàyt/ *n.* a substance produced by hydrolysis

hy·drol·yse *vti.* U.K. = **hydrolyze**

hy·drol·y·sis /hī drólləssiss/ *n.* a chemical reaction in which a compound reacts with water, causing decomposition and the production of two or more other compounds, e.g., the conversion of starch to glucose —**hy·dro·lyt·ic** /hĭdrə líttik/ *adj.* —**hy·dro·lyt·i·cal·ly** *adv.*

hy·dro·lyze /hĭdrə līz/ (**-lyzed, -lyz·ing, -lyz·es**) *vti.* to undergo hydrolysis, or make a substance undergo hydrolysis [Late 19thC. Formed from HYDROLYSIS on the model of ANALYSIS, ANALYZE.] —**hy·dro·lyz·a·ble** *adj.* —**hy·dro·ly·za·tion** /hĭdrəli záysh'n/ *n.*

hy·dro·mag·net·ics /hĭdrō mag néttiks/ *n.* = **magnetohydrodynamics** (*takes a singular verb*) —**hy·dro·mag·net·ic** *adj.*

hy·dro·man·cy /hĭdrə mànsee/ *n.* the attempt to find out about future events or unknown knowledge by studying the appearance or movement of water —**hy·dro·manc·er** *n.* —**hy·dro·man·tic** /hĭdrə mántik/ *adj.*

hy·dro·me·chan·ics /hĭdrō mə kánniks/ *n.* = **hydrodynamics** (*takes a singular verb*) —**hy·dro·me·chan·i·cal** *adj.*

hy·dro·me·du·sa /hĭdrōm dóossə, -dyóo-/ (*plural* **-sae** /hĭdrōmə dóozee, -dóossee/) *n.* a free-swimming marine invertebrate animal, resembling a tiny jellyfish, that is the reproductive stage of a hydroid

hy·dro·mel /hĭdrə mèl/ *n.* a drink made of honey mixed in water. If allowed to ferment, it turns into mead. (*archaic*) [15thC. Via Latin *hydromeli* from Greek *hudromeli*, literally "water honey," from *meli* "honey."]

hy·dro·met·al·lur·gy /hĭdrō mètt'l ùrjee/ *n.* the extraction of metals from ores by treating them with aqueous chemical solutions, including extraction by electrolysis and ion exchange —**hy·dro·met·al·lur·gi·cal** /hĭdrō mètt'l úrjik'l/ *adj.*

hy·dro·me·te·or /hĭdrō meétee ər/ *n.* a weather condition caused by condensation of water in the atmosphere, e.g., rain, snow, or fog —**hy·dro·me·te·or·o·log·i·cal** /hĭdrō meetee ərə lójjik'l/ *adj.* —**hy·dro·me·te·or·ol·o·gist** /-rólləjist/ *n.* —**hy·dro·me·te·or·ol·o·gy** /-rólləjee/ *n.*

hy·drom·e·ter /hī drómmətər/ *n.* a device used to determine the specific gravity, or density, of a liquid, e.g., battery acid. It consists typically of a sealed graduated tube containing a weighted bulb. —**hy·dro·met·ric** /hĭdrə méttrik/ *adj.* —**hy·dro·met·ri·cal·ly** /-kəlee/ *adv.* —**hy·drom·e·try** /hī drómmətree/ *n.*

hy·dro·mor·phic /hĭdrə máwrfik/ *adj.* relating to or typical of a soil that has built up in the presence of excess water

hy·dro·ni·um i·on *n.* the positive ion that is formed by the addition of a proton to a water molecule, usually in solutions of acids. Formula: H_3O^+. [Early 20thC. *Hydronium* coined from HYDRO- + *oxonium*, from OXY- on the model of AMMONIUM.]

hy·drop·a·thy /hī dróppəthee/ *n.* the treatment of injuries or disease by applying water both internally and externally —**hy·dro·path** /hĭdrə pàth/ *n.* —**hy·dro·path·ic** /hĭdrə páthik/ *adj.* —**hy·dro·path·i·cal** /-ik'l/ *adj.* —**hy·dro·path·i·cal·ly** /-kəlee/ *adv.*

hy·dro·per·ox·ide /hĭdrōpə rók sīd/ *n.* an intermediate compound formed during the oxidation of unsaturated organic substances and containing the group -OOH

hy·dro·phane /hĭdrə fàyn/ *n.* a translucent form of opal that has a pearly luster and becomes transparent in water —**hy·droph·a·nous** /hī dróffənəss/ *adj.*

hy·dro·phil·ic /hĭdrə fíllik/ *adj.* dissolving in, absorbing, or mixing easily with water —**hy·dro·phile** /hĭdrə fīl/ *n.* —**hy·dro·phi·lic·i·ty** /hĭdrə fi líssətee/ *n.*

hy·dro·pho·bi·a /hĭdrə fōbee ə/ *n.* **1.** = **rabies 2.** FEAR OF FLUIDS an extremely intense aversion to water, especially the fear of drinking water or other liquids

hy·dro·pho·bic /hĭdrə fōbik/ *adj.* **1.** AFRAID OF WATER relating to or affected by an extreme fear of water **2.** CHEM NOT COMPATIBLE WITH WATER not dissolving in, absorbing, or mixing easily with water —**hy·dro·phobe** /hĭdrəfō bíssətee/ *n.* —**hy·dro·pho·bic·i·ty** /hĭdrə fō bíssətee/ *n.*

hy·dro·phone /hĭdrə fōn/ *n.* an electronic receiver that can pick up sound traveling through water by converting acoustic energy into electromagnetic waves. It is used, e.g., to track submarines.

hy·dro·phyte /hī́drə fīt/ *n.* a plant that will only grow in water or in a very damp environment —**hy·dro·phyt·ic** /hīdrə fíttik/ *adj.*

hy·dro·plane /hī́drə plàyn/ *n.* **1.** FAST BOAT a motorboat designed so that it rises up out of the water at high speed and skims along the surface **2.** = **hydrofoil** *n.* 1 **3.** DIVING PLANE ON SUBMARINE a horizontal diving plane on a submarine, used to control its vertical movement **4.** = **seaplane** ■ *vi.* (**-planed, -plan·ing, -planes**) **1.** SKIM THE SURFACE to skim along on the surface of the water, especially in a hydroplane **2.** SKID ON WET ROAD to skid on a wet road because a film of surface water prevents a vehicle's tires from making firm contact with the road surface

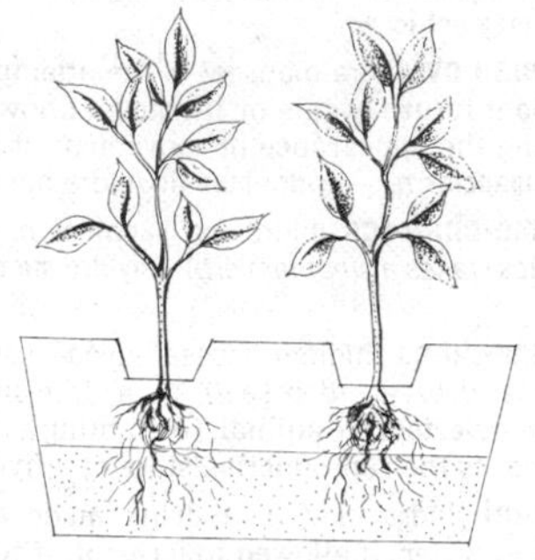

Hydroponics

hy·dro·pon·ics /hīdrə pónniks/ *n.* the growing of plants in a nutrient liquid with or without gravel or another supporting medium (*takes a singular verb*) [Mid-20thC. Coined from HYDRO- + Greek *ponos* "work" + -ICS.] —**hy·dro·pon·ic** *adj.* —**hy·dro·pon·i·cal·ly** *adv.* —**hy·dro·pon·i·cist** *n.* —**hy·dro·pon·ist** /hī dróppənist/ *n.*

hy·dro·pow·er /hī́drə pòwr/ *n.* electric power generated using water power

hy·dro·qui·none /hīdrəkwi nṓn, -kwí nṓn/, **hy·dro·quin·ol** /-àwl/ *n.* a white crystalline compound used as a photographic developer, in paints, in motor oils, and in some medicines. Formula: $C_6H_4(OH)_2$.

hy·dro·scope /hī́drə skṓp/ *n.* an optical instrument for observing objects that are deep beneath the surface of a body of water. It is constructed from a series of mirrors encased in a tube. —**hy·dro·scop·ic** /hīdrə skóppik/ *adj.* —**hy·dro·scop·i·cal** /-k'l/ *adj.* —**hy·dro·scop·i·cal·ly** /-kəlee/ *adv.*

hy·dro·ski /hī́drō skee/ *n.* a hydrofoil on a seaplane, usually ski-shaped and retractable, used to give extra lift on takeoff

hy·dro·sol /hī́drə sàwl/ *n.* a colloidal solution in which the particles are suspended in water [Mid-19thC. Coined from HYDRO- + SOLUTION.] —**hy·dro·sol·ic** /hīdrə sóllik/ *adj.*

hy·dro·space /hī́drə spàyss/ *n.* the area beneath the surface of the seas

hy·dro·sphere /hī́drə sfeer/ *n.* the portion of the earth's surface that is water, including the seas and water in the atmosphere —**hy·dro·spher·ic** /hīdrə sféerik, -sférrik/ *adj.*

hy·dro·stat /hī́drə stàt/ *n.* a device designed to regulate the height of fluid in a column or container

hy·dro·stat·ic /hīdrə státtik/, **hy·dro·stat·i·cal** /-k'l/ *adj.* **1.** OF FLUIDS AT REST relating to, involving, or typical of fluids that are at rest and the forces and pressures they exert **2.** OF HYDROSTATICS relating to, involving, or typical of hydrostatics [Mid-17thC. Origin uncertain: probably from modern Latin *hydrostaticus* or formed from its source Greek *hudrostatēs* "hydrostatic balance," from *statikos* "causing to stand."] —**hy·dro·stat·i·cal·ly** *adv.*

hy·dro·stat·ics /hīdrə státtiks/ *n.* the scientific study of the equilibrium of liquids at rest and the forces and pressures exerted by them (*takes a singular verb*)

hy·dro·tax·is /hīdrə táksiss/ *n.* the response of an organism or cell to the presence of water or moisture, usually detected as movement —**hy·dro·tac·tic** /-táktik/ *adj.*

hy·dro·ther·a·peu·tics /hīdrə therrə pyóotiks/ *n.* the scientific study and theory of the external use of water for healing (*takes a singular verb*) —**hy·dro·ther·a·peu·tic** *adj.*

hy·dro·ther·a·py /hīdrə thérrəpee/ *n.* the treatment of disease by the external use of water, e.g., by exercising weakened limbs in a pool —**hy·dro·ther·a·pist** *n.*

hy·dro·ther·mal /hīdrə thúrm'l/ *adj.* relating to or produced by extremely hot water, as are, e.g., rock formations —**hy·dro·ther·mal·ly** *adv.*

hy·dro·tho·rax /hīdrə tháw ràks/ *n.* an abnormal buildup of fluid in a pleural cavity, e.g., as a result of failing circulation caused by heart disease [Late 18thC. From modern Latin, from Latin *thorax* "chest."] —**hy·dro·tho·rac·ic** /hīdrə thaw rássik/ *adj.*

hy·drot·ro·pism /hī dróttrə pìzzəm/ *n.* movement in a plant, e.g., by roots, toward or away from a source of water —**hy·dro·tro·pic** /hīdrə tróppik/ *adj.* —**hy·dro·tro·pi·cal·ly** /-kəlee/ *adv.*

hy·drous /hī́drəss/ *adj.* **1.** CONTAINING WATER containing water or moisture **2.** MIXED WITH WATER containing or combined chemically with water molecules

hy·drox·ide /hī drók sīd/ *n.* a compound containing the hydroxyl group -OH, specifically an acid or base containing the hydroxyl ion. Formula: OH^-.

hy·drox·ide i·on *n.* = **hydroxyl**

hy·drox·y /hī dróksee/ *adj.* containing one or more hydroxyl groups

hy·drox·y·a·pa·tite /hī dròksee áppə tīt/ *n.* naturally occurring hydrated calcium phosphate, the mineral constituent of bone and enamel. Formula: $Ca_5(PO_4)_3OH$.

hy·drox·yl /hī dróksil/ *n.* the negative ion formed by the attachment of an oxygen atom and a hydrogen atom. Formula: OH^-. [Mid-19thC. Coined from HYDRO- + OXY- + -YL.] —**hy·drox·yl·ic** /hī drok síllik/ *adj.*

hy·drox·yl·a·mine /hī dròksələ meen, hī drok síllə meen, -sə lá meen/ *n.* a colorless crystalline compound that decomposes at room temperature and explodes on heating, used as a reducing agent and in the synthesis of organic molecules. Formula: NH_2OH.

hy·drox·yl·ate /hī dróksə làyt/ (**-at·ed, -at·ing, -ates**) *vt.* to introduce hydroxyl into a compound —**hy·drox·y·la·tion** /hī dròksə láysh'n/ *n.*

hy·drox·yl i·on *n.* = **hydroxyl**

hy·drox·y·pro·line /hī dròksi prṓ leen/ *n.* an amino acid derived from proline residues within protein molecules, occurring in gelatin and collagen

hy·dro·zo·an /hīdrə zṓ ən/ *n.* a marine or freshwater invertebrate animal such as a polyp or jellyfish. Class: Hydrozoa. [Late 19thC. Formed from modern Latin *Hydrozoa*, class name, literally "water animals," from Greek *zōia*, the plural of *zōion* "animal" (source of English *zoology*).]

Hy·drus /hī́drəss/ *n.* a constellation in the southern hemisphere near the south celestial pole

Hyena

hy·e·na /hī éenə/, **hy·ae·na** *n.* a carnivorous scavenging mammal resembling a dog, with a sloping back and loping gait, found in Africa and southern Asia. Family: Hyaenidae. [14thC. Directly or via Old French *hyene* from Latin *hyaena*, from Greek *huaina*, the feminine of *hus* "pig."] —**hy·en·ic** *adj.*

hy·e·tal /hī́ ət'l/ *adj.* relating to rain, or having high rainfall [Mid-19thC. Formed from Greek *huetos* "rain."]

hyeto- *prefix.* rain ○ *hyetograph* [From Greek *huetos*, from *huein* "to rain"]

hy·e·to·graph /hī éttə gràf/ *n.* **1.** RAIN CHART a chart or graph showing the pattern of rainfall in an area **2.** DEVICE THAT MEASURES RAINFALL an instrument that automatically collects rain and measures its amount —**hy·e·to·graph·i·cal·ly** /hī èttə gráffikəlee/ *adv.*

hy·e·tog·ra·phy /hī ə tóggrəfee/ *n.* the scientific study of rainfall, including its distribution and variation over a specific area

Hy·ge·ia /hī jée ə/ *n.* in Greek mythology, the goddess of health. The daughter of Asclepius, she is often represented as a maiden feeding a snake.

hy·giene /hī́ jeen/ *n.* **1.** PRESERVATION OF HEALTH the science dealing with the preservation of health **2.** CLEANLINESS the practice or principles of cleanliness [Late 17thC. Directly or via French *hygiène* from modern Latin *(ars) hygieina*, literally "healthful art," a partial translation of Greek *hugieinē tekhnē*; the first word came ultimately from *hugiēs* "healthy."]

hy·gi·en·ic /hī jénnik, -jéenik/ *adj.* **1.** OF CLEANLINESS relating to the scientific study or principles of cleanliness **2.** PROMOTING HEALTH promoting health or cleanliness **3.** GERM-FREE clean or free from disease-causing microorganisms —**hy·gi·en·i·cal·ly** *adv.*

hy·gi·en·ics /hī jénniks, -jéeniks/ *n.* = **hygiene** *n.* 1 (*takes a singular verb*)

hy·gien·ist /hī jéenist, -jénnist/ *n.* somebody who has studied and become a specialist in the maintenance of hygiene

hygro- *prefix.* moisture, humidity ○ *hygrostat* [From Greek *hugros* "moist." Ultimately from an Indo-European base that is also the ancestor of English *humid*.]

hy·gro·graph /hī́grə gràf/ *n.* an automatic hygrometer that records the humidity of the air

hy·grom·e·ter /hī grómmətər/ *n.* an instrument used to measure humidity —**hy·gro·met·ric** /hīgrə méttrik/ *adj.* —**hy·gro·met·ri·cal·ly** /-kəlee/ *adv.*

hy·groph·il·ous /hī gróffələss/ *adj.* adapted to growing in damp places

hy·gro·phyte /hī́grə fīt/ *n.* PLANTS = **hydrophyte** —**hy·gro·phyt·ic** /hīgrə fíttik/ *adj.*

hy·gro·scope /hī́grə skṓp/ *n.* an instrument that shows changes in the humidity of the air but does not measure the changes

hy·gro·scop·ic /hīgrə skóppik/, **hy·gro·scop·i·cal** /-ik'l/ *adj.* capable of easily absorbing moisture, e.g., from the air —**hy·gro·scop·i·cal·ly** /-kəlee/ *adv.* —**hy·gro·sco·pic·i·ty** /hīgrə skō píssətee/ *n.*

hy·gro·stat /hī́grə stàt/ *n.* = **humidistat**

Hyk·sos /híksōss/ (*plural* **-sos**) *n.* a member of an ancient nomadic Asian group of people, probably of Semitic ancestry, who conquered and ruled Egypt between 1720 B.C. and 1560 B.C. [Early 17thC. Via Greek *Huksōs* from Egyptian *heqa khoswe* "foreign rulers."] —**Hyk·sos** *adj.*

hy·la /hī́lə/ *n.* a tree frog of a genus found all over the world. Genus: *Hyla.* [Mid-19thC. Via modern Latin, genus name, from Greek *hulē* "wood."]

hylo- *prefix.* matter ○ *hylotheism* [From Greek *hulē* "wood, matter"]

hy·lo·mor·phism /hīlə máwr fìzzəm/ *n.* the belief that all material objects are made up of matter, which is only potential, and form, which makes the object an actuality

hy·lo·the·ism /hīlə thée ìzzəm/ *n.* the belief that God and the material world are the same

hy·lo·zo·ism /hīlə zṓ ìzzəm/ *n.* the belief that all matter is living [Late 17thC. Coined from HYLO- + Greek *zōē* "life" + -ISM.] —**hy·lo·zo·ic** /hīlə zṓ ik/ *adj.*

hy·men /hī́mən/ *n.* a thin mucous membrane that completely or partially covers the opening of the vagina [Mid-16thC. Directly or via French from late Latin, from Greek *humēn* "membrane."]

Hy·men *n.* in Greek mythology, the god of marriage, often represented as a youth holding a torch

hy·me·ne·al /hīmə née əl/ *adj.* OF MARRIAGE relating to, involving, or typical of marriage (*literary*) ■ *n.* WEDDING SONG a song or poem celebrating a wedding (*literary*) [Early 17thC. Formed from Latin *hymenaeus* "wedding song, wedding," from Greek *humenaios*, from *Humēn* HYMEN.] —**hy·me·ne·al·ly** *adv.*

hy·me·ni·um /hī méenee əm/ (*plural* **-a** /-ə/ *or* **-ums**) *n.* a layer of spore-bearing structures within or on the surface of the fruiting body of a fungus [Early 19thC. Via modern Latin from Greek *humenion*, literally "small membrane," from *humēn* "membrane" (source of English *hymen*).] —**hy·me·ni·al** *adj.*

hy·me·nop·ter·an /hīmə nóptərən/, **hy·me·nop·ter·on** /-nóptə ròn, -nóptərən/ *n.* an insect such as the wasp, ant, and sawfly that has two pairs of membranous wings and a very thin waist and that lives in socially complex colonies. Order: Hymenoptera. [Mid-19thC. Formed from modern Latin *Hymenoptera*, order name, from the neuter plural of Greek *humenopteros* "membrane-winged," from *humēn* "membrane" + *-pteros* from *pteron* "wing."] —**hy·me·nop·ter·an** *adj.* —**hy·me·nop·ter·ous** *adj.*

Hy·mie /hīmee/ *n.* a highly offensive term for a Jew (*taboo offensive*) [Late 20thC. Alteration of *Hyman*, a Jewish man's name.]

hymn /him/ *n.* **1.** RELIGIOUS SONG a song of praise to God, a god, or a saint **2.** SONG OF PRAISE a song of praise to somebody or something other than a deity ■ *v.* (**hymned, hymn·ing, hymns**) **1.** *vt.* SING IN PRAISE to sing in praise of somebody or something **2.** *vi.* SING HYMNS to sing songs of praise [Pre-12thC. Via Latin *hymnus* from Greek *humnos* "song in praise of gods or heroes," of uncertain origin: perhaps formed from *Humēn* HYMEN.]

hym·nal /hímnəl/ *n.* a book of church hymns

hym·nist /hímnist/ *n.* somebody who composes hymns

hym·no·dy /hímnədee/ (*plural* **-dies**) *n.* **1.** COMPOSING OF HYMNS the composing or singing of hymns **2.** HYMNS COLLECTIVELY hymns collectively, usually a group that share a specific characteristic such as time of composition or use in a particular church [Early 18thC. Via medieval Latin *hymnodia* from Greek *humnōidia* "singing of hymns," from *humnos* "song in praise of gods or heroes" (see HYMN).]

hym·nol·o·gy /him nólləjee/ (*plural* **-gies**) *n.* **1.** STUDY OF HYMNS the study of religious hymns **2.** = **hymnody** —**hym·no·log·ic** /hìmnə lójjik/ *adj.* —**hym·no·log·i·cal** *adj.* —**hym·nol·o·gist** /him nólləjist/ *n.*

hy·oid /hí òyd/ *adj.* OF THE HYOID BONE relating to or invoving the U-shaped hyoid bone ■ *n.* = **hyoid bone** [Early 19thC. Via French *hyoïde* from, ultimately, Greek *huoeidēs* "shaped like the Greek letter upsilon," from *hu* "the letter upsilon."]

hy·oid bone *n.* a U-shaped bone positioned at the base of the tongue and above the thyroid cartilage that supports the tongue and its muscles

hy·o·scine /hí ə seen/ *n.* CHEM = **scopolamine** [Late 19thC. Formed from modern Latin *Hyoscyamus* (see HYOSCYAMINE).]

hy·o·scy·a·mine /hì ə sí ə meen/ *n.* a poisonous alkaloid, resembling atropine and used medicinally in similar ways, that occurs naturally in henbane and belladonna. Formula: $C_{17}H_{23}NO_3$. [Mid-19thC. Formed from modern Latin *Hyoscyamus*, genus name of the henbane, from Greek *huoskuamos*, literally "pig's bean," from the genitive of *hus* "pig" + *kuamos* "bean."]

hyp. *abbr.* **1.** hypotenuse **2.** hypothesis **3.** hypothetical

hyp- *prefix.* = **hypo-** (*used before vowels*)

hyp·a·bys·sal /hìppə bíss'l, hìpə bíss'l/ *adj.* used to describe igneous rocks, especially in the form of dikes or sills, created when molten magma rose to the surface of the earth but solidified before reaching it —**hyp·a·bys·sal·ly** *adv.*

hy·paes·the·sia *n.* U.K. = **hypoesthesia**

hy·pae·thral /hī peethrəl, hi-/, **hy·pe·thral** *adj.* with no roof or a roof that is partly open to the sky, in the style, e.g., of a classical temple [Late 18thC. Formed from Latin *hypaethrus* "in the open air," from Greek *hupaithros*, literally "under the air," from *aithēr* "air" (source of English *ether*).]

hy·pal·lage /hi-, hī pálləjee/ *n.* a figure of speech in which the usual relations of words or phrases are interchanged [Late 16thC. Via late Latin from Greek *hupallagē*, literally "interchange," from *allag-*, the stem of *allassein* "to exchange," from *allos* "other."]

hy·pan·thi·um /hī pánthee əm/ (*plural* **-a** /-ə/) *n.* the flat or cup-shaped area that bears the stamens, petals, and sepals of some plants, e.g., a rose or cherry [Mid-19thC. From modern Latin, literally "structure under the flower," from Greek *anthos* "flower" (source of English *anther*).] —**hy·pan·thi·al** *adj.*

hype[1] /hīp/ *n.* **1.** PUBLICITY greatly exaggerated publicity intended to excite public interest in something such as a movie or theatrical production **2.** SOMEBODY OR SOMETHING OVERPUBLICIZED somebody who or something that is extensively publicized **3.** DECEPTION a deception or dishonest scheme ■ *vt.* (**hyped, hyp·ing, hypes**) **1.** PUBLICIZE to promote somebody or something with intense publicity **2.** ARTIFICIALLY BOOST SALES to boost sales of a pop recording artificially by employing people to buy quantities of it at numerous outlets [Early 20thC. Origin uncertain: partly a back-formation from HYPERBOLE and from slang *hyper* "somebody giving short change" (from HYPER-). First recorded in the senses "instance of short-changing" and "to short-change."]

hype[2] /hīp/ *n.* (*slang*) **1.** HYPODERMIC a hypodermic needle or injection **2.** DRUG ADDICT a drug addict

hyped-up *adj.* highly stimulated or excited, especially by drugs (*slang*) [Early 20thC. *Hyped* formed from a shortening of HYPODERMIC.]

hy·per /hípər/ *adj.* (*informal*) **1.** EXCESSIVELY ACTIVE behaving in an overexcited or hyperactive way **2.** EXCITABLE easily excited, or having a high-strung temperament [Mid-20thC. Shortening of HYPERACTIVE.]

hyper- *prefix.* **1.** over, above, beyond ○ *hyperextension* **2.** excessive, abnormally high ○ *hypertension* [From Greek *huper* "above, beyond." Ultimately from an Indo-European base that is also the ancestor of English *over* and *super.*]

hy·per·a·cid·i·ty /hìpər ə síddətee/ *n.* a condition in which there is abnormal production of stomach acid, usually associated with the formation of a peptic or duodenal ulcer

hy·per·ac·tive /hìpər áktiv/ *adj.* abnormally active, restless, and lacking the ability to concentrate for any length of time, especially as a result of deficit disorder —**hy·per·ac·tion** *n.* —**hy·per·ac·tive·ly** *adv.* —**hy·per·ac·tiv·i·ty** /-ak tívvətee/ *n.*

hy·per·ae·mi·a *n.* U.K. = **hyperemia**

hy·per·aes·the·sia *n.* = **hyperesthesia**

hy·per·bar·ic /hìpər bérrik/ *adj.* relating to, involving, occurring at, or operating at pressures higher than normal [Mid-20thC. Coined from HYPER- + Greek *baros* "heavy" (source of English *barometer*) + -IC.] —**hy·per·bar·i·cal·ly** *adv.*

hy·per·ba·ton /hī púrbə tòn/ *n.* a figure of speech in which the expected word order is inverted for emphasis, e.g., in "you I hate" [Mid-16thC. Via Latin from Greek *huperbaton* "overstepping," from *huperbainein* "to step over," from *bainein* "to step, walk."]

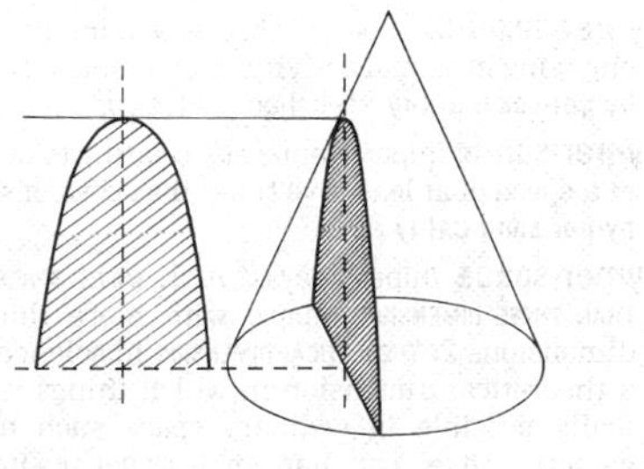

Hyperbola

hy·per·bo·la /hī púrbələ/ (*plural* **-las** *or* **-lae** /hī púrbəlee/) *n.* a conic section formed by a point that moves in a plane so that the difference in its distance from two fixed points in the plane remains constant [Mid-17thC. Via modern Latin from Greek *huperbolē* "excess" (see HYPERBOLE).]

hy·per·bo·le /hī púrbəlee/ *n.* deliberate and obvious exaggeration used for effect, e.g., "I could eat a million of these" [15thC. Via Latin from Greek *huperbolē* "excess," literally "overthrow," from *ballein* "to throw."]

hy·per·bol·ic /hìpər bóllik/, **hy·per·bol·i·cal** /-ik'l/ *adj.* **1.** OF HYPERBOLA relating to, involving, or typical of a hyperbola **2.** OF GEOMETRIC SYSTEM produced by or relating to a geometric system in which two lines can pass through any point in a plane without intersecting a specific line in the same plane **3.** OF HYPERBOLIC FUNCTION connected with or relating to a hyperbolic function **4.** OF HYPERBOLE relating to, involving, or typical of hyperbole —**hy·per·bol·i·cal·ly** *adv.*

hy·per·bol·ic func·tion *n.* any of six functions analogous to trigonometric functions but related to a hyperbola rather than a circle. Hyperbolic functions include the hyperbolic sine, hyperbolic cosine, hyperbolic tangent, hyperbolic cotangent, hyperbolic secant, and hyperbolic cosecant.

hy·per·bo·lize /hī púrbə līz/ (**-lized, -liz·ing, -liz·es**) *vti.* to use deliberate and obvious exaggeration for effect, or describe something in obviously exaggerated terms

hy·per·bo·loid /hī púrbə lòyd/ *n.* a mathematical surface whose sections parallel to one coordinate plane form ellipses and those parallel to the other two coordinate planes form hyperbolas —**hy·per·bo·loid·al** /hī pùrbə lóyd'l/ *adj.*

hy·per·bo·re·an /hìpər báwree ən/ *adj.* **1.** OF FAR NORTHERN REGIONS relating to, typical of, or in the far northern regions **2.** OF ARCTIC PEOPLES relating to or typical of peoples who live in the Arctic [Late 16thC. From late Latin *hyperboreanus*, from Latin *hyperboreus*, from Greek *huperbore(i)os*, from *boreios* "northern" or *Boreas* "north wind."]

Hy·per·bo·re·an *n.* in Greek legend, a member of a people who lived beyond the north wind in a land that was always sunny and warm

hy·per·cal·ce·mia /hìpər kal seemee ə/ *n.* an abnormally high amount of calcium in the blood

hy·per·cap·ni·a /hìpər kápnee ə/ *n.* an abnormally high level of carbon dioxide in the blood [Early 20thC. From modern Latin, literally "condition of excessive smoke," from Greek *kapnos* "smoke."] —**hy·per·cap·nic** *adj.*

hy·per·charge /hípər chaarj/ *n.* a quantized property of elementary particles that is calculated by adding together a particle's baryon number and its strangeness [Mid-20thC. Contraction of *hyperonic charge* (*hyperonic* being formed from HYPERON).]

hy·per·cho·les·ter·ol·e·mi·a /hìpərkə lestərə leemee ə/ *n.* an abnormally high level of cholesterol in the blood —**hy·per·cho·les·ter·ol·em·ic** /hìpərkə lestərə leemik/ *adj.*

hy·per·cor·rect /hìpərkə rékt/ *adj.* **1.** EXCESSIVELY CORRECT too greatly concerned about correctness **2.** SHOWING HYPERCORRECTION showing or being the result of hypercorrection —**hy·per·cor·rect·ly** *adv.* —**hy·per·cor·rect·ness** *n.*

hy·per·cor·rec·tion /hìpərkə rékshən/ *n.* a grammatical mistake or mispronunciation made by correcting something that is not actually wrong, e.g., saying "between you and I" instead of "between you and me"

hy·per·crit·i·cal /hìpər kríttik'l/ *adj.* criticizing somebody or something too severely or too much —**hy·per·crit·i·cal·ly** *adv.* —**hy·per·crit·i·cism** /hìpər krítti sìzzəm/ *n.*

hy·per·cube /hípər kyoob/ *n.* a figure in four or more dimensions with sides that are all of the same length and angles that are all right angles

hy·per·e·mi·a /hìpə reemee ə/ *n.* an abnormally high level of blood in some part of the body —**hy·per·e·mic** *adj.*

hy·per·es·the·sia /hìpərə stheezhə/, **hy·per·aes·the·sia** *n.* an abnormally heightened sensitivity of some part of the body, e.g., the skin, or any of the senses [Mid-19thC. From modern Latin, literally "condition of extreme sensation," from Greek *aisthēsis* "sensation."] —**hy·per·es·thet·ic** /hìpərə sthéttik/ *adj.*

hy·per·eu·tec·tic /hìpəryoo téktik/, **hy·per·eu·tec·toid** /-tòyd/ *adj.* used to describe a compound or alloy that contains a minor component in a higher proportion than in the mixture of the same elements that has the lowest melting point

hy·per·ex·ten·sion /hìpərik sténshən/ *n.* the movement of a limb beyond its normal range —**hy·per·ex·tend** *vt.* —**hy·per·ex·tend·ed** *adj.*

hy·per·fine struc·ture /hípər fìn-/ *n.* the splitting of lines in a spectrum into two or more closely spaced fine lines, caused by magnetic interactions within atoms

hy·per·fo·cal dis·tance /hìpər fōk'l-/ *n.* the distance between a camera lens and the closest object that is in focus when the lens is focused at infinity

hy·per·ga·my /hī púrgəmee/ *n.* a custom in some societies that requires a woman to marry a man of a higher social class than the one to which she belongs

hy·per·gly·ce·mi·a /hìpər glī seemee ə/ *n.* an abnormally high level of sugar in the blood. = **hyperglycemia** —**hy·per·gly·ce·mic** *adj.*

hy·per·gol·ic /hìpər góllik/ *adj.* used to describe a rocket propellant that ignites on contact with an oxidizer [Mid-20thC. Coined from German *Hypergol* "hypergolic fuel," from *hyper-* "hyper-" + *erg-* "work" (from Greek *ergon*) + *-ol* (see -OL).] —**hy·per·gol** /hīpər gàwl/ *n.* —**hy·per·gol·i·cal·ly** /hīpər góllikəlee/ *adv.*

hy·per·hi·dro·sis /hīpər hī drṓsiss/ *n.* excessive sweating, either generalized or localized to a particular part of the body

hy·per·i·cum /hī pérrikəm/ *n.* an herbaceous plant that grows in temperate regions, e.g., St. John's wort. Genus: *Hypericum.* [15thC. Via Latin, genus name, from Greek *hupereikon*, from *huper* "over" + *ereikē* "heath, heather."]

hy·per·in·fla·tion /hīpərin fláysh'n/ *n.* very high and rapid monetary inflation, or the period during which this occurs —**hy·per·in·fla·tion·ar·y** *adj.*

hy·per·in·su·lin·ism /hīpər ínsələ nìzzəm/ *n.* an abnormally high level of insulin in the blood, causing hypoglycemia

Hy·pe·ri·on /hī péeree ən/ *n.* **1.** ASTRON **MOON OF SATURN** the seventh moon of Saturn, discovered in 1848 **2.** MYTHOL **TITAN** in Greek mythology, one of the Titans. He was the son of Gaea and Uranus and the father of Helios, god of the sun, Selene, goddess of the moon, and Eos, goddess of the dawn.

hy·per·ir·ri·ta·bil·i·ty /hīpər irrətə bíllətee/ *n.* an abnormally extreme response to stimuli —**hy·per·ir·ri·ta·ble** /hīpər éerətəb'l/ *adj.*

hy·per·ker·a·to·sis /hīpər kerrə tṓsiss/ *n.* an excessive thickening of the outer layer of the skin —**hy·per·ker·a·tot·ic** /-tóttik/ *adj.*

hy·per·ki·ne·sia /hīpərki néezhə/, **hy·per·ki·ne·sis** /-néessiss/ *n.* **1. ABNORMAL MOVEMENT** abnormally increased movement in a muscle, e.g., in a spasm **2. HYPERACTIVITY** excessive activity in children, e.g., those affected by attention deficit disorder [Mid-19thC. *Hyperkinesis*, literally "extreme movement," coined from HYPER- + Greek *kinēsis* "movement" (see KINESIS); *hyperkinesia*, coined from HYPERKINESIS + -IA.] —**hy·per·ki·net·ic** /-néttik/ *adj.*

hy·per·link /hīpər lìngk/ *n.* a word, symbol, image, or other element in a hypertext document that links to another such element in the same document or in another hypertext document. The hyperlink is activated with a mouse click.

hy·per·li·pe·mi·a /hīpərli péemee ə/ *n.* an excessive level of fats or lipids in the blood —**hy·per·li·pe·mic** *adj.*

hy·per·mar·ket /hīpər maarkət/ *n.* a very large self-service store that sells products usually sold in department stores as well as those sold in supermarkets, e.g., clothes, hardware, electrical goods, and food [Late 20thC. Translation of French *hypermarché*, from *marché* "market," from Latin *mercatus* (see MARKET).]

hy·per·me·di·a /hīpər méedee ə/ *n.* a hypertext system that supports the linking of graphics, audio and video elements, and text. The World Wide Web has many aspects of a complete hypermedia system.

hy·per·me·ter /hī púrmətər/ *n.* a line or metric foot of poetry that has one or more syllables in addition to those usually occurring in a metric foot or completed line of verse [Mid-17thC. Via late Latin *hypermetrus* from Greek *hupermetros* "beyond measure," from *metron* "measure."] —**hy·per·met·ric** /hīpər méttrik/ *adj.* —**hy·per·met·ri·cal** *adj.*

hy·per·me·tro·pi·a /hīpərmə trṓpee ə/, **hy·per·met·ro·py** /-méttrəpee/ *n.* = **hyperopia** (*technical*) [Mid-19thC. From modern Latin, formed from Greek *hupermetros* "beyond measure," from *metron* "measure" (see METER).] —**hy·per·me·tro·pic** /hīpərmə tróppik/ *adj.* —**hy·per·me·tro·pi·cal** *adj.*

hy·perm·ne·sia /hīpərm néezhə/ *n.* an unusually powerful ability to remember exactly, sometimes a symptom of a psychiatric disorder [Mid-19thC. From modern Latin, literally "condition of extreme memory," from Greek *mnēsis* "memory."] —**hy·perm·ne·sic** /hīpərm néezik/ *adj.*

hy·per·nym /hīpərnim/ *n.* LING = **superordinate** *n.* 1

hy·per·on /hīpə ròn/ *n.* a kind of baryon, a comparatively massive elementary particle that may be unstable or partially stable and is short-lived [Mid-20thC. Coined from HYPER- + -ON.]

hy·per·o·pi·a /hīpə rṓpee ə/ *n.* far-sightedness (*technical*) —**hy·per·ope** /hīpə rōp/ *n.* —**hy·per·o·pic** /hīpə róppik/ *adj.*

hy·per·os·to·sis /hīpə ro stṓsiss/ *n.* an abnormal growth or thickening of bone [Mid-19thC. From modern Latin, literally "condition of excessive bone," from Greek *osteon* "bone" (source of English *osteo-*).] —**hy·per·os·tot·ic** /hīpə ro stóttik/ *adj.*

hy·per·par·a·site /hīpər pèrrə sìt/ *n.* a parasite living on another parasite —**hy·per·par·a·sit·ic** /hīpər perrə síttik/ *adj.* —**hy·per·par·a·sit·ism** /hīpər pérrəsi tìzzəm, -pérrə sī-/ *n.*

hy·per·par·a·thy·roid·ism /hīpər perrə thī ròy dìzzəm/ *n.* an abnormally high level of parathyroid hormone in the body, causing various disorders including kidney damage

hy·per·pha·gia /hīpər fáyjə/ *n.* a condition in which somebody compulsively overeats over a long period —**hy·per·phag·ic** /-fájjik/ *adj.*

hy·per·phys·i·cal /hīpər fízzik'l/ *adj.* not governed by the natural laws of physics —**hy·per·phys·i·cal·ly** *adv.*

hy·per·pi·tu·i·ta·rism /hīpərpi tóo itə rìzzəm/ *n.* excessively high activity of the pituitary gland, sometimes causing abnormal bodily growth —**hy·per·pi·tu·i·tar·y** /-tóo i tèrree/ *adj.*

hy·per·plane /hīpər plàyn/ *n.* a figure in hyperspace that is the three-dimensional equivalent of a plane in ordinary space

hy·per·pla·sia /hīpər pláyzhə/ *n.* abnormal growth in a part of the body, caused by an excessive multiplication of cells —**hy·per·plas·tic** /-plástik/ *adj.*

hy·per·ploid /hīpər plòyd/ *adj.* having an extra chromosome or section of a chromosome, e.g., in Down syndrome, in which there is an extra copy or segment of chromosome 21 —**hy·per·ploi·dy** *n.*

hy·perp·ne·a /hīpər née ə, -pərp-/ *n.* unusually deep or fast breathing, e.g., after physical exertion [Mid-19thC. From modern Latin, literally "extreme breathing," from Greek *pnoē* "breathing."] —**hy·perp·ne·ic** *adj.*

hy·per·py·rex·i·a /hīpər pī réksee ə/ *n.* a very high fever [Late 19thC. From modern Latin, literally "extreme fever," from *pyrexia* "fever" (see PYREXIA).] —**hy·per·py·ret·ic** /-réttik/ *adj.* —**hy·per·py·rex·i·al** /-réksee əl/ *adj.*

hy·per·sen·si·tive /hīpər sénsitiv/ *adj.* **1. EASILY UPSET** very easily upset or offended **2.** MED **SUSCEPTIBLE** easily affected by a drug, allergen, or other agent —**hy·per·sen·si·tive·ness** *n.* —**hy·per·sen·si·tiv·i·ty** /-sensi tívvətee/ *n.*

hy·per·sex·u·al /hīpər sékshoo əl/ *adj.* interested in or engaging in sexual activity to an abnormal extent —**hy·per·sex·u·al·i·ty** /-sekshoo állətee/ *n.*

hy·per·son·ic /hīpər sónnik/ *adj.* relating to or moving at a speed of at least five times the speed of sound —**hy·per·son·i·cal·ly** *adv.*

hy·per·space /hīpər spàyss/ *n.* **1.** MATH **SPACE OF MORE THAN THREE DIMENSIONS** space with more than three dimensions **2. THEORETICAL DIMENSION** in science fiction, a theoretical dimension in which things not physically possible in ordinary space such as intergalactic travel can happen —**hy·per·spa·tial** /hīpər spáysh'l/ *adj.*

hy·per·sthene /hīpər sthèen/ *n.* a green, brown, or black pyroxene mineral, consisting of silicate of magnesium and iron [Early 19thC. From French *hypersthène*, literally "extremely strong (mineral)," from Greek *sthenos* "strength."] —**hy·per·sthen·ic** /hīpər sthénnik/ *adj.*

hy·per·sur·face /hīpər sùrfəss/ *n.* a mathematical surface in hyperspace, analogous to a surface in three-dimensional space

hy·per·ten·sion /hīpər ténshən/ *n.* **1. HIGH BLOOD PRESSURE** abnormally high blood pressure **2. ARTERIAL DISEASE** arterial disease accompanied by high blood pressure

hy·per·text /hīpər tèkst/ *n.* a system of storing images, text, and other computer files that allows direct links to related text, images, sound, and other data

hy·per·text mark·up lan·guage *n.* the markup language used for creating documents on the World Wide Web

hy·per·text trans·fer pro·to·col *n.* the client/server protocol that defines how messages are formatted and transmitted on the World Wide Web

hy·per·ther·mi·a /hīpər thúrmee ə/ *n.* abnormally high body temperature, especially when induced for therapeutic reasons [Late 19thC. From modern Latin, literally "condition of extreme heat," from Greek *thermē* "heat."] —**hy·per·ther·mal** *adj.* —**hy·per·ther·mic** *adj.*

hy·per·thy·roid·ism /hīpər thī ròy dìzzəm/ *n.* **1. EXCESSIVE THYROID HORMONES** the overproduction of thyroid hormones at dangerously high levels **2. THYROID CONDITION** the condition in which basal metabolism increases as a result of overactivity of the thyroid gland —**hy·per·thy·roid** *adj.*

hy·per·ton·ic /hīpər tónnik/ *adj.* **1.** MED **EXCESSIVELY TENSE** used to describe a body part, e.g., a muscle or artery, that is under abnormally high tension **2.** CHEM **HAVING HIGHER OSMOTIC PRESSURE** having a higher osmotic pressure than another fluid —**hy·per·to·ni·a** /-tō níssətee/ *n.* —**hy·per·to·nic·i·ty** /-tṓnee ə/ *n.*

hy·per·tro·phy /hī púrtrəfee/ *n.* **1.** BIOL **ENLARGEMENT BY CELL GROWTH** a growth in size of an organ through an increase in the size, rather than the number, of its cells **2. UNNECESSARY COMPLEXITY** exaggerated or unnecessary growth or complexity ■ *vti.* (**-phied, -phy·ing, -phies**) BIOL **GET BIGGER BY CELL GROWTH** to grow larger through an increase in the size, rather than the number, of cells —**hy·per·tro·phic** /hīpər tróffik/ *adj.*

hy·per·ven·ti·late /hīpər vént'l àyt/ (**-lated, -lat·ing, -lates**) *vi.* to breathe unusually deeply or rapidly because of anxiety or organic disease and in excess of the body's requirements, causing too much loss of carbon dioxide

hy·per·ven·ti·la·tion /hīpər vent'l áysh'n/ *n.* unusually deep or rapid breathing, caused by extreme anxiety or an organic disease, that leads to loss of carbon dioxide from the blood and often faintness

hy·per·vi·ta·min·o·sis /hīpər vītəmə nṓssiss/ *n.* a condition in which abnormal effects are caused by taking in too much of one or more vitamins

hy·pe·thral /hi péethrəl/ *adj.* = **hypaethral** (*technical*)

hy·pha /hīfə/ (*plural* **-phae** /hīfee/) *n.* a threadlike part of the vegetative portion of a fungus [Mid-19thC. Via modern Latin from Greek *huphē* "web."] —**hy·phal** *adj.*

hy·phen /hīfən/ *n.* **DASH SHOWING WORD BREAK** a punctuation mark (-) used at the end of a line when a word must be divided, or to link elements in a compound word or phrase ■ *vt.* (**-phened, -phen·ing, -phens**) = **hyphenate** [Early 17thC. Via late Latin from late Greek *huphen* "sign joining two syllables or words" (literally "under one"), from, ultimately, *hupo* HYPO- + *hen*, the neuter of *heis* "one."]

hy·phen·ate /hīfə nàyt/ (**-at·ed, -at·ing, -ates**) *vt.* to separate or join words or parts of words using a hyphen —**hy·phen·a·tion** /hīfə náysh'n/ *n.*

hy·phen·at·ed /hīfə nàytəd/ *adj.* **1. WITH HYPHEN** split or joined by a hyphen **2. BELONGING TO TWO CATEGORIES** belonging to a group of people identified in two ways that may be joined as one term

hypn- *prefix.* = **hypno-** (*used before vowels*)

hyp·na·gog·ic /hìpnə gójjik/, **hyp·no·gog·ic** *adj.* in or relating to the state of drowsiness immediately before sleep [Late 19thC. From French *hypnagogique*, literally "of leading to sleep," from Greek *hupno-* HYPNO- + *agōgos* "leading" (from *agein* "to lead"; see AGONY).]

hyp·na·gog·ic im·age *n.* something of the nature of hallucination seen or imagined by somebody just before falling asleep

hypno- *prefix.* **1.** sleep ○ *hypnopompic* **2.** hypnosis ○ *hypnoanalysis* [From Greek *hupnos*. Ultimately from an Indo-European word meaning "to sleep," which is also the ancestor of English *soporific* and *insomnia*.]

hyp·no·a·nal·y·sis /hìpnō ə nálləssiss/ (*plural* **-ses** /-sèez/) *n.* psychoanalysis carried out on people who are in a state of hypnosis —**hyp·no·an·a·lytic** /hìpnō annə líttik/ *adj.*

hyp·no·gen·e·sis /hìpnō jénnəssiss/ *n.* the process of inducing sleep or a state of hypnosis —**hyp·no·ge·net·ic** /hìpnōjə néttik/ *adj.* —**hyp·no·ge·net·i·cal·ly** /-kəlee/ *adv.*

hyp·no·gog·ic *adj.* = **hypnagogic**

hyp·noid /híp nòyd/, **hyp·noi·dal** /hip nóyd'l/ *adj.* relating to, involving, or resembling sleep or hypnosis

hyp·nol·o·gy /hip nólləjee/ *n.* the scientific study of sleep or hypnosis —**hyp·no·log·ic** /hìpnə lójjik/ *adj.* —**hyp·nol·o·gist** /hip nólləjist/ *n.*

hyp·no·pe·di·a /hìpnə péedee ə/ *n.* sleep-learning (*technical*) [Mid-20thC. Coined from HYPNO- + Greek *paideia* "education" (source of English *encyclopedia*).]

hyp·no·pom·pic /hìpnə pómpik/ *adj.* involving, typical of, or in the state between sleeping and waking [Early 20thC. Coined from HYPNO- + Greek *pompē* "a sending away" (source of English *pomp*) + -IC.]

Hyp·nos /híp nòss/ *n.* in Greek mythology, the god of sleep, and the father of Morpheus, god of dreams [From Greek *Hupnos*, literally "sleep"]

hyp·no·sis /hip nóssiss/ (*plural* **-ses** /-seez/) *n.* **1.** SLEEPLIKE CONDITION a sleeplike condition that can be artificially induced in people, in which they can respond to questions and are very susceptible to suggestions from the hypnotist **2.** PUTTING PEOPLE IN SLEEPLIKE CONDITION the technique or practice of inducing a state of hypnosis in people

hyp·no·ther·a·py /hìpnō thérrəpee/ *n.* the use of hypnosis in treating illness, e.g., in dealing with physical pain or psychological problems —**hyp·no·ther·a·pist** *n.*

hyp·not·ic /hip nóttik/ *adj.* **1.** OF SLEEP OR HYPNOSIS relating to, involving, or producing sleep or hypnosis **2.** SUSCEPTIBLE TO HYPNOSIS susceptible to being hypnotized **3.** FASCINATING so fascinating that the attention of people watching or listening is absorbed completely (*informal*) ■ *n.* **1.** SOMETHING CAUSING SLEEP a drug or other agent that causes sleep or drowsiness **2.** SOMEBODY EASILY HYPNOTIZED somebody who is susceptible to being hypnotized [Early 17thC. Via French *hypnotique* from, ultimately, Greek *hupnōtikos* "putting to sleep," from *hupnoun* "to put to sleep," from *hupnos* "sleep."] —**hyp·not·i·cal·ly** *adv.*

hyp·no·tism /hípnə tìzzəm/ *n.* **1.** = **hypnosis** *n.* 2 **2.** THEORY OF HYPNOSIS the theory and practice of hypnotizing people [Mid-19thC. Shortening of *neuro-hypnotism*.] —**hyp·no·tist** *n.*

hyp·no·tize /hípnə tìz/ (**-tized, -tiz·ing, -tiz·es**) *vt.* **1.** PUT SOMEBODY INTO HYPNOSIS to put somebody into the sleeplike state of hypnosis **2.** FASCINATE to fascinate or charm somebody utterly —**hyp·no·tiz·a·bil·i·ty** /hìpnə tìzə bíllətee/ *n.* —**hyp·no·tiz·a·ble** /hípnə tìzəb'l, hìpnə tíz-/ *adj.* —**hyp·no·ti·za·tion** /hìpnəti záysh'n/ *n.* —**hyp·no·tiz·er** /hípnə tìzər/ *n.*

hy·po[1] /hípō/ *n.* (*plural* **-pos**) HYPODERMIC SYRINGE a hypodermic syringe or injection (*informal*) ■ *vt.* (**-poed, -po·ing, -pos**) GET SOMEBODY OR SOMETHING MOVING to stimulate somebody or something to action in order to achieve some purpose or goal (*dated informal*) [Early 20thC. Shortening of HYPODERMIC.]

hy·po[2] /hípō/ *n.* sodium thiosulfate, used in photographic processing as a fixing agent (*informal*) [Mid-20thC. Shortening of *hyposulfite*, another name for thiosulfate.]

hypo- *prefix.* **1.** under, below ○ *hypodermis* **2.** abnormally low ○ *hypotonia* **3.** in a lower state of oxidation [From Greek *hupo*. Ultimately from an Indo-European word meaning "under," which is also the ancestor of English *up*, *above*, and *opal*.]

hy·po·a·cid·i·ty /hìpō ə síddətee/ *n.* an abnormally low level of acidity, especially in the stomach

hy·po·al·ler·gen·ic /hìpō allər jénnik/ *adj.* not likely to cause an allergic reaction

hy·po·blast /hípə blàst/ *n.* the inner germ layer of an embryo, which develops into the endoderm —**hy·po·blas·tic** /hìpə blástik/ *adj.*

hy·po·cal·ce·mi·a /hìpō kal séemee ə/ *n.* an abnormally low level of calcium in the blood —**hy·po·cal·ce·mic** *adj.*

hy·po·cen·ter /hípə sèntər/ *n.* ARMS = **ground zero** —**hy·po·cen·tral** /hípə séntrəl/ *adj.*

hy·po·chlo·rite /hìpə kláw rìt/ *n.* a salt or ester of hypochlorous acid

hy·po·chlo·rous ac·id /hìpə klàwrəss-/ *n.* a weak unstable greenish-yellow acid that occurs only in solution or in its salts, formed when chlorine dissolves in water. It is commonly used in bleach and disinfectants. Formula: HOCl.

hy·po·chon·dri·a /hìpə kóndree ə/ *n.* IMAGINED ILLNESS an abnormal, usually long-term preoccupation with health and bodily sensations, accompanied by a deluded conviction of having a serious disease without objective evidence ■ plural of **hypochondrium** [Mid-16thC. Via late Latin (plural) "upper abdomen," formerly believed to be the seat of melancholy, from, ultimately, Greek *hupokhondrios*, literally "under the cartilage of the breastbone," from *khondros* "cartilage."]

hy·po·chon·dri·ac /hìpə kóndree àk/ *n.* PSYCHOL SOMEBODY WITH IMAGINARY ILLNESS somebody who is excessively preoccupied with health and persistently believes that he or she is ill or in danger of becoming ill ■ *adj.* **1.** PSYCHOL BELIEVING IN NONEXISTENT ILLNESS excessively preoccupied with health and persistently believing in a nonexistent illness, or relating to the attitudes or state of mind of somebody with this condition **2.** ANAT OF THE HYPOCHONDRIUM relating to, involving, or typical of the hypochondrium —**hy·po·chon·dri·a·cal** /hìpəkən drí ək'l/ *adj.* —**hy·po·chon·dri·a·cal·ly** *adv.*

hy·po·chon·dri·a·sis /hìpəkən drí əssiss/ (*plural* **-as·es** /-seez/) *n.* = **hypochondria** *n.*

hy·po·chon·dri·um /hìpə kóndree əm/ (*plural* **-a** /-dree ə/) *n.* the area of the upper abdomen on either side of the epigastrium below the lower ribs [Mid-17thC. Back-formation from HYPOCHONDRIA (which was originally a plural form).]

hy·poc·o·rism /hì pókə rìzzəm, hìpə káw-/ *n.* **1.** PET NAME a pet name, especially a diminutive or abbreviated form of somebody's full name (*formal*) **2.** USE OF PET NAME the use of a pet name to address somebody, instead of his or her full name [Early 16thC. Via late Latin *hypocorisma* from Greek *hupokorisma*, from *hupokorizesthai* "to play the child," from, ultimately, *korē* "child."] —**hy·po·co·ris·tic** /hìpəkə rístik/ *adj.* —**hy·po·co·ris·ti·cal** *adj.* —**hy·po·co·ris·ti·cal·ly** *adv.*

hy·po·cot·yl /hìpə kòtt'l/ *n.* the part of an embryo plant lying between its cotyledons and its radicle [Late 19thC. Coined from HYPO- + COTYLEDON.] —**hy·po·cot·y·lous** /hìpə kótt'ləss/ *adj.*

hy·poc·ri·sy /hi pókrəssee/ (*plural* **-sies**) *n.* **1.** FEIGNED HIGH PRINCIPLES the false claim to or pretense of having admirable principles, beliefs, or feelings ○ *It would be sheer hypocrisy for them to turn around and do what they criticize in others.* **2.** HYPOCRITICAL ACT an act or instance of hypocrisy ○ *After his hypocrisies became widely known, he decided not to run for reelection.* [12thC. Via Old French *ypocrisie* from, ultimately, Greek *hupokrisis* "acting a part," from *hupokrinesthai* "to dispute subordinately, act a part," literally "to separate under," from *krinein* "to separate."]

hyp·o·crite /híppəkrit/ *n.* somebody who gives a false appearance of having admirable principles, beliefs, or feelings ○ *nothing but a bunch of hypocrites* [12thC. Via Old French *ypocrite* from, ultimately, Greek *hupokritēs* "actor, pretender," from *hupokrinesthai* (see HYPOCRISY).]

hy·po·crit·i·cal /hìppə kríttik'l/ *adj.* showing, originating from or of the nature of hypocrisy ○ *It would be hypocritical of me to congratulate you on defeating me.* —**hyp·o·crit·i·cal·ly** *adv.*

hy·po·cy·cloid /hìpə sí klòyd/ *n.* a curve traced by a point on the circumference of a circle as it rolls along the inside circumference of another circle —**hy·po·cy·cloid·al** /-klóyd'l/ *adj.*

hy·po·derm *n.* = **hypodermis**

hy·po·der·mal /hìpə dúrm'l/ *adj.* **1.** OF HYPODERMIS relating to the layer of fatty tissue (**hypodermis**) beneath the skin **2.** UNDER THE SKIN located beneath the skin

hy·po·der·mic /hìpə dúrmik/ *adj.* ANAT INVOLVING AREA BENEATH SKIN relating to or involving the area of tissue lying beneath the skin ■ *n.* INJECTION OR NEEDLE USED a hypodermic injection, needle, or syringe (*informal*) [Mid-19thC. Coined from HYPO- + Greek *derma* "skin" (source of English *-derm*) + -IC.] —**hy·po·der·mi·cal·ly** *adv.*

hy·po·der·mic in·jec·tion *n.* an injection into tissue under the skin

hy·po·der·mic nee·dle *n.* **1.** NEEDLE FOR INJECTIONS a thin hollow needle used with a syringe, suitable for administering hypodermic injections **2.** SYRINGE COMPLETE WITH NEEDLE a hypodermic syringe to which a needle has been fitted (*informal*)

hy·po·der·mic sy·ringe *n.* a plastic or glass syringe to which a thin hollow needle is attached, used to inject medicine under the skin or to withdraw fluids, especially blood, from under the skin

hy·po·der·mis /hìpə dúrmiss/, **hy·po·derm** /hípə dùrm/ *n.* **1.** ANAT TISSUE UNDER SKIN the layer of fatty tissue beneath the skin **2.** ZOOL SKIN BENEATH ANIMAL'S SHELL the epidermis of some animals, e.g., arthropods, that secretes a shell or other outer covering **3.** BOT CELLS UNDER PLANT SURFACE the usually supportive and protective layer of cells immediately under the outer covering of a plant [19thC. Coined from HYPO- + *-dermis*, on the model of EPIDERMIS.]

hy·po·es·the·sia /hìpō is théezhə/, **hy·pes·the·sia** /hìppə sthéezhee ə/ *n.* an abnormally reduced sensitivity to touch [Late 19thC. From modern Latin, literally "condition of sensation being below normal," from Greek *aisthēsis* "sensation."] —**hy·poes·thet·ic** /hìpō is théttik/ *adj.*

hy·po·eu·tec·tic /hìpə yoo téktik/, **hy·po·eu·tec·toid** /-tòyd/ *adj.* containing less of the minor component in a mixture or alloy than in the mixture of the same elements that has the lowest melting point

hy·po·gas·tri·um /hìpə gástree əm/ (*plural* **-a** /-tree ə/) *n.* the part of the front of the human abdomen that lies below the navel [Late 17thC. Via modern Latin from Greek *hupogastrion* "lower part of the belly," literally "underbelly," from the stem *gastr-* "belly" (source of English *gastric*).] —**hy·po·gas·tric** *adj.*

hy·po·ge·a plural of **hypogeum**

hy·po·ge·al /hìpə jée əl/, **hy·po·ge·an** /-ən/, **hy·po·ge·ous** /-əss/ *adj.* **1.** UNDERGROUND happening or living below ground **2.** BOT REMAINING UNDERGROUND remaining below ground while the stem of the plant grows. ◊ **epigeal** [Late 17thC. Formed from late Latin *hypogeus*, from Greek *hupogeios* "underground," from *gē* "ground, earth" (source of English *geo-*).] —**hy·po·ge·al·ly** *adv.*

hy·po·gene /hípə jèen/ *adj.* used to describe rocks that are formed or lying beneath the earth's surface [Mid-19thC. Coined from HYPO- + -GENE.] —**hy·po·gen·ic** /hìpə jénnik/ *adj.*

hy·pog·e·nous /hì pójjənəss/ *adj.* on or growing on the undersurface of something, e.g., a leaf

hy·po·ge·ous /hìpə jée əss/ *adj.* = **hypogeal**

hy·po·ge·um /hìpə jée əm/ (*plural* **-a** /-ə/) *n.* an underground room or space in an ancient building, or an ancient underground burial chamber [Mid-17thC. Via Latin from Greek *hupogeion*, originally a form of *hupogeios* "underground" (see HYPOGEAL).]

hy·po·glos·sal /hìpə glóss'l/ *adj.* **1.** UNDER THE TONGUE beneath or on the underside of the tongue **2.** RELATING TO HYPOGLOSSAL NERVE relating to or involving the hypoglossal nerve [Mid-19thC. Formed from *hypoglossus* "either of the hypoglossal nerves," from HYPO- + Greek *glōssa* "tongue" (source of English *gloss* "translation").]

hy·po·glos·sal nerve *n.* either of the 12th pair of cranial nerves that serve the muscles of the tongue

hy·po·gly·ce·mi·a /hìpō glì séemee ə/ *n.* the medical condition of having an abnormally low level of sugar in the blood —**hy·po·gly·ce·mic** *adj.*

hy·pog·y·nous /hì pójjənəss/ *adj.* used to describe a flower such as a buttercup that has its petals, sepals, or other parts situated below and apart from its ovary [Early 19thC. Formed from modern Latin *hypogynus*, from *hypo-* "below" + Greek *gunē* "woman," used to mean "pistil."] —**hy·pog·y·ny** *n.*

hy·poid gear /hí pòyd-/ *n.* a type of gear often used in the transmission of motor vehicles, in which a hypocycloidal curve is used in arranging the meshing of the teeth [Early 20thC. Origin uncertain: perhaps a contraction of HYPOCYCLOID.]

hy·po·lim·ni·on /hìpə límnee òn, hìpə límnee ən/ (*plural* **-nia** /-ə/) *n.* the lower and colder layer of water in a lake, largely stagnant and remaining at a constant temperature [Early 20thC. Coined from HYPO- + Greek *limnion* "small lake," from *limnē* "lake."]

hy·po·ma·ni·a /hìpō máynee ə/ *n.* a condition of mild mania or abnormal excitement, especially when part of a bipolar manic-depressive cycle —**hy·po·man·ic** /hìpō mánnik/ *adj.*

hy·po·nas·ty /hípə nàstee/ *n.* greater than normal growth on the underside of a plant part, causing the part to bend upward [Late 19thC. Coined from HYPO- + Greek *nastos* "pressed close, compact."] —**hy·po·nas·tic** /hìpə nástik/ *adj.* —**hy·po·nas·ti·cal·ly** *adv.*

hy·po·nym /hípənim/ *n.* a word whose meaning is both narrower than and included in the meaning of a more general term. The words "tulip" and "rose" are hyponyms of "flower." ◊ **superordinate** —**hy·po·ny·my** /hì pónnə mee/ *n.*

hy·po·phy·sec·to·my /hì pòffi séktəmee/ (*plural* **-mies**) *n.* surgical removal of the pituitary gland

hy·poph·y·sis /hī póffəsiss/ (*plural* **-ses** /-seez/) *n.* the pituitary gland (*technical*) [Late 17thC. Via modern Latin from Greek *hupophusis* "offshoot," literally "growth from under," from *phusis* "growth" (source of English *physic*).] —**hy·po·phys·e·al** /hī póffəsee əl, hīpə fízzee əl/ *adj.*

hy·po·pi·tu·i·ta·rism /hīpōpi to͝o itə rìzzəm/ *n.* failure of the pituitary gland to produce hormones, especially a deficiency in growth hormone, which can result in dwarfism —**hy·po·pi·tu·i·tar·y** /hīpōpi to͝o i tèrree/ *adj.*

hy·po·pla·sia /hìpə pláyzhə/, **hy·po·plas·ty** /hípə plàstee/ *n.* the failure of an organ or body part to grow or develop fully —**hy·po·plas·tic** /hìpə plástik/ *adj.*

hy·po·ploid /hípə plòyd/ *adj.* having a chromosome number slightly less than the diploid number —**hy·po·ploi·dy** *n.*

hy·pop·ne·a /hī pópnee ə, hīpō neé ə/ *n.* breathing that is abnormally shallow and slow [Via modern Latin from Greek, formed from *pnoia* "breathing"] —**hy·pop·ne·ic** /hīpō neé ik/ *adj.*

hy·po·sen·si·tiv·i·ty /hīpō sensi tívvətee/ *n.* an abnormally low sensitivity to stimuli such as allergens —**hy·po·sen·si·tive** /hīpō sénsitiv/ *adj.*

hy·po·sen·si·tize /hīpō sénsi tīz/ (**-tized, -tiz·ing, -tiz·es**) *vt.* to lower somebody's sensitivity to something, e.g., in the treatment of allergies —**hy·po·sen·si·ti·za·tion** /hīpō sensiti záysh'n/ *n.*

hy·pos·ta·sis /hī póstəssiss/ (*plural* **-ses** /-seez/) *n.* **1.** PHILOS **ESSENCE** the essence or reality of something **2.** CHR **ONE OF TRINITY** any of the three persons of the Christian Trinity **3.** CHR **ESSENTIAL NATURE OF JESUS CHRIST** the essential nature of Jesus Christ, in which the divine and the human are believed to be combined **4.** MED **SETTLING OF BODY FLUID** the abnormal settling of fluid in an organ or other part of the body, as a result of poor circulation, in patients kept in bed, and after death [Early 16thC. Via late Latin from Greek *hupostasis* "sediment, foundation," later "essence," from *huphistasthai* "to stand under, support," from *histasthai* "to stand."] —**hy·po·stat·ic** /hīpə státtik/ *adj.* —**hy·po·stat·i·cal** *adj.* —**hy·po·stat·i·cal·ly** *adv.*

hy·pos·ta·tize /hī póstə tīz/ (**-tized, -tiz·ing, -tiz·es**) *vt.* to treat something conceptual as if it is real —**hy·pos·ta·ti·za·tion** /hī pòstəti záysh'n/ *n.*

hy·po·style /hípə stīl/ *adj.* **WITH ROOF ON COLUMNS** with a roof or ceiling that rests on many columns ■ *n.* **COLUMNED SPACE** a building or space with a roof or ceiling that rests on columns [Mid-19thC. From Greek *hupostulos* "resting upon pillars," literally "pillar under," from *stulos* "pillar."]

hy·po·tax·is /hìpə táksiss/ *n.* the subordinate status of one clause in relation to another separated from it by a subordinating conjunction [Late 19thC. From Greek *hupotaxis* "subjection," from *hupotassein* "to arrange under," from *tassein* "to arrange."] —**hy·po·tac·tic** *adj.*

hy·po·ten·sion /hīpō ténshən/ *n.* abnormally low blood pressure —**hy·po·ten·sive** *adj., n.*

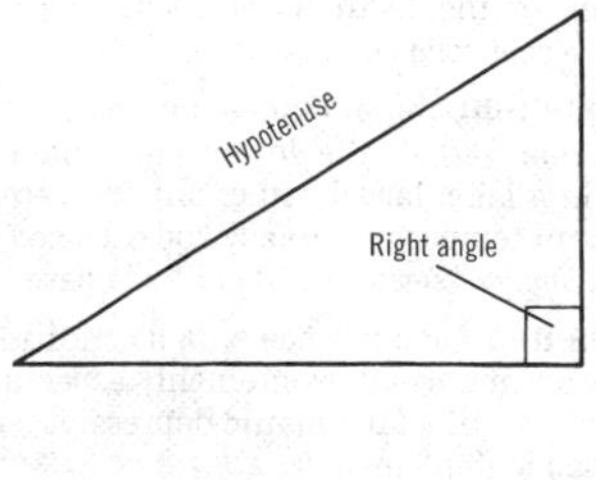

Hypotenuse

hy·pot·e·nuse /hī pótt'n o͞oss/ *n.* the longest side of a right triangle, opposite the right angle [Late 16thC. Via Latin *hypotenusa* from Greek *hupoteinousa* "(line) stretching under (the right angle)," from the present participle of *hupoteinein* "to stretch under," from *teinein* "to stretch."]

hypoth. *abbr.* **1.** hypothesis **2.** hypothetical

hy·po·thal·a·mus /hìpə thálləməss/ (*plural* **-mi** /-mī/) *n.* a central area on the underside of the brain, controlling involuntary functions such as body temperature and the release of hormones —**hy·po·tha·lam·ic** *adj.*

hy·poth·e·cate /hī póthə kàyt/ (**-cat·ed, -cat·ing, -cates**) *vt.* to pledge property or goods as security for a debt without surrendering ownership [Early 17thC. From medieval Latin *hypothecare*, from late Latin *hypotheca* "deposit," from Greek *hupothēkē*, from *hupotithenai* "to deposit as a pledge."] —**hy·poth·e·ca·tion** /hī pòthə káysh'n/ *n.* —**hy·poth·e·ca·tor** /hī póthə kàytər/ *n.*

hy·po·ther·mal /hīpō thúrm'l/ *adj.* used to describe rocks and minerals formed deep underground at high temperatures

hy·po·ther·mi·a /hīpō thúrmee ə/ *n.* **1.** **ABNORMALLY LOW BODY TEMPERATURE** dangerously low body temperature caused by prolonged exposure to cold **2.** **DELIBERATELY REDUCED BODY TEMPERATURE** lower-than-normal body temperature induced medically, e.g., to slow a patient's metabolism during heart surgery [Late 19thC. Coined from HYPO- + Greek *thermē* "heat" (source of English *thermal*) + -IA.] —**hy·po·ther·mic** *adj.*

hy·poth·e·sis /hī póthəssiss/ (*plural* **-ses** /-seez/) *n.* **1.** **THEORY NEEDING INVESTIGATION** a tentative explanation for a phenomenon, used as a basis for further investigation ○ *The hypothesis of the big bang is one way to explain the beginning of the universe.* **2.** **ASSUMPTION** a statement that is assumed to be true for the sake of argument ○ *That is what would logically follow if you accepted the hypothesis.* **3.** LOGIC **ANTECEDENT CLAUSE** the antecedent of a conditional statement [Late 16thC. Via late Latin from Greek *hupothesis* "foundation, base," literally "placing under," from *thesis* "placing."] —**hy·poth·e·sist** *n.*

hy·poth·e·size /hī póthə sīz/ (**-sized, -siz·ing, -siz·es**) *vti.* to offer something as or form a hypothesis ○ *Let us, for the moment, hypothesize that the earth is flat.* —**hy·poth·e·siz·er** *n.*

hy·po·thet·i·cal /hìpə théttik'l/, **hy·po·thet·ic** /-théttik/ *adj.* **1.** **INVOLVING IDEAS OR POSSIBILITIES** existing as or involving something that exists as an unproven idea, theory, or possibility ○ *the hypothetical existence of a Loch Ness monster* **2.** **ASSUMED FOR THE SAKE OF ARGUMENT** assumed or proposed for further investigation ○ *The question is purely hypothetical.* —**hy·po·thet·i·cal·ly** *adv.*

hy·po·thet·i·cal im·per·a·tive *n.* an imperative that depends on a condition, e.g., "be kind to people if they are kind to you." ◊ **categorical imperative**

hy·po·thy·roid /hīpō thī ròyd/ *adj.* relating to, characteristic of, or affected by hypothyroidism

hy·po·thy·roid·ism /hīpō thī roy dìzzəm/ *n.* a deficiency or the bodily condition resulting from a deficiency in the production of thyroid hormones by the thyroid gland, resulting in a slowing of the metabolic rate. A severe deficiency can result in myxedema.

hy·po·ton·ic /hìpə tónnik/ *adj.* **1.** **LACKING MUSCLE TONE** with low or diminished muscle tone or tension **2.** **LOWER IN OSMOTIC PRESSURE** with a lower osmotic pressure than another fluid —**hy·po·to·nia** /hìpə tṓnee ə/ *n.* —**hy·po·to·nic·i·ty** /hīpōtō níssətee/ *n.*

hy·po·ven·ti·late /hìpō vént'l àyt/ (**-lat·ed, -lat·ing, -lates**) *vi.* to breathe in an abnormally slow and shallow way

hy·po·ven·ti·la·tion /hìpō vent'l áysh'n/ *n.* abnormally slow and shallow breathing leading to a dangerous buildup of carbon dioxide in the blood

hy·pox·ae·mi·a *n.* U.K. = **hypoxemia**

hy·po·xan·thine /hìpə zán theen/ *n.* a white powdery substance that is a by-product of metabolism in plants and animals. Formula: $C_5H_4N_4O$.

hy·pox·e·mi·a /hì pok seémee ə/ *n.* inadequate oxygen in the blood [Late 19thC. Coined from HYP- + OXYGEN + -EMIA.] —**hy·pox·e·mic** *adj.*

hy·pox·i·a /hī póksee ə/ *n.* an inadequacy in the oxygen reaching the body's tissues [Mid-20thC. Coined from HYP- + OXYGEN + -IA.] —**hy·pox·ic** *adj.*

hypso- *prefix.* height ○ *hypsometer* [From Greek *hupsos*; ultimately related to *hupo* "under, below" (see HYPO-)]

hyp·sog·ra·phy /hip sóggrəfee/ (*plural* **-phies**) *n.* **1.** **MEASURING AND MAPPING EARTH'S FEATURES** the measurement and mapping of the contours and elevations of natural features of the earth above sea level **2.** **SHOWING EARTH'S FEATURES IN RELIEF** the depiction of the contours and elevations of the natural features on the surface of the land **3.** = **hypsometry** —**hyp·so·graph·ic** /hìpsə gráffik/ *adj.* —**hyp·so·graph·i·cal** *adj.*

hyp·som·e·ter /hip sómmətər/ *n.* **1.** **INSTRUMENT FOR MEASURING ALTITUDE** an instrument that uses the boiling point of water at different altitudes to measure the elevation of a given point on the earth's surface **2.** **INSTRUMENT MEASURING TREE HEIGHT** an instrument for calculating the heights of trees by using the principles of geometric triangulation

hyp·som·e·try /hip sómmətree/ *n.* the measurement of the elevation of land above sea level —**hyp·so·met·ric** /hìpsə méttrik/ *adj.* —**hyp·so·met·ri·cal** *adj.* —**hyp·so·met·ri·cal·ly** *adv.* —**hyp·som·e·trist** /hip sómmətrist/ *n.*

hy·rax /hī ràks/ (*plural* **-rax·es** *or* **-ra·ces** /hīrə seez/) *n.* a small gregarious plant-eating mammal that resembles a rabbit with short ears and has toenails resembling hooves. Hyraxes live around the Mediterranean Sea and in southwestern Asia. Family: Procaviidae. [Mid-19thC. Via modern Latin from Greek *hurax* "shrew mouse," of unknown origin.]

hy·son /hīss'n/ *n.* a Chinese green tea [Mid-18thC. From Chinese *xīchūn*, literally "bright spring."]

Hyssop

hys·sop /híssəp/ *n.* **1.** **AROMATIC HERB** a fragrant blue-flowered plant of Europe and Asia, similar to mint, cultivated since medieval times as a medicinal herb and still used today in aromatherapy and alternative medicine. Latin name: *Hyssopus officinalis.* **2.** **PLANT SIMILAR TO HYSSOP** a plant related to or similar to true hyssop **3.** **BIBLICAL PLANT** an unidentified plant whose twigs are described in the Bible as being used to sprinkle water during Hebrew religious ceremonies [Pre-12thC. Via Latin *hyssopus* from Greek *hussōpos*, of uncertain origin: probably from Semitic.]

hyster- *prefix.* = **hystero-** (*used before vowels*)

hys·ter·ec·to·my /hìstə réktəmee/ (*plural* **-mies**) *n.* a surgical operation to remove a woman's uterus —**hys·ter·ec·to·mize** *vt.*

hys·ter·e·sis /hìstə reéssiss/ *n.* a delayed response by an object to changes in the forces acting on it, especially magnetic forces [Late 19thC. From Greek *husterēsis* "deficiency," from *husterein* "to be behind, come late," from *husteros* "late."] —**hys·ter·et·ic** /hìstə réttik/ *adj.*

hys·ter·i·a /hi steéree ə/ *n.* **1.** **EMOTIONAL INSTABILITY CAUSED BY TRAUMA** an emotionally unstable state brought about by a traumatic experience **2.** **STATE OF EXTREME EMOTION** a state of extreme or exaggerated emotion such as excitement or panic, especially among large numbers of people ○ *press hysteria about the latest scandals* **3.** **LAUGHING OR CRYING** uncontrollable laughter or crying **4.** PSYCHIAT **CONVERSION DISORDER** conversion disorder (*dated*) [Early 19thC. Formed from Latin *hystericus* (see HYSTERIC).]

WORD KEY: CULTURAL NOTE

Studies in Hysteria, a book by Austrian psychologists Joseph Bauer and Sigmund Freud (1895). A pioneering work in the field of psychoanalysis, it suggests that hysterical symptoms are the result of the memory's suppression of earlier traumatic events. The authors recommend that patients recall and confront these experiences in the hope of achieving catharsis.

hys·ter·ic /hi stérrik/ *n.* **SOMEBODY WITH HYSTERIA** somebody affected by hysteria (*dated*) (*sometimes considered offensive*) ■ *adj.* = **hysterical** *adj.* 1, **hysterical** *adj.* 2,

hysterical *adj.* 3 [Mid-17thC. Via Latin *hystericus* from Greek *husterikos* "suffering in the uterus," from *hustera* "uterus" (see HYSTERO-). From the belief that hysteria was caused by malfunction of the uterus.]

hys·ter·i·cal /hi stérrik'l/ *adj.* **1. AFFECTED BY HYSTERIA** in a state of hysteria ○ *hysterical with grief* **2. RELATING TO HYSTERIA** relating to, caused by, or subject to hysteria **3. UNCONTROLLABLE** impossible to hold back or control ○ *hysterical sobbing coming from the next room* **4. EXTREMELY FUNNY** causing uncontrollable laughter (*informal*) ○ *one hysterical sketch after another* — **hys·ter·i·cal·ly** *adv.*

hys·ter·ics /hi stérriks/ *n.* (*takes a singular or plural verb*) **1. LAUGHTER** a state of uncontrollable laughter (*informal*) ○ *had them in hysterics with her stories* **2. STATE OF HYSTERIA** a state of hysteria or an episode of hysterical behavior

hystero- *prefix.* **1.** uterus ○ *hysterotomy* **2.** hysteria ○ *hysterogenic* [From Greek *hustera* "womb." Ultimately from an Indo-European word that is also the ancestor of English *uterus.*]

hys·ter·o·gen·ic /hìstərō jénnik/ *adj.* bringing about a state of emotional instability or hysteria

hys·ter·on prot·er·on /hìstə ròn próttə ròn/ *n.* a figure of speech in which the order of words or phrases is the reverse of what is usual, e.g., "photographed in white and black" [Mid-16thC. Via late Latin from Greek *husteron proteron* "latter first."]

hys·ter·ot·o·my /hìstə róttəmee/ (*plural* **-mies**) *n.* a surgical incision into a woman's uterus, especially in order to perform a cesarean section

Hz *symbol.* hertz

I i

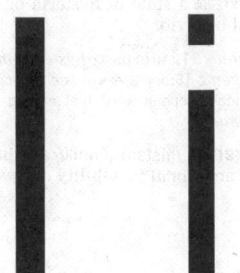

i[1] /ī/ (*plural* **i's**), **I** (*plural* **I's** *or* **Is**) *n.* **1. 9TH LETTER OF ENGLISH ALPHABET** the ninth letter of the modern English alphabet **2. SPEECH SOUND CORRESPONDING TO "I"** the speech sound that corresponds to the letter "I" **3. LETTER "I" WRITTEN** a written representation of the letter "I" **4. ROMAN NUMERAL FOR 1** the Roman numeral for one

i[2] *symbol.* **1.** MATH imaginary unit **2.** one **3.** CHEM van't Hoff's factor

I[1] *pron.* a pronoun used by a speaker or writer to refer to himself or herself (*used as the subject of a verb*) [Old English *ic.* Via prehistoric Germanic from an Indo-European word meaning "I," which is also the ancestor of English *ego* and *egotism.*]

I[2] *symbol.* **1.** electric current **2.** CHEM ELEM iodine **3.** CHEM ionization potential **4.** QUANTUM PHYS isospin **5.** PHYS moment of inertia **6.** one **7.** LOGIC a particular affirmative categorial statement **8.** MATH unit matrix

I[3] *abbr.* **1.** interstate **2.** Italy (*international vehicle registration*)

i. *abbr.* **1.** incisor **2.** indicate **3.** BANKING interest **4.** GRAM intransitive **5.** island **6.** isle

I. *abbr.* **1.** Imperial **2.** (single column) inch (*of an advertisement*) **3.** incumbent **4.** independence **5.** Independent **6.** India **7.** Indian **8.** Inspector **9.** Institute **10.** Instructor **11.** intelligence **12.** International **13.** interpreter **14.** Ireland **15.** Irish **16.** Island **17.** Isle **18.** issue **19.** Italian

-i- used as a connector to join word elements ○ *fossiliferous* [Via Old French from Latin]

IA *abbr.* **1.** infected area **2.** Institute of Actuaries **3.** MAIL Iowa

Ia. *abbr.* Iowa

i.a. *abbr.* in absentia

-ia *suffix.* **1. PLACE NAMES** used to form place names ○ *Australia* ○ *India* **2. LATIN PLURAL** one of the Latin endings that can be used to denote a plural ○ *Saturnalia* **3. DISEASES** used to form names of diseases or medical conditions ○ *dyslexia* **4. CLASSES OR GENERA** used to form words for classes of animals or genera of plants ○ *mammalia* ○ *gardenia* **5. THINGS BELONGING TO SOMETHING** used to form plurals for things that belong to or are associated with something ○ *memorabilia* [Directly or via modern Latin from Latin and Greek]

IAA *abbr.* **1.** indoleacetic acid **2.** International Advertising Association

IAAE *abbr.* Institution of Automotive and Aeronautical Engineers

IAAF *abbr.* International Amateur Athletic Federation

IAB *abbr.* **1.** Industrial Advisory Board **2.** Industrial Arbitration Board **3.** Inter-American Bank

IABA *abbr.* International Amateur Boxing Association

Ia·coc·ca /ī ə kṓkə/, **Lee** (*b.* 1924) U.S. automobile executive. After a 32-year career at Ford, he became the president and chief executive officer of Chrysler Corporation (1978–92), which he rescued from failure. Full name **Lido Anthony Iacocca**

IACP *abbr.* **1.** International Association of Chiefs of Police **2.** International Association of Computer Programmers

IADB *abbr.* **1.** Inter-American Defense Board **2.** Inter-American Development Bank

IAEA *abbr.* International Atomic Energy Agency

IAF *abbr.* Indian Air Force

IAL *abbr.* International Algebraic Language

-ial *suffix.* forms adjectives meaning connected with or belonging to something ○ *secretarial* ○ *imperial* [Directly or via French from Latin *-ialis* and *-iale,* adjective suffixes]

IAM *abbr.* **1.** Institute of Administrative Management **2.** internal auditory meatus

IAMAW *abbr.* International Association of Machinists and Aerospace Workers

i·amb /ī àm/ *n.* a unit of rhythm in poetry, consisting of one short or unstressed syllable or group followed by one long or stressed syllable. "The ploughman homeward plods his weary way" consists of five iambs. [Mid-19thC. Anglicized form of IAMBUS.]

i·am·bic /ī ámbik/ *adj.* **USING IAMBS** relating to or consisting of iambs ■ *n.* **1.** = **iamb 2. POEM CONSISTING OF IAMBS** a poem or a line of poetry written in iambs (*often used in the plural*)

i·am·bic pen·tam·e·ter *n.* the most common rhythm in English poetry, consisting of five iambs in each line. "The quality of mercy is not strained" is an iambic pentameter.

i·am·bus /īám bəss/ (*plural* **-bus·es** *or* **-bi** /-bī/) *n.* = **iamb** [Late 16thC. Via Latin from Greek *iambos* "iamb, lampoon," from *iaptein* "to attack in words." From the tradition that iambic verse was first used by satirists.]

-ian *suffix.* forms adjectives and nouns indicating the condition of belonging to, coming from, being involved in, or being like something ○ *Italian* ○ *Smithsonian* ○ *mathematician* [Directly or via French *-ien* from Latin *-ianus,* which was formed by adding the adjective suffix *-anus* to nouns with stems ending in *i*]

I·ap·e·tus /ī áppətəss/ *n.* a natural satellite of Saturn, discovered in 1671. It is 892 mi./1436 km in diameter and occupies an outer orbit.

IARC *abbr.* International Agency for Research on Cancer

IARU *abbr.* International Amateur Radio Union

IAS *abbr.* **1.** image analysis system **2.** COMPUT immediate access store **3.** AIR indicated air speed

Ia·şi /yaáshee/ city and capital of the county of the same name in eastern Romania, situated on a tributary of the Prut River. Population: 342,994 (1992).

-iasis (*plural* **-iases**) *suffix.* forms words for diseases characterized by or caused by something specified ○ *filariasis* [Coined from -I- + Latin or Greek *-asis,* used to form nouns of state or process]

IATA *abbr.* International Air Transport Association

-iatric *suffix.* forms adjectives that describe a particular field of medicine ○ *psychiatric*

-iatrics *suffix.* forms nouns meaning a particular field of medicine ○ *pediatrics*

i·at·ro·gen·ic /ī àttrə jénnik/ *adj.* used to describe a symptom or illness brought on unintentionally by something that a doctor does or says ○ *iatrogenic disorders* [Early 20thC. Coined from Greek *iatros* "doctor" + -GENIC.] —**i·at·ro·gen·i·cal·ly** *adv.*

-iatry *suffix.* forms nouns meaning a particular field of medicine or medical treatment ○ *podiatry* ○ *psychiatry* [From Greek *-iatreia* "art of healing," from *iatros* "doctor"]

IAU *abbr.* **1.** International Association of Universities **2.** International Astronomical Union

IB *abbr.* **1.** COMM in bond **2.** incendiary bomb **3.** industrial business **4.** International Baccalaureate **5.** invoice book

ib. *abbr.* ibidem

IBA *abbr.* **1.** indolebutyric acid **2.** International Bar Association **3.** Investment Bankers' Association

I·ba·dan /ee baád'n, -daan/ city and capital of Oyo State, southwestern Nigeria, situated 89 mi./143 km northeast of Lagos. Population: 1,295,000 (1992).

IBD *abbr.* **1.** inflammatory bowel disease **2.** ion-beam deposition

I-beam *n.* a metal beam or girder that is shaped like a capital "I" in cross section

I·be·ri·a /ī beéree ə/ *n.* **1.** = **Iberian Peninsula** (the) **2. ANCIENT CAUCASIAN REGION** an ancient region in the Caucasus, roughly equivalent to present-day eastern Georgia

I·be·ri·an /ī beéree ən/ *n.* **1. MEMBER OF ANCIENT PEOPLE** a member of one of the ancient peoples who lived either on the Iberian Peninsula or in the Transcaucasian state of Iberia **2. SOMEBODY FROM IBERIAN PENINSULA** somebody who lives in or was born or raised in Spain or Portugal ■ *adj.* **1. OF ANCIENT IBERIANS** relating to or typical of the ancient peoples who lived either on the Iberian Peninsula or in the Transcaucasian state of Iberia **2. OF IBERIAN PENINSULA** relating to or typical of Spain or Portugal, or their people or culture [Early 16thC. Formed from Latin *Iberia* "land of the Iberes," from Greek *Ibēres* "Spaniards."]

I·be·ri·an Pen·in·su·la /ī beéree ən-/ peninsula in southwestern Europe, divided into Spain and Portugal, together with Gibraltar

Ibero- *prefix.* Iberia or Iberian

Ibex

i·bex /ī bèks/ (*plural* **i·bex** *or* **i·bex·es**) *n.* a wild mountain goat with long knobbly backward-curving horns that lives in Europe, Asia, and northern Africa. Genus: *Capra.* [Early 17thC. From Latin, of uncertain origin.]

IBF *abbr.* International Boxing Federation

IBG *abbr.* interblock gap

I·bib·i·o /i bíbbee ō/ (*plural* **-o** *or* **-os**) *n.* **1.** PEOPLES **MEMBER OF AFRICAN PEOPLE** a member of a people living in southeastern parts of Nigeria, especially in the region around the port of Calabar **2.** LANG **LANGUAGE OF IBIBIO** the language of the Ibibio belonging to the Benue-Congo group of languages. About two million people speak Ibibio. [Early 19thC. From Ibibio.] —**I·bib·i·o** *adj.*

ibid. /íbbid/ *abbr.* ibidem

i·bi·dem /íbbi dèm/ *adv.* used to cite the same book, publication, chapter, or page previously cited [Mid-18thC. From Latin, "in the same place," from *ibi* "there" + *-dem* "that."]

-ibility (*plural* **-ibilities**) *suffix.* = **-ability** [Via French *-ibilité* from the Latin stem *-ibilitat-*, from *-ibilis*]

Ibis

i·bis /íbiss/ (*plural* **i·bis·es** *or* **i·bis**) *n.* a gregarious wading bird with a downward-curving bill. Ibises live in warm and tropical climates. Family: Threskiornithidae. [14thC. Via Latin from, ultimately, Egyptian *hbj*.]

I·bi·za /ee beéthə/ **1.** third largest island in the Balearic group, Baleares Province, Spain, situated in the western Mediterranean Sea approximately 60 mi./96 km from the eastern coast of Spain. Area: 230 sq. mi./596 sq. km. **2.** seaport and capital of the island of Ibiza, situated 80 mi./129 km southwest of Palma. Population: 29,447 (1996).

I·bi·zan hound /ī beéz'n-/ *n.* a smooth-haired dog similar to, but smaller than, a German shepherd, with a light brown or reddish, sometimes spotted, coat. It was originally bred in the Balearic Islands for hunting. [Early 20thC. Named for *Ibiza*, the westernmost of the Balearic Islands.]

-ible *suffix.* = **-able** [From Latin *-ibilis*, adjective suffix]

IBM *abbr.* intercontinental ballistic missile

IBMBR *abbr.* interbank market bid rate

Ibn Sa·ud /ibbən saa oód, -sówd/, **Abdul Aziz, King of Saudi Arabia** (1880?–1953). As the first king of Saudi Arabia (1932–53), he helped to found the Arab League (1945) and opened up his country's oil reserves.

I·bo /eé bō/ (*plural* **I·bo** *or* **I·bos**), **Ig·bo** /íg bō/ (*plural* **-bo** *or* **-bos**) *n.* **1.** PEOPLES **MEMBER OF NIGERIAN PEOPLE** a member of a people living in parts of western Africa, especially in southeastern Nigeria. During the 1960s, the Ibo formed the breakaway state of Biafra. Fighting with Nigerian troops and severe famine led to enormous loss of life and the Ibo capitulated in 1970. **2.** LANG **LANGUAGE OF IBO** a language spoken in southern parts of Nigeria and in some areas of Niger. It is one of the Kwa group of the Niger-Congo family of African languages. Ibo is spoken by about 17 million people. [Mid-18thC. From Ibo.] —**I·bo** *adj.*

IBRD *abbr.* International Bank for Reconstruction and Development

IBS *abbr.* irritable bowel syndrome

Henrik Ibsen

Ib·sen /ibss'n/, **Henrik** (1828–1906) Norwegian playwright. The pioneering psychological realism of such works as *A Doll's House* (1879) and *Hedda Gabler* (1890) had a profound impact on 20th-century drama. Full name **Henrik Johan Ibsen**

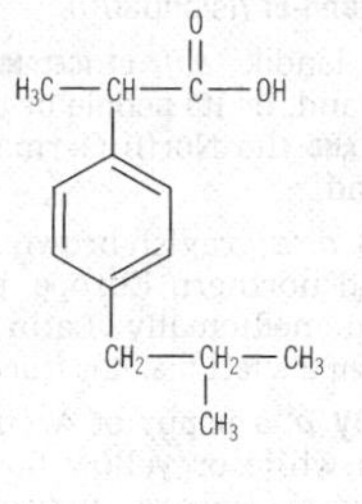

Ibuprofen

i·bu·pro·fen /ībyoo prṓfən/ *n.* a drug used to relieve pain and reduce inflammation, widely used in the treatment of arthritis and rheumatism. It is a member of a class of drugs known as NSAIDs, nonsteroidal anti-inflammatory drugs, which also includes aspirin. Formula: $C_{13}H_{18}O_2$. [Mid-20thC. Coined from ISO- + BUTYL + PROPIONIC + an alteration of PHENYL.]

i/c *abbr.* **1.** in charge (of) **2.** in command

ICA *abbr.* **1.** International Coffee Agreement **2.** International Commodity Agreement **3.** International Cooperation Administration

ICAO *abbr.* **1.** International Civil Aeronautics Organization **2.** International Civil Aviation Organization

Ic·a·rus /íkərəss/ *n.* **1.** MYTHOL **CHARACTER IN GREEK MYTHOLOGY** in Greek mythology, the son of Daedalus, who drowned in the sea while attempting to escape from Crete after the sun melted his wings of wax and feathers **2.** ASTRON **ASTEROID** an asteroid whose orbit is within 19 million mi./30 million km of the sun, closer than any other orbiting object —**I·car·i·an** /i káiree ən/ *adj.*

ICBM *abbr.* intercontinental ballistic missile

ICC *abbr.* **1.** Indian Claims Commission **2.** International Chamber of Commerce **3.** Interstate Commerce Commission

ice /īss/ *n.* **1. FROZEN WATER** water that has frozen into solid form ○ *puddles turning to ice* **2. EXPANSE OF FROZEN WATER** an area, layer, or body of frozen water ○ *a polar bear far out on the ice* **3. SUBSTANCE LIKE ICE** any substance resembling ice, e.g., the frozen form of carbon dioxide, known as dry ice **4. PIECES OF FROZEN WATER** ice, either crushed or in cubes, used to cool drinks or food **5.** FOOD **FROZEN DESSERT** a dessert or snack of crushed ice flavored with sweetened juice **6.** SPORTS **SKATING SURFACE** a prepared frozen surface for ice skaters or ice-hockey players **7. COLDNESS** animosity or excessive formality between people ○ *The room's atmosphere turned to ice when the two adversaries met.* **8. DIAMONDS** diamonds, or jewelry in general, especially stolen merchandise (*slang*) **9.** DRUGS **ILLEGAL DRUG** a concentrated form of the drug methamphetamine (*slang*) **10. ILLEGAL MONEY** money obtained illegally, especially protection money paid to criminals (*slang*) **11.** CRIMINOL **ILLEGAL PROFIT** profit made on the illegal diversion of tickets for the theater, a movie, or a sporting event to a ticket broker (*slang*) ■ *adj.* **MADE OF ICE** made of, containing, using, or for use on ice ○ *an ice cube* ○ *an ice sculpture* ○ *an ice ax* ■ *v.* (**iced, ic·ing, ic·es**) **1.** *vi.* **FREEZE UP** to sustain freezing and the development of a thin coating of ice on the surface ○ *The bridge iced, making it dangerous.* ○ *Bridges ice before roads.* **2.** *vt.* **PUT ICING ON CAKE** to cover something such as a cake with icing **3.** *vt.* **COOL A DRINK** to chill a drink with ice, or stir ice cubes into it **4.** *vt.* **KILL SOMEBODY** to kill somebody (*slang*) **5.** *vt.* HOCKEY **SEND PUCK OUT OF DEFENSIVE TERRITORY** to shoot an ice-hockey puck out of defensive territory and far into the opposing team's territory **6.** *vt.* **MAKE CERTAIN OF SOMETHING** to make certain of something, especially of winning a game (*slang*) ○ *They iced the game with a late field goal.* [Old English *īs*. From prehistoric Germanic, of uncertain origin.] —**ice·less** *adj.* ◇ **break the ice** to overcome the initial restraint felt by people who have just met or who are meeting under awkward circumstances ◇ **cut no ice** to fail to impress or make a difference ◇ **on ice 1.** in abeyance or in a state of being postponed **2.** in a place of safekeeping (*slang*) **3.** being chilled in a freezer, refrigerator, or among ice cubes ◇ **on thin ice** in an unsafe, difficult, or vulnerable situation (*informal*)

WORD KEY: USAGE

ice or **iced**? For most cold beverages, ***iced*** is by far the more common form for the adjective: *iced tea, iced coffee. Ice beer* and *ice wine* are exceptions; here the meaning is not that the drink is being served with ice but that ice figured in the production of it.

ice over *vi.* to become covered with a layer of ice ○ *As soon as the lake iced over, people were out there with their skates.*

ice up *vi.* to become coated with a layer of ice ○ *The car's windshield will ice up if you don't park it in the garage.*

ICE *abbr.* **1.** ice, compress, elevation (*used as a treatment for injuries and bruises*) **2.** Institution of Civil Engineers **3.** internal-combustion engine **4.** International Cultural Exchange

Ice. *abbr.* **1.** Iceland **2.** Icelandic

ice age *n.* any of the periods in the earth's history when temperatures fell worldwide and large areas of the earth's surface were covered with glaciers

Ice Age *n.* the most recent ice age during which most of the northern hemisphere was covered with glaciers, occurring during the Pleistocene epoch

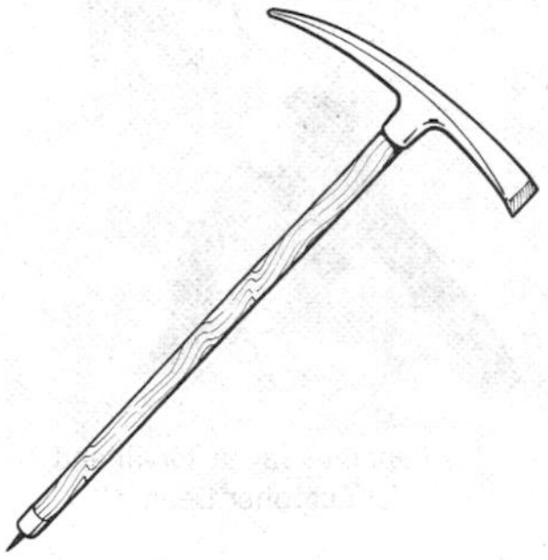

Ice ax

ice ax *n.* a lightweight tool resembling an ax, used by mountaineers to cut handholds and footholds in ice and provide additional balance during a slide down a snow-covered slope

ice bag *n.* a waterproof bag filled with ice and held against an injured part of the body to ease pain or reduce swelling

ice beer *n.* beer brewed by a process that freezes the beer and removes some of the ice, thus increasing the beer's alcohol content

ice·berg /íss bùrg/ *n.* **1. MASS OF FLOATING ICE** a large mounded mass of ice that has broken away from a glacier and floats in the sea, with the greater part of its bulk under the water **2.** FOOD = **iceberg lettuce** (*informal*) **3. SOMEBODY WITH COOL MANNER** somebody who is unemotional or unfriendly (*informal*) [Late 18thC. From Dutch *ijsberg*, literally "ice mountain."]

ice·berg let·tuce *n.* a large round kind of lettuce with pale crisp juicy leaves, somewhat like cabbage leaves, that form a tight head when the lettuce is mature

ice·blink /íss blìnk/ *n.* a yellowish glow in the sky, occurring when sunlight is reflected by a distant ice field

ice·boat /íss bōt/ *n.* **1. BOAT USED ON ICE** a boat or simple frame with runners, usually propelled by a sail and used on ice for recreation or travel **2.** = **icebreaker** *n.* 1 —**ice·boat·er** *n.* —**ice·boat·ing** *n.*

ice·bound /íss bòwnd/ *adj.* unable to move because of being covered with or surrounded by ice

ice·box /íss bòks/ *n.* **1.** = **refrigerator 2. COOL CONTAINER FOR FOOD** an insulated container filled with ice and used to keep food and drinks cool and fresh

ice·break·er /íss bràykər/ *n.* **1.** SHIPPING **SHIP FOR BREAKING ICE** a ship with a reinforced bow used to break up ice and cut a passage through frozen navigable waters **2. SOMETHING THAT RELAXES GROUP** something such as a joke or game used to ease the initial tension, restraint, or awkwardness of a meeting or social gathering

ice·cap /íss kàp/, **ice cap** *n.* a thick permanent covering of ice and snow extending outward in every direction, e.g., from the North and South poles or from a mountain top

ice-cold *adj.* extremely cold

ice cream *n.* a sweet frozen dessert or snack traditionally made with cream and egg yolks and flavored with a variety of fruits or other extracts [Alteration of *iced cream*]

ice-cream chair *n.* a wire chair with a round seat and without arms, once popular in ice-cream parlors and used in a variety of cafés

ice-cream cone *n.* **1.** CONE-SHAPED WAFER a hollow cone-shaped wafer designed to hold a serving of ice cream **2.** CONE-SHAPED WAFER CONTAINING ICE CREAM an ice-cream cone containing a serving of ice cream

ice-cream so·da *n.* a refreshment consisting of ice cream in any kind of soda, sometimes with the addition of a flavored syrup, and served in a tall glass

iced /īst/ *adj.* **1.** CHILLED OR WITH ICE chilled or poured over ice cubes **2.** WITH ICING decorated with icing ○ *iced cinnamon buns*

WORD KEY: USAGE

See Usage note at ***ice.***

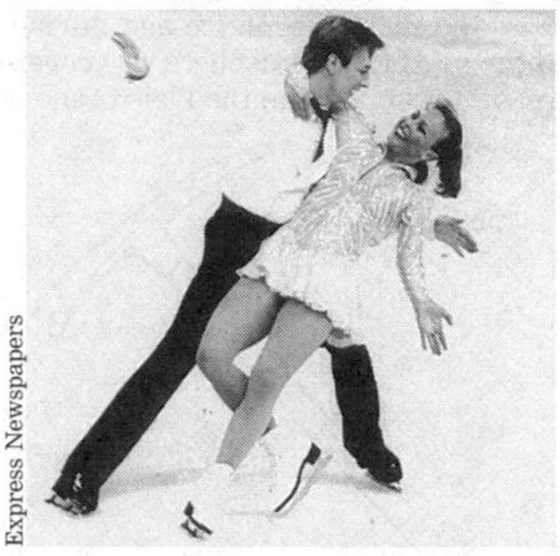

Ice dancing: Jayne Torvill and Christopher Dean

ice danc·ing *n.* figure skating in which a pair of skaters perform routines based on ballroom dancing, and in which the height of lifts is restricted in competition. Competitive ice dancing also requires that the two skaters remain in close physical contact throughout their routine.

ice·fall /īss fòl/ *n.* **1.** FROZEN WATERFALL a waterfall that has frozen solid **2.** SLOPING FACE OF A GLACIER a face of a glacier on which the gradient is so steep that the ice breaks up into a jumble of blocks. ◊ **serac** [Modeled on WATERFALL]

ice field *n.* a large, flat expanse of ice formed where the land surface is level, therefore making it easy for ice to accumalate

ice floe *n.* a sheet of floating ice smaller than an ice field

ice fog *n.* a fog that is made up of ice particles rather than water droplets

ice foot *n.* a permanent band of ice along the coast of a polar region

ice hock·ey *n.* = **hockey**

ice·house /īss hòwss/ (*plural* **-hous·es** /-hòwzəz/) *n.* a building where ice is made, stored, and sometimes sold

Icel. *abbr.* **1.** Iceland **2.** Icelandic

Iceland

Ice·land /īslənd, -land/ island republic in the North Atlantic Ocean, 185 mi./300 km east of Greenland and 620 mi./1,000 km west of Norway. Language: Icelandic. Currency: króna. Capital: Reykjavik. Population: 269,697 (1997). Area: 39,800 sq. mi./103,000 sq. km. Official name **Republic of Iceland** —**Ice·land·er** /īsləndər/ *n.*

Ice·land·ic /īs lándik/ *adj.* OF ICELAND relating to or typical of Iceland, or its people or culture ■ *n.* LANG LANGUAGE OF ICELAND the North Germanic language of modern Iceland

Ice·land moss *n.* a grayish-brown lichen found in the Arctic and northern Europe, grown as a food and also used medicinally. Latin name: *Cetraria islandica.* [From the fact that it is found in ICELAND]

Ice·land pop·py *n.* a poppy of Arctic regions, often grown for its white or yellow flowers on leafless stems. Latin name: *Papaver nudicaule.* [From the fact that it is found in ICELAND]

Ice·land spar *n.* a transparent form of calcite used in optical instruments for its refractive properties [From the fact that it is found in ICELAND]

ice ma·chine *n.* = **icemaker**

ice·mak·er /īss màykər/ *n.* a machine that produces ice cubes, often built into a refrigerator

ice·man /īss màn/ (*plural* **-men** /-mèn/) *n.* **1.** SOMEBODY WHO SELLS OR DELIVERS ICE somebody who sells or delivers ice, in the past primarily to homes, but now chiefly to establishments that sell packaged ice to the public and in large quantities to commercial fishing boats **2.** EXPERT IN ICY CONDITIONS an explorer or mountaineer experienced in traveling on ice

ice milk *n.* a frozen food like ice cream but made with skim milk

ice nee·dle *n.* a tiny needle-shaped ice crystal that forms in cold moist air and gathers with others into masses resembling clouds, often at high altitudes and in otherwise clear weather

I·ce·ni /ī seé nī/ *npl.* an ancient people of Britain who, under Queen Boudicca, attempted to overthrow the Romans in A.D. 61. The Romans fought off the Iceni and Boudicca committed suicide.

ice-out *n.* a thawing of ice covering a lake or other body of water

ice pack *n.* **1.** MED ICE USED FOR AN INJURY an ice-filled cloth or bag held against an injured part of the body to ease pain or reduce swelling **2.** GEOG PACK ICE an area of pack ice

ice pick *n.* a lightweight hand-held pick for chipping away or breaking up ice

ice plant *n.* **1.** PLANTS PLANT WITH THICK LEAVES AND PINK FLOWERS a clump-forming plant with thick, pale-green leaves and flat heads of pink flowers on long stalks. Latin name: *Sedum spectabile.* **2.** PLANT WITH GLISTENING LEAVES a low-growing succulent plant native to southern Africa with pink or white flowers and leaves that are covered with fine protruding sacs that glisten like ice crystals. Latin name: *Mesembryanthemum crystallinum.*

ice point *n.* the temperature, 0°C or 32°F, at which water freezes under a pressure of one atmosphere

ice road *n. Can* a stretch of road that runs on a frozen body of water

ice sheet *n.* a thick covering of ice over a large area that remains for a long period of time

ice shelf *n.* a thick mass of ice covering coastal land and extending out over the sea so that the extended portion floats

ice show *n.* an entertainment performed by skaters on ice

ice skate (**ice skated, ice skating**) *n.* a boot with a metal blade fixed along the length of its sole, allowing the wearer to glide over an ice-covered surface

ice-skate (**ice-skates**) *vi.* to glide over an ice-covered surface on ice skates —**ice-skat·er** *n.*

ice skat·ing *n.* the sport or pastime of using ice skates to glide over an ice-covered surface

ice storm *n.* a rainstorm in conditions so cold that the rain freezes as it hits the ground, forming sheets of ice

ice vol·ca·no *n.* a volcano-like formation composed of plastic ice magma, found on the two moons of Uranus

ice wa·ter *n.* **1.** DRINK OF CHILLED WATER very cold water or water chilled in a refrigerator or with ice cubes, served as a drink **2.** MELTED ICE water produced when ice melts

ICFTU *abbr.* International Confederation of Free Trade Unions

I Ching /ee jíng/ *n.* **1.** CHINESE SYSTEM OF FORTUNE-TELLING an ancient Chinese system of divination, based on a book of Taoist philosophy and expressed in hexagrams chosen at random and interpreted to answer questions and give advice **2.** BOOK OF I CHING the book containing the symbols used in I Ching divination and an accompanying text that the reader may consult for help in interpreting the symbols [Late 19thC. From Chinese, literally "Book of Changes."]

ich·neu·mon fly /ik nóomən-/, **ich·neu·mon wasp, ich·neu·mon** *n.* a slender insect related to and resembling a wasp. The various species are parasites of many insect pests, laying their eggs in insect larvae. Family: Ichneumonidae.

ich·nog·ra·phy /ik nóggrəfee/ (*plural* **-phies**) *n.* **1.** DRAWING GROUND PLANS the art or practice of drawing ground plans of the layout of buildings **2.** GROUND PLAN a ground plan of the layout of a building [Late 16thC. Directly or via French from Latin *ichnographia*, from Greek *ikhnographia*, literally "track-drawing," from *ikhnos* "track."] —**ich·no·graph·ic** /iknə gráffik/ *adj.* —**ich·no·graph·i·cal** *adj.* —**ich·no·graph·i·cal·ly** *adv.*

ich·nol·o·gy /ik nóllәjee/ *n.* the scientific study of fossilized footprints [Mid-19thC. Coined from Greek *ikhnos* "track, footprint" + -LOGY.] —**ich·no·log·i·cal** /iknə lójjik'l/ *adj.*

i·chor /ī kàwr, īkər/ *n.* **1.** MED DISCHARGE FROM SORE a watery or slightly bloody discharge from a wound or an ulcer **2.** MYTHOL GREEK GODS' BLOOD the fluid said to run, instead of body fluid, through the veins of the gods in Greek mythology [Mid-17thC. From Greek *ikhōr*, of unknown origin.] —**i·chor·ous** /īkərəss/ *adj.*

ichth. *abbr.* ichthyology

ich·thus /íkthəss/, **ich·thys** /íkthiss/ *n.* a simple symbol that resembles a fish, consisting of two curves that bisect each other. It is a symbol of Christianity. [From Greek *ikhthus* "fish"]

ichthy- *prefix.* = **ichthyo-** (*used before vowels*)

ichthyo- *prefix.* fish ○ *ichthyology* [Via Latin from, ultimately, Greek *ikhthus* "fish"]

ich·thy·o·fau·na /íkthee ə fáwnnə/ *n.* all fish that live in a particular area —**ich·thy·o·fau·nal** *adj.*

ich·thy·oid /íkthee òyd/ *n.* a fish, or a vertebrate such as a lamprey or hagfish that is similar to a fish —**ich·thy·oid** *adj.* —**ich·thy·oi·dal** /íkthee óyd'l/ *adj.*

ichthyol. *abbr.* ichthyology

ich·thy·ol·o·gy /íkthee óllәjee/ *n.* the branch of zoology that deals with the scientific study of fish —**ich·thy·o·log·ic** /íkthee ə lójjik/ *adj.* —**ich·thy·o·log·i·cal** *adj.* —**ich·thy·o·log·i·cal·ly** *adv.* —**ich·thy·ol·o·gist** /íkthee óllәjist/ *n.*

ich·thy·oph·a·gous /íkthee óffəgəss/ *adj.* eating or feeding on fish

ich·thy·or·nis /íkthee áwrniss/ *n.* a prehistoric toothed bird, similar to a gull, that lived during the Cretaceous period. Genus: *Ichthyornis.* [Late 19thC. From modern Latin, genus name, literally "fish-bird," from Greek *ikhthus* "fish" + *ornis* "bird" (source of English *ornitho-*).]

ich·thy·o·saur /íkthee əsàwr/, **ich·thy·o·sau·rus** /íkthee ə sáwrəss/ (*plural* **-rus·es** *or* **-ri** /-rī/) *n.* a prehistoric reptile with a long snout and paddle-shaped limbs that lived in the sea during the Mesozoic era. Order: Ichthyosauria. [Mid-19thC. From modern Latin *Ichthyosauria*, order name, literally "fish-lizards," from Greek *ikhthus* "fish" + *sauros* "lizard."] —**ich·thy·o·sau·ri·an** /íkthee ə sáwree ən/ *adj.*

ich·thy·o·sis /íkthi óssiss/ *n.* a disease that causes the skin to become dry, thick, and scaly

ich·thys *n.* = **ichthus**

-ician *suffix.* one who practices or specializes in ○ *musician* ○ *statistician* [From Old French *-icien*, from *-ique* (see -IC)]

i·ci·cle /íssik'l/ *n.* **1.** HANGING ICE a hanging tapered rod of ice, formed when dripping water freezes **2.** SOMEBODY VERY RESERVED somebody who is aloof or unemotional (*informal*) **3.** DECORATION ON CHRISTMAS TREE a decoration for Christmas trees resembling an icicle, made of a thin strip of foil or formed from plastic or glass [14thC. From ICE + obsolete *ickle* "icicle," from Old English *gicel*, of prehistoric Germanic origin.]

i·ci·ly /íssilee/ *adv.* in a very aloof or unfriendly manner

i·ci·ness /ísseenəss/ *n.* **1.** BEING COVERED WITH ICE the state of being covered with ice **2.** EXTREME COLDNESS extreme coldness, usually to the point of freezing ○ *the wind's iciness* **3.** UNFRIENDLINESS extreme aloofness or unfriendliness of manner ○ *the iciness of her tone*

ic·ing /íssing/ *n.* **1.** FOOD GLAZING OR FROSTING FOR CAKES a sugar-based decorative coating for cakes, either soft or hardened, made by mixing powdered sugar with water or another binding substance and often other ingredients or flavorings **2.** METEOROL FORMATION OF ICE the formation of ice on surfaces, e.g., on aircraft or ships ○ *Some bridges and overpasses are more predisposed to icing than paved roads.* **3.** HOCKEY SHOOTING PUCK INTO OPPOSING TERRITORY in ice hockey, the action of shooting the puck out of defensive territory and far into the opposing team's territory ◇ **the icing on the cake** something additional that makes something that was already good even better

ic·ing sug·ar *n. U.K.* = **confectioners' sugar**

ICJ *abbr.* International Court of Justice

Ickes /íkəss/, **Harold L.** (1874–1952) U.S. lawyer and public official. He was Franklin D. Roosevelt's Secretary of the Interior (1933–46). Full name **Harold Leclair Ickes**

ick·y /íkee/ (**-i·er, -i·est**) *adj.* (*informal*) **1.** STICKY disgustingly and messily sticky **2.** NASTY generally nasty or unpleasant ○ *I had an icky feeling in their presence.* **3.** SENTIMENTAL sentimental in a silly or childish way ○ *a script with some pretty icky lines* [Early 20thC. Origin uncertain.] —**ick·i·ness** *n.*

ICM *abbr.* **1.** Institute of Credit Management **2.** Intergovernmental Committee for Migrations (*part of the UN*)

Icon: Eastern Orthodox icon of *Christus Acheiropoietus* in the Cathedral of the Assumption, Moscow

i·con /í kòn/ *n.* **1.** **i·con, i·kon** RELIG IMAGE OF HOLY PERSON a holy picture, carving, or statue of Jesus Christ, the Virgin Mary, or a saint, especially an oil painting on a wooden panel, used in worship in the Eastern Orthodox churches **2.** SOMEBODY FAMOUS FOR SOMETHING somebody or something widely and uncritically admired, especially somebody or something symbolizing a movement or field of activity ○ *the all-time rock 'n' roll icon.* **3.** COMPUT PICTURE ON COMPUTER SCREEN a small image on a computer screen that represents something, e.g., a program or device that is activated by a mouse click or a trash bin for unwanted files ○ *Open the program by clicking on its icon.* **4.** COMMUNICATION RECOGNIZABLE SYMBOL a picture or symbol that is universally recognized to be representative of something ○ *The icon of a walking person is the international symbol to indicate that it's safe to cross the street.* **5.** SIGN a word or sign that stands for something else, e.g., the Roman numeral "II" representing the number two [Mid-16thC. Via Latin from Greek *eikōn* "likeness, image." Ultimately from an Indo-European word meaning "to be like."]

icon- *prefix.* = **icono-**

i·con·ic /ī kónnik/ *adj.* **1.** CHARACTERIZED BY FAME relating to or characteristic of somebody or something admired as an icon ○ *Their fame has grown to iconic proportions.* **2.** RELIG TYPICAL OF A RELIGIOUS ICON relating to or characteristic of a religious icon ○ *iconic images* **3.** SCULPTURE CONVENTIONAL made in a conventional style or pose, especially that of ancient Greek statues of athletes —**i·con·i·cal·ly** *adv.*

i·con·ic mem·o·ry *n.* a form of memory in which objects are retained briefly but clearly as a visual image after the stimulus has been removed. It develops between the ages of two and six when a child begins to use images to stand for objects.

icono- *prefix.* icon, image ○ *iconolatry* ○ *iconoscope* [From Greek *eikōn*]

i·con·o·clasm /ī kónnə klàzzəm/ *n.* **1.** CHALLENGE TO TRADITION a challenge to and overturning of traditional beliefs, customs, and values **2.** RELIG BREAKING OF RELIGIOUS IMAGES the destruction of religious images used in worship, or opposition to their use in worship

i·con·o·clast /ī kónnə klàst/ *n.* **1.** SOMEBODY CHALLENGING TRADITION somebody who challenges or overturns traditional beliefs, customs, and values **2.** RELIG DESTROYER OF RELIGIOUS IMAGES somebody who destroys religious images used in worship or is opposed to their use in worship **3.** HIST HERETIC IN GREEK ORTHODOX CHURCH a member of an 8th-century movement in the Greek Orthodox Church that tried to end the use of icons [Mid-17thC. Via medieval Latin *iconoclastes* from medieval Greek *eikonoklastēs* "image-breaker," from Greek *eikōn* (see ICON) + *klan* "to break."] —**i·con·o·clas·tic** /ī kònnə klástik/ *adj.* —**i·con·o·clas·ti·cal·ly** *adv.*

i·co·nog·ra·phy /īkə nóggrəfee/ *n.* **1.** COMMUNICATION SET OF RECOGNIZED IMAGES the set of symbols or images used in a particular field of activity, e.g., music or the movies, and recognized by people as having a particular meaning ○ *In the 1960s, peace signs, long hair, work shirts, and blue jeans were part of the iconography of rebellion.* **2.** PAINTING SYMBOLS IN PAINTING the symbols and images used conventionally in a genre of painting, or the study and interpretation of these symbols and images ○ *the iconography used in Renaissance paintings of the Virgin and Child* **3.** IMAGES OF SOMEBODY OR SOMETHING SPECIFIC the collection, description, or study of images of somebody or something specific —**i·co·nog·ra·pher** *n.* —**i·con·o·graph·ic** /ī kònnə gráffik/ *adj.* —**i·con·o·graph·i·cal** *adj.*

i·co·nol·a·try /īkə nóllətree/ *n.* the worshiping of religious images rather than of what they represent (*disapproving*) —**i·co·nol·a·ter** *n.*

i·co·nol·o·gy /īkə nólləjee/ *n.* the study of artistic images and their symbolism and interpretation —**i·con·o·log·i·cal** /ī kònnə lójjik'l/ *adj.* —**i·co·nol·o·gist** /īkə nólləjist/ *n.*

i·con·o·scope /ī kónnə skōp/ *n.* an early form of television camera tube in which an image is converted into electrical impulses [Mid-19thC. The earliest meaning of the word was "instrument for giving an impression of depth to flat pictures."]

i·co·nos·ta·sis /īkə nóstəssiss/ (*plural* **-ses** /-sēez/), **i·co·nos·tas** /ī kónnə stàss/ (*plural* **-ta·ses** /-tàsseez/) *n.* a screen on which icons are mounted, used in Eastern Orthodox churches to separate the area around the altar from the main part of the church [Mid-19thC. From modern Greek *eikonostasis*, literally "place where images stand."]

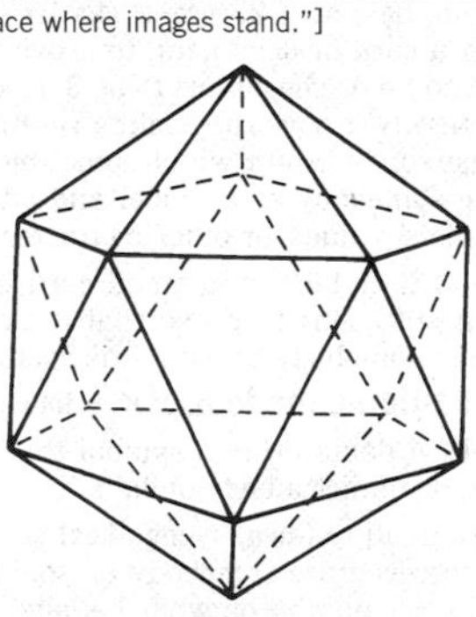
Icosahedron

i·co·sa·he·dron /ī kōssə hēedrən/ (*plural* **-drons** *or* **-dra** /-drə/) *n.* a solid geometric figure having 20 sides or faces [Late 16thC. Via late Latin *icosahedrum* from Greek *eikosaedron*, from *eikosi* "twenty" + *hedra* "base."] —**i·co·sa·he·dral** *adj.*

i·co·si·tet·ra·he·dron /ī kōssə téttrə hēedrən/ (*plural* **-drons** *or* **-dra** /-drə/) *n.* a solid geometric figure having 24 sides or faces [Mid-19thC. Coined from Greek *eikosi* "twenty" + *tetra-* "four" + -HEDRON.]

ICPO *abbr.* International Criminal Police Organization

ICR *abbr.* **1.** COMPUT intelligent character recognition **2.** Institute for Cancer Research

ICRC *abbr.* International Committee of the Red Cross

ICS *abbr.* **1.** installment credit selling **2.** Institute of Chartered Shipbrokers **3.** International Chamber of Shipping **4.** international consultancy service

-ics *suffix.* **1.** SCIENCE forms words meaning a science, art, or knowledge ○ *physics* ○ *mathematics* **2.** ACTIVITY forms words meaning an activity or action ○ *calisthenics* [From -IC + -S; translation of Greek *-ika* "matters pertaining to a certain subject," hence used as name of treatises]

ic·ter·ic /ik térrik/ *adj.* affected with, relating to, or resembling jaundice

ic·ter·us /íktərəss/ *n.* jaundice (*technical*) [Early 18thC. Via Latin from Greek *ikteros*, of unknown origin.] —**ic·ter·ic** /ik térrik/ *adj.*

ic·tus /íktəss/ (*plural* **-tus** *or* **-tus·es**) *n.* **1.** MED SEIZURE a seizure (*technical*) **2.** POETRY STRESS ON SYLLABLES the stress that falls on syllables in poetic rhythm [Early 18thC. From Latin, originally the past participle of *icere* "to strike," of unknown origin.] —**ic·tal** *adj.*

ICU *abbr.* intensive care unit

ic·y /íssee/ (**-i·er, -i·est**) *adj.* **1.** ICE-COVERED covered in ice, or involving the presence of ice **2.** VERY COLD extremely cold, like ice ○ *Your hands are icy.* **3.** UNFRIENDLY very aloof or unfriendly ○ *his reserved manner and icy voice*

id /id/ *n.* in Freudian psychoanalytic theory, the part of the psyche that is unconscious and the source of primitive instinctive impulses and drives. The other parts of the psyche are the ego and the superego. [Early 20thC. From Latin, "it"; translation of German *es*.]

I'd /īd/ *contr.* **1.** I HAD I had ○ *I'd forgotten you were coming.* **2.** I WOULD I would or should

ID[1] *abbr.* **1.** identification **2.** infectious disease(s) **3.** internal diameter **4.** Intelligence Department **5.** **ID, i.d.** ANAT intradermal **6.** MAIL Idaho

ID[2] (**IDed, IDing, IDs**) *vt.* to identify somebody, or check somebody's identity (*informal*) ○ *Police to ID the suspect.*

id. *abbr.* idem

Id. *abbr.* Idaho

-id *suffix.* **1.** INDICATING METEORS forms nouns meaning objects, especially meteors, that appear to come from a specified constellation ○ *Perseids* **2.** PHYS INDICATING PARTICLE forms names for particular kinds of particle or body ○ *energid* **3.** ZOOL INDICATING ANIMAL a member of a zoological family ○ *camelid* **4.** INDICATING DYNASTY a member of a dynasty ○ *Abbasid* [Directly or via French *-ide* from Latin *-ides*, from Greek *-idēs* "offspring of"]

IDA *abbr.* International Development Association

Ida. *abbr.* Idaho

Idaho

I·da·ho /ídəhō/ state in the western United States bordered by Montana, Nevada, Oregon, Utah, Washington, and Wyoming, and British Columbia, Canada. Capital: Boise. Population: 1,210,232 (1997). Area: 83,574 sq. mi./216,456 sq. km. —**Ida·ho·an** *adj., n.*

I·da·ho Falls /ídəhō-/ city in southeastern Idaho, on the Snake River, northeast of Pocatello. Population: 48,079 (1996).

Id al-Ad·ha /id aal áadə/ *n.* an important Islamic annual festival, the Feast of the Sacrifice, commemorating Abraham's sacrifice of the lamb in place of his son Isaac

Id al-Fitr /id aal fíttər/ *n.* an important Islamic annual festival and public holiday, the Feast of Breaking the Fast, marking the end of the Ramadan fast

I·da Mountains /ídə-/ mountain range in northwestern Turkey, southeast of the ancient site of Troy. The highest peak is Mount Gargarus, 5,797 ft./1,767 m.

IDB *abbr.* 1. Industrial Development Bank 2. Inter-American Development Bank

ID card *n.* a card identifying its carrier, having on it such information as name, age, and often an address and a physicial description or photograph (*informal*)

IDD *abbr.* 1. TELECOM international direct dialing 2. insulin-dependent diabetes

IDDD *abbr.* international direct distance dialing

-ide *suffix.* 1. **REFERRING TO CLASS** forms names for classes of elements or compounds ○ *actinides* 2. **NAMES OF ORGANIC COMPOUNDS** forms names for organic compounds derived from other compounds ○ *anhydride* [From OXIDE]

i·de·a /ī deé ə/ *n.* 1. **OPINION** a personal opinion or belief ○ *Do you have any ideas on how the problem should be dealt with?* 2. **SUGGESTION** a thought to be presented as a suggestion ○ *It was her idea to plant daisies.* 3. **IMPRESSION** an impression or knowledge of something ○ *We have no idea how much it would cost.* 4. **PLAN** a realization of a possible way of doing something or of something to be done ○ *Watching the beaver building its dam gave me an idea.* 5. **AIM** the aim or purpose of a project or plan ○ *The idea of the new program is to keep young people in school.* 6. **GIST** the gist or précis of something such as a book, report, project, or plan ○ *give you only a broad idea now, with a detailed outline to follow* 7. **THOUGHT** a thought about or mental picture of something such as a future or possible event ○ *Sometimes the idea of having to speak in public is worse than actually doing it.* 8. **CONCEPT** a concept that exists in the mind only ○ *discussing the idea of morality* 9. **MENTAL IMAGE** a mental image that reflects reality [14thC. Via Latin from Greek, "look," formed from *idein* "to see" (source of English *identity*). The meaning developed in Greek from "appearance" via "image" to "mental image, notion."] —**ide·a·less** *adj.* ◇ **get ideas** to become ambitious or begin thinking undesirable thoughts (*informal*) ◇ **have no idea** to know nothing at all, especially about a particular subject ◇ **what's the big idea?** used, often angrily, to ask about somebody's intention or about what is happening

i·de·al /ī deé əl/ *n.* 1. **PERFECT EXAMPLE** an excellent or perfect example of something or somebody, or something that is considered a perfect example ○ *By her third movie, she had become the world's ideal of beauty and grace.* 2. **PRINCIPLE** a standard or principle to which people aspire ○ *political ideals* 3. **IMAGINARY OBJECT OR CONCEPT** a concept that exists in the imagination only ■ *adj.* 1. **BEST** serving as the best or most perfect example 2. **PERFECT** perfect but existing only in the imagination ○ *In an ideal world, such horrors wouldn't happen.* 3. **EXCELLENT** excellent or perfectly suitable ○ *A later meeting would be ideal for me.* [15thC. Directly or via French *idéal* from late Latin *idealis*, from Latin *idea* "IDEA." The English word originally meant "existing as an archetype."] —**ide·al·less** *adj.* —**ide·al·ness** *n.*

i·de·al gas *n.* a hypothetical gas that obeys the gas laws perfectly at all temperatures and pressures

i·de·al·ism /ī deé ə lìzzəm/ *n.* 1. **BELIEF IN PERFECTION** belief in and pursuit of perfection as an attainable goal ○ *youthful idealism* 2. **LIVING BY HIGH IDEALS** aspiring to or living in accordance with high standards or principles 3. PHILOS **BELIEF THAT MATERIAL THINGS ARE IMAGINARY** the philosophical belief that material things do not exist independently but only as constructions in the mind

i·de·al·ist /ī deé əlist/ *n.* 1. **IMPRACTICAL PERSON** somebody who rejects practical considerations in favor of the pursuit of perfection ○ *too much of an idealist to compromise with her opponents* 2. **SOMEBODY WITH HIGH IDEALS** somebody who aspires to or lives in accordance with high standards or principles 3. PHILOS **BELIEVER IN PHILOSOPHICAL IDEALISM** a believer in a philosophy holding that material objects do not exist independently of the mind —**i·de·al·is·tic** /ī deé ə lístik/ *adj.* —**i·de·al·is·ti·cal·ly** *adv.*

i·de·al·i·ty /ìdee állətee/ *n.* 1. **CONDITION OF BEING IDEAL** the condition or quality of being ideal 2. **STATUS AS IDEA** existence as an idea only, rather than as a concrete object

i·de·al·ize /ī deé ə lìz/ (**-ized, -iz·ing, -iz·es**) *v.* 1. *vt.* **IMAGINE AS PERFECT** to think of or represent somebody or something as being perfect, ignoring any imperfections that exist or may exist in reality ○ *paintings that idealize feminine beauty* 2. *vi.* **FORMULATE IDEALS** to form ideals in the mind ○ *He has a tendency to idealize.* —**i·de·al·i·za·tion** /ī deé əli záysh'n/ *n.* —**i·de·al·iz·er** /ī deé ə lìzər/ *n.*

i·de·al·ly /ī deé əlee/ *adv.* 1. **IN AN IDEAL SITUATION** if everything were perfect or as desired ○ *Ideally, I'd like to finish the job by next week.* 2. **PERFECTLY** in a perfect manner ○ *She is ideally suited to the post.* 3. **THEORETICALLY** in theory or in the imagination

i·de·ate /ídee àyt/ (**-at·ed, -at·ing, -ates**) *vti.* to form an idea of something, or form ideas [Early 17thC. From medieval Latin *ideat-*, the past participle stem of *ideare* "to form an idea or conception," from Latin *idea* "IDEA."] —**i·de·a·tion** /ìdee áysh'n/ *n.* —**i·de·a·tion·al** *adj.* —**i·de·a·tion·al·ly** /-áyshnəlee/ *adv.* —**i·de·a·tive** /ídee ətiv, -àytiv/ *adj.*

i·dée fixe /ee dày féeks/ (*plural* **i·dées fixes** /ee dày féeks/) *n.* an idea that remains fixed and unchanging in the mind and often becomes an obsession [From French, literally "fixed idea"]

i·dée re·çue /ee dày rə sóo, -sǘ/ (*plural* **i·dées re·çues** /ee dày rə sóo, -sǘ/) *n.* a conventional or commonplace idea [From French, literally "received idea"]

i·dem /í dèm, í dèm/ *pron.* the same, especially a book, article, or chapter previously referred to [14thC. From Latin, "same" (see IDENTITY).]

i·dem·po·tent /ī dem pṓt'nt, ì dem-/ *adj.* remaining unchanged when multiplied by itself [Late 19thC. From Latin *idem* "same" (see IDENTITY) + the stem *potent-* "powerful" (source of English *potent*).]

i·den·tic /ī déntik/ *adj.* 1. POL **WITH THE SAME DIPLOMATIC FORM** used to describe diplomatic notes sent, or diplomatic action taken, by two or more governments in exactly the same form 2. **IDENTICAL** identical (*archaic*) [Mid-17thC. From medieval Latin *identicus* "identical," from *ident-*, combining form of Latin *idem* "same" (see IDENTITY).]

i·den·ti·cal /ī déntik'l/ *adj.* 1. **ONE AND THE SAME** being one single person or thing though appearing in different guises or disguises 2. **ALIKE IN EVERY WAY** exactly the same as or equal to something else, or alike in every respect [Late 16thC. Formed from medieval Latin *identicus*, from *ident-*, combining form of Latin *idem* "same" (see IDENTITY).] —**i·den·ti·cal·ly** *adv.* —**i·den·ti·cal·ness** *n.*

i·den·ti·cal rhyme *n.* 1. **RHYME MADE BY WORD REPETITION** a rhyme created by a repeated word 2. = **rime riche**

i·den·ti·cal twin *n.* one of a pair of twins of the same sex and with the same genetic makeup who develop from a single fertilized egg

i·den·ti·fi·ca·tion /ī dèntəfi káysh'n/ *n.* 1. **CONNECTION OF IDENTITY** the action or an act of recognizing and naming somebody or something or otherwise identifying him, her, or it 2. **PROOF OF IDENTITY** something, especially a card or document, to prove that somebody is who he or she claims to be 3. PSYCHOL **STRONG FEELING OF AFFINITY** a powerful feeling of affinity with another person or group, which sometimes involves regarding somebody as a model and adopting his or her beliefs, values, or other characteristics

i·den·ti·fi·ca·tion card *n.* a small card holding information sufficient to prove that a claim or description of somebody bearing it is accurate

i·den·ti·fi·ca·tion pa·rade *n.* *U.K.* = **lineup** *n.* 3

i·den·ti·fi·er /ī déntə fìr/ *n.* a symbol that identifies, indicates, or names a body of data

i·den·ti·fy /ī dénti fì/ (**-fied, -fy·ing, -fies**) *vt.* 1. **RECOGNIZE AND NAME** to recognize somebody or something and to be able to say who or what he, she, or it is 2. **CONSIDER AS THE SAME** to consider two or more things as being entirely or essentially the same [Mid-17thC. Directly or via French *identifier* from medieval Latin *identificare*, literally "to make the same," from *ident-* (see IDENTITY).] —**i·den·ti·fi·a·bil·i·ty** /ī dènti fì ə bíllətee/ *n.* —**i·den·ti·fi·a·ble** /ī dénti fì əb'l/ *adj.* —**i·den·ti·fi·a·bly** *adv.*

identify with *v.* 1. *vt.* **FEEL AFFINITY WITH** to feel a strong sympathetic or imaginative bond with somebody or something and a sense of understanding and sharing his, her, or its nature or concerns 2. **ASSOCIATE ONE THING WITH ANOTHER** to consider somebody or something as closely linked with somebody or something, e.g., a school of thought or political movement (*often passive*)

i·den·ti·ty /ī déntitee/ (*plural* **-ties**) *n.* 1. **WHAT IDENTIFIES SOMEBODY OR SOMETHING** who somebody is or what something is, especially the name somebody or something is known by. ◊ **individuality** 2. **SOMEBODY'S ESSENTIAL SELF** the set of characteristics that somebody recognizes as belonging uniquely to himself or herself and constituting his or her individual personality for life 3. **SAMENESS** the fact or condition of being the same or exactly alike 4. *ANZ* **CELEBRITY** somebody who is well known in a particular field of activity (*informal*) 5. MATH **EQUATION TRUE FOR ALL ITS VARIABLES** a mathematical equation that remains valid whatever values are taken by its variables 6. MATH = **identity element** [Late 16thC. From late Latin *identitas*, from *ident-*, combining form of Latin *idem* "same," from *id* "that."]

i·den·ti·ty card *n.* *U.K.* = **identification card**

i·den·ti·ty cri·sis *n.* 1. **ANXIETY ABOUT SOCIAL ROLE** a period during which somebody feels great anxiety and uncertainty about his or her identity and role in life and society, typically experienced in adolescence or middle age 2. **ANXIETY OF GROUP** a period of anxiety or confusion about the nature, aims, and role of a group, organization, or business

i·den·ti·ty el·e·ment *n.* an element of a set that leaves other elements unchanged when combined with them

i·den·ti·ty ma·trix *n.* a square matrix that has the numeral 1 in each position on the principal diagonal and 0 in all other positions

ideo- *prefix.* forms words whose meaning involves ideas ○ *ideomotor* [Via French from, ultimately, Greek *idea* (see IDEA)]

id·e·o·gram /ídee ə gràm, íddee-/, **id·e·o·graph** /-gràf/ *n.* 1. **SYMBOL IN WRITING SYSTEM** a symbol used in some writing systems, e.g., those of Japan and China, that directly but abstractly represents the thing or concept itself rather than the word for it 2. **GRAPHIC SYMBOL** a symbol or graphic character, e.g., "@" or "&," used to represent a word —**id·e·o·gram·mat·ic** /ìdee əgrə máttik, -máttik/ *adj.* —**id·e·o·gram·mat·i·cal·ly** /-máttikəlee/ *adv.* —**id·e·o·graph·ic** /-gráffik/ *adj.* —**id·e·o·graph·i·cal·ly** /-gráffikəlee/ *adv.*

id·e·og·ra·phy /ìdee óggrəfee, ìddee-/ *n.* the use of graphical symbols to convey ideas

i·de·o·log·i·cal /ìdee ə lójjik'l, ìddee-/, **i·de·o·log·ic** /-lójjik/ *adj.* based on a particular ideology, or relating to an ideology or to ideologies, especially to ideologies that conflict —**id·e·o·log·i·cal·ly** *adv.*

i·de·ol·o·gist /ìdee óllәjist, ìddee-/ *n.* 1. **BELIEVER IN SYSTEM OF IDEAS** somebody who advocates or supports a particular ideology 2. **SOMEBODY WHO WORKS ON BELIEF SYSTEM** somebody who devises or revises an ideology

i·de·o·logue /ídee ə lòg, íddee-/ *n.* an ideologist, especially a particularly zealous or doctrinaire supporter of an ideology [Early 19thC. From French *idéologue*, back-formation from *idéologie* (see IDEOLOGY).]

i·de·ol·o·gy /ìdee óllәjee, ìddee-/ (*plural* **-gies**) *n.* 1. **SYSTEM OF SOCIAL BELIEFS** a closely organized system of beliefs, values, and ideas forming the basis of a social, economic, or political philosophy or program 2. **MEANINGFUL BELIEF SYSTEM** a set of beliefs, values, and opinions that shapes the way an individual or a group such as a social class thinks, acts, and understands the world [Late 18thC. From French *idéologie*, literally "science of ideas," from *idéo-* IDEO- + *-logie* -LOGY.]

i·de·o·mo·tor /ìdee ə mṓtər, ìddee-/ *adj.* used to describe body movements triggered by thoughts rather than by external stimuli

ides /īdz/, **Ides** *npl.* in the ancient Roman calendar, the name given to the 15th day of March, May, July, and October, or the 13th day of any other month (*takes a singular or plural verb*) [12thC. Directly or via French from Latin *idus* (plural), of uncertain origin: perhaps from Etruscan.]

-idine *suffix.* forms names for chemical compounds related to another compound ○ *histidine* [From -IDE + -INE]

idio- *prefix.* forms words whose meaning involves the idea of being private, individual, proper, or distinctive ○ *idiolect* ○ *idiomorphic* [From Greek *idios* "one's own, private." Ultimately from an Indo-European base meaning "self," which is also the ancestor of English *self*, *ethnic*, and *custom*.]

id·i·o·blast /íddee ə blàst/ *n.* a specialized plant cell that differs considerably from others in the same area of tissue. An idioblast is usually thick-walled and lacks chlorophyll. —**id·i·o·blas·tic** /ìddee ə blástik/ *adj.*

id·i·o·cy /íddee əssee/ *n.* 1. **EXTREME LACK OF INTELLIGENCE OR FORESIGHT** extreme lack of intelligence or foresight

2. EXTREMELY UNINTELLIGENT OR THOUGHTLESS ACT an extremely unintelligent or thoughtless act 3. AN OFFENSIVE TERM an offensive term in a now disused classification system for mental disability (*dated offensive*) [Early 16thC. Formed from IDIOT; perhaps modeled on words such as ACCURACY.]

id·i·o·glos·si·a /iddee ə glóssee ə/ *n.* 1. CHILDHOOD SPEECH DEFECT a developmental speech defect in which a child substitutes different sounds for the correct ones, so that speech is intelligible only to parents or others closely involved with the child 2. PRIVATE LANGUAGE the invention and use of language by a child or closely involved siblings such as twins that is unintelligible to anyone else [Late 19thC. Formed from Greek *idioglōssos*, literally "of distinct tongue," from *idios* "distinct" + *glossa* "tongue."]

id·i·o·gram /íddee ə gràm/ *n.* a graphic representation of one or more chromosomes

id·i·o·graph·ic /iddee ə gráffik/ *adj.* concentrating on particular cases and the unique traits or functioning of individuals, rather than on broad generalizations about human behavior. Idiographic research methods in psychology include the case study, which is characterized by the distinctiveness of each case. ◊ **nomothetic**

id·i·o·lect /íddee ə lèkt/ *n.* an individual person's vocabulary and particular and unique way of using language [Mid-20thC. Coined from IDIO- + DIALECT.] —**id·i·o·lec·tal** /iddee ə lékt'l/ *adj.*

id·i·om /íddee əm/ *n.* 1. FIXED EXPRESSION WITH NONLITERAL MEANING a fixed, distinctive, and often colorful expression whose meaning cannot be understood from the combined meanings of its individual words, e.g., "to have somebody in stitches" 2. NATURAL WAY OF USING A LANGUAGE the way of using a particular language that comes naturally to its native speakers and involves both knowledge of its grammar and familiarity with its usage 3. STYLISTIC EXPRESSION OF PERSON OR GROUP the style of expression of a specific individual or group 4. ARTS DISTINGUISHING ARTISTIC STYLE the characteristic style of an artist or artistic group [Late 16thC. Directly or via French *idiome* from late Latin *idioma*, from Greek, "property, peculiarity," from, ultimately, *idios* (see IDIO-).]

id·i·o·mat·ic /iddee ə máttik/, **id·i·o·mat·i·cal** /-máttik'l/ *adj.* 1. CHARACTERISTIC OF NATIVE-SPEAKER USE characteristic of, or in keeping with, the way a language is ordinarily and naturally used by its native speakers 2. OF THE NATURE OF AN IDIOM having a meaning not deducible from the combined meanings of the words that make it up ○ *an idiomatic phrase* 3. ARTS CHARACTERISTIC OF PARTICULAR STYLE characteristic of a particular style, or using a particular and distinctive style, especially in the arts —**id·i·o·mat·i·cal·ly** *adv.* —**id·i·o·mat·ic·ness** *n.*

id·i·o·mor·phic /iddee ə máwrfik/ *adj.* used to describe minerals that occur naturally in the form of fully developed crystals —**id·i·o·mor·phi·cal·ly** *adv.* —**id·i·o·mor·phism** *n.*

id·i·o·path·ic /iddee ə páthik/ *adj.* used to describe a disease or disorder that has no known cause —**id·i·o·path·i·cal·ly** *adv.*

id·i·op·a·thy /iddee óppəthee/ (*plural* **-thies**) *n.* a disease of unknown cause [Late 17thC. Via modern Latin *idiopathia* "primary disease" from Greek *idiopatheia*, from *idio-* "IDIO-" + *-patheia* "-pathy."]

id·i·o·phone /iddee ə fōn/ *n.* a percussion instrument, e.g. a gong or xylophone, that is made from resonating material that does not have to be tuned —**id·i·o·phon·ic** /iddee ə fónnik/ *adj.*

id·i·o·syn·cra·sy /iddee ə síngkrəssee/ (*plural* **-sies**) *n.* 1. QUIRK a way of behaving, thinking, or feeling that is peculiar to an individual or group, especially an odd or unusual one 2. MED UNUSUAL RESPONSE TO SOMETHING an unusual or exaggerated reaction to a drug or food that is not caused by an allergy [Early 17thC. Directly or via French *idiosyncrasie* from Greek *idiosugkrasia*, literally "personal mixing together," from, ultimately, *krasis* "mixing."] —**id·i·o·syn·crat·ic** /iddee əsing kráttik/ *adj.* —**id·i·o·syn·crat·i·cal·ly** /-kəlee/ *adv.*

id·i·ot /íddee ət/ *n.* 1. OFFENSIVE TERM an offensive term that deliberately insults somebody else's intelligence (*insult*) 2. OFFENSIVE TERM an offensive term in a now disused classification system for somebody with an IQ of about 25 or under and a mental age of less than three years (*dated offensive*) [14thC. Via French from, ultimately, Greek *idiōtēs* "private person, layperson lacking specialized knowledge," from *idios* (see IDIO-).]

id·i·ot board *n.* a placard, projector, or continuous roll of paper that prompts a television performer with lines to be spoken (*slang*)

id·i·ot box *n.* television or a television set (*slang*) [*Idiot* from the belief that watching too much television causes stupidity]

id·i·ot card *n.* TV = **idiot board** (*slang*)

id·i·ot·ic /iddee óttik/ *adj.* an offensive term that deliberately insults somebody else's behavior (*insult*) —**id·i·ot·i·cal·ly** *adv.*

id·i·ot light *n.* a warning light (*slang disapproving*) [*Idiot* from the idea that the light is for people who can't figure out the gauges]

id·i·ot-proof *adj.* constructed or designed so as not to fail or go wrong even if misused

id·i·ot sa·vant /iddee ət sa vaánt, -sə vaánt/ (*plural* **id·i·ot sa·vants** /iddee ət sa vaánt, -sə vaánt/ *or* **id·i·ots sa·vants** /iddee ət sa vaánt, -sə vaánt/) *n.* somebody who has a psychiatric disorder or a learning problem but who is exceptionally gifted in one particular area, e.g., rapid mental calculation, architectural drawing, or remembering facts (*sometimes considered offensive*) [From French, literally "learned idiot"]

id·i·ot tape *n.* a tape for a typesetting machine that contains text but no formatting except markers for new paragraphs

i·dle /íd'l/ *adj.* (**i·dler, i·dlest**) 1. NOT WORKING OR IN USE not working, operating, producing, or in use 2. LAZY lazy and unwilling to work 3. FRIVOLOUS serving no serious purpose, or frivolous and a waste of time 4. NOT EARNING MONEY not being used to yield a financial return ○ *idle funds* 5. UNFOUNDED having no basis in fact ○ *idle gossip* 6. INEFFECTIVE unlikely to be carried out or impossible to put into effect ○ *idle threats* 7. SPORTS NOT PLAYING not playing or competing ■ *n.* CARS SPEED OF ENGINE WITH GEAR DISENGAGED the speed of a motor vehicle engine that is running but is not in gear, or the way it runs ■ *v.* (**i·dled, i·dling, i·dles**) 1. *vti.* PASS TIME AIMLESSLY to be lazy and avoid work, or to pass the time lazily doing nothing in particular 2. *vi.* MOVE SLOWLY AND AIMLESSLY to move in slow and lazy or aimless way 3. *vti.* RUN WITHOUT APPLYING POWER to run gently with the gear disengaged, or to allow an engine to do this 4. *vt.* MAKE UNEMPLOYED to make workers unemployed or inactive [Old English *īdel* "worthless, empty," from a prehistoric Germanic word of unknown origin] —**i·dle·ness** *n.* —**i·dly** *adv.*

WORD KEY: SYNONYMS

See Synonyms at ***vain***.

i·dle pul·ley, **i·dler pul·ley** *n.* a freely rotating pulley wheel that guides or takes up slack from a drive belt by pressing against it

i·dler /ídlər/ *n.* 1. LAZY PERSON somebody who avoids work or who spends time in a lazy or relaxed fashion 2. MECH ENG = **idle wheel**

i·dler pul·ley *n.* = **idle pulley**

i·dler wheel *n.* = **idle wheel**

i·dle time *n.* a period during which a device, machine, or employee is temporarily inactive

i·dle wheel, **i·dler wheel** *n.* 1. MECHANISM THAT TRANSMITS MOTION a gear wheel or roller placed between two others to transmit motion between them without changing their speed or direction or to provide support 2. = **idle pulley**

i·do·crase /ídə krayss, ídə kràyz, íddə kràyss, íddə kràyz/ *n.* MINERALS = **vesuvianite** [Early 19thC. From Greek *eidos* "form" (see IDOL) + *krasis* "mixture."]

i·dol /íd'l/ *n.* 1. OBJECT OF ADORATION somebody or something greatly and often fanatically admired and loved (*disapproving*) 2. RELIG OBJECT WORSHIPED AS GOD something, such as a statue or carved image, that is worshiped as a god 3. RELIG FORBIDDEN OBJECT OF WORSHIP in monotheistic religions, any object of worship other than the one God [13thC. Via French *idole* from, ultimately, Greek *eidōlon* "image," from *eidos* "form, shape" (source of English *idyll* and *kaleidoscope*).]

i·dol·a·ter /ī dóllətər/ *n.* 1. WORSHIPER OF IDOLS somebody who worships idols (*disapproving*) 2. EXTREME ADMIRER a fanatical admirer of somebody or something [14thC. Formed from French *idolâtre*, from, ultimately, Greek *eidōlolatrēs*, literally "image worshiper," from *eidōlon* (see IDOL).]

i·dol·a·tress /ī dóllətrəss/ *n.* a woman who worships idols (*dated disapproving*)

i·dol·a·try /ī dóllətree/ *n.* 1. EXTREME ADMIRATION extreme admiration or fanatical devotion to somebody or something 2. IDOL WORSHIP the worship of idols or false gods (*disapproving*) [13thC. Via French *idolâtrie* from, ultimately, Greek *eidōlolatreia*, literally "image-worship," from *eidōlon* (see IDOL).] —**i·dol·a·trous** *adj.* —**i·dol·a·trous·ly** *adv.*

i·dol·ize /íd'l īz/ (**-ized, -iz·ing, -iz·es**) *vt.* 1. ADMIRE FANATICALLY to feel great admiration and respect for, or be fanatically devoted to, somebody or something 2. WORSHIP AS IDOL to worship something or somebody as an idol (*disapproving*) —**i·dol·i·za·tion** /íd'li záysh'n/ *n.* —**i·dol·iz·er** /íd'l īzər/ *n.*

i·dyll /íd'l/, **i·dyl** *n.* 1. EXPERIENCE OF SERENE HAPPINESS an experience or period of serene and carefree happiness, usually in beautiful surroundings and often in the context of a romantic relationship 2. TRANQUIL CHARMING SCENE a scene or event characterized by tranquility, simple beauty, and innocent charm, usually in a rural setting 3. ARTS LITERARY PIECE ABOUT CHARMING RURAL LIFE a short work in verse or prose, a painting, or a piece of music depicting simple pastoral or rural scenes and the life of country folk, often in idealized terms [Late 16thC. Via Latin *idyllium* "pastoral poem" from Greek *eidullion*, literally "small picture," from *eidos* (see IDOL).]

i·dyl·lic /ī díllik/ *adj.* 1. SERENELY BEAUTIFUL AND HAPPY serenely beautiful, untroubled, and happy 2. LIKE AN IDYLL like an idyll, especially in having a simple, unspoiled, and especially rural charm —**i·dyl·li·cal·ly** *adv.*

i·dyl·list /íd'list/, **i·dyl·ist** *n.* a writer, composer, or painter of idylls

IE *abbr.* 1. LING Indo-European 2. ENG industrial engineer 3. ENG industrial engineering

i.e. *abbr.* that is to say [Latin, *id est* "that is"]

-ie *suffix.* 1. one that is small or dear ○ *doggie* ○ *auntie* 2. one having a particular character ○ *sweetie* 3. one having to do with ○ *townie*

-ier *suffix.* = **er**

if /if/ CORE MEANING: a conjunction used to indicate the circumstances that would have to exist in order for an event to happen ○ *You can come with us if you want to.* ○ *Are you thinking of buying a new car? If so, talk to us first.*

1. *conj.* USED IN INDIRECT QUESTIONS used to introduce in indirect speech a question that in direct speech requires the answer "yes" or "no" ○ *He asked the hotel receptionist if it was possible to rent a car.* 2. *conj.* MODIFYING A STATEMENT used to indicate a modification to a statement, usually to add something negative or to indicate that there is less of something than originally expected ○ *The report will be with you at the end of the week, if not before.* ○ *a gallant, if misguided attempt* 3. *conj.* INTRODUCING AN EXCLAMATION used to introduce an exclamation expressing surprise or dismay ○ *If she isn't the most selfish person I've met!* 4. *n.* DOUBT a doubt or uncertainty ○ *The proposal contained too many ifs for us to be enthusiastic about it.* 5. *n.* CONDITION a condition or qualification ○ *I'm not very happy about the ifs that have been put into the contract.* [Old English *gif*, from a prehistoric Germanic word of unknown origin] ◇ **ifs, ands, or buts** excuses or protests ◇ **if only** used to introduce the expression of a hopeless wish or regret ○ *If only you had told me sooner.*

WORD KEY: USAGE

Ambiguous construction: In *We have hundreds, if not thousands, of items in stock*, the *if not* fairly plainly means "or even." In *It's a clever idea, if not a practical one*, it fairly plainly means "although not." But in *He's good-looking, if not really handsome*, it is unclear which of those meanings is intended — at least out of context. Often it is clear what *if not* means only because the context shows what the phrase must mean. Where it will not be clear, another wording is preferable and can be easily found.

IF *abbr.* ELECTRON ENG intermediate frequency

IFC *abbr.* International Finance Corporation (*of the UN*)

I·fe /ée fày/ city in southwestern Nigeria, situated 54 mi./87 km east of Ibadan. Population: 225,500 (1990).

IFF *abbr.* MIL Identification, Friend, or Foe

if·fy /íffee/ (**-fi·er, -fi·est**) *adj.* (*informal*) **1. DUBIOUS OR SUSPICIOUS** of doubtful and probably low quality, not to be relied on, or arousing suspicion **2. DOUBTFUL** doubtful and undecided about something —**if·fi·ness** *n.*

If·ni /éfnee/ former overseas province of Spain, now part of Morocco, situated on the southwestern coast of the country. Sidi Ifni is the only city. Area: 580 sq. mi./1502 sq. km.

IFO *abbr.* identified flying object

I for·ma·tion *n.* in football, an alignment of the offensive team in which all the backs line up in single file behind the center

IFR *abbr.* instrument flight rules

Ig *abbr.* immunoglobulin

IG, I.G. *abbr.* **1.** Inspector General **2.** imperial gallon

IgA *n.* a class of antibodies, found in respiratory and alimentary secretions as well as in saliva and tears, that help the body to neutralize harmful bacteria and viral antigens [Shortening of *immunoglobulin A*]

IGB *abbr. S Africa* illicit gold buying

Ig·bo *n., adj.* = **Ibo**

IgD *n.* a class of antibodies, present on most cell surfaces and predominant in B cells, that help the body to resist antigens. ◊ **B cell** [Shortening of *immunoglobulin D*]

IgE *n.* a class of antibodies, abundant in tissues, that help the body to expel intestinal parasites and cause allergic reactions in response to antigens [Shortening of *immunoglobulin E*]

igg /ig/ (**igged, ig·ging, iggs**) *vt.* to ignore something or somebody (*slang*) [Shortening and alteration]

IgG *n.* a class of antibodies, predominant in serum, that pass through the placental wall into fetal circulation and help to prepare the immune system for the period of infancy [Shortening of *immunoglobulin G*]

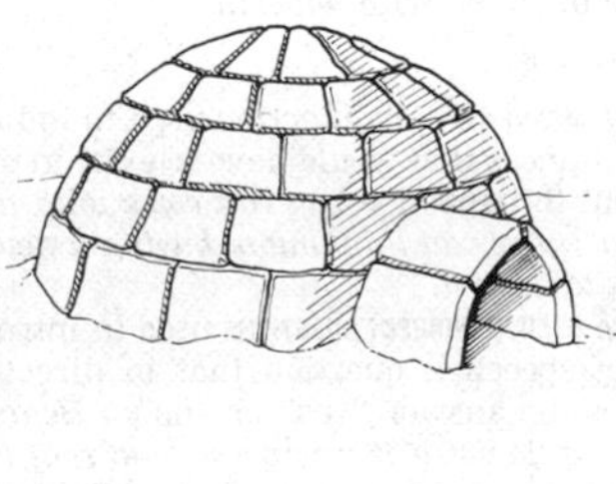

Igloo

ig·loo /íggloo/ *n.* **1. DOME-SHAPED INUIT HOUSE** an Inuit dwelling, usually dome-shaped and built from blocks of packed snow **2. DOME-SHAPED SHELTER** any small dome-shaped shelter or structure [Mid-19thC. From Inuit *iglu* "house."]

IgM *n.* a class of antibodies, circulating in the blood and secretions, that help the body to resist viruses [Shortening of *immunoglobulin M*]

ign. *abbr.* **1.** ignites **2.** ignition **3.** unknown [Latin *ignotus*]

Ig·na·tius (of An·ti·och) /ig nàyshəss-/, **St.** (35?–107) bishop and martyr. He was one of the Apostolic Fathers of the Christian church, and his seven epistles give important historical information about the early church.

Ig·na·tius Loy·o·la /ig nàyshəss loy ólə/, **St.** (1491–1556) Spanish priest who was cofounder of the Society of Jesus (Jesuits) in 1534. He also produced a Jesuit training manual, *Spiritual Exercises* (1548).

ig·ne·ous /ígnee əss/ *adj.* **1. FORMERLY MOLTEN** used to describe rock formed under conditions of intense heat or produced by the solidification of volcanic magma on or below the Earth's surface **2. RELATING TO FIRE** connected with or characteristic of fire (*formal*) [Mid-17thC. Formed from Latin *igneus*, from *ignis* "fire" (see IGNITE).]

ig·nes·cent /ig néss'nt/ *adj.* giving off sparks when struck, as a flint does [Early 19thC. From Latin *ignescent-*, the present participle stem of *ignescere* "to catch fire," from *ignis* "fire" (see IGNITE).]

ig·nes fat·u·i plural of **ignis fatuus**

ig·nim·brite /ígnim brìt/ *n.* a volcanic rock consisting of droplets of lava and glass that were welded together by intense heat [Mid-20thC. Coined from Latin *ignis* "fire" (see IGNITE) + the stem *imbr-* "rain" + -ITE; from its formation from the deposits of a cloud of volcanic ash.]

ig·nis fat·u·us /ígniss fáchoo əss/ (*plural* **ig·nes fa·tu·i** /ígneez fáchoo ī/) *n.* **1.** = **will-o'-the-wisp 2. ILLUSORY THING** something, e.g., a hope or an aim, that proves illusory or leads somebody astray (*literary*) [From Latin, literally "foolish fire"; from its erratic movements]

ig·nite /ig nít/ (**-nit·ed, -nit·ing, -nites**) *v.* **1.** *vti.* **LIGHT FIRE OR BEGIN TO BURN** to set fire to something, or catch fire **2.** *vti.* CHEM **HEAT GAS UNTIL IT BURNS** to heat a gas to the temperature at which it begins to burn **3.** *vt.* **AROUSE EMOTION IN** to cause a strong emotion to arise or show itself in somebody [Mid-17thC. From Latin *ignit-*, the past participle stem of *ignire* "to set on fire," from *ignis* "fire" (source of English *igneous*).] —**ig·nit·a·bil·i·ty** /ig nìtə bíllətee/ *n.* —**ig·nit·a·ble** /ig nítəb'l/ *adj.* —**ig·nit·er** *n.*

ig·ni·tion /ig nísh'n/ *n.* **1.** CHEM **PROCESS OF IGNITING** the process of setting something on fire **2.** MECH ENG **MEANS OF STARTING ENGINE** a mechanism that determines when, where, and how a spark is delivered to an engine cylinder to ignite the fuel and start or run the engine **3.** MECH ENG **SPARK THAT IGNITES FUEL-AIR MIXTURE** a spark in an internal-combustion engine that ignites and explodes a mixture of fuel and air

ig·ni·tion point *n.* the temperature at which a substance begins to burn and will remain alight

ig·no·ble /ig nób'l/ *adj.* **1. DISHONORABLE** dishonorable, ungenerous, and contrary to the high standards of conduct expected of somebody **2. NOT OF THE NOBILITY** not belonging to the nobility (*formal*) [15thC. Directly or via French from Latin *ignobilis*, literally "not noble," from *(g)nobilis* "noble" (see NOBLE).] —**ig·no·bil·i·ty** /ig nō bíllətee/ *n.* —**ig·no·bly** /ig nóblee/ *adv.*

WORD KEY: SYNONYMS

See Synonyms at ***mean***.

ig·no·min·i·ous /ìgnə mínnee əss/ *adj.* **1. SHAMEFUL** involving a total loss of dignity and pride and making somebody or something appear shamefully weak and ineffective **2. DESPICABLE** deserving condemnation and contempt (*formal*) —**ig·no·min·i·ous·ly** *adv.* —**ig·no·min·i·ous·ness** *n.*

ig·no·min·y /ig nómmənee, ígnə mìnnee/ (*plural* **-ies**) *n.* **1. DISGRACE AND DISHONOR** a total loss of dignity and self-respect or an incurring of public disgrace **2. SOMETHING DISGRACEFUL** a disgraceful act (*formal*) [Mid-16thC. Directly or via French *ignominie* from Latin *ignominia*, literally "lacking name," from *nomin-*, the stem of *nomen* "name, reputation."]

ig·no·ra·mus /ìgnə ráyməss/ *n.* an offensive term that deliberately insults somebody else's intelligence level (*insult*) [Late 16thC. Via modern Latin, "we ignore," from Latin, a form of *ignorare* (see IGNORE).]

ig·no·rance /ígnərəns/ *n.* **1. LACK OF KNOWLEDGE** lack of knowledge or education **2. UNAWARENESS** unawareness of something, often of something important

ig·no·rant /ígnərənt/ *adj.* **1. LACKING KNOWLEDGE** lacking knowledge and education in general or in a specific subject **2. UNAWARE** unaware of something ○ *ignorant of the danger* **3. RESULTING FROM LACK OF KNOWING** caused by a lack of understanding or experience ○ *an ignorant mistake* **4.** *Carib* **QUARRELSOME** quarrelsome and aggressive —**ig·no·rant·ly** *adv.*

ig·nore /ig náwr/ (**-nored, -nor·ing, -nores**) *vt.* to refuse to notice or pay attention to somebody or something [Early 17thC. Directly or via French *ignorer* from Latin *ignorare* "not to know, to ignore," ultimately from *(g)noscere* "to know" (source of English *notice*).] —**ig·nor·a·ble** *adj.* —**ig·nor·er** *n.*

I·go·rot /íggə rót, éegə rót/ *n.* (*plural* **-rot** or **-rots**) **PHILIPPINE PEOPLE** a member of a people living in the mountainous northern part of the island of Luzon in the Philippines ■ *adj.* **OF THE IGOROT** relating to or typical of the Igorot or their culture [Early 19thC. From Spanish *Ygolote*, from the local name.]

I·gua·çu /ig waa sóo/ river in southern Brazil and northeastern Argentina. Length: 745 mi./1,200 km.

I·gua·çu Falls waterfalls on the Iguaçu River. In the wet season they form a single waterfall over 2.5 mi./4 km wide and up to 260 ft./80 m high.

i·gua·na /i gwáanə/ (*plural* **-nas** or **-na**) *n.* a large plant-eating tropical lizard, chiefly found in South and Central America, with a serrated fringe or crest running along its back from head to tail. Family: Iguanidae. [Mid-16thC. Via Spanish from Arawak *iwana*.] —**i·gua·ni·an** *adj., n.*

Iguaçu Falls

Iguana

i·guan·o·don /i gwáanə dòn/ *n.* a large long-tailed plant-eating dinosaur of the Jurassic and early Cretaceous periods. Genus: *Iguanodon*. [Early 19thC. Formed from IGUANA + *-odon*, from Greek, variant of the stem *odont-* "tooth"; from the similarity of its teeth to those of an iguana.]

IGY *abbr.* International Geophysical Year

IHC *abbr. NZ* intellectually handicapped child

i.h.p., ihp *abbr.* indicated horsepower

ih·ram /ee ráam/ *n.* **1. WHITE ROBE WORN BY MECCA PILGRIMS** a white cotton robe worn by men when they are pilgrims to Mecca, formed from pieces of cloth wound around the waist and over the shoulder **2. HOLY STATE OF PILGRIM WEARING IHRAM** the state of holiness conferred or symbolized by the wearing of the ihram [Early 18thC. From Arabic *'iḥrām*.]

IHS *abbr.* Iesus Hominum Salvator [Via late Latin from Greek, "Jesus," abbreviation using three letters of Jesus' name in Greek (*Iē(sou)s*)]

IJs·sel·meer /íss'l meer/ shallow freshwater lake in the northern Netherlands that occupies part of what was formerly the Zuider Zee. The IJssel River flows into it.

i·kat /ée kaat/ *n.* a technique for making patterned fabric by using tie-dyed yarn [Mid-20thC. From Malay, literally "to tie, fasten."]

IKBS *abbr.* intelligent knowledge-based system

i·ke·ba·na /ìkə báanə, èeke báanə/ *n.* the Japanese art of arranging flowers in a formal balanced composition [Early 20thC. From Japanese, literally "living flowers."]

I·ke Tai·ga /ée kay tígə/ (1723–76) Japanese painter. His works, using ancient forms of calligraphy, are in the Bunjinga style.

i·kon *n.* = **icon** *n.* 1

IL *abbr.* **1.** MAIL Illinois **2.** Israel (*international vehicle registration*)

il- *prefix.* = **in-** (*used before l*)

ILA *abbr.* International Longshoremen's Association

i·lang-i·lang *n.* = **ylang-ylang**

-ile[1] *suffix.* of, relating to, capable of ○ *pulsatile* ○ *protrusile* [Via Old French from Latin *-ilis*]

-ile[2] *suffix.* a portion of a particular size in a frequency distribution ○ *quartile* ○ *percentile* [Origin uncertain: probably from ILE-[1]]

il·e·a plural of **ileum**

il·e·ac /íllee àk/, **il·e·al** *adj.* relating to the ileum [Early 19thC. Alteration of ILIAC on the model of ILEUM and ILEUS.]

il·e·i·tis /íllee ítiss/ *n.* inflammation of the ileum

il·e·os·to·my /íllee óstəmee/ (*plural* **-mies**) *n.* **1. OPERATION MAKING OPENING TO ILEUM** the surgical operation of making an opening through the abdominal wall into the ileum, so that waste can be discharged out of the body without passing through the colon **2. SURGICAL OPENING TO ILEUM** a surgical opening through the abdominal wall into the ileum

I·le·sa /i láyshə/, **I·le·sha** town in Kwara State, southwestern Nigeria, situated approximately 15 mi./24 km southeast of Oshogbo. Population: 342,000 (1992).

il·e·um /íllee əm/ (*plural* **-a** /-ə/) *n.* the third and lowest portion of the small intestine, extending from the jejunum to the pouch-shaped cecum at the beginning of the large intestine [Late 17thC. From medieval Latin, variant of Latin *ilium* "entrails," perhaps from association with *ileus* "ILEUS."]

il·e·us /íllee əss/ *n.* the inability of the contents of the intestines to pass through them owing to physical obstruction, or muscular inadequacy, often accompanied by extreme pain and vomiting [Late 17thC. Via Latin from Greek *ileos* "colic," of uncertain origin: probably formed from *eilein* "to hold in check."]

i·lex /í lèks/ *n.* **1. PLANT OF HOLLY GENUS** any tree or shrub belonging to a genus whose best-known member is the holly tree. Genus: *Ilex.* **2.** = **holm oak** [From Latin, "holm oak"]

ILGWU, **I.L.G.W.U.** *abbr.* International Ladies' Garment Workers' Union

il·i·a plural of **ilium**

il·i·ac /íllee àk/ *adj.* relating to the ilium and its surroundings [Early 16thC. From late Latin *iliacus* "relating to colic," from Latin *ilia* (see ILIUM).]

Il·i·ad /íllee əd/ *n.* an ancient Greek epic poem, describing the siege and capture of Troy, ascribed to Homer, and probably composed by oral tradition over the centuries prior to 700 B.C. [Early 17thC. Via the Latin stem *Iliad-* from Greek *Ilias* "of Troy," from *Ilion* "Troy."] —**Il·i·ad·ic** /íllee áddik/ *adj.*

Il·i·am·na /íllee ámnə/ volcanic peak in southwestern Alaska, situated on the western side of Cook Inlet. Height: 10,016 ft./3,053 m.

Il·i·am·na, Lake the largest lake in Alaska, situated in the southwest of the state, west of Cook Inlet. Area: 1,022 sq. mi./2,647 sq. km.

il·i·um /íllee əm/ (*plural* **-a** /-ə/) *n.* the wide flat upper portion of the pelvis that is connected to the base of the vertebral column. The ilium is a separate bone at birth but later becomes fused with two other bones to form the hip bone (**innominate bone**). [14thC. From Latin, the classical Latin plural meaning "groin, flanks, entrails." Originally, the English word denoted the "ileum."]

ilk *n.* kind or sort ○ *"save forlorn hopes and their ilk"* (Stephen Crane, *The Red Badge of Courage*; 1895) [Old English *ilca* "same," a compound whose parts are descended from an Indo-European word meaning "same" and a prehistoric Germanic word meaning "form" (also the ancestor of English *each*)]

ill /il/ *adj.* **1. UNWELL** not in good health, having a disease, or feeling unwell or nauseated **2. HARMFUL** resulting in harm, pain, or trouble for somebody or something **3. UNKIND** unkind and unfriendly ○ *ill feeling* **4. UNFAVORABLE** predicting a bad future or outcome **5. MORALLY BAD** resulting from the actual or supposed moral badness of somebody or something ○ *of ill repute* **6. BAD** not up to the expected or required standard, e.g., of behavior or competence ■ *adv.* **1. BADLY** badly, inadequately, or inappropriately ○ *prisoners who were ill treated* **2. UNFAVORABLY** in an adverse or unfavorable way or so as to reflect badly on somebody or something ○ *It boded ill for the future.* **3. WITH DIFFICULTY** only with great difficulty and trouble ○ *She can ill afford the time at present.* ■ *n.* **1. HARM** evil or harm, especially as a fate wished on somebody ○ *don't wish others ill* **2. UNFAVORABLE OPINION** an unfavorable opinion of somebody or something ○ *spoke ill of them* ○ *thought ill of them* **3. MISFORTUNE** trouble or misfortune, or a troublesome or distressing experience (*archaic*) **4. ILLNESS** a disease or sickness (*archaic*) [12thC. From Old Norse *illr* "evil, difficult," *illa* "badly," and *ilt* "evil," of unknown origin. "Unwell" dates from the 15thC.]

I'll /īl/ *contr.* I will or shall

ill. *abbr.* **1.** illustrated **2.** illustration **3.** illustrator

Ill. *abbr.* Illinois

ill-ad·vised *adj.* not wise, prudent, or sensible —**ill-ad·vis·ed·ly** *adv.*

ill-as·sort·ed, **ill-sort·ed** *adj.* mismatched or incompatible

ill at ease *adj.* uncomfortable and nervous

il·la·tion /i láysh'n/ *n.* (*formal*) **1. INFERENCE** an inference drawn to something **2. ACT OR PROCESS OF INFERRING SOMETHING** the act or process of making an inference [Mid-16thC. From the Latin stem *illation-*, from *illat-* (see ILLATIVE).]

il·la·tive /íllətiv, i láy-/ *adj.* **1. INFERENTIAL** involving or relating to the making of inferences (*formal*) **2. STATING INFERENCE** expressing or preceding an inference **3. OF CASE OF FINNISH NOUN** expressing motion toward something. It is usually translated into English using the prepositions "into" or "towards." (*used to describe a noun case in Finnish and some other languages*) ■ *n.* **1. CASE OF FINNISH NOUN** the illative case in Finnish and similar languages **2. SOMETHING THAT STATES INFERENCE** a word, phrase, or morpheme that expresses an inference [Late 16thC. From Latin *illativus*, from *illat-*, the past participle stem of *inferre* "to infer" (see INFER).] —**il·la·tive·ly** *adv.*

Il·la·war·ra /íllə wórrə/ division in southeastern New South Wales, southeastern Australia, situated approximately 30 mi./48 km south of Sydney. Population: 33,478 (1991).

ill-bred *adj.* rude, impolite, or otherwise showing a lack of good manners or the results of a bad upbringing —**ill-breed·ing** *n.*

ill-con·ceived *adj.* not based on good planning, especially not having an aim or goal that is likely to be successfully achieved

ill-con·sid·ered *adj.* done or made unwisely or without sufficient thought about the consequences

ill-de·fined *adj.* not clearly or sharply defined, or not clearly thought out

ill-dis·guised *adj.* apparent or visible, especially in somebody's expression, voice, or manner, because any attempt to conceal it is unsuccessful or perfunctory ○ *her ill-disguised contempt for them*

ill-dis·posed *adj.* having an unfriendly or hostile attitude toward somebody or something

il·le·gal /i léeg'l/ *adj.* **1. LAW AGAINST THE LAW** forbidden by law **2. SPORTS, GAME AGAINST THE RULES** not allowed by the rules of something such as a game **3. COMPUT NOT PERMITTED BY COMPUTER** not permitted in a computer program ■ *n.* **ILLEGAL IMMIGRANT** somebody who has entered a country illegally [Early 17thC. Directly or via French from medieval Latin *illegalis* "not legal," from *legalis* "legal" (see LEGAL).] —**il·le·gal·ly** *adv.*

il·le·gal·i·ty /íllee gállətee/ (*plural* **-ties**) *n.* **1. FACT OF BEING ILLEGAL** the fact of being forbidden by law or by the rules of something **2. UNLAWFUL ACT** an act that is against the law

il·le·gal·ize /i léegə līz/ (**-ized, -iz·ing, -iz·es**) *vt.* to declare officially and by law that something is illegal —**il·le·gal·i·za·tion** /i lèegəli záysh'n/ *n.*

il·leg·i·ble /i léjjəb'l/ *adj.* impossible or very difficult to read —**il·leg·i·bil·i·ty** /i lèjjə bíllətee/ *n.* —**il·leg·i·bly** /i léjjəblee/ *adv.*

il·le·git·i·mate /ílli jítəmət/ *adj.* **1. AGAINST LAW OR RULES** not carried out, made, or constituted in accordance with the law, the rules governing a particular activity, or social norms and customs **2. BORN OUT OF WEDLOCK** born to parents who are not married to each other [Mid-16thC. Formed from late Latin *illegitimus*, from *legitimus* (see LEGITIMATE).] —**il·le·git·i·ma·cy** *n.* —**il·le·git·i·mate·ly** *adv.*

ill-fat·ed *adj.* ending in, or doomed to, disaster

ill-fa·vored *adj.* **1. UNATTRACTIVE** unattractive in appearance, especially having an unattractive face **2. OBJECTIONABLE** offensively objectionable (*literary*) —**ill-fa·vored·ly** *adv.* —**ill-fa·vored·ness** *n.*

ill feel·ing *n.* animosity or resentment toward somebody, something, or each other

ill-found·ed *adj.* with no sound basis in fact or logic

ill-got·ten *adj.* acquired dishonestly or illegally ○ *ill-gotten gains*

ill hu·mor *n.* a bad mood or bad temper —**ill-hu·mored** *adj.*

il·lib·er·al /i líbbərəl, -brəl/ *adj.* **1. NARROW-MINDED** narrow-minded and intolerant of ideas and behavior that vary from an inflexibly conservative standard **2. UNGENEROUS** lacking in generosity (*formal*) [Mid-16thC. Via French from Latin *illiberalis* "sordid, mean" (literally "not liberal"), from *liberalis* "liberal" (see LIBERAL).] —**il·lib·er·al·i·ty** /i lìbbə rállətee/ *n.* —**il·lib·er·al·ly** /i líbbərəlee, -brəlee/ *adv.*

il·lic·it /i líssit/ *adj.* **1. ILLEGAL** not allowed by the law **2. UNACCEPTABLE BY PREVAILING SOCIAL STANDARDS** considered wrong or unacceptable by prevailing social customs or standards [Early 16thC. Directly or via French *illicite* from Latin *illicitus* "not licit," from *licitus* "licit" (see LICIT).] —**il·lic·it·ly** *adv.* —**il·lic·it·ness** *n.*

Il·lil·ou·ette Falls /íllə loo ét-/ waterfall situated in Yosemite National Park, central California. Height: 370 ft./113 m.

Il·li·ma·ni /éelyi maanee/ mountain in western Bolivia, situated south of La Paz. The highest peak is Nevada Illimani, 21,201 ft./6,462 m.

il·lim·it·a·ble /i límmitəb'l/ *adj.* with no limits or bounds (*formal*) —**il·lim·it·a·bil·i·ty** /i lìmmitə bíllətee/ *n.* —**il·lim·it·a·bly** /i límmitəblee/ *adv.*

Il·li·nois[1] /íllə nóy/ *n.* (*plural* **-nois**) **MEMBER OF NORTHERN NATIVE AMERICAN CONFEDERACY** a member of a confederacy of Native North American peoples who originally lived in an area covering northern Illinois, eastern Iowa, and southern Wisconsin, now inhabiting a reservation in northeastern Oklahoma ■ *adj.* **OF ILLINOIS CONFEDERACY** relating to or typical of the Illinois confederacy, its people, or their culture

Illinois

Il·li·nois[2] /ìlə nóy/ **1.** state in north central United States, bordered by Indiana, Iowa, Kentucky, Missouri, Wisconsin, and Lake Michigan. Capital: Springfield. Population: 11,895,849 (1997). Area: 57,918 sq. mi./150,007 sq. km. **2.** river in northern Illinois formed by the joining of the Des Plaines and Kankakee rivers. Length: 420 mi./680 km.

Il·li·nois·an /íllə nóyən, -nóyz'n/, **Il·li·nois·i·an** /-nóyzee ən/ *adj.* relating to or typical of the state of Illinois, or its people or culture

Il·li·nois Wa·ter·way system of rivers and canals in Illinois that connects Lake Michigan at Chicago with the Mississippi River at Grafton. Length: 325 mi./523 km.

il·liq·uid /i líkwid/ *adj.* **1. FIN HARD TO CONVERT INTO CASH** not easily convertible into cash **2. NOT HAVING ENOUGH CASH** without sufficient ready cash —**il·li·quid·i·ty** /ílli kwíddətee/ *n.*

il·lite /í līt/ *n.* a clay mineral of the mica group found in shale and mudstone, consisting of hydrated silicate of potassium and aluminum [Mid-20thC. Named for ILLINOIS[2] (where it was first found).] —**il·lit·ic** /i líttik/ *adj.*

il·lit·er·a·cy /i líttərəssee/ (*plural* **-cies**) *n.* **1. READING INCAPACITY** an inability to read and write **2. LACK OF KNOWLEDGE OF A SUBJECT** lack of education and knowledge in a particular subject **3. ERROR IN SPEECH OR WRITING** a basic or gross error in reading, writing, or speaking that suggests limited knowledge of language or grammar

il·lit·er·ate /i líttərət/ *adj.* **1. UNABLE TO READ AND WRITE** not able to read and write (*offensive*) **2. UNEDUCATED** with an inadequate education in or knowledge of a particular subject, or none at all ○ *artistically illiterate* **3. MAKING MANY LANGUAGE MISTAKES** full of, or making many basic errors in the use of language ○ *illiterate prose* ■ *n.* **SOMEBODY UNEDUCATED** somebody who lacks education and knowledge, especially somebody who cannot read or write (*offensive*) [15thC. From Latin *illiterat(t)us*, literally "not lettered," from *lit(t)eratus* "lettered, learned" (see LITERATE).] —**il·lit·er·ate·ly** *adv.* —**il·lit·er·ate·ness** *n.*

ill-judged *adj.* showing a lack of good judgment or an incorrect assessment of a situation

ill-man·nered *adj.* rude or impolite —**ill-man·nered·ly** *adv.*

ill na·ture *n.* a bad-tempered, unpleasant, or unkind disposition

ill-na·tured *adj.* bad-tempered, unpleasant, or unkind —**ill-na·tured·ly** *adv.* —**ill-na·tured·ness** *n.*

ill·ness /ílnəss/ *n.* **1.** BAD HEALTH a state of bad health **2.** DISEASE OR SICKNESS a disease, sickness, or other such indisposition

il·lo·cu·tion /ìllə kyo͞osh'n/ *n.* an action such as naming, threatening, warning, or promising that is carried out simply by saying the appropriate words [Mid-20thC. Coined by the philosopher J. L. Austin from IL + LOCUTION.] —**il·lo·cu·tion·ar·y** *adj.*

il·log·ic /i lójjik/ *n.* the quality or condition of having no basis in logic

il·log·i·cal /i lójjik'l/ *adj.* **1.** NOT FOLLOWING RULES OF LOGIC not following the rules of logic, or not following logically from a previous premise, statement, or action **2.** UNREASONABLE apparently unreasonable or perverse, especially in not being or not giving the expected response —**il·log·i·cal·i·ty** /i lòjji kálləteel/ *n.* —**il·log·i·cal·ly** /i lójjikəlee/ *adv.*

ill-o·mened *adj.* accompanied by signs suggesting disaster or failure

ill-sort·ed *adj.* = **ill-assorted**

ill-starred *adj.* doomed to end in failure or disaster (*formal*) [From the astrological belief that an unpropitious arrangement of the celestial bodies at the time of a birth or the start of an undertaking predetermined an unhappy outcome]

ill-tem·pered *adj.* having or showing an irritable mood or disposition —**ill-tem·pered·ly** *adv.*

ill-timed *adj.* done or occurring at the wrong time and thus not having the desired effect

ill-treat *vt.* **1.** ABUSE to behave cruelly or unkindly toward a person or animal **2.** MISUSE to misuse something or give something rough treatment —**ill-treat·ment** *n.*

WORD KEY: SYNONYMS

See Synonyms at ***misuse***.

il·lume /i lo͞om/ (**-lumed, -lum·ing, -lumes**) *vt.* to cast illumination onto something (*archaic literary*) [Early 17thC. Contraction of ILLUMINE.]

il·lu·mi·nance /i lo͞ominənss/ *n.* the amount of light, evaluated according to its capacity to produce visual stimulation, that reaches a unit of surface area during a unit of time. It is measured in lux. Symbol E_v

il·lu·mi·nant /i lo͞ominənt/ *n.* SOURCE OF LIGHT something that gives off or provides light ■ *adj.* SHINING giving off light [Mid-17thC. From Latin *illuminant-*, the present participle stem of *illuminare* (see ILLUMINATE).]

il·lu·mi·nate /i lo͞omi nàyt/ (**-nat·ed, -nat·ing, -nates**) *v.* **1.** *vti.* SHINE LIGHT ON SOMETHING to make something visible or bright with light, or be lit up **2.** *vt.* DECORATE WITH LIGHTS to decorate something with lights for a celebration **3.** *vt.* CLARIFY to make something clear, or easier to understand and appreciate **4.** *vt.* PRINTING ADD COLORED ELEMENTS TO PAGE to add colored letters, illustrations, and designs to a manuscript or the borders of a page **5.** *vti.* ENLIGHTEN SOMEBODY to provide somebody with knowledge or with intellectual or spiritual enlightenment (*literary*) (*often passive*) **6.** *vt.* CAUSE TO LOOK HAPPY AND ANIMATED to make something, especially somebody's face, look happy and animated [15thC. From Latin *illuminat-*, the past participle stem of *illuminare* "to light up," ultimately from the stem *lumin-* "light" (source of English *luminous*).] —**il·lu·mi·na·tive** *adj.* —**il·lu·mi·na·tor** *n.*

il·lu·mi·na·ti /i lo͞omi naatee/, **Il·lu·mi·na·ti** *npl.* any one of various groups of people in history claiming to have received special religious or spiritual enlightenment, especially an 18th-century German secret society with deist and republican ideas. The name was also applied to several groups in 18th-century France, a group of religious enthusiasts in 16th-century Spain, and the Rosicrucians. [Late 16thC. Via Italian from Latin, plural of *illuminatus*, past participle of *illuminare* (see ILLUMINATE).]

il·lu·mi·nat·ing /i lo͞omi nàyting/ *adj.* informative and enlightening, often by revealing or emphasizing facts that were previously obscure —**il·lu·mi·nat·ing·ly** *adv.*

AKG London

Illumination: Title page of the manuscript *Augustinus Questiones in Heptateuchon* (8th century)

il·lu·mi·na·tion /i lo͞omi náysh'n/ *n.* **1.** ACT OF ILLUMINATING the provision of light to make something visible or bright, or the fact of being lit up **2.** USABLE LIGHT the amount or strength of light available in a place or for a purpose **3.** CLARIFICATION AND EXPLANATION the process of clarifying or explaining something **4.** ENLIGHTENMENT intellectual or spiritual enlightenment **5.** PRINTING ORNAMENTATION OF PAGE a colored letter, design, or illustration decorating a manuscript or page, or the art or act of decorating written texts **6.** PHYS = **illuminance** —**il·lu·mi·na·tion·al** *adj.*

il·lu·mine /i lo͞omin/ (**-mined, -min·ing, -mines**) *vti.* to illuminate somebody or something, or become illuminated (*literary*) [14thC. Via French *illuminer* from Latin *illuminare* (see ILLUMINATE).] —**il·lu·min·a·ble** *adj.*

il·lu·mi·nism /i lo͞omi nìzzəm/ *n.* the beliefs held by illuminati, especially their belief in or claim to special enlightenment

illus. *abbr.* **1.** illustrated **2.** illustration **3.** illustrator

ill-use *vt.* = **ill-treat** *v.* 1 —**ill-us·age** *n.*

il·lu·sion /i lo͞ozh'n/ *n.* **1.** SOMETHING WITH DECEPTIVE APPEARANCE something that deceives the senses or mind, e.g., by appearing to exist when it does not or appearing to be one thing when it is in fact another **2.** DECEPTIVE POWER OF APPEARANCES the ability of appearances to deceive the mind and senses or the capacity of the mind and senses to be deceived by appearances **3.** FALSE IDEA a false idea, conception, or belief concerning something **4.** PSYCHOL MISTAKEN SENSORY PERCEPTION a misinterpretation of an experience of sensory perception, especially a visual one, where the stimuli are objectively present and the mistaken perception is due to physical rather than psychological causes. ◊ **hallucination 5.** TEXTILES FINE GAUZE a fine gauze used for trimming. ◊ **tulle** [14thC. Via French from, ultimately, Latin *illus-*, past participle stem of *illudere* "to play at," ultimately from *ludus* "play, sport" (source of English *ludicrous*).] —**il·lu·sion·ar·y** *adj.*

il·lu·sion·ism /i lo͞ozh'n ìzzəm/ *n.* the use of pictorial techniques to create illusions. ◊ **trompe l'oeil**

il·lu·sion·ist /i lo͞ozh'nist/ *n.* **1.** MAGICIAN a performer of magical tricks **2.** PAINTING PAINTER WHO MAKES PICTORIAL ILLUSIONS an artist who creates pictorial illusions —**il·lu·sion·is·tic** /i lo͞ozh'n ístik/ *adj.* —**il·lu·sion·is·ti·cal·ly** *adv.*

il·lu·sive /i lo͞ossiv/ *adj.* = **illusory** [Early 17thC. From medieval Latin *illusivus* "deceptive," from the Latin stem *illus-* (see ILLUSION).] —**il·lu·sive·ly** *adv.* —**il·lu·sive·ness** *n.*

il·lu·so·ry /i lo͞ossəree/ *adj.* produced by, based on, or consisting of an illusion [Late 16thC. Directly or via French *illusoire* from ecclesiastical Latin *illusorius* "ironical, of mocking character," from the Latin stem *illus-* (see ILLUSION).] —**il·lu·so·ri·ly** *adv.* —**il·lu·so·ri·ness** *n.*

il·lus·trate /íllə stràyt/ (**-trat·ed, -trat·ing, -trates**) *v.* **1.** *vt.* BE CHARACTERISTIC OF to be a good example of something, or serve to demonstrate something and make it clear ○ *a case that illustrates the need for legislation* **2.** *vti.* FULLY EXPLAIN to clarify something by giving examples or making comparisons **3.** *vt.* ARTS ACCOMPANY WITH PICTURES to provide explanatory or decorative pictures to accompany a printed, spoken, or electronic text ○ *The book was illustrated with diagrams.* [Early 16thC. From Latin *illustrat-*, the past participle stem of *illustrare* "to light up," from *lustrare* (source of English *luster*).] —**il·lus·trat·a·ble** /íllə stràytəb'l/ *adj.* —**il·lus·tra·tor** *n.*

il·lus·tra·tion /íllə stráysh'n/ *n.* **1.** PICTURE THAT COMPLEMENTS TEXT a drawing, photograph, or diagram that accompanies and complements a printed, spoken, or electronic text **2.** SOMETHING THAT HELPS EXPLAIN an example or comparison that helps to clarify or explain something **3.** ARTS PROVISION OF PICTURES ACCOMPANYING TEXT the art or process of producing or providing pictures to accompany a text —**il·lus·tra·tion·al** *adj.*

il·lus·tra·tive /i lústrətiv/ *adj.* serving to illustrate or explain something —**il·lus·tra·tive·ly** *adv.*

il·lus·tri·ous /i lústree əss/ *adj.* extremely distinguished and deservedly famous [Mid-16thC. Formed from Latin *illustris* "bright, famous," from *illustrare* (see ILLUSTRATE).] —**il·lus·tri·ous·ly** *adv.* —**il·lus·tri·ous·ness** *n.*

il·lu·vi·a·tion /i lo͞ovee áysh'n/ *n.* the process by which materials such as colloids and salts are washed from an upper layer of soil to a lower one [Early 20thC. Coined from IL- + *-luviation* (as in ELUVIATION).] —**il·lu·vi·at·ed** *adj.*

il·lu·vi·um /i lo͞ovee əm/ (*plural* **-ums** *or* **-a** /-ə/) *n.* colloids, salts, and other material washed out from an upper to a lower layer of soil [Early 20thC. From modern Latin, from *-luvium* (as in ALLUVIUM).]

ill will *n.* a feeling or attitude of hostility, unfriendliness, or dislike toward somebody ○ *They bore us no ill will.*

ill-wish·er *n.* somebody who wishes misfortune or evil to come to another person

Il·lyr·i·an /i léeree ən/ *n.* **1.** PEOPLES HISTORICAL INHABITANT OF EASTERN ADRIATIC COAST a member of any of the related peoples who, for over a thousand years from the late third century B.C., occupied the Adriatic coastal regions from Albania northward. The Illyrians were conquered by the Romans around 33 B.C. **2.** LANG EXTINCT LANGUAGE OF ILLYRIANS an extinct language that was spoken in Illyria in ancient times. It is agreed that it was an Indo-European language, and generally thought to be related to Albanian. ■ *adj.* CHARACTERISTIC OF ILLYRIA relating to or characteristic of Illyria, its people, or extinct language [Mid-16thC. Formed from Latin *Illyrius*, from *Illyria*.]

il·men·ite /ílmə nìt/ *n.* a mineral, usually found in basic metamorphic and igneous rocks, consisting of a mixed oxide of iron and titanium [Early 19thC. Named for the *Ilmen* Mountains in the southern Urals, Russia, where it was found.]

ILO *abbr.* International Labor Organization

I·lo·i·lo /èelō èelō/ city and capital of Iloilo Province, Philippines, situated in the southeastern part of the Iloilo Strait. Population: 309,505 (1990).

I·lo·rin /i lórrən/ city and capital of Kwara State, southwestern Nigeria, situated approximately 170 mi./274 km northeast of Lagos. Population: 420,000 (1991).

ILS *abbr.* AEROSP instrument landing system

I'm /īm/ *contr.* I am

IM *abbr.* **1.** CHESS International Master **2.** MED intramuscular

im- *prefix.* **1.** = **in-** (*used before b, m, and p*) **2.** = **in** (*used before r*) **3.** = **In** (*used before r*)

im·age /ímmij/ *n.* **1.** ACTUAL OR MENTAL PICTURE a picture or likeness of somebody or something, produced either physically by a sculptor, painter, or photographer, or conjured in the mind **2.** SOMEBODY CLOSELY RESEMBLING SOMEBODY ELSE somebody who or something that is very like somebody or something else in appearance **3.** CONSPICUOUS EXAMPLE an extremely typical or extreme example of something **4.** OPTICS LIKENESS SEEN OR PRODUCED the likeness of somebody or something that appears in a mirror, through a lens, or on the retina of the eye, or that is produced electronically on a screen **5.** LITERAT EXAMPLE OF FIGURATIVE LANGUAGE a figure of speech, especially a metaphor or simile **6.** MATH SET OF FUNCTION'S VALUES the value of a mathematical function corresponding to a specific value of the function's variable ■ *vt.* (**-aged, -ag·ing, -ag·es**) **1.** CREATE IMAGE OF to produce a physical or mental image of something **2.** MED MAKE VISUAL IMAGE OF BODY STRUCTURES to produce a visual representation of bodily structures, using X-rays, ultrasound, radioactivity, heat, or magnetism and, usually, computerized scanning devices, as an aid to diagnosis and treatment **3. PICTURE IN MIND** to form a mental image of something **4. DESCRIBE SOMETHING IN VISUAL TERMS** to describe vivdly or in visual terms **5. TYPIFY** to embody or typify something [12thC. Via French from Latin *imago* "likeness" (source of English *imagine*). Originally "statue, figurine."] —**im·age·a·ble** *adj.* —**im·ag·er** *n.*

image compression *n.* COMPUT a technique based on fractal mathematics for reducing the amount of digitized information needed to store a visual image such as a movie electronically

im·age con·vert·er *n.* an optical-electronic device that reproduces an image formed by invisible radiation such as ultraviolet and infrared on a photoemissive surface as a visible-light image on a luminescent surface

im·age in·ten·si·fi·er *n.* an optical-electronic device that amplifies an image formed by visible radiation on a photoemissive surface to present an enhanced image on a luminescent surface

im·age-mak·er *n.* somebody employed to create a favorable public image of a business, organization, product, or public figure

im·age or·thi·con *n.* a television camera tube in which an electron image on a photoemissive surface is focused onto a target for scanning

im·age·ry /ímmijree/ (*plural* **-ries**) *n.* **1.** LITERAT **METAPHORS AND SIMILES** the figurative language, especially metaphors and similes, used in poetry, plays, and other literary works **2. IMAGES IN THE MIND** a set of mental pictures produced by the memory or imagination or conjured up by a stimulus ○ *Her dreams were filled with surreal imagery.* **3.** ARTS **IMAGES IN ARTISTIC WORK** the pictorial images found in works of art such as paintings and sculptures **4. IMAGES COLLECTIVELY** a group or set of images considered together ○ *studying the CAT-scan imagery*

im·age tube *n.* an optical-electronic device that converts invisible radiation into a visible image, as in an image converter, or amplifies visible radiation into an enhanced image, as in an image intensifier

i·mag·i·na·ble /i májjənəb'l/ *adj.* capable of being conceived or imagined ○ *the worst meal imaginable* —**i·mag·i·na·bil·i·ty** /i màjjənə bíllətee/ *n.* —**i·mag·i·na·bly** /i májjənəblee/ *adv.*

i·mag·i·nar·y /i májjə nèrree/ *adj.* **1. IN THE MIND** existing only in the mind, not in reality **2.** MATH **RELATING TO IMAGINARY NUMBERS** relating to or containing imaginary numbers, or being the coefficient of the imaginary part in a complex number. ◊ **imaginary number, complex number** ■ *n.* MATH = **imaginary number** [14thC. From Latin *imaginarius*, from *imagin-*, the stem of *imago* (see IMAGE).] —**i·mag·i·nar·i·ly** *adv.* —**i·mag·i·nar·i·ness** *n.*

i·mag·i·nar·y num·ber *n.* MATH a complex number in the form $a + ib$ where i is the square root of negative one, and b is not equal to zero. ◊ **real number**

i·mag·i·nar·y part *n.* MATH the real number, b, in the complex number a + ib, where i = $\sqrt{-1}$

i·mag·i·nar·y u·nit *n.* MATH the positive square root of minus one

i·mag·i·na·tion /i màjjə náysh'n/ *n.* **1. ABILITY TO VISUALIZE** the ability to form images and ideas in the mind, especially of things never seen or never experienced directly **2. CREATIVE PART OF THE MIND** the part of the mind where ideas, thoughts, and images are formed **3. RESOURCEFULNESS** the ability to think of ways of dealing with difficulties or problems **4. CREATIVE ACT** an act of creating a semblance of reality, especially in literature —**i·mag·i·na·tion·al** *adj.*

i·mag·i·na·tive /i májjənətiv, -nàytiv/ *adj.* **1. SKILLED AT VISUALIZING OR THINKING ORIGINALLY** good at thinking of new ideas or at visualizing things that have not been seen or experienced **2. ORIGINAL** new and original or not likely to have been easily thought up by somebody else ○ *an imaginative solution to a long-standing problem* **3. TENDING TO FANTASIZE** with a tendency to pretend or fantasize **4. UNLIKELY** seeming untrue, implausible, or unlikely (*often used ironically*) **5. OF THE IMAGINATION** relating to the ability to form images and ideas in the mind, or to think of new things —**i·mag·i·na·tive·ness** *n.*

i·mag·ine /i májjin/ *v.* (**-ined, -in·ing, -ines**) **1.** *vti.* **FORM AN IMAGE IN THE MIND** to form an image or idea of something in the mind ○ *I can just imagine his reaction!* **2.** *vt.* **SEE OR HEAR SOMETHING UNREAL** to see or hear something that is not there, or to think something that is not true ○ *There's nothing there—you're imagining things!* **3.** *vt.* **ASSUME SOMETHING** to suppose or assume something ■ *interj.* **i·mag·ine, i·mag·ine that EXPRESSION OF SURPRISE** used to express surprise [14thC. Via French from Latin *imaginare* "to make an image of" and *imaginari* "to picture to yourself," both formed from *imagin-*, the stem of *imago* (see IMAGE).] —**i·mag·in·er** *n.* —**i·mag·in·ing** *n.*

im·ag·ing /ímməjing/ *n.* **1. TECHNIQUE FOR MAKING IMAGES** any of several often computerized techniques, e.g., X-rays, ultrasound, radioactivity, heat, or magnetism, used to obtain images of bodies or body parts for diagnosis, emergency rescue, or surveillance **2.** PSYCHOL, ALTERN MED **USE OF MENTAL IMAGES** the use of mental images to ease pain, alter the course of disease processes, or help in achieving a goal

im·a·gism /ímmə jìzzəm/ *n.* POETRY a literary movement of early 20th-century U.S. and English poets that sought to modernize poetic language by the use of ordinary language, free verse, and precise everyday imagery —**im·a·gist** *n.* —**im·a·gis·tic** /immə jístik/ *adj.* —**im·a·gis·ti·cal·ly** *adv.*

i·ma·go /i máy gō, i maá gō/ (*plural* **-goes** *or* **-gi·nes** /i máygə neez, i maágə-/) *n.* **1.** INSECTS **SEXUALLY MATURE ADULT INSECT** an insect in its sexually mature adult state **2.** PSYCHOL **IDEALIZED MENTAL PICTURE** in psychoanalysis, an unconscious idealized mental picture, especially of a parent, that is formed early in life and retained in adulthood [Late 18thC. From Latin (see IMAGE).]

i·mam /i maám/ *n.* **1. LEADER OF MOSQUE PRAYERS** a man who leads the prayers in a mosque **2. i·mam, I·mam RELIGIOUS LEADER DESCENDED FROM MUHAMMAD** any of various Islamic religious leaders regarded as direct descendants of Muhammad or Ali and appointed by Allah **3. ISLAMIC COMMUNITY LEADER** a leader of an Islamic community **4. ISLAMIC SCHOLAR** a respected Islamic scholar, especially a founder of a school of theology or law [Early 17thC. From Arabic *'imām*, literally "leader."]

i·mam·ate /i maá màyt, i má-/ *n.* **1. IMAM'S POSITION OR PERIOD OF OFFICE** the title or position of an imam, or the period somebody spends as an imam **2. IMAM'S TERRITORY** the area for which an imam is leader

IMarE *abbr.* Insitute of Marine Engineers

i·ma·ret /i maárət/ *n.* a place providing food and shelter for travelers and pilgrims in Turkey [Early 17thC. Via Turkish from Arabic *'imāra* "building."]

I·mar·i /i maáree/ *n.* a Japanese porcelain that is brightly decorated, especially with a floral design [Late 19thC. Named for the port of *Imari* in Kyushu, Japan, from which it was exported.]

im·bal·ance /im báləns/ *n.* **1. UNEVENNESS OF EMPHASIS** an unevenness, inequality, or bias existing between two or more people or things, especially in their degree of emphasis, proportions, or function **2. STATE OF DISHARMONY** a lack of harmony or an inability to function well or harmoniously, or something causing this state ○ *a hormonal imbalance*

im·be·cile /ímbəss'l, ímbə sīl/ *n.* **1. OFFENSIVE TERM** an offensive term that deliberately insults somebody's level of intellect (*insult*) **2. OFFENSIVE TERM** offensive term in an absolute classification system for an IQ between 25 and 50 and a mental age of between two and seven years (*dated offensive*) [15thC. Via French from Latin *imbecillus*, literally "without support," from *baculum* "stick, staff." The underlying meaning is "weak, powerless."] —**im·be·cil·ic** /imbə síllik/ *adj.* —**im·be·cil·i·ty** /imbə síllətee/ *n.*

im·bed /im béd/ *vt.* = **embed**

im·bibe /im bīb/ (**-bibed, -bib·ing, -bibes**) *v.* **1.** *vti.* **DRINK SOMETHING** to drink something, especially alcohol (*formal or humorous*) **2.** *vt.* **ABSORB IDEAS** to take something into the mind as if drinking a liquid (*literary*) **3.** *vt.* **TAKE SOMETHING IN AS IF DRINKING** to take in something as if drinking it (*literary*) **4.** *vti.* **ABSORB SOMETHING** to absorb moisture, gas, light, or heat (*formal*) [14thC. From Latin *imbibere*, literally "to drink in," from *bibere* "to drink."] —**im·bib·er** *n.*

im·bi·bi·tion /imbə bísh'n, im bī bísh'n/ *n.* CHEM the absorption or adsorption of something, such as liquid or heat, by a mixture (**colloid**) such as a gel [15thC. From the medieval Latin stem *imbibition-* "absorption, infusion," from Latin *imbibere* (see IMBIBE).] —**im·bi·bi·tion·al** *adj.*

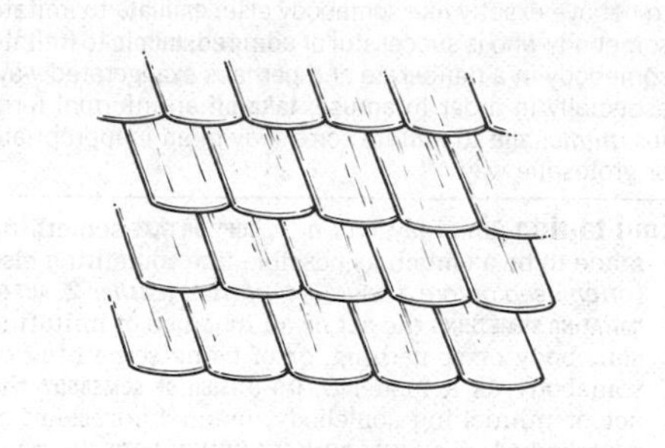

Imbricate

im·bri·cate /ímbrə kàyt/ *adj.* **1.** ARCHIT **CONSISTING OF OVERLAPPING TILES** consisting of overlapping tiles or slates **2.** BOT, ZOOL **OVERLAPPING, LIKE ROOF TILES** used to describe plant or animal parts that overlap in a regular pattern ■ *vti.* (**-cat·ed, -cat·ing, -cates**) **OVERLAP OR BE OVERLAPPING** to lay things so that they overlap in layers, or to be overlapping in layers, in a similar way to roof tiles [Mid-17thC. From Latin *imbricare* "to cover with pantiles," from *imbric-*, the stem of *imbrex* "roof tile," from *imber* "rain."] —**im·bri·cat·ed** *adj.* —**im·bri·ca·tion** /imbrə káysh'n/ *n.*

im·bro·glio /im brólee ō/ (*plural* **-glios**) *n.* a confusing, messy, or complicated situation, especially one that involves disagreement or intrigue (*formal*) [Mid-18thC. From Italian, from *brogliare* "to mix up," probably from Old French *brōoillier* (see BROIL[2]).]

im·brue /im broō/ (**-brued, -bru·ing, -brues**) *vt.* to stain something, especially with blood (*archaic or literary*) [Early 16thC. From Old French *embruer* "to soil or spatter," of uncertain origin: perhaps from assumed Vulgar Latin *imbiberare*, from Latin *bibere* "to drink."]

im·bue /im byoō/ (**-bued, -bu·ing, -bues**) *vt.* **1. FILL WITH A PARTICULAR QUALITY** to make something or somebody rich with a particular quality (*usually passive*) ○ *imbued with a strong sense of patriotism* **2. SOAK SOMETHING WITH SOMETHING** to saturate something with a substance, especially dye (*formal*) [Late 16thC. From Latin *imbuere* "to moisten, stain," of unknown origin.]

IMCO *abbr.* Intergovernmental Maritime Consultative Organization

IMF *abbr.* International Monetary Fund

IMHO *abbr.* in my humble opinion (*used in e-mail communications*)

im·id·az·ole /immə dá zōl/ *n.* an organic white crystalline base that inhibits the action of histamine. Formula: $C_3H_4N_2$. [Late 19thC. Coined from IMIDE + AZO- + -OLE.]

im·ide /í mīd/ *n.* any of a class of organic compounds containing the NH group combined with an acid group and derived from ammonia [Mid-19thC. From French, alteration of *amide* (see AMIDE).] —**i·mid·ic** /i míddik/ *adj.*

im·ine /í meen, ímmin, i meen/ *n.* any of a class of organic compounds containing the NH group combined with a nonacid group and derived from ammonia [Late 19thC. Alteration of AMINE, on the model of IMIDE.]

i·mip·ra·mine /i míppra meen/ *n.* a chemical with a three-ring (**tricyclic**) molecular structure, used as a drug in the treatment of depression. Formula: $C_{19}H_{24}N_2$. [Mid-20thC. Blend of IMINE, PROPYL, and AMINE.]

imit. *abbr.* **1.** imitation **2.** imitative

im·i·ta·ble /ímmitəb'l/ *adj.* capable or worthy of being imitated —**im·i·ta·bil·i·ty** /immitə bíllətee/ *n.*

im·i·tate /ímmi tàyt/ (**-tat·ed, -tat·ing, -tates**) *vt.* **1. MIMIC SOMEBODY** to copy somebody's behavior, voice, or manner, especially in order to make fun of him or her **2. FOLLOW SOMEBODY'S EXAMPLE** to use somebody or something as a model, attempting to copy an existing method, style, or approach **3. BE OR LOOK LIKE SOMETHING** to be or look like something else ○ *a case of life imitating art* **4.** ARTS **COPY THE STYLE OF AN ARTISTIC WORK** to reproduce the style of a work of art, e.g., a piece of literature, painting, or music [Mid-16thC. From Latin *imitari*, of unknown origin.] —**im·i·ta·tor** *n.*

WORD KEY: SYNONYMS

imitate, copy, emulate, mimic, take off, ape

CORE MEANING: to adopt the behavior of another person

imitate the most wide-ranging term; **copy** a term similar in meaning to *imitate*, with the suggestion of attempting to behave exactly like somebody else; **emulate** to imitate somebody who is successful or admired; **mimic** to imitate somebody in a deliberate and perhaps exaggerated way, especially in order to amuse; **take off** an informal term for *mimic*; **ape** to imitate somebody in an inappropriate or grotesque way.

im·i·ta·tion /ìmmi táysh'n/ *n.* **1. COPY OR FAKE** something made to be as much as possible like something else (*often used before a noun*) ○ *imitation leather* **2. ACT OF IMITATING SOMETHING** the act or an instance of imitating somebody or something, or of using something or somebody as a model **3. IMPRESSION OF SOMEBODY** the act of mimicking somebody, or an impression of somebody **4.** MUSIC **REPETITION OF A MUSICAL MOTIF** the repetition of a musical idea such as a melody or rhythmic figure in another part, often at another pitch and sometimes with variation ■ *adj.* **NOT GENUINE** synthetic, intended as a copy of something, or not genuine —**im·i·ta·tion·al** *adj.*

im·i·ta·tive /ìmmi tàytiv/ *adj.* **1. ATTEMPTING TO COPY SOMETHING** designed to be like something else, but usually inferior to the original **2. INVOLVING IMITATION** involving or practicing imitation **3.** = **onomatopoeic** —**im·i·ta·tive·ly** *adv.* —**im·i·ta·tive·ness** *n.*

IMM *n., abbr.* International Monetary Market

im·mac·u·late /i mákyələt/ *adj.* **1. CLEAN** absolutely clean, neat, and free from blemishes **2. FAULTLESS** showing faultless perfection [15thC. From Latin *immaculatus*, literally "without stain," from, ultimately, *macula* "blemish" (source of English *mackle*), of unknown origin.] —**im·mac·u·la·cy** *n.* —**im·mac·u·late·ness** *n.* —**im·mac·u·late·ly** *adv.*

Im·mac·u·late Con·cep·tion *n.* **1. VIRGIN MARY'S SINLESSNESS** the Roman Catholic doctrine that the Virgin Mary's soul was free from the stain of original sin from the moment of her soul's conception. The term does not, contrary to popular belief, refer to the conception of Jesus Christ. **2. FEAST OF THE IMMACULATE CONCEPTION** the feast of the Immaculate Conception, celebrated in the Roman Catholic Church on December 8

im·ma·nent /ímmənənt/ *adj.* **1. WITHIN SOMETHING** existing within or inherent in something (*formal*) **2.** RELIG **EXISTING IN ALL PARTS OF THE UNIVERSE** existing in, and extending into, all parts of the created world [Mid-16thC. From late Latin *immanere*, literally "to dwell within," from Latin *manere* "to remain or dwell."] —**im·ma·nence** *n.* —**im·ma·nen·cy** *n.* —**im·ma·nent·ly** *adv.*

im·ma·nent·ism /ímmənən tìzzəm/ *n.* the belief that God exists in, and extends into all of, the created universe, including the individual —**im·ma·nent·ist** *adj., n.* —**im·ma·nent·is·tic** /ìmmənən tístik/ *adj.*

Im·man·u·el /i mánnyoo əl/, **Em·man·u·el** *n.* the Messiah, referred to in Jewish and Christian scriptures, whom Christians believe to be Jesus Christ [15thC. Via late Latin and Greek from Hebrew *'immānū'ēl*, literally "with us is God."]

im·ma·te·ri·al /ìmmə téeree əl/ *adj.* **1. NOT RELEVANT** lacking relevance or importance **2. HAVING NO PHYSICAL SUBSTANCE** not made of matter or not physically real [14thC. From late Latin *immaterialis*, from *materialis* (see MATERIAL).] —**im·ma·te·ri·al·i·ty** /ìmmə teeree állətee/ *n.* —**im·ma·te·ri·al·ness** *n.* —**im·ma·te·ri·al·ly** *adv.*

im·ma·te·ri·al·ism /ìmmə téeree ə lìzzəm/ *n.* a metaphysical doctrine holding that the material world does not exist except as ideas or perceptions in the mind, or that only spirits and nonphysical things exist

im·ma·te·ri·al·ize /ìmmə téeree ə lìz/ (**-ized, -iz·ing, -iz·es**) *vt.* to take away the physical substance of something and make it spiritual or intangible —**im·ma·te·ri·al·i·za·tion** /ìmmə teeree əli záysh'n/ *n.*

im·ma·ture /ìmmə chóor/ *adj.* **1. NOT FULLY DEVELOPED** young, and not fully grown or developed **2. CHILDISH** lacking the wisdom or emotional development normally associated with adults (*disapproving*) **3. STYLISTICALLY CRUDE AND IMPERFECT** not yet having attained the perfection of a later, or fully developed, style ○ *an example of the artist's immature period* [Mid-16thC. From Latin *immaturus*, literally "not ripe," from *maturus* (see MATURE).] —**im·ma·ture·ly** *adv.* —**im·ma·tur·i·ty** *n.* —**im·ma·ture·ness** *n.*

im·meas·ur·a·ble /i mézhərəb'l/ *adj.* too large or too much to be measured —**im·meas·ur·a·bil·i·ty** /i mèzhərə bíllətee/ *n.* —**im·meas·ur·a·bly** /i mézhərəblee/ *adv.* —**im·meas·ur·a·ble·ness** /-b'lnəss/ *n.*

immed. *abbr.* immediate

im·me·di·ate /i mídee ət/ *adj.* **1. WITHOUT PAUSE OR DELAY** happening or done at first, at once, or without delay ○ *the problem requires immediate attention* **2. NEAREST** nearest in time, space, or relationship ○ *only my immediate family were invited* **3. CURRENT** urgent or pressing, and so needing to be dealt with before anything else **4. HAVING A DIRECT EFFECT** affecting something directly, without anything intervening **5.** PHILOS **KNOWN FROM EXPERIENCE** relating to something that is known about from personal experience or by intuition **6.** LOGIC **DERIVED FROM A SINGLE PREMISE** used to describe an inference derived from a single premise, without any middle term, and often by conversion of a categorial statement. An example is "some cows are brown so some brown things are cows." [14thC. Directly or via French from late Latin *immediatus*, literally "not separated," from Latin *mediatus*, the past participle of *mediare* (see MEDIATE).] —**im·me·di·a·cy** *n.* —**im·me·di·ate·ness** *n.*

im·me·di·ate con·stit·u·ent *n.* the first level into which a linguistic unit is analyzed, e.g., the subject and predicate as parts of a sentence

im·me·di·ate·ly /i mídee ətlee/ *adv.* **1. AT ONCE** without delay or without pausing beforehand **2. VERY CLOSELY** very closely in space or time ■ *conj. U.K.* **AS SOON AS** as soon as, or at the moment that

im·me·mo·ri·al /ìmmə máwree əl/ *adj.* so old that it seems always to have existed ○ *have known them since time immemorial* ○ *immemorial customs of the nation* [Early 17thC. From medieval Latin *immemorialis*, literally "not belonging to memory," from Latin *memoria* (see MEMORY).] —**im·me·mo·ri·al·ly** *adv.*

im·mense /i méns/ *adj.* **1. HUGE** very large in extent or degree ○ *an immense desert* ○ *immense relief* **2. EXCELLENT** very good or showing excellence (*informal*) [15thC. Via French from Latin *immensus*, literally "not measured," from *mensus*, the past participle of *metiri* (see MEASURE).] —**im·mense·ly** *adv.* —**im·mense·ness** *n.* —**im·men·si·ty** *n.*

im·mense·ly /i ménslee/ *adv.* to a huge extent or degree ○ *she was immensely rich*

im·merse /i múrs/ (**-mersed, -mers·ing, -mers·es**) *v.* **1. COMPLETELY COVER SOMETHING IN LIQUID** to put something into a liquid so that the liquid's surface covers it completely **2.** *vt.* CHR **BAPTIZE SOMEBODY** to baptize somebody by lowering the person's head and upper body, or sometimes the whole body, into water **3.** *vr.* **OCCUPY YOURSELF TOTALLY WITH SOMETHING** to become completely occupied with something, giving all your time, energy, or concentration to it [Early 17thC. From Latin *immers-*, the past participle stem of *immergere*, literally "to plunge into," from *mergere* (see MERGE).]

im·mer·sion /i múrsh'n, i múrzh'n/ *n.* **1. COMPLETE INVOLVEMENT** involvement in something that completely occupies all the time, energy, or concentration available **2.** EDUC **METHOD OF LANGUAGE TEACHING** a method of language teaching that involves teachers and students using the foreign language at all times (*often used before a noun*) ○ *an immersion course* **3. PLACING OF SOMETHING UNDER LIQUID** the dipping of something into a liquid so that it is completely covered **4.** CHR **BAPTISM BY DIPPING BODY IN WATER** the practice of baptism by lowering a person's head and upper body, or sometimes the whole body, into water **5.** ASTRON **DISAPPEARANCE OF A CELESTIAL BODY BEFORE AN ECLIPSE** the movement of a celestial body, such as the Moon, into the shadow of another body, causing an eclipse

im·mer·sion·ism /i múrsh'n ìzzəm, -múrzh'n-/ *n.* the belief that immersion is the only true method of baptism

im·mesh /i mésh/ (**-meshed, -mesh·ing, -mesh·es**) *vt.* = **enmesh**

im·mi·grant /ímmigrənt/ *n.* **1. SOMEBODY COMING TO SETTLE IN A COUNTRY** somebody who has come to a country and settled there **2.** BOT, ZOOL **PLANT OR ANIMAL IN A NEW PLACE** a plant or animal that establishes itself in a place where it was not found before ■ *adj.* **SETTLING IN ANOTHER COUNTRY** relating to those who have come to settle in another country

im·mi·grate /ímmi gràyt/ (**-grat·ed, -grat·ing, -grates**) *v.* **1.** *vi.* **COME AND SETTLE IN A COUNTRY** to enter a new country for the purpose of settling there **2.** *vi.* BOT, ZOOL **ARRIVE FROM ELSEWHERE** to become established in a new environment **3.** *vt.* **BRING IN AS A SETTLER** to bring people into a country and settle them as permanent residents there [Early 17thC. From Latin *immigrare*, literally "to move into," from *migrare* (see MIGRATE).] —**im·mi·gra·tor** *n.* —**im·mi·gra·to·ry** /ímmigrə tàwree/ *adj.*

im·mi·gra·tion /ìmmi gráysh'n/ *n.* **1. ARRIVAL OF SETTLERS IN A NEW COUNTRY** the act of people entering into a new country to settle permanently **2. PASSPORT CONTROL** the control point at an airport, seaport, or border crossing where people entering a country must stop to have their passports officially checked **3. Im·mi·gra·tion INS** the United States Immigration and Naturalization Service (**INS**) (*informal*) —**im·mi·gra·tion·al** *adj.*

im·mi·nent /ímminənt/ *adj.* about to happen or threatening to happen [Early 16thC. From Latin *imminere*, literally "to hang over," from *minere* (see EMINENT).] —**im·mi·nence** *n.* —**im·mi·nent·ly** *adv.* —**im·mi·nent·ness** *n.*

im·mis·ci·ble /i míssəb'l/ *adj.* used to describe two or more liquids that will not mix together to form a single homogenous substance [Late 17thC. From late Latin *immiscibilis*, literally "not subject to mixing," from Latin *miscere* "to mix."] —**im·mis·ci·bil·i·ty** /i missə bíllətee/ *n.* —**im·mis·ci·bly** /i míssəblee/ *adv.*

im·mit·i·ga·ble /i míttigəb'l/ *adj.* incapable of being alleviated, weakened, or softened (*literary*) [Late 16thC. From late Latin *immitigabilis*, from Latin *mitigare* (see MITIGATE).] —**im·mit·i·ga·bil·i·ty** /i mìttigə bíllətee/ *n.* —**im·mit·i·ga·ble·ness** /i míttigəb'lnəss/ *n.* —**im·mit·i·ga·bly** /-blee/ *adv.*

im·mit·tance /i mítt'ns/ *n.* the joint concept of electrical admittance and impedance [Mid-20thC. Blend of IMPEDANCE and ADMITTANCE.]

im·mo·bile /i mṓb'l/ *adj.* **1. MOTIONLESS** without moving ○ *he stood perfectly immobile for a few seconds* **2. INCAPABLE OF MOTION** unable to move or be moved [14thC. Via French from Latin *immobilis*, literally "not moving," from *mobilis* (see MOBILE).] —**im·mo·bil·i·ty** /ìmmō bíllətee, ìmmə bíllətee/ *n.*

im·mo·bi·lize /i mṓb'l ìz/ (**-lized, -liz·ing, -liz·es**) *vt.* **1. MAKE MOTIONLESS** to make somebody or something completely still (*often passive*) **2. PUT A MACHINE OUT OF ACTION** to make a machine or device stop working, or adjust or damage it so that it cannot be made to work **3.** MED **KEEP THE BROKEN PART OF A LIMB STILL** to rest a joint, or keep the parts of a fractured limb fixed in place so that they are unable to move **4.** FIN **TAKE OUT OF CIRCULATION** to withdraw money or other capital from circulation to establish a reserve —**im·mo·bi·li·za·tion** /i mōb'li záysh'n/ *n.*

im·mod·er·ate /i móddərət/ *adj.* going beyond what is healthy, moral, appropriate, or socially acceptable (*formal*) [14thC. From Latin *immoderatus*, literally "not restrained," from *moderatus* (see MODERATE).] —**im·mod·er·a·cy** *n.* —**im·mod·er·ate·ly** *adv.* —**im·mod·er·ate·ness** *n.* —**im·mod·er·a·tion** /i mòddə ráysh'n/ *n.*

im·mod·est /i móddəst/ *adj.* **1. BOASTFUL** boasting, or tending to boast a great deal **2. INDECENT** likely to embarrass, offend, or shock people, especially because of open references to sexual matters or exposure of parts of the body that are normally covered [Late 16thC. Directly or via French from Latin *immodestus*, from *modestus* "kept within due measure."] —**im·mod·est·ly** *adv.* —**im·mod·es·ty** *n.*

im·mo·late /ímmə làyt/ (**-lat·ed, -lat·ing, -lates**) *vt.* to kill a person or an animal, e.g., as a ritual sacrifice, or to commit suicide as a protest, especially by burning (*formal*) [Mid-16thC. From Latin *immolare* "to sprinkle with meal," from *mola* "meal, millstone"; from the custom of sprinkling sacrificial victims with meal.] —**im·mo·la·tion** /ìmmə láysh'n/ *n.* —**im·mo·la·tor** /ímmə làytər/ *n.*

im·mor·al /i máwrəl/ *adj.* contrary to accepted moral principles —**im·mor·al·i·ty** /ì maw rállətee/ *n.* —**im·mor·al·ly** /i máwrəlee/ *adv.*

im·mor·al·ist /i máwrəlist/ *n.* somebody who engages in immoral acts, who rejects moral values, or who urges others to behave immorally

im·mor·tal /i máwrt'l/ *adj.* **1. ABLE TO LIVE OR LAST FOREVER** able to have eternal life or existence **2. FAMOUS** very famous and likely to be remembered for a long time ■ *n.* **1. SOMEBODY OR SOMETHING FAMOUS** somebody or something famous that people will remember for a long time (*often used in the plural*) **2. im·mor·tal, Im·mor·tal A GOD** a god who lives for ever, especially a god of ancient Greece or Rome [14thC. From Latin *immortalis*, literally "not subject to death," from *mortalis* (see MORTAL).] —**im·mor·tal·i·ty** /ì mawr tállətee/ *n.* —**im·mor·tal·ly** /i máwrt'lee/ *adv.*

im·mor·tal·ize /i máwrt'l ìz/ (**-ized, -iz·ing, -iz·es**) *vt.* **1.** MAKE SOMEBODY'S MEMORY LIVE ON to make somebody or something famous for a very long time, especially as the subject of a work of art such as a painting, novel, or movie **2.** GIVE ETERNAL LIFE TO to elevate a mortal person to the state of divinity or bestow eternal life on somebody **3.** BIOL CAUSE TO REPRODUCE INDEFINITELY to cause something such as human cells to reproduce indefinitely —**im·mor·tal·i·za·tion** /i màwrt'li záysh'n/ *n.*

im·mor·telle /i màwr tél/ *n.* PLANTS = **everlasting** *n.* 2 [Mid-19thC. From French, shortened from *fleur immortelle*, literally "undying flower."]

im·mo·tile /i mṓt'l/ *adj.* BOT, ZOOL used to describe a plant or animal part that cannot move — **im·mo·til·i·ty** /ìmmō tíllətee/ *n.*

im·mov·a·ble /i móovəb'l/ *adj.* **1.** UNABLE TO BE MOVED fixed in a permanent position, or incapable of being moved **2.** OF FIXED OPINION sticking firmly to an opinion or decision **3.** ALWAYS OCCURRING ON THE SAME DATE used to describe a religious festival that always falls on the same date each year, as does Christmas but not Hannukah ■ *n.* **im·mov·a·ble** LAW BUILDING OR LAND property that consists of land or buildings (*often used in the plural*) —**im·mov·a·bil·i·ty** /i mòovə bíllətee/ *n.* —**im·mov·a·ble·ness** /i móovəb'lnəss/ *n.* —**im·mov·a·bly** /i móovə blee/ *adv.*

immun. *abbr.* **1.** immunity **2.** immunization **3.** immunology

im·mune /i myóon/ *adj.* **1.** IMMUNOL SAFE FROM A PARTICULAR DISEASE protected from getting a particular disease because of natural resistance, resistance acquired after catching the disease before, or resistance conferred by inoculation ○ *immune to smallpox* **2.** IMMUNOL RELATING TO DISEASE RESISTANCE relating to a body's resistance to disease, or the creation of resistance **3.** NOT SUBJECT TO OR RESPONSIBLE FOR exempt from something that others are subject to or made to endure or perform ○ *immune from prosecution* **4.** NOT AFFECTED BY SOMETHING not sensitive or susceptible to something ○ *immune to flattery* [Late 19thC. From Latin *immunis* "exempt from public service," from *munis* "ready for service" (related to English *municipal*.)]

im·mune com·plex, **im·mu·no·com·plex** /ìmmyə nō kómpleks/ *n.* a combination of a disease-causing agent (**antigen**) and its corresponding antibody that plays a role in some types of immune responses and may be associated with autoimmune disease

im·mune re·sponse *n.* **1.** RESPONSE OF THE IMMUNE SYSTEM the overall activity of the body's immune system following the arrival of a disease-causing agent (**antigen**) **2.** BIOLOGICAL DEFENSE SYSTEM OF AN ORGANISM the integrated defense mounted by an organism against a disease-causing agent (**antigen**), including the production of antibodies and white blood cells designed to destroy the antigen or render it harmless

im·mune sys·tem *n.* the interacting combination of all the body's ways of recognizing cells, tissues, objects, and organisms that are not part of itself, and initiating the immune response to fight them

im·mu·ni·ty /i myóonətee/ (*plural* **-ties**) *n.* **1.** IMMUNOL RESISTANCE TO DISEASE a body's ability to resist a particular disease, whether existing naturally or as a result of inoculation or previous infection (**acquired immunity**). In active immunity, the body itself produces appropriate antibodies and lymphocytes, while in passive immunity, antibodies are introduced from another source, as from mother to fetus. ○ *immunity to smallpox* **2.** FREEDOM FROM RESPONSIBILITY OR PUNISHMENT exemption or protection from something unpleasant, such as a duty or penalty, to which others are subject ○ *immunity from prosecution* **3.** LAW EXEMPTION FROM PROSECUTION an exemption from prosecution for somebody who has knowledge of possible criminal activity and may be personally culpable in exchange for giving sufficient information to the police or to a grand jury

im·mu·nize /ímmyə nìz/ (**-nized, -niz·ing, -niz·es**) *vt.* **1.** IMMUNOL MAKE SOMEBODY RESISTANT TO A DISEASE to make somebody resistant to a particular disease, especially by vaccination ○ *immunized against tuberculosis* **2.** GRANT SOMEBODY EXEMPTION give somebody exemption or protection from something that others are subjected to, especially in a criminal matter under investigation —**im·mu·ni·za·tion** /ìmmyəni záysh'n/ *n.* —**im·mu·niz·er** /ímmyə nìzər/ *n.*

immuno- *prefix.* immune, immunity ○ *immunodeficiency* [From IMMUNE]

im·mu·no·as·say /ìmmyə nō á sày, i myòo-/ *n.* the use of disease-causing agents (**antigens**) and their corresponding antibodies to detect and analyze various chemical substances —**im·mu·no·as·say·ist** *n.*

im·mu·no·chem·is·try /ìmmyə nō kémistree, i myòo-/ *n.* the branch of chemistry dealing with the chemical reactions of immunity —**im·mu·no·chem·i·cal** *adj.*

im·mu·no·com·pe·tence /ìmmyə nō kómpət'ns, i myòo-/ *n.* the ability of the body to develop an immune response in the presence of a disease-causing agent (**antigen**) —**im·mu·no·com·pe·tent** *adj.*

im·mu·no·com·plex *n.* IMMUNOL = **immune complex**

im·mu·no·com·pro·mised /ìmmyə nō kómprə mìzd, i myòo-/ *adj.* lacking an adequate immune response as a result of disease, exposure to radiation, or treatment with immunosuppressive drugs

im·mu·no·de·fi·cien·cy /ìmmyə nō di físh'nsee, i myòo-/ (*plural* **-cies**) *n.* the inability, either inborn or acquired, of the body to produce an adequate immune response to fight disease — **im·mu·no·de·fi·cient** *adj.*

im·mu·no·de·pres·sion /ìmmyə nō də présh'n/ *n.* = **immunosuppression**

im·mu·no·di·ag·no·sis /ìmmyə nō dì əg nṓssiss, i myòo-/ (*plural* **-nos·es** /-nṓ sèez/) *n.* the diagnosis of disease by studying the antibodies in a sample of blood serum —**im·mu·no·di·ag·nos·tic** /ìmmyə nō dì əg nóstik, i myòo-/ *adj.*

im·mu·no·e·lec·tro·pho·re·sis /ìmmyə nō i lek trō fə réessiss, i myòo-/ *n.* the separation and identification of proteins using precipitates formed by specific immunological reactions —**im·mu·no·e·lec·tro·pho·re·tic** /ìmmyə nō i lek trō fə réttik, i myòo-/ *adj.* — **im·mu·no·e·lec·tro·pho·ret·i·cal·ly** /-rétti kəlee/ *adv.*

im·mu·no·fluo·res·cence /ìmmyə nō flòo réss'ns, -flàw-, i myòo-/ *n.* the labeling of antibodies or disease-causing agents (**antigens**) with a fluorescent dye in order to identify or locate them in a tissue sample —**im·mu·no·fluo·res·cent** *adj.*

im·mu·no·ge·net·ics /ìmmyə nō jə néttiks, i myòo-/ *n.* the discipline that studies the genetic basis of the immune system. This study is especially important in organ transplantation, where a close genetic match of tissue lowers the likelihood of organ rejection. (*takes a singular verb*) —**im·mu·no·ge·net·ic** *adj.* —**im·mu·no·ge·net·i·cist** /ìmmyə nō jə néttəssist, i myòo-/ *n.*

im·mu·no·gen·ic /ìmmyə nō jénnik, i myòo-/ *adj.* creating immunity or an immune response — **im·mu·no·gen·i·cal·ly** *adv.* —**im·mu·no·gen·ic·i·ty** /ìmmyə nō jə níssətee, i myòo-/ *n.*

im·mu·no·glob·u·lin /ìmmyə nō glóbbyəlin, i myòo-/ *n.* BIOCHEM a glycoprotein with a high molecular weight that acts like an antibody and is produced by white blood cells during an immune response. Immunoglobins are found in blood serum, the respiratory and digestive tracts, and body secretions, and they are grouped into five classes on the basis of their structure and physiological activity.

im·mu·no·he·ma·tol·o·gy /ìmmyə nō hemmə tólləjee, -heemə-, i myòo nō-/ *n.* the discipline concerned with all aspects of immunology relating to the blood, including blood types and blood disorders — **im·mu·no·he·ma·to·log·ic** /ìmmyə nō hemmətə lójjik, -heemə-, i myòo-/ *adj.* —**im·mu·no·he·ma·to·log·i·cal** /ìmmyə nō hemmətə lójjik'l, -heemə-, i myòo-/ *adj.*

immunol. *abbr.* immunology

im·mu·nol·o·gy /ìmmyə nólləjee/ *n.* the scientific study of the way the immune system works in the body, including allergies, resistance to disease, and acceptance or rejection of foreign tissue — **im·mu·no·log·ic** /ìmmyənə lójjik/ *adj.* —**im·mu·no·log·i·cal** /-lójji k'l/ *adj.* —**im·mu·no·log·i·cal·ly** /-lójji kəlee/ *adv.* —**im·mu·nol·o·gist** /-nólləjist/ *n.*

im·mu·no·mod·u·la·tion /ìmmyə nō mojjə láysh'n, i myòo-/ *n.* modification of some aspect of the immune system as part of a treatment, especially the suppression of the immune system in order to encourage the body to accept a transplanted organ — **im·mu·no·mod·u·la·to·ry** /ìmmyə nō mójjələ tàwree, i myòo-/ *adj.*

im·mu·no·path·ol·o·gy /ìmmyə nō pə thólləjee, i myòo-/ *n.* the study of disorders of the immune system and the resulting diseases or allergies — **im·mu·no·path·o·log·ic** /ìmmyə nō pathə lójjik, i myòo-/ *adj.* —**im·mu·no·path·o·log·i·cal** /-lójjik'l/ *adj.* —**im·mu·no·path·ol·o·gist** /ìmmyə nō pə thólləjist, i myòo-/ *n.*

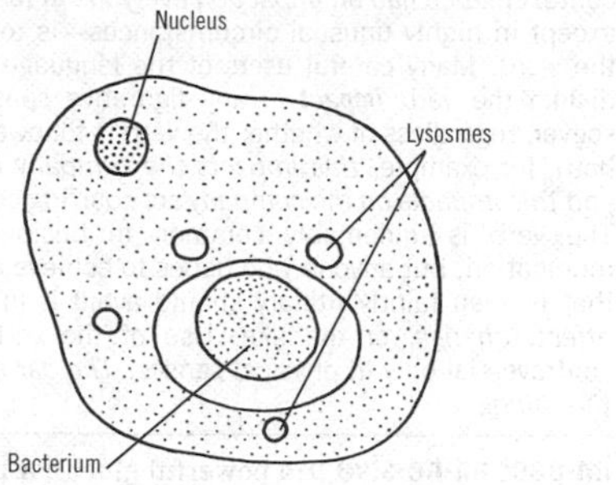

Immunoreaction: Section of immune cell ingesting and degrading disease-causing bacterium

im·mu·no·re·ac·tion /ìmmyə nō ree ákshən, i myòo-/ *n.* the reaction between a disease-causing agent (**antigen**) and its specific antibody, either as the body's immune response or as part of a laboratory procedure —**im·mu·no·re·ac·tive** *adj.* —**im·mu·no·re·ac·tiv·i·ty** /ìmmyə nō ree ak tívvətee, i myòo-/ *n.*

im·mu·no·sup·pres·sion /ìmmyə nō sə présh'n, i myòo-/ *n.* the inhibition of the immune response, usually deliberately by administering drugs to prevent rejection of transplanted organs, but sometimes resulting from disease, as in the case of AIDS —**im·mu·no·sup·pres·sant** *adj.*, *n.* —**im·mu·no·sup·pres·sive** *adj.*, *n.*

im·mu·no·ther·a·py /ìmmyə nō thérrəpee, i myòo-/ *n.* treatment of disease or other disorders by strengthening the body's immune system, e.g., by administering antibodies —**im·mu·no·ther·a·peu·tic** /ìmmyə nō thèrə pyóotik, i myòo nō-/ *adj.*

im·mure /i myóor/ (**-mured, -mur·ing, -mures**) *vt.* **1.** IMPRISON SOMEBODY to confine somebody in prison (*literary*) (*usually passive*) **2.** SHUT SOMEBODY AWAY to shut away or seclude somebody (*formal*) (*often passive*) **3.** ENCLOSE SOMETHING to enclose something in a wall or surround something with walls (*archaic*) [Late 16thC. Directly or via French *emmurer* from Latin *immurare*, literally "to wall in," from *murus* "wall."] —**im·mure·ment** *n.*

im·mu·ta·ble /i myóotəb'l/ *adj.* not changing or not able to be changed [15thC. From Latin *immutabilis*, literally "unchanging," from *mutare* "to change."] — **im·mu·ta·bil·i·ty** /i myòotə bíllətee/ *n.* —**im·mu·ta·ble·ness** *n.* —**im·mu·ta·bly** *adv.*

IMO *abbr.* **1.** International Meteorological Organization **2.** International Miners' Organization **3.** in my opinion (*used in e-mail communications*)

imp /imp/ *n.* **1.** NAUGHTY FAIRY in children's stories, a small mischievous creature resembling a fairy **2.** MISCHIEVOUS CHILD a high-spirited or mischievous child **3.** DEMON a small demon or devil ■ *vt.* (**imped, imp·ing, imps**) REPAIR A HAWK'S FEATHERS to repair the broken wing of a hawk or falcon by grafting on new feathers [Old English *impa* "young shoot, scion" and *impian* "to graft," both ultimately from Greek *emphuein*, literally "to emplant," from *phuein* "to grow, plant"]

IMP *abbr.* **1.** COMPUT interface message processor **2.** BRIDGE International Match Point

imp. *abbr.* **1.** GRAM imperative **2.** GRAM imperfect **3. imp., IMP.** imperial **4.** import **5.** important **6.** imported **7.** importer **8.** imprimatur

Imp. *abbr.* **1.** Imperator **2.** Imperatrix

im·pact *n.* /ím pàkt/ **1.** ACTION OF HITTING the action of one object hitting another **2.** FORCE OF COLLISION the force with which one object hits another **3.** EFFECT the strong effect that something or somebody has ■ *vti.* /im pákt/ (**-pact·ed, -pact·ing, -pacts**) **1.** STRIKE SOMETHING to strike something with force **2.** HAVE AN EFFECT ON SOMETHING to have an immediate and strong effect on something or somebody **3.** PRESS TOGETHER FORCEFULLY to press together with great force [Early

17thC. From Latin *impactus*, the past participle of *impingere* (see IMPINGE).] —**im·pac·tion** *n.*

WORD KEY: USAGE

Impact, noun and verb: The noun ***impact***, in its figurative meaning, should normally convey some sense of powerful or dramatic consequence, and should not just be an alternative word for *effect* or *impression.* To use it in a context like *he had an impact on everyone in the room*—except in highly unusual circumstances—is to devalue the word. Many careful users of the language strongly dislike the verb ***impact*** in any figurative sense whatsoever, regardless of whether the verb is followed by *on*: both, for example, *this impacts the company favorably* and *this impacts on the company* are courting contempt. The verb is undeniably common in business communication, but anyone who hopes to achieve an effect that is even faintly literary should avoid it in favor of *affect, change,* or the like. Use of the verb is uncontroversial only in physical senses: *The car impacted the railing.*

im·pact ad·he·sive *n.* a powerful glue that begins to form a bond as soon as the two coated surfaces are brought together

im·pact·ed /im páktəd/ *adj.* **1.** DENT **WEDGED SIDEWAYS UNDER THE GUM** wedged sideways against a barrier, usually the root of another tooth, and thus unable to break through the gum (*refers to an unerupted tooth*) **2.** MED **WITH BROKEN ENDS JAMMED TOGETHER** with the broken ends jammed tightly together by the initial trauma (*refers to a bone fracture*) **3.** MED **COMPRESSED IN THE INTESTINE TOO TIGHTLY** used to describe feces pressed together so tightly in the intestine that they cannot be eliminated in a bowel movement **4. DIFFICULT TO MOVE** unable to be moved, usually because of being jammed in a narrow space

im·pact print·er *n.* a printing device in which ink is pressed onto the paper by the printing element, as it is in a traditional typewriter

im·pact zone *n.* in surfing, the best and at the same time most dangerous position on a wave, where the water is about to separate into droplets

im·pair /im páir/ (**-paired, -pair·ing, -pairs**) *vt.* to lessen the quality, strength, or effectiveness of something [14thC. Via Old French *empeirier* from assumed Vulgar Latin *empejorare*, literally "to make worse," from Latin *pejor* "worse."] —**im·pair·a·ble** *adj.* —**im·pair·er** *n.*

im·paired *adj.* with something specified that is absent or lessened, either temporarily or permanently (*usually used in combination*) ○ *hearing-impaired*

im·pair·ment /im páirmənt/ *n.* **1. LESSENING OR ABSENCE OF ABILITY** a lessening or the absence of a particular physical or mental function **2. ACT OF DAMAGING SOMETHING** the causing of injury or harm to something, such as the health of a particular area of the body or mind, or the function of a machine

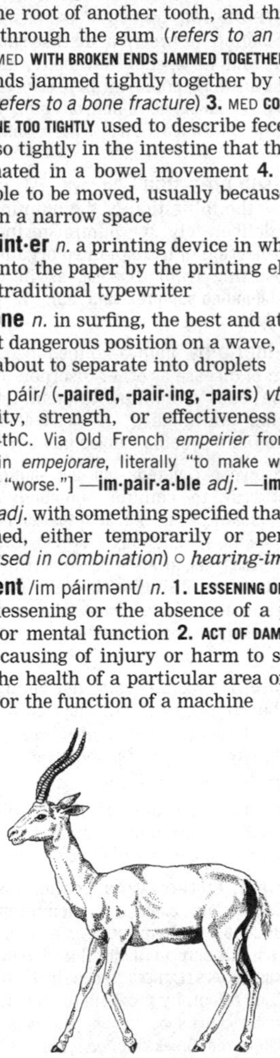

Impala

im·pa·la /im pállə/ (*plural* **-las** *or* **-la**) *n.* a large reddish-brown African antelope with long curved horns that makes spectacular leaps when alarmed. Latin name: *Aepyceros melampus.* [Late 19thC. From Zulu *impala.*]

im·pale /im páyl/ (**-paled, -pal·ing, -pales**), **em·pale** /em páyl/ (**-paled, -pal·ing, -pales**) *vt.* **1. SPEAR** to pierce somebody or something with a pointed object (*often passive*) **2. FENCE IN** to surround something with a fence (*archaic*) **3.** HERALDRY **COMBINE COATS OF ARMS** to combine two coats of arms on a single shield, divided by a vertical stripe (**pale**) [Mid-16thC. Directly or via French *empaler* from medieval Latin *impalare*, literally "to put on a stake," from Latin *palus* "stake."] —**im·pale·ment** *n.* —**im·pal·er** *n.*

im·pal·pa·ble /im pálpəb'l/ *adj.* (*formal*) **1. UNABLE TO BE TOUCHED OR SENSED** not capable of being touched, or not capable of being perceived by the senses **2. HARD TO UNDERSTAND** difficult to understand or grasp [Early 16thC. Directly or via French from late Latin *impalpabilis*, literally "not touchable," from *palpare* "to touch gently."] —**im·pal·pa·bil·i·ty** /im pàlpə bíllətee/ *n.* —**im·pal·pa·bly** /im pálpəblee/ *adv.*

im·pa·na·tion /impə náysh'n/ *n.* according to some denominations of Christianity, the presence of the body and blood of Jesus Christ in bread and wine that has been consecrated for the service of Communion (*formal*) [Mid-16thC. From medieval Latin *impanare* "to embody in bread," from Latin *panis* "bread."]

im·pan·el /im pánn'l/ (**-eled, -el·ing, -els**), **em·pan·el** /em pánn'l/ (**-eled, -el·ing, -els**) *vt.* LAW **1. LIST PEOPLE AS POSSIBLE JURORS** to draw up a list of people to be selected for jury service **2. SELECT A JURY FROM A LIST** to select a jury from a list of eligible persons [15thC. From Anglo-Norman *empaneller* "to put on a list," from *panel* "list," "jury list" (see PANEL).]

im·part /im paárt/ (**-part·ed, -part·ing, -parts**) *vt.* **1. COMMUNICATE** to communicate information or knowledge **2. GIVE A QUALITY TO SOMETHING** to give something a particular quality [Mid-16thC. Via Old French *impartir* from Latin *impartire*, literally "to give a share in," from *pars* "part."] —**im·par·ta·tion** /im paàr táysh'n/ *n.*

im·par·tial /im paársh'l/ *adj.* having no direct involvement or interest and not favoring one person or side more than another —**im·par·ti·al·i·ty** /im paàrshee állətee/ *n.* —**im·par·tial·ly** /im paárshəlee/ *adv.* —**im·par·tial·ness** /-sh'lnəss/ *n.*

im·part·i·ble /im paártəb'l/ *adj.* LAW not to be divided up [Late 16thC. From late Latin *impartibilis*, literally "not divisible," from *partire* (see PART).] —**im·part·i·bil·i·ty** /im paàrtə bíllətee/ *n.* —**im·part·i·bly** /im paártəblee/ *adv.*

im·pass·a·ble /im pássəb'l/ *adj.* **1. IMPOSSIBLE TO USE** impossible to travel on or through, e.g., because of being in bad condition or being blocked by snow **2. IMPOSSIBLE TO OVERCOME** impossible to solve or overcome ○ *impassable obstacles to peace* —**im·pass·a·bil·i·ty** /im pàssə bíllətee/ *n.* —**im·pass·a·ble·ness** /im pássəb'lnəss/ *n.* —**im·pass·a·bly** /-pássə blee/ *adv.*

im·passe /ím pàss/ *n.* **1. BLOCK TO PROGRESS OR AGREEMENT** a point at which no further progress can be made or agreement reached ○ *talks have reached an impasse* **2. ROAD WITHOUT EXIT** a road or passage that has no way out or through, e.g., a dead end or a blockage caused by an accident [Mid-19thC. From French, formed from *im-* "not" + *passer* (see PASS).]

im·pas·sion /im pásh'n/ (**-sioned, -sion·ing, -sions**) *vt.* to arouse strong feelings in somebody (*usually passive*) [Late 16thC. From Italian *impassionnare*, from *passione* "passion," from the late Latin stem *passion-* (see PASSION).]

im·pas·sioned /im pásh'nd/ *adj.* expressing or revealing strong feelings —**im·pas·sioned·ly** *adv.* —**im·pas·sioned·ness** *n.*

im·pas·sive /im pássiv/ *adj.* **1. EXPRESSIONLESS** showing no emotion, especially on the face **2. DEVOID OF ALL EMOTION** feeling no emotions at all, either positive or negative [Early 17thC. The literal meaning is "without suffering or passion."] —**im·pas·sive·ly** *adv.* —**im·pas·sive·ness** *n.* —**im·pas·siv·i·ty** /impə sívvətee/ *n.*

WORD KEY: SYNONYMS

impassive, apathetic, phlegmatic, stolid, stoic, unmoved

CORE MEANING: showing no emotional reponse or interest

impassive suggesting the absence of any outward sign of emotion, whether of facial expression, gesture, or action; **apathetic** often used in a derogatory way and suggesting a failure to respond because of a total lack of interest and a state of inertia; **phlegmatic** a formal word indicating that somebody has the kind of temperament that makes him or her generally unemotional and difficult to arouse; **stolid** describes somebody who is unemotional and not easily excited or upset; **stoic** used showing approval to describe somebody who accepts problems and difficulties without complaining or getting upset; **unmoved** describes somebody's reaction if no emotion, surprise, or excitement is shown in a situation where this would normally have been expected.

im·paste /im páyst/ (**-past·ed, -past·ing, -pastes**) *vt.* to cover something thickly with paint, paste, or crust (*literary*) [Mid-16thC. From Italian *impastare*, literally "to paste on," from *pasta* (see PASTE).] —**im·pas·ta·tion** /im pas táysh'n/ *n.*

im·pas·to /im pás tō, im paás tō/ *n.* **1. TECHNIQUE OF PAINTING THICKLY** the technique of applying paint so thickly that brush or knife strokes can be seen **2. PAINT THICKLY APPLIED** paint applied so thickly that brush or knife strokes can be seen [Late 18thC. From Italian, the past participle of *impastare* (see IMPASTE).]

im·pa·tience /im páysh'ns/ *n.* **1. ANNOYANCE AT WAITING** irritation at having to wait or at somebody or something that causes a wait **2. EAGERNESS** eagerness to do something immediately, and unwillingness to wait

Impatiens

im·pa·tiens /im páysh'nz, -sh'ns/ (*plural* **-tiens**) *n.* a cultivated species of the balsam family, popular as a houseplant and garden plant for its low-growing, numerous colorful flowers. The related wild varieties include touch-me-nots and jewelweed. Latin name: *Impatiens balsamina.* [Late 18thC. Via modern Latin, genus name, from Latin, literally "impatient" (see IMPATIENT); so called because the capsules tend to burst open when touched.]

im·pa·tient /im páysh'nt/ *adj.* **1. ANNOYED AT WAITING** annoyed by being kept waiting or by being delayed **2. EAGER** eager to do something immediately, and unwilling to wait **3. SHOWING IMPATIENCE** showing annoyance at being kept waiting, or eagerness to proceed with something **4. EASILY ANNOYED** unable to tolerate a particular thing and easily annoyed by it ○ *he was impatient of formalities* [14thC. Via French from the Latin stem *impatient-*, literally "not enduring," from *pati* "to suffer."] —**im·pa·tient·ly** *adv.*

im·peach /im peéch/ (**-peached, -peach·ing, -peach·es**) *vt.* **1. ACCUSE AN OFFICIAL OF AN OFFENSE** to charge a serving government official with serious misconduct while in office **2. CAST OUT OF PUBLIC OFFICE** to remove somebody, especially a president, from public office because of having committed high crimes and misdemeanors (*formal*) **3.** LAW **BRING CHARGES AGAINST SOMEBODY** to charge somebody with a crime or misdemeanor **4. DISPARAGE** to question somebody's good character (*formal*) **5.** *U.K.* LAW **ACCUSE OF A SERIOUS CRIME** to accuse somebody of a crime, especially treason or another crime against the state [14thC. Via Old French *empecher* from late Latin *impedicare* "to catch, entangle," from *pedica* "fetter, snare."] —**im·peach·er** *n.* —**im·peach·ment** *n.*

im·peach·a·ble /im peéchəb'l/ *adj.* **1. WORTHY OF A CRIMINAL TRIAL** serious enough for the offender to be brought to trial (*refers to a crime or charge*) ○ *an impeachable offense* **2. ABLE TO BE CHARGED** subject to a charge of crime and therefore liable to being brought to trial —**im·peach·a·bil·i·ty** /im peèchə bíllətee/ *n.*

im·pec·ca·ble /im pékəb'l/ *adj.* **1. PERFECT** so perfect or flawless as to be beyond criticism ○ *she had impeccable taste* **2.** RELIG **FREE FROM SIN** so perfect in character as to be incapable of sinning [Mid-16thC. From Latin *impeccabilis*, literally "not liable to sin," from *peccare* "to sin."] —**im·pec·ca·bil·i·ty** /im pèkə bíllətee/ *n.* —**im·pec·ca·bly** /im pékəblee/ *adv.*

im·pe·cu·ni·ous /impə kyoónee əss/ *adj.* having little or no money, and so unable to lead a comfortable life (*formal*) [Late 16thC. Formed from obsolete *pecunious* "wealthy," from Latin *pecunia* (see PECUNIARY).] —**im·pe·cu·ni·os·i·ty** /impə kyoònee óssətee/ *n.* —**im·pe·cu·ni·ous·ly** /impə kyoónee əsslee/ *adv.* —**im·pe·cu·ni·ous·ness** *n.*

im·pe·dance /im peéd'ns/ *n.* **1. PREVENTION OF PROGRESS** something that delays or prevents progress, or the preventing of progress (*formal*) **2.** ELEC **OPPOSITION TO THE FLOW OF ALTERNATING CURRENT** the opposition in a circuit to the flow of alternating current, consisting of resistance and reactance. Symbol *Z* **3.** ACOUSTICS **RATIO OF SOUND PRESSURE TO VELOCITY** the ratio of the sound pressure in a medium to the velocity of the particles in the medium. ◊ **immittance**

im·pede /im pe̱éd/ **(-ped·ed, -ped·ing, -pedes)** *vt.* to interfere with the movement, progress, or development of something or somebody [Late 16thC. From Latin *impedire* "to shackle the feet" (ultimately related to *pes* "foot").] —**im·ped·er** *n.*

WORD KEY: SYNONYMS

See Synonyms at ***hinder.***

im·ped·i·ment /im péddəmənt/ *n.* **1. IMPAIRMENT** an impairment, especially one affecting speech **2. OBSTACLE** something that hinders progress in some way **3.** LAW **LEGAL OBSTRUCTION** the reason a legal contract, e.g., a marriage, cannot be entered into [14thC. From Latin *impedimentum* "hindrance," from *impedire* (see IMPEDE).] —**im·ped·i·men·tal** /im pèddə mént'l/ *adj.* —**im·ped·i·men·ta·ry** /-méntəree/ *adj.*

im·ped·i·men·ta /im pèddə méntə/ *npl.* **1. OBSTRUCTIONS** obstacles, hindrances, or obstructions to progress (*literary*) **2.** ARMY **MILITARY EQUIPMENT** equipment and baggage carried by soldiers (*formal*) [Early 17thC. From Latin, literally "hindrances," plural of *impedimentum* (see IMPEDIMENT).]

im·pel /im pél/ **(-pelled, -pel·ling, -pels)** *vt.* **1. FORCE TO DO** to force somebody to do something, or make somebody feel the need to do something (*usually passive*) ○ *I felt impelled to protest* **2. CAUSE TO MOVE** to start or keep something or somebody moving in a particular direction (*formal*) [15thC. From Latin *impellere*, literally "to drive toward," from *pellere* "to beat."]

im·pel·ler /im péllər/ *n.* the rotating part that transmits motion in a centrifugal pump, turbine, or blower

im·pend /im pénd/ **(-pend·ed, -pend·ing, -pends)** *vi.* **1. BE CLOSE TO HAPPENING** to be threateningly close to happening (*formal*) **2. HANG MENACINGLY** to hover or hang above something, usually in a threatening way (*literary*) [Late 16thC. From Latin *impendere*, literally "to hang over," from *pendere* "to hang."] —**im·pen·dence** *n.* —**im·pen·den·cy** *n.* —**im·pen·dent** *adj.* —**im·pend·ing** *adj.*

im·pend·ing /im pénding/ *adj.* about to happen

im·pen·e·tra·ble /im pénnətrəb'l/ *adj.* **1. IMPOSSIBLE TO GET IN OR THROUGH** not able to be passed through or entered ○ *The woods formed an impenetrable barrier.* **2. INCOMPREHENSIBLE** impossible to understand or discern ○ *impenetrable legal jargon* **3. CLOSED TO INFLUENCE** not open to intellectual or moral influences, impressions, or ideas [15thC. Via French from Latin *impenetrabilis*, from *penetrabilis* (see PENETRABLE).] —**im·pen·e·tra·bil·i·ty** /im pènnətrə bíllətee/ *n.* —**im·pen·e·tra·bly** /-trə blee/ *adv.*

im·pen·i·tent /im pénnit'nt/ *adj.* **NOT SORRY** having or showing no regret or sorrow for sin or misbehavior ■ *n.* **UNREPENTING PERSON** somebody who is unrepentant [15thC. From the ecclesiastical Latin stem *impaenitent-*, from *paenitent-* (see PENITENT).] —**im·pen·i·tence** *n.* —**im·pen·i·ten·cy** *n.* —**im·pen·i·tent·ly** *adv.*

im·pen·nate /im pé nàyt/ *adj.* used to describe a bird that has small wings that are incapable of supporting flight but are adapted for swimming

imper. *abbr.* GRAM imperative

im·per·a·tive /im pérrətiv/ *adj.* **1. NECESSARY** absolutely necessary or unavoidable ○ *It is imperative that justice is seen to be done.* **2. COMMANDING** forceful and demanding the obedience and respect of others (*formal*) **3.** GRAM **USED FOR GIVING ORDERS** used to express a command or request, e.g., the verb form "come" in "Come here!") ■ *n.* **1. PRIORITY** something that must be done ○ *Preservation of honor is a moral imperative.* **2. im·per·a·tive, im·per·a·tive mood** GRAM **WAY OF COMMANDING** the form of a verb used to give an order **3.** GRAM **VERB EXPRESSING A COMMAND OR REQUEST** a verb in the imperative mood, such as "close" in "Please close the door" [15thC. From late Latin *imperativus*, literally "specially ordered," from Latin *imperare* "to command," from *parare* "to prepare."] —**im·per·a·tive·ly** *adv.* —**im·per·a·tive·ness** *n.*

im·pe·ra·tor /impə ráatər, -ráa tàwr/ *n.* **1. ROMAN GENERAL** a victorious military commander during the time of the Roman Republic **2.** HIST **ROMAN EMPEROR** the head of state of the Roman Empire **3. ABSOLUTE RULER** an absolute ruler or commander [Mid-16thC. From Latin, literally "commander," formed from *imperare* (see IMPERATIVE).] —**im·per·a·to·ri·al** /im pèrrə táwree əl/ *adj.*

im·per·cep·ti·ble /impər séptəb'l/ *adj.* very slight or gradual ○ *an imperceptible touch of the hand* —**im·per·cep·ti·bil·i·ty** /impər sèptə bíllətee/ *n.* —**im·per·cep·ti·bly** /-blee/ *adv.*

im·per·cep·tive /impər séptiv/ *adj.* lacking the ability to notice things or to understand somebody or something —**im·per·cep·tive·ly** *adv.* —**im·per·cep·tive·ness** *n.* —**im·per·cep·tiv·i·ty** /impər sep tívətee/ *n.*

im·per·cip·i·ence /impər síppee əns/ *n.* a lack of perception (*formal*) ○ *the impercipience of the egotist* —**im·per·cip·i·ent** *adj.*

imperf. *abbr.* **1.** GRAM, BOT imperfect **2.** STAMPS imperforate

im·per·fect /im púrfəkt/ *adj.* **1. FAULTY** having a fault or defect **2. NOT COMPLETE** lacking a part **3.** BOT **NOT ABLE TO REPRODUCE** used to describe a flower that lacks either a stamen or a pistil and is therefore unable to reproduce **4.** MUSIC **NOT PERFECT** used to describe a musical interval between the first and third or first and sixth notes of the scale **5.** MUSIC **ENDING ON 5TH NOTE OF SCALE** used to describe a cadence ending on the 5th note of the scale (**dominant**) rather than on the first note (**tonic**) **6.** GRAM **EXPRESSING INCOMPLETE ACTION** used to describe a verb or tense that denotes past action going on but not completed **7.** LAW **UNENFORCEABLE** unable to be enforced ■ *n.* GRAM **1. VERB TENSE** a grammatical tense used for expressing incomplete or habitual action in the past **2. VERB FORM** a form of a verb used to express the imperfect tense [14thC. Alteration of *imperfit*, from French *imparfait*, from Latin *imperfectus*, from *perfectus* "perfect" (see PERFECT).] —**im·per·fect·ly** *adv.* —**im·per·fect·ness** *n.*

im·per·fect fun·gus *n.* a fungus that forms only asexual spores (**conidia**). Order: Fungi Imperfecti.

im·per·fec·tion /impər fékshən/ *n.* **1. FAULT** something that makes a person or thing less than perfect **2. FAULTINESS** the possession of faults or defects

WORD KEY: SYNONYMS

See Synonyms at ***flaw.***

im·per·fec·tive /impər féktiv/ *adj.* **INDICATING INCOMPLETE ACTION** used to describe a verb aspect expressing action that is not completed. ◊ **perfective** ■ *n.* **1. VERB ASPECT** the imperfective aspect of the verb **2. VERB FORM** a verb form belonging to the imperfective aspect —**im·per·fec·tive·ly** *adv.*

im·per·fo·rate /im púrfərət/ *adj.* **1. WITHOUT AN OPENING** with no perforation or opening **2.** ANAT **PARTIALLY OR COMPLETELY CLOSED** lacking an opening of the normal size, especially because of abnormal development **3.** STAMPS **WITH NO HOLES** produced without the perforations that allow easy tearing or division ■ *n.* STAMPS **STAMP WITHOUT PERFORATIONS** a stamp without perforations around it —**im·per·fo·ra·tion** /im pùrfə ráysh'n/ *n.*

im·pe·ri·a plural of **imperium**

im·pe·ri·al /im pe̱éree əl/ *adj.* **1. BELONGING TO EMPIRE OR EMPEROR** concerning or involving an empire or its ruler **2. INDICATING A COUNTRY'S AUTHORITY** involving or relating to the authority of a country over colonies or other countries **3. SUPREMELY POWERFUL** holding supreme power ○ *All are subject to the imperial power of the state.* **4. GRAND** very grand or majestic **5. SUPERIOR** better in quality or larger in size **6.** MEASURE **OF BRITISH NONMETRIC SET OF MEASURES** belonging or conforming to the nonmetric system of weights and measures legally established in Britain that includes the foot, pound, and gallon ■ *n.* **1.** PRINTING **PAPER SIZE** the largest of the traditional U.S. and British paper sizes. The U.S. imperial measures 23 x 33 in./584 x 838 mm and the British imperial 22 x 30 in./559 x 762 mm, untrimmed. **2. RELATIVE OF AN EMPEROR OR EMPRESS** a person belonging to an imperial family (*formal*) **3.** HAIR **SMALL BEARD** a tuft or point of hair grown on the chin or below the lower lip. This style was made fashionable by the French Emperor Napoleon III. **4.** ANTIQUES **TRUNK FOR LUGGAGE** a chest fitted into the top of a coach to store travelers' bags, or the part of a coach's roof where this chest fits **5.** MONEY **OLD RUSSIAN COIN** a former gold coin of Russia worth about eight rubles **6.** BEVERAGES **LARGE WINE BOTTLE** a wine bottle containing the equivalent of eight standard bottles, used for red Bordeaux [14thC. Via French from Latin *imperialis*, from *imperium* "rule, empire" (see EMPIRE).] —**im·pe·ri·al·ly** *adv.*

im·pe·ri·al·ism /im pe̱éree ə lìzzəm/ *n.* **1. BELIEF IN EMPIRE-BUILDING** the policy of extending the rule or influence of a country over other countries or colonies **2. DOMINATION BY AN EMPIRE** the political, military, or economic domination of one country over another **3. TAKEOVER AND DOMINATION** the extension of power or authority over others in the interests of domination ○ *cultural imperialism* —**im·pe·ri·al·ist** *n., adj.* —**im·pe·ri·al·is·tic** /im pe̱éree ə lístik/ *adj.* —**im·pe·ri·al·is·ti·cal·ly** /-kəlee/ *adv.*

im·pe·ri·al moth *n.* a large moth found in North and South America that has yellow wings and purplish-brown markings. Latin name: *Eacles imperialis.* [*Imperial* from its purplish markings, because the color purple was traditionally used for rulers' garments]

Im·pe·ri·al Val·ley valley in southeastern California, part of a larger valley that extends into Mexico. It is a rich agricultural area. Length: 60 mi./97 km.

im·per·il /im pérəl/ **(-iled, -il·ing, -ils)** *vt.* to put something or somebody in danger (*formal*) —**im·per·il·ment** *n.*

im·pe·ri·ous /im pe̱éree əss/ *adj.* haughty and domineering [Mid-16thC. From Latin *imperiosus*, from *imperium* "rule, empire" (see EMPIRE).] —**im·pe·ri·ous·ly** *adv.* —**im·pe·ri·ous·ness** *n.*

im·per·ish·a·ble /im pérrishəb'l/ *adj.* **1. THAT WILL NOT DECAY** not liable to become spoiled, weak, or damaged through time and wear **2. LONG-LASTING** not forgotten or ignored over time (*literary*) ○ *The imperishable quality of great literature distinguishes it from humbler writing.* —**im·per·ish·a·bil·i·ty** /im pèrrishə bíllətee/ *n.* —**im·per·ish·a·ble·ness** /im pérrishəb'lnəss/ *n.* —**im·per·ish·a·bly** /-pérrishə blee/ *adv.*

im·pe·ri·um /im pe̱éree əm/ (*plural* **-ria** /-ree ə/) *n.* **1. SUPREME POWER** supreme or imperial power (*formal*) **2.** LAW **LEGAL RIGHT TO COMMAND** the use of the power of the state to enforce the law **3. EMPIRE** an area controlled by a supreme power (*formal or literary*) [Mid-17thC. From Latin, literally "rule, empire" (see EMPIRE).]

im·per·ma·nent /im púrmənənt/ *adj.* that will change, go away, disappear, or fade —**im·per·ma·nence** *n.* —**im·per·ma·nen·cy** *n.* —**im·per·ma·nent·ly** *adv.*

im·per·me·a·ble /im púrmee əb'l/ *adj.* not permitting the passage of liquid, gas, or other fluid. ◊ **impervious** —**im·per·me·a·bil·i·ty** /im pùrmee ə bíllətee/ *n.* —**im·per·me·a·ble·ness** /im púrmee əb'lnəss/ *n.* —**im·per·me·a·bly** /-púrmee ə blee/ *adv.*

im·per·mis·si·ble /im pùr míssəb'l/ *adj.* that cannot or will not be allowed ○ *Such conduct is impermissible.* —**im·per·mis·si·bil·i·ty** /im pur mìssə bíllətee/ *n.* —**im·per·mis·si·bly** /im pùr míssəblee/ *adv.*

impers. *abbr.* GRAM impersonal

im·per·son·al /im púrsən'l/ *adj.* **1. NOT PERSONALIZED** not referring to individuals or reflecting personalities but focusing on events and facts ○ *an impersonal style of reporting* **2. ANONYMOUS** not considering people as individuals ○ *an impersonal bureaucracy* **3. COLD AND ALIENATING** making a person feel insignificant and ignored as an individual ○ *the service in the restaurant was brisk and impersonal* **4. WITHOUT HUMAN TRAITS** without any human characteristics or personality **5.** GRAM **NOT SPECIFIC** used to describe a clause or construction that includes a personal pronoun that does not refer to a specific person or thing, such as "it is raining" or "you shouldn't drink and drive" —**im·per·son·al·i·ty** /im pùrs'n állətee/ *n.* —**im·per·son·al·ly** /im púrsən'lee/ *adv.*

im·per·son·al·ize /im púrsən'l ìz/ **(-ized, -iz·ing, -iz·es)** *vt.* to make something neutral, lacking in human warmth, or without reference to individuals —**im·per·son·al·i·za·tion** /im pùrsən'li záysh'n/ *n.*

im·per·son·ate /im púrs'n àyt/ **(-at·ed, -at·ing, -ates)** *vt.* **1. MIMIC** to mimic the voice, appearance, and manners of another person, especially in order to entertain **2.** LAW **ACT A PART** to pretend to be another person, especially in order to deceive [Early 17thC. Formed from Latin *persona* "person" (see PERSON), on the model of INCORPORATE.] —**im·per·son·a·tion** /im pùrs'n áysh'n/ *n.* —**im·per·son·a·tor** /im púrs'n àytər/ *n.*

im·per·ti·nence /impúrt'nəns/, **im·per·ti·nen·cy** /impúrt'nənsee/ (*plural* **-cies**) *n.* **1. IMPUDENCE** boldness and rudeness, especially to a superior **2. SOMETHING DISRESPECTFUL** a disrespectful action or comment **3. IRRELEVANCE** lack of relevance to the matter in hand (*formal*)

im·per·ti·nent /im púrt'nənt/ *adj.* (*formal*) **1. BRASH** showing a bold or rude lack of respect, especially to a superior **2. IRRELEVANT** not appropriate or relevant [14thC. Directly or via French from the late Latin stem *impertinent-* "not pertinent," from the Latin stem *pertinent-* "pertinent" (see PERTINENT); "disrespectful" evolved in the 17thC, via the idea of presumptuously going beyond what is relevant to yourself.] —**im·per·ti·nent·ly** *adv.*

im·per·turb·a·ble /impər túrbəb'l/ *adj.* not easily worried, distressed, or agitated ○ *The Captain's imperturbable manner gave the crew confidence.* [15thC. From late Latin *imperturbabilis*, from *perturbare* "to disturb" (see PERTURB).] —**im·per·turb·a·bil·i·ty** /impər turbə bíllətee/ *n.* —**im·per·turb·a·ble·ness** /impərtúrbəb'lnəss/ *n.* —**im·per·turb·a·bly** /-túrbəblee/ *adv.*

im·per·vi·ous /im púrvee əss/ *adj.* **1. NOT RESPONSIVE** remaining unmoved and unaffected by other people's opinions, arguments, or suggestions ○ *He was impervious to the growing resentment among his staff.* **2. NOT LETTING SOMETHING THROUGH** not allowing passage into or through something [Mid-17thC. Formed from Latin *impervius*, from *pervius* (see PERVIOUS).] —**im·per·vi·ous·ly** *adv.* —**im·per·vi·ous·ness** *n.*

im·pe·ti·go /impə tée gō, impə tí gō/ *n.* a contagious infection of the skin characterized by blisters that form yellow-brown scabs. It is caused by staphylococcal and streptococcal bacteria. [14thC. From Latin, where it was formed from *impetere* (see IMPETUS).] —**im·pe·tig·i·nous** /impə tíjjənəss/ *adj.*

im·pe·trate /impə tràyt/ (**-trat·ed, -trat·ing, -trates**) *vt.* to request something in an earnest manner, especially in prayer, or to obtain something in this way (*archaic or formal*) [15thC. From Latin *impetrare* "to achieve or procure," from *patrare* "to bring about" (source of English *perpetrate*).] —**im·pe·tra·tion** /impə tráysh'n/ *n.* —**im·pe·tra·tive** /ímpə tràytiv/ *adj.* —**im·pe·tra·tor** /-tər/ *n.*

im·pet·u·os·i·ty /im pèchoo óssətee/ (*plural* **-ties**) *n.* **1. TENDENCY TO RASHNESS** a tendency to act rashly **2. IMPULSIVE ACTION** an act performed on the spur of the moment after little or no consideration (*formal*)

im·pet·u·ous /im péchoo əss/ *adj.* **1. ACTING IMPULSIVELY** acting on the spur of the moment, without considering the consequences **2. DONE ON IMPULSE** done without thought as a reaction to an emotion or impulse **3. VIOLENT** moving with great force and energy (*literary*) [14thC. Via French *impétueux* from late Latin *impetuosus*, from *impetus* (see IMPETUS).] —**im·pet·u·ous·ly** *adv.* —**im·pet·u·ous·ness** *n.*

im·pe·tus /ímpətəss/ *n.* **1. PUSH** something that provides energy or motivation to accomplish something or to undertake something **2.** PHYS **FORCE** a force that causes the motion of an object to overcome resistance and maintain its velocity [Mid-17thC. From Latin, literally "assault, force," from *impetere* "to assail," from *petere* "to go toward, seek."]

imp. gal., **imp. gall.** *abbr.* imperial gallon

im·pi·e·ty /im pí ətee/ (*plural* **-ties**) *n.* **1.** RELIG **LACK OF RELIGIOUS RESPECT** a lack of due reverence for God or religion **2.** RELIG **UNGODLY ACT** an act that shows a lack of religious respect or devotion **3. LACK OF RESPECT** a lack of respect or dutifulness (*formal or archaic*) [Late 16thC. Directly or via French *impiété* from Latin *impietas*, from *impius* (see IMPIOUS).]

im·pinge /im pínj/ (**-pinged, -pinge·ing, -ping·es**) *vi.* **1. INTERFERE** to affect the limits of something, especially a right or law, often causing some kind of restriction (*formal*) ○ *Members claimed that canceling the ballot impinged on their voting rights.* **2. STRIKE** to strike or hit something ○ *Loud noise can impinge on the eardrum, causing temporary hearing impairment.* [Mid-16thC. From Latin *impingere* "to strike or drive in forcibly," from *pangere* "to drive or fix in" (source of English *page*).] —**im·pinge·ment** *n.* —**im·ping·er** *n.*

im·pi·ous /ímpee əs, im pí əss/ *adj.* **1.** RELIG **SHOWING LACK OF RELIGIOUS RESPECT** not showing due reverence for God or something holy **2. DISRESPECTFUL** showing a lack of respect for somebody or something (*formal or archaic*) [Mid-16thC. Formed from Latin *impius*, from *pius* "pious" (see PIOUS).] —**im·pi·ous·ly** *adv.* —**im·pi·ous·ness** *n.*

imp·ish /ímpish/ *adj.* wicked in a playful way, without causing serious harm —**imp·ish·ly** *adv.* —**imp·ish·ness** *n.*

im·plac·a·ble /im plákəb'l/ *adj.* impossible to pacify or to reduce in strength or force (*formal*) ○ *an implacable foe* ○ *an implacable ice storm* [15thC. From Latin *implacabilis*, from *placabilis* "easily appeased," from *placare* "to calm" (see PLACATE).] —**im·plac·a·bil·i·ty** /implàkə bíllətee/ *n.* —**im·plac·a·ble·ness** /im plákəb'lnəss/ *n.* —**im·plac·a·bly** /-plákəblee/ *adv.*

im·plant *v.* /im plánt/ (**-plant·ed, -plant·ing, -plants**) **1.** *vt.* **ESTABLISH HABITS OR NOTIONS** to fix something deeply in somebody's mind or consciousness as a behavior pattern, thought, or belief **2.** *vt.* **INSERT** to fit or fix something small into something larger, which then encases it ○ *Gold fillings, implanted in his front teeth, flashed when he smiled.* **3.** *vt.* **BURY** to fix something in the ground, especially so that it grows **4.** *vt.* SURG **EMBED** to embed something such as a mechanical device in the body ○ *The hormone pellets are invisibly implanted just below the skin.* **5.** *vi.* GYN **BECOME EMBEDDED** to become embedded in the lining of the womb ■ *n.* /ím plant/ SURG **SOMETHING INSERTED DURING SURGERY** something inserted or embedded in the tissues or organs of the body during a surgical procedure, such as encapsulated drugs or fluid-filled sacs to replace or augment breast tissue —**im·plant·a·ble** *adj.* —**im·plant·er** *n.*

im·plan·ta·tion /implan táysh'n/ *n.* **1. BEING OR BECOMING IMPLANTED** the state of being or process of becoming fixed or embedded in something **2.** SURG **SURGICALLY IMPLANTING IN THE BODY** the insertion or embedding of something into body tissues or organs during a surgical procedure **3.** GYN **ATTACHMENT OF AN EMBRYO** the process by which or stage at which an embryo becomes embedded in the lining of the womb

im·plau·si·ble /im pláwzəb'l/ *adj.* hardly likely to be true —**im·plau·si·bil·i·ty** /im plàwzə bíllətee/ *n.* —**im·plau·si·ble·ness** /im pláwzəb'lnəss/ *n.* —**im·plau·si·bly** /-pláwzəblee/ *adv.*

im·plead /im pléed/ (**-plead·ed, -plead·ing, -pleads**) *vti.* to bring a lawsuit against an individual or organization in court [14thC. From Anglo-Norman *empleder*, ultimately from Old French *plaidier* (see PLEAD).] —**im·plead·a·ble** *adj.* —**im·plead·er** *n.*

im·ple·ment *n.* /ímpləmənt/ **1. TOOL** a useful article of equipment, usually a specially shaped object to do a particular task ○ *writing implements* **2. REQUIREMENT** something needed in order to achieve something (*formal*) ■ *vt.* /implə mént/ (**-ment·ed, -ment·ing, -ments**) **1. CARRY OUT OR FULFILL** to put something into effect or action ○ *The plan has yet to be fully implemented.* **2. GIVE TOOLS TO** to provide or equip somebody with the tools or other means to do something (*formal*) [15thC. From late Latin *implementum* "filling," from Latin *implere*, literally "to fill in," from *plere* "to fill."] —**im·ple·men·tal** /implə ménťl/ *adj.* —**im·ple·men·ta·tion** /impləmən táysh'n/ *n.* —**im·ple·ment·er** /implə mèntər/ *n.*

im·pli·cate /ímpli kàyt/ (**-cat·ed, -cat·ing, -cates**) *vt.* **1. CONNECT WITH SOMETHING** to show that somebody or something played a part in or is connected to an activity, such as a crime **2. IMPLY** to imply or involve something as a consequence (*formal*) ○ *Do you not see that his words implicate an error on my part?* **3. ENTANGLE OR INTERWEAVE** to wreathe, twist, or knit things together (*literary*) [15thC. From Latin *implicat-*, the past participle stem of *implicare* "to entangle, involve" (the original sense in English), from *plicare* "to fold" (source of English *ply*).]

im·pli·ca·tion /impli káysh'n/ *n.* **1. INDIRECT SUGGESTION** something that is implied as a natural consequence of something else ○ *It is important to consider the wider implications of making such a decision.* **2. IMPLICIT UNDERSTANDING** the state of implying or being implied, without being plainly expressed **3. INVOLVEMENT** the involvement or entanglement of somebody in something ○ *his implication in the crime* **4.** LOGIC **LOGICAL RELATION** in logic, a relationship between two propositions that holds when both propositions are true and fails when the first is true but the second is false —**im·pli·ca·tion·al** *adj.*

im·pli·ca·tive /ímpli kàytiv/ *adj.* tending to imply or implicate (*formal*) —**im·pli·ca·tive·ly** *adv.*

im·plic·it /im plíssit/ *adj.* **1. IMPLIED** not stated, but understood in what is expressed ○ *Asking us when we would like to start was an implicit acceptance of our terms.* **2. ABSOLUTE** not affected by any doubt or uncertainty ○ *implicit faith* **3. CONTAINED** present as a necessary part of something ○ *Confidentiality is implicit in the relationship between doctor and patient.* [Late 16thC. Directly or via French *implicite* from Latin *implicitus* "entangled," from *implicare* (see IMPLICATE).] —**im·plic·it·ly** *adv.*

im·plied /im plíd/ *adj.* involved, understood, or suggested without expressly being stated ○ *implied criticisms*

im·plode /im plṓd/ (**-plod·ed, -plod·ing, -plodes**) *vti.* PHYS to collapse inwardly with force, as a result of the external pressure being greater than the internal pressure, or to cause something to collapse inwardly [Late 19thC. Formed from Latin *plodere* "to clap," on the model of EXPLODE.]

im·plore /im pláwr/ (**-plored, -plor·ing, -plores**) *vt.* (*formal*) **1. BEG EARNESTLY** to plead with somebody to do something ○ *The tenants implored their landlord not to sell the building.* **2. REQUEST EARNESTLY** to beg or pray for something [Early 16thC. Directly or via French *implorer* from Latin *implorare* "to call upon with tears," from *plorare* "to weep."] —**im·plo·ra·tion** /implə ráysh'n, im plaw ráysh'n/ *n.* —**im·plo·ra·to·ry** /im pláwrə tàwree/ *adj.* —**im·plor·er** /-pláwrər/ *n.*

im·plor·ing /im pláwring/ *adj.* earnestly asking for something ○ *an imploring look* —**im·plor·ing·ly** *adv.*

im·plo·sion /im plṓzh'n/ *n.* PHYS the violent inward collapse of a vessel or structure resulting from the external pressure being greater than the internal pressure [Late 19thC. Formed from IMPLODE, on the model of EXPLOSION.]

im·plo·sive /im plṓssiv/ *adj.* PHYS indicating or relating to violent inward collapse —**im·plo·sive·ly** *adv.*

im·ply /im plí/ (**-plied, -ply·ing, -plies**) *vt.* **1. SUGGEST** to make something understood without expressing it directly **2. INVOLVE** to involve something as a necessary part or condition ○ *Such impressive exam results imply good teaching and study methods.* [14thC. Via Old French *emplier* from Latin *implicare* "to entangle or involve" (the original sense in English) (see IMPLICATE).]

im·po·lite /impə lít/ *adj.* not showing proper manners or respect [Early 17thC. From Latin *impolitus*, from *politus* "polished" (see POLITE).] —**im·po·lite·ly** *adv.* —**im·po·lite·ness** *n.*

im·pol·i·tic /im póllətik/ *adj.* likely to be disadvantageous and therefore not advisable (*formal*) ○ *It would be impolitic to refuse.* —**im·pol·i·tic·ly** *adv.* —**im·pol·i·tic·ness** *n.*

im·pon·der·a·bil·i·a /im pòndərə bíllee ə/ *npl.* matters or factors whose importance or effect cannot be assessed (*literary*) [Early 20thC. From modern Latin, literally "things that cannot be weighed," ultimately from Latin *ponderare* "to weigh" (see PONDER).]

im·pon·der·a·ble /im póndərəb'l/ *adj.* **NOT MEASURABLE** not quantifiable in terms of importance or effect ○ *Sheer inspiration remains an imponderable force in cultural and technological developments.* ■ *n.* **SOMETHING IMPOSSIBLE TO CALCULATE** an event, factor, or other matter whose importance or effects cannot be calculated (*often used in the plural*) ○ *just another of life's imponderables* —**im·pon·der·a·bil·i·ty** /im pòndərə bíllətee/ *n.* —**im·pon·der·a·ble·ness** /im póndərəb'lnəss/ *n.* —**im·pon·der·a·bly** /-póndərəblee/ *adv.*

im·port *vt.* /im páwrt/ (**-port·ed, -port·ing, -ports**) **1.** COMM **BRING IN FROM ABROAD** to bring something or cause something to be brought in from another country, usually for commercial or industrial purposes **2. BRING IN FROM OUTSIDE** to bring in something, such as knowledge or expertise, from an outside source **3.** COMPUT **TRANSFER DATA** to transfer data from one location to another in a computer or from one computer to another in a computer network, especially when a change of format is required **4. IMPLY** to mean something, often in addition to what is actually expressed (*formal*) ○ *What does the legal motion really import here?* ■ *n.* /ím pawrt/ **1.** COMM **SOMETHING BROUGHT FROM ABROAD** something that is brought into one country from another, usually for commercial or industrial purposes **2. IDEA OR PERSON BROUGHT IN** an idea, practice, or person brought in from the outside ○ *The new accounting system is an import from the private sector.* **3.** COMM **IMPORTATION** the bringing in of something from abroad or an outside source ○ *Most governments forbid the import of such goods.* **4. TRUE SIGNIFICANCE** the meaning or significance of something ○ *a foreign policy decision of great import* [15thC. From Latin *importare* "to carry or bring in," used in medieval Latin to mean "to convey a meaning, be significant," from *portare* "to carry."] —**im·port·a·bil·i·ty** /im pàwrtə bíllətee/ *n.* —**im·port·a·ble** /im páwrtəb'l/ *adj.*

im·por·tance /im páwrt'ns/ *n.* **1. SIGNIFICANCE** considerable value, relevance, or interest ○ *It is difficult to overestimate the importance of this breakthrough to medical science.* **2. HIGH RANK** high position, rank, or reputation in society

im·por·tant /im páwrt'nt/ *adj.* **1. HAVING VALUE OR SIGNIFICANCE** worthy of note or consideration, especially for its interest, value, or relevance ○ *an important scientific discovery* ○ *an important author* **2. HIGH-RANKING** with high social position or influence among people **3. POMPOUS** seeming to assume more status, significance, or value than is actually due ○ *strode into the room with an important air* [15thC. From medieval Latin *important-*, present participle stem of *importare* (see IMPORT).] —**im·por·tant·ly** *adv.*

im·por·ta·tion /ìm pawr táysh'n/ *n.* **1.** COMM **ACT OF IMPORTING** the bringing in of goods or commodities from another country **2. SOMETHING BROUGHT IN FROM ELSEWHERE** any thing, person, or service from another country, separate source, or external organization

im·port·er /im páwrtər/ *n.* a person or company that buys goods or services from abroad and then sells them in the domestic market

im·por·tu·nate /im páwrchoonət/ *adj.* (*formal*) **1. DEMANDING AND PERSISTENT** continually asking for something, especially in a forceful, insistent, or troublesome manner ○ *importunate requests for a loan* **2. URGENT OR PRESSING** requiring immediate attention and action ○ *importunate requests for medical aid* [Early 16thC. Formed from Latin *importunus* (see IMPORTUNE).] —**im·por·tu·nate·ly** *adv.* —**im·por·tu·nate·ness** *n.*

im·por·tune /ìmpər tóon, ìm páwr chən/ *vt.* (**-tuned, -tun·ing, -tunes**) (*formal*) **1. BOTHER INSISTENTLY** to ask somebody continually, repeatedly, or forcefully for something, especially in a troublesome way **2. MAKE AN IMMORAL REQUEST** to ask somebody to have sexual relations in exchange for money ■ *adj.* **IMPORTUNATE** persistent or pressing [Mid-16thC. From French *importuner* or medieval Latin *importunari*, from Latin *importunus* "inconvenient, unseasonable," from *Portunus*, god of harbors (source of English *opportune*).] —**im·por·tu·na·cy** /im páwrchənəssee, ìmpər tóon-/ *n.* —**im·por·tune·ly** /ìmpər tóonlee, im páwrchənlee/ *adv.* —**im·por·tun·er** /ìmpər tóonər, im páwrchənər/ *n.*

im·por·tu·ni·ty /ìmpər tóonətee/ (*plural* **-ties**) *n.* (*formal*) **1. WEARISOME PERSISTENCE** the fact of being troublesomely demanding or insistent **2. PERSISTENT DEMAND** a demand made repeatedly or insistently

im·pose /im pṓz/ (**-posed, -pos·ing, -pos·es**) *v.* **1.** *vt.* **LEVY OR ENFORCE** to lay down something compulsory, such as a tax or a punishment **2.** *vt.* **INSIST ON** to make people agree to something or comply with something by having superior strength or authority ○ *It broke his heart to see Western culture imposed on this dignified people.* **3.** *vti.* **INCONVENIENCE SOMEBODY** to give people extra work or difficulties by forcing your company or your personal concerns on them **4.** *vt.* PRINTING **ARRANGE PAGES** to order the pages of something such as a book or magazine for printing **5.** *vt.* **PASS OFF ON SOMEBODY** to use deceit or fraud to give something to somebody or to persuade somebody to accept something **6.** *vt.* RELIG **LAY ON HANDS** to bless somebody, e.g., in confirmation or ordination, by laying hands on the person's head [15thC. Via French *imposer* (influenced by *poser* "to put") from Latin *imponere* "to place on or into," from *ponere* "to place" (source of English *component*).] —**im·pos·a·ble** *adj.* —**im·pos·er** *n.*

im·pos·ing /im pṓzing/ *adj.* large and stately, creating an impression of grandeur [Mid-17thC. The original meaning was "insistent, dictatorial."] —**im·pos·ing·ly** *adv.* —**im·pos·ing·ness** *n.*

im·po·si·tion /ìmpə zísh'n/ *n.* **1. EXTRA TROUBLE** a request or task, especially a time-consuming one, that is unreasonably expected of somebody **2. ENFORCED DUTY** a tax, fee, or penalty that is imposed on people **3. ESTABLISHING OR ENFORCING OF SOMETHING** the official or legal process of laying down something compulsory such as a tax, fee, or penalty **4.** PRINTING **ARRANGEMENT OF PAGES** the setting up and ordering of pages for printing **5. DECEPTION** a deception or fraud (*literary*) **6.** RELIG **BLESSING** the laying of hands on somebody's head in a religious sacrament such as ordination or confirmation

im·pos·si·bil·i·ty /im pòssə bíllətee/ (*plural* **-ties**) *n.* **1. SOMETHING IMPOSSIBLE** a situation that cannot happen, or anything that cannot exist or cannot be done ○ *Living without water is a physical impossibility.* **2. FACT OF BEING IMPOSSIBLE** the likelihood that something will not happen or cannot be achieved ○ *the impossibility of finding another job close to home*

im·pos·si·ble /im póssəb'l/ *adj.* **1. NOT POSSIBLE** that cannot exist or cannot be done ○ *an impossible task* **2. TOO DIFFICULT** very difficult to deal with and apparently without a solution ○ *The situation was impossible: I couldn't be honest without offending one of them.* **3. UNENDURABLE** unbearably difficult or not possible to endure ○ *the humidity was impossible* **4. NOT BELIEVABLE** ridiculous or unreasonable, because it could not be true [14thC. Directly or via French from Latin *impossibilis*, from *possibilis* "possible" (see POSSIBLE).] —**im·pos·si·ble·ness** *n.*

im·pos·si·bly /im póssəblee/ *adv.* **1. INFURIATINGLY** to an infuriating or intolerable degree (*informal*) **2. EXTREMELY** to an extent that is almost unbelievable ○ *impossibly thin slices* **3. NOT BY ANY MEANS** in a way that could not be done or could not happen

im·post[1] /ím pòst/ *n.* **1.** FIN **CUSTOMS DUTY** a tax or other payment levied on goods brought into a country **2.** HORSERACING **HANDICAP WEIGHT** the weight a horse must carry, including that of the jockey, in a handicap race [15thC. From Italian *imposta*, feminine past participle of *imporre* "to impose" used as a noun, from Latin *imponere* (see IMPOSE).]

im·post[2] /ím pòst/ *n.* ARCHIT the top part of a pillar, column, or wall, which may be decorated or molded and on which a vault or arch rests [Mid-16thC. Via French from, ultimately, Latin *impostus*, *impositus*, the past participle of *imponere* (see IMPOSE).]

im·pos·tor /im póstər/, **im·pos·ter** *n.* somebody who pretends to be somebody else in order to deceive or cheat [Late 16thC. Via French *imposteur* from, ultimately, Latin *impositor*, from *imponere* (see IMPOSE). The underlying sense is of "putting on" a false identity.]

im·pos·tume /im pós choom/ *n.* a cyst or pus-containing abscess found in or on any part of the body (*archaic*) [14thC. From Old French *empostume*, ultimately from Greek *apostēnai* "to withdraw" (referring to the gathering or "withdrawal" of pus into an abscess).]

im·pos·ture /im póschər/ *n.* the act of pretending to be somebody else in order to trick people, or an occasion on which this is done (*formal*) [Mid-16thC. Via French from late Latin *impostura*, literally "a putting on," ultimately from *imponere* (see IMPOSE).]

im·po·tence /ímpət'ns/, **im·po·ten·cy** /ímpət'nsee/ *n.* **1.** MED **SEXUAL INABILITY** the inability of a male to perform sexual intercourse, usually because erection of the penis cannot be achieved or sustained **2. WEAKNESS** the lack of strength or power to do anything ○ *We lamented our impotence as we watched the business gradually deteriorate.*

im·po·tent /ímpət'nt/ *adj.* **1.** MED **SEXUALLY UNABLE** unable to perform sexual intercourse, usually because erection of the penis cannot be achieved or sustained **2. POWERLESS** without the strength or power to do anything effective or helpful [14thC. Via French from the Latin stem *impotent-*, from *potent-* "powerful" (see POTENT).] —**im·po·tent·ly** *adv.*

im·pound /im pównd/ (**-pound·ed, -pound·ing, -pounds**) *vt.* **1. KEEP IN A CONFINED PLACE** to lock something such as an illegally parked car in an enclosure or compound **2.** LAW **TAKE INTO LEGAL CUSTODY** to take goods or possessions into official custody **3.** LAW **WITHHOLD LEGALLY** to withhold something by legal means, especially funds that the law requires to be spent **4.** CIV ENG **HOLD A WATER SUPPLY** to save and collect water in a dam or reservoir [15thC. Literally "to put into a pound," formed from POUND[3] "enclosed place."] —**im·pound·a·ble** *adj.* —**im·pound·age** *n.* —**im·pound·er** *n.* —**im·pound·ment** *n.*

im·pov·er·ish /im póvvərish/ (**-ished, -ish·ing, -ish·es**) *vt.* **1. MAKE POOR** to cause somebody or something to be poor or poorer (*often passive*) **2. SPOIL OR REDUCE IN QUALITY** to take away some part or quality belonging to something, leaving it in a worse or weaker condition ○ *a vocabulary impoverished by technical jargon* **3.** AGRIC **MAKE LESS RICH OR FERTILE** to take away the nutrients and richness from something such as soil [15thC. From Old French *empoveriss-*, a stem of *empov(e)rier*, from *povre* "poor" (see POOR).] —**im·pov·er·ish·er** *n.* —**im·pov·er·ish·ment** *n.*

im·prac·ti·ca·ble /im práktikəb'l/ *adj.* **1. NOT POSSIBLE** that cannot be carried out effectively **2. UNUSABLE** not in a fit condition for use —**im·prac·ti·ca·bil·i·ty** /im pràktikə bíllətee/ *n.* —**im·prac·ti·ca·ble·ness** /im práktikəb'lnəss/ *n.* —**im·prac·ti·ca·bly** /-práktikəblee/ *adv.*

im·prac·ti·cal /im práktik'l/ *adj.* **1. NOT WORKABLE** that will not work effectively or be without problems when put into practice **2. UNABLE TO DO EVERYDAY THINGS** not able to perform practical tasks or deal easily with practical matters ○ *She is a brilliant academic, but completely impractical around the house.* —**im·prac·ti·cal·i·ty** /im pràkti kállətee/ *n.* —**im·prac·ti·cal·ly** /im práktikəlee/ *adv.* —**im·prac·ti·cal·ness** /-práktik'lnəss/ *n.*

im·pre·cate /ímprə kàyt/ (**-cat·ed, -cat·ing, -cates**) *vti.* to call down something bad or harmful, especially a curse, on somebody (*formal*) [Early 17thC. From Latin *imprecari*, from *precari* "to pray" (see PRAY).] —**im·pre·ca·tor** *n.* —**im·pre·ca·to·ry** /ímprəkə tàwree/ *adj.*

im·pre·ca·tion /ìm prə káysh'n/ *n.* (*formal*) **1. CURSE** an oath or curse **2. CURSING SOMEBODY** the calling down of harm on somebody **3. SWEARING** swearing or blasphemy

im·pre·cise /ìmprə síss/ *adj.* not exact or accurate —**im·pre·cise·ly** *adv.* —**im·pre·cise·ness** *n.* —**im·pre·ci·sion** /ìmprə sí<u>zh</u>'n/ *n.*

im·preg·na·ble /im prégnəb'l/ *adj.* **1. IMPOSSIBLE TO BREAK INTO** too strong to be captured or opened by force ○ *an impregnable fortress* **2. UNBEATABLE** unable to be shaken or destroyed by any outside influence ○ *impregnable faith* [15thC. From Old French *imprenable*, which was formed from *prenable* "takeable," from *prendre* "to take," from Latin *prehendere* The *-g-* spelling may have been modeled on words like DEIGN and REIGN.] —**im·preg·na·bil·i·ty** /im prègnə bíllətee/ *n.* —**im·preg·na·ble·ness** /im prégnəb'lnəss/ *n.* —**im·preg·na·bly** /-prégnəblee/ *adv.*

im·preg·nate /im prég nàyt/ *vt.* (**-nat·ed, -nat·ing, -nates**) **1. SATURATE** to incorporate a chemical into a porous material such as wood or cloth, especially by soaking it thoroughly with a liquid (*usually passive*) **2. FILL** make something express or contain a particular quality or idea throughout (*literary*) **3.** BIOL **MAKE PREGNANT** to make a female pregnant ■ *adj.* **1. SATURATED** infused or saturated with something **2.** BIOL **PREGNANT** pregnant or fertilized [Early 17thC. From late Latin *impregnat-*, the past participle stem of *impregnare*, ultimately from Latin *praegnas* "pregnant" (see PREGNANT).] —**im·preg·na·tion** /im prèg náyshn/ *n.* —**im·preg·na·tor** /im prég nàytər/ *n.*

im·pre·sa /im práyzə/ *n.* a design, usually with a motto, representing a particular person or thing, e.g. on a coat of arms (*archaic*) [Late 16thC. From Italian, literally "undertaking, device," from *imprendere* "to undertake," ultimately from Latin *prendere* "to take, grasp."]

im·pre·sa·ri·o /ìmprə saaree ṑ, -séree ṑ/ (*plural* **-os**) *n.* **1. ENTERTAINMENT MANAGER** a producer or promoter of commercial entertainment ventures, especially in musical theater **2. BUSINESS HEAD OF AN OPERA OR BALLET COMPANY** somebody in charge of an opera or ballet company who is responsible for business affairs, contracting artists, and commissioning new works **3. ENTERTAINER** a showman [Mid-18thC. From Italian, "somebody who undertakes," formed from *impresa* (see IMPRESA).]

im·pre·script·i·ble /ìmprə skríptəb'l/ *adj.* impossible to remove or violate [Late 16thC. From medieval Latin *imprescriptibilis*, from Latin *praescript-*, past participle stem of *praescribere* "to direct in writing" (see PRESCRIBE).] —**im·pre·script·i·bil·i·ty** /ìmprə skriptə bíllətee/ *n.* —**im·pre·script·i·bly** /ìmprə skríptəblee/ *adv.*

im·press[1] /im préss/ *v.* (**-pressed, -press·ing, -press·es**) **1.** *vti.* **INFLUENCE DEEPLY OR PLEASE GREATLY** to bring about a strong or lasting effect, usually favorable, on the mind or feelings of somebody (*often passive*) ○ *We were not impressed by the way we were treated.* **2.** *vt.* **MAKE CLEARLY UNDERSTOOD** to make sure that somebody has a clear and lasting understanding, memory, or mental image of something ○ *She impressed on every child that she expected them to tell the truth at all times.* **3.** *vt.* **PRESS A SHAPE INTO SOMETHING** to make a pattern, design, or mark on something by pressing or stamping **4.** *vt.* ELECTRON ENG **APPLY A VOLTAGE** to apply a voltage to an electronic circuit or device ■ *n.* **STAMP** a characteristic mark (*literary*) [14thC. From French *empresser*, from Latin *impressus*, past participle of *imprimere* "to press in," from *premere* "to press" (see PRESS).] —**im·press·er** *n.* —**im·press·i·ble** *adj.* —**im·press·i·bil·i·ty** /im prèssə bíllətee/ *n.* —**im·press·i·bly** /im préssəblee/ *adv.*

im·press[2] (-pressed, -press·ing, -press·es) *vt.* /im préss/ 1. SEIZE to seize by force for public use 2. HIST FORCE TO SERVE to compel people to serve in a navy or army, especially by arbitrary means ○ *It was a common practice to impress seamen from coastal towns.* [Late 16thC. Formed from PRESS[2] "to force into service."]

im·pres·sion /im présh'n/ *n.* 1. WHAT STAYS IN SOMEBODY'S MIND a lasting effect, opinion, or mental image of somebody or something ○ *I made a bad impression by arriving late for the interview.* 2. GENERAL IDEA a belief about or understanding of something ○ *I was under the impression that they were married.* 3. PRESSED-IN SHAPE a pattern, design, or mark made by something hard being pressed onto something softer ○ *The intruder's boots had left an impression in the mud.* 4. ARTS IMITATING OF SOMEBODY entertainment in which a performer mimics the way a well-known person speaks and behaves, usually in a humorous or exaggerated way 5. DENT MOLD TAKEN OF TEETH a mold taken of the teeth and surrounding gums on which dentures, restorations, or dental appliances are constructed 6. PRINTING COPIES OF A BOOK all the copies of a book printed at one time, or the printing of these 7. PRINTING COPY OF A BOOK a printed copy of a book — **im·pres·sion·al** *adj.* —**im·pres·sion·al·ly** *adv.*

im·pres·sion·a·ble /im présh'nəb'l/ *adj.* ready to accept or be impressed by the experiences, opinions, and personalities of other people — **im·pres·sion·a·bil·i·ty** /im prèsh'nə bíllətee/ *n.* —**im·pres·sion·a·ble·ness** /im présh'nəb'lnəss/ *n.*

im·pres·sion·ism /im présh'n ìzzəm/, **Im·pres·sion·ism** *n.* 1. PAINTING SCHOOL OF PAINTING a style of painting that concentrates on the general tone and effect produced by a subject without elaboration of details. Monet and Renoir were practitioners of impressionism. 2. MUSIC MUSIC EXPRESSING IMPRESSIONS AND FEELINGS a style of music, especially of late 19th- and early 20th-century France, characterized by the use of rich harmonies and tones rather than form to express scenes or emotions. Debussy and Ravel were practitioners of impressionism.

im·pres·sion·ist /im présh'nist/ *n.* 1. **im·pres·sion·ist, Im·pres·sion·ist** PAINTING, MUSIC PRACTITIONER OF IMPRESSIONISM an artist or composer who paints pictures or writes music in the style of impressionism, especially one active in France at the end of the 19th century 2. THEATER, TV ENTERTAINER a performer who mimics the way well-known people speak and behave, usually in a humorous and exaggerated way [Late 19thC. In the sense "practitioner of impressionism," from French *impressioniste*, originally a derisive name stemming from the title of Monet's *Impression: soleil levant* "Impression: rising sun."]

im·pres·sion·is·tic /im prèsh'n ístik/ *adj.* 1. UNDETAILED giving a broad picture or general idea rather than an exact description 2. PAINTING, MUSIC LIKE IMPRESSIONIST ART OR MUSIC concerning, involving, or in the style of impressionism or the impressionists in painting or music —**im·pres·sion·is·ti·cal·ly** *adv.*

im·pres·sive /im préssiv/ *adj.* that makes a deep and usually favorable impression on the mind or senses —**im·pres·sive·ly** *adv.* —**im·pres·sive·ness** *n.*

im·press·ment /im présmənt/ *n.* the seizing of property or people and forcing them into public use or service (*formal*) [Late 18thC. Formed from IMPRESS[2].]

im·prest /im prést/ *n.* 1. FIN ADVANCE OF MONEY an advance payment of money, especially to somebody who is to carry out some business for a government 2. FIN LOAN TO DRAW ON a loan, usually in the form of a petty cash account, that can be drawn upon as needed 3. NAVY, MIL ADVANCE PAYMENT a payment formerly made in advance to a British soldier or sailor upon enlistment [Mid-16thC. Formed from obsolete *prest* "loan," from Old French, formed in turn from *prester* "to lend," ultimately from Latin *praesto* "at hand" (source of English *presto*).]

im·pri·ma·tur /imprə maátər, imprə maá toor/ *n.* 1. APPROVAL authority to do, say, or especially print something (*formal*) 2. OFFICIAL LICENSE an authorization allowing a book or other work to be published, now usually confined to works sanctioned by the Roman Catholic Church [Mid-17thC. From Latin, literally "let it be printed."]

im·pri·mis /im prímiss/ *adv.* in the first place (*formal*) [15thC. From Latin, from *in primis*, literally "among the first things."]

im·print *n.* /ím prìnt/ 1. PRESSED-IN SHAPE a pattern, design, or mark that is made by pressing something down on or into something else 2. LASTING EFFECT an effect that remains and is recognizable for a long time ○ *The years of occupation left their imprint on all the inhabitants.* 3. SPECIAL MARK a printed or stamped sign on an object, e.g., to indicate its origin 4. PUBL PRINTED PUBLICATION DETAILS the name and address of the publisher and printer as shown at the front of a book ■ *v.* /im prínt/ (-print·ed, -print·ing, -prints) 1. *vt.* MARK BY PRESSING to put a shape or design on something, e.g., the surface of an object, using a stamp or printing device 2. *vt.* CAUSE TO REMAIN to fix an image, memory, opinion, or idea in a vivid or lasting way ○ *The scene was imprinted on her memory.* 3. *vi.* ZOOL ESTABLISH SOCIAL ATTACHMENTS to learn an attraction to members of the same species or substitutes very early in life. ◊ **imprinting** — **im·print·er** *n.*

im·print·ing /im prínting/ *n.* ZOOL a form of rapid learning very early in a social animal's development that results in strong behavioral patterns of attraction to members of its own species, especially parents. Imprinting was first described by Konrad Lorenz in 1937 when he trained young ducks and geese to follow him and regard him as their mother. [15thC. Originally in the sense "the printing of books"; used by Lorenz to translate his term, German *Prägung*.]

im·pris·on /im prízz'n/ (-oned, -on·ing, -ons) *vt.* to lock somebody up in prison [13thC. From Old French *emprisoner*, from *prison* (see PRISON).] —**im·pris·on·er** *n.* — **im·pris·on·ment** *n.*

im·prob·a·ble /im próbbəb'l/ *adj.* not likely to happen or to be true —**im·prob·a·bil·i·ty** /im pròbbə bíllətee/ *n.* —**im·prob·a·ble·ness** /im próbbəb'lnəss/ *n.* — **im·prob·a·bly** /-próbbəblee/ *adv.*

im·pro·bi·ty /im próbətee/ *n.* lack of moral scruples or honesty (*formal*)

im·promp·tu /im prómp toō/ *adj.* DONE OR SAID SPONTANEOUSLY not prepared or planned in advance ○ *an impromptu speech* ■ *adv.* WITHOUT PRIOR THOUGHT OR PREPARATION in an unrehearsed way ■ *n.* 1. MUSIC SHORT SOLO PIECE a short instrumental piece whose style gives an impression of improvisation. Such pieces were a highly developed and popular form in the 19th century. 2. SOMETHING SPONTANEOUS OR UNREHEARSED something done or said without planning [Mid-17thC. Via French from Latin *in promptu* "at hand, in readiness," from *promptus* (see PROMPT).]

im·prop·er /im próppər/ *adj.* 1. UNSUITABLE not appropriate to the context, the nature of the case, or the purpose in view (*formal*) 2. RUDE not in accordance with accepted good manners or decorum 3. LAW IRREGULAR not in accordance with the accepted standards of something such as a profession ○ *the improper handling of funds* —**im·prop·er·ly** *adv.* — **im·prop·er·ness** *n.*

im·prop·er frac·tion *n.* a fraction in which the numerator is equal to or greater than the denominator, such as 6/4

im·pro·pri·ate /im própree àyt/ *vt.* (-at·ed, -at·ing, -ates) PUT UNDER LAY CONTROL to put ecclesiastical property or tithes in lay hands ■ *adj.* UNDER LAY CONTROL in the hands of laypeople (*refers to ecclesiastical property*) [Early 16thC. From the past participle of Anglo-Latin *impropriare* "to appropriate," ultimately from Latin *proprius* "own" (see PROPER).] —**im·pro·pri·a·tion** /im pròpree áysh'n/ *n.* —**im·pro·pri·a·tor** /im própree àytər/ *n.*

im·pro·pri·e·ty /imprə prí ətee/ (*plural* -ties) *n.* conduct not considered correct, moral, or appropriate in a given context

im·prove /im proōv/ (-proved, -prov·ing, -proves) *v.* 1. *vti.* MAKE OR BECOME BETTER to make something better in quality or condition, or to become better ○ *His health is improving daily.* 2. *vt.* INCREASE THE VALUE OF to make property, such as land or buildings, more valuable 3. *vt.* USE WELL to make good use of or employ something to advantage [Early 16thC. From Anglo-Norman *emprower* "to make a profit" (the original sense in English), from Old French *prou* "profit," from late Latin *prode* "profitable" (see PROUD).] —**im·prov·a·bil·i·ty** /im proōvə bíllətee/ *n.* —**im·prov·a·ble** /im proōvəb'l/ *adj.* — **im·prov·a·ble·ness** /-proōvəb'lnəss/ *n.* —**im·prov·a·bly** /-proōvəblee/ *adv.* —**im·prov·er** /-proōvər/ *n.*

improve on, im·prove up·on *vt.* to do better or be better than a particular thing, especially a previous standard or record ○ *improved on her previous time by four seconds*

im·prove·ment /im proōvmənt/ *n.* 1. GETTING OR MAKING BETTER the process of making something better or of becoming better ○ *an improvement on her past performance* 2. CHANGE OR ADDITION a change or addition that makes something better 3. CHANGE THAT ADDS VALUE a change or addition, especially to real estate, that increases value ○ *home improvements* 4. ADVANCE IN VALUE an increase in value, especially in the value of land or property

im·prov·i·dent /im próvvid'nt/ *adj.* (*formal*) 1. UNCONCERNED ABOUT FUTURE NEEDS failing to put money aside or give any thought to the future 2. WITHOUT FORESIGHT not sensible, cautious, or wise [15thC. Literally "not foreseeing," ultimately from the late Latin stem *provident-* "foreseeing" (see PROVIDENT).] —**im·prov·i·dence** *n.* — **im·prov·i·dent·ly** *adv.*

im·prov·i·sa·tion /im pròvvi záysh'n, ìmprəvi-/ *n.* 1. IMPROVISED PIECE OR PERFORMANCE something performed or done without any preparation or set text to follow 2. CREATING AND PERFORMING SIMULTANEOUSLY the skill or creative process of creating and performing something without any preparation or set text to follow —**im·prov·i·sa·tion·al** *adj.* —**im·prov·i·sa·tion·al·ly** *adv.*

im·pro·vise /ímprə vīz/ (-vised, -vis·ing, -vis·es) *vti.* 1. ARTS MAKE SOMETHING UP ON THE SPOT to act or compose something, especially a sketch, play, song, or piece of music, without any preparation or set text to follow 2. SUBSTITUTE to make a substitute for something out of the materials that happen to be available at the time ○ *If you haven't got a hammer, we'll have to improvise.* [Early 19thC. Directly or via French from Italian *improvvisare*, ultimately from Latin *improvisus* "unforeseen," from *providere* "to foresee" (see PROVIDE).] —**im·prov·i·sa·to·ri·al** /im pròvvizə táwree əl/ *adj.* —**im·prov·i·sa·to·ry** /im próvvizə tàwree, ìmprə vízə-/ *adj.* —**im·pro·vis·er** /ímprə vīzər/ *n.*

im·pru·dence /im proōd'ns/ *n.* a lack of wisdom, judgement, or discretion

im·pru·dent /im proōd'nt/ *adj.* showing no care, forethought, or judgement (*formal*) —**im·pru·dent·ly** *adv.*

im·pu·dence /ímpyəd'ns/, **im·pu·den·cy** /ímpyəd'nsee/ *n.* 1. DELIBERATE RUDENESS behavior that shows a lack of respect and shameless boldness 2. PIECE OF IMPUDENCE a rude or disrespectful remark or act

im·pu·dent /ímpyəd'nt/ *adj.* showing a lack of respect and excessive boldness [14thC. From the Latin stem *impudent-*, from *pudens* "ashamed, modest," present participle of *pudere* "to feel or make ashamed" (source of English *pudendum*).] —**im·pu·dent·ly** *adv.* — **im·pu·dent·ness** *n.*

im·pugn /im pyoōn/ (-pugned, -pugn·ing, -pugns) *vt.* to suggest that somebody or something cannot be trusted or respected (*formal*) ○ *Far be it from me to impugn his motives, but...* [14thC. From Latin *impugnare* "to fight against" (the original sense in English), from *pugnare* "to fight" (see PUGNACIOUS).] —**im·pugn·a·ble** *adj.* —**im·pugn·er** *n.*

im·pulse /ím pùls/ *n.* 1. SUDDEN URGE a sudden desire, urge, or inclination (*often used before a noun*) ○ *an impulsive buy* 2. INSTINCTIVE DRIVE an instinctive drive or natural tendency 3. MOTIVE a motivation or reason for a specific activity 4. FORCE DRIVING SOMETHING FORWARD a driving force producing a forward motion 5. FORWARD MOTION the motion produced by a driving force 6. PHYS FORCE ACTING OVER TIME a measure of momentum arrived at by multiplying the average force acting on a body by the length of time it acts 7. PHYSIOL NERVE OR MUSCLE SIGNAL a progressive wave of biochemically generated energy that travels along a nerve fiber or muscle and stimulates or inhibits activity [Mid-17thC. From Latin *impulsus*, past participle of *impellere* (see IMPEL).]

im·pul·sion /im púlshən/ *n.* 1. ACT OR INSTANCE OF URGING the act of urging or forcing somebody into action, or an instance of this 2. MOVEMENT OR THRUSTING FORCE a movement that comes from being pushed or thrust, or the force that creates this movement 3. SUDDEN DESIRE a sudden desire, inclination, or urge

im·pul·sive /im púlsiv/ *adj.* 1. INCLINED TO ACT ON SUDDEN URGES having a tendency to act on sudden urges or desires 2. SPONTANEOUS based on or motivated by impulse 3. PHYS COMING IN BURSTS acting or coming in short bursts 4. ACOUSTICS SHORT AND PERCUSSIVE used to describe a sound that is of short duration and composed of a wide range of frequencies

—**im·pul·sive·ly** *adv.* —**im·pul·sive·ness** *n.* —**im·pul·siv·i·ty** /im pul sívvətee/ *n.*

im·pu·ni·ty /im pyóonətee/ *n.* exemption from punishment, harm, or recrimination [Mid-16thC. From Latin *impunitas*, from *impunis* "without punishment," from *poena* "punishment."]

im·pure /im pyoor/ *adj.* **1. CONTAMINATED** unclean because containing something harmful **2. ADULTERATED** combined with something of inferior quality **3. SINFUL** tainted with sin **4. HAVING MIXED STYLES** combining a mixture of styles, or derived from more than one source **5.** COLORS **MIXED WITH OTHER COLORS** being mixed with other colors or with black or white [15thC. From Latin *impurus*, from *purus* "pure" (see PURE).] —**im·pure·ly** *adv.* —**im·pure·ness** *n.*

im·pu·ri·ty /im pyóorətee/ (*plural* **-ties**) *n.* **1. LACK OF PURITY** the state or quality of being impure **2. CONTAMINANT** a substance that adulterates or contaminates something ○ *drinking water that was found to contain impurities* **3.** ELECTRON ENG **SOMETHING ADDED TO A SEMICONDUCTOR** a small amount of a substance added to a pure semiconductor to control its electrical conductivity

im·pu·ta·tion /impyə táysh'n/ *n.* **1. ACT OF IMPUTING** the act of accusing somebody of something, or of attributing a result to a particular cause **2. ACCUSATION** an accusation of wrongdoing or an attribution of blame

im·pute /im pyóot/ (**-put·ed, -put·ing, -putes**) *vt.* **1. ATTRIBUTE A BAD ACTION** to attribute a usually undesirable action or event to somebody ○ *"He had married her with that bad past life hidden behind him, and she had no faith left to protest his innocence of the worst that was imputed to him."* (George Eliot, *Middlemarch*; 1872) **2. ATTRIBUTE A QUALITY** to attribute a quality to a person, cause, or source ○ *"it was charity to impute some of her unbecoming indifference to the languor of ill-health"* (Jane Austen, *Emma*; 1816) **3.** LAW **CHARGE SOMEBODY RESPONSIBLE FOR ANOTHER'S CRIME** to bring legal charges against somebody because a person that he or she is responsible for has committed an offense **4.** RELIG **EXTEND A QUALITY TO SOMEBODY ELSE** to regard a quality such as righteousness that applies to somebody as also applying to another person associated with him or her [14thC. Via French *imputer* from Latin *imputare* "to bring into the reckoning," from *putare* "to reckon" (source of English *putative*).] —**im·put·a·ble** *adj.* —**im·pu·ta·tive** *adj.* —**im·put·er** *n.*

impv. *abbr.* GRAM imperative

in /in/ CORE MEANING: a grammatical word indicating that something or somebody is within or inside something ○ (prep) *The dinner's in the oven.* ○ (adv) *I stopped by your house, but you weren't in.*

1. *prep.* **INDICATES A PLACE** indicates that something happens or is situated somewhere ○ *He spent a whole year in Russia.* **2.** *prep.* **INDICATES A STATE** indicates a state or condition that something or somebody is experiencing ○ *The banking industry is in a state of flux.* **3.** *prep.* **INDICATES AFTER** after a period of time that will pass before something happens ○ *She should be well enough to leave in a week or two.* **4.** *prep.* **DURING** indicates that something happens during a period of time ○ *He crossed the desert in 39 days.* **5.** *prep.* **INDICATES HOW SOMETHING IS EXPRESSED** indicates the means of communication used to express something ○ *I managed to write the whole speech in French.* **6.** *prep.* **INDICATES SUBJECT AREA** indicates a subject or field of activity ○ *She graduated with a degree in biology.* **7.** *prep.* **AS A CONSEQUENCE OF** while doing something or as a consequence of something ○ *In reaching for a glass he knocked over the ashtray.* **8.** *prep.* **COVERED BY** indicates that something is wrapped or covered by something ○ *The floor was covered in balloons and toys.* **9.** *prep.* **INDICATES HOW SOMEBODY IS DRESSED** indicates that somebody is dressed in a particular way ○ *She was dressed in a smart suit.* **10.** *prep.* ZOOL **PREGNANT WITH** pregnant with ○ *The cows were in calf.* **11.** *adj.* **FASHIONABLE** fashionable or popular ○ *Inline skates are the in thing.* **12.** *adj.* **INTO OFFICE** indicates that a party or group has achieved or will achieve power or authority ○ *Everyone was very optimistic when the new party got in.* [Old English] ◇ **have it in for, have got it in for** to dislike somebody and want to do that person harm ○ *Ever since I got the job the boss has had it in for me.* ◇ **in between** between ○ *Normal light consists of a wave that vibrates up and down, side to side, and every direction in between.* ◇ **in for** indicates that somebody will experience something, e.g. a surprise or a shock ○ *Little did she know what she was in for.* ◇ **in on** having knowledge about or involvement in something ○ *The whole class was in on the plans for the surprise party.* ◇ **in that** introduces an explanation of a statement ○ *She's unusual for a commuter in that she's never late for work.* ◇ **in with** associated with or friendly with ○ *a reporter perhaps too much in with the politicians to be objective* ○ *He's been getting in with a bad crowd.* ◇ **the ins and outs** all the detailed facts and points about something ○ *I don't know all the ins and outs of the matter, but she's leaving.*

In *symbol.* CHEM ELEM indium

IN *abbr.* MAIL Indiana

in. *abbr.* **in.**, **in** MEASURE inches

-in *suffix.* **1.** a neutral chemical compound ○ *fibroin* ○ *digitalin* ○ *thrombin* **2.** antibiotic ○ *streptothricin* **3.** pharmaceutical ○ *warfarin* **4.** toxic substance ○ *botulin* **5.** antigen ○ *bacterin* **6.** = **-ine** ○ *hyalin* [From IN, Latin *in* "in, into, on, during, against," or *in-* "not"]

in·a·bil·i·ty /innə bíllətee/ *n.* a lack of the ability, means, or power to do something ○ *his inability to face the truth*

in ab·sen·tia *adv.* in the absence of the person or persons concerned (*formal*) [From Latin, literally "in absence"]

in·ac·ces·si·ble /innək séssib'l/ *adj.* **1. DIFFICULT TO GET TO** difficult or impossible to gain access to or reach **2. DIFFICULT TO ACHIEVE** difficult or impossible to afford or attain **3. HARD TO UNDERSTAND** difficult or impossible to understand [15thC. Directly or via French from late Latin *inaccessibilis*, from *accessibilis* "accessible."] —**in·ac·ces·si·bil·i·ty** /innək sessi bíllətee/ *n.* —**in·ac·ces·si·bly** /-séssiblee/ *adv.*

in·ac·cu·ra·cy /in ákyərəssee/ (*plural* **-cies**) *n.* **1. LACK OF ACCURACY** lack of accuracy or correctness **2. MISTAKE** an error or mistake

WORD KEY: SYNONYMS

See Synonyms at ***mistake***.

in·ac·cu·rate /in ákyərət/ *adj.* not accurate or correct —**in·ac·cu·rate·ly** *adv.*

in·ac·tion /in ákshən/ *n.* **1. FAILURE TO ACT** failure to take action when action is necessary ○ *"But in a nation that demands action, Congress has become the master of inaction."* (National Public Telecomputing Network, *Bush speeches in campaign '92*) **2. ABSENCE OF ACTIVITY** lack of activity, especially laziness or idleness

in·ac·ti·vate /in ákti vàyt/ (**-vat·ed, -vat·ing, -vates**) *vt.* to make something inactive or unable to function —**in·ac·ti·va·tion** /in akti váysh'n/ *n.*

in·ac·tive /in áktiv/ *adj.* **1. NOT TAKING ACTION** taking no action or not taking part in action that others are involved in **2. NOT BEING USED OR OPERATED** not in use, or not functioning or operating **3. LAZY OR SEDENTARY** not involving or taking part in physical activity **4.** GEOG **DORMANT** used to describe a volcano that is not erupting but not extinct **5.** MIL **NOT IN ACTIVE SERVICE** not taking part in, or not being used for, active military service **6.** CHEM **INERT** having little or no chemical reactivity **7.** CHEM **HAVING LOW RADIOACTIVITY** having low or zero radioactivity **8.** BIOL **BIOLOGICALLY INERT** having little if any discernible effect on living things as a result of the loss of some property such as the ability to infect or create antigens **9.** MED **NOT DEVELOPING OR GIVING SYMPTOMS** used to describe a disease that is present in the body but not developing or not producing any symptoms —**in·ac·tive·ly** *adv.* —**in·ac·tiv·i·ty** /in ak tívvətee/ *n.*

in·ad·e·qua·cy /in áddəkwəssee/ (*plural* **-cies**) *n.* **1. STATE OF NOT BEING ADEQUATE** the failure to be adequate, e.g., to reach a required or expected standard **2. FAULT** a flaw or weakness that reveals inadequacy

in·ad·e·quate /in áddəkwət/ *adj.* failing to reach an expected or required level or standard ○ *inadequate supplies of food* —**in·ad·e·quate·ly** *adv.*

in·ad·mis·si·ble /in ad míssəb'l/ *adj.* not admissible or allowable, especially in a court of law —**in·ad·mis·si·bil·i·ty** /innədmissə bíllətee/ *n.* —**in·ad·mis·si·bly** /innəd míssəblee/ *adv.*

in·ad·ver·tence /innəd vúrt'ns/, **in·ad·ver·ten·cy** (*plural* **-cies**) *n.* **1. CARELESSNESS** carelessness or lack of attention **2. OVERSIGHT** an oversight or result of carelessness

in·ad·ver·tent /innəd vúrt'nt/ *adj.* **1. RESULTING FROM CARELESSNESS** done unintentionally or without thinking **2. CARELESS** failing to pay enough attention or take enough care [Mid-17thC. Formed from Latin *advertent-*, present participle stem of *advertere* "to turn the mind to" (see ADVERT).]

in·ad·ver·tent·ly /innəd vúrt'ntlee/ *adv.* without intending to or without realizing

in·ad·vis·a·ble /innəd vízəb'l/ *adj.* not to be advised or recommended —**in·ad·vis·a·bil·i·ty** /innəd vīzə bíllətee/ *n.* —**in·ad·vis·a·bly** *adv.*

in ae·ter·num /in ee t-rnəm/ *adv.* eternally or forever (*formal*) [From Latin, literally "in eternal"]

in·al·ien·a·ble /in áylee ənəb'l/ *adj.* not able to be transferred or taken away, e.g., because of being protected by law (*formal*) —**in·al·ien·a·bil·i·ty** /in aylee ənə bíllətee/ *n.* —**in·al·ien·a·bly** /in áylee ənəblee/ *adv.*

in·al·ter·a·ble /in áwltərəb'l/ *adj.* not able to be changed —**in·al·ter·a·bil·i·ty** /in àwltərə bíllətee/ *n.* —**in·al·ter·a·bly** /in áwltərəblee/ *adv.*

in·am·o·ra·ta /i nàmmə raátə/ (*plural* **-tas**) *n.* a woman whom somebody loves or with whom somebody has a romantic relationship (*literary*) [Late 16thC. From Italian, feminine of *inamorato* (see INAMORATO).]

in·am·o·ra·to /i nàmmə raá tō/ (*plural* **-tos**) *n.* a man whom somebody loves or with whom somebody has a romantic relationship (*literary*) [Late 16thC. From Italian, past participle of *inamorare* "to fall in love," from *amore* "love," from Latin *amor* (source of English *amorous*).]

in·ane /i náyn/ *adj.* **1. SILLY OR UNINTELLIGENT** having little sense or importance **2. INSUBSTANTIAL** empty, insubstantial, or void ■ *n.* **EMPTINESS** great emptiness, especially the perceived emptiness of outer space (*archaic*) [Mid-16thC. From Latin *inanis* "empty, lacking sense."] —**in·ane·ly** *adv.* —**in·ane·ness** *n.*

in·an·i·mate /in ánnimət/ *adj.* **1. NOT LIVING** not alive **2. NOT LIVELY** not active, energetic, or lively ○ *"She had relapsed once more into the vacant inanimate creature who had opened the gate to us."* (Wilkie Collins, *The Law and the Lady*; 1875) **3. RELATING TO NOUNS FOR NONLIVING THINGS** belonging to the category of nouns that refer to things and concepts considered to be without life [15thC. From late Latin *inanimatus* "lifeless," from Latin *animatus*, past participle of *animare* "to animate" (see ANIMATE).] —**in·an·i·mate·ly** *adv.* —**in·an·i·mate·ness** *n.*

in·a·ni·tion /innə nísh'n/ *n.* **1. EXHAUSTION DUE TO STARVATION** exhaustion caused by lack of food or water or as a result of disease **2. LETHARGY** lethargy or lack of vitality (*literary*) **3. EMPTINESS** emptiness such as the absence of moral standards or intellectual substance (*formal*) [14thC. From the late Latin stem *inanition-*, from, ultimately, Latin *inanis* (see INANE).]

in·an·i·ty /i nánnətee/ (*plural* **-ties**) *n.* **1. MEANINGLESS QUALITY** meaninglessness or senselessness that suggests a lack of understanding or intelligence **2. SILLINESS** silliness or foolishness **3. SOMETHING INANE** something such as a silly remark that demonstrates or suggests inanity **4. EMPTY QUALITY** emptiness such as the imagined void of outer space (*archaic*)

in·ap·pe·tence /in áppət'ns/, **in·ap·pe·ten·cy** /in áppət'nsee/ *n.* lack of appetite (*formal*) —**in·ap·pe·tent** *adj.*

in·ap·pli·ca·ble /in áppli kəb'l, innə plíkəb'l/ *adj.* not applicable, suitable, or relevant —**in·ap·pli·ca·bil·i·ty** /innəplikə bíllətee, in àpplikə-/ *n.* —**in·ap·pli·ca·bly** /in ápplikəblee/ *adv.*

in·ap·po·site /in áppəzit/ *adj.* unsuitable or out of place (*formal*) —**in·ap·po·site·ly** *adv.* —**in·ap·po·site·ness** *n.*

in·ap·pre·cia·ble /innə préeshəb'l/ *adj.* too small to be noticed or significant —**in·ap·pre·cia·bly** *adv.*

in·ap·pre·cia·tive /innə préeshətiv/ *adj.* feeling or showing no appreciation —**in·ap·pre·cia·tive·ly** *adv.* —**in·ap·pre·cia·tive·ness** *n.*

in·ap·proach·a·ble /innə próchəb'l/ *adj.* impossible to approach —**in·ap·proach·a·bil·i·ty** /innə prōchə bíllətee/ *n.* —**in·ap·proach·a·bly** /innə próchəblee/ *adv.*

in·ap·pro·pri·ate /innə própree ət/ *adj.* not fitting, timely, or suitable —**in·ap·pro·pri·ate·ly** *adv.* —**in·ap·pro·pri·ate·ness** *n.*

in·apt /in ápt/ *adj.* **1. NOT SUITABLE** not suitable or appropriate **2. UNSKILLED** lacking aptitude, capability, or skill —**in·ap·ti·tude** /in ápti tood/ *n.* —**in·apt·ly** *adv.* —**in·apt·ness** *n.*

in·arch /in náarch/ (**-arched, -arch·ing, -arch·es**) *vt.* to graft part of one plant onto another without separating it from its parent [Early 17thC. Coined from IN- + ARCH, because the graft forms an arch between its parent and the new stock.]

in·ar·gu·a·ble /in áargyoo əb'l/ *adj.* impossible to deny or take an opposing view about —**in·ar·gu·a·bly** *adv.*

in·ar·tic·u·late /in aar tíkyələt/ *adj.* **1.** EXPRESSING ONESELF POORLY not good at choosing the right words or speaking fluently **2.** NOT UNDERSTANDABLE not understandable as speech or language **3.** NOT EFFECTIVELY EXPRESSED not clearly or effectively expressed **4.** NOT SPOKEN ABOUT not expressed, or not able to be expressed in words **5.** UNABLE TO SPEAK lacking the power to speak, especially because of feeling strong emotion **6.** ZOOL NOT JOINTED used to describe certain body parts that have no joints or segments, e.g., the bones of the skull **7.** MARINE BIOL HAVING A SHELL WITHOUT A HINGE used to describe a class of brachiopods that have shells without a hinge and are held together only by muscles and the body wall [Early 17thC. Originally in the sense "without joints."] —**in·ar·tic·u·late·ly** *adv.* —**in·ar·tic·u·late·ness** *n.* —**in·ar·tic·u·la·cy** *n.*

in·ar·tis·tic /in aar tístik/ *adj.* **1.** LACKING ARTISTIC SKILL possessing or demonstrating little or no artistic talent **2.** NOT CONFORMING TO THE RULES OF ART not in accordance with the principles of art **3.** NOT INTERESTED IN THE ARTS having no appreciation of or sensitivity to the arts —**in·ar·tis·ti·cal·ly** *adv.*

in·as·much as /innəz múch əz/ *conj.* **1.** BECAUSE used to introduce an explanation or reason ○ *"This was an idle and unpractical question, inasmuch as the answer was not forthcoming"* (Henry James, *Confidence*) **2.** INSOFAR AS used to introduce a comment that limits the extent of something [*Inasmuch* from IN + AS + MUCH, modeled on French *en tant* "in so much"]

in·at·ten·tion /innə ténshən/ *n.* failure to take proper care or give enough attention to something

in·at·ten·tive /innə téntiv/ *adj.* not paying attention or taking enough care —**in·at·ten·tive·ly** *adv.* —**in·at·ten·tive·ness** *n.*

in·au·di·ble /in áwdib'l/ *adj.* not loud enough to be heard —**in·au·di·bil·i·ty** /in áwdi bíllətee/ *n.* —**in·au·di·bly** /in áwdiblee/ *adv.*

in·au·gu·ral /i nóggyərəl/ *adj.* **1.** RELATING TO AN INAUGURATION relating to or marking the official beginning of something **2.** FIRST OF SEVERAL being the first of a series, such as the first issue of a magazine ■ *n.* INAUGURATION OR SPEECH AT AN INAUGURATION an inauguration, or a speech given at such a ceremony [Late 17thC. From French, formed from *inaugurer* "to inaugurate," from Latin *inaugurare* (see INAUGURATE).]

in·au·gu·rate /i nóggyə ràyt/ (**-rat·ed, -rat·ing, -rates**) *vt.* **1.** POL SWEAR FORMALLY INTO OFFICE to place somebody in office with a formal ceremony **2.** OPEN CEREMONIALLY to open or mark the beginning of something such as a new building with a formal ceremony or dedication **3.** PUT INTO OPERATION to initiate something or put it into operation, especially in a formal or official manner [Late 16thC. From Latin *inaugurare* "to foretell the future from birds' flight," later "to install in office after observing the omens," from *augurari* (see AUGUR).] —**in·au·gu·ra·tor** *n.* —**in·au·gu·ra·to·ry** *adj.*

in·au·gu·ra·tion /i nòggyə ráysh'n/ *n.* **1.** POL INDUCTION INTO OFFICE the formal placing of somebody in an official position, especially the President of the United States, or a ceremony held for this purpose **2.** CEREMONIAL OPENING OF SOMETHING a formal ceremony to open or mark the beginning of something such as a new building **3.** PUTTING SOMETHING INTO OPERATION the act of bringing something into service or putting it into operation, or an occasion on which this is done

In·au·gu·ra·tion Day *n.* the day in January following a presidential election, on which the inauguration of a new President of the United States takes place

in·aus·pi·cious /in aw spíshəss/ *adj.* suggesting that the future is not very promising or that success is unlikely —**in·aus·pi·cious·ly** *adv.* —**in·aus·pi·cious·ness** *n.*

in·au·then·tic /in aw théntik/ *adj.* not authentic or genuine —**in·au·then·tic·i·ty** /in awthən tíssətee/ *n.*

inbd. *abbr.* TRANSP inboard

in·be·tween *adj., adv.* INTERMEDIATE falling between others ○ *one of his in-between moods when you don't know what he'll say* ■ *n.* SOMEBODY OR SOMETHING INTERMEDIATE somebody or something that falls between others ○ *the oldest, the youngest, and the in-between*

in·board /ín bàwrd/ *adj.* **1.** LOCATED INSIDE A BOAT'S HULL located inside the hull of a boat, not fitted to the outside **2.** HAVING AN INBOARD ENGINE having an inboard engine ■ *n.* BOAT WITH AN INBOARD MOTOR a boat that has an inboard motor ■ *adv.* AWAY FROM THE SIDES more toward the center of an aircraft or boat than toward the sides or edges

in·born /ín bàwrn/ *adj.* inherited from parents or possessed from birth [Old English. Originally in the sense "native, indigenous"; the current sense dates from the early 16thC.]

in·bound[1] /ín bòwnd/ *adj.* arriving, incoming, or heading toward an airport, port, or station [Late 19thC. From IN + BOUND.]

in·bound[2] (**-bound·ed, -bound·ing, -bounds**) *vti.* in basketball, to put the ball back into play by passing it from out of bounds to a player on the court [Late 20thC. Back-formation from INBOUNDS.]

in·bounds /ín bòwndz/ *adj.* **1.** SPORTS ON THE FIELD OF PLAY within the boundaries of the playing area on a sports field **2.** BASKETBALL RETURNING A BASKETBALL TO PLAY involving returning the basketball into play ○ *on the ensuing inbounds play*

in·bounds line *n.* either of the two broken lines that run the length of a football field

in·breathe /in brée*th*/ (**-breathed, -breath·ing, -breathes**) *vt.* to take something into the airways by breathing in [14thC. Modeled on Latin *inspirare* "to breathe into" (source of English *inspire*).]

in·bred /ín brèd/ *adj.* **1.** INNATE existing naturally, through being possessed from birth or inherited from parents **2.** GENETICS PRODUCED BY INBREEDING produced by the mating of closely related individuals of a species ■ *n.* GENETICS FORM RESULTING FROM INBREEDING a person or an animal whose health and intelligence are affected because his, her, or its ancestors were too closely related to each other

in·breed /ín brèed/ (**-bred, -bred** /ín brèd/, **-breed·ing, -breeds**) *v.* **1.** *vti.* GENETICS MATE CLOSELY RELATED INDIVIDUALS to mate closely related individuals of a species with each other, especially over many generations **2.** *vt.* CREATE OR PRODUCE to cause something to develop in somebody —**in·breed·er** *n.*

in·breed·ing /ín brèeding/ *n.* the mating of closely related individuals of a species, especially over many generations. It may be done deliberately to enhance desired traits in livestock or pets but increases the risk of inherited defects.

in·built *adj.* innate or built-in

inc. *abbr.* **1.** included **2.** including **3.** inclusive **4.** income **5.** incomplete **6. inc., Inc.** BUSINESS incorporated **7.** increase

In·ca /íngkə/ (*plural* **-ca** *or* **-cas**) *n.* a member of a Native South American people whose huge empire, based in Peru and covering the entire Andean region, flourished from the 12th century A.D. until the mid-16th century. The Incas were sophisticated engineers, architects, and artists who had a highly complex social structure. The descendants of the Incas form roughly 50% of today's population of Peru. [Late 16thC. From Quechua, literally "royal person."] —**In·ca** *adj.* —**In·ca·ic** /in káy ik/ *adj.* —**In·can** /íngkən/ *adj.*

in·cal·cu·la·ble /in kálkyələb'l/ *adj.* **1.** TOO GREAT TO MEASURE too great or numerous to be measured **2.** IMPOSSIBLE TO FORESEE too uncertain to assess or plan for in advance —**in·cal·cu·la·bil·i·ty** /in kàlkyələ bíllətee/ *n.* —**in·cal·cu·la·bly** /in kálkyələblee/ *adv.*

in·ca·les·cent /inkə léss'nt/ *adj.* becoming warmer or hotter (*technical*) [Mid-17thC. From Latin *incalescent-*, the present participle stem of *incalescere* "to get hotter," ultimately from *calere* "to be hot" (source of English *chafe*).] —**in·ca·les·cence** *n.*

in cam·er·a *adv., adj.* **1.** IN PRIVATE in private or in secret **2.** IN A COURT CLOSED TO THE PUBLIC in a court from which the public is barred **3.** IN A JUDGE'S CHAMBERS in a judge's private chambers rather than in open court [From late Latin, literally "in the chamber"]

in·can·desce /inkən déss/ (**-desced, -desc·ing, -desc·es**) *vti.* to give off light as a result of being heated to a high temperature, or to cause something to give off light in this way [Late 19thC. Back-formation from INCANDESCENT.]

in·can·des·cence /inkən déss'ns/ *n.* **1.** EMISSION OF LIGHT BY A HOT OBJECT the emission of light by an object as a result of its being heated to a high temperature **2.** LIGHT FROM A HOT OBJECT the light produced by an object heated to a high temperature **3.** EMOTIONAL INTENSITY intensity of emotion such as anger or romantic passion

in·can·des·cent /inkən déss'nt/ *adj.* **1.** GLOWING WITH HEAT emitting light as a consequence of being heated to a high temperature **2.** GLOWING BRIGHTLY shining or glowing brightly **3.** SHOWING INTENSE EMOTION feeling or displaying intense emotion such as anger or romantic passion [Late 18thC. Directly or via French from Latin *incandescere* "to glow," from *candescere* "to become white," from *candidus* (see CANDID).] —**in·can·des·cent·ly** *adv.*

in·can·des·cent lamp *n.* an electric lamp that produces light from an electrically heated filament

in·can·ta·tion /in kan táysh'n/ *n.* **1.** USE OF SUPPOSEDLY MAGIC WORDS the ritual chanting or use of supposedly magic words **2.** SET OF SUPPOSEDLY MAGIC WORDS a set of words spoken or chanted as a supposedly magic spell [14thC. Via French from, ultimately, Latin *incantare* "to chant," from *cantare* "to sing."] —**in·can·ta·tion·al** *adj.*

in·ca·pa·ble /in káypəb'l/ *adj.* **1.** LACKING NECESSARY ABILITY lacking the ability, character, or strength required to do something **2.** NOT GOOD ENOUGH unable to function or perform adequately **3.** IMPOSSIBLE too extreme for something to be possible ○ *damage incapable of being repaired* **4.** LEGALLY INELIGIBLE legally disqualified or ineligible [Late 16thC. Directly or via French from late Latin *incapabilis*, from *capabilis* "capable" (see CAPABLE).] —**in·ca·pa·bil·i·ty** /in kàypə bíllətee/ *n.* —**in·ca·pa·ble·ness** *n.* —**in·ca·pa·bly** /-blee/ *adv.*

in·ca·pac·i·tant /inkə pássit'nt/ *n.* a substance such as tear gas that can temporarily incapacitate somebody, used especially in riot control and biological warfare

in·ca·pac·i·tate /inkə pássi tàyt/ (**-tat·ed, -tat·ing, -tates**) *vt.* **1.** DEPRIVE OF EFFECTIVENESS to deprive somebody or something of power, force, or effectiveness **2.** LAW OFFICIALLY RULE SOMEBODY OUT to disqualify somebody or make somebody legally ineligible —**in·ca·pac·i·ta·tion** /inkə pàssi táysh'n/ *n.*

in·ca·pac·i·ty /inkə pássətee/ (*plural* **-ties**) *n.* **1.** INABILITY OR INEFFECTIVENESS lack of ability, force, or effectiveness **2.** PHYSICAL OR MENTAL CHALLENGE a physical or mental challenge **3.** LEGAL DISQUALIFICATION a legal or official disqualification [Early 17thC. Directly or via French *incapacité* from late Latin *incapacitas*, from Latin *capacitas* "capacity" (see CAPACITY).]

in·cap·su·late *vti.* = **encapsulate**

in·car·cer·ate /in káarsə ràyt/ (**-at·ed, -at·ing, -ates**) *vt.* (*formal*) **1.** IMPRISON to put somebody in prison **2.** CONFINE to place somebody in a place or situation of confinement [Early 16thC. From medieval Latin *incarcerat-*, past participle stem of *incarcerare*, from *carcer* "prison."] —**in·car·cer·a·tion** /in kàarsə ráysh'n/ *n.* —**in·car·cer·a·tor** /in káarsə ràytər/ *n.*

in·car·di·nate /in káard'n àyt/ (**-nat·ed, -nat·ing, -nates**) *vt.* **1.** MOVE A PRIEST TO A NEW DISTRICT to transfer a Roman Catholic priest to a new district under the authority of a different bishop **2.** MAKE A PRIEST A CARDINAL to promote a member of the Roman Catholic clergy to the position of cardinal **3.** MAKE A PRIEST MOST SENIOR to promote a Roman Catholic priest to the position of most senior member of the clergy within a particular church or area [Early 17thC. From late Latin *incardinat-*, past particple stem of *incardinare* "to ordain as chief priest," from Latin *cardinalis* (see CARDINAL).] —**in·car·di·na·tion** /in kàard'n áysh'n/ *n.*

in·car·na·dine /in káarnə dìn, -dìn/ *adj.* CRIMSON of a crimson or blood red color (*literary*) ■ *n.* CRIMSON COLOR the color crimson or the color of blood (*literary*) ■ *vt.* (**-dined, -din·ing, -dines**) MAKE CRIMSON to tinge or stain something crimson or blood red (*literary*) [Late 16thC. Via French from Italian *incarnatino* "carnation," literally "flesh-color," ultimately from the Latin stem *carn-* "flesh" (see CARNAL).]

in·car·nate *adj.* /in káarnət/ **1.** MADE HUMAN having a bodily form, especially a human form **2.** PERSONIFIED being the epitome of something ○ *an advisor who is discretion incarnate* **3.** BOT PINK OR RED used to describe plant parts that are pink or crimson ■ *vt.* /in káar nàyt/ (**-nat·ed, -nat·ing, -nates**) **1.** SHOW IN HUMAN FORM to give something a bodily form, especially a human form **2.** PERSONIFY to be the epitome or personification of something **3.** CAUSE TO HAPPEN to bring about or realize something that exists as an idea or theory only [14thC. From ecclesiastical Latin *incarnatus*, past participle of *incarnari* "to be made flesh," from the Latin stem *carn-* "flesh" (see CARNAL).] —**in·car·na·tor** /in kaár nàytər/ *n.*

in·car·na·tion /in kaar náysh'n/ *n.* **1. PERSONIFICATION OF SOMETHING** somebody or something personifying, representing, or typifying a quality or idea **2. ONE LIFE IN A SERIES OF LIVES** one of a succession of lives or periods spent in the body of a particular animal or person **3. MANIFESTATION OF A GOD** a god's or spirit's appearance in human or animal form

In·car·na·tion *n.* in Christianity, God's taking human form as Jesus Christ

in case ♦ case

in·case *vt.* = encase —**in·case·ment** *n.*

in·cau·tious /in kóshəss/ *adj.* careless, rash, or lacking in caution —**in·cau·tious·ly** *adv.* —**in·cau·tious·ness** *n.* —**in·cau·tion** *n.*

in·cen·di·a·rism /in séndee ə rìzzəm/ *n.* inflammatory talk or provocative behavior designed or likely to cause civil unrest (*formal*)

in·cen·di·ar·y /in séndee èrree/ *adj.* **1.** ARMS **CONTAINING CHEMICALS THAT CAUSE FIRE** containing highly flammable substances that will cause a fire on impact **2. LIKELY TO CATCH FIRE** able to catch fire spontaneously or cause a fire easily **3. INCITING CIVIL UNREST** designed or likely to cause civil unrest **4. RELATING TO ARSON** relating to or involving the illegal burning of property ■ *n.* (*plural* **-ies**) **1. in·cen·di·ar·y, in·cen·di·ar·y bomb** ARMS **BOMB DESIGNED TO CAUSE A FIRE** a bomb or missile containing a highly flammable substance such as napalm, designed to cause a fire on impact **2. SOMEBODY INCITING TROUBLE** somebody who stirs up trouble or violence, especially with political motives (*formal*) **3. ARSONIST** somebody who illegally sets fire to property (*formal*) [15thC. From Latin *incendiarius*, from *incendium* "conflagration," from *incendere* (see INCENSE[1]).]

in·cense[1] /in sèns/ *n.* **1. SUBSTANCE BURNED FOR ITS FRAGRANT SMELL** a substance, usually fragrant gum or wood, that gives off a pleasant smell when burned **2. SMOKE OR FRAGRANCE FROM INCENSE** the smoke or fragrant smell produced when incense is burned **3. FRAGRANCE** a pleasant smell **4. PRAISE** praise or adulation ■ *v.* (**-censed, -cens·ing, -cens·es**) **1.** *vti.* **HONOR A GOD WITH INCENSE** to honor a god by burning incense **2.** *vt.* **PERFUME WITH INCENSE** to perfume something with incense [13thC. Via French *encens* from ecclesiastical Latin *incensum*, a form of *incensus*, past participle of Latin *incendere* "to set fire to," from the base of *candere* "to glow."] —**in·cen·sa·tion** /in sen sáysh'n/ *n.*

in·cense[2] /in séns/ (**-censed, -cens·ing, -cens·es**) *vt.* to make somebody extremely angry [15thC. From French *encenser*, from *encens*, or ecclesiastical Latin *incensare*, from *incensum* (see INCENSE[1]).] —**in·cense·ment** *n.*

in·cense ce·dar *n.* **1. EVERGREEN TREE** a coniferous evergreen tree of the cypress family with resinous scaly leaves, flattened branches, and aromatic wood. Different species occur in the Americas, Asia, and New Zealand. Genera: *Austrocedrus* and *Calocedrus* and *Libocedrus*. **2. FRAGRANT WOOD OF THE INCENSE CEDAR TREE** the aromatic wood of the incense cedar tree, often used to scent rooms or drawers, or to keep away moths. Its resistance to decay makes it useful for decking and fence posts, and it is also used to make pencils.

in·cen·so·ry /in sensəree, in sénsəree/ (*plural* **-ries**) *n.* RELIG = **censer** [Early 17thC. From medieval Latin *incensorium*, from ecclesiastical Latin *incensum* (see INCENSE[1]).]

in·cen·tive /in séntiv/ *n.* **SOMETHING THAT ENCOURAGES SOMEBODY TO ACTION** something that encourages or motivates somebody to do something ■ *adj.* **ENCOURAGING OR MOTIVATING** serving to encourage or motivate somebody [Early 17thC. From Latin *incentivum*, literally "something that sets the tune," ultimately from *incinere* "to sound," from *canere* "to sing."] —**in·cen·tive·ly** *adv.*

WORD KEY: SYNONYMS

See Synonyms at ***motive***.

in·cen·tiv·ize /in sénti vìz/ (**-ized, -iz·ing, -iz·es**) *vt.* to motivate somebody by offering an incentive such as a higher rate of pay (*informal*)

in·cept /in sépt/ (**-cept·ed, -cept·ing, -cepts**) *vi.* *U.K.* UNIV to enroll at a university, especially to begin studying for a master's degree or doctorate (*dated formal*) [15thC. From Latin *incept-*, past participle stem of *incipere* "to begin" (see INCIPIENT).] —**in·cep·tor** *n.*

in·cep·tion /in sépshən/ *n.* **1. BEGINNING** the beginning of something (*formal*) **2.** *U.K.* UNIV **ENROLLMENT AT UNIVERSITY** enrollment as a university student, especially one studying for a master's degree or doctorate (*dated formal*) [15thC. Directly or via French from the Latin stem *inception-*, ultimately from *incipere* (see INCIPIENT).]

in·cep·tive /in séptiv/ *adj.* **1. INITIAL** representing or coming at the beginning of something (*formal*) **2.** LING **EXPRESSING THE IDEA OF STARTING** used to describe a verb or verb form that, in some languages, indicates the beginning of an action ■ *n.* LING **1. INCEPTIVE ASPECT** the inceptive aspect of verbs **2. INCEPTIVE VERB** a verb in the inceptive aspect [Early 17thC. From late Latin *inceptivus*, ultimately from Latin *incipere* (see INCIPIENT).] —**in·cep·tive·ly** *adv.*

in·cer·ti·tude /in súrtə to͞od/ *n.* **1. DOUBT** doubt or uncertainty **2. LACK OF SELF-CONFIDENCE** lack of confidence in yourself [15thC. Directly or via French from late Latin *incertitudo*, from *certitudo* "certitude" (see CERTITUDE).]

in·ces·sant /in séss'nt/ *adj.* continuing for a long time without stopping [15thC. Directly or via French from the late Latin stem *incessant-*, from *cessare* "to stop" (see CEASE).] —**in·ces·san·cy** *n.* —**in·ces·sant·ly** *adv.*

in·cest /in sèst/ *n.* sexual activity between two people who are considered, for moral and genetic reasons, too closely related to have such a relationship. Incest is regarded as a serious taboo in almost every society, although cultures differ as to the extent to which marriages are allowed between relatives. [13thC. From Latin *incestus*, from *castus* (see CHASTE).]

in·ces·tu·ous /in séschoo əss/ *adj.* **1. RELATING TO OR INVOLVING INCEST** relating to or involving a sexual relationship between two people who are considered, for moral and genetic reasons, too closely related to have such a relationship **2. GUILTY OF INCEST** having had a sexual relationship with somebody considered to be too close a relative **3. UNHEALTHILY EXCLUSIVE OF OTHERS** unhealthily intimate or interconnected, especially so as to exclude the involvement or influence of others ○ *an incestuous friendship* **4. BORN OF PARENTS WHO COMMITTED INCEST** born as the result of an incestuous relationship (*archaic*) —**in·ces·tu·ous·ly** *adv.* —**in·ces·tu·ous·ness** *n.*

inch[1] /inch/ *n.* **1.** MEASURE **UNIT OF LENGTH** a unit of length equal to 1/12th of a foot/2.54 cm. Symbol " **2. SMALL AMOUNT** a very small amount, degree, or distance **3.** METEOROL **AMOUNT OF RAIN OR SNOW** a fall of enough rain or snow to cover a surface to a depth of one inch **4.** METEOROL **UNIT OF ATMOSPHERIC PRESSURE** a unit of atmospheric pressure equal to that needed to maintain a mercury column one inch high in a barometer ■ *vti.* (**inched, inch·ing, inch·es**) **MOVE SLOWLY** to move or cause somebody or something to move very slowly or by small degrees [Pre-12thC. From Latin *uncia* "one twelfth," from *unus* "one" (source of English *unit* and *ounce*).]

inch[2] /inch/ *n.* in Scotland and Ireland, a small island (*often used in placenames*) [15thC. From Scottish Gaelic *innis* "island."]

inch·meal /inch me͞el/ *adv.* in very small stages or progressions [Mid-16thC. From INCH[1] + -MEAL.]

in·cho·ate *adj.* /in kō ət/ (*formal*) **1. JUST BEGINNING** just beginning to develop **2. IMPERFECTLY FORMED** only partly formed **3. CHAOTIC** lacking structure, order, or organization [Mid-16thC. From Latin *inchoatus*, past participle of *inchoare*, variant of *incohare* "to begin."] —**in·cho·ate·ly** *adv.* —**in·cho·ate·ness** *n.* —**in·cho·a·tion** /in kō áysh'n/ *n.*

in·cho·a·tive /in kō ətiv/ *adj.*, *n.* GRAM = **inceptive** *adj.* **2**, **inceptive** *n.* **1**, **inceptive** *n.* **2**

inch·worm /inch wùrm/ *n.* the larva of a geometrid moth that has legs only at each end of its body and moves by bringing its rear forward, forming a loop, then moving its front

in·ci·dence /insid'ns/ *n.* **1. RATE OF OCCURRENCE OF SOMETHING** the frequency with which something occurs **2. INSTANCE OR MANNER OF SOMETHING HAPPENING** an instance of something happening, or the manner in which it happens **3.** PHYS, MATH **IMPACT ON A SURFACE** the impact that something moving e.g., a ray of light or a projectile, makes with a surface

in·ci·dent /insid'nt/ *n.* **1. EVENT** something that happens, especially a single event **2. VIOLENT OCCURRENCE** a public occurrence, especially a violent one ○ *an incident outside a nightclub* **3. EVENT WITH POTENTIALLY SERIOUS CONSEQUENCES** an event that may result in a crisis, especially in international matters ■ *adj.* **1. RELATED TO SOMETHING** accompanying something or occurring as a consequence of it (*formal*) **2.** PHYS **COMING INTO CONTACT WITH SURFACE** coming into contact with a surface [15thC. Directly or via French from, ultimately, Latin *incidere* "to fall upon or happen to," from *cadere* "to fall."]

in·ci·den·tal /insi dént'l/ *adj.* **1. RELATED OR ACCOMPANYING** related to or accompanying something more important **2. OCCURRING BY CHANCE** occurring by chance or without intention **3. OCCASIONAL** unimportant or occasional **4. RESULTING FROM SOMETHING** occurring as a result of something (*formal*) ■ *n.* **MINOR ITEM** something that is occasional or unimportant such as a minor expense

in·ci·den·tal·ly /insi dént'lee/ *adv.* **1. BY THE WAY** used to introduce additional information such as something that the speaker has just thought of **2. BY CHANCE** by chance or by accident

in·ci·den·tal mu·sic *n.* music that accompanies the action of a movie, play, or television program, as distinct from theme music or songs that feature in a musical

in·cin·er·ate /in sínnə ràyt/ (**-at·ed, -at·ing, -ates**) *vti.* to burn to ashes, or cause something to burn to ashes, especially in an incinerator [15thC. From medieval Latin *incinerare*, from *ciner-*, stem of *cinis* "ashes."] —**in·cin·er·a·tion** /in sìnnə ráysh'n/ *n.*

in·cin·er·a·tor /in sínnə ràytər/ *n.* a furnace for destroying things by burning them, especially one used to burn waste

in·cip·i·ent /in síppee ənt/ *adj.* beginning to appear or develop [Mid-17thC. From Latin *incipient-*, present participle stem of *incipere* "to undertake or begin," from *capere* "to take."] —**in·cip·i·ence** *n.* —**in·cip·i·ent·ly** *adv.*

in·ci·pit /ínsipit/ *n.* the opening word or words of a medieval manuscript or an early printed book, by which it is often known in the absence of a title [Late 19thC. From Latin, literally "it begins," a form of *incipere* (see INCIPIENT).]

in·ci·sal /in sīz'l/ *adj.* relating to the cutting edge of a tooth [Early 20thC. Formed from INCISOR.]

in·cise /in sīz/ (**-cised, -cis·ing, -cis·es**) *vt.* **1.** SURG **CUT** to cut into something **2.** ARTS **ENGRAVE OR CARVE** to carve or engrave a pattern or design into something [Mid-16thC. From French *inciser*, from Latin *incis-*, past participle stem of *incidere* "to cut into," from *caedere* "to cut."]

in·cised /in sīzd/ *adj.* BOT used to describe a leaf with edges that are deeply and sharply indented

in·ci·sion /in sízh'n/ *n.* **1.** SURG **CUT OR ACT OF CUTTING** a cut or the act of cutting, especially when performed by a surgeon **2.** BOT **LEAF'S DEEPLY INDENTED EDGE** a sharp indentation in the edge of a leaf **3. FACT OF BEING INCISIVE** the fact or quality of being quick to understand or able to express something clearly

in·ci·sive /in sīssiv/ *adj.* **1. QUICK TO UNDERSTAND** quick to understand, analyze, or act **2. EXPRESSING OR EXPRESSED CLEARLY** characterized by clear and direct expression —**in·ci·sive·ly** *adv.* —**in·ci·sive·ness** *n.*

in·ci·sor /in sīzər/ *n.* one of the flat sharp-edged teeth in the front of the mouth, used for cutting and tearing food [Late 17thC. From medieval Latin *dens incisor*, literally "cutter tooth," formed from Latin *incis-* (see INCISE).]

in·ci·ta·tion *n.* = **incitement**

in·cite /in sīt/ (**-cit·ed, -cit·ing, -cites**) *vt.* to stir up feelings in or provoke action by somebody [15thC. Via French *inciter* from Latin *incitare* "to hasten or urge on," from *citare* "to set in motion" (see CITE).] —**in·cit·er** *n.*

in·cite·ment /in sītmənt/, **in·cit·a·tion** *n.* **1. PROVOCATION** the stirring up of feelings or the provoking of action, especially militancy or violence **2. SOMETHING THAT INCITES** something that stirs up feelings or provokes action

in·ci·vil·i·ty /insi villətee/ (*plural* **-ties**) *n.* **1. RUDE BEHAVIOR OR LANGUAGE** rude or impolite behavior or language **2. RUDE ACT OR REMARK** a rude or impolite act or remark [Mid-16thC. From Latin *incivilis*, from *civilis* (see CIVIL).]

incl. *abbr.* **1.** including **2.** inclusive

in·clem·ent /in klémmənt/ *adj.* **1.** METEOROL **NOT PLEASANT OR MILD** unpleasant in being stormy, rainy, or snowy **2. SHOWING LITTLE OR NO MERCY** showing little or no mercy (*formal*) [Mid-16thC. Directly or via French *inclément* from the Latin stem *inclement-*, literally "not clement," from *clement-* (see CLEMENT).] —**in·clem·en·cy** *n.* —**in·clem·ent·ly** *adv.*

in·clin·a·ble /in klīnəb'l/ *adj.* **1.** HAVING A PARTICULAR TENDENCY inclined to behave in a particular way **2.** IN FAVOR likely to agree or approve (*formal*)

in·cli·na·tion /inkli náysh'n/ *n.* **1.** WAY SOMEBODY FEELS ABOUT SOMETHING a feeling that pushes somebody to make a particular choice or decision **2.** TENDENCY a tendency to do or prefer something, or a desire for something **3.** DEVIATION FROM LINE OR PLANE the tilting of something away from a line or surface, or the degree to which is it tilted **4.** SLOPE a sloping surface **5.** TILTING OF SOMETHING a bending of something, e.g., a bowing of the head **6.** GEOM ANGLE ON GRAPH the angle between a line on a graph and the positive direction of the x-axis **7.** GEOM SMALLER ANGLE the smaller angle between two lines or planes **8.** ASTRON ANGLE OF ORBIT the angle between a planet's orbit and the apparent orbit of the Sun in relation to the Earth **9.** PHYS = dip —**in·cli·na·tion·al** *adj.*

in·cline *vti.* /in klīn/ (**-clined, -clin·ing, -clines**) **1.** BE OR MAKE LIKELY TO ACT to tend, or make somebody tend, toward a particular belief or course of action **2.** ANGLE OR BE ANGLED to lie at an angle or put something at an angle **3.** BEND to bend something, especially the head or body when bowing or nodding ■ *n.* /ín klīn/ SLOPE a slope or sloping surface [14thC. Via Old French *encliner* from Latin *inclinare* "to lean toward," from *clinare* "to lean" (source of English *decline*).] —**in·clin·er** /in klīnər/ *n.*

in·clined /in klīnd/ *adj.* **1.** MOTIVATED TO DO SOMETHING moved or persuaded to do something ○ *I'm not inclined to listen to any more of this.* **2.** TALENTED IN A PARTICULAR AREA naturally talented or interested in a particular field or area **3.** SLANTED OR FORMING AN ANGLE sloping or forming an angle with something else

in·cli·nom·e·ter /in klī nómmətər/ *n.* **1.** DEVICE FOR MEASURING INCLINATION an instrument that measures angles or slopes such as the angle of an aircraft relative to the ground **2.** DEVICE FOR FINDING AN INCLINATION an instrument used to determine the angle made by the Earth's magnetic field relative to the horizontal plane [Mid-19thC. Coined from Latin *inclinare* (see INCLINE) + -METER.]

in·close *vt.* = **enclose** —**in·clos·a·ble** *adj.* —**in·clos·er** *n.* —**in·clo·sure** *n.*

in·clude /in klóod/ (**-clud·ed, -clud·ing, -cludes**) *vt.* **1.** CONTAIN to have something as a constituent element **2.** BRING INTO GROUP to make somebody or something part of a group [15thC. From Latin *includere* "to shut in or enclose," from *claudere* "to shut."] —**in·clud·a·ble** *adj.*

WORD KEY: USAGE

See Usage note at ***comprise.***

in·clud·ed /in klóodəd/ *adj.* **1.** CONTAINED WITHIN A GROUP forming part of a group or whole **2.** BOT NOT PROTRUDING used to describe the stamens or carpels of a flower that do not protrude beyond the edges of the petals **3.** GEOM LOCATED BETWEEN INTERSECTING LINES formed by and contained in two intersecting lines —**in·clud·ed·ness** *n.*

in·clud·ing /in klóoding/ *prep.* used to introduce examples of people or things forming part of a specified group or whole ○ *It will cost you $65 including sales tax.*

in·clu·sion /in klóozh'n/ *n.* **1.** PRESENCE IN GROUP the addition of somebody or something to, or the presence of somebody or something in, a group or mixture **2.** SOMEBODY OR SOMETHING INCLUDED somebody or something included in a group or mixture **3.** GEOL SUBSTANCE TRAPPED INSIDE MINERAL a solid, liquid, or gas contained within a mineral or rock **4.** BIOL FOREIGN BODY IN CELL a nonliving mass such as a starch grain or droplet of fat in the cytoplasm or nucleus of a cell **5.** MATH RELATION BETWEEN SETS the relation between two classes or sets when the second is a subset of the first **6.** EDUC TEACHING CHALLENGED CHILDREN IN PUBLIC SCHOOL the practice of teaching mentally and physically challenged children in public school classrooms instead of in separate classrooms [Early 17thC. Formed from the Latin stem *inclus-*, past participle stem of *includere* (see INCLUDE).] —**in·clu·sion·ar·y** *adj.*

in·clu·sion bod·y *n.* MED a mass of virus particles inside a cell, formerly used in the diagnosis of some viral infections

in·clu·sive /in klóossiv/ *adj.* **1.** INCLUDING THE SPECIFIED LIMITS used to indicate that a span of time or a range within a series includes the dates, times, or other items stated at the beginning and end of the span ○ *the period from October 1 to July 31, inclusive* **2.** INCLUDING MANY THINGS including many things or everything **3.** GRAM INCLUDING SPEAKER AND PERSON ADDRESSED used to describe a pronoun that includes the speaker and the person or persons spoken to. In English, "we" is the only inclusive pronoun. ◊ **exclusive 4.** LOGIC BEING TYPE OF SENTENCE IN LOGIC used to describe a sentence in logic (**disjunction**) containing two propositions of which at least one and possibly both can be true. ◊ **exclusive** [Late 16thC. From medieval Latin *inclusivus*, from Latin *inclus-* (see INCLUDE).] —**in·clu·sive·ly** *adv.* —**in·clu·sive·ness** *n.*

in·co·er·ci·ble /in kō úrsəb'l/ *adj.* not giving in to force or pressure from others

incog. *abbr.* incognito

in·cog·i·tant /in kójjit'nt/ *adj.* inconsiderate or thoughtless (*formal*) [Early 17thC. From the Latin stem *incogitant-*, literally "unthinking," from *cogitare* "to think" (see COGITATE).]

in·cog·ni·ta /in kog néetə/ *adj., adv.* with the identity disguised or hidden, e.g., under an assumed name (*used to describe a woman or girl*) [Late 17thC. From Italian, feminine of *incognito* "incognito").] —**in·cog·ni·ta** (*plural* **-tas**) *n.*

in·cog·ni·to /in kog nee tō/ *adj., adv.* IN DISGUISE with the identity disguised or hidden, e.g., under an assumed name ■ *n.* (*plural* **-tos**) **1.** SOMEBODY INCOGNITO somebody who is acting or traveling incognito **2.** DISGUISE the character, disguise, or name assumed by somebody who is incognito [Mid-17thC. Via Italian from Latin *incognitus* "unknown," from *cognitus*, past participle of *cognoscere* "to learn," from *gnoscere* "to know."]

in·cog·ni·zant /in kógnizz'nt/ *adj.* not knowing, realizing, or being aware (*formal*) —**in·cog·ni·zance** *n.*

in·co·her·ence /in kō héerəns/ *n.* a lack of logical organization in the way something is thought out or expressed that makes it difficult to understand

in·co·her·ent /in kō héerənt/ *adj.* **1.** LACKING CLARITY OR ORGANIZATION not clearly expressed or well thought out, and consequently difficult to understand **2.** UNABLE TO SPEAK OR EXPRESS CLEARLY unable to express thoughts or feelings clearly or logically **3.** NOT COHESIVE not sticking together as a mass **4.** PHYS OUT OF PHASE having the same frequency but not the same phase —**in·co·her·ent·ly** *adv.*

in·com·bus·ti·ble /in kəm bústəb'l/ *adj.* NOT COMBUSTIBLE not capable of being burned ■ *n.* SOMETHING INCOMBUSTIBLE an incombustible object, material, or substance [15thC. From medieval Latin *incombustibilis*, from *combustibilis* "combustible" (see COMBUSTIBLE).] —**in·com·bus·ti·bil·i·ty** /inkəm bustə bílləṭee/ *n.* —**in·com·bus·ti·bly** /-bústəblee/ *adv.*

in·come /ín kùm/ *n.* **1.** MONEY RECEIVED OVER PERIOD the amount of money received over a period of time either as payment for work, goods, or services, or as profit on capital **2.** INFLOW a coming in or flowing in [14thC. From Old Norse *innkoma* "arrival"; in later use from IN + COME.]

in·come bond *n.* a bond paying a rate of return in proportion to the issuer's income

in·come tax *n.* a tax paid on money made from employment, business, or capital (*hyphenated when used before a noun*)

in·com·ing /ín kùmming/ *adj.* **1.** ARRIVING arriving, coming in, or entering **2.** TAKING UP NEW JOB about to take up a particular job or office **3.** BEING RECEIVED being received or taken in ■ *n.* ARRIVAL an arrival or entrance (*formal*) ■ **in·com·ings** *npl.* INCOME sums of money earned or received

in·com·men·su·ra·ble /inkə ménsərəb'l, -shərəb'l/ *adj.* **1.** IMPOSSIBLE TO MEASURE not capable of being compared or measured, especially because lacking a common quality necessary for a comparison to be made **2.** MATH HAVING NO COMMON FACTOR having no common factor or measure other than 1 ■ *n.* SOMETHING INCOMMENSURABLE something that cannot be compared or measured, especially a quality or a mathematical value [Mid-16thC. From late Latin *incommensurabilis*, from *commensurabilis* "commensurable."] —**in·com·men·su·ra·bil·i·ty** /inkə ménsərə bíllətee, -shərə-/ *n.* —**in·com·men·su·ra·bly** /inkə ménsərəblee, -ménshə-/ *adv.*

in·com·men·su·rate /inkə ménsərət, -ménshə-/ *adj.* **1.** NOT PROPORTIONATE not proportionate to or up to the level of something **2.** = **incommensurable** *adj.* 1 —**in·com·men·su·rate·ly** *adv.* —**in·com·men·su·rate·ness** *n.*

in·com·mode /inkə mṓd/ (**-mod·ed, -mod·ing, -modes**) *vt.* to bother or inconvenience somebody (*formal*) [Late 16thC. Directly or via French *incommoder* from Latin *incommodare*, from *commodus* "convenient" (see COMMODIOUS).]

in·com·mo·di·ous /inkə mṓdee əss/ *adj.* (*formal*) **1.** UNCOMFORTABLY CRAMPED uncomfortably lacking in space **2.** CAUSING INCONVENIENCE causing trouble or inconvenience —**in·com·mo·di·ous·ly** *adv.* —**in·com·mo·di·ous·ness** *n.*

in·com·mod·i·ty /inkə móddətee/ (*plural* **-ties**) *n.* trouble or inconvenience, or something that causes it (*formal*) [15thC. Via French *incommodité* from ultimately, from Latin *commodus* "convenient" (see COMMODIOUS).]

in·com·mu·ni·ca·ble /inkə myóonikəb'l/ *adj.* **1.** IMPOSSIBLE TO CONVEY not capable of being expressed or conveyed to others **2.** NOT TALKATIVE tending not to say much or give much information away (*archaic*) [Mid-16thC. From late Latin *incommunicabilis* "not to be passed on," from *communicabilis* "communicable."] —**in·com·mu·ni·ca·bil·i·ty** /inkə myóonikə bílləṭee/ *n.* —**in·com·mu·ni·ca·bly** /inkə myóonikəblee/ *adv.*

in·com·mu·ni·ca·do /inkə myóoni kaá dō/ *adj.* prevented by circumstances or by force from communicating with other people [Mid-19thC. From Spanish *incomunicado*, from *incomunicar* "to deprive of communication," from Latin *communicare* (see COMMUNICATE).] —**in·com·mu·ni·ca·do** *adv.*

in·com·mu·ni·ca·tive /inkə myóoni kàytiv, -nikətiv/ *adj.* unwilling to communicate or provide information —**in·com·mu·ni·ca·tive·ly** *adv.* —**in·com·mu·ni·ca·tive·ness** *n.*

in·com·mut·a·ble /inkə myóotəb'l/ *adj.* not able to be changed, exchanged for something else, or reduced in severity (*formal*) [15thC. From Latin *incommutabilis* "unchangeable," from *commutare* (see COMMUTE).] —**in·com·mut·a·bil·i·ty** /inkə myootə bílləṭee/ *n.* —**in·com·mut·a·ble·ness** /inkə myóotəb'lnəss/ *n.* —**in·com·mut·a·bly** *adv.*

in·com·pa·ra·ble /in kómpərəb'l/ *adj.* **1.** UNEQUALED IN QUALITY so excellent, outstanding, or unique as to have no equal **2.** IMPOSSIBLE TO COMPARE WITH SOMETHING ELSE impossible to compare with something else, or with each other, because there is no basis on which a comparison could be made [15thC. Via French from Latin *incomparabilis* "that cannot be equaled," from *comparare* (see COMPARE).] —**in·com·pa·ra·bil·i·ty** /in kòmpərə bílləṭee/ *n.* —**in·com·pa·ra·ble·ness** /in kómpərə b'lnəss/ *n.* —**in·com·pa·ra·bly** *adv.*

in·com·pat·i·bil·i·ty /inkəm pattə bílləṭee/ (*plural* **-ties**) *n.* **1.** INABILITY TO COOPERATE OR COEXIST a basic inability to cooperate, coexist, or function in combination with somebody or something else **2.** CONFLICTING QUALITY a quality or feature that renders somebody or something incompatible with somebody or something else

in·com·pat·i·ble /inkəm páttəb'l/ *adj.* **1.** UNABLE TO COOPERATE OR COEXIST unable to exist, cooperate, blend, or get along with somebody or something else because of basic differences **2.** IMMUNOL LIKELY TO BE REJECTED BY DONOR used to describe a tissue transplant or blood that is likely to be rejected by a recipient's immune system **3.** PHARM NOT SUITABLE FOR USE IN COMBINATION used to describe two or more drugs that should not be used in combination because, e.g., they would counteract each other **4.** BOT NOT ABLE TO BE POLLINATED OR GRAFTED used to describe plants or varieties that cannot be successfully cross-pollinated or grafted onto each other **5.** LOGIC CONTRADICTORY used to describe two propositions that cannot both be true at the same time **6.** MATH MATHEMATICALLY INCONSISTENT not mathematically consistent ■ *n.* SOMEBODY OR SOMETHING INHARMONIOUS somebody or something that is not compatible with somebody or something else [15thC. From medieval Latin *incompatibilis*, from *compati* "to suffer together."] —**in·com·pat·i·ble·ness** *n.* —**in·com·pat·i·bly** *adv.*

in·com·pe·tent /in kómpət'nt/ *adj.* **1.** BAD AT DOING SOMETHING lacking the skills, qualities, or ability to do something properly **2.** LAW LACKING NECESSARY STATUS not having the necessary legal status, validity, or powers for the purpose in question ■ *n.* SOMEBODY BAD AT DOING SOMETHING somebody who lacks the skills, qualities, or ability to do something properly [Late 16thC. Via French *incompétent* from the late Latin stem *incompetent-*, literally "not competent," from *competere* (see COMPETE).] —**in·com·pe·tence** *n.* —**in·com·pe·tent·ly** *adv.*

in·com·plete /inkəm pleet/ *adj.* 1. LACKING A PART lacking something such as a particular part that properly or desirably belongs with it 2. UNFINISHED not yet finished or fully developed 3. FOOTBALL NOT CAUGHT in football, used to describe a forward pass that is dropped or not legally caught by an intended receiver [14thC. From Latin *incompletus*, literally "not finished," from *completus* (see COMPLETE).] —**in·com·plete·ly** *adv.* —**in·com·plete·ness** *n.* —**in·com·ple·tion** /-pleesh'n/ *n.*

in·com·plete frac·ture *n.* a fracture that does not go all the way through a bone

in·com·pli·ant /inkəm plī ənt/ *adj.* unwilling to to be flexible and accommodating or to comply with something (*formal*) —**in·com·pli·ance** *n.* —**in·com·pli·ant·ly** *adv.*

in·com·pre·hen·si·ble /in kòmpri hénsəb'l/ *adj.* 1. BEYOND UNDERSTANDING impossible or very difficult to understand 2. LIMITLESS lacking or incapable of having limits (*archaic*) [14thC. From Latin *incomprehensibilis*, literally "not comprehensible," from *comprehendere* (see COMPREHEND).] —**in·com·pre·hen·si·bil·i·ty** /in kòmpri hensə bíllətee/ *n.* —**in·com·pre·hen·si·ble·ness** /in kòmpri hénsəb'lnəss/ *n.* —**in·com·pre·hen·si·bly** *adv.*

in·com·pre·hen·sion /in kòmpri hénshən/ *n.* an inability or failure to understand, or a state of bewilderment resulting from this

in·com·pre·hen·sive /in kòmpri hénsiv/ *adj.* 1. NOT COMPREHENSIVE limited in scope (*formal*) 2. NOT UNDERSTANDING unable to understand well —**in·com·pre·hen·sive·ly** *adv.* —**in·com·pre·hen·sive·ness** *n.*

in·con·ceiv·a·ble /inkən seévəb'l/ *adj.* 1. UNIMAGINABLE impossible to imagine or to grasp mentally and understand 2. EXTREMELY UNLIKELY so unlikely as to be beyond belief or thought impossible ○ *It's inconceivable that they should have made the same mistake twice.* —**in·con·ceiv·a·bil·i·ty** /inkən seévə bíllətee/ *n.* —**in·con·ceiv·a·ble·ness** /inkən seévəb'lnəss/ *n.* —**in·con·ceiv·a·bly** *adv.*

in·con·cin·ni·ty /inkən sínətee/ *n.* inelegance or unsuitability caused by not being in proportion or not harmonizing with other things (*formal*) [Early 17thC. From Latin *inconcinnitas*, literally "not well joined," from *concinnus* (see CONCINNITY).]

in·con·clu·sive /inkən kloóssiv/ *adj.* not producing a clear-cut result, firm conclusion, or decisive proof of something —**in·con·clu·sive·ly** *adv.* —**in·con·clu·sive·ness** *n.*

in·con·dite /in kóndit, -dīt/ *adj.* crude, poorly constructed, or unpolished (*formal*) [Mid-16thC. From Latin *inconditus*, literally "not put together," from *condere* (see ABSCOND).] —**in·con·dite·ly** *adv.*

in·con·gru·ent /in kóng groo ənt, ìn kon groó ənt/ *adj.* not corresponding in structure or content [15thC. From the Latin stem *incongruent-*, literally "not in agreement," from *congruens*, the present participle of *congruere* (see CONGRUENT).] —**in·con·gru·ence** *n.* —**in·con·gru·ent·ly** *adv.*

in·con·gru·i·ty /inkən groó itee/ (*plural* **-ties**) *n.* 1. INCONGRUOUSNESS the fact of being incongruous 2. SOMETHING OUT OF PLACE something that does not seem to fit in with or be appropriate to its context

in·con·gru·ous /in kóng groo əss/ *adj.* 1. UNSUITABLE OR ODD unsuitable, strange, or out of place in a particular setting or context 2. INCONSISTENT WITH SOMETHING not in accord or consistent with something [Early 17thC. From Latin *incongruus*, literally "not in agreement," from *congruus* (see CONGRUOUS).] —**in·con·gru·ous·ly** *adv.* —**in·con·gru·ous·ness** *n.*

in·con·sec·u·tive /inkən sékyətiv/ *adj.* not following in order one after another —**in·con·sec·u·tive·ly** *adv.* —**in·con·sec·u·tive·ness** *n.*

in·con·se·quent /in kónsəkwənt/ *adj.* not following as a natural or logical result [Late 16thC. From the Latin stem *inconsequent-*, literally "not following," from *consequens*, the present participle of *consequi* (see CONSEQUENT).] —**in·con·se·quent·ly** *adv.*

in·con·se·quen·tial /in kònsi kwénshəl/ *adj.* 1. UNIMPORTANT of little or no importance 2. = **inconsequent** ■ *n.* TRIVIALITY something without importance or significance [Early 17thC. Formed from IN- + CONSEQUENTIAL.] —**in·con·se·quen·ti·al·i·ty** /in kònsi kwenshee állətee/ *n.* —**in·con·se·quen·tial·ness** /in kónsi kwénshəlnəss/ *n.* —**in·con·se·quen·tial·ly** /-kwénshəlee/ *adv.*

in·con·sid·er·a·ble /inkən síddərəb'l/ *adj.* 1. SMALL small in size, amount, or value (*often used with "not"*) 2. UNWORTHY OF CONSIDERATION so unimportant as to be not worth considering (*formal*) [Late 16thC. Directly or via French from late Latin *inconsiderabilis*, literally "unimaginable," from Latin *considerare* (see CONSIDER).] —**in·con·sid·er·a·ble·ness** *n.* —**in·con·sid·er·a·bly** *adv.*

in·con·sid·er·ate /inkən síddərət/ *adj.* lacking thought or consideration for other people and their feelings [15thC. From Latin *inconsideratus*, literally "not thinking," from *consideratus*, the past participle of *considerare* (see CONSIDER).] —**in·con·sid·er·ate·ly** *adv.* —**in·con·sid·er·ate·ness** *n.* —**in·con·sid·er·a·tion** /inkən siddə ráysh'n/ *n.*

in·con·sis·ten·cy /inkən sístənssee/ (*plural* **-cies**), **in·con·sis·tence** *n.* 1. LACK OF CONSISTENCY the fact of being inconsistent 2. INCONSISTENT THING something that contradicts something else or that is not in keeping with it

in·con·sis·tent /inkən sístənt/ *adj.* 1. CONTAINING CONFLICTING OR CONTRADICTORY ELEMENTS containing elements that conflict with or contradict each other 2. VARYING AND UNPREDICTABLE unpredictable or unreliable in being likely to behave differently or achieve a different result if a particular situation is repeated 3. CONFLICTING OR INCOMPATIBLE WITH SOMETHING conflicting with or not corresponding to something such as a rule, principle, or expectation 4. MATH LACKING COMMON VALUES IN AN EQUATION not having a common set of values for the unknowns in an equation —**in·con·sis·tent·ly** *adv.*

in·con·sol·a·ble /inkən sṓləb'l/ *adj.* so deeply distressed that nobody can offer any effective comfort [Late 16thC. Directly or via French from Latin *inconsolabilis*, from *consolare* (see CONSOLE).] —**in·con·sol·a·bil·i·ty** /inkən sṓlə bíllətee/ *n.* —**in·con·sol·a·ble·ness** /inkən sṓləb'lnəss/ *n.* —**in·con·sol·a·bly** *adv.*

in·con·so·nant /in kónsənənt/ *adj.* not in harmony or not compatible with something else (*formal*) —**in·con·so·nance** *n.* —**in·con·so·nant·ly** *adv.*

in·con·spic·u·ous /inkən spíkyə əss/ *adj.* not easily seen or noticed [Early 17thC] —**in·con·spic·u·ous·ly** *adv.* —**in·con·spic·u·ous·ness** *n.*

in·con·stant /in kónstənt/ *adj.* 1. UNFAITHFUL not faithful in relationships (*literary*) 2. CHANGEABLE likely to change frequently and unpredictably [15thC. Directly or via Old French from the Latin stem *inconstant-*, literally "not standing firm," from *constare* (see CONSTANT).] —**in·con·stan·cy** *n.* —**in·con·stant·ly** *adv.*

in·con·test·a·ble /inkən téstəb'l/ *adj.* impossible to question or dispute [Late 17thC. Directly or via French from medieval Latin *incontestabilis*, literally "unanswerable," from *contestari* (see CONTEST).] —**in·con·test·a·bil·i·ty** /inkən testə bíllətee/ *n.* —**in·con·test·a·ble·ness** /-téstəb'lnəss/ *n.* —**in·con·test·a·bly** *adv.*

in·con·ti·nence /in kóntənənss/ *n.* 1. MED INABILITY TO CONTROL URINATION OR DEFECATION an inability to control urination or defecation, so that either may take place involuntarily 2. LACK OF SEXUAL CONTROL lack of sexual restraint or self-control 3. LACK OF MODERATION lack of moderation in an action or emotion (*literary*)

in·con·ti·nent[1] /in kóntənənt/ *adj.* 1. MED UNABLE TO CONTROL BLADDER OR BOWELS unable to control the bladder or bowels and liable to urinate or defecate involuntarily 2. LACKING SEXUAL CONTROL lacking restraint in sexual matters, or engaging in premarital or extramarital sex 3. UNRESTRAINED unrestrained and uncontrolled (*literary*) [14thC. Directly or via French from the Latin stem *incontinent-*, literally "not holding together," from *continere* (see CONTAIN).] —**in·con·ti·nent·ly** *adv.*

in·con·ti·nent[2] /in kóntənənt/ *adv.* immediately, or abruptly and hastily (*archaic*) [15thC. From Old French *incontinent*, from late Latin *in continenti (tempore)* "in continuous (time)" (i.e., without a break), from *continens*, the present participle of *continere* (see CONTAIN).]

in·con·trol·la·ble /inkən trṓləb'l/ *adj.* = **uncontrollable** —**in·con·trol·la·bly** *adv.*

in·con·tro·vert·i·ble /in kóntrə vúrtəb'l/ *adj.* certain, undeniable, and not open to question —**in·con·tro·vert·i·bil·i·ty** /in kóntrə vùrtə bíllətee/ *n.* —**in·con·tro·vert·i·ble·ness** /in kóntrə vúrtəb'lnəss/ *n.* —**in·con·tro·vert·i·bly** *adv.*

in·con·ven·ience /inkən veényənss/ *n.* 1. LACK OF CONVENIENCE the quality or fact of being inconvenient or causing discomfort, difficulty, or annoyance 2. AN ANNOYANCE something that causes difficulties or annoyance ■ *vt.* (**-ienced, -ienc·ing, -ienc·es**) CAUSE DIFFICULTY TO to cause somebody difficulties, especially relatively minor or unnecessary ones, or unwanted extra effort, work, or trouble

in·con·ven·ient /inkən veényənt/ *adj.* causing or involving difficulties or unwanted extra effort, work, or trouble [Mid-17thC. Via Old French from the Latin stem *inconvenient-* "incongruous," literally "not fitting together," from *convenire* (see CONVENE).] —**in·con·ven·ient·ly** *adv.*

in·con·vert·i·ble /inkən vúrtəb'l/ *adj.* FIN 1. NOT EXCHANGEABLE FOR GOLD not exchangeable for gold or silver 2. NOT EXCHANGEABLE FOR FOREIGN CURRENCY not exchangeable for the currency of another country [Mid-17thC. Directly or via French from late Latin *inconvertibilis*, literally "unchangeable," from *convertire* (see CONVERT).] —**in·con·vert·i·bil·i·ty** /inkən vùrtə bíllətee/ *n.* —**in·con·vert·i·ble·ness** /inkən vúrtəb'lnəss/ *n.* —**in·con·vert·i·bly** *adv.*

in·con·vinc·i·ble /inkən vínsəb'l/ *adj.* impossible or very difficult to convince —**in·con·vinc·i·bil·i·ty** /inkən vínsə bíllətee/ *n.* —**in·con·vinc·i·ble·ness** /inkən vínsəb'lnəss/ *n.* —**in·con·vinc·i·bly** *adv.*

in·co·or·di·nate /in kō áwrd'nət/ *adj.* lacking coordination —**in·co·or·di·nate·ly** *adv.*

in·co·or·di·na·tion /inkō àwrd'n áysh'n/ *n.* 1. MED INABILITY TO CONTROL MUSCLES an inability to control voluntary muscular movements 2. INCONSISTENT APPROACH lack of organization or a consistent approach (*formal*)

incorp. *abbr.* incorporated

in·cor·po·rate *v.* /in káwrpə ràyt/ (**-rat·ed, -rat·ing, -rates**) 1. *vti.* JOIN WITH SOMETHING THAT EXISTS to unite or combine something with, or include it within, something already formed 2. *vti.* MERGE THINGS to merge, or to combine one thing with another, so as to form a united whole 3. *vti.* COMM FORM OR BECOME CORPORATION to form a corporation, or to give something the legal form of a corporation 4. *vt.* GIVE REAL FORM TO to give material form to something (*formal*) ■ *adj.* /in káwrpərət/ 1. UNITED merged into a united whole (*formal*) 2. COMM LEGALLY A CORPORATION legally established as a corporation [14thC. From late Latin *incorporare*, literally "to make into a body," from *corpus* "body" (see CORPUS).] —**in·cor·po·ra·ble** /in káwrpərəb'l/ *adj.* —**in·cor·po·ra·tion** /in kàwrpə ráysh'n/ *n.* —**in·cor·po·ra·tive** /in káwrpə ràytiv/ *adj.* —**in·cor·po·ra·tor** /-ràytər/ *n.*

in·cor·po·rat·ed /in káwrpə ràytəd/ *adj.* 1. LEGALLY CONSTITUTED AS A CORPORATION constituted in the legal form of a corporation 2. COMBINED AS ONE WHOLE combined or merged into one thing

in·cor·po·re·al /in kawr páwree əl/ *adj.* 1. WITHOUT PHYSICAL BEING without a physical body, or existing solely as a spirit (*formal*) 2. LAW ATTACHED TO SOMETHING MATERIAL used to describe a legal entity that has no material existence of its own but connected to an actual object such as a patent or copyright [15thC. Formed from Latin *incorporeus*, literally "having no body," from *corpus* "body" (see CORPUS).] —**in·cor·po·re·al·ly** *adv.*

in·cor·rect /inkə rékt/ *adj.* 1. ERRONEOUS wrong, false, or inaccurate 2. UNFITTING not appropriate, suitable, or proper [15thC. Directly or via French from Latin *incorrectus*, literally "uncorrected," from *correct-*, the past participle stem of *corrigere* (see CORRECT).] —**in·cor·rect·ly** *adv.* —**in·cor·rect·ness** *n.*

in·cor·ri·gi·ble /in káwrijəb'l/ *adj.* 1. IMPOSSIBLE TO CHANGE impossible to correct or reform ○ *incorrigible cynics* 2. UNRULY AND UNMANAGEABLE very difficult to control or keep in order ■ *n.* SOMEBODY OR SOMETHING INCORRIGIBLE somebody or something that is impossible or very difficult to change [14thC. Directly or via French from Latin *incorrigibilis*, literally "not able to be corrected," from *corrigere* (see CORRECT).] —**in·cor·ri·gi·bil·i·ty** /in kàwrijə bíllətee/ *n.* —**in·cor·ri·gi·bly** *adv.*

in·cor·rupt /inkə rúpt/ *adj.* 1. UNSULLIED morally pure and uncorrupted (*formal*) 2. NOT DECOMPOSED unaffected by decay or spoiling (*archaic*) 3. FREE OF MISTAKES without errors or alterations (*formal*) [14thC. From Latin *incorruptus*, literally "not destroyed," from *corruptus* (see CORRUPT).] —**in·cor·rup·tion** /inkə rúpshən/ *n.* —**in·cor·rupt·ly** /-rúptlee/ *adv.*

in·cor·rupt·i·ble /inkə rúptəb'l/ *adj.* 1. INCAPABLE OF BEING CORRUPTED incapable of being morally corrupted, especially incapable of being bribed or motivated by selfish or base interests **2.** NOT SUBJECT TO DECOMPOSITION incapable of being affected by decay or decomposition —**in·cor·rupt·i·bil·i·ty** /ìnkə rúptə bíllətee/ *n.* —**in·cor·rupt·i·bly** *adv.*

incr. *abbr.* **1.** increase **2.** increased **3.** increasing **4.** increment

in·crease *vti.* /in kreéss/ (**-creased, -creas·ing, -creas·es**) MAKE OR BECOME LARGER OR GREATER to make something or become larger in number, quantity, or degree ■ *n.* /ín kreèss/ **1.** RISE IN SOMETHING a rise to a greater number, quantity, or degree, or the amount by which something is increased **2.** BECOMING OR MAKING LARGER OR GREATER the process of becoming or of making something larger in number, quantity, or degree, [14thC. Via Old French *encreistre* from Latin *increscere*, from *crescere* "to grow" (see CRESCENT).] —**in·creas·a·ble** *adj.* —**in·creas·er** *n.*

WORD KEY: SYNONYMS

increase, expand, enlarge, extend, augment, intensify, amplify

CORE MEANING: make larger or greater

increase a general word meaning to become larger or greater; **expand** to make larger, usually in scope as well as size. It can also be used to talk about making something such as an account or report seem larger or more substantial by adding more details; **enlarge** make bigger; **extend** to make larger in terms of length or to cause to cover a wider area; **augment** to add to something in order to make it larger or more substantial; **intensify** to cause something such as an emotion or reaction to be stronger or more extreme; **amplify** to make a sound louder. It can also be used to talk about making an effect greater.

in·creas·ing·ly /in kreéssinglee/ *adv.* ever increasing over time ○ *"As Election Day approaches, there is no front-runner, and the insults and accusations from both sides have been increasingly frequent and bellicose."* (Susan K. Livio, *Election '96: Senate Race*; 1996)

in·cre·ate /inkree áyt, in kreé ət/ *adj.* existing without having been created (*archaic or literary*) [Mid-16thC. From Latin *increatus*, literally "not created," from *creatus*, the past participle of *creare* (see CREATE).] —**in·cre·ate·ly** *adv.*

in·cred·i·ble /in kréddəb'l/ *adj.* **1.** BEYOND BELIEF impossible or very difficult to believe **2.** MORE THAN THOUGHT POSSIBLE unexpectedly or astonishingly large or great (*informal*) ○ *There's an incredible amount of food still left.* **3.** AMAZING very surprising ○ *It's incredible how many people have turned up.* **4.** EXCELLENT extraordinarily good, talented, or enjoyable (*informal*) [15thC. From Latin *incredibilis*, literally "not believable," from *credere* "to believe."] —**in·cred·i·bil·i·ty** /in krèddə bíllətee/ *n.* —**in·cred·i·bly** *adv.*

in·cre·du·li·ty /ìnkrə dóolətee/ *n.* a state or feeling of disbelief

in·cred·u·lous /in kréjələss/ *adj.* **1.** UNWILLING TO BELIEVE unable or unwilling to believe something or completely unconvinced by it **2.** SHOWING DISBELIEF showing or characterized by disbelief [Late 16thC. Formed from Latin *incredulus*, literally "not believing," from *credulus* (see CREDULOUS).] —**in·cred·u·lous·ly** *adv.* —**in·cred·u·lous·ness** *n.*

in·cre·ment /íng krə mənt/ *n.* **1.** INCREASE IN SOMETHING an addition to or increase in the amount or size of something, especially one of a series of small, often regular or planned increases **2.** ACT OF INCREASING the act or process of increasing **3.** MATH SMALL CHANGE IN MATHEMATICAL VALUE a small positive or negative change in the value of a mathematical variable or function [15thC. From Latin *incrementum* "growth, increase," from *increscere* (see INCREASE).] —**in·cre·men·tal** /ìngkrə mént'l/ *adj.* —**in·cre·men·tal·ly** *adv.*

in·cre·men·tal·ism /ìng kri mént'lizəm/ *n.* = **gradualism**

in·cres·cent /in kréss'nt/ *adj.* showing a lighted surface area, especially that of the Moon, that is increasing in size [Late 16thC. From Latin *increscere* (see INCREASE).]

in·crim·i·nate /in krímmi nàyt/ (**-nat·ed, -nat·ing, -nates**) *vt.* **1.** MAKE APPEAR GUILTY to provide evidence of somebody's guilt or make somebody appear guilty of a crime or mistake **2.** LAW ACCUSE OF WRONGDOING to accuse somebody of a crime or error [Mid-18thC. From late Latin *incriminat*, the past participle stem of *incriminare*, literally "to make criminal," from *crimen* (see CRIME).] —**in·crim·i·na·tion** /in krìmmi náysh'n/ *n.* —**in·crim·i·na·tor** /in krímmi nàytər/ *n.* —**in·crim·i·na·to·ry** /in krímminə tàwree/ *adj.*

in·cross /ín kràwss/ *n.* INBRED ORGANISM an organism produced through inbreeding within the same strain or breed ■ *vti.* (**-crossed, -cross·ing, -cross·es**) PRODUCE BY INBREEDING to produce an organism by inbreeding or to be produced in this way. ◊ **outcross**

in·crowd *n.* a small, fashionable, and exclusive or influential group, especially one that others want to be part of because of its prestige (*informal*)

in·crust *vti.* = **encrust**

in·crust·a·tion *n.* = **encrustation**

in·cu·bate /íngkyə bàyt/ (**-bat·ed, -bat·ing, -bates**) *v.* **1.** *vti.* ZOOL SIT ON EGGS to keep eggs warm by sitting on them so that the embryos inside can develop and hatch, or to be kept warm in this way **2.** *vti.* MED KEEP BABY IN INCUBATOR to keep a premature or unwell baby inside a controlled environment in order to keep it alive and assist its growth and development, or to be kept in such an environment **3.** *vti.* MICROBIOL GROW MICROORGANISMS IN CONTROLLED ENVIRONMENT to keep cells or microorganisms at a controlled temperature in or on a medium so that they multiply, or to be kept in or such a medium **4.** *vi.* DEVELOP IN FAVORABLE ENVIRONMENT to be kept, or to develop while being kept, in a favorable environment, e.g., under a parent bird's body, in a incubator, or in a growth medium **5.** *vti.* MED BUILD UP DISEASE-PRODUCING GERMS to develop an infection, through the reproduction of germs, to the point at which the first signs of a disease appear, or to be developed in this way **6.** *vti.* GRADUALLY BRING SOMETHING INTO BEING to form or develop something, such as a plan or an idea, slowly and quietly over a period of time, or to be formed or developed in this way [Mid-17thC. From Latin *incubare*, literally "to lie down on," from *cubare* "to lie down."] —**in·cu·ba·tive** *adj.*

in·cu·ba·tion /ìng kyə báysh'n/ *n.* **1.** MED MAINTENANCE OF BABY IN CONTROLLED ENVIRONMENT the keeping of a premature or unwell baby in an environment in which the temperature, humidity, and oxygen levels can be easily controlled **2.** MICROBIOL CONTROLLED GROWTH OF MICROORGANISMS the maintenance of cells or microorganisms under a controlled temperature in or on a medium so that they can multiply **3.** MED GROWTH OF DISEASE-CAUSING MICROORGANISMS the development of an infection inside the body to the point at which the first signs of disease become apparent **4.** GRADUAL DEVELOPMENT the slow development of something, especially through thought and planning **5.** = **incubation period** —**in·cu·ba·tion·al** *adj.*

in·cu·ba·tion pe·ri·od *n.* the period between the time somebody is infected with a disease and the appearance of its first symptoms

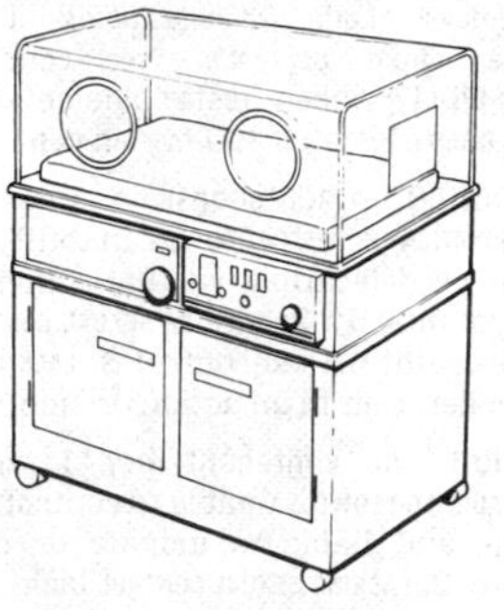

Incubator

in·cu·ba·tor /íng kyə bàytər/ *n.* **1.** MED HOSPITAL APPARATUS FOR PREMATURE BABIES a hospital apparatus, usually a transparent box, in which a premature or unwell baby is kept in a controlled environment to protect it from infection and assist its growth and development. Incubators regulate temperature, humidity, and oxygen levels. **2.** ZOOL DEVICE TO NURTURE SOMETHING an apparatus in which the temperature is kept at a constant level so that eggs can be artificially hatched or cells and microorganisms can multiply in or on a growth medium **3.** SURROUNDINGS FAVORABLE TO PROGRESS a place, organization, or environment that promotes the growth or development of something ○ *"Start-ups looking for cost-efficient office space and support services can consider joining a local business incubator."* (Barbara Sturm, *Taking another look at the charms of Newark, Asbury Park Press*; 1997)

in·cu·bus /íng kyəbəss/ (*plural* **-bi** /íng kyə bì/ *or* **-bus·es**) *n.* **1.** MYTHOL MALE DEMON HAVING SEX WITH WOMEN a male demon that was believed in medieval times to have sexual intercourse with women while they were asleep **2.** CAUSE OF MENTAL DISTRESS something that causes somebody much worry or anxiety, especially a nightmare or obsession (*literary*) [14thC. Via late Latin, "nightmare," from, ultimately, Latin *incubare* "to lie down on." The underlying meaning is "one that lies down on another."]

in·cu·des plural of **incus**

in·cul·cate /in kúl kàyt, ín kul kàyt/ (**-cat·ed** *formal*, **-cat·ed, -cat·ing, -cates**) *vt.* to fix something firmly in somebody's mind through frequent and forceful repetition [Mid-16thC. From Latin *inculcat-*, the past participle stem of *inculcare*, literally "to stamp in," from *calcare* "to step on, press in" (see CAULK).] —**in·cul·ca·tion** /ìn kul káysh'n/ *n.* —**in·cul·ca·tor** /in kúl kàytər, ín kul-/ *n.*

in·cul·pa·ble /in kúlpəb'l/ *adj.* free of guilt and blame (*formal*) [Late 15thC. From late Latin *inculpabilis*, literally "not guilty," from *culpare* (see CULPABLE).] —**in·cul·pa·bil·i·ty** /in kùlpə bíllətee/ *n.* —**in·cul·pa·ble·ness** /in kúlpəb'lnəss/ *n.* —**in·cul·pa·bly** *adv.*

in·cul·pate /in kúl pàyt/ (**-pat·ed, -pat·ing, -pates**) *vt.* to incriminate somebody or put the blame for something on somebody (*formal*) [Late 18thC. From late Latin *inculpat-*, the past participle stem of *inculpare*, literally "to put blame on," from Latin *culpa* "blame, fault" (source of English *culpable* and *culprit*).] —**in·cul·pa·tion** /ìn kul páysh'n/ *n.* —**in·cul·pa·to·ry** /in kúlpə tàwree/ *adj.*

in·cult /in kúlt/ *adj.* (*archaic*) **1.** AGRIC NOT FARMED not used for farming or gardening **2.** UNCOUTH coarse, uncouth, and without culture or refinement [Late 16thC. From Latin *incultus*, literally "uncultivated," from *cultus*, the past participle of *colere* "to inhabit, cultivate, worship."]

in·cum·ben·cy /in kúmbənssee/ (*plural* **-cies**) *n.* (*formal*) **1.** TENURE OF OFFICE the period of time during which somebody occupies an official post **2.** OFFICIAL POST an official position, especially in a church or political organization **3.** EXISTENCE AS A DUTY the obligatory nature of something or the fact of its being a duty or obligation that must be performed **4.** OBLIGATION something such as a duty that is necessary or obligatory

in·cum·bent /in kúmbənt/ *adj.* **1.** OBLIGATORY necessary as a result of a duty, responsibility, or obligation (*formal*) ○ *It is incumbent on me to ensure that our generous hosts should not go unthanked.* **2.** IN OFFICE currently holding a position or office **3.** ON TOP OF SOMETHING resting, lying, or leaning on something (*archaic or technical*) ○ *incumbent strata* ■ *n.* SOMEBODY IN OFFICE somebody currently holding an official post, especially in a church or political organization ○ *He took comfort in the fact that incumbents are often offered the chance of serving a second term of office.* [15thC. From Latin *incumbent-*, the present participle stem of *incumbere*, literally "to lie in or on," from *-cumbere* "to lie down."] —**in·cum·bent·ly** *adv.*

in·cum·ber *vt.* = **encumber**

in·cu·na·ble /in kyóonəb'l/ *n.* = **incunabulum** [Late 19thC. Via French from Latin *incunabulum* (see INCUNABULA).]

in·cu·nab·u·la /ìnkyə nábbyələ/ *npl.* the early stages or beginnings of something (*literary*) [Early 19thC. From Latin, "swaddling clothes, infancy," from *cunae* "cradle." Ultimately from an Indo-European word meaning "place to lie" that is also the ancestor of English *cemetery.*]

in·cu·nab·u·lum /ìnkyə nábyələm/ *n.* PRINTING a book printed from movable type before 1501 [Early 19thC. From Latin, singular of *incunabula* (see INCUNABULA).]

in·cur /in kúr/ (**-curred, -cur·ring, -curs**) *vt.* **1.** EXPERIENCE SOMETHING UNPLEASANT to suffer something such as somebody's anger or a financial loss as a result of an action ○ *incur their wrath* **2.** ACQUIRE A BURDEN to become burdened with something such as a debt [15thC. Via Old French *encourir* from Latin *incurrere*, literally "to run into," from *currere* "to run" (see CURRENT).] —**in·cur·ra·ble** *adj.* —**in·cur·rence** *n.*

in·cur·a·ble /in kyóorəb'l/ *adj.* **1.** IMPOSSIBLE TO CURE not possible to cure **2.** IMPOSSIBLE TO CHANGE not possible to change ■ *n.* SOMEBODY OR SOMETHING IMPOSSIBLE TO CURE somebody or something with an illness or condition that cannot be cured [14thC. Directly or via French from late Latin *incurabilis*, literally "not curable," from *cura* (see

CURE).] —**in·cur·a·bil·i·ty** /in kyo͝orə billətee/ *n.* —**in·cur·a·ble·ness** /in kyo͝orəb'lnəss/ *n.* —**in·cur·a·bly** *adv.*

in·cu·ri·ous /in kyo͝oree əss/ *adj.* showing no curiosity about or interest in something —**in·cu·ri·os·i·ty** /in kyo͝oree óssətee/ *n.* —**in·cu·ri·ous·ly** /in kyo͝oree əsslee/ *adv.* —**in·cu·ri·ous·ness** *n.*

in·cur·rent /in kúrənt/ *adj.* flowing or running inward into something [Late 16thC. From Latin *incurrere* (see INCUR).]

in·cur·sion /in kúrzh'n/ *n.* **1.** RAID a brief, hostile, and usually sudden invasion of somebody's territory **2.** UNWELCOME INTRUSION the act of flowing, running, or intruding into something, usually with unpleasant or damaging effects (*formal*) [15thC. Directly or via Old French from the Latin stem *incursion-*, literally "a running in," from *incurs-*, the past participle stem of *incurrere* (see INCUR).] —**in·cur·sive** /in kúrsiv/ *adj.*

in·cur·vate *vti.* /in kur vàyt, in kúr vàyt/ (**-vat·ed, -vat·ing, -vates**) = **incurve** ■ *adj.* /in kúr vàyt, in kúrvət/ INWARDLY CURVED curved or bending inward [Late 16thC. From Latin *incurvat-*, the past participle stem of *incurvare*, literally "to bend inwards" from *curvus* (see CURVE).] —**in·cur·va·tion** /in kúr váysh'n/ *n.* —**in·cur·va·ture** /in kúrvə cho͝or, in kúrvəchər/ *n.*

in·curve /in kúrv/ *vti.* (**-curved, -curv·ing, -curves**) CURVE INWARD to curve inward, or to give something an inward curve ■ *n.* INWARD CURVE a curve that bends inwards

in·cus /íngkəss/ (*plural* **-cu·des** /ing kyo͞o de͞ez/) *n.* **1.** ANAT SMALL BONE IN THE MIDDLE EAR a small bone, shaped like an anvil, found in the middle ear of mammals between the malleus and stapes bones. ◊ **malleus, stapes 2.** (*plural* **-cus**) METEOROL = **thunderhead** [Mid-17thC. From Latin *incus* "anvil," from, ultimately, *incudere* (see INCUSE).] —**in·cu·dal** /íngkyəd'l, in kyo͞od'l/ *adj.* —**in·cu·date** /íngkyə dàyt, in kyo͞odət/ *adj.*

in·cuse /in kyo͞oz/ *adj.* STAMPED INTO COIN AS A DESIGN hammered, stamped, or impressed on a coin as a design ■ *n.* STAMPED-IN COIN DESIGN a design stamped, hammered, or impressed on a coin ■ *vt.* (**-cused, -cus·ing, -cus·es**) IMPRESS COIN DESIGN to hammer or stamp a design on a coin [Early 19thC. From Latin *incus-*, past participle stem of *incudere*, literally "to hammer on," from *cudere* "to beat."]

IND *abbr.* in God's Name [Latin *in nomine domini*]

ind., **ind** *abbr.* **1.** independence **2.** independent **3.** index **4.** indicative **5.** indirect **6.** industrial **7.** industry

Ind., **Ind** *abbr.* **1.** India **2.** Indian **3.** Indiana **4.** Indies

in·da·mine /in da͞abə/ *n.* an organic base that forms blue or green salts and is used in making dyes [Late 19thC. Coined from IND- + AMINE.]

in·debt·ed /in déttəd/ *adj.* **1.** IN DEBT owing money to somebody **2.** OBLIGATED TO SOMEBODY obliged or grateful to somebody for something such as assistance or a favor received [13thC. Alteration of Old French *endetté*, the past participle of *endetter*, literally "to put in debt," from *dette* (see DEBT).]

in·debt·ed·ness /in déttədnəss/ *n.* **1.** STATE OF BEING IN SOMEBODY'S DEBT the condition of owing money to somebody or owing somebody thanks **2.** AMOUNT OWED the total amount somebody owes

in·de·cen·cy /in de͞ess'nsee/ (*plural* **-cies**) *n.* **1.** OFFENSIVENESS offensiveness according to accepted standards, especially in sexual matters **2.** INDECENT ACT an act that offends against accepted standards of decency

in·de·cent /in de͞ess'nt/ *adj.* **1.** OFFENDING PUBLIC MORAL STANDARDS unacceptable and offensive to accepted standards, especially in sexual matters **2.** IMPROPER inappropriate under the circumstances and disapproved of by others ○ *The funeral was arranged with indecent haste.* [Late 16thC. Directly or via French from the Latin stem *indecent-*, literally "not fitting," from *decens* (see DECENT).] —**in·de·cent·ly** *adv.*

in·de·cent as·sault *n.* a sexual assault on somebody that does not involve rape

in·de·cent ex·po·sure *n.* the criminal offense of deliberately displaying part of the body, usually the genitals, to somebody else in public

in·de·cid·u·ous *adj.* evergreen (*technical*)

in·de·ci·pher·a·ble /indi sífərəb'l/ *adj.* impossible or very difficult to read or understand —**in·de·ci·pher·a·bil·i·ty** /indi sífərə billətee/ *n.* —**in·de·ci·pher·a·ble·ness** /indi sífərəb'lnəss/ *n.* —**in·de·ci·pher·a·bly** *adv.*

in·de·ci·sion /indi sízh'n/ *n.* inability to reach a decision or uncertainty resulting from somebody's inability or refusal to reach a decision [Mid-18thC. From French *indécision*, literally "indecisiveness," from *decision* "decision."]

in·de·ci·sive /indi síssiv/ *adj.* **1.** UNABLE TO DECIDE unable or reluctant to make decisions generally or to come to a decision about something in particular **2.** WITHOUT A CLEAR OUTCOME not producing a clear result, especially a clear victory for somebody —**in·de·ci·sive·ly** *adv.* —**in·de·ci·sive·ness** *n.*

in·de·clin·a·ble /indi klínəb'l/ *adj.* GRAM existing in one form only and having no grammatical inflections, e.g., no plural form [15thC. Via French from Latin *indeclinabilis*, literally "not declinable," from *declinare* (see DECLINE).] —**in·de·clin·a·bly** *adv.*

in·dec·o·rous /in dékərəss/ *adj.* somewhat rude or shocking because of being considered socially unacceptable [Late 17thC. Formed from Latin *indecorus*, literally "not seemly," from *decorus* (see DECOROUS).] —**in·dec·o·rous·ly** *adv.* —**in·dec·o·rous·ness** *n.*

in·de·cor·um /indi káwrəm/ *n.* **1.** IMPROPER BEHAVIOR behavior that offends against what is socially acceptable and polite **2.** INDECOROUS ACT an indecorous action [Late 16thC. From Latin, formed from *indecorus* (see INDECOROUS).]

in·deed /in de͞ed/ CORE MEANING: an adverb indicating agreement with or confirmation of something ○ *He is indeed an actor.* ○ *"Do you know that man?" "Indeed I do."*

adv. **1.** WHAT IS MORE used to introduce a statement that strengthens or adds to a point just made ○ *I am willing, indeed eager, to speak on your behalf.* **2.** FOR EMPHASIS used to give additional emphasis to a descriptive word or phrase (*used at the end of a clause*) ○ *The news, I learned, was grim indeed.* **3.** EMPHASIZE A QUESTION used to emphasize a question and usually to express surprise or doubt at the same time (*often used as a question itself*) [14thC. From IN + DEED; the underlying meaning is "in fact."]

indef. *abbr.* indefinite

in·de·fat·i·ga·ble /indi fáttigəb'l/ *adj.* never showing any sign of getting tired or of relaxing an effort [Early 17thC. Directly or via obsolete French *indéfatigable* from, ultimately, Latin *defatigare* "to tire out," from *fatigare* (source of English *fatigue*).] —**in·de·fat·i·ga·bil·i·ty** /indi fáttigə billətee/ *n.* —**in·de·fat·i·ga·ble·ness** /indi fáttigəb'lnəss/ *n.* —**in·de·fat·i·ga·bly** *adv.*

in·de·fea·si·ble /indi fe͞ezəb'l/ *adj.* LAW impossible to annul, make void, or forfeit —**in·de·fea·si·bil·i·ty** /indi fe͞ezə billətee/ *n.* —**in·de·fea·si·bly** *adv.*

in·de·fec·ti·ble /indi féktəb'l/ *adj.* (*formal*) **1.** ENDURING not affected by decay or failure **2.** FLAWLESS without fault or imperfection [Mid-17thC. Formed from obsolete *defectible* "liable to fail," from late Latin *defectibilis* from *defectus* (see DEFECT).] —**in·de·fec·ti·bil·i·ty** /indi féktə billətee/ *n.* —**in·de·fec·ti·bly** /indi féktəblee/ *adv.*

in·de·fen·si·ble /indi fénsəb'l/ *adj.* **1.** PERMITTING NO EXCUSE too bad or blameworthy to be in any way justified or excused ○ *indefensible conduct* **2.** INVALID not based on fact, proof, or sound reasoning ○ *an indefensible argument* **3.** UNABLE TO BE PROTECTED incapable of being defended from attack —**in·de·fen·si·bil·i·ty** /indi fénsə billətee/ *n.* —**in·de·fen·si·ble·ness** /indi fénsəb'lnəss/ *n.* —**in·de·fen·si·bly** *adv.*

in·de·fin·a·ble /indi fínəb'l/ *adj.* INCAPABLE OF DEFINITION impossible or very difficult to describe, define, or analyze ■ *n.* SOMETHING HARD TO DEFINE something that is impossible or very difficult to describe, define, or analyze —**in·de·fin·a·bil·i·ty** /indi fínə billətee/ *n.* —**in·de·fin·a·ble·ness** /indi fínəb'lnəss/ *n.* —**in·de·fin·a·bly** *adv.*

in·def·i·nite /in déffənət/ *adj.* **1.** UNLIMITED not fixed or limited in length, size, duration, or quantity **2.** NOT CLEAR not clear or not precisely defined or fixed **3.** VAGUE AND UNCERTAIN unable or unwilling to give a clear indication of thoughts or plans **4.** BOT TOO MANY TO COUNT consisting of units that are too numerous to be counted precisely ○ *indefinite stamens* **5.** BOT = **indeterminate** [Mid-16thC. From Latin *indefinitus*, literally "having no limits," from *definire* "to define."] —**in·def·i·nite·ness** *n.*

in·def·i·nite ar·ti·cle *n.* a word such as "a" or "an" in English that designates a noun referring to something that has not been mentioned before and is simply any one of its kind ○ *Choose a book and write a review of it.*

in·def·i·nite in·te·gral *n.* an integral that when differentiated equals a given function

in·def·i·nite·ly /in déffənətlee/ *adv.* **1.** FOR UNSPECIFIED LENGTH OF TIME for a length of time that has no fixed or obvious end **2.** UNSPECIFICALLY OR VAGUELY in a general and unspecific or vague and imprecise way

in·def·i·nite pro·noun *n.* a pronoun, such as "someone," "nothing," or "anything" in English, that does not refer to a particular person or thing

in·de·his·cent /indi híss'nt/ *adj.* not opening up to release seeds when ripe —**in·de·his·cence** *n.*

in·del·i·ble /in délləb'l/ *adj.* **1.** PERMANENT impossible to remove and therefore remaining forever **2.** CONTAINING AN INDELIBLE SUBSTANCE containing indelible ink or lead ○ *an indelible pencil* [15thC. Directly or via French *indélébile* from Latin *indelebilis*, literally "not defaceable," from *delere* "to blot out, deface."] —**in·del·i·bil·i·ty** /in dèllə billətee/ *n.* —**in·del·i·ble·ness** /in déləb'lnəss/ *n.* —**in·del·i·bly** *adv.*

in·del·i·cate /in déllikət/ *adj.* **1.** TACTLESS OR OFFENSIVE tactless, crude, or too frank, and therefore causing or likely to cause offense **2.** PHYSICALLY UNREFINED crude, rough, or coarse in texture or appearance —**in·del·i·ca·cy** *n.* —**in·del·i·cate·ly** *adv.* —**in·del·i·cate·ness** *n.*

in·dem·ni·fy /in démni fì/ (**-fied, -fy·ing, -fies**) *vt.* **1.** INSURE AGAINST LOSS to provide somebody with protection, especially financial protection, against possible loss, damage, or liability **2.** REIMBURSE AFTER LOSS to pay compensation to somebody for damage, loss, or liability incurred [Early 17thC. Formed from Latin *indemnis*, literally "not injured," from *damnum* "injury."] —**in·dem·ni·fi·ca·tion** /in dèmnifi káysh'n/ *n.* —**in·dem·ni·fi·er** /in démni fìr/ *n.*

in·dem·ni·ty /in démnitee/ (*plural* **-ties**) *n.* **1.** INSURANCE protection or insurance against possible loss or damage **2.** LAW EXEMPTION FROM PENALTIES legal exemption from penalties or liabilities **3.** COMPENSATION a compensation paid for loss or damage [15thC. Via French from late Latin *indemnitas* "security for damage," from Latin *indemnis* (see INDEMNIFY).]

in·de·mon·stra·ble /indi mónstrəb'l/ *adj.* impossible to prove or demonstrate (*formal*) —**in·de·mon·stra·bil·i·ty** /indi monstrə billətee/ *n.* —**in·de·mon·stra·ble·ness** /indi mónstrəb'lnəss/ *n.* —**in·de·mon·stra·bly** *adv.*

in·dene /ín de͞en/ *n.* a colorless liquid obtained from coal tar and petroleum that is used in making synthetic resins. Formula: C_9H_8. [Late 19thC. Coined from INDOLE + -ENE.]

in·dent[1] *v.* /in dént/ (**-dent·ed, -dent·ing, -dents**) **1.** *vti.* PRINTING BEGIN LINE IN FROM MARGIN to start a line or row some distance in from the margin **2.** *vt.* FORM RECESS IN to form a deep recess in something (*often passive*) **3.** *vt.* TEAR COPIED DOCUMENT IN HALF to tear a document, especially one containing two copies of the same text, in half along an irregular line **4.** *vt.* NOTCH to make jagged, notched, or serrated edges in something **5.** *vt.* FIT NOTCHED EDGES to join together two notched pieces of something **6.** *vt.* DRAW UP IN DUPLICATE to draw up a document in two or more exact copies **7.** *vt.* CONTRACT AS APPRENTICE to contract somebody as an apprentice (*archaic*) ■ *n.* /ín dènt, in dént/ **1.** PRINTING SPACE SET IN FROM MARGIN a blank space left between the margin and the beginning of a line or row **2.** INDENTURE an indenture (*archaic*) **3.** HISTORY CERTIFICATE FOR INTEREST ON PUBLIC DEBT a certificate issued by the federal or a state government for the principal or interest on public debt at the end of the American Revolution [14thC] —**in·dent·er** /in déntər/ *n.*

WORD KEY: ORIGIN

Etymologically, English has two separate words *indent*, although they have converged to a considerable extent over the centuries (particularly in the virtually shared derivative *indentation*). The one meaning "to make a hole or depression in" is simply a derivative of *dent*. ***Indent*** "to make notches in," however, owes its origin to Latin *dens* "tooth." This formed the basis of an Anglo-Latin verb *indentare* that denoted the drawing up of a contract between two parties on two identical documents that were cut along a matching line of notches or "teeth" that could subsequently be rejoined to prove their authenticity. A particular use of such contracts was between master craftsmen and their trainees, who hence became known as *indentured* apprentices.

in·dent[2] *vt.* /in dént/ (**-dent·ed, -dent·ing, -dents**) MAKE DENT IN to press something inward to form a dent ■ *n.* /ín dènt, in dént/ = **dent** *n.* 1 [14thC. Formed from IN- + DENT.]

in·den·ta·tion /in den táysh'n/ *n.* **1.** NOTCH OR RECESS a notch, recess, or hollowed-out place in something such as an edge, a boundary line, or a coast **2.** JAGGED EDGE a series of notches or recesses, or the edge formed by this **3.** PRINTING LEAVING SPACE AT BEGINNING OF LINE the leaving of space between the margin and the beginning of a line or row, or the blank space left **4.** ACT OF INDENTING the act of indenting something or the fact of being indented

in·den·ture /in déncher/ *n.* **1.** CONTRACT WITH APPRENTICE a contract committing an apprentice or servant to serve a master or employer for a specific period of time (*often plural*) **2.** WRITTEN AGREEMENT a written contract or agreement between two or more parties **3.** DUPLICATE DOCUMENT WITH TORN EDGE a document written in duplicate on a single sheet and torn in half so that the edges of the two resulting copies could be matched up to prove their authenticity **4.** AUTHORIZED LIST an official list or inventory that has been authenticated for use as a voucher **5.** INDENTATION an indentation (*archaic*) ■ *vti.* CONTRACT SOMEBODY FOR SERVICES to commit somebody to work as an apprentice or servant for a specified period of time by means of indentures —**in·den·ture·ship** *n.*

in·den·tured ser·vant *n.* an immigrant to North America during the 17th to 19th centuries who contracted to work for an employer for a number of years in exchange for passage and accommodation

in·de·pend·ence /inde péndenss/ *n.* **1.** FREEDOM FROM CONTROL freedom from dependence on or control by another person, organization, or state **2.** BEGINNING OF POLITICAL FREEDOM the date or point in time when a state achieves its political independence ○ *the first elections since independence*

In·de·pend·ence /inde péndenss/ city and county seat of Montgomery County, southeastern Kansas, situated 97 mi./156 km southeast of Wichita. Population: 9,942 (1990).

In·de·pend·ence Day *n.* a national holiday celebrated on July 4, to commemorate the signing of the Declaration of Independence in 1776

in·de·pend·en·cy /indi péndenssee/ (*plural* **-cies**) *n.* **1.** INDEPENDENCE independence (*archaic*) **2.** FREE TERRITORY an independent state or territory

In·de·pend·en·cy *n.* CHR the principle or policy that each local Christian church or congregation should be free of external ecclesiastical control

in·de·pend·ent /indi péndent/ *adj.* **1.** NOT CONTROLLED BY ANOTHER free from the authority, control, or domination of somebody or something else, especially not controlled by another state or organization and able to self-govern **2.** ABLE TO FUNCTION BY ITSELF able to operate or stand on its own because not dependent on another ○ *Each wheel has an independent suspension system.* **3.** SELF-SUPPORTING not forced to rely on another for money or support **4.** SHOWING CONFIDENCE IN SELF capable of thinking or acting without consultation with or guidance from others **5.** DONE WITHOUT OBSTRUCTION carried out or operating without interference or influence from interested parties ○ *an independent counsel* **6.** SUFFICIENT TO LIVE ON providing the means on which to live without having to work **7. in·de·pend·ent, In·de·pend·ent** POL NOT AFFILATED TO POLITICAL PARTY not a member, representative, or supporter of any political party **8.** MATH NOT SOLVABLE USING SOLUTION TO ANOTHER used to describe a system of equations in which no single equation is necessarily solved using a solution to the others **9.** STATS NOT AFFECTING OTHER VARIABLES in statistics, distributed in such a way that the value taken on by one variable leaves all others unaffected **10.** LOGIC NOT DEPENDENT ON AXIOM OR PROPOSITION not proved from another logical axiom or proposition ■ *n.* **1.** SOMEBODY OR SOMETHING UNAFFECTED BY OTHERS somebody or something that is free from control, dependence, or interference **2. in·de·pend·ent, In·de·pend·ent** POL NON-PARTY POLITICIAN somebody, especially a politician, who is not a member of, does not represent, or does not support any political party —**in·de·pend·ent·ly** *adv.*

In·de·pend·ent *n.* **1.** CHR SUPPORTER OF SELF-GOVERNING CHRISTIAN CHURCH somebody who believes that each Christian church or congregation should be free of external ecclesiastical control. Originally, Independents were members of a religious and political movement in 17th-century England that resulted in the organization of the Baptist and Congregationalist churches. **2.** = **independent** *n.* 2

in·de·pend·ent clause *n.* GRAM a clause that can stand on its own as a sentence, such as "She'll go on vacation" in the sentence "She'll go on vacation if she can get the money."

in·de·pend·ent in·ven·tion *n.* ANTHROP an invention arrived at independently, even though another group of people may have created the same invention in a different place at a different time

in·de·pend·ent var·i·a·ble *n.* **1.** MATH VARIABLE DETERMINING VALUE OF OTHERS the variable in a mathematical statement whose value, when specified, determines the value of another variable or other variables **2.** STATS VARIABLE MANIPULATED IN AN EXPERIMENT a variable that is manipulated in an experiment in order to observe the effect on another variable

in-depth *adj.* giving careful consideration to all details and aspects of a subject —**in depth** *adv.*

in·de·scrib·a·ble /indi skríbeb'l/ *adj.* **1.** IMPOSSIBLE TO DESCRIBE impossible or very difficult to describe ○ *an indescribable sensation* **2.** SO GREAT AS TO DEFY DESCRIPTION so intense or extreme as to defy description ○ *indescribable joy* —**in·de·scrib·a·bil·i·ty** /indi skríbe bíllatee/ *n.* —**in·de·scrib·a·ble·ness** /indí skríbeb'lness/ *n.* —**in·de·scrib·a·bly** *adv.*

in·de·struc·ti·ble /indi strúkteb'l/ *adj.* impossible or very difficult to destroy —**in·de·struc·ti·bil·i·ty** /indi strúkte bíllatee/ *n.* —**in·de·struc·ti·ble·ness** /indi strúkteb'lness/ *n.* —**in·de·struc·ti·bly** *adv.*

in·de·ter·min·a·ble /indi túrmineb'l/ *adj.* **1.** IMPOSSIBLE TO FIND OUT DEFINITELY impossible to determine or ascertain exactly **2.** IMPOSSIBLE TO ANSWER OR SETTLE impossible to resolve, answer, or settle [15thC. From late Latin *indeterminabilis*, literally "not definable," from *determinare* (see DETERMINE).] —**in·de·ter·min·a·ble·ness** *n.* —**in·de·ter·min·a·bly** *adv.*

in·de·ter·mi·na·cy prin·ci·ple *n.* = **uncertainty principle**

in·de·ter·mi·nate /indi túrminet/ *adj.* **1.** NOT KNOWN EXACTLY not known exactly, or impossible to work out **2.** VAGUE not definite, precise, or clear **3.** UNPREDICTABLE without a predictable result or outcome **4.** MATH HAVING NO NUMERICAL MEANING having no numerical value or meaning, e.g., the expressions "0/0" or "0^0" **5.** MATH WITH AN INFINITE NUMBER OF SOLUTIONS having an infinite number of solutions **6.** BOT GROWING AT TIP continuing to grow at the tip of the main stem instead of terminating in a flower bud [14thC. From Latin *indeterminatus*, literally "not defined," from *determinare* (see DETERMINE).] —**in·de·ter·mi·na·cy** *n.* —**in·de·ter·mi·nate·ly** *adv.* —**in·de·ter·mi·nate·ness** *n.* —**in·de·ter·mi·na·tion** /indi turmi náysh'n/ *n.*

in·de·ter·mi·nate sen·tence *n.* a prison sentence that has a wide or unlimited term, e.g., from one to five years, the date of release being determined by the prisoner's conduct and other factors

in·de·ter·mi·nate vow·el *n.* = **schwa**

in·de·ter·min·ism /indi túrmi nìzzem/ *n.* the philosophical theory that human beings have free will and their actions are not always and completely determined by previous events. ◊ **determinism** —**in·de·ter·min·ist** *n.* —**in·de·ter·min·is·tic** /indi turmi nístik/ *adj.*

in·dex /ín dèks/ *n.* (*plural* **-dex·es** *or* **-di·ces** /-di seez/) **1.** PUBL ALPHABETICAL REFERENCE LIST IN BOOK an alphabetical list, usually at the end of a book, of people, places, or topics, giving the numbers of the pages on which they are mentioned **2.** CATALOG an ordered list of the items that make up a set **3.** PUBLICATION LISTING ARTICLES a periodical or book that lists articles or other published works alphabetically by subject or author **4.** INDICATOR an indicator or sign of something ○ *One index of the situation's gravity is the severance of diplomatic relations.* **5.** TECH POINTER a pointer or needle, especially on a piece of scientific equipment **6.** PRINTING PRINTING CHARACTER a character ◊ used by printers to draw attention to a paragraph, section, or note **7.** = **thumb index 8.** MATH = **exponent** *n.* 4 **9.** MATH NUMBER GIVEN AS SUPERSCRIPT a number or variable given as a superscript before a square-root sign showing which root is to be taken **10.** MATH SUBSCRIPT OR SUPERSCRIPT IDENTIFYING AN ELEMENT a subscript or superscript numeral that identifies a particular element or range in a set or sequence **11.** NUMBER EXPRESSING RELATIONSHIP a scale, or a number on a scale, that expresses the price, value, or level of something in comparison to something else or to a previously established base number ■ *v.* **1.** *vti.* MAKE INDEX FOR to compile an index for something such as a book **2.** *vt.* PUT IN AN INDEX to enter something such as a name, title, subject, or quotation in an index **3.** *vt.* INDICATE to be a sign or indicator of something (*formal*) **4.** *vt.* ECON SUBJECT TO INDEXATION to subject a variable such as wages to indexation [Late 16thC. From Latin *index* "forefinger," literally "pointer." Ultimately from an Indo-European base meaning "to show."] —**in·dex·er** *n.*

In·dex *n.* = **Index Librorum Prohibitorum**

in·dex·a·tion /in dek sáysh'n/ *n.* the linking of wages, pensions, or other remuneration to an index representing the cost of living, so that they are automatically adjusted up or down as that rises or falls

in·dex case *n.* the first documented case of an illness in an epidemiological study

in·dex fin·ger *n.* the finger next to the thumb [From Latin *index* "forefinger" (see INDEX)]

in·dex fos·sil *n.* the fossil of an organism that is specific to a particular geologic age and is used for dating or identifying rocks or rock layers in which it is found

in·dex fund *n.* a mutual fund composed of companies listed in an important stock market index in order to match the market's overall performance

In·dex Li·bro·rum Pro·hib·i·to·rum *n.* a list formerly compiled by the Roman Catholic Church of books and publications that Church members were forbidden to read [From Latin, "list of forbidden books"]

in·dex num·ber *n.* a number used to indicate the change in a value or quantity, e.g., a price or unemployment, when compared with the level of that value or quantity at an earlier time. The base level is usually arbitrarily set at 100, and the increase or decrease in index numbers over time is often expressed as a percentage change.

in·dex of re·frac·tion *n.* the ratio of the speed of refracted light in a vacuum or reference medium to its speed in the medium under examination. Symbol *n*

India

In·di·a /índee e/ country in southern Asia, the second largest in the world by population and the seventh largest by area. Language: Hindi, English. Currency: rupee. Capital: New Delhi. Population: 966,783,171 (1997). Area: 1,195,063 sq. mi./3,095,472 sq. km. Official name **Republic of India**

In·di·a ink *n.* **1.** BLACK PIGMENT USED IN INK a black pigment made from lampblack and a binding agent and shaped into cakes or sticks **2.** LIQUID BLACK INK a liquid black ink made from a pigment that is a mixture of lampblack and a binding agent

In·di·a·man /índee emen/ (*plural* **-men** /-men/) *n.* a large merchant sailing ship that was formerly used to transport goods to and from India [Early 18thC. From INDIA + MAN "ship," as in *man of war.*]

In·di·an /índee en/ *n.* **1.** SOMEBODY FROM INDIA somebody who was born or raised in the Republic of India, or who has Indian citizenship **2.** NATIVE AMERICAN a Native American (*offensive*) **3.** *Can* STATUS INDIAN in Canada, somebody of Aboriginal ancestry who is neither Inuit nor Métis ■ *adj.* **1.** RELATING TO INDIA relating to India or its peoples, languages, or culture **2.** RELATING TO NATIVE AMERICANS relating to Native Americans or their languages or cultures (*offensive*) [13thC. From *India*, from, ultimately, Greek, "the region of the Indus river," which came via Old Persian *Hindu* "Indus" from Sanskrit *sindhuḥ*.]

WORD KEY: USAGE

Sensitivity trap: Initially the term ***Indian*** was applied to the earliest inhabitants of the American continents because Columbus and other early European explorers, having arrived at North America's east coast, believed they had reached India by a new route. As a name thus applied in error by conquerors, ***Indian*** may well be regarded as insensitive or even offensive. Some of the people in question prefer to be called *American Indians* and some prefer the term *Native American*, this last choice being the one that is least likely to cause offense.

Indiana

In·di·an·a /indee ánnə/ state in the northcentral United States, bordered by Illinois, Kentucky, Michigan, Ohio, and Lake Michigan. Capital: Indianapolis. Population: 5,864,108 (1997). Area: 36,420 sq. mi./94,327 sq. km. —**In·di·an·an** *n., adj.*

In·di·an a·gent *n.* an official in the United States or, formerly, in Canada, acting as a government representative to communities of Native Americans

In·di·an·ap·o·lis /indee ə náppələss/ capital of Indiana, in the central part of the state, southwest of Fort Wayne on the White River. It is the largest city in the state. Population: 746,737 (1996).

In·di·an bread *n.* any of a number of plants with edible parts used by some Native American peoples as food

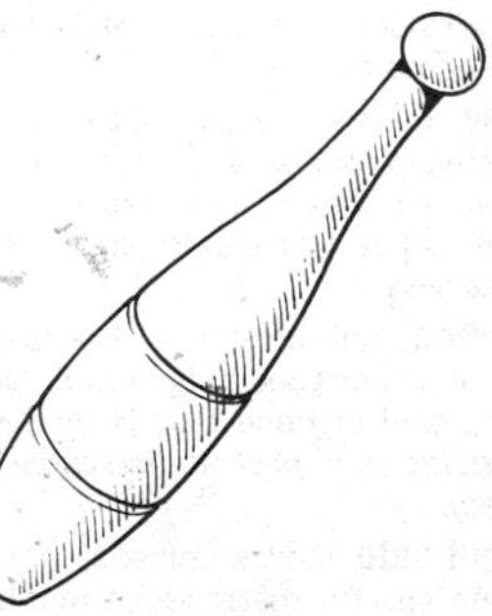
Indian club

In·di·an club *n.* a club shaped like an elongated bottle, used in gymnastics and juggling

In·di·an corn *n.* = **corn** [From its cultivation by Native Americans]

In·di·an file *n.* single file (*dated offensive*) [From a Native American custom of walking in single file]

In·di·an giv·er *n.* somebody who gives something and then asks for its return (*informal offensive*) [Possibly from a Native American custom of exchanging gifts of equal value]

In·di·an hemp *n.* **1.** = **hemp 2. PERENNIAL PLANT** a perennial North American plant of the dogbane family whose roots can be used as a laxative and emetic. Latin name: *Apocynum cannabinum.*

In·di·an ink *n. U.K.* = **India ink**

In·di·an lic·o·rice *n.* = **rosary pea**

In·di·an mal·low *n.* = **flowering maple**

In·di·an meal *n.* = **cornmeal**

In·di·an mus·tard *n.* a wild plant of the mustard family, with yellow flowers and oil-rich seeds. Latin name: *Brassica juncea.*

In·di·an O·cean ocean situated east of Africa, south of Asia, west of Australia, and north of Antarctica. Its greatest known depth is 25,344 ft./7,725 m. Area: 28,350,500 sq. mi./73,427,800 sq. km.

In·di·an paint·brush *n.* a wild plant of the figwort family, found in North America, with brightly colored bracts that look like flowers. Latin name: *Castileja linariaefolia.*

In·di·an pipe *n.* a perennial North American and Asian woodland plant whose single white stem and nodding flower resemble a tobacco pipe. Latin name: *Monotropa uniflora.*

In·di·an po·ny *n.* a small and rugged western North American horse that is often used in crossbreeding

In·di·an pud·ding *n.* a baked pudding made of cornmeal, molasses, milk, and spices

In·di·an red *n.* **1. RED PIGMENT** a red pigment made of iron oxide, used in paint, cosmetics, and polish for gold and silver objects **2. DARK REDDISH-BROWN** a dark reddish-brown color —**In·di·an red** *adj.*

In·di·an re·serve *n. Can* an area of land set aside for a particular Native American group whose members are recognized by the government as Status Indians. ◊ **reservation**

In·di·an rice *n.* = **wild rice**

In·di·an roll·er *n.* a bird of Europe and Asia, related to the kingfisher, that has bright blue wings and a chestnut breast. Latin name: *Coracias benghalensis.*

In·di·an Stan·dard Time *n.* the standard time in India. It is five-and-a-half hours later than Universal Coordinated Time.

In·di·an Sub·con·ti·nent large region in southern Asia, including the countries of Bangladesh, the Republic of India, and Pakistan

In·di·an sum·mer *n.* **1. MILD AUTUMN WEATHER** a period of mild sunny weather occurring in autumn in the northern hemisphere **2. TIME OF CALM** a calm or productive and enjoyable period toward the end of somebody's life or the end of a process, period, or activity [Origin uncertain: perhaps because it was first noticed in areas inhabited by Native Americans]

In·di·an Ter·ri·to·ry *n.* the territory west of the Mississippi River formally ceded to Native American peoples for their resettlement in 1834. It gradually diminished in size and was finally incorporated into Oklahoma in 1907.

In·di·an to·bac·co *n.* a very poisonous North American annual plant of the bluebell family that has oval toothed leaves and small purplish flowers followed by swollen seed capsules. Native American peoples once smoked the leaves as a remedy for respiratory symptoms. Latin name: *Lobelia inflata.*

In·di·an tur·nip *n.* = **jack-in-the-pulpit**

In·di·an-wres·tle (**In·di·an-wres·tled, In·di·an-wres·tling, In·di·an-wres·tles**) *vti.* to attempt to force down an opponent's upraised arm or to throw a standing opponent off balance

In·di·an wres·tling *n.* a form of wrestling in which one opponent attempts to force down another's upraised arm or to throw a standing opponent off balance

In·di·a pa·per *n.* **1. THIN PAPER** a thin fine paper originally made in Asia, used for prints and illustrations **2.** = **Bible paper**

In·di·a print *n.* a fabric made in India that has colorful block patterns on it

In·di·a rub·ber *n.* INDUST rubber (*dated*)

In·dic /índik/ *n.* a group of over 500 languages of the Indian subcontinent, forming a major division of Indo-Iranian that includes Hindi, Urdu, Assamese, Bengali, Gujarati, Sinhalese, Punjabi, Sanskrit, and the Dardic languages. Over 700 million people speak one of the languages classified as Indic. ◊ **Iranian** [Mid-19thC. Via Latin *Indicus* from Greek *Indikos*, from *Indos* "the Indus river."] —**In·dic** *adj.*

indic. *abbr.* **1.** indicating **2.** GRAM indicative **3.** indicator

in·di·can /índi kàn/ *n.* **1. CHEMICAL IN URINE** a substance formed in the intestine by bacterial action and excreted in urine and sweat. High levels in urine may indicate obstruction of the intestine. Formula: $C_8H_6NO_4SK$. **2. CHEMICAL IN PLANTS** an off-white, crystalline, sugar derivative found in plants that was the original source of indigo dye. Formula: $C_{14}H_{17}NO_6$. [Mid-19thC. Coined from Latin *indicum* "indigo" + -AN[1].]

in·di·cant /índi kənt/ *n.* something that indicates something [Early 17thC. From Latin *indicare* (see INDICATE).]

in·di·cate /índi kàyt/ (**-cat·ed, -cat·ing, -cates**) *v.* **1.** *vt.* **POINT TO** to point something out or point to something **2.** *vt.* **SHOW EXISTENCE OR TRUTH OF** to be or provide a sign or symptom of something **3.** *vt.* **REGISTER MEASUREMENT** to register a measurement, e.g., of speed or temperature **4.** *vt.* **SHOW WHAT SOMEBODY THINKS OR INTENDS** to state or show an opinion, feeling, instruction, or intention, especially briefly or indirectly **5.** *vt.* **SHOW WHAT SHOULD BE DONE** to make somebody think that something should be done or used (*usually used in the passive*) ○ *In a case like this, a firm approach is indicated.* **6.** *vti. U.K.* **GIVE SIGNALS AS DRIVER** to signal your intentions to other vehicles when driving, especially before turning or moving to the left or right **7.** *vt.* MED **SHOW PRESENCE OF DISEASE** to point out the presence of, or remedy for, a disease or syndrome [Early 17thC. From Latin *indicare* "to point toward, show," from *dicare* "to proclaim" (source of English *preach* and *abdicate*).] —**in·di·cat·a·ble** *adj.* —**in·di·ca·to·ry** /in díkə tàwree/ *adj.*

in·di·cat·ed horse·pow·er *n.* the theoretical power produced by a reciprocating engine such as a steam or internal-combustion engine, calculated as the power produced before reduction due to friction and mechanical movement. The usable, reduced-power output of the engine is its brake horsepower.

in·di·ca·tion /índi káysh'n/ *n.* **1. SIGN OF SOMETHING** a sign, signal, or symptom that something exists or is true **2. ACT OF INDICATING** an act of indicating or pointing to something **3. READING INSTRUMENT** a reading shown on a measuring instrument **4. SOMETHING NECESSARY OR DESIRABLE** something that is indicated as the right thing to do or use **5.** MED **MEDICAL SIGN** a medical sign or symptom that shows the presence of a disease or a remedy for it —**in·di·ca·tion·al** *adj.*

WORD KEY: SYNONYMS

See Synonyms at ***sign***.

in·dic·a·tive /in díkətiv/ *adj.* **1. INDICATING EXISTENCE OR TRUTH** showing, suggesting, or pointing out that something exists or is true **2.** GRAM **RELATING TO BASIC MOOD OF VERBS** relating to verbs in simple objective statements ■ *n.* GRAM **1. BASIC MOOD OF A VERB** the basic mood of a verb in languages such as English, used for ordinary objective statements **2. VERB IN BASIC MOOD** a verb used in a simple statement of fact —**in·dic·a·tive·ly** *adv.*

in·di·ca·tor /índi kàytər/ *n.* **1. SOMETHING THAT SHOWS WHAT CONDITIONS ARE** something observed or calculated that is used to show the presence or state of a condition or trend **2. MEASURING INSTRUMENT** an instrument or gauge that measures something and registers the measurement **3. SOMETHING GIVING INFORMATION** something such as a light, sign, or pointer that gives information, e.g., about which direction to follow **4.** ECOL = **indicator organism 5.** CHEM **CHEMICAL SHOWING PRESENCE OF SOMETHING** a substance such as litmus that shows the presence or concentration of a particular material or chemical

in·di·ca·tor di·a·gram *n.* a graph showing the variation of pressure and volume in a cylinder of a reciprocating engine

in·di·ca·tor or·gan·ism *n.* an organism whose presence or absence in an environment indicates particular conditions there, e.g., its oxygen level or the presence of a contaminating substance

in·dic·es plural of **index**

in·di·cia plural of **indicium**

in·di·cial /in dísh'l/ *adj.* acting as or relating to a sign or indication of something (*formal*)

in·di·ci·um /in díshəm/ (*plural* **-a** /-shə/) *n.* **1. SIGN OF SOMETHING** a sign indicating the presence or nature of something, e.g., a medical condition **2. SIGN ON BULK MAIL** a printed sign on an item of bulk mail showing the postage paid or canceled [Early 17thC. From Latin, where it was formed from *indic-*, the stem of *index* (see INDEX).]

in·di·co·lite /in díkə līt/ *n.* a blue-colored tourmaline used as a gemstone [Early 19thC. Coined from Latin *indicum* "indigo" + -LITE.]

in·dict /in dít/ (**-dict·ed, -dict·ing, -dicts**) *vt.* **1. FORMALLY CHARGE ACCUSED PERSON** to charge somebody formally with commission of a crime **2. ACCUSE OF A WRONG** to accuse somebody of wrongdoing [14thC. Via Anglo-Norman *enditer* from, ultimately, Latin *indicere* "to proclaim," literally "to say in," from *dicere* "to say." The spelling *indict*, dating from the 17thC., was modelled on medieval

Latin *indictare* "to indict."] —**in·dict·ee** /in dī tée/ *n.* —**in·dict·er** /in dītər/ *n.* —**in·dict·or** *n.*

in·dict·a·ble /in dītəb'l/ *adj.* **1. LIABLE TO INDICTMENT** liable to be charged with a criminal offense **2. MAKING SOMEBODY LIABLE TO INDICTMENT** making somebody liable to be charged with commission of a crime ○ *an indictable offense*

in·dic·tion /in díkshən/ *n.* a cyclical period of 15 years begun during the reign of Constantine the Great in the later Roman Empire at the end of which property was evaluated for taxation [14thC. From the Latin stem *indiction-* "declaration," from *indictus*, past participle of *indicere* "to declare" (see INDICT); from the declaration fixing the valuation on which tax was assessed.]

in·dict·ment /in dītmənt/ *n.* **1. FORMAL ACCUSATION BEFORE GRAND JURY** a formal accusation of a serious crime, presented to a grand jury **2. ACT OF INDICTING SOMEBODY** the act of indicting somebody or the condition of being indicted **3. STATEMENT OR FACT THAT ACCUSES** a statement or indication that something is wrong or somebody is to blame ○ *a stinging indictment of our prison system*

in·die /índee/ *n.* a small independent business enterprise, especially one related to music or film (*slang*) [Early 20thC. Shortening of INDEPENDENT.]

in·dif·fer·ence /in dífərəns, -dífrəns/ *n.* **1. LACK OF INTEREST IN SOMETHING** lack of interest, care, or concern **2. UNIMPORTANCE** lack of importance or significance ○ *It's a matter of complete indifference to me whether you go or stay.* **3. LOW QUALITY** ordinariness or lack of quality

in·dif·fer·ent /in dífərənt, -dífrənt/ *adj.* **1. WITHOUT CARE OR INTEREST** showing no care or concern for, or interest in, somebody or something ○ *She was indifferent to their criticism.* **2. FAVORING NEITHER SIDE** without bias or preference for one person, group, or thing rather than another **3. ONLY AVERAGE** average or low in quality **4.** BIOL **UNDIFFERENTIATED** not specialized or differentiated in cells or tissues **5.** SCI **NEUTRAL** neutral and having no properties that are affected by a process or reaction **6. OF NO IMPORT** lacking importance or significance (*archaic*) [14thC. Directly or via Old French from the Latin stem *indifferent-* "making no difference," from *different-*, present participle stem of *differre* "to differ."]

in·dif·fer·ent·ism /in dífərən tìzzəm, -dífrən tìzzəm/ *n.* the belief that variations in doctrine and practice within a religion are unimportant

in·dif·fer·ent·ly /in dífərəntlee, -dífrəntlee/ *adv.* **1. WITHOUT INTEREST** without showing interest or concern **2. NOT WELL** not very well **3. EQUALLY** without differences or exceptions (*formal*)

in·di·gen *n.* = **indigene**

in·di·gence /índijəns/ *n.* extreme poverty in which the basic necessities of life are lacking (*formal*)

WORD KEY: SYNONYMS

See Synonyms at ***poverty***.

in·di·gene /índi jeèn/, **in·di·gen** /índijən/ *n.* somebody who was born in a place or location or something that was produced in or grows in or belongs naturally to a place or location (*formal*) [Late 16thC. Via French *indigène* from Latin *indigena* "native" (see INDIGENOUS).]

in·di·gen·ize /in díjjə nīz/ (**-ized, -iz·ing, -iz·es**) *vti.* to increase the use of local inhabitants for a task previously done by people from another country, usually the home country of an employing company —**in·di·gen·i·za·tion** /in dìjjəni záysh'n/ *n.*

in·dig·e·nous /in díjjənəss/ *adj.* **1. BELONGING TO A PLACE** originating in and typical of a region or country **2. NATURAL** natural or inborn (*formal*) [Mid-17thC. From Latin *indigena*, literally "born in," from *gignere* "to beget." Ultimately from an Indo-European word that is also the ancestor of English *gender*.] —**in·di·gen·i·ty** /índi jénnətee/ *n.* —**in·dig·e·nous·ly** *adv.*

WORD KEY: SYNONYMS

See Synonyms at ***native***.

in·dig·e·nous peo·ple *n.* the people who occupy a region at the time of its contact with colonial powers or the outside world

in·di·gent /índijənt/ *adj.* **EXTREMELY POOR** lacking the necessities of life, such as food, clothing, and shelter (*formal*) ■ *n.* **DESTITUTE PERSON** somebody who is very poor (*formal*) [14thC. Via Old French from Latin *indigent-*, present participle stem of *indigere*, literally "to lack in," from *egere* "to need."] —**in·di·gent·ly** *adv.*

in·di·gest·ed /índi jéstəd, ìn dī-/ *adj.* not having undergone the process of digestion

in·di·gest·i·ble /índi jéstəb'l, ìn dī-/ *adj.* difficult or impossible to digest [15thC. Directly or via French from late Latin *indigestibilis*, from *digestibilis* "digestible."] —**in·di·gest·i·bil·i·ty** /índi jéstə bíllətee, ìn dī-/ *n.* —**in·di·gest·i·ble·ness** /índi jéstəb'lnəss, ìn dī-/ *n.* —**in·di·gest·i·bly** *adv.*

in·di·ges·tion /índi jéschən, ìn dī-/ *n.* difficulty in digesting food, resulting in such symptoms as belching, heartburn, or stomach pains. Technical name **dyspepsia** [14thC. Directly or via Old French from the late Latin stem *indigestion-*, from *digestion-* (see DIGESTION).]

in·di·ges·tive /índi jéstiv, ìn dī-/ *adj.* experiencing or resulting from indigestion

in·dig·nant /in dígnənt/ *adj.* angry or annoyed at the unfairness or unreasonableness of somebody or something [Late 16thC. From Latin *indignant-*, present participle stem of *indignari* "to regard as unworthy," ultimately from *dignus* "worthy" (see DIGNITY).] —**in·dig·nant·ly** *adv.*

in·dig·na·tion /índig náysh'n/ *n.* anger or annoyance because somebody or something seems unfair or unreasonable [14thC. Directly or via Old French from the Latin stem *indignation-*, from *indignari* (see INDIGNANT).]

WORD KEY: SYNONYMS

See Synonyms at ***anger***.

in·dig·ni·ty /in dígnətee/ (*plural* **-ties**) *n.* a humiliating loss of dignity or self-esteem [Late 16thC. Directly or via French *indignité* from Latin *indignitas*, from *indignus* "unworthy."]

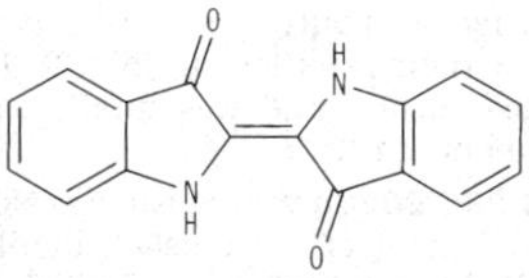

Indigo: Synthetic indigo

in·di·go /índi gō/ *n.* (*plural* **-gos** *or* **-goes**) **1. BLUE DYE** a blue dye, once obtained from plants, but now usually made synthetically **2. PLANT YIELDING INDIGO DYE** a tropical plant of the pea family with fronds of pointed leaves and spikes of red or purple flowers, a source of indigo dye. Genus: *Indigofera*. **3. DEEP PURPLISH-BLUE COLOR** a deep purplish-blue color that lies toward one end of the visible spectrum, between blue and violet ■ *adj.* **DEEP PURPLISH-BLUE** of a deep purplish-blue color [Mid-16thC. Via Portuguese from, ultimately, Greek *indikon*, literally "the Indian substance," a form of *Indikos* "Indian," from *Indos* "the Indus River."]

in·di·go bird *n.* an East African weaverbird, the male of which has deep purplish-black feathers, found in gardens and in the wild. Genus: *Hypochera.*

in·di·go blue *n.* = **indigo**

in·di·go bunt·ing *n.* a North American finch found in hedges and at the margins of woods, the male of which has brilliant indigo feathers. Latin name: *Passerina cyanea.*

in·di·go snake *n.* a large deep-blue snake, found from the southern United States to South America, that preys on small mammals but is harmless to humans. Latin name: *Drymarchon corais.*

in·dig·o·tin /in díggətin, ìndi gót'n/ *n.* = **indigo** *n.* 1 [Mid-19thC. Coined from INDIGO + -IN.]

In·di·o /índi ō/ city in Riverside County, southeastern California, situated southeast of San Bernadino. Population: 36,793 (1990).

in·di·rect /índi rékt/ *adj.* **1. NOT IN STRAIGHT LINE** not in a direct line, course, or path **2. NOT IMMEDIATE OR INTENDED** not occurring as an immediate or intended effect or consequence **3. DEVIOUS** not obvious or straightforward in approach **4. INVOLVING INTERMEDIATE STAGES** not obtained or proceeding from an immediate or straightforward relationship [14thC. Directly or via Old French from medieval Latin *indirectus* "not direct," from Latin *directus* (see DIRECT).] —**in·di·rect·ness** *n.* —**in·di·rect·ly** *adv.*

in·di·rect cost *n.* a business expense that is not directly connected with a particular product or operation

in·di·rect dis·course *n.* = **indirect speech**

in·di·rec·tion /índi rékshən/ *n.* **1. LACK OF DIRECTNESS** lack of directness in a path, course, or procedure **2. AIMLESSNESS** lack of a goal or goals **3. SOMETHING NOT HONEST AND STRAIGHTFORWARD** an approach or action that is devious or deceitful

in·di·rect la·bor *n.* work that is not considered in determining costs per unit in producing or manufacturing something, e.g., work done by clerical or maintenance staff

in·di·rect light·ing *n.* reflected or diffused light used to avoid glare or shadows

in·di·rect ob·ject *n.* the recipient of the action shown by a verb and its direct object, e.g., "the cat" in "She gave the cat a meal"

in·di·rect proof *n.* LOGIC proof of a conclusion by showing that assuming its negation will lead to a contradiction

in·di·rect ques·tion *n.* a question reported in indirect speech, e.g., "He asked why you were not there"

in·di·rect speech *n.* a report of something said or written that conveys what was said, but not the exact words in their original form, as in "She said she would join us later"

in·di·rect tax *n.* a tax levied on goods or services, instead of directly on companies and individuals

in·dis·cern·i·ble /índi súrnəb'l/ *adj.* impossible to see or to understand —**in·dis·cern·i·bil·i·ty** /índi surnə bíllitee/ *n.* —**in·dis·cern·i·ble·ness** /índi súrnəb'lnəss/ *n.* —**in·dis·cern·i·bly** *adv.*

in·dis·ci·pline /in díssiplin/ *n.* lack of control or discipline

in·dis·creet /índi skreét/ *adj.* lacking tact or discretion [15thC. From Latin *indiscretus* "unseparated, undistinguished" (see DISCREET).] —**in·dis·creet·ly** *adv.* —**in·dis·creet·ness** *n.*

in·dis·crete /índi skreét/ *adj.* not divided into parts or appearing to consist of separate parts [Early 17thC. From Latin *indiscretus* "unseparated, undistinguished," from *discretus* (see DISCRETE).] —**in·dis·crete·ly** *adv.* —**in·dis·crete·ness** *n.*

in·dis·cre·tion /índi skrésh'n/ *n.* **1. TACTLESS LACK OF JUDGMENT** lack of tact or good judgment **2. SOMETHING UNWISE** something said or done that is tactless or unwise ○ *apologizing for past indiscretions* —**in·dis·cre·tion·ar·y** *adj.*

in·dis·crim·i·nate /índi skrímmənət/ *adj.* **1. UNSELECTIVE** making no careful distinctions or choices **2. HAPHAZARDLY RANDOM** random, haphazard, or confused —**in·dis·crim·i·nate·ly** *adv.* —**in·dis·crim·i·nate·ness** *n.* —**in·dis·crim·i·na·tion** /índi skrimmə náysh'n/ *n.*

in·dis·crim·i·nat·ing /índi skrímmə nàyting/ *adj.* lacking discrimination or judgment —**in·dis·crim·i·nat·ing·ly** *adv.* —**in·dis·crim·i·na·tive** *adj.*

in·dis·pen·sa·ble /índi spénsəb'l/ *adj.* **1. NECESSARY** necessary, essential, or not to be dispensed with **2. HAVING TO BE FACED** unavoidable, especially as a duty ■ *n.* **ESSENTIAL** something that is essential and cannot be dispensed with —**in·dis·pen·sa·bil·i·ty** /índi spensə bíllətee/ *n.* —**in·dis·pen·sa·ble·ness** /índi spénsəb'lnəss/ *n.* —**in·dis·pen·sa·bly** *adv.*

WORD KEY: SYNONYMS

See Synonyms at ***necessary***.

in·dis·pose /índiss pṓz/ (**-posed, -pos·ing, -pos·es**) *vt.* **1. SICKEN** to make somebody ill (*archaic*) **2. MAKE UNFIT** to make somebody unfit for something (*formal*) **3. MAKE AVERSE TO SOMETHING** to make somebody dislike the prospect of something or be unwilling to do something (*formal*) [Mid-17thC]

in·dis·posed /índiss pṓzd/ *adj.* (*formal*) **1. SICK** too ill to do something **2. UNWILLING TO SAY OR DO SOMETHING** unwilling to say or do something, especially because of a feeling of annoyance

in·dis·po·si·tion /in dispə zísh'n/ *n.* (*formal*) **1. MINOR ILLNESS** an illness that is not serious **2. RELUCTANCE** reluctance or unwillingness to do something

in·dis·put·a·ble /indi spyóotəb'l/ *adj.* impossible to doubt, question, or deny [Mid-16thC. From late Latin *indisputabilis* "not disputable," from Latin *disputabilis* (see DISPUTABLE).] —**in·dis·put·a·bil·i·ty** /indi spyootə bíllətee/ *n.* —**in·dis·put·a·ble·ness** /indi spyóotəb'lnəss/ *n.* —**in·dis·put·a·bly** *adv.*

in·dis·sol·u·ble /indi sóllyəb'l/ *adj.* incapable of being dissolved, broken, or undone —**in·dis·sol·u·bil·i·ty** /indi sollyə bíllətee/ *n.* —**in·dis·sol·u·bly** /-blee/ *adv.*

in·dis·tinct /indi stíngkt/ *adj.* **1. UNCLEAR** giving an unclear impression to the sight or hearing **2. VAGUE** not clearly remembered, understood, or thought out [Mid-16thC. From Latin *indistinctus* "not distinct," from *distinctus* (see DISTINCT).] —**in·dis·tinct·ly** *adv.*

in·dis·tinc·tive /indi stíngktiv/ *adj.* without any distinguishing qualities or features —**in·dis·tinc·tive·ly** *adv.*

in·dis·tin·guish·a·ble /indi stíngwishəb'l/ *adj.* **1. VERY LIKE SOMEBODY OR SOMETHING ELSE** impossible to tell apart from somebody or something else ○ *His handwriting is indistinguishable from his father's.* **2. INDISTINCT** very hard to see, hear, or understand —**in·dis·tin·guish·a·bil·i·ty** /indi stingwishə bíllətee/ *n.* —**in·dis·tin·guish·a·bly** /indi stíngwishəblee/ *adv.*

in·dite /in dīt/ (**-dit·ed, -dit·ing, -dites**) *vt.* to write or compose something such as a poem, letter, or speech (*archaic or literary*) [14thC. From Old French *enditer*, literally "to compose in words in," from, ultimately, Latin *dictare* "to compose in words" (see DICTATE).]

in·di·um /índee əm/ *n.* a soft silvery-colored rare metallic chemical element, often found in zinc and tin ores, used in alloys, transistors, and electroplating. Symbol **In** [Mid-19thC. Coined from INDIGO + -IUM. From two indigo lines in its spectrum.]

indiv., individ. *abbr.* individual

in·di·vid·u·al /indi víjjoo əl/ *n.* **1. PARTICULAR PERSON** a particular person, distinct from others in a group **2. SEPARATE THING** a separate entity or thing **3.** BIOL **SEPARATE ORGANISM** an independent organism separate from a group ■ *adj.* **1. SEPARABLE FROM OTHERS** singular and separable from others in a group or class **2. OF OR FOR ONE PERSON** belong to, relating to, or intended for one person only **3. VERY DISTINCTIVE** strikingly personal, unusual, or distinctive [15thC. From medieval Latin *individualis*, from Latin *individuus* "not divisible," from, ultimately, *dividere* "to divide."]

in·di·vid·u·al·ism /indi víjjoo ə lìzzəm/ *n.* **1. PURSUIT OF PERSONAL GOALS** the pursuit of personal happiness and independence rather than collective goals or interests **2. PERSONAL TRAIT** a personal peculiarity or trait **3.** POL **POLITICAL BELIEF IN IMPORTANCE OF INDIVIDUAL** the belief that society exists for the benefit of the individual, who must not be constrained by government interventions or made subordinate to collective interests

in·di·vid·u·al·ist /indi víjjoo əlist/ *n.* **1. INDEPENDENT THINKER** somebody who thinks or behaves independently **2. BELIEVER IN INDIVIDUALISM** somebody who believes in the social or political philosophy of individualism —**in·di·vid·u·al·is·ti·cal·ly** /indi vijoo ə lístikəlee/ *adv.*

in·di·vid·u·al·i·ty /indi vijoo állətee/ (*plural* **-ties**) *n.* **1. INDIVIDUAL TRAIT OR CHARACTER** a specific personality, character, or characteristic that distinguishes one person or thing from another **2. STATE OF BEING AN INDIVIDUAL** the state or condition of being separate from others

in·di·vid·u·al·ize /indi víjjoo ə līz/ (**-ized, -iz·ing, -iz·es**) *vt.* **1. GIVE INDIVIDUAL CHARACTER TO** to give somebody or something a character that is separate and distinct from other people or things **2. TREAT INDIVIDUALLY** to consider or treat somebody or something specifically, as distinct from other people or things **3. ADAPT TO INDIVIDUAL REQUIREMENTS** to make, adapt, or modify something to suit a particular person —**in·di·vid·u·al·i·za·tion** /indi vijjoo əli záysh'n/ *n.* —**in·di·vid·u·al·iz·er** /indi víjjoo ə līzər/ *n.*

in·di·vid·u·al·ly /indi víjjoo əlee/ *adv.* as a separate person or entity, not as part of a group or class

in·di·vid·u·al med·ley *n.* a swimming race divided into three or four equal parts, in each of which the swimmers must use a particular stroke such as backstroke, breaststroke, or butterfly stroke

in·di·vid·u·ate /indi víjjoo àyt/ (**-at·ed, -at·ing, -ates**) *vt.* to make somebody or something separate and distinct from others (*formal*) [Early 17thC. From medieval Latin *individuat-*, past participle stem of *individuare*, from Latin *individuus* (see INDIVIDUAL).] —**in·di·vid·u·a·tor** *n.*

in·di·vid·u·a·tion /indi vijoo áysh'n/ *n.* **1. ACT OF MAKING SEPARATE** the act or process of making somebody or something separate and distinct from others **2.** PSYCHOL **PROCESS OF PSYCHOLOGICAL DEVELOPMENT** in Jungian psychology, the process of the development of the self, achieved by resolving the conflicts arising at life's transitional stages, in particular the transition from adolescence to adulthood. Jung believed this process could not be completed until middle age.

in·di·vis·i·ble /indi vízzəb'l/ *adj.* **1. NOT SEPARABLE** not capable of being separated into parts ○ *"... one nation indivisible, with liberty and justice for all"* (*Pledge of Allegiance*) **2.** MATH **NOT MULTIPLE OF NUMBER** not capable of being divided by a given number without leaving a remainder [14thC. From late Latin *indivisibilis* "not divisible," from *divisibilis* "divisible."] —**in·di·vis·i·bil·i·ty** /indi vizzə bíllətee/ *n.* —**in·di·vis·i·bly** /indi vízzəblee/ *adv.*

indn. *abbr.* indication

indo- *prefix.* Forms the name of chemical compounds derived from or related to indigo ○ *indoxyl* [From INDIGO]

Indo- *prefix.* **1.** India ○ *Indo-Pacific* **2.** Indic ○ *Indo-Iranian* [From INDIA and INDIC]

Indochina

In·do·chi·na /índō chīnə/ peninsula of southeastern Asia that includes Myanmar, Thailand, Cambodia, Vietnam, Laos, and the Malay Peninsula. In a narrower sense it refers only to Cambodia, Laos, and Vietnam. —**In·do·chi·nese** *adj., n.*

in·doc·ile /in dóss'l/ *adj.* resisting discipline or instruction [Early 17thC. Directly or via French from Latin *indocilis* "difficult to teach," from *docilis* (see DOCILE).] —**in·do·cil·i·ty** /ində síllətee, ìn do-/ *n.*

in·doc·tri·nate /in dóktrə nàyt/ (**-nat·ed, -nat·ing, -nates**) *vt.* to teach somebody a belief, doctrine, or ideology thoroughly and systematically, especially with the goal of discouraging independent thought or the acceptance of other opinions [Early 17thC. From Old French *endoctriner*, literally "to teach in," from medieval Latin *doctrinare* "to teach."] —**in·doc·tri·na·tion** /in dòktrə náysh'n/ *n.* —**in·doc·tri·na·tor** *n.*

In·do-Eu·ro·pe·an /índō yoorə pée ən/ *n.* **1. FAMILY OF EUROPEAN AND ASIAN LANGUAGES** a family of languages conventionally divided into the following branches: Balto-Slavonic, Germanic, Italic, Indo-Iranian, Celtic, Greek, Albanian, Armenian, Anatolian, and Tocharian. This language family, now spoken from India to western Europe, includes many modern languages, e.g., English, French, German, Spanish, Russian, Hindi, and Urdu. ◊ **satem, centum, Proto-Indo-European 2. SPEAKER OF INDO-EUROPEAN LANGUAGE** somebody who speaks any of the Indo-European languages —**In·do-Eu·ro·pe·an** *adj.*

In·do-I·ra·ni·an *n.* a group of languages spoken in the north of the Indian subcontinent and in parts of the Middle East, forming a branch of Indo-European and dividing into two subgroups, Indic and Iranian. About 800 million people speak one of the languages classified as Indo-Iranian. —**In·do-I·ra·ni·an** *adj.*

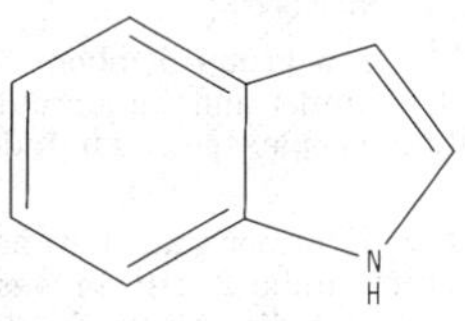

Indole

in·dole /in dōl/, **in·dol** /in dòl/ *n.* a crystalline compound that occurs in plants and in the intestines. It can also be derived from coal tar and is used in perfumes and as a reagent. Formula: C_8H_7N. [Mid-19thC. Coined from IND- + -OLE.]

in·dole·a·ce·tic ac·id /in dōlə sèttik-/ *n.* a plant hormone that stimulates growth and root formation in stems. Formula: $C_{10}H_9NO_2$. [*Indoleacetic* coined from INDOLE + ACETIC]

in·dole·bu·tyr·ic ac·id /indōl byoo tèerik-/ *n.* a synthetic plant hormone that stimulates growth in stems. Formula: $C_{12}H_{13}O_2N$. [*Indolebutyric* coined from INDOLE + BUTYRIC]

in·do·lent /índələnt/ *adj.* **1. LAZY** lethargic and not showing any interest or making any effort **2.** MED **PAINLESS AND SLOW TO CHANGE** used to describe a disease or condition that is slow to develop or be healed, and causes no pain [Mid-17thC. From the late Latin stem *indolent-* "insensitive to pain," from *dolent-*, present participle stem of *dolere* "to suffer pain."] —**in·do·lence** *n.* —**in·do·lent·ly** *adv.*

in·do·meth·a·cin /indō méthəssin/ *n.* a drug used to relieve pain, fever, and inflammation, especially from arthritis. Formula: $C_{19}H_{16}ClNO_4$. [Mid-20thC. Coined from INDOLE + METHYL + ACETIC + -IN.]

in·dom·i·ta·ble /in dómmitəb'l/ *adj.* brave, determined, and impossible to defeat or frighten [Mid-17thC. From late Latin *indomitabilis* "untamable," from *domitare* "to tame" (source of English *daunt*).] —**in·dom·i·ta·bil·i·ty** /in dòmmitə bíllətee/ *n.* —**in·dom·i·ta·ble·ness** /in dómmitəb'lnəss/ *n.* —**in·dom·i·ta·bly** *adv.*

Indon. *abbr.* Indonesian

In·do·ne·sia /ində née<u>zh</u>ə,-néeshə/ island republic of southeastern Asia, the fourth most populous country in the world. It consists of more than 13,670 islands, 6,000 of which are inhabited. Language: Bahasa Indonesia. Currency: rupiah. Capital: Jakarta. Population: 209,774,138 (1997). Area: 741,903 sq. mi./1,919,317 sq. km. Official name **Republic of Indonesia**

In·do·ne·sian /indō née<u>zh</u>'n/ *n.* **1.** PEOPLES **SOMEBODY FROM INDONESIA** somebody who was born or raised in Indonesia, or who is a citizen of Indonesia **2.** LANG = **Bahasa Indonesia** —**In·do·ne·sian** *adj.*

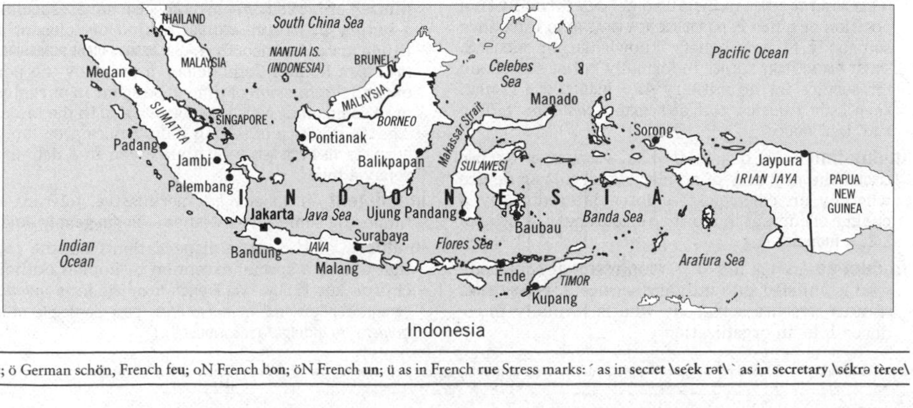

Indonesia

in·door /in dáwr/ *adj.* situated or done within a building [Early 18thC. From IN + DOOR, replacing earlier *within door(s)*; from the use of *door* as a metaphor for building (as in *next door*).]

in·door air qual·i·ty *n.* the condition of the air inside buildings, including the extent of pollution caused by smoking, dust, mites, mold spores, radon, and gases and chemicals from materials and appliances

in·door-out·door *adj.* designed to be used inside or outside a building

in·doors /in dáwrz/ *adv.* into or inside a building [Late 18thC. Formed from INDOOR.]

In·do-Pa·cif·ic *n.* a group of about 700 languages spoken in New Guinea and the surrounding islands. Three million people speak an Indo-Pacific language.

In·dore /in dáwr/ **1.** former state, now part of Madhya Pradesh, central India **2.** city in western Madhya Pradesh, central India, situated 340 mi./547 km northeast of Mumbai (Bombay). Population: 1,086,673 (1991).

in·dorse (**-dorsed, -dors·ing, -dorses**) *vt.* = **endorse**

in·dox·yl /in dóksəl/ *n.* a crystalline compound found in plants and animals that, when oxidized, is a source of indigo dye. Formula: C_8H_7NO. [Late 19thC. Coined from IND- + OXY- + -YL.]

In·dra /índrə/ *n.* in Vedic mythology, a powerful warrior god and the ruler of the sky and weather. He became a subordinate god in later Hindu mythology.

in·draft /ín dràft/ *n.* an inward flow or current of air

in·dri /índree/ *n.* a large rare black-and-white lemur of Madagascar, with large eyes, silky fur, and a rudimentary tail. Latin name: *Indri indri.* [Mid-19thC. From Malagasy *indry!* "look!" or *indry izy!* "there he is!", wrongly taken to be the name of the animal, which in Malagasy is *babakoto*.]

in·du·bi·ta·ble /in do͞obitəb'l/ *adj.* obvious or definitely true, and not to be doubted (*formal*) [Early 17thC. Directly or via French from Latin *indubitabilis* "not doubtful," ultimately from *dubitare* "to doubt" (source of English *doubt*).] —**in·du·bi·ta·bil·i·ty** /in do͞obitə bíllətee/ *n.* —**in·du·bi·ta·bly** *adv.*

induc. *abbr.* induction

in·duce /in do͞oss/ (**-duced, -duc·ing, -duc·es**) *v.* **1.** *vt.* PERSUADE TO DO SOMETHING to persuade or influence somebody to do or think something **2.** *vt.* PSYCHOL PRODUCE MENTAL OR PHYSICAL STATE to cause or bring about a thought, feeling, or physical condition **3.** *vti.* OBSTET HASTEN BIRTH OF BABY to make the process of labor or the birth of a baby start by a medical intervention, usually by administering a drug, before it happens naturally **4.** *vt.* LOGIC REASON FROM OBSERVATION to make a statement based on the observation of facts **5.** *vt.* PHYS PRODUCE BY INDUCTION to produce an electric current or a magnetic field by induction [14thC. From Latin *inducere* "to lead into, persuade," from *ducere* "to lead."]

in·duced drag *n.* the drag force created by the lift of an aircraft

in·duce·ment /in do͞ossmənt/ *n.* **1.** STIMULUS OR INCENTIVE something that gives somebody a reason to do something, especially something that is offered as an incentive **2.** INDUCING ACTION the act of inducing something

WORD KEY: SYNONYMS

See Synonyms at ***motive***.

in·duct /in dúkt/ (**-duct·ed, -duct·ing, -ducts**) *vt.* **1.** FORMALLY ADMIT TO OFFICE to install somebody formally in a position or office **2.** INTRODUCE NEW IDEAS TO to introduce somebody to new beliefs, knowledge, or ideas **3.** ENLIST FOR MILITARY SERVICE to formally enlist somebody for service in the military **4.** = **induce** *v.* 5 [14thC. From Latin *inductus*, past participle of *inducere* "to lead into" (see INDUCE).]

in·duc·tance /in dúktənss/ *n.* **1.** PROPERTY OF ELECTRIC CIRCUIT the property of an electric circuit or device whereby an electromotive force is created by a change of current in it or in a circuit near it. Symbol **L 2.** = **inductor** *n.* 2

in·duct·ee /in dùk teé/ *n.* **1.** MILITARY RECRUIT somebody who is enlisted into military service **2.** PERSON BEING FORMALLY APPOINTED somebody who is formally introduced into an organization

in·duc·tile /in dúkt'l/ *adj.* not pliable or yielding [Mid-18thC. Formed from IN- + DUCTILE.] —**in·duc·til·i·ty** /in dùk tíllətee/ *n.*

in·duc·tion /in dúkshən/ *n.* **1.** PROCESS OF INDUCING SOMETHING the process of inducing a state, feeling, or idea **2.** OBSTET PROCESS OF HASTENING BABY'S BIRTH the act or the process of medically hastening, or inducing, the birth of a baby **3.** ACT OF INDUCTING SOMEBODY the act or process of inducting somebody into a position or an organization **4.** LOGIC CONCLUSION BASED ON EVIDENCE a generalization based on observed instances, or the making of such generalizations, in the usual working method of scientists **5.** PHYS CREATION OF ELECTRIC OR MAGNETIC FORCES the process by which electric or magnetic forces are created in a circuit by being in proximity to an electric or magnetic field or a varying current without physical contact **6.** MIL ACT OF ENLISTING SOMEBODY the act of formally enlisting somebody into military service **7.** EMBRYOL PROCESS IN DEVELOPMENT OF EMBRYO the process by which one part of an embryo affects the development of another, e.g., through the diffusion of hormones **8.** CHEM SYNTHESIS OF ENZYME the process by which the production of an enzyme is stimulated by the increased concentration of the substance it acts on **9.** MATH PROCESS OF MATHEMATICAL PROOF a process for proving propositions with variables limited to positive integers by showing that the smallest instance is true and each following instance is derived from the one before —**in·duc·tion·al** *adj.*

in·duc·tion coil *n.* a transformer that produces an intermittent high-voltage current from a low-voltage direct current by means of several wire windings and, often, a soft iron core

in·duc·tion heat·ing *n.* a process for raising the temperature of a metal by inducing an electric current within it

in·duc·tion mo·tor *n.* an alternating-current electric motor powered by the interaction of a varying magnetic field in its windings with the current induced in the rotor

in·duc·tive /in dúktiv/ *adj.* **1.** PHYS OF ELECTRIC OR MAGNETIC INDUCTION involving, operating by, or caused by electric or magnetic induction **2.** PSYCHOL PRODUCING MENTAL OR PHYSICAL STATE relating to the process of inducing a feeling, idea, or state **3.** LOGIC REACHING A CONCLUSION BASED ON OBSERVATION generalizing to produce a universal claim or principle from observed instances **4.** BIOL AFFECTING ANOTHER EMBRYONIC PART producing an effect on another embryonic part by induction —**in·duc·tive·ly** *adv.* —**in·duc·tive·ness** *n.*

in·duc·tor /in dúktər/ *n.* **1.** AGENT OF INDUCTION somebody or something that inducts **2.** PART OF CIRCUIT GENERATING FORCE a part of an electric circuit, usually a coil, in which an electromotive force is generated by inductance **3.** COMPONENT CAUSING INDUCTANCE an electrical or electronic component designed to cause or work on inductance

in·due (**-dued, -du·ing, -dues**) *vt.* = **endue**

in·dulge /in dúlj/ (**-dulged, -dulg·ing, -dulg·es**) *v.* **1.** *vti.* HAVE OR PERMIT A TREAT to allow somebody or yourself to have or do something enjoyable **2.** *vi.* DRINK ALCOHOL to permit yourself to drink alcohol, especially to excess (*dated informal*) **3.** *vt.* BUSINESS GIVE DEBTOR TIME TO PAY to allow a debtor time to pay a bill [Early 17thC. From Latin *indulgere* "to allow space or time for, give rein to," of unknown origin.] —**in·dulg·er** *n.*

in·dulged /in dúljd/ *adj.* pampered, spoiled, or catered to

in·dul·gence /in dúljənss/ *n.* **1.** YIELDING TO SOMEBODY'S WISH the gratification of or yielding to a wish **2.** SOMETHING ALLOWED AS LUXURY something that somebody lets himself or herself or somebody else have, especially a luxury **3.** TOLERANT ATTITUDE a kind or tolerant attitude toward somebody **4.** CHR REMISSION OF PUNISHMENT FOR SIN in Roman Catholicism, a grant by the pope of partial remission of time to be spent in purgatory or of some other consequence of a sin. In the Middle Ages, a practice of selling indulgences grew up. **5.** BUSINESS TIME FOR REPAYMENT time given to a debtor to repay a bill

in·dul·gent /in dúljənt/ *adj.* permissive, tolerant, or humoring somebody's wishes —**in·dul·gent·ly** *adv.*

in·dult /in dúlt/ *n.* CHR a dispensation from the pope that allows a special exception to Roman Catholic church law [15thC. Via French from late Latin *indultum* "grant, concession," from *indultus*, past participle of *indulgere* "to indulge" (see INDULGE).]

in·du·men·tum /ìndə méntəm, ìndyə-/ (*plural* **-ta** /-tə/ *or* **-tums**), **in·du·ment** /índəmənt, índyə-/ *n.* a covering of hairs on a plant, or of hair, fur, or feathers on an animal [Mid-19thC. From Latin *indumentum* "garment," from *induere* "to put on."]

in·du·pli·cate /in do͞oplì kət, in do͞oplə kàyt/ *adj.* used to describe a bud or leaf that has its edges bent or folded inward, so as to touch but not overlap [Early 19thC. Coined from IN- + DUPLICATE.] —**in·du·pli·ca·tion** /in do͞opli káysh'n/ *n.*

in·du·rate *vti.* /índə rày t/ (**-rat·ed, -rat·ing, -rates**) MAKE OR BECOME HARD to make something hard or to become hard (*literary or technical*) ■ *adj.* /índə rət, in dyo͞orət/ FEELING NO COMPASSION unsympathetic or unfeeling (*literary*) [Mid-16thC. From Latin *indurat-*, past participle stem of *indurare* "to make hard," from *durus* "hard."] —**in·du·ra·tive** /in do͞orətiv/ *adj.*

in·du·ra·tion /ìndə ráysh'n/ *n.* **1.** HARDENING the process of hardening something or of becoming hard (*literary or technical*) **2.** GEOL HARDENING OF GEOLOGICAL SEDIMENT the process by which a soft geological sediment becomes hard **3.** MED HARDNESS IN BODY TISSUE a hardness in body tissue, especially a tumor

In·dus[1] /índəss/ river in Asia. It rises in western Tibet and flows northwest across Jammu and Kashmir and then southwest through Pakistan to the Arabian Sea. Length: 1,800 mi./2,900 km.

In·dus[2] /índəss/ *n.* a faint constellation visible in the Southern Hemisphere

indus. *abbr.* **1.** industrial **2.** industry

in·du·si·um /in do͞ozhee əm, -do͞ozee-/ (*plural* **-a** /-ə/) *n.* **1.** BOT PROTECTIVE COVERING a membrane on the underside of a fern leaf that protects developing spores **2.** BIOL PROTECTING AND COVERING MEMBRANE an enveloping protective membrane [Early 18thC. From Latin, "tunic," from *induere* "to put on (a garment)."] —**in·du·si·al** /in do͞ozh'l, in do͞ozee əl/ *adj.*

in·dus·tri·al /in dústree əl/ *adj.* **1.** OF INDUSTRY relating to, used in, or created by industry **2.** WITH MANY DEVELOPED INDUSTRIES having a large quantity of highly developed industries **3.** OF INDUSTRY'S WORKFORCE relating to or involving workers in industry ■ *n.* MANUFACTURING COMPANY a company or employee engaged in an industry, especially manufacturing ■ **in·dus·tri·als** *npl.* SHARES IN INDUSTRIAL COMPANIES the shares and interest-bearing securities of industrial companies —**in·dus·tri·al·ly** *adv.*

in·dus·tri·al ac·ci·dent *n.* an accident, often causing serious injury, that is job-related in that it usually happens on a work site, e.g., a factory floor or a construction site

in·dus·tri·al ac·tion *n. U.K.* = **job action**

in·dus·tri·al ar·che·ol·o·gy *n.* the study of sites, buildings, and equipment used by industries in the past

in·dus·tri·al arts *n.* a branch of education that develops the skills needed by workers in industry (*takes a singular verb*)

in·dus·tri·al de·sign *n.* the art of designing the shape, size, or appearance of manufactured objects

in·dus·tri·al dis·ease *n.* a disease affecting people as a result of the work they do

in·dus·tri·al en·gi·neer·ing *n.* the study and practice of designing industrial operations

in·dus·tri·al es·pi·o·nage *n.* the secret removal, copying, or recording of confidential or valuable information in a company for use by a rival concern or a competitor

in·dus·tri·al es·tate *n. U.K.* = **industrial park**

in·dus·tri·al·ism /in dústree ə lìzzəm/ *n.* the organization of an economy or a society around extensive manufacturing, rather than around agriculture, the production of handicrafts, or commerce

in·dus·tri·al·ist /in dústree əlist/ *n.* somebody who owns or controls an industrial concern, or has a major share in one

in·dus·tri·al·i·za·tion /in dùstree əli záysh'n/ *n.* the adoption of industrial methods of production and manufacturing by a country or group, with all the associated changes in lifestyle, transport, and other aspects of society

in·dus·tri·al·ize /in dústree ə lìz/ (**-ized, -iz·ing, -iz·es**) *vti.* to adapt a country or group to industrial methods of production and manufacturing, across a wide area, with all the accompanying social changes or to be adapted in this way

in·dus·tri·al mel·a·nism *n.* the increase in the numbers of animals, especially moths, with dark coloration in places where industries create a lot of black smoke and predators more easily feed on lighter individuals

in·dus·tri·al park *n. Aus, U.S.* a large area of land where factories and businesses are concentrated in accordance with local zoning policy

in·dus·tri·al psy·chol·o·gy *n.* the study of human behavior and attitudes in the workplace — **in·dus·tri·al psy·chol·o·gist** *n.*

in·dus·tri·al re·la·tions *npl.* **1.** LINKS BETWEEN WORKERS AND MANAGERS the relationship between management and employees in an industrial company **2.** RELATIONS BETWEEN ORGANIZED MANAGEMENT AND LABOR the relations and procedures between employers' organizations and labor unions that are institutionalized in an industrial society

In·dus·tri·al Rev·o·lu·tion *n.* the social and economic changes in Great Britain, Europe, and the United States that began in the second half of the 18th century and involved widespread adoption of industrial methods of production. The specialization of tasks, the concentration of capital, and the centralization of workforces were important aspects of these changes, which first affected Great Britain.

in·dus·tri·al so·ci·ol·o·gy *n.* the study of relationships and structures in industrial organizations

in·dus·tri·al-strength *adj.* used to describe materials or chemicals that are strong or of a quality suitable for use in industry

in·dus·tri·al un·ion *n.* a labor union made up of workers with different occupations who are all employed in one industry. ◊ **craft union**

In·dus·tri·al Work·ers of the World *n.* an international labor union with socialist aims that was founded in the United States in 1905 and lost influence after the 1920s

in·dus·tri·ous /in dústree əss/ *adj.* hard-working, conscientious, and energetic —**in·dus·tri·ous·ly** *adv.* — **in·dus·tri·ous·ness** *n.*

in·dus·try /índəstree/ (*plural* **-tries**) *n.* **1.** LARGE-SCALE PRODUCTION organized economic activity connected with the production, manufacture, or construction of a particular product or range of products **2.** WIDESPREAD ACTIVITY an activity that many people are involved in, especially one that has become excessively commercialized or standardized ○ *the counseling industry* **3.** HARD WORK diligent hard work (*formal or literary*) [15thC. Directly or via Old French *industrie* from Latin *industria* "diligence," from *industrius* "diligent," literally "building in," from assumed *-struus* "building."]

in·dus·try-wide *adj.* cutting across an entire field of commercial activity

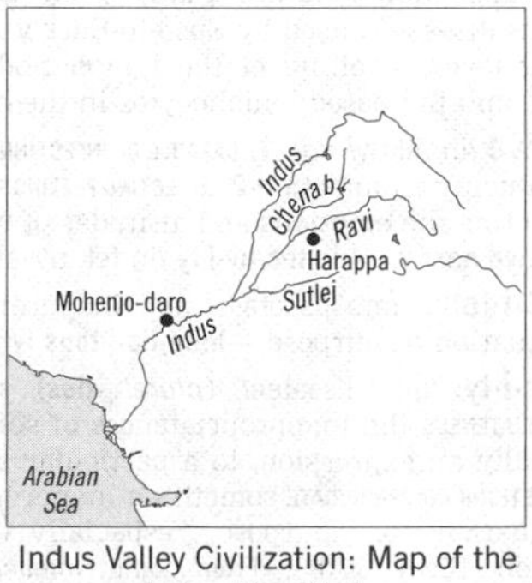

Indus Valley Civilization: Map of the Indus River Valley

In·dus Val·ley Civ·i·li·za·tion *n.* a Bronze-Age civilization that flourished in the lower Indus River Valley, mainly in present-day Pakistan and northern India, from about 2500 to 1700 B.C. It was the earliest known civilization in South Asia and, with Mesopotamia and Egypt, one of the earliest anywhere in the world.

in·dwell /in dwél/ (**-dwelled, -dwell·ing, -dwells**) *vti.* to inhabit, infuse, or abide within a person, community, or place (*literary*) [14thC. Formed from IN- + DWELL.] —**in·dwell·er** *n.*

-ine *suffix.* of, relating to, made of ○ *crystalline* ○ *murrhine* [Directly or via Old French from Latin *-inus* and, ultimately, Greek *-inos*]

in·e·bri·ant /i neébree ənt/ *n.* something that causes drunkenness or intoxication [Early 19thC. Formed from INEBRIATE, on the model of INTOXICANT.]

in·e·bri·ate *v.* /i neébree àyt/ (**-at·ed, -at·ing, -ates**) **1.** *vti.* MAKE INTOXICATED to cause somebody to become drunk or intoxicated **2.** *vt.* EXCITE to make somebody excited or exhilarated (*formal*) ■ *n.* /i neébree ət/ INTOXICATED PERSON somebody who is drunk or intoxicated (*archaic or literary*) ■ *adj.* /i neébree ət/ INTOXICATED drunk or intoxicated (*archaic or literary*) [15thC. From Latin *inebriatus*, past participle of *inebriare*, literally "to make drunk in," from *ebriare* "to make drunk," from *ebrius* "drunk."] —**in·e·bri·a·tion** /i neébree áysh'n/ *n.* —**in·e·bri·e·ty** /ìnnee brí ətee/ *n.*

in·e·bri·at·ed /i neébree àytəd/ *adj.* drunk or intoxicated (*formal*)

in·ed·i·ble /in éddəb'l/ *adj.* unfit for consumption as food —**in·ed·i·bil·i·ty** /in èddə bíllətee/ *n.* —**in·ed·i·bly** *adv.*

WORD KEY: USAGE

See Usage note at ***eatable.***

in·ed·u·ca·ble /in éjjəkəb'l/ *adj.* impossible to educate (*archaic*) —**in·ed·u·ca·bil·i·ty** /in èjjəkə bíllətee/ *n.*

in·ef·fa·ble /in éffəb'l/ *adj.* incapable of being expressed in words (*formal*) [15thC. Directly or via French from Latin *ineffabilis* "unutterable," from, ultimately, *effari* "to speak out," from *fari* "to speak" (source of English *fable*).] —**in·ef·fa·bil·i·ty** /in èffə bíllətee/ *n.* — **in·ef·fa·bly** /in éffəblee/ *adv.*

in·ef·face·a·ble /ìnnə fáyssəb'l/ *adj.* incapable of being erased or removed (*formal*) —**in·ef·face·a·bil·i·ty** /ìnnə fayssə bíllətee/ *n.* —**in·ef·face·a·bly** /ìnnə fáyssəblee/ *adv.*

in·ef·fec·tive /ìnnə féktiv/ *adj.* **1.** NOT PRODUCING DESIRED RESULT not producing the desired result or effect **2.** LACKING COMPETENCE incompetent or inept — **in·ef·fec·tive·ly** *adv.* —**in·ef·fec·tive·ness** *n.*

in·ef·fec·tu·al /ìnnə fék choo əl/ *adj.* **1.** INCOMPETENT OR INDECISIVE not competent, decisive, or authoritative enough to achieve desired aims **2.** INCAPABLE OF GENERATING DESIRED OUTCOME not able to produce a satisfactory outcome —**in·ef·fec·tu·al·i·ty** /ìnnə fek choo állətee/ *n.* —**in·ef·fec·tu·al·ly** /ìnnə fék choo əlee/ *adv.* —**in·ef·fec·tu·al·ness** *n.*

in·ef·fi·ca·cious /in èffi káyshəss/ *adj.* not having a positive or useful effect (*formal*) —**in·ef·fi·ca·cious·ly** *adv.* —**in·ef·fi·ca·cious·ness** *n.* —**in·ef·fi·cac·i·ty** /ìnnefi kássətee/ *n.* —**in·ef·fi·ca·cy** /in éffikəssee/ *n.*

in·ept /i népt/ *adj.* **1.** UNABLE TO HANDLE JOB lacking the competence or skill for a particular task **2.** TOTALLY INAPPROPRIATE not in keeping with what is right or proper for the circumstances [Mid-16thC. From Latin *ineptus*, literally "not suitable," from *aptus* (see APT).] — **in·ep·ti·tude** *n.* —**in·ept·ly** *adv.* —**in·ept·ness** *n.*

in·eq·ua·ble /in ékwəb'l/ *adj.* not fair or uniform [Early 18thC. From Latin *inaequabilis*, from *aequabilis* "equable" (see EQUABLE).]

in·e·qual·i·ty /ìnnə kwáwlətee/ (*plural* **-ties**) *n.* **1.** DIFFERENCE IN STATUS social or economic disparity between people or groups **2.** LACK OF EQUAL TREATMENT unequal opportunity or treatment based on social or economic disparity **3.** STATE OF BEING UNEQUAL the condition or an instance of not being equal **4.** MATH STATEMENT INDICATING UNEQUAL QUANTITIES a mathematical statement indicating that two quantities are not equal, represented by the symbols <, >, and ≠, meaning less than, greater than, and not equal to. An unconditional inequality is one that is true for all values of a variable. A conditional inequality is false for some values of a variable. **5.** UNEVENNESS ON SURFACE variability or unevenness in the surface of something [15thC. From Old French *inequalité*, from, ultimately, Latin *aequalis* (see EQUAL).]

in·eq·ui·ta·ble /in ékwitəb'l/ *adj.* showing bias or favoritism —**in·eq·ui·ta·ble·ness** *n.* —**in·eq·ui·ta·bly** *adv.*

in·eq·ui·ty /in ékwitee/ (*plural* **-ties**) *n.* **1.** UNFAIR TREATMENT lack of fairness or justice (*formal*) **2.** UNFAIR SITUATION OR ACTION a situation or action that is not fair

in·eq·ui·valve /in ékwi vàlv, -eékwi-/, **in·eq·ui·valv·ed** /in ékwi vàlvd, -eékwi-/ *adj.* used to describe a bivalve mollusk whose valves are unequal in size or form [Late 18thC. Coined from IN- + EQUI- + VALVE.]

in·e·rad·i·ca·ble /ìnnə ráddikəb'l/ *adj.* impossible to get rid of —**in·e·rad·i·ca·bil·i·ty** /ìnnə raddikə bíllətee/ *n.* —**in·e·rad·i·ca·ble·ness** /ìnnə ráddikəb'lnəss/ *n.* — **in·e·rad·i·ca·bly** *adv.*

in·er·rant /in érrənt/ *adj.* **1.** INCAPABLE OF MISTAKES incapable of making a mistake (*literary*) **2.** CORRECT containing no mistakes [Mid-17thC. From the Latin stem *inerrant-*, literally "not wandering," from *errare* (see ERR).] —**in·er·ran·cy** *n.*

in·ert /i núrt/ *adj.* **1.** MOTIONLESS not moving or able to move **2.** NON-REACTIVE not readily changed by chemical or biological reaction **3.** SLUGGISH OR UNMOTIVATED lacking in energy or motivation [Mid-17thC. From Latin *inert-*, the stem of *iners*, literally "having no skill," from *ars* "skill, art" . The underlying meaning is "useless, ineffective."] —**in·ert·ly** *adv.* —**in·ert·ness** *n.*

in·ert gas *n.* = **noble gas**

in·er·tia /i núrshə/ *n.* **1.** APATHY inability or unwillingness to move or act **2.** RESISTANCE TO CHANGE the property of a body by which it remains at rest or moving in a straight line unless acted upon by a directional force [Early 18thC. From Latin, "lack of skill, inactivity," formed from *iners* (see INERT).] —**in·er·tial** *adj.* —**in·er·tial·ly** *adv.*

in·er·tial con·fine·ment fu·sion *n.* NUCLEAR PHYS nuclear fusion achieved by firing high-energy lasers or particle beams at small pellets, typically containing deuterium and sometimes also tritium

in·er·tial guid·ance, in·er·tial nav·i·ga·tion *n.* navigation by conversion of the accelerations experienced into distances and directions. It is used on aircraft, spacecraft, or missiles that use devices such as gyroscopes, accelerometers, and computers to calculate and adjust course.

in·es·cap·a·ble /ìnnə skáypəb'l/ *adj.* impossible to avoid —**in·es·cap·a·bly** *adv.*

in es·se /in éssee/ *adj.* having actual existence as opposed to potential existence [From Latin, literally "in existence"]

in·es·sen·tial /ìnnə sénshəl/ *adj.* **1.** NOT ESSENTIAL not absolutely necessary **2.** WITHOUT ESSENCE without substance or being ■ *n.* SOMETHING INESSENTIAL something that is unnecessary —**in·es·sen·ti·al·i·ty** /ìnnə senshee állətee/ *n.*

in·es·sive /in éssiv/ *n.* in the grammar of languages such as Finnish, a case of nouns and pronouns used to indicate the location of something [Late 19thC. Formed from Latin *inesse* "to be in or at," from *esse* "to be."]

in·es·ti·ma·ble /in éstiməb'l/ *adj.* **1.** INCALCULABLE too great to calculate its extent, magnitude, or amount **2.** INVALUABLE of such great worth that a value cannot be placed upon it [14thC. Via French from Latin *inaestimabilis*, literally "not calculable," from *aestimare* (see ESTIMATE).] —**in·es·ti·ma·bil·i·ty** /in èstimə bíllətee/ *n.* — **in·es·ti·ma·ble·ness** /in éstiməb'lnəss/ *n.* —**in·es·ti·ma·bly** *adv.*

in·ev·i·ta·ble /in évvitəb'l/ *adj.* UNAVOIDABLE impossible to avoid or to prevent from happening ■ *n.* SOMETHING CERTAIN something that is certain to happen [15thC. From Latin *inevitabilis*, literally "not avoidable," from *evitare* "to shun."] —**in·ev·i·ta·bil·i·ty** /in èvvitə bíllətee/ *n.* — **in·ev·i·ta·ble·ness** *n.* —**in·ev·i·ta·bly** *adv.*

in·ex·act /ìnnig zákt/ *adj.* **1.** NOT PRECISE not entirely accurate **2.** SLAPDASH not thorough or careful — **in·ex·act·i·tude** *n.* —**in·ex·act·ly** *adv.* —**in·ex·act·ness** *n.*

in·ex·cus·a·ble /ìnnik skyoózəb'l/ *adj.* impossible to pardon or justify [15thC. From Latin *inexcusabilis*, literally "not excusable," from *excusare* (see EXCUSE).] — **in·ex·cus·a·bil·i·ty** /ìnnik skyoozə bíllətee/ *n.* —**in·ex·cus·a·ble·ness** /ìnnik skyoózəb'lnəss/ *n.* —**in·ex·cus·a·bly** *adv.*

in·ex·haust·i·ble /ìnnig zóstəb'l/ *adj.* **1.** EVERLASTING impossible to use up **2.** NOT GETTING TIRED showing no sign of tiring —**in·ex·haust·i·bil·i·ty** /ìnnig zostə bíllətee/ *n.* —**in·ex·haust·i·ble·ness** /ìnnig zóstəb'lnəss/ *n.* — **in·ex·haust·i·bly** *adv.*

in·ex·o·ra·ble /in éksərəb'l/ *adj.* **1.** UNSTOPPABLE impossible to stop (*formal*) **2.** ADAMANT AND PITILESS not moved by anyone's attempts to plead or persuade [Mid-16thC. Via French from, ultimately, Latin *exorare* "to prevail upon," from *orare* "to pray" (see

ORATION).] —**in·ex·o·ra·bil·i·ty** /in èksərə bíllətee/ *n.* —**in·ex·o·ra·ble·ness** /in éksərəb'lnəss/ *n.* —**in·ex·o·ra·bly** *adv.*

in·ex·pe·di·ent /ìnnik spéedee ənt/ *adj.* **1. INCONVENIENT** not convenient or practical **2. INADVISABLE** not recommended or prudent (*formal*) —**in·ex·pe·di·ence** *n.* —**in·ex·pe·di·ent·ly** *adv.*

in·ex·pen·sive /ìnnik spénsiv/ *adj.* not costing much money —**in·ex·pen·sive·ly** *adv.* —**in·ex·pen·sive·ness** *n.*

in·ex·pe·ri·ence /ìnnik spéeree ənss/ *n.* **1. LACK OF EXPERIENCE** the lack of skills or knowledge that people learn over a period of time **2. LACK OF SOPHISTICATION** lack of sophistication about worldly ways [Late 16thC. Via French from late Latin *inexperientia*, literally "lack of experience," from Latin *experientia* (see EXPERIENCE).] —**in·ex·pe·ri·enced** *adj.*

in·ex·pert /in ékspərt/ *adj.* lacking in skill or experience [15thC. Via Old French from Latin *inexpertus*, literally "not experienced," from *expertus*, the past participle of *experiri* (see EXPERIENCE).] —**in·ex·pert·ly** *adv.* —**in·ex·pert·ness** *n.*

in·ex·pi·a·ble /in ékspee əb'l/ *adj.* so bad that it cannot be atoned for [15thC. From Latin *inexpiabilis* "that cannot be atoned for," from *expiare* (see EXPIATE).] —**in·ex·pi·a·ble·ness** *n.* —**in·ex·pi·a·bly** *adv.*

in·ex·plain·a·ble /ìnnik spláynəb'l/ *adj.* impossible to explain

in·ex·pli·ca·ble /ìnnik splíkəb'l, in éksplikəb'l/ *adj.* incapable of being explained or justified [15thC. Directly or via French from Latin *inexplicabilis*, from *explicare* (see EXPLICATE).] —**in·ex·pli·ca·bil·i·ty** /ìnnik splìkə bíllətee, in èksplìkə-/ *n.* —**in·ex·pli·ca·ble·ness** /ìnnik splíkəb'lnəss, in éksplikəb'lnəss/ *n.* —**in·ex·pli·ca·bly** *adv.*

in·ex·plic·it /ìnnik splíssit/ *adj.* not expressed or shown fully, openly, and unambiguously

in·ex·press·i·ble /ìnnik spréssəb'l/ *adj.* impossible to put into words —**in·ex·press·i·bil·i·ty** /ìnnik sprèssə bíllətee/ *n.* —**in·ex·press·i·ble·ness** /ìnnik spréssə b'lnəss/ *n.* —**in·ex·press·i·bly** *adv.*

in·ex·pres·sive /ìnnik spréssiv/ *adj.* conveying no feeling —**in·ex·pres·sive·ly** *adv.* —**in·ex·pres·sive·ness** *n.*

in·ex·pug·na·ble /ìnnik spyóonəb'l/ *adj.* **1. IMPREGNABLE** impossible to take by force **2. UNBEATABLE** impossible to overcome [15thC. Via French from Latin *inexpugnabilis*, from *expugnare*, literally "to fight off," from pugnare "to fight."] —**in·ex·pug·na·bil·i·ty** /ìnnik spyòonə bíllətee/ *n.* —**in·ex·pug·na·ble·ness** /ìnnik spyóonəb'lnəss/ *n.* —**in·ex·pug·na·bly** *adv.*

in·ex·pun·gi·ble /ìnnik spúnjəb'l/ *adj.* impossible to remove or cancel out

in·ex·ten·si·ble /ìnnik sténsəb'l/ *adj.* impossible to stretch to a greater length —**in·ex·ten·si·bil·i·ty** /ìnnik stènsə bíllətee/ *n.*

in ex·ten·so /ìnnik sténsō/ *adv.* at its full length ○ *quote a passage in extenso* [From Latin, literally "at a stretch"]

in·ex·tin·guish·a·ble /ìnnik stíng gwishəb'l/ *adj.* impossible to extinguish or suppress —**in·ex·tin·guish·a·ble·ness** *n.* —**in·ex·tin·guish·a·bly** *adv.*

in·ex·tir·pa·ble /ìnnik stúrpəb'l/ *adj.* impossible to remove or destroy (*literary*) [Early 17thC. From Latin *inex(s)tirpabilis*, from *ex(s)tirpare* (see EXTIRPATE).] —**in·ex·tir·pa·ble·ness** *n.*

in ex·tre·mis /in ik stréemiss/ *adv.* **IN DESPERATE CIRCUMSTANCES** in desperate circumstances, especially at the point of death ■ *adj.* **NEAR DEATH** on the point of death [From Latin, literally "in the extremes"]

in·ex·tri·ca·ble /in ékstrikəb'l, ìnnik stríkəb'l/ *adj.* **1. IMPOSSIBLE TO ESCAPE FROM** impossible to get free from **2. IMPOSSIBLE TO DISENTANGLE** impossible to unentangle or undo **3. HOPELESSLY COMPLEX** hopelessly involved or complex [Mid-16thC. From Latin *inextricabilis* "that cannot be disentangled," from *extricare* (see EXTRICATE).] —**in·ex·tri·ca·bil·i·ty** /in èkstrikə bíllətee, ìnnik strìkə-/ *n.* —**in·ex·tri·ca·ble·ness** /in ékstrikəb'lnəss, ìnnik stríkəb'lnəss/ *n.* —**in·ex·tri·ca·bly** *adv.*

INF *n., abbr.* intermediate-range nuclear forces

inf. *abbr.* **1.** infantry **2.** inferior **3.** BASEBALL infield **4.** BASEBALL infielder **5.** GRAM infinitive **6.** infinity **7.** informal **8.** information **9.** infra

Inf. *abbr.* infantry

in·fal·li·ble /in fálləb'l/ *adj.* **1. NOT ERRING** incapable of making a mistake **2. INCAPABLE OF FAILING** certain not to fail **3.** RELIG **UNERRING IN DOCTRINE** incapable of being mistaken in matters of doctrine and dogma [15thC. From medieval Latin *infallibilis*, from Latin *fallere* "to deceive, disappoint" (source of English *fail*).] —**in·fal·li·bil·i·ty** /in fàllə bíllətee/ *n.* —**in·fal·li·ble·ness** /in fálləb'lnəss/ *n.* —**in·fal·li·bly** *adv.*

in·fa·mous /ínfəməss/ *adj.* **1. NOTORIOUS** having an extremely bad reputation **2. ABOMINABLE** so bad as to earn somebody an extremely bad reputation **3.** LAW **PUNISHABLE BY A SERIOUS PENALTY** punishable by imprisonment or loss of civil rights **4.** LAW **CONVICTED OF INFAMOUS CRIME** convicted of an infamous crime [14thC. From medieval Latin *infamosus*, a variant of Latin *infamis* "of ill repute," literally "having no fame," from *fama* (see FAME).] —**in·fa·mous·ly** *adv.* —**in·fa·mous·ness** *n.*

in·fa·my /ínfəmee/ (*plural* **-mies**) *n.* **1. NOTORIETY** the disgrace to somebody's reputation caused by an infamous act or behavior **2. SHAMEFUL OR CRIMINAL CONDUCT** shameful or criminal conduct or character **3. EVIL DEED** a publicly known infamous act or event **4.** LAW **LOSS OF RIGHTS OR IMPRISONMENT** punishment incurred by being convicted of an infamous crime [15thC. From French *infamie*, from, ultimately, Latin *infamis* (see INFAMOUS).]

in·fan·cy /ínfənsee/ *n.* **1. BABYHOOD** the condition or time of childhood before a baby walks or talks **2. BEGINNING** an early stage of development for an idea, project, or enterprise **3.** LAW **TIME OF BEING MINOR** the condition or time in which a young person is not legally considered an adult

in·fant /ínfənt/ *n.* **1. BABY** a very young child that can neither walk nor talk **2.** LAW **LEGAL MINOR** a young person legally considered a minor ■ *adj.* **JUST BEGINNING** in an early stage of development [14thC. Via French *enfant* from, ultimately, Latin *infans*, literally "not speaking," from *fari* "to speak."] —**in·fant·hood** *n.*

in·fan·ta /in fántə, -faántə/ (*plural* **-tas**) *n.* **1. SPANISH OR PORTUGUESE PRINCESS** in the past, the daughter of a Spanish or Portuguese king **2. INFANTE'S WIFE** the wife of an infante [Late 16thC. From Spanish and Portuguese, feminine of *infante* "INFANTE."]

in·fan·te /in fán tày/ (*plural* **-tes**) *n.* in the past, a son, other than the heir to the throne, of a Spanish or Portuguese king, especially the second son [Mid-16thC. Via Spanish and Portuguese from Latin *infans* "child" (see INFANT).]

in·fan·ti·cide /in fántə sìd/ *n.* **1. MURDER OF INFANT** the killing of an infant **2. KILLING OF BABIES** the practice of killing newborn babies **3. KILLER OF INFANT** somebody who kills an infant —**in·fan·ti·cid·al** /in fàntə sìd'l/ *adj.*

in·fan·tile /ínfən tìl/ *adj.* **1. CHILDISH** showing a lack of maturity **2. RELATING TO INFANTS** relating to infants or infancy **3.** GEOG **IN FIRST STAGE OF EROSION** in the earliest stage of erosion —**in·fan·til·i·ty** /ìnfən tíllətee/ *n.*

in·fan·tile pa·ral·y·sis *n.* poliomyelitis (*dated*)

in·fan·til·ism /in fánt'l ìzzəm, ínfənt'l-/ *n.* **1. SEXUAL AND EMOTIONAL UNDERDEVELOPMENT** a condition of mental or physical underdevelopment, in which a person fails to mature sexually and emotionally **2. CHILDISH BEHAVIOR** childish or immature behavior

in·fan·til·ize /ínfənt'l ìz, in fánt'l-/ (**-ized, -iz·ing, -iz·es**) *vt.* **1. KEEP FROM MATURING** to make somebody infantile or to keep somebody in an infantile state **2. TREAT AS A BABY** to treat somebody as or consider somebody to be infantile —**in·fan·til·i·za·tion** /ìnfənt'li záysh'n, in fànt'li-/ *n.*

in·fant mor·tal·i·ty rate *n.* the number of deaths during the first year of life per thousand live births

in·fan·try /ínfəntree/ (*plural* **-tries**) *n.* the soldiers or a unit of soldiers who are trained to fight on foot [Late 16thC. From French *infanterie*, from, ultimately, Italian *infante* "youth, foot soldier," from Latin *infans* (see INFANT).]

in·fan·try·man /ínfəntrimən/ (*plural* **-men** /-mən/) *n.* a soldier in the infantry

in·fant school *n. U.K.* a school, or part of a school, for children between the ages of four or five and seven. This is the first stage of compulsory education in the U.K.

in·farct /ín faarkt, in faárkt/ *n.* an area of tissue that has recently died as a result of the sudden loss of its blood supply, e.g., following blockage of an artery by a blood clot [Late 19thC. From modern Latin *infarctus*, from the past participle stem of Latin *infarcire*, literally "to cram in," from *farcire* "to stuff."]

in·farc·tion /in faárkshən, in faárkshən/ *n.* **1. INFARCT FORMATION** the formation of an infarct **2.** = **infarct**

in·fat·u·ate /in fáchoo àyt/ (**-at·ed, -at·ing, -ates**) *vt.* to make somebody behave irrationally as a result of a great, often temporary passion for somebody or something [Mid-16thC. From Latin *infatuat-*, the past participle stem of *infatuare*, literally "to make foolish," from *fatuus* "foolish" (source of English *fatuous*).]

in·fat·u·at·ed /in fáchoo àytəd/ *adj.* **1. HOPELESSLY IN LOVE** preoccupied with and foolishly in love with somebody **2. PASSIONATE ABOUT SOMETHING** utterly captivated and obsessed by something —**in·fat·u·at·ed·ly** *adv.*

in·fat·u·a·tion /in fàchoo áysh'n/ *n.* **1. THOUGHTLESS PASSION** a great, often temporary, and irrational passion for somebody or something **2. OBJECT OF SOMEBODY'S INFATUATION** the person or object that somebody is infatuated with

WORD KEY: SYNONYMS

See Synonyms at ***love***.

in·fau·na /in fáwnə/ *npl.* organisms that live in tubes or burrows beneath the surface of the sea floor [Early 20thC. Coined from IN- + FAUNA.] —**in·fau·nal** *adj.*

in·fea·si·ble /in féezəb'l/ *adj.* not practical or easily achieved —**in·fea·si·bil·i·ty** /in fèezə bíllətee/ *n.* —**in·fea·si·ble·ness** /in féezəb'lnəss/ *n.* —**in·fea·si·bly** *adv.*

in·fect /in fékt/ (**-fect·ed, -fect·ing, -fects**) *vt.* **1. CAUSE INFECTION IN** to contaminate or cause infection in somebody or something with a disease-producing agent **2. CAUSE COMMUNICABLE DISEASE IN** to give somebody a communicable disease **3. ENTER PERSON OR ANIMAL** to invade and live in the body of a person or animal (*refers to microorganisms or endoparasites*) **4. AFFECT** to corrupt or adversely affect somebody or something **5. INFLUENCE SOMEBODY'S FEELINGS** to communicate an emotion such as enthusiasm or fear to somebody **6.** COMPUT **CONTAMINATE COMPUTER WITH VIRUS** to copy to a computer system a computer virus that is capable of damaging the system's programs or data [14thC. From Latin *infect-*, the past participle stem of *inficere* "to stain, dye," literally "to dip in," from *facere* "to do, put."] —**in·fect·ed** *adj.* —**in·fec·tor** *n.*

in·fec·tion /in fékshən/ *n.* **1. STATE OF BEING INFECTED** the reproduction and proliferation of microorganisms within the body **2. INFECTING OF OTHERS** the transmission of infectious microorganisms from one person to another **3. INFECTING MICROORGANISM** an infecting microorganism or agent **4. DISEASE** a communicable disease **5. MORAL CORRUPTION** something that corrupts somebody morally **6. TRANSMISSION OF FEELINGS** the communication of emotions or attitudes between people

in·fec·tious /in fékshəss/ *adj.* **1. COMMUNICABLE** used to describe a disease that is capable of being passed from one person to another **2. CAUSED BY BACTERIA** caused by bacteria, viruses, or other microorganisms **3. CAUSING INFECTION** bringing about infection **4. AFFECTING FEELINGS OF OTHERS** capable of affecting the emotions and attitudes of others ○ *an infectious laugh* —**in·fec·tious·ly** *adv.* —**in·fec·tious·ness** *n.*

in·fec·tious hep·a·ti·tis *n.* = **hepatitis A**

in·fec·tious mon·o·nu·cle·o·sis *n.* an acute infectious disease caused by Epstein-Barr virus, producing fever, swelling of the lymph nodes, sore throat, and increased lymphocytes in the blood

in·fec·tive /in féktiv/ *adj.* **1. CAPABLE OF INFECTING** capable of producing an infection **2. AFFECTING FEELINGS** capable of affecting the emotions and attitudes of others —**in·fec·tive·ness** *n.* —**in·fec·tiv·i·ty** /in fek tívvətee/ *n.*

in·fe·lic·i·tous /ìnfə líssətəss/ *adj.* inappropriate to the situation or purpose —**in·fe·lic·i·tous·ly** *adv.*

in·fe·lic·i·ty /ìnfə líssətee/ (*plural* **-ties**) *n.* **1. INAPPROPRIATENESS** the inappropriateness of something, especially an expression, to a particular situation **2. SOMETHING INAPPROPRIATE** something inappropriate to a situation or purpose, especially an expression [Early 17thC. From Latin *infelicitas* "unhappiness," from *felix* "happy." The underlying meaning is "an unfortunate expression."]

in·fer /in fúr/ (**-ferred, -fer·ring, -fers**) *v.* **1.** *vti.* **CONCLUDE SOMETHING ON THE BASIS OF REASONING** to conclude something on the basis of evidence or reasoning **2.** *vt.* **SUGGEST** to suggest or lead to something as a conclusion **3.** *vt.* **IMPLY** to imply or suggest something **4.** *vt.* **GUESS SOMETHING** to make a reasonable guess at something [Early 16thC. From Latin *inferre*, literally "to bring in," from *ferre* "to carry."] —**in·fer·a·ble** *adj.* —**in·fer·a·bly** *adv.* —**in·fer·rer** *n.*

WORD KEY: SYNONYMS
See Synonyms at ***deduce***.

in·fer·ence /ínfərəns/ *n.* **1.** CONCLUSION a conclusion drawn from evidence or reasoning **2.** LOGIC REASONING PROCESS the process of reasoning from a premise to a conclusion **3.** IMPLICATION something that is implied [Late 16thC. From medieval Latin *inferentia*, from Latin *inferre* (see INFER).] —**in·fer·en·tial** /ìnfə rénshəl/ *adj.* —**in·fer·en·tial·ly** *adv.*

in·fe·ri·or /in féeree ər/ *adj.* **1.** LOWER IN STANDING lower or low in rank, standing, or degree **2.** NOT AS GOOD lower in quality or value **3.** MEDIOCRE failing to meet a standard of quality, ability, or achievement **4.** ANAT LOWER IN BODY used to describe a body part or organ situated beneath another similar part **5.** BOT BELOW A CALYX used to describe a plant ovary located below a calyx **6.** ASTRON BETWEEN EARTH AND SUN orbiting or taking place between the Earth and the Sun. Mercury and Venus are designated as inferior planets. **7.** PRINTING PRINTED BELOW THE LINE written or printed at a slightly lower level than the rest of the characters in a line, e.g., the "2" in "CO_2" ■ *n.* **1.** LOWER RANKING PERSON somebody of lower status, rank, or quality **2.** PRINTING SUBSCRIPT CHARACTER a character printed or written below the line [15thC. From Latin, "lower," from *inferus* "below." Ultimately from an Indo-European word meaning "beneath" that is also the ancestor of English *under* and *infernal*.] —**in·fe·ri·or·i·ty** /in fèeree áwrətee/ *n.* —**in·fe·ri·or·ly** /in féeree ərlee/ *adv.*

in·fe·ri·or·i·ty com·plex *n.* an overdeveloped sense of being inferior to others. In extreme cases it can manifest itself in either withdrawn or aggressive social behavior.

in·fer·nal /in fúrn'l/ *adj.* **1.** VERY ANNOYING extremely annoying or unpleasant (*informal*) **2.** RELATING TO UNDERWORLD relating to hell or the underworld **3.** DIABOLICAL IN NATURE so wicked or cruel as to be worthy of hell [14thC. From Old French, from, ultimately, Latin *infernus* "lower, the underworld." Ultimately from an Indo-European word meaning "beneath" that is also the ancestor of English *under* and *inferior*.] —**in·fer·nal·ly** *adv.*

in·fer·no /in fúrnō/ (*plural* **-nos**) *n.* **1.** CONFLAGRATION a fire or a place that is burning fiercely **2.** HELLISH PLACE a place or situation that is reminiscent of hell [Mid-19thC. Via Italian, "hell," from late Latin *infernus* (see INFERNAL).]

WORD KEY: SYNONYMS
See Synonyms at ***fire***.

in·fer·tile /in fúrt'l/ *adj.* **1.** STERILE physically incapable of conceiving offspring **2.** NOT PRODUCING CROPS incapable of producing crops **3.** NOT FERTILIZED used to describe an egg that has not been fertilized [Late 16thC. Directly or via French from late Latin *infertilis*, literally "not bearing," from *fertilis* (see FERTILE).] —**in·fer·tile·ly** *adv.* —**in·fer·til·i·ty** /ìn fur tíllətee/ *n.*

in·fest /in fést/ (**-fest·ed, -fest·ing, -fests**) *vt.* **1.** TAKE OVER PLACE to overrun a place in large numbers and become threatening, harmful, or unpleasant **2.** LIVE AS A PARASITE ON to live as a parasite on or in something [Mid-16thC. Directly or via French *infester* from Latin *infestare* "to attack," from *infestus* "hostile."] —**in·fes·ta·tion** /ìn fess táysh'n/ *n.* —**in·fest·ed** /in féstəd/ *adj.* —**in·fest·er** *n.*

in·fib·u·late /in fíbbyə làyt/ (**-lat·ed, -lat·ing, -lates**) *vt.* to close the vagina partially by stitching it, or closing it with a clasp. The clitoris is often removed at the same time. ◊ **female circumcision** [Early 17thC. From Latin *infibulat-* "to fasten with a pin," from *fibula* (see FIBULA).] —**in·fib·u·la·tion** /in fìbbyə láysh'n/ *n.*

in·fi·del /ínfid'l, ínfi dèl/ *n.* (*disapproving*) **1.** HEATHEN somebody who has no belief in the religion of the speaker or writer, especially Christianity or Islam **2.** NONBELIEVER somebody who has no religious beliefs [15thC. Directly or via French *infidèle* from Latin *infidelis*, literally "unbelieving," from *fidelis* "faithful," from *fides* (see FAITH).]

in·fi·del·i·ty /ìnfi déllətee/ (*plural* **-ties**) *n.* **1.** UNFAITHFULNESS unfaithfulness or disloyalty, especially to a sexual partner **2.** UNFAITHFUL ACT an act of unfaithfulness or disloyalty, especially to a sexual partner **3.** DISBELIEF lack of religious faith (*disapproving*) [14thC. From French *infidélité*, from, ultimately, Latin *infidelis* (see INFIDEL).]

in·field /ín fèeld/ *n.* **1.** BASEBALL DIAMOND the area of a baseball field bounded by home plate and the three bases **2.** BASEBALL PLAYERS IN INFIELD the defensive baseball players in the infield considered together. They are the first, second, and third basemen and the shortstop. **3.** AREA WITHIN A RACETRACK the area bounded by a racetrack **4.** AGRIC, HIST FARMLAND CLOSE TO A FARMHOUSE the farmland close to a farmhouse that is regularly manured and cropped

in·field·er /ín fèeldər/ *n.* a defensive baseball player in the infield

in·fight·ing /ín fìting/ *n.* **1.** INTERNAL SQUABBLING conflict or rivalry between associates or members of the same organization **2.** SPORTS FIGHTING AT CLOSE RANGE boxing or fighting at close range —**in·fight·er** *n.*

in·fil·trate /in fíl tràyt, ínfil-/ *vti.* (**-trat·ed, -trat·ing, -trates**) **1.** BREAK THROUGH SECRETLY to cross or send somebody into enemy territory without the enemy's knowledge ○ *infiltrate troops behind enemy lines* **2.** GET IN POSITION TO DO HARM to establish somebody or become established within a place or organization with the intention of doing harm or gathering information ○ *activists were infiltrated into local parties* **3.** CHEM PERMEATE FLUID THROUGH A SUBSTANCE to pass through a substance by filtration, or make a liquid or gas pass through a substance by filtration ■ *n.* MED ABNORMAL ACCUMULATION a substance such as fat that passes into tissues and cells and forms an abnormal accumulation [Mid-18thC. Formed from IN- + FILTRATE.] —**in·fil·tra·tion** /ìnfil tráysh'n/ *n.* —**in·fil·tra·tive** /ínfil tràytiv, in fíltrətiv/ *adj.* —**in·fil·tra·tor** /in fíl tràytər, ínfil-/ *n.*

infin. *abbr.* GRAM infinitive

in·fi·nite /ínfənit/ *adj.* **1.** NOT MEASURABLE without any limits that can be measured or realized **2.** EXCEEDINGLY GREAT very great in size, number, degree, or extent ○ *he took infinite pains over it* **3.** MATH GREATER THAN ANY ASSIGNED VALUE greater in number, size, or scope than any arbitrarily assigned value **4.** MATH WITH UNLIMITED SPATIAL EXTENT extending indefinitely or having unlimited spatial extent **5.** MATH WITH INFINITELY MANY ELEMENTS having an infinite number of terms or elements **6.** MATH SUPPORTING ONE-TO-ONE RELATIONSHIP able to be put into a one-to-one correspondence with a subset of itself ■ *n.* SOMETHING INFINITE something that is infinite, e.g., space [14thC. Via Old French from Latin *infinitus*, literally "not bounded," from *finitus* "finished, finite."] —**in·fi·nite·ly** *adv.* —**in·fi·nite·ness** *n.*

In·fi·nite *n.* used to refer to God

in·fi·nite loop *n.* a series of instructions in a computer program that repeats endlessly

in·fin·i·tes·i·mal /in finni téssəm'l/ *adj.* **1.** TINY very small in number, amount, or degree **2.** MATH CLOSE TO ZERO able to assume values arbitrarily close to but greater than zero ■ *n.* INFINITESIMAL NUMBER an infinitesimal number or function [Mid-17thC. Formed from modern Latin *infinitesimus* "the number in a series corresponding to infinity" (as when calculating fractions), from Latin *infinitus* (see INFINITE).] —**in·fin·i·tes·i·mal·ly** *adv.*

in·fin·i·tes·i·mal cal·cu·lus *n.* MATH = **calculus** *n.* 1

in·fin·i·tive /in fínnitiv/ *n.* a form of a verb with no reference to a particular tense, person, or subject. In English, an infinitive is usually preceded by the word "to," as in "to see." [15thC. From late Latin *infinitivus*, from Latin *infinitus*, literally "not bounded" (see INFINITE). The underlying meaning is "not limited by person or number."] —**in·fin·i·ti·val** /in finni tív'l/ *adj.* —**in·fin·i·ti·val·ly** /-tívəlee/ *adv.*

in·fin·i·tude /in fínni tòod/ *n.* **1.** BOUNDLESSNESS the infinite nature of something **2.** VERY LARGE NUMBER OF SOMETHING a very great number, degree, or extent of something [Mid-17thC. Formed from Latin *infinitus* "infinite" (see INFINITE), on the model of MAGNITUDE.]

in·fin·i·ty /in fínnitee/ (*plural* **-ties**) *n.* **1.** SOMETHING WITHOUT LIMITS limitless time, space, or distance ○ *beyond the Earth lay infinity* **2.** SOMETHING TOO GREAT TO COUNT an amount or number so great that it cannot be counted ○ *an infinity of stars* **3.** STATE OF BEING INFINITE the state or quality of being infinite **4.** MATH CONCEPT OF BEING ALWAYS UNLIMITED the concept of being unlimited by always being larger than any imposed value or boundary. For some purposes this may be considered as being the same as one divided by zero. **5.** GEOM GEOMETRIC POINT AT INFINITE DISTANCE a part of a geometric figure situated an infinite distance from the observer, e.g., the hypothetical point at which parallel lines meet in Euclidean geometry **6.** OPTICS INFINITELY DISTANT POINT a point sufficiently far from a lens or mirror that the light emitted from it falls in parallel rays on the surface [14thC. From French *infinité*, from, ultimately, Latin *infinitus* (see INFINITE).]

in·firm /in fúrm/ *adj.* **1.** NOT STRONG lacking strength and vitality, e.g. because of sickness or age **2.** IRRESOLUTE lacking firmness of character or a strong will **3.** BUILDING STRUCTURALLY UNSOUND having a structure that is not sound **4.** LAW LEGALLY UNSOUND invalid or not supported, e.g., a title to property or a claim ■ *npl.* PEOPLE WHO ARE NOT STRONG people who lack strength and vitality, e.g. because of sickness or age (*sometimes considered offensive*) [14thC. From Latin *infirmus*, literally "not strong," from *firmus* "firm."] —**in·firm·ly** *adv.* —**in·firm·ness** *n.*

WORD KEY: SYNONYMS
See Synonyms at ***weak***.

in·fir·ma·ry /in fúrməree/ (*plural* **-ries**) *n.* a hospital or area within an institution where sick and injured people are cared for [15thC. From medieval Latin *infirmaria*, from Latin *infirmus* (see INFIRM).]

in·fir·mi·ty /in fúrmətee/ (*plural* **-ties**) *n.* **1.** LACK OF STRENGTH lack of strength and vitality **2.** CHARACTER FLAW a weakness or failing in somebody's character **3.** MINOR ILLNESS any medical condition that causes a lack of strength or vitality

in·fix *vt.* /in fíks/ (**-fixed, -fix·ing, -fix·es**) **1.** FIX SOMETHING FIRMLY IN SOMETHING ELSE to insert something into another thing in order to secure it **2.** INSTILL to secure something firmly in the mind **3.** GRAM PUT AN ELEMENT IN WORD to insert a linking element into a word. In the word acidophilus, "-o-" is an infix. ■ *n.* /ín fìks/ GRAM AFFIX IN MIDDLE an affix inserted into the middle of a word [Early 16thC. Partly from IN + FIX; partly from Latin *infix-*, the past participle stem of *infigere*, literally "to fasten in," from *figere* (see FIX).] —**in·fix·a·tion** /ìn fik sáysh'n/ *n.* —**in·fix·ion** /in fíkshən/ *n.*

infl. *abbr.* **1.** inflammable **2.** inflorescence **3.** influence **4.** influenced

in fla·gran·te de·lic·to /in flə gràntee də líktō/, **in fla·gran·te** *informal adv.* **1.** IN A CRIMINAL ACT in the act of committing an offense **2.** HAVING SEX in the act of having sexual relations, especially illicit sexual relations [From Latin, literally, "in the heat of the crime"]

in·flame /in fláym/ (**-flamed, -flam·ing, -flames**) *v.* **1.** *vt.* PROVOKE A POWERFUL RESPONSE IN to excite somebody to an intense emotion such as anger or jealousy **2.** *vt.* MAKE SOMETHING STRONGER to make something, e.g., anger or jealousy, become more intense **3.** *vti.* SWELL AND TURN RED to become red and swollen, or to make bodily tissue become red and swollen, in response to injury or infection [14thC. Via Old French *enflammer* from Latin *inflammare*, from *flamma* "flame."] —**in·flamed** *adj.* —**in·flam·er** *n.*

in·flam·ma·ble /in flámməb'l/ *adj.* **1.** EASILY SET ON FIRE quickly and easily set on fire and burned. ◊ **flammable 2.** EASILY ROUSED easily made angry or passionate ■ *n.* FLAMMABLE ITEM something that is quickly and easily set on fire and burned [Early 17thC. From medieval Latin *inflammabilis* "liable to inflammation," from Latin *inflammare* (see INFLAME).] —**in·flam·ma·bil·i·ty** /in flàmmə bíllətee/ *n.* —**in·flam·ma·ble·ness** /in flámməb'lnəss/ *n.* —**in·flam·ma·bly** /-flámməblee/ *adv.*

in·flam·ma·tion /ìnflə máysh'n/ *n.* **1.** SWOLLEN REDDENED STATE swelling, redness, heat, and pain produced in an area of the body as a reaction to injury or infection **2.** HEIGHTENING OF EMOTION a heightening or stirring up of emotion

in·flam·ma·to·ry /in flámmə tàwree/ *adj.* **1.** PROVOCATIVE liable to arouse strong emotions, especially anger **2.** MED RELATING TO INFLAMMATION caused or characterized by inflammation —**in·flam·ma·to·ri·ly** *adv.*

in·flat·a·ble /in fláytəb'l/ *adj.* ABLE TO BE BLOWN UP made of expandable material that can be filled with gas or air ■ *n.* BLOWN-UP OBJECT something, e.g., a ball, mattress, or boat, that can be filled with air or gas

in·flate /in fláyt/ (**-flat·ed, -flat·ing, -flates**) *vti.* **1.** EXPAND WITH AIR to fill something, e.g., a ball, mattress or boat, with air or gas, or to be filled with air or gas **2.** MAKE SOMETHING APPEAR GREATER to exaggerate the size or importance of something, or to become exaggerated in size or importance **3.** ECON INCREASE PRICES OR MONEY SUPPLY to cause inflation in prices or the money supply, or to undergo inflation [15thC. From Latin *inflat-*, literally "to blow into," from *flare* (see FLATULENT).] —**in·fla·tor** *n.*

in·flat·ed /in fláytəd/ *adj.* **1.** UNDESERVEDLY GREAT greater than is justified or normal ○ *an inflated sense of her* *own importance* **2.** ECON **EXCESSIVELY HIGH** excessively or abnormally high **3. PRETENTIOUS** exaggerated or pompous in expression **4. BLOWN UP** expanded with air or gas —**in·flat·ed·ly** *adv.* —**in·flat·ed·ness** *n.*

in·fla·tion /in fláysh'n/ *n.* **1.** ECON **HIGHER PRICES** an increase in the supply of currency or credit relative to the availability of goods and services, resulting in higher prices **2. BEING INFLATED** the act of inflating something or the condition of being inflated **3. BEING PUFFED UP WITH PRIDE** being puffed up with pride

in·fla·tion·ar·y /in fláysh'n èrree/ *adj.* relating to or causing economic inflation ○ *inflationary policies*

in·fla·tion·ar·y spi·ral *n.* a continuous economic cycle of higher prices causing higher wages, which in turn cause even higher prices

in·fla·tion·ism /in fláysh'n ìzzəm/ *n.* the advocacy or policy of deliberately causing economic inflation through an increase in the supply of available currency and credit —**in·fla·tion·ist** *adj., n.*

in·flect /in flékt/ (**-flect·ed, -flect·ing, -flects**) *v.* **1.** *vt.* **VARY THE PITCH OF THE VOICE** to change the pitch or tone of the voice **2.** *vti.* GRAM **CHANGE A WORD FORM** to change the form of a word, e.g., to show a change in tense, mood, gender, or number, or to be changed in this way **3.** *vt.* **BEND** to make something turn from a direct line or course [15thC. From Latin *inflectere,* literally "to bend in," from *flectere* (see FLEXIBLE).] —**in·flect·a·ble** *adj.* —**in·flect·ed** *adj.* —**in·flec·tive** *adj.* —**in·flec·tor** *n.*

in·flec·tion /in flékshən/ *n.* **1. CHANGE IN PITCH** a change in the tone or pitch of the voice **2.** GRAM **WORD CHANGE** a change in the form of a word to show a grammatical change such as tense, mood, gender, or number **3.** GRAM **ALTERED FORM OF WORD** an altered form of a word, e.g., one showing a change in tense, mood, gender, or number, or the part of the word that changes in this way **4. BENDING** a turning from a straight line or course, or a more general change in direction **5.** GEOM = **inflection point** —**in·flec·tion·al** *adj.* —**in·flec·tion·al·ly** *adv.* —**in·flec·tion·less** *adj.*

in·flec·tion point *n.* GEOM a point on a curve at which the arc changes from convex to concave or vice versa

in·flexed /in flékst/ *adj.* BOT used to describe a plant part that is bent inward or downward toward the stem [Mid-17thC. Formed from Latin *inflex-,* the past participle stem of *inflectere* (see INFLECT).]

in·flex·i·ble /in fléksəb'l/ *adj.* **1. UNBENDING** adhering firmly to a viewpoint or principle **2. IMPOSSIBLE TO CHANGE** firmly established and impossible to change ○ *an inflexible rule* **3. RIGID** stiff and bent only with difficulty [15thC. From Latin *inflexibilis,* literally "not able to bend," from *flex-,* the past participle stem of *flectere* (see FLEXIBLE).] —**in·flex·i·bil·i·ty** /in flèksə bíllətee/ *n.* —**in·flex·i·ble·ness** /in fléksəb'lnəss/ *n.* —**in·flex·i·bly** *adv.*

in·flex·ion *n.* U.K. = **inflection**

in·flict /in flíkt/ (**-flict·ed, -flict·ing, -flicts**) *vt.* **1. CAUSE SUFFERING** to cause damage, harm, or unpleasantness to somebody or something ○ *inflicted heavy casualties on the enemy forces* **2. FORCE ON SOMEBODY** to impose a burden on another [Mid-16thC. From Latin *inflict-,* the past participle stem of *infligere,* literally "to strike upon," from *fligere* "to hit" (source also of English *conflict, afflict,* and *profligate*).] —**in·flict·a·ble** *adj.* —**in·flict·er** *n.* —**in·flic·tion** *n.* —**in·flic·tive** *adj.*

in-flight *adj.* taking place or provided for passengers during an aircraft journey ○ *in-flight entertainment*

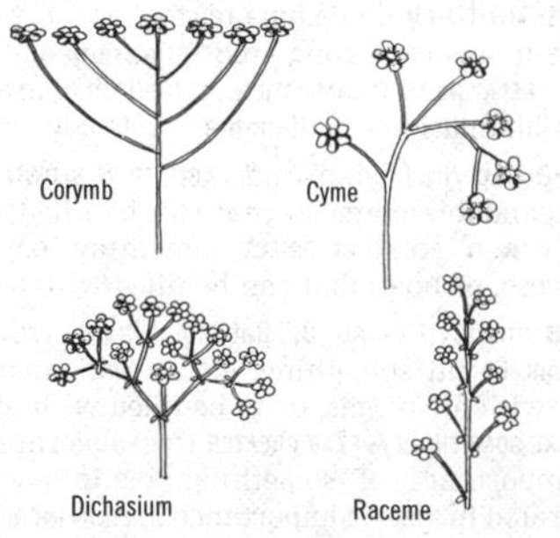

Inflorescence

in·flo·res·cence /in flaw réss'ns, ìnflə-/ *n.* BOT **1. FLOWERING PART OF A PLANT** a flowering structure that consists of more than one flower and usually comprises distinct individual flowers **2. WAY FLOWERS GROW** the arrangement or manner in which flowers develop on a stalk **3. FLOWERING** the budding and flowering of a plant [Mid-18thC. From modern Latin *inflorescentia,* from, ultimately, Latin *inflorescere,* literally "to come into flower," from *florescere* "to begin to flower."]

in·flow /in flō/ *n.* **1. SOMETHING THAT FLOWS IN** something that flows in somewhere ○ *an inflow of fresh water into a lake* **2. INFLUX** an instance or process of something flowing in ○ *the inflow of visitors to the site* **3. PLACE WHERE AN INFLOW OCCURS** the point at which something flows in —**in·flow·ing** *n.*

in·flu·ence /in floo əns/ *n.* **1. EFFECT ON SOMETHING** the effect of something on a person, thing, or event ○ *Picasso's influence on the course of 20th-century art* **2. POWER TO SWAY** the power that somebody has to affect other people's thinking or actions by means of argument, example, or force of personality ○ *She came under the influence of one of her teachers.* **3. SPECIAL ADVANTAGE** the power or authority that comes from wealth, social status, or position **4. SOMEBODY WHO CAN SWAY ANOTHER** somebody or something able to affect the course of events or somebody's thinking or action ○ *He's a bad influence on you.* **5. STARS' EFFECT ON PEOPLE** in astrology, an emanation that is believed to come from the stars and planets and to affect human characteristics, personality, and actions ■ *vt.* (**-enced, -enc·ing, -enc·es**) **1. SWAY** to persuade or sway somebody ○ *What influenced you in your choice of career?* **2. AFFECT** to have the power to affect something ○ *the factors that influence a nation's development* [14thC. From medieval Latin *influentia,* from, ultimately, Latin *influere,* literally "to flow in," from *fluere* (see FLUENT).] —**in·flu·ence·a·ble** *adj.* —**in·flu·enc·er** *n.* ◇ **under the influence** intoxicated by the use of a chemical substance, especially alcohol (*informal*)

in·flu·ent /in floo ənt, in flòo ənt/ *n.* GEOG a stream flowing into a lake or larger river [15thC. From Latin *influent-,* the present participle stem of *influere* (see INFLUENCE).]

in·flu·en·tial /in floo énshəl/ *adj.* having a great deal of power to change something, especially people's behavior —**in·flu·en·tial·ly** *adv.*

in·flu·en·za /in floo énzə/ *n.* **1. WIDESPREAD VIRAL ILLNESS** a viral illness producing a high temperature, sore throat, runny nose, headache, dry cough, and muscle pain. The illness is widespread, especially during winter months, and can sometimes be fatal. **2.** VET **VIRAL ILLNESS OF ANIMALS** a viral disease of domestic animals, usually characterized by fever and respiratory problems [Mid-18thC. Via Italian from medieval Latin *influentia* (see INFLUENCE), apparently from the belief that epidemics were due to the influence of the stars.] —**in·flu·en·zal** *adj.*

in·flux /in flùks/ *n.* **1. ARRIVAL IN LARGE NUMBERS** a sudden arrival of a large number of people or things dealing with the influx of tourists into the city **2. INFLOW** a flowing in, especially of a stream or river [Late 16thC. Via late Latin *influxus* from Latin, the past participle of *influere* (see INFLUENCE).]

in·fo /ínfō/ *n.* information (*informal*) [Early 20thC. Shortening.]

in·fo·bahn /ínfō baan/ *n.* = **information superhighway**

in·fold *vt.* = **enfold**

in·fo·me·di·ar·y /ìnfō meedee èrree/ *n.* a Web site providing specialist information on behalf of both the producers of goods and their customers

in·fo·mer·cial /ínfə múrsh'l, ìnfō-/ *n.* a commercial advertisement on television that is made to appear like a full-length interview or documentary program [Late 20thC. Blend of INFORMATION and COMMERCIAL.]

in·fo·ne·sia /ìfō neezhə/ *n.* an inability to remember an item of information or its location, especially on the Internet (*informal*)

in·form /in fáwrm/ (**-formed, -form·ing, -forms**) *v.* **1.** *vt.* **TELL SOMEBODY SOMETHING** to communicate information or knowledge to somebody (*often passive*) ○ *The police informed us of the accident.* **2.** *vr.* **LEARN ABOUT SOMETHING** to familiarize yourself with a subject **3.** *vi.* **TELL THE POLICE** to give confidential or incriminating information to the authorities about somebody else's activities, especially to the police **4.** *vt.* ARTS **UNDERLIE AND ANIMATE SOMETHING** to be an essential characteristic of something ○ *His religious beliefs inform his entire work.* **5.** *vt.* **GIVE STRUCTURE TO** to give structure or substance to something (*formal*) [14thC. Via Old French *enformer* from Latin *informare,* literally "to give form to," from *forma* (see FORM). The underlying meaning is "to shape somebody's mind, instruct."]

in·for·mal /in fáwrm'l/ *adj.* **1. FREE OF CEREMONY** relaxed and casual rather than ceremonious and stiff **2. UNOFFICIAL** not officially prepared, organized, or sanctioned ○ *The two sides in the conflict held informal talks.* **3. CASUAL AND EVERYDAY** suitable for casual or everyday situations ○ *informal dress* **4.** LANG **COLLOQUIAL** more appropriate in spoken than written form —**in·for·mal·i·ty** /ìn fawr mállətee/ *n.* —**in·for·mal·ly** /in fáwrm'lee/ *adv.*

in·form·ant /in fáwrmənt/ *n.* **1. SOMEBODY WHO SUPPLIES INFORMATION** somebody who gives information to somebody, often a newspaper **2. INFORMER** somebody who gives confidential or incriminating information to the police about somebody **3.** LING, ANTHROP **SOMEBODY PROVIDING LANGUAGE INFORMATION** somebody who provides a researcher with useful cultural or linguistic data for analysis

in for·ma pau·per·is /in fàwrmə páwpəriss/ *adj., adv.* LAW not liable for court costs as an indigent [Late 16thC. From Latin, literally, "in the form of a poor person."]

in·for·ma·tion /ìnfər máysh'n/ *n.* **1. KNOWLEDGE** definite knowledge acquired or supplied about something or somebody ○ *a bulletin giving the latest information on the trial* **2. GATHERED FACTS** the collected facts and data about a particular subject **3. TELEPHONE INFORMATION SERVICE** a telephone service that supplies telephone numbers to the public on request **4. MAKING FACTS KNOWN** the communication of facts and knowledge **5.** COMPUT **COMPUTER DATA** computer data that has been organized and presented in a systematic fashion to clarify the underlying meaning **6.** LAW **FORMAL CRIMINAL ACCUSATION** a formal accusation of a crime brought by a prosecutor, as opposed to an indictment brought by a grand jury —**in·for·ma·tion·al** *adj.* —**in·for·ma·tion·al·ly** *adv.*

in·for·ma·tion age *n.* a period characterized by widespread electronic access to information through the use of computer technology

in·for·ma·tion ap·pli·ance *n.* a small, portable, digital information processing machine designed to function on an electronic network

in·for·ma·tion proc·ess·ing *n.* the organization, manipulation, analysis, and distribution of data, nowadays typically carried out by computers

in·for·ma·tion re·triev·al *n.* the process used to store and retrieve computerized data systematically

in·for·ma·tion sci·ence *n.* the study of the processes involved in the collection, categorization, and distribution of data, particularly with reference to computer data

in·for·ma·tion su·per·high·way *n.* the developing worldwide computer network that includes the Internet, private networks, and proprietary online services. It permits the rapid sending of many different forms of data, including voice, video, and text.

in·for·ma·tion tech·nol·o·gy *n.* the use of technologies from computing, electronics, and telecommunications to process and distribute information in digital and other forms

in·for·ma·tion the·o·ry *n.* the mathematical study of the transmission, reception, storage, and retrieval of information based on the statistical analysis of communication between humans and machines

in·form·a·tive /in fáwrmətiv/ *adj.* providing useful information —**in·form·a·tive·ly** *adv.* —**in·form·a·tive·ness** *n.*

in·form·a·to·ry /in fáwrmə tàwree/ *adj.* providing useful information (*dated*) —**in·form·a·to·ri·ly** *adv.*

in·formed /in fáwrmd/ *adj.* **1. HAVING KNOWLEDGE** showing, having, or based on knowledge or understanding of a situation or subject ○ *informed criticism* **2. FULLY AWARE** based on a proper knowledge and understanding of a situation or subject ○ *an informed decision* —**in·formed·ly** *adv.*

in·formed con·sent *n.* agreement by a patient to undergo an operation or medical treatment or take part in a clinical trial after being informed of and having understood the risks involved

in·form·er /in fáwrmər/ *n.* **1. SECRET PROVIDER OF INFORMATION ABOUT A CRIME** somebody who provides the police or authorities with information about criminal activities **2. PROVIDER OF INFORMATION** somebody or something that provides information about a subject or situation

in·for·mer·cial /ínfər múrsh'l, ìnfə múrsh'l/ *n.* = **infomercial**

in·fo·tain·ment /ínfō táynmənt/ *n.* television programs that deal with serious issues or current affairs in an entertaining way [Late 20thC. Blend of INFORMATION and ENTERTAINMENT.] —**in·fo·tain·er** *n.*

in·fra /ínfrə/ *adv.* a term used in an explanatory note to refer a reader to a point later in a text, especially in the phrase "vide infra" (*formal*) ◊ **supra** [Late 19thC. From Latin.]

infra- *prefix.* below, beneath, inferior ○ *infrasonic* ○ *infraclass* [From Latin *infra* "below." Ultimately from an Indo-European word that is also the ancestor of English *under, inferior,* and *infernal.*]

in·fra·class /ínfrə klàss/ *n.* a taxonomic category of organisms that is above an order and below a subclass

in·fra·cos·tal /ínfrə kóst'l/ *adj.* lying below the ribs

in·fract /in frákt/ (**-fract·ed, -fract·ing, -fracts**) *vt.* to fail to obey or fulfill a law, contract, or agreement [Late 18thC. From Latin *infractus,* the past participle stem of *infringere* "to destroy."] —**in·frac·tor** *n.*

in·frac·tion /in frákshən/ *n.* a failure to obey or fulfill a law, contract, or agreement [15thC. Directly and via Middle French, from Latin *infractio,* from *infractus* (see INFRACT).]

in·fra dig *adj.* below the standard of social behavior that somebody usually maintains (*informal*) [Early 19thC. Shortening of Latin *infra dignitatem.*]

in·fra·hu·man /ínfrə hyóomən/ *adj.* in the system of classifying living organisms, belonging to a lower order than human beings

in·fran·gi·ble /in fránjib'l/ *adj.* (*formal*) **1. IMPOSSIBLE TO BREAK OR SEPARATE** unable to be broken or separated into pieces **2. NOT TO BE IGNORED** unable to be disregarded or violated [Late 16thC. Directly or via French from medieval Latin *infrangibilis,* from *in-* "not" + *frangibilis* "breakable."] —**in·fran·gi·bil·i·ty** /in frànji bíllətee/ *n.* —**in·fran·gi·ble·ness** /in fránjib'lnəss/ *n.* —**in·fran·gi·bly** *adv.*

in·fra·red /ínfrə réd/ *n.* **PORTION OF INVISIBLE SPECTRUM** the portion of the invisible electromagnetic spectrum consisting of radiation with wavelengths in the range 750 nm to 1 mm, between light and radio waves ○ *infrared radiation* ■ *adj.* **RELATING TO INFRARED RADIATION** using, producing, or affected by infrared radiation [Late 19thC. Because it lies below the red end of the visible spectrum.]

in·fra·red as·tron·o·my *n.* the study of celestial objects with wavelengths in the infrared range. Infrared sources within our galaxy include cool gas giants and the galactic center.

in·fra·red pho·tog·ra·phy *n.* photography with film that is sensitive to infrared radiation, used, e.g., for taking pictures at night or in haze and in detecting camouflaged objects

in·fra·son·ic /ínfrə sónnik/ *adj.* **1. RELATING TO SOUND INAUDIBLE TO HUMANS** relating to sound at frequencies below 20 Hz, which cannot be heard by human beings but can be felt as vibration **2. RELATING TO INFRASONIC WAVES OR VIBRATIONS** using or produced by infrasonic waves or vibrations —**in·fra·son·i·cal·ly** *adv.*

in·fra·sound /ínfrə sòwnd/ *n.* sound at frequencies below 20 Hz, which cannot be heard by humans but can be felt as vibration

in·fra·struc·ture /ínfrə strùkchər/ *n.* **1. BASIC ORGANIZATION** the system according to which a company, organization, or other body is organized at the most basic level **2. PUBLIC SERVICES OR SYSTEMS** the large-scale public systems, services, and facilities of a country or region that are necessary for economic activity, including power and water supplies, public transportation, telecommunications, roads, and schools —**in·fra·struc·tur·al** /ínfrə strúkchərəl/ *adj.*

in·fre·quent /in fréekwənt/ *adj.* not appearing, happening, or encountered very often ○ *Her visits became more infrequent.* —**in·fre·quence** *n.* —**in·fre·quen·cy** *n.* —**in·fre·quent·ly** *adv.*

in·fringe /in frínj/ (**-fringed, -fring·ing, -fring·es**) *v.* **1.** *vt.* **DISOBEY OR DISREGARD SOMETHING** to fail to obey a law or regulation or observe the terms of an agreement **2.** *vti.* **ENCROACH ON SOMEBODY'S RIGHTS OR PROPERTY** to take over land, rights, privileges, or activities that belong to somebody else, especially in a minor or gradual way ○ *infringing on our personal freedom* [Mid-16thC. From Latin *infringere* "to damage," from *frangere* "to break" (source of English *fracture*).] —**in·fring·er** *n.*

in·fringe·ment /in frínjmənt/ *n.* **1. BREACH OF A LAW OR RIGHT** a failure to obey a law or regulation **2. ENCROACHMENT** an encroachment on land, rights, privileges, or activities that belong to somebody else, especially in a minor or gradual way

in·fun·dib·u·la plural of **infundibulum**

in·fun·dib·u·li·form /ìnfən díbbyələ fàwrm/ *adj.* used to describe a flower or other plant part that resembles a funnel in shape

in·fun·dib·u·lum /ìnfən díbbyələm/ (*plural* **-la** /-lə/) *n.* a funnel-shaped opening, passage, or structure in vertebrates such as the stalk connecting the pituitary gland to the brain or the opening of a fallopian tube into the ovary [Mid-16thC. From Latin, "funnel," from *infundere* "to pour in" (source of English *infuse*).] —**in·fun·dib·u·lar** *adj.* —**in·fun·dib·u·late** *adj.*

in·fu·ri·ate /in fyóoree àyt/ (**-at·ed, -at·ing, -ates**) *vt.* to make somebody extremely angry [Mid-17thC. From medieval Latin *infuriare,* from *furiare* "to anger," from *furia* "fury."] —**in·fu·ri·at·ed** *adj.* —**in·fu·ri·at·ed·ly** *adv.* —**in·fu·ri·at·ing** *adj.* —**in·fu·ri·at·ing·ly** *adv.*

in·fuse /in fyóoz/ (**-fused, -fus·ing, -fus·es**) *v.* **1.** *vt.* **PERVADE** to fill something with a strong emotion such as hatred, enthusiasm, or desire (*often passive*) **2.** *vt.* **INTRODUCE SOMETHING INTO SOMEBODY'S MIND** to fix an emotion, belief, or quality gradually but firmly in somebody's mind **3.** *vti.* **STEEP IN LIQUID** to soak tea or herbs in liquid in order to extract the flavor or some other property **4.** *vt.* MED **GIVE A LIQUID USING A DRIP** to introduce a solution such as saline, sucrose, or glucose into a vein, body cavity, or the intestinal tract in order to treat or feed somebody using a drip feed. ◊ **transfuse** [15thC. Via Old French *infuser* from, ultimately, Latin *infundere* "to pour in," from *fundere* "to pour."] —**in·fus·er** *n.*

in·fus·i·ble /in fyóozəb'l/ *adj.* **1.** MED **USABLE IN A DRIP FEED** able to be introduced into the body through a drip feed **2. SUITABLE FOR INFUSING** suitable for soaking in liquid to make an infusion ○ *infusible herbs* —**in·fus·i·bil·i·ty** /in fyóozə bíllətee/ *n.*

in·fu·sion /in fyóozh'n/ *n.* **1.** MED **ADMINISTERING OF A LIQUID THROUGH A DRIP FEED** the introduction of a solution such as saline, sucrose, or glucose through a drip feed in order to treat or feed a patient **2.** MED **LIQUID ADMINISTERED THROUGH A DRIP FEED** a solution introduced into the body by infusion **3. LIQUID MADE BY INFUSING SOMETHING** a liquid such as tea that is made by infusing something **4. ACT OF INFUSING SOMETHING** the act of of soaking something in a liquid in order to extract something soluble **5. INTRODUCTION OF SOMETHING NEEDED** the addition of a new or necessary quality or element to something ○ *an infusion of private capital into the project* [14thC. Via Old French from Latin *infusio,* from the past participle stem of *infundere* (see INFUSE).]

-ing[1] *suffix.* **1.** forming the present participle of verbs ○ *raining* **2.** forming adjectives from words other than verbs ○ *swashbuckling* [Alteration of earlier *-ende,* from Old English]

-ing[2] *suffix.* **1.** action or process ○ *rowing* ○ *cooking* **2.** result of or thing connected with an action or process ○ *opening* ○ *planking* ○ *lining* [Old English *-ung, -ing*]

-ing[3] *suffix.* somebody or something that has a particular character ○ *gelding* [Old English, "belonging to, of the line of"]

in·gath·er /in gàthər/ (**-ered, -er·ing, -ers**) *v.* **1.** *vt.* **COLLECT A HARVEST** to gather in a harvest of something **2.** *vi.* **CONVERGE** to come together or assemble (*formal or literary*) —**in·gath·er·er** *n.*

Inge /inj/, **William** (1913–73) U.S. playwright. He is known for his small-town Midwestern dramas such as *Picnic,* which won the Pulitzer Prize in 1953. Full name **William Motter Inge**

in·gen·ious /in jéenyəss/ *adj.* **1. INVENTIVE** possessing cleverness and imagination **2. CLEVER AND EFFECTIVE** clever, original, and effective ○ *an ingenious solution* [15thC. Via Middle French *ingénieux* from Latin *ingeniosus,* from *ingenium* "mind" (source of English *engine*).] —**in·gen·ious·ly** *adv.* —**in·gen·ious·ness** *n.*

in·gé·nue /áNzhə noo/ *n.* **1. UNSOPHISTICATED GIRL OR YOUNG WOMAN** a girl or young woman who is naive and lacks experience or understanding of life **2. NAIVE CHARACTER IN DRAMA** a character in a play or a movie who is a naive inexperienced young woman **3. ACTOR IN ROLE OF INGÉNUE** an actor, especially a young one, who plays or specializes in playing the role of an ingénue [Mid-19thC. Via French from, ultimately, Latin *ingenuus* (see INGENUOUS).]

in·ge·nu·i·ty /ìnjə nóo itee/ (*plural* **-ties**) *n.* cleverness and originality [Late 16thC. From Latin *ingenuitas,* from *ingenuus* (see INGENUOUS).]

in·gen·u·ous /in jénnyoo əss/ *adj.* **1. INNOCENT AND UNWORLDLY** showing innocence and a lack of worldly experience **2. SEEMING HONEST** appearing honest and direct [Late 16thC. From Latin *ingenuus* "native, freeborn, honest," from *gignere* "to beget." Ultimately from an Indo-European word that also produced English *kin.*] —**in·gen·u·ous·ly** *adv.* —**in·gen·u·ous·ness** *n.*

WORD KEY: SYNONYMS

See Synonyms at ***naive.***

In·ger·soll /íng gər sàwl/, **Robert** (1833–99) U.S. orator. He was a noted agnostic, and in his lectures maintained that happiness is the only good. Full name **Robert Green Ingersoll**. Known as **Great Agnostic**

in·gest /in jést/ (**-gest·ed, -gest·ing, -gests**) *vt.* to take something such as food or liquid into the body by swallowing or absorbing it [Early 17thC. From the past participle stem of Latin *ingerere* "to carry in," from *gerere* "to carry."] —**in·ges·tion** *n.* —**in·ges·tive** *adj.*

in·ges·ta /in jéstə/ *npl.* food or liquid taken into the body by swallowing or absorbing (*takes a plural verb*) [Early 18thC. From Latin *ingestus,* the past participle of *ingerere* (see INGEST).]

in·gle /íng g'l/ *n.* a fireplace, or an open fire burning in a fireplace (*archaic*) [Early 16thC. Origin uncertain: perhaps from Gaelic *aingeal* "fire, light."]

in·gle·nook /íng g'l nòok/ *n.* **1. RECESS BESIDE A FIREPLACE** a recess for a seat or bench beside a large fireplace **2. FIRESIDE SEAT** a seat built in an inglenook, especially one of two benches or wing chairs facing each other

In·gle·wood /íng g'l wòod/ city in Los Angeles County, southwestern California, bordering the city of Los Angeles. Population: 110,085 (1994).

In·glis /íng gliss, íng g'lz/, **Charles** (1734–1816) Irish-born Canadian cleric. He was the Church of England's first colonial bishop (1787–95).

in·glo·ri·ous /in gláwree əss/ *adj.* **1. SHAMEFUL** bringing shame or dishonor **2. NOT FAMOUS** not having received recognition, and so unknown or obscure (*archaic or literary*) [Mid-16thC. From Latin *inglorius,* from *gloria* "glory."] —**in·glo·ri·ous·ly** *adv.* —**in·glo·ri·ous·ness** *n.*

in·go·ing /ín gòing/ *adj.* relating to entering a place or taking up a new position

in·got /íng gət/ *n.* **1. METAL CASTING** a metal casting that is shaped for easy working or for recasting, typically in an oblong **2. MOLD FOR CASTING INGOTS** a mold used for the casting of ingots [14thC. Origin uncertain: probably formed from Old English *in* "in" + *gotan,* past participle of *gēotan* "to pour."]

in·got i·ron *n.* very pure iron that is produced in the same way as steel but using methods that reduce the carbon, manganese, and silicon content

in·graft /in gráft/ (**-graft·ed, -graft·ing, -grafts**) *vt.* = **engraft** —**in·graf·ta·tion** /ìn graf táysh'n/ *n.* —**in·graft·ment** *n.*

in·grain *vt.* /in gráyn/ (**-grained, -grain·ing, -grains**) **IMPRESS SOMETHING IN SOMEBODY'S MIND** to impress a feeling, belief, or experience firmly and indelibly in somebody's mind (*usually passive*) ○ *The sight is still ingrained in my memory.* ■ *adj.* /ín gràyn/ **1.** = **ingrained 2.** TEXTILES **PREDYED** dyed before being spun or woven ■ *n.* /ín gràyn/ TEXTILES **1. PREDYED YARN OR FIBER** yarn or fiber that is dyed before being spun or woven **2. PREDYED RUG OR CARPET** a rug or carpet made of yarn or fiber that is dyed before being spun or woven [15thC. Formed from GRAIN, from its application to certain insects and the dye produced by them.]

in·grained /in gráynd/ *adj.* **1. WORKED DEEP INTO SOMETHING** worked into the surface, pores, or fibers of something and very difficult to remove ○ *ingrained dirt* **2. HABITUAL** long-established or confirmed in a habit or practice **3. IMPRESSED IN SOMEBODY'S MIND** firmly fixed in somebody's mind and only removed or challenged with difficulty —**in·grain·ed·ly** /in gráynədlee/ *adv.* —**in·grain·ed·ness** /-ədnəss/ *n.*

in·grate /ín gràyt/ *n.* **UNGRATEFUL PERSON** somebody who does not show or express gratitude (*formal or literary*) ■ *adj.* **UNGRATEFUL** showing no gratitude (*formal or* *literary*) [15thC. Via Old French from Latin *ingratus*, "ungrateful," from *in-* "not" + *gratus* "grateful."]

in·gra·ti·ate /in gráyshee àyt/ (**-at·ed, -at·ing, -ates**) *vr.* to try to enter somebody's favor, especially in order to gain an advantage ○ *It's no use trying to ingratiate yourself with me.* [Early 17thC. From Italian *ingraziare*, from *in grazia* "into favor," from Latin *in gratiam*, from, ultimately, *gratia* "favor" (source of English *grace*).] —**in·gra·ti·a·tion** /in gràyshee áysh'n/ *n.* —**in·gra·ti·a·to·ry** /in gráyshee ətàwree/ *adj.*

in·gra·ti·at·ing /in gráyshee àyting/ *adj.* **1. SEEKING TO PLEASE SOMEBODY** designed to win somebody's approval, especially in order to gain an advantage **2. PLEASING** agreeable or giving pleasure (*archaic or literary*) —**in·gra·ti·at·ing·ly** *adv.*

in·grat·i·tude /in gráttə tòod/ *n.* failure to show or express gratitude [14thC. Directly or via Old French from Latin *ingratitudo*, from *ingratus* "ungrateful," from *gratus* "grateful."]

in·gre·di·ent /in gréedee ənt/ *n.* **1. ITEM IN RECIPE** any of the component parts of a mixture, especially in cooking **2. ELEMENT REQUIRED FOR SOMETHING** any of the different elements required for a situation, relationship, or plan ○ *What are the ingredients for a happy marriage?* [15thC. From, ultimately, Latin *ingredi* "to enter" (source of English *ingress*), from *gradi* "to step."]

In·gres /áNgrə/, **Jean-Auguste-Dominique** (1780–1867) French artist. He was a leading exemplar of neoclassicism in such paintings as *Grande Odalisque* (1814).

in·gress /ín grèss/ *n.* (*formal*) **1. ENTRY** entry into a place **2. RIGHT OF ENTRY** the right to enter a place **3. ENTRANCE** a way of entering a place [15thC. From Latin, "entrance," from *ingredi* "to enter," from *gradi* "to walk."]

in·gres·sive /in gréssiv/ *adj.* **1. OF ENTRY** relating to entry into or the entrance to a place **2.** PHON **PRONOUNCED BY INHALING** used to describe a speech sound that is pronounced by inhaling rather than exhaling **3.** GRAM = **inceptive** *n.* 1, **inceptive** *n.* 2 ■ *n.* PHON **INGRESSIVE SPEECH SOUND** a speech sound pronounced by inhaling ■ *adj., n.* GRAM = **inceptive** *adj.* 2 —**in·gres·sive·ness** *n.*

in·group *n.* a group of people who show loyalty and preferential treatment to one another because they share common interests, beliefs, and attitudes

in·grow·ing /in grṓing/ *adj.* growing or appearing to grow inward. An ingrowing toenail does not actually grow inward: inflamed tissue around the edge of the nail grows over it.

in·grown /ín grṑn/ *adj.* **1.** MED **GROWN INTO THE FLESH** that has or appears to have grown into the flesh. ◊ **ingrowing 2. NATURAL TO SOMEBODY** having become a natural part of somebody's character over a long period of time **3. INWARD-LOOKING** inward-looking and preoccupied with personal or local interests —**in·grown·ness** *n.*

in·growth /ín grṑth/ *n.* **1. GROWTH INTO THE FLESH** growth or apparent growth into the flesh. ◊ **ingrowing 2. SOMETHING INGROWN** something that grows inward, e.g., a hair

in·gui·nal /íng gwən'l/ *adj.* located in or affecting the groin [15thC. From Latin *inguinalis*, from *inguen* "groin."]

in·gulf /in gúlf/ (**-gulfed, -gulf·ing, -gulfs**) *vt.* = **engulf** —**in·gulf·ment** *n.*

in·gur·gi·tate /in gúrji tàyt/ (**-tat·ed, -tat·ing, -tates**) *vt.* to swallow large amounts of food greedily (*formal or literary*) [Late 16thC. From, ultimately, Latin *ingurgitare* "to pour in, gorge yourself," from *gurges* "gulf," from the sense "engulf."] —**in·gur·gi·ta·tion** /in gùrji táysh'n/ *n.*

In·gush /ín gòosh, in gòosh/ (*plural* **-gush·es** *or* **-gush**) *n.* a member of an ethnic group that lives mainly in the Russian provinces of Ingushetia and Chechnya [Early 20thC. From Russian, the name of the former autonomous area.]

INH *tdmk.* a trademark for a drug used to treat tuberculosis

in·hab·it /in hábbit/ (**-it·ed, -it·ing, -its**) *v.* **1.** *vt.* **LIVE IN A PLACE** to live in or occupy a particular place (*often passive*) **2.** *vt.* **BE FOUND** to be found in or pervade something ○ *the fears that inhabited each waking moment* **3.** *vi.* **RESIDE PERMANENTLY** to reside permanently in a place (*archaic*) [14thC. Via Old French *enhabiter* from Latin *inhabitare*, from *habitare* "to possess, dwell," from *habere* "to hold, have" (source of English *habit*).] —**in·hab·it·a·bil·i·ty** /in hàbbitə bíllətee/ *n.* —**in·hab·it·a·ble** /in hábbitəb'l/ *adj.* —**in·hab·i·ta·tion** /in hàbbi táysh'n/ *n.* —**in·hab·it·er** /in hábbitər/ *n.*

in·hab·i·tan·cy /in hábbit'nsee/ (*plural* **-cies**), **in·hab·i·tance** /in hábbit'ns/ *n.* living in a place as an inhabitant (*archaic*)

in·hab·i·tant /in hábbit'nt/ *n.* a person or animal that lives in a particular place or area

in·hab·it·ed /in hábbitəd/ *adj.* lived in, especially by human beings

in·ha·lant /in háylənt/ *adj.* **BREATHED IN** breathed in through the nose or mouth as a medicine or for its soothing effect ■ *n.* **MEDICINE THAT IS INHALED** a substance in the form of a vapor or gas that is inhaled, especially as a medicine or for its soothing effect

in·ha·la·tion /ìnhə láysh'n/ *n.* **1. BREATH TAKEN IN** an intake of breath through the nose or mouth into the lungs **2. SOMETHING INHALED** a substance in the form of a vapor or gas that is inhaled, especially as a medicine or for its soothing effect [Early 17thC. From medieval Latin, from, ultimately, Latin *inhalare*, "to breathe upon" (see INHALE).] —**in·ha·la·tion·al** *adj.*

in·ha·la·tor /ínhə làytər/ *n.* MED **1.** = **respirator 2.** = **inhaler**

in·hale /in háyl/ (**-haled, -hal·ing, -hales**) *vti.* to breathe in, or to draw a gas, liquid, or solid into the lungs through the nose or mouth [Early 18thC. Either by back-formation from INHALATION, or from Latin *inhalare* "to breathe upon," from *halare* "to breathe" (by contrast with EXHALE in English).]

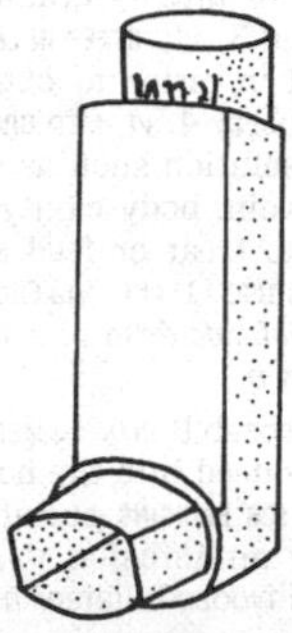

Inhaler

in·hal·er /in háylər/ *n.* **1. DEVICE FOR INHALING MEDICINE** a small device used for inhaling medicine in the form of a vapor or gas in order to ease a respiratory condition such as asthma or to relieve nasal congestion **2. SOMEBODY WHO INHALES** somebody who inhales or who inhales something

in·har·mo·ni·ous /in haar mṓnee əss/ *adj.* **1. DISCORDANT** lacking in harmony or sounding unpleasant **2. UNHAPPY** characterized by disagreement and conflict **3. CLASHING** clashing or not matching —**in·har·mo·ni·ous·ly** *adv.* —**in·har·mo·ni·ous·ness** *n.*

in·har·mo·ny /in haármənee/ *n.* lack of harmony, accord, or agreement

in·haul /ín hàwl/, **in·haul·er** /ín hàwlər/ *n.* a rope used to haul or hold in a sail

in·here /in héer/ (**-hered, -her·ing, -heres**) *vi.* to be a natural and integral part of something (*formal*) [Mid-16thC. From Latin *inhaerere*, from *haerere* "to stick."] —**in·her·ence** /in héerəns, -hérrəns/ *n.* —**in·her·en·cy** *n.*

in·her·ent /in héerənt, -hérrənt/ *adj.* unable to be considered separately from the nature of something because of being innate or characteristic ○ *the risks inherent in investing in the stock market* [Late 16thC. From, ultimately, Latin *inhaerere* "to stick to" (see INHERE).] —**in·her·ent·ly** *adv.*

in·her·it /in hérrit/ (**-it·ed, -it·ing, -its**) *v.* **1.** *vti.* **RECEIVE SOMETHING WHEN SOMEBODY DIES** to become the owner of something when somebody dies in accordance with legal succession or the terms of a will or as the result of a bequest or legacy **2.** *vt.* **RECEIVE A CHARACTERISTIC OR QUALITY FROM A PARENT** to receive a characteristic or quality as a result of its being passed on genetically **3.** *vt.* **GET SOMETHING FROM A PREDECESSOR** to take something over from the person or group who previously lived in a place or did a job [14thC. Via Old French *enheriter* "to make an heir" from late Latin *inhereditare* "to inherit," from *hereditare*, from Latin *heres* "heir."] —**in·her·i·tor** *n.*

in·her·it·a·ble /in hérritəb'l/ *adj.* **1.** LAW = **heritable 2.** BIOL **ABLE TO BE PASSED ON GENETICALLY** used to describe a characteristic or quality that can be transmitted genetically from parent to offspring **3. ABLE TO INHERIT** having the right to inherit something (*archaic*) [15thC. Via Anglo-French *enheritable* "able to be made heir" from Old French *enheriter* "to make an heir" (see INHERIT).] —**in·her·it·a·bil·i·ty** /in hèrritə bíllətee/ *n.* —**in·her·it·a·ble·ness** /in hérritəb'lnəss/ *n.*

in·her·i·tance /in hérrit'ns/ *n.* **1.** LAW **INHERITED WEALTH OR TITLE** money, property, or a title that has been inherited or is to be inherited **2.** LAW **OWNERSHIP OR SUCCESSION BY HEREDITY** hereditary ownership of wealth or a title, or the succession to wealth or a title **3.** LAW **RIGHT TO INHERIT** the right of an heir to inherit wealth or a title when an ancestor dies **4. HERITAGE** something that is inherited from the past **5.** BIOL **TRANSMISSION OF GENETICALLY CONTROLLED CHARACTERISTICS** the transmission of genetically controlled characteristics or qualities from parent to offspring **6.** COMPUT **CREATION OF AN OBJECT WITH THE SAME VARIABLES** a feature of programming whereby a new object can be created from existing objects and, as a consequence of creation, possess the variables and methods of the parent object [15thC. From Old French *enheritaunce*, from *enheriter* "to make an heir" (see INHERIT).]

in·her·i·tance tax *n.* a tax levied on property received by inheritance or legal succession, calculated according to the value of the property received

in·he·sion /in héezh'n/ *n.* the state of being a natural and integral part of something (*formal*) [Mid-17thC. From late Latin *inhaesio*, from the past participle stem of Latin *inhaerere* "to stick."]

in·hib·in /in híbbin/ *n.* a hormone secreted by the testis and ovary that inhibits the pituitary's production of follicle-stimulating hormone and helps control gamete and blood cell production, growth, and development [Mid-20thC. Coined from Latin *inhibere* "to hinder" + -IN.]

in·hib·it /in híbbit/ (**-it·ed, -it·ing, -its**) *vt.* **1. HOLD SOMETHING IN CHECK** to stop something from continuing or developing ○ *changes in spending patterns that are likely to inhibit the growth of the economy* **2. CONSTRAIN** to prevent somebody from behaving or speaking freely or unself-consciously **3.** CHEM **STOP OR RESTRICT A CHEMICAL REACTION** to prevent or slow down a chemical reaction **4.** BIOL **INTERFERE WITH A BODILY PROCESS OR ORGAN** to slow down or adversely affect a bodily process or the action of an organ **5.** ELECTRON ENG **PREVENT A SIGNAL OR EVENT** to prevent a specific signal or event from occurring **6. FORBID SOMETHING** to forbid something (*archaic*) [15thC. From the past participle stem of Latin *inhibere* "to hinder," from *habere* "to hold."] —**in·hib·it·a·ble** *adj.* —**in·hib·i·tive** *adj.*

in·hib·it·ed /in híbbitəd/ *adj.* unable to behave spontaneously or express feelings openly, especially with regard to sexuality and the body —**in·hib·it·ed·ly** *adv.* —**in·hib·it·ed·ness** *n.*

in·hib·it·er *n.* = **inhibitor**

in·hi·bi·tion /ìnnə bísh'n, ìnhə-/ *n.* **1. FEELING THAT INHIBITS SOMEBODY** a feeling or belief that prevents somebody from behaving spontaneously or speaking freely **2. SOMETHING THAT INHIBITS** something that inhibits, or the act of inhibiting **3.** PSYCHOL **INHIBITED MENTAL STATE** a mental state in which somebody's activity or behavior is inhibited. ◊ **repression 4.** PSYCHOL **DIMINISHED RESPONSE TO A STIMULUS** in Pavlovian conditioning, the progressive weakening of a response to a stimulus after repeated presentations of the stimulus **5.** CHEM **IMPEDING CHEMICAL REACTION** the slowing down or prevention of a chemical reaction **6.** BIOL **OBSTRUCTION OF A BODILY PROCESS OR ORGAN** the suppression or blocking of a bodily process or the action of an organ [14thC. Via Old French from Latin *inhibitio*, from *inhibere* "to hinder" (see INHIBIT).]

in·hib·i·tor /in híbbitər/, **in·hib·it·er** *n.* **1.** CHEM **SUBSTANCE SLOWING A CHEMICAL REACTION** a substance that stops or slows a chemical reaction ○ *a rust inhibitor* **2.** BIOCHEM **SUBSTANCE HALTING A BIOLOGICAL PROCESS** a substance that slows or halts a metabolic or physiological process, e.g., by preventing the activity of an enzyme **3. SOMETHING THAT INHIBITS SOMETHING** somebody or something that inhibits somebody or something else

in·hold·ing /ín hṑlding/ *n.* a piece of private land inside a state or national park —**in·hold·er** *n.*

in-home *adj.* available in somebody's home

in·hos·pi·ta·ble /in ho spíttəb'l, in hóspitəb'l/ *adj.* **1. NOT WELCOMING** not welcoming or friendly **2. HARSH** harsh and difficult to live or work in ○ *an inhospitable climate* [Late 16thC. From French, from *in-* "not" + *hospitable* (see HOSPITABLE).] —**in·hos·pi·ta·ble·ness** *n.* —**in·hos·pi·ta·bly** *adv.* —**in·hos·pi·tal·i·ty** *n.*

in-house *adj.* **LOCATED WITHIN A COMPANY** working, carried out, or existing within a company or organization ■ *adv.* **WITHIN A COMPANY** within a company or organization

in·hu·man /in hyóomən/ *adj.* **1. VERY CRUEL** showing great cruelty and a lack of humanity **2. UNFEELING** giving an impression of being cold and unfeeling **3. NOT HUMAN** not seeming to be human, or not typical of human beings [15thC. Directly or via Middle French from Latin *inhumanus*, from *in-* "not" + *humanus* "human."] —**in·hu·man·ly** *adv.* —**in·hu·man·ness** *n.*

in·hu·mane /in hyoo máyn/ *adj.* lacking compassion, and causing excessive suffering [15thC. Originally from INHUMAN; later from IN- + HUMANE.] —**in·hu·mane·ly** *adv.*

in·hu·man·i·ty /in hyoo mánnətee/ (*plural* **-ties**) *n.* **1. GREAT CRUELTY** great cruelty and lack of humanity **2. CRUEL ACT** an act of great cruelty [15thC. Via Old French from Latin *inhumanitas*, from *inhumanus* (see INHUMAN).]

in·hume /in hyóom/ (**-humed, -hum·ing, -humes**) *vt.* to bury a dead body (*formal or literary*) [Early 17thC. From Latin *inhumare*, from *humus* "earth" (source of English *humble*).] —**in·hu·ma·tion** /in hyoo máysh'n/ *n.* —**in·hum·er** /in hyóomər/ *n.*

in·im·i·cal /i nímmik'l/ *adj.* **1. NOT FAVORABLE** unfavorable for something ○ *activities inimical to the public good* **2. HOSTILE** showing hostility [Early 16thC. Via late Latin *inimicalis* from Latin *inimicus* "unfriendly" (source of English *enemy*), from *in-* "not" + *amicus* "friend."] —**in·im·i·cal·i·ty** /i nìmmi kállətee/ *n.* —**in·im·i·cal·ly** /i nímmikəlee/ *adv.* —**in·im·i·cal·ness** /i nímmik'lnəss/ *n.*

in·im·i·ta·ble /i nímmitəb'l/ *adj.* impossible to imitate, especially because of being unique to a particular person or group ○ *she carried it off in her usual inimitable style* [15thC. Directly or via French from Latin *inimitabilis*, from *in-* "not" + *imitabilis* "capable of being imitated."] —**in·im·i·ta·bil·i·ty** /i nìmmitə bíllətee/ *n.* —**in·im·i·ta·ble·ness** /i nímmitəb'lnəss/ *n.* —**in·im·i·ta·bly** *adv.*

in·i·on /ínnee ən/ *n.* ANAT a projection of the occipital bone that forms a slight lump at the back of the skull just above the neck [Early 19thC. From Greek, "nape of the neck."]

in·iq·ui·tous /i níkwitəss/ *adj.* immoral, especially in a way that results in great injustice or unfairness —**in·iq·ui·tous·ly** *adv.* —**in·iq·ui·tous·ness** *n.*

in·iq·ui·ty /i níkwitee/ (*plural* **-ties**) *n.* **1. INJUSTICE OR IMMORALITY** great injustice or extreme immorality **2. IMMORAL ACT** a grossly immoral act [13thC. Via Old French from Latin *iniquitas*, from *iniquus* "unjust," from *in-* "not" + *aequus* "equal" (source of English *equity*).]

init. *abbr.* initial

in·i·tial /i nísh'l/ *adj.* **1. COMING AT THE START** coming first, or present at the beginning of an event or process ○ *My initial feeling was one of shock.* **2. COMING FIRST IN A WORD** relating to or used as the first letter or letters of a word ■ *n.* **1. FIRST LETTER OF A NAME** the first letter of the name of a person, place, or organization **2.** PRINTING **LARGE ORNATE FIRST LETTER** the large and often highly decorative first letter of a verse, paragraph, or page, especially as seen in illuminated manuscripts **3.** BOT **PLANT-TISSUE CELL** a cell in the growing point (**meristem**) of a plant that gives rise to cells that will develop into different plant tissues ■ **in·i·tials** *npl.* **FIRST LETTERS OF SOMEBODY'S NAMES** the first letter of each of the names of a person, place, or organization, used as an abbreviation or means of identification ■ *vt.* (**-tialed, -tial·ing, -tials**) **MARK SOMETHING WITH INITIALS** to sign or mark a document with initials, especially in order to show approval or give authorization [Early 16thC. From Latin *initialis*, from *initium* "beginning" (source of English *commence*).] —**in·i·tial·er** *n.*

in·i·tial·ism /i nísh'l ìzzəm/ *n.* an abbreviation made up of initial letters that are all pronounced separately, e.g., U.N. for United Nations

in·i·tial·ize /i nísh'l īz/ (**-ized, -iz·ing, -iz·es**) *vti.* to prepare a piece of computer hardware or software such as a printer, modem, or timer for use, often by resetting a memory location to its initial value —**in·i·tial·i·za·tion** /i nìsh'li záysh'n/ *n.* —**in·i·tial·iz·er** /i nísh'l īzər/ *n.*

in·i·tial·ly /i nísh'lee/ *adv.* at first or to begin with

in·i·tial pub·lic of·fer·ing *n.* FIN a first-time sale of company securities on a stock exchange to public investors

in·i·tial rhyme *n.* a rhyme at the start of successive lines of verse

In·i·tial Teach·ing Al·pha·bet *n.* an alphabet of 44 symbols, each representing a single sound in English, used to teach children to read

in·i·ti·ate *vt.* /i níshee àyt/ (**-at·ed, -at·ing, -ates**) **1. MAKE SOMETHING START** to cause something, especially an important event or process, to begin ○ *to initiate talks* **2. TEACH SOMEBODY ABOUT SOMETHING NEW** to introduce somebody to a new activity, interest, or area ○ *initiated me into the joys of snowboarding* **3. INTRODUCE SOMEBODY INTO GROUP** to allow somebody take part in a ritual or ceremony in order to become a member of a group, organization, or religion ■ *n.* /i níshee ət/ **1. SOMEBODY INITIATED INTO A GROUP** somebody who has been recently admitted to a group, organization, or religion after participating in a ritual or ceremony **2. SOMEBODY NEWLY INTRODUCED TO SOMETHING** somebody recently introduced to a new activity, interest, or area ■ *adj.* /i níshee ət/ **1. RECENTLY INITIATED** belonging or relating to those who have been recently introduced to a new activity, interest, or area **2. HAVING SECRET OR SPECIAL KNOWLEDGE** knowing the secrets of a group, organization, or religion [Mid-16thC. From the past participle stem of Latin *initiare* "to begin," from *initium* "beginning" (see INITIAL).] —**in·i·ti·a·tor** *n.*

in·i·ti·at·ed /i níshee àytəd/ *npl.* those who know about something that seems difficult or complicated, or who know the secrets of a group, organization, or religion

in·i·ti·a·tion /i nìshee áysh'n/ *n.* **1. ACTION THAT MAKES SOMETHING START** action that causes something, especially an important process or event, to begin ○ *the initiation of legal proceedings* **2. CEREMONY** a usually secret or mysterious ceremony by which somebody is admitted to a group, organization, or religion (*sometimes used before a noun*) ○ *initiation rites* **3. INTRODUCTION TO SOMETHING NEW** the introduction of somebody to a new activity, interest, or area [Late 16thC. From Latin *initiatio*, from the past participle stem of *initiare* "to begin."]

in·i·tia·tive /i níshətiv/ *n.* **1. ABILITY TO ACT ON YOUR OWN** the ability to act and make decisions without the help or advice of other people ○ *You'll just have to use your initiative.* **2. INTRODUCTORY STEP** the first step in a process that, once taken, determines subsequent events ○ *decided to take the initiative* **3. PLAN** a plan or strategy designed to deal with a particular problem ○ *a peace initiative* **4. ADVANTAGEOUS POSITION** a favorable position that allows somebody to take preemptive action or control events ○ *lose the initiative* **5.** POL **RIGHT TO INTRODUCE NEW LEGISLATION** the right to bring a new law or measure before a legislative body **6.** POL **PROPOSAL OF LEGISLATION BY CITIZENS** a process valid in many U.S. states and in Switzerland that allows citizens to propose legislation by petition ■ *adj.* **OF INITIATION** used in or relating to initiation (*formal*) [Late 18thC. Via French from the past participle stem of Latin *initiare* "to begin."] —**in·i·tia·tive·ly** *adv.*

in·i·ti·a·to·ry /i níshee ə tàwree/ *adj.* **1. BEGINNING** occurring at or related to the beginning of something **2. FOR INITIATION** used in or characteristic of an initiation [Early 17thC]

inj. *abbr.* **1.** injection **2.** injury

in·ject /in jékt/ (**-ject·ed, -ject·ing, -jects**) *v.* **1.** *vti.* MED **PUT FLUID INTO THE BODY WITH A SYRINGE** to introduce a drug, vaccine, or other fluid into part of the body using a syringe **2.** *vt.* **FORCE LIQUID OR GAS INTO SOMETHING** to force a liquid or gas through a small opening into a confined space ○ *They inject an insulating foam into the cavity between the walls.* **3.** *vt.* **ADD SOMETHING TO SITUATION** to introduce a particular quality or element into a situation ○ *an attempt to inject a little levity into the proceedings* **4.** *vt.* SPACE TECH **PUT A ROCKET OR SATELLITE IN ORBIT** to put a rocket or satellite in orbit or a spacecraft on a trajectory to its destination [Late 16thC. From, ultimately, Latin *inicere* "to throw in," from *iacere* "to throw" (source of English *ejaculate*).] —**in·ject·a·ble** *adj.*

in·jec·tant /in jéktənt/ *n.* an injected substance

in·jec·tion /in jékshən/ *n.* **1.** MED **INJECTED DOSE OF A DRUG** a dose of a particular drug in liquid form that is injected into the body with a syringe **2.** MED **INTRODUCTION OF FLUID WITH A SYRINGE** the introduction of fluid into the body by means of a syringe **3.** AUTOMOT **SPRAYING FUEL INTO AN ENGINE** the process of spraying fuel through a pump into the inlet manifold or cylinder of an internal-combustion engine, eliminating the need for a carburetor **4. ADDITION OF SOMETHING TO SITUATION** the introduction of a particular quality or element into a situation ○ *a cash injection* **5. PROVISION OF MONEY** a provision of money for a country, organization, project, or person in financial need **6.** ALGEBRA **ONE-TO-ONE MAPPING OF SETS** a one-to-one mapping of two sets such that each element of each set corresponds only to one element of the other set **7.** TECH **INTRODUCTION OF FLUID INTO A CAVITY** a process for introducing a fluid such as a plastic under pressure into a cavity **8.** SPACE TECH **PUTTING A SATELLITE INTO ORBIT** the insertion of an artificial satellite into orbit or a space probe on a trajectory **9.** SPACE TECH **MOMENT OF SATELLITE INSERTION** the moment or place at which insertion of a satellite or probe occurs [15thC. Directly or via Middle French from Latin *injectio*, from *inicere* "to throw in" (see INJECT).]

in·jec·tion mold·ing *n.* a manufacturing process in which heated material (**thermoplastic**) is forced under pressure into a water-cooled mold —**in·jec·tion-mold·ed** *adj.*

in-joke *n.* a joke that is shared and understood by only a particular group of people

in·ju·di·cious /in joo díshəss/ *adj.* lacking in judgment or discretion —**in·ju·di·cious·ly** *adv.* —**in·ju·di·cious·ness** *n.*

In·jun /ínjən/ *n.* an offensive term for a Native American (*dated offensive*) [Late 17thC. Represents colloquial and dialectal pronunciation of INDIAN.]

in·junc·tion /in júngkshən/ *n.* **1.** LAW **COURT ORDER** a court order that requires somebody involved in a legal action to do something or refrain from doing something **2. COMMAND** a command or order, especially from somebody in a position of authority **3. ACT OF ORDERING SOMEBODY** the act of ordering somebody to do or not to do something [15thC. From late Latin *injunctio*, from *injungere* "to enjoin," from *jungere* "to join."]

in·jure /ínjər/ (**-jured, -jur·ing, -jures**) *vt.* **1. HURT SOMEBODY OR SOMETHING** to cause physical hurt or damage to a person, animal, or body part **2. OFFEND SOMEBODY** to cause somebody distress by an unkind action or words **3.** LAW **DO LEGAL WRONG TO SOMEBODY** to wrong somebody by word or deed in such a way that redress by legal means is available **4. DAMAGE SOMEBODY'S REPUTATION** to damage somebody's reputation, career, or chances of success [15thC. Via Old French *injurier* from Latin *injuriare*, from *injuria* (see INJURY).] —**in·jur·a·ble** *adj.* —**in·jur·er** *n.*

WORD KEY: SYNONYMS

See Synonyms at ***harm***.

in·ju·ri·ous /in jóoree əss/ *adj.* **1. CAUSING INJURY** causing harm, hurt, damage, or distress **2. DAMAGING SOMEBODY'S REPUTATION** damaging somebody's reputation, career, or chances of success [15thC. Via Middle French *injurios* from Latin *injuriosus*, from *injuria* (see INJURY).] —**in·ju·ri·ous·ly** *adv.* —**in·ju·ri·ous·ness** *n.*

in·ju·ry /ínjəree/ (*plural* **-ries**) *n.* **1. PHYSICAL DAMAGE** physical damage to the body or a part of the body ○ *they escaped without injury* **2. WOUND** a specific instance of physical damage to part of the body ○ *a serious back injury* **3.** LAW **HARM TO SOMEBODY'S REPUTATION** harm caused to somebody's career or reputation by scandal, rumor, or defamation **4.** LAW **INFRINGEMENT OF SOMEBODY'S RIGHTS** the violation of somebody's rights, against which legal action can be taken [14thC. Via Anglo-Norman from Latin *injuria* "a wrong," from *injurius* "unjust," from *in-* "not" + *jus* "justice."]

in·ju·ry time *n.* extra time allowed at the end of some games, especially soccer and rugby, to compensate for time spent attending to injured players during the game

in·jus·tice /in jústiss/ *n.* unfair or unjust treatment of somebody, or an instance of this [14thC. Via Old French from Latin *injustitia*, from *injustus* "unjust," from *in-* "not" + *justus* "just."]

ink /ingk/ *n.* **1. LIQUID FOR WRITING, DRAWING, OR PRINTING** a colored liquid or paste used for writing, printing, or drawing **2.** ZOOL **LIQUID EJECTED BY OCTOPUS OR SQUID** a dark brown liquid (**sepia**) ejected from a gland (**ink sac**) near the anus by most cephalopods, including the octopus and the squid, to distract predators **3. PRINT PUBLICITY** publicity, especially in the print media (*slang*) ○ *The stunt got him all kinds of ink.* ■ *vt.* **(inked, ink·ing, inks) 1. MARK SOMETHING WITH INK** to write or draw with ink on a piece of paper or other surface **2. ADD INK** to coat something with ink or apply ink to something, usually in preparation for printing **3. SIGN A CONTRACT** to put or obtain a signature on a contract or other document (*informal*) [13thC. Via Old French *enque* from, ultimately, Greek *enkauston* "purple ink," from *enkaiein* "to burn in," from the process of encaustic painting.] —**ink·er** *n.*

ink in *vt.* to go over the pencil lines of a drawing or design in ink

ink·ber·ry /íngk bèrree/ (*plural* **-ries**) *n.* **1. EVERGREEN SHRUB** an upright evergreen shrub native to eastern North America with small black fruits and oblong to oval dark green leaves that may be smooth-edged or have serrated tips. Latin name: *Ilex glabra.* **2. BLACK FRUIT** the small black rounded fruit of an inkberry **3.** BOT = **pokeweed** [Mid-18thC. From the use of the berries for making ink.]

ink·blot /íngk blòt/ *n.* **1. INK STAIN** a stain or spot of spilled ink **2.** PSYCHOL **PATTERN USED IN THE RORSCHACH TEST** any of the ten abstract patterns resembling an inkblot used in the Rorschach test

ink·blot test *n.* PSYCHOL = **Rorschach test**

ink·horn /íngk hàwrn/ *n.* **OLD INK CONTAINER** a small portable ink container made from horn or a similar material and used in former times ■ *adj.* **TOO LEARNED** excessively scholarly in style or language, especially in the use of terms derived from Latin and Greek

in-kind *adj.* **1. IN GOODS OR SERVICES** in the form of goods or services rather than in cash **2. GIVING BACK AN EQUIVALENT AMOUNT** giving something that is equivalent to what has been received

ink-jet print·er *n.* a printer that prints using particles or droplets of electrically charged ink from a matrix of tiny ink jets

in·kle /íngk'l/ *n.* a narrow linen tape used for trimmings, or the yarn used in this tape [Mid-16thC. Origin unknown: possibly from Dutch *enkel* "single," from its narrowness.]

in·kling /íngkling/ *n.* **1. FAINT IDEA** a vague idea or suspicion about a fact, event, or person ○ *I had no inkling that he was unhappy.* **2. HINT** an indication of how to go about something ○ *Could you give me some inkling of where to look?* [Early 16thC. From an obsolete English verb of unknown origin meaning "to utter in an undertone," hence, "to hint."]

ink sac *n.* a large gland with an opening close to the anus of most cephalopods, including the octopus and squid, from which ink (**sepia**) is ejected to distract predators

ink·stand /íngk stànd/ *n.* **1. STAND FOR WRITING MATERIALS** a rack or stand that is kept on a desk and contains bottles of ink, pens, and other writing materials **2.** = **inkwell**

ink·well /íngk wèl/ *n.* a small container for ink, especially one that fits into a hole in a desk

ink·y /íngkee/ (**-i·er, -i·est**) *adj.* **1. COVERED IN INK** consisting of or covered in ink **2. DARK** black or dark blue in color

ink·y cap *n.* a mushroom with a conical cap and gills on the underside that dissolve into an inky black pulp after the spores mature. Species include the common inky cap and the edible shaggymane. Genus: *Coprinus.*

in·lace /in láyss/ *vt.* = **enlace**

in·laid /ín làyd/ *adj.* **1. SET INTO A SURFACE** set into the surface of wood or another material, usually to provide decoration **2. DECORATED** decorated with an inlaid pattern

in·land /ín lànd, ínlənd/ *adj.* **1. NOT NEAR A COAST OR BORDER** in or relating to the part of a country that is not near the coast or a border **2.** *U.K.* **WITHIN A COUNTRY** occurring within a country, rather than between countries ■ *adv.* **IN OR INTO THE INTERIOR OF COUNTRY** in or toward the interior of a country ■ *n.* **INTERIOR OF A COUNTRY** the interior of a country [Old English]

In·land Rev·e·nue *n. U.K.* a British government department responsible for the collection and administration of direct taxes

In·land Sea arm of the Pacific Ocean, in Japan, between the islands of Honshu, Shikoku, and Kyushu. Length: 240 mi./386 km.

in-law *n.* a relative by marriage (*informal*)

in·lay /ín lày/ *vt.* **(-laid, -lay·ing, -lays) 1. SET SOMETHING INTO A SURFACE** to set pieces of material such as wood, ivory, or stone into previously cut slots in a surface to form a decorative pattern **2. DECORATE SOMETHING WITH AN INLAID DESIGN** to decorate something such as a piece of furniture by setting pieces of wood, stone, ivory, or other material into its surface ■ *n.* **1. PIECES OF MATERIAL SET INTO A SURFACE** pieces of material such as wood, ivory, or stone set into the surface of a piece of furniture to form a decorative pattern **2. DECORATIVE PATTERN** a decorative pattern formed by inlaying **3.** DENT **GOLD OR PORCELAIN FILLING FOR TOOTH** a filling made of gold or porcelain that is inserted into a cavity in a tooth and cemented in position —**in·lay·er** /ín láyr/ *n.*

in·let /ín lèt, ínlət/ *n.* **1. NARROW OPENING IN A COASTLINE** a narrow stretch of water reaching inland from a sea or lake **2. STRETCH OF WATER BETWEEN TWO ISLANDS** a narrow stretch of water between two islands **3.** SEW **PIECE OF EXTRA FABRIC** a piece of fabric put into the seam of a garment to make it bigger or for decoration **4.** TECH **PASSAGE OR VALVE** an opening through which liquid or gas enters a machine or other device ■ *vt.* **(-let, -let·ing, -lets)** = **inlay** *v.* 1, **inlay** *v.* 2 [13thC. Originally in the sense "permission to enter."]

in·li·er /ín lìr/ *n.* a rock formation in which older rocks are completely surrounded by younger rocks. ◊ **outlier** [Mid-19thC. Formed from IN- + *lier*, modeled on OUTLIER.]

in-line *adj.* used to describe a device or machine in which similar parts are located together and in a straight line, e.g., the cylinders in an internal-combustion engine

In-line skate

in-line skates *npl.* roller skates with each boot mounted on a single line of three or four narrow wheels

in loc. cit. *adv.* = **loc. cit.**

in lo·co pa·ren·tis /in lṓkō pə réntiss/ *adv.* having or taking on the responsibilities of a parent when dealing with somebody else's child [From Latin]

in·ly /ínnlee/ *adv.* (*literary*) **1. INWARDLY** in an inward way **2. INTIMATELY** with deep or intimate understanding

in·ly·ing /ín lì ing/ *adj.* situated within a country or region

in·mate /ín màyt/ *n.* somebody who has been confined within a prison or a psychiatric hospital [Late 16thC. Formed from IN + MATE "companion."]

in me·di·as res /in mée̱dee əss ráyss/ *adv.* straight in or into the middle of a sequence of events, especially in a literary narrative that has no introduction (*formal*) [From Latin, "into the midst of things"]

in me·mo·ri·am /in mə máwree əm/ *prep.* in memory of or in memory (*used in epitaphs and obituaries*) [From Latin]

in·mesh *vt.* = **enmesh**

in·mi·grant *adj.* **FROM ANOTHER PART OF THE SAME COUNTRY** coming from a different part of the same country ■ *n.* **SOMEBODY FROM WITHIN THE SAME COUNTRY** somebody who travels from a different part of the same country

in·mi·grate **(in·mi·grat·ed, in·mi·grat·ing, in·mi·grates)** *vi.* to travel to a place from a different part of the same country —**in·mi·gra·tion** *n.*

in·most /ín mṓst/ *adj.* = **innermost** [Old English *innemest*, from *inne* "in" + *mest* "most"]

inn /in/ *n.* **1. HOTEL** a place providing food and lodging for travelers (*often used in the names of establishments*) **2. BAR OR RESTAURANT** a bar or restaurant **3.** *U.K.* **RESIDENCE FOR STUDENTS** formerly, a dormitory for students, especially those studying law [Old English from, ultimately, an Indo-European word meaning "in" which is also the source of English *in*]

in·nards /ínnərdz/ *npl.* (*informal*) **1. INTERNAL ORGANS** the internal organs of the body, especially the intestines **2. INTERNAL PARTS OF A MACHINE** the internal working parts of a machine or mechanical device [Early 19thC. Alteration of INWARDS (plural noun).]

in·nate /i náyt/ *adj.* **1. PRESENT FROM BIRTH** relating to qualities that a person or animal is born with **2. INTEGRAL** forming an integral part of something **3.** PHILOS **COMING FROM THE MIND** coming directly from the mind rather than being acquired by experience or from external sources ○ *an innate sense of justice* **4.** BOT **JOINED TO THE FILAMENT BY THE BASE** used to describe an anther that is joined to the filament by its base only **5.** BOT **ORIGINATING WITHIN THE THALLUS** forming an integral part of the thallus [15thC. From Latin *innatus*, the past participle of *innasci* "to be born in," from *nasci* "to be born" (source of English *nature*).] —**in·nate·ly** *adv.* —**in·nate·ness** *n.*

in·nate re·leas·ing mech·a·nism *n.* a process within the central nervous system of animals that, in response to certain stimuli, causes the animal to produce instinctive behavior. An example is the way that chicks of some birds peck at the red dot on the adult's beak.

in·ner /ínnər/ *adj.* **1. NEAR OR CLOSER TO THE CENTER** located near or closer to the center of something ○ *the inner city* **2. BEING OR OCCURRING INSIDE** located or happening on the inside of something ○ *an inner door* **3. OF THE MIND** relating to somebody's private feelings or happening in somebody's mind ○ *his quiet exterior that hid an inner confidence* **4. NOT OBVIOUS** needing to be examined closely or thought about in order to be seen or understood ○ *searching for the inner meaning of the text* **5. PRIVILEGED** most privileged or influential ○ *the inner circle* [Old English *innera*. Ultimately from an Indo-European word meaning "in" that is also the source of English *enter*.] —**in·ner·ly** *adv.* —**in·ner·ness** *n.*

in·ner child *n.* PSYCHOL an adult's conception of himself or herself as a child, often used as a tool in therapeutic processes to explore feelings about the person's childhood

in·ner cit·y *n.* the central or innermost parts of a city, particularly when associated with social problems such as inadequate housing and high levels of crime and unemployment

in·ner-di·rect·ed *adj.* guided by personal beliefs rather than by norms imposed by society

in·ner ear *n.* the fluid-filled part of the ear, including the cochlea, which is responsible for hearing, and the semicircular canals, which control balance

In·ner Light *n.* in Quaker belief, the presence of God as a guiding force within the human soul

in·ner man *n.* the soul or the spiritual or intellectual part of a man. ◊ **inner woman**

In·ner Mon·go·li·a Au·ton·o·mous Re·gion administrative region of northern China, bordered on the north by Russia and Mongolia. Population: 22,840,000 (1995). Area: 454,600 sq. mi./1,177,500 sq. km.

in·ner·most /ínnər mṓst/ *adj.* **1. MOST CENTRAL** most important, private, or personal ○ *innermost thoughts* **2. FARTHEST FROM THE OUTSIDE** taking place or being situated farthest from the outside

in·ner plan·et *n.* any of the four planets Mercury, Venus, Earth, or Mars whose orbits lie closest to the Sun and are within the asteroid belt. ◊ **outer planet**

in·ner prod·uct *n.* MATH = **scalar product**

in·ner·sole /ínnər sṑl/ *n.* a foot-shaped piece of leather, sheepskin, or synthetic material worn inside a shoe or boot to provide a better fit or added warmth. ◊ **insole**

in·ner space *n.* **1. AREA BENEATH THE SURFACE OF THE SEA** the environment that exists beneath the surface of the sea **2. MENTAL REALM** somebody's inner spiritual or psychological depths

in·ner·spring /ínnər spring/ *adj.* used to describe a

mattress that has many helical springs inside a thick padded cover

in·ner tube *n.* a hollow rubber ring filled with compressed air that fits inside a pneumatic tire

in·ner·vate /i núr vàyt, ínnər vàyt/ (**-vat·ed, -vat·ing, -vates**) *vt.* **1. SUPPLY NERVES TO A BODY ORGAN** to distribute nerves to an organ or body part **2. STIMULATE A MUSCLE, ORGAN, OR BODY PART** to cause a muscle, organ, or other part of the body to act —**in·ner·va·tion** /innər váysh'n/ *n.* —**in·ner·va·tion·al** /-váyshən'l, -váyshnəl/ *adj.*

in·ner·wear /ínnər wàir/ *n.* clothing that is worn next to the skin, such as an undershirt or a slip

in·ner wom·an *n.* the soul or the spiritual or intellectual part of a woman. ◊ **inner man**

In·ness /ínniss/, **George** (1825–94) U.S. artist. He is known for his many landscapes such as *Home of the Heron* (1893).

in·ning /ínning/ *n.* **1.** BASEBALL **BASEBALL DIVISION** one of the divisions of a game of baseball or softball during which each team bats until it makes three outs. Nine innings is standard for baseball, seven for softball, but extra innings are played if the score remains tied. **2.** CIV ENG **RECLAMATION OF LAND FROM THE SEA** the reclamation of marshy or flooded land from the sea (*archaic*) [Old English *innung*, from *innian* "to put in," from *in* (see IN). In sports, from the sense of "in possession of the game."]

in·nings /ínningz/ (*plural* **-nings**) *n.* **1.** CRICKET **TURN AT BATTING** the turn of a cricket player or team at batting **2.** CRICKET **RUNS SCORED DURING AN INNINGS** the runs scored during the turn of a cricket player or team at batting **3. PERIOD OF SUCCESS** a period of opportunity or success, or a long active life or career

in·nit /ínnit/ *interj. U.K.* used as a tag question at the end of a statement (*nonstandard*) ○ *Nice weather, innit?* [Mid-19thC. Alteration.]

inn·keep·er /in kèepər/ *n.* somebody who owns or manages an inn

in·no·cence /ínnəs'ns/ *n.* **1.** LAW **ABSENCE OF GUILT** the state of not being guilty of a crime or offense **2.** LAW **LAWFULNESS** the state of being permitted by law **3. HARMLESSNESS** harmlessness in intention **4. FREEDOM FROM SIN** freedom from sin or evil **5. LACK OF WORLDLY EXPERIENCE** a lack of experience of the world, especially when this results in a failure to recognize the harmful intentions of other people **6. IGNORANCE** ignorance of the serious consequences of something such as an act or remark **7. CHASTITY** sexual inexperience **8.** BOT = **blue-eyed Mary** [14thC. Via Old French from Latin *innocentia*, from *innocens* (see INNOCENT).]

in·no·cen·cy /ínnəs'nsee/ (*plural* **-cies**) *n.* an innocent action or quality (*archaic*)

in·no·cent /ínnəs'nt/ *adj.* **1.** LAW **NOT GUILTY** not guilty of a crime or offense **2.** LAW **WITHIN THE LAW** permitted by or acting within the law ○ *an innocent bystander* **3. HARMLESS IN INTENTION** not intended to cause harm ○ *an innocent remark* **4. UNCORRUPTED** pure and uncorrupted by evil, sin, or experience of the world **5. NAIVE** more trusting or naive than most people through lack of experience of life or failure to recognize the motives of others **6. IGNORANT OF SOMETHING** having very little or no knowledge of something ○ *innocent of the finer points of etiquette* **7. LACKING IN SOMETHING** completely lacking in a particular quality ○ *innocent of any artistic skill* ■ *n.* **1. BLAMELESS PERSON** a blameless vulnerable person, especially a very young child **2. NAIVE PERSON** a simple, naive, or inexperienced person [14thC. Via Old French from Latin *innocens*, from *in-* "not" + the present participle of *nocere* "to harm."] —**in·no·cent·ly** *adv.*

In·no·cent III /ínnəss'nt/, **Pope** (1160?–1216). As pope (1198–1216) he exercised considerable power over the European political rulers of the day, launched the Fourth Crusade (1204), and summoned the Fourth Lateran Council (1215).

in·noc·u·ous /i nókyoo əss/ *adj.* **1. UNLIKELY TO OFFEND** not intended to cause offense or provoke a strong reaction and unlikely to do so ○ *an innocuous comment* **2. HARMLESS** harmless in effect ○ *an innocuous white powder* [Late 16thC. From Latin *innocuus*, from *in-* "not" + *nocuus* "hurtful," from *nocere* "to harm."] —**in·noc·u·ous·ly** *adv.* —**in·noc·u·ous·ness** *n.*

in·nom·i·nate /i nómmənət/ *adj.* **1. NAMELESS** without a name (*formal*) **2. UNNAMED** anonymous (*literary*) [Mid-17thC. From late Latin *innominatus*, from *in-* "not" + *nominatus* "NOMINATE."]

in·nom·i·nate ar·ter·y *n.* a short artery rising from the arch of the aorta toward the right upper part of the body. It divides to form the right common carotid artery, which supplies blood to the head, and the right subclavian artery, which supplies blood to the right arm.

in·nom·i·nate bone *n.* a hipbone (*technical*) [Because early anatomists could not think of anything it resembled]

in·nom·i·nate vein *n.* either of two large veins on opposite sides of the neck that join to form the superior vena cava, one of the two veins taking blood to the heart

in·no·vate /ínnə vàyt/ (**-vat·ed, -vat·ing, -vates**) *vti.* to introduce a new way of doing something or a new device [Mid-16thC. From Latin *innovat-*, from *innovare* "to renew," from *novus* "new."]

in·no·va·tion /ínnə váy sh'n/ *n.* **1. ORIGINATION** the act or process of inventing or introducing something new **2. NEW IDEA OR METHOD** something newly invented or a new way of doing things ○ *suspicious of fax machines and other technological innovations* —**in·no·va·tion·al** *adj.*

in·no·va·tive /ínnə vàytiv/ *adj.* new and original or taking a new and original approach [Early 17thC] —**in·no·va·tive·ly** *adv.* —**in·no·va·tive·ness** *n.*

Inns·bruck /ínz bro͝ok/ city, tourist center, and capital of the Tirol Province, western Austria, situated on the Inn River approximately 85 mi./137 km southwest of Salzburg. Population: 118,112 (1991).

In·nu /í no͞o/ (*plural* **-nu**) *n.* **1.** PEOPLES **ONE OF AN ALGONQUIAN PEOPLE** a member of an Algonquian people living in northern Quebec and Labrador **2.** LANG **LANGUAGE OF THE INNU** the Algonquian language of the Innu people —**In.nu** *adj.*

in·nu·en·do /ínnyoo éndō/ (*plural* **-does** *or* **-dos**) *n.* **1. HINT OF SOMETHING IMPROPER** an indirect remark or gesture that usually carries a suggestion of impropriety ○ *"'I suppose Mary Garth admires Mr. Lydgate,' said Rosamond, not without a touch of innuendo."* (George Eliot, *Middlemarch*; 1872) **2.** LAW **INTERPRETATION OF POSSIBLY LIBELOUS LANGUAGE** an interpretation of words that are claimed to be libelous where the meaning is not obvious, in a legal action for libel or slander **3.** LAW **GLOSS FOR A TECHNICAL LEGAL WORD** an explanation of a technical legal word, usually given in brackets [Mid-16thC. From Latin *innuendo* "by intimation," from *innuere* "to nod to, signify."]

in·nu·mer·a·ble /i nyo͞omərəb'l/ *adj.* too many to be counted [14thC. Via Latin *innumerabilis* from, ultimately, *numerus* "number."] —**in·nu·mer·a·bil·i·ty** /i nyo͞omərə bílləte e/ *n.* —**in·nu·mer·a·ble·ness** /i nyo͞omərəb'lnəss/ *n.* —**in·nu·mer·a·bly** /i nyo͞omərəblee/ *adv.*

in·nu·mer·ate /i nyo͞omərət/ *adj.* lacking a basic knowledge of mathematics and unable to use numbers in calculation [Mid-20thC. Formed from NUMERATE.]

in·ob·ser·vance /innəb zúrvəns/ *n.* **1. DISREGARD FOR RULE, LAW, ETC** failure to comply with something, especially a rule, law, or custom **2. LACK OF ATTENTION** lack of heed or attention —**in·ob·ser·vant** *adj.* —**in·ob·ser·vant·ly** *adv.*

in·ob·tru·sive *adj.* = **unobtrusive**

in·oc·u·la·ble /i nókyələb'l/ *adj.* able to be prevented by inoculation —**in·oc·u·la·bil·i·ty** /i nòkyələ bílləte e/ *n.*

in·oc·u·lant /ináw kyə l'nt/ *n.* = **inoculum**

in·oc·u·late /i nókyə làyt/ (**-lat·ed, -lat·ing, -lates**) *vt.* **1.** MED **PROTECT SOMEBODY AGAINST DISEASE** to inject or introduce a serum, antigen, or a weakened form of a disease-producing pathogen into somebody's body in order to create immunity to the disease ○ *inoculated every child against polio* **2.** BIOL **ADD MICROORGANISMS TO A CULTURE** to introduce microorganisms into a culture medium [15thC. From Latin *inoculare* "to graft on a plant part" (the original sense in English), from *oculus* "bud, eye," the underlying idea being "implanting something into an individual."] —**in·oc·u·la·tive** *adj.* —**in·oc·u·la·tor** *n.*

in·oc·u·lum /i nókyələm/ (*plural* **-ula** /-lə/) *n.* material injected into somebody or something to create resistance to a disease [Early 20thC. Formed from Latin *inoculare* "to inoculate" (see INOCULATE), modeled on COAGULUM.]

in·o·dor·ous /in ṓdərəss/ *adj.* having no smell

in·of·fen·sive /ínnə fénsiv/ *adj.* not causing harm, annoyance, or offense ○ *the remark was inoffensive enough* —**in·of·fen·sive·ly** *adv.* —**in·of·fen·sive·ness** *n.*

in·of·fi·cious /ínnə físhəss/ *adj.* LAW violating standards of morality or natural affection, especially failing to give an heir a just, and, in some cases, legally required, share of the inheritance ○ *an inofficious will* [Early 17thC. From Latin *inofficiosus* "undutiful, not obliging," from *officium* "duty."] —**in·of·fi·cious·ly** *adv.* —**in·of·fi·cious·ness** *n.*

İn·ö·nü /éenə nyo͞o/, **Ismet** (1884–1973) Turkish soldier and politician. He was the first premier of the Turkish Republic (1923–37) and its second president (1938–50).

in·op·er·a·ble /in óppərəb'l, -óppre-/ *adj.* **1.** SURG **TOO FAR ADVANCED FOR EFFECTIVE SURGERY** having advanced to a stage at which surgical intervention would serve no useful purpose **2. NOT PRACTICAL** not practical or workable **3.** = **inoperative** *adj.* 1 —**in·op·er·a·bil·i·ty** /in òppərə bílləte e/ *n.* —**in·op·er·a·ble·ness** /in óppərə b'lnəss/ *n.* —**in·op·er·a·bly** *adv.*

in·op·er·a·tive /in óppərətiv, in óppretiv/ *adj.* **1. NOT WORKING** not functioning properly or as usual **2. INEFFECTIVE OR UNENFORCEABLE** not effective or no longer valid or able to be enforced —**in·op·er·a·tive·ly** *adv.* —**in·op·er·a·tive·ness** *n.*

in·op·por·tune /in òppər to͞on/ *adj.* happening at a bad moment or an inconvenient time —**in·op·por·tune·ly** *adv.* —**in·op·por·tune·ness** *n.* —**in·op·por·tu·ni·ty** /in òppər to͞onətee/ *n.*

in·or·di·nate /in áwrd'nət/ *adj.* **1. EXCESSIVE** beyond reasonable limits in amount or degree ○ *"capable of expressing an inordinate degree of unreason"* (Henry James, *Roderick Hudson*; 1876) **2. UNRESTRAINED** showing a lack of restraint or control (*archaic or literary*) [14thC. Via Latin *inordinatus* "not orderly, out of order" from, ultimately, *ordo* "order."] —**in·or·di·na·cy** *n.* —**in·or·di·nate·ly** *adv.* —**in·or·di·nate·ness** *n.*

inorg. *abbr.* inorganic

in·or·gan·ic /in awr gánnik/ *adj.* **1. NOT ANIMAL OR VEGETABLE** composed of minerals rather than living material **2.** CHEM **WITHOUT CARBON** used to describe chemical compounds that contain no carbon, excluding the oxides of carbon, carbon disulfide, cyanides, and their associated acids and salts —**in·or·gan·i·cal·ly** *adv.*

in·or·gan·ic chem·is·try *n.* the branch of chemistry relating to inorganic compounds

in·os·cu·late /in óskyə làyt/ (**-lat·ed, -lat·ing, -lates**) *vti.* to join and blend with something else [Late 17thC. Coined from IN- + Latin *osculare* "to provide with a mouth," from *osculum* "little mouth," from *os* "mouth" (source of *oral* and *orifice*).] —**in·os·cu·la·tion** /in òskyə láysh'n/ *n.*

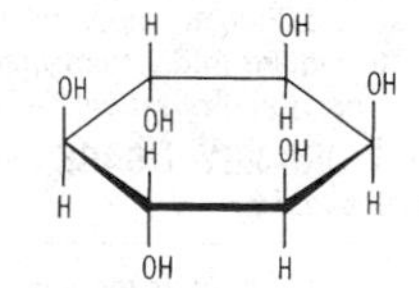

Inositol

in·o·si·tol /i nṓssə tàwl, T-/ *n.* a cyclic alcohol that has nine related forms, one of which occurs in plants and animals and functions as a growth factor. Formula: $C_6H_{12}O_6$. [Late 19thC. Coined from Greek *inos* "sinew" + -ITE + -OL.]

in·o·tro·pic *adj.* having an effect on the force of muscular contraction ○ *an inotropic drug* [Early 20thC. Coined from Greek *inos* "sinew, tendon" + -TROPIC.]

in·pa·tient, **in-pa·tient** *n.* **PERSON STAYING IN HOSPITAL** somebody receiving medical treatment that requires a stay in a hospital ■ *adj.* **FOR INPATIENTS** relating to, designed for, or used by inpatients [Mid-18thC]

in per·pe·tu·um /in pərpétoo əm/ *adv.* LAW forever [From Latin]

in per·so·nam /in pur sṓnəm/ *adj., adv.* LAW made about or directed at a person rather than at property. ◊ **in rem** [From Latin, literally "against a person"]

in pet·to /in péttō/ *adj.* CHR not disclosing publicly the name of a cardinal appointed by the pope [Late 17thC. From Italian, literally "in the breast."]

in·phase /ín fàyz/ *adj.* of the same electrical phase

in pos·se /in póssay/ *adj.* potentially rather than in reality [From Latin]

in·pour·ing /ín pàwring/ *n.* a sudden flowing in of a large amount of something

in-proc·ess *adj.* **1.** UNDERWAY in the process of happening **2.** DURING MANUFACTURING in the process of being manufactured

in pro·pri·a per·so·na /in prŏpree ə pur sṓnə/ *adv.* LAW in person, especially when unrepresented by a lawyer [From Latin, literally "in your own person"]

in·put /ín pòot/ *n.* **1.** CONTRIBUTION a contribution to something, especially comments or suggestions made to a group **2.** SOMETHING GOING IN something that enters a process or situation from the outside and is then acted upon or integrated ○ *dollar input* ○ *sensory input* **3.** ELECTRON ENG ELECTRICITY DRIVING A MACHINE power, electrical energy, or an electric signal that enters a device and is usually recovered in the form of work or some other output effect **4.** COMPUT DATA ENTERED INTO A COMPUTER data entered into a computer for processing **5.** COMPUT COMPUTER TERMINAL a terminal or connection where data enters a computer ■ *v.* (**-put·ted** *or* **-put, -put·ting, -puts**) **1.** *vti.* CONTRIBUTE INFORMATION to provide information to help somebody make a decision (*informal*) **2.** *vt.* COMPUT ENTER DATA to enter data into a computer

in·put/out·put *n.* the hardware or software that controls the passage of information into and out of a computer or computer component

inq. *abbr.* inquiry

in·quest /ín kwèst/ *n.* **1.** FORMAL INVESTIGATION an official inquiry in front of a jury into the facts of a case such as a sudden unexpected death **2.** INQUIRY INTO WHAT WENT WRONG an investigation of the facts of a situation, particularly one that had an undesired outcome (*literary*) [14thC. Via Old French *enqueste* from Latin *inquesta*, which was formed from *inquirere* "to enquire" (source of English *enquire*).]

in·qui·e·tude /in kwī́ ə tòod/ *n.* a worried or restless state of mind (*literary*) [15thC. Via Late Latin *inquietudo* from, ultimately, Latin *quietus* "quiet" (source of English *quiet*).]

in·qui·line /ínkwə lĭn, ínkwəlin/ *n.* an animal that lives in the nest or home of another species [Mid-17thC. Via Latin *inquilinus* "tenant, lodger" from *incolere* "to inhabit," from *colere* "to dwell" (source of English *colony* and *culture*).]

in·quire /in kwī́r/ (**-quired, -quir·ing, -quires**), **en·quire** /en-/ (**-quired, -quir·ing, -quires**) *v.* **1.** *vti.* ASK to ask a question ○ *inquire about a job* ○ *May I inquire to whom I have the honor of speaking?* **2.** *vi.* TRY TO FIND OUT THE FACTS to try to discover the facts of a case [13thC. Via Old French *enquerre* from, ultimately, Latin *inquirere* "to inquire into," from *quaerere* "to seek" (source of English *query* and *question*).] —**in·quir·er** *n.*

WORD KEY: USAGE

See Usage note at ***enquire.***

in·quir·ing /in kwī́ring/, **en·quir·ing** /en-/ *adj.* **1.** EAGER TO LEARN eager to learn new things **2.** LOOKING QUESTIONING appearing to want to know or learn something ○ *an inquiring glance from the attendant* —**in·quir·ing·ly** *adv.*

in·quir·y /in kwī́ree, ínkwəree/ (*plural* **-ies**), **en·quir·y** /en kwī́ree, énkwəree/ (*plural* **-ies**) *n.* **1.** OFFICIAL REVIEW a formal investigation to determine the facts of a case **2.** REQUEST FOR INFORMATION a request for information

in·qui·si·tion /inkwə zísh'n/ *n.* **1.** PERIOD OF INTENSE QUESTIONING a succession of detailed and relentless questions **2.** HARSH INVESTIGATION an inquiry or investigation that is harsh or unfair [14thC. Via Old French *inquisicion* from Latin *inquirere* "to inquire" (see INQUIRE).] —**in·qui·si·tion·al** *adj.* —**in·qui·si·tion·ist** *n.*

In·qui·si·tion *n.* an organization in the Roman Catholic Church founded in the 13th century to find, question, and sentence those who did not hold orthodox religious beliefs. The Spanish Inquisition lasted until the 19th century and was known for its harsh punishments and use of torture.

in·quis·i·tive /in kwízzətiv/ *adj.* **1.** INQUIRING eager for knowledge **2.** TOO CURIOUS too curious about other people's business [14thC. Via Old French from, ultimately, Latin (see INQUIRE).] —**in·quis·i·tive·ly** *adv.* —**in·quis·i·tive·ness** *n.*

in·quis·i·tor /in kwízzitər/ *n.* **1.** INTERROGATOR somebody who asks a succession of relentless and searching or hostile questions **2.** **in·quis·i·tor, In·quis·i·tor** HIST ROMAN CATHOLIC QUESTIONER an official working for the Inquisition [Early 16thC. (See INQUIRE).]

in·quis·i·to·ri·al /in kwìzzə táwree əl/ *adj.* **1.** OF OR LIKE AN INQUISITION resembling a formal inquiry, especially in using rigorous or relentless questioning **2.** HAVING JUDGE AND PROSECUTOR AS THE SAME PERSON used to describe a trial in which one person is both judge and prosecutor —**in·quis·i·to·ri·al·ly** *adv.*

in re /in rée, in ráy/ *prep.* with regard to [From Latin, literally "in the matter of"]

in rem /in rém/ *adj.* LAW made about or directed at property rather than a person. ◊ **in personam** [From Latin, literally "against a thing"]

in·res·i·dence *adj.* officially connected with a university or other institution, often as a teacher or lecturer, but allowed time for original creative work ○ *She completed her book while serving as poet-in-residence at a small college.*

I.N.R.I. *abbr.* Jesus of Nazareth, King of the Jews (*used as an inscription over the head of the crucified Jesus Christ*) [Latin, Iesus Nazarenus Rex Iudaeorum]

in·ro /ín rṑ/ (*plural* **-ro**) *n.* a small ornamented box worn hanging from the sash of a kimono with compartments for holding cosmetics, perfumes, and medicines [Early 17thC. From Japanese *in*, "seal" + *ro*, "basket."]

in·road /ín rṑd/ *n.* RAID a sudden attack on an enemy camp (*archaic*) ■ **in·roads** *npl.* ENCROACHMENT a gradual encroachment on or of something ○ *young companies using electronic sales methods have made inroads into traditional markets* [Mid-16thC. Coined from IN + *road* "a riding, raid."]

in·rush /ín rùsh/ *n.* a sudden flooding or flowing in

INS *abbr.* **1.** Immigration and Naturalization Service **2.** inertial navigation system **3.** International News Service

ins. *abbr.* **1.** MEASURE inches **2.** inscription **3.** **ins., Ins.** inspector **4.** insulation **5.** insurance

in·sal·i·vate /in sálli vàyt/ (**-vat·ed, -vat·ing, -vates**) *vt.* to mix food with saliva in the process of chewing —**in·sal·i·va·tion** /in sàlli váysh'n/ *n.*

in·sa·lu·bri·ous /ìnsə lóobree əss/ *adj.* not pleasant, healthy, or wholesome (*formal*) —**in·sa·lu·bri·ous·ly** *adv.* —**in·sa·lu·bri·ty** /ìnsə lóobritee/ *n.*

in·sane /in sáyn/ *adj.* **1.** PSYCHIAT LEGALLY CONSIDERED AS PSYCHIATRICALLY DISORDERED legally incompetent or irresponsible because of a psychiatric disorder **2.** LACKING REASONABLE THOUGHT showing a complete lack of reason or foresight (*informal*) ■ *npl.* PSYCHIAT PEOPLE LEGALLY CONSIDERED AS PSYCHIATRICALLY DISORDERED persons who are legally incompetent or irresponsible because of a psychiatric disorder (*dated*) [Mid-16thC. From Latin *insanus*, from *sanus* "healthy, sane."] —**in·sane·ly** *adv.* —**in·sane·ness** *n.*

in·san·i·tar·y /in sánnə tèrree/ *adj.* dirty or unhygienic and thus likely to cause disease —**in·san·i·tar·i·ness** *n.* —**in·san·i·ta·tion** /in sànni táysh'n/ *n.*

in·san·i·ty /in sánnətee/ (*plural* **-ties**) *n.* **1.** LACK OF REASON OR GOOD SENSE extreme foolishness or an act that demonstrates it **2.** LAW legal incompetence or irresponsibility because of a psychiatric disorder

in·sa·tia·ble /in sáyshəb'l/ *adj.* always needing more and impossible to satisfy [15thC. Via Old French from, ultimately, Latin *satiare* "to fill" (see SATIATE).] —**in·sa·tia·bil·i·ty** /in sàyshə bíllətee/ *n.* —**in·sa·tia·ble·ness** /in sáyshəb'lnəss/ *n.* —**in·sa·tia·bly** *adv.*

in·sa·ti·ate /in sáyshee ət/ *adj.* insatiable (*literary*) [15thC. From Latin *insatiatus* "not satisfied" (see SATIATE).] —**in·sa·ti·ate·ly** *adv.* —**in·sa·ti·ate·ness** *n.*

in·scape /ín skàyp/ *n.* the distinctive and essential inner quality of something, especially a natural object or a scene in nature [Mid-19thC. Origin uncertain, probably modeled on LANDSCAPE.]

in·scribe /in skrī́b/ (**-scribed, -scrib·ing, -scribes**) *vt.* **1.** PUT WRITING ON SOMETHING to write, print, or engrave words or letters on a surface **2.** WRITE SOMETHING ON A LIST to add a name to a list or book **3.** WRITE A DEDICATION ON SOMETHING to write a signed message to somebody in a book or on a photograph, often when presenting it as a gift **4.** GEOM DRAW A GEOMETRIC FIGURE WITHIN ANOTHER to draw a geometric figure within another so that all of the second figure lies within the first and touches it at as many points as possible ○ *inscribe a circle within a square* [15thC. From Latin *inscribere* "to write on," from *scribere* "to write."] —**in·scrib·a·ble** *adj.* —**in·scrib·er** *n.*

in·scrip·tion /in skrípsh'n/ *n.* **1.** WRITING words or letters written, printed, or engraved on a surface **2.** DEDICATION a signed message written in a book or on a photograph, often when it is being presented as a gift [14thC. Via Latin from *inscribere* "to write on."] —**in·scrip·tion·al** *adj.*

in·scrip·tive /in skríptiv/ *adj.* relating to or constituting an inscription —**in·scrip·tive·ly** *adv.*

in·scru·ta·ble /in skróotəb'l/ *adj.* hard to interpret because not expressing anything obviously ○ *his inscrutable expression* [16thC. Via Old French from ecclesiastical Latin *inscrutabilis*, from Latin *scrutari* "to search, investigate" (source of English *scrutiny*).] —**in·scru·ta·bil·i·ty** /in skròotə bíllətee/ *n.* —**in·scru·ta·ble·ness** /in skróotəb'lnəss/ *n.* —**in·scru·ta·bly** *adv.*

in·seam /in séem/ *n.* **1.** INSIDE PANT LEG SEAM the inner seam of a pair of pants, from the crotch to the bottom of the pant leg **2.** MEASUREMENT OF AN INSEAM the measurement of a pant leg's inner seam [Late 19thC]

in·sect /ín sèkt/ *n.* **1.** ZOOL SMALL SIX-LEGGED ANIMAL an air-breathing invertebrate animal (**arthropod**) that has well-defined segments, e.g., a head, thorax, abdomen, two antennae, three pairs of legs, and usually two sets of wings. There are more than a million species of insects including flies, crickets, bees, beetles, and gnats. Class: Insecta. **2.** SOMETHING LIKE AN INSECT a small animal that resembles an insect, e.g., a spider or centipede (*not used technically*) **3.** CONTEMPTIBLE PERSON an unimportant person viewed with contempt (*insult*) [Early 17thC. Via Latin *insectum* from *insecare* "to cut up," from *secare* "to cut" (source of *dissect*, and *segment*).] —**in·sect·an** /in séktən/ *adj.*

in·sec·tar·i·um /in sek táiree əm/ (*plural* **-ums** *or* **-a** /-ə/), **in·sec·ta·ry** /ín sèktəree, in séktəree/ (*plural* **-ries**) *n.* a place for breeding or observing insects

in·sec·ti·cide /in sékti sīd/ *n.* a chemical substance used to kill insects —**in·sec·ti·cid·al** /in sèkti sī́d'l/ *adj.* —**in·sec·ti·cid·al·ly** *adv.*

in·sec·ti·vore /in sékti vàwr/ *n.* **1.** SMALL INSECT-EATING MAMMAL a small nocturnal mammal that feeds primarily on insects. Moles, shrews, and hedgehogs are all insectivores. **2.** PLANT OR ANIMAL EATING INSECTS any plant or animal that feeds primarily on insects [Mid-19thC. From modern Latin *Insectivora*, name of the order, from *insecta* "insect" (see INSECT) + *-vorus* "-eating."]

in·sec·tiv·o·rous /in sek tívvərəss/ *adj.* **1.** ZOOL FEEDING ON INSECTS feeding on insects, as some birds and small mammals do **2.** BOT ABLE TO TRAP INSECTS adapted for or capable of trapping insects as food, as the pitcher plant does

in·se·cure /ìnsə kyóor/ *adj.* **1.** NOT CONFIDENT anxious and lacking in self-confidence **2.** NOT SAFE unsafe and unprotected ○ *insecure premises that are vulnerable to thieves* **3.** LIKELY TO FALL liable to fall down or fall off ○ *an insecure walkway* [Mid-17thC. From medieval Latin *insecurus*, "unsafe."] —**in·se·cure·ly** *adv.* —**in·se·cure·ness** *n.* —**in·se·cu·ri·ty** /ìnsə kyóorətee/ *n.*

in·se·cu·ri·ty /ìnsə kyóorətee/ (*plural* **-ties**) *n.* **1.** BEING INSECURE the state of being unsafe or insecure **2.** UNSAFE FEELING a state of mind characterized by self-doubt and vulnerability **3.** INSECURE PHENOMENON an instance or cause of being insecure —**in·se·cu·ri·ty** *n.*

in·sel·berg /íns'l búrg/ *n.* an isolated hill or mountain, often heavily eroded on its lower slopes, rising abruptly from a plain [Early 20thC. From German, literally "island mountain."]

in·sem·i·nate /in sémmi nàyt/ (**-nat·ed, -nat·ing, -nates**) *vt.* to put sperm into the reproductive tract of a female [Early 17thC. From Latin *inseminare* "to implant," which was formed from, ultimately, *semen* "seed."] —**in·sem·i·na·tion** /in sèmmi náysh'n/ *n.*

in·sen·sate /in sén sàyt/ *adj.* **1.** WITHOUT FEELING inanimate and thus unable to feel anything **2.** COLD AND HEARTLESS entirely lacking in sympathetic feeling or human kindness (*literary*) **3.** THOUGHTLESS lacking in common sense or reasonable thought (*literary*) [15thC. From ecclesiastical Latin *insensatus* (see SENSATE).] —**in·sen·sate·ly** *adv.* —**in·sen·sate·ness** *n.*

in·sen·si·ble /in sénsəb'l/ *adj.* **1.** = **insensate** *adj.* 1 **2.** NOT CONSCIOUS without feeling or consciousness **3.** NOT AWARE OR RESPONSIVE unaware of or unresponsive to something **4.** UNNOTICEABLE so small or gradual as to be almost imperceptible ○ *an insensible shift in* *emphasis* [14thC. Via Old French from Latin *insensibilis* "imperceptible," from *sensus* "perception" (see SENSE).] —**in·sen·si·bil·i·ty** /in sènsə bíllətee/ *n.* —**in·sen·si·ble·ness** /in sénsəb'lnəss/ *n.* —**in·sen·si·bly** *adv.*

in·sen·si·tive /in sénsətiv/ *adj.* **1. THOUGHTLESS** insufficiently aware of other people's feelings and unable to respond to them appropriately **2. NOT REACTING PHYSICALLY** not responsive to a physical stimulus such as touch or sound **3. INDIFFERENT AND UNRESPONSIVE** indifferent to the importance of something and therefore not responding to it —**in·sen·si·tive·ly** *adv.* —**in·sen·si·tive·ness** *n.* —**in·sen·si·tiv·i·ty** /in sènsə tívvətee/ *n.*

in·sen·tient /in sénshənt/ *adj.* without life, consciousness, or perception —**in·sen·tience** *n.*

in·sep·a·ra·ble /in séppərəb'l, -sépprə-/ *adj.* **1. ALWAYS TOGETHER** sharing a close friendship and always seen or found together ○ *the two girls became inseparable* **2. UNABLE TO BE SEPARATED** so closely linked as to be impossible to consider separately ○ *reading and the ability to spell will seem inseparable* —**in·sep·a·ra·bil·i·ty** /in sèppərə bíllətee, -sèpprə-/ *n.* —**in·sep·a·ra·ble·ness** /in séppərəb'lnəss, -sépprə-/ *n.* —**in·sep·a·ra·bly** *adv.*

in·sert /in súrt/ *vt.* (**-sert·ed, -sert·ing, -serts**) **1. PLACE SOMETHING INSIDE SOMETHING** to put something inside or into something else ○ *insert the screws in the holes already drilled* **2. ADD SOMETHING TO SOMETHING** to add new material to the body of something, especially a text ■ *n.* **1.** PRESS **ADVERTISING SUPPLEMENT IN A MAGAZINE** a supplement in the form of a single sheet or booklet placed inside a magazine or newspaper, usually as advertising **2.** SEW **ADDED PART** a piece of fabric, usually contrasting, that is sewn into a main piece [15thC. From Latin *serere* "to join" (source of English *series*).] —**in·sert·a·ble** *adj.* —**in·sert·er** *n.*

in·ser·tion /in súrsh'n/ *n.* **1. ADDITION** the act of putting something into something else **2. SOMETHING ADDED** material that is inserted into a text **3.** ANAT, BOT **ATTACHMENT POINT** the point of attachment of something, e.g., a leaf to its stem or a muscle to a bone it moves **4.** GENETICS **INSERTED GENETIC MATERIAL** a segment of DNA that is inserted into a gene sequence **5.** SPACE TECH = **injection** *n.* 8, **injection** *n.* 9 —**in·ser·tion·al** *adj.*

in·ser·tion stitch *n.* an embroidery stitch that joins two pieces of fabric together and decorates the gap between them

in-serv·ice *adj.* **1. HAPPENING WHEN EMPLOYED FULL TIME** taking place while somebody is employed full time ○ *an in-service training program* **2. WORKING AS FULL-TIME EMPLOYEE** employed full time, especially in a particular job

in·ses·so·ri·al /in se sáwree əl/ *adj.* used to describe birds that are adapted, or have feet that are adapted, for perching [Mid-19thC. Formed from modern Latin *Insessores*, former name for the order of perching birds, from *insidere* "to sit on" (see INSIDIOUS).]

in·set *vt.* /in sét/ (**-set, -set·ting, -sets**) **PLACE A SMALLER THING IN A LARGER THING** to insert something into a larger thing, e.g., a gem in a ring or a small map in the corner of a larger map ■ *n.* /ín sèt/ **1. SMALL THING PLACED IN SOMETHING LARGER** something inserted into a larger thing ○ *a map of the state with city maps as insets* **2.** GEOG **CHANNEL** a place where something flows in, especially the tide

in·shal·lah /in shállə/, **in·sh'al·lah** *interj.* an expression meaning "if God wills," used to suggest that something in the future is uncertain [Mid-19thC. From Arabic *in šā csq Allāh*, literally "if God wills (it)."]

in·shore /in sháwr/ *adj.* **NEAR THE COAST** near or toward the coast ○ *inshore waters* ■ *adv.* **TOWARD THE COAST** toward the coast from the direction of the sea

in·shrine /in shrín/ (**-shrined, -shrin·ing, -shrines**) *vt.* = **enshrine**

in·side a grammatical word indicating the interior part of something, the part that is enclosed by or surrounded with something, or the place or part within ○ (adv) *I opened the door and looked inside.* ○ (adj) *his inside jacket pocket* ○ (n) *I looked around the room, gnawing the inside of my cheek nervously.* ○ *The jewels are kept inside a locked box.* ■ *adj.* /in síd, ín síd/, *prep.* /in síd, ín síd/ **WITHIN AN ORGANIZATION** happening or coming from within an organization ○ *They had access to inside information about the takeover bid.* ○ *things that were going on inside the committee* ■ *adv., prep.* /in síd, ín síd/ **RELATING TO INNER FEELINGS** indicating emotions that are not expressed ○ *She doesn't like to look inside and face up to what she's really like.* ○ *Seeing her like that had snapped something inside him.* ■ *prep.* /in síd, ín síd/ **WITHIN A TIME** done in a period of time less than the one stated ○ *We managed to completely redecorate the room inside seven hours.* ■ *adj.* /in síd, ín síd/ **AT THE EDGE OF THE ROAD** nearest the edge of the road ■ *adv.* **IN PRISON** serving time in prison (*informal*) ○ *He was inside for three years.* ■ *n.* /in síd/ **1. INNER EDGE** the part of a road or path farthest from the center ○ *was forced to overtake him on the inside* **2. PRIVILEGED ACCESS** a position that gives access to privileged information ○ *information from someone on the inside* ■ **in·sides** *npl.* ANAT **INTERNAL ORGANS** the internal organs of the body, especially the stomach and bowels (*informal*) [15thC] ◇ **inside of** within a particular period of time ◇ **inside out** with the part that is normally inside facing out ◇ **know something inside out** to know something extremely well

in·side ad·dress *n.* the name, title, and street address of the person to whom a business letter is written, as it appears on the letter above the salutation

in·side for·ward *n.* in soccer, one of two offensive players whose position is between the center forward and the wings

in·side in·for·ma·tion *n.* something secret or confidential known only to somebody who holds a position within a corporation or other organization

in·side job *n.* a crime carried out by or with the help of somebody who works for the individual or organization concerned (*informal*)

in·side leg *n.* CLOTHES = **inseam**

in·sid·er /in sídər/ *n.* somebody who is accepted as a member of a group and who knows all about its inner workings

in·sid·er trad·ing, **in·sid·er deal·ing** *n.* profitable trading in securities that is done using access to privileged information. Such trading is usually illegal.

in·side track *n.* **1.** SPORTS **INNER LANE OF RACETRACK** the lane of an oval racetrack nearest the center and thus shorter than the outer lanes **2. POSITION OF ADVANTAGE** an advantageous position

in·sid·i·ous /in síddee əss/ *adj.* slowly and subtly harmful or destructive [Mid-16thC. Via Latin *insidiosus* from *insidiae* "ambush," from *insidere* "to sit on, lie in wait," from *sedere* "to sit" (source of English *sedentary, session, reside,* and *seance*).] —**in·sid·i·ous·ly** *adv.* —**in·sid·i·ous·ness** *n.*

in·sight /ín sìt/ *n.* **1. PERCEPTIVENESS** the ability to see clearly and intuitively into the nature of a complex person, situation or subject **2. CLEAR PERCEPTION** a clear perception of something ○ *thanked him for his remark and told him it was an interesting insight* **3.** PSYCHOL **SELF-AWARENESS** the ability of a person to understand and find solutions to his or her personal problems **4.** PSYCHIAT **PERCEPTION THAT HALLUCINATIONS ARE NOT REAL** the perception, lacking in some psychiatric disorders such as schizophrenia, that symptoms such as delusions and hallucinations are not objective [Old English]

in·sight·ful /in sítfəl, ín sítfəl/ *adj.* containing or capable of clear and subtle perceptions about a subject [Early 20thC] —**in·sight·ful·ly** *adv.* —**in·sight·ful·ness** *n.*

in·sight med·i·ta·tion *n.* = **vipassana**

in·sig·ne /in sígnee/ singular of **insignia** (*literary*)

in·sig·ni·a /in sígnee ə/ (*plural* **-a** *or* **-as**) *n.* **1. OFFICIAL SYMBOL** a badge of authority or membership of a group **2. IDENTIFYING MARK** an identifying mark or sign [Mid-17thC. From Latin *insignis* "marked," from *signum* "sign."]

in·sig·nif·i·cant /in sig nífikənt/ *adj.* **1. WITHOUT IMPORTANCE** too small and unimportant to be relevant ○ *statistically insignificant* **2. WITHOUT MEANING** having little or no meaning **3. POWERLESS** lacking in power or status —**in·sig·nif·i·cance** *n.* —**in·sig·nif·i·cant·ly** *adv.*

in·sin·cere /in sin séer/ *adj.* not genuine and not reflecting true feelings —**in·sin·cere·ly** *adv.* —**in·sin·cer·i·ty** /in sin sérrətee/ *n.*

in·sin·u·ate /in sínnyoo àyt/ (**-at·ed, -at·ing, -ates**) *v.* **1.** *vti.* **IMPLY SOMETHING** to hint at something unpleasant or suggest it indirectly and gradually **2.** *vr.* **WORM YOUR WAY IN** to introduce yourself gradually and cunningly into a position, especially a place of confidence or favor [Early 16thC. From Latin *insinuare*, from *sinus* "curve" (source of English *sine*). The underlying sense is "to work in a roundabout way."] —**in·sin·u·at·ing·ly** *adv.* —**in·sin·u·a·tive** *adj.* —**in·sin·u·a·tor** *n.*

in·sin·u·a·tion /in sìnnyoo áysh'n/ *n.* **1. SLY HINT** something unpleasant artfully and indirectly suggested to another person **2. ACT OF INSINUATING** the act of hinting something unpleasant or suggesting it indirectly and gradually

in·sip·id /in síppid/ *adj.* **1. DULL** dull because lacking in character and lively qualities ○ *"that insipid languor that results from the removal of all passions from the mind"* (David Hume) **2. FLAVORLESS** bland and without flavor [Early 17thC. Directly or via French from late Latin *insipidus* "tasteless," from *sapidus* "having a flavor."] —**in·si·pid·i·ty** /insi píddətee/ *n.* —**in·sip·id·ly** /in síppidlee/ *adv.* —**in·sip·id·ness** *n.*

in·sist /in síst/ (**-sist·ed, -sist·ing, -sists**) *vti.* **1. MAINTAIN SOMETHING AGAINST OPPOSITION** to state or demand something firmly in spite of disagreement or resistance from others ○ *She insisted that he was wrong.* ○ *Please, you must take it, I insist!* **2. DECLARE SOMETHING PERSISTENTLY** to state something firmly and steadfastly ○ *They insist on punctuality.* ○ *he insisted there was nothing to worry about* [Late 16thC. From Latin *insistere* "to persist," from *sistere* "to stand, cause to stand."]

in·sis·tence /in sístəns/, **in·sis·ten·cy** *n.* continued assertion of something despite disagreement from others ○ *the UN's insistence that the resolution must be accepted*

in·sis·tent /in sístənt/ *adj.* **1. PERSISTENT** persistent in maintaining or demanding something ○ *she was most insistent* **2. DEMANDING ATTENTION** persistently calling for or compelling attention ○ *insistent pleas* —**in·sis·tent·ly** *adv.*

in si·tu /in sí too, in sée too/ *adv., adj.* in its natural or original place ○ *a useful tool for studying cell proliferation in situ under normal and pathological conditions* [From Latin]

in·snare *vt.* = **ensnare** —**in·snare·ment** *n.* —**in·snar·er** *n.*

in·so·bri·e·ty /insō brí ətee/ *n.* lack of moderation, especially in drinking

in·so·far as /in sō fáar-/ *conj.* used to introduce a statement that explains or qualifies a previous statement. (*formal*)

insol. *abbr.* insoluble

in·so·late /ín sō làyt/ (**-lat·ed, -lat·ing, -lates**) *vt.* to expose something to sunlight [Early 17thC. From Latin *insolare*, from *sol* "sun" (source of English *solar*).]

in·so·la·tion /ìn sō láysh'n/ *n.* **1. EXPOSURE TO SUNLIGHT** exposure of something to sunlight **2.** MED **SUNSTROKE** sunstroke (*technical*) **3.** ASTROPHYS **RATE OF SOLAR RADIATION** the rate of solar radiation received per unit area

in·sole /ín sōl/ *n.* **1. SHOE LINING** the inner lining of a shoe **2. PAD INSIDE SHOE** a thin removable liner placed inside a shoe to make it warmer or more comfortable or to prevent the buildup of odor

in·so·lent /ínsələnt/ *adj.* showing an aggressive lack of respect in speech or behavior [14thC. From Latin *insolens* "unusual, arrogant," from *solere* "to be accustomed."] —**in·so·lence** *n.* —**in·so·lent·ly** *adv.*

in·sol·u·bi·lize /in sóllyəbə lìz/ (**-lized, -liz·ing, -liz·es**) *vt.* to make something incapable of being dissolved in a liquid —**in·sol·u·bi·li·za·tion** /in sòllyəbəli záysh'n/ *n.*

in·sol·u·ble /in sóllyəb'l/ *adj.* **1. NOT DISSOLVABLE** incapable of being dissolved in a liquid **2. IMPOSSIBLE TO SOLVE** not able to be solved —**in·sol·u·bil·i·ty** /in sòllyə bíllətee/ *n.* —**in·sol·u·ble·ness** /in sóllyəb'lnəss/ *n.* —**in·sol·u·bly** *adv.*

in·solv·a·ble /in sólvə blee/ *adj.* = **insoluble** *adj.* 2 —**in·solv·a·bil·i·ty** /in sòlvə bílətee/ *n.* —**in·solv·a·bly** /in sólvəblee/ *adv.*

in·sol·ven·cy /in sólvənssee/ (*plural* **-cies**) *n.* the condition of being unable to pay debts, or an instance of this

in·sol·vent /in sólvənt/ *adj.* **1.** FIN **BANKRUPT** unable to pay debts **2.** LAW **OF BANKRUPTCY** relating to people or businesses that are bankrupt ■ *n.* FIN **BANKRUPT PERSON** somebody who is unable to pay his or her debts

in·som·ni·a /in sómnee ə/ *n.* inability to fall asleep or to remain asleep long enough to feel rested, especially as a problem continuing over time [Early 17thC. Coined from Latin *insomnis* "sleepless," from *somnus* "sleep."] —**in·som·ni·ac** *adj., n.*

in·so·much as /insō mùch áz/ *conj.* used to introduce an explanation or reason

in·so·much that *conj.* used to indicate the extent to which something is true or is the case

in·sou·ci·ance /in sóossee ənss/ *n.* cheerful lack of anxiety or concern [Early 19thC. Via French from *soucier,* "to care," formed from Latin *solicitare* "to trouble" (source of English *solicit*).]

in·sou·ci·ant /in sóossee ənt/ *adj.* cheerfully unconcerned or unworried about something [Early 19thC. From French, from *souciant,* present participle of *soucier* "to care," from Latin *sollicitare* "to disturb."]

in·soul *vt.* = **ensoul**

insp. *abbr.* **1.** inspected **2. insp., Insp.** inspector

in·spect /in spékt/ (**-spect·ed, -spect·ing, -spects**) *vt.* **1. LOOK AT SOMETHING CRITICALLY** to examine something carefully in order to judge its quality or correctness ○ *She took the cheese out of the refrigerator and inspected it for mold.* **2. SURVEY SOMETHING** to examine or review something officially ○ *The barracks is inspected every day.* [Early 17thC. From Latin *inspicere,* from *specere* "to look at."] —**in·spect·a·ble** *adj.* —**in·spec·tive** *adj.*

in·spec·tion /in spéksh'n/ *n.* **1. CRITICAL EXAMINATION** a critical examination of somebody or something aimed at forming a judgment or evaluation **2. OFFICIAL EXAMINATION** an official and authoritative examination of something ○ *a motor vehicle inspection* [14thC. Via French from, ultimately, Latin *inspect-* (see INSPECT).]

in·spec·tion arms *n.* a position in which a rifle is held diagonally in front of the body with the muzzle pointing upward to the left and the rifle chamber open for inspection

in·spec·tor /in spéktər/ *n.* **1. OFFICIAL EXAMINER** an official who examines something in order to judge its quality or compliance with rules or the law **2. POLICE OFFICER OF MIDDLE RANK** a police officer of the rank above a sergeant and below a superintendent — **in·spec·to·ral** *adj.* —**in·spec·to·ri·al** /in spek táwree əl/ *adj.* —**in·spec·tor·ship** /in spéktər shìp/ *n.*

in·spec·tor·ate /in spéktərət/ *n.* **1. GROUP OF INSPECTORS** a group or department of inspectors **2. INSPECTOR'S DISTRICT** an area supervised by an inspector **3. INSPECTOR'S DUTIES** the office or duties of an inspector

in·spec·tor gen·er·al (*plural* **in·spec·tors gen·er·al**) *n.* **1. HEAD OF INSPECTORS** an official who is the head of an inspectorate **2.** MIL **MILITARY INSPECTOR** a military officer who investigates and reports on organizational matters

in·sphere *vt.* = **ensphere**

in·spi·ra·tion /inspə ráysh'n/ *n.* **1. STIMULUS TO DO CREATIVE WORK** something that stimulates the human mind to creative thought or to the making of art ○ *found inspiration in the landscape around her* **2. THING THAT INSPIRES** somebody or something that inspires somebody ○ *his book is an inspiration to all would-be travellers* **3. CREATIVENESS** the quality of being stimulated to creative thought or activity, or the manifestation of this ○ *a moment of inspiration* **4. GOOD IDEA** a sudden brilliant idea **5.** RELIG **DIVINE INFLUENCE** divine guidance and influence on human beings **6.** PHYSIOL **BREATHING IN** the drawing of air into the lungs [14thC. Via Old French from Latin *inspiratio.*]

in·spi·ra·tion·al /inspə ráyshən'l, -shnəl/ *adj.* **1. BRINGING INSPIRATION** bringing or showing creative stimulus **2. STIMULATING PEOPLE TO ACHIEVE** stimulating people into greater efforts or more enthusiastic or more creative behavior ○ *an inspirational leader* — **in·spi·ra·tion·al·ly** *adv.*

in·spi·ra·tor /inspi ráytər/ *n.* a device for drawing in a gas or vapor [Late 19thC. Formed from INSPIRE.]

in·spir·a·to·ry /in spī́rə tàwree/ *adj.* relating to the process of breathing in, or used in breathing in [Late 18thC. Formed from INSPIRE.]

in·spire /in spī́r/ (**-spired, -spir·ing, -spires**) *v.* **1.** *vti.* **STIMULATE SOMEBODY TO DO SOMETHING** to encourage people into greater efforts or greater enthusiasm or creativity **2.** *vt.* **PROVOKE A FEELING** to arouse a particular feeling in somebody **3.** *vt.* **CAUSE CREATIVE ACTIVITY** to stimulate somebody to do something, especially creative work or the making of art **4.** *vti.* PHYSIOL **BREATHE IN** to inhale air or a gas into the lungs [14thC. Via Old French *enspirer* from Latin *inspirare,* from *spirare* "to breathe" (source of English *spirit*).] —**in·spir·a·ble** *adj.* — **in·spi·ra·tive** *adj.* —**in·spir·er** *n.*

in·spired /in spī́rd/ *adj.* **1. EXTRAORDINARILY GOOD** brilliant and creative ○ *an inspired rendition of a classic song* ○ *she was an inspired teacher* **2. MOTIVATED BY SOMETHING** based on a particular motive or example (*usually used in combination*) ○ *a Jesuit-inspired curriculum*

in·spir·ing /in spī́ring/ *adj.* making somebody feel more enthusiastic, confident, or stimulated — **in·spir·ing·ly** *adv.*

in·spir·it /in spírrit/ (**-it·ed, -it·ing, -its**) *vt.* to give energy or courage to somebody (*archaic or literary*) — **in·spir·it·er** *n.* —**in·spir·it·ing·ly** *adv.*

in·spis·sate /in spí sàyt, ínspi sàyt/ (**-sat·ed, -sat·ing, -sates**) *vti.* to become thicker in consistency or to cause something to thicken, especially by boiling or evaporation [Early 17thC. From Latin *inspissare* "to thicken," from *spissus* "thick."] —**in·spis·sa·tion** /ìnspi sáysh'n/ *n.* —**in·spis·sa·tor** /in spí sàytər, ínspi sàytər/ *n.*

INST *abbr.* in the name of the Holy Trinity [Latin, *in nomine Sanctae Trinitaris*]

inst. *abbr.* **1.** COMM instant **2.** instantaneous **3. inst., Inst.** institute **4. inst., Inst.** institution **5.** institutional

in·sta·bil·i·ty /ìnstə bíllətee/ *n.* **1. BEING UNSTABLE** the quality of being unstable, erratic, or unpredictable **2. NOT STEADY** lack of steadiness or firmness

in·stall /in stáwl/ (**-stalled, -stall·ing, -stalls**), **in·stal** (**-stalled, -stall·ing, -stals**) *v.* **1.** *vt.* **FIT OR CONNECT SOMETHING** to put machinery or equipment into place and make it ready for use **2.** *vt.* COMPUT **LOAD SOFTWARE** to load software onto a computer **3.** *vt.* **PLACE SOMEBODY IN OFFICE** to appoint somebody to a particular position or to induct somebody formally into office **4.** *vr.* **SETTLE IN** to settle yourself comfortably somewhere [15thC. Directly or via Old French *installer* from medieval Latin *installare* "to place in office," from *stallum* "stall."] — **in·stall·er** *n.*

in·stal·la·tion /ìnstə láysh'n/ *n.* **1. ACT OF INSTALLING EQUIPMENT** the process of putting a piece of equipment or machinery in place and setting it up ready for use **2. PLACE WITH EQUIPMENT** a place housing equipment or machinery for a particular use ○ *a communications installation* **3. SOMETHING THAT HAS BEEN INSTALLED** a piece or system of equipment that has been put in place and made ready for use **4.** MIL **MILITARY BASE** a military base or camp ○ *The artillery installation on the island is marked in red on the map.* **5. APPOINTING OF SOMEBODY TO POSITION** the act of appointing somebody to a particular position or of inducting somebody formally into office **6.** ARTS **ART EXHIBIT** an artwork assembled by the artist involving the arrangement of three-dimensional objects or the use of paint and other media directly on walls or floors ○ *an installation using video monitors and empty bottles*

in·stall·ment /in stáwlmənt/, **in·stal·ment** *n.* **1. PARTIAL REPAYMENT** one of a series of sums of money paid at regular intervals to settle a debt **2. PART IN A SERIES** one of the parts of something that appears or is presented at intervals ○ *published in installments* ○ *"The working documents now circulating are but the latest installment of a debate that first surfaced in the 1970s."* (Art Weissman, *Pulse of the People;* 1997) [Mid-18thC. Via Anglo-Norman *estallment* from Old French *estaler* "to fix, place."]

in·stall·ment plan *n.* a system for buying merchandise involving a series of payments at regular intervals instead of a single lump sum

in·stance /ínstəns/ *n.* **1. ILLUSTRATION** an example of a particular situation or event ○ *cited several instances of his being untruthful* **2. EVENT** an occurrence of something ○ *we can overlook it in this instance* **3. REQUEST** a request or demand (*archaic*) **4.** LAW **LEGAL ACTION** a legal proceeding or lawsuit ■ *vt.* (**-stanced, -stanc·ing, -stanc·es**) **1. GIVE AS AN EXAMPLE** to offer something as an example **2. SERVE AS AN EXAMPLE** to serve as an example of something [14thC. Via French *instance* and medieval Latin *instantia* from, ultimately, Latin *instans* "present" (see INSTANT).] ◇ **for instance** as an example ◇ **in the first instance** used to indicate something that is or happens first, before other events or stages (*formal*)

in·stan·cy /ínstənsee/ *n.* **1. URGENCY** the need for something to be done without delay, or insistence that it be done **2. LACK OF DELAY** immediateness or lack of delay

in·stant /ínstənt/ *adj.* **1. IMMEDIATE** happening immediately, without delay ○ *She took an instant dislike to him* . **2.** FOOD **QUICK TO PREPARE** quickly and easily prepared, often premixed, precooked, or powdered ○ *instant coffee* **3. SUDDEN** achieving a particular status very suddenly and effortlessly ○ *the play was an instant success* **4. URGENT AND PRESSING** requiring immediate attention or an immediate response ○ *an instant need for help* **5.** COMM **FROM THIS MONTH** happening in the current month (*dated*) ○ *your letter of the 13th instant* **6. CURRENT** present or current (*archaic*) ■ *n.* **1. SHORT TIME** an extremely brief period of time ○ *for an instant* **2. MOMENT IN TIME** a particular moment in time ○ *The instant I saw his face I knew that something was wrong.* **3.** FOOD **INSTANT PRODUCT** a quickly prepared item of food or drink [15thC. Via Old French from Latin *instare* "to be present," from *stare* "to stand."]

in·stan·ta·ne·ous /ìnstən táynee əss/ *adj.* **1. HAPPENING IMMEDIATELY** occurring immediately or almost immediately **2.** MATH **OF VALUE AT GIVEN INSTANT** indicating the value of something at a given moment in time, expressed as the average value of a varying quantity over an infinitesimally small time interval ○ *instantaneous velocity* [Mid-17thC. Via medieval Latin *instantaneus* from Latin *instans* "present" (see INSTANT).] — **in·stan·ta·ne·i·ty** /in stàntə née itee, ìnstəntə née itee/ *n.* —**in·stan·ta·ne·ous·ly** /ìnstən táynee əsslee/ *adv.* — **in·stan·ta·ne·ous·ness** *n.*

in·stan·ti·ate /in stánshee àyt/ (**-at·ed, -at·ing, -ates**) *vt.* to provide an example to support or explain something [Mid-20thC. Formed from INSTANCE.]

in·stant·ly /ínstəntlee/ *adv.* **1. IMMEDIATELY** immediately and without delay **2. URGENTLY** urgently or insistently (*archaic*) ■ *conj.* **AS SOON AS** happening or done immediately after something else ○ *I phoned instantly I heard you were back.*

in·stant-on *adj.* including a device that allows for a rapid startup, eliminating the need for a warmup period

in·stant re·play *n.* the playing back of a videotape in slow motion, usually to show the movement of a ball or player in a sport shown on television

in·star /ín staar/ *n.* in the life cycle of an arthropod such as an insect, a stage between two successive molts [Late 19thC. From Latin "form, image."]

in·state /in stáyt/ (**-stat·ed, -stat·ing, -states**) *vt.* to establish somebody in office —**in·state·ment** *n.*

in sta·tu quo /in stà too kwṓ, -stày-/ *adv.* in the same state [From Latin *in statu quo ante,* literally "in the (same) state as before"]

in·stau·ra·tion /in staw ráysh'n/ *n.* (*formal*) **1. RENOVATION** the restoration of something that has lapsed or fallen into decay **2. FOUNDING** the founding or establishment of something [Early 17thC. From Latin *instaurare* "to renew" (source of English *store*).]

in·stead /in stéd/ *adv.* as a replacement or substitute for something [13thC. Formed from IN + *stede* "place."] ◇ **instead of** as an alternative to, or substitute for, something

in·step /ín stèp/ *n.* **1.** ANAT **UPPER MIDDLE AREA OF THE FOOT** the arched middle portion of the human foot between the ankle and toes, especially its upper surface **2.** CLOTHES **MIDDLE PART OF A SHOE** the part of a shoe that covers the middle portion of the foot [15thC. Origin unknown.]

in·sti·gate /ínsti gàyt/ (**-gat·ed, -gat·ing, -gates**) *vt.* **1. GET SOMETHING STARTED** to cause a process to start **2. START TROUBLE** to cause trouble, especially by urging somebody to do something destructive or wrong [Mid-16thC. From Latin *instigare.*] —**in·sti·ga·tion** *n.* —**in·sti·ga·tive** *adj.* —**in·sti·ga·tor** *n.*

in·still /in stíl/ (**-stilled, -still·ing, -stills**), **in·stil** (**-stilled, -still·ing, -stils**) *vt.* **1. IMPART SOMETHING GRADUALLY** to impress ideas, principles, or teachings gradually on somebody's mind ○ *I tried to instill self-respect in my students.* **2. DRIP LIQUID INTO SOMETHING** to pour medicine or another liquid into something drop by drop [15thC. From Latin *instillare,* from *stilla* "drop."] — **in·stil·la·tion** /ìnsti láysh'n/ *n.* —**in·still·er** /in stíllər/ *n.* —**in·still·ment** /-mənt/ *n.*

in·stinct /ín stingkt/ *n.* **1. BIOLOGICAL DRIVE** an inborn pattern of behavior characteristic of a species and shaped by biological necessities such as survival and reproduction **2. STRONG NATURAL IMPULSE** a powerful impulse that feels natural rather than reasoned ○ *followed his instincts and took to his heels* **3. KNACK** a natural gift or skill ○ *an instinct for putting people at ease* ■ *adj.* **FILLED** completely filled or imbued with something (*formal*) ○ *a look instinct with com-*

passion [15thC. Via Latin *instinctus* "impulse" from *instinguere* "to incite," from *stinguere* "to sting, goad" (source of English *distinct* and *extinct*).]

in·stinc·tive /in stíngtiv/ *adj.* **1. INVOLUNTARY** relating to, prompted by, or based on a strong natural impulse ○ *an instinctive fear of water* **2. NATURAL** having a particular quality or skill spontaneously and without effort or instruction ○ *an artist with an instinctive feel for color* ○ *an instinctive cook* —**in·stinc·tive·ly** *adv.*

in·stinc·tu·al /in stíngkchoo əl/ *adj.* relating to or prompted by a basic biological need [Early 20thC. Formed from INSTINCT + *-ual*, adjective suffix.] —**in·stinc·tu·al·ly** *adv.*

in·sti·tute /ínsti toot/ *vt.* (**-tut·ed, -tut·ing, -tutes**) **1. START SOMETHING** to start or initiate something in an official or formal way ○ *institute legal proceedings* **2. SET SOMETHING UP** to set up or establish something **3. APPOINT SOMEBODY** to appoint somebody to an office, especially a religious one ■ *n.* **1. ORGANIZATION WITH A SPECIALIZED GOAL** an organization for promoting something, such as art, science, or the well-being of a group **2. PLACE FOR ADVANCED STUDY** an educational institution, especially one concerned with technical subjects **3. RULE** an established principle or rule **4. SEMINAR** a short intensive teaching or study program ■ **in·sti·tutes** *npl.* LAW **LAW SUMMARY** a summary of laws [14thC. From Latin *instituere* "to establish," from *statuere* "to set up," from *stare* "to stand" (source of English *constant* and *stage*).] —**in·sti·tut·er** *n.*

in·sti·tu·tion /ínsti tóosh'n/ *n.* **1. IMPORTANT ORGANIZATION** a large organization such as a college, hospital, or bank that is influential in the community **2. ESTABLISHED PRACTICE** an established law, custom, or practice ○ *the institution of marriage* **3. STARTING OF SOMETHING** the act of initiating or establishing something **4. LONG-ESTABLISHED PERSON OR THING** somebody or something that has been well-known and established in a place for many years (*informal*) **5. PLACE OF CARE OR CONFINEMENT** a place where people who are, e.g., mentally or physically challenged are cared for **6.** FIN **LARGE AND POWERFUL INVESTOR** a large financial organization, e.g., a pension fund, that has considerable resources to make investments ○ *a mutual fund available only to institutions* —**in·sti·tu·tion·al** *adj.* —**in·sti·tu·tion·ally** *adv.* —**in·sti·tu·tion·ar·y** *adj.*

in·sti·tu·tion·al·ism /ínsti tóoshən'l ìzzəm, ìnstə tóoshnə lìzzəm/ *n.* a belief in the merits of established customs and systems —**in·sti·tu·tion·al·ist** *n.*

in·sti·tu·tion·al·ize /ínstə tóoshən'l ìz, ìnstə tóoshnə lìz/ (**-ized, -iz·ing, -iz·es**) *vt.* **1. PUT SOMEBODY INTO AN INSTITUTION** to put somebody into an institution such as an alcohol or drug-treatment facility, a psychiatric hospital, or a prison **2. ESTABLISH SOMETHING AS NORMAL** to make something an established custom or an accepted part of the structure of a large organization or society **3. MAKE INTO OR LIKE INSTITUTION** to convert something into an institution or make something resemble an institution —**in·sti·tu·tion·al·i·za·tion** /ínstə tóoshən'li záysh'n, ìnstə tóoshnəli-/ *n.*

in·sti·tu·tion·al·ized /ínstə tóoshən'l ìzd, ìnstə tóoshnə lìzd/ *adj.* **1. ESTABLISHED AS NORMAL** having become an established custom or an accepted part of the structure of a large organization or society because it has existed for so long **2. DEPENDENT ON THE ROUTINE OF INSTITUTION** lacking the will or ability to think and act independently because of having spent a long time in an institution such as a psychiatric hospital or prison

in·sti·tu·tive /ínsti tootiv/ *adj.* serving to establish or being established —**in·sti·tu·tive·ly** *adv.*

in-store *adj.* happening, available, or situated within a large store, e.g., a supermarket or department store ○ *an in-store bakery*

instr. *abbr.* **1.** instruction **2.** instructor **3.** instrument **4.** GRAM, MUSIC instrumental

in·struct /in strúkt/ (**-struct·ed, -struct·ing, -structs**) *v.* **1.** *vti.* **TRAIN SOMEBODY** to teach somebody a subject or how to do something **2.** *vt.* **DIRECT SOMEBODY** to tell somebody to do something, especially with authority or as an order **3.** *vt.* **GIVE SOMEBODY INFORMATION** to inform somebody about something, especially in a formal or official manner ○ *The judge instructed the jurors as to the points of law applicable in the case.* **4.** *vt.* *U.K.* **OBTAIN LEGAL REPRESENTATION** to ask or authorize a lawyer to act on your behalf and supply him or her with relevant information [15thC. From Latin *instruct-*, the past participle stem of *instruere* "to prepare, equip," from *struere* "to build."] —**in·struct·i·ble** *adj.*

WORD KEY: SYNONYMS

See Synonyms at ***teach***.

in·struc·tion /in strúkshən/ *n.* **1. TEACHING OR THINGS TAUGHT** teaching in a particular subject or skill, or the facts or skills taught ○ *driving instruction* **2. TEACHING PROFESSION OR PROCESS** the profession of teaching or the teaching process **3. ORDER** a spoken or written statement of what must be done, especially delivered formally, with official authority, or as an order ○ *acting on instructions we received* **4.** COMPUT **COMMAND** a code that tells a computer to perform a specific operation ■ **in·struc·tions** *npl.* **1. LIST OF THINGS TO DO** printed information about how to do, make, assemble, use, or operate something ○ *The instructions are printed on the back of the box.* **2.** LAW **JUDGE'S SUMMARY** the information given by a judge to a jury at the end of a case that explains the applicable points of law and summarizes what has to be proved —**in·struc·tion·al** *adj.*

in·struc·tive /in strúktiv/ *adj.* providing useful information or insight into something —**in·struc·tive·ly** *adv.* —**in·struc·tive·ness** *n.*

in·struc·tor /in strúktər/ *n.* **1. TEACHER OR TRAINER** somebody who teaches something, often a sport or a practical skill ○ *a ski instructor* **2. LOW-RANKING COLLEGE TEACHER** a university, college, or community college teacher who is lower in rank than an assistant professor —**in·struc·tor·ship** *n.*

in·stru·ment /ínstrəmənt/ *n.* **1.** SCI **TOOL** a tool or mechanical device, especially one used for precision work in science, medicine, or technology **2.** MUSIC **OBJECT THAT PRODUCES MUSIC** an object used to produce musical notes, e.g., by blowing through an opening, plucking or rubbing its strings, or striking it **3.** MEASURE **MEASURING DEVICE** a device that measures or controls something, such as a speedometer or voltometer **4. MEANS OF DOING SOMETHING** something or somebody used as a means of achieving a desired result or accomplishing a particular purpose (*usually used in the singular*) ○ *The secret police was the state's instrument for controlling the populace.* **5. OBJECT USED FOR SOME PURPOSE** an object that has been or could be used for some purpose (*formal*) ○ *hit on the head by a blunt instrument* **6.** LAW **DOCUMENT** a legal document (*formal*) ■ *vt.* (**-ment·ed, -ment·ing, -ments**) **1.** MUSIC **ARRANGE MUSIC** to write or arrange a piece of music for performance on musical instruments **2.** SCI **SUPPLY WITH MEASURING DEVICES** to equip something with instruments for measurement or control [13thC. Via Old French from Latin *instrumentum*, from *instruere* "to prepare."]

in·stru·men·tal /ínstrə mént'l/ *adj.* **1.** MUSIC **FOR INSTRUMENTS, NOT VOICES** played on one or more musical instruments and not sung or accompanied by singing **2. CONNECTED WITH INSTRUMENTS** done with or produced by an instrument or instruments **3. MAKING SOMETHING HAPPEN** playing an important part in achieving a result or accomplishing a purpose ○ *she was instrumental in getting the legislation passed* **4.** GRAM **INDICATING THE MEANS OF DOING SOMETHING** used to describe a noun case used to indicate that something is used for a purpose or is the means by which something is done **5.** PHILOS **OF INSTRUMENTALISM** relating to instrumentalism ■ *n.* **1.** MUSIC **MUSIC PLAYED BY INSTRUMENTS** a piece of music, or part of a piece of music, that is played by one or more musical instruments and is not sung or accompanied by singing **2.** GRAM **NOUN FORM INDICATING THE MEANS OF DOING SOMETHING** the form (**case**) of a noun indicating that something is used for a purpose or is the means of doing something, or a noun in this form —**in·stru·men·tal·ly** *adv.*

in·stru·men·tal·ism /ínstrə mént'l ìzzəm/ *n.* PHILOS the view that theories are useful tools for making predictions but cannot be literally true or false

in·stru·men·tal·ist /ínstrə mént'list/ *n.* **1.** MUSIC **PLAYER OF INSTRUMENT** somebody who plays a musical instrument **2.** PHILOS **PROPONENT OF INSTRUMENTALISM** a supporter or advocate of instrumentalism ■ *adj.* PHILOS **FOR INSTRUMENTALISM** supporting or advocating instrumentalism

in·stru·men·tal·i·ty /ínstrəmən tállətee, -men-/ (*plural* **-ties**) *n.* (*formal*) **1. ACTION OR USE** somebody's action or the use of somebody or something in getting something done ○ *"But for her instrumentality, the fatal knowledge would not have been imparted."* (Elizabeth Gaskell, *Some Passages from the History of the Chomley Family*; 1865) **2.** POL **SECTION** a subbranch of a department or agency ○ *a department, agency, or instrumentality of the executive, legislative, and judicial branches of the Federal Government* [Mid-17thC]

in·stru·men·tal learn·ing *n.* PSYCHOL a form of learning that takes place as a direct consequence of a reward or pleasant outcome for the learner

in·stru·men·ta·tion /ínstrəmən táysh'n, -men-/ *n.* **1.** MUSIC **ARRANGEMENT FOR MUSICAL INSTRUMENTS** the composition or arrangement of music for performance, in which a combination of musical instruments is specified **2.** MUSIC **MUSICAL INSTRUMENTS USED** the particular instruments that are to perform a piece of music **3. EQUIPMENT FOR CONTROL OR OPERATION** a set of instruments used for a particular purpose, e.g., operating a machine or controlling an aircraft **4. USE OF INSTRUMENTS** the use of instruments as tools or for measurement or control **5. MAKING INSTRUMENTS** the design, development, or manufacture of instruments for use in science, medicine, technology, or industry **6. MEANS** the means or agency through which something is done (*formal*)

in·stru·ment board *n.* = **instrument panel**

in·stru·ment fly·ing *n.* the flying of an aircraft using only information obtained from instruments rather than from what the pilot can see

in·stru·ment land·ing *n.* landing an aircraft while relying on information from instruments rather than from looking out the aircraft's window

in·stru·ment pan·el *n.* a set of instruments mounted at the front of a machine or in front of somebody driving or steering a motor vehicle, aircraft, or ship

in·sub·or·di·nate /ínsə báwrd'nət/ *adj.* **DISOBEDIENT OR REBELLIOUS** refusing to obey orders or submit to authority ■ *n.* **DISOBEDIENT OR REBELLIOUS PERSON** somebody who refuses to obey orders or submit to authority —**in·sub·or·di·nate·ly** *adv.* —**in·sub·or·di·na·tion** /ínsə bawrd'n áysh'n/ *n.*

in·sub·stan·tial /ínsəb stánshəl/ *adj.* **1. SMALL AND WEAK** not very large, solid, or strong **2. NOT TANGIBLE** not existing in reality ○ *an insubstantial apparition* —**in·sub·stan·ti·al·i·ty** /ínsəb stanshee állətee/ *n.* —**in·sub·stan·tial·ly** /-stánshəlee/ *adv.*

in·suf·fer·a·ble /in súffərəb'l/ *adj.* so annoying, unpleasant, or uncomfortable that it is unbearable —**in·suf·fer·a·bly** *adv.* —**in·suf·fer·a·ble·ness** *n.*

in·suf·fi·cien·cy /ínsə físh'nsee/ (*plural* **-cies**) *n.* **1. NOT ENOUGH** a smaller number or lesser amount than is needed ○ *an insufficiency of provisions for a long cruise* **2.** MED **UNFITNESS OR FAILURE** inability or failure to perform competently, adequately, or normally ○ *cardiac insufficiency* **3. FAILURE TO MEASURE UP** a failure to meet some standard or requirement ○ *the insufficiency of the causes presented to explain this phenomenon*

in·suf·fi·cient /ínsə físh'nt/ *adj.* not enough in amount or quality to satisfy some purpose or standard ○ *we were given insufficient notice* —**in·suf·fi·cient·ly** *adv.*

in·suf·flate /ínsə flàyt, in sú flàyt/ (**-flat·ed, -flat·ing, -flates**) *vt.* **1. BLOW INTO SOMETHING** to blow or breathe into something (*formal*) **2.** MED **BLOW SOMETHING INTO A BODY CAVITY** to blow something, e.g., air, powder, or gas, into the lungs or some other body cavity in the course of medical treatment [Late 17thC. Latin *insufflat-*, from *insufflare*, from *sufflare* "to blow up" (source of English *soufflé*).] —**in·suf·fla·tion** /ínsə fláysh'n/ *n.* —**in·suf·fla·tor** /ínsə fláytər/ *n.*

in·su·lant /ínsələnt/ *n.* material that insulates something

in·su·lar /ínsələr, ínsyələr/ *adj.* **1. LIMITED IN OUTLOOK** concerned only with your own country, society, or way of life and not interested in new ideas or different cultures **2. NOT CLOSE TO OTHERS** physically or emotionally removed from others **3. OF ISLANDS** relating to or originating in an island **4.** ANAT **OF ISLANDS OF CELLS** relating to a collection of cells or tissue reminiscent of an island [Mid-16thC. Via French *insulaire* from late Latin *insularis*, from Latin *insula* "island."] —**in·su·lar·ism** *n.* —**in·su·lar·i·ty** /ínsə lérrətee, ìnsyə-/ *n.* —**in·su·lar·ly** /ínsələrlee, ínsyə-/ *adv.*

in·su·late /ínsə làyt, ínsyə-/ (**-lat·ed, -lat·ing, -lates**) *vt.* **1. PREVENT THE PASSAGE OF SOMETHING** to prevent or reduce the passage of heat, electricity, or sound into, from, or through something, especially by surrounding it with some material **2.** **PROTECT OR ISOLATE SOMEBODY** to protect or isolate somebody from something, especially from something unpleasant or undesirable [Mid-16thC. Formed from Latin *insula* "island."]

in·su·lat·ing tape *n. U.K.* = **friction tape**

in·su·la·tion /insə láysh'n, ìnsyə-/ *n.* **1.** **MATERIAL THAT INSULATES** something that prevents or reduces the passage of heat, electricity, or sound, e.g., a special material or a layer of air. Cork, glass fiber, rubber, and plastic are all used as insulation. **2.** **PREVENTION OF CONDUCTION** the act of covering or surrounding something to prevent or reduce the passage of heat, electricity, or sound **3.** **PROTECTION** protection or isolation from something

in·su·la·tive /ínsə làytiv, ínsyə-/ *adj.* preventing or reducing the passage of heat, electricity, or sound

in·su·la·tor /ínsə làytər, ínsyə-/ *n.* a material or device that prevents or reduces the passage of heat, electricity, or sound

in·su·lin /ínsəlin/ *n.* a hormone secreted by the islets of Langerhans in the pancreas that regulates the level of glucose in the blood. Deficiency in production results in diabetes mellitus. [Early 20thC. Coined from Latin *insula* "island" (source of English *isle* and *isolate*), after the "islets of Langerhans."]

in·su·lin shock, **in·su·lin re·ac·tion** *n.* a severe drop in blood sugar resulting from an excess of insulin and marked by sweating, dizziness, trembling, and eventual coma

in·sult *v.* /in súlt/ (**-sult·ed, -sult·ing, -sults**) **1.** *vti.* **BE OFFENSIVE** to say or do something rude or insensitive that offends somebody else **2.** *vt.* **SHOW CONTEMPT** to say or do something suggesting a low opinion of somebody or something ○ *Don't insult me by offering me pity.* ■ *n.* /ín sùlt/ **1.** **OFFENSIVE WORDS OR ACTION** a remark or action that offends somebody, usually because it is rude or insensitive **2.** **SOMETHING SHOWING CONTEMPT** behavior or words implying a low opinion of somebody, e.g., a payment that is much less than expected or deserved ○ *The article is an insult to the intelligence of the reader.* **3.** MED **INJURY OR AN INJURING AGENT** an injury or trauma to the body or something that causes such harm [Mid-16thC. Via French *insulter* from Latin *insultare*, literally "to keep jumping on," which was formed from, ultimately, *salire* "to jump."] —**in·sult·er** *n.*

in·sult·ing /in súlting/ *adj.* causing offense because it is rude or insensitive or suggests a low opinion of somebody or something —**in·sult·ing·ly** *adv.*

in·su·per·a·ble /in sóopərəb'l/ *adj.* impossible to overcome, get rid of, or deal with successfully ○ *battling insuperable odds* [14thC. Via Old French from, ultimately, Latin *superare* "to overcome," from *super* "above" (source of English *superior, sovereign, soprano,* and *sirloin*).] —**in·su·per·a·bil·i·ty** /in sòopərə bíllətee/ *n.* —**in·su·per·a·ble·ness** /in sóopərəb'lnəss/ *n.* —**in·su·per·a·bly** /-sóopərəblee/ *adv.*

in·sup·port·a·ble /insə páwrtəb'l/ *adj.* **1.** **IMPOSSIBLE TO ENDURE** too great, unpleasant, or difficult to bear ○ *an insupportable claim* **2.** **UNJUSTIFIABLE** impossible to justify or defend —**in·sup·port·a·ble·ness** *n.* —**in·sup·port·a·bly** *adv.*

in·sur·a·ble /in shóorəb'l/ *adj.* INSUR able to be covered or protected by insurance —**in·sur·a·bil·i·ty** /in shòorə bíllətee/ *n.*

in·sur·ance /in shóorəns/ *n.* **1.** INSUR **FINANCIAL PROTECTION AGAINST LOSS OR HARM** an arrangement by which a company gives customers financial protection against loss or harm, e.g., theft or illness, in return for payment (**premium**) **2.** **A MONEY PAID BY AN INSURANCE COMPANY** the sum of money that an insurance company pays or agrees to pay if a specified undesirable event occurs **3.** INSUR **PREMIUM** the payment made to obtain insurance ○ *My car insurance has gone up again.* **4.** INSUR **INSURANCE BUSINESS** the commercial business of providing insurance **5.** **MEANS OF PROTECTION** an act, measure, or provision that gives protection against some undesirable event or risk ○ *provided as map as insurance against getting lost* ■ *adj.* SPORTS **PREVENTING AN OPPONENT FROM TYING A GAME** relating to an act of scoring that increases a team's lead to the extent that the other side cannot tie the game in a single play [15thC. Via Old French *enseurance*.]

in·sur·ance pol·i·cy (*plural* **in·sur·ance pol·i·cies**) *n.* a written contract between an insurance company and a person or organization requiring insurance against loss or harm. The insurance policy sets out the terms and conditions of the agreement, specifying the risks for which compensation or costs will be paid.

in·sure /in shóor/ (**-sured, -sur·ing, -sures**) *v.* **1.** *vti.* **COVER SOMETHING WITH INSURANCE** to agree formally that, for a sum of money paid to a company, the company will pay compensation or costs if some specified harm or loss occurs to somebody or something ○ *the ring was insured for $5,000* **2.** *vi.* **PROTECT AGAINST RISK** to get protection from something undesirable that might happen, usually by making contingency plans or taking precautionary or preventive measures **3.** *vt.* = **ensure** [15thC. Variant of ENSURE.]

WORD KEY: USAGE

See Usage note at *assure.*

in·sured /in shóord/ *adj.* **COVERED BY INSURANCE** covered by insurance ■ *n.* **OBJECT OF INSURANCE** somebody or something covered by insurance ○ *the signature of the insured*

in·sur·er /in shóorər/ *n.* a company or individual providing insurance

in·sur·gen·cy /in súrjənsee/ (*plural* **-cies**), **in·sur·gence** /-jənss/ *n.* **1.** **REBELLION** a rebellion or uprising against a government **2.** **STATE OF REBELLION** the state of being in rebellion

in·sur·gent /in súrjənt/ *n.* **1.** **REBEL** somebody who rebels against authority or leadership, especially somebody belonging to a group involved in an uprising against the government or ruler of a country **2.** **POLITICAL REBEL** a member of a political party who rebels against the party leaders or policies ■ *adj.* **REBELLIOUS** rebelling against authority or leadership, especially against the government or ruler of a country [Mid-18thC. From Latin *insurgent-*, formed from *insurgere* "to rise up," from *surgere* "to rise."] —**in·sur·gent·ly** *adv.*

in·sur·mount·a·ble /insər mówntəb'l/ *adj.* impossible to overcome or deal with successfully —**in·sur·mount·a·bil·i·ty** /insər mowntə bíllətee/ *n.* —**in·sur·mount·a·bly** /-mówntəblee/ *adv.*

in·sur·rec·tion /insə rékshən/ *n.* rebellion against the government or rulers of a country, often involving armed conflict [15thC. From the Latin stem *insurrection-*, from *insurgere* "to rise up."] —**in·sur·rec·tion·al** *adj.* —**in·sur·rec·tion·ar·y** *n., adj.* —**in·sur·rec·tion·ism** *n.* —**in·sur·rec·tion·ist** *n., adj.*

in·sus·cep·ti·ble /insə séptəb'l/ *adj.* (*formal*) **1.** **NOT AFFECTED** not likely to be affected or influenced by something **2.** **NOT SUBJECT TO SOMETHING** not able to undergo some process —**in·sus·cep·ti·bil·i·ty** /insə septə bíllətee/ *n.* —**in·sus·cep·ti·bly** /-séptəblee/ *adv.*

in·swing·er /ín swìngər/ *n.* SOCCER a ball kicked, particularly from a corner, that curves through the air toward the goal

int. *abbr.* **1.** intelligence **2.** intercept **3.** interest **4.** interim **5.** interior **6.** GRAM interjection **7.** intermediate **8.** internal **9.** **int., Int.** international **10.** interpreter **11.** intersection **12.** interval **13.** interview **14.** GRAM intransitive **15.** MUSIC introit

in·tact /in tákt/ *adj.* **1.** **NOT DAMAGED** whole and undamaged ○ *Only two of the original plates remained intact.* **2.** **COMPLETE** without any missing parts or elements **3.** ANAT **WITHOUT ANY REMOVED PARTS** having all bodily parts in place and undamaged [15thC. From Latin *intactus* "untouched," which was formed ultimately from *tangere* "to touch" (see TANGIBLE).] —**in·tact·ly** *adv.* —**in·tact·ness** *n.*

in·ta·glio /in tállyō, in taályō/ (*plural* **-glios** *or* **-gli** /-tállyee/) *n.* **1.** **HOLLOWED-OUT DESIGN** a carving made by cutting a hollowed-out design into some material such as stone **2.** **CARVING OF INTAGLIOS** the process or art of carving hollowed-out designs in material such as stone **3.** **CARVED GEM** a gem in which a hollowed-out design has been carved **4.** PRINTING **PRINTING WITH INCISED PLATES** a printing technique in which the design is cut into the plate rather than protruding from it. Intaglio printing includes engraving, etching, and drypoint. **5.** PRINTING **INCISED PRINTING PLATE** a printing plate into which the design is cut or incised [Mid-17thC. Via Italian from, ultimately, *intagliare* "to engrave," from *tagliare* "to cut."]

Barnaby's

Intaglio: Ancient Egyptian granite carving

in·take /ín tàyk/ *n.* **1.** **AMOUNT TAKEN IN** an amount taken in or consumed ○ *increase your intake of fluids* **2.** **TAKING IN SOMETHING** the process of taking in some substance, especially by eating or drinking **3.** **OPENING THROUGH WHICH FLUID PASSES** an opening through which fluid enters a duct or contained area, e.g., that of a jet engine ○ *the fuel intake*

in·tan·gi·ble /in tánjəb'l/ *adj.* **1.** **NONMATERIAL** without material qualities, and so not able to be touched or seen **2.** **HARD TO DESCRIBE** difficult to define or describe clearly, but nonetheless perceived ■ *n.* **SOMETHING UNQUANTIFIABLE** an unquantifiable quality or asset ○ *such intangibles as duty* [Early 17thC. Via medieval Latin *intangibilis*, or formed from TANGIBLE.] —**in·tan·gi·bil·i·ty** /in tànjə bíllətee/ *n.* —**in·tan·gi·ble·ness** /in tánjəb'lnəss/ *n.* —**in·tan·gi·bly** /-tánjəblee/ *adv.*

in·tan·gi·ble as·set *n.* a business asset, e.g., a company's customer goodwill, that is of value although it is not directly quantifiable in terms of goods produced or sold

Massimo Listri/Corbis

Intarsia: Panel (1506) in the Palazzo Ducale, Mantua, Italy

in·tar·si·a /in taársee ə/ (*plural* **-as**) *n.* **1.** CRAFT **WOOD INLAY** wood inlay using different colors of wood, common in the Italian Renaissance **2.** CRAFT **MAKING OF INTARSIAS** the art or process of making intarsias, e.g., for wall panels **3.** KNITTING **WAY OF KNITTING** knitting with two or more colored yarns in which the new color is introduced by twisting around the old, left hanging until it is needed again [Mid-19thC. Via German and Italian from, ultimately, Arabic *tarṣī'*.]

in·te·ger /íntəjər/ *n.* **1.** **WHOLE NUMBER** any positive or negative whole number or zero **2.** **WHOLE THING** a whole unit or entity (*technical*) [Early 16thC. From Latin "complete, whole" (source of English *entire*). Ultimately from an Indo-European base meaning "to touch."]

in·te·gral /íntəgrəl, in téggrəl/ *adj.* **1.** **NECESSARY OR CONSTITUENT** being an essential part of something or any of the parts that make up a whole ○ *Adequate funding is integral to the success of the venture.* ○ *mealtimes are an integral part of family life* **2.** **MADE UP OF PARTS** composed of parts that together make a whole **3.** **COMPLETE** without missing parts or elements **4.** ARITH **OF AN INTEGER** relating to an integer **5.** MATH **RELATING TO INTEGRALS** relating to mathematical integrals or integration ■ *n.* MATH **1.** = **definite integral** **2.** = **indefinite integral** [Mid-16thC. Via French from, ultimately, Latin *integer* "whole."] —**in·te·gral·i·ty** /intə grállətee/ *n.* —**in·te·gral·ly** /íntəgrəlee/ *adv.*

in·te·gral cal·cu·lus *n.* a branch of mathematics dealing with integrals and differential equations, used to determine areas, volumes, and lengths, and in many areas of applied mathematics

in·te·grand /íntə grànd/ *n.* a mathematical function or equation to be integrated [Late 19thC. From Latin *integrandus* "to be integrated," from *integrare* "to integrate," from *integer* "whole."]

in·te·grant /íntəgrənt/ *adj.* **PART OF WHOLE** part of a whole (*formal*) ■ *n.* INTEGRAL PART an integral part of something (*formal*)

in·te·grate (-grat·ed, -grat·ing, -grates) *v.* /íntə gràyt/ **1.** *vti.* FIT IN WITH A GROUP to become an accepted member of a group and its activities, or to help somebody do this **2.** *vti.* MAKE INTO A WHOLE to join two or more objects or make something part of a larger whole, or to become joined or combined in this way **3.** *vt.* MAKE OPEN TO ALL to make a group, community, place, or organization and its opportunities available to all, regardless of race, ethnic group, religion, gender, or social class **4.** *vt.* MATH FIND A MATHEMATICAL INTEGRAL to find the definite or indefinite integral of a function or equation [Mid-17thC. From Latin *integrat-*, from *integrare* "to make whole," from *integer* "whole."] —**in·te·gra·ble** /íntəgrəb'l/ *adj.* —**in·te·gra·bil·i·ty** /ìntəgrə bíllətee/ *n.* —**in·te·gra·tive** /íntə gràytiv/ *adj.*

in·te·grat·ed /íntə gràytəd/ *adj.* **1.** COMBINED OR COMPOSITE made up of elements or parts that work well together ○ *an integrated transportation system* **2.** COMBINING DISSIMILAR THINGS bringing together processes or functions that are normally separate **3.** OPEN TO ALL PEOPLE open to everyone, without restrictions based on race, ethnicity, religion, gender, or social class

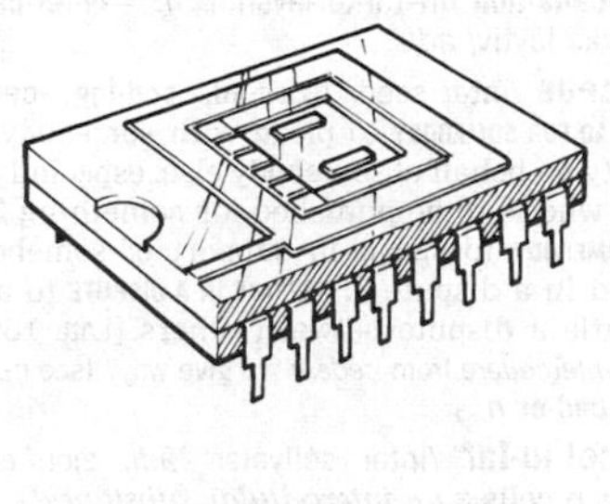

Integrated circuit

in·te·grat·ed cir·cuit *n.* an extremely small complex of electronic components contained on a thin chip or wafer of semiconducting material such as silicon —**in·te·grat·ed cir·cuit·ry** *n.*

in·te·gra·tion /íntə gráysh'n/ *n.* **1.** EQUAL ACCESS FOR ALL the process of opening a group, community, place, or organization to all, regardless of race, ethnicity religion, gender, or social class **2.** ACCEPTANCE INTO A COMMUNITY becoming an accepted member of a group or community **3.** COMBINATION a combination of parts or objects that work together well **4.** MATH MATHEMATICAL OPERATION the mathematical process of finding the solution of a differential equation or a function whose differential equation is known **5.** PSYCHOL ORGANIZATION OF PERSONALITY TRAITS the process of coordinating separate personality elements into a balanced whole or producing behavior compatible with somebody's environment

in·te·gra·tion·ist /íntə gráysh'nist/ *n.* WORKER FOR INTEGRATION a supporter or activist who works to promote and maintain integration ■ *adj.* FAVORING INTEGRATION supporting or promoting racial integration

in·te·gra·tor /íntə gràytər/ *n.* **1.** COMPUT COMPUTER DEVICE a computer component that performs numerical integration to solve differential equations **2.** SOMEBODY OR SOMETHING THAT INTEGRATES somebody or something that brings about integration

in·teg·ri·ty /in téggritee/ *n.* **1.** POSSESSION OF FIRM PRINCIPLES the quality of possessing and steadfastly adhering to high moral principles or professional standards **2.** COMPLETENESS the state of being complete or undivided (*formal*) ○ *the territorial integrity of a nation.* **3.** WHOLENESS the state of being sound or undamaged (*formal*) ○ *Their refusal to participate in the experiment will undermine its integrity.* [15thC. Via Old French from Latin *integritas*, from *integer* "whole."]

in·teg·u·ment /in téggyəmənt/ *n.* an outer protective layer or part of an animal or plant, e.g., a shell, rind, husk, or skin [Early 17thC. Via Latin *integumentum* from *integere* "to cover up," from *tegere* "to cover" (source of English *tile* and *detect*).] —**in·teg·u·men·tal** /in tèggyə mént'l/ *adj.* —**in·teg·u·men·ta·ry** /-méntəree, -méntree/ *adj.*

in·tel·lect /ínt'l èkt/ *n.* **1.** MENTAL ABILITY somebody's ability to think, reason, and understand ○ *appeals to the intellect rather than the emotions* ○ *a highly developed intellect* **2.** INTELLIGENT PERSON a very intelligent and knowledgeable person ○ *The commission called on some of our most notable intellects in its search for solutions.* [14thC. Via Old French from Latin *intellect-*, from *intellegere* "to perceive" (see INTELLIGENT).]

in·tel·lec·tion /ínt'l ékshən/ *n.* (*formal*) **1.** THINKING thinking, reasoning, or other mental activity **2.** RESULT OF THINKING a thought or an idea —**in·tel·lec·tive** /ínt'l éktiv/ *adj.*

in·tel·lec·tu·al /ínt'l ékchoo əl/ *adj.* **1.** RELATING TO THINKING relating to or involving the mental processes of abstract thinking and reasoning rather than the emotions **2.** INTELLIGENT AND KNOWLEDGEABLE having a highly developed ability to think, reason, and understand, especially in combination with wide knowledge **3.** FOR INTELLIGENT PEOPLE intended for, appealing to, or done by intelligent people ○ *intellectual pursuits* ■ *n.* INTELLIGENT PERSON somebody with a highly developed ability to reason and understand, especially if also well educated and interested in the arts or sciences or enjoying activities involving serious mental effort [15thC. Via Old French from late Latin *intellectualis*, from *intellectus* "intellect," from *intellegere* "to perceive" (see INTELLIGENT).] —**in·tel·lec·tu·al·i·ty** /ínt'l ekchoo állətee/ *n.* —**in·tel·lec·tu·al·ly** /-ékchoo əlee/ *adv.*

in·tel·lec·tu·al·ism /ínt'l ékchoo ə lìzzəm/ *n.* **1.** PSYCHOL EXERCISE OF POWER TO THINK the development and use of the ability to think, reason, and understand **2.** TOO MUCH ATTENTION TO THINKING overemphasis on intellectual processes or pursuits **3.** PHILOS BELIEF THAT KNOWLEDGE COMES FROM REASONING the doctrine that all that can truly be called knowledge is derived from reasoning —**in·tel·lec·tu·al·ist** *n.* —**in·tel·lec·tu·al·is·tic** /ínt'l ekchoo ə lístik/ *adj.* —**in·tel·lec·tu·al·is·ti·cal·ly** /-lístikəlee/ *adv.*

in·tel·lec·tu·al·ize /ínt'l ékchoo ə lìz/ (-ized, -iz·ing, -iz·es) *v.* **1.** *vti.* CONSIDER SOMETHING RATIONALLY to analyze, deal with, or explain something by thinking or reasoning exclusively **2.** *vi.* THINK to think or reason **3.** *vti.* MAKE OR BECOME INTELLECTUAL to make somebody or something intellectual or to become intellectual ○ *intellectualized poetry* **4.** *vt.* PSYCHOL REASON AWAY PROBLEMS to protect yourself unconsciously from the emotional stress that would come from dealing with fears or problems by reasoning them away —**in·tel·lec·tu·al·i·za·tion** *n.* —**in·tel·lec·tu·al·iz·er** *n.*

in·tel·lec·tu·al prop·er·ty *n.* original creative work manifested in a tangible form that can be legally protected, e.g., by a patent, trademark, or copyright

in·tel·li·gence /in téllijəns/ *n.* **1.** ABILITY TO THINK AND LEARN the ability to learn facts and skills and apply them, especially when this ability is highly developed **2.** SECRET INFORMATION information about secret plans or activities, especially those of foreign governments, the armed forces, business enemies, or criminals **3.** GATHERING OF SECRET INFORMATION the collection of secret military or political information **4.** PEOPLE GATHERING SECRET INFORMATION an organization that gathers information about the secret plans or activities of an adversary or potential adversary and the people involved in gathering such information **5.** INTELLIGENT SPIRIT an entity capable of rational thought, especially one that does not have a physical form —**in·tel·li·gen·tial** /in tèlli jénshəl/ *adj.*

in·tel·li·gence quo·tient *n.* full form of **IQ**

in·tel·li·genc·er /in téllijənsər/ *n.* somebody who provides or gathers information, especially about secret plans or activities (*archaic*)

in·tel·li·gent /in téllijənt/ *adj.* **1.** MENTALLY ABLE having intelligence, especially to a highly developed degree **2.** SENSIBLE OR RATIONAL showing or resulting from an ability to think and understand things clearly and logically ○ *an intelligent solution* **3.** COMPUT ABLE TO STORE AND PROCESS DATA with built-in electronic processing and data storage ability ○ *an intelligent terminal* **4.** COMPUT SELF-REGULATING programmed to be able to adjust itself to changes in its environment and make deductions from information it processes ○ *an intelligent building* **5.** AWARE aware, knowledgeable, or informed (*formal*) ○ *The President has been made intelligent of the probable consequences of this policy.* [Early 16thC. From Latin *intelligent-*, formed from *intellegere* "to perceive, discern," from *inter-* "between" + *legere* "to choose, read" (source of English *select* and *legible*).] —**in·tel·li·gent·ly** *adv.*

WORD KEY: SYNONYMS

intelligent, bright, quick, smart, clever, able, gifted

CORE MEANING: having the ability to learn and understand

intelligent a general word used to describe a person or animal who is quick to learn and understand; **bright** an informal word used to describe somebody who is mentally alert and responsive; **quick** an informal word emphasizing the ability to recognize or understand things quickly; **smart** an informal word similar to *bright*, but also implying mental resourcefulness; **clever** having the capacity to learn quickly, often implying mental resourcefulness, but also cunning or ingenuity; **able** a word used, especially in educational circles, of children who are intelligent; **gifted** describes somebody who has an exceptional talent, especially somebody artistic or creative. Also used, especially in educational circles, of children who are exceptionally intelligent and learn easily.

in·tel·li·gent·si·a /in tèlli jéntsee ə/ *n.* the most intelligent, intellectual, or highly educated members of a society or community, especially those who are interested in the arts, literature, philosophy, and politics [Early 20thC. Via Russian *intelligentsiya* from Latin *intelligentia* "intelligence."]

in·tel·li·gi·ble /in téllijəb'l/ *adj.* **1.** UNDERSTANDABLE capable of being understood ○ *his ideas were barely intelligible* **2.** PHILOS UNDERSTANDABLE BY THE MIND ALONE perceptible only by the mind, not the senses [14thC. Via Old French from Latin *intelligibilis*, from *intellegere* "to perceive" (see INTELLIGENT).] —**in·tel·li·gi·bil·i·ty** /in tèllijə bíllətee/ *n.* —**in·tel·li·gi·ble·ness** /in téllijəb'lnəss/ *n.* —**in·tel·li·gi·bly** *adv.*

In·tel·sat /ín tel sàt/, **IN·TEL·SAT** *n.* **1.** an international organization whose membership includes the telecommunications agencies of most countries and that owns the communications satellites that orbit the Earth. Full form **International Telecommunication Satellite Organization** **2.** TELECOMMUNICATIONS SATELLITE a telecommunications satellite launched by Intelsat

in·tem·per·ance /in témpərəns, -prəns/ *n.* **1.** EXCESSIVE INDULGENCE the satisfying of an unacceptable or excessive desire, especially excessive drinking of alcohol **2.** LACK OF SELF-CONTROL lack of self-control **3.** METEOROL BAD WEATHER severity of weather conditions or climate (*formal*)

in·tem·per·ate /in témpərət, -prət/ *adj.* **1.** DRINKING TO EXCESS drinking too much alcohol, especially frequently **2.** LACKING SELF-CONTROL having or showing a lack of self-control, especially in expressing feelings or satisfying physical desires **3.** METEOROL TOO HOT OR COLD extremely or unpleasantly hot or cold (*formal*) —**in·tem·per·ate·ly** *adv.* —**in·tem·per·ate·ness** *n.*

in·tend /in ténd/ (-tend·ed, -tend·ing, -tends) *v.* **1.** *vti.* MEAN TO DO SOMETHING to have something in mind as a plan ○ *I really intended to write, but I didn't have time.* **2.** *vt.* DO OR SAY FOR SOME PURPOSE to do, say, or produce something with a particular purpose, use, target, or group of people in mind ○ *a dictionary intended for grade-schoolers* **3.** *vt.* MEAN SOMETHING to signify or indicate something through speech or behavior ○ *What impression did he intend to give us with such a remark?* [14thC. Via Old French from Latin *intendere*, from *in-* "toward" + *tendere* "to stretch."]

in·ten·dance /in téndəns/ *n.* **1.** ADMINISTRATIVE DEPARTMENT a public department or administrative office in some countries **2.** = **intendancy** *n.* 1

in·ten·dan·cy /in téndənsee/ (*plural* -cies) *n.* **1.** WORK OF AN INTENDANT the role or functions of an intendant **2.** INTENDANTS AS A GROUP intendants considered collectively **3.** ADMINISTRATIVE AREA the department or district administered by an intendant

in·ten·dant /in téndənt/ *n.* an official or administrator in some countries, especially in the past in France, Spain, and Portugal, and currently in parts of Latin America [Mid-17thC. Via Old French from Latin *intendent-*, formed from *intendere* (see INTEND).]

in·tend·ed /in téndəd/ *adj.* **1.** ENVISIONED aimed at or designed for ○ *We were unable to reach our intended destination* **2.** PLANNED planned for the future **3.** DELIBERATE said or done deliberately ■ *n.* FUTURE HUSBAND OR WIFE the person to whom somebody is engaged to be married (*dated or humorous*) ○ *a letter from his intended* —**in·tend·ed·ly** *adv.*

in·tend·ing /in ténding/ *adj.* planning or having in mind to be a particular thing ○ *an intending candidate*

in·tend·ment /in téndmənt/ *n.* the meaning of something, especially a word or term, according to law

intens. *abbr.* 1. intensify 2. intensive

in·tense /in téns/ *adj.* 1. EXTREME great, strong, or extreme in a way that can be felt ○ *intense heat* 2. EFFORTFUL OR ACTIVE involving great effort or much activity ○ *showed intense dedication to the task* 3. CONCENTRATED narrowly focused or concentrated ○ *an intense stare* 4. PASSIONATE feeling or showing strong and deeply felt emotions in a serious way ○ *a very intense young student* [15thC. Via Old French from Latin *intensus*, the past participle of *intendere* "to stretch out" (see INTEND).] —**in·tense·ly** *adv.* —**in·tense·ness** *n.*

in·ten·si·fi·er /in ténsə fìr/ *n.* 1. GRAM = **intensive** *n.* 1 2. SOMEBODY OR SOMETHING THAT INTENSIFIES somebody or something that makes something larger, sharper, or stronger

in·ten·si·fy /in ténsə fì/ (-fied, -fy·ing, -fies) *vti.* 1. MAKE OR BECOME GREATER to make something greater or stronger, or to increase in strength or degree ○ *media interest intensified as the week progressed* 2. INCREASE EFFORT OR CONCENTRATION to do something with greater effort or more activity or to become more concentrated —**in·ten·si·fi·ca·tion** /in tènsəfi káysh'n/ *n.*

WORD KEY: SYNONYMS

See Synonyms at ***increase***.

in·ten·sion /in ténshən/ *n.* 1. LOGIC MEANING OF EXPRESSION the meaning of an expression as opposed to what it refers to. The intension of the word "human" is the property of being human, whereas it has as its reference, or extension, human beings as a group. 2. INTENSITY intensity (*formal*) 3. INTENSIFICATION intensification (*formal*) [Early 17thC. From the Latin stem *intension-*, from *intendere* "to stretch out, become tense."] —**in·ten·sion·al** *adj.* —**in·ten·sion·al·ly** *adv.*

in·ten·sion·al ob·ject *n.* LOGIC a concept, property, or proposition as opposed to an individual, set, or truth value, which are the extensional counterparts of intensional objects

in·ten·si·ty /in ténsitee/ (*plural* -ties) *n.* 1. QUALITY OF BEING INTENSE the strength, power, force, or concentration of something ○ *The pain increased in intensity.* 2. INTENSE MANNER a passionate and serious attitude or quality ○ *a rare emotional intensity in her work* 3. PHYS MAGNITUDE OF ENERGY the strength of a source of energy, e.g., light, electricity, or sound, per unit area, mass, or time

in·ten·sive /in ténsiv/ *adj.* 1. CONCENTRATED involving concentrated effort, usually in order to achieve something in a comparatively short time ○ *an intensive course in German* 2. AGRIC INCREASING PRODUCTION relating to a form of agriculture in which scientific and technological methods, e.g., the use of chemicals that boost growth or crop yields, are used to increase productivity 3. MAKING HEAVY USE OF requiring or using a great deal of a particular thing ○ *capital-intensive* 4. GRAM INDICATING HOW MUCH used to describe a word or phrase, e.g., "extremely," that emphasizes or intensifies the word that it modifies ■ *n.* 1. GRAM WORD INDICATING HOW MUCH a word or phrase, e.g., "extremely," that emphasizes or intensifies the word that it modifies 2. QUICK COURSE WITH A LOT OF INFORMATION a course or workshop in which a great deal of information is absorbed in a very short time (*informal*) ○ *She's taken several intensives in personnel management.* —**in·ten·sive·ly** *adv.* —**in·ten·sive·ness** *n.*

in·ten·sive care *n.* 1. CARE OF THE CRITICALLY ILL the monitoring, care, and treatment of patients who are critically ill or critically injured ○ *One of the survivors is still in intensive care.* 2. = **intensive care unit**

in·ten·sive care u·nit *n.* a department of a hospital that is designed and equipped for the monitoring, care, and treatment of critically ill or critically injured patients. The monitoring is usually done by electronic means so that essential corrective action can be taken with a minimum of delay.

in·tent /in tént/ *n.* 1. PLAN OR PURPOSE something planned or the purpose that accompanies a plan (*formal*) ○ *"My intent is to use our attractive domestic market as the basis of a muscular free trade policy that will strengthen America's global economic reach..."* (National Public Telecomputing Network, *Bush speeches in campaign '92*; 1992) 2. LAW STATE OF MIND somebody's state of mind when deliberately committing or planning to commit an illegal act 3. CONNOTATION the meaning or significance of something, especially when it is not explicitly expressed ■ *adj.* 1. WITH FIXED ATTENTION with full attention or effort concentrated or focused on one thing ○ *Intent on her work, she lost track of the time.* 2. DETERMINED showing great determination to do something ○ *They are intent on catching the first shuttle.* [13thC. Via Old French *entent* from, ultimately, Latin *intendere* (see INTEND).] —**in·tent·ly** *adv.* —**in·tent·ness** *n.* ◇ **to all intents and purposes** in effect the same, although not actually the same

in·ten·tion /in ténshən/ *n.* 1. AIM OR OBJECTIVE something that somebody plans to do or achieve ○ *State your intentions.* 2. QUALITY OF PURPOSEFULNESS the quality or state of having a purpose in mind ○ *She acted without intention.* ■ **in·ten·tions** *npl.* SOMEBODY'S MARRIAGE PLANS somebody's plans with respect to marriage (*dated*) ○ *What are your intentions toward my daughter?* [14thC. Via Old French from the Latin stem *intention-*, from *intendere* (see INTEND).]

in·ten·tion·al /in ténshən'l/ *adj.* 1. DELIBERATE done on purpose, not by accident 2. PHILOS INVOLVING THOUGHTS ABOUT OBJECTS involving thoughts, e.g., beliefs or desires, about different kinds of objects, including those that have no actual existence —**in·ten·tion·al·i·ty** /in tènshə nállətee/ *n.* —**in·ten·tion·al·ly** /in ténshən'lee/ *adv.*

in·ter /in túr/ (-terred, -ter·ring, -ters) *vt.* to bury the body or ashes of a cremated body in a grave or tomb (*formal*) [15thC. Via Old French *enterer*, ultimately from IN + Latin *terra* "earth."]

inter. *abbr.* intermediate

inter- *prefix.* 1. between, among ○ *interlinear* ○ *interstate* ○ *intercut* 2. mutual, reciprocal ○ *interweave* 3. involving two or more groups ○ *international* [Directly and via Old French *entre* from Latin *inter* "between, among" (source of English *internal* and *entrails*). Ultimately from an Indo-European word meaning literally "more in."]

in·ter·a·bang /in térrə bàng/ *n.* PRINTING = **interrobang**

in·ter·act /ìntər ákt/ (-act·ed, -act·ing, -acts) *vi.* 1. ACT ON EACH OTHER to have an effect on something else or one another 2. COMMUNICATE OR WORK TOGETHER to be or become involved in communication, social activity, or work with somebody else or one another

in·ter·ac·tant /ìntər áktənt/ *n.* somebody or something that interacts in some way (*formal*)

in·ter·ac·tion /ìntər ákshən/ *n.* 1. COMMUNICATION OR COLLABORATION communication between or joint activity involving two or more people 2. RECIPROCAL ACTION the combined or reciprocal action of two or more things that have an effect on each other and work together 3. PHYS FORCE BETWEEN ELEMENTARY PARTICLES any of the four fundamental forces acting between elementary particles, namely gravitational, electromagnetic, strong, and weak —**in·ter·ac·tion·al** *adj.*

in·ter·ac·tion·ism /ìntər ákshə nìzzəm/ *n.* PHILOS in Western metaphysics, the theory that the mind and the body act on each other

in·ter·ac·tive /ìntər áktiv/ *adj.* 1. COMMUNICATING OR COLLABORATING involving the communication or collaboration of people or things 2. COMPUT WITH USER-MACHINE COMMUNICATION allowing or involving the exchange of information or instructions between a person and a machine such as a computer or a television 3. COMPUT OPERATOR-CONTROLLED operating on instructions entered by somebody at a keyboard or other input device —**in·ter·ac·tive·ly** *adv.* —**in·ter·ac·tiv·i·ty** /ìntər aktívvitee/ *n.*

in·ter·a·gen·cy /ìntər áyjənsee/ *adj.* involving two or more agencies, especially government agencies ○ *an interagency initiative*

in·ter a·li·a /ìntər áylee ə, -áalee ə/ *adv.* among other things (*formal*) ○ *budget funds for two new schools inter alia* [From Latin]

in·ter a·li·os /ìntər áalee ōss, -áylee ōss/ *adv.* among other people (*formal*) [From Latin]

in·ter·al·lied /ìntər ə líd, ìntər á lìd/ *adj.* involving the combined or mutual action of allies, especially in a war

in·ter-A·mer·i·can *adj.* involving two or more countries of North, Central, or South America

in·ter·bank /ìntər bángk/ *adj.* between, connecting, or involving two or more banks

in·ter·breed /ìntər bréed/ (-bred /-bréd/, -bred, -breed·ing, -breeds) *vti.* 1. BREED WITH OTHER GROUPS to produce offspring by mating with a member of a different breed or species, or to mate an animal of one species or variety with one of another 2. BREED WITHIN A NARROW GROUP to breed or make something breed within a closed population or narrow range of types

in·ter·ca·lar·y /in túrkə lèrree, ìntər kállərree/ *adj.* 1. INSERTED INTO THE CALENDAR added to the calendar year to keep calendar years concurrent with solar years. In the Gregorian calendar February 29 is an intercalary day in leap years. 2. INDICATING A YEAR WITH ADDITION used to describe a year to which an intercalary day or month has been added. A leap year is an intercalary year. 3. INSERTED OR INTRODUCED put into something else, or inserted between other parts (*formal*) 4. BOT GROWING IN INTERNODE used to describe a meristem that grows in the internode of a stem [Early 17thC. Via Latin *intercalarius* from *intercalare* (see INTERCALATE).]

in·ter·ca·late /in túrkə làyt/ (-lat·ed, -lat·ing, -lates) *v.* 1. *vt.* INSERT EXTRA TIME INTO THE CALENDAR to insert an extra day or month into a calendar year to keep it consistent with the solar year 2. *vti.* INSERT OR INTRODUCE to place something into something else, inserting it between other elements, or to be placed between other elements (*formal*) [Early 17thC. From Latin *intercalat-*, from *intercalare*, from *calare* "to proclaim."] —**in·ter·ca·la·tion** /in tùrkə láysh'n/ *n.* —**in·ter·ca·la·tive** /in túrkə làytiv/ *adj.*

in·ter·cede /ìntər séed/ (-ced·ed, -ced·ing, -cedes) *vi.* 1. PLEAD FOR SOMEBODY to plead with somebody in authority on behalf of somebody else, especially somebody who is to be punished for something 2. SPEAK FOR SOMEBODY to speak in support of somebody involved in a dispute 3. MEDIATE IN A DISPUTE to attempt to settle a dispute between others [Late 16thC. Via Latin *intercedere* from *cedere* "to give way" (see CEDE).] —**in·ter·ced·er** *n.*

in·ter·cel·lu·lar /ìntər séllyələr/ *adj.* BIOL existing between cells ○ *an intercellular substance*

in·ter·cept *v.* /ìntər sépt/ (-cept·ed, -cept·ing, -cepts) 1. *vti.* INTERRUPT PROGRESS to prevent people or objects from reaching their destination or target by stopping, diverting, or seizing them ○ *the contraband was intercepted by police at the dock* 2. *vt.* SPORTS GET THE BALL in sports, to gain possession of a ball intended for an opponent 3. *vt.* GEOM MARK EXTENT to include part of a curve, surface, or solid between two points or lines ■ *n.* /ìntər sèpt/ 1. MATH DISTANCE BETWEEN THE ORIGIN AND AXIS CROSSING the distance from the origin of a coordinate system to the point where a curve or surface crosses an axis 2. ACT OF INTERCEPTING the intercepting of something, especially a radio transmission, a missile, or an aircraft 3. ASTRON DIFFERENCE BETWEEN CALCULATED AND OBSERVED ALTITUDE the difference between the calculated and observed altitude of a celestial object [15thC. From Latin *intercept-*, formed from *intercipere*, from *capere* "to seize."] —**in·ter·cep·tive** *adj.*

in·ter·cept·er /ìntər séptər/ *n.* = **interceptor**

in·ter·cep·tion /ìntər sépshən/ *n.* 1. INTERCEPTING SOMEBODY OR SOMETHING the act or an instance of intercepting somebody or something 2. SOMETHING INTERCEPTED something intercepted, especially a passed ball that is intercepted by an opponent while it is in the air

in·ter·cep·tor /ìntər séptər/, **in·ter·cept·er** *n.* 1. AIR FORCE FAST FIGHTER PLANE a fast, very maneuverable fighter plane designed to intercept enemy aircraft 2. ARMS GUIDED MISSILE a guided missile designed to intercept enemy missiles or spacecraft 3. ONE THAT INTERCEPTS somebody or something that intercepts

in·ter·ces·sion /ìntər sésh'n/ *n.* 1. INTERCEDING the action of pleading on somebody's behalf 2. TRYING TO RESOLVE CONFLICT the action of attempting to settle a dispute 3. PRAYER OR PETITION prayer to God, a god, or a saint on behalf of somebody or something [15thC. Via Old French from the Latin stem *intercession-*, from *intercedere* (see INTERCEDE).] —**in·ter·ces·sion·al** *adj.* —**in·ter·ces·sor** *n.* —**in·ter·ces·so·ri·al** /ìntərsə sáwree əl/ *adj.* —**in·ter·ces·so·ry** /ìntər séssəree/ *adj.*

in·ter·change /ìntər cháynj/ *v.* (-changed, -chang·ing, -chang·es) 1. *vti.* SWITCH OR SWAP PLACES to put each of two things in the place of the other or to change places with something else 2. *vti.* ALTERNATE OR FOLLOW EACH OTHER to arrange things alternately in a series or to be arranged in this way 3. *vt.* EXCHANGE THINGS to give something to somebody and receive a similar thing from the same person in return ■ *n.* 1. EXCHANGE

OF THINGS an exchange of things, especially ideas, opinions, or information, among people **2.** ALTERNATION the action of alternating or changing places **3.** TRANSP ROAD INTERSECTION a major road junction where vehicles can, by means of access roads, bridges, and underpasses, change from one road to another without stopping or crossing other traffic **4.** TRANSP PLACE WHERE PASSENGERS CHANGE TRANSPORTATION a place where passengers can change from one train or bus to another or between trains and buses [14thC. Via Old French *enterchangier.*] —**in·ter·change·a·bil·i·ty** /ìntər cháynjə bílləteel/ *n.* —**in·ter·change·a·ble** /ìntər cháynjəb'l/ *adj.* —**in·ter·change·a·bly** /-cháynjəblee/ *adv.* —**in·ter·chang·er** /ìntər cháynjər/ *n.*

in·ter·cit·y /ìntər síttee/ *adj.* involving, connecting, or occurring between two or more cities

in·ter·coast·al /ìntər kṓst'l/ *adj.* connecting or occurring between ports on different coasts or two or more coastlines

in·ter·col·le·giate /ìntər kə léejee ət/ *adj.* involving or occurring between the members of two or more colleges or universities ○ *intercollegiate sports*

in·ter·co·lum·ni·a·tion /ìntər kə lumnee áysh'n/ *n.* a system used to space columns in a colonnade, based on the use of their diameters as a measurement

in·ter·com /ìntər kòm/ *n.* a system or device for transmitting sound from one part of a building, aircraft, or ship to another [Mid-20thC. Shortening of *intercommunication system.*]

in·ter·com·mu·nal /ìntər kə myóon'l/ *adj.* existing or occurring between the members of two or more communities

in·ter·com·mu·ni·cate /ìntər kə myóoni kàyt/ (**-cat·ed, -cat·ing, -cates**) *vi.* **1.** TALK TO EACH OTHER to communicate with each other **2.** ALLOW PASSAGE FROM ONE TO ANOTHER to be connected to something else or each other, especially to another room by means of a door in the dividing wall ○ *intercommunicating hotel rooms* —**in·ter·com·mu·ni·ca·tion** /-myooni káysh'n/ *n.* —**in·ter·com·mu·ni·ca·tive** /-myóoni kàytiv/ *adj.* —**in·ter·com·mu·ni·ca·tor** /-myóoni kàytər/ *n.*

in·ter·com·mun·ion /ìntər kə myóonyən/ *n.* **1.** CHR AGREEMENT ALLOWING JOINT COMMUNION an arrangement between different Christian denominations enabling members to receive the Communion at each other's services **2.** CLOSE ASSOCIATION a close association or relationship between people or groups, especially one that involves mutual participation or action

in·ter·con·nect /ìntər kə nékt/ (**-nect·ed, -nect·ing, -nects**) *vti.* **1.** JOIN ONTO ONE ANOTHER to be joined to something else or to a number of joined things, or to make something part of such a network (*often passive*) ○ *the rooms are interconnected to form a suite* **2.** RELATE THINGS to show a relationship between two or more things, or to be related —**in·ter·con·nect·i·ble** *adj.* —**in·ter·con·nec·tion** *n.*

in·ter·con·nec·tive /ìntər kə néktiv/ *adj.* connecting or capable of connecting with something else or with each other —**in·ter·con·nec·tiv·i·ty** /ìntər kə nék tívvətee/ *n.*

in·ter·con·ti·nen·tal /ìntər kontə nént'l/ *adj.* **1.** BETWEEN CONTINENTS involving or occurring between two or more continents **2.** GOING TO ANOTHER CONTINENT going from one continent to another

in·ter·con·ti·nen·tal bal·lis·tic mis·sile *n.* a ballistic missile with a range of about 3,000 to 8,000 nautical miles

in·ter·con·ver·sion /ìntərkən vúrzh'n/ *n.* the conversion of two or more things, e.g., chemicals, into one another —**in·ter·con·vert** *vt.* —**in·ter·con·vert·i·bil·i·ty** /ìntərkən vurtə bílləteel/ *n.* —**in·ter·con·vert·i·ble** /-vúrtəb'l/ *adj.*

in·ter·cool·er /ìntər kóolər/ *n.* a heat exchanger that cools a fluid between successive stages of compression or chemical reaction

in·ter·cos·tal /ìntər kóst'l/ *adj.* situated or occurring between the ribs ○ *an intercostal nerve* [Late 16thC. Coined from Latin *costa* "side, rib."]

in·ter·course /ìntər kàwrs/ *n.* **1.** MUTUAL DEALINGS communication or exchanges between people or groups, especially conversation or social activity **2.** = **sexual intercourse** [15thC. Via Old French *entrecours* "commerce," from Latin *intercursus*, literally "running between," from *currere* "to run" (source of English *courier, current,* and *cursive*).]

in·ter·crop /ìntər krόp/ (**-cropped, -crop·ping, -crops**) *vti.* to grow different crops in the same field, usually in alternate rows, or to plant a crop between the rows of another crop —**in·ter·crop** *n.*

in·ter·cul·tur·al /ìntər kúlchərəl/ *adj.* involving or occurring between different cultures or between people with different cultural backgrounds —**in·ter·cul·tur·al·ly** *adv.*

in·ter·cur·rent /ìntər kúr ənt/ *adj.* **1.** MED OCCURRING DURING OTHER DISEASE occurring during and changing the course of an already existing disease ○ *treating an intercurrent infection* **2.** SIMULTANEOUS OR INTERVENING occurring at the same time as something else or during the period between two other events (*formal*) [Early 17thC. From Latin *intercurrent-*, from *intercurrere*, literally "to run between," from *currere* "to run."] —**in·ter·cur·rence** *n.* —**in·ter·cur·rent·ly** *adv.*

in·ter·cut /ìntər kút/ (**-cut, -cut·ting, -cuts**) *vt.* to alternate scenes or shots of a movie or insert one scene into another during the editing process, usually to show different events taking place at the same time

in·ter·de·nom·i·na·tion·al /ìntər di nommi náyshən'l, -shnəl/ *adj.* involving, occurring between, or open to people from different religious groups

in·ter·den·tal /ìntər dént'l/ *adj.* **1.** DENT BETWEEN THE TEETH existing between or designed for use between teeth **2.** PHON WITH THE TONGUE BETWEEN THE TEETH made by placing the tip of the tongue between the teeth ■ *n.* PHON SOUND MADE WITH TONGUE BETWEEN TEETH a sound made by putting the tip of the tongue between the teeth —**in·ter·den·tal·ly** *adv.*

in·ter·de·part·men·tal /ìntər dee paart mént'l/ *adj.* involving or occurring between different departments of the same organization or the people who work in them —**in·ter·de·part·men·tal·ly** *adv.*

in·ter·de·pend·ent /ìntər di péndənt/ *adj.* **1.** DEPENDING ON EACH OTHER unable to exist or survive without each other ○ *interdependent organisms* **2.** WITH MUTUALLY DEPENDENT ELEMENTS relying on mutual assistance, support, cooperation, or interaction among constituent elements or members —**in·ter·de·pend** *vi.* —**in·ter·de·pend·ence** *n.* —**in·ter·de·pend·ent·ly** *adv.*

in·ter·dict *n.* /ìntər dìkt/ **1.** LAW PROHIBITIVE ORDER a court order that prohibits something **2.** CHR EXCLUSION FROM CHURCH SACRAMENTS a ban imposed by a pope, church council, or bishop that excludes a person, group, or nation from the sacraments of the Roman Catholic Church. In the past the interdict was used to enforce obedience. ■ *vt.* /ìntər díkt/ (**-dict·ed, -dict·ing, -dicts**) **1.** LAW BAN BY LAW to prohibit something or forbid somebody from doing something, especially in accordance with civil or ecclesiastical law **2.** LAW PREVENT ILLEGAL ENTRY to prevent somebody or something from entering a country illegally ○ *Patrols will be increased along the border to interdict smugglers.* **3.** MIL PREVENT ENEMY USE to keep an enemy from using an area by troop movements or other means [13thC. Via Old French *entredit* from Latin *interdictum*, formed from *interdicere* "to prohibit," from *dicere* "to speak."] —**in·ter·dic·tion** /ìntər díkshən/ *n.* —**in·ter·dic·tor** /-tər/ *n.* —**in·ter·dic·to·ry** /-təree/ *adj.*

in·ter·dig·i·tal /ìntər díjjit'l/ *adj.* **1.** ELECTRON ENG MADE OF PARALLEL STRIPS in the form of two series of parallel strips that fit together like the fingers of clasped hands **2.** ANAT BETWEEN THE FINGERS OR TOES between the fingers or toes —**in·ter·dig·i·tal·ly** *adv.*

in·ter·dig·i·tate /ìntər díjji tàyt/ (**-tat·ed, -tat·ing, -tates**) *vti.* to fit together like the fingers of clasped hands or to place or hold objects together in such a pattern —**in·ter·dig·i·ta·tion** /ìntər dijjə táysh'n/ *n.*

in·ter·dis·ci·pli·nar·y /ìntər díssəplə nèrree/ *adj.* involving two or more academic subjects or fields of study

in·ter·est /íntrəst/ *n.* **1.** CURIOSITY OR CONCERN a feeling of curiosity or concern about something that makes the attention turn toward it ○ *an interest in art* **2.** QUALITY THAT ATTRACTS ATTENTION a power, quality, or aspect of something that attracts attention, concern, or curiosity ○ *it's of no interest to me* **3.** ENJOYABLE THING something that somebody enjoys doing (*often used in the plural*) ○ *My leisure interests include sailing, music, reading, and walking.* **4.** BENEFIT OR ADVANTAGE the good, benefit, or advantage of somebody or something ○ *in the interests of peace* **5.** INVOLVEMENT somebody's involvement with something that makes its progress or success important to him or her ○ *took a personal interest in the progress of the project* **6.** FIN BORROWING CHARGE OR PAYMENT FOR MONEY USE a charge made for a loan or credit facility, or a payment made by a bank or other financial institution for the use of money deposited in an account **7.** COMM SHARE IN SOMETHING a legal right to claim a share in something, especially in a business or property, or the business or property itself **8.** CONNECTION a personal or commercial connection with something or somebody, especially when this prevents somebody from being objective or impartial ○ *had to declare a conflict of interest* ■ **in·ter·ests** *npl.* INFLUENTIAL GROUP a group of people in business or society who have the same aims or support the same cause, especially a powerful or influential group ■ *vt.* (**-est·ed, -est·ing, -ests**) **1.** GET SOMEBODY'S ATTENTION to attract or hold somebody's attention or arouse somebody's curiosity or concern ○ *It may interest you to know that the building used to be a mortuary.* **2.** MAKE SOMEBODY WANT SOMETHING to make somebody want to have or buy something, do something, or become involved with something ○ *I tried to interest him in helping with the preparations.* [15thC. Via Old French from Latin "it matters," from *interesse*, literally "to be in the middle," from *esse* "to be."]

in·ter·est·ed /íntrəstəd/ *adj.* **1.** CURIOUS OR CONCERNED paying attention to something or devoting time to something because of curiosity, concern, or enjoyment **2.** WANTING SOMETHING involved or wanting to be involved in something ○ *interested parties can call the toll-free number* **3.** AFFECTED OR INVOLVED having a legal right or share in something or a personal or commercial connection with something —**in·ter·est·ed·ly** *adv.* —**in·ter·est·ed·ness** *n.*

in·ter·est group *n.* **1.** GROUP WITH COMMON PURPOSE a group of people who act or work together in support of a cause **2.** PEOPLE WITH SHARED INTEREST a group of people who share an interest in something such as a subject of study

in·ter·est·ing /íntrəsting/ *adj.* **1.** AROUSING CURIOSITY OR ATTENTION arousing curiosity, attracting or holding attention, or provoking thought **2.** NOT BORING enjoyable because of being varied, challenging, stimulating, or exciting —**in·ter·est·ing·ly** *adv.*

in·ter·face /ìntər fàyss/ *n.* **1.** COMMON BOUNDARY the surface, place, or point where two things touch each other or meet **2.** CHEM BOUNDARY BETWEEN THINGS a common boundary between objects or different phases of a substance ○ *an oil-water interface* **3.** POINT OF INTERACTION the place, situation, or way in which two things or people act together or affect each other or the point of connection between things **4.** COMPUT BOUNDARY ACROSS WHICH DATA PASSES a common boundary shared by two devices, or by a person and a device, across which data or information flows, e.g., the screen of a computer **5.** COMPUT LINKING SOFTWARE software that links a computer with another device, or the set of commands, messages, images, and other elements allowing communication between computer and operator **6.** ELECTRON ENG LINKING DEVICE an electronic device or circuit or other point of contact between two pieces of equipment ■ *vti.* /ìntər fàyss, ìntər fáyss/ (**-faced, -fac·ing, -fac·es**) **1.** HAVE OR GIVE COMMON BOUNDARY to touch or meet at a surface, place, or point, or to make things join in this way **2.** INTERACT to act together or affect each other or to make things or people interact **3.** COMPUT SERVE AS INTERFACE to connect or serve as an interface for two or more pieces of equipment —**in·ter·fa·cial** /ìntər fáysh'l/ *adj.* —**in·ter·fa·cial·ly** /-fáyshəlee/ *adv.*

in·ter·fac·ing /ìntər fàyssing/ *n.* a fabric that is used to stiffen or support collars, cuffs, or other parts of a garment

in·ter·faith /ìntər fáyth/ *adj.* involving or occurring between people of different religious faiths

in·ter·fere /ìntər féer/ (**-fered, -fer·ing, -feres**) *vi.* **1.** HAVE AN UNDESIRABLE EFFECT to delay, hinder, or obstruct the natural or desired course of something ○ *The weather interfered with our plans.* **2.** MEDDLE IN OTHERS' AFFAIRS to participate in the affairs of others, especially by offering unwanted or unhelpful advice or by trying to resolve others' disputes ○ *It's not advisable to interfere in a private quarrel.* **3.** COMMUNICATION CAUSE INTERFERENCE to cause electronic interference **4.** SPORTS OBSTRUCT ILLEGALLY to obstruct, block, or hinder illegally an opponent in sport ○ *a 15-yard penalty for interfering with the pass* **5.** PHYS AFFECT DISPLACEMENT OR AMPLITUDE to act together to increase, decrease, or cancel out displacement or amplitude **6.** EQU **HIT A HOOF AGAINST A LEG** to hit one hoof against the opposite hoof or leg while walking (*refers to horses*) [15thC. Via Old French *s'entreferer* "to strike each other," ultimately from Latin *ferire* "to strike."] —**in·ter·fer·er** *n.*

in·ter·fer·ence /intər féerəns/ *n.* **1. MEDDLING IN OTHERS' AFFAIRS** involvement in something without any invitation or justification ○ *he deeply resented any interference in his private life* **2. HINDRANCE** hindrance or obstruction that prevents a natural or desired outcome **3.** SPORTS **ILLEGAL OBSTRUCTION** the illegal blocking, hindering, or obstruction of an opposing player in some sports **4.** FOOTBALL **LEGAL BLOCKING** in football, the legal blocking of defensive players to protect and make way for the player carrying the ball **5.** COMMUNICATION **SIGNAL THAT INTERFERES** an unwanted signal that disrupts radio, telephone, or television reception **6.** PHYS **PROCESS OF WAVE INTERACTION** a process in lightwave transmission in which two or more waves are superimposed in such a way that they produce higher peaks, lower troughs, or a new wave pattern —**in·ter·fer·en·tial** /intərfə rénshəl/ *adj.* ◇ **run interference 1.** FOOTBALL to carry out legal blocking of defensive players to protect and make way for the player carrying the ball **2.** to contribute help or support to somebody or something, especially by preventing others from acting as a hindrance (*informal*)

in·ter·fer·ing /intər féering/ *adj.* deliberately becoming involved in other people's affairs in a way that is not needed and is unwelcome —**in·ter·fer·ing·ly** *adv.*

in·ter·fe·rom·e·ter /intərfə rómmətər/ *n.* a device that uses an interference pattern to determine wave frequency, length, or velocity —**in·ter·fer·o·met·ric** /intər feerə méttrik/ *adj.* —**in·ter·fer·o·met·ri·cal·ly** /-méttrikəlee/ *adv.* —**in·ter·fe·rom·e·try** /intərfə rómmətree/ *n.*

in·ter·fer·on /intər fée ròn/ *n.* a complex protein (**glycoprotein**) that is produced by cells in response to a virus or bacterium and that inhibits virus development [Mid-20thC. Coined from INTERFERE + -on.]

in·ter·fer·tile /intər fúrt'l/ *adj.* able to interbreed with other species or subspecies and produce viable offspring —**in·ter·fer·til·i·ty** /intər fər tíllətee/ *n.*

in·ter·file /intər fíl/ (**-filed, -fil·ing, -files**) *vt.* to put an item or items among similar items in a file

in·ter·flow /intər fló/ (**-flowed, -flow·ing, -flows**) *vi.* to merge into a single stream

in·ter·flu·ent /intər flóo ənt/ *adj.* **1. FLOWING TOGETHER** merging into a single stream **2. FLOWING BETWEEN** flowing between things or places [Mid-17thC. From Latin *interfluent-*, the present participle stem of *interfluere* "to flow together," from *fluere* "to flow."]

in·ter·fluve /intər flóov/ (*plural* **-fluves**) *n.* **1. LINE SEPARATING DRAINAGE AREAS** the ridge line separating two drainage basins **2. LINE MARKING A DIVIDE IN WATER FLOW** a line joining points on one side of which water will flow to one river while on the other side water will flow to another river [Early 20thC. Back-formation from *interfluvial*.] —**in·ter·flu·vi·al** *adj.*

in·ter·fold /intər fóld/ (**-fold·ed, -fold·ing, -folds**) *vt.* to fold two or more things together

in·ter·fuse /intər fyóoz/ (**-fused, -fus·ing, -fuses**) *vti.* to mingle, blend, or fuse thoroughly, or to mix two or more things in this way [Late 16thC. From Latin *interfus-*, formed from *interfundere*, literally "to pour together," from *fundere* "to pour."] —**in·ter·fu·sion** *n.*

in·ter·ga·lac·tic /intərgə láktik/ *adj.* situated, happening, or moving between galaxies, or involving two or more galaxies —**in·ter·ga·lac·ti·cal·ly** *adv.*

in·ter·gen·er·a·tion·al /intər jennə ráyshən'l, -shnəl/ *adj.* occurring between, involving, or affecting people of two or more generations

in·ter·gla·cial /intər gláysh'l/ *n.* a period of warmer climate separating two periods of glaciation and displaying a characteristic sequence of changes in vegetation. The term is used especially for several such periods that occurred during the Pleistocene epoch, lasting from 1.8 million to 10,000 years ago. ◊ **interstadial** —**in·ter·gla·cial** *adj.*

in·ter·gov·ern·men·tal /intər guvvərn mént'l/ *adj.* involving representatives of or concerning relations between two or more governments —**in·ter·gov·ern·men·tal·ly** *adv.*

in·ter·grade /intər gráyd/ *vi.* (**-grad·ed, -grad·ing, -grades**) ZOOL **CHANGE BY STAGES** to be transformed from one form to another through a series of stages or forms that involve partial transitions ■ *n.* **1. TRANSITIONAL FORM** a transitional form or stage **2.** GEOG **TRANSITIONAL SOIL HORIZON** a transitional soil horizon between two distinctive soils —**in·ter·gra·di·ent** /intər gráydee ənt/ *adj.* —**in·ter·gra·da·tion** /grə dáysh'n/ *n.*

in·ter·group /intər gróop/ *adj.* involving members of two or more racial or social groups, or concerned with relations between groups

in·ter·growth /intər grōth/ *n.* growth of one thing into or within another thing, or among other things, or the result of such growth

in·ter·im /intərim/ *adj.* **1. HAVING TEMPORARY EFFECT** serving as a temporary measure until something more complete and permanent can be established **2.** POL **HOLDING TEMPORARY OFFICE** serving temporarily until a permanent replacement can be elected or appointed ■ *n.* **INTERVENING TIME** a period of time between two occurrences or periods ○ *in the interim* [Mid-16thC. From Latin, "meanwhile."]

in·ter·i·on·ic /intər ī ónnik/ *adj.* situated between or involving two or more ions

in·te·ri·or /in téeree ər/ *n.* **1. INSIDE PART** the inside of something ○ *the interior of the church was dark* **2. INSIDE OF A BUILDING OR ROOM** the inside of a building or room considered especially with regard to its decoration and furnishing **3. PART FARTHEST IN FROM THE EDGE** the part of something that is far or farthest from its edge, boundary, or surface, especially the part of a country or continent that is remote or farthest from the coast **4. PICTURE OF THE INSIDE OF A ROOM** a painting or photograph of the inside of a room **5. INSIDE SET OR SCENE** a setting or actual location that represents the inside of a building, or a scene filmed inside a building ■ *adj.* **1. LOCATED INSIDE** located or occurring inside something, or suitable for the inside of something **2. CENTRAL** remote or farthest from the edge, boundary, or surface of something, especially from the coast of a country or continent **3. OCCURRING IN THE MIND** taking place within somebody's mind and usually not expressed out loud [15thC. Directly or via French *intérieur* from Latin *interior*, literally "more in the midst of," from *inter* "between" (see INTER-).] —**in·te·ri·or·i·ty** /in tèeree áwritee/ *n.* —**in·te·ri·or·ly** /in téeree ərlee/ *adv.*

In·te·ri·or *n.* **COUNTRY'S DOMESTIC AFFAIRS** in the United States and some other countries, the domestic affairs of the nation, especially as opposed to its foreign affairs ■ *adj.* **OF DOMESTIC AFFAIRS** relating to the domestic affairs of a country, especially as opposed to its foreign affairs

in·te·ri·or an·gle *n.* **1. ANGLE INSIDE A POLYGON** the angle formed between two adjacent sides of a polygon and lying in its interior. The sum of the interior angles of any polygon is equal to the number of its sides minus two and multiplied by 180°. **2. ANGLE WITHIN INTERSECTING LINES** any of the four angles formed in the area between two parallel lines by a third line that intersects them (**transversal**)

in·te·ri·or dec·o·ra·tion *n.* **1. PLANNING OF DECORATION** the art or process of planning the decoration and furnishings of a room or building **2. DECORATIONS AND FURNISHINGS** the way that a room or building is decorated and furnished **3. WALLPAPERING AND PAINTING** the skill or trade of somebody who specializes in wallpapering and painting interiors —**in·te·ri·or dec·o·ra·tor** *n.*

in·te·ri·or de·sign *n.* = **interior decoration** —**in·te·ri·or de·sign·er** *n.*

in·te·ri·or mon·o·logue *n.* an extended passage in a story or novel that expresses what a character is thinking and feeling. ◊ **stream of consciousness, soliloquy**

In·te·ri·or Sa·lish (*plural* **In·te·ri·or Sa·lish**) *n.* a member of a Native North American people who originally lived in parts of British Columbia, northern Washington, northern Idaho, and western Montana. Today a small community of approximately 5,000 Interior Salish lives on a reservation in Montana. —**In·te·ri·or Sa·lish** *adj.*

in·te·ri·or-sprung *adj.* *U.K.* = **innerspring**

in·ter·is·land /intər íland/ *adj.* occurring between islands, or involving two or more islands [Mid-19thC]

interj. *abbr.* interjection

in·ter·ject /intər jékt/ (**-ject·ed, -ject·ing, -jects**) *vti.* to say or insert something in a way that interrupts what is being said or discussed [Late 16thC. From Latin *interject-*, the past participle stem of *interjicere* "to interpose," literally "to throw between," from *jacere* "to throw."] —**in·ter·jec·tor** *n.* —**in·ter·jec·to·ry** *adj.*

in·ter·jec·tion /intər jékshən/ *n.* **1. EXCLAMATION EXPRESSING EMOTION** a sound, word, or phrase that expresses a strong emotion such as pain or surprise but otherwise has no meaning **2. COMMENT MADE ABRUPTLY** something said loudly and abruptly or inserted in a text, especially something that interrupts what is being said or discussed —**in·ter·jec·tion·al** *adj.* —**in·ter·jec·tion·al·ly** *adv.*

in·ter·ki·ne·sis /intər ki néessiss, -kī-/ *n.* the period of rest between meiotic cell divisions, similar to the interphase stage in mitosis

in·ter·lace /intər láyss/ (**-laced, -lac·ing, -lac·es**) *v.* **1.** *vti.* **WEAVE TOGETHER** to join together or interweave, often in an intricate pattern, by crossing over each other, or to cause two or more things to do this **2.** *vt.* **BREAK UP SOMETHING WITH SOMETHING ELSE** to break up the flow or relieve the monotony of something by occasionally inserting something different such as jokes in a serious talk [14thC. From Old French *entrelacier*, literally "to lace together," from *lacier* "to lace."] —**in·ter·lace·ment** *n.*

in·ter·laced /intərláyst/ *adj.* ELECTRON ENG refreshing the image on a monitor screen by scanning first all odd and then all even numbered lines

in·ter·laced scan·ning *n.* a technique used in television and computer monitors in which high vertical resolution is achieved by scanning all odd and then all even numbered lines

in·ter·lan·guage /intər làngwidj/ *n.* LANG a form of language typically produced by learners of a second language or foreign language, which combines elements of two or more languages

in·ter·lard /intər laárd/ (**-lard·ed, -lard·ing, -lards**) *vt.* to vary or interrupt speech or writing by interspersing other contrasting words [Mid-16thC. From French *entrelarder* "to mix alternating layers of fat into lean meat," from *larde* "lard."]

in·ter·lay *vt.* /intər láy/ (**-laid,** /intər láyd/ **-laid, -lay·ing, -lays**) **PUT SOMETHING BETWEEN SOMETHING** to lay or layer something between something else ■ *n.* /intər lày/ **INSERTED LAYER** something laid between two surfaces

in·ter·leaf /intər léef/ (*plural* **-leaves** /-léevz/) *n.* an extra sheet or page, usually a blank one, inserted into a book

in·ter·leave /intər léev/ (**-leaved, -leav·ing, -leaves**) *vt.* to add extra sheets or pages, usually blank ones, between the pages of a book, e.g., to allow for notes or to protect illustrations [Mid-17thC. Formed from INTER- + LEAF.]

in·ter·leu·kin /intər lóokin/ *n.* a chemical found in white blood cells that stimulates them to fight infection [Late 20thC. Coined from INTER- + LEUKOCYTE + -IN.]

in·ter·leu·kin-1 *n.* an interleukin secreted by antigen-activated macrophages that stimulates the production of other factors that activate the immune system

in·ter·leu·kin-2 *n.* an interleukin that stimulates T-cells and is used in the treatment of cancer

in·ter·li·brar·y loan /intər līb rerree-/ *n.* **1. BOOK-BORROWING SYSTEM** a system by which libraries and library users can borrow books from other libraries **2. BORROWING OF A BOOK** a borrowing of a book through an interlibrary loan system **3. BOOK BORROWED** a book borrowed through an interlibrary loan system

in·ter·line[1] /intər lín/ (**-lined, -lin·ing, -lines**) *vt.* to write or print words between the lines of writing or printing in a text or document [15thC. From medieval Latin *interlineare*, from Latin *linea* (see LINE[1]).] —**in·ter·lin·e·a·tion** /intər linnee áysh'n/ *n.*

in·ter·line[2] /intər lín/ (**-lined, -lin·ing, -lines**) *vt.* to put an extra lining, usually of a stiffer material, between the fabric and the lining of a piece of clothing [15thC. Formed from INTER- + LINE[2].]

in·ter·lin·e·ar /intər línnee ər/, **in·ter·lin·e·al** /intər línnee əl/ *adj.* **1. INSERTED BETWEEN LINES** inserted between the lines of a text or document **2. HAVING ALTERNATING VERSIONS OF TEXT** written or printed with different versions of the same text on alternate or succeeding lines [14thC. Via medieval Latin *interlinearis* from, ultimately, Latin *linea* (see LINE[1]).] —**in·ter·lin·e·ar·ly** *adv.*

In·ter·lin·gua /íntər líng gwə/ *n.* a made-up language designed to facilitate international communication, based on the common elements of living Latinate languages [Early 20thC. Coined from INTER- + Latin *lingua* "tongue, language."]

in·ter·lin·ing /íntər līning/ *n.* an extra lining inserted between the fabric and lining of a piece of clothing to provide extra thickness or warmth, or the fabric used for this

in·ter·link /íntər língk/ (**-linked, -link·ing, -links**) *vti.* to connect something with something else in several ways, or be connected together in several ways

in·ter·lock /íntər lók/ (**-locked, -lock·ing, -locks**) *vti.* **1. FIT TOGETHER CLOSELY** to fit or fasten two or more things together closely and firmly, especially by means of parts that mesh, hook, or dovetail together, or to be fitted together in this way **2. OPERATE AS A UNIT** to connect together as parts in such a way that all must move or operate if one does, or to be connected in this way ■ *n.* /íntər lòk/ **1. CONNECTING AND COORDINATING DEVICE** a device or mechanism that connects different parts or components of something such as a piece of machinery in order to coordinate and synchronize their action **2. CLOSE CONNECTION** a close connection by means of parts that fit or fasten together closely and firmly **3.** TEXTILES **TIGHTLY-KNITTED FABRIC** a fabric made with tightly-knitted stitches **4.** SEW **CANVAS FOR NEEDLEPOINT** a type of canvas used for needlepoint that has the warp and weft threads knotted together to prevent movement **5.** COMPUT **COMPUTER SECURITY DEVICE** a security device such as a password system designed to prevent unauthorized use of a computer ■ *adj.* TEXTILES **TIGHTLY-KNITTED** knitted with close, tight stitches

in·ter·lock·ing di·rec·tor·ates *npl.* boards of directors that have enough members in common to place the companies that they oversee under the same control

in·ter·loc·u·tor /íntər lókyətər/ *n.* **1. MINSTREL SHOW PERFORMER** a performer in a minstrel show who acted as the presenter and stood in the middle and bantered with the end men **2. SOMEBODY DISCUSSING** somebody who takes part in a discussion or conversation (*formal*) [Early 16thC. From modern Latin, formed from Latin *interlocut-*, the past participle stem of *interloqui* "to interrupt," literally "to speak between," from *loqui* (see LOQUACIOUS).]

in·ter·loc·u·to·ry /íntər lókyə tàwree/ *adj.* **1.** LAW **ISSUED PROVISIONALLY** issued provisionally during a lawsuit **2. INVOLVING DISCUSSION** involving or characteristic of conversation or discussion (*formal*)

in·ter·lop·er /íntər lōpər/ *n.* **1. INTRUDER** somebody who enters a place or joins a group or gathering without any right to do so **2. SOMEBODY WHO INTERFERES** somebody who interferes in other people's affairs, especially selfishly [Late 16thC. Modeled on earlier *landloper* "vagabond," from Middle Dutch *landlooper*, literally "land-runner," from *land* "land" + *loopen* "to run." The word originally meant "an unauthorized trader."]

in·ter·lude /íntər lood/ *n.* **1. INTERVENING PERIOD OF TIME** a relatively short period of time between two longer periods, during which something happens that is different from what has happened before and what follows **2.** ARTS **ENTERTAINMENT DURING A PERFORMANCE BREAK** a short play, piece of music, or other entertainment performed during a break in the performance of a long work [14thC. From medieval Latin *interludium*, literally "in-between-play" (because it was originally performed between the acts of a long medieval mystery play), from Latin *ludus* "play."]

in·ter·mar·riage /íntər mérrij/ *n.* **1. MARRIAGE BETWEEN DIFFERENT GROUPS** marriage between members of different religious, social, or racial groups, or an instance of this **2. MARRIAGE WITHIN A GROUP** marriage between people who belong to the same religious, social, or racial group, or an instance of this [Early 17thC. The word was used earlier in the general sense "marriage."]

in·ter·mar·ry /íntər mérree/ (**-ried, -ry·ing, -ries**) *vi.* **1. MARRY MEMBER OF ANOTHER GROUP** to marry a member of a different religious, social, or racial group **2. MARRY WITHIN A GROUP** to marry within a religious, social, or racial group [Early 17thC. The word was used earlier in the general sense "to marry."]

in·ter·me·di·ar·y /íntər meédee èrree/ *n.* (*plural* **-ies**) **1. GO-BETWEEN** somebody who goes from one person or group to another, carrying messages or trying to bring about agreement **2. MEANS OR MEDIUM** something that functions as a means or medium for bringing something about ■ *adj.* **1. MEDIATING** acting as a messenger or mediator between two or more people or groups **2. LYING IN BETWEEN** lying or occurring between two different forms, states, points, or extremes [Late 18thC. Via French *intermédiaire* from, ultimately, Latin *intermedius* (see INTERMEDIATE[1]).]

in·ter·me·di·ate[1] /íntər meédee ət/ *adj.* **1. BEING IN BETWEEN** lying or occurring between two different forms, states, points, or extremes ○ *an intermediate course* **2.** GEOL **CONTAINING BETWEEN 55% AND 66% SILICA** used to describe an igneous rock with a silica content of between 55 percent and 66 percent ■ *n.* **1. SOMETHING BETWEEN TWO OTHER THINGS** something that lies or occurs between two different forms, states, points, or extremes **2.** = **intermediary** *n.* 1 **3.** CHEM **CHEMICAL FOR FURTHER REACTIONS** a chemical compound that is formed during a chemical reaction and is used in another reaction to obtain another compound **4.** CHEM **SHORT-LIVED CHEMICAL COMPONENT** a molecule, ion, or free radical that exists for a short time during a chemical reaction [15thC. Directly or via French from medieval Latin *intermediatus*, from Latin *intermedius*, from *medius* "middle."] —**in·ter·me·di·ate·ly** *adv.* —**in·ter·me·di·ate·ness** *n.*

in·ter·me·di·ate[2] /íntər meédee àyt/ (**-at·ed, -at·ing, -ates**) *vi.* to act as a go-between or mediator between two or more people or groups [Early 16thC. Formed from INTER- + MEDIATE.] —**in·ter·me·di·a·tion** /íntər meedee áysh'n/ *n.* —**in·ter·me·di·a·tor** /íntər meédee àytər/ *n.*

in·ter·me·di·ate-act·ing *adj.* PHARM having a period of therapeutic activity that is between that of long-acting and short-acting drugs

in·ter·me·di·ate bulk con·tain·er *n.* a portable container for transporting liquids or solids that holds 132 to 264 gallons/500 to 1,000 liters or 1,100 to 3,300 lbs./500 to 1,500 kg. It is intermediate in size between a drum and a tanker load.

in·ter·me·di·ate fre·quen·cy *n.* the frequency that an incoming signal is changed to in a heterodyne receiver prior to amplification

in·ter·me·di·ate host *n.* an animal that is the host for an immature parasite, which then moves on to a different host before reproducing

in·ter·me·di·ate-lev·el waste *n.* radioactive waste from reactors and processing plants that is solidified, mixed with concrete, and stored in drums. These drums are then placed for long-term storage in waste repositories.

in·ter·me·di·ate-range bal·lis·tic mis·sile *n.* a ballistic missile that has a range of 750 to 1,000 mi./1,200 to 1,600 km. ◊ **intercontinental ballistic missile**

in·ter·me·di·ate school *n.* = **junior high, middle school**

in·ter·me·di·ate vec·tor bo·son *n.* an electrically neutral elementary particle that transmits weak interactions between other elementary particles. The three postulated intermediate vector bosons, the W^+, W^-, and Z^0 particles, have all been observed.

in·ter·me·din /íntər meéd'n/ *n.* PHYSIOL = **melanocyte-stimulating hormone** [Mid-20thC. Coined from modern Latin *(pars) intermedia* "intermediate (part) (of the pituitary)" (from Latin *intermedius*) + -IN.]

in·ter·ment /in túrmənt/ *n.* the burial of a dead body or the ashes of a cremated body (*formal*) [14thC. Formed from INTER.]

in·ter·mesh /íntər mésh/ (**-meshed, -mesh·ing, -mesh·es**) *vti.* to engage or mesh with one another, or to cause something such as the teeth of gears to do so

in·ter·me·tal·lic /íntərmə tállik/ *adj.* consisting of two or more metals in specific proportions

in·ter·mez·zo /íntər mét sō/ (*plural* **-zos** *or* **-zi** /-métsee/) *n.* **1. SHORT MOVEMENT IN A LONGER MUSICAL WORK** a short piece of music that is performed between longer movements of an extended musical composition **2. SHORT PIECE OF MUSIC** a short musical composition, usually for solo piano **3.** = **interlude** *n.* 2 [Late 18thC. Via Italian from Latin *intermedius* "intermediate," from *medius* "middle."]

in·ter·mi·na·ble /in túrminəb'l/ *adj.* so long and boring or frustrating as to seem endless ○ *interminable delays* [14thC. Directly or via French from late Latin *interminabilis*, literally "unending," from Latin *terminare* (see TERMINATE).] —**in·ter·mi·na·bil·i·ty** /in tùrmənə bíllətee/ *n.* —**in·ter·mi·na·bly** /in túrmənəblee/ *adv.*

in·ter·min·gle /íntər míng g'l/ (**-gled, -gling, -gles**) *vti.* to mix something together with something else, or to become mixed together ○ *the scents of jasmine and honeysuckle intermingled*

in·ter·mis·sion /íntər mísh'n/ *n.* **1. BREAK IN PERFORMANCE** a break between parts of a musical or theatrical performance or in the showing of a movie in a movie theater **2. PAUSE** a pause in, or temporary discontinuation of, an activity [15thC. Directly or via French from the Latin stem *intermission-*, from *intermiss-*, the past participle stem of *intermittere* (see INTERMIT).]

in·ter·mit /íntər mít/ (**-mit·ted, -mit·ting, -mits**) *vti.* (*formal*) **1. DISCONTINUE** to discontinue doing something temporarily, or to be discontinued temporarily **2. PAUSE** to stop or cause something to stop for a short time or for short intervals [Mid-16thC. From Latin *intermittere* "to interrupt," literally "to send between," from *mittere* (see MISSION).] —**in·ter·mit·ter** *n.* —**in·ter·mit·ting·ly** *adv.*

in·ter·mit·tent /íntər mítt'nt/ *adj.* happening or coming from time to time [Mid-16thC. From Latin *intermittere* "to interrupt" (see INTERMIT).] —**in·ter·mit·tence** *n.* —**in·ter·mit·tent·ly** *adv.*

WORD KEY: SYNONYMS

See Synonyms at ***periodic***.

in·ter·mit·tent clau·di·ca·tion *n.* a cramping pain, induced by exercise and relieved by rest, that is caused by inadequate blood supply to the affected muscles, usually the calves

in·ter·mit·tent cur·rent *n.* a unidirectional current that is interrupted periodically

in·ter·mit·tent fe·ver *n.* a fever that rises and falls and then returns, occurring in diseases such as malaria

in·ter·mix /íntər míks/ (**-mixed, -mix·ing, -mix·es**) *vti.* = **intermingle** [Mid-16thC. From Latin *intermixtus*, the past participle of *intermiscere*, literally "to mix together," from *miscere* (see MIXED).] —**in·ter·mix·a·ble** *adj.*

in·ter·mod·al /íntər mód'l/ *adj.* **TRANSPORTABLE BY VARIOUS MEANS** used to describe containers designed to be transferred from one means of transportation to another while in transit, e.g., from a train to a ship to a truck ■ *n.* **FREIGHT CONTAINER** a container for freight that can be transferred from one means of transportation to another during shipment without being unpacked

in·ter·mod·u·la·tion /íntər mojjə láysh'n/ *n.* the undesired interaction of electronic signals or complex wave components to produce waves with frequencies equal to the sums and differences of integral multiples of the frequencies of the signals

in·ter·mo·lec·u·lar /íntərmə lékyələr/ *adj.* occurring between molecules, or involving two or more molecules —**in·ter·mo·lec·u·lar·ly** *adv.*

in·ter·mon·tane /íntər món tàyn/ *adj.* used to describe basins lying between two mountain ranges, and often filling up with sediment washed down from them [Early 19thC. Formed from INTER- + MONTANE.]

in·ter·mu·ral /íntər myóorəl/ *adj.* involving participants from two or more educational institutions, athletic clubs, or other groups. ◊ **intramural** [Modeled on INTRAMURAL]

in·tern /íntərn/, **in·terne** *n.* **1. JUNIOR HOSPITAL DOCTOR** a junior doctor at a hospital **2. TRAINEE** somebody who works as a low-level assistant or trainee in an occupation in order to gain practical experience ■ *v.* (**-terned, -tern·ing, -terns**) **1.** *vi.* **WORK AS AN INTERN** to work as an intern, especially in a hospital **2.** *vt.* **DETAIN SOMEBODY** to detain somebody in confinement as being a security threat [Mid-19thC. The noun is via French *interne*; the verb via *interner*, both ultimately from Latin *internus* (see INTERNAL).]

in·ter·nal /in túrn'l/ *adj.* **1. LOCATED INSIDE** located within or affecting the inside of something, especially the inside of the body ○ *internal organs* **2. INTENDED FOR USE INSIDE** effective when used or suitable for use inside of something, especially the inside of the body **3. SELF-CONTAINED OR SELF-GENERATING** existing, evident in, or arising from the nature, structure, or qualities that somebody or something has ○ *internal cohesion* **4. OCCURRING WITHIN A COUNTRY** originating, operating, or located within a country's borders

○ *internal affairs* **5.** MENTAL involving or existing within the mind or spirit ○ *internal conflict* **6.** OCCURRING WITHIN AN ORGANIZATION working at or carried out within an organization or institution ○ *internal e-mail* [15thC. Directly or via Old French *internel* from medieval Latin *internalis*, from Latin *internus* "inward, within," from *inter* (see INTER-).] —**in·ter·nal·i·ty** /intər nállətee/ *n.* —**in·ter·nal·ly** /in túrnəlee/ *adv.* —**in·ter·nal·ness** /-n'lnəss/ *n.*

in·ter·nal-com·bus·tion en·gine *n.* an engine in which fuel is burned in combustion chambers within the engine instead of in an external furnace and in which the energy released moves one or more pistons

in·ter·nal en·er·gy *n.* the total kinetic energy of the atoms and molecules of a system plus the potential energy of their mutual interaction. An increase in internal energy manifests as a rise in temperature or a change in phase. Symbol *U*

in·ter·nal·ize /in túrn'l ìz/ (**-ized, -iz·ing, -iz·es**) *vt.* **1.** ADOPT OTHERS' BELIEFS to adopt the beliefs, values, and attitudes of others, either consciously or unconsciously **2.** KEEP A PROBLEM INSIDE to deal with an emotion or conflict by thinking about it rather than expressing it openly —**in·ter·nal·i·za·tion** /in tùrn'li záysh'n/ *n.*

in·ter·nal med·i·cine *n.* the branch of medicine concerned with the diagnosis and nonsurgical treatment of diseases affecting the internal organs, and with preventive medicine

in·ter·nal re·sis·tance *n.* the resistance within a source of electric current such as a cell or generator

in·ter·nal res·pi·ra·tion *n.* the metabolic use of oxygen by a cell to produce energy, resulting in the release of carbon dioxide

In·ter·nal Rev·e·nue Ser·vice *n.* the division of the U.S. Department of the Treasury responsible for the collection of income, excise, and other taxes and the enforcement of the tax laws

in·ter·nal rhyme *n.* a rhyme in which one of the rhyming words is within the line of poetry and the other is at the end of the same line or within the next line

in·ter·nal se·cre·tion *n.* a secretion, especially a hormone, that is absorbed into the blood directly after production

in·ter·nal wave *n.* a waveform that develops below the surface of a body of water where two water masses with different densities meet. An internal wave can develop in an estuary where salt water lies underneath less dense river water.

internat. *abbr.* international

in·ter·na·tion·al /intər náshən'l, -náshnəl/ *adj.* **1.** INVOLVING SEVERAL COUNTRIES involving two or more countries or their citizens **2.** CROSSING NATIONAL BOUNDARIES extending beyond or across national boundaries **3.** OF RELATIONS AMONG NATIONS concerned with relations between nations ■ *n.* **1.** INTERNATIONAL ORGANIZATION an organization that has offices or branches in two or more countries **2.** MEMBER OF AN INTERNATIONAL TEAM a member of a team representing his or her country in an international event —**in·ter·na·tion·al·i·ty** /intər nashə nállətee/ *n.* —**in·ter·na·tion·al·ly** /-náshən'lee, -náshnəlee/ *adv.*

In·ter·na·tion·al *n.* any of four international Socialist, Communist, or Anarchist organizations formed in 1864, 1889, 1919, and 1938 respectively

In·ter·na·tion·al A·tom·ic Time *n.* a precisely determined system of measuring time in which a second is defined in terms of atomic events that are known to a high degree of accuracy

In·ter·na·tion·al Bank for Re·con·struc·tion and De·vel·op·ment *n.* = **World Bank**

In·ter·na·tion·al Bri·gade *n.* any of seven mainly Communist and Socialist forces of volunteers from many different countries that fought on the Republican side during the Spanish Civil War

in·ter·na·tional can·dle *n.* a former unit of luminous intensity, now replaced by the candela

In·ter·na·tion·al Court of Jus·tice *n.* the chief judicial body of the United Nations, empowered to resolve international disputes between member nations who submit a case to the court

In·ter·na·tion·al Crim·i·nal Po·lice Or·ga·ni·za·tion *n.* full form of **Interpol**

In·ter·na·tion·al Date Line *n.* an internationally agreed imaginary line running roughly along the 180° meridian of longitude. To the east of the line the date is one day earlier than to the west.

In·ter·na·tion·al De·vel·op·ment As·so·ci·a·tion *n.* a specialized agency of the United Nations that provides credit to nations on easier terms than the World Bank

In·ter·na·tion·ale /intər nashə nál/ *n.* a revolutionary Socialist song written in France in 1871 and adopted as the anthem of the First, Second, and Third Internationals. A Russian version was the national anthem of the Soviet Union until 1944. [Early 20thC. From French *(chanson) internationale* "international (song)."]

In·ter·na·tion·al Fi·nance Cor·po·ra·tion *n.* a specialized agency of the United Nations that is affiliated with the World Bank and promotes private enterprise in developing nations by providing risk capital

In·ter·na·tion·al Goth·ic *n.* a style of painting and other visual art that emerged in Europe with the increasing exchange of ideas and techniques among European artists toward the end of the 14th century

In·ter·na·tion·al Grand·mas·ter *n.* a chess player who has achieved the highest ranking awarded to a participant in international competitions

in·ter·na·tion·al·ism /intər náshən'l ìzzəm, -náshnə lìzzəm/ *n.* **1.** COOPERATION BETWEEN COUNTRIES a policy or spirit of cooperation and mutual understanding between countries **2.** INTEREST IN OTHER COUNTRIES a willingness and ability to understand and respect the concerns, attitudes, and ways of life of other countries **3.** INTERNATIONAL CHARACTER OR QUALITY the international character or quality of somebody or something

in·ter·na·tion·al·ist /intər náshən'list, -náshnəlist/ *n.* **1.** ADVOCATE OF INTERNATIONAL COOPERATION somebody who favors greater cooperation and understanding between countries **2.** SOMEBODY INTERESTED IN OTHER COUNTRIES somebody who is interested in other countries and understands and respects their peoples' concerns, attitudes, and ways of life **3.** = **international** *n.* **2** ■ *adj.* FAVORING INTERNATIONAL COOPERATION favoring greater cooperation and understanding between countries

in·ter·na·tion·al·ize /intər náshən'l ìz, -náshnə lìz/ (**-ized, -iz·ing, -iz·es**) *vt.* **1.** MAKE SOMETHING INTERNATIONAL to make something international in character, structure, or outlook **2.** PUT SOMETHING UNDER INTERNATIONAL CONTROL to place something under the protection or control of several countries instead of one country —**in·ter·na·tion·al·i·za·tion** /intər nash'nəli záysh'n, -náshnəli záysh'n/ *n.*

in·ter·na·tion·al law *n.* the accepted rules that govern countries in their relations with other countries

In·ter·na·tion·al Mas·ter *n.* a chess player who has achieved a high ranking in international competitions that is below that of an International Grandmaster

In·ter·na·tion·al Mon·e·tar·y Fund *n.* a specialized agency of the United Nations that seeks to promote international monetary cooperation and the stabilization of national currencies and help nations resolve balance of payment problems

In·ter·na·tion·al Morse code *n.* the form of Morse code used internationally

In·ter·na·tion·al Pho·net·ic Al·pha·bet *n.* a system of letters and marks, based for the most part on the letters of the Roman alphabet, that is used internationally to represent the speech sounds of languages

In·ter·na·tion·al Prac·ti·cal Tem·per·a·ture Scale *n.* a scientific temperature scale, expressed in degrees Celsius, that has eleven fixed temperature reference points, including the boiling point of oxygen and the freezing point of gold

in·ter·na·tion·al re·la·tions *npl.* RELATIONS BETWEEN COUNTRIES political and other dealings between two or more countries ■ *n.* STUDY OF RELATIONS BETWEEN COUNTRIES the branch of political science that studies the relations between countries (*takes a singular verb*)

In·ter·na·tion·al Stan·dards Or·ga·ni·za·tion *n.* an international organization established in 1947 to standardize such things as units of measurement and the meanings of technical terms

International Style: Studio building (1925) at the Bauhaus, Dessau, Germany

In·ter·na·tion·al Style *n.* **1.** = **International Gothic 2.** EARLY 20THC ARCHITECTURAL STYLE an early 20th-century architectural style in the United States and Europe that favored the use of simple geometric lines, spacious interiors, and materials such as steel and reinforced concrete

In·ter·na·tion·al Sys·tem of U·nits *n.* an internationally accepted system of units of measurement used for scientific work. The basic units are the meter, kilogram, second, kelvin, mole, ampere, and candela, these being the basic quantities of length, mass, time, temperature, amount of substance, electric current, and luminous intensity.

in·ter·na·tion·al u·nit *n.* an internationally agreed unit of the amount of a biologically active substance such as a hormone or vitamin required to produce a specific response

in·terne *n.* = **intern**

in·ter·nec·ine /intər né seen, ìntər née seen/ *adj.* **1.** INTERNAL occurring within a group or organization **2.** MUTUALLY DESTRUCTIVE damaging or injuring participants on both sides of a conflict or struggle [Mid-17thC. From Latin *internecinus* "deadly," from *internecare* "to exterminate," literally "to kill completely," from *necare* "to kill," from *nex* "death" (source of English *pernicious*).]

WORD KEY: ORIGIN

The original meaning of ***internecine*** is "attended by great slaughter." Its modern connotations of "conflict within a group," which can be traced back to the 18th century (Samuel Johnson in his *Dictionary* (1755) defined it as "endeavoring mutual destruction"), arose from the standard interpretation of *inter-* as "among, between," but in fact in the case of Latin *internecinus* it was being used simply to add emphasis.

in·tern·ee /intər née/ *n.* somebody who is confined in prison, a concentration camp, or other place, especially during a war

in·ter·ne·sia /intər néezhə/ *n.* an inability to remember either the location or information contained in a World Wide Web site (*informal*) [Combination of INTERNET + AMNESIA]

In·ter·net /íntər nèt/ *n.* a network that links computer networks all over the world by satellite and telephone, connecting users with service networks such as e-mail and the World Wide Web

In·ter·net pro·to·col *n.* the standard that controls the routing and structure of data transmitted over the Internet

In·ter·net ser·vice pro·vid·er *n.* a business that provides access to the Internet, usually for a monthly fee. Some large providers offer users a wide range of news, information, and entertainment services.

in·ter·neu·ron /intər nòo ròn/ *n.* a short nerve cell in the central nervous system that connects the nerve cells in a reflex arc, e.g., a sensory nerve to a motor nerve —**in·ter·neu·ro·nal** /intər nóorən'l, ìntər nòo rṓn'l/ *adj.*

in·ter·nist /in túrnist/ *n.* a doctor who specializes in the diagnosis, prevention, and nonsurgical treatment of diseases affecting the internal organs [Early 20thC. Formed from INTERNAL + -IST.]

in·tern·ment /in túrnmənt/ *n.* the confinement of somebody regarded as a security threat in a prison, concentration camp, or other place, especially during a war

in·ter·node /íntər nōd/ *n.* **1.** BOT **STEM SECTION BETWEEN TWO NODES** the part of a plant stem between two nodes **2.** ANAT **NERVE CELL PART** the part of the axon of a nerve cell that lies between the nodes of Ranvier. The internode is covered by the myelin sheath, which is absent at the nodes. [Mid-17thC. From Latin *internodium,* from *nodus* "knot."] —**in·ter·nod·al** /ìntər nṓd'l/ *adj.*

in·ter nos /íntər nṓss/ *adv.* between or among ourselves [From Latin]

in·tern·ship /íntərn shìp/ *n.* the position of an intern or a period of time working as one

in·ter·nun·cial /ìntər núnshəl/ *adj.* **1.** ANAT **CONNECTING** used to describe nerve cells that connect one nerve cell to another **2.** CHR **OF A PAPAL INTERNUNCIO** acting as or connected with an internuncio of the Roman Catholic Church —**in·ter·nun·cial·ly** *adv.*

in·ter·nun·ci·o /ìntər núnsee ō/ (*plural* **-os**) *n.* **1. PAPAL AMBASSADOR** a diplomatic representative of the pope ranking below a nuncio **2. GO-BETWEEN** a messenger or go-between (*formal*) [Mid-17thC. Via Italian *internunzio* from Latin *internuntius,* literally "intermediate messenger," from *nuntius* (see NUNCIO).]

in·ter·o·ce·an·ic /ìntər ōshee ánnik/ *adj.* occurring between or connecting two or more oceans

in·ter·of·fice /ìntər óffiss/ *adj.* occurring between offices or involving two or more offices in the same organization ○ *an interoffice memo*

interp. *abbr.* interpreter

in·ter·per·son·al /ìntər púrsən'l/ *adj.* concerning or involving relationships between people —**in·ter·per·son·al·ly** *adv.*

in·ter·pha·lan·ge·al /ìntərfə lánjee əl/ *adj.* situated between the bones of the fingers or toes

in·ter·phase /íntər fàyz/ *n.* the period during which a cell is not actively dividing, when other activities such as DNA synthesis take place

in·ter·plan·e·tar·y /ìntər plánnə tèrree/ *adj.* situated, happening, or moving between planets or involving two or more planets

in·ter·play /íntər plày/ *n.* the way in which two or more people or things repeatedly act on and react to each other

in·ter·plead /ìntər pleéd/ (**-plead·ed** *or* **-pled, -plead·ed** *or* **-pled** /ìntər pléd/, **-plead·ing, -pleads**) *vi.* to go to trial to resolve which of several claimants has the right to claim money or property held by a third party [Mid-16thC. From Anglo-Norman *enterpleder,* literally "to plead together," from *pleder* (see PLEAD).]

in·ter·plead·er /ìntər pleédər/ *n.* a trial to resolve which of several claimants can sue for money or property held by a third party. The third party institutes an interpleader to avoid several individual proceedings. [Mid-16thC. From Anglo-Norman *enterpleder* (see INTERPLEAD).]

In·ter·pol /íntər pàwl/ *n.* an association of national police forces, established in 1923, that promotes cooperation and mutual assistance in apprehending international criminals and criminals who flee abroad to avoid justice. The headquarters of Interpol is in Paris. Full form **International Criminal Police Organization**

in·ter·po·late /in túrpə làyt/ (**-lat·ed, -lat·ing, -lates**) *v.* **1.** *vt.* **INSERT SOMETHING INTO SOMETHING ELSE** to add something, often something unnecessary, between the existing elements or items of something else **2.** *vt.* **ADD WORDS TO A TEXT** to add a comment or extra words to a written text, often altering or falsifying the meaning **3.** *vt.* **ALTER TEXT** to alter or deliberately falsify a text by adding a comment or extra words to it **4.** *vti.* **INTERRUPT BY SAYING SOMETHING** to say something that interrupts what somebody else is saying **5.** *vt.* MATH **ESTIMATE THE VALUE OF A MATHEMATICAL FUNCTION** to estimate the value of a mathematical function that lies between known values, often by means of a graph [Early 17thC. From Latin *interpolare,* literally "to polish up." The underlying meaning is "to add new material so as make a book appear more recent."] —**in·ter·po·la·tion** /in tùrpə láysh'n/ *n.* —**in·ter·po·la·tive** /in túrpə làytiv/ *adj.* —**in·ter·po·la·tor** /in túrpə làytər/ *n.*

in·ter·pose /ìntər pṓz/ (**-posed, -pos·ing, -pos·es**) *v.* **1.** *vti.* **INTERRUPT BY SAYING SOMETHING** to say something that interrupts what somebody else is saying **2.** *vt.* **PLACE BETWEEN PEOPLE OR THINGS** to place yourself or something else between two people or things **3.** *vti.* **INTERVENE WITH SOMETHING** to intervene or interfere in a situation such as a dispute [Late 16thC. From French *interposer,* an alteration (influenced by *poser* "to place") of Latin *interponere,* literally "to place between," from *ponere* (see POSITION).] —**in·ter·pos·a·ble** *adj.* —**in·ter·pos·al** *n.* —**in·ter·pos·er** *n.* —**in·ter·po·si·tion** /ìntərpə zísh'n/ *n.*

in·ter·pret /in túrprət/ (**-pret·ed, -pret·ing, -prets**) *v.* **1.** *vt.* **FIND THE MEANING OF SOMETHING** to establish or explain the meaning or significance of something **2.** *vt.* **ASCRIBE A MEANING TO** to ascribe a particular meaning or significance to something ○ *I interpreted his gesture as an invitation.* **3.** *vt.* **PERFORM SOMETHING IN PARTICULAR WAY** to perform something such as a play or piece of music in a way that conveys particular ideas or feelings about it **4.** *vti.* LANG **TRANSLATE SOMETHING** to translate what is said in one language into another so that speakers of different languages can communicate **5.** *vt.* COMPUT **EXECUTE A COMPUTER PROGRAM** to convert instructions in a computer program written in a high-level language into machine language and execute them, one instruction at a time [14thC. Directly or via French *interpréter* from Latin *interpretari* "to explain," from *interpret-,* the stem of *interpres* "broker, explainer, translator."] —**in·ter·pret·a·ble** *adj.* —**in·ter·pret·a·bil·i·ty** /in tùrprətə bíllətee/ *n.* —**in·ter·pret·a·bly** /in túrprətəblee/ *adv.*

in·ter·pre·ta·tion /in tùrprə táysh'n/ *n.* **1. ESTABLISHMENT OF MEANING** an explanation or establishment of the meaning or significance of something **2. ASCRIPTION OF PARTICULAR MEANING** an ascription of a particular meaning or significance to something **3. PERFORMANCE OF SOMETHING** the way in which an artistic work, e.g., a play or piece of music, is performed so as to convey a particular understanding of the work **4. TRANSLATION** the oral translation of what is said in one language into another, so that speakers of different languages can communicate —**in·ter·pre·ta·tion·al** *adj.*

in·ter·pre·ta·tive *adj.* = **interpretive**

in·ter·pret·er /in túrprətər/ *n.* **1. TRANSLATOR** somebody who translates orally what is said in one language into another language, so that speakers of different languages can communicate **2. PERFORMER EXPRESSING PARTICULAR IDEAS** somebody who performs something such as a play or piece of music in a way that expresses particular ideas or feelings about it **3.** COMPUT **PROGRAM EXECUTING INSTRUCTIONS** a computer program that translates the instructions in a program written in a high-level computer language into machine language and executes them, processing one instruction at a time —**in·ter·pre·ter·ship** /in túrprətər shìp/ *n.*

in·ter·pre·tive /in túrprətiv/, **in·ter·pre·ta·tive** /in túrprə tàytiv/ *adj.* relating to, involving, or providing an interpretation or explanation of something —**in·ter·pre·tive·ly** *adv.*

in·ter·pre·tive cen·ter *n.* = **visitor center**

in·ter·pro·vin·cial /ìntər prə vínshəl/ *adj.* occurring between provinces, or connecting or involving two or more provinces

in·ter·pu·pil·lar·y /ìntər pyóop'l èrree/ *adj.* between the pupils of the eyes

in·ter·quar·tile range /ìntər kwàwr tīl-, -kwàwrt'l-/ *n.* a measure of the spread of a group of values equal to the difference between the upper limit for the lower quarter and the lower limit for the upper quarter

in·ter·ra·cial /ìntər ráysh'l/ *adj.* occurring between or involving different races —**in·ter·ra·cial·ly** *adv.*

in·ter·re·gion·al /ìntər reéjən'l/ *adj.* occurring between regions or involving two or more regions

in·ter·reg·num /ìntər régnəm/ (*plural* **-nums** *or* **-na** /-régnə/) *n.* **1. TIME BETWEEN ONE REIGN AND THE NEXT** the period of time between the end of one reign or regime and the beginning of the next **2. TIME WITHOUT GOVERNMENT OR CONTROL** a period of time during which there is no government, control, or authority **3. INTERRUPTION** a pause or gap in any continuous activity or series [Late 16thC. From Latin, "period between kingships," from *regnum* (see REIGN). Originally the English word denoted the "temporary authority in place between reigns."] —**in·ter·reg·nal** *adj.*

in·ter·re·late /ìntəri láyt/ (**-lat·ed, -lat·ing, -lates**) *vti.* to have a relationship in which each person or thing depends on or is affected by the others, or to cause persons or things to have such a relationship —**in·ter·re·la·tion** *n.* —**in·ter·re·la·tion·ship** *n.*

in·ter·re·nal /ìntər reén'l/ *adj.* situated between or connecting the kidneys

in·ter·ro·bang /in térrə bàng/, **in·ter·a·bang** *n.* a punctuation mark used at the end of, or sometimes in place of, an utterance that is both question and exclamation, especially to indicate an emphatic rhetorical question or disbelief [Mid-20thC. Blend of INTERROGATION MARK and BANG[1] (printers' slang for an exclamation point).]

interrog. *abbr.* **1.** interrogate **2.** interrogation **3.** interrogative

in·ter·ro·gate /in térrə gàyt/ (**-gat·ed, -gat·ing, -gates**) *vt.* **1. QUESTION SOMEBODY THOROUGHLY** to question somebody thoroughly, often in an aggressive or threatening manner and especially as part of a formal investigation, e.g., in a police station or courtroom **2.** COMPUT **REQUEST A RESPONSE FROM A COMPUTER PART** to transmit a request for information to a device or program with the expectation that an immediate response will trigger further interaction [15thC. From Latin *interrogare,* literally "to ask in the presence of," from *rogare* (see ROGATION).] —**in·ter·ro·ga·tee** /in tèrrə gay teé/ *n.* —**in·ter·ro·ga·tor** /in térrə gàytər/ *n.*

in·ter·ro·ga·tion /in tèrrə gáysh'n/ *n.* **1. THOROUGH QUESTIONING** the act or process of questioning somebody closely, often in an aggressive manner, especially as part of a official investigation or trial **2. QUESTION** a question (*formal*) **3.** COMPUT **TRANSMISSION OF A SIGNAL TO A COMPUTER** the transmission of a signal to a device or program that triggers a response —**in·ter·ro·ga·tion·al** *adj.*

in·ter·ro·ga·tion point, in·ter·ro·ga·tion mark *n.* = **question mark**

in·ter·rog·a·tive /ìntə róggətiv/ *adj.* **1. QUESTIONING** questioning or seeming to question somebody or something **2.** GRAM **USED TO ASK A QUESTION** consisting of or used in asking a question ■ *n.* GRAM **1. WORD USED TO ASK A QUESTION** a word or particle that is used to form a question, e.g., "who," "what," or "where" **2. FORM OF QUESTION** the form of a sentence that is used to ask a question —**in·ter·rog·a·tive·ly** *adv.*

in·ter·rog·a·to·ry /ìntə róggə tàwree/ *adj.* **ASKING A QUESTION** asking a question, used to ask a question, or in the form of a question (*formal*) ■ *n.* (*plural* **-ries**) **1. QUESTION** a question or series of questions **2.** LAW **FORMAL WRITTEN QUESTION** a formal written question asked during a legal proceeding and usually answered under oath —**in·ter·rog·a·to·ri·ly** *adv.*

in·ter·ro·gee /in tèrrə geé, -térrə gee/ *n.* somebody who is being subjected to interrogation

in·ter·rupt /ìntə rúpt/ *v.* (**-rupt·ed, -rupt·ing, -rupts**) **1.** *vti.* **HALT A SPEAKER OR SPEAKER'S UTTERANCE** to halt the flow of a speaker or of a speaker's utterance with a question or remark **2.** *vti.* **DISTURB SOMEBODY OR SOMEBODY'S WORK** to disturb somebody who is busy doing something, causing him or her to stop **3.** *vt.* **CAUSE SOMETHING TO STOP** to cause a break in the flow of something or put a temporary stop to something **4.** *vt.* **TAKE A BREAK FROM** to discontinue doing something temporarily **5.** *vt.* **OBSTRUCT A VIEW** to obstruct or block a view ■ *n.* COMPUT **1. SIGNAL TO SUSPEND OPERATION** a signal to a computer processor to suspend the operation it is currently doing in favor of the operation that produced the interrupt signal **2. INTERRUPT A SIGNAL CIRCUIT** the circuit that conveys an interrupt signal [14thC. From Latin *interrupt-,* the past participle stem of *interrumpere* "to break apart," from *rumpere* (see RUPTURE).] —**in·ter·rupt·i·ble** *adj.* —**in·ter·rup·tive** *adj.* —**in·ter·rup·tive·ly** *adv.* —**in·ter·rupt·er** *n.*

in·ter·rupt·ed ca·dence *n.* MUSIC a cadence that does not end with the expected chord of the tonic but moves from the dominant to the more unstable submediant or subdominant

in·ter·rupt·ed screw *n.* a screw whose thread is broken in one or more places by a lengthwise slot that enables a partial turn to lock or unlock the screw

in·ter·rup·tion /ìntə rúpshən/ *n.* **1. SOMETHING THAT INTERRUPTS** the act of interrupting somebody, or something that interrupts somebody who is saying or doing something **2. BREAK IN ACTIVITY** a pause, break, or temporary halt in an ongoing activity or process

in·ter·scho·las·tic /ìntər skə lástik/ *adj.* occurring between, involving, or representing two or more schools —**in·ter·scho·las·ti·cal·ly** *adv.*

in·ter se /ìntər sáy, -seé/ *adv., adj.* between or among themselves [From Latin]

in·ter·sect /intər sékt/ (**-sect·ed, -sect·ing, -sects**) *v.* **1.** *vti.* CROSS to cross something, or to cross each other **2.** *vt.* GO THROUGH SOMETHING to follow a path across or through something **3.** *vti.* OVERLAP to overlap or have things in common with something or each other **4.** *vti.* GEOM, MATH HAVE POINTS IN COMMON to overlap geometrically so that a point or set of points is common to two or more figures [Early 17thC. From Latin *intersect-*, the past participle stem of *intersecare*, literally "to cut between," from *secare* (see SECTION).]

in·ter·sec·tion /intər sékshən/ *n.* **1.** ACT OF INTERSECTING the act or fact of intersecting **2.** CROSSROADS a place where two roads or paths cross each other **3.** CROSSING POINT the place or point where two things cross each other **4.** OVERLAPPING an overlapping between two things such as different personal interests or political positions **5.** GEOM COMMON POINT a point or set of points common to two or more intersecting geometric figures **6.** MATH SET OF COMMON ELEMENTS a set that consists of all of the elements common to two or more other sets, thus being the largest set contained in all of the others —**in·ter·sec·tion·al** *adj.*

in·ter·ser·vice /intər súrviss/ *adj.* occurring among the various branches of the armed forces

in·ter·ses·sion /intər sèsh'n/ *n.* a period of time, usually about a month, between two college or university semesters or terms during which students sometimes undertake special projects or attend special classes —**in·ter·ses·sion·al** /intər séshən'l, -séshnəl/ *adj.*

in·ter·sex /intər sèks/ *n.* an organism with characteristics of both sexes

in·ter·sex·u·al /intər sékshoo əl/ *adj.* **1.** OCCURRING BETWEEN MALES AND FEMALES occurring between males and females or affecting their relations **2.** ZOOL HAVING MALE AND FEMALE CHARACTERISTICS having characteristics of both sexes —**in·ter·sex·u·al·ism** *n.* —**in·ter·sex·u·al·i·ty** /intər sekshoo állitee/ *n.* —**in·ter·sex·u·al·ly** /-sékshoo əlee/ *adv.*

in·ter·space *n.* /intər spàyss/ SPACE OR INTERVAL a space or interval of time between two things ■ *vt.* /intər spáyss/ (**-spaced, -spac·ing, -spac·es**) **1.** PUT SOMETHING BETWEEN TWO THINGS to put something in the spaces or gaps between things **2.** INSERT SPACES BETWEEN to put spaces or breaks between things —**in·ter·spa·tial** /intər spáysh'l/ *adj.* —**in·ter·spa·tial·ly** /-spáysh'lee/ *adv.*

in·ter·spe·cif·ic /intər spə síffik/ *adj.* **1.** CREATED FROM DIFFERENT SPECIES created by crossing different species **2.** MINERALS OCCURRING BETWEEN DIFFERENT SPECIES occurring between or involving different species

in·ter·sperse /intər spúrs/ (**-spersed, -spers·ing, -spers·es**) *vt.* **1.** BREAK SOMETHING'S CONTINUITY to break up the continuity or flow of something with something else **2.** PUT HERE AND THERE to put or insert something here and there among or in something else [Mid-16thC. From Latin *interspers-*, the past participle stem of *interspergere*, literally "to scatter between," from *spargere* "to scatter" (source also of English *disperse* and *sparse*).] —**in·ter·spers·ed·ly** /intər spúrsədlee/ *adv.* —**in·ter·sper·sion** /-spúrzh'n, -spúrshən/ *n.*

in·ter·sta·di·al /intər stáydee əl/ *adj.* relating to a short period of relatively warmer climate within an ice age [Early 20thC. Coined from INTER- + Latin *stadium* "stage."]

in·ter·state /intər stàyt/ *adj.* OCCURRING BETWEEN STATES occurring between, connecting, or involving two or more states ■ *n.* **in·ter·state, In·ter·state** MAJOR HIGHWAY BETWEEN CITIES a limited-access road that forms part of the federally funded system of highways connecting the major cities of the United States

in·ter·sta·tion /intər stáysh'n/ *adj.* occurring between or connecting stations

in·ter·stel·lar /intər stéllər/ *adj.* situated, happening, or moving between stars, or involving two or more stars

in·ter·ster·ile /intər stérrəl/ *adj.* not capable of interbreeding —**in·ter·ster·il·i·ty** /intər stə rílləteel/ *n.*

in·ter·stice /in túrstiss/ *n.* **1.** SMALL SPACE a small opening, crack, or gap between two things **2.** CRYSTALS A SPACE IN A CRYSTAL LATTICE a gap between neighboring atoms in the lattice of a crystal **3.** ANAT SPACE IN BODY TISSUE a small space in a tissue or between parts of the body [15thC. Via French from Latin *interstitium*, from *intersistere*, literally "to stand still in the middle," from *sistere* "to cause to stand," from *stare* (see STAND).]

in·ter·sti·tial /intər stísh'l/ *adj.* **1.** MINERALS RELATING TO GAPS forming, situated in, or relating to one or more small openings, gaps, or cracks **2.** OCCURRING BETWEEN OTHER MINERALS located in or creating a space between other minerals **3.** CHEM OF A COMPOUND CONTAINING METALS AND NONMETALS relating to a compound, e.g., a carbide, in which ions or atoms of a nonmetal occupy positions in a metal lattice. Interstitial compounds generally have metallic characteristics. **4.** ANAT OCCURRING BETWEEN TISSUES lying between parts of an organ or between groups of cells or tissues. The interstitial cells between mammalian testicles are responsible for secreting male sex hormones. ■ *n.* UNSOLICITED ADVERTISEMENT ON THE INTERNET an unsolicited page of advertisement on the World Wide Web that briefly precedes a selected page —**in·ter·sti·tial·ly** *adv.*

in·ter·tes·ta·men·tal /intər testə mént'l/ *adj.* during, from, or relating to the period between the composition of the last books of the Hebrew Scriptures, called Old Testament by Christians, and the first books of the New Testament of the Bible

in·ter·tex·ture /intər tékschər/ *n.* **1.** INTERWOVEN OBJECT OR MATERIAL an object or material that has been made by interweaving two or more things **2.** INTERWEAVING OR BEING INTERWOVEN an act of interweaving two or more things, or the fact of being interwoven [Mid-17thC. Formed from Latin *intertext-*, the past participle stem of *intertexere*, literally "to weave together," from *texere* (see TEXT).]

in·ter·tid·al /intər tíd'l/ *adj.* occurring within or forming the area between high and low tide levels in a coastal zone —**in·ter·tid·al·ly** *adv.*

in·ter·tri·bal /intər tríb'l/ *adj.* occurring between tribes or involving two or more tribes —**in·ter·trib·al·ly** *adv.*

in·ter·tri·go /intər trígō/ *n.* the inflammation of two skin surfaces that are in constant contact. It is caused by friction or sweat. [Early 18thC. Via Latin, "chafing of the skin," from assumed *interterere*, literally "to rub together," from *terere* "to rub."]

in·ter·trop·i·cal /intər tróppik'l/ *adj.* located or occurring between the Tropic of Capricorn and Tropic of Cancer

in·ter·twine /intər twín/ (**-twined, -twin·ing, -twines**) *vti.* **1.** TWIST OR BE TWISTED TOGETHER to twist two or more things together, or to be or become twisted together or with something else **2.** LINK OR BECOME LINKED TOGETHER to link or involve something with something else, or to become linked or involved with each other ○ *Their lives had intertwined.* —**in·ter·twine·ment** *n.*

in·ter·twist /intər twíst/ (**-twist·ed, -twist·ing, -twists**) *vti.* = **intertwine** *v.* 1

in·ter·un·ion /intər yóonyən/ *adj.* occurring between or involving two or more unions, especially labor unions

in·ter·ur·ban /intər úrbən/ *adj.* occurring between, connecting, or involving two or more towns or cities

in·ter·val /íntərvəl/ *n.* **1.** INTERVENING PERIOD OF TIME a period of time between one event and the next **2.** INTERVENING DISTANCE the distance between one thing and another **3.** MUSIC DIFFERENCE IN MUSICAL PITCH the musical distance between the pitches of two notes **4.** MATH ALL NUMBERS BETWEEN TWO NUMBERS a set containing all the real numbers or points between two specified real numbers or points, which are called the endpoints. If the set includes the endpoints it is a closed interval, and if it excludes the endpoints it is an open interval. [14thC. Via Old French *entreval(e)* from, ultimately, Latin *intervallum*, literally "space between ramparts or palisades," from *vallum* "rampart" (source of English *wall*).] —**in·ter·val·lic** /intər vállik/ *adj.* ◇ **at intervals 1.** at different points in time **2.** at various locations

in·ter·vale /íntərvəl/ *n.* in New England and the Maritime Provinces, a piece of low-lying land between hills or along a river [Mid-17thC. Blend of INTERVAL and VALE.]

in·ter·va·lom·e·ter /intər və lómmətər/ *n.* a device that is designed to activate a mechanism automatically and at regular intervals, especially one that operates a camera shutter [Mid-20thC. Coined from INTERVAL + -METER.]

in·ter·val train·ing *n.* a method of training, especially in athletics, that involves alternating between aerobic and nonaerobic exercise in the same session

in·ter·vene /intər véen/ (**-vened, -ven·ing, -venes**) *vi.* **1.** ACT TO PRODUCE CHANGE to take some action or get involved in something in order to change what is happening, especially to prevent something undesirable ○ *the referee had to intervene to stop the fight* **2.** HAPPEN SO AS TO IMPEDE to occur and as a result stop or delay something from happening **3.** ELAPSE to elapse between one point in time and another ○ *the intervening years* **4.** BE SITUATED IN BETWEEN to be located between two things **5.** BREAK INTO A CONVERSATION to break into a conversation or discussion **6.** LAW ENTER A LAWSUIT to enter a lawsuit as a third party in order to protect your own interests **7.** ECON ACT TO MANIPULATE ECONOMIC MARKETS to take economic action that is designed to counter a trend in a market, especially in order to stabilize a country's currency [Late 16thC. From Latin *intervenire*, literally "to come between," from *venire* (see VENUE).]

in·ter·ven·or /intər véenər/ *n.* a party that enters a lawsuit as a third party in order to protect its interests

in·ter·ven·tion /intər vénshən/ *n.* **1.** ACTION AFFECTING ANOTHER'S AFFAIRS an action undertaken in order to change what is happening or might happen in another's affairs, especially in order to prevent something undesirable **2.** ECON MARKET MANIPULATION economic action that is designed to counter a trend in a market, especially in order to stabilize a country's currency

in·ter·ven·tion·ism /intər vénshə nìzzəm/ *n.* **1.** POL INVOLVEMENT IN ANOTHER COUNTRY'S AFFAIRS political interference or military involvement by one country in the affairs of another **2.** ECON GOVERNMENT INTERFERENCE IN ECONOMIC MATTERS action by a government to influence and improve the country's economic situation or some aspect of it —**in·ter·ven·tion·ist** *n., adj.*

in·ter·ven·tric·u·lar /intər ven tríkyələr/ *adj.* situated or occurring between the ventricles of the heart

in·ter·ver·te·bral /intər vúrtəbrəl/ *adj.* situated or occurring between the vertebrae of the backbone —**in·ter·ver·te·bral·ly** *adv.*

in·ter·ver·te·bral disk *n.* one of the flexible plates of cartilage connecting adjacent vertebrae of the backbone that impart flexibility and act as shock absorbers to protect the spinal cord from impact, e.g., when running

in·ter·view /intər vyoō/ *n.* **1.** MEETING FOR ASKING QUESTIONS a meeting during which somebody is asked questions, e.g., by a prospective employer, a journalist, or a researcher **2.** RECORD OF AN INTERVIEW a transcript, report on, or recording of an interview **3.** SOMEBODY IN AN INTERVIEW somebody who is invited to an interview (*informal*) ■ *v.* (**-viewed, -view·ing, -views**) **1.** *vt.* ASK SOMEBODY QUESTIONS to ask somebody a series of questions in an interview **2.** *vi.* PERFORM IN AN INTERVIEW to speak and answer in a particular way in an interview ○ *she always interviews well* [Early 16thC. From obsolete French *entrevue*, from *entrevoir*, literally "to see each other," from *voir* "to see," from Latin *videre* (see VISIBLE).] —**in·ter·view·a·ble** *adj.*

in·ter·view·ee /intər vyoo ée/ *n.* somebody who is the subject of an interview

in·ter·view·er /intər vyoō ər/ *n.* somebody who conducts an interview or interviews

in·ter vi·vos /intər vée vòss, -vī-/ *adv., adj.* LAW from one living person to another [From Latin, literally "between the living"]

in·ter·vo·cal·ic /intər vō kállik/ *adj.* used to describe a speech sound occurring or inserted between vowels, e.g., between one word that ends with a vowel and another word that starts with a vowel —**in·ter·vo·cal·i·cal·ly** *adv.*

in·ter·war /intər wáwr/ *adj.* occurring between two wars, especially between world wars I and II

in·ter·weave /intər wéev/ (**-wove** /-wṓv/, **-woven** /-wṓv'n/, **-weav·ing, -weaves**) *vti.* **1.** WEAVE TOGETHER to weave something into or with something else, or to be woven together, into, or with something else **2.** COMBINE to combine something with something else, or to be combined with something —**in·ter·weave·ment** *n.* —**in·ter·weav·er** *n.*

in·tes·ta·cy /in téstəsee/ *n.* the condition of having died without having made a legally valid will

in·tes·tate /in té stàyt, in téstət/ *adj.* **1.** LEAVING NO LEGALLY VALID WILL not having made a legally valid will **2.** NOT WILLED TO SOMEBODY not having been assigned to somebody in a legally valid will ■ *n.* SOMEBODY LEAVING

NO LEGALLY VALID WILL somebody who has died without having made a legally valid will [14thC. Directly or via French *intestat* from Latin *intestatus* "not having made a will," from *testari* "to make a will."]

in·tes·ti·nal /in téstən'l/ *adj.* **1. LOCATED IN THE INTESTINES** found in or affecting the intestines **2. THE INTESTINES** characteristic of, forming part of, or relating to the intestines —**in·tes·ti·nal·ly** *adv.*

in·tes·ti·nal flo·ra *npl.* bacteria present in a healthy intestine that complete digestion, synthesize vitamin K, and create an acid environment that prevents infection by harmful bacteria

in·tes·ti·nal for·ti·tude *n.* courage and perseverance (*humorous*)

in·tes·tine /in téstin/ *n.* that part of the digestive system between the stomach and the anus or cloaca that digests and absorbs food. In mammals, the small intestine digests and absorbs food from the stomach, and the large intestine then absorbs most of the remaining water in the food. (*often used in the plural*) [15thC. Via French from, ultimately, Latin *intestinus* "internal," from *intus* "within." Ultimately from an Indo-European word that is also the ancestor of English *endo-*.]

in·thrall *vt.* = **enthrall**

in·throne *vt.* = **enthrone**

in·ti·fa·da /inti faádə/ *n.* the Palestinian uprising in the West Bank and Gaza Strip that started in 1987 in protest against the continued Israeli occupation [Late 20thC. From Arabic *intifāḍa*, literally "a shaking off."]

in·ti·ma·cy /íntəməssee/ (*plural* **-cies**) *n.* **1. CLOSE RELATIONSHIP** a close personal relationship **2. QUIET ATMOSPHERE** a quiet and private atmosphere **3. DETAILED KNOWLEDGE** a detailed knowledge resulting from a close or long association or study **4. PRIVATE UTTERANCE OR ACTION** a private and personal utterance or action **5. SEXUAL ACT** a sexual act or sexual intercourse (*used euphemistically*)

in·ti·mate[1] /íntəmət/ *adj.* **1. CLOSE** having, involving, or resulting from a close personal relationship **2. COZY** quiet and private or secluded, enabling people to feel relaxed with each other **3. PRIVATE AND PERSONAL** so private and personal as to be kept secret or discussed only with a close friend or relative **4. SEXUAL** involving or having a sexual relationship (*used euphemistically*) **5. WORN NEXT TO THE SKIN** intended to be worn next to the skin or in a private setting **6. THOROUGH** very great and detailed as a result of extensive study or close experience ○ *an intimate knowledge of the workings of government* **7. CLOSELY CONNECTED** very close because of the influence of one thing on another ○ *the intimate connection between power and corruption* **8. INNERMOST** relating to or involving the innermost nature of something ■ *n.* **CLOSE FRIEND** a close personal friend [Early 17thC. From late Latin *intimatus*, the past participle of *intimare* (see INTIMATE[2]).] —**in·ti·mate·ly** *adv.* —**in·ti·mate·ness** *n.*

in·ti·mate[2] /íntə màyt/ (**-mat·ed, -mat·ing, -mates**) *vt.* **1. HINT QUIETLY** to hint at something or let something be known in a quiet, indirect, or subtle way **2. ANNOUNCE** to announce something formally (*old*) [Early 16thC. From late Latin *intimare* "to make known," from *intimus* "innermost." Ultimately from the Indo-European word for "in," which is also the ancestor of English *in* and *inter-*.] —**in·ti·mat·er** *n.*

in·ti·ma·tion /íntə máysh'n/ *n.* **1. HINT** a subtle hint or sign of something **2. ANNOUNCEMENT** a formal announcement of something

in·time /aN teém/ *adj.* small, quiet, and private or secluded [Early 17thC. Via French, "intimate," from Latin *intimus* "innermost" (see INTIMATE[2]).]

in·tim·i·date /intímmi dàyt/ (**-dat·ed, -dat·ing, -dates**) *vt.* **1. PERSUADE OR DISSUADE BY FRIGHTENING** to persuade somebody to do something or dissuade somebody from doing something by frightening him or her, e.g., by means violence or blackmail **2. DAUNT** to create a feeling of fear, awe, or inadequacy in somebody [Mid-17thC. From medieval Latin *intimidare*, literally "to put in fear," from Latin *timidus* "fearful."] —**in·tim·i·da·tion** /in tìmmi dáysh'n/ *n.* —**in·tim·i·da·to·ry** /in tímmidə tàwree/ *adj.*

in·tinc·tion /in tíngkshən/ *n.* CHR the act of dipping the Communion bread into the wine so that the person taking Communion receives both [Late 19thC. From the late Latin stem *intinction-* from Latin *intingere* "to dip in," from *tingere* (see TINGE).]

in·tine /in teén/ *n.* the inner wall of a pollen grain or spore [Mid-19thC. Formed from Latin *intimus* "innermost" (see INTIMATE[2]), on the model of "extine."]

intl. *abbr.* international

in·to /in too/ CORE MEANING: a preposition indicating that somebody or something is or moves inside something, either physically or figuratively ○ *I released the balloon into the air.* ○ *in case you get into difficulties* ○ *I decided to go into the army.* ○ *When did you go into partnership with them?*

prep. **1. INDICATES MOVEMENT** moving or putting something from outside to the interior or inner part of something ○ *He stuck his hand into his pocket and pulled out a pencil.* **2. INDICATES MOVEMENT TO THE MIDST OF** indicates that something or somebody moves to the middle of something and becomes part of it or is surrounded by it ○ *He leapt into the water.* **3. INDICATES ENTRY** indicates entering a state, career, or period of time ○ *She decided to go into marketing.* ○ *He went on working until he was well into his seventies.* ○ *The fire department burst into action.* **4. INDICATES CONTACT WITH** indicates coming up against something accidentally ○ *I happened to bump into him last night quite by chance.* **5. INDICATES CHANGE** indicates becoming a new entity, shape, or form as a result of a change or transformation ○ *change water into wine* ○ *The caterpillar changes into a butterfly.* **6. INDICATES RESULT** indicates a situation resulting from somebody's persuasion ○ *My friends talked me into getting this haircut.* **7.** ARITH **INDICATES DIVIDEND** indicates the division of numbers ○ *9 into 63 equals 7.* **8. DIVIDED** indicates that something is divided so that it becomes several smaller parts ○ *She divided the cake into six, and gave each of us a slice.* **9. ENTHUSIASTIC ABOUT** indicates interest in or enthusiasm about something (*informal*) ○ *I was really into tennis that summer.* [Old English *in(n)tō*, from IN + TO]

in·tol·er·a·ble /in tóllərəb'l/ *adj.* **1. IMPOSSIBLE TO BEAR** so bad, difficult, or painful that it cannot be endured ○ *the pain was intolerable* **2. VERY UNPLEASANT** very unpleasant or annoying —**in·tol·er·a·bil·i·ty** /in tòllərə bíllətee/ *n.* —**in·tol·er·a·bly** /-tóllərəblee/ *adv.*

in·tol·er·ant /in tóllərənt/ *adj.* **1. EASILY ANNOYED** easily angered or annoyed when things do not go as expected or desired **2. UNACCEPTING OF DIFFERENCES** refusing to accept people who are different or live differently, e.g., people of different races or religions **3. UNABLE TO TOLERATE SOMETHING** not able to endure or tolerate something —**in·tol·er·ance** *n.* —**in·tol·er·ant·ly** *adv.*

in·to·nate /íntə nàyt/ (**-nat·ed, -nat·ing, -nates**) *vt.* **1. SAY IN PARTICULAR WAY** to say something with a particular tone of voice **2.** PHON **SPEAK WITH VARYING PITCH** to speak with the rising and falling pitch that is typical of ordinary speech **3.** PHON **PRONOUNCE A CONSONANT WITH VOICING** to pronounce a consonant with a vibration of the vocal cords, as English speakers do when they pronounce the consonant "v" as opposed to the consonant "f" [Late 18thC. From medieval Latin *intonat-*, the past participle stem of *intonare* "to intone" (see INTONE).]

in·to·na·tion /íntə náysh'n/ *n.* **1.** PHON **PITCH OF THE VOICE** the rising or falling pitch of the voice when somebody says a word or syllable, or the rising and falling pattern of speech generally **2. INTONING** a saying or chanting of something in a solemn or serious way, or something said or chanted in this way **3.** MUSIC **ACCURACY OF PITCH** accuracy of pitch in performing music **4.** MUSIC **BEGINNING OF A GREGORIAN CHANT** the opening phrase of a Gregorian chant, sung by a soloist or just a few members of the choir —**in·to·na·tion·al** *adj.*

in·to·na·tion con·tour, in·to·na·tion pat·tern *n.* LING the pattern of rising and falling pitch in speech that helps to distinguish between questions, statements, and other types of speech

in·tone /in tṓn/ (**-toned, -ton·ing, -tones**) *v.* **1.** *vt.* **SAY** to say something, especially in a slow and serious or solemn way (*formal*) **2.** *vti.* **CHANT A PRAYER** to recite a prayer or other religious words in a chanting monotone **3.** *vt.* MUSIC **START A GREGORIAN CHANT** to sing the opening phrase of a Gregorian chant [14thC. Directly or via Old French *entoner* from medieval Latin *intonare*, literally "(to sing) in tone," from Latin *tonus* "tone" (see TONE).] —**in·tone·ment** *n.* —**in·ton·er** *n.*

in to·to /in tṓtō/ *adv.* in its entirety or as a whole ○ *The salary's nothing special, but when you consider compensation in toto it's quite attractive.* [From Latin]

in·tox·i·cant /in tóksikənt/ *n.* **INTOXICATING THING** something that causes physical or psychological intoxication, e.g., an alcoholic beverage or great power ■ *adj.* **CAPABLE OF INTOXICATING** capable of making somebody intoxicated

in·tox·i·cate /in tóksi kàyt/ (**-cat·ed, -cat·ing, -cates**) *v.* **1.** *vt.* **MAKE DRUNK OR STUPEFIED** to make somebody drunk with alcohol or stupefied with drugs or other substances **2.** *vt.* **EXCITE** to make somebody intensely excited or overjoyed, often so much so that the person becomes irrational **3.** *vti.* PATHOL **POISON** to poison somebody (*technical*) [15thC. From medieval Latin *intoxicat-*, the past participle stem of *intoxicare* "to poison," from Latin *toxicum* "poison" (see TOXIC).] —**in·tox·i·ca·ble** *adj.* —**in·tox·i·ca·tive** *adj.* —**in·tox·i·ca·tion** /in tòksi káysh'n/ *n.* —**in·tox·i·ca·tor** /in tóksi kàytər/ *n.*

in·tox·i·cat·ed /in tóksi kàytəd/ *adj.* **1. DRUNK** drunk or stupefied (*formal*) **2. EXCITED** intensely excited or overjoyed, often so much so that a person becomes foolish or irrational —**in·tox·i·cat·ed·ly** *adv.*

in·tox·i·cat·ing /in tóksi kàyting/ *adj.* **1. CAPABLE OF MAKING SOMEBODY DRUNK** capable of making somebody drunk or stupefied (*formal*) **2. EXCITING** capable of making somebody intensely excited or overjoyed, often so much so that the person becomes irrational —**in·tox·i·cat·ing·ly** *adv.*

intr. *abbr.* GRAM intransitive

intra- *prefix.* within or inside ○ *intranasal* [Directly or via modern Latin "on the inside, within," from late Latin, from Latin *intra*. Ultimately from an Indo-European word that is also the ancestor of English *enter* and *entero-*.]

in·tra·ar·te·ri·al *adj.* within or introduced into an artery or arteries —**in·tra·ar·te·ri·al·ly** *adv.*

in·tra·ar·tic·u·lar *adj.* within or introduced into a joint of the body

in·tra·a·tom·ic *adj.* existing or occurring within an atom or atoms, rather than between atoms

in·tra·car·di·ac /intrə kaárdee àk/ *adj.* within or introduced into the heart —**in·tra·car·di·al·ly** /-kaárdee əlee/ *adv.*

in·tra·cel·lu·lar /intrə séllyələr/ *adj.* within a cell or cells —**in·tra·cel·lu·lar·ly** *adv.*

in·tra·cer·e·bral /intrə sə reébrəl, -sérrə-/ *adj.* existing or taking place inside the main part of the brain or cerebrum —**in·tra·cer·e·bral·ly** *adv.*

In·tra·coas·tal Wa·ter·way /intrə kṓst'l-/ a system of protected waterways, including rivers, bays, coastal sounds, and canals, in the eastern and southeastern United States, made up of the Atlantic Intracoastal Waterway and the Gulf Intracoastal Waterway. Length: 2,500 mi./4,000 km.

in·tra·com·pany /intrə kúmpənee/ *adj.* within the same company or between employees or divisions of the same company

in·tra·cra·ni·al /intrə kráynee əl/ *adj.* within or introduced into the skull —**in·tra·cra·ni·al·ly** *adv.*

in·trac·ta·ble /in tráktəb'l/ *adj.* **1. STRONG-WILLED AND REBELLIOUS** resisting attempts to control, correct, or influence (*formal*) **2. DIFFICULT TO DEAL WITH** difficult to deal with or solve **3. DIFFICULT TO MANIPULATE** difficult to shape or manipulate [15thC. From Latin *intractabilis*, from *tractabilis* (see TRACTABLE).] —**in·trac·ta·bil·i·ty** /in tràktə bíllətee/ *n.* —**in·trac·ta·bly** /in tráktəblee/ *adv.*

WORD KEY: SYNONYMS

See Synonyms at *unruly*.

in·tra·cu·ta·ne·ous /intrə kyoo táynee əss/ *adj.* = **intradermal** —**in·tra·cu·ta·ne·ous·ly** *adv.*

in·tra·der·mal /intrə dúrm'l/, **in·tra·der·mic** /-mik/ *adj.* within or introduced between the layers of the skin —**in·tra·der·mal·ly** *adv.*

in·tra·der·mal test *n.* a test for immunity or allergic sensitivity involving the injection of small amounts of a test material into the skin through a fine needle. The development of swelling or inflammation at the injection site indicates allergy to the material injected.

in·tra·der·mic *adj.* = **intradermal**

in·tra·dos /intrə dòss, -dŏss, in tráy dòss, -dŏss/ (*plural* **-dos** *or* **-dos·es**) *n.* the inner curve of an arch [Late 18thC. From French, from Latin *intra* "within" + French *dos* "back" (from Latin *dorsum*; see DORSAL).]

in·tra·gen·ic /intrə jénnik/ *adj.* located or occurring within the same gene

in·tra·lin·gual /intrə líng gwəl/ *adj.* occurring within a single language

in·tra·mo·lec·u·lar /intrə mə lékyələr/ *adj.* existing or occurring within a single molecule —**in·tra·mo·lec·u·lar·ly** *adv.*

in·tra·mu·ral /intrə myŏŏrəl/ *adj.* **1. WITHIN SCHOOL OR INSTITUTION** occurring within or involving members of a single school, college, or institution, instead of members of or teams from various institutions **2.** ANAT **WITHIN WALL TISSUE** within the tissue of the wall of a blood vessel or another hollow body part

in·tra·mus·cu·lar /intrə múskyələr/ *adj.* within or into the substance of a muscle —**in·tra·mus·cu·lar·ly** *adv.*

in·tra·na·sal /intrə náyz'l/ *adj.* within or introduced into the nose —**in·tra·na·sal·ly** *adv.*

in·tra·net /intrə nèt/ *n.* a network of computers, especially one using World Wide Web conventions, that can be accessed only by an authorized set of users, e.g., those within a single company

intrans. *abbr.* GRAM intransitive

in·tran·si·gence /in tránsəjəns, -zə-/, **in·tran·si·geance** *n.* firm or unreasonable refusal even to consider changing a decision or attitude

in·tran·si·gent /in tránsəjənt, -zə-/, **in·tran·si·geant** *adj.* **REFUSING TO COMPROMISE** firmly or unreasonably refusing even to consider changing a decision or attitude ■ *n.* **UNYIELDING PERSON** somebody who firmly or unreasonably refuses to compromise or change an attitude or decision, especially in politics (*formal*) [Late 19thC. Via French from Spanish *los intransigentes*, extreme political party (literally "the uncompromising ones"), ultimately from *transigir* "to compromise," from Latin *transigere* "to come to an agreement" (see TRANSACTION).] —**in·tran·si·gent·ly** *adv.*

in·tran·si·tive /in tránzətiv/ *adj.* GRAM **WITH NO DIRECT OBJECT** without a direct object, e.g., the verb "die" in the sentence "He was slowly dying" ■ *n.* GRAM **VERB WITHOUT A DIRECT OBJECT** a verb that does not take a direct object [Early 17thC. From late Latin *intransitivus*, literally "not passing over," from *transitivus* "transitive, passing over."] —**in·tran·si·tive·ly** *adv.* —**in·tran·si·tive·ness** *n.*

in·tra·nu·cle·ar /intrə nóoklee ər/ *adj.* **1.** NUCLEAR PHYS **WITHIN ATOMIC NUCLEUS** existing or occurring within the nucleus of an atom **2.** CELL BIOL **WITHIN CELL NUCLEUS** existing or occurring within the nucleus of a cell

in·tra·oc·u·lar /intrə ókyələr/ *adj.* within or introduced into the inside of the eyeball —**in·tra·oc·u·lar·ly** *adv.*

in·tra·pe·ri·to·ne·al /intrə perrit'n ée əl/ *adj.* within or introduced into the peritoneal cavity —**in·tra·pe·ri·to·ne·al·ly** *adv.*

in·tra·per·son·al /intrə púrsən'l, -púrsnəl/ *adj.* relating to the internal aspects of a person, especially emotions. ◊ **interpersonal** —**in·tra·per·son·al·ly** *adv.*

in·tra·pre·neur /intrə prə núr, -nóor/ *n.* a employee with a flair for innovation and risk-taking who is given unusual freedom to develop products or subsidiary businesses within a company. ◊ **entrepreneur** [Late 20thC. Coined from INTRA- + ENTREPRENEUR.] —**in·tra·pre·neur·i·al** *adj.* —**in·tra·pre·neur·i·al·ism** *n.* —**in·tra·pre·neur·i·al·ly** *adv.*

in·tra·spe·cif·ic /intrə spə síffik/, **in·tra·spe·cies** /-spée shèez, -sèez/ *adj.* existing within a single species or confined to members of one species

in·tra·state /intrə stáyt/ *adj.* existing or occurring within the boundaries of a single state

in·tra·u·ter·ine /intrə yóotərin, -rīn/ *adj.* existing, occurring, or designed to be used inside the womb

in·tra·u·ter·ine de·vice *n.* a plastic or metal device that is inserted into the cavity of the womb in order to prevent pregnancy

in·tra·vas·cu·lar /intrə váskyələr/ *adj.* within the blood vessels or a similar system in animals or plants —**in·tra·vas·cu·lar·ly** *adv.*

in·tra·ve·nous /intrə véenəss/ *adj.* **1. WITHIN VEIN** existing or occurring inside a vein, or administered into a vein **2. USED TO ADMINISTER TREATMENT** used in administering fluids or medicines into the veins —**in·tra·ve·nous·ly** *adv.*

in·tra·ven·tric·u·lar /intrə ven tríkyələr/ *adj.* within or introduced into a ventricle, such as one in the heart or brain —**in·tra·ven·tric·u·lar·ly** *adv.*

in·tra·vi·tal /intrə vīt'l/, **in·tra·vi·tam** /-vee tàm, -wée tàam/ *adj.* occurring in or used on a living cell or organism [Late 19thC. Formed from modern Latin *intra vitam* "within life."] —**in·tra·vi·tal·ly** *adv.*

in·tra·zo·nal /intrə zṓn'l/ *adj.* used to describe a soil that has a well-developed and differentiated set of soil characteristics (**profile**), determined by the nature of the parent material and age of the soil

in·treat *vti.* = **entreat**

in·trench *vti.* = **entrench**

in·trep·id /in tréppid/ *adj.* fearless and persistent in the pursuit of something [Late 17thC. Directly or via French *intrépide* from Latin *intrepidus*, literally "not agitated," from *trepidus* "agitated" (source of English *trepidation*).] —**in·tre·pid·i·ty** /intrə píddətee/ *n.* —**in·trep·id·ly** *adv.*

WORD KEY: SYNONYMS

See Synonyms at ***bold***.

in·tri·ca·cy /intrikəssee/ (*plural* **-cies**) *n.* **1. COMPLEXITY** the complex character of something that has many details, parts, or other elements **2. COMPLEX THING** something that is complex and has many details, parts, or other elements (*often used in the plural*) ○ *the intricacies of quantum chromodynamics*

in·tri·cate /intrikət/ *adj.* **1. WITH MANY PARTS** containing many details or small parts that are skillfully made or assembled **2. COMPLEX AND DIFFICULT** with many interrelated elements, parts, or factors so as to be complex and difficult to understand or resolve [15thC. From Latin *intricatus*, past participle of *intricare* "to entangle, perplex," from *tricae* "impediments, tricks" (see TRICK).] —**in·tri·cate·ly** *adv.* —**in·tri·cate·ness** *n.*

in·tri·gant /intree gaant/, **in·tri·guant** *n.* (*archaic*) **1. SECRET PLOTTER** somebody who devises secret plots or schemes **2. CLANDESTINE LOVER** somebody who carries on a secret love affair

in·trigue *n.* /in treeg, in tréeg/ **1. SECRET PLOTTING** secret scheming or plotting **2. SECRET PLOT** a secret scheme or plot **3. SECRET LOVE AFFAIR** a secret love affair (*archaic*) ■ *v.* /in tréeg/ (**-trigued, -trigu·ing, -trigues**) **1.** *vt.* **INTEREST SOMEBODY** to make somebody greatly interested or curious **2.** *vi.* **SCHEME** to scheme or use underhanded methods to achieve something **3.** *vi.* **HAVE SECRET LOVER** to carry on a secret love affair (*archaic*) [Early 17thC. Via French from Italian *intrigo*, from *intrigare* "to entangle" (source of the verb), from Latin *intricare* (see INTRICATE).] —**in·trigu·er** /in tréegər/ *n.* —**in·trigu·ing·ly** *adv.*

in·trin·sic /in trínzik, -sik/, **in·trin·si·cal** /-zik'l, -sik'l/ *adj.* **1. BASIC AND ESSENTIAL** belonging to something as one of the basic and essential elements that make it what it is **2. OF ITSELF** by or in itself, rather than because of its associations or consequences **3.** ANAT **FOUND IN BODY PART** occurring wholly within or belonging wholly to a part of the body, e.g., an organ [15thC. Via French *intrinsèque* from late Latin *intrinsecus* "inward," from assumed Latin *intrim* "within."] —**in·trin·si·cal·ly** *adv.*

in·trin·sic fac·tor *n.* a protein produced in the stomach that promotes the absorption of vitamin B_{12} in the small intestine. Insufficient intrinsic factor results in pernicious anemia.

in·tro /íntrō/ *n.* an introduction, especially the opening few bars of a piece of pop music (*informal*) [Early 19thC. Shortening.]

intro. *abbr.* 1. introduction 2. introductory

intro- *prefix.* **1.** in, into ○ *intromission* **2.** inward ○ *introvert* [From Latin *intro*; ultimately related to *intra* (see INTRA-)]

introd. *abbr.* 1. introduction 2. introductory

in·tro·duce /intrə dóoss, -dyóoss/ (**-duced, -duc·ing, -duc·es**) *v.* **1.** *vt.* **ACQUAINT WITH SOMEBODY ELSE** to present yourself or another person to somebody else and become acquainted with that person **2.** *vt.* **GIVE AUDIENCE FORETASTE** to tell an audience a little about what or whom they are going to see or hear **3.** *vt.* **BRING IN SOMETHING NEW** to bring something to a place, into existence, or into operation for the first time **4.** *vt.* **CAUSE TO EXPERIENCE SOMETHING NEW** to make somebody aware of something for the first time, or give somebody a first experience of something **5.** *vt.* **PREFACE WITH SOMETHING ELSE** to begin something with a preface of some sort, especially one designed to get people's attention **6.** *vt.* **TALK ABOUT SOMETHING NEW** to mention something for the first time **7.** *vt.* POL **PRESENT LEGISLATION FORMALLY** to present proposed legislation formally to an assembly, so that it can be debated and voted on **8.** *vt.* **INSERT** to insert something into something else **9.** BOT, ZOOL **BRING IN NEW SPECIES** to place or establish an individual or species of plant or animal in a new habitat or environment [15thC. Origin uncertain: either from Latin *introducere* "to lead in," from *ducere* "to lead," or a back-formation from INTRODUCTION.] —**in·tro·duc·er** *n.* —**in·tro·duc·i·ble** *adj.*

in·tro·duc·tion /intrə dúkshən/ *n.* **1. EXPLANATORY SECTION AT BEGINNING** a section at the beginning of a book or of another piece of writing, e.g., one that summarizes what it is about or sets the scene **2. SOMETHING GIVING BASIC FACTS** a book or course of study that gives somebody basic facts or skills in a field **3. MAKING ACQUAINTANCE** the act of formally presenting somebody or yourself to somebody else and becoming acquainted **4. PRESENTATION** the act of presenting somebody or something to an audience, assembly, or other group **5. FIRST EXPERIENCE** somebody's first experience of something **6.** MUSIC **BEGINNING OF PIECE OF MUSIC** the opening passage of a piece of music, or the opening movement in a suite **7. BRINGING IN SOMETHING NEW** the act of bringing something to a place, into existence, into operation, or into an activity for the first time **8. SOMETHING BROUGHT IN** something brought in from elsewhere or created **9. INSERTION** the insertion of something somewhere [14thC. Directly or via French from the Latin stem *introduction-*, from *introduct-*, the past participle stem of *introducere* (see INTRODUCE).]

in·tro·duc·to·ry /intrə dúktəree/ *adj.* **1. GIVING FORETASTE** telling a little about what is to come **2. PROVIDING THE BASICS** providing the basic facts or skills **3. INITIAL** made or used when something begins or is first introduced [14thC. Directly or via Old French *introductoire* from late Latin *introductorius*, from *introduct-* (see INTRODUCTON).] —**in·tro·duc·to·ri·ly** *adv.* —**in·tro·duc·to·ri·ness** *n.*

in·tro·gres·sion /intrə grésh'n/ *n.* the incorporation of genes from one species into the gene pool of another as a result of hybridization [Mid-17thC. Coined from INTRO- + *-gression* as in PROGRESSION, originally in the general sense "going in."] —**in·tro·gres·sant** /intrə gréss'nt/ *adj.* —**in·tro·gres·sive** /-gréssiv/ *adj.*

in·tro·it /ín tròyt, -trō it, -trṓ it/, **In·tro·it** *n.* **1. PART OF ROMAN CATHOLIC MASS** the part of the Roman Catholic Mass consisting of psalm verses and the Gloria Patri, said or sung when the priest first approaches the altar **2. PART OF ANGLICAN SERVICE** a psalm or hymn sung as the minister enters the church at the beginning of the Anglican service of Holy Communion [15thC. Via French from medieval Latin *introitus*, from Latin, "entrance," the past participle of *introire* "to go in," from *ire* "to go."] —**in·tro·it·al** /in trōyt'l, -trṓ it'l/ *adj.*

in·tro·jec·tion /intrə jékshən/ *n.* PSYCHOL the unconscious adoption by somebody of the values or attitudes of somebody else, whom that person wants to impress or be accepted by [Mid-19thC. Coined from INTRO- + *-jection* as in PROJECTION.] —**in·tro·ject** *vt.*

in·tro·mis·sion /intrə mísh'n/ *n.* the inserting or admitting of something into something else (*formal*) [Mid-16thC. Directly or via French from the medieval Latin stem *intromission-*, from, ultimately, Latin *intromittere* (see INTROMIT).] —**in·tro·mis·sive** /intrə míssiv/ *adj.*

in·tro·mit /intrə mít/ (**-mit·ted, -mit·ting, -mits**) *vt.* to cause or allow something to enter something else (*formal*) [15thC. From Latin *intromittere* "to send in," from *mittere* "to send" (see MISSION).] —**in·tro·mis·si·bil·i·ty** /intrə missə bíllətee/ *n.* —**in·tro·mis·si·ble** /-míssəb'l/ *adj.* —**in·tro·mit·ter** *n.*

in·tron /ín tròn/ *n.* a section of DNA in a cell that is not expressed as an amino acid or messenger RNA. ◊ **exon** [Late 20thC. Coined from INTRAGENIC + -ON.]

in·trorse /in tràwrs, in tráwrs/ *adj.* pointing and opening inward, as the anthers of some flowers do, releasing pollen toward the center of the flower [Mid-19thC. From Latin *introrsus*, a contraction of *introversus*, from *versus*, the past participle of *vertere* "to turn."] —**in·trorse·ly** *adv.*

in·tro·spect /intrə spékt, íntrə spèkt/ (**-spect·ed, -spect·ing, -spects**) *vi.* to undertake a detailed mental self-examination of feelings, thoughts, and motives [Late 17thC. Directly or via Latin *introspectare*, literally "to look into repeatedly," from *introspect-*, past participle stem of *introspicere* "to look into," from *specere*.]

in·tro·spec·tion /intrə spékshən/ *n.* the detailed mental self-examination of feelings, thoughts, and motives —**in·tro·spec·tion·al** *adj.*

introspectionism /intrə spékshə nìzzəm/ *n.* = **introspective psychology** —**in·tro·spec·tion·is·tic** *adj.*

in·tro·spec·tive /intrə spéktiv/ *adj.* tending to make or containing a detailed examination of somebody's feelings, thoughts, and motives

in·tro·spec·tive psy·chol·o·gy *n.* a school of psychology concentrating on the study of immediate subjective experience. ◊ **behaviorism**

in·tro·ver·sion /intrə vúrzh'n, -sh'n/ *n.* **1.** PSYCHOL **INTEREST IN SELF** the tendency to be more interested in your own feelings and thoughts than in the people and world around you. ◊ **extroversion** **2.** MED **ORGAN'S TURNING IN ON ITSELF** a turning inward of a hollow organ such as the womb into itself [Mid-17thC. Formed from INTROVERT on the model of such pairs as *evert, eversion.*]

in·tro·vert *n.* /intrə vùrt/ **1. RESERVED PERSON** a shy person who tends not to socialize much **2.** PSYCHOL **SOMEBODY INTERESTED IN OWN SELF** somebody who tends to be more interested in his or her own feelings and thoughts than in other people and the outside world ■ *vt.* /intrə vùrt, intrə vúrt/ (**-vert·ed, -vert·ing, -verts**) **1. TURN INWARD** to direct or turn something inward or in on itself **2.** PSYCHOL **THINK ABOUT OWN THOUGHTS** to direct your mind inward and examine or dwell on your own thoughts, feelings, and motives ■ *adj.* = **introverted** [Mid-17thC. From modern Latin *introvertere*, literally "to turn in," from Latin *vertere* "to turn" (see VERSUS).]

in·tro·vert·ed /intrə vùrtəd, -vúrtəd/ *adj.* **1. SHY** tending to be shy and quiet or ill at ease in a group **2.** PSYCHOL **INTERESTED IN OWN FEELINGS** interested more in your own feelings, thoughts, and motives than in other people and the world around you **3.** MED **TURNED INTO ITSELF** turned into itself or pulled back inside a larger part

in·trude /in tróod/ (**-trud·ed, -trud·ing, -trudes**) *v.* **1.** *vi.* **INVADE SOMEBODY'S PRIVACY** to disturb somebody's peace or privacy by going where you have not been invited or are not welcome **2.** *vi.* **HAVE UNPLEASANT EFFECT** to have an unpleasant or undesired effect on something **3.** *vt.* **ADD SOMETHING UNPLEASANT** to add or mention something inappropriate or unwanted (*formal*) **4.** *vti.* GEOL **MOVE INTO ROCK FORMATION** to move in a molten state into a preexisting rock formation, or force molten rock into a preexisting rock formation [15thC. Partly from Latin *intrudere* "to thrust in," from *trudere* "to thrust"; partly a back-formation from INTRUSION.]

in·trud·er /in tróodər/ *n.* **1. SOMEBODY WHO ENTERS ILLEGALLY** somebody who enters a building or property illegally, usually in order to commit a crime **2. UNWELCOME PERSON** somebody who is somewhere where he or she is not welcome or has not been invited

in·tru·sion /in tróozh'n/ *n.* **1. DISTURBANCE** a disturbing of somebody's peace or privacy by an unwelcome arrival or presence **2. SOMETHING UNWELCOME** an unwelcome presence or effect that disturbs or upsets something **3.** LAW **UNLAWFUL ENTRY** an illegal entry into a place, often by force, in order to commit a crime (*formal*) **4.** GEOL **INTRUDED ROCK** a body of igneous rock, often massive with associated linear dikes and sills, that has moved while molten into older solid rocks with subsequent alteration of those rocks **5.** GEOL **MOVEMENT OF MOLTEN ROCK** the movement of molten rock (**magma**) into preexisting rock [14thC. Directly or via French from the medieval Latin stem *intrusion-*, from Latin *intrus-*, past participle stem of *intrudere* (see INTRUDE).] —**in·tru·sion·al** *adj.*

in·tru·sive /in tróossiv/ *adj.* **1. INTRUDING** causing a disturbance or having an unpleasant effect **2.** GEOL **FORMED BY INTRUSION** used to describe a rock formed by having moved while in a molten state into preexisting rocks **3.** PHON **OF CONNECTING SPEECH SOUND** used to describe a speech sound that is introduced between two words only to facilitate more fluent pronunciation —**in·tru·sive·ly** *adv.* —**in·tru·sive·ness** *n.*

in·trust *vt.* = **entrust**

in·tu·bate /íntyə bàyt/ (**-bat·ed, -bat·ing, -bates**) *v.* MED **1.** *vti.* **INSERT TUBE IN WINDPIPE** to insert a tube through the vocal cords and into the windpipe in order to provide somebody's lungs with oxygen, usually during surgery under anesthesia **2.** *vt.* **INSERT TUBE IN SOMEBODY** to treat somebody by inserting a tube into the windpipe so that oxygen can be supplied to the lungs [Late 19thC. Coined from IN- + Latin *tuba* "tube" + -ATE.] —**in·tu·ba·tion** /intyə báysh'n/ *n.*

in·tu·it /in tóo it/ (**-it·ed, -it·ing, -its**) *vt.* to be aware of or know something without having to think about it or learn it [Mid-19thC. Back-formation from INTUITION.] —**in·tu·it·a·ble** *adj.*

in·tu·i·tion /in too ísh'n/ *n.* **1. KNOWING SOMETHING INSTINCTIVELY** the state of being aware of or knowing something without having to discover or perceive it, or the ability to do this **2. INSTINCTIVE BELIEF** something known or believed instinctively, without actual evidence for it **3.** PHILOS **IMMEDIATE KNOWLEDGE** immediate knowledge of something [15thC. Directly or via French from the late Latin stem *intuition-* "consideration," ultimately from Latin *intueri* "to look upon," from *tueri* "to look."] —**in·tu·i·tion·al** *adj.* —**in·tu·i·tion·al·ly** *adv.*

in·tu·i·tion·ism /in too ísh'n ìzzəm/ *n.* **1.** PHILOS **DOCTRINE OF INTUITIVE PERCEPTION** the doctrine that asserts that a perceived object is intuitively known to be real **2.** ETHICS **ETHICAL PRINCIPLES UNDERSTOOD THROUGH INTUITION** the doctrine that knowledge of goodness or obligation and the principles governing them can be discerned through intuition **3.** LOGIC, MATH **MATHEMATICAL THEORY** a theory in the foundation of mathematics that holds that only proofs constrained by certain restrictions are permitted. ◊ **formalism, logicism**

in·tu·i·tive /in tóo itiv/ *adj.* **1. KNOWN AUTOMATICALLY** known directly and instinctively, without being discovered or consciously perceived **2. KNOWING BY INSTINCT** knowing things instinctively —**in·tu·i·tive·ly** *adv.* —**in·tu·i·tive·ness** *n.*

in·tu·mesce /in too méss/ (**-mesced, -mesc·ing, -mesc·es**) *vi.* to become enlarged or swollen as a result of increased flow of blood or other fluids [Late 18thC. From Latin *intumescere* "to swell up," from *tumescere* (see TUMESCENT).]

in·tu·mes·cence /in too méss'ns/ *n.* **1.** MED **SWELLING WITH FLUID** a swelling or increase in the volume of part of the body as a result of increased flow of blood and other fluids **2.** MED **SWOLLEN PART** a part of the body that is swollen with blood or another fluid **3.** CHEM **SWELLING OF COMPOUND** the swelling of a crystalline compound on heating, often with the release of water vapor —**in·tu·mes·cent** *adj.*

in·tus·sus·cept /intəssə sépt/ (**-cept·ed, -cept·ing, -cepts**) *vti.* to undergo, or cause part of a tubular structure to undergo, a partial sliding into itself, e.g., as part of the intestine sometimes does [Early 19thC. Back-formation from INTUSSUSCEPTION.] —**in·tus·sus·cep·tive** *adj.*

in·tus·sus·cep·tion /intəssə sépshən/ *n.* **1.** MED **TELESCOPING OF TUBULAR ORGAN** a sliding of a portion of a tubular organ into another portion, especially a condition of the bowel in which this happens, creating swelling that leads to obstruction **2.** BOT **CELL WALL GROWTH** the growth of the surface area of a cell wall by the incorporation of particles into the wall [Early 18thC. Directly or via French from the modern Latin stem *intussusception-*, from Latin *intus* "within" + the stem *susception-* "undertaking," from *suscept-* (see SUSCEPTIBLE).]

in·twine *vti.* = **entwine**

in·twist *vt.* = **entwist**

In·u·it /ínnoo it, -yoo-/ (*plural* **-it** *or* **-its**), **In·nu·it** (*plural* **-it** *or* **-its**) *n.* **1.** PEOPLES **ARCTIC OR GREENLAND PEOPLE** a member of any of several aboriginal peoples who live in coastal regions of the Canadian Arctic and in Greenland. The Inuit are related to the Yupik of Alaska and northeastern Siberia. **2.** LANG **LANGUAGE OF INUIT** any of the languages of the Inuit, constituting one of the three branches of the Eskimo-Aleut family of languages. Inuit is spoken by about 60,000 people. ◊ **Inuktitut** [Mid-18thC. From Inuit, the plural of *inuk* "person."] —**In·u·it** *adj.*

WORD KEY: USAGE

See Usage note at ***Eskimo.***

in·uk·shuk *n. Can* rocks piled up to look like a person from a distance, used as a marker or guidepost by the Inuit [From *Inuit*]

I·nuk·ti·tut /i nóokti tòot/ *n.* a language of the Inuit, especially those in the eastern Arctic. ◊ **Inuit** [Late 20thC. From Inuit, literally "the Inuit way."]

in·u·lase /ínnyə làyss, -làyz/ *n.* an enzyme that brings about the breakdown of inulin [Late 19thC. Coined from INULIN + -ASE.]

in·u·lin /ínnyəlin/ *n.* a fructose sugar found in the roots and tubers of various plants and is used medically in a test that assesses whether the kidneys are functioning properly [Early 19thC. Coined from Latin *inula* "elecampane" + -IN.]

in·unc·tion /in úngkshən/ *n.* **1.** MED **RUBBING IN OF OIL** the rubbing in of oil or ointment **2.** RELIG **ANOINTING** the anointing of somebody with oil as part of a religious ceremony (*formal*) [15thC. Via the Latin stem *inunction-* from, *inunguere* "to anoint" (literally "to smear on"), from *unguere* "to smear" (see UNGUENT).]

in·un·date /ínnən dàyt/ (**-dat·ed, -dat·ing, -dates**) *vt.* **1. OVERWHELM** to overwhelm somebody with a huge quantity of things that must be dealt with **2. FLOOD** to flood a place with water [Late 16thC. Back-formation from INUNDATION.] —**in·un·da·tor** *n.* —**in·un·da·to·ry** /i núndə tàwree/ *adj.*

in·un·da·tion /ìnnən dáysh'n/ *n.* **1. FLOOD** a flood of water (*formal*) **2. OVERWHELMING ACCUMULATION** an accumulation of an overwhelming amount of things that somebody has to deal with [15thC. Directly or via Old French *inondacion* from the Latin stem *inundation-*, from *inundare*, literally "to flow onto," ultimately from *unda* "wave" (see UNDULATE).]

In·u·piat /i nóopee àat/ *npl.* an Inuit people who live along the Beaufort Sea and Chukchi coast of the Arctic Ocean [Late 20thC. From Inuit *inuk* "person" + *piaq* "genuine."]

in·ur·bane /in ur báyn/ *adj.* lacking good manners or sophistication —**in·ur·bane·ly** *adv.* —**in·ur·ban·i·ty** /in ur bánnətee/ *n.*

in·ure /i nóor/ (**-ured, -ur·ing, -ures**) *v.* **1.** *vt.* **HARDEN SOMEBODY TO SOMETHING** to make somebody used to something unpleasant over a period of time, so that he or she no longer is bothered or upset by it **2.** *vi.* LAW **COME INTO EFFECT** to come into operation or effect [15thC. From assumed Anglo-Norman *eneurer*, literally "to accustom by use," ultimately from assumed *eure* "use," from Latin *opera* "work."] —**in·ure·ment** *n.*

in·urn /in úrn/ (**-urned, -urn·ing, -urns**) *vt.* **1. PUT ASHES IN URN** to place a cremated body's ashes in an urn **2. BURY** to put a dead body in a grave (*formal*) —**in·urn·ment** *n.*

in u·ter·o /in yóotərō/ *adv., adj.* in or while still inside a woman's uterus [From Latin]

in·u·tile /in yóot'l/ *adj.* pointless or useless (*literary*) [15thC. Via French from Latin *inutilis*, from *utilis* "useful" (see UTILITY).] —**in·u·tile·ly** *adv.* —**in·u·til·i·ty** /innyoo tíllətee/ *n.*

inv. *abbr.* **1.** invariable **2.** invented **3.** invention **4.** inventor **5.** invoice

in vac·u·o /in vákyoo ō/ *adv.* **1.** CHEM **IN VACUUM** in a vacuum **2.** LAW **IN ISOLATION** in isolation, without considering any evidence [From Latin]

in·vade /in váyd/ (**-vad·ed, -vad·ing, -vades**) *v.* **1.** *vti.* **ENTER COUNTRY BY MILITARY FORCE** to enter a country by force with or as an army, especially in order to conquer it **2.** *vt.* **ENTER AND SPREAD THROUGH** to enter and spread throughout something completely **3.** *vt.* **GO SOMEWHERE IN NUMBERS** to enter or be present in a place in great numbers **4.** *vt.* **SPOIL** to spoil something by interfering, interrupting, or reducing it **5.** *vti.* MED **CAUSE DISEASE** to enter and spread gradually throughout a part of the body, causing harm or damage **6.** *vti.* BOT **GROW RAPIDLY AND HARMFULLY** to become established and spread rapidly in an area, crowding out the pre-existing plants [15thC. Directly or via Old French *invader* from Latin *invadere* "to go in;" from *vadere* "to go" (source of English *evade*).] —**in·vad·a·ble** *adj.* —**in·vad·er** *n.*

in·vag·i·nate /in vájjə nàyt/ (**-nat·ed, -nat·ing, -nates**) *vti.* to push the wall of a cavity or hollow organ inward or one section of a hollow organ into another, like a glove finger pushed into itself [Mid-17thC. Back-formation from INVAGINATION.]

in·vag·i·na·tion /in vàjjə náysh'n/ *n.* **1.** MED **PUSHING SOMETHING INSIDE ITSELF** the pushing of something into itself or partially inside out, like a glove finger pushed into itself, or the condition of something that results from this **2.** MED **INVAGINATED ORGAN** a hollow organ or body part that has been pushed back inside itself **3.** CELL BIOL **INFOLDING OF CELL STRUCTURE** the process of folding a portion of a cell structure inward, as when the cell membrane turns inward during phagocytosis **4.** EMBRYOL **FORMING OF HOLLOW GROWTH INSIDE** the pushing inward of a layer of cells to produce a hollow ingrowth in something, as when the wall of the blastula forms the gastrula [Mid-17thC. From medieval Latin *invaginare* "to sheathe," from Latin *vagina* "sheath" (source of English *vagina*).]

in·va·lid[1] /in vállid/ *adj.* **1.** LAW **NOT LEGAL** not legally binding or enforceable **2.** LOGIC **FLAWED** not acceptable or correct because of being based on a mistake or employing flawed reasoning [Mid-16thC. From Latin *invalidus* "not strong," from *validus* "strong" (see VALID).]

in·va·lid[2] /ínvəlid/ *n.* **1.** MED **SOMEBODY WITH CHRONIC DISEASE** somebody who has a chronic disease or a medical disorder and needs care **2. OFFENSIVE TERM** an offensive term for somebody who is physically challenged (*dated offensive*) ■ *adj.* **1.** having a chronic disease or medical disorder **2. FOR SOMEBODY WITH CHRONIC DISEASE** for somebody who has a chronic disease or medical disorder ■ *vt.* (**-va·lid·ed, -va·lid·ing, -val·ids**) **CAUSE TO HAVE CHRONIC DISEASE** to cause somebody to have a chronic disease or medical disorder [Mid-17thC. From INVALID[1].]

in·val·i·date /in vállə dàyt/ (**-dat·ed, -dat·ing, -dates**) *vt.* **1. MAKE NOT LEGAL** to deprive something of its legal force or value **2. SHOW TO BE WRONG** to prove that something is wrong or make something worthless —**in·val·i·da·tion** /in vàllə dáysh'n/ *n.* —**in·val·i·da·tor** *n.*

WORD KEY: SYNONYMS

See Synonyms at ***nullify***.

in·va·lid·ism /ínvələ dìzzəm/ *n.* chronic illness or medical disorder

in·va·lid·i·ty /ìnvə líddətee/ *n.* **1.** LOGIC **UNSOUNDNESS** a lack of soundness or accuracy that results from an error in reasoning **2.** LAW **LACK OF LEGALITY** the condition of not being legally binding or enforceable

in·val·u·a·ble /in vállyoo əb'l/ *adj.* extremely useful or valuable —**in·val·u·a·ble·ness** *n.* —**in·val·u·a·bly** *adv.*

In·var /ín vaar/ *tdmk.* a trademark for an iron, nickel, and carbon alloy that is used for making watch springs

in·var·i·a·ble /in váiree əb'l/ *adj.* **NEVER CHANGING** never changing or varying ■ *n.* MATH **CONSTANT QUANTITY** a mathematical quantity that is a constant —**in·var·i·a·bil·i·ty** /in vàiree ə bíllətee/ *n.* —**in·var·i·a·ble·ness** *n.*

in·var·i·a·bly /in váiree əblee/ *adv.* always or almost always

in·var·i·ant /in váiree ənt/ *adj.* **1.** = **invariable** *adj.* **2.** MATH **UNCHANGING** used to describe a quantity or set of quantities that is not changed by a designated mathematical operation such as the transformation of coordinates ■ *n.* MATH **UNCHANGING RELATIONSHIP** a relationship that is not changed by a designated mathematical operation such as the transformation of coordinates —**in·var·i·ance** *n.* —**in·var·i·an·cy** *n.*

in·va·sion /in váyzh'n/ *n.* **1.** MIL **ATTEMPT TO CONQUER** a hostile entry of an armed force into a country's territory, especially with the intention of conquering it **2. ARRIVAL IN LARGE NUMBERS** the arrival of large numbers of people or things at one time ○ *an invasion of tourists* **3. SPOILING** a spoiling of something by interfering with it or taking some of it away **4. SPREAD OF SOMETHING HARMFUL** the arrival or spread of something that causes damage or harm **5.** MED **SPREAD OF DISEASE** the spread of disease-causing organisms or malignant cells in the body **6.** BOT **AGGRESSIVE SPREAD OF PLANT** the aggressive spread of a plant species in an area, stifling the growth of preexisting species [15thC. Directly or via French from the late Latin stem *invasion-*, from Latin *invas-*, past participle stem of *invadere* (see INVADE).]

in·va·sive /in váyssiv/ *adj.* **1.** MIL **ATTACKING** involving or mounting a military attack on a territory, especially with a view to conquering it **2. INTRUDING** involving an intrusion or infringement, e.g., of somebody's privacy or rights **3.** MED **ATTACKING ADJACENT TISSUE** having or showing a tendency to spread from the point of origin to adjacent tissue, as some cancers do **4.** SURG **INTO PATIENT'S BODY** done by inserting something into or operating on the body through an incision or a natural orifice **5.** BOT **GROWING AGGRESSIVELY** growing aggressively in an area and stifling the growth of preexisting plants —**in·va·sive·ly** *adv.* —**in·va·sive·ness** *n.*

in·vec·tive /in véktiv/ *n.* **ABUSIVE LANGUAGE** an abusive expression, or language used to attack or blame somebody (*formal*) ■ *adj.* **USING ABUSE** using abusive language (*formal*) [15thC. Directly or via French *invectif* from late Latin *invectivus* "abusive," from, ultimately, Latin *invehere* "to carry in," from *vehere* "to carry."] —**in·vec·tive·ly** *adv.* —**in·vec·tive·ness** *n.*

in·veigh /in váy/ (**-veighed, -veigh·ing, -veighs**) *vi.* to speak angrily in criticism of or protest at something (*formal*) [15thC. From Latin *invehere* (see INVECTIVE).] —**in·veigh·er** *n.*

in·vei·gle /in váyg'l/ (**-gled, -gling, -gles**) *vt.* **1. PERSUADE** to charm or entice somebody into doing something that he or she would not otherwise have done ○ *inveigled me into making the trip* **2. OBTAIN BY PERSUASION** to obtain something by persuading somebody to give it [15thC. From Anglo-Norman *envegler*, an alteration of French *aveugler* "to deprive of sight," ultimately from assumed Vulgar Latin *aboculus*, literally "without eye," from Latin *oculus* "eye."] —**in·vei·gle·ment** *n.* —**in·vei·gler** *n.*

in·vent /in vént/ (**-vent·ed, -vent·ing, -vents**) *vt.* **1. CREATE SOMETHING NEW** to be the first to think of, make, or use something **2. MAKE UP** to make up something false, e.g., a false excuse [15thC. From Latin *invent-*, past participle stem of *invenire* "to come upon," from *venire* "to come" (see VENUE).] —**in·vent·a·ble** *adj.*

in·ven·tion /in vénshən/ *n.* **1. CREATED THING** a thing that somebody has created, especially a device or process **2. ACT OF CREATING** the creation of something new **3. LIE** a lie, or the telling of lies (*used euphemistically*) **4. CREATIVE ABILITY** the talent to create new things **5.** MUSIC **SHORT INSTRUMENTAL WORK** a short instrumental work, usually for keyboard, that has two or three parts and employs the technique of counterpoint —**in·ven·tion·al** *adj.* —**in·ven·tion·less** *adj.*

in·ven·tive /in véntiv/ *adj.* **1. SKILLED AT INVENTING** good at creating new things **2. DISPLAYING CREATIVITY** displaying creativity or imagination in its design **3. INVOLVED IN INVENTION** involved in or concerned with invention —**in·ven·tive·ly** *adv.* —**in·ven·tive·ness** *n.*

in·ven·tor /in véntər/ *n.* somebody who invents something, especially a new device or process

in·ven·to·ry /ínvən tàwree/ *n.* (*plural* **-ries**) **1. LIST OF ITEMS** a list of things, especially items of property **2.** ACCT **RECORD OF ASSETS** a record of a business's current assets, including property owned as well as merchandise on hand and the value of work in progress and work completed but not sold **3. ASSETS** a company's assets as a whole, or the value of them **4. STOCK OF GOODS** the merchandise or stock that a store or company has on hand **5. MAKING OF INVENTORY** the act or process or making an inventory, or the period of time when this is done ■ *vt.* (**-ried, -ry·ing, -ries**) **MAKE INVENTORY OF** to make an inventory of items, or enter a particular item in an inventory [15thC. From medieval Latin *inventorium*, an alteration of late Latin *inventarium*, literally "list of what is found," from, ultimately, Latin *invenire* (see INVENT).] —**in·ven·to·ri·a·ble** *adj.* —**in·ven·to·ri·al** /ìnvən táwree əl/ *adj.* —**in·ven·to·ri·al·ly** *adv.*

in·ve·rac·i·ty /ìnvə rássətee/ (*plural* **-ties**) *n.* a lie, or the telling of lies (*formal*)

In·ver·car·gill /ìnvər kaárgəl/ city on the southern coast of the South Island, New Zealand. Situated on the Waihopai River, it is the commercial center of a farming district. Population: 49,306 (1996).

in·ver·ness /ìnvər néss/ *n.* a long overcoat with a rounded collar and a detachable cape [Mid-19thC. Named for INVERNESS.]

In·ver·ness /ìnvər néss/ industrial and market town in northern Scotland, at the northeastern end of the Caledonian Canal. Population: 62,647 (1991).

in·verse *adj.* /in vúrs, ín vùrs/ **1. OPPOSITE OR REVERSING** opposite to or reversing something **2.** MATH **INVOLVING OPPOSITELY AFFECTED VARIABLES** involving two variables that are in a mathematical relationship where, when one increases, the other decreases and vice versa ■ *n.* /ín vùrs, in vúrs/ **1. OPPOSITE** something that is a total opposite **2.** MATH **ELEMENT OF SET** either of two elements of a set that when added together give 0, one being the negative of the other, e.g., 3 and –3 **3.** MATH = **inverse function 4.** LOGIC **OPPOSITE LOGICAL PROPOSITION** a logical proposition in which both the subject and the predicate are the opposite of another proposition [15thC. From Latin *inversus*, past participle of *invertere* "to turn upside down" (literally "to turn inside-out"), from *vertere* "to turn" (see VERSE).] —**in·verse·ly** *adv.*

in·verse func·tion *n.* a mathematical operation or function that exactly reverses another operation or function. Addition and subtraction are inverse functions, as are exponentiation and taking the root of a number.

in·verse·ly pro·por·tion·al *adj.* **1. OPPOSITE** opposite in size, degree, or rate of development **2.** MATH **CHANGING OPPOSITELY BY SAME FACTOR** involving a mathematical relationship in which an increase in one variable by a given factor brings about a decrease by the same factor in another

in·verse square law *n.* a natural law in which the magnitude of a physical quantity varies inversely with the square of its distance from its source. The gravitational attraction exerted by the Sun on the planets and the attraction or repulsion exhibited between two magnets are governed by the inverse square law.

in·ver·sion /in vúrzh'n, -sh'n/ *n.* **1. REVERSAL** a reversing of the order, arrangement, or position of something **2. REVERSED STATE OR THING** a state in which the order, arrangement, or position of something is reversed, or something in such a state **3.** GRAM = **anastrophe 4.** METEOROL **TEMPERATURE INCREASE WITH ALTITUDE** a stable atmospheric condition in which air temperature increases vertically upward through a layer. It is the reverse of normal conditions. **5.** MED **INVERTING OF ORGAN** abnormal positioning of an organ, especially the abnormal turning inward or inside out of an organ. This sometimes happens to the womb after childbirth, when part of it is pulled through the cervical canal. **6.** MATH **INVERTED RATIO** the transformation of a mathematical proportion by inverting the ratio and order of its terms **7.** MUSIC **CHANGING OF INTERVAL BY OCTAVE** a raising of the lower note of an interval, or a lowering of the upper note, by an octave **8.** MUSIC **MOVING OF CHORD TONE** a moving of the root tone of a chord to a position other than the lowest **9.** MUSIC **REVERSING OF MELODY INTERVALS** a converting of all the intervals in a melody from ascending to descending and vice versa **10.** CHEM **PRODUCTION OF OPPOSITE OPTICAL ACTIVITY** a chemical reaction in which an optically active compound gives a product with opposite optical configuration **11.** GENETICS **CHROMOSOMAL MUTATION** a chromosomal mutation in which a block of genes in a segment is in reverse order —**in·ver·sive** *adj.*

in·vert *vt.* /in vúrt/ (**-vert·ed, -vert·ing, -verts**) **1. REVERSE ARRANGEMENT** to reverse the order, position, or arrangement of something **2. MAKE OPPOSITE** to change something to its opposite or contrary **3.** MUSIC **ALTER POSITION OF NOTES** to change the position or arrangement of the musical notes in an interval, chord, or melody to produce inversion **4.** CHEM **CHANGE OPTICAL CONFIGURATION** to convert an optically active isomer into an isomer with the opposite configuration **5.** LOGIC **CONVERT LOGICAL PROPOSITION** to negate both the subject and predicate of a logical proposition ■ *n.* /ín vùrt/ CHEM **PRODUCT OF INVERSION** a substance obtained by optical inversion. ◊ **invert sugar** ■ *adj.* /ín vùrt/ CHEM **OPTICALLY INVERTED** subjected to optical inversion [Mid-16thC. From Latin *invertere* (see INVERSE).] —**in·vert·i·ble** /in vúrtəb'l/ *adj.* —**in·vert·i·bil·i·ty** /in vùrtə bíllətee/ *n.*

in·ver·tase /in vúr tàyss, -tàyz, ínvər-/ *n.* an enzyme that converts sucrose to a mixture of fructose and glucose by catalytic hydrolysis

in·ver·te·brate /in vúrtəbrət, -bràyt/ *n.* **ANIMAL WITHOUT BACKBONE** an animal such as an insect or worm that does not have a backbone ■ *adj.* **1. WITH NO BACKBONE** lacking a backbone or spinal column **2. OF INVERTEBRATES** relating to or consisting of animals that lack backbones **3. LACKING CHARACTER** lacking strength of character [Early 19thC. From modern Latin *invertebratus*, literally "not jointed," from Latin *vertebra* "joint, vertebra" (see VERTEBRA).]

in·vert·ed /in vúrtəd/ *adj.* **1. REVERSED** turned upside down, inside out, or back to front **2.** MUSIC **WITH FUNDAMENTAL NOTE REPOSITIONED** modified so that the fundamental note of the chord is not the lowest note of the chord **3.** MUSIC **WITH NOTES IN MIRROR IMAGE** with the musical notes so arranged that every ascending interval is made descending and vice versa

in·vert·ed com·ma *n. U.K.* = **quotation mark**

in·vert·ed mor·dent *n.* a musical ornament consisting of two notes of the same pitch separated by a third note one step above the others

in·vert·ed pleat *n.* a flat symmetrical pleat formed by folding the fabric to the front on either side of the section being pleated. It is the reverse of a box pleat.

in·vert·er /in vúrtər/ *n.* **1.** SOMETHING THAT INVERTS something or something that inverts or causes an inversion **2.** ELEC ENG DEVICE CONVERTING CURRENT a device that changes direct current into alternating current and is commonly used on boats to operate devices such as radios from batteries

in·vert sug·ar *n.* a mixture of glucose and fructose, obtained by the optical inversion of sucrose, that also occurs naturally in fruits and honey. It is used in the food industry.

in·vest /in vést/ (**-vest·ed, -vest·ing, -vests**) *v.* **1.** *vti.* BUY STOCKS OR BONDS to use money to buy or participate in a business enterprise that offers the possibilty of profit, especially by buying stocks or bonds **2.** *vti.* DEPOSIT MONEY IN BANK to deposit money in a bank or other financial institution in an account that pays interest **3.** *vti.* SPEND MONEY ON PROJECT to spend money on something in the hope of a future return or benefit **4.** *vt.* CONTRIBUTE EFFORT TO SOMETHING to contribute time, energy, or effort to an activity or project, or undertaking in the expectation of a benefit **5.** *vt.* GIVE SOMETHING A QUALITY to give somebody or something a particular quality or characteristic **6.** *vt.* CONFER SOMETHING ON to confer something such as a power or right on a person or group ○ *The charter invests the directors with the right to spend money as they see fit.* **7.** *vi.* MAKE A PURCHASE to use money to buy something, especially something that somebody should be able to use for a relatively long time (*informal*) ○ *It's time this family invested in a new car.* **8.** *vt.* INSTALL IN OFFICIAL ROLE to install somebody formally or ceremoniously in an official position (*formal*) ○ *The prince was invested in a ceremony held at the castle.* **9.** *vt.* ADORN to dress, clothe, or cover somebody or something with a garment or other covering (*literary*) **10.** *vt.* BESIEGE to lay siege to a place (*archaic*) [Mid-16thC. Directly or via French *investir* from Latin *investire* "to clothe (in)," ultimately from *vestis* "clothing" (see VEST). The underlying idea is of "dressing up" your capital.] —**in·vest·a·ble** *adj.*

in·ves·ti·gate /in vésti gàyt/ (**-gat·ed, -gat·ing, -gates**) *v.* **1.** *vti.* CARRY OUT OFFICIAL INQUIRY to carry out a detailed examination or inquiry, especially officially, in order to find out about something or somebody ○ *The local police are investigating a murder.* **2.** *vi.* TAKE A LOOK to take a look or go and see what happened ○ *We heard noises downstairs, so Fred went down to investigate.* [Early 16thC. From Latin *investigare*, literally "to look into for traces," ultimately from *vestigium* "footprint" (see VESTIGE).] —**in·ves·ti·ga·ble** /in véstigəb'l/ *adj.*

in·ves·ti·ga·tion /in vèsti gáysh'n/ *n.* an examination or inquiry into something, especially a detailed one that is undertaken officially

in·ves·ti·ga·tive /in vésti gàytiv/, **in·ves·ti·ga·to·ry** /-gə tàwree/ *adj.* **1.** SPECIALIZING IN INVESTIGATING responsible for or specializing in investigating **2.** USED IN INVESTIGATION used in or relating to investigation ○ *investigative techniques*

in·ves·ti·ga·tor /in vésti gàytər/ *n.* somebody who investigates things as a profession, especially somebody who investigates crimes or prepares official or confidential reports on people or events. ◊ **private detective**

in·ves·ti·ture /in véstə chòor, -chər/ *n.* **1.** INSTALLATION IN POSITION the formal installing of somebody in a position or role, especially an official one, or a ceremony held to mark this **2.** LAY APPOINTMENT OF ROMAN CATHOLIC BISHOPS the appointment of bishops in the Roman Catholic Church by a civil ruler instead of by the Church [14thC. Via medieval Latin *investitura* from, ultimately, Latin *investire* "to clothe (in)" (see INVEST); from clothing the person being installed in the insignia of rank or position.]

in·vest·ment /in véstmənt/ *n.* **1.** FIN USE OF MONEY FOR FUTURE PROFIT the outlay of money, e.g., by depositing it in a bank or by buying stock in a company, with the object of making a profit **2.** FIN MONEY INVESTED an amount of money invested in something for the purpose of making a profit **3.** FIN SOMETHING INVESTED IN something such as a company, endeavor, or object that money is invested in with the goal of making a profit **4.** CONTRIBUTION TO ACTIVITY a contribution of something such as time, energy, or effort to an activity, project, or undertaking, in the expectation of a benefit **5.** PURCHASE a purchase, especially something that somebody should be able to use for a relatively long time (*informal*) **6.** INVESTITURE the formal or ceremonial installing of somebody in a role or position, especially an official one (*formal*) **7.** MIL SIEGE a siege or besieging (*archaic*) **8.** ECON MONEY IN COMPANY'S PROPERTY the outlay of money that a company's existing buildings, equipment, and materials is equivalent to **9.** BIOL OUTER LAYERS OF ORGANISM the outer layers of an animal or organ

in·vest·ment an·a·lyst *n.* somebody who is employed by a stock exchange business to research other companies and areas of investment for clients

in·vest·ment com·pa·ny *n.* a company that holds securities in other companies purely for investment

in·vest·ment trust *n.* a legal arrangement of investors that invests its capital in securities

in·ves·tor /in véstər/ *n.* a person, company, or other organization that has money invested in something, especially one that holds stock in publicly owned corporations

in·vet·er·ate /in véttərət/ *adj.* **1.** HABITUAL fixed in a habit or practice, especially a bad one **2.** FIRMLY ESTABLISHED firmly established and of long standing [14thC. From Latin *inveteratus*, past participle of *inveterare* "to become old," from *veter-*, the stem of *vetus* (source of English *veteran* "old.")] —**in·vet·er·a·cy** *n.* —**in·vet·er·ate·ly** *adv.* —**in·vet·er·ate·ness** *n.*

in·vi·a·ble /in ví əb'l/ *adj.* unable to survive, especially financially or biologically —**in·vi·a·bil·i·ty** /in vì ə bíllətee/ *n.* —**in·vi·a·ble·ness** *n.* —**in·vi·a·bly** *adv.*

in·vid·i·ous /in víddee əss/ *adj.* **1.** PRODUCING RESENTMENT producing resentment or ill feeling, e.g., by unfairly slighting somebody **2.** UNPLEASANT unpleasant because producing or likely to produce jealousy, resentment, or hatred in others [Early 17thC. From Latin *invidiosus*, from *invidia* "ill will," literally "looking at (with malice)," ultimately from *videre* "to look."] —**in·vid·i·ous·ly** *adv.* —**in·vid·i·ous·ness** *n.*

in·vig·i·late /in víjjə làyt/ (**-lat·ed, -lat·ing, -lates**) *vti.* *U.K.* = **proctor** [Mid-16thC. From Latin *invigilare* "to watch, be awake in or on account of," ultimately from *vigil* "watchful" (see VIGIL).]

in·vig·i·la·tor /in víjjə làytər/ *n.* *U.K.* = **proctor**

in·vig·or·ate /in víggə ràyt/ (**-at·ed, -at·ing, -ates**) *vt.* to fill somebody or something with energy or life (*often passive*) [Mid-17thC. Origin uncertain: probably formed from earlier *invigor*, from, ultimately, Old French *envigourer* "to make vigorous," from "vigor."] —**in·vig·or·a·tion** /in vìggə ráysh'n/ *n.* —**in·vig·o·ra·tive** *adj.* —**in·vig·o·ra·tive·ly** *adv.* —**in·vig·or·a·tor** *n.*

in·vig·or·at·ing /in víggə ràyting/ *adj.* filling somebody or something with energy or life —**in·vig·or·at·ing·ly** *adv.*

in·vin·ci·ble /in vínsəb'l/ *adj.* **1.** UNBEATABLE incapable of being defeated or beaten as a result of great strength or skill **2.** TOO DIFFICULT TO OVERCOME so great or difficult as to be impossible to overcome **3.** DEEP-ROOTED too deep-rooted or ingrained to be altered [15thC. Directly or via French from Latin *invincibilis*, from *vincibilis* "conquerable" (see VINCIBLE).] —**in·vin·ci·bil·i·ty** /in vìnsə bíllətee/ *n.* —**in·vin·ci·ble·ness** *n.* —**in·vin·ci·bly** /in vínsəblee/ *adv.*

in·vi·o·la·ble /in ví ələb'l/ *adj.* **1.** UNBREAKABLE secure from infringement or breaking **2.** SECURE FROM ATTACK secure from violence or attack [15thC. Directly or via French from Latin *inviolabilis*, from *violabilis* "that may be injured," from *violare* "to treat violently" (see VIOLATE).] —**in·vi·o·la·bil·i·ty** /in vì ələ bíllətee/ *n.* —**in·vi·o·la·ble·ness** /in ví ələb'lnəss/ *n.* —**in·vi·o·la·bly** *adv.*

in·vi·o·late /in ví ələt/ *adj.* **1.** UNALTERED not subject to change, damage, or destruction **2.** KEPT PURE kept pure, untouched, or unblemished [15thC. From Latin *inviolatus*, from *violat-*, past participle stem of *violare* "to treat violently" (see VIOLATE).] —**in·vi·o·la·cy** /in ví ələssee/ *n.* —**in·vi·o·late·ly** *adv.* —**in·vi·o·late·ness** *n.*

in·vis·i·ble /in vízzəb'l/ *adj.* **1.** IMPOSSIBLE TO SEE not able to be seen with the eyes **2.** HIDDEN hidden from view **3.** MADE TRANSPARENT MAGICALLY impossible to see as a result of magic or pseudoscientific processes **4.** NOT EASILY NOTICED not noticed or detected readily **5.** ECON UNRECORDED STATISTICALLY not reflected or reported in economic statistics, or not recorded statistically ■ *n.* **1.** ACCT ITEM NOT IN FINANCIAL STATEMENT an item not reported in a company's financial statement **2.** SOMEBODY OR SOMETHING INVISIBLE somebody or something that is invisible [14thC. Directly or via French from Latin *invisibilis*, from *visibilis* (see VISIBLE).] —**in·vis·i·bil·i·ty** /in vìzzə bíllətee/ *n.* —**in·vis·i·ble·ness** /in vízzəb'lnəss/ *n.* —**in·vis·i·bly** *adv.*

in·vis·i·ble ink *n.* a liquid used to write something that cannot be seen until the paper is treated in some way, e.g., with heat

in·vi·ta·tion /ìnvi táysh'n/ *n.* **1.** OFFER OF SOMETHING an offer to come or go somewhere, especially one promising pleasure or hospitality, or the making of such an offer **2.** WRITTEN NOTE a note or other message, especially a printed card, that contains an invitation **3.** ENCOURAGEMENT encouragement to do something ■ *adj.* *U.K.* = **invitational**

in·vi·ta·tion·al /ìnvi táyshən'l, -shnəl/ *adj.* **1.** OPEN ONLY TO THOSE INVITED open only to people who have been invited **2.** REQUESTED asked for or requested ■ *n.* EVENT FOR INVITED PEOPLE an event, especially a sports tournament, that is open only to people who have been invited to participate

in·vi·ta·to·ry /in vítə tàwree/ *adj.* inviting or encouraging something

in·vite *vt.* /in vít/ (**-vit·ed, -vit·ing, -vites**) **1.** ASK TO PARTICIPATE to ask somebody to come or go somewhere or to do something **2.** REQUEST to ask for something or say that something should be welcomed ○ *She invited questions from the audience.* **3.** PROVOKE to encourage or provoke something that might not have happened otherwise ○ *an attitude that invites disaster* ■ *n.* /ín vìt/ INVITATION an invitation (*informal*) [Mid-16thC. Directly or via French *inviter* from Latin *invitare*, of uncertain origin: perhaps literally "to be pleasant toward," formed from assumed *vitus* "pleasant."] —**in·vi·tee** /in vì tée/ *n.* —**in·vit·er** /in vítər/ *n.*

in·vit·ing /in víting/ *adj.* suggesting or offering pleasure or enjoyment ○ *Inviting smells were coming from the kitchen.* —**in·vit·ing·ly** *adv.* —**in·vit·ing·ness** *n.*

in vi·tro /in vée trō/ *adj., adv.* in an artificial environment such as a test tube rather than inside a living organism [From Latin, literally "in glass"]

in vi·tro fer·til·i·za·tion *n.* fertilization of an ovum by sperm outside the body when normal conception is not achievable because of a woman's low fertility. After 5 days, this is followed by implantation in the womb.

in vi·vo /in vée vō/ *adj., adv.* existing or carried out inside a living organism, as in a test or experiment [From Latin, literally "in the living"]

in·vo·cate /ínvə kàyt/ (**-cat·ed, -cat·ing, -cates**) *vt.* to appeal to somebody or to God or a spirit for help (*archaic*) [Mid-16thC. From Latin *invocare* "to call upon" (see INVOKE).] —**in·vo·ca·tive** /in vókətiv/ *adj.*

in·vo·ca·tion /ìnvə káysh'n/ *n.* **1.** CALLING UPON HIGHER POWER a calling upon a greater power such as God or a spirit for help **2.** RELIG PRAYER a short prayer forming part of a religious service **3.** QUOTING OF SOMETHING AS A REASON the act of calling upon or quoting something such as a law as a reason or justification **4.** INCANTATION SUPPOSEDLY SUMMONING DEMON a casting of a spell in an attempt to make an evil spirit appear, or the spell itself —**in·vo·ca·tion·al** *adj.* —**in·voc·a·to·ry** /in vókə tàwree/ *adj.*

in·voice /ín vòyss/ *n.* **1.** REQUEST FOR PAYMENT a written record of goods or services provided and the amount charged for them, sent to a customer as a request for payment **2.** SHIPMENT OF GOODS a shipment of goods that is recorded on an invoice ■ *vt.* (**-voiced, -voic·ing, -voic·es**) SEND SOMEBODY AN INVOICE to send somebody an invoice for payment [Mid-16thC. Originally the plural of obsolete *invoy*, from obsolete French *envoy* "sending" (see ENVOY); because the invoice is sent.]

in·voke /in vók/ (**-voked, -vok·ing, -vokes**) *vt.* **1.** CALL UPON GREATER POWER to call upon a greater power such as God or a spirit for help **2.** USE IN SUPPORT to quote, rely on, or use something such as a law in support of an argument or case **3.** ASK FOR to ask or appeal for something **4.** ATTEMPT TO SUMMON DEMON to call upon an evil spirit to appear, e.g., by casting a spell **5.** AROUSE to create or arouse an idea, emotion, or image [15thC. Via French *invoquer* from Latin *invocare* "to call upon," from *vocare* "to call" (see VOCATION).] —**in·vok·er** *n.*

in·vo·lu·cre /ínvə lòokər, ìnvə lóokər/ *n.* a ring of modified leaves beneath a flower or flower cluster, as in dandelion or daisy flowers [Late 16thC. Directly or via French from Latin *involucrum* "wrapper," from *involvere* "to roll into," from *volvere* "to roll."] —**in·vo·lu·cral** /ìnvə lóokrəl/ *adj.* —**in·vo·lu·crate** *adj.*

in·vo·lu·crum /ìnvə lóokrəm/ (*plural* **-cra** /-krə/) *n.* **1.** MED **NEW BONE** a growth of new bone that forms around a mass of dead or infected bone **2.** BOT = **involucre** [Late 17thC. From Latin (see INVOLUCRE).]

in·vol·un·tar·i·ly /in vóllən tèrrilee/ *adv.* without wanting or intending to

in·vol·un·tar·y /in vóllən tèrree/ *adj.* **1. COMPELLED** required or exacted against somebody's will or wishes **2. UNCONTROLLABLE** spontaneous or automatic, and not controlled or controllable by the mind — **in·vol·un·tar·i·ness** *n.*

in·vol·un·tar·y man·slaugh·ter *n.* LAW the accidental and unlawful killing of one human being by another without planning of the killing in advance

in·vol·un·tar·y mus·cle *n.* a muscle that acts independently of the will, especially in reflex functions

in·vo·lute *adj.* /ínvə lòot/ **1. COMPLEX** complicated or intricate **2.** BOT **ROLLING INWARD** having petals or leaves that roll inward at the edges **3.** ZOOL **TIGHTLY WHORLED** used to describe a shell whose axis is hidden by tight whorls ■ *n.* /ínvə lòot/ GEOM **TYPE OF CURVE** a curve traced by the end of a taut thread that cannot be extended as it is wound upon or unwound from another curve ■ *vi.* /ìnvə lóot/ (**-lut·ed, -lut·ing, -lutes**) **BECOME INVOLUTE** to become complex or inwardly rolled, whorled, or curved [Mid-17thC. From Latin *involutus* "intricate" or, in medieval Latin, "rolled inward, forming a spiral," past participle of *involvere* "to enwrap" (see INVOLVE).] —**in·vo·lute·ly** /ínvə lòotlee/ *adv.*

in·vo·lut·ed /ínvə lóotəd/ *adj.* = **involute**

in·vo·lu·tion /ìnvə lóosh'n/ *n.* **1. COMPLICATION** an act of making something complicated or intricate, or the condition of being complicated or intricate **2. SOMETHING COMPLEX** something complicated or intricate **3.** ZOOL **DECLINE IN FUNCTION** a decline or degeneration in the physiological function of an organ **4.** BIOL **INVOLUTE PART** an involute part or structure **5.** PHYSIOL **DECREASE IN SIZE** a return to normal size of a body or body part after expansion **6.** ALGEBRA **RAISING OF QUANTITY TO POWER** the operation of raising a number, variable, or expression to a specified positive integral power, x^n **7.** GRAM **COMPLEX GRAMMATICAL STRUCTURE** a complicated grammatical construction **8.** BIOL **DEVELOPMENTAL PROCESS FORMING TUBE** the process by which certain cells grow inward over the edge of an organ or part until they rejoin the structure to form a tube. The bladder is formed by involution. —**in·vo·lu·tion·al** *adj.*

in·volve /in vólv/ (**-volved, -volv·ing, -volves**) *v.* **1.** *vt.* **CONTAIN SOMETHING** to contain or include as a necessary element of something **2.** *vt.* **CONCERN SOMEBODY** to be a matter that concerns or affects somebody **3.** *vt.* **CAUSE SOMEBODY TO PARTICIPATE** to make somebody part of, or make somebody take part in, an event or ongoing process **4.** *vt.* **IMPLICATE SOMEBODY** to connect a person with something, especially something disreputable **5.** *vt.* **ENGROSS SOMEBODY** to take up somebody's whole attention **6.** *vt.* **COMPLICATE SOMETHING** to make something complicated or difficult to follow (*often passive*) **7.** *vt.* **ENCLOSE SOMETHING** to envelop something (*literary*) (*often passive*) **8.** *vr.* **COIL UP** to coil, wrap, or wind up (*archaic*) [Late 14thC. From Latin *involvere* "to enfold," from *volvere* "to roll" (source of English *evolution* and *vault*).] —**in·volve·ment** *n.* —**in·volv·er** *n.*

in·volved /in vólvd/ *adj.* **1. COMPLICATED** complicated or difficult to follow **2. CONNECTED** connected with or participating in something **3. IN RELATIONSHIP** participating in a romantic or sexual relationship — **in·volv·ed·ly** /in vólvədlee/ *adv.*

in·volv·ing /in vólving/ *adj.* holding the attention ○ *a highly involving storyline*

invt. *abbr.* inventory

in·vul·ner·a·ble /in vúlnərəb'l/ *adj.* **1. UNABLE TO BE HURT** not capable of being wounded, damaged, hurt, or affected ○ *invulnerable to criticism* **2. SAFE FROM ATTACK** not capable of being successfully attacked [Late 16thC. From Latin *invulnerabilis*, from *vulnerare* "to wound" (see VULNERABLE).] —**in·vul·ner·a·bil·i·ty** /in vùlnərə bíllətee/ *n.* —**in·vul·ner·a·ble·ness** /in vúlnərəb'lnəss/ *n.* —**in·vul·ner·a·bly** *adv.*

in·ward /ínwərd/ *adj.* **1. INSIDE** situated within something **2. OF THE MIND OR SPIRIT** relating to or existing in the mind or spirit **3. TOWARD THE INSIDE** toward the inside or center of something ■ *adv.* **1. TOWARD THE INSIDE** moving or facing toward the inside or center of something **2. TOWARD THE MIND OR SPIRIT** toward the mind or spirit ■ *n.* **THE INSIDE** the inner part (*literary archaic*) ○ *"To kiss the tender inward of thy hand"* (William Shakespeare, *Sonnets*; 1609) —**in·ward·ness** *n.*

In·ward Light *n.* = **Inner Light**

in·ward·ly /ínwərdlee/ *adv.* **1. TO YOURSELF** to yourself, or without showing a feeling on the outside **2. TOWARD INSIDE** on or to the inside

in·wards /ínwərdz/ *adv. U.K.* = **inward** ■ *npl.* **INTERNAL ORGANS** the internal organs of the body (*archaic or literary*)

in·weave /in wéev/ (**-wove** /-wṓv/, **-wo·ven** /-wṓv'n/, **-weav·ing, -weaves**) *vt.* to weave something into a fabric or design

in·wind (**-wound, -wound** /-wównd/, **-wind·ing, -winds**) *vt.* = **enwind**

in·wrap *vt.* = **enwrap**

in·wreathe *vt.* = **enwreathe**

in-your-face *adj.* aggressively direct, bold, or exhibitionist (*slang*) ○ *the age of in-your-face political campaigning*

I·o[1] *symbol.* ionium (*archaic*)

I·o[2] /ī ō, ée ō/ *n.* **1.** MYTHOL **WOMAN TURNED INTO HEIFER** in Greek mythology, the daughter of the river god Inachus, turned into a heifer by the god Zeus to protect her from the jealousy of his wife Hera **2.** ASTRON **LARGE MOON OF JUPITER** a large natural satellite of Jupiter, discovered in 1601 by Galileo. It is 2,260 m/3,640 km in diameter and remarkable for being volcanically active. [Via Latin from Greek *Iō*]

I/O *abbr.* COMPUT input/output

IOC *n., abbr.* International Olympic Committee

iod- *prefix.* = **iodo-** (*used before vowels*)

i·o·date /ī ə dàyt/ *n.* a salt of iodic acid. The most important salts are sodium and potassium iodates, which are used in medicine. [Early 19thC. Formed from IODIC ACID.]

i·od·ic /ī óddik/ *adj.* relating to, containing, or caused by iodine, especially with a valence of five

i·od·ic ac·id *n.* a colorless or white crystalline solid that is soluble in water and is used in analytical chemistry and as a disinfectant, deodorant, and antiseptic. Formula: HIO_3.

i·o·dide /ī ə dīd/ *n.* a salt of hydriodic acid that contains the univalent anion ion I^-. Metallic iodides such as silver, sodium, or potassium iodide are employed in photography and in iodized table salt.

i·o·di·nate /ī ədi nàyt/ (**-nat·ed, -nat·ing, -nates**) *vt.* to treat something with iodine or an iodine compound, or add or substitute iodine atoms to or in an organic compound —**i·o·di·na·tion** /ī ədi náysh'n/ *n.*

i·o·dine /ī ə dīn/ *n.* **1.** CHEM **NONMETALLIC CRYSTALLINE HALOGEN ELEMENT** a poisonous, dark gray to purple-black, lustrous, and nonmetallic crystalline element in the halogen family used as a germicide and antiseptic and in the preparation of dyes, pharmaceuticals, and tinctures. Radioactive isotopes of iodine are employed as tracers in medicine and industry and in the diagnosis and treatment of certain diseases. Symbol **I 2.** PHARM **ANTISEPTIC** a mixture of iodine and potassium iodide in alcohol employed as a topical antiseptic [Early 19thC. Formed from French *iode*, from Greek *iōdēs* "violet-colored," from *ion* "violet"; from the purple vapor produced by heated iodine crystals.]

i·o·dize /ī ə dīz/ (**-dized, -diz·ing, -diz·es**) *vt.* to treat or combine something with iodine or an iodine compound —**i·o·di·za·tion** /ī ədi záysh'n/ *n.* —**i·o·diz·er** /ī ə dīzər/ *n.*

iodo- *prefix.* iodine ○ *iodophor* [From French *iode* (see IODINE)]

i·o·do·form /ī ṓdə fàwrm, -óddə-/ *n.* a yellow volatile crystalline compound with a penetrating odor, used as an antiseptic and in ointments for minor skin diseases. Formula: CHI_3. [Mid-19thC. Coined from IODO- + FORMYL.]

i·o·do·phor /ī ṓdə fàwr/ *n.* a substance consisting of iodine and a surface-active agent in solution that slowly releases elemental iodine and can be used as a disinfectant [Mid-20thC. Coined from IODO- + *-phor*, variant of -PHORE.]

i·o·dop·sin /ī ə dópsin/ *n.* a photosensitive violet pigment in the retinal cones of the eye [Mid-20thC. Coined from Greek *iōdēs* "violet-colored" (see IODINE) + OPSIN, on the model of *rhodopsin*.]

i·o·dous /ī ṓdəss, ī ədəss/ *adj.* involving, containing, or caused by iodine

i·o·lite /ī ə līt/ *n.* = **cordierite** [Early 19thC. Coined from Greek *ion* "violet" + -LITE.]

I·o moth *n.* a large yellow North American moth with a large spot resembling an eye on each of its hind wings. Stinging spines appear on its larvae. Latin name: *Automeris io.* [Named for Io, who was tormented by a gadfly; so called because of the stinging spines of the larvae]

i·on /ī ən, ī òn/ *n.* an atom or group of atoms that has acquired an electric charge by losing or gaining one or more electrons [Mid-19thC. From Greek *ion*, literally "moving thing," from the present participle of *ienai* "to go," from the movement of any ion toward the electrode of opposite charge.]

Ion. *abbr.* Ionic

-ion *suffix.* **1.** action or process ○ *eruption* ○ *erosion* **2.** result of an action or process ○ *abrasion* **3.** condition, state ○ *elation* [Via Old French from the Latin stem *-ion-*]

I·o·na /ī ṓnə/ low-lying island off the southwestern tip of Mull, in the Inner Hebrides, western Scotland. Area: 3 sq. mi./8.5 sq. km.

i·on en·gine *n.* a theoretical rocket engine that derives its thrust from the electrostatic acceleration of a stream of positive ions. Because the engine does not provide enough thrust to escape the earth's gravity, it could be used only in space.

Popperfoto

Eugene Ionesco

Io·nes·co /ee ə néskō/, **Eugène** (1909–94) Romanian-born French dramatist. He was one of the chief exponents of the Theater of the Absurd. His plays include *The Chairs* (1952) and *Rhinoceros* (1959).

i·on ex·change *n.* the interchange of ions of the same charge between a solution and a solid in contact with it —**i·on ex·chang·er** *n.*

I·o·ni·a /ī ṓnee ə/ region of ancient western Asia Minor in the Aegean coast that was colonized by the Greeks around 1000 B.C.

I·o·ni·an /ī ṓnee ən/ *n.* **MEMBER OF ANCIENT GREEK PEOPLE** a member of an ancient Greek people who lived in Attica around the 10th century B.C., before spreading out to many of the coastal regions and islands of the Aegean. They established important cultural and trading centers in their new settlements. ■ *adj.* **OF IONIA** relating to or typical of Ionia, or its people, dialect, or culture

I·o·ni·an Is·lands /ī ṓnee ən-/ group of seven Greek islands in the Ionian and Mediterranean seas. Corfu is the capital and largest city in the islands. Population: 191,003 (1991). Area: 891 sq. mi./2,307 sq. km.

I·o·ni·an mode *n.* the medieval musical mode corresponding to the modern C major scale

I·o·ni·an Sea /ī ṓnee ən-/ part of the Mediterranean Sea, situated between the southeastern coast of Italy and western Greece

i·on·ic /ī ónnik/ *adj.* relating to or containing matter in the form of charged atoms or groups of atoms

I·on·ic *n.* **1.** LANG **IONIAN DIALECT** an extinct dialect of Ancient Greek, that was spoken mainly in Ionia **2.** POETRY **METRICAL FOOT** a metrical foot used in classical prosody, consisting of two long syllables followed by two short ones (**greater Ionic**) or two short syllables followed by two long ones (**lesser Ionic**) ■ *adj.* **1.** ARCHIT **OF ARCHITECTURAL ORDER** relating to or typical of the order of architecture characterized by fluted columns and capitals with spiral scroll-shaped ornaments **2.** = **Ionian** *adj.* **3.** POETRY **IN IONIC**

METER relating to, typical of, or expressed in Ionic meter [Early 17thC. From Greek *Iōnikos* "of Ionia."]

I·on·ic or·der *n.* one of the five classical orders of architecture, characterized by fluted columns and capitals with spiral scroll-shaped ornaments

i·on·ic pro·pul·sion *n.* motion produced in reaction to the expulsion of a stream of accelerated ions

i·on im·plan·ta·tion *n.* the use of a stream of electrically accelerated ions to implant impurities on or near the surface of the substrate during the manufacture of a semiconductor

i·o·ni·um /ī ṓnee əm/ *n.* a radioactive isotope of thorium, originally thought to be a new element (*archaic*) Symbol **Io** [Early 20thC. Coined from ION + -IUM, in reference to the supposed new element's ionizing action.]

i·on·i·za·tion /ī əni záysh'n/ *n.* a process in which an atom or molecule loses or gains electrons, acquiring an electric charge or changing an existing charge

i·on·i·za·tion cham·ber *n.* a device used to detect and measure ionizing radiation, consisting of a gas-filled tube with electrodes at each end between which a voltage is maintained. Radiation that ionizes gas molecules in the tube causes a current between the electrodes, the strength of which is a function of the radiation's intensity.

i·on·ize /ī ə nīz/ (**-ized, -iz·ing, -iz·es**) *vti.* to undergo or cause something to undergo ionization —**i·on·iz·a·ble** *adj.*

i·o·none /ī ə nṑn/ *n.* a yellow liquid smelling of violets that is extracted from plants and used in the production of perfumes. Formula: $C_{13}H_{20}O$. [Late 19thC. Coined from Greek *ion* "violet" + -ONE.]

i·on·o·phore /ī ónnə fàwr/ *n.* a chemical compound that increases the permeability of biological membranes to particular ions [Mid-20thC. Coined from ION + -PHORE.]

i·on·o·sphere /ī ónnə sfeer/ *n.* four layers of the Earth's upper atmosphere in which incoming ionizing radiation from space creates ions and free electrons that can reflect radio signals, enabling their transmission around the world [Early 20thC. Coined from ION + -SPHERE.] —**i·on·o·spher·ic** /ī ònnə sféerik, -sférrik/ *adj.* —**i·on·o·spher·i·cal·ly** *adv.*

i·on·o·spher·ic wave *n.* = **sky wave**

i·on pro·pul·sion *n.* = **ionic propulsion**

i·on rock·et *n.* a rocket powered by an ion engine

i·on·to·pho·re·sis /ī òntəfə réessiss/ *n.* the movement of ions through biological material under the influence of an electric current [Early 20thC. Coined from Greek *iont-*, stem of *iōn*, present participle of *ienai* "to go" (see ION) + -PHORESIS.] —**i·on·to·pho·ret·ic** /ī òntəfə réttik/ *adj.* —**i·on·to·pho·ret·i·cal·ly** *adv.*

IOOF *abbr.* Independent Order of Odd Fellows

i·o·ta /ī ṓtə/ *n.* **1. 9TH LETTER OF GREEK ALPHABET** the 9th letter of the Greek alphabet, represented in the English alphabet as "i" or "j." See table at **alphabet** **2. SMALL AMOUNT** a very small amount of something ○ *anyone with an iota of sense* [Early 17thC. Via Latin from Greek *iōta*, from a Semitic source.]

i·o·ta·cism /ī ṓtə sìzzəm/ *n.* the tendency in speakers of modern Greek to use the sound of iota in place of the sound of other vowel characters such as eta or upsilon [Mid-17thC. Via Latin from Greek *iōtakismos*, from *iōta* (see IOTA).]

IOU /ī ō yoó/ *n.* a written acknowledgment of a debt between the writer and somebody else [Representation of "I owe you"]

IOW *abbr.* in other words (*used in e-mail messages*)

I·o·wa /ī əwə/ **1.** state in the north central United States bordered by Illinois, Minnesota, Missouri, Nebraska, South Dakota, and Wisconsin. Capital: Des Moines. Population: 2,852,423 (1997). Area: 56,276 sq. mi./145,754 sq. km. **2.** river in Iowa that flows southeastward, emptying into the Mississippi River near Louisa. Length: 330 mi./530 km.

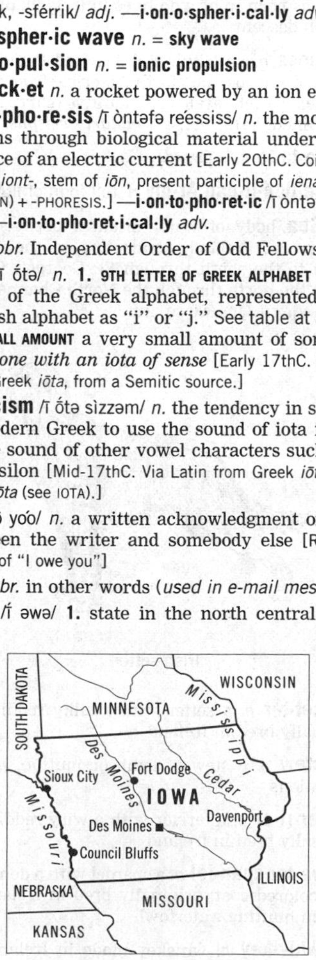

Iowa

I·o·wa Cit·y city in eastern Iowa, on the eastern bank of the Iowa River, northwest of Davenport and southeast of Cedar Rapids. Population: 60,923 (1996).

I·o·wan /ī əwən/ *n.* somebody who lives in or was born or raised in the state of Iowa —**I·o·wan** *adj.*

IP *abbr.* **1.** image processing **2.** BASEBALL innings pitched **3.** Internet protocol

IPA, **I.P.A.** *abbr.* International Phonetic Alphabet

ip·e·cac /íppi kàk/, **ip·e·cac·u·an·ha** /íppi kakyoo ánnə, -ánnyə/ (*plural* **-cacs** *or* **-cac·u·an·has**) *n.* **1.** PLANTS **S AMERICAN SHRUB** a South American shrub, the roots of which are a source of a vomit-inducing medicine (**emetic**). Latin name: *Cephaelis ipecacuanha*. **2.** MED **EMETIC** an emetic made from the dried roots of the ipecacuanha plant [Early 17thC. Via Portuguese from Tupi *ipe-kaâ-guéne*, literally "low plant causing vomit."]

Iph·i·ge·ni·a /íffijə nī ə, -née ə/ *n.* in Greek mythology, a daughter of Agamemnon. He was prepared to sacrifice her to Artemis in order to gain favorable winds for the Greek fleet to sail for Troy. Differing versions of the myth give different accounts of her fate.

IPL *abbr.* initial program load

ipm *abbr.* inches per minute

IPO *abbr.* initial public offering

I·poh /éepō/ city and capital of Perak State, western Malaysia. Population: 382,633 (1991).

ip·pon /í pón/ *n.* a winning point awarded in judo or karate for perfect technique [Mid-20thC. From Japanese.]

ipro·ni·a·zid /íprə nī əzid/ *n.* a compound used as an antidepressant and, formerly, in treating tuberculosis. Formula: $C_9H_{13}N_3O$. [Mid-20thC. Blend of ISOPROPYL and ISONIAZID.]

ips *abbr.* inches per second

ip·se dix·it /ípsi díksit/ *n.* something asserted dogmatically and without proof [Late 16thC. From Latin, "he himself said it," translating Greek *autos epha*, originally used by Pythagoreans in reference to Pythagoras himself.]

ip·si·lat·er·al /ípsə láttərəl/ *adj.* being on or affecting the same side of the body [Early 20thC. Alteration of *ipselateral*, from Latin *ipse* "self, same" + LATERAL.] —**ip·si·lat·er·al·ly** *adv.*

ip·sis·si·ma ver·ba /ip sissəmə vúrbə/ *npl.* the precise words used in something that is quoted [From Latin, "the very words"]

ip·so fac·to /ípsō fáktō/ *adv.* as the result of a particular fact [From Latin, "by the fact itself"]

ip·so ju·re /ípsō jóoree, -yóoree/ *adv.* by reason of a particular law [From Latin, "by the law itself"]

Ips·wich /ípswich/ **1.** city in Queensland, eastern Australia, just outside Brisbane. Population: 117,435 (1996). **2.** town in northeastern Massachusetts, on the Ipswich River, northwest of Gloucester and south of Newburyport. Population: 12,352 (1996).

IQ, **I.Q.** *n.* a measure of somebody's intelligence, obtained through a series of aptitude tests concentrating on different aspects of intellectual functioning. An IQ score of 100 represents "average" intelligence. Full form **intelligence quotient**

i.q. *abbr.* idem quod [Latin, "the same as"]

Iq·bal /ík bal/, **Sir Muhammad** (1875–1938) Indian philosopher, poet, and political leader. He became president of the Muslim League in 1930, and his separatist political philosophy underpinned the eventual formation of Pakistan.

I·qui·que /ee kée kay/ seaport, city, and capital of Tarapacá Region, northern Chile, situated 130 mi./209 km south of the Peruvian border. Population: 145,139 (1992).

I·qui·tos /ee kée tōss/ city and river port in northeastern Peru, situated on the upper Amazon, River 1,268 mi./2,040 km overland northeast of Lima. Population: 266,175 (1993).

Ir *symbol.* iridium

IR *abbr.* **1.** COMPUT information retrieval **2.** infrared (radiation) **3.** SPORTS inside right **4.** international registration **5.** Iran (*international vehicle registration*)

Ir. *abbr.* **1.** Ireland **2.** Irish

IRA[1] *n.* an organization of Irish nationalists originally set up to strive for an independent Ireland by force of arms and still dedicated to achieving the unity of the island of Ireland. Full form **Irish Republican Army**

IRA[2] *n.* a plan that permits individuals to accumulate savings tax free until retirement. Full form **Individual Retirement Account**

i·ra·cund /írə kùnd/ *adj.* easily made angry (*literary*) [Early 19thC. From Latin *iracundus*, from *ira* "anger" + *-cundus* "inclined toward" (source of English *jocund*).] —**i·ra·cun·di·ty** /írə kúndətee/ *n.*

i·ra·de /ee ráadee/ *n.* a written decree of a Muslim ruler, especially, formerly, the Sultan of Turkey [Late 19thC. From Arabic *irādah* "will, desire, wish."]

Iran

I·ran /i rán, i ráan/ republic in southwestern Asia, formerly known abroad as Persia. Language: Farsi. Currency: Iranian rial. Capital: Tehran. Population: 67,540,002 (1997). Area: 636,300 sq. mi./1,648,000 sq. km. Official name **Islamic Republic of Iran**

Iran. *abbr.* Iranian

I·ra·ni·an /i ráynee ən/ *n.* **1.** LANG **LARGE SUBGROUP OF INDO-EUROPEAN LANGUAGES** a group of languages spoken in the region northeast of the Persian Gulf. It is a subgroup of the Indo-Iranian branch of Indo-European, and includes Baluchi, Kurdish, and Farsi. About 70 million people speak an Iranian language. **2.** PEOPLES **SOMEBODY FROM IRAN** somebody who was born or raised in Iran, or who is a citizen of Iran —**I·ra·ni·an** *adj.*

Iraq

I·raq /i rák, i ráak/ republic in southwestern Asia, bordered by Turkey, Iran, Saudi Arabia, Kuwait, the Persian Gulf, Jordan, and Syria. Language: Arabic. Currency: Iraqi dinar. Capital: Baghdad. Population: 22,219,289 (1997). Area: 169,235 sq. mi./438,317 sq. km. Official name **Republic of Iraq**

I·ra·qi /i rákee, i ráakee/ *n.* **1.** PEOPLES **SOMEBODY FROM IRAQ** somebody who was born or raised in Iraq, or who is a citizen of Iraq **2.** LANG **ARABIC DIALECT OF IRAQ** the modern dialect of Arabic spoken in Iraq —**I·ra·qi** *adj.*

i·ras·ci·ble /i rássəb'l/ *adj.* **1. QUICK-TEMPERED** easily provoked to anger or outbursts of temper **2. SHOWING ANGER** showing or typical of anger [Mid-16thC. Via French from Latin *irascibilis* "quick to anger, irritable," from *irasci* "to grow angry," from *ira* "anger."] —**i·ras·ci·bil·i·ty** /i ràssə bíllətee/ *n.* —**i·ras·ci·ble·ness** /i rássəb'lnəss/ *n.* —**i·ras·ci·bly** *adv.*

i·rate /ī ráyt/ *adj.* **1. VERY ANGRY** feeling great anger **2. INDICATING ANGER** showing or typical of great anger [Mid-19thC. From Latin *iratus* "enraged," past participle of *irasci* "to grow angry."] —**i·rate·ly** *adv.* —**i·rate·ness** *n.*

Ir·a·wad·i = **Irrawaddy**

IRBM *abbr.* intermediate-range ballistic missile

ire /īr/ *n.* a feeling or display of deep anger or fury (*literary*) [13thC. Via French from Latin *ira* "anger," of uncertain origin.] —**ire·ful** *adj.*

WORD KEY: SYNONYMS

See Synonyms at *anger.*

Ire. *abbr.* Ireland

Ireland

Ire·land /írlənd/ **1.** island in northwestern Europe, in the North Atlantic Ocean, west of Great Britain. It comprises the Republic of Ireland and the British province of Northern Ireland. Area: 32,599 sq. mi./84,431 sq. km. **2.** republic occupying the southern, central, and northwestern parts of the island of Ireland. Language: English, Irish Gaelic. Currency: punt. Capital: Dublin. Population: 3,606,952 (1997). Area: 27,133 sq. mi./70,273 sq. km. Official name **Republic of Ireland**

Ire·land, North·ern ◆ **Northern Ireland**

i·ren·ic /ī rénnik, ī reénik/, **i·ren·i·cal** /ī rénnik'l, ī reénik'l/ *adj.* promoting or intended to promote peace (*literary*) [Mid-19thC. From Greek *eirēnikos* "peaceable, peaceful," from *eirēnē* "peace."] —**i·ren·i·cal·ly** *adv.*

i·ren·ics /ī rénniks, ī reéniks/ *n.* a branch of theology that seeks to promote unity between different churches and religious groups (*takes a singular verb*)

I·ri·an Jay·a /írree ən jī ə/ province of Indonesia, consisting of the western half of the island of New Guinea and including islands off its northern and northwestern coasts. Former name **West New Guinea**

irid- *prefix.* = **irido-** (*used before vowels*)

ir·i·da·ceous /írri dáyshəss/ *adj.* relating or belonging to the family of flowering plants that includes the iris and crocus. Family: Iridaceae.

ir·i·dec·to·my /írri déktəmee/ (*plural* **-mies**) *n.* the surgical removal of part of the iris of the eye

ir·i·des·cent /írri déss'nt/ *adj.* **1. HAVING RAINBOW COLORS** marked by or showing rainbow colors that appear to move and change as the angle at which they are seen changes **2. LUSTROUS** having a lustrous or brilliant appearance or quality —**ir·i·des·cence** *n.* —**ir·i·des·cent·ly** *adv.*

i·rid·ic[1] /i ríddik, ī-/ *adj.* relating to, involving, or containing the element iridium [Mid-19thC. Formed from IRIDIUM.]

i·rid·ic[2] /i ríddik, ī-/ *adj.* relating to or typical of the iris of the eye [Late 19thC. Formed from IRID-.]

i·rid·i·um /i ríddee əm/ *n.* a brittle silver-white metallic chemical element that forms hard corrosion-resistant alloys used in pen nibs, jewelry, watch and compass pivot bearings, surgical instruments, electrical contacts, and chemical crucibles. The international kilogram standard maintained in Paris is made of an alloy of 10 parts iridium and 90 parts platinum. Symbol **Ir** [Early 19thC. From modern Latin, formed from IRID-, from the rainbow colors of the metal when dissolved in hydrochloric acid.]

irido- *prefix.* **1.** iris ○ *iridotomy* ○ *iridaceous* **2.** rainbow ○ *iridescent* **3.** iridium ○ *iridosmine* [Via Latin from, ultimately, Greek *irid-*, the stem of *iris* (see IRIS)]

i·rid·o·cyte /i riddə sīt, ī-/ *n.* a cell in the skin of fish and certain cephalopods that contains guanine and causes iridescence

ir·i·dol·o·gy /írri dóllәjee/ *n.* a technique in alternative medicine by which diagnosis of various bodily disorders is claimed to be possible by examination of the fine structure of the iris of the eye —**ir·i·dol·o·gist** *n.*

ir·i·dos·mine /írri dóz meen/, **ir·i·dos·mi·um** /-dózmee əm/ *n.* an ore and natural alloy of iridium and osmium in which the osmium content exceeds 35 percent, with traces of platinum, rhodium, ruthenium, iron, and copper [Early 19thC. Blend of IRIDIUM and OSMIUM.]

ir·i·dot·o·my /írri dóttəmee/ (*plural* **-mies**) *n.* a surgical operation in which the iris of the eye is cut into, nowadays using a laser

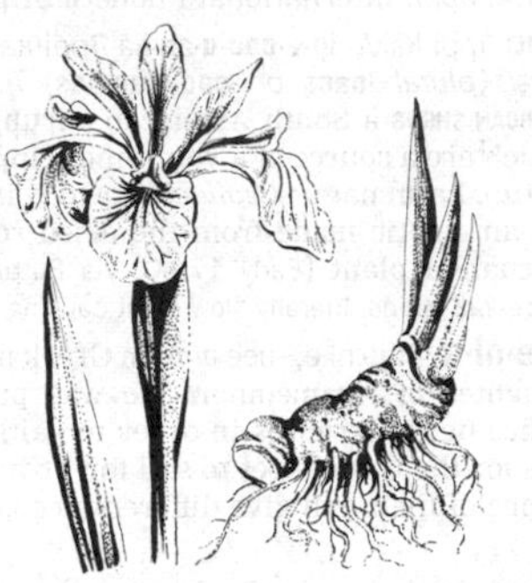

Iris

i·ris /íriss/ *n.* **1.** ANAT **PART OF EYE** the colored part of the eye that consists of a muscular diaphragm surrounding the pupil and regulating the light entering the eye by expanding and contracting the pupil **2.** PLANTS **FLOWERING PLANT** a plant with long sword-shaped leaves and large brightly colored flowers. Genus: *Iris.* **3.** METEOROL **RAINBOW** a rainbow (*literary*) **4.** COLORS **RAINBOW SHOW OF COLORS** a show of colors of various hues, like a rainbow **5.** PHOTOGRAPHY = **iris diaphragm** [15thC. Directly, or via modern Latin, from Greek *Iris, iris,* rainbow (or the messenger-goddess personifying it), iris of the eye, the flower iris.]

iris in *vi.* to open up the iris diaphragm of a camera gradually in order to expand the picture area

iris out *vi.* to close the iris diaphragm of a camera gradually in order to contract the picture area until the image darkens completely. Irising out was formerly a common way to end a film or sequence.

i·ris di·a·phragm *n.* a diaphragm consisting of adjustable thin plates that control the size of an aperture, especially one used in a camera to control the amount of light allowed to enter

I·rish /írish/ *adj.* **1. OF IRELAND** relating to or typical of Ireland, or its people or culture **2.** LANG **OF IRISH GAELIC** relating to the Irish Gaelic language **3.** LANGUAGE **OF ENGLISH DIALECT OF IRELAND** relating to the dialect of English spoken in Ireland ■ *npl.* PEOPLES **PEOPLE FROM IRELAND** people who were born or raised in Ireland, or who have Irish citizenship ■ *n.* LANG = **Irish Gaelic** [13thC. Formed from *Īr-*, stem of Old English *Īras* "inhabitants of Ireland," of uncertain origin: probably ultimately from Old Irish *Ériu* "Ireland."] —**I·rish·ness** *n.*

I·rish bug·gy *n.* a wheelbarrow (*regional*)

WORD KEY: REGIONAL NOTE

This is a Rocky Mountain term that recurs from Montana to Texas, with scattered instances in California. Variants are *Irish automobile, Irish car,* and *Irish locomotive.*

I·rish cof·fee *n.* a hot drink of sweetened coffee containing Irish whiskey and topped with cream

I·rish elk *n.* any of various extinct giant large-antlered Eurasian deer of the Pleistocene epoch. Genus: *Megaloceros.*

I·rish Eng·lish *n.* the variety of English spoken in Ireland —**I·rish Eng·lish** *adj.*

WORD KEY: WORLD ENGLISH

The English language as used in Ireland since at least the 16th century. For some observers, the terms *Irish English, Anglo-Irish,* and *Hiberno-English* mean much the same; for others, the term ***Irish English*** refers to English throughout Ireland, Anglo-Irish refers to a variety which originated among settlers from England (and has been especially associated with a Dublin élite), and Hiberno-English refers to usage markedly influenced by Irish Gaelic, although all commentators agree that it is difficult to draw a clear line between the various kinds of ***Irish English.*** Northern Irish English is generally regarded as a distinct variety of ***Irish English*** (but is not usually contrasted with a "Southern Irish English"). Within Northern Ireland, Ulster Scots derives from the settlement (or as it was called at the time, "plantation") of Scottish Protestants in the North from the early 17th century onward. ***Irish English*** is generally "rhotic" (that is, *r* is pronounced in words such as *art, door,* and *worker*) and "retroflex" (that is, with the tip of the tongue curled back and raised); the "wh" in words like *why* and *what* is pronounced as "hw," so that *whales* and *Wales* are clearly distinguished; words like *three* and *those* are commonly pronounced like "tree" and "dose" and words like *leave* and *tea* as "lave" and "tay." There are distinctive grammatical forms influenced by Irish Gaelic. First, forms like these are used for emphasis and increased focus: "It's a fine man he is,""It was to help her I went," and "It's himself was the best player." Second is the use of *after* and *-ing* to mark an action just completed: "She's after helping them this very morning." The third is the omission of *yes* and *no* in answers: "Did you come yesterday? – I did"; "Can you see him now? – We can." Vocabulary adapted from Gaelic includes the now internationally current *banshee* (from *bean sidhe* "fairy woman"), *colleen* ("young woman," from *cailín*), *kitter* ("left-handed," from *citeóg*), *shillelagh* (a thick stick, from the town of the same name); and *whiskey* or *whisky* (both originally from Gaelic *uisge beatha* "water of life").

I·rish Gael·ic *n.* an official language of the Republic of Ireland, spoken mainly in the western parts of the country. It is one of the Goidelic group of the Celtic branch of Indo-European. Irish Gaelic is spoken by about 5,000 people as a first language, with approximately a million others using it as a second language. —**I·rish Gael·ic** *adj.*

I·rish harp *n.* a small diatonic harp constructed with a hollowed willow soundbox

I·rish·ism /íri shìzzəm/ *n.* an expression or custom common among the Irish

I·rish·man /írishmən/ (*plural* **-men** /-mən/) *n.* a man who was born in or who lives in Ireland, or who is of Irish descent

I·rish moss *n.* an edible red seaweed found on the coasts of Europe and North America, from which a complex carbohydrate food additive (**carrageenan**) is obtained. Latin name: *Chondrus crispus.*

I·rish po·ta·to *n.* = **potato**

I·rish Re·pub·li·can Ar·my *n.* full form of **IRA**

I·rish Sea body of water situated between Great Britain and Ireland, connecting to the Atlantic Ocean to the south through St. George's Channel and to the north through the North Channel. Area: 40,000 sq. mi./103,600 sq. km.

Irish setter

I·rish set·ter *n.* a setter with a silky reddish coat, originally bred in Ireland

I·rish stew *n.* a stew of lamb or mutton, potatoes, and onions

I·rish ter·ri·er *n.* a terrier with a wiry reddish coat, originally bred in Ireland

I·rish wa·ter span·iel *n.* a spaniel with a dense curly liver-colored coat, originally bred in Ireland. It is used in hunting waterfowl.

I·rish whis·key *n.* whiskey made in Ireland, principally of barley

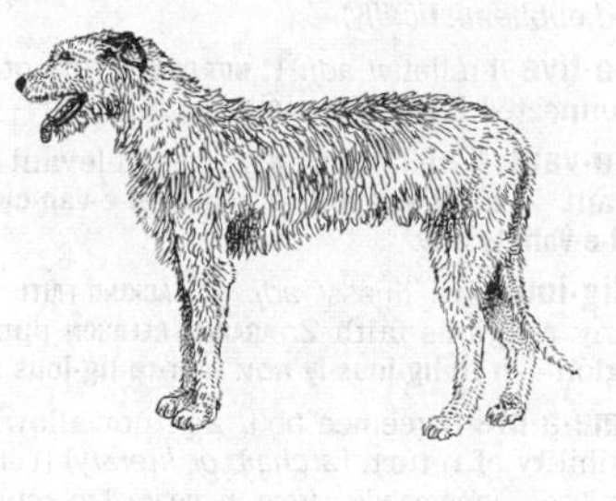

Irish wolfhound

I·rish wolf·hound *n.* a large powerful hound with a rough shaggy coat, belonging to an ancient breed originally developed in Ireland. The Irish wolfhound is the tallest breed of dog in the world.

I·rish·wom·an /írish wòommən/ (*plural* **-en** /-wìmmin/) *n.* a woman who was born in or who lives in Ireland, or who is of Irish descent

i·ri·tis /ī rítiss/ *n.* inflammation of the iris of the eye [Early 19thC. Coined from IRIS + -ITIS.] —**i·rit·ic** /ī ríttik/ *adj.*

irk /urk/ (**irked, irk·ing, irks**) *vt.* to annoy somebody slightly, especially by being tedious [14thC. Earliest sense "to grow weary or vexed"; originally northern English; origin uncertain: perhaps from Old Norse *yrkja* "to work."]

WORD KEY: SYNONYMS

See Synonyms at ***annoy*** and ***bother.***

irk·some /úrksəm/ *adj.* slightly annoying, especially by being tedious —**irk·some·ly** *adv.* —**irk·some·ness** *n.*

Ir·kutsk /ur kóotsk, eer-/ city in southern Siberian Russia and capital of Irkutsk Oblast. It is situated on the Angara River, 45 mi./72 km from the southwestern shore of Lake Baikal. Population: 639,000 (1992).

IRL *abbr.* **1.** Republic of Ireland (*international vehicle registration*) **2.** in real life (*used in e-mail messages*)

IRO *abbr.* **1.** International Refugee Organization **2.** International Relief Organization

i·ro·ko /i rṓkō/ (*plural* **-kos**) *n.* **1.** TREES **AFRICAN TREE** a hardwood tree of tropical Africa. Genus: *Chlorophora.* **2.** INDUST **HARD AFRICAN WOOD** the hard brown wood of the iroko tree, often used as a substitute for teak [Late 19thC. From Yoruba.]

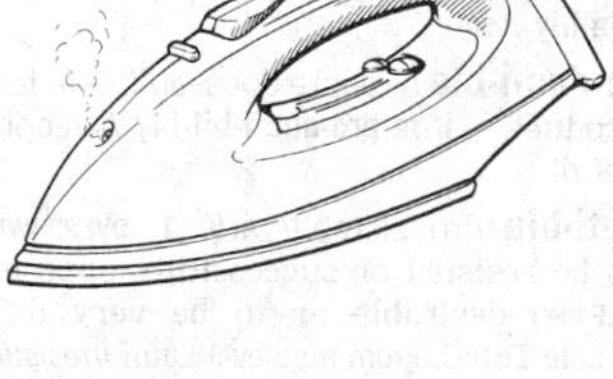

Iron

i·ron /írn/ *n.* **1.** CHEM ELEM **METALLIC ELEMENT** a heavy magnetic malleable ductile lustrous silvery-white metallic element used for a variety of engineering and structural products. It is also present in very small quantities in the blood. It is the fourth most abundant element in the earth's crust and is believed to make up 80 percent of the planet's core. Symbol **Fe 2. HARSH CHARACTER** a strong, unyielding, or hard aspect of somebody's nature **3. HEATED TOOL** any of various tools made of iron or steel, usually heated before and during use ○ *a soldering iron* **4.** HOUSEHOLD **CLOTHES PRESSER** a small, usually electrical, appliance with a handle and a flat metal base that is heated for use in pressing clothes and sometimes contains water to make steam **5.** GOLF **METAL-HEADED GOLF CLUB** any of various golf clubs with metal heads, differentiated by numbers that indicate different angles of the face and lengths of the shaft **6.** EQU = **stirrup 7. HANDGUN** a handgun, especially a revolver (*archaic slang*) ○ *a shooting iron* **8.** TECH **COMPUTER HARDWARE** computer hardware, especially older and larger mainframes (*slang*) ○ *a company with some big iron* ■ **i·rons** *npl.* **RESTRAINTS FOR THE ARMS OR LEGS** manacles or fetters for restraining the arms or legs ■ *adj.* **1. MADE OF IRON** relating to or made of iron **2. VERY STRONG** very strong or hard **3. TOUGH** very robust or tough **4. UNYIELDING** very determined, unyielding, or cruel ■ *v.* (**i·roned, i·ron·ing, i·rons**) **1.** *vti.* HOUSEHOLD **PRESS CLOTHES** to press clothes or other fabrics with an iron to remove wrinkles **2.** *vt.* **COVER WITH IRON** to cover or clad something with iron **3.** *vt.* CRIMINOL **FETTER PRISONER** to place fetters on a prisoner (*archaic*) [Old English *īren*, from a prehistoric Germanic word of uncertain origin: probably via Celtic from, ultimately, an Indo-European word that is also the ancestor of English *ore*] —**i·ron·ness** *n.* ◇ **have several irons in the fire** to be involved in several different activities at the same time ◇ **pump iron** to do weight-lifting exercises for bodybuilding or fitness (*slang*) ◇ **strike while the iron is hot** to act while circumstances are favorable for a successful outcome

iron out *vt.* **1. SMOOTH SOMETHING** to smooth away wrinkles in a garment or fabric using an iron **2. SETTLE OR RESOLVE SOMETHING** to settle a dispute or resolve a problem by removing difficulties

i·ron age *n.* in Greek and Roman mythology, an era regarded as the third and last step in humankind's degeneration from the golden age

I·ron Age *n.* the period following the Bronze Age from about 1500 B.C. onward in the Middle East, during which iron was increasingly used in making tools and weapons

i·ron·bark /írn baàrk/ *n.* any of several species of Australian eucalyptus trees noted for their hard rough bark, e.g., red ironbark. Latin name: *Eucalyptus sideroxylon.*

i·ron blue *n.* an insoluble compound used as a blue pigment in paint, ink, and paper dyeing, and in fertilizers. Formula: $Fe_7C_{18}N_{18} \cdot 10H_2O$.

i·ron·bound /írn bòwnd/ *adj.* **1. DECORATED WITH IRON** wrapped or decorated with iron bands **2. HARSH** stern or unyielding **3. RUGGED** edged or enclosed with rocks (*literary*) ○ *an ironbound coast*

i·ron·clad /írn klàd/ *adj.* **1. COVERED OR PROTECTED WITH IRON** covered with iron, especially as a protection or armor **2. STRONG** strong, firm, or unyielding **3. IRREFUTABLE** not capable of being attacked or refuted ○ *an ironclad alibi* ■ *n.* **ARMORED SHIP** a 19th-century wooden warship armored with metal plates

I·ron Cross *n.* the highest German military decoration, instituted in Prussia in 1813 and awarded during World Wars I and II

i·ron cur·tain *n.* an impenetrable barrier to understanding, awareness, or agreement

I·ron Cur·tain *n.* the militarized border between the Communist bloc and western Europe during the Cold War, or the policy of isolation that prevented western and eastern Europeans from traveling or communicating freely. The Iron Curtain existed from the end of World War II until the fall of eastern European Communist governments between 1989 and 1991. ○ *"From Stettin in the Baltic to Trieste in the Adriatic, an iron curtain has descended across the continent."* (Sir Winston Churchill *Fulton, Missouri, Speech*; 1946)

i·ron gray *adj.* of a dark gray color with a greenish hue —**i·ron gray** *n.*

i·ron hand *n.* strict, harsh, or despotic control —**i·ron·hand·ed** /írn hándəd/ *adj.* —**i·ron·hand·ed·ness** *n.*

i·ron horse *n.* a steam-powered railroad locomotive (*dated*)

i·ron·ic /ī rónnik/, **i·ron·i·cal** *adj.* relating to, characterized by, using, or containing irony —**i·ron·i·cal·ly** *adv.* —**i·ron·i·cal·ness** *n.*

i·ron·ing /írning/ *n.* **1. PRESSING CLOTHES** the act of pressing clothes or other fabrics to remove wrinkles **2. CLOTHES** clothes that have been ironed or have to be ironed

i·ron·ing board *n.* a covered, often padded board on legs on which clothes are ironed

i·ron·ize /írə nīz/ (**-ized, -iz·ing, -iz·es**) *v.* **1.** *vi.* **USE IRONY** to use irony or be ironic **2.** *vt.* **MAKE SOMETHING IRONIC** to give something an ironic tone, or make something ironic in nature

i·ron lung *n.* an airtight metal cylinder encasing a patient up to the neck, formerly used to provide help in breathing by alternating air pressure within the cylinder

i·ron maid·en *n.* a medieval instrument of torture consisting of a hinged box shaped like a human body and lined with spikes that impale somebody placed inside as it is closed

i·ron man *n.* **1. STRONG MAN** a man of great physical strength and endurance **2.** *ANZ, U.S.* **MEN'S SPORTS COMPETITION** an athletic competition for men held at a beach and including a variety of disciplines such as surfing, canoeing, swimming, and running

i·ron·mon·ger /írn mùng gər, -mòng-/ *n. U.K.* somebody who deals in tools and other articles made chiefly of metal —**i·ron·mon·ger·y** *n.*

i·ron ox·ide *n.* any of the natural or synthetic compounds of iron and oxygen

i·ron pan *n.* a hard layer below the surface of sand or gravel in which iron salts from percolating water have precipitated, cementing the grains of the material together

i·ron py·rites /írn pī ríts/ *n.* = **pyrite**

i·ron ra·tion *n.* a ration of food designed to be used in an emergency, especially by military personnel

i·ron·side /írn sīd/ (*plural* **-sides**) *n.* a man of great physical strength or endurance

i·ron·sides *n.* = **ironside**

i·ron·stone /írn stōn/ *n.* **1.** GEOL **IRON-BEARING SEDIMENTARY ROCK** any sedimentary rock that contains a large amount of iron ore **2.** CERAMICS **WHITE POTTERY** a hard and durable variety of white pottery

i·ron·weed /írn wèed/ *n.* any of various American weeds with purplish flowers and alternate leaves. Genus: *Vernonia.*

i·ron wom·an *n. ANZ, U.S.* an athletic competition for women held at a beach and including a variety of disciplines such as surfing, canoeing, swimming, and running

i·ron·wood /írn wòod/ (*plural* **-woods** *or* **-wood**) *n.* **1.** TREES **TREE WITH HARD WOOD** any of a range of trees that have very hard wood, e.g., the hornbeam **2.** INDUST **HARD WOOD** the very hard wood of an ironwood tree

i·ron·work /írn wùrk/ *n.* something made of iron, e.g., a gate, especially when it is decorative

i·ron·work·er /írn wùrkər/ *n.* **1. WORKER IN IRONWORKS** somebody employed in an ironworks **2. MAKER OF IRONWORK** somebody who produces ironwork

i·ron·works /írn wùrks/ *n.* a factory where iron is smelted or large metal goods are made (*takes a singular verb*)

i·ro·ny /írənee/ (*plural* **-nies**) *n.* **1. HUMOR BASED ON OPPOSITES** a type of humor based on using words to suggest the opposite of their literal meaning **2. SOMETHING HUMOROUS BASED ON CONTRADICTION** something said or written that uses sardonic humor **3. INCONGRUITY** incongruity between what actually happens and what might be expected to happen, especially when this disparity seems absurd or laughable **4. INCONGRUOUS THING** something that happens that is incongruous with what might be expected to happen, especially when this seems absurd or laughable **5.** = **dramatic irony 6.** = **Socratic irony** [Early 16thC. Via Latin *ironia* from Greek *eirōneia* "pretended ignorance," formed from *eirōn* "dissembler," of uncertain origin: perhaps formed from *eirein* "to say."]

Ir·o·quoi·an /ìrrə kwóy ən/ *n.* **1.** LANG **NATIVE NORTH AMERICAN FAMILY OF LANGUAGES** a family of Native North American languages spoken by Iroquois peoples of eastern North America. Its many languages include Mohawk, Seneca, Cherokee, and Huron. **2.** PEOPLES **MEMBER OF NATIVE NORTH AMERICAN PEOPLE** a member of any of the Native North American peoples who speak an Iroquoian language —**Ir·o·quoi·an** *adj.*

Ir·o·quois /írrə kwòy/ (*plural* **-quois**) *n.* a member of a former confederacy of six Native North American peoples, the Mohawk, Oneida, Seneca, Onondaga, Cayuga, and Tuscarora. Originally settled along the Hudson River Valley, many Iroquois now live in urban areas. [Mid-17thC. Via French from Algonquian.] —**Ir·o·quois** *adj.*

IRQ *abbr.* Iraq (*international vehicle registration*)

ir·ra·di·ant /i ráydee ənt/ *adj.* radiating light or shining brightly [Early 16thC. From Latin *irradiant-*, present participle stem of *irradiare* (see IRRADIATE).]

ir·ra·di·ate /i ráydee àyt/ (**-at·ed, -at·ing, -ates**) *vt.* **1. EXPOSE SOMETHING TO RADIATION** to expose somebody or something to or treat somebody or something with radiation or streams of particles **2. PRESERVE FOOD** to treat food with electromagnetic radiation to kill microorganisms and slow down the process of ripening and gradual deterioration or rotting **3. LIGHT SOMETHING UP** to make something brighter by shining light onto it **4. MAKE SOMETHING INTELLIGIBLE** to make something intellectually clear **5.** = **radiate** *v.* 4 [Early 17thC. From Latin *irradiat-*, past participle stem of *irradiare* "to illumine, send out beams," ultimately from *radius* "ray, beam."] —**ir·ra·di·a·tive** *adj.* —**ir·ra·di·a·tor** *n.*

ir·ra·di·a·tion /i ràydee áysh'n/ *n.* **1. IRRADIATING** the act of irradiating somebody or something, or the state of being irradiated **2. LIGHTING EFFECT** the visual effect by which a brightly lit thing appears larger against a dark background **3.** MED **MEDICAL RADIATION** the medical use of radiation, e.g., X-rays, gamma rays, or neutrons

ir·rad·i·ca·ble /i ráddikəb'l/ *adj.* incapable of being eradicated [Early 18thC. From medieval Latin *irradicabilis*, from Latin *radicare*, "to take root," wrongly understood as "to root out."] —**ir·rad·i·ca·bly** *adv.*

ir·ra·tion·al /i ráshən'l, i ráshnəl/ *adj.* **1. LACKING IN REASON** contrary to or lacking in reason or logic **2. LACKING IN LOGIC** unable to think logically **3. UNABLE TO THINK CLEARLY** lacking the normal ability to think clearly, especially because of shock or injury to the brain **4.** MATH **CONTAINING IRRATIONAL NUMBER** used to describe an expression that contains an irrational number **5.** POETRY **CONTAINING METRIC IRREGULARITY** used to describe an irregularity in the meter of a classical poem, usually where there is a long foot instead of a short one ■ *n.* **1. IRRATIONAL PERSON** somebody who is unable to think and reason clearly or logically **2.** MATH = **irrational number** [15thC. From Latin *irrationalis*, from *rationalis* "endowed with reason" (see RATIONAL).] —**ir·ra·tion·al·i·ty** /i ràsh'n állətee/ *n.* —**ir·ra·tion·al·ly** /i ráshən'lee, i ráshnəlee/ *adv.* —**ir·ra·tion·al·ness** /-nəss/ *n.*

ir·ra·tion·al·ism /i ráshən'l ìzzəm, i ráshnə lìzzəm/ *n.* **1. ABSENCE OF REASON** the state of lacking reason or logic **2. BELIEF IN FEELINGS** the belief that feelings and intuition are more important than reason —**ir·ra·tion·al·is·tic** /i ráshən'lístik, i ráshnəlístik/ *adj.*

ir·ra·tion·al num·ber *n.* any real number that cannot be expressed as the exact ratio of two integers, e.g., $\sqrt{2}$ and π

Ir·ra·wad·dy /ìrrə wóddee/, **Ir·a·wad·i** principal river of Myanmar (Burma). Length: 1,300 mi./2,100 km.

ir·real /i reé əl/ *adj.* illusory or not actually existing —**ir·re·al·i·ty** /ìrree állətee/ *n.*

ir·re·claim·a·ble /ìrri kláyməb'l/ *adj.* not able to be reclaimed ○ *an irreclaimable desert* ○ *irreclaimable damages* —**ir·re·claim·a·bil·i·ty** /ìrri kláymə bíllətee/ *n.* —**ir·re·claim·a·ble·ness** /ìrri kláyməb'lnəss/ *n.* —**ir·re·claim·a·bly** *adv.*

ir·rec·on·cil·a·ble /i rèkən sīləb'l, i rékən sīləb'l/ *adj.* **1. INCOMPATIBLE** not capable of being made to agree or coexist with something else **2. UNRESOLVABLE** incapable of being resolved **3. IMPLACABLE** determinedly hostile and unwilling to accept compromise ■ *n.* **1. IMPLACABLE PERSON** somebody who is determinedly hostile or will not accept compromise **2. INCOMPATIBLE IDEA** any one of two or more ideas, beliefs, or principles that cannot be made to agree or coexist —**ir·rec·on·cil·a·bil·i·ty** /i rèkən sīlə bíllətee/ *n.* —**ir·rec·on·cil·a·ble·ness** /-sīləb'lnəss, -sīləb'lnəss/ *n.* —**ir·rec·on·cil·a·bly** *adv.*

ir·re·cov·er·a·ble /ìrri kúvvərəb'l/ *adj.* **1. INCAPABLE OF BEING REGAINED** impossible to get back or regain **2. INCAPABLE OF BEING REPAIRED** impossible to repair or remedy —**ir·re·cov·er·a·ble·ness** *n.* —**ir·re·cov·er·a·bly** *adv.*

ir·re·deem·a·ble /ìrri deéməb'l/ *adj.* **1.** FIN **UNABLE TO BE PAID OFF** that cannot be ended by paying off the principal **2.** FIN **NOT CONVERTIBLE INTO COINS** that cannot be converted into coins **3.** FIN **NOT RECOVERABLE** that cannot be made good once lost **4.** CHR **INCAPABLE OF REDEMPTION** refusing to reform and unable to be saved **5. NOT REPAIRABLE** impossible to repair —**ir·re·deem·a·bil·i·ty** /ìrri deemə bíllətee/ *n.* —**ir·re·deem·a·ble·ness** /ìrri deéməb'lnəss/ *n.* —**ir·re·deem·a·bly** *adv.*

ir·re·den·ta /ìrri déntə/ *n.* a territory that was once part of one country but is now ruled by another and is subject to claims that it should be returned to its former country [Early 20thC. From Italian *(Italia) irredenta* (see IRREDENTIST.)]

ir·re·den·tist /ìrri déntist/ *n.* a member of a group of people who support the return to their country of territories that used to belong to it but are now under foreign rule —**ir·re·den·tism** *n.*

Ir·re·den·tist *n.* a member of an Italian organization founded in 1878 that advocated the adding to Italy of Italian-speaking territories that were under foreign control at that time [Late 19thC. From Italian *irredentista*, from *(Italia) irredenta* "unrecovered (Italy)," from *redento* "redeemed," from Latin *redemptus* (see REDEMPTION).]

ir·re·duc·i·ble /ìrri dóossəb'l/ *adj.* **1. INCAPABLE OF BEING DECREASED** not able to be made smaller **2. INCAPABLE OF SIMPLIFICATION** not able to be simplified or simplified further **3.** MATH **IMPOSSIBLE TO FACTOR INTO LESSER POLYNOMIALS** used to describe a polynomial that cannot be factored into two polynomials of a lesser degree **4.** MATH **IMPOSSIBLE TO REDUCE TO RATIONAL EXPRESSION** used to describe a radical that cannot be reduced to a rational expression —**ir·re·duc·i·bil·i·ty** /ìrri dóossə bíllətee/ *n.* —**ir·re·duc·i·ble·ness** /ìrri dóossəb'lnəss/ *n.* —**ir·re·duc·i·bly** *adv.*

ir·re·flex·ive /ìrri fléksiv/ *adj.* used to describe a relation in which, if a has the relation to b, then b does not have the relation to a

ir·re·form·a·ble /ìrri fáwrməb'l/ *adj.* **1. INCAPABLE OF REFORM** incapable of being reformed **2. INCAPABLE OF ALTERATION** impossible to revise or alter —**ir·re·form·a·bil·i·ty** /ìrri fáwrmə bíllətee/ *n.*

ir·ref·ra·ga·ble /i réffrəgəb'l/ *adj.* not able to be refuted or disputed (*formal*) [Mid-16thC. From late Latin *irrefragabilis*, from Latin *refragari* "to oppose, contest."] —**ir·ref·ra·ga·bil·i·ty** /i rèffrəgə bíllətee/ *n.* —**ir·ref·ra·ga·ble·ness** /-nəss/ *n.* —**ir·ref·ra·ga·bly** *adv.*

ir·re·fran·gi·ble /ìrrə fránjəb'l/ *adj.* **1. INCAPABLE OF BEING DISOBEYED** impossible to disobey or violate (*formal*) **2. INCAPABLE OF BEING BROKEN** impossible to break or smash (*formal*) **3.** PHYS **INCAPABLE OF BEING REFRACTED** used to describe visible light or other radiation that cannot be refracted —**ir·re·fran·gi·bil·i·ty** /ìrrə franjə bíllətee/ *n.* —**ir·re·fran·gi·ble·ness** /ìrrə fránjəb'lnəss/ *n.* —**ir·re·fran·gi·bly** *adv.*

ir·ref·u·ta·ble /ìrrə fyóotəb'l, i réffyə-/ *adj.* impossible to refute or disprove [Early 17thC. From late Latin *irrefutabilis*, from Latin *refutare* "to refute."] —**ir·ref·u·ta·bil·i·ty** /ìrrə fyootə bíllətee, i rèffyə-/ *n.* —**ir·ref·u·ta·ble·ness** /ìrrə fyóotəb'lnəss, i réffyə-/ *n.* —**ir·ref·u·ta·bly** *adv.*

irreg. *abbr.* irregular

ir·re·gard·less /ìrri gaárdləss/ *adv.* = **regardless** (*nonstandard*) [Early 20thC. Origin uncertain: probably a blend of IRRESPECTIVE and REGARDLESS.]

WORD KEY: USAGE

Nonstandard usage: A moment's thought will reveal that since the prefix *ir-* means "not" (as it does in *irrespective*), and the suffix *-less* means "without," ***irregardless*** is an illogical double negative. As such it is to be avoided, in favor of *irrespective* or *regardless.*

ir·reg·u·lar /i réggyələr/ *adj.* **1. NOT OF UNIFORM APPEARANCE** not even, uniform, or symmetrical in appearance **2. OCCURRING AT ODD INTERVALS OF TIME** not occurring at equally spaced intervals of time **3. NONCONFORMING** not conforming to common practices **4. BEHAVING UNACCEPTABLY** not conforming to accepted rules or standards of behavior **5. UNAUTHORIZED** not conforming to law or social conventions **6.** MIL **UNOFFICIAL** not forming part of an official military body **7.** GRAM **NOT FORMED BY USUAL GRAMMATICAL RULES** not following the usual rules of word formation **8.** MED **CONSTIPATED** not having a regular daily bowel movement (*used euphemistically*) **9.** COMM **SUBSTANDARD** not meeting the manufacturer's standards for goods but still salable **10.** BOT **HAVING ASYMMETRICAL PARTS** not having symmetrical parts ■ *n.* **1.** MIL **SOLDIER NOT PART OF REGULAR FORCES** a soldier who is not part of of an official military body **2.** COMM **SUBSTANDARD ITEM** an item of merchandise that does not meet the manufacturer's standards but is still salable (*often used in the plural*) [15thC. Via Old French *irreguler* from medieval Latin *irregularis* "breaking a rule," from *regularis* "of a rule" (see REGULAR).] —**ir·reg·u·lar·ly** *adv.*

ir·reg·u·lar·i·ty /i règgyə lérrətee/ (*plural* **-ties**) *n.* **1. BEING IRREGULAR** the state of being irregular **2. IRREGULAR THING** something irregular, e.g., a bump in a road **3. UNAUTHORIZED THING** something unauthorized or unacceptable by usual standards **4.** MED **CONSTIPATION** the state of not having a regular daily bowel movement (*used euphemistically*)

ir·rel·a·tive /i réllətiv/ *adj.* **1. NOT CONNECTED** not related or connected **2. NOT APPLICABLE** not relevant

ir·rel·e·vant /i rélləvənt/ *adj.* not relevant or important —**ir·rel·e·vance** *n.* —**ir·rel·e·van·cy** *n.* —**ir·rel·e·vant·ly** *adv.*

ir·re·lig·ious /ìrri líjjəss/ *adj.* **1. LACKING FAITH** lacking in any religious faith **2. AGAINST RELIGION** opposed to religion —**ir·re·lig·ious·ly** *adv.* —**ir·re·lig·ious·ness** *n.*

ir·re·me·a·ble /i reémee əb'l/ *adj.* not allowing any possibility of return (*archaic or literary*) [Late 16thC. From Latin *irremeabilis*, from *remeare* "to return."] —**ir·re·me·a·bly** *adv.*

ir·re·me·di·a·ble /ìrri meédee əb'l/ *adj.* impossible to remedy or make right [Mid-16thC. From late Latin *irremediabilis* "incurable," from *remediare* "to cure."] —**ir·re·me·di·a·ble·ness** *n.* —**ir·re·me·di·a·bly** *adv.*

ir·re·mis·si·ble /ìrri míssəb'l/ *adj.* **1. UNPARDONABLE** not able to be pardoned or excused **2. OBLIGATORY** not able to be avoided or postponed [15thC. Directly or via French from ecclesiastical Latin *irremissibilis* "unpardonable," from Latin *remiss-*, past participle stem of *remittere* "to forgive" (see REMISSION).] —**ir·re·mis·si·bil·i·ty** /ìrri missə bíllətee/ *n.* —**ir·re·mis·si·ble·ness** /ìrri míssəb'lnəss/ *n.* —**ir·re·mis·si·bly** *adv.*

ir·re·mov·a·ble /ìrri móovəb'l/ *adj.* incapable of being removed —**ir·re·mov·a·bil·i·ty** /ìrri moovə bíllətee/ *n.* —**ir·re·mov·a·ble·ness** /ìrri móovəb'lnəss/ *n.* —**ir·re·mov·a·bly** *adv.*

ir·rep·a·ra·ble /i réppərəb'l/ *adj.* not able to be repaired or fixed ○ *did irreparable damage to the computer* [15thC. Directly or via Old French from Latin *irreparabilis* "not to be recovered," from *reparare* "to recover" (source of *repair*).] —**ir·rep·a·ra·bil·i·ty** /i rèppərə bíllətee/ *n.* —**ir·rep·a·ra·ble·ness** /i réppərəb'lnəss/ *n.* —**ir·rep·a·ra·bly** *adv.*

ir·re·peal·a·ble /ìrri peéləb'l/ *adj.* not able to be repealed (*formal*) —**ir·re·peal·a·bil·i·ty** /ìrri peelə bíllətee/ *n.* —**ir·re·peal·a·ble·ness** /ìrri peéləb'lnəss/ *n.* —**ir·re·peal·a·bly** *adv.*

ir·re·place·a·ble /ìrri pláyssəb'l/ *adj.* not able to be replaced —**ir·re·place·a·bil·i·ty** /ìrri playssə bíllətee/ *n.* —**ir·re·place·a·ble·ness** /ìrri pláyssəb'lnəss/ *n.* —**ir·re·place·a·bly** *adv.*

ir·re·press·i·ble /ìrri préssəb'l/ *adj.* not able to be controlled ○ *irrepressible high spirits* —**ir·re·press·i·bil·i·ty** /ìrri pressə bíllətee/ *n.* —**ir·re·press·i·ble·ness** /ìrri préssəb'lnəss/ *n.* —**ir·re·press·i·bly** *adv.*

ir·re·proach·a·ble /ìrri prṓchəb'l/ *adj.* not incurring any reproach or criticism [Mid-17thC. From French *irréprochable*, from *réprochable* "reproachable."] —**ir·re·proach·a·bil·i·ty** /ìrri prōchə bíllətee/ *n.* —**ir·re·proach·a·ble·ness** /ìrri prṓchəb'lnəss/ *n.* —**ir·re·proach·a·bly** *adv.*

ir·re·pro·duc·i·ble /i reeprə dóossəb'l/ *adj.* impossible to reproduce —**ir·re·pro·duc·i·bil·i·ty** /i reeprə doossə bíllətee/ *n.*

ir·re·sis·ti·ble /ìrri zístəb'l/ *adj.* **1. OVERPOWERING** not able to be resisted or successfully opposed **2. VERY DESIRABLE** so desirable as to be very difficult to resist [Late 16thC. From medieval Latin *irresistibilis*, from Latin *resistere* "to oppose, resist."] —**ir·re·sis·ti·bil·i·ty** /ìrri zistə bíllətee/ *n.* —**ir·re·sis·ti·ble·ness** /ìrri zístəb'lnəss/ *n.* —**ir·re·sis·ti·bly** *adv.*

ir·re·sol·u·ble /ìrri zóllyəb'l/ *adj.* incapable of being solved, reconciled, or explained [Mid-17thC. From Latin *irresolubilis* "indissoluble," from *resolvere* "to melt, thaw, dissolve."] —**ir·re·sol·u·bil·i·ty** /ìrri zollyə bíllətee/ *n.* —**ir·re·sol·u·bly** /ìrri zóllyəblee/ *adv.*

ir·res·o·lute /i rézzə lòot/ *adj.* unsure and unable to make decisions —**ir·res·o·lute·ly** *adv.* —**ir·res·o·lute·ness** *n.* —**ir·res·o·lu·tion** /i rèzzə lóosh'n/ *n.*

ir·re·solv·a·ble /ìrri zólvəb'l/ *adj.* **1. IMPOSSIBLE TO RESOLVE INTO COMPONENT PARTS** not able to be broken down into different parts **2. INCAPABLE OF SOLUTION** not able to be solved —**ir·re·solv·a·bil·i·ty** /ìrri zolvə bíllətee/ *n.* —**ir·re·solv·a·ble·ness** /ìrri zólvəb'lnəss/ *n.* —**ir·re·solv·a·bly** *adv.*

ir·re·spec·tive /ìrri spéktiv/ *adj.* without considering or regarding something —**ir·re·spec·tive·ly** *adv.* ◇ **irrespective of** without consideration or regardless of

WORD KEY: USAGE

See Usage note at ***irregardless.***

ir·re·spon·si·ble /ìrri spónsəb'l/ *adj.* **1. NOT CARING** not having or showing any care for the consequences of personal actions **2.** LAW **INCAPABLE OF RESPONSIBILITY** not capable of assuming responsibility **3. NOT ACCOUNTABLE** not answerable to a higher authority (*archaic*) ■ *n.* **IRRESPONSIBLE PERSON** somebody who behaves irresponsibly —**ir·re·spon·si·bil·i·ty** /ìrri sponsə bíllətee/ *n.* —**ir·re·spon·si·ble·ness** /ìrri spónsəb'lnəss/ *n.* —**ir·re·spon·si·bly** *adv.*

ir·re·spon·sive /ìrri spónsiv/ *adj.* not responding quickly or favorably —**ir·re·spon·sive·ly** *adv.* —**ir·re·spon·sive·ness** *n.*

ir·re·triev·a·ble /ìrri treévəb'l/ *adj.* **1. INCAPABLE OF RECOVERY** impossible to find or recover **2. INCAPABLE OF REPAIR** impossible to repair or fix —**ir·re·triev·a·bil·i·ty** /ìrri treévə bíllətee/ *n.* —**ir·re·triev·a·ble·ness** /ìrri treévəb'lnəss/ *n.* —**ir·re·triev·a·bly** *adv.*

ir·rev·er·ence /i révvərənss/ *n.* **1. DISRESPECT** lack of respect or veneration **2. DISRESPECTFUL THING** something said or done that is disrespectful

ir·rev·er·ent /i révvərənt/ *adj.* lacking in respect [Mid-16thC. From Latin *irreverent-*, from the present participle stem of *revereri* "to revere, respect" (see REVERE).] —**ir·rev·er·ent·ly** *adv.*

ir·re·vers·i·ble /ìrri vúrsəb'l/ *adj.* impossible to reverse or undo —**ir·re·vers·i·bil·i·ty** /ìrri vursə bíllətee/ *n.* —**ir·re·vers·i·ble·ness** /ìrri vúrsəb'lnəss/ *n.* —**ir·re·vers·i·bly** *adv.*

ir·rev·o·ca·ble /i révvəkəb'l/ *adj.* not able to be revoked, undone, or changed [14thC. Directly or via French *irrévocable* from Latin *irrevocabilis* "that cannot be recalled or altered," from *revocare* "to recall," later "retract" (see REVOKE).] —**ir·rev·o·ca·bil·i·ty** /i rèvvəkə bíllətee/ *n.* —**ir·rev·o·ca·ble·ness** /i révvək əb'lnəss/ *n.* —**ir·rev·o·ca·bly** *adv.*

ir·ri·gate /írri gàyt/ (**-gat·ed, -gat·ing, -gates**) *vt.* **1.** AGRIC **SUPPLY AREA WITH WATER** to bring a supply of water to a dry area, especially in order to help crops to grow **2.** MED **WASH SOMETHING OUT** to make water or liquid medication flow through or over a body part or wound **3. REFRESH SOMETHING** to make something fresh [Early 17thC. From Latin *irrigat-*, past participle stem of *irrigare*, literally "to water in," from *rigare* "to water."] —**ir·ri·ga·ble** /írrigəb'l/ *adj.* —**ir·ri·ga·tion** /ìrri gáysh'n/ *n.* —**ir·ri·ga·tion·al** /-gáyshnəl/ *adj.* —**ir·ri·ga·tive** /írri gàytiv/ *adj.* —**ir·ri·ga·tor** *n.*

ir·ri·ta·ble /írritəb'l/ *adj.* **1. EASILY ANNOYED** easily annoyed or exasperated **2.** MED **SENSITIVE** extremely sensitive, especially to inflammation **3.** BIOL **RESPONSIVE TO STIMULI** used to describe an organism that is able to respond to stimuli [Mid-17thC. From Latin *irritabilis* "easily enraged," from *irritare* "to provoke, aggravate."] —**ir·ri·ta·bil·i·ty** /ìrritə bíllətee/ *n.* —**ir·ri·ta·ble·ness** /írritəb'lnəss/ *n.* —**ir·ri·ta·bly** *adv.*

ir·ri·ta·ble bow·el syn·drome *n.* a condition of the bowel in which there is recurrent pain with constipation or diarrhea or alternating attacks of these

ir·ri·tant /írritənt/ *adj.* **CAUSING IRRITATION** causing irritation, especially physical irritation ■ *n.* **ANNOYANCE** something that causes irritation [Early 17thC. From Latin *irritant-*, present participle stem of *irritare* "to provoke, aggravate."] —**ir·ri·tan·cy** *n.*

ir·ri·tate /írri tàyt/ (**-tat·ed, -tat·ing, -tates**) *v.* **1.** *vti.* **ANNOY SOMEBODY** to cause somebody to feel annoyance or exasperation, or cause annoyance or exasperation **2.** *vt.* MED **INFLAME BODY PART** to stimulate a body part excessively, causing a painful reaction, e.g., inflammation **3.** *vt.* BIOL **STIMULATE ORGANISM** to stimulate an organism so as to provoke a response [Mid-16thC. From Latin *irritat-*, past participle stem of *irritare* "to provoke, aggravate."] —**ir·ri·tat·ing** *adj.* —**ir·ri·tat·ing·ly** *adv.* —**ir·ri·ta·tive** *adj.* —**ir·ri·ta·tor** *n.*

WORD KEY: SYNONYMS

See Synonyms at ***annoy.***

ir·ri·ta·tion /ìrri táysh'n/ *n.* **1. ANNOYANCE** a feeling of annoyance or exasperation **2. ACT OF ANNOYING** the act of causing annoyance or exasperation **3. SOMEBODY OR SOMETHING ANNOYING** something who or somebody that causes annoyance or exasperation **4.** MED **REACTION TO IRRITANT** a painful reaction, especially an inflammation, caused by an irritant **5.** MED **INFLAMING** the act of causing a painful reaction, especially an inflammation

ir·rupt /i rúpt/ (**-rupt·ed, -rupt·ing, -rupts**) *vi.* **1. ENTER ABRUPTLY** to enter suddenly or violently **2. INCREASE QUICKLY** to increase suddenly and rapidly, e.g., in number [Mid-19thC. From Latin *irrupt-*, past participle stem of *irrumpere* "to break into a place," from *rumpere* "to break" (source of English *rupture*).] —**ir·rup·tion** /i rúpshən/ *n.*

ir·rup·tive /i rúptiv/ *adj.* **1. BREAKING IN** entering suddenly, or likely to enter suddenly **2.** GEOL **INJECTED INTO ROCK** used to describe igneous rock that is injected forcibly into preexisting rock formations —**ir·rup·tive·ly** *adv.*

IRS *abbr.* Internal Revenue Service

Ir·tysh /ir tísh/ ➧ **Ob'**

Ir·vine /úr vīn, úrvīn/ city in southwestern California, situated just southeast of Santa Ana. Population: 125,624 (1994).

Cook Neilson

John Irving

Ir·ving /úrving/, **John** (*b.* 1942) U.S. novelist. His works include *The World According to Garp* (1978) and *The Hotel New Hampshire* (1981).

Ir·ving, Washington (1783–1859) U.S. writer. The first U.S. author to achieve international renown, he is best known for *The Sketch Book* (1819–20), which includes the stories "Rip Van Winkle" and "The Legend of Sleepy Hollow."

Ir·ving·ton /úrvingtən/ **1.** town in northeastern New Jersey, situated southwest of and adjoining Newark. Population: 61,018 (1990). **2.** village in Westchester County, New York, situated on the Hudson River 22 mi./35 km north of New York City

is 3rd person present singular of **be**

IS *abbr.* **1.** COMPUT information services **2.** Iceland (*international vehicle registration*)

is. *abbr.* **1.** island **2.** isle

Is. *abbr.* **1.** BIBLE Isaiah **2.** GEOG Island (*used in placenames*) **3.** GEOG Isle (*used in placenames*)

is- *prefix.* = **iso-** (*used before vowels*)

ISA *abbr.* International Standard Atmosphere

Isa. *abbr.* BIBLE Isaiah

Is·a·bel·la I /ìzzə béllə/, **Queen of Castile and León** (1451–1504). The heir to the crown of Castile and León, she married Ferdinand of Aragón (1469), bringing about the unification of Spain. As queen of Castile and León (1474–1504), she supported the Inquisition, expelled the Jews from Spain, and defeated Granada, the last Moorish kingdom in Spain. She sponsored Christopher Columbus's voyages. Known as **Isabella the Catholic**

Is·a·bel·la II, Queen of Spain (1830–1904). She ruled from 1833 until she was deposed in 1868. Her reign was marked by political turmoil and insurrection.

is·a·gog·ics /ìssə gójjiks/ *n.* introductory studies, especially introducing the Bible in its literary and historical contexts (*takes a singular verb*) —**is·a·goge** /íssə gōjee, ìssə gōjee/ *n.*

I·sa·iah /ī záy ə/ *n.* **1. HEBREW PROPHET** a Hebrew prophet who lived in the latter half of the 8th century B.C. He was the earliest of the major prophets. **2. BOOK IN BIBLE** a book in the Bible that contains prophecies and apocalyptic material. It is traditionally thought to have been written by Isaiah. See table at **Bible**

is·al·o·bar /ī sállə baar/ *n.* a contour line on a weather chart joining places where equal changes in atmospheric pressure occurred during a given time interval [Early 20thC. Coined from IS(O)- + ALLO- + Greek *baros* "weight," on the model of ISOBAR.]

i·sa·tin /íssət'n/ *n.* a water-soluble compound related to indigo and indole that crystallizes as orange needles and is used in the maufacture of vat dyes. Formula: $C_8H_5NO_2$. [Mid-19thC. Coined from Greek *isatis* "woad" + -IN.] —**i·sa·tin·ic** /ìssə tínnik/ *adj.*

ISBN *abbr.* International Standard Book Number

is·chae·mi·a *n.* U.K. = **ischemia**

is·che·mi·a /i skeémee ə/ *n.* an inadequate supply of blood to a part of the body, caused by partial or total blockage of an artery —**i·sche·mic** *adj.*

Is·chi·a /ískee ə/ island in west central Italy, situated in the Tyrrhenian Sea between the Gulf of Gaeta and the Bay of Naples. Its highest point is Monte Epomeo, 2,589 ft./789 m. Population: 17,600 (1990). Area: 18 sq. mi./47 sq. km.

is·chi·um /ískee əm/ (*plural* **-a** /-ə/) *n.* the lowest and rearmost of the three bones that make up each half of the pelvis [Early 17thC. Via Latin from Greek *iskhion* "hip joint."] —**is·chi·al** *adj.*

ISD *abbr.* international subscriber dialing

ISDN *n.* a digital telephone network that can transmit both voice and data messages. Full form **Integrated Services Digital Network**

-ise *suffix.* *U.K.* = **-ize**

is·en·trope /íss'n trōp, íz'n-/ *n.* a line on a graph or chart linking points of equal entropy [Back-formation from ISENTROPIC]

is·en·tro·pic /ìss'n tróppik, ìz'n-/ *adj.* **1. HAVING CONSTANT ENTROPY** used to describe a reaction or process that takes place without a change in entropy **2. OF ISENTROPE** relating to an isentrope —**is·en·tro·pi·cal·ly** *adv.*

-ish *suffix.* **1.** characteristic of, like, tending to ○ *churlish* ○ *babyish* ○ *bookish* **2.** of or relating to, from ○ *Gaulish* **3.** somewhat, approximately ○ *bluish* ○ *latish* [Old English *-isc*, of prehistoric Germanic origin]

Ish·er·wood /íshər wŏŏd/, **Christopher** (1904–86) British writer. He described prewar Berlin in two volumes of short stories, *Mr Norris Changes Trains* (1935) and *Goodbye to Berlin* (1939). Full name **Christopher William Bradshaw Isherwood**

Ish·ma·el /íshmee əl, ísh màyl/ *n.* **1. OUTCAST IN BIBLE** in the Bible, the son of Abraham, expelled into the desert after the birth of his brother Isaac, the forebear of twelve desert tribes. Muslims regard themselves as his descendants. (Genesis 16–21) **2. OUTCAST** an outcast (*literary*)

Ish·ma·el·ite /íshmee ə līt, ísh mayə līt/ *n.* **1. DESCENDANT OF ISHMAEL** a descendant of Abraham's son Ishmael **2.** = **Ishmael** *n.* 2 (*literary*) —**Ish·ma·el·it·ish** *adj.* —**Ish·ma·el·it·ism** *n.*

Ish·tar /ísh taar/ *n.* in Babylonian and Assyrian mythology, the queen of heaven and goddess of fertility. Tammuz was her consort. She was worshiped throughout the Middle East under various names, including the Phoenician Astarte.

i·sin·glass /íz'n glàss, ízing-/ *n.* **1.** INDUST **GELATIN USED IN ADHESIVES** a transparent or translucent gelatin made from the air bladders of various fish, especially the sturgeon, and used as a clarifying agent and in adhesives and jellies **2.** GEOL = **mica** [Mid-16thC. By folk etymology from obsolete early Dutch *huysenblas* "sturgeon's bladder" (from *huysen* "sturgeon" + *blas* "bladder"), applied to the bladder's gelatinous product.]

I·sis[1] /íssiss/ *n.* in Egyptian mythology, the goddess of fertility, generally depicted wearing a cow's horns bearing a golden disk representing the sun. She was the wife of her brother Osiris and the mother of Horus.

I·sis[2] /íssəss/ alternative name for the Thames River around Oxford, England

Is·ken·de·run /eess kéndə roon/, **Is·ken·de·ron** city in southern Turkey, on the southeastern shore of the Gulf of Iskenderun, situated approximately 60 mi./96 km southeast of Adana. Population: 154,807 (1990).

isl. *abbr.* **1.** island **2.** isle

Is·lam /is laam, iz-, íz laam, ís-/ *n.* **1. MUSLIM RELIGION** the religion of Muslims, based upon the teachings of Muhammad during the 7th century and now the second largest of the great religions in number of believers **2. MUSLIM WORLD** Muslim people, their culture, or their countries considered collectively [Early 17thC. From Arabic *islām*, literally "submission (to God)," from the base of *aslama* "he surrendered" (source of English *Muslim* and *salaam* "peace").] —**Is·lam·ic** /is laamik, iz-/ *adj.*

Is·lam·a·bad /iz laámmə bad/, **Is·lām·ā·bād** city and capital of Pakistan, situated northeast of Rawalpindi. Population: 204,364 (1981).

Is·lam·ism /íssla mìzzəm, ízz-/ *n.* = **Islam** *n.* 1

Is·lam·ize /íssla mīz, ízzlə-/ (**-ized, -iz·ing, -iz·es**) *vt.* **1.** CONVERT TO ISLAM to convert people or countries to Islam **2.** MAKE SUBJECT TO ISLAMIC LAW to cause people, institutions, or countries to follow Islamic law —**Is·lam·i·za·tion** /ísslәmi záysh'n, ìzzlәmi-/ *n.*

is·land /ílənd/ *n.* **1.** GEOG LAND SURROUNDED BY WATER an area of land, smaller than a continent, that is completely surrounded by water (*often used in placenames*) **2.** SOMETHING LIKE AN ISLAND something that is like an island because it is isolated or surrounded by something different ○ *"No man is an island, entire of itself."* (John Donne, *Devotions upon Emergent Occasions*; 1624) **3.** ANAT ISOLATED BODY PART a body part or group of cells that is different in construction from its surroundings ■ *vt.* (**-land·ed, -land·ing, -lands**) **1.** MAKE SOMETHING INTO AN ISLAND to form something into an island **2.** ISOLATE SOMEBODY to cause somebody to feel isolated, e.g., from contact with peers or colleagues **3.** SET WITH ISLANDS to provide a stretch of water with islands (*literary*) [Old English *īegland*, from *īeg* "island" (ultimately from an Indo-European word meaning "water") + LAND]

WORD KEY: ORIGIN

Despite their similarity, ***island*** and *isle* have completely different origins. ***Island*** goes back to Old English, whereas *isle* comes from Latin *insula*, meaning "island." The resemblance is due to a 16th-century change in the spelling of ***island*** under the influence of the semantically close *isle*.

is·land arc *n.* an arc-shaped chain of islands, usually found in an area of volcanic or seismic activity

is·land·er /íləndər/ *n.* somebody who lives on an island

is·land-hop *vi.* to travel from island to island within the same chain, especially as part of a vacation (*informal*)

is·lands of Lang·er·hans /-laángər haàns/ *npl.* = **islets of Langerhans**

Is·lands of the Bless·ed *npl.* MYTHOL = **Hesperides**

Is·lay /ílə, ī lay/ the southernmost island of the Inner Hebrides, western Scotland. Area: 235 sq. mi./609 sq. km.

isle /īl/ *n.* an island, often a small one (*literary*) [13thC. From Old French *ile* (the variant *isle* later influenced the English word), from Latin *insula* (source of English *insulate* and *peninsula*).]

Isle of Man ➧ **Man, Isle of**

Isle of Wight ➧ **Wight, Isle of**

Isle Roy·ale Na·tion·al Park /-ròy əl-/ national park in northwestern Michigan, on Isle Royale and nearby islands in Lake Superior. Area: 571,790 acres/231,395 hectares.

is·let /ílət/ *n.* a small isle or island

is·lets of Lang·er·hans /-laángər haàns/ *npl.* clusters of endocrine cells found in the pancreas that secrete insulin and glucagon

Is·lip /ízlip/ **1.** town in Suffolk County, southeastern New York, situated on Long Island. Population: 299,587 (1994). **2.** village in Oxfordshire, central England, approximately 6 mi./10 km north of Oxford

ism /ízzəm/ (*plural* **isms**) *n.* a movement, doctrine, or system of belief (*informal*) [Late 17thC. From -ISM.]

-ism *suffix.* **1.** action, process ○ *mesmerism* ○ *volcanism* **2.** characteristic behavior or manner ○ *despotism* **3.** state, condition ○ *conservatism* ○ *gangsterism* **4.** abnormal state ○ *caffeinism* **5.** doctrine, system of beliefs ○ *defeatism* ○ *Calvinism* **6.** prejudice ○ *sexism* **7.** distinctive feature or trait ○ *Southernism* ○ *vulgarism* [Via Old French *-isme* and Latin *-ismus* from Greek *-ismos*]

Is·ma·i·li /ìzmə éelee, ìz maa-, ìsmə-, ìs maa-/ *n.* a member of a branch of Shiite Muslims whose members believe that Ismail, son of the sixth imam, was the true seventh imam [Mid-19thC. From Arabic, formed from the proper name *'Ismā'īl*.]

Is·ma·i·liy·ya /ìzmə éelee ə/ city in northeastern Egypt, situated on Lake Timsah. It is the halfway station on the Suez Canal. Population: 255,000 (1992).

is·n't /ízz'nt/ *contr.* is not ○ *It isn't ready yet.*

ISO *abbr.* **1.** International Standards Organization **2.** in search of

iso- *prefix.* **1.** equal, uniform ○ *isoelectric* ○ *isogloss* **2.** isomeric ○ *isooctane* **3.** of or for different members of the same species ○ *isoagglutination* [From Greek *isos* "equal," of unknown origin]

i·so·ag·glu·ti·na·tion /íssō əgloot'n áysh'n/ *n.* the clumping together (**agglutination**) of red blood cells in one individual induced by antibodies in the serum of another individual of the same species —**i·so·ag·glu·ti·na·tive** /íssō əglóot'n àytiv/ *adj.*

i·so·ag·glu·ti·nin /íssō ə glóot'nin/ *n.* an antibody from one individual that causes the clumping together (**agglutination**) of red blood cells in another individual of the same species but of a different blood group

i·so·bar /íssə baàr/ *n.* **1.** METEOROL LINE SHOWING WEATHER PATTERNS a line drawn on a weather map that connects places with equal atmospheric pressure. Isobars are often used collectively to indicate the movement or formation of weather systems. **2.** PHYS ATOM WITH THE SAME MASS NUMBER one of two or more atoms or elements having the same mass number but different atomic numbers [Mid-19thC. From Greek *isobaros*, literally "of equal weight."] —**i·so·bar·ism** *n.*

i·so·bar·ic /íssə bérrik/ *adj.* **1.** WITH CONSTANT ATMOSPHERIC PRESSURE having constant or equal atmospheric pressure **2.** OF ISOBARS relating to isobars

i·so·bar·ic spin *n.* PHYS = **isospin**

i·so·bath /íssō bàth/ *n.* a line on a map of the sea that connects points that are at the same depth [Late 19thC. Coined from ISO- + Greek *bathos* "depth."] —**i·so·bath·ic** /íssō báthik/ *adj.*

i·so·bu·tane /íssō byoō tàyn/ *n.* a colorless gaseous hydrocarbon that is an isomer of butane and is used especially as a fuel and refrigerant. Formula: C_4H_{10}.

i·so·car·box·a·zid /íssō kaar bóksəzid/ *n.* a substance used as an antidepressant drug. Formula: $C_{12}H_{13}N_3O_2$. [Mid-20thC. Formed from ISO- + a contraction of CARBONYL + OX- + HYDRAZIDE, elements of its chemical name.]

i·so·cheim /íssə kīm/, **i·so·chime** *n.* a line on a weather map connecting places that have the same average temperature in winter [Mid-19thC. Coined from ISO- + Greek *kheima* "winter weather."] —**i·so·cheim·al** /íssə kīm'l/ *adj.* —**i·so·cheime·nal** /-kīmən'l/ *adj.*

i·so·chro·mat·ic /íssə krō máttik/ *adj.* **1.** = **orthochromatic 2.** WITH EQUAL COLOR OR WAVELENGTH having the same color or wavelength of light

i·soch·ro·nous /ī sókrənəss/, **i·soch·ro·nal** /-krən'l/ *adj.* **1.** WITH EQUAL FREQUENCY having the same frequency or periodicity **2.** MEASURED AT OR LASTING THE SAME TIME measured or occurring at the same time, or lasting for the same length of time —**i·soch·ro·nous·ly** *adv.*

i·soch·ro·ous /ī sókrō əss/ *adj.* having the same color throughout [Mid-19thC. Coined from ISO- + Greek *khros* "color."]

i·so·cli·nal /íssə klīn'l/ *adj.* **1.** WITH THE SAME SLOPE having the same inclination or slope **2.** GEOL HAVING PARALLEL SIDES having the sides of a geological fold parallel to one another ■ *n.* **1.** = **isocline 2.** = **isoclinic line**

i·so·cline /íssə klīn/ *n.* **1.** FOLD OF ROCK STRATA a geologic fold with rock beds that slope in the same direction **2.** = **isoclinic line** [Late 19thC. From Greek *isoklinēs* "equally balanced," literally "leaning equally," from *klinein* "to lean."]

i·so·clin·ic /íssə klínnik/ *adj.* = **isoclinal**

i·so·clin·ic line *n.* a line on a map connecting points on the Earth's surface that have the same magnetic dip

i·so·cy·a·nate /íssə sī ə nàyt/ *n.* a chemical compound used in resins and adhesives, containing the chemical group -NCO

i·so·cy·a·nide /íssə sī ə nīd/ *n.* a colorless liquid with a very unpleasant odor that contains the chemical group -NC

i·so·di·a·met·ric /íssō dī ə méttrik/ *adj.* with diameters or axes of equal length

i·so·dose /íssə dòss/ *n.* a dose of radiation of equal intensity applied to more than one part of the body as a medical treatment

i·so·dy·nam·ic /íssō dī námmik/ *adj.* **1.** WITH EQUAL STRENGTH having the same strength or intensity **2.** SHOWING EQUAL MAGNETIC INTENSITY connecting points on a map of the Earth's surface that have the same magnetic intensity [Mid-19thC. Formed from Greek *isodunamos*, literally "of equal power" + -IC.]

i·so·e·lec·tric /íssō i léktrik/ *adj.* having exactly the same electric potential

i·so·e·lec·tron·ic /íssō i lek trónnik/ *adj.* with the same number of electrons or the same outer atomic structure —**iso·e·lec·tron·i·cal·ly** *adv.*

i·so·en·zyme /íssō én zīm/ *n.* one of two or more enzymes that are different chemically but function in the same way —**i·so·en·zy·mat·ic** /íssō enzi máttik/ *adj.* —**i·so·en·zy·mic** /íssō en zímmik/ *adj.*

i·so·ga·mete /íssō gá meet, -gə méet/ *n.* a gamete physically identical to another with which it unites to form a zygote —**i·so·ga·met·ic** /íssōgə méttik/ *adj.*

i·sog·a·my /ī sóggəmee/ *n.* the fusion of isogametes in some algae and fungi during reproduction

i·so·gen·eic /íssōjə née ik/ *adj.* = **syngeneic** [Mid-20thC. Alteration of ISOGENIC.]

i·so·gen·ic /íssə jénnik/ *adj.* having identical genes ○ *an isogenic line* [Mid-20thC. Coined from ISO- + Greek *genea* "race, stock."]

i·sog·e·nous /ī sójjənəss/ *adj.* **1.** WITH THE SAME ORIGIN used to describe bodily organs or parts that have the same or a similar origin **2.** = **isogenic** —**i·sog·e·ny** *n.*

i·so·gloss /íssə glòss/ *n.* a line on a language map that surrounds an area within which a linguistic usage, e.g., a dialectal word, is found [Early 20thC. Formed from ISO- + Greek *glossa* "language."] —**i·so·gloss·al** /íssə glóss'l/ *adj.* —**i·so·glos·sic** /-glóssik/ *adj.* —**i·so·glot·tal** /-glótt'l/ *adj.* —**i·so·glot·tic** /-glóttik/ *adj.*

i·sog·o·nal *adj.* = **isogonic**

i·sog·o·nal line *n.* = **isogonic line**

i·so·gone *n.* = **isogonic line**

i·so·gon·ic /íssə gónnik/, **i·sog·o·nal** /ī sóggən'l/ *adj.* WITH EQUAL ANGLES having equal angles ■ *n.* = **isogonic line** [Mid-19thC. Formed from Greek *isogōnios* "equiangular."]

i·so·gon·ic line *n.* a line on a map of the Earth's surface connecting places of equal magnetic declination

i·so·graft /íssə gràft/ *n.* a tissue graft taken from an individual genetically identical to the recipient of the graft, e.g., from an identical twin

i·so·gram /íssə gràm/ *n.* = **isoline**

i·so·hel /íssə hèl/ *n.* a line on a map connecting places that receive the same number of hours of sunshine in the course of a year [Early 20thC. Coined from ISO- + Greek *hēlios* "sun."]

i·so·hy·et /íssə hī ət/ *n.* a line on a map connecting places that receive the same amount of rainfall in the course of a year [Late 19thC. Coined from ISO- + Greek *huetos* "rain."] —**i·so·hy·et·al** *adj.*

i·so·la·ni (*plural* **-nis**) *n.* CHESS = **isolated pawn**

i·so·late *vt.* /íssə làyt/ (**-lat·ed, -lat·ing, -lates**) **1.** SEPARATE SOMEBODY FROM OTHERS to separate a person or place from others of the same type **2.** MED QUARANTINE SOMEBODY to keep somebody who is infected away from others to prevent the spread of a contagious disease **3.** CUT A PLACE OFF to make a place unreachable from the surrounding area ○ *Heavy snowfalls have temporarily isolated the town.* **4.** FIND A CAUSE OF SOMETHING to discover which of a number of possible causes or factors is responsible for a particular phenomenon or problem ○ *He isolated the failure to a bug in the software.* **5.** BIOL SEPARATE OUT to separate out a chemical or biological material such as a virus or bacterium in order to identify and study it **6.** ELECTRON ENG INSULATE AN ELECTRONIC DEVICE to prevent a circuit or device from interacting with another or with an outside stimulus ■ *n.* /íssələt/ **1.** LONE PERSON OR GROUP a person or group separated or cut off from others **2.** BIOL, CHEM MICROORGANISM GROWN IN A LABORATORY a sample of biological material, especially a microorganism, that has been cultured for study **3.** LING ONLY LANGUAGE OF A FAMILY a language that is the only known surviving member of its language family [Early 19thC. Back-formation from ISOLATED, from French *isolé*, ultimately from late Latin *insulatus* "made into an island," from Latin *insula* "island" (see INSULAR).] —

i·so·la·ble /íssələb'l/ *adj.* —**i·so·lat·a·ble** /íssə láytəb'l/ *adj.* —**i·so·la·tor** *n.*

i·so·lat·ed /íssə làytəd/ *adj.* **1. OFF BY ITSELF** far away from other inhabited areas or buildings **2. ALONE OR LONELY** without enough social contact, friends, or support **3. RARE** happening singly, rarely, or only once and unlikely to recur or prove a continuing problem ○ *an isolated incident*

i·so·lat·ed pawn *n.* in chess, a pawn that is not supported by other pawns of the same color on adjacent files

i·so·lat·ing /íssə làyting/ *adj.* LING = **analytic**

i·so·la·tion /íssə láysh'n/ *n.* **1. SEPARATION FROM OTHERS** the process of separating somebody or something from others, or the fact of being alone and separated from others **2. GEOGRAPHIC REMOTENESS** remoteness from other inhabited areas or buildings ◇ **in isolation 1.** separate from other related factors or things ○ *we have to look at the problem in isolation* **2.** alone and physically separated from other people

i·so·la·tion·ism /íssə láysh'n ìzzəm/ *n.* **1.** POL **AVOIDANCE OF INTERNATIONAL RELATIONS** a government policy based on the belief that national interests are best served by avoiding economic and political alliances with other countries **2.** MUSIC **TYPE OF ELECTRONIC AMBIENT MUSIC** a type of electronic ambient music that is generally produced without beats, creating a soothing ambience with unusual sounds —**i·so·la·tion·ist** *n., adj.*

i·so·la·tive /íssə làytiv/ *adj.* **1.** PHON **RELATING TO PHONETIC CHANGES** relating to a sound change that occurs in all phonetic environments such as in the Great Vowel Shift **2. CAUSING ISOLATION** causing somebody or something to be separated or cut off

i·so·lec·i·thal /íssə léssithəl/ *adj.* used to describe the eggs of mammals and some other vertebrates in which the yolk is evenly distributed throughout the egg

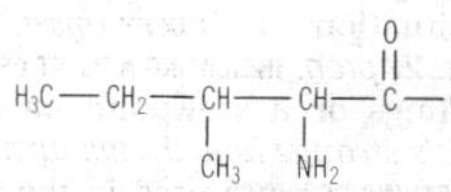

Isoleucine

i·so·leu·cine /íssə lóoss'n/ *n.* an amino acid, obtained by animals from their diet, that is an isomer of leucine and is found in most proteins. Formula: $C_6H_{13}NO_2$.

i·so·lex /íssə lèks/ *n.* a line on a language map that surrounds an area within which a particular word is used [Early 20thC. Coined from ISO- + Greek *lexis* "word."]

i·so·line /íssō līn/ *n.* a line on a map connecting points with the same value for variables such as temperature or air pressure

i·so·lo·gous /ī sólləgəss/ *adj.* used to describe two organic compounds that have the same molecular structure but different atoms of the same valence [Mid-19thC. Formed from ISO- + Greek *logos* "ratio."]

i·so·mag·net·ic /íssō mag néttik/, **i·so·mag·net·ic line** *n.* a line on a map connecting points of the same magnetic force —**i·so·mag·net·ic** *adj.*

i·so·mer /íssəmər/ *n.* **1. CHEMICALLY IDENTICAL MOLECULE WITH A DIFFERENT STRUCTURE** one of two or more molecules that have the same number of atoms but have different chemical structures and therefore different properties **2. NUCLIDE WITH A DIFFERENT ENERGY STATE** one of two or more nuclides that have the same mass number and atomic number but different energy states and half-lives [Mid-19thC. Formed from Greek *isomerēs*, literally "sharing equally."] —**i·so·mer·ic** /íssə mérrik/ *adj.*

i·som·er·ase /ī sómmə ràyss, -ràyz/ *n.* an enzyme that converts one isomer into another

i·som·er·ism /ī sómmə rìzzəm/ *n.* **1. EXISTENCE OF ISOMERS** the existence of two or more molecules that are isomers **2. EXISTENCE OF NUCLIDES THAT ARE ISOMERS** the existence of two or more nuclides that are isomers

i·som·er·ize /ī sómmə rìz/ (-ized, -iz·ing, -iz·es) *vti.* to change something into an isomer or become an isomer —**i·som·er·i·za·tion** /ī sòmməri záysh'n/ *n.*

i·som·er·ous /ī sómmərəss/ *adj.* ZOOL, BIOL with parts that are similar in number, markings, or other characteristics

i·so·met·ric /íssə méttrik/, **i·so·met·ri·cal** /íssə méttrik'l/ *adj.* **1. EQUAL** equal in dimension or measurement **2.** PHYSIOL **INVOLVING PUSHING THE MUSCLES AGAINST SOMETHING** used to describe exercises in which muscles are put under tension but not allowed to contract **3.** CRYSTALS **WITH THREE EQUAL AXES** used to describe a crystalline system that has three equal axes at right angles to one another **4.** POETRY **WITH LINES OF THE SAME LENGTH** having the same number of metrical feet in each line of poetry **5.** ENG **PROJECTED AT THE SAME ANGLE TO AXES** projected so that the plane of projection of a three-dimensional drawing is at an equal angle to each of the three axes of the object drawn [Mid-19thC. Formed from Greek *isometria*, literally "equality of measure."] —**i·so·met·ri·cal·ly** *adv.*

i·so·met·rics /íssə méttriks/ *n.* a form of exercise in which the muscles are pushed against something fixed or against other muscles to strengthen them (*takes a singular or plural verb*)

i·so·me·tro·pi·a /íssōmə trṓpee ə/ *n.* a condition of equal refraction in both eyes [Coined from Greek *isometros* "of equal measure" (from *metron* "measure") + -OPIA]

i·som·e·try /ī sómmətree/ (*plural* **-tries**) *n.* **1. EQUAL MEASUREMENTS** equality of measure **2.** MATH **GEOMETRIC TRANSFORMATION** a geometric transformation such as the rotation of a plane in which the distance between any two points is preserved

i·so·morph /íssə màwrf/ *n.* a substance or organism that exhibits similarity in form or appearance to others (**isomorphism**)

i·so·mor·phic /íssə máwrfik/ *adj.* **1.** BIOL **LOOKING LIKE ANOTHER ORGANISM** having the same form or appearance as another organism or the same organism at a different stage in its life cycle **2.** MATH **CORRESPONDING** used to describe mathematical sets with a one-to-one correspondence so that an operation such as addition or multiplication in one produces the same result as the analogous operation in the other **3.** CHEM = **isomorphous** —**i·so·mor·phi·cal·ly** *adv.*

i·so·mor·phism /íssə máwr fìzzəm/ *n.* **1.** BIOL **SIMILARITY IN ORGANISMS** similarity in form or appearance between organisms of different ancestry or between different stages in the life cycle of the same organism **2.** MATH **CORRESPONDENCE BETWEEN SETS** a one-to-one correspondence between sets such that an operation such as addition or multiplication in one produces the same result as the analogous operation in the other **3.** CHEM **SIMILARITY BETWEEN CHEMICALS** similarity in crystalline form between chemicals

i·so·mor·phous /íssə máwrfəss/ *adj.* used to describe a chemical compound that is able to crystallize in a form similar to another chemical compound

i·so·ni·a·zid /íssə nī́ əzid/ *n.* a colorless crystalline compound used to treat tuberculosis. Formula: $C_6H_7N_3O$. [Mid-20thC. Formed from ISO- + a contraction of NICOTINIC + HYDRAZIDE, elements of its chemical name.]

i·so·oc·tane /íssō ók tàyn/ *n.* a flammable isomer of octane used to determine the octane number of fuel. Formula: $(CH_3)_3CCH_2$.

i·so·pach /íssə pàk/ *n.* a line on a map of the Earth's surface connecting points where a rock stratum has equal thickness [Early 20thC. Coined from ISO- + Greek *pakhus* "thick."]

i·so·phone /íssə fōn/ *n.* a line on a language map surrounding an area within which a particular pronunciation is used

i·so·pi·es·tic /íssō pī éstik/ *adj.* METEOROL = **isobaric** [Coined from ISO- + Greek *piezein* "to press, squeeze"] —**i·so·pi·es·ti·cal·ly** *adv.*

i·so·pleth /íssə plèth/ *n.* METEOROL = **isoline** [Early 20thC. From Greek *isoplēthēs*, literally "equal in quantity."] —**i·so·pleth·ic** /íssə pléthik/ *adj.*

i·so·pod /íssə pòd/ *n.* a small invertebrate animal with a flattened body and seven pairs of legs. Sow bugs are isopods but most are marine. Order: Isopoda. [Mid-19thC. From modern Latin *Isopoda*, order name, literally "equal foot," from the Greek stem *pod-* "foot."] —**i·so·po·dan** /ī sóppəd'n/ *adj.* —**i·so·po·dous** /ī sóppədəss/ *adj.*

i·so·pre·na·line /íssə prénn'lin, íssə prénn'l een/ *n.* PHARM = **isoproterenol** [Mid-20thC. Contraction of *N-isopropylnoradrenaline*, its chemical name.]

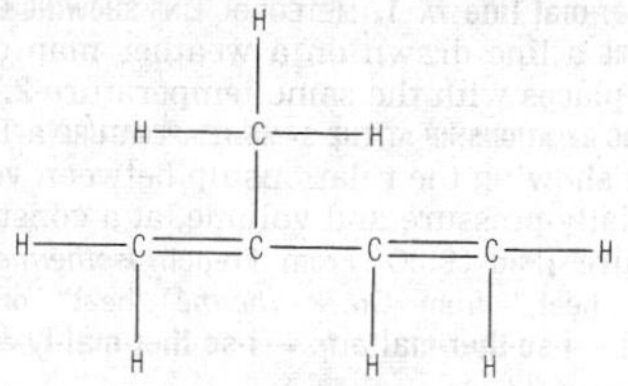

Isoprene

i·so·prene /íssə preen/ *n.* a colorless flammable liquid hydrocarbon used in making synthetic rubber. Formula: C_5H_8. [Mid-19thC. Formed from ISO- + a contraction of *prophylene*, its chemical name.]

iso·pro·pa·nol /íssə prṓpə nòl/ *n.* = **isopropyl alcohol**

iso·pro·pyl /íssə prṓp'l/ *n.* a chemical radical isomer of propyl. Formula: C_3H_7.

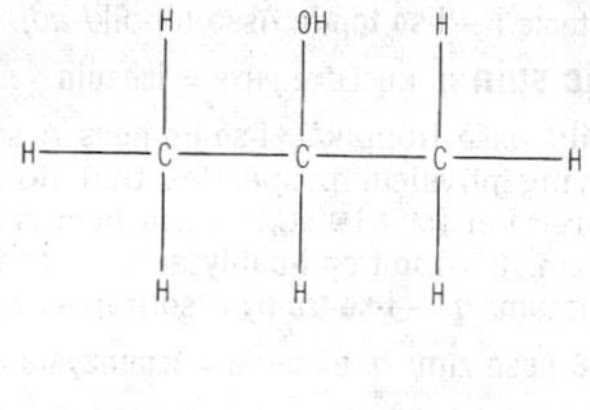

Isopropyl alcohol

iso·pro·pyl al·co·hol *n.* a colorless flammable alcohol used in antifreeze and rubbing alcohol and as a solvent.

i·so·pro·ter·e·nol /íssəprō térrə nàwl/ *n.* a compound used as a bronchodilator in the treatment of asthma. Formula: $C_{11}H_{17}NO_3$. [Mid-20thC. Contraction of *N-isopropylarterenol*, its chemical name.]

ISO rat·ing *n.* a measure of the sensitivity to light of a material such as photographic film or paper

i·so·rhy·thm /íssə rithəm/ *n.* a technique of musical composition of the 14th and 15th centuries that uses a repeated rhythmic pattern —**i·so·rhyth·mic** /íssə ríthmik/ *adj.*

i·sos·ce·les /ī sóssə leez/ *adj.* **1. WITH TWO OUT OF THREE EQUAL SIDES** used to describe a triangle in which two of the three sides are of equal length **2. WITH TWO OUT OF FOUR EQUAL SIDES** used to describe a trapezoid in which the two nonparallel sides are of equal length [Mid-16thC. From late Latin, from Greek *isoskelēs*, literally "equally legged."]

i·so·seis·mal /íssə sī́zməl/, **i·so·seis·mic** /íssə sī́zmik/ *adj.* **WITH EQUAL EARTHQUAKE INTENSITY** relating to or showing equal strength of earthquake shock ■ *n.* **LINE SHOWING EQUAL STRENGTH OF EARTHQUAKE** a line on a map connecting points of equal strength of earthquake shock

i·sos·mot·ic /ìs oz móttik/ *adj.* CHEM relating to or exerting equal osmotic pressure —**i·sos·mot·i·cal·ly** *adv.*

i·so·spin /íssə spìn/ *n.* a quantum characteristic of baryons and mesons that relates to the number of different values of electric charge they can have. Symbol I [Mid-20thC. Shortening of ISOBARIC SPIN and ISOTOPIC SPIN.]

i·sos·ta·sy /ī sóstəssee/ *n.* a state of equilibrium between forces such as accumulated ice pushing down on a section of the Earth's surface and those pushing up from below [Late 19thC. Formed from ISO- + Greek *stasis* "station, stoppage."] —**i·so·stat·ic** /íssə státtik/ *adj.* —**i·so·stat·i·cal·ly** /-státtikalee/ *adv.*

i·so·tach /ísə tàk/ *n.* a line on a weather map connecting points where the wind speed is equal [Mid-20thC. Coined from ISO- + Greek *takhos* "speed."]

i·so·tac·tic /ìsə táktik/ *adj.* used to describe a polymer that exhibits a repetitive stereochemical structure [Mid-20thC. Formed from ISO- + Greek *taktos* "ordered."]

i·so·therm /ísə thùrm/, **i·so·ther·mal** /ìsə thúrm'l/, **i·so·ther·mal line** *n.* **1.** METEOROL **LINE SHOWING EQUAL TEMPERATURE** a line drawn on a weather map that connects places with the same temperature **2.** PHYS **LINE SHOWING RELATIONSHIP AT THE SAME TEMPERATURE** a line on a graph showing the relationship between variables, especially pressure and volume, at a constant temperature [Mid-19thC. From French *isotherme*, literally "equal heat," from Greek *thermē* "heat" or *thermos* "hot."] —**i·so·ther·mal** *adj.* —**i·so·ther·mal·ly** *adv.*

i·so·tone /ísə tōn/ *n.* either of two or more atoms with the same number of neutrons but different atomic numbers

i·so·ton·ic /ìsə tónnik/ *adj.* **1.** PHYSIOL **OF MUSCLE TENSION AND CONTRACTION** relating to the contraction and shortening of a muscle under relatively constant tension, e.g., in weightlifting **2.** CHEM = **isosmotic 3.** PHYSIOL **DESIGNED TO RESUPPLY THE BODY** specially formulated to supply the body's chemical needs in situations in which minerals and fluids are used up by the body, e.g., during vigorous exercise —**i·so·ton·i·cal·ly** *adv.* —**i·so·to·nic·i·ty** /ìsə tō níssətee/ *n.*

i·so·tope /ísə tōp/ *n.* either of two or more forms of a chemical element with the same atomic number but different numbers of neutrons [Early 20thC. Coined from ISO- + Greek *topos* "place," so called because isotopes of the same name occupy the same place in the periodic table.] —**i·so·top·ic** /ìsə tóppik/ *adj.*

i·so·top·ic spin *n.* NUCLEAR PHYS = **isospin**

i·so·tro·pic /ìsə tróppik/, **i·so·tro·pous** /ī sóttrəpəss/ *adj.* having physical properties that do not vary with direction [Mid-19thC. Formed from ISO- + Greek *tropos* "turn."] —**i·so·trop·i·cal·ly** *adv.* —**i·so·trop·ism** /ī sóttrə pìzzəm/ *n.* —**i·so·tro·py** /ī sóttrəpee/ *n.*

i·so·zyme /ísə zīm/ *n.* BIOCHEM = **isoenzyme**

ISP *abbr.* Internet service provider

Isr. *abbr.* Israel

Israel

Is·ra·el /ízree əl/ republic in southwestern Asia formed in 1948 as a Jewish state in the historic region of Palestine, on the eastern shore of the Mediterranean Sea. Language: Hebrew, Arabic. Currency: shekel. Capital: Jerusalem. Population: 5,534,670 (1997). Area: 8,000 sq. mi./20,700 sq. km. Official name **State of Israel** —**Is·rae·li** *n., adj.*

Is·ra·el·ite /ízzree ə lìt/ *n.* **1. MEMBER OF AN ANCIENT HEBREW PEOPLE** a member of the ancient Hebrew people descended from the biblical patriarch Jacob **2. SOMEBODY FROM ANCIENT ISRAEL** somebody who was born in or lived in the ancient kingdom of Israel [14thC. Via late Latin *Israelita*, from Greek *Israēlitēs*, from Hebrew *yisrē'ēlī*, from *Yiśrā'ēl*.] —**Is·ra·el·it·ic** /ìzzree ə líttik/ *adj.*

Is·ra·fil /ízzrə feel/, **Is·ra·fel, Is·ra·feel** *n.* according to the Koran, the archangel who will herald the end of the world by sounding a trumpet on the Day of Judgment [From Hebrew, "God heals"]

Is·sa·char /ísə kaar/ *n.* **1. JACOB'S SON** in the Bible, a son of Jacob and Leah **2. TRIBE DESCENDED FROM ISSACHAR** one of the twelve tribes of Israel, descended from Issachar [Via late Latin from Greek, from Hebrew *Yiśśākhār*]

Is·sei /ee sáy/ (*plural* **-sei**), **is·sei** (*plural* **-sei**) *n.* a Japanese immigrant to the United States or Canada. ◊ **Nisei, Sansei** [Early 20thC. From Japanese, literally "first generation."]

ISSN *abbr.* International Standard Serial Number

is·su·a·ble /íshoo əb'l/ *adj.* **1. ALLOWED TO BE ISSUED** authorized to be made available for sale or use **2. CAPABLE OF BEING LITIGATED** able to be litigated or debated **3. ACCRUABLE** able to be accrued —**is·su·ab·ly** *adv.*

is·su·ance /íshoo əns/ *n.* the act of distributing something or giving something out officially

is·su·ant /íshoo ənt/ *adj.* in heraldry, displaying an animal rising up from something with only its upper body showing

is·sue /íshoo/ *n.* **1. SUBJECT OF CONCERN** a topic for discussion or of general concern ○ *I want to raise several issues at the meeting.* **2. MAIN SUBJECT** the central or most important topic in a discussion or debate ○ *The real issue is education.* **3.** LAW **LEGAL MATTER IN A DISPUTE** a legal matter in dispute between two parties **4.** PUBL **COPY OF A PUBLICATION** a copy of a magazine or newspaper published on a particular date **5.** COMM **OFFICIAL RELEASE OF SOMETHING** a set of things such as new stamps or bonds that are made available for sale by an official body at a particular time **6.** FIN **STOCK MADE AVAILABLE** a series of items such as stock in a company that becomes available at the same time **7. ALLOTTING OF SOMETHING** distribution of something by an official body ○ *the issue of parking permits* **8. OFFICIAL ALLOTMENT** something officially distributed or supplied, or a specific amount of something officially supplied ○ *government issue rations* **9.** LAW **PROGENY** the offspring of a person ○ *died without issue* **10. FINAL OUTCOME** a final outcome or conclusion of a matter that is usually a solution to a problem or difficulty (*dated*) ○ *Let's bring our differences to an issue.* **11.** MED **DISCHARGE FROM WOUND** pus or blood coming from an open wound or ulcer **12.** FIN **PROFIT FROM PROPERTY** profits made from owning land or buildings **13. SOURCE OF A FLOW** a place from which something flows ■ *v.* (**-sued, -su·ing, -sues**) **1.** *vt.* **SUPPLY SOMETHING** to supply or distribute something officially **2.** *vt.* **ANNOUNCE SOMETHING PUBLICLY** to make public something such as a bulletin, statement, or warning, or deliver it officially to somebody ○ *The mayor's office issued a press release.* **3.** *vt.* COMM **RELEASE SOMETHING FOR SALE** to make a set of things such as new stamps or bonds available for sale at a particular time **4.** *vt.* PUBL **PUBLISH SOMETHING** to publish something such as a newspaper, magazine, or book **5.** *vi.* **ORIGINATE** to emerge or come out from somewhere ○ *Smoke issued from the burning building.* **6.** *vi.* **ARISE FROM A CONDITION** to result from or be produced by a particular thing or situation ○ *Our conclusions issue from analysis of the data.* **7.** *vi.* FIN **ADD UP AS GAIN** to accrue in the form of interest or profit **8.** *vi.* **RESULT IN** to have as a result (*archaic*) [13thC. From Old French, ultimately from Latin *exitus*, past participle of *exire* "to go out" (see EXIT).] —**is·sue·less** *adj.* —**is·su·er** *n.* ◇ **at issue** under discussion or to be decided ◇ **take issue with somebody** to disagree with somebody about something

is·sue price *n.* the price of new securities when they are first offered to the public

Is·syk-Kul /íssik kŏŏl/ lake in northeastern Kyrgyzstan. It has a maximum depth of 2,300 ft./700 m. Area: 2,360 sq. mi./6,100 sq. km.

IST *abbr.* **1.** information sciences technology **2.** insulin shock therapy

-ist *suffix.* **1.** somebody who practices a particular skill or profession ○ *psychologist* ○ *etymologist* **2.** somebody who follows a particular belief or school of thought ○ *idealist* **3.** somebody associated with a particular action or thing ○ *archivist* ○ *oboist* [Via Old French and Latin from, ultimately, Greek *-istēs*] —**-istic** *suffix.*

Is·tan·bul /is tan bŏŏl, -taan-/, **İs·tan·bul** the largest city in Turkey, situated in the northwest of the country. Population: 7,615,000 (1994). Former name **Byzantium, Constantinople**

Isth., **isth.** *abbr.* isthmus

isth·mi plural of **isthmus**

isth·mi·an /ísmee ən/ *adj.* GEOG **OF AN ISTHMUS** relating to, shaped like, or living in an isthmus joining two larger areas of land ■ *n.* **INHABITANT OF ISTHMUS** somebody who lives on an isthmus [Early 17thC. Formed from Latin *isthmius*, from Greek *isthmios*.]

Isth·mi·an *adj.* relating to the Isthmus of Panama or the Isthmus of Corinth

Isth·mi·an Games *npl.* a sports festival held in ancient Greece on the Isthmus of Corinth that included horseracing and chariot racing

isth·mic /ísmik/ *adj.* relating to an isthmus in the body ○ *an isthmic constriction*

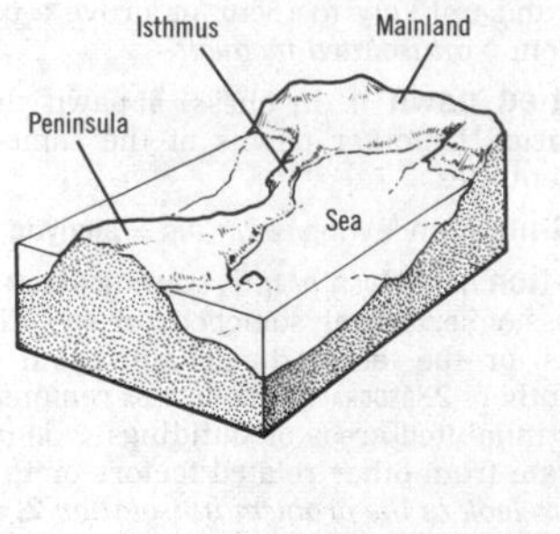

Isthmus

isth·mus /ísməss/ (*plural* **-mus·es** *or* **-mi** /ís mī/) *n.* **1.** GEOG **NARROW CONNECTING STRIP OF LAND** a narrow strip of land that joins two larger areas of land ○ *The isthmus connects the continents of North and South America.* **2.** ANAT **PASSAGE BETWEEN BODY PARTS** a narrow connection or passage between parts of the body [Mid-16thC. Via Latin, from Greek *isthmos* "island."] —**isth·moid** /ís mòyd/ *adj.*

is·tle /ísslee, íst-/, **ix·tle** *n.* a strong fiber from some tropical American plants such as agave or yucca, used to make rope, baskets, and carpets [Mid-19thC. Via American Spanish *ixtle*, from Nahuatl *ixtli*.]

Is·tri·a /ístree ə/ peninsula in northwestern Croatia and southwestern Slovenia, projecting into the Adriatic Sea. Area: 1,500 sq. mi./3,885 sq. km.

ISV *abbr.* International Scientific Vocabulary

it CORE MEANING: a pronoun used to refer to an object or an animal, and sometimes a baby ○ *It's a lovely baby.* ○ *They've had the dog a week, and they still haven't thought of a name for it.*

1. *pron.* **INDICATING A PARTICULAR SITUATION** used to refer to a situation just described, or to an unspecified or implied situation ○ *He's very upset, but he won't talk about it.* **2.** *pron.* **INDICATING A POINT OF VIEW** used to indicate feelings or a viewpoint on a particular situation ○ *It's strange how things turn out.* **3.** *pron.* **INDICATING SOMETHING REPORTED** used in the formation of passive sentences reporting a situation ○ *It was reported that several people had been arrested.* **4.** *pron.* **INDICATING WEATHER** used as the subject of verbs such as "be," "get," "seem," and "feel" in order to describe something about the environment, e.g., the temperature or the weather ○ *It's cold and rainy.* **5.** *pron.* **INDICATING TIME** used to state the time, e.g., the time of day, the month, the year, or the season ○ *It's six o'clock.* **6.** *pron.* **INDICATING A DESCRIPTION OF AN EXPERIENCE** used to refer to life or a particular experience ○ *What's it like being famous?* **7.** *pron.* **EMPHASIZING A FOLLOWING CLAUSE** used to draw attention to the person, thing, or clause that immediately follows ○ *It's you who's always complaining!* ○ *It isn't that I don't care.* **8.** *pron.* **INDICATING A CRISIS** the crucial or ultimate point, the perfect situation, person, or thing, or the death or end of somebody or something ○ *When the car turned over I really thought that was it.* **9.** *pron.* **ATTRACTIVE OR SELLING QUALITY** a quality considered by somebody to be the most important, e.g., talent, charm, sex appeal, or profitability (*informal*) ○ *You either have it or you don't.* **10.** *pron.* **SEX** sexual intercourse (*slang*) **11.** *n.* GAME **PLAYER IN CHILDREN'S GAMES** in children's informal games, the player who must do something to the others, e.g., run after and touch them in the game of tag ○ *You're it!* [Old English *hit*, from a prehistoric Germanic base that is also the ancestor of English *he*]

IT *abbr.* information technology

ITA *abbr.* **ITA, I.T.A.** initial teaching alphabet

ital. *abbr.* **1.** italic **2.** italics

Ital. *abbr.* **1.** Italian **2.** Italy

I·tal·ian /i tállyən/ *n.* **1.** PEOPLES **SOMEBODY FROM ITALY** somebody who was born or raised in Italy, or who has Italian citizenship **2.** LANGUAGE **LANGUAGE OF ITALY** the official language of Italy and one of the official languages of Switzerland, belonging to the Romance subgroup of the Italic branch of the Indo-European languages. There are about 60 million native speakers of Italian and approximately 60 million using it as a second language. ■ *adj.* **OF ITALY** relating to Italy, or its people or culture [14thC. From Italian *italiano* "of Italy," from *Italia* "Italy."]

I·tal·ian·ate /i tállyə nàyt/ *adj.* expressed, done, or made in an Italian style or character

I·tal·ian dress·ing *n.* a salad dressing typically made with oil and vinegar, garlic, and oregano

I·tal·ian·esque /i tàllyə nésk/ *adj.* = **Italianate**

I·tal·ian grey·hound *n.* a dog resembling a miniature greyhound, belonging to a breed originating in Italy

I·tal·ian·ism /i tállyə nìzzəm/ *n.* something that comes from or is typical of Italy, e.g., a word or phrase that is derived from Italian

I·tal·ian·ize /i tállyə nīz/ (**-ized, -iz·ing, -iz·es**) *vti.* to make something Italian in character, or become Italian in character —**I·tal·ian·i·za·tion** /i tàllyəni záysh'n/ *n.*

I·tal·ian sixth *n.* a three-note chord consisting of an augmented sixth chord and a major third above the root of the chord, used for modulation and for providing color

I·tal·ian son·net *n.* = **Petrarchan sonnet**

i·tal·ic /i tállik/ *adj.* **1. HAVING PRINTED LETTERS SLOPING TO THE RIGHT** printed in or using letters that slope to the right. Italic letters are used, e.g., in book titles or to show emphasis. **2. SLOPING TO RIGHT** handwritten in letters that slope to the right ■ *n.* **ITALIC LETTER** a printed letter that slopes to the right, or a font that uses such letters (*often used in the plural*) [Late 16thC. From the introduction of the style by an Italian printer from Venice in 1501. Originally denoting handwriting.]

I·tal·ic *n.* **BRANCH OF THE INDO-EUROPEAN LANGUAGE FAMILY** a branch of the Indo-European language family that includes many former languages of Italy, including Latin and Umbrian ■ *adj.* **1. OF ITALIC** relating to the language family Italic **2. ANCIENT ITALIAN** dating from or used in ancient Italy

I·tal·i·cism /i tálli sìzzəm/ *n.* a word or phrase that is borrowed from Italian

i·tal·i·cize /i tálli sīz/ (**-cized, -ciz·ing, -ciz·es**) *vt.* to print a word, letter, or document in italics, or change words to an italic font —**i·tal·i·ci·za·tion** /i tàllissi záysh'n/ *n.* —**i·tal·i·cized** /i tálli sīzd/ *adj.*

I·tal·o·phile /i tállō fīl/ *n.* somebody who loves Italy, Italians, or the Italian way of life —**I·tal·o·phil·i·a** /i tàllō fíllee ə/ *n.*

Italy

It·a·ly /ítt'lee/ republic in southern Europe. Its mainland area projects as a peninsula into the Mediterranean Sea, and it includes, among others, the islands of Elba, Sicily, and Sardinia. Language: Italian. Currency: lira. Capital: Rome. Population: 56,830,508 (1997). Area: 116,341 sq. mi./301,323 sq. km. Official name **Italian Republic**

I·tar Tass /ée taar tass/, **I·TAR-Tass** *n.* a Russian news agency founded in 1992 to replace Tass, the news agency of the former Soviet Union [Late 20thC. An acronym of Russian *Informatsionnoe telegrafnoe agentsvo Rossii* "Information Telegraph Agency of Russia" + TASS.]

itch /ich/ *v.* (**itched, itch·ing, itch·es**) **1.** *vti.* **WANT TO SCRATCH** to have, produce, or cause somebody to feel an irritating sensation on the body that provokes a desire to scratch the skin **2.** *vi.* **BE ANXIOUS TO DO SOMETHING** to be very eager or impatient to do something **3.** *vt.* **SCRATCH ITCHY SKIN** to scratch the skin where it itches (*nonstandard*) ■ *n.* **1. FEELING OF WANTING TO SCRATCH** an irritating sensation in the body that provokes a desire to scratch the skin **2. LONGING FOR SOMETHING** a restless or uneasy desire for something **3. MED ITCHY SKIN DISORDER** a skin disorder such as scabies that causes the skin to itch [Old English *giccan*, from prehistoric Germanic] —**itch·i·ness** *n.* —**itch·ing** *n.* —**itch·y** *adj.*

itch mite *n.* a tiny parasite that burrows into the skin and causes the disease scabies in humans. Latin name: *Sarcoptes scabiei.*

it'd /íttəd/ *contr.* **1. IT WOULD** it would **2. IT HAD** it had

-ite[1] *suffix.* **1.** mineral, rock, ore, soil, fossil ○ *carnotite* ○ *nummulite* **2.** descendant or follower of ○ *Hamite* ○ *Hussite* **3.** native or resident of ○ *Israelite* ○ *urbanite* **4.** organ, body part, cell, protozoan ○ *sporozoite* **5.** commercial product, explosive ○ *cordite* **6.** product of a chemical process ○ *evaporite* [Via Old French and Latin from Greek *-itēs*]

-ite[2] *suffix.* salt or ester of an acid with a name ending in *-ous* ○ *phosphite* [Alteration of -ATE]

i·tem /ítəm/ *n.* **1. ONE IN A COLLECTION** a single thing in a group or collection of things **2. ONE OF A LIST** one in a list of things **3. BROADCAST OR PUBLISHED REPORT** a piece of information in a news report, e.g., in a newspaper or on television **4. ACCT BOOKKEEPING ENTRY** one entry in a set of financial accounts **5. COUPLE IN A RELATIONSHIP** a couple who are linked in a romantic or sexual relationship (*informal*) ■ *adv.* **INTRODUCING AN ITEM IN LIST** used to introduce an item in a list [Late 16thC. From Latin *item* "likewise," from *ita* "thus, so." Originally used before each article in a list, hence "separate thing."]

i·tem·ize /ítə mīz/ (**-ized, -iz·ing, -iz·es**) *v.* **1.** *vt.* **LIST INDIVIDUAL THINGS** to list all of a set of related things ○ *an itemized bill* **2.** *vi.* **FIN LIST DEDUCTIONS ON A TAX RETURN** to list separately on a tax return all deductions from taxable income ○ *Unless you want to itemize, you can use the easier, shorter tax form.* —**i·tem·i·za·tion** /ìtəmi záysh'n/ *n.* —**i·tem·iz·er** /ítə mīzər/ *n.*

it·er·ance /íttərəns/ *n.* = **iteration** *n.* 1 [Early 17thC. Formed from Latin *iterare* (see ITERATE.]

it·er·ant /íttərənt/ *adj.* marked by repetition or recurrence [Early 17thC. Formed from *iterant-*, present participle stem of Latin *iterare* (see ITERATE.]

it·er·ate /íttə ràyt/ (**-at·ed, -at·ing, -ates**) *vt.* to say or do the same thing again [Mid-16thC. From Latin *iterare* "to repeat," from *iterum* "again."]

it·er·a·tion /ìttə ráysh'n/ *n.* **1. REPETITION** an instance or the act of doing something again **2. MATH STEP-BY-STEP PROCESS** a process of achieving a desired result by repeating a sequence of steps and successively getting closer to that result **3. COMPUT REPETITION OF STEPS** the repetition of a sequence of instructions in a computer program until a result is achieved

it·er·a·tive /íttə ràytiv/ *adj.* **1. MATH, LOGIC** = **recursive 2. COMPUT REPEATING STEPS** using repeated routines in a loop as part of a computer program **3. GRAM** = **frequentative 4. REPETITIVE** repeating again and again —**it·er·a·tive·ly** *adv.*

Ith·a·ca /íthəkə/ **1.** island in western Greece, the traditional site of the legendary kingdom of Odysseus. Population: 3,646 (1981). Area: 37 sq. mi./96 sq. km. **2.** city in south central New York, south of Cayuga Lake and northwest of Binghamton. Population: 28,507 (1996).

ith·y·phal·lic /ìthə fállik/ *adj.* **1. OF HYMNS TO BACCHUS** relating to or composed in the meter used in hymns to the ancient Greek god Bacchus **2. SHOWING AN ERECT PENIS IN ART** in sculpture, painting, or other art, having or showing an erect penis ■ *n.* **HYMN** a hymn composed in ithyphallic meter [Early 17thC. Via late Latin *ithyphallicus*, from, ultimately, Greek *ithuphallos* "phallus carried in procession at festivals of Bacchus," literally "straight phallus."]

i·tin·er·an·cy /ī tínnərənsee/, **i·tin·er·a·cy** /-rəssee/ *n.* **1. REQUIREMENT TO TRAVEL IN JOB** the fact of traveling, or necessity to travel, from place to place, especially as part of an occupation or profession **2. PEOPLE WITH A CIRCUIT TO COVER** people such as judges or preachers who move from place to place on a circuit **3. CHR SYSTEM OF MOVING CLERGY BETWEEN CHURCHES** a system for rotating clergy, especially within the Methodist Church

i·tin·er·ant /ī tínnərənt/ *adj.* **TRAVELING ON THE JOB** traveling from place to place, especially to find work or as a part of work ■ *n.* **SOMEBODY WHO MOVES AROUND** somebody who moves from place to place [Late 16thC. From late Latin *itinerant-*, present participle stem of *itinerari* "to journey," from Latin *itiner-* (see ITINERARY).] —**i·tin·er·ant·ly** *adv.*

i·tin·er·ar·y /ī tínnə rèrree/ *n.* (*plural* **-ies**) **1. LIST OF PLACES TO BE VISITED** a plan for a journey listing different places in the order in which they are to be visited **2. RECORD OF A JOURNEY** a written record of a journey to visit different places **3. GUIDEBOOK** a guidebook for travelers ■ *adj.* **INTENDED FOR TRAVELING** intended or used for the purpose of traveling [15thC. From late Latin *itinerarius*, from Latin *itiner-*, stem of *iter* "journey, way."]

i·tin·er·ate /ī tínnə ràyt/ (**-at·ed, -at·ing, -ates**) *vi.* to move from place to place on a circuit (*refers to a judge or preacher*) [Early 17thC. From late Latin *itinerari*, from Latin *itiner-* (see ITINERARY).] —**i·tin·er·a·tion** /ītìnə ráysh'n/ *n.*

-itis *suffix.* **1.** inflammation, disease ○ *retinitis* **2.** excessive interest in ○ *spectatoritis* [From Greek]

it'll /ítt'l/ *contr.* it will ○ *It'll be so good to see you.*

ITO *abbr.* International Trade Organization

I·to Ja·ku·chu /éetō ja kóo chōō/ (1716–1800) Japanese artist. He is known for his meticulously detailed paintings of birds, flowers, and fish.

-itol *suffix.* polyhydric alcohol ○ *inositol* [Coined from -ITE[1] + -OL 1]

its /its/ *adj.* used to indicate that something belongs or relates to something ○ *The park changed its policy.* [Late 16thC. Coined from IT + -'s (possessive).]

it's /its/ *contr.* **1. IT IS** it is ○ *It's perfect.* **2. IT HAS** it has ○ *It's been rebuilt.*

it·self /it sélf/ CORE MEANING: a reflexive pronoun used to refer back to the subject of a verb or for emphasis *pron.* **1. USED TO REFER BACK TO SOMETHING** used to refer back to the subject of a verb ○ *His ignorance finally revealed itself.* **2. USED TO EMPHASIZE SOMETHING** used to emphasize the thing that is referred to ○ *The house itself was cheap compared to the land.* **3. ITS NORMAL SELF** the way it usually feels or behaves ○ *The dog's not itself since we moved to the city.*

it·sy-bit·sy /ítsee bítsee/, **it·ty-bit·ty** /íttee bíttee/ *adj.* extremely small (*informal*) [Alteration of LITTLE + BIT]

ITU *abbr.* **1.** MED intensive therapy unit **2.** International Telecommunication Union

I·tur·bi·de /ée tōōr bée day/, **Agustín de** (1783–1824) Mexican general. A leader of Mexico's independence movement, he declared himself emperor (1822–23), but was forced to abdicate and was executed.

ITV *abbr.* instructional television

IU *abbr.* **1.** immunizing unit **2.** PHARM international unit

IUCD *abbr.* intrauterine contraceptive device

IUD *abbr.* intrauterine device

-ium *suffix.* chemical element, radical, or ion ○ *californium* [From modern Latin, an alteration of *-um*]

IV[1] *abbr.* **IV 1.** intravenous **2.** intravenously

IV[2] /ī vée/ (*plural* **IVs** *or* **IV's**) *n.* **1. MEDICAL INJECTION OF LIQUID** the injection of quantities of a therapeutic fluid such as blood, plasma, saline, or glucose directly into somebody's vein at an adjustable rate **2. EQUIPMENT FOR INJECTING A LIQUID** the equipment used to administer an IV [Mid-20thC. Abbreviation of INTRAVENOUS.]

i.v. *abbr.* invoice value

I·van III /ív'n/, **Grand Prince of Muscovy** (1440–1505). As the grand duke of Muscovy (1462–1505), he declared himself "sovereign of all Russia" (1472) and greatly expanded his empire. He ended Muscovy's subjection to the Tatars (1480). Known as **Ivan the Great**

I·van IV, Tsar of Russia (1530–84). The grand duke of Moscow, he became the first tsar of Russia (1547–84). He expanded his empire into the Urals and Siberia and instigated major internal reforms, but he is remembered in history for the extreme despotism of his last twenty years. Known as **Ivan the Terrible**

I·va·no·vo /i vaánəvə/ city in central Russia, situated approximately 145 mi./233 km northeast of Moscow. Population: 482,000 (1992).

I've /īv/ *contr.* I have

-ive *suffix.* tending to or performing ○ *illustrative* [Via Old French from Latin *-ivus*]

Ives /īvz/, **Charles E.** (1874–1954) U.S. composer. He was an early proponent of modernism in works such as *Three Places in New England* (1903–14), which combine and distort fragments of marches, hymns, and popular songs. Full name **Charles Edward Ives**

Ives, James Merritt (1824–95) U.S. lithographer. He was a partner in the New York lithographic firm Currier & Ives, famous for their colored prints of 19th-century social and domestic life.

IVF *abbr.* in vitro fertilization

i·vied /ívveed/ *adj.* covered or overgrown with ivy

i·vo·ry /ívəree/ *n.* (*plural* **-ries**) **1.** MATERIAL OF ELEPHANT'S TUSKS a hard cream-colored substance (**dentine**) that forms the tusks of animals such as the elephant, walrus, and sperm whale and was formerly used to carve small decorative objects **2.** SOMETHING MADE OF IVORY an object made of ivory, e.g., a figurine of a person or animal **3.** COLORS **CREAMY WHITE** a creamy-white color, like that of an elephant's tusk ■ **i·vo·ries** *npl.* **1.** PIANO KEYS the keys of a piano (*informal*) **2.** TEETH somebody's teeth (*slang*) **3.** DICE dice (*slang*) ■ *adj.* CREAM-COLORED of a creamy white color, like that of an elephant's tusk [13thC. Via Old French *ivurie* from Latin *ebur*, of uncertain origin: probably ultimately from Egyptian *ab* "ivory, elephant."]

i·vo·ry-billed wood·peck·er *n.* a large, nearly extinct woodpecker of the southern United States and Cuba that has black-and-white plumage, a red crest in the male, and an ivory-colored bill. Latin name: *Campephilus principalis.*

i·vo·ry black *n.* a black pigment made from burnt ivory

I·vo·ry Coast /ívəree-/ former name for **Côte d'Ivoire**

i·vo·ry gull *n.* a small white Arctic gull that nests on rocky cliffs and winters on the edge of the pack ice. Latin name: *Pagophila eburnea.*

i·vo·ry nut *n.* the hard white nut of the ivory palm, the inner part (**endosperm**) of which is used in making buttons or other small items

i·vo·ry palm, **i·vo·ry-nut palm** *n.* a low-growing palm tree of Brazil and Peru that yields ivory nuts. Latin name: *Phytelephas macrocarpa.*

i·vo·ry tow·er *n.* a state or situation in which somebody is sheltered from the practicalities or difficulties of ordinary life [Translation of French *tour d'ivoire*] —**i·vo·ry-tow·ered** *adj.*

I.V.R. *abbr.* international vehicle registration

Ivy

i·vy /ívee/ (*plural* **i·vies** *or* **i·vy**) *n.* **1.** EVERGREEN CLIMBING PLANT an evergreen climbing plant with woody stems and green, green-and-yellow, or green-and-white leaves that grows easily on walls or trees or along the ground. Genus: *Hedera.* **2.** PLANT SIMILAR TO THE IVY any climbing plant that resembles the true ivy, e.g., the Boston ivy, Japanese ivy, poison ivy, or ground ivy **3.** MOUNTAIN LAUREL the mountain laurel, an evergreen shrub with leathery poisonous leaves (*regional*) [Old English *īfig*, from a prehistoric Germanic word of uncertain origin]

WORD KEY: REGIONAL NOTE

In the sense "mountain laurel," *ivy* is used mainly in Appalachia, from Virginia and Kentucky to the Carolinas and Georgia, but also in New England, notably Connecticut and Massachusetts.

I·vy League *n.* GROUP OF PRESTIGIOUS U.S. UNIVERSITIES a group of prestigious and respected universities in the northeastern United States consisting of Brown, Columbia, Cornell, Dartmouth, Harvard, Princeton, the University of Pennsylvania, and Yale ■ *adj.* OF THE IVY LEAGUE relating to the Ivy League or students of the universities of the Ivy League ○ *an Ivy League education* [*Ivy* from the presumption that the universities walls were ivy-clad on account of their great age] —**I·vy Leagu·er** *n.*

i.w. *abbr.* inside width

I·wo /éewō/ city in southwestern Nigeria, just north of Ibadan. Population: 319,500 (1991).

IWW *abbr.* Industrial Workers of the World

Ix·i·on /íksee òn, íksee ən/ *n.* in Greek mythology, a king of Thessaly who was bound to a perpetually turning wheel by Zeus as punishment for making sexual advances to Hera

Ix·ta·cal·co /eesta kálkō/ industrial city in south central Mexico, situated just south of Mexico City. Population: 448,357 (1990).

ix·tle *n.* = **istle**

I·yar /ée yaar/ *n.* the second month of the Jewish religious calendar and the eighth month of the Jewish civil calendar, falling approximately in April and May [Mid-18thC. From Hebrew *iyyār.*]

-ize *suffix.* **1.** to cause to be, make ○ *formalize* **2.** to treat with or as ○ *chromize* ○ *lionize* **3.** to become, become like ○ *crystallize* **4.** to engage in ○ *extemporize* [Via Old French *-iser* and Latin *-izare* from Greek *-izein*] —**-ization** *suffix.*

I·zhevsk /i zhéfsk/ city and capital of Udmurtia, eastern Russia, located on the Izh River. Population: 650,700 (1992).

Iz·mir /izmeer/, **İz·mir** city and seaport in western Turkey. Population: 1,757,414 (1990). Former name **Smyrna**

Iz·mit /ízmit/, **İz·mit** city in northwestern Turkey, situated on the Gulf of Izmit. Population: 256,882 (1990).

iz·zard /ízzərd/ *n.* the letter "z" (*archaic*) [Mid-18thC. Alteration of ZED.]

Jj

j[1] /jay/ (*plural* **j's**), **J** (*plural* **J's** *or* **Js**) *n.* **1. 10TH LETTER OF ENGLISH ALPHABET** the tenth letter of the modern English alphabet **2. SPEECH SOUND CORRESPONDING TO LETTER "J"** the speech sound that corresponds to the letter "J" **3. LETTER "J" WRITTEN** a written representation of the letter "J"

j[2] *symbol.* **1.** the imaginary number –1 **2.** the unit vector parallel to the y-axis **3. j, J** PHYS electric current density

j[3], **J** *abbr.* PHYS joule

J *abbr.* CARDS jack

J., j. *abbr.* **1.** PRESS Journal **2.** LAW Judge **3.** LAW Justice

JA *abbr.* **1.** BANKING joint account **2.** COMM Junior Achievement

Ja. *abbr.* January

J.A. *abbr.* Judge Advocate

jab /jab/ *vti.* (**jabbed, jab·bing, jabs**) **1. PUNCH SHARPLY** to make a short punching movement, or push something with a short punching movement **2. MAKE SHORT FAST PUNCH** to make a short fast punch at an opponent, e.g., in boxing ■ *n.* **1. PUNCHING MOVEMENT** a short sharp punching movement **2. SHORT SHARP PUNCH** a short sharp punch, as used in boxing **3.** *Aus, U.K.* = **shot**[1] *n.* 14 (*informal*) [Early 19thC. Originally a Scottish variant of *job* "to pierce, thrust," an imitation of the sound of a brief forcible action.]

Jab·al·pur /jùbb'l pòor/ city in central India. It is a major commercial center. Population: 739,961 (1991). Former name **Jubbulpore**

jab·ber /jábbər/ *vti.* (**-bered, -ber·ing, -bers**) **TALK VERY FAST** to talk or say something rapidly, so that it is incomprehensible ■ *n.* **RAPID SPEECH** rapid speech that is incomprehensible [15thC. Supposedly imitative of the sound made by somebody talking in this way.] —**jab·ber·er** *n.*

jab·ber·wock·y /jábbər wòkee/ (*plural* **-ies**) *n.* speech or writing that is meaningless and often deliberately whimsical or humorous [Early 20thC. From "Jabberwocky," nonsense poem by English writer **Lewis Carroll**, from his book *Through the Looking Glass* (1872).]

Jabiru

jab·i·ru /jábbə ròo, jábbə ròo/ (*plural* **-rus** *or* **-ru**) *n.* **1. LARGE WHITE TROPICAL STORK** a large tropical stork of Central and South America that has white plumage and a naked head. Latin name: *Jabiru mycteria.* **2. LARGE BLACK-AND-WHITE AUSTRALIAN STORK** a large black-and-white stork inhabiting the north and east of Australia. Latin name: *Xenorhynchus asiaticus.* [Late 18thC. From Tupi-Guarani *jabirú* "swollen-necked," with reference to the large neck typical of the tropical storks.]

Jab·i·ru /jábbirə/ town in northern Australia, situated inside Kakadu National Park in the Northern Territory. It is a mining town and tourist resort. Population: 1,694 (1996).

jab·o·ran·di /jàbbə rándee/ (*plural* **-dis** *or* **-di**) *n.* **1. TROPICAL AMERICAN SHRUB** a tropical American shrub of the rue family. Genus: *Pilocarpus.* **2. DRIED LEAVES USED AS MEDICINE** the dried leaves of the jaborandi tree that yield the drug pilocarpine [Early 17thC. From Portuguese, from Tupi-Guarani *jaburandi,* literally "somebody who spits," from the increased saliva of those who chew the leaves.]

ja·bot /zha bṓ, zhá bō/ (*plural* **-bots**) *n.* **1. RUFFLE ON WOMEN'S CLOTHING** an edging of ruffles at the upper front of a blouse or dress **2. RUFFLE ON MEN'S CLOTHING** formerly, a set of ruffles attached to the neckband and falling in tiers down the front of a man's shirt [Early 19thC. From French, "bird's crop," "shirt-frill," of uncertain origin: probably from a Proto-Romance base meaning "crop, gullet."]

ja·bot·i·ca·ba /jə bòtti kaábə/ (*plural* **-bas** *or* **-ba**) *n.* a Brazilian evergreen tree of the myrtle family cultivated for its clusters of fruit. Latin name: *Myrciaria cauliflora.* [Early 17thC. Via Portuguese from Tupi *iauoti'kaua.*]

ja·cal /hə kaál/ *n.* a thatched hut of the southwestern United States and Mexico that has walls made of stakes driven into the ground and daubed with mud [Mid-19thC. Via Mexican Spanish from Nahuatl *xacalli,* a contraction of *xamitl calli* "adobe house."]

Jacamar

jac·a·mar /jákə maar/ (*plural* **-mars** *or* **-mar**) *n.* a South and Central American bird with a very long bill and bright blue or green feathers. Jacamars feed on insects and butterflies and lay their eggs in holes in the ground. Family: Galbulidae. [Early 19thC. From French, of uncertain origin: probably from Tupi.]

ja·ça·na /jákənə/, **ja·ca·na** (*plural* **-nas** *or* **-na**) *n.* TREES a water bird found in tropical and subtropical parts of the world that has short rounded wings and tail and long toes that enable it to walk on floating plants. Male jaçanas incubate the eggs and raise the young birds. Family: Jacanidae. [Mid-18thC. Via Portuguese *jaçanã* from Tupi-Guarani *jasanã.*]

jac·a·ran·da /jàkə rándə/ (*plural* **-das** *or* **-da**) *n.* **1.** TREES **PLANT WITH FERNY LEAVES** a tree or shrub of tropical America with ferny leaves, purple flowers, and pleasant smelling wood. Genus: *Jacaranda.* **2.** INDUST **WOOD FROM JACARANDA** the pleasant smelling wood of the jacaranda tree [Mid-18thC. From Portuguese, from Tupi-Guarani *jakara'na.*]

Jaçana

ja·cinth /jáyssinth/ (*plural* **-cinths** *or* **-cinth**) *n.* = **hyacinth** [13thC. From Old French *iacinte* or medieval Latin *iacintus,* an alteration of Latin *hyacinthus* (see HYACINTH).]

jack[1] /jak/ *n.* **1.** MECH ENG **DEVICE FOR LIFTING SOMETHING HEAVY** a portable device that uses a mechanical or hydraulic lifting system to raise heavy objects, especially cars, a short distance **2.** CARDS **PLAYING CARD** a playing card ranking between a ten and a queen, with a picture of a young man on it **3.** ELEC ENG **ELECTRICAL SOCKET** a female socket designed to receive a male plug for completing a circuit **4.** GAME **OBJECT USED IN JACKS** a small, usually metal object with six points that is used in the game of jacks **5.** BOWLING **TARGET BALL USED IN LAWN BOWLING** a small, usually white ball that players aim at in lawn bowling **6.** ZOOL **MALE ANIMAL** the male of various animals, especially the donkey **7.** = **jackrabbit 8.** NAUT **FLAG ON A SHIP** a small flag displayed to indicate the nationality of a ship **9.** ZOOL **TROPICAL FISH** a warm-water marine fish that has a forked tail. Genus: *Caranx.* **10. MONEY** money (*slang*) **11. APPLEJACK** applejack **12.** COOK **DEVICE THAT TURNS SPIT** a device that mechanically turns a spit over an open fire **13. LABORER** a laborer, or somebody who does odd jobs (*usually used in combination*) **14.** NAUT **BRACE ON MAST** either one of a pair of wooden braces (**crosstrees**) at the head of a topgallant mast used to hold the mast stays away from the mast ■ *v.* (**jacked, jack·ing, jacks**) **1.** *vt.* MECH ENG **RAISE SOMETHING WITH JACK** to raise a heavy object a short distance using a jack **2.** *vti.* HUNT **HUNT AT NIGHT WITH LIGHT** to hunt or fish for game at night using a jacklight as a lure **3.** *vt.* CRIMINOL **ROB SOMEBODY** to steal something, especially a car, from somebody (*slang*) **4.** *vt.* **PRY SOMETHING OPEN** to open something by prying it apart (*slang*) ○ *Who jacked the door?* [14thC. Originally a nickname for *John,* hence a name for an ordinary man, hence applied to things taking the place of a man or saving human labor.] ◇ **every man jack** *U.K.* every single person

jack around *vi.* to waste time, loaf, or act irresponsibly (*slang*) ○ *Stop jacking around and get to work!*

jack in, jack in·to *vt.* to connect somebody or something electronically to something (*slang*) ○ *We're jacked into the Internet.*

jack off *vti.* to masturbate yourself or somebody else (*slang taboo*)

jack up *v.* **1.** *vt.* MECH ENG **LIFT SOMETHING WITH JACK** to use a jack to lift a heavy object, especially a motor vehicle, off the ground **2.** *vt.* **INCREASE AMOUNT OF SOMETHING** to increase something, especially a price or salary, often to an unreasonably high level **3.** *vti.* DRUGS **INJECT ILLEGAL DRUGS** to inject a drug, especially heroin, intravenously (*slang*)

jack[2] /jak/ *n.* = **jak**

jack[3] /jak/ *n.* a short sleeveless coat of armor used in the Middle Ages made of canvas covered with metal plates [14thC. Via Old French *jaque* from Spanish or Portuguese *jaco*, of uncertain origin: perhaps from Arabic *shakk*.]

Jack /jak/ *n.* **1.** USED TO ADDRESS UNKNOWN MAN used to address a man who is a stranger ○ *Hey, Jack, what time is it?* **2.** NAVY = **jack-tar** *n.* (*dated informal*)

Jackal

jack·al /jákəl/ (*plural* **-als** *or* **-al**) *n.* **1.** ZOOL **WILD ANIMAL RESEMBLING DOG** a wild mammal resembling a dog, with long legs, large ears, and a bushy tail. It lives in Africa and southern Asia, and eats small animals, insects, and plants. Genus: *Canis.* **2.** CRIMINOL **SWINDLER** somebody who works with others to deceive people, especially to swindle them out of money [Early 17thC. From Turkish *çakal*, from Persian *šagāl*.]

jackanapes /jákə nayps/ (*plural* **jackanapes**) *n.* **1. IMPUDENT PERSON** somebody who behaves in an impudent, self-centered way (*dated*) **2. MISCHIEVOUS CHILD** a child who behaves mischievously or impertinently (*dated*) **3. MONKEY** a monkey (*archaic*) [Early 16thC. Originally *Jack Napes*, of uncertain origin: perhaps a playful name for a tame ape, with "n" added by misdivision of *an ape*.]

jackass /ják ass/ *n.* **1.** ZOOL **MALE ASS** a male donkey or ass (*slang*) **2. OFFENSIVE TERM** an offensive term that deliberately insults somebody's intelligence (*slang insult*) [Early 18thC. *Jack* from JACK[1].] —**jackassery** *n.*

jack bean *n.* a tropical American climbing plant of the pea family that is grown in the southern United States mainly for forage. It has clusters of purple flowers that produce long pods with edible seeds. Latin name: *Canavalia ensiformis.*

jackboot /ják boot/ *n.* **1.** MIL **MILITARY BOOT** a type of sturdy long black leather boot that comes up to, or over, the knee, worn especially by the military in Nazi Germany **2. HARSH TREATMENT** military or other rule that is characterized by cruelty, oppression, or arbitrary aggression [Late 17thC. *Jack* of uncertain origin: probably from *jack*, a medieval iron-plated battle jacket.]

jack-by-the hedge (*plural* **jack-by-the-hedges**) *n.* the garlic mustard plant

jack cheese *n.* = **Monterey Jack**

jack crevalle *n.* a spiny-finned edible fish that is common off the western coast of Florida, where it is economically important. Latin name: *Caranx hippos.*

jackdaw /ják daw/ *n.* a large noisy bird of the crow family native to Europe and Asia. It is renowned for stealing things, especially shiny objects, which it hides or takes back to its nest. Latin name: *Corvus monedula.* [Mid-16thC. Literally "untidy Jack" (see DAW).]

jacked /jakt/ *adj.* highly stimulated and wide awake (*slang*) ○ *jacked on coffee*

jack·et /jákət/ *n.* **1.** CLOTHES **SHORT COAT** a short, usually hip-length or waist-length coat, sometimes forming part of a suit. It usually has long sleeves, pockets, lapels, and fastens at the front with buttons or a zipper. **2.** CLOTHES **PROTECTIVE CLOTHING** something that is worn on the upper part of the body for protection or support **3.** RECORDING **RECORD COVER** a decorated protective cover for a record or CD that usually lists the performers and contents **4.** PUBL = **dust jacket** **5.** FOOD **POTATO SKIN** the outer skin of an unpeeled cooked potato, especially a baked one **6.** COMPUT **FLOPPY DISK CASING** the casing of a floppy disk **7.** COMM **FOLDER** a strong envelope or folder for holding papers or documents **8.** ENG **BOILER COVER** a cover or outer casing designed to insulate a boiler **9.** INDUST **OUTER CASING OF PIPE** an outer casing around a pipe that can be filled with steam or hot water to keep the contents of the pipe warm **10.** ARMS **OUTER CASING OF BULLET** an outer casing on certain bullets and other types of ammunition **11.** SPORTS **COAT IDENTIFYING RACING DOG** a distinctive colored coat for an animal, especially a racing greyhound ■ *vt.* (**-et·ed, -et·ing, -ets**) **PUT JACKET ON SOMETHING** to put a jacket on somebody or something, e.g., a book or record [15thC. From French *jaquet*, diminutive of Old French *jacque* "tunic," from *jacques* "peasant," from the common name *Jacques*; because peasants wore the garments.]

jack·fish /ják fish/ (*plural* **-fish** *or* **-fish·es**) *n.* a pike, especially a young or small one [Late 16thC. *Jack* from JACK[1] in the meaning of "small."]

Jack Frost *n.* a personification of frost, very cold wintry weather, or the effects that frost or cold weather can produce

jack·fruit /ják froot/ (*plural* **-fruit** *or* **-fruits**) *n.* **1.** TREES **TROPICAL ASIAN TREE** a large tree native to tropical Asia, where it is cultivated for its fine-grained yellowish wood and large edible fruits. Latin name: *Artocarpus heterophyllus.* **2.** FOOD = **jak** [Mid-19thC. *Jack* from Portuguese *jaca* (see JAK).]

jack·ham·mer /ják hammər/ *n.* a hand-held power tool, usually powered by compressed air and used for splitting or drilling rock, or for breaking up paved areas [*Jack* from JACK[1] in the meaning of "small"]

jack-in-the-box (*plural* **jacks-in-the-box** *or* **jack-in-the-box·es**) *n.* a child's toy consisting of a puppet on a spring inside a box. The puppet jumps out when a mechanism is triggered, often by opening the lid.

jack-in-the-pul·pit *n.* a woodland plant of eastern North America that produces a thick spike of tiny flowers (**spadix**) surrounded by a sheath. Latin name: *Arisaema triphyllum.*

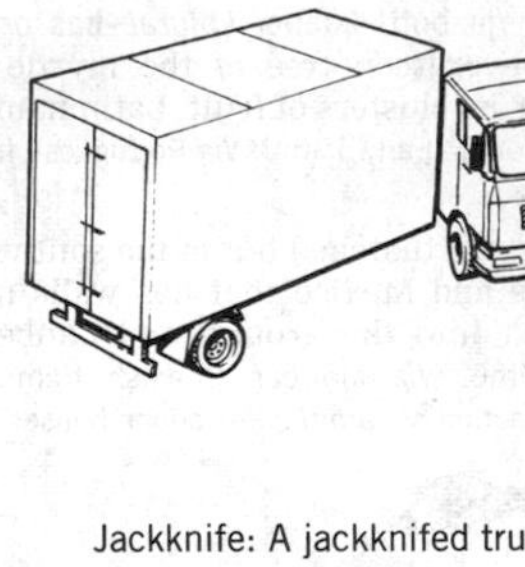

Jackknife: A jackknifed truck

jack·knife /ják nīf/ *n.* (*plural* **-knives** /-nīvz/) **1. POCKETKNIFE** a large pocketknife **2.** SWIMMING **DIVE** a dive in which the diver jumps, bends the body at the waist while keeping the legs together and straight, then straightens out to enter the water headfirst ■ *vi.* (**-knifed, -knif·ing, -knifes**) **1.** TRANSP **FOLD TRAILER IN ON CAB** to come to a halt with the trailer at an angle to the cab, as a result of sudden braking or swerving at speed (*refers to tractor-trailers*) ○ *The truck struck a patch of ice and jackknifed.* **2.** SWIMMING **DO JACKKNIFE DIVE** to perform a jackknife dive [Early 18thC. *Jack* of uncertain origin: perhaps from JACK[1].]

jack·leg /ják leg/ *adj.* *Southern U.S.* **1. UNTRAINED** untrained or incompetent ○ *jackleg plumbers* **2. UNSCRUPULOUS** unscrupulous and untrustworthy ○ *a jackleg insurance salesman* ■ *n.* *Southern U.S.* **INCOMPETENT PERSON** somebody who is incompetent or untrustworthy [Mid-17thC. Coined from JACK[1] + *-leg*, as in BLACKLEG.]

jack·light /ják līt/ *n.* **LIGHT FOR HUNTING** a light used for fishing or hunting at night, usually illegally ■ *vi.* (**-lit** *or* **-light·ed, -lit** /-lit/, **-lights**) **USE JACKLIGHT** to hunt or fish at night using a jacklight [Late 19thC. *Jack* from *jack* "vessel covered with pitch and used for carrying oil or coal to be burned for light."]

jack mack·er·el *n.* a torpedo-shaped edible fish of the jack family, native to Pacific coastal waters, with a body bluish-green on top and silvery underneath. Latin name: *Trachurus symmetricus.*

jack-of-all-trades (*plural* **jacks-of-all-trades**) *n.* somebody who can do various kinds of work

jack-o'-lan·tern *n.* **1. LANTERN MADE FROM PUMPKIN** a lantern made from a hollowed-out pumpkin that has facial features cut out of it, used as a part of Halloween decoration **2.** = **will-o'-the-wisp**

jack pine *n.* a pine tree of northern North America that has a narrow trunk, short needles arranged in pairs, and curving cones. It has soft wood that is used especially for paper pulp. Latin name: *Pinus banksiana.*

jack plane *n.* a large carpentry plane used for rough planing of wood and other surfaces [*Jack* from JACK[1] in the sense of "instrument"]

jack·pot /ják pot/ *n.* **1.** GAMBLING **CASH PRIZE** an amount of money won in a competition or lottery, or as a payout from a slot machine or other kind of gambling machine **2.** CARDS **TOTAL AMOUNT BET ON POKER HANDS** an accumulated stake in poker games that can be competed for only by players holding a pair of jacks or a better hand [Late 19thC. *Jack* from the necessity of holding a pair of jacks or better to compete for the pot in poker.] ◇ **hit the jackpot** to achieve great success, especially financially

jack rab·bit *n.* a large hare native to the prairies of western North America, with long hind legs and extremely long ears. Genus: *Lepus.* [*Jack* from JACKASS, because of its long ears]

jack·rab·bit start *n.* a fast acceleration of a motor vehicle from a standing position (*regional informal*)

Jack Rus·sell /jak rúss'l/, **Jack Rus·sell ter·ri·er** *n.* a small terrier with short legs and a white coat with patchy markings in black, brown, or tan, or a combination of these colors [Early 20thC. Named for John *(Jack) Russell* (1795–1883), the English clergyman who introduced the breed.]

jacks /jaks/ *n.* a game involving picking up small metal or plastic pieces in a particular sequence between bouncing or throwing and catching a ball (*takes a singular verb*) [Early 19thC. Shortening of JACKSTONES.]

jack·screw /ják skroo/ *n.* = **screwjack**

jack·shaft /ják shaft/ *n.* a short shaft that transmits power from a motor or engine to a machine

jack·smelt /ják smelt/ (*plural* **-smelts** *or* **-smelt**) *n.* an edible and commercially important fish of the silverside family, found in North Pacific coastal waters of North America. Latin name: *Atherinopsis californiensis.*

jack·snipe /ják snīp/ (*plural* **-snipe** *or* **-snipes**) *n.* a small wading bird with a fairly short bill and legs and dark plumage. It breeds in swamps and bogs in the far north of Europe and Asia. Latin name: *Limnocryptes minimus.* [So called because of its small size (see JACK[1])]

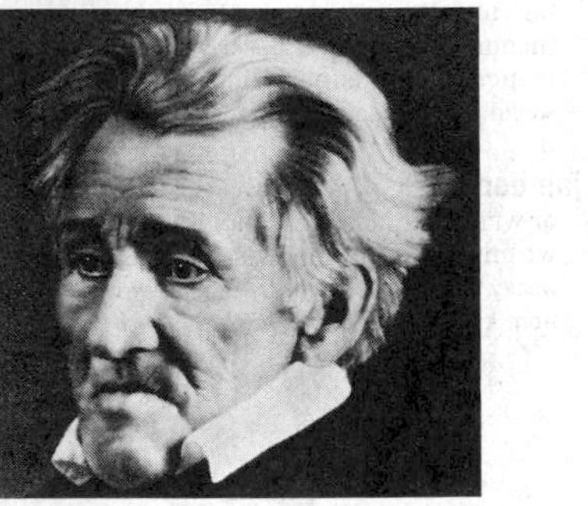

Library of Congress

Andrew Jackson

Jack·son /jáks'n/, **Andrew** (1767–1845) U.S. statesman and 7th President of the United States. His army defeated the British at New Orleans during the War of 1812. As Democratic president (1829–37), he opposed the Bank of America and greatly strengthened the presidency. Known as **Old Hickory**

Jack·son, Glenda (*b.* 1936) British actor and politician. She played in numerous Royal Shakespeare Company productions and in films, winning two Academy Awards, before becoming a Labour MP (1992).

Jack·son, Jesse (*b.* 1941) U.S. civil rights leader, clergyman, and politician. He was closely associated with civil rights leader Martin Luther King and the Southern Christian Leadership Conference in the 1960s, and later twice ran for the Democratic presidential nomination (1984, 1988) at the head of his own political organization, the Rainbow Coalition. Full name **Jesse Louis Jackson**

Jack·son, Mahalia (1911–72) U.S. singer. She helped to popularize gospel music during the 1940s and 1950s.

Jack·son, Michael (*b.* 1958) U.S. entertainer. He was the youngest brother in The Jackson Five before embarking on a successful solo singing career. His album *Thriller* (1982) broke sales records.

Jack·son, Robert Houghwout (1892–1954) U.S. jurist. An associate justice on the U.S. Supreme Court (1941–54), he was chief U.S. prosecutor at the Nuremburg war crimes trials (1945–46).

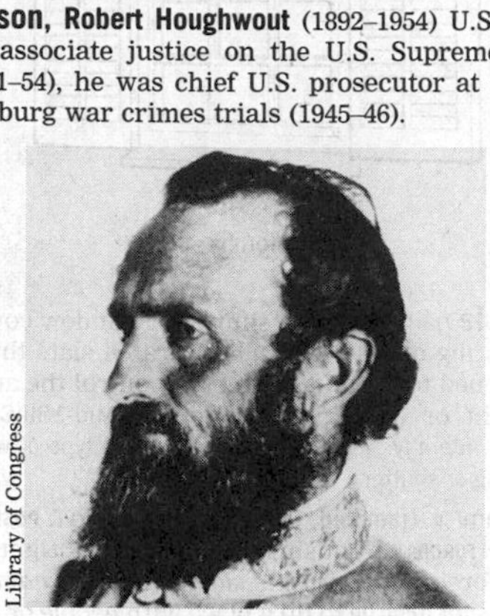

Library of Congress

Stonewall Jackson

Jack·son, Stonewall (1824–63) U.S. general. He was one of the most successful Confederate commanders during the Civil War. Real name **Thomas Jonathan Jackson**

Jack·son Day *n.* January 8, a legal holiday celebrated in Louisiana marking Andrew Jackson's victory over the British in the Battle of New Orleans in 1815

Jack·son Hole valley in northwestern Wyoming, east of the Teton Range and partly in Grand Teton National Park. Length: 50 mi./80 km.

Jack·so·ni·an /jak sṓnee ən/ *adj.* relating to Andrew Jackson's presidential term or policies, especially his advocacy of greater public involvement in politics. —**Jack·so·ni·an** *n.* —**Jack·so·ni·an·ism** *n.*

Jack·son·ville /jáks'n vil/ city in northeastern Florida. It is a major commercial and cultural center. Population: 665,070 (1994).

jack·stay /ják stay/ *n.* **1.** ROD TO SECURE SAIL a rod attached to a horizontal beam **(yard)** on a mast, used for securing a sail **2.** SUPPORT a support for the ring **(parrel)** that holds a boom to a mast

jack·stone /ják stōn/ *n.* a small piece of metal or plastic used in the game of jacks

jack·stones /ják stōnz/ *n.* = **jacks** (*takes a singular verb*) [Early 19thC. Named with reference to the small size of the "stones" (see JACK[1]), originally little pebbles or bones.]

jack·straw /ják straw/ *n.* **1.** THIN PLAYING STICK a small thin stick used in the game of jackstraws **2.** **jack·straws** GAME OF SKILL a game that involves trying to remove a small thin stick **(jackstraw)** from a pile of others without disturbing any of the rest of them (*takes a singular verb*) [Late 16thC. Named because of its small size and also for *Jack Straw,* a 14thC English political rebel, with the sense of "worthless person"; also "man of straw."]

jack-tar, Jack Tar *n.* a sailor (*dated informal*) [JACK[1] with the sense "everyman," *tar* from shortening of *tarpaulin,* used to make the sailors' hats]

Jack the Rip·per /jàk t͟hə rĭppər/ (*fl.* 1880s) British murderer. He was the notorious unknown killer of six prostitutes in London's East End between August and November 1888.

jack-up rig *n.* an offshore oil rig with a floating hull and retractable legs that can be lowered to the seabed for support

Ja·cob /jáykəb/ *n.* in the Bible, the son of Isaac and Rebekah, and the grandson of Abraham. He tricked his brother, Esau, out of his father's blessing, and had a vision of ascent into heaven that came to be called "Jacob's ladder" (Genesis 25–35).

Jac·o·be·an /jàkə beé ən, jàykə beé ən/ *adj.* **1.** HISTORY OF JAMES I relating to King James I or to the period of his English reign (1603–25). **2.** FURNITURE OF FURNITURE STYLE in the style of furniture fashionable during the reign of King James I. Pieces were typically quite bulky and were usually made from dark carved oak, often with Gothic motifs. **3.** ARCHIT OF ARCHITECTURAL STYLE in the style of architecture produced during the reign of King James I. It is transitional between the Gothic and Renaissance periods, retaining some Gothic motifs, but also anticipating the reverence for the classical that typifies later design. ■ *n.* HISTORY CONTEMPORARY OF JAMES I somebody, especially a prominent person, who lived during the reign of King James I of England [Late 18thC. From ecclesiastical Latin *Jacobus* "James."]

Jac·o·be·an lil·y *n.* a flowering plant of the amaryllis family that is native to Mexico, widely cultivated for its bright-red, single flower. Latin name: *Sprekelia formosissima.* [Named in honor of St. James.]

jac·o·bin /jákəbin/ *n.* a variety of pigeon with feathers over the neck and head that grow in the opposite direction to the others, giving it the appearance of having a hood [Late 17thC. From French *jacobine,* femininine of *Jacobin* (see JACOBIN).]

Jac·o·bin /jákəbin/ *n.* **1.** HISTORY FRENCH REVOLUTIONARY EXTREMIST a member of a group of left-wing extremists founded during the French Revolution. In 1793, they overthrew the more moderate republicans, the Girondists, and this allowed Robespierre, the leader of the group, to begin the Reign of Terror and to install revolutionary measures. **2.** POL LEFT-WING EXTREMIST a political radical, especially one who holds extreme left-wing views **3.** CHR FRIAR a French Dominican friar ■ *adj.* HISTORY OF FRENCH JACOBINS relating to the Jacobins of the French Revolution, or to their policies [From Old French, from ecclesiastical Latin *Jacobus,* originally a Dominican friar associated with the church of St. Jacques in Paris, where the Jacobins were established.] —**Jac·o·bin·ic** /jàkə bínnik/ *adj.* —**Jac·o·bin·i·cal** *adj.* —**Jac·o·bin·i·cal·ly** *adv.* —**Jac·o·bin·ism** /jákəbiniz'm/ *n.*

Jac·o·bite /jákə bīt/ *n.* **1.** HISTORY SUPPORTER OF JAMES II somebody who supported the Roman Catholic King James II of England and his descendants in the Stuart claim to the British throne **2.** CHR EASTERN CHURCH MEMBER a member of any of the Monophysite churches, especially of Syria ■ *adj.* HISTORY OF JACOBITES relating to the Stuart claim to the British throne or to those who supported the Stuart claim [Late 17thC. From ecclesiastical Latin *Jacobus* (see JACOBEAN).] —**Jac·o·bit·ic** /jàkə bíttik/ *adj.* —**Jac·o·bit·i·cal** *adj.* —**Jac·o·bit·ism** /jákə bītiz'm/ *n.*

Ja·cob's lad·der *n.* **1.** NAUT ROPE LADDER a ladder, used especially on ships, whose rungs are held together by ropes or chains, thus allowing it to be rolled up and stored in a small space **2.** PLANTS N AMERICAN PLANT a North American wild or garden plant that has blue or white flowers and leaves divided into several leaflets in an arrangement similar to a ladder. Genus: *Polemonium.* [Named with reference to the story of Jacob's vision of a ladder reaching to heaven (Genesis 28 :12)]

Ja·cob's staff *n.* a medieval instrument for measuring distance [Alludes to St. James (ecclesiastical Latin *Jacobus* "James"), one of whose symbols is a pilgrim's staff, or to the staff of Jacob (Genesis 30:10).]

jac·o·net /jákə net/ *n.* a cotton fabric that is like muslin but slightly heavier and is used for clothing and bandages [Mid-18thC. Anglicization of *Jagannāth(purī)* in India, where it originated.]

jac·quard /jəkaard/ *n.* **1.** WEAVING TECHNIQUE a technique for producing intricate patterns in material by means of punched cards that give instructions to use or withhold various colors of thread **2.** LOOM ATTACHMENT a loom attachment with punched cards that makes jacquard patterns **3.** = **jacquard loom** **4.** PATTERNED MATERIAL a fabric that has been woven with a jacquard pattern [Mid-19thC. Named for its inventor J. M. JACQUARD.]

Jac·quard /jə kaárd/, **Joseph Marie** (1752–1832) French inventor. His invention of the jacquard loom (1801–08), the first mechanical loom for weaving complex patterns, was an inspiration for modern computer programming.

jac·quard loom *n.* a loom with an attachment for making jacquard patterns

Jacques-Car·tier /zhaák kàartee áy/ river that flows south into the St. Lawrence River just south of Quebec City in southern Quebec, Canada. Length: 70 mi./113 km.

Jacques-Car·tier, Mount mountain in eastern Canada, on the Gaspé Peninsula. It is Quebec's second-highest point. Height: 4,160 ft./1,268 m.

jac·ti·ta·tion /jàktə táysh'n/ *n.* **1.** MED UNCONTROLLED THRASHING a state of thrashing around uncontrollably, usually brought on by extremely high temperature, or occasionally by psychiatric disorders **2.** LAW HARMFUL LIE a false boast or claim, especially one that is intended to harm another **3.** BOASTING the act of boasting or exaggerating (*literary*) [Mid-17thC. From Latin *jactitare* "to bring forward in public, boast," literally "to throw repeatedly over and over," from, ultimately, Latin *jacere* "to throw."]

Ja·cuz·zi /jə kóozee/ *tdmk.* a trademark for a whirlpool bath with a system of underwater jets that deliver water under pressure in order to massage and invigorate the body

jade[1] /jayd/ *n.* **1.** SEMIPRECIOUS STONE either of two different minerals, nephrite or jadeite, varying in color from a deep green through yellow and brown to white, mainly used for making ornaments and jewelry (*often used before a noun*) ○ *a jade necklace* **2.** JADE OBJECTS objects made of jade, collectively ○ *a collector of jade* ■ *n., adj.* COLORS = **jade green** [Late 16thC. Via French *l'ejade* from Spanish *piedra de ijada* "stone of the flanks," thought to cure pain in the renal areas, ultimately from Latin *ilia* "flanks."]

WORD KEY: ORIGIN

Despite ***jade***'s close association with China and Japan, its name has no Asian connections. It is of Latin origin, and started life as a description of the stone's medical applications. Latin *ilia* denoted the "sides of the lower torso," the "flanks," the part of the body where the kidneys are situated. A derivative of it passed eventually into Spanish as *ijada.* It was thought in former times that jade could cure pain in the renal area, so the Spanish called it *piedra de ijada,* literally "stone of the flanks." In due course this was reduced to simply *ijada.* French took it over as *ejade,* but subsequently *l'ejade* "the jade" became *le jade,* from which English ***jade*** is derived. (***Jade***'s alternative name, *nephrite,* is based on the same idea: it comes from Greek *nephros* "kidney").

jade[2] /jayd/ *n.* **1.** TIRED OLD HORSE an old horse, especially one that is worn out through overwork **2.** OFFENSIVE TERM an offensive term for a woman that deliberately insults her temperament or her morality (*offensive insult*) ■ *vti.* (**jad·ed, jad·ing, jades**) MAKE OR BECOME EXHAUSTED to wear somebody out or become exhausted, especially through overwork [14thC. Origin unknown.]

jad·ed /jáydəd/ *adj.* **1.** BORED no longer interested in something, often because of having been overexposed to it **2.** TIRED exhausted, especially through overwork —**jad·ed·ly** *adv.* —**jad·ed·ness** *n.*

jade green *n.* a pale milky green color, like that of some types of jade —**jade-green** *adj.*

jade·ite /jáy dīt/ *n.* a usually greenish pyroxine mineral consisting of sodium aluminum silicate, occurring only in metamorphic rocks. It is the source of the most precious jade and is found mainly in Myanmar. —**ja·dit·ic** /jay dĭttik/ *adj.*

jade plant *n.* a plant with thick fleshy leaves the color of jade, native to southern Africa and Asia and widely cultivated as a houseplant. Latin name: *Crassula argentea.*

j'a·doube /zha dóob, zhaa-/ *interj.* an expression used by a chess player who is about to adjust a piece on the board, to ensure that this will not be counted as an official move [Early 19thC. From French, literally "I dub" (touch on the shoulder).]

jae·ger /yáygər/ *n.* **1.** BIRDS PREDATORY SEA BIRD any of several mostly brownish or grayish predatory sea birds with narrow wings, found in the northern Pacific and Atlantic. Genus: *Stercorarius.* **2.** HUNT HUNTER a hunter, especially in Germany and Switzerland [Mid-19thC. Anglicization of German *Jäger* "huntsman," from *jagen* "to hunt, pursue."]

Ja·én /ha áyn/ capital city of Jaén Province in southern Spain. It is an industrial center. Population: 101,938 (1991).

Jaf·fa /jáffə/, **Jaf·fa or·ange** *n.* a variety of large thick-skinned juicy orange [Late 19thC. Named for *Jaffa* (TEL-AVIV YAFO), where this fruit was first cultivated.]

Jaff·na /jáafnə/ port and capital city of Northern Province, in northern Sri Lanka. Population: 129,000 (1990).

jag[1] /jag/ *n.* **1.** JAGGED PROJECTION a sharp projection, especially of rock **2.** NOTCH a notch or indentation in something, e.g., a leaf (*archaic*) **3.** TEAR IN CLOTHING a deliberate tear in a garment or piece of material that reveals a different material underneath (*archaic*) ■ *v.* (**jag·ged, jag·ging, jags**) **1.** *vt.* **CUT SOMETHING UNEVENLY** to cut notches in something, or cut something unevenly **2.** *vi.* **ZIGZAG** to zigzag or move in jerks (*informal*) [14thC. Origin uncertain, possibly from, ultimately, Arabic *az-zagaye* "lance, javelin."]

jag[2] /jag/ *n.* (*informal*) **1. PERIOD OF INTOXICATION** a period of intoxication by drugs or alcohol **2. DRUNKEN STATE** the state of being intoxicated from drugs or alcohol **3. BINGE** a period of time spent doing something in an uncontrolled or excessive way [Late 16thC. Origin unknown.]

J.A.G., JAG *abbr.* Judge Advocate General

Ja·gan /yaágən/, **Cheddi** (1918–97) Guyanan statesman. As the first prime minister of British Guiana (1961–69), he was instrumental in gaining Guyanan independence (1966). He was Guyana's president (1992–97).

jag·ged /jággəd/ *adj.* **1. POINTY** having sharp protruding parts or points ○ *jagged peaks of the distant mountains* **2. UNEVEN** having rough and uneven edges or surfaces ○ *a hastily drawn, jagged portrait* —**jag·ged·ly** *adv.* —**jag·ged·ness** *n.*

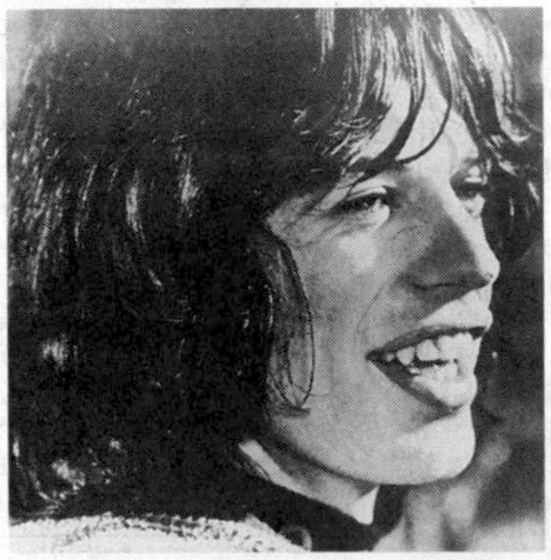

Mick Jagger

Jag·ger /jággər/, **Mick** (*b.* 1943) British rock musician and songwriter. He founded, with Keith Richards, the Rolling Stones, and wrote many of their hits, including "Satisfaction" (1965). Full name **Michael Phillip Jagger**

jag·ger·y /jággəree/ *n.* unrefined brown sugar made in Southeast Asia from the sap of the date palm [Late 16thC. From Portugese *xagara*, from, ultimately, Sanskrit *śarkarā* "sugar."]

jag·gy /jággee/ (**-gi·er, -gi·est**) *adj.* jagged (*informal*)

Jaguar

jag·uar /jág waar/ *n.* a large cat related to the leopard but with a shorter tail and black spots inside black rings on its tawny coat. It lives mainly in the forests of southern North America, Central America, and northern South America. Latin name: *Panthera onca.* [Early 17thC. From Portuguese, from Tupi *jaguara* and Guarani *yaguará* "carnivorous animal."]

jag·ua·run·di /jàggwə rúndee, jaágwə-/, **jag·ua·ron·di** /jàggwə róndee, jaágwə-/ *n.* a small slender cat of Central and South America that has a brownish, grayish, or reddish coat and small ears. It is occasionally also found in the southwestern United States. Latin name: *Felis yagouaroundi.* [Mid-19thC. Coined from Portuguese *jaguar* (see JAGUAR) + *undi* "dark."]

Jah /jaa/ *n.* God, especially in Rastafarianism [Mid-16thC. From Hebrew *Yāh*, a shortening of *Yahweh* "Jehovah."]

Jah·veh, Jah·weh *n.* = **Yahweh**

jai a·lai /hī́ lī, hī́ ə lī/ *n.* a Latin American game similar to handball, played with baskets fastened to the arm for catching and throwing the ball. ◊ **pelota** [Early 20thC. From Spanish, from Basque *jai* "festival" + *alai* "merry."]

jail /jayl/ *n.* **1. PLACE WHERE CRIMINALS ARE KEPT** a secure place for keeping people found guilty of minor crimes or awaiting legal judgment **2. LIFE AS A PRISONER** the state of being kept in a jail ○ *sentenced to three years jail.* ◊ **prison** ■ *vt.* (**jailed, jail·ing, jails**) **1. SEND SOMEBODY TO JAIL** to sentence somebody to spend time in a jail ○ *The judge jailed her for three months.* **2. LOCK SOMEBODY IN JAIL** to keep somebody in a jail or other secure place ○ *prisoners who were jailed in a dungeon* [13thC. Via Old French *jaiole*, from Latin *caveola*, diminutive of *cavea* "cage."]

jail·bait /jáyl bayt/ *n.* an offensive term for a minor under the age of consent who is sexually desirable to somebody older (*slang offensive*)

jail·bird /jáyl burd/ *n.* a current or former prisoner, especially somebody with more than one experience of prison (*slang*)

jail·break /jáyl brayk/ *n.* a forceful escape from jail or prison

jail·er /jáylər/, **jail·or** *n.* somebody who is in charge of prisoners in a jail, or who is in overall charge of a jail

jail·house /jáyl howss/ *n.* a jail (*informal*)

jail·house law·yer *n.* a prisoner who has studied law while serving time in order to be able to conduct legal proceedings in person rather than through a lawyer

jail·or *n.* = **jailer**

Jain /jīn/, **Jai·na** /jīnə/ *n.* **BELIEVER IN JAINISM** somebody who believes in or practices Jainism ■ *adj.* **OF JAINISM** relating to Jains or Jainism [Late 18thC. From Hindi, from Sanskrit *jaina* "of a conqueror."]

Jain·ism /jīniz'm/ *n.* an ancient branch of Hinduism that rejects the notion of a supreme being and advocates a deep respect for all living things. Some adherents refuse to wash for fear of killing creatures on the body. —**Jain·ist** *adj.*

Jai·pur /jī poor/ capital city of Rajasthan State, northern India. It is a major commercial and manufacturing center. Population: 1,454,678 (1991).

jak /jak/, **jack** *n.* the large greenish bulbous fruit produced by the jackfruit tree. It can weigh up to 60 lb./27 kg and has highly nutritious seeds. [Late 16thC. Via Portuguese *jaca* from Malayalam *cakka*.]

Ja·kar·ta /jə kaártə/ capital and largest city of Indonesia, located in the center of the country, on the northwestern coast of the island of Java. Population: 9,160,5000 (1995). Former name **Batavia**

jake leg *n.* permanent inability to move, caused by drinking contaminated alcoholic drink or alcoholic drink that has not been properly distilled [*jake* from *jake* alcoholic drink made from "Jamaica ginger"]

jakes /jayks/ (*plural* **jakes·es** *or* **jakes**) *n. U.K., U.S.* an outhouse (*regional archaic informal*) [Mid-16thC. Origin uncertain: perhaps from the male forename *Jacques*, or *Jack's* (see JACK[1]).]

Ja·lal·a·bad /jə laálə baad/, **Ja·lāl·ā·bād** city in eastern Afghanistan, on the Kabul River

Ja·land·har /jə lúndər/ ◗ **Jullunder**

jal·ap /jálləp, jaáləp/ *n.* a Mexican twining plant of the convolvulus family, the dried tubers of which have a purgative effect. Latin name: *Ipomoea purga.* [Mid-17thC. Via French from an abbreviation of Spanish *purga de Jalapa*, named after the Mexican city of *Jalapa*, where the plant flourished.] —**jal·ap·ic** /jə láppik/ *adj.*

ja·la·pe·ño /haálə páyn yō/ (*plural* **-ños**), **ja·la·pe·ño pep·per** *n.* a small hot pepper that is green or red when ripe and is used extensively in Mexican cooking. Latin name: *Capsicum annuum.* [Mid-20thC. From Mexican Spanish.]

ja·lop·y /jə lóppee/ (*plural* **-ies**) *n.* a rickety or battered old car (*dated informal*) [Early 20thC. Origin unknown.]

Jalousie

jal·ou·sie /jálləssee/ *n.* a shutter or window covering consisting of a set of angled parallel slats that can be opened to various degrees to control the amount of light or air passing through [Mid-18thC. From French, literally "jealousy," by extension a type of window-covering or shutter.]

jam[1] /jam/ *v.* (**jammed, jam·ming, jams**) **1.** *vt.* **PUSH SOMETHING IN FORCIBLY** to push something into a tight space with force ○ *jammed the clothes into the hamper* **2.** *vt.* **FILL SOMETHING UP** to fill a place with people or things pressed closely together ○ *The fans jammed the streets to see their heroes.* ○ *jammed the refrigerator with delicacies* **3.** *vti.* **STOP WORKING** to cause a piece of machinery or equipment to stick or stop working, or undergo such a stoppage ○ *The photocopier jammed when I was in the middle of using it.* **4.** *vt.* **BLOCK SOMETHING UP** to block up something that functions as an exit, passage, or means of escape ○ *Leaves had jammed the gutters and downspouts.* **5.** *vt.* BROADCAST **INTERFERE WITH BROADCASTING SIGNALS** to block a radio or TV signal, usually by broadcasting other signals on the same frequency **6.** *vt.* TELECOM **OVERWHELM SWITCHBOARD** to overwhelm a switchboard with telephone calls **7.** *vt.* **PUT ON BRAKES HARD** to apply the brakes of a car suddenly and hard **8.** *vt.* RECORDING **MAKE TAPE IMPOSSIBLE TO COPY** to put a blocking device on something, especially a prerecorded videotape, in order to prevent it from being copied **9.** *vt.* **CRUSH PART OF BODY** to injure a part of the body, especially by squeezing or mashing it ○ *I jammed my finger in the door.* **10.** *vi.* MUSIC **IMPROVISE MUSIC TOGETHER** to play music, especially jazz, rock, or pop, in an improvised way, often in a group ■ *n.* **1. = traffic jam 2. DIFFICULT SITUATION** a difficult, awkward, or embarrassing situation (*informal*) ○ *a cash shortage that's gotten the company into a jam* **3. STOPPAGE** an instance of something being blocked or prevented from functioning ○ *a paper jam in the photocopier* **4.** BROADCAST **SIGNAL BLOCKAGE** a blockage of radio or television signals [Early 18thC. Origin uncertain, perhaps imitative of the action of pushing. Music senses perhaps from Mandingo and Black West African English *jama* "crowd gathering," and Wolof *jaam* "enslaved person."] —**jam·ma·ble** *adj.* —**jam·mer** *n.*

jam[2] /jam/ *n.* a spread made from fruit boiled with sugar. Pectin is often added to help it set. [Mid-18thC. Origin uncertain: possibly from the idea of crushing or "jamming" fruit into jars.]

Jam. *abbr.* **1.** Jamaica **2.** BIBLE James

JAMA *abbr.* Journal of the American Medical Association

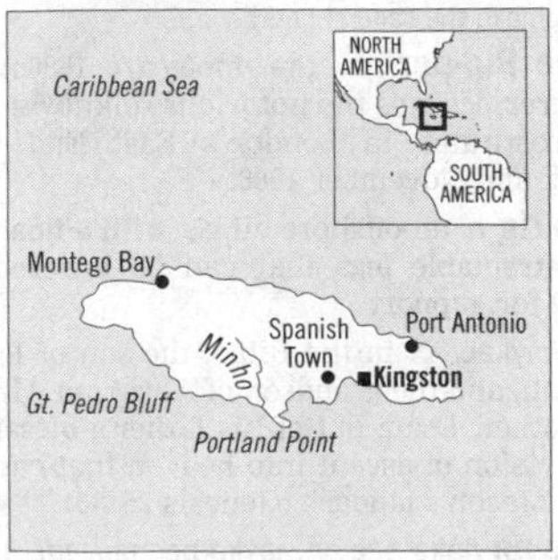

Jamaica

Ja·mai·ca /jə máykə/ island country situated south of Cuba in the northern Caribbean Sea. It is the third largest island of the Greater Antilles. Language: English. Currency: Jamaican dollar. Capital: Kingston. Population: 2,615,581 (1997). Area: 4,244 sq. mi./10,991 sq. km. —**Ja·mai·can** *n., adj.*

Ja·mai·ca pep·per *n.* = **allspice** *n.* 2

Ja·mai·ca rum *n.* a slowly fermented rum that has a dark color and a strong flavor

jamb /jam/, **jambe** *n.* **1. UPRIGHT SUPPORT** either of the upright parts of a door or window frame or the sides of a fireplace **2. INSIDE SURFACE** the inside vertical face of an opening [14thC. Via Italian *gamba* or Old French *jambe* "leg," from, ultimately, Greek *kampē* "bend, joint."]

jam·ba·lay·a /jámbə lī́ ə/ *n.* a Creole dish of rice with a mixture of fish and meat such as shrimp, chicken, ham, and spicy sausage [Late 19thC. Via Louisiana French from Provençal *jambalaia* "stewed mixture of rice and fowl."]

Jam·bi /jáambee/ city and port in western Indonesia, on the island of Sumatra. It is the capital of Jambi Province. Population: 301,359 (1990).

jam·bo·ree /jàmbə rée/ *n.* **1. BIG CELEBRATION** a large-scale planned celebration with various events and entertainments **2. INTERNATIONAL MEETING OF SCOUTS** a large gathering of members of the Boy Scouts, often on an international scale [Mid-19thC. Origin uncertain.]

James /jaymz/, **St.** (*d.* A.D. 62?). One of the 12 apostles, he was the son of Alphaeus. (Matthew 10:3). Known as **St. James the Less**

James[1] /jaymz/ *n.* in the Bible, an epistle believed to have been written by James, a brother or relative of Jesus Christ

James, St. (*fl.* 1st century A.D.) One of the 12 apostles, he was a member of the inner circle of Jesus Christ's disciples. He was the son of Zebedee and Salome and the brother of St. John. (Matthew 4:21). Known as **St. James the Great**

James, St. (*fl.* 1st century A.D.) He was a relative of Jesus Christ, and is identified in the New Testament as a leader of the early Christian church in Jerusalem. (Mark 6:3). Known as **St. James the Just**

James[2] river in western Virginia, formed at Iron Gate by the joining of the Cowpasture and Jackson rivers. Length: 340 mi./547 km.

James I, King of Aragón (1208–76). He captured the Balearic Islands (1229–35) and Valencia (1238) from the Moors. Known as **James the Conqueror**

James I, King of England, Scotland, and Ireland (1566–1625). He was king of Scotland as James VI (1567–1625), and succeeded to the English throne in 1603. He authorized the King James Bible.

James II, King of England, Scotland, and Ireland (1633–1701). His Roman Catholicism occasioned political conflict before and during his reign (1685–88), and he was deposed in the Revolution of 1688 by his nephew and son-in-law William III.

James, Henry (1843–1916) U.S. writer. He described the collision of American innocence and European worldliness in novels such as *The Portrait of a Lady* (1881) and *The Golden Bowl* (1909). He was the brother of William James.

James, Jesse (1847–82) U.S. outlaw. He robbed banks and trains between Missouri and Texas, and was killed in a shootout. Full name **Jesse Woodson James**

Express Newspapers

P. D. James

James, P. D., Baroness James of Holland Park (*b.* 1920) British novelist. Her best-selling crime novels include *The Black Tower* (1975) and *Original Sin* (1994). Full name **Phyllis Dorothy James**

James, William (1842–1910) U.S. philosopher and psychologist. The brother of Henry James, he developed the philosophy of pragmatism, and encouraged an empirical approach to psychology.

James Bay southern extension of Hudson Bay, between western Québec and northeastern Ontario, Canada. Area: 12,350 sq. mi./32,000 sq. km.

James·i·an /jáymzee ən/ *adj.* relating to or characteristic of the style of Henry James, e.g., in containing long complex sentences, or describing emotional states and relationships in minute detail

James·town /jáymz town/ city in southwestern New York, east of Lake Chautauqua and southwest of Buffalo. Population: 33,154 (1996).

James·town Is·land island in eastern Virginia, on the James River. It was the site of Jamestown village.

James VI ➧ **James I**

ja·min·der *n.* = **zamindar**

jam·mies /jámmiz/ *npl.* pajamas (*informal*) (*often used by or to children*) [Late 20thC. Shortening and alteration.]

Jam·mu and Kash·mir /jùmmoo-/ section of the disputed territory of Kashmir in the northern part of the Indian subcontinent that has been under Indian control since 1972

jam·my /jámmee/ (**-mi·er, -mi·est**) *adj.* covered in or filled with jam

jam-pack *vt.* to fill a container or place extremely tightly or to capacity (*informal*)

jam ses·sion *n.* a period of time spent making improvised music, especially jazz, rock, or pop music, as practice, for fun, or to experiment with new songs or techniques

Jam·shed·pur /jaámshed pöór/ city in eastern India, on the Subarnarekha River, in Bihār State. Population: 478,950 (1991).

Jan, Jan. *abbr.* January

Jane Doe *n.* **1. ANONYMOUS WOMAN** a woman or girl, especially one who is involved in legal proceedings and whose identity is not known or is being protected **2. ORDINARY WOMAN** an average woman affected by everyday events [Modeled on JOHN DOE]

Jane·ite /jáyn īt/ *n.* somebody who is an expert on or admirer of the life and works of the English novelist, Jane Austen

Janes·ville /jáynz vil/ city in southern Wisconsin. It is the seat of Rock County. Population: 52,133 (1990).

jan·gle /jáng g'l/ *vti.* (**-gled, -gling, -gles**) **1. MAKE A METALLIC SOUND** to make a harsh metallic noise, or cause something made of metal to make such a noise ○ *heard his keys jangling* **2. IRRITATE SOMEBODY'S NERVES** to put somebody's nerves on edge, or be tense and on edge ○ *The shock jangled her nerves.* ■ *n.* **1. METALLIC SOUND** a harsh metallic noise **2. ARGUMENT** a disagreement or quarrel (*dated*) [13thC. From Old French *jangler* "to chatter," of uncertain origin: possibly from prehistoric Germanic.] —**jan·gler** *n.* —**jan·gly** *adj.*

jan·is·sar·y /jánnə serree/ (*plural* **-ies**), **jan·i·zar·y** /-zerree/ (*plural* **-ies**) *n.* **1.** HIST **TURKISH SOLDIER** a member of the Turkish sultan's elite personal guard from the 14th century until 1826. Janissaries were recruited from Christians in the Balkans and disbanded as part of 19th-century reforms. **2. DEVOTED FOLLOWER** a loyal follower or supporter [Early 16thC. Via French *janissaire* from, ultimately, Turkish *yeniçeri*, literally "new troops."]

jan·i·tor /jánnətər/ *n.* **1.** *U.S., Can, Scotland* **CLEANING AND MAINTENANCE PERSON** somebody whose job is to look after the cleaning and maintenance of a building, especially a school or an apartment building **2. DOORKEEPER** a doorkeeper (*archaic*) [Mid-16thC. From Latin, "door person," from *janua* "door." The caretaking sense developed in the early 18thC.] —**jan·i·to·ri·al** /jànnə táwree əl/ *adj.*

jan·i·zar·y *n.* = **janissary**

Jan May·en /yaa mī́ ən/ island of Norway, lying between Norway and Greenland in the Arctic Ocean. Area: 144 mi./373 km. Length: 39 mi./63 km.

Jan·sen·ism /jánsəniz'm/ *n.* a religious movement of the 17th and 18th centuries based on the theological views of Cornelius Jansen, who maintained that there can be no good act without divine will or the grace of God [Mid-17thC. Named for Cornelius *Jansen* (1585–1638), Bishop of Ypres in France.] —**Jan·sen·ist** *n.* —**Jan·sen·is·tic** /jànsə nístik/ *adj.* —**Jan·sen·is·ti·cal** *adj.*

jan·sky /jánskee/ (*plural* **-skys**) *n.* a unit used to indicate the strength of radio sources in astronomy, equal to 10^{-26} watts per square meter per hertz. Symbol **Jy** [Mid-20thC. Named for Karl JANSKY.]

Jan·sky /jánskee/, **Karl** (1905–50) U.S. engineer. He discovered radio waves in outer space (1931), so laying the foundation of radio astronomy. Full name **Karl Guthe Jansky**

Jan·u·ar·y /jánnyoo erree/ (*plural* **-ys**) *n.* the first month of the year in the Gregorian calendar. It is 31 days long. [Pre-12thC. From Latin *Januarius (mensis)*, first month of the Roman year, literally "month of Janus," from *Janus* (see JANUS).]

Ja·nus /jáynəss/ *n.* **1.** MYTHOL **ROMAN GOD SHOWN WITH TWO FACES** the Roman god of beginnings, of the past and the future, and of gates, doorways, and bridges, and of peace. He is traditionally depicted as having two faces looking in opposite directions, suggesting not only vigilance, but also fair-mindedness. Unusually, he has no Greek counterpart. **2.** ASTRON **SATELLITE OF SATURN** the tenth satellite of Saturn

Ja·nus-faced *adj.* insincere or hypocritical (*literary*)

JAP /jap/ *n.* an offensive term for a Jewish girl or woman that deliberately insults her ethnic background, upbringing, and character (*slang insult*) Abbr of **Jewish American Princess**

Jap. *abbr.* Japanese

ja·pan /jə pán/ *n.* **1. BLACK VARNISH** a lacquer that, when used to coat wood or metal, gives a glossy black finish **2. VARNISHED OBJECTS** decorative work that has been coated with japan or a similar kind of varnish ■ *vt.* (**-panned, -pan·ning, -pans**) **APPLY JAPAN TO SOMETHING** to varnish an object with japan [Late 17thC. Named after JAPAN, where it was originally made.]

Japan

Ja·pan /jə pán/ constitutional monarchy in eastern Asia, comprising four large islands and more than 1,000 lesser adjacent islands. Language: Japanese. Currency: yen. Capital: Tokyo. Population: 125,688,711 (1997). Area: 145,850 sq. mi./377,750 sq. km.

Ja·pan, Sea of sea lying between Japan and mainland Asia, connected to the Sea of Okhotsk, the Pacific Ocean, and the East China Sea. Area: 390,000 sq. mi./1,000,000 sq. km.

Ja·pan clo·ver *n.* an annual plant originally native to China and Japan, but now widely grown in the southeastern United States as a forage crop. It has compound leaves divided into many leaflets and small pink flowers. Latin name: *Lespedeza striata.*

Ja·pan Cur·rent ➧ **Kuroshio**

Jap·a·nese /jàppə néez, jáppə neez/ *n.* (*plural* **-nese**) **1.** PEOPLES **SOMEBODY FROM JAPAN** somebody who was born or raised in Japan, or who has Japanese citizenship **2.** LANG **OFFICIAL LANGUAGE OF JAPAN** the official language of Japan, also spoken in parts of Brazil and North America. Its linguistic affiliations are disputed. Some linguists consider it to be an isolate, others relate it to the Altaic family or to Korean. About 126 million people speak Japanese. ■ *adj.* **OF JAPAN OR JAPANESE** relating to or typical of Japan, or its people, culture, or language

Jap·a·nese an·drom·e·da *n.* an ornamental shrub originally native to Japan but now widely grown for its early-blooming clusters of white bell-shaped flowers. Latin name: *Pieris japonica.*

Jap·a·nese bee·tle *n.* a shiny green and brown scarab beetle that was accidentally introduced into the eastern United States where it has become a serious pest. The larvae eat the roots of grasses and cereal crops and the adults feed on leaves and fruits.

Jap·a·nese ce·dar *n.* an evergreen tree of the bald cypress family, cultivated in China and Japan for its soft wood. Latin name: *Cryptomeria japonica.*

Jap·a·nese clo·ver *n.* = **Japan clover**

Jap·a·nese gar·den *n.* a garden designed according to formal Japanese rules, distinguished by its use of foliage plants, rocks, sand, and wooden garden paths, bridges, and pavilions

Jap·a·nese i·ris *n.* an ornamental plant originally native to Japan, but now widely grown for its large-petaled, brightly colored red flowers. Latin name: *Iris kaempferi.*

Jap·a·nese ma·ple *n.* a small Asian maple that is widely cultivated for its reddish deeply lobed leaves and purple flowers. Latin name: *Acer palmatum.*

Jap·a·nese mil·let *n.* a coarse Asian annual grass that has edible seeds and is grown for fodder. Latin name: *Echinochloa frumentacea.*

Jap·a·nese per·sim·mon *n.* **1.** TREES **ASIAN FRUIT TREE** an Asian tree that produces large edible red or orange fruit. Latin name: *Diospyros kaki.* **2.** FOOD **FRUIT OF JAPANESE PERSIMMON** the large edible red or orange fruit of the Japanese persimmon tree. It is bitter when unripe and retains its green calyx even when ripe.

Jap·a·nese plum *n.* **1.** TREES **ASIAN PLUM TREE** a widely cultivated Asian tree with yellow or red fruit. Latin name: *Prunus salicina.* **2.** FOOD **FRUIT OF JAPANESE PLUM** the fruit of the Japanese plum tree, often pickled and used in cooking, or dried as a health food

Jap·a·nese quince *n.* an Asian ornamental shrub of the rose family cultivated for its bright red or pink flowers and edible round white, yellow, or green fruit. Latin name: *Chaenomeles japonica.*

Jap·a·nese rad·ish *n.* = **daikon**

Jap·a·nese um·brel·la pine *n.* a coniferous tree native to central Japan, widely grown elsewhere for ornament. Its leaves grow in pairs fused along their entire lengths and arranged in whorls like the ribs of an umbrella. Latin name: *Sciadopitys verticillata.*

Ja·pan wax, Ja·pan tal·low *n.* a hard yellow wax obtained from certain berries. It is used in making candles, matches, soap, polish, food packaging, and as a substitute for beeswax.

jape /jayp/ *n.* **JEST** a joke or an act of mischief (*archaic*) ■ *vti.* **(japed, jap·ing, japes) MAKE MISCHIEF** to joke, trick, or make fun of something (*archaic*) [14thC. From Old French *japer* "to yelp," influenced by *gaber* "to mock."] —**jap·er** *n.* —**jap·er·y** *n.*

Ja·pheth /jáyfith/ *n.* in the Bible, the third son of Noah and brother of Shem and Ham. He was traditionally regarded as the ancestor of a number of non-Semitic peoples of the Mediterranean (Gen 10:1–5).

Jap·lish /jáplish/ *n.* Japanese with many adoptions of English words, phrases, or idioms [Mid-20thC. Blend of JAPANESE and ENGLISH.]

ja·pon·i·ca /jə pónnikə/ *n.* **1.** = **Japanese quince 2.** = **camellia** *n.* 1 [Early 19thC. From modern Latin, feminine form of *Japonicus* "of Japan."]

jar[1] /jaar/ *n.* **1. STORAGE CONTAINER** a cylindrical container, usually one that has a wide mouth and a lid but no spout, typically made of glass, plastic, or earthenware ○ *pickle jars* **2.** = **jarful** [Late 16thC. Via French *jarre* from Arabic *jarra.*]

jar[2] /jaar/ *v.* **(jarred, jar·ring, jars) 1.** *vti.* **SHAKE** to start vibrating, or cause something to start vibrating ○ *When the furnace comes on it jars the table.* **2.** *vti.* **IRRITATE** to have an irritating or upsetting effect on somebody's nerves or mind ○ *Her constant moaning jars my nerves.* **3.** *vt.* **DISTURB SOMEBODY** to have a sudden unsettling effect on somebody ○ *He needs something to jar him out of his reverie.* **4.** *vti.* **GRATE** to make, or cause something to make, a harsh grating noise **5.** *vi.* **CLASH** to look or seem bad or inappropriate in the context of something else ○ *The ultramodern dormitories jar with the older, Gothic classroom buildings.* ■ *n.* **1. PHYSICAL JOLT** an act of knocking against something with a sudden blow **2. GRATING SOUND** a harsh grating noise [Late 15thC. Origin uncertain: probably in some part imitative of discordant sound.] —**jar·ring** *adj.* —**jar·ring·ly** *adv.*

jar[3] /jaar/ *n.* the state of being open or ajar (*archaic*) [Late 17thC. Later form of CHAR, from Old English *cerr* "turn (of work)."]

jar·di·nière /jaàrd'n eér, jaàrd'n eer, jaàrd'n yáir, jaàrd'n yair/ *n.* a large, usually decorative flower pot or other holder for plants [Mid-19thC. From French, literally "woman gardener."]

jar·ful /jaár fòol/ *n.* the amount a jar holds, or the contents of a jar

jar·gon[1] /jaárgən/ *n.* **1. SPECIALIST LANGUAGE** language that is used by a particular group, profession, or culture, especially when the words and phrases are not understood or used by other people ○ *typesetters' jargon* **2. UNINTELLIGIBLE LANGUAGE** pretentious or meaningless language (*disapproving*) ○ *Cut the jargon and get to your point.* **3.** = **pidgin** [14thC. From Old French *jargoun,* of uncertain origin.] —**jar·gon·eer** /jaàrgə neér/ *n.* —**jar·gon·ist** /jaárgənist/ *n.* —**jar·gon·is·tic** /jaàrgə nístik/ *adj.*

jar·gon[2] /jaar gón/, **jar·goon** /jaar goòn/ *n.* a colorless, pale, or smoky zircon [Mid-18thC. Via French from Italian *giargone* and, ultimately, from Persian *zargūn* "gold-colored."]

jar·gon·ize /jaárgə nīz/ **(-ized, -iz·ing, -iz·es)** *v.* **1.** *vt.* **TURN LANGUAGE INTO JARGON** to convert ordinary language into jargon **2.** *vi.* **USE JARGON** to talk in jargon —**jar·gon·i·za·tion** /jaàrgənə záysh'n/ *n.*

jar·goon *n.* = **jargon**[2]

jar·head /jaár hed/ *n.* a nickname for a U.S. Marine (*slang*) [Perhaps from the shape of the hat once worn by marines]

ja·ri *n.* = **zari**

jarl /yaarl/ *n.* a chieftain or nobleman in medieval Scandinavia [Early 19thC. From Old Norse *jarl* "earl," of unknown origin.] —**jarl·dom** *n.*

ja·ro·site /járrə sīt/ *n.* a secondary mineral in iron-containing ores, yellow to brown in color and consisting of a hydrous sulfate of iron and potassium [Mid-19thC. Named for the *Jarosa ravine* in southern Spain, where it was first found.]

jar·rah /járrə/ *n.* **1.** TREES **AUSTRALIAN TREE** a eucalyptus tree of southwestern Australia with dark reddish hard wood. Latin name: *Eucalyptus marginata.* **2.** INDUST **JARRAH WOOD** the timber of the jarrah tree, used in flooring and building [Mid-19thC. From Aboriginal *djarryl, jerrhyl.*]

Jas. *abbr.* James

Jasmine

jas·mine /jázmin/ (*plural* **-mine** *or* **-mines**), **jes·sa·mine** /jéssəmin/ (*plural* **-mine** *or* **-mines**) *n.* **1. SCENTED PLANT** a tropical or subtropical climbing plant with fragrant white, yellow, or red flowers. Jasmines are often grown as house or garden plants, and for use in making perfumes. Genus: *Jasminum.* **2. SCENT** perfume made from the oil of a variety of jasmine **3.** = **Carolina jasmine** [Mid-16thC. Via French *jasmin, jessemin* from, ultimately, Persian *yāsaman.*]

jas·mine tea *n.* black tea flavored with jasmine blossoms

Ja·son /jáyss'n/ *n.* in Greek mythology, a prince who led a group of heroes on his ship, the *Argo,* on a quest to obtain the Golden Fleece and bring it back to Greece

jas·pé /zha spáy/ *adj.* used to describe fabric that resembles jasper, especially in being streaked or veined with different colors [Mid-19thC. From French past participle of *jasper* "to marble."]

jas·per /jáspər/ *n.* an impure form of chalcedony usually colored red by iron impurities, used for jewelry and ornaments [13thC. Via Anglo-French *jaspre* from Latin *iaspidem,* from Greek *iaspis* "jasper," from, ultimately, a Semitic source.]

Jas·per Na·tion·al Park /jàspər-/ national park in western Alberta, Canada, in the Rocky Mountains. Area: 4,200 sq. mi./10,900 sq. km.

Jat /jaat/ *n.* a member of an Indo-European people living in the Punjab, other areas of northwestern India, and parts of Pakistan [Early 17thC. From Hindi *Jāt.*]

ja·to /jáy tō/, **JATO** *n.* an auxiliary jet or rocket designed to aid the combined thrust of aircraft jet engines during takeoff. Full form **jet-assisted takeoff**

jaun·dice /jáwndiss/ *n.* **1. ILLNESS CAUSING YELLOW SKIN** a condition in which there is yellowing of the whites of the eyes, skin, and mucous membranes, caused by bile pigments in the blood. It is a symptom of liver diseases such as hepatitis and cirrhosis, or of a blocked bile duct, and sometimes occurs temporarily in new-born babies whose livers are slightly immature. Technical name **icterus 2. CYNICAL STATE OF MIND** an attitude that is characterized by cynical hostility, jealousy, or prejudice ■ *vt.* **(-diced, -dic·ing, -dic·es) 1. MAKE SOMEBODY CYNICAL** to alter somebody's attitude for the worse, especially when it results in cynical hostility, jealousy, or prejudice **2. AFFECT SOMEBODY WITH JAUNDICE** to affect somebody with jaundice, as a symptom of liver disease [14thC. From Old French *jaunice,* from *jaune* "yellow."] —**jaun·diced** *adj.*

jaunt /jawnt/ *n.* **EXCURSION** a trip, especially a short one taken for fun or pleasure ■ *vi.* **(jaunt·ed, jaunt·ing, jaunts) TAKE SHORT TRIP** to go on a short journey, usually for pleasure [Late 16thC. Origin unknown.]

jaunt·ing car *n.* a lightweight two-wheeled open vehicle pulled by a single horse and having lengthwise seats positioned so that passengers either face each other or sit back-to-back. It was formerly widely used in Ireland.

jaun·ty /jáwntee/ **(-ti·er, -ti·est)** *adj.* **1. CAREFREE** happy, carefree, and confident **2. CASUAL** perky and casually fashionable **3. POLITE** genteel and mannerly (*archaic*) [Mid-17thC. From French *gentil* "polite, kind." The sense of "carefree" did not develop until late 17thC.] —**jaun·ti·ly** *adv.* —**jaun·ti·ness** *n.*

Jav. *abbr.* **1.** Javanese **2. Jav., jav.** SPORT javelin

java /jaávə/ *n.* coffee, especially brewed coffee as opposed to instant coffee (*informal*) [Mid-19thC. From JAVA[2].]

Ja·va[1] /jaávə/ island in southeastern Asia, the most populous island in Indonesia. Population: 114,733,500 (1995). Area: 120,000 sq. mi./310,000 sq. km.

Ja·va[2] /jaávə/ *n.* a variety of rich coffee grown on Java and the surrounding islands

Ja·va[3] /jaávə/, *tdmk.* a high-level computer programming language that allows small application programs to be downloaded from a server to a client along with the data that each program processes

Ja·va man *n.* a fossil human found in Java and elsewhere in Indonesia, taken to be from the Paleolithic Age. The body and limbs of Java man are very similar to those of Homo sapiens, but the brain and skull are smaller.

Jav·a·nese /jaàvə neéz/ (*plural* **-nese**) *n.* **1.** PEOPLES **SOMEBODY FROM JAVA** somebody who was born or who lives on the Indonesian island of Java **2.** LANG **LANGUAGE SPOKEN ON JAVA** a language spoken on the Indonesian island of Java. It belongs to the Western branch of the Austronesian family of languages. Over 70 million people speak Javanese. —**Jav·a·nese** *adj.*

Ja·va spar·row *n.* a small Indonesian weaverbird that has gray and pink feathers and a stout red beak, popular as a cage and aviary bird. Latin name: *Padda oryzivora.*

jave·lin /jávvlən, -vələn/ *n.* **1. SPEAR** a long thin piece of wood, plastic, or metal with a pointed end, used as a weapon or thrown in field competitions **2. THROWING CONTEST** a field event in which competitors try to throw a javelin as far as possible [15thC. Via Middle French *javeline,* diminutive of Old French *javelot,* possibly from, ultimately, a Celtic source, ancestor of Welsh *gaflach* "feathered lance."]

ja·ve·li·na /haàvə leénə/ *n.* ZOOL = **peccary** [Early 19thC. Alteration of Spanish *jabalina,* the feminine of *jabalí* "wild boar," from Arabic *jabalī.*]

Ja·velle wa·ter /jə vèl-, zhə vèl-/, **Ja·vel wa·ter** *n.* a solution of sodium hypochlorite, used as a bleach and disinfectant. Formula: NaOCl. [Early 19thC.

Named for *Javelle*, a village on the outskirts of Paris, where the solution was first used.]

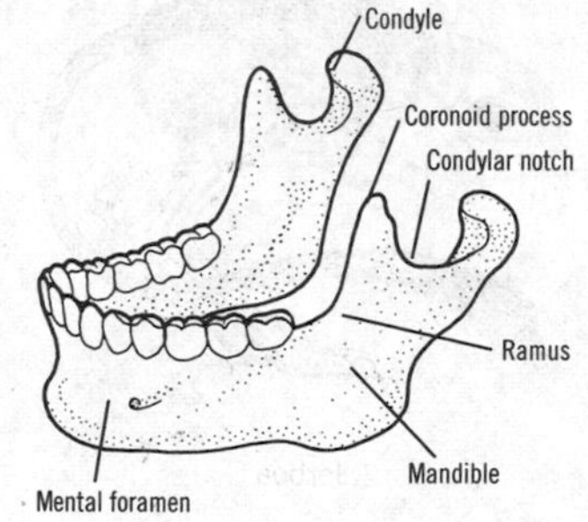

Jaw

jaw /jaw/ *n.* **1.** ZOOL **TOOTHBEARING BONE** either of the upper or lower bones that anchor the teeth and form the structural basis of the mouth in vertebrates. In humans and other higher vertebrates, the upper jaw is known as the maxilla and the lower the mandible. **2.** ZOOL **INVERTEBRATE BITING PART** an invertebrate body part with a function or structure similar to a vertebrate jaw **3.** MECH ENG **GRIPPING PART** either of two hinged parts of a tool or machine used to grip objects securely **4. FACE PART** the lower, mobile part of the human face ○ *a strong square jaw* **5. IMPUDENCE** cocky or impudent talk (*slang*) **6. LONG TALK** a long conversation or discussion (*slang*) **7. MORALIZING TALK** a moralizing talk or lecture (*slang*) ■ **jaws** *npl.* **1.** GEOG **NATURAL ENTRANCE** a narrow opening in something such as a cave, gorge, canyon, or other natural feature **2. DANGEROUS PLACE** a situation that is dangerously close to something horrible or frightening ■ *vi.* **(jawed, jaw·ing, jaws) TALK AT LENGTH** to talk or gossip, usually at length (*slang*) ○ *Quit your jawing about travel arrangements and let's get going.* [14thC. Origin uncertain: possibly from Old French *joe* "cheek," or from a prehistoric Germanic word, ancestor of *chew*.] —**jaw·less** *adj.*

jaw·bone /jáw bōn/ *n.* **BONE IN JAW** a bone in the jaw, especially the lower jaw. ◊ **mandible, maxilla** ■ *vt.* **(-boned, -bon·ing, -bones) PERSUADE SOMEBODY FORCEFULLY** to coerce somebody to comply with something by using the authority of high office (*informal*) —**jaw·bon·er** *n.*

jaw·bon·ing /jáw bōning/ *n.* an act or the process of coercing compliance by imposing authority (*informal*)

jaw·break·er /jáw braykər/ *n.* **1.** FOOD **HARD CANDY** a large round hard piece of candy (*informal*) **2.** CONSTR **CRUSHING MACHINE** a machine that crushes rocks using powerful jaws **3.** LANGUAGE **UNPRONOUNCEABLE WORD** a long word that is difficult to pronounce (*informal*)

jawed /jáwd/ *adj.* having jaws of a particular kind (*used in combination*) ○ *slack-jawed*

jaw·line /jáw līn/ *n.* the shape of somebody's lower jaw

Jaws of Life *tdmk.* a trademark for a pneumatically operated metal device resembling pincers that is inserted into the body of a severely damaged motor vehicle and then opened to access people trapped inside

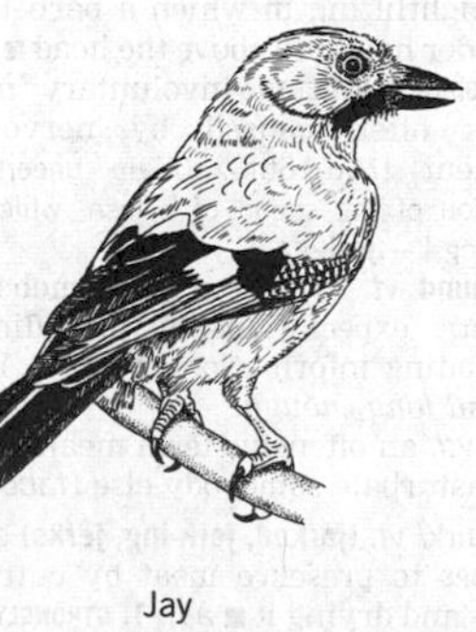

Jay

jay[1] /jay/ *n.* **1.** BIRDS **NOISY BIRD** any of several related birds of the crow family that are typically noisy, often brightly colored, and known for their intelligence. Family: Corvidae. **2. SOMEBODY THOUGHTLESSLY TALKATIVE** a heedless or chattering person (*informal*) [13thC. Via Old French *jay* from Latin *gaius*, of uncertain origin: perhaps from the male forename *Gaius*.]

jay[2] /jay/ *n.* a marijuana cigarette (*slang*)

Jay /jay/, **John** (1745–1829) U.S. jurist. He was president of the Second Continental Congress (1778–79) and negotiated the Treaty of Paris (1783) that ended the Revolution. He was the first chief justice of the Supreme Court (1789–95).

Jay·cee /jay sée/ *n.* in North America, Australia, and New Zealand, a member of a junior chamber of commerce, an organization for young people that promotes leadership and business skills [Mid-20thC. From the initial letters of *Junior Chamber*.]

Jay·hawk·er /jáy hawkər/ *n.* a nickname for somebody who was born or who lives in Kansas

jay·vee /jay vée/ *n., abbr.* **1.** Junior Varsity ■ *n.* **2. JUNIOR VARSITY PLAYER** a member of a junior varsity team

jay·walk /jáy wawk/ **(-walked, -walk·ing, -walks)** *vi.* to cross a street anywhere other than at designated crossing places. It is a violation of law in some places, though rarely enforced. [Early 20thC. Based on JAY in the sense "heedless person."] —**jay·walk·er** *n.* —**jay·walk·ing** *n.*

jazz /jaz/ *n.* **1. SYNCOPATED POPULAR MUSIC** popular music that originated among Black people in New Orleans in the late 19th century and is characterized by syncopated rhythms and improvisation. It has developed various styles. Jazz originally drew on ragtime, gospel, Black spiritual songs, West African rhythms, and European harmonies. **2. STUFF** unnamed related things or belongings (*slang*) ○ *a new motorcycle and all the jazz that comes with it* **3. BLATHER** information or ideas regarded as untrue, misconceived, or misleading (*slang disapproving*) ○ *Don't be fooled if she starts giving you that jazz about being broke.* **4. LIVELINESS** animated enthusiasm or vivacity (*slang*) ■ *v.* **(jazzed, jazz·ing, jazz·es) 1.** *vi.* **PLAY OR DANCE TO JAZZ** to play or dance to jazz music **2.** *vi.* **EXAGGERATE** to engage in exaggeration (*slang*) **3.** *vt.* **LIE TO SOMEBODY** to tell lies or a lie to somebody (*slang*) ○ *Stop jazzing me and tell me where you really were!* [Early 20thC. Origin uncertain: perhaps from Bantu *jaja*, earlier *jas* "to make dance, excite, exaggerate."] —**jazz·er** *n.*

WORD KEY: ORIGIN

The term ***jazz*** originated in the southern United States (it is first recorded in 1909, applied to a type of ragtime dance), and it is tempting to speculate that its ancestor crossed the Atlantic on the slave ships from Africa. This may have cropped up earlier in U.S. English in the form *jasm*, meaning "energy," which is first recorded in 1860. The link has not been established, but it adds weight to the idea that "liveliness, lively activity" (which probably also lies behind the word's sexual connotatons) is the ancestral meaning of ***jazz***, rather than any musical application. In the absence of any certain origin, various colorful alternative theories have been put forward – for example, that ***jazz*** came from the nickname of a certain Jasbo Brown, an itinerant musician along the banks of the Mississippi (*Jasbo* perhaps being an alteration of *Jasper*).

jazz up *vt.* **1. ENHANCE** to make somebody or something more interesting or decorative (*informal*) ○ *jazzed up his wardrobe with some Hawaiian shirts* **2.** MUSIC **ENLIVEN MUSIC** to make a piece of music more lively, especially by quickening the tempo or adding improvisations

jazz age *n.* the era that immediately followed World War I and lasted until the beginning of the Depression, during which jazz increased in popularity. It was a reaction to the austerity and hardship of the war and was characterized by extravagance and hedonism.

jazz band *n.* a band that plays jazz, usually consisting of five or more instruments including one or more solo wind instruments and a rhythm section consisting of piano, double bass, and drums

jazz·fest /jáz fest/ *n.* a festival of jazz music

jazz-fu·sion *n.* = **jazz-rock**

jazz·man /jáz man, jázmən/ (*plural* **-men** /-mən/) *n.* a man who plays or writes jazz music

jazz-rock *n.* jazz music that incorporates elements of rock music, especially its heavy, repetitive beats and electronic amplification

jazz·y /jázzee/ **(-i·er, -i·est)** *adj.* **1. SHOWY** showy, bright, and colorful (*slang*) **2. JAZZED UP TO APPEAL** exaggerated and unrestrained, especially in an attempt to make something more appealing (*slang*) **3. LIKE JAZZ** in the style of jazz music, especially with the syncopated rhythms of jazz —**jazz·i·ly** *adv.* —**jazz·i·ness** *n.*

Jb. *abbr.* BIBLE Job

J-bar *n.* a metal bar that is suspended from an overhead cable, used to tow a single skier up a slope ○ *rode to the summit on the J-bar*

JC *abbr.* junior college

J.C. *abbr.* **1.** Jesus Christ **2.** Julius Caesar

JCC *abbr.* Jewish Community Center

JCL *n.* a powerful computer language for writing a script used to control the execution of programs in batch processing systems. Full form **job control language**

J.C.S., JCS *abbr.* MIL Joint Chiefs of Staff

jct. *abbr.* junction

JD[1] *abbr.* **1.** Juris Doctor **2.** Justice Department **3. JD, J.D.** juvenile delinquent

JD[2] symbol **Jordan dinar**

Jdt. *abbr.* BIBLE Judith

jeal·ous /jélləss/ *adj.* **1. ENVIOUS** feeling bitter and unhappy because of another's advantages, possessions, or luck **2. SUSPICIOUS OF RIVALS** feeling suspicious about a rival's or competitor's influence, especially in regard to a loved one **3. WATCHFUL** possessively watchful of something ○ *keeps a jealous watch on his research* **4. DEMANDING LOYALTY** demanding exclusive loyalty or adherence (*archaic*) ○ *a jealous god.* [13thC. Via Old French *gelos* from Latin *zelosus*, from, ultimately, Greek *zelos* "jealousy," also "enthusiasm" (source of English *zeal*).] —**jeal·ous·ly** *adv.* —**jeal·ous·ness** *n.*

jeal·ous·y /jéllәssee/ *n.* **1. BEING JEALOUS** jealous feelings or behavior **2.** (*plural* **-ies**) **JEALOUS IMPULSE** an instance of feeling jealous ○ *a man of many jealousies*

jean /jeen/ *n.* a strong twill cotton that is used in making work clothes, uniforms, overalls, and jeans ○ *a jean jacket* [15thC. Via Old French *Janne* from medieval Latin *Janua*, the Italian city (Genoa) where the cloth was first made. Known in 16thC England as "jean fustian."]

jeans /jeenz/ *npl.* casual pants with raised seams and often with back pockets sewn on, made from denim, jean, or some other strong fabric

je·bel /jébb'l/, **dje·bel, ge·bel** *n.* a hill or mountain in the Middle East or North Africa (*often used in place names*) [Mid-19thC. From Arabic *jabal* "mountain."]

Jeep /jeep/ *tdmk.* a trademark for a four-wheel-drive vehicle suitable for rough terrain

jeep·ers /jéepərz/, **jeep·ers creep·ers** *interj.* used to express surprise (*dated informal*) [Early 20thC. Alteration of JESUS.]

jeep·ney /jéepnee/ (*plural* **-neys**) *n.* a Jeep or similar vehicle that has been converted into a jitney, used in the Philippines as a form of public transport [Mid-20thC. Blend of JEEP and JITNEY.]

jeer /jeer/ *vti.* **(jeered, jeer·ing, jeers) EXPRESS DERISION VOCALLY** to shout or laugh at somebody or something as an expression of disgust, scorn, or other displeasure ■ *n.* **DERISIVE SHOUT** a mocking or scornful laugh or shout [Mid-16thC. Origin uncertain: perhaps from Dutch *gieren* "to cry, roar (with laughter)."] —**jeer·er** *n.* —**jeer·ing·ly** *adv.*

jeez /jeez/ *interj.* used to express surprise, enthusiasm, or annoyance (*slang*) [Early 20thC. From a shortening of JESUS.]

Jef·fers /jéffərz/, **Robinson** (1887–1962) U.S. poet. His eloquent verse expresses contempt for human society. His work includes a successful adaptation of *Medea* (1946). Full name **John Robinson Jeffers**

Jef·fer·son /jéffərss'n/, **Thomas** (1743–1826) U.S. statesman and 3rd President of the United States. He was the author of the Declaration of Independence. As Democratic Republican president (1801–09), he strengthened the executive branch of government.

Jef·fer·son Day *n.* April 13, the day Thomas Jefferson was born, designated as a public holiday in Alabama in memory of him, and often celebrated by the Democratic Party with fundraising dinners

Jef·frey pine /jéffri-/ *n.* a pine tree of the western United States that has long needles grouped in

Thomas Jefferson

threes. Latin name: *Pinus jeffreyi.* [Mid-19thC. Named for John *Jeffrey,* Scottish plant collector.]

Jef·fries /jéffreez/, **Jim** (1875–1953) U.S. boxer. He held the world heavyweight championship (1899–1905). Full name **James Jackson Jeffries**

je·had *n.* = **jihad**

Je·hosh·a·phat /jə hóshə fàt, -hósə-/ *n.* in the Bible, a king of Judea who succeeded Asa and formed an alliance with Ahab of Israel against Syria. (1, 2 Kings; 2 Chronicles).

Je·ho·vah /jə hṓvə/ *n.* JUD-CHR = **God** [Mid-16thC. From medieval Latin *Iehoua,* mistaken transliteration of *YHWH,* using vowel points of Hebrew *ădōnāy* "my lord," incorrectly supposed substitution for the name too sacred to pronounce.]

Je·ho·vah's Wit·ness *n.* a member of a religious group that believes in the imminence of Jesus Christ's personal reign on Earth and rejects secular law where it appears to conflict with the divine. Jehovah's Witnesses reject the doctrine of the Trinity.

Je·ho·vist /jə hṓvist/ *n.* **1.** = **Yahwist 2. INTERPRETER OF BIBLICAL WORD** somebody who believes that the Hebrew word "YHVH" in the Bible was pronounced like "Jehovah" —**Je·ho·vism** *n.* —**Je·ho·vis·tic** /jə hō vístik, jèe hō vístik/ *adj.*

je·ju·nal /jə jóon'l/ *adj.* relating to the middle part of the small intestine (**jejunum**)

je·june /jə jóon/ *adj.* **1. BORING** uninteresting and intellectually undemanding **2. CHILDISH** lacking maturity or sophistication ○ *jejune chatter about concepts beyond their understanding* **3. WITHOUT PROPER NOURISHMENT** lacking or not providing proper nourishment **4. BARREN** not very fertile [Early 17thC. From Latin *jejunus* "fasting, meager." The late 19thC sense "childish" arose perhaps from a mistaken belief that "jejune" came from Latin *juvenis* or French *jeune* "young."] —**je·june·ly** *adv.* —**je·june·ness** *n.*

je·jun·os·to·my /ji joo nóstəmee/ (*plural* **-mies**) *n.* **1. OPENING UP OF PART OF INTESTINE** a surgical operation that creates access from the outside of the body into the middle part of the small intestine (**jejunum**) so that nourishment can be directly introduced **2. OPENING INTO INTESTINE** the opening formed in a jejunostomy

je·ju·num /jə jóonəm/ *n.* the section of the small intestine that is situated between the duodenum and the ileum and whose main function is the absorption of nutrients from digested food [Mid-16thC. From medical Latin, from Latin *jejunus* "fasting," so called because it is usually found to be empty after death.]

Je·kyll and Hyde /jék'l ən hīd/ (*plural* **Je·kyll and Hydes**) *n.* somebody who has two distinct personalities, one good and the other evil [Late 19thC. From *The Strange Case of Dr. Jekyll and Mr. Hyde,* 1886, by R. L. Stevenson.]

jell /jel/ (**jelled, jell·ing, jells**) *v.* **1.** *vti.* **SOLIDIFY** to become, or cause a substance to become, set or firm **2.** *vti.* **TAKE SHAPE** to become, or cause something to become, fixed or more definite in shape or form **3.** *vi.* **GET ON WELL TOGETHER** to bond in a way that gives rise to mutual cooperation ○ *"It's fun being with a bunch of guys who are fighting through adversity and jelling together."* (*The Philadelphia Inquirer*; 1997) [Mid-18thC. Back-formation from JELLY.]

jel·la·ba /jéllәbə, jə laábə/, **djel·la·ba** *n.* a unisex coverall garment with a hood, of a type worn in Morocco and other parts of North Africa [Early 19thC. From Moroccan Arabic *jellāb(a).*]

jel·lied /jéllid/ *adj.* set in jelly, or covered with a thin layer of jelly ○ *jellied tomato salad*

jel·li·fy /jéllə fī/ (**-fied, -fy·ing, -fies**) *vti.* to turn, or cause a substance to turn, into jelly —**jel·li·fi·ca·tion** /jèlləfə káysh'n/ *n.*

Jell-O /jéllō/ *tdmk.* a trademark for a gelatin-based dessert

jel·ly /jéllee/ *n.* (*plural* **-lies**) **1. FRUIT JUICE BOILED TO SPREADABLE CONSISTENCY** a fruit preserve that is made by boiling fruit juice, sugar, and sometimes pectin until it has a semisolid consistency **2. THICKENED MEAT STOCK** a savory semisolid food made from gelatin boiled with meat stock ○ *calf's foot jelly* **3. SUBSTANCE WITH JELLY CONSISTENCY** any substance that has the consistency of jelly, especially a pharmaceutical preparation ■ *vti.* (**-lied, -ly·ing, -lies**) **THICKEN** to set, or cause something to set, into a jelly [14thC. Via Old French *gelee* "frost, jelly," from Latin *gelare* "to freeze" (source of English *congeal*).] ◇ **turn to jelly** to feel shaky because of extreme fear, nervousness, or exhaustion (*informal*)

jel·ly·bean /jéllee been/ *n.* a small bean-shaped fruit candy with a hard coating and a soft jelly center

jel·ly·fish /jéllee fish/ (*plural* **-fish·es** *or* **-fish**) *n.* **1.** MARINE BIOL **STINGING MARINE ANIMAL** an invertebrate marine animal that, in its reproductive stage, has a nearly transparent gelatinous body shaped like an umbrella with trailing tentacles bearing stinging cells. Phylum: Coelenterata. **2.** MARINE BIOL **MARINE ANIMAL LIKE JELLYFISH** any of various invertebrate marine animals that have bodies similar to that of a true jellyfish, including cnidarians, ctenophores, and siphonophores **3. WEAK PERSON** somebody who lacks strength of character (*informal*) ○ *I'm afraid I'm just a jellyfish when it comes to making decisions.*

jel·ly fun·gus (*plural* **jel·ly fun·gus·es** *or* **jel·ly fun·gi**) *n.* any of various fungi that grow on trees and have a gelatinous fruiting body. Order: Tremellales.

jel·ly roll *n.* a long cylindrical cake made by rolling up a thin rectangle of light sponge spread with jelly

jem·my /jémmee/ *n.* (*plural* **-mies**) *U.K.* = **jimmy n.** ■ *vt.* (**-mied, -my·ing, -mies**) *U.K.* = **jimmy v.** [Early 19thC. From *Jemmy,* familiar form of the name *James.*]

je ne sais quoi /zh-nə say kwaá/ *n.* an indefinable quality that makes somebody or something more attractive or interesting [Mid-17thC. From French, literally "I do not know what."]

Jen·ner /jénnər/, **Bruce** (*b.* 1949) U.S. athlete. He won the gold medal in the decathlon at the 1976 Olympic games.

jen·net /jénnit/, **gen·et** *n.* **1. DONKEY** a female donkey **2. HORSE** a small Spanish riding horse [15thC. Via French *genet,* from, ultimately, Spanish Arabic *Genētī* "light horseman."]

jen·ny /jénnee/ (*plural* **-nies**) *n.* **1.** ZOOL **DONKEY** a female donkey **2.** BIRDS **BIRD** a female bird (*often used before a noun*) ○ *a jenny wren* **3.** MARINE BIOL **FEMALE CRAB** a female crab. ◊ **jimmy 4.** MANUF = **spinning jenny** [Early 17thC. From diminutive of names *Jane, Jennifer,* and a feminine version of *Jack,* often used to designate a tool or piece of machinery.]

Je·no·lan Caves /jə nṓlən-/ cave system in southeastern New South Wales, Australia. Located in the Blue Mountains National Park, the limestone cave system is a major tourist attraction.

jeop·ard /jéppərd/ (**-ard·ed, -ard·ing, -ards**) *vt.* to put somebody or something in jeopardy (*archaic*) [15thC. Back-formation from JEOPARDY.]

jeop·ard·ize /jéppər dīz/ (**-ized, -iz·ing, -iz·es**) *vt.* to put somebody or something at risk of being harmed or lost ○ *jeopardizing the entire mission through his indiscretion*

jeop·ard·y /jéppərdee/ *n.* **1. DANGER** the risk of loss, harm, or death ○ *The entire project is in jeopardy.* **2.** LAW **CHANCE OF BEING CONVICTED** the risk of being convicted when put on trial for a crime. ◊ **double jeopardy** [14thC. From Old French *jeu* (from Latin *jocus* "pastime") + *parti* (past participle of *partir* "to divide"), literally "even or divided game."]

Jer. *abbr.* **1.** BIBLE Jeremiah **2.** Jersey **3.** Jerusalem

Jerboa

jer·bo·a /jər bṓ ə/ (*plural* **-as**) *n.* **1. SMALL RODENT OF ASIA AND AFRICA** a small nocturnal rodent that lives in arid regions of Asia and Africa and has large ears, a long tufted tail, and long hind legs adapted for leaping. Family: Dipodidae. **2. SMALL MARSUPIAL OF CENTRAL AUSTRALIA** a small marsupial with long hind legs and a long bushy tail that lives in central desert areas of Australia. Genus: *Antechinomys.* [Mid-17thC. Via modern Latin *jerboa* from Arabic *yarbū'(a)* (variant *jarbū*).]

jer·e·mi·ad /jèrrə mī əd/ *n.* a long recitation of mournful complaints (*literary*) [Late 18thC. From French *jérémiade,* from *Jérémie* "Jeremiah" (see JEREMIAH).]

Jer·e·mi·ah /jèrrə mī ə/ *n.* **1. HEBREW PROPHET** a Hebrew prophet who lived in Judah in the 7th and 6th centuries B.C. and was persecuted for prophesying the fall of Judah and Jerusalem and the Israelites' captivity in Babylon **2. BOOK OF THE BIBLE** the book of the Bible that contains the prophecies of Jeremiah. See table at **Bible 3. NEGATIVE PERSON** somebody with a gloomy outlook on the present and future

Je·rez de la Fron·te·ra /he rèss də laa frun táirə/ city in southwestern Spain, in Cádiz Province, Andalucía. It is the world's sherry wine capital. Population: 182,939 (1991).

Jer·i·cho /jérrikō/ town in the West Bank, in the Jordan Valley. It is regarded as the world's oldest town, with remains dating back to 8000 B.C. and, according to the Bible, was destroyed by Joshua after he led the Israelites back from captivity in Egypt (Joshua 3–8). Population: 25,000 (1994).

jerk[1] /jurk/ *v.* (**jerked, jerk·ing, jerks**) **1.** *vt.* **PULL SUDDENLY** to pull somebody or something with a sudden strong movement ○ *He jerked her back from in front of the speeding car.* **2.** *vti.* **MOVE JOLTINGLY** to proceed, or cause something or somebody to proceed, with bumps and jolts ○ *The car jerked forward.* **3.** *vi.* PHYSIOL **MOVE IN SPASM** to move in response to muscular spasms (*refers to parts of the body*) **4.** *vt.* **SAY SOMETHING ABRUPTLY** to utter words or sounds suddenly and forcefully, e.g., from excitement **5.** *vt.* COOK, COMM **MAKE ICE CREAM REFRESHMENTS** to prepare and serve ice cream sodas, sundaes, and other refreshments at a soda fountain ■ *n.* **1. SUDDEN PULL** a sudden and forceful pulling movement ○ *giving the door a jerk* **2. JOLTING MOTION** an abrupt jolting or jarring motion ○ *moving in jerks* **3.** PHYSIOL **TWITCH** a spasmodic movement in a muscle **4. OFFENSIVE TERM** an offensive term referring contemptuously to somebody who behaves foolishly (*slang insult*) **5.** GYM **OVERHEAD LIFT IN WEIGHTLIFTING** a lift in weightlifting in which a barbell is thrust from shoulder height to above the head ■ **jerks** *npl.* PHYSIOL **SPASMODIC MOVEMENTS** involuntary muscular movements often caused by nervousness or excitement [Mid-16thC. Origin uncertain: possibly an imitation of the sound of a lash, which was its original meaning.] —**jerk·er** *n.*

jerk around *vt.* to encourage somebody to have unrealistic expectations by providing dishonest or misleading information (*slang*) ○ *You've jerked me around long enough.*

jerk off *vti.* an offensive term meaning to masturbate, or masturbate somebody else (*taboo offensive*)

jerk[2] /jurk/ *vt.* (**jerked, jerk·ing, jerks**) COOK **PRESERVE MEAT IN STRIPS** to preserve meat by cutting it into long strips and drying it ■ *adj.* **1. STRONGLY FLAVORED AND SPICY** made with strongly flavored spices, including hot peppers and allspice, as a marinade or rub for grilled meats **2. SPICY AND GRILLED** marinated in a jerk sauce and grilled [Early 18thC. Via American Spanish *charquear* from, ultimately, Quechua (Peruvian) *echarquini* "to prepare dried meat."]

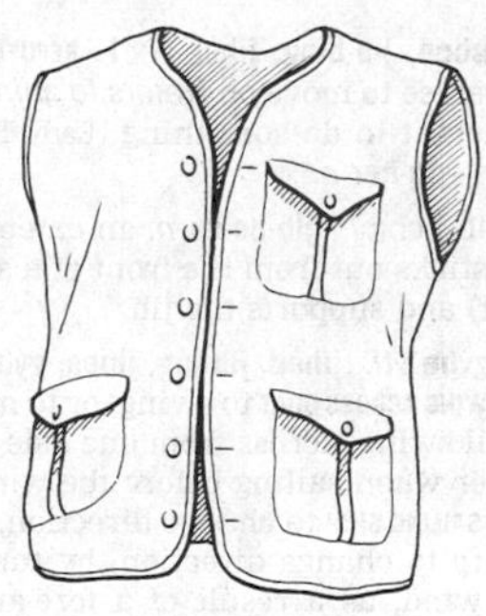

Jerkin

jer·kin /júrkin/ *n.* **1.** JACKET a sleeveless coat or jacket worn by men or women **2.** LEATHER TUNIC a man's close-fitting sleeveless tunic, often made of leather, worn in the 16th and 17th centuries [Early 16thC. Origin unknown.]

jerk·wa·ter /júrk wàwtər, -waàtər/ *adj.* **1.** SMALL AND UNIMPORTANT remote from population centers and considered insignificant and backward (*insult*) **2.** LACKING SIGNIFICANCE lacking consequence or significance [Because water had to be supplied to early trains in remote places with a bucket on a rope]

jerk·y[1] /júrkee/ (**-i·er, -i·est**) *adj.* **1.** IRREGULAR moving irregularly with sudden stops and starts **2.** LACKING GOOD SENSE lacking good sense or reason (*informal*) —**jerk·i·ly** *adv.* —**jerk·i·ness** *n.*

jerk·y[2] /júrkee/ *n.* meat cut into thin strips and dried [Mid-19thC. From American Spanish *charqui*, from Quechua *echarqui* "dried flesh in long strips."]

WORD KEY: REGIONAL NOTE

This is a Western term, used from the Dakotas and Texas to the Pacific states, now generalized as a commercial snack food.

jer·o·bo·am /jèrrə bṓ əm/ *n.* a large wine or champagne bottle holding the equivalent of four standard wine bottles, 108 fl. oz/3 l, or a Bordeaux wine bottle equivalent to six bottles, 162 fl. oz/4.5 l [Early 19thC. Named for *Jeroboam*, "a mighty man of valor" (I Kings 11:28).]

Jer·o·bo·am I /jèrrə bṓ əm/ (*fl.* 10th century B.C.) King of Israel. He was the first king of the ten northern tribes of Israel (922–901 B.C.) (1,2 Kings; 2 Chronicles).

Jer·o·bo·am II (*fl.* 8th century B.C.) King of Israel. He reigned from 786 to 746 B.C. (2 Kings13–15).

Jer·ry /jérree/ (*plural* **-ries**) *n. U.K.* an offensive term referring to a German person, especially a German soldier in World War II (*dated slang insult*) [Early 20thC. Alteration of GERMAN.]

jer·ry-build /jérri bìld/ (**-built** /jérri bìlt/, **-build·ing, -builds**) *vt.* to build something as quickly and cheaply as possible, with little regard for quality [Mid-19thC. *Jerry* of unknown origin.] —**jer·ry-build·er** *n.* —**jer·ry-build·ing** *n.*

jer·ry can *n.* a flat-sided can with a capacity of approximately 5 gal./19 l of liquid, originally of German design and used in World War II [*Jerry* a shortening of GERMAN]

jer·sey /júrzee/ (*plural* **-seys**) *n.* **1.** TEXTILES SOFT KNITTED CLOTHING MATERIAL a knitted fabric, usually made with a plain or stocking stitch, used for making clothing **2.** CLOTHES SWEATER a knitted woolen pullover [Late 16thC. Named for JERSEY, where the fabric was originally made.]

Jer·sey[1] /júrzee/ the largest and southernmost of the Channel Islands in the English Channel, a dependency of the British crown. Language: English, French. Capital: St. Helier. Population: 84,082 (1991). Area: 45 sq. mi./117 sq. km.

Jer·sey[2] /júrzee/ (*plural* **-seys**) *n.* a pale brown dairy cow that produces particularly creamy milk, belonging to a breed originating on the island of Jersey

Jer·sey Cit·y city and port in northeastern New Jersey. It is an industrial center. Population: 226,022 (1994).

Je·ru·sa·lem /jəróo sə ləm, jəróo zə-/ historic city lying at the intersection of Israel and the West Bank. The whole of the city is claimed by Israel as its capital, but this is disputed internationally. Population: 602,100 (1997).

Je·ru·sa·lem ar·ti·choke *n.* **1.** FOOD ROOT VEGETABLE the edible tuber of a North American species of sunflower plant that has reddish-brown knobbly skin and white flesh and is eaten cooked as a vegetable **2.** PLANTS PLANT WITH EDIBLE TUBERS a perennial North American sunflower whose edible tubers are called Jerusalem artichokes. Latin name: *Helianthus tuberosus.* [*Jerusalem* from Italian *girasole*, from *girare* "to turn" + *sole* "sun"]

Je·ru·sa·lem cher·ry *n.* a plant of the nightshade family, native to South America and widely grown as a houseplant for its white flowers and inedible orange or red berries. Latin name: *Solanum pseudocapsicum.*

Je·ru·sa·lem crick·et *n.* a large flightless nocturnal cricket with short spiny legs, found in arid regions of the southwestern United States. Latin name: *Stenopelmatus fuscus.*

Je·ru·sa·lem oak *n.* a strong-smelling plant of the goosefoot family that grows as a weed in the northern United States and Canada. Latin name: *Chenopodium botrys.*

Je·ru·sa·lem thorn *n.* a thorny tropical American shrub of the pea family with pinnate leaves and long clusters of yellow flowers. Latin name: *Parkinsonia aculeata.*

Jer·vis Bay /júrvəss-/ harbor in southeastern Australia, on the eastern coast of New South Wales. The headland on its southern side is part of the Australian Capital Territory. Area: 60 sq. mi./160 sq. km.

jess /jess/ *n.* FALCON'S LEASH STRAP a short strap with a ring for attaching a leash, fastened around one of the legs of a falcon or other trained bird of prey ■ *vt.* (**jessed, jess·ing, jess·es**) FIT BIRD WITH JESS to put a jess on a bird [14thC. Via Old French *ges*, a form of *get* "act of throwing," from, ultimately, Latin *jacere* "to throw."]

jest /jest/ *n.* **1.** JOKE something done or said in a playful joking manner (*literary or humorous*) ○ *Forgive my little jest.* **2.** SOMETHING JOKED ABOUT an object of scorn or derision (*archaic*) ■ *vti.* (**jest·ed, jest·ing, jests**) **1.** BE WITTY to act, write, or speak cleverly or humorously about something (*literary or humorous*) **2.** MAKE FUN OF SOMEBODY to treat somebody with derision or scorn (*archaic*) [13thC. Via Old French *geste* "romantic exploit" from Latin *gerere* "to behave, perform," of unknown origin. Originally "entertainment, heroic poem."] ◇ **in jest** as a joke

jest·er /jéstər/ *n.* **1.** ENTERTAINER an entertainer employed at a medieval court to amuse the monarch and guests ○ *the court jester* **2.** SOMEBODY WHO JOKES somebody who is inclined to joke with others

Jes·u·it /jézhoo it, jézzoo it/ *n.* **1.** MEMBER OF ROMAN CATHOLIC RELIGIOUS ORDER a member of the Society of Jesus, a Roman Catholic religious order engaged in missionary and educational work worldwide. The order was founded by Saint Ignatius of Loyola in 1534 with the aim of defending Catholicism against the Reformation. ◊ **Society of Jesus 2. Jes·u·it, jes·u·it** OFFENSIVE TERM an offensive term referring to somebody regarded as crafty or scheming, especially somebody who uses deliberately ambiguous or confusing words to deceive others (*slang insult*) ■ *adj.* OF JESUITS belonging or relating to the members of the Society of Jesus ○ *a Jesuit priest* [Mid-16thC. From French *jésuite* or modern Latin *Jesuita*, literally "follower of Jesus," from *Jesus.*] —**Jes·u·it·ic** /jèzhoo íttik, jèzzoo-/ *adj.* —**Jes·u·it·i·cal** *adj.* —**Jes·u·it·i·cal·ly** *adv.* —**Jes·u·it·ism** /jézhoo ə tìzz'm, jézzoo-/ *n.* —**Jes·u·it·ry** *n.*

Je·sus Christ /jéezəss <krīst/, **Je·sus** *n.* **1.** BIBLE FOUNDER OF CHRISTIANITY a Jewish religious teacher who lived from about 4 B.C. to A.D. 33. His life and teachings form the basis of Christianity. Christians believe he is the Son of God. **2.** HUMAN EMBODIMENT OF DIVINE in Christian Science, the highest human embodiment of the divine idea ■ *interj.* SWEARWORD used as a swearword (*slang offensive*)

Je·sus freak *n.* an offensive term referring contemptuously to somebody who belongs to a youthful evangelical Christian group that is contemporary in tone (*dated slang offensive*)

jet[1] /jet/ *n.* **1.** AIR AIRCRAFT an aircraft powered by jet engines (*often used before a noun*) ○ *a jet landing strip* **2.** PRESSURIZED STREAM OF FLUID a thin concentrated stream of liquid, air, or gas that is forced under pressure from a small nozzle or opening **3.** HOLE THROUGH WHICH FLUID IS FORCED a small opening or nozzle for letting out a stream of fluid **4.** AIR = **jet engine** (*often used before a noun*) ○ *using jet technology* ■ *v.* (**jet·ted, jet·ting, jets**) **1.** *vi.* TRANSP TRAVEL BY AIR to travel by air, especially by modern passenger aircraft ○ *always jetting off to business meetings* **2.** *vti.* FLOW FORCEFULLY IN THIN STREAM to be emitted, or emit something, in a thin powerful stream ○ *Water jetted from the broken pipe.* [Late 16thC. Via Old French *jeter* "to throw," from, ultimately, Latin *jacere* "to throw."]

WORD KEY: ORIGIN

Jet was originally used in English to mean "to protrude, stick out." This sense is best preserved in the related *jetty* "projecting pier," while the underlying meaning "to throw" is still present in the related *jettison* "things thrown overboard." ***Jet*** began to be used for "to spurt out in a forceful stream" in the 17th century. The notion of using such a stream to create forward motion was first encapsulated in the term "jet propulsion" in the mid-19th century, but it did not take concrete form for nearly a hundred years (the term *jet engine* is not recorded until 1943). Other English words descended from Latin *jacere* include *abject, dejected, eject, inject, interject, jetsam, jettison, jetty, object, project, reject, subject*, and *trajectory*.

jet[2] /jet/ *n.* **1.** MINERALS BLACK MINERAL a dense black variety of the mineral lignite, cut and polished and used for jewelry and other ornaments (*often used before a noun*) ○ *a jet necklace* **2.** COLORS JET BLACK jet black [14thC. Via Old French *jaiet*, from Latin *gagates*, from Greek *Gagatēs*, named for *Gagai*, the town in Asia Minor where it was found.]

jet·bead /jét beed/ *n.* an ornamental shrub of the rose family with white flowers and shiny black berries. Latin name: *Rhodotypos scandens.*

jet black *n.* a very dark black color —**jet-black** *adj.*

jet boat *n.* a boat powered by an engine that produces a pressurized stream of water directed backward

je·té /zhə táy/ *n.* a ballet leap from one leg to the other in which one leg is stretched forward and the other backward [Mid-19thC. From French, past participle of *jeter* "to throw."]

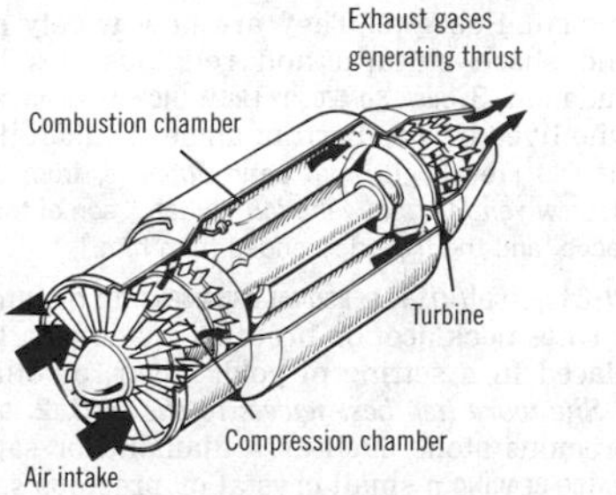

Jet engine: Cutaway view

jet en·gine *n.* an engine, especially one used to propel aircraft, that produces forward thrust by means of a rearward discharge of fluid, usually combustion gases

jet lag *n.* an internal physical disturbance experienced by air travelers on flights across different time zones. It affects the body's internal clock, disrupting sleeping patterns, eating schedules, and body temperature. —**jet-lagged** *adj.*

jet·lin·er /jét lìnər/ *n.* a large passenger airplane powered by jet engines [Mid-20thC. Blend of JET[1] and AIRLINER.]

jet plane *n.* an airplane powered by jet engines

jet-pro·pelled *adj.* powered by means of engines that use jet propulsion

jet pro·pul·sion *n.* forward thrust that results from the rearward discharge of a jet of fluid, especially a jet engine's combustion gases

jet·sam /jétsəm/ *n.* **1.** SHIPPING SHIP'S DISCARDED CARGO cargo or equipment that either sinks or is washed ashore after being thrown overboard to lighten the load of a ship in distress. ◊ **flotsam 2.** DISCARDED THINGS things that have been discarded as useless or unwanted [Late 16thC. Contraction of JETTISON.]

jet set *n.* wealthy people who travel internationally on a regular basis, especially in pursuit of pleasure (*dated informal*) [*Jet* because they supposedly travel on jets] —**jet·set·ter** *n.* —**jet·set·ting** *n.*

Jet Ski *tdmk.* a trademark for a jet-propelled personal watercraft

jet stream *n.* **1.** METEOROL **HIGH-LEVEL WINDS** a strong permanent high-altitude wind current that moves east in a meandering pattern, affecting the development and movement of weather systems **2.** AEROSP **JET ENGINE EXHAUST** a flow of exhaust gases produced by a jet engine

jet·ti·son /jéttiss'n/ *vt.* (**-soned, -son·ing, -sons**) **1.** SHIPPING **THROW SOMETHING OVERBOARD** to throw something from a ship, aircraft, or vehicle **2. REJECT SOMETHING** to discard or abandon something, e.g., an idea or project ○ *plans that had to be jettisoned* ■ *n.* **1. REJECTION** the discarding or rejecting of something **2.** SHIPPING **SHIP'S DISCARDED CARGO** the cargo and equipment thrown from a distressed ship to lighten it [15thC. From Anglo-Norman *getteson* "throwing cargo overboard" (to lighten a ship), from, ultimately, Latin *jectare* "to throw about."] —**jet·ti·son·a·ble** *adj.*

jet·ty[1] /jéttee/ (*plural* **-ties**) *n.* **1. BREAKWATER** a wall or other barrier built out into a body of water to shelter a harbor, protect a shoreline from erosion, or redirect water currents **2. DOCK** a landing pier [15thC. From Old French *jetee*, literally "something thrown (up as a breakwater)," from *jeter* (see JET[1]).]

jet·ty[2] /jéttee/ *adj.* as black as or as shiny as the mineral jet —**jet·ti·ness** *n.*

Jet·way /jét way/ *tdmk.* a trademark for an enclosed telescoping walkway between an airplane and a terminal building, through which passengers can embark and disembark

jeu d'e·sprit /zhṑo de spreé/ (*plural* **jeux d'e·sprit** /zhṑo de spreé/) *n.* a witticism, especially one that appears in a work of literature (*literary*) [Early 18thC. From French, literally "game of spirit or wit."]

jeu·nesse do·rée /zhoo nèss daw ráy/ *n.* young people who enjoy wealth and privilege (*literary*) [Mid-19thC. From French, literally "gilded youth."]

Jew /joo/ *n.* **1.** RELIG **BELIEVER IN JUDAISM** somebody whose religion is Judaism **2.** PEOPLES **MEMBER OF SEMITIC PEOPLE** a member of a Semitic people descended from the ancient Hebrews. They are now widely dispersed and share cultural and religious ties based on Judaism. **3.** HIST **SOMEBODY FROM ANCIENT JUDAH** somebody who lived or was born in ancient Judah [Pre-12thC. Via Old French *giu* from Latin *Judaeus*, from, ultimately, Hebrew *yĕhūdī*, from *yĕhūdāh* "Judah," son of the patriarch Jacob, and the tribe descended from him.]

jew·el /jṓo əl/ *n.* **1. PERSONAL ORNAMENT** an ornament, e.g., a ring, necklace, or bracelet, made of a gemstone placed in a setting of gold, silver, or other metal ○ *She wore her best jewels to the ball.* **2. GEMSTONE** a precious stone such as a diamond or sapphire **3. WATCH BEARING** a small crystal or precious stone used as a bearing in a watch **4. SOMEBODY OR SOMETHING PRIZED** a fine example of a particular type of person or thing ○ *Her new teacher's such a jewel!* ■ *vt.* (**-eled** *or* **-elled, -el·ing** *or* **-el·ling, -els**) **ADORN SOMETHING WITH JEWELS** to equip or decorate something with jewels [13thC. Via Anglo-Norman *juel* from *jeu* "game," from Latin *jocus* (source of English *joke*).] ◇ **the jewel in the crown** the best or most outstanding example of something

jew·el bee·tle *n.* an Australian beetle with an iridescent body that gives it a superficial resemblance to a gemstone. Family: Buprestidae.

jew·el·er /jṓo ə lər/, **jew·el·ler** *n.* somebody who makes, sells, or repairs jewelry

jew·el·fish /jṓo əl fish/ (*plural* **-fish·es** *or* **-fish**) *n.* a brightly colored African fish that is popular as an aquarium fish. Latin name: *Hemichromis bimaculatus.* ["Jewel" from its irregular speckling of emerald green or sapphire]

jew·el·ler *n.* = **jeweler**

jew·el·ry /jṓo əlree/ *n.* articles worn on the body for decoration, e.g., necklaces, bracelets, earrings, and rings (*often used before a noun*) ○ *a jewelry box*

jew·el·weed /jṓo əl weéd/ (*plural* **-weeds** *or* **-weed**) *n.* a North American plant with spurred yellow, orange, or white flowers and seed pods that burst open to the touch when mature. Genus: *Impatiens.* [*Jewel* from the earring shape of the flowers and the silver sheen of the underside of the leaf in water]

Jew·ess /jṓo əss/ *n.* an offensive term referring to a Jewish woman or girl (*dated offensive*)

Jew·ett /jṓo it/, **Sarah Orne** (1849–1909) U.S. writer. Her novels and short stories, set on the coast of her native Maine, are leading examples of the regional literature of her time.

jew·fish /jṓo fish/ (*plural* **-fish·es** *or* **-fish**) *n.* a large dark spotted fish of the grouper family that has rough scales and is found in warm and tropical seas. Latin name: *Epinephelus itajara.* [Said to have been so called because it was a "clean" fish in accordance with Jewish dietary law]

Jew·ish /jṓo ish/ *adj.* **1. OF JUDAISM** relating to or practicing Judaism **2. OF JEWS** belonging or relating to a people descended from the ancient Hebrews —**Jew·ish·ly** *adv.* —**Jew·ish·ness** *n.*

Jew·ish cal·en·dar *n.* the lunar calendar of the Jewish religious year. It has 12 months, with 13 in leap years, and dates from 3761 B.C., considered the year of Creation.

Jew·ry /jṓoree/ (*plural* **-ries**) *n.* Jewish people in general, or the Jewish religion

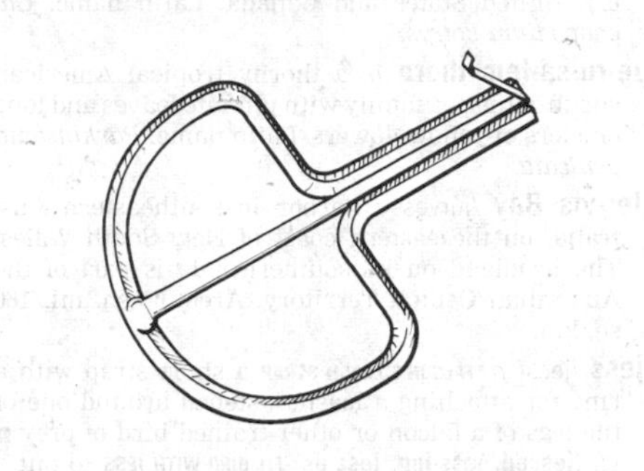

Jew's harp

jew's harp *n.* a small musical instrument held between the teeth and played by plucking a protruding metal tongue. It has a soft twanging sound. [The reason for the name is unknown]

Jez·e·bel /jézzə bel/ *n.* **1.** BIBLE **BIBLICAL PRINCESS** a Phoenician princess who lived in the 9th century B.C. The Bible describes how, as the wife of King Ahab, she introduced tyranny and idolatry into Israel. **2. Jez·e·bel, jez·e·bel OFFENSIVE TERM** an offensive term that deliberately insults a woman's sexual activity or interactions (*offensive*)

JFK *abbr.* **1.** John Fitzgerald Kennedy **2.** John Fitzgerald Kennedy International Airport

jg, j.g. *abbr.* MIL junior grade

Jhan·si /jaánssee/, **Jhān·si** capital city of Jhansi District, central India, in Uttar Pradesh State. Population: 301,304 (1991).

Jhe·lum /jeéləm/ river in northwestern India and northeastern Pakistan. It runs through the Indian city of Srinagar.

JHVH, JHWH *n.* BIBLE = **YHWH**

Jiang Qing /jyaáng chíng/ (1914–91) Chinese political activist. She was the third wife of Mao Zedong, and was one of the prime movers of China's Cultural Revolution (1966–76). Alternate name **Chiang Ch'ing**

Jiang·su /jyaáng sóo/ province in eastern China, bordering on the Yellow Sea. Capital: Nanjing. Population: 70,210,000 (1994). Area: 39,600 sq. mi./102,600 sq. km.

Jiang·xi /jyaáng sheé/ inland province of southeastern China. Capital: Nanchang. Population: 40,150,000 (1994). Area: 63,600 sq. mi./164,800 sq. km.

Jiang Ze·min /jyaáng zay mín/ (*b.* 1926) Chinese statesman. He succeeded Deng Xiaoping as paramount leader of China when he became president in 1993.

jiao /jow/ (*plural* **jiao**) *n.* **1. CURRENCY UNIT IN CHINA** a subunit of currency in China, worth one tenth of a yuan. See table at **currency** **2. BILL WORTH ONE JIAO** a bill worth one jiao [Mid-20thC. From Chinese *jiăo*.]

jib[1] /jib/ *n.* SAILING a small triangular sail in front of the main or only mast on a sailing ship [Mid-17thC. Origin unknown.] ◇ **the cut of somebody's jib** somebody's manner and general appearance

jib[2] /jib/ *n.* INDUST the projecting arm of a crane [Mid-18thC. Origin uncertain: perhaps a shortening and alteration of GIBBET.]

jib[3] /jib/ (**jibbed, jib·bing, jibs**) *vi.* **1. REFUSE TO MOVE** to stop and refuse to move on (*refers to animals*) **2. BALK** to be reluctant to do something [Early 19thC. Origin uncertain.] —**jib·ber** *n.*

jib boom /jíb bòom/, **jib·boom** *n.* an extension of the spar that sticks out from the front of a sailing ship (**bowsprit**) and supports the jib

jibe[1] /jīb/, **gybe** *vti.* (**jibed, jib·ing, jibes; gybed, gyb·ing, gybes**) **1. SWING ACROSS BOAT** to swing, or to make a fore-and-aft sail swing, across from one side of the boat to the other when sailing before the wind **2. CHANGE DIRECTION IN SAILING SHIP** to change direction, or cause a sailing ship to change direction, by turning away from the wind, as a result of a fore-and-aft-sail's jibing ■ *n.* SAILING **SAIL SHIFT OR DIRECTION CHANGE** a sudden shift of a sail back and forth, or a change in the direction a ship is sailing [Late 17thC. From Dutch *gijben*.]

jibe[2] /jīb/ (**jibed, jib·ing, jibes**) *vi.* to conform or agree with something or with one another (*informal*) [Early 19thC. Origin unknown.]

jibe[3] *n.*, *vti.* = **gibe**

ji·ca·ma /heékəmə/ *n.* the starchy tuberous root of a tropical plant of the pea family, eaten raw in salads or cooked as a vegetable. Latin name: *Pachyrhizus erosus.* [Early 17thC. Via Mexican Spanish *jícama*, from Nahuatl *xicama*.]

Ji·car·il·la /heekə reéyə/ (*plural* **-la** *or* **-las**) *n.* a member of a Native American Apache people who originally lived in a large area across central and southwestern North America. Today the Jicarilla live in northern New Mexico. [Mid-19thC. From Mexican Spanish, literally "small calabash tree," from *jicara* "calabash tree," from Nahuatl *xicalli* "container made from the fruit of the calabash tree."] —**Ji·car·il·la** *adj.*

Jid·dah /jéddə/, **Jed·da** city and port in western Saudi Arabia, on the Red Sea, in Al Hijaz state. Population: 1,600,000 (1994 estimate).

jif·fy /jíffee/, **jiff** /jif/ *n.* the shortest of moments (*informal*) ○ *I'll be with you in a jiffy.* [Late 18thC. Origin uncertain: perhaps from Bantu *tshipi* "short."]

Jif·fy *tdmk.* a trademark for a padded mailing envelope

jig /jig/ *n.* **1.** DANCE **LIVELY DANCE** a lively folk dance in triple time, especially one with kicking or jumping steps ○ *an Irish jig* **2.** MUSIC **DANCING MUSIC** a piece of music to which a jig is danced **3.** WOODWORK, INDUST **DEVICE FOR HOLDING PIECE OF WORK** the part of a woodworking or metalworking machine that holds the object to be worked on and guides the cutting or drilling tool **4.** ANGLING **WIGGLY FISHING LURE** a fishing lure made to attract a fish's attention through its motion as it is jerked around in the water **5.** MINING **MINERAL-WASHING DEVICE** a device that cleans and separates coal or other excavated minerals from waste material by shaking and washing ■ *v.* (**jigged, jig·ging, jigs**) **1.** *vti.* **JERK AROUND QUICKLY** to move around, or cause something to move around, in a quick jerky way **2.** *vi.* DANCE **DANCE A JIG** to dance a lively folk dance in triple time, especially one with kicking or jumping steps **3.** *vt.* WOODWORK, INDUST **CUT OR DRILL SOMETHING WITH JIG** to cut or drill a piece of work using a jig as a guide **4.** *vti.* ANGLING **FISH WITH JIG** to fish, or catch a fish, using a jig **5.** *vt.* MINING **CLEAN AND SEPARATE MINERALS WITH JIG** to wash and separate coal or other excavated minerals with a jig [Mid-16thC. Noun of unknown origin. Verb of uncertain origin: perhaps from French *giguer* "to dance," from *gigue* "fiddle," from a prehistoric Germanic word.]

jig·ger[1] /jíggər/ *n.* **1.** MEASURE, BEVERAGES **MEASURE FOR ALCOHOLIC SPIRITS** a measure used for alcoholic spirits, equal to approximately 1.5 fl. oz **2.** WOODWORK, INDUST **JIG OPERATOR** somebody who operates a mechanical jig **3. SOMETHING OR OTHER** an object whose name is not known or cannot be recalled (*informal*) **4.** ANGLING = **jig** *n.* 4 **5.** *Can* ANGLING **FISHING LINE** a short line attached to an unbaited hook, used to catch squid or cod by a jerking motion **6.** SAILING **SAIL AT BOAT'S STERN** a small sail near the stern of a small sailing boat **7.** SAILING = **jiggermast** **8.** ENG **DEVICE WORKING WITH JERKING MOTION** a mechanical device, e.g., a drill, that operates with a jerking movement

jig·ger[2] *n.* INSECTS = **chigoe** *n.* 1 [Late 18thC. Alteration of CHIGGER.]

jig·ger·mast /jíggər màst/ *n.* **1. SMALL REAR MAST** the shorter mast near the stern of a small sailing boat

2. FOURTH MAST BACK on a four-masted sailing ship, the mast nearest the stern

jig·ging grounds *n. Can* ANGLING an area of shallow water where fish or squid can be caught using a jigger

jig·gle /jígg'l/ *vti.* (**-gled, -gling, -gles**) TO WIGGLE to move, or cause something to move, in small rapid movements in any direction ○ *He jiggled the handle.* ■ *n.* WIGGLY MOVEMENT a rapid back-and-forth or up-and-down motion ○ *giving the key a quick jiggle in the lock* [Mid-19thC. Blend of JIG and JOGGLE.] —**jig·gly** *adj.*

jig·saw /jíg saw/ *n.* **1.** LEISURE JIGSAW PUZZLE a jigsaw puzzle **2.** CONSTR POWER SAW FOR CURVES a machine saw with a narrow blade, used for cutting curves and shapes ■ *vt.* (**-sawed, -sawed** *or* **-sawn, -saw·ing, -saws**) CONSTR CUT SOMETHING USING JIGSAW to cut or shape something using a jigsaw ■ *adj.* WITH COMPLEX STRUCTURE with many interrelating parts or elements forming a complex whole ○ *the jigsaw nature of politics*

jig·saw puz·zle *n.* **1.** LEISURE PICTURE CUT INTO PIECES a puzzle in the form of interlocking irregularly shaped pieces that make a picture when fitted together **2.** COMPLEX WHOLE something that is made up of many interconnecting parts ○ *help the police to figure out this jigsaw puzzle of a crime*

ji·had /ji haád/, **je·had** *n.* **1.** ISLAMIC CAMPAIGN AGAINST NONBELIEVERS a campaign waged by Muslims in defense of the Islamic faith against individuals, organizations, or countries regarded as hostile to Islam **2.** HOSTILE CAMPAIGN any hostile campaign, e.g., a series of political advertisements attacking an adversary [Mid-19thC. From Arabic *jihād* "effort."]

Ji·lin /jéelín/ province in Manchuria, northeastern China. The southeast of the province borders Russia and North Korea. Capital: Changchun. Population: 25,740,000 (1994). Area: 72,200 sq. mi./187,000 sq. km.

jil·lion /jíllyən/ *n.* a number or amount too great to specify (*informal*) [Mid-20thC. Imaginative formation modeled on BILLION.]

jilt /jilt/ *vt.* (**jilt·ed, jilt·ing, jilts**) REJECT A LOVER to break off a romantic relationship with somebody abruptly ■ *n.* SOMEBODY WHO REJECTS A LOVER somebody who abruptly breaks off a relationship with a lover [Mid-17thC. Origin unknown. Originally "to deceive, cheat."]

Jim Crow /jìm krṓ/, **jim crow** *n.* **1. Jim Crow, jim Crow, Jim Crow·ism, jim Crow·ism** RACIAL DISCRIMINATION the practice of discriminating against Black people, especially by operating systems of public segregation (*informal*) **2.** TABOO OFFENSIVE TERM a highly offensive taboo word referring to a Black person (*taboo offensive*) [Mid-19thC. From *Jim Crow*, a Black character in the early 19thC plantation song of that name.]

jim-dan·dy /jìm dándee/ (*plural* **jim-dan·dies**) *n.* something that is exceptionally good of its kind (*informal*) [Late 19thC. From *Jim*, familiar form of the forename James, + DANDY.] —**jim-dan·dy** *adj.*

jim·jams /jím jàmz/ *npl.* (*informal*) **1.** DELIRIUM TREMENS an attack of delirium tremens **2.** NERVOUSNESS an attack of nervous anxiety [Late 19thC. Plural of obsolete *jimjam* "trivial article, knick-knack," a playful formation.]

jim·mies /jímmeez/ *npl.* small pieces of chocolate or candy sprinkled on top of ice-cream

jim·my /jímmee/ *n.* (*plural* **-mies**) **1.** LEVER FOR PRYING SOMETHING OPEN a short crowbar used as a lever, usually for prying things open **2.** MARINE BIOL MALE CRAB a male crab. ◊ **jenny** ■ *vt.* (**-mied, -my·ing, -mies**) OPEN SOMETHING WITH JIMMY to force something open using a jimmy [Mid-19thC. Alteration of JEMMY.]

jim·son·weed /jíms'n weed, jímps'n-/ *n.* a tall poisonous weed of the nightshade family, with large trumpet-shaped white or purple flowers, foul-smelling foliage, and spiny capsule fruits. Latin name: *Datura stramonium.* [Late 17thC. Alteration of *Jamestown*, Virginia, where it was first observed.]

Ji·nan /jée naán/ city and capital of Shandong Province on the Huang He, eastern China. Population: 2,320,000 (1991).

jin·gle /jíng g'l/ *n.* **1.** METALLIC TINKLE a light musical noise like that of small bells or pieces of metal being shaken together **2.** TUNE ASSOCIATED WITH SOMETHING ADVERTISED a catchy tune or verse, usually one that is played repeatedly to advertise something ■ *v.* (**-gled, -gling, -gles**) **1.** *vti.* MAKE A TINKLING SOUND to make, or cause something to make, a light musical noise like that of small bells or pieces of metal being shaken together ○ *He jingled the coins in his pocket.* **2.** *vi.* HAVE AN EASILY REMEMBERED SOUND to have a sound or rhyme that is catchy or repetitious [14thC. An imitation of the sound of small metallic objects shaken together.] —**jin·gly** *adj.*

jin·go /jíng gō/ (*plural* **-goes**) *n.* a zealous patriot, especially somebody who advocates hostility toward other countries [Late 17thC. Origin uncertain: originally a conjurers' term. The modern sense derives from the use of "by jingo!" in the refrain of a hawkish popular song of the late 19thC.] —**jin·go·ish** *adj.* ◇ **by jingo!** used to express surprise or annoyance (*dated informal*)

jin·go·ism /jíng gō ìzzəm/ *n.* zealous patriotism expressing itself especially in hostility toward other countries —**jin·go·ist** *adj., n.* —**jin·go·is·tic** /jìng gō ístik/ *adj.* —**jin·go·is·ti·cal·ly** *adv.*

WORD KEY: ORIGIN

The context of the coining of ***jingoism*** was British foreign policy of the late 1870s: the Prime Minister, Benjamin Disraeli, favored sending in gunboats to halt the advance of the Russian fleet out of their own waters into the Mediterranean; this gave rise to a music-hall song, written in 1878 by G.W. Hunt, the refrain of which went: "We don't want to fight, yet by Jingo! if we do, We've got the ships, we've got the men, and got the money too"; opponents of the policy picked up on the word *jingo* and used it as an icon of blind patriotism.

Jin·ja /jínjə/ city in southeastern Uganda, in the Eastern Region, on Lake Victoria. Population: 60,979 (1991).

jink /jingk/ *vi.* (**jinked, jink·ing, jinks**) DODGE to make quick sideways movements in order to evade somebody or something ■ *n.* DODGING MOVEMENT a quick evasive movement or maneuver [Late 17thC. Origin uncertain: perhaps an imitation of a sudden movement.]

Jin·nah /jínnə/, **Muhammad Ali** (1876–1948) Indian and Pakistani statesman. He became president of the Muslim League in India in 1935. His campaign for a separate Muslim state resulted in the creation of Pakistan in 1947, when he became the state's first president and governor-general.

jin·ni /jínnee/ (*plural* **jinn** /jin/), **djin·ni** (*plural* **djinn**) *n.* in Islamic mythology, a spirit that can take on various human and animal forms and makes mischievous use of its supernatural powers. ◊ **genie** [Early 19thC. From Arabic *jinn*, plural of *jinnī*. The plural form is popularly thought of as the singular.]

Jin Nong /jìn náwng/ (1687–1764?) Chinese artist. He frequently incorporated calligraphy into his paintings, which are often of fruits and plants.

jin·rik·sha /jin ríkshə/, **jin·rick·sha** *n.* = **rickshaw** [Late 19thC. From Japanese *jin* "man" + *riki* "strength" + *sha* "vehicle."]

jinx /jingks/ *n.* CAUSE OF MISFORTUNE an unseen force that is thought to bring bad luck, or somebody or something, e.g., a curse, that is thought to bring bad luck ○ *There must be a jinx on this expedition.* ■ *vt.* (**jinxed, jinx·ing, jinx·es**) BRING MISFORTUNE ON SOMETHING to bring a supposed unseen force of misfortune to bear on something or somebody ○ *the feeling that they had been jinxed in some way* [Early 20thC. Origin uncertain: probably from earlier *jynx* "the wryneck bird," from its use in witchcraft.] —**jinxed** *adj.*

ji·pi·ja·pa /héepee haápə/ *n.* a stemless plant native to Central and South America that resembles a palm and has large leaves that are used to make panama hats. Latin name: *Carludovica palmata.* [Mid-19thC. Named for *Jipijapa*, a town in Ecuador where it is found.]

JIT *abbr.* MANAGEMT just-in-time

jit·ney /jítnee/ (*plural* **-neys**) *n.* **1.** INEXPENSIVE SMALL BUS a small bus that takes passengers on a regular route for a small fare **2.** NICKEL a nickel (*archaic slang*) [Early 20thC. Origin unknown. The bus was so named for its low fare (five cents).]

jit·ter /jíttər/ *vi.* (**-tered, -ter·ing, -ters**) BEHAVE NERVOUSLY to behave in a nervous or restless way (*informal*) ■ *n.* ELEC ENG **1.** RAPID SIGNAL FLUCTUATION an undesired rapid movement of electrical signals or images, e.g., on a television or oscilloscope screen, because of circuit instability or faulty components **2.** DISTORTION IN DIGITIZED INFORMATION a distortion in digitally transmitted or recorded sound or images, caused when two devices are not perfectly synchronized, e.g., the recording and playback devices of audio recordings ■ **jit·ters** *npl.* NERVOUS ATTACK feelings of extreme nervousness and agitation (*informal*) ○ *He's got the jitters about his interview tomorrow.* [Early 20thC. Origin uncertain: perhaps from Mandingo *ji-to* "frightened," from *ji* "to be afraid."]

jit·ter·bug /jíttər bùg/ *n.* **1.** FAST DANCE a fast energetic jazz dance for couples that was popular in the 1940s **2.** JITTERBUG DANCER somebody who dances the jitterbug ■ *vi.* (**-bugged, -bug·ging, -bugs**) DANCE JITTERBUG to dance the jitterbug [Mid-20thC. Origin uncertain: perhaps from Mandingo *jitobaga* "frightened person" (see JITTER), or *bug* from BUG "insect." Originally "jittery person."]

jit·ter·y /jíttəree/ *adj.* **1.** NERVOUS feeling nervous or agitated **2.** JERKY making rapid jumpy movements —**jit·ter·i·ness** *n.*

Ji·va·ro /heévə rṓ/ (*plural* **-ro** *or* **-ros**) *n.* **1.** PEOPLES MEMBER OF NATIVE S AMERICAN PEOPLE a member of a Native South American people living in the tropical forests of Ecuador and northeastern Peru. Their ancestors were noted for their ritual of shrinking and preserving the heads of enemies they had killed. **2.** LANG LANGUAGE OF JIVARO the language spoken by the Jivaro. It belongs to the Equatorial branch of the Andean-Equatorial family of American languages. Jivaro is spoken by about 20,000 people. [Mid-19thC. From Spanish *jíbaro*, of uncertain origin: probably from Jivaro *Shuara*.] —**Ji·va·ro** *adj.*

jive /jīv/ *n.* **1.** MUSIC JAZZ MUSIC jazz or swing music, especially that of the 1930s and 1940s **2.** DANCE LIVELY DANCING STYLE a very lively, uninhibited style of popular dancing, often with a man swinging and throwing a woman. It was originally done to jazz music, and later to rock and roll. **3.** LANGUAGE JAZZ MUSICIANS' JARGON the special terminology and slang used by jazz musicians (*slang*) **4.** INSINCERE TALK smooth talk that is often deceptive or insincere (*slang*) ■ *v.* (**jived, jiv·ing, jives**) **1.** *vi.* DANCE DANCE JIVE to dance in the lively, often acrobatic style associated with jazz music, and later with rock and roll **2.** *vi.* LANGUAGE TALK JIVE to use the special terminology and slang of jazz musicians (*slang*) **3.** *vti.* FLATTER WITH SMOOTH TALK to flatter or deceive somebody with insincere talk (*slang*) ○ *I know when you're jiving me.* ■ *adj.* INSINCERE lacking sincerity or honesty (*slang*) ○ *His comments are so jive!* [Early 20thC. Origin uncertain: perhaps from Wolof *jev* "to talk about somebody not present, especially disparagingly."] —**jiv·er** *n.*

JJ, JJ. *abbr.* **1.** BIBLE Judges **2.** LAW Justices

Jl. *abbr.* **1.** BIBLE Joel **2.** journal **3.** July

Jm. *abbr.* BIBLE James

Jn. *abbr.* BIBLE John

j.n.d. *abbr.* PSYCHOL just noticeable difference

jnr., Jnr. *abbr.* junior

jnt. *abbr.* joint

jo /jō/ (*plural* **joes**) *n. Scotland* somebody whom somebody else loves (*dated*) [Early 16thC. Scottish form of JOY.]

Joan of Arc /jōn əv aárk/, **St.** (1412–31) French patriot. She led the French to victory against the English, but was captured and burned at the stake as a heretic. She is the patron saint of France.

João Pes·so·a /zhwŏng pe sṓ ə/ capital city of Paraíba State, in northeastern Brazil. It is a leading trade center. Population: 497,214 (1991). Former name **Parahyba**

job /job/ *n.* **1.** PAID OCCUPATION an activity such as a trade or profession that somebody does regularly for pay, or a paid position doing this ○ *She's got a new job.* **2.** TASK something that remains to be done or dealt with ○ *I have several jobs to do this afternoon.* **3.** ASSIGNMENT an individual piece of work of a particular nature ○ *We managed to complete the job in under a week.* **4.** FUNCTION the role that somebody or something fulfils ○ *It's her job to look after the finances.* **5.** DIFFICULTY something that is difficult to accomplish ○ *I had quite a job getting it to start.* **6.** QUALITY OF WORK DONE a completed piece of work of a particular quality ○ *They did a very good job on the exterior.* **7.** OBJECT an object of some kind, especially a manufactured item (*informal*) ○ *one of those big four-wheel-drive jobs* **8.** CRIME a criminal act, especially a robbery (*informal*) ○ *a bank job* **9.** COMPUT PROGRAMMING TASK a computer programming task run as a single application or unit ■ *v.* (**jobbed, job·bing, jobs**) **1.** *vi.* WORK OCCASIONALLY to take occasional or casual work ○ *He jobs as a gardener from time to time.* **2.** *vti.* DEAL IN WHOLESALE MERCHANDISE to buy and sell merchandise as a wholesaler or agent **3.** *vt.* DISTRIBUTE WORK TO OTHERS to subcontract portions of contract work to others

○ *job out the plumbing work on the house* **4.** *vi.* **PROFIT FROM PUBLIC OFFICE** to make a private gain from working in a public position [Mid-16thC. Origin uncertain: perhaps from obsolete *job* "piece," of unknown origin.] ◇ **on the job** engaged in working

WORD KEY: SYNONYMS

job, assignment, task, chore, duty

CORE MEANING: a piece of work to be done

job a general word used to describe both a piece of work that somebody has chosen to do or one that he or she is obliged to do, for example, because it is part of his or her employment. It can also be used to talk about somebody's employment; **assignment** a set piece of work given to somebody as part of the workload of an occupation or course of study, often with the requirement to finish it within a fixed period of time. It can also be used to mean a post or position that has been allocated to somebody; **task** a piece of work that requires effort, often imposed by an employer or someone in authority or by circumstances, but sometimes self-imposed. It is usually either quite short in duration or else has to be finished within a certain time; **chore** a relatively short undertaking, either imposed by somebody in authority or self-imposed, requiring effort and indicating some kind of routine. It is often used to indicate that something is considered tedious and even unpleasant; **duty** used to describe something that has to be done because of obligations to other individuals or to society.

Job[1] /jōb/ *n.* in the Bible, a righteous man whose faith withstood severe testing by God ○ *have the patience of Job*

Job[2] /jōb/ *n.* the book of the Bible that describes Job's afflictions and eventual reward. See table at **Bible**

job ac·tion *n.* a short-term action by workers, e.g., a slowdown, to achieve demands or protest policies

job·ber /jóbbər/ *n.* **1. SOMEBODY TAKING OCCASIONAL OR CASUAL WORK** somebody who does piecework or work on a job by job basis **2.** COMM **WHOLESALER** a wholesaler to retailers

job·ber·y /jóbbəree/ *n.* the corrupt practice of making private gains from public office, or an instance of this

Job Corps *n.* a U.S. government training program for youths to enable them to obtain employment

job de·scrip·tion *n.* an official written description of the responsibilities and requirements of a specific job, often one agreed between employer and employee

job·hold·er /jób hōldər/ *n.* somebody who has a regular job

job-hop (**job-hopped, job-hop·ping, job-hops**) *vi.* to change jobs frequently, especially working for different companies (*informal*) —**job-hop·per** *n.* —**job-hop·ping** *n.*

job-hunt (**job-hunt·ed, job-hunt·ing, job-hunts**) *vi.* to look for a job (*informal*) —**job hunt·er** *n.*

job·less /jóbləss/ *adj.* **UNEMPLOYED** without a job ■ *npl.* **PEOPLE WITHOUT JOBS** unemployed people considered collectively —**job·less·ness** *n.*

job lot *n.* a miscellaneous collection of articles, especially ones that are bought or sold together ○ *I bought it as a job lot.*

job-re·lat·ed ill·ness *n.* = **industrial disease**

Jobs /jobz/, **Steve** (*b.* 1955) U.S. entrepreneur. He cofounded Apple Computer Company (1976), which produced the first "user-friendly" home computer. Full name **Steven Paul Jobs**

Job's com·fort·er *n.* somebody who, though appearing or intending to comfort a distressed person, only succeeds in worsening the situation [From the friends who came to "comfort" Job in his affliction, counseling him: "despise not thou the chastening of the Almighty" (Job 5:17)]

job-shar·ing *n.* the dividing up of the responsibilities of a single full-time job between two or more part-time workers —**job-share** *n., vi.*

Job's tears *n.* (*plural* **Job's tears**) **TROPICAL GRASS PLANT** a tropical Asian grass plant with hard white spherical leaves that are used as beads. Latin name: *Coix lacryma-jobi.* ■ *npl.* **WHITE LEAVES USED AS BEADS** the hard white leaves of Job's tears, used as beads [From its round shiny leaves that resemble tears]

jock[1] /jok/ *n.* (*informal*) **1. JOCKEY** a jockey **2. DISC JOCKEY** a disc jockey [Late 18thC. Shortening.]

jock[2] /jok/ *n.* (*informal*) **1. ATHLETE** an athlete, especially a male athlete in college **2. JOCKSTRAP** a jockstrap **3. MACHO MAN** a man with macho attitudes [Mid-20thC. Shortening of JOCKSTRAP.]

jock[3] /jok/ (**jocked, jock·ing, jocks**) *vi. Carib* an offensive term meaning to masturbate (*taboo offensive*) [Origin unknown: perhaps originally in the sense "genitals"]

jock·ey /jókee/ *n.* (*plural* **-eys**) **1. RIDER OF RACEHORSE** somebody who rides racehorses, especially professionally **2. WORKER WITH OR OPERATOR OF SOMETHING** somebody whose work involves the use or operation of a particular device, vehicle, or object (*informal*) ○ *We desk jockeys need to get out and exercise more.* ■ *v.* (**-eyed, -ey·ing, -eys**) **1.** *vti.* **RIDE RACEHORSE** to ride a racehorse, especially as a professional jockey **2.** *vi.* **TRY TO GAIN ADVANTAGE** to maneuver in order to gain an advantage ○ *watch them all jockeying for promotion* **3.** *vt.* **MANIPULATE** to trick somebody, usually for personal gain ○ *felt she has been jockeyed into doing work for which he gets credit* **4.** *vti.* **CHANGE POSITIONS SKILLFULLY** to change position using skillful maneuvers ○ *jockey a motorcycle through traffic* [Late 16thC. Originally a familiar form of the Scottish personal name *Jock*, indicating "boy, underling," later "horse dealer" and hence "horseback rider."]

Jock·ey *tdmk.* a trademark for underwear

jock·ey box *n.* the glove compartment in an automobile's dashboard (*regional*)

WORD KEY: REGIONAL NOTE

This is a Western usage, especially of the Upper Rocky Mountain states, but is recorded as far south as Texas.

jock itch *n.* a fungal infection of the skin in the groin area, especially in men and boys

jock·strap /jók stràp/ *n.* an elasticated belt with a pouch at the front, worn by sportsmen to support their genitals or to keep a protective cup in place [Late 19thC. *Jock* from slang *jock* "genitals," of unknown origin.]

jo·cose /jō kṓss/ *adj.* (*literary*) **1. FOND OF JOKING** with a playful joking disposition **2. HUMOROUS** playfully humorous in style [Late 17thC. From Latin *jocosus* "full of joking," from *jocus* "joke" (source of English *joke*).] —**jo·cose·ly** *adv.* —**jo·cose·ness** *n.* —**jo·cos·i·ty** /jō kóssətee/ *n.*

joc·u·lar /jókyələr/ *adj.* **1. FOND OF JOKING** with a playful joking disposition **2. HUMOROUS** intended to be funny [Early 17thC. From Latin *jocularis*, literally "of a little joke," from, ultimately, *jocus* "joke" (source of English *joke*).] —**joc·u·lar·i·ty** /jòkyə lérrətee/ *n.* —**joc·u·lar·ly** *adv.*

joc·und /jókənd/ *adj.* cheerful and full of good humor (*literary*) [14thC. Via Old French *jocond* (influenced by Latin *jocus* "joke") from Latin *jucundus*, from *juvare* "to please, help."] —**jo·cun·di·ty** /jə kúndətee/ *n.* —**joc·und·ly** *adv.*

Jodh·pur /jod pŏŏr/ city in northwestern India, in the state of Rajasthan. Population: 648,621 (1991).

jodh·purs /jódpərz/ *npl.* riding breeches that are wide at the hip and narrow around the calves, often with reinforced patches at the knee and thigh where the rider's legs grip the horse [Late 19thC. Named for JODHPUR.]

Jo·do·in /zhō dwáN/, **Claude** (1913–75) Canadian labor leader. He was the first president of the Canadian Labor Congress (1956–66).

Joe /jō/, **joe** *n.* an ordinary man (*informal*) [Late 18thC. Familiar shortening of forename *Joseph.*]

Joe Bloggs /jō blógz/ *n. U.K.* = **Joe Blow** (*informal*)

Joe Blow *n. U.S., Can, Aus* the average man in the street

joe-boat /jṓ bōt/ *n.* a small rowboat (*regional*) [Of uncertain origin; perhaps after JOHNBOAT]

WORD KEY: REGIONAL NOTE

This is a Lower Ohio valley term, used especially in Kentucky.

Jo·el /jṓ əl, jōl/ *n.* **1. HEBREW PROPHET** a Hebrew prophet who lived in the 6th century B.C. **2. BOOK OF THE BIBLE** the book of the Bible that contains the prophecies of Joel, dating from the years following the Israelites' Babylonian exile. See table at **Bible**

joe-pye weed /jṓ pī́-/ *n.* a tall North American perennial plant with whorled leaves and clusters of small pink or purple flower heads. Latin name: *Eupatorium maculatum* and *Eupatorium purpureum.* [Early 19thC. According to tradition, named for *Joe Pye*, a Native American who mistakenly gathered it in place of the healing herb boneset; the gods turned him into this plant.]

Joe Six-Pack *n.* the ordinary working man (*slang*) [*Six-Pack* because such a man supposedly buys six-packs of beer]

jo·ey /jṓ ee/ *n. Aus* a young animal, especially a kangaroo still young enough to be carried in its mother's pouch [Mid-19thC. From Aboriginal *joè.*]

Jof·frey /jóffree/, **Robert** (1930–88) U.S. choreographer and ballet dancer. He founded the Joffrey Ballet (1954), and is known for his imaginative experimental works. Born **Abdulla Jaffa Anver Bey Khan**

jog[1] /jog/ *v.* (**jogged, jog·ging, jogs**) **1.** *vi.* **TROT** to run at a slow steady pace ○ *He jogged across the road to the shop.* **2.** *vi.* FITNESS **RUN FOR EXERCISE** to run at a slow steady pace as a fitness exercise ○ *She jogs around the park every morning.* **3.** *vt.* **NUDGE SOMETHING** to give a light push or shake to something ○ *thought the photo might have jogged your memory* **4.** *vi.* **GO SLOWLY BUT STEADILY** to move along at a slow steady pace ○ *The little steam train jogged along the track.* **5.** *vi.* **PLOD** to progress at a slow dull pace ○ *How are things? – Oh, you know: jogging along.* ■ *n.* **1.** FITNESS **SPELL OF RUNNING** a spell of slow steady running for exercise ○ *I'm going for a quick jog.* **2. NUDGE** a light push or shake **3. SLOW SPEED** a slow steady pace or motion ○ *moving along at a jog* [Mid-16thC. Origin uncertain: perhaps an alteration of *shaggen* "to jolt." Originally "shake up" or "throw up with a push or jerk."]

jog[2] /jog/ *n.* **SHARP TURN** a sharp turn or angle ○ *We took a jog to the left.* ■ *vi.* (**jogged, jog·ging, jogs**) **MAKE SHARP TURN** to make a sharp turn or angle ○ *The path jogs toward the south.* [Early 18thC. Origin unknown.]

jog·ging /jógging/ *n.* a fitness or recreational activity that involves running at a moderate pace, often over long distances

jog·gle /jógg'l/ *n.* **1. SHAKING ACTION** a gentle shaking motion or action **2.** BUILDING **MASONRY JOINT** a joint between two pieces of masonry or concrete, in which a projection on one fits into a recess of the other ■ *v.* (**-gled, -gling, -gles**) **1.** *vti.* **SHAKE** to shake something gently ○ *The table joggled and my soda spilled all over.* **2.** *vt.* BUILDING **JOIN WITH JOGGLE** to join pieces of masonry or concrete with a joggle [Early 18thC. Of uncertain origin: perhaps, in building senses, literally "little jog," ultimately from JAG "projecting point"; in shaking senses, perhaps literally "to jog repeatedly," from JOG[1].]

Jog·ja·kar·ta /jòg jə kaártə/ city in southwestern Indonesia, on the island of Java. Population: 412,400 (1990).

jog trot *n.* **1. SLOW RUNNING PACE** a slow steady running pace **2. BORING PACE** a dull steady pace of life ○ *things going on at a jog trot*

Jo·han·nes·burg /jō haánnəss bùrg/ city in northeastern South Africa, capital of Gauteng Province. It grew up as the center of a goldmining region. Population: city 712,507 (1991).

Jo·han·nine /jō hánnīn/ *adj.* relating to the apostle John or to the books of the Bible attributed to him [Mid-19thC. Formed from late Latin *Joannes* "John."]

john /jaan/ *n.* **1. TOILET** a toilet (*informal*) ○ *Where's the john?* **2. PROSTITUTE'S CUSTOMER** a man who is a prostitute's customer (*slang*) [Early 20thC. From *John*, forename.]

John /jon/, **King of England** (1167–1216). The youngest son of Henry II, he succeeded his brother Richard I as king (1199–1216). He was forced to issue the Magna Carta in 1215 after demands by the barons of England for constitutional reform. Known as **John Lackland**

John, St. (*d.* 101?) Judean apostle. He was one of the 12 disciples of Jesus Christ, and helped organize the early church throughout Palestine and Asia Minor. By tradition he is the author of the fourth Gospel, three Epistles, and Revelations in the Bible.

John *n.* See table at **Bible 1. GOSPEL IN THE BIBLE** the fourth of the gospels of the Bible in which the life and teachings of Jesus Christ are described. It is thought to have been written by St. John. **2. EPISTLE OF BIBLE** any of the three books of the Bible written in epistle form and traditionally attributed to St. John.

John II, King of France (1319–64). He came to the throne in 1350. He was captured by the English (1356) but allowed to return to France to raise a ransom.

Failing to do so, he returned to captivity. Known as **John the Good**

John VI, King of Portugal (1769–1826). He fled to Brazil following Napoleon's invasion of Portugal (1807), became King in 1816, and returned to Portugal in 1821. He granted Brazil independence (1822).

John (the Bap·tist), St. (8? B.C.–A.D. 27?) Judean prophet. He is described in the gospels as the cousin and precursor of Jesus Christ. He was beheaded at the behest of Salome.

John /jaan/, **Sir Elton** (*b.* 1947) British rock singer and pianist. His partnership with lyricist Bernie Taupin produced a string of international hit songs. Real name **Reginald Dwight**

John Bar·ley·corn *n.* the personification of alcoholic drink (*literary or humorous*)

john·boat /jón bōt/ *n.* a narrow boat with a flat bottom and squared-off ends that is paddled or poled in shallow waterways [Early 20thC. *John*, forename.]

John Bull *n.* **1. ENGLAND PERSONIFIED** the personification of England and the English people **2. ENGLISHMAN** an individual Englishman, especially one regarded as embodying Englishness [Late 18thC. Named for a character representing the English nation in *Law is a Bottomless Pit* (1712), by J. Arbuthnot.] —**John Bul·lish** *adj.* —**John Bul·lish·ness** *n.* —**John Bul·lism** *n.*

John Chry·sos·tom /jòn kríssəstəm/, **St.** (349–407) Syrian-born preacher. He was called "chrysostomos" (golden-mouthed) because of his oratory. He became patriarch of Constantinople (398–403) but was exiled because of his campaigning against vice.

John Doe *n.* **1. ORDINARY MAN** an average man affected by everyday events (*informal*) **2.** LAW **UNNAMED MAN** a man or boy in a legal proceeding whose identity is either not known or not revealed

John Do·ry *n.* an edible deep-sea fish with a large flat olive-yellow body, long dorsal spines, and large jaws, found in the eastern Atlantic and the Mediterranean. Latin name: *Zeus faber.* [Mid-18thC. *John*, forename.]

Johne's dis·ease /jṓnəz-/ *n.* a chronic disease of sheep, cattle, and other domestic animals, with symptoms of diarrhea and loss of weight, caused by a bacterium that is related to the tuberculosis bacterium [Early 20thC. Named for H. A. *Johne* (1839–1910), German veterinary surgeon, who first described it.]

John Han·cock *n.* somebody's signature (*informal*) [Name of the U.S. statesman who was the first to sign the Declaration of Independence; he signed it in large bold writing]

John Hen·ry *n.* **1. BLACK FOLKLORE HERO** an African American hero in U.S. folklore, renowned for his great strength. He died after beating a steam drill in a contest of endurance. **2. SIGNATURE** somebody's signature (*informal*) [In the sense "signature" modeled on JOHN HANCOCK]

john·ny /jónnee/ (*plural* **-nies**) *n.* a short gown that ties at the back, worn in hospitals by patients [Late 17thC. Diminutive of *John*, first name, originally in the sense "man, boy."]

john·ny·cake /jónni kàyk/ *n. Northeast U.S.* a flat cornbread either baked or fried on a griddle

John·ny Ca·nuck *n. Can* a personification of Canada, in the form of a strong clean-cut young man, often a lumberjack

John·ny-come-late·ly (*plural* **John·ny-come-late·lies** *or* **John·nies-come-late·ly**) *n.* a recent arrival at a place, group, position, or point of view (*informal*) ○ *these Johnny-come-latelies and their "new" ideas*

John·ny-jump-up *n.* a common pansy grown for its small multicolored flowers. Latin name: *Viola tricolor.*

John·ny-on-the-spot *n.* somebody who is always ready to be of assistance

John·ny Reb *n.* a Confederate soldier in the Civil War (*archaic informal*) [Mid-19thC. Shortening of *Johnny Rebel*, the name for a Confederate supporter.]

John Paul I /jòn páwl/, **Pope** (1912–78). He died 34 days after becoming pope in 1978. Born **Albino Luciani**

John Paul II, Pope (*b.* 1920). In 1978 he became both the first-ever Polish-born pope and the first non-Italian pope since 1522 and is regarded as a traditionalist within the Roman Catholic Church. Born **Karol Wojtyta**

Johns /jonz/, **Jasper** (*b.* 1930) U.S. artist. His work was an important influence on pop art, and features such imagery as the U.S. flag.

Popperfoto

Amy Johnson

John·son /jónss'n/, **Amy** (1903–41) British flyer. She made record solo flights to Australia (1930), Tokyo (1932), and the Cape of Good Hope and back (1936). She flew the Atlantic in 1936 with her husband and was killed in an air crash.

John·son, Andrew (1808–75) U.S. statesman and 17th President of the United States. A Democrat, he was Lincoln's vice president (1865), and succeeded to the presidency after Lincoln's assassination in April 1865. As president (1865–69), he survived an impeachment by Republicans opposed to his conciliatory Reconstruction policies.

John·son, Jack (1878–1946) U.S. boxer. He became the first African American to win the world heavyweight boxing championship (1908). Full name **Arthur John Johnson**

John·son, James Weldon (1871–1938) U.S. poet and writer. He is best known for his novel *The Autobiography of an Ex-Colored Man* (1912).

The White House

Lyndon Baines Johnson and Lady Bird Johnson

John·son, Lyndon Baines (1908–73) U.S. statesman and 36th President of the United States. A Democrat, he was John F. Kennedy's vice president and became president when Kennedy was assassinated, winning a full term the following year. During his presidency (1963–69), increased U.S. involvement in the Vietnam War made him unpopular, and diverted attention from his program of social reform.

John·son, Magic (*b.* 1959) U.S. basketball player. He played guard for the Los Angeles Lakers (1979–91), and is regarded as one of the greatest players of the game. Real name **Earvin Johnson, Jr.**

John·son, Philip (*b.* 1906) U.S. architect. His eclectic designs include the AT&T headquarters (1984) in New York City. Full name **Philip Cortelyou Johnson**

John·son, Richard Mentor (1780–1850) U.S. statesman and vice president of the United States (1837–41). He was a vice president in Martin van Buren's democratic administration.

John·son, Samuel (1709–84) English critic, poet, and lexicographer. His works include his *Dictionary of the English Language* (1755), an edition of Shakespeare (1765), and *Lives of the Poets* (1779–81). He founded two periodicals, *The Rambler* (1750–52) and *The Idler* (1758–60), and his witty conversation is recorded in Boswell's biography of him.

John·son, Thomas (1732–1819) U.S. jurist. He served as an associate justice on the U.S. Supreme Court (1791–93).

John·son, Walter (1887–1946) U.S. baseball player. One of the greatest major league pitchers, he was elected to the Baseball Hall of Fame (1936). Known as **The Big Train.** Full name **Walter Perry Johnson**

John·son grass *n.* a coarse perennial variety of sorghum grass, native to Mediterranean regions and often grown as forage. Latin name: *Sorghum halepense.* [Named for William *Johnson*, an Alabama planter]

John·so·ni·an /jon sṓnee ən/ *adj.* relating to Samuel Johnson or his works, or written in his style.

John·ston /jonstən/ town in northeastern Rhode Island, west of Providence. Population: 26,551 (1996).

John·ston, Albert Sidney (1803–62) U.S. Confederate general. He led the Confederate army at the battle of Shiloh, in which he was killed.

John·ston, Joseph Eggleston (1807–91) U.S. Confederate general. He helped to win the First Battle of Bull Run (1861), but was unsuccessful in defending Vicksburg (1862) and Atlanta (1864).

Johns·town /jónz town/ city in south central Pennsylvania, in Cambria County. It is a manufacturing center. Population: 28,134 (1990).

Jo·hor Strait /jə hàwr-/ narrow strait running between Singapore and Malaysia. Previously known as **Johore Strait**

joie de vi·vre /zhwaà də veévrə/ *n.* energy and love of life [Late 19thC. From French, literally "joy of living."]

join /joyn/ *v.* (**joined, join·ing, joins**) **1.** *vti.* **BRING OR COME TOGETHER** to meet, or make two or more things meet, and become linked or united **2.** *vt.* **FIX TOGETHER** to put or fix two or more things together ○ *join the wing to the body with glue* **3.** *vt.* **MAKE CONNECTION BETWEEN THINGS** to establish a connection between two or more things, e.g., by drawing a line between them ○ *join the dots* **4.** *vti.* **BECOME PART OF GROUP** to become a member of something such as a club, social group, company, team, or other organization ○ *I've joined the Mountaineering Club.* **5.** *vt.* **DO THE SAME AS SOMEBODY** to agree to do the same as somebody ○ *I'm sure my colleagues will want to join me in thanking you for your visit today.* **6.** *vt.* **UNITE PEOPLE IN PARTNERSHIP** to bring two or more people into a partnership, e.g., a marriage **7.** *vt.* **MEET SOMEBODY** to go to meet somebody ○ *I'll join you later.* **8.** *vt.* **SHARE SOMEBODY'S COMPANY** to enter into the company of another person ○ *Do you mind if I join you?* **9.** *vti.* **BE ADJACENT** to be next to something or to each other ○ *This room joins the bathroom.* ■ *n.* **JOINT** a place where two or more things have been joined ○ *You can hardly see the join.* [13thC. Via Old French *joign-*, present stem of *joindre*, from Latin *jungere* "to join" (source of English *juncture* and *junta*).] —**join·a·ble** *adj.*

WORD KEY: ORIGIN

The Indo-European ancestor of ***join*** is also the ultimate source of English *adjust, conjugal, jostle, joust, jugular, juxtapose, subjugate, yoga,* and *yoke.*

join up *vi.* to enlist as a member of one of the armed forces, especially at the outbreak of hostilities

join·der /jóyndər/ *n.* **1. ACT OF JOINING** a joining or bringing together of two things (*formal*) **2.** LAW **JOINING OF LEGAL PARTIES** a joining of two parties in a single lawsuit **3.** LAW **COMBINING OF LEGAL PROCEEDINGS** a joining of two causes of action or two defenses in a lawsuit **4.** LAW **ACCEPTANCE OF ISSUE** a formal acceptance of an issue offered in a lawsuit [Early 17thC. Via Anglo Norman from Old French *joindre* "to join."]

join·er /jóynər/ *n.* **1. WOODWORKER IN CONSTRUCTION INDUSTRY** somebody who is trained or skilled in making the wooden components of buildings, especially the finished woodwork, e.g., door frames and window frames **2. ENTHUSIASTIC PARTICIPANT** somebody who readily joins clubs, societies, and organizations (*informal*)

join·er·y /jóynəree/ *n.* **1. FINISHED WOODWORK IN BUILDINGS** the visible finished woodwork in a building, e.g., door frames and window frames **2. JOINER'S WORK** the work of a joiner, or the techniques that a joiner uses

joint /joynt/ *n.* **1.** ANAT **JUNCTION BETWEEN BONES** any of the parts of the body, e.g., the knee, elbow, or skull, where bones are connected. Many joints have supporting ligaments, protective cartilage, and a particular range of movement, while others, e.g., those between the bones of the vault of the skull, are immobile. **2.** ZOOL **JUNCTION BETWEEN SEGMENTS OF IN-**

VERTEBRATE BODY any of the points of connection between movable segments of the body in an insect, spider, crab, or other invertebrate **3.** BOT **DIVIDING POINT ON PLANT STEM** the place on a plant stem from which a leaf or branch grows **4.** GEOL **CRACK IN ROCK** a crack or fissure in rock, without any looseness or displacement of the surrounding mass **5.** PUBL **HINGE OF BOOK COVER** either of the creases between the spine and the front and back covers of a book, especially a hardback **6. PLACE WHERE PARTS ARE JOINED** the place where parts or pieces of something are joined together **7.** COOK **PIECE OF MEAT** a large piece of meat prepared and cooked for several people, especially one that is roasted **8. BAR OR NIGHTCLUB** a place of entertainment, e.g., a nightclub, especially one considered cheap or disreputable (*slang*) **9. PRISON** prison or similar penal institution (*slang*) **10. A PLACE** a building or dwelling (*slang*) **11.** DRUGS **MARIJUANA CIGARETTE** a cigarette containing marijuana (*slang*) ■ *adj.* **1. DONE TOGETHER** done or produced together with others ○ *A joint statement was issued by the three party leaders.* **2. SHARING SAME ROLE** sharing the same role or position with another person or body ○ *My brother and I were appointed joint executors of her will.* **3. OWNED IN COMMON** owned in common by two or more people or concerns ○ *joint assets* **4. COMBINED** existing and operating in combination ○ *the joint ravages of the weather and the pollution* ■ *v.* **(joint·ed, joint·ing, joints) 1.** *vt.* **FIT TOGETHER** to fit or put parts together by means of a joint **2.** *vt.* COOK **DIVIDE INTO PIECES** to cut a carcass into pieces of meat for cooking **3.** *vt.* WOODWORK **PLANE EDGE OF BOARD** to plane and shape the edge of a board so that it fits with another edge to form a joint **4.** *vi.* BOT **FORM JOINTS DURING GROWTH** to form joints in the stem during the growth process (*refers to cereal plants*) [13thC. From French, past participle of *joindre* "to JOIN."] —**joint·ed** *adj.* —**joint·ing** *n.* ◇ **out of joint 1.** dislocated or painfully displaced **2.** in a bad mood **3.** disturbed or disrupted, usually as a result of some major change or upheaval

joint ac·count *n.* a bank account held in the names of more than one person, typically spouses or partners

Joint Chiefs of Staff *npl.* the most important military advisory group to the President of the United States consisting of the Chiefs of Staff of the Army and Air Force, the commandant of the Marine Corps, and the Chief of Naval Operations

joint de·fense *n.* a defense strategy in which two or more defendants join and cooperate with one another, their attorneys working together and sharing information. Such defendants can assert attorney-client privilege not only with respect to statements made in confidence to their own attorneys, but also to attorneys to codefendants.

joint·er /jóyntər/ *n.* **1.** BUILDING **TOOL FOR SHAPING MORTAR** a tool for pointing the mortar in brickwork or stonework after it has been laid **2.** WOODWORK **PLANE FOR SHAPING JOINTS** a long plane used to shape the edges of planks into joints

joint grass *n.* a creeping grass that roots at the nodes, or joints, in the stem. Latin name: *Paspalum distichum.*

joint·ly /jóyntlee/ *adv.* in conjunction with, or in cooperation with, a person or organization ○ *The copyright is jointly owned by the composer and the publisher.*

join·tress /jóyntrəss/ *n.* LAW a woman on whom property has been settled by her husband at the time of their marriage

joint stock *n.* FIN stock held jointly, especially in a joint-stock company, a commercial enterprise whose capital is in shares that individual holders may transfer without the consent of the whole body

join·ture /jóynchər/ *n.* LAW an estate or property settled by a husband on his wife at the time of their marriage, to take effect in the event of his death

joint ven·ture *n.* **1. JOINTLY UNDERTAKEN BUSINESS ENTERPRISE** a business enterprise jointly undertaken by two or more companies, who share the initial investment, risks, and profits **2.** CRIMINOL, LAW **ILLEGAL ACTION BY TWO PARTIES** an illegal or criminal action that is undertaken by two or more parties

joint·worm /jóyntwurm/ *n.* the larva of some wasps that forms a weakening swelling at the stem joint of a cereal plant. Family: Eurytomidae.

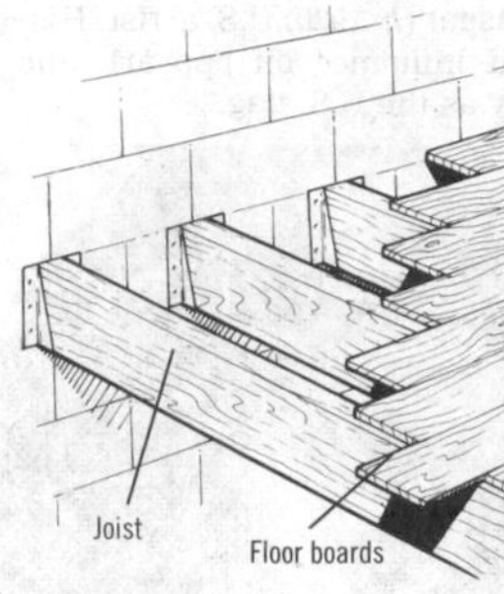

Joist

joist /joyst/ *n.* any of the parallel beams of wood, metal, or concrete that support a floor, roof, or ceiling [14thC. Via Old French *giste* "beam supporting a bridge" from, ultimately, Latin *jacere* "to lie down" (source of English *adjacent*).]

jo·jo·ba /hōh'bə/ (*plural* **-bas**) *n.* **1.** PLANTS **DESERT SHRUB YIELDING COSMETIC OIL** a desert shrub or small tree native to Mexico, Arizona, and California, with edible seeds that yield a waxy oil used in shampoos and other cosmetics. Latin name: *Simmondsia chinensis.* **2.** COSMETICS **COSMETIC OIL** the oil derived from the jojoba tree, used in shampoos and other cosmetics (*often used before a noun*) [Early 20thC. Via Mexican Spanish from a Native American word.]

joke /jōk/ *n.* **1. FUNNY STORY** a funny story, anecdote, or piece of wordplay that gets passed round and repeated **2. SOMETHING FUNNY SAID OR DONE** anything said or done to make people laugh ○ *dressed up the dog in a hat and sunglasses as a joke* **3. FUNNY EVENT** a funny event or circumstance, or something to laugh at **4. SOMETHING INADEQUATE** somebody or something that is laughably inadequate or absurd (*slang*) ○ *The surroundings were pleasant enough but the food was a joke.* ■ *v.* **(joked, jok·ing, jokes) 1.** *vti.* **MAKE JOKES** to tell funny stories, or say or do things to make somebody laugh **2.** *vi.* **NOT TO BE SERIOUS** to be trying to be amusing, rather than serious or in earnest ○ *We knew he was only joking.* [Late 17thC. From Latin *jocus* "jest, wordplay" (source of English *jocular, juggle,* and *jeopardy*). Originally slang.]

jok·er /jōkər/ *n.* **1. TELLER OR PLAYER OF JOKES** somebody who frequently makes jokes or plays jokes on other people **2.** CARDS **CARD BEARING PICTURE OF JESTER** an extra playing card in a deck, bearing a picture of a jester, that in some games can be substituted for other cards **3. AMUSING ECCENTRIC PERSON** an amusing, entertaining, or entertainingly eccentric person (*slang*) **4. THOUGHTLESS OR INCONSIDERATE PERSON** somebody whose thoughtless or inconsiderate action is highly annoying (*slang*) ○ *I'm looking for the joker who double-parked outside my front door.* **5.** LAW, POL **DISABLING CLAUSE** a clause or phrase surreptitiously slipped into a legislative bill or legal contract with the purpose of compromising its effect or making it unworkable ◇ **the joker in the deck** an unpredictable element that makes planning or projections difficult (*slang*)

jok·ey /j'kee/ (**-i·er, -i·est**), **jok·y** *adj.* good-humored and amusing, or full of jokes —**jok·ily** *adv.* —**jok·i·ness** *n.*

jok·ing·ly /j'kinglee/ *adv.* with the intention of making a joke rather than a serious comment or suggestion

jok·y *adj.* = **jokey**

jol·ie laid·e /Zhawli léd/ (*plural* **jol·ies laid·es**) *n.* a woman whose facial features are not pretty in conventional terms, but nevertheless have a distinctive harmony or charm [From French, from *jolie* "pretty" + *laide* "ugly"]

Jo·li·et /jṓ lee èt/ city in northeastern Illinois, southeast of Aurora and southwest of Chicago. Population: 86,749 (1996).

Jo·li·ot-Cu·rie /zhō lyṓ kyóoree/, **Irène** (1897–1956) French physicist. She was joint winner of the Nobel Prize in chemistry (1925) with her husband, Frédéric Joliot-Curie, for producing the first radioisotope artificially. Born **Irène Curie**

Jol·li·et /jṑlee ét/, **Jo·li·et, Louis** (1645–1700) French-Canadian explorer. With Father Jacques Marquette he charted the upper reaches of the Mississippi River (1673).

jol·li·fi·ca·tion /jòllifi káysh'n/ *n.* the activities of people who are enthusiastically celebrating something in a happy, friendly way [Early 19thC. Formed from JOLLY.]

jol·li·fy /jólli fī/ (**-fied, -fy·ing, -fies**) *vt.* to make somebody cheerful or create a festive atmosphere in something [Early 19thC. Formed from JOLLY.]

jol·li·ty /jóllətee/ *n.* cheerful, joking, or celebratory behavior [13thC. From Old French *jolite,* from *joli* (see JOLLY).]

jol·ly /jóllee/ *adj.* (**-li·er, -li·est**) **1. FRIENDLY AND CHEERFUL** friendly and cheerful, especially in a hearty or exuberant way ○ *a jolly pink-cheeked woman* **2. HAPPY** happily festive in tone or mood (*dated*) **3.** *U.K.* **ENJOYABLE** bringing pleasure or enjoyment (*dated informal*) ○ *A picnic would be jolly.* ■ *adv. U.K.* **VERY** used to emphasize the extent to which something is good or bad (*dated informal*) ○ *jolly nice of you to come* [13thC. From Old French *joli* "merry, pleasant, pretty," of uncertain origin: perhaps from Old Norse *jól* "yule."] ◇ **get your jollies** to get pleasure out of something (*slang*)

jolly along *vt. U.K.* to keep somebody happy or cooperative by using flattery or encouragement (*informal*) ○ *Try to jolly her along a little bit longer*

jolly up *vt. U.K.* to make a person, place, or situation more lively or cheerful (*dated informal*)

jol·ly·boat /jóllibōt/ *n.* a small boat carried on a larger ship, often one kept hoisted at the stern of the ship [Late 17thC. Origin of "jolly" uncertain: possibly related to YAWL.]

Jolly Roger

Jol·ly Rog·er *n.* the flag traditionally flown by a pirate ship, depicting a white skull and crossbones against a black background [Late 18thC. Origin unknown: *Roger* perhaps from slang use to denote a man or a rogue.]

Jol·son /jṓlss'n/, **Al** (1886–1950) Lithuanian-born U.S. entertainer. He was known for his minstrel-style singing in blackface makeup. He starred in the first talking movie, *The Jazz Singer* (1927). Born **Asa Yoelson**

jolt /jōlt/ *v.* (**jolt·ed, jolt·ing, jolts**) **1.** *vti.* **SHAKE OR JERK VIOLENTLY** to shake or jerk suddenly and violently, or to make somebody or something shake or jerk suddenly and violently, especially as a result of a sudden movement **2.** *vt.* **SHAKE OR DISLODGE** to knock or shake somebody or something violently enough to cause unsteadiness or loss of balance ○ *A major earthquake jolted the city.* **3.** *vt.* **STARTLE INTO REALITY** to startle somebody out of a daydream, fantasy, or other state of semiawareness **4.** *vi.* **BUMP UP AND DOWN** to bump up and down or shake from side to side while moving ■ *n.* **1. SHOCK OR REMINDER** an emotional shock or a sharp reminder **2. VIOLENT MOVEMENT** a sudden, violent movement or blow ○ *The train moved off again with a series of jolts.* [Late 16thC. Origin unknown: perhaps an alteration of Middle English *jollen* "to knock" or *jot* "to bump."] —**jolt·ing·ly** *adv.* —**jolt·y** *adj.*

Jon. *abbr.* BIBLE Jonah

Jo·nah[1] /j'nə/ *n.* **1. HEBREW PROPHET** in the Bible, a Hebrew prophet of the 8th century B.C. who was swallowed by a great fish and vomited out three days later, unharmed **2. BOOK IN THE BIBLE** a book in the Bible that tells the story of Jonah, whose preaching caused the Assyrians to repent their wickedness. See table at **Bible**

Jo·nah[2] /j'nə/ *n.* somebody who is regarded as a bringer of bad luck —**Jo·nah·esque** *adj.*

Jon·a·than[1] /j'nəthən/ *n.* **1.** FOOD **NORTH AMERICAN APPLE** a North American variety of red-skinned dessert apple **2. NEW ENGLANDER** a citizen or resident of New England, especially in the early to mid-19th century (*archaic humorous*) **3.** HIST, NAUT **YANKEE SHIP** a New England-registered naval vessel (*archaic slang*) [Late 18thC. From "Brother Jonathan," the name George WASHINGTON used to address Connecticut governor Jonathan Trumbull.]

Jon·a·than[2] /j'nəthən/ *n.* in the Bible, the eldest son of King Saul and close friend of David, who was killed in battle against the Philistines (1 Samuel 13–2 Samuel 21)

jones /jōnz/ *n.* **1. DRUG ADDICTION** an addiction, especially a heroin addiction (*slang*) **2. WITHDRAWAL** drug withdrawal symptoms, especially from heroin (*slang*) **3. HABITUAL CRAVING** an all-consuming craving or desire for something (*slang*) **4. jones, Jones PENIS** a penis (*taboo*) [Late 20thC. Origin unknown.]

Jones /jōnz/, **Bobby** (1902–71) U.S. amateur golfer. He won several major tournaments (1923–29) and the Grand Slam (1930). Full name **Robert Tyre Jones, Jr.**

Jones, James (1921–77) U.S. writer. He is known for his war novel *From Here to Eternity* (1951).

Jones·bor·o /jónzbərə/ city in northeastern Arkansas, northwest of West Memphis. Population: 52,656 (1996).

jon·gleur /ZhōN glúr/ *n.* a wandering minstrel of medieval times who traveled around singing the compositions of troubadours or reciting epic poems in noble households or royal courts [Late 18thC. Via French from, ultimately, Latin *joculator* "jester," from *joculari* (see JUGGLE).]

Jön·kö·ping /yőn chö ping/ city and capital of Jönköping County, in southern Sweden. Population: 113,557 (1993).

Jon·quière /zhōN kyáir/ city in eastern Canada, in Chicoutimi County, southern Québec Province. Population: 56,603 (1996).

Jonquil

jon·quil /j'ngkwəl/ *n.* a flowering plant native to southern Europe that is a variety of narcissus. It has intensely fragrant, golden-yellow, short-tubed flowers, is widely cultivated as an ornamental, and is also used in perfumery. Latin name: *Narcissus jonquilla.* [Early 17thC. Via modern Latin *jonquilla* or French *jonquille* from Spanish *junquillo* "little rush," from *junco* (see JUNCO). So called because of its resemblance to a rush.]

Jon·son /jónss'n/, **Ben** (1573–1637) English playwright and poet. His plays include brilliant comedies such as *Volpone* (1606) as well as classical tragedies. He was poet laureate (1616–25). Full name **Benjamin Jonson**

Jop·lin /jóplin/, **Scott** (1868–1917) U.S. composer. He is best known for his ragtime piano music.

Jor·dan /jáwrd'n/ **1.** kingdom in the Middle East, bordered by Syria, Iraq, Saudi Arabia, the Gulf of Aqaba, Israel, and the West Bank. Language: Arabic. Currency: Jordanian dinar. Capital: Amman. Population: 4,322,255 (1997). Area: 34,578 sq. mi./89,556 sq. km. Official name **Hashemite Kingdom of Jordan** **2.** river in southwestern Asia that rises in the Anti-Lebanon Mountains of Lebanon and flows south through the Sea of Galilee before emptying into the Dead Sea. Length: 200 mi./320.

Jor·dan, Michael (*b.* 1963) U.S. basketball player. He played for the Chicago Bulls from 1984, and is considered by many to be the greatest player in basketball history. Known as **Air Jordan**

Scott Joplin

Jordan

Jor·dan al·mond *n.* **1. SPANISH ALMOND** a large Spanish variety of almond chiefly cultivated around and exported from Malaga **2. CANDY ALMOND** a Jordan almond or other almond with a hard sugar coating [15thC. *Jordan* is an alteration of French or Spanish *jardin* "garden" (see GARDEN).]

Jor·dan curve *n.* in mathematics, any simple closed curve, e.g., a circle or an ellipse [Early 20thC. Named for the French mathematician M. E. C. *Jordan* 1838–1922.]

Jor·dan curve the·o·rem *n.* in geometry, a theorem holding that every simple closed curve divides a plane into two regions and serves as their boundary

Jor·da·nian *n.* **SOMEBODY FROM JORDAN** somebody who was born or raised in Jordan, or who is a citizen of Jordan ■ *adj.* **OF JORDAN** relating to or typical of Jordan, or its people or culture

jo·rum /jáwrəm/, **jo·ram** *n.* a large drinking bowl or its contents (*archaic*) [Mid-18thC. Origin uncertain: perhaps named for *Joram*, who took silver, gold, and brass vessels to King David (II Samuel 8:10).]

jo·seph /jṓzəf/ *n.* a woman's 18th-century riding cloak with a short cape [Mid-17thC. From the coat that *Joseph* left behind in fleeing, Potiphar's wife (Genesis 39:13).]

Jo·seph /jṓzəf/ (1840?–1904) U.S. Native American leader. As chief of the Nez Percé he resisted white encroachment in the western United States. Born **In-mut-too-yah-lat-lat ("thunder coming up from the water over the land")**. Known as **Chief Joseph**

Jo·seph *n.* in the Bible, the son of Jacob and Rachel. He was given a coat of many colors and sold into slavery in Egypt by his jealous brothers (Genesis 30–50).

Jo·seph, St. (*fl.* 1st century B.C.) Biblical figure. In the New Testament he is described as a carpenter of Nazareth and the husband of Mary, the mother of Jesus Christ.

Jo·seph II, Holy Roman Emperor (1741–90). He was the son of Francis I and Maria Theresa. As emperor (1765–90), he saw his reforms frustrated by insurrection and the distractions of war.

Jo·seph Bo·na·parte Gulf /jōsəf bṓnə paart-/ inlet of the Timor Sea on the north coast of Australia, extending from Western Australia into the Northern Territory. It is 200 mi./320 km wide.

Jo·sé·phine /jṓzə feen/, **Empress of the French** (1763–1814). She married the future Napoleon I in 1796 and was empress from 1804 until the childless marriage was dissolved in 1809. Born **Marie Joséphine Rose Tascher de la Pagerie**

Jo·seph of Ar·i·ma·the·a /jṓzəf əv àrrə mə thée ə/, **St.** (*fl.* 1st century A.D.) According to the Bible, he asked Pontius Pilate for the body of Jesus Christ, and buried it in his own tomb (Matthew 27).

Jo·seph·son ef·fect /jṓzəfs'n-/ *n.* the passage of an electric current through a thin insulating layer between two superconducting metals [Late 20thC. Named for the British physicist Brian David *Josephson* b.1940, who predicted it.]

Jo·seph·son junc·tion *n.* in electrical or electronic circuits, a junction that utilizes the Josephson effect, consisting of two superconducting materials separated by a thin insulating layer. In a computer memory, a Josephson junction acts as a high-speed switch.

josh /josh/ (**joshed, josh·ing, josh·es**) *v.* (*informal*) **1.** *vti.* **TEASE SOMEBODY** to make fun of somebody in a friendly, good-humored way **2.** *vi.* **JOKE OR BANTER** to joke or indulge in banter with somebody [Mid-19thC. Origin unknown: perhaps from *Josh* Billings, pseudonym of U.S. humorist.] —**josh·er** *n.* —**josh·ing·ly** *adv.*

Josh. *abbr.* Joshua

Josh·u·a /jóshooə/ *n.* the book of the Bible that contains a narrative of the Hebrew invasion and partition of Canaan under Joshua's command. See table at **Bible**

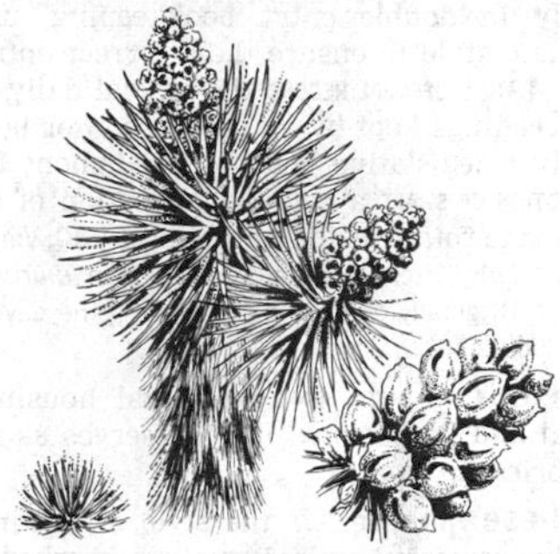
Joshua tree

Josh·u·a tree *n.* a small tree-shaped yucca with sword-shaped leaves and clusters of white flowers that is native to deserts of the southwestern United States. Latin name: *Yucca brevifolia.* [Mid-19thC. Origin uncertain: probably named for JOSHUA, because the tree's branching shape resembles someone brandishing a spear (Joshua 8:18).]

Jo·si·ah /jō sī́ ə/, **King of Judah** (648?–609 B.C.). He is credited in the Old Testament with restoring the worship of Jahweh, and was killed by the Assyrians at the Battle of Megiddo.

joss /joss/ *n.* an image or statue representing a Chinese deity [Early 18thC. Via Javanese *dejos* from Portuguese *deus* "god," from Latin.]

joss house *n.* a Chinese shrine or temple containing images or statues of deities

joss stick *n.* incense in the form of a stick of dried paste

jos·tle /jóss'l/ (**-tled, -tling, -tles**) *vti.* to knock or bump against somebody, or to push or elbow somebody deliberately, sometimes as an expression of aggression or hostility ○ *We managed to jostle our way to the front.* [Mid-16thC. Formed from JOUST; the underlying sense is of repeatedly coming together.] —**jos·tler** *n.*

jot /jot/ *vt.* (**jot·ted, jot·ting, jots**) **WRITE QUICKLY** to write something down hastily for later reference ○ *jotted down the title in her notebook* ■ *n.* **TINY BIT** a very small amount [15thC. Via Latin from Greek *iōta* (see IOTA).]

jo·ta /khṓtə/ *n.* a fast Spanish dance, performed with castanets in 3/4 time, usually to a voice and guitar accompaniment. It is the traditional dance of Aragon. [Mid-19thC. From Spanish.]

jot·ting /jótting/ *n.* a hastily written note, comment, or observation

Jo·tun /jṓ tun/, **Jo·tunn** *n.* a member of a race of giants with supernatural powers in Norse mythology

Jo·tun·heim /jṓtun hīm/ *n.* the home of the giants in Norse mythology [From Old Norse *Jotunheimar*]

jou·al /zhoō ál, zhoō aál/, **joo·al** *n.* *Can* a nonstandard, mainly urban dialect of Canadian French containing many English words. It is also spoken in parts of Maine. [Mid-20thC. Via dialectal Canadian French from French *cheval* "horse."]

joule /jool/ *n.* the International System unit of energy or work, equal to the work done when the application point of a one newton force moves one meter in the direction of application. Symbol **J** [Late 19thC. Named for the British physicist James Prescott *Joule* 1818–89.]

Joule ef·fect /jo͞ol-/ *n.* an increase in heat resulting from the passage of a current through a conductor [Late 19thC (see JOULE)]

jounce /jownss/ *vti.* **(jounced, jounc·ing, jounc·es) MOVE WHILE BOUNCING** to bounce up and down and rock from side to side while moving, or to make somebody or something move in this way ■ *n.* **BOUNCING MOVEMENT** a jolting, swaying, bouncing, or rocking movement [15thC. Origin unknown.] —**jounc·y** *adj.*

jour. *abbr.* **1.** journal **2.** journalist **3.** journeyman

jour·nal /júrn'l/ *n.* **1.** PUBL **MAGAZINE OR PERIODICAL** a magazine or periodical, especially one published by a specialist or professional body for its members, containing information and contributions relevant to their area of activity ○ *a medical journal* **2. DIARY** somebody's written daily record of personal experiences **3.** ACCT **PRELIMINARY RECORD OF FINANCIAL TRANSACTIONS** a book for recording daily transactions, especially in double entry bookkeeping, using a formulaic style to ensure their correct entry in a ledger **4.** POL **OFFICIAL RECORD** the official daily record of proceedings kept by an association or body, especially a legislative body or parliament **5.** MECH ENG **SECTION OF SHAFT** a cylindrical section of a shaft designed to rotate inside a bearing [14thC. Via French, literally "daily," from, ultimately, late Latin *diurnalis* (see DIURNAL). Originally denoted a book listing the daytime canonical hours.]

jour·nal box *n.* MECH ENG the metal housing of a journal and its bearing. It often serves as a place for lubricant.

jour·nal·ese /jùrn'léez/ *n.* the style of writing supposedly associated with journalists, marked by the use of formulaic expressions (*disapproving*)

jour·nal·ism /júrnəlìzəm/ *n.* **1. REPORTING NEWS FOR THE MEDIA** the profession of gathering, editing, and publishing news reports and related articles for newspapers, magazines, television, or radio **2. NEWS GATHERING AND REPORTING AS A GENRE** writing or reporting for the media as a literary genre or style

jour·nal·ist /júrnəlist/ *n.* somebody who works as a writer or editor for a newspaper or magazine or for television or radio

jour·nal·is·tic /jùrnə lístik/ *adj.* relating to journalism or similar in style to journalism —**jour·nal·is·ti·cal·ly** *adv.*

jour·nal·ize /júrnə līz/ **(-ized, -iz·ing, -iz·es)** *vti.* to keep a journal or record something in a journal (*formal*) —**jour·nal·i·za·tion** /jùrnə lī záysh'n/ *n.* —**jour·nal·iz·er** /júrnə līzər/ *n.*

jour·ney /júrnee/ *n.* (*plural* **-neys**) **1. TRIP SOMEWHERE** a trip or expedition from one place to another **2. PROCESS OF DEVELOPMENT** a gradual passing from one state to another regarded as more advanced, e.g., from innocence to mature awareness ○ *a spiritual journey* ■ *vi.* **(-neyed, -ney·ing, -neys) TRAVEL** to travel to a place or over a particular distance ○ *We are journeying into the unknown.* [12thC. Via Old French *journee* "day, day's work or travel" (the original senses in English), from, ultimately, Latin *diurnus* (see DIURNAL).] —**jour·ney·er** *n.*

jour·ney cake *n. New England* = **johnnycake**

jour·ney·man /júrnimən/ (*plural* **-men**) *n.* (*often used before a noun*) **1. QUALIFIED ARTISAN** an artisan who has completed an apprenticeship and is fully trained and qualified but still works for an employer ○ *a journeyman electrician* **2. SOMEBODY WITH ORDINARY COMPETENCE** somebody who is a competent and reliable performer or exponent, without being brilliant or outstanding ○ *a good journeyman violinist* [15thC. Literally, someone qualified to work for a daily wage rather than as an apprentice.]

joust /jowst/ *n.* **MEDIEVAL TOURNAMENT** a form of combat in medieval times held between two mounted knights in full armor who charged at and tried to unseat each other with a lance ■ *vi.* **(joust·ed, joust·ing, jousts) 1. ENGAGE IN A JOUST** to take part in a joust **2. ENGAGE IN A CONTEST** to take part in a contest against others ○ *candidates jousting for ninety minutes in a televised debate* [13thC. Via Old French *jouster* "bring together" from, ultimately, Latin *juxta* "close, beside" (source of English *adjust* and *juxtaposition*).] —**joust·er** *n.*

J'Ou·vert /jo͝ováy/ *n. Carib* the Monday that is the eve of Mardi Gras, when the festivities begin [From French *jour ouvert*, literally "the day having been opened"]

Jove /jōv/ *n.* = **Jupiter** (*literary*) [14thC. Via the stem of Latin *Jovem* from Old Latin *Jovis* (source of English *Jupiter*).] ◇ **by Jove** used to convey surprise, or to emphasize a conviction (*dated*)

jo·vi·al /jṓvee əl/ *adj.* cheerful in mood or disposition [Late 16thC. Via French from Latin *jovialis*, from *Jovis* (see JOVE).] —**jo·vi·al·i·ty** /jòvee álitee/ *n.* —**jo·vi·al·ly** /jṓvee əlee/ *adv.* —**jo·vi·al·ness** /jóvee əlnəss/ *n.*

Jo·vi·an /jṓvee ən/ *adj.* **1.** MYTHOL **RELATING TO GOD JUPITER** associated with or characteristic of the god Jupiter **2.** ASTRON **RELATING TO THE PLANET JUPITER** relating to the planet Jupiter

Jo·vi·an plan·et *n.* any one of the four major planets, Jupiter, Uranus, Saturn, or Neptune

jowl[1] /jowl/ *n.* **1. JAW** the jaw, especially the lower jaw **2. CHEEK** a cheek, especially a prominent one [Old English *ceafl*, ultimately from a prehistoric Germanic word]

jowl[2] /jowl/ *n.* **1. HANGING PART OF A DOUBLE CHIN** a flaccid, plump fold of flesh under somebody's chin **2. HANGING FLESH UNDER AN ANIMAL'S CHIN** a dewlap under the neck of cattle or a wattle on the neck of a bird [Old English *ceole*, ultimately from a prehistoric Germanic word]

jowl·y /jówlee/ **(-i·er, -i·est)** *adj.* with a fold of flesh hanging under the neck —**jowl·i·ness** *n.*

joy /joy/ *n.* **1. GREAT HAPPINESS** feelings of great happiness or pleasure, especially of an elevated or spiritual kind **2. SOMETHING THAT BRINGS HAPPINESS** a pleasurable aspect of something, or something that is seen as a source of happiness ○ *His little granddaughter was a great joy to him.* ■ *v.* **(joyed, joy·ing, joys) 1.** *vti.* **REJOICE OR GLADDEN** to derive joy from something, or to give somebody joy (*archaic or literary*) **2.** *vt.* **ENJOY** to delight in or enjoy something (*archaic literary*) [12thC. Via French *joie* from, ultimately, Latin *gaudere* "to rejoice."]

joy·ance /jóy ənss/ *n.* feelings or expressions of joy (*archaic or literary*)

James Joyce

Joyce /joyss/, **James** (1882–1941) Irish novelist. His innovative techniques, as in *Ulysses* (1922) and *Finnegans Wake* (1939), make him one of the most influential modern writers. Full name **James Augustine Aloysius Joyce**

joy·ful /jóyf'l, jóyfo͝ol/ *adj.* **1. FEELING OR SHOWING JOY** full of joy, or feeling, expressing, or showing joy **2. WELCOME** bringing or causing joy —**joy·ful·ly** *adv.* —**joy·ful·ness** *n.*

joy·less /jóyləss/ *adj.* lacking in warmth or happiness —**joy·less·ly** *adv.* —**joy·less·ness** *n.*

Joy·ner-Ker·see /jòynər kúrzee/, **Jackie** (*b.* 1962) U.S. track and field champion. She won Olympic gold medals in the heptathlon (1988 and 1992). Born **Jacqueline Joyner**

joy·ous /jóy əss/ *adj.* **1. EXPRESSING JOY** full of joy, especially of a fervent and unrestrained nature **2. GIVING JOY** making people happy or joyful —**joy·ous·ly** *adv.* —**joy·ous·ness** *n.*

joy·pop /jóy pŏp/ **(-popped, -pop·ping, -pops)** *vi.* to take illicit drugs occasionally rather than habitually (*slang*) [Mid-20thC] —**joy·pop·per** *n.*

joy·rid·ing /jóy rīding/ *n.* a crime involving stealing a car and driving it dangerously at high speed [Early 20thC] —**joy·ride** *n., vi.* —**joy·rid·er** *n.*

joy·stick /jóystik/ *n.* **1. VEHICLE'S CONTROL LEVER** the control lever of an aircraft or of a small motor-powered vehicle **2.** COMPUT **LEVER CONTROLLING A CURSOR** a hand-held control stick that allows a player to control the movements of a cursor on a VDU screen or a symbol in a video game

J.P., JP *abbr.* Justice of the Peace

J par·ti·cle *n.* = **J/psi particle**

JPG *n.* COMPUT a format for encoding high-resolution graphic images as computer files for storage and transmission. Abbr of **Joint Photographic Group**

Jpn. *abbr.* **1.** Japan **2.** Japanese

J/psi par·ti·cle *n.* an unstable elementary particle of the meson group. It has a large mass, about 6,000 times that of an electron, and is thought to be formed from charmed quarks. [*J* and *psi* represent the 23rd letter of the Greek alphabet]

jr. *abbr.* junior

Jr. *abbr.* **1.** BIBLE Jeremiah **2.** Junior

JRC *abbr.* Junior Red Cross

JROTC *abbr.* Junior Reserve Officers Training Corps

J.S.D. *abbr.* Doctor of Juristic Science [Latin, *Juris Scientiae Doctor*]

jt. *abbr.* joint

Juan Car·los /waan kaarlōss, hwaan-/, **King of Spain** (*b.* 1938). He became king following the death of General Franco (1975), presiding over Spain's rapid transition to democracy.

Juan de Fu·ca, Strait of /waan də fo͞okə/ body of water lying between Washington State and Vancouver Island, Canada, connecting the Strait of Georgia and Puget Sound to the Pacific Ocean. Length: 100 mi./160 km.

Juá·rez /waar ez, hwaar ez/, **Benito Pablo** (1806–72) Mexican statesman and national hero. He fought against the government of General Santa Anna and served as president of Mexico (1861–63 and 1867–72).

ju·ba /jo͞obə/ *n.* formerly in the South, a lively rustic dance with much clapping and thigh-slapping, the word "juba" being repeated as a refrain [Mid-19thC. Origin unknown.]

Ju·ba /jo͞obə/ city in southern Sudan on the White Nile River

ju·bi·lant /jo͞obilənt/ *adj.* feeling or expressing great delight over a success, achievement, or victory [Mid-17thC. From Latin *jubilantem*, present participle of *jubilare* (see JUBILATE).] —**ju·bi·lant·ly** *adv.*

ju·bi·late /jo͞obə layt/ **(-lat·ed, -lat·ing, -lates)** *vi.* to feel or express immense joy (*archaic*) [Early 17thC. From Latin *jubilatus*, the past participle of *jubilare* "to call out, to shout for joy."]

Ju·bi·la·te /jo͞obə láytee, yooba-/ *n.* Psalm 100, which is sung as a canticle in the Roman Catholic and Anglican churches. In the Latin version it begins, "Jubilate Deo"(Rejoice in the Lord).

ju·bi·la·tion /jo͞obə láysh'n/ *n.* uninhibited rejoicing in the celebration of a victory or success [14thC. From the Latin *jubilationem*, from *jubilare* (see JUBILATE).]

ju·bi·lee /jo͞obəlee, jo͞obəlée, jo͞obəlee/ *n.* **1. SPECIAL ANNIVERSARY** a significant anniversary of an important event such as a wedding **2. JOYFUL TIME** a time or season of celebration **3.** CHR **YEAR OF INDULGENCE SET BY THE POPE** in the Roman Catholic Church, a period set by the Pope, traditionally every 25 years, in which forgiveness of sins is granted in return for acts of piety or repentance **4.** JUDAISM **YEAR OF RESTITUTION** in Jewish history, a year of restoration or restitution that was proclaimed every fifty years by a countrywide blast of trumpets. During the period, land was left uncultivated, enslaved people were emancipated, and land that had been sold reverted to its former owner. **5. JUBILATION** an act or period of jubilation (*archaic*) [14thC. Via French *jubilé* from Latin *jubilaeus (annus)* "(year) of jubilee," from, ultimately, Hebrew *yōbēl*, literally "ram," from the ram's horn with which the year of jubilee was proclaimed.]

Jud. *abbr.* BIBLE **1.** Judges **2.** Judith

Judaeo- *prefix.* = **Judeo-**

Ju·dah = **Judea**

Ju·da·ic /joo dáy ik/, **Ju·da·i·cal** /joo dáy ik'l/ *adj.* belonging to or relating to Judaism or Jews [15thC. Via Latin *Judaicus* from Greek *Ioudaikos*, from *Ioudaios* (see JEW).] —**Ju·da·i·cal·ly** *adv.*

Ju·da·i·ca /joo dáy ikə/ *npl.* the Jewish religion, customs, and culture, or artifacts and historical and literary materials that relate to them (*formal*) [Early 20thC. From Latin, neuter plural of *Judaicus* (see JUDAIC).]

Ju·da·ism /jōō day ìzzəm/ *n.* **1. RELIGION OF THE JEWS** the religion of the Jews that has its basis in the Bible and the Talmud. In Judaism, God is the creator of everything and the source of all goodness. **2. JEWISH WAY OF LIFE** Jewish religious practices, customs, and culture as a way of life [14thC. Via ecclesiastical Latin *Judaismus* from Greek *Ioudaismos*, from *Ioudaios* (see JEW).] —**Ju·da·is·tic** *adj.*

Ju·da·ize /jōō day īz/ (**-ized, -iz·ing, -iz·es**) *v.* **1.** *vi.* **ADOPT JUDAISM** to adopt the Jewish religion and Jewish cultural practices **2.** *vt.* **MAKE SOMETHING JEWISH** to give something a Jewish character [Late 16thC. Via ecclesiastical Latin *judizare* from Greek *ioudizein*, from *Ioudaios* (see JEW).] —**Ju·da·i·za·tion** /jōō day əzáysh'n/ *n.*

ju·das /jōōdəss/, **ju·das hole** *n.* a peephole or very small window, e.g., in a door [Mid-19thC. Named for JUDAS.]

Ju·das /jōōdəss/ *n.* **1. DISCIPLE WHO BETRAYED JESUS CHRIST IN THE BIBLE** one of Jesus Christ's disciples in the new Testament who betrayed him by identifying him with a kiss to the Jewish leaders in exchange for thirty pieces of silver (Luke 22) **2. TRAITOR** a traitor, especially somebody who betrays a close friend or a cause or belief (*literary*)

Ju·das tree *n.* = **redbud** [Mid-17thC. Named for JUDAS from the popular notion that he hanged himself from this tree, and also an alteration of JUDEA, from which the tree originates.]

jud·der /júddər/ *vi.* (**-dered, -der·ing, -ders**) **SHAKE VIOLENTLY** to shake or vibrate violently and rapidly, or to move while shaking ■ *n.* **VIOLENT SHAKING** a violent, rapid vibration or shaking motion [Mid-20thC. An imitation of the sound.]

Jude /jood/ *n.* **1. APOSTLE OF JESUS CHRIST** one of the twelve Apostles of Jesus Christ, he was the brother of James and author of the New Testament Book of Jude **2. BOOK OF THE NEW TESTAMENT** the last epistle of the New Testament, probably written in the late 1st century. It reminds Christians of the importance of keeping their faith. See table at **Bible**

Ju·de·a /joo dée ə/, **Ju·dae·a, Ju·dah** /jōōdə/ region in southwestern Asia, incorporating parts of Israel and the West Bank

Judeo- *prefix.* Jewish, Judaism ○ *Judeo-Christian* [Via Latin *Judaeus* from Greek *Ioudaios* (see JEW)]

Ju·de·o-Chris·ti·an /joo dàyo-/ *adj.* in the shared tradition of Judaism and Christianity or combining their common beliefs

Ju·de·o-Span·ish, **Ju·dez·mo** /joo dézmō/ *n.*, *adj.* = **Ladino**

Judg. *abbr.* BIBLE Judges

judge /juj/ *n.* **1.** LAW **A SENIOR OFFICIAL IN A COURT OF LAW** a high-ranking court officer, formerly a lawyer, who supervises court trials, instructs juries, and pronounces sentences **2. ADJUDICATOR** a person, sometimes one of several, appointed to assess entries or performances in a competition and decide on the winner or winners **3. SOMEBODY GIVING AN INFORMED OPINION** somebody who has an ability to assess quality or give an informed opinion in a particular area of knowledge or experience ○ *a good judge of character* ○ *a fine judge of a horse* **4.** JUDAISM **JEWISH WARRIOR LEADER** in Jewish history, any of a succession of warrior leaders who each temporarily held supreme power in Israel between Joshua's death and Saul's succession ■ *v.* (**judged, judg·ing, judg·es**) **1.** *vt.* LAW **ACT AS A LEGAL JUDGE** to act as the judge of a legal case **2.** *vt.* **BE JUDGE IN A CONTEST** to act as a judge in a competition or, as an adjudicator, to pronounce officially on the entries **3.** *vti.* **ASSESS** to assess the quality of something or estimate probabilities ○ *Each proposal has to be judged on its own merits.* **4.** *vt.* **CONSIDER OR RECKON** to form an opinion of somebody or something, especially after thought or consideration ○ *She was judged to have the best qualifications.* **5.** *vti.* **ESTIMATE** to measure by guesswork, using the eye or some other sense as a rough guide ○ *You can't always judge people's ages by their voices.* **6.** *vt.* **CONDEMN** to criticize or condemn somebody on moral grounds [12thC. Via Old French *juge* from, ultimately, Latin *judex*, literally "one who speaks the law," from *jus* "law, right" (source of English *just*).] —**judg·er** *n.*

judge ad·vo·cate *n.* a military officer-lawyer who advises commanders on points of law, especially the Uniform Code of Military Justice, and who may function as defense counsel or prosecutor at courts-martial

judge·ment *n.* = **judgment**

Judges *n.* a book of the Bible that tells the story of the Israelites from Joshua's death in the 13th century B.C. to Samuel's birth in the 11th century B.C. (*takes a singular verb*) See table at **Bible**

judg·ment /jújmənt/, **judge·ment** *n.* **1.** LAW **VERDICT** the decision arrived at and pronounced by a court of law **2.** LAW **OBLIGATION RESULTING FROM A VERDICT** an obligation such as a debt that arises as a result of a court's verdict, or a document setting out an obligation of this kind **3. DECISION OF A JUDGE** the decision reached by one or more judges in a contest ○ *The judgment of the panel must be regarded as final.* **4. DECISION ON A DISPUTED MATTER** an opinion formed or decision reached in the case of a disputed, controversial, or doubtful matter **5. DISCERNMENT OR GOOD SENSE** the ability to form sound opinions and make sensible decisions or reliable guesses ○ *someone with shrewd commercial judgment* **6. OPINION** an opinion formed or given after consideration ○ *a snap judgment* **7. ESTIMATE BASED ON OBSERVATION** an estimate of something such as speed or distance, made with the help of the eye or some other sense **8. JUDGING OF SOMETHING** the judging of a case or a contest **9. DIVINE PUNISHMENT** a misfortune regarded as a divine punishment for folly or sin (*archaic or humorous*) ○ *defeat regarded as a judgment from God for the leader's pride* **10.** LOGIC **ACT OF MAKING A STATEMENT** the mental act of making or understanding a positive or negative proposition about something, e.g., in "a chihuahua is a dog" or "a lobster is not an insect" [13thC. From Old French *jugement*, from *jugier* "to judge" (see JUDGE).]

Judg·ment *n.* **1. GOD'S JUDGMENT ON AN INDIVIDUAL** in Roman Catholic belief, God's decision at the instant of somebody's death on whether the soul is to be saved or damned **2. GOD'S JUDGMENT ON HUMANITY** in Jewish, Islamic, and other Christian traditions, God's final judgment of humankind (**the Last Judgment**), which is to take place at the end of the world

judg·men·tal /jujméntʼl/ *adj.* tending to judge or criticize the conduct of other people —**judg·men·tal·ly** *adv.*

Judg·ment Day *n.* in Jewish, Christian, and Islamic belief, the day at the end of the world when God delivers his final judgment on humankind

ju·di·ca·ble /jōōdikəb'l/ *adj.* capable of being or liable to be tried in a court of law [Mid-17thC. From late Latin *judicabilis*, from *judicare* (see JUDICATURE).]

ju·di·ca·tor /jōōdi kàytər/ *n.* somebody who judges or who acts as a judge (*formal*) [Mid-18thC. Via late Latin from Latin *judicare* (see JUDICATURE).]

ju·di·ca·to·ry /jōōdikətàwree/ *adj.* **ju·di·ca·to·ry, ju·di·ca·to·rial** LAW **RELATING TO A LEGAL SYSTEM** relating to a legal system, or to judges or judgment ■ *n.* (*plural* **-ries**) LAW **LEGAL SYSTEM** a system of administering justice (*formal*) [Late 16thC. From, ultimately, Latin *judicare* (see JUDICATURE).]

ju·di·ca·ture /jōōdikəchoor/ *n.* **1. ADMINISTERING OF JUSTICE** the administration or dispensation of justice **2. JUDGE'S OFFICE** the power or office of a judge, or a judge's tenure of office **3. JUDGE'S AREA OF AUTHORITY** the area of authority of a judge or a court of law **4. BODY OF JUDGES** a body of judges or of people holding judicial power **5. SYSTEM OF LAW COURTS** a law court, or a system of law courts [Mid-16thC. Via medieval Latin *judicatura* from, ultimately, Latin *judicare* "to judge," from *judex* (see JUDGE).]

ju·di·cial /joo dísh'l/ *adj.* **1. RELATING TO JUDGES** relating or belonging to a body of judges or to the system that administers justice **2. RELATING TO COURT JUDGMENTS** relating to judges in performance of their duties, or to judgment in a court of law **3. ENFORCED BY A LAW COURT** enforced or sanctioned by a court of law **4. APPROPRIATE TO JUDGES** appropriate to a judge or expected of a judge [14thC. From Latin *judicialis*, from *judicium* "legal proceedings," from *judex* (see JUDGE).] —**ju·di·cial·ly** *adv.*

ju·di·cial ac·tiv·ism *n.* the doctrine that the judicial branch, especially the federal courts, may interpret the Constitution by deviating from legal precedent as a means of effecting legal and social change

ju·di·cial re·view *n.* **1. RE-EXAMINATION BY JUDGES** a reassessment or re-examination by judges of a decision or proceeding by a lower court or a government department **2. CONSTITUTIONAL FACILITY FOR REVIEWING LEGISLATION** a constitutional right of the court system in some countries to review and cancel government legislation that is held to have been passed illegally

ju·di·cial sep·a·ra·tion *n.* = **legal separation**

ju·di·ci·ar·y /joo díshee èree/ *n.* (*plural* **-ies**) **1. GOVERNMENT BRANCH DISPENSING JUSTICE** the branch of a country's central administration that is concerned with dispensing justice **2. COURT SYSTEM** a country's system of law courts **3. JUDGES IN GENERAL** a country's body of judges ■ *adj.* **RELATING TO JUDGES** relating to courts, judges, and judgment [15thC. From Latin *judiciarius*, from *judicium* (see JUDICIAL).]

ju·di·cious /joo díshəss/ *adj.* showing wisdom, good sense, or discretion, often with the underlying aim of avoiding trouble or waste ○ *a little judicious pruning* [Late 16thC. Via French *judicieux* from Latin *judicium* (see JUDICIAL).] —**ju·di·cious·ly** *adv.* —**ju·di·cious·ness** *n.*

Ju·dith /jōōdəth/ *n.* **1. HEROINE IN THE BIBLE** in the Bible, a Jewish woman who saved the city of Bethulia by beheading the general Holofernes **2. BOOK OF THE BIBLE** a book in the Roman Catholic version of the Bible and the Protestant Apocrypha that tells the story of Judith's heroism in saving her people. See table at **Bible**

Barnaby's

Judo

ju·do /jōōdō/ *n.* a Japanese martial art in which opponents use balance and body weight, with minimal physical effort, to throw or pin each other or hold each other in a lock. Judo was developed from jujitsu, a samurai art, by Jigoro Kano (1860–1938). [Late 19thC. From Japanese, literally "gentle way."] —**ju·do·ist** *n.*

ju·do·gi /jōōdo gée/ *n.* the costume worn by participants in judo, made of thick white cotton and consisting of a loose jacket secured by a belt and loose pants. The color of belt indicates the participant's grade, from the white belt worn by a beginner through various colors to black belt. [Mid-20thC. From Japanese.]

ju·do·ka /jōōdō kə/ (*plural* **-kas** *or* **-ka**) *n.* somebody who practices the art of judo or who is an expert in it [Mid-20thC. From Japanese.]

Ju·dy /jōōdee/ *n.* the wife of Punch in a traditional Punch-and-Judy puppet show

jug /jug/ *n.* **1. LARGE LIQUID-CONTAINER** a large container for liquids, typically of earthenware or glass, with a handle and a narrow mouth usually closed with a cork **2. LIQUID CONTAINED IN A JUG** the quantity of liquid held in a jug **3. PRISON** prison or jail (*humorous*) **4. OFFENSIVE TERM** an offensive term for a woman's breast (*slang*) (*considered offensive by many people*) ■ *vt.* (**jugged, jug·ging, jugs**) **STEW IN AN EARTHENWARE POT** to stew meat in a deep earthenware pot [15thC. Origin uncertain: perhaps from *Jug*, an old diminutive of the name *Joan*, sometimes given as a nickname to a girl thought not good-looking.]

ju·gate /júg gayt, júggət/ *adj.* **1.** BOT **WITH PAIRED LEAFLETS** used to describe leaves that consist of paired leaflets attached to a single leaf stalk **2.** COINS **WITH OVERLAPPING PROFILES** used to describe heads or busts on coins that are superimposed in profile one on another [Late 19thC. From Latin *jugatus*, past participle of *jugare* "to join together."]

jug band *n.* a blues or jazz band featuring jugs as instruments, played by blowing across their rims

Ju·gend·stil /yōōgənd shtéel/ *n.* the equivalent in Germany and Austria of art nouveau, a style of design that influenced all the visual arts in Europe during the late 19th and early 20th centuries. It is characterized by curvilinearity and the stylization of forms. [Early 20thC. From German, formed from *Jugend* "youth" (the name of a magazine) + *Stil* "style."]

jug·ger·naut /júggər nàwt/ *n.* **1.** CRUSHING FORCE a force that is relentlessly destructive, crushing, and insensitive **2.** *U.K.* HUGE TRUCK a very large long truck for transporting goods in bulk [Mid-19thC. From JUGGERNAUT.]

WORD KEY: ORIGIN

It used to be said, apocryphally, that worshipers of Krishna threw themselves under the wheels of the ***Juggernaut*** wagon in an access of religious ecstasy, so ***juggernaut*** came to be used metaphorically in English for an "irresistible crushing force." The pejorative British application to large trucks did not become firmly established until the late 1960s.

Jug·ger·naut /júggər nawt/ *n.* a form of the Hindu god Krishna. A statue of Juggernaut is pulled through the Indian town of Puri every year on a huge chariot during the festival of Rathayatra. [Mid-17thC. From Sanskrit *Jagannātha*, literally "protector of the world."]

jug·gle /júgg'l/ (**-gled, -gling, -gles**) *v.* **1.** *vti.* KEEP SEVERAL OBJECTS IN THE AIR to keep several objects in motion in the air at the same time by throwing them and catching them in quick succession **2.** *vt.* HAVE DIFFICULTY HOLDING SOMETHING to keep adjusting your grip or stance in order to balance objects being held ○ *I was juggling coffee and a plate of sandwiches in one hand.* **3.** *vt.* FIT INTO A SCHEDULE to try to make something fit into a satisfactory pattern or schedule by careful arranging ○ *parents juggling careers and family life* **4.** *vt.* REARRANGE DATA to manipulate data in order to deceive ○ *juggling the company's books* [14thC. Back-formation from JUGGLER.] —**jug·gler·y** *n.*

Corbis/Hulton-Deutsch Collection

Juggler

jug·gler /júgglər, júgg'lər/ *n.* somebody who can juggle, especially an entertainer who juggles for a living [Pre-12thC. Via Old French *jogler* from Latin *joculator* "jester," from *jocus* (see JOKE).]

jug·u·lar /júggyələr/ *n.* ANAT = **jugular vein** ■ *adj.* **1.** ANAT RELATING TO THE NECK relating to or situated close to the neck or throat **2.** ZOOL WITH PELVIC FINS FURTHER FORWARD used to describe a fish that has pelvic fins in front of the pectoral fins [Late 16thC. From late Latin *jugularis*, from Latin *jugulum* "collarbone, throat," from *jugum* (see YOKE).] ◇ **go for the jugular** to make an attack that is intended to be highly destructive and conclusive (*informal*)

jug·u·lar vein *n.* any one of four pairs of veins in the neck that drain blood from the head. A larger internal vein is flanked by an external vein on either side of the neck.

ju·gum /jóogəm/ *n.* **1.** INSECTS PART OF AN INSECT'S FOREWING a lobe that sticks out from the base of the forewing of some insects in order to couple it with the hindwing during flight **2.** BOT PAIR OF LEAFLETS a pair of opposed leaflets in a compound leaf [Mid-19thC. From Latin (see YOKE).]

jug wine *n.* a modest, inexpensive wine packaged and sold in a large bottle

juice /jooss/ *n.* **1.** LIQUID FROM FRUIT OR VEGETABLES the extractable liquid that is contained in fruit or vegetables, or a drink made from this liquid ○ *lemon juice* **2.** LIQUID FROM COOKING MEAT the liquid that comes from a piece of meat when it is roasted or otherwise cooked **3.** POWER electric power (*informal*) **4.** BODILY FLUID a natural fluid or secretion of the body **5.** LIQUID EXTRACT any liquid extract or essence, especially from biological material ○ *Pure penicillin was isolated from mold juice.* **6.** MONEY OR INFLUENCE money or influence gained through or utilized in the service of corrupt or criminal activities (*slang*) **7.** ALCOHOL alcoholic drink (*slang*) **8.** LOAN OR INTEREST money lent at an extortionate rate of interest, or the interest extorted (*slang*) ■ *vt.* (**juiced, juic·ing, juic·es**) EXTRACT JUICE FROM to extract the juice from a fruit or vegetable [13thC. Via French *jus* from Latin, "broth, sauce, vegetable juice."] ◇ **stew in your own juice** *or* **juices** to have to suffer the consequences of your actions without any help from others

juice up *vt.* to make something or somebody more lively, exciting, or interesting (*slang*) ○ *juice the party up by bringing in a live band*

juice·head /jóoss hèd/ *n.* a heavy drinker or an alcoholic (*slang*)

juic·er /jóossər/ *n.* **1.** GADGET TO EXTRACT JUICE a kitchen appliance, usually electrically powered, for extracting the juice from fruit or vegetables **2.** ALCOHOLIC an alcoholic or habitual drunkard (*slang*)

juic·y /jóossee/ (**-i·er, -i·est**) *adj.* **1.** SUCCULENT containing a lot of juice **2.** PROVIDING INTEREST repaying effort by providing plenty of stimulation and food for thought ○ *I like getting my teeth into a nice juicy problem.* **3.** TITILLATING containing scenes or details that evoke interest because of their sensational nature (*informal*) **4.** LUCRATIVE extremely profitable or productive (*informal*) —**juic·i·ly** *adv.* —**juic·i·ness** *n.*

ju·jit·su /joo jítsoo/, **jiu·jit·su** *n.* a Japanese system of unarmed fighting devised by the samurai, or the martial art based on it. Judo, aikido, and karate are all developments of jujitsu. [Late 19thC. From Japanese *jūjutsu*, literally "gentle skill."]

ju·ju /jóojoo/ *n.* **1.** OBJECT WITH SUPPOSED MAGICAL POWERS an object revered among some West African peoples for the magical powers that it is thought to possess **2.** SUPPOSED MAGIC POWER OF A JUJU the magical or supernatural power associated with a juju **3.** SPELL EFFECTED BY A JUJU a spell put on something or somebody by means of a juju [Early 17thC. From Hausa, of uncertain origin: probably from French *joujou* "plaything," from *jouer* "to play," from Latin *jocari*.] —**ju·ju·ism** *n.*

ju·jube /jóojoob/ *n.* **1.** TREE WITH RED FRUITS a tree belonging to the buckthorn family that has small yellow flowers and plum-shaped dark red edible fruits. It has been cultivated throughout Asia since ancient times. Latin name: *Ziziphus jujuba.* **2.** FRUIT OF THE JUJUBE TREE the plum-shaped fruit of the jujube tree, which is sometimes dried like a date **3.** CHEWY CANDY a chewy, usually fruit-flavored, candy made of gum or gelatin [14thC. Directly or via French from medieval Latin *jujuba* from, ultimately, Greek *ziziphos*.]

juke /jook/ *vti.* (**juked, juk·ing, jukes**) FAKE to move deceptively so as to induce an opponent to move in a way that brings about an advantage (*slang*) ■ *n.* JUKEBOX a jukebox (*dated slang*) [Mid-20thC. Origin uncertain: probably from Gullah, literally "disorderly, wicked," of West African origin.]

juke·box (*plural* **-box·es**) *n.* a coin-operated machine that automatically plays selected records or compact discs

juke joint *n.* a roadhouse where music is played on a jukebox for dancing (*informal*)

Jul. *abbr.* July

ju·lep /jóoləp/ *n.* = **mint julep** [14thC. Via Old French or medieval Latin from, ultimately, Persian *gulāb* "rosewater."]

Jul·ian /jóolyən/ *adj.* **1.** OF JULIUS CAESAR relating to or typical of Julius Caesar **2.** OF THE JULIAN CALENDAR relating to or reckoned according to the Julian calendar

Jul·ian cal·en·dar *n.* the twelve-month solar calendar introduced by Julius Caesar in 46 B.C., consisting of 365 days, with an extra day every four years. It was replaced by the Gregorian calendar in 1582. ◊ **Gregorian calendar**

Jul·ian date *n.* COMPUT in computer programming, a date expressed as the number of days since January 1 of the current year

ju·li·enne /jóolee èn, zhóolee èn/ *adj.* CUT THINLY used to describe food, usually vegetables, cut into long thin matchstick strips ■ *n.* CLEAR SOUP WITH VEGETABLE STRIPS a clear soup containing vegetables cut into thin matchstick strips ■ *vt.* (**-enned, -en·ning, -ennes**) CUT INTO THIN STRIPS to cut vegetables into thin matchstick strips [Early 18thC. From French, from the first name *Jules* or *Julien*.]

Ju·li·et /jóoleeət/ *n.* **1.** ASTRON SMALL INNER MOON OF URANUS a small inner natural satellite of Uranus, discovered in 1986 by the spacecraft Voyager 2. It is 52 mi./84 km in diameter. **2.** COMMUNICATION CODE FOR J a code word for the letter "J," used in international radio communications

Ju·li·et cap *n.* a round close-fitting crocheted net cap for women, sometimes set with pearls. It was fashionable in the 1920s, 1930s, and 1950s for brides and bridesmaids. [Early 20thC. From the heroine of Shakespeare's *Romeo and Juliet*.]

Jul·lun·dur /júlləndər/ city in northwestern India, a major industrial center. Population: 519,530 (1991).

Ju·ly /joo lī/ (*plural* **-lies**) *n.* the seventh month of the year in the Gregorian calendar, made up of 31 days [12thC. Via *julie* from Latin *Julius* (referring to Julius CAESAR, who was born in July).]

Ju·ma·da /jŏomaadaa/ *n.* in the Muslim calendar, either the fifth or the sixth lunar month in the year [Late 18thC. From Arabic *jumādā*, from *jamada* "to freeze."]

ju·mar /jóomər/ *n.* ROPE CLIP a clip or clamp used in rock climbing or ice climbing that runs freely up a slack rope but tightens around the rope in response to weight applied from below ■ *vi.* (**-mared, -mar·ing, -mars**) CLIMB USING JUMARS to climb using jumar clamps [Mid-20thC. Origin unknown.]

jum·ble /júmb'l/ *vti.* (**-bled, -bling, -bles**) **1.** PUT THINGS OUT OF ORDER to mix things together indiscriminately so that they are no longer neat or ordered **2.** MIX THINGS UP MENTALLY to mix things up in the mind ■ *n.* MUDDLED MASS an untidy or disorganized mass of objects, images, or ideas ○ *His thoughts were all in a jumble.* [Early 16thC. Origin uncertain: perhaps thought to suggest the action.]

jum·ble sale *n. U.K.* = **rummage sale**

jum·bo /júmbō/ *n.* **1.** LARGE THING something or somebody that is extra large (*often used before a noun*) ○ *a jumbo helping* **2.** AIR = **jumbo jet** [Early 19thC. From the name of a very large elephant at London Zoo, sold in 1882 to Barnum and Bailey's circus. Perhaps from MUMBO-JUMBO.]

jum·bo jet *n.* a large wide-bodied commercial aircraft capable of carrying several hundred passengers

Jum·na /júmnə/ river in northern India flowing south into the Ganges River at Allahabad. Length: 95 mi./153 km.

jump /jump/ *v.* (**jumped, jump·ing, jumps**) **1.** *vi.* LEAVE A SURFACE WITH BOTH FEET to bend the knees and push the whole body quickly up off a surface or the ground **2.** *vt.* GET OVER to pass from one side of something to the other by jumping ○ *jump the fence* **3.** *vti.* SPORTS JUMP AS A SPORTING SKILL in various sports such as riding and skiing, to perform a movement in which the whole body leaves the ground ○ *Make sure you have your skis parallel before you attempt to jump.* **4.** *vi.* MOVE QUICKLY to move quickly in a particular direction ○ *Jump in and I'll give you a lift home.* **5.** *vi.* OBEY IMMEDIATELY to carry out orders immediately (*informal*) ○ *When she speaks, you jump.* **6.** *vi.* RISE SUDDENLY to rise or increase suddenly by a large amount ○ *The Nikkei Index jumped 35 points.* **7.** *vt.* AMBUSH to ambush somebody by attacking unexpectedly (*informal*) ○ *The guy jumped me.* **8.** *vi.* AIR MAKE A PARACHUTE DESCENT to make a descent by parachute from an aircraft **9.** *vi.* MOVE JERKILY to move jerkily, in contrast to progressing smoothly or keeping still ○ *Interference was making the picture jump.* **10.** *vi.* START IN SURPRISE to give a start of surprise or fright ○ *The noise made me jump.* **11.** *vti.* RAIL LEAVE THE TRACK to come off the track accidentally (*refers to trains*) **12.** *vt.* START BEFORE PERMITTED to start moving before a red light changes green or a starter's gun fires (*informal*) **13.** *vt.* BOARD ILLEGALLY to board a train surreptitiously with the intention of traveling on it without paying (*informal*) **14.** *vi.* MAKE A MENTAL LEAP to make an illogical mental leap ○ *His mind keeps jumping from one thing to another.* **15.** *vt.* VIOLATE AN ENGAGEMENT BY LEAVING to abscond or desert in violation of an engagement, contract, or undertaking **16.** *vti.* OMIT to omit the intervening parts of something, especially passages of a text, sometimes inadvertently **17.** *vt.* USURP OWNERSHIP to usurp ownership of a piece of land, especially a mining claim, on the grounds that the owner has abandoned it or not fulfilled the conditions of ownership **18.** *vt.* BOARD GAMES PASS A PIECE OVER AN OPPONENT'S PIECE in checkers, to capture an opponent's playing piece by passing a piece over it into an empty square **19.** *vt.* OFFENSIVE TERM an offensive term meaning to have sexual intercourse with a woman (*offensive slang*) **20.** *vti.* BRIDGE RAISE A BID to raise a partner's bid to indicate a strong hand **21.** *vt.* **HELP TO JUMP** to support or lift somebody who is jumping over something or down from something (*archaic*) ○ *"In all their walks he had had to jump her from the stiles."* (Jane Austen, *Persuasion*; 1818) ■ *n.* **1. JUMPING MOVEMENT** a jumping movement or the distance jumped ○ *a winning jump of 26 feet* **2.** SPORTS **OBSTACLE OR APPARATUS USED IN JUMPING** a specially constructed obstacle or other piece of apparatus for use in competitive jumping, e.g., a fence in steeplechasing or a platform from which skiers take off **3. LEAP OF A PARTICULAR DISTANCE IN SPORTS** in field events, a leap of a particular distance or height, or the action of attempting or completing such a leap **4. SUDDEN RISE** a sudden steep rise or increase in an amount ○ *a jump in property prices* **5. START OF SURPRISE** an involuntary movement made when startled **6. SUDDEN TRANSITION** a sudden transition or change of direction, representing a break in continuity or logical progression **7. PARACHUTE DESCENT** a descent by parachute from an aircraft **8.** BRIDGE = **jump bid 9.** BOARD GAMES **JUMP OVER AN OPPONENT'S PIECE** in checkers, the move of jumping an opponent's piece and capturing it **10.** MATH **DISCONTINUOUS NUMERIC INCREASE** a point at which a function or a curve undergoes a sudden or major transition [Early 16thC. Origin uncertain: perhaps an imitation of the sound of jumping feet hitting the ground, suggested by *bump* and *thump*.] —**jump·a·ble** *adj.* ◇ **jump to it** to hurry up and carry out orders or instructions (*informal*)

jump at *vt.* to accept a chance or opportunity eagerly ○ *would jump at the chance*

jump on *vt.* to make a sudden physical or verbal attack on somebody (*informal*) ○ *jumped on the students for missing easy questions*

jump up *vi.* to get to your feet immediately

jump ball *n.* a restarting of play in a basketball game, in which the referee throws the ball up high between two opponents who each try to tip it toward a team member

jump bid *n.* in bridge, a bid of one more than is necessary to raise the existing bid

jump boot *n.* a paratrooper's boot

jump cut *n.* in movies and television, a sudden abrupt change from one sequence to another

jump·er[1] /júmpər/ *n.* **1. SLEEVELESS OUTER DRESS** a sleeveless dress designed for wearing over a blouse or sweater ○ *She was wearing a plaid jumper with a long-sleeved white blouse.* **2.** *U.K.* = **sweater** [Mid-17thC. Origin uncertain: probably from "jump," an alteration of *jupe*, a man's short coat, worn in the 17th and 18th centuries.]

jump·er[2] /júmpər/ *n.* **1. PERSON OR ANIMAL THAT JUMPS** a person or animal that jumps or is trained to jump competitively **2.** BASKETBALL = **jump shot** (*informal*) **3.** ELEC **WIRE FOR MAKING A CONNECTION** a short length of wire for making an electrical connection or for cutting out part of a circuit

jump·er ca·bles *npl.* a pair of electric cables used to start the engine of a vehicle that has a dead battery by connection to a live battery

jump·ers /júmpərz/ *npl.* a child's one-piece playsuit made of pants and a bibbed top or bodice

jump·ing bean *n.* a seed of some Mexican shrubs when it contains the larva of a small moth. The larva feeds on the seed pulp, making the seed move jerkily. The movements intensify if the seed is warmed, e.g., in the palm of the hand.

jump·ing gene *n.* a genetic element that can move from place to place within the chromosomes of an organism. These elements occur in bacteria, plants, and animals and their insertion may inactivate functional genes, causing a type of mutation.

jump·ing jack *n.* **1. WARMUP EXERCISE** a warmup exercise in which the legs are flung apart while the hands are clapped or swung above the head **2. PUPPET** a flat wooden or cardboard puppet whose limbs are worked by a string or a sliding stick

jump·ing mouse *n.* a rodent that looks like a mouse but has long hind legs and a long tail. It is found in Northern temperate regions. Family: Zapodidae.

jump·ing-off place, **jump·ing-off point** *n.* a very remote place, especially a point at the edge of civilization beyond which lies the wilderness

jump·ing-off point *n.* **1. BASE FOR A TRIP** a place from which to begin a trip **2. BASIS FOR BEGINNING** a basis on which to begin an enterprise or a discussion **3.** = **jumping-off place**

jump·ing plant louse *n.* a small insect that is a weak flier but has enlarged hind legs for jumping. Found worldwide, it feeds on the sap of plants. Family: Psyllidae.

jump·ing spi·der *n.* a spider found mostly in the tropics that fixes on its prey using an enlarged central pair of eyes, then pounces by rapidly extending its legs. The jumping mechanism depends on sudden elevation in the spider's internal body pressure, and they can achieve distances of several inches. Family: Salticidae.

jump jet *n.* a jet aircraft that takes off and lands vertically

jump leads *npl. U.K.* = **jumper cables**

jump·mas·ter *n.* somebody who is in charge of military paratroopers or civilian parachutists and determines when they will jump from an aircraft

jump-off *n.* **1. START** the start of something such as a race or a military attack **2.** SHOWJUMPING **DECIDING ROUND OF A JUMPING CONTEST** a final extra round of a jumping competition, e.g., one in horseback riding in which all the riders who have had clear rounds compete against the clock —**jump off** *vi.*

jump pass *n.* a pass that one basketball player makes to another while in mid-jump

jump rope *n.* a rope that is swung around and jumped over in children's games and adult exercises

jump seat *n.* a folding seat between the front and back seats of a limousine or similarly large vehicle, or a seat like this for temporary use in an aircraft or train

jump shot *n.* a basketball shot made with one or both hands by a player who is at the highest point of a jump —**jump shoot·er** *n.*

jump-start *vt.* (**jump-start·ed, jump-start·ing, jump-starts**) **START A VEHICLE USING JUMPER CABLES** to start a motor vehicle by attaching it to an external battery using jumper cables ■ *n.* **ACTION OF JUMP-STARTING A VEHICLE** a jump-starting of a motor vehicle

jump·suit /júmp soot/, **jump suit** *n.* **1. WOMAN'S ONE-PIECE SUIT** a woman's casual one-piece suit combining top and pants **2. PARACHUTIST'S GARMENT** a protective zippered one-piece suit combining long pants and jacket, worn by a parachutist when jumping

jump·y /júmpee/ (**-i·er, -i·est**) *adj.* **1. JITTERY** very nervous or anxious **2. MOVING ERRATICALLY** moving jerkily or erratically —**jump·i·ly** *adv.* —**jump·i·ness** *n.*

jun. *abbr.* junior

Jun. *abbr.* June

jun·co /júngkō/ (*plural* **-cos**) *n.* a small North American finch with grayish plumage, a pink bill, and white outer tail feathers. Genus: *Junco.* [Early 18thC. Via Spanish from Latin *juncus* "rush."]

junc·tion /júngkshən/ *n.* **1. PLACE WHERE THINGS JOIN** a place where two or more objects, e.g., roads or railroad routes, join, meet, or cross **2.** *U.K.* TRANSP = **intersection 3.** ELEC ENG **ELECTRICAL CONNECTION** a connection between electrical wires or cables **4.** PHYS **LAYER BETWEEN METALS** a layer of metal separating two metals with different properties and serving as a contact between them, especially in a thermocouple **5.** ELECTRON ENG **SEMICONDUCTOR CONTACT** a point in a semiconductor device at which regions with different electrical properties come into contact with each other **6. STATE OR ACT OF JOINING** the joining of things or their joined state [Early 18thC. From the Latin stem *junction-*, from *jungere* "to join" (source of English *join* and *junta*).] —**junc·tion·al** *adj.*

junc·tion box *n.* an enclosed and protected box inside which electrical circuits are interconnected or branched for distribution

Junc·tion Cit·y /jùngksh'n-/ city in north central Kansas, at the junction of the Republican and Smoky Hill rivers. Population: 17,659 (1996).

junc·ture /júngkshər/ *n.* **1. POINT IN TIME** a point in time, especially an important or critical one **2. JOINING PLACE** a place where two or more things join (*formal*) **3. JOINING OF THINGS** the joining of one thing with another or their joined state (*formal*) **4.** LING **BREAK BETWEEN WORDS** the break between one spoken word and another or the pronunciation features that help a listener to recognize the break, distinguishing, e.g., between "gray day" and "grade A" [14thC. From Latin *junctura* "joint," from *jungere* "to join."]

June /joon/ *n.* the sixth month of the year in the Gregorian calendar, made up of thirty days [Pre-12thC. Via French *juin* from Latin *(mensis) junius* "(month) of Juno."]

Ju·neau /jŏŏnō/ capital of the state of Alaska and a port city on the Gastineau Channel, opposite Douglas Island. Population: 29,756 (1996).

June bee·tle *n.* = **June bug**

June·ber·ry /jŏŏn bèrree/ (*plural* **-ries**) *n.* = **serviceberry** *n.* **1, serviceberry** *n.* **2** [Mid-19thC. From the month when it blooms.]

June bug *n.* a large brown North American flying beetle that is seen in late spring and feeds on leaves. The larvae feed on roots. Subfamily: Melolonthinae.

Carl Gustav Jung

Jung /yŏŏng/, **Carl Gustav** (1875–1961) Swiss psychiatrist. He broadened Freud's interpretation of the unconscious, and introduced the concepts of introvert and extrovert types and the collective unconscious. —**Jung·i·an** *adj., n.*

Jung Chang /jŏŏng cháng/ (*b.* 1952) Chinese-born U.S. author of *Wild Swans* (1993), an account of her family's experience in communist China.

Jung·frau /yŏŏng fròw/ mountain in southern Switzerland. Height: 13,642 ft./4,158 m.

jun·gle /júng'l/ *n.* **1. TROPICAL FOREST** an area of tropical rainforest covered with vegetation so dense that it is largely impenetrable **2. THICKLY COVERED AREA** any area covered with dense vegetation **3. TANGLE** a tangled or confused mass **4. COMPLEX MATTER** a frustratingly or impenetrably complex system **5. HARSH PLACE** a harsh environment characterized by fierce competitiveness or struggle for survival **6. HOBO CAMP** a place where homeless people camp (*dated slang*) [Late 18thC. Via Hindi *jangal*, literally "wasteland," from Sanskrit *jāṅgala* "dry."]

jun·gle fe·ver *n.* a severe form of malaria common in tropical regions, especially Southeast Asia

jun·gle fowl *n.* any of various species of wild Asian birds related to the pheasant. Jungle fowl are thought to be the ancestors of the modern domestic fowl. Genus: *Gallus.*

jun·gle gym *n.* a framework of interlocking metal, wooden, or plastic bars on which children can climb [Originally a trademark]

jun·ior /jŏŏnyər/ *adj.* **1. RELATING TO YOUTH OR CHILDHOOD** relating to youth, childhood, or children **2. jun·ior, Ju·nior YOUNGER** younger in age, especially when referring to the younger of two family members, e.g., father and son, who share the same name **3. LOW IN RANK** of relatively low rank or with relatively little experience **4. SMALLER** smaller than the standard or expected size **5.** EDUC **OF THIRD-YEAR STUDENTS** relating to or involving students in the third year of high school or college **6.** *U.K.* EDUC **FOR CHILDREN BETWEEN 7 AND 11** relating to or involving schoolchildren between the ages of 7 and 11 ○ *junior school* ■ *n.* **1. YOUNGER PERSON** a person younger than another being referred to ○ *My sister is three years my junior.* **2. LOW-RANKING PERSON** somebody of relatively low rank or little experience **3. CHILD** a young person, especially somebody younger than a teenager **4. jun·ior, Jun·ior WAY OF ADDRESSING BOY** a form of address used for a boy or young man, affectionately to the son in a family or condescendingly to a stranger (*informal*) (*offensive in some contexts*) **5.** EDUC **THIRD-YEAR STUDENT** a student in the third year of high school or college **6.** *U.K.* EDUC **JUNIOR-SCHOOL STUDENT** a pupil in a junior school **7.** CLOTHES **CLOTHING SIZE** a range of clothing sizes for teenage girls and slender women [13thC. From Latin, "younger," formed from *juvenis* "young."]

jun·ior col·lege *n.* a college offering students a two-year course of study that either terminates in an associate degree or corresponds to the first two years at a four-year college

jun·ior high, jun·ior high school *n.* a school that is intermediate between elementary school and high school, embracing grades six or seven through eight or nine. School districts often replace junior high schools with middle schools when demographic factors increase the number of younger students. ◊ **middle school**

jun·ior mid·dle·weight *n.* **1. BOXING WEIGHT** in professional boxing, a weight class that is lighter than middleweight and heavier than welterweight, for boxers weighing between 147 and 154 lb./67 and 71 kg **2. BOXER** a boxer who fights at junior middleweight

jun·ior miss *n.* a girl or young woman in her teenage years (*dated*)

jun·ior var·si·ty *n.* a high-school or college sports team that competes at a level below varsity

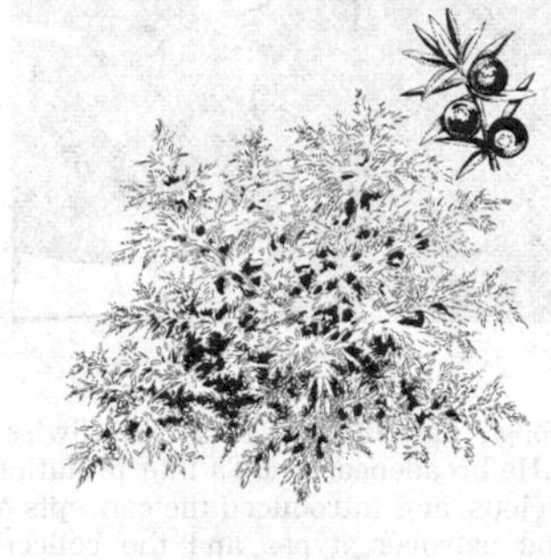

Juniper

ju·ni·per /jóonipər/ *n.* **1. EVERGREEN PLANT BEARING CONES RESEMBLING BERRIES** an evergreen tree or shrub with small purple cones resembling berries that yield juniper oil, used to flavor gin. Genus: *Juniperus.* **2. OIL FROM JUNIPER** the oil from juniper berries [14thC. From Latin *juniperus.*]

junk[1] /jungk/ *n.* **1. USED GOODS FOR SALE** secondhand goods offered for sale (*informal*) **2. RUBBISH** discarded things, or things regarded as worthless or causing clutter (*informal*) **3. CHEAP STUFF** cheap and poorly made goods (*informal*) **4. NONSENSE** meaningless or worthless talk (*informal*) **5. HEROIN** narcotics, especially heroin (*slang*) ■ *vt.* **(junked, junk·ing, junks) DISCARD** to get rid of something as useless (*informal*) [14thC. Origin uncertain: perhaps via Old French *jonc* "rush" from Latin *juncus.* Originally in the meaning "old rope"(perhaps from the use of rushes to make ropes).]

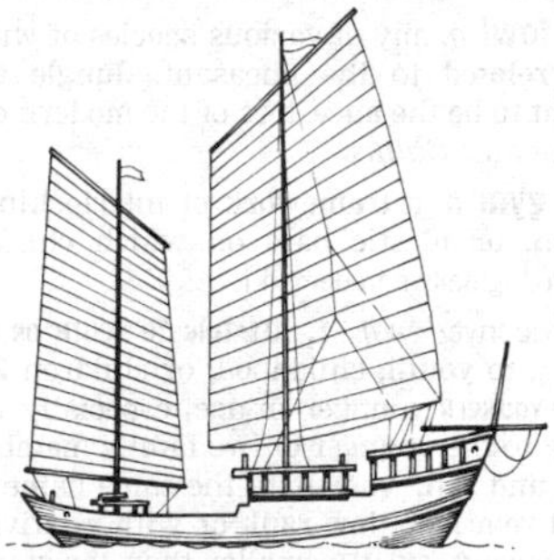

Junk

junk[2] /jungk/ *n.* a flat-bottomed sailing boat, popular in Chinese waters, that is high at the stern and has squarish sails, each supported on several battens [Mid-16thC. Via Portuguese *junco* or Dutch *jonk* from Malay *jong.*]

junk bond *n.* an investment bond that offers the possibility of a high return but at a high risk

junk·er /júngkər/ *n.* a vehicle that is so old and in such bad repair that it might as well be scrapped (*slang*)

Jun·ker /yóongkər/ *n.* **1. PRUSSIAN ARISTOCRAT** any of the aristocratic landowners in Prussia, who continued to exercise great political power well into the 20th century **2. OFFENSIVE TERM** an offensive term for a German army officer or official who is considered to be arrogant and dictorial (*offensive*) [Mid-16thC. From German *Junker,* literally "young lord."] —**Jun·ker·dom** *n.* —**Jun·ker·ism** *n.*

jun·ket /júngkət/ *n.* **1. EXPENSE-PAID TRIP** a trip taken by at somebody else's expense, especially one taken by a politician at public expense **2. AMUSING OCCASION** an outing, excursion, or party of any kind **3. FOOD SET MILK DESSERT** a dessert made from milk that has been set with rennet ■ *v.* **(-ket·ed, -ket·ing, -kets) 1.** *vti.* **HOLD PARTY** to hold a party or entertain somebody with a party **2.** *vi.* **HAVE EXPENSE-PAID TRIP** to go on an expense-paid trip, especially one paid for with public money [14thC. From French *jonquette,* from *jonc* "rush," from Latin *juncus.* From being made or served on rushes.] —**jun·ket·er** *n.*

junk food *n.* food that does not form part of a well-balanced diet, especially highly processed, high-fat snack items eaten in place of or in addition to regular meals

junk·ie /júngkee/, **junk·y** (*plural* **-ies**) *n.* **1. DRUG ADDICT** a drug addict, especially somebody addicted to heroin (*slang*) **2. ENTHUSIAST** somebody whose interest in or liking for something resembles an addiction (*informal*) ○ *a baseball junkie*

junk mail *n.* unsolicited mail, especially advertising material

junk·man /júngk man/ *n.* a dealer in objects of little value that others have discarded (*dated*)

junk shop *n.* **1. STORE SELLING USED GOODS** a store selling a variety of secondhand goods **2. LOW-QUALITY ANTIQUE STORE** a second-rate antique store

junk·y /júngkee/ *adj.* **(-i·er, -i·est) WORTHLESS** of very low quality or very little value ■ *n.* = **junkie**

junk·yard /júngk yaard/ *adj.* **AGGRESSIVE** aggressive and fearsome (*slang*) ○ *a junkyard litigator* ■ *n.* **PLACE WHERE JUNK COLLECTED** a place where junk is collected before being sold or processed

junk·yard dog *n.* a particularly vicious and combative animal, especially a chained dog (*slang*)

Ju·no /jóon ō/ (*plural* **-nos**) *n.* **1.** MYTHOL **ROMAN GODDESS** in Roman mythology, the queen of the gods and wife of Jupiter. Greek equivalent **Hera 2. QUEENLY WOMAN** a woman of queenly bearing and imposing beauty —**Ju·no·esque** /jòonō ésk/ *adj.*

jun·ta /hóontə/ (*plural* **-tas**) *n.* **1.** POL **NEW RULERS AFTER COUP** a group of military officers who have taken control of a country following a coup d'état (*takes a singular or plural verb*) **2. SECRET GROUP** a small group of people, especially one secretly assembled for a common goal (*takes a singular or plural verb*) **3.** POL **LATIN AMERICAN GOVERNMENT BODY** in some parts of Central and South America, a council or other legislative body within the government [Early 17thC. Via Spanish or Portuguese from, ultimately, Latin *jungere* "to join."]

jun·to /júntō/ *n.* = **junta** *n.* 2 [Early 17thC. Alteration of JUNTA.]

Ju·pi·ter /jóopitər/ *n.* **1.** MYTHOL **ROMAN GOD** in Roman mythology, the king of the gods. Greek equivalent **Zeus 2.** ASTRON **LARGEST PLANET** the largest planet in the solar system, fifth in order from the sun [12thC. From Latin, from the stem *Jov-* "Jove" + *pater* "father."]

Ju·ra /zhóorə/ department in east central France, in the province of Franche-Comté. Area: 1,951 sq. mi./5,053 sq. km.

ju·ral /jóorəl/ *adj.* **1.** LAW **RELATING TO LAW** relating to law or the administration of justice **2. RELATING TO RIGHTS** relating to rights or obligations (*formal*) [Mid-17thC. Formed from the Latin stem *jur-* "law."] —**ju·ral·ly** *adv.*

Ju·ra Moun·tains mountain range situated on the border between France and Switzerland. The highest point is Crêt de la Neige, 5,636 ft./1,718 m. Length: 200 mi./320 km.

Ju·ras·sic /joo rássik/ *n.* GEOL the period of geologic time during which dinosaurs flourished and birds and mammals first appeared, extending from 210 million years to 140 million years ago. It is the middle period of the Mesozoic era. [Mid-19thC. From French *Jurrassique,* from *Jura* "Jura."] —**Ju·ras·sic** *adj.*

ju·rat /jóoràt/ *n.* **1. AFFIDAVIT STATEMENT** a closing statement on an affidavit, giving details of the parties to it, the witnesses, and the place and time of signing **2. MAGISTRATE** a magistrate in France or the Channel Islands [15thC. From medieval Latin *juratus,* literally "sworn man," from *jurare* (see JURY).]

ju·rid·i·cal /joorídik'l/, **ju·rid·ic** /-dik/ *adj.* relating to judges, to the administration of the law, or to law in general —**ju·rid·i·cal·ly** *adv.*

ju·rid·i·cal days *npl.* days on which law courts are in session

ju·ris·con·sult /jòoriskónsùlt, -kənsúlt/ *n.* an expert in law who gives advice on legal matters, especially in relation to public or international law [Early 17thC. From Latin *jurisconsultus,* literally "skilled in law."]

ju·ris·dic·tion /jòorisdíksh'n/ *n.* **1.** LAW **LEGAL AUTHORITY** the authority to enforce laws or pronounce legal judgments **2. RANGE OF LEGAL AUTHORITY** the area over which legal authority extends **3. AUTHORITY** power or authority generally [13thC. Via Old French *jurediction* from the Latin stem *jurisdiction-,* from *jus* "law" + *dictio* "saying" (source of English *diction*).] —**ju·ris·dic·tion·al** *adj.* —**ju·ris·dic·tion·al·ly** *adv.* —**ju·ris·dic·tive** *adj.*

jurisp. *abbr.* jurisprudence

ju·ris·pru·dence /jòorispróod'nss/ *n.* **1. THEORY OF LAW** the philosophy or science of law **2. LEGAL SYSTEM** a system of law or the body of laws applied in a particular country or state **3. BRANCH OF LAW** a branch of law or the law as it applies to a particular area of life —**ju·ris·pru·den·tial** /jòorisproodénsh'l/ *adj.* —**ju·ris·pru·den·tial·ly** *adv.*

ju·ris·pru·dent /joorispróod'nt/ *adj.* **LEGALLY EXPERT** knowledgeable in the science or philosophy of law ■ *n.* = **jurist** [Early 17thC. Via obsolete French from the late Latin stem *jurisprudent-,* from *jus* "law" + *prudens* "wise" (source of English *prudent*).]

ju·rist /jóorist/ *n.* an expert in the science or philosophy of law, especially a judge or legal scholar [15thC. Directly or via French from medieval Latin *jurista,* from *jus* "law, right."] —**ju·ris·tic** /jooristik/ *adj.* —**ju·ris·ti·cal** *adj.* —**ju·ris·ti·cal·ly** *adv.*

ju·ror /jóorər/ *n.* **1.** LAW **JURY MEMBER** a member of a jury, especially in a court of law **2. SOMEBODY TAKING OATH** somebody who has sworn an oath, e.g., an oath of allegiance (*formal or literary*) [14thC. Via Anglo-Norman *jurour* and Old French *jureor* from Latin *jurator,* from *jurare* (see JURY).]

ju·ry /jóoree/ (*plural* **-ries**) *n.* **1.** LAW **PEOPLE DECIDING LEGAL CASE** a group of people, usually twelve people, chosen to give a verdict on a legal case that is presented before them in a court of law **2. PEOPLE JUDGING COMPETITION** a group of people who judge a competition [14thC. Via Anglo-Norman and Old French *juree* "oath, inquest" from, ultimately, Latin *jurare* "to swear," from *jus* "law, right."]

ju·ry box *n.* the part of a court where the jury sits

ju·ry du·ty *n.* service as a member of a jury in a court of law. = **jury service**

ju·ry·man /jóorimən/ (*plural* **-men** /-mən/) *n.* a man who is on a jury in a court of law

ju·ry nul·li·fi·ca·tion *n.* the process whereby a jury in a criminal case effectively nullifies a law by acquitting a defendant regardless of the weight of evidence against him or her

ju·ry-rig **(ju·ry-rigged, ju·ry-rig·ging, ju·ry-rigs)** *vt.* to build something in a makeshift way or fit something out, especially a boat, with makeshift equipment [*jury* of uncertain origin: probably via Old French *ajurie* "aid" from Latin *adjutare* "to aid"]

ju·ry·wom·an /jóori wòomən/ (*plural* **-en** /jóori wímmin/) *n.* a woman who is on a jury in a court of law

jus gen·ti·um /yòoss géntee əm/ *n.* international law [From Latin, literally "law of nations"]

jus san·gui·nis /yooss sáng gwənəss/ *n.* the principle in law according to which children's citizenship is determined by the citizenship of their parents [From Latin, literally "right of blood"]

jus·sive /jússiv/ *adj.* GRAM = **imperative** [Mid-19thC. Formed from Latin *juss-,* the past participle stem of *jubere* "to command."]

jus so·li /yòoss sōlee/ *n.* the principle in law according to which children's citizenship is determined by the place of their birth [From Latin, literally "right of soil"]

just /just/ *adv.* **1. IN THE IMMEDIATE PAST** a very short time ago ○ *The train just left.* **2. AT THIS MOMENT** indicating that somebody will begin doing something, or something will start happening now (*used also with "about to" and "going to"*) ○ *I was just about to tell you.* **3. ONLY** only or merely the thing, amount, or situation mentioned ○ *This is just a warning.* **4. BARELY** by only a small degree or margin ○ *I arrived just in time.* **5. USED FOR EMPHASIS** used to emphasize a statement, usually in order to express an emotion ○ *It's just plain wrong.* **6. EXACTLY** precisely the thing, amount, or situation mentioned ○ *It's just what you need.* ■ *adj.* 1. FAIR AND IMPARTIAL acting with fairness and impartiality 2. MORALLY CORRECT done, pursued, or given in accordance with what is morally right 3. REASONABLE valid or reasonable [14thC. Via French *juste* from Latin *justus*, from *jus* "law, right."] —**just·ly** *adv.* —**just·ness** *n.* ◇ **just about** used to indicate that something is the case, but only by a very small degree or amount ◇ **just a moment** *or* **second** *or* **minute** used to ask someone to wait for a short time ◇ **just now** 1. a very short time ago 2. at this very moment ◇ **just so** 1. used to express agreement with or confirmation of a statement that has just been made 2. done or arranged precisely ○ *They wanted the room decorated just so.*

just-folks *adj.* friendly and informal or unpretentious (*informal*) ○ *has a just-folks attitude*

jus·tice /jústiss/ *n.* 1. FAIRNESS fairness or reasonableness, especially in the way people are treated or decisions are made 2. LAW APPLICATION OF LAW the legal system or the act of applying or upholding the law 3. LAW VALIDITY validity in law 4. GOOD REASON sound or good reason 5. JUDGE a judge, especially of a higher court [12thC. Via French from Latin *justitia*, from *justus* "JUST."] ◇ **bring somebody to justice** to arrest somebody to be tried in a court of law ◇ **do justice to somebody** *or* **something** 1. to deal with somebody or something fairly 2. to convey the true qualities, especially the merits, of somebody or something ◇ **do yourself justice** to display your own abilities fully or perform to your full potential (*often used in the negative*)

Jus·tice /jústiss/ village in northeast Illinois, southeast of Downers Grove, and a western suburb of Chicago. Population: 11,439 (1996).

jus·tice of the peace *n.* somebody, usually without legal training or qualifications, who is appointed to judge minor cases such as speeding violations, perform marriages, and administer oaths

jus·ti·ci·a·ble /jùstíshəb'l/ *adj.* 1. LIABLE FOR TRIAL able or required to be tried in a court of law 2. CAPABLE OF BEING SETTLED IN COURT able to be settled by applying the principles of law —**jus·ti·ci·a·bil·i·ty** /jùstìshə bíllətee/ *n.*

jus·ti·ci·ar·y /jùstíshee əree/ *adj.* relating to the administration of law

jus·ti·fi·a·ble /jústifì əb'l/ *adj.* capable of being shown as reasonable or merited according to accepted standards —**jus·ti·fi·a·bil·i·ty** /jùstifì əbíllətee/ *n.* —**jus·ti·fi·a·ble·ness** *n.* —**jus·ti·fi·a·bly** *adv.*

jus·ti·fi·a·ble hom·i·cide *n.* killing that is deemed to be lawful, especially because it is carried out in self-defense or as the only way to prevent a crime

jus·ti·fi·ca·tion /jùstifi káysh'n/ *n.* 1. SOMETHING THAT JUSTIFIES something, e.g., a reason or circumstance, that justifies an action or attitude 2. GIVING OF REASONS FOR SOMETHING the act of justifying something 3. PRINTING ALIGNMENT OF MARGINS adjustment of the lengths of spaces between and within words in text in order to make both left and right margins align 4. CHR CHRISTIAN DOCTRINE the Christian belief that people are absolved from all sin if they believe in Jesus Christ [14thC. Directly or via French from the late Latin stem *justification-*, from *justificare* (see JUSTIFY).]

jus·tif·i·ca·to·ry /ju stífikə tàwree/, **jus·ti·fi·ca·tive** /jústifi kàytiv/ *adj.* serving or acting to justify something [Late 16thC. From medieval Latin *justificatorius*, from late Latin *justificare* (see JUSTIFY).]

jus·ti·fy /jústi fì/ (**-fied, -fy·ing, -fies**) *vt.* 1. MAKE REASONABLE to serve as an acceptable reason or excuse for something (*often passive*) 2. GIVE SOMEBODY REASON to give somebody an acceptable reason for taking a particular action (*often passive*) 3. EXPLAIN to give a reason or explanation why something was done 4. PRINTING ALIGN MARGINS OF to adjust the lengths of spaces between and within words in text in order to make both the left and right margins align 5. CHR FREE FROM SIN to free somebody from sinfulness through faith in Jesus Christ or by the grace of Jesus Christ 6. LAW GIVE LEGAL REASON FOR to provide a good reason in law for something, especially for committing the offense that is the subject of a criminal charge [14thC. Via French *justifier* from Latin *justificare* "to act justly, justify," from Latin *justus* "JUST."]

just-in-time *n.* a manufacturing and stock-control system in which goods are produced and delivered as they are required. It is designed to eliminate waste and avoid the need for large inventories.

jut /jut/ *vti.* (**jut·ted, jut·ting, juts**) STICK OUT to stick out, or make something stick out, especially beyond the surface or edge of something ■ *n.* PROJECTING PART something that sticks out [Mid-16thC. Alteration of JET[1].] —**jut·ting** *adj.*

jute /joot/ *n.* 1. INDUST FIBER coarse fiber from the bark of an Asian tree that is used for making sacking and rope 2. PLANTS PLANT either of two Asian plants of the linden family that provide jute. Genus: *Corchorus.* [Mid-18thC. Via Bengali *jhuto* from Sanskrit *jūṭah* "matted hair."]

Jute /joot/ *n.* MEMBER OF GERMANIC PEOPLE a member of a Germanic people from around the Rhine estuary who invaded parts of southeastern England during the fifth century A.D. They settled in Kent and the Isle of Wight, where they soon became the dominant people. ◊ **Angle, Saxon** ■ *adj.* RELATING TO JUTES relating to or typical of the Jute people or their culture [Pre-12thC. From Latin *Jutae*, of Germanic origin.]

Jut·land /jút lənd/ peninsula in northern Europe, containing all of mainland Denmark. The base of the peninsula is part of Germany. Length: 210 mi./338 km.

ju·ve·nes·cent *adj.* (*literary*) 1. YOUTHFUL youthful or young-looking 2. BECOMING A CHILD growing out of infancy and into childhood [Early 19thC. From Latin *juvenescere* "to grow up."] —**ju·ve·nes·cence** *n.*

ju·ve·nile /jo͞ovə n'l/ *adj.* 1. YOUTHFUL young or youthful 2. RELATING TO YOUNG PEOPLE relating to, intended for, or suitable for young people ○ *a juvenile court* 3. IMMATURE immature or childish ○ *juvenile behavior* 4. BIOL NOT YET MATURE used to describe a plant or animal that has not yet reached maturity 5. BIRDS SEXUALLY IMMATURE used to describe a bird that has developed contour feathers but is not yet sexually mature 6. GEOL FROM WITHIN THE EARTH used to describe water or gas that has risen to the surface from within the Earth for the first time ■ *n.* 1. YOUNGSTER a young person 2. BIOL IMMATURE ANIMAL OR PLANT an animal or plant that has not yet reached maturity 3. THEATER ACTOR SUITED TO YOUTHFUL PARTS an actor who plays youthful roles 4. PUBL BOOK FOR CHILDREN a book intended to be read by young people [Early 17thC. From Latin *juvenilis*, from *juvenis* "young."] —**ju·ve·nile·ly** *adv.* —**ju·ve·nile·ness** *n.*

ju·ve·nile de·lin·quent *n.* a young person who habitually breaks the law, especially somebody repeatedly charged with vandalism or other antisocial behavior —**ju·ve·nile de·lin·quen·cy** *n.*

ju·ve·nile hor·mone *n.* a hormone present in insect larvae that regulates the form of the larva after each molt. The levels of it eventually fall to allow the larva to be transformed into the adult insect.

ju·ve·nil·i·a /jo͞ovənílee ə, jo͞ovənílyə/ *npl.* works produced in a writer's, artist's, or composer's youth, especially before a mature style has developed

ju·ve·nil·i·ty /jo͞ovə nílətee/ *n.* 1. JUVENILE QUALITY juvenile quality or state 2. IMMATURITY foolishly immature behavior 3. ACT OF IMMATURITY an act of foolishly immature behavior (*often used in the plural*)

jux·ta·pose /júkstəpṑz/ (**-posed, -pos·ing, -pos·es**) *vt.* to place two or more things together, especially in order to suggest a link between them or emphasize the contrast between them [Mid-19thC. From French *juxtaposer*, from Latin *juxta* "close" + French *poser* "POSE."] —**jux·ta·po·si·tion** /jùkstəpə zísh'n/ *n.* —**jux·ta·po·si·tion·al** *adj.*

JV *abbr.* 1. COMM joint venture 2. junior varsity

J.W.V. *n., abbr.* Jewish War Veterans

Jy *symbol.* Jansky

Jy·sai·tha /jáyssətə/ *n.* INDIAN RELIG in the Hindu calendar, the third month of the year, made up of 29 or 30 days and occurring at about the same time as May and June

Kk

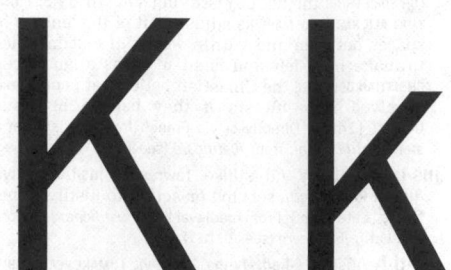

k[1] /kay/ (*plural* **k's**), **K** (*plural* **K's** *or* **Ks**) *n.* **1.** **11TH LETTER OF THE ENGLISH ALPHABET** the eleventh letter of the modern English alphabet **2.** **SPEECH SOUND CORRESPONDING TO LETTER "K"** the speech sound that corresponds to the letter "K" **3.** **LETTER "K" WRITTEN** a written representation of the letter "K"

k[2] *abbr.* **1.** karat **2.** kilo- **3.** knight **4.** knit **5.** SAILING knot

k[3] MATH symbol unit coordinate vector along the z-axis

K[1] *abbr.* **1.** COMPUT kilobyte **2.** kilometer (*informal*) **3.** EDUC kindergarten **4. K, K.** CARDS, CHESS king **5. K, K.** MUSIC Köchel (*preceding a number in Köchel's catalogue of Mozart's works*) **6.** knight **7.** one thousand **8.** FIN one thousand dollars **9.** BASEBALL strikeout

K[2] *symbol.* **1.** PHYS kaon **2.** PHYS kelvin **3.** PHYS kinetic energy **4.** CHEM ELEM potassium

K-12 *n.* the school system from kindergarten through twelfth grade ○ *a need for K-12 funding* [Shortening of KINDERGARTEN through twelfth grade]

K2 /kày tōō/ the second highest mountain in the world. It is situated in the Karakorum Range of the western Himalayas on the border between China and the disputed territory of Jammu and Kashmir. Height: 28,251 ft./8,611 m.

ka[1] /kaa/ *n.* in ancient Egypt, the soul of a dead person, said to be able to reside in a statue of that person after death [Late 19thC. From Ancient Egyptian.]

ka[2] *symbol.* cathode

Kaa·ba /kaábə/ *n.* a square building inside the great mosque in Mecca, containing a sacred stone (**Black Stone**) said to have been given by God. It is the most holy site in the Islamic religion. [Early 17thC. From Arabic, literally "the square house."]

ka·bab *n.* = **kebab**

kab·a·la *n.* = **cabala**

Ka·bar·di·an /kə baárdee ən, kə baárdyən/ *n.* **1.** PEOPLES **MEMBER OF A RUSSIAN PEOPLE** a member of a people who live in an area to the north of the Caucasus Mountains in southern European Russia **2.** LANG **LANGUAGE OF SOUTHERN RUSSIA** a language spoken in an area to the north of the Caucasus Mountains in southern European Russia. It belongs to the Abkhazo-Adyghean group of the Caucasian family of languages and is spoken by about 300, 000 people. [Late 19thC. From Russian *Kabarda*, a place name.] —**Ka·bar·di·an** *adj.*

kab·ba·lah *n.* = **cabala**

kab·i·nett /kàbi nét/, **Kab·i·nett** *n.* the lowest grade of high-quality German table wine, typically dry to medium dry [Early 20thC. From German *Kabinettwein*, literally "cabinet wine"; because the wine was originally kept in a special cellar.]

ka·bob *n.* = **kebab**

ka·bu·ki /kə bóokee/ *n.* traditional Japanese drama in which male actors play both male and female parts [Late 19thC. From Japanese *ka* "song" + *bu* "dance" + *ki* "art, skill."]

Ka·bul /kaá bóol, kə bóol/ capital city of Afghanistan, located in the center of the country. Population: 1,424,400 (1988).

Ka·byle /kə bī́l/ (*plural* **-byles** *or* **-byle**) *n.* **1.** PEOPLES **MEMBER OF A N AFRICAN PEOPLE** a member of a Berber people who live in northeastern Algeria **2.** LANG **N AFRICAN LANGUAGE** a Berber language spoken in northeastern Algeria. It belongs to the Afro-Asiatic family of African languages and is spoken by about three million people. [Mid-18thC. Probably from Arabic *kabā'il* "tribes."] —**Ka·byle** *adj.*

Kabuki

ka·chi·na /kə cheénə/ (*plural* **-nas**) *n.* **1.** **NATIVE AMERICAN SPIRIT** any one of the spirits believed by the Native American Hopi people to be the ancestors of human beings **2.** **FIGURE OF A KACHINA** a representation of a kachina, usually either a carved wooden doll or a costumed performer in a ceremonial dance [Late 19thC. From Hopi *kacina* "supernatural."]

ka·dai·tcha *n.* = **kurdaitcha**

Kad·dish /kaádish/ (*plural* **-dish·im** /kaadíshim/) *n.* a prayer recited at the close of the sections of Jewish religious services, and by close relatives of a deceased person at times of mourning and anniversaries of the death [Early 17thC. From Aramaic *qaddīš* "holy."]

Ka·du·na /kə dóonə/ capital of Kaduna State, north central Nigeria, situated about 90 mi./145 km north of the national capital, Abuja. Population: 309,600 (1992).

kaf·fee·klatsch /kóffee klàch, -klòch/ *n.* = **coffee klatch** [Late 19thC. From German, from *Kaffee* "coffee" + *Klatsch* "gossip."]

Kaf·fir /káffər/, **Kaf·ir** *n.* **1.** *S Africa* **OFFENSIVE TERM** a highly offensive term referring to a Black African person (*taboo insult*) **2. Kaf·fir, kaf·fir OFFENSIVE TERM** an offensive term referring to a person who is not a Muslim (*slang insult*) **3.** LANG **XHOSA** the Xhosa language (*dated*) [Mid-16thC. From Arabic *kāfir* "unbeliever, infidel."]

kaf·fir corn, **kaf·ir corn** *n.* a variety of sorghum cultivated in southern Africa for its grain, used to make beer and as a fodder crop (*sometimes considered offensive*)

kaf·fi·yeh /kə feé ə, kaa feé ə/ *n.* a cotton headdress fastened by a band and worn by Arab men

kaf·ir *n.* = **kaffir corn**

Kaf·ir *n.* = **Kaffir**

kaf·ir corn *n.* = **kaffir corn**

Kaf·i·ri /káfəree/ *n.* the language of the Nuri people of Pakistan and Afghanistan. It belongs to the Dardic branch of the Indo-Aryan family of languages. [Early 20thC. See KAFFIR.]

Kaf·ka /kaáfkə/, **Franz** (1883–1924) Czech novelist. His dreamlike works, such as *The Trial* (1925) and *The Castle* (1926), are full of oppression and despair. His major novels were published posthumously by his friend, Max Brod, against Kafka's wishes.

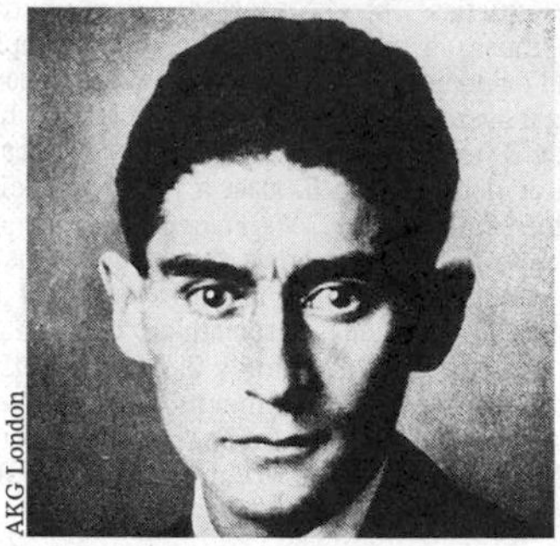

Franz Kafka

Kaf·ka·esque /kaàfkə ésk/ *adj.* **1.** **OF KAFKA'S WORK** relating to or typical of the work of Franz Kafka **2.** **IMPERSONAL AND OVERCOMPLEX** characterized by seemingly pointless, impersonal, and often disturbing overcomplexity

kaf·tan *n.* = **caftan**

Ka·fu·e /kaa fóo ay/ river in central Zambia, a tributary of the Zambezi. It rises near Zambia's northern border with the Democratic Republic of the Congo. Length: 980 mi./1,570 km.

Ka·go·shi·ma /kàgō sheémə, kàagō-/ seaport and capital of Kagoshima Prefecture on the southern coast of Kyushu, Japan. Population: 536,752 (1990).

ka·gu /kaá góo/ *n.* a large grayish flightless bird found only on the Pacific island of New Caledonia. It is now nearly extinct. Latin name: *Rhynochetos jubatus.* [Mid-19thC. From Melanesian.]

ka·ha·wai /kaáhə wī/ (*plural* **-wais** *or* **-wai**) *n.* a large marine fish of the perch family, similar in appearance to the salmon. It is found in Australia and New Zealand. Latin name: *Arripis trutta.* [Mid-19thC. From Maori.]

ka·hi·ka·te·a /kīkə teé ə, kàkə teé ə/ *n.* a tall evergreen tree that is native to New Zealand and is an important source of timber. Latin name: *Podocarpus dacrydioides.* [Early 19thC. From Maori.]

Frida Kahlo: Photographed in 1930 by Edward Weston

Kah·lo /kaál ō/, **Frida** (1907–54) Mexican painter. She is known for her idiosyncratic self-portraits that incorporate elements and subject matter inspired by Mexican folk art and her personal life. She was married to the Mexican painter Diego Rivera.

Ka·hu·lui /kaà hoo lóo ee/ community in Maui County, Hawaii, on the northern coast of Maui Island. Population: 16,889 (1990).

ka·hu·na /kə hóonə/ *n.* **1.** **IMPORTANT PERSON** an important or influential person (*informal*) **2.** **HAWAIIAN SHAMAN** a

Hawaiian priest or witch doctor [Late 19thC. From Hawaiian.]

kai·ak *n.* = **kayak**

Kai·e·teur Falls /kī̀ ə to͝or-/ falls in central Guyana, on the Potaro branch of the Essequibo River. Height: 740 ft./225 m.

kaif *n.* = **kif**

Kai·feng /kī̀ féng/ city in northern China, in the Huang He valley of northern Henan Province. Population: 507,763 (1990).

Kai·lu·a /kī lo͞o ə/ community in Honolulu County, Hawaii, on the southeastern coast of Oahu Island. Population: 36,818 (1990).

kai·nite /kī́ nī̀t, káy-/ *n.* a variously colored mineral that is a sulfate and chloride of magnesium and potassium. It is a source of potassium and is often used as a fertilizer. [Mid-19thC. From German *Kainit*, from Greek *kainos* "new, recent."]

Kai·pa·ra Har·bour /kī pàa raa-/ wide harbor on the northwestern coast of the North Island, New Zealand. Area: 200 sq. mi./520 sq. km.

Kai·rou·an /kər wáan/ city in northern Tunisia, capital of Al Qayrawan Governate. Called the City of a Hundred Mosques, it is one of the holiest Muslim cities. Population: 102,600 (1992).

kai·ser /kī́zər/ *n.* any one of the former German, Austrian, or Austro-Hungarian emperors, especially the German emperor Wilhelm II, who ruled Germany during World War I [Old English *cāsere*] —**kai·ser·dom** *n.* —**kai·ser·ism** *n.*

Kai·ser /kī́zər/, **Henry J.** (1882–1967) U.S. industrialist. He was involved in the construction, shipbuilding, automobile, steel, aluminum, and chemical industries. Full name **Henry John Kaiser**

kai·ser·in /kī́zərin/ *n.* a German empress or the wife of a German emperor [Late 19thC. From German, feminine form of KAISER.]

kai·ser roll *n.* a crusty round roll, often sprinkled with poppy or sesame seeds, made by folding corners of a square up until they meet

ka·ka /kaákə/ *n.* a species of parrots found in New Zealand and having a long gray bill and greenish-brown plumage. Latin name: *Nestor meridionalis.* [Late 18thC. From Maori.]

Ka·ka·du Na·tion·al Park /kaákə doo-/ national park in the Northern Territory, Australia. Area: 7,770 sq. mi./20,000 sq. km.

Kakapo

ka·ka·po /kaákə pṑ/ (*plural* **-pos**) *n.* a large flightless nocturnal parrot with green plumage, native to New Zealand. It looks similar to an owl and is now rare. Latin name: *Strigops habroptilus.* [Mid-19thC. From Maori.]

ka·ke·mo·no /kaákə mṓ nṑ/ (*plural* **-nos**) *n.* a Japanese wall hanging in the form of a tall narrow scroll, weighted at the base with a roller and decorated with a painting or with a text in ornamental handwriting [Late 19thC. From Japanese, from *kake-* "to hang" + *mono* "thing."]

ka·ki *n.* = **Japanese persimmon** [Early 18thC. From Japanese.]

kak·is·toc·ra·cy /kàkə stókrəssee/ (*plural* **-cies**) *n.* government by the most unscrupulous or unsuitable people, or a state governed by such people [Early 19thC. From Greek *kakistos* "worst" + -CRACY.]

ka·la-a·zar /kaálə ə zaár/ *n.* a severe, often fatal tropical fever caused by a parasite that enters the body via a sandfly bite. Symptoms include acute anemia, weight loss, and an enlarged liver and spleen. [Late 19thC. From Assamese, from *kala* "black" + *āzār* "disease."]

Kalachakra /kaálə chùkrə/ *n.* a mandala, traditionally constructed out of grains of sand, depicting Buddhist deities in a portrayal of time. The mandala is destroyed shortly after construction to illustrate the Buddhist teaching of impermanence.

Ka·la·ha·ri De·sert /kaálə haáree-/ arid and semiarid region in southern Africa. It occupies much of Botswana and parts of Namibia and South Africa. Area: 275,000 sq. mi./712,000 sq. km.

Ka·la·ha·ri Gems·bok Na·tion·al Park /-khemzbok-/ national park in northwestern South Africa. Area: 3,703 sq. mi./9,591 sq. km.

kal·an·choe /kàllən kṓ ee/ *n.* any one of various species of tropical African succulent plants often grown as potted plants for their shiny leaves and clusters of small bright red, pink, or white flowers. Genus: *Kalanchoe.* [Mid-19thC. Via modern Latin from French, ultimately from Chinese *gāláncài.*]

Ka·lash·ni·kov /kə laáshni kòf/ *n.* a Russian-manufactured semiautomatic assault rifle that is widely used by popular weapon among terrorists and paramilitary organizations [Late 20thC. From Russian, named for M. T. *Kalashnikov*, its developer.]

Ka·lat /kə laát/, **Ka·lāt** town in western Pakistan, principal town of the Kalat region, in Baluchistan Province. Population: 11,000 (1981).

Kale

kale /kayl/ *n.* **1. VARIETY OF CABBAGE** a hardy heartless variety of cabbage with darkgreen curly leaves. Latin name: *Brassica oleracea acephala.* **2. MONEY** money (*slang*) [14thC. Scottish variant of COLE.]

ka·lei·do·scope /kə lī́də skṑp/ *n.* **1. OPTICAL TOY** an optical toy consisting of a cylinder with mirrors and colored shapes inside that create shifting symmetrical patterns when the end is rotated **2. COMPLEX SCENE OR PATTERN** a complex, colorful, and shifting pattern or scene **3. COMPLEX SET OF EVENTS** a complex set of events or circumstances [Early 19thC. Coined from Greek *kalos* "beautiful" + *eidos* "form" + -SCOPE, literally "observer of beautiful forms," coined by Sir David Brewster (1781–1868), its inventor.] —**ka·lei·do·scop·ic** /kə lī̀də skópik/ *adj.* —**ka·lei·do·scop·i·cal·ly** *adv.*

kal·ends *npl.* = **calends**

Kale·yard School *n.* a group of Scottish writers, active from the late 19th to the early 20th century, who wrote romantic portrayals of life in the Scottish Lowlands [*Kaleyard* "kitchen garden (of a small cottage)," from KALE + YARD; from the writers' portrayal of local town life]

Kal·goor·lie-Boul·der /kalgo͞orlee-/ city in southern Western Australia, a goldmining center. Population: 28,087 (1996).

ka·lif *n.* = **caliph**

Ka·li·man·tan /kàlə mántàn/ region of the Republic of Indonesia, occupying the southern portion of the island of Borneo. Population: 10,470,800 (1995). Area: 209,500 sq. mi./542,700 sq. km.

ka·lim·ba /kə límbə/ *n.* an African instrument consisting of tuned metal or bamboo bars of varying lengths attached to a soundboard. The bars are plucked to give sound. [Mid-20thC. From Bantu.]

Ka·li·nin /kə leénən/ former name for **Tver** (1933–90)

Ka·li·nin·grad /kə leénin graád/ city in western Russia, on the Pregolya River. It is the capital of Kaliningrad Oblast. Population: 406,000 (1990). Former name **Königsberg** (until 1946)

Ka·li Yu·ga /kàllee yo͞ogə, kùllee-/ *n.* in Hindu philosophy, the age of decadence. It is the fourth and last age in the Hindu cycle of the world. [From Sanskrit]

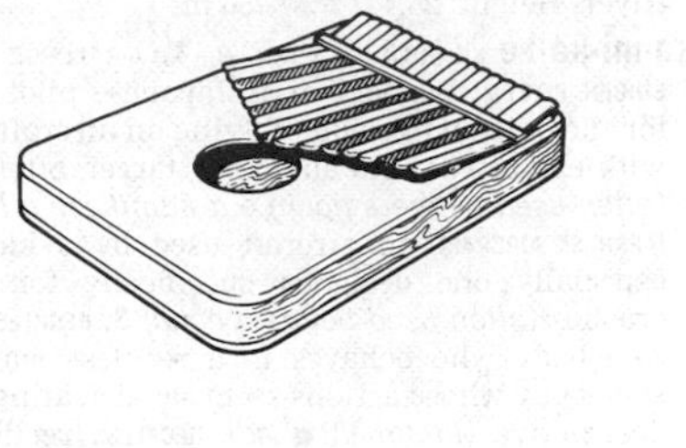

Kalimba

kal·li·krein /kàlə kreé ən, kə líkree ən/ *n.* an enzyme present in blood, urine, and body tissue that, when activated, dilates blood vessels

Kal·mar /kaálmaàr/ port city in southern Sweden, the capital of Kalmar county. It is situated on Kalmarsund opposite the island of Öland. Population: 58,420 (1995).

kal·mi·a /kálmee ə, kálmyə/ *n.* a flowering evergreen shrub, native to North America, that has poisonous leaves and belongs to the heath family. The mountain ash is a kalmia. Genus: *Kalmia.* [Mid-18thC. From modern Latin, genus name, named for the Swedish botanist Pehr *Kalm* (1716–79).]

Kal·myck /kál mìk, kal mík/, **Kal·muk** /kálmùk, kal múk/ *n.* (*plural* **-mycks** *or* **-myck;** *plural* **-muks** *or* **-muk**) **1.** PEOPLES **MEMBER OF A SW RUSSIAN PEOPLE** a member of a people who live in an autonomous region of southwest Russia. They migrated from northeastern China during the 17th century. **2.** LANG **MONGOLIAN LANGUAGE** the language spoken by the Kalmyck. It belongs to the Mongolian branch of the Altaic family of languages and is spoken by about 150, 000 people. ■ *adj.* **1.** LANGUAGE **OF THE LANGUAGE OF THE KALMYCK** relating to the Kalmyck language **2.** PEOPLES **OF THE KALMYCK** relating to the Kalmyck or their culture [Early 17thC. From Russian *Kalmyk.*]

kal·pa /kálpə, kúlpə/ *n.* in Hindu philosophy, an immeasurably long period of time. Its length is variable, sometimes described as one complete cycle of the world (**yuga**), sometimes as 1,000 cycles. [Late 18thC. From Sanskrit.]

kal·pak *n.* CLOTHES = **calpac**

ka·ma /kaámə/ *n.* sexual pleasure as the third of the four Hindu goals of life [From Sanskrit *kāma* "love, desire"]

ka·maa·i·na /kaámə ī́nə/ (*plural* **-nas**) *n.* somebody who is a long-time resident of Hawaii [Early 20thC. From Hawaiian, from *kama* "child" + *āina* "land."]

ka·ma·cite /kámmə sī̀t/ *n.* an alloy of nickel and iron found in meteorites [Late 19thC. From Greek *kamak-*, *kamax* "vine pole" + -ITE.]

Ka·ma·ku·ra /kaámə ko͝orə/ city southwest of Tokyo, on Sagami Bay, in Kanagawa Prefecture, southeastern Honshu, Japan. Population: 174,307 (1993).

ka·ma·la /kaámmələ, kámmələ/ *n.* **1. EAST INDIAN TREE** an East Indian tree that belongs to the spurge family. Latin name: *Mallotus philippinensis.* **2. POWDER** a powder obtained from seeds of the kamala, used as a dye and formerly used to treat worm infestations [Early 19thC. From Sanskrit, probably of Dravidian origin.]

Ka·ma·su·tra /kaámə so͞otrə/ *n.* an ancient Sanskrit text giving instruction on the art of lovemaking [Late 19thC. From Sanskrit, from *kāma* "love, desire" + *sūtra* "precept."]

Kam·chat·ka Pen·in·su·la /kam chàt kə-/ large peninsula of eastern Russia that separates the Sea of Okhotsk from the Bering Sea and the Pacific Ocean. Area: 200,000 sq. mi./518,000 sq. km.

kame /kaym/ *n.* a ridge of sand and gravel left by a melting glacier [Late 18thC. From Scottish *kame* "comb."]

Ka·me·ha·me·ha I /kə màyəmáy ə/, **King of Hawaii** (1758–1819). He became king of the island of Hawaii in 1782, united all the Hawaiian islands (1810), and ruled until his death. Known as **Kamehameha the Great**

Ka·met, Mount /kú mày-/ mountain in the Himalayas, in northern India, near the source of the Jamna River. Height: 25,447 ft./7,756 m.

ka·mi·ka·ze /kaàmi kaàzee/ *n.* **1.** AIR FORCE **JAPANESE SUICIDE PILOT** a World War II Japanese pilot trained for the suicide mission of flying an aircraft packed with explosives into an enemy target, often a ship (*often used before a noun*) ○ *a kamikaze pilot* **2.** AIR **JAPANESE AIRCRAFT** an aircraft used by a kamikaze, especially one designed specifically for suicide crashes (*often used before a noun*) **3. RECKLESS PERSON** somebody who behaves in a reckless way, often somebody whose actions seem self-defeating or self-destructive (*informal*) ■ *adj.* **RECKLESS** reckless, especially seeming to invite failure or self-destruction (*informal*) [Late 19thC. From Japanese, literally "divine wind."]

Kam·loops /kám loòps/ city in southern British Columbia, Canada. It is a transportation and commercial hub. Population: 74,394 (1996).

Kam·pa·la /kaam paàlə/ capital city of Uganda, situated in the southern part of the country, near Lake Victoria. Population: 773,463 (1991).

Kam·pu·che·a /kàmpoò cheè ə/ former name for **Cambodia** (1975–89) —**Kam·pu·che·an** *n., adj.*

ka·na /kaànə/ *n.* **1. JAPANESE WRITING SYSTEM** one of the writing systems used in Japanese. Symbols represent syllables and are often used in conjunction with Japanese pictorial symbols (**kanji**) to change the form of words. ◊ **hiragana, katakana 2. SYMBOL** any one of the syllabic symbols used in kana [Early 18thC. From Japanese.]

Ka·nak /kə naàk/ *n.* somebody who was born in or is a citizen of the French overseas territory of New Caledonia in the South Pacific, and who supports independence from France [Early 20thC. From French *canaque*, of uncertain origin: probably from English *Kanaka* (see KANAKA).] —**Ka·nak** *adj.*

Ka·na·ka /kə naàkə, kə nákə/ *n.* **HAWAIIAN CITIZEN** somebody who was born in or is a citizen of Hawaii, especially somebody of Polynesian descent ■ *adj.* **OF THE KANAKAS** relating to or typical of the Kanakas or their culture [Mid-19thC. From Hawaiian, "person, human being."]

kan·a·my·cin /kànnə míss'n/ *n.* an antibiotic obtained from a bacterium found in soil, effective against a wide range of serious infections that are resistant to other safer antibiotics [Mid-20thC. From modern Latin *kanamyceticus*.]

Ka·nan·ga /kə naàng gə/ city in the southern Democratic Republic of Congo, capital of Kasai-Occidental Region. Population: 393,030 (1994). Former name **Luluabourg**

Kan·a·rese /kànnə reèz, -reèss/ *n.* (*plural* **-rese**) **1.** PEOPLES **MEMBER OF AN INDIAN PEOPLE** a member of a people living in southwestern India, mainly in the Kanara region **2.** LANG = **Kannada** ■ *adj.* PEOPLES, GEOG **OF KANARA REGION** relating to the region of Kanara in southwestern India, or its people or culture

Ka·na·wha /kə naà wə/ river in west central West Virginia. It rises in northwestern North Carolina and joins the Ohio River at Point Pleasant. Length: 97 mi./156 km.

Ka·na·za·wa /kaànə zaàwə/ city and seaport in northern Honshu, Japan. Population: 442,868 (1990).

kan·ban /kaàn baàn/ *n.* **1. ORDER CARD** in the just-in-time manufacturing and stock-control system, a card bearing an order for goods, sent to a manufacturer or supplier **2.** = **just-in-time** [Late 20thC. From Japanese "billboard, sign."]

Kan·chen·jun·ga /kùnchən júng gə, -joòng-/ the third highest mountain in the world. It is situated in the Himalayas, on the border between Nepal and Sikkim, India. Height: 28,208 ft./8,598 m.

Kan·da·har /kaàndə haàr, kùndə-/ city in southern Afghanistan. It is the capital of Kandahar Province and the country's commercial center. Population: 225,500 (1988).

Kan·din·sky /kan dínskee/, **Wassily** (1866–1944) Russian painter. One of the earliest exponents of pure abstraction in art, he wrote *Concerning the Spiritual in Art* (1912), the first treatise on this subject. He taught at the Bauhaus school of design in Weimar and Dessau, Germany (1922–33).

Kan·dy /kándee/ city in central Sri Lanka, capital of Central Province. Population: 104,000 (1990).

Wassily Kandinsky: Photographed at the Bauhaus, Dessau, Germany (1930?)

Kane /kayn/, **Paul** (1810–71) Irish-born Canadian artist. His paintings depict Native North American life in northwestern Canada.

Ka·ne·o·he /kaà nee ō hee/ community in Honolulu County, Hawaii, on the southeastern coast of Oahu Island. Population: 35,448 (1990).

kan·ga /káng gə/, **khan·ga** *n.* a brightly colored and decorated piece of cotton cloth that women wrap around the body as a garment, originally and especially in East Africa [Mid-20thC. From Kiswahili.]

Kangaroo

kan·ga·roo /kàng gə roó/ (*plural* **-roos**) *n.* a large leaping animal with powerful hind legs, short forelegs, and a long tail. It is marsupial and is native to Australia and New Guinea. Family: Macropodidae. [Late 18thC. From Aboriginal.]

kan·ga·roo court *n.* an unofficial or mock court set up spontaneously for the purpose of delivering a judgment arrived at in advance, usually one in which a disloyal cohort's fate is decided

kan·ga·roo paw *n.* an Australian plant with downy green-and-red flowers. Genus: *Anigozanthos.*

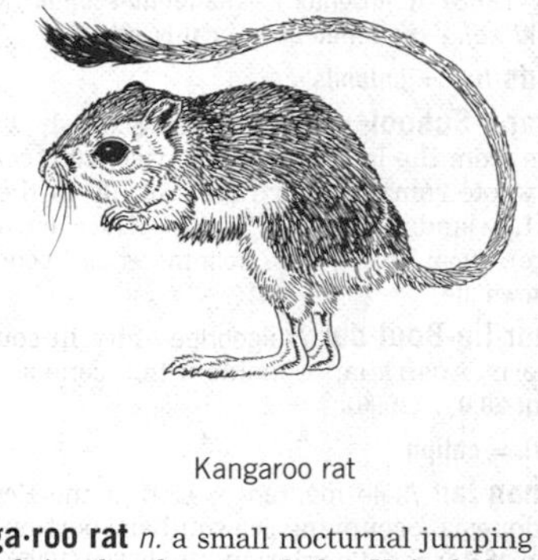
Kangaroo rat

kan·ga·roo rat *n.* a small nocturnal jumping rodent found in the deserts of the United States and Mexico. It has a long tail and long hind limbs. Genus: *Dipodomys.*

kan·ga·roo vine *n.* a climbing vine of Australia with shiny green or mottled leaves. Latin name: *Cissus antarctica.*

Ka·Ng·wa·ne /kaà əng gwaànay/ former homeland in northeastern South Africa, created in 1971 and abolished in 1994

kan·ji /kaánjee/ (*plural* **-ji** *or* **-jis**) *n.* **1. JAPANESE WRITING SYSTEM** a Japanese writing system that uses pictorial characters based largely on Chinese ideograms **2. WRITTEN CHARACTER** any one of the characters used in the kanji writing system [Early 20thC. From Japanese, from *kan* "Chinese" + *ji* "letter, character."]

Kan·ka·kee /kàngkə keè/ city in northeastern Illinois, on the Kankakee River, northeast of Urbana and southwest of Chicago. Population: 27,217 (1996).

Kan·na·da /kaànədə/ *n.* **INDIAN LANGUAGE** a language spoken in some of the southern states of India. It belongs to the Dravidian family of languages and is spoken by about 44 million people. ■ *adj.* **RELATING TO KANNADA** relating to the Kannada language

Ka·no /kaànō/ capital of Kano State, northern Nigeria. Population: 699,900 (1992).

Ka·no Ma·sa·no·bu /kaànō masənṓboo/ (1453–90) Japanese artist. He founded the Kano school of painting and based his style on that of Chinese ink painting.

Ka·no Mo·to·no·bu /kaànō mōtōnṓboo/ (1476–1539) Japanese artist. He continued the style of his father Kano Masanobu, and introduced the firm brush line used in later Kano painting.

Kan·pur /kaán poòr, kaan poòr/, **Kān·pur** city in Uttar Pradesh State, northern India, on the Ganges River. Population: 1,958,282 (1991).

Kans. *abbr.* Kansas

Kan·sa /kánzə, kánsə/ (*plural* **-sas** *or* **-sa**) *n.* **1.** PEOPLES **MEMBER OF A NATIVE AMERICAN PEOPLE** a member of a Native American people who originally lived in parts of eastern and central Kansas. Today the population lives mainly in eastern Oklahoma. **2.** LANG **NATIVE AMERICAN LANGUAGE** a Native American language spoken in eastern Oklahoma. It belongs to the Siouan group of the Hokan Siouan family of languages. —**Kan·sa** *adj.*

Kansas

Kan·sas /kánzəss/ state in the western part of the central United States, bordered by Colorado, Missouri, Nebraska, and Oklahoma. Capital: Topeka. Population: 2,594,840 (1997). Area: 82,282 sq. mi./213,110 sq. km. —**Kan·san** *n., adj.*

Kan·sas City /kànzəss-/ city in northeastern Kansas. It is directly across the state line from Kansas City, Missouri. Population: 142,654 (1996).

Kan·sas Cit·y jazz *n.* a style of bigband jazz music characterized by blues motifs and a relaxed beat

Kant /kant, kaant/, **Immanuel** (1724–1804) German philosopher. He is a seminal figure in Western philosophy whose major work is *Critique of Pure Reason* (1781). —**Kant·i·an** /kántee ən/ *adj.* —**Kant·i·an·ism** /kántee ə nìzzəm/ *n.*

kan·zu /kán zoò/ (*plural* **-zus**) *n.* a long garment resembling a robe, usually white and with long sleeves, worn by men in East Africa [Early 20thC. From Kiswahili.]

ka·o·lin /káy əlin/, **ka·o·line** *n.* fine white clay used in making porcelain and ceramics and in medicine as an absorbent, e.g., in treatments for diarrhea [Early 18thC. From Chinese *gāoling*, literally "high hill," named for the hill where it is found.]

ka·o·lin·ite /káy əli nìt/ *n.* a white or gray mineral that consists of a silicate of aluminum and is the main constituent of kaolin. Formula: $Al_2Si_2O_5(OH)_4$. —**ka·o·lin·it·ic** /kày əli níttik/ *adj.*

ka·on /káy òn/ *n.* an unstable elementary particle produced as a result of high-energy particle collision. It occurs in both charged and neutral forms and helps to hold protons and neutrons together inside a nucleus. Symbol **K** [Mid-20thC. From *K-meson*, its earlier name.]

ka·pell·meis·ter /kə pél mīstər/ *n.* the director of a modern choir or, in former times, the director of the orchestra, choir, or opera in the household of a German prince [Mid-19thC. From German, from *Kappelle* "court orchestra" + *Meister* "master."]

kaph /kaáf/ *n.* the eleventh letter of the Hebrew alphabet, represented in the English alphabet as "k" or, at the end of a word, as "kh." See table at **alphabet** [Early 19thC. From Hebrew, literally "the palm of the hand."]

ka·pok /káy pòk/ *n.* silky fiber obtained from the seed covering of a tropical tree, with numerous uses in the textile industry, e.g., as a stuffing and padding material [Mid-18thC. From Malay.]

ka·pok bush *n.* a small Australian deciduous tree with bright yellow flowers. Genus: *Cochlospermum.*

Ka·po·si's sar·co·ma /kə pòsseez saar kṓmə/ *n.* a cancer of connective tissue that causes purplish-red patches on the skin, most commonly found in equatorial Africa and in AIDS patients [Late 19thC. Named for the Hungarian dermatologist M. K. *Kaposi* (1837–1902), who described it.]

kap·pa /káppə/ *n.* the tenth letter in the Greek alphabet, represented in the English alphabet as "k" or "c." See table at **alphabet** [From Greek]

ka·put /kaa pŏŏt, -pŏŏt, kə-/ *adj.* broken, incapacitated, or not functioning (*informal*) [Late 19thC. Via German *kaputt* from French *capot,* part of a phrase that refers to losing all tricks in the game of piquet.]

Ka·ra·chay-Cher·kes·sia /kèrrachī chər késsyə/ autonomous republic in southwestern European Russia, bordering Georgia. Cherkessk is the capital. Population: 434,100 (1994). Area: 5,444 sq. mi./14,100 sq. km.

Ka·ra·chi /kə raáchee/ seaport and largest city of Pakistan, located in the south of the country. Population: 5,180,562 (1981).

Kar·a·ism /kérrə ìzzəm/ *n.* the beliefs of a Jewish denomination **(Karaites)** founded in the 8th century. Its members accept the Bible as the sole source of religious law and reject the Oral and Rabbinical Law. [Late 19thC. From Hebrew *qĕrāīm* "Karaites," from *qārā'* "to read."] —**Kar·aite** *n.*

Hulton-Deutsch Collection/Corbis

Herbert von Karajan

Ka·ra·jan /kaárə yaán/, **Herbert von** (1908–89) Austrian conductor. He was the music director of the Berlin Philharmonic Orchestra (1955–89) and director of the Vienna State Opera (1955–64).

Ka·ra-Kal·pak /kèrrə kál pak/ (*plural* **Ka·ra-Kal·paks** *or* **Ka·ra-Kal·pak**) *n.* **1.** PEOPLES **MEMBER OF A PEOPLE OF UZBEKISTAN** a member of a people who live mainly in the Kara-Kalpak Autonomous Republic in northwestern Uzbekistan **2.** LANG **TURKIC LANGUAGE** a Turkic language spoken by the Kara-Kalpak. It belongs to the Altaic family of languages and is spoken by about 300,000 people. [Early 18thC. From Kirghiz, from *kara* "black" + *kalpak* "cap."] —**Ka·ra-Kal·pak** *adj.*

Ka·ra·ko·ram Range /kàrrə káwrəm-/ mountain range in the western Himalayas, south central Asia. Its highest peak is K2, 28,250 ft./8,611 m.

kar·a·kul /kérrəkəl/, **car·a·cul** *n.* **1.** SHEEP a hardy sheep of a breed from Central Asia, the lambs of which have a soft curly black coat **2.** FLEECE the furry wool from karakul lambs, used especially for making fur coats [Mid-19thC. From Russian, from, in turn, the name of an oasis in Uzbekistan and two lakes in Tajikistan, perhaps ultimately from Turkish.]

Ka·ra Kul /kèrrəkŏŏl/ two lakes in eastern Tajikistan, high on the Pamir plateau near the border with China, Great Kara Kul and Little Kara Kul

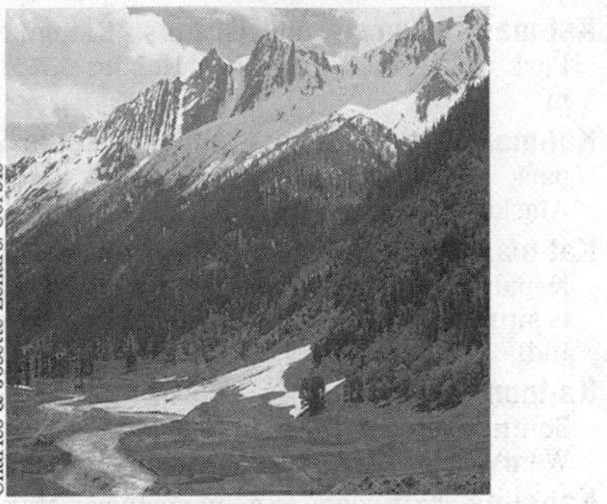

Charles & Josette Lenars/Corbis

Karakoram Range: View of the Sind Valley

kar·a·o·ke /kèrree ṓkee/ *n.* a form of entertainment in which amateur singers sing popular songs accompanied by prerecorded music from a machine that may also display the words on a video screen [Late 20thC. From Japanese, from *kara* "empty" + *oke* an abbreviation of *ōkesutora* "orchestra."]

Ka·ra Sea /kaárə-/ sea bordering the northwestern coast of Siberian Russia. It is an arm of the Arctic Ocean. Area: 300,000 sq. mi./777,000 sq. km.

kar·at /kérrət/ *n.* a unit of proportion of gold in an alloy equal to 1/24 part of pure gold

Barnaby's

Karate

ka·ra·te /kə raátee/ *n.* a traditional Japanese form of unarmed combat, now widely popular as a sport, in which fast blows or kicks are used [Mid-20thC. From Japanese, from *kara* "empty" + *te* "hand."] —**ka·ra·te·ist** *n.*

ka·ra·te·ka /kə raátə kaà/ *n.* somebody who practices karate or is an expert in karate [From Japanese, literally "karate person"]

Kar·ba·la /kaárbələ/, **Kar·ba·lā'** city in central Iraq, on the edge of the Syrian Desert. Population: 184,600 (1985).

Ka·re·li·an /kə reélee ən, -ly ən/ *n.* **1.** LANG **FINNISH DIALECT** a dialect of Finnish spoken in the northeastern European region of Karelia that formerly belonged to Finland but is now an autonomous republic. It is spoken by around 120,000 people. **2.** PEOPLES **CITIZEN OF THE KARELIAN REPUBLIC** a native or citizen of the Karelian Republic —**Ka·re·li·an** *adj.*

Ka·ren /kə rén, kə rén/ (*plural* **-rens** *or* **-ren**) *n.* **1.** PEOPLES **MEMBER OF AN ASIAN PEOPLE** a member of a people who live mainly in southern and eastern Myanmar, formerly Burma **2.** LANG **ASIAN LANGUAGE** any of the Tibeto-Burman languages spoken in southern and eastern Myanmar. It belongs to the Sino-Tibetan language family and around two million people speak it. [Mid-18thC. From Burmese *ka-reng* "wild, unclean man."] —**Ka·ren** *adj.*

Ka·ri·ba, Lake /-kə reébə/ artificial lake on the border between Zambia and Zimbabwe, southern Africa. It was created by building the Kariba Dam across the Zambezi River. Area: 2,000 sq. mi./5,180 sq. km.

Karl-Marx-Stadt /kaarl maárks shtaát/ former name for **Chemnitz** (1953–90)

Kar·loff /kaár làwf/, **Boris** (1887–1969) British actor. He appeared in numerous U.S. horror films, notably as the monster in the film *Frankenstein* (1931). Real name **William Henry Pratt**

Kar·lo·vy Va·ry /kaárləvee vaáree/ city in the northwestern Czech Republic, situated on the Ohře River, west of Prague. Population: 56,292 (1991).

Karls·ru·he /kaárlz rŏŏ ə/ industrial and university city in Baden-Württemberg State, southwestern Germany. Population: 277,700 (1994).

kar·ma /kaármə/ *n.* **1.** EASTERN RELIG **EASTERN PHILOSOPHY** the Hindu and Buddhist philosophy according to which the quality of people's current and future lives is determined by their behavior in this life **2.** **ATMOSPHERE** the atmosphere radiated by a place, situation, person, or object (*informal*) **3.** **DESTINY** destiny or fate in general [Early 19thC. From Sanskrit *karman* "fate, action."] —**kar·mic** *adj.*

Kar·nak /kaár nàk/ village in eastern Egypt, on the Nile River, occupying part of the ancient city of Thebes

Kar·na·ta·ka /kər naátəkə/, **Kar·nā·ta·ka** state in southern India. Capital: Bangalore. Population: 48,150,000 (1994). Area: 74,051 sq. mi./191,791 sq. km. Former name **Mysore**

Kar·na·tak mu·sic /kər naátək-/, **Kar·nat·ic mu·sic** *n.* the classical music of southern India, which often accompanies dance

Kar·ok /kə rók/ (*plural* **-oks** *or* **-ok**) *n.* **1.** PEOPLES **MEMBER OF A NATIVE AMERICAN PEOPLE** a member of a Native American people living mainly in northwestern California **2.** LANG **HOKAN LANGUAGE** a Hokan language spoken in parts of northwestern California. It belongs to the Hokan Siouan family of Native American languages. [Mid-19thC. From Karok *karuk* "upstream."] —**Ka·rok** *adj.*

ka·roo /kə rŏŏ/ (*plural* **-roos**) *n.* an arid plateau in southern Africa

Ka·roo /kə rŏŏ/, **Kar·roo** semidesert plateau regions in Western Cape Province, South Africa. Area: 100,000 sq. mi./259,000 sq. km.

kar·oss /kə róss/ *n.* a blanket made of animal skins, used in southern Africa as either a cloak or a mattress [Mid-18thC. From Afrikaans *karos,* perhaps from Nama.]

Kar·rath·a /kə raáthə/ town on the western coast of Western Australia, an industrial center. Population: 10,057 (1996).

karst /kaarst/ *n.* a limestone landscape, characterized by caves, fissures, and underground streams [Late 19thC. From German *der Karst.*] —**karst·ic** *adj.*

Kart·ti·ka /kaártəkə/ *n.* in the Hindu calendar, the eighth month of the year, made up of 29 or 30 days and occurring about the same time as October to November

Ka·rum·ba /kərúmbə/ fishing port on the Gulf of Carpentaria in northwestern Queensland, Australia. Population: 1,043 (1996).

karyo- *prefix.* cell nucleus ○ *karyoplasm* [Via modern Latin from Greek *karuon* "nut, kernel"]

kar·y·og·a·my /kèrree óggəmee/ *n.* the fusion of cell nuclei that occurs during fertilization [Late 19thC. Coined from KARY(O)- + -GAMY.] —**kar·y·o·gam·ic** /kèrree ə gámmik/ *adj.*

kar·y·o·gram /kérree ə gràm/ *n.* a photograph or diagram of the chromosomes of a cell in sequence [Mid-20thC. Coined from KARY(O)- + -GRAM.]

kar·y·o·ki·ne·sis /kèrree ōkə neéssəss/ *n.* BIOL = **mitosis** [Late 19thC] —**kar·y·o·ki·net·ic** *adj.*

kar·y·ol·o·gy /kèrree óllәjee/ *n.* the study of cell nuclei, especially with reference to chromosomes [Late 19thC] —**kar·y·o·log·ic** /kèrree ə lójjik/ *adj.* —**kar·y·o·log·i·cal** /-lójjik'l/ *adj.* —**kar·y·ol·o·gist** /kèrree óllәjist/ *n.*

kar·y·o·lymph /kérree ə lìmf/ *n.* BIOL = **nuclear sap** [Late 19thC]

kar·y·o·plasm /kérree ə plàzzəm/ *n.* = **nucleoplasm** [Late 19thC] —**kar·y·o·plas·mic** /kèrree ə plázzmik/ *adj.*

kar·y·o·some /kérree ə sōm/ *n.* a thickened mass of chromatin in a cell nucleus [Late 19thC]

kar·y·o·type /kérree ə tīp/ *n.* **1.** **CHARACTERISTICS OF CELL CHROMOSOMES** the appearance and characteristics of the chromosomes of a cell, especially size, number, and form **2.** CELL BIOL **PHOTOMICROGRAPH OF CELL CHROMOSOMES** a photomicrograph in which a cell's chromosomes are arranged according to size and classification ■ *vt.* (**-typed, -typ·ing, -types**) **DETERMINE CELL'S KARYOTYPE** to determine the karyotype of a cell [Early 20thC] —**kar·y·o·typ·ic** /kèrree ə típpik/ *adj.* —**kar·y·o·typ·i·cal** /-típpik'l/ *adj.* —**kar·y·o·typ·i·cal·ly** *adv.*

kas·bah *n.* = **casbah.**

ka·sha /kaáshə/ *n.* **1. BUCKWHEAT PORRIDGE** a dish of cooked buckwheat resembling porridge, originally from Eastern Europe **2. BUCKWHEAT** the buckwheat from which kasha is made [Early 19thC. From Russian.]

Kash·mir /kásh meer/ disputed territory in the northern part of the Indian subcontinent. ◊ **Jammu and Kashmir, Kashmir [Azad]**

Kash·mir, Azad /-aá zàd/ section of the disputed territory of Kashmir in the northern part of the Indian subcontinent that has been under Pakistani control since 1972

Kash·mir·i /kash meéree, kazh-/ *n.* **1.** PEOPLES **SOMEBODY FROM KASHMIR** somebody who was born in or who is a citizen of Kashmir in Central Asia **2.** LANG **DARDIC LANGUAGE** the official state language of Kashmir, also spoken in neighboring areas. It is a Dardic language that belongs to the Indic group of languages and is spoken by about five million people. ■ *adj.* **OF KASHMIR** relating to Kashmir, its people, language, or culture

kash·ruth /kaáshrəth, kaash ro͞ot/, **kash·rut** *n.* **1. JEWISH LAWS** the body of Jewish laws that relate to the preparation and fitness of foods and to items such as textiles and ritual scrolls to be used by Jewish people **2. FITNESS FOR USE BY JEWISH PEOPLE** the fitness of an item for use by Jewish people, as determined by reference to kashruth [Early 20thC. From Hebrew "fitness" especially "ritual fitness."]

Kas·kas·ki·a[1] /kəs káskee ə/ (*plural* **-kask·ias** *or* **-kas·ki·a**), **Kas·kas·ki·as** *n.* a member of a Native American people, one of the six that form the Illinois Confederacy —**Kas·kas·ki·as** *adj.*

Kas·kas·ki·a[2] /kəskás kee ə/ river in Illinois. It flows southwestward into the Mississippi River. Length: 320 mi./515 km.

Kas·pa·rov /káspə ràwf/, **Garry** (*b.* 1963) Armenian chess player. He became world champion following his defeat of Anatoly Karpov in 1985. Full name **Garry Kimovich Kasparov.** Born **Garri Weinstein**

Kas·sa·la /kə saálə/, **Kas·sa·lā** city in northeastern Sudan. Population: 98,751 (1983).

Kas·sel /káss'l/, **Cas·sel** city in west central Germany. Population: 201,900 (1994).

ka·ta /kaá taá/ *n.* a sequence of movements in some martial arts such as karate, used either for training or to demonstrate technique [Mid-20thC. From Japanese, literally "model, pattern."]

ka·ta·ba·sis /kàttə bássiss/ (*plural* **-bas·es** /-bá seez/) *n.* a retreat, particularly of a military kind (*literary*) [Mid-19thC. From Greek, from *kata* "down" + *basis* "going."]

kat·a·bat·ic /kàttə báttik/ *adj.* used to describe a wind that moves down a slope, produced by the cooling of air at higher altitudes [Late 19thC. From Greek *katabatikos*, from *katabainein* "to go down."]

ka·tab·o·lism *n.* = **catabolism**

Ka·tah·din, Mount /kə taá dən/ mountain in northern Maine, in Baxter State Park. The highest of its several summits is Baxter Peak, 5,267 ft./1,605 m.

ka·ta·ka·na /kaàtə kaánə/ *n.* a syllabic form of writing in Japanese that is used principally to transliterate non-Japanese words. ◊ **kana, hiragana** [Early 18thC. From Japanese, from *kata* "side" + KANA.]

Kath·ak /kútək/ *n.* a form of classical dancing from northern India, used to tell a story [Mid-20thC. From Sanskrit *kathaka* "storyteller," from *kathā* "story."]

Kath·a·ka·li /kaàtə kaálee/ *n.* a form of drama from southern India that interprets stories from Hindu classical literature by combining dance and mime [Early 20thC. From Malayalam *kathakali*, from Sanskrit *kathā* "story" + Malayalam *kali* "play."]

Ka·tha·rev·u·sa /kaàthə révvoo saá/ *n.* a form of modern Greek, used in literature as opposed to everyday speech and writing, that employs some of the features of classical Greek. ◊ **Demotic** [Early 20thC. From Greek *kathareuousa*, ultimately from Greek *katharos* "pure."]

Kath·e·rine /káthrən/ town in north central Northern Territory, Australia, a center of beef production, fruit-growing, and tourism. Population: 7,979 (1996).

Kath·e·rine Gorge series of sandstone gorges cut by the Katherine River in the Northern Territory of Australia, northeast of Katherine

Kath·man·du = **Katmandu**

Kat·mai, Mount /kát mì/ volcano in Katmai National Park and Preserve, Alaska. Height: 6,715 ft./2,047 m.

Kat·mai Na·tion·al Park and Pre·serve national park on the Alaska Peninsula, southwestern Alaska. Area: 4,093,240 acres/1,656,475 hectares.

Kat·man·du /kàt man do͞o/, **Kath·man·du** capital city of Nepal, located in the central part of the country. It is situated about 55 mi./89 km from the border with India. Population: 419,073 (1991).

Ka·toom·ba /kə to͝ombə/ town in southeastern New South Wales, Australia. Population: 17,700 (with Wentworth Falls) (1996).

Kat·si·na /kaatseénə/ city in northern Nigeria, the capital of Katsina State. Population: 186,900 (1992).

Kat·te·gat /káttə gàt/ strait between the southwestern coast of Sweden and the eastern coast of the Jutland peninsula, Denmark. Length: 140 mi./225 km.

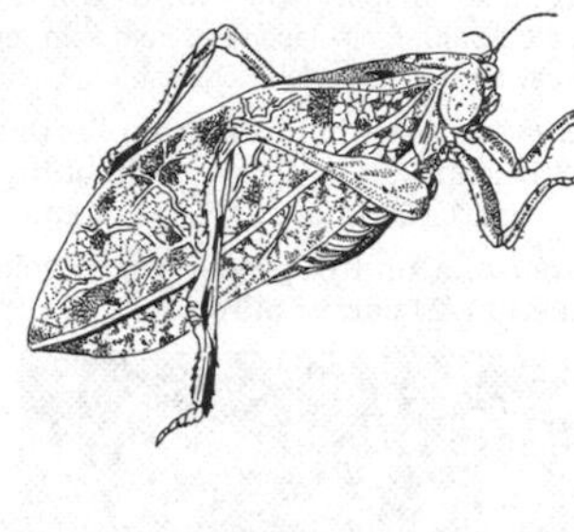

Katydid

ka·ty·did /káytee dìd/ *n.* a large green grasshopper that is native to North America and has very long antennae. The males make a shrill sound. Genus: *Microcentrum.* [Late 18thC. An imitation of the sound produced by the male when it rubs its front wings together.]

Ka·tyn For·est /ka teén/ forest in western European Russia, near Smolensk

katz·en·jam·mer /kátsən jàmmər/ *n.* (*dated informal*) **1. HANGOVER** a hangover **2. BLUES** a bewildered or discouraged state **3. DIN** a loud and confused noise [Mid-19thC. From German, from *Katze* "cat" + *Jammer* "distress."]

Kau·ai /ków wì/ fourth largest island in Hawaii, the northernmost of the main islands. Area: 552 sq. mi./1,431 sq. km.

Kauf·man /káwfmən/, **George S.** (1889–1961) U.S. playwright and director. He cowrote many Broadway comedies, such as *Animal Crackers* (1928) and *Stage Door* (1936). Full name **George Simon Kaufmann**

Kau·nas /kównəss/ industrial city in central Lithuania, situated about 60 mi./97 km west of Vilnius. Population: 415,300 (1995).

Ka·un·da /kaa o͞ondə/, **Kenneth** (*b.* 1924) Zambian statesman. He was president of Zambia from independence in 1964 until 1991. Full name **Kenneth David Kaunda**

kau·ri /kówree/ *n.* **1.** TREES **NEW ZEALAND TREE** a large evergreen tree, native to New Zealand, that has oval leaves and is valued for its strong timber. Latin name: *Agathis australis.* **2.** INDUST **TIMBER** the light-colored wood from the kauri tree **3.** = **kauri gum** [Early 19thC. From Maori.]

kau·ri gum, **kauri resin** *n.* the brittle resin of the kauri tree that is usually found in fossilized form and is used mainly in varnishes

ka·va /kaávə/ *n.* **1.** PLANTS **POLYNESIAN SHRUB** a Polynesian shrub that has clusters of small flowers and belongs to the pepper family. Latin name: *Piper methysticum.* **2.** BEVERAGES **DRINK** a narcotic drink made from the roots of the kava plant [Late 18thC. From Tongan, literally "bitter."]

Kaw /kaw/ *n.* (*plural* **Kaw** *or* **Kaws** /kaws/), *adj.* PEOPLES, LANG = **Kansa**

Ka·wa·ba·ta /kàawə baáttə/, **Yasunari** (1899–1972) Japanese novelist. His works include *Snow Country* (1956) and *Thousand Cranes* (1959). He won the 1968 Nobel Prize in literature.

Ka·wa·gu·chi /kaàwə go͞ochee/ city north of Tokyo in Saitama Prefecture, southeastern Honshu, Japan. Population: 438,680 (1990).

Ka·wa·sa·ki /kaàwə saákee/ city south of Tokyo beside Tokyo Bay in Kanagawa Prefecture, Honshu, Japan. Population: 1,173,603 (1990).

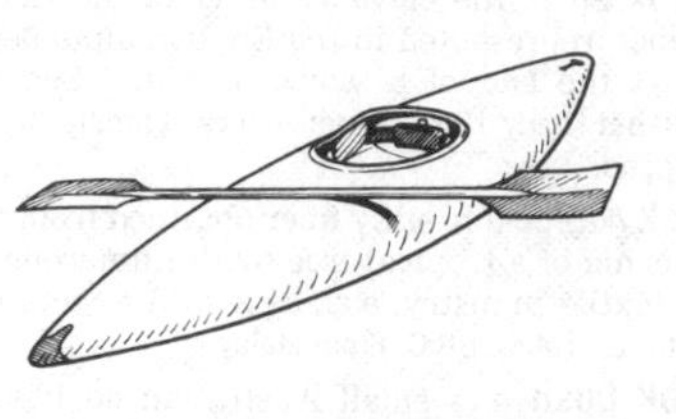

Kayak

kay·ak /kí àk/, **kai·ak** *n.* **1. SPORTS CANOE** a lightweight fiberglass canoe used for leisure and in competitive sport **2. ANIMAL-SKIN BOAT** a traditional Inuit boat for one or two people using double-bladed paddles. It is narrow and pointed and consists of a light frame covered with skins. ■ *vti.* (**-aked, -ak·ing, -aks**) **TRAVEL BY KAYAK** to travel or race in a kayak [Mid-18thC. From Inuit *qayaq.*] —**kay·ak·er** *n.*

kay·o /kày ó/ *n.* (*plural* **-os**) **KNOCKOUT** a knockout, especially in boxing (*slang*) ■ *vt.* (**-oed, -o·ing, -os**) **KNOCK SOMEBODY OUT** to knock somebody out, especially in boxing (*slang*) [Early 20thC. The pronunciation of KO, a shortening of KNOCKOUT.]

Kay·se·ri /kìzəreé/ city in central Turkey, near Mount Argaeus. It is the capital of Kayseri Province. Population: 421,362 (1990).

ka·za·chok /kàzzə cháwk/ *n.* a Russian folk dance in which high kicks are made from a squatting position [Early 20thC. From Russian, a diminutive of *kazak* "Cossack."]

Ka·zakh /kə zák, -zaák/, **Ka·zak** *n.* **1.** PEOPLES **MEMBER OF AN ASIAN PEOPLE** a member of a Turko-Tatar people of Central Asia, most of whom live in Kazakhstan and who are predominantly Muslim **2.** LANG **OFFICIAL LANGUAGE OF KAZAKHSTAN** the official language of Kazakhstan in Central Asia, also spoken in parts of Mongolia, China, and Afghanistan. It belongs to the Turkic branch of languages and is spoken by about eight million people. [Mid-19thC. From Russian, from Kazakh *kazak.*] —**Ka·zakh** *adj.*

Kazakhstan

Ka·zakh·stan /kàzək staán, kə zaák-/ republic in Central Asia, bounded by Russia, China, Kyrgyzstan, Uzbekistan, Turkmenistan, and the Caspian Sea. Language: Kazakh. Currency: tenge. Capital: Astana. Population: 16,881,793 (1997). Area: 1,049,155 sq. mi./2,717,300 sq. km. Official name **Republic of Kazakhstan**

Ka·zan /kə zaán/, **Elia** (*b.* 1909) Turkish-born U.S. stage and film director and novelist. He won Academy Awards for directing *Gentleman's Agreement* (1947) and *On the Waterfront* (1954). Real name **Elia Kazanjoglous**

ka·zat·sky /kəzaátskee/ (*plural* **-skies**), **ka·zat·ske** *n.* DANCE = **kazachok**

Kaz·bek /kaáz bek/ peak on the border of Russia and Georgia in the Caucasus Mountains. Height: 16,526 ft./5,037 m.

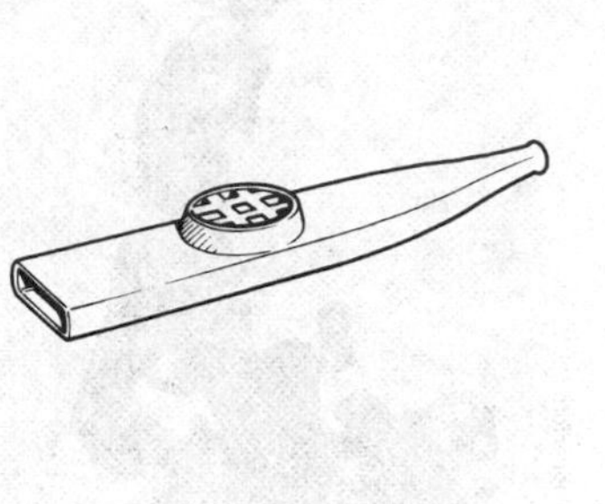

Kazoo

ka·zoo /kə zoō/ (*plural* **-zoos**) *n.* a toy instrument that makes a buzzing sound, consisting of a tube with a mouthpiece and a hole covered by a thin diaphragm [Late 19thC. An imitation of the sound produced by the instrument.]

KB *abbr.* **1.** COMPUT kilobyte **2.** CHESS king's bishop

KBP *abbr.* CHESS king's bishop's pawn

kbyte *n., abbr.* COMPUT kilobyte

kc *abbr.* PHYS kilocycle

K.C. *abbr.* **1.** Kansas City **2.** Kennel Club **3.** King's Counsel **4.** Knight of Columbus

kcal *abbr.* kilocalorie

kea /keé ə/ *n.* a large New Zealand parrot with brownish-green feathers that lives in mountainous regions and feeds mainly on insects. Latin name: *Nestor notabilis.* [Mid-19thC. From Maori.]

Kear·ny /kaárnee/, **Stephen Watts** (1794–1848) U.S. army officer. He helped to capture New Mexico and California during the Mexican War (1846–48).

Keat·ing /keéting/, **Paul** (*b.* 1944) Australian statesman. He was Labor prime minister of Australia (1991–96). Full name **Paul John Keating**

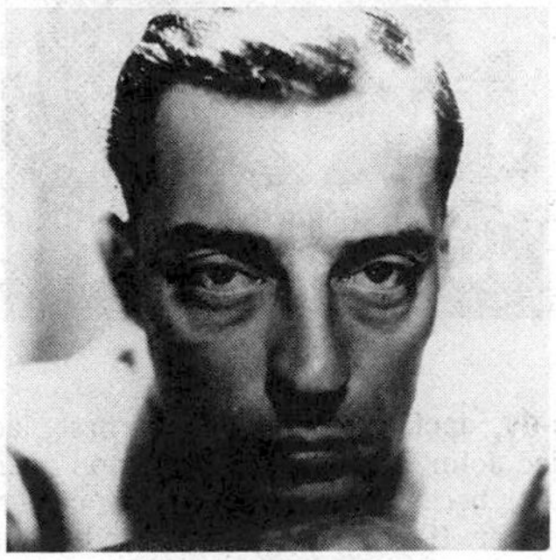

Buster Keaton

Kea·ton /keét'n/, **Buster** (1895–1966) U.S. silent film comedian. He was a deadpan acrobatic clown in many classic silent films such as *The General* (1927). Real name **Joseph Francis Keaton**

Keats /keets/, **John** (1795–1821) English poet. His lyrical intensity made him one of the most influential of the romantic poets. His great odes were collected in *Lamia, Isabella, The Eve of St Agnes, and Other Poems* (1820). —**Keats·i·an** /keétsee ən/ *adj.*

ke·bab /kə baáb/, **ka·bob** /kə bób/, **ka·bab** *n.* a selection of small pieces of tender food, e.g., poultry, meat, fish, or seafood, threaded onto a stick and grilled [Late 17thC. From Arabic *kabāb.*]

Ke·dah /kéddə/ state in northwestern Malaysia, on the Malay Peninsula. Capital: Alor Setar. Area: 3,660 sq. mi./9,479 sq. km.

kedge /kej/ *vti.* (**kedged, kedg·ing, kedg·es**) MOVE A VESSEL to move a vessel by pulling on a rope or cable attached to a light anchor, or to move in this way ■ *n.* **kedge, kedge an·chor** LIGHT ANCHOR a light anchor, especially one that is lodged some distance from a vessel so that the vessel can be pulled toward it [15thC. Origin uncertain: perhaps from CADGE in an earlier sense "to tie or bind."]

ked·ger·ee /kéjjə reé, kéjjə reé/ *n.* **1.** INDIAN DISH a spicy dish of Indian origin, made from lentils, rice, and sometimes fish **2.** DISH OF RICE, FISH, AND EGGS a dish of British origin based on Indian kedgeree, consisting of spiced rice with flaked smoked fish and hard-boiled eggs [Mid-17thC. From Hindi *khicṛī.*]

keel /keel/ *n.* **1.** NAUT SHIP'S STRUCTURAL ELEMENT the main structural element of a ship, stretching along the center line of its bottom from the bow to the stern. It may be made of wood or steel and sometimes extends farther downward into the water to provide extra stability. **2.** AIR AIRCRAFT'S STRUCTURAL ELEMENT any structure that looks or acts like a ship's keel, such as the main structural element of an aircraft's fuselage **3.** BIOL RIDGELIKE PART a ridge-shaped part of an organism **4.** NAUT SHIP a ship (*literary*) ■ *vti.* (**keeled, keel·ing, keels**) NAUT CAPSIZE to capsize a vessel, or to capsize [14thC. From Old Norse *kjölr.*] ◇ **on an even keel** in a stable, steady condition

keel over *v.* **1.** *vi.* COLLAPSE to collapse or fall over, often through exhaustion or illness (*informal*) **2.** *vti.* NAUT = **keel**

keel·age /keélij/ *n.* a docking fee for merchant ships, charged by a port

keel·boat /keél bōt/ *n.* a covered river boat with a keel and shallow draft but no sail, propelled by rowing, poling, or towing, and used for transporting freight [Late 17thC. Formed from KEEL.]

keel·haul /keél hàwl/ (**-hauled, -haul·ing, -hauls**) *vt.* **1.** DRAG SOMEBODY UNDER A BOAT to drag somebody on a rope from one side of a vessel to the other under the keel as a form of punishment **2.** REBUKE SOMEBODY to reprimand somebody severely (*informal*) [Mid-17thC. From Dutch *kielhalen.*]

keel·son /keélsən, kéllsən/, **kel·son** /kéllsən/ *n.* a metal or wooden beam attached to the upper side of a boat's keel to reinforce it [13thC. Origin uncertain: probably from Old Norse *kjölsvīn* or from Low German *kielsvīn.*]

keen[1] /keen/ *adj.* **1.** INTENSE intense and lively ○ *keen competition* **2.** SENSITIVE finely tuned and able to sense minor differences, distinctions, or details ○ *a keen sense of smell* **3.** ENTHUSIASTIC very eager and willing ○ *not very keen on the idea* **4.** ACUTE quick to understand things ○ *a keen sense of humor* **5.** SHARP with a sharp cutting edge (*literary*) ○ *a keen razor* **6.** BITING extremely cold and penetrating ○ *a keen wind* **7.** VERY GOOD fine or very good (*dated slang*) ○ *a keen new bike* [Old English *cēne* "brave, clever." Ultimately from a prehistoric Germanic word.] —**keen·ly** *adv.* —**keen·ness** *n.*

keen[2] /keen/ *vi.* (**keened, keen·ing, keens**) HOWL IN GRIEF to cry out or wail in grief, especially while lamenting the dead ■ *n.* LAMENT a lamentation for a dead person (*literary*) [Early 19thC. From Irish *caoinim* "I wail."] —**keen·er** *n.*

Keene /keen/ city in southwestern New Hampshire. Population: 22,430 (1990).

keep /keep/ *v.* (**kept** /kept/, **keep·ing, keeps**) **1.** *vti.* POSSESS to hold or maintain something in your possession ○ *The sample is yours to keep.* **2.** *vt.* MAINTAIN THE CONDITION OF SOMETHING to maintain something or somebody in a particular place or condition ○ *Keep your arm up.* **3.** *vt.* STORE SOMETHING to store something in a place when it is not in use ○ *He keeps the keys in a drawer.* **4.** *vti.* CONTINUE to cause somebody or something to continue in a particular way or activity, or to continue in a particular way ○ *It keeps working even in a power failure.* **5.** *vt.* SAFEGUARD INFORMATION to refrain from telling a secret or other information ○ *keep a secret* **6.** *vt.* SAVE SOMETHING to save something for later use or withhold something from use ○ *Keep some in reserve.* **7.** *vt.* BE TRUE TO SOMETHING to fulfill a promise or other verbal commitment ○ *keep your word* **8.** *vt.* FULFILL A RELIGIOUS DUTY to observe a religious obligation ○ *keep Kosher* ○ *keep the sabbath* **9.** *vt.* MAINTAIN A RECORD to create or maintain something as a written record ○ *keep a diary* **10.** *vi.* STAY to remain in a particular condition ○ *The stove will keep warm for a while after the fire goes out.* **11.** *vi.* MAINTAIN A COURSE to follow a particular course or direction ○ *Keep right until you see a big yellow barn.* **12.** *vi.* NOT SPOIL to remain fresh or in a usable condition ○ *That fish won't keep in this hot weather.* **13.** *vi.* CONTINUE to do something repeatedly or continue to do something ○ *Keep smiling!* **14.** *vi.* NOT REQUIRE ATTENTION to be able to be postponed ○ *I think the dusting will keep till tomorrow.* **15.** *vt.* HAVE SOMETHING FOR SALE to have something in stock in order to sell it ○ *Do you keep chainsaw blades?* **16.** *vt.* DETAIN SOMEBODY to make somebody wait or prevent somebody from going ○ *Could I keep you for a moment?* **17.** *vt.* LOOK AFTER SOMEBODY OR SOMETHING to take care of a person or animal, providing what is required to live ○ *We've never kept pets.* **18.** *vt.* HAVE AS LIVESTOCK to raise an animal for profit ○ *keep cattle* **19.** *vt.* EMPLOY SOMEBODY to employ somebody, especially in a household ○ *keep servants* **20.** *vt.* RUN A BUSINESS OR HOUSEHOLD to maintain a business, house, or other establishment ○ *He keeps house for the General.* **21.** *vt.* SUPPORT FINANCIALLY to provide financially for a spouse or lover (*dated*) ■ *n.* **1.** MAINTENANCE food and lodging, or whatever somebody needs to live ○ *work for your keep* **2.** CASTLE PART a stronghold, or the innermost fortified part of a castle [Old English *cēpan* "to take, observe," of unknown origin] ◇ **for keeps** permanently or forever (*informal*) ◇ **keep it up** to continue to do something ◇ **keep something to yourself** to refrain from revealing ◇ **keep yourself to yourself** to avoid mixing or communicating with other people

keep at *vt.* **1.** CONTINUE DOING SOMETHING to persevere with something, especially something difficult or strenuous **2.** PESTER SOMEBODY to persist in asking somebody to do something (*informal*) ○ *They kept at me to do more and more work in less and less time.*

keep away *v.* **1.** *vt.* KEEP SOMEBODY OR SOMETHING DISTANT to prevent somebody or something from going near somebody or something **2.** *vi.* NOT APPROACH to avoid going near something or somebody

keep back *vt.* **1.** NOT TELL SOMETHING to refrain from telling or revealing something **2.** WITHHOLD SOMETHING FOR LATER USE to hold something in reserve for later use or for another purpose **3.** RESTRAIN SOMETHING to restrain or confine something to a limit

keep down *v.* **1.** *vt.* OPPRESS SOMEBODY OR SOMETHING to maintain somebody or something in an inferior position or in a state of oppression **2.** *vt.* MAINTAIN SOMETHING AT A LOW LEVEL to maintain something at a low level, position, or number ○ *keep the costs down* **3.** *vi.* STAY LOW to stay in a place or position where you cannot be seen **4.** *vt.* NOT VOMIT SOMETHING to hold food or drink in your stomach without vomiting ○ *He hasn't been able to keep anything down since the operation.*

keep from *vt.* **1.** HIDE SOMETHING FROM SOMEBODY to refrain from disclosing something to somebody **2.** RESTRAIN SOMEBODY to prevent somebody from doing something **3.** SAFEGUARD SOMEBODY to protect somebody from something ○ *kept us from harm*

keep in *vt.* to repress something that you feel

keep off *v.* **1.** *vt.* PREVENT CONTACT to prevent something or somebody from having direct contact with something or somebody else **2.** *vti.* NOT TOUCH to refrain from direct contact with something or somebody ○ *Keep off the grass!* **3.** *vti.* NOT CONSUME to prevent somebody from consuming something or to refrain from consuming something ○ *I was told to keep off caffeine.* **4.** *vti.* NOT TALK ABOUT to prevent somebody from discussing something or to refrain from discussing something ○ *we kept off the topic of money*

keep on *v.* **1.** *vi.* CONTINUE to continue ○ *They just kept on, even after we told them to stop.* **2.** *vt.* NOT TAKE SOMETHING OFF to continue wearing something **3.** *vt.* NOT DISMISS SOMEBODY to continue to employ somebody

keep out *vti.* to prevent somebody from entering or to refrain from entering a place

keep out of *vti.* **1.** PREVENT EXPOSURE to prevent somebody or something from exposure to something, or to avoid exposure to something ○ *keep it out of the rain* **2.** AVOID INVOLVEMENT to prevent somebody's involvement in something, or to avoid involvement in something ○ *Keep out of her way.*

keep to *vt.* to adhere without deviation to a plan, course, or subject

keep up *v.* **1.** *vt.* MAINTAIN THE PRESENT LEVEL OF to maintain something at its present level, not letting it fall or subside ○ *Keep up the good work.* **2.** *vi.* STAY EVEN WITH to go as fast or make the same progress as somebody else **3.** *vt.* MAINTAIN SOMETHING IN GOOD CONDITION to make sure that something stays in good condition ○ *has a beautiful home but doesn't really keep it up* **4.** *vt.* DELAY SOMEBODY'S SLEEP OR BEDTIME to prevent somebody from sleeping or going to bed at night ○ *The music from the party kept us up till dawn.*

keep up with *vt.* **1.** REMAIN INFORMED ABOUT SOMETHING to remain abreast of something that undergoes continuous change or progress **2.** STAY IN CONTACT WITH to stay in contact with somebody, especially by letter ○ *I still keep up with a few friends from school.*

keep-a-way *n.* GAME = **monkey in the middle**

keep·er /keépər/ *n.* **1.** CARETAKER somebody in charge of a building or small business (*usually used in combination*) ○ *a lighthouse keeper* **2.** WARDEN somebody whose job is to look after or protect animals **3.** CRIMINOL PRISON GUARD somebody who is responsible for guarding other people, especially in a prison **4. SOMEBODY KEEPING SOMETHING** somebody who keeps or maintains something ○ *a good record keeper* **5. SOMETHING WORTH KEEPING** something that is worth keeping, especially a fish that is large enough to be legally caught and retained (*informal*) **6.** FOOTBALL **PLAY IN FOOTBALL** in football, a play in which the quarterback runs toward the goal with the ball **7.** SPORTS **GOALKEEPER** a goalkeeper (*informal*) **8.** PHYS **IRON BAR PLACED ACROSS A MAGNET'S POLES** an iron or steel bar placed across the poles of a permanent horseshoe magnet when it is not in use, to close the magnetic circuit and prevent demagnetization

keep·ing /kéeping/ *n.* **1. LOOKING AFTER** the act of looking after or caring for somebody or something **2. CHARGE** somebody's charge, custody, or possession ○ *It's in the bank's keeping.* ◇ **in keeping with** consistent with or suitable for something ◇ **out of keeping with** not consistent with or suitable for something

keep·sake /kéep sàyk/ *n.* a small item or gift kept because it evokes memories of somebody or something [Late 18thC. The underlying meaning is of something to be kept "for the sake of" the giver.]

kees·hond /káyss hàwnt, -hònd/ (*plural* **-honds** *or* **-hon·den** /-hàwndən/) *n.* a dog with a dense shaggy blackish-gray coat and a tightly curled tail, belonging to a breed developed in the Netherlands [Early 20thC. From Dutch, literally "Kees dog," from *Kees* (a pet form of the name *Cornelis* "Cornelius") + *hond* "dog."]

kees·ter *n.* = **keister**

kef *n.* DRUGS = **kif**

Ke·fau·ver /kée fàwvər/, **Estes** (1903–63) U.S. politician. He chaired a Senate committee on organized crime (1950–51), and was unsuccessful Democratic candidate for vice president (1956). Full name **Carey Estes Kefauver**

kef·fi·yeh /kə fée ə/ *n.* = **kaffiyeh**

ke·fir /ke féer/ *n.* a creamy drink made from fermented cow's milk [Late 19thC. Via Russian from Old Turkic *köpür* "milk."]

Kef·la·vik /kéfləveek, kyébləveek/ town in southwestern Iceland, situated about 22 mi./35 km southwest of Reykjavik. Population: 7,605 (1995).

keg /keg/ *n.* **1. SMALL BARREL** a small barrel used for storing liquids **2. CONTENTS OF A KEG** the amount that a keg can hold **3. NAIL WEIGHT UNIT** a unit of weight used for nails, equivalent to 100 lb./45.5kg **4. BEER BARREL** an aluminum barrel that is used for storing and transporting beer ■ *vt.* (**kegged, keg·ging, kegs**) **STORE BEER IN A BARREL** to put or store beer in a small barrel [Early 17thC. Alteration of *cag* from, ultimately, Old Norse *kaggi.*]

keg·ler /kégglər/, **kege·ler** *n.* somebody who takes part in the sport of bowling (*informal*) [Mid-20thC. From German *kegeln* "to bowl."]

keis·ter /kéestər/, **kees·ter** *n.* the buttocks (*humorous slang*) [Late 19thC. Origin unknown.]

Kei·tel /kît'l/, **Wilhelm** (1882–1946) German field marshal. Hitler's chief military adviser during World War II, he was executed for war crimes in 1946.

Ke·jim·ku·jik Na·tion·al Park /kejim kóojik-/ national park and wildlife preserve in southern Nova Scotia, Canada, established in 1974. Area: 156 sq. mi./403 sq. km.

Ke·ku·lé for·mu·la /kékyə lay-/ *n.* the representation of a benzene molecule as a hexagonal ring with alternating single and double bonds linking six carbon atoms, each linked to one hydrogen atom at the vertices [Mid-20thC. Named for the German physicist Friedrich August *Kekulé* (1829–96), who devised it.]

Kel·logg /kél àwg/, **John** (1852–1943) U.S. surgeon and food manufacturer. During the 1890s he and his brother William developed the process of making corn flakes. Full name **John Harvey Kellog**

Kel·ly /kéllee/, **Gene** (1912–96) U.S. movie actor, dancer, and director. He is best known for starring in and co-directing *Singing in the Rain* (1952). Full name **Eugene Curran Kelly**

Kel·ly, Grace (1929–82) U.S. movie actor. She starred in motion pictures such as *High Noon* and *Rear Window* before retiring in 1956 to marry Prince Rainier of Monaco. Full name **Grace Patricia Kelly**

kel·ly green *adj.* of a bright vibrant green color [From the common Irish surname "Kelly"] —**kelly green** *n.*

ke·loid /kée lòyd/ *n.* an area of raised pink or red fibrous scar tissue at the edges of a wound or incision [Mid-19thC. From French *chéloïde, kéloïde,* from Greek *khēlē* "crab claw."] —**ke·loid·al** /kee lóyd'l/ *adj.*

Ke·low·na /kə lṓnə/ city in south central British Columbia, Canada, 60 mi./97 km north of the U.S. border. Population: 89,442 (1996).

kelp /kelp/ *n.* **1. BROWN SEAWEED** brown seaweed with thick broad fronds. Order: Laminariales. **2. SEAWEED ASH** the ash from kelp or other seaweeds, used as a source of potash and iodine [14thC. Origin unknown.]

kel·pie[1] /kélpee/, **kel·py** (*plural* **-pies**) *n.* in Scottish folklore, a malicious water spirit that takes the form of a horse and lures people to death by drowning [Late 17thC. Origin uncertain: perhaps from Gaelic *cailpeach* "colt, bullock."]

kel·pie[2] /kélpee/ *n.* a smooth-haired dog of an Australian breed of sheepdog [Early 20thC. Named for *King's Kelpie*, the female dog that founded the breed.]

Kel·sey /kélssee/, **Henry** (1667?–1724) English explorer. He trekked across the Canadian plains from Hudson Bay to present-day Alberta (1690–92).

kel·son *n.* NAUT = **keelson**

kelt /kelt/ *n.* a salmon that has returned to the river of its birth and recently spawned. In most species, the kelts do not survive, but Atlantic salmon can return to the ocean to spawn another season. [14thC. Origin unknown.]

Kelt *n., adj.* = **Celt** —**Kelt·ic** *adj.*

kel·vin /kélvin/ *n.* **UNIT OF ABSOLUTE TEMPERATURE** the SI unit of absolute temperature, equal to 1/273.16 of the absolute temperature of the triple point of water, equivalent to one degree Celsius. A temperature in kelvin may be converted to Celsius by subtracting 273.16. Symbol **K** ■ *adj.* **ON THE KELVIN SCALE** relating to or measured on the Kelvin scale [Early 20thC. Named for the British physicist William Thomson, first Baron KELVIN.]

Kel·vin /kélvin/, **William Thomson, 1st Baron** (1824–1907) British physicist. He did pioneering work in thermodynamics and electricity and devised the absolute temperature scale. His work helped develop the law of the conservation of energy. Full name **William Thomson, 1st Baron Kelvin of Largs**

Kel·vin scale *n.* a temperature scale on which zero is the lowest possible temperature and the triple point of water is defined as 273.16K. It is based on heat transfer between two sections of a reversible heat engine. [Late 19thC. Named for William Thomson, first Baron KELVIN.]

Ke·me·ro·vo /kèmmə rṓvə/ city in southern Siberian Russia. It is the capital city of Kemerovo Oblast, on the Tom' River. Population: 521,000 (1990).

kemp /kemp/ *n.* a short coarse hair or fiber [14thC. From Old Norse *kampr* "beard, whisker."] —**kemp·y** *adj.*

Kemp·sey /kémpsee/ town in northeastern New South Wales, Australia, a center of agriculture, timber production, and light industry. Population: 8,630 (1996).

kempt /kempt/ *adj.* neat in appearance and well looked after (*archaic*) [Old English *cemd*, from the past participle of *cemban* "to comb." Ultimately from a prehistoric Germanic word that is also the ancestor of English *comb.*]

ken /ken/ *n.* **KNOWLEDGE** somebody's knowledge or understanding ○ *It's beyond my ken.* ■ *vti.* (**kenned** *or* **kent** /kent/, **kenned** *or* **kent, ken·ning, kens**) *Scotland* **KNOW** to know somebody or something [Old English *cennan* "to make known." Ultimately from an Indo-European word that is also the ancestor of English *can* and *know.*]

Ken. *abbr.* Kentucky

Ken·dal /kénd'l/ market town in the Lake District, Cumbria, northwestern England. Population: 23,710 (1991).

Ken·dal green /kénd'l-/ *n.* **GREEN WOOLEN CLOTH** a coarse thick green woolen cloth similar to tweed ■ *adj.* **LIGHT GRAYISH GREEN** of a light grayish-green color [14thC. Named for the town of KENDAL, where the cloth was made.]

Ken·dall /kénd'l/, **Edward Calvin** (1886–1972) U.S. biochemist. He won the Nobel Prize in physiology or medicine (1950) for his research on hormones such as cortisone.

Popperfoto

Kendo

ken·do /kén dṓ/ *n.* a Japanese martial art in which people fence using bamboo sticks instead of swords [Early 20thC. From Japanese, literally "way of the sword."]

Ken·ne·bec /kénnəbèk/ river in western Maine that flows south from Moosehead Lake to the Atlantic Ocean. Length: 164 mi./264 km.

Ken·ne·dy, Cape ◆ **Cape Canaveral**

Ken·ne·dy, Mount /kénnədee/ mountain in the St. Elias Range in southwestern Yukon Territory, Canada. Height: 13,905 ft./4,238 m.

Ken·ne·dy, Edward M. (*b.* 1932) U.S. politician. He became a senator in 1962 and unsuccessfully ran for the Democratic presidential nomination in 1980. John F. Kennedy and Robert F. Kennedy were his brothers. Known as **Ted Kennedy.** Full name **Edward Moore Kennedy**

John F. Kennedy Library

Jackie Kennedy

Ken·ne·dy, Jackie (1929–94) U.S. first lady. She married John F. Kennedy in 1953 and as first lady (1961–63) became an international celebrity and style-setter. Her great dignity after her husband's assassination increased public admiration for her. She married Greek shipping magnate Aristotle Onassis in 1968, and after his death in 1975 worked in publishing in New York and continued her lifelong patronage and promotion of the arts. Born **Jacqueline Lee Bouvier.** Full name **Jacqueline Lee Kennedy-Onassis.** Known as **Jackie O**

Ken·ne·dy, John F. (1917–63) U.S. statesman and 35th president of the United States. His Democratic administration (1961–63) pursued liberal reforms at home and a hard-line Cold War policy abroad. He was assassinated in Dallas. Full name **John Fitzgerald Kennedy.** Known as **Jack Kennedy**

Ken·ne·dy, Joseph P. (1888–1969) U.S. businessman and government official. He was the father of John F., Robert F., and Edward M. Kennedy. He was ambassador to Britain (1938–40). Full name **Joseph Patrick Kennedy**

Ken·ne·dy, Robert F. (1925–68) U.S. politician. Attorney general (1961–64) during the Democratic administration of his brother John F. Kennedy, he was assassinated during his 1968 presidential campaign. Full name **Robert Francis Kennedy.** Known as **Bobby Kennedy**

Ken·ne·dy, William (*b.* 1928) U.S. writer. He won a Pulitzer Prize for his novel *Ironweed* (1983).

ken·nel /kénn'l/ *n.* **1. DOG BOARDING OR BREEDING PLACE** a place where dogs are bred and trained and where people can leave their dogs while they are away **2.** = **doghouse 3. ANIMAL'S LAIR** the lair of a wild animal such as a fox **4. PACK OF DOGS** a pack of hounds or dogs **5. HOVEL** a small house in bad condition (*archaic*) ■

vti. **(-neled, -nel·ing, -nels)** PUT OR STAY IN A KENNEL to put a dog into a kennel or to stay in a kennel [14thC. Via assumed Anglo-Norman *kenil* from, ultimately, Latin *canis* "dog" (source of English *canine.*]

Ken·nel·ly-Heav·i·side lay·er /kénnəlee héevəsīd-/ *n.* PHYS = **E layer** [Early 20thC. Named for the U.S. electrical engineer, Arthur Edwin *Kennelly* (1861–1939) and the British physicist, Oliver *Heaviside* (1850–1925).]

Ken·neth I /kénnith/, **King of Scotland** (*fl.* mid-9th century) Around 846 he united the kingdoms of the Scots and the Picts, becoming the first king of Scotland. Known as **Kenneth MacAlpin**

ke·no /kéenō/ *n. U.S., Aus* a game of chance in which players wager on a set of numbers to be drawn at random. It is operated for profit by many states and gaming authorities. [Early 19thC. Via French *quine* "set of five winning numbers" from Latin *quini* "five each," from *quinque* "five."]

Ke·no·sha /kə nṓ shə/ industrial city in southeastern Wisconsin, on Lake Michigan. Population: 80,352 (1990).

ke·no·sis /kə nṓssiss/ *n.* according to Christian belief, Jesus Christ's act of partially giving up his divine status in order to become a man, as recorded in Philippians 2: 6–7 [Late 19thC. From Greek *kenōsis* "an emptying," from the phrase in *Philippians 2:7 heauton ekenōse* "emptied himself."] —**ke·not·ic** /kə nóttik/ *adj.*

Ken·sett /kénsət/, **John Frederick** (1818–72) U.S. artist. Noted for his detailed landscapes, he was a member of the Hudson River School.

kent *Scotland* past participle, past tense of **ken**

Kent /kent/, **Rockwell** (1882–1971) U.S. artist. He is known for his stark woodcut illustrations and landscape paintings.

ken·te, ken·te cloth *n.* a handwoven cloth from Ghana, usually very brightly colored [Mid-20thC. From Twi, literally "cloth."]

ken·tia /kénntee ə/, **ken·tia palm** *n.* a tall-growing palm tree that is native to Lord Howe Island, Australia, and is widely cultivated for its decorative foliage. Latin name: *Howea forsterana.* [Late 19thC. Coined from modern Latin, named for the British plant collector, William *Kent.*]

Ken·tish /kéntish/ *adj.* **1.** OF THE ENGLISH COUNTY OF KENT from or relating to the English county of Kent **2.** LANG OF THE KENTISH DIALECT relating to the Kentish dialect ■ *n.* LANG OLD ENGLISH DIALECT a dialect of Old English spoken in the extreme southeast of England, probably from around the 5th century A.D., recorded in written form from around the 7th century A.D. It continued to be spoken in the area into the Middle English period, but was increasingly overtaken by the form of English that developed from the dialect known as East Midlands. ◊ **Anglian, West Saxon**

kent·ledge /kéntlij/ *n.* scrap iron or other heavy material used as permanent ballast on ships [Early 17thC. From Old French *quintelage* "ballast," from *Old French quintal* (see QUINTAL).]

Kentucky

Ken·tuck·y[1] /ken túkee/ state in the east central United States, bordered by Illinois, Indiana, Missouri, Ohio, Tennessee, Virginia, and West Virginia. Capital: Frankfort. Population: 3,908,124 (1997). Area: 40,411 sq. mi./104,664 sq. km. —**Ken·tuck·ian** *n., adj.*

Ken·tuck·y[2] river in central Kentucky that flows northwestward to join the Ohio River at Carrolton. Length: 259 mi./417 km.

Ken·tuck·y blue·grass *n.* a grass native to Africa, Europe, and Asia, naturalized in North America and widely used for pastureland and lawns. Latin name: *Poa pratensis.*

Ken·tuck·y cof·fee tree *n.* a deciduous tree of the legume family with brown pods and compound leaves that is native to eastern North America. Its pulpy seeds were formerly used as a coffee substitute. Latin name: *Gymnocladus dioica.*

Ken·tuck·y Der·by *n.* a race for three-year-old horses that has been run annually since 1875 at Churchill Downs in Louisville, Kentucky. It is held on the first Saturday in May.

Ken·tuck·y ri·fle *n.* a muzzleloading rifle developed in the 18th century and widely used on the American frontier

Kenya

Ken·ya /kényə/ republic in eastern Africa. It became independent from the United Kingdom in 1963. Language: English, Swahili. Currency: Kenyan shilling. Capital: Nairobi. Population: 27,838,597 (1997). Area: 224,961 sq. mi./582,646 sq. km. Official name **Republic of Kenya** —**Ken·yan** *n., adj.*

Ken·ya, Mount extinct volcano in central Kenya, the second highest mountain in Africa. Height: 17,057 ft./5,199 m.

Ken·yon /kényən/, **Dame Kathleen** (1906–78) British archeologist. She is famous for her excavations at Jericho and Jerusalem.

Keogh plan /kée ō-/ *n.* a retirement plan for the self-employed and their employees [Late 20thC. Named for the U.S. politician, Eugene James *Keogh* (d. 1989).]

Ke·o·kuk /kéeə kùk/ city in southeastern Iowa on the Mississippi River. Population: 12,315 (1996).

keph·a·lin *n.* BIOL = **cephalin**

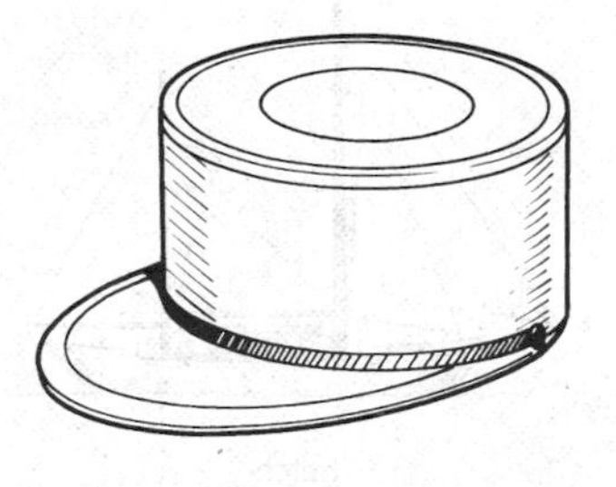

Kepi

ke·pi /káypee, képpee/ *n.* a French military hat with a round flat top and a visor [Mid-19thC. Via French *képi* from Swiss German *Käppi*, literally "little cap."]

Ke·pler /képplər/ *n.* a crater on the Moon in Oceanus Procellarum, 20 mi./32 km in diameter. It is the center of a large bright system of rays on the lunar surface.

Kep·ler /képlər/, **Johannes** (1571–1630) German astronomer. His three laws of planetary motion include his finding that the planets move around the sun in elliptical orbits.

Ke·pler's laws *npl.* three mathematical statements that describe the movement of the planets in their orbits around the Sun. The first two laws were published in 1609 and the third a decade later. [Late 18thC. Named for the German astronomer, Johannes KEPLER, who discovered them.]

kept past tense, past participle of **keep** ■ *adj.* SUPPORTED supported financially by a lover especially a married one

Ker·a·la /kérrələ/ state in southwestern India. Capital: Trivandrum. Population: 30,555,000 (1994). Area: 15,005 sq. mi./38,864 sq. km.

kerat- *prefix.* = **kerato-** (*used before vowels*)

ker·a·tec·to·my /kèrrə téktəmee/ (*plural* **-mies**) *n.* surgical removal of part of the cornea

ker·a·tin /kérrətin/ *n.* a fibrous insoluble protein that is the main structural element in hair, nails, feathers, and hooves [Mid-19thC. Coined from the stem of Greek *keras* "horn" + -IN.] —**ke·rat·i·nous** /ke rátt'nəss/ *adj.*

ker·a·tin·i·za·tion /kèrrətəni záysh'n/ *n.* the deposition of keratin in skin cells, e.g., in hair and nails, giving them the texture of horn

ker·a·tin·ize /kérrəti nīz/ (**-ized, -iz·ing, -iz·es**) *vti.* to convert something into keratin, or become keratin

ker·a·ti·tis /kèrrə tītiss/ *n.* inflammation and swelling of the cornea

kerato- *prefix.* **1.** hornlike tissue ○ *keratose* **2.** cornea ○ *keratoplasty* [From Greek *kerat-*, the stem of *keras* "horn." Ultimately from an Indo-European base that is also the ancestor of English *horn, corn,* and *cranium.*]

ker·a·toid /kérrə tòyd/ *adj.* like horn in texture or appearance

ker·a·top·a·thy /kèrrə tóppəthee/ *n.* any non-inflammatory disorder of the cornea

ker·a·to·plas·ty /kérrə tō plàstee/ (*plural* **-ties**) *n.* plastic surgery on the cornea, especially corneal grafting —**ker·a·to·plas·tic** /kèrrə tō plástik/ *adj.*

ker·a·tose /kérrə tōss/ *adj.* having a hornlike skeleton, as some sponges have

ker·a·to·sis /kèrrə tṓssiss/ (*plural* **-ses** /-seez/) *n.* **1.** HORNLIKE GROWTH growth of hard hornlike tissue on the skin **2.** HORNLIKE PART a hornlike growth on the skin —**ker·a·tot·ic** /kèrrə tóttik/ *adj.*

ker·a·tot·o·my /kèrrə tóttəmee/ (*plural* **-mies**) *n.* a surgical cutting of the cornea

kerb /kurb/ *n. U.K.* = **curb** ■ *vt.* (**kerbed, kerb·ing, kerbs**) *U.K.* = **curb** [Mid-17thC. Variant of CURB, in the sense "an enclosing framework."]

Kerch /kurch/ city and seaport in southern Ukraine, on the eastern shore of the Crimean Peninsula. Population: 176,000 (1990).

ker·chief /kúrchif, kúr cheef/ *n.* a square scarf for women, worn around the neck or as a headscarf [13thC. From Anglo-Norman *courchef* or Old French *cuevre-chef*, literally "cover-head."] —**ker·chiefed** *adj.*

Ke·ren·sky /kərénskee/, **Aleksandr Fyodorovich** (1881–1970) Russian revolutionary leader. He was the head of the 1917 provisional government of Russia from July until the Bolshevik takeover in November 1917.

kerf /kurf/ *n.* a cut or the width of a cut made by an ax, saw, or cutting tool [Old English *cerf.* Ultimately from a prehistoric West Germanic word that is also the ancestor of English *carve.*]

ker·fuf·fle /kər fúff'l/ *n. U.K.* a noisy disturbance or commotion (*informal*) [Early 19thC. Origin uncertain: perhaps from Gaelic *car* "twist" + Scots *fuffle* "fuss."]

Ker·gue·len Is·lands /kúrgələn-/ island group in the southern Indian Ocean, consisting of one main island and about 300 smaller islands and islets. Area: 2,700 sq. mi./6,993 sq. km.

Ker·ma·dec Is·lands /kər mádək-/ island group in the southern Pacific Ocean, a dependency of New Zealand. Area: 13 sq. mi./34 sq. km.

Ker·man /kur maan/, **Ker·mān** city in southeastern Iran, the capital of Kerman Province. Population: 311,643 (1991).

ker·mes /kúr meez, kúrməss/ (*plural* **-mes**) *n.* **1.** INSECTS RED DYESTUFF the dried bodies of female scale insects of the genus *Kermes*, used to produce a purplish-red dye **2.** TREES = **kermes oak** [Late 16thC. Via French *kermès* from Arabic *ḳirmiz* "kermes beetle" (source of English *crimson*).]

kermes oak *n.* a small evergreen oak tree native to Europe and Asia that provides a habitat for the scale insects used to make kermes. Latin name: *Quercus coccifera.*

ker·mis /kúrmiss/, **kir·mess, ker·mess** *n.* **1.** COUNTRY FAIR an annual country fair that used to be held in the

Netherlands and northern Germany **2. FUNDRAISING FESTIVAL** a festival or fair held to collect money for charity [Late 16thC. From Dutch, literally "mass on the anniversary of the church's dedication," from *kerk* "church" + *misse* "mass." From the fair held on this day.]

kern[1] /kurn/ *n.* **PART OF A CHARACTER** the part of a typographic character that projects beyond the body ■ *v.* (**kerned, kern·ing, kerns**) **1.** *vti.* **BRING TYPE TOGETHER** to eliminate white space between adjacent letters that may appear too widely separated on a line **2.** *vt.* **OVERLAP ADJACENT CHARACTERS** to join adjacent printed characters or make them overlap [Late 17thC. Via French *carne* "corner" from, ultimately, Latin *cardo* "hinge" (source of English *cardinal*).]

kern[2] /kurn/, **kerne** *n.* a medieval Irish or Scottish light infantryman [14thC. From Irish *ceithearn.*]

Kern /kurn/, **Jerome** (1885–1945) U.S. composer. He wrote numerous Broadway musicals, including *Show Boat* (1927). His songs include "Ol' Man River" and "Smoke Gets in Your Eyes." Full name **Jerome David Kern**

ker·nel /kúrn'l/ *n.* **1.** PLANTS **EDIBLE CORE** the edible content of a nut or fruit stone **2.** PLANTS **CEREAL GRAIN** the grain of a cereal that contains a seed and husk **3. CENTRAL PART** the central or most important part of something ○ *a kernel of self-belief that never wavered* **4.** PHYS **ATOM STRIPPED OF ITS ELECTRONS** a positively charged atomic nucleus that has lost its valence electrons **5.** COMPUT **KEY PORTION OF AN OPERATING SYSTEM** the core portion of a computer's operating system that resides in the memory and performs essential functions such as controlling the memory and files and allocating system resources [Old English *cyrnel* "little seed," from CORN]

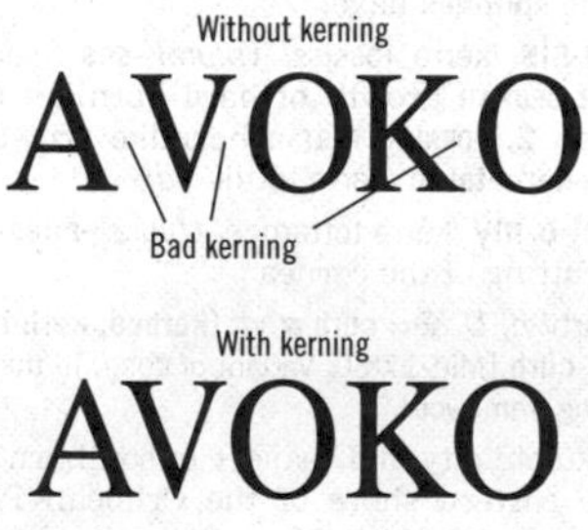

Kerning

kern·ing /kúrning/ *n.* the addition or removal of space between individual characters in a piece of typeset text to improve its appearance or alter its fit

kern·ite /kúr nìt/ *n.* a colorless or white crystalline mineral that is composed of hydrated sodium borate and is a souce of borax and other boron compounds [Early 20thC. Named for *Kern* County, California, where it was discovered.]

ker·o·gen /kérrəjən/ *n.* a fossilized insoluble organic material found in some sedimentary rocks, e.g., oil shales, yielding petroleum products when heated [Early 20thC. Coined from Greek *kēros* "wax" + -GEN.]

ker·o·sene /kérrə seen, kèrrə séen/, **ker·o·sine** *n.* a colorless flammable oil distilled from petroleum and used as a fuel for jet engines, heating, cooking, and lighting [Mid-19thC. Coined from Greek *kēros* "wax" + -ENE or -INE.]

Ker·ou·ac /kérrə wàk/, **Jack** (1922–69) U.S. novelist. He was a leading figure in the 1950s Beat Generation, and his best-known novel is *On the Road* (1957). Full name **Jean Louis Kerouac**

ker·plunk /kər plúngk/ *adv., interj.* used to imitate the sound made by something heavy falling suddenly (*informal*) [An imitation of the sound]

Kerr ef·fect /káar-, kúr-/ *n.* **1. DOUBLE REFRACTION** the property of some transparent substances that makes them refract doubly when placed in an electric field **2. ELLIPTICAL POLARIZATION OF REFLECTED LIGHT** the elliptical polarization of plane polarized or unpolarized light when reflected from the polished pole of a magnetized material [Early 20thC. Named for the Scottish physicist, John *Kerr* (1824–1907), who discovered it.]

Ker·ry[1] /kérree/ (*plural* **-ries**) *n.* a small black bull or dairy cow belonging to a breed that originated in Ireland [Mid-19thC. Named for County KERRY, where the breed originated.]

Ker·ry[2] /kérree/ county in Munster Province, southwestern Republic of Ireland. Population: 125,863 (1996). Area: 1,815 sq. km/4,701 sq. km.

Ker·ry blue ter·ri·er, **Ker·ry blue** *n.* a terrier with a dense but soft wavy bluish-gray coat, belonging to a breed that originated in Ireland [Early 20thC. Named for County KERRY, where the breed originated.]

ker·sey /kúrzee/ *n.* a smooth woolen fabric used for making coats [14thC. Named for the village of *Kersey* in Suffolk, England.]

ker·sey·mere /kúrzee meer/ *n.* a fine soft woolen cloth with a fancy twill weave [Late 18thC. Alteration of CASSIMERE by association with KERSEY.]

Ker·tész /kərtésh/, **André** (1894–1985) Hungarian-born U.S. photographer. One of the founders of photojournalism, he is known for his realistic and sensitive scenes of everyday life.

ke·ryg·ma /kə rígmə/ *n.* the proclamation of Jesus Christ's teachings, especially as taught in the Gospels [Late 19thC. From Greek *kērugma*, from *kērussein* "to proclaim."] —**ker·yg·mat·ic** /kèrrig máttik/ *adj.*

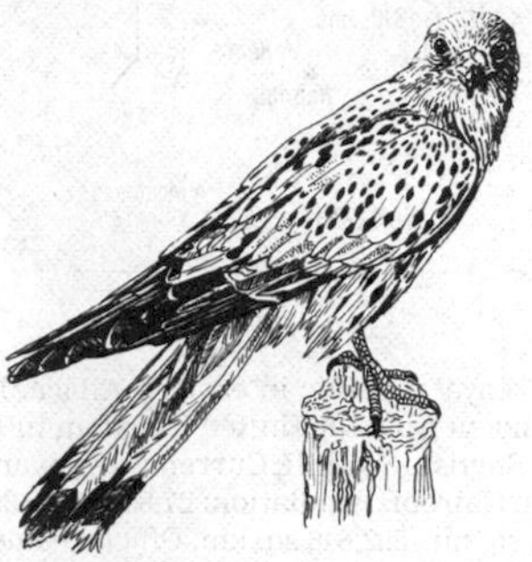

Kestrel

kes·trel /késtrəl/ *n.* a small European and Asian falcon that feeds on small mammals. It can hover in the wind before diving on its prey. Genus: *Falco.* [14thC. Origin uncertain: probably via a dialectal form of French *crécerelle* "rattle," from Latin *crepitacillum*, literally "small rattle," from *crepitare* "to rattle."]

ket- *prefix.* = **keto-** (*used before vowels*)

ke·ta·mine /kéttə meen/ *n.* a white crystalline powder used as a general anesthetic in human and veterinary medicine. Formula: $C_{13}H_{16}ClNO$.

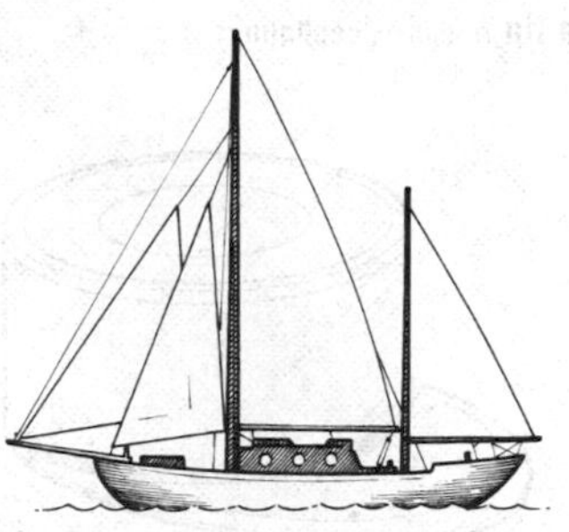

Ketch

ketch /kech/ *n.* a small sailboat with two masts [Mid-17thC. Origin uncertain: probably from CATCH.]

ketch·up /kéchəp/, **catch·up** /káchəp, kéchəp/, **cat·sup** /kátsəp, káchəp, kéchəp/ *n.* a thick sauce, made with tomatoes, that is served cold as a condiment [Late 17thC. Origin uncertain: probably via Malay *kēchap* "fish sauce" from Chinese (Cantonese) *k'ē chap* "sauce."]

ke·tene /kée teen/ *n.* a strong-smelling colorless highly reactive toxic gas used as an agent to attach an acetyl group to an organic compound. Formula: C_2H_2O. [Early 20thC. From KETONE + -ENE.]

keto-, **ket-** *prefix.* indicating a chemical compound containing a keto group, C=O, such as ketone ○ *ketosteroid* [From KETONE]

ke·to form /kée tō-/ *n.* one of two interconvertible forms of an organic compound, characterized by a carbonyl group attached to two alkyl groups

ke·to·gen·e·sis /kée tō jénnəssiss/ *n.* the formation or stimulation of the production of ketone bodies, as happens in diabetes —**ke·to·gen·ic** /kée tō jénnik/ *adj.*

ke·tone /kée tōn/ *n.* an organic compound characterized by a carbon atom doubly bonded to an oxygen atom and to two carbon atoms. The simplest ketone is acetone, an important industrial solvent. [Mid-19thC. From German *Keton*, an alteration of *Aketon* "acetone."] —**ke·ton·ic** /kee tónnik/ *adj.*

ke·tone bod·y *n.* a substance containing ketones produced by fatty acid metabolism. The concentration of ketone bodies in blood and urine increases in starvation, diabetes, and pregnancy.

ke·tone group *n.* the carbonyl group, containing carbon atoms doubly bonded to an oxygen atom and linked to the carbon atoms of two other organic groups, a characteristic of all ketones

ke·to·nu·ri·a /keetō nóoree ə/ *n.* the presence of ketones in the urine, a dangerous feature of severe and uncontrolled diabetes

ke·tose /kée tōss/ *n.* a carbohydrate that contains a ketone group

ke·to·sis /kee tóssiss/ *n.* the condition resulting from overproduction of ketone bodies —**ke·tot·ic** /kee tóttik/ *adj.*

ke·tox·ime /kee tók seem/ *n.* an organic compound containing a nitrogen atom bonded to a hydroxyl group and a carbon atom, which is bonded to two ketones. It is produced by the reaction between hydroxylamine and a ketone.

ket·tle /kétt'l/ *n.* **1. TEAKETTLE** a teakettle **2. METAL POT** a metal pot used for cooking, usually one with a lid ○ *a fish kettle* **3.** GEOL **BASIN IN A GLACIAL DRIFT DEPOSIT** a steep-sided basin, often a lake or swamp, in a glacial drift deposit, caused by the melting of an ice mass left behind as the glacier retreated [Old English *cetel.* Ultimately via a prehistoric Germanic word from Latin *catillus* "small cooking pot."]

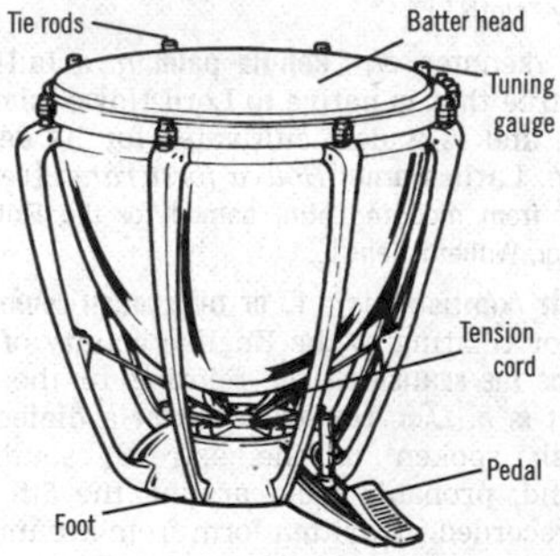

Kettledrum

ket·tle·drum /kétt'l drùm/ *n.* a percussion instrument consisting of a large copper or brass drum covered with a parchment skin. Pitch is altered by screws and pedals that increase or decrease the skin's tension. —**ket·tle·drum·mer** *n.*

ket·tle hole *n.* GEOL = **kettle** *n.* 3

ket·tle of fish *n.* **1. DIFFICULT SITUATION** an undesirable situation, usually one caused by somebody's negligence or incompetence **2. TYPE OF PERSON OR SITUATION** a situation or person to be dealt with (*informal*) ○ *That's a different kettle of fish altogether.*

keV *abbr.* kiloelectron unit

kev·el[1] /kévv'l/ *n.* a sturdy bitt or bollard for securing the heavier cables on a ship [13thC. Via Old Norman French *keville* "pin, peg" from Latin *clavicula* "small key" (source of English *clavicle*).]

kev·el[2] /kévv'l/ *n.* a two-headed hammer, one head with a sharp edge, the other with a point, used for breaking up or shaping stone [Origin unknown]

Kev·lar /kév laar/ *tdmk.* a trademark for a reinforcing material used in bulletproof vests and tires

Ke·wa·nee /ki wáa nee/ city in northwestern Illinois, northwest of Peoria and southeast of Moline. Population: 12,684 (1996).

kew·pie /kyóopee/ *n.* a plump doll with rosy cheeks and a curl of hair on its head [Originally a trademark]

key[1] /kee/ *n.* **1. INSTRUMENT FOR LOCKING AND UNLOCKING** a metal bar with notches or grooves that, when inserted into a lock and turned, operates the lock's mechanism **2. DOOR OR LOCK OPENER** a device such as a plastic card with an encoded magnetic strip that operates a door or lock **3.** MUSIC **INSTRUMENT FEATURE** the levers on a keyboard instrument that sound a note when pressed, or the metal buttons on a woodwind instrument that alter a note's pitch **4.** MUSIC **MUSICAL SCALE** a system of related notes in a scale beginning on a particular note ○ *in the key of E* **5. INSTRUMENT FOR WINDING UP** a fitted tool that is turned repeatedly to wind up, set, or calibrate a mechanism **6. MEANS** a way or means of achieving something ○ *Continuity of effort is the key to success.* **7. IMPORTANT ASPECT** the aspect of something that, once understood, provides a full understanding or explanation of the whole ○ *The key to this riddle lies in the subtle meanings of the words used.* **8. STRATEGIC PLACE** a place that is strategically vital in gaining access to or controlling a larger area ○ *Istanbul is the key to the Bosporus.* **9. LIST OF ANSWERS** a list of the answers to a test or exercise **10. KEYBOARD BUTTON** any of the buttons on a typewriter's or computer's keyboard or keypad that perform an operation when pressed **11.** ELEC ENG **DEVICE FOR OPERATING CIRCUITS** a small manual device for opening, closing, or switching circuits ○ *a telegraph key* **12.** BASKETBALL **BASKETBALL COURT AREA** the area at the ends of a basketball court between the base line and the foul line **13.** MUSIC **MAIN NOTE OF A SCALE** the note on which a musical scale begins **14.** MUSIC **TONAL CENTER** the main tonal center of a musical work, as defined by the relationships between the notes of a scale and the scale's main note **15.** ARTS **MOOD OF AN ART WORK** the general mood or style of a work of art, literature, or music **16. PITCH OR QUALITY** the pitch or quality of an expressive sound, especially the voice ○ *answered in thoughtful key* **17.** MAPS **EXPLANATORY LIST** an explanatory list of the symbols or abbreviations used on a map or diagram **18. CRYPTOGRAPHIC FEATURE** in cryptography, the sequence of symbols or characters that defines the makeup of an encoding mechanism **19. EXPLANATORY TEXT** a text that provides additional information on, or an explanation of, a work of literature, art, or music **20.** ENG **METAL WEDGE OR PIN** a metal wedge or pin used to lock together two structural or mechanical components, e.g., a shaft and a hub, to prevent movement relative to each other **21.** COMPUT **DATABASE FEATURE** a field in a database record that uniquely identifies that record **22.** ARCHIT = **keystone** *n.* 1 **23.** BIOL **OUTLINE OF CHARACTERISTICS** an outline of the characteristics of an organism, used for taxonomic identification **24.** PHOTOGRAPHY, PAINTING **IMAGE FEATURE** the tonal value of an image with regard to lightness, darkness, or color intensity **25.** CONSTR **SURFACE PREPARATION** the preparing of a surface, usually by making it rough or grooved so that paint or some other finish will stick to it **26.** BOT **WINGED FRUIT** a dry winged fruit like that of an ash or elm tree ■ *adj.* **CRUCIAL** vital in achieving understanding or success ○ *the key points in the report* ■ *v.* **(keyed, key·ing, keys) 1.** *vt.* **PROVIDE SOMETHING WITH AN EXPLANATION** to provide something with an explanatory list or text **2.** *vt.* MUSIC **REGULATE AN INSTRUMENT'S PITCH** to regulate the pitch of a musical instrument **3.** *vt.* **ADAPT SOMETHING** to bring something in line with or make something consistent with something else (*often passive*) ○ *We want these ads keyed to an upscale clientele.* **4.** *vti.* COMPUT **TYPE** to use the keyboard of a computer, or input data using it ○ *a solid hour of keying* **5.** *vt.* PRINTING **MARK ARTWORK** to mark artwork, or anything to be reproduced, with symbols that will allow different parts to be correctly aligned for reproduction **6.** *vt.* **LOCK SOMETHING** to lock or adjust something with a key **7.** *vt.* BUILDING **PUT A KEYSTONE IN AN ARCH** to provide an arch with a keystone **8.** *vt.* BIOL **IDENTIFY SOMETHING** to identify an organism or specimen [Old English *cǣg*, of unknown origin]

key in *vt.* to enter data, e.g., a password or PIN, by typing on a keyboard or keypad

key[2] /kee/ *n.* a small low island of sand or coral, especially in the Gulf of Mexico or the Caribbean [Late 17thC. Via Spanish *cayo* from French *quai* (see QUAY).]

key[3] /kee/ *n.* DRUGS a kilogram of marijuana, heroin, or cocaine (*slang*) [Mid-20thC. Shortening of KILOGRAM.]

Key /kee/, **Francis Scott** (1779–1843) U.S. poet and lawyer. He wrote the lyrics to "The Star Spangled Banner" (1814), adopted as the U.S. national anthem in 1931.

key·board /kée bàwrd/ *n.* **1. SET OF KEYS** a set of keys laid out in a row or rows, e.g., on a computer, typewriter, piano, or organ **2.** MUSIC **MUSICAL INSTRUMENT** a musical instrument that has a keyboard, especially an electronic instrument ■ *vti.* **(-board·ed,**

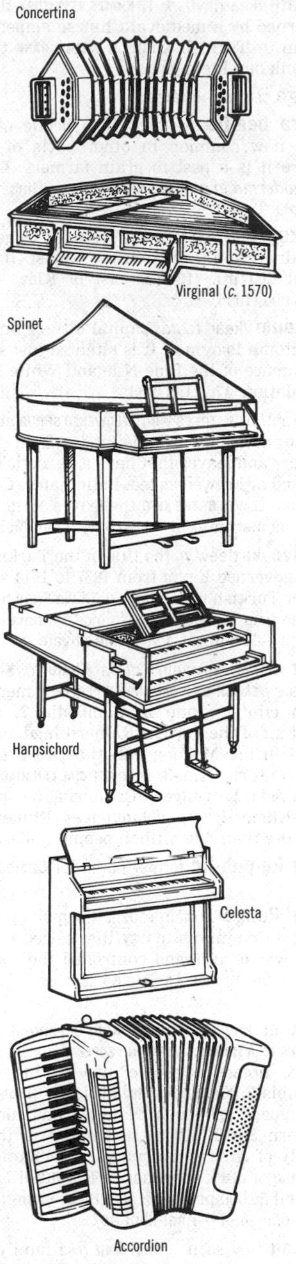

Keyboard: Historical keyboard instruments

-board·ing, -boards) COMPUT **INPUT DATA** to enter information into a computer using a keyboard

key·board·er /kée bàwrdər/ *n.* somebody who operates the keyboard of a computer or typesetting machine

key·board·ist /kée bàwrdist/ *n.* a musician who plays a keyboard instrument

key card *n.* a card, usually made of plastic with an encoded magnetic strip, giving access to a door or mechanism

key club *n.* **1. PRIVATE CLUB** a private country club, nightclub, or restaurant to which each member has a key **2. STUDENT ORGANIZATION** an organization for high school students who participate in community service projects

key deer *n.* a small white-tailed deer native to the Florida Keys that survives only in game preserves. Latin name: *Odocoileus virginianus clavium.*

keyed up *adj.* in a state of great excitement, tension, or nervousness (*informal*)

key es·crow *n.* a system for encrypting computer data in which the decoding key is held by a third party

key fruit *n.* BOT = **key**[1]

key grip *n.* the chief grip in a film or stage crew

key·hole /kée hòl/ *n.* **1. HOLE IN A LOCK** the small hole in a lock into which a key fits **2.** BASKETBALL = **key**[1] *n.* 4

key·hole saw *n.* a handsaw with a stiff narrow pointed fine-toothed blade, used to make small-radius curved and internal cuts

key·hole sur·ger·y *n.* surgery performed using instruments that can be introduced into the body through a very small hole and manipulated externally, thus avoiding the need for major incisions

Key Lar·go /-laárgō/ one of the largest of the Florida Keys, in southeastern Florida, at Biscayne Bay. Length: 30 mi./48 km.

key light *n.* the main studio or stage light that sets the overall level of light intensity for something that is being filmed, videotaped, or photographed

key lime, Key lime *n.* a small tart lime grown in the Florida Keys and Caribbean islands

key lime pie, Key lime pie *n.* a pie made from sweetened condensed milk flavored and thickened with juice from key limes

key-man in·sur·ance *n.* a life insurance policy on an important executive in a business, with the business as the beneficiary

key mon·ey *n.* **1. DEPOSIT ON ACCOMMODATION** a fee paid by a prospective tenant to a landlord or landlady in order to secure a tenancy **2. MONEY PAID FOR AN APARTMENT** money paid, usually secretly, to a building owner or manager, or to the current tenant, in order to secure an apartment

Keynes /kaynz/, **John Maynard, 1st Baron Keynes of Tilton** (1883–1946) British economist. He proposed the influential theory that government spending must compensate for insufficient business investment in times of recession. —**Keynes·i·an** *n., adj.* —**Keynes·i·an·ism** *n.*

key·note /kée nòt/ *n.* **1. MAIN THEME** the central or most important point or theme of something **2.** MUSIC = **tonic** *n.* 5 ■ *adj.* **MOST IMPORTANT** containing or outlining the most important themes or policies ■ *v.* **(-not·ed, -not·ing, -notes) 1.** *vti.* **DELIVER A SPEECH** to deliver an important speech to a convention or meeting **2.** *vt.* **NOTE IMPORTANT POINTS** to outline an important policy in a speech or report [Mid-18thC, in the sense "first note of a scale," hence, the one that decides what follows]

key·note ad·dress *n.* = **keynote speech**

key·not·er /kée nòtər/ *n.* somebody who delivers the most important speech at a conference or political convention

key·note speech, key·note ad·dress *n.* the most important speech at a conference or political convention

key·pad /kée pàd/ *n.* **1. SMALL KEYBOARD** a small keyboard, e.g., on a calculator or television remote control, usually with numbers rather than letters on the keys **2. PART OF A KEYBOARD** the part of a computer keyboard in which the number and command keys are grouped

key·pal *n.* somebody with whom regular email is exchanged [Modeled on PENPAL]

key·punch /kée pùnch/ *n.* **MACHINE FOR PUNCHING HOLES** a machine, operated by keyboard, that punches holes in cards or paper for use in a data-processing system. Once the primary means of computer input, the keypunch has been made largely obsolete by the computer keyboard. ■ *vti.* **(-punched, -punch·ing, -punch·es) TO PUNCH HOLES FOR DATA ENTRY** to use a keypunch to punch holes in a card or paper tape for data entry into a computer —**key·punch·er** *n.*

key ring /kée rìng/ *n.* a metal ring used for keeping keys together, often with a decorative or identifying attachment

key sig·na·ture *n.* a group of sharps or flats printed on the staffs at the beginning of a piece of music to show the key in which it is to be played

key·stone /kée stòn/ *n.* **1.** ARCHIT **CENTRAL STONE IN AN ARCH** the wedge-shaped stone at the highest point of an arch that locks the others in place **2. SUPPORTING ELEMENT** something on which other interrelated things depend ○ *friendly alliances that are the keystone of the country's security*

WORD KEY: CULTURAL NOTE

The Keystone Kops, a group of comic characters who appeared in a number of silent movies by Mack Sennett (1884–1960). A bumbling police squad dressed in oversized uniforms, the Kops usually featured in slapstick chase sequences characterized by superb sight gags and acrobatic stunts.

key·stroke /keé strȯk/ *n.* the pressing down of one of the keys on a keyboard, thus activating it

key·way /keé wày/ *n.* a longitudinal slot in two structural or mechanical components, e.g., in the hub or shaft of a wheel, into which a metal wedge or pin can be inserted. When the slots are filled, the two components are locked together so that they will not turn relative to one another.

Key West city in southern Florida, situated on the island of the same name. It is a port and a resort. Population: 24,832 (1990).

key·word /keé wùrd/, **key word** *n.* **1. REFERENCE POINT** a word used as a reference point for further information or as an indication of the contents of a document **2. CODE WORD** a word that is used as a key to a code **3.** COMPUT **WORD WITH A SPECIAL MEANING TO A COMPUTER** a sequence of letters and numbers, often in the form of a common word, with special significance in the context of a computer database or programming or command language

kg *symbol.* kilogram

KGB *n.* the secret police of the former Soviet Union [From Russian, from *Komitet Gosudarstvennoĭ Bezopasnosti* "Committee of State Security"]

kgf *symbol.* kilogram-force

Kha·ba·rovsk /kəbaár əfsk/ city in eastern Russia, the administrative center of Khabarovsk Territory. Population: 634,500 (1992).

khad·dar /kaádər/, **kha·di** /kaádee/ *n.* a cotton cloth from India that has a plain weave [Early 20thC. From Panjabi *khaddar* or Hindi *khādar, khādī.*]

khak·i /kákee, kaákee/ *adj.* COLORS **BROWNISH-YELLOW** of a dull brownish-yellow color ■ *n.* **1.** COLORS **BROWNISH-YELLOW** a dull brownish-yellow color **2.** TEXTILES **BEIGE CLOTH** a tough beige-colored fabric often used for making military uniforms ■ **khak·is** *npl.* **TROUSERS OR UNIFORM** a pair of trousers or a uniform made of khaki [Mid-19thC. Via Urdu *kakī* "dust-colored" from, ultimately, Persian *ḵāk* "dust."] —**khak·i** *adj.*

kha·lif *n.* = **caliph**

Khal·sa /kaálsə/ *n.* a strict Sikh religious order founded in 1699 by Guru Gobind Singh [Late 18thC. Via Urdu from, ultimately, Arabic *ḵāliṣ* "pure."]

kham·sin /kam seén/ *n.* a dry dusty hot southerly wind that blows from the Sahara across Egypt and over the Red Sea from March to May [Late 17thC. From Arabic *ḵamāsīn*, from *ḵamsīn* "fifty" (because it blows for about fifty days).]

khan[1] /kaan, kan/ *n.* **1. MEDIEVAL TITLE** a medieval title formerly used by Mongol and Turkish rulers in various parts of Asia (*usually added to a name*) ○ *Genghis Khan* **2. TITLE OF RESPECT IN CENTRAL ASIA** a title of respect taken by various dignitaries in Central Asian countries ○ *the Aga Khan* [14thC. Via Old French *chan* or medieval Latin *ca(a)nus* from Turkic *ḵān* "lord, ruler."]

khan[2] /kaan, kan/ *n.* an inn in Turkey and some other Central Asian countries [14thC. From Persian *ḵān.*]

Popperfoto

Imran Khan

Khan /kaan/, **Imran** (*b.* 1952) Pakistan cricketer. He was four times captain of Pakistan's national team between 1982 and his retirement from cricket in 1992, and also played for Sussex and Worcestershire. Full name **Imran Ahmad Khan Niazi**

khan·ate /kaá nàyt/ *n.* **1. KHAN'S TERRITORY** the territory governed by a medieval Chinese emperor or Mongolian or Turkish khan **2. KHAN'S RANK** the position or rank of a khan

khan·ga CLOTHES = **kanga**

khap·ra bee·tle /kaáprə-/ *n.* a beetle of Southeast Asia now common in other parts of the world, where it is a pest to grain farmers. Latin name: *Trogoderma granarium.* [*Khapra* via Hindi from Sanskrit *khapara* "thief"]

Khar·kov /kaár kàwf/ the second largest city in Ukraine, capital of Kharkov Oblast. It is situated about 260 mi./418 km east of Kiev. Population: 1,576,000 (1995).

Khar·toum /kaar to͞om/ capital city of Sudan and of Khartoum Province. It is situated just south of the confluence of the Blue Nile and White Nile rivers. Population: 476,218 (1983).

khat /kaat/ *n.* **1.** TREES **WHITE-FLOWERED SHRUB** an evergreen shrub native to Arabia and Africa with white flowers and leaves that have a narcotic effect when chewed or brewed as tea. Latin name: *Catha edulis.* **2.** DRUGS **LEAVES OF THE KHAT** the leaves of the khat plant, used as a stimulant [Mid-19thC. From Arabic *ḳāt.*]

khe·dive /kə deév/ *n.* the title of the Turkish viceroys who governed Egypt from 1867 to 1914 while it was under Turkish rule [Mid-19thC. Via French and Ottoman Turkish from Persian *ḵadiiw* "prince," ultimately from *ḵudā* "god."] —**khe·di·val** *adj.* —**khe·di·vate** *n.*

Khmer /kmair, kə máir/ (*plural* **Khmer** *or* **Khmers**) *n.* **1.** PEOPLES **MEMBER OF A CAMBODIAN PEOPLE** a member of the main ethnic group in Cambodia **2.** HIST an inhabitant of the ancient Khmer kingdom that flourished in the Mekong valley between the 9th and 13th centuries A.D. **3.** LANG **OFFICIAL LANGUAGE OF CAMBODIA** the official language of Cambodia, belonging to the Mon-Khmer group of languages. Khmer is spoken by more than five million people. —**Khmer** *adj.*

Khmer Re·pub·lic former name for **Cambodia** (1970–75)

Khmer Rouge /kmàir ro͞ozh, kə màir-/ *n.* the Cambodian Communist party that seized power in the civil war of 1975 and controlled the country until 1979 [From Khmer *Khmer* "Kampuchea" + French *rouge* "red"]

Khoi·khoi /kóy kòy/ (*plural* **-khoi** *or* **-khois**) *n.* **1.** PEOPLES **MEMBER OF A NOMADIC AFRICAN PEOPLE** a member of a formerly nomadic people now living mainly in Namibia **2. Khoikhoi, Khoi Khoi** LANG **NAMIBIAN LANGUAGE** a language spoken in Namibia and some parts of western South Africa, belonging to the Khoisan family of African languages and characterized by the use of click consonants. Khoikhoi is spoken by around 55,000 people. [Late 18thC. From Nama, literally "men of men."] —**Khoi·khoi** *adj.*

Khoi·san /kóy saán/, **Khoi-San** *n.* a family of around fifty languages, including Khoikhoi, San, Kwadi, and Sandawe, spoken in parts of Namibia and Botswana and notable for the use of click consonants [Mid-20thC. Blend of KHOIKHOI and SAN.]

Kho·mei·ni /kōmáynee/, **Ruhollah, Ayatollah** (1900–89) Iranian religious leader. He led an Islamic revolution that overthrew the shah (1979), and as virtual head of state introduced a constitution and administration based on Islamic law.

Khru·shchev /kro͞osh chef, -chawf/, **Nikita** (1894–1971) Soviet statesman. In 1953, after Stalin's death, he became first secretary of the Communist Party, and embarked on a programme of destalinization. He was ousted in 1964. The Cuban missile crisis occurred during his administration. Full name **Nikita Sergeyevich Khrushchev**

Khul·na /ko͞olnə/ city and river port in southwestern Bangladesh. It is situated about 90 mi./145 km southwest of Dhaka. Population: 545,849 (1991).

khus·khus /kúskəss/, **khus-khus** BOT = **vetiver** [Early 19thC. From Urdu and Persian *ḵasḵas.*]

Khy·ber Pass /kíbər-/ mountain pass in western Asia, the most important pass connecting Afghanistan and Pakistan

kHz *abbr.* kilohertz

KIA *abbr.* killed in action

Ric Ergenbright/Corbis

Khyber Pass

Ki·a·ma /kī ámmə/ coastal town in southeastern New South Wales, Australia, an administrative center and tourist resort. Population: 11,711 (1996).

ki·ang /kee aáng/ *n.* a large wild ass native to the Tibetan plateau and the Himalayas. Latin name: *Equus hemionus kiang.* [Mid-19thC. From Tibetan *kyang.*]

kib·be /kíbbə/ *n.* a Middle Eastern dish made with ground lamb, pine nuts, and spices [Mid-20thC. From Arabic *kubbah.*]

kib·ble /kíbb'l/ *n.* **GROUND MEAL** meal that has been ground into small pieces and then formed into pellets, especially for pet food ■ *vt.* **(-bled, -bling, -bles) GRIND SOMETHING** to grind something, e.g., grain, into small pieces [Late 18thC. Origin unknown.]

kib·butz /ki bo͝ots, ki bo͝ots/ (*plural* **-but·zim** /-bo͝ot seém, -bo͝ot-/) *n.* communal farm or factory in Israel run collectively and dedicated to the principle that production work and domestic work are of equal value [Mid-20thC. From modern Hebrew *qibbūṣ* "gathering."]

kib·butz·nik /ki bo͝otsnik, -bo͝ots-/ *n.* somebody who lives and works on a kibbutz

kibe /kīb/ *n.* a chapped or swollen area of skin, usually on the heel and often ulcerated, caused by exposure to cold [14thC. Origin unknown.]

Ki·bei /kee báy/ (*plural* **-bei**) *n.* somebody born in the United States of Japanese parents and educated in Japan [From Japanese, literally "to go home"]

ki·bit·ka /ki bítkə/ *n.* **1.** TRANSP **RUSSIAN SLED** a covered sled or wagon in Russia **2. TATAR TENT** a tent made of felt used by the Tatars of Central Asia **3. TATAR FAMILY** a family of Tatars [Late 18thC. From Russian.]

kib·itz /kíbbits/ (**-itzed, -itz·ing, -itz·es**) *vi.* (*informal*) **1. INTERFERE** to interfere or give unwanted advice, especially when watching a card game **2. CHAT** to chat [Early 20thC. Via Yiddish from German *kiebitsen.*] —**kib·itz·er** *n.*

kib·lah /kíbblə/ *n.* the direction of Mecca that Muslims must face when praying [Mid-17thC. From Arabic *ḳibla*, literally "that which is opposite."]

ki·bosh /kī bòsh, ki bósh/ (**-boshed, -bosh·ing, -bosh·es**) *vt.* to put a stop to something [Mid-19thC. Origin unknown.] ◇ **put the kibosh on something** to prevent something from happening or from being successful (*informal*)

kick /kik/ *v.* (**kicked, kick·ing, kicks**) **1.** *vti.* **STRIKE WITH THE FOOT** to strike something or somebody with the foot **2.** *vti.* **MOVE WITH THE FOOT** to make something move by striking it with the foot ○ *kick a ball around* **3.** *vti.* **MAKE A THRASHING MOVEMENT** to make a thrashing movement with the legs, e.g., when fighting or swimming ○ *Hold onto the side of the pool and kick your legs as hard as you can.* **4.** *vti.* **RAISE THE LEG HIGH** to raise the leg up high in a swift movement, e.g., in a dance **5.** *vi.* ARMS **RECOIL** to recoil when fired (*refers to firearms*) **6.** *vti.* SPORTS **SCORE GOAL** in various football games, to score a field goal by kicking **7.** *vi.* **OBJECT** to show disapproval or object to something by not cooperating (*informal*) ○ *He kicked against the restrictions.* **8.** *vr.* **BLAME** to be irritated with yourself (*informal*) ○ *I'm kicking myself for missing the deadline.* ■ *n.* **1. BLOW WITH THE FOOT** a blow with the foot **2. LEG MOVEMENT** a thrashing movement with the leg ○ *a swimming kick* **3. RAISING OF THE LEG** a swift raising of the leg, e.g., in a dance ○ *a high kick* **4.** SPORTS **KICKING OF A BALL** the striking of a ball with the foot ○ *opted for a kick instead of a pass* **5. PLEASURE** an exciting, pleasurable, or satisfying feeling (*informal*) ○ *She really gets a kick out of appearing on stage.* **6.**

POWER power or strength ○ *That sauce has quite a kick to it.* **7.** TEMPORARY INTEREST a temporary interest, especially a strongly absorbing interest (*informal*) ○ *They're on some kind of a health food kick right now.* **8.** ARMS RECOIL OF A GUN the backward thrust of a gun when it is fired [14thC. Origin unknown.] —**kick·a·ble** *adj.* ◇ **a kick in the pants** a reprimand given to somebody who is not showing enough enthusiasm or effort (*informal*)

kick around *v.* **1.** *vt.* MISTREAT SOMEBODY to treat somebody badly and unfairly (*informal*) **2.** *vt.* DISCUSS SOMETHING to discuss a topic or range of topics in an informal way (*informal*) **3.** *vti.* TRAVEL AIMLESSLY to travel around a place without any fixed plans **4.** *vi.* BE SOMEWHERE to remain forgotten or neglected (*informal*)

kick back *v.* **1.** *vti.* PAY A BRIBE to pay money illegally in order to buy concessions or favors (*informal*) **2.** *vi.* RECOIL SUDDENLY to recoil suddenly and unexpectedly (*informal*) **3.** *vi.* ARMS RECOIL to recoil when fired (*refers to guns*) **4.** *vi.* RELAX to relax comfortably (*informal*)

kick in *v.* **1.** *vi.* TAKE EFFECT to start to take effect or come into operation (*informal*) ○ *I'll feel better once the antibiotics kick in.* **2.** *vti. U.S., ANZ* CONTRIBUTE to contribute toward the cost of something (*informal*) **3.** *vi.* DIE to die (*slang*)

kick off *v.* **1.** *vi.* FOOTBALL START PLAY in football, to start play by kicking the ball to the receiving team **2.** *vti.* BEGIN to start something or to begin (*informal*) ○ *Let's kick off tonight's show with our first guest.* **3.** *vi.* DIE to die (*slang*)

kick out *vt.* to throw somebody out or send somebody away (*informal*)

kick over *vi.* to turn over or begin to fire (*slang; refers to engines*)

kick up *v.* (*informal*) **1.** *vt.* CAUSE SOMETHING to cause or instigate something, usually something undesirable ○ *kick up a fuss* **2.** *vt.* INTENSIFY to increase in force or intensity **3.** *vi.* GIVE TROUBLE to misbehave or malfunction

Kick·a·poo /kíkə poo/ (*plural* **-poo** *or* **-poos**) *n.* **1.** PEOPLES MEMBER OF A NATIVE NORTH AMERICAN PEOPLE a member of a Native North American people who inhabited southwestern Wisconsin before moving to Illinois during the 18th century. Kickapoo communities exist today in Kansas, Oklahoma, and Texas. **2.** LANG LANGUAGE OF THE KICKAPOO an Algonquian language spoken in parts of Oklahoma and Kansas, and along the Texas-Mexico border, one of the Algonquian-Wakashan family of Native North American languages. Kickapoo is spoken by about 4,000 people. [Late 17thC. From Kickapoo *kiikaapoa*.] —**Kick·a·poo** *adj.*

kick·back /kík bàk/ *n.* **1.** BRIBE a sum of money paid illegally in order to gain concessions or favors **2.** REACTION a strong or violent reaction (*informal*)

kick·ball /kík bàwl/ *n.* a children's game similar to baseball but using a large, inflated ball that is kicked instead of batted

kick·board /kík bàwrd/ *n.* SWIMMING a small buoyant board held by a swimmer in order to stay afloat while practicing kicking techniques

kick·box·ing /kík bòksing/ *n.* a form of boxing that involves kicking as well as punching —**kick·box·er** *n.*

kick·er /kíkər/ *n.* **1.** SOMEBODY THAT KICKS somebody that kicks, especially a football player **2.** CATCH a disadvantage that is often hidden or unexpected (*informal*) ○ *The price isn't bad, but the kicker is that he wants it all in cash.* **3.** AUTOMATIC INCREASE an increase that makes something such as a pension or labor contract more valuable **4.** SOMETHING THAT KICKS something, especially a firearm, that kicks or recoils

kick·ing /kíking/ *adj.* excellent, exciting, or very enjoyable (*slang*)

kick·off /kík àwf/ *n.* **1.** FOOTBALL START OF A GAME in football, the kicking of the ball at the beginning of a game, half, or after a touchdown or field goal **2.** START OF SOMETHING the start of something or the time when something starts (*informal*) **3.** SOCCER START OF MATCH in soccer, the place kick from the center spot that begins the game **4.** SOCCER STARTING TIME the time at which a game of soccer is due to start **5.** a beginning (*informal*) ○ *the kickoff of their European tour*

kick plate *n.* a metal plate attached to the face of a door at foot level to protect it

kick pleat *n.* an inverted pleat at the lower back of a straight skirt to prevent the wearer from being hampered when walking

kick·shaw /kík shàw/ *n.* (*archaic*) **1.** TRINKET a trinket of little value **2.** FOOD DELICACY an exotic food delicacy [Late 16thC. From French *quelque chose* "something."]

kick·sin' /kíksin/ *n. Carib* playing around and not acting seriously (*informal*)

kick·stand /kík stànd/ *n.* a pivoting metal bar on a bicycle or motorcycle that can be pushed down into contact with the ground to keep the vehicle upright when it is stationary [Mid-20thC. So called because it is raised and lowered with the foot.]

kick-start *vt.* (**kick-start·ed, kick-start·ing, kick-starts**) **1.** MOTORCYCLES START A MOTORCYCLE to start the engine on a motorcycle by stepping down hard on the kick-starter **2.** START SOMETHING QUICKLY to start or restart a process or activity quickly and forcefully ○ *policies designed to kick-start an ailing economy* ■ *n.* **1.** MOTORCYCLES = **kick-starter 2.** FORCEFUL START a course of action that quickly and forcefully starts or restarts a process or activity (*informal*)

kick-start·er *n.* **1.** MOTORCYCLES STARTING PEDAL the pedal on a motorcycle that starts the engine when it is kicked downward **2.** INITIAL BOOST something, e.g., a large amount of money, that gets a project off to an unusually good start

kick turn *n.* in skiing, a standing 180° turn made by swiveling each ski separately

kick·up /kík ùp/ *n.* a noisy commotion or protest (*informal*)

kick wheel *n.* a mechanical potter's wheel that is turned by a foot-operated treadle

kick·y /kíkee/ (**-i·er, -i·est**) *adj.* thrilling and unusual (*slang*) [Late 18thC. Originally in the sense "lively, teasing."]

kid[1] /kid/ *n.* **1.** CHILD a young child (*informal*) **2.** YOUTH a young person (*informal*) **3.** TERM OF ADDRESS used as an informal term of address (*informal*) ○ *Here's looking at you, kid.* **4.** YOUNG GOAT a young goat, antelope, or similar animal **5.** INDUST SOFT LEATHER soft leather made from the skin of a young goat ■ *adj.* YOUNGER younger, especially of two siblings (*informal*) ○ *his kid sister* ■ *vti.* (**kid·ded, kid·ding, kids**) BEAR YOUNG to give birth to a young goat [12thC. From Old Norse *kið*.]

WORD KEY: SYNONYMS

See Synonyms at ***youth***.

kid[2] /kid/ (**kid·ded, kid·ding, kids**) *v.* **1.** *vti.* SAY SOMETHING FOR FUN to say something that is not true, especially as a joke or to tease somebody **2.** *vt.* DECEIVE SOMEBODY to deceive or mislead somebody (*informal*) ○ *don't kid yourself* [Late 16thC. From KID[1].] —**kid·der** *n.*

Kidd /kid/, **William** (1645?–1701) Scottish-American pirate. He was hired to suppress piracy in the Indian Ocean (1695), but made his own attacks on merchant vessels (1697–99) and was later hanged. Known as **Captain Kidd**

Kid·der·min·ster /kíddər mìnstər/, **Kid·der·min·ster car·pet** *n.* a type of ingrain carpet originally made in Kidderminster, England

kid·die /kíddee/, **kid·dy** (*plural* **-dies**) *n.* a small child (*informal*) [Late 16thC]

kid·do /kíddō/ (*plural* **-dos** *or* **-does**) *n.* **1.** YOUNG PERSON a child, young person, or friend (*slang*) **2.** TERM OF ADDRESS used as an informal term of address, especially to a young person (*informal*)

Kid·dush /kíddəsh, ki dóosh/ (*plural* **-dush·im** /ki doo shéem/), **kid·dush** (*plural* **-dush·im**) *n.* **1.** BLESSING in Judaism, a special blessing, usually for wine, said before a meal on the eve of the Sabbath or a holiday in order to consecrate the festival **2.** RECEPTION a reception following the recitation of the Kiddush for the congregants, at which drinks and snacks are served [Mid-18thC. From Hebrew *qiddūš* "sanctification."]

kid·dy *n.* = **kiddie** (*informal*)

kid glove *n.* a glove of soft leather made from the skin of a young goat —**kid**

kid-glove /kíd glùv/, **kid-glove** *adj.* displaying tact and sensitivity

kid·lit /kid lit/ *n.* literature for children (*informal*) [Late 20thC. Shortening.]

Kid·man /kídmən/, **Nicole** (*b.* 1967) Hawaiian-born Australian actor. She has starred in movies such as *To Die For* (1994) and *Portrait of a Lady* (1996).

kid·nap /kíd nàp/ (**-napped** *or* **-naped, -nap·ping** *or* **-nap·ing, -naps**) *vti.* to take somebody away by force and hold him or her prisoner, usually for ransom [Mid-17thC. From KID[1] + *nap* "to steal," of uncertain origin: perhaps a variant of NAB. From the practice of abducting children to provide servants for U.S. plantations.] —**kid·nap·per** *n.*

kid·nap·ping /kíd nàpping/, **kid·nap·ing** *n.* the action or crime of forcefully taking away and holding somebody prisoner, usually for ransom

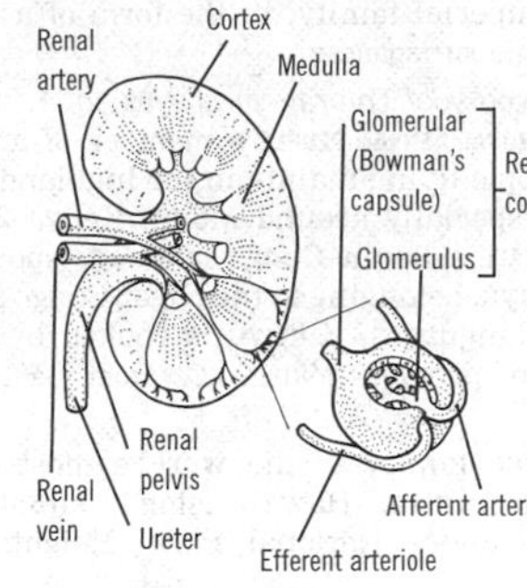

Kidney

kid·ney /kídnee/ (*plural* **-neys**) *n.* **1.** ANAT WASTE-REMOVING VERTEBRATE ORGAN either of a pair of organs in the abdomen of vertebrates that filter waste liquid resulting from metabolism of the blood, which is subsequently excreted as urine **2.** ZOOL INVERTEBRATE ORGAN the organ in invertebrates that filters waste material for excretion **3.** FOOD ANIMAL KIDNEY AS FOOD the kidney of a pig, calf, ox, or lamb, eaten as meat **4.** KIND a kind, type, or disposition (*dated*) ○ *a person of a very different kidney* [14thC. Origin unknown: perhaps formed from Old English *cod* "bag."]

kid·ney bean *n.* **1.** FOOD PULSE OF THE HARICOT FAMILY a small, usually dark red, edible bean shaped like a kidney **2.** PLANTS PLANT PRODUCING KIDNEY BEANS a widely cultivated annual plant that produces kidney beans. Latin name: *Phaseolus vulgaris.*

kid·ney-shaped *adj.* in the shape of an oval with a concavity in one side ○ *a kidney-shaped swimming pool*

kid·ney stone *n.* a small hard mass that forms in the kidney, consisting mainly of phosphates, oxylates, and urates

kid·skin /kídd skìn/ *n.* = **kid**[1] *n.* **5**

kid stuff *n.* (*informal*) **1.** SOMETHING FOR CHILDREN something considered suitable only for children or immature people **2.** SOMETHING EASY OR BORING something that is very easy or very boring

kid·vid /kíd vìd/ *n.* a video for children (*informal*) [Late 20thC. Shortening.]

Kiel /keel/ city and seaport in north central Germany, the capital of the state of Schleswig-Holstein situated north of Hamburg. Population: 247,700 (1994).

kiel·ba·sa /kil báassə, keel-/ *n.* a spicy smoked sausage, originally made in Poland [Mid-20thC. Via Polish from, ultimately, Turkic *kūl bastī* "roast pressed meat."]

Kiel Ca·nal canal in northwestern Germany connecting the North and Baltic seas. Length: 60 mi./97 km.

kier /keer/ *n.* a vat in which yarn or cloth is bleached or dyed [Late 16thC. From Old Norse *ker* "tub."]

Kier·ke·gaard /kéerkə gaàrd/, **Søren** (1813–55) Danish philosopher. His religious philosophy is concerned with individual existence, choice, and commitment, and has profoundly influenced theology and the existential philosophers. His books include *The Concept of Irony* (1841) and *Either/Or* (1843). Full name **Søren Aabye Kierkegaard**

kie·ser·ite /kéezə rìt/ *n.* a white to yellow crystalline mineral that consists of hydrated magnesium sulfate and is found in large amounts in some salt residues [Mid-19thC. Named for the German physician, Dietrich *Kieser* (1779–1862).]

Ki·ev /kée ev/ capital and largest city of Ukraine, located in the north centre of the country. Population: 2,646,000 (1993).

kif /kif, keef/, **kef** /kef, keef, kayf/, **kaif** /kayf/ *n.* marijuana especially in North Africa [Early 19thC. From Arabic *kayf, kef* "pleasure."]

Ki·ga·li /ki gaalee/ capital city of Rwanda, situated on a plateau in the center of the country, just south of the equator. Population: 234,500 (1993).

kike /kīk/ *n.* a highly offensive taboo term referring to a Jewish person (*taboo offensive*) [Early 20thC. Origin unknown.]

Ki·kon·go /kee kóng gō/ *n.* LANG = **Kongo**[1] *n.* 2 [Late 19thC. From Kikongo.]

ki·ku·mon /kíkə mòn, keekə-/ *n.* the emblem of the Japanese imperial family, in the form of a chrysanthemum [From Japanese]

Ki·ku·yu /ki koo yoo/ (*plural* **-yu** *or* **-yus**) *n.* **1.** PEOPLES **MEMBER OF A RURAL KENYAN PEOPLE** a member of an agricultural people living mainly in the highland areas of Kenya, especially around Mount Kenya **2.** LANG **AFRICAN LANGUAGE** a Benue-Congo language spoken in parts of Kenya, belonging to the Niger-Congo family of African languages. Kikuyu is spoken by about five million people. [Mid-19thC. From Bantu.] —**Ki·ku·yu** *adj.*

Ki·lau·e·a /kee low áy ə/ the world's most active volcano, on central Hawaii Island, situated in Hawaii Volcanoes National Park. Height: 4,090 ft./1,247 m.

kil·der·kin /kíldərkin/ *n.* **1. OLD LIQUID MEASUREMENT** an obsolete British measurement for liquids, equivalent to about 18 gallons or 68 liters **2. CASK** a cask with a capacity of one kilderkin [14thC. From Middle Dutch *kinderkin*, literally "small quintal."]

ki·lim /ki leem, keelim/ *n.* a Middle Eastern rug with richly colored geometric patterns, woven like tapestry, with no pile [Late 19thC. Via Turkish *Kilim* from Persian *gelīm*, coarse-woven blanket.]

Mount Kilimanjaro: View from Amboseli National Park

Kil·i·man·ja·ro, Mount /kìllәmәn jaarō/ the highest mountain in Africa, located in northeastern Tanzania. Height: 19,340 ft./5,895 m.

kill[1] /kil/ *v.* (**killed, kill·ing, kills**) **1.** *vti.* **CAUSE SOMEBODY TO DIE** to cause the death of a person or an animal ○ *They were killed in a car accident.* **2.** *vt.* **RUIN SOMETHING** to cause something to end or be ruined ○ *The remark killed the conversation.* **3.** *vt.* **HURT PART OF SOMEBODY'S BODY** to cause severe physical pain or discomfort to somebody (*informal*) ○ *My feet are killing me!* **4.** *vt.* **OVERPOWER SOMETHING SUBTLE OR LESS STRONG** to destroy or severely damage an essential, often delicate quality in something by superimposing something stronger ○ *Her perfume killed the scent of the roses.* **5.** *vt.* **TIRE SOMEBODY OUT** to exhaust somebody completely (*informal*) ○ *These stairs kill me every time.* **6.** *vr.* **OVEREXERT YOURSELF** to push yourself too hard (*informal; often used ironically*) ○ *She was killing herself to get the job done on time.* **7.** *vt.* **TURN SOMETHING OFF** to disconnect the power to something electrical or mechanical so that it stops working (*informal*) ○ *kill the engine* **8.** *vt.* **MAKE TIME PASS** to use up spare time in some activity (*informal*) ○ *They killed a couple of hours at the mall.* **9.** *vt.* PUBL **CUT TEXT** to delete a piece of text from a publication or remove a particular amount from a text (*slang*) ○ *We had to kill half a column to make space for the ad.* **10.** *vt.* **BLOCK A PLAN** to prevent a proposal from going through, e.g., the passing of a congressional bill ○ *The bill was killed in the Appropriations Committee.* **11.** *vti.* **BOWL SOMEBODY OVER** to have an overpowering effect on somebody, e.g., causing extreme admiration, helpless laughter, or utter amazement (*informal*) ○ *dressed to kill* **12.** *vt.* **DRINK ALL OF SOMETHING** to finish off a bottle of something, usually an alcoholic beverage (*slang*) **13.** *vt.* FOOTBALL **MAKE A BALL DEAD** in football, to stop the ball so that it is no longer in play (*informal*) **14.** *vt.* SPORTS **HIT A BALL HARD** to hit a ball very hard **15.** *vt.* RACKET GAMES **MAKE A BALL UNRETURNABLE** in racket games, to hit the ball so hard, with such skill, or in such a direction that your opponent has no chance of returning it ■ *n.* **1. KILLING** the moment or an act of killing something, especially prey or game, or the bull at the end of a bullfight **2.** HUNT **PREY** the prey killed by an animal or human being **3.** MIL **DESTRUCTION OF ENEMY VEHICLE** the destroying of an enemy vehicle such as a plane, ship, or tank (*slang*) [13thC. From assumed Old English *cyllan*, from a prehistoric Germanic word that is also the ancestor of English *quell*.]

WORD KEY: SYNONYMS

kill, murder, assassinate, execute, put to death, slaughter, slay, put to sleep

CORE MEANING: to deprive of life

kill a general word used to talk about causing the death of a person or animal; **murder** to take the life of another person in an intentional and often premeditated way that constitutes a serious criminal act; **assassinate** to murder a public figure by means of a sudden surprise attack, often for political or religious reasons; **execute** to take somebody's life in accordance with a legal death sentence. It is also used to refer to the instant or summary killing of an enemy, often for political or military reasons; **put to death** to deliberately take somebody's life, especially in accordance with a legal death sentence; **slaughter** to kill animals for food, especially animals that have been bred on a farm. It can also be used to refer to brutal and violent killing, usually on a large scale; **slay** a formal or literary word used to refer to killing a person or animal in an intentional and violent way; **put to sleep** a euphemism used to talk about the humane killing of sick or injured animals, especially when done by a vet.

kill off *vt.* **1. COMPLETELY DESTROY SOMETHING** to destroy something utterly, or destroy the remaining members of a group of people or creatures ○ *The spray killed off all the aphids.* **2.** TV, LITERAT **GET RID OF A CHARACTER** to write in the death of a character, especially in a serial or soap opera

kill[2] /kil/ *n.* a stream, channel, or waterway (*regional or archaic*) [Mid-17thC, From Dutch *kil*, "river bed, channel"]

WORD KEY: REGIONAL NOTE

The term ***kill*** meaning "a waterway" endures today mainly in place names in New York (*Catskill* and *Peekskill*) and New Jersey (*Paulins Kill*).

Kil·lar·ney /ki laarnee/ city and tourist center in the southwestern Republic of Ireland, situated by the Lakes of Killarney. Population: 9,950 (1991).

kill·deer /kíl deer/ *n.* a large North American plover that has brown and white plumage, two black breast bands, and a distinctive noisy cry. Latin name: *Charadrius vociferus*. [Mid-18thC. An imitation of the bird's call.]

kill·er /kíllər/ *n.* **1. SOMEBODY OR SOMETHING THAT KILLS** somebody or something that kills other people or animals intentionally, especially one that does this more than once ○ *a killer crocodile* **2. SOMETHING VERY DIFFICULT** something that is very demanding or difficult (*informal*) ○ *This aerobics class is a killer.* **3. DESTRUCTIVE FORCE, PERSON, OR ORGANISM** somebody or something that destroys or is fatal ○ *A killer storm hit the nation on Sunday.* **4. EXCEPTIONAL THING** something that is excellent or exceptional (*slang*) ○ *a killer performance*

kill·er app *n.* COMPUT a computer application of outstanding power, originality, or market reach (*slang*)

kill·er bee *n.* an Africanized bee (*informal*)

kill·er cell *n.* a T cell that is part of the body's immune system and attacks cells having specific antigens on their surface, e.g., cancer cells and those infected with a virus

kill·er in·stinct *n.* **1. URGE TO KILL** a tendency, capacity, or urge to kill **2. STRONG WILL TO WIN** an overpowering drive to succeed, e.g., in business deals or sports, whatever the cost may be to other people

kill·er T cell *n.* = **killer cell**

Killer whale

kill·er whale *n.* a black-and-white toothed whale inhabiting colder seas. It grows up to 25 ft./7.62 m long, has a tall dorsal fin, and feeds mainly on fish and squid. Latin name: *Orcinus orca*.

kill fee *n.* payment made to a writer, photographer, artist, or illustrator by a publisher who has decided not to publish the contracted work

kil·lick /kíllik/, **kil·lock** /kíllək/ *n.* a small anchor, especially one made of a heavy stone [Early 17thC. Origin unknown.]

Kil·lie·cran·kie, Pass of /kìlli krángkee/ wooded pass in Perth and Kinross, central Scotland

kil·li·fish /kíllee fish/ *n.* a fish about the size of a minnow that inhabits fresh and brackish water and is used as an aquarium fish, as bait, and in mosquito control. Family: Cyprinodontidae. [Early 19thC. *Killi* of uncertain origin: perhaps from New York dialect *kill* "creek, channel," from Dutch *kil* "channel."]

kill·ing /kílling/ *n.* **1. SLAYING** the act of causing the death of a human being or an animal **2. QUICK PROFIT** a large and quick profit (*informal*) ○ *made a killing on the hog futures market* ■ *adj.* **1. EXHAUSTING** totally exhausting **2. FATAL** causing or resulting in death ○ *We expect a killing frost tonight.* **3. GIVING PLEASURE** providing extreme pleasure or very good (*slang*) **4. INTENSE** very intense (*slang*) —**kill·ing·ly** *adv.*

kill·ing fields *npl.* the site of mass slaughter, e.g., of civilians

WORD KEY: CULTURAL NOTE

The Killing Fields, a movie by British director Roland Joffe (1984). Through the true story of U.S. journalist Sydney Schanberg's attempts to trace the Cambodian aide he was forced to leave behind after the fall of Phnom Penh in 1975, Joffe portrays the atrocities perpetrated on the Cambodian people by the Khmer Rouge regime between 1975 and 1978. References such as "the killing fields of Bosnia" clearly take their linguistic cues from this movie title.

kill·joy /kíl jòy/ *n.* somebody whose behavior prevents other people from having a good time

kil·lock *n.* SAILING = **killick**

kill shot *n.* RACKET GAMES in racket games, a shot that is hit so hard or accurately that it cannot be returned

Kil·mer /kílmər/, **Joyce** (1886–1918) U.S. poet. He is known for his lyric poem "Trees" (1913). He was killed in World War I. Full name **Alfred Joyce Kilmer**

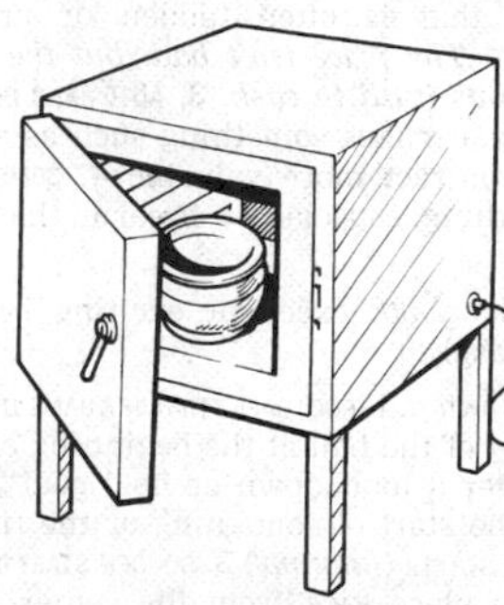

Kiln: Pottery kiln

kiln /kiln/ *n.* **INDUSTRIAL OVEN** a specialized oven or furnace used for industrial processes such as firing clay for pottery or bricks and for drying materials such as hops or timber ■ *vt.* (**kilned, kiln·ing, kilns**) **PROCESS SOMETHING IN A KILN** to dry, fire, or bake something in a kiln [Pre-12thC. From Latin *culina*, a variant of *coquina* (source of English *kitchen*).]

ki·lo /keélō/ *n.* 1. KILOGRAM a kilogram (*informal*) Symbol **k** 2. COMMUNICATION **CODE WORD FOR LETTER "K"** a code word for the letter "K," used in international radio communications [Mid-19thC. Shortening.]

kilo- *prefix.* 1. a thousand (10^3) ○ *kilogram* 2. a binary thousand ○ *kilobyte* [Via French from Greek *khilioi* "thousand"]

kil·o·bit /kíllə bìt/ *n.* COMPUT 1,024 bits

kil·o·byte /kíllə bìt/ *n.* COMPUT 1,024 bytes

kil·o·cal·o·rie /kíllə kàlləree, -kàllree/ *n.* = **calorie**

kil·o·cy·cle /kíllə sìk'l/ *n.* a kilohertz (*dated*)

kil·o·gram /kíllə gràm/ *n.* the basic unit of mass in the SI system, equal to 1,000 grams or 2.2046 lbs. Symbol **kg**

kil·o·gram-me·ter *n.* a unit of energy measuring how much work a kilogram force does across a distance of one meter in the direction of the applied force

kil·o·hertz /kíllə hùrts/ *n.* 1,000 hertz

ki·lom·e·ter /ki lómmətər/ *n.* 1,000 meters or 0.621 miles

kil·o·ton /kíllə tùn/ *n.* 1. **1,000 TONS** 1,000 tons 2. **MEASURE OF EXPLOSIVE CAPABILITY** an explosive force equal to 1,000 tons of TNT

kil·o·volt /kílə vòlt/ *n.* 1,000 volts

kil·o·watt /kíllə wòt/ *n.* 1,000 watts

kil·o·watt-hour *n.* a unit of energy equal to the work done by one kilowatt in one hour

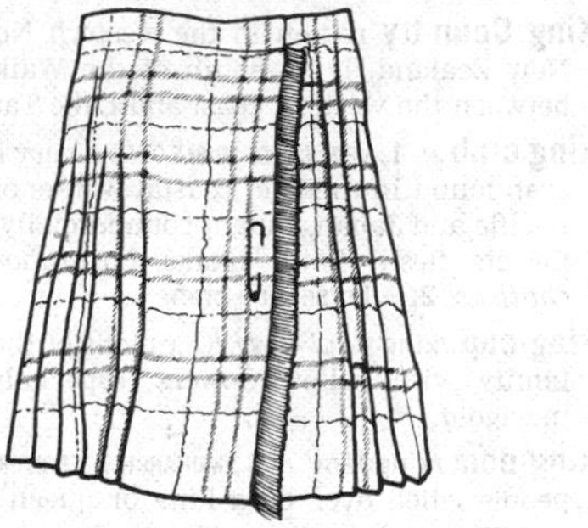

Kilt

kilt /kilt/ *n.* an approximately knee-length wraparound tartan garment that is part of the traditional Scottish highland dress for men. A variant of it is worn by women and girls. [Mid-18thC. From dialect *kilt* "to tuck up, gird," of Scandinavian origin.]

kil·ter /kíltər/ *n.* good working order or condition ○ *The well pump is out of kilter.* [Mid-17thC. Variant of earlier *kelter*, of unknown origin.]

Kim·ber·leys, The /kímbər leez/ plateau region of northwestern Western Australia, near the border with the Northern Territory. The highest point is Mount Hann, 2,545 ft./776 m. Area: 140,000 sq. mi./360,000 sq. km.

kim·ber·lite /kímbər lìt/ *n.* a form of igneous rock, found especially in South Africa, composed mainly of peridotite and often containing diamonds [Late 19thC. Named for *Kimberley*, South Africa, a diamond-mining center.]

kim·chi /kímchee/ *n.* a pickle made with vegetables such as cabbage and white radish seasoned with chili, garlic, and ginger, regarded as the national dish of Korea [Late 19thC. Via Korean *kimch'i* from, ultimately, Chinese.]

Kim Il Sung /kìm il súng/ (1912–94) North Korean statesman. As supreme leader of North Korea (1948–94) he tried to reunite Korea in the Korean War (1950–53), and developed a cult of his own personality. Born **Kim Song Ju**

ki·mo·no /kə mṓnə, ki mṓnō/ (*plural* **-nos**) *n.* 1. **TRADITIONAL JAPANESE GARMENT** a loose, floor-length, traditional Japanese garment that has wide sleeves, wraps in front, and is fastened with a sash 2. **WESTERN GARMENT** a Western garment, especially a robe, similar to the Japanese kimono [Late 19thC. From Japanese, formed from *ki* "wear" + *mono* "thing."] —**ki·mo·noed** *adj.*

Kim Young Sam /kìm yung saám/ (*b.* 1927) South Korean statesman. He was president (1993–98) and worked to eliminate corruption in government.

Kimono

kin /kin/ *n.* 1. **FAMILY GROUP** somebody's relatives as a group (*takes a plural verb*) 2. **GROUP OR CLASS** a member of a group that shares characteristics with another group ○ *Starfishes and sea urchins are kin.* 3. **BLOOD RELATION** somebody related by blood ○ *He's not kin, but we consider him one of the family.* ■ *adj.* **RELATED** related to somebody ○ *I'm kin to them through my grandmother.* [Old English *cyn(n)*. Ultimately from an Indo-European word that is also the ancestor of English *gender, genre, genetic,* and *genesis.*]

-kin *suffix.* little, dear ○ *limpkin* [Origin uncertain: probably from Middle Dutch *-ki(j)n*]

ki·na /keénə/ *n.* 1. **CURRENCY OF PAPUA NEW GUINEA** the main unit of currency of Papua New Guinea, equal to 100 toeas. See table at **currency** 2. **COIN WORTH A KINA** a coin worth a kina [Late 20thC. From Tok Pisin.]

Ki·n·a·ba·lu, Mount /kìnnəbə lóō/ mountain in Malaysia in the state of Sabah, in northern Borneo. It lies in Kinabalu National Park. Height: 13,455 ft./4,101 m.

ki·nase /kí nàyss, -nàyz/ *n.* any of a group of enzymes that catalyze the transfer of a phosphate group from ATP [Early 20thC. Formed from KINETIC + -ASE.]

kin·cob /kín kòb, kíng-/ *n.* an Indian silk embroidered with gold or silver thread [Early 18thC. From Urdu and Persian *kamkāb* "gold or silver brocade," an alteration of *kamkā* "damask silk," ultimately from Chinese words meaning "gold" and "flower."]

kind[1] /kīnd/ *adj.* 1. **COMPASSIONATE** having a generous, warm, compassionate nature 2. **GENEROUS** showing generosity or compassion 3. **AGREEABLE OR SAFE** not harsh, unpleasant, or likely to have destructive effects ○ *a detergent that is kind to the environment* 4. **CARING** showing courtesy or caring about somebody (*formal*) ○ *my kindest regards to your family* 5. **LOVING** full of love (*archaic*) [Old English *gecynde* "innate," "natural," from a prehistoric Germanic word that is also the ancestor of English *kin*]

WORD KEY: USAGE

See Usage note at ***kindly***.

kind[2] /kīnd/ *n.* 1. **GROUP OF INDIVIDUALS THAT SHARE FEATURES** a group or class of individuals connected by shared characteristics ○ *What kind of fruit is this?* 2. **SOMETHING INFERIOR** an example of something, especially if it is seen as inferior or doubtful ○ *Well, you could say it's a kind of tool, but how would you use it?* 3. **ESSENCE OF SOMETHING** the primary character of something that determines the class to which it belongs 4. **WAY** way or manner (*archaic*) ◇ **kind of** rather, to some extent, or in a way (*informal*) ○ *She seemed kind of upset when I talked to her.* ◇ **in kind** 1. with goods or services and not money 2. with something of the same sort that was given ○ *If they attack us, they'll be paid back in kind.* ◇ **of a kind** 1. like something else in some respects but not enough to be satisfactory 2. alike, or belonging to the same sort

WORD KEY: USAGE

These kind of When ***kind of*** is followed by a plural word, there is a temptation to precede the whole phrase with a corresponding plural such as *these* or *those*, so that *this kind of thing* becomes *these kind of things*. However, such expressions (and ones on the same pattern employing *sort* or *type*) are widely regarded as ungrammatical. *These kinds of things* or *things of this kind* is to be preferred.

WORD KEY: USAGE

See Synonyms at ***type***.

kin·da /kíndə/ *contr.* kind of (*nonstandard*) ○ *It's kinda strange.* [Early 20thC. Alteration.]

kin·der·gar·ten /kíndər gaàrt'n, -gaàrd'n/ *n.* a school or class for young children, usually between the ages of four and six, immediately before they begin formal education [Mid-19thC. From German, literally "children's garden."] —**kin·der·gart·ner** *n.*

kind·heart·ed /kīnd haártəd/ *adj.* 1. **FRIENDLY AND GENEROUS BY NATURE** sympathetic and kind ○ *She's too kind-hearted to be angry with you for long.* 2. **ARISING FROM KINDNESS** showing or arising from a sympathetic and generous nature ○ *a kindhearted gesture* [Mid-16thC] —**kind·heart·ed·ly** *adv.* —**kind·heart·ed·ness** *n.*

Kin·di, al- /kíndee/, (801?–873?) Arabian Islamic philosopher. He translated Aristotle into Arabic and formulated the theology of the Mutazilites.

kin·dle[1] /kínd'l/ (**-dled, -dling, -dles**) *vti.* 1. **START BURNING** to set something alight, or to begin to burn 2. **BRIGHTEN OR GLOW** to make something glow, or to become bright 3. **IGNITE EMOTION OR INTEREST** to become aroused, or to arouse feelings or interest ○ *The program kindled his interest in antiquarian books.* [12thC. From Old Norse *kynda* "to catch fire," influenced by Old Norse *kyndill* "torch, candle."] —**kin·dler** *n.*

kin·dle[2] *n.* ZOOL **BROOD OF NEWBORN ANIMALS** a brood or a litter, e.g., of kittens ■ *vi.* (**kin·dled, kind·ling, kin·dles**) ZOOL **GIVE BIRTH** to give birth, especially to baby rabbits

kind·li·ness /kíndleenəss/ *n.* the quality or state of being friendly and generous

kin·dling /kíndling/ *n.* 1. **FIRE-LIGHTING MATERIAL** something such as a bunch of small dry twigs used to start a fire because it burns easily 2. **MAKING SOMETHING BURN** the act of making something start to burn 3. **STIRRING UP OF EMOTION** the arousal of somebody's interest or feelings

kind·ly /kíndlee/ *adj.* (**-li·er, -li·est**) 1. **FRIENDLY AND GENEROUS BY NATURE** sympathetic and kind 2. **SHOWING SYMPATHY** arising from or showing a sympathetic and generous nature 3. **PLEASANT** pleasant, mild, or comfortable ■ *adv.* 1. **PLEASE** used in polite requests ○ *Kindly take your seats* 2. **IN A KIND WAY** showing kindness and considerateness ○ *He kindly accompanied me home.* 3. **TOLERANTLY** with tolerance and patience ○ *She kindly disregarded their lack of skill during the first few days.* [Old English]

WORD KEY: USAGE

Often misplaced modifier: ***Kindly*** is not restricted just to *kindness* as such but may also mean, approximately, "please." In either case it should modify the action or thing wished for, not some other part of the sentence. Surely the intention of, for example, *May we kindly request that patrons take their seats ...* is not to point out how kind *we* are in making the request but to encourage patrons to be so kind as to sit down. Thus the sentence should be reworded as *May we request that patrons kindly take their seats.*

kind·ness /kíndnəss/ *n.* 1. **ABILITY TO BEHAVE KINDLY** the practice of being or the capability to be sympathetic and compassionate 2. **COMPASSIONATE ACT** an act that shows consideration and caring ○ *How can we thank you for your many kindnesses?*

kin·dred /kíndrəd/ *adj.* 1. **SIMILAR TO SOMEBODY OR SOMETHING** close to somebody or something else because of similar qualities or interests ○ *the kindred relationship between neuroscience and neurology* 2. **RELATED BY BLOOD** related to somebody by blood (*formal*) ○ *the search for someone kindred to him* ■ *n.* 1. **AFFINITY** closeness to somebody not related to you by blood based, e.g., on similarity of character or interests ○ *a sense of kindred between the two candidates* 2. **BLOOD RELATIONSHIP** relationship by blood or, less strictly, by marriage ○ *occasions that reinforce the ties of kindred* 3. **SOMEBODY'S FAMILY** somebody's relatives as a group (*takes a plural verb*) 4. **CLAN** a family or group of closely related families, e.g., in the Celtic kin-based social system [12thC. Originally spelled *kinrede* (with later appearance of "d" between "n" and "r"), from KIN + Old English *r_æden* "condition."] —**kin·dred·ness** *n.* —**kin·dred·ship** *n.*

kin·dred spir·it *n.* somebody who is close to you in character, interests, and temperament

kine /kīn/ *npl.* cows or cattle (*archaic*) [Old English *cȳna* "of the cows," a plural form of *cū*, an earlier form of COW]

kin·e·mat·ics /kìnnə máttiks/ *n.* a branch of physics that deals with the motion of a body or system without reference to force and mass (*takes a singular verb*) [Mid-19thC. Formed from Greek *kinēmat-*, the stem of *kínēma*, "motion, movement."] —**kin·e·mat·ic** *adj.* —**kin·e·mat·i·cal·ly** *adv.*

kin·e·scope /kínnə skṑp/ *n.* **1.** = **television tube 2.** **RECORDED TELEVISION PROGRAM** a film of a transmitted television program ■ *vt.* (**-scoped, -scop·ing, -scopes**) **FILM A TELEVISION PROGRAM** to make a film of a transmitted television program [Mid-20thC. Formerly a trademark, formed from KINETIC + -SCOPE.]

ki·ne·sics /kə nēésiks, kī-, -nēéziks/ *n.* the study of the ways in which people use body movements, e.g., shrugging, to communicate without speaking (*takes a singular verb*) [Mid-20thC. Formed from Greek *kinēsis* (see KINESIS).]

ki·ne·si·ol·o·gy /kə nēéssee óllǝjee, -nēézee-/ *n.* **1.** **STUDY OF THE MOTION OF THE BODY** the study of the mechanics of motion with respect to human anatomy **2.** ALTERN MED **ALTERNATIVE THERAPY** a system of muscle testing that reveals and corrects musculoskeletal imbalances and identifies food sensitivities [Late 19thC. Formed from Greek *kinēsis* (see KINESIS).] —**ki·ne·si·ol·o·gist** *n.*

ki·ne·sis /kə nēéssiss, kī-/ *n.* the movement of a cell or organism in response to a stimulus such as light. Such movement can be in any direction and its rate depends on the intensity of stimulation. [Early 20thC. From Greek *kinēsis*, "movement, motion," from *kinein* "to move" (source of English *cinema* and *telekinesis*).]

-kinesis *suffix.* **1.** motion, activity ○ *psychokinesis* **2.** cell division ○ *diakinesis* [From Greek *kinēsis*, from *kinein* "to move" (see KINETIC)]

kin·es·the·sia /kìnnəss theézhə/, **kin·es·the·sis** /kìnnəss theéssiss/ *n.* ANAT the perception or sensing of the motion, weight, or position of the body as muscles, tendons, and joints move [Late 19thC. From Greek *kinein* "to move" (see KINESIS) + *aisthēsis* "sensation."] —**kin·es·thet·ic** /kìnnəss théttik/ *adj.* —**kin·es·thet·i·cal·ly** *adv.*

kin·e·the·od·o·lite /kìnnə thee ódd'l īt/ *n.* an optical instrument that contains a movie camera and provides continuous footage of a moving target, e.g., a missile or satellite, along with its altitude and trajectory [Mid-20thC. Formed from KINESIS + THEODOLITE.]

ki·net·ic /ki néttik/ *adj.* relating to, caused by, or producing motion [Mid-19thC. From Greek *kinētikos*, "for putting in motion," from *kinein*, "to move" (see KINESIS).]

ki·net·ic art *n.* art, especially sculpture, with parts that move, e.g., when blown by the wind or activated by electricity —**ki·net·ic art·ist** *n.*

ki·net·ic en·er·gy *n.* the energy that a body or system has because of its motion. Symbol *T*, E_k

ki·net·ics /ki néttiks/ *n.* (*takes a singular verb*) **1.** PHYS = **dynamics** *n.* 3 **2.** CHEM **BRANCH OF CHEMISTRY** a branch of chemistry that studies rates of reactions

kineto- *prefix.* motion, movement ○ *kinetosome* [From Greek *kinetos* "moving," from *kinein* "to move" (see KINETIC)]

ki·net·o·plast /kə néttə plàst/ *n.* a small cell body outside the nucleus and near the base of the flagellum in some protozoans

kine·to·some /kə néttə sṑm/ *n.* BIOL = **basal body**

kin·folk /kín fṑk/ *npl.* somebody's relatives

king /king/ *n.* **1.** **MAN OR BOY SOVEREIGN** a man or boy who rules as a monarch over an independent state **2.** **CHIEF** a ruler of a specific group ○ *Jupiter was king of the Roman gods* **3.** **BEST EXAMPLE OF ITS KIND** any animal considered as the best, strongest, or biggest of its kind ○ *The lion is variously called the king of beasts or the king of the jungle.* **4.** **PREEMINENT MAN IN SPECIFIC SPHERE** the principal man or preeminent male figure in a specific field ○ *King of the talk/chat shows.* **5.** CARDS **HIGH FACE CARD** any of the four cards in a deck, one in each suit, that carries the picture of a king **6.** CHESS **PRINCIPAL CHESS PIECE** the most important piece in chess, whose capture wins the game **7.** BOARD GAMES **CROWNED PIECE IN CHECKERS** a piece in the game of checkers that has reached the far side of the board and has been crowned, and may therefore move in any direction ■ *vt.* (**kinged, king·ing, kings**) **1.** BOARD GAMES **CROWN A PLAYING PIECE** to make a piece into a king **2.** **CROWN SOMEBODY KING** to make somebody a king [Old English *cyning*, from a prehistoric Germanic word that is also the ancestor of English *kin*]

King /king/ *n.* a title used to denote God or Jesus Christ [Old English]

Express Newspapers

B. B. King

King /king/, **B. B.** (*b.* 1925) U.S. blues musician. He led a blues revival in the 1960s and his rhythm-and-blues hits include "The Thrill is Gone" (1970) and the album *Live at Cook Country* (1971). Real name **Riley B. King**

Popperfoto

Billie Jean King

King, Billie Jean (*b.* 1943) U.S. tennis player. Between 1961 and 1979 she won a record 20 Wimbledon titles. She also won numerous other titles in the United States, France, and Australia. She became the first president of the Women's Tennis Association in 1974.

King, Larry (*b.* 1933) U.S. broadcaster. He is known for his interviews of public figures, especially politicians.

AKG London

Martin Luther King, Jr.

King, Martin Luther, Jr. (1929–68) U.S. civil rights leader and clergyman. His nonviolent demonstrations against racial inequality led to civil rights legislation. He was awarded the Nobel Peace Prize in 1964 and was assassinated four years later in Memphis, Tennessee.

King, Stephen (*b.* 1947) U.S. writer. His horror tales such as *Carrie* (1973) have been hugely successful, and many have been made into motion pictures. Full name **Stephen Edwin King**

King, William Lyon Mackenzie (1874–1950) Canadian statesman. He was Liberal prime minister of Canada (1921–26, 1926–30, 1935–48).

King, William Rufus de Vane (1786–1853) U.S. statesman and vice president of the United States (1853). A Democrat, he died six weeks after taking up office.

king·bird /kíng bùrd/ *n.* a large American songbird that belongs to the tyrant flycatcher family of birds. Genus: *Tyrannus.*

king·bolt /kíng bṑlt/ *n.* a vertical bolt that joins the body of a carriage, wagon, or railroad car to the front axle

King Charles span·iel *n.* a small spaniel of a breed with a markedly domed head, snub nose, bulging eyes, floppy ears, and a tan or black coat with white patches [Late 19thC. Named after CHARLES II of England, who was partial to the breed.]

King cobra

king co·bra *n.* a very large poisonous cobra of Southeast Asia and the Philippines that eats other reptiles and can reach a length of 18 ft./5.5 m. Latin name: *Ophiophagus hannah.*

King Coun·try region in the western North Island, New Zealand, lying south of the Waikato region between the western coast and Lake Taupo

king crab *n.* **1.** **VERY LARGE EDIBLE CRAB** a very large edible crab found in the cold coastal waters of the North Pacific and Japan, caught commercially and prized for its flesh. Latin name: *Paralithoides camtschaticus.* **2.** = **horseshoe crab**

king·cup /kíng kùp/ *n. U.K.* a plant of the buttercup family with yellow flowers, especially a marsh marigold

king·dom /kíngdəm/ *n.* **1.** **MONARCH'S TERRITORY** a state or people ruled over by a king or queen **2.** **SPHERE OF ACTIVITY** a realm or area of activity in which a particular thing is thought to dominate ○ *the kingdom of professional tennis* **3.** SCI **HIGHEST CLASSIFICATION FOR NATURAL THINGS** any of the three groups, animal, vegetable, and mineral, into which natural organisms and objects are traditionally, as opposed to scientifically, divided [Old English]

king·dom come *n.* **1.** **THE NEXT WORLD** the next world, or the state after death **2.** **END OF THE WORLD** the point at which the world comes to an end (*informal*) [Late 18thC. From the phrase *Thy kingdom come* in the Lord's Prayer (Matt. 6:10), where *come* is subjunctive, literally "May Thy kingdom come."]

king·fish /kíng fish/ *n.* **1.** ZOOL **LARGE EDIBLE FISH** a large edible game fish that lives in the warm coastal waters of the Atlantic Ocean. Genus: *Menticirrhus.* **2.** ZOOL = **king mackerel 3.** ZOOL = **opah 4.** **POWERFUL MAN** somebody very powerful, especially a man who has no challengers to his authority (*slang*) ○ *He's the kingfish in this two-bit town.*

Kingfisher

king·fish·er /kíng fishər/ *n.* a brightly colored bird that usually has a short tail, a long stout bill, and sometimes a crest. It feeds on fish, insects, and other prey. Family: Alcidinidae. [15thC. Originally *king's fisher.*]

King Is·land island off the northwestern coast of Tasmania, Australia. It is known for its dairy produce. Population: 1,882 (1996). Area: 421 sq. mi./1,091 sq. km.

King James Bi·ble, **King James Ver·sion** *n.* a version of the Bible published in England in 1611 and authorized by James I for use in the Church of England

king·let /kíngglət/ *n.* **1.** BIRDS **SMALL N AMERICAN BIRD** a small North American bird that is related to the gnatcatchers and to European warblers and has a black-edged yellow or reddish crown. Genus: *Regulus.* **2. PETTY RULER** a minor king, e.g., of a contemptibly small or unimportant kingdom (*insult*)

king·ly /kínglee/ (**-li·er, -li·est**) *adj.* **1. MAGNIFICENT** stately and grand, as befits a king ○ *a kingly posture* **2. ROYAL** having or relating to the rank of king ○ *kingly duties* —**king·li·ness** *n.*

king mack·er·el *n.* a mackerel that lives in the warm waters of the Atlantic Ocean and is often caught for sport. Latin name: *Scomber cavalla.*

king·mak·er /kíng màykər/ *n.* somebody with the power and connections to influence who is appointed to important positions, usually within a government

King·man /kíngmən/ city in northwestern Arizona, east of Bullhead City. Population: 17,270 (1996).

king-of-arms (*plural* **kings-of-arms**) *n. U.K.* a title given to principal heralds in the British colleges of arms

king of kings, **King of Kings** *n.* **1.** CHR **GOD OR JESUS CHRIST** a title used for God or Jesus Christ **2. SUPREME MONARCH** a male monarch who rules over other, subordinate kings

King Peak mountain in the St. Elias Range of southwestern Yukon Territory, Canada. Height: 17,130 ft./5,221 m.

king pen·guin *n.* a large penguin that lives mainly on islands near the Antarctic Circle. Latin name: *Aptenodytes patagonica.*

king·pin /kíng pìn/ *n.* **1. LEADER** the most important person in a group or place (*informal*) **2.** AUTOMOT **PART OF AXLE** a pivot pin that secures an axle to an axle beam and allows a vehicle to be steered **3.** LEISURE **FRONT PIN IN A BOWLING ARRANGEMENT** the pin at the apex of a layout of the pins in tenpin bowling, which must be struck at a certain angle if all the pins are to be knocked down

king post *n.* a vertical post that joins the apex of a triangular roof truss to the cross-beam. ◊ **queen post**

Kings /kingz/ *n.* either of two books of the Bible, Kings I and II, that relate the histories of Israel and the kings of Judah (*takes a singular verb*) [Old English]

king salm·on *n.* = **Chinook salmon**

King's Bench *n. U.K.* LAW the term used for the Queen's Bench Division, a division of the British supreme court system when the reigning monarch is a man or boy

Kings Can·yon canyon in central Australia, near Alice Springs in the Northern Territory

Kings Can·yon Na·tion·al Park national park in the Sierra Nevadas in east central California. Its main features are two canyons of the Kings River and a grove of giant sequoias. Area: 461,901 acres/186,925 hectares.

King's Coun·sel *n. U.K.* LAW the term used for a Queen's Counsel when the reigning monarch is a man or boy

King's Eng·lish *n.* standard written or spoken English, especially in British English, described as the most correct form of the language. It is called the Queen's English when the reigning monarch is a woman.

king's ev·i·dence *n. U.K.* LAW the term used for queen's evidence when the reigning monarch is a man or boy

king·ship /kíng shìp/ *n.* the office, power, or authority of a king

king-size, **king-sized** *adj.* **1. EXTRA BIG** larger, wider, or longer than the standard version of the same thing **2.** FURNITURE **FULL-SIZE** used to describe an extra-large size of bed, 76 in. x 80 in., or bedding made to fit this size of bed **3. VERY GREAT** very great in intensity, scope, or difficulty (*informal*) ○ *a king-size job to finish this weekend*

king snake *n.* a nonpoisonous North American constricting snake ranging from 2 ft./0.6 meters to 6 ft./1.8 meters in length and preying on small animals and other snakes. Genus: *Lampropeltis.*

king's ran·som *n.* an enormous sum of money

King·ston /kíngstən/ **1.** chief seaport, largest city, and capital of Jamaica, located on the southeastern coast of the island at the foot of the Blue Mountains. Population: 538,100 (1995). **2.** city on Lake Ontario at the mouth of the St. Lawrence River, in southeastern Ontario Province, Canada. Population: 143,416 (1996). **3.** city in eastern New York, on the Hudson River, in the Catskill Mountain foothills. Population: 22,195 (1996).

King·wa·na /king waánə/ *n.* a Bantu language spoken in parts of Zaire and widely used as a lingua franca. It is related to Swahili and is a member of the Niger-Congo family of languages. —**King·wa·na** *adj.*

king·wood /kíng wòod/ *n.* **1. HARD PURPLISH WOOD** the hard fine-grained purplish wood of a Brazilian tree, used in cabinetwork **2. LEGUMINOUS TREE** the leguminous tree that yields kingwood. Latin name: *Dalbergia cearensis.*

ki·nin /kínin/ *n.* BIOCHEM **1. BLOOD HORMONE** a polypeptide hormone in the blood that causes dilation of blood vessels and contraction of smooth muscle **2.** = **cytokinin** [Mid-20thC. Origin uncertain: possibly a shortening of BRADYKININ.]

kink /kingk/ *n.* **1. TIGHT COIL** a tight twist or coil in an otherwise straight section of something such as rope, string, or wire **2. MINOR DIFFICULTY IN SOMETHING** a slight difficulty or holdup in the progress of something (*informal*) **3. MUSCULAR SPASM** a sudden spasm in a muscle, especially a crick in the neck (*informal*) **4. ECCENTRICITY** something that is eccentric or peculiar in somebody's personality or behavior **5. ODD IDEA** a quirky, odd idea or impulse (*informal*) ○ *She got a kink in her head to swim across the Chesapeake Bay alone.* **6. SEXUAL ODDITY** an unusual sexual practice, especially one that might be considered deviant (*slang*) ■ *vti.* (**kinked, kink·ing, kinks**) **MAKE OR BECOME FULL OF TWISTS** to put a kink in something, or develop a kink [Late 17thC. From Low German *kinke* "twist in a rope."]

kink·a·jou /kíngkə jòo/ *n.* a tree-dwelling fruit-eating mammal that lives in Central and South America. It is related to the raccoon and has a long prehensile tail, brownish fur, and large eyes. Latin name: *Potos flavus.* [Late 18thC. Via French *quincajou* from, ultimately, an Algonquian word meaning "wolverine."]

kink·y /kíngkee/ (**-i·er, -i·est**) *adj.* **1. TIGHTLY COILED** full of tight coils ○ *kinky copper wire* **2. SEXUALLY ODD** being or engaging in unusual sexual practices that may be considered deviant (*slang*) **3. ECCENTRIC** behaving in an unusual, idiosyncratic way (*informal*) **4. SEXUALLY PROVOCATIVE** intended to be provocative or sexually alluring, usually by being deliberately unusual or bizarre (*slang*) —**kink·i·ly** *adv.* —**kink·i·ness** *n.*

kin·ni·kin·nick /kìnnikə ník/ *n.* **1. DRIED LEAVES FOR SMOKING** a mixture of the dried leaves of some plants, bark, and sometimes tobacco, smoked in the past by some Native Americans **2. PLANT USED FOR SMOKING** a plant such as sumac or dogwood used for making kinnikinnick [Late 18thC. Ultimately from an Algonquian word meaning "mixture."]

ki·no /keé nō/ (*plural* **-nos**) *n.* a red astringent substance resembling resin, obtained by tapping any of several unrelated trees and used medicinally and for tanning in parts of Africa, India, Australia, and the West Indies [Early 19thC. From a West African language.]

Ki·no /keén ō/, **Eusebio Francisco** (1645–1711) Italian Jesuit missionary and explorer. He explored and mapped parts of Mexico and what is now the southwestern United States.

kin se·lec·tion *n.* ZOOL natural selection that favors self-sacrificing behavior toward relatives because, even if the individual dies, those relatives that survive will carry some of its genes

Kin·sey /kínzee/, **Alfred** (1894–1956) U.S. biologist. He is best known for his studies of male (1948) and female (1953) sexuality (the so-called *Kinsey Reports*). Full name **Alfred Charles Kinsey**

kins·folk *npl.* somebody's relatives

Kin·sha·sa /kin shaássə/ capital city of the Democratic Republic of the Congo, situated on the southern bank of the Congo River. Population: 4,655,313 (1994). Former name **Léopoldville** (until 1966)

kin·ship /kín shìp/ *n.* **1. HUMAN RELATIONSHIP** relationship by blood or marriage to another or others **2. RELATEDNESS OF THINGS** relatedness through having characteristics in common, or through coming from the same origin ○ *kinship between Italic and Celtic languages*

kins·man /kínzmən/ (*plural* **-men** /-mən/) *n.* a man or boy who is somebody's relative (*formal*) [12thC. From Old English *cynnes mann(um).*]

Kin·ston /kínstən/ city in North Carolina, near the Atlantic Ocean. Population: 25,295 (1990).

kins·wom·an /-wòommən/ (*plural* **-en** /-wìmmin/) *n.* a woman or girl who is somebody's relative (*formal*) [14thC. Modeled on KINSMAN.]

Kin·tyre /kin tír/ peninsula of western Scotland, between the Firth of Clyde and the Atlantic Ocean The Mull of Kintyre is its southernmost tip. Length: 40 mi./64 km.

ki·osk /keé òsk, kee ósk/ *n.* **1. SMALL ROOFED STREET BOOTH** a small permanent or temporary structure on a sidewalk from which items such as newspapers and candy can be bought **2. SMALL STRUCTURE FOR ADVERTISING** a cylindrical structure that stands at an intersection of walkways or sidewalks or on the street, used to post advertisements and announcements of events **3. MIDDLE EASTERN GAZEBO** a small open pavilion in the Middle East, especially in a garden [Early 17thC. Via French *kiosque* from Turkish *kōşk* "villa," from Persian *kūšk* "villa, palace."]

Ki·o·wa /kí əwàw, kí ə waà/ (*plural* **-wa** *or* **-was**) *n.* **1.** PEOPLES **MEMBER OF A NATIVE NORTH AMERICAN PEOPLE** a member of a once-nomadic Native North American people who originally lived in Montana and migrated to an area near the Black Hills. Today, most Kiowa live on a reservation in Oklahoma, which they share with a small community of Kiowa Apache. **2.** LANG **LANGUAGE OF THE KIOWA** the language of the Kiowa people [Early 19thC. Via American Spanish *Caygua* from Kiowa *kygú* (plural).] —**Ki·o·wa** *adj.*

Ki·o·wa A·pach·e *n.* PEOPLES **MEMBER OF A NATIVE NORTH AMERICAN PEOPLE** a member of a Native North American people who originally lived with the Kiowa on the southern Great Plains, sharing a common history and culture, but speaking a different language ■ *adj.* LANG **RELATING TO KIOWA APACHE** relating to the Kiowa Apache people, or their language or culture

kip[1] /kip/ *n. U.K.* **1. SLEEP** a sleep or a nap (*informal*) **2. BED** a bed or other place to sleep (*slang*) ■ *vi.* (**kipped, kip·ping, kips**) *U.K.* **SLEEP OR NAP** to sleep or take a nap, often in a makeshift bed (*informal*) [Mid-18thC. From Danish *kippe* "cheap inn."]

kip[2] /kip/ *n.* a unit of weight equivalent to 1,000 lb./455 kg [Early 20thC. Formed from an abbreviation of KILO + POUND.]

kip[3] /kip/ (*plural* **kip**) *n.* **1. UNIT OF CURRENCY IN LAOS** the main unit of currency of Laos, equal to 100 at. See table at **currency** **2. COIN WORTH A KIP** a coin worth one kip [Mid-20thC. From Thai.]

kip[4] /kip/ *n.* a hide taken from an immature animal, especially a calf or a lamb [14thC. From Middle Dutch or Middle Low German, "bundle (of hides)."]

Kip·ling /kípling/, **Rudyard** (1865–1936) British writer and poet. His books, many with Indian settings, include *The Jungle Books* (1894, 1895) and *Kim* (1901). He won the 1907 Nobel Prize in literature.

kip·per /kíppər/ *n.* **1. SALMON** a male salmon during the spawning season **2. SMOKED HERRING** a fish, usually a herring, that has been cleaned, split open, and then salted and smoked ■ *vt.* (**-pered, -per·ing, -pers**) **SMOKE FISH** to cure fresh fish, especially herring, by salting and smoking it (*usually passive*) [Old English *cypera* "spawning salmon," of uncertain origin: perhaps from *coper* "copper" (from the color of the fish)] —**kip·per·er** *n.*

kir /keer/, **Kir** *n.* an alcoholic drink made by adding cassis to dry white wine [Mid-20thC. Named after Canon Félix *Kir* (1876–1968), mayor of Dijon, France, who supposedly invented the drink.]

Kir·giz *n.* LANG, PEOPLES = **Kyrgyz**

Ki·ri·ba·ti /keérrə baàtee/ independent state in the west central Pacific Ocean, part of Micronesia. Language: English. Currency: Australian dollar. Capital: Tarawa. Population: 82,449 (1997). Area: 313 sq. mi./811 sq. km. Official name **Republic of Kiribati**

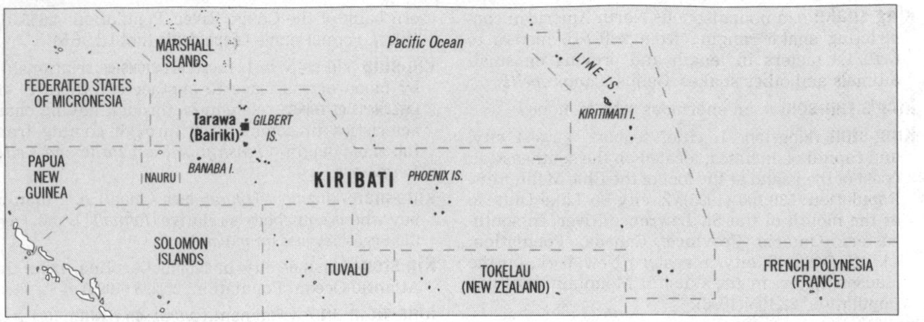

Kiribati

Kir·i·ti·ma·ti /kìrrətee máatee/ island forming part of Kiribati Republic. It is the largest atoll in the Pacific Ocean. Population: 2,537 (1990). Area: 150 sq. mi./388 sq. km.

kirk /kurk/ *n. Scotland* a church [12thC. From Old Norse *kirkja*, from Old English *cir(i)ce*, an earlier form of CHURCH.]

Kirk *n. Scotland* the Church of Scotland, the largest Presbyterian Church in Scotland

Kirk·land Lake /kùrklənd-/ town in northern Ontario, Canada, a former goldmining center

Kir·li·an pho·tog·ra·phy /kèerlee ən-/ *n.* PHOTOGRAPHY a photographic process that records the radiation emitted by or the aura surrounding an object in a high-frequency electric field [Late 20thC. Named after Semyon D. and Valentina K. *Kirlian*, Russian technicians who invented the process.]

Kir·man /keer maán/ *n.* a Persian carpet or rug [Late 19thC. Named after *Kirman*, a province in Iran where the rugs were originally made.]

kir·mess *n.* = **kermis**

Ki·rov /keé ràwf/ city in northeastern European Russia, capital of Kirov Oblast. Population: 487,000 (1990). Former name **Vyatka**

Ki·ro·vo·hrad /ki róvvə gràd/ city in central Ukraine, situated southeast of Kiev. Population: 278,000 (1995).

kirsch /keersh/, **kirsch·was·ser** /keérsh vaàssər/ *n.* a clear brandy distilled from black cherries, especially in Germany and France [Early 19thC. From German, a shortening of *Kirschwasser*, literally "cherry-water," from *Kirsche* "cherry," from assumed Vulgar Latin *cerasia* (source of English *cherry*).]

kir·tle /kúrt'l/ *n.* **1.** WOMAN'S DRESS a long gown or skirt worn by women from the Middle Ages to the 17th century **2.** 16THC MAN'S COAT a long tunic or coat worn by men until the 16th century [Old English *cyrtel* "short coat," via prehistoric Germanic from, ultimately, Latin *curtus* "short, cut short"]

Ki·ru·na /keérə naà/ city in Norrbotten County, northern Sweden, a region rich in high-quality iron ore. Population: 26,173 (1995).

Ki·san·ga·ni /keèsaan gaánee/ capital of Orientale Region, in northern Democratic Republic of the Congo. Population: 417,517 (1994).

kish·ke /kíshkə/ *n.* a Jewish dish consisting of a chicken's or cow's intestine stuffed with flour meal, onion, and fat, and then boiled and roasted [Mid-20thC. From Yiddish, from Slavic.]

Kis·ka Is·land /kískə-/ island in the Aleutian Islands, southwestern Alaska, the largest and westernmost of the Rat Islands. Area: 110 sq. mi./285 sq. km.

Kis·lev /kísslef/ *n.* the third month of the year in the Jewish civil calendar, and the ninth month in the religious year. It has either 29 or 30 days. [From Hebrew *Kislēw*]

kis·met /kíz mèt, kízmət/ *n.* **1.** FATE fate or destiny **2.** ISLAM ALLAH'S WILL the will of Allah [Mid-19thC. Via Turkish from Persian *ḳismat*, from Arabic *ḳisma(t)* "lot, portion," from *ḳasama* "he divided, allotted."]

kiss /kiss/ *v.* (**kissed, kiss·ing, kiss·es**) **1.** *vti.* BRUSH OR CARESS WITH THE LIPS to touch somebody or something with the lips, either gently or passionately **2.** *vti.* CUE GAMES GLANCE AGAINST ONE ANOTHER in cue games, to touch each other gently while one ball is passing the other, or to touch another ball while passing it **3.** *vt.* SIDESWIPE to clip or brush against an object while in a moving vehicle (*informal*) **4.** *vt.* TOUCH SOMETHING GENTLY to touch or brush against something lightly (*usually passive*) ○ *oranges kissed by the California sun* ■ *n.* **1.** CARESS DONE WITH THE LIPS a gentle or passionate touch with the lips **2.** GENTLE PASSING TOUCH a very light, almost imperceptible touch in passing ○ *She felt the kiss of the evening breeze on her skin.* **3.** FOOD SMALL PIECE OF CANDY a very small piece of soft candy, sometimes individually wrapped in foil [Old English *cyssan* "to kiss," from *coss* "kiss," the old form of the noun] —**kiss·a·ble** *adj.*

kiss off *v.* (*slang*) **1.** *vt.* REJECT SOMEBODY OR SOMETHING to reject somebody or something abruptly ○ *The boss kissed off that idea fast.* **2.** *vt.* BE FORCED TO YIELD SOMETHING to be compelled to give something up ○ *We had to kiss the trip off for lack of money.* **3.** *vi.* GO AWAY to leave immediately or leave somebody alone

kiss and tell *n.* a book, article, or broadcast interview in which the author or interviewee publicly relates past sexual intimacy with somebody

kiss-and-tell *adj.* revealing an earlier sexual experience with somebody else, especially when the information, considered to be confidential, is made public (*informal*)

kiss curl *n. U.K.* = **spit curl**

kiss·er /kíssər/ *n.* **1.** SOMEBODY WHO KISSES somebody who kisses, especially in a particular way ○ *not much of a kisser* **2.** MOUTH somebody's mouth (*slang*)

Kis·sim·mee /kissimèe/ river in central Florida that runs south into Lake Okeechobee. Length: 140 mi./225 km.

kiss·ing bug *n.* INSECTS = **conenose**

kiss·ing cous·in *n.* somebody who is distantly related but known well enough to be kissed on meeting

kiss·ing dis·ease *n.* infectious mononucleosis (*informal*)

Kis·sin·ger /kíssinjər/, **Henry** (*b.* 1923) German-born U.S. statesman. National security adviser and then secretary of state under Nixon and Ford, he helped to negotiate an end to the Vietnam War, for which he shared the 1973 Nobel Peace Prize. His "shuttle diplomacy" was aimed at bringing peace between Israel and Arab states. Full name **Henry Alfred Kissinger**

kiss of death *n.* something or somebody whose presence will bring failure or disaster to something [From the passage in the Bible (Mark 14:44–46) in which Judas kissed Jesus Christ, thereby betraying him]

kiss of life *n.* (*informal*) **1.** ARTIFICIAL RESPIRATION mouth-to-mouth resuscitation **2.** SOMETHING THAT REVIVES SOMETHING ELSE something that revives or restores an enterprise or, less commonly, somebody's spirits

kiss of peace *n.* a gesture, usually either a kiss or handshake, used as a sign of Christian fellowship during Communion

kist *n.* ARCHEOL = **cist**

Ki·su·mu /ki sóomoo/ city in southwestern Kenya, on Lake Victoria, a port and capital of Nyanza Province. Population: 201,100 (1991).

Ki·swa·hi·li /keè swaa heèlee/ *n.* a Bantu language spoken by the Swahili people of coastal East Africa and used as a lingua franca throughout East and Central Africa [Mid-19thC. From Bantu, coined from *ki-*, a prefix, + *Swahili*.]

kit /kit/ *n.* **1.** SET OF THINGS FOR USE TOGETHER a set of articles, tools, or equipment used for a particular purpose **2.** CONTAINER FOR SET the container for a set of things ○ *a sewing kit* **3.** SPECIAL CLOTHING AND EQUIPMENT a special set of clothing and equipment assembled for a member of the armed forces or a sportsperson **4.** SET OF PARTS FOR ASSEMBLING a set of parts ready to be put together ○ *a model of a Porsche made from a kit* [14thC. From Dutch *kitte* "tankard, jug." Originally in the meaning "wooden tub."]

kit out *vt. U.K.* to provide somebody with the clothes, and sometimes also equipment, needed to do something

Ki·ta·kyu·shu /keètə kyóoshoo/, **Ki·ta·kyū·shū** industrial city at the northern tip of Kyushu Island, in Fukuoka Prefecture, Japan. Population: 1,026,455 (1990).

Ki·ta·sa·to Shi·ba·sa·bu·ro /keè taa saàto sheè baasə bóoro/ (1852–1931) Japanese bacteriologist. He isolated the bacteria that cause tetanus, anthrax, dysentery, and bubonic plague.

kit bag *n.* a canvas bag, usually cylindrical, for holding military gear or a similar bag used by civilians, carried on the shoulder

kitch·en /kíchən/ *n.* a room or part of a room or building in which food is prepared and cooked [Pre-12thC. From Latin *coquina* (source of English *cuisine*), and derived from *coquere*, source of English *cook*.]

kitch·en cab·i·net *n.* an informal unelected group of advisors to a head of government who are often believed to have more influence than the official cabinet

Kitch·e·ner /kích'nər/ industrial city located southwest of Toronto in southern Ontario, Canada. Population: 178,240 (1996).

kitch·en·ette /kìchə nét/ *n.* a very small room, or part of another room, equipped and furnished as a kitchen

kitch·en gar·den *n.* a garden in which vegetables, herbs, and sometimes fruit are grown for the use of a household

kitch·en mid·den *n.* an area of an archeological site that contains domestic refuse such as food waste, broken pottery, and pieces of other household artifacts, indicating long-term human occupation

kitch·en po·lice *npl.* enlisted soldiers assigned to work in a kitchen, usually as a punishment

kitch·en·ware /kíchən wàir/ *n.* utensils used in the kitchen, including pots and pans, mixing bowls, cutting boards, knives, spoons, and gadgets

kite /kīt/ *n.* **1.** TOY FOR FLYING IN WIND a light framework covered in a thin light material, flown for fun in the wind at the end of a long string **2.** BIRDS SMALL SLIM HAWK a small slim hawk that has long pointed wings and a forked tail. Family: Accipitridae. **3.** SAILING LIGHT SAIL a light sail used in addition to a ship's standard sails **4.** FIN FAKE FINANCIAL TRANSACTION a negotiable bill, e.g., a check, that is fraudulently used to sustain credit by representing a fictitious monetary transaction (*slang*) **5.** FIN BAD CHECK a check that is fraudulently written against an account containing insufficient funds and dated so as to allow the perpetrator to take advantage of the time lag required for clearing ■ *v.* (**kit·ed, kit·ing, kites**) **1.** *vti.* FIN PASS BAD CHECKS to write and pass bad checks in order to sustain credit on a temporary basis, all the time using to advantage the period between writing them and their clearing (*slang*) **2.** *vi.* GLIDE AS IF FLYING to glide and soar like a kite [Old English. From Old English *cȳta* "kite, bittern."] —**kit·er** *n.* ◇ **fly a kite 1.** to do something or speak about something in order to test public opinion on it (*slang*) **2.** to issue a fraudulent financial document such as a check without having enough funds to cover it (*slang*) ◇ **high as a kite 1.** extremely excited or elated (*informal*) **2.** extremely intoxicated or drug-affected (*informal*)

kit fox *n.* a small slender fox of the western United States that has large ears. It is often regarded as a subspecies of the swift fox. Latin name: *Vulpes macrotis.* [Early 19thC. *Kit* of uncertain origin: probably from *kit*, a shortening of KITTEN.]

kith /kith/ *n.* somebody's friends and acquaintances (*dated*) ◇ **kith and kin** somebody's friends and relatives

ki·tha·ra /kíthərə/ *n.* = **cithara**

Kit·i·mat /kíttə màt/ seaport on Douglas Channel in western British Columbia, Canada. Population: 11,136 (1996).

kitsch /kich/ *n.* **1.** ARTISTIC VULGARITY sentimentality, tastelessness, or ostentation in any of the arts ○ *The book jackets were pure kitsch.* **2.** VULGAR OBJECTS collectively, decorative items that are regarded tasteless, sentimental, or as ostentatious in style ○ *tourist* *shops full of kitsch* [Early 20thC. From German, derived from *kitschen* "to throw together (a work of art)."] —**kitsch·y** *adj.*

kit·ten /kítt'n/ *n.* **YOUNG CAT** a young cat ■ *vi.* **(-tened, -ten·ing, -tens) GIVE BIRTH TO CATS** to give birth to young cats [14thC. Via Old French *chitoun*, diminutive of *chat* "cat."] ◇ **have kittens** to become angry, excited, or nervous about something (*informal*)

kit·ten heel *n.* (*usually plural*) **1. LOW HEEL** a low heel on a woman's shoe **2. LOW HEELED SHOE** a woman's shoe with a low heel

kit·ten·ish /kítt'nish/ *adj.* **1. FRISKY** behaving in a lively and playful way, as a kitten does **2. FLIRTATIOUS** coyly flirtatious —**kit·ten·ish·ly** *adv.* —**kit·ten·ish·ness** *n.*

kit·ti·wake /kítti wàyk/ (*plural* **-wake** *or* **-wakes**) *n.* a gull of northern regions that nests on cliffs and winters on open oceans. Latin name: *Rissa tridactyla* and *Rissa brevirostris.* [Mid-17thC. An imitation of the bird's call.]

kit·ty[1] /kíttee/ (*plural* **-ties**) *n.* a kitten or cat (*informal*) [Early 18thC. Shortening and alteration of KITTEN.]

kitty[2] /kíttee/ (*plural* **kit·ties**) *n.* **1. JOINT POOL OF MONEY** a fund of money contributed to by a group of people and used to buy something in common **2.** CARDS, GAMBLING **PROPORTION OF THE OVERALL POT IN POKER** a portion of the total amount of money bet by all the players on each hand of poker **3.** GAMBLING **POOL OF BETS** the amount of money that has been bet by the players in a game **4.** CARDS = **widow** *n.* 4 [Early 19thC. Originally "small bowl." See KIT.]

kit·ty-cor·nered, kit·ty-cor·ner *adv., adj.* = **cater-cornered**

Kit·ty Hawk /kíttee hawk/ town in northeastern North Carolina, on the Atlantic Ocean. It is the site of the Wright Brothers National Memorial. Population: 1,937 (1990).

Ki·twe /kít wày/ copper-mining town in north central Zambia, north of Lusaka. Population: 338,207 (1990).

ki·va /keévə/ *n.* an underground or partly underground chamber, usually with a hole at the top that lets in daylight, used by the men in a Pueblo community for ceremonial or formal meetings [Late 19thC. From Hopi *kíva*.]

Ki·vu, Lake /keévoo/ freshwater lake in the Great Rift Valley of Africa, between western Rwanda and eastern Democratic Republic of the Congo. Area: 1,040 sq. mi./2,700 sq. km.

Ki·wa·nis /ki wáaniss/ *n.* a North American-based association of men's clubs that encourages community service

Kiwi

ki·wi /keéwee/ *n.* (*plural* **-wi** *or* **-wis**) **1.** BIRDS **FLIGHTLESS BIRD OF NEW ZEALAND** a nocturnal flightless bird with a long slender beak and no tail that is found only in New Zealand, where it is also the national emblem. Genus: *Apteryx.* **2. ki·wi, Ki·wi** PEOPLES **SOMEBODY FROM NEW ZEALAND** somebody who comes from or lives in New Zealand (*informal*) **3.** BOT **CHINESE VINE WITH EDIBLE FRUIT** a Chinese vine that bears edible fruit with a greenish-brown fuzzy skin and sweet green pulp. Latin name: *Actinidia chinensis.* **4.** FOOD = **kiwi fruit** ■ *adj.* **RELATING TO NEW ZEALAND** relating to or typical of New Zealand, its people, or culture (*informal*) [Mid-19thC. From Maori, an imitation of the bird's cry.]

ki·wi fruit *n.* the fruit of the kiwi plant, which has a greenish-brown fuzzy skin and sweet green pulp

kj, kJ *abbr.* kilojoule

KJV *abbr.* BIBLE King James Version

Kiwi fruit

KKK, K.K.K. *abbr.* Ku Klux Klan

KKt *abbr.* CHESS king's knight

KKtP *abbr.* CHESS king's knight's pawn

kl *symbol.* kiloliter

KL *abbr.* Kuala Lumpur

Kla·gen·furt /klaágən fòort/ city and capital of Kärnten Province, southern Austria. It is situated about 62 mi./100 km southwest of Graz. Population: 89,415 (1991).

Klai·pe·da /klīpidə/ port and city in western Lithuania, on the coast of the Baltic Sea. Population: 202,800 (1995).

Klam·ath /klámməth/ (*plural* **-ath** *or* **-aths**) *n.* **1. A MEMBER OF A NATIVE AMERICAN PEOPLE** a member of a Native American people who lived in Oregon and northern California, in part of the Cascade Range, and were culturally connected to the Modoc **2. MEMBER OF KLAMATH** a member of the Klamath people [Early 19thC. From Chinook *łámał* "Klamath."] —**Klam·ath** *adj.*

Klam·ath River /klàmməth-/ river in the states of Oregon and California, flowing from Upper Klamath Lake into the Pacific Ocean. Length: 250 mi./400 km.

Klan /klan/ *n.* the Ku Klux Klan (*informal*) —**Klan·ism** *n.*

Klans·man /klánzmən/ (*plural* **-men** /-mən/) *n.* a member of the Ku Klux Klan

klatch /klach/ *n.* ➧ **coffee klatch** (*regional*)

WORD KEY: REGIONAL NOTE

Klatch and its fuller forms *coffee klatch* and *kaffee klatch* are fairly widespread, but centered in German settlements of the Upper Midwest and the western Great Lakes regions.

klav·ern /klávvərn/ *n.* a local unit of the Ku Klux Klan [Early 20thC. Formed from an abbreviation of *klan* + CAVERN.]

Klax·on /kláksən/ *n.* a trademark for a loud electric horn

Klee /klay/, **Paul** (1879–1940) Swiss painter. His imaginative and often witty works, some inspired by children's paintings and drawings, had a great influence on modern art.

Kleen·ex /kleé nèks/ *tdmk.* a trademark for a soft facial tissue

Klein /klīn/, **A. M.** (1909–72) Canadian poet and novelist. His works are concerned with Jewish culture and history. Full name **Abraham Moses Klein**

Calvin Klein

Klein, Calvin (*b.* 1942) U.S. fashion designer. After establishing his own company in 1968, he became known for his understated, sophisticated designs. Full name **Calvin Richard Klein**

Klein, Melanie (1882–1960) Austrian psychoanalyst. She pioneered studies in child psychoanalysis using free-play therapy. She moved to England in 1926.

Klein bot·tle /klīn-/ *n.* a one-sided surface formed by inserting the small open end of a tapered tube through the side of the tube and upward until it is contiguous with the larger end [Mid-20thC. Named for Felix *Klein* (1849–1925), German mathematician.]

Klem·per·er /klémpərər/, **Otto** (1885–1973) German conductor. Noted for his interpretations of Beethoven, Mozart, and Mahler, he moved to the United States in 1933, where he conducted the Los Angeles Symphony Orchestra. From 1959 he conducted the Philharmonia Orchestra of London.

klepht /kleft/ *n.* one of the Greeks who resisted Turkish rule in Greece from 1456 to 1832 and who lived in the mountains as outlaws and brigands [Early 19thC. From modern demotic Greek *klephtēs* "thief," from Greek *kleptēs*.] —**kleph·tic** *adj.*

klep·to·ma·ni·a /klèptə máynee ə/ *n.* an obsessive urge to steal, especially when there is no economic necessity

klep·to·ma·ni·ac /klèptə máynee àk/ *n.* somebody who has an obsessive urge to steal, especially when there is no economic necessity —**klep·to·ma·ni·a·cal** /klèptəmə nī ək'l/ *adj.*

klick /klik/ *n.* a kilometer (*informal*) [Mid-20thC. Origin unknown.]

klieg light /kleég-/ *n.* a very powerful carbon-arc light used in the past in making movies [Early 20thC. Named for John H. *Kliegl* (1869–1959) and Anton T. *Kliegl* (1872–1927), German-born U.S. lighting experts and inventors.]

Klimt /klimt/, **Gustav** (1862–1918) Austrian painter. Founder of the Vienna Secession school of painting (1897), he created richly decorated portraits of women.

Kline /klīn/, **Franz** (1910–62) U.S. artist. He is known for his abstract expressionist paintings, which have large black forms on a white background. Full name **Franz Josef Kline**

Klippel /klīppel/, **Robert** (*b.* 1920) Australian sculptor. His works include assemblages made with scraps of metal.

klip·spring·er /klíp sprìngər/ *n.* a small agile antelope with large ears that lives in mountainous regions of Africa. Latin name: *Oreotragus oreotragus.* [Late 18thC. From Afrikaans, literally "cliff-springer, rock-jumper."]

Klu·ane Na·tion·al Park Re·serve /kloo àyn-/ national park in southwestern Yukon Territory, Canada. It includes Canada's highest peak, Mt. Logan. Area: 8,500 sq. mi./22,000 sq. km.

kludge /klooj/, **kluge** *n.* **PATCHED SOLUTION** a makeshift combination of hardware and software put together to solve a computing problem, that, while effective, is usually inelegant and not suitable for manufacture (*slang*) ■ *vt.* **(kludged, kludg·ing, kludges; kluged, klug·ing, kluges) FIX SOMETHING WITH A KLUDGE** to solve a computing problem using a kludge (*slang*) [Mid-20thC. Formed on the model of BOTCH and FUDGE.] —**kludg·y** *adj.*

klutz /kluts/ *n.* (*slang insult*) **1. OFFENSIVE TERM** an offensive term referring to somebody who is regarded as physically or socially clumsy **2. OFFENSIVE TERM** an offensive term referring to somebody who is regarded as unintelligent [Mid-20thC. Via Yiddish *klots* "wooden beam" from German *Klotz* "clod."] —**klutz·i·ness** *n.* —**klutz·y** *adj.*

kly·stron /klī stròn/ *n.* an electron tube that uses an electric field to generate and amplify microwaves [Mid-20thC. Coined from Greek *klus-*, stem of *kluzein* "to wash or break over," + -TRON.]

km *abbr.* kilometer

K-mes·on *n.* = **kaon**

km/h *abbr.* kilometers per hour

kmph *abbr.* kilometers per hour

kmps *abbr.* kilometers per second

kn, kn. *abbr.* **1. kn.** SAILING knot **2.** MONEY krona **3.** MONEY krone

KN *abbr.* CHESS king's knight

knack /nak/ *n.* **1. SKILL** an easy, clever way of doing something or handling a problem ○ *I can't get the knack of this software.* **2. PARTICULAR ABILITY** a particular skill, especially one that might be innate or intuitive and therefore difficult to teach ○ *You certainly have a knack with children.* **3.** INGENIOUS DEVICE a device or mechanism that is ingeniously constructed (*archaic*) **4.** KNICKKNACK small usually decorative item (*archaic*) [14thC. Origin uncertain: perhaps from or related to *Dutch* and Low German *knak* "sharp blow, crack," an imitation of the sound. Originally "trick, deception."]

WORD KEY: SYNONYMS

See Synonyms at ***talent.***

knack·er /nákər/ *n. U.K.* **1.** SOMEBODY WHO KILLS HORSES FOR PROFIT somebody who makes a living by buying old, worn-out, or injured horses, slaughtering them, and selling their parts, e.g., their flesh and hide **2.** DEMOLITION MERCHANT somebody who makes a living by buying unwanted buildings, demolishing them, and selling their materials for scrap [Early19thC. Originally "saddler, harness maker," of uncertain origin: probably from Scandinavian.]

knack·ered /nákərd/ *adj. U.K.* totally exhausted, broken-down, or about to collapse (*slang*) [Late 19thC. Formed from KNACKER.]

knack·wurst /naák wùrst, -wŏŏrst/, **knock·wurst** /nók wùrst/ *n.* a spicy smoked European sausage similar to a frankfurter but shorter and thicker [Mid-20thC. From German, literally "crack-sausage" (because its skin cracks open when bitten), formed from *knacken* "to crack."]

knap /nap/ (**knapped, knap·ping, knaps**) *vt.* to chisel or hammer something such as a stone so that it breaks into flakes [15thC. Origin uncertain: probably from Low German or Dutch *knappen* "to crack," an imitation of the sound.] —**knap·per** *n.*

knap·sack /náp sàk/ *n.* a cloth or leather bag with shoulder straps, designed for carrying personal items and supplies on a hiker's back [Early 17thC. From Low German, literally "eating sack," from *knappen* "to bite, eat" + *Sack* "sack."]

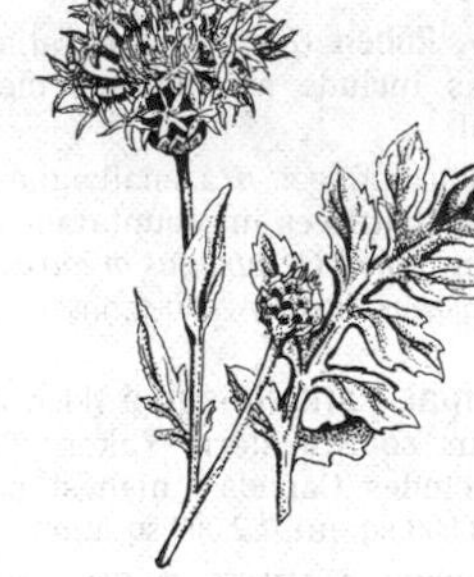

Knapweed

knap·weed /náp weèd/ (*plural* **-weeds** *or* **-weed**) *n.* a thistle plant with purple flowers grouped in a head, and spiny parts just below them. Latin name: *Centaurea nigra.* [Early 16thC. Alteration of Middle English *knopwed*, literally "knob-weed," from *knop* "knob," from the shape of its cluster of flowers.]

knar /naar/ *n.* a knot on a tree or in wood [13thC. Origin uncertain: perhaps from Middle Dutch or Middle Low German *knorre.*] —**knarred** *adj.* —**knarr·y** *adj.*

knave /nayv/ *n.* **1.** CUNNING UNTRUSTWORTHY MAN a man who is dishonest and deceitful (*archaic insult*) **2.** MAN SERVANT a man who works as a servant (*archaic*) **3.** MAN OF LOW BIRTH a man of low social position (*archaic*) **4.** CARDS = **jack**[1] *n.* 2 [Old English *cnafa* "boy, male servant," from prehistoric Germanic] —**knav·ish** *adj.* —**knav·ish·ly** *adv.* —**knav·ish·ness** *n.*

knav·er·y /náyvəree/ *n.* an action, or behavior, that is dishonest or deceitful (*archaic*)

knead /need/ (**knead·ed, knead·ing, kneads**) *v.* **1.** *vti.* WORK DOUGH UNTIL SMOOTH to fold, press, and stretch a soft substance such as dough or clay, working it into a smooth uniform mass **2.** *vt.* MASSAGE MUSCLES to rub, squeeze, or press a part of the body with the hands, e.g., in order to relax the muscles **3.** *vt.* SHAPE SOMETHING WITH THE HANDS to make or shape something out of a soft substance by kneading it [Old English *cnedan.* Ultimately from an Indo-European word meaning "to bend" that is also the ancestor of English *knob* and *knar.*] —**knead·a·ble** *adj.* —**knead·er** *n.*

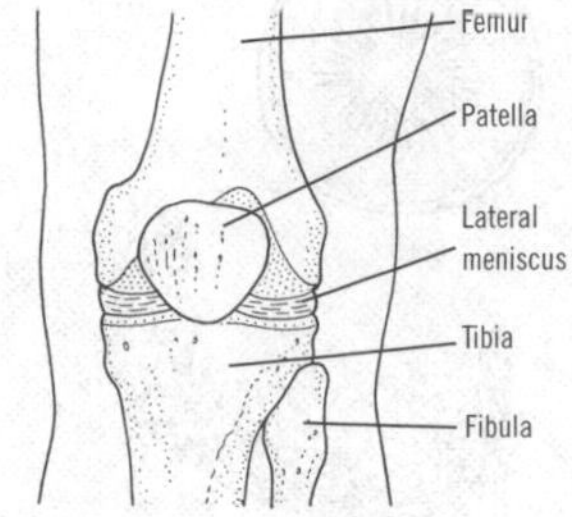

Knee

knee /nee/ *n.* **1.** ANAT MIDDLE JOINT OF THE HUMAN LEG the joint of the human leg between the thigh and the lower leg, where the femur and the tibia meet, covered in front by the kneecap (**patella**) **2.** ANAT WIDER AREA AROUND THE KNEE JOINT the general area surrounding the knee joint **3.** UPPER LEG the upper surface of the thigh of somebody sitting down ○ *Come and sit on my knee.* **4.** CLOTHES PART OF PANTS SURROUNDING THE KNEE the part of a piece of clothing, especially pants, that fits around the knee **5.** ZOOL LEG JOINT IN ANIMALS the joint between the upper and lower parts of the hind legs in four-legged vertebrates and of the legs in birds **6.** TREES GROWTH ABOVE WATER FROM A ROOT a woody outgrowth from the roots of some trees that grow in saturated soils or standing water, which protrudes above the surface and enables them to breathe **7.** OBJECT THAT LOOKS LIKE A KNEE something that resembles the human knee, e.g., a bent pipe ■ *vt.* (**kneed, knee·ing, knees**) HIT SOMEBODY WITH THE KNEE to strike somebody with the knee [Old English *cnēow.* Ultimately from an Indo-European word meaning "to bend" that is also the ancestor of English *genuflect.*] ◇ **bring somebody to his** *or* **her knees** to reduce somebody to a state of abject weakness and vulnerability or force somebody to admit defeat

knee ac·tion *n.* a type of front-wheel suspension in an automobile that allows each wheel to move independently in a vertical direction

knee breech·es *npl.* = **breeches**

knee·cap /neè kàp/ *n.* **1.** FLAT BONE OVER THE KNEE JOINT a flat triangular bone located at the front of the knee. It protects the knee joint. Technical name **patella 2.** = **kneepad** ■ *vt.* (**-capped, -cap·ping, -caps**) CRIMINOL SHOOT SOMEBODY IN THE KNEES to shoot somebody deliberately in the knees as a punishment in order to cause lasting difficulty in standing or walking (*informal*)

knee-deep *adj.* **1.** IN AS HIGH AS THE KNEES standing or sunk in something that reaches up to the knees ○ *be knee-deep in mud* **2.** AS HIGH AS THE KNEES reaching up to the knees ○ *The river was only knee-deep.* **3.** EXTREMELY INVOLVED IN SOMETHING completely occupied by or entangled in something ○ *knee-deep in paperwork*

knee-high *adj.* UP TO THE KNEES reaching up to the knees ■ *n.* SOCK REACHING KNEE a sock or stocking that comes up as high as the knee

knee·hole /neè hōl/ *n.* a hole made for the knees in a desk or other piece of furniture

knee jerk *n.* an involuntary contraction of the thigh muscle that produces a sudden extension of the leg, usually in response to a light rap on the tendon below the kneecap

knee-jerk *adj.* (*informal disapproving*) **1.** NOT THOUGHT THROUGH given or occurring immediately and automatically, without thinking, and usually expressing habitual attitude or prejudice ○ *a knee-jerk opinion* **2.** REACTING PREDICTABLY tending to respond in the same way to any situation ○ *a knee-jerk political hack*

kneel /neel/ (**knelt** /nélt/ *or* **kneeled, knelt** *or* **kneeled, kneel·ing, kneels**) *vi.* to rest on, or get down on, one or both knees [Old English *cnēowlian*, from *cnēow*, an earlier form of KNEE]

knee·pad /neè pàd/ *n.* a covering that protects the knee from injury, especially during sports

knee·pan /neè pàn/ *n.* = **kneecap** *n.* 1

knee sock *n.* a sock that reaches to the knee

knell /nel/ *n.* **1.** SLOW BELL RING the sound of a bell rung slowly, associated with solemnity or mourning, used to announce a death or funeral **2.** OMINOUS SIGNAL something that signals death, disaster, or the end of something (*literary*) ■ *v.* (**knelled, knell·ing, knells**) **1.** *vti.* RING A BELL to ring a bell slowly, or produce a slow ringing sound, especially as a sign of mourning or to announce a death or funeral **2.** *vt.* SIGNAL SOMETHING OMINOUS to announce or signal something such as a death, disaster, or the end of something (*literary*) [Old English *cnyll*, from *cnyllan* "to strike." Ultimately from an Indo-European word that is also the ancestor of English *knock* and *knuckle.*]

knelt past participle, past tense of **kneel**

Knes·set /knéssət/, **Knes·seth** *n.* the parliamentary legislature of Israel. It has one legislative chamber with supreme authority. [Mid-20thC. From Hebrew, literally "gathering."]

knew past tense of **know**

Knick·er·bock·er /níkər bòkər/ *n.* **1.** DESCENDANT OF DUTCH IN NEW YORK somebody descended from the early Dutch settlers of New York **2.** SOMEBODY FROM NEW YORK somebody who is a native of or lives in the state of New York (*informal*) [Early 19thC. Named for Diedrich *Knickerbocker*, fictitious author of Washington Irving's *History of New York.*]

knick·er·bock·ers /níkər bòkərz/ *npl.* loose-fitting short breeches gathered at or just below the knee [Mid-19thC. Origin uncertain: perhaps from their resemblance to the Dutchmen's knee breeches in Cruikshank's illustrations to Washington Irving's *History of New York.*]

knick·ers /níkərz/ *npl.* **1.** = **knickerbockers 2.** *U.K.* PANTIES women's or girl's underpants [Late 19thC. Shortening.]

knick·knack /ník nàk/, **nick·nack** *n.* a small decorative ornament or object [Late 16thC. Formed from a reduplication of KNACK. From the earlier meaning "petty trick, artifice."]

knick·point /ník pòynt/ *n.* a point along a river's length at which it suddenly begins to flow in a steeper course [Early 20thC. Partial translation of German *Knickpunkt*, from *Knick* "bend, kink" + *Punkt* "point."]

knife /nīf/ *n.* (*plural* **knives** /nīvz/) **1.** TOOL FOR CUTTING OR SPREADING a tool with a usually sharp blade and a handle, used for cutting, slicing, or spreading **2.** ARMS STABBING WEAPON a knife with a handle and a sharpened blade specifically made to be a weapon ■ *v.* (**knifed, knif·ing, knifes**) **1.** *vt.* CRIMINOL STAB SOMEBODY to stab or cut somebody with a knife **2.** *vt.* BETRAY SOMEBODY to try to bring about somebody's downfall in a devious or dishonest way (*informal*) **3.** *vi.* MOVE WITH A SWIFT SMOOTH MOTION to move quickly, forcefully, and cleanly through something ○ *The hawk knifed through the air.* [Pre-12thC. Origin uncertain: perhaps via Old French *canif* from Basque *kanibet* or *ganibet*, from Latin *canna* "reed" + Basque *bedoi* "billhook," *egitai* "sickle," or *ebaille* "cutter."] —**knif·er** *n.* ◇ **under the knife** undergoing surgery (*informal*)

knife-edge *n.* **1.** KNIFE'S CUTTING EDGE the cutting edge of the blade of a knife **2.** OBJECT LIKE THE EDGE OF KNIFE an object that is sharp, thin, and narrow **3.** CRITICAL TIME IN A SITUATION a decisive and precarious point in a situation at which it is finely balanced between different possibilities or outcomes ○ *with the future of the project on a knife-edge* **4.** TECH FULCRUM FOR A PRECISE INSTRUMENT a metal wedge whose narrow edge is used as a fulcrum for a scale beam or a lever in a precision instrument

knight /nīt/ *n.* **1.** HIST MEDIEVAL MOUNTED SOLDIER OF LOW RANK in earlier medieval Europe, a tenant of a feudal lord who was required to serve as a soldier on horseback **2.** HIST MEDIEVAL SOLDIER OF HIGH RANK in later medieval Europe, a soldier of noble rank raised to a privileged military status by his king after serving as a page and squire **3.** POL MAN WITH THE TITLE "SIR" a man who holds a nonhereditary title conferred by a ruler for personal achievement or public service. A British knight has the title "Sir" before his name. **4.** MEMBER OF A BROTHERHOOD a man who belongs to a special group or organization, especially a religious or secret brotherhood **5.** CHAMPION OF A CAUSE a fervent supporter or defender of a cause or belief **6.** PROTECTOR OF A WOMAN a man who is protective of and devoted to a woman **7.** CHESS HORSE'S HEAD CHESS PIECE a chess piece shaped like a horse's head that moves two squares horizontally and one vertically or two vertically and one horizontally. Symbol **N** ■ *vt.* (**knight·ed, knight·ing, knights**) MAKE A MAN A KNIGHT to bestow a knighthood on a man [Old English *cniht* "boy, male attendant," from prehistoric Germanic]

knight bach·e·lor (*plural* **knights bach·e·lors** *or* **knights bach·e·lor**) *n.* a British knight of the lowest rank who is not a member of any of the orders of knighthood

knight-er·rant (*plural* **knights-er·rant**), **knight er·rant** (*plural* **knights er·rant**) *n.* **1. WANDERING MEDIEVAL KNIGHT** a medieval knight who traveled around looking for adventure **2. ADVENTUROUS ROMANTIC** a man preoccupied with ideas of adventure and romance —**knight-er·rant·ry** *n.*

knight·head /nît hèd/ *n.* either of two upright timbers supporting the inner end of the bowsprit of a sailing ship, to which mooring cables or ropes are sometimes attached [Early 18thC. From the fact that it often had a carving of a male head.]

knight·hood /nît hòod/ *n.* **1. POSITION OF KNIGHT** the rank, title, or occupation of a knight **2. CHIVALRY AND HONOR** the qualities of chivalry, bravery, and honor, thought to be characteristic of a knight **3. KNIGHTS** knights considered as a group [Old English]

knight·ly /nîtlee/ (**-li·er, -li·est**) *adj.* relating to knights, or characteristic of a knight, especially in being noble and chivalrous [Old English] —**knight·li·ness** *n.*

Knight of Co·lum·bus *n.* a member of a benevolent and fraternal organization of Roman Catholic men, founded in 1882 [Late 19thC. Named for Christopher *Columbus*.]

Knight of Pyth·i·as *n.* a member of a benevolent and fraternal organization for men, founded in the 1860s

Knight of the Mac·ca·bees (*plural* **Knights of the Mac·ca·bees**) *n.* a member of a benevolent organization, founded in Canada in 1878

Knights of the Round Ta·ble *npl.* an order of knights said to have been created by King Arthur that figures prominently in Arthurian legends and chivalric poems [The *Round Table* was where the knights sat. It was circular so that no knight would be seated in a position of superiority.]

Knight Tem·plar (*plural* **Knights Tem·plar**) *n.* **1.** HIST **MEMBER OF A MEDIEVAL CHRISTIAN MILITARY ORDER** a member of a Christian military order that was founded in Jerusalem in 1119 to protect pilgrims after the First Crusade. The order grew wealthy and influential from banking activities before being suppressed by the Pope in 1312. **2.** FREEMASONRY **U.S. FREEMASON** a member of a Masonic order in the United States

knish /kə nísh/ *n.* a piece of dough filled with meat, cheese, or potato, baked or fried, and eaten as a snack or appetizer, especially in Jewish-American cooking [Mid-20thC. Via Yiddish from Russian.]

knit /nit/ *v.* (**knit·ted** *or* **knit, knit·ting, knits**) **1.** *vti.* **INTERLOCK YARN LOOPS TO MAKE GARMENT** to interlock loops of yarn, using either long needles or a machine, or to make a garment, fabric, or other item by this method **2.** *vti.* **USE A KNIT STITCH** to use a basic plain stitch that forms a flat vertical loop on the front of the piece of knitting ○ *Knit one, purl one.* ◊ **purl 3.** *vti.* **UNITE** to bring people or things together, or come together, in a close association **4.** *vi.* MED **BECOME HEALED** to grow together again after a fracture (*refers to a broken bone*) **5.** *vti.* **BRING THE BROWS CLOSER TOGETHER** to draw the brows together, or be drawn together, in a frown ■ *n.* **1. SOMETHING MADE BY KNITTING** a knitted garment or fabric **2. WAY OF KNITTING** a method or style of knitting a garment or fabric **3. PLAIN STITCH** a basic knitting stitch that forms a flat vertical loop on the face of something being knitted. ◊ **purl** [Old English *cnyttan* "to tie in knots," from a prehistoric Germanic word that is also the ancestor of English *knot*] —**knit·ta·ble** *adj.* —**knit·ter** *n.*

knit·ting /nítting/ *n.* **1. PRODUCTION OF KNITTED ITEMS** the act or process of making knitted items or fabric by hand-held needles or by machine **2. SOMETHING BEING KNITTED** an item that is in the process of being knitted

knit·ting nee·dle *n.* a long slim rod with a dull point, used in pairs in knitting

knit·wear /nít wàir/ *n.* garments made from knitted fabric

knives plural of **knife**

knob /nob/ *n.* **1. ROUNDED HANDLE OR DIAL** a rounded projecting part attached to a door, drawer, appliance, or other object, used as a handle or a dial or switch **2. ROUNDED PROJECTION** any rounded lump or part projecting from the surface of something **3.** GEOG **HILL** a rounded hill [14thC. From Middle Low German *knobbe* "knot, knob, bud."]

knob·by /nóbbee/ (**-bi·er, -bi·est**) *adj.* having small hard rounded parts sticking out from the surface [Mid-17thC. Formed from *knobble* "small knob," from KNOB.]

knob·ker·rie /nób kèrree/, **knob·stick** /nób stìk/ *n.* a short wooden stick with a knob at one end, used by some South African peoples as a weapon [Mid-19thC. Formed from KNOB + a variant of *kierie*, on the model of Afrikaans *knopkierie*.]

knock /nok/ *v.* (**knocked, knock·ing, knocks**) **1.** *vi.* **HIT REPEATEDLY** to strike loudly against something such as a door with the knuckles or an object in order to attract attention ○ *Someone's knocking at the door.* **2.** *vi.* **MAKE A LOUD NOISE BY COLLIDING** to produce a loud and usually repetitive noise by hitting something ○ *disturbed by a branch knocking against the window all night.* **3.** *vti.* **DEAL BLOW** to strike somebody or something with a hard blow ○ *knock in a nail* **4.** *vt.* **PUT IN A PARTICULAR STATE WITH BLOW** to cause something or somebody to be in a particular state, e.g., unconscious or flat on the floor, with a blow ○ *He knocked me off balance.* **5.** *vti.* **COLLIDE OR CAUSE SOMETHING TO COLLIDE** to hit against something, especially accidentally, or cause something to hit against something else ○ *The glass broke when I knocked it against the table.* **6.** *vt.* **MAKE SOMETHING BY STRIKING** to produce something, especially a hole, by means of repeated blows **7.** *vt.* **CRITICIZE SOMEBODY OR SOMETHING** to criticize or find fault with somebody or something (*slang*) ○ *Don't knock it until you've tried it.* **8.** *vi.* AUTOMOT **PRODUCE REPEATED RAPPING SOUND** to make a regular rapping noise that is usually caused by faulty fuel combustion (*refers to a vehicle or its engine*) **9.** *vi.* CARDS **END CARD GAME** to end a game, especially gin rummy, by striking the table before laying down a hand in which those cards not in sets total less than a specified amount ■ *n.* **1. BLOW OR COLLISION** a blow struck against somebody or something or a collision with somebody or something **2. SOUND OF KNOCKING** the sound made by somebody or something hitting something, especially repeatedly **3.** AUTOMOT **REPEATED RAPPING SOUND IN ENGINE** a regular rapping noise made by an engine and usually caused by faulty fuel combustion **4. CRITICISM** a disparaging or critical comment about somebody or something (*slang*) **5. BAD EXPERIENCE** a painful, damaging, or distressing experience (*informal*) [Old English *cnocian*, of uncertain origin: thought to be imitative of the sound] ◇ **knock somebody cold** to make somebody unconscious with a blow (*informal*) ◇ **knock somebody dead** to amaze and delight somebody with the quality of a performance (*informal*) ◇ **knock something on the head** to put an end to something or prevent it from developing any further (*informal*)

knock around, knock a·bout *v.* (*informal*) **1.** *vt.* **BEAT SOMEBODY** to abuse somebody physically **2.** *vti.* **TRAVEL AROUND** to travel to different places, or to different places within a specific area, especially without a specific itinerary **3.** *vt.* **HAVE A RELAXING TIME** to relax by doing nothing in particular **4.** *vi.* **SPEND TIME** to spend time habitually in the company of somebody **5.** *vt.* **DISCUSS SOMETHING SPECULATIVELY** to dicuss something casually in order to hear different views **6.** *vt.* **KICK A BALL AROUND** to kick, hit, or throw a ball in an informal game

knock back *vt.* (*informal*) **1.** BEVERAGES **GULP A DRINK DOWN** to drink something, especially alcohol, very quickly **2. COST SOMEBODY MUCH MONEY** to cost somebody a large amount of money ○ *The repairs knocked me back $500.*

knock down *vt.* **1. MAKE SOMEBODY OR SOMETHING FALL** to cause somebody or something to fall to the ground by striking or pushing **2. DISMANTLE SOMETHING** to take something apart for shipping or storage **3. PRONOUNCE SOMETHING SOLD** to show that something has been sold at an auction by striking a surface with a gavel **4. CUT PRICE OF** to reduce the price of something (*informal*) ○ *furniture knocked down by 50%* **5. MAKE SOMEBODY CUT PRICE** to persuade somebody to reduce the price of something **6.** BUSINESS **EARN** to earn a particular amount of money as salary or wages (*informal*) **7.** BASKETBALL **MAKE A BASKET** to score a basket in basketball (*informal*)

knock off *v.* **1.** *vti.* **STOP WORKING** to finish work at the end of the day, or to stop working or doing something in order to take a break (*informal*) **2.** *vt.* **CUT PRICE OF** to decrease the price of something by a particular amount **3.** *vt.* **DEDUCT SOMETHING** to deduct something from something, especially an amount from a price or a number of points from a score or total **4.** *vt.* **PRODUCE SOMETHING WITH EASE OR SPEED** to make or deal with something easily and quickly (*informal*) ○ *knocks off six or seven articles a month* **5.** *vt.* CRIMINOL **KILL SOMEBODY** to kill somebody, especially intentionally (*slang*) **6.** *vt.* CRIMINOL **ROB PLACE** to rob a bank, store, or other business (*slang*) **7.** *vt.* COMM **MAKE CHEAP COPY OF PRODUCT** to produce a cheap, sometimes illegal copy of a well-known product (*slang*) **8.** *vt.* **PLAGIARIZE SOMETHING** to copy somebody else's work (*slang*) ◇ **knock it off** used to demand that somebody stop doing or saying something (*slang*)

knock out *vt.* **1. DEFEAT OPPOSING BOXER WITH PUNCH** in boxing, to knock an opponent down for a count of ten, thus winning the match **2. MAKE SOMEBODY UNCONSCIOUS BY HITTING** to cause somebody to lose consciousness by striking him or her **3. STUPEFY SOMEBODY WITH DRUGS OR ALCOHOL** to cause somebody to lose consciousness or fall asleep by means of drugs or alcohol **4.** SPORTS **ELIMINATE OPPONENT FROM TOURNAMENT** to eliminate an opponent or team from a competition by winning a match or game **5. MAKE SOMETHING USELESS** to destroy something or make it inoperable ○ *The storm knocked out our electricity.* **6. TIRE SOMEBODY OUT** to exhaust somebody completely (*informal*) **7. PRODUCE SOMETHING WITH EASE OR SPEED** to make or do something easily or quickly **8.** BASEBALL **REPLACE A PITCHER** to cause a baseball pitcher's removal from a game by getting several hits **9. PLEASE OR IMPRESS SOMEBODY GREATLY** to overwhelm somebody with excitement or pleasure (*informal*) ○ *That music really knocks me out.*

knock over *vt.* **1. MAKE SOMEBODY FALL** to cause somebody or something to fall by striking or pushing ○ *knocked my cup of coffee over* **2. ASTOUND SOMEBODY** to overwhelm somebody with amazement or shock (*informal*) **3. ROB A PLACE** to rob a bank, store, or other business (*informal*)

knock together *vt.* to make something quickly, without much preparation, and often with little care (*informal*)

knock up *vt.* an offensive term meaning to make a woman pregnant (*slang offensive*)

knock·a·bout /nókə bòwt/ *n.* SAILING **SMALL SAILBOAT** a small sailboat with a mainsail, jib, and keel but no bowsprit ■ *adj.* **1. USING SLAPSTICK** characterized by boisterous physical activity **2. STURDY AND INFORMAL** suitable for rough or casual activities

knock·down /nók dòwn/ *n.* **1. OVERWHELMING BLOW** a powerful emotional or physical blow **2. PRICE DROP** a reduction in the price of something **3. EASILY DISASSEMBLED OBJECT** something such as a piece of furniture that is made so that it can be taken apart easily ■ *adj.* **1. VERY POWERFUL** having an overwhelmingly powerful or very damaging effect **2. EASILY DISASSEMBLED** made to be taken apart easily **3. DISCOUNTED** reduced or very cheap ○ *a knockdown price*

knock·down-drag·out /nòk dòwn drág òwt/, **knock-down-drag-out** *adj.* fought violently or argued bitterly and without mercy —**knock·down-drag·out** *n.*

knock·er /nókər/ *n.* **1. FIXTURE FOR KNOCKING ON DOOR** a metal fixture attached with hinges to the door of a house, used for knocking on the door **2. CRITIC** somebody who finds fault with somebody or something, especially unfairly (*informal*) ■ **knock·ers** *npl.* **OFFENSIVE TERM** an offensive term for a woman's breasts (*slang offensive*)

knock-knee *n.* **PERMANENT CONDITION OF LEGS** a condition in which the legs are permanently bent so that the knees are close together and the ankles are spread far apart ■ **knock-knees** *npl.* **KNEES TURNED INWARD** the knees of somebody with knock-knee —**knock-kneed** *adj.*

knock·off /nók àwf/ *n.* an inexpensive, sometimes illegal copy of a piece of well-known or popular merchandise (*informal*)

knock·out /nók òwt/ *n.* **1.** BOXING **PUNCH WINNING A BOXING MATCH** in boxing, a punch that knocks an opponent down for a count of ten and so wins a contest **2. BLOW CAUSING SOMEBODY TO BECOME UNCONSCIOUS** a blow that knocks somebody unconscious **3.** BOXING **BOXING MATCH WON BY A KNOCKOUT** a victory in a boxing match by a knockout **4. SOMEBODY OR SOMETHING STUNNING** somebody or something extremely attractive, good-looking, or enjoyable (*informal*)

knock·out drops *npl.* a solution, usually containing chloral hydrate, secretly put in a drink to make somebody unconscious (*informal*)

knock·wurst *n.* = **knackwurst**

knoll[1] /nōl/ *n.* a small rounded hill or mound [Old English *cnoll*, from a prehistoric Germanic base that is also the ancestor of English *knot*] —**knoll·y** /nṓlee/ *adj.*

knoll[2] /nōl/ *n., vti.* (**knolled, knoll·ing, knolls**) knell (*archaic*) [14thC. Ultimately from a prehistoric Germanic base that is also the ancestor of English *knell*.]

knop /nop/ *n.* a small decorative knob [14thC. From Middle Low German or Middle Dutch *knoppe* "knob, knot, button."] —**knopped** *adj.*

Knos·sos /nósəss, knóssəss/ ruined city in northern Crete, the center of the Minoan civilization from about 3000 B.C. to 1100 B.C.

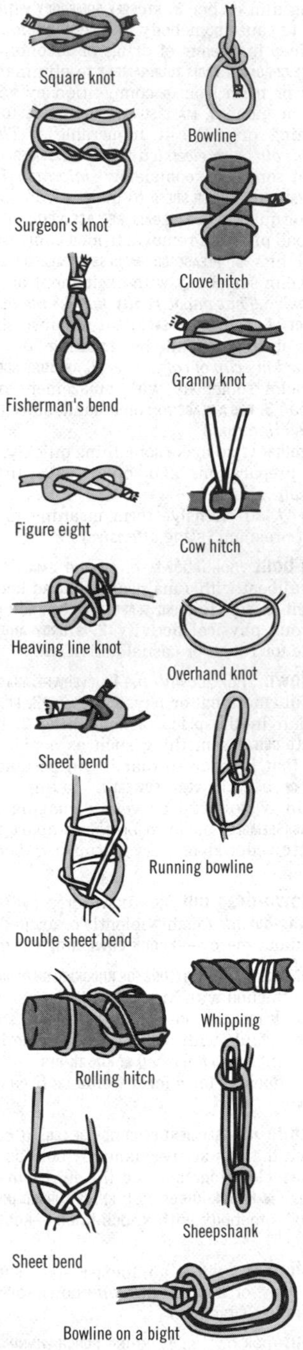

Knot

knot[1] /not/ *n.* **1.** OBJECT MADE BY TYING A STRAND a usually hard, lump-shaped object formed when a strand of something, e.g., string or rope, is interlaced with itself or another strand and pulled tight. Knots are mainly used for tying pieces of string, rope, or thread together or securing them to other objects. **2.** WAY OF TYING A LENGTH OF MATERIAL any of a number of set ways of joining or securing lengths of rope, thread, or other strands by tying the material together or around itself **3.** A TANGLE a tightly tangled mass of strands that are hard to separate **4.** DECORATION SHAPED LIKE A KNOT a piece of material such as ribbon or braid tied in a knot or bow and used as a decoration **5.** HARD PATCH ON A TREE a hard patch on a tree out of which a branch or stem grows **6.** DARK SWORL IN LUMBER a hard dark colored patch in cut wood at a point where a branch or stem formerly grew out of the tree **7.** LUMP ON A TREE a lump on a tree trunk or branch **8.** MED LUMP IN THE BODY a node, ganglion, lump, or swelling in the body **9.** UNIT OF NAUTICAL OR AIR SPEED a unit of measurement for the speed at which a ship or aircraft travels, equivalent to one nautical mile per hour, approximately 1.15 statute mph/1.85 km per hour **10.** NAUT INDICATOR FOR MEASURING A SHIP'S SPEED a division on a log line used for calculating the speed of a ship **11.** NAUT = **nautical mile** **12.** TIGHT GROUP a number of people or things grouped closely together **13.** TENSE FEELING a feeling of tightness or anxiety **14.** PROBLEM a difficult or complex problem ■ *v.* (**knot·ted, knot·ting, knots**) **1.** *vti.* MAKE A KNOT to tie something in a knot, or be tied with a knot **2.** *vti.* TO TANGLE to tangle something, or become tangled **3.** *vt.* MAKE SOMETHING WITH A PATTERN OF KNOTS to produce something, e.g., a piece of macramé, that consists of a pattern of decorative knots **4.** *vti.* BECOME TENSE to become, or to cause something to become, tight or tense with anxiety or fear ○ *My stomach knotted up.* [Old English *cnotta*, from a prehistoric Germanic word meaning "round lump," which is also the ancestor of English *knit* and *knoll*] —**knot·ter** *n.* ◇ **tie the knot** to get married (*informal*)

knot[2] /not/ *n.* a small sandpiper that migrates to the Arctic to breed. Latin name: *Calidris canutus* and *Calidris tenuirostris.* [15thC. Origin unknown.]

knot gar·den *n.* an herb or flower garden that has its plants arranged in an intricate pattern and sometimes also has trees and bushes trimmed in decorative designs

knot·grass /nót gràss/ (*plural* **-grass·es** *or* **-grass**) *n.* a creeping plant with prominent nodes on its stems and small pink flowers, considered a troublesome weed. Knotgrass was at one time widely used herbally in an infusion to treat asthma. Latin name: *Polygonum aviculare.* [Early 16thC. "Knot" from KNOT[1], from its knotted stem.]

knot·hole /nót hōl/ *n.* a hole in wood where a knot has fallen out or been removed

knot·ted /nóttəd/ *adj.* **1.** TIED OR TANGLED IN KNOTS tied in a knot, tangled up in knots, or made using decorative knots **2.** WOODWORK = **knotty** *adj.* 2 **3.** BOT HAVING STEMS WITH SWELLINGS used to describe a plant that has stems with swellings resembling knots

knot·ty /nóttee/ (**-ti·er, -ti·est**) *adj.* **1.** FULL OF KNOTS full of tied or tangled knots **2.** WOODWORK MARKED WITH KNOTS containing or marked with many knots. Also called **knotted** **3.** PUZZLING OR COMPLEX very difficult to understand or solve —**knot·ti·ly** *adv.* —**knot·ti·ness** *n.*

knot·ty pine *n.* pine wood that has many knots in it, used especially for paneling and making furniture

knot·weed /nót wèed/ (*plural* **-weeds** *or* **-weed**) *n.* = **knotgrass**

knout /nowt/ *n.* LEATHER WHIP a leather whip used for flogging ■ *vt.* (**knout·ed, knout·ing, knouts**) BEAT SOMEBODY WITH KNOUT to flog somebody using a knout [Mid-17thC. Via French and Russian *knut* from Old Norse *knútr* "knot."]

know /nō/ (**knew** /noo/, **known** /nōn/, **know·ing, knows**) *v.* **1.** *vti.* HOLD INFORMATION IN THE MIND to have information firmly in the mind or committed to memory ○ *They know the names of all the U.S. presidents.* **2.** *vti.* BE CERTAIN ABOUT SOMETHING to believe firmly in the truth or certainty of something ○ *I know she wouldn't be late without a good reason.* **3.** *vti.* REALIZE SOMETHING to be or become aware of something ○ *I didn't know you cared.* **4.** *vt.* COMPREHEND SOMETHING to have a thorough understanding of something through experience or study ○ *know computers* **5.** *vt.* HAVE ENCOUNTERED SOMEBODY OR SOMETHING BEFORE to be acquainted, associated, or familiar with somebody or something ○ *I have known John for years.* **6.** *vt.* RECOGNIZE DIFFERENCES to be able to perceive the differences or distinctions between things or people ○ *old enough to know right from wrong* **7.** *vt.* IDENTIFY SOMEBODY OR SOMETHING BY A CHARACTERISTIC to recognize somebody or something by a distinguishing characteristic or attribute ○ *I'd know him anywhere by his peculiar laugh.* **8.** *vt.* HAVE SEX WITH SOMEBODY to have sexual intercourse with somebody (*archaic*) [Old English *cnāwan*. Ultimately from an Indo-European word that is also the ancestor of English *can* and *cognition*.] —**know·a·ble** *adj.* —**know·er** *n.* ◇ **in the know** possessing information that is secret or known only to a small group of people ◇ **you know** used to fill a pause, add emphasis to a statement, or elicit a response from the listener (*informal*) ◇ **you never know** used to indicate that the outcome of events is uncertain and it is possible that something that seems unlikely could happen

know-all *n. U.K.* = **know-it-all** (*informal*)

know-how *n.* the practical ability and knowledge necessary to do something (*informal*)

know·ing /nṓ ing/ *adj.* **1.** INDICATING PRIVATE KNOWLEDGE suggesting that somebody knows a secret or something that others are unaware of ○ *a knowing smile* **2.** ASTUTE aware of things and able to act cleverly and judge shrewdly **3.** SHOWING INTELLIGENCE having knowledge, information, or understanding **4.** INTENTIONAL done on purpose —**know·ing·ly** *adv.* —**know·ing·ness** *n.*

know-it-all *n.* somebody who professes to know more or better than anyone else about everything (*informal*)

knowl·edg·a·ble *adj.* = **knowledgeable**

knowl·edge /nóllij/ *n.* **1.** INFORMATION IN MIND general awareness or possession of information, facts, ideas, truths, or principles ○ *Her knowledge and interests are extensive.* **2.** SPECIFIC INFORMATION clear awareness or explicit information, e.g., of a situation or fact ○ *I believe they have knowledge of the circumstances.* **3.** ALL THAT CAN BE KNOWN all the information, facts, truths, and principles learned throughout time ○ *With all our knowledge, we still haven't found a cure for the common cold.* **4.** LEARNING THROUGH EXPERIENCE OR STUDY familiarity or understanding gained through experience or study ○ *knowledge of nuclear physics* **5.** INTERCOURSE sexual intercourse (*archaic*) [14thC. Origin uncertain: probably from obsolete *knowlechen* "to acknowledge," ultimately from Old English *cnāwan* "to know" + *-l_æcan*, from *-lāc*, noun suffix (source of English *wedlock*.]

WORD KEY: SYNONYMS

knowledge, erudition, information, learning, scholarship, wisdom

CORE MEANING: what can be known

knowledge used to talk about what can be known by means of study as well as what can be known through observation, investigation, reasoning, and experience; **erudition** advanced academic learning, often of a specialized or difficult nature; **information** facts or data; **learning** what is known through formal study, especially when this is of quite an advanced nature; **scholarship** advanced academic learning, especially when this is specialized; **wisdom** knowledge or learning, but also the ability to use these prudently and to combine them with experience and good judgment.

knowl·edge·a·ble /nóllijəb'l/, **knowl·edg·a·ble** *adj.* possessing or showing a great deal of knowledge, awareness, or intelligence —**knowl·edge·a·bil·i·ty** /nòllijə bíllətee/ *n.* —**knowl·edge·a·ble·ness** /nóllijəb'lnəss/ *n.* —**knowl·edge·a·bly** *adv.*

knowl·edge base *n.* **1.** COMPUT DATA USED FOR PROBLEM SOLVING the computerized data in an expert system required for solving problems in a particular area **2.** NECESSARY FACTS FOR SOLVING PROBLEM the facts required for solving a problem or problems

knowl·edge in·dus·try *n.* businesses that specialize primarily in data processing or the development and use of information technology

known /nōn/ past participle of **know** ■ *adj.* ESTABLISHED generally recognized as or proven to be something ○ *a known criminal* ■ *n.* CERTAINTY a fact or piece of information that is certain ○ *separate the knowns from the unknowns*

know-noth·ing *n.* **1.** SOMEBODY WITHOUT KNOWLEDGE somebody who is considered ignorant or uninformed (*often used before a noun*) **2.** SOMEBODY WHO IS AGNOSTIC somebody who believes that it is impossible to know anything for certain, especially the existence of God —**know-noth·ing·ism** *n.*

Know-Noth·ing *n.* a member of a U.S. political party of the 1850s that opposed the participation of immigrants and Roman Catholics in political affairs, and whose members denied knowledge of the party —**Know-Noth·ing·ism** *n.*

Knox /noks/, **Henry** (1750–1806) U.S. military leader. During the Revolution he commanded the American artillery. He served as secretary of war (1785–94).

Knt *abbr.* CHESS knight

knuck·le /núk'l/ *n.* **1.** ANAT **FINGER JOINT** a joint of a finger, especially a joint connecting a finger to the hand **2. ROUNDED PROJECTION WHEN A FIST IS MADE** one of the rounded projections above a knuckle that appears on the back of a hand when a fist is made (*often used in the plural*) **3.** COOK **PIECE OF MEAT NEAR THE KNEE** a cut of meat consisting of the lower joint from the hind leg of a calf, pig, or lamb **4.** MECH ENG **HINGE PIVOT** the cylindrical part of a hinge through which the pin passes **5.** MECH ENG = **knuckle joint** *n.* 2 ■ **knuck·les** *npl.* ARMS = **brass knuckles** ■ *v.* (**-led, -ling, -les**) **1.** *vt.* **APPLY KNUCKLES TO** to rub, hit, or press something with the knuckles ○ *knuckled her eyes in disbelief* **2.** *vi.* GAME **HAVE KNUCKLES ON GROUND PLAYING MARBLES** to have the knuckles on the ground when shooting a marble with the thumb pressed into the bent forefinger [14thC. From Middle Low German *knökel*, literally "small bone," ultimately from a prehistoric Germanic word meaning "small bone."] —**knuck·ly** /núklee/ *adj.*

knuckle down *vi.* to work hard and conscientiously at something (*informal*)

knuckle under *vi.* to give in to force or pressure used against you

knuck·le·ball /núk'l bàwl/ *n.* in baseball, a slow pitch with little spin and an unpredictable flight, produced by releasing the ball from the knuckles and the thumb or the tips of two or three fingers —**knuck·le·ball·er** *n.*

knuck·le·bone /núk'l bōn/ *n.* any knobby bone forming part of a joint in the human finger (*informal*)

knuck·le·dust·er *n. U.K.* = **brass knuckles**

knuck·le·head /núk'l hèd/ *n.* an offensive term referring to somebody who is regarded as unintelligent or thoughtless (*slang insult*) —**knuck·le·head·ed** /nùk'l héddəd/ *adj.*

knuck·le joint *n.* **1.** ANAT **FINGER JOINT** a joint of the human finger **2.** MECH ENG **HINGE FASTENING TWO RODS TOGETHER** a hinge with a pin that fastens the ends of two rods together, allowing movement in one plane only

knuck·ler /núklər/ *n.* = **knuckleball**

knuck·le sand·wich *n.* a blow with the fist to the mouth (*slang*)

knur /nur/ *n.* a bump or knot on a tree trunk or in wood [15thC. Origin uncertain: perhaps a variant of KNAR.]

knurl /nurl/ *n.* **1. BUMP OR KNOB** a small hard knob or protuberance **2. RIDGE USED FOR GRIPPING** a ridge, especially one in a series that run along the edge of something, e.g., those on a thumbscrew that make it easier to grip ■ *vt.* (**knurled, knurl·ing, knurls**) **PUT RIDGES ON** to give ridges to something, especially to make it easier to grip [Early 17thC. Origin uncertain: probably literally "small knur," formed from KNUR.] —**knurl·y** /núrrlee/ *adj.*

KO /kay ṓ/ *n.* (*plural* **KO's**) **KNOCKOUT** a knockout, especially in boxing (*informal*) ■ *vt.* (**KO'd, KO'ing, KO's**) **KNOCK SOMEBODY OUT** to knock somebody out, especially in boxing (*informal*) [Early 20thC. From the initial letters of *knock out*.]

ko·a /kṓ ə/ (*plural* **ko·as** *or* **ko·a**) *n.* **1. HAWAIIAN ACACIA TREE** an acacia tree that is native to Hawaii and has spreading branches, gray bark, and hard wood valued as timber. Latin name: *Acacia koa*. **2. WOOD OF THE KOA TREE** the red or golden-brown hard wood of the koa tree, used to make furniture [Early 19thC. From Hawaiian.]

ko·a·la /kō áalə/, **ko·a·la bear** *n.* an Australian marsupial that resembles a small bear and has gray fur, a round face, and large ears. It lives in eucalyptus trees, feeding almost exclusively on their leaves. Latin name: *Phascolarctos cinereus*. [Late 18thC. From Dharuk (an Aboriginal language of southwestern Australia) *kūl(l)a*.]

Koala

ko·an /kṓ àan/ (*plural* **-ans** *or* **-an**) *n.* a Zen Buddhist riddle used to focus the mind during meditation and to develop intuitive thinking [Mid-20thC. From Japanese *kōan*, from Chinese *gōngàn* "official business."]

kob /kob, kōb/ (*plural* **kobs** *or* **kob**) *n.* a large antelope of Central and West Africa with orange-brown fur. It lives in open grasslands near swamps or rivers. Latin name: *Kobus kob*. [Late 18thC. From Wolof *kooba*.]

Ko·be /kṓbee, kṓbày/, **Kō·be** capital of Hyogo Prefecture, and seaport on Osaka Bay, southern Honshu Island, Japan. Population: 1,477,410 (1990).

Ko·blenz /kṓ blènts/ city in the Rhineland-Palatinate, west central Germany, south of Bonn. Population: 109,600 (1994).

ko·bo /kṓ bō/ (*plural* **-bo** *or* **-bos**) *n.* **1. NIGERIAN CURRENCY** a subunit of currency in Nigeria, 100 of which are worth one naira. See table at **currency 2. COIN WORTH A KOBO** a coin worth a kobo [Late 20thC. From Nigerian English, alteration of COPPER.]

ko·bold /kṓbəld/ *n.* in German folklore, a mischievous elf that lives in houses or a gnome that haunts underground places, especially mines [Mid-19thC. From German, variant of *Kobalt* (see COBALT).]

Ko·buk Val·ley Na·tion·al Park /kṑ búk-/ national park located entirely north of the Arctic Circle in northwestern Alaska. Area: 1,750,737 acres/708,498 hectares.

Ko·dak /kṓ dàk/ *tdmk.* a trademark for a hand-held camera invented by George Eastman in 1888 and for photographic supplies such as film

Ko·di·ak[1] /kṓdee àk/ (*plural* **-aks** *or* **-ak**), **Ko·di·ak bear** *n.* a brown bear of the coastal areas and nearby islands of Alaska and British Columbia. Latin name: *Ursus middendorffi*. [Late 19thC. Named for KODIAK ISLAND.]

Ko·di·ak[2] /kṓdee àk/ city in southern Alaska, on northeastern Kodiak Island, south of Anchorage. Population: 7,677 (1996).

Ko·di·ak Is·land island in the Gulf of Alaska, southwestern Alaska, noted for its Kodiak bears and marine life. Area: 3,465 sq. mi./8,974 sq. km.

Ko·et·su Hon·'A·mi /ko èttsoo hōnaámee/ (1558–1637) Japanese artist. A founder member of the revivalist Rimpa school, he was noted for his paintings, calligraphy, pottery, and patronage of the arts.

K of C *abbr.* Knight of Columbus

K of P *abbr.* Knight of Pythias

kohl /kōl/ *n.* a chemical preparation used by women, especially in Asia and the Middle East, to darken the rims of their eyelids. It usually consists of powdered antimony sulphide or lead sulphide. [Late 18thC. From Arabic *kuhl* (see ALCOHOL).]

Kohl /kōl/, **Helmut** (*b.* 1930) German statesman. As Christian Democratic chancellor (1982–98), he played the leading role in German reunification (1990).

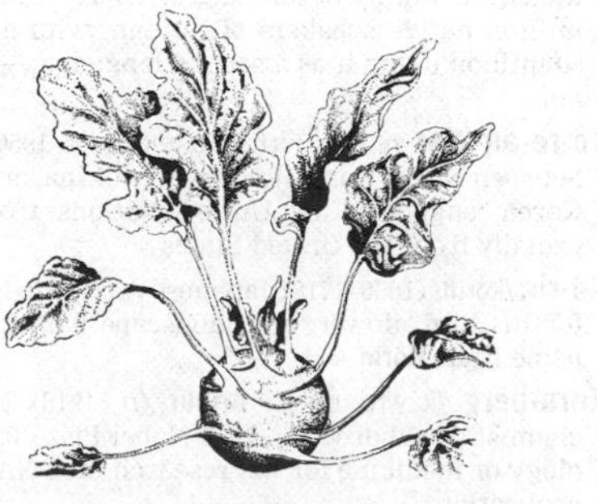

Kohlrabi

kohl·ra·bi /kōl raábee, -rábbee/ (*plural* **-bies**) *n.* **1. CABBAGE PLANT WITH A THICK EDIBLE STEM** a kind of cabbage with an edible swollen stem similar to a turnip and short leaf stalks sprouting vertically from it. Latin name: *Brassica oleracea caulorapa* and *Brassica oleracea gongylodes*. **2. VEGETABLE RESEMBLING A TURNIP** the thick stem of the kohlrabi plant that is eaten as a vegetable [Early 19thC. Via German from the plural of Italian *cavolo rapa*, from medieval Latin *caulorapa*, ultimately from Latin *caulis* "cabbage" + *rapa* "turnip."]

koi /koy/ (*plural* **koi**), **koi carp** *n.* a carp native to Japan and the temperate regions of eastern Asia that is popular as an aquarium or ornamental pond fish because of its red-gold or white coloring. Latin name: *Cyprinus carpio*. [Early 18thC. From Japanese.]

koi·ne /koy náy, kóynee/ *n.* **1.** = **lingua franca 2. STANDARD DIALECT** a dialect or regional variant of a language that becomes the standard language for a wider population of speakers [Late 19thC. From Greek *koinē*, a form of *koinos* "common, ordinary."]

Koi·ne /koy náy, kóynee/ *n.* the form of Greek, derived primarily from the Attic dialect, that became the standard language for Greek-speaking people during the Hellenistic period

ko·ka·nee /kō kánnee/ (*plural* **-nees** *or* **-nee**), **ko·ka·nee salmon** *n.* ZOOL a landlocked form of sockeye salmon native to lakes from western North America to Siberia and Japan, but widely introduced to other areas. Latin name: *Oncorhynchus nerka*. [Late 19thC. From Shuswap *kəknǽxw*.]

Ko·ko·mo /kṓ kə mṑ/ industrial city in north central Indiana, on Wildcat Creek, directly north of Indianapolis. Population: 45,785 (1996).

Ko·ko Nor /kṑkō náwr/ = **Qinghai Hu**

kok-sa·ghyz /kṑksə géez/ (*plural* **kok-sa·ghyz·es**), **kok-sa·gyz** (*plural* **kok-sa·gyz·es**) *n.* a dandelion found in Central Asia that has fleshy roots that are a source of rubber. Latin name: *Taraxacum kok-saghyz*. [From Russian *kok-sagyz*, from Turkic *kök* "root" + *sagiz* "gum, resin"]

ko·la (*plural* **-las** *or* **-la**) *n.* = **cola**

ko·la nut *n.* = **cola nut**

Ko·la Penin·sula /kṑlə-/ peninsula in northwestern European Russia, between the Barents Sea and the White Sea. Area: 40,000 sq. mi./100,000 sq. km.

Ko·lar Gold Fields /kō laár-/ city in southern Karnataka State, southern India, near Bangalore. Population: 156,398 (1991).

Kol·ha·pur /kṓl haa pòor/ city in Maharashtra State, southwestern India. Population: 405,118 (1991).

ko·lin·sky /kə línskee/ (*plural* **-skies**) *n.* **1.** ZOOL **WEASEL WITH TAWNY FUR** a weasel of northern Europe and Asia that has dark tawny fur and is sometimes considered to be a subspecies of the European mink. Latin name: *Mustela sibirica*. **2.** TEXTILES **KOLINSKY FUR** the fur of the kolinsky weasel [Mid-19thC. From Russian *kolinskiĭ* "of Kola," named for *Kola*, a port in northwestern Russia.]

kol·khoz /kol káwz/ (*plural* **kol·khoz·es** *or* **kol·khoz** *or* **kolkhoz·y** /kol káwzee/), **kol·koz** (*plural* **-koz·es** *or* **-koz** *or* **-koz·y**) *n.* a collective farm in the former Soviet Union [Early 20thC. From Russian, from *kol(lektivnoe) khoz(yaĭstvo)* "collective farm."]

kol·khoz·nik /kol káwznik/ *n.* a worker on a collective farm in the former Soviet Union

Kol Nid·re /kōl ní drày, kàwl nee dráy/ *n.* the prayer recited at the opening of the service on the eve of Yom Kippur. It asks that all unfulfilled vows to God be nullified and that all transgressions be forgiven. [Late 19thC. From Aramaic *kol nidrē*, literally "all the vows," the opening words of the prayer.]

ko·lo /kṓlō/ (*plural* **-los**) *n.* a Serbian folk dance in which one or more dancers perform in the center of a circle of other dancers [Late 18thC. From Serbo-Croat, "wheel."]

Ko·lon·ia /kəlṓneeə/ the largest town in the Federated States of Micronesia, and capital of Pohnpei island state. Population: 6,169 (1989).

Ko·ly·ma Range /kəléemə-/ mountain range in northeastern Siberian Russia. Length: 1,300 mi./2,100 km.

ko·ma·tik /kómmətik, kō máttik/ *n.* an Inuit sled with wooden crossbars tied to the runners with rawhide [Early 19thC. From Inuit *qamutik*.]

kom·bu /kóm bòo/ *n.* a type of kelp sold dried and used in Japanese cooking [Late 19thC. From Japanese.]

Komodo dragon

Ko·mo·do drag·on /kə mṓ dṓ-/, **Ko·mo·do liz·ard** *n.* a large monitor lizard found only on the island of Komodo, east of Java. It is the largest living lizard and can grow to a length of 10 ft./3 m. Latin name: *Varanus komodoensis.*

ko·mon·dor /kómmən dàwr/ *n.* a large dog with a long matted white coat, belonging to a Hungarian breed that is traditionally used for herding sheep or as a watchdog [Mid-20thC. From Hungarian.]

Kom·so·mol /kómsə màwl, kòmsə máwl/ *n.* a Communist organization for young people in the former Soviet Union [Mid-20thC. From Russian, coined from *Kommunisticheskiĭ Soyuz Molodëzhi* "Communist Union of Youth."]

Kom·so·molsk /kòmsə máwlsk/ city in far eastern Russia, on the Amur River. Population: 318,600 (1992).

Kon·go[1] /kóng gṓ/ (*plural* **-gos** *or* **-go**) *n.* **1.** PEOPLES **MEMBER OF AN AFRICAN PEOPLE** a member of a people who live along the lower part of the Congo River in west central Africa **2.** LANG **LANGUAGE OF KONGO PEOPLE** the Bantu language spoken by the Kongo people, in southern Congo and northern Angola. There are about seven million native speakers of Kongo, with approximately two million more people using it as a common language. [Mid-19thC. From Kikongo.] —**Kon·go** *adj.*

Kon·go[2] /kóng gṓ/ former kingdom in central Africa that flourished from the 14th to 16th centuries in the area between present-day Gabon and northern Angola

Kö·nigs·berg /kṓnigz bùrg/ former name for **Kaliningrad** (until 1946)

Kon·ka·ni /kóngkənee/ *n.* a dialect of Marathi spoken in coastal Maharashtra in western India [Late 19thC. From Marathi *kōkṇī.*]

Koo /koo/, **Vi Kyuin Wellington** (1888–1985) Chinese statesman and diplomat. He represented China at the United Nations (1946), and followed the Chinese Nationalist government when it retreated to Taiwan. Born **Ku Wei-chun**

koo·doo *n.* = **kudu**

kook /kook/ *n.* somebody whose behavior is considered unpleasantly eccentric (*slang insult*) [Mid-20thC. Origin uncertain: probably a shortening of CUCKOO.]

Kookaburra

kook·a·bur·ra /kóökə bùrrə/ (*plural* **-ras** *or* **-ra**) *n.* a large kingfisher of Australia and nearby islands, known for its loud call that sounds like laughter. Latin name: *Dacelo novaeguineae* and *Dacelo leachii.* [Mid-19thC. From Wiradhuri *gugubarra.*]

kook·y /kóökee/ (**-i·er, -i·est**) *adj.* considered to be unpleasantly eccentric (*slang insult*) —**kook·i·ly** *adv.* —**kook·i·ness** *n.*

Koo·ning /kóöning/, **Willem de** (1904–97) Dutch-born U.S. painter. Although he was a leading abstract expressionist, many of his works nevertheless include elements of the human form.

Koo·te·nay[1] /kóöt'nàỳ/, **Koo·te·nai** river of the northwestern United States and southwestern Canada. It rises in the Rocky Mountains of southeastern British Columbia, flows into the United States, then reenters Canada through Kootenay Lake into the Columbia River. Length: 407 mi./655 km.

Koo·te·nay[2], **Koo·te·nai** *n.*, *n.* = **Kutenai**

Koo·te·nay Na·tion·al Park national park in the Rocky Mountains of southeastern British Columbia, Canada. Area: 543 sq. mi./1,406 sq. km.

ko·peck /kṓ pèk/, **kopek, co·peck** *n.* **1. SUB-UNIT OF RUSSIAN CURRENCY** a sub-unit of currency in Russia and some other countries of the former Soviet Union, worth one hundredth of a rouble. See table at **currency 2. COIN WORTH ONE KOPECK** a coin worth one kopeck [Early 17thC. From Russian *kopeika,* literally "little lance," from the figure of a czar bearing a lance on the coins.]

koph /kof/, **qoph** *n.* the 19th letter of the Hebrew alphabet, represented in the English alphabet as "q." See table at **alphabet** [From Hebrew *qōph*]

kop·pa /kóppə/ *n.* the 17th letter of the ancient Greek alphabet, represented in the English alphabet as "q." Though obsolete in Greek, it was later adopted by the Romans as the letter "q." [Late 19thC. From Greek.]

Kor. *abbr.* **1.** Korea **2.** Korean

Ko·ran /kə ráan, kaw-/, **Qur·'an** *n.* the sacred text of Islam, believed by Muslims to record the revelations of God to Muhammad [Early 17thC. From Arabic *ḳur'ān* "recitation, reading," from *ḳara'a* "to read, recite."] —**Ko·ran·ic** /kə ráanik, kə ránnik, kaw-/ *adj.*

Kor·do·fan /kawr dō fáan/ former province in central Sudan

Kor·do·fan·i·an /kàwrdə fánnee ən/ *n.* **AFRICAN LANGUAGE GROUP** a small group of languages spoken in southern Sudan that is considered either to be distinct from other African languages or to be a branch of the Niger-Congo family ■ *adj.* **1. OF KORDOFANIAN LANGUAGES** relating to the Kordofanian group of languages **2. RELATING TO KORDOFAN** relating to or typical of Kordofan [Named for the former province of KORDOFAN]

Ko·re·a, North /kə rée ə, kō rée ə/ country in northeastern Asia that occupies the northern portion of the Korean Peninsula. Language: Korean. Currency: won. Capital: Pyongyang. Population: 23,904,124 (1996). Area: 46,540 sq. mi./120,538 sq. mi. Official name **Democratic People's Republic of Korea**

Ko·re·a, South country in northeastern Asia that occupies the southern portion of the Korean Peninsula. Language: Korean. Currency: won. Capital: Seoul. Population: 45,948,811 (1997). Area: 38,328 sq. mi./99,268 sq. km. Official name **Republic of Korea**

Ko·re·an /kə rée ən/ *n.* **1.** PEOPLES **SOMEBODY FROM NORTH OR SOUTH KOREA** somebody who was born or raised in or is a citizen of North or South Korea **2.** LANG **LANGUAGE OF NORTH AND SOUTH KOREA** the official language of North and South Korea, also spoken in parts of China, Japan, and Asiatic Russia. It is often assigned to the Altaic family of languages. There are about 60 million native speakers of Korean, with a further 60 million using it as a second language. —**Ko·re·an** *adj.*

Ko·re·an War *n.* a war that lasted from 1950 to 1953 between North Korea, and its ally China, and South Korea, supported by United Nations troops, especially from the United States

Kō·rin /kṓrin/ (1658–1716) Japanese artist. He is known for his bird, flower, and landscape paintings. Full name **Ogata Kōrin**

Korn·berg /káwrn bùrg/, **Arthur** (*b.* 1918) U.S. biochemist. He shared the 1959 Nobel Prize for physiology or medicine for his research on DNA and its replication.

Ko·ror /kə ráwr/ island and administrative center of the Republic of Palau, in the western Pacific Ocean. Population: 11,552 (1997). Area: 8 sq. mi./21 sq. km.

Kor·sa·koff's psy·cho·sis /káwrsə kòfs sī kṑssiss, káwrsə kàwfs sī kṑssiss/, **Kor·sa·koff's syn·drome** *n.* now called **Wenicke-Korsakoff syndrome** [Early 20thC. Named for the Russian psychiatrist S. S. *Korsakoff* (1854–1900).]

ko·ru·na /káwrə nàa/ (*plural* **-run** *or* **-ru·nas**) *n.* **1. UNIT OF CZECH AND SLOVAK CURRENCY** a unit of currency in the Czech Republic and Slovakia. See table at **currency 2. COIN WORTH ONE KORUNA** a coin worth one koruna [Early 20thC. From Czech, "crown."]

Kos·ci·us·ko, Mount /kòzzee úskō/ the highest mountain in Australia, located in the Snowy Mountains in southeastern New South Wales. Height: 7,310 ft./2,228 m.

Koś·ci·us·ko /kòssee úsk ō/, **Tadeusz** (1746–1817) Polish national hero. He served with Washington in the Revolution, and in 1794 led a revolt for Polish independence.

ko·sher /kṓshər/ *adj.* **1.** JUDAISM **RITUALLY PURE** used to describe food that has been prepared so that it is fit and suitable under Jewish law **2.** JUDAISM **PREPARING OR SELLING KOSHER FOOD** preparing or selling foods that are fit and suitable under Jewish law **3. LAWFUL OR PROPER** allowed by law or regarded as correct or proper (*informal*) ○ *Something's not kosher about his handling of the situation.* **4. REAL** genuine, not false or fake (*informal*) ■ *vt.* (**-shered, -sher·ing, -shers**) JUDAISM **PREPARE KOSHER FOOD** to prepare food in a way that is fit and suitable under Jewish Law [Mid-19thC. From Hebrew *kāšēr* "fit, proper."]

Ko·so·vo /káwssəvṓ/ region in southwestern Serbia, in the Federal Republic of Yugoslavia, with a mainly ethnic Albanian population. The administrative center is Pristina. Population: 1,956,196 (1991). Area: 4,203 sq. mi./10,887 sq. km. —**Ko·so·van** *n., adj.* —**Ko·so·var** *n., adj.*

Ko·sy·gin /kə séegin/, **Alexey** (1904–80) Soviet statesman. He was chairman of the Council of Ministers of the Soviet Union, a position equivalent to that of premier, from 1964 to 1980. Full name **Alexey Nikolayevich Kosygin**

Ko·ta Ba·ha·ru /kṓtə baároo/ city on the northeastern coast of the Malay Peninsula, Malaysia, and capital of Kelantan State. Population: 220,000 (1991).

Ko·ta Kin·a·ba·lu /kṓtə kinəbə loo/ city in eastern Malaysia. It is the capital of Sabah State, on the South China Sea. Population: 55,997 (1993). Former name **Jesselton**

Ko·tex /kṓ tèks/ *tdmk.* a trademark for sanitary pads and tampons

ko·to /kṓtō/ (*plural* **-tos**) *n.* a Japanese musical instrument similar to a zither, with 7 to 13 usually silk strings stretched over a convex wooden sounding board. It is plucked using three picks worn on the thumb, index finger, and middle finger. [Late 18thC. From Japanese.]

Kou·fax /kṓf aks/, **Sandy** (*b.* 1935) U.S. baseball player. He pitched for the Brooklyn (later Los Angeles) Dodgers (1955–66) , and won the Cy Young Award (1963, 1965, 1966). Full name **Sanford Koufax**

kou·miss, kou·mis *n.* = **kumiss**

kou·prey /kóo pràỳ/ (*plural* **-preys** *or* **-prey**) *n.* an endangered species of wild ox found in Cambodia and Vietnam that has a blackish brown body with white markings on its back and feet. Latin name: *Bos sauveli.* [Mid-20thC. From Khmer.]

Kous·se·vitz·ky /kòossə vítskee/, **Serge** (1874–1951) Russian-born U.S. conductor. He conducted the Boston Symphony Orchestra (1924–49). Full name **Serge (or Sergey) Alexandrovitch Koussevitzky**

Kow·loon /kòw lóon/ town in Hong Kong Special Administrative Region, southeastern China, on the northern side of Hong Kong harbor. Population: 1,990,000 (1994).

kow·tow /kow tów, ków tòw/ *vi.* (**-towed, -tow·ing, -tows**) **1. KNEEL TO SHOW RESPECT** formerly, in China, to kneel and touch the forehead to the ground in order to show respect, awe, or submission **2. BE SERVILE** to behave in an extremely submissive way in order to please somebody in a position of authority ■ *n.* **1. ACT OF KNEELING TO SHOW RESPECT** a show of respect or worship made by kneeling and touching the forehead to the ground **2. SERVILE ACT** an extremely submissive act aimed at pleasing somebody in a position of authority [Early 19thC. From Chinese *kētóu,* literally "strike head."] —**kow·tow·er** *n.*

KP[1] (*plural* **KPs** *or* **KP's**) *n.* MIL = **kitchen police**

KP[2] *symbol.* CHESS king's pawn

K.P. *abbr.* Knight of Pythias

kph, k.p.h. *abbr.* kilometers per hour

Kr *symbol.* krypton

KR *symbol.* CHESS king's rook

kr. *abbr.* **1.** krona **2.** króna **3.** krone

kraal /kraal/ *n. S Africa* **1. AFRICAN VILLAGE WITHIN STOCKADE** a traditional rural village in Africa, usually consisting of a number of huts surrounded by a stockade (*sometimes considered offensive*) **2. CATTLE PEN** a pen or other enclosure for livestock, especially cattle [Mid-18thC. Via Afrikaans from Portuguese *curral*, from Nama.]

kraft /kraft/, **kraft pa·per** *n.* a type of tough, usually brown, paper made from chemically treated wood pulp and used to make bags and wrapping paper [Early 20thC. From a shortening of Swedish *kraftpapper*, literally "strength paper."]

krait /krīt/ *n.* an extremely poisonous snake, native to Southeast Asia and nearby islands, that has brightly colored bands on its back. Genus: *Bungarus.* [Late 19thC. From Hindi *karait.*]

Kra·ka·tau /kràkə tów/, **Kra·ka·to·a** /kràkə tṓ ə/ **1.** small volcanic island in southwestern Indonesia, in the Sunda Strait between Java and Sumatra. Area: 6 sq. mi./16 sq. km. **2.** volcano on the island of Krakatau, whose eruption in 1883 destroyed most of the island and caused thousands of deaths. Height: 2,667 ft./813 m.

kra·ken /kraákən/ *n.* in Norwegian folklore, a huge sea monster shaped like a giant squid. Norwegian fishermen have periodically reported sightings since the 16th century. [Mid-18thC. From Norwegian.]

kram /kram/ *n.* articles of little value (*regional*) [From German *Kram* "rubbish," or Norwegian *kram* "junk, trash, trifles"]

WORD KEY: REGIONAL NOTE

Kram is a Wisconsin word.

Kra·mer /kráymər/, **Jack** (*b.* 1921) U.S. tennis player. He won the U.S. singles championship (1946, 1947) and the Wimbledon men's singles championships (1947). Full name **John Albert Kramer**

Kras·ner /kráznər/, **Lee** (1908–84) U.S. artist. She was one of the abstract expressionists, and was married to Jackson Pollock.

Kras·no·dar /krəsnə daár/ city and port in southwestern Russia. It is the administrative center of Krasnodar Territory. Population: 634,500 (1992). Former name **Yekaterinodar** (until 1922)

Kras·no·yarsk /krəsnə yaársk/ city in southern Siberian Russia. It is the administrative center of Krasnoyarsk Territory. Population: 925,000 (1992).

Krater

kra·ter /kráytər/, **cra·ter** *n.* in ancient Greece, a large two-handled bowl, used to mix wine with water [Mid-18thC. Via Latin *crater* from Greek *kratēr* "mixing bowl," from *kerannunai* "to mix" (source of English *idiosyncracy*).]

K ra·tion *n.* an emergency food ration consisting of one prepared meal, supplied to U.S. soldiers fighting in World War II [Mid-20thC. Named for the American physiologist Ancel Benjamin *Keyes* (born 1904).]

kraut /krowt/ *n.* = **sauerkraut** [Mid-19thC. From German "vegetable, cabbage."]

Kraut /krowt/ *n.* an offensive term referring to a German (*slang offensive*) [Early 20thC. From German, "vegetable, cabbage." From the stereotype of Germans as eaters of sauerkraut.] —**Kraut** *adj.*

Krebs cy·cle /krébz-/ *n.* a sequence of biochemical reactions occurring in cell structures (**mitochondria**) of living organisms whereby energy is obtained from the oxidation of acetic acid and related compounds derived from food [Mid-20thC. Named for the British biochemist Sir Hans *Krebs.*]

Krei·sler /krī́sslər/, **Fritz** (1875–1962) Austrian-born U.S. violinist and composer. He was one of the most noted violinists of his generation, and wrote numerous pieces for violin.

krem·lin /krémmlin/ *n.* a fortress or citadel in any Russian city [Mid-17thC. Via French from Russian *kreml* "citadel."]

Krem·lin *n.* **1. WALLED COMPOUND IN MOSCOW** the walled citadel in Moscow in which cathedrals, palaces, and the offices of the Russian government are located. The outer walls date back to the 15th century. **2. FORMER SOVIET GOVERNMENT** the government of the former Soviet Union

Krem·lin·ol·o·gy /krèmmlə nólləjee/ *n.* the study of the government and policies of the former Soviet Union —**Krem·lin·o·log·i·cal** /-nə lójjik'l/ *adj.* —**Krem·lin·ol·o·gist** /-nólləjist/ *n.*

krep·lach /krépplәkh/ *npl.* a Jewish dish consisting of triangles or squares of pasta filled with liver or meat that are boiled and served in soup [Late 19thC. From Yiddish *kreplech*, the plural of *krepel*, from German dialect *Kräppel* "fried pastry, fritter."]

kreut·zer /króytsər/, **kreu·zer** *n.* a small silver or copper coin used in Germany, Austria, and Hungary from the 13th to the mid-19th centuries [Mid-16thC. From German *Kreuzer*, from *Kreuz* "cross"; modeled on medieval Latin *denarius crucigerus*, literally "cross-bearing penny."]

krill /kril/ (*plural* **krill**) *n.* a tiny marine crustacean resembling a shrimp. It is the primary food of baleen whales and other animals that filter their food from seawater. Order: Euphausiacea. [Early 20thC. From Norwegian *kril* "small fry of fish."]

krim·mer /krímmər/ *n.* whitish or pale gray fur that is made from the soft curly wool of lambs from the Crimean Peninsula [Mid-19thC. From German, where it was formed from *Krim* "Crimea."]

Kri·o /kreé ō/ (*plural* **-os**) *n.* **1.** LANG **CREOLE LANGUAGE OF SIERRA LEONE** a creole language spoken in Sierra Leone, especially in and around the capital, Freetown. It is based on English, with a strong Yoruba influence. About 50,000 people speak Krio as a first language, and a further 200,000 use it as a second language. **2.** PEOPLES **SOMEBODY WHO SPEAKS KRIO** somebody who speaks Krio [Mid-20thC. Origin uncertain: probably an alteration of CREOLE.] —**Kri·o** *adj.*

kris /krees/ *n.* a Malay and Indonesian dagger with a wavy two-edged blade [Late 16thC. From Malay *keris.*]

Krish·na /kríshnə/ *n.* in Hindu religion, the eighth incarnation of the god Vishnu, often depicted as a young cowherd [From Sanskrit *kṛṣṇa*] —**Krish·na·ism** *n.*

Kriss Kring·le /krìss kríng g'l/ *n.* = **Santa Claus** [Mid-19thC. Alteration of German dialect *Christkindl*, literally "Christmas child, Christmas present."]

Kris·tof·fer·son /kri stófərsən/, **Kris** (*b.* 1936) U.S. singer, songwriter, and film actor. He is known for his country-and-western songs, and films such as *Heaven's Gate* (1980).

Kri·voy Rog /kri vòy ráwk/, **Kri·voi Rog** city and major iron-producing center in south central Ukraine. Population: 724,000 (1991).

KRL *n.*, *abbr.* COMPUT knowledge representation language

kro·na /krṓnə/ (*plural* **-nor** /krṓnər/) *n.* **1. UNIT OF CURRENCY IN SWEDEN** the standard unit of currency in Sweden, worth 100 öre. See table at **currency 2. UNIT OF CURRENCY IN FAEROE ISLANDS** the standard unit of currency in the Faeroe Islands, worth 100 öre. See table at **currency 3. COIN WORTH ONE KRONA** a coin worth one krona [Late 19thC. From Swedish, "crown."]

kró·na /krṓnə/ (*plural* **-nur** /krṓnər/), **kro·na** (*plural* **-nur**) *n.* **1. UNIT OF CURRENCY IN ICELAND** the standard unit of currency in Iceland, worth 100 aurar. See table at **currency 2. COIN WORTH ONE KRÓNA** a coin worth one króna [Late 19thC. From Icelandic, "crown."]

kro·ne /krṓnə/ (*plural* **-ner** /krṓnər/) *n.* **1. UNIT OF CURRENCY IN DENMARK** the standard unit of currency in Denmark, worth 100 øre. See table at **currency 2. UNIT OF CURRENCY IN NORWAY** the standard unit of currency in Norway, worth 100 øre. See table at **currency 3. COIN WORTH ONE KRONE** a coin worth one krone **4.** (*plural* **-nen**) **OLD GERMAN COIN** a gold coin formerly used in Germany, equivalent to 10 marks **5. OLD UNIT OF AUSTRIAN CURRENCY** the standard unit of currency in Austria from 1892 until 1925, or a coin representing it [Late 19thC. From Danish and German, "crown."]

Kro·neck·er del·ta /krṓ nèkər-/ *n.* a mathematical function of two variables that takes on only two values: 0 when the variables are unequal, and 1 when the variables are equal [Early 20thC. Named for the mathematician Leopold *Kronecker* (died 1891).]

kro·ner plural of **krone**

kro·nor plural of **krona**

Kron·stadt /krṓn shtat/, **Kronsh·tadt** military port on Kotlin Island in the Gulf of Finland, in northwestern European Russia. Population: 44,400 (1994).

kró·nur plural of **króna**

kroon /kroon/ (*plural* **kroons** *or* **kroon·i** /kroónee/) *n.* **1. UNIT OF ESTONIAN CURRENCY** the standard unit of currency in Estonia, worth 100 sents. See table at **currency 2. COIN WORTH ONE KROON** a coin worth one kroon [Early 20thC. From Estonian "crown."]

Kru·ger Na·tion·al Park /kroógər-/ national park in northeastern South Africa, bordering Mozambique, established in 1928. Area: 7,523 sq. mi./19,485 sq. km.

Kru·ger·rand /kroógə rànd, -raànd/ *n.* a South African gold coin weighing one ounce, intended mostly to be purchased as an investment [Mid-20thC. From KRUGER + RAND.]

Kru·gers·dorp /kroógərz dawrp/ city in Gauteng Province, northeastern South Africa, near Johannesburg. Population: 93,000 (1991).

krumhorn *n.* = **crumhorn**

krumm·holz /kroóm hōlts/ (*plural* **-holz**) *n.* the stunted trees that grow just above the timberline on a mountain, or the high-altitude zone in which they grow [Early 20thC. From German, "elfin-wood," literally "crooked wood."]

krumm·horn /kroóm hàwrn/ *n.* = **crumhorn**

Krutch /kruch/, **Joseph Wood** (1893–1970) U.S. critic and naturalist. He is known for his literary biographies and nature writings.

kryp·ton /kríp tòn/ *n.* a colorless inert gaseous chemical element found in small quantities naturally in the atmosphere and used in fluorescent lamps and lasers. Symbol **Kr** [Late 19thC. From Greek *krupton*, a form of *kruptos* "hidden, concealed."]

KS *abbr.* **1.** Kansas **2.** Kaposi's sarcoma

K se·lec·tion *n.* a process of natural selection that leads to a lowering of the birthrate when the population of a species approaches the maximum number that the environment can sustain [From *K*, the constant for carrying capacity in the population growth equation]

Ksha·tri·ya /kshá ttree ə, kə sháttree ə/ *n.* **1. HINDU CASTE** the second of the four Hindu castes, originally a royal and warrior caste. In modern times, its members are professionals, administrators, or military personnel. **2. MEMBER OF KSHATRIYA CASTE** a member of the Kshatriya caste [Late 18thC. From Sanskrit *kṣatriya*, from *kṣatra* "rule."]

kt *abbr.* PHYS kiloton

Kt, Kt. *abbr.* knight

kt., kt *abbr.* **1.** CHESS knight **2.** NAUT, AEROSP knot

K.T. *abbr.* Knight Templar

Kua·la Lum·pur /kwaàllə loóm p'oor/ capital city of Malaysia, located on the southern Malay Peninsula. Population: 1,145,075 (1991).

Ku·blai Khan /koóblī kaán/ (1215–94) Mongol leader and emperor of China. He completed the conquest of China begun by his grandfather Genghis Khan, and founded the Yuan dynasty (1279).

Ku·brick /kyoóbrik/, **Stanley** (1928–99) U.S. film director. His varied films include *Lolita* (1962), *Dr. Strangelove* (1964), and *2001: A Space Odyssey* (1968).

ku·chen /koókən, koókhən/ (*plural* **-chen**) *n.* any cake that has been raised with yeast [Mid-19thC. From German, "cake."]

Ku·ching /koó ching/ city in Malaysia. It is the capital of Sarawak State, on the island of Borneo. Population: 147,729 (1991).

ku·dos /koó dōz/ *n.* praise, credit, or glory for an achievement (*takes a singular verb*) ○ *The president deservedly got the kudos for the success of the negotiations.* [Late 18thC. From Greek, "praise, renown."]

WORD KEY: USAGE

Careful writers and speakers avoid the pseudosingular form *kudo.*

ku·du /ko͝o do͞o/ (*plural* **-dus** *or* **-du**), **koo·doo** (*plural* **-doos** *or* **-doo**) *n.* a large antelope native to Africa. The male has long spiraling horns. Latin name: *Tragelaphus strepsiceros* and *Tragelaphus imberbis.* [Late 18thC. Via Afrikaans *koedoe* from Xhosa *i-qudu.*]

kud·zu /kúd zo͞o/ (*plural* **-zus**) *n.* a hardy vine from eastern Asia that has compound leaves, purplish flowers, and roots that contain a nourishing starch used medicinally. It was introduced into the United States to stop the erosion of the soil in the South, but now grows out of control. Latin name: *Pueraria lobata.* [Late 19thC. From Japanese *kuzu.*]

Ku·fic /ko͞ofik/, **Cu·fic** *adj.* USING ANGULAR ARABIC ALPHABET used to describe an early angular style of Arabic writing used for Koranic manuscripts and inscriptions ■ *n.* KUFIC SCRIPT the Arabic alphabet written in Kufic script [Early 18thC. Named for the ancient city of *Kufa,* south of Baghdad, because the script was attributed to the scholars there.]

ku·gel /ko͝og'l/ *n.* a casserole in Jewish cuisine, often of noodles or potatoes [Mid-19thC. From Yiddish, "ball," from Middle High German; probably from its traditional mound shape.]

Kui·per belt /kīpər-/ *n.* a ring of small celestial bodies orbiting through the outer solar system, beyond the farthest planets, Neptune and Pluto. It is believed that the Kuiper belt is a source of comets.

Ku Klux Klan /ko͞o klùks klán/ *n.* **1.** 19THC WHITE SUPREMACIST GROUP a terrorist secret society organized in the South after the Civil War that used violence and murder to promote its white supremacist beliefs **2.** 20THC WHITE SUPREMACIST GROUP a white supremacist organization founded in Georgia in 1915. Its secret membership, supremacist views, and terrorist methods are similar to those of the 19th-century Ku Klux Klan. [Mid-19thC. Origin uncertain: perhaps from Greek *kuklos* "circle" + a variant of CLAN.]

kuk·ri /ko͝okree/ (*plural* **-ris**) *n.* a large knife with a sharp curved blade that gets broader toward the point, used by the Gurkhas in Nepal for hunting and fighting [Early 19thC. From Nepali *khukuri.*]

ku·lak /koo laák, -lák/ *n.* a wealthy landowning peasant in Russia during the time between the emancipation of the serfs and the Russian Revolution [Late 19thC. Via Russian, literally "fist, tight-fisted person," from Turkic *ḳol* "hand."]

Kul·tur /ko͝ol to͝or/ *n.* **1.** CULTURE culture or civilization in general **2.** HIST GERMAN CULTURE German culture, regarded as superior and used as a vehicle of German imperialism during the Hohenzollern and Nazi regimes [Early 20thC. Via German from Latin *cultura* or French *culture* "culture."]

Kul·tur·kampf /ko͝ol to͝or kaàmpf/ *n.* **1.** HIST GERMAN CONFLICT BETWEEN CHURCH AND STATE the struggle between the German government under Bismarck and the Roman Catholic Church over control of education, marriage, and Church appointments. It lasted from 1871 to 1887 and ended in compromise. **2.** DISPUTE BETWEEN CHURCH AND STATE any struggle between a religion and a government [Late 19thC. From German *Kultur* "culture" + *Kampf* "struggle."]

Ku·ma·mo·to /ko͞oma mṓtō/ capital city of Kumamoto Prefecture, on western Kyushu Island, Japan. Population: 579,306 (1990).

Ku·ma·si /koo maássee/ capital of the Ashanti Region, central Ghana. It is situated northwest of Accra. Population: 399,300 (1990). Former name **Coomassie**

ku·miss /koo míss, ko͞omiss/, **kou·miss, kou·mis** *n.* slightly alcoholic, fermented, and sour-tasting milk from a mare or camel, drunk by some of the peoples of western and Central Asia [Late 16thC. Via French *koumis,* German, Polish *kumys,* or Russian from Tartar *kumiz.*]

küm·mel /kímm'l/, **kum·mel** *n.* a colorless liqueur or cordial that is flavored with cumin and caraway seeds and is made primarily in the Baltic region [Mid-19thC. From German, literally "caraway seed," from Old High German *kumīn* "cumin."]

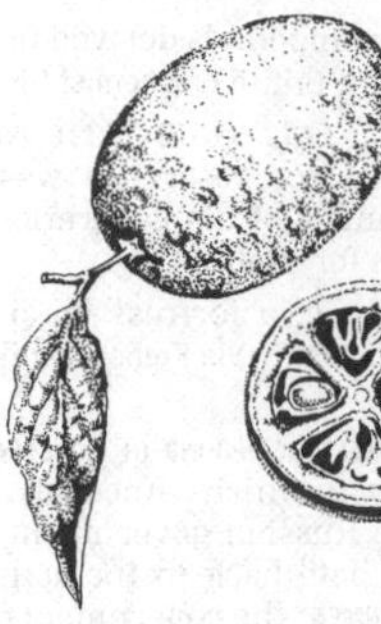

Kumquat

kum·quat /kúm kwòt/, **cum·quat** *n.* **1.** FRUIT-BEARING TREE a Chinese evergreen shrub or small tree of the rue family, with small yellow edible fruit. Genus: *Fortunella.* **2.** EDIBLE FRUIT the sweet edible fruit of a kumquat shrub or tree. It is like a very small orange and is often used in preserves. [Late 17thC. From Chinese (Cantonese) *kam kwat,* literally "gold orange."]

kun·da·li·ni /ko͝ondə le͞enee, kùndə-/ *n.* vital energy that Hindus believe lies dormant at the base of the spine until it is called into action, e.g., through yoga, to be used in seeking enlightenment [Late 19thC. From Sanskrit *kuṇḍalinī,* literally "snake," from the idea that it is like a coiled snake.]

Kung fu: Bruce Lee

kung fu /kung fo͞o, ko͝ong-/ *n.* a Chinese form of self-defense in which fluid, circular movements of the arms and legs are used to attack an opponent [Late 19thC. From Chinese *gongfu,* literally "merit-master."]

Kun·lun Moun·tains /ko͝on lo͝on-/ mountain range in western China. India claims territory in the western area. Height: 25,338 ft./7,723 m. Length: 1,500 mi./2,400 km.

Kun·ming /ko͝on míng/ capital city of Yunnan Province and trade and transportation center of southwestern China. Population: 1,520,000 (1991).

kunz·ite /ko͝ont sīt/ *n.* a reddish-purple variety of the mineral spodumene, used as a gemstone [Early 20thC. Named for George F. *Kunz* 1856–1932, a U.S. gem expert.]

Kuo·min·tang /kwṑmin táng, kwàwmin-/ *n.* the political party that established China as a republic in 1911, ruled China from 1928 to 1947 until defeated by the Communists, and then withdrew to rule in Taiwan [Early 20thC. From Chinese *guómíndǎng,* literally "national people's party."]

Ku·ra /ko͞o raá/ river in the Transcaucasia Region. It flows through Turkey, Georgia, and Azerbaijan, and empties into the Caspian Sea. Length: 940 mi./1,500 km.

kur·cha·tov·i·um /kùrchə tṓvee əm/ *n.* the name given to the element rutherfordium in the former Soviet Union [Mid-20thC. Named for I. V. *Kurchatov* (1903–60), a Russian nuclear physicist.]

Kurd /kurd/ *n.* a member of a largely Islamic people who live in an area straddling the borders of Iraq, Turkey, and Iran [Early 17thC. From Kurdish.]

kur·dai·tcha /kər dīchə/, **ka·dai·tcha** /kə dīchə/ *n.* among Aboriginal peoples of central Australia, a sorcerer who was responsible for avenging the death of a kinsman [Late 19thC. From Aboriginal.]

Kurd·ish /kúrdish/ *n.* LANGUAGE OF THE KURDS an Iranian language spoken in parts of Turkey, Iraq, Iran, Armenia, and Syria. It belongs to the Indo-Iranian branch of the Indo-European family of languages. About 10 million people speak Kurdish. ■ *adj.* OF KURDISH PEOPLE OR LANGUAGE relating to the Kurds, their language, or their culture [Early 19thC]

Kurdistan

Kurd·i·stan /kúrdə stàn/, **Kurd·i·stān** region in southwestern Asia, considered the homeland of the Kurdish people and encompassing parts of Turkey, Iraq, Iran, Armenia, and Syria. Population: 26,000,000 (early 1990s).

kur·gan /koor gaán, -gán/ *n.* a burial mound built by a prehistoric culture of eastern Europe and northern Iran [Late 19thC. From Russian.]

Ku·ro·shi·o /ko͞o rṓshi ō/ warm current in the Pacific Ocean, flowing from the Philippines northeastward along the eastern coast of Japan

kur·ra·jong /kúr ə jàwng, kúrrə-/ *n.* a small or medium-sized tree that grows throughout eastern Australia, has yellowish or red bell-shaped flowers, and yields a tough fiber. Latin name: *Brachychiton populneum.* [Early 19thC. From Aboriginal.]

Kursk /ko͝orsk/ city in western Russia, the capital of Kursk Oblast, and a mining center. Population: 430,000 (1990).

kurta /ko͝ortə/ *n.* a long loose collarless shirt worn by men in India [Early 20thC. From Urdu and Persian *kurtah.*]

kur·to·sis /kər tṓssiss/ (*plural* **-ses** /-tṓ se͞ez/) *n.* a measure of the extent to which a frequency distribution is concentrated about its mean [Early 20thC. From Greek *kurtōsis,* "a bulging, curvature," from *kurtos* "bulging, bent."]

ku·ru /ko͝orroo/ *n.* a fatal degenerative disease of the central nervous system that affects some tribes in New Guinea. Similar to Creutzfeldt-Jakob disease, it is believed to derive from the practice of eating the brains of an ancestor. [Mid-20thC. From a name in New Guinea, literally "trembling, shivering."]

ku·rus /kə ro͞osh/ (*plural* **-rus**) *n.* **1.** see table at **currency** **2.** COIN WORTH ONE KURUS a coin worth one kurus [Late 19thC. From Turkish.]

Kusch /ko͝osh/, **Polykarp** (1911–93) German-born U.S. physicist. He shared a Nobel Prize (1955) for establishing the magnetic moment of the electron.

Kush *n.* = **Cush**

Kus·ko·kwim /kúskə kwìm/ river in southwestern Alaska, rising in the Alaska Range and flowing into the Bering Sea. Length: 724 mi./1,170 km.

Kutch, Rann of /kuch/ region of mud flats and salt marshes in western India and southern Pakistan. Area: 8,100 sq. mi./21,000 sq. km.

Ku·te·nai /ko͞ot'n ày, -ée/ (*plural* **-nai** *or* **-nais**), **Koo·te·nai** (*plural* **-nai** *or* **-nais**), **Koo·te·nay** (*plural* **-nay** *or* **-nays**) *n.* **1.** PEOPLES MEMBER OF A NATIVE AMERICAN PEOPLE a member of a Native American people living principally in Montana, Idaho, and British Columbia **2.** LANG KUTENAI LANGUAGE the language of the Kutenai people [Early 19thC. From Blackfoot *Kotonáai-.*] — **Ku·te·nai** *adj.*

Ku·wait /koo wáyt/ Islamic constitutional monarchy in southwestern Asia, located at the northwestern tip of the Persian Gulf. It is bordered by Iraq and Saudi Arabia. Language: Arabic. Currency: Kuwaiti dinar. Capital: Kuwait City. Population: 1,834,269 (1997). Area: 6,880 sq. mi./17,818 sq. km. Official name **State of Kuwait** —**Ku·wait·i** *n., adj.*

Ku·wait Cit·y capital city of Kuwait, situated on the southern shore of Kuwait Bay in the Persian Gulf. Population: 31,241 (1993).

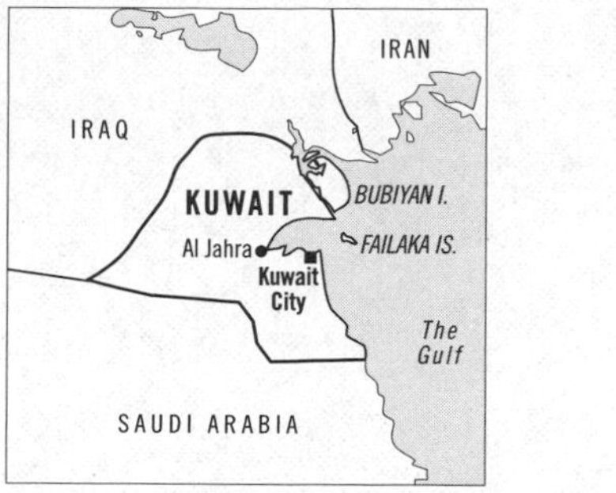

Kuwait

Kuz·nets /ko͞oz nèts/, **Simon** (1901–85) Russian-born U.S. economist. He received the Nobel Prize for economics (1971) for developing the concept of the gross national product (GNP).

kV, kv *abbr.* kilovolt

kvass /kə vaáss, kfaass/, **kvas, quass** *n.* an alcoholic drink similar to beer, made in Russia and Eastern European countries from rye or barley or from stale bread [Mid-16thC. From Russian *kvas*.]

kvetch /kvech/ *vi.* (**kvetched, kvetch·ing, kvetch·es**) **COMPLAIN INCESSANTLY** to grumble and complain about things all the time (*informal*) ■ *n.* (*informal*) **1. SOMEBODY INCESSANTLY COMPLAINING** somebody who is always grumbling and complaining about things **2. COMPLAINT** a complaint about something [Mid-20thC. Via Yiddish *kvetsh* (noun) and *kvetshn* (verb) from German *Quetsche* "crusher" and *quetschen* "to crush, squeeze."]

kW, kw *abbr.* kilowatt

Kwa /kwaa/ *n.* a group of languages in the Niger-Congo family that are spoken in West Africa, and include Yoruba and Ibo [Mid-19thC. From Kwa.] —**Kwa** *adj.*

kwa·cha /kwaáchə/ *n.* **1. ZAMBIAN UNIT OF CURRENCY** the standard unit of currency in Zambia, worth 100 ngwee. See table at **currency 2. MALAWIAN CURRENCY UNIT** the standard unit of currency in Malawi, worth 100 tambala. See table at **currency 3. COIN OR BILL WORTH ONE KWACHA** a coin or bill worth one kwacha [Mid-20thC. From Bantu, "dawn."]

Kwa·ki·utl /kwaákee ō͝ot'l/ (*plural* **-utl** *or* **-utls**) *n.* **1.** PEOPLES **MEMBER OF NATIVE AMERICAN PEOPLE** a member of a Native American people who live on Vancouver Island and parts of the adjacent coast of British Columbia **2.** LANG **LANGUAGE OF THE KWAKIUTL PEOPLE** the Wakashan language of the Kwakiutl people [Mid-19thC. From Kwakiutl *Kwágut*.] —**Kwa·ki·utl** *adj.*

Kwang·ju /kwaáng jo͞o/ city in southwestern South Korea. It is the capital of South Chŏlla Province. Population: 1,257,504 (1995).

kwan·za /kwaánzə/ (*plural* **-zas** *or* **-za**) *n.* **1. ANGOLAN CURRENCY UNIT** the standard unit currency in Angola, worth 100 lwei. See table at **currency 2. COIN OR BILL WORTH ONE KWANZA** a coin or bill worth one kwanza [Late 20thC. Origin uncertain: perhaps from Swahili, literally "first," or named for *Kwanza* (Cuanza), the name of a river in Angola.]

Kwan·zaa /kwaánzə/, **Kwan·za** *n.* a cultural and harvest festival celebrated by African Americans from December 26 to January 1 [Late 20thC. From Swahili, literally "first" (possible source of English *kwanza*).]

kwa·shi·or·kor /kwaáashee áwr kàwr/ *n.* a type of malnutrition in children caused by inadequate intake of protein, common in African children weaned on to a traditional cornmeal diet [Mid-20thC. From a local name in Ghana, literally "red boy" (from the symptomatic reddening of the hair).]

Kwa·Zu·lu /kwaa zo͞oloo/ former homeland in South Africa, part of the province of KwaZulu-Natal since 1994

Kwa·Zu·lu-Na·tal /kwaa zo͞oloo náytaal/ province in southeastern South Africa, established in 1994. Capital: Pietermaritzburg. Population: 8,713,100 (1995). Area: 35,348 sq. mi./91,548 sq. km.

kWh, kW-hr *abbr.* kilowatt-hour

KWIC /kwik/ *abbr.* COMPUT key word in context

KWOC *abbr.* COMPUT key word out of context

Ky., KY *abbr.* Kentucky

ky·ack /kī àk/ *n.* a double packsack designed to be slung across a packsaddle, with one sack on either side of the saddle [Early 20thC. Origin unknown.]

ky·a·nite /kī ə nīt/, **cy·a·nite** /sī ə-/ *n.* a bluish aluminosilicate mineral that is found as thin-bladed crystals or in masses in rocks that have been metamorphosed at high pressure, used as a gemstone and as a refractory [Late 18thC. Formed from Greek *kuan(e)os* "dark blue."]

ky·a·nize /kī ə nīz/ (**-nized, -niz·ing, -niz·es**) *vt.* to preserve wood against decay by treating it with a corrosive sublimate [Mid-19thC. Named for J .H. *Kyan* (1774–1850), the Irish inventor of the process.]

kyat /chaat/ *n.* **1. MYANMAR CURRENCY UNIT** the standard unit of currency in Myanmar, worth 100 pyas. See table at **currency 2. COIN OR BILL WORTH ONE KYAT** a coin or bill worth one kyat [Mid-20thC. From Burmese.]

ky·lix /kīliks, kílliks/ (*plural* **-lic·es** /-lə keèz/) *n.* a shallow two-handled cup, often with a footed stem, used in ancient Greece [Mid-19thC. From Greek *kulix*.]

ky·mo·graph /kīmə gràf/ *n.* a device for recording variations in motion or pressure, e.g. of blood, consisting typically of a stylus and a rotating drum [Mid-19thC. Coined from Greek *kumo-* (from *kuma* "wave") + -GRAPH.] —**ky·mo·graph·ic** /kīmə gráffik/ *adj.* —**ky·mog·ra·phy** /kī móggrəfee/ *n.*

Kym·ry *npl.* = **Cymry**

Kyo·to /kyṓtō/ manufacturing center and capital of Kyoto Urban Prefecture, southern Honshu Island, Japan. Population: 1,461,000 (1990).

ky·pho·sis /kī fóssiss/ *n.* a permanent curving of the spine that makes somebody look hunched over [Mid-19thC. From Greek *kuphōsis*, from *kuphos* "bent, hunchbacked."] —**ky·phot·ic** /kī fóttik/ *adj.*

Kyp·ri·a·nou /kìpree aán oo/, **Spyros** (*b.* 1932) Cypriot statesman. He succeeded Archbishop Makarios as president of Cyprus (1977–88).

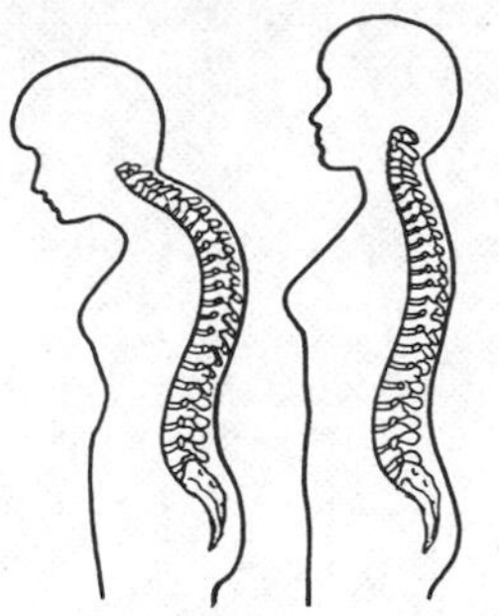
Kyphosis

Kyr·gyz /keer geéz/, **Kir·ghiz** (*plural* **Kyr·gyz** *or* **Kir·ghiz**) *n.* **1.** PEOPLES **ASIAN NOMAD** a member of a traditionally nomadic people living in Kyrgyzstan and Siberia **2.** LANG **KYRGYZ LANGUAGE** the Turkic language of the Kyrgyz

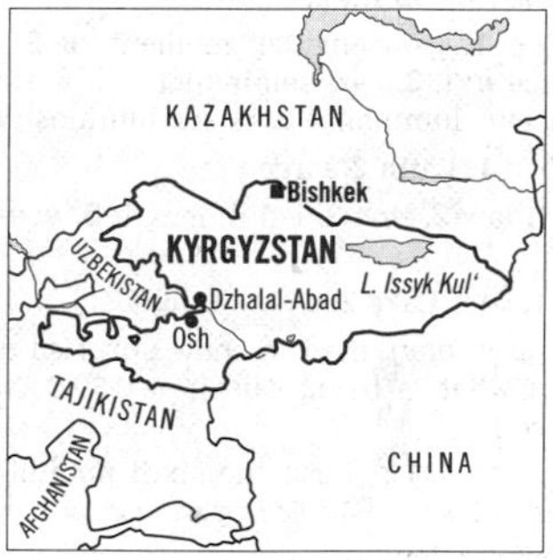

Kyrgyzstan

Kyrg·yz·stan /keérgi stàn/ republic in Central Asia, bordered by Kazakhstan, China, Tajikistan, and Uzbekistan. Language: Kyrgyz, Russian. Currency: som. Capital: Bishkek. Population: 4,512,809 (1997). Area: 76,640 sq. mi./198,500 sq. km. Official name **Kyrgyz Republic**

Kyr·i·e /keéree àyl/, **Kyr·i·e e·le·i·son** /keéree ay ə láy sòn, -ə láyss'n/ *n.* **1.** CHR **FORM OF PRAYER** a form of prayer that begins with the words "Lord have mercy," used in the Roman Catholic, Greek Orthodox, and Anglican churches **2.** MUSIC **MUSICAL SETTING FOR THE KYRIE** a musical setting for the Kyrie, often forming part of a sung Mass [Via medieval Latin from Greek *Kuriē eleēson* "Lord, have mercy"]

Kyu·shu /kee ó͞o shoo, kyó͞o shoo/, **Kyū·shū** island of Japan, the most southerly of the four major Japanese islands. Population: 13,269,000 (1990). Area: 16,279 sq. mi./42,164 sq. km.

Ll

l[1] /el/, **L** *n.* **1. 12TH LETTER OF THE ALPHABET** the 12th letter of the modern English alphabet **2. SOUND OF THE LETTER "L"** the sound of a spoken letter "L" **3. SOMETHING SHAPED LIKE "L"** something that has the same shape as a capital letter "L"

l[2] *abbr.* latitude

L[1], **l** *n.* the Roman numeral for 50

L[2] *symbol.* **1.** PHYS angular momentum **2.** PHYS inductance *n.* 1. **3.** PHYS self-inductance **4.** PHYS latent heat **5.** PHYS luminance **6.** ASTRON luminosity

L[3], **L.** *abbr.* **1.** Latin **2.** large

l. *abbr.* **1.** law **2.** line **3.** left **4.** length **5.** MONEY lira **6.** AIR lift

L. *abbr.* **1.** MAPS Lake **2.** SPORTS League

la[1] /laa, law/ *interj.* used to show surprise or to emphasize what is being said [Late 16thC. Natural exclamation.]

la[2] /laa/, **lah, laa** *n.* MUSIC the sixth note of a major scale in solfeggio [Middle English, from medieval Latin]

La *symbol.* lanthanum

LA *abbr.* **1. LA, L.A.** Los Angeles **2. LA, La.** Louisiana

laa·ger /laágər/, **la·ger** *n.* **CAMP PROTECTED BY WAGONS** a camp protected by a circle of wagons, used in the past by the Boers in South Africa ■ *vti.* **(-gered, -ger·ing, -gers) MAKE A PROTECTED CAMP** to form wagons into a circle to make a protected camp [Mid-19thC. Alteration of obsolete Afrikaans *lager*, of uncertain origin: probably from German *Lager* "camp, bed, storeroom" (source of English *lager*[1]).]

La Argentina /la aarjən teénə/ (1888?–1936) Argentine dancer. She reestablished Spanish dancing as a popular art form in the 20th century.

lab /lab/ *n.* a laboratory (*informal*) [Late 19thC. Shortening.]

Lab. *abbr.* Labrador

La·ban /laábən/, **Rudolf von** (1879–1958) Hungarian dancer and choreographer. He devised a method of notating dance movements and founded several dance schools, including the Laban Centre, London, England.

la·ba·no·ta·tion /laàbə nō táysh'n/ *n.* a method of notating dance movements in detail, including the placement of the dancer's body, direction of movement, tempo, and dynamics [Mid-20thC. Named for Rudolf von LABAN who invented it, LABAN being blended with NOTATION.]

lab·a·rum /lábbərəm/ (*plural* **-ra** /-rə/) *n.* a military banner carried before Roman emperors, especially one with Christian symbols that was carried in front of Constantine the Great as a sign of his conversion to Christianity [Early 17thC. From late Latin, of unknown origin.]

lab·da·num /lábdənəm/, **la·da·num** /lád'nəm/ *n.* a bitter resinous gum extracted from various rockroses and used in flavorings and perfumes [Early 16thC. From medieval Latin, an alteration of Latin *ladanum*, from Greek *lēdanon*, from *lēdon* "mastic."]

la·bel /láyb'l/ *n.* **1. INFORMATIVE ITEM ATTACHED TO SOMETHING** a piece of paper, fabric, or plastic attached to something to give instructions about it or identify it **2. DESCRIPTIVE WORD OR PHRASE** a word or phrase used to describe a person or group **3.** RECORDING, COMM **NAME OF A RECORD COMPANY** the name of a record company, especially when displayed on a record, CD, or cassette **4. BRAND** a brand name of some items of fashion ○ *always wore designer labels* **5.** COMPUT **IDENTIFIER FOR PART OF A COMPUTER PROGRAM** a number or word that acts as a unique identifier for a part of a computer program **6.** HERALDRY **HERALDIC DESIGN** a figure on a heraldic shield consisting of a horizontal band with pendants and identifying the person to whom it belongs as an eldest son **7.** CHEM **SOMETHING USED TO IDENTIFY A CHEMICAL** a substance, usually a radioactive isotope or dye, that can be traced to identify a compound as it undergoes a chemical reaction or assimilation ■ *vt.* **(-beled** *or* **-belled, -bel·ing** *or* **-bel·ling, -bels) 1. ATTACH A LABEL TO** to attach a label to something as identification or to give instructions **2. USE A DESCRIPTIVE WORD FOR** to describe somebody or something using a particular word or phrase ○ *resented being labeled as either liberal or progressive* **3.** CHEM **ATTACH A CHEMICAL LABEL TO** to make a chemical substance identifiable with a label such as a radioactive isotope or dye [13thC. From Old French, "ribbon, fillet, fringe," of uncertain origin; probably ultimately from a prehistoric Germanic base that is also the ancestor of English *lap*.] —**la·bel·er** *n.*

la·bel·lum /lə béllәm/ (*plural* **-la** /-lə/) *n.* **1.** BOT **LARGE ORCHID PETAL** the petal of an orchid that is its lowest and largest and forms a lip **2.** INSECTS **INSECT'S FEEDING PART** the lobe at the end of an insect's proboscis that it uses for feeding on liquids [Early 19thC. From Latin, "small lip," from *labrum* "lip" (source of English *labrum*).]

la·bi·a plural of **labium**

la·bi·al /láybee əl/ *adj.* **1.** ANAT **INVOLVING LIPS OR LABIA** in, on, close to, or involving the lips or the labia **2.** PHON **WITH LIPS CLOSED** pronounced with the lips closed or nearly closed as, e.g., in the sounds "b" and "p" **3.** MUSIC **MOVING AIR ACROSS A LIPLIKE EDGE** used to describe an instrument or organ pipe that produces sound by the movement of air across a sharp edge ■ *n.* **1.** PHON **SOUND PRONOUNCED WITH LIPS CLOSED** a speech sound pronounced with the lips closed or nearly closed as, e.g., in "b" and "p" **2.** MUSIC **INSTRUMENT WITH A LIPLIKE EDGE** an instrument or organ pipe in which sound is produced by the movement of air across a sharp liplike edge [Late 16thC. From medieval Latin *labialis*, from Latin *labia* "lips."] —**la·bi·al·ly** *adv.*

la·bi·al·ize /láybee ə līz/ (**-ized, -iz·ing, -iz·es**) *vt.* to pronounce a sound with the lips rounded —**la·bi·al·i·za·tion** /làybee əli záysh'n/ *n.*

la·bi·a ma·jo·ra /làybee ə mə jáwrə/ *npl.* the two thick outer folds of skin that surround the clitoris, the opening of the urethra, and the opening of the vagina of women and girls [From modern Latin, literally "larger lips"]

la·bi·a mi·no·ra /làybee ə mə náwrə/ *npl.* the two small folds of skin that lie immediately inside the labia majora of women and girls and join at the front to form the hood of the clitoris [From modern Latin, literally "smaller lips"]

la·bi·ate /láybee ət, -àyt/ *adj.* **1. WITH A DIVIDED SET OF PETALS** used to describe a flower such as a snapdragon that has its set of petals (**corolla**) divided into two unequal and overlapping parts **2. OF THE MINT FAMILY** belonging to the mint family ■ *n. U.K.* **PLANT OF THE MINT FAMILY** any plant belonging to the mint family, which includes nettles, snapdragons, rosemary, and thyme. Labiates have square stems and aromatic leaves. Family: Labiatae. [Early 18thC. From modern Latin *labiatus*, from Latin *labium* "lip."]

la·bile /láyb'l, -bīl/ *adj.* **1. CHANGEABLE** liable to change **2.** CHEM **UNDERGOING FREQUENT CHANGE** readily or frequently undergoing chemical or physical change ○ *a labile compound* [15thC. From late Latin *labilis* "prone to slip," from Latin *labi* "to fall, slip" (source of English *lapse*). The original English sense was "prone to lapse."]

labio- *prefix.* lips, labial ○ *labiodental* [From Latin *labium* (see LABIUM)]

la·bi·o·den·tal /làybee ō dént'l/ *adj.* **WITH THE UPPER TEETH ON THE LOWER LIP** pronounced with the upper teeth resting on the inside of the lower lip, as in the sounds "f" and "v" ■ *n.* **LABIODENTAL CONSONANT** a labiodental speech sound

la·bi·o·na·sal /làybee ō náyz'l/ *adj.* **PRONOUNCED LIKE "M"** pronounced with the lips closed and the air being pushed through the nose, as in the sound "m" ■ *n.* **LABIONASAL CONSONANT** a labionasal speech sound

la·bi·o·ve·lar /làybee ō veélər/ *adj.* **PRONOUNCED LIKE "KW"** pronounced by constricting the back of the mouth and closing the lips, as in the sound "kw" ■ *n.* **LABIOVELAR CONSONANT** a labiovelar speech sound

la·bi·um /láybee əm/ (*plural* **-a** /-ə/) *n.* **1.** ANAT **FOLD AROUND WOMEN'S GENITALIA** any of the four folds, two inner (**labia minora**) and two outer (**labia majora**), that surround a woman's or girl's genital organs **2.** INSECTS **INSECT MOUTHPART** a mouthpart of some insects, formed from a fused pair of appendages **3.** BOT **LIP OF A FLOWER** the lower lip of the corolla of a labiate flower **4. ANY LIP** any part that looks or functions like a lip [Late 16thC. From Latin, "lip."]

lab·lab /láb làb/ *n.* BOT = **hyacinth bean** [Early 19thC. From Arabic *lablāb*.]

la·bor /láybər/ *n.* **1. PHYSICAL WORK** work done using the strength of the body ○ *sentenced to two years' hard labor* **2. WORKERS COLLECTIVELY** the workers, especially manual workers, in a country, company, or industry considered as a group (*often used before a noun*) ○ *labor relations* **3. SUPPLY OF WORK** the supply of work or workers for a particular job, industry, or employer **4. LABOR UNIONS COLLECTIVELY** labor unions collectively and the movement that built and supported them **5. PARTICULAR PIECE OF WORK** a particular piece of work, especially a difficult or long one (*often used in the plural*) ○ *the labors of Hercules* **6.** OBSTET **PROCESS OF CHILDBIRTH** the process of giving birth to a baby from when the contractions start to the baby's delivery, or the time taken for this process (*often used before a noun*) ○ *labor pains* ■ *v.* **(-bored, -bor·ing, -bors) 1.** *vi.* **WORK HARD** to work hard, especially at physical work ○ *labored all day in the hot sun* **2.** *vi.* **STRUGGLE TO DO SOMETHING** to struggle to do something very difficult or very tiring ○ *labored over the questions for several hours* **3.** *vi.* **OPERATE WITH DIFFICULTY** to have difficulty in running or functioning smoothly, e.g., because of being overloaded or defective (*refers to engines or machines*) **4.** *vi.* **MOVE WITH DIFFICULTY** to move with difficulty or great effort ○ *We labored up to the summit.* **5.** *vi.* OBSTET **GIVE BIRTH** to be in the process of giving birth to a baby **6.** *vi.* NAUT **PITCH AND ROLL** to pitch and roll heavily at sea (*refers to ships*) **7.** *vt.* **OVEREMPHASIZE** to continue trying to express or emphasize something when it is unnecessary ○ *There's no need to labor the point.* [14thC. Via Old French *labo(u)r* from Latin *labor* "toil, pain" (source of English *elaborate*), perhaps literally "stumbling under a burden."] ◇ **labor of love** something demanding or difficult that is done just for pleasure rather than for money

labor under *vt.* to be at a disadvantage because of believing something to be true that is not ○ *She had been laboring under the misconception that the problem was solved.*

lab·o·ra·to·ry /lábbrə tàwree/ (*plural* **-ries**) *n.* **1. ROOM FOR TEACHING SCIENCE** a room or place with appropriate equipment for teaching science or doing scientific work **2. PLACE FOR SCIENTIFIC RESEARCH** a facility, or a room in a facility, where research and testing is carried out **3.** **ACADEMIC PERIOD FOR DOING SCIENCE** a period in school when students work in a laboratory [Early 17thC. Via medieval Latin *laboratorium* "place for work" from, ultimately, Latin *laborare* "to work," from *labor* (see LABOR).]

la·bor camp *n.* a prison where the prisoners have to do hard physical work under a harsh, typically cruel, regime

La·bor Day *n.* **1.** **U.S. AND CANADIAN PUBLIC HOLIDAY** a national holiday observed in the United States and Canada on the first Monday in September in honor of working people **2.** = **May Day**

la·bored /láybərd/ *adj.* done with obvious effort or difficulty rather than naturally or gracefully

la·bor·er /láybərər/ *n.* somebody who works at a job that requires physical strength and stamina

la·bor force *n.* = **workforce**

la·bor-in·ten·sive *adj.* involving a relatively high number of workers or greater costs for labor than for other areas such as materials, machines, or design ○ *a labor-intensive industry*

la·bo·ri·ous /lə báwree əss/ *adj.* **1.** **NEEDING EFFORT** requiring a great deal of effort **2.** **NOT FLUENT** showing signs of effort or difficulty rather than naturalness or fluency, especially in speech or writing **3.** **ENJOYING WORK** happy or likely to work hard and long [14thC. Originally in the sense "hard-working, industrious."] —**la·bo·ri·ous·ly** *adv.* —**la·bo·ri·ous·ness** *n.*

WORD KEY: SYNONYMS

See Synonyms at ***hard.***

la·bor·ite /láybə rìt/ *n.* somebody who belongs to or actively supports a labor union or the labor movement

la·bor un·ion *n.* an organization of wage earners that is set up to serve and advance its members' interests in terms of wages, benefits, and working hours and conditions

la·bour *n., vti.* U.K. = **labor**

WORD KEY: SYNONYMS

See Synonyms at ***work.***

WORD KEY: CULTURAL NOTE

Love's Labour's Lost, a play by English dramatist William Shakespeare (1594–95). Ferdinand, King of Navarre, and three of his lords agree to forgo the company of women in order to devote themselves to study. The arrival of the Princess of France and three of her ladies upsets their plans, giving rise to lively comedy and witty and poetic dialogue.

La·bour Par·ty *n.* a British political party founded in 1900 to support the rights and interests of working people

la·bra plural of **labrum**

Lab·ra·dor[1] /lábbrə dàwr/ *n.* a large dog with a short thick black, brown, or yellow coat, originally bred to fetch killed or injured game during a hunt. Labradors were first bred in Newfoundland. [Early 20thC. Named for LABRADOR, where the breed's stock originated.]

Lab·ra·dor[2] /lábbrə dàwr/ mainland portion of the eastern Canadian province of Newfoundland. It abuts Quebec to the west and south and the Atlantic Ocean on the east. Area: 114,618 sq. mi./296,860 sq. km.

Lab·ra·dor Cur·rent cold ocean current that flows south past western Greenland and eastern Labrador and Newfoundland, Canada, to join the Gulf Stream

lab·ra·dor·ite /lábbrə daw rìt/ *n.* a variety of plagioclase feldspar, the color of which shifts between blue and green depending on the angle it is seen from [Named for LABRADOR, where it was found]

Lab·ra·dor Pen·in·su·la large peninsula in eastern Canada. The region includes much of Quebec and the mainland portion of Newfoundland. Area: 625,000 sq. mi./1,619,000 sq. km.

Lab·ra·dor re·triev·er *n.* = **Labrador**[1]

Lab·ra·dor Sea arm of the Atlantic Ocean that separates Labrador in eastern Canada from Greenland and the Atlantic Ocean

Lab·ra·dor tea *n.* a low-growing evergreen shrub native to northern North America. It has bell-shaped flowers and leaves that are used in making a tea. Latin name: *Ledum groenlandicum.*

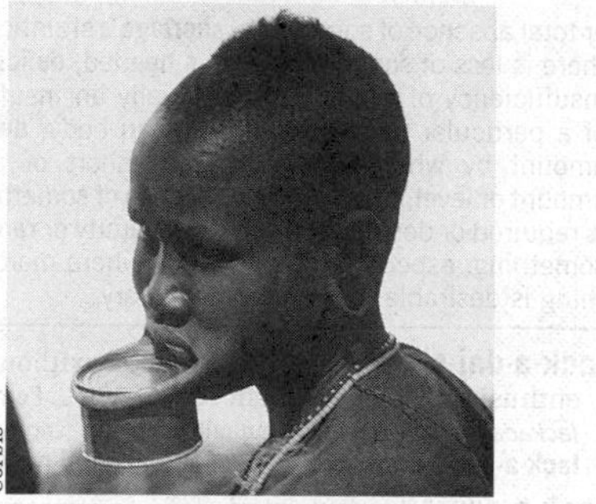

Corbis

Labret

la·bret /láybrət/ *n.* an ornament made of bone, shell, or other materials that is worn pierced through the lip, especially by some peoples in East Africa and South America [Mid-19thC. Formed from Latin *labrum* "lip" (source of English *labial*).]

la·brid /láybrid, láb-/ *n.* a fish belonging to the wrasse family, many species of which are colorful tropical coral reef fish. Family: Labridae. [From modern Latin *Labridae*, family name, from *Labrus*, genus name]

la·brum /láybrəm, láb-/ (*plural* **-bra** /-brə/) *n.* a projecting upper mouthpart of some arthropods [Early 18thC. Via modern Latin from Latin, "lip" (source of English *labial*).]

La·bu·an /lə bóoən, laa bóoaan/ island in Malaysia, situated off the northern coast of Borneo, northeast of Singapore. Capital: Victoria. Population: 54,307 (1991). Area: 40 sq. mi./100 sq. km.

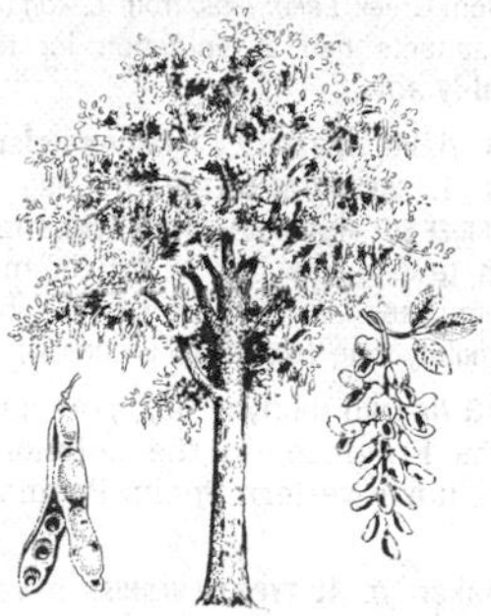

Laburnum

la·bur·num /lə búrnəm/ *n.* a European or Asian tree or shrub with hanging sprays of bright yellow flowers and poisonous leaves, bark, and seeds. Genus: *Laburnum.* [Mid-16thC. From Latin, "broad-leaved bean trefoil," of uncertain origin: perhaps from Etruscan.]

lab·y·rinth /lábbərinth/ *n.* **1.** **CONFUSING NETWORK** a place with a lot of crisscrossing or complicated passages, tunnels, or paths in which it would be easy to become lost **2.** **SOMETHING VERY COMPLICATED** something that is made up of many different parts that is complicated and hard to understand ○ *You need legal advice to guide you through the labyrinth of regulations.* **3.** ANAT **INNER EAR** a structure consisting of connected cavities or canals, especially the inside of the ear [14thC. Directly or via French from Latin *labyrinthus*, from Greek *laburinthos*, of uncertain origin: perhaps "royal structure," formed from Lydian *labrus* "two-edged axe," a symbol of royal power.]

Lab·y·rinth *n.* in Greek mythology, the maze designed by Daedalus for King Minos of Crete to confine the Minotaur

lab·y·rinth fish *n.* a fish with a specialized labyrinthine breathing organ that allows it to breathe air out of water. Family: Anabantidae.

lab·y·rin·thine /làbbə rínthin, -theen, -thìn/, **lab·y·rin·thi·an** /làbbə rínthee ən/ *adj.* **1.** **CONSISTING OF A CONFUSING NETWORK** consisting of or resembling a labyrinth of passages or paths ○ *a labyrinthine maze of backstreets* **2.** **EXTREMELY COMPLICATED** extremely complicated and therefore difficult to understand

lab·y·rin·thi·tis /làbbərin thítiss/ *n.* an illness in which the inner ear becomes inflamed, causing a loss of balance and nausea

lab·y·rin·tho·dont /làbbə rínthə dònt/ *n.* an extinct amphibian resembling the crocodile that lived in the Late Paleozoic and Early Mesozoic eras. Order: Labyrinthodontia. [Mid-19thC. From modern Latin *Labyrinthodontia*, order name, literally "labyrinth-toothed" (from the amphibians' labyrinthine dental structure), from Greek *laburinthos* (see LABYRINTH).]

lac[1] /lak/ *n.* a resinous substance secreted by an insect (**lac insect**), used in the past in the manufacture of shellac [15thC. Via Portuguese *lac(c)a* and medieval Latin *lac* from Persian *lāk* and Hindi *lākh*, from Sanskrit *lākṣā*, literally "red dye" (source of English *lacquer*), an alteration of *rākṣā*.]

lac[2] *n.* = **lakh**

lac·co·lith /lákə lith/ *n.* a massive intrusion of igneous rock between beds of sedimentary rock, creating a dome-shaped structure [Late 19thC. Coined from Greek *lakkos* "pond, pit, reservoir" + -LITH.] —**lac·co·lith·ic** /làkə líthik/ *adj.* —**lac·co·lit·ic** /làkə líttik/ *adj.*

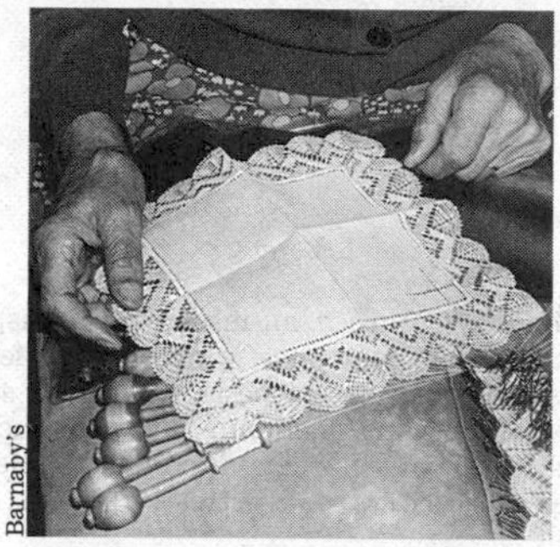

Barnaby's

Lace

lace /layss/ *n.* **1.** TEXTILES **DELICATE FABRIC WITH PATTERNED HOLES** a delicate fabric made by weaving cotton, silk, or a synthetic yarn in a pattern that leaves small holes between the threads (*often used before a noun*) ○ *a lace shawl* **2.** CLOTHES **CORD USED TO TIE EDGES TOGETHER** a long cord that is used to tie two parts of a garment, shoe, or boot together and is threaded through holes or round hooks **3.** MIL **BRAID ON MILITARY UNIFORMS** ornamental gold or silver braid used on military officers' uniforms and hats ■ *vt.* (**laced, lac·ing, lac·es**) **1.** **FASTEN USING LACES** to tie the edges of something with holes or hooks together by threading laces through the holes or around the hooks, pulling the edges close, and knotting the laces **2.** **THREAD A LACE THROUGH HOLES** to thread a lace or cord through holes or around hooks **3.** **DECORATE WITH LACE** to decorate or trim something with lace **4.** **ADD ALCOHOL TO A DRINK** to add a small amount of alcohol or a drug to a drink or to food ○ *eggnog laced with rum* **5.** **ADD A SMALL AMOUNT TO** to add an amount of something to something else to enhance it ○ *It was an intelligent article, laced with wit.* **6.** **STREAK WITH A DIFFERENT COLOR** to mark something with streaks of a different color **7.** **BEAT** to beat or thrash somebody (*informal*) **8.** **INTERTWINE** to intertwine something with something else, e.g., fingers [12thC. Via Old French *laz* "net, string" (the original English senses) from assumed Vulgar Latin *lacium*, from Latin *laqueus* "noose, snare" (source of English *lasso*).] —**lace·like** *adj.*

lace into *vt.* **1.** **FASTEN INTO A GARMENT** to fasten a corset or close-fitting garment around somebody by lacing it up **2.** **ATTACK VERBALLY OR PHYSICALLY** to attack somebody verbally or physically (*informal*)

lace up *vt.* to fasten or tighten the laces of something such as a boot or corset

lace bug *n.* a small bug with a delicate lacy vein pattern on its wings. Family: Tingitidae.

Lac·e·dae·mo·ni·an /làssədə mṓnee ən/ *adj.* relating to the ancient Greek city of Sparta [Mid-16thC. Formed from Latin *Lacedaemonius* or Greek *Lakedaimonios* "of Lacedaemon (ancient name of an area including Sparta), Spartan."] —**Lac·e·dae·mo·ni·an** *n.*

lac·er·ate *vt.* /lássə ràyt/ (**-at·ed, -at·ing, -ates**) **1.** **CUT JAGGEDLY** to cut or gash the skin so that the wound is deep with irregular edges **2.** **DISTRESS DEEPLY** to distress somebody deeply or agonizingly ■ *adj.* /lássərət, lássə ràyt/ BOT **WITH JAGGED EDGES** used to describe leaves or petals that have jagged or irregular edges [15thC. From Latin *lacerat-*, the past participle stem of *lacerare* "to tear to pieces," from *lacer* "torn, mangled."]

lac·er·a·tion /làssə ráysh'n/ *n.* **1.** **DEEP JAGGED CUT** a deep and jagged cut in the flesh **2.** **SOMETHING THAT WOUNDS** something that is deeply wounding to the feelings

La·cer·ta /lə súrtə/ *n.* a small constellation in the northern hemisphere

lac·er·tid /lə súrtid/ *n.* a lizard such as the common wall lizard or green lizard of Europe with rough irregular scales and bony plates on its skull. Family: Lacertidae. [Late 19thC. Formed from Latin *lacerta* "lizard."]

lace-up *n.* a shoe or boot that fastens with laces — **lace-up** *adj.*

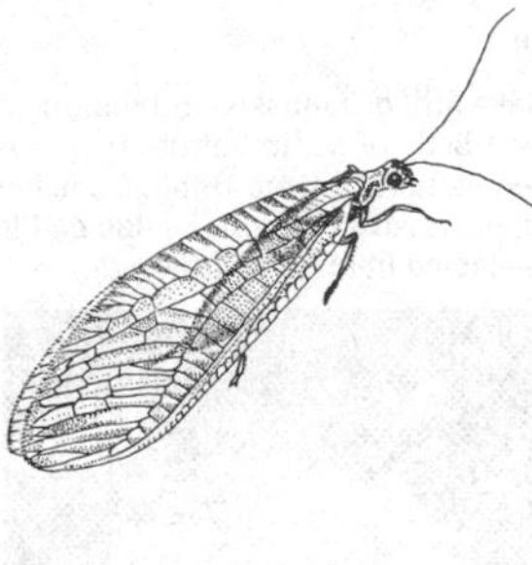

Lacewing

lace·wing /láyss wìng/ *n.* an insect with transparent wings and long antennae whose larvae feed on aphids and other insect pests. There are several species of lacewing, including the green lacewing and the brown lacewing. Superfamily: Hemerobioidea. [From the fine network of veins in its wings, likened to lace]

Lachaise /lə sháyz/, **Gaston** (1882–1935) French-born U.S. sculptor. He is known for his large representations of nude figures, such as *Standing Woman* (1930–33), and portrait busts.

lach·es /láchəz, láychəz/ *n.* LAW negligence or delay in doing something, especially in pursuing a legal claim [14thC. Via Anglo-Norman *laches(se)* "negligence," from Old French *lasche* "lax, lazy," from, ultimately, Latin *laxus* "wide, loose, relaxed" (source of English *lax* and *lease*).]

Lach·e·sis /lákəssiss/ *n.* one of the three Fates in Greek mythology

Lach·lan /laák lən/ river in south central New South Wales, Australia. Length: 920 mi./1,480 km.

lach·ry·mal *adj.* **1.** CRYING relating to tears or weeping (*literary*) **2.** ANAT = **lacrimal**

lach·ry·ma·tion *n.* PHYSIOL = **lacrimation**

lach·ry·ma·tor *n.* = **lacrimator**

lach·ry·ma·to·ry /lákrəmə tàwree/ *n.* (*plural* **-ries**) BOTTLE FOR TEARS a small bottle of a kind found in ancient tombs, thought in the past to have contained the tears of mourners ■ *adj.* = **lacrimatory**

lach·ry·mose /lákrə mòss/ *adj.* (*literary*) **1.** CRYING crying, or tending to cry easily and often **2.** SAD so sad as to make people cry [Early 18thC. From Latin *lacrimosus*, from *lacrima* "tear."] —**lach·ry·mose·ly** *adv.* —**lach·ry·mos·i·ty** /làkrə mόssətee/ *n.*

lac·ing /láyssing/ *n.* **1.** LACE THAT FASTENS a lace that fastens **2.** ALCOHOL ADDED TO DRINK a small amount of alcohol or a drug added to a drink or to food **3.** BEATING a beating or thrashing (*informal*)

la·cin·i·ate /lə sínnee ət, -àyt/, **la·cin·i·at·ed** /lə sínnee àytəd/ *adj.* BOT, ZOOL having a fringed, jagged, or lobed border [Mid-17thC. Formed from Latin *lacinia* "fringe, flap, edge."] —**la·cin·i·a·tion** /lə sìnnee áysh'n/ *n.*

lac in·sect *n.* a southern Asian insect, the female of which secretes a substance (**lac**) that was used in the past to make shellac. Latin name: *Laccifer lacca.*

lack /lak/ *n.* **1.** SHORTAGE OR ABSENCE OF SOMETHING a shortage or complete absence of a particular thing ○ *Lack of sleep makes it difficult to concentrate.* **2.** SOMETHING ABSENT something that is needed but is in short supply or missing ■ *vt.* (**lacked, lack·ing, lacks**) **1.** NOT HAVE not to have something that is needed ○ *the project lacked funding* **2.** NOT HAVE ENOUGH to have too little of something ○ *What he lacks in patience, he makes up for in drive.* [13thC. Origin uncertain: probably from assumed Old English *lac*, from a prehistoric Germanic base that also produced English *leak*.]

WORD KEY: SYNONYMS

lack, shortage, deficiency, deficit, want, dearth

CORE MEANING: an insufficiency or absence of something

lack a general word used to talk about an insufficiency or total absence of something; **shortage** a situation where there is less of something than is needed; **deficiency** an insufficiency of something, especially an insufficiency of a particular nutrient in the human body; **deficit** the amount by which something falls short of a target amount or level; **want** a lack or absence of something that is required or desirable; **dearth** the scarcity or rareness of something, especially in a situation where more of that thing is desirable rather than necessary.

lack·a·dai·si·cal /làkə dáyzik'l/ *adj.* without much enthusiasm, energy, or effort [Mid-18thC. Formed from *lackadaisy* "alas, alack," an alteration of LACKADAY.] —**lack·a·dai·si·cal·ly** *adv.* —**lack·a·dai·si·cal·ness** *n.*

lack·a·day /lákə dày/ *interj.* used to express regret, disapproval, or dismay (*archaic*) [Late 17thC. Shortening of the phrase *alack-a-day* (from ALACK).]

lack·ey /lákee/ *n.* (*plural* **-eys**) **1.** OBEDIENT FOLLOWER somebody excessively willing to obey another's orders **2.** MAN SERVANT a man servant, especially a footman or valet who wears a uniform (*archaic*) ■ *vti.* (**-eyed, -ey·ing, -eys**) ACT AS LACKEY to act as a servant, especially a footman [Early 16thC. From French *laquais*, of uncertain origin: perhaps ultimately from Arabic *al-kāḍī* "the judge" (source of English *alcalde*).]

lack·lus·ter /lák lùstər/ *adj.* lacking energy, excitement, enthusiasm, or passion

lack·lus·tre /lák lùstər/ *adj.* U.K. = **lackluster**

La·co·ni·a /lə kṓnee ə/ region in Ancient Greece that occupied much of the Peloponnesus. The capital city was Sparta.

la·con·ic /lə kónnik/, **la·con·i·cal** /lə kónnik'l/ *adj.* using very few words [Mid-16thC. Via Latin *Laconicus* "of Laconia" from Greek *Lakōnikos*, from *Lakōn* (see LACONIA), whose inhabitants had a reputation for terseness.] —**la·con·i·cal·ly** *adv.*

lac·o·nism /lákə nìzzəm/, **la·con·i·cism** /lə kónni sìzzəm/ *n.* **1.** BREVITY IN SPEECH the use of very few words **2.** BRIEF BUT MEANINGFUL STATEMENT something that is said in few words but is full of meaning [Late 16thC. From Greek *lakōnismos* "imitation of Spartan manners," ultimately from *Lakōn* (see LACONIC).]

La Co·ru·ña /làa kō roṓnyə/ city, port, and capital of La Coruña Province, in the autonomous region of Galicia, northwestern Spain. Population: 254,822 (1995).

lac·quer /lákər/ *n.* **1.** TYPE OF VARNISH a varnish made from the sap of an eastern Asian tree and used to give a protective surface, especially to wood **2.** GLOSSY SYNTHETIC COATING a hard, glossy, clear or colored coating made up of resins or cellulose derivatives and a plasticizer in a volatile solvent **3.** = **hair spray** ■ *vt.* (**-quered, -quer·ing, -quers**) APPLY LACQUER TO to apply lacquer to or spray lacquer on something [Late 16thC. From obsolete French *lacre* "sealing wax," an alteration of Portuguese *la(c)ca* "lac" (see LAC).] —**lac·quer·er** *n.*

lac·quer tree *n.* a poisonous sumac tree of Southeast Asia whose sap is used to make lacquer. Latin name: *Rhus verniciflua.*

AKG London

Lacquerware: Japanese lacquered box (1890)

lac·quer·ware /lákər wàir/, **lac·quer·work** /lákər wùrk/ *n.* ornamental objects, usually of wood, that have been coated with lacquer and sometimes inlaid

lac·ri·mal /lákrəməl/, **lach·ry·mal** *adj.* relating to, involving, or typical of tears, the glands that produce tears, or the ducts through which they drain [15thC. From medieval Latin *lacrimalis, lachrymalis*, from Latin *lacrima* "tear."]

lac·ri·mal duct *n.* the passage carrying tears into the nose

lac·ri·mal gland *n.* a gland in the outer corner of the eye that produces tears

lac·ri·ma·tion /làkrə máysh'n/, **lach·ry·ma·tion** *n.* the production of tears in the eyes, especially excessive production as in crying or in reaction to a foreign body

lac·ri·ma·tor /lákrə màytər/, **lach·ry·ma·tor** *n.* a substance such as tear gas that makes tears form in the eyes

lac·ri·ma·to·ry /lákrəmə tàwree/, **lach·ry·ma·to·ry** *adj.* causing the eyes to produce tears

Popperfoto

Lacrosse

la·crosse /lə kráwss/ *n.* a sport, originated by Native North Americans, in which two teams of ten players use sticks with a net pouch at one end (**crosse**) to throw and catch a small hard rubber ball. The aim is to score a goal by throwing the ball into the opposing team's goalnet. (*often used before a noun*) ○ *a lacrosse stick* [Early 18thC. From Canadian French *(jeu de) la crosse*, literally "(game of) the hooked stick," *crosse* "hooked stick, crosier" ultimately from a prehistoric Germanic word that also produced English *crook*.]

La Crosse /lə kráws/ city in western Wisconsin, situated at the junction of the Mississippi, Black, and La Crosse rivers. Population: 51,003 (1990).

lact- *prefix.* = **lacto-** (*used before vowels*)

lac·tal·bu·min /lák tal byoṓmən/ *n.* a protein in milk and whey that contains all the amino acids needed in the human diet

lac·tase /lák tàyss, -tàyz/ *n.* an enzyme found in the intestines of young mammals and in yeasts that breaks down lactose into glucose and galactose [Late 19thC. Formed from LACTOSE.]

lac·tate[1] /lák tàyt/ (**-tat·ed, -tat·ing, -tates**) *vi.* to produce milk in the body (*refers to female mammals*) [Late 19thC. Back-formation from LACTATION.]

lac·tate[2] /lák tàyt/ *n.* a chemical compound that is a salt or ester of lactic acid [Late 18thC. Formed from LACTIC.]

lac·ta·tion /lak táysh'n/ *n.* **1.** PRODUCTION OF MILK the production of milk by the mammary glands **2.** PERIOD OF MILK PRODUCTION the period during which milk is produced by the mammary glands [Mid-17thC. Directly or via French from, ultimately, Latin *lactare* "to suckle," from *lact-*, the stem of *lac* "milk" (see LACTO-).] —**lac·ta·tion·al** *adj.*

lac·te·al /láktee əl/ *adj.* **1.** OF MILK relating to milk or milk production **2.** ANAT CARRYING MILKY FLUID carrying or containing a milky fluid (**chyle**) ○ *a lacteal vessel* ■ *n.* ANAT LYMPHATIC VESSEL any lymphatic vessel that originates in the small intestine and carries a milky fluid (**chyle**) to the thoracic duct [Mid-17thC. Formed from Latin *lacteus* "of milk," from *lact-*, the stem of *lac* "milk" (see LACTO-).] —**lac·te·al·ly** *adv.*

lac·tes·cent /lak téss'nt/ *adj.* **1.** BOT, ZOOL SECRETING A MILKY SUBSTANCE used to describe plants and insects that secrete a milky substance **2.** RESEMBLING MILK looking like milk, or becoming milky [Mid-17thC. From Latin *lactescent-*, the present participle stem of *lactescere* "to turn to milk" from *lactere* "to be milky," from *lact-*, the stem of *lac* "milk" (see LACTO-).] —**lac·tes·cence** *n.*

lac·tic /láktik/ *adj.* relating to or derived from milk [Late 18thC]

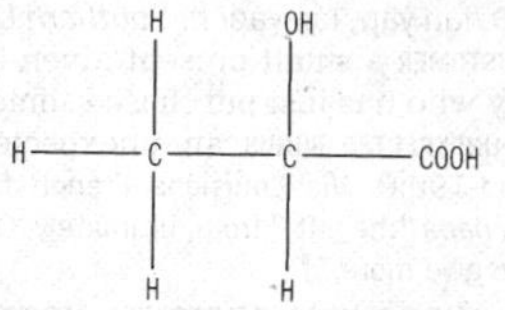

Lactic acid

lac·tic ac·id *n.* a colorless organic acid produced in muscles and found in sour milk. It is used as a preservative, in dyeing, and in making adhesives and pharmaceuticals. Formula: $C_3H_6O_3$.

lac·tif·er·ous /lak tíffərəss/ *adj.* **1.** ANAT **CAPABLE OF PRODUCING MILK** carrying or producing milk, or capable of producing milk ○ *a lactiferous duct* **2.** BOT **PRODUCING A MILKY JUICE** used to describe a plant that produces a milky juice (**latex**) [Late 17thC. Coined from LACTO- + -IFEROUS.] —**lac·tif·er·ous·ness** *n.*

lacto- *prefix.* **1.** milk ○ *lactometer* **2.** lactic acid ○ *lactate* **3.** lactose ○ *lactase* [From Latin *lact-*, the stem of *lac* "milk"; ultimately related to Greek *gala* (source of English *galaxy*)]

lac·to·ba·cil·lus /làktō bə sílləss/ (*plural* **-li** /-lī/) *n.* a rod-shaped bacterium that produces lactic acid through fermentation. Genus: *Lactobacillus.*

lac·to·fla·vin /làktə fláyvən/ *n.* BIOCHEM = **riboflavin**

lac·to·gen·ic /làktə jénnik/ *adj.* causing the mammary glands to produce milk

lac·to·glob·u·lin /làktō glóbbyələn/ *n.* any one of a group of globular proteins that occur in milk

lac·tom·e·ter /lak tómmətər/ *n.* an instrument that is used to measure the density of milk. It is a kind of hydrometer.

lac·tone /lák tōn/ *n.* any one of several chemical compounds derived from hydroxy acids, often occurring as the odor-bearing component of a plant product —**lac·ton·ic** /lak tónnik/ *adj.*

lac·to·pro·tein /làktō prṓ teen/ *n.* any protein that is present in milk

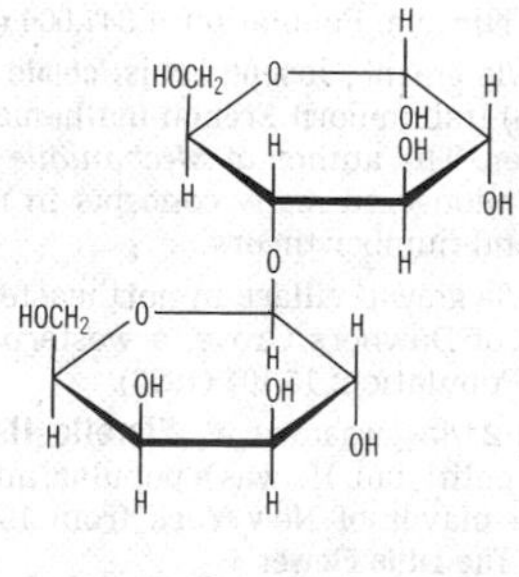

Lactose

lac·tose /lák tōss, -tōz/ *n.* **1.** **SUGAR IN MILK** a sugar (**disaccharide**) found in milk that breaks down into glucose and galactose and creates lactic acid through fermentation. **2.** **COMMERCIAL FORM OF LACTOSE** a white crystalline form of lactose extracted from whey and used commercially in food products and pharmaceuticals

lac·tose in·tol·er·ance *n.* a condition resulting from low activity or absence of the enzyme lactase, which is responsible for the digestion of milk sugar. It is common in people of Asian and African descent.

lac·to·veg·e·tar·i·an /làktō vejjə táiree ən/ *n.* somebody who eats vegetables, grains, fruit, nuts, and milk products but not meat or eggs

la·cu·na /lə kyṓnə, -kṓnə/ (*plural* **-nae** /-nee/ *or* **-nas**) *n.* **1.** **GAP** a gap or place where something is missing, e.g., in a manuscript or a line of argument (*literary*) **2.** ANAT **SMALL PIT OR CAVITY** a small pit or cavity, e.g., in bone or cartilage [Mid-17thC. From Latin, "hole, pit," from *lacus* "pond" (source of English *lagoon* and *lake*).] —**la·cu·nal** *adj.*

la·cu·nar /lə kyṓnər, -kṓnər/ *n.* **1.** **CEILING WITH SUNKEN PANELS** a ceiling that has sunken panels in it **2.** **SUNKEN PANEL IN A CEILING** a decorative sunken panel in a ceiling ■ *adj.* MED **OF BODILY CAVITIES** relating to pits or cavities in tissue, e.g., in bone or cartilage, especially ones that are abnormal [Late 17thC. From Latin, from *lacuna* (see LACUNA).]

la·cus·trine /lə kústrən/ *adj.* **1.** **OF LAKES** relating to lakes **2.** **FOUND IN OR NEAR LAKES** growing, living, or formed in or at the edge of a lake [Early 19thC. Formed either from French or Italian *lacustre* or from their source, Latin *lacus* "lake" (see LACUNA) (on the model of Latin *palustris* "marshy").]

lac·y /láyssee/ (**-i·er, -i·est**) *adj.* **1.** **MADE OF LACE** made of or decorated with lace **2.** **LOOKING LIKE LACE** having the appearance of lace ○ *The sky was filled with lacy clouds.* —**lac·i·ly** *adv.* —**lac·i·ness** *n.*

lad /lad/ *n.* **1.** **YOUNG MAN** a boy or young man **2.** **MAN** any man (*informal*) [13thC. Origin uncertain: perhaps from a Scandinavian source Originally "man of lowly status."]

lad·a·num *n.* = **labdanum**

lad·der /láddər/ (**-dered, -der·ing, -ders**) *n.* **1.** **DEVICE WITH RUNGS TO CLIMB ON** a portable piece of equipment with rungs attached to sides made of metal, wood, or rope, used for climbing up or down **2.** **PATH TO ADVANCEMENT** a series of hierarchical levels on which somebody moves up or down within an organization or society ○ *She joined the firm at a fairly low level but quickly moved up the ladder.* **3.** SPORTS, GAME **LIST OF RANKED PLAYERS** a list of contestants in an ongoing sports or games competition, arranged according to ability [Old English *hlǣd(d)er.* From, ultimately, an Indo-European base meaning "to lean," which also produced English *incline, lid,* and *enclitic.*]

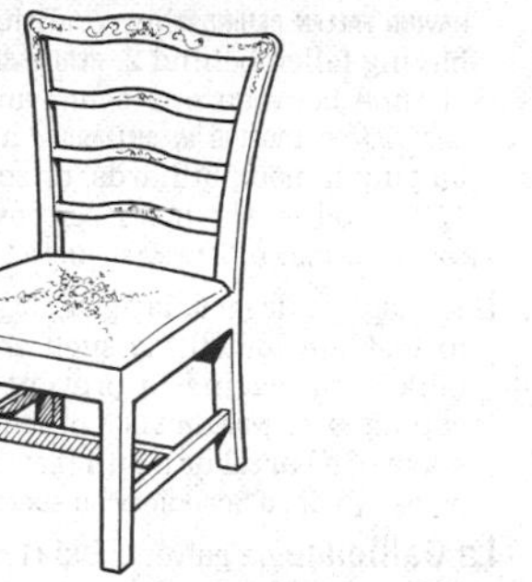
Ladder-back

lad·der·back *n.* **1.** **CHAIR WITH A BACK SHAPED LIKE A LADDER** a chair with a back formed by horizontal slats between the two vertical parts that form the sides **2.** **TALL CHAIR BACK** a chair back formed by horizontal slats between the two vertical parts that form the sides —**lad·der-back** *adj.*

lad·der tour·na·ment *n.* a tournament based on a list of ranked players in a game or sport, whereby each player may challenge the player on the next one or two higher rungs

lad·der truck *n.* = **hook-and-ladder truck**

lad·die /láddee/ *n.* a boy or young man (*informal*) ○ *How old are you, laddie?*

lade /layd/ (**lad·ed, lad·en** /láyd'n/ *or* **lad·ed, lad·ing, lades**) *v.* **1.** *vti.* **LOAD UP A SHIP WITH CARGO** to take on cargo or freight, or load up a ship with cargo or freight **2.** *vti.* **REMOVE LIQUID WITH A LADLE** to remove a measure of liquid using a ladle **3.** *vt.* **LOAD** to load something, or place a heavy burden on somebody (*dated*) [Old English *hladan* (source of English *ladle*), from a prehistoric Germanic base that also produced English *ballast*]

la-de-da *adj.* = **la-di-da**

lad·en past participle of **lade** ■ *adj.* **1.** **HEAVILY LOADED** carrying a load, usually a heavy load (*often used in combination*) ○ *He was laden down with shopping bags.* ○ *fruit-laden boughs* **2.** **OPPRESSED BY SOMETHING** weighed down by a problem or an unpleasant feeling such as doubt or unhappiness ○ *laden with guilt*

la-di-da, la-de-da *adj.* speaking or behaving in a way that is affectedly upper-class (*informal*) [Late 19thC. An imitation of the sound of affectedly refined pronunciation.]

la·dies /láydeez/ *n. U.K.* = **ladies room** (*informal*) (*takes a singular verb*)

la·dies' man, la·dy's man *n.* a man who enjoys being with women and flirting with them

la·dies room, la·dies' room *n.* a women's restroom

la·dies' tress·es, la·dy's tress·es *n.* an orchid with slender spiral spikes of small white flowers. Genus: *Spiranthes.* (*takes a singular or plural verb*)

La·din /lə deén/ *n.* a language spoken in some valleys in northern Italy, belonging to the Rhaeto-Romance subgroup of Romance languages. It has about 25,000 speakers. [Mid-19thC. Via Rhaeto-Romance from Latin *Latinus* "Latin" (see LATIN).]

lad·ing /láyding/ *n.* freight or cargo being transported from one place to another

La·di·no /lə deénō/ (*plural* **-nos**) *n.* **1.** LANG **SPANISH-HEBREW LANGUAGE** a language based on Spanish with Hebrew elements, spoken by some Sephardic Jews. It is usually written in a form of Hebrew script. **2.** **La·di·no, la·di·no** PEOPLES **SPANISH-SPEAKING NATIVE CENTRAL AMERICAN** somebody of indigenous or partially Spanish ancestry in Central America who speaks Spanish [Late 19thC. Via Spanish from Latin *Latinus* "Latin" (see LATIN). Recorded earlier (mid-19thC) of a vicious or unmanageable animal.]

la·di·no clo·ver *n.* a large variety of white clover grown as forage [Early 20thC. Via Italian from Latin *Latinus* "Latin" (see LATIN).]

la·dle /láyd'l/ *n.* **LONG SPOON WITH A DEEP BOWL** a spoon with a long handle and a deep bowl, used to serve soup and other liquids ■ *vt.* (**-dled, -dling, -dles**) **SERVE USING A LADLE** to serve food such as soup onto a plate using a ladle [Old English *hlædel,* from *hladan* "to load" (see LADE)]

ladle out *vt.* to give out generous or overgenerous amounts of something, especially something intangible (*informal*) ○ *ladled out praise*

Lad·o·ga, Lake /laá dəgə/ the largest lake in Europe, in northwestern Russia, northeast of St. Petersburg. Its outlet is the Neva River, which connects it with the Gulf of Finland. Area: 7,100 sq. mi./18,390 sq. km.

la·dy /láydee/ (*plural* **-dies**) *n.* **1.** **WOMAN** a woman, especially when addressed as part of a group ○ *Ladies and gentlemen, please take your seats.* **2.** **REFINED WOMAN** a woman of refined family background or upbringing **3.** **POLITE DIGNIFIED WOMAN** a woman who behaves very politely and with dignity **4.** **WIFE OR USUAL WOMAN COMPANION** a man's wife or usual woman companion (*informal*) **5.** **WOMAN FEUDAL SUPERIOR** a woman who, in medieval Europe, was a powerful land or property owner with authority over an area, castle, or community, e.g., a manor **6.** **COCAINE** the drug cocaine (*slang*) [Old English *hlǣfdīge* 'woman in charge of a household, queen' (literally 'bread-kneader'), from *hlāf* 'bread' (source of English *loaf*) + a prehistoric Germanic base meaning "to knead"]

La·dy *n. U.K.* **1.** **TITLE FOR A WOMAN** used as an alternative title for a marchioness, countess, viscountess, or baroness **2.** **COURTESY TITLE FOR A WOMAN** used as a courtesy title for the daughter of an earl, marquess, or duke **3.** **FORM OF ADDRESS FOR A WOMAN** used as a form of address for the wife of a viscount, earl, marquess, baron, barnoet, or knight, and the daughter of a duke, marquess, or earl

la·dy bee·tle *n.* = **ladybug**

la·dy·bird bee·tle, la·dy·bird *n.* = **ladybug**

la·dy boun·ti·ful *n.* a woman who makes generous and well-publicized charitable donations

la·dy·bug /láydee bùg/ *n.* a small round flying beetle that has red or orange outer wings with black spots. It eats aphids and other insects. Family: Coccinellidae. [Named for *(Our) Lady,* the Virgin Mary]

La·dy Chap·el, la·dy chap·el *n.* a chapel dedicated to Mary, mother of Jesus Christ, that is inside a cathedral or church

La·dy Day *n. U.K.* the feast of the Annunciation, March 25

la·dy·fin·ger /láydee fing gər/ *n.* a small finger-shaped sponge cake, several of which are often used to surround molded desserts

la·dy·fish /láydee fish/ (*plural* **-fish** *or* **-fish·es**) *n.* **1.** **LARGE SILVERY GAMEFISH** a large silvery fish that lives in tropical seas. It is related to the tarpon and is prized as a gamefish. Latin name: *Elops saurus.* **2.** = **bonefish**

la·dy friend *n.* a man's regular woman companion, or a woman a man is seen with (*informal*) (*sometimes considered offensive*)

la·dy-in-wait·ing (*plural* **la·dies-in-wait·ing**) *n.* a woman who is an attendant for a queen or princess

la·dy-kill·er *n.* a man who is extremely attractive to women

la·dy·like /láydee lìk/ *adj.* behaving or done in the polite dignified way expected of an upper-class woman ○ *not a very ladylike thing to whine*

la·dy·love /láydee lùv/ *n.* a woman that a man is in love with (*dated*)

la·dy luck, La·dy Luck *n.* luck or good fortune personified as a woman (*informal*) (*sometimes considered offensive*)

La·dy of the Lake *n.* a supernatural woman who plays various roles in Arthurian legend, sometimes considered to be the same person as Vivian, the lover of Merlin

la·dy·ship /láydee shìp/, **La·dy·ship** *n.* a title used when addressing or referring to a woman with the title of "Lady"

la·dy slip·per *n.* = **lady's slipper**

la·dy's man *n.* = **ladies' man**

La·dy·smith /láydee smìth/ town in KwaZulu-Natal Province, eastern South Africa, scene of a famous siege (1899–1900) during the Boer War. Population: 25,102 (1985).

Lady's slipper

la·dy's slip·per, la·dy slip·per *n.* a North American orchid with reddish, purple, or yellow flowers that look like slippers. Genus: *Cypripedium.*

la·dy's smock *n.* = **cuckooflower**

Lady's thumb

la·dy's thumb *n.* a weedy plant of Europe and Asia belonging to the buckwheat family that has pink or purplish flowers and long leaves with a dark spot resembling a thumbprint. Latin name: *Polygonum persicaria.*

la·dy's tress·es *n.* = **ladies' tresses**

La·er·tes /lay úr teèz, -áir teèz/ *n.* in Greek mythology, the father of Odysseus

la·e·trile /láy ə trìl, -trəl/ *n.* a drug extracted from peach pits that has been used in treating cancer but with no proven effectiveness

lae·vo·ro·ta·tory *adj.* U.K. = **levorotatory**

La Farge /lə faárzh/, **John** (1835–1910) U.S. artist and critic. He is known for his landscapes, murals, and work in stained glass.

La·fay·ette /làfee yét/ **1.** city in west central Indiana, situated on the Wabash River, southwest of Kokomo. Population: 44,344 (1996). **2.** city in southern Louisiana, situated north of Abbeville and southwest of Baton Rouge. Population: 104,899 (1996).

La·fay·ette /làfee yét/, **Marie Joseph Paul Yves Roch Gilbert du Motier, Marquis de** (1757–1834) French soldier and politician. He fought against the British in the Revolution, and then took part in the French Revolution. He became a politician in the French post-revolutionary government.

laff /laf/ *n.* a laugh (*slang*)

Laf·fer curve /láffər-/ *n.* a graph summarizing the fact that tax revenues are low for very high and for very low tax rates, thus demonstrating that raising tax rates beyond an optimum point will discourage investment and decrease tax revenues [Late 20thC. Named for Arthur B. *Laffer* (b. 1942), U.S. economist.]

Laf·fite /lə feét/, **Jean** (1780?–1825?) French-born U.S. pirate. He helped defend New Orleans against Britain in the War of 1812.

La Follette /lə fó llət/, **Robert Marion** (1855–1925) U.S. senator. He led the progressive wing of the Republican Party, often opposing the leadership in the cause of reform.

Lafontaine /lə fon táyn/, **Sir Louis Hippolyte** (1807–64) Canadian politician. He is credited with launching responsible government and was, jointly, the first prime minister of the united province of Canada.

lag[1] /lag/ *vi.* (**lagged, lag·ging, lags**) **1. FALL BEHIND COMPARED WITH OTHERS** to go, develop, or progress more slowly than somebody or something similar so as to fall back or fall behind **2. SLACKEN** to decrease in strength or intensity ○ *Interest in the scandal has never lagged.* **3.** CUE GAMES **DECIDE THE ORDER OF PLAY** to decide who is to play first in pool or billiards by having each player rebound a ball from the top cushion as close as possible to the hand rail ■ *n.* **1. POSITION OF HAVING FALLEN BEHIND** the condition or an instance of having fallen behind **2. PERIOD BETWEEN EVENTS** a period of time between one event and a related event **3.** CUE GAMES **LAGGING IN BILLIARDS** an act or instance of lagging in pool, billiards, or some other game [Early 16thC. Origin uncertain: perhaps from a Scandinavian source (compare Norwegian dialect *lagga* "to go slowly").]

lag[2] /lag/ *vt.* (**lagged, lag·ging, lags**) **INSULATE WITH LAGGING** to insulate something such as a pipe or hot water tank with lagging to prevent freezing or heat escaping ■ *n.* **WOODEN STRIP** a strip of wood such as a stave of a barrel or a lath [Late 17thC. Origin uncertain: probably from a Scandinavian source.]

La Gallienne /là galyén/, **Eva** (1899–1991) British-born U.S. actor. She was known for her roles in plays by Ibsen and Chekhov. She also directed and taught acting.

lag·an /lággən/, **li·gan** /lígən/ *n.* cargo or wreckage lying on the sea bed, often with a buoy attached so that it can be recovered [Mid-16thC. From Old French, of uncertain origin: perhaps from Old Norse *lagn-*, the stem of *lögn* "net" (related to English *lay*[1]).]

La·gan Valley /lágən-/ region in southeastern Northern Ireland, near Belfast, and an Area of Outstanding Natural Beauty

Lag b'O·mer /laàg bṓmər/ *n.* a minor Jewish festival celebrated on the 18th day of Iyar, being the 33rd day of the Omer, the period following Passover. On this day some of the restrictions on activities imposed during the Omer are lifted. [From Hebrew, literally "thirty-third in the Omer," from *lāḡ* "thirty-third" (pronunciation of the letters LG that symbolize this number) + *bā* "in the" + *ōmer* "Omer"]

la·ger[1] /laágər/ *n.* a type of light-colored beer made with a low proportion of hops, usually stored for a period after brewing [Mid-19thC. Shortening of *lager beer*, a partial translation of German *Lager-Bier*, from *Lager* "storehouse" + *Bier* "beer."]

la·ger[2] *n.* = **laager**

lag·gard /lággərd/ *n.* **SOMEBODY OR SOMETHING FALLING BEHIND** somebody who or something that falls behind and does not keep up with others ■ *adj.* **RELUCTANT** slow or reluctant to do something [Early 18thC. Formed from LAG[1].] —**lag·gard·ly** *adv., adj.* —**lag·gard·ness** *n.*

lag·ging /lágging/ *n.* **1. INSULATION TO STOP HEAT FROM ESCAPING** insulating material used to keep heat from escaping, especially around a pipe or hot water tank **2.** BUILDING **SUPPORTING FRAME** a wooden frame used in building, especially to support an arch while it is being built

lag·ging in·di·ca·tor, lag·ging ec·o·nom·ic in·di·ca·tor *n.* an economic statistic that typically reflects how the economy was rather than how it is or will be

la·gniappe /lan yáp, lán yàp/ *n. Southern U.S.* **1. PRESENT GIVEN TO CUSTOMER** a small present given by a store to somebody who has just purchased something in the store **2. UNEXPECTED BONUS** an unexpected bonus or extra [Mid-19thC. Via Louisiana French from American Spanish *la ñapa* "the gift," from, ultimately, Quechua *yapay*, literally "to give more."]

WORD KEY: REGIONAL NOTE

Lagniappe is primarily a Louisiana French term, although it is derived from American Spanish and Quechua. With scattered incidence to the east and west, recurrent forms outline the New Orleans area, where it is most common, across Lower Mississippi and East Texas.

lag·o·morph /lággə màwrf/ *n.* any plant-eating mammal with two pairs of incisors in the upper jaw specialized for gnawing, e.g., the rabbit, hare, and pika. Order: Lagomorpha. [Late 19thC. From modern Latin *Lagomorpha*, order name, from, ultimately, Greek *lagōs* "hare" + *morphē* "shape, form."] —**lag·o·mor·phic** /làggə máwrfik/ *adj.* —**lag·o·mor·phous** /-máwrfəss/ *adj.*

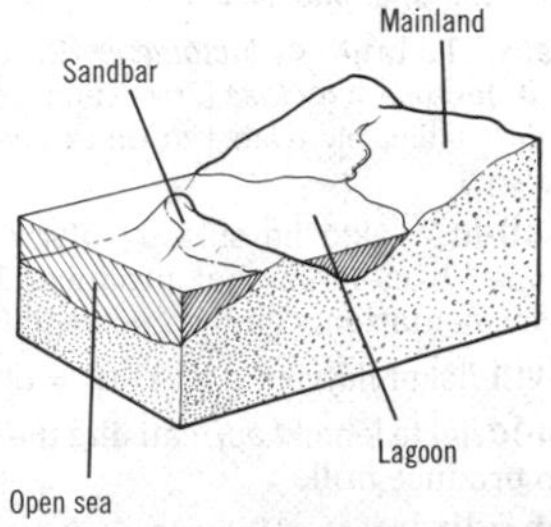

Lagoon

la·goon /lə goón/ *n.* **1. PARTLY-ENCLOSED AREA OF SEAWATER** a coastal body of shallow water formed where low-lying rock, sand, or coral presents a partial barrier to the open sea **2. SMALL LAKE** a small lake adjoining a larger one **3. HUMAN-MADE POOL OF WATER** a shallow body of water or other liquid, created by or near an industrial or waste site [Early 17thC. Via Italian or Spanish *laguna* and French *lagune* from Latin *lacuna* "hole, pit, pond" (see LACUNA).] —**la·goon·al** *adj.*

La·gos /láy gòs/ the largest city, chief port, and former capital of Nigeria. Population: 1,347,000 (1992).

La·grange /lə graánj/, **Joseph Louis, comte de l'Empire** (1736–1813) Italian-born French mathematician and astronomer. The author of *Méchanique analytique* (1788), he pioneered many concepts in mechanics, algebra, and number theory.

La Grange /lə gráynj/ village in northeastern Illinois, northeast of Downers Grove, a western suburb of Chicago. Population: 15,104 (1996).

La Guar·di·a /lə gwaárdee ə/, **Fiorello Henry** (1882–1947) U.S. politician. He was a popular, and populist, reforming mayor of New York from 1933 to 1945. Known as **The Little Flower**

La·gu·na Beach /la goónə-/ city in Orange County, southwestern California, situated 27 mi./43 km southeast of Long Beach. Population: 23,170 (1990).

La·gu·na Hills /la goónə-/ city in Orange County, southwestern California. Population: 46,731 (1990).

La·gu·na Ni·guel /lə goónə neejèl/ city in Orange County, southwestern California. Population: 56,681 (1994).

lah *n.* MUSIC = **la**[2]

La Ha·bra /lə haábrə/ city in Orange County, southwestern California, situated 19 mi./31 km northeast of Long Beach. Population: 51,266 (1990).

la·har /laá haàr/ *n.* a landslide or mudflow of volcanic debris, especially after a heavy rainfall [Early 20thC. From Javanese.]

Lah·nda /laándə/ *n.* a language spoken in Pakistan, related to Punjabi. It belongs to the Indic branch of the Indo-European family of languages. [Early 20thC. From Punjabi *lahandā*, literally "western."] —**Lah·nda** *adj.*

La·hore /lə háwr/ city and capital of Punjab Province, northeastern Pakistan, about 160 mi./257 km southeast of Islamabad. Population: 2,952,689 (1981).

Lah·ti /laáttee/ industrial city in southern Finland, north of Helsinki. Population: 95,119 (1995).

LAIA *n.* a trade association formed by Argentina, Bolivia, Brazil, Chile, Colombia, Ecuador, Mexico, Paraguay, Peru, Uruguay, and Venezuela in 1980. Full form **Latin American Integration Association**

la·ic /láy ik/, **la·i·cal** /láy ik'l/ *adj.* relating to or involving followers of a religion who are not clergy [Mid-16thC. Via late Latin *laicus* from Greek *laikos* "of the people," from *laos* "people" (source of English *lay*).] —**la·i·cal·ly** *adv.*

la·i·cize /láy i sīz/ (**-cized, -ciz·ing, -ciz·es**) *vt.* to remove something from control or governance by the church or the clergy and give control of it to the lay community —**la·i·ci·za·tion** /lày issi záysh'n/ *n.*

laid past tense, past participle of **lay**[1]

laid-back *adj.* very relaxed, easygoing, and unworried (*informal*) —**laid-back·ness** *n.*

laid pa·per *n.* a paper with a watermark of fine lines on it that are produced in the manufacturing process

Lai·lat-ul-Qa·dr /láy lat ōōl kaádər/ *n.* an Islamic festival, the Night of Power, celebrating the sending down of the Koran to Muhammad and occurring on the 27th of Ramadan

Laing /lang/, **R. D.** (1927–89) Scottish psychiatrist. His radical views on schizophrenia were set out in *The Divided Self* (1960). Other books include *The Politics of Experience* (1967) and *The Politics of the Family* (1971). Full name **Ronald David Laing**

lair /lair/ *n.* **1. WILD ANIMAL'S DEN** a place where a wild animal rests or sleeps **2. PLACE TO BE ALONE IN** a retreat or hideaway (*informal*) ■ *vti.* (**laired, lair·ing, lairs**) **GO TO A LAIR** to go to a lair, or be taken or made to go to a lair (*refers to an animal*) [Old English *leger* "act of lying, bed, grave." Ultimately from an Indo-European word that also produced English *lager*[1], *lay*[1], and *beleaguer*.]

laird /laird/ *n.* *Scotland* somebody who owns land, especially a large estate [14thC. Variant of LORD.]

lais·sez-faire /lè say fáir, lè zày-/, **lais·ser-faire** *n.* **1. PRINCIPLE OF NO REGULATION OF INDUSTRY** the principle that the economy works best if private industry is not regulated and markets are free **2. REFUSAL TO INTERFERE** refusal to interfere in other people's affairs, or the practice of letting people do as they wish [From French, literally "allow to do"]

lais·sez-pas·ser /-paa sáy/, **lais·ser-pas·ser** *n.* a document that permits the holder to travel freely, especially one given in lieu of a passport [From French, literally "allow to pass"]

la·i·ty /láy itee/ *npl.* **1. LAYPEOPLE RATHER THAN CLERGY** the followers of a religion who are not clergy **2. PEOPLE NOT IN A PARTICULAR PROFESSION** all the people who are not members of a specific profession, as distinguished from those who are members [15thC. Formed from LAY[2].]

La·ius /láy əss, lī́ əss/ *n.* a king of Thebes in Greek mythology, mistakenly killed by his son Oedipus

lake[1] /layk/ *n.* **1. INLAND BODY OF WATER** a large body of water surrounded by land **2. POOL OF LIQUID** a large pool of liquid that has collected or spilled somewhere ○ *A lake of hot grease covered the floor by the stove.* [Pre-12thC. Directly and via Old French *lac* from Latin *lacus* "pond" (source of English *lacuna* and *lagoon*).]

WORD KEY: CULTURAL NOTE

The Lady of the Lake, a poem by Scottish writer Sir Walter Scott (1810). Set in early 16th-century Scotland, it describes the eventful courtship of Ellen, daughter of outlawed chieftain James of Douglas, who lives at Loch Katrine (the lake of the title). Regarded as one of Scott's finest works, it is admired for its satisfying plot, strong characterization, and charming songs."Hail to the Chief who in triumph advances!", canto II, stanza 19, is a famed line in this work.

lake[2] /layk/ *n.* **1. TRANSLUCENT PIGMENT** a bright translucent pigment that can be of different colors, made by combining an organic dye with a metallic hydroxide or other inorganic substance **2. RED PIGMENT** a red pigment made by combining cochineal with a metallic compound [Early 17thC. Variant of LAC.]

Lake Dis·trict /láyk dìstrikt/ region of mountains and lakes in Cumbria, northwestern England. The district extends about 30 mi./50 km from north to south and 25 mi./40 km from east to west.

WORLD'S LARGEST LAKES

1		Caspian Sea
	Area	[143,000 sq. mi. / 370,000 sq. km]
	Location	*Europe/Asia*
2		Lake Superior
	Area	[31,700 sq. mi. / 82,100 sq. km]
	Location	*North America*
3		Lake Victoria
	Area	[26,830 sq. mi. / 69,490 sq. km]
	Location	*Africa*
4		Lake Huron
	Area	[23,000 sq. mi. / 59,600 sq. km]
	Location	*North America*
5		Lake Michigan
	Area	[22,300 sq. mi. / 57,800 sq. km]
	Location	*North America*
6		Lake Tanganyika
	Area	[12,700 sq. mi. /32,900 sq. km]
	Location	*Africa*
7		Great Bear Lake
	Area	[12,270 sq. mi. /31,790 sq. km]
	Location	*North America*
8		Lake Baikal
	Area	[12,200 sq. mi. /31,500 sq. km]
	Location	*Asia*
9		Aral Sea
	Area	[12,050 sq. mi. /31,220 sq. km]
	Location	*Asia*
10		Lake Nyasa
	Area	[8,683 sq. mi. /22,490 sq. km]
	Location	*Africa*

lake dwell·ing *n.* a home or settlement built on a platform supported by wooden posts over or by a shallow lake or river edge, especially in prehistoric times —**lake dwell·er** *n.*

lake ef·fect *n.* the effect that a large lake such as any of the Great Lakes has on the local weather

Lake For·est /làyk fórrist/ suburban city in northeastern Illinois, situated on the shore of Lake Michigan 30 mi./50 km north of Chicago. Population: 18,296 (1996).

lake·front /láyk frùnt/ *n.* the land along the shores of a lake

Lake George /làyk jáwrj/ historic village and county seat of Warren County, eastern New York State, situated on the southern end of Lake George 40 mi./64 km northeast of Amsterdam. Population: 3,211 (1990).

Lake Hav·a·su City /layk hàvvə sōō-/ city in Mohave County, Arizona, situated on Lake Havasu on the Colorado River, bordering California. Population: 39,503 (1996).

lake her·ring *n.* a food fish related to the whitefish and found in the Great Lakes. Latin name: *Coregonus artedii.*

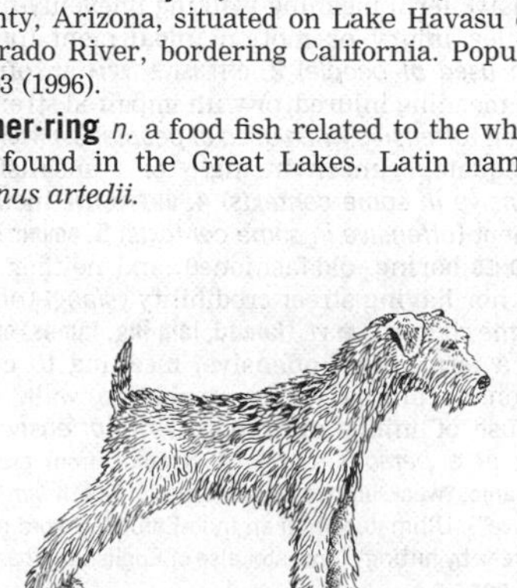

Lakeland terrier

Lake·land ter·ri·er /láyklənd-/ *n.* a wire-haired terrier with a black and tan coat, originally bred in England for foxhunting [Early 20thC. Named for *Lakeland*, a name for the Lake District in northwestern England, where the breed originated.]

Lake of the Woods /làyk əv thə wōōdz/ lake in central North America, on the border between the United States and Canada. It includes hundreds of wooded islands. Area: 1,695 sq. mi./4,390 sq. km.

Lake Po·ets *n.* the poets Wordsworth, Coleridge, and Southey, who lived in the Lake District in northwestern England in the early 19th century

lak·er /láykər/ *n.* **1.** SHIPPING **VESSEL SAILING ON LAKES** a boat or ship that is used on lakes rather than the sea **2.** ZOOL **FISH LIVING IN A LAKE** a fish living in a lake rather than the sea, e.g., a lake trout

lake·shore /láyk shàwr/ *n.* = **lakefront**

lake·side /láyk sīd/ *n.* = **lakefront**

lake trout *n.* **1. N AMERICAN FISH** a fish of the salmon family, native to deep North American lakes. Latin name: *Salvelinus namaycush.* **2.** *U.K.* = **brown trout**

Lake Worth /làyk wúrth/ city in Palm Beach County, southeastern Florida, situated on Lake Worth 6 mi./10 km south of West Palm Beach. Population: 28,564 (1990).

lakh /laak/ (*plural* **lakhs** *or* **lakh**), **lac** (*plural* **lacs** *or* **lac**) *n.* *S Asia* the number 100,000, used especially for referring to sums of rupees [Early 17thC. Via Hindi *lākh* from Sanskrit *lakṣam* "mark, token, 100,000."]

La·ko·ta /lə kṓtə/ *n.* (*plural* **-tas** *or* **-ta**), *adj.* PEOPLES = **Teton** [Mid-19thC. From Lakota *lakhóta.*]

laks /laks/ *n.* smoked salmon

lak·sa /láksə/ *n.* a Malaysian or Singaporean rice noodle, slightly thicker than spaghetti, often served in a spicy fish sauce or soup

Lak·shmi /lúkshmee/, **Lak·smi** *n.* the Hindu goddess of prosperity, wealth, and royalty, and wife of the god Vishnu

la·ky /láykee/ *adj.* of a reddish or crimson color similar to a red form of the pigment lake

la·lang /laá laang/ *n.* a tall coarse tropical grass that grows in the Malay Archipelago. Latin name: *Imperata arundinacea.* [Late 18thC. From Malay.]

la·la·pa·loo·za *n.* = **lollapalooza** (*informal*)

-lalia *suffix.* speech, speech disorder ○ *echolalia* [From Greek *lalia* "talk," from *lalein* "to talk"]

La·lique glass /lə leék-/ *n.* ornamental frosted glassware decorated with bas-relief figures, fruits, and flowers, designed by the French Art Nouveau craftsperson René Lalique

Lal·lans /lállənz/, **Lal·lan** /lállən/ *adj.* relating to or typical of the Lowlands of Scotland or any of the dialects of Scots spoken there [Early 18thC. Variant of *Lowlands*, LOWLAND.]

lal·la·tion /la láysh'n/ *n.* a mispronunciation of "r," especially one that sounds like "l" [Mid-17thC. From Latin *lallare* "to sing a lullaby."]

lal·ly·gag *vi.* = **lollygag**

lam[1] /lam/ (**lammed, lam·ming, lams**) *v.* (*informal*) **1.** *vti.* **HIT HARD** to hit somebody or something hard **2.** *vi.* **SPEAK ANGRILY** to speak angrily to somebody [Late 16thC. Origin uncertain: perhaps from Scandinavian.]

lam[2] /lam/ *n.* **HASTY ESCAPE** a hasty escape, especially to avoid arrest ■ *vi.* (**lammed, lam·ming, lams**) **ESCAPE HASTILY** to escape or run away, especially from the law (*informal*) [Late 19thC. From LAM[1]. The phrase *beat it* "to run away" has a similar origin.] ◇ **on the lam** making a hasty escape, especially from the law (*informal*)

lam. *abbr.* laminated

Lam. *abbr.* BIBLE Lamentations

la·ma /laámə/ *n.* **1. BUDDHIST MONK** a Tibetan or Mongolian Buddhist monk **2. TITLE FOR A REINCARNATED BUDDHIST** a title used for those individuals who are believed to be the reincarnations of a Bodhisattva [Mid-17thC. Alteration of Tibetan *bla-ma.*]

La·ma·ism /laámə ìzzəm/ *n.* a form of Mahayana Buddhism practiced in Tibet and Mongolia that has non-Buddhist elements from India and from Bön, an older nature-worshipping religion. Lamaist monks, or lamas, are led by the Dalai Lama, a temporal as well as spiritual ruler. —**La·ma·ist** *n., adj.* —**La·ma·is·tic** /laámə ístik/ *adj.*

La Man·cha /laa maánchə/ barren plateau region in south central Spain

Lamar /lə ma̋ar/, **Lucius Quintus Cincinnatus** (1825–93) U.S. jurist. He served on the U.S. Supreme Court twice, 1885 to 1889 and 1893 to 1897, and was a strong advocate of the rights of the states.

La·marck /lə ma̋ark/, **Jean Baptiste, Chevalier de** (1744–1829) French naturalist and evolutionist. His theory that evolution proceeded by the inheritance of acquired characteristics was superseded by Darwin's theory of natural selection. —**La·marck·i·an** *adj., n.*

La·marck·ism /lə ma̋ar kìzzəm/ *n.* the evolutionary theory of the French naturalist Jean Baptiste Lamarck that holds that evolution proceeds through the inheritance of characteristics acquired by individual organisms, e.g., through intensive use —**La·marck·i·an** *n., adj.*

la·ma·ser·y /la̋amə sèrree/ (*plural* **-ies**) *n.* a Tibetan or Mongolian monastery of lamas [Mid-19thC. From French *lamaserie*, literally "lama dwelling," from *lama* LAMA.]

La Mauricie National Park /laa màwri sée-/ national park situated due west of Quebec City, in the Laurentian Mountains, southern Quebec, Canada. Area: 206 sq. mi./536 sq. km.

La·maze /lə ma̋az/ *n.* a method of natural childbirth by which a woman is physically and psychologically prepared through prenatal training. Lamaze encourages the use of controlled breathing and the participation of the woman's partner during the process of childbirth. [Mid-20thC. Named for the French physician Fernand *Lamaze* (1890–1957), its originator.]

lamb /lam/ *n.* **1.** ZOOL **YOUNG SHEEP** an immature sheep, especially one under a year old and without permanent teeth **2. MEAT OF A LAMB** the meat of an immature sheep that is under a year old **3.** = **lambskin 4. SOMEBODY MEEK AND MILD** somebody who is gentle and innocent, especially a baby or small child **5. SOMEBODY EASILY DECEIVED** somebody who is easily cheated, especially financially ■ *vti.* (**lambed, lamb·ing, lambs**) AGRIC **BEAR A LAMB** to give birth to a lamb [Old English, of prehistoric Germanic origin] ◇ **like a lamb to the slaughter** calmly and without resistance going to face something unpleasant, difficult, or dangerous

Lamb /lam/, **Charles** (1775–1834) British essayist. He was a prose stylist of great clarity whose books include *Essays of Elia* (1823). Pseudonym **Elia**

Lam·ba /lámbə, la̋ambə/ *n.* a language spoken in parts of Benin that belongs to the Gur branch of Niger-Congo languages. Lamba is spoken by about 29,000 people. [Early 20thC. From Bantu.] —**Lam·ba** *adj.*

lam·ba·da /lam ba̋adə/ *n.* **1. LATIN AMERICAN DANCE** an athletic erotic dance originating in Brazil, in which partners hold each other close and gyrate their hips in unison **2. BRAZILIAN DANCE MUSIC** the fast, rhythmic music for the lambada [Late 20thC. From Brazilian Portuguese, literally "a beating, a lashing."]

Lam·ba·ré·né /làmbə réenee, loNbə ráynay/ capital of Moyen-Ogooué Region, western Gabon. Population: 42,316 (1993).

lam·baste /lam báyst/ (**-bast·ed, -bast·ing, -bastes**), **lam·bast** /-bást/ (**-bast·ed, -bast·ing, -basts**) *vt.* **1. CRITICIZE STRONGLY** to criticize somebody or something severely **2. WHIP** to beat or whip somebody (*archaic*) [Mid-17thC. From LAM^{1} + BASTE "to beat."]

lamb·da /lámdə/ *n.* **1. 11TH LETTER OF GREEK ALPHABET** the 11th letter of the Greek alphabet, represented in the English alphabet as "l." See table at **alphabet 2.** ANAT **JUNCTION IN SKULL** the point of junction at the center of the back of the cranium between the rear plate of the cranium (**occipital bone**) and the two upper plates (**parietal bones**). This junction is said to resemble the Greek capital letter lambda. ◊ **lambdoid** [Early 17thC. From Greek.]

lamb·da cal·cu·lus *n.* a descriptive theory of functions and the way they combine, used as the basis for certain high-level computer programming languages

lamb·da·cism /lámdə sìzzəm/ *n.* the erroneous substitution of "l" for "r" in speech [Mid-17thC. Via late Latin from Greek *la(m)bdakismos*, from *la(m)bda* (see LAMBDA).]

lamb·da par·ti·cle *n.* = **lambda hyperon**

lamb·doid /lám dòyd/, **lamb·doidal** /lam dóyd'l/ *adj.* used to describe the suture that joins bones at the back of the skull, shaped like the Greek capitalized lambda

lam·bent /lámbənt/ *adj.* **1. GLEAMING** softly gleaming or glowing (*literary*) **2. PLAYING OVER A SURFACE** flickering or playing as a flame over a surface without burning it (*literary*) **3. BRILLIANTLY LIGHT** having a light but brilliant touch [Mid-17thC. From Latin *lambent-*, the present participle stem of *lambere* "to lick." Ultimately from an Indo-European word that is also the ancestor of English *lap*^{3}.] —**lam·ben·cy** *n.* —**lam·bent·ly** *adv.*

lam·bert /lámbərt/ *n.* an SI unit of surface brightness (**luminance**) equivalent to one lumen per square centimeter [Late 19thC. Named for Johann Heinrich *Lambert* (1728–77), German scientist, in honor of his work on the measurement of light intensity and absorption.]

Lam·beth walk /làmbəth-/, **Lam·beth Walk** *n.* a lively ballroom dance originating and popularized in England during the 1930s [Mid-19thC. Named for a street in *Lambeth*, a borough in southern London.]

lam·bie /lámmee/ *n. Carib* tenderized conch flesh used for food

lamb·ing /lámming/ *n.* **1. BIRTH OF LAMBS** the birth of lambs, or the season when they are born **2. DELIVERY OF BABY LAMBS** the work of helping ewes give birth to lambs

lamb·kill /lám kil/ (*plural* **-kills** *or* **-kill**) *n.* BOT = **sheep laurel**

lamb·kin /lámkin/ *n.* an infant lamb, sometimes used as a term of endearment for a baby or small child

Lamb of God *n.* Jesus Christ, seen as a sacrifice whose crucifixion and resurrection redeemed humankind

lam·bre·quin /lámbrəkin, -bər-/ *n.* **1.** HOUSEHOLD **ORNAMENTAL HANGING** a decorative strip of drapery, hung along the top of a doorway, window, shelf, or mantelpiece **2.** HIST **SCARF ATTACHED TO A KNIGHT'S HELMET** a veil, scarf, or piece of drapery attached to a knight's helmet to protect it from heat and rust **3.** HERALDRY = **mantling 4.** CERAMICS **ORNAMENTAL BORDER ON A VASE** a decorative border near the top of a vase [Early 18thC. Via French from assumed Dutch, literally "small veil," from *lamper* "veil."]

Lam·brus·co /lam bro͞os kō/ *n.* a sweet sparkling red or white wine from northern Italy [Mid-20thC. Via Italian from Latin *labruscum* "fruit of the wild grape Vitis labrusca," from *labrusca*, the species name.]

lamb·skin /lám skìn/ *n.* **1. WOOLLY LAMB'S PELT** the woolly pelt of a lamb, used for making or trimming winter clothing **2. LAMB'S HIDE** the hide of a lamb, prepared as leather

lamb's let·tuce *n.* BOT = **corn salad** [Translation of its old Latin name *lactuca agnina*]

lamb's quar·ters *n.* BOT = **pigweed**

lambs·wool, **lamb's wool** *n.* fine soft wool, especially the wool sheared from a year-old lamb, often used for knitwear

Lambton /lámtən/, **John George, 1st Earl of Durham** (1792–1840) British colonial administrator. He served briefly as governor-general of Canada (1838). His report on the status of Canada paved the way for eventual self-government.

lame^{1} /laym/ *adj.* (**lam·er, lam·est**) **1. OFFENSIVE TERM** an offensive term meaning walking unevenly because of a leg injury or motion impairment (*offensive when used of people*) **2. OFFENSIVE TERM** an offensive term meaning injured, or with impaired strength or motion (*offensive when used of people*) **3. UNCONVINCING** inadequate, unconvincing, or unsatisfactory (*offensive in some contexts*) **4. INEFFECTIVE** ineffectual or inept (*offensive in some contexts*) **5. BORING AND OLD-FASHIONED** boring, old-fashioned, and neither streetwise nor having street credibility (*slang*) (*offensive in some contexts*) ■ *vt.* (**lamed, lam·ing, lames**) **OFFENSIVE TERM** a term, often offensive, meaning to cause a person or animal to be unable to walk evenly because of injury or impairment (*offensive when used of a person*) [Old English *lama*, from prehistoric Germanic, "weak-limbed" (source also of Dutch *lam* "unable to move"). Ultimately from an Indo-European word meaning "to break by hitting" (ancestor also of English *lambaste*).] —**lame·ness** *n.*

lame^{2} /laym/ *n.* a thin plate of metal, especially one of the overlapping metal plates of which medieval armor was made from the mid-14th century [Late 16thC. Via French from Latin *lamina* (see LAMINA).]

la·mé /la máy/ *n.* a fabric that has metallic threads, especially gold or silver, interwoven with silk, wool, or cotton [Early 20thC. From French, "worked with silver and gold thread," from Old French *lame* "thin metal plate," from Latin *lamina* (see LAMINA).]

lame·brain /láym bràyn/ *n.* an offensive term that deliberately insults somebody's intelligence (*informal insult*) —**lame·brained** *adj.*

la·med /la̋a mèd/, **la·medh** *n.* the 12th letter of the Hebrew alphabet, represented in the English alphabet as "l." See table at **alphabet** [Mid-17thC. From Hebrew *lāmĕdh*.]

lame duck *n.* **1.** POL **OUTGOING OFFICEHOLDER WITH WEAKENED POWER** an elected official or group left seemingly powerless after a successor has been elected but has not yet taken over **2.** POL **OFFICEHOLDER UNABLE TO BE REELECTED** an elected official who either will not or may not legally run for another term in office and has reduced power or effectiveness **3. SOMEBODY OR SOMETHING WEAK** somebody who or something that is weak, inadequate, or unfortunate, especially somebody requiring special help

la·mel·la /lə méllə/ (*plural* **-lae** /-lee/) *n.* **1.** ANAT **THIN PIECE OF BONE** any thin flat structure of bone or tissue **2.** FUNGI **PART OF FUNGUS** a gill of a fungus **3.** BOT **CONNECTIVE LAYER** a cementing layer between two plant cells **4.** CONSTR **STRUCTURAL PART OF VAULT** a structural part of wood, metal, or reinforced concrete that is crisscrossed to form a vault [Late 17thC. From Latin, literally "small thin plate," from *lamina* (see LAMINA).] —**la·mel·lar** *adj.* —**la·mel·lar·ly** *adv.*

la·mel·late /lə mé làyt, lə méllət, lámmə làyt/ *adj.* arranged in, composed of, or resembling layers —**lam·el·la·ted** /lámmə làytəd/ *adj.* —**lam·el·la·tion** /làmmə láysh'n/ *n.*

lamelli- *prefix.* lamella ○ *lamelliform* [From LAMELLA]

la·mel·li·branch /lə mélli brànk/ *n.* ZOOL = **bivalve** [Mid-19thC. From modern Latin *Lamellibranchia*, genus name, from Latin *lamella* (see LAMELLA) + Greek *bragkhia* "gills."] —**la·mel·li·branch·i·ate** /lə mèlli bránkee ət, lə mèlli bránkee àyt/ *adj., n.*

la·mel·li·corn /lə mélli kàwrn/ *adj.* **WITH LAYERED SEGMENTED ANTENNAE** used to describe a beetle such as the dung beetle, stag beetle, or chafer that has antennae composed of layered segments ■ *n.* **LAMELLICORN BEETLE** a beetle with layered antennae [Mid-19thC. From modern Latin *Lamellicornia*, former family name, from Latin *lamella* (see LAMELLA) + *cornu* "horn."]

la·mel·li·form /lə mélli fàwrm/ *adj.* shaped like a thin plate or scale [Early 19thC. Coined from LAMELLA + -FORM.]

lame·ly /láymlee/ *adv.* inadequately, unconvincingly, or ineptly

la·ment /lə mént/ *vti.* (**-ment·ed, -ment·ing, -ments**) **1. BE SAD ABOUT SOMETHING** to express sorrow about something **2. EXPRESS DISAPPOINTED REGRET** to express regret, annoyance, or disappointment ○ *She was lamenting the lack of funding for her project.* ■ *n.* **1. EXPRESSION OF SADNESS** an expression of grief or sorrow **2. EXPRESSION OF REGRET** an expression of regret or disappointment **3.** MUSIC, POETRY **WORK LAMENTING A DEATH** a song or poem of mourning [Mid-16thC. Directly or via French from Latin *lamentari*, from *lamenta* "laments." Ultimately from an Indo-European word, imitative of the sound of crying (ancestor also of English *lullaby*).] —**la·ment·er** *n.* —**la·ment·ing·ly** *adv.*

la·men·ta·ble /lə méntəb'l, lámməntəb'l/ *adj.* **1. DISAPPOINTINGLY BAD** unsatisfactory, pitiful, or deplorable **2. MOURNFUL** sad and mournful (*literary*) —**la·men·ta·ble·ness** *n.* —**lam·en·ta·bly** *adv.*

lam·en·ta·tion /làmmən táysh'n/ *n.* an act or expression of grief or sorrow [14thC. Directly or via French from, ultimately, Latin *lamentari* (see LAMENT).]

Lam·en·ta·tions /làmmən táysh'nz/ *n.* a book of the Bible written in the form of elegies, according to tradition, by Jeremiah (*takes a singular verb*) See table at **Bible**

la·ment·ed /lə méntəd/ *adj.* dead or departed and grieved for —**la·ment·ed·ly** *adv.*

La Me·sa /lə méesə/ city in San Diego County, southwestern California, situated 8 mi./13 km east of San Diego. Population: 52,931 (1990).

la·mi·a /láymee ə/ (*plural* **-as** *or* **-ae** /-ee/) *n.* in Greek and Roman mythology, a blood-sucking witch who takes the form of a serpent to threaten children [14thC. Via Latin from Greek, "mythical monster, carnivorous fish." Ultimately from an Indo-European word meaning "nocturnal spirits," which is also the ancestor of English *lemures*.]

lam·i·na /lámmənə/ (*plural* **-nae** /-nee/ *or* **-nas**) *n.* **1.** THIN LAYER a thin plate, layer, or flake **2.** BOT LEAF BLADE the blade or flat part of a leaf **3.** ZOOL PROTECTIVE PLATE INSIDE A HOOF in hoofed mammals, any of the parallel layers of sensitive tissue just inside the hard exterior of the hoof [Mid-17thC. From Latin, "plate, leaf" (source of English *lamé* and *omelette*).]

lam·i·nal /lámmən'l/ *adj.* articulated using the blade or flat part of the tongue

lam·i·nar flow /lámmənər-/ *n.* a type of flow in a liquid or gas in which neighboring layers do not mix and flow at different velocities

lam·i·nar·i·a /làmmə náiree ə/ *n.* a large brown seaweed (**kelp**) that has broad, flat fronds. Genus: *Laminaria.* [Mid-19thC. From modern Latin *Laminaria*, genus name, from Latin *lamina* (see LAMINA), from the thin appendages.]

lam·i·nar·in /làmmə náirin/ *n.* a carbohydrate occurring in brown algae [Mid-20thC. Formed from modern Latin *Laminaria* (see LAMINARIA).]

lam·i·nate /lámmə nàyt/ *v.* (**-nat·ed, -nat·ing, -nates**) **1.** *vt.* COVER SOMETHING WITH A THIN LAYER to cover something with a thin sheet of protective material, e.g., plastic or metal **2.** *vt.* BOND LAYERS TOGETHER to bond sheets or layers together so as to produce a strong and durable composite material ○ *Wood veneers were laminated to produce a cheap and durable alternative to expensive hardwoods for furniture-making.* **3.** *vt.* METALL FORM METAL INTO THIN LAYERS to roll or beat metal into thin sheets **4.** *vti.* SEPARATE INTO LAYERS to split something, or be split, into thin layers ■ *n.* MATERIAL MADE UP OF BONDED LAYERS a product composed of layers or sheets bonded together ■ *adj.* IN LAYERS composed of or with layers —**lam·in·a·ble** *adj.* —**lam·i·na·tor** *n.*

lam·i·nat·ed /lámmə nàytəd/ *adj.* **1.** MADE OF BONDED LAYERS composed of layers bonded together **2.** COVERED WITH A THIN LAYER covered with a thin layer of plastic or metal

lam·i·na·tion /làmmə náysh'n/ *n.* **1.** PROCESS OF BONDING LAYERS the bonding together of thin layers of materials to form a composite material **2.** FORMATION OF LAYERS the formation of layers in something **3.** THIN LAYER a thin layer in something (*technical*) **4.** THINLY-LAYERED STRUCTURE a structure composed of thin layers **5.** ELEC ENG THIN STEEL PLATE IN TRANSFORMER CORE one of a number of thin steel or iron plates that are held together to form a transformer core

lam·i·nec·to·my /làmmə néktəmee/ (*plural* **-mies**) *n.* a surgical operation to remove one or more sides of the rear arches of a spinal vertebra and gain access to the spinal cord or spinal nerve roots

Lam·ing·ton Na·tion·al Park /làmmingtən-/ national park in southeastern Queensland, Australia

Lam·ing·ton Pla·teau high mountain plateau situated in the Macpherson Range, Lamington National Park, Queensland, Australia

lam·i·ni·tis /làmmə nítiss/ *n.* inflammation of the sensitive plates of tissue in a hoof, especially a horse's hoof, usually causing lameness. It is one of the most serious equine hoof diseases.

La Mi·ra·da /laa mə raadə/ city in Los Angeles County, southwestern California, situated 13 mi./21 km southeast of Los Angeles. Population: 40,452 (1990).

Lam·mas /lámməss/ *n.* **1.** CHR CHRISTIAN RELIGIOUS FEAST ON AUGUST 1 a Christian religious feast on August 1 to celebrate St Peter's deliverance from prison **2.** CALENDAR AUGUST 1 the first day of August, originally celebrated in England as a harvest festival. In Scotland Lammas was formerly one of the quarter days. [Old English *hlāfmæsse*, from earlier forms of LOAF + MASS "liturgy"; altered through folk etymology by association with LAMB]

lam·mer·gei·er /lámmər gīr/, **lam·mer·gey·er** *n.* a large rare vulture found in mountainous areas in southern Europe, Africa, and Asia, with dark wings and dark feathers that resemble a beard around its beak. Latin name: *Gypaetus barbatus.* [Early 19thC. From German *Lämmergeier*, literally "lambs' vulture," because it can prey upon animals of that size.]

La Mothe /la mót/, **Antoine Laumet de, Sieur de Cadillac** (1658–1730) French-born Canadian colonial administrator. He founded present-day Detroit (1701) and served as the governor of Louisiana (1710–17).

lamp /lamp/ *n.* **1.** DEVICE PRODUCING ELECTRIC LIGHT a device that produces electric light **2.** DEVICE PRODUCING LIGHT a device that burns oil, gas, or wax to produce light **3.** RADIATION SOURCE a device that supplies ultraviolet light or infrared heat radiation, especially for medical or cosmetic treatment ○ *sun lamp* **4.** SOURCE OF ENLIGHTENMENT a source of enlightenment or inspiration (*literary*) [12thC. Via French and Latin from Greek *lampas* "burning torch," later "oil lamp," from *lampein* "to shine" (source of English *lantern*).]

lam·pas /lámpəss/ *n.* an ornately patterned cloth resembling damask, especially one made of silk, that is used for upholstery [Mid-19thC. From French, of uncertain origin: perhaps from or related to obsolete Dutch *lampers* "a kind of crape."]

lamp·black /lámp blàk/ *n.* a fine powdery form of carbon that is deposited when oils containing carbon are burned. It is used as a pigment, a printing ink, and in electrodes.

lamp·brush chro·mo·some /lámp brush-/ *n.* an enlarged chromosome covered with fine loops of chromatin, observed during cell division in many organisms [*Lampbrush* a loose translation of German *Lampencylinderputzer*, literally "lamp-glass cleaner," coined by J. Rückert because it resembles a brush for the inside of a lampshade.]

lamp chim·ney *n.* a glass cover that is placed over the wick of an oil or kerosene lamp to protect and control the flame

lam·per eel /lámpər-/ *n.* = **lamprey** [Early 16thC. *Lamper* probably from a variant of LAMPREY.]

lamp glass *n.* = **lamp chimney**

lam·pi·on /lámpee ən/ *n.* a small oil lamp, usually with a tinted glass chimney, formerly popular as a carriage light [Mid-19thC. Via French from Italian *lampione*, literally "large lamp," from *lampa* "lamp," from French *lampe* (see LAMP).]

lamp·light /lámp līt/ *n.* the light cast by a lamp —**lam·plit** *adj.*

lamp·light·er /lámp lītər/ *n.* **1.** SOMEBODY EMPLOYED TO LIGHT STREET LAMPS somebody who was employed to light the gas lamps along a street in times before the introduction of electricity **2.** DEVICE FOR LIGHTING LAMPS a device used to light lamps

Lampman /lámpmən/, **Archibald** (1861–99) Canadian poet. He was best known for his nature poems.

lamp oil *n.* **1.** OIL FOR LAMPS oil suitable as lamp fuel **2.** KEROSENE kerosene (*regional*)

lam·poon /lam po͞on/ *n.* SATIRICAL ATTACK IN WRITING OR VERSE a piece of satirical writing or verse ridiculing somebody or something ■ *vt.* (**-pooned, -poon·ing, -poons**) SATIRIZE WITH RIDICULE to use ridicule as a way of satirizing somebody or something in a piece of writing [Mid-17thC. From French *lampon*, of uncertain origin: perhaps from *lampons* "let us drink!" (used as a refrain in songs), a form of *lamper* "to gulp down."] —**lam·poon·er** *n.* —**lam·poon·er·y** *n.* —**lam·poon·ist** *n.*

lamp·post /lámp pōst/, **lamp post** *n.* a post or pillar that supports a streetlight

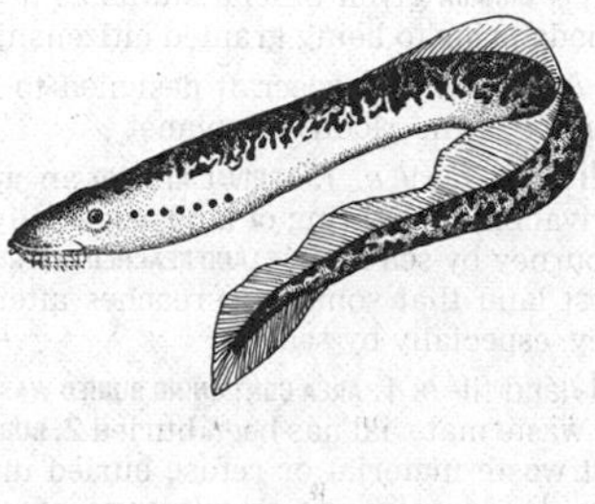

Lamprey

lam·prey /lámpree/ (*plural* **-preys**), **lam·prey eel** *n.* a freshwater jawless fish that has a round sucking mouth for attaching itself to other fish and, in the case of adults, feeding parasitically on their blood. Family: Petromyzontidae. [13thC. Via Old French *lampreie* from medieval Latin *lampreda* (source also of English *limpet*), perhaps from *lampetra*, literally "stone-licker," because it clings to rocks with its mouth.]

lam·pro·phyre /lámprə fīr/ *n.* an igneous rock that occurs mainly as an intrusion or dike containing large crystals, especially of biotite and mica [Late 19thC. From German, literally "shining porphyry."]

lamp·shade /lámp shàyd/ *n.* a cover, typically decorative, used to moderate and direct artificial light from a lamp

lamp shell *n.* = **brachiopod** [From its resemblance to an ancient oil lamp and its wick]

lamp·work·ing /lámp wùrking/ *n.* the process or technique of forming glass items made of rods and tubes by heating them with an oxygen-gas flame

La·mut /lə mo͝ot/ *n.* a language spoken in parts of eastern Siberia, belonging to the Manchu-Tungus branch of the Altaic languages. Lamut is spoken by about 12,000 people. [Early 18thC. Via Russian from Evenki, literally "those living by the sea," from *lamu* "sea."] —**La·mut** *adj.*

LAN /lan/ *abbr.* COMPUT local area network

la·nai /lə nī/ (*plural* **-nais**) *n.* in Hawaii, an open roofed porch or veranda, often used as a living room [Early 19thC. From Hawaiian.]

la·nate /láy nàyt/ *adj.* covered with or consisting of woolly hairs [Mid-18thC. From Latin *lanatus*, from *lana* "wool" (source of English *lanolin*).]

lan·ça·do /làn sádō/ (*plural* **-dos**) *n.* a collection point in the interior of Africa for Portuguese trade, from the 16th century on, that linked African economies to the commercial centers on the Atlantic coast [From Portuguese, "launching point"]

Lan·cas·ter /láng kəstər/, **Burt** (1913–94) U.S. actor. His movies include *From Here To Eternity* (1953), *Elmer Gantry* (1960), *The Swimmer* (1968), and *Local Hero* (1983).

Lan·cas·tri·an /lang kástree ən/ *adj.* **1.** BELONGING TO LANCASHIRE belonging or relating to Lancashire or Lancaster in England **2.** HIST CONNECTED WITH THE LANCASTER ROYAL FAMILY belonging to or supporting the royal house of Lancaster, especially during the 15th-century Wars of the Roses ■ *n.* **1.** SOMEBODY FROM LANCASHIRE IN ENGLAND somebody who was born or raised or who lives in Lancashire or Lancaster in England **2.** HIST PARTISAN OF THE LANCASTER ROYAL FAMILY somebody who belonged to or supported the royal house of Lancaster, especially during the Wars of the Roses when the Yorkists and Lancastrians fought for the throne of England

lance /lans/ *n.* **1.** LONG CAVALRY SPEAR a long weapon with a metal point carried by cavalry in battle **2.** HUNT HUNTING OR FISHING SPEAR a long pointed spear used in hunting or fishing **3.** METALL METAL-PIERCING DEVICE a thin metal tube or pipe through which a stream of oxygen is directed at a heated metal surface in order to pierce it **4.** SURG LANCET a lancet (*archaic*) ■ *vt.* (**lanced, lanc·ing, lanc·es**) MED PIERCE SOMETHING WITH A SHARP INSTRUMENT to pierce flesh with a sharp instrument to let out pus [13thC. Via French from Latin *lancea* (source of English *launch*), of uncertain origin: probably from Celtic.]

lance cor·po·ral *n.* **1.** MARINE RANK a Marine who ranks above private first class but below corporal **2.** RANK OF NONCOMMISSIONED OFFICER the first rank above private soldier in the British army or the Royal Marines [From obsolete *lancepesade* "officer of lowest rank," via Old French from Old Italian *lancia spezzata*, literally "broken lance," hence "old soldier"]

lance·let /lánslət/ *n.* a small slender translucent marine animal that is related to the ancestors of all vertebrate animals and lives buried in sand. Subphylum: Cephalochordata. [Mid-16thC. Originally used for "lancet," it disappeared in the 17thC but was revived in the modern sense in the 19thC.]

Lan·ce·lot /lánsələt/ *n.* in Arthurian legend, the most famous of King Arthur's knights and the lover of Queen Guinevere

lan·ce·o·late /lánsee ələt, -ə làyt/ *adj.* tapering to a point like the head of a lance ○ *lanceolate leaves* [Mid-18thC. From late Latin *lanceolatus*, from Latin *lanceola*, literally "small lance," from *lancea* "lance" (see LANCE).] —**lan·ce·o·late·ly** *adv.*

lanc·er /lánsər/, **Lanc·er** *n.* a soldier on horseback armed with a lance

lanc·ers /lánsərz/ *n.* (*takes a singular verb*) **1.** DANCE SQUARE DANCE a square dance for 8 or 16 couples, originally a 19th-century quadrille **2.** MUSIC MUSIC FOR THE LANCERS the music for the lancers, a square dance

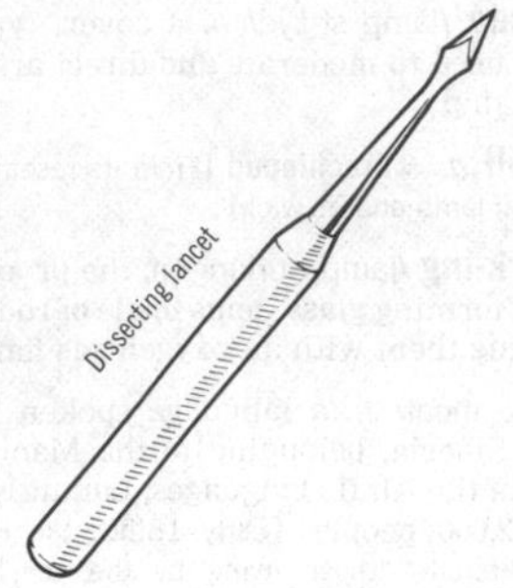

Lancet

lan·cet /lánsət/ *n.* **1.** SURG **SCALPEL** a scalpel (*archaic*) **2.** ARCHIT = **lancet arch 3.** ARCHIT = **lancet window**

lan·cet arch *n.* a narrow arch that comes steeply to a point, typical in Gothic architecture

lanc·et·ed /lánsətəd/ *adj.* **1. WITH POINTED OPENINGS** built with lancet arches or lancet windows, as in Gothic architecture **2. WITH A POINTED TOP** with an arched, steeply pointed top

lan·cet fish *n.* a long-bodied carnivorous deep-sea fish with a long dorsal fin and sharp teeth. Latin name: *Alepisauridae.* [From the sharpness of the fins]

Lancet window

lan·cet win·dow *n.* a window formed as one or more slender pointed arches

lance·wood /láns wŏŏd/ (*plural* **-woods** *or* **-wood**) *n.* **1.** TREES **TROPICAL TREE** a tropical tree of the Americas, especially the West Indies, that yields a tough elastic wood. Latin name: *Oxandra lanceolata.* **2.** INDUST **WOOD OF THE LANCEWOOD TREE** the tough flexible wood of the lancewood tree, used for making fishing rods, bows, and in cabinetmaking [From the use of the wood in objects like fishing rods]

lan·ci·form /lánsə fàwrm/ *adj.* shaped like a lance

lan·ci·nate /lánsə nàyt/ (**-nated, -nat·ing, -nates**) *vt.* to stab or pierce something (*archaic*) [Early 17thC. From Latin *lancinere* "to tear."] —**lan·ci·na·tion** /lànsə náysh'n/ *n.*

lan·ci·nat·ing /lánsə nàyting/ *adj.* producing a stabbing or piercing sensation (*formal*)

Lancs /langks/ *abbr.* Lancashire

land /land/ *n.* **1. SOLID EARTH** the solid part of the earth's surface not covered by a body of water **2. EARTH FOR USE** a part of the earth's surface of a particular kind or that is used for a particular purpose ○ *low-lying land* ○ *agricultural land* **3. COUNTRYSIDE** ground used for agriculture, or rural or agricultural areas as distinguished from villages, towns, or cities ○ *He had worked on the land all his life.* **4. OWNED GROUND** an area of ground that somebody owns ○ *publicly owned land* ○ *What are you doing on my land?* **5. HOMELAND** a territory, country, or nation inhabited by those who regard it as their home ○ *her native land* **6. AREA NOTABLE FOR SOMETHING** an area, domain, or realm that is notable for something ○ *She's living in the land of make-believe.* **7. SMOOTH PARTS OF GROOVED AREA** the unindented parts of a grooved surface, e.g., a ridge between grooves in the bore of a rifle **8.** AGRIC **UNFURROWED SOIL** the parts of the ground between furrows in a plowed field ■ *v.* (**land·ed, land·ing, lands**) **1.** *vi.* AIR **ARRIVE BY PLANE** to arrive by aircraft ○ *We land at 8:43.* **2.** *vti.* AIR **SET DOWN AIRCRAFT** to come down, or bring an aircraft down, onto water or solid ground, especially at an airport ○ *The Baltimore plane landed five minutes ago.* **3.** *vt.* **OBTAIN SOMETHING** to win, obtain, secure, or be awarded something desired ○ *He finally landed the job he wanted.* **4.** *vti.* TRANSP **GO OR PUT SOMETHING ASHORE** to arrive on shore from a ship, or put something ashore from a ship ○ *We decided to land and explore the port.* **5.** *vt.* **HIT SOMEBODY OR SOMETHING** to succeed in hitting somebody or something ○ *She landed a blow on his head.* **6.** *vi.* **COME DOWN THROUGH THE AIR** to come down, or bring somebody or something down, from a height ○ *The ball shot up and landed on the roof.* **7.** *vti.* **END UP SOMEWHERE UNPLEASANT** to end up or cause somebody or something to end up in an undesirable place or situation ○ *It could land him in jail.* **8.** *vi.* **APPEAR UNEXPECTEDLY** to appear in an undesired and unexpected way ○ *One problem after another landed in our lap.* **9.** *vt.* ANGLING **CATCH AND BRING A FISH IN** to catch a fish and get it onto a boat or solid ground [Old English, from a prehistoric Germanic word apparently meaning "particular (enclosed) area," which is also the ancestor of English *lawn*] ◇ **back to the land** relating to moving from a city to a rural area and taking up a simple life ◇ **be in the land of the living** to be alive (*humorous*) ◇ **see out how the land lies, find out how the land lies** to assess a situation before taking action

land on *vt.* to criticize somebody severely

land up *vi. U.K., Can* to finally get to a place or situation after a series of events or circumstances (*informal*) ○ *land up on the streets*

land with *vt. U.K., Can* to give somebody something to do or deal with, especially because no one else wants to do it (*informal*) ○ *I was landed with the bill.*

Land *interj.* used for Jesus Christ (*dated*) (*used euphemistically*) ○ *Land sakes, why did you do that?* [Alteration of LORD]

Land /land/, **Edwin Herbert** (1909–91) U.S. inventor and entrepreneur. He invented the Polaroid Land camera (1947) and founded and headed a major corporation for its development (1937–82).

land a·gent *n.* somebody who arranged the sale or settlement of North American public lands in the 19th and early 20th century

lan·dau /lán dòw/ (*plural* **-daus**) *n.* a four-wheeled horse-drawn carriage with a top that may be let down or folded back and a raised seat for the driver [Mid-18thC. Named for *Landau*, a town in Bavaria, Germany, where it was first made.]

lan·dau·let /làndə lét/, **lan·dau·lette** *n.* **1. SMALL CARRIAGE** a small horse-drawn landau **2. AUTOMOBILE WITH A REAR FOLDING TOP** an automobile that has a convertible top for the back seat, while the front seat is either roofed or open

land bank *n.* a bank that issues loans using the borrower's property as security

land bridge *n.* a tract of land that connects continents, permitting the passage of people and animals

land crab *n.* any crab that lives mainly on land and breeds in the sea

land·ed /lándəd/ *adj.* **1. OWNING LAND** possessing land, especially a large rural property **2. CONSISTING OF LAND** consisting of a large area of land **3.** *Can* **OFFICIALLY A RESIDENT OF CANADA** given official status as a resident in Canada prior to being granted citizenship

land·er /lándər/ *n.* a spacecraft designed to land on the surface of the Moon or a planet

land·fall /lánd fàwl/ *n.* **1. ARRIVAL AT LAND** an approach to, arrival on, or sighting of land, especially after a long journey by sea **2. FIRST LAND REACHED AFTER A JOURNEY** the first land that somebody reaches after a long journey, especially by sea

land·fill /lánd fìl/ *n.* **1. AREA CONTAINING BURIED WASTE** a site where waste material has been buried **2. BURIED WASTE MATERIAL** waste material or refuse buried under the soil for landscaping or as a means of safe and sanitary waste disposal **3. BURIAL OF WASTE MATERIAL** the disposal of waste material or refuse by burying it in natural or excavated holes or depressions

land·form /lánd fàwrm/ *n.* a natural physical feature of the earth's surface, e.g., a valley, mountain, or plain

land·grab·ber /lánd gràbbər/ *n.* somebody who seizes land unfairly or illegally —**land·grab** *n.*

land grant *n.* a grant of public land, especially for the establishment of a state university

land·grave /lánd gràyv/ *n.* **1. COUNT WITH REGIONAL JURISDICTION** in Germany, from the 13th century to 1806, a count who had jurisdiction over a region **2. TITLE OF SOME GERMAN PRINCES** a title given to certain princes in central Germany after 1806 [Early 16thC. From Middle Low German, literally "land count," from *land* "land" + *grave* "count, nobleman."]

land·hold·er /lánd hòldər/ *n.* the owner or occupant of a piece of land —**land·hold·ing** *n., adj.*

land·ing /lánding/ *n.* **1. ACT OF COMING TO THE GROUND** the act of reaching, touching, or alighting on the ground, e.g., after a jump or fall **2. ARRIVAL ON LAND** an arrival on the ground after having been in the air or at sea **3. PLACE FOR LOADING OR UNLOADING** a place for loading or unloading passengers or goods, especially from a ship ○ *There are good landings at most of the villages along the coast.* **4.** BUILDING **LEVEL AREA BETWEEN STAIRS** a platform between flights of stairs or the floor at the top or foot of a flight of stairs

land·ing beam *n.* a radio beam emitted by a beacon at a landing field that enables incoming aircraft to make a landing

land·ing craft *n.* a low open flat-bottomed boat designed for landing troops and equipment on shore from a ship

land·ing field *n.* a place where aircraft can land and take off

land·ing gear *n.* the wheels or floats and related mechanisms that are used by an aircraft or spacecraft when taking off and landing

land·ing net *n.* a baglike net fitted on a frame that is used by anglers to scoop up a hooked fish

land·ing speed *n.* the minimum speed at which an aircraft has to be flying in order to land safely

land·ing stage *n.* a floating or fixed wooden platform, used for loading or unloading passengers and goods from a boat

land·ing strip *n.* = **airstrip**

land·la·dy /lánd làydee/ (*plural* **-dies**) *n.* **1. WOMAN WHO RENTS PROPERTY** a woman who owns property that she rents to tenants **2. WOMAN WHO RENTS OUT LODGINGS** a woman who owns or runs a place offering accommodations, e.g., a rental house, apartment, or duplex

länd·ler /léndlər/ (*plural* **-ler**) *n.* **1.** DANCE **SLOW GERMAN DANCE** a dance of southern Germany and Austria in slow triple time, in which couples clap and whirl round. The ländler was a forerunner of the waltz. **2.** MUSIC **MUSIC FOR LÄNDLER** a slow rustic waltz as the music for the ländler [Late 19thC. From German, literally "something connected with Landl," from *Landl*, a part of Austria, where the dance was first popular.]

land·less /lándləss/ *adj.* without having the ownership of land —**land·less·ness** *n.*

land·line /lánd lìn/ *n.* a telecommunications cable laid overland

land·locked /lánd lòkt/ *adj.* **1.** GEOG **SURROUNDED BY LAND** closed in completely or almost completely by land **2.** ZOOL **LIVING WITH NO ACCESS TO SEA** adapted to life in a freshwater environment, with no access to the ocean, though being a species historically found in the ocean

land·lord /lánd làwrd/ *n.* **1. MAN WHO RENTS PROPERTY** a man who owns property that he rents to tenants **2. MAN WHO RENTS OUT LODGINGS** a man who owns or runs a place offering accommodations, e.g., a rental house, apartment, or duplex

land·lub·ber /lánd lùbbər/ *n.* somebody who is awkward aboard a ship because of a lack of experience at sea —**land·lub·ber·ly** *adj.*

land·mark /lánd maàrk/ *n.* **1. SOMETHING PROMINENT THAT IDENTIFIES A LOCATION** a prominent structure or geographic feature that identifies a location and serves as a guide to finding it **2. SOMETHING THAT REPRESENTS IMPORTANT NEW DEVELOPMENT** an event, idea, or item that represents a significant or historic development **3. SOMETHING PRESERVED FOR HISTORIC IMPORTANCE** a structure or site identified and preserved because of its historical significance **4. BOUNDARY MARKER** a conspicuous object, e.g., a tree or stone, that is recognized as marking the boundary of a piece of land ■ *adj.* **HIGHLY SIGNIFICANT** marking a significant change or turning point in something, especially the law ○ *a landmark ruling*

land·mass /lánd màss/ *n.* a very large unbroken area of land, e.g., a continent or large island

land·mine /lánd mìn/ *n.* **1. BURIED EXPLOSIVE DEVICE** an explosive mine that is laid just under the surface of the ground and detonates if disturbed by pressure or the proximity of something such as metal **2.** TRAP a trap that is difficult to see (*informal*) ○ *That process seems simple, but it's loaded with landmines.*

land of·fice *n.* a government office that administers and records the sale and transfers of public land

land-of·fice bus·i·ness *n.* a highly successful trade in something (*informal*) [From the offices in new U.S. territories for selling land to settlers quickly and cheaply]

land of milk and hon·ey *n.* **1.** BIBLE **FERTILE LAND PROMISED TO ISRAELITES** a land of prosperity and plenty promised by God to the Israelites **2.** **ANY FERTILE REGION** a rich and fertile area, or region of plenty (*literary*)

land of Nod *n.* an imaginary place where people go in order to sleep (*informal humorous*) [Pun, from the Bible, *Genesis* 4:16, after Cain has killed Abel: "Then Cain went away. . .and dwelt in the land of Nod, east of Eden"]

Landon /lándən/, **Alfred Mossman** (1887–1987) U.S. politician. As Republican nominee he lost the presidential election to Franklin D. Roosevelt in 1936.

land·own·er /lánd ōnər/ *n.* somebody who owns land —**land·own·er·ship** *n.* —**land·own·ing** *n., adj.*

land-poor *adj.* lacking funds because all available money has been spent to acquire land

landrail *n.* = **corncrake** [From RAIL "bird"]

Land Ro·ver *tdmk. U.K.* a trademark for a four-wheel-drive vehicle

land·scape /lánd skàyp/ *n.* **1.** **VISUALLY DISTINCT SCENERY** an expanse of scenery of a particular type, especially as much as can be seen by the eye **2.** **PAINTING OF VIEW** a painting, drawing, or photograph of scenery, especially rural scenery **3.** **THE PAINTING OR DRAWING OF SCENERY** the branch of art dealing with the painting, drawing, or photography of scenery **4.** **GENERAL SITUATION OF ACTIVITY** the general situation providing the background to a particular type of activity ○ *the economic landscape* **5.** **RANGE OF MENTAL CONCERNS** any characteristic group of intellectual or imaginative features (*literary*) ■ *adj.* PRINTING **PRINTED WITH LONG SIDES HORIZONTAL** photographed or printed so that the long sides of a picture or the lines of text are parallel to the long sides of a rectangular page ○ *It's best to print most tables in landscape.* ◊ **portrait** ■ *vt.* (**-scaped, -scap·ing, -scapes**) ENVIRON **MAKE LAND LOOK BETTER** to enhance the appearance of land by altering its contours and planting trees and shrubs for aesthetic effect (*often passive*) ○ *The property was beautifully landscaped.* [Late 16thC. Anglicization of Dutch *landschap*, literally "condition of being land," from *land* "land." Originally used in painting.]

land·scape ar·chi·tect *n.* somebody employed to plan and design an environment, especially with the aim of making new buildings, roads, and other structures compatible with their natural surroundings —**land·scape ar·chi·tec·ture** *n.*

land·scape gar·den·er *n.* somebody who designs and lays out grounds and gardens —**land·scape gar·den·ing** *n.*

land·scap·er /lánd skàypər/ *n.* somebody who alters grounds or gardens for aesthetic effect

land·scap·ist /lánd skàypist/ *n.* an artist who specializes in painting landscapes

Land's End /làndz énd/ cliff and headland in Cornwall, England that forms the extreme southwestern tip of Great Britain

land·shark /lánd shaàrk/ *n.* somebody who profits by unethical dealings in land (*informal insult*)

land·side /lánd sīd/ *n.* AGRIC the flat part of a plow that faces unbroken land as it moves

land·sknecht /laànts kə nékht/ *n.* a mercenary foot soldier in Europe during the 16th century, especially a German pikeman [Early 17thC. From German, literally "servant of the country." By folk etymology "lands" has often been misunderstood as "lance."]

lands·leit /laànts līt/ plural of **landsman**

land·slide /lánd slīd/ *n.* **1.** **SUDDEN COLLAPSE OF LAND** the collapse of part of a mountainside or cliff so that it descends in a disintegrating mass of rocks and earth **2.** **MASS OF LOOSENED ROCK AND EARTH** a disintegrating mass of rock and earth that suddenly descends from a mountainside or cliff **3.** POL **CONSPICUOUS TRIUMPH** an overwhelming victory, especially in an election

Lands·mål /laàndz maàl/ *n.* an official form of the Norwegian language derived from the rural dialects of Norwegian spoken in the west and north of the country and standardized during the mid-19th century. ◊ **Bokmål** [Late 19thC. From Norwegian, literally "country language."]

lands·man[1] /lándzmən/ (*plural* **-men**) *n.* somebody who lives and works on land rather than at sea

lands·man[2] /laàntsmən/ (*plural* **-leit** /-līt/) *n.* a fellow Jew, usually one from the same district or area, originally in Eastern Europe [Mid-20thC. Via Yiddish, from Middle High German *lantsman*, literally "man from the (same) country," plural *lantsliute*.]

Land·stei·ner /lánd stīnər/, **Karl** (1868–1943) Austrian pathologist. He was awarded the Nobel Prize in medicine (1930) for developing the ABO blood group classification system.

Land·sturm /laànt shtoòrm/ *n.* **1.** **MILITARY DRAFT** in some European countries a general draft of people for conscription into the armed forces **2.** **CONSCRIPTED FORCE** in some European countries, a military force of people drafted from the general population [Early 19thC. From German, literally "land storm."]

Land·tag /laàn taàk/ *n.* the legislative assembly of a German or Austrian state [Late 16thC. Via German, from, ultimately, Middle High German *lanttac*, literally "land day."]

land·ward /lándwərd/ *adj.* **FACING LAND** facing toward the land ■ *adv.* **TOWARD LAND** in the direction of land

land·wards /lándwərdz/ *adv.* in the direction of land

Land·wehr /laànt vàir/ *n.* in German-speaking countries, a reserve military force [Early 19thC. From German, literally "national defense."]

land yacht *n.* a wind-driven vehicle resembling a boat with a mast, sails, and three wheels, for use on beaches or other hard surfaces

lane /layn/ *n.* **1.** TRANSP **TRACK INTO WHICH ROAD IS DIVIDED** a division of a road, street, or highway wide enough for a single line of motor vehicles **2.** BOWLING **STRIP OF FLOOR IN BOWLING ALLEY** the long strip of polished wooden flooring along which balls are rolled in a bowling alley **3.** SPORTS **TRACK ASSIGNED TO RACER** a track assigned to a competitive runner on a racing track or a swimmer in a swimming pool **4.** **NARROW STREET** a narrow path, road or street, typically in older town areas or in the countryside, often enclosed by walls or hedges **5.** BASKETBALL **DIVISION OF BASKETBALL COURT** an area of a basketball court extending from the free-throw line to just below the basket **6.** AIR = **air lane** **7.** SHIPPING **SHIPPING ROUTE** a route assigned to a ship on a journey, especially through a congested area of sea [Old English, of unknown origin] ◇ **in the fast lane** at a fast, hectic, or stressful pace associated with success and achievement

lang /lang/, **k.d.** (*b.* 1961) Canadian-born U.S. singer. She is equally adept at country-and-western and popular songs. Full name **Kathryn Dawn Lang**

Fritz Lang

Lang, Fritz (1890–1976) German-born U.S. movie director. He made many Hollywood movies, but is best known for the silent film *Metropolis* (1921) and the German-language *M* (1931).

lang. *abbr.* language

Lange /lang/, **Dorothea** (1895–1965) U.S. photographer. Her documentary photographs of the Great Depression and migrant workers in southern states, had a huge impact.

Lange, Jessica (*b.* 1950) U.S. movie actor. She won Academy Awards for *Tootsie* (1982) and *Blue Sky* (1994).

Lan·gi *n.* = **Lango**

lang·lauf /laàng lòwf/ *n.* **1.** = **cross-country skiing** **2.** **CROSS-COUNTRY SKIING CONTEST** a contest in cross-country skiing [Early 20thC. From German, literally "long run," from *lang* "long" + *Lauf* "a run" (from, ultimately, a prehistoric Germanic word that is also the ancestor of English *leap*).] —**lang·lauf·er** *n.*

lang·ley /lánglee/ (*plural* **-leys**) *n.* a unit of solar radiation equivalent to one calorie per square centimeter [Mid-20thC. Named for Samuel P. LANGLEY.]

Lang·ley /lánglee/, **Samuel Pierpont** (1834–1906) U.S. aviation pioneer. In 1896 he successfully launched two unmanned aircraft.

Lang·muir /láng myoòr/, **Irving** (1881–1957) U.S. chemist. He received a Nobel Prize in chemistry (1932) for his research on surface reactions of solids.

Lan·go /laàng gō/ (*plural* **-gos** *or* **-go**), **Lan·gi** /laàng gee/ (*plural* **-gis** *or* **-gi**) *n.* **1.** PEOPLES **MEMBER OF UGANDAN PEOPLE** a member of a Nilotic people who live in northern Uganda **2.** LANG **LANGO LANGUAGE** the language of the Lango people, belonging to the Chari-Nile branch of Nilo-Saharan languages. Lango is spoken by about half a million people. [Early 20thC. From Nilotic.] —**Lan·go** *adj.*

Lan·go·bard /láng gə baard/ *n.* = **Lombard** *n.* 2 [Late 18thC. From late Latin *Langobardus* (see LOMBARD).]

Lan·go·bar·dic /làng gə baàrdik, -gō-/ *n.* a dialect of Old High German spoken by the ancient Lombards

lan·gouste /laan goóst/ *n.* = **spiny lobster** [Mid-20thC. Via French from Old Provençal *lagosta*, from, ultimately, Latin *locusta* "locust, crustacean" (source also of English *locust*).]

lan·gous·tine /laàng goo stéen, laàng goo stéen/ *n.* a large prawn or small lobster of the North Atlantic [Mid-20thC. Via French, from, ultimately, Latin *locusta* "locust, crustacean."]

lan·grage /lángrij/, **lan·gridge** *n.* shot consisting of a case filled with fragments of iron, formerly used for tearing the sails and rigging of enemy ships [Mid-18thC. Origin unknown.]

Lan·gre·nus /lan gréenəss/ *n.* a plain on the Moon with a complex central peak located on the eastern edge of the Mare Fecunditatis, 82 mi./132 km in diameter

Lang·try /lángtree/, **Lillie** (1853–1929) British actress. She was the first woman of high social standing to go on the stage in Great Britain. She became the mistress of the Prince of Wales (later Edward VII). Born **Emilie Charlotte Le Breton**

lan·guage /láng gwij/ *n.* **1.** **SPEECH OF GROUP** the speech of a country, region, or group of people, including its diction, syntax, and grammar **2.** **COMMUNICATION WITH WORDS** the human use of spoken or written words as a communication system **3.** **SYSTEM OF COMMUNICATION** a system of communication with its own set of conventions or special words **4.** **NONVERBAL COMMUNICATION BETWEEN ANIMALS** a nonverbal form of communication used by birds and animals **5.** **NONVERBAL COMMUNICATION BETWEEN HUMANS** the use of signs, gestures, or inarticulate sounds to communicate something **6.** **SPECIALIST VOCABULARY** the characteristic forms of expression used by those in a specified group or sphere of activity **7.** **STYLE OF VERBAL EXPRESSION** the verbal style by which people express themselves ○ *the language of diplomacy* **8.** COMPUT = **programming language** [13thC. Via French *langage*, from *langue* "tongue," from, ultimately, Latin *lingua*, literally "tongue," hence "language" (source of English *linguistics*).] ◇ **speak the same language** to have values and interests in common with somebody so that it is possible to communicate effectively

WORD KEY: SYNONYMS

language, vocabulary, tongue, idiolect, dialect, slang, jargon, parlance, lingo, -speak, -ese

CORE MEANING: communication by words

language the way human beings communicate using words, whether written or spoken. It is also used for the particular system of communication used by a specific country, nation, or community; **vocabulary** the body of words that make up a particular language. It can also be used to refer to the words used to talk about a particular subject; **tongue** the particular language used by a specific country, nation, or community; **idiolect** the particular language or speech habits of an individual; **dialect** the specific way a language is used in a particular area of a country or among those in a particular part of a community when this is distinct in some way from the language spoken generally in that nation or community; **slang** the words, expressions, and turns of phrase used by a particular group of people, especially when these are considered nonstandard; **jargon** the words associated with a particular specialized activity or group or used in a particular situation, especially in order to suggest that they are technical or difficult for an ordinary person to understand; **parlance** a formal and fairly old-fashioned word for the words and expressions usually associated with a particular group of people; **lingo** an informal word for the words or way of speaking associated with a particular, usually specialized, group of people; **-speak** a suffix added to nouns to describe the specific way words are used by a particular group of people or in a particular context. It is used especially to suggest that this way of speaking or writing is made deliberately hard for ordinary people to follow; **-ese** a suffix added to nouns to describe the words and speech patterns associated with a particular person or group of people, especially when the words have been coined or the speech is hard to understand, for example, in the speech of journalists.

lan·guage arts *npl.* a range of skills taught in school that are designed to give students proficiency in using their native language, including all forms of written and verbal expression

lan·guage lab·o·ra·to·ry *n.* a room equipped with audio or multimedia equipment for use in learning languages

langue /laang/ *n.* language regarded as a communication system and the common property of a speech community (*technical*) ◊ **parole** [14thC. Via French from Latin *lingua* (see LANGUAGE). The modern technical sense dates from the early 20thC.]

langue de chat /laáng də shaá/ (*plural* **langues de chat** /laáng də shaá/) *n.* a small narrow flat cookie often coated with chocolate [From French, literally "cat's tongue"]

langue d'oc /laaNg dáwk/ *n.* the group of French dialects, usually thought of as including Provençal, spoken in southern parts of medieval France [From French, literally "language of "oc"," from the use of *oc* (from Latin *hoc*) for "yes"]

langue d'oïl /laaNg dóyl/ *n.* the group of French dialects spoken in the northern part of medieval France [From French, literally "language of "oïl"," from the use of *oïl* (from Latin *hoc ille*) for "yes"]

lan·guet /láng gwət, lang gwét/ *n.* something, e.g., a part in a machine or instrument, that is shaped like a tongue [14thC. From Old French *languete*, literally "small tongue," from *langue* "tongue," from Latin *lingua* (see LANGUAGE).]

lan·guid /láng gwid/ *adj.* **1.** WITHOUT ENERGY lacking vigor and energy **2.** SLUGGISH sluggish or slow-moving **3.** LISTLESS listless and indifferent [Late 16thC. Directly or via French from Latin *languidus*, from *languere* (see LANGUISH).] —**lan·guid·ly** *adv.* —**lan·guid·ness** *n.*

lan·guish /láng gwish/ (**-guished, -guish·ing, -guish·es**) *vi.* **1.** BE NEGLECTED OR DEPRIVED to undergo hardship as a result of being deprived of something, typically independence, freedom, or attention **2.** BECOME LESS SUCCESSFUL to decline steadily, becoming less vital, strong, or successful **3.** PINE FOR SOMETHING to long for something that is being denied [14thC. From Old French *languiss-*, the stem of *languir*, from, ultimately, Latin *languere* "to be weak or faint."] —**lan·guish·er** *n.* —**lan·guish·ing** *n., adj.* —**lan·guish·ing·ly** *adv.* —**lan·guish·ment** *n.*

lan·guor /lángər, láng gər/ *n.* **1.** TIREDNESS a pleasant feeling of weariness or weakness **2.** LISTLESSNESS IN SPEECH OR BEHAVIOR listlessness and indifference in speech or behavior **3.** HEAVINESS IN ATMOSPHERE an oppressive heaviness or sultriness in the air [13thC. Via Old French from Latin, from *languere* (see LANGUISH).]

lan·guor·ous /lángərəss, láng gərəss/ *adj.* **1.** WEAK AND RELAXED lazily or pleasantly lacking vigor and vitality **2.** LISTLESS listless and indifferent **3.** SLUGGISH slow-moving or sluggish —**lan·guor·ous·ly** *adv.* —**lan·guor·ous·ness** *n.*

lan·gur /lan góor/ *n.* a slender, leaf-eating monkey of Southeast Asia with a long tail, bushy eyebrows, and a chin tuft. Genus: *Presbytis.* ◊ **leaf monkey** [Early 19thC. Via Hindi *langūr* from Sanskrit *lāngūla* "having a tail."]

lan·iard *n.* = **lanyard**

la·ni·a·ry /láynee àiree/ *adj.* FOR TEARING FOOD adapted for tearing food ○ *laniary teeth* ■ *n.* TOOTH FOR TEARING FOOD a tooth adapted for tearing food [Early 19thC. From Latin *laniarius*, literally "of a butcher," from *lanius* "butcher," from *laniare* "to tear."]

Lanier /lə neér/, **Sidney** (1842–81) U.S. poet and lecturer. He is known for his melodic poems.

la·nif·er·ous /lə níffərəss/, **la·nig·er·ous** *adj.* wool-bearing or wool-covered [Mid-17thC. Formed from Latin *lanifer*, from *lana* "wool" (source of English *lanolin*).]

lank /langk/ *adj.* **1.** ELONGATED long and slender **2.** LIMP limp and straight ○ *lank hair* [Old English *hlanc* "lean," from a prehistoric Germanic word meaning "flexible" that is also the ancestor of English *flinch* and *link*] —**lank·ly** *adv.* —**lank·ness** *n.*

lank·y /lángkee/ (**-i·er, -i·est**) *adj.* tall and thin in a bony, ungracefully angular way —**lank·i·ly** *adv.* —**lank·i·ness** *n.*

lan·ner /lánnər/ (*plural* **-ners** *or* **-ner**) *n.* a large falcon found in Africa, Southeast Asia, and the Mediterranean region, the female of which is used especially in falconry. Latin name: *Falco biarmicus.* [13thC. From French *lanier*, of uncertain origin: perhaps from Old French, "cowardly," because it flies slowly and was therefore thought to lack courage.]

lan·ner·et /lánnə rèt, lànnə rét/ (*plural* **-ets** *or* **-et**) *n.* a male lanner, smaller than the female and used in falconry

lan·o·lin /lánn'lin/, **lan·o·line** /lánn'l een/ *n.* a fat extracted from sheep's wool, often used as a base in ointments and skin medications [Late 19thC. Coined from Latin *lana* "wool" (ultimately from an Indo-European word that is also the ancestor of English *wool*) + *oleum* "oil" (source of English *oil*).]

lans·for·dite /lánsfər dìt/ *n.* a crystallized hydrate of magnesium carbonate occurring as stalactites [Late 19thC. Formed from *Lansford*, the name of a town in Pennsylvania where it was found.]

Lan·sing /lánsing/ **1.** village in northeastern Illinois, on the Illinois-Indiana border south of Calumet City. It is a southern suburb of Chicago. Population: 28,664 (1996). **2.** capital of Michigan, a manufacturing city in the south central part of the state. Population: 127,812 (1994).

lan·ta·na /lan tánnə/ (*plural* **-nas** *or* **-na**) *n.* a shrub of the vervain family that is native to the tropical Americas and has bright aromatic spikes of yellow, orange, or blue and violet flowers. Genus: *Lantana.* [Late 18thC. Via modern Latin, genus name, from Italian dialect *lantana* "wayfaring tree," which it resembles.]

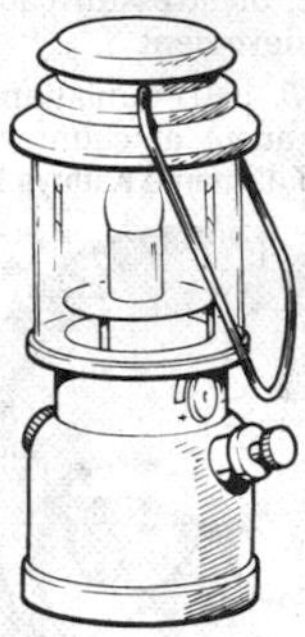

Lantern

lan·tern /lántərn/ *n.* **1.** PORTABLE LAMP a portable case with transparent or translucent sides that protects and holds a lamp **2.** LIGHTHOUSE ROOM a room containing the large lamp at the top of a lighthouse **3.** ARCHIT STRUCTURE WITH WINDOWS a structure with windows on all sides, resembling a lantern, e.g., one at the top of a dome [13thC. Via French from, ultimately, Greek *lamptēr* "torch, lamp," from *lampein* "to shine" (source also of English *lamp*).]

lan·tern-eyed fish *n.* a marine fish with luminous organs under each eye that it can turn off and on at will. Family: Anomalopidae.

lan·tern fish *n.* a small bony deep-sea fish with rows of luminous spots along its body. Family: Myctophidae.

lan·tern fly *n.* a tropical insect with an elongated head that resembles a lantern and was formerly thought to emit light. Family: Fulgoridae.

lan·tern jaw *n.* a long bony lower jaw, typically projecting beyond the upper jaw —**lan·tern-jawed** *adj.*

lan·tern pin·ion *n.* a gearwheel used in clocks and watches that has two circular disks connected by cylindrical pins

lan·tern slide *n.* a transparent slide, typically made of glass, for projection onto a screen by a slide projector or magic lantern

lan·tha·nide /lánthə nìd/ *n.* any of the chemical elements in the lathanide series of rare earths [Early 20thC. Coined from LANTHANUM + -IDE.]

lan·tha·nide se·ries *n.* a group of the rare earths that range from lanthanum at atomic number 57 to lutetium at atomic number 71

lan·tha·num /lánthənəm/ *n.* a silvery ductile metallic element resembling aluminum that belongs to the rare earth series and used in the manufacture of glass. Symbol **La** [Mid-19thC. Coined from Greek *lanthanein* "to lie hidden" (because it was discovered hidden in cerium oxide).]

la·nu·gi·nous /lə nóojənəss/, **la·nu·gi·nose** /-nōss/ *adj.* covered with downy hairs [Late 16thC. Formed from Latin *lanuginosus*, from *lanugo* (see LANUGO).] —**la·nu·gi·nous·ness** *n.*

la·nu·go /lə nóo gō/ (*plural* **-gos** *or* **-go**) *n.* a covering of soft downy hairs, especially those on a developing human fetus or newborn infant [15thC. From Latin, from *lana* "wool" (source of English *lanolin*).]

lan·yard /lánnyərd/, **lan·iard** *n.* **1.** MIL, SCOUTING CORD WORN AROUND THE NECK a cord worn around the neck by military and naval personnel or by Boy Scouts and Girl Scouts for carrying something such as a whistle or penknife **2.** NAUT SHORT ROPE ABOARD SHIP a short rope or cord used to hold or fasten something on a ship **3.** ARMS CORD FOR FIRING A CANNON a cord tied to the breech mechanism of a cannon and used to fire it [14thC. Anglicization (influenced by YARD "spar") of French *lanière* "strap," from, ultimately, *lasne*, of uncertain origin: perhaps a blend of *laz* "string" (source of English *lace*) and *nasle* "lace."]

Lan·za·rot·e /lanzə róttee/ the easternmost island of the Canary Islands, Las Palmas Province, Spain, situated northeast of Grand Canary in the Atlantic Ocean. Population: 76,413 (1995). Area: 335 sq. mi./862 sq. km.

La·oc·o·ön /lay ókō òn/, **La·oc·o·on** *n.* a Trojan priest of Apollo who warned the Trojans about the Wooden Horse and was killed along with his two sons by sea serpents after he gave his warning

la·od·i·ce·an /lay òddə seé ən/, **La·od·i·ce·an** *adj.* UNCOMMITTED lacking in religious or political commitment ■ *n.* SOMEBODY LACKING INTEREST somebody who is lukewarm or indifferent, especially about religion or politics [Early 17thC. Formed from Latin *Laodicea*, modern-day western Turkey, whose Christians were rebuked for indifference (the Bible, *Revelation*, 3:16: "...you are lukewarm, and neither cold nor hot").]

Laos

La·os /lowss, láy òss/ independent state of Southeast Asia, bounded by China, Vietnam, Cambodia, Thailand, and Myanmar. It is the only landlocked nation in Southeast Asia. Language: Lao. Currency: new kip. Capital: Vientiane. Population: 5,116,959 (1997). Area: 91,400 sq. mi./236,800 sq. km. Official name **Lao People's Democratic Republic** —**La·o·tian** *n., adj.*

Lao-tzu /lòw dzóo/ (570?–490? B.C.) Chinese philosopher. He is credited with originating Taoism, described in the seminal *Tao-te Ching*. Known as **Master Lao**

lap[1] /lap/ *n.* **1.** TOP OF SOMEBODY'S THIGHS WHEN SITTING the level area provided by the upper surface of the thighs of somebody who is seated **2.** CLOTHES PART OF CLOTHING RESTING ON THE THIGHS the part of a garment that hangs loosely across the thighs of somebody seated **3.** GEOG **VALLEY** a hollow in the contours of land, especially the gap between hills [Old English *læppa* "flap of a garment, lobe," from a prehistoric Germanic word that is perhaps also the ancestor of English *label*] —**lap·ful** *n.* ◇ **drop in** *or* **into your lap** to be given as something welcome and unexpected ◇ **drop (something) in somebody's lap** to become or make something somebody's responsibility ◇ **in the lap of luxury** in great luxury and comfort ◇ **in the lap of the gods** beyond human control or influence

lap[2] /lap/ *n.* **1. ONE CIRCUIT OF A TRACK** a single circuit of a racetrack or running track, or one length of a swimming pool **2. STAGE IN SOMETHING** a phase in an extended project, enterprise, or journey **3. OVERLAPPING PART** an overlapping part of something **4. LENGTH GOING ONCE AROUND A REEL** a length of fabric, thread, or rope that goes once around a roller, drum, or reel **5.** TECH **POLISHING DISK** a rotating disk for cutting or polishing something such as glass or gemstones ■ *v.* **(lapped, lap·ping, laps) 1.** *vt.* **PASS COMPETITORS BY A COMPLETE CIRCUIT** to overtake a competitor on a racetrack or running track or in a swimming pool after having completed at least one circuit or pool length more than he or she has **2.** *vi.* **COMPLETE ONE TRACK CIRCUIT** to run one complete circuit around a track or to swim one length of a swimming pool **3.** *vt.* **WRAP IN SOMETHING** to enfold or enwrap somebody in something (*literary*) (*often passive*) **4.** *vti.* **OVERLAP** to overlap something (*literary*) **5.** *vt.* **POLISH OR CUT HARD SURFACES** to polish or cut something hard such as glass, metal, or gemstones **6.** *vt.* **FORM FIBERS INTO A BAND** to arrange fibers so that they lie one against the other and form a band [14thC. From LAP[1], perhaps from the meaning "folds of a garment." The modern sense "circuit of track" evolved from "something wrapped," via "overlapping part."] —**lap·per** *n.*

lap[3] /lap/ *vti.* **(lapped, lap·ping, laps) 1. lap, lap up DRINK SOMETHING WITH THE TONGUE** to drink a liquid by scooping it into the mouth with the tongue **2. WASH GENTLY AGAINST A SURFACE** to flow or splash gently against a surface ■ *n.* **1. PROCESS OF DRINKING SOMETHING WITH TONGUE** the action of drinking liquid by scooping small amounts of it into the mouth with the tongue **2. SOUND OF MOVING LIQUID** the sound of a liquid gently flowing or splashing against something [Old English *lapian*, from, ultimately, a prehistoric Germanic word] —**lap·per** *n.*

lap up *v.* **1.** *vti.* = **lap**[3] *v.* 1 **2.** *vt.* **DRINK EAGERLY** to drink or eat something enthusiastically **3.** *vt.* **ENJOY EAGERLY** to enjoy something eagerly and uncritically

La Pal·ma /lə paálmə/ **1.** city in Orange County, southwestern California, situated 16 mi./26 km southeast of Los Angeles. Population: 15,392 (1990). **2.** town, port, and capital of Darién Province, eastern Panama, situated on an inlet of the Gulf of Panama 100 mi./161 km southeast of Panama City. Population: 1,634 (1980). **3.** one of the Canary Islands, Spain, situated off the north coast of Africa. Population: 82,183 (1995). Area: 280 sq. mi./725 sq. km.

lap·a·ro·scope /láppərə skōp/ *n.* an instrument in the shape of a tube that is inserted through the abdominal wall to give an examining doctor a view of the internal organs

lap·a·ros·co·py /làppə róskəpee/ (*plural* **-pies**) *n.* examination of the internal organs of the abdomen using a laparoscope [Mid-19thC. Coined from Greek *lapara* "flank" + -SCOPY.] —**lap·a·ro·scop·ic** /làppərə skóppik/ *adj.* —**lap·a·ros·co·pist** *n.*

lap·a·rot·o·my /làppə róttəmee/ (*plural* **-mies**) *n.* a surgical incision through the abdominal wall made to allow investigation of an abdominal organ or diagnosis of an abdominal disorder [Mid-19thC. Coined from Greek *lapara* (see LAPAROSCOPY) + -TOMY.]

La Paz /lə páz, laa páss/ capital city of Bolivia, located in the western part of the country. Population: 711,036 (1992).

lap belt *n.* a safety belt that is fitted to the seat of a motor vehicle and fastens across the lap

lap·board /láp bàwrd/ *n.* a thin flat board that is laid across the knees to serve as a table or writing surface

lap-chart *n.* a record of each lap made by a motor vehicle in a race, showing each vehicle's exact position

lap dan·cer *n.* a stripteaser who performs an erotic dance close to or in the lap of a customer —**lap danc·ing** *n.*

lap desk *n.* a portable writing surface that fits over or on somebody's lap

lap·dog /láp dòg/ *n.* **1. SMALL PET DOG** a small gentle-natured dog **2. MINION** somebody who is willing to say or do anything at another's command, especially in an organization or institution

la·pel /lə pél/ *n.* either of the two folded-back front edges of a jacket that are continuous with the collar [Mid-17thC. Diminutive of LAP[1] (in the earlier meaning of "part of a garment that projects and can be folded over").] —**la·pelled** *adj.*

lap·i·dar·y /láppi dàiree/ *adj.* **1. ENGRAVED ON STONE** engraved in stone or on a gemstone **2. OF ENGRAVING GEMSTONES** relating to the art of engraving gemstones **3. DIGNIFIED AND ELEGANT** careful, elegant, and dignified in style (*formal*) ■ *n.* (*plural* **-ies**) **CUTTER OF PRECIOUS STONES** somebody who is expert at cutting, polishing, and engraving gemstones [14thC. From Latin *lapidarius* "of stone," later "stone-cutter," from *lapid-*, the stem of *lapis* "stone" (source of English *lapis lazuli*), of uncertain origin; perhaps Mediterranean.]

lap·i·date /láppi dàyt/ (**-dated, -dat·ing, -dates**) *vt.* (*literary*) **1. STONE SOMEBODY** to throw stones at somebody **2. STONE SOMEBODY TO DEATH** to stone somebody to death, especially as a punishment for wrongdoing [Early 17thC. From Latin *lapidare*, from the stem *lapid-* (see LAPIDARY).] —**lap·i·da·tion** /làppi dáysh'n/ *n.*

la·pil·lus /lə píllәss/ (*plural* **-li** /-lī/) *n.* a small fragment of lava thrown from a volcano [Mid-18thC. From Latin, "small stone," from *lapis* (see LAPIDARY).]

la·pis laz·u·li /làppiss lázzyə lī, -lázhə lī, làppiss lázzyəlee/ *n.* **BLUE GEMSTONE** a deep blue semiprecious stone that is chiefly composed of lazurite and is used in making jewelry ■ *adj.* COLORS **DEEP BLUE** of the same deep brilliant blue as lapis lazuli [Literally "stone of lapis lazuli"; from Latin *lapis* "stone" + medieval Latin *lazuli* "of lapis lazuli," from, ultimately, Persian *lāžward* (source of English *azure*)]

Lap·ith /láppith/ (*plural* **-iths** *or* **-i·thae** /-pithee/) *n.* in Greek mythology, a member of a people of Thessaly who fought the drunken centaurs at the wedding of their king, Pirithous. The contest of the Lapiths and centaurs was a frequent theme in Greek sculpture and appeared notably in the metope frieze on the Parthenon at Athens. [Early 17thC. Via Latin *Lapithae* "people of Thessaly," from Greek *Lapithai*.]

lap joint *n.* a joint made by overlapping the ends of two parts or pieces and fastening them together —**lap-joint·ed** *adj.*

Lap·land /láplənd/ region largely within the Arctic Circle, extending across the northern parts of Norway, Sweden, Finland, and the Kola Peninsula of Russia —**Lap·lan·der** *n.*

La Pla·ta /laa plaá taa/ city and capital of Buenos Aires Province, eastern Argentina. Population: 520,647 (1991).

Lapp /lap/ *n.* (*offensive*) **1.** PEOPLES **OFFENSIVE TERM** an offensive term for a member of the Sami people of northern Europe **2.** LANG **OFFENSIVE TERM** a name now considered offensive for the language of the Sami [Late 16thC. From Swedish, of uncertain origin.] —**Lapp** *adj.*

lapped joint *n.* = **lap joint**

lap·pet /láppət/ *n.* **1.** CLOTHES **FOLD OR FLAP ON CLOTHING** a loose fold or flap of clothing on a garment **2.** ZOOL **LOOSE FLESHY PART** a lobe or hanging flap of flesh such as a cow's dewlap or the wattle on a bird's head [15thC. Formed from LAP[1] + -ET.]

lap·pet moth *n.* a large purplish-brown moth whose furry larvae have flaps along their sides. Latin name: *Gastropacha quercifolia.*

lap robe *n.* a small rug that wraps around the knees

lapse /laps/ *n.* **1. ERROR** a momentary fault or failure in behavior or morality **2. GAP IN CONTINUITY** a break in the continuity of something **3. PERIOD** a passage of time **4.** LAW **FAILURE TO ACT IN TIME** a failure to exercise a right within a specified period of time, e.g., the failure to buy a property before the termination of an option to buy ■ *vi.* **(lapsed, laps·ing, laps·es) 1. GRADUALLY COME TO A STOP** to come to an end or stop doing something gradually **2.** LAW **BECOME VOID** to become null and void through disuse, negligence, or death **3. DECLINE** to decline in value, quality, or conduct ○ *Their standards have lapsed.* **4. LOSE SIGNIFICANCE** to decline gradually, becoming less important **5.** = **elapse** [14thC. From Latin *lapsus* "falling, failure," from the past participle stem of *labi* "to fall, slip" (source of English *collapse*).] —**laps·a·ble** *adj.* —**laps·er** *n.* ◇ **lapse from grace** a failure in moral conduct or religious belief

lapse into *vi.* **1. SLIDE INTO A CONDITION** to revert to a previous state, especially of quiet or inactivity **2. RETURN TO PREVIOUS HABITS** to revert to a previous habit or way of life, often an undesirable one

lapsed /lapst/ *adj.* **1. NO LONGER FAITHFUL TO SOMETHING** no longer committed to something, especially religious faith or observance **2. EXPIRED** expired or terminated

lapse rate *n.* the rate at which the temperature of the atmosphere falls as altitude increases

lap·strake /láp stràyk/ *adj.* = **clinker-built** ■ *n.* **CLINKER-BUILT BOAT** a boat built with overlapping planks [Late 18thC. From LAP[2] + STRAKE.]

Lap·tev Sea /láptef-/ a section of the Arctic Ocean, situated off the northern coast of Siberian Russia

lap·top /láp tòp/ *n.* a small portable personal computer, especially a battery operated one, usually consisting of a hinged outer case that opens to reveal a screen set in the upper part and a compact keyboard set in the lower part. ◊ **palmtop, notebook**

La Pu·en·te /laá pōōéntee/ city in Los Angeles County, southwestern California, situated northeast of Long Beach. Population: 36,955 (1990).

La·pu·tan /lə pyōōt'n/ *adj.* concentrating on absurdly impractical ideas or projects, often to the exclusion of things that need to be done [Mid-19thC. Formed from *Laputa*, an island in Jonathan Swift's *Gulliver's Travels* where the inhabitants were given to unrealistic, fanciful hopes and plans.]

lap·wing /láp wing/ (*plural* **-wings** *or* **-wing**) *n.* a bird in the plover family that has a long crest and spurs and is noted for its shrill cry and erratic flight. Genus: *Vanellus.* [Old English *hleapewince* (altered by folk etymology), literally "leaping from side to side," from LEAP + an assumed word that is also the ancestor of *wink*]

La Quin·ta /laa kwíntə/ city in Riverside County, southern California. Population: 17,241 (1990).

lar /laar/ (*plural* **lar·es** /láireez, laáreez/) *n.* a protective god or a statue of a protective god in an ancient Roman household [Late 16thC. From Latin.]

Lar·a·mie /lárrəmee/ city in Albany County, southeastern Wyoming. It is the site of the University of Wyoming. Population: 26,687 (1990).

lar·bo /laár bō/ *n.* molasses cooled in snow (*regional*)

WORD KEY: REGIONAL NOTE

Larbo is an old-fashioned New Hampshire term.

lar·board /laár bàwrd, -bərd/ *n.* the port or left side of a vessel (*archaic*) [Late 16thC. Alteration of *laddeborde*, literally "loading side."]

lar·ce·ny /laársənee/ *n.* the unlawful taking and removal of another person's property [15thC. Via Anglo-Norman, from, ultimately, Latin *latrocinium*, "theft, robbery," from *latro*, "thief," from Greek *latron*, "pay, wages."] —**lar·ce·ner** *n.* —**lar·ce·nist** *n.* —**lar·ce·nous** *adj.* —**lar·ce·nous·ly** *adv.*

WORD KEY: SYNONYMS

See Synonyms at ***theft***.

larch /laarch/ (*plural* **larch·es** *or* **larch**) *n.* **1. TREE OF PINE FAMILY** a deciduous tree of the pine family that has clusters of leaves resembling needles and egg-shaped cones. Genus: *Larix.* **2. LARCH WOOD** the durable wood of the larch tree [Mid-16thC. Via Middle High German *larche*, from, ultimately, Latin *larix*.]

larch saw·fly *n.* a small insect resembling a wasp and native to northern forests where its larvae are infamous for defoliating large stands of larches. Latin name: *Nematus erichsonii.*

lard /laard/ *n.* **WHITE COOKING FAT** white, slightly soft, rendered pork used in cooking and baking, and as a base in some ointments and perfumes ■ *v.* **(lard·ed, lard·ing, lards) 1.** *vti.* **ADD LARD TO MEAT BEFORE COOKING** to thread strips of fat or fatty bacon through holes made in a lean cut of meat to keep the meat moist while cooking **2.** *vt.* **INCLUDE EXTRA WORDS** to include an unnecessary or undesirable amount of additional material in a speech or piece of writing [14thC. From French *lard*, "bacon," from Latin *lar(i)dum*.]

lar·der /laárdər/ *n.* **1. FOOD STORAGE PLACE** a cool place, especially a small room or large cupboard, used for storing food **2. FOOD SUPPLY** a supply of food [13thC. Via Anglo-Norman from , ultimately, Latin *lar(i)dum* "lard."]

lar·der bee·tle *n.* a small beetle whose larvae eat dried meats, cheese, and other animal products. Genus: *Dermestes.*

lard·ing nee·dle *n.* a long thick metal needle that grips one end of a strip of fat to allow it to be threaded through lean meat to keep it moist while cooking

Lard·ner /laárdnər/, **Ring** (1885–1933) U.S. humorist and writer. He is known for his satirical short stories. Full name **Ringgold Wilmer Lardner**

La·re·do /la reédō/ city in southern Texas, on the border with Mexico. Population: 149,914 (1994).

lar·ee /laáree/ *n.* **1.** see table at **currency** **2. COIN WORTH ONE LAREE** a coin worth one laree [Late 16thC. From Persian *lārī*, from *Lār*, the name of a town on the Persian Gulf.]

lar·es plural of **lar**

lar·es and pe·nates *npl.* **1. HOUSEHOLD GODS** the household deities of the ancient Romans. The lares were believed to protect the household from danger, while the penates were believed to bring wealth. **2. VALUABLES** a family's treasured or valuable possessions (*dated*) [Late 16thC. From Latin.]

large /laarj/ (**larg·er, larg·est**) *adj.* **1. VERY BIG** comparatively big in size, number, or quantity, or bigger in size, number, or quantity than is usual or expected **2. OF TALL HEAVY BUILD** tall and well-built, heavy set, broad, or overweight **3. SPACIOUS** occupying a comparatively big space or a bigger space than is usual or expected ○ *a large house* **4. IMPORTANT** significant or general in scope, extent, or effect ○ *a large view of the subject* **5. GENEROUS** generous in spirit or attitude **6.** NAUT **FAVORABLE** blowing in a favorable direction ○ *a large wind* **7. VULGAR** coarse or vulgar (*archaic*) [12thC. Via Old French from Latin *larga*, the feminine form of *largus*, "large, copious."] — **large·ness** *n.* ◇ **at large 1.** as a widely based and general group of people **2.** escaped or free and possibly dangerous ◇ **by and large** speaking generally

large cal·o·rie *n.* = **Calorie**

large-heart·ed *adj.* generous, kind, or understanding —**large-heart·ed·ness** *n.*

large in·tes·tine *n.* the end section of the alimentary canal reaching from ileum to anus, and consisting of the cecum, colon, and rectum. Its function is to extract water and form feces.

large·ly /laárjlee/ *adv.* **1. PRINCIPALLY** for the most part or mainly **2. ON A GRAND SCALE** on a big or grand scale

large-mind·ed *adj.* characterized by a liberal attitude —**large-mind·ed·ly** *adv.* —**large-mind·ed·ness** *n.*

large·mouth bass /laárj mowth-/ *n.* a large blackish-green freshwater bass of North America that has a large mouth extending behind the eye and is popular as a game fish. Latin name: *Micropterus salmoides.*

large-print *adj.* set in type that is bigger than normal for the benefit of partially sighted readers ○ *a large-print book*

larg·er-than-life *adj.* very confident, impressive, flamboyant, and likely to attract attention (*not hyphenated when used after a verb*)

large-scale *adj.* **1. BIG AND DETAILED** comparatively big in size and showing a lot of detail **2. EXTENSIVE** extensive in scope or scale

large-scale in·te·gra·tion *n.* the process of integrating a large number of circuits, often several thousand, on a silicon chip

lar·gesse /laar jéss/, **lar·gess** *n.* **1. GENEROSITY** the generous giving of gifts, money, or favors **2. GIFTS** the gifts, money, or favors given as a result of somebody's largesse **3. LIBERALITY** generosity or liberality, especially in spirit or attitude [13thC. Via French, from, ultimately, Latin *largus* (see LARGE).]

large-toothed as·pen *n.* a deciduous tree found in eastern North America. Latin name: *Populus grandidentanta.*

lar·ghet·to /laar géttō/ *adv.* **MODERATELY SLOWLY** at a fairly slow tempo, but slightly faster than largo (*used as a musical direction*) ■ *n.* (*plural* **-tos**) MUSIC **PIECE OF LARGHETTO MUSIC** a larghetto movement or musical piece [Early 18thC. From Italian, literally "little largo," from *largo* (see LARGO).] —**lar·ghet·to** *adj.*

larg·ish /laárjish/ *adj.* quite big, rather than enormous

lar·go /laár gō/ *adv.* **FAIRLY SLOWLY** at a fairly slow and broad tempo, more slowly than lento but faster than grave (*used as a musical direction*) ■ *n.* (*plural* **-gos**) **PIECE OF LARGO MUSIC** a largo movement or musical piece [Late 17thC. From Italian, literally "broad."] —**lar·go** *adj.*

lar·i·at /lérree ət/ *n.* **1.** = **lasso 2. ROPE FOR TETHERING AN ANIMAL** a tethering rope, especially one used to hold a grazing animal in one place [Mid-19thC. From Spanish *la reata*, "the rope," from *reatar*, "to tie again," utimately from Latin *aptare*, "to adjust, fit" (source of English *apt*).]

Lark

lark[1] /laark/ *n.* a small songbird with brownish plumage, found worldwide and noted for its song. Family: Alaudidae. [Old English *lāferce*, earlier *lǣwerce*, ultimately of unknown origin]

lark[2] /laark/ *n.* **1. MISCHIEVOUS ADVENTURE** adventurous or risky fun **2. AMUSING PRANK** a good-humored prank ■ *vi.* (**larked, lark·ing, larks**) **ACT MISCHIEVOUSLY** to behave in a mischievous, annoying, or irresponsible manner [Early 19thC. Origin uncertain: perhaps an alteration of obsolete *laik* "to play," via Old English *lācan* from prehistoric Germanic.]—**lark·ish** *adj.* —**lark·ish·ness** *n.* —**lark·y** *adj.*

lark·spur /laárk spùr/ *n.* any delphinium plant with spikes of pink, white, or blue flowers. Genus: *Delphinium.* [From the resemblance of the spurred flowers to the unusually long hind claws of the lark]

Lark·spur /laárk spùr/ city in Marin County, western California, situated approximately 280 mi./725 km northwest of San Francisco. Population: 11,070 (1990).

La Ro·chelle /laa rəshél/ seaport, tourist center, and capital of Charente-Maritime Department, Poitou-Charentes region, western France. Population: 71,117 (1990).

lar·ri·gan /lérrigən/ *n.* a knee-high boot with the leg part made of oiled leather, worn especially by lumberjacks, trappers, and woodsmen [Late 19thC. Origin uncertain: perhaps taken from the name of its first maker or wearer.]

lar·rup /lérrəp/ *vt.* (**-ruped, -rup·ing, -rups**) **BEAT SOMEBODY** to beat or flog a person or animal ■ *n.* **THRASHING** a blow, especially one delivered with a lot of force [Early 19thC. Origin uncertain.] —**lar·ru·per** *n.*

Larson /laárss'n/, **Gary** (*b.* 1950) U.S. cartoonist. His comic strip "The Far Side," dating from 1980, is characterized by whimsical, absurd, and macabre animal characters.

lar·um /lérrəm/ *n.* an alarm (*archaic*) [Mid-16thC. Variant of ALARM.]

lar·va /laárvə/ (*plural* **-vae** /-vee/ *or* **-vas**) *n.* **1.** INSECTS **IMMATURE INSECT** the wingless immature worm-shaped form of many insects that develops into a pupa or chrysalis before becoming an adult insect **2.** ZOOL **IMMATURE AMPHIBIAN OR FISH** the immature, early-stage form of frogs and other animals that undergo marked changes during metamorphosis [Mid-17thC. From Latin, "ghost, apparition, mask."] —**lar·val** *adj.*

lar·vi·cide /laárvə sīd/ *n.* a chemical used to kill larvae —**lar·vi·cid·al** /laárvə sīd'l/ *adj.*

laryng- *prefix.* = **laryngo-** (*used before vowels*)

la·ryn·ge·al /lə rínjee əl, lèrrən jeé əl, lə rínjəl/ *adj.* **1.** ANAT **RELATING TO THE LARYNX** belonging to, relating to, situated in, or affecting the larynx **2.** PHON **PRODUCED AT THE LARYNX** used to describe a speech sound produced in the region of the larynx ■ *n.* PHON **CONSONANT** a sound made in the region of the larynx, especially a sound similar to "/h/" that some linguists believe was used by speakers of Proto-Indo-European [Late 18thC. Formed from modern Latin *laryngeus*, from the stem *laryng-* (see LARYNX).] —**la·ryn·ge·al·ly** *adv.*

lar·yn·gec·to·my /lèrrən jéktəmee/ (*plural* **-mies**) *n.* the surgical removal of all or part of the larynx

la·ryn·ges plural of **larynx**

lar·yn·gi·tis /lèrrən jítiss/ *n.* inflammation of the larynx, usually accompanied by hoarseness and coughing —**lar·yn·git·ic** /lèrrən jítik/ *adj.*

laryngo- *prefix.* larynx ○ *laryngotomy* [Via modern Latin from Greek *larugg-*, the stem of *larugx*]

lar·yn·gol·o·gy /lèrrəng góllәjee/ *n.* a branch of medicine dealing with diseases and conditions of the larynx and vocal cords —**lar·yn·go·log·ic** /lə rìng gə lójjik/ *adj.* —**lar·yn·go·log·i·cal·ly** /-lójjik'lee/ *adv.* —**lar·yn·gol·o·gist** /lèrrəng góllәjist/ *n.*

la·ryn·go·phar·ynx /lə rìng gō férringks/ (*plural* **-pha·ryn·ges** /-fə rínjeez/ *or* **-phar·ynx·es**) *n.* the part of the throat immediately behind the voice box or larynx, and extending downward to the top of the gullet or esophagus

la·ryn·go·scope /lə ríng gə skōp/ *n.* a medical instrument consisting of a short metal or plastic tube fitted with a tiny light bulb, used when examining the larynx. Its most common use is for viewing the entrance to the larynx when inserting a breathing tube during surgery.

lar·yn·gos·co·py /lèrrəng góskəpee/ (*plural* **-pies**) *n.* an examination of the entrance to, or interior of, the larynx, for the purpose of diagnosis or to facilitate the passage of a tube through the larynx —**la·ryn·go·scop·ic** /lə rìng gə skóppik/ *adj.* —**la·ryn·go·scop·i·cal·ly** /-skóppikəlee/ *adv.* —**la·ryn·go·scop·ist** /lèrrəng góskəpist/ *n.*

la·ryn·go·to·my /lèrrəng góttəmee/ (*plural* **-mies**) *n.* a surgical procedure in which an incision is made in the larynx

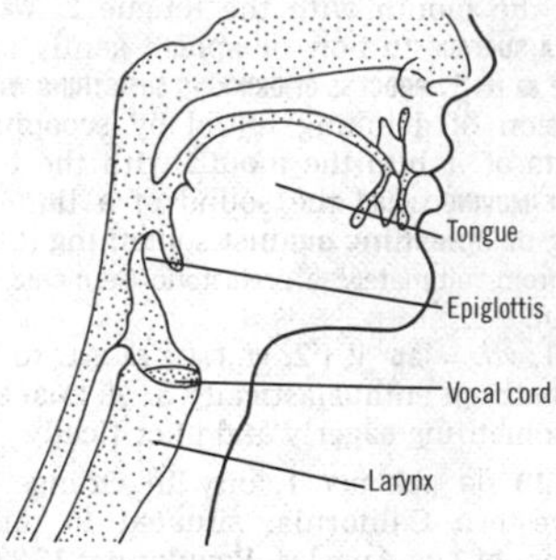

Larynx

lar·ynx /lérringks/ (*plural* **la·ryn·ges** /lə rín jeez/ *or* **lar·ynx·es**) *n.* the cartilaginous box-shaped part of the respiratory tract between the level of the root of the tongue and the top of the trachea. In humans and certain other air-breathing vertebrates it is the organ of voice production, containing the vocal cords. [Late 16thC. Via modern Latin, from Greek *larugx*.]

la·sa·gna /lə zaányə/ (*plural* **-gnas** *or* **-gne**), **la·sa·gne** (*plural* **-gnes** *or* **-gne**) *n.* **1. PASTA DISH** a dish of Italian origin consisting of alternate layers of pasta sheets and filling, especially alternating pasta, tomato sauce, cheese, and usually ground meat, baked in the oven. Various fish, poultry, or vegetable sauces or fillings may also be used. **2. SHEETS OF PASTA** thin flat sheets of fresh or dried pasta, which are generally layered with sauces or other ingredients, then baked [Mid-19thC. Via Italian, from, ultimately, Latin *lasanum*, "cooking vessel."]

La Salle /lə sál/ industrial city in La Salle County, north central Illinois, 51 mi./82 km northeast of Peoria. Population: 9,717 (1990).

La Salle, René Robert Cavelier, Sieur de (1643–87) French explorer. He navigated the Mississippi River to its mouth, and tried to colonize the area for France.

las·car /láskər/, **Las·car** *n.* an Indian or Southeast Asian sailor, army servant, or artilleryman (*dated*) [Early 17thC. From Persian and Urdu *laškarī* "soldier," from *laškar* "army, camp."]

Las Casas /laass kaássəss/, **Bartolomé de** (1474–1566) Spanish missionary. He was the first person to be ordained as a priest in America (1512). Known as **Apostle of the Indians**

Las·caux /la skṓ/ site of an underground cave, called Grotte de Lascaux, in southwestern France, that contains outstanding examples of Stone Age art

las·civ·i·ous /lə sívvee əss/ *adj.* **1. LEWD** showing a desire for, or unseemly interest in, sex **2. EROTIC** provoking or exciting lust [15thC. From late Latin *lasciviosus*, from, ultimately, Latin *lascivus* "lustful."] —**las·civ·i·ous·ly** *adv.* —**las·civ·i·ous·ness** *n.*

Las Cru·ces /laas kroóssiss/ city in southern New Mexico, situated north of El Paso, Texas, and Juarez, Mexico. Population: 74,779 (1996).

lase /layz/ (**lased, las·ing, las·es**) *vi.* to emit the type of single-wavelength radiation produced by a laser [Mid-20thC. Back-formation from LASER.]

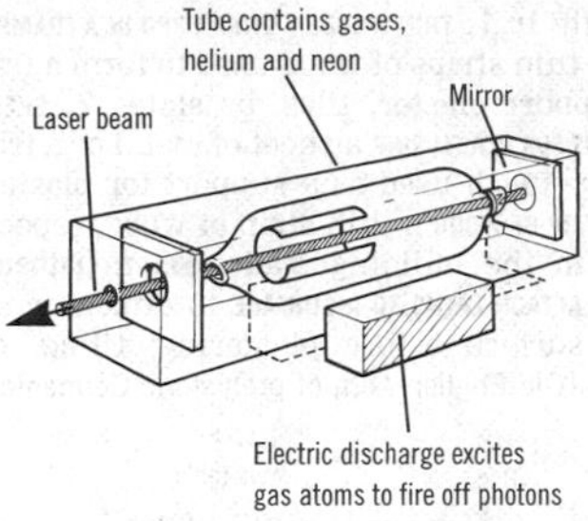

Laser

la·ser /láyzər/ *n.* a device that utilizes the ability of certain substances to absorb electromagnetic energy and re-radiate it as a highly focused beam of synchronized single-wavelength radiation [Mid-20thC. Acronym formed from *Light Amplification by Stimulated Emission of Radiation*.]

la·ser disk *n.* = **optical disk**

la·ser dop·pler flow·me·ter *n.* MED an instrument that measures blood flow through the arteries and veins, used to help detect narrowing of the arteries and the presence of blood clots

la·ser print·er *n.* a computer printer that uses a focused laser beam to place an image on a photosensitive drum, which uses an electrostatic charge to transfer the image to paper

lash[1] /lash/ *n.* **1. STROKE WITH A WHIP** a stroke with a whip or some other long flexible object, often one of several given as a punishment **2. EYELASH** an eyelash **3. MOVEMENT LIKE A WHIP** a movement like that of a whip being cracked ○ *The lion gave a lash of its tail.* **4. END OF A WHIP** the flexible end of a whip **5. SEVERE SCOLDING** a severe reproof or verbal attack ○ *He felt the full lash of his father's tongue.* **6. IMPACT OF SOMETHING** a strong or powerful, often continuous, impact of something, especially a natural element, against a surface ○ *the lash of waves onto the beach* ■ *v.* (**lashed, lash·ing, lash·es**) **1.** *vti.* **SMASH ONTO SOMETHING** to have a strong or powerful, often continuous, impact on a surface ○ *Heavy seas lashed the shore.* **2.** *vti.* **CRITICIZE SOMEBODY** to criticize somebody or something severely ○ *She lashed into her critics.* **3.** *vt.* **WHIP SOMEBODY** to hit somebody or something with a whip or an object like a whip, often repeatedly as a form of punishment ○ *Prisoners were lashed severely.* **4.** *vti.* **FLICK TO AND FRO** to flick something from side to side sharply so that it moves like a whip, or move in this way ○ *The cat lashed its tail angrily.* **5.** *vt.* **INCITE PEOPLE** to encourage strong emotion such as anger in others, especially in a crowd ○ *The fans had lashed themselves into a fever of enthusiasm.* [14thC. Origin uncertain: possibly an imitation of the sound made by a whip or rope swung through the air.] —**lash·er** *n.*

lash out *vi.* **1. SUDDENLY ATTACK VERBALLY** to attack somebody or something verbally and suddenly **2. SUDDENLY ATTACK PHYSICALLY** to start suddenly to attack somebody or something with uncontrolled movements

lash[2] /lash/ (**lashed, lash·ing, lash·es**) *vt.* to tie something tightly or securely to another object [15thC. Origin uncertain; perhaps from Low German.] —**lash·er** *n.*

lash·ing[1] /láshing/ *n.* **1. FLOGGING** a beating with a whip or something resembling a whip **2. SEVERE SCOLDING** a severe rebuke or critical attack

lash·ing[2] /láshing/ *n.* rope, string, or cord used for securing things

lash·ings /láshingz/ *npl. U.K.* generous or plentiful amounts of something

Lash·kar /lásh kaar/ city in Madhya Pradesh, central India

Las·kin /láskin/, **Bora** (1912–84) Canadian lawyer and judge. He served as chief justice of Canada (1973–84).

Las Pal·mas /laas paálməss/ city, seaport, and capital of Las Palmas Province, northeastern Grand Canary Island, Spain. Population: 342,030 (1991).

La Spe·zia /laa spéetseeə/ naval base, port city, and capital of La Spezia Province, Liguria Region, northwestern Italy. Population: 103,008 (1990).

lass /lass/ *n.* **1. YOUNG WOMAN** a girl or young woman (*sometimes considered offensive*) **2. GIRLFRIEND** a girlfriend or sweetheart [14thC. Origin uncertain: probably related to Old Norse *laskura* "unmarried."]

Las·sa fe·ver /laássə-/ *n.* an infectious, often fatal, viral disease of West Africa marked by high fever, muscle pain, ulcers of the mucous membranes, headaches, hemorrhaging, and heart and kidney failure [Late 20thC. Named for *Lassa*, Nigerian village where the disease first appeared.]

Las·sen Vol·can·ic Na·tion·al Park /làssən-/ national park in northeastern California, established in 1907. Its main feature is the volcanic Lassen Peak, 10,457 ft./3,187 m high. Area: 106,372 acres/43,049 hectares.

las·sie /lássee/ *n. N England, Scotland* a girl or young woman (*informal*) (*sometimes considered offensive*)

las·si·tude /lássi toòd/ *n.* a state of weariness accompanied by listlessness or apathy [15thC. Via French from Latin *lassitudo*, from *lassus* "weary."]

las·so /lássō, la soó/ *n.* (*plural* **-sos**) **ROPE WITH A SLIDING NOOSE** a long stiff piece of rope or cord with a sliding noose at one end, used especially for catching horses and cattle ■ *vt.* (**-soed, -soing, -sos**) **CAPTURE AN ANIMAL WITH A LASSO** to use a lasso or other length of rope to catch a horse, cow, or other animal [Mid-18thC. Via Spanish *lazo*, from Latin *laqueus* "noose" (source of English *lace*).] —**las·so·er** /lássō ər/ *n.*

last[1] /last/ CORE MEANING: a grammatical word indicating that something is the most recent or final of all ○ (adj) *She was married last April.* ○ (adj) *Johnny turned and took a last look at the band.* ○ (adv) *Allow me to apologize for the uncomfortable circumstances under which we last met.* ○ (adv) *He got to the meeting last.* ○ (pron) *Her new album's even better than the last.*

1. *adj., pron.* **MOST RECENT** occurring most recently ○ (adj) *I saw him last Tuesday.* ○ (pron) *This flood may turn out to be even worse than the last.* **2.** *adj., pron.* **AFTER ALL THE OTHERS** being or occurring after all the others ○ (adj) *He is believed to be the last person to see her before she left.* ○ (pron) *Your first complaint may well be your last.* **3.** *adj., pron.* **ONLY REMAINING** the final or only person, thing, or part remaining ○ (adj) *This machine just ate my last dollar!* ○ (pron) *Here – finish up the last of the cake.* **4.** *adj., pron.* **LEAST SUITABLE** least suitable, appropriate, or likely ○ (adj) *She's the last person we want on this project.* ○ (pron) *I am the last to criticize you in any way.* **5.** *adj.* **RELATING TO THE END** relating to the end of somebody's life ○ *The priest performed the last rites.* **6.** *adv.* **MOST RECENTLY** on the most recent occasion ○ *When I last spoke to them they sounded fine.* **7.** *adv.* **AFTER ALL THE OTHERS** after all the others in a series or order **8.** *adv.* **FINALLY** as the final point ○ *Last, I'd like to mention all the people who helped to make this evening a success.* **9.** *n.* **FINAL MOMENT** the final moment, especially of life ○ *She remained cheerful to the last.* [Old English *latost* (adv.) "after all the others," of prehistoric Germanic origin] ◇ **at last** finally or in the end ○ *I've found you at last – I've been looking everywhere.* ◇ **at long last** eventually, after a long delay or many difficulties ○ *They fought the case for years and at long last got some compensation.* ◇ **breathe your last** to die ○ *I was by her side when she breathed her last.* ◇ **every last** everything without exception ○ *They ate it up, every last piece of it.* ◇ **last but not least** the final thing to be mentioned but important nevertheless ○ *And of course, last but not least, we thank the staff of customer relations.* ◇ **the last of somebody** *or* **something 1.** the last remaining person, thing, or part of something, or the last in a sequence ○ *That's the last of the bread – I'll get some more tomorrow.* **2.** somebody's final contact with or news of somebody or something ○ *You haven't heard the last of this – I'm going to complain.*

WORD KEY: CULTURAL NOTE

The Last of the Mohicans, a novel by writer James Fenimore Cooper (1826). The most popular of Cooper's evocative accounts of frontier life, it is set in mid-18th-century North America during the wars between Britain and France. It describes the attempts of frontiersman Hawkeye and his Mohican companions, Chingachook and Uncas, the last of their people, to protect a British family from the French and their Huron allies.

last[2] /last/ (**last·ed, last·ing, lasts**) *vti.* to continue to be used or available for a period of time ○ *The provisions lasted for ten days.* ○ *The fruit lasted us a week.* [Old English *læstan* "to last, follow." The underlying idea is of following a track.]

last out *vt.* **1. BE SUFFICIENT FOR SOMETHING** to be an adequate supply for a particular length of time ○ *I think we've got enough food to last out the week.* **2. REMAIN ALIVE** to survive for a particular length of time ○ *The vet said she didn't think Prince would last out the night.*

last[3] /last/ *n.* a wooden or metal block shaped like a human foot that a shoemaker or cobbler uses for making and repairing footwear [Old English *lǣste*, from *lāst* "sole of the foot, footprint," from a prehistoric Germanic verb meaning "to follow," which is also the ancestor of *last*[2]]

last[4] /last/ *n. U.K.* a unit of measurement that has different values in different contexts including the values of 80 bushels and two tons [Old English *hlæst*, "load"]

last-born *adj.* **YOUNGEST** youngest in a particular family ■ *n.* **YOUNGEST CHILD** the youngest in a particular family

last call *n.* a bartender's request for last drink orders before closing time (*informal*)

last-ditch *adj.* done or taken when all other options have been exhausted

last-gasp *adj.* done as a last measure when all other options have failed

last hur·rah *n.* a final appearance, performance, or effort [Mid-20thC. Taken from *The Last Hurrah*, title of a novel by Edwin O'Connor.]

last-in, first-out *n.* ACCT a method of accounting in which it is assumed that the most recently purchased items in an inventory are the first to be sold

last·ing /lásting/ *adj.* **PERMANENT** continuing for a very long time or indefinitely ■ *n.* **SHOE MATERIAL** a strong durable twill fabric, mostly used for the uppers of shoes —**last·ing·ly** *adv.* —**last·ing·ness** *n.*

Last Judg·ment *n.* = **Judgment Day**

last·ly /lástlee/ *adv.* as the final thing at the end of a series

last min·ute *n.* the latest time that it is possible to do something and still be in time —**last-min·ute** *adj.*

last name *n.* = **surname**

last or·ders *npl., interj. U.K.* = **last call**

last re·sort *n.* something tried or done when everything else has failed

last rites *npl.* **1. ROMAN CATHOLIC CEREMONY FOR SOMEBODY DYING** in the Roman Catholic Church, religious rites performed for somebody who is close to death **2. RELIGIOUS BURIAL RITES** in Christianity, religious rites accompanying a burial or funeral

last spike, Last Spike *n.* the final section completing a rail line, symbolized by the final spike driven to secure the rails

last straw *n.* a minor annoyance that, because it comes at the end of a series of other misfortunes, turns out to be the thing that makes a situation unbearable [From the fable of the camel whose back was broken by the last straw added to its load]

Last Sup·per *n.* the last meal that Jesus Christ ate with his disciples before his crucifixion, commemorated by Christians in the Communion ceremony

last word *n.* **1. FINAL REMARK IN A DISCUSSION** the final thing to be said, especially at the end of an argument, disagreement, or discussion **2. ULTIMATE DECISION** the final decision on something **3. BEST** the best of its kind ○ *the last word in convenience*

Las Ve·gas /laas váygəss/ city in southern Nevada, a center for tourism and gambling. It is famous for the extravagant neon-lighted resort hotels, casinos, and bars that line its main street, known as "The Strip." Population: 327,878 (1994).

lat. *abbr.* latitude

Lat. *abbr.* **1.** Latin **2.** Latvia **3.** Latvian

Lat·a·ki·a /làttə keé ə/ city and seaport, capital of Latakia Governorate, northwestern Syria. Population: 303,000 (1994).

latch /lach/ *n.* **1. DEVICE FOR KEEPING DOORS SHUT** a device for holding a door, gate, or other opening closed consisting of a movable or liftable bar that drops into a hole or notch **2. DOOR LOCK** a door lock that needs a key to be opened from the outside but not the inside ■ *vt.* **(latched, latch·ing, latch·es) LOCK SOMETHING WITH A LATCH** to close or lock something with a latch [Old English *læccan,* "to grasp, clasp, seize." Ultimately from an Indo-European word that is also the ancestor of English *lasso.*]

latch onto *vt.* (*informal*) **1. GET** to get hold of something **2. REMAIN CONSTANTLY IN SOMEBODY'S COMPANY** to remain constantly in somebody's company even if the person would prefer other company or solitude **3. BECOME INTERESTED IN SOMETHING** to become particularly interested in something

latch·et /láchət/ *n.* a leather thong for tying a shoe or sandal (*archaic*) [14thC. From Old French *lachet,* dialectal variant of *lacet,* literally "little string," from *laz* "string" (see LACE).]

latch·key /lách keé/ (*plural* **-keys**) *n.* a key for lifting a latch, especially one on an outside door or gate

latch·key child, latch·key kid *n.* a child who returns from school to an empty home because the adults in the family are still at work

latch·string /lách strìng/ *n.* a string attached to a latch and passed through a hole in a door to allow somebody to open it from the other side

late /layt/ *adj.* **(lat·er, lat·est) 1. AFTER AN EXPECTED TIME** happening or arriving after an expected or arranged time ○ *Hurry up or we'll be late!* **2. AFTER THE USUAL TIME** happening or done after the normal or usual time ○ *a late lunch* **3. NEAR THE END OF A PERIOD** near the end of a particular period of time ○ *The meeting is scheduled for late morning.* **4. INTO THE NIGHT** well into the evening or night ○ *It's late – time for bed.* **5. DEAD** having died, especially fairly recently ○ *my late grandfather* **6. UP UNTIL RECENTLY** having recently, but no longer, done something, lived somewhere, or belonged to a group or organization ○ *That reporter, late of the European bureau, is now moving to Southeast Asia.* **7. DONE TOWARD THE END OF A CAREER** produced near the end of somebody's career or life ○ *a late Degas* ■ *adv.* **(lat·er, lat·est) 1. NOT ON TIME** after an expected or arranged time ○ *He arrived late.* **2. BEYOND THE USUAL TIME** after the usual or normal time ○ *She had to work late.* **3. NEAR THE END OF A PERIOD** toward the end of a period of time ○ *These birds tend to nest late in the year.* **4. WELL INTO EVENING** at or until a point well into the evening or night ○ *Their flight is due late on Friday.* **5. RECENTLY** relatively recently ○ *She didn't pack her bags until as late as yesterday.* [Old English *læt.* Ultimately from an Indo-European word meaning "to let go," which is also the ancestor of English *let, liege,* and *lassitude.*] —**late·ness** *n.* ◇ **of late** recently

WORD KEY: USAGE

When to use ***late*** for the deceased. In obituaries or death announcements the person in question is hardly ever described as *the late*. ... Nor is it usual for somebody who died centuries ago to be described that way. In references to a deceased person, when is it time to start and stop using ***late***? The word's purpose is to serve as a reminder that the person in question is no longer living. In an obituary, that much is obvious, so ***late*** is not needed. Nor is it needed in historical contexts, except to indicate that somebody was dead by a given time: *By 1800 Thomas Jefferson's late wife, Martha....*

WORD KEY: SYNONYMS

See Synonyms at ***dead***.

late blight *n.* a disease of potatoes, caused by a fungus, in which both tubers and foliage decay

late·com·er /làyt kúmmər/ *n.* **1. SOMEBODY ARRIVING LATE** somebody who arrives late for an event **2. RECENT CONVERT** somebody who has participated in or started appreciating something only recently

late de·vel·op·er *n.* a child whose potential in some or all aspects of school work develops later than is the case for the majority of his or her contemporaries

la·teen /lə teén, la-/ *adj.* used to describe a triangular sail hung on a yard attached to a small mast, or a ship with such a sail [Mid-16thC. From French *(voile) latine,* literally "Latin (sail)," ultimately from Latin *latinus,* so called because it was used in the Mediterranean.]

la·teen-rigged *adj.* using a lateen sail

late Greek *n.* the form of the Greek language used from around the 3rd to the 9th centuries A.D.

late He·brew *n.* the form of the Hebrew language used from around the 12th to the 18th centuries A.D.

late Lat·in *n.* the written form of Latin used from around the 3rd to the 7th centuries A.D.

late·ly /láytlee/ *adv.* within the last few days or weeks or not too long ago

lat·en /láyt'n/ **(-ened, -en·ing, -ens)** *vti.* to grow late, or make something late

la·ten·cy /láyt'nsee/ *n.* the state or condition of being latent

la·ten·cy pe·ri·od *n.* = **latent period**

La Tène /la tén/ *adj.* ARCHEOL relating to an Iron-Age culture that flourished in Europe from the fifth to the first century B.C. [Late 19thC. Named for *La Tène,* the district in Switzerland where the remains were first found.]

la·tent /láyt'nt/ *adj.* **1. HIDDEN** present or existing, but in an underdeveloped or unexpressed form **2.** BIOL **DORMANT** dormant or undeveloped but able to develop normally under suitable conditions **3.** PSYCHOANAL **PRESENT BUT UNEXPRESSED** present in the unconscious but not consciously expressed [Early 17thC. From Latin *latent-,* present participle stem of *latere,* "to be hidden."]

la·tent con·tent *n.* the content of a dream that is hidden or repressed, and is represented in symbols

la·tent heat *n.* the heat that is absorbed or emitted when a substance undergoes a physical phase change but that does not make the substance change temperature. Symbol *L*

la·tent im·age *n.* the invisible image recorded on light-sensitive materials such as photographic film or paper but not yet developed

la·tent pe·ri·od *n.* **1.** PHYSIOL **TIME BETWEEN STIMULUS AND RESPONSE** the interval between the application of a stimulus and the start of a response **2.** MED **DISEASE INCUBATION PERIOD** the incubation period of a disease **3.** PSYCHOANAL **THEORETICAL CHILDHOOD DEVELOPMENTAL STAGE** in Freudian theory, a period between five or six years of age and adolescence when sexual interest is suppressed

la·tent print *n.* a fingerprint that is left at a crime scene and remains invisible until chemically treated

lat·er /láytər/ comparative of **late** ■ *adv.* **AFTER** after a particular period of time, the present time, or the time being discussed

lat·er·al /láttərəl/ *adj.* **1. AT THE SIDE** belonging to, relating to, located at, or affecting the side **2. SIDEWAYS IN A CAREER, RATHER THAN UP** involving transfer to a different position in an organization or career, but without greater status or advancement **3.** PHON **PRODUCED WITH AN INCOMPLETE OBSTRUCTION OF AIR** produced with the tip of the tongue touching the alveolar ridge so that air moves around the outside of one or both sides of the tongue. The only lateral sound in English is /l/. ■ *n.* **1. PART AT THE SIDE** a part, appendage, movement, or object at the side of something **2.** PHON **LATERAL SPEECH SOUND** a lateral speech sound such as /l/ in English **3.** FOOTBALL **SIDEWAYS OR BACKWARD FOOTBALL PASS** a sideways or backward pass in football ■ *vti.* **(-aled, -al·ing, -als)** FOOTBALL **PASS A BALL SIDEWAYS** to pass the ball sideways or backward in football [15thC. From Latin *lateralis,* from *later-,* stem of *latus* "side."] —**lat·er·al·ly** *adv.*

lat·er·al bud *n.* a bud that develops in the angle between a leaf and a stem

lat·er·al·i·za·tion /làttərəli záysh'n/ *n.* the localization of the control center for a particular function, e.g., speech, on the right or left side of the brain

lat·er·al line *n.* a line of sensory pores along the head and sides of fish and some amphibians that detect pressure, current variations, and vibrations

lat·er·al think·ing *n.* a way of solving problems by unconventional or apparently illogical means rather than using a traditionally logical approach

lat·er·ite /láttə rìt/ *n.* a reddish mixture of clayey iron and aluminium oxides and hydroxides formed by the weathering of basalt under humid, tropical conditions. There are extensive deposits in India. [Early 19thC. Coined from Latin *later* "brick" + -ITE.] —**lat·er·it·ic** /làttə ríttik/ *adj.*

lat·est /láytəst/ superlative of **late** ■ *adj.* **NEWEST** newest, most recent, or most up-to-date ■ *n.* **MOST UP-TO-DATE VERSION** the newest, most recent, or most up-to-date news, fashion, or version of something (*informal*)

la·tex /láy tèks/ (*plural* **-ti·ces** /-sèez/ *or* **-tex·es**) *n.* **1. PLANT SAP** a milky white liquid produced by some plants such as the rubber tree, whose sap is used to make rubber **2. MIXTURE OF PLASTIC PARTICLES IN WATER** a suspension of rubber or plastic (**polymer**) particles in water, used to make emulsion paints, adhesives, and other products [Mid-17thC. From Latin, "liquid, watery fluid."]

la·tex paint *n.* paint with a latex binder

lath /lath/ *n.* **1. THIN WOODEN STRIP USED IN A FRAMEWORK** one of the thin strips of wood used to form a framework to support plaster, tiles, or slates **2. SHEET OR WIRE SUPPORT FOR PLASTERING** a sheet of metal or a framework of wire mesh used as a support for plasterwork **3. THIN STRIP OF WOOD** a thin strip of wood, especially one used in the building trades ■ *vt.* **(lathed, lathing, laths) ATTACH LATHS TO A SURFACE** to attach or nail laths to a surface before plastering, tiling, or fixing slates [Old English *lætt,* of prehistoric Germanic origin]

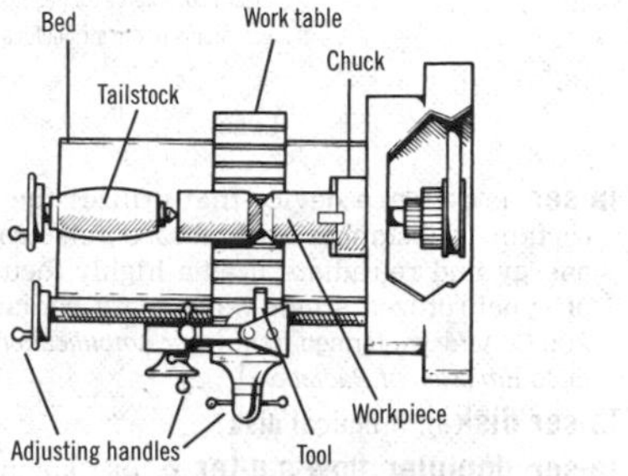

Lathe

lathe /layth/ *n.* **TURNING TOOL** a machine for working wood or metal, in which the piece being worked is held and rotated while a cutting tool is applied to it ■ *vt.* **(lathed, lath·ing, lathes) SHAPE SOMETHING WITH A LATHE** to shape wood or metal using a lathe [14thC. Origin uncertain: probably from Old Danish *lad,* "framework for supporting work."]

lath·er /láthər/ *n.* **1. SOAPY FROTH** foam that is produced by soap or detergent used with water **2. SWEATY FROTH** white foam produced during periods of extremely heavy sweating, especially by horses **3. AGITATED STATE** a state of agitation or nervous anxiety (*informal*) ■ *v.* **(-ered, -er·ing, -ers) 1.** *vti.* **PRODUCE LATHER** to produce a lather using a soap or detergent **2.** *vt.* **COAT WITH LATHER** to coat something with lather [Old English *lēaþor.* Ultimately from an Indo-European word meaning "to wash," which is also the ancestor of English *lotion, latrine,* and *deluge.*] —**lath·er·y** *adj.*

lath·y·rism /láthə rìzzəm/ *n.* a neurological disease of humans and domestic animals, caused by eating certain legumes and characterized by lack of strength in or inability to move the legs. The legumes responsible for the disease are of the genus *Lathyrus.* [Late 19thC. Formed from modern Latin *Lathyrus,* genus name, from Greek *lathuros,* a species of vetch.]

la·ti·ces plural of **latex**

la·tic·i·fer /la tíssəfər/ *n.* a duct that produces latex in some plants [Early 20thC. From Latin *latici-,* the stem of *latex,* "liquid, watery fluid."] —**lat·i·cif·er·ous** /làtti síffərəss/ *adj.*

lat·i·fun·di·um /làttə fúndee əm/ (*plural* **-a** /-ə/) *n.* in ancient Rome, an agricultural estate, especially one that was worked by enslaved laborers [Mid-17thC. From Latin, from *latus* "broad" + *fundus* "landed estate."]

lat·i·go /láttə gō, laátə gō/ (*plural* **-gos** *or* **-goes**) *n.* a strap for tightening the girth on a Western saddle [Late 19thC. From Spanish, "strap, whip, cinch."]

Lat·in /látt'n/ *n.* **1.** LANG **ANCIENT ROMAN LANGUAGE** the extinct Indo-European language of ancient Rome and its empire, also adopted across medieval Europe as the language of education, government, law, the Church, the aristocracy, and cultured society. The Romance languages developed from Vulgar Latin, and its prominence during medieval times led to Latin-derived words entering the vocabularies of other European languages. **2.** PEOPLES **SOMEBODY FROM ANCIENT LATIUM** somebody who was born or lived in ancient Latium in western central Italy **3.** PEOPLES **SOMEBODY SPEAKING A ROMANCE LANGUAGE** somebody who speaks any of the languages derived from Latin, especially somebody living in Latin America or southern Europe ■ *adj.* **1.** LANG **OF THE LATIN LANGUAGE** relating to the Latin language **2.** PEOPLES **RELATING TO PEOPLE SPEAKING ROMANCE LANGUAGES** relating to any of the peoples using languages derived from Latin, especially those peoples living in Latin America or in southern Europe **3.** CHR **RELATING TO THE ROMAN CATHOLIC CHURCH** belonging or relating to the Roman Catholic Church **4.** LANG **WRITTEN IN THE ROMAN ALPHABET** written in or relating to the Roman alphabet [Pre-12thC. From Latin *Latinus* "of the people of Latium, Roman," from *Latium*, an ancient region of western central Italy.]

Lat·i·na /lə téenə/ *n.* a woman or girl of Latin American descent who was born in or is a citizen of the United States [Mid-20thC. From American Spanish, feminine of *Latino* (see LATINO).]

Lat·in al·pha·bet *n.* = **Roman alphabet**

Lat·in A·mer·i·ca **1.** the entire western hemisphere south of the United States **2.** those countries of the Americas that developed from the colonies of Spain, Portugal, and France

Lat·in A·mer·i·can *n.* **1. SOMEBODY FROM LATIN AMERICA** somebody who was born in or is a citizen of any of the countries of Latin America **2. LATIN AMERICAN LIVING IN U.S.** somebody of Latin American descent who was born in or is a citizen of the United States

La·tin-A·mer·i·can *adj.* relating to any of the countries of Latin America, or their peoples or cultures

Lat·in A·mer·i·can·ist *n.* somebody who is an expert in or is studying Latin America, especially its literature, culture, music, or history

Lat·in·ate /látt'n àyt/ *adj.* derived from, relating to, or characteristic of Latin

Lat·in Church *n.* = **Roman Catholic Church**

Lat·in cross *n.* an upright cross in which the lowest limb is longer than the other three, often associated with Christianity

Lat·in·ism /látt'n ìzzəm/ *n.* a word or phrase e.g., "ipso facto," that has been borrowed from Latin

Lat·in·ist /láttnist/ *n.* somebody who is an expert in or student of the Latin language

La·tin·i·ty /lə tínnətee/ *n.* a style or level of expertise in using Latin

Lat·in·ize /látt'n ìz/ (**-ized, -iz·ing, -iz·es**) *vt.* **1.** LANG **TRANSLATE SOMETHING INTO LATIN** to translate something into Latin, or give a Latin form to something such as a name **2.** LANG **TRANSCRIBE SOMETHING INTO THE ROMAN ALPHABET** to transcribe words into the Roman alphabet from another alphabet **3.** CHR **MAKE SOMETHING LIKE THE ROMAN CATHOLIC CHURCH** to adopt the practices of, or make practices more like those of, the Roman Catholic Church **4.** HIST **MAKE PEOPLE MORE ROMAN** to make people adapt to Roman customs and styles —**Lat·in·i·za·tion** /làtt'ni záysh'n/ *n.* —**Lat·in·iz·er** /látt'n ìzər/ *n.*

La·ti·no /lə tée nō/ (*plural* **-nos**) *n.* **1. SOMEBODY FROM LATIN AMERICA** somebody who was born in or is a citizen of any of the countries of Latin America **2. LATIN AMERICAN LIVING IN U.S.** somebody of Latin-American descent who was born in or is a citizen of the United States [Mid-20thC. From American Spanish, (perhaps via a shortening of *latinoamericano*), from Spanish, "Latin, a Latin," from Latin *Latinus* (see LATIN).]

Lat·in Quar·ter area in central Paris on the Left Bank of the Seine River, noted for educational and cultural pursuits

lat·ish /láytish/ *adj.* **FAIRLY LATE** fairly late, or later than is desirable or expected ○ *a latish supper* ■ *adv.* **AT A FAIRLY LATE TIME** at a fairly late time, or later than is desirable or expected ○ *They arrived latish.*

la·tis·si·mus dor·si /la tìssəməss dáwr sì/ (*plural* **la·tis·si·mi dor·si**) *n.* either of the two broad triangular muscles along the sides of the back [Shortening of modern Latin *musculus latissimus dorsi*, literally "broadest muscle of the back"]

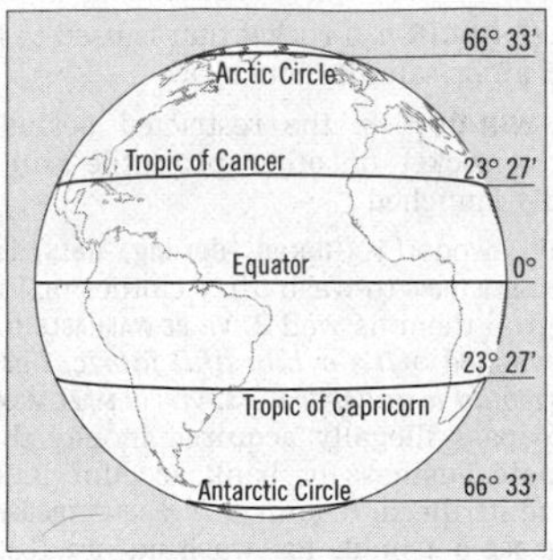

Latitude

lat·i·tude /láttə tòod/ *n.* **1.** GEOG **IMAGINARY LINE AROUND THE EARTH** an imaginary line joining points on the Earth's surface that are all of equal distance north or south of the equator. ◊ **longitude 2.** GEOG **AREA OF THE EARTH'S SURFACE** a region of the Earth's surface near a particular latitude (*often plural*) ○ *snow showers in the northerly latitudes.* ◊ **longitude 3. ROOM TO MANEUVER** enough scope or leeway for some freedom of choice, action, or thinking ○ *It's a very creative job, allowing me a great deal of latitude.* **4.** PHOTOGRAPHY **DEGREE OF TOLERANCE OF EXPOSURE ERROR** the degree of over- or underexposure that light-sensitive material can accommodate and still provide an acceptable image [14thC. From Latin *latitudo*, "breadth, width," from *latus* "broad."] —**lat·i·tu·din·al** /làttə tòod'nəl/ *adj.* —**lat·i·tu·di·nal·ly** *adv.*

lat·i·tu·di·nar·i·an /làttə tood'n érree ən/ *adj.* **TOLERANT** allowing some freedom in attitude, beliefs, behavior, or interpretation, especially in religious matters ■ *n.* **SOMEBODY TOLERANT** somebody who believes in or advocates a latitudinarian approach, especially in religious matters [Mid-17thC. Formed from Latin *latitudin-*, stem of *latitudo* (see LATITUDE).]

lat·ke /látkə/ *n.* a fried flat cake of grated potato made by moistening finely grated potato with beaten egg and frying it until golden brown on both sides. It is an Eastern European and particularly a Jewish specialty. [Early 20thC. From Yiddish, from, ultimately, Russian *latka*, "earthenware cooking vessel, something cooked in a latka."]

Latona /lə tṓnə/ *n.* MYTHOL in Roman mythology, the mother of Apollo and Diana by Jupiter. Greek equivalent **Leto**

lat·o·sol /láttə sàwl/ *n.* a soil variety that is common in tropical or subtropical regions and is rich in iron and aluminum [Mid-20thC. Coined from LATERITE + -SOL.]

la·trine /lə tréen/ *n.* a toilet, especially a communal one on a military base [13thC. From Latin *latrina*, contraction of *lavatrina* (see LAVATORY).]

Latrobe /lə trṓb/, **Benjamin Henry** (1764–1820) British-born U.S. architect. He designed and rebuilt part of the Capitol building in Washington, D.C. (1803 and 1814).

-latry *suffix.* worship ○ *iconolatry* [From Greek *latreia* "service, worship"]

lat·te /laá tə/ *n.* an espresso coffee with frothy steamed milk

lat·ter /láttər/ *n.* **SECOND OF TWO** the second of two people or things that have been mentioned, or that are being considered or referred to ○ *She went out with Joe and Sam, eventually marrying the latter.* ◊ **former** ■ *adj.* **1. CLOSING** near the end of something, or nearer to the end than the beginning ○ *spent the latter part of the day relaxing by the pool* **2. LATER** more recent or more advanced in time ○ *In his latter years he became very forgetful.* [Old English *lætra* (adjective) and *lator* (adverb), comparatives of *læt*, an earlier form of LATE]

lat·ter-day *adj.* resembling a particular person or type of person from the past ○ *thought of himself as a latter-day Roosevelt*

Lat·ter-day Saint *n.* a member of the Church of Jesus Christ of Latter-day Saints, founded by Joseph Smith in 1830 and centered in Salt Lake City, Utah

lat·ter·ly /láttərlee/ *adv.* recently, or in the most recent period ○ *He was quite ill for a while, but latterly seems to have returned to normal.*

lat·tice /láttiss/ *n.* **1. CRISS-CROSS FRAMEWORK** an interwoven open-mesh frame made by crisscrossing strips of wood, metal, or plastic to form a pattern **2. SOMETHING MADE FROM LATTICE** something such as a door, gate, or fence that is made from or consists of a lattice **3. INTERWOVEN FORM** a representation of a lattice framework, especially a heraldic one **4. ARRANGEMENT OF POINTS** a regular geometric arrangement of points or objects, e.g., the atoms in a crystal ■ *vti.* (**-ticed, -tic·ing, -tices**) **PROVIDE A LATTICE** to make, decorate something with, or provide a lattice [14thC. From Old French *lattis*, from *latte* "lath," from a prehistoric Germanic word.]

lat·tice·work /láttəs wurk/ *n.* = **lattice** *n.* 1

La Tuque /lə tòok/ resort town with a hydroelectric power station in Quebec Province, eastern Canada, situated northwest of Quebec City. Population: 13,165 (1996).

Latvia

Lat·vi·a /laátvee ə/ republic bordering the Baltic Sea in northeastern Europe. It is one of the Baltic States. Language: Latvian. Currency: lat. Capital: Riga. Population: 2,421,163 (1997). Area: 24,600 sq. mi./63,700 sq. km. Official name **Republic of Latvia**

Lat·vi·an /látvee ən/ *n.* **1.** PEOPLES **SOMEBODY FROM LATVIA** somebody who was born or raised in, or who is a citizen of Latvia **2.** LANG **OFFICIAL LANGUAGE OF LATVIA** the official language of Latvia, also spoken in western parts of European Russia, belonging to the Balto-Slavic branch of Indo-European languages. Latvian is spoken by about two million people. —**Lat·vi·an** *adj.*

laud /lawd/ *vt.* (**laud·ed, laud·ing, lauds**) **PRAISE SOMEBODY** to glorify somebody or praise somebody highly ■ *n.* **1. GREAT PRAISE** high praise, acclaim, or glorification (*formal*) **2.** MUSIC **SONG OF PRAISE** a hymn of praise or glorification **3.** CHR **MORNING PRAYER** the first prayer of the day in some Christian churches, especially the Roman Catholic Church (*often used in the plural*) [14thC. From Old French *laude*, from Latin *laud-*, the stem of *laus*, "praise."] —**laud·er** *n.*

laud·a·ble /láwdəb'l/ *adj.* admirable and worthy of praise —**laud·a·bil·i·ty** /làwdə bíllətee/ *n.* —**laud·a·ble·ness** /láwdəb'lnəss/ *n.* —**laud·a·bly** /láwdəblee/ *adv.*

lau·da·num /láwd'nəm/ *n.* a solution of opium in alcohol, formerly used to treat pain [Mid-16thC. Origin uncertain: perhaps from Latin *ladanum*, "juice of a shrub."]

laud·a·tion /law dáysh'n/ *n.* great praise and acclaim, often in the form of a eulogy (*formal*)

laud·a·to·ry /láwdə tàwree/, **laud·a·tive** /láwdətiv/ *adj.* expressing praise or admiration

Lau·der·dale Lakes /làwdər dàyl-/ city in Broward County, southeastern Florida. Population: 27,341 (1990).

laugh /laf/ *v.* (**laughed, laugh·ing, laughs**) **1.** *vti.* **MAKE SOUNDS EXPRESSING AMUSEMENT** to make sounds from the throat while breathing out in short bursts or gasps as a way of expressing amusement **2.** *vt.* **BRING TO PARTICULAR STATE BY LAUGHING** to cause somebody or yourself to be in a particular state by laughing long and hard ○ *We both laughed ourselves silly.* **3.** *vi.* **MOCK** to mock somebody or something **4.** *vi.* **SHOW CONTEMPT** to express amusement, contempt, or disrespect for something ○ *laugh in the face of adversity* **5.** *vi.* ZOOL **MAKE A NOISE LIKE LAUGHTER** to make a noise that sounds like somebody laughing (*refers to some birds and mammals*) ■ *n.* **1. SOUND MADE WHEN LAUGHING** a series of sounds made when somebody laughs **2. SOMETHING FUNNY OR ENJOYABLE** a time of great fun and enjoyment, or something that gives fun and enjoyment (*informal*) ○ *had a real laugh with Bob and Patty* **3. SOMEBODY FUNNY** somebody who is funny or entertaining ○ *You'll like him; he's a real laugh.* [Old English *hlæhhan*] —**laugh·er** *n.* ◇ **have the last laugh** to be proved right or successful after being treated with disbelief, lack of confidence, or scorn

laugh down *vt.* to reject something with contemptuous laughter ○ *The entire committee laughed down the new design.*

laugh off *vt.* to trivialize or treat as amusing something serious or important ○ *Later we laughed the incident off as just a silly mistake.*

laugh·a·ble /láffəb'l/ *adj.* so inadequate as to cause laughter or ridicule —**laugh·a·bly** *adv.*

laugh·ing gas *n.* = **nitrous oxide** (*informal*)

laugh·ing gull *n.* a common black-headed gull found from eastern North America to northern South America that has a high-pitched song resembling a human laugh. Latin name: *Larus atricilla.*

laugh·ing jack·ass *n.* = **kookaburra** (*dated*)

laugh·ing·ly /láffinglee/ *adv.* with laughter that shows amusement or contempt at something or somebody funny or ridiculous ○ *She laughingly dismissed this idea and changed the subject.*

laugh·ing·stock *n.* somebody whose behavior has made him or her an object of ridicule or fun

laugh·ter /láftər/ *n.* **1.** ACT OF LAUGHING the sound or an act of laughing **2.** HAPPINESS EXPRESSED BY LAUGHING happiness or fun expressed by laughing [Old English *hleahtor*]

Laugh·ton /láwt'n/, **Charles** (1899–1962) British-born U.S. actor. He acted on stage and screen, winning an Academy Award for *The Private Life of Henry VIII* (1933).

laugh track *n.* recorded laughter added to the soundtrack of a radio or television program

launce /lawns/ *n.* = **sand launce** [Early 17thC. A variant of LANCE, from its slender shape.]

Launce·ston /láwn stən/ city and port in northern Tasmania, Australia, situated where the North Esk and South Esk rivers join to form the Tamar River. Population: 67,701 (1996).

launch[1] /lawnch/ *vt.* (**launched, launch·ing, launch·es**) **1.** SPACE TECH, MIL FIRE A ROCKET INTO THE AIR to send a rocket, missile, or spacecraft into the air or the upper atmosphere **2.** NAUT PUT A CRAFT TO SEA to push or put a vessel into the water so that it is ready to sail **3.** NAUT LAUNCH A SHIP FOR THE FIRST TIME to send a newly built vessel into the water for the first time, usually with a special ceremony **4.** BEGIN A CAMPAIGN to begin an attack, campaign, investigation, or other carefully planned activity ○ *The police have launched an investigation.* **5.** MARKETING PUT A PRODUCT ON SALE to put a new product on sale to the public and begin promoting it **6.** THROW SOMETHING WITH GREAT FORCE to throw or propel something, especially forcefully ■ *n.* **1.** MARKETING START FOR A NEW PRODUCT an occasion such as a party at which a new product is launched ○ *the launch of her new book* **2.** SPACE TECH, MIL TIME WHEN A ROCKET IS LAUNCHED the occasion when a rocket, missile, or spacecraft is launched **3.** NAUT TIME WHEN A SHIP IS LAUNCHED the occasion when a boat or ship is launched, especially for the first time **4.** START OF A CAMPAIGN the start of something, especially a carefully planned activity such as a military offensive, an investigation, or a campaign [14thC. From Anglo-Norman *launcher*, a variant of Old French *lancier*, "to wound with a lance, pierce," from *lance* (see LANCE).]

launch into *vt.* to begin a particular activity suddenly and enthusiastically ○ *The professor launched into yet another of his theories about how dinosaurs became extinct.*

launch[2] /lawnch/ *n.* **1.** LARGE MOTORBOAT a large powerful motorboat **2.** SMALL MOTORBOAT ON A LARGE SHIP a small motorboat carried on a large ship **3.** LARGEST BOAT ON AN OLD WARSHIP the largest boat formerly carried by a man-of-war [Late 17thC. From Spanish *lancha*, "pinnace," perhaps of Malay origin.]

launch com·plex *n.* a site containing the people and equipment needed for a rocket, missile, or spacecraft launch

launch·er /láwnchər/ *n.* a device or platform for firing something such as a rocket or missile

launch pad, **launch·ing pad** *n.* **1.** PLATFORM FOR LAUNCHING ROCKETS a platform, usually in a launch complex, from which a rocket, missile, or spacecraft is launched **2.** STARTING POINT FOR SUCCESS a starting point from which great or successful progress is made, e.g., in somebody's career

launch ve·hi·cle *n.* a rocket that is used to launch a spacecraft or satellite into space

launch win·dow *n.* the restricted period during which a rocket or other projectile can be successfully launched

laun·der /láwndər/ *v.* (**-dered, -der·ing, -ders**) **1.** *vt.* WASH AND IRON SOMETHING to wash dirty clothes or linen and, often, iron them as well **2.** *vi.* BE WASHABLE to be able to be washed ○ *It's a beautiful fabric, but I doubt that it would launder well.* **3.** *vt.* FIN MAKE MONEY APPEAR LEGAL to pass illegally acquired money through a legitimate business or bank account in order to disguise its illegal origins ■ *n.* MINING TROUGH USED FOR WASHING ORE a trough for washing ore [Late 16thC. From *launder* "somebody who washes linen," contraction of *lavender*, ultimately from Latin *lavare*, "to wash" (see LAVATORY).] —**laun·der·er** *n.*

laun·der·ette /làwndə rét/ *n.* a laundry, usually self-service, containing coin-operated washing and drying machines [Mid-20thC. Coined from LAUNDER + -ETTE.]

laun·dress /láwndrəss/ *n.* a woman who does washing and ironing, especially one who does other people's washing and ironing as a way of earning a living (*dated*) [Mid-16thC. Formed from *launder* "somebody who washes linen" (see LAUNDER).]

Laun·dro·mat /láwndrə màt/ a service mark for a self-service coin-operated commercial laundry

laun·dry /láwndree/ (*plural* **-dries**) *n.* **1.** DIRTY WASH dirty clothes or linen put aside to be washed and ironed **2.** CLEAN WASH freshly washed clothes or linen **3.** WASHING AND IRONING PLACE a place, especially a commercial establishment or a communal room in a building, where clothes and linen can be washed and ironed [Early 16thC. Shortening of obsolete *lavendry*, ultimately from Latin *lavare*, "to wash" (see LAVATORY).]

laun·dry list *n.* a lengthy list of items, usually things wanted or needed

Laun·fal /láwnfəl/ *n.* in the legend of King Arthur, one of the knights at the court

Laur·a·sia /lawráyzhə, -shə/ the northern part of the ancient continent of Pangaea, a hypothetical ancient landmass that included what would become North America, Greenland, northern and central Europe, and most of Asia

lau·re·ate /láwree ət/ *n.* **1.** AWARD WINNER somebody who has been awarded a prize or is recognized for outstanding achievement in the arts or sciences **2.** = **poet laureate** ■ *adj.* **1.** DESERVING HONOR deserving honor or distinction **2.** CROWNED WITH LAUREL crowned with laurel as a sign of honor (*literary*) **3.** MADE OF LAUREL made of laurel leaves or branches [14thC. From Latin *laureatus*, from *laurea* "laurel tree" from, ultimately, *laurus* (see LAUREL).] —**lau·re·ate·ship** *n.*

lau·rel /láwrəl/ *n.* **1.** PLANTS MEDITERRANEAN EVERGREEN TREE a small evergreen tree that grows in southern Europe and has glossy aromatic leaves and dark purple or black berries. Latin name: *Laurus nobilis.* **2.** PLANTS TREE OR SHRUB RESEMBLING LAUREL any tree or shrub whose leaves, aroma, or berries are similar to those of the laurel, e.g., the mountain laurel and cherry laurel **3.** HIST WREATH OF LEAVES the leaves of the laurel woven into a wreath and used as a mark of honor or victory in ancient times, e.g., to crown the winners of athletic events ■ **lau·rels** *npl.* HONOR FOR ACHIEVEMENT honor won for an achievement ■ *vt.* (**-reled** *or* **-relled, -rel·ing** *or* **-rel·ling, -rels**) **1.** CROWN WITH LAUREL to crown somebody with laurel as a sign of honor (*literary*) **2.** GIVE SOMEBODY AWARD to honor somebody with an award or prize [14thC. Via Old French *lorier* from Latin *laureola* "small laurel branch," from *laurus* "laurel tree."] ◇ **look to your laurels** to watch out that you do not lose a successful or winning position because of a better performance by somebody else ◇ **rest on your laurels** to be satisfied with your success and do nothing to improve on it

WORD KEY: REGIONAL NOTE

The term ***laurel*** identifies three different trees in the Eastern United States. From Massachusetts and Pennsylvania through Tennessee to Florida and westward to Mississippi, it may mean "magnolia." In the eastern states, it may mean "mountain laurel." In the Upper South, especially North Carolina, it may mean "rhododendron."

Lau·rel /láwrəl/ city in west central Maryland, on the Patuxent River, southwest of Baltimore and northeast of Washington, D.C. Population: 18,718 (1996).

Laurel and Hardy

Laurel, Stan (1890–1965) British-born U.S. comedian. His partnership with Oliver Hardy was the first Hollywood movie comedy duo. Laurel was the "thin one" whose clumsiness was always getting them into trouble. Real name **Arthur Stanley Laurel Jefferson**

Laurence /láwr'nss/, **Margaret** (1926–87) Canadian writer. Her novels, set in western Canada, are characterized by strong-minded women. Real name **Jean Margaret Wemyss**

Laurens /láwrənz/, **Henry** (1724–92) U.S. patriot. He led the Continental Congress (1777–78) and fought against the British.

Lau·ren·tian Moun·tains /law rènshən-/ range that runs north of the St. Lawrence River in southern Quebec Province, Canada. Height: 3,905 ft./1,190 m.

Lau·ren·tian Pla·teau = **Canadian Shield**

lau·ric ac·id /làwrik-/ *n.* a crystalline fatty acid found mainly in coconut and laurel oils and used in making soaps, insecticides, cosmetics, and lauryl alcohol. Formula: $C_{12}H_{24}O_2$. [Late 19thC. *Lauric* formed from modern Latin *Laurus*, genus name, from Latin, "laurel."]

Lau·ri·er /láwree ày/, **Sir Wilfrid** (1841–1919) Canadian lawyer, journalist, and statesman. He served as prime minister of Canada (1896–1911).

lau·ryl al·co·hol *n.* a crystalline solid that is insoluble in water and is used to make detergents. Formula: $C_{12}H_{27}O$. [Early 20thC. Coined from a shortening of *lauric* (see LAURIC ACID) + -YL.]

Lau·sanne /lō zán, lō zaán/ capital of Vaud Canton, western Switzerland, on Lake Geneva. Population: 123,266 (1994).

lav /lav/ *n. U.K.* a toilet (*informal*) [Early 20thC. Shortening of LAVATORY.]

la·va /laávə, lávvə/ *n.* **1.** MOLTEN ROCK FLOWING FROM A VOLCANO molten rock that flows from a volcano or from a fissure on land or on the ocean floor. The molten rock originates in the Earth's mantle. **2.** ROCK FULL OF SMALL AIR HOLES rock formed by the rapid cooling and hardening of lava. It usually has many small air holes caused by escaping volcanic gases. [Mid-18thC. Via Italian from Neapolitan dialect, of unknown origin.]

la·va·bo /le váy bō, lə vaá bō/ (*plural* **-boes**) *n.* **1.** **la·va·bo, La·va·bo** CHR RELIGIOUS RITUAL a priest's ritual washing of the hands and reciting from the Psalms during the Communion service in some Christian churches **2.** BASIN ATTACHED TO A WALL a basin with a water tank above attached to a wall, often used as a planter **3.** PLACE FOR WASHING IN A MONASTERY a place for washing in a monastery [Mid-18thC. From Latin, "I will wash," a form of *lavare* (see LAVATORY).]

lav·age /lə vaázh, lávvij/ *n.* the washing out of a hollow body organ, e.g., the stomach, using a flow of water [Late 18thC. Formed from French *laver* "to wash."]

La·val /lə vál/ city in Île-Jésus County, southern Quebec, Canada, situated on Île-Jésus just north of Montreal. Population: 330,393 (1996).

La·val, Francois-Xavier de Montmorency (1623–1708) French-born Canadian cleric. He was the first Roman Catholic bishop of Quebec (1659–85).

la·va-la·va *n.* a rectangular piece of printed cotton worn wrapped around the waist by the people of Samoa and other parts of Polynesia [Late 19thC. From Samoan.]

lav·a·liere /làvvə léer, laàvə-/ *n.* NECKLACE a pendant on a chain worn around the neck ■ *vt.* (**-liered, -lier·ing, -lieres**) GIVE A LAVALIERE TO SOMEBODY to give a lavaliere, especially one with the emblem of a fraternity, usually to a sweetheart as a symbol of attachment [Late 19thC. Named for Louise de *la Valière*, lover of Louis XIV, with whose reign certain fashions were associated.] —**lav·a·liered** *adj.*

lav·a·te·ra /làvə teérə, lə vaátərə/ (*plural* **-ras** *or* **-ra**) *n.* a plant or shrub such as the tree mallow with pink, white, or purple flowers that is native to Europe but naturalized in California. Genus: *Lavatera.* [Mid-18thC. From modern Latin, genus name, named for the brothers *Lavater*, 17th and 18thC Swiss doctors and naturalists.]

la·va·tion /lə váysh'n/ *n.* washing or cleansing (*formal*) [15thC. Formed from Latin *lavare* "to wash" (source of English *lotion, dilute,* and *deluge*).]

lav·a·to·ry /lávvə tàwree/ (*plural* **-ries**) *n.* **1. TOILET** a toilet or a small room containing a toilet **2. WASHROOM** a room or building with washing and toilet facilities **3. WASHBASIN** a bowl or basin with a faucet and drain [14thC. From late Latin *lavatorium*, from Latin *lavare* (see LAVATION).] —**lav·a·to·ri·al** /làvvə táwree əl/ *adj.*

lave /layv/ (**laved, lav·ing, laves**) *vt.* **1. WASH SOMETHING** to wash or bathe something (*archaic or literary*) **2. FLOW AGAINST** to lap or flow against something (*archaic or literary*) **3. SOOTHE SOMEBODY OR SOMETHING** to soothe somebody or something (*archaic or literary*) **4. POUR SOMETHING** to pour something out (*archaic*) [Pre-12thC. From Latin *lavare* "to wash."]

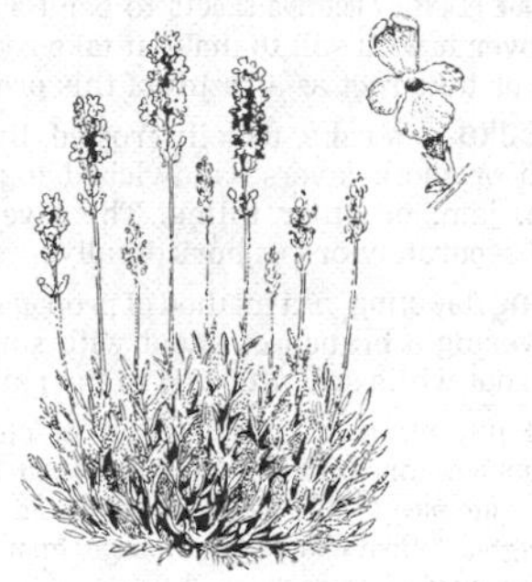

Lavender

lav·en·der /lávvəndər/ *n.* **1.** PLANTS **FRAGRANT PLANT** a plant that has clusters of fragrant bluish-purple flowers used in making a fragrant oil. Latin name: *Lavendula officinalis.* **2.** HOUSEHOLD **FLOWERS AND LEAVES** the dried flowers and leaves of the lavender plant used to perfume clothes and linen **3.** COLORS **PALE PURPLE COLOR** a pale purple color tinged with blue ■ *adj.* COLORS **PALE PURPLE** of a pale purple color tinged with blue [14thC. Via Anglo-Norman *lavendre* from medieval Latin *lavendula*, of uncertain origin: perhaps formed from *lividus* "bluish, livid."]

lav·en·der wa·ter *n.* perfume or toilet water made from the flowers of the lavender plant

la·ver1 /láyvər/ *n.* **1.** JUDAISM **JEWISH CEREMONIAL BASIN** a large basin in the temple in Jerusalem and in modern synagogues used for ritual washing **2. WASHBASIN** a basin to wash in (*archaic*) [14thC. Via Old French *laveor* from late Latin *lavatorium* (see LAVATORY).]

la·ver2 /láyvər/ *n.* a dried edible seaweed of the red algae family. Genus: *Porphyra.* [12thC. From Latin.]

La·ver /láyvər/, **Rod** (*b.* 1938) Australian tennis player. He is the only man to have won the tennis grand slam twice (1962 and 1969).

lav·ish /lávvish/ *adj.* **1. ABUNDANT** given or produced in abundance or to excess **2. GENEROUS** giving or spending generously or to excess ■ *vt.* (**-ished, -ish·ing, -ish·es**) **BE EXTRAVAGANT WITH SOMETHING** to give or spend something generously or to excess [15thC. From Old French *lavasse* "torrential rain," from *laver* "to wash, pour."] —**lav·ish·er** *n.* —**lav·ish·ly** *adv.* —**lav·ish·ness** *n.*

La·voi·sier /lə vwaá zyày, laav waa zyáy/, **Antoine Laurent** (1743–94) French chemist. He disproved the phlogiston theory of combustion and published the first proper table of the chemical elements. He was guillotined during the Reign of Terror.

law /law/ *n.* **1. BINDING OR ENFORCEABLE RULE** a rule of conduct or procedure recognized by a community as binding or enforceable by authority **2. PIECE OF LEGISLATION** an act passed by a legislature or similar body **3. LEGAL SYSTEM** the body or system of rules recognized by a community that are enforceable by established process ○ *You are forbidden by law to enter the premises.* **4. CONTROL OR AUTHORITY** the control or authority resulting from the observance and enforcement of a community's system of rules ○ *Nobody is above the law.* **5. BRANCH OF KNOWLEDGE** the branch of knowledge or study concerned with the rules of a community and their enforcement ○ *went to school to study law* **6. AREA OF LAW** the body of law relating to a particular subject or area **7.** = **common law 8. LAWYERS** the legal profession **9. LEGAL ACTION** legal action or proceedings **10. LAW ENFORCEMENT AGENT OR AGENCY** a person or organization responsible for enforcing the law, especially the police **11.** SCI **STATEMENT OF SCIENTIFIC TRUTH** a statement of a scientific fact or phenomenon that is invariable under given conditions ○ *the laws of physics* **12.** MATH **MATHEMATICAL PRINCIPLE** a general relationship that is assumed or proved to exist between expressions **13. GENERAL RULE OR PRINCIPLE** a general rule or principle that is thought to be true or held to be binding [Pre-12thC. From Old Norse *lög* "laws," from *lag* "something set down," from a prehistoric Germanic word meaning "to put," which is also the ancestor of English *lay.*] ◇ **be a law unto yourself** refuse to obey the rules, conventions, or suggestions made or upheld by others ◇ **lay down the law** to express an opinion in an overbearing or dogmatic way ◇ **take the law into your own hands** to try to obtain revenge or justice without involving the police, courts, or usual legal procedures

Law *n.* **1.** JUD-CHR **DIVINE WILL** the principles set out in the Bible, especially the Pentateuch, said to be the divine will. ◊ **Law of Moses, Mosaic Law 2.** JUDAISM = **Pentateuch**

law-a·bid·ing *adj.* voluntarily and habitually obeying the law

law and or·der *n.* **1. ENFORCEMENT OF LAW** the strict enforcement of the law (*hyphenated before a noun*) ○ *law-and-order issues* **2. SOCIAL STABILITY** the stability created by the observance and enforcement of the law within a community

law clerk *n.* somebody, often a student or novice lawyer, working as an assistant to a judge or lawyer

law court *n.* a court where legal cases are heard

law·ful /láwf'l/ *adj.* **1. PERMITTED BY LAW** not forbidden by the law **2. AUTHORIZED BY LAW** authorized or recognized by the law **3. OBEYING THE LAW** obeying or conforming to the law —**law·ful·ly** *adv.* —**law·ful·ness** *n.*

law·giv·er /láw givvər/ *n.* **1. SOMEBODY WHO GIVES LAWS TO A COMMUNITY** somebody who gives a code of laws to a people, e.g., from a source considered to be divine **2.** = **lawmaker**

law·less /láwləss/ *adj.* **1. UNREGULATED** uncontrolled or unregulated **2. AGAINST THE LAW** contrary to the law **3. WITHOUT LAW** having no laws —**law·less·ly** *adv.* —**law·less·ness** *n.*

law·mak·er /láw màykər/ *n.* somebody who drafts laws and causes them to be put into effect

law·man /láw màn, -mən/ (*plural* **-men** /-mèn, -mən/) *n.* an officer responsible for enforcing the law, e.g., a sheriff

law mer·chant *n.* the principles and rules governing commercial transactions, which originated in English common law and are codified in U.S. law

lawn1 /lawn/ *n.* an area of closely mowed grass, sometimes part of a yard [Mid-16thC. Alteration of *laund*, from Old French *launde* "wooded district, heath," from Celtic.]

lawn2 /lawn/ *n.* a fine light fabric used for clothing and household linen. It is usually made of cotton, sometimes mixed with polyester. [15thC. Named for *Laon*, town in France known for linen manufacture.] —**lawn·y** *adj.*

lawn bowl·ing *n.* a game played on a lawn in which the players roll balls toward a smaller target ball, trying to come as close as possible

Lawn·dale /láwn dàyl/ city in Los Angeles County, southwestern California, situated east of Manhattan Beach. Population: 27,331 (1990).

lawn mow·er *n.* a machine, often power-operated, that cuts grass with rotating blades

lawn par·ty *n.* a party held in a garden or yard

lawn ten·nis *n.* a game for two or four players played on a hard or grass court of standard dimensions in which the players hit balls with rackets across a central net

law of av·er·ag·es *n.* **1. PRINCIPLE ON EFFECT OF PROBABILITY LAWS** the principle that over the long term laws of probability will influence all events that are subject to them **2. PRINCIPLE THAT THINGS MUST EVEN OUT** the unscientific but reasonable assumption that things are bound to change some time ○ *We have had bad weather for our vacation for the past six years, so by the law of averages we should get some sunshine this year.*

law of di·min·ish·ing re·turns *n.* the principle that a continual increase in effort or investment does not lead to a continual increase in output or results

law of ef·fect *n.* the theory that behavior that is rewarded is more likely to be repeated than behavior that is not rewarded. This theory was put forward by the U.S. psychologist Edward Lee Thorndike.

law of large num·bers *n.* the principle that a large sample is more likely than a smaller sample to have the characteristics of the whole

Law of Mos·es *n.* = **Mosaic Law**

law of na·tions *n.* = **international law**

law of na·ture *n.* a broadly applicable principle relating to natural phenomena

law of par·si·mo·ny *n.* = **Occam's razor**

law of sup·ply and de·mand *n.* the economic principle that the price charged for a product is determined by the level of demand and the quantity available

law of the jun·gle *n.* aggressive or competitive behavior based on the principle that self-interest and survival are of prime importance

law of the sea *n.* the international rules that govern the use of the oceans, derived from custom, treaties, and judicial decisions

law of war *n.* a rule or body of rules that governs the rights and duties of those engaged in international war

Law·rence /láwr'nss/ **1.** city in eastern Kansas, on the Kansas River, west of Kansas City and east of Topeka. Population: 71,887 (1996). **2.** city in northeastern Massachusetts, on the north bank of the Merrimack River, southwest of Haverhill and northeast of Lowell. Population: 68,807 (1996).

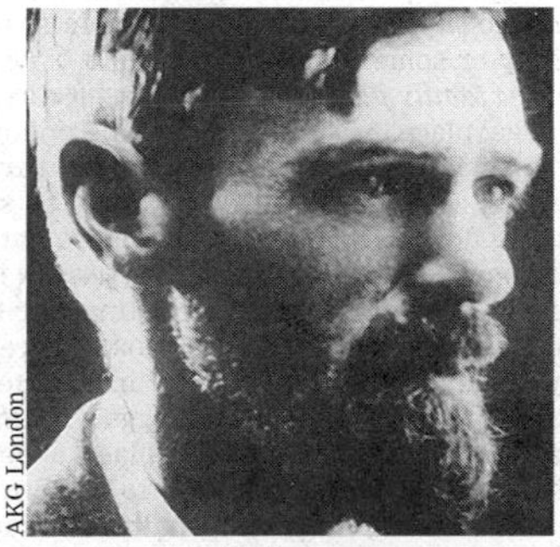

AKG London

D. H. Lawrence

Law·rence, D. H. (1885–1930) British writer. His novels include *Sons and Lovers* (1913), *Women in Love* (1921), and *Lady Chatterley's Lover* (1928). Full name **David Herbert Lawrence**

Barnaby's

Gertrude Lawrence

Law·rence, Gertrude (1898–1952) British actor. She starred in comedies and musical revues in London and New York, including *Blithe Spirit* (1945) and several other plays by her friend, Sir Noel Coward, as well as the film *The King and I* (1951). Born **Gertrud Alexandra Dagmar Lawrence Klasen**

Law·rence, Jacob Armstead (*b.* 1917) U.S. artist. His paintings, e.g., *The Migration of the Negro* (1940–41), explore the African American experience in U.S. history.

law·ren·ci·um /law rénsee əm/ *n.* a short-lived radioactive metallic element that was first produced artificially from californium and later from other elements. The symbol Lw was used for lawrencium at first but in 1963 it was changed to Lr. Symbol **Lr** [Mid-20thC. Named for Ernest O. *Lawrence*, U.S. physicist who first produced it.]

Law·son /láwss'n/, **Nigel, Baron Lawson of Blaby** (*b.* 1932) British politician. He was chancellor of the exchequer (1983–89).

law·suit /láw sòot/ *n.* a legal action brought between two private parties in a court of law

law·yer /láwyər/ *n.* somebody who is professionally qualified to give legal advice to others and represent them in court —**law·yer·like** *adj.* —**law·yer·ly** *adj.*

law·yer·ing /láwyəring/ *n.* the work of the legal profession

lax /laks/ *adj.* **1. NOT STRICT** not strict or careful enough **2. NOT TENSE** not tight or tense **3.** PHYSIOL **WITH TENDENCY TO DIARRHEA** not easily controlled and producing loose feces **4.** PHON **PRONOUNCED WITH RELAXED MUSCLES** pronounced with the muscles of the jaw relaxed rather than tense, as, e.g., is the "a" in "hat" [14thC. From Latin *laxus* "loose."] —**lax·ly** *adv.* —**lax·ness** *n.*

lax·a·tion /lak sáysh'n/ *n.* the action of making something loose, or the process of becoming loose

lax·a·tive /láksətiv/ *n.* a drug or other substance that promotes bowel movements, either by irritating the lower colon or by bulking the stool [14thC. From Old French *laxatif*, from medieval Latin *laxativus* "loosening," from Latin *laxare* "to loosen," from *laxus* "loose."] —**lax·a·tive** *adj.*

lax·i·ty /láksitee/ *n.* the condition or fact of being not strict or careful enough

lay[1] /lay/ *v.* (**laid** /layd/, **lay·ing, lays**) **1.** *vt.* **SET SOMETHING DOWN** to put something down, often carefully, in a horizontal position ○ *I laid the files on my desk.* **2.** *vt.* **PUT IN RESTING POSITION** to place somebody or something in a position of rest ○ *It was time to lay the baby down for a nap.* **3.** *vt.* **BURY SOMEBODY** to bury somebody or something in the ground ○ *They laid him in the family plot.* **4.** *vt.* **PLACE SOMETHING ON SURFACE** to arrange, place, or spread something on, over, or along a surface ○ *They are laying the carpet tomorrow.* **5.** *vt.* **PRESS SOMETHING DOWN FLAT** to smooth something down, or make something lie flat ○ *The cat laid back its ears.* **6.** *vt.* **ARRANGE THINGS ON TABLE** to prepare a table for a meal by setting out the required items **7.** *vt.* **ARRANGE FUEL FOR FIRE** to prepare a fire by arranging the fuel, usually in a grate **8.** *vti.* **PRODUCE EGGS** to produce or deposit eggs ○ *All the hens are laying.* **9.** *vti.* BETTING **BET** to place a bet with somebody **10.** *vt.* **IMPOSE SOMETHING** to impose something as a burden, duty, or penalty ○ *lay a tariff on imported products* **11.** *vt.* **ATTRIBUTE** to impute or attribute something ○ *He laid the blame on me.* **12.** *vt.* **BRING TO BEAR** to bring something to bear ○ *laid emphasis on the fact that we must study to excel* **13.** *vt.* **DEVISE SOMETHING** to devise, organize, or prepare something **14.** *vt.* **MAKE PREPARATIONS** to prepare something as a basis **15.** *vt.* **BRING SOMETHING INTO CERTAIN STATE** to bring something into a particular state ○ *Their scheme was laid bare.* **16.** *vt.* **OFFENSIVE TERM** an offensive term meaning to have sexual intercourse with somebody (*slang offensive*) **17.** *vt.* **ARRANGE STRANDS OF ROPE** to twist strands together to make a rope or cable **18.** *vt.* MIL **PUT CANNON IN POSITION** to establish the direction and elevation of a cannon or a battery of cannon **19.** *vt.* AGRIC **TREAT HEDGE TO KEEP IT THICK** to partially cut through some of the branches of a hedge, bending them over horizontally and pegging them to the ground to keep the hedge thick and dense ○ *hedge laying* **20.** *vi.* **LIE DOWN** to be in or adopt a lying position (*nonstandard*) ○ *Lay down on the sofa and have a rest.* **21.** *vi.* **PUT EFFORT INTO SOMETHING** to apply effort vigorously to a task ○ *The rowing team laid to their oars.* **22.** *vi.* NAUT **BE IN OR GO TO POSITION** to put a boat in a specified position, or move in a specified direction ■ *n.* **1. WAY SOMETHING LIES** the way or position in which something lies ○ *wanted to inspect the lay of the property* **2. OFFENSIVE TERM** an offensive term for a partner in sexual intercourse (*slang offensive*) **3. OFFENSIVE TERM** an offensive term for sexual intercourse (*slang offensive*) **4. TWIST OF ROPE OR CABLE STRANDS** the arrangement of strands in a rope or cable, determined by the number, length, angle, and direction of twist **5. TERMS OF EMPLOYMENT** terms of employment or purchase **6.** FIN **SHARE OF PROCEEDS** a share in the proceeds of a whaling expedition [Old English *lecgan*, from a prehistoric Germanic word meaning "to put," which is also the ancestor of English *lie* "to rest horizontally"] ◇ **be laid low** to become ill or incapacitated ◇ **lay it on (thick)** to exaggerate greatly, especially in order to flatter somebody ◇ **lay yourself open to something** to put yourself in a position that will make you liable to be blamed, criticized, or attacked

lay aside *vt.* **1. ABANDON SOMETHING** to give up on or abandon something ○ *"Be not the first by whom the new are tried, nor the last to lay the old aside."* (Alexander Pope, *An Essay on Criticism*; 1711) **2. SAVE SOMETHING** to put something away for the future

lay away *vt.* **1. SAVE SOMETHING** to put something away for the future **2. SET SOMETHING ASIDE** to set merchandise aside for future delivery

lay before *vt.* to present something for consideration by somebody

lay by *vt.* to set something aside for the future

lay down *v.* **1.** *vt.* **SURRENDER SOMETHING** to put down, surrender, or sacrifice something **2.** *vt.* **DECIDE ON RULE** to formulate a rule or principle **3.** *vt.* **STORE FOR FUTURE** to acquire and store something for future use **4.** *vt.* BETTING **PLACE BET** to place a bet **5.** *vt.* MIL **DELIVER MILITARY FIRE** to deliver a concentration of military fire **6.** *vi.* **LIE DOWN** to lie down in a horizontal position (*nonstandard*)

lay in *vt.* to acquire and store something for future use

lay into *vt.* **1. CRITICIZE SOMEBODY** to attack somebody forcefully in words (*informal*) **2. HIT SOMEBODY** to attack somebody forcefully with blows

lay off *v.* **1.** *vt.* **TERMINATE THE EMPLOYMENT OF SOMEBODY** to stop employing somebody, often temporarily, when there is insufficient work to be done **2.** *vti.* **STOP DOING SOMETHING** to stop doing or using something (*informal*) **3.** *vti.* **STOP IRRITATING SOMEBODY** to stop bothering somebody (*informal*) **4.** *vt.* **MEASURE OR MARK SOMETHING OFF** to measure off a distance, or mark out the boundaries of something **5.** *vt.* BETTING **REDUCE RISK ON BET** to reduce risk as a bookmaker by placing all or part of a bet with another bookmaker

lay on *vt.* **1. APPLY SOMETHING** to apply something by spreading it **2. APPLY OR USE TO EXCESS** to apply, administer, or use something in an exaggerated manner **3. PROVIDE SOMETHING SPECIAL** to provide or arrange something, often in an elaborate or extravagant manner

lay out *vt.* **1. SPREAD SOMETHING OUT FOR DISPLAY** to arrange things, or spread things out for display **2. PLAN OR DESIGN SOMETHING** to plan or design something in detail **3. PREPARE SOMEBODY FOR BURIAL** to prepare a body for burial **4. KNOCK UNCONSCIOUS** to knock somebody unconscious (*informal*) **5. SPEND MONEY** to spend money, especially in large quantities

lay over *vi.* to make a brief stop during a journey

lay to *vi.* to make a ship or boat stop, e.g., by turning a sailing vessel into the wind

lay up *vt.* **1. STORE FOR FUTURE** to store something for future use **2. CONFINE SOMEBODY WITH INJURY OR ILLNESS** to prevent somebody from leading a normal active life, usually temporarily because of injury or illness **3. STOP USING SHIP OR BOAT** to take a ship or boat out of service, usually temporarily, e.g., by moving it to a dry dock for maintenance or repairs

lay[2] /lay/ *adj.* **1. NOT BELONGING TO CLERGY** belonging to or involving the people of a church who are not members of the clergy **2. UNTRAINED** without expertise or professional training in a particular field [14thC. Directly or via Old French *lai* from late Latin *laicus* "secular" (see LAIC).]

lay[3] /lay/ *n.* **1.** POETRY **POEM FOR SINGING** a short narrative poem that is sung **2.** MUSIC **SONG** a medieval lyric or narrative song [13thC. From Old French *lai*, of unknown origin.]

lay[4] past tense of **lie**

lay·a·bout /láy ə bòwt/ *n.* a lazy person who loafs around and does no work

lay at·tend·ant *n.* in Buddhist monasteries, somebody who is responsible for taking care of tasks that the monks are forbidden to undertake

lay·a·way /láy ə wày/ *n.* a method of purchasing something in which the purchaser pays a deposit and the seller keeps the goods until full payment is made

lay·back /láy bàk/ *n.* a way of climbing a vertical crack in a rock by leaning back and pulling on one side of the crack and pushing against the other side with the feet

lay broth·er *n.* in a Christian religious order, a man who has taken vows, but does not take part in the full liturgical program and serves as an ancillary or manual worker

lay-by (*plural* **lay-bys**) *n.* *U.K.* a short strip of ground alongside a main road where vehicles can stop for a short time

lay days *npl.* the time allowed in port for a ship to load or unload its cargo without extra payment

lay·er /láyr/ *n.* **1. FLAT COVERING OR SHEETLIKE THICKNESS** a single thickness of something that lies over or under something or between other similar thicknesses **2. SOMEBODY WHO LAYS SOMETHING** somebody whose work is laying something such as tile or brick (*usually used in combination*) **3.** ZOOL **LAYING HEN** a hen that lays eggs **4.** GARDENING **ROOTED PLANT SHOOT** a branch or shoot that has been bent over and covered with soil to make it take root and grow into a new plant ■ *v.* (**-ered, -er·ing, -ers**) **1.** *vti.* **MAKE LAYERS OF SOMETHING** to apply or arrange things as separate thicknesses, or form into separate thicknesses **2.** *vt.* HAIR **CUT HAIR IN DIFFERENT LENGTHS** to cut somebody's hair in overlapping sections of different lengths, usually in order to give shape to a hairstyle **3.** *vt.* GARDENING **PROPAGATE PLANT BY ROOTING SHOOTS** to bend a shoot over and cover it with soil to make it take root as a new plant, or take root as a result of this procedure

lay·er cake *n.* a cake, usually frosted, that consists of two or more layers sandwiched together with cream, jam, or other filling. The layers may be baked separately or cut horizontally.

lay·er·ing /láy əring/ *n.* a method of propagating plants by covering a branch or shoot with soil so that it takes root while still attached to the parent plant

lay·ette /lay ét/ *n.* a complete set of clothing and accessories for a newborn baby [Mid-19thC. From French, literally "small drawer," from Old French *laie* "drawer, box," from Middle Dutch *laege*, from a prehistoric Germanic word meaning "load."]

lay fig·ure *n.* **1. ARTIST'S DUMMY** a jointed model of the human body used by artists **2. COMPLIANT PERSON** a submissive or insignificant person

lay·ing on of hands *n.* placing the hands on somebody's head in certain religious ceremonies or rituals, e.g., in ordination and faith healing

Lay·lat al-Mi·raj /lày lat al mi raáj/ *n.* an Islamic festival, the Night of Ascent, celebrating the ascent of Muhammad to heaven and held on the 27th of Rajab [From Arabic, literally "night of the ascent"]

lay·man /láymən/ (*plural* **-men** /-mən/) *n.* **1. SOMEBODY WITHOUT SPECIALIST KNOWLEDGE** somebody who is not trained or expert in a particular area ○ *a law book for the layman* **2.** RELIG **NONORDAINED PERSON** somebody who does not belong to the clergy

lay·off /láy àwf/ *n.* **1. DISMISSAL OF EMPLOYEES** a dismissal of employees, usually temporary **2. PERIOD OF UNEMPLOYMENT** the time during which employees are out of work

lay of the land *n.* the general appearance or state of an area or situation presenting itself to somebody (*informal*)

lay·out /láy òwt/ *n.* **1. WAY THINGS ARE ARRANGED** the way component parts or individual items are arranged **2. DESIGN SHOWING RELATIVE POSITIONS** a design or plan showing the way things are arranged **3.** DESIGN **DESIGN OF PRINTED MATTER** the design or arrangement of all the elements of printed material, e.g., an advertisement or the pages of a book **4.** DESIGN **PAGE SHOWING DESIGN** a page or pages showing the design for printed material **5.** DESIGN **DESIGNING OF PRINTED MATERIAL** the art of designing printed material **6. LARGE ESTABLISHMENT** a residence, business establishment, or other property, especially one that is large or elaborate ○ *a new high-tech manufacturing layout* **7. SET OF TOOLS** a set or kit of tools (*dated*) **8.** GYMNASTICS **GYMNASTIC POSITION** a position in the air in which the performer's body is straight with the arms extended

lay·o·ver /láy ōvər/ *n.* a brief stop during a journey

lay·per·son /láy pùrs'n/ (*plural* **-peo·ple** /-peèp'l/) *n.* **1. SOMEBODY WITHOUT SPECIALIST KNOWLEDGE** somebody who is not trained or expert in a particular area ○ *Such concepts are difficult for laypeople to understand.*

2. NONORDAINED PERSON somebody who does not belong to the clergy

lay read·er *n.* a lay member of a church, especially an Anglican church or the Roman Catholic Church, who is authorized to read some parts of the service

Layton /láyt'n/, **Peter** (*b.* 1912) Canadian poet. His poems depict the experience of Jewish Canadians.

lay-up *n.* a basketball shot made close to the basket, usually made one-handed and by bouncing the ball off the backboard

lay·wom·an /láy wŏŏmmən/ (*plural* **-en** /-wìmmin/) *n.* **1.** WOMAN WITHOUT SPECIALIST KNOWLEDGE a woman who is not trained or expert in a particular area **2.** RELIG NONORDAINED WOMAN a woman who does not belong to the clergy

la·zar /lázzər, láyzər/ *n.* a poor and sick person, especially somebody affected by leprosy (*archaic*) [13thC. Via medieval Latin *lazarus* from Latin *Lazarus*, name of the beggar "full of sores" described in Luke 16:20.]

laz·a·ret·to /làzzə réttō/ (*plural* **-tos**), **laz·a·ret** /-rét/, **laz·a·rette** *n.* **1.** MED HOSPITAL FOR CONTAGIOUS DISEASES a hospital for the treatment of contagious diseases such as leprosy, especially in former times **2.** MED QUARANTINE FACILITY a building or ship used to hold people during a period of quarantine **3.** SHIPPING SHIP'S STORAGE SPACE a storage space below deck near the stern of a ship [Mid-16thC. Via Italian *lazzaretto*, blend of *lazzaro* "leper" (see LAZAR) and Venetian dialect *nazareto*, hospital in Venice named for Santa Maria di *Nazaret* "St. Mary of Nazareth."]

Laz·a·rus /lázzərəss/, **Emma** (1849–87) U.S. writer. She wrote the poem "The New Colossus" (1883) as an ode to the Statue of Liberty.

laze /layz/ (**lazed, laz·ing, laz·es**) *v.* **1.** *vi.* TAKE IT EASY to relax and do no work ○ *I just lazed in the shade with a book.* **2.** *vt.* IDLE to pass time idly ○ *laze the day away* [Late 16thC. Back-formation from LAZY.]

laze around *vti.* to relax, doing nothing that requires effort

laz·u·lite /lázzə lìt, lázhə-/ *n.* a rare blue mineral, a phosphate of aluminum, iron, and magnesium, that has a glassy luster and is used as a gem [Early 19thC. Coined from *(lapis) lazuli* + -ITE.]

laz·u·rite /lázzə rìt, lázhə rìt/ *n.* a rare deep violet-blue or greenish blue mineral, primarily a silicate of sodium and aluminum, that is the main constituent of the semiprecious gemstone lapis lazuli [Late 19thC. Via medieval Latin *lazur* from Arabic *lāzaward* "(lapis) lazuli."]

la·zy /láyzee/ (**-zi·er, -zi·est**) *adj.* **1.** NOT WANTING TO WORK unwilling to do any work or make an effort **2.** CONDUCIVE TO IDLENESS contributing to an unwillingness to work or make an effort ○ *a lazy spring day* **3.** SLOW moving slowly ○ *a lazy river* **4.** AGRIC UPSIDE DOWN shown as a brand on livestock as a letter or number rotated 90 degrees from an upright position ○ *a lazy H* [Mid-16thC. Origin uncertain: perhaps from Low German *lasich* "feeble, tired."] —**la·zi·ly** *adv.* —**la·zi·ness** *n.*

la·zy·bones /láyzee bōnz/ (*plural* **-bones**) *n.* somebody who is lazy or without ambition (*informal*)

la·zy dai·sy stitch *n.* a single unattached chain stitch in embroidery, often worked in a circle to resemble the petals of a flower

la·zy eye *n.* **1.** IMPAIRED VISION an eye disorder in which vision is impaired for no apparent reason, or an eye affected by this disorder (*not used technically*) ◆ **amblyopia 2.** CONVERGENT SQUINT a disorder in which the eyes appear to be looking in different directions, or an eye affected by this disorder

la·zy Su·san *n.* a revolving tray holding a selection of items such as cheeses or sauces, usually placed in the middle of a dining table

la·zy tongs *npl.* tongs that can be used to grasp objects at a distance, usually by bringing together the handles to extend the jointed arms

LB *abbr.* linebacker

lb. *abbr.* pound

L-band *n.* the range of frequencies of electromagnetic waves from 390 megahertz to 1550 megahertz used for radar. Other bands in the microwave spectrum used for radar are designated S, X, and K.

LBJ *abbr.* Lyndon Baines Johnson

LBO *abbr.* leveraged buyout

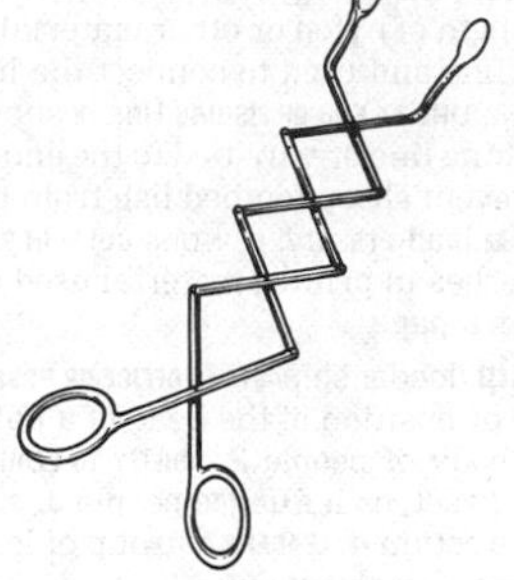

Lazy tongs

lbs. *abbr.* pounds

lc, l.c. *abbr.* **1.** PRINTING lower case **2.** loco citato

LC *abbr.* **1.** landing craft **2. LC, L.C.** Library of Congress

L/C, l/c *abbr.* letter of credit

LCD *abbr.* liquid-crystal display

l.c.d. *abbr.* least common denominator

l'chaim /lə k͟hī im/, **le·chayim** *interj.* GOOD HEALTH a word used to express good wishes just before drinking an alcoholic drink ■ *n.* SMALL DRINK OF ALCOHOL a small drink of alcohol used to toast somebody or something

LCL *abbr.* **1.** less-than-carload lot **2.** less-than-container load

LCM *abbr.* landing craft, mechanized

l.c.m. *abbr.* least common multiple

L.Cpl. *abbr.* lance corporal

LCS *abbr.* landing craft, support

LCV *abbr.* longer combination vehicle

LD *abbr.* **1.** EDUC learning disability **2.** EDUC learning-disabled **3.** PHARM lethal dose

ld. *abbr.* **1.** PRINTING lead **2.** load

Ld. *abbr.* **1.** COMM Limited (company) **2.** Lord

LD50 *n.* a toxicological test in which the dose that kills 50% of a group of test animals is calculated. This test has been criticized by animal protection organizations and by many scientists, but it is still used.

LDC *abbr.* less-developed country

ldg. *abbr.* **1.** landing **2.** loading

Ldg. *abbr.* Leading

LDL *abbr.* low-density lipoprotein

L-do·pa *n.* a natural substance that stimulates the production of dopamine in the brain and is used to treat Parkinson's disease [Mid-20thC. From the initial letters of *levorotatory*, and of DI- + OXY- + PHENYL + ALANINE, the chemical names.]

LDS *abbr.* **1.** Latter-day Saints **2.** praise be to God forever

lea /lee, lay/ *n.* **1. lea, ley** GRASSLAND a grassy field or meadow (*literary*) **2.** AGRIC SOWN GRASS a field sown with grass [Old English *lēah* "meadow, clearing"]

lea. *abbr.* **1.** MEASURE league **2.** leather

leach /leech/ *v.* (**leached, leach·ing, leach·es**) **1.** *vt.* REMOVE SOMETHING BY DISSOLUTION to remove soluble components from a solid mixture by the use of a solvent **2.** *vi.* LOSE SOLUBLE MATERIAL to lose soluble material by dissolution **3.** *vti.* DEPRIVE OR BE DEPRIVED OF SOMETHING take something away slowly, or be slowly taken away ○ *have the joy leached from life* ■ *n.* **1.** CONTAINER USED IN LEACHING a porous container used to hold a solid mixture through which a solvent is run in order to remove soluble components **2.** MIXTURE USED IN LEACHING a solid mixture through which a solvent is run in order to remove soluble components **3.** LIQUID CONTAINING LEACHED SUBSTANCE a solution containing a substance leached from a solid mixture [Old English *leccan*, from a prehistoric Germanic word that is also the ancestor of English *lake*] —**leach·a·bil·i·ty** /leéchə bíllətee/ *n.* —**leach·er** /leéchər/ *n.*

leach·ate /leé chàyt/ *n.* **1.** SOLUTION FORMED BY LEACHING a liquid containing soluble material removed from a solid mixture through which the liquid has passed **2.** LIQUID WASTE IN LANDFILL the liquid produced in a landfill from the decomposition of waste within the landfill

Lea·cock /leé kòk/, **Stephen** (1869–1944) British-born Canadian writer. He was best known for his satirical short stories and essays, including *Literary Lapses* (1910). Full name **Stephen Butler Leacock**

lead[1] /leed/ *v.* (**led, lead·ing, leads**) **1.** *vti.* GUIDE SOMEBODY to show the way to others, usually by going ahead of them ○ *He led us down the mountain.* **2.** *vti.* BE THE WAY SOMEWHERE to be the route or direction that goes to a particular place or in a particular direction ○ *That street leads to the school.* **3.** *vt.* BRING SOMEBODY OR SOMETHING to bring somebody or something along with physical guidance, e.g., by holding somebody's hand or pulling a horse's reins **4.** *vt.* COMMAND OTHERS to control, direct, or command others ○ *He led an infantry division during the Korean War.* **5.** *vt.* BE IN CHARGE OF SOMETHING to have a principal part or guiding role in something **6.** *vt.* MUSIC BE PRINCIPAL MUSICIAN to be the principal performer of an orchestra or of a section of an orchestra **7.** *vt.* INFLUENCE SOMEBODY TO DO SOMETHING to cause somebody to think or act in a particular way ○ *I was led to believe the house had been sold.* **8.** *vi.* RESULT IN SOMETHING to bring about a particular outcome ○ *Her hard work ultimately led to stardom.* **9.** *vt.* LIVE LIFE to go through life or spend time in a particular way ○ *We all lead very busy lives.* **10.** *vt.* BE AT THE START to be at the beginning or front of something ○ *Your name leads the waiting list.* **11.** *vti.* BE AHEAD OF OTHERS to be ahead in a race or competition ○ *be leading in the election* **12.** *vt.* BE MOST SUCCESSFUL to be the most successful at something and set an example to others ○ *a city that leads the nation in the fight against crime* **13.** *vti.* DANCE GUIDE DANCE PARTNER to guide a partner in a dance **14.** *vt.* LAW ASK WITNESS LEADING QUESTION to suggest to a witness an answer to a question by phrasing the question in a way that will elicit the desired response **15.** *vt.* CHANNEL OR CONVEY SOMETHING to guide something through a passage such as a conduit or channel **16.** *vti.* CARDS PUT DOWN FIRST CARD to play the first card in a trick in a card game, often requiring others to play a card of the same suit if they can **17.** *vi.* BOXING AIM THE FIRST BLOW to direct the first of a series of punches **18.** *vi.* BASEBALL LEAVE BASE EARLY to leave a base as a runner before a pitch in baseball **19.** *vt.* AIM AHEAD OF SOMETHING to aim something such as a missile or ball at a point in front of a moving target to allow for the time of flight ■ *n.* **1.** FRONT POSITION OR PRINCIPAL ROLE the front position, first place, or principal role **2.** FORWARD POSITION a position ahead of all competitors ○ *Portugal took the lead at the halfway stage.* **3.** FRONT-RUNNER somebody or something ahead of all competitors **4.** DISTANCE BETWEEN FIRST AND SECOND the margin by which somebody or something is ahead of all competitors ○ *She had a narrow lead as the runners entered the last lap.* **5.** ARTS STAR ROLE IN PERFORMANCE a principal role in a play, motion picture, or show ○ *He will play the male lead in the movie version.* **6.** ARTS SOMEBODY WITH STAR ROLE somebody who has a principal role in a play, motion picture, or show **7.** ROLE OF SOMEBODY IN COMMAND the role of somebody who directs or guides others ○ *take the lead in a discussion* **8.** PRECEDENT an example or precedent ○ *follow his lead* **9.** TIP OR CLUE a piece of helpful or useful information ○ *The police are following up a number of leads.* **10.** PRESS INTRODUCTION TO NEWS ITEM an introduction to a news story **11.** PRESS HEADLINE ITEM the most important story in a newspaper or news broadcast ○ *The conflict should make the lead in all tomorrow's papers.* **12.** = **leash** *n.* 1 **13.** ELEC WIRE CONDUCTING ELECTRICITY an insulated electrical conductor used to connect two points in a circuit, e.g., a cable connecting an appliance to a source of electricity **14.** GEOL WATER CHANNEL THROUGH ICE a water channel through an ice field **15.** NAUT DIRECTION OF ROPE the direction in which a rope runs **16.** CARDS FIRST CARD PLAYED the first card played in a trick in a game **17.** CARDS RIGHT TO PUT DOWN FIRST CARD the right to play a card first in a trick in a game **18.** BASEBALL POSITION OF BASE RUNNER a position taken by a runner off one base of a baseball diamond toward another **19.** BOXING PUNCH an attacking punch **20.** DISTANCE AHEAD OF MOVING TARGET the distance a missile, ball, or other projectile is aimed in front of a moving target to allow for the time of flight **21.** GEOL = **lode** [Old English *lǣdan*, from a prehistoric Germanic word that is also the ancestor of English *load*]

WORD KEY: SYNONYMS

See Synonyms at ***guide***.

lead off *v.* **1.** *vi.* BEGIN to begin doing something **2.** *vt.*

BASEBALL **BE FIRST BATTER** to be the first batter in a baseball or softball lineup or inning

lead on *vt.* **1. ENTICE SOMEBODY WITH FALSE PROMISE** to lure somebody with an offer or promise that is later withdrawn **2. PERSUADE SOMEBODY TO MISBEHAVE** to persuade somebody to do something foolish or wrong ○ *She doesn't let the older kids lead her on.*

lead up to *vt.* **1. PREPARE** to prepare the way for something **2. APPROACH SUBJECT INDIRECTLY** to approach a subject gradually or indirectly

lead[2] /led/ *n.* **1.** CHEM ELEM **CHEMICAL ELEMENT** a heavy bluish gray metallic chemical element that bends easily. It is used in car batteries, pipes, solder, and as a radiation shield. It usually occurs in the mineral galena. Symbol **Pb 2. DEVICE FOR MEASURING DEPTH** a weight on the end of a line used to measure the depth of water **3.** ANGLING **WEIGHT FOR FISHING LINE** a lead weight used on a fishing line **4.** ARMS **AMMUNITION FOR GUNS** bullets or shot for firearms (*informal*) **5. GRAPHITE IN A PENCIL** a long thin stick of graphite used in a pencil for writing or drawing **6.** PRINTING **STRIP BETWEEN LINES OF TYPE** in traditional hot metal printing, a thin strip of metal between lines of type that creates the space between lines on the printed page ■ **leads** *npl.* CRAFT **LEAD STRIPS BETWEEN GLASS PANES** strips of lead used to hold the small glass panes in place in a decorative window or art object ■ *vt.* (**lead·ed, lead·ing, leads**) **1. COVER SOMETHING WITH LEAD** to cover, fill, or weight something with lead **2.** PRINTING **INSERT STRIP BETWEEN LINES OF TYPE** to put a thin strip of metal between lines of type to create a space on the printed page **3.** CRAFT **SECURE GLASS USING LEADS** to hold small panes of glass together with strips of lead [Pre 12thC. Ultimately from a prehistoric Germanic word of uncertain origin: probably from Celtic, and originally meaning "to flow" (referring to the metal's low melting point).] —**lead·less** *adj.* —**lead·y** *adj.*

lead ac·e·tate *n.* a poisonous crystalline compound used in making paints and varnishes and as a mordant in dyeing and printing cottons. Formula: $Pb(C_2H_3O_2)_2 \cdot 3H_2O$.

lead ar·se·nate *n.* a poisonous crystalline compound used as an insecticide. Formula: $Pb_3(AsO_4)_2$.

lead az·ide *n.* a crystalline compound used as a detonator in explosives. Because of its sensitivity, lead azide must be submerged in water when transported. Formula: $Pb(N_3)_2$.

lead bal·loon *n.* a total failure ○ *went over like a lead balloon*

Leadbelly /léd bèllee/ (1885?–1949) U.S. singer and guitarist. His work influenced folk, jazz, and popular music. Real name **Huddie William Ledbetter**

lead car·bon·ate *n.* a poisonous white solid used as a pigment in paints. Formula: $PbCO_3$.

lead chro·mate *n.* a poisonous yellow crystalline substance used as a pigment. Formula: $PbCrO_4$.

lead crys·tal *n.* glass containing a high proportion of lead, used to make decorative items, especially tableware

lead di·ox·ide *n.* a poisonous brown crystalline compound used in batteries and explosives, and as a mordant in dyeing textiles. Formula: PbO_2.

lead·ed /léddəd/ *adj.* **1. CONTAINING LEAD** containing or treated with lead or a compound of lead **2.** CRAFT **WITH SMALL PANES SECURED BY LEAD** containing many small panes of glass held together with strips of lead

lead·en /lédd'n/ *adj.* **1. OF LEAD** made of lead **2. DULL AND GRAY** of a dull gray color, like lead ○ *leaden skies* **3. TIRED AND HEAVY** tired, heavy, and hard to move ○ *My legs felt stiff and leaden from miles of walking.* **4. SLOW** sluggish or labored ○ *a leaden pace* **5. LIFELESS** lacking spirit or vitality ○ *leaden prose* —**lead·en·ly** *adv.* —**lead·en·ness** *n.*

lead·er /leédər/ *n.* **1. SOMEBODY WHOM PEOPLE FOLLOW** somebody who guides or directs others by showing them the way or telling them how to behave **2. SOMEBODY OR SOMETHING IN THE LEAD** somebody or something in front of all others, e.g., in a race or procession **3. SOMEBODY IN CHARGE OF OTHERS** the head of a nation, political party, legislative body, or military unit **4.** MUSIC **PRINCIPAL MUSICIAN** the principal performer of an orchestra or of a section of an orchestra **5.** MUSIC **MUSICAL CONDUCTOR** a conductor of a band or group **6.** *U.K.* PRESS = **editorial 7.** MARKETING = **loss leader 8.** BOT **MAIN STEM** the main growing shoot of a tree or shrub **9.** RECORDING **BLANK END OF TAPE** a short strip of blank film or recording tape at the beginning or end of a reel, used for threading **10.** ANGLING **LINE CONNECTING HOOK** a short length of nylon or other material attached to a fishing line and used to connect the lure or hook **11.** ANGLING **LINE AT END OF FISHING LINE** a short length of heavy fishing line or wire tied to the end of the main line to prevent sharp-toothed fish from breaking off the hook ■ **lead·ers** *npl.* PRINTING **GUIDE IN PRINTED MATTER** dots or dashes in printed material used to guide the eye across a page

lead·er·ship /leédər shìp/ *n.* **1. OFFICE OR POSITION OF LEADER** the office or position of the head of a political party or other body of people **2. ABILITY TO LEAD** the ability to guide, direct, or influence people **3. GUIDANCE** guidance or direction **4. LEADERS** a group of leaders (*takes a singular or plural verb*)

lead glass *n.* glass that contains a high proportion of lead oxide. It is used to make decorative objects and optical components.

lead-in *n.* **1. INTRODUCTORY REMARK** an introduction to something such as an item on television or a topic for discussion **2.** BROADCAST **ANTENNA WIRE** a wire that connects an outside antenna with a transmitter or receiver

lead·ing[1] /leéding/ *adj.* **1. PROMINENT** most important or well known **2. AHEAD** ahead of all others, e.g., in a race or procession

lead·ing[2] /lédding/ *n.* **1.** CRAFT **GLASS FRAMING** lead strips around small panes in windows or art objects ○ *The leading in the stained-glass window needs repair.* **2.** PRINTING **LINE SPACING** the spacing between lines of type in traditional hot metal printing

lead·ing ec·o·nom·ic in·di·ca·tor *n.* an economic variable that tends to show the direction of future economic activity

lead·ing edge *n.* **1. MOST ADVANCED POSITION** the forefront of development in technology, science, or some other field (*hyphenated when used before a noun*) **2.** AIR **FRONT EDGE** the forward edge of an aircraft wing, propeller, or airfoil **3.** HOUSEHOLD **INNER EDGE OF CURTAIN** the vertical edge of a curtain that faces the middle of the window

lead·ing la·dy *n.* the actor who has the principal female role in a play or motion picture

lead·ing light *n.* somebody who influences or sets an example to others

lead·ing man *n.* the actor who has the principal male role in a play or motion picture

lead·ing note *n. U.K.* = **leading tone**

lead·ing ques·tion *n.* a question asked in a way that prompts the desired answer, e.g., "Do you think the government should be wasting taxpayers' money on such a venture?"

lead·ing tone *n.* the seventh tone of the diatonic scale

lead line *n.* a line, weighted at one end, used to measure the depth of water. The line is usually marked at intervals to make measurement easier.

lead mon·ox·ide *n.* a yellow or reddish yellow poisonous lead compound used in making storage batteries, pottery, glass, and rubber, and as a pigment in paints. Formula: PbO.

lead·off /leéd àwf/ *n.* the first move or action in a series, or somebody who begins something

lead·plant /léd plànt/ *n.* a North American shrub with hairy grayish leaves, thought by early miners to indicate the presence of lead. Latin name: *Amorpha canescens.*

lead poi·son·ing *n.* **1. POISONING CAUSED BY LEAD** poisoning from the absorption of lead into the body, the chronic form of which can cause damage to the nervous system, brain, liver, and gastrointestinal tract **2. BULLET WOUND** injury or death from a bullet wound (*slang*)

lead screw *n.* a threaded shaft that controls the movement of a machine part, e.g., the tool carriage of a lathe

leads·man /lédzmən/ (*plural* **-men** /-mən/) *n.* somebody who uses a lead line to measure the depth of water

lead tet·ra·eth·yl *n.* = **tetraethyl lead**

lead time *n.* **1. ADVANCE NOTICE** the length of time in advance of a deadline that somebody must know or have something **2. TIME TO COMPLETE PROCESS** the time needed to do something measured from start to finish, e.g., from design to production or from placing an order to delivery of the goods ○ *How much lead time do you need?*

Lead·ville /léd vìl/ city and county seat of Lake County, central Colorado, situated in the Rocky Mountains, southwest of Denver. Population: 2,629 (1990).

lead·wort /léd wùrt, -wàwrt/ *n.* a tropical plant grown in gardens for its spikes of blue, white, or red flowers. Genus: *Plumbago.*

leaf /leef/ *n.* (*plural* **leaves** /leevz/) **1.** BOT **PLANT PART FOR PHOTOSYNTHESIS** any of the flat green parts that grow in various shapes from the stems or branches of plants and trees and whose main function is photosynthesis **2.** BOT **FOLIAGE** the foliage of a plant or tree, or the time when a plant or tree has leaves **3. LEAVES AS CROP** a crop in the form of leaves **4.** PUBL **PAPER IN BOOK** any of the sheets of paper that make up a book **5. VERY THIN METAL FOIL** a very thin sheet of metal such as gold or silver used, e.g., to decorate an art object **6.** FURNITURE **PART OF TABLE TOP** a hinged or removable section of a table top **7.** BUILDING **PART OF DOOR** a hinged or sliding section of a door, shutter, or gate **8. PART OF SPRING IN VEHICLE** one of the metal strips that form a spring in a vehicle suspension system (**leaf spring**) ■ *vi.* (**leafed, leaf·ing, leafs**) BOT **GROW LEAVES** to put out new leaves [Old English *lēaf*, from a prehistoric Germanic word that is probably also the ancestor of English *lobby* and *lodge*] —**leaf·less** *adj.* ◇ **take a leaf out of somebody's book** to follow somebody's usually good example ◇ **turn over a new leaf** to start to behave in a more acceptable way

leaf through *vt.* to turn the pages of a book or magazine quickly and casually

leaf·age /leéfij/ *n.* leaves or foliage

leaf bee·tle *n.* a beetle, e.g., the Colorado potato beetle or the flea beetle, that feeds on the leaves of plants and can be destructive to cultivated crops. Family: Chrysomelidae.

leaf·bird /leéf bùrd/ *n.* a forest-dwelling bird of Southeast Asia with a long curved bill and bold black and green or yellow markings. Family: Aegithinidae.

leaf but·ter·fly *n.* a butterfly of southern and southeastern Asia that resembles a leaf. Genus: *Kallima.*

leaf cha·fer *n.* a scarab beetle that eats the leaves of grape vines and many garden plants. Genus: *Macrodactylus.*

leaf curl *n.* a disease of plants that causes the leaves to curl

leaf·cut·ter ant /leéf kùttər-/ *n.* a tropical American ant that cuts leaves into pieces to use as fertilizer for the fungi it grows in its nest for food. Genus: *Atta.*

leaf·cut·ter bee *n.* a common solitary bee that usually nests in the ground or in a natural cavity and lines its nest with pieces of leaves. Family: Megachilidae.

leaf fat *n.* the dense layers of fat surrounding the kidneys, especially a hog's kidneys, often used for making lard

leaf fish *n.* a tropical freshwater fish that is laterally flat so that it appears like a floating dead leaf. Family: Nandidae.

leaf·hop·per /leéf hòppər/ *n.* a slender spindle-shaped leaping insect found worldwide that sucks the sap from plants and spreads plant diseases. Family: Cicadellidae.

leaf in·sect *n.* an insect with a flat body that resembles a leaf in shape and color, found mainly in southern Asia. Family: Phyllidae.

leaf lard *n.* a high-quality lard made from the fat surrounding the kidneys of hogs (**leaf fat**)

leaf·let /leéflət/ *n.* **1.** PUBL **FREE PRINTED MATERIAL** a sheet of printed paper, usually folded, that is distributed free as part of an advertising or information campaign **2.** BOT **SMALL LEAF** a small or young leaf **3.** BOT **PART OF LEAF** any of the divisions of a compound leaf ■ *vti.* (**-let·ed** *or* **-let·ted, -let·ing** *or* **-let·ting, -lets**) **DISTRIBUTE LEAFLETS** to hand out or distribute leaflets in a particular place or to a particular group of people

leaf·le·teer /leéflə teér/, **leaf·le·ter** /leéflə tər/ *n.* somebody who writes or distributes leaflets

leaf min·er *n.* any insect whose larvae tunnel into and feed on leaf tissue, including several species of very small moths and a particular species of fly. Family: Agromyzidae.

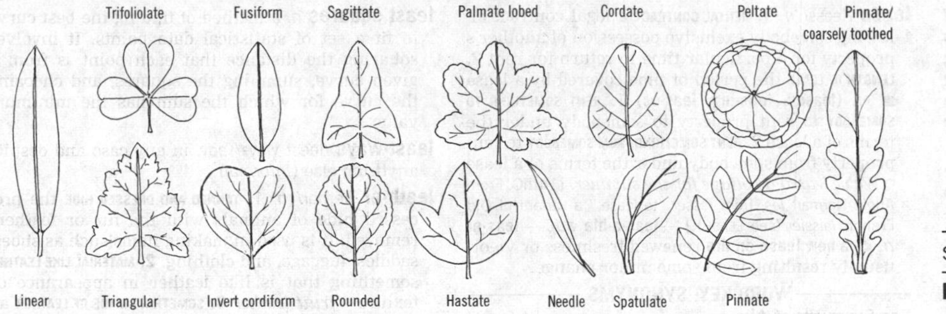

Leaf

leaf mold *n.* **1.** COMPOST OR SOIL nitrogen-rich compost or soil that consists mainly of decomposed leaves **2.** GROWTH ON LEAVES a fungal growth on leaves

leaf mon·key *n.* a leaf-eating Asian monkey related to the langurs. Genus: *Presbytis.* ◊ **langur**

leaf pri·mor·di·um *n.* a group of cells that develop into a leaf

leaf roll *n.* a viral disease of potatoes that is transmitted by aphids and causes the leaves to curl upward

leaf roll·er *n.* a small moth whose larvae roll leaves to protect themselves while they eat them

leaf scar *n.* the mark left on a stem when a leaf falls

leaf sheath *n.* the part at the bottom of the leaf that surrounds the stem in grasses

leaf spot *n.* a fungal or bacterial plant disease that causes discolored spots to develop on leaves

leaf spring *n.* a spring made of several curved metal strips of different lengths **(leaves)** bracketed together, used in automobile suspension systems

leaf·stalk /leéf stàwk/ *n.* a stalk by which a leaf is attached to a stem. Technical name **petiole**

leaf trace *n.* the structure that carries fluid between the main stem and the base of the leaf in plants

leaf ty·er *n.* = **leaf roller**

leaf·y /leéfee/ (-i·er, -i·est) *adj.* **1.** WITH MANY LEAVES covered with or having many leaves **2.** WITH MANY TREES THAT HAVE LEAVES with many trees and therefore a lot of foliage **3.** PRODUCING LEAVES producing broad leaves as distinct from blades or needles **4.** WITH EDIBLE LEAVES having edible leaves ○ *leafy vegetables* —**leaf·i·ness** *n.*

leaf·y spurge *n.* a tall perennial plant that is native to Europe but naturalized in the northern United States and Canada. It is found growing in patches along roadsides. Latin name: *Euphorbia esula.*

league[1] /leeg/ *n.* **1.** GROUP WITH COMMON GOALS an association of nations, states, organizations, or businesses with common interests or goals **2.** SPORTS GROUP OF SPORTS CLUBS an association of sports clubs or teams that compete with each other **3.** LEVEL OF SKILL a level of performance or skill ○ *Her painting is not in the same league as yours.* ■ *vti.* **(leagued, leagu·ing, leagues)** FORM INTO LEAGUE to join with others for a common interest or goal, or bring people together for such a purpose [15thC. Via French *ligue* "pact, agreement" from Italian *liga,* variant of *lega,* ultimately from Latin *ligare* "to bind"; spelling later influenced by Italian *lega.*] ◇ **in league (with somebody)** collaborating with somebody, usually for a questionable purpose

league[2] /leeg/ *n.* a measure of distance of variable length, usually about 3 mi./5 km, no longer in general use [14thC. Directly or via French dialect *lega* (from Old French *legue*) from late Latin *leuca,* from late Greek *leugā,* ultimately from Gaulish.]

League of Na·tions *n.* an alliance of nations established in 1920 to promote world peace and cooperation that was replaced by the United Nations in 1946. It was first proposed by President Woodrow Wilson after World War I, though the United States never joined, and became increasingly ineffective in the 1930s.

leagu·er[1] /leégər/ *n.* (*archaic*) **1.** SIEGE a siege **2.** BESIEGING ARMY CAMP the camp of a besieging army ■ *vt.* **(-ered, -er·ing, -ers)** BESIEGE to besiege a place (*archaic*) [Late 16thC. From Dutch *leger* "camp."]

lea·guer[2] /leégər/ *n.* a member of a sports league

leak /leek/ *n.* **1.** HOLE OR CRACK an unintentional hole or crack that permits something such as liquid, gas, or light to escape or enter **2.** ACCIDENTAL ESCAPE OR ENTRY the accidental escape or unwanted entry of something, usually by way of an unintentional hole or crack **3.** ESCAPING LIQUID OR GAS something that escapes through an unintentional hole or crack **4.** ELEC ACCIDENTAL ESCAPE OF ELECTRICITY a place through which an electric current escapes accidentally, or the resulting loss of electricity **5.** MEANS OF ESCAPE a means of escape, or the resulting loss ○ *We need to plug the leak in our finances.* **6.** DISCLOSURE OF SECRETS an unofficial release of confidential information, usually to the media **7.** ACT OF URINATION an act of urination (*slang*) ■ *vti.* **(leaked, leak·ing, leaks) 1.** LET SOMETHING IN OR OUT to let something escape or enter accidentally, or escape or enter in this way **2.** DISCLOSE SECRETS OR BE DISCLOSED to release confidential information unofficially or covertly, usually to the media, or become publicly known in such a way ○ *She leaked the details of the deal to the press.* [15thC. Origin uncertain: perhaps via Old Norse *leka* or Middle Dutch *lek* from, ultimately, a prehistoric Germanic word meaning "deficiency."] —**leak·er** *n.*

leak out *vi.* to become known unintentionally, or be disclosed unofficially

leak·age /leékij/ *n.* **1.** ESCAPE OR ENTRANCE OF SOMETHING a gradual escape or entrance of something such as oil, gas, or electric current by a leak **2.** SOMETHING THAT ESCAPES OR ENTERS an amount of something that escapes or enters by leaking **3.** DISCLOSURE OF SECRETS the unofficial release of confidential information, usually to the media

Lea·key /leékee/, **Louis** (1903–72) British archeologist and paleontologist. He pioneered research into human ancestry at Olduvai Gorge in Tanzania, discovering several key hominid fossils. Full name **Louis Seymour Bazett Leakey**

Lea·key, Richard (*b.* 1944) Kenyan-born British archeologist and paleontologist. He continued his parents' research into human ancestry in Africa, becoming director of the Kenyan Wildlife and Conservation Management Service (1989). Full name **Richard Erskine Frere Leakey**

leak·proof /leék proof/ *adj.* **1.** DESIGNED NOT TO LEAK designed to prevent any of the contents from escaping or anything unwanted from entering **2.** NOT DISCLOSING SECRETS not allowing breaches in secrecy or confidentiality (*informal*)

leak·y /leékee/ (-i·er, -i·est) *adj.* **1.** LEAKING letting liquid or gas in or out accidentally through holes or cracks **2.** NOT SECURE allowing breaches in secrecy or confidentiality (*informal*) —**leak·i·ly** *adv.* —**leak·i·ness** *n.*

lean[1] /leen/ *v.* **(leaned, lean·ing, leans) 1.** *vi.* BEND OR INCLINE to be in or move to a position that is at an angle to the vertical **2.** *vti.* REST SOMETHING OR BE SUPPORTED to rest against something for support, or rest something against something else **3.** *vi.* TEND TOWARD SOMETHING to have a preference or inclination for a particular thing or course of action ■ *n.* TILTED POSITION a position that is at an angle to the vertical [Old English *hleonian.* Ultimately from an Indo-European word meaning "slope," which is also the ancestor of English *decline, incline,* and *ladder.*]

lean on *vt.* **1.** DEPEND ON SOMEBODY to be dependent on somebody **2.** GET SUPPORT FROM SOMEBODY to gain moral support from somebody ○ *You can always lean on me.* **3.** INTIMIDATE SOMEBODY INTO DOING SOMETHING to put pressure on somebody to do something (*informal*)

lean[2] /leen/ *adj.* **1.** WITHOUT EXCESS FAT having no excess fat **2.** NOT FATTY having little or no fat ○ *lean meat* **3.** NOT PRODUCTIVE not productive or profitable ○ *lean harvest* **4.** ECONOMICAL AND EFFICIENT not using any more resources than necessary ○ *He is able to compete because he runs a lean business.* **5.** MINING WITH FEW MINERALS low in mineral content ○ *lean ore* **6.** LOW IN COMBUSTIBLE MATERIAL used to describe a mixture of fuel and air that is low in combustible material ○ *lean fuel mixture* ■ *n.* MEAT WITHOUT FAT meat with little or no fat [Old English *hl_æne,* from prehistoric Germanic] —**lean·ly** *adv.*

WORD KEY: SYNONYMS

See Synonyms at ***thin.***

Lean /leen/, **Sir David** (1908–91) British movie director. He won Academy Awards for *Bridge on the River Kwai* (1957), and *Lawrence of Arabia* (1962).

lean-burn *adj.* designed to run on a mixture that has a high proportion of air to fuel in order to reduce air pollution ○ *a lean-burn engine*

lean·ing /leéning/ *n.* an inclination or tendency toward something such as a particular set of opinions

Leaning Tower of Pisa

Lean·ing To·wer of Pi·sa the bell tower of Pisa Cathedral, Italy, built between 1173 and 1350 and well-known for its tilt. It is 180 ft./55 m high and leans more than 16 ft./5 m from the perpendicular.

lean-to (*plural* **lean-tos**) *n.* **1.** OUTBUILDING BUILT AGAINST WALL an outbuilding with a slanted roof that rests against the wall of a larger building **2.** SLOPE-ROOFED SHELTER a shelter or small building with a roof that slopes in one direction, often reaching the ground

leap /leep/ *v.* **(leaped** *or* **leapt** /lept/, **leap·ing, leaps) 1.** *vi.* JUMP FORCEFULLY to make a jump with a long or high arc ○ *She leaped over the stream with ease.* **2.** *vi.* MOVE AS IF BY JUMPING to move abruptly, as if by jumping up or across something ○ *The dog leaped into her arms.* **3.** *vi.* ABRUPTLY SWITCH TO SOMETHING to move abruptly to a new thought or action ○ *The reporters leaped to the conclusion that wrongdoing had occurred.* **4.** *vi.* GO UP SUBSTANTIALLY to increase suddenly and sizably ○ *Stock prices leaped to new highs.* **5.** *vt.* JUMP SOMETHING to jump over an obstacle ○ *didn't think he could leap the stream* **6.** *vt.* MAKE ANIMAL JUMP to cause an animal to jump over something ■ *n.* **1.** ARCHING JUMP a long high jump **2.** DISTANCE OF JUMP the distance covered by a leap ○ *a leap of almost eight feet* **3.** PLACE TO JUMP a place over or from which to leap **4.** LARGE INCREASE a sudden and sizable increase ○ *The market has made many leaps this quarter.* **5.** MUSIC MUSICAL INTERVAL a large interval in music [Old English *hlēapan.* From a prehistoric Germanic word meaning "to run," which is also the ancestor of English *lope, gallop,* and *loafer.*] —**leap·er** *n.* ◇ **a leap in the dark** an action taken without knowing what the outcome or consequences will be ◇ **in** *or* **by leaps and bounds** extremely rapidly

leap at *vt.* to be quick to accept or take advantage of something ○ *He leaped at the chance to play the lead in the movie.*

leap out at *vt.* to be suddenly or immediately obvious to somebody ○ *The answer just leaps out at you.*

leap·frog /leép fròg/ *n.* VAULTING GAME a game in which players take turns bending over so that another player can vault over them with the legs wide apart and the hands placed on their backs ■ *v.* **(-frogged, -frog·ging, -frogs) 1.** *vti.* PLAY LEAPFROG to vault over somebody in the game of leapfrog **2.** *vt.* VAULT OVER SOMEBODY OR SOMETHING to vault over a person or obstacle in a style similar to that used in the game of leapfrog **3.** *vti.* PASS EACH OTHER ALTERNATELY to take turns passing each other ○ *The two drivers were leapfrogging down the racetrack.* **4.** *vi.* ADVANCE QUICKLY to advance quickly in status or position, usually bypassing competitors or colleagues ○ *She started the day in seventh place but soon leapfrogged into first.* **5.** *vt.* CIRCUMVENT SOMETHING to evade something by passing around it **6.** *vt.* MIL ADVANCE MILITARY UNITS BY TURN to advance military units by having one engage the enemy while the other passes around the battle [From the players' resemblance to jumping frogs]

leap sec·ond *n.* a second added at the end of June or December to a timekeeping system in order to keep measured time synchronized with the movement of the earth around the sun [Modeled on LEAP YEAR]

lea·pt past tense, past participle of **leap**

leap year *n.* a year with an extra day, February 29, added to make up the difference between the 365-day calendar and the actual duration of the earth's orbit of the sun. Leap years occur every four years, except for years ending in "00" that are not divisible by 400. [Origin uncertain: probably so called because in such years any given date falls two days later than in the preceding year, instead of one as in a normal year]

Lear /leer/, **Edward** (1812–88) British writer and artist. His limericks and cartoons for children were first published in *A Book of Nonsense* (1846).

learn /lurn/ (**learned** *or* **learnt** /lurnt/, **learned** *or* **learnt, learn·ing, learns**) *v.* **1.** *vti.* COME TO KNOW SOMETHING to acquire knowledge of a subject or skill through education or experience ○ *I'm learning to play piano.* **2.** *vti.* FIND OUT SOMETHING to gain information about somebody or something ○ *I just learned that Jim is arriving tomorrow.* **3.** *vt.* MEMORIZE SOMETHING to memorize something, e.g., facts, a poem, a piece of music, or a dance ○ *I have to learn the periodic table for my exam.* **4.** *vt.* TEACH SOMEBODY SOMETHING to teach a topic or skill to somebody (*nonstandard*) [Old English *leornian.* Ultimately from an Indo-European word meaning "track," which also produced English *lore* and *last*². The underlying idea is "to follow a course of instruction."] —**learn·a·ble** *adj.*

learn·ed /lúrnəd/ *adj.* **1.** HIGHLY EDUCATED well-educated and very knowledgeable ○ *a learned professor* **2.** EDUC SCHOLARLY showing or requiring much education and knowledge **3.** LAW HONORABLE used in addressing lawyers in court ○ *my learned colleague* **4.** /lúrnd/ PSYCHOL ACQUIRED, NOT INSTINCTUAL used to describe behavior or knowledge that is acquired through training or experience rather than being instinctual [14thC. Originally the past participle of LEARN in the sense "to teach."] —**learn·ed·ly** /lúrnədlee/ *adv.* —**learn·ed·ness** *n.*

learn·ed help·less·ness *n.* somebody's failure to take action to make his or her life better, arising from a sense of not being in control

learn·er's per·mit *n.* a driver's license for those who have not yet passed a driving test, and subject to various restrictions

learn·ing /lúrning/ *n.* **1.** ACQUIRING OF KNOWLEDGE the acquisition of knowledge or skill **2.** EDUC ACQUIRED KNOWLEDGE knowledge or skill gained through education ○ *a man of great learning* **3.** PSYCHOL CHANGE IN KNOWLEDGE a relatively permanent change in, or acquisition of, knowledge, understanding, or behavior

learn·ing curve *n.* **1.** RATE OF LEARNING the rate at which a new subject or skill is learned **2.** EDUC GRAPH PLOTTING LEARNING OUTCOMES a graph that shows the relation between the rate at which knowledge or a skill is learned and the time spent acquiring it

learn·ing dis·a·bil·i·ty *n.* a condition that either prevents or significantly hinders somebody from learning basic skills or information at the same rate as most people of the same age

learn·ing-dis·a·bled *adj.* prevented or hindered by a learning disability from learning basic skills or information at the same rate as most people of the same age (*not hyphenated when used after a verb*) ○ *materials aimed specifically at learning-disabled children*

learn·ing the·o·ry *n.* the theory that behavior can be explained in terms of how people and animals learn to respond to a stimulus, e.g., learning by rewards and punishments (**operant conditioning**) and learning by association (**classical conditioning**)

learnt past tense, past participle of **learn**

lear·y *adj.* = **leery**

lease /leess/ *n.* **1.** RENTAL CONTRACT a legal contract allowing somebody exclusive possession of another's property for a particular time in return for rent **2.** LENGTH OF LEASE the period of time covered by a lease ■ *vt.* (**leased, leas·ing, leas·es**) **1.** RENT SOMETHING TO SOMEBODY to rent property to somebody under the terms of a lease **2.** RENT SOMETHING FROM SOMEBODY to rent property from somebody under the terms of a lease ○ *We've leased a cottage for the summer.* [14thC. From Anglo-Norman *les,* from *lesser* "to lease," a variant of Old French *laissier* (see LEASH).] —**leas·a·ble** *adj.* —**leas·er** *n.* ◇ **a new lease on life** renewed freshness or vigor, usually resulting from some minor change

WORD KEY: SYNONYMS

See Synonyms at ***hire.***

lease·back /leéss bàk/ *n.* an arrangement in which a property is sold and then leased to its former owner by its new owner

lease·hold /leéss hòld/ *n.* **1.** RENTING OF PROPERTY the holding of a property through a lease **2.** RENTED PROPERTY a property that is leased —**lease·hold·er** *n.*

leash /leesh/ *n.* **1.** LINE USED TO CONTROL ANIMAL a strap, chain, or rope used to control the animal it is attached to, especially one used when walking a dog. *Also called* **lead 2.** RESTRAINT something that controls or restrains somebody ○ *Our supervisor keeps us on a short leash.* **3.** THREE ANIMALS TOGETHER a set of three animals of one type, especially hounds ■ *vt.* (**leashed, leash·ing, leash·es**) **1.** FIT WITH LEASH to attach a leash to an animal ○ *Leash your dog!* **2.** RESTRAIN SOMETHING to restrain your emotions or impulses or the emotions or impulses of somebody under your control [13thC. From Old French *laisse,* from *laissier* "to let go," from Latin *laxare,* literally "to loosen," from *laxus* (see LAX).]

leash law *n.* a law requiring owners to keep their dogs on a leash in public places

least /leest/ CORE MEANING: the smallest or lowest quantity or degree

1. *adj., adv., pron.* SMALLEST AMOUNT POSSIBLE a smaller amount than anything or anyone else ○ *He went up the steps without showing the least anxiety.* ○ *what I liked the least of all* ○ *The least said the soonest mended.* **2.** *adv.* LESS OF A QUALITY THAN OTHERS having less of a particular quality than most other people or things ○ *one of the least appealing movies of the year* **3.** *adj.* EXTREMELY SMALL used to emphasize that something is so small as to be virtually nonexistent ○ *She had not the least idea of what was going on with me.* **4.** *adv.* TO A SMALLER DEGREE indicates that something happens or is true to a smaller degree than at any other time ○ *I had been appointed to take charge while I least expected anything of the sort.* **5.** *pron.* THE MINIMUM used to indicate the minimum that should be done in a situation ○ *The least you can do is to make yourself thoroughly acquainted with the procedure.* [Old English *lǣst,* a contraction of *lǣsest,* from *lǣs* "less"] ◇ **at least 1.** not less than a specified amount ○ *It'll take at least two days to finish.* ○ *We travelled at least forty-five miles without a rest.* **2.** in any case and despite anything else ○ *At least you've got a job, which is more than I have.* **3.** indicates a correction or change ○ *The answer seemed right, or at least close enough.* ◇ **least of all** emphasizes that a negative applies to one case in particular ○ *No one must know of our discovery – least of all our competitors.* ◇ **not (in) the least** not in the slightest ○ *The only noteworthy point about him was of the negative sort – he was not in the least like his sister.* ○ *I'm not the least bit tired.* ◇ **not least** emphasizes something particularly important ○ *It is too early to be sure, not least because the weather may change.* ◇ **to say the least** without exaggerating or overstating the case ○ *We were, to say the least, surprised at her rudeness.*

least com·mon de·nom·i·na·tor *n.* the lowest multiple shared by all the denominators in a set of fractions

least com·mon mul·ti·ple *n.* the lowest whole number that is divisible without a remainder by all of the members of a set of numbers

least fly·catch·er *n.* a small grayish bird of eastern North America that flies from branches to catch flying insects. Latin name: *Empidonax minimus.* [So called because it is slightly smaller than the other "Empidonax" flycatchers]

least squares *n.* a method of finding the best curve to fit a set of statistical data points. It involves squaring the distance that each point is from a given curve, summing the squares, and choosing the curve for which the sum has the minimum value.

least·ways /leést wàyz/ *adv.* in any case and despite anything else (*informal*)

leath·er /léthər/ *n.* **1.** TANNED AND DRESSED HIDE the processed hide of animals with the fur or feathers removed. It is used in making items such as shoes, saddles, luggage, and clothing. **2.** MATERIAL LIKE LEATHER something that is like leather in appearance or texture ○ *fruit leather* **3.** SOMETHING MADE OF LEATHER an item or part of an item that is made of leather **4.** ZOOL DOG'S EARFLAP the flap of a dog's ear ■ **leath·ers** *npl.* CLOTHES MOTORCYCLISTS' LEATHER CLOTHING the protective leather jacket, trousers, boots, and gloves worn by motorcyclists ■ *adj.* **1.** MADE OF LEATHER made of leather or a material that looks like leather **2.** INVOLVING SADOMASOCHISM OR FETISHISM wearing, or for people who wear, leather clothing as a symbol of interest in sadomasochism or as a fetish ■ *vt.* (**-ered, -er·ing, -ers**) **1.** COVER SOMETHING IN LEATHER to give something a covering of leather **2.** PUNISH SOMEBODY PHYSICALLY to beat a person or animal severely, especially by using a leather strap (*dated informal*) [Old English *lether-.* Ultimately from an Indo-European word that is also the ancestor of Irish *leathar* and Welsh *lledr.*]

Leatherback

leath·er·back /léthər bàk/ *n.* the largest of the living sea turtles, which has a flexible shell ridged with bone and covered with leathery skin. Latin name: *Dermochelys coriacea.*

leath·er·leaf /léthər leéf/ (*plural* **-leaves** /-leévz/) *n.* an evergreen bog shrub of North America with small white flowers and leathery leaves. Latin name: *Chamaedaphne calyculata.*

leath·ern /léthərn/ *adj.* made of leather or a material that looks like leather (*archaic*)

leath·er·neck /léthər nèk/ *n.* a member of the United States Marine Corps (*slang*) [From the leather collar that was formerly part of the uniform]

leath·er·wear /léthər wàir/ *n.* clothing and accessories made of leather [Modeled on *sportswear* or *footwear*]

leath·er·wood /léthər wòod/ *n.* **1.** TREES TREE WITH YELLOW FLOWERS a small deciduous tree of eastern North America with pliable branches and bark and small yellow flowers. Latin name: *Dirca palustris.* **2.** PLANTS = **titi**¹

leath·er·work /léthər wùrk/ *n.* **1.** DECORATING OF LEATHER the craft of sculpting, cutting, or burning designs into leather **2.** DECORATED LEATHER items made from leather, especially decorated leather —**leath·er·work·er** *n.* —**leath·er·work·ing** *n.*

leath·er·y /létharee/ *adj.* looking or feeling like leather, especially having a grainy surface or a tough unyielding consistency —**leath·er·i·ness** *n.*

leave¹ /leev/ (**left** /left/, **left, leav·ing, leaves**) *v.* **1.** *vti.* DEPART to go away from a person or place ○ *I leave the office at five o'clock daily.* **2.** *vt.* LET SOMEBODY CONTINUE DOING SOMETHING to go away from somebody in order to allow that person to do something ○ *You run along and leave me to my paperwork.* **3.** *vt.* CAUSE SOMETHING TO REMAIN to give something to somebody or put something in a place before departing ○ *I left my number with Dan.* **4.** *vt.* LET SOMETHING REMAIN BEHIND ACCIDENTALLY to forget to bring something away from a place ○ *I must have left my keys at the office.* **5.** *vt.* GIVE SOMETHING IN WILL to bequeath something as a legacy ○ *He plans to leave all his money to charity.*

6. *vt.* PRODUCE SOMETHING THAT REMAINS to cause a residue, trace, or mark to remain ○ *The snails left trails on the path.* **7.** *vt.* NOT CHANGE CONDITION OF SOMETHING to allow something or somebody to remain unchanged in a certain state ○ *I left my coat on.* ○ *Leave your sister alone.* **8.** *vt.* HAVE SOMETHING REMAINING to cause an amount to remain by removing some amount or part ○ *Six minus four leaves two.* **9.** *vt.* SET SOMETHING ASIDE to save or keep something for somebody's use ○ *I left some cake for you.* **10.** *vt.* DESERT SOMEBODY OR SOMETHING to abandon a person or place ○ *She has left the city to live in the country.* **11.** *vt.* HAVE SOMEBODY AS SURVIVOR to be survived by somebody after death ○ *He leaves a wife and two young sons.* **12.** *vti.* GIVE UP POSITION IN SOMETHING to end participation in a group or activity ○ *She left that job for a better one.* **13.** *vt.* GIVE JOB TO ANOTHER to transfer control of or responsibility for something to somebody ○ *Leave the typing to me.* **14.** *vt.* REJECT SOMETHING to reject something offered ○ *That's the best I can offer, take it or leave it.* [Old English *lǣfan.* Ultimately from an Indo-European word meaning "to stick" and "fatty substance," which is also the ancestor of English *life* and *liver.*] ◇ **leave go** *or* **hold of somebody** *or* **something 1.** to stop holding somebody or something (*nonstandard*) ○ *Leave go of my arm!* **2.** to stop bothering somebody, or stop interfering in a situation ◇ **leave it at that** to do or say no more about something ◇ **leave somebody** *or* **something alone** to avoid bothering or becoming involved with somebody or something ◇ **leave much to be desired** to be highly unsatisfactory ◇ **leave somebody to himself** *or* **herself** to go away and allow somebody to be alone (*often passive*) ◇ **leave well enough alone** to leave a situation as it is rather than risk making it worse

leave behind *vt.* **1.** PROGRESS FASTER THAN SOMEBODY OR SOMETHING to travel or progress faster than somebody or something (*often passive*) **2.** FORGET ABOUT SOMETHING to dismiss something from the mind ○ *She left her worries behind as she headed for the Bahamas.*

leave off *v.* **1.** *vi.* CEASE to stop doing something ○ *Leave off chatting and listen for a change!* **2.** *vt.* STOP USING SOMETHING to stop doing or making use of something ○ *You can leave your coats off as it's so warm.*

leave out *vt.* to fail to include somebody or something, whether by choice or accident ○ *I felt left out of the party.*

leave[2] /leev/ *n.* **1.** PERIOD OF PERMITTED ABSENCE time off from work or duty, with official permission ○ *He'll get a month's paternity leave.* **2.** PERMISSION permission to do something (*formal*) ○ *He was given leave to present his proposal.* **3.** FAREWELL the act of saying goodbye to somebody ○ *We took leave of our host and went on to the next party.* [Old English *lēaf*, literally "pleasure, approval." Ultimately from an Indo-European word meaning "to desire," which is also the ancestor of English *love, believe,* and *furlough.*] ◇ **take leave of your senses** to become entirely irrational or lose all sense of reality

leave[3] /leev/ (**leaved, leav·ing, leaves**) *vi.* to grow foliage ○ *The oak has started to leave.* [13thC. Formed from LEAF.]

leav·en /lévv'n/ *n.* **leav·en, leav·en·ing 1.** RISING AGENT a substance used to make dough rise, especially yeast or other fermenting agents **2.** SOMETHING THAT ENLIVENS something that lightens the weight or mood of something (*literary*) ○ *with a leaven of wit* ■ *vt.* (**-ened, -en·ing, -ens**) **1.** MIX YEAST IN SOMETHING to add leaven to dough **2.** MAKE FOOD RISE to cause bread or cake to rise using leaven **3.** ENLIVEN SOMETHING to lighten the atmosphere or mood of something (*literary*) ○ *His story leavened the mood of the gathering.* [14thC. Via Old French *levain* from assumed Vulgar Latin *levamen*, from Latin *levare* "to raise."]

Leav·en·worth /lévv'n wùrth/ city in northeastern Kansas. It is home to Leavenworth Federal Penitentiary. Population: 39,431 (1996).

leave of ab·sence *n.* **1.** PERMISSION TO BE ABSENT permission to have time off from work or another duty for a specified period ○ *I requested a leave of absence so that I could take a finance course.* **2.** TIME AWAY FROM WORK the time spent away from work or another duty with leave of absence ○ *His leave of absence included the Christmas holidays.*

leaves plural of **leaf**

leave-tak·ing *n.* a saying of goodbye before leaving somebody (*literary*) ○ *After a teary leave-taking, we set off.*

leav·ings /leévingz/ *npl.* something that somebody has left behind or that is left over from something, usually of little value

Leav·is /leéviss/, **F. R.** (1895–1978) British literary critic. He stressed the moral value of the study of literature. He edited the journal *Scrutiny* (1932–53), and wrote *The Great Tradition* (1948), as well as studies of Dickens and D. H. Lawrence. Full name **Frank Raymond Leavis**

Leb·a·nese /lèbbə neéz, -neéss/ (*plural* **-nese**) *n.* somebody who was born or raised in Lebanon, or who has Lebanese citizenship —**Leb·a·nese** *adj.*

Lebanon

Leb·a·non /lébbənən, -nòn/ **1.** republic on the eastern coast of the Mediterranean Sea, in southwestern Asia. Language: Arabic. Currency: Lebanese pound. Capital: Beirut. Population: 3,111,828 (1997). Area: 4,036 sq. mi./10,452 sq. km. Official name **Lebanese Republic 2.** village and county seat of Warren County, southwestern Ohio, situated 18 mi./29 km east of Hamilton. Population: 10,453 (1990). **3.** city in Grafton County, western New Hampshire, situated 19 mi./31 km north of Claremont. Population: 12,183 (1990). **4.** city and county seat of Wilson County, central Tennessee, situated 31 mi./50 km east of Nashville. Population: 15,208 (1990).

Leb·a·non, Mount mountain in western Massachusetts, situated in Berkshire and Middlesex counties

le·bens·raum /láybənz ròwm, láybəns-/ *n.* **1.** ADDITIONAL TERRITORY CLAIMED BY NAZIS additional land in Eastern Europe that the Nazi government claimed was necessary for the continued political and economic development of Germany **2.** SPACE FOR GROWTH adequate room for life or development [Early 20thC. From German, "living space."]

leb·ku·chen /láyb kòokən, láyp kòokhən/ (*plural* **-chen**) *n.* a rich decorated German gingerbread, traditionally baked in a wide variety of shapes and sizes for Christmas and other celebrations [Early 20thC. Via German from Middle High Geman *lebekuoche*, from *lebe* "loaf" + *kuoche* "cake."]

Le·bow·a /lə bṓ ə/ former homeland in northern South Africa, created in 1969 for the northern Sotho people

Le Carré /lə ka ráy/, **John** (*b.* 1931) British novelist. His popular spy novels include *Tinker, Tailor, Soldier, Spy* (1974) and *Smiley's People* (1980). Real name **David John Moore Cornwell**

lech /lech/, **letch** *n.* (*informal*) **1.** LECHER a lecher **2.** INTENSE DESIRE a lustful desire for somebody **3.** INSTANCE OF LECHERY an act or instance of lechery [Late 18thC. Origin uncertain: probably a back-formation from LECHER.]

Le Chate·lier's prin·ci·ple /lə shàtt'l yáyz-/ *n.* the principle that a change affecting a chemical equilibrium is offset by compensatory changes in other components of the equilibrium, thus producing little overall effect [Early 20thC. Named for the French chemist Henri Louis *Le Chatelier* (1850–1936), who formulated it.]

le·chayim *interj., n.* = **l'chaim**

lech·er /léchər/ *n.* a man who behaves lewdly and lustfully in a way regarded as distasteful (*disapproving*) [12thC. From Old French *lecheor*, from *lechier*, literally "to lick." Ultimately of Germanic origin.]

lech·er·ous /léchərəss/ *adj.* expressing or displaying lewdness in a way regarded as distasteful —**lech·er·ous·ly** *adv.* —**lech·er·ous·ness** *n.*

lech·er·y /lécharee/ *n.* lustful behavior especially by a man that is regarded as distasteful [12thC. From Old French *lecherie*, from *lecheor* (see LECHER).]

lech·we /leéchwee/ *n.* **1.** S AFRICAN ANTELOPE an African antelope found mainly in marshes and by rivers in Botswana and Zambia. It has long narrow hooves and long backward-pointing horns. Latin name: *Kobus leche.* **2.** NILE REGION ANTELOPE an African antelope with a white shoulder patch, found in the wetlands of the upper Nile valley. Latin name: *Kobus megaceros.* [Mid-19thC. Of uncertain origin: probably from Sesotho *lets'a.*]

lec·i·thin /léssəthin/ *n.* a waxy substance (**phospholipid**) that consists of choline and fatty acids and occurs widely in plants and animals. Lecithin is used as an emulsifier in foods and commercial products. [Mid-19thC. From French *lécithine*, from Greek *lekithos* "egg yolk," of unknown origin.]

lec·i·thin·ase /léssəthi nàyss, -nàyz/ *n.* = **phospholipase**

Le Corbusier

Le Cor·bu·sier /lə kawr boo zyáy/ (1887–1965) Swiss-born French architect and designer. His dictum that "a house is a machine for living in" formed one of the bases of his own work and of functionalism. Pseudonym of **Charles-Édouard Jeanneret**

lect /lekt/ *n.* a variety within a language, having its own rules [Late 20thC. Back-formation from DIALECT.]

lect. *abbr.* **1.** lecture **2.** lecturer

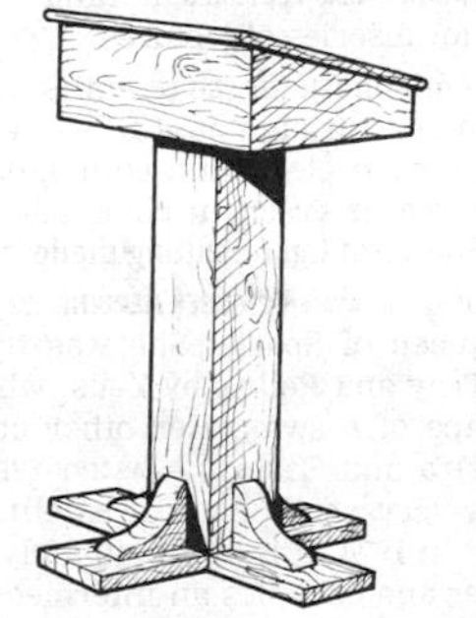

Lectern

lec·tern /léktərn/ *n.* **1.** READING STAND FOR SCRIPTURES a tall slender table with a slanted top on which an open book can rest, used in churches and temples for reading scriptures to the congregation **2.** READING STAND FOR SPEAKER a stand with a slanted top on which a book or lecture notes can rest before a standing speaker. It may be free-standing or be placed on a table or desk. [14thC. Via Old French *letrun* and medieval Latin *lectrinum* from late Latin *lectrum*, from Latin *lect-*, the past participle stem of *legere* "to read" (see LEGIBLE).]

lec·tin /léktin/ *n.* a plant protein that binds to particular sugars [Mid-20thC. Formed from Latin *lect-*, the past participle stem of *legere* "to choose, read" (see LEGIBLE).]

lec·tion /lékshən/ *n.* **1.** TEXTUAL VARIANT a variant reading of a text in a particular edition or translation **2.** CHR BIBLE READING a passage from the Bible that is set to be read on a particular day as part of the liturgy of a Christian service [Early 17thC. Via the Latin stem *lection-* "reading," from, ultimately, *legere* (see LEGIBLE).]

lec·tion·ar·y /léksha nèrree/ (*plural* **-ies**) *n.* a schedule of readings from the Bible for church services during the course of the year, or a book containing such readings

lec·tor /léktər, -tàwr/ *n.* **1.** UNIV UNIVERSITY LECTURER a university lecturer **2.** CHR SCRIPTURE READER somebody who reads passages from the Bible to the congregation at a religious service or to a religious community during meals [14thC. From Latin, literally "reader," from *lect-*, the past participle stem of *legere* (see LEGIBLE).]

lec·ture /lékchər/ *n.* **1.** INSTRUCTIONAL SPEECH an educational speech on a particular subject made before an audience ○ *I missed the lecture on Shakespeare's use of irony.* **2.** TEACHING SESSION a session of a class at which a lecture is given ○ *The course involves two lectures and two lab sessions per week.* **3.** REPRIMAND a lengthy reprimand or scolding concerning something ○ *The teacher lectured the students on their tardiness.* ■ *v.* (**-tured, -tur·ing, -tures**) **1.** *vti.* GIVE EDUCATIONAL SPEECH to deliver a speech before a group of people as a method of instruction ○ *He lectures on stress management all over the country.* **2.** *vi.* BE UNIVERSITY LECTURER to be employed as a lecturer at a university ○ *She lectures at the University.* **3.** *vt.* REPRIMAND SOMEBODY to reprimand somebody by making a speech about how a person should behave ○ *lecturing the congregation about church attendance* [13thC. Via French from medieval Latin *lectura*, literally "reading," from Latin *lect-*, the past participle stem of *legere* (see LEGIBLE).]

lec·ture hall *n.* a large room with tiered or auditorium-style seating, or a building, used for holding lectures

lec·tur·er /lékchərər/ *n.* **1.** UNIV UNIVERSITY TEACHER IN UNITED STATES a teacher in a college or university who neither has tenure nor is a full member of the faculty **2.** *U.K.* UNIV UNIVERSITY TEACHER IN THE UNITED KINGDOM somebody who works as a teacher in higher education in a British university and whose position is lower than that of a professor **3.** INFORMATIVE SPEAKER somebody who gives an informative speech on a particular topic, especially as a profession ○ *a lecturer's tour*

lec·ture·ship /lékchər ship/ *n.* **1.** POSITION OF LECTURER IN UNITED STATES the position of a lecturer at a college or university in the United States, especially a nontenured teaching position at a college or university **2.** *U.K.* BRITISH ACADEMIC POST a post at the rank of lecturer in a British institution of higher education ○ *The University has three lectureships open.* **3.** FINANCE FOR LECTURES a fund that provides financing for a series of lectures

LED *n.* a semiconductor that emits light when a current passes through it. LEDs are used as indicator lights on electronic equipment. They are commonly red or green in color and very energy efficient. Full form **light-emitting diode**

Le·da /leédə/ *n.* **1.** MYTHOL GREEK HEROINE in Greek mythology, a queen of Sparta. She was the mother of Helen of Troy and Pollux by Zeus, who wooed her in the shape of a swan. Her other children were Clytemnestra and Castor. **2.** ASTRON VERY SMALL MOON OF JUPITER a very small natural satellite of Jupiter discovered in 1974. It is approximately 6 mi./10 km in diameter and occupies an intermediate orbit.

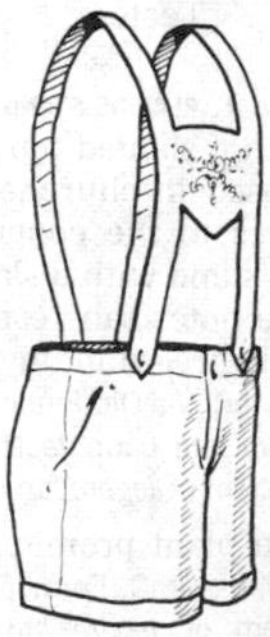

Lederhosen

le·der·ho·sen /láydər hōz'n/ *npl.* a pair of Bavarian leather shorts, usually with suspenders, worn by men and boys [Mid-20thC. From German, "leather trousers."]

ledge /lej/ *n.* **1.** ARCHIT NARROW SHELF AGAINST WALL a narrow shelf or molding attached to a wall that serves a decorative or protective purpose **2.** GEOG FLAT SURFACE PROJECTING FROM ROCK FACE a narrow flat projecting rock shelf, e.g., on the vertical surface of a cliff **3.** OCEANOG UNDERWATER RAISED SURFACE a raised surface underwater such as a reef or ridge, especially one found near a shore **4.** MINING ROCK LAYER a layer of ore-bearing rock [Mid-16thC. Origin uncertain: possibly a variant of LAY[1]. The word's earliest meaning was "crossbar."] —**ledged** *adj.* —**ledg·y** *adj.*

ledg·er /léjjər/ *n.* **1.** ACCT FINANCIAL RECORD BOOK a book or page with columns for debits and credits, on which to transcribe financial records **2.** HORIZONTAL GRAVESTONE a gravestone that lies flat on the ground **3.** CONSTR SCAFFOLDING BEAM a horizontal beam in a scaffolding that is attached to the uprights and supports the beams (**putlogs**) [Early 16thC. Of uncertain origin: probably formed from *leggen*, an earlier form of LAY[1].]

ledg·er board *n.* **1.** HORIZONTAL RAIL a horizontal board, especially the top rail of a fence **2.** JOIST-SUPPORTING BOARD a narrow horizontal board attached to a row of studs to support joist ends

ledg·er line (*plural* **ledg·er lines** *or* **leg·er lines**) *n.* a short line added above or below a musical staff to accommodate notes that are higher or lower than those on the staff

Le·duc /lə do͝ok/ town in Alberta, Canada, situated 20 mi./32 km south of Edmonton. Population: 13,970 (1991).

lee /lee/ *n.* **1.** NAUT SHIP SIDE AWAY FROM WIND the side of a ship away from the source of the wind **2.** PROTECTIVE COVER shelter from the elements when the wind is blowing ○ *in the lee of the wall* ■ *adj.* NAUT AWAY FROM WIND on or toward the side of a ship, natural feature, or object that is away from the wind [Old English *hlēo* "shelter." Ultimately from an Indo-European word meaning "warm" that is also the ancestor of English *lukewarm*, *calorie*, and *chowder*.]

Lee /lee/, **Ann** (1736–84) British-born U.S. religious leader. She led the English Shakers to America (1774).

Lee, Charles (1731–82) British-born U.S. army officer. He left the British Army to fight with the Americans in the American Revolution.

Lee, Francis Lightfoot (1734–97) U.S. politician. A member of the Continental Congress (1775–79), he signed the Declaration of Independence (1776).

Lee, Gypsy Rose (1914–70) U.S. entertainer. The musical *Gypsy* was based on her life as a striptease artist. Born **Louise Rose Hovick**

Lee, Henry (1756–1818) U.S. soldier and politician. He was governor of Virginia (1792–95) and a member of congress (1799–1801).

Lee, Richard Henry (1732–94) U.S. politician. He moved the motion in the Continental Congress that led to the writing of the Declaration of Independence (1776), of which he was a signatory.

Library of Congress

Robert E. Lee

Lee, Robert E. (1807–70) U.S. general. He commanded the Confederate army during the last three years of the Civil War, and surrendered to Ulysses S. Grant at Appomattox Courthouse. Full name **Robert Edward Lee**

Lee, Spike (*b.* 1957) U.S. movie writer and director. His movies, including *Do the Right Thing* (1989) and *Malcolm X* (1992), are concerned with racial issues. Real name **Shelton Jackson Lee**

lee·board /leé bàwrd/ *n.* either of two movable wooden or metal shelves on the outside of a ship's hull that prevent sideways movement caused by the wind [So called because the board on the boat's leeward side is lowered into the water to prevent making leeway]

leech[1] /leech/ *n.* **1.** ZOOL BLOOD-SUCKING WORM a freshwater worm that sucks blood or eats flesh. One species has been used in medical treatments to bleed patients or to eat away putrid flesh from a wound. Class: Hirudinea. **2.** SOMEBODY WHO EXPLOITS SOMEBODY ELSE somebody who clings to or takes advantage of somebody else e.g., for financial support **3.** DOCTOR a physician (*archaic informal*) ■ *v.* (**leeched, leech·ing, leech·es**) **1.** *vt.* MED BLEED SOMEBODY USING LEECHES to bleed a patient using leeches **2.** *vt.* DRAIN OFF SOMETHING to draw off or deplete a supply of something **3.** *vi.* EXPLOIT SOMEBODY to cling to or take advantage of somebody e.g., for financial support (*informal*) [Old English *lǣce*, of uncertain origin: possibly identical with *lǣce* "physician," originally perhaps "speaker of spells," ultimately from an Indo-European base meaning "to speak" that also produced English *lecture*]

leech[2] /leech/, **leach** *n.* **1.** VERTICAL SAIL EDGE a vertical edge of a square sail **2.** EDGE OF SAIL AWAY FROM MAST the edge of a fore-and-aft sail that is farthest from the mast or stay [15thC. Origin uncertain: possibly from Middle Low German *līk* "leech line." Ultimately from an Indo-European word meaning "to bind" that is also the ancestor of English *rely* and *furl*.]

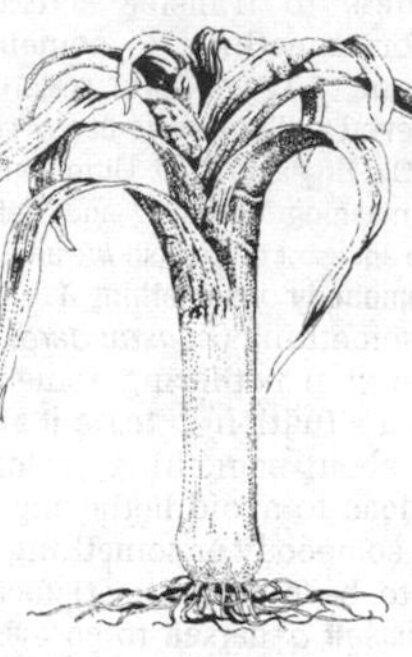

Leek

leek /leek/ *n.* an edible plant with dark green leaves rising from a close-set white base. It is related to the onion and has a flavor similar to it. The leek is one of the national symbols of Wales. Latin name: *Allium porrum.* [Old English *lēac* (source also of English *garlic*), of prehistoric Germanic origin)]

Lee Kuan Yew /leé kwaán yo͞o/ (*b.* 1923) Singaporean statesman. He was the first prime minister of Singapore (1959–90).

leer /leer/ *vi.* (**leered, leer·ing, leers**) LOOK LASCIVIOUSLY to look or smile in a way that suggests unpleasantly lustful or malicious intent ■ *n.* LASCIVIOUS LOOK an unpleasantly lustful or malicious look or smile [Mid-16thC. Origin uncertain: probably from an obsolete word meaning "cheek," from Old English *hlēor*.]

leer·y /leeree/ (**-i·er, -i·est**), **lear·y** (**-i·er, -i·est**) *adj.* regarding somebody or something with suspicion ○ *I'm leery of anyone who approaches me on the street.* [Early 18thC. Origin uncertain: probably formed from LEER in the obsolete meaning "cheek, side of the face," with the underlying meaning "looking sideways."] —**leer·i·ness** *n.*

lees /leez/ *npl.* sediment that settles in wine or another alcoholic beverage during fermentation [14thC. Via Old French *lie* from medieval Latin *lia*, probably of Celtic origin.]

lee shore *n.* a shore that is in the direction away from the wind, relative to a ship

Leeu·win, Cape /loo ín/ headland in southwestern Western Australia, the most southwesterly point on the continent

lee·ward /leéwərd/; (*nautical*) /lo͞o ərd/ *adj.* AWAY FROM WIND on or toward a location, especially the side of a ship, that is away or sheltered from the wind. ◊ **windward** ■ *n.* PLACE AWAY FROM WIND a place or direction away or sheltered from the wind. ◊ **windward**

Lee·ward Is·lands /leéwərd-/ chain of islands in the West Indies, between the Atlantic Ocean and the Caribbean Sea. The principal islands include Antigua, Guadeloupe, Montserrat, and St. Kitts. Area: 1,237 sq. mi./3,297 sq. km.

lee·way /leé wày/ *n.* **1.** LATITUDE FOR VARIATION the permissible margin for variation or deviation from something **2.** SAILING, AEROSP DEVIATION FROM COURSE the sideways movement of a ship or aircraft from its course, caused by strong winds

left[1] /left/ *adj.* **1.** WEST WHEN FACING NORTH on or toward the west when somebody or something is facing north ○ *Her left leg is broken.* **2. left, Left** POL ADVOCATING POLITICAL AND SOCIAL CHANGE supporting liberal, socialist, or communist political and social changes or reform **3.** GEOG ON LEFT WHEN LOOKING DOWNSTREAM on the river bank to the left of somebody facing downstream **4.** THEATER TO RIGHT OF AUDIENCE on or relating to that part of a stage that is to the left of somebody standing on it and facing the audience ○ *Exit stage left.* ■ *adv.* **ON LEFT SIDE** on or toward the left side of somebody or something ○ *The pole is leaning left a bit.* ■ *n.* **1. LEFT SIDE** the left side of somebody or something ○ *The house is on your left.* **2. left, Left** POL **LIBERALS, SOCIALISTS AND COMMUNISTS** people who support liberal, socialist, or communist political and social changes or reform **3.** BOXING **LEFT-HANDED PUNCH** a blow delivered with the left hand ○ *took a hard left to the jaw* **4.** BOXING **LEFT-HANDED PUNCHING ABILITY** a boxer's left hand with respect to its ability to deliver a punch ○ *He's got a good left.* **5.** BASEBALL = **left field** [13thC. From Old English *lyft-* "weak," of unknown origin.]

left[2] past tense, past participle of **leave**

left a·tri·o·ven·tric·u·lar valve *n.* = **mitral valve**

Left Bank area in central Paris, south of the Seine River

left-brain *adj.* relating to or involving skills or knowledge such as analytical or linguistic ability that are believed to be associated with the left half of the cerebrum —**left brain** *n.*

left face *n., interj.* a military command to turn 90° to the left, or the execution of that command

left field *n.* **1.** BASEBALL **SECTION OF OUTFIELD** the part of the outfield in baseball that is to the batter's left **2.** BASEBALL **OUTFIELDER'S POSITION** the position held by the baseball player who is responsible for fielding balls that are hit to left field **3. VERY UNUSUAL POSITION** a position that is so different from mainstream beliefs that it is not generally taken seriously (*informal*) ◇ **out in left field** extremely bizarre or wrong (*informal*)

left field·er *n.* BASEBALL a baseball player who is responsible for fielding balls hit to left field

left-hand *adj.* **1. TO LEFT** on or toward the left **2. FOR LEFT HAND** intended for or done by the left hand

left-hand·ed *adj.* **1. USING LEFT HAND** using the left hand, instead of the right, for tasks such as writing and reaching for and manipulating objects. About ten percent of the population is naturally left-handed. **2.** SPORTS **STARTING SWING FROM LEFT** swinging from the left to the right **3. DONE WITH LEFT HAND** done using the left hand **4. NOT SINCERE** ironic and insincere ○ *a left-handed compliment* **5. CLUMSY** lacking skill or grace **6. TURNING RIGHT TO LEFT** spiraling toward the left **7.** LAW = **morganatic** ■ *adv.* **1. WITH LEFT HAND** with the left hand, especially when it is used instead of the right for tasks such as writing **2. WITH LEFT-HANDED SWING** with a swing that moves from the left to the right —**left-hand·er** *n.*

left-hand·er *n.* somebody who uses the left hand for tasks such as writing and reaching for and manipulating objects

left·ie /léftee/ *n.* = **lefty**

left·ish /léftish/ *adj.* tending to be relatively left-wing in politics

left·ism /léf tìzzəm/, **Left·ism** *n.* the advocating of liberal, socialist, or communist political and social change or reform —**left·ist** *adj., n.*

left-lug·gage of·fice *n. U.K.* = **baggage check**

left·most /léft mōst/ *adj.* in the position farthest to the left

left·o·ver /léft ōvər/ *adj.* **REMAINING UNUSED** remaining after the rest of something has been used or eaten ■ *n.* **SOMETHING REMAINING** something that remains or was not used ■ **left·o·vers** *npl.* **SAVED FOOD** food remaining from a previous meal or meals, saved and served again or made into a new dish ○ *I made this soup from leftovers.*

left·ward /léftwərd/ *adj.* **GOING OR BEING LEFT** moving toward or located on the left ■ *adv.* **left·ward, left·wards TO OR AT LEFT** toward or on the left

left wing *n.* POL a subgroup of a larger organization that is more liberal or radical than the rest of the organization —**left-wing** *adj.* —**left-wing·er** *n.*

left·y /léftee/, **left·ie** *n.* (*plural* **-ies**) (*informal*) **1.** POL **LEFTIST** somebody with left-wing beliefs **2. LEFT-HANDER** somebody who is left-handed ○ *How many lefties are on the team?* ■ *adv.* **WITH LEFT HAND** with the left hand or in a left-handed way (*informal*) ○ *He bats lefty.*

leg /leg/ *n.* **1.** ANAT **LOWER LIMB** any of the limbs that animals and people use for standing, walking, running, or jumping, either including or excluding the foot **2.** FURNITURE, BUILDING **SUPPORTING POLE** a part of an object that looks like a leg and is used to support it ○ *a table leg* **3.** FOOD **MEAT FROM ANIMAL'S OR FOWL'S LEG** the meat, including the bone, from the back hindquarter of a four-legged animal, or from the leg of a bird, that is cooked and eaten as food **4. BRANCH OF OBJECT** one of the extensions of a branched object **5.** CLOTHES **CLOTHING FOR LEG** the portion of a piece of clothing that covers all or part of the leg ○ *pants leg* **6.** GEOM **RIGHT-ANGLE SIDE OF TRIANGLE** either of the two sides of a right triangle that extends from the right angle **7. SECTION OF TRIP** a part of a trip that is separated from other parts by a period of rest, or by a change in direction or the manner of travel **8.** SAILING **SAILING COMPLETED ON ONE TACK** the distance traveled by a boat on a single tack **9.** SPORTS **RELAY RACE PORTION** one of the parts of a relay race that a single athlete completes **10. GESTURE OF RESPECT** a bow in honor of a superior made by extending one straight leg forward and bending the back leg **11.** SPORTS **PORTION OF SPORTS COMPETITION** one of stages, events, or games that is part of a larger competition but is treated independently of the other parts and has its own winner ■ **legs** *npl.* WINE **WINE CLINGING TO GLASS** the vertical trails of wine that cling to the side of a glass after wine has been swirled around in it. The length and movement of these trails are taken as an indication of the wine's body. ■ *vt.* NAUT **MOVE BOAT THROUGH TUNNEL** to move a canal boat through a tunnel by lying on the deck and pushing off the roof or walls of the tunnel with the legs (*archaic*) [13thC. From Old Norse *leggr*, of unknown origin.] ◇ **a leg up 1.** a push or lift up onto or over something **2.** an advantage over others ◇ **have legs** to be of long or lasting duration ◇ **leg it** to walk or run (*informal*) ◇ **not have a leg to stand on** to have nothing to justify or support an attitude or position (*informal*) ◇ **on your last legs** on the verge of collapse or breakdown ◇ **pull somebody's leg** to tell somebody something untrue in teasing or for fun (*informal*) ◇ **shake a leg 1.** to hurry up (*usually used as a command*) **2.** to dance (*dated informal*) ◇ **stretch your legs** to go for a walk after a period of being seated or stationary

leg. *abbr.* **1.** legal **2.** legate **3.** MUSIC legato **4.** legislation **5.** legislative **6.** legislature

leg·a·cy /léggəssee/ *n.* (*plural* **-cies**) **1. BEQUEST MADE IN WILL** money or property that is left to somebody in a will **2. SOMETHING FROM PAST** something that is handed down or remains from a previous generation or time ■ *adj.* **OUTDATED OR DISCONTINUED** associated with something that is outdated or discontinued [14thC. Via Old French *legacie* "office of a delegate" from medieval Latin *legatia*, from Latin *legatus* (see LEGATE).]

le·gal /leég'l/ *adj.* **1. LAW-RELATED** relating to the law or to courts of law **2. OF OR FOR LAWYERS** relating to lawyers or to law as a profession **3. UNDER THE LAW** established under the law, or by common law or legislation ○ *the legal age of consent* **4. PERMITTED BY LAW** allowed under the law ○ *Parking on the grass isn't legal.* **5. ESTABLISHED BY LAW COURT** recognized or established by a court of law, rather than a court of equity **6. OLD ENOUGH UNDER LAW** older than a minimum age established by law for some activities such as driving (*informal*) [15thC. Via French from Latin *legalis*, from *leg-*, the stem of *lex* "law."]

WORD KEY: SYNONYMS

legal, lawful, decriminalized, legalized, legitimate, licit

CORE MEANING: used to describe something that is permitted, recognized, or required by law

legal permitted, recognized, or required by law; **lawful** a less commonly used word meaning the same as "legal"; **decriminalized** no longer categorized as a criminal offence; **legalized** previously categorized as illegal and now declared legal; **legitimate** legally acceptable; **licit** a very formal and now rarely used word meaning the same as "legal".

WORD KEY: ORIGIN

The Latin stem *leg-*, from which ***legal*** is derived, is also the source of English *allegation, colleague, college, delegate, legacy, legislate, legitimate, loyal,* and *privilege.*

le·gal age *n.* the age, according to the law, after which somebody is considered to be an adult

le·gal aid *n.* legal advice or representation that is provided by an organization at low or no cost to people who cannot afford to pay for legal services

le·gal cap *n.* ruled white writing paper used by lawyers that is 8½ in./216 mm by 14 in./350 mm to 16 in./406 mm, with the fold at the top

le·gal ea·gle *n.* a lawyer, especially a skillful or successful one (*slang*) [Rhyming expression of uncertain origin, perhaps from the keenness of vision for which the eagle is known]

le·gal·ese /leég'l eéz, -eéss/ *n.* language that is typically used in legal documents and is generally considered by lay people to be difficult to understand

le·gal hol·i·day *n.* a day established as a holiday by law, when government offices, schools, and post offices are typically closed. Legal holidays usually commemorate an event or person and many businesses close as well.

le·gal·ism /leég'l ìzzəm/ *n.* **1. ADHERENCE TO LETTER OF LAW** strict adherence to a literal interpretation of a law, rule, or religious or moral code **2.** LAW **LAW TERM** a word or phrase in legal jargon **3.** CHR **BELIEF IN NECESSITY OF GOOD DEEDS** the belief that good deeds are required for entrance into Heaven —**le·gal·ist** *n.* —**le·gal·is·tic** /leég'l ístik/ *adj.* —**le·gal·is·ti·cal·ly** *adv.*

le·gal·i·ty /lee gálləteе/ (*plural* **-ties**) *n.* **1. CONFORMITY TO LAW** the state of being in accordance with the law ○ *the legality of the corporation's activities* **2. OBEYING OF LAW** the observance of the law **3. LEGAL REQUIREMENT** something required by law, especially when a technical detail (*often used in the plural*) ○ *We have to take care of certain legalities before opening the business.*

le·gal·ize /leég'l ìz/ (**-ized, -iz·ing, -iz·es**) *vt.* to make an activity legal by making or changing a law —**le·gal·i·za·tion** /leég'li záysh'n/ *n.*

le·gal pad *n.* a pad of yellow ruled paper measuring 8½ in./216 mm by 14 in./356 mm, typically used by lawyers

le·gal re·serves, **le·gal re·serve** *npl., n.* an amount of money that a financial organization such as a bank or insurer is required to keep as security against debts

le·gal sep·a·ra·tion *n.* separation of a married couple that is recognized by a court of law, or the court decree establishing such a separation. This is often required as a first step toward divorce.

le·gal-size *adj.* having the size of a piece of legal pad paper, 8½ in./216 mm by 14 in./350 mm, or a size that is appropriate to hold such paper

le·gal ten·der *n.* the currency that is valid for the payment of a debt and must be accepted by a creditor

Le·gas·pi /lə gásspee/, **Le·gaz·pi** city and capital of Albay Province, Philippines, situated at the head of Albay Gulf. Population: 121,120 (1990).

leg·ate /léggət/ *n.* **1.** CHR **POPE'S REPRESENTATIVE** an emissary of the Pope, especially one who represents the Vatican in other countries **2.** POL **GOVERNMENT REPRESENTATIVE** an official representative of a government, especially a diplomat **3.** HIST **PROVINCIAL GOVERNOR'S ASSISTANT** in the ancient Roman Republic, an assistant to a provincial governor **4.** HIST **COMMANDER OF ROMAN LEGION** in the ancient Roman Empire, a legion commander who was sometimes also a provincial governor [12thC. Via French from Latin *legatus*, from the past participle of *legare* "to send as an envoy, bequeath" (source also of English *colleague, delegate,* and *relegate*).] —**leg·ate·ship** *n.* —**leg·a·tine** /léggə teen, -tīn/ *adj.*

leg·a·tee /lèggə teé/ *n.* somebody who inherits a bequest under the terms of a will

le·ga·tion /lə gáysh'n/ *n.* **1. DIPLOMAT'S RESIDENCE** the official local residence of a senior diplomat assigned to a country. It ranks below an embassy in importance. **2. DIPLOMATIC STAFF** the staff of a legation **3. DIPLOMATS ON MISSION** a group of representatives sent on a mission, especially a diplomatic mission **4. SENDING OF DIPLOMATIC REPRESENTATIVE** the sending of a representative on a diplomatic mission **5. DIPLOMATIC MISSION** a mission performed by a diplomatic representative **6. LEGATE'S POSITION** the status or office of a legate [14thC. Directly or via French from, ultimately, Latin *legare* "to send as an envoy" (source of English *legate*).]

le·ga·to /lə gaá tō/ *adv.* **SMOOTHLY** in a smooth, even manner, often indicated in a musical score by a curved line (**slur**) connecting the notes to be so played (*used as a musical direction*) ■ *n.* (*plural* **-tos**) **LEGATO PIECE OF MUSIC** a piece of music, or a section of a piece, played legato [Mid-18thC. From Italian, literally "tied together."] —**le·ga·to** *adj.*

le·ga·tor /lə gáytər/ *n.* somebody who has made a will to pass on property to somebody else

leg·end /léjjənd/ *n.* **1.** OLD STORY a story that has been passed down for generations, especially one that is presented as history but is unlikely to be true **2.** OLD STORIES a group of stories presented as history but unlikely to be true **3.** MODERN MYTH a popular myth that has arisen in modern times **4.** CELEBRITY somebody famous admired for a particular skill or talent **5.** INSCRIPTION an inscription on an object, especially a title or motto **6.** PUBL CAPTION a caption for an illustration **7.** MAPS MAP KEY an explanation of the symbols used on a map (*dated*) [14thC. Via French *légende* from medieval Latin *legenda*, literally "things to be read," from Latin *legere* (see LEGIBLE).]

leg·en·dar·y /léjjən dèrree/ *adj.* **1.** BELONGING TO LEGEND described or commemorated in a legend ○ *the legendary figure of Hercules* **2.** CONTAINING LEGENDS retold for generations as history but unlikely to be completely or even partially true ○ *the legendary tales of ancient warriors* **3.** LIKE SOMETHING IN LEGEND appropriate for a legend ○ *an organization of legendary proportions* **4.** FAMOUS very famous in contemporary society —**leg·en·dar·i·ly** *adv.*

leg·end·ry /léjjəndree/ (*plural* **-ries**) *n.* a collection or group of legends

Léger /lay zhay/, **Fernand** (1881–1955) French painter. One of the founders of the Cubist movement, he developed a personal style that used rounded and cylindrical forms.

Léger, Jules (1913–80) Canadian government official. He was governor-general of Canada (1974–79).

leg·er·de·main /lèjjərdə máyn/ *n.* **1.** ARTS = **sleight of hand 2.** SHOW OF SKILL a display of skill or cleverness, especially for deceitful purposes ○ *a dazzling display of political legerdemain* [15thC. From French *léger de main*, literally "light of hand."]

le·ges plural of **lex**

-legged *suffix.* **1.** with a particular number of legs ○ *four-legged* **2.** with a particular type of legs ○ *bandy-legged*

leg·ging /légging/ *n.* PROTECTIVE COVERING FOR LOWER LEG a protective covering made of a strong material that is wrapped around the lower leg by laborers and players in certain sports ■ **leg·gings** *npl.* **1.** CLOSE-FITTING PANTS women's pants or footless tights made of elastic material that fit very closely to the legs and hips **2.** PROTECTIVE OUTER PANTS waterproof or insulated outer pants that are worn for protection from snow, rain, and cold

leg·gy /léggee/ (**-gi·er, -gi·est**) *adj.* **1.** WITH LONG LEGS having very long legs in relation to the rest of the body **2.** WITH SHAPELY LEGS having long good-looking legs **3.** BOT SPINDLY IN GROWTH with long thin stems that have few and widely spaced leaves

leg·horn /lég hàwrn, -gərn/ *n.* **1.** BLEACHED STRAW fine bleached straw made from a type of Italian wheat **2.** STRAW FABRIC a fabric made from plaited leghorn straw **3.** STRAW HAT a hat made from leghorn straw [Mid-18thC. Named for the city of *Leghorn* (Livorno) in Italy, where the wheat originated.]

Leg·horn /lég hàwrn, -gərn/ *n.* a small domestic fowl from the Mediterranean region that is noted for its rapid production of white eggs [Mid-18thC. Named for the city of *Leghorn* (Livorno) in Italy, where the bird originated.]

leg·i·ble /léjjəb'l/ *adj.* **1.** ABLE TO BE READ clear enough to be read **2.** ABLE TO BE RECOGNIZED capable of being easily understood or recognized (*archaic*) [15thC. From late Latin *legibilis*, from *legere* "to collect, read." Ultimately from an Indo-European base meaning "to gather, speak."] —**leg·i·bil·i·ty** /lèjjə bíllətee/ *n.* —**leg·i·ble·ness** /léjjəb'lnəss/ *n.*

WORD KEY: ORIGIN

The Latin word *legere*, from which ***legible*** is derived, is also the source of English *coil, collect, cull, elect, elegant, intelligent, lecture, legend, legion, lesson, neglect,* and *select.*

le·gion /leéjən/ *n.* **1.** HIST ROMAN ARMY DIVISION in ancient Rome, an army division of 3,000 to 6,000 soldiers, including cavalry **2.** MIL LARGE BODY OF SOLDIERS a large military unit, especially an army ○ *the French Foreign Legion* **3.** MIL ORGANIZATION OF EX-MILITARY PERSONNEL an association of ex-servicemen and ex-servicewomen ○ *the American Legion* **4.** MULTITUDE a large number of people or things ○ *Their complicated affairs are managed by a legion of accountants.* ■ *adj.* MANY very numerous ○ *dissatisfied customers and their legion complaints* [12thC. Via Old French from the Latin stem *legion-*, from *legere* "to gather, choose" (see LEGIBLE); the underlying meaning was "picked troops."]

le·gion·ar·y /leéjə nèrree/ *adj.* OF OR FORMING LEGION belonging to, typical of, or forming a legion ■ *n.* (*plural* **-ies**) SOLDIER IN LEGION a member of a legion, especially a Roman legion. ◊ **legionnaire** *n.* 1

le·gion·ar·y ant *n.* = **army ant**

le·gion·naire /leèjə náir/, **Le·gion·naire** *n.* **1.** SOMEBODY IN LEGION a soldier in a legion, especially the French Foreign Legion. ◊ **legionary** *n.* **2.** SOMEBODY IN AMERICAN LEGION a member of the American Legion [Early 19thC. From French *légionnaire*, from *légion* (see LEGION).]

Le·gion·naires' dis·ease *n.* a virulent and sometimes fatal form of pneumonia caused by a bacterium and spread mainly by the water droplets in air conditioning systems [From the first recognized occurrence of the disease at an American Legion convention in Philadelphia in 1976]

Le·gion of Hon·or *n.* a French order of merit awarded for illustrious military or civil service. It was established by Napoleon in 1802.

Le·gion of Mer·it *n.* an American military decoration awarded to military personnel from any country for exceptional and outstanding service

legis. *abbr.* **1.** legislation **2.** legislative **3.** legislature

leg·is·late /léjji slàyt/ (**-lat·ed, -lat·ing, -lates**) *v.* **1.** *vi.* MAKE LAWS to write and pass laws **2.** *vt.* BRING SOMETHING ABOUT BY MAKING LAWS to make laws or rules designed to bring about some action or condition ○ *No one can legislate good manners.* [Early 18thC. Back-formation from LEGISLATOR.]

leg·is·la·tion /lèjji sláysh'n/ *n.* **1.** MAKING OF LAWS the process of writing and passing laws **2.** LAW OR LAWS a law or laws passed by an official body, especially a govermental assembly

leg·is·la·tive /léjji slàytiv/ *adj.* **1.** RELATING TO LAWMAKING involved in the writing and passing of laws **2.** RELATING TO LAWMAKING BODY relating to or part of a legislature **3.** ENACTED BY LAW created by governmental legislation ○ *There is no legislative solution to this problem.* —**leg·is·la·tive·ly** *adv.*

leg·is·la·tive as·sem·bly, Leg·is·la·tive As·sem·bly *n.* **1.** U.S. LAWMAKING BODY the two-chambered legislature of some U.S. states **2.** LOWER HOUSE OF BRITISH COMMONWEALTH LEGISLATURE the lower house of a two-chambered state legislature in some British Commonwealth countries, especially that of some Australian states **3.** SINGLE-CHAMBER BRITISH COMMONWEALTH LEGISLATURE a single-chamber legislature, especially the legislature of most Canadian provinces and some Australian states **4.** GROUP WITH POWER TO PASS LAWS any official body with law- or rule-making powers

leg·is·la·tive coun·cil, Leg·is·la·tive Coun·cil *n.* **1.** COMMITTEE OF STATE SENATORS AND REPRESENTATIVES a permanent committee consisting of members of both houses of a two-chambered state legislature who discuss issues of common concern and plan a legislative program for the next session **2.** UPPER HOUSE IN TWO-CHAMBERED LEGISLATURE the upper house of the two-chambered legislature in some British Commonwealth countries, e.g., in most Indian and Australian states **3.** LEGISLATURE IN FORMER BRITISH COLONY the single-chamber legislature of some former British colonies

leg·is·la·tor /léjji slàytər/ *n.* somebody who writes and passes laws, especially as a member of a legislature [15thC. From Latin *legis lator* "proposer of a law," from *lex* "law" + *lat-*, the past participle stem of *ferre* "to bring."] —**leg·is·la·to·ri·al** /lèjjislə táwree əl/ *adj.* —**leg·is·la·tor·ship** /léjji slaytər shìp/ *n.*

leg·is·la·ture /léjji slàychər/ *n.* an official body, usually chosen by election, with the power to make, change, and repeal laws [Late 17thC. Formed from LEGISLATOR, on the model of JUDICATURE.]

le·gist /leéjist/ *n.* a specialist in law, especially classical law [15thC. Via French *légiste* from, ultimately, the Latin stem *leg-* (see LEGAL).]

le·git /lə jít/ *adj.* **1.** LEGAL complying with the law (*slang*) **2.** HONEST AND TRUTHFUL telling the truth and not trying to deceive (*slang*) ○ *Is his story legit?* **3.** THEATER PRESENTING SERIOUS DRAMAS performing professionally produced dramatic theater that is considered to be serious art, in contrast to such forms as burlesque, revues, and musical comedy (*informal*) [Late 19thC. Shortening of LEGITIMATE.]

le·git·i·mate *adj.* /lə jíttimət/ **1.** LAW LEGAL complying with the law, or under the law ○ *legitimate tax deductions* **2.** CONFORMING TO ACKNOWLEDGED STANDARDS complying with recognized rules, standards, or traditions ○ *not a legitimate excuse for missing school* **3.** NOT SPURIOUS well-reasoned and sincere ○ *We have legitimate reasons for worrying about the quality of our water.* **4.** BORN IN WEDLOCK born of legally married parents **5.** POL, LAW WITH RIGHT OF INHERITANCE having the right to inherit something, such as the throne in a monarchy **6.** THEATER RELATING TO SERIOUS PROFESSIONAL DRAMA performing or involving professionally produced dramatic works that are considered to be serious art, in contrast to such forms as burlesque, revues, and musical comedy ■ *vt.* /lə jítti màyt/ (**-mat·ed, -mat·ing, -mates**) **1.** LAW LEGALIZE SOMETHING to make somebody or something lawful, by making, changing, or repealing laws or by decree **2.** PROVE SOMETHING TO BE LAWFUL to argue or prove that a claim or action is lawful or reasonable [15thC. Via medieval Latin *legitimatus*, the past participle of *legitimare* "to make legal," from Latin *legitimus* "lawful," from *lex* "law" (see LEGAL).] —**le·git·i·ma·cy** *n.* —**le·git·i·mate·ly** *adv.* —**le·git·i·mate·ness** *n.* —**le·git·i·ma·tion** /lə jìtti máysh'n/ *n.* —**le·git·i·mat·or** *n.*

le·git·i·ma·tize /lə jíttimə tīz/ (**-tized, -tiz·ing, -tiz·es**) *vt.* = **legitimate** *v.* 1, **legitimate** *v.* 2 —**le·git·ima·ti·za·tion** /lə jìttiməti záysh'n/ *n.*

le·git·i·mist /lə jíttimist/ *n.* **1.** MONARCHIST somebody who believes in political rule by inheritance or in a particular person's claim to legitimate inheritance of a throne **2.** HIST BOURBON SUPPORTER a supporter of the Bourbon claimants to the French throne in the 19th century [Mid-19thC. From French *légitimiste*, from *légitime* "legitimate," from Latin *legitimus* (see LEGITIMATE).] —**le·git·i·mist** *adj.* —**le·git·i·mism** *n.*

le·git·i·mize /lə jítti mīz/ (**-mized, -miz·ing, -miz·es**) *vt.* = **legitimate** *v.* 1, **legitimate** *v.* 2 [Mid-19thC. Formed from Latin *legitimus* (see LEGITIMATE).] —**le·git·i·mi·za·tion** /lə jìttimi záysh'n/ *n.* —**le·git·i·miz·er** *n.*

leg·man /lég màn, légmən/ (*plural* **-men** /-mèn, -mən/) *n.* **1.** ERRAND RUNNER somebody employed in an office to run errands and gather information **2.** COMMUNICATION NEWS REPORTER a reporter who gathers information for a story, especially from firsthand sources

Leg·o /léggō/ *tdmk.* a trademark for a toy consisting of plastic building blocks and other components

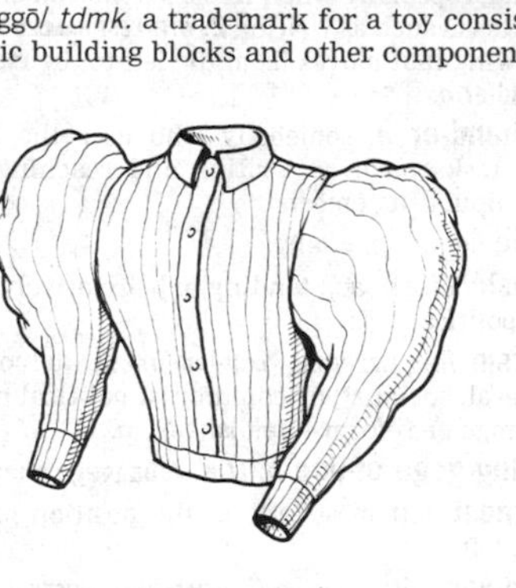

Leg-of-mutton

leg-of-mut·ton, leg-o'-mut·ton *adj.* shaped like a sharply tapered triangle

leg·room /lég ro͝om, -ro͞om/ *n.* space in front of a seat for somebody's legs, especially enough space to stretch out and move the legs

Le Guin /lə gwín/, **Ursula** (*b.* 1929) U.S. writer. Her science fiction novels include *The Left Hand of Darkness* (1969). Born **Ursula Kroeber**

leg·ume /lé gyo͞om, lə gyo͞om/ *n.* **1.** PLANTS LEGUMINOUS PLANT a plant that has pods as fruits and roots that bear nodules containing nitrogen-fixing bacteria **2.** FOOD SEED OR POD OF LEGUMINOUS PLANT a seed, pod, or other part of a legume, used as food [Mid-17thC. Via French *légume* from Latin *legumen* "bean," of uncertain origin.]

le·gu·mi·nous /lə gyo͞omeenəss/ *adj.* **1.** OF LEGUME PLANT FAMILY belonging to or typical of the family of plants that has pods as fruits and roots that bear nodules containing nitrogen-fixing bacteria **2.** LIKE LEGUMES resembling a leguminous plant or its seed pods [Mid-17thC. From Latin *leguminosus*, from *legumin-*, the stem of *legumen* "bean."]

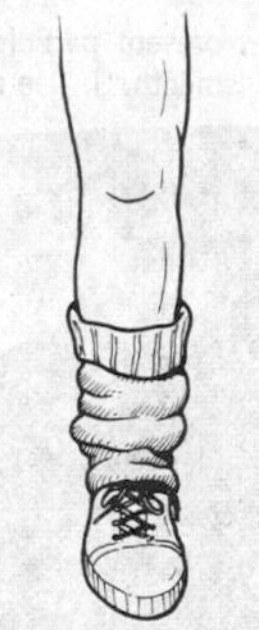

Legwarmer

leg·warm·er /lég wàwrmər/ *n.* a knit tube that covers the calf and sometimes also the top of the foot, and is typically worn by a dancer during practice (*usually used in the plural*)

leg·work /lég wùrk/ *n.* preparatory research for a project that is usually physically demanding or involves a lot of walking (*informal*)

Le Ha·vre /lə haávrə/ city in Seine-Maritime Department, Haute-Normandie Region, northwestern France. Population: 197,219 (1990).

Lehrer /láirər/, **Tom** (*b.* 1928) U.S. teacher and songwriter. A university professor, he became a successful entertainer in the 1960s with his humorous songs, many of them political satires.

le·hu·a /lay hoō ə/ (*plural* **-as**) *n.* **1.** TREES **RED-FLOWERED POLYNESIAN TREE** a common evergreen shrub of the Pacific Islands that has large red flowers. Latin name: *Metrosideros collinus.* **2.** PLANTS **RED FLOWER** the red flower of the lehua tree [Late 19thC. From Hawaiian.]

lei[1] /lay, láy ee/ (*plural* **leis**) *n.* a garland of flowers, especially one worn around the neck in Hawaii and other parts of Polynesia [Mid-19thC. From Hawaiian.]

lei[2] plural of **leu**

Leib·niz /līb nits/, **Leib·nitz, Gottfried Wilhelm von, Baron** (1646–1716) German philosopher and mathematician. The first president of the Prussian Academy of Sciences, he discovered calculus (independently of Newton) and contributed to the sciences of mechanics, optics, and logic, and to probability theory. —**Leib·niz·i·an** /līb nítsee ən/ *adj., n.*

Lei·den /līd'n/, **Ley·den** university city in Zuid-Holland Province, western Netherlands. Population: 114,892 (1994).

Leif Ericson /leef érrikss'n/ (975–1020) Icelandic explorer. He sailed from the Norse settlement in Greenland to become one of the first Europeans to reach North America. His story is told in the Icelandic *Eiriks Saga.*

Vivien Leigh

Leigh /lee/, **Vivien** (1913–67) British actor. She won Academy Awards for her perfomances in *Gone with the Wind* (1939) and *A Streetcar Named Desire* (1951).

Lein·ster /lénstər/ historic province in the eastern Republic of Ireland. Population: 1,921,835 (1996). Area: 7,580 sq. mi./19,633 sq. km.

Leip·zig /līpsig/ city and cultural center in east central Germany, known for its international trade fairs. Population: 487,700 (1994).

leish·man·i·a·sis /leeshmə nī əssiss/ *n.* an infection such as kala-azar and some other skin diseases that are caused by a protozoan that is a parasite in the tissue of vertebrates [Early 20thC. Formed from modern Latin *Leishmania*, genus name, from the name of the Scottish pathologist Sir William Boog *Leishman* (1865–1926), who identified it.]

leis·ter /leestər/ *n.* **THREE-PRONGED FISH SPEAR** a stick with three prongs, used for spearing fish ■ *vt.* (**-tered, -ter·ing, -ters**) **CATCH FISH WITH LEISTER** to catch fish using a three-pronged spear [Mid-16thC. From Old Norse *ljóstr*, from *ljósta* "to strike," of unknown origin.]

lei·sure /leezhər, lézhər/ *n.* time during which somebody has no obligations or work responsibilities, and therefore is free to engage in enjoyable activities [13thC. Via Old French dialect *leisour* "permission," literally "to be allowed," a variant of *leisir*, from Latin *licere* (see LICENSE.] ◇ **at your leisure** at the time and pace that suits you ◇ **gentleman** *or* **lady** *or* **man** *or* **woman of leisure** used to describe a man or woman who does not have to work for a living (*humorous*) ○ *a lady of leisure*

lei·sured /leezhərd, lézhərd/ *adj.* **1. NOT HAVING TO WORK** having a lot of free time, especially as a result of having enough money not to have to work for a living **2.** = **leisurely**

lei·sure·ly /leezhərlee, lézh-/ *adj.* **lei·sure·ly, lei·sured SLOW AND RELAXED** relaxed, unhurried, and enjoyable, usually because done during free time ○ *a leisurely stroll in the park* ■ *adv.* **IN UNHURRIED WAY** in a slow and relaxed manner —**lei·sure·li·ness** *n.*

lei·sure so·ci·e·ty *n.* a society in which a greater proportion of people's time is spent in leisure than in work

lei·sure suit *n.* a man's casual outfit, usually made of synthetic double-knit fabric, consisting of a jacket resembling a shirt and matching pants, first popular in the 1970s

lei·sure·wear /leezhər wàir, lézhər-/ *n.* comfortable informal clothing such as a sweat suit, appropriate for relaxation or play

leit·mo·tif /līt mō teef, līt mō teef/, **leit·mo·tiv** *n.* **1.** MUSIC **THEMATIC PASSAGE OF MUSIC** a musical theme that recurs in the course of a work to evoke a particular character or situation, especially typical of the operas of Richard Wagner **2. MAIN RECURRING THEME** a recurring theme, e.g., in literature or history [Late 19thC. From German, literally "leading motif," from *leiten* "to lead" + *Motiv* "motif" (from French *motif*).]

Lei·zhou Pen·in·su·la /lày jō-/ peninsula in southwestern Guangdong Province, southeastern China

lek[1] /lek/ *n.* **1. ALBANIAN CURRENCY UNIT** the basic currency unit of Albania. See table at **currency 2. COIN WORTH ONE LEK** a coin worth one lek [Early 20thC. From Albanian, named for the Albanian lawgiver *Lek* Dukagjin.]

lek[2] /lek/ *n.* an area of ground that some birds such as the black grouse use as a stage for communal breeding displays and courtship during the mating season [Late 19thC. Origin uncertain: perhaps from Swedish *leka* "to play."]

lek·var /lék vaar/ *n.* a spread made of prunes or apricots, often used as pastry filling [Mid-20thC. Via Hungarian *lekvár* from, ultimately, late Latin *electuarium* (see ELECTUARY).]

LEM /lem/ *abbr.* lunar excursion module

le·man /lémmən, leemən/ (*plural* **-mans**) *n.* somebody loved, e.g., a sweetheart or lover (*archaic*) [12thC. Variant of *leofman*, literally "beloved person," from LIEF + MAN.]

Le Mans /lə móN, lə maaN/ capital of Sarthe Department, Pays de la Loire Region, northern France. Population: 148,465 (1990).

Lemay /lə máy/, **Léon-Pamphile** (1837–1918) Canadian writer. Some of his French-language poetry was collected in *Les Vengeances* (1875). His novels include *L'Affaire Sougraine* (1884).

lem·ma[1] /lémmə/ (*plural* **-mas** *or* **-ma·ta** /-mətə/) *n.* **1.** LOGIC **ASSUMPTION FOR THE SAKE OF ARGUMENT** a proposition that is assumed to be true in order to test the validity of another proposition **2.** PUBL **SUBJECT HEADING** a heading that indicates the topic of a work or passage **3.** PUBL **GLOSSARY WORD** a term that is defined in a glossary [Late 16thC. Via Latin from Greek *lēmma*, literally "something taken (for granted)."]

lem·ma[2] /lémmə/ *n.* the lower of two bracts surrounding the flower of a grass [Mid-18thC. From Greek, "husk," from the past participle of *lepein* "to peel" (source of English *lepton*). Ultimately from an Indo-European word that is also the ancestor of English *leper.*]

lem·ma·ta plural of **lemma**[1]

Lemming

lem·ming /lémming/ *n.* **1.** ZOOL **SUBARCTIC RODENT** a rodent with a small thick furry body and furry feet that lives in subarctic regions. Lemmings are noted for their mass migrations in search of food during population explosions, which has given rise to the myth that they flock to the sea to drown themselves. Genus: *Lemmus* and *Dicrostonyx.* **2. DOOMED CONFORMIST** a member of a large group of people who blindly follow one another on a course of action that will lead to destruction for all of them [Early 18thC. From Norwegian, of uncertain origin.]

Lem·mon /lémmən/, **Jack** (*b.* 1925) U.S. actor. His many movies include the Academy Award-winning *Mr. Roberts* (1955) and *Save the Tiger* (1973). Full name **John Uhler Lemmon III**

lem·nis·cus /lem nískəss/ (*plural* **-ci** /lem ní sī, -kī, -kee/) *n.* a bundle of fibers, especially a bundle of nerve fibers [Mid-19thC. Via Latin from Greek *lēmniskos* "ribbon," of unknown origin.]

Lem·nos /lémnoss/ island in eastern Greece, in the Aegean Sea, near the Dardanelles. Population: 15,721 (1981).

Lemon

lem·on /lémmən/ *n.* **1.** FOOD **YELLOW OR GREEN CITRUS FRUIT** a yellow or, in some climates, green oval citrus fruit with a thick fragrant rind and sour juicy flesh **2.** TREES **TREE THAT BEARS LEMONS** the tree with glossy almond-shaped leaves and spiky branches that bears lemons. Latin name: *Citrus limon.* **3.** COLORS **PALE YELLOW COLOR** a pale yellow color typical of the rind of a ripe lemon **4. DEFECTIVE PRODUCT** something that is defective or disappointing, especially a car that does not run properly (*informal*) ■ *adj.* **OF A PALE YELLOW COLOR** having the pale yellow color typical of the rind of a ripe lemon [14thC. Via French *limon* from, ultimately, Arabic *līmūn*.]

lem·on·ade /lémmə nàyd/ *n.* **1. DRINK MADE FROM LEMONS** an uncarbonated soft drink made from fresh lemons, sugar, and water **2. DRINK OF LEMONADE** a drink of lemonade ○ *ordered a lemonade and two coffees*

lem·on·ade ber·ry *n.* a Californian evergreen shrub with leathery leaves, clusters of small pink flowers, and acidic dark red fruit that is used as a flavoring for drinks. Latin name: *Rhus integrifolia.*

lem·on balm *n.* a widely-cultivated plant of the mint family native to southern Europe that has small white or pinkish flowers and lemon-scented leaves. It has long been used in food, as well as in herbal medicines to promote relaxation and sleep. Latin name: *Melissa officinalis.*

lem·on·bel·ly *n.* a Chesapeake Bay female blue crab, so-called for its yellow underside (*regional*)

WORD KEY: REGIONAL NOTE
The term is used in coastal Maryland and Virginia. A variant name is *lemon crab.*

lem·on drop *n.* a lemon-flavored piece of hard candy

lem·on·grass /lémmən gràss/ *n.* a grass native to southern India that is cultivated in the tropics for a lemon-scented oil distilled from its leaves, and for use as a flavoring in cooking. Latin name: *Cymbopogon citratus.*

lem·on law *n.* a law requiring anyone who sells or manufactures a faulty motor vehicle either to replace or repair it or to refund the buyer's money (*informal*)

lem·on sole *n.* an edible flatfish found in the northeastern Atlantic and the North Sea. Latin name: *Microstomus kitt.*

lemon-squeez·er *n.* = **reamer**

lem·on ver·be·na, lem·on ver·vain *n.* a widely cultivated South American shrub with small lavender-colored flowers and lance-shaped leaves that produce a lemony fragrance when crushed. The leaves and flower tops may be dried and used as a herbal tea. Latin name: *Lippia triphylla.*

lem·on·y /lémmənee/ *adj.* like a lemon in taste, smell, or color

lem·on yel·low *n.* a pale yellow color typical of the rind of a ripe lemon —**lem·on-yel·low** *adj.*

Le Moyne /lə mwán/, **Charles, Sieur de Longueuil and de Chateauguay** (1626–85) French-born Canadian colonist. The father of Charles, he settled in Canada in 1641, worked among the Indians, and then oversaw his extensive estate.

Le Moyne, Charles, Baron de Longueuil (1656–1729) Canadian soldier and politician. He was commandant general of Canada (1711) and governor of Montreal (1724–29).

lem·pi·ra /lem péerə/ *n.* **1. HONDURAN CURRENCY UNIT** the basic currency unit of Honduras. See table at **currency 2. BILL WORTH ONE LEMPIRA** a bill worth one lempira [Mid-20thC. Named for *Lempira*, a 16th-century chieftain who fought against the Spanish conquerors of Honduras.]

Lemur

le·mur /léemər/ *n.* a primate with a long snout, large ears, and a long tail, found only in Madagascar and nearby islands. Family: Lemuridae. ◊ **ring-tailed lemur** [Late 18thC. Via modern Latin from Latin *lemures* (see LEMURES), because it is nocturnal.]

lem·u·res /lémmyə rèez, lémmə ràyss/ *npl.* in ancient Rome, the spirits of the dead (*literary*) [Mid-16thC. From Latin, literally "shades of the dead."]

Le·na /léenə/ river in Siberian Russia that rises in southern Siberia and flows northward before emptying into the Laptev Sea, an arm of the Arctic Ocean. Length: 2,680 mi./4,313 km.

lend /lend/ (**lent** /lent/, **lent, lend·ing, lends**) *v.* **1.** *vt.* **LET SOMEBODY BORROW SOMETHING** to allow somebody to take or use something on the understanding that it will be returned later **2.** *vti.* **GIVE SOMEBODY MONEY FOR LIMITED TIME** to allow a person or business to use a sum of money for a specified period of time, usually on condition that a charge (**interest**) is paid in return ○ *The bank lent us money at a good interest rate.* **3.** *vt.* **ADD SOMETHING** to give a certain quality or character to something ○ *The candles lend an air of intimacy to the room.* [Old English *lǣnan.* Ultimately from a prehistoric Germanic word (ancestor also of English *loan*).] —**lend·able** *adj.* —**lend·er** *n.* ◇ **lend itself to something** to be suitable for a particular purpose or occasion

lend·ing li·brar·y *n.* a library or department of a library where the public can borrow books, and often audio tapes, video tapes, and CDs

Len·dl /lénd'l/, **Ivan** (*b.* 1960) Czechoslovakian-born U.S. tennis player. Between 1981 and 1987 he won many international tournaments, including the French Open, the U.S. Open and the Grand Prix Masters.

le·nes plural of **lenis**

L'Engle /léng'l/, **Madeleine** (*b.* 1918) U.S. author. *A Wrinkle in Time* (1962), her novel for young readers, won the Newbery Medal (1963). Born **Madeleine L'Engle Camp**

Popperfoto

Suzanne Lenglen: Photographed playing at Wimbledon (1922)

Len·glen /léN gləN/, **Suzanne** (1899–1938) French tennis player. The women's champion of France for several years (1920–23, 1925–26) and Olympic champion (1920), she also won several Wimbledon titles.

length /length/ *n.* **1. DISTANCE FROM END TO END** the distance along something from end to end, or a measurement taken of this distance ○ *The length of the garden is 25 yards.* **2. QUALITY OF LONGNESS** the condition or state of being long ○ *The garden is designed to give a sense of length and openness.* **3. HOW LONG SOMETHING TAKES** the time something lasts or takes from beginning to end ○ *The length of the second act is about 75 minutes.* **4. HOW LONG SOMETHING IS** how long something is when measured from beginning to end ○ *The second volume is a massive 400 pages in length.* **5. LONG PIECE OF SOMETHING** a piece of something long and narrow ○ *a length of copper piping* **6. UNIT OF MEASUREMENT** a piece of something such as cloth that is measured or bought in units of a standard size ○ *bought three lengths of fabric* **7.** SWIMMING **END TO END IN SWIMMING POOL** the distance from one end of a swimming pool to the other **8. SET DISTANCE** a particular distance, e.g., between two points **9.** FASHION **HOW LONG GARMENT IS** how high the hem of a coat, skirt, or dress is above the ground or below the wearer's waist, or how much of the wearer's legs it shows **10.** SPORTS **WINNING DISTANCE** in something such as a boat race or horse race, the distance between two competitors, measured according to how long a single boat or horse is ○ *two lengths ahead with only 100 yards to go* **11.** PHON **HOW LONG SOUND TAKES TO MAKE** the amount of time required to articulate a vowel or syllable [Old English *lengþ*, ultimately from a prehistoric Germanic word that is also the ancestor of English *long*] ◇ **at length 1.** in great detail and for a long time (*formal*) **2.** after some time or following a delay

-length *suffix.* extending all the way to a particular part of something ○ *shoulder-length hair*

length·en /léngthən/ (**-ened, -en·ing, -ens**) *vti.* to make something longer, or become longer ○ *The weeks lengthened into months and still no news came.* —**length·en·er** *n.*

length·wise /léngth wìz/, **length·ways** /-wàyz/ *adv., adj.* in relation to something's length from end to end ○ *attempting to force the suitcase into the trunk lengthwise*

length·y /léngthee/ (**-i·er, -i·est**) *adj.* lasting for a long time, especially excessively long —**length·i·ly** *adv.* —**length·i·ness** *n.*

le·ni·en·cy /léenee ənsee/, **le·ni·ence** /-ənss/ *n.* **1. LENIENT TREATMENT** punishment, judgment, or action that is not too severe **2. GENTLENESS OR TOLERANCE** the personal characteristic or quality of being lenient

le·ni·ent /léenee ənt/ *adj.* showing tolerance or mercy in dealing with crime or misbehavior [Mid-17thC. From Latin *lenient-*, present participle stem of *lenire* "to soothe," from *lenis* "smooth."] —**le·ni·ent·ly** *adv.*

AKG London

Vladimir Ilyich Lenin

Le·nin /lénnin/, **Vladimir Ilyich** (1870–1924) Russian revolutionary leader. Founder of the Soviet Union, he led the Bolshevik revolution in October 1917. He was the first leader of the Soviet communist regime, but became less active after suffering a stroke in 1922. Born **Vladimir Ilyich Ulyanov**

Le·nin·a·khan /lènninə kaán/ former name for **Gyumri** (1924–90)

Len·in·grad /lénnin gràd/ former name for **St. Petersburg** (1924–90)

Len·in·ism /lénnə nìzzəm/ *n.* the political, social, and economic theories of Lenin, which he developed from Marxist theory —**Len·in·ist** *n., adj.*

Len·in Peak /lènnin-/ mountain in the Trans-Alai Range of the Pamirs, situated in Tajikistan. Height: 23,508 ft./7,165 m. Former name **Mount Kaufman**

le·nis /léenəss, láy-/ *adj.* **PRONOUNCED USING LITTLE BREATH** used to describe a consonant produced using fairly little breath and muscle power ■ *n.* (*plural* **-nes** /-neez/) **LENIS CONSONANT** a consonant that is produced using fairly little breath and muscle power [Early 20thC. From Latin, literally "smooth."]

le·ni·tion /lə nísh'n/ *n.* the use of fairly little breath and muscle power when articulating consonants [Early 20thC. From Latin *lenis* "smooth."]

len·i·ty /lénnitee/ *n.* action or treatment that is lenient (*formal*) [15thC. Directly or via Old French *lenite* from Latin *lenitas*, from *lenis* "smooth."]

Len·non /lénnən/, **John** (1940–80) British singer, songwriter, and musician. A member of the Beatles, he had a songwriting partnership with Paul McCartney that revolutionized popular music. His most distinctive solo recording was "Imagine" (1971). He was murdered in 1980.

le·no /lée nō/ (*plural* **-nos**) *n.* **1. TYPE OF OPEN WEAVE** a type of open weave created in textiles by twisting together pairs of warp threads to lock the weft threads in place **2. FABRIC** a fabric made using a leno weave [Late 18thC. From French *linon*, from *lin* "flax," from Latin *linum.*]

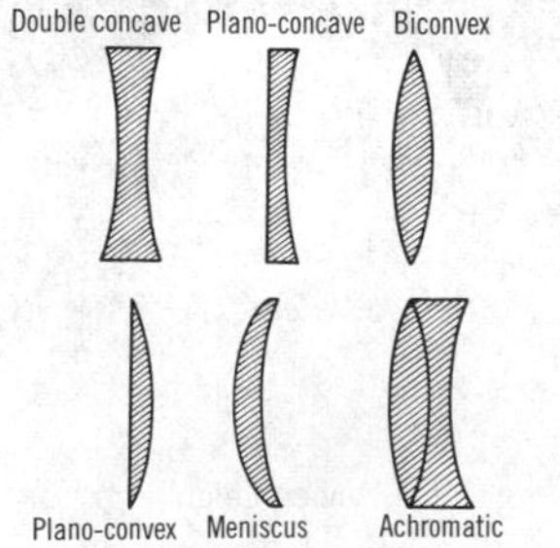

Lens: Cross sections of different lenses

lens /lenz/ *n.* **1.** OPTICS **TRANSPARENT PIECE OF GLASS FOR FOCUSING** a piece of curved and polished glass or other transparent material that forms an image by refracting and focusing light passing through it **2.** OPTICS **SYSTEM OF LENSES** a system of two or more lenses that is used in an optical instrument such as a telescope or camera **3.** OPHTHALMOL = **contact lens 4.** ANAT **LIGHT-FOCUSING PART OF THE EYE** the part of the eye that focuses light to produce an image on the light-sensitive cells of the retina. It is nearly spherical and convex on both sides, and sits behind the pupil.

5. TECH **BEAM-FOCUSING DEVICE** a device that focuses a beam of electrons or radiation other than light ■ *vt.* (**lensed, lens·ing, lens·es**) CINEMA **FILM SOMETHING** to record a motion picture on film [Late 17thC. From Latin, literally "lentil" (so called because of its shape).]

lent past participle, past tense of **lend**

Lent /lent/ *n.* the period of 40 weekdays before Easter observed in some Christian churches as a period of prayer, penance, fasting, and self-denial. This period, starting on Ash Wednesday in Western churches, commemorates the 40 days that Jesus Christ spent fasting in the wilderness. [13thC. Shortening of LENTEN.]

Lent·en /léntən/, **lent·en** *adj.* happening in or suitable for Lent, especially in being meager [Old English *lencten* "spring" (in which Lent falls in the northern hemisphere). Ultimately from a prehistoric Germanic word (ancestor also of English *long,* referring to the lengthening days of spring).]

len·tic /léntik/ *adj.* relating to or inhabiting still or slow-moving water [Mid-20thC. Formed from Latin *lentus* "slow, calm."]

len·ti·cel /lénti sèl/ *n.* a pore in the outer layer of a woody plant stem, through which gases pass from inside the stem to the atmosphere, or vice versa [Mid-19thC. From modern Latin *lenticella,* literally "little lentil," from Latin *lens* "lentil."] —**len·ti·cel·late** /lènti séllət/ *adj.*

len·tic·u·lar /len tíkyələr/ *adj.* **1. OF LENSES** relating to a lens or lenses **2. LENS-SHAPED** shaped like a biconvex lens in having two convex faces [15thC. From Latin *lenticularis,* from *lenticula* (see LENTIL).]

len·til /lént'l/ *n.* **1.** PLANTS **PLANT WITH EDIBLE SEEDS** a plant of the pea family native to the Mediterranean area and to western Asia and grown for its edible seeds. Latin name: *Lens culinaris.* **2.** FOOD **SEED** a seed of the lentil plant that is lens-shaped, brown, gray, or black on the outside and yellow or orange inside, and rich in protein [14thC. Via French *lentille* from, ultimately, Latin *lenticula,* literally "little lentil," from *lens* "lentil."]

len·tisk /lén tìsk/ *n.* = **mastic tree** [14thC. From Latin *lentiscus.*]

len·tis·si·mo /len tíssə mō, -téssə-/ *adv.* very slowly (*used as a musical direction*) [Early 20thC. From Italian, superlative of *lento* (see LENTO).] —**len·tis·si·mo** *adj.*

len·ti·vi·rus /léntə vìrəss/ *n.* a retrovirus causing illness that characteristically does not produce symptoms until some time after infection [Late 20thC. Coined from Latin *lentus* "slow" + -I- + VIRUS.]

len·to /lén tō/ *adv.* **SLOWLY** at a slow tempo (*used as a musical direction*) ■ *n.* (*plural* **-tos**) **LENTO PIECE OF MUSIC** a piece of music, or a section of a piece, to be played lento [Early 18thC. Via Italian from Latin *lentus* "slow."] —**len·to** *adj.*

Le·o /lée ō/ (*plural* **-os**) *n.* **1. FIFTH SIGN OF THE ZODIAC** the fifth sign of the zodiac, represented by the lion and lasting from approximately July 23 to August 22. Leo is classified as a fire sign and is ruled by the sun. **2. SOMEBODY BORN UNDER LEO** somebody whose birthday falls between July 23 and August 22 [Pre-12thC. From Latin, literally "lion."] —**Le·o** *adj.*

Leo I /lée ō/, **St.** (400?–461) Pope. He summoned the Council of Chalcedon in 451 and was proclaimed a doctor of the church in 1574. Known as **Leo the Great**

Leo III, Emperor (680?–741) Byzantine monarch. He revitalized the Byzantine Empire, founded the Isaurian dynasty, and issued a legal code, the *Ecloga.*

Leo IX, St. (1002–54) Pope. During his reforming reign (1049 –54), papal authority was strengthened, and this led to the Great Schism of 1054. Real name **Bruno of Egisheim**

Leo X, Pope (1475–1521). An important patron of the arts, as Pope (1513–21) he initiated the rebuilding of St. Peter's Basilica, Rome. Real name **Giovanni de Medici**

Leo XIII, Pope (1810–1903). He upheld the authority of the papacy and promoted learning. His encyclical of 1896 declared Episcopalian orders invalid. Real name **Vincenzo Gioacchino Pecci**

Leom·in·ster /léminstər/ **1.** city in central Massachusetts, southeast of Fitchburg and north of Worcester. Population: 39,263 (1996). **2.** town in Herefordshire, England. Population: 9,543 (1991).

Le·ón /lay ón/ **1.** city and capital of León Province, in the Castile-León autonomous region of northwestern Spain. Population: 147,780 (1995). **2.** industrial city in central Mexico, founded in 1576. Population: 758,279 (1990).

Le·o·nard /lénnərd/, **Sugar Ray** (*b.* 1956) U.S. boxer. He won various boxing titles in five different weight categories, mainly in the 1980s. Real name **Ray Charles Leonard**

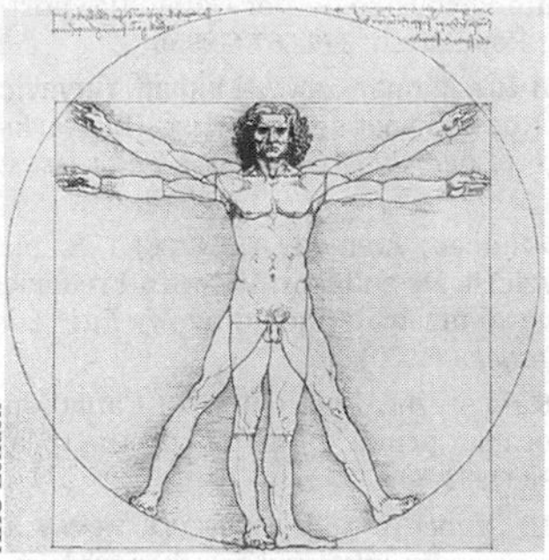

AKG London

Leonardo da Vinci: *Vitruvian Man* (1490?)

Le·o·nar·do da Vin·ci /lée ə naàr dō də vínchee/ (1452–1519) Italian painter, sculptor, architect, engineer, and scientist. One of the great masters of the High Renaissance, his works include the *Mona Lisa* (1503–06), and *The Last Supper* (1495–97).

le·one /lee ṓn/ *n.* **1. CURRENCY UNIT OF SIERRA LEONE** the basic currency unit of Sierra Leone. See table at **currency** **2. BILL WORTH ONE LEONE** a bill worth one leone [Mid-20thC. From the name of Sierra *Leone.*]

Le·on·i·an /lee ṓnee ən/ *n.* ZODIAC = **Leo** *n.* 2

le·o·nine /lée ə nìn/ *adj.* relating to or characteristic of a lion, e.g., in strength or appearance [14thC. Directly or via French from Latin *leoninus,* from *leo* "lion."]

Le·o·nine /léeə nìn/ *n.* ZODIAC = **Leo** *n.* 2

Le·on·tief /lee ón tee èf/, **Wassily** (*b.* 1906) Russian-born U.S. economist. He received a Nobel Prize in economics (1973) for his development of the input-output economic theory.

Leopard

leop·ard /léppərd/ *n.* **1.** ZOOL **LARGE SPOTTED CAT** a large slender member of the cat family found in Africa and parts of Asia. It has a fawn to orange red coat spotted with black rosettes. Leopards are generally solitary and nocturnal, living in scrub or forest and hunting a wide range of prey, including antelope, snakes, fish, and birds. Latin name: *Panthera pardus.* ◊ **panther, snow leopard, clouded leopard 2.** HERALDRY **HERALDIC FIGURE OF WALKING LION** an image of a lion viewed from the side facing left, with its head turned toward the viewer and one front leg raised [13thC. Via Old French from, ultimately, late Greek *leopardos,* from *leōn* (see LION) + *pardos* (see PARD).]

WORD KEY: CULTURAL NOTE

The Leopard, a novel by Italian writer Giuseppe Tomasi di Lampedusa (1958). Set in late 19th-century Sicily, it describes the social and political changes resulting from the unification of Italy from the point of view of a local nobleman, Prince Salina. In addition to its political and historical insights, the novel is admired for its evocative descriptions of the Sicilian landscape and its moving and poetic meditations on mortality.

leop·ard cat *n.* a small wild cat with spots like those of a leopard, found in southern and eastern Asia. Latin name: *Felis bengalensis.*

leop·ard·ess /léppərdəss/ *n.* a female leopard, usually an adult one

leop·ard lil·y *n.* a plant native to the southwestern United States that is cultivated for its showy orange red flowers with black-speckled petals. Latin name: *Lilium pardalinum.*

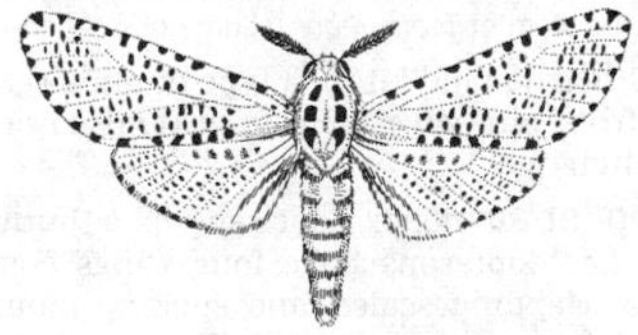

Leopard moth

leop·ard moth *n.* a large white moth with black spots that is found in Europe, Asia, North Africa, and North America. The caterpillars bore into trees, causing damage, and may be considered pests. Latin name: *Zeuzera pyrina.*

leop·ard's bane *n.* a European and Asian plant with clusters of yellow flowers resembling daisies on long stalks. Leopard's banes are cultivated as ornamentals and also grow wild. Genus: *Doronicum.*

leop·ard seal *n.* a seal with a spotted dark gray back and paler belly that lives as a solitary hunter in Antarctic waters, feeding mainly on penguins. Latin name: *Hydrurga leptonyx.*

Le·o·pold I /lée ə pòld/, **Holy Roman Emperor, King of Bohemia, and King of Hungary** (1640–1705). As Holy Roman Emperor (1658–1705), King of Bohemia (1656–1705), and King of Hungary (1655–87) he led wars against France and the Ottoman Turks, and made efforts to extend Habsburg territory.

Le·o·pold II, Grand Duke of Tuscany and Holy Roman Emperor (1747–92) Austrian monarch. While Holy Roman Emperor (1790–92) he formed an alliance with Prussia against France to aid Marie Antoinette, his sister, during the French Revolution.

Le·o·pold II, King of Belgium (1835–1909). During his reign (1865–1909), Belgium annexed the Congo Free State, which became the Belgian Congo.

Le·o·pold III, King of Belgium (1901–83). He became king in 1934, but went into exile after the invasion by Germany during World War II. He abdicated in 1951.

Lé·o·pold·ville /lée ə pōld vìl/ former name for **Kinshasa** (until 1966)

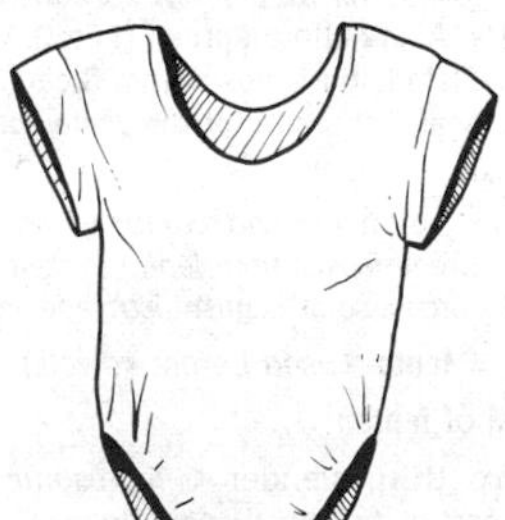

Leotard

le·o·tard /lée ə taàrd/ *n.* **TIGHT GARMENT FOR GYMNASTS OR ATHLETES** a tight-fitting one-piece elastic garment that covers the torso and is worn especially by dancers, gymnasts, and acrobats ■ **le·o·tards** *npl.* **DANCER'S ONE-PIECE GARMENT** a one-piece, close-fitting garment, covering the body from the neck or waist to the feet, worn by male and female dancers [Late 19thC. Named for the French trapeze artist Jules *Léotard* (1830–70), its inventor.]

Lep·cha /lépchə/ (*plural* **-chas** *or* **-cha**) *n.* **1.** PEOPLES **MEMBER OF PEOPLE OF INDIA** a member of a people who live in the northeastern Indian state of Sikkim **2.** LANG **LANGUAGE OF INDIA** a language spoken in the northeastern Indian state of Sikkim. It belongs to the Tibeto-Burman branch of Sino-Tibetan languages. Lepcha is spoken by about 65,000 people. [Early 19thC. From Nepali *lāpche*.] —**Lep·cha** *adj.*

lep·er /léppər/ *n.* **1.** SOMEBODY WITH LEPROSY somebody affected with leprosy **2.** SOMEBODY AVOIDED somebody who is ignored or disliked by the rest of society [14thC. Via French *lèpra* from Latin *lepra* "leprosy" (the original sense in English), from Greek *lepros* (see LEPROUS).]

lepido- *prefix.* flake, scale ○ *lepidolite* [From Greek *lepid-*, the stem of *lepis, lepos* (source of English *leper*)]

le·pid·o·lite /lə pídd'l ìt/ *n.* a type of mica ranging in color from pinkish purple to gray, used as an ore of lithium

lep·i·dop·ter·an /lèppi dóptərən/ *n.* a butterfly or moth. Lepidopterans have four wings covered in tiny overlapping scales, and sucking mouthparts. Their larvae are caterpillars. Order: Lepidoptera. [Mid-19thC. From modern Latin *Lepidoptera*, order name, from Greek *lepis* "scale" + *pteron* "wing."]

lep·i·dop·ter·ist /lèppi dóptərist/ *n.* somebody who studies or is an expert in butterflies and moths

lep·i·do·si·ren /lèppi dō sīrən/ *n.* an eel-shaped South American freshwater fish that can breathe air using a pair of lungs that it has in addition to its gills. It spends the dry season lying dormant in a burrow. Latin name: *Lepidosiren paradoxa.*

lep·i·dote /léppi dōt/ *adj.* covered in small scaly leaves [Mid-19thC. Via modern Latin *lepidotus* from Greek *lepidōtos*, from *lepis* "scale."]

lep·re·chaun /léprə kàwn/ *n.* in Irish folklore, a small man with magical powers, often dressed in green, who works as a shoemaker and is believed to know where treasure is hidden [Early 17thC. From Irish *leipreachán*, literally "small body."] —**lep·re·chau·nish** *adj.*

lep·ro·sar·i·um /lèprə sáiree əm/ (*plural* **-ums** *or* **-a** /-ə/) *n.* a hospital for the treatment of patients with leprosy [Mid-19thC. From late Latin *leprosus* (see LEPROUS).]

lep·rose /lé prōss/ *adj.* = **leprous** *adj.* 2 [Mid-19thC. Directly from or via late Latin *leprosus* (see LEPROUS).]

lep·ro·sy /léprəssee/ (*plural* **-sies**) *n.* a tropical disease that mainly affects the skin and nerves, and can cause tissue change. Leprosy is transmitted following close personal contact and has a long incubation period (1–30 years). It can now be cured if treated with a combination of drugs. [Mid-16thC. From LEPROUS (influenced by earlier *lepry* "leprosy"), from LEPER.] —**lep·rot·ic** /lə próttik/ *adj.*

lep·ro·sy gourd *n.* = **balsam pear**

lep·rous /léprəss/ *adj.* **1.** OF LEPROSY having or relating to leprosy **2.** WHITE AND SCALY resembling the physical symptoms of leprosy, especially in being pale or scaly ○ *a leprous white deposit spreading across the cellar walls.* Also called **leprose** [12thC. Via Old French *lepro(u)s* and late Latin *leprosus* from Greek *lepros* "scaly," from *lepos* "scale" (because of the white scales that form on the skin).]

-lepsy *suffix.* seizure ○ *narcolepsy* [Via modern Latin *-lepsia* from Greek *lepsis*, from *lēp-*, the stem of *lambanein* "to seize" (source also of English *astrolabe* and *syllable*)]

lept- *prefix.* = **lepto-** (*used before vowels*)

lep·ta plural of **lepton**[1]

lepto- *prefix.* thin, slender ○ *leptosome* [From Greek *leptos*, the past participle of *lepein* "to peel" (see LEMMA)]

lep·to·ceph·a·lus /lèp tō séffələss/ (*plural* **-li** /-lì/) *n.* the larva of some bony fishes such as the eel that has a markedly different appearance to that of the adult fish. The eel larva has a leaf-shaped, almost transparent body, in contrast to the long thin form of the adult eel. Genus: *Anguilla.* [Mid-18thC. From modern Latin, from Greek *leptos* "fine, small" + *kephalē* "head."]

lep·ton[1] /lép tòn/ (*plural* **-ta** /-tə/) *n.* **1.** GREEK MONETARY UNIT a monetary unit of Greece, used only in calculations. **2.** OLD COIN WORTH ONE LEPTON an ancient Greek coin worth one lepton [Early 18thC. From Greek *leptos* "small."]

lep·ton[2] /lép tòn/ *n.* a fundamental subatomic particle such as the electron, muon, neutrino, and their antiparticles that interacts only weakly with other particles [Mid-20thC. Coined from Greek *leptos* "small" + -ON.] —**lep·ton·ic** /lep tónnik/ *adj.*

lep·to·spi·ro·sis /lèptə spī rṓssiss/ *n.* a disease affecting human beings and domestic animals caused by spiral-shaped bacteria (**spirochetes**) of the genus *Leptospira*, sometimes with fever, jaundice, and kidney failure. In human beings a significant form of the disease is Weil's disease. [Early 20thC. Formed from modern Latin *Leptospira*, genus name, literally "small coil."]

Lé·ri·da /láy reédə, -ridə/ capital of Lérida Province in the autonomous region of Catalonia, northeastern Spain. Population: 114,367 (1995).

Ler·mon·tov /lúrmən tawf/, **Mikhail Yuryevich** (1814–1841). Russian poet and novelist. His works include *A Hero of our Time* (1840) and *The Circassian Boy* (1840).

Ler·ner /lúrnər/, **Alan Jay** (1918–86) U.S. playwright and lyricist. He collaborated with Frederick Loewe on several musicals including *My Fair Lady* (1956) and *Camelot* (1960).

Le·sage /lə saázh/, **Jean** (1912–80) Canadian lawyer. He became prime minister of the province of Quebec (1962–66).

les·bi·an /lézbee ən/ *n.* HOMOSEXUAL WOMAN a woman who is sexually attracted to other women ■ *adj.* OF LESBIANS involving or relating to lesbians [From the poems of SAPPHO of *Lesbos*]

Les·bi·an *n.* SOMEBODY FROM LESBOS somebody who was born or raised on the Greek island of Lesbos ■ *adj.* **1.** OF LESBOS relating to the Greek island of Lesbos **2.** OF THE POETRY OF SAPPHO relating to the writings of the poet Sappho of the 6th century B.C., who was from Lesbos

les·bi·an·ism /lézbee ə nìzzəm/ *n.* sexual attraction and sexual relations between women

Les·bos /léz boss/ island, in eastern Greece, in the Aegean Sea, situated 6 mi./10 km off the coast of Turkey. Population: 104,620 (1981). Area: 632 sq. mi./1,637 sq. km.

Les Cayes /lay káy/ town and seaport in southwestern Haiti, west of Port-au-Prince. Population: 36,000 (1994).

lese maj·es·ty /leez májjəstee/, **lèse ma·jes·té** *n.* **1.** DISRESPECT TO AUTHORITY disrespect toward the authority or dignity of somebody or something **2.** ACT OF TREASON a criminal offense against a ruler or head of state [15thC. Via French from Latin *laesa majestas*, literally "violated majesty."]

le·sion /leézh'n/ *n.* **1.** CHANGE DUE TO ILLNESS OR INJURY a physical change in a body part that is the result of illness or injury **2.** WOUND a wound, especially an area of skin that is broken or infected [15thC. Via French from the Latin stem *laesion-*, from the past participle stem of *laedere* "to injure."]

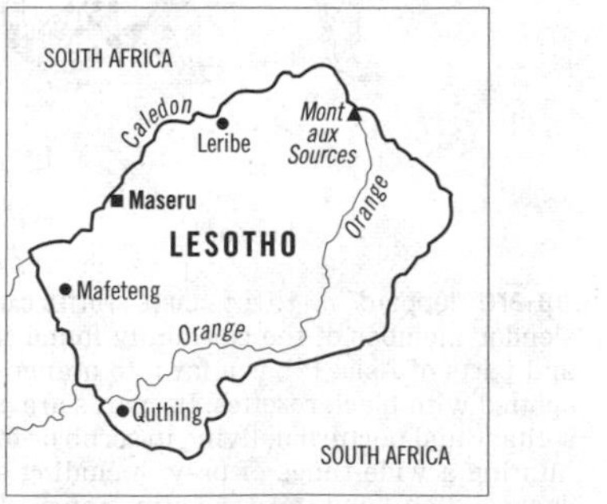

Lesotho

Le·so·tho /lə sṓtō, -sóotoo/ country in southern Africa, bordered on all sides by South Africa. It became independent from Britain in 1966. Language: English. Currency: loti. Capital: Maseru. Population: 2,049,275 (1997). Area: 11,720 sq. mi./30,355 sq. km. Official name **Kingdom of Lesotho**

les·pe·de·za /lèspə deézə/ (*plural* **-zas** *or* **-za**) *n.* a plant of the pea family with leaves having three leaflets that is grown for forage and to control erosion [Late 19thC. From modern Latin, genus name, from an alteration of the name of Vincente Manuel de Céspedes, 18th-century Spanish governor of eastern Florida.]

less /less/ CORE MEANING: a grammatical word used to indicate a smaller amount of something

1. *adj., pron.* SMALLER AMOUNT a smaller amount or proportion of something ○ *New cars tend to emit less air pollution.* ○ *Last month less of her salary was taken up with household expenses.* **2.** *adv.* TO A SMALLER DEGREE to a smaller extent or degree ○ *Demanding? I've never known a less demanding patient!* ○ *I see her much less than I used to.* **3.** *prep.* MINUS indicating that a number or amount is subtracted from a previously mentioned number or amount ○ *Total: $500, less $50 expenses.* ○ *I earned $45,000 last year, less tax and insurance.* [Old English *lǣssa*, ultimately of prehistoric Germanic origin] ◇ **less than** not having a particular quality ○ *Her whole attitude towards me has been less than pleasant.* ◇ **no less** expressing surprise or admiration at the importance of somebody or something ○ *He had borrowed money at Homburg from no less a person than Lord Montbarry.* ○ *The author says our whole universe, no less, is only one of many.* ◇ **much** *or* **still** *or* **even less** emphasizing that something is done or happens to a smaller extent than something mentioned in the previous statement (*used after a negative statement*) ○ *She could not fix her attention on any object or feel sensations, much less have conscious thoughts.*

-less *suffix.* **1.** without, lacking ○ *headless* ○ *restless* **2.** unable to be ○ *fathomless* [From Old English *lēas* "without"; related to *los* (see LOSS)]

les·see /le seé/ *n.* somebody who is granted a lease for property [15thC. From Anglo-Norman, the past participle of *lesser* (see LEASE).]

less·en /léss'n/ (**-ened, -en·ing, -ens**) *vti.* to make something less, or become less

less·er /léssər/ *adj., adv.* less significant, or smaller in size or amount

Less·er Bai·ram *n.* an Islamic festival held each year at the end of Ramadan

less·er car·pen·ter bee *n.* a small usually black solitary bee that bores extensive nests out of solid wood. Family: Ceratinidae.

less·er cel·an·dine *n.* a plant of the buttercup family found in woodland and damp locations in Europe and Asia. It has heart-shaped leaves and yellow flowers that grow on individual stems. Latin name: *Ranunculus ficaria.*

less·er corn·stalk bor·er *n.* a moth caterpillar that bores into corn stems and can be a crop pest in warm and temperate regions of North and South America. Latin name: *Elasmopalpus lignosellus.*

less·er o·men·tum *n.* ◆ **omentum**

less·er peach tree bor·er, **less·er peach bor·er** *n.* a moth caterpillar, found especially in the southern United States, that bores into the trunks and branches of peach and other fruit trees. Latin name: *Synanthedon pictipes.*

Les·ser Slave Lake /lèssər sláyv-/ lake in central Alberta, Canada, northwest of Edmonton. It empties through the Lesser Slave River into the Athabasca River. Area: 451 sq. mi./1,168 sq. km.

less·er yel·low·legs (*plural* **less·er yel·low·legs**) *n.* a sandpiper with long yellow legs that breeds in North America and overwinters in South America. It is usually found in marshes and on mudflats. It resembles the greater yellowlegs but is smaller with a shorter narrower bill. Latin name: *Tringa flavipes.* ◊ **greater yellowlegs**

Doris Lessing

Les·sing /léssing/, **Doris** (*b.* 1919) British novelist. Her works such as *The Grass is Singing* (1950), *Children of Violence* (1952–69), and *The Golden Notebook* (1962) explore political and social themes. Born **Doris May Tayler**

les·son /léss'n/ *n.* **1.** INSTRUCTION PERIOD a period of time spent teaching or learning a subject ○ *I'm old enough to start taking driving lessons.* **2.** MATERIAL

TAUGHT material to be taught or studied **3. NEW OR BETTER KNOWLEDGE** some useful knowledge or sense that results from direct experience ○ *I think there's a lesson there for all of us – think ahead.* **4. USEFUL EXPERIENCE** something that acts as an example, punishment, or warning by teaching something not previously understood or accepted **5. REBUKE** a strong criticism or reproof, usually instructing or reminding somebody how to behave correctly ○ *I need to give him a lesson in how to behave properly.* **6. les·son, Les·son** CHR **BIBLE PASSAGE** a passage from the Bible that is read out to the congregation during a church service ○ *Today's lesson is from the book of Matthew.* ■ *vt.* **(-soned, -son·ing, -sons) 1. INSTRUCT** to teach somebody **2. CRITICIZE FOR WRONGDOING** to scold somebody for doing something wrong [12thC. Via French *leçon* from Latin *lectio* "reading," formed from *legere* "to read" (source also of English *lecture*). The underlying sense is "something to read or listen to."]

les·sor /lé sàwr/ *n.* somebody who grants somebody else a lease on property [14thC. From Anglo-Norman *lessour*, from *lesser* (see LEASE).]

lest /lest/ *conj.* in order to prevent something happening, especially something causing fear ○ *must stay out of sight lest we be discovered* [Old English *þȳ lǣs þe*, literally "by which less that"]

let[1] /let/ **(let, let·ting, lets)** *vt.* **1. NOT PREVENT** to allow something to happen or somebody to do something ○ *You should let him explain what happened.* ○ *I won't let anything get in the way of us living a happy life together.* ○ *I never let myself worry about the future.* **2. PERMIT** to give somebody permission to do something ○ *I want to go to the disco but Dad won't let me.* **3. EXPRESSING A SUGGESTION** used to express a suggestion, an offer, or an order ○ *Let's eat – I'm starving.* ○ *Let me take that bag for you – you must be exhausted.* ○ *Let the show go on!* **4.** *U.K.* **MAKE SOMETHING PASS SOMEWHERE** to allow or make something pass from one place to another ○ *You need to let some air out of those tires.* ○ *Open the window and let some fresh air in.* **5. EXPRESSING RESIGNATION** used to indicate that you do not care what happens or what somebody does, even though it may be unpleasant ○ *Let them do their worst.* ○ *If he wants to leave then let him – see if I care!* **6.** MATH, LOGIC **MAKE AS A MATHEMATICAL ASSUMPTION** used to introduce an assumption or hypothesis ○ *Let the point P be on a line L.* **7.** COMM LAW **RENT OUT PROPERTY** to allow people to use land, rooms, or a building in return for rent **8.** *Ireland* **UTTER** to utter something (*informal*) [Old English *lǣtan* "to leave behind, let alone, allow." Ultimately from an Indo-European word meaning "to let go," which is also the ancestor of English *late* and *let*.] ◇ **let alone** used to introduce something that is even less likely or probable than what has just been mentioned ◇ **let go (of something)** to stop holding something ◇ **let yourself go 1.** to start acting in a much more relaxed or less inhibited way than usual **2.** to stop caring about your appearance

WORD KEY: SYNONYMS

See Synonyms at ***hire***.

let down *vt.* **1. LOWER SOMETHING** to move something, or allow something to move, to a lower position ○ *It was getting dark, so she let down the blinds.* **2. DISAPPOINT SOMEBODY** to disappoint somebody by not meeting expectations ○ *Sorry to let you down, but I won't be able to make it tonight.* **3. LENGTHEN GARMENT** to lengthen clothing or part of a piece of clothing by shortening the hem ○ *let down the sleeves of the coat* **4. ALLOW HAIR TO HANG DOWN** to undo long hair so it falls to its full length

let in *vt.* **1. ALLOW SOMEBODY ENTRANCE** to allow somebody to enter somewhere such as a building or a room ○ *They refused to let her in the house.* **2. ALLOW WATER OR AIR IN** to allow water or air into something that is meant to be sealed ○ *Their boat had hit a rock and was letting in water.*

let in for *vt.* to become involved in something that turns out to be more difficult or complicated than expected (*informal*) ○ *didn't realize what I was letting myself in for*

let in on *vt.* to allow somebody to know about something

let into *vt.* **1. ALLOW TO ENTER** to allow somebody to enter somewhere **2. ALLOW TO JOIN A CLUB** to allow somebody to join an organization or club

let off *vt.* **1. EXCUSE SOMEBODY FROM PUNISHMENT** to allow somebody to avoid something such as an unpleasant task or a punishment ○ *I'll let you off this time, but you'd better behave from now on.* **2. LET A PASSENGER GET OUT** to allow somebody to get off a vehicle such as a bus or train

let on *v.* **1.** *vi.* **SHARE A SECRET** to share a secret with somebody ○ *He didn't let on that he was very rich.* **2.** *vi.* **PRETEND** to make somebody believe something that is not true ○ *She let on that she was upset, but she wasn't really that bothered.* **3.** *vt.* **LET A PASSENGER GET ON** to allow somebody to board a vehicle such as a bus or train

let out *v.* **1.** *vt.* **MAKE A LOUD YELL** to make a loud or piercing sound using the voice ○ *let out a scream* **2.** *vt.* **RELEASE SOMEBODY OR SOMETHING** to set a person or animal free from being confined or trapped **3.** *vt.* **RELEASE SOMEBODY FROM PRISON** to release somebody from prison early or temporarily **4.** *vt.* **ALLOW SOMEBODY TO LEAVE** to allow somebody to leave someplace such as a building or room **5.** *vt.* **ENLARGE A GARMENT** to make a piece of clothing, or a specific part of it, wider than it was before **6.** *vt.* **SPREAD INFORMATION** to allow previously secret information to become more widely known **7.** *vi.* **END AND RELEASE STUDENTS** to come to an end and release students at the end of a session or term ○ *classes let out in early June* **8.** *vt.* **LET PROPERTY** to make a place available for letting ○ *They have recently let out a suite of rooms on the third floor.*

let through *vt.* to allow somebody or something to pass through a crowd ○ *Cars were pulling over to let an ambulance through.*

let up *vi.* **1. BECOME SLOWER** to become slower, calmer, or quieter ○ *Once the rain lets up a bit we'll have a look outside.* **2. RELAX** to stop working hard or being angry ○ *He never lets up, does he.*

let up on *vt.* to treat somebody or something in a more relaxed, gentle, or kind way

let[2] /let/ *n.* **1. REPLAYED SERVICE SHOT** in games such as tennis and squash, a service in which the ball is obstructed and the service has to be played again **2. REPLAYED POINT** the point that is replayed because of a let **3. DIFFICULTY OR OBSTACLE** something that prevents somebody from doing something, or makes it more difficult (*archaic*) [12thC. From Old English *lettan* "to hinder or obstruct." Ultimately from an Indo-European word that is also the ancestor of English *let*[1].]

-let *suffix.* **1.** small one ○ *wavelet* **2.** something worn on ○ *anklet* [From Old French *-elet*, from *-el* "small one" (from Latin *-ellus*) + *-et* (see -ET)]

letch *n., vi.* = **lech**

let·down /lét dòwn/ *n.* **1. DISAPPOINTMENT** an occasion when somebody or something disappoints expectations, or the feeling of disappointment that results ○ *After all the hype the concert was a bit of a letdown.* **2.** AIR **DESCENT OF AN AIRCRAFT** the descent of an aircraft in preparation for landing, before the actual landing approach

le·thal /léethəl/ *adj.* **1. DEADLY** causing or able to cause death **2. HARMFUL** causing disaster or destruction ○ *a move that was lethal to his career* [Late 16thC. From Latin *lethalis*, from *lethum*, an alteration of *letum* "death," by association with Greek *lēthē* "forgetfulness, oblivion."] — **le·thal·i·ty** /lee thálətee/ *n.* —**le·thal·ly** /léethəlee/ *adv.*

WORD KEY: SYNONYMS

See Synonyms at ***deadly***.

le·thal dose *n.* the amount of a drug or other substance that will cause death when administered. ◊ **median lethal dose**

le·thar·gic /lə thaárjik/ *adj.* **1. TIRED** physically slow and mentally dull as a result of tiredness, disease, or drugs **2. CAUSING LETHARGY** causing a state of physical slowness and mental dullness —**le·thar·gi·cal·ly** *adv.*

leth·ar·gy /léthərjee/ *n.* **1. TIREDNESS** a state of physical slowness and mental dullness as a result of tiredness, disease, or drugs **2. LACK OF ENERGY** lack of energy, activity, or enthusiasm [14thC. Via Old French *litargia* from, ultimately, Greek *lēthargia*, from *lēthargos* "forgetful," from *lēthē* "forgetfulness, oblivion."]

Leth·bridge /léth brìj/ city in southern Alberta, Canada. It is the cultural and economic center of the surrounding agricultural area. Population: 63,053 (1996).

le·the /leéthee/ *n.* a dreamy state of forgetfulness or unconsciousness (*literary*) —**le·the·an** *adj.*

Le·the *n.* in Greek and Roman mythology, a river in Hades whose water made those who drank it forget their past [Mid-16thC. Via Latin from Greek *lēthē* "forgetfulness, oblivion."] —**Le·the·an** *adj.*

Le·to /leé tō/ *n.* in Greek mythology, the mother of Apollo and Artemis by Zeus. Roman equivalent **Latona**

Lett /let/ *n.* PEOPLES = **Latvian** *n.* 1 [Late 16thC. Via German *Lette* from Latvian *Latvi*.]

let·ter /léttər/ *n.* **1. MESSAGE SENT BY MAIL** a piece of handwritten, typed, or printed text addressed to a particular person or organization and typically sent by mail **2. SYMBOL USED TO SPELL WORDS** each of a set of written or printed symbols representing a particular sound or set of sounds in a language and used for spelling words **3.** SPORTS **BADGE OF EXCELLENCE IN SPORTS** a badge consisting of the initial letter of the name of a school awarded for excellence, especially in varsity sports **4.** PRINTING **FONT** a typeface or font ■ *v.* **(-tered, -ter·ing, -ters) 1.** *vt.* **WRITE ON SOMETHING** to write letters or words on something such as a sign **2.** *vi.* SPORTS **EARN A LETTER** to earn a badge of excellence at a school, especially in varsity sports [13thC. Via French *lettre* from Latin *littera* "letter of the alphabet," used in the plural to mean "document, epistle, literature" (source of English *literature* and *obliterate*).]

let·ter bomb *n.* an envelope with an explosive device inside it, addressed and sent through the mail and designed to blow up when it is opened

let·ter·box /léttər bòks/ *n. U.K.* **1.** = **mailbox 2.** = **maildrop**

let·ter car·ri·er *n.* somebody who delivers letters or other mail

let·tered /léttərd/ *adj.* **1. WITH LETTERS WRITTEN ON IT** marked with letters of the alphabet **2. EDUCATED** knowledgeable and cultured, especially in literary matters **3. LITERATE** able to read and write

let·ter·form /léttər fàwrm/ *n.* the shape of a letter of the alphabet

let·ter·head /léttər hèd/ *n.* **1. PRINTED NAME AND ADDRESS ON STATIONERY** a printed heading for official stationery, usually containing a company's name, address, telephone and fax numbers, and often including a logo and other details **2. HEADED NOTEPAPER** a piece of writing paper with a printed letterhead

let·ter·ing /léttəring/ *n.* **1. PIECE OF WRITING** letters of the alphabet written, printed, inscribed, or painted on something **2. ACT OF WRITING** the physical process of forming letters, or the way somebody forms letters

let·ter·man /léttər màn, -mən/ (*plural* **-men** /-mèn, -mən/) *n.* a secondary or college student who has earned a letter for excellence in an activity, especially a varsity sport

let·ter of cred·it *n.* a letter from a bank, usually for presentation to another branch or bank, authorizing it to issue credit or money to the person named

let·ter of in·tent *n.* a signed statement outlining an intention to form an agreement or arrangement

let·ter of in·tro·duc·tion *n.* a letter written by somebody to introduce one person to another

let·ter-per·fect *adj.* without any incorrect words or misspellings

let·ter·press /léttər prèss/ *n.* **1. PRINTING BY USE OF PRESSURE** a printing technique that transfers ink by pressing raised type onto paper **2. PRINTED MATERIAL** material that is printed using the letterpress technique **3.** *U.K.* **TEXT** text as opposed to illustrations

let·ter-qual·i·ty *adj.* of a quality high enough to be compared to conventional printing

let·ters /léttərz/ *n.* (*takes a singular or plural verb*) **1. LITERATURE** literature or literary culture **2. KNOWLEDGE** knowledge and education

let·ters cre·den·tial *npl.* = **letters of credence**

let·ters of ad·min·is·tra·tion *npl.* an official court order appointing somebody as the administrator of a deceased person's estate when no valid will exists

let·ters of cre·dence *npl.* an official document presented to a government in order to authenticate the official status of a diplomatic representative of another country (*formal*)

let·ters of mar·que *npl.* **1. LICENSE TO SEIZE FOREIGN PROPERTY** a formal document issued by one country authorizing one of its private citizens to take possession of goods, or sometimes citizens, belonging to another country **2. LICENSE TO ARM A SHIP** an official document issued by one country authorizing one of its citizens to fit a ship with weapons in order to attack or seize another country's ships and cargo

let·ters pat·ent *npl.* an official document stating that somebody has been granted the exclusive right to make and sell a new product. Letters patent are issued by the government and specify the length of time a patent will remain valid. (*formal*)

let·ters tes·ta·men·tar·y *npl.* an official document authorizing somebody to assume the responsibilities and duties of executor of the will of a deceased person (*formal*)

Let·tish /léttish/ *n.* LANG = **Latvian** *n.* 2 —**Let·tish** *adj.*

let·tre de ca·chet /lèttrə də kaa sháy/ (*plural* **let·tres de ca·chet** /lèttrə-/) *n.* a letter, sealed with the royal seal, authorizing the arrest and indefinite imprisonment of somebody who has offended the monarch (*archaic formal*) [Early 18thC. From French, literally "letter of seal."]

let·tuce /léttəss/ *n.* **1.** **PLANT GROWN FOR ITS EDIBLE LEAVES** a common plant that is widely grown for its edible leaves, which are usually eaten in salads. Genus: *Lactuca*. **2.** **PAPER MONEY** paper money as opposed to coins (*slang*) [13thC. Via Old French *letuës* from Latin *lactuca*, from *lac* "milk" (source of English *lactate*), from the milky sap of its stalk.]

let·tuce bird *n.* the goldfinch (*regional*)

WORD KEY: REGIONAL NOTE

As well as ***lettuce bird***, the goldfinch is also called *salad bird* and *thistle bird*, all three related to its feeding habits. These terms have a scattered occurrence in Midland territory, especially Indiana.

let·up /lét ùp/ *n.* a pause, especially in something unpleasant ○ *I can take criticism, but with her there's no letup.*

le·u /lé ōō/ (*plural* **lei** /lay/) *n.* **1.** **ROMANIAN CURRENCY UNIT** the basic currency unit of Romania. See table at **currency** **2.** **BILL WORTH A LEU** a bill worth a leu [Late 19thC. From Romanian, literally "lion."]

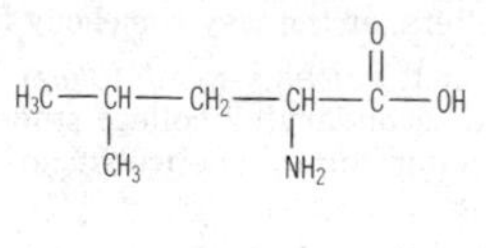

Leucine

leu·cine /lóo seen/ *n.* a white crystalline essential amino acid that is one of the chemical constituents of proteins. Formula: $C_6H_{13}NO_2$. [Early 19thC. Formed from Greek *leukos* "white."]

leu·cite /lóo sīt/ *n.* a white or gray mineral consisting of a silicate of aluminum and potassium, found in igneous rocks and used as a source of aluminum and of potash for fertilizers [Late 18thC. Formed from Greek *leukos* "white."]

leuco- *prefix.* = **leuko-**

leu·co·blast *n.* = **leukoblast**

leu·co·cyte *n.* = **leukocyte**

leuco·cy·to·sis *n.* = **leukocytosis**

leu·co·der·ma *n.* = **leukoderma**

leu·co·dys·tro·phy *n.* = **leukodystrophy**

leu·co·ma *n.* = **leukoma**

leu·co·pe·ni·a *n.* = **leukopenia**

leu·co·plak·i·a *n.* = **leukoplakia**

leu·co·plast /lóokə plàst/, **leu·co·plas·tid** /lóokə plástid/ *n.* a common minute colorless body (**plastid**) found inside plant cells and used for storing food

leu·cor·rhe·a *n.* = **leukorrhea**

leu·co·sis *n.* = **leukosis**

leu·cot·o·my *n.* = **leukotomy**

leu·co·tri·ene *n.* = **leukotriene**

leu·kae·mi·a *n.* *U.K.* = **leukemia**

leu·ke·mi·a /loo kéemee ə/ *n.* a type of cancer in which white blood cells displace normal blood. This leads to infection, shortage of red blood cells (**anemia**), bleeding, and other disorders, and often proves fatal. Certain types of childhood leukemias respond well to treatment, which includes drugs (**chemotherapy**) and radiotherapy. [Mid-19thC. Coined from LEUKO- + -EMIA.] —**leu·ke·mic** *adj.*

leuko-, **leuco-** *prefix.* **1.** white, pale, colorless ○ *leukoplakia* **2.** leukocyte ○ *leukopenia* **3.** white matter of the brain ○ *leukodystrophy* [From Greek *leukos* "white, clear." Ultimately from an Indo-European base denoting lightness, which is also the ancestor of English *light*[1], *lucid*, and *lunar*.]

leu·ko·blast /lóokə blàst/, **leu·co·blast** *n.* an immature white blood cell (**leukocyte**)

leu·ko·cyte /lóokə sīt/, **leu·co·cyte** *n.* a white blood cell (*technical*) —**leu·ko·cyt·ic** /lóokə síttik/ *adj.* —**leu·ko·cy·toid** /-sī tòyd/ *adj.*

leuko·cy·to·sis /lóokə sī tṓssiss/, **leu·co·cy·to·sis** *n.* a marked increase in the number of white blood cells (**leukocytes**), usually because of infection or disease —**leu·ko·cy·tot·ic** /lóokə sī tóttik/ *adj.*

leu·ko·der·ma /lóokə dúrmə/, **leu·co·der·ma** *n.* a condition in which absence of pigmentation causes white patches to develop on the skin. It may be inherited or due to other, often unknown, causes. [Late 19thC. Coined from LEUKO- + Greek *derma* "skin."] —**leu·ko·der·mal** *adj.*

leu·ko·dys·tro·phy /lóokō dístrəfee/, **leu·co·dys·tro·phy** *n.* a degenerative disease of nerve fibers or white matter that impairs brain function, sight, and motion, leading to death, often at an early age. It involves progressive loss of the fatty myelin layer surrounding the nerve fibers.

leu·ko·ma /loo kṓmə/, **leu·co·ma** *n.* a dense white scar on the cornea of the eye, caused by disease or injury [Early 18thC. Via modern Latin from Greek *leukōma* "white tumor," from *leukos* "white."]

leu·ko·pen·i·a /lóokə péenee ə/, **leu·co·pe·ni·a** *n.* an abnormal reduction in the number of white blood cells (**leukocytes**) —**leu·ko·pe·nic** *adj.*

leu·ko·plak·i·a /lóokə pláykee ə, -plák-/, **leu·co·plak·i·a** *n.* a precancerous condition that is seen as small thickened white patches, usually inside the mouth or vulva. It requires expert management if cancer is to be avoided. Oral leukoplakia may be caused by smoking or by alcohol abuse. [Late 19thC. Coined from LEUKO- + Greek *plax* "flat surface."]

leu·kor·rhe·a /lóokə rée ə/, **leu·cor·rhe·a** *n.* thick whitish or yellowish discharge from the vagina —**leu·kor·rhe·al** *adj.*

leu·ko·sis /loo kṓssiss/, **leu·co·sis** *n.* any animal disease in which the blood contains an abnormally high number of white blood cells (**leukocytes**) [Early 18thC. From Greek *leukōsis*, from *leukon* "to make white," from *leukos* "white."]

leu·kot·o·my /loo kóttəmee/ (*plural* **-mies**), **leu·cot·o·my** (*plural* **-mies**) *n.* a surgical operation that involves cutting nerve fibers, especially in the frontal lobes of the brain. It is now rarely performed, and only as a treatment for severe psychiatric disorders.

leu·ko·tri·ene /lóokə trī een/, **leu·co·tri·ene** *n.* a substance that functions as a powerful but short-range chemical messenger in various body systems, including the circulatory, nervous, and immune systems. Leukotrienes help regulate the state of blood vessels and airways, and influence the activities of certain white blood cells. [Late 20thC. Coined from LEUKO- + *triene* "chemical compound containing three double bonds" (coined from TRI- + -ENE).]

lev /lev/ (*plural* **lev·a** /lévvə/) *n.* **1.** **BULGARIAN CURRENCY UNIT** the basic unit of currency of Bulgaria. See table at **currency** **2.** **BILL WORTH A LEV** a bill worth one lev [Late 19thC. From Bulgarian, a variant spelling of *lăv* "lion," probably ultimately from Greek *leōn*.]

Lev. *abbr.* BIBLE Leviticus

lev- *prefix.* = **levo-**, **laev-** (*used before vowels*)

Le·vant /lə vánt/ former name for the region in the eastern Mediterranean comprising modern-day Lebanon, Israel, and parts of Syria and Turkey [15thC. From French, literally "rising" (referring to the point where the sun rises).] —**Le·van·tine** /lévv'n tīn, -teen, lə ván-/ *n.*, *adj.*

le·vant·er /lə vántər/ *n.* a strong easterly wind that blows in the western Mediterranean area, especially in the late summer

le·va·tor /lə váytər/ *n.* **1.** ANAT **MUSCLE FOR LIFTING** a muscle that helps to lift the body part to which it is attached **2.** SURG **SURGICAL INSTRUMENT FOR LIFTING** a surgical instrument used to lift up a body part, especially a bone or a tooth [Early 17thC. From Latin, literally "lifter," from *levare* (see LEVER).]

lev·ee[1] /lévvee/ *n.* **1.** **NATURAL EMBANKMENT BESIDE A RIVER** a natural embankment alongside a river, formed by sediment during times of flooding **2.** **ARTIFICIAL EMBANKMENT BESIDE A RIVER** an artificial embankment alongside a river, built to prevent flooding of the surrounding land ■ *vt.* (**-eed**, **-ee·ing**, **-ees**) **BUILD A LEVEE** to provide a river with an embankment to prevent flooding

lev·ee[2] /lévvee/ *n.* **1.** **MORNING VISITING TIME** an occasion when a noble or royal receives visitors informally soon after getting up in the morning **2.** **ROYAL RECEPTION FOR MEN** a court reception at which a prince or sovereign receives men visitors. It is usually held in the early afternoon. [Late 17thC. From French *levé*, variant of *lever* "rising," from *lever* "to rise" (see LEVER).]

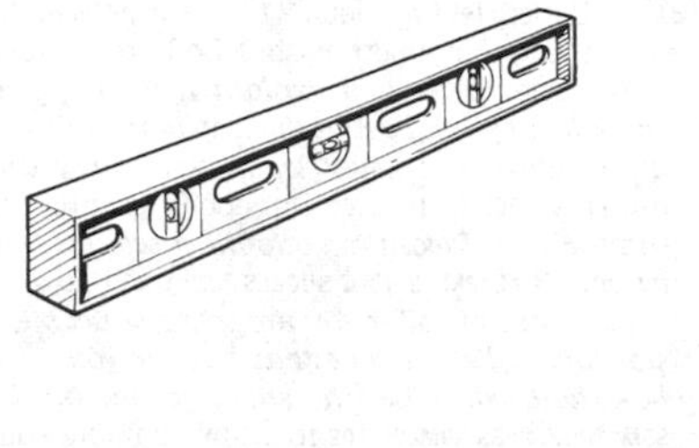

Level

lev·el /lévv'l/ *adj.* **1.** **NOT SLOPING** flat and horizontal, with an even surface or top **2.** **EQUAL** equal to or even with another individual or group in rank, ability, or condition ○ *The two teams have drawn level after six games.* **3.** **STEADY** steady, consistent, or unchanging **4.** **UNWAVERING** not blinking or looking away, and showing penetrating or determined calm **5.** = **level-headed** **6.** **OF A PARTICULAR LEVEL** relating to or characteristic of a particular rank or condition (*usually used in combination*) **7.** **EVEN** smooth or even ○ *We wanted a house with a completely level lawn.* **8.** **ALONGSIDE** next to or alongside somebody or something else ○ *His car drew level as we approached the bend.* ■ *n.* **1.** **HEIGHT FOR MEASUREMENT** a position, line, or flat surface according to which height is measured ○ *10,000 feet above sea level* **2.** **STATED HEIGHT** a particular height ○ *flying below the level of the tree tops* **3.** **HEIGHT OF A SURFACE FROM BOTTOM** the height of a surface from the ground or from the bottom of its container ○ *The level of the river had fallen alarmingly during the summer.* **4.** **RANK OR SCALE** a particular position in a range of relative scales or values ○ *playing tennis at the professional level* **5.** **ASPECT** a quality or aspect of something ○ *It's a movie that works well on a number of different levels.* **6.** **AMOUNT** the amount or concentration of something ○ *My job has a low stress level but few prospects.* **7.** **POSITION OF A PARTICULAR FLOOR** the relative position of a particular floor or other plane in a structure, e.g., a building or bridge ○ *The storeroom is down on the second level.* **8.** CONSTR **TOOL FOR DETERMINING LEVELNESS** a calibrated glass tube containing liquid with an air bubble in it, mounted in a frame and used for measuring whether surfaces are horizontal **9.** CIV ENG **SURVEYING INSTRUMENT** an instrument used in surveying to measure the relative heights of different points in the landscape **10.** CIV ENG **MEASUREMENT OF HEIGHT** in surveying, a measurement taken of the relative heights of different points in a landscape **11.** **HORIZONTAL SURFACE** a horizontal surface or area of land ■ *v.* (**-eled** *or* **-elled**, **-el·ing** *or* **-el·ling**, **-els**) **1.** *vt.* **FLATTEN SOMETHING EVENLY** to make something even, flat, and horizontal ○ *We spent days leveling the ground before we could build anything.* **2.** *vt.* **DEMOLISH AND FLATTEN SOMETHING** to completely destroy a building, place, or area and leave it flattened ○ *The village had been leveled by the hurricane.* **3.** *vt.* **KNOCK SOMEBODY DOWN** to knock somebody to the ground, especially with a punch or blow (*informal*) ○ *leveled him with one punch* **4.** *vti.* **MAKE OR BECOME EQUAL** to make two things or people equal in position or of the same standard or value, or become equal in position, standard or value ○ *Another goal in the final few minutes leveled the scores again.* **5.** *vti.* AIM A GUN to aim or point a weapon ○ *He leveled his pistol at the target.* **6.** *vt.* DIRECT ATTENTION AT SOMEBODY to direct criticism or an attack toward somebody in a purposeful way ○ *Criticism has been leveled at a number of prominent politicians.* **7.** *vi.* BE HONEST WITH SOMEBODY to speak frankly and honestly to somebody (*informal*) ○ *I'd better level with you right now – I'm leaving the company and going it alone.* **8.** *vti.* MEASURE THE ELEVATION OF LAND in surveying, to measure the elevation of an area of land ■ *n.* MINING a horizontal tunnel in a mine [14thC. Via Old French *livel* "tool for determining levelness" (the earliest sense in English) from, ultimately, Latin *libra* "balance, scales" (source of English *Libra*, the zodiac sign).] —**lev·el·ly** *adv.* —**lev·el·ness** *n.* ◇ **on the level** honest and trustworthy (*informal*)

level off *vti.* **1. lev·el off, lev·el out** FLY LEVEL WITH THE GROUND to make an aircraft fly level with the ground, especially after climbing or descending ○ *We passed through the clouds and eventually leveled off at about 10,000 feet.* **2.** BECOME STEADY to reach a level and become stable and unchanging ○ *Stock prices seem to have leveled off.*

lev·el cross·ing *n.* *U.K.* = **grade crossing**

lev·el·er /lévv'lər/, **lev·el·ler** *n.* **1.** SOMETHING THAT MAKES SITUATIONS MORE EQUAL something that makes situations or people more equal, especially by removing distinctions based on status or privilege ○ *Time is a great leveler; we all end up the same way in the end.* **2.** BELIEVER IN EQUALITY somebody who wants to make everyone in society more equal

lev·el-head·ed *adj.* remaining rational and fully in control in difficult situations or emergencies —**lev·el-head·ed·ly** *adv.* —**lev·el-head·ed·ness** *n.*

lev·el·ing screw *n.* one of usually several screws on the bottom of something such as a scientific instrument or a washing machine that can be adjusted to make the piece of equipment stand level

lev·el·ler *n.* = **leveler**

Lev·el·ler *n.* a member or supporter of a radical Parliamentarian movement during the English Civil War, calling for religious tolerance, legal equality, a universal male vote, and the abolition of the monarchy. The movement was later suppressed by Cromwell.

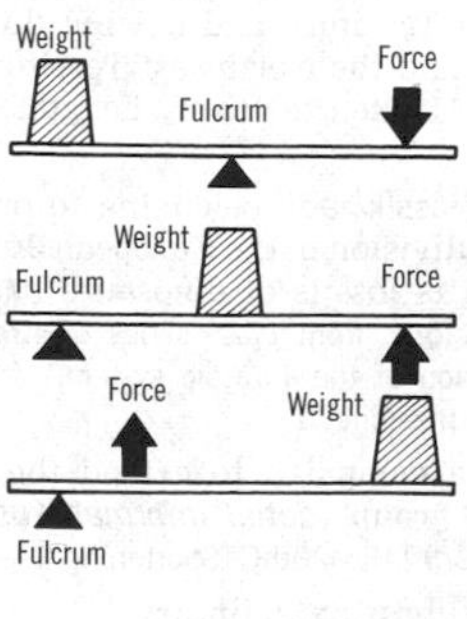

Lever

lev·er /lévvər, léevər/ *n.* **1.** RIGID BAR USED FOR LEVERAGE a rigid bar that pivots about a point (**fulcrum**) and is used to move or lift a load at one end by applying force to the other end **2.** DEVICE OR MACHINE a mechanical device or machine that operates using leverage **3.** WAY OF ACHIEVING SOMETHING a device, tactic, or situation that can be used to advantage ■ *vt.* (**-ered, -er·ing, -ers**) MOVE WITH A LEVER to move something using a lever [13thC. Via Anglo-Norman, literally "something that raises," from Old French *lever* "to rise or raise," from Latin *levare*, from *levis* "light" (source of English *levity*).]

lev·er·age /lévvərij/ *n.* **1.** ACTION OF A LEVER the action of a lever pivoting about a point **2.** MECHANICAL ADVANTAGE the mechanical advantage gained by using a lever **3.** POWER TO GET THINGS DONE power over other people, especially something that gives an advantage but is not referred to openly ○ *He uses the leverage his age gives him with the more junior employees.* **4.** FIN BORROWING OF MONEY TO PURCHASE COMPANY the borrowing of money to purchase a company, relying on it to make enough profit to cover the interest payable on the loan **5.** FIN PROPORTION OF CAPITAL AS DEBT the ratio of a company's debt capital to the value of its ordinary shares ■ *vti.* (**-aged, -ag·ing, -ag·es**) FIN BORROW MONEY HOPING TO MAKE MORE to borrow money in order to buy a company, relying on it to make enough profit to cover the interest payable on the loan

lev·er·aged buy·out *n.* a takeover strategy in which a controlling proportion of a company's shares is bought using borrowed money, the collateral for which is assets belonging to the purchased company

Le Ver·en·drye /lə vèrraaN drée/, **Sieur Pierre Gaultier de Varennes de** (1685–1749) Canadian explorer and fur trader. He explored and established forts in western Canada and the United States from 1731.

lev·er·et /lévvərət/ *n.* a young hare, especially one less than a year old [14thC. From Anglo-Norman, literally "little hare," from *levre* "hare," from Latin *lepus*.]

Le·vesque /lə vék/, **Rene** (*b.* 1922) Canadian journalist and political leader. He founded the Parti Québecois (1968), whose primary goal is Quebec's sovereignty, and became prime minister of the province (1976–85).

Le·vi /léev ī/ *n.* in the Bible, the third son of Jacob and patriarch of the house of Levi (Genesis 29:34)

lev·i·a·ble /lévvee əb'l/ *adj.* **1.** ABLE TO BE TAXED able to have a tax imposed **2.** ABLE TO BE LEVIED capable of being levied

le·vi·a·than /lə ví əthən/ *n.* **1. Le·vi·a·than, le·vi·a·than** MONSTER in the Bible, a large beast or sea monster **2.** SOMETHING HUGE something extremely large and powerful in comparison with others of its kind **3.** WHALE a whale or other large sea animal (*literary*) ○ *A leviathan from the icy deeps crashed ashore one night.* [14thC. Via late Latin from Hebrew *liwyāṯān*.]

WORD KEY: CULTURAL NOTE

Leviathan, a treatise by English philosopher Thomas Hobbes (1651). Hobbes's major work is a defense of the principle of absolute monarchy. It argues that human beings can only live in peace if they agree to subject themselves to a single, absolute ruler. Since this ruler should be answerable only to God, the church too must be subject to civil authority.

lev·i·gate /lévvi gàyt/ (**-gat·ed, -gat·ing, -gates**) *v.* **1.** *vt.* GRIND MINERAL INTO POWDER to grind a mineral into a fine powder with water, forming a smooth paste or slurry **2.** *vt.* SEPARATE PARTICLES IN LIQUID to separate fine particles from coarser ones by suspending them in a liquid **3.** *vti.* FORM A MIXTURE to form a smooth uniform liquid mixture, e.g., a paste or gel [15thC. From Latin *levigat-*, the past participle stem of *levigare* "to polish or make smooth."] —**lev·i·ga·tion** /lèvvi gáysh'n/ *n.*

Le·vi-Mont·al·ci·ni /làyvee mónt'l cheénee/, **Rita** (*b.* 1901) Italian-born U.S. neurobiologist. She shared a Nobel Prize (1986) for research into growth factor in human development.

Le·vine /lə veén/, **James Lawrence** (*b.* 1943) U.S. pianist and conductor. He was made principal conductor of the Metropolitan Opera in New York City (1973), and later became its artistic director (1986).

lev·i·rate /lévvərət, -ràyt, léev-/ *n.* the practice or requirement of marriage of a widow to the brother of her deceased husband. This custom was practiced in ancient Jewish society and is common in parts of Africa today. [Early 18thC. From Latin *levir* "husband's brother."] —**lev·i·rat·ic** /lèvvə ráttik, lèevə-/ *adj.*

Le·vi-Strauss /lay vee strówss/, **Claude Gustave** (*b.* 1908) French social anthropologist. A proponent of structuralism, he originated the thesis that all cultures have a common framework.

Levit. *abbr.* Leviticus

lev·i·tate /lévvi tàyt/ (**-tat·ed, -tat·ing, -tates**) *v.* **1.** *vti.* RISE IN THE AIR to rise and float in the air, or make something rise and float in the air, seemingly in defiance of gravity **2.** *vt.* MED SUPPORT A PATIENT ON AIR to support a patient on a cushion of air during treatment for severe burns [Late 17thC. From Latin *levis* "light," modeled on *gravitate*. Originally "to make light."] —**lev·i·ta·tor** *n.*

lev·i·ta·tion /lèvvi táysh'n/ *n.* the act of rising into or floating something in the air without visible means of support —**lev·i·ta·tion·al** *adj.*

Le·vite /lée vīt/ *n.* a member of the tribe of Levi, chosen to assist the priests of the Temple. The Levites were descended from Jacob's son Levi and constituted one of the twelve tribes of Israel. [14thC. Via ecclesiastical Latin *levita* from Greek *leuitēs*, named for *Levi* "Levi."]

Le·vit·i·cal /lə víttik'l/ *adj.* **1.** OF THE LEVITES belonging or relating to the Levites **2.** OF THE BOOK OF LEVITICUS relating to the book of Leviticus, especially those portions containing laws relating to ritual or moral precepts

Le·vit·i·cus /lə víttikəss/ *n.* a book of the Bible, the third book of the Pentateuch, containing the priestly tradition of the Levites. It continues from the end of the book of Exodus and is traditionally attributed to Moses. [14thC. From late Latin, literally "of the Levites," ultimately from Greek *leuitēs* (see LEVITE).]

Lev·it·town /lévit tòwn/ **1.** town in Nassau County, New York, situated on Long Island. Population: 53,286 (1990). **2.** town in Bucks County, Pennsylvania. Population: 55,362 (1990).

lev·i·ty /lévvətee/ *n.* **1.** FLIPPANCY remarks or behavior intended to be amusing, especially when they are out of keeping with a serious occasion **2.** BUOYANCY lightness in weight (*archaic*) [Mid-16thC. From Latin *levitas*, from *levis* "light."]

le·vo /lée vò/ *adj.* = **levorotatory** [Mid-20thC. Shortening.]

levo- *prefix.* **1.** leftward, counterclockwise ○ *levorotation* **2.** levorotatory ○ *levulose* [Via French *lévo-* from Latin *laevus* "left"]

le·vo·do·pa /leevə dṓpə, lèvvə-/ *n.* full form of **L-dopa** [Late 20thC. Coined from LEVO- + DOPA (see L-DOPA).]

le·vo·ro·ta·tion /leevə rō táysh'n/ *n.* a rotation to the left or counterclockwise, especially of the plane of polarized light

le·vo·ro·ta·to·ry /leevə rṓtə tàwree/ *adj.* **1.** WITH COUNTERCLOCKWISE MOTION turning or circling in a counterclockwise direction or to the left **2.** TURNING POLARIZED LIGHT COUNTERCLOCKWISE turning the plane of polarized light in a counterclockwise direction

lev·u·lose /lévvyə lòss, -lòz/ *n.* = **fructose** [Late 19thC. Coined from LEVO- + -ULE + -OSE.]

lev·y /lévvee/ *v.* (**-ied, -y·ing, -ies**) **1.** *vt.* POL IMPOSE A TAX to use government authority to impose or collect a tax **2.** *vt.* MIL RAISE AN ARMY to enlist troops for military service, often by force **3.** *vt.* DECLARE WAR to declare war on somebody **4.** *vi.* LAW SEIZE PROPERTY TO FULFILL A JUDGMENT to seize property in accordance with a legal ruling ■ *n.* (*plural* **-ies**) **1.** TAX money raised under government authority **2.** THE RAISING OF TAX the act of collecting taxes under government authority **3.** MIL ARMY a group of soldiers drafted under government authority **4.** MIL CONSCRIPTION the act of drafting soldiers under government authority [15thC. From French *lever* "to raise or rise," from Latin *levare* (see LEVER).] —**lev·i·er** *n.*

lewd /lood/ *adj.* showing an inordinate interest in sex or sexual excitement (*disapproving*) [Old English *lǣw(e)de* "lay, not in holy orders," of unknown origin. The current sense evolved via Middle English meanings "not educated, ignorant" and "crude, vulgar, vile."] —**lewd·ly** *adv.* —**lewd·ness** *n.*

Lew·in /loo in/, **Kurt** (1890–1947) German-born U.S. psychologist. He pioneered research in behavior, personality, and group dynamics.

lew·is /loo iss/ *n.* an iron attachment consisting of linked pieces that fit into a dovetailed opening in a stone, used to grip heavy stones before lifting them [Mid-18thC. Origin uncertain: probably from French *lous*, plural of *lou(p)* "kind of siege engine," literally "wolf," from Latin *lupus* (see LUPUS).]

Lew·is /loo iss/, **Carl** (*b.* 1961) U.S. athlete. He won nine Olympic gold medals for 100- and 200-meter races and the long jump between 1984 and 1996.

Lew·is, C. S. (1898–1963) Irish-born British critic, scholar, and novelist. He wrote books on moral and religious issues, e.g., *The Screwtape Letters* (1942), and a children's book series known as *The Chronicles of Narnia* (1950–56). Full name **Clive Staples Lewis**

Lew·is, Gilbert Newton (1875–1946) U.S. chemist. He was noted for his research in chemical energy and for his pioneering methods.

Lew·is, Jerry (*b.* 1926) U.S. actor, screenwriter, movie director, and movie producer. He formed a comic duo with Dean Martin, with whom he made 18 movies, and later starred in his own movies. Real name **Joseph Levitch**

Lew·is, Meriwether (1774–1809) U.S. explorer. With William Clark he explored territory between the Mississippi River and the Pacific Ocean (1804–06).

Lew·is, Sinclair (1885–1951) U.S. novelist. The author of *Babbitt* (1922) and other novels that pillory middle-class life in the United States, he won a Nobel Prize in literature (1930). Full name **Harry Sinclair Lewis**

Lew·is ac·id *n.* a substance that can accept a pair of electrons from a base to form a covalent bond [Mid-20thC. Named for Gilbert Newton *Lewis*, who introduced the concept.]

Lew·is gun *n.* a gas-powered machine gun with a circular magazine, first used in World War I [Early 20thC. Named for the U.S. soldier Colonel Isaac Newton *Lewis* (1858–1931), who invented it.]

lew·is·ite /lóo i sīt/ *n.* a colorless or brownish oily poisonous liquid used in gaseous form in chemical warfare during World War I. Formula: $C_2H_2AsCl_3$. [Early 20thC. Named for the U.S. chemist Winford Lee *Lewis* (1878–1943), who developed it.]

lew·is·son /lóo əss'n/ *n.* = **lewis**

Lew·is·ton /lóo istən/ **1.** city in northwestern Idaho, where the Clearwater River joins the Snake River near Washington State. Population: 30,271 (1996). **2.** city in southwestern Maine, on the eastern bank of the Androscoggin River across from Auburn. Population: 36,830 (1996).

lex /leks/ (*plural* **le·ges** /lée jeez/) *n.* a named law or set of laws (*formal*) [Late 18thC. From Latin, literally "law."]

lex. *abbr.* lexicon

lex·eme /lék seem/ *n.* a fundamental unit of the vocabulary of a language, e.g., "make," which may exist in a number of different forms, e.g., "make, makes, making, maker, made" [Mid-20thC. Coined from LEXICON + -EME.]

lex·i·ca plural of **lexicon**

lex·i·cal /léksik'l/ *adj.* **1.** OF WORDS relating to the individual words that make up the vocabulary of a language **2.** OF A LEXICON relating to a lexicon or lexicography [Mid-19thC. Formed from Greek *lexikos* (see LEXICON).] —**lex·i·cal·i·ty** /lèksi kállətee/ *n.* —**lex·i·cal·ly** /léksikəlee/ *adv.*

lex·i·cal·i·za·tion /lèksik'li záysh'n/ *n.* **1.** MAKING A WORD FROM EXISTING WORDS the creation of a single word out of existing words, usually in order to express something previously conveyed by several words or a phrase, e.g., "shoplifting" **2.** WORD FORMED FROM EXISTING WORDS a single word created by lexicalization

lex·i·cal·ize /léksik'l īz/ (**-ized, -iz·ing, -iz·es**) *vti.* to form a single word or be formed as a single word from existing words in order to express something previously conveyed by several words or a phrase, e.g., "shoplifting"

lex·i·cal mean·ing *n.* the meaning of the base word in the set of inflected forms (**paradigm**). In the paradigm "throw, throws, throwing, threw, thrown," the lexical meaning is "throw."

lexicog. *abbr.* **1.** lexicography **2.** lexicographical

lex·i·cog·ra·phy /lèksi kóggrəfee/ *n.* the writing and editing of dictionaries [Mid-17thC. Coined from Greek *lexikos* (see LEXICON) + -GRAPHY.] —**lex·i·cog·ra·pher** *n.* —**lex·i·co·graph·ic** /lèksikə gráffik/ *adj.* —**lex·i·co·graph·i·cal·ly** *adv.*

lex·i·col·o·gy /lèksi kólləjee/ *n.* the branch of linguistics dealing with the use and meanings of words and the relationships between items of vocabulary [Early 19thC. Coined from Greek *lexikos* (see LEXICON) + -LOGY.] —**lex·i·co·log·i·cal** /lèksikə lójjik'l/ *adj.* —**lex·i·co·log·i·cal·ly** *adv.* —**lex·i·col·o·gist** /lèksə kólləjist/ *n.*

lex·i·con /léksəkən, -kòn/ (*plural* **-cons** *or* **-ca** /-kə/) *n.* **1.** DICTIONARY a reference book with an alphabetized listing of words and their meanings, especially one dealing with an ancient language **2.** VOCABULARY the entire stock of words belonging to a branch of knowledge or known by somebody [Early 17thC. Via modern Latin from Greek *lexikon*, literally "of words," from, ultimately, *lexis* "word," from *legein* "to speak."]

lex·i·gra·phy /lek síggrəfee/ *n.* a system of writing in which each character stands for a word [Early 19thC. From Greek *lexis* (see LEXICON) + -GRAPHY.]

Lex·ing·ton /léksingtən/ **1.** city in Fayette County, in northern central Kentucky. The surrounding area is a leading world center for horse breeding and sales. Population: 225,366 (1990). **2.** town in northeastern Massachusetts, northwest of Boston. It is the site of the first battle of the Revolution in 1775. Population: 29,484 (1996).

lex·is /léksiss/ *n.* the entire stock of words in a language [Mid-20thC. From Greek (see LEXICON).]

lex ta·li·o·nis /-tállee óniss/ *n.* the legal principle that proscribes retaliating in kind for crimes committed [From Latin, literally "law of retaliation"]

ley /lay, lee/ (*plural* **leys**) *n.* **1.** = **lea 2.** AGRIC LAND PUT DOWN TO GRASS an area of arable land temporarily put down to grass **3.** VERY OLD PATH any of many ancient paths in Britain that led from hilltop to hilltop and touched on water sources and places of worship

Ley·den jar /líd'n-/ *n.* an early device for condensing static electricity consisting of a glass jar coated inside and outside with metal foil and with a conducting rod passing through an insulated stopper [Mid-18thC. From *Leyden*, former spelling of LEIDEN, where it was invented.]

ley line *n.* in the United Kingdom, a straight line linking ancient landmarks and places of worship, believed to follow the course of former routes and popularly associated with mystical phenomena

Lez·ghi·an /lézgee ən/ *n.* a language spoken in an area around the Caspian Sea belonging to the Dagestanian branch of Caucasian languages. Lezghian is spoken by about 300,000 people. [Mid-19thC. From Russian *Lezgin*.] —**Lez·ghi·an** *adj.*

lf *abbr.* **1.** light face **2.** low frequency

LF *abbr.* **1.** BASEBALL left field **2.** BASEBALL left fielder **3.** RADIO low frequency

L-form *n.* a bacterium that lacks cell walls [*L* from the *Lister* Institute in London, England, where it was first isolated]

LG *abbr.* Low German

lg. *abbr.* **1.** large **2.** long

LH *abbr.* luteinizing hormone

l.h. *abbr.* left hand

Lha·sa /laásse, lássə/ city and capital of the autonomous region of Tibet, southwestern China. Population: 106,885 (1990).

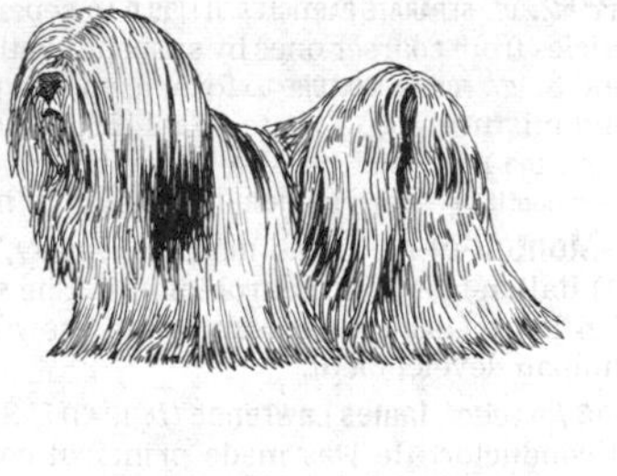

Lhasa apso

Lha·sa ap·so (*plural* **Lha·sa ap·sos**) *n.* a small dog of a Tibetan breed with a long straight coat, hair that falls heavily over the eyes, and a fluffy tail that curls over the back [Early 20thC. From LHASA + *Apso*, the Tibetan name of the breed.]

LHD *abbr.* Litterarum Humaniorum Doctor

lher·zo·lite /lúrzə līt/ *n.* a coarse-grained rock containing minerals high in iron and magnesium that is believed to originate in the earth's mantle

LHRH *abbr.* luteinizing hormone-releasing hormone

li[1] *abbr.* link

li[2] /lee/ (*plural* **li**) *n.* a traditional Chinese unit of distance, now standardized at 547 yd./500 m [Late 16thC. From Chinese *lǐ*.]

Li *symbol.* lithium

L.I. *abbr.* Long Island

li·a·bil·i·ty /lī ə bíllətee/ *n.* (*plural* **-ties**) **1.** LAW OBLIGATION UNDER THE LAW legal responsibility for something, especially costs or damages **2.** DEBT anything for which somebody is responsible, especially a debt **3.** DISADVANTAGE something that holds somebody back or causes trouble **4.** SOMEBODY WHO IS A BURDEN somebody who prevents a successful outcome or causes social embarrassment **5.** LIKELIHOOD OF SOMETHING likelihood or probability of something happening ■ **li·a·bil·i·ties** *npl.* ACCT MONEY OWED all debts and other financial obligations that appear on a balance sheet

li·a·ble /lī əb'l/ *adj.* **1.** LAW RESPONSIBLE having legal responsibility for something, especially costs or damages **2.** LIKELY likely to experience or do something, often something unpleasant or hazardous [15thC. Origin uncertain: probably formed from French *lier* (see LIAISON).]

li·aise /lee áyz/ (**-aised, -ais·ing, -ais·es**) *vi.* to establish or maintain close cooperation with somebody [Early 20thC. Back-formation from LIAISON (originally military slang).]

li·ai·son /lée ay zòn, lee áy-/ *n.* **1.** COORDINATION the exchange of information or the planning of joint efforts by separate groups or individuals, often of military units **2.** COORDINATOR somebody who is responsible for maintaining communication between one group or office and another **3.** UNMARRIED LOVE AFFAIR a romantic and sexual relationship between people who are not married to each other **4.** LING PRONOUNCED CONSONANT LINKING TWO WORDS in spoken French, the pronunciation of the usually silent final consonant of a word when it is followed by another word beginning with a vowel **5.** FOOD SOMETHING USED TO THICKEN A LIQUID a thickening agent such as egg yolks or flour used in soups and sauces [Mid-17thC. From French, formed from *lier* "to bind," from Latin *ligare* (source of English *ligature*).]

li·an·a /lee aánə, -ánnə/, **li·ane** /-áan, -án/ *n.* a woody climbing tropical vine [Late 18thC. From French *liane*, originally "clematis" of uncertain origin: perhaps formed from *lier* (see LIAISON).] —**li·a·noid** /lee aá nòyd, -á-/ *adj.*

Liao /lyow/ river in northeastern China. Length: 700 mi./1,125 km.

Liao·ning /lyòw níng/ province in the historic region of Manchuria, northeastern China. Shenyang is the capital. Population: 40,670,000 (1994). Area: 58,300 sq. mi./151,000 sq. km.

Liao·yang /-yaáng/, **Liao-yang** city in Liaoning Province, northeastern China, situated 35 mi./56 km south of Shenyang. Population: 492,559 (1990).

Li·a·quat A·li Khan /lee ə kwaát aallee kaán/ (1895–1951) Pakistani statesman. The first prime minister of Pakistan (1947–51), he was assassinated while in office.

li·ar /lī́r/ *n.* somebody who tells lies

li·ard /lee aárd, -aár/ *n.* a coin of small value formerly used in various European countries, including France [Mid-16thC. From French, of unknown origin.]

Li·ard /lée ərd/ river of western Canada, rising in the Yukon Territory and flowing through British Columbia and the Northwest Territories, where it joins the Mackenzie River. Length: 700 mi./1,115 km.

Li·as·sic /lī ássik/ *adj.* belonging to or dating from the oldest division of the European Jurassic period, noted for its fossils of dinosaurs [Mid-19thC. From French *liassique*, from *Lias* "series of strata forming the lowest division of the Jurassic system," from Old French *liais* "hard limestone."]

lib /lib/ *n.* a campaign to extend the rights of an oppressed group (*dated informal*) (*usually used in combination*) [Mid-20thC. Shortening.] —**lib·ber** *n.*

lib. *abbr.* **1.** librarian **2.** library

Lib. *abbr.* **1.** Liberal **2.** Liberalism

li·ba·tion /lī báysh'n/ *n.* **1.** RELIG POURING OF LIQUID AS A RELIGIOUS OFFERING the pouring out of a liquid such as wine or oil as a sacrifice to a god or in honor of a dead person **2.** RELIG SOMETHING POURED OUT AS A SACRIFICE a liquid such as wine or oil poured out as a religious offering **3.** ALCOHOLIC DRINK an alcoholic drink (*humorous*) [14thC. From the Latin stem *libation-*, from *libare* "to pour out."] —**li·ba·tion·al** *adj.*

Lib·by /líbbee/, **Willard Frank** (1908–80) U.S. chemist. He received the Nobel Prize in chemistry (1960) for his discovery of radiocarbon dating.

li·bel /līb'l/ *n.* **1.** LAW DEFAMATION a false and malicious published statement that damages somebody's reputation. Libel can include pictures and any other representations that have public or permanent form. **2.** ATTACKING SOMEBODY'S REPUTATION the making of false and damaging statements about somebody **3.** LAW WRITTEN STATEMENT the plaintiff's written statement in a case under admiralty law or in an ecclesiastical court ■ *vt.* (**-beled, -bel·ing, -bels**) **1.** DEFAME to publish false and malicious statements that damage somebody's reputation **2.** ATTACK to give a false and damaging account of somebody **3.** LAW BRING A SUIT FOR LIBEL to bring a suit for libel against somebody under admiralty law or in an ecclesiastical court [14thC. Via Old French from Latin *libellus* "little book," diminutive of *liber* (see LIBRARY). Originally "written declaration," later "something setting out the grounds for a lawsuit."] —**li·bel·ant** *n.* —**li·bel·ee** /lība lée/ *n.* —**li·bel·er** *n.* —**li·bel·ist** /līb'list/ *n.* —**li·bel·ous** *adj.* —**li·bel·ous·ly** *adv.*

WORD KEY: SYNONYMS

See Synonyms at ***malign.***

Lib·er·a·ce /lìbbər áachee/ (1919–87) U.S. entertainer. A performer of popular piano pieces, he was distinguished by his flamboyant attire and lavish presentations. Real name **Wladziu Valentino Liberace**

lib·er·al /líbbərəl, líbbrəl/ *adj.* **1. BROAD-MINDED** tolerant of different views and standards of behavior in others **2.** POL **PROGRESSIVE POLITICALLY OR SOCIALLY** favoring gradual reform, especially political reforms that extend democracy, distribute wealth more evenly, and protect the personal freedom of the individual **3. GENEROUS** generous with money, time, or some other asset ○ *My great-aunt was liberal in her bequests.* **4. GENEROUS IN QUANTITY** large in size or amount ○ *a liberal helping* **5.** LANG **NOT LITERAL** not limited to the literal meaning in translation or interpretation **6.** ARTS **CULTURALLY ORIENTED** concerned with general cultural matters and broadening of the mind rather than professional or technical study ○ *a liberal education* **7.** HIST **OF POLITICAL LIBERALISM** relating to a political ideology of liberalism ■ *n.* **LIBERAL PERSON** somebody who favors tolerance or reform [14thC. Via French from Latin *liberalis,* from *liber* "free" (source of English *liberty*). The underlying sense is "suitable for a free (later wellbred) person."]

WORD KEY: SYNONYMS

See Synonyms at ***generous.***

Lib·er·al *adj.* **OF A LIBERAL PARTY** supporting, belonging to, or associated with a Liberal Party, e.g., in the United Kingdom, Canada, or Australia ■ *n.* **MEMBER OF A LIBERAL PARTY** somebody who is a member of or supports a Liberal Party, e.g., in the United Kingdom, Canada, or Australia

lib·er·al arts *npl.* **1. EDUCATION IN CULTURALLY ORIENTED SUBJECTS** college and university subjects that are intended to provide students with general cultural knowledge, e.g., languages, literature, history, and philosophy **2. MEDIEVAL EDUCATION** the medieval studies known as the trivium and quadrivium

lib·er·al de·moc·ra·cy *n.* a political system that has free elections, a multiplicity of political parties, political decision made through an independent legislature, and an independent judiciary, with a state monopoly on law enforcement

lib·er·al·ism /líbbərə lìzzəm, líbbrə-/ *n.* **1.** POL **PROGRESSIVE VIEWS** a belief in tolerance and gradual reform in moral, religious, or political matters **2.** POL **POLITICAL THEORY STRESSING INDIVIDUALISM** a political ideology with its beginnings in western Europe that rejects authoritarian government and defends freedom of speech, association, and religion, and the right to own property **3.** ECON **FREE-MARKET ECONOMICS** an economic theory in favor of free competition and minimal government regulation **4.** CHR **CHRISTIAN THEOLOGICAL MOVEMENT** a movement in modern Protestantism stressing intellectual freedom and the moral content of Christianity over the doctrines of traditional theology —**lib·er·al·ist** *n.* —**lib·er·al·is·tic** /lìbbərə lístik, lìbbrə-/ *adj.*

lib·er·al·i·ty /lìbbə rállətee/ *n.* **1. GENEROSITY** generous provision of money, time, or some other asset **2. LARGENESS** largeness in size or amount **3. BROAD-MINDEDNESS** tolerance of different views and standards of behavior in others

lib·er·al·ize /líbbərə līz, líbbrə-/ (**-ized, -iz·ing, -iz·es**) *vti.* to reform and become less strict, or reform something and make it less strict —**lib·er·al·i·za·tion** /lìbbərəli záysh'n, lìbbrəli-/ *n.* —**lib·er·al·iz·er** /líbbərə līzər, líbbrə-/ *n.*

lib·er·al·ly /líbbərəlee, líbbrə-/ *adv.* **1. GENEROUSLY** giving money, time, or some other asset with generosity **2. IN LARGE AMOUNTS** in large quantities or amounts

lib·er·al·ness /líbbərəlnəss, líbbrəl-/ *n.* = **liberality**

Lib·er·al Par·ty *n.* **1. FORMER U.K. POLITICAL PARTY** one of the main British political parties that evolved from the Whigs and eventually merged with the Social Democratic Party in 1988 to form the Social and Liberal Democratic Party. The Social and Liberal Democrats later became known as the Liberal Democrats. **2.** *Can* **MAJOR CANADIAN POLITICAL PARTY** a major Canadian political party at both the national and provincial levels that first came to power nationally in 1873

lib·er·ate /líbbə ràyt/ (**-at·ed, -at·ing, -ates**) *vt.* **1. SET SOMEBODY FREE PHYSICALLY** to release an individual, group, population, or country from political or military control or from any severe physical constraint **2. RELEASE SOMEBODY FROM SOCIAL STEREOTYPING** to set somebody free from traditional socially imposed constraints such as those arising from stereotyping by gender or age **3. STEAL** to steal something (*informal*) **4.** CHEM **RELEASE GAS DURING A CHEMICAL REACTION** to free something such as a gas from combination in a chemical compound during a chemical reaction [Late 16thC. From Latin *liberare,* from *liber* "free."]

lib·er·at·ing·ly /líbbə ràytinglee/ *adv.* in such a way as to induce a feeling of liberation, especially from traditional socially imposed constraints such as those arising from stereotyping by age or gender

lib·er·a·tion /lìbbə ráysh'n/ *n.* **1. BEING SET FREE** the process or state of being liberated ○ *When I left that job, I had a tremendous feeling of liberation.* **2. RELEASE FROM SOCIAL STEREOTYPING** gaining equal rights for a particular group by setting its members free from traditional socially imposed constraints such as those arising from sexual or ageist stereotyping ○ *My career wouldn't have been possible without women's liberation.* —**lib·er·a·tion·ist** *n., adj.*

lib·er·a·tion the·ol·o·gy *n.* a movement in Roman Catholic religious teaching that argues that the Church should work actively together with socialists to combat social, political, and economic oppression. The movement is international but especially active in Latin America and bases its case on Jesus Christ's ministry to the poor and outcast in society. —**lib·er·a·tion the·o·lo·gi·an** *n.*

lib·er·a·tor /líbbə ràytər/ *n.* somebody who sets others free

Liberia

Li·be·ri·a /lī béeree ə/ republic in western Africa, on the North Atlantic Ocean. Language: English. Currency: Liberian dollar. Capital: Monrovia. Population: 2,602,068 (1997). Area: 38,250 sq. mi./99,067 sq. km. Official name **Republic of Liberia** —**Li·ber·i·an** *adj., n.*

lib·er·tar·i·an /lìbbər táiree ən/ *n.* **1.** PHILOS **ADVOCATE OF INDIVIDUAL RESPONSIBILITY** somebody who believes in the doctrine of free will **2.** POL **ADVOCATE OF INDIVIDUAL FREEDOM** somebody who believes that people should have complete freedom of thought and action and should not be subject to the authority of the state [Late 18thC. Formed from LIBERTY, modeled on words such as UNITARIAN.] —**lib·er·tar·i·an·ism** *n.*

lib·er·tine /líbbər teèn/ *n.* somebody, usually a man, who indulges in pleasures that are considered immoral and who has sexual relationships with many people [14thC. From Latin *libertinus,* from *libertus* "somebody freed from slavery," from *liber* "free." The underlying sense is of somebody unrestrained.] —**lib·er·tin·age** *n.* —**lib·er·tin·ism** *n.*

lib·er·ty /líbbərtee/ (*plural* **-ties**) *n.* **1. RIGHT TO CHOOSE** the freedom to think or act without being constrained by necessity or force **2. FREEDOM** freedom from captivity or slavery **3.** POL **BASIC RIGHT** any of the political, social, and economic rights that belong to the citizens of a state or to all people (*often used in the plural*) ◊ **civil liberties 4. BREACH OF ETIQUETTE** an action or remark that violates the polite distance usually left between individuals and that may strike the person at whom it is directed as insultingly familiar [14thC. Via French *liberté* from Latin *libertas,* from *liber* "free."] ◇ **at liberty 1.** free or freed after a period of imprisonment or other constraint **2.** free or allowed to do something ◇ **take liberties with 1.** behave inappropriately toward somebody, especially by way of excessive familiarity or sometimes sexual harrassment **2.** to be deliberately inaccurate when dealing with facts (*disapproving*) ◇ **take the liberty** be bold enough to do something, sometimes without permission

WORD KEY: CULTURAL NOTE

Liberty Leading the People, a painting by French artist Eugene Delacroix (1830). Inspired by a scene witnessed by Delacroix during the 1830 uprisings in Paris, this mixture of allegory and realism shows a young woman leading a ragged band of rebels over razed barricades. Delacroix's declaration of solidarity with the revolutionary cause, it is also a powerful symbol of freedom and the struggle against oppression. The painting is sometimes called *Liberty on the Barricades.*

WORD KEY: CULTURAL NOTE

On Liberty, an essay by English philosopher John Stuart Mill (1859). A work that has inspired civil libertarians around the world, it examines the relationship between the rights of the individual and the power of the state. Mill argues for freedom of thought and expression, asserting that the only valid restrictions on the rights of individuals are those that protect the rights of others.

lib·er·ty cap *n.* a soft cone-shaped cap fitting tightly on the head and falling to one side, worn as a symbol of freedom by French revolutionaries and in the United States before 1800. It was first worn in ancient Rome, where it was given to people who were set free from slavery.

Lib·er·ty Is·land island in New York Bay, southeastern New York. It is the site of the Statue of Liberty. Area: 12 acres/5 hectares. Formerly **Bedloe's Island** (until 1956)

lib·er·ty pole *n.* a tall flagpole to the top of which a liberty cap or the flag of a new republic is attached

lib·er·ty ship *n.* a type of cargo ship mass-produced in the United States during World War II

li·bid·i·nous /li bídd'nəss/ *adj.* having or expressing strong sexual desires (*formal*) [15thC. From Latin *libidinosus,* from *libido* "desire, lust."] —**li·bid·i·nous·ly** *adv.* —**li·bid·i·nous·ness** *n.*

li·bi·do /li beè dō/ (*plural* **-dos**) *n.* **1. SEX DRIVE** sexual drive **2.** PSYCHOANAL **EMOTIONS THEORETICALLY LINKED TO SEXUALITY** in some theories, the psychic and emotional energy in somebody's psychological makeup that is related to the basic human instincts, especially the sex drive [Early 20thC. From Latin, literally "desire, lust."] —**li·bid·i·nal** /lə bídd'nəl/ *adj.* —**li·bid·i·nal·ly** *adv.*

Li·bra /leébrə, lī-/ *n.* **1.** ASTRON **CONSTELLATION IN THE SOUTHERN HEMISPHERE** a small constellation in the southern hemisphere between Virgo and Scorpio **2.** ZODIAC **SEVENTH SIGN OF THE ZODIAC** the seventh sign of the zodiac represented by a pair of scales and lasting from approximately September 23 to October 22. Libra is classified as an air sign and its ruling planet is Venus. **3. SOMEBODY BORN UNDER LIBRA** somebody whose birthday falls between September 23 and October 22 [Pre-12thC. From Latin, literally "balance, scales."] —**Li·bra** *adj.*

Li·bran /lībrən, leébrən/ *n.* = **Libra** *n.* 3 —**Li·bran** *adj.*

li·brar·i·an /lī bráiree ən/ *n.* somebody who works in or is in charge of a library [Late 17thC. Formed from Latin *librarius* (see LIBRARY), literally "of books," also "scribe, somebody concerned with books."]

li·brar·i·an·ship *n.* = **library science**

li·brar·y /līb rèrree, lībraree/ (*plural* **-ies**) *n.* **1. PLACE WHERE BOOKS ARE KEPT** the room, building, or institution where a collection of books or other research materials is kept **2. COLLECTION OF THINGS** a collection of books, newspapers, records, tapes, or other materials that are valuable for research **3.** COMPUT **COLLECTION OF SOFTWARE** a collection of things for use on a computer, e.g., programs or diskettes, or a collection of routines or instructions used by a computer program [14thC. Via French *librairie* from, ultimately, Latin *libraria* "bookshop," literally "of books," from, ultimately, *liber* "book" (literally "inner bark of a tree," once used as writing material).]

li·brar·y e·di·tion *n.* a set of books published in a

series that are either by a single author or on the same subject and are alike in size and format

Li·brar·y of Con·gress *n.* the national library of the United States, located in Washington, D.C. and founded by an Act of Congress in 1800. It contains more than 28 million books and pamphlets as well as presidential papers, music, photographs, and recordings.

li·brar·y paste *n.* thick white glue made from starch that is used on paper and lightweight cardboard

li·brar·y sci·ence *n.* the study of libraries and their administration, including techniques of research and principles of organization

li·bra·tion /lī bráysh'n/ *n.* a real or apparent oscillation in the orbit of one celestial body as seen from the one around which it orbits, especially as seen in the Moon from the Earth [Early 17thC. From the Latin stem *libration-*, from *librare* "to balance," from *libra* "balance, scales."] —**li·brate** *vi.* —**li·bra·tion·al** *adj.*

lib·ret·ti plural of **libretto**

li·bret·tist /li bréttist/ *n.* somebody who writes the words of a dramatic musical work such as an opera or musical

li·bret·to /li bré tō/ (*plural* **-tos** *or* **-ti** /-tee/) *n.* the words of a dramatic musical work such as an opera, including both the spoken and the sung parts [Mid-18thC. From Italian, literally "little book," from *libro* "book," from Latin *liber* (see LIBRARY).]

Li·bre·ville /leébrə vìl/ city, chief port, and capital of Gabon, on the Gulf of Guinea. Population: 365,650 (1993).

Lib·ri·um /líbbree əm/ *tdmk.* a trademark for the long-acting benzodiazepine drug chlordiazepoxide, used to treat anxiety, alcohol withdrawal symptoms, and sometimes insomnia

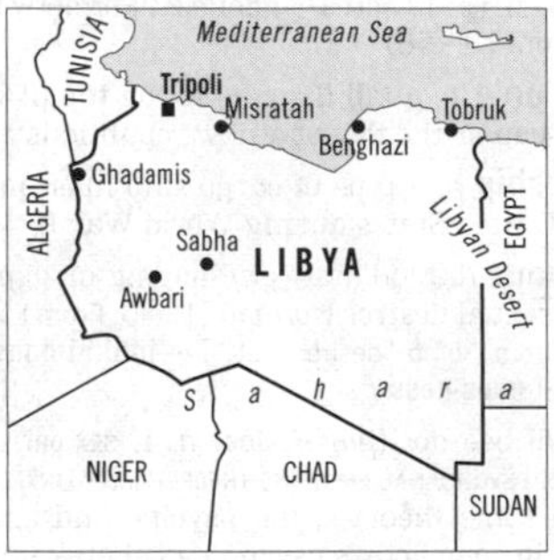

Libya

Lib·y·a /líbbee ə/ country in northern Africa, south of the Mediterranean Sea. It became independent as a kingdom in 1951. Language: Arabic. Currency: Libyan dinar. Capital: Tripoli. Population: 5,484,202 (1997). Area: 678,400 sq. mi./1,757,000 sq. km. Official name **Socialist People's Libyan Arab Jamahiriyah**

Lib·y·an /líbbyən/ *n.* **1.** PEOPLES **SOMEBODY FROM LIBYA** somebody who was born or raised in Libya, or who is a citizen of Libya **2.** LANG **LANGUAGE OF ANCIENT LIBYA** an extinct language formerly spoken in ancient Libya, belonging to the Nilo-Hamitic branch of Nilo-Saharan languages [15thC. Formed from Latin *Libya* "Libya."] —**Lib·y·an** *adj.*

Lib·y·an Des·ert desert, the northeastern section of the Sahara, extending from eastern Libya into southwestern Egypt and the extreme northwestern part of Sudan

lice plural of **louse**

li·cence[1] /líss'nss/ *n.* LAW = **license** [14thC. Via French from Latin *licentia* "freedom," later "authority, permission," from *licere* "to be allowed."]

li·cence[2] *n.* U.K. = **license**

li·cense /líss'ns/ *n.* **1. PERMIT** a printed document that gives official permission to a specific person or group to own something or do something **2.** LAW **LEGAL AUTHORIZATION** official permission to do something, either from a government or under a law or regulation **3. CHANCE TO DO SOMETHING** the opportunity to do something, especially when this goes beyond normal limits ○ *a license to print money* **4. PERMISSION TO BEND TRUTH** the freedom of a writer or artist to rearrange the facts of ordinary life in order to make a more striking effect ○ *artistic license* **5. LACK OF RESTRAINT** freedom in behavior or speech that exceeds what is considered appropriate ■ *vt.* (**-censed, -cens·ing, -cens·es**) **FORMALLY ALLOW** to give official mission for somebody to do something or for activity to take place (*often passive*) ○ *He was censed to practice medicine in the United States.* [14thC. Via French from Latin *licentia* "freedom," later "authority, permission," from *licere* "to be allowed."] —**li·cens·a·ble** *adj.* —**li·cens·er** *n.* —**li·cen·sor** *n.*

li·censed prac·ti·cal nurse *n.* in the United States, a nurse trained to provide routine nursing care but allowed to perform more complex tasks only under the direction of a registered nurse or a doctor

li·cens·ee /lìss'n seé/ *n.* somebody who has been granted official permission to do something

li·cense plate *n.* a thin flat piece of metal showing the registration number of a vehicle, usually attached just above the front and back bumpers

li·cen·sure /líss'nshər, -shoor/ *n.* the act of granting a license, especially to practice a profession

li·cen·ti·ate /lī sénshee ət/ *n.* **1. SOMEBODY AUTHORIZED IN A PROFESSION** somebody who has been granted a license to practice a particular profession or teach a particular skill **2. QUALIFICATION OF A LICENTIATE** the qualification awarded to a licentiate in a specific profession or to teach a specific skill ○ *He has a licentiate in music.* **3. ACADEMIC DEGREE** a degree awarded by some European universities that ranks one step below that of a doctorate **4. SOMEBODY WITH A LICENTIATE DEGREE** somebody holding the degree of licentiate **5.** CHR **PRESBYTERIAN PREACHER** somebody licensed to preach but not perform the sacraments in a Presbyterian church, usually a trainee minister who has not yet been ordained [15thC. From medieval Latin *licentiatus*, past participle of *licentiare* "to permit," from Latin *licentia* (see LICENSE).]

li·cen·tious /lī sénshəss/ *adj.* pursuing desires aggressively and selfishly, unchecked by morality especially in sexual matters (*formal disapproving*) [15thC. From Latin *licentiosus*, from *licentia* (see LICENSE).] —**li·cen·tious·ly** *adv.* —**li·cen·tious·ness** *n.*

li·chee *n.* = **lychee**

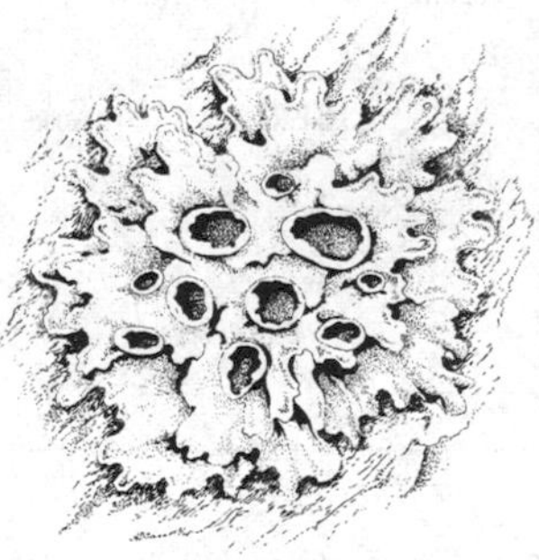

Lichen

li·chen /líkən/ (*plural* **-chen** *or* **-chens**) *n.* a gray, green, or yellow plant appearing in often flat patches on rocks and other surfaces that is a complex organism consisting of fungi and algae growing together in symbiosis [Early 17thC. Via Latin from Greek *leikhēn*.] —**li·chened** *adj.* —**li·chen·i·form** /lī kénni fàwrm, líkəni-/ *adj.* —**li·chen·oid** /líkə nòyd/ *adj.* —**li·chen·ous** *adj.*

li·chen·ol·o·gy /lìkə nólləjee/ *n.* the scientific study of lichens —**li·chen·ol·o·gist** *n.*

lich-gate *n.* = **lych-gate**

Lich·ten·stein /líktən stīn/, **Roy** (1923–97) U.S. painter, graphic artist, and sculptor. A major figure in pop art, he is noted for his paintings featuring enlarged comic-strip images.

Roy Lichtenstein

lic·it /líssit/ *adj.* allowed by law [15thC. From Latin *licitus*, past participle of *licere* "to be allowed."] —**lic·it·ly** *adv.* —**lic·it·ness** *n.*

WORD KEY: SYNONYMS

See Synonyms at *legal*.

lick /lik/ *v.* (**licked, lick·ing, licks**) **1.** *vt.* **PASS THE TONGUE OVER SOMETHING** to move the tongue across the surface of something, either to wet or clean it or as a way to move something into the mouth **2.** *vti.* **BRUSH AGAINST SOMETHING** to touch or lightly move against something **3.** *vt.* **BEAT SOMEBODY** to give somebody a physical beating (*informal*) **4.** *vt.* **DEFEAT A COMPETITOR** to defeat somebody easily or thoroughly (*informal*) ■ *n.* **1. MOVEMENT OF THE TONGUE OVER SOMETHING** a movement of the tongue across the surface of something **2. QUICKLY APPLIED COATING** a quick coat of something, especially paint ○ *a lick of paint* **3. BIT OF SOMETHING** a small amount of something (*informal*) **4. PUNCH** a punch or blow (*informal*) **5.** MUSIC **BRIEF IMPROVISATION** a distinctive few notes or short phrase in pop music or jazz, often improvised (*informal*) **6. NATURAL SALT LICKED BY ANIMALS** an exposed natural deposit of salt that animals lick **7.** VET **MEDICINAL BLOCK FOR ANIMALS** a block of salt or chemical material to be licked by domestic animals as medicine [Old English *liccian*, from a prehistoric Germanic word that is also the ancestor of English *lecher*] —**lick·er** *n.*

lick·er·ish /líkərish/, **liquorish** *adj.* (*archaic*) **1. GREEDY** taking an excessive or unfair amount, without concern for the needs of others **2. LECHEROUS** continually thinking about sex or trying to make sexual contact with others [15thC. An alteration of *lickerous*, from an Anglo-Norman variant of French *lecheros* "lecherous" (see LECHEROUS).]

lick·e·ty-split /líkəti splít/ *adv.* very quickly (*informal*) [*Lickety* is a playful lengthening of LICK]

lick·ing /líking/ *n.* (*informal*) **1. BEATING** a beating or spanking **2. DEFEAT** a severe defeat or setback

lick·spit·tle /lík spìtt'l/ *n.* somebody who fawns on social superiors or powerful people (*literary insult*)

lic·o·rice /líkərish/ (*plural* **-rice**) *n.* **1.** PLANTS **PLANT WITH A SWEET ROOT** a perennial plant growing near the Mediterranean that has spiked blue feathery leaves and a root with a sweet flavor. Latin name: *Glycyrrhiza glabra.* **2.** FOOD **KIND OF CANDY** a dense rubbery candy that is usually made in black or red strips or twisted ropes and flavored with the root of the licorice plant **3. ROOT OF THE LICORICE PLANT** the dried black root of the licorice plant or an extract made from it, used as a laxative and in confectionery and brewing [12thC. Via Anglo-Norman *lycorys* from, ultimately, Greek *glukurrhiza*, from *glukus* "sweet" + *rhiza* "root" (source of English *rhizome*).]

lic·tor /líktər/ *n.* one of a group of minor officials in ancient Rome whose duties included carrying the fasces as a symbol of authority and clearing the way for the chief magistrates [14thC. From Latin, of uncertain origin: perhaps formed from *ligare* "to bind."]

lid /lid/ *n.* **1. TOP FOR A CONTAINER** a cover of a container that can be removed or raised on a hinge to open the container **2.** = **eyelid 3. RESTRAINT** a restraint or control on something that keeps it within acceptable bounds (*informal*) ○ *He promised to put a lid on manufacturing costs.* **4.** BIOL = **operculum** *n.* 3 **5.** DRUGS **OUNCE OF MARIJUANA** a quantity of marijuana, usually an ounce (*slang*) [Old English *hlid*. Ultimately from an Indo-European word meaning "cover, something that bends over," which is also the ancestor of English *lean*, *client*, and *climax*.]

li·dar /lī daar/ *n.* a device, similar in operation to radar, that uses pulses of laser light to analyze atmospheric phenomena [Mid-20thC. Blend of LIGHT[1], DETECTION, and *ranging*.]

Li·di·ce /líddə chay, -see/ village in western Czechoslovakia, in what is now the Czech Republic. It was the scene of a retaliatory massacre of villagers by German forces during World War II.

lid·less /líddləss/ *adj.* having no eyelids

Li·do /leé dō/ island reef in northeastern Italy, separating the Venice Lagoon from the Adriatic Sea. It is a beach resort.

li·do·caine /lídə kàyn/ *n.* a synthetic local anesthetic drug that may be given by injection or applied to a surface. It can also be given intravenously to control heart irregularities. [Mid-20thC. Coined from ACETANILIDE + -CAINE.]

lie[1] /lī/ *vi.* (**lay** /lay/, **lain** /layn/, **ly·ing**, **lies**) **1.** RECLINE to stretch out on a surface that is slanted or horizontal, ○ *She was lying on the sofa.* **2.** BE PLACED FLAT ON A SURFACE to be positioned on and supported by a horizontal surface ○ *A book lay open on his bedside table.* **3.** BE LOCATED SOMEWHERE to be located in a particular place ○ *Mexico lies south of the United States.* **4.** BE BURIED to be buried in a particular place ○ *Here lies Martha, beloved daughter of John and Mary.* **5.** BE IN A PARTICULAR STATE to be or continue to be in a particular condition or state ○ *It lay hidden for years.* **6.** BE IN A PARTICULAR DIRECTION to extend or be in a particular direction ○ *The city lies beneath us, glittering with a thousand lights.* **7.** BE IN STORE to be still to come ○ *A great deal of hard work lies ahead of us.* **8.** STAY UNDISTURBED to remain undiscussed or undisturbed ○ *Let sleeping dogs lie.* **9.** LAW BE ACCEPTABLE IN LAW to be acceptable as an assertion or as evidence in court ■ *n.* **1.** ZOOL ANIMAL'S RESTING PLACE a place where an animal returns to rest or hide **2.** GOLF POSITION OF A GOLF BALL the position of a golf ball after it comes to rest on a golf course or putting green ○ *The ball has quite a good lie, in spite of being in the rough.* [Old English *licgan*. Ultimately from an Indo-European word that is also the ancestor of English *ledge, lager,* and *litter.*]

lie around *vti.* to sit around doing nothing in particular (*informal*)

lie back *vi.* to relax by stretching out flat on the back or reclining in a chair, especially one that tilts backward

lie down *vi.* **1.** LIE ON A SURFACE to stretch out flat **2.** REST IN BED to rest, especially in bed ○ *I need to lie down for an hour or two.* **3.** REMAIN PASSIVE to do nothing or make no response ○ *I'm not going to take this lying down.*

lie off *vti.* to stay close to the shore or to another ship

lie to *vi.* to remain motionless, facing the wind

lie with *v.* **1.** *vt.* BE THE RESPONSIBILITY OF SOMEBODY to be the responsibility of a particular person or persons **2.** *vi.* HAVE SEX WITH SOMEBODY to have sexual intercourse with somebody (*archaic*)

lie[2] /lī/ *vi.* (**lied**, **ly·ing**, **lies**) **1.** DELIBERATELY SAY SOMETHING UNTRUE to say something that is not true in a conscious effort to deceive somebody ○ *He lied about his age in order to get into the army.* **2.** BE DECEPTIVE to give a false impression ○ *Don't forget that appearances can lie.* ■ *n.* **1.** FALSEHOOD a false statement made deliberately ○ *She told me she wasn't seeing anyone else, but that was a lie.* **2.** WRONG IMPRESSION a false impression created deliberately ○ *I'm beginning to feel that my whole life is a lie.* [Old English *lēogan* "to lie" and *lyge* "a lie," both ultimately from a prehistoric Germanic word that is also the ancestor of English *warlock*]

WORD KEY: SYNONYMS

lie, untruth, falsehood, fabrication, fib, white lie

CORE MEANING: something that is not true

lie used to describe a written or spoken statement that is not true; **untruth** a more formal word meaning the same as "lie"; **falsehood** a formal or literary word meaning the same as "lie"; **fabrication** a statement, story, or account devised with intent to deceive; **fib** an informal word for a minor or trivial lie, often used by or about children; **white lie** a minor harmless lie, usually told to avoid hurting somebody's feelings.

Lieb·frau·milch /leeb frow milk/ *n.* a slightly sweet German white wine from the Rhine region [Mid-19thC. From German, from *lieb* "dear" + *Frau* "lady" (referring to the Virgin Mary, patroness of the convent where it was first produced) + *Milch* "milk."]

Liech·ten·stein /líkt'n stīn/ small independent principality in central Europe, lying between Switzerland, with which it has close ties, and Austria. Language: German. Currency: Swiss franc. Capital: Vaduz. Population: 31,389 (1997). Area: 62 sq. mi./160 sq. km. Official name **Principality of Liechtenstein**

lied /leed/ (*plural* **lie·der** /leédər/) *n.* a German folk or art song, especially an art song of the 19th century with a solo voice part and interwoven piano accompaniment of equal importance. Schubert, Brahms, and Schumann are major composers of lieder. (*usually used in the plural*) [Mid-19thC. From German, literally "song."]

lie de·tec·tor *n.* a device for finding out whether somebody is telling the truth during questioning. It

Liechtenstein

has sensors that measure changes in blood pressure and pulse, which are supposed to reflect the uneasiness caused by lying.

lief /leef, leev/ *adv.* WILLINGLY readily or without reluctance (*archaic*) ■ *adj.* (*archaic*) **1.** WILLING ready or desirous **2.** BELOVED dear or treasured [Old English *lēof*. Ultimately from a prehistoric Germanic word that is also the ancestor of English *leave*[2] and *love.*]

liege /leej, leezh/ *n.* **1.** FEUDAL LORD a lord or sovereign who deserves loyalty and service under feudal law **2.** VASSAL a vassal or subject who owes loyalty and service to a lord or sovereign under feudal law ■ *adj.* LOYAL faithful or loyal (*archaic*) [13thC. Via French *lige* from medieval Latin *leticus*, from *letus* "colonist with limited freedom," of uncertain origin: probably from a prehistoric Germanic word meaning "free."] —**liege·dom** *n.*

Li·ège /lee áyzh, ly ezh/ city and capital of Liège Province, eastern Belgium. Population: 190,525 (1996).

liege·man /leéjmən, leézh-, -màn/ (*plural* **-men** /-mən/) *n.* **1.** = **liege** *n.* 2 **2.** LOYAL FOLLOWER a faithful or loyal follower

lien /leen, leé ən/ *n.* the legal right to keep or sell somebody else's property as security for a debt [Mid-16thC. Via French from, ultimately, Latin *ligamen* "bond," from *ligare* "to bind."]

lie of the land *n. U.K.* = **lay of the land** (*informal*)

Lierne

li·erne /lee úrn/ *n.* a reinforcing rib in the vaulting of a Gothic cathedral or other roofed structure [Mid-19thC. From French, formed from *lier* "to bind," from Latin *ligare.*]

lieu /loo/ *n.* place or stead (*archaic*) [Mid-16thC. Via French from Latin *locus* "place" (source of English *locate*).] ◇ **in lieu** instead of something else already mentioned or that is usual in the current situation

Lieut. *abbr.* Lieutenant

lieu·ten·ant /loo ténnənt/ *n.* **1.** DEPUTY somebody who acts as an assistant to or in place of somebody else **2.** MIL ARMY OFFICER the rank below captain in the British, Australian, and Canadian armies and in the United States Army, Marine Corps and Air Force. ◊ **first lieutenant, second lieutenant 3.** NAVY NAVY OFFICER the rank below lieutenant commander in the United States, British, Australian, and Canadian navies **4.** EMERGENCIES POLICE OFFICER OR FIREFIGHTER an officer in a United States or Canadian police department or a United States fire department ranking below a captain [14thC. From French, literally "somebody who holds a place," from *lieu* (see LIEU) + *tenant* (see TENANT).] —**lieu·ten·an·cy** *n.*

lieu·ten·ant colo·nel *n.* an officer in the United States Army, Air Force, or Marine Corps and in the British Army ranking above a major and below a colonel

lieu·ten·ant com·man·der *n.* an officer in the U.S. Navy or Coast Guard and in the British Navy ranking above a lieutenant and below a commander

lieu·ten·ant gen·er·al *n.* an officer in the U.S. Army, Air Force, or Marine Corps and in the British Army ranking above a major general and below a general

lieu·ten·ant gov·er·nor *n.* **1.** STATE OFFICIAL an elected official in a state government ranking just below the governor **2.** CANADIAN PROVINCIAL OFFICAL an official appointed by the federal Canadian government who acts for the Crown as the representative of the British monarch in a province —**lieu·ten·ant gov·er·nor·ship** *n.*

lieu·ten·ant jun·ior grade (*plural* **lieu·ten·ants jun·ior grade**) *n.* an officer in the U.S. Navy or Coast Guard ranking above an ensign and below a lieutenant

life /līf/ (*plural* **lives** /līvz/) *n.* **1.** EXISTENCE IN THE PHYSICAL WORLD the quality that makes living animals and plants different from dead organisms and inorganic matter. Its functions include the ability to take in food, adapt to the environment, grow, and reproduce. **2.** LIVING INDIVIDUAL a living being, especially a person, often used when referring to the number of people killed in an accident or a war (*usually used in the plural*) ○ *Two hundred lives were lost in the crash.* **3.** LIVING THINGS CONSIDERED TOGETHER a group of living things, usually of a particular kind ○ *She was an expert on plant life in the Amazon.* **4.** WHOLE TIME SOMEBODY IS ALIVE the entire period during which somebody is, has been, or will yet be alive ○ *All my life I've wanted to learn to fly.* **5.** TIME WHEN SOMETHING FUNCTIONS the period during which something continues to function ○ *Cheap batteries usually have short lives.* **6.** SOME PART OF SOMEBODY'S LIFE a particular aspect of somebody's life ○ *social life* **7.** HUMAN ACTIVITY human existence or activity in general ○ *real life* **8.** LIFE IMPRISONMENT life imprisonment (*informal*) **9.** WAY IN WHICH SOMEBODY LIVES the character or conditions of an individual's existence ○ *Most people in this city lead hard lives.* **10.** CHARACTERISTIC WAY OF LIVING a way of living that is characteristic of a particular place or group ○ *country life* **11.** BIOGRAPHY an account of a somebody's life, usually in writing, but sometimes in other media such as film, video, or radio ○ *He was the author of the "Life of Galileo."* **12.** VITALITY animation and vitality, or something that produces animation or vitality ○ *We liked him because he was so full of life.* **13.** ARTIST'S SUBJECT something real used as a subject by an artist, especially human models, who are often nude ○ *She always insisted on painting from life.* [Old English *lif*, from a prehistoric Germanic word that is also the ancestor of English *live, delay,* and *liver*] ◇ **get a life** to do something to improve your situation or change your lifestyle for the better (*slang*)

WORD KEY: CULTURAL NOTE

The Life of Samuel Johnson, a biography by Scottish writer James Boswell (1791). Generally considered the finest biography in the English language, it is a rounded, revealing, and respectful portrait of one of the great scholars of the day. But its greatness also derives from its vivid descriptions of contemporary society and the candid revelations of its author.

life-and-death *adj.* extremely important or serious, especially when somebody's life is at stake ○ *a life-and-death struggle*

life as·sur·ance *n. U.K.* = **life insurance**

life belt *n.* a belt made of material that floats, worn by people taking part in water sports such as sailing to keep them from sinking or drowning

life·blood /līf blŭd/ *n.* **1.** BLOOD NECESSARY FOR LIFE blood when considered as necessary in maintaining life (*literary*) **2.** SOMETHING VITAL TO A WHOLE something that is vitally important to the welfare of a larger entity ○ *Donations are the lifeblood of this organization.*

life·boat /līf bōt/ *n.* **1.** BOAT USED IN EMERGENCIES any of a number of small boats kept on the deck or railings of a larger ship, for use if the ship has to be abandoned **2.** RESCUE BOAT a boat used for rescuing people from ships in trouble at sea

life buoy *n.* a ring-shaped float used in an emergency to keep somebody's head and shoulders above water until help arrives

life cri·sis *n.* a major disruptive event that happens in somebody's lifetime, e.g., bereavement or divorce

life cy·cle *n.* **1.** STAGES OF DEVELOPMENT OF A LIVING ORGANISM the series of changes of form and activity that a living organism undergoes from its beginning through its development to sexual maturity ○ *the life cycle of the snail* **2.** ALL STAGES OF DEVELOPMENT the complete process of change and development during somebody's lifetime or the useful life of something such as an organization, institution, or manufactured product

life ex·pec·tan·cy *n.* the number of years that somebody can be expected to live, according to statistics ○ *The rise in life expectancy can be traced to advances in nutrition and medical care.*

life force *n.* = **élan vital**

life form *n.* **1.** BIOL ADULT SPECIMEN the characteristic form of an organism at maturity **2.** SOMETHING ALIVE any living organism ○ *They scanned the surface of the planet for life forms.*

life·guard /lɪ̄f gaàrd/ *n.* somebody trained in rescue techniques whose job is to watch over swimmers at a beach or swimming pool and save those in danger of drowning

life his·to·ry *n.* **1.** BIOL ENTIRE STAGES OF LIFE all the changes experienced by a living organism, from its conception to its death **2.** SOMEBODY'S LIFE STORY the story of somebody's life **3.** SOCIOL SOMEBODY'S LIFE STORY USED FOR RESEARCH an account of the life of an individual derived from oral or documentary evidence and used in social research. It may shed light on issues of social concern or add to the sum of knowledge about society and social institutions.

life im·pris·on·ment *n.* a punishment in which somebody convicted of a crime must remain in prison for the rest of his or her life. It may be shortened for good behavior, but it normally remains a very lengthy period.

life in·sur·ance *n.* a plan under which regular payments are made to a company during somebody's lifetime, and in return the company pays a specified sum to the person's beneficiaries after the person's death

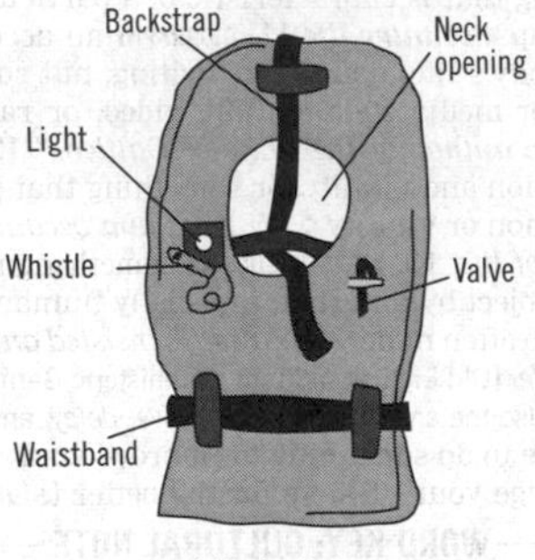

Life jacket

life jack·et *n.* a sleeveless jacket made of light material or filled with air, used to keep somebody afloat in water. Also called **life vest**

life·less /lɪ̄fləss/ *adj.* **1.** DEAD dead, or seeming to be dead **2.** WITHOUT LIFE not capable of supporting life **3.** DULL lacking excitement or animation —**life·less·ly** *adv.* —**life·less·ness** *n.*

WORD KEY: SYNONYMS

See Synonyms at ***dead***.

life·like /lɪ̄f lɪ̄k/ *adj.* looking alive, or representing real life accurately

life·line /lɪ̄f lɪ̄n/ *n.* **1.** SHIPPING SAFETY CABLE a rope or cable used for safety in dangerous maneuvers, especially at sea, e.g., attached to a diver's helmet or stretched along the deck of a boat **2.** VITAL LINK a means of communication or support that is extremely important to the survival of an isolated person or group

life list *n.* a bird-watcher's record of all the species of birds sighted in a lifetime

life·long /lɪ̄f làwng/ *adj.* lasting the whole of a lifetime

life mask *n.* a cast made of a living person's face, using plaster or another soft substance that hardens when it dries

life peer *n.* somebody who is given a title and place in the British House of Lords that cannot be passed on to descendants —**life peer·age** *n.*

life pre·serv·er *n.* **1.** OBJECT MADE OF BUOYANT MATERIAL a ring, belt, or jacket made of material that floats in water, designed to prevent drowning by keeping the wearer's head and shoulders above water **2.** *U.K.* WEAPON USED FOR HITTING SOMEBODY a hand weapon consisting of metal stitched into one end of a length of thick flexible leather, used to hit or batter somebody

lif·er /lɪ̄fər/ *n.* (*informal*) **1.** SOMEBODY SERVING A LIFE SENTENCE somebody sentenced to life imprisonment **2.** MIL CAREER MEMBER OF THE MILITARY somebody who spends an entire career in one of the armed forces

life raft *n.* a raft usually made of inflatable plastic designed for use during an emergency at sea

life·sav·er /lɪ̄f sàyvər/ *n.* somebody who or something that provides help at a time of great need (*informal*)

life·sav·ing /lɪ̄f sàyving/ *adj.* RESCUING OR REVIVING used to rescue people or keep them alive ■ *n.* SWIMMING RESCUING OF PEOPLE techniques or efforts to rescue people from danger, especially from drowning

life sci·ence *n.* a principal branch of science concerned with plants, animals, and other living organisms and including biology, botany, and zoology (*often used in the plural*)

life sen·tence *n.* a court verdict that condemns a convicted felon to life in prison for the rest of his or her life. It may be shortened for good behavior, but it normally remains a very lengthy sentence.

life-size *adj.* being the size of the original in life

life span *n.* **1.** EXPECTED LENGTH OF LIFE the length of time that a member of a particular species can be expected to remain alive **2.** LENGTH OF TIME SOMETHING LASTS the length of time that something can be expected to last or function

life span psy·chol·o·gy *n.* a field of psychology that studies human development from birth through death

life·style /lɪ̄f stɪ̄l/ *n.* the way of life that is typical of a person, group, or culture

life-sup·port *adj.* designed to keep somebody alive in an environment such as space that does not support life or to maintain breathing, heartbeat, and other vital functions in somebody who is seriously ill

life-sup·port sys·tem *n.* **1.** TECHNICAL EQUIPMENT PROVIDING NORMAL LIVING CONDITIONS a piece of technical equipment that is designed to provide normal living conditions when these are not available, especially in space **2.** TECHNICAL EQUIPMENT TAKING OVER BODY FUNCTION a piece of technical equipment that temporarily performs a vital body function, e.g., respiration, when somebody's own organ cannot because of injury or disease

life's work *n.* = **lifework**

life ta·ble *n.* = **mortality table**

life-threat·en·ing *adj.* very dangerous or serious with the possibility of death as an outcome

life·time /lɪ̄f tɪ̄m/ *n.* **1.** TIME REMAINING ALIVE the length of time that somebody or something remains alive **2.** TIME THAT SOMETHING REMAINS USEFUL the length of time that something remains useful or in working order **3.** LONG TIME an extremely long time (*informal*)

life vest *n.* = **life jacket**

life·work /lɪ̄f wùrk/ *n.* something that is the product, result, or culmination of somebody's working life

life zone *n.* an area with a characteristic or identifiable set of animal or plant life forms

LIFO /lɪ̄fō/ *abbr.* last in, first out

lift[1] /lift/ *v.* (**lift·ed, lift·ing, lifts**) **1.** *vt.* RAISE SOMETHING to carry or raise something from one position to another, higher position **2.** *vi.* MOVE HIGHER to move to a higher level **3.** *vt.* MOVE SOMETHING UPWARD to direct something upward ○ *lifting her eyes from the book* **4.** *vi.* GO UPWARD to move, especially mechanically, in an upward direction ○ *Just press the button, and the car trunk will lift automatically.* **5.** *vt.* TAKE SOMETHING FROM A PLACE to grasp something and move it somewhere else ○ *She lifted the CD from the rack.* **6.** *vt.* CARRY IN AN AIRCRAFT to transport somebody or something in an aircraft ○ *The rescue helicopter lifted the stranded climbers to safety.* **7.** *vt.* MAKE SOMETHING INVALID to revoke something or make something no longer apply ○ *The government has decided to lift the trade restrictions.* **8.** *vt.* SURG REMOVE WRINKLES SURGICALLY to perform cosmetic surgery on a face to tighten the skin and so reduce wrinkling, or on a woman's breasts to reduce or eliminate sagging **9.** *vti.* CHEER SOMEBODY OR BECOME CHEERED to make somebody happier or more cheerful, or become happier or more cheerful ○ *His low spirits lifted after a few songs.* **10.** *vi.* DIMINISH to clear, disappear, or become less severe ○ *I think we should wait until this fog lifts.* **11.** *vt.* STEAL SOMETHING to steal something or take something away without the owner's permission or knowledge (*informal*) ○ *A pickpocket lifted my wallet.* **12.** *vt.* PLAGIARIZE SOMEBODY'S WORK to take and use somebody else's work without attributing it to its creator (*informal*) ○ *She was accused of lifting her first two paragraphs from a report on someone's Web pages.* **13.** *vt.* SPORTS HIT BALL HIGH INTO THE AIR to hit a baseball or golf ball high into the air **14.** *vt.* MAKE SOMETHING BE HEARD to make something be heard, or make something be heard more easily or clearly ○ *The choir lifted their voices in song.* **15.** *vt.* IMPROVE SOMETHING to raise the level of a performance, or enhance a skill ○ *She managed to lift her grades last semester.* **16.** *vt.* FIN PAY BACK MONEY to pay something back, especially a debt, mortgage, or another obligation **17.** *vt.* RAISE SOMEBODY OR SOMETHING'S STATUS to have the effect of raising somebody or something in terms of status, respect, or public or official estimation ○ *Her latest novel has lifted her into the league of best-selling authors.* **18.** *vt.* MIL STOP A MILITARY ASSAULT to cease the firing of artillery or naval guns during a combat operation or assault so as to allow ground personnel to move forward **19.** *vt.* AGRIC, GARDENING HARVEST to dig up a plant for its edible underground tubers ○ *lift potatoes* **20.** *vt.* AGRIC, GARDENING DIG UP A PLANT FOR TRANSPLANTING to dig up a plant in order to transplant it ■ *n.* **1.** RISE IN SPIRITS a rise in spirits, mood, or emotions that can often be attributed to a specific cause ○ *audiences turning to feel-good movies to give themselves a lift* **2.** RIDE IN A VEHICLE a free ride as a passenger in somebody else's motor vehicle (*informal*) ○ *Do you want a lift to the airport?* **3.** CLOTHES SOMETHING ADDED TO A SHOE a layer of something that is put inside a shoe or added to the heel of a shoe to make the wearer appear taller (*dated*) **4.** AEROSP UPWARD FORCE ACTING ON AN AIRCRAFT the combination of forces that act to cause an aircraft to leave the ground and stay in the air **5.** ICE SKATING, DANCE RAISING A PARTNER IN THE AIR an act of raising a partner in pairs skating or ice dancing into the air as part of a choreographed sequence **6.** RAISING OF SOMEBODY OR SOMETHING a placing of somebody or something in a higher position **7.** DEGREE OF RISE the degree or distance by which something rises ○ *a moderate lift in temperature* **8.** FORCE NEEDED TO RAISE SOMETHING the power or force available, necessary, or used for raising something **9.** WEIGHT RAISED a weight or an amount of something that is or can be raised **10.** *U.K.* = **elevator.** ◊ **chair lift, ski lift** **11.** AEROSP FORCE MAKING A HOT-AIR BALLOON RISE the force, usually provided by heated air, that makes a hot-air balloon or airship rise into the sky **12.** CLOTHES = **heeltap** *n.* **2** **13.** MECH ENG MECHANICAL RAISING DEVICE a typically hydraulic-powered device that is designed to raise heavy objects such as motor vehicles off the ground **14.** MINING AMOUNT OF EXTRACTED ORE the amount of ore extracted from a seam **15.** MINING WATER PUMPS USED IN MINING a set of pumps used to pump water out of a mineshaft to the surface [12thC. From Old Norse *lypta*, from a prehistoric Germanic word that is also the ancestor of English *loft*.] —**lift·a·ble** *adj.* —**lift·er** *n.*

WORD KEY: SYNONYMS

See Synonyms at ***raise***.

lift off *vi.* to leave a launch pad and head upward into the atmosphere (*refers to spacecraft*)

lift[2] /lift/ *n.* a surgical operation to alter a part of the body for cosmetic effect (*informal*) ○ *Who did your lift?* [Shortening of FACE LIFT]

lift·gate /lift gàyt/ *n.* a rear panel that opens upward, especially a station wagon's rear door

lift·off /lift àwf/ *n.* **1.** MOMENT WHEN A ROCKET LEAVES A LAUNCH PAD the time when a rocket or spacecraft leaves the launch pad **2.** INITIAL THRUST SENDING A ROCKET FROM THE GROUND the initial thrust that sends a rocket or spacecraft upward from the launch pad into the atmosphere

lig·a·ment /líggəmənt/ *n.* **1.** TOUGH TISSUE CONNECTING BODY PARTS a sheet or band of tough fibrous tissue that connects bones or cartilage at a joint or supports an organ, muscle, or other body part **2.** CONNECTOR something that forms a connection or bond [14thC.

From Latin *ligamentum*, from *ligare* "to bind."] —**lig·a·ment·al** /lìggə mént'l/ *adj.* —**lig·a·men·ta·ry** /-méntəree/ *adj.* —**lig·a·men·tous** /-méntəss/ *adj.*

WORD KEY: ORIGIN

The Latin word *ligare*, from which ***ligament*** is derived, is also the source of English *ally, liable, liaison, lien, oblige, religion*, and *rely*.

li·gan *n.* NAUT = **lagan**

li·gand /lígənd, líggənd/ *n.* an atom, molecule, group, or ion that is bound to a central atom of a molecule forming a complex [Mid-20thC. From Latin *ligandus*, from *ligare* "to bind."]

li·gase /lī gàyss, -gàyz/ *n.* an enzyme that joins two molecules, especially in living organisms [Mid-20thC. From Latin *ligare* "to bind" (see LIGAMENT).]

li·gate /lī gàyt/ (**-gat·ed, -gat·ing, -gates**) *vt.* to bind something or tie something up (*formal or technical*) [Late 16thC. From Latin *ligare* "to bind" (see LIGAMENT).] —**lig·a·tive** /líggətiv/ *adj.*

li·ga·tion /lī gáysh'n/ *n.* **1.** SURG **SURGICAL TYING** the tying of something with a surgical ligature **2. SOMETHING USED FOR TYING** something that is used for binding things or tying things up (*formal*)

lig·a·ture /líggəchər, líggə choor/ *n.* **1. SOMETHING USED FOR TYING** something that is used for binding things or tying things up **2. TYING PROCESS** the process of binding something or tying something up **3. BOND** a unifying link or bond (*formal*) **4.** SURG **SURGICAL THREAD FOR TYING OFF A DUCT** a piece of surgical thread used to tie off a duct or blood vessel in order to cut off the supply of body fluid normally running through it **5.** PRINTING, LING **CHARACTER CONSISTING OF JOINED LETTERS** a character or piece of type, e.g., æ, that consists of two or more letters joined together **6.** MUSIC = **tie** *n.* **8** **7.** MUSIC **SYMBOL IN MEDIEVAL MUSIC** a symbol indicating a group of notes to be sung to one syllable in the notation of medieval music **8.** MUSIC **REED-HOLDER ON WOODWIND INSTRUMENT** on a woodwind instrument, a band, usually made of metal, that holds the reed to the mouthpiece [14thC. Via Old French from, ultimately, Latin *ligare* "to bind" (see LIGAMENT).]

li·ger /lígər/ *n.* the offspring that results from breeding a male lion with a female tiger. ◊ **tigon** [Mid-20thC. Blend of LION and TIGER.]

light[1] /līt/ *n.* **1. ENERGY PRODUCING BRIGHTNESS** the energy producing a sensation of brightness that makes seeing possible **2. QUALITY OF LIGHT** a particular kind or quality of brightness ○ *We won't get good photographs in this fading light.* **3. ARTIFICIAL SOURCE OF LIGHT** an artificial source of illumination, e.g., an electric lamp or a candle ○ *turn the light on* **4.** PHYS **VISIBLE ELECTROMAGNETIC RADIATION** electromagnetic radiation in the range visible to the human eye, between approximately 4,000 and 7,700 angstroms **5.** PHYS **ELECTROMAGNETIC RADIATION** electromagnetic radiation that has wavelengths of any length **6. PATH THAT LIGHT TAKES** the path that light takes, or somebody's share or access to light ○ *asked her to move out of my light* **7. DAYLIGHT** the condition of brightness created by the rays of the sun during the day ○ *keep filming while there's still some light left* **8. DAWN** the arrival of the sun's brightness at the beginning of the day ○ *get up before light to go running* **9.** ARTS **REPRESENTATION OF LIGHT IN ART** the representation of light or the effect it has in a work of art **10. TRAFFIC SIGNAL** a signal that controls the movement of traffic ○ *Turn right at the first set of lights.* **11. GENERAL NOTICE** general or public notice, attention, or knowledge ○ *facts that only recently came to light* **12. WAY SOMETHING IS VIEWED** the manner in which somebody or something is regarded, especially by the public ○ *Those actions have shown the commission in an exceptionally bad light.* **13. SOMETHING THAT IGNITES SOMETHING** a source of fire, especially a match **14. GLEAM IN SOMEBODY'S EYE** a glint in somebody's eye that is taken to indicate a particular mood or expression ○ *had a mischievous light in her eye* **15. ENTRY IN A CROSSWORD GRID** an entry in the grid of a cryptic crossword **16. EYESIGHT** somebody's general ability to see (*archaic*) **17.** BUILDING **WINDOW** a window or other opening in a building, designed to let sunlight in. ◊ **ancient lights** ■ *adj.* **1. FULL OF BRIGHTNESS** full of illumination, or relatively well lit ○ *a light airy room* **2. PALE** of a relatively pale shade ○ *decorated in light green* **3. WITH MILK** served with milk or cream added ○ *Do you want your coffee light or black?* ■ *v.* (**lit** /lit/ *or* **light·ed, lit** *or* **light·ed, light·ing, lights**) **1.** *vti.* **START BURNING** to begin to burn, or cause something to begin to burn ○ *still trying to light the grill?* **2.** *vt.* **ILLUMINATE** to illuminate, brighten, or shine on something ○ *Hundreds of stars lit the night sky.* **3.** *vt.* **GIVE SOMETHING AN ANIMATED LOOK** to give somebody's eyes or face a happy or animated look ○ *A playful smile lit his face.* **4.** *vt.* **LEAD SOMEBODY WITH A LIGHT** to lead or direct somebody with a source of illumination such as a flashlight ○ *The usher lit the way to our seats.* ○ *I'll light you down the path to the road.* [Old English *lēoht.* Ultimately from an Indo-European word that is also the ancestor of English *lucid* and *illuminate.*] ◇ **bring something to light** to reveal something ◇ **come to light** to be revealed ◇ **go out like a light** to fall asleep very quickly and deeply (*informal*) ◇ **in the light of, in light of** taking into consideration what is known, or what has just been said or found out ◇ **the light of day** the early hours of daylight, especially at dawn ◇ **the light of somebody's life** the person somebody cherishes the most ◇ **punch** *or* **put somebody's lights out** to give somebody a severe beating ◇ **see the light 1.** to have a sudden understanding or appreciation of something **2.** to be converted to a faith, belief, or point of view ◇ **see the light of day** to be published or made publicly known ◇ **shed** *or* **throw** *or* **cast light on something** make it possible or easier to understand something

light into *vt.* to attack somebody or something either verbally or physically (*informal*)

light out *vi.* to leave a place in a hurry (*informal*)

light up *v.* **1.** *vti.* **LIGHT A CIGARETTE OR PIPE** to light something such as a cigarette, cigar, or pipe and begin smoking it **2.** *vt.* **ILLUMINATE SOMETHING** to cast light on somebody or something **3.** *vti.* **MAKE OR BECOME CHEERFUL** to become, or cause something or somebody to become, animated or cheerful **4.** *vi.* **BEGIN SHINING** to start to shine

light[2] /līt/ *adj.* **1. NOT HEAVY** weighing comparatively little **2. LIGHTWEIGHT** made of thin fabric ○ *light summer apparel* **3. LESS SEVERE THAN POSSIBLE** considered less severe or harsh than might have been the case ○ *a light sentence* **4. NOT FORCEFUL** performed with little physical force ○ *She felt a light tap on her shoulder.* **5. EASY TO DO** involving relatively little effort or exertion ○ *a little light weeding* **6. EASILY DIGESTED** easily digested or not very filling ○ *a light snack* **7. light, lite** FOOD **LOW IN CALORIES** low in calories, especially containing less than the usual amount of sugar or fat **8. CONSUMING LITTLE OF SOMETHING** consuming something in small quantities only ○ *a light eater* **9. NOT DENSE** low in density or intensity ○ *only a light shower* **10. EASILY AWAKENED** easily awakened or disturbed when asleep ○ *a light sleeper* **11. NOT INTELLECTUALLY DEMANDING** not meant for serious study or contemplation ○ *some light vacation reading* **12. light, lite** BEVERAGES **LOW IN ALCOHOL** having a very low alcohol content **13. UNIMPORTANT** of relatively little importance or seriousness ○ *a light, throwaway remark* **14. WEIGHING TOO LITTLE** weighing less than is correct or less than would be expected ○ *This sack is a couple of ounces light.* **15. NIMBLE** moving with grace, nimbleness, and agility ○ *She's very light on her feet.* **16.** FOOD **FLUFFY AND WELL RISEN** of a light, flaky, fluffy, and well-risen consistency ○ *a very light pastry* **17. SHORT OF SOMETHING** lacking the usual or expected quantity of something ○ *a nice guy, if a little light on brains* **18. UNWORRIED** not burdened by worries or troubled ○ *a light heart* **19. DIZZY** slightly dizzy or not quite thinking clearly, e.g., because of fatigue, alcohol or drugs ○ *a light head* **20. MANUFACTURING SMALL PRODUCTS** involved in the manufacture of comparatively small products, especially consumer goods made without the use of heavy machinery **21.** WINE **DELICATELY FLAVORED** having a fresh delicate flavor ○ *a light rosé* **22. CARRYING SMALL WEIGHTS** designed to carry something that is relatively low in weight or relatively small in bulk ○ *a light delivery van* **23.** ARMY **NOT HEAVILY ARMED** carrying only hand-held weapons ○ *a light infantry brigade* **24. NOT LOADED** not containing or carrying a full load **25.** AGRIC, GARDENING **EASILY WORKED** loose, well aerated, and therefore easily worked ○ *light soil* **26.** CHEM **WITH A LOW BOILING POINT** having a relatively low boiling point **27.** PHON **UNSTRESSED** used to describe a syllable that is not stressed or accented **28.** BRIDGE **OF LOW VALUE** used to describe a bid in bridge that is made on a fewer than normal number of points **29.** BRIDGE **WITH TOO FEW TRICKS** used to describe a bridge player who has taken too few tricks to make a contract **30. IMMORAL** with low moral standards, especially relating to sexual behavior (*archaic*) ■ *adv.* **1. WITH LITTLE LUGGAGE** with only a small amount of luggage ○ *to travel light* **2. LENIENTLY** in a casual or lenient way ○ *Go light on him – he didn't mean to break the window.* ■ *vi.* (**light·ed** *or* **lit** /lit/, **light·ed** *or* **lit, light·ing, lights**) **1. COME TO REST** to come to rest on a branch after flight (*refers to birds*) **2. GET DOWN FROM A VEHICLE** to get down from a horse, vehicle, or other form of transportation (*dated*) [Old English *lēocht.* Ultimately from an Indo-European word that is also the ancestor of English *levity* and *lung.*] ◇ **make light of something** to treat something as unimportant

Light *n.* **1.** JUD-CHR **GOD** God as a source of spiritual illumination and strength **2.** CHR = **Inner Light**

light ad·ap·ta·tion, light ad·ap·tion *n.* the rapid changes that occur in the eye to permit vision when moving from darkness to light. The pupil constricts and the retina is bleached of visual pigment, making it less sensitive to light. —**light-a·dapt·ed** *adj.*

light air *n.* a wind of between 1 and 3 miles/1.6 and 4.8 km per hour, classified as force one on the Beaufort scale

light air·craft *n.* = **light plane**

light bread *n. Southern U.S.* white bread

WORD KEY: REGIONAL NOTE

The term ***light bread*** is used in the southern United States from the Atlantic coast to Texas, with scattered incidence in the Rocky Mountain and Pacific states.

light breeze *n.* a wind of between 4 and 7 mi./6.4 and 11 km per hour, classified as force two on the Beaufort scale

light bulb *n.* a source of artificial light in the form of a near-spherical glass case containing a filament that emits light when an electric current is passed through it. The filament is usually made of tungsten and is surrounded by argon or neon.

light chain *n.* the shorter of the two main polypeptides that make up an antibody molecule. ◊ **heavy chain**

light-e·mit·ting di·ode *n.* full form of **LED**

light·en[1] /līt'n/ (**-ened, -en·ing, -ens**) *vti.* **1. MAKE OR BECOME LESS HEAVY** to become less heavy, or make something less heavy **2. BECOME OR MAKE SOMETHING LESS BURDENSOME** to become, or cause something to become, less of a burden or chore **3. BECOME OR MAKE SOMETHING MORE CHEERFUL** to become or make somebody or something become more relaxed or lively ○ *The mood of the gathering lightened a little.*

lighten up *vi.* to become less gloomy, serious, or angry (*informal*)

light·en[2] /līt'n/ (**-ened, -en·ing, -ens**) *v.* **1.** *vti.* **MAKE OR BECOME PALE** to become, or cause something to become, pale or paler in color **2.** *vi.* **GLOW** to give off shining or glowing illumination **3.** *vi.* **FLASH** to flash across the sky (*refers to lightning*) **4.** *vt.* **ENLIGHTEN** to enlighten (*archaic*)

light·en·ing /līt'ning/ *n.* the process or time during late pregnancy when the fetal head begins to descend into the mother's pelvis resulting in a lessening of pressure on the diaphragm

light·er[1] /lītər/ *n.* **1. SMALL DEVICE FOR LIGHTING CIGARETTES** a small typically gas-filled container with a flint or other spark-producer that produces a flame used for lighting something that is smoked such as a cigarette, cigar, or pipe **2. SOMEBODY OR SOMETHING THAT LIGHTS SOMETHING** a person or device that lights, illuminates, or ignites something (*usually used in combination*) ○ *a firelighter*

light·er[2] /lītər/ *n.* **FLAT-BOTTOMED CARGO BOAT** a flat-bottomed open cargo boat or barge, used especially for taking goods to or from a larger vessel when it is being loaded or unloaded ■ *vt.* (**-ered, -er·ing, -ers**) **TRANSPORT BY LIGHTER** to transport cargo using a lighter [14thC. Origin uncertain: possibly formed from LIGHT[2], or possibly from Dutch *lichter*, which was formed from *lichten* "to lighten, unload."]

light·er-than-air *adj.* **WEIGHING LESS THAN AIR** used to describe aircraft such as hot-air balloons and dirigibles that weigh less than the air they displace ■ *n.* **AIRCRAFT WEIGHING LESS THAN AIR** an aircraft, e.g., a hot-air balloon or a dirigible, that weighs less than the air it displaces

light·face /līt fàyss/ *adj.* **light·face, light-faced NOT BOLD** having characters formed from relatively narrow lines (*refers to printed type*) ■ *n.* **LIGHTFACE TYPE** printed type that is lightface

light·fast /līt fàst/ *adj.* used to describe a dye or dyed fabric whose shade or color is unchanged by exposure to light, especially sunlight [Early 20thC. Modeled on COLORFAST.] —**light·fast·ness** *n.*

light-fin·gered *adj.* **1.** LIKELY TO STEAL THINGS skilled at and likely to try shoplifting, pickpocketing, or petty stealing **2.** NIMBLE WITH THE FINGERS able to move the fingers quickly and nimbly, and therefore good at doing intricate jobs —**light-fin·gered·ness** *n.*

light fly·weight *n.* **1.** WEIGHT CATEGORY IN AMATEUR BOXING a weight category in amateur boxing for competitors whose weight does not exceed 106 lbs./48 kg **2.** LIGHT FLYWEIGHT BOXER an amateur boxer who competes at light flyweight level

Light·foot /lĭt fo͝ot/, **Gordon** (*b.* 1938) Canadian-born U.S. folk-pop singer and writer. His songs include "If You Could Read My Mind"(1971).

light-foot·ed, **light·foot** *adj.* able to walk or run with light agile easy-flowing steps —**light-foot·ed·ly** *adv.* —**light-foot·ed·ness** *n.*

light-hand·ed *adj.* having a steady, delicate touch —**light-hand·ed·ly** *adv.* —**light-hand·ed·ness** *n.*

light·head·ed /lĭt héddəd/ *adj.* **1.** DIZZY OR EUPHORIC slightly dizzy or euphoric, e.g. as an effect of caffeine, alcohol, or fatigue **2.** SILLY having a tendency to behave in a frivolous or immature way —**light·head·ed·ly** *adv.* —**light·head·ed·ness** *n.*

light·heart·ed /lĭt haártəd/ *adj.* **1.** HAPPY AND RELAXED not weighed down with worries or troubles **2.** ENJOYABLE entertaining in an amusing carefree way —**light·heart·ed·ly** *adv.* —**light·heart·ed·ness** *n.*

light heav·y·weight *n.* **1.** BOXING WEIGHT CATEGORY IN PROFESSIONAL BOXING a weight category in professional boxing for competitors who weigh between 160 and 175 lbs./72.5 and 79.5 kg **2.** BOXING WEIGHT CATEGORY IN AMATEUR BOXING a weight category in amateur boxing for competitors who weigh between 165 and 179 lbs./75 and 81 kg **3.** WRESTLING WEIGHT CATEGORY IN WRESTLING a weight category in wrestling for competitors who weigh between 192 and 214 lbs./87 and 97 kg. ◊ **heavyweight, middleweight 4.** BOXING BOXER COMPETING AT LIGHT HEAVYWEIGHT a professional or amateur boxer who competes at light heavyweight level **5.** WRESTLING WRESTLER COMPETING AT LIGHT HEAVYWEIGHT a wrestler who competes at light heavyweight level. ◊ **heavyweight, middleweight**

Lighthouse

light·house /lĭt hòws/ (*plural* **-houses** /-hòwzəz/) *n.* a strategically placed coastal building, often a tall round tower, with a powerful flashing light, designed to guide sailors or warn them of dangers such as rocks

WORD KEY: CULTURAL NOTE

To the Lighthouse, a novel by English writer Virginia Woolf (1927). Typical of Woolf's more experimental novels in its unusual structure and use of stream-of-consciousness narrative, it is set at the vacation home of the Ramsay family on a Scottish island. Through the relationship between Mrs. Ramsay and a young painter, Lily Briscoe, Woolf explores the changing roles and attitudes of contemporary women.

light-in·de·pend·ent re·ac·tion *n.* BOT = **dark reaction**

light·ing /lĭting/ *n.* **1.** TYPE OF LIGHT light of a particular quality or type, or the equipment that produces it ○ *subdued lighting* ○ *lighting fixtures* **2.** EQUIPMENT FOR PROVIDING ARTIFICIAL LIGHT the equipment used for providing artificial light and light effects on a theater stage or a television or movie set **3.** EFFECT PRODUCED BY LIGHTS the overall effect produced by the lights used on a theater stage or a television or movie set **4.** QUALITY OF LIGHT IN ARTWORK the amount or type of light in a photograph, painting, or other artwork

light·ly /lĭtlee/ *adv.* **1.** WITH LITTLE FORCE without exerting much pressure, force, or weight **2.** WITH LEVITY without seriousness **3.** SPARINGLY in small or sparing amounts **4.** GRACEFULLY in an easy graceful way

light me·ter *n.* PHOTOGRAPHY = **exposure meter**

light mid·dle·weight *n.* ◊ **junior middleweight 1.** WEIGHT CATEGORY IN AMATEUR BOXING a weight category in amateur boxing for competitors who weigh between 148 and 157 lbs./67 and 71 kg **2.** AMATEUR BOXER COMPETING AT LIGHT MIDDLEWEIGHT an amateur boxer who competes at light middleweight level

light-mind·ed *adj.* not capable of thinking seriously, or not likely to think about serious issues —**light-mind·ed·ly** *adv.* —**light-mind·ed·ness** *n.*

light·ness[1] /lĭtnəss/ *n.* **1.** ILLUMINATION the illumination of something relative to its surroundings **2.** OPTICS INTENSITY OF LIGHT OR COLOR the attribute of an object or a color that enables an observer to quantify the amount of light it appears to reflect

light·ness[2] /lĭtnəss/ *n.* **1.** RELATIVE SLIGHTNESS OF WEIGHT the condition of something that weighs relatively little **2.** RELATIVE SLIGHTNESS OF FORCE the condition of something that has relatively little force ○ *lightness of touch* **3.** EASE OR DELICACY the ease or delicacy with which something is done **4.** NIMBLENESS ease and rapidity of movement **5.** UNTROUBLED STATE total freedom from worry and trouble **6.** LEVITY lack of the seriousness that is required or expected

light·ning /lĭtning/ *n.* FLASH OF LIGHT IN THE SKY flashes of light seen in the sky when there is a discharge of atmospheric electricity in the clouds or between clouds and the earth, usually occurring during a thunderstorm ■ *adj.* FAST very fast and often very sudden [14thC. Variant of *lightening*, formed from LIGHTEN[2].]

light·ning ar·rest·er *n.* a device, often an antenna, that protects a piece of electrical equipment from damage by lightning or some other electrical surge by diverting the electricity to the ground

light·ning bug *n.* = **firefly**

light·ning chess *n.* a fast form of chess in which players either have a limited time to make each move or have to complete all their moves within a set time

light·ning con·duc·tor *n. U.K.* = **lightning rod**

light·ning rod *n.* **1.** DEVICE PROTECTING A BUILDING FROM LIGHTNING a metal rod attached to the highest point of a building or other structure to protect it from lightning by conducting the lightning to the ground **2.** FOCUS OF PUBLIC FEELINGS somebody who attracts public disapproval or criticism, thus diverting attention from other issues

light op·er·a *n.* = **operetta**

light or·gan *n.* ZOOL = **photophore**

light pen *n.* **1.** COMPUT PEN-SHAPED COMPUTER DEVICE a pen-shaped light-sensitive device used to manipulate information on a computer screen by touching the screen directly **2.** *U.K.* COMM = **bar-code reader**

light plane *n.* an aircraft with a takeoff weight that does not exceed 12,500 lbs./5,670 kg, especially a privately operated one

light pol·lu·tion *n.* excessive artificial light, especially street lighting in towns and cities that prevents people from seeing the night sky clearly

light re·ac·tion *n.* an initial stage in photosynthesis when light energy is absorbed by chlorophyll and converted into chemical energy that is stored as ATP (**adenosine triphosphate**). It also generates NADPH, a substance that, like ATP, is essential for subsequent stages of photosynthesis.

light re·flex *n.* the normal contracting of the pupil of the eye in response to increased light

lights /lĭts/ *npl.* the lungs of domestic animals, especially those of hogs, sheep, or cattle when they are used in making pet food or, occasionally, food for people [Pre-12thC. From LIGHT[2], because the lungs are full of air and therefore light.]

light-sen·si·tive *adj.* affected in some way by the presence of light, as are some materials such as photographic film or silicon sheets

light·ship /lĭt shìp/ *n.* a ship with a bright flashing light that functions as a lighthouse, especially one that is anchored in a place where a permanent structure would be impracticable

light show *n.* **1.** DISPLAY OF MOVING LIGHTS a spectacle in the form of a display of colorful moving lights, often a feature of a live pop or rock concert **2.** COLORED LIGHTS SYNCHRONIZED WITH RECORDED MUSIC a form of entertainment in which moving colored lights are synchronized with recorded music, usually synthesized instrumental music. ◊ **son et lumière**

light·some[1] /lĭtsəm/ *adj.* (*archaic or literary*) **1.** HAPPY AND CAREFREE feeling and displaying happiness and freedom from worry **2.** FRIVOLOUS devoid of seriousness **3.** GRACEFUL with a graceful lightness of movement [15thC. Formed from LIGHT[2].] —**light·some·ly** *adv.* —**light·some·ness** *n.*

light·some[2] /lĭtsəm/ *adj.* (*archaic or literary*) **1.** EMITTING LIGHT producing plenty of light **2.** WELL LIT flooded with light [14thC. Formed from LIGHT[1].]

lights out *n.* **1.** TIME WHEN PEOPLE MUST SLEEP the time at night when people, especially those in the armed forces, prison, boarding schools, and other institutions, are supposed to go to sleep **2.** SIGNAL SOUNDED AT LIGHTS OUT a bugle call, gong, or other signal sounded at lights out

light-struck *adj.* used to describe photographic material that has become fogged through being accidentally exposed

light sty·lus *n.* COMPUT = **light pen** *n.* 1

light wa·ter *n.* PHYS ordinary water, as opposed to heavy water

light·weight /lĭt wàyt/ *adj.* **1.** NOT HEAVY IN WEIGHT OR TEXTURE relatively light in weight and in texture **2.** LACKING INTELLECTUAL DEPTH fairly frivolous or trivial and requiring little or no intellectual effort ■ *n.* **1.** INSIGNIFICANT PERSON OR THING somebody or something regarded as insignificant or without influence, often in a particular area ○ *a political lightweight* **2.** BOXING WEIGHT CATEGORY IN PROFESSIONAL BOXING a weight category in professional boxing for competitors who weigh between 130 and 135 lbs./59 and 61 kg **3.** BOXING WEIGHT CATEGORY IN AMATEUR BOXING a weight category in amateur boxing for competitors who weigh between 126 and 132 lbs./57 and 60 kg **4.** BOXING BOXER COMPETING AT LIGHTWEIGHT a boxer who competes at lightweight level **5.** WRESTLING WEIGHT CATEGORY IN WRESTLING a weight category in wrestling for competitors who weigh between 115 and 126 lbs./52 and 57 kg **6.** WRESTLING WRESTLER WHO COMPETES AT LIGHTWEIGHT a wrestler who competes at lightweight level

light wel·ter·weight *n.* **1.** WEIGHT CATEGORY IN AMATEUR BOXING a weight category in amateur boxing for competitors who weigh between 132 and 140 lbs./60 and 63.5 kg **2.** AMATEUR BOXER COMPETING AT LIGHT WELTERWEIGHT an amateur boxer who competes at light welterweight level

light·wood /lĭt wo͝od/ *n.* resinous pine used for kindling (*regional*)

WORD KEY: REGIONAL NOTE

Lightwood, meaning "kindling," is also called *fat lightwood* and *lighterd*, the latter reflecting a common South Midland pronunciation.

light-year, **light year** *n.* UNIT OF DISTANCE IN ASTRONOMY a unit of distance in astronomy equal to the distance that light travels in a vacuum in one mean solar year, approximately 5.88 trillion mi./9.46 trillion km ■ **light years** *npl.* LONG WAY a very long way in time, distance, or some other quantity or quality (*informal*)

lign- *prefix.* = **ligni-** (*used before vowels*)

lig·ne·ous /lígnee əss/ *adj.* consisting of wood, or with the appearance or texture of wood [Early 17thC. From Latin *ligneus*, from *lignum* "wood" (see LIGNI-).]

ligni- *prefix.* wood ○ *lignicole* [From Latin *lignum* "wood, firewood," literally "something gathered." Ultimately from an Indo-European base meaning "to collect," which is also the ancestor of English *select* and *logic*.]

lig·ni·cole /lígnə kōl/, **lig·ni·co·lous** /lig níkələss/ *adj.* living or growing in or on wood [Mid-19thC. Coined from LIGNI- + Latin *colere* "to inhabit."]

lig·ni·fy /lígnə fī/ (**-fied, -fy·ing, -fies**) *vti.* to become woody and relatively rigid as lignin is deposited in cell walls, or to make plant parts woody in this way [Early 19thC. Formed from Latin *lignum* "wood" (see LIGNI-).] —**lig·ni·fi·ca·tion** /lìgnəfi káysh'n/ *n.*

lig·nin /lígnin/ *n.* the complex polymer that is laid down in plant cell walls to give plant parts varying degrees of rigidity. It is the major component of wood, and enables, e.g., the trunk of a tree to support the weight of the crown. [Early 19thC. From Latin *lignum* "wood."]

lig·nite /líg nìt/ *n.* = **brown coal** [Early 19thC] —**lig·nit·ic** /lig níttik/ *adj.*

ligno- *prefix.* wood ○ *lignocellulose* [From Latin *lignum* "wood" (see LIGNI-)]

lig·no·caine /lígnə kàyn/ *n. U.K.* = **lidocaine** [Mid-20thC. Coined from Latin "wood."]

lig·no·cel·lu·lose /lìgnō séllyə lòss, -lòz/ *n.* a substance that gives strength to the woody tissues of plants and is formed by the combination of lignin and cellulose

lig·num vi·tae /lìgnəm vítee/ *n.* **1.** TREES **TROPICAL AMERICAN TREE** a tropical American tree that has purple or blue flowers and is grown commercially for its timber. Latin name: *Guaiacum oficinale* and *Guaiacum sanctum.* **2.** INDUST **WOOD OF THE LIGNUM VITAE TREE** the valuable hard resinous heavy wood from the lignum vitae tree [Late 16thC. From Latin, literally "wood of life" (from the medicinal uses of the wood and its resin).]

lig·ro·in /líggrō in/ *n.* a solvent in the form of a flammable liquid mixture of hydrocarbons. It is obtained by the distillation of petroleum. [Late 19thC. Origin unknown.]

lig·u·la /líggyələ/ (*plural* **-lae** /-lèe/ *or* **-las**) *n.* **1.** INSECTS **PART OF AN INSECT'S LIP** the tip of the lower lip (**labium**) of an insect, which typically has four lobes **2.** BOT = **ligule** *n.* 1 [Mid-18thC. From Latin, "strap," a variant of *lingula*, literally "little tongue," from *lingua* "tongue" (see LINGUA).] —**ligu·lar** *adj.*

lig·u·late /líggyə làyt/ *adj.* **1.** **STRAP-SHAPED** shaped like a strap **2.** BOT **WITH A LIGULE** used to describe a plant that has a ligule, or to describe a plant part in the form of a ligule

lig·ule /líggyool/ *n.* **1.** **lig·ule, lig·u·la** **OUTGROWTH ON A LEAF IN GRASSES** an outgrowth at the junction of the leaf sheath and leaf blade in a grass, typically a membranous or scaly flap but in some grasses a ring of hairs **2.** **STRAP-SHAPED EXTENSION OF A FLORET** the strap-shaped extension of florets found in the flower heads of some members of the daisy family and in some grasses [Early 19thC. From Latin *ligula* (see LIGULA).]

Li·gu·ri·an Sea /li gŏoree ən-/ part of the Mediterranean Sea, bordering northwestern Italy

lik·a·ble /líkəb'l/, **like·a·ble** *adj.* pleasant and friendly and, therefore, easy to like —**lik·a·bil·i·ty** /lìkə bíllətee/ *n.* —**lik·a·ble·ness** /líkəb'lnəss/ *n.*

Li·ka·si /li kaássee/ mining and industrial city in the southeastern part of the Democratic Republic of the Congo. Population: 299,118 (1994).

like[1] /lìk/ CORE MEANING: a preposition indicating that two things or people are similar or share some of the same features, qualities, or characteristics; it also introduces an example of the set of things or people that have just been mentioned ○ *Vivid red phone booths, looking like London imports, stood nearby.*

1. *prep.* **RESEMBLING** having a resemblance to somebody or something ○ *She wrapped the towel like a turban on her head.* ○ *He looks like the hero type to me!* **2.** **SUCH AS** as a typical instance or example of ○ *She won't go to public places like movie theaters.* ○ *I bought things like fishing tackle and waders.* **3.** **INDICATES CHARACTERISTICS** indicates qualities, characteristics, or features (*often used in questions*) ○ *What's it like, being a mother?* ○ *When you go on like this, you know what you sound like?* **4.** **TYPICAL OF** in a manner typical or characteristic of somebody or something (*often negative*) ○ *It's not like him to be this late home.* **5.** **INCLINED TOWARD** having a tendency or desire for something ○ *I felt like screaming when I found the kitchen floor flooded.* **6.** **WITH A SUGGESTION OF** as though something might happen ○ *It looks like rain this morning.* **7.** *conj.* **AS** in the same way or manner as something ○ *To ski like she does requires great athletic ability.* **8.** **AS IF** as though or as if (*nonstandard*) ○ *Butch hops out of the car like it was on fire.* ○ *Like I'd tell you a secret!* **9.** *adv.* **IN A PARTICULAR WAY** in a particular way or manner (*informal*) ○ *He fixed the chair like new.* **10.** **USED AS FILLER OR FOR EMPHASIS** used especially in conversation as a filler or for emphasis (*nonstandard*) ○ *You're, like, feeling stressed today, aren't you?* ○ *There were, like, hundreds of people there.* **11.** **INTRODUCES DIRECT SPEECH** used informally to introduce what somebody says (*nonstandard*) ○ *Susan is like "It's not for me" and Brandon is like, "You had me worried" and Susan is like, "Don't worry, I'm not going anywhere."* **12.** *n.* **SOMETHING SIMILAR** a thing or set of things similar to another ○ *window boxes, planters, flower pots, and the like* **13.** **COUNTERPART** one person or thing that is regarded as similar or almost identical to another ○ *Have you ever tasted the like of this cheesecake?* ○ *We won't see his like again in this decade.* **14.** *adj.* **ALIKE** having exactly the same or almost identical qualities or characteristics ○ *These two cats are as like as though they were of the same litter.* ○ *The new laws affect hospitals, nursing homes, clinics, and other like institutions.* [12thC. From Old Norse *líkr*, shortening of *glíkr*, from a prehistoric Germanic word that is also the ancestor of English *alike, each*, and *frolic*.] ◇ **like as not** to a probable or likely extent ○ *Like as not he'll show up very late.* ◇ **the likes of** people or things of the particular sort ○ *Such luxuries aren't for the likes of us.*

like[2] /lìk/ *v.* (**liked, lik·ing, likes**) **1.** *vt.* **ENJOY** to regard something as enjoyable ○ *I like cross-country skiing.* ○ *Do you like prunes?* **2.** *vt.* **CONSIDER PLEASANT** to regard somebody as pleasant and enjoy that person's company ○ *I like a man with a sense of humor.* ○ *Do you like your new teacher?* **3.** *vt.* **WANT** to want to have or do something ○ *Would you like some coffee?* ○ *I'd like to meet your brother.* **4.** *vt.* **REGARD IN A POSITIVE WAY** to have a positive opinion about something or somebody ○ *How do you like her prose style?* **5.** *vi.* **HAVE A PREFERENCE** to have a specified or unspecified preference or inclination ○ *We can leave later than seven if you like.* ○ *If you like, I'll show you around the house.* ■ *n.* **PREFERENCE** something that is preferred over others ○ *a full litany of her likes and dislikes* [Old English *lician* "to please"; related to Old Norse *líkr* (see LIKE[1])]

WORD KEY: CULTURAL NOTE

As You Like It, a play by English dramatist William Shakespeare (1599?). Based on Thomas Lodge's romance ***Rosalynde*** (1590), it is one of Shakespeare's most charming romantic comedies. Its complex plot revolves around Rosalind, daughter of wicked Duke Ferdinand. Her love for a young knight, Orlando, results in her being banished to the forest, where she is eventually reunited with her lover. The oft-used expression "All the world's a stage" comes from Act II, scene vii, line 139 of this play.

like[3], **liked** *vi. Southern U.S.* to be on the verge or point of doing or almost doing a particular thing (*informal*) ○ *I like to have died when I saw her in that getup.* [15thC. From LIKE[1]. Originally "to make in a particular likeness, to pretend."]

-like *suffix.* resembling or characteristic of ○ *workmanlike* [From LIKE[1]]

like·li·hood /líklee hŏŏd/ *n.* **1.** **DEGREE OF PROBABILITY** the chance of something happening **2.** **PROBABLE EVENT** something that is likely to happen ◇ **in all likelihood** very probably

like·ly /líklee/ *adj.* (**-li·er, -li·est**) **1.** **PROBABLE** that will probably happen **2.** **PLAUSIBLE** fit to be believed (*often used ironically*) **3.** **SUITABLE** appropriate for a specified activity or purpose **4.** **PROMISING** with a good chance of success or victory **5.** pleasant or good-looking (*regional*) ○ *a likely young woman* ■ *adv.* **PROBABLY** to a probable degree or extent ○ *It will very likely snow tomorrow.* [14thC. From Old Norse *(g)líkligr*, from *líkr* (see LIKE[1]). The underlying sense is "like the truth, apparently."] ◇ **(as) likely as not** very probably

WORD KEY: USAGE

Adverbial uses: The most traditional usage calls for the adverb ***likely*** never to be used without a qualifier such as *quite* or *very*: *He will very likely attend the meeting.* This stricture has been increasingly ignored, so that sentences like *He will likely attend* are now common.

like-mind·ed *adj.* sharing the same or similar views, opinions, tastes, values, or outlook —**like-mind·ed·ness** *n.*

lik·en /líkən/ (**-ened, -en·ing, -ens**) *vt.* to compare something or somebody with another, especially in order to point out the similarities

like·ness /líknəss/ *n.* **1.** **REPRESENTATION OF SOMEBODY OR SOMETHING** a representation of somebody or something, e.g. a painting or statue, often considered in terms of how accurately it represents the person or thing **2.** **SIMILARITY** similarity of appearance among or between people or things [Old English *(ge)līknes*, formed from the base that also produced *alike*]

Lik·ert scale /líkərt skàyl/ *n.* PSYCHOL a scale measuring the degree to which people agree or disagree with a statement, usually on a 3-, 5-, or 7-point scale [Mid-20thC. Named for Rensis *Likert* (1903–81), U.S. psychologist.]

like·wise /lík wìz/ *adv.* **1.** **IN THE SAME WAY** in the same or a similar way **2.** **ALSO** used to state that the same applies in a second or subsequent case ○ *She works as a teacher; her brother likewise.* [15thC. Contraction of *in like wise* "in like or similar manner."]

lik·ing /líking/ *n.* **1.** **FONDNESS** a feeling of enjoying something or finding it pleasant **2.** **PREFERENCE** personal taste or choice [14thC. From LIKE[2].]

WORD KEY: SYNONYMS

See Synonyms at ***love***.

li·ku·ta /lee kŏŏtə/ (*plural* **ma·ku·ta** /maa kŏŏtə/) *n.* **1.** **MINOR UNIT OF CURRENCY** a subunit of currency of the Democratic Republic of Congo, 100 of which are worth one new zaire. See table at **currency** **2.** **LIKUTA COIN** a coin worth one likuta [Mid-20thC. From Kikongo, literally "the cloth" (a piece of cloth formerly being used as a unit of currency).]

li·lac /lílək/ (*plural* **-lacs** *or* **-lac**) *n.* **1.** TREES **FLOWERING TREE** a European and Asian shrub or small tree with strongly perfumed sprays of white, pink, or pale purple flowers. It is a member of the olive family. Genus: *Syringa.* **2.** PLANTS **BLOSSOM OF LILAC** a pink, white, or pale purple blossom from the lilac tree or shrub **3.** COLORS **PALE PINKISH-PURPLE COLOR** a pale pinkish-purple color with a tinge of blue [Early 17thC. Via French from, ultimately, Persian *līlak*, literally "bluish."] —**li·lac** *adj.*

li·lan·ge·ni /li laáng gènnee/ (*plural* **em·a·lan·ge·ni** /èmmə laang génnee/) *n.* **1.** **UNIT OF CURRENCY** the basic unit of currency of Swaziland, worth 100 cents. See table at **currency** **2.** **LILANGENI COIN** a coin worth one lilangeni [Late 20thC. From Bantu.]

lil·i·a·ceous /lìllee áyshəss/ *adj.* used to describe plants that belong to the lily family [Mid-18thC. From late Latin *liliaceus*, from Latin *lilium* (see LILY).]

Lil·ith /líllith/ *n.* **1.** **PREDECESSOR TO EVE** in Hebrew Scripture, the first woman, believed to have been created before Eve **2.** **EVIL SPIRIT OF A WOMAN** in Jewish folklore, an evil spirit of a woman, believed to lurk in deserted places and attack children

Li·li·u·o·ka·la·ni /lə lèe ō kə laánee/, **Queen of Hawaii** (1838–1917). She was the last native sovereign to govern Hawaii before its annexation by the United States, which she strongly opposed.

Lille /leel/ industrial city and capital of Nord Department, Nord-Pas-de-Calais Region, northern France. Population: 178,301 (1990).

Lil·li·pu·tian /lìllə pyóosh'n/, **lil·li·pu·tian** *n.* **SMALL PERSON OR THING** a person or thing that is unusually small in height ■ *adj.* **1.** **TINY** unusually small **2.** **TRIVIAL OR PETTY** of little or no importance or significance [Mid-18thC. From the name of the imaginary country of *Lilliput* in *Gulliver's Travels* (1726) by Jonathan Swift, whose people were only 15 cm./6 in. high.]

Li·long·we /li lóng way/ capital and second largest city of Malawi. Population: 395,500 (1994).

lilt /lilt/ *n.* **1.** **VARIATION IN VOICE PITCH** a pleasant rising and falling variation in the pitch of a person's voice **2.** **CHEERFUL PIECE OF MUSIC** a cheerful song or piece of music, especially one that is easy to sing along with **3.** **BOUNCY STEP** a light bouncy way of walking, often taken as an indication of a cheerful disposition ■ *v.* (**lilt·ed, lilt·ing, lilts**) **1.** *vti.* **SAY OR SING SOMETHING CHEERFULLY** to say, sing, or play something in a cheerful way, often with pleasant variations in pitch **2.** *vi.* **WALK BOUNCILY** to walk or move in a bouncy cheerful way [14thC. Origin uncertain. Originally "to sound an alarm or raise your voice," later "to strike up a song."] —**lilt·ing** *adj.*

lil·y /líllee/ *n.* (*plural* **-ies**) **1.** PLANTS **PERENNIAL PLANT** a perennial plant that has layered bulbs, blade-shaped leaves, and single, large, sometimes trumpet-shaped flowers. The flowers often have spotted petals and conspicuous protruding stamens. Genus: *Lilium.* **2.** PLANTS **PLANT RESEMBLING A LILY** a plant that resembles the lily but is not necessarily related to it, e.g., the lily of the valley, the arum lily, or the water lily **3.** PLANTS **FLOWER OF THE LILY PLANT** a flower of any of the lily plants ○ *Julia chose lilies for her wedding bouquet.* **4.** HERALDRY = **fleur-de-lis** *n.* 1 **5.** **WHITE OR PURE THING** somebody or something that is particularly white or

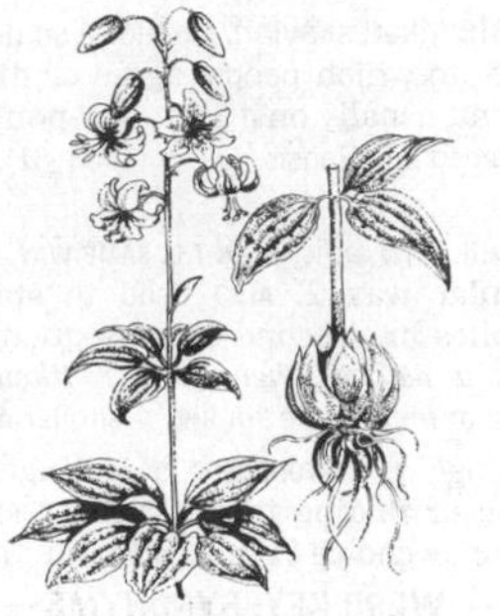

Lily

pure (*dated*) ■ *adj.* PALE unusually pale in color or shade [Pre-12thC. From Latin *lilium*, of uncertain origin: probably ultimately from a pre-Indo-European Mediterranean language.] ◇ **gild the lily** to try to improve something that is good or beautiful enough

lil·y i·ron *n.* a harpoon that has a detachable head with barbs on it, used especially in swordfishing [From its shape, thought to resemble the leaves of a lily]

lil·y-liv·ered *adj.* lacking in courage (*literary*) [From the idea that a cowardly person's liver is pale through lack of bile, once thought to engender courage]

lil·y of the val·ley (*plural* **lil·ies of the val·ley** *or* **lil·y of the val·ley**) *n.* a small ornamental flowering plant with two long, oval, dark green leaves and small, white or pale pink, sweet-scented, bell-shaped drooping flowers growing from a single spike. All parts of the plant, which is grown throughout North America, Europe, and Asia, are poisonous, including the bright red berries. Genus: *Convallaria.* [Translation of Latin *lilium convallium*, name of an unidentified plant in the Bible]

lil·y pad *n.* a floating leaf of a water lily

lil·y-white *adj.* **1.** PALE AND UNBLEMISHED unusually pale in tone and free from blemishes **2.** PREJUDICED AGAINST BLACK PEOPLE discriminating against or excluding people of African American origin (*disapproving*) (*sometimes considered offensive*) **3.** UNMIXED characterized by complete or extreme absence of admixture

Li·ma[1] /leéma/ *n.* COMMUNICATION a code word for the letter "L," used in international radio communications

Li·ma[2] /leéma/ capital city of Peru, situated in the west central part of the country, on the Pacific Ocean and adjacent to the Rímac River in an arid coastal region. Population: 6,400,000 (1991).

li·ma bean /límə-/ *n.* **1.** PLANTS PLANT OF THE BEAN FAMILY a plant of the bean family, originally native to tropical America but now widely grown throughout the United States for its edible seeds that develop inside flat pods. Latin name: *Phaseolus limensis* and *Phaseolus lunatus.* **2.** FOOD SEED OF THE LIMA BEAN the pale green edible seed produced by the lima bean plant. ◊ **butter bean** [Mid-18thC. Named for LIMA[1], the capital of Peru.]

lim·a·cine /límmə seen, límə-/ *adj.* **1.** OF THE SLUG FAMILY belonging or relating to the slug family of invertebrate terrestrial mollusks **2.** LIKE A SLUG resembling a slug in appearance or movement [Late 19thC. Formed from the Latin stem *limac-* "slug, snail."]

lim·a·çon /leémə sáwN, límmə sòn/ *n.* a heart-shaped mathematical curve that is generated by a point on a line that intersects with a circle and rotates about a point on the circle [Late 19thC. From French, literally "snail shell," ultimately from the Latin stem *limac-* "slug, snail."]

Li·mas·sol /leemaásōl/ city and port in southern Cyprus. It is the capital of Limassol District. Population: 143,400 (1994).

limb[1] /lim/ (**limb·ed, limb·ing, limbs**) *n.* **1.** BODY PART an arm, leg, or similar appendage, e.g. a wing or flipper **2.** LARGE BRANCH any of the major branches of a tree **3.** ASSOCIATED PERSON OR ORGANIZATION somebody or something that is affiliated with a larger group or organization **4.** PART STICKING OUT a part that sticks out, e.g., on a building or a mountain range [Old English *lim*] —**limbed** *adj.* —**limb·less** *adj.* ◇ **go out on a limb** to express a viewpoint that risks being controversial ◇ **out on a limb** in an isolated position, without support

limb[2] /lim/ *n.* **1.** ASTRON RIM OF A PLANET the illuminated edge of the Sun, the Moon, or a planet **2.** MATH ARC-SHAPED SCALE ON A MEASURING DEVICE an arc-shaped scale on an instrument that measures angles such as a sextant **3.** BOT END OF A PLANT PART the expanded end of a plant part, especially of a sepal, petal, or leaf **4.** BOT RIM OF A FLOWER the flared outer rim of a bell- or trumpet-shaped flower **5.** ARCHERY PART OF A BOW either of the two halves of a bow used in archery [14thC. Directly or via French *limbe* from Latin *limbus* (see LIMBUS).]

lim·bate /lím bàyt/ *adj.* used to describe flowers that are a different color at the edges ○ *limbate carnations* [Early 19thC. From late Latin *limbatus*, from Latin *limbus* "limbus" (see LIMBUS).]

lim·ber[1] /límbər/ *adj.* **1.** SUPPLE AND AGILE able to move with elastic ease and nimble quickness **2.** FLEXIBLE able to be bent easily ■ *vti.* (**-bered, -ber·ing, -bers**) MAKE OR BECOME FLEXIBLE to become, or cause something to become, flexible or supple [Mid-16thC. Origin uncertain: probably from LIMBER[2], from its ease of movement.] —**lim·ber·ness** *n.*

limber up *vi.* to do gentle physical exercises to loosen and warm the muscles prior to taking part in more strenuous physical activity

lim·ber[2] /límbər/ *n.* VEHICLE FOR TRANSPORTING A LARGE GUN a two-wheeled vehicle that forms the detachable front part of a gun carriage. It was also used for transporting ammunition and other supplies on the battlefield. ■ *vt.* (**-bered, -ber·ing, -bers**) ATTACH TO A LIMBER to attach a gun or other piece of field equipment to a limber [Early 17thC. Origin uncertain: perhaps via French *limon* "shaft of a cart" from Celtic or a prehistoric Germanic word that is also the ancestor of *limb*.]

lim·bi plural of **limbus**

lim·bic /límbik/ *adj.* ANAT **1.** OF OR NEAR A LIMBUS belonging to a limbus or situated in or near a limbus **2.** OF THE LIMBIC SYSTEM belonging to or situated in the limbic system [Late 19thC. From French *limbique*, ultimately from Latin *limbus* (see LIMBUS).]

lim·bic sys·tem *n.* an interconnected system of brain nuclei associated with basic needs and emotions, e.g., hunger, pain, pleasure, satisfaction, sex, and instinctive motivation. The most primitive part of the brain, it is situated close to the inner wall of each cerebral hemisphere and includes the brain system concerned with the sense of smell.

lim·bo[1] /límbō/ *n.* **1. Lim·bo, lim·bo** CHR PLACE FOR SOULS OF UNBAPTIZED CHILDREN in Roman Catholic theology, the place that is believed to be home to the souls of children who have died before baptism, and the souls of the righteous who died before Jesus Christ. Although they are barred from entry to heaven, they are not condemned to the eternal suffering of hell. **2.** STATE OF OBLIVION a state in which somebody or something is neglected or is simply left in oblivion **3.** PRISON a place for the confinement of prisoners (*archaic*) [14thC. From Latin, literally "on the border (of hell)," where limbo was thought to be, a form of *limbus* (see LIMBUS).] ◇ **in limbo** in a state of uncertainty or of being kept waiting

lim·bo[2] /límbō/ *n.* (*plural* **-bos**) WEST INDIAN DANCE UNDER A BAR a West Indian dance that involves bending the body backward from the knees and moving under a horizontal bar or rope that is put into progressively lower positions (*often used before a noun*) ○ *a limbo dancer* ■ *vi.* DANCE THE LIMBO to dance the limbo [Mid-20thC. Alteration of LIMBER[1].]

Lim·burg·er /lím bùrgər/, **Lim·burg·er cheese, Lim·burg cheese** /lìm burg-/ *n.* a soft white Belgian cheese noted for its characteristically strong smell and taste [Mid-19thC. From Dutch or German, literally "from Limburg," a province of northwestern Belgium, where it was first made.]

lim·bus /límbəss/ (*plural* **-bi** /-bī/) *n.* the edge of various organs or body parts, e.g., the area in the eyeball where the cornea and sclera meet [15thC. From Latin, literally "edge, border."]

lime[1] /līm/ *n.* **1.** CHEM CALCIUM OXIDE the chemical calcium oxide **2.** AGRIC, GARDENING CALCIUM USED FOR IMPROVING SOIL any of several forms of calcium, especially calcium hydroxide, used for improving soil that has a low calcium content **3.** HUNT BIRDLIME the substance birdlime ■ *vt.* (**limed, lim·ing, limes**) **1.** AGRIC, GARDENING SPREAD CALCIUM ON to spread calcium, often in the form of ground limestone, on soil in order to reduce its acidity **2.** BUILDING PAINT WITH WHITEWASH to cover a surface with whitewash **3.** HUNT SMEAR WITH BIRDLIME to smear twigs or branches with birdlime in order to catch small birds **4.** HUNT CATCH BIRDS OR ANIMALS USING BIRDLIME to catch small birds or animals using birdlime or some other sticky substance [Old English *līm*, from a prehistoric Germanic word that is also the ancestor of English *slime, loam,* and *slippery*] —**lim·y** *adj.*

lime[2] /līm/ *n.* **1.** TREES EVERGREEN TREE a small evergreen citrus tree, originally native to Asia, but now widely grown for its small green fruits. Latin name: *Citrus aurantifolia.* **2.** FOOD SMALL GREEN FRUIT the small acid-tasting citrus fruit of the lime tree that has a thin green rind and pale green juicy flesh (*often used before a noun*) ○ *lime juice* ■ *adj.* COLORS LIME-GREEN lime-green [Mid-17thC. Via French from, ultimately, Arabic *līma* "citrus fruit" (source of English *lemon*).]

lime[3] /līm/ *n.* **1. lime, lime tree** TREES = **linden 2.** INDUST WOOD the wood of the linden tree [Early 17thC. Alteration of *line*, ultimately from Old English *linde* (probable source of English *linden*).]

lime[4] /līm/ (**limed, lim·ing, limes**) *vi. Carib* to spend time lazily (*slang*) [Late 20thC. Back-formation from offensive *limey* "low-class Causasian person."]

lime·ade /lī máyd/ *n.* a nonalcoholic drink made from or tasting of lime juice

lime-green *adj.* having the pale green color of a lime

lime·kiln /līm kìln/ *n.* an oven that is used for heating limestone to produce quicklime

lime·light /līm līt/ *n.* **1.** FOCUS OF ATTENTION the focus of attention or public interest **2.** THEATER LAMP IN WHICH QUICKLIME IS HEATED a type of lamp in which quicklime is heated to produce a brilliant light. It was used in theaters as an early form of stage lighting. **3.** LIGHT PRODUCED BY LIMELIGHT the light that a limelight lamp produces

lime·light·er /līm lītər/ *n.* somebody who wants and enjoys celebrity status

lim·er·ick /límmərik/ *n.* a five-line humorous poem with regular meter and rhyme patterns, often dealing with a risqué subject and typically opening with a line such as "There was a young lady called Jenny." Lines one, two, and five rhyme with each other and have three metrical feet, and lines two and four rhyme with each other and have two metrical feet, giving the poem a catchy bouncy rhythm. [Early 19thC. Said to derive from the Victorian custom of singing nonsense songs with this rhyme scheme, with the refrain "will you come up to LIMERICK."]

Lim·er·ick /límmərik/ **1.** port and chief city of Limerick County, southwestern Republic of Ireland. Population: 75,436 (1991). **2.** county in the southwestern Republic of Ireland, in Munster Province. Population: 112,975 (1996). Area: 1,039 sq. mi./2,686 sq. km.

limes /lī meez/ (*plural* **lim·i·tes** /límmə teez/) *n.* a boundary or boundary wall, especially one that marked the outskirts of territory held by the ancient Romans [Mid-16thC. From Latin (see LIMIT).]

lime·stone /līm stōn/ *n.* sedimentary rock formed from the skeletons and shells of marine organisms that consists chiefly of calcium carbonate and is used widely in construction and in making lime and cement

lime tree *n.* = **lime**[3] *n.* 1

lime tree loop·er *n.* a North American moth whose inchworm larvae are destructive to citrus trees. Latin name: *Erannis tiliaria.*

lime·wa·ter /līm wàwtər, -wòttər/ *n.* **1.** CHEM CALCIUM HYDROXIDE IN WATER a clear alkaline solution of calcium hydroxide in water, used in skin lotions and as an antacid **2.** GEOL WATER CONTAINING CALCIUM SALTS water that is naturally high in dissolved calcium carbonate or calcium sulfate

lim·ey /līmee/ *n. U.S., Can, ANZ* (*sometimes considered offensive*) **1.** BRITISH PERSON a name, sometimes considered offensive, for a British person, originally a British sailor (*slang offensive*) **2.** BRITISH SHIP a name, sometimes considered offensive, for a British commercial or naval vessel (*slang*) ■ *adj. U.S., Can, ANZ* BRITISH a term, sometimes considered offensive, meaning belonging or relating to the United Kingdom (*slang offensive*) [Late 19thC. Shortening of *lime-juicer* (because sailors in the British Navy were made to drink lime juice to prevent scurvy).]

lim·i·nal /límmin'l/ *adj.* belonging to the point of conscious awareness below which something cannot be experienced or felt [Late 19thC. Formed from Latin *limin-*, stem of *limen* "threshold."]

lim·it /límmit/ *n.* **1. FARTHEST POINT, DEGREE, OR AMOUNT** the farthest point, degree, amount, or boundary, especially one that cannot or should not be passed or exceeded ○ *impose a spending limit* **2. MAXIMUM OR MINIMUM AMOUNT ALLOWED** the maximum or minimum amount, or the largest or lowest quantity, that is available or allowed ○ *an upper age limit of 12 years* **3. BOUNDARY OF AN AREA** the boundary or edge of an area, or something that marks a boundary or edge (*often used in the plural*) ○ *the city limits* **4. RESTRICTION** a feature or circumstance that restricts what can be done ○ *a time limit* **5.** GAMBLING **MAXIMUM MONEY ALLOWED IN BETTING** the maximum amount of money that can be staked at any one time in various games of chance **6.** MATH **MAXIMUM OF A MATHEMATICAL FUNCTION** a numerical value approached by a mathematical function as the independent variable of the function approaches infinity or some specified value **7.** MATH **VALUE SPECIFYING AN INTEGRAL'S RANGE** one of the two given values specifying the range over which a definite integral is evaluated ■ *vt.* **(-it·ed, -i·ting, -its) 1. RESTRICT** to restrict something or somebody in number or quantity, or restrict something to a specified group ○ *had to limit the number of guests because of space problems* **2. BE BOUNDARY TO** to be or act as a boundary to a specified area [14thC. From Latin *limit-*, stem of *limes*, literally "ridge of land separating fields," later "boundary."] —**lim·it·a·ble** *adj.* ◇ **be the limit** to be so bad as to be almost beyond what somebody is able or prepared to tolerate

lim·i·tar·y /límmi tèrree/ *adj.* (*archaic*) **1. RESTRICTED** on which limits are imposed **2. RESTRICTIVE** imposing limits of some kind

lim·i·ta·tion /lìmmi táysh'n/ *n.* **1. RESTRICTION** an imposed restriction that cannot be exceeded or sidestepped ○ *limitations on the height of vehicles* **2. RESTRICTING FLAW** a disadvantage or weakness in a person or thing (*often used in the plural*) ○ *One of the limitations of the program is the amount of memory it requires.* **3. SETTING OF A LIMIT** the act of limiting something ○ *damage limitation* **4.** LAW **MAXIMUM DELAY ALLOWED** a stated period of time within which a legal action must start **5.** LAW **LEGAL RESTRICTION** a legal restriction on the powers that somebody has

lim·it down *n.* FIN under futures exchange rules, the point reached by a commodity price that has fallen by the maximum amount allowed in a single day's trading

lim·it·ed /límmitəd/ *adj.* **1. WITH A LIMIT IMPOSED** on which some form of limit or restriction is imposed ○ *we have limited space available* **2. LACKING FULL SCOPE** existing at below the full degree or extent, usually far below ○ *limited powers* **3. OF RELATIVELY LITTLE TALENT** with talents or skills that fall short of what is expected or required **4.** POL **LACKING FULL AUTHORITY** lacking a full range of powers, especially because of constitutional or legal limitations **5. lim·it·ed, Lim·it·ed** COMM **WITH RESTRICTED STOCKHOLDER LIABILITY** used to describe a British-registered company or other business enterprise whose stockholders' liability for any debts or losses is restricted **6.** TRANSP **STOPPING AT ONLY A FEW PLACES** used to describe a passenger train or bus that stops at only a few places along a route and carrying a relatively small number of people ■ *n.* TRANSP **BUS OR TRAIN MAKING FEW STOPS** a bus or train that stops at only a few places on its route and carries a relatively small number of passengers —**lim·i·ted·ly** *adv.* —**lim·i·ted·ness** *n.*

lim·it·ed-ac·cess high·way *n.* = **expressway**

lim·it·ed com·pa·ny *n.* a British-registered company in which the stockholders' liability for any debts or losses is restricted

lim·it·ed e·di·tion *n.* an edition, especially of a book or an art print, of which only a set number of copies have been made. This has the effect of increasing the item's exclusivity value. (*hyphenated before a noun*) ○ *limited-edition prints*

lim·it·ed li·a·bil·i·ty *n.* an investor's liability for no greater a proportion of a company's debt than is represented by the value of his or her financial stake in the business

lim·it·ed part·ner *n.* a business partner who has no management responsibility and whose liability for company debts is limited to his or her financial stake —**lim·it·ed part·ner·ship** *n.*

lim·it·ed war *n.* a war in which it is not the aim of the participants to defeat or destroy the enemy totally, especially a war in which nuclear weapons are available but are not used

lim·it·er /límmitər/ *n.* **1.** ELECTRON ENG **CIRCUIT THAT LIMITS OUTPUT** an electronic circuit that limits the amplitude of an output wave to a specified value **2. SOMETHING IMPOSING A LIMIT** somebody or something that has a restricting effect

lim·i·tes plural of **limes**

lim·it·ing /límmiting/ *adj.* **1. IMPOSING RESTRICTIONS** imposing limits of some kind, especially limits on the scope for development, progress, or improvement ○ *a limiting factor* **2.** GRAM **IDENTIFYING, NOT DESCRIBING** identifying rather than describing the referent of a noun, as the possessive adjective "your" does in the phrase "your house." The term "limiting adjective" is now rarely used, having been superseded by the term "determiner."

lim·it·less /límmitləss/ *adj.* very great in amount, extent, or degree ○ *limitless resources* —**lim·it·less·ly** *adv.* —**lim·it·less·ness** *n.*

lim·it or·der *n.* FIN an order instructing an investment broker to buy or sell something at a set price or better within a certain period of time

lim·it point *n.* MATH a point in a set of mathematical points, such that for every neighborhood around the point at least one other point in the set is contained in the neighborhood

lim·it·ro·phe /límmə trōf/ *adj.* on or close to the border of a country or region (*formal*) [Late 16thC. Via French from late Latin *limitrophus*, literally "supporting a boundary," from the Latin stem *limit-* "boundary."]

lim·it up *n.* FIN under futures exchange rules, the point reached by a commodity price that has risen by the maximum amount allowed in a single day's trading

limn /lim/ **(limned, limn·ing, limns)** *vt.* (*literary*) **1. DRAW OR PAINT** to draw or paint a picture of somebody or something, especially in outline **2. DESCRIBE** to describe something in words [15thC. Alteration of *lumine* "to illustrate a manuscript," from Old French *luminer*, ultimately from Latin *luminare* "to illumine," from *lumin-* "light."] —**limn·er** *n.*

lim·net·ic /lim néttik/ *adj.* relating to or living in the deep open water of a freshwater pond or lake [Late 19thC. Formed from Greek *limnētēs* "living in marshes," from *limnē* "marshy lake."]

lim·nol·o·gy /lim nóllǝjee/ *n.* the scientific study of lakes and other bodies of fresh water, including their physical and biological features [Late 19thC. Coined from Greek *limnē* "marshy lake" + -LOGY.] —**lim·no·log·i·cal** /limnə lójjik'l/ *adj.* —**lim·no·log·i·cal·ly** /-lójjiklee/ *adv.* —**lim·nol·o·gist** /lim nóllǝjist/ *n.*

lim·o /límmō/ (*plural* **-os**) *n.* a limousine (*informal*) [Mid-20thC. Shortening.]

Li·moges[1] /lee mṓzh/ *n.* a fine porcelain made in the town of Limoges, France, since the 19th century [Mid-19thC. From *French*.]

Li·moges[2] /lee mṓzh/ town and capital of Haute-Vienne Department and Limousin Region, central France. Population: 136,407 (1990).

Li·mon /li mṓn/, **José Arcadio** (1908–72) Mexican-born U.S. dancer and choreographer. In 1947 he founded the José Limon American Dance Company.

lim·o·nene /límmə neen/ *n.* a liquid unsaturated hydrocarbon that smells like lemon and is found in the essential oils of citrus fruits and peppermint. It is used as a wetting agent and in making resins. Formula: $C_{10}H_{16}$. [Mid-19thC. From German *Limonen*, from *Limone* "lemon."]

li·mo·nite /límə nīt/ *n.* a hydrated iron oxide ore that varies in color from dark brown to yellow [Early 19thC. From German *Limonit*, from Greek *leimōn* "meadow," modeled on earlier German *Wiesenerz* "limonite," literally "meadow ore."] —**li·mo·nit·ic** /līmə níttik/ *adj.*

Li·mou·sin /límmə zeen, lì moo záN/ *n.* a breed of large hardy beef cattle that originated in Limousin, a former province of central France [Late 20thC. From French.]

lim·ou·sine /límmə zeen, lìmmə zeen/ *n.* **1. LARGE AUTOMOBILE** a large luxurious automobile, usually chauffeur-driven, with a partition between the chauffeur and passengers **2. TRANSPORTATION TO AIRPORT** a vehicle used to transport passengers to and from an airport, usually between a hotel and airport [Early 20thC. From French, feminine of *Limousin*, "caped cloak worn by cart drivers of the Limousin area," hence "vehicle with roofed passenger compartment."]

limp[1] /limp/ *vi.* **(limped, limp·ing, limps) 1. WALK UNEVENLY** to walk with an uneven step, usually because of having an injured leg **2. PROCEED WITH DIFFICULTY** to move or continue with great difficulty ○ *The business limped through the recession.* ■ *n.* **IMPAIRED GAIT** a way of walking or running that involves a motion impairment, either slight or more extensive (*offensive in some contexts*) [Late 16thC. Origin uncertain: possibly a back-formation from obsolete *limphalt* "motion impaired," from Old English *lemphealt*, from *lemp* (of uncertain origin) + HALT "motion impaired."] —**limp·er** *n.*

limp[2] /limp/ *adj.* **1. FLEXIBLE** without stiffness or rigidity **2. WEAK** without strength, power, or firmness ○ *a limp handshake* **3. LACKING FORCE** without energy, vitality, or enthusiasm **4.** PUBL **NOT STIFFENED BY BOARDS** used to describe a book cover that is not stiffened by boards but is made of more durable material than a paperback **5. UNCONVINCING** not very convincing [Early 18thC. Origin uncertain: possibly related to Middle High German *lampen* "to hang down."] —**limp·ly** *adv.* —**limp·ness** *n.*

lim·pet /límpət/ (*plural* **-pets** *or* **-pet**) *n.* a marine gastropod mollusk that has a low rough conical shell and clings to rocks [Pre-12thC. Via medieval Latin *lampreda* from late Latin *lampetra* (source also of English *lamprey*), of uncertain origin: probably literally "lick-rock."]

lim·pet mine *n.* an explosive device that can be attached to the hull of a ship

lim·pid /límpid/ *adj.* **1. CLEAR** clear and transparent **2. LUCID** expressing something in a way that is clear and easy to understand ○ *limpid prose* **3. UNWORRIED** emotionally calm and composed [Early 17thC. Directly or via French *limpide* from Latin *limpidus* "clear," of uncertain origin.] —**lim·pid·i·ty** /lim píddətee/ *n.* —**lim·pid·ly** /límpidlee/ *adv.* —**lim·pid·ness** /límpidnəss/ *n.*

limp·kin /límpkin/ (*plural* **-kins** *or* **-kin**) *n.* a wading bird with a long neck, a long curved bill, long legs, and short rounded wings. It lives in marshes in South America and southeastern North America. Latin name: *Aramus guarauna.* [Late 19thC. Coined from LIMP[1] + -KIN, from the bird's limping walk.]

Lim·po·po /lim pṓpō/ river in southeastern Africa. Length: 1,100 mi./1,800 km.

limp-wrist·ed *adj.* an offensive term meaning effeminate (*insult*) [From the stereotypic attitude offensively associated with effeminate or gay men, with hands relaxed from raised wrists]

lim·u·lus /límmyələss/ (*plural* **-li** /-lee/ *or* **-lus**) *n.* a member of a group of arthropods that includes the horseshoe crab. Genus: *Limulus.* [Mid-19thC. Via modern Latin from Latin, "somewhat sidelong," from *limus* "sidelong, oblique"; from the crab's sideways motion.]

lim·y /līmee/ **(-i·er, -i·est)** *adj.* **1. COVERED WITH BIRDLIME** smeared with birdlime **2. OF LIME** consisting of, containing, or similar to lime

lin. *abbr.* **1.** lineal **2.** linear

lin·ac /línn ak/ *n.* PHYS = **linear accelerator** [Mid-20thC. Shortening.]

lin·age /línij/, **line·age** *n.* **1. NUMBER OF PRINTED LINES** the number of lines in a printed text **2. PAYMENT BY THE LINE** a fixed payment per line of printed text made to the author

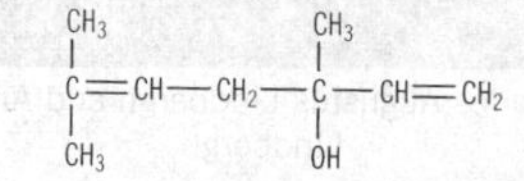

Linalool

lin·al·o·ol /li nállō àwl, línnə lòol/, **lin·al·ol** /línnə lòl/ *n.* a colorless liquid with a pleasant smell that is found in many essential plant oils. It is used in making perfumes. [Late 19thC. Coined from Mexican Spanish *linaloē* "lignaloes" + -OL.]

Lin Biao /lìn byów/ (1907?–71) Chinese military and political leader. He successfully commanded Communist forces during the Chinese Civil War, and died in an air crash after a failed coup attempt. Real name **Lin Yu-yung**

linch·pin /línch pin/, **lynch·pin** *n.* **1. PIN TO STOP A WHEEL COMING OFF** a pin placed crosswise through an axle to prevent a wheel from coming off **2. ESSENTIAL ELEMENT** somebody or something that is an essential element in the success of something such as a team or a plan [14thC. From obsolete *linch* "linchpin," from Old English *lynis,* + PIN.]

Lin·coln[1] /língkən/ *n.* a heavy-fleeced sheep of a breed originally developed in Lincolnshire, England, and raised mainly for its meat

Lin·coln[2] /língkən/ historic cathedral city in eastern England. Population: 84,300 (1995).

Abraham Lincoln

Lin·coln, Abraham (1809–65) U.S. statesman and 16th president of the United States. He led the Union to victory in the Civil War and abolished slavery. He was assassinated while attending a theater performance. —**Lin·coln·esque** /lìngkə nésk/ *adj.*

Lin·coln green *adj.* of a bright green color [Early 16thC. Named for the city of LINCOLN, where cloth of this color was originally manufactured.] —**Lin·coln green** *n.*

Lin·col·ni·a·na /ling kōnee áanə, -ánnə/ *n.* objects, writings, or anecdotes relating to the life of Abraham Lincoln

linc·tus /língktəss/ (*plural* **-tus·es**) *n.* a medicinal syrup given to relieve coughs and soothe sore throats [Late 17thC. From medieval Latin, "(medicine) for licking," from Latin *lingere* "to lick."]

Lind /lind/**, Jenny** (1820–87) Swedish soprano. The best known singer of her day, she established the Mendelssohn Scholarships and various charities. Known as **The Swedish Nightingale**

lin·dane /lín dàyn/ *n.* a white poisonous crystalline powder that biodegrades very slowly, used to kill insects and weeds. Formula: $C_6H_6Cl_6$. [Mid-20thC. Named for Dutch chemist Teunis van der *Linden.*]

Charles Augustus Lindbergh and Anne Lindbergh

Lind·bergh /línd bùrg/**, Charles Augustus** (1902–74) U.S. aviator and engineer. In 1927 he became the first person to fly solo across the Atlantic, which he described in *The Spirit of St Louis* (1953). Known as **Lucky Lindy**

lin·den /líndən/ (*plural* **-dens** *or* **-den**) *n.* a deciduous hardwood tree of the northern hemisphere with heart-shaped leaves and fragrant cream-colored flowers, grown for its soft lumber and for shade. Genus: *Tilia.* [Late 16thC. Origin uncertain: perhaps from *linden* "made of limewood," from *lind* "lime tree."]

Lind·say /línzee/, **Vachel** (1879–1931) U.S. poet. He wrote *General Booth Enters into Heaven* (1913) and *The Congo* (1914). Full name **Nicholas Vachel Lindsay**

lin·dy /líndee/ (*plural* **-dies**), **lin·dy hop** *n.* a lively dance for couples that is a kind of jitterbug [Early 20thC. From *Lindy,* nickname of Charles Augustus LINDBERGH.]

line[1] /līn/ *n.* **1. LONG NARROW MARK** a long narrow mark or stroke made on or in a surface **2. TRACED PATH OF POINT** an imaginary path that has length but not width, traced by a moving point **3. PEOPLE OR THINGS WAITING** a row of people or things waiting for a turn at something or for admittance to a place **4.** GEOM **ONE-DIMENSIONAL ELEMENT** a straight geometric element that has length but not width or thickness and whose identity is determined by two points **5. ROW** a row of people or things **6. FACIAL MARK** a wrinkle or crease in the skin of the face (*often used in the plural*) **7. BORDER** a boundary or division between two properties, jurisdictions, or political units **8.** SPORTS **CONFINING BOUNDARY** a long narrow mark that shows the boundary of any of the divisions of a playing area or race track **9.** PRINTING **ROW OF PRINT** a row of words or numbers on a page or other surface ○ *a few lines of doggerel* **10. DIRECTION** a path or direction of movement **11. SHAPE** the characteristic shape or contour of something (*often used in the plural*) **12. THIN ROPE** a length of rope or wire **13.** TRANSP **ROUTE** a rail, sea, or air route served by a transport organization **14.** TRANSP **TRANSPORT COMPANY** a company that runs a regular service of buses, ships, or aircraft on a route **15.** RAIL **TRACK** the track on which a railroad train runs **16.** RAIL **FIXED RAILROAD ROUTE** a particular part of a railroad network **17.** MUSIC **PART OF STAFF** any of the five horizontal marks that make up a staff **18.** ELEC **ELECTRIC CABLE** a cable used for transmitting electric power or electronic messages **19.** MUSIC **MELODY** the notes that make up a melody **20.** COMMUNICATION **CONNECTION** a telephone connection **21.** FOOTBALL **FOOTBALL PLAYERS** either of the two rows of opposing football players facing each other on either side of the line of scrimmage **22.** COMM **TYPE OF MERCHANDISE** a particular type of product or merchandise **23.** FOOTBALL = **line of scrimmage 24. POLICY** a policy, a way of thinking, or a version of something ○ *What's the government line on this?* **25. SERIES** a series of people, usually in the same family, who follow one another in the same job or role ○ *the last in a long line of musicians* **26. BRIEF MESSAGE** a short written message ○ *Why not drop me a line?* **27. USEFUL INFORMATION** useful information or an insight into something **28. SPECIALIZED FIELD** a particular area of interest, work, activity, or expertise **29. LIMIT** any limit or division ○ *a thin line between happiness and misery* **30. APPROACH** a course or approach followed in doing something ○ *must decide what line to take before the meeting* **31. DECEIVING TALK** something said to deceive, impress, or attract somebody (*informal*) ○ *gave me that old line about the dog eating his report card* **32. ODDS** odds for wagering **33.** MIL **POSITIONED FORMATION** a formation of troops, ships, weapons, or fortifications positioned in a place (*often used in the plural*) ○ *behind enemy lines* **34.** THEATER **ACTOR'S WORDS** the words spoken that make up an actor's part (*often used in the plural*) **35.** MIL **FIGHTING FORCE** the military or naval units of a country that actually go into battle **36.** ELECTRON ENG **NARROW BAND OF FREQUENCIES** a narrow band of frequencies in an electromagnetic spectrum **37.** GEOG **EQUATOR** the equator (*dated*) **38.** TV **PART OF TELEVISION PICTURE** any of the horizontal scans that make up the picture on a television screen **39.** DRUGS **AMOUNT OF A DRUG** a portion of a drug, such as cocaine, scraped into a long thin row to be inhaled (*slang*) **40.** INSUR **KIND OR AMOUNT OF INSURANCE** a class or type of insurance, or the amount of insurance an underwriter will sell to cover a specific risk ■ *v.* (**lined, lin·ing, lines**) **1.** *vt.* **MARK A LINE ON SOMETHING** to mark something with lines **2.** *vt.* **ARRANGE ALONG AN EDGE** to arrange or be arranged along the edge or length of something **3.** *vti.* BASEBALL **HIT A LINE DRIVE** to hit a line drive in baseball [Pre-12thC. Directly or via Old French *ligne* from Latin *linea* "linen string, line," a form of *lineus* "made of linen," from *linum* "flax, linen."] —**lin·a·ble** *adj.* ◇ **all along the line** throughout or at every stage in something ◇ **draw the line** to restrict or set limits at a particular point ◇ **hold the line 1.** to keep a telephone connection open while waiting to speak to somebody **2.** MIL to resist a military attack without giving ground or allowing a formation to be broken **3.** to be firm under pressure in maintaining an existing condition or situation (*informal*) ◇ **in line 1.** arranged in an orderly row **2.** in keeping with a policy or obedient to a set of rules ◇ **in line for** likely to receive something such as a promotion or position ◇ **in line with** in agreement or conformity with something ◇ **lay it on the line** to speak about something frankly (*informal*) ◇ **lay** *or* **put something on the line** to risk by some action the loss of something valuable (*informal*) ◇ **off line** temporarily not connected in an electronic communications system ◇ **on line** connected in an electronic communications or other system ◇ **out of line 1.** rude and disrespectful (*informal*) **2.** unruly or out of control (*informal*) ◇ **read between the lines** to deduce something that is not made explicit (*informal*) ◇ **toe the line** to comply with what is expected

line out *vi.* BASEBALL to be put out when at bat by hitting a line drive that is caught by a fielder

line up *v.* **1.** *vti.* **FORM A ROW** to form a row or form people or things into a row **2.** *vi.* **FORM A LINE** to form a line to wait for a turn **3.** *vt.* **PROVIDE** to organize, provide, or make something available to somebody ○ *had lined up a program of entertainments for us* **4.** *vti.* **ALIGN THINGS** to align two or more things or be in alignment

line[2] /līn/ (**lined, lin·ing, lines**) *vt.* **1. REINFORCE** to cover or reinforce the inside or unexposed surface of something ○ *a jacket lined with silk* **2. COVER** to completely cover something with something else ○ *The walls were lined with books.* **3. FILL** to fill or supply something with something else ○ *a good hot meal to line your stomach* [14thC. From obsolete *line* "spun or woven flax," from Old English *līn,* from or related to Latin *linum* "flax" (source of LINE[1]); from the frequent use of linen to line garments.]

lin·e·age[1] /línnee ij/ *n.* **1. LINE OF DESCENT** the line of descent from an ancestor to a person or family **2. RELATED GROUP OF PEOPLE** a group of people related by descent from a common ancestor [14thC. From French *lignage,* from *ligne* "line," (see LINE[1]).]

lin·e·age[2] /línij/ *n.* = **linage**

lin·e·al /línnee əl/ *adj.* in or from a direct line from an ancestor —**lin·e·al·ly** *adv.*

lin·e·a·ment /línnee əmənt/ *n.* **1. FACIAL FEATURE** a feature or contour of a face (*literary*) **2. CHARACTERISTIC FEATURE** a characteristic feature, especially of something immaterial (*literary*) **3.** GEOL **FEATURE OF LAND** a major topographical feature, such as a long fault plane, that reveals something about its subsurface [15thC. From Latin *lineamentum* "line," from *lineare* "to make straight," from *linea* "line."]

lin·e·ar /línnee ər/ *adj.* **1. RELATING TO LINES** relating to, consisting of, or using lines **2. RELATING TO A STRAIGHT LINE** relating to a straight line or capable of being represented by a straight line **3. CHANGING PROPORTIONALLY** changing proportionally and representable on a graph as a straight line (*refers to variables*) ○ *There's no linear relation between mortality and size.* **4. UNIMAGINATIVE** developed sequentially from the obvious without in-depth understanding ○ *takes a somewhat linear approach to the problem* **5.** ARTS **WITH CLEARLY DEFINED LINES** dominated by clearly defined lines rather than relying on the effects of color **6.** MATH **OF THE FIRST DEGREE** about or in the first degree relative to a mathematical variable **7.** ELECTRON ENG **WITH OUTPUT VARYING AS INPUT DOES** with an output that varies directly with the input **8.** BOT **LONG AND NARROW** used to describe a leaf that is long and narrow —**lin·e·ar·i·ty** /línnee áirətee/ *n.* —**lin·e·ar·ly** *adv.*

Lin·e·ar A /línnee ər-/ *n.* an undeciphered writing system, dating from about 1500 B.C. and found on clay remains in Crete

lin·e·ar ac·cel·er·a·tor *n.* a device that propels charged particles in straight paths by using alternating high-frequency voltages

lin·e·ar al·ge·bra *n.* a branch of algebra dealing with linear transformations, vector spaces, matrices, and determinants

Lin·e·ar B *n.* an early form of Greek that dates from about 1400 B.C., found on clay remains in Crete and the Greek mainland, and deciphered about 1952

lin·e·ar e·qua·tion *n.* an equation with no variable raised to a power

lin·e·ar func·tion *n.* = **linear transformation**

lin·e·ar in·duc·tion mo·tor *n.* = **linear motor**

lin·e·ar·ize /línnee ə rìz/ (**-ized, -iz·ing, -iz·es**) *vt.* to form or project something into a line —**lin·e·ar·i·za·tion** /lìnnee əri záysh'n/ *n.*

lin·e·ar meas·ure *n.* any system or unit used to measure length

lin·e·ar mo·tor *n.* an electric motor in which the motion between the rotor and stator is linear so that thrust is produced along a straight line

lin·e·ar per·spec·tive *n.* a form of perspective in which drawings or paintings are given apparent depth by showing parallel lines as converging on the horizon

lin·e·ar pro·gram·ming *n.* MATH a method of finding the maximum and minimum values of a linear transformation using variables that are subject to constraints

lin·e·ar trans·for·ma·tion *n.* a mathematical transformation in which the resulting variables are neither multiplied together nor raised to any power

lin·e·a·tion /lìnnee áysh'n/ *n.* **1. ARRANGEMENT OF LINES** division into or arrangement of lines **2. OUTLINE** the outline of an image

line·back·er /lín bàkər/ *n.* a football player who takes a position near and behind the defensive line —**line·back·ing** *n.*

line breed·ing *n.* the deliberate mating of closely related individuals in order to retain characteristics of a common ancestor

line cut *n.* a photoengraving made from a line drawing

line danc·ing *n.* a style of dancing to country and western music, in which dancers follow the same steps in rows rather than as couples —**line dance** *n., vi.* —**line danc·er** *n.*

line draw·ing *n.* a drawing done entirely in lines, with tones shown by the thickness or closeness of the lines

line drive *n.* in baseball or softball, a ball batted so that it moves fast, straight, and low

line en·grav·ing *n.* an engraving in which lines are cut by hand into a metal plate from which the print is made

line i·tem *n.* an item of financial or other data presented on a separate line, such as in a ledger or an annual report

line judge *n.* = **linesman** *n.* 2

line·man /línmən/ (*plural* **-men** /-mən/) *n.* **1.** COMMUNICATION **SOMEBODY MAINTAINING PHONE OR POWER LINES** somebody who installs or repairs telephone or power lines **2.** FOOTBALL **FOOTBALL PLAYER** in football, a player on the forward line, especially a center, guard, tackle, or tight end

lin·en /línnən/ (*plural* **-en** *or* **-ens**) *n.* **1. FABRIC MADE FROM FLAX** a thread or durable fabric made from the spun fibers of flax **2. THINGS MADE FROM LINEN** clothes, table coverings, underwear, or bedclothes made from linen or cotton (*often used in the plural*) [Old English *līnen* "made of flax," from *līn* "flax" (source of English *linseed*). Ultimately from an Indo-European word that is also the ancestor of English *line* and English *lingerie*.]

lin·en pa·per *n.* fine paper that is made from flax fibers, or given a finish to resemble linen

line of cred·it *n.* = **credit line**

line of·fi·cer *n.* an officer who serves in combat

line of fire *n.* **1. PATH OF FIRED PROJECTILE** the path taken by a bullet or missile fired from a weapon **2. EXPOSED POSITION** a position exposed to a threat, attack, or criticism

line of force *n.* an imaginary curve whose tangent at any point is that of the electric or magnetic field that is operating there

line of scrim·mage *n.* in football, an imaginary line across the field at which the ball rests and where the players of the opposing teams line up facing each other for a play

line of sight *n.* **1. LINE FROM EYE TO OBJECT** an imaginary line from an observer to a distant object **2.** OPTICS = **line of vision 3.** TELECOM **UNOBSTRUCTED TRANSMITTING PATH** a straight path, unobstructed by the horizon, between a transmitting and receiving antenna

line print·er *n.* a printing device that prints a line at a time rather than one character at a time

lin·er[1] /línər/ *n.* **1.** TRANSP **PASSENGER SHIP OR PLANE** a passenger ship or airplane run by a shipping line or airline **2.** COSMETICS = **eyeliner 3.** BASEBALL = **line drive**

lin·er[2] /línər/ *n.* **1. LINING** something used as a lining or padding **2.** RECORDING = **jacket** *n.* 3 **3.** ENG **PROTECTIVE SLEEVE FOR COMPONENT** a protective sleeve, usually made of metal, fitted inside or outside a cylindrical component

lin·er·board /línər bàwrd/ *n.* a thick stiff cardboard used for containers, especially corrugated boxes

lin·er notes *npl.* printed information about a recording that appears on the cover or as part of the packaging

line score *n.* the score of a baseball game giving the runs scored by both teams in each inning as well as the total number of runs, hits, and errors

lines·man /línzmən/ (*plural* **-men** /-mən/) *n.* **1.** SPORTS **REFEREE'S ASSISTANT** in soccer, tennis, and ice hockey, an official who assists the head official, referee, or umpire, e.g., by deciding whether or not the ball has gone out of play **2.** FOOTBALL **FOOTBALL OFFICIAL** an official in football who watches for infringements, marks the downs, and places the ball in position **3.** *U.K.* COMMUNICATION = **lineman** *n.* 1

lines·per·son /línz pùrs'n/ (*plural* **-sons**) *n.* in tennis, soccer, ice hockey, and football, an official who assists the referee

line squall *n.* a strong storm advancing along a weather front

line storm *n.* = **equinoctial storm**

lines·wom·an /línz wòomən/ (*plural* **-en** /-wìmmin/) *n.* in tennis, soccer, ice hockey, and football, a woman official who assists the head official, referee, or umpire, e.g., by deciding whether or not the ball has gone out of play

line-up /lín ùp/, **line-up** *n.* **1.** SPORTS **LIST OF PLAYERS** a list of players in a team together with the positions they play **2.** TV **TELEVISION SCHEDULE** a programming schedule of a television network **3.** CRIMINOL **PEOPLE ASSEMBLED BY POLICE** a group of people, including a crime suspect, assembled by the police so that a witness or victim of the crime can identify the person responsible for the crime **4. GROUP UNITED IN A PURPOSE** a group of people or organizations recruited for a cause or common purpose such as raising funds for a charity

ling[1] /ling/ (*plural* **ling** *or* **lings**) *n.* an edible fish that is related to the cod and is found off the coasts of Greenland and northern Europe. Genus: *Molva.* [13thC. Origin uncertain.]

ling[2] /ling/ *n.* = **heather** *n.* 1 [Old English *lyng*, of unknown origin]

-ling[1] *suffix.* **1.** one connected with or resembling ○ *hatchling* **2.** small one ○ *princeling* ○ *spiderling* [Old English]

-ling[2] *suffix.* in a particular manner or condition ○ *darkling* [Old English]

Lin·ga·la /ling gáalə/ *n.* a language belonging to the Bantu group of Benue-Congo languages and used as a lingua franca in Zaire. More than 10 million speakers use Lingala as a second language. [Early 20thC. From Bantu.]

lin·gam /líng gəm/ *n.* a stylized phallus, used to represent the Hindu god Shiva [Early 18thC. From Sanskrit *liṅga* "mark, phallus."]

ling·cod /líng kòd/ (*plural* **-cod** *or* **-cods**) *n.* a spiny-finned large-mouthed fish that lives in the North Pacific Ocean and is caught for food and sport. Latin name: *Ophidion elongatus.* [Mid-20thC. From LING + COD.]

lin·ger /líng gər/ (**-gered, -ger·ing, -gers**) *v.* **1.** *vi.* **DELAY LEAVING** to put off leaving a place because you are reluctant to go **2.** *vi.* **WAIT AROUND** to wait around or move about a place slowly and idly **3.** *vi.* **BE BARELY ALIVE** to remain alive, although very weak, while gradually dying **4.** *vi.* **TAKE TIME TO DO SOMETHING** to take longer than is usual to do something, e.g., to complete a task or look at somebody or something, usually because you are enjoying yourself ○ *Her eyes lingered on the letter.* **5.** *vi.* **PERSIST** to remain fixed in the mind or noticed by the senses for a long time **6.** *vt.* **PASS TIME** to pass time in a relaxed or uneventful way [13thC. Literally "to delay repeatedly," formed from Middle English *lengen* "to delay," from, ultimately, Old Norse *lengja* "to lengthen."] —**lin·ger·er** *n.*

lin·ge·rie /láanzhə ráy, láanzhəree, láaNzh-/ *n.* women's underwear and nightgowns [Early 19thC. From French, literally "things made of linen," from *linge* "linen," from Latin *lineus* "made of flax."]

lin·ger·ing /líng gəring/ *adj.* **1. DRAWN-OUT** long and drawn-out, especially with pain **2. SLOW** done slowly in order to prolong something as long as possible **3. PERSISTING IN THE MIND** remaining for some time in the thoughts or mind —**lin·ger·ing·ly** *adv.*

lin·go /líng gō/ (*plural* **-goes**) *n.* a language that is not the speaker's native language or a specialized set of terms requiring to be learned like a language (*informal*) [Mid-17thC. Origin uncertain: perhaps an alteration of *lingua* in LINGUA FRANCA; or via Portuguese *lingoa* or Provençal *lingo* from, ultimately, Latin *lingua* "tongue."]

lin·gon·ber·ry /líng gən berree/ (*plural* **-ry** *or* **-ries**) *n.* = **cowberry** [Mid-20thC. "Lingon" from Swedish *lingon* "mountain cranberry."]

lin·gua /líng gwə/ (*plural* **-guae** /-gwee/) *n.* the tongue or a part resembling one [Late 17thC. From Latin, "tongue."]

lin·gua fran·ca /-frángkə/ (*plural* **lin·gua fran·cas** *or* **lin·guae fran·cae** /-kee/) *n.* **1. LANGUAGE USED FOR CONVENIENCE** a language or mixture of languages used for communication by people who speak different first languages **2. TRADERS' LANGUAGE IN MEDITERRANEAN** the mixed language used chiefly by merchants throughout the Mediterranean ports until the 18th century, consisting mainly of Italian with elements of French, Spanish, Greek, Arabic, and Turkish [Late 17thC. From Italian, literally "Frankish tongue."]

lin·gual /líng gwəl/ *adj.* **1. OF THE TONGUE** relating to, using, or similar to the tongue **2. OF LANGUAGE** relating to language or languages [Mid-17thC. From medieval Latin *lingualis*, from Latin *lingua* "tongue, language."] —**lin·gual·ly** *adv.*

lin·gui·ne /ling gwéenee/, **lin·gui·ni** *n.* a type of pasta consisting of long narrow flat strips [Mid-20thC. From Italian *linguine*, plural of *linguina*, literally "little tongue," from *lingua* "tongue," from Latin.]

lin·guist /líng gwist/ *n.* **1. SPEAKER OF SEVERAL LANGUAGES** somebody who speaks several languages or finds it easy to learn languages **2. STUDENT OF LINGUISTICS** somebody who studies linguistics [Late 16thC. Formed from Latin *lingua* "tongue, language."]

lin·guis·tic /ling gwístik/ *adj.* **1. OF LANGUAGE** relating to language or languages **2. OF LINGUISTICS** relating to linguistics —**lin·guis·ti·cal·ly** *adv.*

lin·guis·tic at·las *n.* a collection of maps showing the distribution of varying language features in a region

lin·guis·tic form *n.* an identifiable unit of speech such as a word, prefix, phrase, or sentence

lin·guis·tic ge·og·ra·phy *n.* the study of regional variation in speech —**lin·guis·tic ge·og·ra·pher** *n.*

lin·guis·tics /ling gwístiks/ *n.* the systematic study of language (*takes a singular verb*)

lin·gu·late /língyə làyt/ *adj.* shaped like a tongue [Mid-19thC. From Latin *lingulatus*, from *lingula*, literally "little tongue," from *lingua* "tongue."]

lin·i·ment /línnəmənt/ *n.* a liquid such as one containing alcohol and camphor, rubbed into the skin to relieve aches or pain [15thC. From late Latin *linimentum*, from Latin *linire* "to smear."]

li·nin /línin/ *n.* a connective material in a cell nucleus [Mid-19thC. Coined from Greek *linon* "thread" + -IN.]

lin·ing /líning/ *n.* a layer or a material used to cover, protect, or insulate the inner or unexposed surface of something [14thC. Formed from LINE[2].]

link[1] /lingk/ *n.* **1. PART OF A CHAIN** any of the connected rings or loops that make up a chain, or something resembling a loop in a chain **2. CONNECTION** something that ties, connects, or relates two or more things **3.** ACCESSORIES = **cuff link 4.** TRANSP **ROUTE** any part of a transportation system, especially a connection between major routes **5.** COMMUNICATION **UNIT FOR COMMUNICATING BROADCASTS** a broadcasting unit or system used to relay radio or television signals, e.g., a transmitter, receiver, or relay station **6.** MEASURE **SURVEYOR'S UNIT OF LENGTH** a unit of length used in surveying equal to 7.92 in./20.12 cm, and one hundredth of a chain ■ *vti.* (**linked, link·ing, links**) **CONNECT** to connect, join, or associate somebody or something with another or to become joined with another [14thC. From Old Norse *hlekkr* "link," from a prehistoric Germanic word meaning "bending."] —**link·er** *n.*

link[2] /lingk/ *n.* a burning torch used in the past to give light [Mid-16thC. Origin uncertain: perhaps from medieval Latin *linchinus* "candle," alteration of Latin *lichinus* "wick," from Greek *lukhnos* "light."]

link·age /língkij/ *n.* **1. LINK** a link or connection or the fact of being connected **2. DIPLOMATIC PROCEDURE** a procedure in diplomacy that requires progress toward an overall objective to depend on concessions made by the various parties on other related issues **3.** TECH **SYSTEM OF INTERCONNECTED PARTS** a system of interconnected rods, springs, or levers that transmit motion in a mechanism **4.** GENETICS **ASSOCIATED GENES** the proximity of two or more genes on a chromosome, which tends to cause them to be inherited together

link·age group *n.* two or more genes on a chromosome that tend to be inherited as a group

linked list *n.* chain of items of data each of which is associated with a pointer to the next, and sometimes also to the previous one

Lin·kö·ping /lín chŏ ping/ industrial city and capital of Östergötland County, southeastern Sweden. Population: 131,370 (1995).

links /lingks/ *n.* (*takes a singular or plural verb*) **1. GOLF COURSE** a golf course **2.** *Scotland* **UNDULATING SANDY AREA** an area of gently undulating sandy ground near a seashore [Old English *hlincas*, plural of *hlinc* "ridge," of uncertain origin: possibly formed from *hlinian* "to lean"]

Lin·nae·an /li neé ən/ *adj.* relating to the system devised by Linnaeus for classifying plants and animals under two names, one referring to the genus and one to the species [Mid-18thC. From Carolus LINNAEUS, who devised the system.]

Lin·nae·us /li neé əss/, **Carolus** (1707–78) Swedish naturalist. A pioneer of taxonomy, he devised the standard system of binomial nomenclature for plants and animals. Real name **Carl von Linné**

lin·net /línnət/ (*plural* **-nets** *or* **-net**) *n.* a small brownish songbird of the finch family that lives in Europe, Africa, and Asia. The male has a red breast and forehead. Latin name: *Carduelis cannabina.* [Early 16thC. From Old French *linette*, from *lin* "flax," from Latin *linum*; from the bird's diet of flaxseed.]

li·no·cut /línō kùt/ *n.* a print made from a design that has been cut in relief into a piece of linoleum and mounted on a block of wood, or the design itself

li·no·le·ate /li nṓlee àyt/ *n.* any salt or ester of linoleic acid [Mid-19thC. Coined from *linoleic* (see LINOLEIC ACID) + -ATE.]

li·no·le·ic ac·id /linnə leè ik-/ *n.* a colorless liquid, essential to human nutrition, found in linseed and other natural oils and used in making soaps, emulsifiers, and quick-drying oils. Formula: $C_{18}H_{32}O_2$. [*Linoleic* coined from Latin *linum* "flax" + OLEIC]

lin·o·len·ic ac·id /linnə lènnik-/ *n.* a colorless liquid found in linseed and other natural oils, essential to human nutrition, and used in making paints and synthetic resins. Formula: $C_{18}H_{30}O_2$. [Translation of German *Linolensäure*, coined from *Linolsäure* "linoleic acid," with insertion of *-en*, equivalent to -ENE]

li·no·le·um /li nṓlee əm/ *n.* a tough washable floor covering, made from canvas or other material coated under heat and pressure with powdered cork, rosin, and linseed oil [Late 19thC. Originally a trademark, from Latin *linum* "flax" + *oleum* "oil."]

lin·sang /lín sàng/ (*plural* **-sangs** *or* **-sang**) *n.* **1. ASIAN ANIMAL LIKE A GENET** a carnivorous mammal related to and resembling the civet and genet that lives in forests in southern Asia and has spotted or banded fur and a long tail. Genus: *Prionodon.* **2. AFRICAN ANIMAL** an animal similar to the Asian linsang that lives in forests in West Africa. Genus: *Poiana.* [Early 19thC. From Javanese *lingsang.*]

lin·seed /lín seed/ *n.* = **flaxseed** [Old English *līnsǣd*, from *līn* "flax" (see LINEN) + *sǣd*, an earlier form of SEED]

lin·seed oil /lín seèd-/ *n.* oil pressed from flaxseed, used in making linoleum and in paints and inks to help them dry more quickly

lin·sey-wool·sey /línzi wŏolzee/ *n.* a coarse cloth made from linen interwoven with wool or cotton [15thC. Origin uncertain: possibly from *lyn*, from Old English *līn* "flax" (see LINSEED) + *wolle*, an earlier form of WOOL, with *-sey* for a rhyme.]

lin·stock /lín stòk/ *n.* a long staff with a forked end designed to hold a lighted match, used in the past to fire cannons [Mid-16thC. From Dutch *lontstok*, from *lont* "match" (altered perhaps by association with *lint*) + *stok* "stick."]

lint /lint/ *n.* **1. THREAD OR FLUFF** little pieces of thread or fluff **2. COTTON FIBERS** the fibers that surround unprocessed cotton seeds **3. MATERIAL FOR COVERING WOUNDS** a soft absorbent material made from cotton or linen, used to dress wounds [14thC. Origin uncertain: perhaps from Old French *linette*, literally "small flax," from *lin* "flax," from Latin *linum* (see LINE[1]).] —**lint·y** *adj.*

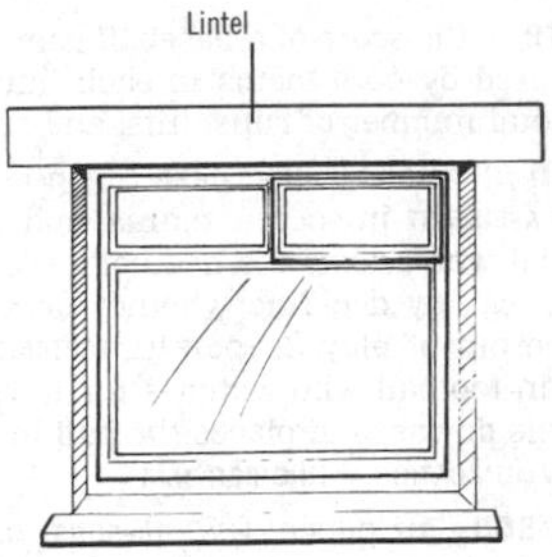

Lintel

lin·tel /línt'l/ *n.* a horizontal beam that supports the weight of the wall above a window or door [14thC. From Old French, from Latin *limitaris* "relating to a boundary," from the stem *limit-* "boundary" (confused with popular Latin *liminaris* "of a threshold").]

lint·er /líntər/ *n.* **MACHINE FOR REMOVING COTTON FIBERS** a machine for removing fibers sticking to cottonseeds ■ **lint·ers** *npl.* **UNWANTED COTTON FIBERS** fibers that stick to cottonseeds

Lin Yu·tang /lìn yŏo táng/ (1895–1976) Chinese-born U.S. philologist. He brought together Chinese and western culture in his novels, and worked on the standard system of romanizing Chinese script.

Linz /lints/ capital of Upper Austria Province, northern Austria. Population: 203,044 (1991).

Lion

li·on /lī ən/ *n.* **1.** ZOOL **BIG WILD PREDATORY CAT** a large wild member of the cat family that lives in Africa and India in extended family groups and hunts cooperatively for prey. It has a tawny yellow coat and the males have a shaggy mane. Latin name: *Panthera leo.* **2. SOMEBODY BRAVE AND STRONG** somebody who is very brave, strong, or fierce **3. CELEBRITY** somebody who is admired and celebrated [13thC. Via Anglo-Norman *liun* and the Latin stem *leon-* from Greek *leōn*, of uncertain origin: probably from a Semitic language.]

Li·on *n.* **1.** ASTRON, ZODIAC = **Leo 2. CHARITY CLUB MEMBER** a member of a Lions Club

li·on dance *n.* a traditional Chinese ritual performed to bring good luck, especially at Chinese New Year, in which two men dance costumed in a large ornamental artificial lion head and body

li·on·ess /lī ənəss/ *n.* a female lion

li·on·fish /lī ən fish/ (*plural* **-fish** *or* **-fish·es**) *n.* a scorpion fish that lives in the tropical Pacific Ocean and has a striped body, long spiny fins, and venomous dorsal spines. Genus: *Pterois.*

li·on·heart·ed /lī ən haártəd/ *adj.* very brave

Lionfish

li·on·ize /lī ə nīz/ (**-ized, -iz·ing, -iz·es**) *vt.* to make somebody into a celebrity or treat somebody like a celebrity [Early 19thC. From the notion of a lion as something unusual or celebrated in a place, and therefore worth going to see.] —**li·on·i·za·tion** /lī əni záysh'n/ *n.* —**li·on·iz·er** *n.*

Li·ons Club *n.* any club belonging to the International Association of Lions Clubs, an organization founded in the United States in 1917 to promote fellowship and service in local communities

li·on's share *n.* the largest part or share of something [Late 18thC. From Aesop's story in which a lion joins a hunt with other animals and by means of spurious reasoning and intimidation gets the whole kill for himself.]

lip /lip/ *n.* **1.** ANAT **PART OF MOUTH** either of two fleshy folds around the mouth that help control eating, drinking, and the production of sounds by the mouth **2. SOMETHING LIKE A LIP** something like a lip, especially an edge or rim of something hollow **3.** LANGUAGE **IMPERTINENCE** impudent or disrespectful talk (*slang*) **4.** ANAT **PART OF VULVA** any of the two sets of folds of skin (**labia**) at the opening of the vulva ■ *vt.* (**lipped, lip·ping, lips**) **1.** GOLF **STRIKE RIM WITH GOLF BALL** to putt a golf ball so that it strikes the lip of a cup, but does not go in **2. TOUCH WITH LIPS** to touch something with the lips **3. FORM LIP OF** to form or be a lip of something [Old English *lippa.* Ultimately from an Indo-European word meaning "lip" that is also the ancestor of English *labial.*] ◇ **bite your lip 1.** to stop yourself from saying something you feel moved to say (*informal*) **2.** to show that you are angry (*informal*) ◇ **button your lip** to stop speaking, not begin speaking, or to keep a secret (*slang*) ◇ **give somebody a fat lip** to punch somebody hard in the mouth (*slang*) ◇ **stiff upper lip** *U.K.* a brave and composed bearing, with no giving way to emotion (*informal*)

Li·pan /li paán/ *n.* a member of a Native North American people who originally occupied lands in Texas and who now live mainly in New Mexico

lip·ase /lī pàyss, -pàyz/ *n.* an enzyme produced by the liver, pancreas, or stomach, or by plant seeds that breaks down fats

lip balm *n.* an ointment used on the lips, often in stick form, especially to relieve chapping or dryness

Lip·chitz /lípshits/, **Jacques** (1891–1973) Lithuanian-born French sculptor. The Cubist style of his early work was replaced by more sensual sculpture, much of it innovative and experimental.

lip·ec·to·my /li péktəmee, lī-/ (*plural* **-mies**) *n.* the surgical removal of fatty tissue from beneath the skin

li·pe·mi·a /li peémee ə/ *n.* the presence of excessive fat in the blood

Li Peng /leè péng/ (*b.* 1928) Chinese statesman. Having become prime minister in 1987, he crushed the prodemocracy movement that had occupied Tiananmen Square (1989).

lip gloss, **lip-gloss** *n.* a cosmetic used on the lips to make them look shiny

lip·id /líppid, lípid/, **lip·ide** /lí pìd, lī-/ *n.* any of a group of organic compounds consisting of fats, oils, and related substances that, along with proteins and carbohydrates, are the structural components of living cells. In addition to fats the group includes waxes, oils, sterols, triglycerides, phosphatides, and phospholipids. [Early 20thC. From French *lipide*, which was coined from Greek *lipos* "fat" (see LIPO-) + French *-ide*, equivalent to -ID.] —**lip·id·ic** /li píddik/ *adj.*

Lip·iz·zan·er /lìppit saánər/, **Lip·piz·an·er** *n.* a compact, usually white or gray horse, belonging to a breed often used in equestrian displays [Early 20thC. From German, literally "of Lipizza," named for *Lipizza*, a place near Trieste in Italy where the stud producing these horses was located.]

lip lin·er *n.* a cosmetic, usually in soft pencil form, used to outline the lips before lipstick is applied

Li Po /lee pṓ/ (701–762) Chinese poet. His work is known for its lyrical beauty and precise imagery. Also known as **Li Bo, Li Taipo**

lipo- *prefix.* fat, fatty tissue ○ *lipolysis* [From Greek *lipos* "fat." Ultimately from an Indo-European base meaning "to stick" that is also the ancestor of English *live*[1] and *liver*[1].]

li·po·gen·e·sis /lìppə jénnəssiss/ *n.* the formation of fatty acids in the body

lip·o·ic ac·id /li pṓ ik-/ *n.* a fatty acid that contains sulfur, metabolizes carbohydrates in the body, and, as part of the vitamin B complex, contributes to growth

lip·oid /lí pòyd, lī́-/ *adj.* **FATTY** containing or resembling fat ■ *n.* **SUBSTANCE LIKE FAT** a substance such as wax that is similar to fat —**li·poi·dal** /li póyd'l, lī-/ *adj.*

li·pol·y·sis /li póllәssiss/ *n.* the breakdown of fats into other compounds —**lip·o·lyt·ic** /lìppə líttik, lī̀pə-/ *adj.*

li·po·ma /li pṓmə, lī-/ (*plural* **-mas** *or* **-ma·ta** /-mətə/) *n.* a benign tumor made up of fatty tissue —**li·pom·a·tous** /li pómmətəss, lī-/ *adj.*

lip·o·phil·ic /lìppə fíllik, lī̀pə-/ *adj.* with a chemical affinity for lipids

lip·o·pol·y·sac·cha·ride /lìppō polli sákə rīd, lī̀pō-/ *n.* a carbohydrate consisting of a sugar chemically linked to a lipid

lip·o·pro·tein /lìppō prṓ teen, lī̀pō-/ *n.* a protein that contains a lipid molecule and carries lipids in the bloodstream

lip·o·some /líppə sōm, lī́pə-/ *n.* a tiny artificial sac formed from one or more layers of lipid, used medicinally to carry a drug, vaccine, or enzyme to targeted cells in the body

lip·o·suc·tion /líppə sùkshən, lī́pə-/ *n.* cosmetic surgery in which fat is removed from under the skin by vacuum suction

lip·o·trop·ic /lìppō tróppik, lī̀pō-/ *adj.* preventing or reducing the accumulation of fat in the liver

lip·o·tro·pin /lìppō trṓpin, lī̀pō-/ *n.* either of two hormones produced in the pituitary gland that play a part in using up fat reserves in the body and are a source of endorphins

-lipped *suffix.* having a particular kind of lip or lips

Lip·piz·an·er *n.* = **Lipizzaner**

Lipp·mann /lípmən/, **Walter** (1889–1974) U.S. journalist. He was joint founder of the liberal magazine *New Republic* (1914), and won two Pulitzer Prizes.

lip·py /líppee/ (**-pi·er, -pi·est**) *adj.* tending to say impudent things (*informal*)

lip-read /líp reed/ (**lip-read** /-red/, **lip-read·ing** /líp reeding/, **lip-reads** /líp reedz/) *vti.* to understand what is said by watching how somebody's lips move rather than by listening —**lip-read·er** *n.*

lip-read·ing *n.* understanding spoken words by watching lip movements, rather than by listening

lip salve *n. U.K.* = **lip balm**

Lip·scomb /lípskəm/, **William Nunn, Jr.** (*b.* 1919) U.S. chemist. He conducted pioneering research on the molecular structure and chemical bonding of boron compounds.

lip ser·vice *n.* support or agreement that does not appear to be sincere because the words spoken are not followed up by appropriate action or behavior

lip·stick /líp stìk/ *n.* an oily cosmetic in stick form, in a plastic or metal tube, used to color the lips

lip-synch /-singk/ (**lip-synched, lip-synch·ing, lip-synchs**), **lip-sync** (**lip-synced, lip-sync·ing, lip-syncs**) *vti.* to pretend to sing or speak by moving lips in synchronization with a recorded song or speech, or to perform a song or speech in this way

Lip·ton /líptən/, **Seymour** (1903–86) U.S. sculptor. His innovative works are constructed of sheet metals hammered into shape.

lip·u·ri·a /li pyŏoree ə/ *n.* the abnormal presence of fat in the urine [Late 19thC. From modern Latin, from Greek *lipos* "fat" + *ouron* "urine."]

liq. *abbr.* **1.** liquid **2.** liquor

li·quate /lī́ kwàyt/ (**-quat·ed, -quat·ing, -quates**) *vt.* to heat an alloy or ore to a temperature high enough to separate the constituents with the lowest melting point from the rest [Mid-17thC. From Latin *liquat-*, past participle stem of *liquare* "to liquefy."] —**li·qua·tion** /lī kwáysh'n/ *n.*

liq·ue·fa·cient /lìkwə fáysh'nt/ *n.* **SOMETHING THAT TURNS SOMETHING TO LIQUID** something that liquifies or helps to liquify something else ■ *adj.* **TURNING SOMETHING TO LIQUID** capable of liquifying or helping to liquify something [Mid-19thC. From Latin *liquefacient-*, present participle stem of *liquefacere* (see LIQUEFY).]

liq·ue·fac·tion /lìkwə fákshən/ *n.* the process of liquifying something or the state of having been liquified [14thC. From the late Latin stem *liquefaction-*, from Latin *liquefacere* (see LIQUEFY).]

liq·ue·fied pe·tro·le·um gas *n.* a mixture of petroleum gases liquefied under pressure and mainly used as heating or engine fuel

liq·ue·fy /líkwə fī/ (**-fied, -fy·ing, -fies**), **liq·ui·fy** (**-fied, -fy·ing, -fies**) *vti.* to become or cause something to become liquid [14thC. Via French *liquéfier* from Latin *liquefacere*, from *lique-*, stem of *liquere* "to be liquid" (source of English *liquid* and *liquor*) + *facere* "to make, render."] —**liq·ue·fi·a·ble** *adj.* —**liq·ue·fi·er** *n.*

li·ques·cent /li kwéssənt/ *adj.* becoming or tending to become liquid [Early 18thC. From Latin *liquescent-*, present participle stem of *liquescere* "to become liquid," from *liquere* "to be liquid."] —**li·ques·cence** *n.* —**li·ques·cen·cy** *n.*

li·queur /li kúr, -kyŏŏr/ *n.* a sweet flavored alcoholic drink usually considered an after-meal beverage [Mid-18thC. Via French from Latin *liquor* "fluid."]

liq·uid /líkwid/ *n.* **1.** SCI **FLOWING SUBSTANCE** a substance in a condition in which it flows, that is a fluid at room temperature and atmospheric pressure, and whose shape but not volume can be changed **2.** LING **FRICTIONLESS CONSONANT** a consonant that is pronounced without friction and is capable of being prolonged like a vowel. In modern English, "l" and "r" are liquids. ■ *adj.* **1.** **CONSISTING OF A LIQUID** relating to, characteristic of, or consisting of a liquid or liquids **2.** **SMOOTH AND FLUENT** moving or produced in a smooth and fluent way **3.** FIN **CONVERTIBLE TO CASH** easily converted into cash **4.** **CLEAR** clear and shining **5.** LING **ARTICULATED WITHOUT FRICTION** used to describe a consonant that is articulated without friction and capable of being prolonged like a vowel [14thC. Via Old French *liquide* from Latin *liquidus* "fluid," from *liquere* "to be fluid."] —**liq·uid·ly** *adv.* —**liq·uid·ness** *n.*

liq·uid air *n.* a pale blue mixture of gases, mainly oxygen and nitrogen, that has been cooled and liquefied to be used in manufacturing pure gases and as a refrigerant

liq·uid·am·bar /lìkwi dámbər/ (*plural* **-bars** *or* **-bar**) *n.* a tree of North and Central America and Asia that exudes a yellowish aromatic balsam. Genus: *Liquidambar*. [Late 16thC. From modern Latin, genus name, irregularly formed from Latin *liquidus* (see LIQUID) + medieval Latin *ambar* "amber."]

liq·ui·date /líkwi dàyt/ (**-dat·ed, -dat·ing, -dates**) *v.* **1.** *vti.* FIN **PAY DEBT** to pay a debt or other financial obligation **2.** *vti.* COMM **SHUT DOWN A BUSINESS** to shut down a business, paying off its liabilities from its assets, or to cease trading as a business in this way **3.** *vt.* FIN **CASH ASSETS** to turn assets into cash **4.** *vt.* **KILL** to kill or dispose of somebody [Mid-16thC. From late Latin *liquidat-*, past participle stem of *liquidare* "to melt, make clear," ultimately from Latin *liquere* "to be liquid or clear."] —**liq·ui·da·tion** /lìkwi dáysh'n/ *n.*

liq·ui·da·tor /líkwi dàytər/ *n.* somebody appointed to oversee the liquidation of a business

liq·uid crys·tal *n.* a liquid that changes between being clear and cloudy depending on variations in temperature or applied voltage and is used in some types of display unit

liq·uid-crys·tal dis·play *n.* a display of numbers or letters in a calculator, watch, or other electronic device, created by applying electricity to cells made of liquid crystal to make some of them look darker

li·quid·i·ty /li kwíddətee/ *n.* **1.** **STATE OF BEING LIQUID** the state or quality of being liquid **2.** FIN **ASSETS CONVERTING EASILY TO CASH** assets that can easily be converted into cash

liq·uid·ize /líkwi dīz/ (**-ized, -iz·ing, -iz·es**) *v.* **1.** *vti.* **TURN TO LIQUID** to become liquid or cause something to become liquid **2.** *vt.* **TURN TO LIQUID IN LIQUIDIZER** to make something solid into a liquid using a liquidizer

liq·uid meas·ure *n.* any unit or system of units for measuring liquid volume or capacity

liq·uid par·af·fin *n. U.K.* = **mineral oil**

liq·uor /líkər/ *n.* **1.** BEVERAGES **ALCOHOLIC BEVERAGE** an alcoholic drink, especially of the type produced by distillation, e.g., whiskey, rather than of the type produced by fermentation, e.g., wine or beer **2.** COOK **COOKING LIQUID** a reduced liquid or juice left after cooking food, used as a sauce or as a basis for sauces **3.** PHARM **SOLUTION OF DRUG** a concentrated solution of a drug in a liquid, usually water **4.** BEVERAGES, FOOD TECH **WATER IN WHICH MALT IS STEEPED** warm water added to malt in order to produce wort in the brewing process ■ *vti.* (**-uored, -uor·ing, -uors**) BEVERAGES, FOOD TECH **STEEP MALT IN WATER** to steep malt in warm water in order to form wort in the brewing of beer [13thC. Via Old French from Latin.]

liq·uored up *adj.* drunk (*informal*)

liq·uor store *n.* a store that sells alcoholic beverages for consumption off the premises

li·ra /leérə/ (*plural* **-re** /leér ay, -rə/) *n.* **1.** **ITALIAN UNIT OF CURRENCY** the standard unit of currency of Italy, worth 100 centesimi. See table at **currency** **2.** **TURKISH UNIT OF CURRENCY** the standard unit of currency of Turkey, worth 100 kurus **3.** **COIN WORTH ONE LIRA** a coin worth one lira [Early 17thC. Via Italian from, ultimately, Latin *libra*, a measure of weight.]

Lis·bon /lízbən/ capital and largest city of Portugal. Population: 681,063 (1991).

lisle /līl/ *n.* a strong smooth fine cotton thread or fabric used for making gloves and stockings [Mid-16thC. Named for the town of *Lisle* (Lille) in northern France, where it was originally made.]

lisp /lisp/ *n.* **1.** **SPEECH DEFECT** a minor speech defect in which the sounds "s" and "z" are pronounced like the soft "th" sound in "third" or "thick." Small children whose front teeth have not come in yet often have a temporary lisp. **2.** **SPEECH SOUND** the sound produced when "s" and "z" are pronounced like the soft "th" sound in "third" or "thick" ■ *vti.* (**lisped, lisp·ing, lisps**) **1.** **PRONOUNCE "S" LIKE "TH"** to pronounce something or speak so that "s" and "z" are pronounced like the soft "th" sound in "third" or "thick" **2.** **SPEAK LIKE A CHILD** to speak in a childish or halting way [Old English *wlyspian*, of prehistoric Germanic origin; ultimately an imitation of the sound] —**lisp·er** *n.* —**lisp·ing** *adj., n.* —**lisp·ing·ly** *adv.*

LISP /lisp/ *n.* a high-level computer programming language, widely used in artificial intelligence research, that converts data into lists [Mid-20thC. Contraction of *List Processing (language)*.]

lis·some /líssəm/, **lis·som** *adj.* **1.** **GRACEFULLY FLEXIBLE** slender and able to bend easily and gracefully **2.** **QUICK AND GRACEFUL IN MOVING** quick, light, and graceful in movement [Late 18thC. Alteration of LITHESOME.] —**lis·some·ly** *adv.* —**lis·some·ness** *n.*

list[1] /list/ *n.* **1.** **ORDERED SERIES** a series of related words, names, numbers, or other items that are arranged in order, one after the other ○ *a list of people to call* **2.** COMPUT **SET OF DATA** an ordered set of data ■ *v.* (**list·ed, list·ing, lists**) **1.** *vt.* **ARRANGE ITEMS AS ORDERED SERIES** to arrange a series of related words, names, numbers, or other items one after the other ○ *She listed the things she intended to get done that afternoon.* **2.** *vt.* **INCLUDE IN ORDERED SERIES** to include somebody or something in a series of words, numbers, or other items arranged one after the other ○ *He's listed among the founding members in the club brochure.* **3.** *vt.* **CATEGORIZE SOMEBODY** to place somebody in a category or classification ○ *She lists herself as a club member but never attends meetings.* **4.** *vt.* STOCK EXCH **ADMIT SECURITY TO EXCHANGE** to admit a security for trading on an exchange **5.** *vti.* COMM **SET OFFICIAL PRICE** to set an official retail price, e.g., in a catalog or advertisement, that can often be discounted by the retailer **6.** *vti.* **ENLIST** to enlist or enlist somebody (*archaic*) [Late 16thC. From French *liste*, ultimately of prehistoric Germanic origin.]

list[2] /list/ *vti.* (**list·ed, list·ing, lists**) **LEAN TO ONE SIDE** to lean or make a ship lean to one side ■ *n.* **SIDEWAYS TILT** an inclination to one side, especially one developed by a ship [Mid-17thC. Origin unknown.]

list[3] /list/ *n.* **1.** STRIP OF MATERIAL a band or strip of cloth or other material, especially one forming a border (*archaic*) **2.** TRIMMED STRIP OF WOOD a narrow strip of wood, especially sapwood, trimmed from a board or plank (*archaic*) **3.** AGRIC FURROWS FORMING RIDGE a ridge of earth formed by two furrows plowed side by side **4.** ARCHIT = **fillet** *n.* 3 **5.** TEXTILES SELVAGE a selvage (*archaic*) ■ **lists** *npl.* HIST, MIL FENCED AREA IN TOURNAMENT an area of combat in a medieval tournament enclosed by a fence of high stakes ■ *vt.* (**list·ed, list·ing, lists**) **1.** COVER SOMETHING WITH STRIP OF MATERIAL to cover or border something with a band or strip of cloth or other material **2.** CUT STRIP OF WOOD to cut a narrow strip of wood, especially sapwood, from a board or plank (*archaic*) **3.** AGRIC FORM RIDGE FROM FURROWS to plow together two furrows of earth to form a ridge [Old English *līste*. From a prehistoric Germanic word meaning "band, strip" that is also the ancestor of English *list*[1].] ◇ **enter the lists** to begin to take part in a fight or argument

list[4] /list/ (**list·ed, list·ing, lists**) *vti.* to listen (*archaic*) [Old English *hlystan*]

list[5] /list/ *vt.* (**list·ed, list·ing, lists**) (*archaic*) **1.** WISH SOMETHING to choose, wish, or like something **2.** PLEASE SOMEBODY to give pleasure to somebody ■ *n.* DESIRE a choice, wish, or liking (*archaic*) [Old English *lystan*. Ultimately from an Indo-European base meaning "to be eager" that is also the ancestor of English *lust* and *lascivious*.]

list·ed /lístəd/ *adj.* **1.** INCLUDED IN LIST included in a list, catalog, or directory ○ *a listed phone number* **2.** STOCK EXCH TRADABLE ON EXCHANGE placed on a list of securities that may be traded on an exchange [Formed from LIST[1]]

lis·tel /líst'l/ *n.* ARCHIT = **fillet** *n.* 3 [Late 16thC. From Italian *listello*, literally "small border," from *lista* "border"; ultimately of the same prehistoric Germanic origin as English *list*[2].]

lis·ten /líss'n/ *vi.* (**-tened, -ten·ing, -tens**) **1.** MAKE CONSCIOUS EFFORT TO HEAR to concentrate on hearing somebody or something ○ *We listened for the sound of the geese overhead.* **2.** PAY ATTENTION to pay attention to something and and take it into account ○ *She wouldn't listen to my advice.* ■ *n.* ACT OF HEARING an act of making an effort to hear something (*informal*) ○ *Why not give their new CD a listen?* [Old English *hlysnan* (influenced by LIST[4]). Ultimately from an Indo-European word meaning "to hear" that is also the ancestor of English *list*[4] and *loud*.]

listen in *vi.* **1.** EAVESDROP to listen to other people, sometimes without their knowing it **2.** LISTEN TO RADIO to listen to a radio broadcast **3.** MONITOR TELECOMMUNICATIONS to monitor radio or telephone communications

listen up *vi.* to pay attention or listen carefully (*slang*)

lis·ten·a·ble /líss'nəb'l/ *adj.* pleasant to listen to or suitable for listening to —**lis·ten·a·bil·i·ty** /lìss'nə bíllətee/ *n.*

lis·ten·er /líss'nər/ *n.* somebody who listens, especially somebody who tunes in to a radio broadcast

lis·ten·er·ship /líss'nər shìp/ *n.* the number or kind of people who listen to a radio broadcast, program, or station

lis·ten·ing post *n.* **1.** FORWARD POSITION an advanced position near enemy lines from which troops can detect the enemy's movements **2.** MONITORING PLACE a post or area where information or intelligence is gathered

lis·ter /lístər/ *n.* a plow that heaps earth on both sides of a furrow [Late 17thC. Formed from LIST[3].]

List·er /lístər/, **Joseph, 1st Baron** (1827–1912) British surgeon. His discoveries in antisepsis, which led to the use of carbolic acid during operations, greatly reduced surgical mortality.

lis·te·ri·a /lə stéeree ə/ *n.* a rod-shaped aerobic parasitic bacterium that causes disease, especially listeriosis. Genus: *Listeria.* [Mid-20thC. From modern Latin, genus name, formed from the name of Joseph LISTER.]

lis·te·ri·o·sis /lə stéeree óssiss/ *n.* a disease of the nervous system of mammals, birds, and occasionally humans that can cause fever, meningitis, miscarriage, or premature birth and is spread by eating food contaminated with listeria [Mid-20thC]

list·ing /lísting/ *n.* **1.** SOMETHING ENTERED IN LIST an entry in a list, catalog, or directory **2.** LIST a list, catalog, or directory **3.** COMPUT PRINTOUT a printout of a computer file or program **4.** STOCK EXCH PLACE ON OFFICIAL LIST OF SECURITIES a place on an official list of securities that can be traded on an exchange ■ **list·ings** *npl.* ARTS, COMMUNICATION LISTS OF EVENTS published lists of movies, plays, or other cultural events, containing information such as times, locations, and ticket prices [Mid-17thC. Formed from LIST[1].]

list·less /lístləss/ *adj.* lacking energy, interest, or the willingness to make an effort [15thC. Formed from LIST[5], literally "without pleasure."] —**list·less·ly** *adv.* —**list·less·ness** *n.*

Lis·ton /lístən/, **Sonny** (1917?–70) U.S. boxer. As world heavyweight champion (1962–64), he was noted for his power and physical stature. Real name **Charles Liston**

list price *n.* a published or advertised retail price of something that can often be discounted by the seller

list·serv /líst sùrv/ *n.* a free service available on the internet that is like a forum that allows users to discuss a subject via e-mail

Franz Liszt

Liszt /list/, **Franz** (1811–86) Hungarian pianist, composer, and conductor. His compositions, including *A Faust Symphony* (1857), arrangements, and transcriptions for piano, influenced other composers. He was a brilliant virtuoso pianist.

lit[1] past participle of **light**[1] *v.* 2. past tense of **light**[1] *v.* 1

lit[2] *adj.* drunk (*slang*)

lit. *abbr.* **1.** liter **2.** literal **3.** literally **4.** literary **5.** literature

lit·a·ny /lítt'nee/ (*plural* **-nies**) *n.* **1.** CHR PRAYERS DURING WORSHIP a series of sung or spoken liturgical prayers or requests for the blessing of God, including invocations from a priest or minister and responses from a congregation **2.** LONG REPETITIOUS LIST a long and repetitious list of things such as complaints or problems ○ *recited a litany of complaints about the system* [13thC. Via Old French *letanie* from, ultimately, Greek *litaneia* "prayer," from *litanos* "entreating," from *litē* "supplication," of unknown origin.]

Lit.B. = **Litt.B.**

li·tchi *n.* = **lychee**

lit. crit. *abbr.* literary criticism

Lit.D. = **Litt.D.** [Shortening of Latin *Litterarum Doctor*]

lite /līt/ *adj.* low in alcohol, calories, sugar, or fat (*used especially in labeling or advertising foods and beverages*) [Mid-20thC. Variant of LIGHT.]

-lite *suffix.* mineral, rock, fossil ○ *halite* ○ *coprolite* [Via French from, ultimately, Greek *lithos* "stone"]

li·ter /léetər/ *n.* a unit of volume equal to 1 cubic decimeter or 1.056 liquid quarts [Late 18thC. Via French *litre* from, ultimately, Greek *litra*, a unit of measure.]

lit·er·a·cy /líttərəssee, líttrəssee/ *n.* **1.** ABILITY TO READ AND WRITE the ability to read and write to a competent level **2.** SKILL IN PARTICULAR SUBJECT knowledge of or training in a particular subject or area of activity ○ *computer literacy*

lit·er·al /líttərəl/ *adj.* **1.** WORD FOR WORD exactly following the order or meaning of an original word or text **2.** FOLLOWING BASIC MEANING adhering strictly to the basic meaning of an original word or text without further elaboration or interpretation ○ *a literal reading of the story of Noah* **3.** USED TO EMPHASIZE TRUTH OF SOMETHING a word used to emphasize that something is true ○ *That's the literal truth.* **4.** FACTUAL AND UNIMAGINATIVE simple in a clear unimaginative way that sticks to the facts and avoids embellishment ○ *a literal account of the incident for the court* **5.** USING ALPHABETICAL LETTERS involving or expressed by letters of the alphabet [14thC. Via Old French from Latin *literalis*, from *littera* "letter" (source of English *letter*).] —**lit·er·al·ness** *n.*

lit·er·al·ism /líttərə lìzzəm/ *n.* **1.** FAITHFULNESS TO EXPLICIT MEANING strict adherence to the basic or primary meaning of a word or text **2.** REALISM the realistic representation of something in art or literature —**lit·er·al·ist** *n.* —**lit·er·al·is·tic** /líttərə lístik/ *adj.* —**lit·er·al·is·ti·cal·ly** /-lístiklee/ *adv.*

lit·er·al·ly /líttərəlee/ *adv.* **1.** STRICTLY ADHERING TO BASIC MEANING in a way based on the explicit meaning of a word or text **2.** USED TO EMPHASIZE a word used to emphasize another word or a phrase (*informal*) ○ *I was literally freezing.*

lit·er·ar·y /líttə rèree/ *adj.* **1.** RELATING TO LITERATURE relating to literature, writing, or the study of literature **2.** FORMALLY EXPRESSED typical of literature rather than everyday speech **3.** PROFESSIONALLY INVOLVED WITH LITERATURE involved with literature or writing as a profession **4.** KNOWLEDGEABLE ABOUT LITERATURE well-read or knowledgeable about literature [Mid-17thC. From Latin *literarius* "having to do with letters," from *littera* "letter" (source of English *letter*).] —**lit·er·ar·i·ly** *adv.* —**lit·er·ar·i·ness** *n.*

lit·er·ar·y a·gent *n.* somebody whose job is to negotiate business contracts on behalf of an author

lit·er·ar·y ex·ec·u·tor *n.* somebody who is appointed to manage literary property on behalf of an author's estate

lit·er·ate /líttərət/ *adj.* **1.** ABLE TO READ AND WRITE having the ability to read and write **2.** KNOWLEDGEABLE having a good understanding of a particular subject ○ *Children have to become computer-literate.* **3.** WELL-EDUCATED AND WELL-READ well-educated and cultured, particularly with respect to literature or writing **4.** SKILLFULLY WRITTEN showing skill in the techniques of writing ○ *a literate account of the voyage* ■ *n.* **1.** SOMEBODY CAPABLE OF READING AND WRITING somebody who is able to read and write **2.** SOMEBODY WITH EXTENSIVE EDUCATION somebody who is well-educated, learned, or cultured [15thC. From Latin *litteratus* "lettered, acquainted with literature," from *littera* "letter" (source of English *letter* and *literature*).] —**lit·er·ate·ly** *adv.* —**lit·er·ate·ness** *n.*

lit·er·a·ti /líttə ráatee/ *npl.* (*formal*) **1.** HIGHLY EDUCATED PEOPLE intellectuals or the educated class **2.** PEOPLE DEEPLY INVOLVED IN LITERATURE authors and other people closely or professionally involved with literature and the arts [Early 17thC. Directly or via Italian from Latin *litterati*, literally "lettered people," from *littera* "letter."]

lit·er·a·tim /líttə ráytim/ *adv.* word for word (*formal*) [Mid-17thC. From medieval Latin, "by the letter."]

lit·er·a·tion /lìttə ráysh'n/ *n.* the representation of sounds or words by means of alphabetical letters [Early 20thC. Formed from Latin *littera* "letter" (source of English *letter*).]

lit·er·a·tor /líttə ràytər/ *n.* a littérateur (*archaic*) [Mid-17thC. From Latin, "teacher of letters," from *littera* "letter."]

lit·er·a·ture /líttərəchər, líttrəchər, -chòor/ *n.* **1.** WRITTEN WORKS WITH ARTISTIC VALUE written works such as fiction, poetry, drama, and criticism that are recognized as having important or permanent artistic value **2.** BODY OF WRITTEN WORKS the body of written works of a culture, language, people, or period of time ○ *Russian literature* **3.** WRITINGS ON SPECIFIC SUBJECT the body of published work concerned with a particular subject ○ *scientific literature* **4.** PRINTED INFORMATION printed matter that gives information, in the form of, e.g., brochures or flyers **5.** PRODUCTION OF LITERARY WORKS the creation of literary work, especially as an art or occupation [14thC. Via Old French from Latin *litteratura*, from *litteratus* "lettered" (see LITERATE).]

lith. *abbr.* **1.** lithograph **2.** lithography

Lith. *abbr.* **1.** Lithuania **2.** Lithuanian

lith- *prefix.* = **litho-** (*used before vowels*)

-lith *suffix.* **1.** mineral, rock, stone ○ *batholith* **2.** stone structure or implement ○ *megalith* ○ *microlith* **3.** calculus, concretion ○ *otolith* [Via modern Latin *-lithus* from Greek *lithos* "stone," of unknown origin]

lith·arge /lì thaárj, li thaárj/ *n.* = **lead monoxide** [14thC. Via Old French *litarge* from, ultimately, Greek *litharguros*, literally "stone-silver," from *lithos* "stone" + *arguros* "silver."]

lithe /līth/ (**lith·er, lith·est**) *adj.* able to move or bend the body lightly and gracefully ○ *a lithe gymnast* [Old English *līþe* "gentle." Ultimately from an Indo-European word meaning "flexible," which is also the ancestor of English *linden* and *relent*.] —**lithe·ly** *adv.* —**lithe·ness** *n.*

lithe·some /líthsəm/ *adj.* lithe (*archaic or literary*)

lith·i·a /líthee ə/ *n.* = **lithium oxide** [Early 19thC. Alteration of earlier *lithion* (on the model of words such as SODA, from Greek *lithos* "stone."]

li·thi·a·sis /li thí əssiss/ *n.* the formation or presence of stones formed by mineral concretions in the body, e.g., in the kidney, gallbladder, pancreas, or salivary glands [Mid-17thC. Via modern Latin from Greek, from *lithos* "stone."]

lith·ic[1] /líthik/ *adj.* **1.** GEOL **MADE OF STONE** consisting of stone **2.** MED **RELATING TO STONES IN BODY** relating to undesirable mineral concretions in the body, e.g., kidney stones [Late 18thC. From Greek *lithikos*, from *lithos* "stone."]

lith·ic[2] /líthik/ *adj.* CHEM relating to lithium [Early 19thC. Formed from LITHIUM.]

-lithic *suffix.* of a particular stage in human beings' use of stone implements ○ *Neolithic* [Formed from Greek *lithos* "stone"]

lith·i·fy /líthə fì/ (**-fied, -fy·ing, -fies**) *vti.* to change, or change something, from loose sediments into solid rock [Late 19thC. Formed from Greek *lithos* "stone."] —**lith·i·fi·ca·tion** /lìthəfi káysh'n/ *n.*

lith·i·um /líthee əm/ *n.* a soft silver-white chemical element that is the lightest metal known, used in alloys, ceramics, and batteries, and in compounds as a medical treatment for manic-depressive disorders. Symbol **Li** [Early 19thC. Coined from LITHIA + -IUM.]

lith·i·um car·bon·ate *n.* a white crystalline salt used in ceramics and glass and medicinally to treat manic-depressive disorders. Formula: Li_2CO_3.

lith·i·um flu·o·ride *n.* a white, slightly water-soluble powder used in making ceramics. Formula: LiF.

lith·i·um-ion bat·ter·y *n.* a lightweight battery charged with lithium atoms that provides more energy for a longer time than a standard battery

lith·i·um ox·ide *n.* a white alkaline solid that absorbs carbon dioxide and water vapor and is used in ceramics and glass. Formula: Li_2O.

litho., **lithog.** *abbr.* **1.** lithograph **2.** lithography

litho- *prefix.* **1.** stone ○ *lithosphere* **2.** calculus, concretion ○ *lithotomy* [From Greek *lithos* "stone," of unknown origin]

lith·o·gen·ous /li thójjənəss/ *adj.* secreting stony deposits (*refers to organisms such as coral*)

lith·o·graph /líthə gràf/ *n.* **LITHOGRAPHIC PRINT** a print made by lithography ■ *vti.* (**-graphed, -graph·ing, -graphs**) **MAKE PRINT USING LITHOGRAPHY** to make a print using the lithography process [Early 19thC. Back-formation from LITHOGRAPHY.]

li·thog·ra·phy /li thóggrəfee/ *n.* a printing process using a plate on which only the image to be printed takes up ink. The nonprinting area is treated to repel ink. [Early 19thC. From German *Lithographie*, from Greek *lithos* "stone" + *graphein* "to write"; so called because the printing plate was originally a porous stone.] —**li·thog·raph·er** *n.* —**lith·o·graph·ic** /lìthə gráffik/ *adj.* —**lith·o·graph·i·cal·ly** *adv.*

lith·oid /lí thòyd/, **lith·oid·al** /-thóyd'l/ *adj.* consisting of or resembling stone [Mid-19thC. From Greek *lithoeidēs*, from *lithos* "stone."]

li·thol·o·gy /li thóllǝjee/ *n.* **1.** **STUDY OF ROCKS** the scientific study of rocks **2.** **CHARACTERISTICS OF ROCKS** the physical characteristics of a rock or a rock formation —**lith·o·log·i·cal** /lìthə lójjik'l/ *adj.* —**lith·o·log·i·cal·ly** /-lójjikəlee/ *adv.* —**li·thol·o·gist** /li thólləjist/ *n.*

lith·o·phane /líthə fàyn/ *n.* a piece of thin translucent porcelain or china with an intaglio design [Late 19thC. Coined from LITHO- + -PHANE.]

lith·o·phyte /líthə fìt/ *n.* **1.** **PLANT GROWING ON ROCK** a plant that grows on rock and absorbs nutrients from the atmosphere **2.** **STONY ORGANISM** an organism such as a coral that is composed in part of stony material —**lith·o·phyt·ic** /lìthə fíttik/ *adj.*

lith·o·pone /líthə pōn/ *n.* a white pigment that is a mixture of barium sulfate and zinc sulfide and is used in making paints and linoleum [Late 19thC. Coined from Greek LITHO- + *ponos* "product."]

lith·o·sol /líthə sàwl/ *n.* a type of soil with poorly defined horizons that consists mainly of partially weathered rock fragments [Early 20thC. Coined from LITHO- + Latin *solum* "soil."]

lith·o·sphere /líthə sfeer/ *n.* the solid outer layer of the Earth above the asthenosphere, consisting of the crust and upper mantle —**lith·o·sphe·ric** /líthə sfeèrik, lìthə sférrik/ *adj.*

li·thot·o·my /li thóttəmee/ (*plural* **-mies**) *n.* the surgical removal of a stone from an organ or duct of the body, especially the urinary tract or bladder —**lith·o·tom·ic** /lìthə tómmik/ *adj.* —**lith·o·tom·ist** /li thóttəmist/ *n.*

lith·o·trip·sy /líthō trìpsee/ *n.* the fragmentation of a stone in the urinary system or gallbladder, e.g., with ultrasound shock waves, so that the gravel can be passed naturally [Mid-19thC. Coined from LITHO- + Greek *tripsis* "rubbing, crushing."]

lith·o·trip·ter /líthō trìptər/ *n.* a device that breaks up kidney stones using ultrasound shock waves [Early 19thC. Alteration of earlier *lithotriptor*, from, ultimately, Greek *lithon thruptika* "capable of pulverizing stones," from *lithos* "stone" + *thruptein* "to crush."]

Lithuania

Lith·u·a·ni·a /lìthoo áynee ə/ republic bordering the Baltic Sea in northeastern Europe. Language: Lithuanian. Currency: litas. Capital: Vilnius. Population: 3,617,104 (1997). Area: 25,200 sq. mi./65,300 sq. km. Official name **Republic of Lithuania**

Lith·u·a·ni·an /lìthoo áynee ən/ *n.* **1.** PEOPLES **SOMEBODY FROM LITHUANIA** somebody who was born or lives in Lithuania **2.** LANG **OFFICIAL LANGUAGE OF LITHUANIA** the official language of Lithuania, also spoken in western parts of European Russia, belonging to the Balto-Slavonic branch of Indo-European languages. Lithuanian is spoken by about four million people. —**Lith·u·a·ni·an** *adj.*

lit·i·ga·ble /líttigəb'l/ *adj.* able to be pursued in court

lit·i·gant /líttigənt/ *n.* somebody engaged in a lawsuit —**lit·i·gant** *adj.*

lit·i·gate /lítti gàyt/ (**-gat·ed, -gat·ing, -gates**) *vti.* to contest or be involved in a lawsuit [Early 17thC. From Latin *litigat-*, past participle stem of *litigare*, from *lit-*, the stem of *lis* "lawsuit" + *agere* "to drive, pursue."] —**lit·i·ga·tor** *n.*

lit·i·ga·tion /lìtti gáysh'n/ *n.* **1.** **EXISTENCE OF LAWSUIT** the act or process of bringing about or contesting a lawsuit or all lawsuits collectively ○ *The matter is in litigation.* **2.** **LAWSUIT** a lawsuit (*technical*)

li·ti·gious /li tíjjəss/ *adj.* **1.** **RELATING TO LEGAL ACTION** relating to litigation **2.** **INCLINED TO GO TO LAW** tending or wanting to take legal action ○ *a litigious person* **3.** **QUARRELSOME** inclined to quarrel or argue (*formal*) [14thC. From French *litigieux*, from, ultimately, Latin *litigium* "litigation," from *litigare* "to quarrel" (see LITIGATE).] —**li·ti·gious·ly** *adv.* —**li·ti·gious·ness** *n.*

lit·mus /lítməss/ *n.* a powdery substance obtained from lichens that is used to indicate whether something is an acid or a base, turning red in acids and blue in bases [14thC. From Old Norse *litmosi*, from *litr* "dye" + *mosi* "moss."]

lit·mus pa·per *n.* a strip of paper treated with litmus, used to find out if something is an acid or a base

lit·mus test *n.* **1.** **TEST TO IDENTIFY ACID OR BASE** a test in which litmus is used to find out if something is an acid or a base **2.** **TEST DETERMINED BY SINGLE FACTOR** a test in which a single factor determines the outcome ○ *The candidate's stance on free trade was a litmus for the nomination.*

li·to·tes /lítə teez, líttə teez, lī tṓ teez/ (*plural* **-tes**) *n.* a deliberate understatement, such as an affirmative statement formed by a negation of the contrary, as in the sentence "I am not unmindful of your devotion" [Late 16thC. Via late Latin from Greek *litotēs*, from *litos* "simple, plain."]

li·tre *n. U.K.* = **liter** [Late 18thC. Via French from, ultimately, Greek *litre*, a unit of measure.]

Litt.B., **Lit.B.** *abbr.* **1.** Bachelor of Letters **2.** Bachelor of Literature [From Latin *Litterarum Baccalaureus*]

Litt.D., **Lit.D.** *abbr.* **1.** Doctor of Letters **2.** Doctor of Literature [From latin *Litterarum Doctor*]

lit·ter /líttər/ *n.* **1.** **SCATTERED TRASH** pieces of trash that have been carelessly left on the ground, especially in a public place or the outdoors **2.** **MESSY STATE OR PLACE** a large number of objects that have been scattered around untidily or a place that is in a messy state ○ *I found her working away in the litter of her study.* **3.** ZOOL **ANIMAL OFFSPRING** a group of young animals born at the same time from the same mother **4.** AGRIC **BEDDING FOR ANIMALS** material such as hay or straw that is used as bedding for animals **5.** **MATERIAL FOR PET'S TOILET BOX** a dry absorbent substance, often in the form of granules, that is spread in a shallow container where a pet, especially a cat, can urinate or defecate when indoors **6.** **GROUND SURFACE OF FOREST** the surface layer of a forest floor, consisting of partly decomposed leaves and twigs **7.** **STRETCHER WITH LONG SHAFTS** a piece of cloth stretched between two long poles on either side that is used to carry a sick person or a dead body (*dated*) **8.** HIST **COUCH FOR CARRYING PASSENGER** a couch with poles on either side, used to transport a single passenger on people's shoulders or on animals. It is often enclosed with curtains. ■ *v.* (**-tered, -ter·ing, -ters**) **1.** *vti.* **DROP TRASH** to make a place, especially a public place or the outdoors, messy by leaving pieces of trash behind **2.** *vt.* **COVER PLACE WITH SCATTERED OBJECTS** to put a place in disorder by leaving scattered objects in it ○ *Toys littered the playroom floor.* **3.** *vt.* **FILL WITH THINGS** to fill something with or contain many examples of a particular thing ○ *an essay littered with spelling mistakes* **4.** *vti.* ZOOL **HAVE YOUNG** to give birth to young (*refers to animals*) **5.** *vt.* AGRIC **SUPPLY ANIMAL WITH BEDDING** to provide an animal with hay or straw for bedding [14thC. Via Anglo-Norman *litere* from medieval Latin *lectaria*, from Latin *lectus* "bed." Ultimately from an Indo-European word meaning "to lie," which is also the ancestor of English *lie*[1].] —**lit·ter·er** *n.*

lit·tér·a·teur /lìttərə túr/ *n.* somebody closely involved with literature, especially a professional writer (*archaic*) [Early 19thC. Via French from Latin *litterator*, from *littera* "letter."]

lit·ter·bug /líttər bùg/ *n.* somebody who leaves litter, especially in public places or outdoors (*informal*)

lit·ter·mate /líttər màyt/ *n.* one of several animal young born or reared in the same litter

lit·tle /lítt'l/ (**-tler, -tlest**) CORE MEANING: an adjective meaning "small" or "young," or a grammatical word indicating that something exists in small quantities ○ (adj) *It was only a very little mistake!* ○ (adj) *He was helping the little boy put on his boots.* ○ (adj) *I'll bring my little sister with me.* ○ (adj) *There was a little food left.* ○ (adj) *There was little chance of winning.*

1. *adj.* **SMALL** small or of less than average size ○ *He gave her a little Christmas tree ornament.* **2.** *adj.* **YOUNG** young ○ *I met her when she was just a little girl.* **3.** *adj.* **YOUNGER** refers to a younger sister or brother ○ *My little sister is always causing problems.* **4.** *adj.* **SMALL AND PLEASANT** small in a pleasant or good looking way ○ *a cute little button nose* ○ *one of his sweet little habits* **5.** *adj.* **SHORT** short or quick ○ *Wait a little while.* ○ *He turned and gave them a little nod.* **6.** *adj.* **TRIVIAL** of no importance ○ *It's the little things that count when you're sharing a house with somebody.* **7.** *adj., pron.* **A SMALL AMOUNT** a small amount of something (*used after "a"*) ○ (adj) *She was given a little alimony and a little child support.* ○ *We paid only a little for it.* ○ *A little of what you desire does you good.* **8.** *adj., pron.* **NOT MUCH** only a very small amount ○ (adj) *The cleanups had little or no effect on the environment.* ○ *She would eat very little.* ○ *Little of what was said meant much to me.* **9.** *adv.* **HARDLY** hardly or not at all ○ *He little knew what was in store for him.* **10.** *adv.* **NOT OFTEN** on rare occasions ○ *We visit him very little these days.* [Old English *lȳtel*. From a prehistoric Germanic base meaning "small," which is also the ancestor of English *lout*.] ◇ **little by little** gradually; by small degrees ○ *Little by little I grew too drowsy to think – then too lazy to go on walking.* ◇ **no little** considerable ○ *They commenced eating with no little appetite.* ◇ **not a little** a lot ○ *I was pretty shocked and not a little embarrassed.* ◇ **quite a little** to a considerable degree or extent ○ *The rest* *of the evening was quite a little triumph for her.* ◇ **think little of** to have a low opinion of ○ *I have learned not to think little of anyone else's beliefs.*

Lit·tle /lítt'l/, **Rich** (*b.* 1938) Canadian impressionist. His impressions of contemporary figures, especially Richard Nixon, made him popular on Canadian and U.S. television.

lit·tle auk *n.* = **dovekie**

Lit·tle Bear *n.* = **Ursa Minor**

Lit·tle Big·horn /lítt'l bíg hawrn/ river in southern Montana. (**General George Custer**) and his army were defeated by Native Americans on its banks in 1876. Length: 90 mi./145 km.

lit·tle-bit·ty *adj.* extremely small (*informal*)

Lit·tle Di·o·mede /lítt'l dí ə meed/ the smaller of two islands situated in the middle of the Bering Strait between Alaska and Russia. It belongs to the United States. Area: 2.4 sq. mi./6 sq. km.

Lit·tle Dip·per *n.* = **Ursa Minor**

Lit·tle Falls /lítt'l fáwlz/ city and county seat of Morrison County, central Minnesota, situated 25 mi./40 km south of Brainerd. Population: 6,041 (1990).

lit·tle fin·ger *n.* the smallest finger of the human hand, located farthest from the thumb

lit·tle folk *npl.* = **little people** *npl.* **2**

Little grebe

lit·tle grebe *n.* a small diving bird with brown plumage, the smallest European grebe. Latin name: *Tachybaptus ruficollis.*

lit·tle green man *n.* an imaginary person from outer space (*humorous*)

lit·tle guy *n.* an average person, as opposed to an important or wealthy one ○ *felt that big business was always trampling on the little guy*

lit·tle hours, **Lit·tle Hours** *npl.* the hours of prime, terce, sext, and nones in the divine office to be recited every day by members of Roman Catholic orders

Lit·tle John *n.* in English legend, a particularly tall and strong member of Robin Hood's band of men

Lit·tle League *n.* a baseball league for boys and girls from 8 to 12 years old, divided into administrative bodies for the United States, Canada, South America, the Far East, and Europe —**Little Leaguer** *n.*

lit·tle mag·a·zine *n.* a literary magazine primarily made up of work by writers who have yet to become established, usually having a limited circulation and a small format

lit·tle man *n.* **1.** = **little guy 2. SMALL BUSINESS PERSON OR INVESTOR** somebody who operates a small business or invests on a small scale

Lit·tle Mis·sou·ri /lítt'l mizŏŏree/ river in the northwestern United States, rising in Wyoming, flowing eastward into the Missouri River. Length: 560 mi./9,012 km.

lit·tle·neck, **lit·tle·neck clam** *n.* a small young quahog clam, often eaten raw [Mid-19thC. Named for *Little Neck* Bay, Long Island, New York, where the clams were once plentiful.]

lit·tle of·fice, **Lit·tle Of·fice** *n.* CHR a Roman Catholic office similar to but shorter than a divine office, especially a liturgical service of psalms and prayers to the Virgin Mary

lit·tle owl *n.* a small owl, native to Europe, Africa, and Asia, that eats insects and small rodents and has speckled brown feathers, a broad head, and a low forehead. Genus: *Athene noctua.*

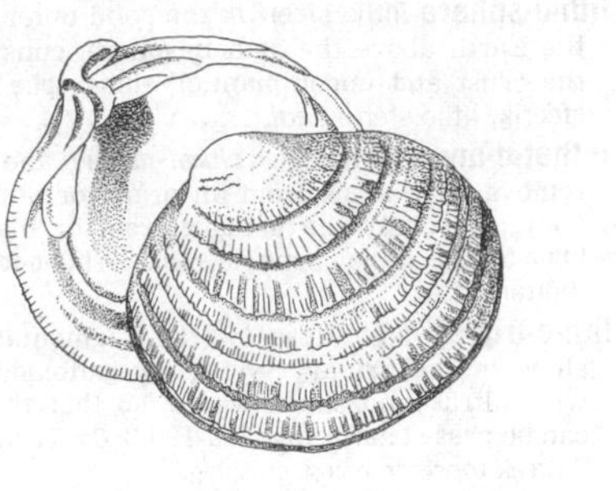

Littleneck

lit·tle peo·ple *npl.* **1. PEOPLE LACKING MONEY AND POWER** people who are typical in having a small or average income and minimal power and influence **2. SMALL SUPERNATURAL BEINGS** tiny imaginary or mythological beings such as fairies, elves, and leprechauns **3. CHILDREN** small children (*informal*)

Lit·tle Richard (*b.* 1935) U.S. pianist and singer. A pioneer of rock-and-roll, his performance of songs such as "Tutti Frutti" and "Good Golly Miss Molly" made them classics of the genre. Real name **Richard Wayne Penniman**

Lit·tle Rock /lítt'l rŏk/ capital of Arkansas and port in central Arkansas, on the Arkansas River. Population: 175,752 (1996).

lit·tle slam *n.* the winning of 12 out of the 13 tricks in a deal in the game of bridge

lit·tle the·a·ter *n.* **1. SMALL EXPERIMENTAL THEATER** a small, usually noncommercial theater that produces experimental drama **2. EXPERIMENTAL NONCOMMERCIAL DRAMA** a form of noncommercial drama emphasizing experimental work **3. THEATER GROUP IN SMALL TOWN** an amateur theatrical group that puts on plays in small cities and towns

lit·tle toe *n.* the fifth and smallest toe of the human foot, located farthest from the big toe

Lit·tle·ton /lítt'ltən/ city and county seat of Arapahoe County, central Colorado, situated 8 mi./13 km south of Denver. Population: 33,685 (1990).

lit·tle wom·an *n.* an offensive term for a wife (*dated offensive*)

lit·to·ral /líttərəl/ *adj.* **1. ON OR NEAR A SHORE** on or near a shore, especially the zone between the high and low tide marks **2. SHORE-LIVING** living on or near a shore ■ *n.* **SHORE** a shore or coastal region [Mid-17thC. From Latin *littoralis*, from *litor-*, the stem of *litus* "shore."]

lit up *adj.* drunk (*slang*)

li·tur·gi·cal /li túrjik'l/, **li·tur·gic** /li túrjik/ *adj.* **1. OF LITURGY** relating to liturgy **2. RELATING TO WORSHIP** relating to religious worship or to a service of worship, especially the Communion —**li·tur·gi·cal·ly** *adv.*

li·tur·gics /li túrjiks/ *npl.* the study of public worship or liturgies (*takes a singular verb*)

li·tur·gi·ol·o·gy /lə tùrjee áwləjee/ *n.* = **liturgics** —**li·tur·gi·ol·o·gist** *n.*

lit·ur·gist /líttərjist/ *n.* **1. SOMEBODY WHO STUDIES LITURGIES** somebody who studies or compiles liturgies **2. PRACTITIONER OF LITURGY** somebody who practices the liturgy **3. SUPPORTER OF LITURGIES** somebody who favors using liturgies —**lit·ur·gism** *n.* —**lit·ur·gis·tic** /líttər jístik/ *adj.*

lit·ur·gy /líttərjee/ (*plural* **-gies**) *n.* a form and arrangement of public worship laid down by a church or religion [Mid-16thC. Via Old French *liturgie* from, ultimately, Greek *leitourgia* "public worship service," from *leitourgos* "public servant," from *leitos* "public" + *ergon* "work."]

Lit·ur·gy (*plural* **-gies**), **liturgy** (*plural* **liturgies**) *n.* the form of service used to celebrate Communion in a Christian denomination, especially the Eucharist in Eastern churches

Liu Shaoqi /lyŏŏ shòw chée/ (1898–1969) Chinese political leader. He became vice-chairman of the communist party in 1959 but was forced from office during the Cultural Revolution (1966–69). Alternate name **Liu Shao-ch'i**

liv·a·ble /lívvəb'l/, **live·a·ble** *adj.* **1. COMFORTABLE** comfortable or suitable for living in ○ *a very livable apartment* **2. WORTH LIVING** endurable and worthwhile ○ *It's very tense at home, but still livable.* **3. ENJOYABLE AS LIVING COMPANION** enjoyable to live with —**liv·a·ble·ness** *n.* —**liv·a·bil·i·ty** /lìvvə bíllətee/ *n.*

live[1] /liv/ (**lived, liv·ing, lives**) *v.* **1.** *vi.* **BE ALIVE** to be alive or have life **2.** *vi.* **STAY ALIVE** to remain alive or to continue living ○ *lived through a serious illness last year* **3.** *vi.* **MAKE A HOME** to reside in a particular place or way ○ *He lived in Bangkok for two years.* ○ *She lives alone.* **4.** *vti.* **LEAD CERTAIN TYPE OF EXISTENCE** to have a particular kind of life ○ *live comfortably* **5.** *vi.* **MAKE A LIVING** to earn or make a living ○ *She wants to be an actor but lives by waiting on tables.* **6.** *vti.* **FULLY ENJOY LIFE** to enjoy life to the fullest ○ *He really knows how to live.* **7.** *vi.* **CONTINUE** to persist or continue ○ *Her fame lives on.* **8.** *vt.* **EXPERIENCE** to experience or go through something ○ *earthquake survivors living a nightmare* **9.** *vti.* **MAKE LIFE CONFORM** to make your life conform to something such as a philosophy or religion ○ *lived her faith* ○ *lived by strict rules* **10.** *vi.* **BE KEPT SOMEWHERE** to be found or kept in a particular place (*informal*) ○ *The spare car keys live in this drawer.* [Old English *libban, lifian.* Ultimately from an Indo-European word meaning "fat, to stick," which is also the ancestor of English *lipo-*; in prehistoric Germanic it developed the sense "to continue, live."] ◇ **live and let live** to be tolerant of others ◇ **live it up** to live or celebrate in an extravagant way (*slang*)

WORD KEY: SYNONYMS

See Synonyms at ***living.***

live down *vt.* to live in a blameless or commendable way long enough for something shameful to be forgotten

live in *vi.* to live at your place of work

live off, live on *vt.* to depend on somebody or something as a source of financial support or for a livelihood ○ *He lived off his parents.* ○ *They live on a small private income.*

live on *vt.* **1.** = **live off 2. EAT TO SURVIVE** to eat a certain type of food in order to survive or thrive ○ *The koala lives on eucalyptus leaves.*

live out *v.* **1.** *vt.* **DO SOMETHING PREVIOUSLY IMAGINED** to do in reality what had previously only been imagined or fantasized about ○ *live out a dream* **2.** *vt.* **LIVE UNTIL END OF PERIOD** to spend the rest of your life or a period of time in a certain manner or place **3.** *vi.* **LIVE SOMEWHERE OTHER THAN WORKPLACE** to live away from the place where you work

live through *vt.* to experience and survive something difficult or dangerous

live together *vi.* to share the same home and have a sexual relationship without being married

live up to *vt.* to meet somebody's expectations or desires, or match somebody's good example

live with *vt.* to accept or tolerate something difficult or unpleasant ○ *The house is tiny, but we'll just have to live with it.*

live[2] /līv/ *adj.* **1. LIVING** alive or living **2. BROADCAST AS IT HAPPENS** broadcast while an event is happening ○ *Tonight's show is live from Paris.* **3. IN PERSON** appearing or performing in front of an audience or in person, rather than recorded or filmed ○ *I'd rather dance to live music.* **4. RECORDED DURING PERFORMANCE** recorded while a performance is happening ○ *live footage of the concert* **5. RELEVANT TO CURRENT CONCERNS** relevant to current interests or concerns ○ *a live topic* **6.** ELEC **CONNECTED TO POWER SOURCE** connected to an electrical power source ○ *a live wire* **7. CHARGED WITH EXPLOSIVE** containing an explosive and able to be used ○ *live ammunition* **8.** SPORTS **IN PLAY** used to describe a ball, such as a baseball or a football, that remains in play because officials have not halted action (*informal*) **9. BURNING** burning or glowing ○ *live coals* **10.** GEOL **ACTIVE** used to describe a volcano that is still active **11. BRIGHT OR VIVID** bright or brilliant, especially in terms of color **12. WITH LIVING BACTERIA** made using living bacteria ○ *live yogurt cultures* **13. HIGHLY RESONANT** with highly resonant or reverberant acoustics **14.** GEOL **FOUND AS ORIGINAL ROCK** used to describe a rock or mineral that is found free and not mined or quarried ■ *adv.* **1. IN PERSON** in front of an audience or in person ○ *performing live here tomorrow night* **2. BROADCAST WHILE EVENT HAPPENS** broadcast at exactly the same time as a performance or event happens ○ *a live transmission* [Mid-16thC. Shortening of ALIVE.]

live·bear·er *n.* a fish that gives birth to living young, rather than producing eggs —**live·bear·ing** *adj.*

live birth *n.* the birth of a living infant —**live-born** *adj.*

lived-in *adj.* **1.** SLIGHTLY UNTIDY BUT HOMEY with a comfortable but slightly worn or untidy look that it is consistent with actual or current occupation **2.** CAREWORN showing the effects of life's experiences

liv·e·do /li veédō, lī veédō/ (*plural* **-dos**) *n.* a bluish-black patch of discolored skin caused by the settling of blood, especially after death [From modern Latin, formed from Latin *livere* (see LIVID), on the model of COMEDO]

live fire *adj.* using live ammunition and loaded weapons, usually for military tests or training

live-for·ev·er *n.* **1.** = **houseleek 2.** = **orpine** [So called because it lives for a long time]

live-in *adj.* **1.** LIVING AT PLACE OF WORK living in your place of employment ○ *a live-in nanny* **2.** SHARING HOME sharing a home with a sexual partner —**live-in** *n.*

live·li·hood /lívlee hoŏd/ *n.* work done to earn a living, or whatever provides a source of income [13thC. Alteration (influenced by LIVELY and -HOOD) of Old English *līflād* "way of living," from *līf* "life" + *lād* "way."]

live load *n.* the variable load or weight borne by a structure such as a bridge, in addition to its own weight

live·long[1] /lív làwng/ *adj.* used to emphasize how long a period of time seems to last or how tedious it feels (*literary*) ○ *We worked all the livelong day.* [14thC. From LIEF + LONG, literally "dearly long," influenced by LIVE[1].]

live·long[2] *n.* PLANTS = **orpine** [Late 16thC. From LIVE[1] + LONG; from its longevity.]

live·ly /lívlee/ (**-li·er, -li·est**) *adj.* **1.** FULL OF ENERGY full of life and energy ○ *two lively children* **2.** ANIMATED animated, exciting, or intellectually stimulating ○ *A lively discussion ensued.* **3.** ENTHUSIASTIC active and enthusiastic ○ *Pat takes a lively interest in local politics.* **4.** FULL OF MOVEMENT full of activity or movement ○ *a lively dance* **5.** VIVID clear, distinct, and vivid ○ *possessed a lively recollection of the events of that summer* **6.** BRILLIANT IN COLOR bright and colorful in a good looking way **7.** REFRESHING stimulating or refreshing ○ *a lively little breeze* **8.** SPRINGY bouncy or springy ○ *a lively ball* **9.** SAILING RESPONSIVE very responsive to the helm [Old English *līflīc* "life-like"] —**live·li·ly** *adv.* —**live·li·ness** *n.* ◇ **look lively, step lively** hurry up and get going

li·ven /lív'n/ (**-vened, -ven·ing, -vens**) *vti.* to become, or make somebody or something, lively or cheerful ○ *What can we do to liven up the party?* ○ *At the sound of its trainer's voice, the sick horse livened considerably.* [Early 18thC. Formed from LIFE.] —**li·ven·er** *n.*

live oak *n.* **1.** EVERGREEN OAK OF SOUTHERN UNITED STATES an evergreen oak of Mexico and the southern United States that has a short broad trunk and shiny leaves. The live oak is the state tree of Georgia. Latin name: *Quercus virginianus.* **2.** WOOD OF LIVE OAK the hard strong wood of the live oak tree [From LIVE[2]; from its being evergreen]

live one *n.* **1.** = **live wire** *n.* **1** (*informal slang*) **2.** DUPE somebody who is easily cheated or duped (*informal*)

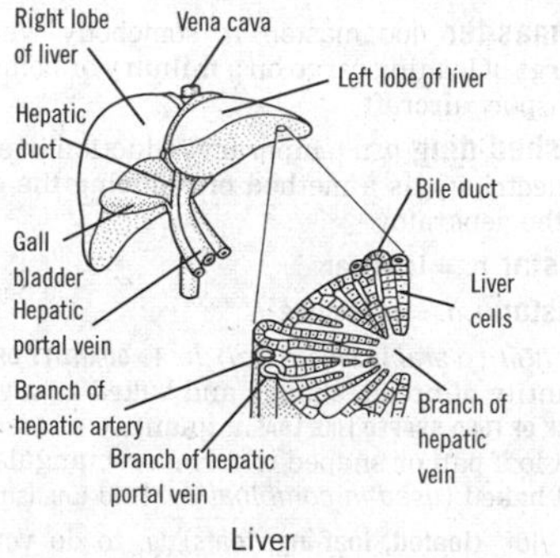

Liver

liv·er[1] /lívvər/ *n.* **1.** ANAT LARGE VITAL ORGAN a vascular glandular organ in vertebrates that secretes bile, stores and filters blood, and takes part in many metabolic functions, e.g., the conversion of sugars into glycogen. The liver is reddish-brown, multilobed, and in humans is located in the upper right part of the abdominal cavity. **2.** INVERTEBRATE ORGAN any of various glandular organs of invertebrates that are involved with digestion and metabolism **3.** LIVER CONSIDERED AS FOOD the liver of an animal or fish eaten as food or taken as medicine **4.** COLORS DARK BROWN COLOR a dark brown color with a tinge of red or gray ■ *adj.* COLORS OF DARK BROWN COLOR of a dark brown color with a tinge of red or gray [Old English *lifer.* Ultimately from an Indo-European word meaning "fat, to stick," later "to continue," hence "life"; the liver was once thought to be the organ that made blood.]

liv·er[2] /lívvər/ *n.* somebody who lives in a specified way ○ *a fast liver* [14thC. Formed from LIVE[1].]

liv·er fluke *n.* a parasitic worm that infests the liver of mammals, including humans. Latin name: *Fasciola hepatica.*

liv·er·ied /lívvəreed/ *adj.* wearing a livery ○ *the monarch's liveried attendants*

liv·er·ish /lívvərish/, **liv·er·y** /lívvəree, lívvree/ *adj.* **1.** IRRITABLE bad-tempered or irritable **2.** LIKE LIVER resembling liver, especially in color (*informal*) **3.** WITH LIVER DISORDER affected by a liver disorder — **liv·er·ish·ness** *n.*

Liv·er·more /lívvər màwr/ city in Alameda County, western California, situated 23 mi./37 km east of San Francisco Bay. Population: 56,741 (1990).

Liv·er·pool /lívvər pōol/ port and university city in northwestern England, on the Mersey River. Population: 470,800 (1995).

Liv·er·pud·li·an /lìvvər púddlee ən/ *n.* somebody who lives in or comes from Liverpool, England [Mid-19thC. Formed from an alteration of LIVERPOOL, substituting *puddle* for *pool.*] —**Liv·er·pud·li·an** *adj.*

liv·er sau·sage *n. U.K.* = **liverwurst**

liv·er spot *n.* a usually dark brown patch of pigmentation on the skin, usually occurring later in life. It is caused by an aggregation of cells containing melanin. [From its color]

liv·er·wort /lívvər wùrt, -wàwrt/ *n.* a small dense green plant that grows on moist surfaces and resembles moss. Class: Hepaticae. [Old English *liferwyrt*, a translation of medieval Latin *hepatica.* So called from its lobed shape, thought to resemble the liver.]

liv·er·wurst /lívvər wùrst/ *n.* a sausage containing cooked ground liver. It is usually eaten cold as a spread. [Mid-19thC. Partial translation of German *Leberwurst* "liver sausage."]

liv·er·y[1] /lívvəree, lívvree/ (*plural* **-ies**) *n.* **1.** UNIFORM an identifying uniform worn by members of a group or trade, especially men and boys who are servants of a household or feudal retainers **2.** UNIFORMED GROUP the members of a group or trade who wear a livery (*archaic*) **3.** CHARACTERISTIC APPEARANCE a distinctive coloring, marking, dress, or outward appearance (*literary*) **4.** PROFESSIONAL CARE OF HORSES the care, feeding, and stabling of horses for money **5.** RENTING OF HORSES the business of renting out horses **6.** = **livery stable 7.** BUSINESS THAT RENTS VEHICLES a company that rents vehicles such as cars, bicycles, or boats [14thC. From Old French *livree* "delivery," from, ultimately, Latin *liberare* "to liberate," from *liber* "free" (see LIBERAL).]

liv·er·y[2] *adj.* = **liverish**

liv·er·y·man /lívvəreemən, lívvreemən/ (*plural* **-men**) *n.* somebody who owns or works in a livery stable

liv·er·y stable, **livery** (*plural* **liveries**) *n.* **1.** STABLE THAT RENTS OUT HORSES a stable where horses and carriages are kept for rent **2.** PLACE THAT STABLES HORSES a stable that accommodates and looks after horses for their owners

live·stock /lív stòk/ *n.* animals raised for food or other products, or kept for use, especially farm animals such as meat and dairy cattle, pigs, and poultry

live trap *n.* a trap designed to catch a wild animal without injuring it

live wire *n.* **1.** ELEC WIRE CONNECTED TO POWER SOURCE a wire connected to a source of voltage **2.** ENERGETIC PERSON somebody who is keen and energetic (*informal*)

liv·ey·ere /liv yáir/ *n. Can* a permanent resident of Newfoundland [Mid-19thC. Variant of *livier* "lifelong tenant," from LIFE + -IER.]

liv·id /lívvid/ *adj.* **1.** FURIOUS very angry **2.** WITH BLUISH BRUISED COLOR bluish or discolored as a result of bruising **3.** ASHEN very pale, especially when this is not natural **4.** GRAYISH tinged with gray [15thC. Directly or via Old French from Latin *lividus*, from *livere* "to be bluish in color." Ultimately from an Indo-European word that is also the ancestor of English *sloe.*] —**li·vid·i·ty** /li víddətee/ *n.* —**liv·id·ly** /lívvidlee/ *adv.*

liv·ing /lívving/ *adj.* **1.** ALIVE alive, not dead **2.** LIKE THE REAL THING realistic or true to life ○ *a living likeness* **3.** INTERESTING AND RELEVANT interesting in a way that is relevant and useful ○ *make history a living subject* **4.** SUITABLE FOR DOMESTIC LIFE designed for living in, especially for social and recreational activities ○ *lots of living space in the home* **5.** STILL USED still used or in existence ○ *a living language* **6.** NATURAL in a natural condition or place ○ *living water* ■ *n.* **1.** MONEY OR MEANS OF EARNING a means of earning money to live on, or the money somebody earns to live on ○ *What do you do for a living?* **2.** MAINTENANCE OF WAY OF LIFE a means of sustaining or maintaining a way of life ○ *improve your standard of living* **3.** MANNER OF LIFE quality of life or the way in which it is lived ○ *likes country living* ■ *npl.* THOSE WHO ARE ALIVE people who are alive (*takes a plural verb*)

WORD KEY: SYNONYMS

living, alive, live, animate, extant

CORE MEANING: having life or existence

living used to indicate that a person is not dead. It can also be used to describe something such a language or way of life that has not died out; **alive** used to indicate that a person, animal, or plant is not dead. It can also be used to indicate that a feeling of vitality is strong in a person; **animate** a formal word used to indicate that something is alive. It is also used to describe things such as animals and plants that live, as opposed to things such as rocks, water, or buildings that do not; **extant** a formal word emphasizing the continuing existence or survival of something.

liv·ing death *n.* a life or period of time that is full of misery or pain

liv·ing do·nor *n.* somebody who, while still alive, donates all or part of an organ for transplantation

liv·ing fos·sil *n.* an organism that is virtually unchanged from early geologic time and belongs to a group whose other members are extinct. Gingko trees and coelacanths are living fossils.

liv·ing pic·ture *n.* = **tableau vivant**

liv·ing room *n.* a room in a house where people usually relax or entertain guests

liv·ing stan·dard *n.* = **standard of living**

Liv·ing·ston /lívvingstən/, **Henry Brockholst** (1757–1823) U.S. jurist. He was an officer in the Revolution and served on the U.S. Supreme Court (1806–23).

Liv·ing·ston, Philip (1716–78) U.S. patriot, businessman, and philanthropist. He was one of the signatories of the Declaration of Independence (1776).

Liv·ing·ston, Robert (1654–1728) Scottish-born American patriot and statesman. He was a major figure in New York colonial politics after 1695.

Liv·ing·ston, Robert R. (1746–1813) U.S. patriot and statesman. After independence he became the first U.S. secretary of foreign affairs (1781–83), and negotiated the Louisiana Purchase.

Liv·ing·ston, William (1723–90) U.S. statesman. He opposed British policies in colonial New York, and was one of the signatories of the Declaration of Independence (1776).

Liv·ing·stone /lívving stən/ city and tourist center in southern Zambia, north of the Victoria Falls. Population: 82,218 (1990).

Liv·ing·stone /lìvving stón/, **David, Dr.** (1813–73) British doctor, missionary, and explorer. One of the most important explorers of the African interior, he was the first European to visit many areas of the continent.

liv·ing wage *n.* a wage that will allow a worker to support a family in reasonable comfort

liv·ing will *n.* a document, typically signed in advance while in good health, in which somebody declines to be kept alive artificially by life-support systems in case of a terminal illness

Li·vo·ni·a /li vónee ə/ ancient Baltic region, comprising most of present-day Estonia and Latvia. Russia annexed it in 1721. —**Livo·ni·an** /lə vónee ən/ *adj., n.*

Li·vor·no /lee váwrnō/ port and industrial city in the Tuscany Region, central Italy. Population: 166,394 (1992). English **Leghorn**

li·vre /leévrə/ *n.* an old unit of French currency, equivalent to a pound of silver [Mid-16thC. Via French from Latin *libra* "pound."]

Li·vy /lívvee/ (59 B.C.–A.D. 17) Roman historian. His *History of Rome*, ranging from the foundation of the city in 753 B.C. to 9 B.C., was the basis for the Western tradition of historical writing, and remained the primary source of information about Rome until the 18th century. Full name **Titus Livius**

lix·iv·i·ate /lik sívvee àyt/ (**-at·ed, -at·ing, -ates**) *vti.* CHEM to leach (*dated*) [Mid-17thC. From late Latin *lixiviare*, from Latin *lixivium* (see LIXIVIUM).] —**lix·iv·i·al** *adj.* —**lix·iv·i·a·tion** /lik sìvvee áysh'n/ *n.*

lix·iv·i·um /lik sívvee əm/ (*plural* **-ums** *or* **-a** /-ə/) *n.* a solution, e.g., lye, obtained by leaching [Mid-17thC. From late Latin, from Latin *lixivius* "made into ashes or lye," from *lix* "lye."]

Lizard

liz·ard /lízzərd/ *n.* **1. FOUR-LEGGED REPTILE** a reptile with a long scaly body, movable eyelids, a long tapering tail, and four legs, typically living in hot dry regions. Lizards include the gecko, iguana, chameleon, and horned toad. Suborder: Sauria. **2. LARGE REPTILE RESEMBLING LIZARD** any large reptile with four legs and a tapering tail that resembles the lizard, e.g., the alligator, crocodile, or certain dinosaurs **3. LEATHER MADE FROM LIZARD SKIN** leather made from the skin of a lizard [14thC. Via Old French *lesard* from Latin *lacertus* "lizard," of unknown origin.]

liz·ard·fish *n.* a slender, large-mouthed, predatory marine fish that has a head shaped like that of a lizard. Family: Synodontidae.

Lju·blja·na /lyoŏ blaánaa/ capital of Slovenia, in the central part of the country, near Trieste. Population: 269,972 (1994).

ll, **ll.** *abbr.* lines

'll *after a vowel* /l/; *after a consonant* /'l/ *contr.* **1. WILL** will **2. SHALL** shall

LL *abbr.* **1.** late Latin **2.** Low Latin

Llama

lla·ma /laámə/ *n.* **1. SHAGGY-COATED LONG-NECKED MAMMAL** a shaggy-coated long-necked cud-chewing South American mammal related to the camel, kept to carry loads. It yields wool, leather, milk, and meat, and is believed to be a domesticated variety of the guanaco. Genus: *Llama*. **2. WOOL** the shaggy wool of a llama **3. CLOTH FROM LLAMA WOOL** cloth made from the wool of a llama [Early 17thC. Via Spanish from Quechua.]

lla·no /laánō/ (*plural* **-nos**) *n.* a large open grassy plain, especially in Latin America and the southwestern United States [Early 17thC. Via Spanish from, ultimately, Latin *planus* "flat, level" (see PLAIN).]

LL.B. *abbr.* Bachelor of Laws [Shortening of Latin *Legum Baccalaureus*]

LL.D. *abbr.* Doctor of Laws [Shortening of Latin *Legum Doctor*]

LL.M. *abbr.* Master of Laws [Shortening of Latin *Legum Magister*]

Lloyd /loyd/, **Harold** (1893–1971) U.S. comedian. He made almost 500 silent movies and talking pictures, including *Safety Last* (1923), many of which featured stunts and chase sequences. Full name **Harold Clayton Lloyd**

Popperfoto

David Lloyd George

Lloyd George /lòyd jáwrj/, **David, 1st Earl of Dwyfor** (1863–1945) British statesman. As the last Liberal prime minister of the United Kingdom (1916–22), he was a strong wartime leader during World War I. He granted home rule to Ireland (1920).

Lloyd Web·ber /lòyd wébbər/, **Andrew, Lord Lloyd Webber of Sydmonton** (*b.* 1948) British composer. His popular stage musicals include *Jesus Christ Superstar* (1971), *Cats* (1981), and *Phantom of the Opera* (1986).

lm *symbol.* lumen

LMT *abbr.* local mean time

ln *symbol.* natural logarithm

LNG *abbr.* liquefied natural gas

lo /lō/ *interj.* used to draw attention to something (*archaic or literary*) [Old English *lā*]

loach[1] /lōch/ *n.* a freshwater fish of Europe and Asia. It is related to the carp and has a long slender body with barbels around its mouth. Family: Cobitidae. [14thC. From Old French *locke*, of uncertain origin: perhaps ultimately from Celtic.]

loach[2] *n.* a U.S. army light helicopter (*informal*) [Mid-20thC. Origin uncertain.]

load /lōd/ *n.* **1. SOMETHING CARRIED OR TRANSPORTED** something that is carried by an animal, person, or vehicle, especially something heavy or bulky **2. AMOUNT CARRIED IN ONE TRIP** the amount of material, goods, or people that are carried in one trip (*often used in combination*) ○ *delivered a boatload of passengers to the island* **3. WORK DEMANDED OF SOMEBODY OR SOMETHING** the amount of work that a person or machine is required to do ○ *unhappy about his teaching load this term* **4. MENTAL BURDEN** something that makes somebody feel mentally weighed down, e.g., responsibility, worry, or guilt ○ *carrying around a load of guilt* **5. QUANTITY THAT MACHINE CAN COPE WITH** the amount that can be handled by a machine at one time, especially the amount of clothes that can be handled by a washing machine **6.** ARMS **SINGLE CHARGE FOR GUN** a single charge of ammunition for a firearm **7.** ELEC **AMOUNT OF DRAWN ELECTRICAL POWER** the amount of electrical power that is drawn from a line or source **8.** ELEC **DEVICE DRAWING ELECTRICAL POWER** any device to which electrical power is delivered **9.** MECH ENG **FORCE AND WEIGHT ON STRUCTURE** the total force and weight that a structure, e.g., a bridge, is designed to withstand. For a bridge this includes the dynamic loads of traffic, wind, snow, and ice and the static load of the bridge's own weight. **10.** MECH ENG **WORK REQUIRED OF MECHANICAL DEVICE** the work required of or placed on an engine or machine, measured in kilowatts or horsepower **11.** FIN **CHARGE ADDED TO MUTUAL SHARE PRICE** a charge that is added to the price of some mutual fund shares as a commission or marketing cost ■ **loads** *npl.* **LARGE AMOUNT OR NUMBER** a large amount or a lot of (*informal*) ○ *We had loads of guests at the party.* ■ *adv.* **loads VERY MUCH** very much or a great deal (*informal*) ○ *feeling loads better* ■ *v.* (**load·ed, load·ing, loads**) **1.** *vti.* ARMS **PUT ROUNDS IN GUN** to put ammunition into a firearm ○ *loaded the rifle* **2.** *vti.* TRANSP **PUT SOMETHING ON VEHICLE** to put cargo or passengers on a vehicle, ship, or aircraft or to have cargo or passengers put on ○ *The aircraft is now loading.* **3.** *vt.* **PUT SOMETHING IN MACHINE** to put into a machine the items that it will work on, e.g., clothes for washing **4.** *vt.* **PUT SOMETHING ON PERSON OR ANIMAL** to put a load on an animal or give a load to a person so that it can be carried **5.** *vt.* BASEBALL **PUT RUNNERS ON ALL THREE BASES** to cause runners to occupy first, second, and third bases (*often passive*) ○ *hit a home run with the bases loaded* **6.** *vti.* PHOTOGRAPHY, TECH **PUT SOMETHING IN CAMERA** to put a film, plate, or tape in a camera or to take in a film, plate, or tape **7.** *vt.* COMPUT **PUT PROGRAM IN COMPUTER** to transfer data or a program to the main memory of a computer **8.** *vt.* COMPUT **PUT DISK IN DRIVE ON COMPUTER** to put a disk or tape in a drive on a computer **9.** *vt.* FIN **ADD EXTRA CHARGE TO INSURANCE PREMIUM** to add an extra charge to an insurance premium, e.g., because of an increased risk **10.** *vt.* MECH ENG **INCREASE WORK REQUIRED OF ENGINE** to increase the work required from an engine or motor **11.** *vt.* ELEC **INCREASE ELECTRIC OUTPUT OF GENERATOR** to increase the output produced by or drawn from a circuit or generator **12.** *vt.* GAMBLING **WEIGHT ONE SIDE OF DIE** to weight one side of each die in a pair or one side of a roulette wheel so that it has a bias toward a certain number [Old English *lād* "course, way, carrying." Ultimately from an Indo-European word meaning "to go ahead," which is also the ancestor of *lead*[1] and *lode*.] ◇ **a load of** used to say emphatically that something is ridiculous or nonsensical (*informal*) ○ *a load of nonsense* ◇ **get a load of** to look at or listen to something or somebody (*slang*) ◇ **load the dice 1.** to arrange things in advance to create an unfair bias in favor of or against somebody (*informal*) **2.** GAMBLING to add weight to a die so that it always falls on a particular side (*informal*) ◇ **a load off your mind** a relief from anxiety or worry

load·ed /lṓdəd/ *adj.* **1. WITH FULL LOAD** carrying a full load **2.** ARMS **CONTAINING AMMUNITION** containing bullets or other ammunition and ready to fire **3. WITH HIDDEN IMPLICATION** with a hidden or secondary implication designed to trick somebody into making an admission or commitment ○ *That is a loaded question.* **4. RICH** extremely rich (*slang*) ○ *Her parents are loaded.* **5. DRUNK** very drunk (*slang*) **6. INTOXICATED BY DRUGS** under the influence of drugs (*slang*) **7.** GAMBLING **WEIGHTED UNFAIRLY** with one side weighted to prevent dice or a roulette wheel from operating randomly **8. WITH MANY EXTRAS** supplied with many luxurious extras ○ *a top-of-the-line car that's really loaded*

load fac·tor *n.* **1. AIRCRAFT PAYLOAD** the payload of an aircraft for a particular flight, expressed as a percentage of the maximum allowable payload **2. LOAD DIVIDED BY WEIGHT OF AIRCRAFT** an external load divided by the weight of an aircraft

load·ing /lṓding/ *n.* **1. WEIGHT CARRIED** a load or weight carried **2.** INDUST **FILLER** material added to something to improve certain properties or add weight **3.** INSUR **ADDITIONAL INSURANCE PREMIUM** an additional insurance premium or higher rating incurred by items that are more valuable or at greater risk **4.** ELEC **ADDITION OF INDUCTANCE** the addition of inductance to a transmission line to improve its performance over a given frequency band

load line *n.* = **Plimsoll line**

load·mas·ter /lṓd màstər/ *n.* somebody who is in charge of loading cargo on a military or commercial transport aircraft

load shed·ding *n.* a temporary reduction in a supply of electricity as a method of reducing the demand on the generator

load·star *n.* = **lodestar**

load·stone *n.* = **lodestone**

loaf[1] /lōf/ (*plural* **loaves** /lōvz/) *n.* **1. QUANTITY OF BREAD** a quantity of bread, shaped and baked as a whole **2. BLOCK OF FOOD SHAPED LIKE LOAF** a quantity of food baked in a loaf pan or shaped to form a rectangular block and baked (*used in combination*) [Old English *hlāf*]

loaf[2] /lōf/ (**loafed, loaf·ing, loafs**) *vi.* to do very little and spend time in a lazy, wasteful way [Mid-19thC. Origin uncertain: probably a back-formation from LOAFER.]

loaf·er /lṓfər/ *n.* a lazy person who avoids work and wastes time [Mid-19thC. Origin uncertain: perhaps from German *Landläufer* "vagabond," from *Land* "country" + *laufen* "to run."]

Loaf·er *tdmk.* a trademark for an open casual leather shoe like a moccasin but having a wide flat heel

loam /lōm/ *n.* **1.** GARDENING **FERTILE WORKABLE SOIL** an easily-worked fertile soil consisting of a mixture of clay, sand, and silt and sometimes also organic matter

2. BUILDING **CLAY AND SAND MIXED FOR BUILDING** a mixture of moist clay and sand used for making bricks and in plastering ■ *vt.* **(loamed, loam·ing, loams)** BUILDING **USE LOAM IN BUILDING JOB** to use loam in the process of covering, filling, or coating something [Old English *lām* "clay, earth." Ultimately from an Indo-European base meaning "slippery," which is also the ancestor of English *slime* and *slip*.] —**loam·y** *adj.*

loan /lōn/ *n.* **1. MONEY LENT** an amount of money given to somebody on the condition that it will be paid back later **2. LENDING** the act of letting somebody use something temporarily **3.** LING = **loanword** ■ *vt.* **(loaned, loan·ing, loans) LEND** to allow somebody to borrow something on the condition that it is returned ○ *Loan me five bucks, will you?* [12thC. From Old Norse *lán*. Ultimately from an Indo-European word meaning "to leave," which is also the ancestor of English *lend* and *relinquish*.] ◇ **on loan 1.** being lent or borrowed **2.** working at a temporary location because additional help or expertise is needed there

loan shark *n.* somebody who lends money at excessively high rates of interest

loan·shark·ing /lṓn shaàrking/ *n.* the activity or business of lending money at excessively high rates of interest

loan trans·la·tion *n.* a word or expression that enters a language as a direct translation from another [Translation of German *Lehnübersetzung*]

loan·word /lṓn wùrd/, **loan word** *n.* a word from one language that has become part of everyday usage in another, often with slight modification [Late 19thC. Translation of German *Lehnwort*.]

loath /lōth, lōth/, **loth** *adj.* unwilling or reluctant to do something [Old English *lāþ* "loathsome"]

WORD KEY: SYNONYMS

See Synonyms at ***unwilling***.

loathe /lōth/ **(loathed, loath·ing, loathes)** *vti.* to dislike somebody or something intensely [Old English *lāþian*. Ultimately from an Indo-European base meaning "to despise."] —**loath·er** *n.*

loath·ing /lṓthing/ *n.* intense dislike of somebody or something —**loath·ing·ly** *adv.*

WORD KEY: SYNONYMS

See Synonyms at ***dislike***.

loath·ly[1] /lṓthlee, lṓthlee/ *adv.* reluctantly or unwillingly (*archaic*) [Old English *lāþlice*]

loath·ly[2] /lṓthlee, lṓthlee/ *adj.* loathsome (*archaic*) [Old English *lāþlic*]

loath·some /lṓthsəm/ *adj.* arousing intense dislike and disgust —**loath·some·ness** *n.*

loaves plural of **loaf**[1]

lob /lob/ *v.* **(lobbed, lob·bing, lobs) 1.** *vti.* SPORTS **HIT BALL IN HIGH ARC** to hit or throw a ball in a high curving trajectory **2.** *vt.* **THROW CASUALLY** to throw something in a casual careless way ■ *n.* **1.** SPORTS **HIGH ARCHING SHOT** a ball hit or thrown in a high curving path **2.** TENNIS **BALL OVER TENNIS PLAYER'S HEAD** a ball that travels over the head of a tennis player [Late 16thC. Origin uncertain: probably from Low German.] —**lob·ber** *n.*

WORD KEY: SYNONYMS

See Synonyms at ***throw***.

lo·bar /lṓbər, -bàar/ *adj.* ANAT relating to or affecting a lobe, e.g., in the lungs

lo·bate /lṓ bàyt/, **lo·bat·ed** *adj.* **1.** BIRDS **HAVING LOBED TOES** having toes with rounded flaps on either side, as grebes have **2.** BOT, ZOOL **WITH OR LIKE LOBES** having or resembling a lobe or lobes —**lo·bate·ly** *adv.*

lob·ber /lóbbər/, **lop·per** /lóppər/ *n.* clabber (*regional dated*) [Probably from an obsolete verb from Old Norse *hlaup* "coagulation"]

WORD KEY: REGIONAL NOTE

Lobber is also called *lobber milk*, *lopper milk*, and *labberd milk*. In the East, the old-fashioned term is restricted mainly to New York State, Connecticut, and New Jersey, with a striking enclave in the Great Lakes state of Michigan.

lob·by /lóbbee/ *n.* (*plural* **-bies**) **1.** ARCHIT **ENTRANCE AREA IN PUBLIC BUILDING** a large entrance hall or foyer immediately inside the door of a hotel, theater, or other public building **2.** POL **PUBLIC AREA IN LEGISLATIVE BUILDING** a public area in or near a legislative building where people can meet and petition their political representatives **3.** POL **GROUP TRYING TO INFLUENCE POLICY** a group of campaigners and representatives of particular interests who try to influence political policy on a particular issue (*takes a singular or plural verb*) ○ *the welfare lobby* **4.** *U.K.* POL **BRITISH VOTING CORRIDOR** either of the two rooms in the British Parliament where members of both houses of Parliament vote for or against bills and proposals ■ *vti.* **(-bied, -by·ing, -bies)** POL **PETITION POLITICIANS OR INFLUENTIAL PEOPLE** to attempt to persuade a political representative or influential person to support or fight a particular cause [Mid-16thC. From medieval Latin *lobia* "cloister, covered walk." Ultimately from a prehistoric Germanic word denoting a roof made of bark, which is also the ancestor of English *lodge*.] —**lob·by·er** *n.*

lob·by·gow /lóbbee gòw/ *n.* a messenger or errand boy, especially in the Chinese area of a city (*slang*) [Early 20thC. Origin unknown.]

lob·by·ist /lóbbee ist/ *n.* somebody who is paid to lobby political representatives on a particular issue —**lob·by·ism** *n.*

lobe /lōb/ *n.* **1.** ANAT **EARLOBE** an earlobe **2.** ANAT **ROUNDED BODY PART** a rounded division or projection of an organ or part in the body, especially in the lungs, brain, or liver **3. ROUNDED PROJECTING PART** a rounded part that projects from the main body of something **4.** BOT **ROUNDED PLANT PART** a rounded segment on a leaf that is not divided all the way to the midrib [15thC. Via late Latin *lobus* from Greek *lobos* "lobe, pod."]

lo·bec·to·my /lō béktəmee/ (*plural* **-mies**) *n.* the surgical removal of a lobe, e.g., of the lungs, liver, or thyroid

lobe·fin /lṓb fìn/ *n.* ZOOL = **crossopterygian** —**lobe·finned** *adj.*

lo·be·li·a /lō beélyə, -beélee ə/ *n.* a plant that is widely grown for its two-lipped blue, red, or white flowers. Some varieties of lobelia are low-growing or trailing annuals, while others are tall perennials with lance-shaped leaves. Genus: *Lobelia*. [Mid-18thC. Named for Matthias de *Lobel* 1538–1616, Flemish botanist and physician to James I of England.]

Lo·bi·to /lō beétō/ city and port in western Angola. Population: 150,000 (1983).

Lo·bi·to Bay arm of the Atlantic Ocean, western Angola

lob·lol·ly pine /lób lòllee-/, **lob·lol·ly** *n.* a pine found in the southeastern United States that has reddish brown flaky bark, long needles grouped in threes, and oblong cones. Genus: *Pinus taeda*. [From earlier *lobololly* "thick gruel," of uncertain origin (perhaps from dialect *lob* "to bubble while boiling," an invitation of the sound + dialect *lolly* "soup"); possibly from its growing where the ground is swampy or muddy, or perhaps from the consistency of its pulp when cooked to make paper]

lo·bo /lṑ bṓ/ (*plural* **-bos**) *n.* = **gray wolf** [Mid-19thC. Via Spanish from Latin *lupus* (see LUPINE[2]).]

lo·bo·la /lṓbələ/, **lo·bo·lo** *n.* a payment, often in cattle, made by a groom's family to his bride's family before their wedding in some parts of southern and eastern Africa [Mid-19thC. Of Bantu origin.]

lo·bot·o·mize /lə bóttə mìz/ **(-mized, -miz·ing, -miz·es)** *vt.* **1. PERFORM BRAIN SURGERY** to carry out a surgical operation in which nerves to the prefrontal lobe of the brain are severed **2. CAUSE TO FEEL APATHETIC OR SLUGGISH** to make somebody feel sluggish, mentally numb, or lacking in energy or vitality (*informal*)

lo·bot·o·my /lə bóttəmee/ (*plural* **-mies**) *n.* a prefrontal lobotomy (*dated*) [Mid-20thC. Coined from LOBE + -TOMY.]

lob·scouse /lób skòwss/ *n.* a stew of meat and vegetables thickened with hardtack, traditionally eaten by sailors [Early 18thC. Origin uncertain.]

lob·ster /lóbstər/ *n.* **1.** ZOOL **EDIBLE SEA CREATURE** a hard-shelled edible marine crustacean that has a pair of large pincers, five pairs of limbs, eyes on stalks, and long antennae. Family: Homaridae. **2.** ZOOL **SPINY LOBSTER** a crustacean that is similar in appearance to the true lobster but without the two large pincers, especially the spiny lobster. Family: Palinuridae. **3. LOBSTER'S FLESH AS FOOD** the flesh of a lobster as food. The tail meat and meat extracted from the claws is particularly valued for its fine, slightly sweet flavor. ■ *vi.* **(-stered, -ster·ing, -sters) CATCH LOBSTERS** to fish for lobsters [Old English *loppestre*, of uncertain origin: probably an alteration of Latin *locusta* "locust, crustacean," influenced by *loppe* "spider" and nouns ending in *-ster*]

lob·ster·man /lóbstərmən/ (*plural* **-men**) *n.* **1. CATCHER OF LOBSTERS** somebody who catches lobsters for a living **2. LOBSTERING BOAT** a boat designed for catching lobsters

lob·ster New·burg /-noō bùrg/ *n.* lobster meat cooked in a rich sherry sauce with butter and cream and usually served on small pieces of toast or croutons or in a pastry shell [Early 20thC. Origin uncertain, possibly from *Newburgh*, city in New York state.]

lob·ster pot *n.* a trap in the form of a basket, used for catching lobsters

lob·ster shift *n.* the night shift of a factory, newspaper, or other workplace

lob·ster ther·mi·dor *n.* cooked lobster with a wine and cream sauce served in the shell with a topping of melted cheese [Late 19thC. *Thermidor* from *Thermidor* (1891), play by the French dramatist Victorien Sardou (1831–1908).]

lob·u·late /lóbbyə làyt/ *adj.* having or made up of small lobes ○ *a lobulate organ* —**lob·u·la·tion** /lòbbyə láysh'n/ *n.*

lob·ule /lób yoōl/ *n.* **1. SMALL LOBE** a small lobe **2. SECTION OF LOBE** a section or division of a lobe [Late 17thC. Formed from LOBE, on the model of GLOBULE.] —**lob·u·lar** *adj.* —**lob·u·late** /lóbbyə làyt/ *adj.* —**lob·u·lose** /lóbbyə lōss/ *adj.* —**lob·u·lar·ly** /lóbbyələrlee/ *adv.*

lob·worm /lób wùrm/ *n.* = **lugworm** [Mid-17thC. *Lob* from obsolete sense "something hanging," (see LOB).]

lo·cal /lṓk'l/ *adj.* **1. IN NEARBY AREA** relating to, situated in, or providing a service for a particular area, especially the area near home or work ○ *the local school* **2. TYPICAL OF PARTICULAR AREA** typical of, or only found in, a particular area ○ *the local dialect* **3. NOT WIDESPREAD** not covering a wide area or the whole country ○ *There have been local outbreaks of the disease.* **4.** POL **RELATING TO GOVERNMENTAL REGION** relating to a comparatively small region that controls some aspects of practical government such as housing or education ○ *local elections* **5.** MED **AFFECTING SMALL PART** affecting only a specific part of the body ○ *local infection* **6.** TRANSP **STOPPING EVERYWHERE** stopping at all the stations or bus stops on a route ○ *a local train* **7.** TELECOM **TO A PHONE NUMBER NEARBY** made to a phone number within a fairly small radius and therefore not itemized on a phone bill ○ *a phone for local calls only* **8.** COMPUT **PROCESSED WITHIN THE SAME COMPUTER OR NETWORK** performed, processed, or transmitted within the same computer or one in a readily accessible network ■ *n.* **1. SOMEBODY WHO COMES FROM PARTICULAR AREA** somebody who lives in a particular area, was born there, or has lived there for a long time **2.** TRANSP **STOPPING TRAIN OR BUS** a train or bus that stops at all the stations or stops on the route **3.** MED **LOCAL ANESTHETIC** a local anesthetic (*informal*) **4.** POL **BRANCH OF ORGANIZATION** a local branch or office, especially of a labor union [14thC. Via French from late Latin *localis*, from Latin *locus* "place."] —**lo·cal·ly** *adv.* —**lo·cal·ness** *n.*

lo·cal an·es·thet·ic *n.* a drug, usually given by injection, that eliminates pain, though not necessarily all sensation, in a particular area of the body without affecting consciousness

lo·cal ar·e·a net·work *n.* a network of personal computers and peripheral devices linked by cable and able to share resources

lo·cal au·thor·i·ty *n. U.K., NZ* = **local government**

lo·cal col·or *n.* unusual or traditional features of a particular place that make it interesting

lo·cale /lō kál/ *n.* the place in which something happens or in which the action in a book or movie takes place [Late 18thC. Alteration of French *local* "local," on the model of MORALE.]

lo·cal gov·ern·ment *n.* **1. GOVERNMENT OF LOCAL AREA** the government of a town, city, county, or region at a local level by locally elected politicians ○ *worked in local government all his life* **2. ELECTED OFFICIALS AT LOCAL LEVEL** an organization of people, most of whom are elected, that governs an area smaller than a state, usually a county, district, or town

lo·cal·ism /lṓk'l ìzzəm/ *n.* **1. LOCAL IDIOM OR TRADITION** a phrase, expression, or custom peculiar to the people in a particular area **2. EXCESSIVE INTEREST IN LOCAL AFFAIRS** interest in local matters and customs rather than in national or global issues, sometimes resulting in a limited perspective —**lo·cal·ist** *n.*

lo·cal·i·ty /lō kállətee/ (*plural* **-ties**) *n.* **1. PARTICULAR PLACE** a particular place, district, or neighborhood

2. SITUATION IN SPACE OR TIME the fact of being situated at a particular point in space or time

lo·cal·ize /lṓk'l ìz/ (**-ized, -iz·ing, -iz·es**) *v.* **1.** *vti.* **CONFINE OR BE CONFINED TO PLACE** to become confined to or restrict something to a particular area **2.** *vt.* **FIND LOCATION OF** to find the source or location of something **3.** *vt.* **DECENTRALIZE CONTROL OF** to transfer power or control from a central authority to local bodies —**lo·cal·iz·a·ble** *adj.* —**lo·cal·i·za·tion** /lṓk'li záysh'n/ *n.*

lo·cal op·tion *n.* the power granted to a local government to decide whether to implement a particular policy, especially with regard to the sale of alcohol

Lo·car·no /lo kaárnō/ town and resort in Ticino Canton, southern Switzerland. Population: 14,765 (1992).

lo·cate /lṓ kàyt, lō káyt/ (**-cat·ed, -cat·ing, -cates**) *v.* **1.** *vt.* **FIND** to discover where something is **2.** *vi.* **ESTABLISH BUSINESS IN PLACE** to establish a residence or business in a particular place **3.** *vt.* **POSITION** to put something in a particular place [Early 16thC. From Latin *locat-*, past participle stem of *locare* , from *locus* "place."] —**lo·cat·a·ble** *adj.* —**lo·cat·er** *n.*

lo·cat·ed /lṓ kàytəd, lō káytəd/ ◇ **be located** to exist or be found in a particular place

lo·ca·tion /lō káysh'n/ *n.* **1. POSITION** the site or position of something **2.** CINEMA **MOVIE SETTING** a place away from a studio where scenes for a movie are shot ○ *The movie was shot on location in Scotland.* **3. DISCOVERY** the discovery of something ○ *A metal detector is an essential aid in the location of buried treasure.* **4. POSITIONING OF SOMETHING** the positioning or siting of something or somebody in a particular place —**lo·ca·tion·al** *adj.*

loc·a·tive /lókətiv/ *adj.* **INDICATING PLACE OR DIRECTION** with the grammatical ending or form that indicates place or direction ■ *n.* **1. GRAMMATICAL CASE** the grammatical case indicating place or direction **2. WORD IN LOCATIVE CASE** a word or expression in the locative case [Early 19thC. Coined from LOCATE, on the model of NOMINATIVE and ACCUSATIVE.]

lo·ca·tor /lṓ kàytər, lō káytər/ *n.* **1. SOMEBODY WHO DECIDES LAND BOUNDARIES** somebody who establishes the boundaries of a piece of land or a mining claim **2. FINDING AID** a device that helps somebody locate something, such as a table or index

loc. cit., **in loc. cit.** *adv.* in the place cited. Full form **loco citato**

loch /lok, lawkh/ *n. Scotland* **1. LAKE** a lake **2. ARM OF SEA** a narrow arm of the sea stretching inland [14thC. From Scottish Gaelic. Ultimately from an Indo-European word denoting a body of water, which is also the ancestor of English *lake*.]

loch·an /lókən, láwkhən/ *n. Scotland* a small lake or pool [Late 17thC. From Scottish Gaelic, literally "small loch."]

lo·chi·a /lṓkee ə, ló-/ *n.* the normal vaginal discharge of cell debris and blood after childbirth [Late 17thC. From Greek *lokhia*, from *lokhos* "childbirth." Ultimately from an Indo-European base meaning "to lie," which is also the ancestor of English *lie* and *lay*.] —**lo·chi·al** *adj.*

lo·ci plural of **locus**

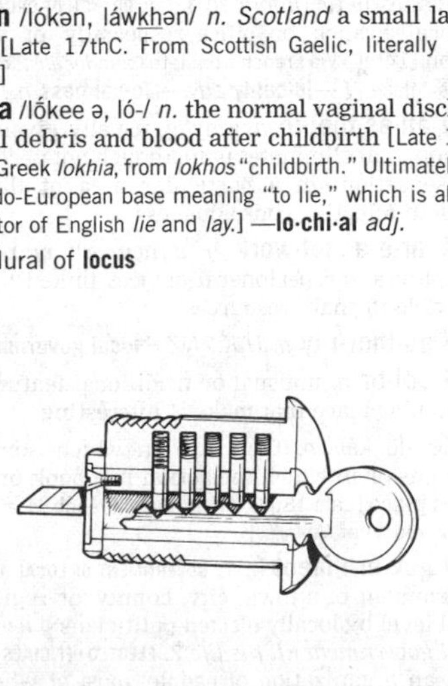

Lock: Cross section of a key-operated lock

lock[1] /lok/ *n.* **1. FASTENING MECHANISM** a mechanism used to fasten or secure a door, window, or lid, especially one operated by a key **2.** TRANSP **GATED SECTION OF CANAL** a short section of a canal or river with gates at each end and a mechanism for letting water in and out. Boats enter the lock and are raised or lowered as the water level is altered and then exit to a higher or lower section of the waterway. **3.** WRESTLING **WRESTLING HOLD** a wrestling hold in which a wrestler twists or puts pressure on part of the other wrestler's body **4.** ARMS **GUN PART** the part of a gun that makes the charge explode **5. BLOCKING DEVICE** a device, e.g., one operated by a password, that prevents an unauthorized person from using something **6. FIRM POSSESSION** firm possession or control of something ○ *a manufacturer with lock on the market for luxury trucks* **7.** ENG **AIRLOCK** an airlock ■ *v.* (**locked, lock·ing, locks**) **1.** *vti.* **FASTEN USING LOCK** to fasten something or become fastened using a lock **2.** *vt.* **PUT IN A SECURE PLACE** to put something into a safe place or container that can be locked ○ *Her diamonds are locked in a safe deposit box.* **3.** *vt.* **SECURE PLACE** to make a building or vehicle secure by locking the doors and windows **4.** *vt.* COMPUT **PREVENT UNAUTHORIZED USE OF** to prevent something from being used by an unauthorized person, e.g. via software **5.** *vti.* **FIX OR BE FIXED IN PLACE** to become fixed in one position, or fix something in one position, so that it cannot move normally **6.** *vt.* **HOLD FIRMLY** to hold somebody tightly ○ *locked in a passionate embrace* **7.** *vt.* **TRAP IN A DIFFICULT SITUATION** to put somebody in a situation or conflict from which it is difficult to escape ○ *locked into a lengthy argument* **8.** *vt.* TRANSP **PUT LOCKS ON WATERWAY** to put locks on a stretch of canal or river **9.** *vi.* TRANSP **GO THROUGH CANAL LOCKS** to go through a series of locks on a boat, or take a boat through a series of locks **10.** *vt.* PRINTING **SECURE TYPE IN PRESS** to secure metal type in a press **11.** *vt.* FIN = **lock up** *v.* **4** [Old English *loc*] —**lock·able** *adj.* ◇ **lock, stock, and barrel** completely

lock away *vt.* = **lock up** *v.* **1**, **lock up** *v.* **2**

lock in *vt.* **1. PREVENT FROM LEAVING** to prevent somebody from leaving a room or building by locking the door **2. FIX** to fix something at a particular level for a long period ○ *locked in a good rate on their mortgage*

lock on *vti.* MIL to find a target and track it automatically, or to make a radar or missile find and track a target

lock out *vt.* **1. PREVENT FROM ENTERING** to prevent somebody from entering a place by locking the door **2. DENY ACCESS TO WORKPLACE** to prevent workers from entering their workplace, usually as a strategy in an industrial dispute

lock up *v.* **1.** *vt.* **IMPRISON** to put somebody into prison, a secure hospital, or other institution that deprives him or her of freedom **2.** *vt.* **STORE IN A SECURE PLACE** to put valuables in a secure locked place **3.** *vti.* **SECURE BUILDING** to make a building secure by locking all the doors and windows **4.** *vt.* FIN **INVEST IN LONG-TERM PLAN** to put money into a form of savings or investment that does not allow easy access to the funds

lock[2] /lok/ *n.* **1. PIECE OF HAIR** a group of hairs that hang together, on somebody's head or cut off **2.** TEXTILES **WISP OF FIBER** a small bunch of wool, cotton, or other fiber ■ **locks** *npl.* **HAIR** somebody's hair (*literary*) [Old English *locc*]

lock·age /lókij/ *n.* **1. PASSAGE THROUGH LOCK** the passage of a boat through a canal or river lock **2. FEE** a fee paid by a boat to pass through a lock **3. LOCKS** a number of locks on a canal or river

lock·box /lók bòks/ *n.* a strong, lockable box for securing items, such as a (**strongbox**), safe-deposit box or post office box

Locke /lok/, **John** (1632–1704) English philosopher. He developed the doctrine of empiricism according to which knowledge was acquired by experience, not by intuition.

lock·er /lókər/ *n.* **1. LOCKABLE COMPARTMENT** a small lockable cupboard or compartment where personal belongings can be left, e.g., at a swimming pool, gym, school, or workplace **2. FREEZER** a walk-in food freezer **3. TRUNK** a trunk or low chest, used for storage **4. SOMEBODY OR SOMETHING THAT LOCKS** a person who or device that locks something

Lock·er·bie /lókərbee/ town in Dumfries and Galloway, southwestern Scotland. In 1988 an airliner was destroyed over the town by a terrorist bomb, killing all the passengers and crew and 11 of the town's residents. Population: 3,982 (1991).

lock·er room *n.* a room containing lockers, where people change their clothes for sports or swimming

lock·er-room *adj.* typical of or suitable only for a men's locker room ○ *telling locker-room jokes*

lock·et /lókət/ *n.* a small decorative metal case with a hinged cover containing a picture or memento, worn on a neck chain or bracelet [14thC. From Old French *locquet*, literally "small latch," from *loc* "latch," ultimately of prehistoric Germanic origin.]

lock·jaw /lók jàw/ *n.* **1.** = **trismus 2.** = **tetanus** [Early 19thC. From the muscle spasms in the jaw that affect sufferers.]

lock·keep·er /lók keepər/, **lock·mas·ter** /lók màstər/ *n.* somebody employed to look after or control a lock on a waterway and collect any fees payable. Traditionally, the lockkeeper lives in a house close to the lock.

lock·nut /lók nùt/ *n.* **1. SECOND NUT TIGHTENED ON A FIRST** a second nut tightened on a first to prevent it from loosening **2. SELF-LOCKING NUT** a nut designed to lock itself in place once tightened

lock-on *n.* MIL the point at which a radar or missile locates and starts to track a target

lock·out /lók òwt/ *n.* the preventing of workers from entering their workplace, a tactic sometimes used by management in an industrial dispute

Lock·port /lók pàwrt/ city in western New York, northeast of Niagara Falls and west of Rochester. Population: 23,300 (1996).

lock·ram /lókrəm/ *n.* a coarse linen fabric [15thC. From French *locrenan*, an alteration of *Locronan*, a village in Brittany where the cloth was made.]

lock·smith /lók smìth/ *n.* somebody who makes or sells locks and keys and repairs and installs locks. A locksmith can also open a lock when the owner has lost the key or locked himself or herself out.

lock·step /lók stèp/ *n.* **1.** MIL **CLOSE MILITARY MARCHING** a form of military marching with soldiers close together and all moving forward with the same foot at the same time **2. MINDLESS ROUTINE** a process or routine that is standardized and inflexible ○ *"It's a lockstep process, and if at any point the virus makes a mistake, the host will almost certainly kill it."* (Virginia Morell, *The Killer Cat Virus that Doesn't Kill Cats, Discover Magazine July 1995*)

lock stitch *n.* the usual stitch made by a sewing machine, formed by the thread above the fabric interlocking with the bobbin thread

lock·up /lók ùp/ *n.* **1. PLACE WITH PRISON CELLS** a small prison, a block of cells at a police station, or a similar place where prisoners are kept for a short time **2. SECURING OF BUILDING** the securing of a building by locking it **3. TIME FOR LOCKING BUILDING** the time at which a building is locked **4.** FIN **LONG INVESTMENT** a long-term investment (*informal*)

lo·co[1] /lṓ kō/ *adj.* **WILDLY IRRATIONAL** wildly irrational (*informal*) ■ *n.* (*plural* **-cos**) **1.** BOT = **locoweed 2.** VET = **loco disease** ■ *vt.* (**-coed, -co·ing, -cos**) **1.** AGRIC **POISON ANIMAL** to poison an animal with locoweed **2. MAKE SOMEBODY WILDLY IRRATIONAL** to make somebody wildly irrational (*informal*) [Late 19thC. From Spanish, "irrational," of uncertain origin: perhaps from Arabic *laqwā* "thoughtless."]

lo·co[2] /lṓ kō/ *adj.* indicating that the performer should return to playing notes in the original register, negating a previous direction that they should be played an octave higher [Early 19thC. From Italian, literally "at the place."] —**lo·co** *adv.*

lo·co ci·ta·to /lṓ kō sī táy tò, lṓ kō si taá tò/ *adv.* full form of **loc. cit.** [From Latin, "in the place cited"]

lo·co dis·ease *n.* a disease of cattle, sheep, and horses in the western United States and Canada, caused by eating locoweed. It affects the animals' nervous systems, with symptoms of weakness, trembling, and inability to move. Also called **loco**

lo·co·mote /lṓkə mṓt/ (**-mot·ed, -mot·ing, -motes**) *vi.* to move under your own power [Mid-19thC. Back-formation from LOCOMOTION.]

lo·co·mo·tion /lṓkə mṓsh'n/ *n.* movement or the power to move from one place to another [Mid-17thC. From Latin *loco* "from a place" + MOTION.]

lo·co·mo·tive /lṓkə mṓtiv/ *n.* RAIL **RAIL ENGINE** a railroad engine ■ *adj.* **1. MOVABLE** able to move about freely **2. RELATING TO LOCOMOTION** relating to, allowing, or aiding in the ability to move ○ *locomotive organs* [Early 17thC. From modern Latin *locomotivus*, from Latin *loco* "from a place" + late Latin *motivus* "moving" (see MOTIVE).]

lo·co·mo·tor /lṓkə mṓtər/ *adj.* relating to or aiding in locomotion ○ *locomotor hyperactivity* [Late 19thC. From Latin *loco* "from a place" + MOTOR.]

lo·co·mo·tor a·tax·i·a *n.* MED = **tabes dorsalis**

Locomotive

lo·co·mo·to·ry /lṑkə mṓtəree/ *adj.* able to move independently

lo·co·weed /lṓkō weed/ *n.* a perennial plant of the pea family, found in western North America. Animals that eat it can contract loco disease. Genera: *Oxytropis* and *Astragalus.* Also called **loco** [Late 19thC. From LOCO[1] + WEED.]

loc·u·lar /lókyələr/, **loc·u·late** /-yələt, -yə làyt/ *adj.* separated into small chambers or cavities that are divided by membranes —**loc·u·la·tion** /lòkyə láysh'n/ *n.*

loc·ule /ló kyoōl/, **loc·u·lus** /lókyələss/ (*plural* **-li** /-lī/) *n.* a small cavity, chamber, or cell in a plant or animal [Late 19thC. Via French from Latin *loculus*, literally "small place," from *locus* "place."]

lo·cum /lṓkəm/, **lo·cum te·nens** /-ténnənz/ (*plural* **lo·cum te·nen·tes** /-tə nén teēz/) *n.* somebody, especially a member of the clergy, who stands in to do the job of another who is away or unwell [Mid-17thC. From medieval Latin *locum tenens* "one holding the place," from Latin *locus* "place" + *tenere* "to hold."]

lo·cus /lṓkəss/ (*plural* **lo·ci** /lṓ sī, lóssee, lṓkee/) *n.* **1.** PLACE a place where something happens **2.** MATH SET OF POINTS a set of points, the positions of which satisfy a set of algebraic conditions **3.** GENETICS GENE POSITION the position of a gene in a chromosome [Early 18thC. From Latin, "place" (source of English *local* and *locate*), of unknown origin.]

lo·cus clas·si·cus /-klássikəss/ (*plural* **lo·ci clas·si·ci** /-klássi sī/) *n.* a much-quoted passage from an authoritative or standard text [From Latin, "classical place"]

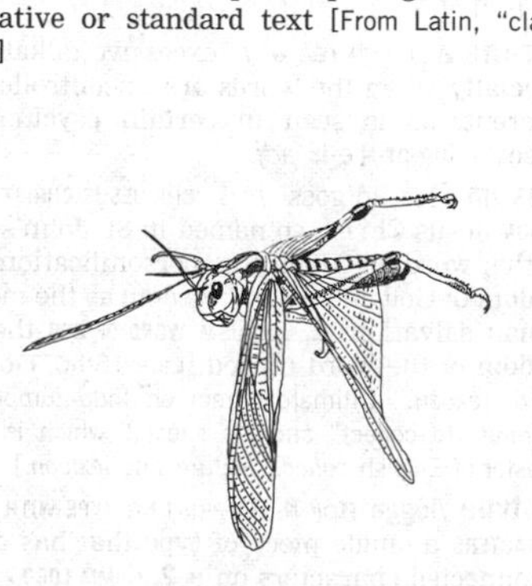

Locust

lo·cust /lṓkəst/ *n.* **1.** INSECTS SWARMING GRASSHOPPER a grasshopper found in warm regions that often swarms and devours crops and vegetation. Family: Acrididae. **2.** INSECTS = **seventeen-year locust 3.** TREES DECIDUOUS N AMERICAN TREE a North American deciduous tree with hanging clusters of fragrant flowers, compound leaves, thorns, and long seed pods. Genus: *Robinia.* **4.** TREES POD-BEARING TREE a pod-bearing tree of the pea family, including honey locust, swamp locust, and carob **5.** INDUST HARD WOOD the hard yellowish wood of a locust tree [14thC. Via French from Latin *locusta* "locust" (source also of English *lobster*); in sense 4, from the supposed resemblance of the pod to a locust.]

lo·cu·tion /lō kyoōsh'n, lə kyoōsh'n/ *n.* **1.** PHRASE a phrase or expression typically used by a group of people **2.** STYLE OF SPEECH the way in which somebody speaks [15thC. Directly or via French from, ultimately, Latin *locut-*, the past participle stem of *loqui* "to speak."]

Lod /lod/ city in Israel, situated 23 mi./37 km northwest of Jerusalem. Population: 45,500 (1992).

lode /lōd/ *n.* **1.** GEOL DEPOSIT OF ORE a deposit or vein of ore **2.** ABUNDANT SUPPLY an abundant supply of something [Old English *lād*, literally "something that leads" (see LOAD)]

lo·den /lṓd'n/ *n.* **1.** TEXTILES THICK WATERPROOF WOOLEN CLOTH a thick waterproof woolen cloth used for coats and jackets **2.** COLORS DARK GREEN the dark-green color of loden cloth [Early 20thC. From German.] —**lo·den** *adj.*

lode·star /lṓd stàar/, **load·star** *n.* **1.** THE NORTH STAR the North Star (**Polaris**), used for navigation or as a reference position in astronomy **2.** GUIDING PRINCIPLE something that somebody uses as a model or principle to guide behavior (*literary*) [14thC. From LODE in the obsolete sense "course, leading" + STAR.]

lode·stone /lṓd stōn/, **load·stone** *n.* **1.** GEOL MAGNETITE magnetite or a piece of magnetite with magnetic properties **2.** ATTRACTION somebody or something that attracts others like a magnet [Early 16thC. From LODE in the obsolete sense "way, leading," from the use of the stone's magnetic properties as a guide + STONE.]

lodge /loj/ *n.* **1.** LEISURE COUNTRY BUILDING a cabin or other building in the country providing temporary accommodation, e.g., as a vacation home or a temporary shelter for campers, walkers, skiers, or hunters **2.** LEISURE BUILDING IN VACATION COMPLEX the main building or all the buildings in a vacation complex, usually providing meals, overnight accommodation and over guest services. Lodges, including park lodges, hunting lodges, and ski lodges are usually located in or near mountains or tourist attractions. **3.** LEISURE INN OR HOTEL a large house or hotel **4.** BRANCH OF UNION OR ORGANIZATION a local branch or chapter of a fraternal organization or union **5.** MEETING HALL a hall or other meeting place used by a branch of a society **6.** NATIVE AMERICAN DWELLING a dwelling traditionally used by Native American people, e.g., a wigwam, hogan, or longhouse **7.** SMALL GATEKEEPER'S HOUSE in Britain, a small house in the grounds of a large country house or park, usually near the main gate, traditionally occupied by a gatekeeper, gardener, or estate worker **8.** ZOOL BEAVER'S DEN the den of certain animals, especially the dome-shaped structure built by a beaver ■ *v.* (**lodged, lodg·ing, lodg·es**) **1.** *vt.* REGISTER COMPLAINT OR APPEAL to make a formal complaint, accusation, or appeal by handing the documents to the appropriate authority **2.** *vt.* DEPOSIT SOMETHING IN SAFE PLACE to put something somewhere or give it to somebody for safekeeping **3.** *vti.* STICK OR GET STUCK to become jammed or embedded somewhere, or to jam or embed something somewhere ○ *His head was lodged between the railings.* **4.** *vi.* LIVE IN SOMEBODY'S HOUSE to live in somebody's house, free or as a paying guest (*dated*) **5.** *vt.* PUT IN ACCOMMODATIONS to place somebody in temporary accommodations ○ *They were evacuated and lodged in a nearby school overnight.* **6.** *vt.* GIVE SOMEBODY POWER TO ACT to invest somebody with the power or authority to do something ○ *powers that are lodged with the cabinet* **7.** *vti.* AGRIC BEAT CROPS FLAT to flatten crops, or be flattened by the wind and rain [13thC. From Old French *loge* "hut." Ultimately from a prehistoric Germanic word denoting a roof made of bark, which is also the ancestor of English *lobby.*]

Lodge /loj/, **Henry Cabot** (1850–1924) U.S. politician. As Republican leader in the Senate, he promoted U.S. entry into World War I but opposed the League of Nations (1919).

lodge·ment *n.* = **lodgment**

lodge·pole pine /lój pōl-/ *n.* a tall pine of western North America that has paired needles and two types of cones, one of which releases seeds only after a forest fire. Genus: *Pinus contorta.* [From Native North Americans' use of the trees' trunks as supports for their lodges]

lodg·er /lójjər/ *n.* **1.** PAYING GUEST somebody who rents a room in another person's house, sharing the accommodation with the owner (*dated*) ○ *"...the small kitchen in which she cooked the food for her lodgers"* (Jack London, *The People of the Abyss*; 1905) **2.** SOMEBODY LODGING SOMETHING somebody who lodges something, e.g., a complaint

lodg·ing /lójjing/ *n.* ACCOMMODATION somewhere to stay temporarily ○ *We asked where we could find lodging for the night.* ■ **lodg·ings** *npl.* RENTED ROOM a room or rooms in a boarding house or private home available for rent (*dated*)

lodg·ing house *n. U.K.* = **rooming house** (*dated*)

lodg·ment /lójmənt/, **lodge·ment** *n.* **1.** ACCUMULATION OR BLOCKAGE a build-up of something, especially when this causes a blockage **2.** MIL FOOTHOLD IN ENEMY TERRITORY a small area of land that has been captured and held on the edge of enemy territory **3.** LODGING the lodging of somebody or something

Lo·di /lṓdī/ **1.** city in San Joaquin County, central California, situated 12 mi./19 km north of Stockton. Population: 51,874 (1990). **2.** borough in Bergen County, northeastern New Jersey, situated 5 mi./8 km southeast of Paterson. Population: 22,355 (1990).

lod·i·cule /lóddi kyoōl/ *n.* any of the tiny scales at the base of the ovary of the flower of certain grasses [Mid-19thC. From Latin *lodicula*, literally "small coverlet," from *lodix* "blanket," of uncertain origin.]

Lodz /loōj, lodz/, **Łódź** industrial city in central Poland, situated about 75 mi./121 km southwest of Warsaw. Population: 825,600 (1995).

Loeb /lōb/, **Jacques** (1859–1924) German-born U.S. physiologist. He produced pioneering work in artificial parthenogenesis, and conducted important research in physiology and psychology.

lo·ess /less, luss, lṓ əss/ *n.* a fine-grained yellowish brown deposit of soil left by the wind. The loess deposited by winds from Central Asia provided the basis for productive farming in early China. [Mid-19thC. From German *Löss*, from, ultimately, Swiss German *lösch* "loose."]

Loewe /lō/, **Frederick** (1904–88) U.S. composer. His musical comedies, produced in collaboration with Alan Jay Lerner, include *My Fair Lady* (1956).

Loe·wi /lṓ ee/, **Otto** (1873–1961) German pharmacologist. He shared a Nobel Prize in chemistry (1936) for his work on the chemical transmission of nerve impulses.

Lo·fo·ten Is·lands /lṑ fōt'n-/ chain of two groups of rock islands, northwestern Norway, in the Norwegian Sea. The southernmost group is the Lofoten, and the Vesterålen are to the north. Population: 26,241 (1970). Area: 1,600 sq. mi./4,044 sq. km.

loft /loft/ *n.* **1.** UPPER FLOOR OF BARN the upper floor of a barn or stable, used for storing hay ○ *a hay loft* **2.** GALLERY a gallery or balcony, especially the gallery where the organ is situated in a church ○ *the organ loft* **3.** *U.K.* ROOF SPACE the area between the ceiling of the top floor of a building and the roof (*often used before a noun*) **4.** BUILDING UPPER FLOOR OF WAREHOUSE OR FACTORY an upper floor of a commercial building such as a factory or warehouse, typically converted to residential or studio use **5.** BUILDING ELEVATED ROOM IN HOUSE a platform, reachable by a ladder or stairs, that serves as an extra room in a high-ceilinged house **6.** GOLF SLANTING ANGLE ON GOLF CLUB the angle of the face of a golf club designed to drive the ball high into the air **7.** TEXTILES THICKNESS OF FABRIC the thickness and fluffiness of fabric, especially as an indication of its warmth ■ *vt.* (**loft·ed, loft·ing, lofts**) **1.** SPORTS HIT BALL HIGH to hit a ball in a high arching path **2.** KEEP IN LOFT to store something in a loft [Pre-12thC. From Old Norse *lopt* "air, upstairs room." Ultimately from a prehistoric Germanic word meaning "air, sky," which is also the ancestor of English *lift.*]

loft·y /lóftee/ (**-i·er, -i·est**) *adj.* **1.** HAUGHTY behaving in a falsely superior or haughty manner **2.** EXALTED exalted and refined **3.** HIGH-RANKING of the highest rank or status **4.** VERY HIGH very high or tall ○ *lofty peaks*

log[1] /log/ *n.* **1.** PIECE CUT FROM TREE a section of the trunk or a thick branch of a tree that has been cut for fuel or building material **2.** TRANSP RECORD OF JOURNEY a record of a journey made by a ship or aircraft, detailing all events, or the book in which it is kept **3.** RECORD OF EVENTS any detailed record of events **4.** NAUT DEVICE FOR MEASURING SPEED a float attached to a ship by a line, formerly used for measuring the ship's speed ■ *v.* (**logged, log·ging, logs**) **1.** *vt.* TRANSP RECORD EVENT IN LOG to record information or an event in a log ○ *The computer will log all these transactions automatically.* **2.** *vti.* FELL TREES to cut down the trees growing on a particular area of land **3.** *vti.* CUT UP TREE FOR LOGS to cut up a tree to produce logs for fuel or building **4.** *vt.* TRAVEL PARTICULAR DISTANCE OR SPEED to travel a particular distance, time, or speed that is then recorded in a log ○ *These checks are made routinely once the aircraft has logged 100,000 miles.* **5.** *vt.* HAVE WORK TIME IN CREDIT to spend time or accumulate a certain number of hours, especially for a job, that are usually recorded somewhere [14thC.

Origin unknown.] ◇ **sleep like a log** to sleep very soundly

log in *vti.* = **log on**

log off, log out *vi.* COMPUT to end a session on a computer by typing in the appropriate command

log on, log in *vti.* COMPUT to gain access to a computer system by entering a name and password or other appropriate commands

log out *vi.* = **log off**

log[2] /log/ *n.* a logarithm (*informal*) [Mid-17thC. Shortening.]

Lo·gan, Mount /lṓgən/ the highest peak in Canada, located in the Saint Elias Range in southwestern Yukon Territory. Height: 19,551 ft./5,959 m.

Lo·gan, Sir William Edmond (1798–1875) Canadian geologist. He was a founder and the first director of the Geological Survey of Canada (1842–69).

Loganberry

lo·gan·ber·ry /lṓgən bèrree/ (*plural* **-ries**) *n.* **1.** PLANTS **PLANT WITH EDIBLE FRUIT** a prickly trailing hybrid plant native to the western United States and northwest Mexico, cultivated for its edible fruit. Latin name: *Rubus ursinus loganobaccus.* **2. PURPLISH-RED FRUIT** the purplish-red fruit obtained from the loganberry, similar to a large raspberry [Late 19thC. Named for James H. *Logan* (1841–1928), U.S. horticulturist who first cultivated the plant.]

lo·ga·oed·ic /lòggə ēédik/ *adj.* used to describe a poem or line of verse in which different metrical feet are mixed to give an effect like speech or prose [Mid-19thC. Via late Latin from Greek *logaoidikos*, from *logos* "speech" + *aoidē* "song."]

log·a·rithm /lóggə ri̱thəm/ *n.* the power to which a base must be raised to equal a given number. For example, the logarithm of 8 to the base 2 is 3, since $2^3 = 8$. [Early 17thC. From modern Latin *logarithmus*, from Greek *logos* "word, proportion" (see LOGOS) + *arithmos* "number" (see ARITHMETIC).] —**log·a·rith·mic** /lòggə ríthmik/ *adj.* —**log·a·rith·mi·cal·ly** *adv.*

log·book /lóg bo͝ok/ *n.* a book containing a record of a journey made by a ship or aircraft [Late 17thC. So called because it recorded all *loggings*, measurements of the ship's speed.]

log cab·in *n.* **1. LOG HOUSE** a simple house made with logs **2.** SEW **PATCHWORK DESIGN** a patchwork design formed from blocks that are made up of strips of fabric attached around each side of a central square

loge /lōzh/ *n.* **1. FRONT OF BALCONY** the area in a theater at the front of the upper level **2. BOX IN THEATER** a small private enclosure or box in a theater [Mid-18thC. Via French from Old French, "hut" (see LODGE).]

log·ger /lóggər/ *n.* a person or company in the business of harvesting trees for wood

log·ger·head /lóggər hèd/ *n.* **1.** ZOOL = **loggerhead turtle 2.** BIRDS = **loggerhead shrike 3.** MECH ENG **TOOL FOR HOT LIQUIDS** a tool consisting of a ball or bulb on a long handle that can be heated and used to melt pitch **4. UNINTELLIGENT PERSON** somebody perceived as unintelligent (*archaic*) [Late 16thC. Origin uncertain: probably from *logger* "block of wood for hobbling a horse" (from LOG[1]) + HEAD.] ◇ **at loggerheads** involved in a quarrel or feud

log·ger·head shrike *n.* BIRDS a North American shrike that has gray plumage, black and white wings and tail, a black facial mask, and a hooked beak. Latin name: *Lanius ludovicianus.*

log·ger·head tur·tle *n.* a large flesh-eating sea turtle that lives in warm waters and has a large head and rounded shell. Latin name: *Caretta caretta.*

Loggia

log·gi·a /láwjee ə/ (*plural* **-gi·as** *or* **-gie** /láw jày/) *n.* **1. COVERED BALCONY AND WALKWAY** a covered open-sided walkway, often with arches, along one side of a building **2. THEATER BALCONY** a balcony in a theater [Mid-18thC. Via Italian from Old French *loge* (see LODGE).]

log·ging /lógging/ *n.* the job of felling, trimming, and transporting trees

lo·gi·a plural of **logion**

log·ic /lójjik/ *n.* **1.** PHILOSOPHY **THEORY OF REASONING** the branch of philosophy that deals with the theory of deductive and inductive arguments and aims to distinguish good from bad reasoning **2. SYSTEM OF REASONING** any system of or an instance of reasoning and inference **3. SENSIBLE ARGUMENT AND THOUGHT** sensible rational thought and argument rather than ideas that are influenced by emotion or whim **4. REASONING OF PARTICULAR FIELD** the principles of reasoning relevant to a particular field **5. INESCAPABLE RELATIONSHIP AND PATTERN OF EVENTS** the relationship between certain events, situations, or objects, and the inevitable consequences of their interaction **6.** COMPUT **CIRCUIT DESIGN** the circuit design and principles used by a computer in its operation [14thC. Via French *logique* from, ultimately, Greek *logikē (tekhnē)* "(art) of reason," from *logos* (see LOGOS).]

log·i·cal /lójjik'l/ *adj.* **1. SENSIBLE AND BASED ON FACTS** based on facts, clear rational thought, and sensible reasoning **2. ABLE TO THINK RATIONALLY** able to think sensibly and come to a rational conclusion based on facts rather than emotion **3.** PHILOSOPHY **OF PHILOSOPHICAL LOGIC** relating to philosophical logic —**log·i·cal·i·ty** /lòjji kállətee/ *n.* —**log·i·cal·ness** /lójjik'lnəss/ *n.*

log·i·cal at·om·ism *n.* the philosophical theories of Bertrand Russell and Ludwig Wittgenstein's early period that analyze a proposition in terms of its relation to certain philosophically basic propositions

log·i·cal con·se·quence *n.* a proposition that is implied by valid reasoning from true propositions

log·i·cal con·stant *n.* a connective expression such as "not," "or," "if … then," or "if and only if" that is used in formal logic

log·i·cal·ly /lójjikəlee/ *adv.* **1. WITH REGARD TO REASON** in a rational well-reasoned way ○ *consider sth logically* **2. USING REASON** using good or rational reasoning ○ *Your conclusion follows logically.*

log·i·cal pos·i·tiv·ism *n.* a theory in linguistic philosophy that holds that in order for a sentence to be cognitively meaningful, it has to be verifiable

log·i·cal truth *n.* a proposition that is necessarily true

log·ic bomb *n.* a piece of software that interferes with the proper working of the computer's operating system

log·ic cir·cuit *n.* a computer switching circuit that performs operations on input signals

lo·gi·cian /lō jísh'n/ *n.* somebody whose special training is in philosophical logic

log·i·cism /lójji sìzzəm/ *n.* the theory at the base of mathematics that mathematics is reducible to logic broadly construed to include set theory

lo·gi·on /lójee òn, -gee-/ (*plural* **-a** /-əl/) *n.* a saying attributed to Jesus Christ that is not in the New Testament [Late 19thC. From Greek, "oracle," from *logos* (see LOGOS).]

lo·gis·tic[1] /lə jístik, lō-/ *adj.* relating to an uninterpreted calculus or system of symbolic logic [Early 17thC. From medieval Latin *logisticus*, from, ultimately, Greek *logos* "reckoning, calculation" (see LOGOS).] —**lo·gis·ti·cian** /lòji stísh'n/ *n.*

lo·gis·tic[2] /lə jístik, lō-/, **lo·gis·ti·cal** /-ik'l/ *adj.* **1. RELATING TO TRANSPORTING OF THINGS** involving the planning and management of how things are moved, especially military forces or industrial goods **2. INVOLVING COMPLICATED ORGANIZATION** involving the planning and management of any complex task [Mid-20thC. From French *logistique* (see LOGISTICS).] —**lo·gis·ti·cal·ly** *adv.*

lo·gis·tics /lə jístiks, lō jístiks/ *n.* (*takes a singular or plural verb*) **1. ORGANIZATION OF COMPLEX TASK** the planning and implementation of a complex task **2. MOVEMENT MANAGEMENT** the planning and control of the flow of goods and materials through an organization or manufacturing process **3.** MIL **ORGANIZATION OF TROOP MOVEMENTS** the planning and organization of the movement of troops, their equipment, and supplies [Late 19thC. Formed from French *logistique*, from *loger* "to lodge," from Old French *loge* (see LODGE).]

log·jam /lóg jàm/ *n.* **1. DEADLOCK** a situation where something is blocked or at a standstill and is unable to progress **2. RIVER BLOCKAGE** a blockage caused by floating logs in a river

log line *n.* a line from a ship trailing a floating log to determine the ship's speed

lo·go /lṓ gō/ (*plural* **-gos**) *n.* a design used by an organization on its letterhead, advertising material, and signs as an emblem by which the organization can easily be recognized [Mid-20thC. Shortening of LOGOGRAM and LOGOTYPE.]

logo- *prefix.* word, thought, speech ○ *logotype* [From Greek *logos* (see LOGOS)]

log·o·gram /lóggə gràm/, **log·o·graph** /lóggə gràf/ *n.* a symbol that represents the meaning of a whole word or phrase, e.g., the symbols used in shorthand, or the symbol "&" used instead of the word "and" —**log·o·gram·mat·ic** /lòggəgrə máttik/ *adj.* —**log·o·gram·mat·i·cal·ly** *adv.*

log·o·griph /lóggə grìf/ *n.* a word puzzle, especially an anagram [Late 16thC. From French *logogriphe*, from Greek *logos* (see LOGOS) + *griphos* "fishing-basket," hence "anything intricate, riddle."]

lo·gom·a·chy /lō gómməkee/ (*plural* **-chies**) *n.* an argument about the use or meaning of words [Mid-16thC. From Greek *logomakhia*, from *logomakhein* "to fight with words," from *logos* "word" (see LOGOS) + *makhē* "battle."]

log·or·rhe·a /lòggə réé ə/ *n.* excessive talkativeness, especially when the words are uncontrolled or incoherent, as is seen in certain psychiatric illnesses —**log·or·rhe·ic** *adj.*

Lo·gos /lṓ gòss, ló gòss/ *n.* **1.** CHR **JESUS CHRIST AS DIVINE WISDOM** Jesus Christ, so named in St. John's Gospel, as the word of God, the personification of the wisdom of God and divine wisdom as the means for human salvation. **2.** JUDAISM **WORD OF GOD** the divine wisdom of the word of God [Late 16thC. From Greek, "word, reason." Ultimately from an Indo-European base meaning "to collect" and "to speak," which is also the ancestor of English *collect*, *lecture*, and *lexicon*.]

lo·go·type /lóggə tìp/ *n.* **1.** PRINTING **TYPE WITH DIFFERENT CHARACTERS** a single piece of type that has different unconnected characters on it **2.** COMM **LOGO** a logo

log·roll /lóg rōl/ (**-rolled, -roll·ing, -rolls**) *vti.* to trade votes with political colleagues to support one another's interests [Mid-19thC. Back-formation from LOGROLLING.]

log·roll·ing /lóg rōling/ *n.* **1.** POL **EXCHANGE OF POLITICAL SUPPORT** the striking of a deal between colleagues in a legislature whereby support is given to a piece of legislation on the understanding that the favor will be returned at a later date ○ *"The national interest will lose out to the logrolling tradeoffs of Congressional business."* (National Public Telecomputing Network, *Bush speeches in campaign '92*; 1992) **2. MUTUAL SUPPORT** mutual praise, support, or favors **3.** SPORTS **BALANCING GAME** a game played by lumberjacks in which players have to balance on spinning floating logs [Early 19thC. From the former custom of neighbors helping each other to clear land by rolling logs to burn them.]

-logue *suffix.* speech ○ *monologue* [Via French from Greek *-logos* "speaking," from *logos* "word" (see LOGOS)]

log·wood /lóg wo͝od/ *n.* **1. SPINY TREE THAT GIVES DYE** a spiny tree of the pea family that grows in the West Indies and Central America and yields a dye from the heart of the wood. Latin name: *Haematoxylon campechianum.* **2.** INDUST **WOOD GIVING DYE** the wood of the logwood from which a purplish-red dye is obtained [Late 16thC. So called because the tree's wood was imported in log form.]

lo·gy /lógee/ (**-gi·er, -gi·est**) *adj.* without any energy or enthusiasm [Mid-19thC. Origin uncertain: perhaps from Dutch *log* "heavy," or a variant of *loggy* "heavy, dull" (from LOG).]

-logy *suffix.* **1.** speech, expression ○ *haplology* **2.** science, study ○ *musicology* [Directly and via French from, ultimately, Greek *-logia*, from *logos* "word, reason" and from *-logos* "speaking" (see LOGOS)]

loin /loyn/ *n.* **1.** ANAT **BACK BETWEEN RIBS AND HIPS** the area on each side of the backbone of a human or animal between the ribs and hips **2.** FOOD **MEAT CUT FROM LOIN OF ANIMAL** a prime cut of tender meat taken from the backbone and rib area of a pig, lamb, or calf. The meat is sold either as joints or cut into chops. ■ **loins** *npl.* **AREA BELOW WAIST** the hips and the front of the body below the waist, considered as the part of the body that should be covered and as the site of the sexual organs (*literary*) [14thC. Via Old French *loigne* from, ultimately, Latin *lumbus* (source of English *lumbar, sirloin,* and *lumbago*).] ◇ **gird (up) your loins** to prepare yourself to do something difficult and challenging

loin·cloth /lóyn klòth/ *n.* a cloth covering the hips and the genital area

Loire /lwaar/ the longest river in France, rising in the Cévennes mountains, southeastern France. Length: 634 mi./1,020 km.

loi·ter /lóytər/ (**-tered, -ter·ing, -ters**) *vi.* **1. STAND AROUND IDLY** to stand around without any obvious purpose (*disapproving*) **2. PROCEED SLOWLY** to do something in a slow lazy way, often stopping to rest [15thC. Origin uncertain: possibly from Middle Dutch *loteren* "to totter, linger."] —**loi·ter·er** *n.*

Lo·ki /lṓkee/ *n.* MYTHOL in Norse mythology, a handsome giant god who was the embodiment of evil

LOL *abbr.* laughing out loud (*used in e-mail messages*)

Lo·li·ta /lō leétə/ *n.* a young teenage girl regarded or depicted as the object of sexual desire [Mid-20thC. From the name of the main character in *Lolita* (1958), a novel by Vladimir Nabokov.]

loll /lol/ (**lolled, loll·ing, lolls**) *vi.* **1. LOUNGE IN A RELAXED WAY** to relax in a reclining or leaning position **2. DROOP** to droop or hang down in a loose floppy way [14thC. Origin uncertain: possibly from Middle Dutch *lollen* "to doze."]

Lol·land /lóllənd/ island of southeastern Denmark, situated in the Baltic Sea. Population: 72,026 (1994). Area: 479 sq. mi./1,241 sq. km.

lol·la·pa·loo·za /lòlləpə lóozə/, **lal·a·pa·loo·za, lal·la·pa·loo·za** *n.* somebody or something that is wonderful or amazing (*slang*) [Early 20thC. Origin unknown.]

lol·li·pop /lóllee pòp/, **lol·ly·pop** *n.* a piece of hard candy attached to a stick [Late 18thC. Origin uncertain: perhaps from dialect *lolly* "tongue" (formed from LOLL) + POP.]

lol·lop /lólləp/ (**-loped, -lop·ing, -lops**) *vi.* **1. MOVE IN BOUNCY UNCONTROLLED WAY** to move along in a bouncy relaxed clumsy way **2.** *U.K.* **LOUNGE ABOUT** to loll or lounge about [Mid-18thC. Formed from LOLL, under the influence of GALLOP.] —**lol·lop·y** *adj.*

lol·ly /lóllee/ (*plural* **-lies**) *n.* **1.** *U.K.* **LOLLIPOP** a lollipop (*informal*) **2.** *U.K.* **MONEY** money (*informal*) **3.** *Aus* **CANDY** a piece of candy [Mid-19thC. Shortening of LOLLIPOP.]

lol·ly·gag /lóllee gàg/ (**-gagged, -gag·ging, -gags**), **lal·ly·gag** *vi.* to have fun, or waste time in a lazy idle way (*dated*) [Mid-19thC. Origin unknown.]

lol·ly·pop *n.* = **lollipop**

lo·ma /lṓmə/ *n.* a rounded hill or ridge [Mid-19thC. From Spanish, feminine of *lomo* "back, ridge," from Latin *lumbus* "loin."]

Lo·max /lṓ màks/, **Alan** (*b.* 1915) U.S. ethnomusicologist. He was noted for his work in the collection of folk songs, in collaboration with his father John Lomax.

Lo·max, John (1867–1948) U.S. ethnomusicologist. He was noted for his work in the collection of American folk songs, in collaboration with his son Alan Lomax.

Lom·bard /lóm baàrd, lúm-/ *n.* **1. SOMEBODY FROM LOMBARDY** somebody who was born in or who lives in Lombardy in Italy **2. ANCIENT ITALIAN** a member of an ancient Germanic people who settled in northern Italy during the 6th century A.D., where they soon became the dominant people

Lom·bar·di /lom baárdee/, **Vince** (1913–70) U.S. football coach. As head coach and then general manager, he led the Green Bay Packers to two Super Bowl victories (1967, 1968). Full name **Vincent Thomas Lombardi**

Lom·bar·dy /lómbərdee, lúm-/ region in northern central Italy, a major commercial and industrial center —**Lom·bar·dic** /lom baárdik, lum-/ *adj.*

Lom·bar·dy pop·lar *n.* a variety of poplar that has upright branches and a tall, narrow shape. Latin name: *Populus nigra italica.*

Lom·bok /lom bók/ island of the Lesser Sunda Islands, West Nusa Tenggara Province, southern Indonesia, situated east of Bali. Population: 2,403,399 (1990). Area: 2,000 sq. mi./5,180 sq. km.

Lo·mé /lō mày/ capital and largest city of Togo, situated on the Bight of Benin, close to the Ghana border. Population: 450,000 (1990).

lo·ment /lṓ mènt/ *n.* a pod or fruit of certain plants that splits and separates at maturity into one-seeded segments [Mid-19thC. From Latin *lomentum* "cosmetic made of bean-meal," from *lavare* "to wash."]

Lom·poc /lóm pòk/ city in Santa Barbara County, southwestern California, situated near the Pacific Ocean 45 mi./72 km northwest of the city of Santa Barbara. Population: 37,649 (1990).

Lon·don /lúndən/ **1.** capital city of the United Kingdom of Great Britain and Northern Ireland. It is one of the world's leading financial, industrial, and cultural centers. Population: 6,967,000 (1994). Area: 610 sq. mi./1,580 sq. km. **2.** city in Middlesex County, southwestern Ontario, Canada, on the Thames River. Population: 325,646 (1996). —**Lon·don·er** *n.*

Lon·don, Jack (1876–1916) U.S. writer. He wrote realist and humanitarian novels, including *The Call of the Wild* (1903), which was inspired by his experiences in the Klondike. Full name **John Griffith London**

Lon·don·der·ry /lúndən dèree/ **1.** city in northwestern Northern Ireland, officially called Derry until it was fortified by people from London, England, in 1613. Population: 72,334 (1991). **2.** former county of Northern Ireland

lone /lōn/ *adj.* **1. SOLITARY** having no one else around **2. ONLY** only or sole **3. ISOLATED** situated in an isolated position **4. SINGLE** without a husband, wife, or partner **5. LONELY** lonely and having no companions (*literary*) [14thC. Shortening of ALONE by mistaken division of *al one* "all by yourself" as *a lone*.]

lone hand *n.* **1.** CARDS **HAND PLAYED WITHOUT PARTNER** a hand played in some card games without help from a partner, or a player without a partner **2. SOMEBODY OPERATING ALONE** somebody who lives or works alone

lone·ly /lṓnlee/ (**-li·er, -li·est**) *adj.* **1. FEELING ALONE** having or causing a feeling of being alone and sad **2. ISOLATED** isolated and rarely visited **3. LACKING SUPPORT** lacking companionship, aid, or encouragement **4. SOLITARY** having no one or nothing else around (*literary*) —**lone·li·ly** *adv.* —**lone·li·ness** *n.*

lone·ly-hearts *adj.* relating to people who are looking for a partner for a romantic relationship

lon·er /lṓnər/ *n.* somebody who prefers to be alone

lone·some /lṓnsəm/ *adj.* **1. SAD FROM BEING ALONE** feeling sad, or causing a feeling of sadness, because of being alone **2. DESOLATE** isolated from human habitation **3. ALONE** having no one or nothing else around —**lone·some·ly** *adv.* —**lone·some·ness** *n.*

lone wolf *n.* somebody who prefers to be alone

long[1] /lawng/ *adj.* **1. EXTENDING CONSIDERABLE DISTANCE** extending a relatively great length or height **2. GOING ON FOR LENGTHY PERIOD** lasting for an extended period of time **3. HAVING MANY ITEMS** containing a relatively large number of parts or individual items **4. OF SPECIFIED LENGTH** of a specified length, height, total, number, or duration ○ *a book 300 pages long* **5. LONGER THAN IT IS WIDE** with a greater length than width ○ *Look in the long box, not the square one.* **6. BEYOND WHAT IS WANTED** extending in time or space beyond what is considered normal, reasonable, or desirable **7. MORE DISTANT OR LENGTHY** the more or most distant or lengthy of two or more things ○ *the long way home* **8. ABLE TO REACH CONSIDERABLE DISTANCE** capable of reaching or traveling far ○ *a long fly ball* **9. SEEMING TO LAST FOREVER** appearing to be or take more time than is really the case ○ *a long hour waiting* **10. GOING FAR BACK IN TIME** extending back in time ○ *a long memory* **11. EXTENSIVE** exhaustive and critical ○ *Take a good long look at yourself.* **12. RISKY** with an uncertain outcome **13. HAVING PLENTY OF SOMETHING** possessing enough or more than enough of something (*informal*) ○ *a politician who is long on rhetoric* **14.** FIN **HOLDING STOCK IN ANTICIPATION OF RISE** used to describe shares and other securities or commodities that are held with the expectation that prices will rise **15.** PHON **DRAWN OUT IN PRONUNCIATION** used to describe a speech sound that is relatively drawn out **16.** PHON **DESCENDED FROM LONG VOWEL** used to describe an English vowel sound that is historically descended from vowels that were drawn out in pronunciation, e.g., the ones in English "beet" and "bite" **17.** POETRY **ACCENTED** used to describe a syllable in accentual verse that is stressed **18.** POETRY **OF GREATER METRICAL DURATION** used to describe a syllable in quantitive verse that is the one of the two types that is of greater duration ■ *adv.* **1. FOR LONG TIME** for or during a lengthy period of time ○ *Have you been here long?* **2. FAR** at or to a great distance ○ *hit the ball long* **3. FOR CERTAIN TIME** for or during a particular length of time ○ *work all day long* **4. AT ANOTHER TIME** at a time much later or earlier than the time specified ○ *long after he left* **5. AFTER CERTAIN TIME** beyond a particular time ○ *Don't stay longer than two hours.* **6.** STOCK EXCH **IN LONG STOCK POSITION** in a long position in securities or commodities ■ *n.* **1. A LONG TIME** a lengthy period of time ○ *Will you be visiting for long?* **2.** PHON **LONG SOUND** a long syllable or sound **3.** CLOTHES **SIZE FOR TALL PEOPLE** a garment or garment size designed for somebody tall [Old English, from a prehistoric Germanic base that is also the ancestor of English *linger, Lent, lunge,* and *long*[2]] ◇ **any longer** for any further time ◇ **as or so long as 1.** during the time that **2.** because of the fact that **3.** on the condition that ◇ **before long** before much time passes ◇ **no longer** as until the present but not for any further time ◇ **not long for** something with little time remaining for something ◇ **so long** good-bye (*informal*) ◇ **the long and the short of it** the basic idea or facts

WORD KEY: SYNONYMS

See Synonyms at ***want***.

long[2] /lawng/ (**longed, long·ing, longs**) *vi.* to have a strong desire or yearning for somebody or something, especially somebody or something unattainable or not within immediate reach [Old English *langian*, from a prehistoric Germanic base that is also the ancestor of English *long*[1]. The meaning "yearn" developed from "grow long" via "seem long."]

Long /long/, **Huey P.** (1893–1935) U.S. politician. As governor of Louisiana (1928–32) and member of the U.S. Senate (1932–35), he was noted for his oratory and populist views. Full name **Huey Pierce Long**

long. *abbr.* longitude

long-a·go *adj.* relating to or in the distant past ○ *long-ago civilizations*

lon·gan /lάwng gən/, **lun·gan** /lúng-/ *n.* **1. FRUIT** a small juicy fruit with a yellowish brown exterior, white juicy flesh, and a large black seed. The dried fruit is often used as a Chinese health food or cooked with herbal medicine. **2. EVERGREEN TREE** an evergreen tree of tropical and subtropical Asia that has small yellowish-white flowers and small white-fleshed fruits. Latin name: *Euphoria longan.* [Mid-18thC. From Chinese *lóngyan*, literally "dragon's eye" (which the fruit is thought to resemble).]

lon·ga·nim·i·ty /làwngə nímmətee/ *n.* patience and serenity in suffering (*archaic*) [14thC. From late Latin *longanimitas*, from *longanimus*, literally "long-minded," from *animus* "mind."] —**lon·gan·i·mous** /lawng gánniməss/ *adj.*

long-a·wait·ed *adj.* hoped for and expected for a considerable time

Long Beach 1. city in Los Angeles County, southwestern California, situated on San Pedro Bay. Population: 433,852 (1994). **2.** city in Nassau County, southeastern New York, situated off the southern shore of Long Island 21 mi./34 km southeast of New York City. Population: 33,510 (1990).

long·boat /láwng bṓt/ *n.* the longest boat, usually a seaworthy rowing boat, carried on board a sailing ship, especially a merchant ship

long bone *n.* any long cylindrical limb bone in vertebrates that contains marrow and ends in an enlarged head that unites to form a joint with another bone

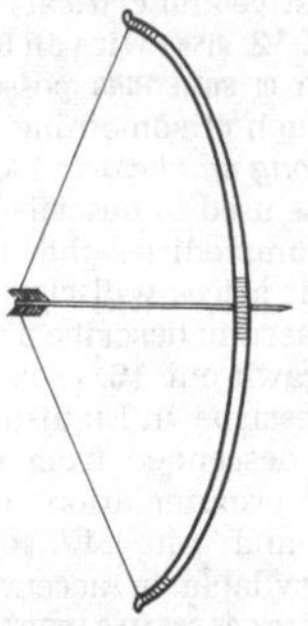

Longbow

long·bow /láwng bō/ *n.* a large powerful hand-drawn bow made from a long piece of slightly curved wood and a bowstring, used, especially in medieval England, for hunting and in warfare

long·bow·man /láwng bōmən/ (*plural* **-men** /-mən/) *n.* an archer who used a longbow, especially in medieval England

Long Branch city in Monmouth County, eastern New Jersey, situated on the Atlantic Ocean 21 mi./34 km southeast of Perth Amboy. Population: 28,658 (1990).

long-case clock *n.* = **grandfather clock**

long-chain *adj.* used to describe a molecule or substance that has a relatively long chain of atoms, especially carbon atoms

long-day *adj.* requiring long periods of daylight, usually more than 12 hours, followed by short nights in order to mature and flower

long-dis·tance *adj.* **1. FOR LONG WAY** traveling or extending a relatively long way **2.** TELECOM **BETWEEN DISTANT PHONES** relating to or providing telephone service between places that are far apart **3. BETWEEN DISTANT PLACES** occurring between places that are far apart ○ *a long-distance romance* ■ *n.* TELECOM **PROVISION OF LONG-DISTANCE TELEPHONE SERVICES** the business of providing long-distance telephone services ■ *adv.* TELECOM **USING LONG-DISTANCE LINE** using a long-distance telephone line

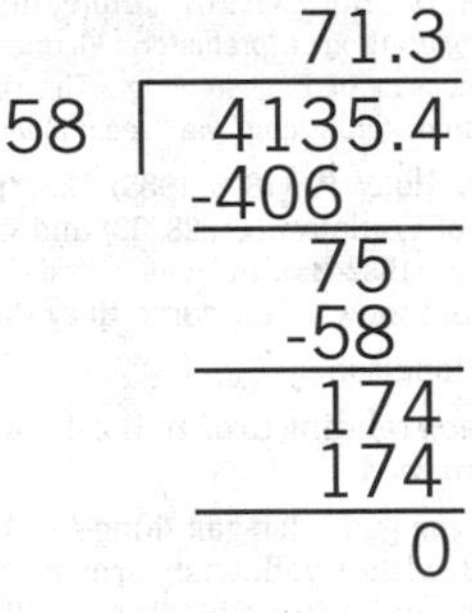

Long division

long di·vi·sion *n.* a method or instance of dividing one number by another in which each step is written out in full

long doz·en *n.* a set of 13 items

long-drawn-out *adj.* going on for an undesirably long period of time

long-eared owl *n.* a medium-sized owl with distinctive pointed ear tufts that lives in coniferous forests in Europe, Asia, and North America. Latin name: *Asio otus.*

lon·ge·ron /lónjə ròn/ *n.* a main structural component of an airplane's fuselage that runs from one end of the airplane to the other [Early 20thC. From French, literally "beam," ultimately from Latin *longus* "long."]

lon·gev·i·ty /lon jévvətee/ (*plural* **-ties**) *n.* **1. LONG LIFE** long duration of life **2. DURATION OF LIFE** the length of a person's or animal's life **3. CAREER SPAN** the length of somebody's employment or career [Early 17thC. From late Latin *longaevitas*, from Latin *longaevus*, literally "of a long age," from *aevum* "age."] —**lon·ge·vous** /lon jeévəss/ *adj.*

long face *n.* a facial expression showing unhappiness, disappointment, or seriousness —**long-faced** *adj.*

Long·fel·low /láwng fèlō/, **Henry Wadsworth** (1807–82) U.S. poet. He wrote many romantic verse narratives, including "The Song of Hiawatha" (1855) and "Paul Revere's Ride" (1863).

long green *n.* money, especially paper money (*informal*)

long·hair /láwng hàir/ *n.* **1. SOMEBODY DEDICATED TO ARTS AND MUSIC** somebody dedicated to the arts and especially to classical music (*informal*) **2. IMPRACTICAL INTELLECTUAL** an intellectual who is unconcerned with practical matters (*informal*) **3. LONG-HAIRED MAN** somebody with long hair, especially a hippie man (*dated informal disapproving*) **4.** ZOOL **CAT WITH LONG FUR** a domestic cat with long fur —**long·haired** *adj.*

long·hand /láwng hànd/ *n.* **1. HANDWRITING IN FULL** words and letters written by hand in full, rather than in shorthand **2. CURSIVE WRITING** cursive writing

long haul *n.* (*informal*) **1. LENGTHY PERIOD** a long period of time **2. LOT OF WORK** a long-lasting job or ordeal **3. LONG DISTANCE** an extensive distance

long-haul *adj.* relating to travel or transportation over long distances

long·head·ed /lawng héddəd/ *adj.* perceptive and wise (*archaic or literary*) [From the belief that a long head indicated wisdom]

long·horn /láwng hàwrn/ (*plural* **-horns** *or* **-horn**) *n.* **1.** **U.S. RED COW WITH LONG HORNS** a red or variegated cow with long horns, belonging to a breed of beef cattle of Spanish origin that was once very common in the southwestern United States **2. COW WITH LONG HORNS** a cow belonging to a breed that has long horns **3. U.S. CYLINDRICAL CHEESE** a mild U.S. cylinder-shaped Cheddar cheese

long-horned bee·tle *n.* a beetle with long antennae, long legs and a narrow, often brightly colored body. The larvae of many species are wood borers. Family: Cerambycidae.

long-horned grass·hop·per *n.* a large, usually green grasshopper with long antennae and often a characteristic song. Family: Tettigoniidae.

long horse *n.* GYMNASTICS = **vaulting horse**

long·house /láwng hòwss/ (*plural* **-hous·es** /-zəz/) *n.* **1. COMMUNAL DWELLING OF NATIVE NORTH AMERICANS** a long bark-covered communal dwelling place built by some Native North American peoples, especially the Iroquois. It had compartments for families around central meeting areas. **2. COMMUNAL DWELLING** a communal dwelling housing entire extended families and found, e.g., in Borneo or Sarawak

long hun·dred·weight *n. U.K.* = **hundredweight** *n.* 2

lon·gi·corn /lónji kàwrn/ *n. U.K.* = **long-horned beetle** ■ *adj.* **WITH LONG ANTENNAE** having long antennae [Mid-19thC. From modern Latin *Longicornia*, literally "long-horned ones," former scientific name, from Latin *cornu* "horn."]

long·ing /láwnging/ *n.* **YEARNING** a persistent and strong desire, usually for somebody or something unattainable or not within immediate reach ■ *adj.* **SHOWING YEARNING** expressing yearning or desire —**long·ing·ly** *adv.*

Long Is·land the largest island in the continental United States, southeastern New York . Queens and Brooklyn, two boroughs of New York City, are situated here. Population: 6,861,474 (1990). Area: 1,682 sq. mi./4,356 sq. km.

Long Is·land Sound body of salt water situated between the southern shore of Connecticut and the northern shore of Long Island, New York. Area: 1,299 sq. mi./3,364 sq. km.

lon·gi·tude /lónji tòod/ *n.* ◊ **latitude 1. ANGULAR DISTANCE FROM PRIME MERIDIAN** the angular distance east or west of the prime meridian that stretches from the north pole to the south pole and passes through Greenwich, England. Longitude is measured in degrees, minutes, and seconds. **2. AREA OF EARTH'S SURFACE** a region near a particular longitude [14thC. From Latin *longitudo* "length" (the original sense in English), from *longus* "long."]

lon·gi·tu·di·nal /lònji tóod'nəl/ *adj.* **1. GOING FROM TOP TO BOTTOM** extending from the top to the bottom of something **2. OVER TIME** relating to development over a period of time **3. OF LONGITUDE** relating to longitude or length —**lon·gi·tu·di·nal·ly** *adv.*

lon·gi·tu·di·nal wave *n.* a wave, e.g., a sound wave, that is propagated in the same direction in which the particles of the medium vibrate

long johns *npl.* underpants with full-length legs, or one-piece underwear covering the torso, arms, and legs [*Johns* from the name *John*]

long jump *n.* a field event in which competitors jump for distance, usually from a running start into a sand pit

long-last·ing *adj.* continuing for a long time

long·leaf pine /láwng leef-/ *n.* **1.** TREES **U.S. PINE TREE** a pine tree native to the southeastern United States, that has long needles grouped in threes, long cones, heavy resinous wood, and orange-brown bark. It is highly valued as a source of lumber, pulp, and turpentine. Latin name: *Pinus palustris.* **2.** INDUST **WOOD FROM LONGLEAF PINE** the wood of the longleaf pine, used for lumber

long-lived *adj.* living, lasting, or enduring for a long time

long-lost *adj.* not seen for a long period of time (*humorous*)

Long·mea·dow /láwng mèdō/ town in southern Massachusetts, on the Connecticut River just north of the Massachusetts-Connecticut border, south of Springfield. Population: 14,864 (1996).

long meas·ure *n.* **1.** MEASURE = **linear measure 2.** = **long meter**

long me·ter *n.* POETRY a four-line stanza in which the second and fourth lines always rhyme and the first and third sometimes rhyme. It is often used for hymns.

Long·mont /láwngmont/ city in Boulder County, northern Colorado, situated 30 mi./48 km north of Denver. Population: 51,555 (1990).

long pig *n.* human flesh as eaten by cannibals [Translation of a Polynesian name]

long-play·ing rec·ord *n.* full form of **LP**

long-range *adj.* **1. EXTENDING WELL INTO THE FUTURE** extending a long time into the future **2. TRAVELING LONG DISTANCES** able to travel long distances **3.** ARMS **ABLE TO HIT DISTANT TARGET** relating to weapons that are capable of hitting a target a considerable distance away

Lon·greach /láwng rèech/ town in central Queensland, Australia, a cattle grazing center and the headquarters of Qantas between 1921 and 1930. Population: 3,766 (1996).

long·ship /láwng shìp/ *n.* a narrow wooden ship with oars and a large square sail used by the Vikings

long·shore /láwng shàwr/ *adj.* living, working, or situated on the coast [Early 19thC. Shortening of ALONGSHORE.]

long·shore·man /láwng shàwrmən/ (*plural* **-men** /-mən/) *n.* somebody whose job is to load and unload cargo vessels in a port

long shot *n.* **1. SOMEBODY OR SOMETHING UNLIKELY TO WIN** somebody or something that is unlikely to win a race or competition **2.** GAMBLING **BET UNLIKELY TO WIN** a bet on somebody or something that is unlikely to win a race or competition **3. VENTURE UNLIKELY TO SUCCEED** a venture, guess, or possibility that has little chance of success, although, if successful, it would be very profitable or rewarding **4.** PHOTOGRAPHY **CAMERA SHOT OF DISTANT OBJECT** a camera shot taken some distance from the object or scene [Originally in the meaning of "shot fired at a distance"] ◇ **(not) by a long shot** (not) in any way at all (*informal*)

long-sight·ed *adj.* = **farsighted** —**long-sight·ed·ly** *adv.* —**long-sight·ed·ness** *n.*

long·some /láwngsəm/ *adj.* extremely long and boring (*archaic*)

long·spur /láwng spùr/ (*plural* **-spurs** *or* **-spur**) *n.* a bunting native to the northern United States, Canada, and the Arctic that has brownish plumage and long-clawed hind toes. Genera: *Calcarius* and *Rhyncophanes.*

long-stand·ing *adj.* having existed or been going on for a long period of time

Long·street /láwng street/, **James** (1821–1904) U.S. soldier. A Mexican War veteran, he was one of Robert E. Lee's most senior Confederate generals during the Civil War. His indecisiveness at the Battle of Gettysburg (1863) was widely blamed for the Confederate loss there.

long-suf·fer·ing *adj.* PATIENTLY ENDURING patient and enduring in the face of suffering or difficulty ■ *n.* PATIENT ENDURANCE patience and endurance in the face of suffering or difficulty —**long-suf·fer·ing·ly** *adv.*

long suit *n.* **1.** CARDS SUIT OF MOST CARDS the suit to which the majority of cards in a player's hand belongs **2.** FINEST QUALITY somebody's strongest quality or talent (*informal*)

long-tailed duck *n.* = **oldsquaw**

long term *n.* the period of time continuing from now long into the future

long-term *adj.* **1.** IN FUTURE relating to or affecting a time long into the future **2.** ACCT WITH LONGER ACCOUNTING PERIOD with or relating to an accounting period of longer than one year **3.** FIN MATURING IN NUMBER OF YEARS maturing only after a long time, usually a number of years **4.** LONG-LASTING continuing for a long period of time

long·time /láwng tìm/ *adj.* having continued in existence for a long period of time

Long Tom *n.* **1.** LONG-BARRELED CANNON USED BY NAVY a swivelling cannon with a long barrel, used in the past by the navy **2.** LONG-RANGE CANNON USED BY ARMY a long-range cannon used by the army. In the United States, the term has usually designated some 155mm howitzers.

long ton *n.* = **ton**[1] *n.* 2

Lon·gueuil /long gáyl/ city in southern Québec Province, Canada, situated on the St. Lawrence River. Population: 127,977 (1996).

lon·gueur /lawng gúr/ *n.* a period of boredom, e.g., a boring passage in a book or a boring scene in a dramatic work (*literary*) [Late 18thC. From French, literally "length," from *long* "long," from Latin *longus*.]

long view *n.* the consideration of how events or circumstances are likely to develop in the long term

Long·view /láwng vyoo/ city in Cowlitz County, southwestern Washington State. Population: 31,499 (1990).

long·ways /láwng wàyz/ *adj.*, *adv.* = **lengthwise**

long-wind·ed *adj.* **1.** USING TOO MANY WORDS tediously wordy in speech or writing **2.** NOT EASILY BECOMING SHORT OF BREATH capable of doing physical exercise for a relatively long period of time without getting short of breath —**long-wind·ed·ly** *adv.* —**long-wind·ed·ness** *n.*

WORD KEY: SYNONYMS

See Synonyms at ***wordy***.

long·wise /láwng wìz/ *adj.*, *adv.* = **lengthwise**

Long·year·by·en /lóng yeer byen/ town in the Svalbard archipelago of Norway, north of the Arctic Circle

loo[1] /loo/ (*plural* **loos**) *n.* *U.K.* a toilet or bathroom (*informal*) [Mid-20thC. Origin uncertain.]

WORD KEY: ORIGIN

The most widely claimed source of *loo* is *gardy loo* (based on pseudo-French *gare de l'eau* "mind the water"), used in 18th-century Edinburgh to warn passers-by when a chamber pot was about to be emptied into the street below. However, this is chronologically unlikely, as there is no evidence of *loo* being used for "toilet" before the 1930s. Other possible candidates include *Waterloo* (the link with "water" gives this some plausibility) and *louvre*, from the use of slatted screens for a makeshift lavatory. The likeliest source is perhaps French *lieux d'aisances*, literally "places of ease," hence "toilet," possibly picked up by British service personnel in France during World War I.

loo[2] /loo/ (*plural* **loos**) *n.* **1.** CARDS GAMBLING CARD GAME a gambling card game in which players place the money they are betting in a pool **2.** GAMBLING BET IN POOL AT LOO a bet placed in the pool in a game of loo [Late 17thC. From French *lantur(e)lu*, the meaningless refrain of a popular song, later the name of the card game.]

loo·fa /lóofə/, **loo·fah**, **luf·fa** /lóofə, lúffə/ *n.* **1.** NATURAL SPONGE a sponge made from the dried fibrous interior of an oblong fruit of a tropical gourd **2.** TROPICAL VINE a tropical vine of the gourd family that bears the large oblong fruits from which loofah sponges are made. Genus: *Luffa*. [Late 19thC. From Arabic *lūfa*.]

look /lòok/ *v.* (**looked, look·ing, looks**) **1.** *vti.* DIRECT EYES to turn the eyes toward or on something **2.** *vi.* USE EYES TO SEARCH to use the eyes to examine, watch, or find somebody or something ○ *We looked everywhere.* **3.** *vi.* SEEM AS SPECIFIED to appear in a specified way ○ *He looks tired.* **4.** *vi.* CONSIDER SOMETHING to direct the attention toward something in order to consider it ○ *Let's look at the entire situation.* **5.** *vt.* FIT SOMETHING BY APPEARANCE to have an appearance that is in accordance with something ○ *He looks his age.* **6.** *vi.* USE EYES IN SPECIFIED WAY to use the eyes in a specified way ○ *He looked intently at the ball.* **7.** *vi.* FACE SPECIFIED WAY to face a specified direction or have a specified view ○ *The room looks over the lake* **8.** *vi.* TEND TOWARD SOMETHING to show a tendency or inclination ○ *The outcome looks good.* **9.** *vt.* EXPRESS SOMETHING to communicate something by an expression ○ *She looked her anger at all of us.* **10.** *vi.* PAY ATTENTION used to tell somebody to pay attention or see something ○ *Look, why don't we split the difference?* ○ *Look! There he goes!* ■ *n.* **1.** ACT OR INSTANCE OF LOOKING an act or instance of looking, e.g., to examine, watch, or find something ○ *Take a look at this.* **2.** WAY SOMEBODY OR SOMETHING APPEARS an impression conveyed by a manner or quality ○ *He has the look of someone enjoying himself.* **3.** EXPRESSION a facial expression that communicates something ○ *a meaningful look* **4.** FASHION an appearance, style, or fashion, especially of dress or hairstyle ■ **looks** *npl.* OUTWARD APPEARANCE somebody's outward physical appearance, especially if it is pleasing ○ *good looks* [Old English *lōcian*, from prehistoric Germanic]

look after *vt.* to care for or be responsible for somebody or something

look ahead *vi.* to think about or plan for the future

look back *vi.* to think about the past or past experiences

look down on, look down up·on *vt.* to regard or treat somebody or something as inferior or with contempt

look for *vt.* **1.** SEARCH FOR to try to find somebody or something **2.** EXPECT to hope for or anticipate something ○ *We're looking for a successful year.* **3.** EXPECT SOMEBODY'S ARRIVAL to expect somebody to arrive at a certain time (*informal*) ○ *We're looking for the grandchildren at noon next Friday.*

look forward to *vt.* to anticipate a future event with excitement or pleasure

look in *vi.* to pay a short visit (*informal*)

look into *vt.* to carry out a careful investigation of something such as a possibility, problem, or crime

look on *v.* **1.** *vi.* WATCH to be a spectator or witness **2.** *vt.* REGARD SOMEBODY OR SOMETHING to regard somebody or something in a particular way

look out *vi.* to be careful to avoid danger

look out for *vt.* **1.** KEEP WATCH FOR SOMEBODY OR SOMETHING to watch for somebody or something to appear (*informal*) **2.** TAKE CARE OF SOMEBODY OR SOMETHING to take particular care of somebody or something

look over *vt.* to inspect or examine somebody or something either quickly or carefully

look through *vt.* to fail to acknowledge somebody's presence, either intentionally or unintentionally

look to *vt.* **1.** EXPECT SOMEBODY TO DO SOMETHING to hope or expect that somebody or something will do or provide something **2.** WANT OR HOPE to want or hope to do something (*informal*) ○ *if you're looking to upgrade your computer*

look up *v.* **1.** *vt.* SEARCH FOR IN REFERENCE BOOK to search for information, e.g., by consulting a reference book **2.** *vi.* IMPROVE to become better **3.** *vt.* VISIT SOMEBODY to locate somebody, especially for a visit

look upon *vt.* = **look on** *v.* 2

look up to *vt.* to have respect and admiration for somebody

look-a-like *n.* somebody or something that looks like somebody or something else (*informal*)

look·down /lòok dòwn/ (*plural* **-downs** *or* **-down**) *n.* a silvery marine fish in the jack family found in Atlantic waters, with a compressed body, a steeply sloping face, and eyes high on the head. Latin name: *Selene vomer*.

look·er /lòokər/ *n.* **1.** SOMEBODY WHO WATCHES somebody who watches, especially an observer or spectator **2.** SOMEBODY GOOD LOOKING a good looking person, especially a girl or woman (*informal*) (*sometimes considered offensive*)

look·er-on (*plural* **look·ers-on**) *n.* = **onlooker**

look-in *n.* a visit of short duration (*informal*)

look·ing glass *n.* a mirror (*archaic*)

look·ing-glass *adj.* characterized by the complete reversal of everything normal (*literary*) [From *Through the Looking Glass* (1871) by Lewis Carroll]

look·out /lòok òwt/ *n.* **1.** CAREFUL WATCH an act of watching carefully for somebody or something **2.** SOMEBODY WATCHING FOR DANGER somebody who watches carefully for any signs of attack or danger **3.** PLACE GIVING GOOD VIEW a place or structure that affords a good view for observation **4.** PROBLEM a problem or concern (*informal*) ○ *That's your lookout.*

look-see *n.* a brief look or inspection (*informal*)

look-up *n.* a computer procedure in which a term or value is matched against a table of stored information

loom[1] /loom/ *vi.* (**loomed, loom·ing, looms**) **1.** BE SEEN AS LARGE SHAPE to appear as a large or indistinct, and sometimes menacing, shape **2.** BE ABOUT TO HAPPEN to be imminent, often in a threatening way ■ *n.* APPEARANCE OF SOMETHING LARGE an appearance of something, usually something large and threatening (*literary*) [Mid-16thC. Origin uncertain: perhaps from Low Dutch, or from a Scandinavian language.]

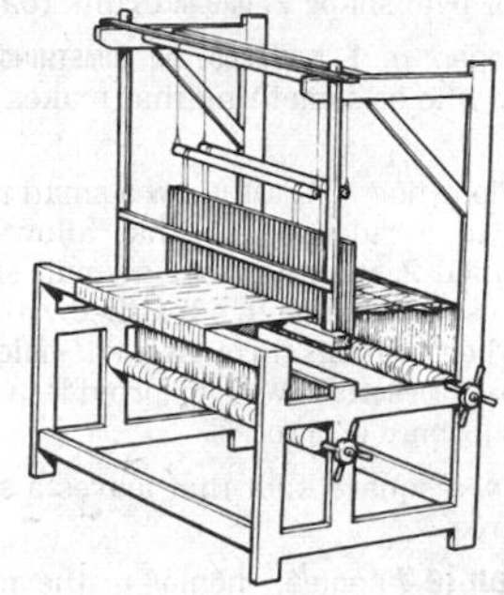

Loom

loom[2] /loom/ *n.* **1.** INDUST WEAVING APPARATUS a hand-operated or machine-operated device for weaving thread or yarn into cloth **2.** NAUT MIDDLE PART OF OAR the middle part of an oar between the blade and the handle [Old English *gelōma* "implement, tool" (source of English *heirloom*), of unknown origin]

loon[1] /loon/ *n.* a fish-eating diving bird found in northern regions of the northern hemisphere. It has a short tail, webbed feet, smooth black-and-white plumage, and a distinctive laughing call. Genus: *Gavia*. [Mid-17thC. Origin uncertain: perhaps ultimately from Old Norse *lómr* "loon," also a name for several other diving birds.]

loon[2] /loon/ *n.* **1.** OFFENSIVE TERM an offensive term that deliberately insults somebody's mental condition or intelligence (*informal*) **2.** *Scotland* BOY a boy or young man [15thC. Origin unknown. In the first sense, influenced by LOON[1] (because of the bird's call), or by LOONY.]

loon·ie /lóonee/, **loon** /loon/ *n.* *Can* a Canadian one-dollar coin with an image of a loon on the back (*informal*) [Late 20thC. Formed from LOON[1].]

loon·y /lóonee/, **loon·ey, lun·y** *adj.* (**-i·er, -i·est**) **1.** OFFENSIVE TERM an offensive term meaning irrational (*informal offensive*) **2.** SILLY silly, thoughtless or strange (*informal*) ○ *loony ideas* ■ *n.* (*plural* **-ies**; *plural* **-eys**) **1.** OFFENSIVE TERM an offensive term that deliberately insults somebody's intelligence and ability to act rationally (*informal insult*) **2.** SOMEBODY SILLY somebody who behaves in an eccentric or thoughtless way (*informal*) (*often considered offensive*) [Mid-19thC. Shortening and alteration of LUNATIC.] —**loon·i·ly** *adv.* —**loon·i·ness** *n.*

loon·y bin *n.* a highly offensive term for a hospital for people who have psychiatric disorders (*informal offensive*)

loop[1] /loop/ *n.* **1.** CIRCLE OR OVAL MADE WITH STRING a circular or oval shape formed by a line or something such as a piece of string that curves back over itself **2.** CIRCLE OR OVAL FOR FASTENING OR HOLDING something that has a closed or nearly closed circular or oval shape and is often used to carry or fasten something **3.** CONTRACEPTIVE DEVICE a contraceptive device in the shape of a loop of plastic or metal that is placed in a woman's womb **4.** ELEC CLOSED CIRCUIT a closed electric circuit **5.** COMPUT SET OF COMMANDS IN COMPUTER PROGRAM a set of instructions in a computer program that is repeated a certain number of times or until a certain objective has been achieved **6.** AIR FLIGHT MANEUVER a flight maneuver in which a plane flies vertically in a circle ○ *to loop the loop* **7.** CINEMA PIECE OF FILM OR TAPE a piece of film or tape joined at both ends to allow repeated use of images or sound, especially in dubbing procedures 8. CRIMINOL COMMON FINGERPRINT PATTERN the most common pattern of a human fingerprint formed by U-shaped ridges 9. ICE SKATING SKATING JUMP AND TURN a jump in which a skater takes off from the outer back edge of a blade, turns in the air, and lands again on the same blade's outer back edge ■ *v.* **(looped, loop·ing, loops)** 1. *vti.* MAKE LOOP to form or make something form the shape of a loop 2. *vt.* to fasten, join, or arrange something using a loop 3. *vi.* CURVE to move in a curved path [14thC. Origin uncertain: perhaps from Irish *lúb* "loop, bend."] ◇ **in** *or* **out of the loop** belonging or not belonging to the people who are decision-makers or are fully informed (*informal*) ◇ **knock** *or* **throw somebody for a loop** to surprise, shock, or upset somebody (*informal*)

loop[2] /loop/ *n.* a loophole in a wall (*archaic*) [14thC. Origin uncertain.]

looped /loopt/ *adj.* 1. FORMED INTO LOOP formed into a circular or oval shape 2. DRUNK drunk (*dated slang*)

loop·er /lóopər/ *n.* 1. SOMEBODY OR SOMETHING THAT LOOPS somebody who or something that makes loops 2. = **inchworm**

loop·hole /lóop hòl/ *n.* 1. GAP IN LAW a small mistake or omission in a rule or law that allows it to be circumvented 2. MIL SLIT IN WALL a small slit or hole in a wall, especially one in a fortified wall for firing guns or other weapons through ■ *vt.* **(-holed, -hol·ing, -holes)** MAKE LOOPHOLES IN WALL to provide a wall with loopholes [Formed from LOOP[2]]

loop knot *n.* a square knot that leaves a single loop hanging free

loop of Hen·le /-hénlee, -hénlə/ *n.* the part of the kidney tubule in birds and mammals that forms a loop between the cortex and medulla [Mid-19thC. Named for the German anatomist and pathologist Friedrich Gustav *Henle* (1801–85).]

loop·y /lóopee/ **(-i·er, -i·est)** *adj.* 1. HAVING LOOPS consisting of loops 2. OFFENSIVE TERM an offensive term for somebody considered to be irrational (*offensive*)

loose /looss/ *adj.* 1. NOT FIRMLY FIXED not firmly fastened or fixed in place ○ *a loose floorboard* 2. SLACK not fastened or pulled tight ○ *a loose knot* 3. NOT TIGHT-FITTING baggy and not fitting closely 4. FREE allowed to move around freely without any restraint 5. NOT PACKAGED not enclosed in a container or bound together ○ *loose tea* 6. NOT FIRMLY PACKED not compact or dense in texture or arrangement ○ *loose soil* 7. IMPRECISE not exact, literal, or precise ○ *a loose translation* 8. FLEXIBLE not strictly controlled or organized ○ *a loose arrangement* 9. AVAILABLE not earmarked for a particular purpose ○ *loose funds* 10. RELAXED relaxed or free from tension (*informal*) 11. IRRESPONSIBLE lacking restraint or a sense of propriety (*dated*) ○ *loose talk* 12. PROMISCUOUS having many sexual partners (*dated*) 13. TOO FLUID too fluid in consistency ○ *loose stools* 14. ACCOMPANIED BY PHLEGM accompanied by the production of phlegm or mucus ○ *a loose cough* ■ *adv.* FREELY freely or without restraint ■ *v.* **(loosed, loos·ing, loos·es)** 1. *vt.* SET FREE to release a person or animal from restraint or confinement 2. *vt.* UNTIE KNOT to undo, untie, or unfasten something 3. *vti.* MAKE SOMETHING LESS TIGHT to make something less tight, or be made less tight 4. *vti.* FIRE MISSILE to fire an arrow, bullet, or other missile (*literary*) 5. *vt.* RELEASE FROM OBLIGATION to release somebody from an obligation or pressure [12thC. From Old Norse *lauss*, from a prehistoric Germanic word that is also the ancestor of English *-less*.] —**loose·ly** *adv.* —**loose·ness** *n.* ◇ **be on the loose** 1. to be free from confinement, e.g., a prison 2. to be free from responsibilities and having a good time (*informal*)

loose·box /lóoss bòks/ *n. U.K.* = **box stall**

loose can·non *n.* somebody who behaves unpredictably or indiscreetly, often causing trouble for colleagues or associates (*slang*)

loose cov·er *n. U.K.* = **slipcover**

loose end *n.* a small part of something, e.g., a project or a story, that has not been completed or fully explained (*informal*) (*often used in the plural*) [Literally referring to the loose end of a string left hanging] ◇ **at loose ends** not knowing what to do with yourself, either because you have nothing to do or because you are in an unusual situation (*informal*)

loose-fill *n.* a lightweight, puffy foam packing material, often shaped like a peanut

loose-joint·ed *adj.* 1. AGILE agile and supple in movement 2. WITH MOBILE JOINTS having joints that fit loosely or that are very mobile —**loose-joint·ed·ness** *n.*

loose-leaf *adj.* with pages that can be removed and replaced easily

loose-limbed *adj.* having supple legs and arms

loose-meat sand·wich *n.* a sandwich on a bun with shredded meats (*regional*)

WORD KEY: REGIONAL NOTE

The term ***loose-meat sandwich*** is most common in the Upper Midwest, especially Iowa.

loos·en /lóoss'n/ **(-ened, -en·ing, -ens)** *v.* 1. *vti.* BECOME OR MAKE LESS TIGHT to become or make something become less tight or fixed 2. *vt.* UNTIE HAIR OR KNOT to untie something such as hair or a knot 3. *vt.* RELAX CONTROL OVER SOMEBODY OR SOMETHING to lessen control, pressure, or strictness 4. *vt.* MAKE BOWELS MORE REGULAR to make somebody's bowel movements more fluid or regular

loosen up *v.* 1. *vti.* WARM UP to do exercises or exercise muscles or joints in order to become more limber, e.g., prior to strenuous activity 2. *vi.* RELAX to become less tense, strict, or serious

loose smut *n.* a disease of cereal grasses in which powdery spore masses replace the grain head

loose·strife /lóoss strìf/ (*plural* **-strifes** *or* **-strife**) *n.* 1. PLANT WITH YELLOW FLOWERS a plant of the primrose family with clusters of yellow flowers. Genus: *Lysimachia.* 2. PLANT WITH PURPLE FLOWERS a plant with spikes of purple flowers. Genus: *Lythrum.* [Mid-16thC. Literal translation of Latin *lysimachia* (as if from Greek *lusis* "loosening" ["ending"] + *makhē* "battle"), named for *Lysimachus*, Greek physician and discoverer of the plant.]

loose-tongued *adj.* liable to gossip or reveal information that should not be told (*informal*)

loot /loot/ *n.* 1. MIL SPOILS OF WAR OR RIOT money or goods that have been pillaged during wartime or a riot 2. CRIMINOL STOLEN GOODS money or goods that have been stolen or obtained illegally 3. MONEY money (*informal*) 4. LOT OF PRESENTS OR PURCHASES a large amount of goods that have been bought or given on one occasion (*informal*) ■ *vti.* **(loot·ed, loot·ing, loots)** STEAL LOOT FROM to steal valuables from a place during wartime or a riot [Mid-19thC. From Hindi *lūṭ*.] —**loot·er** *n.*

lop[1] /lop/ *vt.* **(lopped, lop·ping, lops)** 1. CUT BRANCH OFF TREE to cut a branch off a tree cleanly 2. CUT OFF SOMETHING to cut off something, e.g., hair or a limb, with one stroke 3. GET RID OF SOMEBODY OR SOMETHING to eliminate somebody or something as superfluous 4. TAKE AMOUNT OFF PRICE to deduct an amount from a price ■ *n.* CUT-OFF BRANCH a branch that has been cut off [Early 16thC. From or related to archaic *lop* "smaller branches and twigs of a tree," of uncertain origin: perhaps literally "things stripped off."] —**lop·per** *n.*

lop[2] /lop/ **(lopped, lop·ping, lops)** *v.* 1. *vti.* DROOP to hang or allow something to hang loosely 2. *vi.* MOVE AWKWARDLY to move with an awkward slouching posture [Late 16thC. Thought to suggest the action of flopping about.]

lope /lōp/ *v.* **(loped, lop·ing, lopes)** 1. *vi.* RUN IN LONG EASY STRIDES to run in a relaxed and easy way, taking long strides 2. *vti.* CANTER to canter or to make a horse canter with a long easy stride ■ *n.* LONG-STRIDING GAIT a relaxed and easy gait with long strides [13thC. Ultimately from Old Norse *hlaupa* "to leap."] —**lop·er** *n.*

lop-eared *adj.* used to describe domestic rabbits, dogs, and goats that have loosely hanging ears

Ló·pez Por·til·lo /lòp ez pawr tée ō/, **José** (*b.* 1920) Mexican statesman. As president of Mexico (1976–82), he attempted to make the country more financially independent of the United States.

lo·pho·phore /lóffə fàwr, lṓfə fàwr/ *n.* a circular or horseshoe-shaped structure of tentacles around the mouth of a bryozoan or brachiopod that is used for capturing food [Mid-19thC. Coined from Greek *lophos* "crest" + -PHORE.]

lop·o·lith /lóppə lìth/ *n.* a basin-shaped body of igneous rock formed by the penetration of magma between existing layers of rock [Early 20thC. Coined from Greek *lopas* "basin" + -lith.]

lop·per *n.* = **lobber** (*regional*)

lop·sid·ed /lóp sìdəd, lop sídəd/ *adj.* 1. SLOPING leaning or drooping to one side 2. UNBALANCED unevenly balanced because one side is larger, stronger, or heavier than the other [Early 18thC. "Lop" from LOP[2].]

lo·qua·cious /lō kwáyshəss/ *adj.* tending to talk a great deal (*formal*) [Mid-17thC. Formed from Latin *loquaci-*, stem of *loquax*, from *loqui* "to speak" (source of English *ventriloquist*).]

WORD KEY: SYNONYMS

See Synonyms at ***talkative***.

lo·quat /lṓ kwaat, -kwàt/ (*plural* **-quats** *or* **-quat**) *n.* 1. ORNAMENTAL ORIENTAL TREE a small ornamental evergreen tree native to China and Japan with reddish wooly branches, sweet-smelling white flowers, and edible fruit. Latin name: *Eriobotrya japonica.* 2. FRUIT OF LOQUAT TREE the small pear-shaped orange-yellow sweet but slightly tangy fruit of the loquat tree, eaten raw or used in cooking [Early 19thC. From Chinese *luh kwat*, literally "rush orange."]

lo·ran /láw ràn/ *n.* a long-distance radio navigation system by which a ship or aircraft determines its position using radio signals sent out by two ground stations [Mid-20thC. Acronym formed from "long-range navigation."]

AKG London

Federico García Lorca

Lor·ca /láwrkə/, **Federico García** (1898–1936) Spanish poet and playwright. A popular poet and powerful dramatist, he was assassinated by Nationalists during the Spanish Civil War. His works include *Blood Wedding* (1933) and *The House of Bernarda Alba* (1936).

lord /lawrd/ *n.* 1. POWERFUL MAN a man who has considerable power, authority, or influence over others, e.g., a business tycoon 2. ARISTOCRAT a man who is a member of the nobility, especially in Great Britain 3. FEUDAL SUPERIOR in medieval Europe, a powerful land- or property-owner, with authority over an area, castle, or community, e.g., the lord of a manor ■ *vti.* **(lord·ed, lord·ing, lords)** ACT IN A SUPERIOR WAY to act in a superior, masterful, or bullying way toward others [Old English *hlāford*, contraction of *hlāfweard*, literally "loaf-guardian," from *hlāf*, an earlier form of LOAF (source of English *lady*)] ◇ **lord it (over somebody)** to act in a superior, masterful, or bullying way toward other people (*disapproving*)

Lord *n.* 1. CHRISTIAN GOD a title Christians give to God or specifically to Jesus Christ 2. JEWISH GOD a title that Jews give to God 3. *U.K.* TITLE FOR A MAN used as an alternate title for a marquess, earl, viscount, or baron 4. *U.K.* COURTESY TITLE FOR A MAN used as a courtesy title for the younger son or sons of a marquess, or duke 5. *U.K.* FORM OF ADDRESS FOR A MAN used as a form of address for an earl, viscount, or baron, and for the younger son of a duke or marquess 6. TITLE OF HIGH-RANKING OFFICIAL a title given to some high-ranking British officials ■ *interj.* EXPRESSING SURPRISE used to express surprise, concern, or annoyance about something (*informal*) ■ **Lords** *npl.* HOUSE OF LORDS the House of Lords [Old English]

Lord Chan·cel·lor *n.* the cabinet minister in the British government who is the Speaker in the House of Lords and the official in charge of the judiciary in England and Wales

lord·ing /láwrding/ *n.* (*archaic*) 1. MEMBER OF NOBILITY a gentleman or member of the nobility 2. YOUNG LORD a young lord [Old English]

lord·ling /láwrdling/ *n.* an insignificant lord

lord·ly /láwrdlee/ *adj.* **(-li·er, -li·est)** 1. ARROGANT arrogant, aloof, and behaving in a superior way 2. IMPRESSIVE very grand, magnificent, and suitable for a lord ■ *adv.* IN GRAND MANNER in the manner of a lord (*archaic*) —**lord·li·ness** *n.*

Lord May·or *n.* the mayor of the City of London and some other large British boroughs and cities, e.g. York

Lord of Hosts *n.* the Christian God

Lord of Mis·rule *n.* in Europe in the 15th and 16th centuries, somebody appointed to organize celebrations and sporting events, especially at Christmas

Lord of the Flies *n.* = **Beelzebub** [Literal translation of Hebrew *ba'al zebūb* (see BEELZEBUB)]

lor·do·sis /lawr dṓssiss/ (*plural* **-dos·es** /-dṓ seez/) *n.* **1.** MED **CURVATURE OF BACK** an unusual inward curving of the spine in the lower part of the back, which may be medically significant **2.** ZOOL **ARCHING OF BACK DURING SEX** an inward arching of the back of female mammals during sexual stimulation [Early 18thC. Via modern Latin from Greek *lordōsis*, from *lordos* "bent backward."] —**lor·dot·ic** /lawr dóttik/ *adj.*

Lord Pro·tec·tor *n.* = **Protector**

lords-and-la·dies *n.* = **cuckoopint** (*takes a singular verb*) [Said to be because some plants have dark spadices (the "lords") and some light (the "ladies")]

Lord's Day *n.* the Christian Sabbath

lord·ship /láwrd shìp/ *n.* the position held by, land owned by, or period of tenure of, a lord (*formal*)

Lord·ship *n.* in the United Kingdom, a respectful way to refer to or address a judge, bishop, or some nobles

Lord's Prayer *n.* the most important prayer in Christianity, which Jesus Christ taught to his disciples according to the Gospels of Luke and Matthew

Lord's Sup·per *n.* = **Holy Communion** [So called because Holy Communion commemorates the LAST SUPPER of Jesus Christ and his disciples]

Lord's Ta·ble *n.* the altar or communion table in a Protestant church

lord·y /láwrdee/ *interj.* used to express surprise, shock, or disappointment (*dated informal*)

lore¹ /lawr/ *n.* **1. KNOWLEDGE HANDED DOWN VERBALLY** acquired knowledge or wisdom on a particular subject, e.g., local traditions, handed down by word of mouth and usually in the form of stories or historical anecdotes **2. KNOWLEDGE FROM TEACHING OR EXPERIENCE** knowledge that has been acquired through teaching or experience **3. TEACHING** teaching, or something that has been taught (*archaic*) [Old English *lār* "teaching, learning," from a prehistoric Germanic word that is also the ancestor of English *learn*]

lore² /lawr/ *n.* **1.** BIRDS **PART BETWEEN BIRD'S EYES AND BEAK** the part on either side of a bird's head between its eyes and the base of the bill **2.** ZOOL **AREA ON SNAKE'S OR FISH'S FACE** the area on a snake's or a fish's face between its eyes and its mouth [Early 17thC. From Latin *lorum* "strap, thong" (the original sense in English). The underlying meaning is "flat surface."]

Lo·re·lei¹ /láwrə lī/ *n.* a legendary beautiful woman said to live on a rock near the Rhine and lure sailors onto the rocks with enchanting songs

Lo·re·lei² /láwrə lī/ jutting cliff overlooking the Rhine River, between Mainz and Koblenz, western central Germany. Height: 390 ft./120 m.

Loren /lə rén/, **Sophia** (*b.* 1934) Italian actor. Her movie career includes both Italian comedies, often with Marcello Mastroianni, and work in Hollywood. Real name **Sofia Scicolone**

Lo·rentz-Fitz·ger·ald con·trac·tion /làwrənts fits jérrəld-/ *n.* the consequence of relativity that causes a reduction in length of an object traveling at a speed approaching that of light

Lo·renz /lṓ rents, láw-/, **Konrad** (1903–89) Austrian zoologist and ethologist. He founded the science of ethology, and his research on animal behavior included work on imprinting in birds and on human and animal aggression. He shared the Nobel Prize in physiology or medicine in 1973. Full name **Konrad Zacharias Lorenz**

lor·gnette /lawrn yét/ *n.* a pair of glasses or opera glasses with a short handle at the side [Early 19thC. From French, formed from *lorgner* "to squint, peer at," ultimately from a prehistoric Germanic word.]

lo·ri·ca /law rīkə, lə-/ (*plural* **-cae** /-rī sèe/) *n.* **1.** BIOL **PROTECTIVE SHELL** a lightweight loose-fitting external shell that protects ciliated or flagellated protozoans **2.** HIST, ARMS **PIECE OF ROMAN ARMOR** a protective metal or leather garment covering the chest and back, worn

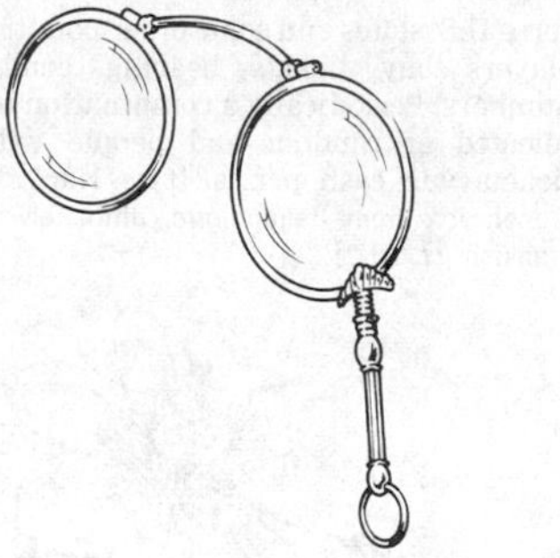

Lorgnette

by the ancient Romans [Early 18thC. From Latin, literally "breastplate," formed from *lorum* "strap, thong."]

lor·i·keet /láwri kèet/ (*plural* **-keets** *or* **-keet**) *n.* a small brightly-colored long-necked parrot native to Australia and other Pacific Islands that has a bristle-tipped tongue for extracting nectar and pollen from flowers. Genera: *Trichoglosus* and *Glossopsitta.* [Late 18thC. Formed from LORY, modeled on *parakeet.*]

lo·ris /láwriss/ (*plural* **-ris**) *n.* a small slow-moving nocturnal tree-dwelling primate native to tropical regions of southern Asia that has large eyes, dense wooly fur, a vestigial index finger, and no tail [Late 18thC. From French, of uncertain origin: perhaps from obsolete Dutch *loeris* "clown, fool," ultimately from Latin *lurid* "pale" (source of English *lurid.*)]

lorn /lawrn/ *adj.* forsaken or forlorn (*archaic literary*) [13thC. Past participle of *lese* "to lose," from Old English *-lēosan* (source of English *forlorn*).]

lor·ry /láwree/ (*plural* **-ries**) *n. U.K.* = **truck** [Mid-19thC. Origin uncertain: perhaps from the name *Laurie*; or from northern English dialect *lurry* "to haul," of unknown origin.]

lo·ry /láwree/ (*plural* **-ries** *or* **-ry**) *n.* a small brightly-colored parrot native to Australia and Indonesia that has a bristle-tipped tongue for extracting nectar and pollen from flowers. It has a heavier build than the lorikeet. Subfamily: Loriidae. [Late 17thC. From Malay *lori.*]

LOS *abbr.* **1.** length of stay **2.** line of scrimmage **3.** line of sight

Los Al·a·mi·tos /los àlə mèetōss/ city in Orange County, southwestern California, situated east of Long Beach. Population: 11,676 (1990).

Los Al·a·mos /los àllə mōss/ city in Los Alamos County, central New Mexico, situated approximately 35 mi./55 km northwest of Santa Fe. Population: 11,455 (1990).

Los Al·tos /los áltəss/ city in Santa Clara County, western California, situated southeast of Palo Alto. Population: 26,303 (1990).

Los An·ge·les /los ánjələss, -lèez/ city and county seat of Los Angeles County, southwestern California. Located on the Pacific Ocean, it is the second most populous city in the United States. Population: 3,448,613 (1994).

lose /looz/ (**lost** /lawst/, **los·ing, los·es**) *v.* **1.** *vt.* **MISLAY** to be unable to find something, often only temporarily **2.** *vti.* **FAIL TO WIN** to fail to win a victory, e.g., in a contest, argument, war, game, or in court **3.** *vt.* **HAVE SOMETHING TAKEN AWAY** to cease to possess or have something, e.g., a job or home **4.** *vt.* **MAKE SOMEBODY FAIL TO WIN** to be the cause of somebody's failure to win something ○ *The goalie's inexperience lost us the match.* **5.** *vt.* **NOT USE TO ADVANTAGE** to waste or fail to take advantage of something, e.g., time or an opportunity **6.** *vt.* **BE UNABLE TO CONTROL SOMETHING** to be unable to control or maintain something ○ *He loses his composure easily.* **7.** *vt.* **EXPERIENCE REDUCTION IN SOMETHING** to experience a reduction in something, e.g., weight or heat **8.** *vt.* **BE UNABLE TO FIND WAY** to be unable to find the way ○ *lost his way* **9.** *vt.* **CEASE HAVING QUALITY** to cease having a quality, belief, attitude, or characteristic ○ *He's lost the will to live.* **10.** *vt.* **CEASE HAVING ABILITY OR SENSE** to cease having a particular ability or sense, e.g., through illness or an accident ○ *He lost his sight in the war.* **11.** *vt.* **NO LONGER SEE OR HEAR SOMEBODY** to be unable to see or hear somebody or something any longer **12.** *vt.* **HAVE LOVED ONE DIE** to suffer the loss of somebody through death, e.g., a loved one, a patient, or a baby **13.** *vt.* **LEAVE SOMEBODY FOLLOWING BEHIND** to escape from or leave behind somebody who is in pursuit **14.** *vt.* **CONFUSE SOMEBODY** to fail to make somebody understand something ○ *You've lost me there.* **15.** *vti.* **RUN SLOW** to be or become slow by an amount of time (*refers to a timepiece*) [Old English *losian* "to perish, destroy, or lose," formed from *los* (see LOSS)] —**los·a·ble** *adj.* —**los·a·ble·ness** *n.* ◇ **lose it 1.** to become removed from reality (*informal*) **2.** to be unable to maintain emotional control or composure (*informal*)

lose out *vi.* to fail to win or obtain something in a competition or rivalry (*informal*)

los·er /lóozər/ *n.* **1. SOMEBODY WHO HAS NOT WON** a person or team that has failed to win a particular contest **2. SOMEBODY UNSUCCESSFUL OR UNLUCKY** somebody who is unsuccessful or unlucky and seems destined to fail repeatedly **3. SOCIAL MISFIT** somebody who is unable or unwilling to adjust to society (*informal insult*)

Losey /lṓzee/, **Joseph** (1909–84) U.S. movie director. His works explored social issues and criticized American society. In 1951 he was blacklisted as left wing and moved to Europe. Full name **Joseph Walton Losey**

Los Ga·tos /los gáttəss/ town in Santa Clara County, western California, situated 8 mi./13 km southwest of San Jose. Population: 27,357 (1990).

los·ings /lóozingz/ *npl.* money or possessions that are lost, especially through gambling

loss /lawss/ *n.* **1. FACT OF NO LONGER HAVING SOMETHING** the fact of no longer having something or of having less of something **2. SOMEBODY OR SOMETHING LOST** somebody or something that has been lost **3. DEATH** the death of somebody **4. MONEY SPENT IN EXCESS OF INCOME** the amount of money by which a company's or person's expenses exceed income or profit (*often used in the plural*) **5. SAD FEELING** a feeling of sadness, loneliness, or emptiness at the absence of somebody or something **6. REDUCTION** a reduction in the level of something, especially in the body ○ *weight loss* **7. INSTANCE OF LOSING CONTEST** an instance of losing a competition, race, or contest **8.** ELEC **DROP IN POWER CAUSED BY RESISTANCE** a drop in power caused by resistance in an electric circuit **9. INSTANCE OR AMOUNT OF CLAIM** an instance or the amount of a claim made by an insurance policyholder [Old English *los* "ruin, destruction," from a prehistoric Germanic word that is also the ancestor of English *lease, lorn,* and *loose.* In later use a back-formation from LOST.] ◇ **at a loss** uncertain what to say or do ◇ **cut your losses** to withdraw from a situation in which there is no possibility of winning

loss ad·just·er *n. U.K.* = **adjuster**

loss lead·er *n.* an item sold at a price below its cost in the hope that customers who buy it will also buy other things

loss ra·tio *n.* the ratio of the losses paid out in a year by an insurance company against the income from premiums

lost /lawst/ *v.* past tense, past participle of **lose** ■ *adj.* **1. MISLAID** unable to be found temporarily **2. UNABLE TO FIND THE WAY** unable to find the way to a place **3. NOT USED PROPERLY** wasted or not taken advantage of **4. UNAPPRECIATED** not understood or appreciated by somebody **5. LACKING CONFIDENCE** unable to cope with a job or situation, usually because of inexperience of lack of confidence **6. GONE** no longer in existence or use **7. PREOCCUPIED** completely absorbed or involved in something **8. CONFUSED BY SOMETHING COMPLICATED** confused or bewildered by something complicated or poorly explained **9. DESTROYED** destroyed or killed **10. LACKING MORALS** morally or spiritually past hoping for (*formal*) ◇ **get lost** used to tell somebody in a blunt and rude way to go away (*slang*)

lost and found *n.* an area or container in a public building such as a theater or school, where personal possessions that have accidentally been left behind are kept for reclaiming by their owners

lost cause *n.* somebody who cannot be influenced to change, or something that cannot succeed

Lost Gen·er·a·tion, **lost gen·er·a·tion** *n.* the group of authors, including Ernest Hemingway and F. Scott Fitzgerald, who came to prominence shortly after World War I.

lost prop·er·ty, **lost prop·er·ty of·fice** *n. U.K.* = **lost and found**

lost tribes *n.* the ten Hebrew tribes that separated from the other two to create a kingdom in northern Israel after Solomon's death. They were defeated by the Assyrians in 721 B.C. and may have become assimilated, but legend predicts their return.

lost wax *n.* a method of casting metal in which a wax model is coated with a material with a high melting point. The wax is melted and replaced by the molten metal.

lot /lot/ *pron.* **MANY** a large number of people or things ■ *n.* **1. A SET** a set or group of things or people **2. ITEMS IN AUCTION** an item or group of items on sale at an auction ○ *I bought the silver as one lot.* **3. GROUP** a particular group of people (*informal*) ○ *Don't expect any help from that lot.* **4. DESTINY** the things somebody has or experiences in life ○ *our lot in life* **5. PIECE OF LAND** a small area of land that has fixed boundaries ○ *a vacant lot* **6.** CINEMA **FILM STUDIO** a film studio together with the land that belongs to it ■ **lots** *npl.* **LARGE NUMBERS OR LARGE AMOUNT** large numbers of people or things, or a large amount ○ *Lots of us went.* ○ *I've got lots left.* ■ *adv.* **1. TO A GREAT EXTENT** to a great extent or degree ○ *Fishing has changed a lot in the last century.* **2. OFTEN** often or much of the time ○ *We went out to restaurants a lot.* **3. lots MUCH** a great deal (*informal*) ○ *I'm feeling lots better, thanks.* [Old English *hlot* "one of a set of objects used to make decisions by chance," also "share assigned by lot," hence "somebody's destiny decided by fate"] ◇ **a bad lot** an unpleasant or disreputable person ○ *Don't have anything to do with him: he's a bad lot.* ◇ **draw lots, cast lots** to choose something at random, e.g. a straw or piece of paper, to determine an outcome ○ *We cast lots to decide who should go first.* ◇ **the lot** everything, or everything considered as one ○ *Money, looks, brains...she's got the lot.*

WORD KEY: USAGE

a lot or **alot**? The superficial similarity of ***a lot*** to adjectives and adverbs like *alone* and *aloud* gives rise to a temptation to treat the expression as one word. This is substandard usage. Even in informal English ***lot*** should be treated as a noun, which may be used either in the plural (*I have lots of ideas*) or as a singular after the indefinite article ***a*** (*Thanks a lot*).

Lot /lot/ in the biblical Book of Genesis, the son of Haran, brother of Abraham. He is mentioned as Lut in the Koran.

Lot /lō/ **1.** department in Midi-Pyrénées Region, southwestern France, known for its scenic beauty. Population: 155,816 (1990). Area: 2,014 sq. mi./5,217 sq. km. **2.** river in southwestern France. Length: 300 mi./483 km.

lo·ta /lṓtə/, **lo·tah** *n.* a small round water container, usually made of brass or copper, used in the Indian subcontinent [Early 19thC. From Hindi *loṭā*.]

loth /lōth, lō*th*/ *adj.* = **loath**

Lo·thair II /lō tháir/, **King of Germany and Holy Roman Emperor** (1075–1137). His election as king of Germany (1125) led to a war between two rival families, the Guelphs and the Ghibellines.

Lo·thar·i·o /lō thérree ō/ (*plural* **-os**), **lo·thar·i·o** *n.* a man who attempts to persuade women to enter sexual affairs with him (*literary*) [Mid-18thC. The name of such a character in *The Fair Penitent* (1703), a tragedy by Nicholas Rowe.]

lo·ti /lṓtee/ (*plural* **ma·lo·ti** /maa lṓtee/) *n.* **1. AFRICAN MONETARY UNIT** the basic unit of currency in the southern African country of Lesotho. See table at **currency** **2. BILL WORTH A LOTI** a bill worth a loti [Late 20thC. From Sesotho, named for the *Maloti* mountains in Lesotho.]

lo·tic /lṓtik/ *adj.* used to describe ecological communities that live in swift-flowing water [Early 20thC. Formed from Latin *lotus*, past participle of *lavare* "to wash."]

lo·tion /lṓsh'n/ *n.* a thick liquid preparation that is applied to the skin for cosmetic or medical reasons [14thC. Directly or via French from the Latin stem *lotion-*, from *lot-*, past participle stem of *lavare* "to wash."]

lot·ter·y /lóttəree/ (*plural* **-ies**) *n.* **1.** GAMBLING **GAMBLING GAME** a large-scale gambling game, usually organized to raise money for a public cause, in which numbered tickets are sold and a draw is held to select the winning numbers **2. SITUATION WHERE OUTCOME DEPENDS ON CHANCE** an activity, situation, or enterprise with an outcome dependent on chance [Mid-16thC. Origin uncertain: probably ultimately from Dutch *loterij*, from *lot* "lot."]

lot·to /lóttō/ (*plural* **-tos**) *n.* **1. GAME RESEMBLING BINGO** a game resembling bingo, in which numbers are called at random and players try to be the first to cover all the corresponding numbers on their cards **2. lot·to, Lot·to STATE-RUN LOTTERY** a state-run lottery in some U.S. states and some other countries, in which players buy tickets bearing combinations of numbers. Periodically a combination of numbers is selected at random and people with matching tickets win cash prizes. [Late 18thC. Directly or via French *loto* from Italian *lotto*, ultimately from assumed Frankish *lot* "lot."]

Lotus

lo·tus /lṓtəss/ (*plural* **-tus·es** *or* **-tus**) *n.* **1. MYTHOLOGICAL FRUIT CAUSING DROWSINESS** a fruit in Greek mythology that made people who ate it feel a pleasant drowsiness **2. MYTHOLOGICAL PLANT BEARING LOTUS FRUIT** a plant in Greek mythology that bore the lotus fruit, thought to be the date or jujube **3. SACRED WATER LILY** a white water lily, native to tropical Africa and Asia, that was sacred to the ancient Egyptians. Latin name: *Nymphaea lotus.* **4. SACRED PINK WATER LILY** a water lily native to Asia and Australia with large leaves and fragrant pink flowers, regarded as sacred in India, China, and Tibet. Latin name: *Nelumbo nucifera.* **5. PLANT OF PEA FAMILY** a plant of the pea family with yellow, pink, or white flowers. Genus: *Lotus.* **6.** RELIG, ARTS **LOTUS FLOWER IN SACRED ART** a representation of the flower of either of the sacred lotus plants, common in ancient Egyptian, Hindu, and Buddhist sacred art [15thC. Via Latin from Greek *lōtos*, applied by ancient writers to a variety of plants.]

lo·tus-eat·er *n.* **1. LAZY AND INDULGENT PERSON** somebody who leads a lazy and self-indulgent life **2.** MYTHOL **SOMEBODY STUPEFIED BY EATING LOTUS** somebody who, in the *Odyssey*, lived in a state of idle stupor after feeding on the legendary lotus

Lotus position: Seated *Buddha*, Uttar Pradesh, northern India

lo·tus po·si·tion *n.* a sitting position, used especially in yoga and meditation, in which the legs are crossed in such a way that each foot rests on top of the other leg's thigh [[*Lotus*] from the supposed resemblance of the position to a lotus blossom]

Lou·ang·phra·bang /loo àang praa baáng/ city in northern Laos, on the Mekong River. Population: 68,399 (1985).

louche /loosh/ *adj.* disreputable or of doubtful morality [Early 19thC. Via French, "cross-eyed, shady," from Latin *luscus* "one-eyed," of unknown origin.]

loud /lowd/ *adj.* **1. HIGH IN VOLUME** high in volume of sound **2. EXPRESSING SOMETHING NOISILY** expressing something forcefully and frequently ○ *loud protests* **3. VISUALLY SHOCKING** shockingly bright in color or bold in design ○ *a loud shirt* **4. OFFENSIVE** noisy, coarse, and offensive ■ *adv.* **LOUDLY** in a loud way [Old English *hlūd*. Ultimately from an Indo-European word meaning "to hear," which also produced English *listen* and *leer*. The underlying idea is of something that is heard.] —**loud·ly** *adv.*

loud·en /lówd'n/ (**-ened, -en·ing, -ens**) *vti.* to become louder, or to make a sound louder

loud·hail·er /lòwd háylər/ *n. U.K.* = **bullhorn**

loud·mouth /lówd mòwth/ (*plural* **-mouths** /-mòwthz/) *n.* somebody who talks a lot and loudly, especially gossiping or boasting (*informal*) —**loud·mouthed** /lówd mòw*th*d, -mòwtht/ *adj.*

loud·ness /lówdnəss/ *n.* **1. DEGREE OF SOUND VOLUME** the degree of volume of sound **2.** PHYS **VOLUME PERCEIVED BY EAR** the magnitude of the physiological effect produced when a sound stimulates the ear **3.** HOUSEHOLD **RELATIVE LEVEL OF BASS TO TREBLE** the relative level of bass to treble in high-fidelity equipment that is adjusted depending on the overall volume level

Lou·don·ville /lówdən vil/ town in Albany County, eastern New York, situated just north of the city of Albany. Population: 10,822 (1990).

loud ped·al *n.* = **sustaining pedal**

loud·speak·er /lòwd spéekər/ *n.* an electronic or electromagnetic device used to convert electrical energy into sound energy, providing the audible sound in equipment such as televisions, radios, CD players, and public-address systems

Lou Geh·rig's dis·ease /lòo gérrigz-/ *n.* = **amyotrophic lateral sclerosis** [Mid-20thC. Named for Henry *Louis Gehrig* (1903–41), U.S. baseball player who died from the disease.]

lough /lok, lawkh/ *n. Ireland* **1. LAKE** a lake **2. LONG NARROW INLET** a long inlet of the sea [13thC. Origin uncertain: probably ultimately from Old Irish *loch* "lake," perhaps via obsolete Welsh *llwch*.]

Lou·ie /lòo ee/ *n.* a left turn (*informal*) ○ *Hang a Louie!*

lou·is *n.* = **louis d'or**

Lou·is XIV /lòo ee/, **King of France** (1638–1715). He was a strong military leader and patron of the arts whose long reign (1642–1715) saw a great strengthening of the monarchy. Known as **the Sun King**

Lou·is XV, King of France (1710–74). His weak leadership and despotic rule (1715–74) contributed to the crisis that led to the French Revolution.

Lou·is XVI, King of France (1754–93). Coming to the throne (1774) when France was impoverished, he was deposed during the French Revolution and executed.

Lou·is /lòo iss/, **Joe** (1914–81) U.S. boxer. He was the world heavyweight champion from 1937 to 1942. Known as **the Brown Bomber**

Lou·is·bourg /lòo iss bùrg/ former town in Cape Breton Island, eastern Nova Scotia, Canada. It is now Canada's largest national historic site.

lou·is d'or /lòo ee dáwr/ (*plural* **lou·is d'or**), **lou·is** /lòo ee/ (*plural* **-is**) *n.* **1. OLD FRENCH COIN** a gold coin of France used from the 17th century to the Revolution **2. FRENCH POST-REVOLUTION COIN** a former gold coin worth 20 francs used in France after the Revolution [Mid-17thC. From French, *louis d'or*, literally "louis of gold," named after *Louis* XIII of France, during whose reign the coin was first issued.]

Louisiana

Lou·i·si·an·a /loo èezee ánə/ state in the southern United States bordering the Gulf of Mexico, Texas, Arkansas, and Mississippi. Capital: Baton Rouge. Population: 4,351,769 (1997). Area: 49,651 sq. mi./128,595 sq. km. —**Lou·i·si·an·an** *n., adj.*

Lou·is Phi·lippe /lòo ee fə léep/, **King of the French** (1773–1850). Proclaimed king after the July Revolution (1830), he ruled as a constitutional monarch until the Revolution of 1848. Known as **the Citizen King**

Lou·is·ville /loǒo i vil, loǒo ee vìl/ city in northern Kentucky, on the Ohio River at Kentucky's border with Indiana. The largest city in the state, it is the site of Churchill Downs, home of the Kentucky Derby, a thoroughbred horse race run each May. Population: 260,689 (1996).

lounge /lownj/ *v.* (**lounged, loung·ing, loung·es**) **1.** *vi.* **LIE OR SIT LAZILY** to sit or act in a casual, relaxed way **2.** *vti.* **PASS TIME LAZILY** to pass time in a relaxed or lazy way ○ *lounged the afternoon away* ■ *n.* **1. PUBLIC ROOM FOR RELAXING** a room in a public building or vehicle, e.g., a hotel, airport, or ship, in which people may relax or wait **2. SITTING ROOM IN HOUSE** a sitting or living room in a house **3. ROOM WHERE COCKTAILS SERVED** a room in a hotel or restaurant where cocktails are served **4.** FURNITURE **BACKLESS COUCH WITH HEADREST** a couch without a back but with a headrest at one end [Early 16thC. Origin uncertain: perhaps from obsolete *lungis* "lanky foolish fellow, slow person," from French *longis*, from Latin *Longinus*, apocryphal name of the Roman centurion who pierced Jesus Christ's side.]

lounge car *n.* = **club car**

lounge liz·ard *n.* **1. MAN FREQUENTING CLASSY VENUES** a man who goes to places or events attended by the rich and famous, especially in order to approach wealthy women (*slang insult*) **2. LOUNGE FREQUENTER** a frequent patron of cocktail lounges (*slang*) [Origin uncertain: probably an alliterative formation based on the negative associations of reptiles]

loung·er /lównjər/ *n.* **1. SOMEBODY WHO LOUNGES AROUND** somebody who typically sits or walks in an especially casual relaxed way **2.** FURNITURE **COMFORTABLE CHAIR OR COUCH** an extendable chair or a lightweight, usually adjustable, couch designed to be comfortable for the user

lounge·wear /lównj wàir/ *n.* clothing designed to be worn when relaxing, usually at home

loup /loop/, **lowp** *vti.* (**louped, loup·ing, loups; lowped, lowp·ing, lowps**) *Scotland* **LEAP** to leap or jump ■ *n. Scotland* **LEAP** a leap or a jump [14thC. From Old Norse *hlaupa* (see LEAP).]

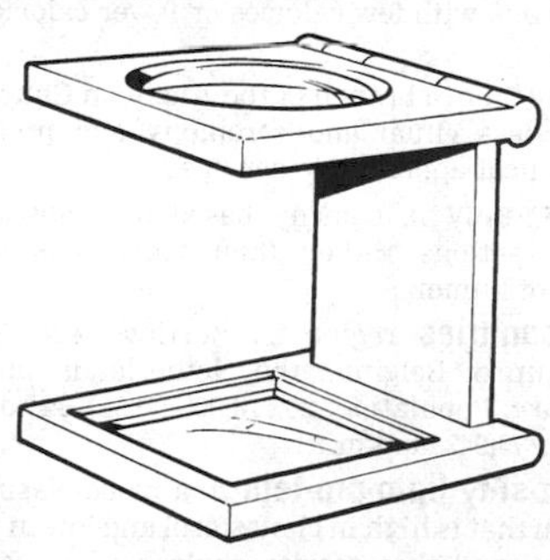

Loupe

loupe /loop/ *n.* a magnifying glass used especially by jewelers and watchmakers [Late 19thC. From French, "flawed gem," of uncertain origin: probably from prehistoric Germanic.]

loup-ga·rou /loō gə roō, -gaa roō/ (*plural* **loups-ga·rous**) *n.* a werewolf (*dated*) [Late 16thC. From French, from Old French *leu* "wolf" (from Latin *lupus*) + *garoul* "werewolf," from a prehistoric Germanic word meaning literally "man-wolf."]

Lourdes /loōrd, loōrdz/ town and place of pilgrimage in Hautes-Pyrénées Department, Provence-Alpes-Côte-d'Azur Region, southwestern France. Population: 16,301 (1990).

louse /lowss/ *n.* (*plural* **lice** /līss/) **1. PARASITIC INSECT** a small wingless insect that lives as a parasite on humans and other animals.There are sucking lice, e.g. head and body lice, and biting lice, e.g., bird lice. **2. SMALL INVERTEBRATE ANIMAL** a small invertebrate animal, e.g., a wood louse (*often used in combination*) **3.** (*plural* **lous·es**) **OFFENSIVE TERM** an offensive term that deliberately insults somebody's behavior and attitude toward others (*informal insult*) ■ *vt.* (**loused, lous·ing, lous·es**) MED = **delouse** [Old English *lūs*. Ultimately from an Indo-European word meaning "louse." Celtic languages also have words meaning "louse" from this ancestor.]

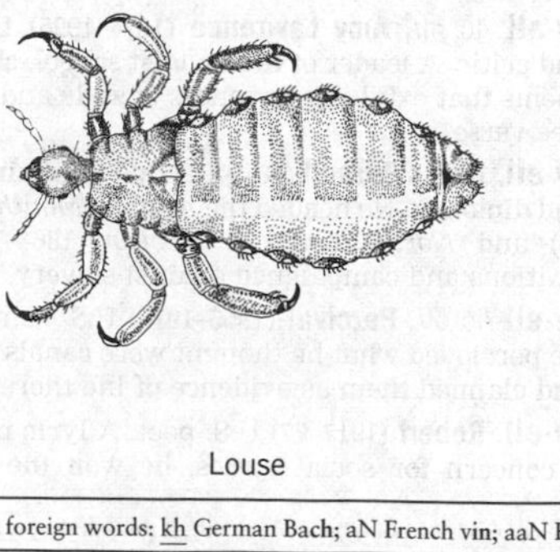

Louse

louse up *vti.* to mishandle a situation or task so it is ruined (*informal*)

louse fly *n.* a parasitic fly that clings to birds and mammals with strong bristly legs and is typically wingless. Family: Hippoboscidae.

louse·wort /lówss wùrt, -wàwrt/ *n.* a plant of the snapdragon family that is native to northern regions and has feathery leaves and spikes of white, yellow, or pinkish-purple flowers. Genus: *Pedicularis.* ◊ **wood betony** [From the belief that sheep feeding on it became infested with lice]

lous·y /lówzee/ (**-i·er, -i·est**) *adj.* **1. INFERIOR** inferior or second-rate (*informal*) **2. UNPLEASANT** unpleasant or unacceptable (*informal*) ○ *a lousy way to treat sb* **3. ILL** painful or in bad health (*informal*) **4. HAVING A LOT OF SOMETHING** having a large amount of something (*informal*) ○ *His parents are lousy with money.* **5. LOUSE-INFESTED** infested with lice —**lous·i·ly** *adv.* —**lous·i·ness** *n.*

lout[1] /lowt/ *n.* an offensive term that deliberately insults the behavior and attitude of somebody, especially a young man (*informal insult*) [Mid-16thC. Origin uncertain: perhaps from LOUT[2] "to bend." The original meaning was "unintelligent person," so the underlying idea seems to be of an awkward person who stoops or slouches.]

lout[2] /lowt/ (**lout·ed, lout·ing, louts**) *vi.* to bow or bend (*archaic*) [Old English *lūtan*. Ultimately from an Indo-European word meaning "small," which is also the ancestor of English *little*. The underlying idea is of making yourself smaller by bending down.]

lout·ish /lówtish/ *adj.* marked by crude and unpleasant behavior —**lout·ish·ly** *adv.* —**lout·ish·ness** *n.*

Lou·vain /loo váN/ town in central Belgium, near Brussels, famous for its old buildings and churches. Population: 87,132 (1996).

Louver

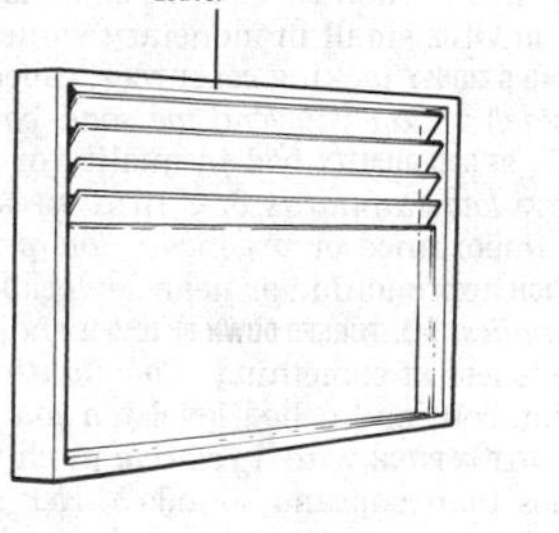

Louver

lou·ver /loōvər/, **lou·vre** *n.* **1. FRAME WITH HORIZONTAL SLATS** a frame on a door or window supporting spaced horizontal slats angled to admit air and light but not rain **2. SLAT IN LOUVER** an individual slat in a louver **3. ANY SLATTED OPENING** any slatted opening, generally for ventilation or cooling **4. ROOF STRUCTURE RELEASING SMOKE** a structure such as a lantern or turret on the roof of a building, especially a medieval building, that allows smoke to escape [14thC. From Old French *lover* "skylight," of uncertain origin: probably from prehistoric Germanic.] —**lou·vered** *adj.*

Louvre /loōvrə, loōvər/ *n.* a museum in Paris, France, that contains the national art collection, including such famous works as the *Mona Lisa* and *Venus de Milo.* Located in the former palace of the kings of France, the museum opened to the public in 1793.

lov·a·ble /lúvvəb'l/, **love·a·ble** *adj.* attracting or worthy of love or affection —**lov·a·bil·i·ty** /lùvvə bíllətee/ *n.* —**lov·a·ble·ness** /lúvvəb'lnəss/ *n.* —**lov·a·bly** *adv.*

lov·age /lúvvij/ *n.* a perennial herb, native to the Mediterranean, with greenish flowers. It is cultivated for its small aromatic fruit used in seasoning. Latin name: *Levisticum officinale.* [14thC. Alteration (by folk etymology from LOVE and obsolete *ache* "parsley") of Old French *levesche*, from late Latin *levisticum (apium)* "Ligurian (parsley)," variant of *ligusticum* "of Liguria," region in Italy.]

lo·vat /lúvvət/ *n.* a color that is a muted dusty mixture of green and yellow or green and blue [Early 20thC. Origin uncertain: probably named for Thomas Alexander Fraser, Lord *Lovat* (1802–75), Scottish nobleman who popularized tweeds in muted colors as hunters' dress.]

love /luv/ *n.* **1. VERY STRONG AFFECTION** an intense feeling of tender affection and compassion ○ *Young children need unconditional love.* **2. PASSIONATE ATTRACTION AND DESIRE** a passionate feeling of romantic desire and sexual attraction **3. SOMEBODY MUCH LOVED** somebody who is loved romantically ○ *He was her first real love.* **4. ROMANTIC AFFAIR** a romantic affair, possibly sexual **5. STRONG LIKING** strong liking for or pleasure gained from something ○ *his love of music* **6. SOMETHING ELICITING ENTHUSIASM** something that elicits deep interest and enthusiasm in somebody ○ *Music was his greatest love but he also liked ballet.* **7. BELOVED** used as an affectionate word to somebody loved **8.** *U.K.* **TERM OF FRIENDLY ADDRESS** used as a friendly term of address, usually to a woman (*informal*) ○ *Here's your change, love.* **9.** CHR **GOD'S LOVE FOR HUMANITY** the mercy, grace, and charity shown by God to humanity **10.** CHR **WORSHIP OF GOD** the worship and adoration of God **11.** SPORTS, GAME **SCORE OF ZERO** a score of zero in sports and games, e.g., tennis, squash, and whist ■ *v.* (**loved, lov·ing, loves**) **1.** *vti.* **FEEL TENDER AFFECTION FOR** to feel tender affection for somebody, e.g., a close relative or friend, or for something such as a place, an ideal, or an animal **2.** *vti.* **FEEL DESIRE FOR** to feel romantic and sexual desire and longing for somebody **3.** *vt.* **LIKE VERY MUCH** to like something or like doing something very much ○ *I love watching old movies on TV.* **4.** *vt.* **SHOW KINDNESS TO** to feel and show kindness and charity to somebody ○ *love one another or love your neighbor* **5.** *vt.* **HAVE SEXUAL INTERCOURSE WITH** to have sexual intercourse with somebody (*dated*) [Old English *lufian*, from *lufu* "love" (source of the noun). Ultimately from an Indo-European word meaning "to love," which is also the ancestor of English *libido, belief,* and *leave* "absence."]

WORD KEY: USAGE

See Usage note at ***enamored.***

WORD KEY: SYNONYMS

love, liking, affection, fondness, passion, infatuation, crush

CORE MEANING: a strong positive feeling toward somebody or something

love used to describe a very strong, positive feeling toward somebody or something. It is used especially to talk about strong romantic or sexual feelings between people; **liking** used to talk about positive feelings toward somebody or something. These feelings are not as strong as those suggested by "love"; **affection** used to describe warm friendly caring feelings between people. It can also be used to talk about a liking for something such as a place; **fondness** used in a similar way to "affection" to talk about feelings between people. It can also be used to describe a strong liking of or preference for something; **passion** used to describe an exceptionally intense love for somebody, usually of a strong sexual nature. It can also be used to refer to a strong liking or enthusiasm for something, sometimes of an excessive nature; **infatuation** used to describe an intense but short-lasting and often unrealistic love for somebody, usually of a romantic or sexual nature; **crush** used to describe somebody's strong feeling of attraction toward a person with whom he or she is not having a relationship. It is used especially to talk about teenagers and young people.

love af·fair *n.* **1. SEXUAL OR ROMANTIC RELATIONSHIP** a sexual or romantic relationship between people who are not married to one another or who do not live together in a permanent relationship **2. INTENSE LIKING FOR SOMETHING** an intense liking or enthusiasm for something ○ *his love affair with the movies*

love ap·ple *n.* = **tomato** [Translation of French *pomme d'amour* and German *Liebesapfel*, perhaps from the reputed aphrodisiac properties of the tomato]

love beads *npl.* a necklace of colored beads, first popular with hippies in the 1960s

love·bird /lúv bùrd/ *n.* **1.** BIRDS **SMALL PARROT** a small greenish short-tailed African parrot, noted for close bonding and mutual preening between mates. They are popular as cage birds. Genus: *Agapornis.* **2. LOVER**

a lover, especially one who is publicly affectionate (*usually used in the plural*) [From the fact that the pairs display very affectionate behavior]

love·bite /lúv bìt/ *n. U.K.* = **hickey**

Love Ca·nal /lùv kənál/ region near Niagara Falls, New York, declared an official disaster area due to toxic waste

love child *n.* the child of parents who are not married to each other

Love·craft /lúv kràft/, **H. P.** (1890–1937) U.S. writer. His horror and fantasy novels and short stories only became popular after his death. Full name **Howard Phillips Lovecraft**

love feast *n.* **1.** CHR **SYMBOLIC CHRISTIAN MEAL** a symbolic meal shared among Christians as a symbol of love and charity **2. GOODWILL MEAL** a meal held with the intention of stimulating goodwill

love han·dles *npl.* two regions of fat located at either side of the back just above the pelvis (*humorous informal*)

love-in *n.* a relatively large gathering in which participants experience feelings of love and mutual support (*dated*)

love-in-a-mist *n.* an erect Mediterranean annual plant of the buttercup family with white or pale blue flowers surrounded by very fine bracts, giving the flowers a delicate appearance. Latin name: *Nigella damascena.* [*[Mist]* from the mass of threadlike bracts that surrounds the flower]

Love·joy /lúv jòy/, **Elijah Parish** (1802–37) U.S. abolitionist and editor. He promoted the antislavery movement through the *Observer* newspaper, from 1833 to his murder in 1837.

love knot *n.* a knot or bow of ribbon used to symbolize love

Love·land /lúvlənd/ city in Larimer County, northern Colorado, situated 12 mi./19 km south of Fort Collins. Population: 37,352 (1990).

love·less /lúvləss/ *adj.* **1. EMPTY OF LOVE** devoid of love ○ *a loveless marriage* **2. NOT SHOWING LOVE** not exhibiting or giving love ○ *a loveless glance* **3. UNLOVED** not receiving love ○ *a loveless child*

love·lock /lúv lòk/ *n.* a long lock of hair separated from the rest by a ribbon, worn forward over the shoulder in the 16th century, or worn on the forehead in later periods

love·lorn /lúv làwrn/ *adj.* terribly unhappy because of unrequited love or difficulties with love —**love·lorn·ness** *n.*

love·ly /lúvlee/ *adj.* (**-li·er, -li·est**) **1. BEAUTIFUL AND PLEASING** beautiful and pleasing, especially in a harmonious way **2. DELIGHTFUL** very enjoyable or pleasant **3. CARING** loving or friendly and caring **4. ATTRACTING LOVE** attracting or inspiring love in others ■ *n.* (*plural* **-lies**) **SOMEBODY OR SOMETHING GOOD-LOOKING** somebody who or something that is very good-looking, especially a woman (*often used in the plural, sometimes considered offensive*) [Old English *luflic.* The word originally meant "affectionate" and "lovable"; the modern sense "beautiful" did not develop until the late 13thC.] —**love·li·ness** *n.*

WORD KEY: SYNONYMS

See Synonyms at ***good looking***.

love·mak·ing /lúv màyking/ *n.* **1. SEXUAL ACTIVITY** sexual activity between lovers, especially sexual intercourse **2. COURTSHIP** courtship or wooing (*dated*)

love po·tion *n.* a magical drink intended to stimulate sexual desire in the person who consumes it, for the person who gives it

lov·er /lúvvər/ *n.* **1. SEXUAL PARTNER** somebody's sexual partner, especially if the two are not married to each other **2. SOMEBODY HAVING LOVE AFFAIR** either of two people involved in a love affair (*often used in the plural*) **3. SOMEBODY DEVOTED TO PARTICULAR THING** somebody who is devoted to or very much likes a particular thing (*often used in combination*) ○ *opera-lovers* —**lov·er·ly** /lúvvərlee/ *adj., adv.*

WORD KEY: CULTURAL NOTE

Lady Chatterley's Lover, a novel by English writer D. H. Lawrence (1928). Lawrence's last novel, it describes an aristocratic woman's search for love and sexual satisfaction after her husband is crippled in war. The novel's notoriety, and the fact that the publishers of the first unexpurgated British edition were prosecuted for obscenity in 1960, has obscured its many qualities, including its insightful analysis of contemporary social and political values.

lov·er's knot *n.* = **love knot**

love seat *n.* a small sofa that seats two people

love·sick /lúv sìk/ *adj.* listless or distracted because of love —**love·sick·ness** *n.*

lov·ey-dov·ey /lùvvi dúvvee/ *adj.* showing affection in an excessive or excessively sentimental way (*informal*) [From pet-forms of LOVE and DOVE]

lov·ing /lúvving/ *adj.* **1. SHOWING AFFECTION** showing or feeling affection **2. DONE WITH CAREFUL ATTENTION** done with enjoyment and careful attention —**lov·ing·ly** *adv.* —**lov·ing·ness** *n.*

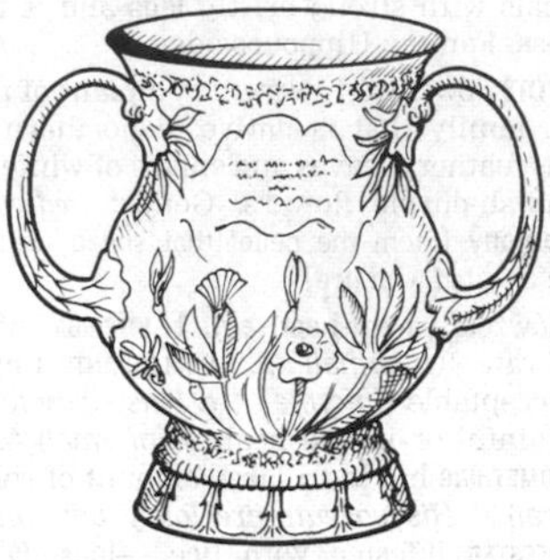

Loving cup

lov·ing cup *n.* **1. TWO-HANDLED DRINKING VESSEL** a large drinking vessel with two or more handles, sometimes passed between people at a banquet **2.** SPORTS **ORNAMENTAL VESSEL** an ornamental vessel with two handles awarded to the winner of a sports contest [From the former use of the vessel in ceremonial drinking at banquets. Two people always stood up together, one to drink and the other to "defend" the drinker.]

lov·ing-kind·ness *n.* tender compassion

low[1] /lō/ *adj.* **1. CLOSE TO THE GROUND** located close or closer than usual to the ground or the base of something ○ *The sinking sun was low in the sky.* **2. WITHOUT GREAT HEIGHT** relatively little in height between the top and bottom ○ *a low fence* **3. BELOW AVERAGE** below the average or expected degree, amount, or intensity ○ *The lowest rainfall in fourteen years.* **4. CONTAINING SMALL AMOUNT** having or containing a relatively small amount ○ *low in calories* **5. WITH LITTLE MONETARY VALUE** small in monetary value ○ *low prices* **6. LACKING MONEY** lacking resources, especially money (*informal*) ○ *Can you lend me some cash, I'm a bit low.* **7. OF BAD QUALITY** bad in quality or having little value ○ *low standards* **8. OF LITTLE IMPORTANCE** having little importance or urgency ○ *low priority* **9. NEAR DEPLETION** approaching or near depletion ○ *We're low on supplies.* **10. TURNED DOWN OR DIMMED** adjusted so that there is less of something ○ *low lighting* **11. QUIET** at a quiet, soft, or hushed level ○ *a low murmur* **12.** MUSIC **DEEP IN PITCH** with a relative pitch that is closer to bass than soprano sounds ○ *Her singing voice was a low soprano* **13. SMALL** small or relatively small ○ *a low risk* **14. NEAR BOTTOM OF SCALE** near the beginning or bottom of something measured on a scale ○ *The temperature was in the low 80s.* **15. DISPIRITED** melancholy, hopeless, or dispirited ○ *in low spirits* **16. LACKING PHYSICAL STRENGTH** lacking in physical strength or vitality ○ *feeling low after a dose of flu* **17.** CLOTHES **SHOWING NECK AND CHEST** cut to show more than usual of the wearer's neck and bosom ○ *a low neckline* **18.** AUTOMOT **PROVIDING SLOW SPEED** providing a relatively slow speed ○ *a low gear* **19. LACKING STATUS** lacking status or rank, or closer to the bottom of a class system **20. UNCOMPLIMENTARY** unfavorable or uncomplimentary ○ *a low opinion of someone* **21. UNPRINCIPLED** without principles or morals **22. VULGAR** full of vulgarity or coarseness **23.** GEOG **NEAR EQUATOR** near to the equator **24.** BIOL **NOT COMPLEX** simple in organic structure **25.** PHON **PRONOUNCED WITH LOW TONGUE** pronounced with the tongue lying low on the bottom of the mouth ○ *a low vowel* ■ *adv.* **1. IN LOW POSITION** in or to a low position, state, degree, or level ○ *Turn the gas down low.* **2. NEAR GROUND** near or nearer to the ground ○ *flew low over the trees* **3. WITH A DEEP PITCH** with a low or deep pitch ○ *Play it a half-step lower.* **4. QUIETLY** in a soft or quiet way **5. AT SMALL PRICE** at a low or small price ■ *n.* **1. SOMETHING LOW** something such as a position or degree that is low ○ *Sales dropped to an all-time low.* **2.** METEOROL **BAD WEATHER REGION** a region of low barometric pressure that results in bad weather **3. UNHAPPY PERIOD** an unhappy or unfortunate experience or period of somebody's life [12thC. From Old Norse *lágr.* Ultimately from an Indo-European word meaning "to lie," which also produced English *lie*[1], *lager*[1], and *fellow.* The underlying idea is of lying flat.] —**low·ness** *n.*

WORD KEY: SYNONYMS

See Synonyms at ***mean***.

low[2] /lō/ *n.* **MOOING SOUND OF COW** a characteristic mooing sound made by a cow or similar animal ■ *vti.* (**lowed, low·ing, lows**) **MOO** to make a mooing sound [Old English *hlōwan* "to bellow" (used of cows). Ultimately from an Indo-European word meaning "to shout," which also produced English *clamor* and *declare.*]

low·ball /lṓ bàwl/ (**-balled, -bal·ling, -balls**) *vti.* to deliberately quote a price or estimate that is lower than the eventual cost [From the card game *lowball*, a game of draw poker in which the player with the lowest-ranking hand wins the pot]

low beam *n.* the headlight beam of a road vehicle that illuminates the road near the vehicle

low blow *n.* an unfair comment or blow (*informal*) [From boxing, where it is prohibited to strike the opponent anywhere other than on the upper body or head]

low·born /lṓ bàwrn/ *adj.* being of common rather than aristocratic parentage

low·boy /lṓ bòy/ *n.* a low chest of drawers, often with cabriole legs, that is similar to the lower part of a highboy [Late 19thC. Modeled on TALLBOY.]

low·bred /lṓ brèd/ *adj.* with a rude and vulgar manner (*insult*)

low·brow /lṓ bròw/ *adj.* **UNSOPHISTICATED** unsophisticated or trivial and not requiring intellectual effort to be understood or appreciated (*disapproving*) ■ *n.* **UNSOPHISTICATED PERSON** somebody who has unsophisticated or unintellectual tastes [Early 20thC. Modeled on HIGHBROW.]

low-cal *adj.* with few calories or fewer calories than usual

Low Church *n.* a branch of the Anglican Church that favors less ritual and ceremony and prefers an evangelical approach to services

low com·e·dy *n.* comedy based on slapstick and coarse actions rather than more sophisticated forms of humor

Low Coun·tries region in northwestern Europe, made up of Belgium, the Netherlands, and Luxembourg. Population: 26,016,000 (1995). Area: 28,550 sq. mi./73,943 sq. km.

low-den·si·ty lip·o·pro·tein *n.* a blood-plasma lipoprotein that is high in cholesterol and low in protein content, and that carries cholesterol to cells and tissue. High levels are associated with the development of atherosclerosis.

low·down /lṓ dòwn/ *n.* significant information about somebody or something, especially information that is not widely known (*informal*) ○ *waiting for someone to give us the lowdown* [Early 20thC. Origin uncertain: from either *low down* "very low" or *low-down* "contemptible"; perhaps because it was considered improper to impart such information.]

low-down *adj.* (*informal*) **1. MEAN** mean and contemptible **2. VERY DISHEARTENED** very disheartened

low earth or·bit *n.* an orbit that is nearer to the Earth than a geostationary orbit. Satellites in such an orbit are usually part of a global mobile telephone system.

Low·ell /lṓ əl/ city in northeastern Massachusetts, at the junction of the Concord and Merrimack rivers. Population: 100,973 (1996).

Low·ell /lṓ əl/, **Amy Lawrence** (1874–1925) U.S. poet and critic. A leader of the imagist school, she wrote poems that exhibit a terseness of style and a use of free verse.

Low·ell, James Russell (1819–91) U.S. magazine editor and diplomat. He headed the *Atlantic Monthly* (1857–61) and *North American Review* (1864–72) publications and campaigned against slavery.

Low·ell /lṓ əl/, **Percival** (1855–1916) U.S. astronomer. He percieved what he thought were canals on Mars and claimed them as evidence of life there.

Low·ell, Robert (1917–77) U.S. poet. A lyric poet with a concern for social issues, he won the Pulitzer

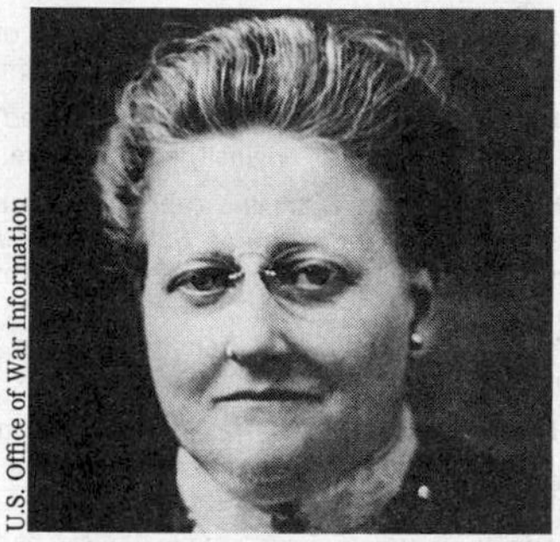
U.S. Office of War Information

Amy Lawrence Lowell

Prize for *"Lord Weary's Castle"* (1946). Full name **Robert Traill Spence Lowell, Jr.**

low-end *adj.* inexpensive compared to a group of similar products

low·er[1] /lṓ ər/ *v.* (**-ered, -er·ing, -ers**) **1.** *vt.* **BRING TO LOWER LEVEL** to move something down to a lower level or to move something downward ○ *lower the flag* **2.** *vti.* **REDUCE OR FALL** to reduce something or fall in quantity, quality, or value ○ *Interest rates have been lowered by the Federal Reserve Bank.* **3.** *vt.* **REDUCE IN DEGREE** to reduce something in degree **4.** *vt.* **LOOK DOWNWARD** to move the head or eyes downward ○ *She lowered her eyes.* **5.** *vr.* **HUMILIATE YOURSELF** to reduce your dignity or the respect in which you are held ○ *I wouldn't lower myself to discuss it.* **6.** *vt.* **REDUCE VOLUME OF SOUND** to reduce the volume of sound that something produces ○ *lower your voice* **7.** *vt.* MUSIC **REDUCE SOUND PITCH** to bring a sound to a lower pitch **8.** *vt.* PHON **MODIFY VOWEL SOUND** to change the sound of a vowel by pushing the tongue to the bottom of the mouth ■ *adj.* **1. BELOW SOMETHING** physically below another thing, especially one of the same type ○ *the lower lip* **2. REDUCED OR LESS** reduced or less in amount ○ *agreed to work for lower wages* **3. CLOSER TO BOTTOM** closer to the bottom or base of something ○ *camped on the lower slopes of the mountain* **4. OF LESS IMPORTANCE** of less importance or inferior status ○ *lower rank* **5.** GEOL **EARLIER IN GEOLOGICAL PERIOD** relating to the earlier part of a geological period or system **6.** ZOOL **LESS ADVANCED** less advanced in terms of development or complexity **7. FARTHER FROM SOURCE** indicating that part of a river that is farthest away from the source ○ *the lower Rio Grande* ■ *n.* **SOMETHING LOWER** something that is the lower of two or more things [12thC. Comparative of LOW[1], literally "more low."]

low·er[2] /lŏr, lowr/ *vi.* (**-ered, -er·ing, -ers**) **1. BE OVERCAST** to be overcast and threatening storms or heavy rain **2. LOOK ANGRY** to look angry or sullen ■ *n.* **SCOWL** a scowl or miserable look [13thC. Origin uncertain.] —**low·er·ing** *adj.* —**low·er·ing·ly** *adv.*

low·er bound *n.* a number that is less than or equal to all the members of a set

Low·er Cal·i·for·ni·a /lṓ ər kàlli fáwrnee ə/ = **Baja California**

Low·er Can·a·da /lṓ ər kánnədə/ southern portion of present-day Quebec. It was a British province separate from Upper Canada from 1791 to 1840.

Low·er Car·bon·if·er·ous *n.* = **Mississippian** *n.* 2

low·er·case *adj.* **NOT CAPITAL** written in small rather than capital form ○ *written with a lowercase "p"* ■ *vt.* (**-cased, -cas·ing, -cas·es**) **PUT IN SMALL LETTERS** to put typescript or written material in lowercase form ■ *n.* **SMALL LETTERS NOT CAPITALS** the small rather than capital form of letters ○ *The advertisement was striking for its use of lowercase.* [Late 17thC. From compositors' practice of keeping types for small letters in the lower of a pair of type cases.]

low·er cham·ber *n.* = **lower house**

low·er class *n.* the social group considered to occupy the lowest position in a hierarchical society, typically composed of manual workers and their families

low·er·class·man /lṓr klássmən/ (*plural* **-men**) *n.* = **underclassman**

low·er deck *n.* the next deck in a ship above the hold

low·er house, **lower chamber** *n.* one of two legislative houses, generally more directly representative and larger than the other house

low·er·most /lṓr mṓst/ *adj.* very lowest

low·er world *n.* the dwelling place of the dead, often considered to be beneath the ground

low·est com·mon de·nom·i·na·tor *n.* **1.** = **least common denominator 2. UNDISCERNING PUBLIC** the mass of ordinary people, particularly when considered to have low critical standards and to lack taste

low·est com·mon mul·ti·ple *n.* = **least common multiple**

low fre·quen·cy *n.* a radio frequency ranging from 30 to 300 kilohertz

Low Ger·man *n.* the German dialects that are spoken in northern regions of Germany. Low German dialects differ in their development from the High German dialects that gave rise to standard German and are generally regarded as forming a separate language. ◊ **Middle Low German** ["Low" from the fact that the language is spoken in the low-lying part of Germany near the seacoast]

low-grade *adj.* **1. INFERIOR IN QUALITY** bad or inferior in quality or grade **2.** MED **MILD** used to describe a medical condition, especially a fever, that is mild and not serious

low-impact *adj.* **1. NOT STRENUOUS** not requiring a lot of energy or effort **2. CAUSING LITTLE DAMAGE TO THE ENVIRONMENT** causing little or no damage to the surrounding environment

low·ing *n.* = **low**[2]

low-key, **low-keyed** *adj.* **1. RESTRAINED** restrained and understated in character ○ *a relatively low-key campaign* **2. SUBDUED IN COLOR** subdued or of low intensity, particularly in color **3.** PHOTOGRAPHY, PAINTING **DARK-TONED** used to describe a photograph or painting made up of dark tones and containing few highlights

low·land /lṓlənd/ *n.* land that is relatively flatter or lower than adjacent land —**low·land** *adj.*

low-lev·el *adj.* **1. LOW DOWN** situated or done at a low or lower than usual level **2. LOW IN STATUS** relatively low in terms of importance, status, expertise, or intensity

low-lev·el lan·guage *n.* COMPUT any computer-oriented programming language such as assembly language, in which the instructions are written in a code closer to machine code than to human language

low·life /lṓ līf/ *n.* **1. CRIMINAL OR ASSOCIATE** a criminal or somebody who associates with criminals (*informal*) **2. SOMEBODY IMMORAL** somebody who is disreputable and immoral (*insult*) **3. CRIMINAL OR IMMORAL PEOPLE** people with criminal tendencies or extremely low morals, regarded as a group (*informal insult*) —**low·life** *adj.*

low·ly /lṓlee/ *adj.* (**-li·er, -li·est**) **1. LOW IN STATUS** low in rank, status, or importance **2. MEEK** with a meek and humble way of behaving **3. SIMPLE AND MODEST** simple, plain, and modest in character ■ *adv.* (**-li·er, -li·est**) **1. IN MEEK WAY** in a humble or meek way **2. AT LOW VOLUME** at a subdued pitch or volume —**low·li·ness** *n.*

low-ly·ing *adj.* at a lower level or closer to sea level than neighboring ground

low-maintenance *adj.* requiring only a little attention or effort to maintain (*informal*) ◊ **high-maintenance**

Low Mass, **low mass** *n.* a plain Mass celebrated in a Roman Catholic or Anglican church that is recited, not sung

low-mind·ed *adj.* thinking or behaving in a coarse vulgar way —**low-mind·ed·ly** *adv.* —**low-mind·ed·ness** *n.*

low-necked *adj.* cut to have a low neckline

low-pass fil·ter *n.* an electronic filter that blocks signals above a specified cutoff frequency but allows those below it to pass through unchanged

low-pitched *adj.* **1. LOW IN PITCH** low in pitch or tonal range ○ *a low-pitched hum* **2. SHALLOW IN SLOPE** with a shallow slope ○ *a low-pitched roof*

low-pres·sure *adj.* **1.** PHYS **NEEDING LITTLE PRESSURE** having, exerting, or working under little pressure **2. RELAXED** relaxed, easygoing, or presenting little stress

low pro·file *n.* a way of behaving in which somebody deliberately seeks to avoid attention or publicity ○ *keep a low profile*

low-pro·file *adj.* **1. AVOIDING ATTENTION** deliberately avoiding attention or publicity **2.** AUTOMOT **WIDE RELATIVE TO HEIGHT** having a wide tread relative to its radial height ○ *low-profile tires*

low re·lief *n.* = **bas-relief** [Translation of French *bas-relief*]

low rid·er *n.* **1. CUSTOMIZED CAR WITH LOW CHASSIS** a car on which the springs have been shortened, so that the body of the car is closer to the ground than usual **2.** *Southwest U.S.* **DRIVER OF LOW RIDER** somebody who drives a low rider

low rise *n.* a building consisting of only a few stories [Modeled on HIGH-RISE] —**low-rise** *adj.*

low-slung *adj.* closer to the ground or the floor than usual

low spir·its *npl.* a state of unhappiness, hopelessness or despondency ○ *The search party was in low spirits after three days.* —**low-spir·it·ed** *adj.* —**low-spir·it·ed·ly** *adv.* —**low-spir·it·ed·ness** *n.*

Low Sun·day *n.* the Sunday after Easter [Origin uncertain: "Low" probably in contrast to the "high" feast of Easter Sunday]

low tech *n.* low technology [Shortening of LOW TECHNOLOGY] —**low-tech** *adj.*

low tech·nol·o·gy *n.* simple technology, especially that used to make basic items or perform basic tasks

low-ten·sion *adj.* capable of carrying low voltage or operating under low-voltage conditions

low-test *adj.* having low volatility and a high boiling point ○ *low-test gasoline*

low tide *n.* **1. LOWEST TIDE LEVEL** a tide at its lowest level, or the time of day when this occurs **2. WORST POINT** a lowest or worst point

low wa·ter *n.* = **low tide** *n.* 1

low-wa·ter mark *n.* **1. LOWEST LEVEL OF WATER** the lowest level reached by a body of tidal or fresh water **2. LINE MARKING LOW-WATER MARK** a natural or artificial line marking a low-water mark **3. LOWEST POINT** a lowest or most difficult point

lox[1] /loks/ *n.* smoked salmon [Mid-20thC. Via Yiddish *laks* from Middle High German *Lachs* "salmon." Ultimately from an Indo-European word meaning "salmon."]

lox[2] /loks/ *n.* liquid oxygen, especially when used as an oxidizer for rocket fuel [Early 20thC. From *l(iquid) o(xygen) (e)x(plosive)*; later misinterpreted by folk etymology as from *l(iquid) ox(ygen)*.]

lox·o·ce·mus py·thon /loksə sēeməss-/ *n.* a stout burrowing snake found on the Pacific coast of Mexico. It is considered by many to be the only member of the python family in the New World. Latin name: *Loxocemus bicolor*.

lox·o·drome /lóksə drṓm/ *n.* = **rhumb line** [Late 19thC. Back-formation from LOXODROMIC.]

lox·o·drom·ic /lòksə drómmik/, **lox·o·drom·i·cal** /lòksə drómmik'l/ *adj.* relating to a map in which the rhumb lines appear straight, or to the rhumb lines on such a map [Late 17thC. From French *loxodromique*, from Greek *loxos* "oblique," of unknown origin, + *dromos* "course" (source of English *-drome*).] —**lox·o·drom·i·cal·ly** *adv.*

lox·o·drom·ic curve *n.* = **rhumb line**

loy·al /lóy əl/ *adj.* **1. FAITHFUL** remaining faithful to a country, person, ruler, government, or ideal **2. EXPRESSING LOYALTY** expressing or relating to loyalty [Mid-16thC. Via French from Old French *loial*, variant of *leial*, from Latin *legalis* "legal" (see LEGAL). The underlying idea is of faithfully carrying out legal obligations.] —**loy·al·ly** *adv.* —**loy·al·ness** *n.*

loy·al·ist /lóy əlist/ *n.* somebody who firmly supports a country, ruler, or government —**loy·al·ism** /lóy ə lìzzəm/ *n.*

Loy·al·ist /lóy əlist/ *n.* **1. AMERICAN WHO SUPPORTED BRITISH** an American who supported the British during the American Revolution **2. SPANISH CIVIL WAR SUPPORTER OF GOVERNMENT** a supporter of the republican government during the Spanish Civil War **3.** *U.K.* POL **SUPPORTER OF ULSTER UNION WITH BRITAIN** a Northern Ireland Protestant who wishes to continue Northern Ireland's political union with Britain

loy·al·ty /lóy əltee/ (*plural* **-ties**) *n.* **1. STATE OF BEING LOYAL** the quality or state of being loyal **2. FEELING OF DUTY** a feeling of devotion, duty, or attachment to somebody or something (*often used in the plural*) [14thC. From Old French *loialté*, from *loial* "loyal" (see LOYAL).]

loz·enge /lózzənj/ *n.* **1.** PHARM **MEDICATED TABLET** a medicated tablet or candy that is dissolved in the mouth, especially to soothe the throat **2.** MATH **DIAMOND SHAPE** a diamond-shaped figure **3.** HERALDRY **DIAMOND-SHAPED IMAGE** a diamond-shaped design or device on heraldic arms [14thC. From Old French *losenge* "windowpane, small square cake," of uncertain origin: perhaps related to Spanish *losa* "slab" and ultimately from Gaulish or Iberian.] —**loz·enged** /lózzənjd/ *adj.*

Lo·zi /lózee/ (*plural* **-zis** *or* **-zi**) *n.* a language of western Zambia, related to Sotho. About 450 thousand people speak Lozi. [Mid-20thC. From Bantu.] —**Lo·zi** *adj.*

LP *n.* **LONG-PLAYING RECORD** a long-playing phonograph record that turns at $33\frac{1}{3}$ revolutions per minute ■ *abbr.* low pressure

LPG *abbr.* liquefied petroleum gas

LPGA *abbr.* Ladies Professional Golf Association

LPM, lpm *abbr.* lines per minute (*refers to a computer printer*)

LPN, L.P.N. *abbr.* licensed practical nurse

LPS *abbr.* lipopolysaccharide

Lr *symbol.* lawrencium

LR *abbr.* living room (*in advertisements*)

LRV *abbr.* light rail vehicle

L.S. *abbr.* locus sigilli (*on documents*) [Latin, "the place of the seal"]

LSAT /él sàt/ *abbr.* Law School Admissions Test

LSD *n.* a hallucinogenic drug made from lysergic acid that was used experimentally as a medicine and is taken as an illegal drug [From German *L(yserg)s(äure)-D(iäthylamid)* "lysergic acid diethylamide"]

LSI *abbr.* ELECTRON ENG large-scale integration

LT *abbr.* ELEC ENG low tension

lt. *abbr.* light

Lt. *abbr.* Lieutenant

l.t. *abbr.* local time

LTC *abbr.* Lieutenant Colonel

Lt. Col. *abbr.* Lieutenant Colonel

Lt. Comdr. *abbr.* Lieutenant Commander

Ltd., ltd. *abbr.* limited (liability) (*used after the name of a British company*)

Lt. Gen. *abbr.* Lieutenant General

Lt. Gov. *abbr.* Lieutenant Governor

LTJG *abbr.* lieutenant junior grade

Lu *symbol.* lutetium

Lu·a·la·ba /lòo aa laá baa/ headstream of the Congo River in southeastern Democratic Republic of the Congo. Length: 1,100 mi./1,800 km.

Lu·an·da /loo ándə/ seaport and capital of Angola, situated in the northwestern part of the country, on the Atlantic Ocean. Population: 2,250,000 (1995).

lu·au /lóo òw/ *n.* a Hawaiian feast, usually with music and entertainment [Mid-19thC. From Hawaiian *lū'au.*]

Lu·ba /lóobə/ (*plural* **-bas** *or* **-ba**) *n.* **Lu·ba, Lu·ba-Lu·lua** a group of languages or dialects of southern Congo, around Kinshasa. Luba has about 8 million speakers and belongs to the Bantu group of Benue-Congo languages. [Late 19thC. From Bantu.] —**Luba** *adj.*

lub·ber /lúbbər/ *n.* **1.** **CLUMSY OR UNINTELLIGENT PERSON** a big person who is clumsy or unintelligent (*insult*) **2.** **LANDLUBBER** a landlubber [14thC. Origin uncertain: perhaps from *lob* "lout," from Low Dutch; or from Old French *lobeor* "swindler, parasite," from *lober* "to deceive," perhaps from Frankish *lobon* "to praise."] —**lub·ber·ly** *adj., adv.*

lub·ber line, lub·ber's line *n.* a mark on a ship's compass that indicates the vessel's heading [*Lubber* from the fact that the line made steering easier for the inexperienced helmsman]

lub·ber's hole *n.* a space in a platform around a mast, allowing a sailor to climb through the space and stand on the platform [*Lubber's* from the idea that the hole was for inexperienced sailors who were too frightened to climb by way of the ropes at the edge of the platform]

lub·ber's line *n.* = **lubber line**

lube /loob/ *n. U.S., Aus* **LUBRICANT** a lubricant (*informal*) ■ *vt.* (**lubed, lub·ing, lubes**) *U.S., Aus* **LUBRICATE** to apply lubricant to something (*informal*)

Lu·bitsch /lóobich/, **Ernst** (1892–1947) German-born U.S. actor and movie director. He started making movies in Germany, then moved to Hollywood as a director of comedies and costume epics.

Lu·blin /lóoblin/ city in southeastern Poland, situated about 95 mi./153 km southeast of Warsaw. Population: 353,300 (1995).

lu·bri·cant /lóobrikənt/ *n.* **1.** **FRICTION-REDUCING SUBSTANCE** a substance, typically oil or grease, applied to a surface to reduce friction between moving parts **2.** **ELEMENT EASING DIFFICULT SITUATION** somebody or something that eases or facilitates a solution to a potentially difficult or awkward situation —**lu·bri·cant** *adj.*

lu·bri·cate /lóobri kàyt/ (**-cat·ed, -cat·ing, -cates**) *v.* **1.** *vti.* **APPLY LUBRICANT** to apply an oily or greasy substance to something in order to reduce friction to moving parts **2.** *vt.* **MAKE SLIPPERY** to make something slippery **3.** *vt.* **MAKE SOMETHING RUN SMOOTHLY** to make something run smoothly and without problems [Early 17thC. From, ultimately, Latin *lubricare*, from *lubricus* "slippery" (source of English *lubricious*). Ultimately from an Indo-European word meaning "to slide," which also produced English *sleeve.*] —**lu·bri·ca·tion** /lóobri káysh'n/ *n.* —**lu·bri·ca·tion·al** *adj.* —**lu·bri·ca·tive** /lóobri kàytiv/ *adj.*

lu·bri·ca·tor /lóobri kàytər/ *n.* **1.** **DEVICE FOR APPLYING LUBRICANT** a device for applying a lubricant to moving parts **2.** **SOMEBODY WHO EASES SITUATION** somebody who is diplomatic and able to ease a difficult situation

lu·bri·cious /loo bríshəss/, **lu·bri·cous** /lóobrikəss/ *adj.* (*literary*) **1.** **LEWD OR OBSCENE** lewd, obscene, or intended to be sexually exciting **2.** **SLIPPERY** slippery or oily [Late 16thC. Formed from Latin *lubricus* "slippery" (see LUBRICATE). Former meanings of the word include "slippery" and "fickle."] —**lu·bri·cious·ly** *adv.*

lu·bric·i·ty /loo bríssətee/ *n.* behavior that is obscene or unchaste (*literary*) [15thC. Directly or via French from late Latin *lubricitas*, from Latin *lubricus* "slippery" (see LUBRICATE).]

lu·bri·cous *adj.* = **lubricious**

Lu·bum·ba·shi /lòoboom baáshee/ industrial city and mining center in Katanga Region, southeastern Democratic Republic of the Congo. Population: 851,381 (1994). Former name **Elizabethville**

Lu·ca·nia, Mount /loo káynee ə/ mountain in the Saint Elias Range, southwestern Yukon Territory, Canada, near the Alaskan border. Height: 17,147 ft./5,226 m.

lu·carne /loo kaárn/ *n.* a dormer window [Mid-16thC. Via French from Provençal *lucana*, of uncertain origin: perhaps from prehistoric Germanic.]

Lu·cas /lóokəss/, **George** (*b.* 1944) U.S. movie director and producer. After directing *American Graffiti* (1973) and the first *Star Wars* trilogy (1977–83), he built up a pioneering special effects company.

Luc·ca /lóokə/ historic town and capital of Lucca Province, Tuscany Region, north-central Italy. Population: 100,508 (1992).

Luce /looss/, **Henry Robinson** (1898–1967) U.S. editor and publisher. The magazines and periodicals he founded include *Time* (1923), which he edited until 1964.

lu·cent /lóoss'nt/ *adj.* **1.** **LUMINOUS** shining with a glowing light **2.** **TRANSLUCENT** translucent or clear [15thC. From Latin, the present participle stem of *lucere* "to shine" (see LUCID).] —**lu·cen·cy** *n.* —**lu·cent·ly** *adv.*

lu·cerne /loo súrn/ *n. U.K.* = **alfalfa** [Mid-17thC. Via French from modern Provençal *luzerno*, originally "glow-worm," from Latin *lucerna* "lamp," from *lucere* "to shine" (see LUCID). Perhaps from the plant's shiny seeds.]

Lu·cerne /loo súrn/ city and capital of Lucerne Canton, central Switzerland. It is a tourist center. Population: 61,656 (1994).

Lu·cerne, Lake of lake and popular tourist region in central Switzerland. Area: 44 sq. mi./114 sq. km.

lu·cid /lóossid/ *adj.* **1.** **EASILY UNDERSTOOD** clear and easily understood ○ *a lucid explanation* **2.** **SHINING** emitting light **3.** **RATIONAL AND MENTALLY** rational and mentally clear, especially only for a period between episodes of delirium or psychosis [Late 16thC. From Latin *lucidus*, from *lucere* "to shine," from the stem *luc-* "light" (source of English *elucidate* and *translucent*). Ultimately from an Indo-European word that also produced English *lunar.*] —**lu·cid·i·ty** /loo síddətee/ *n.* —**lu·cid·ness** /lóossidnəss/ *n.* —**lu·cid·ly** /-lee/ *adv.*

Lu·cid /lóossid/, **Shannon Wells** (*b.* 1943) U.S. astronaut and biochemist. One of the first women astronauts from the United States, she flew on several space missions, including five months on the Russian space station Mir.

lu·ci·fer /lóossəfər/ *n.* a friction match (*dated*) [Mid-19thC. From *lucifer match*, originally a brand name.]

Lu·ci·fer /lóossəfər/ *n.* **1.** **SATAN** a rebellious archangel who is held to be the same as Satan **2.** **THE MORNING STAR** the planet Venus appearing before sunrise as the morning star [Pre-12thC. From Latin, "the planet Venus," literally "light-bearing," from the stem *luc-* "light" (see LUCID).]

lu·cif·er·ase /lóossəfə ràyss, -ràyz/ *n.* an enzyme that aids the oxidation of luciferin in the cells of organisms that emit light

lu·cif·er·in /loo síffərin/ *n.* a substance found in the cells of bioluminescent organisms, e.g., glowworms and fireflies, that on oxidation emits bluish-green light with very little heat

lu·cif·er·ous /loo síffərəss/ *adj.* bringing or emitting light

Lu·ci·na /loo sínə/ *n.* in Roman mythology, Juno in her capacity as goddess of childbirth

Lu·cite /lóo sìt/ *tdmk.* a trademark for polymethyl methacrylate

luck /luk/ *n.* **1.** **GOOD FORTUNE** good fortune ○ *a stroke of luck* **2.** **CHANCE** the arbitrary distribution of events or outcomes ○ *a game of luck* **3.** **EVENT DETERMINED BY CHANCE** something that seems to happen by chance rather than as a logical consequence **4.** **FORTUNATE OR UNFORTUNATE EVENT** something fortunate or unfortunate that happens to somebody, or a series of such events ○ *Just my luck!* **5.** **SOMETHING BEARING LUCK** an event, action, or object regarded as bringing good or bad luck ○ *It's said to be bad luck to walk under ladders.* [15thC. Origin uncertain: probably from Low German *luk*. The word was most likely borrowed as a gambling term.]

luck into *vt.* to obtain something desirable or experience something pleasurable by chance

luck out *vi.* to be lucky enough to succeed by chance

luck·i·ly /lúkilee/ *adv.* as a result of or the occasion for good luck

luck·less /lúkləss/ *adj.* without success or fortune —**luck·less·ly** *adv.* —**luck·less·ness** *n.*

Luck·now /lúk now/ capital of Uttar Pradesh State, northern India, situated in the Ganges valley, about 40 mi./64 km northeast of Kanpur. Population: 1,592,010 (1991).

luck·y /lúkee/ (**-i·er, -i·est**) *adj.* **1.** **FORTUNATE** having good fortune ○ *You were lucky not to be seriously injured.* **2.** **BRINGING GOOD FORTUNE** producing or bringing good fortune ○ *lucky charm* **3.** **RESULTING FROM GOOD LUCK** as a result of good luck ○ *lucky escape* —**luck·i·ness** *n.*

WORD KEY: SYNONYMS

lucky, fortunate, happy, providential

CORE MEANING: relating to advantage or good fortune

lucky used to describe something that brings success or advantage. It can also be used to describe the person who gains the success or advantage, especially when this seems to happen by chance; **fortunate** used to describe something that brings success and advantage, or the person who gains the success or advantage, especially when this is to a greater degree than was expected or deserved; **happy** an old-fashioned or literary word used in the same way as "lucky" or "fortunate"; **providential** used to describe something that happens at a favorable time, for example, because it presents an opportunity or the means to do something.

WORD KEY: CULTURAL NOTE

Lucky Jim, a novel by English writer Kingsley Amis (1954). The protagonist of this satire on academic life, Jim Dixon, is a junior lecturer at a provincial university and the plot revolves around his problematic relationships with his employers, colleagues, and girlfriend. While some critics condemned the book's amorality, many regarded Jim as a symbol of social protest.

luck·y dip *n. U.K.* = **grab bag**

lu·cra·tive /lóokrətiv/ *adj.* producing profit or wealth [15thC. From Latin *lucrativus*, from *lucrari* "to gain," from *lucrum* "gain" (see LUCRE). The word once also meant "covetous."] —**lu·cra·tive·ly** *adv.* —**lu·cra·tive·ness** *n.*

lu·cre /lóokər/ *n.* money, wealth, or profit (*dated or humorous*) ○ *filthy lucre* [14thC. Directly or via French from Latin *lucrum* "gain" (source of English *lucrative*). Ultimately from an Indo-European word that also produced English *guerdon* and *galore*.]

lu·cu·bra·tion /lóokyə bráysh'n/ *n.* **1.** **PIECE OF LEARNED WRITING** a written work resulting from prolonged study, often having a scholarly or pedantic style (*usually used in the plural*) **2.** **LONG STUDY** long hard study, especially at night [Late 16thC. From the Latin stem *lucubration-*, ultimately from *lucubrare* "to compose at night," from the stem *luc-* "light" (see LUCID). The underlying idea is of working by lamplight.] —**lu·cu·brate** /lóokyoo bràyt/ *vi.*

lu·cu·lent /lóokyələnt/ *adj.* **1.** **UNDERSTANDABLE** easy to understand **2.** **GLOWING** shining or glowing [15thC. From Latin *luculentus*, from the stem *luc-* "light" (see LUCID).]

Lu·cul·lan /loo kúllən/ *adj.* lavish or overindulgent, especially with regard to food [Mid-19thC. From Latin *Lucullanus*, from (Licinius) *Lucullus*, a Roman general of the 1stC B.C. famous for his lavish banquets.]

Lud·dite /lú dìt/ *n.* **1.** **OPPONENT OF NEW TECHNOLOGY** somebody who opposes technological or industrial innovation **2.** HIST **19C PROTESTER AGAINST TECHNOLOGY** a worker involved in protests in Britain in the 1810s against new factory methods of production and in favor of traditional methods of work [Early 19thC. Origin uncertain: according to tradition, named for Ned *Ludd*, an 18th-century farm worker in Leicestershire, England, who destroyed two stocking frames in a fit of rage.] —**Lud·dite** *adj.* —**Lud·dism** /lú dìzzəm/ *n.*

lu·di·crous /lóodikrəss/ *adj.* utterly ridiculous because of being absurd, incongruous, impractical, or unsuitable [Early 17thC. Formed from Latin *ludicrus*, from *ludus* "play."] —**lu·di·crous·ly** *adv.* —**lu·di·crous·ness** *n.*

WORD KEY: ORIGIN

The Latin word *ludus*, from which ***ludicrous*** is derived, is also the source of English *allude*, *collude*, *delude*, *elude*, and *illusion*.

Lud·low /lúdlō/ town in southwestern Massachusetts, on the Chicopee River, directly northeast of Springfield and southwest of Worcester. Population: 18,786 (1996).

Lud·wigs·ha·fen /lóodvigs haàfən/ port in Rhineland-Palatinate State, southwestern Germany, situated on the western bank of the Rhine River, opposite Mannheim. Population: 168,100 (1994).

lu·es /lóo eez/ *n.* syphilis [Mid-17thC. From Latin, "plague." Ultimately from an Indo-European word meaning "to loosen," which also produced English *loose*, *forlorn*, and *dissolve*.]

luff /luf/ *v.* **(luffed, luff·ing, luffs) 1.** *vt.* **SAIL TOO CLOSE TO WIND** to bring a boat closer in to the wind, or to sail too close to the wind, so that the sails flap **2.** *vi.* **FLAP** to flap when a boat is in a position too close to the wind (*refers to a sail*) ■ *n.* **FRONT EDGE OF SAIL** the front edge of a sail [12thC. From Old French *lof*, of uncertain origin: probably from Low German *lōf* or Dutch *loef* "windward side of a ship."]

Luft·waf·fe /lóoft vaàfə/ *n.* the German Air Force [Mid-20thC. From German, literally "air weapon."]

lug[1] /lug/ *vt.* **(lugged, lug·ging, lugs) 1.** **PULL SOMETHING WITH EFFORT** to carry or pull something that is heavy or bulky, using great effort **2.** **INTRODUCE IRRELEVANTLY INTO DISCUSSION** to introduce irrelevant material into a discussion or conversation ■ *n.* **ACT OF PULLING A LOAD** the effort or action of pulling something very heavy [15thC. Origin uncertain: probably from a Scandinavian language.The underlying idea would be of something that can be pulled or grasped.]

lug[2] /lug/ *n.* **1.** **PROJECTING PART** a projecting part, especially one by which something can be moved, rotated, or supported **2.** **PROJECTION FOR ELECTRICAL CONTACT** a small metal projection to which an electrical conductor or wire may be attached, usually by soldering or using mechanical pressure **3.** **SMALL PROJECTION IMPROVING TRACTION** a small projection on a tire or shoe that helps provide traction **4.** **FRUIT OR VEGETABLE BOX** a box for vegetables or fruit **5.** **CLUMSY MAN** a man, especially one who is unintelligent or clumsy (*informal insult*) [14thC. Origin uncertain: probably from a Scandinavian language.]

lug[3] /lug/ *n.* = **lugsail** [Mid-19thC. Shortening of LUGSAIL.]

lug[4] /lug/ *n.* = **lugworm** *n.* [Early 17thC. Origin unknown.]

Lu·gan·da /loo gándə, loo gaándə/ *n.* = **Ganda** [Late 19thC. From Bantu.]

Lu·ga·no /loo gaá no/ town and tourist center in Ticino Canton, southern Switzerland. Population: 26,025 (1992).

Lu·ga·no, Lake lake in southern Switzerland and northern Italy. Area: 19 sq. mi./49 sq. km.

luge /loozh/ *n.* **RACING TOBOGGAN** a racing toboggan on which the riders lie on their backs with their feet pointing forward ■ *vi.* **(luged, lug·ing, luges)** **RACE ON LUGE** to race on a luge [Late 19thC. Via Swiss French from medieval Latin *sludia*, of uncertain origin: perhaps from Gaulish, and ultimately from an Indo-European word that also produced English *sled*.] —**lug·er** *n.*

Lu·ger /lóogər/ *tdmk.* a trademark for a German automatic pistol

lug·gage /lúggij/ *n.* suitcases, bags, and other items for carrying somebody's belongings during a journey [Late 16thC. Formed from LUG[1] "to carry," on the model of BAGGAGE. The original meaning was "inconveniently heavy baggage."]

lug·gage rack *n.* **1.** **FRAME ON TOP OF CAR** a frame attached to the top of a motor vehicle, used for carrying things, especially luggage ○ *The tent can go on the luggage rack.* **2.** **OVERHEAD FRAME FOR LUGGAGE** an overhead frame in a train, bus etc. for passengers to keep small items of luggage.

lug·ger /lúggər/ *n.* a small boat for fishing or pleasure sailing that is rigged with a lugsail [Mid-18thC. Origin uncertain: perhaps formed from *lug-* in LUGSAIL, or possibly from Dutch *logger*, from *loggen* "to fish with a drag-net."]

lug nut *n.* a large nut that screws onto a heavy bolt, especially one used to attach a wheel to a motor vehicle

Lu·go·si /loo gṓssee/, **Bela** (1884–1956) Hungarian-born U.S. actor. He starred in numerous horror movies, and was especially closely identified with the title role in *Dracula* (1931). Real name **Bela Ferenc Denzso Blasko**

lug·sail /lúgs'l, lúg sàyl/ *n.* a four-sided sail bent on a yard that crosses the mast at an angle [Late 17thC. Origin uncertain: "lug" probably from LUG[2].]

lu·gu·bri·ous /loo góobree əss, lə-/ *adj.* extremely mournful, sad, or gloomy [Early 17thC. Formed from Latin *lugubris*, from *lugere* "to mourn." Ultimately from an Indo-European word meaning "to break." The underlying idea seems to be of breaking down emotionally.] —**lu·gu·bri·ous·ly** *adv.* —**lu·gu·bri·ous·ness** *n.*

lug·worm /lúg wùrm/ *n.* a segmented marine worm that burrows in sandy shores, has rows of tufted gills, and is often used as fishing bait. Genus: *Arenicola.* [Early 19thC. "Lug" from LUG[4].]

Lu·hansk /loo haánsk/, **Lu·hans'k** industrial city in eastern Ukraine. Population: 504,000 (1991).

Luke /look/ *n.* the third book of the New Testament in which the life and teachings of Jesus Christ are described. It is believed to have been written by St. Luke. See table at **Bible**

Luke /look/, **St.** (*fl.* 1st century A.D.) evangelist companion to St. Paul. Perhaps a physician, he was by tradition author of the biblical Acts of the Apostles and the third Gospel.

luke·warm /lóok wàwrm/ *adj.* **1.** **WARM** just slightly warm, especially of food or drink that is expected to be hot (*disapproving*) **2.** **SHOWING LITTLE ENTHUSIASM** showing or having little enthusiasm, interest, support, or conviction [14thC. "Luke" from obsolete *luke* "lukewarm," of uncertain origin: perhaps a variant of dialect *lew* "lukewarm," from Old English *hlēo* "warm," of unknown origin.] —**luke·warm·ly** *adv.* —**luke·warm·ness** *n.*

Luks /looks/, **George Benjamin** (1867–1933) U.S. artist. A member of the artistic group called the Eight, he produced realistic paintings of urban deprivation.

Lu·le·å /lóo le ō/ seaport at the head of the Gulf of Bothnia, northern Sweden. Population: 71,106 (1995).

lull /lul/ *v.* **(lulled, lull·ing, lulls) 1.** *vt.* **SOOTHE OR CALM SOMEBODY** to soothe or calm a person or animal, especially by using gentle sounds or motions **2.** *vt.* **MAKE SOMEBODY FEEL SAFE** to give somebody a false sense of security so that an unpleasant situation takes the person by surprise ○ *They lulled us into thinking we still had time.* **3.** *vi.* **BECOME CALM** to become calm or calmer ■ *n.* **PERIOD OF CALM** a brief interval of calm or decreased activity [14thC. Origin uncertain: probably an imitation of the sounds used to sing a child to sleep.]

lull·a·by /lúllə bì/ *n.* (*plural* **-bies**) **1.** **GENTLE SONG** a gentle song for soothing a child, especially into sleep **2.** **MUSIC FOR LULLABY** instrumental music in the style of a lullaby ■ *vt.* **(-bied, -by·ing, -bies)** **SOOTHE CHILD WITH LULLABY** to soothe a child with a lullaby [Mid-16thC. From obsolete *lulla* "lullaby," an imitation of the sounds used to sing a child to sleep + *-by*, as in BYE-BYE.]

lu·lu /lóo loo/ *n.* a remarkable or outstanding person, object, or idea (*slang*) [Late 19thC. Alteration (perhaps with influence from *Lulu*, pet-form of the name *Louise*, female name) of earlier *looly*, of unknown origin, used in the admiring phrase "looliest looly of the loolies."]

Lu·lu·a·bourg /lóo lóo ə boorg/ former name for **Kananga**

lum·ba·go /lum báy gō/ *n.* pain in the lower or lumbar region of the back [Late 17thC. From Latin, where it was formed from *lumbus* "loin."]

lum·bar /lúmbər, -baar/ *adj.* relating to or situated in the loins or the small of the back [Mid-17thC. From medieval Latin *lumbaris*, from Latin *lumbus* "loin" (source of English *loin* and *sirloin*).]

lum·ber[1] /lúmbər/ *n.* **1.** **LOGS SAWED FOR USE** trees that have been sawed and prepared for use in building, woodworking, or cabinetmaking **2.** *U.K.* **UNWANTED OBJECTS** large objects that are not being used and are stored out of sight ■ *v.* **(-bered, -ber·ing, -bers) 1.** *vti.* **TURN TREES INTO LUMBER** to cut down the trees in a region and convert them into salable lumber **2.** *vt. U.K.* **BURDEN SOMEBODY WITH TASK** to burden somebody with something unpleasant or unwanted, especially a responsibility or a task (*informal*) **3.** *vt. U.K.* **PILE THINGS TOGETHER** to pile things together haphazardly [Mid-16thC. Originally "disused articles of furniture," of uncertain origin: perhaps literally "things that impede movement," from LUMBER[2], influenced by obsolete *lumber* "pawnbroking establishment" (filled with disused property), variant of LOMBARD.] —**lum·ber·er** *n.*

lum·ber[2] /lúmbər/ **(-bered, -ber·ing, -bers)** *vi.* to move clumsily or heavily [14thC. Origin uncertain: perhaps from a Scandinavian language.]

lum·ber·jack /lúmbər jàk/ *n.* **1.** **FELLER OF TREES** somebody who cuts down trees and transports the lumber **2.** CLOTHES = **lumberjacket** [Mid-19thC. *Jack* from JACK "man, laborer."]

lum·ber·jack·et /lúmbər jàkət/, **lum·ber·jack** *n.* a work jacket made from thick, warm material, usually brightly colored with a checked pattern [Mid-20thC. From its being of a type worn by lumberjacks.]

lum·ber·man /lúmbərmən/ (*plural* **-men**) *n.* somebody who buys and sells lumber

lum·ber·yard /lúmbər yaàrd/ *n.* a business that sells or stores lumber and sometimes other building materials

lu·men /lóomən/ (*plural* **-mens** *or* **-mi·na** /lóomənə/) *n.* **1.** PHYS, MEASURE **UNIT OF LUMINOUS FLUX** the SI unit of luminous flux, equal to the amount of light crossing a unit area at a unit distance from a light source of luminous intensity of one candela. Symbol **lm** **2.** ANAT **SPACE WITHIN TUBE** the space inside any tubular structure in the body, e.g., an intestine, artery, or vein **3.** BOT **CAVITY IN PLANT** the cavity within a plant cell wall [Late 19thC. From Latin, "light, opening" (see LUMINOUS).]

Lu·met /loo mét/, **Sidney** (*b.* 1924) U.S. actor, director, and screenwriter. Among his greatest successes are *Murder on the Orient Express* (1974), *Dog Day Afternoon* (1975), and *Network* (1976).

Lu·mière /lóomyaír/, **Auguste** (1864–1948) French inventor. He and his brother Louis invented the cinema camera and projector, and produced the first film, *La sortie des usines Lumière* (1895).

Lu·mière, Louis (1862–1954) French inventor. He and his brother Auguste invented the cinema camera and projector, and made the first film, *La sortie des usines Lumières* (1895).

lu·mi·nance /lóomənəns/ *n.* **1.** **QUALITY OF BEING LUMINOUS** the condition or quality of emitting or reflecting light. Symbol *L* **2.** MEASURE **MEASURE OF BRIGHTNESS** a measure of the brightness of a surface equal to to the amount of luminous flux arriving at, passing through, or leaving a unit area of surface. It is measured in candelas per square meter. [Late 19thC. Formed from *luminant* "luminous," from Latin *luminant-*, the present participle stem of *luminare* "to illuminate," from the stem *lumin-* "light" (see LUMINOUS).]

lu·mi·nar·i·a /lo͞omə náiree ə/ (*plural* **-as**) *n. Southwest U.S.* a small candle set inside a paper bag that has been weighted with sand, usually placed outdoors with others as a Christmas decoration [Mid-20thC. Via Mexican Spanish and Spanish, "decorative light," from late Latin, "lamp," originally plural of *luminarium* (see LUMINARY).]

lu·mi·nar·y /lo͞omə nèrree/ *n.* (*plural* **-ies**) **1. EMINENT PERSON** an eminent or famous person **2. SUN, MOON, OR STAR** an object, especially a celestial body, that emits light (*literary*) ■ *adj.* **CHARACTERIZED BY LIGHT** relating to or characterized by light [15thC. Directly or via Old French *luminarie* from late Latin *luminarium*, from the Latin stem *lumin-* "light" (see LUMINOUS).]

lu·mi·nesce /lo͞omə néss/ (**-nesced, -nesc·ing, -nesc·es**) *vi.* to emit light by phosphorescence, fluorescence, or bioluminescence [Late 19thC. Back-formation from *luminescent* (see LUMINESCENCE).]

lu·mi·nes·cence /lo͞omə néss'ns/ *n.* **1. LIGHT EMISSION WITHOUT HEAT** the emission of light produced by means other than heat (**incandescence**), e.g., phosphorescence, fluorescence, or bioluminescence **2. LIGHT FROM LUMINESCENCE** the light emitted by luminescence [Late 19thC. From *luminescent*, which was coined from the Latin stem *lumin-* "light" (see LUMINOUS) + -ESCENT.] —**lu·mi·nes·cent** *adj.*

lu·mi·nif·er·ous /lo͞omə nífferəss/ *adj.* generating or giving off light [Early 19thC. Coined from the Latin stem *lumin-* "light" (see LUMINOUS) + -FEROUS.]

lu·mi·nos·i·ty /lo͞omə nóssətee/ (*plural* **lu·mi·nos·i·ties**) *n.* **1. STATE OF BEING LUMINOUS** the state or quality of being luminous **2.** ASTRON **ENERGY RADIATED BY CELESTIAL OBJECT** the energy radiated per second by a celestial body. Symbol *L* **3.** PHYS **STRENGTH OF LIGHT EMITTED** the visual perception of the extent to which an object emits light **4. SOMETHING LUMINOUS** something that emits light

lu·mi·nous /lo͞omənəss/ *adj.* **1. LIGHT-EMITTING** emitting or reflecting light **2. BRIGHT** startlingly bright ○ *luminous orange* **3. ILLUMINATED** brightly illuminated **4. UNDERSTANDABLE** clear and easy to understand **5. INSPIRING** enlightened and inspiring **6.** PHYS **RELATING TO LIGHT** evaluated on the basis of the visual sensation produced in an observer rather than energy measurements [15thC. Directly or via French from Latin *luminosus*, from the stem *lumin-* "light, opening" (source of English *lumen* and *illuminate*).] —**lu·mi·nous·ly** *adv.* —**lu·mi·nous·ness** *n.*

lu·mi·nous en·er·gy *n.* the total amount of light emitted by a source. Symbol Q_v

lu·mi·nous flux *n.* the rate of emission of light evaluated by the visual sensation it produces. Symbol Φ_v

lu·mi·nous in·ten·si·ty *n.* the amount of light emitted by a source in a particular direction. Symbol I_v

lum·mox /lúmməks/ *n.* somebody who is clumsy or unintelligent (*informal insult*) [Early 19thC. Origin unknown.]

lump[1] /lump/ *n.* **1. SOLID CHUNK** a small irregularly shaped solid mass or piece **2. TUMOR** a tumor or other swelling in the body **3. SUGAR CUBE** a small cube of solid sugar **4. LARGE AND CLUMSY PERSON** somebody who is large and unintelligent or clumsy (*informal insult*) ○ *He's a big lump of a boy.* ■ **lumps** *npl.* **HARDSHIP** harsh, often undeserved, criticism, punishment, or hardship (*informal*) ○ *You have to take your lumps like everyone else.* ■ *v.* (**lumped, lump·ing, lumps**) **1.** *vt.* **GROUP THINGS TOGETHER CARELESSLY** to consider people, ideas, or objects as a single group, often without good reason ○ *All the students were lumped together as lazy.* **2.** *vi.* **MOVE HEAVILY** to move in a heavy and clumsy manner ○ *He lumped along.* ■ *adj.* **IN LUMPS** in small cubes or lumps ○ *lump sugar* [14thC. Origin uncertain. The underlying idea seems to be of something coarse or shapeless.]

lump[2] /lump/ (**lumped, lump·ing, lumps**) *vt.* to endure something unpleasant that cannot be changed (*informal*) ○ *like it or lump it* [Late 16thC. Origin unknown. The original sense was "to look sulky"; the meaning "to tolerate" dates from the mid-19thC.]

lump·ec·to·my /lum péktəmee/ (*plural* **-mies**) *n.* a surgical operation for breast cancer in which the surgery is limited to the removal of the visible and palpable tumor only [Late 20thC. Coined from LUMP, on the model of MASTECTOMY.]

lum·pen /lúmpən, lo͝om-/ *adj.* (*disapproving*) **1. MARGINALIZED** living, or regarded as living, on the margins of society **2. NOT EDUCATED OR ENLIGHTENED** stupidly content with a life regarded as intellectually empty and socially inferior ■ *npl.* **LUMPEN PEOPLE** people regarded by others as lumpen (*disapproving*) (*takes a plural verb*) [Mid-20thC. Back-formation from LUMPENPROLETARIAT, with the meaning influenced by LUMP.]

lum·pen·pro·le·tar·i·at /lùmpən prōlə táiree ət, lo͝om-/ *n.* (*takes a singular or plural verb*) **1.** POL **PERMANENT UNDERCLASS** in Marxist analysis, people regarded as living on the margins of society, particularly criminals, homeless people, and the long-term unemployed **2. LOWER-CLASS PEOPLE** people from the lowest social class who are regarded as too content with a life supposedly intellectually empty and socially inferior (*disapproving*) [Early 20thC. From German, formed from *Lumpen*, plural of *Lump* "ragamuffin" + French *prolétariat*(see PROLETARIAT).]

lump·fish /lúmp fìsh/ (*plural* **-fish·es** *or* **-fish**) *n.* a marine fish of northern waters that has a short scaleless body covered with rows of thorny lumps. Its roe is eaten as a cheaper alternative to caviar. Family: Cyclopteridae. [Early 17thC. *Lump*, from Middle Dutch *lumpe* "cod," of uncertain origin: perhaps ultimately the same word as LUMP[1], referring to the fish's lumpy shape.]

lump·ish /lúmpish/ *adj.* **1. MOVING AWKWARDLY** tending to move awkwardly or slowly and heavily **2. UNINTELLIGENT AND LETHARGIC** with no intelligence, energy, or enthusiasm (*insult*) —**lump·ish·ly** *adv.* —**lump·ish·ness** *n.*

lump·suck·er /lúmp sùkər/ *n.* = **lumpfish** [Mid-18thC. From obsolete *lump* "lumpfish" + SUCKER.]

lump sum *n.* an amount of money that is given in a single payment, rather than being divided into smaller periodic payments

lump·y /lúmpee/ (**-i·er, -i·est**) *adj.* **1. WITH LUMPS** having or filled with lumps, especially when lumps are unwanted, e.g., in the upholstery of a chair or the mattress of a bed **2. LACKING SMOOTHNESS OF TEXTURE** used to describe semiliquid foods, e.g., sauces and soups, that lack the normal appetizing smoothness of texture **3. CUMBERSOME** with a cumbersome quality or appearance **4. CHOPPY** having or exhibiting short choppy waves —**lumpily** *adv.* —**lump·i·ness** *n.*

lump·y jaw *n.* = **actinomycosis**

Lu·mum·ba /lo͝o mo͞ombə/, **Patrice** (1925–61) Congolese statesman. The first prime minister of the Republic of the Congo (1960–61), his tenure was marked by civil war.

Lu·na /lo͞onə/ *n.* **1.** MYTHOL **ROMAN MOON GODDESS** the goddess of the Moon in Roman mythology. Greek equivalent **Selene 2.** CHEM **SILVER** the element silver in alchemy (*archaic*) [14thC. From Latin, "moon" (see LUNAR).]

lu·na·cy /lo͞onəssee/ (*plural* **lu·na·cies**) *n.* **1. THOUGHTLESSNESS** unintelligent, inconsiderate, or misguided behavior, or an example of it **2. OFFENSIVE TERM** an offensive former term for any psychiatric disorder that rendered patients legally incompetent and required them to be taken into care. This obsolete term has never been used by physicians in medical or psychiatric contexts. (*archaic offensive*) [Mid-16thC. Formed from LUNATIC.]

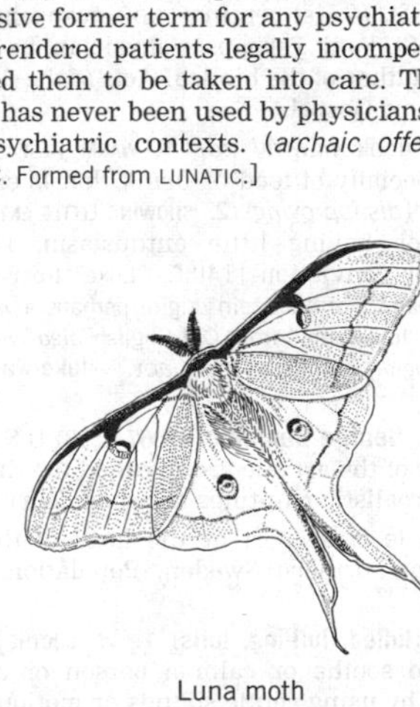

Luna moth

lu·na moth *n.* a large North American moth that has spotted light-green wings with long thin extensions at the back that look like tails. Latin name: *Actias luna.* [From Latin, "moon" (see LUNAR); so called because of the crescent-shaped spots on the moth's wings]

UPI/Corbis-Bettmann

Lunar: A lunar rover used by astronaut James Irwin on the Moon (1971)

lu·nar /lo͞onər/ *adj.* **1.** ASTRON **RELATING TO MOON** relating to a moon or its movement around a planet, especially the Moon in relation to the Earth **2.** SPACE TECH **USED FOR TRAVEL TO THE MOON** for use in space travel to or on the Moon **3. CRESCENT-SHAPED** in the shape of a crescent moon **4. PALE** pale and cold-looking, as the Moon is compared to the Sun [15thC. From Latin *lunaris*, from *luna* "moon" (source of English *lunatic*). Ultimately from an Indo-European word meaning "light," which is also the ancestor of English *light, luminous*, and *lucid*.]

lu·nar caus·tic *n.* silver nitrate, especially when formed into small sticks (*archaic*)

lu·nar cy·cle *n.* a principal means of establishing a calendar, based on the cycles of the Moon. The Muslim calendar is based on the lunar cycle.

lu·nar e·clipse *n.* an eclipse of the Moon caused by the Earth passing between the Sun and the Moon and casting its shadow on the Moon

lu·nar ex·cur·sion mod·ule *n.* = **lunar module**

lu·nar·i·an /loo náiree ən/ *n.* in mythology and science fiction, an inhabitant of the Moon [Early 18thC. Formed from Latin *lunaris* (see LUNAR).]

lu·nar mod·ule *n.* a small spacecraft used to travel from an orbiting command module to the surface of the Moon and back

lu·nar month *n.* **1. PERIOD BETWEEN NEW MOONS** the time between one new moon and the next, a period of about 29.5 days. It is the time the Moon takes to make one complete orbit of the Earth. **2. 28-DAY PERIOD** a period of four weeks

Lu·nar New Year *n.* the Chinese New Year, which usually occurs at a point between late January and mid-February

lu·nar·scape /lo͞onər skàyp/ *n.* a rugged barren landscape of strange rock formations, similar to the surface of the Moon

lu·nar year *n.* a period of 12 lunar months

lu·nate /lo͞o nàyt/ *adj.* **lu·nate, lu·nat·ed CRESCENT-SHAPED** shaped like a crescent moon ■ *n.* ANAT = **lunate bone** [Late 18thC. From Latin *lunatus*, from *luna* "moon" (see LUNAR).]

lu·nate bone *n.* a bone of the wrist that articulates with the bones of the forearm [From the bone's shape]

lu·na·tic /lo͞onətik/ *adj.* **1. THOUGHTLESS** thoughtless, ridiculous, or reckless **2. OFFENSIVE TERM** an offensive term formerly meaning affected by psychiatric disorder (*offensive*) ■ *n.* **1. OFFENSIVE TERM** an offensive term for somebody who has a psychiatric disorder (*offensive*) **2. IRRESPONSIBLE PERSON** somebody who behaves in a wildly reckless manner (*informal*) ○ *the lunatic who ran a red light and hit our car* [13thC. Via French *lunatique* from late Latin *lunaticus*, literally "moonstruck," from Latin *luna* "moon" (see LUNAR). From the belief that the changing phases of the moon caused periodic symptoms.]

lu·na·tic fringe *n.* people whose views are regarded as eccentrically radical (*insult*)

lu·na·tion /loo náysh'n/ *n.* = **lunar month** *n.* 1 [14thC. From the medieval Latin stem *lunation-*, from Latin *luna* "moon" (see LUNAR).]

lunch /lunch/ *n.* **1. MIDDAY MEAL** a meal eaten in the middle of the day, especially a light meal that is not the main meal of the day (*often used before a noun*) **2. FOOD EATEN AT MIDDAY** the food prepared and eaten at the midday meal ○ *Our lunch was soup and salad.* **3.** *Carib* **AFTERNOON TEA** mid-afternoon tea, or an afternoon snack (*dated*) ■ *vi.* (**lunched, lunch·ing, lunch·es**) **EAT LUNCH** to eat lunch, especially a specified kind of lunch eaten somewhere other than at home [Early 19thC. Shortening of LUNCHEON.] ◇ **out to lunch** displaying thoughtlessness or unusual behavior that suggests a loss of touch with reality (*slang insult*)

WORD KEY: USAGE

See Usage note at ***dinner.***

WORD KEY: CULTURAL NOTE

The Naked Lunch, a novel by writer William Burroughs (1959). This controversial portrayal of drug abuse was written by Burroughs in Tunisia as he attempted to free himself of his own addiction. It consists of a series of surreal episodes linked by themes and characters and described in language that is by turns clinical, hallucinatory, poetic, and scatological.

lunch·box /lúnch bòks/ *n.* a container for sandwiches or other foods carried somewhere, e.g., to work, to eat for lunch

lunch count·er *n.* a long counter where sandwiches and snacks are served and sold, especially at lunchtime

lunch·eon /lúnchən/ *n.* **1. LUNCH** lunch (*formal*) **2. MIDDAY GATHERING WITH FOOD** an organized gathering in the middle of the day, with invited guests being served a meal and often offered some form of entertainment, e.g., a guest speaker [Mid-17thC. Origin uncertain: probably an alteration of earlier *nuncheon* "snack," from NOON + obsolete *schench* "drink," under the influence of obsolete *lunch* "piece of bread."]

lunch·eon·ette /lùnchə nét/ *n.* a small fairly simple restaurant serving full lunch menus and snacks, and often breakfast

lunch·eon meat *n.* processed meat, e.g., ham, sold in a loaf or sliced, and usually eaten cold

lunch·meat *n.* = **luncheon meat**

lunch·pail *n.* = **lunchbox**

lunch·room /lúnch ròom, -ròom/ *n.* **1. ROOM FOR EATING LUNCH** a room in a school or office where people can buy lunch or eat a packed lunch **2.** = **luncheonette**

lunch·time /lúnch tìm/ *n.* the time, around the middle of the day, when lunch is usually eaten (*often used before a noun*)

Lund /lund/ historic city in southern Sweden, situated about 11 mi./18 km northeast of Malmö. Population: 96,557 (1995).

Lun·da /lóondə, lóondə/ *n.* a Bantu language spoken in western parts of Central Africa, especially in Zaïre. It belongs to the Benue-Congo branch of Niger-Congo languages. Lunda is spoken by about 82,000 people. [Late 19thC. From Bantu.] —**Lun·da** *adj.*

lune /loon/ *n.* **1.** GEOM **CRESCENT AREA ON PLANE OR SPHERE** a crescent-shaped area on the surface of a plane or sphere defined by two semicircles whose common end points are diametrically opposed **2.** CHR = **lunette** *n.* **6** [Early 18thC. Via French from Latin *luna* "moon" (see LUNAR); so called because its shape resembles a crescent moon.]

lu·nette /loo nét/ *n.* **1. CRESCENT-SHAPED OBJECT** any object that has a crescent shape **2.** ARCHIT **WINDOW IN DOMED CEILING** an arch-shaped window at the height of a domed ceiling **3.** ARCHIT **SEMICIRCULAR PANEL** a semicircular panel on a wall, containing a window, painting, or frieze **4. VEHICLE'S TOWING RING** a metal ring on a vehicle to which a rope can be attached for towing **5.** GEOG **CRESCENT-SHAPED MOUND OF SILT** a crescent-shaped mound of fine silt or clay similar in form to a sand dune, found especially near the edge of a temporary lake **6.** CHR **CONTAINER USED IN ROMAN CATHOLIC MASS** in the Roman Catholic Church, a crescent-shaped container in which the consecrated bread is placed during a Mass [Late 16thC. Via French, literally "little moon," from, ultimately, Latin *luna* (see LUNAR).]

lung /lung/ *n.* **1. RESPIRATORY ORGAN IN VERTEBRATES** in air-breathing vertebrate animals, either of the paired spongy respiratory organs, situated inside the ribcage, that transfer oxygen into the blood and remove carbon dioxide from it (*often used before a noun*) **2. RESPIRATORY ORGAN IN INVERTEBRATES** any of various respiratory organs found in invertebrate animals, especially the highly vascular region of the mantle cavity in some terrestrial snails [Old English. Ultimately, from an Indo-European base meaning "light," which is also the ancestor of English *light*[2].] ◇ **at the top of your lungs** extremely loudly (*informal*)

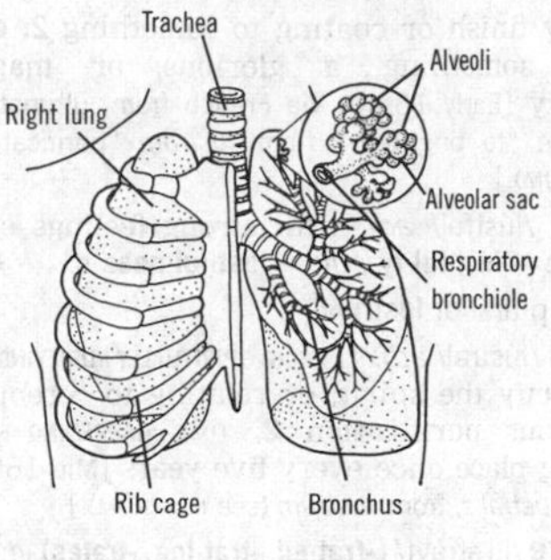

Lung

lun·gan *n.* = **longan**

lunge /lunj/ *n.* **1. SUDDEN FORWARD MOVEMENT** a sudden strong attacking movement forward **2.** FENCING **QUICK THRUST** a sudden thrust made at an opponent ■ *vi.* **(lunged, lung·ing, lung·es) 1. MOVE SUDDENLY FORWARD THREATENINGLY** to make a sudden attacking movement, thrusting forward **2.** FENCING **MAKE A QUICK THRUST** to execute a sudden thrust at an opponent, especially with the sword or epee extended parallel to the floor [Mid-18thC. Alteration of French *allonger,* via Old French *alongier* "to lengthen" from, ultimately, Latin *longus* "long." The underlying meaning is "to lengthen one's reach."]

lung·fish /lúng fìsh/ (*plural* **-fish·es** *or* **-fish**) *n.* any of various bony fishes of Australia, Africa, and South America that inhabit freshwater swamps and pools and have one or two lungs for breathing air as well as gills. They often become inactive and cocoon themselves in mud during the dry season. Order: Dipneusti.

lun·gi /lóong gee, lóonjee/, **lun·gyi** *n.* a long piece of cloth, often brightly colored, traditionally worn by men as a loincloth in the Indian subcontinent and like a skirt by men and women in Myanmar [Early 17thC. Via Hindi *lungī* from Persian.]

lung·worm /lúng wùrm/ *n.* a parasitic nematode worm that inhabits the lungs of mammals and birds, sometimes causing coughs or respiratory distress

lung·wort /lúng wùrt, -wawrt/ *n.* **1. WOODLAND PLANT** any of various perennial woodland plants native to Europe and Asia that have clusters of purple or blue tubular flowers, often pink as buds. They were used in the past to treat respiratory disorders. Genus: *Pulmonaria.* **2. PLANT OF BORAGE FAMILY** any of various plants belonging to the borage family that have dangling clusters of blue flowers. They are found in northern temperate regions. Genus: *Mertensia.* **3. LICHEN RESEMBLING LUNG TISSUE** a lichen that bears a superficial resemblance to lung tissue. It is dark green when wet and pale greenish-brown when dry. It was used in the past to treat lung diseases. Latin name: *Lobaria pulmonaria.* [Old English *lungenwyrt.* So called from the belief that such plants cured lung disorders.]

lun·gyi *n.* = **lungi**

lu·ni·so·lar /lòonee sṓlər/ *adj.* relating to both the Sun and the Moon, especially to the gravitational pull of both the Sun and the Moon

lu·ni·ti·dal in·ter·val /lòonee tíd'l-/ *n.* the time between the moon's passing a given point and the next high tide at that point

lunk·er /lúngkər/ *n.* something, especially a game fish, that is very big compared with other things of the same type (*informal*) [Early 20thC. Origin unknown.]

lunk·head /lúngk hèd/ *n.* somebody considered to be unintelligent (*insult*) [Mid-19thC. Origin uncertain: probably an alteration of LUMP[1] + HEAD.]

Lunt /lunt/, **Alfred** (1893–1977) U.S. actor and director. Appearing in plays with his wife Lynn Fontanne, he enjoyed a successful career as a comedy actor. Full name **Alfred David Lunt**

lu·nu·la /lóonyələ/ (*plural* **-lae** /-lee/), **lu·nule** /lóon yoòl/ *n.* ANAT a semicircular mark, especially the white crescent-shaped area at the base of the fingernail (*technical*) [Late 16thC. From Latin, literally "small moon," from *luna* (see LUNAR).] —**lu·nu·lar** *adj.* —**lu·nu·late** /-làyt/ *adj.*

Lu·o /lóo ō/ (*plural* **-o** *or* **-os**) *n.* **1.** PEOPLES **MEMBER OF AFRICAN PEOPLE** a member of an African people who migrated from the Upper Nile Valley, establishing a dynasty among the Bantu-speaking people in the lake region of eastern Africa, around Bunyoro **2.** LANG **LANGUAGE SPOKEN IN KENYA AND TANZANIA** a language spoken in parts of Kenya and Tanzania that belongs to the Nilotic branch of Nilo-Saharan languages. Luo is spoken by about six million people. [Early 20thC. From Luo.] —**Lu·o** *adj.*

Luo·yang /lwō yaáng/ city in Henan Province, northern China, situated on the Luo River. It alternated with Xian as the capital of ancient China, and after 1948 became a major industrial center. Population: 1,190,000 (1991).

lu·pine[1] /lóopən/, **lu·pin** *n.* any of various annual or perennial plants that have tall spikes of flowers and seeds in pods. They are native to the northern hemisphere. Genus: *Lupinus.* [14thC. From Latin *lupinus* "wolflike" (see LUPINE[2]).]

lu·pine[2] /lóo pìn/ *adj.* **1. RELATING TO A WOLF** relating to wolves, or resembling a wolf **2. RAVENOUS** wildly hungry or greedy in behavior or character [Mid-17thC. From Latin *lupinus,* from *lupus* "wolf." Ultimately, from the Indo-European word for "wolf," which is also the ancestor of English *wolf* and *lycanthrope.*]

lu·pu·lin /lóopyəlin/ *n.* a sticky yellow powder found in hop cones and containing the resins and essential oils that give beer its bitter taste. It was formerly used as a sedative. [Early 19thC. Formed from modern Latin *lupulus,* species name, from Latin, "hop plant," literally "little wolf," from *lupus* "wolf."]

lu·pus /lóopəss/ *n.* **1.** = **lupus erythematosus 2.** = **lupus vulgaris** [Late 16thC. From Latin, "wolf." So called because people having the disease were thought to look as if they had been attacked by a wolf.]

lu·pus er·y·the·ma·to·sus /-èrrə theemə tṓssəss, -themmə-/ *n.* either of two inflammatory diseases affecting connective tissue. One **(discoid lupus erythematosus)** is largely confined to the skin, the other **(systemic lupus erythematosus)** affects the joints and internal organs. [*[Erythematosus]* via modern Latin from Greek *eruthēma* (see ERYTHEMA)]

lu·pus vul·gar·is /-vul gáiriss/ *n.* tuberculosis of the skin in which reddish-brown patches develop on the face, leading to tissue destruction and scarring [From modern Latin, "common lupus"]

lurch[1] /lurch/ *vi.* **(lurched, lurch·ing, lurch·es) 1. MOVE VIOLENTLY** to lean or pitch suddenly to one side **2. MOVE UNSTEADILY** to move along unsteadily, swaying from side to side ■ *n.* **SUDDEN SIDEWAYS MOVEMENT** a sudden unbalanced movement to the side [Late 17thC. Origin unknown.] —**lurch·ing·ly** *adv.*

lurch[2] /lurch/ *n.* in the card game cribbage, the state of being left with less than 30 points or half the winner's score at the end of a game [14thC. Origin uncertain: perhaps a back-formation from *lurching* "decisive defeat at 'lorche'" (a game resembling backgammon), from obsolete French *lourche,* of uncertain origin.] ◇ **leave somebody in the lurch** to leave somebody in a difficult or embarrassing situation and offer no help

lurch·er /lúrchər/ *n.* **1.** *U.K.* **HUNTING DOG** a long-limbed crossbred dog that has predominant greyhound features, especially one used by poachers for catching rabbits **2. PETTY CRIMINAL** somebody who engages in petty thieving or poaching (*archaic*) [Early 16thC. From *lurch* "to lurk," of uncertain origin: probably a variant of LURK.]

lure /loor/ *vt.* **(lured, lur·ing, lures) 1. ENTICE** to persuade somebody to go so somewhere or do something by offering something tempting **2. RECALL FALCON** to persuade a falcon to return by swinging a device in the air to attract its attention ■ *n.* **1. SOMETHING THAT ENTICES** something that attracts or entices somebody to do something or go somewhere **2. ATTRACTION** the attractive or tempting quality that something has **3. DEVICE ATTRACTING FISH** a device attached to a fishing line to attract fish **4. DEVICE FOR RECALLING FALCON** a device swung through the air to attract or recall a falcon, usually a leather bag attached to the end of a line [13thC. From Old French *luere,* of Germanic origin.] —**lur·er** *n.*

Lur·ex /lóo rèks/ *tdmk.* a trademark for a plastic-coated metallic thread or fabric made from this

Lu·ri·a /lóoree ə/, **Isaac ben Solomon** (1534–72) Palestinian mystic and scholar. He founded a school of Cabbalistic thought. Known as **The Lion**

Lu·ri·a, Salvador (1912–91) Italian-born U.S. biologist. He won a Nobel Prize in physiology or medicine (1969) for his research into the way viruses reproduce. Full name **Salvador Edward Luria**

lu·rid /lŏŏrid/ *adj.* **1.** HORRIFYING OR SHOCKING sensational and shocking, with graphic details of horror, devastation, or violence **2.** UNATTRACTIVELY BRIGHT of a sickeningly intense brightness or boldness of color ○ *a lurid green* **3.** GLOWING UNNATURALLY glowing with an unnaturally vivid brightness **4.** PALLID with a pale sickly complexion [Mid-17thC. From Latin *luridus* "pale yellow, ghastly," of unknown origin.] —**lu·rid·ly** *adv.* —**lu·rid·ness** *n.*

Lu·rie /lŏŏree/, **Alison** (*b.* 1926) U.S. novelist and scholar. Many of her novels deal with middle-class discontent. She won the Pulitzer Prize for fiction (1985).

lurk /lurk/ (**lurked, lurk·ing, lurks**) *vi.* **1.** MOVE OR WAIT FURTIVELY to move about furtively, or wait in a concealed position or a shadowy corner, especially with the intention of doing something wrong ○ *a figure lurking in the bushes* **2.** EXIST UNSUSPECTED to exist as an unsuspected threat or danger **3.** COMPUT READ BUT NOT SEND MESSAGES to read messages sent to an online discussion forum without contributing (*slang*) [13thC. Origin uncertain: probably of Low German or Scandinavian origin.] —**lurk·er** *n.* —**lurk·ing** *adj.*

Lur·lei = **Lorelei**

Lu·sa·ka /loo saákə/ capital city of Zambia, situated in the southern central part of the country, about 90 mi./145 km northeast of Kariba Dam, on the Zimbabwe border. Population: 982,362 (1989).

lus·cious /lúshəss/ *adj.* **1.** SWEET AND JUICY with a rich, sweet, and juicy taste **2.** ROMANTIC AND EMOTIONAL written in a dramatic and romantic style with a strong appeal to the emotions and senses **3.** DESIRABLE very desirable physically, especially with a strong and direct sexual presence (*informal*) [14thC. Alteration of earlier *licious*, of uncertain origin: possibly a shortening of DELICIOUS.] —**lus·cious·ly** *adv.* —**lus·cious·ness** *n.*

lush[1] /lush/ *adj.* **1.** GROWING VIGOROUSLY producing a lot of vigorous rich young growth **2.** WITH RICH TASTE tasting rich, sweet, and juicy **3.** LUXURIOUS with luxurious decoration and furnishings **4.** IN A DRAMATIC STYLE written in a dramatic style that is intended to produce an emotional response **5.** SEXY voluptuously sensual in appearance or behavior (*informal*) [15thC. Origin uncertain: probably an alteration of *lache* "loose, weak," via Old French, "soft," from, ultimately, Latin *laxus* "loose."] —**lush·ly** *adv.* —**lush·ness** *n.*

lush[2] /lush/ *n.* **1.** HEAVY DRINKER somebody who regularly drinks too much alcohol (*slang disapproving*) **2.** ALCOHOL alcoholic drink (*slang*) ■ *vi.* (**lushed, lush·ing, lush·es**) DRINK HEAVILY to drink too much alcohol regularly (*slang disapproving*) [Late 18thC. Origin unknown.]

Lu·shun /lŏŏ shŏŏn/, **Lü-shun** town and seaport in Liaoning Province, northeastern China, situated opposite the northern coast of Shangdong. Former name **Port Arthur**

Lu·si·ta·ni·a /lŏŏssi táynee ə/ ancient region and Roman province, corresponding approximately to present-day Portugal and the Spanish provinces of Salamanca and Cáceres —**Lu·si·ta·ni·an** *adj., n.*

lust /lust/ *n.* **1.** SEXUAL DESIRE the strong physical desire to have sex with somebody, usually without associated feelings of love or affection **2.** EAGERNESS great eagerness or enthusiasm for something ○ *the lust for power* ■ *vi.* (**lust·ed, lust·ing, lusts**) **1.** DESIRE SEXUALLY to feel a strong desire to have sex with somebody **2.** BE EAGER FOR SOMETHING to have a very strong desire to obtain something [Old English, "pleasure, desire." Ultimately, from an Indo-European word meaning "to be eager," which is also the ancestor of English *lascivious*.]

lus·ter /lústər/ *n.* **1.** SOFT SHEEN a soft sheen of reflected light, especially from metal that has been polished gently **2.** SHININESS a bright and shiny condition or tone **3.** SPLENDOR the glory and magnificence of a great achievement **4.** POLISH polish or wax used to give something a shiny finish **5.** CHANDELIER a chandelier or candelabrum made of cut glass, designed to reflect the light **6.** GLASS PENDANT ON CHANDELIER any of the decorative pieces of cut glass hanging from a chandelier **7.** CERAMICS GLAZE ON POTTERY an opalescent metallic glaze on pottery, especially porcelain **8.** MINERALS LIGHT REFLECTED BY A MINERAL the quality and amount of light reflected from the surface of a mineral. This is one of the ways in which a mineral is defined, the highest degree of luster being splendent. **9.** TEXTILES GLOSSY FABRIC fabric with a sheen or glossy surface **10.** TIME = **lustrum** *n.* **1** ■ *vt.* (**-tered, -ter·ing, -ters**) **1.** IMPART GLOSSY FINISH TO to impart a glossy finish or coating to something **2.** GLORIFY to give something a glorious or magnificent quality [Early 16thC. Via French from, ultimately, Latin *lustrare* "to brighten," from *lustrum* "purification" (see LUSTRUM).]

lust·ful /lústf'l/ *adj.* with strong feelings of sexual desire —**lust·ful·ly** *adv.* —**lust·ful·ness** *n.*

lus·tra plural of **lustrum**

lus·tral /lústrəl/ *adj.* **1.** RELIG SPIRITUALLY PURIFYING serving to purify the spirit, or relating to ceremonies of religious purification **2.** TIME HAPPENING FIVE-YEARLY taking place once every five years [Mid-16thC. From Latin *lustralis*, from *lustrum* (see LUSTRUM).]

lus·trate /lú stràyt/ (**-trat·ed, -trat·ing, -trates**) *vt.* to make somebody or something spiritually pure by means of a special religious ceremony [Early 17thC. From Latin *lustrare* "to purify by lustral rites," from *lustrum* (see LUSTRUM).] —**lus·tra·tion** /lu stráysh'n/ *n.* —**lus·tra·tive** /lústrətiv/ *adj.*

lus·tre *n., vt.* U.K. = **luster**

lus·trous /lústrəss/ *adj.* with a soft shine or gloss —**lus·trous·ly** *adv.* —**lus·trous·ness** *n.*

lus·trum /lústrəm/ (*plural* **-trums** *or* **-tra** /-trə/) *n.* (*formal*) **1.** TIME FIVE-YEAR PERIOD a period of five years **2.** HIST ROMAN PURIFICATION purification of the entire ancient Roman people, taking place every five years after the census [Late 16thC. From Latin, "purification." Probably ultimately from an Indo-European word meaning "light, bright."]

lust·y /lústee/ (**-i·er, -i·est**) *adj.* **1.** STRONG AND HEALTHY in extremely good physical health, especially possessing great stamina and strength **2.** ENERGETIC full of energy, vitality, and enthusiasm **3.** LUSTFUL stongly desiring sex —**lust·i·ly** *adv.* —**lust·i·ness** *n.*

lu·sus na·tu·rae /lŏŏssəss nə tŏŏree/ (*plural* **lu·sus na·tu·rae** *or* **lu·sus·es na·tu·rae**) *n.* something that has developed abnormally (*literary*) [From Latin, literally "sport of nature"]

Lute

lute[1] /loot/ *n.* a plucked musical instrument that is similar to the guitar but has a pear-shaped body with a flat front. It was popular from the 14th to the 17th century. [13thC. Via Old French *lut* from, ultimately, Arabic *al-'ūd*.]

lute[2] /loot/ *n.* **1.** BUILDING SEALANT USED IN THE CONSTRUCTION INDUSTRY any substance, e.g., clay or cement, used for sealing apertures, joints, or porous surfaces in the construction industry **2.** COOK FLOUR AND WATER PASTE a paste of flour and water used in cooking as a seal, e.g., to keep a casserole lid on tight **3.** DENT PASTE USED IN DENTISTRY a paste used in dentistry to attach a crown or cap onto a tooth ■ *vt.* (**lut·ed, lut·ing, lutes**) SEAL WITH LUTE to seal, pack, or coat something using lute [14thC. Directly or via French from medieval Latin *lutum*, from Latin, "mud, potter's clay." Ultimately from an Indo-European word meaning "dirt," which is also the ancestor of English *pollute*.]

lu·te·al /lŏŏtee əl/ *adj.* relating to the stage of the menstrual cyle between the formation of a yellow mass of tissue (**the corpus luteum**) after the release of an ovum and the start of the next period [Early 20thC. Coined from Latin *luteus* "yellow" + -AL.]

lu·te·fisk /lŏŏtə fisk/, **lut·fisk** /lŏŏt fisk/ *n.* a Scandinavian dish of dried cod, preserved in potash lye, then skinned, boned, and boiled [Early 20thC. From Norwegian, from *lut* "lye" + *fisk* "fish."]

lu·te·in /lŏŏtee in, -teen/ *n.* **1.** YELLOW PIGMENT IN EGG YOLK the yellowish pigment found in egg yolk, some algae, and many plants, as well as in the tissue (**corpus luteum**) formed following the release of an ovum **2.** DRIED TISSUE a powdered preparation of the tissue (**corpus luteum**) formed following the release of an ovum [Mid-19thC. Formed from Latin *luteus* "yellow."]

lu·te·in·iz·ing hor·mone /lŏŏtee i nīzing-, lŏŏti nīzing-/ *n.* a hormone produced by the pituitary gland. It causes the ovary to produce one or more eggs, to secrete the hormone progesterone, and to form the corpus luteum. In the male, the luteinizing hormone promotes the secretion of male sex hormones by the testes.

lu·te·in·iz·ing hor·mone-re·leas·ing hor·mone, lu·te·in·iz·ing hor·mone-re·leas·ing fac·tor *n.* a hormone, released by the hypothalamus, that triggers the secretion of luteinizing hormone by the anterior lobe of the pituitary gland. It is now known to be identical with gonadotropin-releasing hormone.

lu·te·nist /lŏŏt'nist/ *n.* somebody who plays the lute [Early 17thC. From medieval Latin *lutanista*, from *lutana* "lute," of uncertain origin: probably from Old French *lut* (see LUTE[1]).]

lu·te·ti·um /loo téeshee əm/ *n.* a silvery-white metallic chemical element that belongs to the rare-earth series. It is used as a catalyst in the nuclear industries. Symbol **Lu** [Early 20thC. Formed from Latin *Lutetia*, an ancient name for Paris, the native city of the French chemist Georges Urbains (1872–1938), who discovered the element.]

Lu·ther /lŏŏthər/, **Martin** (1483–1546) German theologian and religious reformer. His 95 theses against papal indulgences (1517) launched the Protestant Reformation.

Lu·ther·an /lŏŏthərən/ *n.* ADHERENT OF LUTHERANISM a Christian who is a member of the Protestant church established by Martin Luther (**the Lutheran Church**) ■ *adj.* RELATING TO LUTHERANISM relating or belonging to Lutheranism

Lu·ther·an·ism /lŏŏthərə nìzzəm/ *n.* the first form of Protestantism, founded by Martin Luther in 16th-century Germany. It focuses on the teachings of Jesus Christ and stresses individual faith over collective church authority. Spreading first through northern Europe, particularly Scandinavia, it now has adherents worldwide.

lu·thi·er /lŏŏtee ər/ *n.* somebody who makes and repairs violins and other stringed instruments [Late 19thC. From French, formed from *luth* "lute," from Old French *lut* (see LUTE[1]).]

lu·tist /lŏŏtist/ *n.* = **lutenist**

lutz /luts, lŏŏts/ *n.* a figure-skating jump from the back edge of one skate, landing on the back edge of the other, with one or more full rotations [Mid-20thC. Origin uncertain: possibly an alteration of the name of the Swiss figure skater Gustave Lussi (born 1898), who introduced the jump.]

Lu·wi·an /lŏŏ ee ən/ *n.* an extinct Anatolian language belonging to the Indo-European group of languages [Early 20thC. Translation of German *Luwisch*, from *Luwia* "Luvia," the name of an ancient region of Asia Minor where the language was used.] —**Luwian** *adj.*

lux /luks/ (*plural* **lu·ces** /lŏŏ seez/) *n.* the SI unit of illumination, equal to one lumen per square meter. Symbol **lx** [Late 19thC. From Latin *lux* "light" (source of English *lucid*).]

Lux. *abbr.* Luxembourg

lux·ate /lúk sàyt/ (**-at·ed, -at·ing, -ates**) *vt.* to displace the bones of a joint (*technical*) [Early 17thC. From Latin *luxare*, from *luxus* "dislocated." Ultimately from an Indo-European word meaning "to turn away," which is also the ancestor of English *lock*, *luxury*, and *leek*.] —**lux·a·tion** /luk sáysh'n/ *n.*

Lux·em·bourg /lúksəm bùrg/ **1.** country in western

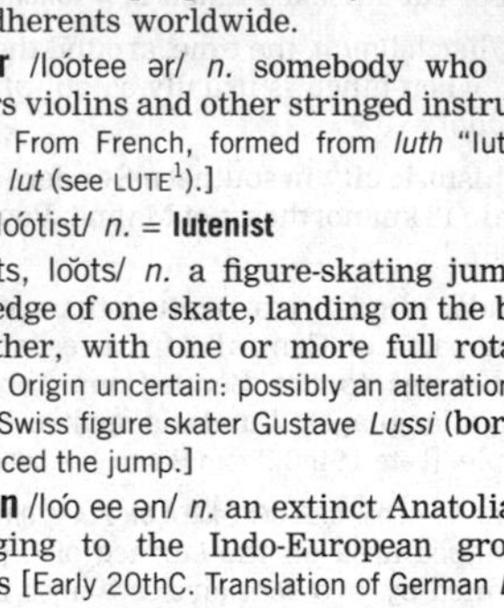

Luxembourg

Europe bordered by Belgium, Germany, and France. Language: Luxembourgish. Currency: Luxembourg franc. Capital: Luxembourg (City). Population: 420,415 (1997). Area: 998 sq. mi./2,586 sq. km. Official name **Grand Duchy of Luxembourg** **2.** the largest and southernmost province of Belgium. Population: 241,339 (1996). Area: 1,714 sq. mi./4,440 sq. km. —**Lux·em·bourg·er** *n.*

Lux·em·bourg City capital of Luxembourg, situated in the southern central part of the country. Population: 76,446 (1995).

Lux·em·bourg·ish /lúksəm bùrg ish/ *n.* the official language of Luxembourg, a form of German with many French elements —**Lux·em·bourg·ish** *adj.*

Rosa Luxemburg

Lux·em·burg /lúksəm bùrg/, **Rosa** (1871–1919) Polish-born German political activist. With Karl Liebknecht she founded the Spartacus League (1916), which became the German Communist Party. She was murdered by German soldiers.

Lux·or /lúk sawr, lóok-/ town on the eastern bank of the Nile River, eastern central Egypt. Population: 146,000 (1992).

lux·ul·yan·ite /luk sóolyə nīt/ *n.* a rare type of granite that contains needles of tourmaline in quartz and feldspar [Late 19thC. Named for the village of *Luxullian* in Cornwall, England, where it was first found.]

lux·u·ri·ant /lug zhóoree ənt, luk shóoree-/ *adj.* **1.** LUSH with a lot of young rich healthy growth ○ *luxuriant ground cover* **2.** GROWING PROFUSELY growing thickly and profusely ○ *a luxuriant mane of dark curly hair* **3.** ELABORATE written in an elaborate, showy, and dramatic style **4.** PRODUCTIVE producing vast quantities of something **5.** LUXURIOUS of a luxurious rich character [Mid-16thC. From Latin *luxuriant-*, the present participle stem of *luxuriare* (see LUXURIATE).] —**lux·u·ri·ance** *n.* —**lux·u·ri·ant·ly** *adv.*

lux·u·ri·ate /lug zhóoree àyt, luk shóoree-/ (**-at·ed, -at·ing, -ates**) *vi.* **1.** DERIVE GREAT ENJOYMENT to enjoy something in a self-indulgent way, taking great pleasure from the luxury and comfort that it offers **2.** GROW VIGOROUSLY to grow vigorously and successfully [Early 17thC. From Latin *luxuriat-*, the past participle stem of *luxuriare*, from *luxuria* "profusion, excess."]

lux·u·ri·ous /lug zhóoree əss, luk shóoree-/ *adj.* **1.** COMFORTABLE AND EXPENSIVE very comfortable, with high-quality expensive furnishings or fabrics **2.** ENJOYING LUXURY with a liking for luxury, or used to living in luxury —**lux·u·ri·ous·ly** *adv.* —**lux·u·ri·ous·ness** *n.*

lux·u·ry /lúgzhəree, lúkshəree/ (*plural* **lux·u·ries**) *n.* **1.** PLEASURABLE SELF-INDULGENT ACTIVITY an activity that gives great pleasure, especially one only rarely indulged in **2.** NONESSENTIAL ITEM an item that is desirable but not essential, and often expensive or hard to get (*often used before a noun*) **3.** GREAT COMFORT expensive high-quality surroundings, and the great comfort that they provide (*often used before a noun*) [14thC. Via Old French *luxurie* from Latin *luxuria* "profusion, excess," from *luxus* "dislocated."]

Lu·zon /loo zón/ the largest island in the Philippines, situated in the northern part of the country. Population: 30,759,000 (1990). Area: 40,420 sq. mi./104,687 sq. km.

Lv *abbr.* lev

LV *abbr.* Latvia (*international vehicle registration*)

lv. *abbr.* MIL leave

Lv. *abbr.* BIBLE Leviticus

Lviv /lə vív/, **L'viv, Lvov** /lə vóf/ industrial city in western Ukraine, capital of Lviv Oblast. Population: 806,000 (1995).

LVN, L.V.N. *abbr.* licensed vocational nurse

LW *abbr.* low water

lwei /lway/ (*plural* **lweis** *or* **lwei**) *n.* a subunit of currency in Angola. See table at **currency** [Late 20thC. Of Bantu origin.]

LWM *abbr.* low water mark

lx *symbol.* lux

-ly *suffix.* **1.** like, having the characteristics of ○ *brotherly* ○ *kindly* **2.** in a particular manner ○ *briefly* **3.** recurring at a particular interval of time ○ *monthly* [The adjective is from Old English *-līc*; the adverb from Old English *-līce*. Both ultimately from an Indo-European word meaning "body, form," which is also the ancestor of English *like* and *alike*.]

ly·ase /lī àyss, -àyz/ *n.* any of a group of enzymes that catalyze either the formation of a double bond within a chemical compound, or the addition of a chemical group at a double bond [Mid-20thC. Coined from Greek *luein* "to loosen" (see LYSIS).]

ly·can·thrope /líkən thròp, lī kán-/ *n.* a werewolf (*literary*) [Early 17thC. Via modern Latin from Greek *lukanthrōpos*, from *lukos* "wolf" + *anthrōpos* "human being."]

ly·can·thro·py /lī kánthrəpee/ *n.* in horror stories and legends, the transformation of a person into a wolf

ly·ce·um /lī sée əm/ *n.* **1.** BUILDING FOR PUBLIC EVENTS a building where concerts, lectures, and other public events take place (*usually used in names of buildings*) **2.** SPONSOR an organization that arranges or sponsors public events and entertainment [Late 16thC. Via Latin from Greek *Lukeion (gymnasion)*, name of the school near Athens where Aristotle taught, which was named for the nearby temple of Apollo *Lukeios*.]

ly·chee /léechee/, **li·tchi, li·chee** *n.* **1.** FOOD CHINESE FRUIT a small round sweet and juicy Chinese fruit with whitish translucent pulp and a red heart-shaped crust **2.** TREES CHINESE TREE the tree that lychees grow on. Latin name: *Litchi chinensis.* [Late 16thC. From Mandarin Chinese *lìzhī*.]

lych-gate /lích-/, **lich-gate** *n.* a covered gateway into a churchyard. Traditionally, pallbearers would rest the coffin there before carrying it into the church. [15thC. From Old English *līc* "body, corpse" + GATE.]

Ly·ci·an /líshee ən, lísh'n/ *n.* **1.** PEOPLES SOMEBODY FROM LYCIA somebody from the ancient region of Lycia, in Asia Minor **2.** LANG EXTINCT LANGUAGE OF LYCIANS an extinct language spoken by the ancient Lycians, belonging to the Anatolian group of languages [Late 16thC. Formed from Latin *Lycia* "Lycia," from Greek *Lukia*.] —**Ly·ci·an** *adj.*

ly·co·po·di·um /lìkə pṓdee əm/ *n.* **1.** MOSS WITH BRANCHING STEMS a plant that is a kind of club moss, with long branching stems covered in small leaves. It has small spore-carrying cones. Genus: *Lycopodium.* **2.** FLAMMABLE POWDER a flammable powder, composed of spores of lycopodium and other club mosses, used in the past as a coating for pills and suppositories, in fireworks, and in foundry work [Early 18thC. From modern Latin, genus name, from Greek *lukos* "wolf" + the stem *pod-* "foot"; so called because of the plant's clawlike foot.]

Ly·cra /líkrə/ *tdmk.* a trademark for a lightweight elastic polyurethane fabric that is widely used in the manufacture of clothing, particularly sportswear and swimwear

lyd·dite /lí dīt/ *n.* a powerful explosive consisting mainly of picric acid mixed with 10 percent nitrobenzene and 3 percent petroleum jelly. It is used in shells. [Late 19thC. Named for the town of *Lydd* in Kent, England, where the explosive was first tested.]

Lyd·i·a /líddee ə/ ancient country in the northwestern part of present-day Turkey, on the Aegean Sea. It reached its peak of wealth in the 7th and 6th centuries B.C. before being conquered by Cyrus the Great of Persia about 546 B.C.

Lyd·i·an /líddee ən/ *n.* **1.** PEOPLES SOMEBODY FROM LYDIA somebody from the ancient region of Lydia **2.** LANG EXTINCT LANGUAGE OF LYDIANS an extinct language spoken by the Lydians, belonging to the Anatolian group of languages ■ *adj.* RELATING TO LYDIA relating to ancient Lydia, or to its people, culture, or langauge [15thC. Formed from Latin *Lydius*, from Greek *Ludios* "Lydia."]

lye /lī/ *n.* a strong solution of sodium hydroxide or potassium hydroxide in water, used in industrial drain and oven cleaners [Old English *lēag*. Ultimately from an Indo-European word meaning "to wash," which is also the ancestor of English *lather, lotion*, and *deluge*.]

Ly·ele /lyé lày/ *n.* a language spoken in parts of Burkina Faso, belonging to the Gur branch of Niger-Congo languages. Lyele is spoken by about 60,000 people. —**Ly·ele** *adj.*

ly·gus bug /lígəss-/ *n.* a plant-eating insect that is especially common in North America, where it is a pest of cotton and other crops. Genus: *Lygus.* [*[Lygus]*, modern Latin, genus name, of uncertain origin: probably from Greek *lugos* "chaste-tree, withy"]

ly·ing present participle of **lie**[1], **lie**[2]

ly·ing-in (*plural* **ly·ings-in**) *n.* the period of time leading up to and immediately following childbirth, during which women used to be confined to bed (*archaic*) (*often used before a noun*)

Lyme dis·ease /līm-/ *n.* an infectious bacterial disease transmitted by ticks, in which skin rash, fever, and headache precede arthritis and nervous disorder [Late 20thC. Named for the town of *Lyme*, Connecticut, where it was first reported.]

lyme grass /līm-/ *n.* a perennial grass with broad bluish-green leaves that is found on sand dunes in northern temperate regions. It is sometimes planted to help stabilize shifting dunes. Latin name: *Elymus arenarius.* [Origin of *lyme* uncertain: perhaps from LIME, from the plant's binding properties]

lymph /limf/ *n.* a fluid containing white cells, chiefly lymphocytes, that is drained from tissue spaces by the vessels of the lymphatic system. It can transport bacteria, viruses, and cancer cells. Colorless in hue, lymph draining the intestines can turn opalescent from fatty globules absorbed from a meal. [Late 17thC. Directly or via French from Latin *lympha* "water," of uncertain origin: probably an alteration of Greek *numphē* "bride, nymph."]

lymph- *prefix.* = **lympho-** (*used before vowels*)

lym·phad·e·nop·a·thy /lim fàdd'n óppəthee, lìmfəd'n-/ (*plural* **-thies**) *n.* any disease, disorder, or enlargement of the lymph nodes [Early 20thC. Coined from LYMPHO- + ADENO- + -PATHY, literally "lymph gland disease."]

lym·phat·ic /lim fáttik/ *adj.* **1.** PHYSIOL RELATING TO THE LYMPH SYSTEM relating to lymph or the lymphatic system **2.** SLUGGISH without any energy or enthusiasm ■ *n.* PHYSIOL VESSEL TRANSPORTING LYMPH a vessel that transports or contains lymph

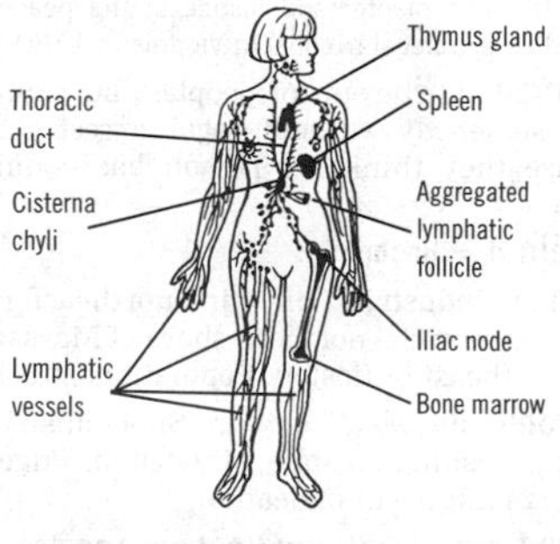

Lymphatic system

lym·phat·ic sys·tem *n.* a network of vessels that transport fluid, fats, proteins, and lymphocytes to the bloodstream as lymph, and remove microorganisms and other debris from tissues

lymph gland *n.* a popular but inaccurate term for a lymph node

lymph node *n.* any of numerous oval bodies, distributed throughout the lymphatic system, that produce and house lymphocytes and filter microorganisms and other particles from lymph. The function of these nodes is to reduce the risk of infection.

lympho- *prefix.* lymph, lymphocyte, lymphatic system ○ *lymphocytosis* [From LYMPH]

lym·pho·blast /límfə blàst/ *n.* an immature cell that develops into a lymphocyte

lym·pho·blas·tic /lìmfə blástik/ *adj.* relating to the production of lymphocytes

lym·pho·blas·tic leu·ke·mi·a *n.* a disease in which there is great overproduction of immature lymphocytes

lym·pho·cyte /límfə sìt/ *n.* an important cell class in the immune system that produces antibodies to attack infected and cancerous cells, and is responsible for rejecting foreign tissue. It is a kind of white blood cell.

lym·pho·cy·to·sis /lìmfō sī tṓssiss/ *n.* an abnormal increase in the number of lymphocytes in the bloodstream. It occurs in some chronic infections, some forms of leukemia, and other diseases.

lym·pho·gran·u·lo·ma ve·ne·re·um /lìmfō grannyə lṓmə və neéree əm/ *n.* a sexually transmitted disease caused by a bacterial infection, in which there is swelling of the genital lymph nodes and, especially in men, a genital ulcer. It occurs mainly in tropical and subtropical regions. [From modern Latin, literally "venereal granuloma of the lymph nodes"]

lym·phoid /lím fòyd/ *adj.* relating to lymph, lymphatic tissue, or the lymphatic system

lym·pho·kine /límfə kìn/ *n.* any of various soluble substances released by lymphocytes during an immune response that influence the behavior of other immune cells. Lymphokines are now included in the more general class of cytokines. (*dated*) [Mid-20thC. Coined from LYMPHO- + Greek *kinein* "to move" (see KINETIC).]

lym·pho·ma /lim fṓmə/ (*plural* **-mas** *or* **-ma·ta** /-mətə/) *n.* a malignant tumor originating in a lymph node, e.g., Hodgkin's disease or any of the range of cancers known as non-Hodgkin's lymphomas

lym·pho·poi·e·sis /lìmfō poy eéssiss/ *n.* the production of lymphocytes, which occurs mainly in the bone marrow, thymus, lymph nodes, spleen, and tonsils —**lym·pho·poi·et·ic** /lìmfō poy éttik/ *adj.*

lynch /linch/ (**lynched, lynch·ing, lynch·es**) *vt.* to seize somebody believed to have committed a crime and put him or her to death immediately and without trial, usually by hanging [Early 19thC. From LYNCH LAW.] —**lynch·er** *n.* —**lynch·ing** *n.*

Lynch /linch/, **David** (*b.* 1946) U.S. movie director. His distinctively bizarre and surreal work includes the movies *Eraserhead* (1977) and *Blue Velvet* (1986) and the cult television series *Twin Peaks* (1989–90).

Lynch, Thomas, Jr. (1749–79) U.S. patriot. He signed the Declaration of Independence (1776), and was a member of the Continental Congress (1776–77).

lynch law *n.* the condemnation and punishment of somebody by a mob or self-appointed group without a legal trial [Early 19thC. Named for Capt. William *Lynch* (1724–1820), a planter and justice of the peace who organized an extralegal tribunal in Virginia in 1780.]

lynch mob *n.* a group of people who capture and hang somebody without legal arrest and trial, because they think the person has committed a crime

lynch·pin *n.* = **linchpin**

Lynn /lin/ industrial city in northeastern Massachusetts, on the northern shore of Massachusetts Bay, northeast of Boston. Population: 80,563 (1996).

Lynn·wood /lín wo͝od/ city in Snohomish County, central Washington state, situated on Puget Sound 15 mi./24 km north of Seattle

Lyn·wood /lín wo͝od/ city in Los Angeles County, southwestern California, on the Los Angeles River. Population: 61,945 (1990).

Lynx

lynx /links/ (*plural* **lynx** *or* **lynx·es**) *n.* a short-tailed cat found in northern coniferous forests, with a lightly mottled yellowish- to reddish-brown coat and tufted ears. Genus: *Lynx.* ◊ **bobcat, caracal** [14thC. Via Latin from Greek *lugx*, of uncertain origin. Perhaps, ultimately, from an Indo-European word meaning "light," referring to the animal's shining eyes.]

lynx-eyed *adj.* with very good eyesight

lyo- *prefix.* dissolution, dispersion ○ *lyophobic* [From Greek *luein* "to loosen, dissolve" (see LYSIS)]

ly·ol·y·sis /lī óllәssiss/ *n.* the reaction of a salt with a solvent to form an acid and a base

Ly·on = **Lyons**

Ly·on /lī ən/, **Mary Mason** (1797–1849) U.S. educator. She pioneered higher education for women, founding the Mount Holyoke Female Seminary (1837), which became Mount Holyoke College (1893).

Ly·on·nais /lee əN áy/ historic region of France, comprising the present-day Loire and Rhône departments

ly·on·naise /lī ə náyz/ *adj.* cooked with onions, or containing fried onions [Early 19thC. From French (*à la*) *lyonnaise* "in the manner of Lyons."]

Ly·ons /lee óN/, **Ly·on** capital of the Rhône Department and the Rhône-Alps Region, eastern central France. Population: 422,444 (1990).

ly·o·phil·ic /lī ə fíllik/ *adj.* used to describe a finely dispersed solid (**colloid**) that forms a stable dispersion

ly·oph·i·lize /lī óffə lìz/ (**-lized, -liz·ing, -liz·es**) *vt.* to freeze-dry something (*technical*) —**ly·oph·i·li·za·tion** /lī òffəli záysh'n/ *n.* —**ly·oph·i·liz·er** /lī óffə lìzər/ *n.*

ly·o·pho·bic /lī ə fṓbik/ *adj.* used to describe a finely dispersed solid (**colloid**) that forms an unstable dispersion

ly·rate /lī ràyt, lī́rət/ *adj.* **1. LYRE-SHAPED** in the shape of a lyre **2.** BOT **WITH ROUNDED APEX** used to describe a leaf that has a broad rounded apex and small lateral lobes at the base [Mid-18thC. Formed from Latin *lyra* (see LYRE).]

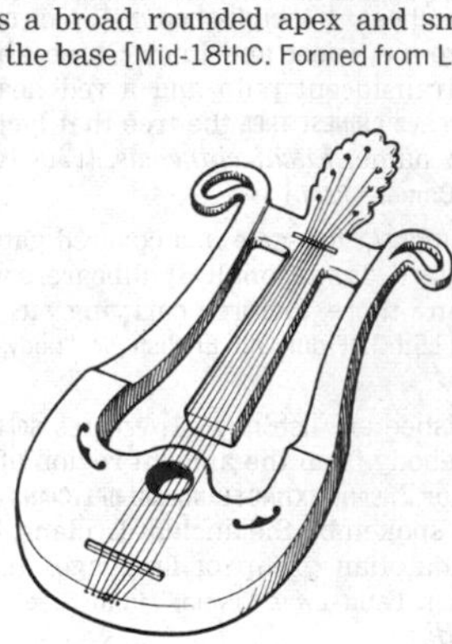

Lyre

lyre /līr/ *n.* a plucked string instrument associated with ancient Greece and consisting of a U-shaped frame with a crossbar from which the strings stretch down to the soundbox [12thC. Via Old French from, ultimately, Greek *lura*, of unknown origin.]

lyre·bird /līr bùrd/ *n.* either of two ground-dwelling birds found in the mountain forests of southeastern Australia. The males have long tail feathers that form into a lyre shape during courtship. Family: Menuridae.

lyr·ic /lírrik/ *adj.* **1.** POETRY **EXPRESSING PERSONAL FEELINGS** relating to poetry that often has a musical quality and expresses personal emotions or thoughts ○ *a lyric poet* **2.** MUSIC **WITH LIGHTNESS OF VOICE** singing with a voice that has a light quality and a vocally undramatic delivery **3.** MUSIC **WITH LIGHTNESS OF MUSICAL QUALITY** having or played with a light smooth nondramatic quality that suggests singing **4.** MUSIC **RELATING TO THE LYRE** relating to or written for the lyre, or for accompaniment by the lyre ■ *n.* **1.** MUSIC **SONG WORDS** the words of a song, especially a popular song (*often used in the plural*) **2.** POETRY **SHORT PERSONAL POEM** a short poem expressing personal feelings or thoughts [Late 16thC. Via French from, ultimately, Greek *lurikos* "singing to the lyre," from *lura* "lyre."]

lyr·i·cal /lírrik'l/ *adj.* **1.** POETRY, MUSIC = **lyric** *adj.* 1, **lyric** *adj.* 2, **lyric** *adj.* 3 **2. GUSHINGLY COMPLIMENTARY** wildly enthusiastic and emotional about something ○ *critics waxing lyrical about the new exhibition* —**lyr·i·cal·ly** *adv.* —**lyr·i·cal·ness** *n.*

lyr·i·cism /lírrə sìzzəm/ *n.* **1.** POETRY, MUSIC **LYRIC STYLE** a lyric style in poetry or music **2. ENTHUSIASTICALLY EMOTIONAL EXPRESSION** emotional and enthusiastic expressions of feelings or opinions

lyr·i·cist /lírrəsist/ *n.* **1.** MUSIC **SONGWRITER** somebody who writes words for songs, especially popular songs **2.** POETRY **LYRIC POET** a writer of lyric poems

lyr·ist /lírrist/ *n.* **1. LYRE PLAYER** somebody who plays the lyre **2.** = **lyricist** *n.* 1 [Mid-17thC. Via Latin *lyrista* from Greek *luristēs*, from *lura* "lyre."]

lys- *prefix.* = **lyso-** (*used before vowels*)

lyse /līss, līz/ (**lysed, lys·ing, lys·es**) *vti.* to undergo, or cause cells to undergo, destruction by disruption of the bounding membrane (**lysis**) [Early 20thC. Back-formation from LYSIS.]

Ly·sen·ko /li séngk ō/, **Trofim Denisovich** (1898–1976) Russian geneticist and agronomist. His belief that acquired characteristics can be inherited were at odds with accepted Mendelian theory.

Ly·sen·ko·ism /lī séng kō ìzzəm/ *n.* a biological doctrine, presented by T. D. Lysenko in the 1930s, maintaining that environmental characteristics acquired by an organism during its lifetime can be inherited by its offspring. This form of neo-Lamarckism, disputed by most biologists, found favor with Stalin and maintained a damaging influence over Soviet genetics until the mid-1960s.

ly·ser·gic ac·id /li sùrjik-, lī-/ *n.* a crystalline acid extracted from the ergot fungus and soluble in most organic solvents. Formula: $C_{16}H_{16}N_2O_2$. [Coined from LYSO- + ERGOT + -IC]

ly·ser·gic ac·id di·eth·yl·am·ide *n.* full form of **LSD**

ly·sin /lī́ssin/ *n.* an agent, e.g., an enzyme or antibody, that is able to destroy cells by disruption of the bounding membrane (**lysis**) [Early 20thC. Formed from LYSIS.]

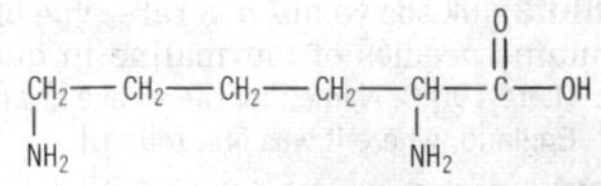

Lysine

ly·sine /lī seèn, lī́ssin/ *n.* an amino acid that occurs in nature as a component of proteins. It is an essential nutrient in the diet of people and animals. [Late 19thC. From German *Lysin*, from Greek *lusis* "loosening" (see LYSIS).]

ly·sis /lī́ssiss/ (*plural* **lys·es** /lī seèz/) *n.* **1.** BIOL **DESTRUCTIVE DISRUPTION OF CELLS** the destruction of cells by disruption of the bounding membrane, allowing the cell contents to escape **2.** MED **GRADUAL REDUCTION OF DISEASE SYMPTOMS** a gradual reduction in severity of a patient's signs and symptoms during the course of a disease [Mid-16thC. Via Latin, "loosening," from Greek *lusis*, from *luein* "to loosen."]

-lysis *suffix.* **1.** dissolution, decomposition, disintegration ○ *thermolysis* **2.** hydrolysis ○ *proteolysis* [Via modern Latin from Greek *lusis* (see LUSIS)]

lyso- *prefix.* lysis ○ *lysosome* [From LYSIS]

ly·so·gen /lī́səjən/ *n.* **1. VIRUS-RELEASING BACTERIUM** a bacterium that is capable of releasing a bacterium-destroying virus (**bacteriophage**) **2. ANTIGEN STIMULATING CELL-DESTROYING AGENTS** an agent, particularly an antigen, that provokes the production of cell-destroying agents (**lysins**) by cells of the immune system

ly·so·gen·ic /lìssə jénnik/ *adj.* used to describe a bacterium that is capable of producing and releasing a bacterium-destroying virus (**bacteriophage**) in response to certain stimuli

ly·sog·e·nize /lī sójjə nìz/ (**-nized, -niz·ing, -niz·es**) *vt.* to convert a bacterium to a lysogenic state by infection with a bacterium-destroying virus (**bacteriophage**)

ly·sog·e·ny /lī sójjənee/ *n.* the ability of a bacterial cell to produce and release a bacterium-destroying virus (**bacteriophage**) in response to certain stimuli

ly·so·some /líssə sṑm/ *n.* a membrane-bound cavity in living cells that contains enzymes that are responsible for degrading and recycling molecules. They can deal with material both originating within the cell and entering from outside, and are especially important in the immune cells that ingest and degrade bacteria. —**ly·so·so·mal** /lìssə sṓm'l/ *adj.*

ly·so·zyme /líssə zīm/ *n.* an enzyme, found in tears, saliva, other body fluids, and egg white, that weakens the cell walls of some bacteria and thus contributes to their ultimate destruction. It was the first enzyme to have its three-dimensional structure determined. [Early 20thC. Coined from LYSO- + ENZYME.]

-lyte *suffix.* a substance that can be decomposed by a particular process ○ *electrolyte* [From Greek *lutos* "soluble," from the past participle of *luein* (see LYSIS)] — **-lytic** *suffix.*

Lyth·am St. Anne's /líthəm saynt ànz/ popular seaside resort in western Lancashire, on the northwestern coast of England. Population: 40,866 (1991).

lyt·ic /líttik/ *adj.* relating to, resulting from, or causing the destruction of cells by disruption of the bounding membrane (**lysis**) [Late 19thC. From Greek *lutikos* "able to loosen," from *luein* (see LYSIS).]

-lyze *suffix.* to cause or undergo lysis ○ *plasmolyze* [Back-formation from -LYSIS]

LZ *abbr.* MIL landing zone

M m

m[1] /em/ (*plural* **m's**), **M** (*plural* **M's** *or* **Ms**) *n.* **1. 13TH LETTER OF ENGLISH ALPHABET** the 13th letter of the modern English alphabet **2. SPEECH SOUND CORRESPONDING TO LETTER "M"** the speech sound that corresponds to the letter "M" **3. LETTER "M" WRITTEN** a written representation of the letter "M" **4. m, M** PRINTING **EM** an em dash

m[2] *symbol.* **1.** magnetic moment **2.** MEASURE meter **3.** TIME minute *or* minutes **4.** PHYS mass **5.** milli- **6.** million ■ *abbr.* **7.** PHYS modulus ■ *symbol.* **8.** PHYS mutual inductance

M, m *abbr.* **1.** BIBLE Maccabees **2.** MONEY Mark **3.** CHEM mass **4.** Master **5.** CLOTHES medium (*used of clothes size*) **6.** mega- **7.** Member **8.** LOGIC middle term **9.** million **10.** CHEM molar **11.** motorway **12.** thousand (*used as a Roman numeral*)

m. *abbr.* **1. M.** male **2.** manual **3.** married **4.** GRAM masculine **5.** medium **6.** mile **7.** TIME minute **8.** CALENDAR month

M. *abbr.* **1.** majesty **2.** male **3.** Manitoba **4.** March **5.** May **6.** medieval **7.** middle **8.** MONEY mill **9.** Monday **10.** Monsieur **11.** mountain

M0 *n.* an assessment of the amount of money in public circulation, the money represented by banks' balances, and the money held in banks' tills (**narrow money**)

M1 *n.* an assessment of the amount of money in coins, notes, and checking accounts

M-1 ri·fle *n.* a .30 caliber rifle invented by John C. Garand and adopted by the U.S. Army in 1936.

M2 *n.* an assessment of the amount of money in coins, currency, checking accounts, savings accounts, and deposits

M3 *n.* an assessment of the amount of money in M1, M2, and also large denomination repurchase agreements, institutional money market accounts, and certain Eurodollar time deposits

ma /maa/ (*plural* **mas**) *n.* **1. MOTHER** a word used to refer to a mother or to address your own mother (*informal*) **2. WOMAN PAST MIDDLE AGE** a way of addressing or referring to a woman past middle age (*often considered offensive*) [Early 19thC. Shortening of MAMA.]

mA *symbol.* milliampere(s)

MA, M.A. *abbr.* **1.** Massachusetts **2.** Maritime Administration **3.** PSYCHOL mental age **4.** Military Academy **5.** military assistant

M.A., MA *abbr.* Master of Arts [Latin *Magister Artium*]

ma'am /mam/ *n.* **1. FORMAL FORM OF ADDRESS** used when addressing royal women or other women of high status (*formal*) **2. RESPECTFUL FORM OF ADDRESS** used when addressing a woman in a polite and respectful way (*dated informal*) [Mid-17thC. Contraction of MADAM.]

ma-and-pa *adj.* = **mom-and-pop** (*informal*)

maar /maar/ (*plural* **maars** *or* **maa·re** /maaree/) *n.* a broad flat volcanic crater formed by a single explosive eruption and often filled with water [Early 19thC. Via German dialect, "crater lake," from, ultimately, Latin *mare* "sea."]

Ma'a·riv /maariv/, **Maa·riv** *n.* in Judaism, the evening service of prayer [Late 20thC. From Hebrew *ma'ărībh* "evening prayer."]

Maa·sai *n., adj.* = **Masai**

Maas·tricht /maastrikht/, **Maes·tricht** capital of Limburg Province, in the southeastern Netherlands. Population: 118,102 (1994).

Maas·tricht Trea·ty *n.* a treaty signed in Maastricht in late1991 by heads of the 12 member states of the European Community that set out a framework for increased political and economic integration. It was ratified in 1993.

Maat /maat/ *n.* in Egyptian mythology, the goddess of the underworld who tests the value of a person's soul after death by weighing the heart on an ostrich feather

maat·jes her·ring *n.* = **matjes herring**

Mab /mab/ *n.* in Celtic mythology, the god of light, who mediates between humankind and the divine

M.A.B.E. *abbr.* Master of Agricultural Business and Economics

mabe pearl /máyb-/ *n.* a cultured pearl with a flat base and a rounded top [Origin unknown]

mac /mak/, **mack** *n. U.K.* a mackintosh (*informal*) [Early 20thC. Shortening.]

Mac /mak/ *n. U.S., Scotland* used as an informal way of addressing a man whose name is not known (*informal*) [Mid-20thC. From the Scottish name element MAC- = Mac or Mc.]

MAC /mak/ *n.* **1. TELEVISION TRANSMISSION SYSTEM** a system for transmitting pictures to color televisions using satellites. Full form **multiplexed analog component** ■ *n., abbr.* **2.** Municipal Assistance Corporation

Mac. *abbr.* BIBLE Maccabees

ma·ca·bre /mə kaabrə, -br/ *adj.* including gruesome and horrific details of death and decay [15thC. From French *(danse) macabre*, a dance in which Death lured people to dance until they dropped dead. Of uncertain origin: probably an alteration of *danse Macabé*, a translation of medieval Latin *chorea Machabaeorum* "dance of the Maccabees," originally probably a representation of the slaughter of the Maccabees in a medieval mystery play.]

ma·ca·co /mə kaakō/ (*plural* **-cos**) *n.* a lemur, especially a species of lemur in which the male is black and the female brown [Mid-18thC. From French *mococo*, of uncertain origin: perhaps from Malagasy *maka* "lemur."]

mac·ad·am /mə káddəm/ *n.* a smooth hard road surface made from small pieces of stone, usually mixed with tar or asphalt, in compressed layers [Early 19thC. Named for the Scottish civil engineer John Loudon McAdam (1756–1836), who developed the system.]

mac·a·da·mi·a /màkə dáymee ə/ *n.* an evergreen tree found in Australia and Southeast Asia that has clusters of white flowers and is cultivated for its edible nuts. Genus: *Macadamia.* [Early 20thC. From modern Latin, named for the Scottish-born Australian chemist John *Macadam* (1827–65).]

mac·a·da·mi·a nut, **mac·a·da·mi·a** *n.* an edible, round, hard-shelled, waxy nut with a mild creamy flavor, produced by the macadamia tree

mac·ad·am·ize /mə káddə mīz/ (**-ized, -iz·ing, -iz·es**) *vt.* to build or surface a road with macadam —**mac·ad·am·i·za·tion** /mə kàddəmi záysh'n/ *n.* —**mac·ad·am·iz·er** /mə káddə mīzər/ *n.*

Mc·Ad·oo /mə káddoo/, **William Gibbs** (1863–1941) U.S. businessman and statesman. He twice unsuccessfully sought a Democratic U.S. presidential nomination (1920 and 1924).

ma·caque /mə kák, -kaak/ (*plural* **-caques** *or* **-caque**) *n.* a short-tailed, sturdily built monkey that inhabits wooded or rocky areas of Asia and northern Africa. Genus: *Macaca.* [Late 17thC. Via French from, ultimately, Bantu *makaku*, literally "some monkeys."]

mac·a·ro·ni /màkə rṓnee/ *n.* **1. SMALL PASTA TUBES** hollow tubular pasta, usually produced in short lengths **2.** (*plural* **-nis** *or* **-nies**) **WELL-TRAVELED DANDY** an affected, foppish young man of 18th-century Britain who adopted the fashions, manners, and customs of the other countries he had visited [Late 16thC. From Italian dialect *maccarone* "macaroni, dumpling," of uncertain origin; probably from Greek *makaria* "food made from barley."]

Macaque

mac·a·ron·ic /màkə rónnik/ *adj.* **1. MIXING LANGUAGES IN VERSE** used to describe verse containing words and phrases from everyday language mixed with Latin or other foreign words and phrases, or with vernacular terms with Latinate endings added, usually for comic effect **2. RELATING TO A MIXTURE OF LANGUAGES** relating to or involving a combination of two or more languages ■ *n.* **MACARONIC VERSE** a macaronic poem or macaronic poetry in general [Early 17thC. Via modern Latin from MACARONI.] —**mac·a·ron·i·cal·ly** *adv.*

mac·a·roon /màkə ro͞on/ *n.* a cookie made from sugar and egg whites, with ground almonds or pieces of dried coconut folded in [Late 16thC. Via French *macaron* from Italian dialect *maccarone* (see MACARONI).]

Mac·Ar·thur /mík aarthər/, **Douglas, General** (1880–1964) U.S. soldier. He played a key role in U.S. military affairs in Japan and the Philippines during World War II, and in Korea (1950–51).

Ma·cas·sar /mə kássər/, **Ma·cas·sar oil** *n.* an oily substance formerly used to make the hair smooth and shiny [Early 19thC. Named for MAKASSAR, from where the ingredients for the hair oil were claimed to have come.]

Ma·cau /mə kówl/, **Ma·cao** Portuguese territory in southern China, on the South China Sea, west of Hong Kong. Population: 497,000 (1996). Area: 6.7 sq. mi./17.4 sq. km.

ma·caw /mə káw/ (*plural* **-caws** *or* **-caw**) *n.* a large parrot with a long tail and brilliant plumage found in Central and South America. Genus: *Anodorhynchus.* [Early 17thC. From Portuguese *macao*, of unknown origin.]

Mac·beth /mək béth/, **King of Scotland** (c. 1005–57). After murdering Duncan I in 1040, he held the throne until he was killed by Duncan's son, Malcolm III, in 1057.

Macc. *abbr.* BIBLE Maccabees

Mac·ca·bees /mákəbeez/ *npl.* **1. FOLLOWERS OF JUDAS MACCABEUS** the followers of Judas Maccabeus, who led the revolt of the Jews against Syria in 168 B.C. The victory of the Maccabees is celebrated at Hannukah. **2. BOOKS OF JEWISH HISTORY** four books of Jewish history. The first two of these are included in the Apocrypha. [14thC. Via Latin *Maccabaeus* from Greek *Makkabaios*, a name given to Judas, perhaps from the Hebrew *maqqeḇet* "hammer."] —**Mac·ca·be·an** /màkə bée ən/ *adj.*

Mc·Car·thy /mə kaárthee/, **Joseph R.** (1908–57) U.S. politician. A Republican U.S. senator (1947–57), he instigated highly publicized Senate hearings in the early 1950s into Communist subversion of the U.S. government. His often unsubstantiated charges and extreme methods led to a Senate censure, and the period is often referred to as "the McCarthy era." Full name **Joseph Raymond McCarthy**

Mc·Car·thy, Mary (1912–89) U.S. writer and critic. She was best known for her novel *The Group* (1969). Full name **Mary Therese McCarthy**

Mc·Car·thy·ism /mə kaárthee ìzzəm/ *n.* **1. PUBLIC ACCUSATION OF COMMUNIST SYMPATHIES** the practice of publicly accusing somebody, especially somebody in government or the media, of subversive or Communist activities or sympathies, especially without real evidence to substantiate this **2. UNFAIR ACCUSATION OR INVESTIGATION OF PEOPLE** the practice of using unsubstantiated accusations or unfair methods of investigation to discredit people [Mid-20thC. Named for Joseph R. McCARTHY, who pursued this policy.] —**Mc·Car·thy·ist** *n., adj.* —**Mc·Car·thy·ite** *n., adj.*

Mc·Cart·ney /mə kaártnee/, **Sir Paul** (*b.* 1942) British singer and songwriter. He was a founder member, singer, and bass guitarist of the *Beatles* (1959–70), cowriting most of their songs with John Lennon. He later formed the band Wings (1971–81) with his wife, Linda. Full name **Sir James Paul McCartney**

Mc·Clel·lan /mə kléllən/, **George Brinton** (1826–85) U.S. Union army commander. He lost his bid for the U.S. presidency to Abraham Lincoln (1864).

Mc·Clin·tock /mə klíntək, -òk/, **Barbara** (1902–92) U.S. botanist and geneticist. Her research into genetics and DNA won her a Nobel Prize (1983).

Mc·Cor·mack /mə káwrmək, -ak/, **John** (1884–1945) Irish-born U.S. tenor. He was noted for his solo performances of Irish folk songs, and also enjoyed a successful career as an opera singer.

Mc·Cor·mick /mə káwrmik/, **Cyrus Hall** (1809–84) U.S. inventor. He patented a mechanical reaping machine (1834), which had a major impact on agriculture.

Mc·Coy /mə kóy/ [Early 20thC. Origin uncertain: perhaps an alteration of *Mackay*, as the title of the chief of a branch of the Mackay clan, whose leadership was regularly disputed.] ◇ **the real McCoy** somebody or something that is genuine (*informal*)

WORD KEY: ORIGIN

Among the suggested origins of the phrase ***the real McCoy*** are that it may be an alteration of *the Reay Mackay*, a title applied to Lord *Reay*, the name of the chief of the northern branch of the Scots *Mackay* clan, the leadership of which was disputed by various branch factions; that it may be from Mackay, a whiskey named for its makers A. and M. *Mackay* of Glasgow (once referred to as *the clear McCoy*); and that it may be from the professional name of the U.S. welterweight boxing champion Kid *McCoy* (real name Norman Selby (1873–1940), so named to distinguish himself from another boxer of the same name.

Mc·Crae /mə kráy/, **John** (1872–1918) Canadian poet. He was best known for his war poem "In Flanders Fields" (1915).

Mc·Cul·lers /mə kúllərz/, **Carson** (1917–67) U.S. writer. Her novels include Southern Gothic tales such as *Ballad of the Sad Café* (1951). Born **Lula Carson Smith**

Mc·Cul·lough /mə kúllək, -əkh/, **Colleen Margaretta** (*b.* 1937) Australian novelist. Her novel *The Thorn Birds* (1977) was an international bestseller.

Mac·don·ald /mək dónn'ld/, **Sir John Alexander** (1815–91) Scottish-born Canadian lawyer, businessman, and politician. He was the first prime minister of Canada (1867–73 and 1878–91).

Mac·don·ald, John Sandfield (1812–72) Canadian lawyer and political leader, who served as the premier of Ontario (1867–71).

Mac·Dow·ell /mək dów əl, mək dṓ əl/, **Edward Alexander** (1861–1908) U.S. composer. He produced romantic piano music such as *Woodland Sketches* (1896).

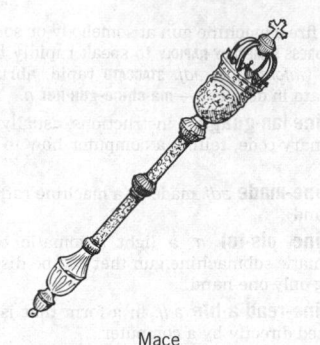

mace[1] /mayss/ *n.* **1. CEREMONIAL STAFF OF OFFICE** a stick or rod, usually with an ornamental head, carried by certain officials on ceremonial occasions as a symbol of authority **2. SPIKED METAL CLUB** a medieval weapon in the form of a heavy club with a round spiked metal head **3.** = **macebearer 4. EARLY BILLIARD CUE** an early form of the modern billiard cue [13thC. Via Old French from, ultimately, Latin *mateola* "mallet."]

Mace

mace[2] /mayss/ *n.* a spice made from the covering of the nutmeg seed, used in the form of dried blades or as a yellow-orange powder [13thC. Via Anglo-Norman *macis* from Latin *macir*, the name of an oriental spice. The form "macis" was understood as a plural, and a new supposedly singular form made.]

Mace *tdmk.* a trademark for Chemical Mace, an aerosol used to immobilize an attacker for a brief time

mace·bear·er /máyss bàirər/ *n.* an official who carries a mace on ceremonial occasions

Maced. *abbr.* **1.** Macedonia **2.** Macedonian

mac·é·doine /màssə dwaán/, **mac·e·doine** *n.* **1. MIXED CHOPPED FRUITS** a salad of small diced pieces of fruit, often in syrup or jelly **2. MIXED CHOPPED VEGETABLES** a mixture of diced vegetables served hot or cold as a garnish, appetizer, or side dish **3. MEDLEY** a mixed-up jumble or medley (*literary*) [Early 19thC. From French *Macédoine* "Macedonia," the underlying idea being of a mixture of the different peoples ruled by ALEXANDER the Great of Macedonia.]

Mac·e·don = **Macedonia 2**

Mac·e·do·ni·a /màssə dṓnee ə/ **1.** republic in the Balkan region of southeastern Europe. Formerly part of the Federal People's Republic of Yugoslavia, it became independent in 1991. Language: Macedonian. Currency: dinar. Capital: Skopje. Population: 1,980,000 (1996). Area: 9,928 sq. mi./25,713 sq. km. **2. Mac·e·do·ni·a, Mac·e·don** /mássədən, -dòn/ ancient kingdom in northern Greece, centralized under Philip II, who, with his son, Alexander the Great, created a vast empire in the 4th century B.C. **3.** region in modern Greece, situated in the northeastern part of the country ■ *n.* **BULGARIAN DISTRICT** a district in southwestern Bulgaria

Mac·e·do·ni·an /màssə dṓnee ən/ *n.* **1. SOMEBODY FROM THE REPUBLIC OF MACEDONIA** somebody who was born in or is a citizen of the Republic of Macedonia **2. SOMEBODY FROM MODERN GREEK MACEDONIA** somebody who was born in or is a citizen of the modern Greek region of Macedonia **3. SOMEBODY FROM ANCIENT MACEDONIA** somebody who was born in or was a citizen of the ancient kingdom of Macedonia **4. LANGUAGE OF REPUBLIC OF MACEDONIA** the official language of the Republic of Macedonia, also spoken in Albania, Bulgaria, and Greece. It belongs to the Balto-Slavonic branch of Indo-European languages and is spoken by about two million people. **5. LANGUAGE OF ANCIENT MACEDONIA** an extinct language formerly spoken in ancient Macedonia. Its relationship with other European languages remains unclear. [Mid-16thC] —**Mac·e·do·ni·an** *adj.*

Mc·En·roe /mákən rṑ/, **John** (*b.* 1959) U.S. tennis player. He was four times winner of the U.S. Open (1979, 1980, 1981, and 1984) and won the Wimbledon men's singles title three times (1981, 1983, and 1984). Full name **John Patrick McEnroe, Jr.**

Mc·En·tire /mákən tìr/, **Reba** (*b.* 1955) U.S. country-and-western singer. This popular singer rejected the "countrypolitan" style in favor of a return to traditional country music values.

mac·er·ate /mássə ràyt/ *vti.* (**-at·ed, -at·ing, -ates**) **1. SOFTEN BY SOAKING** to soften something by soaking it in liquid or to become soft by soaking in liquid **2. SEPARATE BY SOAKING** to make something break up into pieces or into its various parts by soaking it in liquid, or to break up in this way **3. MAKE SOMETHING THIN OR WASTE AWAY** to make somebody or something thin or lean, or to become thin or lean, especially by starvation or fasting ■ *n.* **SOMETHING PRODUCED BY SOAKING** something prepared by soaking in a liquid [Mid-16thC. From Latin *macerat-*, the past participle stem of *macere* "to soften."] —**mac·er·at·er** *n.* —**mac·er·a·tive** *adj.* —**mac·er·a·tion** /màssə ráysh'n/ *n.*

Mc·Gil·li·vray /mə gíllivree, -ray/, **Alexander** (1759–93) Native American leader. His Treaty of New York (1790) helped to maintain the independence of his people, the Creek.

Mc·Gil·li·vray /mə gíllə vràyl/, **William** (1764–1825) Scottish-born Canadian fur-trade merchant. He was chief director of the North West Company, who fought in the War of 1812 at the capture of Detroit.

Mc·Gov·ern /mə gúvvərn/, **George** (*b.* 1922) U.S. statesman. A Democratic U.S. representative (1956–61) and senator (1963–81), he was a leading opponent of the Vietnam War. He lost a populist run for the presidency to Richard Nixon by a landslide in 1972. Full name **George Stanley McGovern**

Mc·Guf·fey /mə gúffee/, **William Holmes** (1800–73) U.S. educator and writer. He wrote a series of influential reading texts called the *Eclectic Readers* (1836–57).

Mac·Guf·fin /mə gúffin/ *n.* in a movie , play, or book, something that starts or drives the action of the plot, but later turns out to be unimportant [Mid-20thC. Coined by Alfred HITCHCOCK.]

Mach *n.* = **Mach number**

Mach /makh/, **Ernst** (1838–1916) Austrian physicist and philosopher. He was noted for his pioneering work in ballistics. The Mach number and Mach angle are named for him.

mach. *abbr.* **1.** machine **2.** machinery **3.** machinist

Ma·cha /maáchə, máchə/ *adj.* *Spanish* in a woman, having or showing characteristics conventionally regarded as typically male, especially physical strength, courage and aggressiveness (*slang*) [Feminine form of MACHO or perhaps shortened and altered from *machisma*]

Ma·cha·do de As·sis /ma shàddoo də a séss/, **Joachim Maria** (1839–1908) Brazilian novelist, poet, and critic. Author of *Dom Casmurro* (1899), he founded the Brazilian Academy of Letters (1896).

mache /ma sháy/, **mâche** *n.* = **corn salad** [Late 17thC. From French.]

Machete

ma·chet·e /mə shéttee, -chéttee/ *n.* a large heavy broad-bladed knife used as a weapon or as a tool for cutting a way through vegetation, especially in Central and South America and the West Indies [Late 16thC. From Spanish, literally "little sledgehammer," from macho "sledge hammer," ultimately from Latin *mateola* "mallet" (source of English MACE[1]).]

Mach·i·a·vel·li /màkee ə véllee, mà kya véllee/, **Niccolò** (1469–1527) Italian historian, statesman, and philosopher. He wrote several works on statecraft, of which *The Prince* (1532) had a huge influence in his own time and later.

Mach·i·a·vel·li·an /màkee ə véllee ən/ *adj.* **1. CUNNING AND UNSCRUPULOUS** using clever trickery, amoral methods, and expediency to achieve a desired goal, especially in politics (*disapproving*) **2. RELATING TO MACHIAVELLI** relating to or characteristic of the statesman and political philosopher Niccolò Machiavelli [Mid-16thC. From the advice in the writings of Niccolò MACHIAVELLI.] —**Mach·i·a·vel·li·an** *n.* —**Mach·i·a·vel·li·an·ism** /màkee ə véllee ə nìzzəm/ *n.* —**Mach·i·a·vel·list** /-véllist/ *n., adj.*

Mach·i·a·vel·li·an in·tel·li·gence *n.* in psychology, social intelligence, especially the intelligence that involves deception and the formation of coalitions

ma·chic·o·late /mə chíkə làyt/ (**-lat·ed, -lat·ing, -lates**) *vt.* to provide a castle wall with projecting galleries along its top [Late 18thC. Via Anglo-Latin, from, ultimately, Provençal *machacol*, literally "neck-crusher," presumably because of the effect on those underneath.]

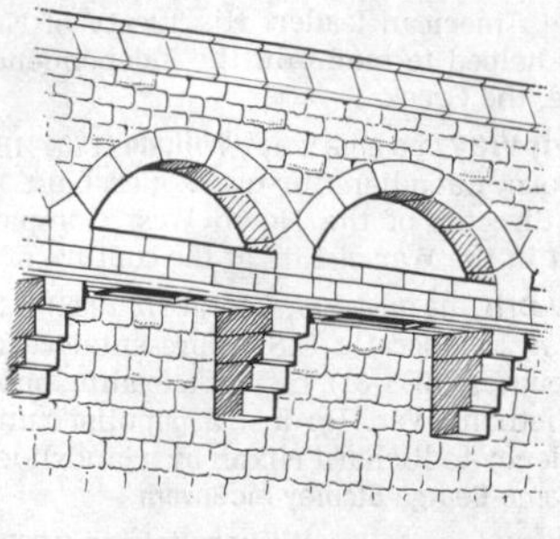

Machicolation

ma·chic·o·la·tion /mə chìkə láysh'n/ *n.* **1. GALLERY ON TOP OF CASTLE WALL** a projecting gallery on top of a castle wall, supported by a row of arches and containing openings through which rocks and boiling oil could be dropped on attackers **2. OPENING IN MACHICOLATION** an opening in the floor of a machicolation **3. ROW OF ARCHES** an ornamental row of supported arches that project from a building

mach·i·nate /mákə nàyt, máshə-/ (**-nat·ed, -nat·ing, -nates**) *vti.* to devise secret, cunning, or complicated plans and schemes to achieve a goal or to cause harm to others [Late 16thC. From Latin *machinat-*, past participle stem of *machinari*, from *machina* (see MACHINE).] —**mach·i·na·tor** *n.*

mach·i·na·tion /màkə náysh'n, màshə-/ *n.* **1. PLOTTING OR INTRIGUE** the devising of secret, cunning, or complicated plans and schemes **2. PLOT OR INTRIGUE** a secret, cunning, or complicated plan or scheme designed to achieve a particular end

ma·chine /mə shéen/ *n.* **1.** MECH ENG **MECHANICAL DEVICE** a device with moving parts, often powered by electricity, used to perform a task, especially one that would otherwise be done by hand ○ *a washing machine* **2.** MECH ENG **SIMPLE UNPOWERED DEVICE** a simple device used to overcome resistance at one point by applying force at another point, e.g., a lever, pulley, or an inclined plane **3. POWERED FORM OF TRANSPORTATION** an engine-driven means of transportation, e.g., an aircraft, car, or motorcycle **4.** POL **GROUP OF PEOPLE IN CONTROL** an organized group of people that controls or directs something, especially a political group ○ *the party machine* **5. COMPLEX SYSTEM** a complex system structured so as to accomplish a specific goal ○ *the war machine* **6. SOMEBODY WHO BEHAVES MECHANICALLY** somebody who acts or works like a mechanical device, e.g., somebody who is very efficient or who shows no emotion or initiative ○ *an editing machine* **7.** THEATER **DEVICE TO PRODUCE STAGE EFFECTS** a mechanical device used in the theater, especially in classical drama, to create special effects such as the entrance of a supernatural being **8.** LITERAT **LITERARY DEVICE** somebody or something introduced into a work of literature to produce an effect or to resolve the plot ■ *v.* (**-chined, -chin·ing, -chines**) **1.** *vti.* **WORK WITH POWER-DRIVEN TOOL** to cut, shape, or finish a piece of work using a power-driven tool such as a lathe or drilling device, or to be cut, shaped, or finished in this way **2.** *vt.* **USE MACHINE ON SOMETHING** to make or do something using a machine [Mid-16thC. Via Old French from Latin *machina*, "device, engine, contrivance" from, ultimately, Greek *mēkhanē* (source of English *mechanic*), from Greek *mēkhos* "contrivance, means."] —**ma·chin·a·bil·i·ty** /mə shèenə bíllətee/ *n.* —**ma·chin·a·ble** /mə shéenəb'l/ *adj.* —**ma·chine·less** /mə shéenləss/ *adj.* —**ma·chine·like** *adj.*

ma·chine bolt *n.* a bolt with a square or hexagonal head, usually of heavy duty construction for use in aircraft and automobiles

ma·chine code *n.* = **machine language**

ma·chine fin·ish *n.* = **mill finish**

ma·chine gun *n.* an automatic weapon that fires rapidly and repeatedly without requiring separate squeezes on the trigger each time

ma·chine-gun *vt.* (**ma·chine-gunned, ma·chine-gun·ning, ma·chine-guns**) **1. SHOOT SOMEBODY WITH MACHINE GUN** to shoot or kill somebody with a machine gun, or to fire a machine gun at somebody or something **2. ADDRESS SOMEBODY RAPIDLY** to speak rapidly to somebody (*informal*) ■ *adj.* **STACCATO** rapid, abrupt, and staccato in delivery —**ma·chine-gun·ner** *n.*

ma·chine lan·guage *n.* instructions, usually written in binary code, telling a computer how to process data

ma·chine-made *adj.* made by a machine rather than by hand

ma·chine pis·tol *n.* a light automatic or semiautomatic submachine gun that can be discharged using only one hand

ma·chine-read·a·ble *adj.* in a form that is able to be used directly by a computer

ma·chin·er·y /mə shéenəree/ *n.* **1.** MECH ENG **MECHANICAL PARTS** the aggregate parts that make up a machine or group of machines **2.** MECH ENG **MACHINES** machines collectively or in general **3. SYSTEM OF MACHINES** a system of machines working together **4. SET OF PROCEDURES** an interconnected series of processes that works like a mechanical system to produce a particular result **5. LITERARY DEVICES** literary devices used for effect, especially in poetry, or to resolve the plot of a play or book

ma·chine screw *n.* a slotted or hexagonal-headed screw with a standardized thread used to connect machine parts together

ma·chine shop *n.* a workshop where various materials, especially metals, are cut, shaped and worked, often to tight specifications using machine tools

ma·chine tool *n.* a machine such as a lathe or grinder, used for shaping and finishing metals and other solid materials —**ma·chine-tooled** *adj.*

ma·chine trans·la·tion *n.* the translation of text from one language to another by computer

ma·chine-wash (**ma·chine-washed, ma·chine-wash·ing, ma·chine-wash·es**) *vt.* to wash something in a washing machine

ma·chine-wash·a·ble *adj.* able to be washed in a washing machine without being damaged

ma·chin·ist /mə shéenist/ *n.* **1. SOMEBODY WHO MACHINES SOMETHING** somebody whose job involves machining something or operating a machine or machine tool, especially in a factory **2. MACHINE MAKER OR REPAIRER** somebody who makes or repairs machines **3. U.S. NAVY POSITION** a Navy petty officer who is assigned to a ship's engine room **4.** THEATER **OPERATOR OF MECHANICAL STAGE EFFECTS** somebody who is in charge of the machinery used to create theatrical effects (*archaic*)

ma·chis·mo /mə kízmō, mə chízmō/ *n.* an exaggerated sense or display of masculinity, emphasizing characteristics that are conventionally regarded as typically male, usually physical strength and courage, aggressiveness, and lack of emotional response [Mid-20thC. From Mexican Spanish, formed from *macho* (see MACHO).]

Mach·me·ter /maák meetər/ *n.* an instrument for measuring the Mach number of an aircraft

Mach num·ber /maák-/ *n.* the speed of an object relative to the speed of sound. An aircraft traveling at twice the speed of sound has a Mach number of 2. [Early 20thC. Named for Ernst MACH, because of his work in aerodynamics.]

ma·cho /maáchō, máchō/ *adj.* **STEREOTYPICALLY MASCULINE** having or showing characteristics conventionally regarded as typically male, especially physical strength and courage, aggressiveness, and lack of emotional response ■ *n.* (*plural* **-chos**) **STEREOTYPICALLY MASCULINE MALE** a male who displays conventionally typical masculine characteristics [Early 20thC. From Mexican Spanish *macho* "male plant or animal, masculine, vigorous" from Spanish "male, masculine," from Latin *masculus* (source of English *masculine* and *male*).] —**ma·cho·ism** *n.*

Ma·chu Pic·chu *n.* the ruins of a large ancient Inca city in the Andes in southern Peru, discovered in 1911. It is well known for its architecture and system of terraces.

mach·zor /maak záwr, maakh-/ *n.* = **mahzor**

mac·in·tosh *n.* = **mackintosh**

Mack /mak/, **Connie** (1862–1956) U.S. baseball manager. He guided the Philadelphia Athletics to five world championships (1910–30).

Machu Picchu

Mack·ay /məkay/ salt lake in central Australia, on the border between Western Australia and the Northern Territory. Area: 1,370 sq. mi./3,550 sq. km.

Mc·Kean /mə kéen/, **Thomas** (1734–1817) U.S. jurist and statesman. He was a signatory of the Declaration of Independence (1776) and governor of Pennsylvania (1799–1808).

Mac·ken·zie /mə kénzee/ river in the Northwest Territories, Canada. Its main stream originates in Great Slave Lake. Length: 1,060 mi./1,705 km.

Mac·ken·zie, Sir Alexander (1764–1820) Scottish explorer. He was founder of the fur-trading North West company. He explored western Canada from the Arctic to the Pacific and was the first to cross North America overland.

Mac·ken·zie, Alexander (1822–92) Canadian statesman. He was the first Liberal prime minister of the Dominion of Canada (1873–78). During his term the Canadian Supreme Court was established.

Mac·Ken·zie, William Lyon (1795–1861) Canadian insurgent and politician. He was leader of the Rebellion of 1837, advocating independent government for Toronto. He became a member of the Canadian assembly (1850–58).

Mac·ken·zie Moun·tains mountain range in western Canada that spans the border between the Northwest Territories and the Yukon Territory. Keele Peak is the highest peak, 9,750 ft./2,972 m. Length: 497 mi./800 km.

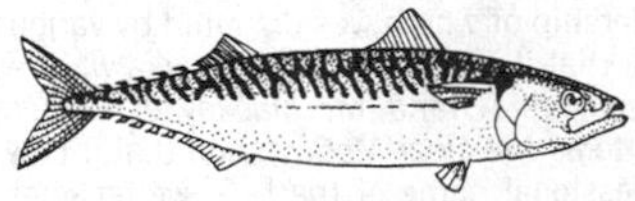

Mackerel

mack·er·el /mákrəl/ (*plural* **-els** *or* **-el**) *n.* **1. OILY FOOD FISH OF NORTHERN ATLANTIC** a bony oily food fish of northern Atlantic coastal waters that has a greenish-blue body with dark blue bars and a forked tail. Latin name: *Scomber scombrus*. **2. FISH LIKE MACKEREL** any fish that is similar to the mackerel, e.g., the Spanish mackerel. Family: Scombridae. [13thC. From Anglo-Norman, of unknown origin.]

mack·er·el breeze *n.* a breeze strong enough to disturb the surface of the water

mack·er·el shark *n.* a large fierce shark with a pointed snout, related to the great white shark, mako shark, and porbeagle. Family: Lamnidae.

mack·er·el sky *n.* a sky covered with cirrocumulus or altocumulus clouds in a pattern that resembles the markings on a mackerel (*regional*)

Mc·Kim /mə kím/, **Charles Follen** (1847–1909) U.S. architect. His designs include the Boston Public Library (1887).

Mack·i·nac, Straits of /máki nak/ channel in Michigan, connecting Lake Huron and Lake Michigan. Length: 30 mi./48 km.

Mack·i·nac Is·land island in northern Michigan, in the Straits of Mackinac, between Michigan's northern and southern peninsulas. Area: 6 sq. mi./16 sq. km.

mack·i·naw /mákə nàw/ *n.* **1. HEAVY WOOLEN FABRIC** a thick heavy woolen cloth, usually with a plaid design **2. SHORT HEAVY COAT** a short double-breasted coat made from mackinaw or a similar fabric **3.** = **Mackinaw blanket 4.** NAUT **FLAT-BOTTOMED BOAT** a boat with a pointed bow, a square stern, and a flat bottom, formerly used on the Great Lakes [Early 19thC. Named for the fort, once an important trading post, which once stood on the site of Mackinaw City, northern Michigan.]

Mack·i·naw blan·ket *n.* a thick blanket made of heavy woolen cloth, sometimes striped, formerly used by Native Americans, trappers, or traders in the northern and western parts of North America

Mack·i·naw trout (*plural* **Mack·i·naw trout** *or* **Mack·i·naw trouts**) *n.* = **lake trout** *n.* 1

Barnaby's

Mount McKinley

Mc·Kin·ley, Mount /mə kínlee/ the highest mountain in North America, in Denali National Park and Preserve, south central Alaska. Height: 20,320 ft./6,194 m.

Library of Congress

William McKinley

Mc·Kin·ley, William (1843–1901) U.S. statesman and 25th president of the United States (1897–1901). Shortly after election to his second term he was assassinated by anarchist Leon Czolgosz.

Mac·kin·non /mə kínnən/, **Catherine** (*b.* 1946) U.S. legal scholar. A pioneer in changing the legal attitude toward sex discrimination, she wrote the influential *Sexual Harassment of Working Women* (1979).

mack·in·tosh /mákin tàwsh/, **mac·in·tosh** *n. U.K.* **1. RAINCOAT** a waterproof coat worn for protection against the rain, originally one made from rubberized fabric (*dated*) **2. WATERPROOF FABRIC** a waterproof fabric, especially rubberized cotton [Mid-19thC. Named for the Scottish inventor Charles *Macintosh* (1766–1843), who patented a waterproof rubberized cloth.]

Mack·in·tosh /mákin tosh/, **Charles Rennie** (1868–1928) British architect and interior designer. Noted for his art nouveau designs, he worked primarily on buildings and interiors in and around Glasgow, Scotland.

mack·le /mák'l/ *n.* **PRINTING ERROR** a blurred or double impression caused by the movement of paper or type during the printing process ■ *vti.* **BLUR IMAGE** to cause a printed impression to blur, or to appear blurred [Late 16thC. Either directly or via French from Latin *macula* "spot, stain."]

Mac·Laine /mə kláyn/, **Shirley** (*b.* 1934) U.S. movie actress. Sister of Warren Beatty, she has appeared in many films, including *Terms of Endearment*

AKG London

Charles Rennie Mackintosh

(1983), and has worked in television. Real name **Shirley MacLean Beatty**

mac·le /mák'l/ *n.* **1.** MINERALS = **chiastolite 2.** CRYSTALS **TWINNED CRYSTAL** a crystal that is twinned **3. DISCOLORED SPOT IN CRYSTAL** a discolored spot within a crystal [Early 19thC. Via French from Latin *macula* "spot, mesh."]

Mac·lean, Alistair (1922–87) British novelist. Many of his adventure stories, set in different parts of the world, were made into movies.

Mac·Leish /mə kléesh/, **Archibald** (1892–1982) U.S. poet, playwright, and public official. He won a Pulitzer Prize for his poetic biblical drama *J.B.* (1958).

Mac·Len·nan /mə klénnən/, **Hugh** (1907–90) Canadian writer, known for his novels and critiques of Canadian life as in *Barometer Rising* (1941). Full name **John Hugh MacLennan**

Mc·Lu·han /mə klóoən/, **Marshall** (1911–80) Canadian-born U.S. critic and theorist. His writings dealt with the effects of media technology on the public. Full name **Herbert Marshall McLuhan**

Popperfoto

Harold Macmillan

Mac·mil·lan /mək míllən/, **Harold, 1st Earl of Stockton** (1894–1986) British statesman. He became prime minister of the United Kingdom (1957–63). His two successful terms of office were marred by the John Profumo scandal (1963). Full name **Maurice Harold Macmillan**

Mc·Na·ma·ra /màknə márrə/, **Robert** (*b.* 1916) U.S. business executive and public official. He left the presidency of Ford Motor Company to serve as secretary of defense (1961–67) during the Vietnam War, which he championed while in office. He was later president of the World Bank (1968–81). Full name **Robert Strange McNamara**

Ma·comb /mə kṓm/ city in western Illinois, east of Keokuk and southwest of Peoria. Population: 18,069 (1996).

ma·con /maa káwN/, **Ma·con, Mâcon** *n.* a red or white wine from the Mâcon area in central France

Ma·con /máykən/ city in central Georgia. It is the seat of Bibb county. Population: 109,191 (1994).

Mâ·con capital of Saône-et-Loire Department, in Burgundy, east central France. Population: 106,612 (1990).

Ma·coun /mə kóon/, **John** (1831–1920) Irish-born Canadian field naturalist. His collection of flora and fauna formed the basis of the National Museum of Natural Sciences.

Mac·Phail /mək fáyl/, **Agnes Campbell** (1890–1954) Canadian politician. She was a member of parliament (1921–40) and of the Ontario legislature (1943–45 and 1948–51).

Mc·Pher·son /mək féersən/ city in central Kansas, south of Saline and northwest of Wichita. Population: 12,746 (1996).

Mc·Pher·son /mək fúrss'n/, **Aimee Semple** (1890–1944) Canadian-born U.S. preacher. She founded the Church of the Four Square Gospel (1927) and was one of the first evangelists to use the radio. Born **Aimee Elizabeth Kennedy**

Mac·quar·ie, Lake /mə kwáwree/ coastal lake in New South Wales, Australia. It is bordered by residential areas as well as centers of energy production and tourism. Area: 43 sq. mi./110 sq. km.

Mac·quar·ie Har·bour large natural harbor in western Tasmania, Australia. Area: 110 sq. mi./285 sq. km.

Mac·quar·ie Is·land uninhabited Australian island located in the Southern Ocean, 835 mi./1,300 km southeast of Tasmania. Area: 50 sq. mi./128 sq. km.

Mc·Queen /mə kwéen/, **Steve** (1930–80) U.S. actor. He achieved his greatest success in tough-guy and loner roles in movies such as *The Magnificent Seven* (1960) and *Bullitt* (1968). Full name **Terence Steven McQueen**

macr- *prefix.* = **macro-** (*used before vowels*)

mac·ra·mé /màkrə máy/ *n.* pieces of string or cord knotted together to form a coarse ornamental lacy pattern, or something made using this method [Mid-19thC. Via Turkish *makrama* "towel, handkerchief, tablecloth," from Arabic *miḳrama* "bed cover." Macramé work was first mainly used to make fringes on items such as towels.]

mac·ro /mákrō/ (*plural* **-ros**) *n.* a single computer instruction that initiates a series of additional instructions for a computer to perform [Mid-20thC. From MACRO-.]

macro- *prefix.* **1.** large, inclusive ○ *macrocyte* ○ *macroclimate* **2.** long ○ *macrobiotics* [From Greek *makros.* Ultimately from an Indo-European base meaning "long, thin," which is also the ancestor of English *meager* and *emaciate.*]

mac·ro·bi·ot·ics /màkrō bī óttiks/ *n.* a vegan diet of seeds, grains, and organically grown fruit and vegetables, said to prolong life and balance the body's systems by adjusting the amount and kind of food eaten (*takes a singular verb*) [Late 18thC. From Greek *makrobiotos,* literally "long life."] —**mac·ro·bi·ot·ic** *adj.*

mac·ro·ceph·a·ly /màkrō séffəlee/, **mac·ro·ce·pha·li·a** /màkrō sə fáylee ə/ *n.* the condition of having a head that is excessively large [Mid-19thC. Formed from MACRO and -CEPHALY.] —**mac·ro·ce·phal·ic** /màkrō sə fállik/ *adj.* —**mac·ro·ceph·a·lous** /-séffələss/ *adj.*

mac·ro·cli·mate /mákrō klīmət/ *n.* the general climate of a large region such as a continent —**mac·ro·cli·mat·ic** /màkrō klī máttik/ *adj.* —**mac·ro·cli·mat·i·cal·ly** /-kəlee/ *adv.*

mac·ro·cosm /mákrə kòzzəm/ *n.* a complex structure such as the world or the universe considered as a single entity that contains numerous similar smaller-scale structures [Early 17thC. From medieval Latin *macrocosmus,* from Greek *makro-* (see MACRO-) + *kosmos* "world."] —**mac·ro·cos·mic** /màkrə kózmik/ *adj.* —**mac·ro·cos·mic·al·ly** /-kózmiklee/ *adv.*

mac·ro·cyte /mákrō sīt/ *n.* an unusually large red blood cell that commonly occurs in cases of anemia [Late 19thC. Coined from MACRO- + -CYTE.] —**mac·ro·cyt·ic** /màkrō síttik/ *adj.*

mac·ro·cy·to·sis /màkrō sī tóssiss/ *n.* the presence of abnormally large red cells in the blood —**mac·ro·cy·tot·ic** /màkrō sī tóttik/ *adj.*

mac·ro·ec·o·nom·ics /màkrō eekə nómmiks, -ekə-/ *n.* a branch of economics that focuses on the general features and processes that make up a national economy and the ways in which different segments of the economy are connected (*takes a singular verb*) —**mac·ro·ec·o·nom·ic** *adj.* —**mac·ro·e·con·o·mist** /màkrō i kónnəmist/ *n.*

mac·ro·e·con·o·my /màkrō ikónnəmee/ *n.* the economy viewed as a whole and in terms of all those factors that control its overall performance ○ *Employment rates did not respond to the macroeconomy as expected.* [Combination of MACRO + ECONOMY]

mac·ro·ev·o·lu·tion /màkrō evvə lóosh'n/ *n.* evolution theorized to occur over a long period of time, producing major changes in species and other taxonomic groups —**mac·ro·ev·o·lu·tion·ar·y** *adj.*

mac·ro·fos·sil /mákrō fóss'l/ *n.* a fossil that is large enough to be observed or examined without the aid of a microscope

mac·ro·gam·ete /màkrō gá meet, màkrō gə meet/ *n.* the larger, usually female sex cell (**gamete**) in a pair of conjugating cells of a heterogamous species

mac·ro·glob·u·lin /màkrō glóbbyəlin/ *n.* **1. SOLUBLE PROTEIN WITH HIGH MOLECULAR WEIGHT** a soluble protein in the blood with a high molecular weight, typically seen in some diseases **2. SOLUBLE PROTEIN WITH NORMAL MOLECULAR WEIGHT** a soluble protein in the blood with a normal molecular weight

mac·ro·glob·u·lin·e·mi·a /màkrō globbyələ neemee ə/ *n.* a condition marked by an increase of macroglobulins in the blood

mac·ro·graph /mákrō gràf/ *n.* a drawing, photograph, or other representation in which something appears at its actual size or larger [Late 19thC. Coined from MACRO- + -GRAPH.] —**mac·ro·graph·ic** /màkrō gráffik/ *adj.* —**ma·crog·ra·phy** /ma króggrəfee/ *n.*

mac·ro·in·struc·tion /màkrō in strúksh'n/ *n.* COMPUT = **macro**

mac·ro lens *n.* a lens used for close-up photography that produces a lifesize or larger image on film, with a minimum of 1:1 object-to-image ratio

mac·ro·mere /mákrō meer/ *n.* a large yolk-filled cell formed from the unequal splitting of a fertilized egg [Late 19thC. Coined from MACRO- + BLASTOMERE.]

mac·ro·mol·e·cule /màkrō móllə kyool/ *n.* a large molecule, e.g., that of a protein or polymer, made up of smaller elements connected to one another —**mac·ro·mo·lec·u·lar** /màkrō mə lékyələr/ *adj.*

ma·cron /máy kròn, máykrən, má kròn/ *n.* **1.** PHON **MARK INDICATING LONG SOUND** a short horizontal line placed over a vowel sound to indicate that it is long or stressed. Macrons are used in some languages, some phonetic transcription systems, and in the study or analysis of poetic meter. **2.** POETRY **LONG OR STRESSED SYLLABLE** a stressed syllable in a foot of verse, marked with a macron [Mid-19thC. From Greek literally "long thing," from *makros* "long."]

mac·ro·nu·cle·us /màkrō nooklee əss/ (*plural* **-i** /-ī/) *n.* the larger of two nuclei in most ciliate protozoans, involved in nonreproductive functions such as feeding and metabolism —**mac·ro·nu·cle·ar** *adj.*

mac·ro·nu·tri·ent /màkrō nootree ənt/ *n.* a chemical element, e.g., nitrogen, carbon, or potassium, needed in large amounts by plants for normal growth and development

mac·ro·phage /mákrō fàyj/ *n.* a large cell that is present in blood, lymph, and connective tissues, removing waste products, harmful microorganisms, and foreign material from the bloodstream [Late 19thC. Coined from MACRO +-PHAGE.] —**mac·ro·phag·ic** /màkrō fájjik/ *adj.*

mac·ro·pho·tog·ra·phy /màkrō fə tóggrəfee/ *n.* close-up photography that produces images on the film that are lifesize or larger than life

mac·ro·phys·ics /màkrō fízziks/ *n.* a branch of physics that studies systems and objects large enough to be easily observed (*takes a singular verb*)

mac·ro·phyte /mákrō fìt/ *n.* a plant large enough to be studied and observed using the unaided eye, especially an aquatic plant [Early 20thC. Coined from MACRO- + -PHYTE.] —**mac·ro·phyt·ic** /màkrō fíttik/ *adj.*

ma·crop·sia /mə krópsee ə/ *n.* a condition in which everything perceived by the eye appears to be larger than it really is, often as a result of a retinal disease or a brain disorder [Late 19thC. Coined from MACRO- + Greek *opsia* "seeing."]

mac·ro·scop·ic /màkrō skóppik/, **mac·ro·scop·i·cal** /màkrō skóppik'l/ *adj.* **1. VISIBLE TO NAKED EYE** large enough to be seen and examined without the aid of magnifying equipment **2. COMPREHENSIVE** relating to or concerned with large units [Late 19thC. From MACRO-, modeled on MICROSCOPIC.] —**mac·ro·scop·i·cal·ly** *adv.*

mac·ro·scop·ic a·nat·o·my *n.* = **gross anatomy**

mac·ro·so·ci·ol·o·gy /màkrō sōssee óllәjee/ *n.* the branch of sociology concerned with the study and analysis of societies in their entirety —**mac·ro·so·ci·o·log·i·cal** *adj.*

mac·ro·spo·ran·gi·um /màkrō spaw ránjee əm/ (*plural* **-a**) *n.* BIOL = **megasporangium** [Late 19thC. From modern Latin, formed from MACRO- + Greek *spora* "spore" + *aggeion* "vessel."]

mac·ro·spore /màkrō spáwr/ *n.* BIOL = **megaspore**

mac·ro·struc·ture /mákrō strùkchər/ *n.* a structure, e.g., that of a metal, large enough to be seen or examined with little or no magnification —**mac·ro·struc·tu·ral** /màkrō strúkchərəl/ *adj.*

mac·u·la /mákyələ/ (*plural* **-lae** /mákyə lee/ *or* **-las**) *n.* **1.** PHYSIOL **SMALL SPOT ON SKIN** a small pigmented spot on the skin that is neither raised nor depressed **2.** OPHTHALMOL **YELLOW SPOT NEAR RETINA** a small yellowish spot in the middle of the retina that provides the greatest visual acuity and color perception **3.** ASTRON **SUNSPOT** a sunspot (*technical*) [14thC. From Latin, "spot, stain."] —**mac·u·lar** /mákyələr/ *adj.*

mac·u·la lu·te·a (*plural* **mac·u·lae lu·te·ae**) *n.* = **macula** *n.* 2 ["Lutea" from Latin *luteus* "yellow"]

mac·u·late /mákyə làyt/ *vt.* (**-lat·ed, -lat·ing, -lates**) (*archaic or literary*) **1. STAIN SOMEBODY OR SOMETHING** to mark somebody or something with a spot, blotch, or blemish **2. MAKE SOMEBODY OR SOMETHING IMPURE** to defile or pollute somebody or something ■ *adj.* **mac·u·late, mac·u·lat·ed** (*archaic or literary*) **1. STAINED** marked with spots, blotches, or blemishes **2. IMPURE** defiled, polluted, or impure [15thC. From Latin *maculat-*, past participle stem of *maculare*, from *macula* "spot."]

mac·u·la·tion /màkyə láysh'n/ *n.* **1. SPOTTED MARKINGS** the pattern of spots on some animals and plants **2. STAINING OR BEING STAINED** the act of marking something with a spot, blotch, or blemish, or the state of being marked in this way (*archaic or literary*)

mac·ule[1] /mákyool/ *n.* = **macula** *n.* 1 [Mid-19thC. Either directly or via French from Latin *macula* "spot, stain."]

mac·ule[2] /mákyəl/ *n.* PRINTING = **mackle**

mad /mad/ *adj.* (**mad·der, mad·dest**) **1. VERY ANGRY** affected by great displeasure or anger **2. OFFENSIVE TERM** an offensive term meaning affected with psychiatric disorder (*offensive*) **3. VERY UNWISE OR RASH** lacking common sense and not reasoning logically (*insult*) (*offensive in some contexts*) **4. WILDLY EXCITED** completely unrestrained and out of control (*offensive in some contexts*) ○ *went mad after the last-minute victory* **5. FRANTIC** done with great haste, excitement, or confusion (*offensive in some contexts*) **6. RAMBUNCTIOUS** very exciting or boisterous (*offensive in some contexts*) **7. SEIZED BY UNCONTROLLABLE EMOTION** overcome with a violent emotion (*offensive in some contexts*) **8. PASSIONATE ABOUT SOMETHING** very fond of, enthusiastic about, or interested in something, often to the exclusion of everything else (*often used in combination, offensive in some contexts*) **9. ABNORMALLY AGGRESSIVE** used to describe an animal that is abnormally aggressive or ferocious (*disapproving*) (*offensive in some contexts*) **10. RABID** having rabies ■ *vti.* (**mad·ded, mad·ding, mads**) **MAKE OR BECOME IRRATIONAL OR FURIOUS** to make somebody furiously angry or insane or to become furiously angry or irrational (*archaic*) (*offensive in some contexts*) [Old English *gemǣd* "deprived of reason," that was formed from *gemād* "irrational," from, ultimately, an Indo-European ancestor meaning "change" (source of English *mutate*)] —**mad·dish** *adj.* ◇ **like mad** with great speed or energy (*offensive in some contexts*)

MAD *abbr.* **1.** PSYCHIAT major affective disorder **2.** MIL mutual assured destruction

Mad. *abbr.* Madagascar

Madag., **Mad.** *abbr.* Madagascar

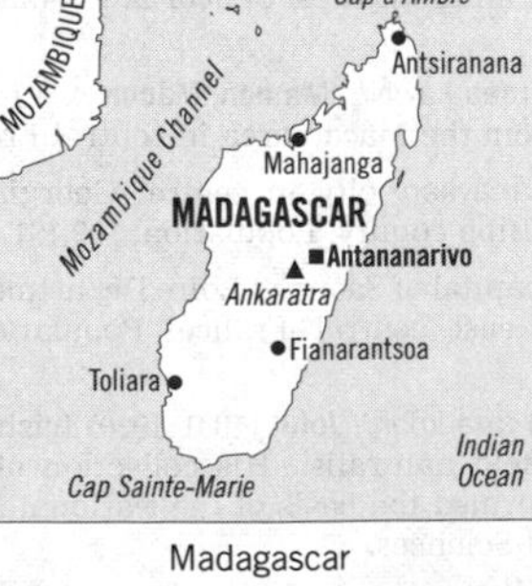

Madagascar

Mad·a·gas·car /màddə gáskaar/ island republic separated from southeastern mainland Africa by the Mozambique Channel. Language: Malagasy, French. Currency: Malagasy franc. Capital: Antananarivo. Population: 13,671,000 (1996). Area: 226,658 sq. mi./587,041 sq. km. Official name **Democratic Republic of Madagascar**. Former name **Malagasy Republic** —**Mada·gas·can** *adj.*, *n.*

Mad·a·gas·car aq·ua·ma·rine *n.* a type of blue beryl found in Madagascar, used as a gemstone

Mad·a·gas·car per·i·win·kle *n.* a perennial plant of India and Madagascar that is poisonous to domestic animals. It has white or pink flowers and produces various substances used to treat cancer. Latin name: *Catharanthus roseus.*

mad·am /máddəm/ *n.* **1.** (*plural* **mes·dames**) **USED TO ADDRESS A WOMAN** a polite term of address for a woman, especially a customer in a store, restaurant, or hotel (*formal*) **2. WOMAN RUNNING A BROTHEL** a woman who manages a brothel [13thC. From Old French *ma dame* "my lady," from, ultimately, Latin *mea domina* (source of English *Madonna*).]

Mad·am /máddəm/ (*plural* **Mes·dames** /may dám, -daám/ *or* **Mad·ams**) *n.* **1. USED TO ADDRESS WOMAN IN LETTER** used at the beginning of a formal letter to a woman, especially one whose name is not known (*formal*) **2. USED TO ADDRESS WOMAN OFFICIAL** used before the name of a woman's official position as a term of address ○ *Madam President*

Ma·dame /máddəm, mə daám/ (*plural* **Mes·dames** /may dám, -daám/), **ma·dame** (*plural* **mes·dames**) *n.* the title of a Frenchwoman or French-speaking woman, especially if married, used before her name or as a polite term of address

WORD KEY: CULTURAL NOTE

Madame Bovary, a novel by French writer Gustave Flaubert (1857). It tells the story of Emma Bovary, a young married woman who seeks refuge from the mundanity of her provincial life in a series of reckless affairs. The novel's frank depiction of middle-class society and its almost scientific analysis of human behavior made it a pioneering work of modern realism.

mad·cap /mád kàp/ *adj.* acting or done without caring or stopping to think about possible consequences [Late 16thC. "Cap" used to represent the head.] —**mad·cap** *n.*

mad cow dis·ease *n.* VET = **BSE**

MADD /mad/ *abbr.* Mothers Against Drunk Driving

mad·den /mádd'n/ (**-dened, -den·ing, -dens**) *vti.* **1. MAKE OR BECOME ANGRY** to make a person or animal extremely angry, or to become extremely angry (*usually passive*) **2. MAKE OR BECOME IRRATIONAL OR FURIOUS** to make somebody irrational or furious, or to become irrational or furious

mad·den·ing /mádd'ning/ *adj.* **1. CAUSING ANGER** causing anger, impatience, or frustration **2. CAUSING INTENSE ANNOYANCE AND DISTRESS** causing intense annoyance and distress —**mad·den·ing·ly** *adv.* —**mad·den·ing·ness** *n.*

mad·der[1] comparative of **mad**

mad·der[2] /máddər/ *n.* **1. HERB WITH RED ROOT** a perennial Eurasian herb that has open clusters of small yellow flowers and a red fleshy root. Latin name: *Rubia tinctorum.* **2. ROOT YIELDING DYE** the root of the madder plant, formerly used for obtaining a red dye by fermentation **3. RED DYE** a red dye formerly obtained from the root of the madder plant **4. RED PIGMENT** a red pigment obtained from alizarin, used in dyes, inks, and paints **5.** COLORS **REDDISH-PURPLE** a deep reddish-purple color ■ *adj.* COLORS **OF REDDISH-PURPLE** deep reddish-purple in color [Old English *mædere*, ultimately from a prehistoric Germanic word]

mad·dest superlative of **mad**

mad·ding /mádding/ *adj.* acting in a way that suggests or reveals the presence of a psychiatric disorder (*archaic*)

WORD KEY: CULTURAL NOTE

Far from the Madding Crowd, a novel by English writer Thomas Hardy (1874). The first of Thomas Hardy's *Wessex Novels*, it is the story of a capricious, forceful young woman, Bathsheba Everdene, and her attempts to improve her social position through marriage. It was made into a movie by John Schlesinger in 1967.

mad-dog skull·cap *n.* a North American perennial plant that has clusters of two-lipped blue or white flowers and is used as an antispasmodic. Latin name: *Scutellaria lateriflora.*

made *v.* **1.** past tense of **make 2.** past participle of **make** ■ *adj.* **1.** ARTIFICIALLY PRODUCED produced by artificial means **2.** CONTRIVED fictitious, invented, or contrived (*dated*) **3.** SUCCESSFUL certain of achieving success **4.** ACCEPTED INTO CRIMINAL GROUP accepted as a member of an underworld crime syndicate (*slang*) ◇ **be made for somebody** *or* **something** to be ideally suited to somebody or something ◇ **have it made, got it made** to be in a position to succeed at something without obstacles or serious problems (*informal*)

Ma·dei·ra /mə dérrə, mə deérə/ *n.* a sweet or dry wine fortified with brandy, made on the island of Madeira and usually served as a dessert wine or after a meal

Ma·dei·ra Is·lands /mə deérə/ group of islands with many resorts in the eastern North Atlantic Ocean. Population: 256,000 (1992). Area: 286 sq. mi./741 sq. km.

Ma·dei·ra vine *n.* a tropical South American ornamental vine with small fragrant flowers. Latin name: *Anredera cordifolia.*

mad·e·leine /máddələn, máddə làyn/ *n.* **1.** SMALL PLAIN SPONGE CAKE a small light whisked sponge cake baked in an individual shell-shaped pan **2.** SPONGE CAKE WITH JAM AND COCONUT a sponge cake that is cooked in a small cup-shaped mold, coated in raspberry jam, rolled in desiccated coconut, and topped with a glacé cherry [Mid-19thC. Probably named for the 19th-century French pastry cook Madeleine Paulmier.]

mad·e·moi·selle /màdmwə zél, màdmə zél/ (*plural* **mes·de·moi·selles** *or* **mad·e·moi·selles**) *n.* **1. Mad·e·moi·selle, mad·e·moi·selle** TITLE OF FRENCHWOMAN the title of a French woman or French-speaking young or unmarried woman, used before her name or as a polite term of address (*sometimes considered offensive*) **2.** FRENCHWOMAN a young Frenchwoman or French-speaking woman **3.** WOMAN FRENCH TEACHER a woman French teacher or French governess (*dated*) **4.** ZOOL = **silver perch** [15thC. From Old French *ma demoiselle* "my damsel."]

made-to-or·der *adj.* **1.** CUSTOM-MADE made in accordance with a customer's specifications or requirements **2.** PERFECTLY SUITABLE perfectly suitable or exactly as required

made-up *adj.* **1.** UNTRUE lacking any basis in fact or reality **2.** WEARING COSMETICS having applied cosmetics to the face **3.** ASSEMBLED completely put together and prepared

mad·house /mád hòwss/ (*plural* **-hous·es** /-zəz/) *n.* **1.** OFFENSIVE TERM an offensive term for hospital or residential facility for people who have psychiatric disorders (*offensive*) **2.** SCENE OF CHAOS OR CONFUSION a place where there is much noise and activity and little order or control (*informal*) (*sometimes considered offensive*)

Mad·i·son /máddissən/ **1.** river in southwestern Montana, joining the Gallatin and Jefferson rivers to form the Missouri River. Length: 180 mi./241 km. **2.** capital city of Wisconsin, situated in the south central part of the state. Population: 194,586 (1994). **3.** town in southern Connecticut. Population: 15,485 (1990). **4.** city in northern New Jersey. Population: 15,763 (1994).

Library of Congress

James Madison

Mad·i·son, James (1751–1836) U.S. statesman and 4th president of the United States. He played a leading role in the Constitutional Convention (1787), and enjoyed two terms as president (1809–17).

Mad·i·son Av·e·nue *n.* the center of the U.S. advertising and public-relations industries, or the U.S. advertising industry itself [Named for the street in New York that is the center of the advertising industry]

mad·ly /máddlee/ *adv.* **1.** INTENSELY with an extraordinary degree of intensity or devotion **2.** WILDLY in a wild and uncontrolled way **3.** TO NO PURPOSE with great haste or activity but without accomplishing much **4.** WILDLY wildly and with intense emotion **5.** RASHLY in a rash or thoughtless way **6.** WITH SIGNS OF MENTAL DISTRESS like somebody who is affected by a psychiatric disorder

mad·man /mád màn, -mən/ (*plural* **-men** /-mèn, -mən/) *n.* an offensive term for a man with a psychiatric disorder (*offensive*)

mad mon·ey *n.* a small amount of money set aside for some unlikely occurrence or for frivolous self-indulgence (*informal*)

mad·ness /mádnəss/ *n.* **1.** OFFENSIVE TERM offensive term for psychiatric disorder (*offensive*) **2.** RASHNESS rash or thoughtless behavior **3.** ANGER great anger or fury **4.** EXCITEMENT great enthusiasm or excitement

Madonna

Ma·don·na /mə dónnə/ (*b.* 1959) U.S. pop singer and actor. Her career, which started in the early 1980s, shows an ability to change her style and image ahead of current trends. Full name **Madonna Louise Veronica Ciccone**

Barnaby's

Madonna: Byzantine mosaic, Athens, Greece

Ma·don·na /mə dónnə/ *n.* **1.** VIRGIN MARY the Virgin Mary, mother of Jesus Christ **2. Ma·don·na, madonna** IMAGE OF VIRGIN MARY a picture, statue, or other artistic representation of the Virgin Mary **3.** SPIRITUAL SAINTLIKE WOMAN a woman portrayed as exhibiting characteristics such as saintliness, patience, or spirituality (*informal*) [Late 16thC. From obsolete Italian *ma donna* "my lady" from Latin *mea domina* (source of Madam).]

Ma·don·na lil·y *n.* an eastern Mediterranean plant widely cultivated for its white trumpet-shaped flowers that produce an oil used in the making of perfume. Latin name: *Lilium candidum.* [Traditionally regarded as a symbol of purity, and often included in pictures of the Madonna]

mad·ras /máddrəss, mə drǎss/ *n.* **1.** STRONG FINE CLOTH a strong fine fabric of cotton or silk, often with a woven striped or checked design **2.** LIGHT CLOTH a light cotton or rayon fabric used to make curtains **3.** BRIGHTLY COLORED SCARF a scarf, handkerchief, or other article made from brightly colored cotton or silk [Early 19thC. Named for MADRAS in southeastern India, where the products were made.]

Mad·ras /mə drǎss/ former name for **Chennai**

mad·ra·sa /mə drássə/ *n.* a school for the study of Islamic religion and thought, especially the Koran [Mid-17thC. From Arabic, literally "place to study."]

mad·re·pore /máddrə pàwr/ *n.* a reef-building coral that lives in tropical waters. Genus: *Madreporaria.* [Mid-18thC. Via French or modern Latin from Italian *madrepora*, from *madre* "mother" and either *poro* "pore, tufa" (from late Latin *porus* "passageway, pore") or Latin *porus* "calcerous stone" (from Greek *poros*).] —**mad·re·po·ral** /máddrə páwrəl/ *adj.* —**mad·repo·ri·an** /-páwree ən/ *adj.* —**mad·re·por·ic** /-páwrik/ *adj.* —**mad·re·por·it·ic** /-pə ríttik/ *adj.*

mad·re·por·ite /màddrə páw rīt/ *n.* a porous plate in an echinoderm that takes in water to the vascular system [Early 19thC. From MADREPORE.]

Ma·drid /mə dríd/ capital and largest city of Spain, located in the center of the country. Population: 3,029,734 (1995).

mad·ri·gal /máddrig'l/ *n.* **1.** MUSIC ENGLISH PART SONG a song with parts for several usually unaccompanied voices that was popular in England in the 16th and 17th centuries **2.** MUSIC MEDIEVAL ITALIAN SONG a secular Italian song of the 13th and 14th centuries, written for two or three unaccompanied voices singing in harmony **3.** POETRY LYRIC POEM a short pastoral or love poem suitable for singing as a madrigal [Late 16thC. Via *Italian* from Latin *matricalis* literally "of the mother," but used in late Latin to mean "uncomplicated" , from *matrix* (see MATRIX). A madrigal was originally a simple unaccompanied song or poem.] —**mad·ri·ga·lesque** /màddrigə lésk/ *adj.* —**mad·ri·ga·li·an** /màddri gáylee ən/ *adj.* —**mad·ri·gal·ist** /máddrigəlist/ *n.*

ma·dri·lène /máddri lèn, màddri lén, máddri làyn, màddri láyn/, **ma·dri·lene** *n.* a clear soup flavored with tomato, usually served cold [Early 20thC. Via French from Spanish *madrileño* "of Madrid."]

ma·dro·ña /mə drṓnə/, **ma·dro·ño** /mə drṓ nō/ (*plural* **-ños**) *n.* a North American evergreen tree of the heath family, with smooth bark, shiny leathery leaves, white flowers, edible red berries, and wood often used to make furniture. Latin name: *Arbutus menziestii.* [Mid-19thC. From Spanish.]

mad tom *n.* a small North American freshwater catfish that has poisonous pectoral spines, a long adipose fin, and a rounded dorsal fin. It is common in the east central United States. Genus: *Noturus.* (*slang offensive*) [Short for "mad tom cat," since the fish inflicts nasty wounds with its poisonous spines]

Ma·du·ra /mə dóorə/ island in southwestern Indonesia, off the northeastern coast of Java. Population: 2,832,900 (1989). Area: 2,042 sq. mi./5,290 sq. km.

Ma·du·rai /məd yóorī/ historic city and pilgrimage center in southern India. Population: 951,696 (1991).

ma·du·ro /mə dóorō/ (*plural* **-ros**) *n.* a dark strong cigar [Late 19thC. From Spanish "ripe, mature."]

mad·wom·an /mád wòommən/ (*plural* **-en** /-wìmmin/) *n.* an offensive term for a woman with a psychiatric disorder (*offensive*)

mad·wort /mád wùrt, -wàwrt/ (*plural* **-worts** *or* **-wort**) *n.* a low-growing Eurasian herb of the borage family that has small blue flowers. Latin name: *Asperugo procumbens.* [Late 16thC. A translation of the modern Latin ALYSSUM "removing rabies" because the plant was believed to cure the bites of rabid dogs.]

Mae·ce·nas /mī seénəss/ (*plural* **-nas**) *n.* a rich patron of the arts (*literary*)

mael·strom /máylstrəm/ *n.* **1.** WHIRLPOOL an exceptionally large or violent whirlpool **2.** TURBULENT OR VIOLENT SITUATION a situation marked by confusion, turbulence, strong feelings, violence, or destruction [Late 17thC. From early modern Dutch, formed from *maalen* "to grind, whirl round" + *stroom* "stream."]

Mael·strom /máyl strəm/ marine whirlpool in northwestern Norway between two islands of the Lofoten Islands

mae·nad /meé nàd/ *n.* **1.** WOMAN MEMBER OF DIONYSIAN CULT in ancient Greece, a woman who belonged to the cult of Dionysus and took part in orgiastic rites **2.** WILDLY EXCITED WOMAN a woman affected by wild, uncontrollable emotion [Late 16thC. Via Latin from Greek *Mainad-*, stem of *Mainas*, from *mainesthai* "to rave."] —**mae·nad·ic** /mee náddik/ *adj.* —**mae·nad·i·cal·ly** /-kəlee/ *adv.* —**mae·nad·ism** /meénə dìzzəm/ *n.*

ma·es·to·so /mī stṓ sṓ/ *adv.* AT STATELY TEMPO in a dignified or majestic manner (*used as a musical direction*) ■ *n.* (*plural* **-sos**) MAESTOSO PIECE OF MUSIC a section of a piece of music played maestoso [Early

18thC. Via Italian, literally "majestic," ultimately from Latin *majestas* "majesty" (see MAJESTY).] —**ma·es·to·so** *adj.*

maes·tro /mī́strō/ (*plural* **-tros** *or* **-tri** /mī́stree/) *n.* somebody who is regarded as an expert in an art or skill, especially a skilled or distinguished musician, conductor, composer, or music teacher [Early 18thC. Via Italian, literally "master," from Latin *magister* (source of English *magistrate*).]

maes·tro di cap·pel·la /-dee kə péllə/ (*plural* **maes·tri di cap·pel·la**) *n.* formerly, somebody in charge of a group of musicians, especially a chapel choir or the private orchestra of a royal court or noble household, especially in 17th century Italy ["di capella" Italian "of the chapel"]

Mae West /may wést/, **mae west** *n.* (*informal*) **1. INFLATABLE LIFE JACKET** an inflatable life jacket, especially one issued to U.S. pilots during World War II **2. PARACHUTE MALFUNCTION** a parachute malfunction in which a suspension line goes over the top of the canopy, creating what appears to be a huge brassiere [Mid-20thC. So called because the shape of the inflated jacket reminded airmen of the large bosom of Mae WEST.]

maf·fick·ing /máffiking/ *n. U.K.* a boisterous and extravagant public celebration (*archaic*) [Early 20thC. A playful coinage based on MAFEKING, following the wild celebrations when news of the relief of the town, which had been beseiged during the Boer War, reached London in 1900 (see MAFIKENG).] —**maf·fick** *vi.* —**maf·ficker** *n.*

Ma·fi·a /maáfee ə, máffee ə/ *n.* **1. CRIMINAL ORGANIZATION** a secret criminal organization originating in Sicily that spread to mainland Italy and the United States and is involved in international drug-dealing, racketeering, gambling, and prostitution **2. ma·fi·a, Ma·fi·a MUTUALLY SUPPORTIVE CLIQUE** a close-knit or influential group of people who work together and protect one another's interests or the interests of a particular person [Mid-19thC. From the Sicilian dialect of Italian, "bragging, blustering, boldness" especially of the type shown by the Mafia.]

maf·ic /máffik/ *adj.* relating to or being a dark-colored igneous group of minerals that have a high magnesium and iron content [Early 20thC. Coined from MAGNESIUM + FERRIC.]

Maf·i·keng /máffi kèng/ town in north central South Africa, formerly known as Mafeking. Population: 6,900 (1994).

Ma·fi·o·so /maàfee ṓssō, maàfee ṓzō/ (*plural* **-si** /maàfee ṓssee, maàfee ṓzee/ *or* **-sos**), **ma·fi·o·so** *n.* a member of the Mafia [Late 19thC. From Italian, formed from *mafia* (see MAFIA).]

mag /mag/ *n.* PUBL = **magazine** *n.* 1 (*informal*) [Early 19thC. Shortening.]

mag. *abbr.* **1.** PUBL magazine **2.** magnesium **3.** magnet **4.** magnetic **5.** magnetism **6.** magnitude **7.** magnum

mag·a·zine /mággə zeén/ *n.* **1.** PUBL **PERIODICAL PUBLICATION** a publication issued at regular intervals, usually weekly or monthly, containing articles, stories, photographs, advertisements, and other features, with a page size that is usually smaller than that of a newspaper but larger than that of a book **2.** *U.K.* BROADCAST, TV **PROGRAM CONTAINING ASSORTED ITEMS** a television or radio program made up of an assortment of short factual items, often of interest to a particular group of people **3.** ARMS **BULLET OR CARTRIDGE HOLDER** a detachable container for cartridges or bullets that can be quickly inserted or removed from a gun **4.** MIL **STOREHOUSE FOR MILITARY SUPPLIES** a structure on land or a part of a ship where weapons, ammunition, explosives, and other military equipment or supplies are stored **5.** ARMS **STOCK OF AMMUNITION** a stock of ammunition or other supplies kept in a storehouse **6.** PHOTOGRAPHY **SLIDE HOLDER** a container designed to hold a number of photographic slides and feed them automatically through a projector **7.** PHOTOGRAPHY **LIGHT-TIGHT FILM CONTAINER** a container that is used for loading film into a camera without exposing it to light **8. SUPPLY DEVICE** a device or container attached to a machine that holds or supplies necessary material [Late 16thC. Via French *magazin* from Italian *magazzino*, from Arabic *makzan* "storehouse." The sense "periodical publication" developed by way of the idea of a storehouse of information.]

Mag·da·le·na /màgdə láynə/ major river of Colombia. It flows north from the Andes into the Caribbean Sea. Length: 960 mi./1,540 km.

Mag·da·lene /mágdələn, mágdə leén/ *n.* = **Mary Magdalene**

Mag·de·burg /mágdə burg/ capital of Madgeburg District, Saxony-Anhalt State, north central Germany. Population: 269,500 (1994).

Ma·gel·lan, Strait of /mə géllən-/ channel between the southernmost tip of the South American mainland and the island of Tierra del Fuego

Ma·gel·lan /mə géllən/, **Ferdinand** (1480?–1521) Portuguese explorer. He was the first person to circumnavigate the earth, and the first European to cross the Pacific Ocean.

Mag·el·lan·ic Cloud /màjjə lánnik-/ *n.* either of two small galaxies near the south celestial pole that are irregularly shaped and closest to the Milky Way [Early 17thC. Named for Ferdinand MAGELLAN, whose crew discovered them during the first voyage around the world.]

Ma·gen Da·vid /maágən dáyvid/, **Mo·gen Dovid** *n.* = **Star of David** [From Hebrew literally "shield of David"]

ma·gen·ta /mə jéntə/ *n.* **1.** COLORS **PURPLISH-PINK** a brilliant purplish-pink color that, together with cyan and yellow, is one of the three primary colors used in printing and photographic processing **2.** CHEM = **fuchsin** ■ *adj.* COLORS **OF PURPLISH-PINK** brilliant purplish-pink in color [Mid-19thC. Named for Magenta in Northern Italy where a major battle was fought shortly before the discovery of the dye.]

mag·gid /maágid/ (*plural* **-gid·im** /maa geédim/) *n.* a popular teacher traveling among the Ashkenazi Jewish communities of Eastern Europe [Late 19thC. From Hebrew *maggīḏ* "narrator."]

mag·gio·re /maa jṓ rày/ *n.* a section of a fugue or set of variations in the major mode that occurs especially after a section in a minor [Late 19thC. From Italian, "major."]

Mag·gio·re, Lake /mə jáwree/ lake that lies partly in the Ticino Canton, Switzerland, and partly in the Lombardy Region of northern Italy. Area: 82 sq. mi./212 sq. km.

mag·got /mággət/ *n.* **1. INSECT LARVA** the worm-shaped larva of any of various members of the fly family, e.g., the housefly, found in decaying matter and used as bait in fishing **2. SOMEBODY DESPICABLE** a name for somebody who is despised (*insult slang*) **3. FANCY** a fanciful notion or idea (*archaic*) [14thC. Possibly from earlier maddock "worm, maggot," ultimately from a prehistoric Germanic word.]

mag·got·y /mággətee/ (**-i·er, -i·est**) *adj.* full of or containing maggots

Mag·ha *n.* INDIAN RELIG in the Hindu calendar, the 11th month of the year, made up of 29 or 30 days and falling in approximately January to February [Late 20thC. From Hindi.]

Ma·ghreb /múgrəb/, **Ma·ghrib** loosely defined region in northwestern Africa, centered on Algeria, Morocco, and Tunisia

ma·gi plural of **magus**

Ma·gi /máy jī, májjī/ *npl.* in the Bible, the three wise men, known as Caspar, Melchior, and Balthazar, who came to Bethlehem from the east to celebrate the birth of Jesus Christ. (Matthew 2: 1–12). [Plural of MAGUS] —**Ma·gi·an** /máyjee ən, máyjən/ *adj., n.* —**Ma·gi·an·ism** /-jə nìzzəm/ *n.*

mag·ic /májjik/ *n.* **1. CONJURING TRICKS** conjuring tricks and illusions that make apparently impossible things seem to happen, usually performed as entertainment **2. INEXPLICABLE THINGS** a special, mysterious, or inexplicable quality, talent, or skill ○ *watched the dancer's feet work their magic* **3. SUPPOSED SUPERNATURAL POWER** a supposed supernatural power that makes impossible things happen, or that gives somebody control over the forces of nature. Magic is used in many cultures for healing, keeping away evil, seeking the truth, and for vengeful purposes. **4. PRACTICE OF MAGIC** the use of supposed supernatural power to make impossible things happen ■ *adj.* **1. OF OR FOR MAGIC** relating to magic or used in the working of magic ○ *a magic potion* **2. PARTICULARLY IMPORTANT** particularly important or desirable ○ *reach the magic figure of 100 points* ■ *vt.* (**-icked, -ick·ing, -ics**) **SUBJECT SOMETHING TO MAGIC** to make somebody or something seem to appear, disappear, change, or move by using magic [14thC. Via Old French *magique* from, ultimately, Greek *magikē*, which in turn was formed, ultimately, from *magos* (see MAGUS).] ◇ **like magic 1.** inexplicably, as though by magic **2.** rapidly **3.** without obstacles or difficulties

WORD KEY: CULTURAL NOTE

The Magic Mountain, a novel by German writer Thomas Mann (1924). It describes young engineer Hans Castorp's lengthy stay in a Swiss TB clinic. The clinic is a microcosm of European society at the time of World War I, with a cosmopolitan group of patients reflecting a range of contemporary political, philosophical, and scientific viewpoints.

mag·i·cal /májjik'l/ *adj.* **1. APPARENTLY PRODUCED BY MAGIC** made or created by or as if by magic **2. WONDERFUL** so beautiful or pleasing as to seem supernaturally created —**mag·i·cal·ly** *adv.*

mag·i·cal re·al·ism *n.* = **magic realism**

mag·ic bul·let *n.* **1. MIRACLE DRUG** a drug that cures a serious disease with no undesirable side effects on the patient **2. EASY SOLUTION** a quick and easy solution for a difficult problem, or a means of accomplishing the impossible

mag·ic car·pet *n.* in fairy stories, a carpet that flies through the air and is used as a form of transportation

ma·gi·cian /mə jísh'n/ *n.* **1. CONJURER OR ILLUSIONIST** an entertainer who performs conjuring tricks and illusions **2. SOMEBODY WHO SUPPOSEDLY PRACTICES SORCERY** somebody who uses supposed supernatural powers to perform magic **3. SOMEBODY WITH EXCEPTIONAL ABILITY** somebody who has extraordinary skill, power, or ability

Mag·ic Mark·er *tdmk.* a trademark for a highlighting pen that comes in various colors of ink

mag·ic mush·room *n.* a fungus that contains a hallucinogenic substance (*informal*)

mag·ic num·ber *n.* any of the numbers 2, 8, 20, 28, 50, 82, and 126 that represent the number of protons or neutrons in very stable atomic nuclei

mag·ic re·al·ism, **mag·i·cal re·al·ism** *n.* a style of art or literature that depicts fantastic or mythological subjects in a realistic manner —**mag·ic re·al·ist** *n.*

5	0	7
6	4	2
1	8	3

Magic square

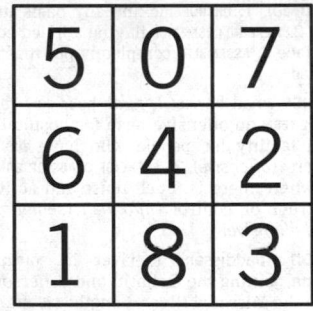

mag·ic square *n.* a square containing rows and columns of numbers arranged in such a way that each horizontal, vertical, and diagonal line has the same sum

mag·ic wand *n.* **1. STICK USED BY MAGICIAN** a small thin stick used by a sorcerer or conjurer while performing magic **2. SOMETHING ABLE TO WORK WONDERS** something fanciful or make-believe that would, if it existed, be able to solve a difficult or impossible problem immediately

Ma·gi·not line /mázhə nō-, maázhə nṓ-/ *n.* **1. FORTIFICATIONS ON FRANCO-GERMAN BORDER** a line of fortifications constructed by the French along the border between France and Germany before World War II that failed to stop the German army from invading **2. INEFFECTIVE DEFENSE** an ineffective defensive strategy that is relied on with unthinking confidence [Mid-20thC. Named for André *Maginot* (1877–1932) who was French Minister of War when it was built.]

mag·is·te·ri·al /màjjə steéree əl/ *adj.* **1. DIGNIFIED** showing great authority and dignity **2. DOMINEERING** behaving in an overbearing or dictatorial way **3. MASTERLY AND AUTHORITATIVE** produced by or characteristic of a teacher, scholar, or expert **4. OF MAGISTRATE** relating to or characteristic of a magistrate [Early 17thC] —**mag·is·te·ri·al·ly** *adv.* —**mag·is·te·ri·al·ness** *n.*

mag·is·te·ri·um /màjji steeree əm/ *n.* the authority of the church in the Roman Catholic tradition to teach religious doctrine [Late 16thC. From Latin, formed from *magister* "master" (source of English *magistrate*).]

mag·is·tra·cy /májjistrəsee/ (*plural* **-cies**) *n.* **1.** OFFICE OF MAGISTRATE the position or function of a magistrate **2.** MAGISTRATE'S TERM OF OFFICE the term of office of a magistrate **3.** AREA OF MAGISTRATE'S JURISDICTION the district over which a magistrate has the power and authority to administer justice **4.** MAGISTRATES COLLECTIVELY magistrates considered as a group

mag·is·tral /májjistrəl/ *adj.* **1.** OF MAGISTRATE relating to or characteristic of a magistrate **2.** OF EXPERT relating to or characteristic of an expert or scholar **3.** PRINCIPAL OR DETERMINING used to describe a line of fortifications that determines the position of other lines ■ *n.* MAGISTRAL LINE OF FORTIFICATIONS a line of fortifications that determines the position of other lines —**mag·is·tral·i·ty** /màjji strállətee/ *n.* —**mag·is·tral·ly** /májjistrəlee/ *adv.*

mag·is·trate /májji stràyt, májjistrət/ *n.* **1.** LOWER COURT JUDGE a judge in a lower court whose jurisdiction is limited to the trial of misdemeanors and the conduct of preliminary hearings on more serious charges **2.** LOCAL LAW OFFICER a minor law officer or member of a local judiciary with extremely limited powers, e.g., a justice of the peace who deals with moving vehicular violations [14thC. From Latin *magistratus*, formed in turn from *magister* "master" (source of English *mister* and *master*).] —**mag·is·trate·ship** *n.*

mag·lev /mág lèv/, **Mag·lev** *n.* an electrically operated high-speed train that glides above a track by means of a magnetic field **(magnetic levitation)** [Late 20thC. A blend of MAGNETIC and LEVITATION.]

mag·ma /mágmə/ (*plural* **-mas** *or* **-ma·ta** /mag maátə/) *n.* **1.** GEOL MOLTEN ROCK molten rock deep within the earth from which igneous rock is formed by solidification at or near the earth's surface **2.** CHEM PASTE OR SUSPENSION a soft paste or thick suspension made from fine solid particles mixed with liquid [15thC. Via Latin from Greek, formed from *massein* "to knead"; the underlying idea being of a mixture kneaded together.] —**mag·mat·ic** /mag máttik/ *adj.*

mag·ma cham·ber *n.* an underground cavity that contains magma, often located below a volcano

Mag·na Car·ta /màgnə kaártə/, **Mag·na Char·ta** *n.* **1.** CHARTER GRANTING RIGHTS charter establishing the rights of English barons and free citizens, granted by King John at Runnymede in 1215 and regarded as the basis of civil and political liberty in England **2.** DOCUMENT ACKNOWLEDGING RIGHTS a document that recognizes or guarantees rights, privileges, or liberties [From Latin literally "great charter"]

mag·na cum lau·de /màgnə kum lówdə, -lówdee/ *adv., adj.* at the second of three levels of commendation for those who achieve excellent grades in coursework, especially graduates of North American universities and colleges that have honors programs involving theses. ◊ **cum laude, summa cum laude** [From Latin, literally "with great praise"]

Mag·na Grae·cia /màgnə greéshə/ *n.* in ancient times, the parts of southern Italy and Sicily that contained numerous Greek colonies [From Latin, literally "great Greece"]

mag·na·nim·i·ty /màgnə nímmətee/ (*plural* **-ties**) *n.* **1.** NOBLE-SPIRITEDNESS great generosity or noble-spiritedness **2.** NOBLE-SPIRITED ACT a generous or noble-spirited act [14thC. Via French *magnanimité* from Latin *magnanimitas*, from *magnanimus* (see MAGNANIMOUS).]

mag·nan·i·mous /mag nánnəməss/ *adj.* very generous, kind, or forgiving [Late 16thC. From Latin *magnanimus*, formed from *magnus* "great" and *animus* "mind."] —**mag·nan·i·mous·ly** *adv.* —**mag·nan·i·mous·ness** *n.*

WORD KEY: SYNONYMS

See Synonyms at ***generous***.

mag·nate /mág nàyt, mágnət/ *n.* somebody who has a lot of wealth and power, especially somebody in business or industry [15thC. From late Latin *magnat-*, stem of *magnas*, from Latin *magnus* "great."] —**mag·nate·ship** *n.*

mag·ne·sia /mag neézhə, mag neéshə/ *n.* CHEM = **magnesium oxide** [14thC. Via medieval Latin from Greek *magnēsia* "mineral from Magnesia" in Asia Minor (source of English *magnet*.)] —**mag·ne·sial** /mag neézh'l, mag neésh'l/ *adj.* —**mag·ne·sian** /-neézh'n, -neésh'n/ *adj.* —**mag·ne·sic** /-neéssik/ *adj.*

mag·ne·site /mágnə sìt/ *n.* a white or colorless magnesium carbonate that occurs naturally and is used in making refractories and as a source of magnesium oxide [Early 19thC. From MAGNESIA.]

mag·ne·si·um /mag neézee əm/ *n.* a light silver-white metallic element that occurs naturally in compounds and is used in alloys, metallurgy, photography, and fireworks. Symbol **Mg** [Early 19thC. From MAGNESIA.]

mag·ne·si·um car·bon·ate *n.* a white crystalline salt found naturally as dolomite and magnesite and used in antacids, glass, and refractories. Formula: $MgCO_3$.

mag·ne·si·um hy·drox·ide *n.* a white crystalline powder used as an antacid and laxative. Formula: $Mg(OH)_2$.

mag·ne·si·um ox·ide *n.* a white powder found naturally as periclase and used as an antacid and laxative and in refractories, cements, electrical insulation, and fertilizers. Formula: MgO.

mag·ne·si·um sul·fate *n.* a colorless crystalline salt used in medicine, fertilizers, and various manufacturing processes. Formula: $MgSO_4$.

mag·net /mágnət/ *n.* **1.** PIECE OF METAL THAT ATTRACTS METAL a piece of metal, often bar-shaped or U-shaped, that has the power to draw iron or steel objects toward it and to hold or move them **2.** ELECTROMAGNET an electromagnet **3.** SOURCE OF GREAT ATTRACTION somebody or something that has a great power of attraction over people [15thC. Directly or via Old French *magnete*, from Latin *magnete*, from Greek *Magnēs lithis* "stone from Magnesia," an ancient city in Asia Minor at which magnetic stone was mined.]

mag·net·ic /mag néttik/ *adj.* **1.** HAVING POWER OF MAGNET able to attract iron or steel objects **2.** ABLE TO BE MAGNETIZED able to be magnetized, or able to be attracted by a magnet **3.** RELATING TO MAGNETISM relating to, involving, or produced by magnetism **4.** USING MAGNET OR MAGNETISM containing or using a magnet or magnetism **5.** POWERFULLY CHARMING having a great power of attraction over people ○ *a magnetic personality* **6.** OF EARTH'S MAGNETISM relating to the Earth's magnetism ○ *magnetic North Pole* —**mag·net·i·cal·ly** *adv.*

mag·net·ic bot·tle *n.* a strong magnetic field used to confine plasma in nuclear fusion experiments

mag·net·ic bub·ble *n.* a small movable magnetic region in a thin film of magnetic material, used to store data in computer memory

mag·net·ic com·pass *n.* an instrument used to indicate magnetic north and other directions, containing a magnetic needle that swings horizontally around a circle marked in degrees or with the points of the compass

mag·net·ic dec·li·na·tion *n.* the angle between magnetic north and true north at a particular point on the Earth's surface

mag·net·ic disk *n.* COMPUT a computer disk consisting of one or more thin magnetically etched plates

mag·net·ic ep·och *n.* a long period of geological time between reversals of the earth's magnetic field

mag·net·ic e·qua·tor *n.* an imaginary line that lies near the geographical equator and passes through all points where a magnetic needle has no dip

mag·net·ic field *n.* a region of space surrounding a magnetized body or current-carrying circuit in which the resulting magnetic force can be detected

mag·net·ic flux *n.* the strength of a magnetic field represented by lines of force. Symbol Θ

mag·net·ic flux den·si·ty *n.* the strength of a magnetic field multiplied by the porosity of a medium, measured in teslas or gauss. Symbol *B*

mag·net·ic head *n.* an electromagnetic device to read, write, or erase data on a magnetic medium

mag·net·ic in·duc·tion *n.* = **magnetic flux density**

mag·net·ic lev·i·ta·tion *n.* a system of high speed rail travel using magnetism both to suspend and to propel trains above and along the track. ◊ **maglev**

mag·net·ic me·rid·i·an *n.* an imaginary line around the Earth's surface that passes through both magnetic poles

mag·net·ic mine *n.* an underwater mine equipped with magnetic sensors that cause it to detonate when a large metal object, usually a ship, passes into its magnetic field

mag·net·ic mir·ror *n.* = **magnetic bottle**

mag·net·ic mo·ment *n.* a vector quantity representing the torque experienced by a magnetic system in a magnetic field. Symbol *m*

mag·net·ic nee·dle *n.* thin bar of magnetized metal used in navigational instruments, mounted or suspended so that it swings freely in a horizontal circle and indicates the direction of the Earth's magnetic poles

mag·net·ic north *n.* the direction of the north magnetic pole, indicated by the needle of a magnetic compass

mag·net·ic pole *n.* **1.** END OF A MAGNET either of the two points at the end of a magnet where the magnet's field is most intense **2.** REGION NEAR A GEOGRAPHIC POLE either of the two regions on the Earth's surface near the geographic poles where the Earth's magnetic field is most intense

mag·net·ic re·cord·ing *n.* **1.** STORING DATA ON A MAGNETIZED MEDIUM the storage of analog or digital data on a magnetized medium, e.g., audio, video or computer data on tape, disk, or cards **2.** SURFACE CONTAINING A MAGNETIC RECORDING a surface on which information has been magnetically recorded

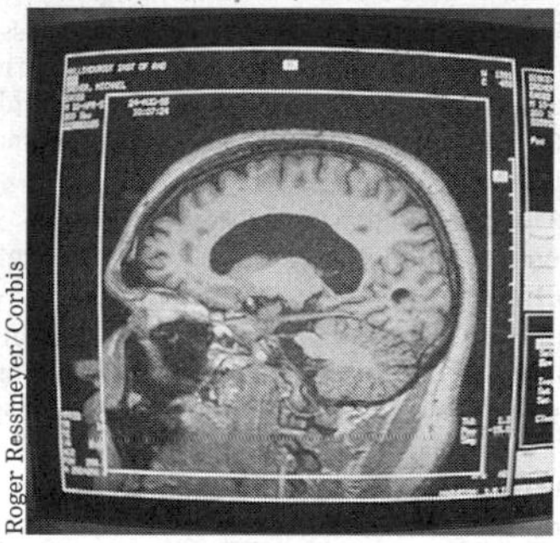

Roger Ressmeyer/Corbis

Magnetic resonance imaging of human head

mag·net·ic res·o·nance im·ag·ing *n.* an imaging technique, useful in diagnosing certain diseases, that uses electromagnetic radiation to obtain images of the body's soft tissues, e.g., the brain and spinal cord. The body is subjected to a powerful magnetic field, allowing tiny signals from atomic nuclei to be detected and then processed and converted into images by a computer.

mag·net·ic storm *n.* a disturbance in the Earth's magnetic field associated with charged particles from solar flares and sunspot activity

mag·net·ic stripe, **mag·net·ic strip** *n.* a strip of magnetic medium on a plastic card such as a credit card, encoded with information

mag·net·ic sus·cep·ti·bil·i·ty *n.* a number that characterizes the magnetization of a substance when it is subjected to a magnetic field

mag·net·ic tape *n.* a thin ribbon of material, usually plastic, coated with iron oxide and used to record sounds, images, or data. It is the tape used in audio and video cassettes, and on computers with tape drives.

mag·net·ic tran·si·tion tem·per·a·ture *n.* = **Curie point**

mag·net·ic var·i·a·tion *n.* = **magnetic declination**

mag·net·ism /mágnə tìzzəm/ *n.* **1.** PHYS ATTRACTION OF MAGNETS FOR IRON the phenomenon of physical attraction for iron, inherent in magnets or induced by a moving electric charge or current **2.** PHYS MAGNETIC FIELD FORCE the force exerted by a magnetic field **3.** ATTRACTION the strong attractiveness of something, e.g., the power of somebody's personality to influence others ○ *"He was a born boon companion, with a magnetism which drew good humor from all around him."* (Arthur Conan Doyle, *The Valley of Fear*; 1915)

mag·net·ite /mágnə tìt/ *n.* a common black magnetic mineral consisting of iron oxide. It is an important ore of iron. Formula: Fe_3O_4.

mag·net·ize /mágnə tìz/ (**-ized, -iz·ing, -iz·es**) *v.* **1.** *vti.* PHYS **MAKE OR BECOME MAGNETIC** to become magnetic, or to make an object or material magnetic **2.** *vt.* **ATTRACT SOMEBODY STRONGLY** to hold a strong attraction for somebody ○ *prospectors magnetized by the possibility of finding gold in the hills* **—mag·net·iz·a·ble** *adj.* **—mag·net·i·za·tion** /màgnəti záysh'n/ *n.* **—mag·net·iz·er** *n.*

mag·ne·to /mag néetō/ (*plural* **-tos**) *n.* a small alternator that uses permanent magnets to generate a spark in an internal-combustion engine, especially in marine and aircraft engines [Late 19thC. Shortening of *magnetoelectric machine*.]

magneto- *prefix.* magnetic field ○ *magnetograph* [From MAGNET]

mag·ne·to·graph /mag néetō gràf/ *n.* an instrument used to record variations in a magnetic field, usually that of the Earth

mag·ne·to·hy·dro·dy·nam·ics /mag neetō hīdrō dī námmiks/ *n.* the study of magnetic and electric fields in relation to the movement of electrically conducting fluids, e.g., plasmas and molten metal (*takes a singular verb*) **—mag·ne·to·hy·dro·dy·nam·ic** *adj.*

mag·ne·tom·e·ter /màgnə tómmətər/ *n.* a device for measuring the direction and intensity of a magnetic field

mag·ne·to·mo·tive force /mag neetō mōtiv-/ *n.* a force that produces magnetic flux. Symbol F_m

mag·ne·ton /mágnə tòn/ *n.* a unit that expresses the combined force and direction of a magnetic field (**magnetic moment**), e.g., the magnetic field of an atom or elementary particle [Early 20thC. Coined from MAGNETIC + -ON.]

mag·ne·to·pause /mag néetə pàwz/ *n.* the region between the magnetosphere and outer space

mag·ne·to·sphere /mag néetō sfeer/ *n.* the region surrounding a celestial body, e.g., the Earth, in which charged particles are trapped and affected by the body's magnetic field **—mag·ne·to·spher·ic** /mag neetō sférrik, -sfeerik/ *adj.*

mag·ne·tron /mágnə tròn/ *n.* an vacuum tube in which the flow of electrons is manipulated by electric and magnetic fields to generate microwaves. The microwave radiation produced is either pulsed, for use in radar applications, or continuous, as required for microwave cooking. [Early 20thC]

mag·net school *n.* a public school specializing in a particular area, e.g., languages or technology, in addition to providing general education. It draws students from inside and outside the local area, and serves as a way of integrating the student population and of providing innovative or alternative education.

mag·nif·ic /mag níffik/, **mag·nif·i·cal** /-níffik'l/ *adj.* (*archaic*) **1. MAGNIFICENT** magnificent **2. BIG AND IMPOSING** large in size and impressive in appearance **3. USING IMPRESSIVE WORDS** using high-sounding vocabulary, often for effect [15thC. Directly, or via Old French *magnifique*, from Latin *magnificus*, literally "performing great actions," from *magnus* "great" (see MAGNIFY).] **—mag·nif·i·cal·ly** *adv.*

Mag·nif·i·cat /mag níffi kàyt/ *n.* **1. HYMN OF THE VIRGIN MARY** the Virgin Mary's hymn of praise to God, taken from and sung or chanted in church **2. HYMN OF PRAISE** any hymn of praise sung or chanted in church [12thC. From Latin, literally "(my soul) magnifies," a form of *magnificare* (see MAGNIFY), from the opening word of the Latin version.]

mag·ni·fi·ca·tion /màgnəfi káysh'n/ *n.* **1.** OPTICS **INCREASING OF APPARENT SIZE** the process of causing an object or image to appear larger than it really is, especially by using a lens or microscope **2. INCREASING OF ACTUAL SIZE** the process of increasing the size or magnitude of something **3. GROWTH IN IMPORTANCE** the increasing of the importance attributed to somebody or something **4.** OPTICS **DEGREE OF ENLARGEMENT** the amount by which an image is made bigger **5. ENLARGED COPY OF SOMETHING** a copy of a map, photograph, or other image that has been made larger than the original **6. RATIO** the size of the image of an object, expressed as a ratio of its actual size

mag·nif·i·cence /mag níffiss'nss/ *n.* **1. GREAT BEAUTY** the impressive beauty or grandeur of somebody or something **2. RICHNESS OF APPEARANCE** the great richness and splendor of somebody or something, usually indicating great wealth [14thC. Directly, or via Old French, from Latin *magnificentia*, from the stem *magnificent-* (see MAGNIFICENT).]

mag·nif·i·cent /mag níffiss'nt/ *adj.* **1. BEAUTIFUL** beautiful, impressive, and splendid in appearance ○ *a magnificent view of Rome from our balcony* **2. EXCEPTIONAL** exceptionally good of its kind **3. VERY GOOD** excellent (*informal*) ○ *The response to the appeal has been magnificent.* [15thC. Directly, or via Old French, from Latin *magnificent-*, stem of *magnificus*, literally "performing great actions," from *magnus* "great" (see MAGNIFY).] **—mag·nif·i·cent·ly** *adv.*

WORD KEY: CULTURAL NOTE

The Magnificent Ambersons, a film by director Orson Welles (1942). Based on a novel by Booth Tarkington, it is set in the U.S. Midwest during the industrial revolution and contrasts the declining fortunes of the upper-class Amberson family with the rise of a young entrepeneur. Despite suffering savage cuts at the hands of the studio, it is regarded as one of Welles's masterpieces.

mag·nif·i·co /mag níffikō/ (*plural* **-coes** *or* **-cos**) *n.* **1. MAGNATE** a rich or powerful person **2.** HIST **VENETIAN NOBLEMAN** a nobleman of the Venetian Republic [Late 16thC. From Italian, literally "magnificent."]

mag·ni·fy /mágnə fì/ (**-fied, -fy·ing, -fies**) *v.* **1.** *vt.* OPTICS **INCREASE THE APPARENT SIZE OF SOMETHING** to cause something to appear larger than it is, especially by using a microscope or lens ○ *a virus magnified 50,000 times* **2.** *vt.* **INCREASE THE ACTUAL SIZE OF SOMETHING** to increase the size or magnitude of something **3.** *vt.* **INCREASE THE IMPORTANCE OF SOMETHING** to increase the importance attributed to somebody or something ○ *The complexities of today's medicine only magnify the need for better hospital management.* **4.** *vt.* **OVERSTATE THE IMPORTANCE OF SOMEBODY OR SOMETHING** to cause somebody or something to appear more important than is in fact the case ○ *He tried to magnify his plight by complaining to the media about unfair stories.* **5.** *vi.* **HAVE AN ENLARGING ABILITY** to have the ability to increase the size or magnitude of something **6.** *vt.* RELIG **PRAISE GOD** to give praise or thanks to God (*formal*) ○ *"my heart doth magnify his holy name" (The Book of Mormon [part 1])* [14thC. Directly, or via Old French *magnifier*, from Latin *magnificare*, literally "to make greater," ultimately, from *magnus* "great" (source of English *major* and *maxim*).] **—mag·ni·fi·a·ble** *adj.* **—mag·ni·fi·er** *n.*

mag·ni·fy·ing glass *n.* a convex lens in a frame with a handle, used to make objects viewed through it appear larger

mag·nil·o·quent /mag níllәkwәnt/ *adj.* employing impressive words and an exaggeratedly solemn and dignifed style [Mid-17thC. Formed from Latin *magniloquus*, which in turn was coined from *magnus* "great" + *-loquus* "speaking."] **—mag·nil·o·quent·ly** *adv.* **—mag·nil·o·quence** *n.*

Mag·ni·to·gorsk /mag neetə gáwrsk/ city in southwestern Siberian Russia, on the Ural River. Population: 427,000 (1995).

mag·ni·tude /mágnə tood/ *n.* **1. GREATNESS OF SIZE** greatness of size, volume, or extent ○ *computing the magnitude of heavenly bodies* **2. IMPORTANCE** the importance or significance of something ○ *the magnitude of the discovery* **3. STATUS** great personal importance or status ○ *a person of her magnitude* **4.** GEOL **MEASURE OF EARTHQUAKE SIZE** a measure of the energy of an earthquake, specified on the Richter scale **5.** MATH **NUMBER ASSIGNED TO A MATHEMATICAL QUANTITY** a numerical value that describes the amount of something, usually expressed in terms of a multiple of standard units, or the item measured in this way **6.** ASTRON **BRIGHTNESS OF A CELESTIAL BODY** a numerical measure of the apparent brightness of a celestial body, on a scale in which a lower number represents greater brightness [14thC. From Latin *magnitudo*, from *magnus* "great" (see MAGNIFY).] **—mag·ni·tu·di·nous** /màgnə tood'nəss/ *adj.*

mag·no·lia /mag nṓlyə/ (*plural* **magnolia** *or* **mag·no·lias**) *n.* **1. FLOWERING TREE** any one of a group of evergreen or deciduous trees or shrubs that typically have large simple leaves and showy yellow, white, pink or green flowers. Native to North America and Asia, they are widely cultivated as ornamentals. Magnolias were among the first plants to have flowers, some 100 million years ago. Genus: *Magnolia.* **2. FLOWER** the flower of a magnolia **3.** COLORS **BEIGE** a creamy-white color [Mid-18thC. Named in honor of the French professor of botany Pierre *Magnol* (1638–1715).] **—mag·no·lia** *adj.*

mag·num[1] /mágnəm/ (*plural* **-nums**) *n.* **1. LARGE WINE BOTTLE** a wine bottle that holds approximately 1.5 liters, the equivalent of two normal bottles **2. CONTENTS OF MAGNUM** the volume of liquid contained in a magnum [Late 18thC. From Latin, a form of *magnus* "large."]

WORD KEY: ORIGIN

The Latin word *magnus*, from which **magnum** is derived, is also the source of English *magnanimous, magnate, magnificent, magnify,* and *magnitude.*

mag·num[2] /mágnəm/ *adj.* **WITH A LARGER CHARGE** used to describe firearms cartridges that have a larger charge and casing and are thus more high-powered than other gun cartridges of the same caliber ■ *n.* **POWERFUL GUN** a gun capable of shooting magnum cartridges

mag·num o·pus *n.* a great work of art or literature, especially the finest work produced by one individual [From Latin, "great work"]

Ma·gog *n.* ♦ **Gog and Magog**

ma·got /ma gṓ, mággət/ *n.* **1.** ZOOL **BARBARY APE** a Barbary ape **2.** SCULPTURE **CROUCHING FIGURINE** a crouching, often grotesque figurine in the Japanese or Chinese style [Early 17thC. From Old French *magos*, a kind of monkey, from *Magog* "Magog" (see GOG AND MAGOG), the biblical giant used as an emblem of ugliness in medieval romance.]

Magpie

mag·pie /mág pì/ *n.* **1.** BIRDS **CHATTERING BLACK-AND-WHITE BIRD** a gregarious bird of the crow family with vivid black-and-white plumage, a long wedge-shaped tail, and a chattering call. Genus: *Pica.* **2.** BIRDS **AUSTRALIAN BIRD** a large, widely distributed, black-and-white Australian bird with a melodious song. Latin name: *Gymnorhina tibicen.* **3. TALKATIVE PERSON** an incurable chatterer (*informal*) **4. AVID COLLECTOR** an enthusiastic or compulsive collector, especially of small objects (*informal*) [Late 16thC. From *Mag*, a shortening of the name *Margaret*, + PIE. It is not known why the "mag" part was added.]

M.Agr. *abbr.* Master of Agriculture

Ma·gritte /maa greet/, **René** (1898–1967) Belgian painter. A leading member of the Belgian surrealists, his work consists of strange juxtapositions of ordinary objects and parodies of famous paintings. Full name **René François Gislain Magritte**

Mag·say·say /maag sī sī/, **Ramon** (1907–57) Philippine statesman. He led the Huk Rebellion against Communist rule, and served as president of the Philippines (1953–57).

mag tape *n.* magnetic tape (*informal*)

ma·guey /ma gáy, mág wày/ *n.* **1. TROPICAL PLANT** any one of various plants cultivated in Mexico and other tropical regions for their fiber or as a source of an alcoholic drink called pulque. Genus: *Agave.* **2. FIBER** fiber from the stalks of maguey plants [Mid-16thC. Via Spanish from Taino.]

ma·gus /máygəss/ (*plural* **-gi** /máy jì/) *n.* **1. ZOROASTRIAN PRIEST** a priest in the ancient Persian religion of Zoroastrianism **2. MAN WITH MAGICAL POWERS** a man with supernatural or magical powers, especially in ancient times [Early 17thC. Via Latin from Greek *magos*, from Old Persian *maguš*.] **—ma·gi·an** /máyjee ən/ *adj.* **—ma·gi·an·ism** /-jee ə nìzzəm/ *n.*

WORD KEY: CULTURAL NOTE

The Magus, a novel by English writer John Fowles (1966). The plot concerns a young teacher, Nicholas Urfe, who takes a job on a Greek island and finds himself lured into an elaborate fiction staged by a wealthy resident, Maurice Conchis. Fowles uses this enigmatic story to explore the nature of individual identity and freedom of choice.

Ma·gus (*plural* **-gi**) *n.* BIBLE in the Bible, one of the men, traditionally three in number, who followed a star to Bethlehem to worship the baby Jesus Christ. They are often called the Three Wise Men or the Three Kings. (*literary*) ◊ **Caspar, Melchior, Balthazar**

Mag·yar /mág yaar, maag-/ (*plural* **-yars** *or* **-yar**) *n.* **1.** PEOPLES **MEMBER OF A HUNGARIAN PEOPLE** a member of the Hungarian people that forms the largest population group of Hungary **2.** LANG = **Hungarian** [Late 18thC. From Hungarian.] —**Mag·yar** *adj.*

Ma·hab·ha·ra·ta /mə haa baarətə/ *n.* one of India's two great national epic poems, written in Sanskrit from about 300 B.C. It tells of the great war in northern India between the Pandava and Kaurava families. The "Bhagavad-Gita" is the most important section of the Mahabharata. [Late 18thC. From Sanskrit, literally "the great history of the Bharata dynasty."]

Ma·ha·janga /maa zhaang/ port on the northwestern coast of Madagascar. Population: 100,807 (1993).

ma·ha·leb /maahə lèb/ *n.* a tree whose seeds are used in Middle Eastern cookery. It belongs to the rose family and is used as a grafting stock in the United States. Latin name: *Prunus mahaleb.* [Mid-16thC. Via French from Arabic *maḥaleb.*]

Ma·hal·lat al Ku·bra /mə haalə el kōbrə/ industrial city in the central Nile delta, northern Egypt. Population: 408,000 (1992).

Ma·han /mə hán/, **Alfred Thayer** (1840–1914) U.S. naval officer. He devised theories about naval power, published in *The Influence of Sea Power upon History 1660–1783* (1870).

ma·ha·ra·jah /maahə raajə, -raazhə/, **ma·ha·ra·ja** *n.* an Indian prince, higher in rank than a rajah, especially the ruler of one of the former Native States of India [Late 17thC. From Sanskrit, formed from *mahā* "great" + *rājān* "raja" (see RAJ).]

ma·ha·ra·ni /maahə raanee/ *n.* **1.** **MAHARAJAH'S WIFE** the wife of a maharajah **2.** **INDIAN PRINCESS** an Indian princess, higher in rank than a rani, especially the ruler of one of the former Native States of India [Mid-19thC. From Hindi, formed from Sanskrit *mahā* "great" + *rājñī.*]

Ma·ha·rash·tra /maa hə raashtrə/ state in western India, situated in the northwestern part of the Deccan plateau. Capital: Mumbai. Population: 85,865,000 (1994). Area: 118,799 sq. mi./307,690 sq. km.

ma·ha·ri·shi /maahə reeshee/ *n.* a Hindu religious teacher [Late 18thC. From Sanskrit *maharṣi* from *mahā* "great" + *ṛṣi* "inspired sage."]

ma·hat·ma /mə haatmə, -hát-/ *n.* in India, a title bestowed on somebody who is deeply revered for wisdom and virtue [Late 19thC. From Sanskrit *mahātman*, formed from *mahā* "great" + *ātman* "soul."]

Ma·ha·ya·na /maahə yaanə/ *n.* the branch of Buddhism that includes Tibetan, Chinese, and Zen Buddhism, developed around A.D. 1. It stresses compassion for all sentient beings and universal salvation. [Mid-19thC. From Sanskrit, formed from *mahā* "great" + *yanā* "vehicle."]

Mah·di /maadee/ *n.* **1.** In Islamic belief, a prophet or messiah who is expected to appear in the world sometime before it ends, somebody fulfilling a messianic role **2.** somebody fulfilling a messianic role [Early 19thC. From Arabic *al-mahdī*, literally "he who is rightly guided," from *hadā* "to lead in the right way."] —**Mah·dism** *n.* —**Mah·dist** *n.*

Ma·hé /moháy/ the largest island in the Republic of Seychelles, in the western Indian Ocean. Population: 59,500 (1987). Area: 57 sq. mi./148 sq. km.

Mah·fouz /maa fooz/, **Naguib** (*b.* 1911) Egyptian novelist and screenwriter. He is author of *The Cairo Trilogy* (1956–57) and other works that explore Egyptian society and culture.

Ma·hi·can /mə heekən/, **Mo·hi·can** /mō heekən/ *n.* **1.** PEOPLES **MEMBER OF A NATIVE AMERICAN CONFEDERACY** a member of a Native American confederacy of peoples formerly lived in the upper Hudson River Valley from the Catskill Mountains north to Lake Champlain. Their descendants live in Wisconsin and Oklahoma. **2.** LANGUAGE **MAHICAN LANGUAGE** the Algonquian language spoken by the Mahican people, belonging to the Algonquian-Wakashan group of Native American languages [Early 17thC. From Mahican *muhheakunneuw*, literally "people of the tidal water."] —**Ma·hi·can** *adj.*

ma·hi·ma·hi /maahee maahee/ *n.* an edible marine tropical fish that has a bright blue body and long dorsal fin. Latin name: *Coryphaena hippurus.* [From Hawaiian]

mah·jongg /maa zhóng, -jóng/, **mah·jong** *n.* a game of Chinese origin using 144 small tiles bearing various designs, played by four people around a square table. The winning player is the first one who completes a specified pattern using 13 tiles. [Early 20thC. From Chinese dialect *ma jiang*, literally "sparrows."]

Mah·ler /maalər/, **Gustav** (1860–1911) Czech-born Austrian composer and conductor. He is best known for his songs and large-scale orchestral works, many of them involving voices, as in *Das Lied von der Erde* (1908).

Mah·mud II /maa mood/ (1785–1839) Turkish national leader. He was the sultan of the Ottoman Empire (1808–39).

Mah·mud of Ghaz·ni /-gaaznee/ (971–1030) Afghan sultan. He developed Ghazni into a center of power and culture, through conquest.

ma·hog·a·ny /mə hóggənee/ (*plural* **-nies**) *n.* **1.** **TROPICAL HARDWOOD TREE** any one of several evergreen hardwood trees native to tropical America but widely cultivated for their red-brown wood. Genus: *Swietenia.* **2.** **REDDISH-BROWN HARDWOOD** the hard reddish-brown wood of any mahogany tree, used in the construction industry and for making furniture **3.** COLORS **REDDISH BROWN** a dark reddish-brown color [Mid-17thC. From obsolete Spanish *mahogani*, of uncertain origin: perhaps a Mayan language.] —**ma·hog·a·ny** *adj.*

ma·ho·nia /mə hōnee ə/ *n.* any one of various evergreen shrubs native to America and Asia that typically have spiny leaflets and clusters of small yellow flowers and are widely cultivated as ornamentals. Genus: *Mahonia.* ◊ **Oregon grape** [Early 19thC. Named for the U.S. botanist Bernard *McMahon* (1775–1816).]

ma·hout /mə hówt/ *n.* in South and Southeast Asia, somebody who trains, drives, and takes care of elephants [Mid-17thC. Via Hindi *mahāut* from Sanskrit *mahāmātra* "high official, elephant-keeper," from *mahā* "great" + *mātra* "measure."]

Mah·rat·ta *n.* = **Maratha**

Mah·rat·ti *n.* = **Marathi**

mah·zor /maakh zawr, maakh záwr/ (*plural* **-zor·im** /maakh záwrim, maakh zaw reem/), **mach·zor** (*plural* **-zor·im** *or* **-zors**) *n.* a Jewish prayer book that details the rituals prescribed for festivals and holidays [Mid-19thC. From Hebrew *maḥzōr.*]

maid /mayd/ *n.* **1.** **WOMAN SERVANT** a woman servant, e.g., one working in a hotel **2.** **YOUNG UNMARRIED WOMAN** a young unmarried woman (*archaic or literary*) (*sometimes considered offensive*) **3.** **UNMARRIED WOMAN** an unmarried woman past middle age (*often considered offensive*) **4.** **VIRGIN** a woman who has never had sexual intercourse (*archaic or literary*) [12thC. Shortening of MAIDEN.]

maid·en /máyd'n/ *n.* **1.** **YOUNG UNMARRIED WOMAN** a young unmarried woman (*sometimes considered offensive*) **2.** **VIRGIN** a woman who has never had sexual intercourse (*archaic or literary*) **3.** HIST **GUILLOTINE** in 16th and 17th-century Scotland, a guillotine used to execute criminals **4.** HORSERACING **HORSE YET TO WIN** a horse that has never won a race ■ *adj.* **1.** **FIRST** done for the very first time (*offensive in some contexts*) ○ *a maiden voyage* **2.** **UNTOUCHED** still in its original, unused, untouched, or unexplored condition (*literary*) (*offensive in some contexts*) **3.** HORSERACING **FOR HORSES YET TO WIN** for horses that have never won a race [Old English *mægden* from a prehistoric Germanic ancestor meaning "young woman"]

maid·en·hair fern /máyd'n hair-/ *n.* any one of various ferns with slender dark stems and delicate fronds of numerous leaflets. Native to warm moist regions worldwide, they are widely cultivated as ornamentals. Genus: *Adiantum.*

maid·en·hair tree *n.* = **ginkgo**

maid·en·head /máyd'n hèd/ *n.* (*literary*) **1.** **HYMEN** the hymen **2.** **VIRGINITY** a woman's virginity [13thC. Coined from MAIDEN + *-head*, a variant of HOOD.]

maid·en·hood /máyd'n hood/ *n.* the period of a woman's life before marriage or before becoming sexually active (*literary*) (*sometimes considered offensive*) [Old English]

maid·en·ly /máyd'nlee/ *adj.* of, like, or thought suitable for a maiden —**maid·en·li·ness** *n.*

maid·en name *n.* the former surname of a woman who has assumed her husband's surname

maid·hood /máyd hood/ *n.* maidenhood (*literary*) [Old English]

maid-in-wait·ing (*plural* **maids-in-wait·ing**) *n.* a young, usually unmarried lady-in-waiting

Maid Mar·i·an /mayd máiree ən/ *n.* in English legend, the beautiful young noblewoman loved by Robin Hood

maid of hon·or *n.* **1.** **BRIDE'S ATTENDANT** the bride's main unmarried honor attendant **2.** **ROYAL ATTENDANT** an unmarried woman of noble birth who attends a queen or princess

maid·ser·vant /máyd sùrvənt/ *n.* a woman servant, especially one working in a large private house (*archaic*)

Maid·u·gu·ri /màydo gooree/ city in Borno State, northeastern Nigeria. Population: 289,100 (1992).

ma·ieu·tic /may yootik, mī-/, **ma·ieu·ti·cal** /may ootik'l/ *adj.* PHILOS Socratic (*technical*) [Mid-17thC (Late 17thC.) From Greek *maieutikos*, literally "acting as midwife," ultimately, from *maia* "midwife"]

mai·gre /máygər, mégrə/ *adj.* CHR **1.** **CONTAINING NO FLESH** containing no meat and therefore suitable for eating on days when abstinence from meat is prescribed by the Roman Catholic Church **2.** **PRESCRIBED FOR ABSTINENCE FROM MEAT** used to describe a day when abstinence from meat is prescribed by the Roman Catholic Church [Late 17thC. From French, literally "lean."]

mail[1] /mayl/ *n.* **1.** **ITEMS SENT** the letters, cards, periodicals, and packages that are handled and distributed in a postal system ○ *Is there any mail for me?* **2.** **POSTAL SYSTEM** the system that handles the collection and delivery of mail (*often used before a noun*) ○ *send it by mail* **3.** **SPECIFIC MAIL COLLECTION OR DELIVERY** a particular collection or delivery of letters, cards, periodicals, and packages ○ *It came in yesterday's mail.* **4.** **VEHICLE DELIVERING MAIL** a car, train, ship, aircraft, or other vehicle used to collect and deliver mail **5.** COMPUT = **e-mail** ■ *vt.* (**mailed, mail·ing, mails**) **SEND SOMETHING BY MAIL** to send a letter, card, periodical, or package by mail [13thC. Via Old French *male* "bag, trunk" from a prehistoric Germanic word meaning "bag, wallet." Originally in the meaning of "bag," hence "letters carried in a bag."] —**mail·a·ble** *adj.*

mail[2] /mayl/ *n.* **1.** HIST **ARMOR** a kind of flexible armor made of interlocking metal rings or overlapping plates **2.** ZOOL **HARD BODY COVERING** the hard protective body covering of some animals, e.g., turtles and crabs ■ *vt.* (**mailed, mail·ing, mails**) **COVER THE BODY WITH MAIL** to cover or protect the body with mail ○ *a mailed torso* [13thC. Via French *maille* "mesh" from Latin *macula* "spot, holes in a net" (source of English *immaculate*).]

mail·bag /máyl bàg/ *n.* **1.** **BAG FOR TRANSPORTING MAIL** a bag used for transporting mail, typically a sack made of coarse material **2.** **MAIL CARRIER'S BAG** a large bag, usually with a shoulder strap, used by mail carriers **3.** **MAIL RECEIVED** mail received by a person or organization (*informal*) ○ *This week's mailbag is bursting with complaints about the schedule change.* [Early 19thC. From MAIL[1].]

mail·box /máyl bòks/ *n.* **1.** **PUBLIC COLLECTION BOX FOR MAILING LETTERS** a box in a public place where letters can be left for later collection by a mail carrier **2.** **BOX FOR RECEIVING MAIL** a container into which mail is delivered **3.** COMPUT **MESSAGE STORAGE FILE** an area of computer memory designated for messages, especially those sent by e-mail ○ *Your online mailbox is empty.* [Early 19thC. From MAIL[1].]

mail car·ri·er *n.* a post office employee who delivers mail to homes and businesses

mail·drop *n.* **1.** **CONTAINER FOR MAIL** a container into which delivered mail is placed **2.** **DELIVERY PLACE** a place where messages or packages can be left for later pickup by somebody else, often secretly and prearranged

mailed fist *n.* the threat of military force (*literary*) [*Mailed* from MAIL[2]]

mail·er /máylər/ *n.* **1.** **MAIL CONTAINER** a carton or tube for sending objects of a particular kind through the mail **2. MAIL SENDER** a person or organization that uses the postal system ○ *Mailers of valuables are advised to insure them.* **3. SOMEBODY WHO PREPARES MAIL** somebody whose job it is to address, stamp, weigh, and sort items for mailing **4. MACHINE THAT PREPARES MAIL** a machine that seals, stamps, and sorts letters into piles **5. ADVERTISEMENT** an advertising leaflet sent with a letter [Late 19thC. Formed from MAIL[1].]

Mail·er /máylər/, **Norman** (*b.* 1923) U.S. writer. A novelist and journalist, many of his works have been concerned with sociopolitical or popular cultural themes. *Armies of the Night* won the Pulitzer Prize (1968).

mail·ing /máyling/ *n.* **1. SOMETHING SENT BY MAIL** a letter, card, or package sent by mail ○ *send out a mailing advertising the service* **2. BATCH OF LETTERS** mail sent by one sender at one particular time ○ *a big mailing to her constituents in that county* ■ *adj.* **FOR MAIL** suitable for or associated with mail ○ *a mailing label* ○ *mailing costs* [Late 19thC. Formed from MAIL[1].]

mail·ing ad·dress *n.* an address to which mail can be delivered

mail·ing list *n.* a list, typically computerized, of names and addresses to which advertising material or information can be mailed

mail·lot /maa yṓ/ *n.* **1.** TEXTILES **STRETCHY FABRIC** a soft stretchable jersey fabric **2.** CLOTHES **LEOTARD OR TIGHTS** a leotard or a pair of tights made of maillot, worn for dancing or gymnastics **3.** CLOTHES **SWIMSUIT** a woman's one-piece bathing suit made of stretchy fabric, especially one with a high-cut leg **4. CLOSE-FITTING TOP** a tight-fitting knitted top or jersey [Late 19thC. From French, from Old French, "swaddling clothes," from *maille* "mesh" (see MAIL[2]).]

mailman /máyl màn, -mən/ (*plural* **mail·men** /-mèn, -mən/) *n.* a man who delivers mail [Late 19thC. From MAIL[1].]

mail merge *n.* the process of creating a series of individual documents on a computer by combining a list of different names and addresses with a single body of text

mail or·der *n.* **1. SELLING BY MAIL** a method of buying and selling goods by mail (*hyphenated before a noun*) ○ *a mail-order catalogue* **2. PURCHASE ORDER** an order for goods to be sent by mail

mail·room /máyl ròom, -rōōm/ *n.* a room in an organization where mail is sorted, prepared, and distributed [Late 19thC. From MAIL[1].]

mail slot *n.* a narrow opening in a door through which a mail carrier can push envelopes, cards, and periodicals [Mid-20thC. From MAIL[1].]

maim /maym/ (**maimed, maim·ing, maims**) *vt.* to inflict a severe and permanent wound on a person or animal, especially one that renders a limb unable to move ○ *maimed by a land mine* [14thC. From Old French *mahaignier* (source of English *mangle* and *mayhem*), of uncertain origin: perhaps, ultimately, from Germanic.]

main /mayn/ *adj.* **1. PRINCIPAL** greatest in size or importance ○ *the main reason we're here* **2. UTMOST** exerted to the full or the utmost ○ *main force* **3.** NAUT **OF A MAINMAST** on or relating to a sailing ship's mainmast ■ *n.* **1. LARGE PIPE OR CABLE** a large and important pipe or line for the distribution of water, gas, or electricity ○ *a ruptured water main* **2. SEA** the open sea (*archaic or literary*) **3. MAINLAND** the mainland (*archaic*) [Old English *mægen*, influenced by Old Norse *magn*, from a prehistoric Germanic word meaning "to have power," which is also the ancestor of English *may* and *might*] ◇ **in the main** largely or in general

Main /mīn, mayn/ river in south central Germany. Length: 307 mi./494 km.

main chance *n.* somebody's chief opportunity or best interest ○ *have an eye to the main chance*

main course *n.* the most substantial dish eaten at a meal with several courses

main drag *n.* the principal street of a town or city (*slang*)

Maine /mayn/ state in the northeastern United States, bordered by New Hampshire, Quebec and New Brunswick Provinces, Canada, and the Atlantic Ocean. Capital: Augusta. Population: 1,242,051 (1997). Area: 33,128 sq. mi./85,802 sq. km.

Maine coon, Maine coon cat *n.* a large, long-haired North American cat of a breed with a bold striped pattern, usually brown with black stripes

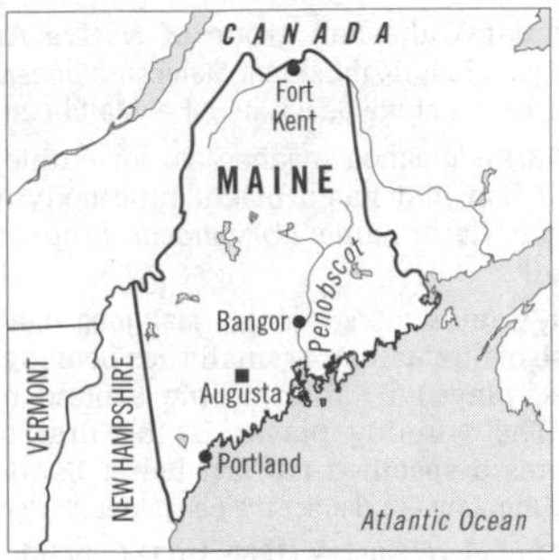

Maine

main·frame /máyn frày m/ *n.* a fast powerful computer with a large storage capacity that has a number of terminals for individual users connected to it

main·land /máynlənd, -lànd/ *n.* a continent's or country's principal landmass, as distinct from its islands and sometimes excluding peninsulas (*often used before a noun*) ○ *a ferry from the mainland* —**main·land·er** *n.*

main line *n.* **1.** RAIL **PRINCIPAL RAIL ROUTE** a major rail route between two cities, often joined by branch lines along its length **2.** DRUGS **PRINCIPAL VEIN** a major vein in the arm or leg into which drugs may be injected (*slang*)

main·line /máyn līn/ *vti.* (**-lined, -lin·ing, -lines**) (*slang*) **1.** DRUGS **TAKE DRUGS INTRAVENOUSLY** to inject an illicit drug, especially heroin or cocaine, intravenously **2. CONSUME EXCESSIVELY** to consume or be affected by something excessively ■ *adj.* **1. ESTABLISHED** well established, accepted, or mainstream ○ *mainline charitable organizations* **2.** RAIL **OF A MAIN RAIL LINE** situated on or relating to a main rail line ○ *a mainline station* —**main·lin·er** *n.* —**main·lin·ing** *n.*

main·ly /máynlee/ *adv.* to a large extent or in most cases ○ *bacteria that live mainly in the small intestine*

main man *n.* somebody's best, most trusted and respected man mentor or friend (*slang*)

main·mast /máyn màst, máynməst/ *n.* the principal mast on a sailing ship with more than one mast, usually either the foremost mast or the second from the bow

main mem·o·ry *n.* the random access memory of a computer, which executes instructions in real time

main·sail /máynsəl, máyn sàyl/ *n.* the largest and most important sail on a sailing ship

main se·quence *n.* a grouping of stars that consists of most of the known stars in the universe, represented on a graph of luminosity (**Hertzsprung-Russell diagram**) as a diagonal band

main·spring /máyn sprìng/ *n.* **1. SPRING IN A WATCH OR CLOCK** the largest and most important spring in the mechanism of a watch or clock **2. CHIEF REASON FOR ACTION** the driving or motive force behind something such as a course of action

main squeeze *n.* a current boyfriend or girlfriend (*slang*)

main·stay /máyn stày/ *n.* **1. CHIEF SUPPORT** somebody or something that plays the most important role in a particular group, place, or situation ○ *Tourism is the mainstay of the country's economy.* **2.** SAILING **ROPE SECURING SHIP'S MAINMAST** the strong rope that secures the mainmast on a sailing ship

main stem *n.* the principal waterway of a river, excluding its tributaries

main·stream /máyn strèem/ *n.* **MAIN CURRENT OF THOUGHT OR BEHAVIOR** the ideas, actions, and values that are most widely accepted by a group or society ○ *views well outside those of the mainstream* ■ *adj.* **REFLECTING THE NORM** reflecting the most widely accepted views of a nation or culture and therefore not exceptional, extreme, or avant-garde ○ *The scandal, previously ignored by the mainstream media, is now on the front pages.* ■ *vti.* (**-streamed, -stream·ing, -streams**) EDUC **ENROLL SPECIAL STUDENTS IN GENERAL CLASSES** to enroll students with physical challenges or learning difficulties in general school classes —**main·stream·er** *n.*

main·stream·ing /máyn strèeming/ *n.* EDUC the practice of educating special students in regular classes

main street *n.* the most important street in a small town

Main Street *n.* people living in small towns, considered as a group and often described as conservative and unsophisticated ○ *Main Street will never accept those fashions.*

main·tain /mayn táyn/ (**-tained, -tain·ing, -tains**) *v.* **1.** *vt.* **MAKE SOMETHING CONTINUE** to make a situation or course of action continue in the same way as before ○ *maintained a semblance of normal procedures even with half the staff out sick* **2.** *vt.* **KEEP SOMETHING IN WORKING ORDER** to ensure that something continues to work properly by checking it regularly and making repairs and adjustments if required ○ *gives years of service if maintained properly* **3.** *vt.* **PROVIDE SOMEBODY WITH FINANCIAL SUPPORT** to provide somebody with the money required for a reasonable standard of living ○ *She maintains a big family on a tight budget.* **4.** *vt.* **KEEP SOMEBODY ALIVE** to keep a person or animal alive by providing food and other basic necessities ○ *maintained the injured animal in a cage over the winter* **5.** *vt.* **DECLARE SOMETHING TO BE TRUE** to insist on the truth of something in the face of challenge or disbelief ○ *He maintains that she knew all along.* **6.** *vt.* **SPEAK IN FAVOR OF SOMETHING** to defend an opinion, idea, or argument against criticism ○ *The governor continues to maintain his position on cleaning up the environment.* **7.** *vt.* MIL **DEFEND A PLACE** to defend a place against physical attack ○ *The unit maintained its position in spite of heavy enemy shelling.* **8.** *vi.* **KEEP GOING** to continue in the present state or situation without losing control (*informal*) ○ *Until the reorganization is complete, we're maintaining, and that's about it.* [13thC. Via Old French *maintener*, from assumed late Latin *manutenere*, literally "to hold in the hand," from Latin *manus* "hand" (source of English *manual*).] —**main·tain·a·bil·i·ty** /mayn tàynə bíllətee/ *n.* —**main·tain·a·ble** *adj.* —**main·tain·er** *n.*

main·te·nance /máyntənənss/ *n.* **1. CONTINUING REPAIR WORK** work that is done regularly to keep a machine, building, or piece of equipment in good condition and working order (*often used before a noun*) ○ *We take the car in for maintenance every six months.* **2. CONDITION** working order ○ *a car in a poor state of maintenance* **3. MAINTAINING OF SOMETHING** the continuation or preservation of something ○ *behavior that threatens the maintenance of our security* **4. PROVISION OF FINANCIAL SUPPORT** the provision of enough money to provide the things necessary for a decent lifestyle, e.g., clothes, food, and a place to live ○ *responsible for the maintenance of two retired parents* **5. MEANS OF SUPPORT** the money that somebody has to pay for necessities such as food, clothing, and a place to live ○ *Family maintenance takes a big bite out of our budget.* **6.** LAW **INTERFERENCE IN LEGAL ACTION** improper or unlawful meddling in a lawsuit by a party typically with no legal standing in the matter

Mainz /mīnts/ historic city and river port in southwestern Germany, on the Rhine River. Population: 185,300 (1994).

ma·iol·i·ca *n.* = **majolica**

Mai·son·neuve /màyz on núrv, mèz oN núrv/, **Paul de Chomedey, Sieur de** (1612–76) French administrator. He was the founder of Montreal (1642) and the governor of Montreal Island (1642–65).

Mait·land /máytlənd/ city in eastern New South Wales, Australia, a center of coal mining, light industry, and agriculture. Population: 50,108 (1996).

mai·tre d' /màytrə dée/ *n.* a maitre d'hotel (*informal*)

mai·tre d'ho·tel /màytrə dō tél/ (*plural* **mai·tres d'ho·tel** /màytrə dō tél/) *n.* **1. HEADWAITER** a headwaiter in a restaurant or a hotel dining room **2. HEAD MAN SERVANT** the senior man servant in a large household [Mid-16thC. From French, literally "master of house."]

maize /mayz/ *n. U.K.* = **corn** [Mid-16thC. Directly, or via French *maïs*, from Spanish *maís*, from Taino *mahis*.]

Maj. *abbr.* Major

ma·jes·tic /mə jéstik/ *adj.* **1. IMPRESSIVE** greatly impressive in appearance ○ *a majestic seascape showing the masts of twenty tall ships under full sail* **2. DIGNIFIED** showing great dignity and grandeur ○ *a majestic inclination of the head* —**ma·jes·ti·cal·ly** *adv.*

maj·es·ty /májəstee/ *n.* **1. DIGNITY** a deeply impressive dignified quality ○ *a duchess whose majesty was clearly present in her every move* **2. POWER** supreme authority and power **3. SPLENDOR** awesomely large size or splendor ○ *the majesty of the Rocky Mountain* *peaks* **4.** ROYALTY royal status (*archaic*) [13thC. Via Old French *majesté* from Latin *majestas*, from the stem of *major* (see MAJOR).]

Maj·es·ty (*plural* **-ties**) *n.* the title used to address or refer to a king or queen

Maj. Gen. *abbr.* Major General

maj·lis /maj líss/ *n.* an assembly or parliament in various countries in North Africa and the Middle East [Early 19thC. From Arabic, "place of session," from *jalasa* "to be seated."]

Majolica

ma·jol·i·ca /mə jóllikə, -yólli-/, **ma·iol·i·ca** *n.* Italian earthenware that is coated with a tin oxide glaze and highly decorated [Mid-16thC. From Italian, an old form of the name of the island of *Majorca*.]

ma·jor /máyjər/ *n.* **1.** MIL MILITARY RANK a military rank immediately below that of lieutenant colonel in many armed forces around the world, including the British and United States armies and the United States Air Force and Marine Corps **2.** MIL OFFICER somebody who holds the rank of major **3.** LAW SOMEBODY OF LEGAL AGE somebody who has reached the age at which a person is deemed fully responsible for his or her actions **4.** *U.S., Can, ANZ* EDUC COURSE CONCENTRATION the field of study in which a college or university student chooses to specialize ○ *a major in philosophy* **5.** *U.S., Can, ANZ* EDUC STUDENT IN A SPECIALTY a student studying a particular academic specialty ○ *a math major* **6.** MUSIC MUSICAL KEY OR HARMONY a key or harmony based on a musical scale that has intervals of a semitone between the third and fourth and the seventh and eighth notes (**major scale**) ■ **ma·jors** *npl.* SPORTS MAJOR LEAGUES the major leagues, such as in football or baseball ■ *adj.* **1.** OF HIGH STANDING greater in importance than most others ○ *a major recording artist* **2.** SIGNIFICANT of considerable degree or significance ○ *major bridge repairs ahead* **3.** SERIOUS of great severity ○ *a major illness* **4.** LARGE great in number or proportion ○ *A major part of the meeting was devoted to agreeing on our report.* **5.** LAW AT THE AGE OF MAJORITY of the age at which a person is deemed fully responsible for his or her actions **6.** EDUC OF A PRINCIPAL SUBJECT relating to a subject studied as a specialty **7.** MUSIC DESCRIBING A MUSICAL SCALE used to describe a musical scale that has intervals of a semitone between the third and fourth and the seventh and eighth notes **8.** MUSIC DESCRIBING A MUSICAL INTERVAL used to describe the interval between the keynote of a major scale and any other note in it, excluding the perfect intervals ○ *a major sixth* **9.** MUSIC DESCRIBING A KEY used to describe a key that is based on a major scale ○ *in B major* ■ *vi.* (**-jored, -jor·ing, -jors**) *U.S., Can, ANZ* EDUC STUDY SOMETHING AS A COURSE CONCENTRATION to make a particular subject the main field of study ○ *She majored in economics.* [13thC. From Latin, "greater," from *magnus* "great" (source of English *mayor* and *majesty*).]

Ma·jor /máyjər/, **John** (*b.* 1943) British statesman. As Conservative prime minister (1990–97), he worked toward peace talks with Northern Ireland but was troubled by party splits on the issue of closer European integration.

Ma·jor·ca /mə yáwrkə/ largest of the Balearic Islands, an autonomous region of Spain, in the western Mediterranean Sea. Population: 736,885 (1994). Area: 1,405 sq. mi./3,640 sq. km. —**Ma·jor·can** *n., adj.*

ma·jor-do·mo /màyjər dṓ mō/ (*plural* **ma·jor-do·mos**) *n.* **1.** CHIEF MAN SERVANT the chief man servant in a large household, especially a royal or noble household, responsible for managing domestic affairs **2.** MAKER OF ARRANGEMENTS somebody responsible for managing the affairs of others, and making arrangements for others (*humorous*) [Late 16thC. Via French, Italian, and Spanish from medieval Latin *major domus* literally "chief of the house," from Latin *magnus* (see MAJOR) and *domus* "house" (source of English *domestic*).]

ma·jor·ette /màyjə rét/ *n.* a girl or young woman who marches in front of a marching band, twirling a baton

ma·jor gen·er·al (*plural* **ma·jor gen·er·als**) *n.* **1.** HIGH MILITARY RANK a military rank immediately below that of lieutenant general in many armed forces around the world, including the British and United States Armies, and the United States Air Force and Marine Corps **2.** MILITARY OFFICER a military officer holding the rank of major general

ma·jor his·to·com·pat·i·bil·i·ty com·plex *n.* a cluster of genes occurring in humans and other animals that determines the recognizable pattern on the surface of the body's cells. This determines the extent to which an individual's immune system will accept or reject tissue from another individual.

ma·jor·i·tar·i·an /mə jàwri táiree ən/ *adj.* FROM MAJORITY RULE resulting from or based on rule by the majority in any given group ■ *n.* SUPPORTER OF MAJORITY RULE somebody who believes that a group should be ruled in the way chosen by the majority of its members — **ma·jor·i·tar·i·an·ism** *n.*

ma·jor·i·ty /mə jáwritee/ (*plural* **-ties**) *n.* **1.** GREATER NUMBER OF PEOPLE OR THINGS most of the people or things in a large group (*takes a singular or plural verb*) ○ *The majority of women now work.* **2.** DIFFERENCE IN NUMBER OF VOTES the number of votes by which the winning party or group beats the opposition ○ *swept to power with an overwhelming majority* **3.** GROUP IN POWER the most powerful party or group voting together in a legislature ○ *The Democrats were the majority in Congress for many years.* **4.** LAW AGE OF LEGAL RESPONSIBILITY the age, generally either 18 or 21, at which somebody is legally responsible and can assume civil duties and rights such as serving on a jury or voting ○ *Until you've reached the age of majority you can't buy a car without a co-signer.* **5.** MIL RANK OF MAJOR the military rank of major **6.** PRE-EMINENCE superior position or status (*archaic*)

ma·jor·i·ty lead·er *n.* the head of the majority party in a legislature

ma·jor·i·ty mi·nor·i·ty *n.* a majority of people in a particular area who belong to a minority group overall ○ *a majority minority district*

ma·jor·i·ty rule *n.* control of an organization or institution according to the wishes or votes of the majority of its members

ma·jor league *n.* **1.** BASEBALL MAIN BASEBALL LEAGUE either of the two main professional baseball leagues **2.** SPORTS TOP SPORTS LEAGUE a top league of professional football, ice hockey, and basketball teams ■ **ma·jor leagues** *npl.* HIGH PLACES the highest spheres of influence (*informal*) ○ *a politician operating in the major leagues*

ma·jor-league *adj.* **1.** OF MAJOR SPORTS LEAGUE relating to or being a team member of a major sports league ○ *major-league ice hockey* **2.** OF HIGHEST LEVEL being at the top of any field of activity (*informal*) ○ *a major-league law firm* —**ma·jor-lea·guer** *n.*

ma·jor·ly /máyjərlee/ *adv.* in a large degree or to a great extent (*informal*)

ma·jor med·i·cal *n.* health insurance that covers most if not all of the costs incurred during a serious illness, including a hospital stay

ma·jor or·der *n.* in the Roman Catholic Church, one of the higher holy orders of bishop, priest, deacon, or subdeacon

ma·jor pen·al·ty *n.* in sports such as ice hockey and lacrosse, a player's removal from the game for five minutes for a serious violation of the rules

ma·jor scale *n.* a musical scale with intervals of a semitone between the third and fourth notes and the seventh and eighth notes and whole tones between all other consecutive notes. Major scales potentially have a bright and joyful quality. ◊ **minor scale**

ma·jor suit *n.* in bridge and some other card games, spades or hearts, owing to their greater scoring potential

ma·jus·cule /mə jú skyo͞ol, májjə-/ *n.* a large letter used in writing or printing, e.g., a capital letter or any of the large rounded letters (**uncials**) used in ancient manuscripts [Early 18thC. Via French from Latin *majuscula (littera)*, literally "somewhat larger (letters)," from *major* (see MAJOR).] —**ma·jus·cu·lar** /mə júskyələr/ *adj.*

Mak·a·lu /múkəloo/ mountain in the Himalayas, on the Nepal-China border, estimated to be the fourth or fifth highest in the world. Height: 27,824 ft./ 8,481 m.

Ma·ka·ri·os /mə kaáree oss/, **Archbishop** (1913–77) Cypriot cleric and statesman. Orthodox archbishop of Cyprus (1950–74) and first president of Cyprus (1959–77), he was noted for his efforts to unify Greek and Turkish Cypriots. Real name **Mihail Christodolou Mouskos**

Ma·ka·ro·va /màkə rṓvə/, **Natalia** (*b.* 1940) Russian-born U.S. dancer. A member of the American Ballet Theater, she won a Tony award in the revival of *On Your Toes* (1983).

Ma·kas·sar /mə kássər/ former name for **Ujungpandang**

make /mayk/ *v.* (**made** /mayd/, **made, mak·ing, makes**) **1.** *vt.* DO used with a range of nouns to describe an action, where "make" is used rather than a more specific verb ○ *She made no effort whatsoever to pass her exams.* **2.** *vt.* SAY to say or deliver a statement or speech ○ *He made an emotional speech about his parents' struggle to get ahead in a new country.* **3.** *vt.* CONSTRUCT to assemble something from constituent parts ○ *The exhibit contains items made out of recyclable materials.* **4.** *vt.* INDUST MANUFACTURE to manufacture something as a business ○ *The company makes surgical instruments.* **5.** *vt.* COOK PRODUCE BY COMBINING INGREDIENTS to prepare food or drink by mixing and usually cooking a number of ingredients ○ *Let's make soup.* **6.** *vt.* FORM WITH MOTION to form something by performing the movements that it requires ○ *She made the signs for "I'll see you later".* ○ *He made a circular motion with his hands.* **7.** *vt.* FORMULATE to form something in the mind ○ *These politicians have made a tacit commitment to try to solve the problem.* **8.** *vt.* UNDERSTAND to comprehend the meaning or truth of something ○ *I couldn't make anything of her last remark.* **9.** *vt.* RECKON to reckon or estimate something ○ *What time do you make it?* **10.** *vt.* BRING ABOUT to cause a condition or situation to arise or exist ○ *The state made it illegal to sell fireworks.* ○ *Some people here have made this a personal issue.* **11.** *vt.* CHANGE SOMEBODY OR SOMETHING to transform somebody or something into something else ○ *They made old clothes into patchwork quilts.* **12.** *vt.* APPOINT to appoint somebody to a particular role or position ○ *She's made me her deputy.* **13.** *vt.* PROVIDE to provide something out of what already exists ○ *Make room for one more.* ○ *Can you make change for a dollar?* **14.** *vt.* CAUSE SOMEBODY TO ACT to cause somebody to do something or act in a particular way ○ *I made him realize how wrong he'd been.* ○ *You made me lose my place.* **15.** *vt.* FORCE to force somebody or something to do something or act in a particular way ○ *You can't make me wear that dress.* **16.** *vt.* CAUSE TO EXIST FOR REASON to cause somebody or something to exist for a particular reason (*usually passive*) ○ *She was made to be a star.* **17.** *vt.* EARN to earn or be paid a specified sum of money ○ *He makes $50,000 from rental properties.* **18.** *vt.* CAUSE SOUND TO BE HEARD to produce or give rise to a sound ○ *She made a choking noise in her throat.* **19.** *vt.* ARRANGE FOR USE to arrange something properly for later use ○ *He made the bed carefully.* **20.** *vt.* SCHEDULE MEETING to fix a meeting or time ○ *Let's make a date for Friday.* **21.** *vt.* SPORTS SCORE to score a goal or points in a game ○ *made a touchdown* **22.** *vt.* REPRESENT SOMETHING to count as one in a series ○ *That makes the third time he's lied to me.* **23.** *vt.* AMOUNT TO to amount to a total ○ *Five and three make eight.* **24.** *vt.* HAVE NECESSARY QUALITIES FOR SOMETHING to have the qualities required to be something ○ *She'll make a very good doctor.* **25.** *vt.* DEVELOP RELATIONSHIP to acquire a friend, enemy, or acquaintance ○ *They made friends right away.* **26.** *vt.* CAUSE TO SUCCEED to cause somebody to be successful, or cause something to seem successful ○ *the novel that made her career* **27.** *vt.* REACH A PLACE to reach or arrive at a place ○ *I'm not sure we can make the island in this tub.* **28.** *vt.* BE IN TIME FOR to be in time to do something or for something to happen ○ *We can make the 10:05 if we hurry.* **29.** *vt.* COVER DISTANCE to travel a particular distance ○ *They made only five miles a day on the ascent.* **30.** *vt.* BE INCLUDED IN to succeed in being included or mentioned in something ○ *He made captain just last Saturday.* ○ *stories that never make* *the national news* **31.** *vi.* **SIGNAL INTENTIONS** to act so as to indicate what is coming ○ *They made as if to leave.* **32.** *vt.* **ACHIEVE SEX WITH SOMEBODY** to succeed in having sex with somebody (*dated slang*) **33.** *vt.* BRIDGE **FULFILL BRIDGE CONTRACT** to fulfill a contract in a game of bridge by winning the required number of tricks **34.** *vt.* CARDS **WIN TRICK IN CARDS** to win a trick in a card game **35.** *vt.* ELECTRON ENG **CLOSE A CIRCUIT** to close an electric circuit **36.** *vi.* AGRIC **MATURE** to dry and mature (*refers to hay*) ■ *n.* **1. BRAND** a brand of something, e.g., an appliance, car, or machine ○ *Specify the make and model of the car.* **2. PROCESS AND OUTPUT** the process of making something, or the amount or number made **3. BUILD OR APPEARANCE** the way that something has been made, or the size or shape it naturally has (*literary*) ○ *a woodland cabin of rustic make* **4. SORT** a type with reference to character (*archaic or literary*) ○ *What make of man is he?* **5. IDENTIFICATION** the identification of somebody or something, usually made with the help of police records or information (*slang*) ○ *The police got a make on him from their records.* [Old English *macian*. Ultimately, from an Indo-European word meaning "kneading," which is also the source of English *magma* and *match*.] —**mak·a·ble** *adj.* ◇ **make believe** to pretend ◇ **make certain, make sure** to do what is necessary to ensure something ○ *Make sure the door is locked.* ◇ **make do (with something)** to use something that is an unsatisfactory substitute or temporary alternative for the real thing ◇ **make it 1.** to be successful (*informal*) ○ *You'll never make it as an actor.* **2.** to succeed in getting somewhere ○ *We finally made it to the top of the hill.* **3.** to be able to attend ○ *I can't make it to the party tonight.* ◇ **make like** to imitate (*informal*) ○ *She made like she was doing the breaststroke.* ◇ **on the make 1.** trying hard to gain a profit or advantage, especially using underhand or dishonest means (*informal*) **2.** looking for or making efforts to persuade somebody to be a sexual partner (*slang*)

WORD KEY: SYNONYMS

make, produce, create, fashion, manufacture

CORE MEANING: to bring something into existence

make to bring something into existence; **produce** to make something in large quantities or in a commercial setting; **create** to make something using imagination and artistic skill or to cause something such as a job or opportunity to exist; **fashion** to make something by shaping and working raw materials, especially when only using the hands or hand-held tools; **manufacture** to make something in large numbers, usually in a factory using machinery, or, showing disapproval, to make something quickly and cynically, especially something that normally requires time and artistic skill.

make after *vt.* to chase after somebody or something

make away *vi.* = **make off**

make away with *vt.* **1. STEAL** to steal something and abscond with it ○ *They made away with the week's receipts.* **2. ABDUCT** to carry somebody off by force **3. GET RID OF** to destroy or get rid of something incriminating ○ *We think someone's made away with the DNA evidence in the lab.* **4. KILL** to kill somebody (*dated*)

make for *vt.* **1. MOVE TOWARD** to move quickly in the direction of somebody or something ○ *The reporters made for the courtroom.* **2. HAVE AS RESULT** to result in a particular situation ○ *This plan will make for a successful product launch.*

make off *vi.* to leave a place quickly, usually with good reason

make off with *vt.* = **make away with**

make out *v.* **1.** *vt.* **SEE OR HEAR INDISTINCTLY** to see or hear somebody or something but not clearly ○ *I could just make out her profile in the darkness.* **2.** *vt.* **COMPREHEND** to identify or understand something ○ *I can't make out the suspect's motive.* **3.** *vt.* **COMPLETE IN WRITING** to write necessary information such as the date and the recipient's name on a bill or similar document ○ *The deed is made out in my spouse's name.* **4.** *vt.* **SUGGEST** to suggest or imply something that may not be true ○ *The kids make him out to be a real tyrant.* **5.** *vt.* **ARGUE IN SUPPORT OF** to try to prove something is true or valid by giving good reasons ○ *made out a case for keeping the work in-house* **6.** *vi.* **MANAGE** to perform in a situation ○ *How did you make out on the test?* **7.** *vi.* **ENGAGE IN SEXUAL ACTIVITIES WITHOUT INTERCOURSE** to kiss and caress somebody as an expression of sexual desire (*slang*) **8.** *vi.* **HAVE SEX** to have sexual intercourse (*slang*)

make over *vt.* **1.** LAW **MAKE SOMEBODY ELSE OWNER OF SOMETHING** to transfer the ownership of money or property to somebody, usually in a legal document ○ *half of her estate was made over to her cousin* **2.** SEW **REFASHION GARMENT** to alter or remodel a garment **3. CHANGE APPEARANCE OF SOMEBODY OR SOMETHING** to make major changes to the way somebody or something looks

make up *v.* **1.** *vt.* **MAKE READY** to get something ready, especially by putting a number of items together ○ *I've made up a box lunch.* **2.** *vt.* **JOIN TO FORM SOMETHING** to combine with other people or objects to form a whole ○ *a group made up of four men and six women* **3.** *vt.* **CONSTITUTE** to form part of something ○ *Women make up more than half the country's workforce.* **4.** *vt.* **INVENT** to invent an excuse, fact, or story ○ *made the whole story up to shock her parents* **5.** *vti.* THEATER **PREPARE FOR PERFORMANCE** to prepare somebody or yourself for an acting performance by applying cosmetics and fitting costumes necessary for assuming a given role ○ *It takes her two hours to make up for the role.* **6.** *vt.* COSMETICS **PUT ON FACIAL COSMETICS** to apply cosmetics to your own face or somebody else's face **7.** *vt.* **COMPLETE** to make a number or amount complete ○ *You three pay $10 each and I'll make up the rest.* **8.** *vt.* EDUC **TAKE EXAM OR COURSE AGAIN** to take an examination or course of study again because of absence or failure ○ *make up a French exam* **9.** *vti.* **RESOLVE A QUARREL** to become friends again after a quarrel ○ *Haven't you two made up yet?* **10.** *vt.* PRINTING **ARRANGE LAYOUT OF PAGE** to arrange columns of print and illustrations on a page **11.** *vi.* **COMPENSATE** to compensate for a failing such as a disappointment, deficiency, or shortcoming ○ *I'll buy lunch to make up for being late.*

make up to *vt.* **1. TRY TO GAIN SOMEBODY'S FAVOR** to try to gain somebody's favor by behaving in a flattering and attentive way ○ *making up to the general manager's assistant* **2. BEHAVE FLIRTATIOUSLY** to flirt with somebody

make with *vt.* to start doing, using, or producing something (*slang*) ○ *Hey, let's make with the party, huh?*

make-be·lieve *n.* imaginary situations or events that somebody, especially a child playing, pretends are true (*often used before a noun*) ○ *watching them in their make-believe world*

make-do *n.* (*plural* **make-dos**) **SUBSTITUTE** a substitute, often an inferior one ■ *adj.* **SUBSTITUTING** temporarily substituting for something else ○ *a make-do set of draperies in a furnished apartment*

make·fast /máyk fàst/ *n.* a strong ring, post, or buoy to which a boat or ship is moored

make-or-break *adj.* likely to result in either complete success or complete failure

make·o·ver /máyk òvər/ *n.* **1. CHANGE OF PHYSICAL APPEARANCE** an alteration of the way somebody looks, usually including changes in hairstyle and in style of makeup and clothes **2. REMODELING** a remodeling of something that completely changes the way it looks

mak·er /máykər/ *n.* **1. CREATOR OR CAUSE** somebody who creates something or is the source or cause of it (*often used in combination*) ○ *a maker of mischief* **2. PRODUCER OF GOODS** a person or organization that produces goods (*often used in combination*) ○ *a maker of mid-priced textiles* **3.** LAW **SIGNER OF DOCUMENT** somebody who signs a promissory note

Mak·er *n.* God, regarded as the creator of everything (*literary*)

make·shift /máyk shìft/ *adj.* **SUBSTITUTING** providing a temporary and usually inferior substitute ■ *n.* **SUBSTITUTE** a temporary and usually inferior substitute [Mid-16thC. From *to make shift* "to try all means."]

make·up /máyk ùp/, **make-up** *n.* **1. COSMETICS** cosmetic products, especially for the face, e.g., lipstick and mascara (*often used before a noun*) ○ *Slap on a little makeup and you'll feel better.* **2.** THEATER **THEATRICAL COSMETICS** the cosmetics and costumes that actors wear to alter their appearance on stage (*often used before a noun*) ○ *makeup department* **3.** THEATER **APPLYING ACTORS' COSMETICS** the application of actors' cosmetics and other appearance-altering accessories, e.g., false hair (*often used before a noun*) ○ *working in makeup* **4. COMBINATION OF PARTS OR QUALITIES** the way parts or qualities combine or are arranged, especially in somebody's personality ○ *Self-deprecation is an intrinsic part of her makeup.* **5.** PRINTING **ARRANGEMENT OF TYPE** the arrangement of typographic elements on a page **6.** EDUC **SPECIAL EXAM** a special examination arranged for students who failed or missed the previous one

make·weight /máyk wàyt/ *n.* **1. ADDITIONAL WEIGHT** something placed on a scale to bring a weight up to a required level **2. EXTRA OBJECT** a counterbalancing object, or one that fills in a required number of objects

make-work *n.* unimportant or needless work assigned to prevent idleness

ma·ki·mo·no /maáki mṓnō/ (*plural* **-nos**) *n.* a horizontal Japanese scroll decorated with paintings or calligraphy [Late 19thC. From Japanese, "a scroll," literally "something rolled up."]

mak·ing /máyking/ *n.* **1. CREATIVE ACTIVITY** the activity of somebody who makes something ○ *during the making of the movie* **2. CAUSE OF SUCCESS** something that causes somebody's success or progress ○ *a book that was the making of her career* ◇ **in the making** in the process of being made, formed, or developed

mak·ings /máykingz/ *npl.* **1. REQUIRED INGREDIENTS** the things required to make something, especially a dish of food **2. POTENTIAL** the qualities required to become a particular thing ○ *has the makings of a good lawyer*

ma·ko shark /maákō-/ *n.* a slender blue-gray shark with a sharp nose and ferocious teeth, found in southern oceans. It can exceed 13 ft./4 m in length and is prized as a game fish. Genus: *Isurus.* [*Mako* from Maori]

Ma·kur·di /mə kúrdee/ town in northern Benue State, eastern central Nigeria. Population: 111,410 (1992).

ma·ku·ta plural of **likuta**

Mal. *abbr.* **1.** BIBLE Malachi **2.** Malay **3.** Malayan **4.** Malaysia **5.** Malaysian

mal- *prefix.* **1.** bad, badly ○ *malpractice* **2.** abnormal or inadequate ○ *malnutrition* [Via Old French from Latin *malus* "bad" (source of English *malice, malady, malaria*, and *dismal*) and *male* "badly"]

Mal·a·bar Coast /mállәbaar-/ region on the southwestern coast of India, that stretches from Goa southward and includes most of Kerala State

mal·ab·sorp·tion /màl әb sáwrpshәn, -záwrp-/ *n.* the inadequate absorption of nutrients from digested food in the alimentary canal, especially by the small intestine in celiac disease

malac- *prefix.* = **malaco-** (*used before vowels*)

ma·lac·ca /mә lákә/, **ma·lac·ca cane, Ma·lac·ca, Ma·lac·ca cane** *n.* **1. RATTAN PALM STEM** the stem of the rattan palm, used to make walking sticks **2. RATTAN WALKING STICK** a walking stick made from the stem of the rattan palm [Mid-19thC. Named for MALACCA.]

Ma·lac·ca /mә lákә/ former name for **Melaka**

Ma·lac·ca, Strait of strait in southeastern Asia connecting the Andaman Sea with the South China Sea. Length: 500 mi./800 km.

Mal·a·chi /mállә kì/ *n.* **1. HEBREW PROPHET** an unidentified Hebrew prophet who wrote in the 5th century B.C., usually referred to by this name **2. BOOK OF THE BIBLE** a book of the Bible containing writings by Malachi. See table at **Bible**

mal·a·chite /mállә kìt/ *n.* a green naturally-occurring carbonate of copper, used as a decorative stone and a source of copper. Formula: $Cu_2CO_3(OH)_2$. [14thC. Via Old French *melochite* from, ultimately, Greek *molokhitis*, a stone similar in color to the mallow leaf, from *malakhē* "mallow."]

malaco- *prefix.* soft ○ *malacophyllous* [From Greek *malakos*. Ultimately from an Indo-European word that is also the ancestor of English *mild, melt*, and *mulch*.]

mal·a·col·o·gy /màllә kóllәjee/ *n.* the branch of zoology that involves the study of mollusks [Mid-19thC. Via French from, ultimately, modern Latin *Malacozoa* "soft-bodied creatures," from Greek *malakos* (see MALACO-).] —**mal·a·co·log·i·cal** /màllәkә lójjik'l/ *adj.* —**mal·a·col·o·gist** /-kóllәjist/ *n.*

mal·a·cos·tra·can /màllә kóstrәkәn/ *n.* a member of a common group of crustaceans that usually have stalked eyes, a carapace, and a tail fan formed from the rear limbs. The group includes the lobster, crab, wood louse, and krill. Subclass: Malacostraca. [Mid-19thC. Formed from modern Latin *Malacostraca*, order name, from Greek *malakos* "soft" + *ostrakon* "shell."] —**mal·a·cos·tra·can** *adj.*

mal·ad·ap·ta·tion /màl a dap táysh'n, -addәp-/ *n.* unsuitable or ineffective adaptation to a particular situation, function, or purpose

mal·a·dap·ted /màllə dáptəd/ *adj.* unsuitable for or poorly adapted to a particular situation, function, or purpose

mal·a·dap·tive /màllə dáptiv/ *adj.* **1.** BADLY OR INCOMPLETELY ADAPTED unsuitable for or poorly adapted to a particular situation, function, or purpose **2.** NOT CONDUCIVE TO ADAPTATION not facilitating or encouraging adaptation —**mal·a·dap·tive·ly** *adv.*

mal·ad·just·ed /màllə jústəd/ *adj.* unable to cope with everyday social situations and personal relationships —**mal·ad·just·ment** *n.*

mal·ad·min·is·tra·tion /màlləd minni stráysh'n/ *n.* incompetent or dishonest management or administration, especially in public affairs —**mal·ad·min·is·ter** /màlləd mínnistər/ *vt.*

mal·a·droit /màllə dróyt/ *adj.* clumsy or insensitive in speech or behavior (*formal*) [Late 17thC. From French, literally "not adept," from *adroit* (see ADROIT).] —**mal·a·droit·ly** *adv.* —**mal·a·droit·ness** *n.*

mal·a·dy /mállədee/ (*plural* **-dies**) *n.* **1.** ILLNESS a physical or psychological disorder or disease **2.** PROBLEM a condition or situation that is problematic and requires a remedy [13thC. Via French *maladie* from, ultimately, Latin *male habitus* "in bad condition."]

ma·la fi·de /màllə fídee/ *adj., adv.* done insincerely or dishonestly (*formal*) [Early 17thC. From Latin.]

Má·la·ga /málləgə/ city, seaport, and holiday resort in southern Spain, on the Mediterranean Sea. It is the center of the Costa del Sol, a major tourist region. Population: 532,425 (1995).

Mal·a·gas·y /màllə gássee/ (*plural* **-y** *or* **-ies**) *n.* **1.** PEOPLES SOMEBODY FROM MADAGASCAR somebody who was born on or is a citizen of Madagascar **2.** LANG OFFICIAL LANGUAGE OF MADAGASCAR one of the official languages of Madagascar, belonging to the Western branch of Austronesian languages. Malagasy is spoken by about 12 million people. [Mid-19thC. Variant of MADAGASCAR.] —**Mal·a·gas·y** *adj.*

Mal·a·gas·y Re·pub·lic former name for **Madagascar** (1958–75)

ma·la·gue·ña /màllə gáynyə, maàlə-/, **ma·la·gue·na** *n.* **1.** DANCE SPANISH DANCE a Spanish dance that is similar to the fandango **2.** MUSIC SPANISH TUNE a Spanish folk song or tune similar to a fandango [Late 19thC. From Spanish, literally from MALAGA, a city in southern Spain.]

mal·aise /mə láyz, ma-, -léz/ *n.* **1.** MED FEELING OF ILLNESS a general feeling of illness or sickness without any specific diagnostic significance **2.** GENERAL FEELING OF DISCONTENT a general feeling of worry, discontent, or dissatisfaction, often resulting in lethargy [Mid-18thC. From French, literally "ill ease," from *aise* (see EASE).]

Mal·a·mud /mállәmood/, **Bernard** (1914–86) U.S. novelist and short-story writer. Known for his parables of Jewish life, he won a Pulitzer Prize for *The Fixer* (1966).

mal·a·mute /màllə myoot/, **mal·e·mute** *n.* an Alaskan dog with a thick gray, black, or white coat, used especially for pulling sleds [Late 19thC. From Inupiaq *malimiut*, the name of an Alaskan people who developed the breed.]

Ma·lang /mállang/ city in southwestern Indonesia, on the island of Java. Population: 548,193 (1989).

mal·a·pert /màllə pùrt/ *adj.* SAUCY OR BRAZEN impudent or bold in speech or behavior (*archaic or literary*) ■ *n.* SAUCY OR BRAZEN PERSON somebody who is impudent or bold in speech or behavior (*archaic or literary*) [15thC. Via Old French, literally "not experienced," from, ultimately, Latin *expertus* (see EXPERT). The meaning was influenced in Old French by association with *apert* "saucy."] —**mal·a·pert·ly** *adv.* —**mal·a·pert·ness** *n.*

mal·ap·por·tioned /màllə páwrsh'nd/ *adj.* used to describe a distribution of representatives within a legislative body that is unequal or unfair —**mal·ap·por·tion·ment** *n.*

mal·a·prop /màllə pròp/ *n.* = **malapropism** *n.* **2**

mal·a·prop·ism /màllə pro pìzzəm/ *n.* **1.** UNINTENTIONAL USE OF WRONG WORD the misuse of a word through confusion with another word that sounds similar, especially when the effect is ridiculous **2.** EXAMPLE OF MALAPROPISM an instance of using malapropism [Early 19thC. Formed from the name of Mrs. *Malaprop* (from MALAPROPOS), a character in Richard Sheridan's play *The Rivals*, who often confused words in this way.] —**mal·a·prop·ist** /màllə pròppist/ *n.*

mal·a·pro·pos /màl apprə pṓ, ma lápprə pṑ/ *adj.* OUT OF PLACE not appropriate to the situation in which something is done or said (*formal*) ■ *adv.* INAPPROPRIATELY OR INOPPORTUNELY in an inappropriate way or at an inopportune moment (*formal*) [Mid-17thC. From French *mal à propos* "ill-suited to the purpose."]

ma·lar /máylər/, **ma·lar bone** *adj.* OF THE CHEEK OR CHEEKBONE relating to the cheek, the cheekbone, or the side of the head ■ *n.* CHEEKBONE the cheekbone [Late 18thC. From modern Latin *malaris*, from Latin *mala* "jaw, cheekbone," of unknown origin.]

Mä·lar·en /máy laar ən/ lake in southeastern Sweden. Stockholm lies on its eastern shore. Area: 440 sq. mi./1,140 sq. km.

ma·lar·i·a /mə láiree ə/ *n.* an infectious disease caused by a parasite that is transmitted by the bite of infected mosquitoes. Common in hot countries, the disease is characterized by recurring chills and fever. [Mid-18thC. From Italian *malaria* "bad air," which was once thought to be the cause of the disease.] —**ma·lar·i·al** *adj.* —**ma·lar·i·an** *adj.* —**ma·lar·i·ous** *adj.*

ma·lar·i·ol·o·gy /mə làiree óllәjee/ *n.* the scientific study of malaria —**ma·lar·i·ol·o·gist** *n.*

ma·lar·key /mə laarkee/, **ma·lar·ky** *n.* nonsense or rubbish, especially insincere talk (*informal*) [Early 20thC. Origin unknown.]

mal·ate /má làyt, máy-/ *n.* a chemical compound that is a salt or ester of malic acid

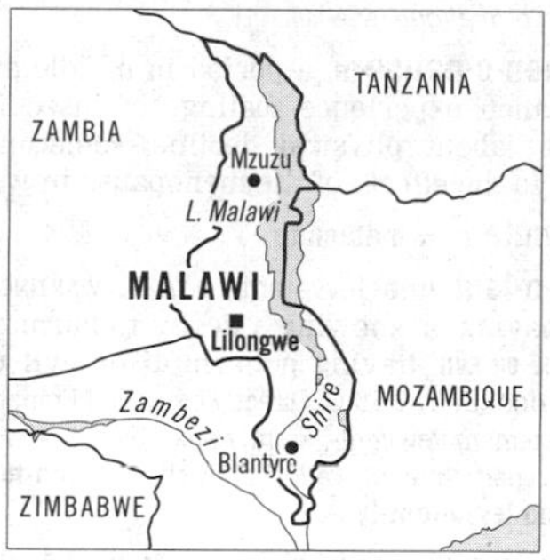

Malawi

Ma·la·wi /məlaawee/ republic in southeastern Africa. Language: English. Currency: kwacha. Capital: Lilongwe. Population: 9,453,000 (1996). Area: 45,747 sq. mi./118,484 sq. km. Official name **Republic of Malawi**. Former name **Nyasaland** —**Ma·la·wi·an** *n., adj.*

Ma·la·wi, Lake = **Nyasa, Lake**

Ma·lay /mə láy, máy lày/ *n.* **1.** PEOPLES MEMBER OF SE ASIAN ETHNIC GROUP a member of an ethnic group that inhabits the Malay Peninsula, Indonesia, and other islands of the Malay Archipelago and the Philippines **2.** LANG LANGUAGE OF MALAYSIA a language spoken in Malaysia, also spoken in parts of Singapore, Borneo, Sumatra, Java, and surrounding areas. It belongs to the Western branch of Austronesian languages. Malay is the native tongue of about 22 million speakers, with approximately 100 million people using it as a second language. ■ *adj.* **1.** PEOPLES OF MALAYS relating to the Malay people, or their language or culture **2.** GEOG OF MALAYSIA relating to the Malay Peninsula, Malaysia, or the Malay Archipelago [Late 16thC. From Malay *malayu, melayu*.] —**Ma·lay·an** *n., adj.*

Ma·la·ya, Fed·er·a·tion of /mə láy ə/ former state in the Malay Peninsula. It was incorporated into the Federation of Malaysia in 1963.

Mal·a·ya·lam /màllə yaaləm/ *n.* a Dravidian language that is the official language of the Indian state of Kerala. Malayalam is spoken by about 30 million people. [Early 19thC. From Malayalam *Malayālam*, literally "mountain man."] —**Mal·a·ya·lam** *adj.*

Ma·lay Ar·chi·pel·a·go the world's largest system of island groups, comprising over 20,000 islands, mainly in Indonesia and the Philippines. Area: 1.1 million sq. mi./2.8 million sq. km.

Ma·lay Pen·in·su·la peninsula in southeastern Asia that includes parts of Myanmar, Thailand, and Malaysia

Ma·lay·sia /mə láyzhə, -láyshə/ constitutional monarchy in southeastern Asia, on the South China Sea, comprising the southern portion of the Malay Peninsula and parts of the Island of Borneo. Language: Bahasa Malaysia. Currency: ringgit. Capital: Kuala Lumpur. Population: 17,566,982 (1991). Area: 127,320 sq. mi./329,758 sq. km. Official name **Federation of Malaysia** —**Ma·lay·sian** *n., adj.*

Ma·lay·sian Eng·lish *n.* a variety of English spoken in Malaysia

WORD KEY: WORLD ENGLISH

The English language as used in Malaysia since the formation of the nation-state in 1963. Prior to independence from Britain the term *Anglo-Malay* was used, indicating the influence of the Malay language. From the earlier period come such general English words of Malay origin as *amok, durian, kampong, mango, orang-utan, sago,* and *sarong*. Malaysian English is "rhotic" (i.e., "r" is pronounced in such words as *art, door,* and *worker*). There is a tendency toward full vowels in all syllables (e.g. *7* pronounced "seh-ven," not "sevn"), and a reduction in consonant clusters at the ends of words ("muss" for *must*, "bes" for *best*, "liv" *lived*, "relac" *relax*). In grammar, reflexive pronouns are used for emphasis, often without the verb to be, as in "Himself sick," and certain general-purpose particles are used, such as *lah*, indicating informality and intimacy, as in "Can do it lah?" ("Can you do it?"). There is considerable hybridization between Malay and English, as in: "She wanted to beli some barang-barang" ("She wanted to buy some things"). See ANGLO-HYBRID, SINGAPOREAN ENGLISH.

Mal·colm III /málkəm/, **King of Scotland** (c. 1031–93). He became king after killing Macbeth in 1057 and ruled until his death. He made peace with the King of England, William I (the Conqueror), in 1072.

Malcolm X

Mal·colm X (1925–65) U.S. political activist. He was a prominent member of the Black Muslims and founder of the Organization of Afro-American Unity (1964). After moderating his views on Black separatism, he was assassinated. Born **Malcolm Little**

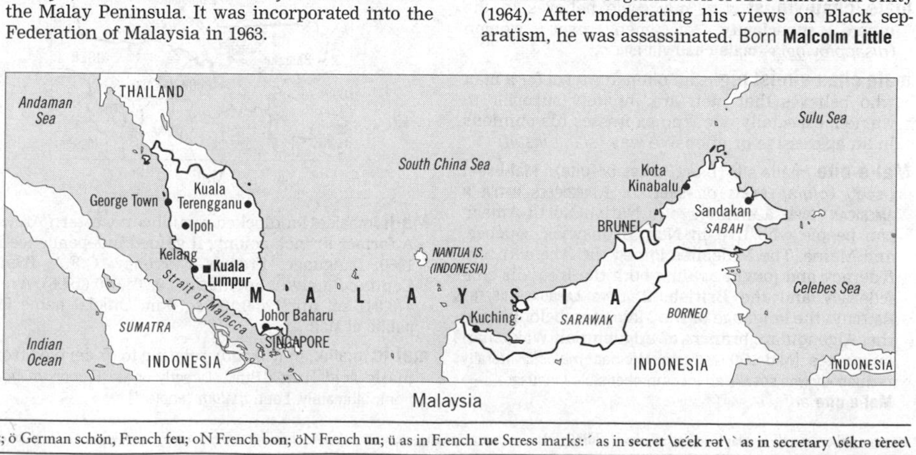

Malaysia

mal·con·tent /málkən tènt/ *n.* **DISCONTENTED PERSON** somebody who is discontented or dissatisfied with a particular state of affairs, e.g., a political system, or with things in general ■ *adj.* **NOT CONTENT** discontented or dissatisfied with something, especially a political system [Late 16thC. From French, literally "ill contented," from *content* (see CONTENT).] —**mal·con·tent·ed** /màlkən téntəd/ *adj.* —**mal·con·tent·ed·ly** *adv.* —**mal·con·tent·ed·ness** *n.*

mal de mer /màl də máir/ *n.* = **seasickness** [Late 18thC. From French, literally "sea sickness."]

Mal·den /máwldən/ city in northeastern Massachusetts, a northern suburb of Boston. Population: 52,749 (1996).

mal·dis·tri·bu·tion /màl distri byo͞osh'n/ *n.* unequal and unfair distribution of something, especially resources or wealth

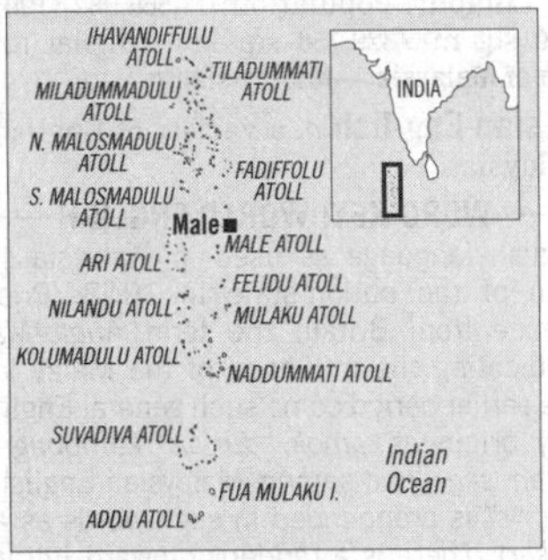

Maldives

Mal·dives /máwl deevz, mál dīvz/ island republic in southern Asia, located southwest of the southern tip of India. Language: Divehi. Currency: rufiyaa. Capital: Male. Population: 270,758 (1996). Area: 115 sq. mi./298 sq. km. Official name **Republic of the Maldives** —**Mal·div·an** *n., adj.*

male /mayl/ *adj.* **1.** ZOOL **PRODUCING SPERM** relating or belonging to the sex that produces sperm to fertilize female eggs **2.** **RELATING TO MEN OR BOYS** relating to, involving, or traditionally characteristic of men or boys. ◊ **masculine 3.** BIOL **FERTILIZING FEMALE SEX CELL** capable of fertilizing a female reproductive cell (**gamete**) during sexual reproduction **4.** BOT **BEARING ONLY STAMENS** used to describe a flower or plant that bears stamens but not pistils and does not produce fruit or seeds **5.** ENG **MACHINE PART OR FITTING** used to describe a projecting part such as a bolt or plug that is designed to fit into a hollow part or socket that is the female counterpart ■ *n.* **1.** BIOL **MALE PERSON OR ANIMAL** a person or animal belonging to the sex that produces sperm **2.** BOT **PLANT WITH MALE FLOWERS ONLY** a plant that has only male flowers [14thC. Via Old French from Latin *masculus* (source of English *masculine*), from *mas* "male person," of unknown origin.] —**male·ness** *n.*

Ma·le /maá lee/ capital city of the Maldives, on the Male atoll. Population: 62,973 (1995).

male al·to (*plural* **male al·tos**) *n.* = **countertenor**

ma·le·ate /máy lee àyt, -ət/ *n.* any salt or ester of maleic acid

Ma·le·bo Pool /mə làybō-/ broad section of the Congo River. Area: 174 sq. mi./450 sq. km. Former name **Stanley Pool**

male chau·vin·ist *n.* a man who believes in the innate superiority of men over women (*disapproving*) —**male chau·vin·ism** *n.*

male chau·vin·ist pig *n.* an offensive term for a man who believes that men are innately superior to women, especially one who expresses his opinions in an aggressive or offensive way (*slang insult*)

Mal·e·cite /málla sīt/ (*plural* **-cites** *or* **-cite**), **Mal·i·seet** /-seet/ (*plural* **-seets** *or* **-seet**) *n.* **1.** PEOPLES **NATIVE N AMERICAN PEOPLE** a member of a Native North American people who live in New Brunswick, Quebec, and Maine. The Malecites joined the Abenaki confederacy and fought against both the Iroquois confederacy and the British. **2.** LANG **LANGUAGE OF THE MALECITES** the language of the Malecites, belonging to the Algonquian branch of Algonquian-Wakashan languages [Mid-19thC. From Micmac *mali:sit*, literally "somebody who speaks an incomprehensible language."] —**Mal·e·cite** *adj.*

mal·e·dict /mállə dìct/ *vti.* (**-dict·ed, -dict·ing, -dicts**) **CURSE SOMEBODY OR SOMETHING** to utter a curse against somebody or something (*literary*) ■ *adj.* **ACCURSED** cursed or deserving to be cursed (*archaic*) [Early 17thC. From Latin *maledicere* (see MALEDICTION).]

mal·e·dic·tion /màllə díkshən/ *n.* (*formal*) **1.** **CURSE** a curse **2.** **SLANDER** slander or evil talk about somebody [14thC. From the Latin stem *malediction-*, from *maledicere* "to speak ill of," from *dicere*).] —**mal·e·dic·tive** *adj.*

mal·e·fac·tor /mállə fàktər/ *n.* somebody who does wrong, especially a criminal (*formal*) [15thC. From Latin, formed from *male facere* "to do evil."] —**mal·e·fac·tion** /màllə fákshən/ *n.*

male fern *n.* a fern whose rhizomes and scaly stalks are used to make a resin that expels tapeworms. Latin name: *Dryopteris filix-mas.*

ma·lef·ic /mə léffik/ *adj.* having a harmful or evil effect or influence (*formal*) [Mid-17thC. From Latin *maleficus*, literally "evil-doing," from *male* "badly."]

ma·lef·i·cent /mə léffiss'nt/ *adj.* causing harm or doing evil intentionally, or capable of such acts [Mid-17thC. Back-formation from earlier *maleficence*, from Latin *maleficentia*, literally "evil doing," from *male* "badly."] —**ma·lef·i·cence** *n.*

ma·le·ic ac·id /mə lee ik-/ *n.* a colorless crystalline solid used in the manufacture of polymers. Formula: $C_4H_4O_4$. [*Maleic* from French *maléique*, an alteration of *malique* (see MALIC)]

male men·o·pause *n.* a period in middle age when some men experience feelings of insecurity and anxiety about physical decline, sometimes compared to the effects of the menopause in women

mal·e·mute *n.* = **malamute**

ma·lev·o·lent /mə lévvələnt/ *adj.* **1.** **WANTING TO CAUSE HARM** having or showing a desire to harm others **2.** **HARMFUL OR EVIL** having a harmful or evil effect or influence [Early 16thC. Directly or via Old French from the Latin stem *malevolent-*, from *male* "badly" + *volens*, the present participle of *velle* "to wish."] —**ma·lev·o·lence** *n.* —**ma·lev·o·lent·ly** *adv.*

mal·fea·sance /mal feez'nss/ *n.* (*formal*) **1.** **MISCONDUCT** wrong or illegal conduct, especially in politics or the civil service. ◊ **misfeasance, nonfeasance 2.** **UNLAWFUL ACT** an unlawful act, especially one committed by a politician or civil servant [Late 17thC. From Anglo-Norman *malfaisance*, from Old French *malfaire* "to do ill," from Latin *malefacere*.] —**mal·fea·sant** *adj., n.*

mal·for·ma·tion /màl fawr máysh'n/ *n.* abnormality in the shape or structure of something

mal·formed /màl fáwrmd/ *adj.* abnormal in shape or structure

mal·func·tion /mal fúngkshən/ *vi.* (**-tioned, -tion·ing, -tions**) **FAIL TO WORK NORMALLY** to fail to function in the correct or normal way, or stop working altogether, usually because of a fault or bad design ■ *n.* **FAILURE TO WORK NORMALLY** a breakdown or failure to function in the correct or normal way, usually because of a fault or bad design

Mali

Ma·li /maálee/ landlocked republic in western Africa. A former French colony, it gained independence in 1960. Language: French. Currency: C.F.A. franc. Capital: Bamako. Population: 9,204,000 (1996). Area: 478,841 sq. mi./1,240,192 sq. km. Official name **Republic of Mali**

mal·ic /mállik, máylik/ *adj.* relating to or derived from malic acid [Late 18thC. Directly or via French *malique* from, ultimately, Latin *malum* "apple."]

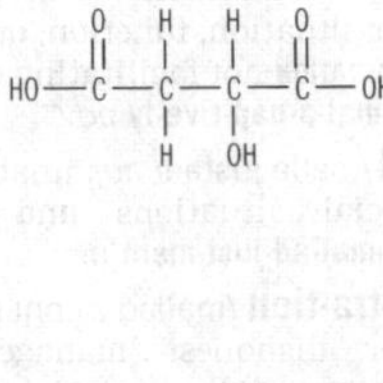
Malic acid

mal·ic ac·id *n.* a colorless crystalline solid found in fruits such as apples. Formula: $C_4H_6O_5$.

mal·ice /málliss/ *n.* **1.** **WISH TO HARM OTHERS** the desire to cause harm to another or others, or to see somebody in pain **2.** LAW **INTENT TO HARM OTHERS** the intention to commit an unlawful act that will result in harm to others and does not have excusable cause [Via French from Latin *malitia*, from *malus* (see MAL-)]

ma·li·cious /mə líshəss/ *adj.* motivated by or resulting from a desire to cause harm or pain to others —**ma·li·cious·ly** *adv.* —**ma·li·cious·ness** *n.*

ma·li·cious mis·chief *n.* deliberate destruction of or damage to somebody's property

ma·lign /mə līn/ *vt.* (**-ligned, -lign·ing, -ligns**) **DEFAME OR SPEAK BADLY OF SOMEBODY** to say or write bad or unpleasant things about somebody or something, especially things that are potentially damaging and may not be true ■ *adj.* **1.** **HARMFUL OR EVIL** harmful or evil in nature, effect, or intention **2.** **WISHING TO HARM OTHERS** having or showing a desire to cause harm or pain to others [15thC. Via French from, ultimately, Latin *malignus*, literally "of evil kind."] —**ma·lign·er** *n.* —**ma·lign·ly** *adv.*

WORD KEY: SYNONYMS

malign, cast aspersions, defame, slander, libel, vilify

CORE MEANING: to say or write something damaging about somebody

malign to criticize somebody in a spiteful and false or misleading way; **cast aspersions** to make remarks or comments that challenge somebody's reputation; **defame** to make an attack on somebody's good name or reputation with a view to damaging or destroying it; **slander** in legal terms, to make spoken false damaging accusations about somebody injurious to the person's reputation; **libel** in legal terms, to make false damaging accusations about somebody in writing, signs, or pictures; **vilify** to make viciously defamatory statements about somebody.

ma·lig·nan·cy /mə lígnənsee/ (*plural* **-cies**) *n.* **1.** **ma·lig·nan·cy, ma·lig·nance** **STATE OF BEING MALIGNANT** the condition or quality of being malignant **2.** MED **CANCEROUS GROWTH** a tumor that invades surrounding tissue and may spread to distant parts of the body by way of the lymphatic system or the circulation of the blood

ma·lig·nant /mə lígnənt/ *adj.* **1.** **WANTING TO DO EVIL** full of hate and showing a desire to harm others **2.** **HARMFUL** likely to cause harm **3.** MED **LIKELY TO GROW OR SPREAD** used to describe a tumor that invades the tissue around it and may spread to other parts of the body **4.** MED **LIKELY TO CAUSE DEATH** used to describe a disease or condition that is liable to cause death or serious disablement unless effectively treated [Mid-16thC. From late Latin *malignare* "to plot against," from Latin *malignus*, literally "of evil kind."] —**ma·lig·nant·ly** *adv.*

ma·lig·ni·ty /mə lígnətee/ (*plural* **-ties**) *n.* **1.** **DESIRE TO DO EVIL** intense hatred and a strong desire to harm others **2.** **INTENTIONALLY HARMFUL ACT** an intentionally harmful or evil act **3.** **HARMFUL POTENTIAL** potential to cause harm or death

ma·lines /mə leen/, **ma·line** *n.* **1.** **NETTING USED IN DRESSMAKING** thin stiff net with hexagonal holes that is used in dressmaking **2.** = **Mechlin** [Mid-19thC. From French, named for the city of *Malines* (Mechlin) in Belgium.]

ma·lin·ger /mə líng gər/ (**-gered, -ger·ing, -gers**) *vi.* to pretend to be ill, especially in order to avoid work (*disapproving*) [Late 18thC. From French *malingre* "sickly," of unknown origin.] —**ma·lin·ger·er** *n.*

Ma·lin·ke /mə língkee/ (*plural* **-ke** *or* **-kes**) *n.* **1.** PEOPLES **MEMBER OF W AFRICAN PEOPLE** a member of a people who live in parts of West Africa, especially in the Ivory Coast, Mali, Senegal, and Gambia. The Malinke have traditionally used cowrie shells as a medium of exchange. **2.** LANG **LANGUAGE OF THE MALINKE** the language of the Malinke, belonging to the Mande branch of Niger-Congo languages. Malinke is spoken by about four million people. [Late 19thC. From Malinke.] —**Ma·lin·ke** *adj.*

Mal·i·seet *n., adj.* = **Malecite**

mal·i·son /mállisś'n, málliz'n/ *n.* a curse (*archaic*) [13thC. Via Old French *maleiçon* from the Latin stem *malediction-* (see MALEDICTION).]

mall /mawl/ *n.* **1. LARGE INDOOR SHOPPING COMPLEX** a large enclosed building complex containing shops, restaurants, and other businesses and facilities serving the general public **2. SHADY AVENUE** a sheltered and shady avenue or promenade **3.** BUILDING **PEDESTRIAN SHOPPING AREA** an urban shopping area along a street that is closed to traffic **4.** *Northeast U.S.* TRANSP **STRIP OF LAND BETWEEN ROADWAYS** a paved or grassy strip of land between two roadways **5.** GAME, HIST **PALL-MALL ALLEY** in former times, an alley used for playing the game of pall-mall [Mid-17thC. Shortening of PALL-MALL, formerly a popular game. The sense "shopping complex" comes from the name of *The Mall* in London, a former pall-mall alley that became a fashionable promenade.]

Mallard

mal·lard /mállərd/ (*plural* **-lards** *or* **-lard**) *n.* a wild duck found in most parts of the northern hemisphere. The male has a dark green head with a white ring around the neck. Latin name: *Anas platyrhynchos.* [14thC. From Old French, of uncertain origin: perhaps formed from *male* (see MALE).]

mal·le·a·ble /mállee əb'l/ *adj.* **1. ABLE TO BE SHAPED AND BENT** used to describe a metal or other substance that can be shaped or bent without breaking **2. EASILY INFLUENCED** easily persuaded or influenced by others [14thC. Via Old French from, ultimately, Latin *malleus* "hammer" (see MALLEUS).] —**mal·le·a·bil·i·ty** /màllee ə bíllətee, màllə-/ *n.* —**mal·le·a·ble·ness** /mállee əb'lnəss/ *n.* —**mal·le·a·bly** *adv.*

WORD KEY: SYNONYMS

See Synonyms at ***pliable.***

mal·lee /mállee/ *n.* **1. SHRUBBY EUCALYPTUS** a low-growing eucalyptus tree that flourishes in desert regions of Australia. Genus: *Eucalyptus.* **2. THICKET OF MALLEE TREES** a group of mallee trees growing closely together [Mid-19thC. From an Australian Aboriginal language.]

mal·le·muck /mállə mùk/ *n.* a sea bird such as the fulmar, petrel, or albatross [Late 17thC. From Dutch *mallemok*, literally "stupid gull."]

mal·le·o·lus /mə leé ələss/ (*plural* **-li** /-lī/) *n.* either of the hammer-shaped bony protuberances at the sides of the ankle joint that project from the lower end of the tibia and fibula [Early 17thC. From Latin, literally "little hammer," from *malleus* (see MALLEUS).] —**mal·le·o·lar** *adj.*

mal·let /mállət/ *n.* **1. TOOL SIMILAR TO HAMMER** a tool with a large usually wooden or metal head that is used for driving another tool such as a chisel, or for striking or molding a material **2.** SPORTS **STICK USED IN CROQUET OR POLO** a long stick with a cylindrical head, used to hit the ball in the games of croquet and polo **3.** MUSIC **HAMMER USED TO PLAY PERCUSSION INSTRUMENT** a small hammer often with a padded head used for playing musical instruments such as the marimba, xylophone, drums, and chimes [15thC. From French *maillet*, literally "small hammer," from *mail* (see MAUL).]

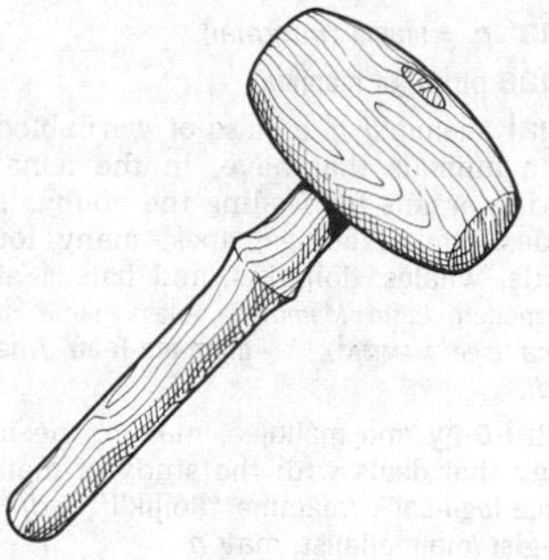

Mallet

mal·le·us /mállee əss/ (*plural* **-i** /-ī/) *n.* a hammer-shaped bone, the outermost of three small bones in the middle ear that transmit sound waves from the eardrum to the inner ear. ◊ **incus, stapes** [Mid-17thC. From Latin, "hammer" (source of English *mallet* and *malleable*). Ultimately from an Indo-European word meaning "to crush," which is also the ancestor of English *meal*[1] and *molar*[1].]

mal·low /mállō/ (*plural* **-lows** *or* **-low**) *n.* **1. FLOWERING PLANT** a wild or cultivated plant with pink, purple, or white flowers, fine hairs on its stem and leaves, and disk-shaped fruit. Genus: *Malva.* **2. PLANT RELATED TO MALLOW** a plant resembling or related to the true mallow. ◊ **rose mallow, marshmallow** [Pre-12thC. From Latin *malva.*]

malm /maam/ *n.* **1.** GEOL **TYPE OF LIMESTONE** a limestone that is grayish in color and crumbles easily **2.** GEOL **CHALKY SOIL** a chalky soil produced by the crumbling of malm **3.** BUILDING **MIXTURE OF CLAY AND CHALK** a mixture of clay and chalk used to make bricks [Old English *mealm.* Ultimately from an Indo-European base meaning "to pound, grind," which is also the ancestor of English *meal.*]

Mal·mö /málmō/ industrial city and port in southwestern Sweden, opposite Copenhagen on the Danish side of the Øresund. Population: 245,699 (1996).

malm·sey /maamzee/ *n.* a dark fortified wine produced in Madeira, the sweetest type of Madeira wine [14thC. Via Middle Dutch from medieval Latin *malmasia*, named for the town of *Monemvasia* in southern Greece, where it was originally made.]

mal·nour·ished /mal núrrisht/ *adj.* having a diet that leads to physical harm through inadequacy, inappropriateness, or excess —**mal·nour·ish·ment** *n.*

mal·nu·tri·tion /màl noo trísh'n/ *n.* a lack of healthy foods in the diet or an excessive intake of unhealthy foods, leading to physical harm

mal·oc·clu·sion /màllə kloózh'n/ *n.* an undesirable relative positioning of the upper and lower teeth when the jaw is closed —**mal·oc·clud·ed** *adj.*

mal·o·dor·ous /mal ṓdərəss/ *adj.* smelling unpleasant or offensive —**mal·o·dor·ous·ly** *adv.* —**mal·o·dor·ous·ness** *n.*

ma·lo·nic ac·id /mə lṓnik ássid, mə lònnik-/ *n.* a colorless crystalline solid obtained from sugar beet. It is used in the manufacture of pharmaceuticals. Formula: $C_3H_4O_4$. [From French *malonique*, an alteration of *malique* (see MALIC)]

ma·lo·ti plural of **loti**

Mal·pigh·i·an cor·pus·cle /mal pàjjee ən-/, **Mal·pigh·i·an bod·y** *n.* a cluster of small blood vessels enclosed in a capsule (**Bowman's capsule**) at the end of each of the tiny urine-secreting tubules (**nephrons**) of the kidney [Mid-19thC. Named for the Italian physician and anatomist Marcello *Malpighi* (1628–94).]

Mal·pigh·i·an lay·er *n.* the deepest layer of the outermost part of the skin (**epidermis**), now called the basal cell layer (*dated*) [See MALPIGHIAN CORPUSCLE]

Mal·pigh·i·an tu·bule, Mal·pigh·i·an tube *n.* a narrow tube in the body of an insect that serves as an organ of excretion [See MALPIGHIAN CORPUSCLE]

mal·po·si·tion /màl pə zísh'n/ *n.* the undesirable position of something, especially a part of the body or a fetus in the womb —**mal·posed** /mal pṓzd/ *adj.*

mal·prac·tice /mal práktiss/ *n.* **1. WRONG OR NEGLIGENT CONDUCT OF PROFESSIONAL** illegal, unethical, negligent, or immoral behavior by somebody in a professional or official position, resulting in a failure to fulfill the duties or responsibilities associated with that position **2. EXAMPLE OF MALPRACTICE** an act or instance of malpractice —**mal·prac·ti·tion·er** /màl prak tísh'nər/ *n.*

malt /mawlt/ *n.* **1. GRAIN USED TO MAKE ALCOHOLIC DRINKS** grain such as barley that has begun germination by being soaked in water. It is used chiefly in brewing and distilling to make beer and whiskey. **2.** *U.K.* = **malt whiskey 3.** = **malt liquor 4.** = **malted milk** *n.* **2** ■ *v.* (**malt·ed, malt·ing, malts**) **1.** *vti.* **CHANGE GRAIN INTO MALT** to make cereal grain into malt by soaking it in water to start germination and then drying it in a kiln, or undergo this process **2.** *vt.* **MAKE OR MIX SOMETHING WITH MALT** to make something with malt, or add malt to something [Old English *mealt*, of prehistoric Germanic origin]

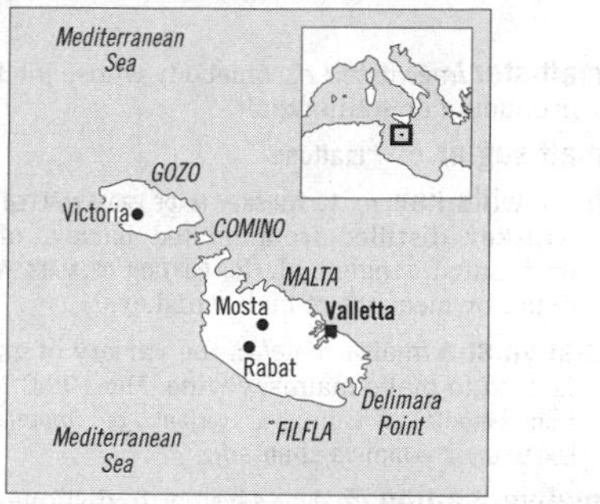

Malta

Mal·ta /máwltə/ republic consisting of two main islands and nearby islets in the central Mediterranean Sea. It became independent from Britain in 1964. Language: Maltese, English. Currency: Maltese lira. Capital: Valletta. Population: 373,000 (1996). Area: 122 sq. mi./316 sq. km. Official name **Republic of Malta**

Mal·ta fe·ver *n.* = **brucellosis** [Named for MALTA, because the disease was once common in the Mediterranean area]

mal·tase /máwl tàyss, -tàyz/ *n.* an enzyme that breaks down maltose into glucose

malt·ed milk, malt·ed *n.* **1. POWDER USED TO MAKE DRINK** a soluble powder made from dried milk and malted grain **2. DRINK MADE FROM MALTED MILK** a drink made from malted milk, whole milk, ice cream, and flavoring

Mal·tese /mawl teéz, -teéss/ (*plural* **-tese**) *n.* **1.** PEOPLES **SOMEBODY FROM MALTA** somebody who was born on or is a citizen of Malta **2.** LANG **LANGUAGE OF MALTA** one of the official languages of Malta, belonging to the Semitic branch of Afro-Asiatic languages and featuring a large number of words adopted from Italian. Maltese is spoken by about 300,000 people. **3.** ZOOL **MALTESE DOG OR CAT** a Maltese dog or Maltese cat —**Mal·tese** *adj.*

Mal·tese cat *n.* a domestic cat with short, silky, bluish gray hair

Mal·tese cross *n.* a cross with four arms resembling arrowheads that taper toward the center

Mal·tese dog *n.* a small breed of dog with long white silky hair and dark eyes

mal·tha /málthə, máwl-/ *n.* a black viscous bitumen that is a naturally occuring mixture of hydrocarbons [Early 17thC. Via Latin from Greek, a mixture of pitch and wax.]

Mal·thus /málthəss/, **Thomas Robert** (1766–1834) British economist. His theory of population growth led to fears that the rising number of living people would produce widespread famine. He advocated birth control as a means of combating poverty.

malt liq·uor *n.* an alcoholic drink that is brewed from malt, especially one having a higher alcohol content than most beer or ale

mal·tose /máwl tōss, -tōz/ *n.* a white crystalline sugar formed from starch by enzymes and used as a sweetener and nutrient. Formula: $C_{12}H_{22}O_{11}$. [Mid-19thC. Formed from MALT.]

mal·treat /mal treét/ (**-treat·ed, -treat·ing, -treats**) *vt.* to treat somebody or something badly or cruelly, usually through neglect or abuse [Early 18thC. From French *maltraiter*, literally "to treat badly," from *traiter* (see TREAT).] —**mal·treat·er** *n.* —**mal·treat·ment** *n.*

WORD KEY: SYNONYMS

See Synonyms at ***misuse.***

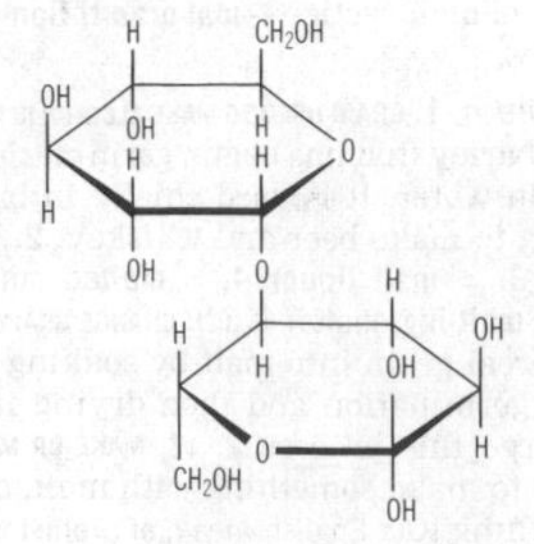

Maltose

malt·ster /máwltstər/ *n.* somebody whose job involves producing or selling malt

malt sug·ar *n.* = **maltose**

malt whis·key *n.* **1.** WHISKEY MADE FROM MALTED BARLEY a whiskey distilled from malted barley, often one designated single-malt **2.** PORTION OF MALT WHISKEY a drink or measure of malt whiskey

mal·va·si·a /màlvə zée ə/ *n.* the variety of grape that is used to make malmsey wine [Mid-19thC. Via Italian from medieval Latin, a variant of *malmasia* (see MALMSEY).] —**mal·va·si·an** *adj.*

mal·ver·sa·tion /màlvər sáysh'n/ *n.* dishonest or unethical conduct by somebody in a professional position or public office, often involving bribery, extortion, or embezzlement (*formal*) [Mid-16thC. Via French from, ultimately, Latin *male versari* "to behave badly."]

ma·ma /maáamə, mámmə/, **mam·ma** *n.* **1.** MOTHER mother (*informal*) (*usually used by or to children*) **2.** WOMAN OR WIFE a woman, especially somebody's girlfriend or wife (*slang*) (*sometimes considered offensive*) [Late 16thC. From children's first attempts at speech.]

Ma·mar·o·neck /maámarōnek/ village in southeastern New York, on Long Island Sound, a suburb of New York City. Population: 17,325 (1990).

ma·ma's boy *n.* an offensive term that deliberately insults a man's strength of character, courage, or independence (*informal insult*)

mam·ba /maámbə/ *n.* a large venomous snake found in tropical Africa, especially a green or black snake that lives in trees. Genus: *Dendroaspis.* [Mid-19thC. From Zulu *imamba.*]

mam·bo /maám bō/ *n.* (*plural* **-bos**) **1.** DANCE DANCE RESEMBLING RUMBA a modern Latin American dance originating in Cuba, similar to the rumba **2.** MUSIC MUSIC FOR MAMBO the music for the mambo. It is in 4/4 time and has strong accents on the backbeats. ■ *vi.* (**-boed, -bo·ing, -bos**) DANCE THE MAMBO to dance the mambo [Mid-20thC. From American Spanish, of uncertain origin.]

Mam·e·luke /mámmə lòok/, **Mam·luk** /mámlook/ *n.* a member of a former military caste, originally comprising enslaved Turks, that ruled Egypt from the 13th century to the 16th, remaining powerful until the early 19th century [Early 16thC. Via French from Arabic *mamlūk* "enslaved person," from *malaka* "to possess."]

Mam·et /mámmit/, **David** (*b.* 1947) U.S. playwright, and movie director. His work, e.g., the movie *Glengarry Glen Ross*, often focuses on the alienation of lower middle-class life.

ma·mey /maa mée/ (*plural* **-meys**) *n.* **1.** TREES W INDIAN TREE a tree that grows in the West Indies, bears large edible fruit, and has white fragrant flowers. Latin name: *Mammea americana.* **2.** FOOD RED-SKINNED FRUIT the edible fruit of the mamey tree that has red skin, yellow flesh, and poisonous seeds [Late 16thC. Via American Spanish *mamei* from Taino.]

mamm- *prefix.* = **mammo-** (*used before vowels*)

mam·ma[1] /mámmə/ (*plural* **-mae** /má mee/) *n.* the milk-secreting organ of female mammals, e.g., a woman's breast or a cow's udder. It includes the mammary gland and associated exterior structures such as the nipple or teat. (*technical*) [Pre-12thC. From Latin. Ultimately from an Indo-European word meaning "mother," ultimately from children's first attempts at speaking.] —**mam·mate** /má màyt/ *adj.* —**mam·mi·form** /mámmi fàwrm/ *adj.*

mam·ma[2] *n.* = **mama** (*informal*)

mam·mae plural of **mamma**[1]

mam·mal /mámm'l/ *n.* a class of warm-blooded vertebrate animals that have, in the female, milk-secreting organs for feeding the young. The class includes human beings, apes, many four-legged animals, whales, dolphins, and bats. [Early 19thC. From modern Latin *Mammalia*, class name, from Latin *mamma* (see MAMMA[1]).] —**mam·ma·li·an** /mə máylee ən/ *adj.*

mam·mal·o·gy /mə mállәjee, ma-/ *n.* the branch of zoology that deals with the study of mammals —**mam·ma·log·i·cal** /màmmə lójjik'l/ *adj.* —**mam·mal·o·gist** /mə mállәjist, ma-/ *n.*

mam·ma·plas·ty *n.* = **mammoplasty**

mam·ma·ry /mámməree/ *adj.* relating or belonging to the milk-secreting organ of a female mammal, e.g., the breast or udder [Late 17thC. Formed from MAMMA[1].]

mam·ma·ry gland *n.* a large milk-producing gland in female mammals that consists of a network of ducts and cavities leading to a nipple or teat. Mammary glands usually occur in pairs.

mam·mee /maa mée/ *n.* = **mamey** *n.* 1 [Variant of MAMEY]

mam·mee ap·ple *n.* = **mamey** *n.* 2

mam·mif·er·ous /mə míffərəss, ma-/ *adj.* having mammary glands [Early 19thC. Coined from MAMMA[1] + -FEROUS.]

mam·mil·la /mə míllə, ma-/ (*plural* **-lae** /-lee/) *n.* **1.** NIPPLE a nipple or teat **2.** PART RESEMBLING NIPPLE a protuberance or organ that resembles a nipple or teat [Late 17thC. From Latin, literally "little breast," from *mamma* (see MAMMA[1]).] —**mam·mil·lar·y** /mámmə lèrree/ *adj.*

mam·mil·late /mámmə làyt/, **mam·mil·lat·ed** /-làytəd/ *adj.* **1.** HAVING NIPPLES having nipples or protrusions that resemble nipples **2.** LIKE A NIPPLE resembling a nipple in shape or function

mammo- *prefix.* breast ○ *mammogram* [From Latin *mamma* (see MAMMA)]

mam·mog·ra·phy /ma móggrəfee/ *n.* X-ray examination of the breast, used for the early detection of developing tumors, especially cancerous ones —**mam·mo·graph·ic** /màmmə gráffik/ *adj.*

mam·mon /mámmən/ *n.* wealth and riches considered as an evil and corrupt influence (*disapproving*) [14thC. Via late Latin from, ultimately, Aramaic *māmōnā* "riches."] —**mam·mon·ism** *n.* —**mam·mon·ist** *n.*

Mam·mon *n.* the personification of wealth portrayed as a false god in the Bible

mam·mo·plas·ty /mámmə plàstee/ (*plural* **-ties**), **mam·ma·plas·ty** (*plural* **-ties**) *n.* plastic surgery performed on a woman's breast to alter the shape or size, e.g., as reconstruction following a mastectomy or as cosmetic surgery

mam·moth /mámməth/ *n.* (*plural* **-moths** *or* **-moth**) **1.** EXTINCT ELEPHANT a large extinct elephant that had long curved tusks and was covered with hair. It existed mainly in the northern hemisphere and died out more than 10,000 years ago. Genus: *Mammuthus.* **2.** SOMETHING ENORMOUS something that is a particularly large example of its kind ■ *adj.* VERY LARGE of very great size or extent [Early 18thC. From obsolete Russian *mámot*, ultimately from a Siberian language.]

WORD KEY: ORIGIN

In its original Siberian language (possibly Ostyak) ***mammoth*** meant literally "earth, soil": the first remains of ***mammoths*** to be found were dug out of the frozen soil of Siberia, and it came to be believed that the animals burrowed in the earth. The adjectival use of ***mammoth*** for "huge" dates from the early 19th century.

Mam·moth Cave Na·tion·al Park national park in southwestern Kentucky, established in 1941. More than 300 mi./480 km of its multilevel cave system, the longest in the world, have been explored. Area: 52,830 acres/21,380 hectares.

mam·my /mámmee/ (*plural* **-mies**) *n.* **mam·my, mam·mie** mother (*informal*) (*usually used by or to children*) [Early 16thC. Variant of MAMMA[2].]

Ma·mo·ré /maamóray/ river in northern Bolivia, flowing northward into the Madeira River on the Brazilian border. Length: 1,200 mi./1,900 km.

mamz·er /maámzər/ (*plural* **-er·im** /maámzə réem/) *n.* **1.** CHILD BORN OF ADULTERY OR INCEST in Jewish religious law, a child born of an adulterous or incestuous relationship **2. mamz·er, mom·ser, momz·er** OFFENSIVE TERM an offensive term for an untrustworthy or despicable person (*slang insult*) [Mid-16thC. Via late Latin from Hebrew *mamzēr.*]

man /man/ *n.* (*plural* **men** /men/) **1.** ADULT MALE HUMAN an adult male human being **2.** PERSON a person, regardless of sex or age (*often considered offensive*) ○ *a six-man crew* **3.** PARTICULAR TYPE OF MAN an adult male human being with a particular occupation, responsibility, background, or nationality (*usually used in combination*) ○ *the TV repairman* ○ *I'm not a dogs man.* **4.** HUMAN RACE the human race in general (*often considered offensive*) **5.** ZOOL MODERN OR EARLIER HUMAN BEING a member of the group that comprises modern humans and their ancestors. Genus: *Homo.* (*sometimes considered offensive*) **6.** EMPLOYEE OR WORKER an employee or worker of either sex (*often considered offensive*) **7.** MIL MALE MEMBER OF ARMED FORCES a male member of the armed forces, especially one who is not an officer (*usually used in the plural*) **8.** SERVANT a man who is a servant (*dated*) **9.** VIRILE PERSON the personification of qualities traditionally associated with the male sex, including courage, strength, and aggression, or somebody with such qualities **10.** HUSBAND OR MAN COMPANION a husband, or a man who is a woman's companion or lover (*slang*) **11.** TERM OF ADDRESS a term of address to a person of either sex (*slang*) (*sometimes considered offensive*) ○ *Cool it, man!* **12. man, Man** AUTHORITY FIGURE somebody in a position of authority, or a group that is seen as having an unfair advantage or undue power over others (*slang*) (*sometimes considered offensive*) ○ *in trouble with the Man* **13.** GAME PIECE USED IN BOARD GAMES a piece used in playing board games such as checkers **14.** HIST MEDIEVAL VASSAL in feudal societies of the early Middle Ages, an adult male human who swore allegiance to a lord in return for help and protection **15.** NAUT SHIP a ship, especially one of a particular kind (*used in combination*) ○ *man-of-war* ■ *vt.* (**manned, man·ning, mans**) (*often considered offensive*) **1.** SUPPLY SOMETHING WITH WORKERS to provide something with workers, operators, or military personnel **2.** BE READY FOR ACTION to be ready to operate or defend something ■ *interj.* USED FOR EMPHASIS used to add emphasis (*slang*) (*sometimes considered offensive*) ○ *Man, that was exciting!* [Old English *man(n).* Ultimately from an Indo-European word meaning "person, man," which is also the ancestor of English *manikin, mensch,* and *muzhik.*] ◇ **as a man, as one man** unanimously or without exception (*often considered offensive*) ◇ **be your own man** to have the resources or confidence to be responsible for yourself or your actions (*often considered offensive*) ◇ **to a man** everyone, without any exceptions (*often considered offensive*)

WORD KEY: USAGE

See Usage note at ***person.***

WORD KEY: ORIGIN

The etymologically primary sense of ***man*** is "human being, person," and that is what it generally meant in Old English: the sexes were usually distinguished by *wer* "man" (which survives probably in WEREWOLF) and *wīf* (source of modern English WIFE) or *cwene* "woman." But during the Middle English and early modern English periods "male person" gradually came to the fore, and today ***man*** is decidedly on the decline (helped on its way by those who feel that the usage discriminates against women).

MAN *abbr.* metropolitan area network

man. *abbr.* manual

Man. *abbr.* PAPER Manila *or* Manila paper ■ *abbr.* Manitoba

ma·na /maánə/ *n.* NZ a life force associated with ritual power and high social status, especially in Polynesia and Melanesia [Mid-19thC. From Maori.]

man a·bout town (*plural* **men a·bout town**), **man-a·bout-town** (*plural* **men-a·bout-town**) *n.* a sophisticated and cultured man who socializes in fashionable circles (*dated*)

man·a·cle /mánnək'l/ *n.* RING AROUND PRISONER'S WRIST either of a pair of metal rings joined by a chain and fastened around the wrists of a prisoner to be restrained (*usually used in the plural*) ■ *vt.* (**-cled, -cling, -cles**) PUT MANACLES ON SOMEBODY to restrain somebody using manacles [14thC. Via French *manicle* "handcuff" from Latin *manicula*, from *manus* "hand."]

man·age /mánnij/ (**-aged, -ag·ing, -ag·es**) *v.* **1.** *vti.* **ACHIEVE SOMETHING WITH DIFFICULTY** to succeed in doing something, especially something that seems difficult or impossible ○ *I finally managed to open the door.* **2.** *vi.* **COPE IN DIFFICULT SITUATION** to survive or continue despite difficulties, especially a lack of resources ○ *He manages with very little money.* **3.** *vti.* BUSINESS **ADMINISTER OR RUN SOMETHING** to be in charge of something such as a store, department, or project and be responsible for its smooth running and for any personnel employed ○ *manages a department of 25 people* **4.** *vt.* **HANDLE AND CONTROL SOMETHING** to handle and keep control of something such as a weapon or tool ○ *could manage a computer without difficulty* **5.** *vt.* **DISCIPLINE OR CONTROL PERSON OR ANIMAL** to keep control of a person or animal, or a number of people or animals, especially when they are wild or unruly **6.** *vt.* BUSINESS **BE SOMEBODY'S MANAGER** to guide the career and control the business affairs of somebody such as a professional entertainer or athlete [Mid-16thC. Via Italian *maneggiare* "to train a horse" from, ultimately, Latin *manus* "hand."]

man·age·a·ble /mánnijəb'l/ *adj.* able to be handled or controlled without much difficulty —**man·age·a·bil·i·ty** /mànnijə bíllətee/ *n.* —**man·age·a·ble·ness** /mánnijəb'lnəss/ *n.* —**man·age·a·bly** *adv.*

man·aged care *n.* a system of managing medical care in which nonmedical administrators such as insurance companies or HMOs control and limit the provison of such things as procedures and medicines

man·age·ment /mánnijmənt/ *n.* **1.** **ADMINISTRATION OF BUSINESS** the organizing and controlling of the affairs of a business or a particular sector of a business **2.** **MANAGERS AS A GROUP** managers and employers considered collectively, especially the directors and executives of a business or organization **3.** **HANDLING OF SOMETHING SUCCESSFULLY** the act of handling or controlling something successfully **4.** **SKILL IN HANDLING OR USING SOMETHING** the skillful handling or use of something such as resources —**man·age·men·tal** /mànnij mént'l/ *adj.*

man·age·ment in·for·ma·tion sys·tem *n.* a system for gathering the financial, production, and other information that managers need to operate a business, especially a system that is computerized

man·ag·er /mánnijər/ *n.* **1.** **SOMEBODY WHO MANAGES BUSINESS** somebody who is responsible for directing and controlling the work and personnel of a business, or of a particular department within a business **2.** **SOMEBODY WHO CONTROLS SOMEBODY'S BUSINESS AFFAIRS** somebody who organizes and controls somebody's business affairs, especially those of a professional actor, singer, or other entertainer **3.** **SOMEBODY ORGANIZING AFFAIRS OF ATHLETE** somebody who organizes and controls the training of an individual athlete or of a team **4.** SPORTS **STUDENT IN CHARGE OF TEAM'S EQUIPMENT** a student who takes care of the equipment and records of a high school or college sports team under the supervision of a coach **5.** **SOMEBODY WHO MANAGES SOMETHING WELL** somebody who handles or controls something such as resources, especially one who does so with skill **6.** **PROGRAM FOR BASIC COMPUTER OPERATIONS** a computer program designed to carry out the basic functions of a computer's operations —**man·ag·er·ship** *n.*

man·a·ger·i·al /mànni jéeree əl/ *adj.* involving or characteristic of a manager or management, especially in business —**man·a·ge·ri·al·ly** *adv.*

man·ag·ing ed·i·tor *n.* an editor of books, newspapers, or other publications who is responsible for the administration of the editorial process

Ma·na·gua /mə nàagwə/ capital city of Nicaragua, located in the west of the country, near the Pacific Ocean. Population: 1,500,000 (mid-1990s).

Ma·na·gua, Lake lake in western Nicaragua, and the country's second largest. It is drained by the Tipitapa River. Area: 405 sq. mi./1,049 sq. km.

man·a·kin /mánnəkin/ *n.* a small South American bird with a short bill and bright colorful plumage. Family: Pipridae. [Early 17thC. Variant of MANIKIN.]

Ma·na·ma capital city of Bahrain, situated in the northeastern part of the country. Population: 136,999 (1991).

ma·ña·na /maa nyàanə/ *adv.* **1.** **TOMORROW** on the day following the present day **2.** **LATER** at some unspecified time in the future [Mid-19thC. Via Spanish, "morning, tomorrow," from, ultimately, Latin *mane* "in the morning."]

Man·a·pou·ri, Lake /màanə pòoree/ lake in the southwestern part of the South Island, New Zealand. At 1,455 ft./444 m deep, it is the deepest lake in New Zealand. Area: 55 sq. mi./142 sq. km.

Ma·nas·sas /mə nássəss/ independent city in northeastern Virginia. It was the site of two Confederate victories at the Civil War battles of Bull Run in 1861 and 1862.

man-at-arms (*plural* **men-at-arms**) *n.* a soldier, especially a medieval mounted soldier who was heavily armed

man·a·tee /mánnə tèe/ *n.* a large plant-eating mammal found in warm Atlantic coastal waters. It has front flippers and a broad flattened tail. Genus: *Trichechus.* [Mid-16thC. Via Spanish *manatí* from Carib *manáti* "breast."]

Man·a·wa·tu-Wang·a·nu·i /mànə wàa too wòng gə nòoee/ administrative region of New Zealand, situated in the southwestern part of the North Island. Population: 229,989 (1996). Area: 9,775 sq. mi./25,317 sq. km.

Mance /maNss, maanss/, **Jeanne** (1606–73) French-born Canadian missionary. She was the founder of the Hotel-Dieu Hospital, Montreal (1642).

Man·ches·ter /mán chestər/ **1.** city in northwestern England. Population: 432,600 (1995). **2.** historic town in central Connecticut. Population: 52,208 (1994). **3.** the largest city in New Hampshire, located in the south of the state. Population: 96,640 (1994).

Man·ches·ter ter·ri·er *n.* a small terrier with a short-haired coat that is mainly black with tan patches [Named for the city of MANCHESTER England, where the breed originated]

man-child (*plural* **men-chil·dren**) *n.* a male child (*literary*)

man·chi·neel /mànchə nèel/ (*plural* **-neels** *or* **-neel**) *n.* a tropical American tree of the spurge family that has poisonous apple-shaped fruit and milky sap that causes blistering. Latin name: *Hippomane mancinella.* [Mid-17thC. Via French *mancenille* from Spanish *manzanilla*, literally "little apple," from *manzana* "apple," ultimately from Latin *matiana*, a kind of apple, named after *Matia*, a Roman gens.]

Man·chu /man chòo/ (*plural* **-chu** *or* **-chus**) *n.* **1.** PEOPLES **MANCHURIAN INVADERS OF CHINA** a member of a people who originally came from Manchuria and invaded China in the 17th century, establishing a powerful dynasty that lasted until the beginning of the 20th century **2.** LANG **LANGUAGE SPOKEN IN CHINA** a language spoken in northeastern parts of the People's Republic of China. It belongs to the Manchu-Tungus branch of Altaic languages. Manchu is spoken by about 20,000 people. [Late 17thC. From Manchu, literally "pure."] —**Man·chu** *adj.*

Man·chu·ri·a historic mountainous region of northeastern China comprising the modern-day provinces of Heilongjiang, Jilin, and Liaoning —**Man·chu·ri·an** *n., adj.*

Man·chu-Tun·gus *n.* a group of languages spoken in northern parts of the People's Republic of China and eastern parts of Asian Russia. It forms a branch of the Altaic family of languages. About 50,000 people speak one of the Manchu-Tungus languages. —**Man·chu-Tun·gus·ic** *adj.*

Man·cu·ni·an /man kyòonee ən/ *n.* somebody who was born in, or who lives in, the city of Manchester, in northwestern England [Early 20thC. Formed from Latin *Mancunium* "Manchester."] —**Man·cu·ni·an** *adj.*

-mancy *suffix.* divination ○ *geomancy* [Via Old French *-mancie* from, ultimately, Greek *mantis* (see MANTIC)]

Man·dae·an /man dèe ən/, **Man·de·an** *n.* **1.** RELIG **WORSHIPER OF JOHN THE BAPTIST** a member of a Gnostic religious group who believe themselves to be descendants of John the Baptist. The group originated in Jordan and still exists in Iraq and Iran. **2.** LANG **LANGUAGE OF MANDAEAN TEXTS** a form of Aramaic used in Mandaean sacred writings [Late 18thC. Formed from Mandaean *mandaia* "having knowledge," from *manda* "knowledge."] —**Man·dae·an** *adj.* —**Man·dae·an·ism** *n.*

Mandala

man·da·la /mándələ/ *n.* **1.** INDIAN RELIG **BUDDHIST OR HINDU SYMBOL** a geometric or pictorial design usually enclosed in a circle, representing the entire universe. It is used in meditation and ritual in Buddhism and Hinduism. **2.** PSYCHOANAL **SYMBOL REPRESENTING SELF** in Jungian psychology, a symbol representing the self and harmony within the individual [Mid-19thC. From Sanskrit *maṇḍalam* "circle."] —**man·dal·ic** /man dállik/ *adj.*

Man·da·lay /màndə láy/ city and transportation center on the Irrawaddy River in central Myanmar. Population: 532,949 (1983).

man·da·mus /man dáyməss/ (*plural* **-mus·es**) *n.* an order from a high court to a lower court or to an authority instructing it to perform a specific action or duty [Mid-16thC. From Latin, literally "we command."]

Man·dan /mán dàn/ (*plural* **-dan** *or* **-dans**) *n.* **1.** PEOPLES **MEMBER OF NATIVE AMERICAN PEOPLE** a member of a Native American people of North Dakota who originally occupied lands along the Missouri River and who now mainly live on the Fort Berthold Reservation near Lake Sakakawea **2.** LANG **MANDAN LANGUAGE** the language of the Mandan, belonging to the Siouan branch of Hokan-Siouan languages. Mandan is spoken by about 1,200 people. [Late 18thC. From North American French *Mandane*, of uncertain origin: probably from Dakota *mawátāna*.]

man·da·rin[1] /mándərin/ *n.* **1.** **FORMER HIGH-RANKING CHINESE OFFICIAL** in the Chinese Empire, a member of any of the nine highest ranks of public officials, attained by examinations **2.** **HIGH-RANKING CIVIL SERVANT** a high-ranking civil servant or bureaucrat with wide-ranging powers **3.** **INFLUENTIAL MEMBER OF ELITE GROUP** an influential member of an elite group, especially a literary or intellectual group [Late 16thC. Via Spanish *mandarín* and Portuguese *mandarim* from, ultimately, the Sanskrit stem *mantrin-* "counselor," from *mantraḥ* "counsel" (see MANTRA).] —**man·dar·i·nate** /mándəri nàyt/ *n.* —**man·da·ri·nic** /màndə rínnik/ *adj.* —**man·da·ri·nism** /mándəri nìzzəm/ *n.*

man·da·rin[2] /mándərin/ *n.* **1.** **CITRUS FRUIT RESEMBLING A SMALL ORANGE** a small citrus fruit, similar in size to a tangerine but with a loose orange skin that is easy to peel, especially a variety with a yellow-orange skin **2.** **SMALL CITRUS TREE** a small citrus tree that originated in China and is cultivated for its edible fruit. Latin name: *Citrus reticulata.* [Late 18thC. Via French *mandarine* from, ultimately, Spanish *mandarín* (see MANDARIN[1]), so called because of its color, likened to that of mandarins' yellow robes.]

Man·da·rin, **Man·da·rin Chi·nese** *n.* the official language of the People's Republic of China, also spoken by people of Chinese descent in various parts of the world. It belongs to the Chinese branch of Sino-Tibetan languages. Mandarin Chinese is spoken by about 800 million people as a first language and one hundred million people as a second language. —**Man·da·rin Chi·nese** *adj.* —**Man·da·rin** *adj.*

man·da·rin col·lar *n.* a narrow collar that stands up from a close-fitting neckline and opens at the front

man·da·rin duck *n.* an Asian duck with a crested head and colorful plumage. The male has one enlarged showy orange feather on each wing, which it uses in displays. Latin name: *Aix galericulata.*

man·da·rin or·ange *n.* = **mandarin**[2] *n.* 1

man·da·tar·y /mándə tèrree/ (*plural* **-ies**) *n.* a person or state that has been given a mandate

man·date /mán dàyt/ *n.* **1.** **AUTHORITATIVE ORDER** an official command or instruction from an authority **2.** POL **SUPPORT FOR GOVERNMENT FROM ELECTORATE** the authority bestowed on a government or other body by an

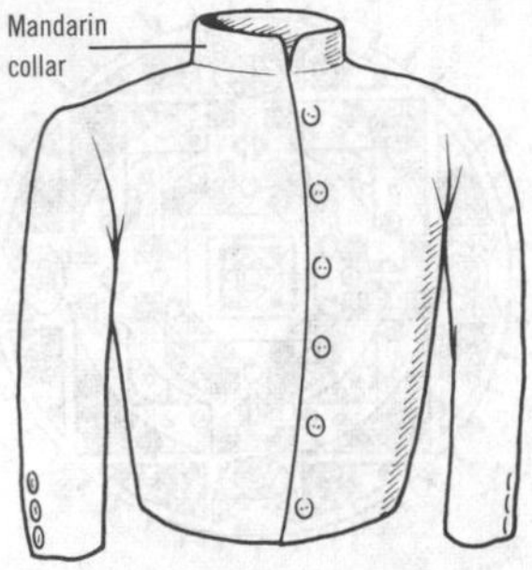

Mandarin collar

Mandarin duck

electoral victory, effectively authorizing it to carry out the policies for which it campaigned ○ *The party in power has a clear mandate for reform.* **3.** LAW **AGREEMENT FOR FREE SERVICE** a contract by which somebody agrees to perform a service without payment **4.** LAW **INSTRUCTION FROM SUPERIOR COURT OR OFFICIAL** an order from a superior court or official to a lower one **5.** HIST **REGION RULED BY OUTSIDE POWER** any of the territories that were placed by the League of Nations under the administration of one of its European member states after World War I **6.** HIST **COMMISSION TO ADMINISTER STATE** the power conferred by the League of Nations on a member state to administer a region ■ *vt.* (**-dat·ed, -dat·ing, -dates**) **1.** INTERNAT LAW **ASSIGN COLONY TO A NATION** to assign a territory or region to a particular nation under a mandate **2. MAKE SOMETHING MANDATORY** to require or order something by making it mandatory ○ *The law mandates systematic tracking and reporting of hazardous wastes.* [Early 16thC. From Latin *mandatum*, from the past participle of *mandare*, literally "to give into somebody's hand," ultimately from the Indo-European word for "hand."] —**man·da·tor** *n.*

man·dat·ed ter·ri·tory *n.* = **mandate** *n.* 5

man·da·to·ry /mándə tàwree/ *adj.* **COMPULSORY** needing to be done, followed, or complied with, usually because of being officially required **2. WITH POWER OF MANDATE** resembling or having the power of a mandate **3.** INTERNAT LAW **AUTHORIZED TO ADMINISTER TERRITORY** having a mandate to administer a region or territory ■ *n.* = **mandatary** —**man·da·to·ri·ly** *adv.*

man·da·to·ry min·i·mum *n.* a minimum sentence that must be imposed for a particular crime, without consideration of mitigating circumstances

man-day *n.* the work done by one person in one day

Man·de /maán dày/ (*plural* **-de** *or* **-des**) *n.* **1. GROUP OF WEST AFRICAN LANGUAGES** a group of around 20 languages spoken in western Africa, especially in Sierra Leone, Mali, Guinea, and the Ivory Coast. It is a branch of the Niger-Congo family of languages. About nine million people speak one of the Mande languages. **2. MANDE SPEAKER** a member of any of the West African groups that speak a Mande language [Late 19thC. From Mande, literally "little mother."] —**Man·de** *adj.*

Man·de·an *n., adj.* = **Mandaean**

Man·de·la /man déllə, -dáylə/, **Nelson** (*b.* 1918) South African statesman. After a long incarceration as a political prisoner (1964–90), in 1994 he became the first Black president of the Republic of South Africa.

Man·de·la, Winnie (*b.* 1934) South African political activist. She married Nelson Mandela in 1958 (divorced 1996), and continued his work after his imprisonment. She was convicted of a kidnapping charge in 1991. Born **Nkosikazi Nomzamo Madikizela**

South African Embassy

Nelson Mandela

man·di·ble /mándib'l/ *n.* **1.** ANAT **LOWER JAW OF VERTEBRATE** the lower jaw of a person or animal, usually containing a single bone (*technical*) **2.** BIRDS **BIRD'S BEAK** the upper or lower part of a bird's beak **3.** ZOOL **INSECT'S MOUTHPART** either of a pair of parts in insects and similar animals used for biting and cutting food [Mid-16thC. Directly or via Old French from late Latin *mandibula*, from Latin *mandere* "to chew" (source of English *manger* and *mange*).] —**man·dib·u·lar** /man díbbyələr/ *adj.* —**man·dib·u·late** /man díbbyələt, -làyt/ *adj., n.*

Man·din·go /man díng gō/ (*plural* **-gos** *or* **-goes** *or* **-go**) *n.* **1.** PEOPLES **A MEMBER OF A WEST AFRICAN PEOPLE** a member of any of several peoples that live in parts of western Africa, especially along the Niger River valley **2.** LANG **WEST AFRICAN LANGUAGE GROUP** a group of languages spoken in parts of western Africa, especially along the Niger River valley. It forms a subgroup of the Mande branch of Niger-Congo languages. About six million people speak one of the Mandingo languages. [Early 17thC. From Mandingo, from Mande *mandi* (see MANDE).] —**Man·din·go** *adj.*

man·do·lin /màndə lín, mánd'lin/ *n.* a stringed instrument of the lute family with a pear-shaped body and four or more pairs of strings, usually played with a plectrum [Early 18thC. Via French from Italian *mandolino*, literally "small lute," from *mandola* "mandola."] —**man·do·lin·ist** /màndə línnist/ *n.*

man·drake /mán dràyk/ *n.* **1. PLANT OF NIGHTSHADE FAMILY** a plant of Europe and Asia that has yellow or purplish flowers and a forked root resembling a human body. It was formerly believed to have magical powers and a drug was prepared from the root. Latin name: *Mandragora officinarum*. **2.** = **May apple** *n.* 2 [14thC. Alteration of medieval Latin *mandragora*, under the influence of MAN (from the shape of the plant's root) and DRAKE "dragon" (from its emetic and narcotic properties).]

man·drel /mándrəl/, **man·dril** *n.* **1. TAPERED SHAFT FOR SECURING WORK TO** a tapered shaft or arbor to which work is secured during machining or turning, e.g., on a lathe **2. CORE ROD** a rod around which materials such as metal or glass are molded, forged, or shaped **3. SHAFT FOR MOUNTING TOOL** a shaft on which a tool such as a dentist's drill or machining tool is mounted [Early 16thC. Origin uncertain.]

man·drill /mándril/ *n.* a large baboon of western Africa with a beard, mane, and crest. The male also has a brilliant ribbed blue, white, and scarlet muzzle. Latin name: *Mandrillus sphinx*. [Mid-18thC. Said to be coined from MAN and DRILL[4].]

Man·du·rah /mán doorə/ coastal town in southwestern Western Australia, on the Peel Inlet south of Perth. Population: 35,945 (1996).

mane /mayn/ *n.* **1.** ZOOL **HAIR ON ANIMAL'S NECK** long hair on the head and neck of an animal such as a lion or horse **2. PERSON'S LONG HAIR** a large amount of thick long hair on somebody's head (*literary or informal*) [Old English *manu*] —**maned** *adj.*

man-eat·er /mán eetər/ *n.* **1.** ZOOL **MAN-EATING ANIMAL** an animal such as a tiger or great white shark that eats or is thought to eat human flesh **2. CANNIBAL** somebody who eats human flesh **3. OFFENSIVE TERM** an offensive term for a woman who pursues men in order to make them her lovers and then discards them (*offensive*) —**man-eat·ing** *adj.*

maned wolf *n.* a wild South American member of the dog family with long legs, a shaggy yellowish-red coat and black markings on the neck and legs. Latin name: *Chrysocyon brachyurus*.

ma·nège /ma nézh/, **ma·nege** *n.* **1. ART OF RIDING** the art of riding or training horses **2. TRAINED HORSE'S MOVEMENTS** the movements that a horse has been trained to make **3. RIDING SCHOOL** a school where people are taught to ride and horses trained [Mid-17thC. From French, from Italian *maneggio*, from *maneggiare* (see MANAGE).]

ma·nes /maá nàyz, máy neez/, **Ma·nes** *n.* **HONORED GHOST** the revered spirit of a dead person (*literary*) (*takes a singular verb*) ■ *npl.* **SPIRITS OF ANCESTORS** in ancient Roman religious belief, the divine spirits of the dead (*takes a plural verb*) [14thC. From Latin, literally "good ones," from *manus* "good."]

AKG London

Édouard Manet: Portrait drawing by Edgar Degas

Ma·net /mán ay/, **Édouard** (1832–83) French painter. His innovative work such as *The Bar at the Folies-Bergère* (1882) contributed to the development of impressionism.

ma·neu·ver /mə noovər/ *n.* **1. SKILLED MOVEMENT** a movement or action that requires skill or dexterity **2.** MIL **MILITARY MOVEMENT** a planned movement of one or several military or naval units **3. DEVIOUS ACT** an action, especially a devious or deceptive one, done to gain advantage ○ *one of his little maneuvers to try to stay in total control* **4.** TRANSP **CHANGE OF COURSE** a controlled change of course of a vehicle or vessel ■ **ma·neu·vers** *npl.* MIL **MILITARY EXERCISES** large-scale military exercises used for training or practice ■ *v.* (**-vered, -ver·ing, -vers**) **1.** *vti.* **MOVE SKILLFULLY** to move or cause something to move skillfully **2.** *vti.* MIL **DO MILITARY EXERCISES** to perform or cause somebody or something to perform military maneuvers **3.** *vt.* **MANIPULATE SOMEBODY OR SOMETHING** to manipulate somebody or something to gain advantage ○ *trying to maneuver her into agreeing* **4.** *vi.* **BEHAVE DEVIOUSLY** to use devious means in order to gain advantage ○ *various candidates maneuvering for party leadership* [15thC. Via French *manoeuvre* "manipulation" from Old French *maneuvre* "manual labor," from medieval Latin *manuoperare* "to work with the hands," from Latin *manus* "hand."] —**ma·neu·ver·a·bil·i·ty** /mə noovərə bíllətee/ *n.* —**ma·neu·ver·a·ble** /-noovərəb'l/ *adj.* —**ma·neu·ver·er** *n.*

man Fri·day (*plural* **man Fri·days** *or* **men Fri·day**) *n.* a man acting as an assistant or servant who is loyal and able to do many things [Named for the loyal servant of the title character in the 1719 novel *Robinson Crusoe* by Daniel Defoe]

man·ful /mánfəl/ *adj.* brave, strong, and resolute, as a man is conventionally supposed to be —**man·ful·ly** *adv.* —**man·ful·ness** *n.*

man·ga /máng gə/ *n.* a Japanese style of comic books or animated cartoons, often very violent or erotic

man·ga·bey /máng gə bày, -bee/ (*plural* **-beys**) *n.* a large agile African monkey with a long tail, slender body, and white eyelids. Genus: *Cercocebus*. [Late 18thC. Named for the *Mangabey* region in Madagascar, to which monkeys of this genus were wrongly believed to be native.]

Man·ga·lore /màng gə láwr/ city and seaport in southwestern India, on the Arabian Sea. Population: 272,819 (1991).

mangan- *prefix.* manganese ○ *manganous* [From MANGANESE]

man·ga·nate /máng gə nàyt/ *n.* any mixed-metal salt containing manganese and oxygen in the form of an anion [Mid-19thC. Coined from MANGANESE + -ATE.]

man·ga·nese /máng gə neez, -neess/ *n.* a brittle grayish-white metallic chemical element found in pyrolusite and rhodonite and used in strengthening steel and alloys. Symbol **Mn** [Late 17thC. Via French and Italian from medieval Latin *magnesia* "magnesia."]

man·ga·nese nod·ule *n.* a stony nodule rich in manganese, found on the ocean floor

man·ga·nese steel *n.* steel containing 11 to 14 percent manganese, used to make drills and crushing blades and tools

man·gan·ic /man gánnik/ *adj.* containing or derived from manganese, especially with a valence of three or six [Mid-19thC. Formed from MANGANESE.]

man·ga·nite /máng gə nīt/ *n.* a grayish crystalline mineral consisting of a hydroxide of manganese [Early 19thC. Coined from MANGANESE + -ITE.]

man·ga·nous /máng gənəss/ *adj.* containing or derived from manganese, especially with a valence of two

mange /maynj/ *n.* an infectious skin disease of animals and sometimes humans that is caused by mites and results in hair loss, scabs, and itching [15thC. From French *manjue* "itch," from Old French *mangier* "to eat," from Latin *manducare* (see MANGER).]

man·gel /máng g'l/, **man·gel-wur·zel** /-wùrz'l/, **man·gold** /máng g'ld, -gōld/, **man·gold-wur·zel** *n.* a large yellow or reddish variety of beet that is grown as food for livestock. ◊ **beet** [Late 18thC. From German *Mangoldwurzel* "beet root."]

man·ger /máynjər/ *n.* a trough from which livestock eat [14thC. From Old French *mangeoire*, from *mangier* "to eat," from Latin *manducare* "to chew," from, ultimately, *mandere* (source of English *mange* and *mandible*).]

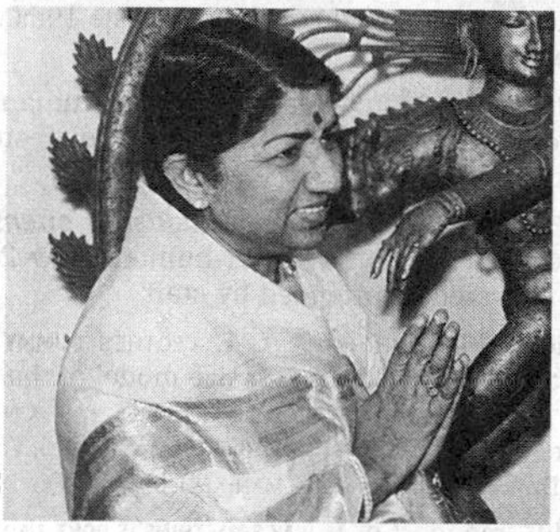

Popperfoto

Lata Mangeshkar

Man·gesh·kar /man gésh kaar/, **Lata** (*b.* 1929) Indian singer. She provided playback singing voices in Hindi films for more than 30 years, making over 30,000 recordings before retiring in 1984. Full name **Lata Dinanath Mangeshkar**

mange·tout /moNzh tōō/, **mange·tout pea** *n.* U.K. = **snow pea** [Early 19thC. From French, literally "eat-all."]

man·gle[1] /máng g'l/ (**-gled, -gling, -gles**) *vt.* **1.** DESTROY SOMEBODY OR SOMETHING BY CRUSHING to mutilate or disfigure somebody or something by violent tearing, cutting, or crushing **2.** RUIN SOMETHING to spoil or ruin something through carelessness or ineptitude ○ *a reading that mangled the rhythm of the poem* [14thC. From Anglo-Norman *mahangler*, of uncertain origin: perhaps literally "to maim repeatedly," from Old French *mahaigner* "to maim," from, ultimately, assumed Vulgar Latin *mahagnare* "to wound."] —**man·gler** *n.*

man·gle[2] /máng g'l/ *n.* **1.** MACHINE FOR PRESSING FABRIC a large machine for pressing sheets or fabric by means of two heated rollers through which the material is passed **2.** *U.K.* = **wringer** ■ *vt.* (**-gled, -gling, -gles**) PUT SOMETHING THROUGH A MANGLE to put washing through a mangle in order to squeeze out water [Late 17thC. From Dutch *mangelstok* "mangling roller," of uncertain origin: ultimately perhaps from Greek *magganon* "war engine" (see MANGONEL) or assumed Vulgar Latin *mahagnare* "to wound" (see MANGLE[1]).]

man·go /máng gō/ (*plural* **-goes** *or* **-gos**) *n.* **1.** TROPICAL ASIAN EVERGREEN TREE a tropical Asian evergreen tree of the cashew family, grown for its edible fruit. Latin name: *Magifera indica.* **2.** SWEET RED FRUIT the mango tree's red or green fruit with juicy, sweet, orange-yellow pulp [Late 16thC. Via Portuguese *manga* and Malay *mangga* from Tamil *mānkāy* "mango -tree fruit."]

man·gold, **man·gold-wur·zel** *n.* = **mangel**

man·go·nel /máng gə nèl/ *n.* a medieval military machine used for hurling stones at an enemy [13thC. Via Old French *mangonel(le)* from medieval Latin *manganellus* "little war-engine," ultimately from Greek *magganon* "war engine, axis of pulley."]

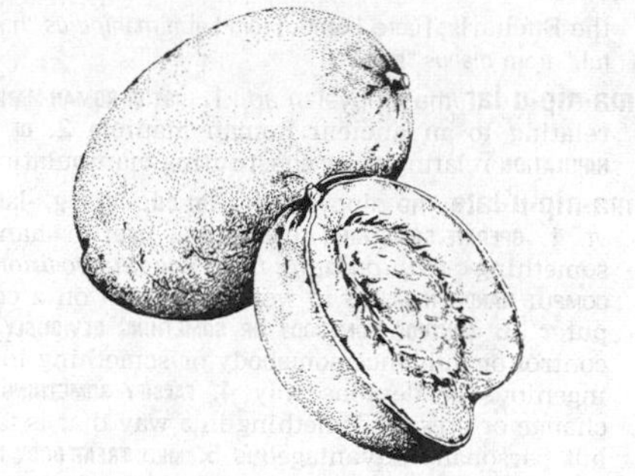

Mango

man·go·steen /máng gə stēen/ *n.* **1.** EVERGREEN TREE OF SOUTHEAST ASIA an evergreen tree native to Southeast Asia that has leathery leaves and large edible fruit. Latin name: *Garcinia mangostana.* **2.** REDDISH-BROWN FRUIT the fruit with a hard reddish-brown rind and sweet juicy pulp that the mangosteen tree produces [Late 16thC. From Malay *manggustan*, an alteration of *manggis.*]

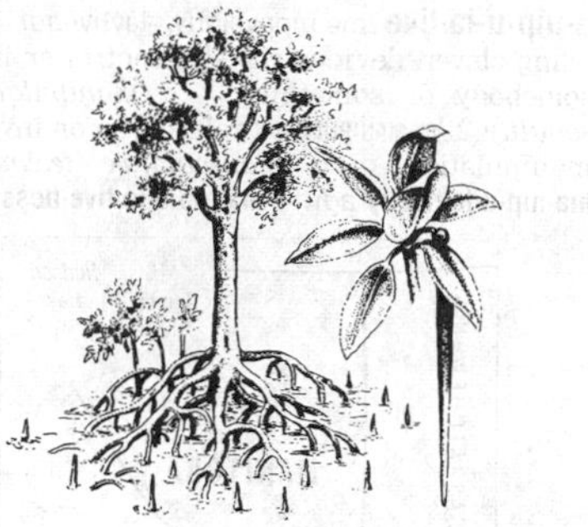

Mangrove

man·grove /mán grōv, máng-/ *n.* a tropical evergreen tree or shrub with intertwined roots and stems resembling stilts that grows in dense groves along tidal coasts. Genus: *Rhizophora.* [Early 17thC. Blend of Portuguese *mangue* or Spanish *mangle*, from Taino, and GROVE.]

mang·y /máynjee/ (**-i·er, -i·est**) *adj.* **1.** HAVING MANGE affected by or caused by mange **2.** SCRUFFY having a dirty or shabby appearance (*informal*) —**mang·i·ly** *adv.* —**mang·i·ness** *n.*

man·han·dle /mán hànd'l/ (**-dled, -dling, -dles**) *vt.* **1.** HANDLE SOMEBODY OR SOMETHING ROUGHLY to pull or push somebody or something around roughly **2.** MOVE SOMETHING BY HAND to move something using human strength alone rather than machinery

Man·hat·tan[1] /man hátt'n/, **man·hat·tan** *n.* a cocktail made from sweet vermouth, whiskey , and a dash of bitters [Late 19thC. Named for MANHATTAN, where it was invented.]

Man·hat·tan[2] /man hátt'n/ **1.** borough and main economic hub of New York City, occupying Manhattan Island at the northern end of New York Bay together with several adjacent areas. Population: 1,487,536 (1990). Area: 31 sq. mi./80 sq. km. **2.** city in northeastern Kansas, northeast of Junction City and northwest of Topeka. Population: 42,117 (1996).

Man·hat·tan Beach /man hátt'n-/ city in southwestern California, in Los Angeles County, on the Pacific Ocean. Population: 33,288 (1994).

Man·hat·tan clam chow·der *n.* a soup made from clams, vegetables, and tomatoes

Man·hat·tan·ize /man hátt'n īz/ (**-ized, -iz·ing, -iz·es**) *vt.* to change the appearance of a city by constructing skyscrapers close together —**Man·hat·tan·i·za·tion** /man hàtt'ni záysh'n/ *n.*

Man·hat·tan Proj·ect *n.* the top-secret research and development in several places in the United States that led to the successful construction and detonation of the first atomic bombs [Mid-20thC. From *Manhattan District*, the codename that was given to the research project.]

man·hole /mán hōl/ *n.* an opening with a detachable cover that gives access to an enclosed area, especially a sewer, drain, or tank

man·hood /mán hòod/ *n.* **1.** STATE OF BEING A MAN the state of being an adult male human **2.** TRADITIONAL MANLINESS the qualities and attributes conventionally thought to be appropriate to a man, especially physical strength, courage, and determination **3.** MEN men considered collectively ○ *the nation's manhood* **4.** PENIS a man's penis (*literary or humorous*)

man-hour *n.* the amount of work that can be done by one person in one hour, used as a means of assessing requirements, production, and performance ○ *the number of man-hours lost through sickness*

man·hunt /mán hùnt/ *n.* an organized search, especially by the police, for an escaped criminal or other wanted person —**man·hunt·er** *n.*

ma·ni·a /máynee ə/ *n.* **1.** OBSESSION an excessive and intense interest in or enthusiasm for something **2.** PSYCHIATRIC DISORDER psychiatric disorder characterized by excessive physical activity, rapidly changing ideas, and impulsive behavior [14thC. Via late Latin from Greek *mania* "loss of reason," from *mainesthai* "to rage." Ultimately from an Indo-European word meaning "think."]

-mania *suffix.* excessive enthusiasm for or attachment to ○ *pyromania* [From MANIA]

ma·ni·ac /máynee àk/ *n.* **1.** OFFENSIVE TERM an offensive term for somebody who behaves in such an uncontrolled manner as to appear to be affected by mania (*offensive*) **2.** ENTHUSIAST somebody who has an excessive and intense interest in or enthusiasm for a particular thing **3.** OFFENSIVE TERM an offensive term for somebody affected by mania (*offensive*) ■ *adj.* = **maniacal** [Late 16thC. Via late Latin *maniacus* from late Greek *maniakos*, from *mania* (see MANIA).]

ma·ni·a·cal /mə nī ək'l/ *adj.* (*offensive*) **1.** OFFENSIVE TERM an offensive term meaning so uncontrolled as to appear to be affected by mania **2.** OFFENSIVE TERM an offensive term meaning or indicative of mania —**ma·ni·a·cal·ly** *adv.*

man·ic /mánnik/ *adj.* **1.** RELATING TO MANIA relating to or affected by mania **2.** HECTIC extremely or excessively busy (*informal*) (*sometimes considered offensive*) **3.** OVEREXCITED in a state of abnormally high excitement, especially because of tension (*informal*) [Early 20thC. Coined from MANIA + -IC.] —**man·i·cal·ly** *adv.*

man·ic-de·pres·sive *n.* PERSON WITH BIPOLAR DISORDER somebody affected by bipolar disorder ■ *adj.* CHARACTERISTIC OF BIPOLAR DISORDER typical of or affected by bipolar disorder

man·ic-de·pres·sive dis·or·der, **man·ic-de·pressive ill·ness** *n.* = **bipolar disorder**

Man·i·chae·ism /mànni kée ìzzəm/, **Man·i·che·ism** *n.* **1.** RELIG ANCIENT DUALIST BELIEF SYSTEM a religious doctrine based on the separation of matter and spirit and of good and evil that originated in 3rd-century Persia and combined elements of Zoroastrianism, Buddhism, Christianity, and Gnosticism **2.** CHR CHRISTIAN RELIGIOUS DUALISM a heretical Christian belief in the separate nature of mattter and spirit [Early 17thC. Formed from late Latin *Manichaeus*, from, ultimately, *Manes*, (216?–276?), name of the Persian founder of this belief system.] —**Man·i·chae·an** /mànni kée ən/ *adj.* —**Man·i·chee** /mánni kee/ *n.*

man·i·cot·ti /mànni kóttee/ *n.* a dish of large pasta tubes that are usually stuffed with a ricotta or meat filling and then baked [Mid-20thC. From Italian, literally "sleeves."]

man·i·cure /mánni kyòor/ *n.* COSMETICS HAND AND NAIL COSMETIC TREATMENT a cosmetic treatment for the hands and nails that usually involves shaping and polishing the fingernails, pushing back the cuticles, and treating rough skin ■ *vt.* (**-cured, -cur·ing, -cures**) **1.** TREAT HANDS AND NAILS to treat the hands and fingernails by cutting, shaping, and polishing the nails, and softening the hands **2.** CUT AND SHAPE SOMETHING CAREFULLY to cut and shape something with great care and precision [Late 19thC. Via French from Latin *manus cura* "hand care."]

man·i·cur·ist /mánni kyòorist/ *n.* somebody whose job is to give people manicures

man·i·fest /mánnə fèst/ *adj.* OBVIOUS clear to see or understand ■ *v.* (**-fest·ed, -fest·ing, -fests**) **1.** *vt.* SHOW SOMETHING CLEARLY to make something evident by showing or demonstrating it very clearly **2.** *vi.* APPEAR to appear or be revealed **3.** *vt.* INCLUDE SOMETHING IN CARGO LIST to include something in a ship's cargo list ■ *n.* **1.** SHIP'S CARGO LIST a list giving details of a ship's cargo, its destination, and other particulars for customs purposes **2. PLANE OR TRAIN'S CARGO LIST** a list of cargo or passengers on a plane or train [14thC. Directly or via Old French from Latin *manifestus* "apprehensible" (literally "seized by hand"), from *manus* "hand" and *festus* "seizable."] —**man·i·fest·a·ble** *adj.* —**man·i·fest·ly** *adv.* —**man·i·fest·ness** *n.*

man·i·fes·ta·tion /mànnə fes táysh'n/ *n.* **1. ACT OF SHOWING SOMETHING** an act of showing or demonstrating something **2. STATE OF BEING MANIFESTED** the state or condition of being shown or perceptible **3. SIGN** an indication that something is present, real, or exists ○ *one of the first manifestations of the disease* **4. PUBLIC DEMONSTRATION** a public demonstration, usually over a political issue **5. MATERIALIZATION** a supposed appearance in visible form by a spiritual being **6. VISIBLE FORM OF DIVINE BEING** a visible form in which a divine being, idea, or person is believed to be revealed or expressed —**man·i·fes·ta·tional** *adj.*

man·i·fest con·tent *n.* in dream analysis, the overt meaning of a dream remembered by the dreamer on waking that requires analysis to interpret its latent content or real meaning

Man·i·fest Des·ti·ny *n.* the 19th-century doctrine according to which the United States was believed to have the God-given right to expand into and possess the whole of the North American continent

man·i·fes·to /mànnə féstō/ (*plural* **-tos** *or* **-toes**) *n.* a public written declaration of principles, policies, and objectives, especially one issued by a political movement or candidate [Mid-17thC. From Italian, where it was formed from *manifestare* "to make evident," ultimately from Latin *manifestus* (see MANIFEST).]

man·i·fold /mánnə fòld/ *adj.* **1. MANY AND VARIOUS** of many different kinds ○ *The reasons for the crisis are manifold.* **2. HAVING MANY FORMS** having many parts, forms, or applications ○ *a manifold political system* ■ *n.* **1.** ENG **CHAMBER WITH PORTS** a chamber or pipe with several openings for receiving or distributing a fluid or gas, such as the intake or exhaust manifolds of an internal-combustion engine **2.** MATH **TOPOLOGICAL SPACE** a topological space or surface satisfying specific conditions ■ *vt.* (**-fold·ed, -fold·ing, -folds**) **1. MULTIPLY** to multiply something **2. MAKE COPIES OF SOMETHING** to make several copies of a book or page [Old English *manigfeald*, from earlier forms of MANY + FOLD] —**man·i·fold·er** *n.* —**man·i·fold·ly** *adv.* —**man·i·fold·ness** *n.*

man·i·kin /mánnikin/, **man·ni·kin** *n.* **1.** CLOTHES = **mannequin** *n.* 1 **2. ANATOMICAL MODEL OF HUMAN BODY** an anatomical model of the human body, used in teaching art or medicine **3. OFFENSIVE TERM** an offensive term for a very short man (*offensive*) [Mid-16thC. From Dutch *manneken* "little man," from *man* "man."]

ma·nil·a /mə nílla/, **Ma·nil·la** *adj.* **MADE OF MANILA PAPER** made of manila paper ○ *a manila envelope* ■ *n.* **1. CIGAR** a cigar made in Manila **2.** = **Manila hemp 3.** = **Manila paper** [Late 17thC. Named for the port of *Manila*, the capital of the Philippines.]

Ma·nil·a /mè níllə/ capital city of the Philippines, located on the coast of Luzon Island. Population: 1,601,234 (1990).

Ma·nil·a Bay /mə níllə-/ bay of the South China Sea in the northern Philippines, on Luzon Island. Area: 770 sq. mi./2,000 sq. km. Length: 37 mi./60 km.

Ma·nil·a hemp, **Ma·nil·la hemp** *n.* a strong fiber obtained from the Philippine abaca plant and used in making rope and paper [Mid-19thC. Named for MANILA.]

Ma·nil·a pa·per, **Ma·nil·la pa·per** *n.* a strong pale-brown paper with a smooth surface, made from Manila hemp and used for wrapping or for envelopes [Late 19thC. Named for MANILA, where it was originally made.]

ma·nille /mə níl/ *n.* CARDS the second-best trump in the card games ombre and quadrille [Late 17thC. Via French from Spanish *malilla* "little bad (card)."]

man in the moon *n.* the imaginary being behind the apparent face on the moon when it is full

man in the street, **man on the street** *n.* the average person, as opposed to an expert, celebrity, or prominent person

man·i·oc /mánni òk/ *n.* = **cassava** [Mid-16thC. From Tupi *mandioca* (influenced by French *manihot*), from Guarani *mandio*.]

man·i·ple /mánnəp'l/ *n.* **1.** HIST **PART OF ROMAN LEGION** in the ancient Roman army, a subdivision of a legion, containing 60 or 120 men **2.** CHR **FORMER ECCLESIASTICAL ADORNMENT** a silk band or folded napkin formerly worn on the left arm of somebody administering the Eucharist [Late 16thC. From Latin *manipulus* "handful," from *manus* "hand."]

ma·nip·u·lar /mə níppyələr/ *adj.* **1.** HIST **OF ROMAN MANIPLE** relating to an ancient Roman maniple **2. OF MANIPULATION** relating to or constituting manipulation

ma·nip·u·late /mə níppyə làyt/ (**-lat·ed, -lat·ing, -lates**) *vt.* **1. OPERATE SOMETHING** to operate, use, or handle something ○ *manipulating the crane into position* **2.** COMPUT **HANDLE NUMBERS** to work with data on a computer **3. CONTROL SOMEBODY OR SOMETHING DEVIOUSLY** to control or influence somebody or something in an ingenious or devious way **4. FALSIFY SOMETHING** to change or present something in a way that is false but personally advantageous **5.** MED **TREAT BODY PART USING HANDS ONLY** to treat a part of the body, or to move a part such as a joint during examination, using the hands only [Early 19thC. Back-formation from *manipulation*, from French, where it was formed from *manipule*, literally "handful," from Latin *manipulus* (see MANIPLE). Originally "digging for silver ore," hence "skillful handling."] —**ma·nip·u·la·bil·i·ty** /mə nìppyələ bíllətee/ *n.* —**ma·nip·u·la·ble** /mə níppyələb'l/ *adj.* —**ma·nip·u·lat·a·ble** /-làytəb'l/ *adj.* —**ma·nip·u·la·tion** /mə nìppyə láysh'n/ *n.* —**ma·nip·u·la·tor** *n.* —**ma·nip·u·la·to·ry** *adj.*

ma·nip·u·la·tive /mə níppyələtiv, -làytiv/ *adj.* **1. DEVIOUS** using clever, devious ways to control or influence somebody or something ○ *a manipulative personality* **2. OF MANIPULATION** relating to or involved in manipulation ○ *a manipulative technique* —**ma·nip·u·la·tive·ly** *adv.* —**ma·nip·u·la·tive·ness** *n.*

Manitoba

Man·i·to·ba /mànni tṓbə/ province in south central Canada, the easternmost of Canada's three Prairie provinces. Capital: Winnipeg. Population: 1,145,200 (1997). Area: 250,947 sq. mi./649,950 sq. km. —**Man·i·to·ban** *adj.*, *n.*

Man·i·toba, Lake /manitṓbə/ lake in southern Manitoba, Canada. It discharges through the Dauphin River to Lake Winnipeg. Area: 1,798 sq. mi./4,659 sq. km.

man·i·tou /mánni tòo/, **man·i·tu, man·i·to** /-tṑ/ (*plural* **-tos**) *n.* a supernatural force or spirit believed by Algonquian peoples to suffuse various living things and inanimate objects [Late 16thC. From Narragansett *manittówock*.]

Man·i·tou·lin Is·lands /màni tòolin-/ archipelago on the border between the United States and Canada, in northern Lake Huron. They include Manitoulin Island, the world's largest freshwater island.

Ma·ni·za·les /mànni thaalayss/ city in western Colombia. It is the capital of Caldas Department, in the Andes mountains. Population: 329,844 (1993).

man jack *n.* a single individual (*informal*) (*often considered offensive*)

Man·ki·e·wicz /máng kye vich/, **Joseph L.** (1909–93) U.S. movie director and screenwriter. He won Academy Awards for *A Letter to Three Wives* (1949) and *All About Eve* (1950). Full name **Joseph Lee Mankiewicz**

Man·kil·ler /mánkilər/, **Wilma** (*b.* 1945) U.S. Native American leader. She was the first woman chief of the Cherokee Nation (1985–95).

man·kind /mán kīnd/ *n.* **1. ALL HUMAN BEINGS** human beings considered collectively (*often considered offensive*) **2. MEN, NOT WOMEN** men considered collectively, as distinct from women (*dated*)

Man·ley /mánnlee/, **Michael** (1923–97) Jamaican statesman. He served twice as prime minister of Jamaica (1972–80, and 1989–92). Full name **Michael Norman Manley**

man·ly /mánlee/ (**-li·er, -li·est**) *adj.* **1. CONVENTIONALLY TYPICAL OF A MAN** having or showing and qualities conventionally thought to be typical of or appropriate to a man, especially physical strength or courage **2. CONSIDERED APPROPRIATE FOR A MAN** considered suitable or appropriate for a man —**man·li·ness** *n.*

man-made /mán màyd/, **man·made** *adj.* made by human beings and not occurring naturally (*often considered offensive*)

Mann /man, maan/, **Thomas** (1875–1955) German-born U.S. novelist and critic. His work, much of which explores the relationship between society and the creative artist, earned him the Nobel Prize in literature (1929).

man·na /mánnə/ *n.* **1.** BIBLE **DIVINELY PROVIDED SUSTENANCE** in the Bible, food provided miraculously to feed the Israelites in the wilderness **2. UNEXPECTED BENEFIT** something very welcome or of great benefit that comes unexpectedly **3.** TREES **SWEET SUBSTANCE FROM ASH TREE** a sweet substance, used in the past as a laxative, exuded by the European ash tree **4.** INSECTS **SWEET INSECT SUBSTANCE** a sweet substance excreted by a scale insect that feeds on the tamarisk and eaten by ants [Pre-12thC. Via late Latin from, ultimately, Hebrew *mān*.]

Mann Act *n.* a 1910 federal law that criminalized the interstate transportation of women for immoral purposes

man·nan /má nàn, mánnən/ *n.* a complex carbohydrate found in the cell walls of some plants such as the ivory nut and carob bean [Late 19thC. Coined from MANNOSE + -AN.]

Man·nar, Gulf of /mə naár/ arm of the Indian Ocean between the southern tip of India and western Sri Lanka

manned /mand/ *adj.* (*often considered offensive*) **1. HAVING PEOPLE ABOARD** having a human crew **2. HAVING STAFF** operated or attended by staff

man·ne·quin /mánnikin/ *n.* **1.** CLOTHES **DUMMY FOR DISPLAYING CLOTHES** a usually life-size model of the human body used to display or fit clothes **2.** FASHION **MODEL** a model (*dated*) **3.** ARTS = **lay figure** [Mid-18thC. Via French from Dutch *manneken* (see MANIKIN).]

man·ner /mánnər/ *n.* **1. WAY SOMETHING IS DONE** the way in which something is done or happens ○ *His manner of doing things is often a little unconventional.* **2. WAY OF BEING** the characteristic way in which somebody behaves ○ *had a capricious manner about him* **3. TYPE** a type or kind ○ *What manner of insect makes this hole?* **4. STYLE OF WORK OF ART** the style in which a work of art is executed ○ *painted in the manner of Vermeer* ■ **man·ners** *npl.* **1. SOCIAL BEHAVIOR** social behavior, especially in terms of what is considered correct or unacceptable **2. CUSTOMS AND PRACTICES** the customs and practices of a particular society or period in time ○ *18th-century manners* [12thC. Via Anglo-Norman *manere* "way of handling," from Latin *manuarius* "of the hand," from *manus* "hand."] ◇ **in a manner of speaking** in some ways, though not exactly or not in all ways ◇ **to the manner born** naturally adapted to something as though accustomed to it from birth

man·nered /mánnərd/ *adj.* **1. AFFECTED** characterized by affected mannerisms ○ *her mannered tones* **2. BEHAVING IN PARTICULAR WAY** behaving in a particular way or having manners of a particular kind (*usually used in combination*) ○ *an ill-mannered child*

man·ner·ism /mánnə rìzzəm/ *n.* **1. IDIOSYNCRASY** a particular gesture, habit, or way of doing something ○ *one of his odd little mannerisms* **2. AFFECTED BEHAVIOR** affected or exaggerated speech, behavior, or writing —**man·ner·is·tic** /mànnə rístik/ *adj.* —**man·ner·is·ti·cal·ly** *adv.*

Man·ner·ism /mánnə rìzzəm/, **man·ner·ism** *n.* a style of art and architecture, predominant in Italy in the late 16th century, characterized by stylized and elongated forms and the pursuit of a representation of idealized beauty —**Man·ner·ist** *adj.*, *n.*

man·ner·less /mánnərləss/ *adj.* having or showing bad manners —**man·ner·less·ness** *n.*

man·ner·ly /mánnərlee/ *adj.* **POLITE** well-mannered or polite ■ *adv.* **POLITELY** in a well-mannered or polite way (*archaic*) ○ *"A child should always say what's true, And speak when he is spoken to, And behave mannerly at table; At least as far as he is able."* (Robert Louis Stevenson, *A Child's Garden of Verse*; 1885) —**man·ner·li·ness** *n.*

Mann·heim /mán hīm/ city and riverport in southwestern Germany, on the Rhine River. Population: 317,300 (1994).

Mann·heim school *n.* a style of orchestral and string playing associated with the rise of the Classical period, developed at the court of Mannheim in the 18th century [Named for MANNHEIM]

man·ni·kin *n.* = **manikin**

Man·ning /mánning/ river in eastern New South Wales, Australia. Length: 140 mi./225 km.

man·nish /mánnish/ *adj.* **1. LIKE OR FOR A MAN** resembling or suitable for a man instead of a woman (*often considered offensive*) **2. TYPICAL OF A MAN** considered characteristic of a man [Old English] —**man·nish·ly** *adv.* —**man·nish·ness** *n.*

man·ni·tol /mánni tàwl/, **man·nite** /má nīt/ *n.* a sweet white crystalline alcohol found in some plants and used as a sweetener, dietary supplement, diuretic, and in kidney testing. Formula: $C_6H_{14}O_6$. [Late 19thC. Formed from MANNA.] —**man·nit·ic** /mə níttik/ *adj.*

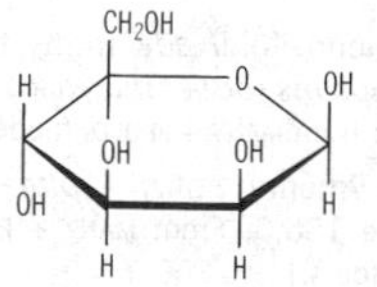

Mannose

man·nose /má nòss/ *n.* a plant sugar obtained from manna and mannitol. Formula: $C_6H_{12}O_6$. [Late 19thC. Coined from MANNITE + -OSE.]

ma·no /maánō/ (*plural* **-nos**) *n.* the stone held in the hand when grinding grain on a stone block (**metate**) [Early 20thC. From Spanish, from Latin *manus* "hand."]

ma·no a ma·no /maánō aa maánō/ *n.* (*plural* **ma·nos a ma·nos**) **1. FACE-TO-FACE CONFRONTATION** a face-to-face confrontation between opposing people or sides **2. BULLFIGHT IN WHICH MATADORS TAKE TURNS** a bullfight during which two competing matadors take turns fighting several bulls each ■ *adj., adv.* **COMPETING DIRECTLY** competing directly with somebody or something [Late 20thC. From Spanish, literally "hand to hand."]

ma·noeu·vre *vti., n.* U.K. = **maneuver**

man of God *n.* **1. CLERGYMAN** a man who is a member of the clergy **2. SAINT** a saint or godly man

man of let·ters *n.* a man who is a writer or scholar (*literary*)

man of straw *n. U.K.* = **straw man**

man of the cloth (*plural* **men of the cloth**) *n.* a man who is a member of the clergy

man-of-war /mánnə wáwr/ (*plural* **men-of-war** /ménnə-/), **man o'war** (*plural* **men o'war** /mènnə-/) *n.* **1.** = **warship 2.** MARINE BIOL = **Portuguese man-of-war**

man-of-war bird, man-o'-war bird *n.* = **frigate bird**

ma·nom·e·ter /mə nómmətər/ *n.* an instrument used to measure the pressure of a gas [Mid-18thC. From French *manomètre*, from Greek *manos* "thin, rare" + an equivalent French form of METER.] —**man·o·met·ric** /mànnə méttrik/ *adj.* —**man·o·met·ri·cal·ly** *adv.* —**ma·nom·e·try** /mə nómmətree/ *n.*

man on horse·back (*plural* **men on horse·back**) *n.* **1. MILITARY STRONGMAN** a powerful man, usually a member of a nation's armed forces, who uses his popularity and influence to become the head of state, often in a dictatorship **2. DICTATOR** a military dictator

man·or /mánnər/ *n.* **1. NOBLE'S HOUSE AND LAND** a house and the land surrounding it, owned by a medieval noble **2. FORMER INHERITABLE LAND** in North America before 1776, an area of land in some colonies with hereditary rights granted by royal charter to the proprietor **3.** = **manor house** [13thC. Via Anglo-Norman *maner* from Old French *maneir* "dwelling place," ultimately from Latin *manere*, "to remain, stay."] —**ma·no·ri·al** /mə náwree əl/ *adj.*

WORD KEY: ORIGIN

The Latin word *manere*, from which ***manor*** is derived, is also the source of English *maisonette, manse, mansion, menagerie, permanent*, and *remain*.

man·or house *n.* the residence of the lord or lady of a manor

man·pow·er /mán pòwr/ *n.* power in terms of the number of people available or needed to do something

man·qué /maaN káy/ *adj.* having wanted unsuccessfully to be or do something ○ *an artist manqué* [Late 18thC. From French, past participle of *manquer* "to fail, lack."]

man·sard /mán saard/ *n.* the part of a building enclosed by a mansard roof [Mid-18thC. From French, named for François *Mansard*, (1598–1666), the architect credited with designing buildings with roofs of this type.]

Mansard roof

man·sard roof *n.* a roof that slopes on all four sides, with each side divided into a gentle upper slope and a steeper lower slope

manse /mans/ *n.* **1. CHRISTIAN MINISTER'S HOUSE** a house provided for a church minister by some Christian denominations, especially in the Presbyterian Church **2. LARGE HOUSE** a large, stately house [Late 15thC. From medieval Latin *mansus* "unit of land," from Latin *manere* (see MANOR).]

Man·sell, Nigel (*b.* 1953) British motor racing driver. He won the World Grand Prix Formula One Championship (1992) and then started racing in the United States, where he won the Indy Car Championship (1993).

man·ser·vant /mán sùrvənt/ (*plural* **men·ser·vants** /mén sùrvənts/) *n.* a man who is a servant, especially somebody's valet

Mans·field, Mount /mánzfeeld/ mountain in northern Vermont in the Green Mountains, the highest point in the state. Height: 4,393 ft./1,339 m.

Mans·field /mánz feeld/, **Jayne** (1933–67) U.S. movie-actor. As a movie comedienne she played leading roles in *The Girl Can't Help It* (1956) and *Will Success Spoil Rock Hunter?* (1957). Real name **Vera Jayne Palmer**

Mans·field /mánss feeld/, **Katherine** (1888–1923) New Zealand-born British writer. She was a major figure in the development of the short-story form. Pseudonym of **Katherine Mansfield Beauchamp**

man·sion /mánshən/ *n.* **1. LARGE HOUSE** a large and stately house **2.** ZODIAC **DIVISION OF ZODIAC** any one of the 28 divisions of the zodiac through which the moon passes successively each month [14thC. Via Old French, "dwelling place," from Latin *manere* "to remain, stay" (source of English *manor* and *remain*).]

man-sized, man-size *adj.* **1. LARGE** larger than the ordinary size ○ *a man-sized appetite* **2. BIG ENOUGH FOR MAN** the same size as or big enough for a man ○ *a man-sized hole in the fence*

man·slaugh·ter /mán slàwtər/ *n.* the unlawful killing of one human being by another without advance planning

man's man (*plural* **men's men**) *n.* a man who prefers the company of other men to that of women (*informal*)

Man·son /mánssən/, **Charles** (*b.* 1934) U.S. cult leader and murderer. Founder of the "Manson Family," he was sentenced to death for ritual murders carried out in California in 1969, but his sentence was later commuted to life imprisonment by a Supreme Court ruling.

man·sue·tude /mánswə tood/ *n.* a meek or gentle attitude or behavior (*archaic*) [14thC. Via Old French or directly from Latin *mansuetudo*, from *mansuetus* "tame," literally "accustomed to the hand," from *suescere* "to accustom."]

Man·su·ra /man soórə/ city in northeastern Egypt, in the Nile delta. Population: 371,000 (1992).

man·ta /mántə/ *n.* **1.** ZOOL **LARGE WARM-WATER RAY** a large warm-water ray with wide pectoral fins, a long tail, and two fins resembling horns that project from the head. Family: Mobulidae. **2.** *Southwest U.S.* TEXTILES **SQUARE OF ROUGH CLOTH** a square piece of rough cloth, used as a cape, shawl, or horse blanket [Late 17thC. From Spanish, literally "blanket, mantle" (because the ray is traditionally caught in a blanketlike fishtrap).]

man-tai·lored *adj.* cut and styled like men's suits ○ *She favors man-tailored suits for the office.*

man·ta ray *n.* ZOOL = **manta** *n.* 1

man·tel /mánt'l/ *n.* an ornamental frame around a fireplace, usually made of stone or wood [15thC. From MANTLE.]

man·tel·et /mánt'lət, mántlət/, **mant·let** /mántlət/ *n.* a short cape worn by women in the 19th century

man·tel·piece /mánt'l peess/, **man·tle·piece** *n.* the mantel of a fireplace, especially its projecting top

man·tel·shelf /mánt'l shèlf/ (*plural* **-shelves** /-shèlvz/), **man·tle·shelf** (*plural* **-shelves**) *n.* the projecting top of the mantel of a fireplace, used as a shelf

man·tel·tree /mánt'l tree/, **man·tle·tree** *n.* a stone or beam that acts as a support for the masonry above a fireplace

man·tic /mántik/ *adj.* relating to or having powers of divination or prophecy [Mid-19thC. From Greek *mantikos*, from *mantis* "prophet," from *mainesthai* "to rage" (see MANIA).] —**man·tic·al·ly** *adv.*

man·tid /mántis/, **man·tis** *n.* = **mantis**

man·til·la /man teéyə, -tíllə/ *n.* **1. LACE HEADSCARF** a lace scarf that covers the head and shoulders, often worn by women in church, especially in Spain and Latin America **2. SHORT CLOAK** a short light cape [Early 18thC. From Spanish, "little mantle."]

man·tis /mántiss/ (*plural* **-tis·es** *or* **-tes** /-teez/) *n.* a large, usually green insect that feeds on other insects and has a long body, large eyes, and strong grasping front legs that it holds up at rest. Family: Mantidae. [Mid-17thC. Via modern Latin from Greek, literally "prophet" (see MANTIC). From the insect's forelegs, the position of which suggests an attitude of prayer.]

man·tis crab *n.* = **squilla**

man·tis·sa /man tíssə/ *n.* the fractional part of a logarithm, to the right of the decimal point [Mid-17thC. From Latin, "makeweight," of ultimately unknown origin, perhaps from Etruscan.]

man·tis shrimp *n.* = **squilla**

man·tle /mánt'l/ *n.* **1. TRANSFERRED OR INHERITED POSITION** a role or position, especially one that can be passed from one person to another (*formal*) ○ *assumed the mantle of the Presidency* **2. COVERING** something that envelops or covers something else (*literary*) ○ *a mantle of snow* **3.** CLOTHES **SLEEVELESS CLOAK** a loose sleeveless cloak **4. WIRE MESH FOR GAS LIGHT** a small circle of wire mesh in a gas or oil lamp that gives out incandescent light when heated by the flame it surrounds **5.** ZOOL **SHELL-PRODUCING GLAND** a layer of epidermis in a mollusk or brachiopod with glands that secrete a shell-producing substance **6.** BIRDS **FEATHERS** the back, inner-wing, and shoulder-area (**scapular**) plumage of a bird **7.** GEOL **CENTRAL PART OF EARTH** the part of the Earth or another planet that lies between the crust and core **8.** = **mantel** ■ *v.* (**-tled, -tling, -tles**) **1.** *vt.* **COVER SOMETHING** to cover something with a mantle or with something resembling a mantle ○ *hilltops mantled with snow* **2.** *vi.* **FLUSH** to become flushed (*refers to sb's face*) ○ *His puffy face mantled in angry red blotches.* [Pre-12thC. Via Old French *mantel* from Latin *mantellum* "cloak" (source of English *mantelpiece* and *dismantle*), of uncertain origin: perhaps ultimately from Celtic.]

Man·tle /mánt'l/, **Mickey** (1931–95) U.S. baseball player. He played center field for the New York Yankees (1951–69) where his many achievements included a Triple Crown in batting, home runs, and runs batted in. Full name **Mickey Charles Mantle**

man·tle·piece /mánt'l peess/ *n.* = **mantelpiece**

man·tle·shelf *n.* = **mantelshelf**

mant·let /mántlət/ *n.* = **mantelet**

man·tle·tree *n.* = **manteltree**

mant·ling /mántling/ *n.* ornamental drapery around a shield on a coat of arms

man-to-man *adj.* **1. HONEST AND INTIMATE** honest and intimate and treating somebody as an equal ○ *a man-to-man talk* **2.** SPORTS **PAIRING PLAYERS** in sports such as basketball, having each defensive player of one team guard a corresponding offensive player of the other team (*sometimes considered offensive*) ○ *a man-to-man defense* —**man-to-man** *adv.*

Man·toux test /man tóo-/ *n.* a test to determine whether somebody has ever had the tuberculosis infection and so has a measure of immunity to the disease [Mid-20thC. Named for the French physician Charles *Mantoux* (1877–1947), its inventor.]

man·tra /mántrə/ *n.* **1.** RELIG **HOLY WORD IN MEDITATION** a sacred word, chant, or sound that is repeated during meditation to facilitate spiritual power and transformation of consciousness **2. OFTEN REPEATED EXPRESSION OR IDEA** an expression or idea that is repeated, often without thinking about it, and closely associated with something [Late 18thC. From Sanskrit, literally "thought," from *man* "to think."]

man·trap /mán tràp/ *n.* an illegal trap set to catch poachers or trespassers on private land, usually in the form of a metal device that snaps shut onto somebody's leg

man·tu·a /mánchoo ə, -too ə/ *n.* a woman's gown, fitted above the waist, with an open front and draped skirt to show the underskirt, worn in Europe in the late 17th and 18th centuries [Late 17thC. Alteration of *manteau*, modeled on MANTUA, which was famous for fabric production.]

Man·tu·a /mán choo ə/ historic city in northern Italy, a tourist and agricultural. Population: 52,205 (1993).

man·u·al /mánnyoo əl/ *adj.* **1. USING HANDS** relating to, done with, or involving the hands ○ *manual dexterity* **2. PHYSICAL** involving physical rather than mental exertion ○ *manual tasks* **3. OPERATED BY PERSON** operated by human effort rather than by a machine, computer, or type of power ○ *switching to manual control* ■ *n.* **1. HANDBOOK** a book that contains information and instructions about the operation of a machine or how to do something **2.** MUSIC **KEYBOARD PLAYED WITH HANDS** an organ or harpsichord keyboard that is played with the hands alone **3.** ARMS **RIFLE DRILL** a drill or exercise in the use of a hand-held weapon ○ *cadets practicing the manual of arms* [15thC. Via French *manuel* or directly from Latin *manualis* "of the hand," from *manus* "hand."] —**man·u·al·ly** *adv.*

WORD KEY: ORIGIN

The Latin word *manus*, from which ***manual*** derives, is also the source of English *amanuensis, command, demand, emancipate, manacle, manage, mandate, manifest, manipulate, manner, maneuver, manufacture, manure, mastiff, maundy*, and *remand*.

man·u·al al·pha·bet *n.* an alphabet in which various finger movements and positions stand for letters, used with other hand signs by hearing-impaired people

man·u·al trans·mis·sion *n.* a vehicle transmission that requires the driver to shift gears using a clutch

ma·nu·bri·um /mə nóobree əm/ (*plural* **-nub·ria** /-ree ə/ *or* **-nu·bri·ums**) *n.* a handle-shaped anatomical part, e.g., the upper part of the sternum or part of the inner ear [Mid-17thC. From Latin, "handle," from *manus* "hand."] —**ma·nu·bri·al** *adj.*

Ma·nuel I Com·nen·us /man wèl kom néenəss/ (1122–80) Byzantine emperor. He reigned from 1143 to 1180 and expanded his empire to the west.

manuf., **manufac.** *abbr.* **1.** manufacture **2.** manufactured **3.** manufacturer

man·u·fac·to·ry /mànnyə fáktəree/ (*plural* **-ries**) *n.* a factory (*archaic*) [Early 17thC. Formed from MANUFACTURE, modeled on FACTORY.]

man·u·fac·ture /mànnyə fákchər/ *v.* (**-tured, -tur·ing, -tures**) **1.** *vti.* INDUST **TO PRODUCE SOMETHING INDUSTRIALLY** to make something into a finished product using raw materials, especially on a large industrial scale ○ *built up a business manufacturing lightweight metal goods* **2.** *vt.* BIOCHEM **MAKE BODY CHEMICAL** to produce a substance needed by the body ○ *Bile is manufactured in the liver.* **3.** *vt.* **PRODUCE MECHANICALLY** to produce something in the manner of a machine, without creativity **4.** *vt.* **INVENT** to invent or make something up ○ *manufactured an excuse to get out the meeting* ■ *n.* **1.** INDUST **PRODUCTION OF GOODS** the production of finished goods from raw materials, especially on a large industrial scale ○ *engaged in the manufacture of arms for the military* **2.** COMM **PRODUCT** something that has been produced from raw materials, especially on a large industrial scale **3.** BIOCHEM **MAKING OF BODY CHEMICAL** the production of a substance needed by the body [Mid-16thC. Via French from Italian *manifattura* "something made by hand," from Latin *manu factum* "made by hand," from *manus* "hand" + *facere* "to make."] —**man·u·fac·tur·a·ble** *adj.* —**man·u·fac·tur·al** *adj.*

WORD KEY: SYNONYMS

See Synonyms at ***make***.

man·u·fac·tured home *n.* **1. PREFABRICATED DWELLING** a dwelling produced in prefabricated sections that are then quickly erected on site **2.** = **mobile home**

man·u·fac·tured hous·ing *n.* prefabricated dwellings as a group

man·u·fac·tur·er /mànnyə fákchərər/ *n.* a factory, individual, or organization that produces finished goods from raw materials, especially on a large industrial scale

man·u·mit /mànnyə mít/ (**-mit·ted, -mit·ting, -mits**) *vt.* to free somebody from slavery (*formal*) [14thC. From Latin *manumittere*, from *manu emittere*, literally "to send out from your hand."] —**man·u·mis·sion** /mànnyə mísh'n/ *n.* —**man·u·mit·ter** *n.*

ma·nure /mə nóor/ *n.* **FERTILIZER MADE FROM DUNG** animal excrement, often mixed with straw, used as fertilizer for soil ■ *vt.* (**-nured, -nur·ing, -nures**) **FERTILIZE WITH MANURE** to spread manure on land or soil to fertilize it [14thC. Via Anglo-Norman from Old French *manouvrer* "to work with the hands," from medieval Latin *manuoperare* (see MANEUVER). Originally "to cultivate, manage land."] —**ma·nur·er** *n.*

WORD KEY: ORIGIN

When English originally took the word **manure** over from Anglo-Norman, its connotations of manual labor had been channeled into the management of land, and in particular the cultivation of land. It was not until the middle of the 16th century that the noun **manure** came to denote "dung spread in cultivating the land." The related MANEUVER, reborrowed from French in the 18th century, has remained in more refined use.

ma·nus /máynəss, máanəss/ (*plural* **-nus**) *n.* the wrist and hand of humans or the carpus and forefoot of other vertebrates (*technical*) [Early 16thC. From Latin, "hand."]

man·u·script /mánnyə skrìpt/ *n.* **1. HANDWRITTEN BOOK** a book or other text written by hand, especially one written before the invention of printing ○ *rare medieval manuscripts* **2. AUTHOR'S ORIGINAL TEXT** an author's text for a book, article, or other piece of written work as it is submitted for publication **3. HANDWRITING** handwriting as opposed to the printed word ○ *a manuscript version of the text* [Late 16thC. From medieval Latin *manuscriptus* "written by hand," from *scribere* "to write" (source of English *inscription* and *scribble*).]

Manx /mangks/ *adj.* **OF ISLE OF MAN** relating the Isle of Man, its people, language, or culture ■ *n.* **OLD ISLE OF MAN LANGUAGE** a language formerly spoken on the Isle of Man, belonging to the Goidelic group of the Celtic branch of Indo-European languages. The last native speaker died in the 1970s, but it survives especially in legal documents and is kept alive as the second language of the island by the Manx Society. ■ *npl.* **MANX PEOPLE** the people of the Isle of Man [Early 16thC. Alteration of assumed Old Norse *manskr*, from Old Irish *Manu* "Isle of Man."]

Manx cat, **manx cat** *n.* a short-haired, tailless, domestic cat [From the origin of the breed in the Isle of Man]

Manx·man /mángksmən/ (*plural* **-men** /-mən/) *n.* a man who comes from or lives on the Isle of Man

Manx shear·wa·ter *n.* an Atlantic seabird with black plumage on its upper parts and white plumage on its underparts that nests in burrows on rocky islands. Latin name: *Puffinus puffinus.*

Manx·wom·an /mángks wòommən/ (*plural* **-en** /-wìmmin/) *n.* a woman who comes from or lives on the Isle of Man

man·y /ménnee/ CORE MEANING: a considerable number of people or things ○ (det) *Many people own their homes.* ○ (det) *Not many people know about this.* ○ (pron) *Many believe that the matter will never come to trial.* ○ (pron) *Many of you may have heard this.* ○ (adj) *He was among the many visitors to this town.* **1.** *det., pron., adj.* **A CONSIDERABLE NUMBER** a considerable number of people or things ○ (det) *Many children are in the park today.* ○ (pron) *He is a friend to many.* ○ (pron) *Many of us agree with you.* ○ (adj) *Among his many faults is self-importance.* **2.** *det., pron.* **A LARGE NUMBER** a large number of people or things (*used after "so," "too," "not," "as" or "that"*) ○ (det) *She has so many clocks, she can't be sure exactly what time it is.* ○ (det) *I've just seen too many government studies that don't move quickly enough.* ○ (det) *There aren't that many people who would agree with you.* ○ (pron) *Help yourself – you can have as many as you like.* **3.** *det.* **EACH OF A CONSIDERABLE NUMBER** each of a considerable number (*used before "a,""an" or "another"*) ○ *The situation has caused them many a sleepless night.* ○ *We did better than many another regiment.* **4.** *pron.* **THE MAJORITY** the majority of people ○ *All these advantages should be available to the many – not just the few.* [Old English *manig*. Ultimately from an Indo-European word meaning "many, often."]

man·y·fold /ménni fòld/ *adv.* many times over ○ *The nation's problems have increased manyfold.* [Late 19thC. Coined from MANY + -FOLD, modeled on MANIFOLD.]

man·y·plies /ménni plìz/ (*plural* **-plies**) *n.* = **omasum** [Late 18thC. From MANY + PLY, because of the organ's many folds.]

man·y-sid·ed *adj.* having a large number of sides, aspects, or abilities —**man·y-sid·ed·ness** *n.*

man·y-val·ued log·ic *n.* a system of logic in which propositions may have values in addition to true or false

man·za·nil·la /mànzə néeyə, -níllə/ *n.* a pale dry Spanish sherry [Mid-19thC. From Spanish, literally "camomile," because its smell resembles camomile.]

Mao·ism /mów ìzzəm/ *n.* the Marxist-Leninist doctrines, teachings, and policies of the former Chinese Communist leader Mao Zedong —**Mao·ist** *n., adj.*

Mao jack·et /mów-/ *n.* a plain tunic-style jacket with a stand-up collar worn by Chairman Mao Zedong and the Chinese people under his regime

Mao·ri /mówree/ (*plural* **-ri**) *n.* **1.** PEOPLES **MEMBER OF NEW ZEALAND PEOPLE** a member of a people living in New Zealand and on the Cook Islands. The Maori are believed to have originated on various Polynesian islands and to have migrated to New Zealand using canoes before the 14th century A.D. **2.** LANG **MAORI LANGUAGE** the language of the Maori people, belonging to the Eastern branch of Austronesian languages. Maori is spoken by about 300,000 people. [Mid-19thC. From Maori.] —**Mao·ri** *adj.*

Mao·ri·land /mówri lànd/ *n.* New Zealand (*archaic*) [From the fact that the Maoris were the land's original inhabitants] —**Mao·ri·lan·der** *n.*

Mao suit *n.* a style of suit consisting of plain loose-fitting trousers and a tunic-style jacket with a stand-up collar worn by Chairman Mao Zedong and the Chinese people under his regime

Mao Zedong

Mao Ze·dong /mòw tsay tóong/, **Mao Tse-tung** (1893–1976) Chinese statesman. Leader of the Long March in the Chinese Civil War (1934), he became the first president of Communist China (1949–67).

map /map/ *n.* **1. GEOGRAPHIC DIAGRAM** a visual representation that shows all or part of the Earth's surface with geographic features, urban areas, roads, and other details **2.** DIAGRAM OF STARS a representation of the stars or the surface of a planet, usually in the form of a diagrammatical drawing **3.** DRAWING SHOWING ROUTE OR LOCATION a diagrammatical drawing of something such as a route or area made to show the location of a place or how to get there **4.** MATH = **function** *n.* 6 ■ *vt.* **(mapped, map·ping, maps)** **1.** CREATE MAP OF SOMETHING to represent a geographic or other defined area on a map ○ *mapping the heavens* **2.** DISCOVER AND SHOW to discover something and create a visual representation of it **3.** BIOL NOTE GENE SEQUENCE to determine and record the sequence of encoded information on a gene or chromosome **4.** MATH MATCH SET ELEMENTS to assign an element in one set to an element in another through a mathematical correspondence [Early 16thC. From medieval Latin *mappa (mundi)*, literally "sheet (of the world)," from Latin *mappa* "towel, sheet" (source of English *napkin* and *apron*).] —**map·pa·ble** *adj.* —**map·per** *n.* ◇ **on the map** so as to be famous or important (*slang*) ◇ **off the map** so as to be no longer famous or important (*slang*)

map out *vt.* to construct something such as a plan in detail

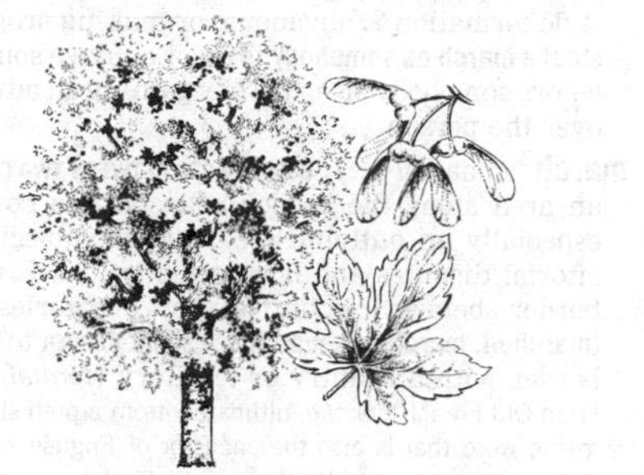

Maple

ma·ple /máyp'l/ *n.* **1.** TREES DECIDUOUS TREE WITH WINGED SEEDS a deciduous tree of northern temperate regions that has opposite leaves and winged seeds occurring in pairs. Genus: *Acer*. **2.** INDUST WOOD FROM MAPLE the hard wood from the maple tree, used to make furniture and flooring **3.** FOOD SUGAR MAPLE FLAVOR the flavor of the processed sap of the sugar maple [Old English *mapul*-]

Ma·ple Leaf *n.* the Canadian flag, showing a stylized red maple leaf on a white background between vertical red bars

ma·ple sug·ar *n.* a sugar made by boiling down the sap of the sugar maple

ma·ple syr·up *n.* a sweet syrup made from the sap of the sugar maple, or from various other sugars and artificially flavored with maple

map·mak·er /máp màykər/ *n.* somebody who makes maps —**map·mak·ing** *n.*

map·ping /mápping/ *n.* **1.** MAKING OF MAPS the act or process of making maps **2.** MATH = **function** *n.* 6

Map·ple·thorpe /máyp'l thàwrp/, **Robert** (1946–89) U.S. photographer. Acclaimed for his elegant photographic technique and experimentation with printing, light, and color, he was controversial for the sexually explicit content of his work.

map pro·jec·tion *n.* a representation of or way of representing a three-dimensional object on a two-dimensional surface

Ma·pu·che /mə po͝ochee/ (*plural* **-che** *or* **-ches**) *n.* **1.** PEOPLES MEMBER OF NATIVE S AMERICAN PEOPLE a member of a subgroup of the Araucanian people of central Chile and areas of western Argentina, known for their resistance to Spanish and Chilean rule **2.** LANG MAPUCHE LANGUAGE the language of the Mapuche people, belonging to the Araucanian family. About 400,000 people speak Mapuche. —**Ma·pu·che** *adj.*

Ma·pu·to /mə po͞otō/ capital city of Mozambique, situated on Delagoa Bay in the southeastern part of the country. Population: 1,098,000 (1991).

ma·quette /ma két/ *n.* a small model of a planned sculpture or architectural work [Early 20thC. Via French from Italian *macchietta* "little spot," from Latin *maculare* "to spot, stain" (source of English *immaculate*).]

ma·qui·la·do·ra /mə kèe laa dáw raa, maa-/ *n.* an assembly plant in Mexico run by the United States or other foreign interests. Parts are shipped to

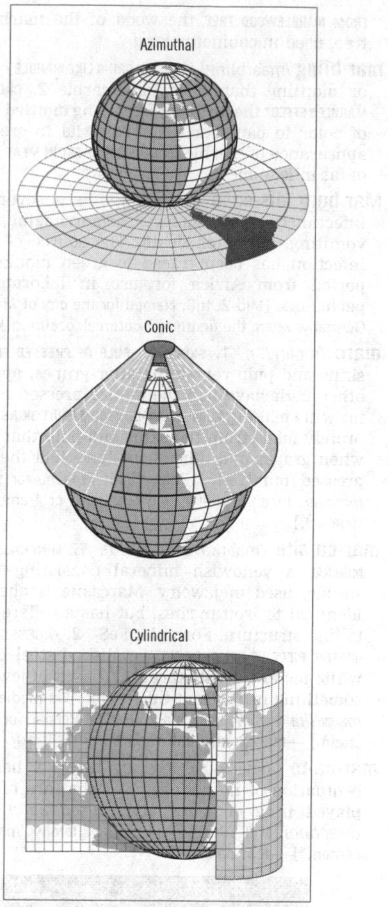

Map projection

Mexico, products are assembled, and finished goods are returned for sale in the markets of origin. [Late 20thC. From Mexican Spanish, where it was formed from *maquilar* "to assemble."]

ma·quil·lage /maakee áazh/ *n.* makeup, or the art of applying makeup [Late 19thC. From French, from *maquiller* "to make up face," from Old French *masquiller* "to stain."]

ma·quis /ma kée, maa-/ (*plural* **-quis**) *n.* **1.** DENSE COASTAL VEGETATION dense shrubby vegetation of Mediterranean coastal regions **2. ma·quis, Ma·quis** HIST FRENCH RESISTANCE the underground French Resistance movement that fought against the German occupying forces during World War II **3. ma·quis, Ma·quis** HIST = **Maquisard** [Mid-19thC. Via French from Italian *macchia*, literally "spot," from Latin *macula* (from the vegetation's resemblance to spots). "French Resistance" from the use of the maquis countryside for hiding.]

Ma·qui·sard /màkee zaárd, -zaár/ *n.* a member of the World War II French Resistance movement [Mid-20thC. From French, where it was formed from MAQUIS.]

mar /maar/ **(marred, mar·ring, mars)** *vt.* to spoil or detract from something [Old English *merran* "to waste, spoil," from prehistoric Germanic]

mar. *abbr.* **1.** maritime **2.** married

Mar., Mar *abbr.* March

ma·ra /mə raá/ *n.* a large long-legged member of the cavy family that resembles a hare and is native to the Argentine pampas. Latin name: *Dolichotis patagonum*. [Mid-19thC. From American Spanish *mará*.]

Ma·ra /maá raa/ *n.* in Buddhism, a force of evil, sometimes conceived of as a being [Late 19thC. From Sanskrit *Māra* "death," from the stem *mr-* "to die."]

mar·a·bou /mérrə bo͞o/, **mar·a·bout** *n.* **1.** BIRDS LARGE AFRICAN STORK a large African carrion stork that has dark gray plumage and a short naked neck with a pink pouch at the front. Latin name: *Leptoptilos crumeniferus*. **2.** MARABOU FEATHERS down taken from the tail of the marabou and used as trimming for clothes **3.** TEXTILES RAW SILK a fine white raw silk [Early 19thC. Via French from Arabic *murābit* "holy man," because the stork was considered holy by Muslims.]

Marabou

mar·a·bout /mérrə bo͞o/ *n.* **1.** MUSLIM HERMIT OR MONK a Muslim hermit, monk, or holy man, especially in North Africa **2.** TOMB OF MARABOUT the tomb or a shrine of a marabout that is often a destination for pilgrims [Early 17thC. Via French and Portuguese from Arabic *murābit*, from *ribāt* "frontier post," because hermits would go to such places to gain merit.]

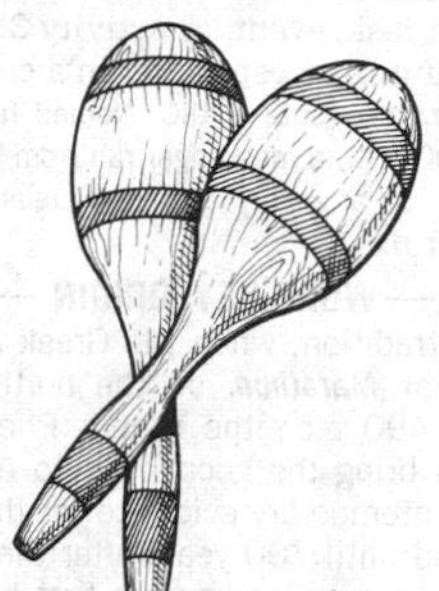

Maracas

ma·ra·ca /mə raákə/ *n.* a percussion instrument usually shaken in pairs as an accompaniment to Latin American music and consisting of a hollow rattle filled with small pebbles or beans [Early 17thC. Via Portuguese *maracà* from Tupi *maráka*.]

Ma·ra·cai·bo, Lake large shallow lake in northwestern Venezuela. It is the largest lake in South America. Area: 5,140 sq. mi./13,300 sq. km.

Ma·ra·cay /màrra káy/ city in northern Venezuela, and capital of the state of Aragua, in the central highlands. Population: 538,616 (1990).

Mar·a·do·na /márrə dónnə/, **Diego** (*b.* 1960) Argentinian soccer player. An outstanding midfielder and goal-scorer, he captained Argentina to World Cup victory in 1986.

ma·ra·ging steel /maá ràyjing-/ *n.* a strong, low-carbon, martensitic steel formed by aging and heating and containing up to 25 percent nickel with lesser amounts of titanium, aluminum, and niobium [*Maraging* from a blend of MARTENSITE and AGE]

Mar·a·jó /màrra zhṓ/ island in Brazil, in Para State, in the delta of the River Amazon. Area: 15,500 sq. mi./40,100 sq. km.

Ma·ra·ñón /màrra nyṓn/ river in South America, flowing northward from the Andes into the River Amazon. Length: 879 mi./1,415 km.

ma·ran·ta /mə rántə/ *n.* a tropical American plant, widely cultivated for its variegated thin leaves. Genus: *Maranta*. [Early 19thC. From modern Latin *Maranta*, named for Bartolomeo *Maranta*, an Italian herbalist of the 16thC.]

ma·ras·ca /mə ráskə/ *n.* a cultivated variety of the sour cherry tree that produces the fruit used to make maraschino. Latin name: *Prunus cerasus*. [Mid-19thC. From Italian, alteration of *amarasca*, from *amaro* "bitter."]

mar·a·schi·no /mèrrə skéenō, -shéenō/ (*plural* **-nos**) *n.* a cordial distilled from marasca cherries [Late 18thC. From Italian, where it was formed from *marasca* (see MARASCA).]

mar·a·schi·no cher·ry *n.* a bright red cherry preserved in a sweet syrup flavored with maraschino or an imitation of this, used especially as an addition to cocktails or to decorate cakes

ma·ras·mus /mə rázməss/ *n.* a gradual wasting away of the body, generally associated with severe malnutrition or inadequate absorption of food and occurring mainly in young children [Mid-17thC. From modern Latin, from Greek *marasmos* "wasting, decay," from *marainein* "to waste away."] —**ma·ras·mic** *adj.*

Ma·ra·tha /mə ráatə, -ráttə/, **Ma·rat·ta, Mah·rat·ta** *n.* a member of a people living mainly in the Deccan plateau in the Indian state of Maharashtra [Mid-18thC. From Marathi *marāthā*, or Hindi *marhattā*, from Sanskrit *Mahārāṣṭra* "great kingdom."]

Ma·ra·thi /mə ráatee, -ráttee/, **Mah·rat·ti** *n.* **LANGUAGE SPOKEN IN MAHARASHTRA** a language belonging to the Indo-Iranian branch of Indo-European languages and spoken mainly in the Indian state of Maharashtra, where it is the state language. Marathi is spoken by about 70 million people. ■ *adj.* **OF MAHARASHTRA** relating to the Indian state of Maharashtra, its people, language, or culture [Late 17thC. From Marathi *marāṭhī*, from Sanskrit *Mahārāṣṭrī*, from *Mahārāṣṭra* (see MARATHA).]

mar·a·thon /mérrə thòn/ *n.* **1. LONG-DISTANCE RACE** a long-distance footrace run over a distance of 26 mi. 385 yds./42.195 km **2. LENGTHY AND DIFFICULT TASK** a lengthy and difficult task, event, or activity **3. ENDURANCE TEST** a test of endurance, especially in a competition ○ *a dance marathon* [Late 19thC. Named for MARATHON in Greece. In 490 B.C., a messenger ran from there to Athens, bearing news of a victory against Persian invaders.] —**mar·a·thon·er** *n.*

WORD KEY: ORIGIN

According to tradition, when the Greek army defeated the Persians at ***Marathon***, on the northeastern coast of Attica, in 490 B.C., the runner Pheidippides was dispatched to bring the good news to Athens (in fact there is no contemporary evidence for the story, which is not recorded until 700 years after the event). When the modern Olympic Games were first held, in Athens in 1896, a long-distance race was introduced to commemorate the ancient feat, run over a course supposedly equal in distance to the journey from ***Marathon*** to Athens (about 22 mi.35 km. The present distance was established at the 1948 Olympics in London, England).

Mar·a·thon /mérrə thòn/ plain in Attica, northeast of Athens, Greece. It was the site of an important Greek victory over the Persians in 490 B.C.

Ma·rat·ta *n.* = **Maratha**

ma·raud /mə ráwd/ (**-raud·ed, -raud·ing, -rauds**) *vti.* to rove around carrying out violent attacks or looking for plunder, or to raid a place in search of plunder [Late 17thC. From French *marauder*, from *maraud* "rogue, vagabond."] —**ma·raud·er** *n.*

ma·raud·ing /mə ráwding/ *adj.* roving around carrying out violent attacks or looking for plunder ○ *marauding pirates cruising the high seas*

mar·ble /maárb'l/ *n.* **1.** INDUST **DENSE CRYSTALLIZED ROCK** a form of limestone transformed through the heat and pressure of metamorphism into a dense, variously colored, crystallized rock used in building, sculpture, and monuments **2.** SCULPTURE **MARBLE SCULPTURE** a sculpture made from marble ○ *the Elgin Marbles* **3. SOMETHING RESEMBLING MARBLE** something that resembles marble in being cold, hard, smooth, or white (*literary*) **4.** GAME **SMALL GLASS BALL** a small hard ball, usually made of glass, used in the game of marbles **5. GAME WITH GLASS BALLS** a game, played mainly by children, in which small hard balls are rolled on the ground with the aim of hitting the opponent's ball (*takes a singular verb*) ■ **mar·bles** *npl.* **WITS** mental abilities or sense of reality (*slang*) ■ *vt.* (**-bled, -bling, -bles**) **COLOR SOMETHING WITH MOTTLED STREAKS** to color something, usually paper, with mottled streaks to give the appearance of marble ○ *an 18th-century volume with marbled endpapers* [12thC. Via Old French *marbre* and Latin *marmor* from Greek *marmaros*, "hard, shiny stone" (influenced by *marmairein* "to shine").] —**mar·bly** *adj.*

mar·ble cake *n.* a type of cake made with two different flavors of sponge, often chocolate and plain, dropped into the same cake pan and very lightly mixed before baking

Mar·ble·head /maárb'l hed/ resort town in northeastern Massachusetts, on the northern shore of Massachusetts Bay, southwest of Gloucester. Population: 19,973 (1996).

mar·ble·wood /maárb'l wòòd/ *n.* **1.** TREES **MALAYSIAN TREE** a Malaysian tree with mottled black-banded wood. Latin name: *Diospyros marmorata.* **2.** INDUST **WOOD FROM MARBLEWOOD TREE** the wood of the marblewood tree, used in cabinetmaking

mar·bling /maárbling/ *n.* **1. COLORING LIKE MARBLE** coloring or mottling that looks like marble **2. CREATION OF MARBLED EFFECT** the process of applying mottled streaks of color to paper or other material to create the appearance of marble **3. STREAKS OF FAT IN MEAT** streaks of fat in lean meat

Mar·burg dis·ease /maár bùrg-/ *n.* a severe viral infection causing high fever, hemorrhaging, rashes, vomiting, and often death. The source of human infection has been traced to green monkeys imported from Africa for use in laboratory experiments. [Mid-20thC. Named for the city of *Marburg* in Germany, where the first major outbreak occurred.]

marc /maark/ *n.* **1. SKINS AND PULP OF PRESSED FRUIT** the skins and pulp remaining after grapes, apples, or other fruit have had their juice pressed out, e.g., for wine making **2.** WINE **BRANDY FROM FRUIT SKINS AND PULP** brandy made from the skins and pulp that remain when grapes and other fruit have had their juice pressed out [Early 17thC. From French, formed from *marcher*, in an earlier sense "to tread or trample" (see MARCH[1]).]

mar·ca·site /maárkə sìt, -zìt/ *n.* **1.** MINERALS **YELLOW MINERAL** a yellowish mineral consisting of iron sulfide, used in jewelry. Marcasite is chemically identical to iron pyrites, but has a different crystalline structure. Formula: FeS_2. **2.** ACCESSORIES **DECORATIVE PIECE OF POLISHED METAL** polished steel or other white metal cut with facets and used in jewelry, or something made from this [15thC. Via medieval Latin *marcasita* from Arabic *marḳašīṯa*, of Persian or Aramaic origin.] —**mar·ca·sit·i·cal** /maárkə síttik'l/ *adj.*

mar·ca·to /maar kaá tō/ *adv.* with a heavy accentuation of individual notes that are often also played in a detached style (*used as a musical direction*) [Mid-19thC. From Italian, literally "marked, accented."] —**mar·ca·to** *adj.*

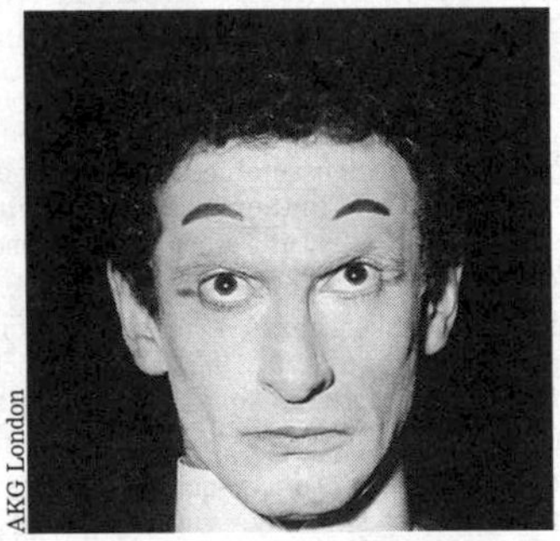

Marcel Marceau

Mar·ceau /maar sṓ/, **Marcel** (*b.* 1923) French mime artist. His white-faced character, Bip, became for a time synonymous with mime.

mar·cel /maar sél/ *n.* **mar·cel, mar·cel wave WAVY HAIRSTYLE** a women's hairstyle, popular in the 1920s, consisting of regular, deep waves created with curling irons ■ *vt.* (**-celled, -cell·ing, -cels**) **STYLE HAIR IN A MARCEL** to style somebody's hair in a marcel [Late 19thC. Named for the French hairdresser François *Marcel* Grateau (1852–1936), who devised the method.]

mar·ces·cent /maar séss'nt/ *adj.* remaining attached to a plant when withered [Early 18thC. From Latin *marcescent-*, the present participle stem of *marcescere*, literally "to begin to wither," from *marcere* "to wither, decay."]

march[1] /maarch/ *v.* (**marched, march·ing, march·es**) **1.** *vi.* **WALK IN MILITARY FASHION** to walk with regular formalized movements of the arms and legs at a steady rhythmic pace, often in a military formation **2.** *vti.* **MOVE IN MILITARY-STYLE FORMATION** to proceed somewhere, or direct a body of people or troops to proceed somewhere, on foot, in a disciplined military or military-style formation ○ *marched the troops off to battle* **3.** *vi.* MIL **SET OFF** to set off, usually on foot, on a military campaign or expedition ○ *Our orders are to march at daybreak.* **4.** *vi.* **WALK WITH DETERMINATION** to walk quickly and with an air of determination ○ *She marched into the store and demanded to see the manager.* **5.** *vt.* **FORCE SOMEBODY TO GO SOMEWHERE** to force somebody to go along with you somewhere, usually by physically taking hold of the person ○ *Police marched the suspects into the jail.* **6.** *vi.* **WALK TO PROTEST OR PUBLICIZE SOMETHING** to take part in a protest march or demonstration ○ *A huge crowd marched in support of the needy.* **7.** *vi.* **PASS STEADILY** to pass steadily or inexorably ○ *Time marches on.* ■ *n.* **1. ACT OR EXTENT OF MARCHING** a journey on foot, especially under military discipline or in a military formation ○ *After a four-hour march, they arrived back at the camp.* **2. MARCHING SPEED** a particular speed or style of marching ○ *The funeral procession advanced at a slow march.* **3. WALK FOR PROTEST OR PUBLICITY** a political demonstration or protest, in the form of an organized walk in procession by a group of people to a place in support of a particular cause ○ *Police estimated that about 20,000 people took part in yesterday's march against world hunger.* **4. MOVEMENT FORWARD** a steady forward movement or progression ○ *the march of time* **5.** MUSIC **MUSIC IN MARCHING RHYTHM** a piece of music especially written or suitable to accompany marching, usually with a regular emphatic beat and in a military style [14thC. From Old French *marchier*, ultimately from a prehistoric Germanic word meaning "to measure off, mark out" that is also the ancestor of English *mark* and *margin*.] —**march·er** *n.* ◇ **on the march 1.** proceeding somewhere on foot, especially purposefully and in a military or military-style formation **2.** advancing or making progress ◇ **steal a march on somebody** to do or achieve something before somebody else, thereby gaining an advantage over the person

march[2] /maarch/ *n.* **1. BORDER AREA BETWEEN TWO COUNTRIES** an area along the border between two countries, especially an outlying area that is subject to territorial disputes and hostile incursions **2. BORDER** a border between countries or territories ■ *vi.* (**marched, march·ing, march·es**) **SHARE BORDER** to share a border with a country or territory (*formal*) [13thC. From Old French *marche*, ultimately from a prehistoric Germanic word that is also the ancestor of English *mark*. The underlying sense is of territory marked out.]

March /maarch/ *n.* in the Gregorian calendar, the third month of the year, made up of 31 days [Via Anglo-Norman from Latin *Martius (mensis)* "(month) of Mars"]

March /maarch/, **Fredric** (1897–1975) U.S. stage and movie actor. He won Academy Awards for *Dr. Jekyll and Mr. Hyde* (1932) and *The Best Years of Our Lives* (1946). Real name **Fredric Ernest McIntyre Bickell**

March. *abbr.* Marchioness

M.Arch. *n., abbr.* Master of Architecture

mar·che·sa /maar káyzə/ (*plural* **-se** /-zày/) *n.* an Italian marchioness, holding the title either in her own right or as the wife or widow of a marchese [Late 18thC. From Italian, feminine of *marchese* (see MARCHESE).]

march·ese /maar káy zày/ (*plural* **mar·che·si** /-zee/) *n.* an Italian marquess, a nobleman of a rank between a prince and a count [Early 16thC. Via Italian from medieval Latin *(comes) marcensis* "count of the border," from *marca* "border," of prehistoric Germanic origin; ultimately related to English *mark*[1].]

march·ing or·ders *npl.* **1. DISMISSAL** a summary dismissal or request to leave (*informal*) **2.** MIL **ORDERS TO MARCH** orders to soldiers to set off on a military campaign or expedition

mar·chio·ness /maárshənəss, maárshə néss/ *n.* in Great Britain and Ireland, a noblewoman ranking between duchess and countess, or the wife or widow of a marquess [Late 16thC. Via medieval Latin *marchionissa* from, ultimately, *marca* "borderland," of prehistoric Germanic origin.]

march·land /maárch lànd, -lənd/ *n.* an area along the border between two countries [Mid-16thC. Formed from MARCH[2].]

march·pane /maárch pàyn/ *n.* marzipan (*archaic*) [15thC. Origin uncertain: possibly via obsolete French *marcepain* from, ultimately, Italian *marzapane* (see MARZIPAN).]

march-past *n.* a formal parade by troops or other people who march in formation past somebody who reviews them from a stand or other vantage point

Mar·ci·a·no /maàrssee aánō, -ánnō/, **Rocky** (1923–69) U.S. boxer. At the end of his four years holding the heavyweight title (1952–56), he was the only heavyweight champion to retire undefeated. Real name **Rocco Francis Marchegiano**

Mar·co·ni /maar kṓnee/, **Guglielmo** (1874–1937) Italian electrical engineer. He pioneered the practical development of radio signaling. In 1909 he shared the

Nobel Prize in physics for his work in wireless telegraphy.

Mar·co·ni rig *n.* = **Bermuda rig** [Named for Guglielmo MARCONI, comparing the rig's unusually tall mast with early radio towers] —**Mar·co·ni-rigged** *adj.*

Mar·cy, Mount /máarssee/ peak in the Adirondack Mountains, northeastern New York. It is the highest point in the state, 5,344 ft./1,629 m.

Mar·dal Wa·ter·fall waterfall in Norway, one of the highest in the world. Height: 1,696 ft./517 m.

Mar·di Gras /máardee graá/ (*plural* **Mar·dis Gras** /máardee graá/) *n.* **1.** CHR **TUESDAY BEFORE LENT** the name given in France and many other places to Shrove Tuesday, the last day before the beginning of Lent in the Christian calendar **2.** LEISURE **CARNIVAL BEFORE LENT** in some places, a carnival held or ending on the day before the beginning of Lent, in the Christian calendar, often celebrated with costumes, parades, balls, and other festivities [From French, literally "fat Tuesday" (the day on which rich foods were used up before Lent)]

Mar·duk /máar dòok, máar dùk/ *n.* in Babylonian mythology, the god who defeated the great goddess Tiamat and created humankind

mare[1] /mair/ *n.* an adult female horse, or adult female of a species closely related to the horse such as the zebra [Old English *mearh.* Ultimately from an Indo-European word meaning "horse."]

ma·re[2] /maá rày, máaree/ (*plural* **-ri·a** /-ree ə/ *or* **-res**) *n.* any of the large dark plains on the surface of the Moon, or any similar area on Mars [Mid-19thC. From Latin, "sea" (source of English *marine*). Ultimately from an Indo-European word that is also the ancestor of English *mere, marsh, morass,* and *meerschaum.*]

ma·re clau·sum /maá ray kláwssəm, -klów sòom, maári kláwssəm, -klów sòom/ *n.* a sea or other area of water that is under the jurisdiction of one country and closed to all others [From Latin, literally "closed sea," the title of a work (1635) by John Selden defending the right of a single nation to control parts of the sea]

Ma·re Cris·i·um /maá ray kríssee əm/ *n.* a lunar lowland plain surrounded by high mountains, approximately 270 × 350 mi./435 × 565 km. Visible with the unaided eye as a dark area near the Moon's eastern edge.

Ma·re Fe·cun·di·ta·tis /maá ray fe kùndi taátiss/ *n.* a lunar lowland region of irregular shape. It is visible with the unaided eye as a dark area southeast of Mare Tranquillitatis.

Ma·re Fri·gor·is /maá ray fri gáwriss/ *n.* a long narrow lunar lowland region near to the north pole. It is just visible as a dark area north of Mare Imbrium and Mare Serentitatis.

Ma·re Hu·mor·um /maá ray hyoo máwrəm/ *n.* a lunar lowland plain, approximately 260 mi./420 km across. It is just visible with the unaided eye as a dark area near the Moon's southwestern edge.

Ma·re Im·bri·um /maá ray ímbree əm/ *n.* a large round lunar lowland plain, approximately 775 mi./1250 km across. It is easily visible with the unaided eye as a large dark area in the Moon's northwest quadrant.

ma·re li·be·rum *n.* an area of sea that is open to the ships of all countries [Mid-17thC. From Latin, literally "free sea," the title of a treatise (1609) by the Dutch jurist Hugo Grotius, defending free access to the ocean by all nations.]

mar·em·ma /mə rémmə/ (*plural* **-me** /-mee/) *n.* an area of marshy ground near the sea, especially in Italy [Mid-19thC. Via Italian from, ultimately, Latin *maritimus,* from *mare* "sea."]

Ma·re Nec·tar·is /maá ray nek taáriss/ *n.* a rounded lunar lowland plain, approximately 250 mi./400 km across. It is visible with the unaided eye as a dark area south of Mare Tranquillitatis.

Ma·ren·go /mə réng gṑ/ *adj.* browned in oil and cooked in a sauce of tomatoes, mushrooms, garlic, onion, and white wine ○ *chicken Marengo* [Mid-19thC. Named for the village of *Marengo* in northern Italy, where such a dish is said to have been served to Napoleon in 1800.]

ma·re nos·trum /maá ray nóstrəm, -nó stròom, maári nóstrəm, -nó stròom/ *n.* an area of sea that is under the jurisdiction of one country or shared by two or more countries [From Latin, literally "our sea" (the Roman name of the Mediterranean)]

Ma·re Nu·bi·um /maá ray nyóobee əm/ *n.* a lunar lowland region that is irregularly shaped. It is visible with the unaided eye as a dark area near the center of the Moon's south west quadrant.

Ma·re O·ri·en·tale /maá ray àwree en taálee/ *n.* a round lunar lowland region on the side of the Moon that is furthest from the Earth

Ma·re Se·ren·i·ta·tis /maá ray sə rènni taátiss/ *n.* a large rounded lunar lowland plane where Apollo 17 landed. It is approximately 360 × 425 mi./580 × 680 km and easily visible in the Moon's north east quadrant.

mare's nest *n.* **1.** **COMPLICATED SITUATION** a complicated or muddled situation **2.** **DISCOVERY FOUND TO BE VALUELESS** a discovery at first thought to be important or valuable but subsequently found to be an illusion, a hoax, or valueless [Late 16thC]

mare's-tail *n.* **1.** METEOROL **STRAND OF CLOUD** a long wispy strand of cloud (*usually used in the plural*) **2.** PLANTS **WATER PLANT** a water plant that has erect, partially submerged stems with narrow leaves and insignificant flowers. Latin name: *Hippuris vulgaris.*

Ma·re Tran·quil·li·ta·tis /maá ray trang kwìlli taátiss/ *n.* a large irregularly-shaped lunar lowland plain, approximately 405 × 560 mi./650 × 900 km, where Apollo 11 made the first crewed lunar landing in 1969

Mar·fan syn·drome /máar fan-/, **Mar·fan's syn·drome** /máar fans-/ *n.* a hereditary disorder that affects the body's connective tissues [Mid-20thC. Named for the French pediatrician A. B. J. *Marfan* (1858–1942).]

marg. *abbr.* **1.** margin **2.** marginal

Mar·gar·et /máargrət, -ərət/, **St., Queen of Scotland** (1046?–93). Sister of Edgar (the Aetheling) and wife of Malcolm Canmore, she instigated reforms in the Celtic Church.

Mar·gar·et, Princess, Countess of Snowdon (*b.* 1930). The younger sister of Elizabeth II, Queen of the United Kingdom, she was the first president of the Royal Ballet.

Mar·gar·et of An·jou (1430?–82) Queen of England. She was the wife of Henry VI of England, and led the Lancastrians in the Wars of the Roses.

mar·gar·ic /maar gérrik/, **mar·garitic** /maárgə ríttik/ *adj.* resembling a pearl or pearls (*formal*) [Early 19thC. Via French *margarique* from, ultimately, Greek *margaron* "pearl."]

mar·ga·rine /máarjərin/ *n.* a yellow fat for spreading and cooking that usually consists of a blend of vegetable oils or animal fats mixed with water, vitamins, coloring, flavoring, and other ingredients. Originally produced as a butter substitute and considered inferior to it in all uses, it is now a food in its own right. [Late 19thC. From French.]

mar·ga·ri·ta /maárgə reétə/ *n.* a cocktail made with tequila, lemon or lime juice, and an orange-flavored liqueur, typically served in a chilled glass whose rim has been dipped into salt [Early 20thC. From Spanish, from the name *Margarita.*]

mar·ga·rit·ic *adj.* = **margaric**

Mar·gas·ir·sa *n.* in the Hindu calendar, the ninth month of the year, made up of 29 or 30 days and occurring about the same time as November to December

Mar·gate /máar gayt/ city in southeastern Florida, a suburb of Fort Lauderdale. Population: 47,450 (1994).

mar·gay /máar gày/ *n.* a wild cat not much bigger than a domestic cat with coloring and markings similar to those of a leopard, found in the rainforests of Central and South America. Latin name: *Felis wiedi.* [Late 18thC. Via French from Portuguese *maracaj'a,* from Tupi *marakaya.*]

mar·gent /máarjənt/ *n.* a margin or edge (*archaic or literary*)

mar·gin /máarjin/ *n.* **1.** **BLANK SPACE AT SIDE OF PAGE** a blank space on the left or right edge, or the top or bottom, of a written or printed page ○ *comments scribbled in the margin* **2.** **LINE DOWN SIDE OF PAGE** a straight line drawn down the left- or right-hand side of a page to separate a narrow section from the main part ○ *Draw a margin about one inch from the edge of the paper.* **3.** **OUTER EDGE** the edge of something, especially the outer edge, or the area close to it ○ *dark-green leaves with reddish margins* **4.** **PART FARTHEST FROM CENTER** that part of anything, e.g., a society or organization, that is least integrated with its center, least often considered, least typical, or most vulnerable (*often used in the plural*) ○ *people living on the margins of society* **5.** **LIMIT** a boundary indicating the limit beyond which something should not go or below which something should not fall (*often used in the plural*) ○ *beyond the margins of good taste* **6.** **DIFFERENCE BETWEEN ONE AMOUNT AND ANOTHER** the difference between two amounts or scores ○ *She won by a margin of only 270 votes.* **7.** **ADDITIONAL AMOUNT** an amount over and above what is strictly necessary, included, e.g., for safety reasons or to allow for mistakes or delays ○ *They left no margin for error.* **8.** COMM **PROFIT** the profit on a transaction, or the amount by which the price of something exceeds its cost ○ *We've cut our margins to the absolute bare minimum.* **9.** FIN **BROKER'S LOSS COVER** the amount or percentage deposited with a stockbroker by a client to cover possible losses on transactions made on account **10.** FIN **DIFFERENCE BETWEEN LOAN AND COLLATERAL VALUES** the difference between the face value of a loan and the value of the collateral given to secure the loan **11.** ECON **LOWEST ACCEPTABLE PROFIT** the minimum profit that a business must make in order to remain viable ■ *vt.* (**-gined, -gin·ing, -gins**) **1.** **CREATE MARGIN AROUND** to create a margin around something **2.** FIN **PLACE AS DEPOSIT WITH BROKER** to place something such as collateral with a broker as a deposit [14thC. From Latin *margin-,* the stem of *margo.* Ultimately from an Indo-European word meaning "boundary, border" that is also the ancestor of English *mark*[1] and *march*[1].]

mar·gin·al /máarjin'l/ *adj.* **1.** **IN A MARGIN** written in a margin **2.** **SMALL IN SCALE** very small in scale or importance ○ *You can ignore any marginal discrepancies you find.* **3.** **IRRELEVANT** not of central importance or relevance ○ *In what follows, I have ignored everything that is marginal to my main thesis.* **4.** **ON THE FRINGE** operating or existing on the fringes of a group or movement ○ *a marginal group with no political base* **5.** **VERY LOW** at or close to the lowest acceptable or viable limit ○ *a marginal standard of living* **6.** ECON **BARELY COVERING COSTS** barely able to cover the costs of production when sold or when producing goods for sale **7.** AGRIC **DIFFICULT TO CULTIVATE** difficult to cultivate and therefore only brought into use if profits are high enough to make it worth the effort ○ *marginal land* —**mar·gin·al·i·ty** /maárji nállətee/ *n.*

mar·gi·na·li·a /maárji náylee ə, maárji náylyə/ *npl.* notes written in a margin

mar·gin·al·ize /máarjin'l ìz/ (**-ized, -iz·ing, -iz·es**) *vt.* to take or keep somebody or something away from the center of attention, influence, or power —**mar·gin·al·i·za·tion** /maárjin'li záysh'n/ *n.*

mar·gin·al·ly /máarjin'lee/ *adv.* **1.** **SLIGHTLY** very slightly **2.** **BARELY** only just or barely

mar·gin·al u·til·i·ty *n.* ECON the increase in utility prompted by one extra unit of a given service or product

mar·gin·ate /máarji nàyt/ *vt.* (**-at·ed, -at·ing, -ates**) **ADD MARGIN TO** to add a margin to something, or provide something with a margin ■ *adj.* **mar·gin·ate, mar·gin·at·ed** BIOL **WITH DIFFERENT EDGE** with a border or edge of a different color or pattern ○ *a marginate leaf* —**mar·gin·a·tion** /maárji náysh'n/ *n.*

mar·gra·vate /máargrə vàyt/, **mar·gra·viate** /maar gráyvee ət, -gráyvee àyt/ *n.* **1.** **MARGRAVE'S TERRITORY** the territory ruled by a margrave or margravine **2.** **RANK OF MARGRAVE** the rank or position of a margrave or margravine

mar·grave /máar gràyv/ *n.* in the past, a German nobleman of a rank equivalent to a British marquess [Mid-16thC. From Middle Dutch *markgrave,* literally "count of the border."] —**mar·gravial** *adj.*

mar·gra·vi·ate *n.* = **margravate**

mar·gra·vine /maárgrə veén/ *n.* in the past, a German noblewoman, equal in rank to a British marchioness, who is the wife or widow of a margrave or who holds the rank in her own right [Late 17thC. From Dutch *markgravin,* feminine of *markgraaf* "margrave."]

mar·gue·rite /maárgə reét, -gyə reét/ *n.* a widely cultivated garden plant from the Canary Islands that has a flower resembling a daisy with narrow white or pale yellow petals radiating from a yellow center. Latin name: *Chrysanthemum frutescens.* [Early 17thC. From French, from the female name *Marguerite.*]

ma·ri·a plural of **mare**[2]

ma·ri·a·chi /maaree aachee, mèrree-/ (*plural* **-chis**) *n.* **1.** MEXICAN STREET BAND a Mexican street band usually consisting of stringed instruments, especially violins and guitars, but sometimes also including brass instruments and singers **2.** MARIACHI BAND MEMBER a member of a mariachi band **3.** MARIACHI MUSIC traditional Mexican folk music as played by a mariachi band [Mid-20thC. From Mexican Spanish, of uncertain origin: perhaps from French *mariage* "wedding," because such bands probably played at weddings.]

Mar·i·an /máiree ən/ *adj.* **1.** CHR OF VIRGIN MARY relating to, characteristic of, or devoted to Mary, the mother of Jesus Christ **2.** HIST OF MARY relating to any Mary other than the Virgin Mary, especially Mary Queen of Scots or Queen Mary I of England ■ *n.* CHR DEVOTEE OF VIRGIN MARY somebody who is especially devoted to Mary, the mother of Jesus Christ

Mar·i·an·a Is·lands /màrree aanə-/ island group in the western Pacific Ocean, south of Japan and east of the Philippines. It comprises the island of Guam and the Commonwealth of the Northern Mariana Islands. Area: 370 sq. mi./958 sq. km.

Ma·ri·a·nao /mÀarja naa ō/ city in western Cuba, on the northern coast, in City of Havana Province. Population: 133,016 (1989).

Mar·i·an·a Trench /màrree aanə-/ the deepest ocean trench, in the western Pacific Ocean, stretching from northwest of the Mariana Islands to southwest of Guam. Length: 1,554 mi./2,500 km.

Mar·i·anne /mèrree án/ *n.* an image of a woman personifying the French republic, e.g., on French coins, usually depicted in a light flowing robe and wearing the Phrygian cap of liberty [Late 19thC. From French.]

Ma·ri·a The·re·sa /mə rèe ə tə ráyzə/, **Archduchess of Austria and Queen of Hungary and Bohemia** (1717–80). Her succession as ruler of the Hapsburg dominions led to the War of the Austrian Succession (1740–48) and the Seven Years' War (1756–63).

Ma·ri·a The·re·sa dol·lar *n.* a silver coin minted in 1780 and used in the Middle East [Named for MARIA THERESA, whose image appears on it]

Ma·ri·co·pa /mèrri kṓpə/ (*plural* **-pa** *or* **-pas**) *n.* **1.** PEOPLES MEMBER OF NATIVE N AMERICAN PEOPLE a member of a Native North American people that live in Arizona where they share reservation lands with the Pima **2.** LANG MARICOPA LANGUAGE the language of the Maricopa people —**Ma·ri·co·pa** *adj.*

mar·i·cul·ture /mérrə kùlchər/ *n.* the cultivation of sea animals and plants in their usual habitats, generally for commercial purposes [Early 20thC. Coined from Latin *mari-* (stem of *mare* "sea") + CULTURE.] —**mar·i·cul·tur·al** /mèrrə kúlchərəl/ *adj.* —**mar·i·cul·tur·ist** /mèrrə kúlchərist/ *n.*

Ma·rie An·toi·nette /mə rèe àntwə nét/, **Queen of France** (1755–93). The wife of Louis XVI, she was unpopular for promoting the interests of her native Austria and for her extravagance. She was captured after attempting to escape the French Revolution, imprisoned, and guillotined.

Ma·rie Byrd Land /maaree búrd-/ unclaimed ice-covered region in Antarctica, on the Amundsen Sea, in the southern Pacific Ocean

Ma·rie de Méd·i·cis /mə rèe də méddi chee/, **Queen of France** (1573–1642). As widow of Henry IV of France, she became regent during Louis XIII's minority. Political intrigue resulted in her exile in 1630.

Ma·rie Ga·lante /maa rèegaa lóNt/ island in the French West Indies, in the Caribbean Sea. It is a dependency of Guadeloupe. Population: 3,757 (1982). Area: 61 sq. mi./158 sq. km.

Ma·rie-Lou·ise (of Austria) /mə rèe loo éez-/, **Empress of France** (1791–1847). She was Napoleon Bonaparte's second wife.

Mar·i·et·ta /màree éttə/ city in northwestern Georgia, 20 mi./32 km northwest of Atlanta. Population: 50,290 (1994).

mar·i·gold /mérrə gṑld/ *n.* a common garden plant, native to tropical America, with scented stems and strikingly rich yellow or orange flowers. Genus: *Tagetes.* [14thC. From the name *Mary* (referring to the Virgin Mary) + Old English *golde* "marigold, corn marigold"; so called because of its medicinal properties.]

Marigold

mar·i·gram /mérrə gràm/ *n.* a printed record of tide levels at a particular place [Late 19thC. Coined from Latin *mari-*, stem of *mare* "sea"(+ -GRAM).]

mar·i·graph /mérrə gràf/ *n.* an instrument for recording tide levels [Mid-19thC. Coined from Latin *mari-*, the stem of *mare* "sea"(+ -GRAPH).]

ma·ri·jua·na /mèrrə hwaanə, -waanə/, **mar·i·hua·na** *n.* **1.** DRUGS DRUG FROM HEMP the dried flowers and leaves of the Indian hemp plant, smoked or eaten as a drug **2.** PLANTS HEMP PLANT the Indian hemp plant that is the source of the drugs marijuana and cannabis. Latin name: *Cannabis sativa.* [Late 19thC. From Mexican Spanish *mariguana, marihuana,* of unknown origin.]

ma·rim·ba /mə rímbə/ *n.* a large musical instrument like a xylophone, with resonators made from metal or hollow gourds beneath the bars, used especially in African and Latin American music [Early 18thC. From Portuguese, of Bantu origin.] —**ma·rim·bist** *n.*

ma·ri·na /mə réenə/ *n.* a harbor specially designed to cater to the needs of pleasure boats and their owners [Early 19thC. Via Italian or Spanish, "seashore," from, ultimately, Latin *marinus,* from *mare* "sea."]

Ma·ri·na /mə réenə/ city in Monterey County, California. Population: 15,433 (1994).

mar·i·nade *n.* /mèrrə náyd/ FLAVORINGS FOR FOOD BEFORE COOKING a liquid or paste made with ingredients such as vinegar, wine, oil, spices, and herbs, in which food is soaked or allowed to stand to give extra flavor and tenderness before cooking ■ *vti.* /mérrə nàyd/ (**-nad·ed, -nad·ing, -nades**) = **marinate** [Early 18thC. Via French from, ultimately, Italian *marinare* or Spanish *marinar* (see MARINATE).]

ma·ri·na·ra /mèrrə nérrə, maarə naarə/ *adj.* **1.** MADE WITH TOMATOES AND GARLIC made with tomatoes and garlic, often with other ingredients such as onions, parsley, capers, or olives, to serve on pasta or as a pizza topping ○ *marinara sauce* **2.** WITH MARINARA SAUCE served with marinara sauce ○ *spaghetti marinara* [Mid-20thC. From Italian *alla marinara* "in sailor style," from *marinaro* "sailor," from *marino* "marine," from Latin *marinus,* from *mare* "sea."] —**ma·ri·na·ra** *n.*

mar·i·nate /mérrə nàyt/ (**-nat·ed, -nat·ing, -nates**) *vti.* to soak or stand, or leave food to soak or stand, in a marinade before cooking [Mid-17thC. From Italian *marinare* or Spanish *marinar* "to pickle in brine," both from Latin *(aqua) marina* "sea (water), brine," feminine of *marinus,* from *mare* "sea."] —**mar·i·na·tion** /mèrrə náysh'n/ *n.*

ma·rine /mə réen/ *adj.* **1.** INSUR OF THE SEA relating to, found in, or living in the sea **2.** NAUT NAUTICAL relating to ships or sailing **3.** MIL OF SEAGOING SOLDIERS relating to soldiers who serve at sea as well as on land ■ *n.* **1. ma·rine, Ma·rine** MIL SEAGOING SOLDIER a soldier who serves at sea as well as in the air and on land, e.g., a member of the U.S. Marine Corps **2.** SHIPPING NATION'S COMMERCIAL FLEET a fleet of merchant or naval ships and their crews (*formal*) **3.** PAINTING SEA SCENE a painting or photograph of a seascape, ship, or scene at sea [14thC. Via French from Latin *marinus,* from *mare* "sea" (see MARE[2]).] ◇ **tell that to the marines** used to express disbelief (*slang*)

ma·rine ar·chi·tect *n.* somebody specially trained to design ships —**ma·rine ar·chi·tec·ture** *n.*

ma·rine bi·ol·o·gy *n.* the branch of biology that deals with the plants and animals of the oceans —**ma·rine bi·ol·o·gist** *n.*

Ma·rine Corps *n.* a branch of the United States armed forces, trained to operate on land, at sea, and in the air, and especially in amphibious assaults. The Marine Corps comes under the authority of the Secretary of the Navy.

ma·rine en·gi·neer *n.* somebody who attends to the engines and other heavy machinery on board a ship or any other offshore structure

mar·i·ner /mérrənər/ *n.* somebody who sails or navigates vessels at sea [13thC. Via Anglo-Norman or French *marinier* from Latin *marinarius,* from *marinus* from *mare* "sea."]

WORD KEY: CULTURAL NOTE

The Rime of the Ancient Mariner, a poem by the English writer Samuel Taylor Coleridge (1798). A cautionary tale of sin and redemption, it describes a curse placed on a sailor after he kills an albatross that has led his ship out of danger. The vessel is becalmed and the rest of the crew die of thirst. After his rescue, the sailor is compelled to repeat his story for the remainder of his days. The expressions "Water, water, every where/ Nor any drop to drink" and "He prayest best who loveth best/ All things both great and small" come from Part II, stanza 9, and Part VII, stanza 23 respectively, of this poem.

ma·rin·ière *adj.* cooked with a little wine, herbs, and chopped onion or shallot, in a closed pan, so that the main ingredient, which is usually mussels, is partly poached and partly steamed ○ *mussels marinière* [From French, literally "sailor-style," possibly a translation of Italian *marinara* (see MARINARA)]

Mar·i·ol·a·try /mèrree óllətree/ *n.* extreme devotion to Mary, the mother of Jesus Christ [Early 17thC. Coined from Latin *Maria* "Mary" + -LATRY.] —**Mar·i·ol·a·ter** *n.* —**Mar·i·ol·a·trous** *adj.*

Mar·i·ol·o·gy /mèrree óllәjee/ *n.* the study of the doctrines and beliefs concerning Mary, the mother of Jesus Christ [Mid-19thC. Coined from Latin *Maria* "Mary" + -LOGY.] —**Mar·i·o·log·i·cal** /mèrree ə lójjik'l/ *adj.* —**Mar·i·ol·o·gist** /-óllәjist/ *n.*

Mar·i·on /máree ən/ city in southern Illinois, just east of Orchard Lake and Carbondale and southeast of Herrin. Population: 15,619 (1996).

Mar·i·on /máree ən/, **Francis** (1732–95) U.S. military officer. He engaged in successful anti-British guerrilla tactics during the Revolution (1775–83). Known as **Swamp Fox**

mar·i·o·nette /mèrree ə nét/ *n.* a puppet operated by means of strings attached to its hands, legs, head, and body [Early 17thC. From French, literally "little Mary," from *Marion,* of the same meaning.]

mar·i·po·sa /mèrrə pṓssə, -pṓzə/ *n.* a western North American plant of the lily family that grows from a bulb and bears brightly colored flowers resembling tulips. Genus: *Calochortus.* [Mid-19thC. From Spanish, literally "butterfly" (because of its brightly-colored flowers).]

Ma·ris /márriss/, **Roger** (1934–85) U.S. baseball player. He played for the New York Yankees (1960–66). He broke Babe Ruth's home run record and was named Most Valuable Player in the American League in 1960 and 1961. Full name **Roger Eugene Maris**

Mar·ist /mérrist/ *n.* a member of either of two Roman Catholic orders, the Society of Mary or Marist Fathers, and the Little Brothers of Mary or Marist Brothers [Late 19thC. From French *mariste,* from *Marie* "Mary."] —**Mar·ist** *adj.*

mar·i·tage /mérritij/ *n.* **1.** RIGHT OF LORD TO ARRANGE MARRIAGE the right of a feudal lord to choose the husband or wife of a vassal's heir **2.** FINE PAID TO FEUDAL LORD money paid to a feudal lord in return for his not exercising his right to choose the husband or wife of a vassal's heir [Early 16thC. From medieval Latin *maritagium,* a latinized form of French *mariage,* from *marier* (see MARRY).]

mar·i·tal /mérrət'l/ *adj.* **1.** OF MARRIAGE relating to marriage or the marriage of a particular couple **2.** OF HUSBANDS relating to a husband or husbands (*formal*) [15thC. From Latin *maritalis,* from *maritus* "married" (source also of English *marry*[1]).] —**mar·i·tal·ly** *adv.*

mar·i·time /mérrə tīm/ *adj.* **1.** SHIPPING OF THE SEA relating to the sea, shipping, sailing in ships, or living and working at sea **2.** CLOSE TO THE SEA situated or living close to the sea **3.** METEOROL INFLUENCED BY THE SEA influenced by the sea, and therefore generally temperate and with relatively small variations in seasonal temperatures [Mid-16thC. Directly or via French from Latin *maritimus,* from *mare* "sea" (see MARE[2]).]

Mar·i·time Prov·inc·es, Mar·i·times collective name for the eastern Canadian provinces of New Brunswick, Nova Scotia, and Prince Edward Island —**Mar·i·tim·er** *n.*

Ma·ri·tsa /mə reétsə/ river in southeastern Europe, in the Balkan Peninsula. Length: 300 mi./480 km.

Ma·ri·u·pol /maree oòpəl/ city in southeastern Ukraine, on the Sea of Azov. Population: 510,000 (1996).

mar·jo·ram /maárjərəm/ *n.* a Mediterranean herb that has small purple or white flowers and aromatic leaves, often used as a seasoning in cookery and salads. Latin name: *Origanum majorana*. [14thC. Via Old French *marjorane* from medieval Latin *majorana*, of unknown origin.]

mark[1] /maark/ *n.* **1.** **SPOT, SCRATCH, OR DIRT** a colored, discolored, or dirty patch, a scratch, dent, or impression, either deliberately or accidentally made, that makes a usually small area of a surface visibly different from the rest ○ *The hot plate left a mark on the table.* **2.** **SYMBOL** a recognizable sign or symbol used, e.g., to indicate ownership, the quality or origin of goods, or punctuation in a piece of writing (*often used in combination*) ○ *a question mark* **3.** **SUBSTITUTE FOR SIGNATURE** a cross or other symbol used in place of a signature by somebody who cannot write **4.** **INDICATION OF FEELING** an action, gesture, or other outward sign of somebody's feeling or attitude ○ *a mark of respect* **5.** **SIGN OF INFLUENCE OR INVOLVEMENT** something that is evidence of somebody's or something's influence on or involvement in something ○ *He left his mark on the firm.* **6.** **IDENTIFYING FEATURE OR CHARACTERISTIC** a distinctive and identifying feature or characteristic ○ *That perfect finish is the mark of the true professional.* **7.** **INDICATION OF CORRECTNESS OR QUALITY** a number, letter, or percentage indicating somebody's assessment of something, e.g., the correctness or quality of answers to examination questions or somebody's performance in a gymnastic or ice-skating contest ○ *She always gets top marks in English.* **8.** **INDICATOR OF POSITION OR EXTENT** any object, sign, or line used to indicate the position, extent, or amount of something ○ *the high-water mark* **9.** **AMOUNT** the amount, distance, or level reached by something ○ *The temperature is way above the 90 degree mark.* **10.** **STANDARD** the desired or required standard for something ○ *Your work is simply not up to the mark these days.* **11.** **TYPE** a model or variety, e.g., of a car, aircraft, or weapon, usually distinguished from earlier or later models by a number **12.** ARMS **TARGET** a target, or something that somebody aims at with a weapon ○ *He missed the mark.* **13.** **GOAL** a goal or standard that somebody wishes to achieve **14.** CRIMINOL **VICTIM OF CRIME** the victim or intended victim of a theft or swindle (*slang*) ○ *an easy mark* **15.** NAVIG **GUIDE TO POSITION OR DIRECTION** a conspicuous object or another point of reference that serves as a visual guide to somebody when proceeding in a particular direction or carrying out an action **16.** SPORT **STARTING LINE** the starting line for a race **17.** SPORTS **RUNNER'S STARTING POSITION** an individual runner's starting position for a race **18.** BOXING **MIDDLE OF STOMACH** the middle of an opponent's stomach **19.** SPORTS = **jack**[1] *n.* 5 **20.** SAILING **SOMETHING THAT INDICATES DEPTH OF WATER** a knot or other marker used to indicate intervals of fathoms on a sounding line **21.** HIST **COMMON LAND** in medieval Germany and England, land held in common by the members of a community ■ *v.* (**marked, mark·ing, marks**) **1.** *vti.* **MAKE OR GET SPOTS OR SCRATCHES** to make or get a colored or discolored patch, dent, scratch, or other mark on something, either accidentally or deliberately ○ *The mugs have marked the table.* **2.** *vt.* **PUT MARK OR SYMBOL ON SOMETHING** to put a recognizable sign or symbol or write on something, e.g., to show ownership, to indicate price, or to give a warning or instruction ○ *All items of clothing must be clearly marked with the student's name.* **3.** *vt.* **MAKE CLEARLY IDENTIFIABLE** to make something clearly visible, recognizable, or traceable by putting a mark on it ○ *I've marked on the map where our house is.* **4.** *vt.* **INDICATE WHERE SOMETHING IS OR HAPPENED** to be an indicator showing where something is situated, how far it extends, or where an event took place ○ *This monument marks their last resting place.* **5.** *vt.* **BE OR INDICATE POINT OF CHANGE** to indicate that a significant point in time or in a process has been reached ○ *It marks the end of an era in American theater.* **6.** *vt.* **GIVE PROMINENCE TO EVENT** to do something to celebrate or give prominence to a particular event ○ *We should do something really special to mark their 50th anniversary* **7.** *vt.* **SELECT FOR SPECIAL ATTENTION** to select or destine somebody or something for particular attention or treatment ○ *He was always marked out for success.* **8.** *vt.* **CHARACTERIZE** to characterize, distinguish, or set somebody or something apart in some way ○ *The originality of her approach marks her as a candidate of real distinction.* **9.** *vt.* **ASSESS AND INDICATE QUALITY OR CORRECTNESS** to assess the quality or correctness of something and indicate the assessment by means of a mark such as a check or cross, a letter, number, or percentage ○ *marking exam papers* **10.** *vt.* **ASSESS THE WORK OF SOMEBODY** to assess the quality or correctness of the work or performance of somebody and indicate the assessment by means of a mark ○ *marked him high on the test* **11.** *vt.* **TAKE NOTICE OF** to pay attention to something or somebody (*often used as a command*) ○ *Mark my words: this'll make them sit up and take notice.* **12.** *vt.* **SEE SOMETHING** to see or notice something (*archaic*) **13.** *vt.* SPORTS **STAY CLOSE TO PLAYER** in games such as soccer and field hockey, to stay close to an attacking player in the opposing team to prevent the player from receiving the ball or scoring **14.** *vti.* SPORTS **KEEP SCORE** to keep a note of the score [Old English *mearc* "boundary, marker." Ultimately from an Indo-European word meaning "boundary," which is also the ancestor of English *march* and *margin*.] ◇ **mark time 1.** to continue marching in rhythm without moving forward **2.** to do something that makes no contribution toward achieving a goal or ambition while awaiting an opportunity to make progress ◇ **make your mark** to achieve recognition or success, usually in a particular field ◇ **mark you** *U.K.* used to call somebody's attention to a point or remark that you are making ◇ **on your mark** used as a command to runners to take up their starting positions ready for the start of a race ◇ **quick off the mark, slow off the mark** quick or slow to begin, react to, or understand something ◇ **up to the mark** of an acceptable standard or quality, or at an acceptable level ◇ **wide of the mark, off the mark** inaccurate or incorrect

mark down *vt.* **1.** **LOWER PRICE** to lower the price of something **2.** **MAKE WRITTEN NOTE** to make a written note of something somewhere **3.** **GIVE LOWER MARK** to reduce the mark given to something or somebody in a test, examination, or contest, as a result of a mistake or inadequacy ○ *You get marked down for bad spelling.* **4.** **CHARACTERIZE** to form an opinion as to the character or likely behavior of somebody

mark off *vt.* **1.** **SEPARATE ONE AREA FROM ANOTHER** to separate one area from another by means of a boundary line or barrier **2.** **PUT A MARK ON SOMETHING** to put a mark such as a check, cross, or line beside, through, or around something, to show that it has been dealt with or to highlight it

mark out *vt.* to draw lines or use some other method to indicate the boundaries and divisions of something, especially the playing area for a game or a racecourse

mark up *vt.* **1.** BUSINESS **INCREASE PRICE** to increase the price of something, especially to provide the seller with a profit **2.** PUBL **MARK CORRECTIONS AND INSTRUCTIONS ON TEXT** to prepare a piece of written work for printing or rekeying by making corrections to it or adding instructions to the typesetters or keyboarders **3.** EDUC **INCREASE GRADES OR SCORES AWARDED** to increase the grades awarded to somebody on a test, examination, or contest

mark[2] /maark/ *n.* **1.** MONEY = **deutsche mark 2.** MONEY **OLD COIN IN ENGLAND AND SCOTLAND** a former unit of currency in England and Scotland that was worth 13 shillings and 4 pence, or two thirds of a pound **3.** MEASURE **UNIT OF WEIGHT** formerly, a unit of weight equivalent to 8 oz/227 gr that was used for weighing gold and silver [Old English *marc*, a unit of weight. From a prehistoric Germanic word (ancestor also of English *mark*[1]). In the sense "Deutschmark": late 19thC, from German.]

Mark /maark/, **St.** (*fl.* 1st century) apostle. A disciple of St. Peter and one of the apostles of Jesus Christ, he is credited with writing the New Testament Gospel of Mark.

Mark *n.* the second of the gospels in the Bible in which the life and teachings of Jesus Christ are described. It is thought to have been written by St. Mark. See table at **Bible**

mark·down /maárk down/ *n.* a reduction in price

marked /maarkt/ *adj.* **1.** **NOTICEABLE** very noticeable ○ *a marked contrast* **2.** **SINGLED OUT** singled out for surveillance, suspicion, hostility, or an unpleasant fate ○ *a marked man* **3.** **WITH MARK ON BACK** having a concealed identifying mark that makes it easier to use when cheating in card games or performing conjuring tricks ○ *marked cards* **4.** LING **WITH DISTINCTIVE LINGUISTIC FEATURE** having an extra or less usual distinctive linguistic feature —**mark·ed·ness** /maárkədnəss/ *n.*

mark·ed·ly /maárkədlee/ *adv.* to a significant extent

mark·er /maárkər/ *n.* **1.** **INDICATOR OF POSITION, PRESENCE, OR ROUTE** an object or sign that indicates the position or presence of something or the direction in which somebody is to go **2.** **SOMETHING THAT MAKES MARKS** something used to make marks, especially a felt-tip pen **3.** **IOU** a debt to be paid off (*slang*) **4.** SPORTS **SCOREKEEPER** somebody who keeps a note of the score in certain games, e.g., pool and billiards, or something that shows the score **5.** EDUC **SOMEBODY WHO ASSESSES STUDENTS' ANSWERS** somebody who grades examination papers or student exercises **6.** SPORTS **PLAYER MARKING ANOTHER** in games such as football and field, hockey, a player who stays close to an attacking player in the opposing team to prevent the player from receiving the ball or scoring

mar·ket /maárkət/ *n.* **1.** COMM **GATHERING FOR BUYING AND SELLING** a gathering of people who sell things, especially food or animals, in a place open to the public or other buyers, especially a gathering that is held regularly ○ *a cattle market* **2.** **MARKET BUILDING OR PLACE** a building or open space where a market is regularly held **3.** COMM **COLLECTION OF SHOPS OR STALLS** a number of small shops or stalls, housed in the same building and sometimes all selling the same type of goods, belonging to different, independent traders **4.** COMM **SHOP** a shop, especially one that sells goods or food of a particular type **5.** FIN **SUPPLY AND DEMAND** the whole area of economic activity where buyers are in contact with sellers and in which the laws of supply and demand operate. Besides being considered as the arena for buying and selling, the market is often thought of as a controlling or regulatory force affecting both economic and political affairs. ○ *market forces* **6.** FIN **BUYING AND SELLING OF PARTICULAR COMMODITY** the trade in, or buying and selling of, a particular commodity ○ *the futures market* **7.** COMM **REGION OR GROUP CONSIDERED AS CUSTOMERS** a geographic area or a section of the population, considered from the point of view of the amount of goods than can be sold to it ○ *the teenage market* **8.** COMM **DEMAND** the demand for a particular type of goods or service being offered for sale ○ *You've got to go out and create a market if you want to succeed.* **9.** ECON **TOTAL AMOUNT OF PRODUCT SOLD** the total amount of a particular product sold within a particular geographical area or over a particular period of time **10.** STOCK EXCH = **stock market** ○ *Prices rose on the New York and Chicago markets this morning* **11.** FIN **TRADING IN STOCKS** trading in stocks and commodities ○ *The market was very slow this morning but picked up later.* **12.** FIN **PRICES OR EXCHANGE RATES** the prices or rates of exchange offered for stocks or commodities ○ *The market fell this morning but rallied later.* ■ *vt.* (**-ket·ed, -ket·ing, -kets**) MARKETING **OFFER FOR SALE** to offer something for sale, or sell something, especially by using advertising and other techniques to attract buyers ○ *If this is marketed in the right way, it'll sell very well.* [Pre-12thC. Via Old French dialect from, ultimately, Latin *mercatus*, from the past participle of *mercari* "to buy," from *merx* "goods" (source of English *merchant* and *commerce*).] —**mar·ket·er** *n.* ◇ **come onto the market** to become available for customers to buy ◇ **in the market (for something)** interested in buying or ready to buy something ◇ **on the market** available for customers to buy ◇ **on the open market** where goods are freely available and prices are subject mainly to the law of supply and demand ◇ **put something on the market** to offer something for sale

mar·ket·a·ble /maárkətəb'l/ *adj.* **1.** COMM **SUITABLE FOR SELLING** fit to be sold ○ *a highly marketable property* **2.** **IN DEMAND** in demand and therefore relatively easy to sell ○ *skills that are readily marketable* **3.** FIN **CONVERTIBLE INTO CASH** able to be converted into cash quickly, but at a price that is determined by the market in that commodity ○ *marketable value* —**mar·ket·a·bil·i·ty** /maárkətə bíllətee/ *n.* —**mar·ket·a·ble·ness** /maárkətəb'lnəss/ *n.* —**mar·ket·a·bly** *adv.*

mar·ket bas·ket *n.* **1.** **GROCERY CART** a supermarket or grocery store cart **2.** **SELECTION OF FOODS FOR STATISTICAL FAMILY** a selection of foods representing the requirements of a statistical household of 3.2 people or a family of four, the cost of which is a factor in cost-of-living statistics

mar·ket e·con·o·my *n.* an economy where prices and wages are determined mainly by the market and the laws of supply and demand, rather than being regulated by a government

mar·ket·eer /maàrkə tèer/ *n.* **1.** COMM **SOMEBODY WHO TRADES AT MARKET** somebody who buys or sells things either at a market or in ordinary trade **2.** POL **SUPPORTER OF TYPE OF MARKET** somebody who advocates or supports a particular type of market (*usually used in combination*) ○ *a free marketeer*

mar·ket gar·den *n.* a plot of ground or small farm where fruit, vegetables, and sometimes flowers are grown for sale rather than for the grower's own use —**mar·ket gar·den·er** *n.* —**mar·ket gar·den·ing** *n.*

mar·ket·ing /maàrkəting/ *n.* **1. SELLING OF PRODUCTS OR SERVICES** the business activity of presenting products or services to potential customers in such a way as to make them eager to buy. Marketing includes such matters as the pricing and packaging of the product and the creation of demand by advertising and sales campaigns. **2.** FOOD, COMM **GROCERY SHOPPING** the buying of household provisions

mar·ket·ing board *n. Can, U.K.* an organization set up by a government to promote and regulate the sale of a particular agricultural product, e.g., grain, dairy products, or poultry

mar·ket·ing mix *n.* the particular mixture of marketing techniques, e.g., pricing, packaging, and advertising, used to promote the sale of a product

mar·ket lead·er *n.* a company or brand that has a very large, or the largest, share of the market for a particular product

mar·ket mak·er *n.* a dealer who buys and sells securities such as stocks

mar·ket or·der *n.* an order instructing a broker to buy or sell an asset immediately at the best prevailing price

mar·ket·place /maàrkət plàyss/ *n.* **1. OPEN SPACE FOR MARKET** an open space where a market is held **2.** COMM **SPHERE OF TRADING** the commercial sphere where buying and selling takes place and the laws of supply and demand operate **3. SETUP WHERE IDEAS CAN BE DISCUSSED** a forum in which ideas are exchanged, discussed, and compete for recognition

mar·ket price *n.* the price at which something is currently being bought by the majority of customers

mar·ket re·search *n.* the gathering and analysis of information about what people want or like, or what they actually buy —**mar·ket re·search·er** *n.*

mar·ket share *n.* the proportion of the total sales of a product secured by one particular company or brand

mar·ket town *n.* a town in which a market is held regularly, usually the chief town of a farming area

mar·ket val·ue *n.* the amount that a seller could expect to obtain for property or goods sold on the open market

Mark·ham /maàrkəm/, **Edwin Ansan** (1852–1940) U.S. poet. His social protest poem "The Man with the Hoe" (1899) made him nationally famous. Full name **Charles Edward Ansan Markham**

mar·khor /maàr kàwr/ (*plural* **-khors** *or* **-khor**) *n.* the largest wild goat, which has a reddish-brown coat, spiral horns, and a shaggy beard on the male, and is found in the Himalayas. Latin name: *Capra falconeri.* [Mid-19thC. From Persian *mār-kwār*, literally "serpent-eater."]

mark·ing /maàrking/ *n.* **1.** ZOOL **MARK OR MARKS** a mark or pattern of marks that occurs naturally, e.g., on an animal's coat (*often used in the plural*) **2.** AIR **AIRCRAFT IDENTIFYING MARK** an identifying mark, usually a colored symbol, on an aircraft (*often used in the plural*) **3.** EDUC **ASSESSMENT AND GRADING OF WRITTEN WORK** a teacher's correction and assessment of students' written work

mark·ing ink *n.* a type of ink used for writing on such things as clothes and bed linen because it does not wash out

mark·ka /maàr kaà, maàrkaà/ (*plural* **-kaa** *or* **-kas**) *n.* **1.** see table at **currency 2. COIN WORTH A MARKKA** a coin worth one markka [Early 20thC. Via Finnish from Swedish *marka.*]

Dame Alicia Markova: In *Mr. Puppet* with Anton Dolin

Mar·ko·va /maar kốvə/, **Dame Alicia** (*b.* 1910) British ballerina. She was a cofounder of the London Festival Ballet (1950) and director of the Metropolitan Opera Ballet (1963–69). Real name **Lillian Alicia Marks**

Mar·kov chain /maàr kàwv-/ *n.* a random process in which events are discrete rather than continuous and the future development of each event is independent of all historical events or dependent only on the immediately preceding event [See MARKOV PROCESS]

Mar·kov proc·ess *n.* a continuous random process in which the probability of occurrence of each random event in a series is independent of all historical events or dependent only on the immediately preceding event [Named for the Russian mathematician A. A. *Markov*, who developed it.]

marks·man /maàrksmən/ (*plural* **-men** /-mən/) *n.* **1. SOMEBODY SKILLED IN SHOOTING** somebody who is able or trained to shoot accurately, especially with a firearm **2. SOMEBODY CONSIDERED GOOD OR BAD SHOT** somebody considered from the point of view of his or her ability to shoot accurately —**marks·man·ship** *n.*

marks·wo·man /maàrks wòommən/ (*plural* **-men** /-wìmmin/) *n.* **1. WOMAN SKILLED IN SHOOTING** a woman who is able or trained to shoot accurately, especially with a firearm **2. WOMAN CONSIDERED GOOD OR BAD SHOT** a woman considered from the point of view of her ability to shoot accurately

markup *n.* COMM the difference between the manufacturing cost or wholesale price of an item and its selling price, that is, the amount added to provide the seller with a profit

marl[1] /maarl/ *n.* GEOL **MIXTURE OF CLAY AND LIME** a naturally occurring fine crumbly mixture of clay and limestone, often containing shell fragments and sometimes other minerals. Marls are used as fertilizer and to soften water. ■ *vt.* (**marled, marl·ing, marls**) AGRIC **FERTLIZE WITH MARL** to add marl to soil as a fertilizer [14thC. Via Old French *marle* from medieval Latin *margila*, from Latin *marga* "marl" on the model of *argilla* "white clay."] —**mar·la·cious** /maar láyshəss/ *adj.* —**marl·y** /maàrlee/ *adj.*

marl[2] /maarl/ (**marled, marl·ing, marls**) *vt.* to bind something with a light two-stranded rope [Early 18thC. From Dutch *marlen*, literally "to keep binding," from Middle Dutch *marren* "to bind" (source of English *marline*).]

Mar·ley /maàrlee/, **Bob** (1945–81) Jamaican musician. His music, much of which he wrote himself, established reggae internationally as an important part of pop music.

mar·lin[1] /maàrlin/ (*plural* **-lins** *or* **-lin**) *n.* a large food and game fish found in warm and tropical regions of the Atlantic and Pacific oceans that has a very long thin upper jaw, like a spear. It can reach 14 ft./4.5 m in length and 1500 lbs/680 kg in weight. Family: Istiophoridae. [Early 20thC. Shortened from *marlinspike*, from the shape of its upper jaw.]

mar·lin[2] *n.* = **marline**

mar·line /maàrlin/, **mar·lin** *n.* a light two-stranded rope, used especially for binding around larger ropes to prevent them from fraying [15thC. Via Dutch *marlijn*, literally "binding line," and *marling* "binding," both ultimately from Middle Dutch *marren* "to bind."]

mar·line·spike /maàrlin spìk/, **mar·lin·spike** *n.* a pointed metal tool used to separate strands of rope that are being spliced [Early 17thC. Alteration (under the influence of MARLINE) of earlier *marlingspike*, from MARL[2] + SPIKE.]

mar·lite /maàr lìt/ *n.* a rock with the same composition as marl but with a harder, more resistant texture [Late 18thC. Formed from MARL[1].] —**mar·lit·ic** /maar líttik/ *adj.*

marl·stone /maàrl stòn/ *n.* = **marlite**

mar·ma·lade /maàrmə làyd/ *n.* FOOD **CITRUS FRUIT JELLY** a clear or thick preserve made with citrus fruits, usually containing the shredded rind of the fruit, and traditionally made with bitter Seville oranges ■ *adj. U.K.* ZOOL **WITH ORANGE FUR** used to describe cats with orange fur, or orange fur streaked with yellow or brown [15thC. Via French *marmelade* "quince jam" from Portuguese *marmelada*, from *marmelo* "quince," from, ultimately, Greek *melimēlon*, literally "honey-apple," denoting a kind of apple grafted onto the quince.]

mar·ma·lade box *n.* the reddish-brown edible fruit of the genipap tree

mar·ma·lade plum *n.* the edible brownish fruit of the marmalade tree, with sweet, slightly spicy, reddish flesh

mar·ma·lade tree *n.* a tree found in Central America, Mexico, and the southern United States, with brownish edible fruit (**marmalade plums**). Latin name: *Calocarpum sapota.*

mar·mite /maàr mìt, maar mèet/ *n.* a deep earthenware or metal cooking pot with a close-fitting lid, used for making soups, stews, or stock [Early 19thC. Via French from Old French, literally "hypocritical" (perhaps because the food is concealed), from *marmouser* "to murmur" + *mite* "cat," both imitations of sounds.]

mar·mo·re·al /maar máwree əl/ *adj.* made of marble, or like marble, especially in being white, cold, or aloof and impressive (*formal*) [Late 18thC. Formed from Latin *marmoreus*, from *marmor* (see MARBLE).] —**mar·mo·re·al·ly** *adv.*

mar·mo·set /maàrmə sèt, -zèt/ (*plural* **-sets** *or* **-set**) *n.* a small monkey that lives in Central and South America and has soft thick fur, tufts of fur around its head and ears, a long tail, and clawed digits. Family: Callithricidae. [14thC. From French *marmouset* "grotesque figure," of uncertain origin.]

mar·mot /maàrmət/ (*plural* **-mots** *or* **-mot**) *n.* a large brownish stout-bodied rodent of the squirrel family that lives on the ground and in burrows and is found throughout North America, Europe, and northern Asia. One species of American marmot is known as the woodchuck or groundhog. Genus: *Marmota.* [Early 17thC. From French *marmotte*, of uncertain origin.]

mar·o·cain /mérrə kàyn, mèrrə káyn/ *n.* a ribbed crepe fabric [Early 20thC. From French, literally "Moroccan."]

Mar·o·nite /mérrə nìt/ *adj.* belonging or relating to the Christian Uniat Church of Lebanon, an Eastern Catholic church [Early 16thC. From medieval Latin *Maronita*, from the name of the 4thC Syrian hermit *Maro*, who founded the group.] —**Mar·o·nite** *n.*

Ma·roo·chy·dore /maroòchee dàwr/ coastal town in southeastern Queensland, Australia, located at the mouth of the Maroochy River. Population: 36,406 (1996).

ma·roon[1] /mə roòn/ *adj.* **DEEP PURPLISH RED** of a deep purplish-red color with a tinge of brown ■ *n.* **DEEP PURPLISH RED COLOR** a deep purplish-red color tinged with brown [Late 18thC. Via French *marron* "large sweet chestnut" from, ultimately, medieval Greek *maraon.* So called because of the color of the nut's inner skin.]

ma·roon[2] /mə roòn/ *vt.* (**-rooned, -roon·ing, -roons**) **1.** NAUT **LEAVE IN LONELY PLACE** to put somebody ashore on a lonely island or coast and leave the person there with no means of escape **2. LEAVE SOMEBODY ISOLATED** to leave somebody somewhere with no means of getting away ■ *n.* **1. ma·roon, Ma·roon** PEOPLES **DESCENDANT OF PEOPLE ESCAPED FROM SLAVERY** a descendant of people escaped from slavery in Guyana and the remoter parts of the West Indies **2. MAROONED PERSON** somebody who has been marooned, especially on a desert island [Mid-17thC. From French *marron* "fugitive from slavery," shortening of American Spanish *cimarrón* "wild, untamed," probably from *cima* "peak."]

mar·o·quin /mérrəkin/ *n.* morocco leather, used especially for bookbindings and shoes [Early 16thC. From French, formed from *Maroc* "Morocco," probably under the influence of Spanish *marroquin* "Moroccan, morocco leather."]

Marq. *abbr.* **1.** Marquess **2.** Marquis

marque /maark/ *n.* a brand or make of product, especially a make of luxury or high-performance car [Early 20thC. From French, formed from *marquer* "to mark or brand," ultimately of prehistoric Germanic origin.]

mar·quee /maar kée/ *n.* **1. COVERING LIKE ROOF** a permanent canopy, often of metal and glass, projecting out over the entrance to a large building such as a hotel or theater **2. LARGE TENT** a very large tent with straight sides that can be rolled up or removed, used for large gatherings such as parties, meetings, sales, and exhibitions [Late 17thC. Alteration of French *marquise* (see MARQUISE), which also denoted a canopy erected over the tent of a nobleman or officer to distinguish it from others.]

Mar·que·sas Is·lands /maar káyssəss-/ group of volcanic islands in French Polynesia, 740 mi./1,200 km north of Tahiti, in the Pacific Ocean. Population: 7,538 (1988). Area: 492 sq. mi./1,274 sq. km.

mar·quess /ma̋arkwəss/ *n.* in Great Britain and Ireland, a nobleman ranking between a duke and an earl [15thC. From Old French *marchis*, from *marche* "border land" (see MARCH[2]).] —**mar·ques·sate** /ma̋arkwə sàyt, -zàyt/ *n.*

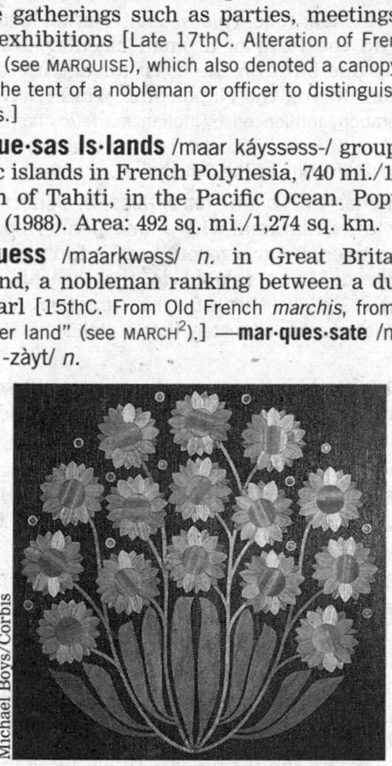

Marquetry

mar·que·try /ma̋arkətree/, **mar·que·terie** *n.* **1. DECORATIVE DESIGNS MADE OF INLAID MATERIALS** designs or pictures made of thin pieces of wood, metal, shell, or other materials, inlaid in a wood veneer and often applied as decoration to pieces of furniture **2. CRAFT OF MAKING MARQUETRY** the craft of making marquetry designs or pictures [Mid-16thC. From French *marqueterie*, from *marqueter* "to variegate," from *marquer* "to mark or brand."]

Mar·quette /maar két/, **Jacques** (1637–75) French Jesuit missionary and explorer. He explored the Mississippi River basin (1673–74) with Louis Jolliet. Known as **Père Marquette**

Már·quez /ma̋ar kez/, **Gabriel García** (*b.* 1928) Colombian writer. In novels such as *100 Years of Solitude* (1967) and *Love in the Time of Cholera* (1985), he developed a distinctive style of fantasy blended with realism. He won the Nobel Prize in literature in 1982.

mar·quis /ma̋arkwiss, -kée/ (*plural* **-quis·es** /ma̋arkwissəz/ *or* **-quis** /maar kéez/) *n.* in various European countries, a nobleman ranking above a count [14thC. From Old French, an alteration of Old French *marchis* (see MARQUESS).] —**mar·quis·ate** /ma̋arkwəzət, -wessət/ *n.*

Mar·quis /ma̋arkwiss/, **Don** (1878–1937) U.S. writer. He is best known for his humorous poems supposedly written by a cockroach called Archy. Full name **Donald Robert Perry Marquis**

mar·quise /maar kéez/ *n.* **1. NOBLEWOMAN** in various European countries, a noblewoman ranking above a countess, or the wife or widow of a marquis **2.** = **marquee** *n.* 1 **3.** CRAFT **POINTED OVAL GEM** a gem cut into the shape of a pointed oval and usually faceted **4.** ACCESSORIES **RING WITH POINTED OVAL** a ring set with a pointed oval gem, or a cluster of stones arranged in a pointed oval shape [Early 17thC. From French, feminine of MARQUIS.]

mar·qui·sette /ma̋arkə zét, -kwə zét/ *n.* a fine woven fabric, often made of cotton or silk, that is used for making curtains and mosquito nets [Early 20thC. From French, literally "little marquise."]

Mar·ra·kesh /màrrə késh/, **Mar·ra·kech** city in western Morocco, on the fertile Haouz Plain, at the foot of the High Atlas Mountains. Population: 602,000 (1994).

Mar·ra·no /mə ra̋a nō/ (*plural* **-nos**) *n.* in the Middle Ages, a Jew from Spain or Portugal who converted to Christianity under duress and without conviction, and who continued to practice Judaism in secret [Late 16thC. From Spanish, literally "pig" (because of the Jewish prohibition against pork), of uncertain origin: probably from Arabic *mahram* "something forbidden" (because of the Islamic prohibition against pork).]

mar·riage /mérrij/ *n.* **1. LEGAL RELATIONSHIP BETWEEN SPOUSES** a legally recognized relationship, established by a civil or religious ceremony, between two people who intend to live together as sexual and domestic partners **2. PARTICULAR MARRIAGE RELATIONSHIP** a married relationship between two specific people, or an individual's relationship with an individual spouse **3. JOINING IN WEDLOCK** the joining together in wedlock of two people **4. MARRIAGE CEREMONY** the ceremony in which two people are joined together formally in wedlock **5. UNION OF TWO THINGS** a close union, blend, or mixture of two things ○ *Civilization is based on the marriage of tradition and innovation.* **6.** CARDS **KING AND QUEEN OF SAME SUIT** a combination of the king and queen of the same suit, in card games such as pinochle and bezique [13thC. From French *mariage*, from *marier* (see MARRY).]

mar·riage·a·ble /mérrijəb'l/ *adj.* suitable or ready for marriage, or old enough to be married —**mar·riage·a·bil·i·ty** /mèrrijə bíllətee/ *n.* —**mar·riage·a·ble·ness** /mérrijəb'lnəss/ *n.*

mar·riage coun·sel·ing *n.* advice given by professionals to help married couples who are having difficulties in their relationship to solve their problems

mar·riage of con·ven·ience *n.* a marriage between two people that is intended to serve a practical, financial, or political purpose and is not based on their love for each other [Translation of French *mariage de convenance*, literally "marriage for expediency"]

mar·ried /mérreed/ *adj.* **1. HAVING A SPOUSE** having a wife or husband ○ *married people* **2. JOINED IN MARRIAGE** joined together in marriage ○ *get married* **3. RELATING TO MARRIAGE** arising out of or connected with marriage ○ *her married name* **4. COMPLETELY DEDICATED TO SOMETHING** completely dedicated to something and devoting a lot of time and effort to it ○ *married to her job* ■ **mar·rieds** *npl.* **MARRIED PEOPLE** people who are married ○ *young marrieds*

mar·ron gla·cé /ma ròN glə sáy, mə ròN-/ (*plural* **mar·rons gla·cés** /ma ròN glə sáy, mə ròN-/) *n.* a chestnut cooked and preserved in sugar syrup, drained and then coated with a sugar glaze finish [From French, literally "iced chestnut"]

mar·row /mérrō/ *n.* **1.** ANAT **SOFT TISSUE IN BONES** soft red or yellow fatty tissue that fills the central cavities of bones. Red marrow is the site of blood cell production. **2. ESSENCE** the essence, core, or key part of something (*literary*) **3. VITALITY** vigor or vitality (*archaic*) **4.** *U.K.* FOOD = **marrow squash** *n.* 1 **5.** (*plural* **-rows** *or* **-row**) *U.K.* PLANTS = **marrow squash** *n.* 2 [Old English *mærh*. Ultimately from an Indo-European word meaning "marrow."] ◇ **to the marrow (of your bones)** used to emphasize how intensely or deeply somebody is affected by something, especially the cold or an unpleasant experience ○ *I was chilled to the marrow.*

mar·row·bone /mérrō bōn/ *n.* a hollow bone that contains edible marrow, traditionally considered to be a culinary delicacy

mar·row·fat /mérrō fàt/, **mar·row·fat pea** *n.* a particularly large type of pea, or the variety of pea plant on which it grows [Mid-18thC. From an earlier sense denoting a substance like tallow, obtained by boiling down marrow, which the pea's texture resembles.]

mar·row pea *n.* = **marrowfat**

mar·row squash *n.* **1.** FOOD **LARGE LONG GREEN VEGETABLE** a large long cylindrical vegetable with a tough green or green and yellow rind, creamy-white flesh, and a core of seeds that is usually scraped out before it is eaten **2.** PLANTS **MARROW SQUASH PLANT** a plant in the cucumber family that produces marrow squash as fruit. Latin name: *Cucurbita pepo.*

mar·ry[1] /mérree/ (**-ried, -ry·ing, -ries**) *v.* **1.** *vti.* **TAKE SOMEBODY IN MARRIAGE** to commit yourself to somebody, or yourselves to each other, formally in marriage **2.** *vt.* LAW, RELIG **JOIN IN MARRIAGE** to officiate at somebody's marriage ceremony and give legal sanction or a religious blessing to the marriage **3.** *vt.* LAW **GIVE IN MARRIAGE** to give somebody, usually a child or ward, to somebody in marriage, or bring about his or her marriage to somebody **4.** *vt.* **ACQUIRE BY MARRIAGE** to acquire something, especially money, by marrying somebody who has it ○ *wanted to marry wealth and power, and got both* **5.** *vti.* **COMBINE SUCCESSFULLY** to combine successfully, or match things with each other that combine successfully ○ *The meat and the spices marry well.* **6.** *vti.* = **marry up 7.** *vt.* NAUT **MATCH TWO PIECES OF ROPE TOGETHER** to match two pieces of rope together, especially before splicing them together [13thC. Via French *marier* from Latin *maritare*, from *maritus* "married person, husband," literally "somebody who has a wife."] —**mar·rier** *n.*

marry into *vt.* to become part of something, or gain something, through marriage

marry off *vt.* to find a husband or wife for somebody, especially a child of yours, often to serve your own ends or to free yourself from responsibility for the person

marry up *vti.* to fit and join together, or make two things fit and join together

mar·ry[2] /mérree/ *interj.* used to add emphasis to a statement, or to convey surprise or indignation (*archaic*) [Late 16thC. Alteration of *Mary* the mother of Jesus Christ.]

mar·ry·ing /mérree ing/ *adj.* likely or inclined to get married

Mars: View of the surface of Mars from the Sojourner rover (1997)

Mars /maarz/ *n.* **1.** MYTHOL **ROMAN GOD OF WAR** in Roman mythology, the god of war and the father of Romulus, the founder of Rome. Greek equivalent **Ares 2.** ASTRON **PLANET 4TH FROM THE SUN** the third smallest planet in the solar system and the fourth planet from the Sun. Mars has two small satellites and its surface is a reddish-orange color.

Mar·sa·la /maar sa̋alə/ *n.* a sweet or dry dark red fortified wine from Sicily [Early 19thC. Named for the Sicilian port of *Marsala*, from which it was exported.]

Wynton Marsalis

Mar·sa·lis /maar sa̋aliss/, **Wynton** (*b.* 1961) U.S. musician and bandleader. His skill on the trumpet has won him renown in jazz and classical music.

Mar·sei·llaise /ma̋arssə yéz, -ə láyz/ *n.* the French national anthem, written in Strasbourg in 1792 by Claude-Joseph Rouget de Lisle, a captain in the French revolutionary army. Originally called "War Song of the Army of the Rhine," its present name derives from its popularity with army units from Marseilles, the first to sing it in Paris.

mar·seille /maar sáy, -sáyl/, **mar·seilles** *n.* a heavy cotton fabric with a raised pattern, used for such things as bedspreads [Mid-18thC. Named for MARSEILLES, from which it was exported.]

Mar·seilles /maar sáy/, **Mar·seille** the leading port and capital of Bouches-du-Rhône Department, Provence-Alpes-Côtes d'Azur Region, southern France. Population: 1,230,936 (1990).

marsh /maarsh/ *n.* an area of low-lying waterlogged land, often beside water, that is poorly drained and liable to flood, difficult to cross on foot, and unfit for agriculture or building [Old English *merisc.* From a prehistoric Germanic word that is also the ancestor of English *mere, morass, meerschaum,* and *mermaid;* ultimately from an Indo-European word that also produced English *marine.*]

Marsh /maarsh/, **Dame Ngaio** (1899–1982) New Zealand writer and theater director. She wrote more than 30 crime novels, and played an important part in the development of live theater in New Zealand. Full name **Dame Edith Ngaio Marsh**

Marsh, Othniel Charles (1831–99) U.S. paleontologist. He discovered many dinosaur fossils in North America. He strongly supported Darwin's theory of evolution.

Marsh, Reginald (1898–1954) U.S. painter. He depicted scenes of New York City life in works such as *The Bowery* (1930).

mar·shal /ma͡arsh'l/ *n.* **1.** MIL **HIGH RANK OR HIGH-RANKING OFFICER** an officer of the highest rank in some armies and air forces **2. SOMEBODY IN CHARGE OF EVENT** somebody in charge of or controlling an event or gathering such as a parade, ceremony, or sports competition **3. PARADE HONOREE** somebody who is the honoree in a parade, and who usually rides in a vehicle at the head of the lines of marchers and floats **4.** LAW **FEDERAL LAW ENFORCEMENT OFFICER** a federal law enforcement officer who carries out court orders in a given federal judicial district and whose duties are similar to those of a local sheriff **5. CITY LAW OFFICER** a municipal law enforcement officer in some U.S. cities ○ *The city marshal's office delivered the subpoenas.* **6. SENIOR FIRE OR POLICE OFFICER** the head of the fire or police departments in some U.S. cities ■ *v.* (**-shaled** *or* **-shalled, -shal·ing** *or* **-shal·ling, -shals**) **1.** *vt.* **ARRANGE** to arrange things in an appropriate order so that they can be used effectively ○ *marshal your thoughts* **2.** *vti.* MIL **GATHER AND ORGANIZE TROOPS** to gather troops together and organize them, or gather together and organize, before embarking on a military campaign or expedition **3.** *vt.* **GATHER TOGETHER** to gather people together and organize them into an effective body ○ *marshal your supporters* **4.** *vt.* **GUIDE OR LEAD** to guide or lead somebody carefully or in an officious or ceremonious way **5.** *vti.* **ACT AS MARSHAL** to act as a marshal at something such as a ceremony, parade, or sports event [13thC. From Old French *mareschal* "royal court official"; ultimately from a prehistoric Germanic word meaning "groom," literally "horse-servant."] —**mar·shal·cy** *n.* —**mar·shal·er** *n.* —**mar·shal·ship** *n.*

mar·shal·ing yard *n.* an area occupied by many parallel railroad tracks, where railroad cars are made up into trains

Mar·shall /ma͡arsh'l/, **George C.** (1880–1959) U.S. military commander and politician. As secretary of state he initiated the Marshall Plan (1948) to coordinate European economic recovery after World War II. Full name **George Catlett Marshall**

Mar·shall, John (1755–1835) U.S. jurist and statesman. He established the principle of judicial review while serving as U.S. chief justice (1801–35).

Mar·shall, Thurgood (1908–93) U.S. civil rights lawyer and U.S. Supreme Court justice. As chief counsel of the NAACP Legal Defense Fund (1939–61), he won nearly every civil rights case he argued, including the landmark *Brown v. Board of Education* (1954) that ended racial segregation in public schools. He was a consistently liberal voice on the U.S. Supreme Court (1967–91).

Mar·shall Is·lands republic consisting of 34 islands in the central North Pacific Ocean. Population: 60,652 (1997). Area: 70 sq. mi./181 sq. km. Official name **Republic of the Marshall Islands**

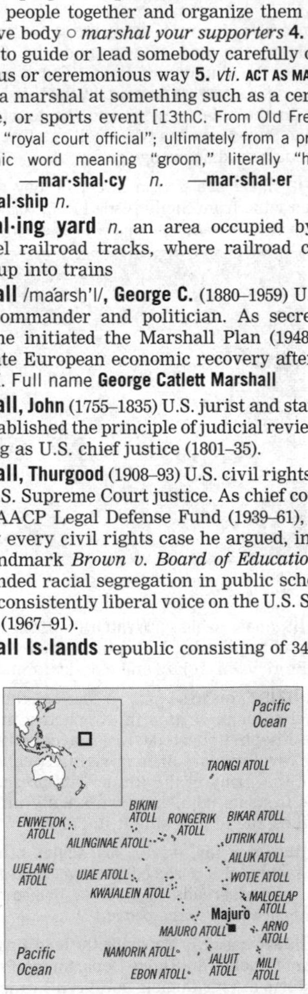

Marshall Islands

Mar·shall Plan *n.* a program of loans and other economic assistance provided by the U.S. government between 1947 and 1952 to help western European nations rebuild after World War II [Mid-20thC. Named for George C. MARSHALL, who proposed it.]

Mar·shall·town /ma͡arshəl tòwn/ city in central Iowa, on the Iowa River, northeast of Des Moines and west of Cedar Rapids. Population: 25,321 (1996).

marsh el·der *n.* a coarse shrubby composite plant with unisexual flowers and greenish flower heads, found growing in marshy areas of eastern and central North America, especially in salt marshes. Genus: *Iva.*

marsh fe·ver *n.* = **malaria**

marsh gas *n.* a gas, consisting mostly of methane, formed by the decomposition of plant matter in the absence of air, e.g., in marshes. Spontaneous combustion of marsh gas is usually supposed to be the cause of the phenomenon known as a will-o'-the-wisp or ignis fatuus.

marsh har·ri·er *n.* a long-winged long-tailed hawk, the largest of the harriers, found mainly in Europe and Asia, almost always in marshland and reedbeds. Latin name: *Circus aeruginosis.*

marsh hawk *n.* = **northern harrier**

marsh hen *n.* a wading bird that inhabits marshy areas and belongs to the family of birds that includes the rail, coot, and gallinule. Family: Rallidae.

marsh·land /ma͡arsh lànd, ma͡arshlənd/ *n.* marshy ground, or an area or expanse of it

marsh·mal·low /ma͡arsh mèllō/ *n.* **1. SOFT SPONGY CANDY** a soft spongy candy made from sugar syrup, starch, gelatin, egg whites, flavoring, and setting agents, formerly made from the root of the marshmallow plant **2. marsh·mal·low, marsh mal·low EUROPEAN HERB** a perennial shrubby European plant that grows in marshes and has pink flowers and sticky roots that were used in confections and medicine. It is now naturalized in marshes of eastern North America. Latin name: *Althacea officinalis.* —**marsh·mal·low·y** *adj.*

marsh mar·i·gold *n.* a plant of the buttercup family that grows in swampy areas of Europe and North America and has round or kidney-shaped leaves and bright yellow flowers. Latin name: *Caltha palustris.*

marsh tit *n.* a small European bird belonging to the tit family that has brownish-gray wings and a black cap and is found in wooded, but not necessarily marshy, areas. Latin name: *Parus palustris.*

marsh tread·er *n.* a slender aquatic insect with an elongated head that crawls on floating vegetation and the surface of water, preying on mosquito larvae and tiny crustaceans. Family: Hydrometridae.

marsh·y /ma͡arshee/ (**-i·er, -i·est**) *adj.* wet, soft, and muddy underfoot, or consisting of marshland —**marsh·i·ness** *n.*

mar·su·pi·al /maar so͞opee əl/ *n.* a mammal, e.g., a kangaroo, wombat, oppossum, or koala, having no placenta and bearing immature young that are developed in a pouch on the mother's abdomen. Order: Marsupialia. [Late 17thC. From modern Latin *marsupialis,* from *marsupium* (see MARSUPIUM).] —**mar·su·pi·al·ian** /maar so͞opee áylee ən/ *adj.* —**mar·su·pi·an** /-so͞opee ən/ *adj.*

mar·su·pi·al frog *n.* any one of several species of tree frog in which the female carries the eggs in a pouch on her back

mar·su·pi·um /maar so͞opee əm/ (*plural* **-a** /-pee ə/) *n.* a pouch on the abdomen of most marsupials that encloses the mammary glands and in which the animal's newly born offspring complete their development [Mid-17thC. Via Latin from Greek *marsupion,* "pouch," literally "little purse," from *marsippos* "purse," perhaps of Iranian origin.]

mart /maart/ *n.* a market, salesroom, or large store [15thC. Via Dutch, an obsolete variant of *markt,* from Latin *mercatus* (see MARKET).]

Mart. *abbr.* Martinique

Mar·ta·ban, Gulf of /ma͡artə ba͡an/ inlet of the Andaman Sea, east of the Irrawaddy delta, southeastern Myanmar

mar·ta·gon /ma͡artəgən/, **mar·ta·gon lil·y** *n.* a lily native to Europe and Asia with mottled pinkish-purple flowers. Latin name: *Lilium martagon.* [15thC. Via French from, ultimately, Turkish *marṭağān,* a kind of turban, which the flower is thought to resemble.]

mar·te·lé /ma͡art'l áy/, **mar·tel·la·to** /ma͡art'l a͡a tō/ *adv.* with the strings played in a strongly accented way (*used as a musical direction*) [Late 19thC. From French, literally "hammered."]

Mar·tel·lo /maar téllō/ (*plural* **-los**), **Mar·tel·lo tow·er** *n.* a fort in the form of a small circular tower, especially one built on the coast for defense against invasion during the Napoleonic Wars [Early 19thC. An alteration, influenced by Italian *martello* "hammer," of Cape *Mortella* in Corsica, where such a tower was captured with great difficulty by the British fleet in 1794.]

mar·ten /ma͡art'n/ (*plural* **-ten** *or* **-tens**) *n.* a short-legged bushy-tailed mammal with a long slender body that lives in trees, is carnivorous, and is found in northern forests. It is related to the weasel. Genus: *Martes.* [13thC. Via Middle Dutch *martren* from, ultimately, Old French *martre,* ultimately from a prehistoric Germanic word.]

mar·ten·site /ma͡art'n zìt/ *n.* the hard solid solution of iron and carbon used in making hardened steel tools [Late 19thC. Named for the German metallurgist Adolf *Martens* (1850–1914).]

Mar·tha /ma͡arthə/ *n.* in the Bible, the sister of Mary and Lazarus, and friend of Jesus Christ (Luke 10: 38–42)

Mar·tha's Vine·yard /ma͡arthəz vín yərd/ island in southeastern Massachusetts, in the Atlantic Ocean, near Cape Cod. It is a popular summer resort. Area: 108 sq. mi./280 sq. km.

Mar·tí /ma͡artee/, **José Julian** (1853–95) Cuban revolutionary leader and poet. He fought for Cuban independence from Spain and wrote many poems and essays on the theme of political freedom.

mar·tial /ma͡arsh'l/ *adj.* **1. OF SOLDIERS AND WAR** typical of or suitable for soldiers, the military life, or war **2. WARLIKE** warlike and fierce [14thC. Directly or via French from Latin *martialis,* from *Mars,* the god of war.] —**mar·tial·ism** *n.* —**mar·tial·ist** *n.* —**mar·tial·ly** *adv.* —**mar·tial·ness** *n.*

mar·tial art *n.* a system of combat and self-defense, e.g., judo or karate, developed especially in Japan and Korea and now usually practiced as a sport

mar·tial law *n.* the control and policing of a civilian population by military forces and according to military rules, imposed, e.g., in wartime or when the civilian government no longer functions

Mar·tian /ma͡arsh'n/ *adj.* **OF THE PLANET MARS** found on, typical of, or originating from the planet Mars ■ *n.* **INHABITANT OF MARS** a supposed inhabitant of the planet Mars [14thC. Directly or via Old French *martien* from Latin *Martianus,* from *Mart-,* the stem of *Mars* "Mars."]

mar·tin /ma͡art'n/ *n.* a bird of the swallow genus with a notched or square tail, e.g., the house martin or the purple martin [15thC. Origin uncertain: possibly referring to St. *Martin* of Tours, perhaps because the birds migrate around the time of his feast day in mid-November.]

Mar·tin V /ma͡artin t͟hə fífth/, **Pope** (1368–1431). His election in 1417, at the Council of Constance, ended the Great Schism. He reunified the Western Church and the Papal States.

Mar·tin /ma͡artin/, **Glenn Luther** (1886–1955) U.S. airplane manufacturer. He designed the China Clipper and the Hawaiian Clipper, as well as World War II bombers.

Mar·tin, Steve (*b.* 1945) U.S. comedian and actor. He became known for his appearances on television's *Saturday Night Live* during the 1970s and for numerous movie comedies.

mar·ti·net /ma͡art'n ét/ *n.* **1. MILITARY DISCIPLINARIAN** a military officer who demands absolute adherence to military rules and behavior by subordinates and peers **2. RIGID DISCIPLINARIAN** somebody who imposes strict discipline on others [Late 17thC. Named for Jean *Martinet* (died 1672), who introduced drills into the French army.] —**mar·ti·net·tish** *adj.*

Mar·ti·nez /maar te͞enəz/ city in western California. It is the seat of Contra Costa County. Population: 31,808 (1990).

mar·tin·gale /ma͡art'n gàyl/ *n.* **1.** EQU **PART OF A HORSE'S HARNESS** a strap of a horse's harness connecting the girth to the reins to keep the horse from throwing its head back **2. mar·tin·gale, mar·tin·gale shroud** NAUT **PART OF A SAILING SHIP'S RIGGING** a rope or cable that supports the forward-projecting spar (**bowsprit**) on some sailing ships **3.** GAMBLING **GAMBLING SYSTEM** gambling in which the stakes are doubled after each loss [Late 16thC. From French, of uncertain origin: perhaps from modern Provençal *marte(n)gal* "inhabitant of Martiques (in Provence)" or an alteration of Spanish *almártaga* "rein."]

mar·ti·ni /maar teénee/ *n.* a cocktail made of gin or vodka with vermouth [Late 19thC. From Italian *Martini*, the surname of a winemaker.]

Mar·tin·ique /maártə neék, maárt'n eék/ island in the eastern Caribbean Sea, an overseas department of France. Population: 363,031 (1990). Area: 425 sq. mi./1,102 sq. km.

Mar·tin Lu·ther King Day *n.* the third Monday in January, designated a public holiday in many states to commemorate the life and work of Martin Luther King

Mar·tins /maártinz/, **Peter** Danish-born U.S. dancer and choreographer. He became director of the New York City Ballet in the 1980s.

Mar·tins·burg /maártənz bùrg/ city in northeastern West Virginia, in the Shenandoah Valley, southwest of Hagerstown, Maryland. Population: 14,541 (1996).

mart·let /maártlət/ *n.* **1.** BIRDS **HOUSE MARTIN** a house martin (*archaic or literary*) **2.** HERALDRY **BIRD SYMBOL ON A COAT OF ARMS** on coats of arms, a footless bird used to represent a fourth son [Early 16thC. From French *martelet*, alteration of *martinet*, pet form of the male name *Martin*.]

mar·tyr /maártər/ *n.* **1. SOMEBODY PUT TO DEATH** somebody who chooses to die rather than deny religious or political beliefs **2. SOMEBODY WHO MAKES SACRIFICES** somebody who makes sacrifices or suffers greatly in order to advance a cause or principle **3. SOMEBODY IN PAIN** somebody who experiences frequent or constant pain as a result of something **4. SOMEBODY SEEKING ATTENTION** somebody who complains a great deal in order to get sympathy from others ■ *v.* (**-tyred, -tyr·ing, -tyrs**) **1.** *vt.* **KILL SOMEBODY FOR HOLDING BELIEFS** to kill somebody for refusing to deny religious or political beliefs **2.** *vr.* **MAKE SACRIFICES FOR SOMETHING** to make sacrifices or endure hardship for something [Pre-12thC. Via ecclesiastical Latin from Greek *martur* "witness."]

mar·tyr·dom /maártərdəm/ *n.* **1. BEING A MARTYR** the state of having been killed for refusing to deny religious or political beliefs **2. DEMISE OF A MARTYR** the actual death of a martyr **3. SACRIFICES AND ENDURANCE** the hardship and endurance involved in making sacrifices for a cause

Ma·ru·ya·ma Ok·y·o /marroo yaámə ōki ō/ (1733–95) Japanese artist. He was founder of the Maruyama school of painting. Born **Maruyama Mondo**

mar·vel /maárv'l/ *n.* **1. WONDERFUL THING** something that inspires awe, amazement, or admiration ○ *one of the marvels of the Ancient World* **2. SOMEBODY SKILLFUL OR HELPFUL** somebody who is very good at something, often somebody who gives much-needed help ■ *vt.* (**-veled, -vel·ing, -vels**) **BE AMAZED** to be very impressed, surprised, or bewildered ○ *I could only marvel at her stamina.* [13thC. Via French *merveille* from Latin *mirabilis* "wonderful," from *mirari* "to wonder at something" (see MIRACLE).]

Mar·vell /maárvəl/, **Andrew** (1621–78) English poet and politician. A metaphysical poet, he also wrote verse satires vigorously opposing the post-Restoration government.

mar·vel·ous /maárvələss/, **mar·vel·lous** *adj.* **1. AMAZINGLY IMPRESSIVE** extraordinarily wonderful ○ *a marvelous example of Baroque architecture* **2. EXTREMELY GOOD** very good or pleasing ○ *It was marvelous to see them all again.* —**mar·vel·ous·ly** *adv.* —**mar·vel·ous·ness** *n.*

Marx /maarks/, **Karl** (1818–83) German philosopher. His books, especially the *Communist Manifesto* (1848) and *Das Kapital* (1867, 1885, 1894), were the basis of Communism.

Marx Broth·ers /maárks brùthərz/ U.S. comedians. Chico (born Leonard, 1891–1961), Groucho (born Julius Henry, 1895–1977), and Harpo (born Adolph, 1888–1964), the three most prominent of the brothers, appeared in comedy films such as *A Night at the Opera* (1935) known for their anarchic verbal and visual humor. Groucho later hosted the television game show *You Bet Your Life* (1950–61). Two

Karl Marx

other brothers, Gummo (born Milton, 1893–1977) and Zeppo (born Herbert, 1901–79), appeared in some of the Marx Brothers' early work.

Marx·i·an /maárksee ən/ *adj.* = **Marxist** *adj.*

Marx·ism /maárk sìzzəm/ *n.* **1. MARX'S THEORIES** the political and economic theories of Karl Marx and Friedrich Engels, in which class struggle is a central element in the analysis of social change in Western societies **2. POLITICS BASED ON MARX'S THEORIES** political ideology based on the theories of Karl Marx and Friedrich Engels

Marx·ism-Len·in·ism *n.* Marxism with the inclusion of Lenin's idea that imperialism is the final stage of capitalism, and Lenin's shifting of the focus of class struggle from industrialized to nonindustrialized societies. ◊ **Leninism** —**Marx·ist-Len·in·ist** *n., adj.*

Marx·ist /maárksist/ *n.* **FOLLOWER OF MARXISM** somebody who supports or practices Marxism ■ *adj.* **OF OR SUPPORTING MARXISM** relating to, supporting, or implementing Marxism

Mar·y /máiree/, **Queen of the United Kingdom** (1867–1953). A great-granddaughter of King George III, she was the queen consort of George V and the mother of Edward VIII and George VI. She is remembered especially for her charitable and relief work during World War II. Known as **Mary of Teck**

Mar·y, St. Mother of Jesus Christ. Christians believe that she conceived Jesus without human contact, through the direct intervention of God. In Islam she is venerated as Maryan.

Mar·y I, Queen of England and Ireland (1516–58). She was the daughter of Henry VIII and Catherine of Aragon. As queen (1553–58) she tried to restore Roman Catholicism in England, and to cement union with Spain by marrying Philip II (1554).

Mar·y II, Queen of England, Scotland, and Ireland (1662–94). After the Glorious Revolution (1688) she was made coregent with her husband William III (Prince of Orange), during whose absences she governed as regent.

Mary (Queen of Scots): Anonymous 16th-century portrait

Mar·y (Queen of Scots) (1542–87). The daughter of James V of Scotland, she was dowager queen of France when her marriage to Lord Darnley (1565) gave her a claim to the English throne. Elizabeth I imprisoned her in England after 1568 and signed the warrant under which she was executed for treason in 1587. Born **Mary Stuart**

Mar·y Jane /màiri jáyn/ *n.* marijuana (*slang*) [Early 20thC. Origin uncertain: possibly from Spanish *Maria Juana*, by folk etymology from *mariguana* (see MARIJUANA).]

Mar·y Janes *tdmk.* a trademark for shoes and boots, especially low-cut patent-leather shoes for girls with a strap fastening near the ankle at the side

Mar·y·knol·ler /máiri nōlər/ *n.* a member of the Catholic Foreign Mission Society of America [Mid-20thC. Named for *Maryknoll*, New York, where the Society was founded.]

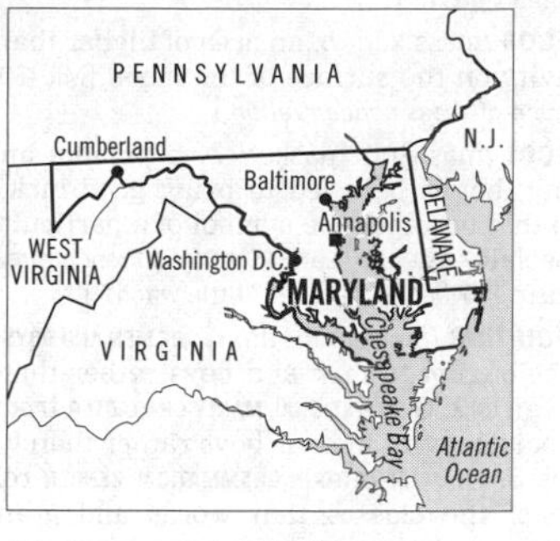

Maryland

Mar·y·land /mérrilənd/ state in the eastern United States, bordered by Delaware, the District of Columbia, Pennsylvania, Virginia, West Virginia, and the Atlantic Ocean. Capital: Annapolis. Population: 5,094,289 (1997). Area: 10,455 sq. mi./27,089 sq. km. —**Mar·y·land·er** *n.*

Mar·y Mag·da·lene *n.* in the Bible, a follower of Jesus Christ, who cured her of evil spirits (Luke 8:2)

mar·zi·pan /maárzə pàn, maártsə-/ *n.* a sweet paste made of ground almonds and sugar, often with egg whites or yolks, used as a layer in cakes or molded into ornamental shapes [15thC. Via German from Italian *marzapane* "type of box," originally for candy or coins. Ultimately from Arabic *mawtabān*, literally "enthroned king."]

WORD KEY: ORIGIN

Arabic *mawtabān* meant literally "enthroned king." It was used by the Saracens as the name of a medieval Venetian coin that had a figure of the seated Christ on it. In the Italian dialect of Venice the word became *matapan*, and eventually, in general Italian, *marzapane*; and its meaning supposedly progressed from the "coin" via "measure of weight or capacity," "box of such capacity," and "such a box containing confectionery" to "the contents of such a box." After English originally acquired the word (possibly via French) it became anglicized to *marchpane*, and that remained the standard form until the 19th century. Around this time ***marzipan*** was borrowed from German. This was an alteration of Italian *marzapane*, based on the misconception that it came from Latin *marci panis* "St. Mark's bread."

Ma·sa·da /mə saádə/ ancient ruined fortress in Israel, on a mountaintop 30 mi./48.3 km southeast of Jerusalem, southwest of the Dead Sea

Ma·sai /maa sí, maá sì/ (*plural* **-sai** *or* **-sais**), **Maa·sai** (*plural* **-sai** *or* **-sais**) *n.* **1.** PEOPLES **MEMBER OF AN E AFRICAN PEOPLE** a member of a people who live in East Africa, mainly in Kenya and Tanzania. Characteristically tall and slender, the Masai are a pastoral people with strong warrior traditions. **2.** LANG **LANGUAGE OF THE MASAI** the Nilotic language of the Masai, from the Nilo-Saharan family of languages. About 700,000 people speak Masai. —**Ma·sai** *adj.*

ma·sa·la /mə saálə/ *n. S Asia* casual conversation (*informal*) [Late 18thC. From Urdu *maṣālaḥ*.]

Mas·ba·te /maa baátee/ island in the central Philippines, in Masbate Province. Area: 1,562 sq. mi./4,046 sq. km.

masc. *abbr.* GRAM masculine

mas·car·a /ma skérrə, mə-/ *n.* **EYELASH COSMETIC** thick colored paste applied to the eyelashes with a fine brush to darken them and give the appearance of greater length and thickness ■ *vt.* (**-car·aed, -car·aing, -car·as**) **PUT ON MASCARA** to apply mascara to eyelashes [Late 19thC. Origin uncertain: probably from Spanish or Italian *maschera* (see MASK).]

Mas·ca·rene Is·lands /màskəreén-/ group of islands east of Madagascar in the Indian Ocean, including Réunion, Mauritius, and Rodrigues. Population: 1,798,000 (1996).

mas·car·po·ne /maàs kaar pṓnee, -pṓn/ *n.* a rich fatty unsalted Italian cream cheese with a spreadable texture [Mid-20thC. From Italian, literally "rich whey cheese."]

mas·cle /máskəl/ *n.* a design on coats of arms in the form of a lozenge with a lozenge-shaped hole in the middle [13thC. Via Anglo-Norman from, ultimately, Latin *macula* "mesh."]

mas·con /máss kòn/ *n.* an area of higher-than-normal gravity on the surface of the moon [Mid-20thC. Contraction of *mass concentration.*]

mas·cot /más kòt, máskət/ *n.* a person, animal, or thing that is believed to bring good luck, usually one that becomes the symbol of a particular group, especially a team [Late 19thC. Via French *mascotte* from modern Provençal *mascotto* "little witch."]

mas·cu·line /máskyəlin/ *adj.* **1. OF MEN AND BOYS** relating or belonging to men and boys rather than women and girls **2. OF TRADITIONAL MANLY CHARACTER** traditionally associated with men or boys rather than women or girls **3.** GRAM **OF CERTAIN GRAMMATICAL GENDER** relating to one of the classes that words and grammatical forms are divided into in some languages **4.** MUSIC **CONCLUDING ON AN ACCENTED BEAT** ending on a beat that is accented ■ *n.* GRAM **MASCULINE GENDER** the masculine gender, or a word or form in the masculine gender [14thC. Via French from, ultimately, Latin *masculinus,* from *masculus.*] —**mas·cu·line·ly** *adv.* —**mas·cu·line·ness** *n.*

mas·cu·line ca·dence *n.* MUSIC a closing section of music (**cadence**) that ends on a strong beat

mas·cu·line end·ing *n.* **1.** POETRY **STRESSED LINE ENDING** a stressed syllable that ends a line of poetry **2.** GRAM **ENDING MARKING MASCULINE GENDER** an ending that marks a word as belonging to the masculine gender in some languages

mas·cu·line rhyme *n.* POETRY a rhyme between two monosyllabic words, e.g., "gab" and "blab," or between the final stressed syllables of polysyllabic words, e.g., "connive" and "survive"

mas·cu·lin·i·ty /màskyə línnətee/ *n.* **1. CONDITION OF MALE HUMAN** the state of being a man or boy **2. TRADITIONAL MANLY QUALITIES** those qualities conventionally supposed to make a man a typical or excellent specimen of manhood, traditionally physical strength and courage

mas·cu·lin·ize /máskyələ nīz/ (**-ized, -iz·ing, -iz·es**) *vt.* **1. MAKE SOMETHING SEEM MALE** to give something or somebody features conventionally associated with maleness **2. PRODUCE MALE CHARACTERISTICS IN FEMALE** to cause a female animal or a plant to acquire male sexual characteristics, e.g., as a result of administering steroids —**mas·cu·lin·i·za·tion** /màskyələni záysh'n/ *n.*

Mase·field /máyss feèld/, **John** (1878–1967) British poet. The author of vigorous narrative verse, collected in *Salt Water Ballads* (1902) and other volumes, he was named poet laureate in 1930.

ma·ser /máyzər/ *n.* a device used in radar and radio astronomy to boost the strength of microwaves [Mid-20thC. Acronym formed from *Microwave Amplification by Stimulated Emission of Radiation.*]

Mas·er·u /mə sáiroo/ capital of Lesotho, situated on the Caledon River, near the border with South Africa. Population: 130,000 (1992).

mash /mash/ *n.* **1.** BEVERAGES **GRAIN AND WATER MIX** a fermentable mixture of hot water and grain, usually barley or wheat, from which alcohol is brewed or distilled **2.** AGRIC **ANIMAL FOOD** a mixture of ground feeds for livestock or poultry **3. PULPY MASS** the consistency of a soft pulp ■ *vt.* (**mashed, mash·ing, mash·es**) **1. SOAK GRAIN** to soak grain in hot water to make a mash for brewing or for feeding to animals **2. MAKE PULP OF** to squash something into a pulpy mass **3. CRUSH SOMETHING** to crush or grind something (*informal*) **4. MAKE ADVANCES** to make sexual advances toward somebody, especially as a man to a woman (*dated slang*) [Old English *masc* "mash for brewing," ultimately from an Indo-European word that is also the ancestor of English *mix* and *promiscuous*]

MASH /mash/, **M.A.S.H.** *abbr.* mobile army surgical hospital

WORD KEY: CULTURAL NOTE

*M*A*S*H*, a movie by director Robert Altman (1970). Set in a Mobile Army Surgical Hospital during the Korean War, this dark satire focuses on a group of eccentric medics who combat the horrors of war with cynicism, ribald humor, and practical jokes. The movie gave rise to a long-running television series that made household names of characters such as Hawkeye Pierce, Hot Lips Houlihan, and Major Frank Burns.

mash·er /máshər/ *n.* a man who inflicts his attentions on a woman (*dated slang*)

mash·gi·ah /maash geè aàkh/ (*plural* **-him** /maash geè khim, maàsh gee kheèm/), **mash·gi·ach** (*plural* **-chim**) *n.* an Orthodox rabbi, or a man appointed or approved by such a rabbi, who inspects slaughterhouses, meat markets, and restaurants to check that kosher food has been properly prepared and served [Mid-20thC. From Hebrew *mašgīaḥ* "supervisor."]

mash·ie /máshee/ *n.* an obsolete golf club similar to the modern five-iron [Late 19thC. Origin uncertain: perhaps via French *massue* "club" from, ultimately, late Latin *mattea* "mace."]

mash·ie nib·lick *n.* an obsolete golf club similar to the modern six-iron

Ma·sho·na /mə shṓnə/ *n., adj.* = **Shona**

mask /mask/ *n.* **1. COVERING FOR THE FACE** a covering for the eyes, mouth, or whole face **2. CONCEALING THING** something that conceals or disguises something else, e.g., true motives or feelings **3. FACELIKE ORNAMENT** a representation of a face used as an ornament or decoration **4.** ZOOL **ANIMAL'S FACE MARKINGS** the face or facial markings of some animals, e.g., foxes and raccoons **5.** MIL **CONCEALMENT FOR TROOPS** a natural or artificial feature that hides military troops and installations from an enemy **6.** ELECTRON ENG **TEMPLATE FOR ELECTRONIC CHIPS** a template used to control the pattern of conducting material deposited or etched onto a semiconductor chip **7.** COSMETICS **BEAUTY TREATMENT** a facial preparation used to tighten the skin and remove impurities, applied to the skin as a paste and allowed to dry before being removed **8.** PHOTOGRAPHY **PHOTOGRAPHIC GUARD** a guard, often a sheet of paper, placed over areas of unexposed photographic film to stop light from hitting it ■ *vt.* (**masked, mask·ing, masks**) **1. HIDE SOMETHING** to conceal or disguise something, e.g., an unpleasant smell or a true intention **2.** PHOTOGRAPHY **SHIELD PART OF SOMETHING** to cover part of a surface using masking tape before painting or spraying **3.** PHOTOGRAPHY **SHIELD PHOTOGRAPHIC FILM FROM LIGHT** to prevent stray or unwanted light from reaching areas of unexposed photographic film, either using hands or a special shield **4.** CHEM **STOP CHEMICAL FROM REACTING** to prevent a chemical substance from reacting by the addition of another chemical [Early 16thC. Via French *masque* from late Latin *masca* "ghost, mask," of uncertain origin: perhaps from Arabic *maskara* "buffoon."] —**mask·a·ble** *adj.*

masked /maskt/ *adj.* **1. WEARING A MASK** with the face covered in order to prevent recognition **2.** MED **NOT DETECTABLE** used to describe diseases and symptoms that are present but not yet perceptible **3.** BOT = **personate 4.** ZOOL **WITH MARKINGS LIKE A MASK** with markings on the head or around the eyes that resemble a mask

masked ball *n.* a ball at which people wear masks

masked hun·ter *n.* a central European insect, belonging to the assassin bug family, introduced to the southern United States, that usually preys on household insects, but occasionally bites humans. Latin name: *Reduvius personatus.*

mask·er /máskər/ *n.* somebody who wears a mask at a masked ball

mask·ing /másking/ *n.* **1.** PHYSIOL **COVERING ONE SENSE WITH ANOTHER** the hiding or screening of one sensory process, e.g., hearing, by another, e.g., sight **2.** THEATER **SCENERY HIDING STAGE** scenery that is used to hide a part of the stage from the audience

mask·ing tape *n.* easy-to-remove adhesive tape used to cover parts of a surface that are not meant to be painted

Mas·low /mázzlō, másslō/, **Abraham Harold** (1908–70) U.S. psychologist. He developed the principles of humanistic psychology, most notably in *Toward a Psychology of Being* (1962).

mas·och·ism /mássə kìzzəm/ *n.* **1. SEXUAL PLEASURE ACHIEVED THROUGH HUMILIATION** sexual gratification achieved by humiliation and the acceptance of physical and verbal abuse **2. NEED FOR PAIN** the psychological disorder in which somebody needs to be emotionally or physically abused in order to be sexually satisfied **3. SEARCH FOR ABUSIVE SEXUAL PARTNERS** the active seeking out of sexual partners who will dominate, humiliate, and physically and verbally abuse **4. ENJOYMENT OF HARDSHIP** the tendency to invite and enjoy misery of any kind, especially in order to be pitied by others or perhaps admired for forbearance [Late 19thC. Named for the Austrian novelist Leopold von Sacher-Masoch (1836–95), who described such sexual practices.] —**mas·o·chist** *n.*

mas·och·is·tic /mássə kístik/ *adj.* **1. OF OR FEELING MASOCHISM** relating to or experiencing the desire to be humiliated and abused by others in order to feel sexually fulfilled **2. LIKING AND INVITING MISERY** tending to invite and enjoy misery —**mas·och·is·ti·cal·ly** *adv.*

ma·son /máyss'n/ *n.* **SOMEBODY WORKING WITH STONE** somebody who makes things out of stone, e.g., buildings or statues, or who prepares stone for builders to use ■ *vt.* (**-soned, -son·ing, -sons**) **BUILD USING STONE** to build or strengthen something using stone [12thC. From Old Norman French *machun* or Old French *masson,* of uncertain origin: probably from a prehistoric Germanic word that is also the ancestor of English *make.*]

Ma·son /máyssən/ *n.* = **Freemason**

Ma·son /máyss'n/, **George** (1725–92) American patriot. He influenced the Declaration of Independence (1776) and argued for the Bill of Rights (1791).

ma·son bee *n.* any solitary bee that builds nests of sand or clay held together with saliva

Ma·son Ci·ty /máysən-/ city in northern Iowa, north of Iowa Falls and northwest of Cedar Falls. Population: 28,972 (1996).

Ma·son-Dix·on Line /màyss'n díks'n-/ *n.* the boundary that separated Pennsylvania from Maryland and Virginia, regarded as the dividing line between free and slave states before the Civil War [Named for the 18thC surveyors Charles *Mason* and Jeremiah *Dixon*]

ma·son·ic /mə sónnik/ *adj.* relating to stonemasons or their work —**ma·son·i·cal·ly** *adv.*

Ma·son·ic *adj.* relating to Freemasons or Freemasonry

Ma·son·ite /máyssə nīt/ *tdmk.* a trademark for fiberboard products used as insulation, paneling, and partitions in buildings

Ma·son jar *n.* a wide-mouthed glass jar with a lid that screws or clips on and forms a vacuum seal, used for preserving food, especially fruits and vegetables [Late 19thC. Named for its inventor, John *Mason* (1832–1902).]

ma·son·ry /máyss'nree/ *n.* **1. MASON'S TRADE** the trade of a mason **2. MASON'S WORK** the work done by a mason **3. STONEWORK** the stone or brick parts of a building or other structure

Ma·son·ry /máyssənree/ *n.* Freemasonry

ma·son wasp *n.* a solitary wasp that builds mud nests or digs out nests in old mortar. Genus: *Odynerus.*

Ma·sor·ete /mássə reèt/, **Ma·sor·ite** /mássə rīt/ *n.* one of the scholars who produced the traditional text of the Hebrew Bible (**Masoretic text**) [Late 16thC. Via French or modern Latin *Massoreta* from a misuse of Hebrew *māsōreṯ*).]

Mas·o·ret·ic /mássə réttik/ *adj.* used to describe or relating to the traditional text of the Hebrew Bible

Mas·o·ret·ic text *n.* the traditional text of the Hebrew Bible, revised and annotated by Jewish scholars between the 6th and 10th centuries A.D.

Ma·sor·ite *n.* = **Masorete**

masque /mask/ *n.* **1. PERFORMANCE** a dramatic entertainment similar to opera, popular in England in the 16th and 17th centuries, in which masked performers represented mythological or allegorical characters **2. TEXT OF MASQUE** the music and words written for a masque **3.** = **masquerade** *n.* 1 [Early 16thC. From French (see MASK).]

mas·quer /máskər/ *n.* = **masker**

mas·quer·ade /màskə ráyd/ *n.* **1. PARTY WITH MASKS** a party at which masks and costumes are worn, whether an informal gathering of friends or a formal ball **2. DISGUISING COSTUME** a costume worn to a masquerade **3. DISGUISING PRETENSE** a pretense or disguise ■ *vi.* (**-ad·ed, -ad·ing, -ades**) **1. PRETEND** to pretend to be somebody or something else **2. WEAR A COSTUME** to wear a particular costume to a party [Late 16thC. Via French *mascarade* from Italian *mascherata,* from *maschera* MASK.] —**mas·quer·ad·er** *n.*

mass /mass/ *n.* **1. LUMP** a body of matter that forms a whole but has no definable shape **2. COLLECTION** a collection of many individual parts ○ *The garden is a mass of weeds.* **3.** **GREAT UNSPECIFIED QUANTITY** a large but unspecified number or quantity ○ *I have masses of work to do.* **4.** **MAJOR PART** the greater part or majority ○ *The mass of respondents oppose the legislation.* **5.** PHYS **PHYSICAL QUANTITY** the property of an object that is a measure of its inertia, the amount of matter it contains, and its influence in a gravitational field. Symbol *m* **6.** PAINTING **AREA OF PAINTING** a large area of a painting where the light, shade, or color is uniform **7.** PHARM **MIXTURE CONTAINING DRUGS** a thick paste containing drugs that is made into pills **8.** MINING **DEPOSIT OF ORE** an irregular deposit of ore that does not occur in veins ■ *vti.* **(massed, mass·ing, mass·es)** **COLLECT** to gather or be gathered in a mass ○ *Troops are massing on the border.* ■ *adj.* **1.** **OF A LARGE NUMBER** made up of or containing a large number ○ *a mass demonstration* **2.** **GENERAL** broadly general, in scope or effect ○ *The mass effect is rather disappointing.* [14thC. Via French *masse* and Latin *massa* from Greek *maza* "barley cake."]

mass in *vt.* to fill in areas of color or shade in a drawing or painting

Mass, **mass** *n.* **1.** **CHRISTIAN CEREMONY** in the Roman Catholic Church and some Protestant churches, the religious ceremony of the Communion **2.** **MUSICAL SETTING OF MASS** a part of the text of a Roman Catholic Mass set to music, to be sung by a choir [Pre-12thC. Via ecclesiastical Latin *missa* from, ultimately, Latin *mittere* "send away."]

Mass. *abbr.* Massachusetts

Mas·sa·chu·sett /màssə chóossət/ (*plural* **-sett** *or* **-setts**), **Mas·sa·chu·set** (*plural* **-set** *or* **-sets**) *n.* **1.** PEOPLES **MEMBER OF NATIVE N AMERICAN PEOPLE** a member of a Native North American people who used to live in the Massachusetts Bay area **2.** LANG **EXTINCT N AMERICAN LANGUAGE** an extinct Native North American language formerly spoken in an area around Massachusetts Bay and belonging to the Algonquian branch of Algonquian-Wakashan languages. It died out in the 17th century when disease wiped out the entire population of its speakers. —**Mas·sa·chu·sett** *adj.*

Massachusetts

Mas·sa·chu·setts /màssə chóossəts/ state in the northeastern United States, bordered by Connecticut, New Hampshire, New York, Rhode Island, Vermont, and the Atlantic Ocean. Capital: Boston. Population: 6,117,520 (1997). Area: 8,262 sq. mi./ 21,399 sq. km. Official name **Commonwealth of Massachusetts**

Mas·sa·chu·setts Bay inlet of the Atlantic Ocean, eastern Massachusetts

mas·sa·cre /mássəkər/ *n.* **1.** **KILLING OF MANY PEOPLE** the vicious killing of large numbers of people or animals **2.** **BAD DEFEAT** a contest in which one side is badly beaten (*informal*) ■ *vt.* **(-cred, -cring, -cres)** **1.** **KILL IN LARGE NUMBERS** to kill large numbers of people or animals **2.** **DEFEAT SOMEBODY COMPLETELY** to defeat somebody completely, especially in a sports contest (*informal*) [Late 16thC. From French, "butchery," of unknown origin.] —**mas·sa·crer** *n.*

mas·sage /mə saázh, -saáj/ *n.* **RUBBING OF THE BODY** a treatment that involves rubbing or kneading the muscles, either for medical or therapeutic purposes or simply as an aid to relaxation ■ *vt.* **(-saged, -sag·ing, -sag·es)** **1.** **RUB SOMEBODY'S MUSCLES** to rub or knead somebody's muscles **2.** **MANIPULATE DECEPTIVELY** to manipulate statistics or other information in order to create a more suitable or falsely impressive result ○ *They massaged the figures.* **3.** **ENHANCE** to give something a boost with kind or uplifting treatment, especially somebody's ego with flattery [Late 19thC. From French, from *masser* "to massage," of uncertain origin: perhaps from Arabic *masaha* "to stroke" or Portuguese *amassar* "to knead."] —**mas·sag·er** *n.*

mas·sage par·lor *n.* **1.** **PLACE FOR MASSAGE** a place that provides massages to paying customers **2.** **BROTHEL** a place that offers sex services for money, including sexual massages

Mas·sa·pe·qua /màssə peékwə/ city in New York, in Nassau county. Population: 22,018 (1990).

mas·sa·sau·ga /màssə sáwgə/ *n.* a small North American rattlesnake that has variable coloring. Latin name: *Sistrurus catenatus.* [Mid-19thC. Alteration of *Mississagi*, a river in southeastern Ontario, Canada.]

Mas·sa·soit /mássə soyt/ (1580?–1661) Native North American leader. He negotiated peace with the pilgrims of Plymouth Colony, and shared the first Thanksgiving feast (1621).

mass bal·ance *n.* a mathematical equation, table, or quantitative chart showing the mass inputs and outputs of a process, plant, or machine, the principle being that what goes in must come out

mass com·mu·ni·ca·tion, **mass com·mu·ni·ca·tions** *n.* communication by means of broadcasting and newspapers, that reaches all or most people in society

mass·cult /máss kùlt/ *n.* culture as it is presented and interpreted by the mass media (*informal*) [Shortening of *mass culture*]

mass de·fect *n.* the difference between the mass of an isotope and the element's mass number

mas·sé /ma sáy/ *n.* a shot in cue games in which the cue is held almost vertically to strike the cue ball off center, making it curve around one ball to hit another [Late 19thC. From French, from *masse* (see MACE[1]).]

Mas·se·na /mə seénə/ village in northeastern New York State, near the St. Lawrence River. Population: 11,867 (1994).

mass-en·er·gy e·quiv·a·lence *n.* the principle in the theory of relativity that mass and energy are equivalent and interchangeable according to the equation $E = mc^2$

Mas·se·net /mássə nay/, **Jules Emile Frédéric** (1842–1912) French composer. Famous for his opera *Manon* (1884), he also wrote oratorios, cantatas, and orchestral pieces.

mass·es /mássiz, mássəz/ *npl.* ordinary people in society, as distinct from political leaders, aristocracy, or educated people

mas·se·ter /mə seétər, ma-/ *n.* a muscle in the cheek that moves the jaws during chewing [Late 16thC. From Greek *masētēr*, from *masasthai* "to chew."] —**mas·se·ter·ic** /màssə térrik/ *adj.*

mas·seur /ma súr, mə súr, ma sóor/ *n.* a man who gives massages professionally [Late 19thC. From French, from *masser* (see MASSAGE).]

mas·seuse /ma sóoz/ *n.* a woman who gives massages professionally [Late 19thC. From French, feminine of *masseur* (see MASSAGE).]

mass ex·tinc·tion *n.* the destruction of a whole species by force of nature such as climate change, volcanic eruption, or an asteroid collision, thought by many scientists to account for the end of dinosaurs

Mas·sey /mássee/, **Charles Vincent** (1887–1967) Canadian statesman and diplomat. He was Canada's first native-born governor general (1952–59).

Mas·sey, Raymond (1896–1983) Canadian actor. He starred for many years as Dr. Gillespie in TV's long-running *Dr. Kildare* series and played the title role in the movie *Abe Lincoln in Illinois* (1938). Full name **Raymond Hart Massey**

mas·si·cot /mássi kòt, -kō/ *n.* a yellow mineral consisting of lead oxide, or a powdered form of it used as a pigment [15thC. From French, of uncertain origin: probably from Italian *marzacotto* "potter's glaze," perhaps ultimately of Arabic or Greek origin.]

mas·sif /ma seéf/ *n.* **1.** **MOUNTAINS** a large mountain mass, or a group of connected mountains that form a mountain range **2.** **EARTH'S CRUST** a part of the Earth's crust that is surrounded by faults and may be shifted or displaced by tectonic movements [Early 16thC. From French (see MASSIVE).]

Mas·sif Cen·tral /màssif sen traál/ highland region in south central France

mas·sive /mássiv/ *adj.* **1.** **UNUSUALLY LARGE** large in comparison with what is typical or usual ○ *gained a massive amount of weight* **2.** **BULKY** large, solid, and heavy **3.** **LARGE-SCALE** extremely large in amount, degree, or scope **4.** MINERALS **DEVOID OF VISIBLE CRYSTALS** with no visible crystalline structure **5.** GEOL **HOMOGENOUS** used to describe rock that is of the same composition throughout, as distinct from being layered [15thC. Via French *massif* and Old French *massiz* from, ultimately, Latin *massa* (see MASS).] —**mas·sive·ness** *n.*

Mas·sive, Mount /mássiv/ mountain in central Colorado in the Sawatch Range. Height: 14,421 ft./4,396 m.

mass lei·sure *n.* the everyday leisure pursuits of the majority of a population, an aspect of popular culture. It is shaped by and shapes the values, behaviors, and economics of societies and cultures.

mass·less /mássləss/ *adj.* with a mass of zero

mass-mar·ket *adj.* **APPEALING TO WIDEST CLIENTELE** designed for sale to as wide a range of people as possible, rather than to a particular group in society ■ *vt.* **SELL SOMETHING TO MANY PEOPLE** to sell something to as many people as possible by advertising and promoting it widely

mass me·di·a *n.* all of the communications media that reach a large audience, especially television, radio, and newspapers (*takes a singular or plural verb*)

mass noun *n.* a noun representing something that cannot be counted, e.g., "water," or something that can only be counted if the meaning is a single type or serving, e.g., "coffee"

mass num·ber *n.* CHEM the number of protons and neutrons in the nucleus of an atom of a particular substance. Symbol *A*

mass-pro·duce *vt.* to manufacture a product in very large quantities in factories, especially using mechanization and assembly-line methods —**mass pro·duc·er** *n.*

mass pro·duc·tion *n.* the manufacturing of products on a large scale in factories, especially using mechanization and assembly-line methods

mass so·ci·e·ty *n.* a society in which the national or global nature of the influences on life, e.g., mass production and the mass media, has stripped the population of its diversity

mass spec·tro·graph *n.* CHEM an instrument that separates atoms and molecules according to their mass and that records the resulting mass spectrum

mass spec·trum *n.* CHEM a record of the chemical constituents of a substance separated according to their mass and presented as a spectrum

mast[1] /mast/ *n.* **1.** NAUT **VERTICAL SUPPORT** a vertical spar that supports sails, rigging, or flags on a ship **2.** **UPRIGHT POLE** a vertical pole **3.** BROADCAST **BROADCAST TOWER** a tall broadcasting antenna **4.** NAVY = **captain's mast** ■ *vti.* **(mast·ed, mast·ing, masts)** NAVY **SUBJECT TO CAPTAIN'S MAST** to subject somebody charged with a usually shipboard or on-base crime or infringement to a disciplinary hearing **(captain's mast)**, or undergo such a hearing [Old English *mæst*, ultimately from Indo-European] ◇ **at half mast 1.** partway down a flagpole, usually as a sign of respect following a death ○ *flags flying at half mast* **2.** partway up or down from the usual position at which something is worn (*informal humorous*) ○ *pants at half mast* ◇ **before the mast** serving as an ordinary sailor or apprentice seaman

mast[2] /mast/ *n.* AGRIC the nuts of certain trees, such as beech, oak, and chestnut, especially when used as food for hogs [Old English *mæst* "fodder." Ultimately from a prehistoric Germanic word meaning "meat."]

mast- *prefix.* breast, nipple, mammary gland ○ *mastitis* [From Greek *mastos*, of unknown origin]

mas·ta·ba /mástəbə/, **mas·ta·bah** *n.* an ancient Egyptian mudbrick tomb built with a flat base, sloping sides, and a flat roof. Its design inspired the pyramids. [Early 17thC. From Arabic *maṣṭaba.*]

mas·tal·gia /ma stáljə, ma stáljee ə/ *n.* pain in the breast

mast cell *n.* a large cell in connective tissue consisting of granules that release histamine and heparin during allergic reactions [From German *Mast* "fattening, feeding"]

mas·tec·to·my /ma stéktəmee/ (*plural* **-mies**) *n.* the surgical removal of a breast, usually as a treatment for breast cancer [Early 20thC. Coined from Greek *mastos* "breast" + -ECTOMY.]

mas·ter /mástər/ *n.* **1.** BOSS a man in a position of authority, e.g., over a business, servants, or an animal **2.** SOMEBODY HIGHLY SKILLED somebody who has great skill in a particular area **3.** SOMEBODY IN CONTROL somebody or something controlling or influencing events or other things (*sometimes considered offensive*) **4.** ABSTRACT CONTROL an abstract idea or force that is thought of as having control or influence (*sometimes considered offensive*) **5.** INDUST SKILLED WORKER somebody who is highly skilled in a trade or craft and is qualified to teach apprentices (*usually used in combination*) **6.** ORIGINAL COPY an original copy of something such as a recording tape or a stencil, from which other copies can be made **7.** GAME PLAYER AT HIGH LEVEL somebody who has reached a level of excellence in some games, especially chess or bridge, reckoned by number of games or points won in major tournaments. ◆ **International Master** **8.** LEADER somebody whose philosophy or religious belief has attracted followers (*sometimes considered offensive*) **9.** NAUT SHIP'S OFFICER the captain of a merchant ship **10.** LAW SPECIALIST ASSISTING JUDGE a specialist, sometimes a retired judge, who assists a court by making a report to the judge presiding over a case, often a highly complex case **11.** VICTOR somebody who defeats another (*literary*) **12.** COMPUT, MECH ENG CONTROLLING MACHINE a device or computer that controls the operation of one or more other connected devices or computers (*sometimes considered offensive*) ■ *adj.* (*sometimes considered offensive*) **1.** MAIN devised to operate on the broadest level ○ *a master plan for flood evacuations* **2.** CONTROLLING controlling the operation of everything or of all others **3.** PRINCIPAL biggest or primary among several ○ *redecorated the master bedroom* ■ *vt.* (**-tered, -ter·ing, -ters**) **1.** LEARN SOMETHING to become highly skilled in something, or acquire a complete understanding of it **2.** CONTROL SOMETHING to learn to control feelings or behavior (*sometimes considered offensive*) **3.** CONTROL SOMEBODY to break the will of a person or animal (*sometimes considered offensive*) **4.** RECORDING MAKE MASTER RECORDING to produce a master recording [Pre-12thC. Via Old English *mægister* and Old French *maistre* from Latin *magister* "chief" (source of English *magistrate*), from *magis* "more."] —**mas·ter·less** *adj.*

Mas·ter *n.* **1.** PREFIX TO BOY'S NAME a title sometimes prefixed to a boy's surname in formal circumstances **2.** RELIG RELIGIOUS TEACHER a title used to address a man who is a religious leader or teacher (*sometimes considered offensive*) **3.** MISTER Mister (*archaic*)

mas·ter-at-arms (*plural* **mas·ters-at-arms**) *n.* a noncommissioned officer aboard a naval vessel who is responsible for maintaining order and enforcing discipline in the ship's company

mas·ter build·er *n.* an especially accomplished builder, especially one licensed to employ others as labor (*sometimes considered offensive*)

mas·ter chief pet·ty of·fi·cer *n.* the highest noncommissioned rank in the U.S. Navy or Coast Guard, or a person holding it

mas·ter class *n.* a class given by an acknowledged expert in a particular field (*sometimes considered offensive*)

mas·ter·ful /mástərfəl/ *adj.* **1.** EXPERT demonstrating exceptional skill or ability in a specific area (*sometimes considered offensive*) **2.** SHOWING LEADERSHIP showing the ability or tendency to lead others —**mas·ter·ful·ly** *adv.* —**mas·ter·ful·ness** *n.*

mas·ter key *n.* a key that will open all the locks in a particular set or place

mas·ter·ly /mástərlee/ *adj.* demonstrating outstanding skill —**mas·ter·li·ness** *n.*

mas·ter·mind /mástər mīnd/ *n.* CHIEF PLANNER somebody who plans, organizes, and oversees a complex operation ■ *vt.* (**-mind·ed, -mind·ing, -minds**) OVERSEE OPERATION to plan, organize, and oversee a complex operation

Mas·ter of Arts *n.* a degree in a nonscience subject, usually awarded after one or two years of postgraduate study

mas·ter of cer·e·mo·nies *n.* somebody who performs the duties of a host at a formal event, making the opening speech and introducing other speakers or performers (*sometimes considered offensive*)

Mas·ter of Sci·ence *n.* a degree in a science subject, usually awarded after one or two years of postgraduate study

mas·ter·piece /mástər peess/ *n.* **1.** GREAT ARTISTIC WORK an exceptionally good piece of creative work, e.g., a book, film, or performance **2.** ARTIST'S BEST WORK the best piece of work by a particular artist or craftsperson **3.** WORK EARNING RECOGNITION BY GUILD the piece of work presented to a medieval guild to show that its maker was worthy of the rank of master craftsman [Early 17thC. Formed on the model of Dutch *meesterstuk* or German *Meisterstück*.]

mas·ter race *n.* a group of people who consider themselves a race superior to all others, especially the Aryans in the ideology of Nazi Germany (*offensive in some contexts*)

Mas·ters /mástərz/, **Edgar Lee** (1869–1950) U.S. poet. He is best known for his free-verse small-town epic *Spoon River Anthology* (1915).

Mas·ter's de·gree *n.* a college degree with the title Master, usually awarded after one or two years of postgraduate study

mas·ter ser·geant *n.* **1.** NONCOMMISSIONED RANK a senior noncommissioned rank in the U.S. Army, Air Force, Marine Corps, and certain other military groups, ranking immediately below the most senior noncommissioned rank **2.** HOLDER OF RANK somebody in a U.S. military organization who holds the rank of master sergeant

mas·ter·sing·er /mástər singər/ *n.* = **Meistersinger** [Early 19thC. An Anglicization of MEISTERSINGER.]

Mas·ter·son /mástərssən/, **Bat** (1853–1921) Canadian-born U.S. sheriff. He was based in Dodge City, Kansas (1887–79) where he also worked as a journalist. Born **Bartholomew Masterson**. Full name **William Barclay Masterson**

mas·ter·stroke /mástər strōk/ *n.* a brilliant idea or very clever tactic

Mas·ter·ton /mástərtən/ town in the south of the North Island, New Zealand. Population: 19,954 (1996).

mas·ter·work /mástər wùrk/ *n.* = **masterpiece** *n.* 1, **masterpiece** *n.* 2

mas·ter·y /mástəree/ *n.* **1.** EXPERT SKILL expert knowledge or outstanding ability **2.** COMPLETE CONTROL total control over somebody or something (*sometimes considered offensive*)

mast·head /mást hèd/ *n.* **1.** PRESS NEWSPAPER'S TITLE AS DISPLAYED the name of a newspaper or magazine as it appears in large letters on the front cover **2.** PRESS NEWSPAPER INFORMATION the list that provides information about staff, owners, and circulation in a newspaper or magazine, usually printed on the first page **3.** SAILING MAST'S TOP the top of a mast

mas·tic /mástik/ *n.* **1.** RESIN an aromatic resin produced by a Mediterranean tree, used to make lacquer, varnish, adhesives, and condiments **2.** INDUST CEMENT a flexible cement used as a filler, adhesive, or sealant in woodwork, plaster, or brickwork **3.** BEVERAGES LIQUOR a liquor in which mastic gum is used as a flavoring **4.** TREES = **mastic tree** *n.* [14thC. Via French from, ultimately, Greek *mastikhan* "to grind the teeth." So called because the resin of the mastic tree can be chewed.]

mas·ti·cate /másti kàyt/ (**-cat·ed, -cat·ing, -cates**) *v.* **1.** *vti.* CHEW FOOD to grind and pulverize food inside the mouth, using the teeth and jaws **2.** *vt.* GRIND TO A PULP to grind or crush something until it turns to pulp [Mid-17thC. Via the past participle stem of Latin *masticare* from Greek *mastikhan* "to grind the teeth."] —**mas·ti·ca·ble** *adj.* —**mas·ti·ca·tion** /màsti káysh'n/ *n.* —**mas·ti·ca·tor** /másti kàytər/ *n.*

mas·ti·ca·to·ry /mástikə tàwree/ *adj.* OF CHEWING relating to chewing ■ *n.* (*plural* **-ries**) MED MEDICINE a medicine made to be chewed in order to increase the production of saliva

mas·tic tree *n.* a small Mediterranean evergreen shrub belonging to the cashew family, grown for its resin. Latin name: *Pistachia lentiscus.*

Mastiff

mas·tiff /mástif/ *n.* a breed of large powerful smooth-haired dogs, often tan or grayish with a dark face [14thC. Via Old French *mastin* from, ultimately, Latin *mansuetus* literally "used to the hand," from *manus* "hand."]

mas·tiff bat *n.* a snub-nosed bat found in most of the warm regions of the world. It has narrow wings and brown, gray, or black fur. Family: Molossidae.

mas·tig·ure /másti gyòor/ *n.* a lizard of northern Africa and the Middle East that blocks its burrow with its very spiny tail. Genus: *Uromastix.* [Mid-19thC. Coined via modern Latin from Greek *mastix* "whip" + *oura* "tail."]

mas·ti·tis /ma stítiss/ *n.* inflammation of a woman's breast or an animal's udder, usually as a result of bacterial infection [Mid-19thC. Coined from MASTO- + -ITIS.] —**mas·tit·ic** /ma stíttik/ *adj.*

mas·to·don /mástə dòn/ *n.* a large extinct mammal that resembled an elephant, with shaggy hair and two sets of tusks. Genus: *Mastodon.* [Early 19thC. Coined from MASTO- + Greek *odōn* "tooth." So called because it had nipple-shaped tubercles on its molars.] —**mas·to·don·ic** /màstə dónnik/ *adj.* —**mas·to·don·tic** /-tik/ *adj.*

mas·toid /máss tòyd/ *adj.* **1.** NIPPLE-SHAPED shaped like a nipple or breast **2.** OF MASTOID PROCESS relating to the mastoid process ■ *n.* ANAT = **mastoid process** [Mid-18thC. Via French *mastoïde* or modern Latin *mastoides* from Greek *mastoeidēs*, from *mastos* "breast."]

mas·toid bone *n.* = **mastoid process**

mas·toid cell *n.* an air-filled space in the mastoid process

mas·toid·ec·to·my /màss toy déktəmee/ (*plural* **-mies**) *n.* a surgical operation to remove part of an infected mastoid process to allow pus to drain off and prevent infection from spreading to the meninges

mas·toid·i·tis /màss toy dítəss/ *n.* inflammation of the mastoid process and mastoid cells

mas·toid proc·ess *n.* a bony protuberance on the skull, found behind the ear in many vertebrates, including humans

Mas·troi·an·ni /màst roy yánnee/, **Marcello** (1924–96) Italian movie actor. Specializing in romantic or bittersweet comedy, he worked with many of the great Italian directors, including Federico Fellini in *La Dolce Vita* (1960).

mas·tur·bate /mástər bàyt/ (**-bat·ed, -bat·ing, -bates**) *vti.* to give oneself or somebody else sexual pleasure by stroking the genitals, usually to orgasm [Mid-19thC. From the past participle of *masturbari*, of uncertain origin: perhaps from *manu stuprare* "to defile with the hand."] —**mas·tur·ba·tor** *n.*

mas·tur·ba·tion /màstər báysh'n/ *n.* the stroking of genitals for sexual pleasure, usually to orgasm

mas·tur·ba·to·ry /mástərbə tàwree/ *adj.* relating to or for the purpose of masturbation

ma·sur·i·um /mə sóoree əm/ *n.* the metallic element technetium (*dated*) [Early 20thC. From German, named for *Masuria*, a region of northeastern Poland.]

mat[1] /mat/ *n.* **1.** PIECE OF CARPET flat material placed on a floor for decoration or protection or for wiping the feet **2.** SPORTS, LEISURE PIECE OF PADDED MATERIAL a piece of padded material placed on the floor for use in some sports and activities, e.g., to absorb the impact of falling in judo **3.** HOUSEHOLD PROTECTIVE COVER a piece of fabric or board that protects tables and other surfaces from damage by heat or scratching, e.g., placed under hot dinner plates or ornaments **4.** THICK MASS any thick or interwoven mass, e.g., a tangle of hair ■ *vti.* (**mat·ted, mat·ting, mats**) FORM TANGLED MASS to make something into or become a thick tangled mass [Pre-12thC. From Latin *matta,* of uncertain origin: probably from a Phoenician word.]

mat[2] /mat/ *n.* **1.** ARTS **PICTURE BORDER** a border of stiff material placed around a picture to act as a simple frame or as a decorative edge within a frame **2. mat, matte NONGLOSS FINISH** a dull or nonglossy finish, e.g., on paintwork or photographic prints ■ *vt.* **(mat·ted, mat·ting, mats) FRAME WITH MAT** to put a mat around a picture ■ *adj.* **mat, matte HAVING MAT FINISH** with a mat finish [Variant of MATT from French, "dull"]

mat., **mat** *abbr.* matinée

M.A.T. *abbr.* Master of Arts in Teaching

Mat·a·be·le·land /màttə beélə land/ region in southern Zimbabwe

Ma·ta·di /mə taádee/ capital of Bas-Congo Region, western Democratic Republic of the Congo. Population: 172,730 (1994).

mat·a·dor /máttə dàwr/ *n.* **1. BULLFIGHTER** the main bullfighter, whose job is to kill the bull **2.** CARDS **HIGH CARD** one of the highest playing cards in some games such as skat **3.** GAME **DOMINO GAME** a variety of the game of dominoes in which the dots on adjacent halves must total seven [Late 17thC. From Spanish, from *matar* "to kill," of uncertain origin: perhaps from late Latin *mattare* "to beat senseless" or Persian *māt* "dead."]

mat·a·gou·ri /màttə góoree/ (*plural* **-ris**) *n.* a thorny bush that forms thickets in open areas of New Zealand. Latin name: *Discaria toumatou.* [Mid-19thC. Alteration of Maori *tumatakuru.*]

Ma·ta Ha·ri /maátə haáree/ (1876–1917) Dutch dancer and spy. Through her liaisons with high-ranking officers, she gathered intelligence for the Germans during World War I. She was executed by the French. Real name **Margaretha Geertruida Zelle**

Ma·ta Ha·ri /maátə haáree/ *n.* a valuable food fish in the tropical Pacific and Indian oceans that looks like a snapper with a scaleless head. Latin name: *Lethrinus nebulosis.* [From MATA HARI, formed from Malay *mata* "eye" + *hari* "day"]

mat·ai /maá tī/ (*plural* **-ais**) *n.* a cone-bearing evergreen tree found in New Zealand with bluish bark and small narrow leaves that grow in two rows. Its wood is often used for flooring. Latin name: *Podocarpus spicatus.* [Mid-19thC. From Maori.]

Ma·ta·mo·ros /màttə máwrəss/ city and port in northeastern Mexico, near the mouth of the Rio Grande and across the river from Brownsville, Texas. Population: 266,065 (1990).

match[1] /mach/ *n.* **1. CONTEST** a contest between opponents, especially a sports contest **2. SOMETHING SIMILAR** somebody who or something that resembles another in certain qualities **3. AN EQUAL** somebody or something capable of competing equally with another **4. GOOD COMPLEMENT** something that combines well with something else **5. MARITAL PARTNERSHIP** a partnership in wedlock **6. POTENTIAL PARTNER** somebody who is thought to be a suitable marriage or romantic partner **7. COUNTERPART** somebody who or something that is identical to another or is one half of a pair ■ *v.* **(matched, match·ing, match·es) 1.** *vt.* **BE ALIKE** to be similar or identical to somebody or something **2.** *vt.* **COMPETE EQUALLY** to be as good, or sometimes as bad, as somebody or something else **3.** *vti.* **COMBINE WELL** to make a suitable or pleasing combination, or put things together to make such a combination **4.** *vt.* **BE IN HARMONY** to correspond with something or reflect certain features **5.** *vt.* **FIND SOMETHING THAT COMBINES** to find something that makes a suitable accompaniment **6.** *vti.* **JOIN CLEANLY** to fit or join something smoothly **7.** *vt.* **PLACE IN OPPOSITION** to provide somebody or something with an opponent **8.** *vti.* **TOSS COINS** to toss coins to see which sides land face up in order to determine a choice or decision **9.** *vt.* **MARRY SOMEBODY** to give or join somebody in marriage (*archaic*) [Old English *gemæcca* "spouse, lover." Ultimately from a prehistoric Germanic word that is also the ancestor of English *make.*] —**match·a·bil·i·ty** /màchə bíllətee/ *n.* —**match·a·ble** /máchəb'l/ *adj.* —**match·er** *n.*

match[2] /mach/ *n.* **1. STICK PRODUCING FIRE** a thin stick of wood whose tip is coated with a combustible material that ignites when scraped against a rough surface, used to light a fire, candle, or gas appliance **2.** ARMS **EXPLOSIVES FUSE** a slow-burning fuse used in cannons and explosives [14thC. Via Old French *meiche* from, ultimately, Greek *muxa* "lampwick" (original sense in English).]

match·board /mách bàwrd/ *n.* a board that has a tongue along one edge and a groove along the other so that it can be fitted together with other boards

match·book /mách bòok/ *n.* a small cardboard folder with safety matches inside and a striking surface usually on the outside

match·box /mách bòks/ *n.* a small cardboard box for matches, with a striking surface along one or both sides

match·less /máchləss/ *adj.* so outstandingly great as to have no rival —**match·less·ly** *adv.* —**match·less·ness** *n.*

match·lock /mách lòk/ *n.* **1. TRIGGER** an old trigger mechanism in guns that ignited the powder with a slow-burning fuse **2. GUN** a gun equipped with a matchlock

match·mak·er /mách màykər/ *n.* somebody who tries to arrange romantic partnerships or marriages, either professionally or informally

match play *n.* a method of golf scoring in which the number of holes won is counted rather than the number of strokes —**match play·er** *n.*

match point *n.* **1.** SPORTS **FINAL POINT** the final point needed to win a match, especially in tennis and other racket games **2.** BRIDGE **SCORING UNIT** a unit used for scoring in bridge tournaments

match·stick /mách stìk/ *n.* **STEM OF MATCH** the wooden part of a match ■ *adj.* **1. MADE FROM MATCHES** built of matchsticks **2. LIKE STICKS IN THINNESS** in the form of thin strips or simple lines

match·up /mách ùp/ *n.* a matching of two people or two teams in a competitive sport

mate[1] /mayt/ *n.* **1.** SHIPPING **DECK OFFICER** a deck officer ranking below the master on a merchant ship, or the rank the officer holds **2.** NAVY **PETTY OFFICER** a petty officer in the U.S. Navy who is assistant to a warrant officer, or the rank the officer holds **3. PARTNER IN SEX OR WEDLOCK** a sexual or marriage partner **4. SKILLED WORKER'S HELPER** an assistant to a skilled worker ○ *a plumber's mate* **5. SOMETHING THAT MATCHES** one of a pair of things that belong together **6. BREEDING PARTNER** either of a pair of animals that breed together **7.** *U.K.* **FRIEND** a friend, also used as a friendly, or sometimes hostile, form of address to a man ■ *v.* **(mat·ed, mat·ing, mates) 1.** *vti.* **BREED** to come together or be brought together to breed **2.** *vi.* **HAVE SEX** to engage in sex **3.** *vt.* **CONNECT TWO OBJECTS** to combine or connect two things **4.** *vti.* **MARRY** to join or become joined in marriage (*informal or humorous*) [14thC. From Middle Low German *gemate.* Ultimately from a prehistoric Germanic word that is also the ancestor of English *meat.* The underlying sense is "somebody you share food with."] —**mate·less** *adj.*

mate[2] *n., vt.* **(mat·ed, mat·ing, mates)** CHESS = **checkmate** [14thC. (See CHECKMATE).]

ma·té /maá tày, maa táy/ *n.* **1.** TREES **EVERGREEN TREE** a South American evergreen tree widely grown for its leaves that are used to make a tea. Latin name: *Ilex paraguariensis.* **2.** BEVERAGES **STIMULATING DRINK** a popular South American milky drink containing caffeine that is made from the dried leaves of the maté tree [Early 18thC. Via Spanish from Quechua *mati.*]

mat·e·lote /mátt'l ŏt, maátə lŏt/ *n.* a chunky fish stew made with wine [Early 18thC. Via French, "sailor," from Middle Dutch *mattenoot* "bed companion."]

ma·ter /máytər/ *n. U.K.* mother (*dated informal or humorous*) [Late 16thC. From Latin (see MOTHER).]

WORD KEY: ORIGIN

The Latin word from which *mater* derives is also the source of English *madrigal, material, maternal, matriculate, matrimony, matrix, matron,* and *matter.* Its ultimate Indo-European ancestor also produced English *metropolis* and *mother.*

ma·ter·fa·mil·i·as /màytər fə míllee ass/ (*plural* **-tres·fa·mil·i·as** /mày trayz-/) *n.* a woman described in her role as head of a household or as the mother of her children (*literary*) [Mid-18thC. From Latin, literally "mother of the family."]

ma·te·ri·al /mə téeree əl/ *n.* **1. SOMETHING USED IN MAKING ITEMS** the substance used to make things **2. INFORMATION** information such as facts, notes, and research, used in the making of a book, movie, or other work **3.** TEXTILES **FABRIC** woven flat cloth or fabric **4. SOMEBODY SUITABLE** somebody regarded in terms of his or her suitability to perform a certain job or do a task ○ *She's certainly executive material.* ■ **ma·te·ri·als** *npl.* **EQUIPMENT** the tools and other things needed to perform a particular task ■ *adj.* **1. PHYSICAL** relating to or consisting of solid physical matter ○ *the material universe* **2. WORLDLY** relating to physical well-being rather than emotional or spiritual well-being ○ *material comforts* **3. PERTINENT** relevant or important **4.** LAW **IMPORTANT IN COURT** important to a case that is being tried in court ○ *testimony that is material to the case* **5.** PHILOSOPHY **OF CONTENT NOT FORM** relating to the substance of reasoning rather than the form it takes [14thC. Via French *matériel* from late Latin *materialis,* from Latin *materia* (see MATTER).] —**ma·te·ri·al·i·ty** /mə téeree állətee/ *n.* —**ma·te·ri·al·ness** /mə téeree əlnəss/ *n.*

ma·te·ri·al·ism /mə téeree ə lìzzəm/ *n.* **1.** PHILOSOPHY **THEORY OF THE PHYSICAL** the theory that physical matter is the only reality and that psychological states such as emotions, reason, thought, and desire will eventually be explained as physical functions **2. FOCUS ON POSSESSIONS** devotion to material wealth and possessions at the expense of spiritual or intellectual values

ma·te·ri·al·ist /mə téeree əlist/ *n.* **1. SOMEBODY CONCERNED ABOUT POSSESSIONS** somebody who is concerned with material wealth and possessions at the expense of spiritual and intellectual values **2.** PHILOSOPHY **SUPPORTER OF PHILOSOPHICAL MATERIALISM** somebody who supports the view that physical matter is the only reality and that psychological states will eventually be explained as physical functions ■ *adj.* = **materialistic**

ma·te·ri·al·is·tic /mə téeree ə lístik/ *adj.* concerned with material wealth and possessions at the expense of spiritual and intellectual values —**ma·te·ri·al·is·ti·cal·ly** *adv.*

ma·te·ri·al·ize /mə téeree ə līz/ (**-ized, -iz·ing, -iz·es**) *v.* **1.** *vi.* **BECOME REAL** to become real or become fact **2.** *vti.* **ASSUME PHYSICAL FORM** to assume, or cause a ghost or spirit to assume, a physical form **3.** *vi.* **APPEAR** to appear suddenly, as if out of nowhere —**ma·te·ri·al·i·za·tion** /mə téeree əli záysh'n/ *n.*

ma·te·ri·al·ly /mə téeree əlee/ *adv.* **1. MUCH** in a real sense or to a significant degree **2. PHYSICALLY** in terms of material wealth and possessions

ma·te·ri·als sci·ence *n.* the study of the features and applications of the different materials used in science and technology such as metals, plastics, and ceramics

ma·té·ri·el /mə téeree él/, **ma·te·ri·el** *n.* the supplies, weapons, and equipment associated with a military force [Early 19thC. From French (see MATERIAL).]

ma·ter·nal /mə túrn'l/ *adj.* **1. OF OR LIKE A MOTHER** belonging or relating to motherhood, a mother, or mothers in general ○ *maternal pride* **2. CARING** kind, caring, and protective in a motherly way ○ *a very maternal person* **3. ON OR FROM THE MOTHER'S SIDE** relating to or inherited from the mother or the mother's side of a family ○ *Her maternal grandfather was Polish.* [15thC. Via French *maternel* from assumed Vulgar Latin *maternalis,* from Latin *maternus,* from *mater* (see MATTER).] —**ma·ter·nal·ism** *n.* —**ma·ter·nal·is·tic** /mə tùrn'l ístik/ *adj.* —**ma·ter·nal·ly** /mə túrn'lee/ *adv.*

ma·ter·ni·ty /mə túrnətee/ *n.* **1. MOTHERHOOD** the condition of being a mother ○ *Maternity did not affect the progress of her career.* **2. MOTHERLY CHARACTERISTICS** the characteristics and emotions traditionally associated with being a mother such as loving kindness and protectiveness **3. HOSPITAL SECTION CARING FOR NEWBORNS** a ward, floor, or other section of a hospital where mothers and newborn babies are cared for ■ *adj.* **OF OR FOR PREGNANCY OR BIRTH** relating to or provided for pregnancy, pregnant women, or women who have just given birth ○ *maternity clothes* [Early 17thC. Via French *maternité* from, ultimately, Latin *maternus* (see MATERNAL).]

ma·ter·ni·ty leave *n.* paid or unpaid leave from work that a woman is entitled to take before, at, and after the time that she has a child

ma·ter·ni·ty ward *n.* a hospital ward for the care of newly delivered babies and their mothers, often also with beds for pregnant women who need medical attention before having their babies

mat·ey /máytee/ *adj.* (**-i·er, -i·est**) *U.K.* **FRIENDLY** friendly, especially in a way that is familiar or seems insincere ○ *Those two have been very matey lately.* ■

n. (*informal*) **1.** TERM OF ADDRESS FOR UNKNOWN MAN used by a man to address another man he does not know **2.** FRIEND a man who is another man's friend and companion —**mat·i·ness** *n.*

math /math/ *n.* mathematics [Late 19thC. Shortening.]

math. *abbr.* 1. mathematical 2. mathematically 3. mathematician 4. mathematics

math·e·mat·ic /màthə máttik/ *adj.* MATHEMATICAL mathematical (*archaic or literary*) ■ *n.* MATH mathematics (*archaic*) [14thC. Directly or via French *mathématique* from Latin *mathematicus*, from, ultimately, the Greek stem *mathēmat-* "something learned," related to *manthanein* "to learn."]

math·e·mat·i·cal /màthə máttik'l/ *adj.* **1.** OF MATHEMATICS belonging to, relating to, or used in mathematics **2.** ACCURATE as accurate as if calculated by mathematics ○ *crafted the strategy with mathematical precision* **3.** WORKED OUT BY MATHEMATICS calculated or proved by mathematics ○ *It's a mathematical certainty that two numbers in the set will be the same.* **4.** GOOD AT MATHEMATICS skilled in mathematics ○ *more artistic than mathematical* [15thC. Formed from French *mathématique* or its source Latin *mathematicus* (see MATHEMATIC).] —**math·e·mat·i·cal·ly** *adv.*

math·e·mat·i·cal ex·pec·ta·tion *n.* = **expected value**

math·e·mat·i·cal in·duc·tion *n.* = **induction** *n.* 9

math·e·ma·ti·cian /màthəmə tísh'n/ *n.* a student or expert in mathematics, or somebody whose job involves mathematics

math·e·mat·ics /màthə máttiks/ *n.* **1.** MATH STUDY OF RELATIONSHIPS USING NUMBERS the study of the relationships among numbers, shapes, and quantities. It uses signs, symbols, and proofs and includes arithmetic, algebra, calculus, geometry, and trigonometry. (*takes a singular verb*) **2.** CALCULATIONS the calculations involved in a process, estimate, or plan (*takes a plural verb*) ○ *I like the idea, but the mathematics of it are beyond me.* [Late 16thC. Formed from MATHEMATIC, probably modeled on French *(les) mathématiques*, a rendering of Latin *mathematica*, from, ultimately, Greek *mathēmat-* (see MATHEMATIC).]

math·e·ma·tize /máthəmə tīz/ (**-tized, -tiz·ing, -tiz·es**) *vt.* to consider something in, or reduce it to, purely mathematical terms ○ *Members of the Institute were apt to mathematize everything, including their social lives.* —**math·e·ma·ti·za·tion** /màthəməti záysh'n/ *n.*

Math·er /máthər, máythər/, **Cotton** (1663–1728) U.S. puritan minister and theologian. He published 469 works on witchcraft, ethics, religion, natural history, medicine and science, and championed inoculations against smallpox.

Math·er /máythər, máth-/, **Increase** (1639–1723) U.S. puritan minister. Father of Cotton Mather, he was president of Harvard College (1685–1701). He campaigned against the prevailing witchcraft hysteria of the day.

Ma·thew·son /máthyoossən/, **Christy** (1880–1925) U.S. baseball player. He played as pitcher for the New York Giants (1901–16) and set the record for the most wins. Full name **Christopher Mathewson**. Nickname **Big Six**

maths /maths/ *n. U.K.* = **math** (*informal*) [Early 20thC. Contraction.]

Ma·thu·ra /mútərə/ capital city of Mathura District, Uttar Pradesh State, northern India. Population: 226,850 (1991).

Ma·til·da /mə tíldə/ (1102–67) English princess. Though the daughter and acknowledged heir of Henry I of England, the throne was seized by Stephen and she was never crowned queen.

ma·til·i·ja pop·py /mə tíllee hàa-/ *n.* a perennial Californian and Mexican herb of the poppy family that produces a single large white flower. Latin name: *Romneya coulteri.* [Named for Matilija Canyon in California]

mat·in /mátt'n/, **mat·in·al** /mátt'nəl/ *adj.* belonging or relating to matins, or taking place during matins [13thC. From French *matines* (see MATINS).]

mat·i·née /màtt'n áy/, **mat·i·nee** *n.* **1.** AFTERNOON PERFORMANCE a performance of a play, concert, or motion picture that is given during the day, especially in the afternoon, often with cheaper seats than the evening performance **2.** MIDDAY OR AFTERNOON EVENT an event or social occasion taking place at midday or in the afternoon ○ *The Senior Center holds a matinée dance on the first Saturday of each month.* [Mid-19thC. From French, literally "morning," because it takes place in the daytime, from *matin* (see MATINS).]

mat·i·née i·dol *n.* an actor, especially a good-looking man movie star of the 1930s and 1940s who was attractive to matinée audiences formed mostly of women (*dated*)

mat·ins /mátt'nz/ *n.* **1.** **mat·ins, Mat·ins** CHR MORNING LITURGY in the Roman Catholic Church, the morning hours of the Divine Office **2.** CHR MORNING PRAYER in the Church of England, the ceremony of morning prayer **3.** CHR HOURS BEFORE VIGIL in some Roman Catholic monastic communities, the hours before a Vigil **4.** DAWN CHORUS a morning song, especially one sung by birds (*literary*) [13thC. Via French *matines* from, ultimately, Latin *matutinus* "of the morning," from *Matuta* "goddess of dawn" (related to *maturus*, source of English *mature*).]

AKG London

Henri Matisse: Photographed in 1948 working on his paper cut-outs

Ma·tisse /mə téess/, **Henri** (1869–1954) French artist. A leader of the fauve group from 1904, and an influential 20th-century artist, he used bold colour to create rhythmical forms and a flat perspective, later working with brightly colored cut-out paper on canvas. Full name **Henri Émile Benoît Matisse**

mat·jes her·ring /maàtyəss-/, **maat·jes her·ring** *n.* a filet or filets of herring, especially of a young herring that has not spawned, that is lightly salted, usually sweetened with sugar and flavored with spice, and eaten raw with onions [Partial translation of Dutch *maatjesharing*, literally "maiden's herring," from *maatjes* "maiden's," from its use for young herring, + *haring* "herring"]

Mat·o Gros·so /màttō gróssō/ state in southwestern Brazil. Population: 2,020,581 (1991). Area: 340,000 sq. mi./881,000 sq. km.

Ma·to·po Hills /mə tṓpə-/ region of granite hills in southwestern Zimbabwe. Area: 1,250 sq. mi./3,240 sq. km.

matri- *prefix.* mother, maternal ○ *matrilineal* ○ *matriarchy* [From Latin *matr-*, the stem of *mater* (see MATER)]

ma·tri·arch /máytree aàrk/ *n.* **1.** WOMAN HEAD OF A FAMILY OR GROUP a woman who is recognized as being the head of a family, community, or people **2.** STRONG SENIOR WOMAN a woman, usually a grandmother, who is highly respected by her family and to whom the family turns for advice and help **3.** WOMAN IN A POWERFUL POSITION a woman who holds a position of dominance, authority, or respect [Early 17thC. Formed from Latin *matri-* (see MATRI-), on the model of *patriarch.*] —**ma·tri·ar·chic** /-aàrkik/ *adj.*

ma·tri·ar·chal /màytree aàrk'l/ *adj.* **1.** IN WHICH WOMEN HOLD POWER used to describe a society in which power and property are held by women and handed down through matrilineal descent **2.** CONTROLLED BY WOMEN controlled or dominated by women **3.** WITH THE TRADITIONAL QUALITIES OF A STRONG WOMAN showing strength and assurance as the most respected woman in a group ○ *My grandmother was a powerful, matriarchal figure.* **4.** OF MATRIARCHS relating to a matriarch or to matriarchs in general —**ma·tri·ar·chal·ism** *n.*

ma·tri·ar·chate /máytree aàr kàyt, máytree aàrkət/ *n.* = **matriarchy** *n.* 2 [Late 19thC. Formed from MATRIARCH on the model of *patriarchate.*]

ma·tri·ar·chy /máytree aàrkee/ (*plural* **-chies**) *n.* **1.** SOCIAL ORDER WHERE WOMEN HAVE POWER a form of social order where women are in charge and are recognized as the heads of families, with power, lineage, and inheritance passing, where possible, from mothers to daughters **2.** COMMUNITY WHERE WOMEN HAVE POWER any community, society, or social group that is based on matriarchy **3.** ORGANIZATION WHERE WOMEN HAVE POWER any form of organization or government where women have power [Late 19thC. Modeled on PATRIARCHY.]

ma·tri·ces plural of **matrix**

mat·ri·cide /máttrə sīd/ *n.* **1.** KILLING OF OWN MOTHER the act of murdering your own mother **2.** KILLER OF OWN MOTHER somebody who has murdered his or her own mother [Late 16thC. Directly or via French from Latin *matricidium*, from *matr-* (see MATRI-).] —**mat·ri·ci·dal** /màttrə sīd'l/ *adj.*

mat·ri·cli·nous /màttrə klīnəss/, **mat·ro·cli·nous, mat·ro·cli·nal** /màttrə klīnəl/ *adj.* having obvious characteristics that are inherited predominantly from the woman parent

ma·tric·u·lant /mə tríkyələnt/ *n.* = **matriculate** *n.* [Mid-19thC. From medieval Latin *matriculant-*, the present participle stem of *matriculare* (see MATRICULATE).]

ma·tric·u·late *v.* /mə tríkyə làyt/ (**-lat·ed, -lat·ing, -lates**) **1.** *vt.* ADMIT SOMEBODY AS STUDENT to admit a student to membership of a college or university **2.** *vi.* BE ENROLLED AS A STUDENT to be enrolled at a college or university, after meeting the academic standard required to be accepted for a course of further education ■ *n.* /mə tríkyələt, mə tríkyə làyt/ SOMEBODY ENROLLED somebody who has matriculated [Late 16thC. From assumed medieval Latin *matriculare*, from *matricula*, literally "little list," from *matrix* (see MATRIX).] —**ma·tric·u·la·tion** /mə trìkyə láysh'n/ *n.* —**ma·tric·u·la·tor** /mə tríkyə làytər/ *n.*

mat·ri·lin·e·age /màttrə línnee ij/ *n.* the line of genealogical relationship or descent that follows the women's side of a family

mat·ri·lin·e·al /màttrə línnee əl/ *adj.* **1.** FOLLOWING THE FEMALE LINE used to describe the line of genealogical relationship or descent that follows the female side of a family **2.** RELATED THROUGH MOTHERS used to describe a group that is related by descent through mothers **3.** COMING THROUGH THE WOMEN'S LINE inherited or traced through the women's line of descent —**mat·ri·lin·e·al·ly** *adv.*

mat·ri·lo·cal /màttrə lṓk'l/ *adj.* **1.** INVOLVING A MOVE TO A WIFE'S FAMILY HOME used to describe a form of marriage in which, after the wedding, the bridegroom moves to his new wife's family home **2.** INVOLVING LIVING WITH A WIFE'S FAMILY used to describe a culture in which young men live with their brides' families after marriage —**mat·ri·lo·cal·ly** *adv.*

mat·ri·mo·ni·al /màttrə mṓnee əl/ *adj.* belonging or relating to marriage or to a particular marriage [15thC. Directly or via French from Latin *matrimonialis*, from *matrimonium* (see MATRIMONY).] —**mat·ri·mo·ni·al·ly** *adv.*

mat·ri·mo·ny /máttrə mōnee, máttrəmənee/ *n.* **1.** MARRIED STATE the state or condition of being married **2.** MARRIAGE CEREMONY the religious ceremony of marriage [13thC. Directly or via Anglo-Norman *matrimonie* from Latin *matrimonium*, literally "state of motherhood" (because of the association of marriage with parenthood), from *matri-* (see MATRI-).]

matrimony vine *n.* any one of several shrubs cultivated for their bright berries and purple flowers. Genus: *Lycium.*

ma·trix /máytriks/ (*plural* **-tri·ces** /-seèz/ *or* **-trix·es**) *n.* **1.** SUBSTANCE THAT CONTAINS SOMETHING a substance in which something is embedded or enclosed **2.** SITUATION IN WHICH SOMETHING DEVELOPS a situation or set of circumstances that allows or encourages the origin, development, or growth of something ○ *The matrix of video and computers is producing new forms of art.* **3.** BIOL TISSUE-FORMING SUBSTANCE the substance that exists between cells and from which tissue, e.g., cartilage and bone, develops **4.** PHYSIOL TISSUE AT THE BASE OF THE NAIL the thickened tissue at the base of a fingernail, toenail, or tooth from which a new nail or tooth grows **5.** GEOL SOIL OR ROCK CONTAINING SOMETHING the soil or rock in which something such as a fossil, crystal, or mineral is embedded. ◊ **gangue** **6.** METALL MAIN PART OF AN ALLOY the main metal component in an alloy **7.** MATH ARRAY OF MATHEMATICAL ELEMENTS a rectangular array of mathematical elements, e.g., the coefficients of linear equations, whose rows and columns can be combined with those of other arrays to solve problems **8.** COMPUT NETWORK OF CIRCUIT ELEMENTS a network of circuit elements, e.g., transistors and resistors **9.** PRINTING METAL TYPE MOLD a metal mold from which type is cast in the hot-metal process **10.** MANUF MOLD MADE FROM A RAISED SURFACE a mold made by taking the impression of a raised surface in a substance such as plastic, used in stereotyping or electrotyping **11.** RECORDING **PHONOGRAPH RECORD MOLD** a mold used in the production of phonograph records **12.** MECH ENG **BED OR SURROUND OF MATERIAL** a bed or surround of material that gives protection or absorbs a force **13. WOMB** the womb (*archaic*) [14thC. Directly or via French *matrice* from Latin *matrix* "womb" (the original sense in English), later "list," from, ultimately, *mater* "mother." The underlying idea is of something growing.]

ma·trix sen·tence *n.* the main clause in a complex sentence

matro- *prefix.* = **matri-**

ma·tro·cli·nal *adj.* = **matriclinous**

ma·tro·cli·nous *adj.* = **matriclinous**

ma·tron /máytrən/ *n.* **1. MATURE WOMAN** a woman, especially a married woman of middle age or later, who has had children and is thought of as being mature, sensible, and of good social standing **2. WOMAN WARDEN** a woman who is a warden in a women's correctional institution **3.** *U.K.* **SUPERVISOR** a woman in charge of the medical and housekeeping arrangements in an institution, e.g., a British boarding school **4.** *U.K.* **HEAD NURSE** a woman who is head of the nursing staff in a hospital, nursing home, or other medical institution, equivalent to a nursing director (*no longer used technically*) [14thC. Directly or via French *matrone* from Latin *matrona*, from *matr-* (see MATRI-).] —**ma·tron·al** *adj.* —**matron·hood** *n.* —**ma·tronship** *n.*

ma·tron·ly /máytrənlee/ *adj.* **1. LIKE A MATRON** having qualities associated with a matron, especially dignity and placidity **2. MATURE AND FULL-FIGURED** mature and plump, especially with a large bosom **3. OF A MATRON** relating to or typical of a matron ○ *matronly duties* —**ma·tron·li·ness** *n.*

ma·tron of hon·or *n.* a married woman who is the chief attendant at the wedding of a woman friend or relative

mat·ro·nym·ic /màttrə nímmik/, **met·ro·nym·ic** /mèttrə nímmik, mèetrə-/ *adj.* a name derived from a mother or a matrilineal ancestor [Late 18thC. Formed from Latin *matr-* (see MATRI-).]

Mat·su Is·lands /maá tsoō-/ island group in Taiwan, close to the Chinese mainland

Ma·tsu·ya·ma /maàt soō yaámə/ industrial city in southwestern Japan, on the island of Shikoku. Population: 443,322 (1990).

matte[1] /mat/ *n., adj.* = **mat**[2] *n.* **2**, **mat**[2] *adj.*

matte[2] /mat/ *n.* **1. MIXTURE OF METAL SULFIDES** a mixture of metal sulfides formed during the smelting of sulfide ores, e.g., ores of copper or nickel **2. DEVICE OBSCURING PART OF IMAGE** a mask used for obscuring part of an image so that another image can be put on top of the original. ◊ **matte shot** [Mid-19thC. From French (see MAT), used as a noun.]

matte[3] *n., adj.* = **matt**

mat·ted /máttəd/ *adj.* **1. TANGLED** forming a thick tangled mass ○ *Long-haired cats need lots of brushing to prevent their coats from becoming matted.* **2. WITH MATS** covered with mats or matting

mat·ter /máttər/ *n.* **1. SOMETHING UNDER CONSIDERATION** something that is being considered or needs to be dealt with ○ *This is a matter for serious thought.* **2. SUBSTANCE** a substance or material of a particular kind ○ *reading matter* **3.** PHYS **MATERIAL SUBSTANCE** the material substance of the universe that has mass, occupies space, and is convertible to energy **4. PRINTED TEXT** text or other material that is printed ○ *cheaper rates for printed matter* **5. SUBJECT OF SPEECH OR WRITING** the subject that is dealt with in speech or writing, as opposed to its presentation ○ *The subject matter was well presented.* **6.** PHILOSOPHY **WHAT IS PERCEIVED BY THE MIND** in Cartesian philosophy, something that is extended in space and persists through time, and is contrasted with mind **7.** LAW **SOMETHING TO BE PROVED** a case to be proved or resolved in a court of law ○ *Who is the defendant in this matter?* **8.** MED **BODILY DISCHARGE** something such as pus that is discharged from the body ■ **mat·ters** *npl.* **CIRCUMSTANCES** the current situation or circumstances ○ *We were both under a lot of stress, which didn't improve matters.* ■ *vi.* **(-tered, -ter·ing, -ters) 1. HAVE IMPORTANCE** to be important ○ *The only thing that matters is for you to get better.* **2. MAKE DIFFERENCE** to make a difference ○ *It doesn't matter how you tell her, just make sure she knows.* **3.** MED **PRODUCE PUS** to form or discharge pus [12thC. Directly or via Anglo-Norman *mater(i)e* and French *matière*, from Latin *materia* "timber, stuff of which something is made," later "subject, topic," from *mater* "mother."] ◇ **for that matter** as far as that is concerned ◇ **a matter of opinion** a subject about which there are varying views ◇ **something** *or* **nothing is** *or* **nothing the matter** something is wrong ○ *What's the matter with the toaster?*

WORD KEY: SYNONYMS

See Synonyms at ***subject.***

Popperfoto

Matterhorn

Mat·ter·horn /máttər hàwrn/ steep pyramid-shaped peak in southwestern Switzerland, near the Italian border. Height: 14,692 ft./4,478 m.

mat·ter-of-fact *adj.* **1. RATIONAL** straightforward and not fanciful or emotional ○ *I admired her matter-of-fact approach to life.* **2. FACTUAL** dealing with facts and not emotions or opinions ○ *The report gave a very matter-of-fact account of the incident.* —**mat·ter-of-fact·ly** *adv.* —**mat·ter-of-fact·ness** *n.*

mat·ter·y /máttəree/ *adj.* secreting or discharging pus

matte shot *n.* in filmmaking, a visual effect that is achieved by masking out part of an image using a matte and superimposing another image so that it combines with the rest of the original

Matt·hau /mát ow/, **Walter** (*b.* 1920) U.S. actor. He is best known for his part in both stage and movie versions of *The Odd Couple* (1965, 1968). He won an Academy Award for *The Fortune Cookie* (1966). Real name **Walter Matasschanskayasky**

Mat·thew /máthyoo/, **St.** (*fl.* 1st century) Arabian apostle. He is credited with writing the Gospel According to Matthew.

Mat·thew *n.* the first of the gospels of the Bible in which the life and teachings of Jesus Christ are described. It is thought to have been written by St. Matthew. See table at **Bible**

Mat·thew Walk·er *n.* a type of knot made in the strands at the end of a rope [Mid-19thC. Probably the name of the person who invented or introduced it.]

Mat·thi·as /mə thí əss/ *n.* in the Bible, the disciple chosen to replace Judas as one of the 12 apostles of Jesus Christ (Acts 1:15–26)

Mat·thi·as Cor·vin·us /mə thí əss kawr vínəss/, **King of Hungary** (1443–90). His acquisition of Austria and various provinces made him a powerful ruler. He was also a patron of the arts.

mat·ting[1] /mátting/ *n.* **1. MATERIAL WOVEN FROM NATURAL FIBERS** a coarse material woven from natural fibers such as hemp or grass and used especially to make mats or other coverings ○ *coconut matting* **2. MATS** mats, taken collectively ○ *Matting is integral to Japanese interior design.* **3. LAYER OF NATURAL MATERIALS** a bed or layer formed by natural materials, e.g., by fallen leaves in a forest ○ *We walked throught the pines on a matting of needles.* **4. MAKING MATS** the process of making a mat or mats

mat·ting[2] /mátting/ *n.* **1. DULL SURFACE** a surface that is dull or without sheen **2. DULLING OF SURFACE** the process of giving a surface, especially a metallic one, a dull finish

mat·tock /máttək/ *n.* a tool like a pickax with one end of its blade flattened at right angles to its handle and used for loosening soil and cutting through roots [Pre-12thC. Origin uncertain: perhaps from assumed Vulgar Latin *matteuca* "club."]

mat·tress /mátrəss/ *n.* **1. PAD FOR SLEEPING ON** a large pad on which to sleep, usually containing springs or a material such as foam rubber, flock, horsehair, or straw. Some modern mattresses have electronic controls that allow them to tilt into different positions. **2. INFLATABLE PAD** a large pad that can be filled with air or water and used as a bed or for floating on, e.g., in a pool **3.** CONSTR **FOUNDATION** a slab or platform used as a foundation for a building [13thC. Via Old French *materas*, from, ultimately, Arabic *al-matraḥ* "carpet, cushion, bed," from the practice of sleeping on cushions, copied by Europeans from Arabs during the Crusades.]

mat·u·rate /máchə ràyt/ **(-rat·ed, -rat·ing, -rates)** *vti.* to mature, ripen, or develop, or develop or ripen something [Mid-16thC. Origin uncertain: either from Latin *maturare* (see MATURE) or a back-formation from MATURATION.] —**mat·u·ra·tive** *adj.*

mat·u·ra·tion /màchə ráysh'n/ *n.* **1. PROGRESS TO MATURITY** the process of becoming mature, ripe, or more developed **2. PROCESS OF MAKING SOMETHING MORE MATURE** the process of ripening or developing something, or of making it more mature **3.** BIOL **PROCESS OF CELL DEVELOPMENT** the process in which immature cells in the ovary and testes develop into ova and spermatozoa [14thC. Directly or via French from the medieval Latin stem *maturation-*, from, ultimately, *maturare* (see MATURE).] —**mat·u·ra·tion·al** *adj.*

mat·u·ra·tion di·vi·sion *n.* the process of cell division by which the ova and spermatozoa are developed

ma·ture /mə chóor/ *adj.* **1. ACTING OR SEEMING LIKE AN ADULT** showing mental, emotional, or physical characteristics that are typical of a fully developed adult person ○ *Philip is only 12 but he's very tall and already quite mature.* **2. EXPERIENCED** showing qualities gained by development and experience ○ *in the author's mature writings* **3. ADULT** adult or fully grown ○ *a mature animal capable of breeding* **4.** BIOL **FULLY DEVELOPED** fully developed to a complete or final stage **5.** FOOD, WINE **OLD AND OF GOOD FLAVOR** old enough to have acquired the maximum flavor ○ *mature cheddar* **6. IN LATER LIFE** no longer young ○ *They specialize in vacations for mature travelers.* **7. ADULT** made up of or suitable only for adults ○ *Because of the subject matter of this movie it is recommended for mature audiences only.* **8. INVOLVING SERIOUS THOUGHT** involving or reached by a period of serious thought ○ *On mature reflection, I feel it would be wiser to sell.* **9.** FIN **DUE FOR PAYMENT** used to describe a financial arrangement that has reached a previously set or mutually agreed-on time limit and is therefore due for payment or repayment ○ *mature bonds* **10.** COMM **NOT SUBJECT TO MAJOR CHANGE** no longer subject to the instability of early development or expansion ○ *Hydroelectric power is a mature industry in the region.* **11.** GEOL **IN THE MIDDLE OF AN EROSION CYCLE** used to describe a natural feature or landform that is in the middle stages of an erosion cycle ■ *v.* **(-tured, -tur·ing, -tures) 1.** *vti.* **DEVELOP** to go through, or make something or somebody go through, a developmental process ○ *Children begin to mature at different ages.* **2.** *vi.* FIN **FALL DUE FOR PAYMENT** to reach a previously set or mutually agreed-on time limit and therefore fall due for payment or repayment (*refers to a financial arrangement*) ○ *When will those Treasury bonds mature?* **3.** *vti.* **DEVELOP INTO SOMETHING FINISHED** to become fully worked out, or work something out fully, especially through long consideration ○ *The plan had matured over the intervening months.* [14thC. Directly or via French from Latin *maturus* "ripe, mature, timely, early" (source also of Old French *mur*, which produced English *demure*). The underlying idea is of "earliness, calmness."] —**ma·ture·ly** *adv.* —**ma·ture·ness** *n.*

ma·ture-on·set di·a·be·tes *n.* = **noninsulin-dependent diabetes**

ma·ture stu·dent *n.* a student aged 25 or over who has gone into higher education later than is usual, especially after working or raising a family

ma·tur·i·ty /mə chóorətee/ *n.* **1. FULL GROWTH OR DEVELOPMENT** the state or condition of being fully grown or developed ○ *Girls tend to reach maturity earlier than boys.* **2.** FIN **TIME FOR REPAYMENT** the time when a financial arrangement falls due for payment or repayment **3.** FIN **READINESS FOR REPAYMENT** the state of a financial arrangement when it falls due for payment or repayment **4. MATURE STATE** the condition of being ripe, fully aged, or fully grown, especially mentally or emotionally ○ *I'm amazed at the maturity shown by these young people.* **5.** GEOL **MATURE STATE OF A LANDFORM** the stage in the development of a landform at which there is maximum relief and drainage is well developed [15thC. Directly or via French *maturité* from Latin *maturitas*, from *maturus* (see MATURE).]

ma·tu·ti·nal /mə to͞ot'nəl, màchə tī́n'l/ *adj.* relating to or happening in the morning or in the early part of the day (*formal*) [Mid-16thC. From late Latin *matutinalis*, from *Matuta*, goddess of the dawn.] —**ma·tu·ti·nal·ly** *adv.*

MATV *abbr.* master antenna television

mat·zo /maátsə/, **mat·zoh** *n.* (*plural* **-zos** *or* **-zoth;** *plural* **-zohs** *or* **-zoth**) UNLEAVENED BREAD unleavened bread that is traditionally eaten during Passover in commemoration of the unleavened bread eaten by Hebrews escaping from slavery in Egypt ■ *adj.* OF OR FOR MATZO made from or like matzo, or used to make matzo ○ *matzo meal* ○ *matzo balls* [Mid-19thC. Via Yiddish *matse* from Hebrew *maṣṣāh*.]

mat·zoth plural of **matzo**

maud·lin /máwdlin/ *adj.* overly or tearfully sentimental, especially because affected by alcohol [Early 16thC. Via French *Madeleine* "Madeleine," from, ultimately, Greek *Mariaē Magdalēnē* "Mary Magdalene," because she was commonly represented in medieval art weeping in repentance.] —**maud·lin·ism** *n.* —**maud·lin·ly** *adv.* —**maud·lin·ness** *n.*

Mau·i /mówee/ the second largest island of Hawaii, consisting of two oval peninsulas connected by an isthmus. Population: 100,374 (1990). Area: 727 sq. mi./1,884 sq. km.

maul /mawl/ *vt.* (**mauled, mauling, mauls**) **1.** ASSAULT OR ATTACK SOMEBODY to beat, batter, or tear at a person or animal ○ *He got mauled in the ring by a better boxer.* **2.** HANDLE SOMEBODY OR SOMETHING ROUGHLY to handle somebody or something too roughly or clumsily ○ *Children may need to be taught not to maul their pets.* **3.** CRITICIZE SOMEBODY OR SOMETHING FIERCELY to criticize somebody or something severely or mercilessly ○ *Despite being a box-office success, her new movie was mauled by the critics.* **4.** to split wood using a large heavy hammer and a wedge ■ *n.* **1.** CONSTR PILE-DRIVING HAMMER a large heavy hammer, usually with a wooden head, that is used for driving in piles, stakes, or wedges **2.** LOG-SPLITTING HAMMER a heavy hammer that has one side of the head shaped like a wedge, making it suitable for splitting logs or wood [13thC. Via Old French *mail* "hammer" (source of English *mallet*) from Latin *malleus* (source of English *malleable* and *mall* "shopping precinct"). Originally in the sense "to strike with a hammer."] —**maul·er** *n.*

Maul·din /máwldin/, **Bill** (*b.* 1921) U.S. cartoonist. He is known for his cartoons of World War II seen from the combat soldier's point of view, particularly via his two characters Willie and Joe. Full name **William Henry Mauldin**

Mau Mau /mów mòw/ *npl.* a secret Kenyan organization set up in 1952 with the aim of forcing European settlers from the land and ending British rule in Kenya [Mid-20thC. From Kikuyu.]

mau-mau /mow mów/ (**mau-maued, mau-mauing, mau-maus**) *vt.* **mau-mau** (**mau-mauing, mau-maus**) to confront somebody, e.g., a public official or bureaucrat, with the intent of gaining concessions, benefits, or advantage through intimidation (*slang*)

Mau·na Ke·a /màwnə keé ə/ dormant volcano in Hawaii, on northern Hawaii Island. It is the highest point in the state, 13,796 ft./4,205 m.

Mau·na Lo·a /màwnə lṓ ə, mównə-/ active volcano on Hawaii Island. It is one of the world's largest volcanoes. Height: 13,680 ft./4,170 m.

maund *n.* a unit of weight used in the Indian subcontinent, with a value that varies from place to place but is often equal to 82 lb./37 kg [Late 16thC. From Arabic *mann*.]

maun·der /máwn dər/ (**maun·dered, maun·der·ing, maunders**) *v.* **1.** *vti.* SAY SOMETHING VAGUE OR INCOHERENT to talk or say something in a vague, rambling, or incoherent way **2.** *vi.* MOVE OR ACT WITHOUT PURPOSE to move or act in a vague, aimless, or directionless way [Early 17thC. Origin uncertain: perhaps formed from earlier *maund* "to beg" in the literal sense of "to keep on begging," or perhaps an imitation of the sound of muttering.] —**maunderer** /máwn dər ər/ *n.*

maun·dy /máwn dee/ *n.* a ceremony held in some Christian churches on Maundy Thursday that involves an actual or symbolic washing of people's feet in commemoration of Jesus Christ's washing of his disciples' feet (John 13:3–34) [13thC. Via Old French *mandé* from Latin *mandatum* "commandment" (source also of English *mandate*), in *mandatum novum* "new commandment," the first words of an antiphon sung in the ceremony.]

Maun·dy /máwn dee/ *n.* the distribution of Maundy money by the British sovereign

Maun·dy mon·ey *n.* specially minted silver coins that the British sovereign distributes in a church ceremony on Maundy Thursday

Maun·dy Thurs·day *n.* the Thursday before Easter Sunday, observed in Christian belief in commemoration of the Last Supper. ◊ **Holy Thursday**

Guy de Maupassant

Mau·pas·sant /mṓ pass oN, mṑ pass aáN/, **Guy de** (1850–93) French novelist and short-story writer. His short stories have been particularly influential and are written with a direct realism, portraying ordinary people in extraordinary situations. Full name **Henri René Albert Guy de Maupassant**

Mauritania

Mau·ri·ta·ni·a /màw rə táynee ə/ republic in northwestern Africa. It became independent from France in 1960. Language: Arabic, French. Currency: ouguiya. Capital: Nouakchott. Population: 2,333,000 (1996). Area: 397,955 sq. mi./1,030,700 sq. km. Official name **Islamic Republic of Mauritania** —**Mau·ri·ta·ni·an** *n., adj.*

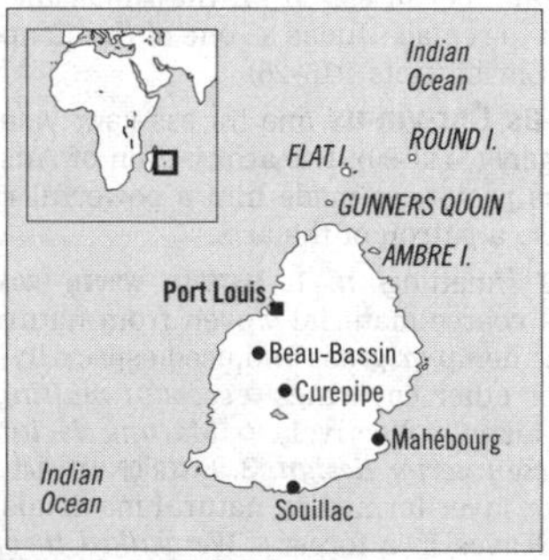

Mauritius

Mau·ri·tius /mə ríshəss/ island republic in the western Indian Ocean consisting of the islands of Mauritius and Rodrigues and some islets. Language: English. Currency: Mauritian rupee. Capital: Port Louis. Population: 1,141,000 (1996). Area: 790 sq. mi./2,045 sq. km. Official name **Republic of Mauritius** —**Mau·ri·tian** /ma ríshən/ *n., adj.*

Mau·ser /mówzər/ *tdmk.* a trademark for a repeating rifle and other firearms

mau·so·le·um /màwzə leé əm, màwssə-/ (*plural* **-ums** *or* **-a** /-leé ə/) *n.* **1.** TOMB a large tomb, especially one that is ornately decorated or made from expensive stone **2.** BUILDING CONTAINING TOMBS a building, often a highly decorated or elaborate one, that houses a tomb or several tombs **3.** GLOOMY INTERIOR a large gloomy oppressive room or building ○ *I can't study in the library; it's a mausoleum.* [15thC. Via Latin from Greek *Mausōleion* "tomb of Mausolus" (a 4th-century B.C. king of Caria in Asia Minor), built in 353 B.C. at Halicarnassus (now Bodrum in Turkey).] —**mau·so·le·an** *adj.*

mauve /mōv/ *n.* a pale color between purple and blue or pink [Mid-19thC. Via French from Latin *malva* "mallow plant" (source of English *mallow*); from the color of its flowers.] —**mauve** *adj.*

ma·ven /máyvən/, **ma·vin** *n.* somebody who is an expert or knowledgeable enthusiast in a particular field [Mid-20thC. Via Yiddish *meyvn* from Hebrew *mēḇīn*, literally "somebody who understands."]

mav·er·ick /mávvərik, mávvrik/ *n.* **1.** INDEPENDENT PERSON somebody who holds independent views and who refuses to conform to the accepted or orthodox thinking on a subject **2.** AGRIC UNBRANDED ANIMAL an unbranded animal, especially a calf that has become separated from its mother and herd. By convention, it can become the property of whoever finds it and brands it. [Mid-19thC. Origin uncertain: probably named for Samuel Augustus *Maverick* (1803–70), a Texas cattle owner who did not brand some of his calves.]

ma·vin *n.* = **maven**

ma·vis /máyviss/ *n.* a songthrush (*literary*) [14thC. From French *mauvis*, of uncertain origin: probably formed from *mauve* "gull," from Old English *mǣw* (source of English *mew*).]

maw /maw/ *n.* **1.** ANIMAL'S MOUTH the mouth, jaws, throat, or stomach of an animal, especially a carnivorous animal that devours food greedily **2.** GREEDY PERSON'S MOUTH the mouth, throat, or stomach of a greedy person (*informal*) **3.** GAPING HOLE anything that seems like a gaping hole that devours things or people ○ *the ravenous maw of readers' expectations* [Old English *maga* "stomach." From a prehistoric Germanic word that is also the ancestor of Welsh *megin* "bellows" and Lithuanian *makas* "purse," the underlying idea being "bag."]

mawk·ish /máwkish/ *adj.* **1.** SENTIMENTAL sentimental, especially in a contrived or offputting way **2.** BLAND OR UNPLEASANT bland or unappetizing in taste or smell [Mid-17thC. Formed from earlier *mawk* "maggot," from Old Norse *maðkr*. Originally in the sense "nauseated, lacking appetite."] —**mawk·ish·ly** *adv.* —**mawk·ish·ness** *n.*

Maw·lid al-Na·bi /màwlid al naábee/ *n.* in Islam, the celebrations held in honor of the prophet Muhammad's birthday, which falls on the 12th day of the month of Rabi I [From Arabic, literally "birthday of the prophet"]

max /maks/ *n.* MAXIMUM the maximum limit or amount of something (*informal*) ○ *I could lend you $100, but that's my max.* ■ *adj.* MOST most or highest (*slang*) ○ *Turn up the volume to get the max effect.* ■ *adv.* AT THE MOST as a maximum (*slang*) ○ *We were offered $200 max.* ■ *vi.* (**maxed, max·ing, max·es**) REACH THE HIGHEST LIMIT to come to the point that it is impossible to exceed (*slang*) ○ *The car maxes at 120 mph.* [Mid-19thC. Shortening of MAXIMUM.]

max out *vti.* to reach a limit in a personal attribute or ability, or reach the limit of a resource (*slang*) ○ *started strong but maxed out after 12 hours* ○ *I maxed out my credit card last week.*

max. *abbr.* maximum

max·i /máksee/ *n.* **1.** ANKLE-LENGTH PIECE OF CLOTHING an ankle-length coat, skirt, or dress **2.** CRIMINOL MAXIMUM SECURITY PRISON a maximum security prison (*informal*) ■ *adj.* ANKLE-LENGTH used to describe an article of clothing that is ankle-length. ◊ **mini** [Mid-20thC. From MAXIMUM.]

max·il·la /mak síllə/ (*plural* **-lae** /-leé/ *or* **-las**) *n.* **1.** UPPER JAW OF VERTEBRATES either of a pair of bones that are fused at the midline and together form the upper jawbone in vertebrates **2.** MOUTHPART OF ARTHROPODS a mouthpart that is one of one or two pairs behind the mandibles of arthropods [Late 17thC. Directly and via Old French *maxille* from Latin *maxilla*, literally "little jaw," from *mala* "jaw."] —**max·il·lar·y** *adj.*

max·il·li·ped /mak síllə pèd/ *n.* one of the six specialized feeding appendages arranged in pairs and located just behind the maxillae on the heads of crustaceans [Mid-19thC. Coined from MAXILLA + -I- + -PED.] —**max·il·li·ped·ar·y** /mak sillə péddəree, -peédəree/ *adj.*

max·il·lo·fa·cial /mak sìllō fáysh'l/ *adj.* relating to, located in, or affecting the face in the region of the upper jaw [Early 20thC. From MAXILLA + FACIAL.]

max·im /máksim/ *n.* **1.** SAYING a succinct or pithy saying that has some proven truth to it **2.** GENERAL RULE a general rule, principle, or truth [15thC. Via French from medieval Latin *maxima*, literally "largest," used as a noun (a shortening of *maxima propositio* "largest proposition," hence "fundamental axiom"), a form of *maximus* (see MAXIMUM).]

Max·im *n.* = **Maxim gun**

Max·im /máksim/, **Sir Hiram** (1840–1916) U.S.-born British engineer and inventor. He is best known for inventing the Maxim gun, an automatic machine gun.

max·i·ma plural of **maximum**

max·i·mal /máksim'l/ *adj.* **1.** CONSTITUTING A MAXIMUM relating to or constituting a maximum **2.** BEST POSSIBLE the best or greatest possible —**max·i·mal·ly** *adv.*

max·i·mal·ist /máksimәlist/ *n.* somebody who is determined to achieve a political aim, by direct action or intervention if necessary, and is unwilling to compromise [Early 20thC. Formed from MAXIMAL on the model of Russian *maksimalist*.] —**max·i·ma·list** *adj.*

Max·i·mal·ist *n.* a member of a Russian group that, in the early 20th century, advocated terrorist action to get rid of the tsar and the setting up of a temporary proletarian dictatorship

Max·im gun *n.* an early single-barreled machine gun that was cooled by an outer casing containing water [Late 19thC. Named for Sir Hiram MAXIM who invented it.]

Max·i·mil·ian /màksi míllee әn/, **Archduke of Austria** (1832–67). He was made Emperor of Mexico by Napoleon III of France in 1863, but was executed by Mexican republicans.

Max·i·mil·ian I, Holy Roman Emperor (1459–1519). He made the Hapsburg Dynasty a major power through diplomacy and marriage policy.

max·i·min /máksimin/ *n.* **1.** MATH LARGEST OF A SET the largest of a set of minimum values **2.** STRATEGY OF INCREASING SMALLEST ADVANTAGE in game theory, a strategy of attempting to maximize the smallest possible advantage [Mid-20thC. Blend of MAXIMUM and MINIMUM; modeled on MINIMAX.]

max·i·mize /máksi mīz/ (**-mized, -miz·ing, -miz·es**) *vt.* **1.** INCREASE SOMETHING TO THE MAXIMUM to make something as large as possible ○ *You can maximise the picture by clicking on this button.* **2.** REGARD SOMETHING AS MOST IMPORTANT to attach the greatest importance to something ○ *Historians maximize the treaty's benefits to trade and tend not to mention its political costs.* **3.** MATH FIND A FUNCTION'S LARGEST VALUE to find or work out the largest value of a function —**max·i·mi·za·tion** /màksimi záysh'n/ *n.* —**max·i·miz·er** /máksi mīzәr/ *n.*

max·i·mum /máksimәm/ *n.* (*plural* **-ma** /-mә/ *or* **-mums**) **1.** GREATEST POSSIBLE AMOUNT the largest or greatest amount, number, extent, or degree possible or allowed ○ *The stadium seats a maximum of 60,000.* **2.** HIGHEST AMOUNT OR LEVEL REACHED the largest amount, level, or value that something variable can reach or reaches during a period ○ *Even at its maximum, the noise did not exceed legal levels.* **3.** MATH LARGEST NUMBER the largest number in a set **4.** MATH FUNCTION'S GREATEST VALUE the greatest value that a continuous function can attain over a specific interval **5.** ASTRON TIME OF A STAR'S GREATEST BRIGHTNESS the interval during which a variable star is most luminous **6.** ASTRON VARIABLE STAR'S MAGNITUDE the magnitude of a variable star at its greatest ■ *adj.* GREATEST POSSIBLE of the greatest possible or permitted amount or value ○ *visual effects with maximum impact* ○ *Maximum occupancy in this building is 235.* ■ *adv.* AT THE MAXIMUM at the maximum extent ○ *The hall seats 400 maximum.* [Mid-16thC. Directly or via French from modern Latin, a form of Latin *maximus* "greatest" (used as a noun), from *magnus* "great" (source of English *magnify*).]

max·i·mum-se·cu·ri·ty *adj.* protected or made secure by tight and elaborate security arrangements ○ *a maximum-security prison*

ma·xixe /mә shéesh, -shéeshә/ *n.* **1.** DANCE BRAZILIAN DANCE a Brazilian dance performed in duple time **2.** MUSIC MUSIC FOR MAXIXE music suitable for a maxixe [Early 20thC. From Brazilian Portuguese.]

max·well /máks wèl, mákswәl/ *n.* the centimeter-gram-second unit of magnetic flux, equal to the flux over one square centimeter perpendicular to a magnetic field of one gauss. Symbol **Mx** [Late 19thC. Named for James Clerk *Maxwell* (1831–79), a Scottish physicist.]

may[1] /may/ (**might** /mīt/, **may**) CORE MEANING: a modal verb indicating that something could be true, or could have happened, or will possibly happen in the future ○ *I may not be able to meet you.* ○ *He may have been working too hard.* ○ *A verdict may be announced today.*

v. **1.** INDICATES POSSIBILITY indicates that something is possibly true ○ *I may have left my book on the bus.* **2.** INDICATES THAT SOMETHING COULD HAPPEN indicates that something could have happened, or could happen in the future ○ *The crash may well have been caused by faulty brakes.* ○ *The comet may be remembered best for its nonscientific impact.* **3.** INDICATES PERMISSION indicates that somebody is asking somebody for permission or giving somebody permission to do something (*formal*) ○ *"May I leave the table?" "No, you may not."* **4.** INDICATES A RIGHT indicates that somebody has a legal or moral right to do something ○ *You may withdraw money from this account at any time.* **5.** INDICATES REQUESTS OR SUGGESTIONS indicates polite requests, suggestions, or offers ○ *May I remind you of our earlier agreement?* ○ *May I help you with that bag?* **6.** INDICATES A WISH indicates that somebody wishes for something very strongly (*formal*) ○ *May God bless us, every one.* [Old English *mæg*, a form of *magan* "to be able." Ultimately from an Indo-European base that is also the ancestor of English *machine* and *magic*.] ◇ **come what may** whatever happens ○ *He swore that, come what may, he would never let her out of his sight again.*

WORD KEY: USAGE

See Usage note at ***can***.

may[2] /may/ *n. U.K.* = **may blossom** [From MAY, this being the month in which it comes into flower]

May *n.* in the Gregorian calendar, the fifth month of the year, made up of 31 days [12thC. Via French *mai* from Latin *Maius*, a form of *Maia* "Maia" (a fertility goddess).]

May, Cape /may/ cape at the southern tip of New Jersey, at the entrance to Delaware Bay

ma·ya /maá yә/ *n.* **1.** ILLUSION OF MATERIAL WORLD in Hinduism, the material world, considered in reality to be an illusion **2.** ABILITY TO CREATE ILLUSION in Hinduism, the ability to create illusion through supernatural, magical, or sacred power [Late 18thC. From Sanskrit *māyā*.] —**ma·yan** *adj.*

Ma·ya[1] /maá yaa/ (*plural* **-ya** *or* **-yas**) *n.* **1.** PEOPLES MEMBER OF A CENTRAL AMERICAN PEOPLE a member of a Native American people of Central America and southern Mexico whose classical culture featured highly developed mathematics, religion, writing, and monumental architecture. It flourished from the 4th to the 8th century A.D., and was in decline by the 12th century. **2.** LANG NATIVE AMERICAN LANGUAGE a Mayan language spoken in parts of Mexico, Guatemala, and Belize. Maya is spoken by about half a million people. [Early 19thC. Via Spanish from Maya.] —**Ma·ya** *adj.*

Ma·ya[2] /maá yә/ *n.* the mother of the Buddha, by a miraculous virgin birth

Ma·ya·güez /maà yaa gwáyz/ city and seaport in western Puerto Rico. Population: 100,937 (1996).

AKG London

Vladimir Mayakovsky

Ma·ya·kov·sky /maàyә káwfskee/, **Vladimir** (1893–1930) Russian poet and propagandist. He wrote propaganda for the Bolsheviks after the Russian Revolution, but later fell from favor and committed suicide. Full name **Vladimir Vladimirovich Mayakovsky**

Ma·yan /maá yәn/ *adj.* OF THE MAYA relating to the Maya, their classical culture, or their language ■ *n.* **1.** PEOPLES MEMBER OF THE MAYA a member of the Maya people **2.** LANG GROUP OF CENTRAL AMERICAN LANGUAGES a group of Native Middle American languages spoken in parts of Mexico, Guatemala, and Belize. It forms a branch of the Penutian family of languages.

Ma·ya·pán /maà yaa paán/ ruined ancient Mayan city in southeastern Mexico, in Yucatan State

May ap·ple *n.* **1.** PLANT WITH A SINGLE YELLOW FRUIT a plant of the barberry family that grows in eastern North America. It has a single white flower that produces an oval yellowish fruit with edible pulp. Other parts of the plant, notably the roots, leaves, and seeds, are poisonous. Latin name: *Podophyllum peltatum.* **2.** FRUIT OF MAY APPLE PLANT the edible fruit of the May apple plant [Because the fruit is produced in the month of May]

may·be /máybee/ *adv.* **1.** PERHAPS expresses uncertainty ○ *Maybe I'm being too optimistic, but I really think we can get the best players.* **2.** NEITHER YES NOR NO used to give a response that is neither yes nor no ○ *"So do you want to come with us or not?" "Well, maybe."* **3.** INTRODUCES SUGGESTIONS used to introduce advice or suggestions ○ *Maybe you should ask her what she means before you jump to conclusions.* **4.** APPROXIMATELY indicates an approximate estimation, e.g. of frequency or a number ○ *The coastal glacier gives off large icebergs maybe every three or four years.* ○ *The forests in this region are no more than 60, maybe 70, years old.* [14thC. From the phrase *(it) may be*.]

May bee·tle *n.* **1.** = **June bug 2.** *U.K.* = **cockchafer** [Because they appear in late spring]

may blos·som *n. U.K.* the flower of the hawthorn

May bug *n.* **1.** = **June bug 2.** *U.K.* = **cockchafer** [See MAY BEETLE]

may·day /máy dày/ *n.* the internationally recognized communications distress call, used especially by ships and aircraft [Early 20thC. Representing the pronunciation of French *m'aider* in *venez m'aider* "come and help me!"]

May Day *n.* **1.** SPRING FESTIVAL the first of May, traditionally a time for celebrating the coming of spring, often with dancing around a maypole, sports, and other festivities **2.** HOLIDAY IN RECOGNITION OF WORKERS the first of May, a national holiday in some countries in recognition of the importance of workers, and a time when workers march and demonstrate to show their solidarity. It is called Labor Day in many countries, but in the United States Labor Day is in early September.

May·er /máy әr/, **Louis Burt** (1885–1957) Russian-born U.S. movie producer. He created and ran the Metro-Goldwyn-Mayer movie studio (1924–51). Real name **Lazar Meir**

may·est *v.* = **mayst**

may·flow·er /máy flòwr/ (*plural* **-ers** *or* **-er**) *n.* **1.** PLANT THAT FLOWERS IN MAY any of various plants that flower in May **2.** = **trailing arbutus**

may·fly /máy flī/ (*plural* **-flies**) *n.* **1.** INSECTS SHORT-LIVED INSECT any one of various insects that live as adults for only a few days, typically having two or four pairs of flimsy wings and two or three long slender tail appendages. The female lays her eggs in fresh water, where the larvae develop without a chrysalis stage. Order: Ephemeroptera. **2.** ANGLING FISHING FLY a fishing fly that looks like a mayfly [Mid-17thC. From a mistaken belief that they appear only in May.]

may·hap /máy hàp/ *adv.* perhaps (*archaic*) [Mid-16thC. From the phrase *it may hap* "it may happen (by chance)."]

may·hem /máy hèm/ *n.* **1.** CHAOS absolute chaos or severe disruption (*informal*) ○ *Whenever the teacher left the room, it was mayhem.* **2.** LAW SERIOUS AND DELIBERATE INJURY malicious injury that disfigures or disables a person [15thC. Via Anglo-Norman *mahem* and Old French *mahaing* "mutilating injury" (the original sense in English), from, ultimately, assumed Vulgar Latin *mahagnare* "to injure" (source also of English *maim*).]

may·ing /máy ing/, **May·ing** *n.* May Day celebrations, or participation in them

may·n't /maynt/ *contr.* may not

may·o /máy ò/ (*plural* **-os**) *n.* mayonnaise (*informal*) [Mid-20thC. Shortening.]

Ma·yo /máy ō/, **William Worral** (1819–1911) U.S. physician and surgeon. He ran St. Mary's Hospital in Minnesota, which later became the Mayo Clinic.

may·on·naise /máy ə nàyz, mà
y ə náyz/ *n.* a rich creamy sauce or dressing made from egg yolks, vegetable oil, vinegar, lemon juice, and spices, and served with salads, sandwiches, and other foods [Early 19thC. Origin uncertain: probably from French.]

WORD KEY: ORIGIN

There are several conflicting theories about the origin of *mayonnaise*, among them that it is an alteration of *bayonnaise*, as if the sauce originated in Bayonne, in southwestern France; that it was derived from the French verb *manier* "to stir"; and that it goes back to Old French *mayou* "egg yolk." But the early variant spelling *mahonnaise* suggests that it originally meant literally "of Mahon," and that the sauce was so named to commemorate the taking of Port Mahon, the capital of the island of Minorca, by the duc de Richelieu in 1756.

Ma·yon Vol·ca·no /ma yŏn-/ active volcano in the northeastern Philippines, on Luzon Island, beside the city of Legaspi. Height: 7,943 ft./2,421 m.

may·or /máyər/ *n.* the person elected to be head of government in a city, town, or borough in many countries including the United States, and in the United Kingdom except for Scotland [13thC. Via French *maire* from Latin *major*, literally "more great" (source also of English *major*), from *magnus* "great" (source of English *maximum*).] —**may·or·al** *adj.* —**may·or·ship** *n.*

WORD KEY: CULTURAL NOTE

The Mayor of Casterbridge, a novel by English writer Thomas Hardy (1886). It is the tragic story of Michael Henchard, a laborer whose success in business raises him to the position of mayor of his hometown, but who then loses his fortune as a result of a petty dispute with his assistant. An instructive character study, it is also a revealing portrait of contemporary rural mores.

may·or·al·ty /máyərəl tee/ (*plural* **-ties**) *n.* **1. MAYOR'S OFFICIAL POSITION** the official position held by a mayor ○ *The mayoralty was fiercely contested.* **2. MAYOR'S PERIOD IN OFFICE** the length of time that a mayor holds office ○ *a five-year mayoralty* ○ *one of the longest mayoralties in New York history*

may·or·ess /máyərəss/ *n.* the wife of a mayor (*dated*)

Ma·yotte /ma yáwt/ island in the western Indian Ocean near Madagascar, an overseas dependency of France. One of the Comoros islands, it stayed under French control when the remaining islands declared independence in 1975. Language: French. Currency: French franc. Capital: Mamoudzou. Population: 108,000 (1996). Area: 144 sq. mi./373 sq. km.

may·pole /máy pōl/ *n.* a tall pole that is traditionally erected for May Day celebrations, usually decorated with flowers and with long colored ribbons attached at the top. Dancers each take hold of the end of a ribbon and dance around the pole so that the ribbons become wrapped around the pole, forming colored patterns.

may·pop /máy pòp/ *n.* **1. CLIMBING PLANT WITH EDIBLE FRUIT** a climbing plant of the southeastern United States that has purple and white flowers, three-lobed leaves, and edible but somewhat tasteless yellow fruit. Latin name: *Passiflora incarnata.* **2. FRUIT OF THE MAYPOP PLANT** the fruit of the maypop plant [Mid-19thC. Alteration of earlier *maycock*, a kind of melon, from obsolete *maracock* "maypop," of uncertain origin: perhaps from Virginian Algonquian.]

May queen *n.* a young woman chosen, often for her beauty and charm, to reign over a May Day celebration

Mays /máyz/, **Willie** (*b.* 1931) U.S. baseball player. Considered one of the greatest players of all time, he was the first player to hit 300 home runs and steal 300 bases. Full name **Willie Howard, Jr Mays**. Known as **the Say Hey Kid**

mayst /mayst/, **may·est** *v.* 2nd person present singular of **may**[1] (*archaic*)

may·weed /máy wēed/ *n.* a straggly weed of the daisy family that has foul-smelling leaves and white flowers resembling daisies. Latin name: *Anthemis cotula.* [Mid-16thC. *May* an alteration of earlier *maythe* "mayweed, camomile," from Old English *magoþe*.]

May wine *n.* **1. WINE FLAVORED WITH WOODRUFF** a white wine flavored with woodruff **2. WINE PUNCH FLAVORED WITH WOODRUFF** a punch of champagne, claret, and other wines flavored with woodruff [Translation of German *Maiwein*]

ma·zal·tov /maáz'l tàwv/, **ma·zal tov** *interj.* = **mazeltov**

Maz·a·rin /mázər ìn, ma za ráN/, **Jules, Cardinal** (1602–61) Italian-born French clergyman and statesman. He virtually governed France during the minority of Louis XIV, when his absolutist policies resulted in the antiroyalist rebellions known as the Fronde (1648–53). He negotiated the Peace of Westphalia (1648) and the Treaty of the Pyrenees (1659), ending major European wars. Born **Giulio Raimondo Mazzarino**

Ma·za·tlán /maàzatlaán/ city, seaport, and tourist resort in western Mexico. Population: 314,345 (1990).

Maz·da·ism /mázdə ìzzəm/, **Maz·de·ism** *n.* RELIG = **Zoroastrianism** [Late 19thC. Formed from Avestan *mazdā*, from *Ahura Mazda*, the name of the supreme god of ancient Persian religion.]

maze /mayz/ *n.* **1. PUZZLE MADE OF CONNECTING PATHS** an area of interconnected weaving paths that is difficult to find a way through, especially one in a garden with hedges between the paths or one designed for laboratory animals **2. PUZZLE OF TRACING A ROUTE THROUGH LINES** a diagrammatic version of a maze, where the object is to arrive at a specific point by tracing a route with a pen or pencil **3. CONFUSING NETWORK OF PATHS** a network, especially of paths, streets, or passageways, that a walker or driver might easily become lost in ○ *a maze of narrow passageways* **4. CONFUSING MUDDLE** any confusing tangle or muddle, e.g., of regulations or procedures, that is difficult to negotiate ○ *a maze of official rules* ■ *vt.* (**mazed, maz·ing, maz·es**) *Southern U.S., U.K.* **ASTONISH SOMEBODY** to astonish, stun, or stupefy somebody (*regional*) [13thC. Shortening of AMAZE, originally in the sense "to stupefy, daze."]

ma·zel·tov /maáz'l tàwv/, **ma·zel tov, ma·zal·tov, ma·zal tov** *interj.* used to express good wishes or congratulations [Mid-19thC. From modern Hebrew *mazzāl ṭōḇ*, literally "good star."]

Mazer

ma·zer /máyzər/ *n.* a large drinking cup or bowl, usually made from hardwood or metal (*archaic*) [13thC. Via Old French *masere* "kind of hardwood, maple," and perhaps reinforced by Middle Dutch *maeser* "maple," from prehistoric Germanic. Originally, "hardwood (such as maple) for making cups."]

ma·zour·ka *n.* = **mazurka**

ma·zu·ma /mə zóomə/ *n.* money, especially cash or loose change (*informal*) [20th C. From Yiddish.]

ma·zur·ka /mə zúrkə, -zóorkə/, **ma·zour·ka** *n.* **1.** DANCE **LIVELY POLISH DANCE** a Polish national dance, similar to the polka **2.** MUSIC **MUSIC FOR A MAZURKA** a piece of music composed for or suitable for the mazurka, usually in three-four time and having several repeated sections [Early 19thC. Origin uncertain: probably via Russian from Polish *mazurek* "dance of an inhabitant of Mazovia (an ancient part of Poland)," from *mazur* "inhabitant of Mazovia."]

maz·y /máyzee/ (**-i·er, -i·est**) *adj.* **1. LIKE A MAZE** tangled and interwoven like a maze **2. CONFUSING** confusing or complicated —**maz·i·ly** *adv.* —**maz·i·ness** *n.*

maz·zard /mázzərd/ *n.* **1.** TREES **WILD CHERRY TREE** a wild sweet cherry tree that fruit growers often use as grafting stock for cultivated varieties of cherry. Latin name: *Prunus avium.* **2.** HOUSEHOLD = **mazer** (*archaic*) [Late 16thC. Origin uncertain.]

mb *abbr.* millibar

MB *abbr.* **1.** Bachelor of Medicine **2.** Manitoba **3.** COMPUT megabyte **4.** Medal of Bravery

M.B.A., MBA *abbr.* Master of Business Administration

Mba·bane /əmba baánee/ town and capital of Swaziland, located in the western part of the country near the border with South Africa. Population: 42,000 (1992).

mbi·ra /əm beérə/ *n.* an African musical instrument that has a resonating box, often a hollow gourd, with tuned strips of wood or metal attached to it that are plucked using the thumbs [Late 19thC. From Bantu.]

MBO *abbr.* **1.** management by objectives **2.** management buyout

Mbu·ji-Ma·yi /əmbóojə mí ee/ town in south central Democratic Republic of the Congo, the capital of Kasai-Oriental Region. Population: 806,475 (1994).

Mbyte *abbr.* COMPUT megabyte

mc *abbr.* millicurie

Mc *symbol.* megacycle

MC *abbr.* **1.** Marine Corps **2.** master of ceremonies **3.** Medical Corps **4.** Midheaven **5.** Military Cross

M.C. *abbr.* Member of Congress

MCAT *abbr.* Medical College Admissions Test

mCi *symbol.* millicurie

M.Com. *abbr.* Master of Commerce

MCP *abbr.* male chauvinist pig (*informal insult*)

MCPO *abbr.* master chief petty officer

Md *symbol.* mendelevium

MD *abbr.* **1.** Maryland **2.** medical department **3.** Doctor of Medicine **4.** BANKING memorandum of deposit **5.** muscular dystrophy **6.** musical director

Md. *abbr.* Maryland

M.D. *abbr.* Doctor of Medicine

m/d[1] *abbr.* COMM months after date

m/d[2], **M/d** *abbr.* months after date

M-day *abbr.* mobilization day

M.Div. *abbr.* Master of Divinity

Mdm. *abbr.* Madam

MDMA *n.* the drug Ecstasy. Full form **methylenedioxymethamphetamine**

M.D.S. *abbr.* Master of Dental Surgery

mdse. *abbr.* merchandise

MDT *abbr.* Mountain Daylight Time

me[1] /mee/ *pron.* **1. THE SPEAKER OR WRITER** used to refer to the speaker or writer ○ *asked her to do me a big favor* ○ *Listen to me!* ○ *Was it me?* **2. PERSONALITY OF THE SPEAKER OR WRITER** used to refer to the personality of the speaker or writer, or something that may express it (*informal*) ○ *I don't think I like this hat; it isn't really me.* **3. MYSELF** myself (*informal*) ○ *I'll get me a new boyfriend, see if I don't.* [Old English *mē, me.* Ultimately from an Indo-European word that is also the ancestor of English *mine*, French *me*, Greek *me, emé*, Welsh and Irish *mi*, and German *mich*.]

me[2] *n.* MUSIC = **mi**

Me *symbol.* methyl

ME *abbr.* **1.** Maine **2.** mechanical engineer **3.** Methodist Episcopal **4.** Middle English **5.** mining engineer **6.** Most Excellent

Me. *abbr.* Maine

M.E. *abbr.* Middle English

me·a cul·pa /mày ə kóol paá/ *interj.* **EXPRESSING GUILT OR FAULT** used to express an admission of your own guilt (*formal or humorous*) ■ *n.* **FORMAL APOLOGY** a formal apology or acknowledgment of responsibility or guilt ○ *His grudging mea culpa failed to soothe feelings.* [From Latin, literally "(through) my fault," these words being taken from the prayer of confession in the Roman Catholic Church's Latin liturgy]

mead[1] /meed/ *n.* an alcoholic drink made by fermenting honey with water, often with added spices [Old English *me(o)du.* Ultimately from an Indo-European word meaning "honey, sweet drink," which is also the ancestor of Greek *methu* "wine" (source of English *amethyst*).]

mead[2] /meed/ *n.* a meadow (*archaic or literary*) [Old English *mæd* (see MEADOW)]

Mead, Lake /meed/ artificial lake in Arizona and Nevada, formed by the Hoover Dam across the Colorado River. Area: 233 sq. mi./603 sq. km.

Mead, George Herbert (1863–1931) U.S. philosopher and social psychologist. He developed theories of self and self-consciousness.

Popperfoto

Margaret Mead

Mead, Margaret (1901–78) U.S. anthropologist. In such influential books as *Coming of Age in Samoa* (1928) she formalized her field work research on child care, adolescence, and sexual behavior in North American society and nonindustrial societies.

Meade, George Gordon (1815–72) U.S. Union general. He commanded the Army of the Potomac (1863–65) in the Revolution.

mead·ow /méddō/ *n.* **1.** GRASSY FIELD a grassy field used for producing hay or for grazing domestic livestock **2.** GRASSY AREA an area of low-lying grassland, especially a marshy one near a river [Old English *mǣdwe*, a form of *mǣd*, from, ultimately, an Indo-European base meaning "to cut grass with a scythe," which is also the ancestor of English *mow*] —**mead·ow·y** *adj.*

mead·ow beau·ty *n.* any of several related low-growing perennial plants with pretty purple flowers that grow in marshy ground in North America. Genus: *Rhexia*.

mead·ow fern *n.* = **sweet gale**

mead·ow fes·cue *n.* a perennial grass that grows throughout Europe and Asia and has shiny leaves and stem bases that are surrounded by brown sheaths. Latin name: *Festuca pratensis*.

mead·ow grass·hop·per *n.* a large green grasshopper with delicate wings that look like leaves and help it to remain concealed among foliage. Latin name: *Tettigonia viridissima*.

mead·ow·land /méddō lànd/ *n.* a large area of land that is made up of meadows

mead·ow·lark /méddō laàrk/ (*plural* **-larks** *or* **-lark**) *n.* either of two related North American songbirds of the blackbird family that have brown speckled feathers, a yellow breast, and a black crescent-shaped mark just under the bill. Genus: *Sturnella*.

mead·ow mouse *n.* a field mouse or vole

mead·ow mush·room *n.* an edible mushroom that grows in European grassland. It has a white cap, a white stem, and pink gills that turn to brown as it matures. Latin name: *Agaricus campestris*.

mead·ow nem·a·tode *n.* any of several parasitic nematode worms that infest and destroy the roots of plants. Genus: *Pratylenchus*.

mead·ow rue *n.* any of several plants related to the buttercup, with small yellow flowers. They grow in Northern temperate zones. Genus: *Thalictrum*.

mead·ow saf·fron *n.* = **autumn crocus**

mead·ow·sweet /méddō sweèt/ (*plural* **-sweets** *or* **-sweet**) *n.* **1.** N AMERICAN PLANT any of several North American plants of the rose family that have clusters of small white flowers. Genus: *Spiraea*. **2.** EUROPEAN PLANT WITH CREAMY-WHITE FLOWERS a tall European perennial plant of the rose family that grows in damp and marshy places and has clusters of tiny creamy-white flowers with a sweet smell. Latin name: *Filipendula ulmaria*. ◊ **dropwort**

mea·ger /méegər/, **mea·gre** *adj.* **1.** UNSATISFACTORILY SMALL unsatisfactory in quantity, substance, or size ○ *a company that is notorious for paying meager salaries* **2.** OF BAD QUALITY bad and unsatisfying in quality, strength, or effectiveness ○ *The street outside my window furnished meager entertainment.* **3.** THIN very thin, especially through malnutrition or illness [14thC. Via Anglo-Norman *megre*, French *maigre* "lean, thin," from Latin *macr-*, the stem of *macer* (source of English *emaciate*).] —**mea·ger·ly** *adv.* —**mea·ger·ness** *n.*

meal[1] /meel/ *n.* **1.** FOOD EATEN AT ONE TIME a substantial amount of food, often more than one course, that is provided and eaten at one time **2.** TIME FOR EATING FOOD any of the usual occasions, e.g., breakfast or lunch, when a substantial amount of food is provided and eaten [Old English *mǣl* "measure, mealtime." Ultimately from a prehistoric Germanic word, ancestor also of German *mal* "time, occasion."] ◇ **make a meal of something 1.** to put more time or effort into something than is usual or necessary (*informal*) **2.** to exaggerate the importance, intensity, or severity of something (*informal*)

meal[2] /meel/ *n.* **1.** GROUND GRAIN the edible part of a cereal crop that has been ground to a powder **2.** GROUND-UP SUBSTANCE any substance ground to a fine or coarse powder ○ *fish meal* [Old English *melu*. Ultimately from an Indo-European base meaning "to crush, grind," which is also the ancestor of English *maul*, *mill*, and *molar*.]

meals on wheels *n.* a service, usually provided by a social work department or charity, whereby hot meals are brought to seniors, physically challenged people, or housebound people (*takes a singular verb*)

meal tick·et *n.* **1.** DEPENDABLE SOURCE OF MONEY OR SUPPORT somebody who or something that can be counted on, or is exploited for financial gain or support (*informal*) **2.** TICKET FOR MEAL a ticket that entitles the holder to a meal

meal·time /meél tìm/ *n.* the time when a meal is usually or regularly served

meal·worm /meél wùrm/ (*plural* **-worms** *or* **-worm**) *n.* the larva of various beetles that feeds on stored grain or flour and can cause severe damage and loss. Genus: *Tenebrio*.

meal·y /meélee/ (**-i·er, -i·est**) *adj.* **1.** LIKE MEAL powdery or granular, like meal or grain ○ *mealy potatoes* **2.** MADE OF MEAL containing, made of, or covered with meal **3.** DAPPLED with a spotted or dappled hide or coat **4.** PALE exceptionally pale, especially through malnutrition or illness —**meal·i·ness** *n.*

meal·y bug *n.* any of various scale insects that are covered with a white powdery secretion and feed on plants, often causing significant damage to citrus crops and greenhouse plants. Family: Pseudococcidae.

meal·y-mouthed *adj.* wary of speaking plainly or openly, especially of admitting unpleasant truths (*disapproving*)

mean[1] /meen/ (**meant** /ment/, **mean·ing, means**) *vt.* ◊ **means 1.** HAVE A PARTICULAR SENSE to indicate or represent a particular sense ○ *I don't know what half these words mean.* ○ *When he raises his hand, it means he's making a bid.* **2.** INTEND TO EXPRESS SOMETHING to intend or be intended to express a particular idea in speech or writing ○ *That's not quite what I meant.* ○ *Just what's that supposed to mean?* **3.** INTEND TO DO SOMETHING to have an intention to do something ○ *I didn't mean to upset you.* ○ *I've been meaning to call you for weeks.* **4.** EXPRESS AN OPINION OR INTENTION to be expressing a definite opinion or intention in what you say ○ *She says she's resigning, and I think this time she means it.* **5.** BE A CAUSE OR SIGN OF SOMETHING to be a cause or indication of something ○ *The strike will mean a hard winter for many families.* ○ *A red sunset means fine weather.* **6.** GO WITH SOMETHING to accompany or be associated with something ○ *For Sam, summer meant golf.* [Old English *mǣnan*. Ultimately from an Indo-European base that is also the ancestor of English *mind*.]

mean[2] /meen/ *adj.* **1.** UNKIND unkind or malicious ○ *You hurt her feelings – that was a mean thing to do.* **2.** CRUEL cruel and bad-tempered ○ *He can be pretty mean at times.* **3.** SHABBY shabby and poor-looking ○ *streets full of small mean houses* **4.** EXCELLENT excellent or skillful (*informal*) ○ *He plays a mean sax.* **5.** BASE base or unworthy **6.** HUMBLE of low social position (*archaic*) ○ *living among the poor and mean* **7.** UNCOMFORTABLE uncomfortable or disagreeable ○ *This is the meanest climate I've ever lived in.* **8.** *U.K.* NOT GENEROUS unwilling to spend money on other people ○ *the meanest person I know* [Old English *mǣne*, from *gemǣne* "shared by everyone." Ultimately from a prehistoric Germanic word (ancestor also of German *gemein*). The modern sense evolved via "inferior."]

WORD KEY: SYNONYMS

mean, nasty, vile, low, base, ignoble

CORE MEANING: referring to somebody or something below normal standards of decency

mean used to describe people or their attitudes and behavior when they are unkind, unfair, or spiteful; **nasty** a general word used to describe somebody or something extremely unpleasant, offensive, or spiteful; **vile** used to emphasize that somebody or something is utterly despicable or wicked; **low** used to describe somebody or something dishonorable or despicable. It is used especially to describe behavior or actions that seem to take advantage of somebody; **base** a formal or literary word meaning dishonorable or despicable; **ignoble** a formal word used to describe somebody or something that seems to have no admirable or worthy qualities at all. It can be used to suggest that somebody's behavior is unworthy of him or her.

mean[3] /meen/ *n.* ◊ **means 1.** MATH INTERMEDIATE VALUE a value that is intermediate between other values, e.g., an average or expected value **2.** MATH MEDIUM TERM OF A PROPORTION either the second or third term of a proportion **3.** MIDDLE WAY a medium or moderate alternative or course of action, in the middle of a range of possibilities ○ *We need to find the mean between these extremes.* ■ *adj.* ◊ **means 1.** MEDIUM medium or intermediate in size, strength, or quality **2.** IN AN INTERMEDIATE POSITION occupying an intermediate position in a range ○ *Speech was achieved in 74.3% of patients within a mean time interval of 63 days.* [14thC. Via Old French *meien* from Latin *medianus* (see MEDIAN).]

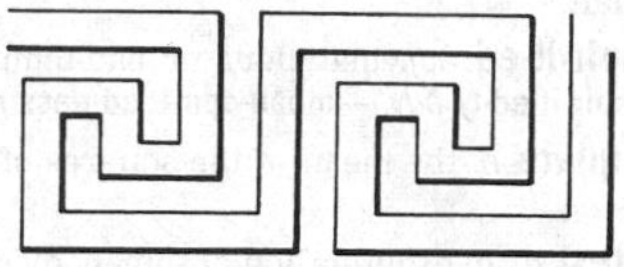

Meander

me·an·der /mee ándər/ *vi.* (**-dered, -der·ing, -ders**) **1.** FOLLOW A TWISTING ROUTE to follow an indirect route or course, especially one with a series of twists and turns ○ *The river meanders to the sea.* **2.** WANDER SLOWLY AND AIMLESSLY to move in a leisurely way, especially for pleasure or because of a lack of motivation ○ *meandering through the park* ■ *n.* **1.** RELAXED WALK a slow leisurely walk or journey ○ *We went for a meander in the woods.* **2.** TWIST OR BEND a twist or bend in something, especially a river, path, or street **3.** TWISTING ROUTE an indirect course or route, especially one that twists and turns ○ *We followed the meanders of the path.* **4.** ARTS ORNAMENTAL DESIGN an ornamental design, popular in ancient Greek art and architecture, made by a continuous line that forms square shapes by doubling back on itself [Late 16thC. Directly or via French from Latin, "winding course" , from Greek *maiandros*, from the name of a river (now called the Büyük Menderes) in Turkey.] —**me·an·der·er** *n.* —**me·an·der·ing·ly** *adv.* —**me·an·drous** /mee ándrəss/ *adj.*

mean de·vi·a·tion *n.* in statistics, the mean of the absolute values of the differences between individual values and the mean or median, used as a measure of dispersion

mean dis·tance *n.* the average distance between an orbiting celestial object and the object it is orbiting

mean free path *n.* the average distance a gas molecule travels before it collides with another molecule or the containing vessel. Symbol **small lambda**

mean·ie /meénee/, **mean·y** (*plural* **-ies**) *n.* a mean, bad-tempered, small-minded person (*informal*)

mean·ing /meéning/ *n.* **1.** WHAT SOMETHING MEANS what a word, sign, or symbol means ○ *Do you know the meaning of this word?* **2.** WHAT SOMEBODY WANTS TO EXPRESS what somebody intends to express ○ *I want to make my meaning very clear.* **3.** WHAT SOMETHING SIGNIFIES what something signifies or indicates ○ *I could not fathom the meaning of their glances.* **4.** INNER IMPORTANCE psychological or moral sense, purpose, or significance ○ *an empty life without meaning* ■ *adj.* SIGNIFICANT conveying a significance that is not directly expressed ○ *A meaning silence followed these words.*

mean·ing·ful /meéningfəl/ *adj.* **1.** WITH MEANING having a discernible meaning ○ *To me, that is not a meaningful expression.* **2.** SIGNIFICANT conveying a meaning or significance that is not directly expressed ○ *She gave me a meaningful glance.* **3.** ADDING VALUE TO LIFE adding significance, meaning, or purpose to somebody's life ○ *I'm not claiming that we have a deep and meaningful relationship, but we do have fun.* —**mean·ing·ful·ly** *adv.* —**mean·ing·ful·ness** *n.*

mean·ing·less /meéningləss/ *adj.* **1.** WITHOUT MEANING having no discernible meaning ○ *a meaningless scrawl* **2.** WITHOUT PURPOSE lacking purpose or significance ○ *Offering to help now could be a meaningless gesture* —**mean·ing·less·ly** *adv.* —**mean·ing·less·ness** *n.*

mean le·thal dose *n.* SCI = **median lethal dose**

means /meenz/ *n.* SOMETHING ENABLING SOMEBODY TO DO SOMETHING something that is available and makes it possible for somebody to do something (*takes a singular or plural verb*) ○ *You can't live out there alone with no means of transportation* ■ *npl.* AVAILABLE MONEY the money and other resources that somebody has to live on ○ *It'll be impossible to find a house in this area that's within their means.* [From MEAN³] ◇ **by all means** used as a polite way to give permission ◇ **by no means** used to emphasize a negative ○ *You were by no means the worst player.*

means of pro·duc·tion *npl.* in Marxism, the raw materials, tools, machinery, and other necessities required in the manufacturing process

mean so·lar day *n.* the constant interval between two successive transits of the mean sun across the meridian

mean-spir·it·ed *adj.* malicious or bad-tempered —**mean-spir·it·ed·ly** *adv.* —**mean-spir·it·ed·ness** *n.*

mean square *n.* the mean of the squares of a set of values

means test *n.* an examination of somebody's income and savings, carried out in order to determine whether the criteria for a type of assistance or financial aid are met —**means test·ing** *n.*

mean sun *n.* in timekeeping, an imaginary sun that moves uniformly in the celestial equator taking the same time to complete a circuit as the real sun takes in the ecliptic

meant past participle, past tense of **mean**¹

mean time *n.* time measured with reference to the mean sun crossing a given meridian

mean·time /meén tìm/ *n.* the intervening period of time between two events, or from now until something else happens ○ *I'll start dinner now and in the meantime you can have an apple.* ○ *I'll come as soon as I can; just wait there for the meantime.* ○ *Repairs will be done tomorrow and meantime please don't use the sink.*

mean·while /meén hwìl/ *adv.* **1.** DURING A PERIOD during the period of time between two events ○ *I'll meet you later; meanwhile I'll leave you to your food.* **2.** WHILE SOMETHING IS HAPPENING at the same time as something is happening ○ *I tried to keep everybody calm, meanwhile struggling to open the car door.*

mean·y *n.* = **meanie**

meas. *abbr.* **1.** measure **2.** measurement

mea·sles /meéz'lz/ *n.* **1.** CONTAGIOUS VIRAL DISEASE a very contagious acute viral disease with symptoms that include a high temperature, sore throat, and a bright red rash of small spots that spread to cover the whole body. The presence of small white spots, known as Koplik's spots, in the mouth on the inside of the cheeks a few days before the rash appears is often used as a diagnostic symptom of the disease. (*takes a singular or plural verb*) **2.** MEASLES SPOTS the spots that are characteristic of measles [14thC. Origin uncertain: probably from Middle Low German *masele* or Middle Dutch *masel* "spot, blemish," and by folk etymology from earlier *mesel* "leper."]

mea·sly /meézlee/ (**-sli·er, -sli·est**) *adj.* **1.** VERY LITTLE AND POINTLESS ridiculously or disappointingly small or inadequate (*informal*) ○ *He tipped me a measly dime.* **2.** HAVING MEASLES infected with measles [The sense "inadequate" evolved from "infected with measles" via "spotty"]

meas·ur·a·ble /mézhərəb'l/ *adj.* capable of being measured or perceived [13thC. Via French *mesurable* from late Latin *mensurabilis* (source of English *mensurable*), from, ultimately, Latin *mensura* (see MEASURE.] —**meas·ur·a·bil·i·ty** /mèzhərə bíllətee/ *n.* —**mea·sur·a·ble·ness** /mézhərəb'lnəss/ *n.* —**meas·ur·a·bly** /-əblee/ *adv.*

meas·ure /mézhər/ *n.* **1.** SIZE the size or extent of something, especially in comparison with a known standard **2.** SYSTEM FOR DETERMINING SIZE a particular system used to determine the dimensions, area, volume, or weight of something **3.** STANDARD USED FOR FIGURING SIZE a standard used for determining the dimensions, area, volume, or weight of something **4.** WAY OF EVALUATING a way of evaluating something, or a standard against which something can be compared **5.** UNIT IN A SYSTEM a unit in a system that is used to determine the dimensions, area, volume, or weight of something **6.** ACTION TAKEN an action taken to make something happen or prevent something (*often used in the plural*) ○ *to take precautionary measures* **7.** SOMETHING USED TO FIGURE QUANTITY something used to determine a quantity, e.g., a ruler, or a spoon or small container that holds a known volume **8.** STANDARD AMOUNT OF SOMETHING a standard amount of something, e.g., of an alcoholic beverage poured into a glass for drinking **9.** DEGREE OF SOMETHING an extent or amount that is limited, appropriate, or has its size specified ○ *Their help contributed in no small measure to our success.* **10.** LIMITS a limit or limits, especially one that is reasonable or appropriate ○ *His rage had no measure.* **11.** MUSIC = **bar**¹ *n.* 14 **12.** LAW LAW a bill to be enacted into law, or a law that has been enacted **13.** POETRY POETIC METER the rhythm or meter of a piece of poetry **14.** POETRY METRICAL FOOT a foot or unit of meter in poetry **15.** DANCE a dance (*archaic*) ■ **meas·ures** *npl.* MINING, GEOL ROCK LAYERS strata of rock, especially when they contain a particular material ■ *v.* (**-ured, -ur·ing, -ures**) **1.** *vt.* FIND SIZE, LENGTH, QUANTITY, OR RATE to find out the size, length, quantity, or rate of something using a suitable instrument or device **2.** *vt.* ASSESS EFFECT OR QUALITY to assess the effect or quality of something, often against a standard ○ *You can't measure a hospital just by its facilities.* **3.** *vt.* BE A PARTICULAR SIZE, LENGTH, QUANTITY to be a particular size, length, quantity, or rate **4.** *vt.* DETERMINE SOMEBODY'S SIZE FOR CLOTHES to determine somebody's size in order to make a garment or garments that will fit ○ *She was being measured for her wedding dress.* **5.** *vt.* COMPARE SIZE OR QUALITY to compare the size, effect, or quality of something with another thing ○ *The champion needs to measure his skill against a worthy challenger.* **6.** *vt.* ADJUST FOR EFFECT to adjust something so that it is suitable or effective ○ *He measured his punch exactly to catch his opponent on the jaw.* **7.** *vi.* JOURNEY to travel a particular distance (*archaic*) [12thC. Via French *mesure* from Latin *mensura*, from *mens-* the past participle stem of *metiri* "to measure."] —**meas·ur·er** *n.* ◇ **beyond measure** very greatly, or to an enormous extent ◇ **for good measure** as something extra to the amount required, especially to make sure of something ◇ **get** *or* **have** *or* **take somebody's measure** to arrive at an accurate assessment of somebody's qualities or abilities

WORD KEY: ORIGIN

The Latin stem *mens-*, from which ***measure*** derives, is also the source of English *commensurate, dimension,* and *immense.*

WORD KEY: CULTURAL NOTE

Measure for Measure, a play by English dramatist William Shakespeare (1604). Set in the court of the Duke of Vienna, this tragicomedy tells of a sister's attempts to win clemency for her brother, who has been condemned to death for the relatively minor crime of permissive behavior. It deals broadly with morality and the nature of justice.

measure off *vt.* **1.** MEASURE A LENGTH FOR CUTTING to determine a particular length of something so that this amount may be cut off **2.** MARK OFF AN AREA to find or mark the limits of an area

measure out *vt.* **1.** MEASURE AN AMOUNT FOR USE to take a particular amount from a larger amount of something for use **2.** MARK OFF AREA to find or mark the limits of an area

measure up *vi.* to be good enough to meet a standard ○ *Her new play didn't measure up to expectations.*

meas·ured /mézhərd/ *adj.* **1.** UNHURRIED OR REASONABLE slow, deliberate, or carefully considered ○ *spoke in measured tones* **2.** ADJUSTED FOR EFFECT adjusted to be suitable or effective ○ *a measured response to the criticism* **3.** BY MEASUREMENT determined as a result of measuring ○ *a measured mile* —**meas·ured·ly** *adv.* —**meas·ured·ness** *n.*

meas·ure·less /mézhərləss/ *adj.* too great to be measured ○ *"Through caverns measureless to man"* (Samuel Taylor Coleridge, *Kubla Khan;* 1816) —**meas·ure·less·ly** *adv.* —**mea·sure·less·ness** *n.*

meas·ure·ment /mézhərmənt/ *n.* **1.** SIZE OF SOMETHING MEASURED the size, length, quantity, or rate of something that has been measured **2.** BODY DIMENSION MEASURED FOR CLOTHING the size of a part of somebody's body, especially used to fit or make clothing (*often used in the plural*) **3.** MEASURING OF SOMETHING an act of measuring something

meas·ur·ing worm /mézhəring-/ *n.* = **inchworm**

meat /meet/ *n.* **1.** EDIBLE ANIMAL FLESH the flesh of an animal that is considered edible, especially a mammal or bird **2.** EDIBLE PART the edible part of anything, e.g., a coconut **3.** IMPORTANT PART the essence or important part of something ○ *the meat of the argument* **4.** MATERIAL FOR THOUGHT material that is interesting or stimulates thought ○ *There is plenty of meat in the book.* [Old English *mete* "food." Ultimately from an Indo-European word meaning "measure," which is also the ancestor of English *measure*, the underlying idea being "measured portion of food."] —**meat·less** *adj.* ◇ **meat and drink** something that somebody particularly enjoys

WORD KEY: ORIGIN

The sense of ***meat*** as "animal flesh (eaten as food)" developed in the 13th century, but the original English sense "food" still survives in phrases such as "meat and drink" and "one man's meat is another man's poison" (and is also seen in the word's relatives Danish *mad*, Icelandic *matur*, and Swedish *mat*).

meat and po·ta·toes *n.* the most basic or important idea or aspect of something (*takes a singular or plural verb*) —**meat-and-po·ta·toes** *adj.*

meat·ball /meét bàwl/ *n.* **1.** GROUND MEAT IN A BALL SHAPE ground meat that is shaped into a small round ball, usually with seasonings and a binding ingredient such as breadcrumbs or egg, and then cooked **2.** OFFENSIVE TERM an offensive term that deliberately insults somebody's intelligence or energy (*slang insult*)

meat·head /meét hèd/ *n.* somebody who is unintelligent or imperceptive (*informal insult*)

meat hook *n.* HOOK FOR HANGING MEAT CARCASSES a large hook used for hanging carcasses of meat ■ **meat hooks** *npl.* HANDS the hands or fists (*slang*)

meat loaf *n.* a mixture of ground meat and other ingredients, usually cooked in a loaf pan and served hot or cold

meat mar·ket *n.* a place where people go to find sexual partners, such as a bar or nightclub (*slang*)

meat·pack·ing /meét pàking/ *n.* the industry that deals with the slaughtering and butchering of meat —**meat·pack·er** *n.*

me·a·tus /mee áytəss/ (*plural* **-tus·es** *or* **-tus**) *n.* a body opening, e.g., the passage in the ear that leads to the eardrum [15thC. From Latin, "passage, channel," the past participle of *meare* "to go, pass" (source of English *permeate*).]

meat·y /meétee/ (**-i·er, -i·est**) *adj.* **1.** CONTAINING OR TASTING OF MEAT containing a high proportion of meat or tasting strongly of meat **2.** INTERESTING AND THOUGHT-PROVOKING full of interesting and thought-provoking material ○ *a meaty role* **3.** FLESHY OR MUSCLED big and fleshy or muscular —**meat·i·ness** *n.*

mec·ca /mékə/ *n.* a place that is an important center for a particular activity or that is visited by a great many people

Mec·ca /mékə/ city in western Saudi Arabia, the birthplace of Muhammad. It is considered by Muslims the most sacred of the holy cities of Islam. Population: 1,500,000 (1994).

mech. *abbr.* **1.** mechanical **2.** mechanics **3.** mechanism

mechan- *prefix.* = **mechano-** (*used before vowels*)

me·chan·ic /mə kánnik/ *n.* a skilled worker who is employed to repair or operate machinery or engines [Mid-16thC. Directly or via French *mechanique* from Latin *mechanicus*, from, ultimately, Greek *mēkhanē* (see MACHINE).]

me·chan·i·cal /mə kánnik'l/ *adj.* **1.** MACHINE-OPERATED operated by or using a machine or mechanism **2.** INVOLVING A MACHINE OR ENGINE involving or located in or on a machine or engine ○ *mechanical failure* **3.**

MEASUREMENTS

SI Metric System

The SI (Système Internationale d'Unités) is founded on seven base units that can be multiplied or divided by each other to yield derived units. Values of the base and derived units can be increased or decreased by using SI prefixes indicating decimal multiplication factors. Units and prefixes are assigned internationally accepted symbols.

Base Units

Name	Physical Quantity	Symbol
meter	length	m
kilogram	mass	kg
second	time	s
ampere	electric current	A
kelvin	thermodynamic temperature	K
mole	amount of substance	mol
candela	luminous intensity	cd

Derived Units With Special Names and Symbols

Name	Physical Quantity	Symbol
becquerel	radioactivity	Bq
coulomb	electric charge	C
degree Celsius	temperature	˚C
farad	electric capacitance	F
gray	absorbed radiation dose	Gy
henry	inductance	H
hertz	frequency	Hz
joule	energy, work	J
lumen	luminous flux	lm
lux	illumination	lx
newton	force	N
ohm	electric resistance	Ω
pascal	pressure, stress	Pa
radian	plane angle	rad
siemens	electric conductance	S
sievert	radiation dose equivalent	Sv
steradian	solid angle	sr
tesla	magnetic flux density	T
volt	electric potential difference	V
watt	power	W
weber	magnetic flux	Wb

Some Derived Units Without Special Names and Symbols

Name	Physical Quantity	Symbol
ampere per meter	magnetic field strength	A/m
cubic meter	volume	m^3
henry per meter	permeability	H/m
joule per kelvin	heat capacity, entropy	J/K
kilogram per cubic meter	mass density	kg/m^3
meter per second	linear speed	m/s
meter per second squared	linear acceleration	m/s^2
mole per cubic meter	concentration of substance	mol/m^3
newton meter	moment of force, torque	N·m
radian per second	angular speed	rad/s
square meter	area	m^2
volt per meter	electric field strength	V/m
watt per meter kelvin	thermal conductivity	W/(m·K)
watt per steradian	radiant intensity	W/sr

Prefixes

Multiplication Factor			Name	Symbol
1 000 000 000 000 000 000 000 000	or	10^{24}	*yotta-*	Y
1 000 000 000 000 000 000 000	or	10^{21}	*zetta-*	Z
1 000 000 000 000 000 000	or	10^{18}	*exa-*	E
1 000 000 000 000 000	or	10^{15}	*peta-*	P
1 000 000 000 000	or	10^{12}	*tera-*	T
1 000 000 000	or	10^{9}	*giga-*	G
1 000 000	or	10^{6}	*mega-*	M
1 000	or	10^{3}	*kilo-*	k
100	or	10^{2}	*hecto-*	h
10	or	10^{1}	*deca-* or *deka-*	da
0.1	or	10^{-1}	*deci-*	d
0.01	or	10^{-2}	*centi-*	c
0.001	or	10^{-3}	*milli-*	m
0.000 001	or	10^{-6}	*micro-*	µ
0.000 000 001	or	10^{-9}	*nano-*	n
0.000 000 000 001	or	10^{-12}	*pico-*	p
0.000 000 000 000 001	or	10^{-15}	*femto-*	f
0.000 000 000 000 000 001	or	10^{-18}	*atto-*	a
0.000 000 000 000 000 000 001	or	10^{-21}	*zepto-*	z
0.000 000 000 000 000 000 000 001	or	10^{-24}	*yocto-*	y

Other Units Used With the SI

Some units technically outside of the SI are nevertheless employed with it due to their practical or special significance or because they are already in wide use. Excepting the electronvolt, litre, tex, and tonne, prefixes are not used with these units. The tonne does not take prefixes indicating a multiplication factor of less than ten.

Name	Symbol	Quantity	SI Equivalent
astronomical unit	–	length	≈ 149.598 Gm
barn	b	area	= 100 fm^2
day, mean solar	d	time	= 86 400 s
degree	˚	plane angle	= (Π/180) rad
electronvolt	eV	energy	≈ 0.160 217 7 aJ
hectare	ha	area	= 10 000 m^2 or 1 hm^2
hour, mean solar	h	time	= 3600 s
knot	kn	linear speed	= 1852 m/h
liter	L or l	volume	≈ 1 dm^3 or 1000 cm^3
millibar	mbar	pressure	= 0.1 kPa
minute, mean solar	min	time	= 60 s
minute	'	plane angle	= (Π/10 800) rad
nautical mile	M	length	= 1852 m
parsec	pc	length	≈ 30.857 Pm
revolution	r	plane angle	= 2Π rad
second	"	plane angle	= (Π/648 000) rad
tex	tex	linear density	= 1 mg/m
tonne	t	mass	= 1000 kg or 1 Mg
unified atomic mass unit	u	mass	≈ 1.660 540 2 yg
year	a	time	= 31.536 Ms (calendar) = 31.556 926 Ms (solar) = 31.558 150 Ms (sidereal)

Conversion of Common SI Units

Conversions for some common SI units or those used with the SI to Imperial or U.S. Customary units are given below.

SI Unit	Conversion
length	
micrometer	= 0.000 039 37 inches
millimeter	= 0.039 37 inches
centimeter	= 0.3937 inches
meter	= 39.37 inches or ≈ 1.094 yards
kilometer	≈ 0.621 miles
area	
square millimeter	≈ 0.001 55 square inches
square centimeter	≈ 0.155 square inches
square meter	≈ 1.196 square yards or 10.76 square feet
hectare	≈ 2.471 acres
square kilometer	≈ 0.386 square miles
volume or capacity	
cubic millimeter	≈ 0.000 061 cubic inches
cubic centimeter or milliliter	≈ 0.0610 cubic inches, 0.0352 Imp. fl.ounces, or 0.0338 U.S. fl. ounces
cubic decimeter or liter	≈ 61.0 cubic inches, 0.880 Imp. quarts, 1.057 U.S. liquid quarts, or 0.908 U.S. dry quarts
cubic meter	≈ 1.308 cubic yards
mass	
gram	≈ 0.0353 ou. avoirdupois or 0.0322 ou. troy
kilogram	≈ 2.205 pounds avoirdupois
tonne	≈ 2205 pounds avoirdupois
temperature	
degree Celsius	(˚C × 1.8) + 32 = degrees Fahrenheit

Foot-Pound-Second and Troy Systems

The Imperial and U.S. Customary systems are the last foot-pound-second systems still used nationally in everyday trade and commerce, while the troy system of weights continues to find use in the precious metals market, chiefly in North America. All have been supplanted by the SI in scientific and technical work and in nearly all international trade.

Imperial and U.S. Customary System Units

Units of the Imperial and U.S. Customary systems are equal except for some units of volume and capacity.

Unit	Relation	Conversion
length		
inch	–	= 25.4 mm
foot	12 inches	= 0.3048 m
yard	3 feet, 36 inches	= 0.9144 m
rod	5½ yards, 16½ feet	= 5.0292 m
furlong	220 yards, ⅛ mile	≈ 0.201 km
mile (statute)	1760 yards, 5280 feet	≈ 1.609 km
area		
square inch	–	= 645.16 mm^2
square foot	144 sq. inches	= 929.0304 cm^2
square yard	9 sq. feet	≈ 0.836 m^2
acre	4840 sq. yards	≈ 0.405 ha
volume or capacity		
cubic inch	–	≈ 16.387 cm^3
cubic foot	1728 cubic inches	≈ 28.316 dm^3
cubic yard	27 cubic feet	≈ 0.765 m^3
(Imperial)		
fluid ounce	–	≈ 28.413 cm^3
pint	20 Imp fl. ou.	≈ 0.568 dm^3
quart	2 Imp. pints	≈ 1.136 dm^3
gallon	4 Imp. quarts	≈ 4.546 dm^3
peck	8 Imp. quarts	≈ 9.092 dm^3
bushel	4 Imp. pecks	≈ 36.369 dm^3
barrel	36 Imp. gallons	≈ 163.7 dm^3
(U.S., liquid)		
fluid ounce	–	≈ 29.573 cm^3
pint	16 U.S. fl. ou.	≈ 0.473 dm^3
quart	2 U.S. fl. pints	≈ 0.946 dm^3
gallon	4 U.S. fl. quarts	≈ 3.785 dm^3
barrel, wine	31½ U.S. gallons	≈ 119.2 dm^3
barrel, oil	42 U.S. gallons	≈ 0.159 m^3
(U.S., dry)		
pint	–	≈ 0.551 dm^3
quart	2 U.S. dry pints	≈ 1.101 dm^3
peck	8 U.S. dry quarts	≈ 8.810 dm^3
bushel	4 pecks	≈ 35.239 dm^3
weight or mass		
ounce	–	≈ 28.349 g
pound (avoirdupois)	16 ounces	≈ 0.454 kg
stone (U.K.)	14 pounds	≈ 6.350 kg
hundred-weight(U.K.)	112 pounds	≈ 50.80 kg
(long) ton (U.K.)	2240 pounds	≈ 1.016 Mg
(short) ton (U.S.)	2000 pounds	≈ 0.907 Mg
(troy)		
ounce	–	≈ 31.103 g
pound	12 ou. troy	≈ 373.242 g
temperature		
degree Fahrenheit	(˚F – 32) ÷ 1.8 = degrees Celsius	

Some Volumetric Measurement Comparisons

Imperial Units	In U.S. Units	In SI Units
1 U.K. fluid ounce	≈ 0.961 U.S. fluid ounce	≈ 28.413 cm^3
1 U.K. pint	≈ 1.201 U.S. liquid pint	≈ 0.568 dm^3
1 U.K. pint	≈ 1.032 U.S. dry pint	≈ 0.568 dm^3
1 U.K. gallon	≈ 1.201 U.S. gallon	≈ 4.546 dm^3

U.S. Units	In Imperial Units	In SI Units
1 U.S. fluid ounce	≈ 1.041 U.K. fluid ounce	≈ 29.573 cm^3
1 U.S. liquid pint	≈ 0.833 U.K. pint	≈ 0.473 dm^3
1 U.S. gallon	≈ 0.833 U.K. gallon	≈ 3.785 dm^3
1 U.S. dry pint	≈ 0.969 U.K. pint	≈ 0.551 dm^3

LACKING HUMAN QUALITIES done automatically or as if by a machine instead of a thinking and feeling human being ○ *His playing was mechanical.* **4.** UNDERSTANDING MACHINES having an aptitude for using or understanding machines ○ *I'm not very mechanical* **5.** INVOLVING PHYSICAL FORCES relating to, involving, or done by physical forces ○ *mechanical erosion* **6.** PHYS OF MECHANICS relating to, involving, or typical of the science of mechanics ○ *mechanical energy* **7.** PHILOS = **mechanistic** ■ *n.* PRINTING MATERIAL READY FOR PRINTING copy consisting of type proofs and artwork that is laid out and ready to be photographed or electronically scanned for the purpose of preparing printing plates —**me·chan·i·cal·ly** *adv.* —**me·chan·i·cal·ness** *n.*

me·chan·i·cal draw·ing *n.* **1.** DRAWING OF MACHINERY TO SCALE a drawing done to scale using specialized instruments, e.g., a sketch showing machinery or an architectural plan **2.** PROCESS OF DRAWING the process of making mechanical drawings

me·chan·i·cal en·gi·neer·ing *n.* the branch of engineering that deals with the design, production, and use of machinery and tools, as well as the generation and transmission of heat and mechanical power —**me·chan·i·cal en·gi·neer** *n.*

me·chan·i·cal pen·cil *n.* a pencil with replaceable lead that may be advanced as needed

me·chan·i·cal weath·er·ing *n.* the breakdown of rocks and minerals by physical agents such as frost, wind, and tree roots, with no chemical alteration

me·chan·ics /mə kánniks/ *n.* **1.** STUDY OF ENERGY AND FORCES the branch of physics and mathematics that deals with the effect of energy and forces on systems (*takes a singular verb*) **2.** MAKING AND RUNNING OF MACHINES the application of the science of mechanics to the design, making, and operating of machines (*takes a singular or plural verb*) ■ *npl.* HOW SOMETHING WORKS OR IS DONE the details of how something works or the way it is done (*takes a plural verb*) ○ *She's a strategic player who really understands the mechanics of the game.*

mech·a·nism /mékə nìzzəm/ *n.* **1.** TECH MACHINE PART a machine or part of a machine that performs a particular task **2.** SOMETHING LIKE A MACHINE something that is not a machine but is like one or is studied as if it were one ○ *the fragile mechanism of the planet's ecology* **3.** METHOD OR MEANS a method or means of doing something ○ *Interest rates are only one mechanism for controlling inflation.* **4.** WAY THAT SOMETHING WORKS the methods, procedures, or processes involved in how something works or is done ○ *the mechanism of international diplomacy* **5.** PSYCHOL INSTINCTIVE BEHAVIORAL REACTION a natural unconscious reaction or type of behavior that comes into action when somebody is faced with a particular situation ○ *defense mechanisms* **6.** PHILOS PHILOSOPHICAL THEORY the philosophical theory that all natural phenomena, including human behavior, can be explained by physical causes and processes [Mid-17thC. From modern Latin *mechanismus*, from Greek *mēkhanē* (see MACHINE).]

mech·a·nist /mékənist/ *n.* PHILOS somebody who believes that all natural phenomena, including human behavior, can be explained by physical causes and processes [Early 17thC. Formed from MECHANIC.]

mech·a·nis·tic /mèkə nístik/ *adj.* **1.** PHILOS EXPLAINING BEHAVIOR MECHANICALLY explaining human behavior or other natural processes in terms of physical causes and processes **2.** LIKE A MACHINE typical of a machine rather than a thinking and feeling human being **3.** PHYS OF THE SCIENCE OF MECHANICS relating to, involving, or typical of the science of mechanics —**mech·a·nis·ti·cal·ly** *adv.*

mech·a·nize /mékə nīz/ (**-nized, -niz·ing, -niz·es**) *vt.* **1.** USE MACHINERY TO DO SOMETHING to change a process so that it is performed by machinery rather than human or animal labor **2.** EQUIP WITH MACHINERY to equip a place of work or a workforce with machines to do work previously done by human or animal labor **3.** MIL EQUIP AN ARMY WITH TRACKED VEHICLES to equip an armed force with tracked armored vehicles [Late 17thC. Formed from MECHANIC.] —**mech·a·ni·za·tion** /mèkəni záysh'n/ *n.* —**mech·a·nized** /mékə nīzd/ *adj.* —**mech·a·niz·er** /-nīzər/ *n.*

mechano- *prefix.* **1.** mechanical ○ *mechanoreceptor* **2.** machinery ○ *mechanize* [From Greek *mēkhanē* (see MACHINE)]

mech·a·no·chem·is·try /mèkənō kémmistree/ *n.* the branch of chemistry concerned with the conversion of chemical energy into mechanical work —**mech·a·no·chem·i·cal** /mèkənō kémmik'l/ *adj.*

mech·a·no·re·cep·tor /mèkənō ri séptər/ *n.* a sensory receptor of a nerve that responds to pressure, vibration, or some other mechanical stimulus —**mech·a·no·re·cep·tion** *n.* —**mech·a·no·re·cep·tive** *adj.*

mech·a·no·ther·a·py /mèkənō thérrəpee/ *n.* the treatment of injuries through mechanical means such as massage and exercise machines —**mech·a·no·ther·a·pist** *n.*

Mech·lin /méklin/, **Mech·lin lace** *n.* a type of bobbin lace made at Mechlin, Belgium [15thC. Named for *Mechlin*, the former English name of the Belgian city *Mechelen*, where it was first made.]

me·co·ni·um /mi kṓnee əm/ *n.* the dark greenish feces that have collected in the intestines of an unborn baby and are released shortly after birth [Early 17thC. Via Latin, "poppy juice," hence "newborn baby's feces" (because of the similarity in color), from Greek *mēkōnion* "poppy juice," from *mēkōn* "poppy."]

me·cop·ter·an /mə kóptərən/ *n.* an insect with long legs and wings and a structure resembling a beak at the front of the head, e.g. the scorpion fly. Order: Mecoptera. [Formed from modern Latin *Mecoptera*, order name, from Greek *mēkos* "length" + *ptera* "wings"] —**me·cop·ter·ous** *adj.*

Med /med/ *n.* the Mediterranean Sea (*informal*)

med. *abbr.* **1.** medical **2.** medicine **3.** medieval **4.** medium

M.Ed. *abbr.* Master of Education

mé·dail·lon /mày da yáwN/ (*plural* **-lons**) *n.* = **medallion** *n.* 3 (*often used in the plural*) [Early 20thC. From French, plural of *médaillon* (see MEDALLION).]

me·da·ka /mə daákə/ *n.* a small Japanese freshwater fish of the killifish family that is popular as an aquarium fish. Latin name: *Oryzias latipes.* [Mid-20thC. From Japanese, literally "eye-high."]

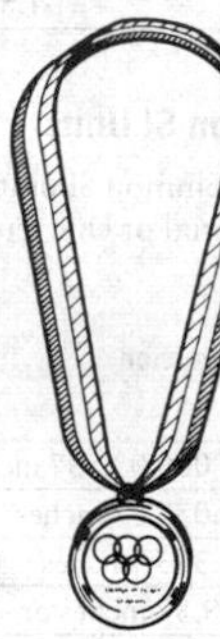

Medal

med·al /médd'l/ *n.* **1.** PIECE OF METAL GIVEN AS AN AWARD a small flat piece of metal, usually shaped like a coin and stamped with an inscription or design, awarded to somebody for outstanding achievement or bravery or to commemorate something **2.** RELIGIOUS IMAGE WORN AS ACCESSORY a cut and shaped piece of metal on which a religious image is often stamped, worn as a pin or on a chain ■ *vi.* (**-aled** *or* **-alled, -al·ing** *or* **-al·ling, -als**) WIN A MEDAL to win a medal in a competition ○ *She medaled in the javelin throw.* [Late 16thC. Via French from, ultimately, assumed Vulgar Latin *medalia* "coins worth half the value of a denarius," from, ultimately, late Latin *medialis* "medial" (source of English *middle*).] —**me·dal·lic** /mə dállik/ *adj.*

Med·al for Merit *n.* a medal awarded by the U.S. government to civilians for outstanding service

med·al·ist /médd'list/ *n.* **1.** SOMEBODY AWARDED A MEDAL somebody who has been awarded a medal, especially in a sports competition **2.** MEDAL DESIGNER, MAKER, OR COLLECTOR somebody who designs, makes, collects, or is an expert on medals **3.** GOLF WINNER OF A MEDAL PLAY TOURNAMENT a golfer who wins a medal play tournament

me·dal·lion /mə dállyən/ *n.* **1.** MEDAL a large medal **2.** LARGE DECORATIVE METAL DISK a large metal disk worn as an ornament, usually on a chain around the neck **3.** COOK ROUND THIN FOOD SLICE a round thin slice or portion of meat or another food **4.** ARTS ROUND DECORATION ON SOMETHING a round or oval decoration on something, e.g., a building, vase, or piece of material [Mid-17thC. Via French *médaillon* from Italian *medaglione*, literally "large medal," from *medaglia* (see MEDAL).]

med·al·list /médd'list/ *n.* U.K. = **medalist**

Med·al of Free·dom *n.* an award given to U.S. civilians for outstanding achievement

Med·al of Hon·or *n.* = **Congressional Medal of Honor**

med·al play *n.* GOLF a way of scoring in golf in which the total number of strokes taken for the round is counted rather than the number of holes won

Me·dan /máy daan/ industrial city in western Indonesia on the island of northern Sumatra. Population: 1,730,052 (1990).

Med·a·war /méddəwər/, **Sir Peter** (1915–87) Brazilian-born U.K. zoologist and immunologist. He shared a Nobel Prize in physiology or medicine (1960) for his work on immunology in organ transplants and skin grafts. Full name **Sir Peter Brian Medawar**

med·dle /médd'l/ (**-dled, -dling, -dles**) *vi.* to interfere or become involved in somebody else's concerns or with something that is somebody else's property (*disapproving*) ○ *I don't mean to meddle, only to offer advice.* ○ *Who's been meddling with the settings on my computer?* [13thC. Via Old French *me(s)dler* (variant of *mesler*), from assumed Vulgar Latin *misculare* "to mix thoroughly."] —**med·dler** *n.*

med·dle·some /médd'lsəm/ *adj.* tending to interfere in other people's business (*disapproving*) —**med·dle·some·ly** *adv.* —**med·dle·some·ness** *n.*

Mede /meed/ *n.* a member of an Indo-European people who ruled an empire northwest of Persia in ancient times [Via Latin *Medi*, plural of *Medus*]

Me·de·a /mə deé ə/ *n.* in Greek mythology, a woman with magical powers who was the daughter of the king of Colchis. She helped Jason steal the Golden Fleece and, when he deserted her, killed their children in revenge.

Me·del·lín /màydə yeén/ major city and capital of Antioquia Department in west central Colombia. Population: 1,621,356 (1995).

med·e·vac /méddə vàk/ *n.* **1.** MEDICAL EVACUATION OF INJURED the removal of injured people from the scene of their injury to the nearest hospital or place of treatment **2.** HELICOPTER USED TO EVACUATE INJURED an aircraft, especially a helicopter, used to take injured people from the scene of their injury to the nearest hospital or place of treatment ■ *vt.* (**-vaced, -vac·ing, -vacs**) EVACUATE AN INJURED PERSON to evacuate somebody who is injured in order to take them to a hospital or place of treatment [Mid-20thC. Blend of MEDICAL and EVACUATION.]

med·fly /méd flì/ (*plural* **-flies**) *n.* a Mediterranean fruit fly (*informal*)

Med·ford /médfərd/ **1.** city in northeastern Massachusetts, a northwestern suburb of Boston. Population: 56,190 (1996). **2.** city in Oregon, the administrative seat of Jackson County. Population: 52,611 (1994).

Med. Gr. *abbr.* medieval Greek

me·di·a[1] /meédee ə/ *n.* TELEVISION, NEWSPAPERS, AND RADIO COLLECTIVELY the various means of mass communication thought of as a whole, including television, radio, magazines, and newspapers, together with the people involved in their production (*takes a singular or plural verb*) ■ plural of **medium** [Early 20thC. Plural of MEDIUM.]

me·di·a[2] /meédee ə/ (*plural* **-ae** /-ee/) *n.* **1.** ANAT LAYER OF A BLOOD VESSEL the middle, muscular layer of the wall of a blood or lymph vessel **2.** INSECTS VEIN IN AN INSECT'S WING a primary vein in an insect's wing [Mid-19thC. From Latin, "middle," the feminine of *medius* (see MEDIUM).]

Me·di·a /meédee ə/ ancient country corresponding to modern-day northeastern Iran —**Me·di·an** *adj., n.*

me·di·a cir·cus *n.* a situation in which members of the media vie with each other in covering an event so that the coverage overwhelms the event and distorts its importance (*informal disapproving*)

me·di·a·cy /meédee əssee/ *n.* the condition of being intermediate or of having an intermediate effect [Mid-19thC. Formed from MEDIATE.]

me·di·ae plural of **media**

me·di·ae·val *adj.* = **medieval**

me·di·ae·val·ism *n.* = **medievalism**

me·di·ae·val·ist *n.* = **medievalist**

me·di·a e·vent *n.* something that attracts great attention from the mass media, often arranged specifically for that purpose

me·di·a·gen·ic /meédee ə jénnik/ *adj.* appealing or attractive when covered by the media and thus highly suitable for media exposure

me·di·al /meédee əl/ *adj.* **1.** AT THE MIDDLE situated in or toward the middle **2.** ORDINARY not extreme or exceptional but average **3.** STATS = **median** *adj.* 2 **4.** ZOOL NEAR THE MEDIAN PLANE near the median plane of an organism or body part **5.** LING IN THE MIDDLE OF A LANGUAGE UNIT occurring between the first and last positions in a word or linguistic unit (**morpheme**) ■ *n.* PHON SOUND BETWEEN STRONG AND SOFT a speech sound midway between a strong sound (**fortis**) and a soft sound (**lenis**) [Late 16thC. From late Latin *medialis,* from Latin *medius* (see MEDIUM).] —**me·di·al·ly** *adv.*

me·di·an /meédee ən/ *n.* **1.** MIDDLE POINT a point, line, part, or plane that is in the middle **2.** TRANSP = **median strip 3.** STATS MIDDLE OF ORDERED VALUES the middle value in a set of statistical values that are arranged in ascending or descending order **4.** STATS MIDPOINT IN A FREQUENCY DISTRIBUTION the value in a frequency distribution above and below which values with equal total frequencies appear **5.** GEOM LINE DIVIDING A TRIANGLE a line connecting a vertex of a triangle and the midpoint of the opposite side **6.** GEOM LINE DIVIDING A TRAPEZOID a line connecting the midpoints of the nonparallel sides of a trapezoid ■ *adj.* **1.** IN, TO, OR THROUGH THE MIDDLE in, toward, or passing through the middle **2.** STATS OF OR AS A STATISTICAL MEDIAN relating to, involving, or constituting a statistical median **3.** ZOOL IN THE MIDDLE OF A BILATERAL ANIMAL lying in the plane that divides a bilaterally symmetrical animal into right and left halves [14thC. Directly or via French *(veine) médiane* "median (vein)" (the original sense in English), from Latin *medianus* "median," from *medius* (see MEDIUM).] —**me·di·an·ly** *adv.*

me·di·an le·thal dose *n.* the dose of something, e.g., a drug or ionizing radiation, that, in a specified period of time, will kill half the experimental animals to whom it is given

me·di·an plane *n.* a vertical plane that divides a bilaterally symmetrical animal into right and left halves

me·di·an strip *n. U.S., Aus* a strip of land down the center of a road that separates lanes of traffic traveling in opposite directions

me·di·ant /meédee ənt/ *n.* the third note of a major or minor musical scale, and the harmony built upon this note [Mid-18thC. Via French *médiante* from, ultimately, late Latin *mediare* "to be in the middle" (source of English *mediate*), from Latin *medius* (see MEDIUM).]

me·di·as·ti·num /meédee ə stínəm/ (*plural* **-na** /-stínə/) *n.* in mammals, the region of the chest between the lungs that contains the heart, trachea, and other organs [15thC. Via medieval Latin, "medial," the neuter form of *mediastinus,* from Latin, "common servant," from *medius* (see MEDIUM).] —**me·di·as·ti·nal** *adj.*

me·di·a stud·ies *n.* a field of academic work that examines the role and operation of the mass media (*takes a singular or plural verb*)

me·di·ate *v.* /meédee àyt/ (**-at·ed, -at·ing, -ates**) **1.** *vi.* INTERVENE TO RESOLVE CONFLICT to work with both sides in a dispute in an attempt to help them reach an agreement ○ *mediating between the government and the rebels* **2.** *vt.* OVERSEE ATTEMPTS TO SOLVE A DISPUTE to oversee an attempt to solve a dispute by working with both sides to help them reach an agreement ○ *appointed to mediate the talks* **3.** *vt.* ACHIEVE AGREEMENT BETWEEN DISPUTING GROUPS to achieve a solution, settlement, or agreement by working with both sides in a dispute ○ *negotiators have mediated a ceasefire* **4.** *vt.* PHYSIOL TRANSFER to act as a medium that transfers something from one place to another **5.** *vi.* BE BETWEEN to be between two stages, ideas, times, or things ■ *adj.* /meédee ət/ DEPENDING ON INTERMEDIATE ACTION involving or depending on an intermediary or an intermediate action [15thC. Partly from late Latin *mediare* "to halve, be in the middle, mediate," from Latin *medius* (see MEDIUM), and partly by back-formation from MEDIATION.] —**me·di·ate·ly** *adv.* —**me·di·ate·ness** *n.* —**me·di·a·tive** /meédee àytiv/ *adj.*

me·di·a·tion /meédee áysh'n/ *n.* **1.** INTERVENTION TO SETTLE A DISPUTE the intervention by a third party between two sides in a dispute in an attempt to help them reach an agreement **2.** PHYSIOL ACTION AS MEDIUM the action a medium that transfers something from one place to another [14thC. Directly or via Old French *mediacion* from the late Latin stem *mediation-,* from, ultimately, Latin *mediare* (see MEDIATE).]

me·di·a·tize /meédee ə tìz/ (**-tized, -tiz·ing, -tiz·es**) *vt.* to take control of another country but allow its ruler to retain his or her title and have some role in governing the country [Early 19thC. Via French *médiatiser* from, ultimately, late Latin *mediare* (see MEDIATE).] —**me·di·a·ti·za·tion** /meédee əti záysh'n/ *n.*

me·di·a·tor /meédee àytər/ *n.* **1.** SOMEBODY HELPING END A DISPUTE somebody who works with both sides in a dispute in an attempt to help them reach an agreement **2.** PHYSIOL SUBSTANCE ACTING AS A MEDIUM a substance that acts as a medium in transferring something from one place to another in the body [14thC. Directly or via French *médiateur* from ecclesiastical Latin *mediator,* from late Latin *mediare* (see MEDIATE).] —**me·di·a·to·ri·al** /meédee ə táwree əl/ *adj.* —**me·di·a·to·ri·al·ly** *adv.*

med·ic /méddik/ *n.* **1.** DOCTOR a doctor or medical student (*informal*) **2.** MIL MEMBER OF AN ARMY MEDICAL CORPS an enlisted or noncommissioned member of a military medical corps [Mid-17thC. From Latin *medicus* (see MEDICINE). Perhaps also by back-formation from MEDICAL.]

med·ic /méddik/, **med·ick** *n.* a plant of the pea family that has three-lobed leaves and is often used as fodder. Genus: *Medicago.* [14thC. Via Latin *medica* from Greek *Mēdikē (poa),* literally "Median (poppy)," *Media* being the name of an ancient southwestern Asian country (present-day northwestern Iran).]

Med·i·caid /méddi kàyd/ *n.* a program funded by the U.S. and state governments that pays the medical expenses of people who are unable to pay some or all of their own expenses. ◊ **Medicare** [Mid-20thC. Blend of MEDICAL and AID.]

med·i·cal /méddik'l/ *adj.* INVOLVING MEDICINE relating to, involving, or used in medicine or treatment given by doctors ■ *n.* PHYSICAL EXAMINATION TO DETERMINE HEALTH a physical examination by a doctor to check a patient's state of health [Mid-17thC. Directly or via French from medieval Latin *medicalis,* from Latin *medicus* (see MEDICINE).]

med·i·cal ex·am·in·er *n.* a physician who is appointed by a state or local government to establish the cause of somebody's death, especially in cases where death is not the result of natural causes

med·i·cal food *n.* an attractively packaged, bite-size dose of medication configured, e.g., as a piece of candy [Mid-20thC]

med·i·cal ju·ris·pru·dence *n.* = **forensic medicine**

med·i·cal mall *n.* a complex of facilities under one roof offering diagnostics, primary and outpatient care, a pharmacy, and therapy along with banks, drycleaners, and restaurants for patients and their families [Mid-20thC]

me·dic·a·ment /mə díkəmənt, méddikə-/ *n.* a substance used to treat an illness [15thC. Directly or via French from Latin *medicamentum,* from *medicari* (see MEDICATE).]

Med·i·care /méddi kàir/ *n.* **1.** PUBLIC HEALTH CARE FOR SENIOR CITIZENS a health insurance program in the United States under which medical care and hospital treatment for people over 65 is partially paid by the government **2.** AUSTRALIAN HEALTH INSURANCE SCHEME in Australia, the national health insurance scheme, which is funded by a tax levy [Mid-20thC. Blend of MEDICAL and CARE.]

med·i·cate /méddi kàyt/ (**-cat·ed, -cat·ing, -cates**) *vt.* **1.** MED GIVE MEDICINE TO SOMEBODY to treat a patient with a drug (*often passive*) **2.** PHARM ADD A DRUG TO SOMETHING to add a drug to something, e.g., an antibacterial agent to a soap, or an anesthetic to a throat lozenge [Early 17thC. Origin uncertain: either from Latin *medicari* "to heal, cure," later "to treat," from *medicus* (see MEDICINE); or by back-formation from MEDICATION.] —**med·i·cat·ed** *adj.* —**med·i·ca·tive** *adj.*

med·i·ca·tion /mèddi káysh'n/ *n.* **1.** DRUG a drug used to treat an illness **2.** TREATMENT WITH MEDICINE treatment of an illness using drugs [15thC. Directly or via French from, ultimately, Latin *medicari* (see MEDICATE).]

Med·i·ce·an /mèddee seéən/ *adj.* relating to the Medici family and the period of their rule over Florence and Tuscany

Med·i·ci /méddə cheè/, **Cosimo de'** (1389–1464) Italian banker and statesman. He established the Medici as virtual rulers of Florence without holding public office himself, and was a patron of the arts and learning. Known as **Cosimo the Elder**

Med·i·ci, Cosimo I de', 1st Grand Duke of Tuscany (1519–74). He became the sovereign ruler of Florence (1570) and established firm autocratic control over Florence and Tuscany.

Med·i·ci, Lorenzo de' (1449–92) Italian statesman. He was the virtual ruler of the Florentine Republic, a poet, and a patron of the arts. Known as **Lorenzo The Magnificent**

med·i·cide *n.* physician-assisted suicide (*informal*)

me·dic·i·nal /mə díss'n'l, -dísnəl/ *adj.* **1.** CAPABLE OF TREATING ILLNESS having properties that can be used to treat illness ○ *a medicinal plant* **2.** INTENDED TO IMPROVE SOMEBODY'S WELLBEING intended to improve somebody's physical or emotional wellbeing in the way a medicine does ○ *a drink taken for medicinal purposes* **3.** LIKE MEDICINE like medicine, especially in having a bitter taste [14thC. Directly or via French from Latin *medicinalis,* from *medicina* (see MEDICINE).] —**me·dic·i·nal·ly** *adv.*

me·dic·i·nal leech *n.* a large European freshwater leech that lives on blood. In the past doctors used it in bloodletting, and it is still occasionally used to prevent coagulation. Latin name: *Hirudo medicinalis.*

med·i·cine /méddəssin/ *n.* **1.** DRUG FOR TREATING ILLNESS a drug or remedy used for treating illness ○ *cough medicine* **2.** TREATMENT OF ILLNESS the diagnosis and treatment of illnesses, wounds, and injuries **3.** TREATMENT USING DRUGS the treatment of illness or injury using drugs rather than surgery **4.** MEDICAL PROFESSION the profession of treating illness as a doctor **5.** ANTHROP RITUAL PRACTICE OR SACRED OBJECT a ritual practice or sacred object believed, especially by Native Americans, to control supernatural powers or work as a preventive or remedy of illness [12thC. Directly or via Old French from Latin *medicina* "practice of medicine," formed from *medicus* "doctor," from *mederi* "to heal."]

med·i·cine ball *n.* a large heavy ball that people throw to one another as a strength-building exercise

med·i·cine chest *n.* a small cupboard or chest where medicines, bandages, and other things used in treating illness or injury are stored

med·i·cine dance *n.* a ceremonial religious dance performed by an aboriginal group or individual to obtain supernatural assistance for something, e.g., to cure illness

Med·i·cine Hat /méddəssin hàt/ city in southeastern Alberta, Canada, on the South Saskatchewan River. Population: 46,783 (1996).

med·i·cine lodge *n.* a wooden building used by some Native American peoples for rituals, e.g., ceremonial curing

med·i·cine man *n.* somebody who is believed to heal others by using supernatural powers, especially among Native American peoples

med·i·cine show *n.* a traveling show, especially in the United States in the 19th century, in which medicines were sold to the people who came to see the entertainments

med·ick *n.* PLANTS = **medic**

med·i·co /méddi kō/ (*plural* **-cos**) *n.* a doctor or medical student (*informal*) [Late 17thC. Via Italian from Latin *medicus* (see MEDICINE).]

me·di·e·val /meédee eév'l, méddee-/, **me·di·ae·val** *adj.* **1.** OF THE MIDDLE AGES relating to, involving, belonging to, or typical of the Middle Ages in Europe **2.** OLD-FASHIONED old-fashioned, especially because lacking modern enlightened attitudes ○ *Some of the attitudes in the industry were positively medieval.* [Early 19thC. Formed from modern Latin *medium aevum* "middle age."] —**me·di·e·val·ly** *adv.*

me·di·e·val Greek *n.* the form of Greek used between the 7th and 13th centuries —**Me·di·e·val Greek** *adj.*

me·di·e·val·ism /meédee eév'l ìzzəm, mèddee-/, **me·di·ae·val·ism** *n.* **1.** CUSTOMS AND BELIEFS OF THE MIDDLE AGES the customs, practices, or beliefs during the Middle Ages in Europe **2.** DEVOTION TO THE MIDDLE AGES devotion to the spirit or beliefs of the Middle Ages in Europe **3.** SOMETHING FROM THE MIDDLE AGES a belief, custom, or style from or like one from the Middle Ages

me·di·e·val·ist /meédee eév'list, mèddee-/, **me·di·ae·val·ist** *n.* somebody who studies, teaches the history of, or has special knowedge of the Middle Ages in Europe

me·di·e·val Lat·in *n.* the form of Latin used in Europe during the Middle Ages —**Me·di·e·val Lat·in** *adj.*

me·di·na /mə deénə/, **Me·di·na** *n.* the oldest part of many North African cities [Early 20thC. From Arabic, literally "town."]

Me·di·na /mə deénə/ city in western Saudi Arabia, the site of the Mosque of the Prophet that houses the tomb of Muhammad. Population: 500,000 (1990).

me·di·o·cre /meè dee ṓkər, meè dee ṑkər/ *adj.* adequate but not very good [Late 16thC. Directly or via French from Latin *mediocris*, literally "middle of a rugged mountain," hence "in a middle state," from *medius* "middle" + *ocris* "rugged mountain."]

me·di·oc·ri·ty /meèdee ókrətee/ (*plural* **-ties**) *n.* **1.** AVERAGENESS a quality that is acceptable but not very good ○ *His poetry seldom rises above the level of mediocrity.* **2.** MEDIOCRE PERSON somebody who is not particularly good at anything [15thC. Directly or via French *médiocrité* from Latin *mediocritas*, from *mediocris* (see MEDIOCRE).]

Medit. *abbr.* Mediterranean

med·i·tate /méddi tàyt/ (**-tat·ed, -tat·ing, -tates**) *v.* **1.** *vi.* EMPTY OR CONCENTRATE THE MIND to empty the mind of thoughts, or concentrate the mind on one thing, in order to develop the mind or spirit, aid contemplation, or relax **2.** *vi.* THINK CAREFULLY ABOUT SOMETHING to think about something calmly, seriously, and for some time **3.** *vt.* PLAN SOMETHING to plan or consider doing something [Mid-16thC. Origin uncertain: either from Latin *meditare*, literally "to keep on measuring," related to *mederi* "to cure" (source of English *remedy*); or by back-formation from MEDITATION.] —**med·i·ta·tor** *n.*

med·i·ta·tion /mèddi táysh'n/ *n.* **1.** EMPTYING OR CONCENTRATION OF THE MIND the emptying of the mind of thoughts, or concentration of the mind on just one thing, in order to aid mental or spiritual development, contemplation, or relaxation **2.** PONDERING OF SOMETHING the act of thinking about something deeply and carefully, or an instance of such thinking **3.** SERIOUS STUDY OF A TOPIC an extended and serious study of a particular topic [15thC. Directly or via French from the Latin stem *meditation-*, from, ultimately, *meditari* (see MEDITATE).] —**med·i·ta·tion·al** *adj.* —**med·i·ta·tive** /méddi tàytiv/ *adj.* —**med·i·ta·tive·ly** *adv.* —**med·i·ta·tive·ness** *n.*

Med·i·ter·ra·ne·an /mèddi tə ráynee ən/ *n.* **1.** MEDITERRANEAN SEA OR SURROUNDING AREA the Mediterranean Sea or the lands bordering it ○ *vacationing in the Mediterranean* **2.** SOMEBODY FROM THE AREA OF THE MEDITERRANEAN SEA somebody who lives in or comes from a region bordering the Mediterranean Sea ■ *adj.* **1.** IN OR NEAR THE MEDITERRANEAN SEA in the Mediterranean Sea, or in a region that borders it **2.** TYPICAL OF MEDITERRANEANS typical of the people living in a region that borders the Mediterranean Sea **3.** METEOROL WITH HOT SUMMERS AND WARM WINTERS having hot summers and warm winters, with most of the rainfall occurring in the winter **4.** ANTHROP WITH DARK HAIR AND OLIVE SKIN resembling people from countries around the Mediterranean Sea, who often have dark hair and olive complexions

Med·i·ter·ra·ne·an fe·ver *n.* = **brucellosis** [Because it is commonly contracted in that region]

Med·i·ter·ra·ne·an flour moth *n.* a small gray moth, common worldwide, whose larvae feed on grain and grain products. Latin name: *Anagasta kuehniella.*

Med·i·ter·ra·ne·an fruit fly *n.* a black-and-white two-winged fly that spread worldwide from the Mediterranean region. It lays its eggs in citrus and other types of fruit, which the maggots then destroy. Latin name: *Ceratitis capitata.*

Med·i·ter·ra·ne·an Sea inland sea of Europe, Asia, and Africa, linked to the Atlantic Ocean at its western end by the Strait of Gibraltar. Area: 969,000 sq. mi./2,510,000 sq. km.

me·di·um /meédee əm/ *adj.* **1.** NEITHER LARGE NOR SMALL of middling size or dimensions, neither large nor small ○ *a man of medium build* **2.** COOK BETWEEN RARE AND WELL-DONE cooked so that the meat is brown on the outside but slightly pink and moist inside ■ *n.* (*plural* **-dia** /meédee ə/ *or* **-di·ums**) **1.** STATE BETWEEN EXTREMES an intermediate state or condition halfway between two extremes **2.** MEANS OF MASS COMMUNICATION one of the means of mass communication such as television, radio, or newspapers **3.** VEHICLE FOR IDEAS a means of conveying ideas or information ○ *French is the medium of instruction in all subjects.* **4.** SUBSTANCE CONVEYING SOMETHING a substance through which something is carried or transmitted **5.** PARANORMAL SOMEBODY SUPPOSEDLY COMMUNICATING WITH DEAD somebody who is supposedly able to convey messages between the spirits of the dead and living people **6.** MEANS OF ACHIEVING SOMETHING the means by which something is carried out or achieved **7.** COMPUT MATERIAL HOLDING DATA any form of material on which data is stored or printed, e.g., paper, tape, or disk **8.** BIOL PRESERVING SUBSTANCE a substance in which specimens of animals and plants are preserved or mounted **9.** BIOL = **culture medium** **10.** BIOL NATURAL ENVIRONMENT a substance or the environment in which an organism naturally lives or grows **11.** ARTS TYPE OF ART a method that an artist uses or a category, e.g., sculpture, in which an artist works **12.** ARTS ARTIST'S MATERIALS the materials that an artist uses in creating a work **13.** INDUST SOLVENT a solvent mixed with a pigment or paint to make it thinner **14.** PAPER PAPER SIZE any of several similar sizes of paper, especially 18.5 in. by 23 in./47 cm by 58.5 cm [Late 16thC. From Latin, the neuter of *medius* "middle."]

WORD KEY: ORIGIN

The Latin word *medius*, from which ***medium*** is derived, is also the source of English *immediate, intermezzo, mean, media, mediate, medieval, mediocre, meridian, mezzanine, mitten,* and *moiety.*

me·di·um fre·quen·cy *n.* a radio frequency lying between 300 and 3,000 kilohertz

me·di·um of ex·change *n.* something commonly recognized in a country or community as a standard of value and used in the same way as money, e.g., gold

me·di·um shot *n.* a filmed view, midway between long shot and closeup, that shows a standing person from the waist up or the full body of a sitting person ○ *a medium shot of the two characters in conversation*

med·lar /méddlər/ *n.* **1.** TREES TREE WITH APPLE-SHAPED FRUIT a small tree of the rose family, native to Europe and Asia, that has white flowers, long oblong leaves, and small apple-shaped fruit. Latin name: *Mespilus germanica.* **2.** FOOD FRUIT OF THE MEDLAR TREE the small apple-shaped fruit of the medlar tree. It can be eaten raw when overripe but is more often used to make preserves. [14thC. Via Old French *medler*, from *medle* "medlar fruit" (a variant of *mesle*), from, ultimately, Greek *mespilē*.]

Med. Lat. *abbr.* medieval Latin

med·ley /méddlee/ (*plural* **-leys**) *n.* **1.** MUSIC MUSICAL SEQUENCE OF DIFFERENT SONGS a continuous piece of music consisting of two or more different tunes or songs played one after the other **2.** MIXTURE OF THINGS a mixture or assortment of various things **3. med·ley, med·ley re·lay** SWIMMING SWIMMING RACE USING DIFFERENT STROKES a relay swimming race in which each team member must use a different stroke **4. med·ley, med·ley re·lay** SPORTS RELAY RACE WITH DIFFERENT LENGTHS a relay race in which each member of a team runs a different length [14thC. Via Old French *medlee* (variant of *meslee* "mêlée," source of English *melee*), ultimately from medieval Latin *misculare* "to mix thoroughly."]

me·dul·la /mə dúllə/ (*plural* **-las** *or* **-lae** /-leē/) *n.* **1.** BIOL INNERMOST STRUCTURE the innermost area of a part or organ of an animal or plant ○ *the adrenal medulla* **2.** ANAT = **medulla oblongata** **3.** BOT = **pith** *n.* 2 [14thC. From Latin, "pith, marrow," of uncertain origin: perhaps formed from *medius* (see MEDIUM).] —**me·dul·lar** *adj.*

me·dul·la ob·lon·ga·ta /mə dùllə ob long gaátə/ (*plural* **me·dul·la ob·lon·gatas** *or* **me·dul·lae ob·lon·ga·tae** /mə dù lee ob long gaátee/) *n.* the lowermost part of the brain in vertebrates. It is continuous with the spinal cord and controls involuntary vital functions such as those involved with the heart and lungs. [From Latin, literally "prolonged marrow"]

med·ul·lar·y ray /mə dùlləree-/ *n.* any one of the bands or sheets of connective tissue that radiate between the pith and bark in the stems of some higher woody plants

med·ul·lar·y sheath *n.* ANAT = **myelin sheath**

med·ul·lat·ed /médd'l àytəd, méjjə làytəd/ *adj.* **1.** ANAT = **myelinated** **2.** BIOL WITH MEDULLA having a medulla ○ *medullated fibers*

med·ul·lo·blas·to·ma /mə dùllō bla stṓmə/ (*plural* **-mas** *or* **-ma·ta** /-tə/) *n.* a rapidly growing malignant tumor of the central nervous system arising in the brain. It occurs especially in children. [Early 20thC. Coined from MEDULLA + BLASTO- + -OMA.]

me·dus·a /mə dóozə, -dóossə/ (*plural* **-as** *or* **-ae** /-dóozee, -dóossee/) *n.* **1.** REPRODUCTIVE STAGE OF JELLYFISH the free-swimming reproductive stage of an animal such as a jellyfish, during which it has a transparent umbrella-shaped body with tentacles **2.** = **jellyfish** [Mid-18thC. Via modern Latin, the genus name, from, ultimately, Greek *Medousa* "Medusa," from the resemblance of the tentacles to the snakes on Medusa's head.] —**me·du·san** *adj.*

Medusa: Ancient Roman mosaic, Sousse, France

Me·du·sa *n.* in Greek mythology, a Gorgon who could turn to stone anyone who looked at her. She was killed by Perseus. —**Me·du·san** *adj.*

me·du·soid /mə doo zòyd, -sòyd/ **1.** *adj.* LIKE A MEDUSA relating to, typical of, or like a medusa **2.** *n.* = **medusa** *n.* 1 [Mid-19thC. Coined from MEDUSA + -OID.]

Med·way /méd wày/ river in southeastern England, flowing through Kent to the Thames Estuary. Length: 70 mi./112 km.

meed /meed/ *n.* something given as a reward or compensation (*archaic or literary*) [Old English *mēd* "price, bribe, compensation," of prehistoric Germanic origin]

meek /meek/ *adj.* **1.** MILD showing mildness or quietness of nature **2.** COWED showing submissiveness and lack of initiative or will [12thC. From Old Norse *mjúkr* "soft, pliant." Ultimately from a prehistoric Germanic stem meaning "soft," which is also the ancestor of English *muck*.] —**meek·ly** *adv.* —**meek·ness** *n.*

Meerkat

meer·kat /meér kàt/ *n.* a burrowing South African mongoose with four-toed feet and a grayish coat with faint black markings. Meerkats live in colonies and often stand erect near their burrows. Latin name: *Suricata suricatta.* [Early 19thC. Via Afrikaans from, ultimately, Middle Low German *meerkatte*, literally "sea-cat," from *meer* "sea" + *katte* "cat," of uncertain origin: perhaps an alteration of an Asian word.]

meer·schaum /meérshəm, meér shàwm/ *n.* **1.** MINERAL RESEMBLING CLAY a fine whitish mineral, hydrous magnesium silicate, that resembles clay and is found in the Mediterranean region **2. meer·schaum, meer·schaum pipe** PIPE WITH A MEERSCHAUM BOWL a tobacco pipe with a bowl made of meerschaum [Late 18thC. From German, literally "sea-foam," from *Meer* "sea" + *Schaum* "foam," a translation of Persian *kef-i-daryā* "sea-foam," from its frothy appearance.]

meet[1] /meet/ *v.* (**met** /met/, **meet·ing, meets**) **1.** *vti.* COME ACROSS SOMEBODY to encounter somebody without having arranged to do so beforehand ○ *Guess who I met in the supermarket?* **2.** *vti.* GET TOGETHER to get together with somebody by arrangement ○ *We could meet for lunch tomorrow.* **3.** *vti.* ENCOUNTER SOMEBODY FOR FIRST TIME to encounter somebody or be introduced for the first time ○ *It's exactly a year since they met.* **4.** *vt.* **GREET SOMEBODY** to go somewhere to greet or fetch somebody who is arriving there ○ *I'll come and meet you at the airport.* **5.** *vi.* **GATHER FOR DISCUSSION** to gather in a place to discuss something ○ *The committee meets monthly.* **6.** *vti.* **JOIN SOMETHING** to join, cross, or be adjacent to something or each other ○ *where the two roads meet* **7.** *vti.* **TOUCH SOMETHING** to come into contact with something, or bring two objects into contact ○ *I can't get the two ropes to meet.* **8.** *vti.* **EXPERIENCE SOMETHING** to experience something, e.g., a difficulty, challenge, or success ○ *All our attempts met with failure.* **9.** *vt.* **SATISFY SOMETHING** to cope with, satisfy, or fulfill what is required **10.** *vt.* **AGREE** to come to an agreement on something ○ *I think we can meet you on that price.* **11.** *vti.* **LOOK AT SOMETHING** to look at or confront something, or look at or confront each other ○ *Their glances met.* **12.** *vti.* **COMPETE OR FIGHT WITH SOMEBODY** to come together to compete or fight with somebody else ○ *The two teams have already met this year.* **13.** *vt.* **RESPOND IN A PARTICULAR WAY** to respond to a situation with a particular type of behavior ○ *He met success and failure with equal indifference.* **14.** *vi.* **OCCUR TOGETHER** to happen or come together in the same place or person ○ *The extremes of creativity and irresponsibility meet in this genius.* ■ *n.* SPORTS **SPORTS OCCASION** an occasion at which numbers of competitors and spectators come together [Old English *mētan* "to come upon, fall in with, find, find out." Ultimately from a prehistoric Germanic base meaning "meeting," which is also the ancestor of English *moot.*] —**meet·er** *n.*

meet up *vi.* to get together with somebody

meet² /meet/ *adj.* suitable or fitting for a particular situation (*archaic*) [Old English *gemǣte.* Ultimately from a prehistoric Germanic base meaning "to measure," which is also the ancestor of English *mete out.* Originally also, "having the correct dimensions."] —**meet·ly** *adv.*

meet·ing /méeting/ *n.* **1.** **GATHERING OF PEOPLE FOR DISCUSSION** an occasion when people gather together to discuss something **2.** **GROUP AT A MEETING** the people attending a meeting ○ *The speaker stood up to address the meeting.* **3.** **OCCASION WHEN SOMEBODY MEETS SOMEBODY ELSE** an occasion when somebody encounters somebody else, either accidentally or by arrangement **4.** CHR **OCCASION FOR WORSHIP** a regular occasion when a group of people, especially Quakers, gather for worship

meet·ing·house /méeting hòwss/ *n.* a room or building where some religious groups, especially Quakers, meet to worship

mef·e·nam·ic ac·id /meffə nàmmik-/ *n.* a drug used to reduce inflammation and to relieve the pain of rheumatoid arthritis and menstruation [Mid-20thC. *Mefenamic* coined from METHYL + *-fen-* (an alteration and shortening of PHENYL) + *am-* (a shortening of *amino-*) + *-ic* (a shortening of *benzoic*).]

meg /meg/ *n.* a megabyte (*informal*)

meg- *prefix.* = **mega-** (*used before vowels*)

me·ga /meggə/ *adj.* extremely good or successful (*slang*) ○ *This is going to be mega!*

mega- *prefix.* **1.** one million (10^6) ○ *megavolt* **2.** COMPUT a binary million (2^{20}) ○ *megabyte* **3.** very large ○ *megadose* **4.** very great or excellent (*slang*) ○ *megastar* **5.** to a great extent (*slang*) ○ *megarich* [From Greek *megas* "great." Ultimately from an Indo-European word meaning "large," which is also the ancestor of English much, magnitude, major, and maharajah.]

meg·a·bar /méggə baar/ *n.* a unit of pressure equal to one million bars

meg·a·bit /méggə bit/ *n.* **1.** **1,048,576 BITS** 2^{20} (= 1,048,576) bits **2.** COMPUT **MILLION BITS** one million bits

meg·a·buck /méggə bùk/ *n.* **MILLION DOLLARS** a million dollars (*slang*) ■ **meg·a·bucks** *npl.* **LARGE AMOUNT OF MONEY** a large unspecified amount of money (*slang*) ○ *an actor earning megabucks in Hollywood*

meg·a·byte /méggə bīt/ *n.* **1.** **1,048,576 BYTES** a unit of computer memory or disk storage space equal to 1,048,576 bytes **2.** **MILLION BYTES** one million bytes

meg·a·ceph·a·ly /mèggə séffəlee/ *n.* = **macrocephaly** —**meg·a·ce·phal·ic** /mèggəsə fállik/ *adj.* —**meg·a·ceph·a·lous** /mèggə séffələss/ *adj.*

meg·a·cy·cle /méggə sīk'l/ *n.* = **megahertz**

meg·a·death /méggə dèth/ *n.* one million deaths, used as a unit for recording deaths in a nuclear war

meg·a·dose /méggə dòss/ *n.* a very large dose of a medical drug or food supplement

Me·gae·ra /mə jéerə/ *n.* in Greek mythology, one of the Furies. ◊ **Alecto, Tisiphone**

meg·a·faun·a /mèggə fáwnə/ *n.* all the animals in a certain place that are larger than microscopic size —**meg·a·faun·al** *adj.*

meg·a·gam·ete /méggə gà meet/ *n.* = **macrogamete**

meg·a·hertz /méggə hùrts/ (*plural* **-hertz**) *n.* one million hertz. Symbol **MHz**

meg·a·kar·y·o·cyte /mèggə kérree ə sīt/ *n.* a large cell in bone marrow that fragments to produce blood platelets

meg·a·lith /méggə lith/ *n.* an enormous stone, usually standing upright or forming part of a prehistoric structure —**meg·a·lith·ic** /mèggə líthik/ *adj.*

megalo- *prefix.* exceptionally large ○ *megalocardia* [From Greek *megal-*, the stem of *megas* (see MEGA-)]

meg·a·lo·blast /méggəlō blàst/ *n.* an abnormally large red blood cell that has failed to mature properly, found especially in people affected by anemia

meg·a·lo·blas·tic a·ne·mi·a /meggəlō blàstik-/ *n.* a form of anemia in which the red blood cells are abnormally large because they fail to mature properly. It includes the type formerly known as pernicious anemia. [*Megaloblastic* formed from MEGALOBLAST]

meg·a·lo·car·di·a /mèggəlō kárdee ə/ *n.* = **cardiomegaly**

meg·a·lo·ceph·a·ly /mèggəlō séffəlee/ *n.* = **macrocephaly** —**meg·a·lo·ce·phal·ic** /mèggəlō sə fállik/ *adj.* —**meg·a·lo·ceph·a·lous** /mèggəlō séffələss/ *adj.*

meg·a·lo·ma·ni·a /mèggəlō máynee ə, mèggələ-/ *n.* **1.** **GREED FOR POWER** the enjoyment of having power over other people and the craving for more of it (*disapproving*) **2.** PSYCHIAT **PSYCHIATRIC DISORDER WITH DELUSIONS OF POWER** a psychiatric disorder in which the patient experiences delusions of great power and importance —**meg·a·lo·ma·ni·ac** *n., adj.* —**meg·a·lo·ma·ni·a·cal** /mèggəlō mə nī́ ək'l/ *adj.* —**meg·a·lo·ma·ni·a·cal·ly** /-kəlee/ *adv.*

meg·a·lop·o·lis /mèggə lóppəliss/ *n.* **1.** **AREA CONTAINING LARGE CITIES** an area in which there are several large cities whose suburbs meet or nearly meet **2.** **VERY LARGE CITY** an extremely large and populous city [Mid-19thC. Coined from MEGALO- + Greek *polis* "city."] —**meg·a·lop·o·lis·tic** /mèggə loppə lístik/ *adj.* —**meg·a·lo·pol·i·tan** /mèggələ póllit'n/ *adj.*

meg·a·lo·saur /méggələ sàwr/ *n.* a very large carnivorous dinosaur of the Jurassic and early Cretaceous periods. Genus: *Megalosaurus.* [Mid-19thC. Anglicization of modern Latin *megalosaurus*, from MEGALO- + Greek *sauros* "lizard" (source of English *dinosaur*).] —**meg·a·lo·sau·ri·an** /mèggələ sáwree ən/ *adj.*

-megaly *suffix.* abnormal enlargement ○ *hepatomegaly* [From modern Latin *-megalia*, from Greek *megal-* (see MEGALO-) + *-ia* (see -Y)]

Meg·an's Law /mégganz-/ *n.* LAW an amendment to the Violent Crime Control and Law Enforcement Act of 1994, requiring community notification when a paroled or released sex offender who has been convicted of that crime moves into a neighborhood [Late 20thC. Named for *Megan* Kanka, a seven-year-old girl killed by a convicted child molester who had moved into her New Jersey neighborhood.]

meg·a·phone /méggə fòn/ *n.* **FUNNEL-SHAPED DEVICE TO AMPLIFY THE VOICE** a device shaped like a funnel, used to channel the voice in a certain direction and increase its volume ■ *vti.* (**-phoned, -phon·ing, -phones**) **SPEAK THROUGH A MEGAPHONE** to speak using a megaphone or to say something through one —**meg·a·phon·ic** /mèggə fónnik/ *adj.* —**meg·a·phon·i·cal·ly** *adv.*

meg·a·plex /méggə plèks/ *n.* a large movie theater complex housing at least fifteen screens, often with the same movie playing simultaneously in three or four of the theaters

meg·a·pode /méggə pòd/ *n.* a large Australasian ground-dwelling bird that builds a large mound of earth in which to incubate its eggs. Family: Megapodiidae. [Mid-19thC. From modern Latin *Megapodius*, genus name, from MEGA- + modern Latin *-podius*, masculine of *-podium* "-pod."]

me·gap·o·lis /mə gáppəliss/ *n.* = **megalopolis** *n.* 1 [Mid-17thC. Coined from MEGA- + Greek *polis* "city."]

Meg·a·ra /méggarə/ historic town in southern Greece. It once rivaled ancient Athens in power. Population: 26,562 (1991).

meg·a·ron /méggə ròn/ (*plural* **-ra**) *n.* the largest room in a house built during the Mycenean period of ancient Greek civilization [Late 19thC. From Greek, "large room, hall, sanctuary, shrine."]

meg·a·scop·ic /mèggə skóppik/ *adj.* = **macroscopic** —**meg·a·scop·i·cal·ly** /mèggə skóppikəlee/ *adv.*

meg·a·spore /méggə spàwr/ *n.* the larger of two kinds of spore produced by seed plants and some ferns that develops into a female gametophyte. ◊ **microspore**

meg·a·spo·ro·gen·e·sis /mèggə spawrə jénnəssiss/ *n.* the formation and maturing of the large spores known as megaspores

meg·a·star /méggə staar/ *n.* somebody who is very famous, especially an entertainer who is extremely popular

meg·a·there /méggə theer/ *n.* a large extinct American ground sloth that lived in the Miocene and Pleistocene epochs. Family: Megatheriidae. [Mid-19thC. Anglicization of modern Latin *Megatherium*, the genus name, from Greek *mega-* "large" + *thērion* "animal."] —**meg·a·the·ri·an** /mèggə théeree ən/ *adj.*

meg·a·ton /méggə tùn/ *n.* **1.** **UNIT OF EXPLOSIVE POWER** a unit of explosive power, e.g., in a nuclear weapon, that is equivalent to one million tons of TNT **2.** **MILLION TONS** one million tons —**meg·a·ton·ic** /mèggə túnnik/ *adj.* —**meg·a·ton·nage** /méggə túnnij/ *n.*

meg·a·vi·ta·min /mèggə vī́təmin/ *n.* a dose of a vitamin or vitamins that is much higher than the normal dose —**meg·a·vi·ta·min** *adj.*

meg·a·volt /méggə vòlt/ *n.* one million volts —**meg·a·volt·age** *n.*

meg·a·watt /méggə wòt/ *n.* one million watts —**meg·a·watt·age** /méggə wòttij/ *n.*

Me·gid·do /mə géedō/ ruined ancient city in northern Israel, thought to be the predicted site of the battle of Armageddon described in the Bible

me·gil·lah /mə gíllə/ (*plural* **-lahs** *or* **-loth** /-lōt/) *n.* **1.** JUDAISM **HEBREW SCROLL** a scroll containing part of the Hebrew Bible, especially the scroll containing the Book of Esther **2.** **OVERLY ELABORATE ACCOUNT** an overly elaborate and unnecessarily lengthy account of something [Mid-17thC. From Hebrew, literally "roll, scroll," from *gālal* "roll."]

meg·ilp /mə gílp/, **mag·ilp** *n.* a mixture of linseed oil and mastic varnish or turpentine, used as a solvent for oil paints [Mid-18thC. Origin unknown.]

me·grim /méegrim/ *n.* (*archaic*) **1.** MED **MIGRAINE** a migraine headache **2.** **WHIM** a sudden change of mind, or something about which somebody is briefly enthusiastic (*often used in the plural*) ■ **me·grims** *npl.* **MELANCHOLY** a spell of melancholy or low spirits (*archaic*) [15thC. Variant of MIGRAINE.]

mei·bo·mi·an cyst /mī bōmee ən-/ *n.* a painless swelling in the eyelid, somewhat like a pea, caused by blockage of the outlet duct of a meibomian gland and the resulting accumulation of fatty secretion [See MEIBOMIAN GLAND]

mei·bo·mi·an gland *n.* any of the sebaceous glands in the eyelid [Early 19thC. Named for Heinrich *Meibom* (1638–1700), a German anatomist who discovered it.]

Meighen /máygən/, **Arthur** (1874–1960) Canadian lawyer, businessman, and statesman. He was prime minister of Canada (1920–21 and 1926).

Mei·ji /may jée, mày jée/ *n.* the reign of the Japanese emperor Meiji Tenno (1867–1912), a period of extensive reform, including the abolition of feudalism [Late 19thC. From Japanese, literally "enlightened government."]

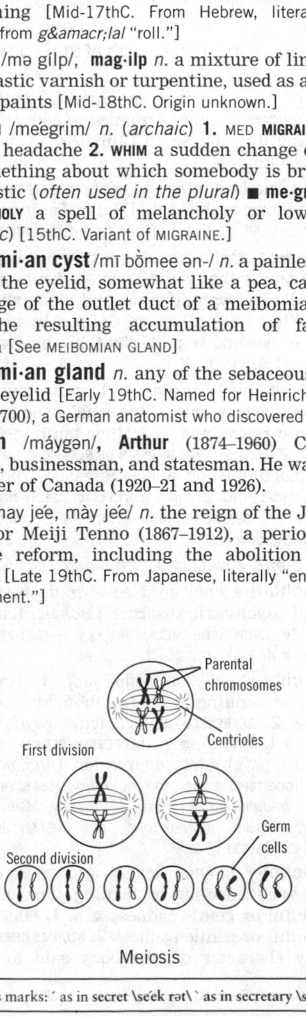

Meiosis

Mei·ji Ten·no /ténnō/, **Emperor of Japan** (1852–1912). During a long reign (1867–1912), he modernized Japanese industry and introduced a new constitution (1889). Born **Mutsuhito**

mei·o·sis /mī óssiss/ *n.* **1.** CELL BIOL **PROCESS OF CELL DIVISION** in organisms that reproduce sexually, a process of cell division during which the nucleus divides into four nuclei, each of which contains half the usual number of chromosomes **2.** LITERAT = **litotes** [Mid-16thC. Via modern Latin from, ultimately, Greek *meiōn* "less." Originally meaning "litotes."]

AKG London

Golda Meir

Me·ir /mī ər, may éer/, **Golda** (1898–1978)Russian-born Israel national leader. She entered the Labor government of Israel in 1949 and served as prime minister from 1969 until 1974, when she resigned after the Yom Kippur War (1973).

Meis·sen[1] /míss'n/ *n.* fine and delicate porcelain as made in Meissen since the early 18th century

Meis·sen[2] /míssən/ town in east central Germany, famous for its porcelain manufacture. Population: 36,800 (1989).

Meis·ter·sing·er /místər sìngər/ (*plural* **-ers** *or* **-er**) *n.* somebody who belonged to one of the German guilds for poets and musicians in the 14th, 15th, and 16th centuries. A Meistersinger had completed an apprenticeship and composed original work. [Mid-19thC. From German, literally "master-singer."]

Mek·nés /mèk nés/ city and former capital of Morocco, located in the north of the country. Population: 401,000 (1993).

Me·kong /mee kóng/ major river in southeastern Asia, flowing through a number of countries before emptying into the South China Sea. Length: 2,600 mi./4,200 km.

Me·la·ka /mə lákə/ city and seaport in Malaysia, on the southern coast of the Malay Peninsula. Population: 295,999 (1991). Former name **Malacca**

mel·a·leu·ca /mèllə lóokə/ *n.* a tree or shrub of the myrtle family that is native to Australia and grows especially in swampy areas and along rivers. One species has naturalized in California and Florida and has become a pest plant in the Everglades. Genus: *Melaleuca.*

mel·a·mine /méllə meen/ *n.* **1.** CHEM **COMPOUND USED IN RESINS** a white crystalline solid used in making synthetic resins and in leather tanning. Formula: $C_3H_6N_6$. **2.** INDUST **TYPE OF RESIN OR PLASTIC** a resin made from melamine, or a plastic made from such a resin [Mid-19thC. Origin uncertain: probably from German *Melamin,* a substance obtained from the distillation of ammonium thiocyanate.]

melan- *prefix.* = **melano-** (*used before vowels*)

mel·an·cho·li·a /mèllən kólee ə/ *n.* depression as a form of psychiatric disorder (*archaic*) [Early 17thC. From late Latin (see MELANCHOLY).] —**mel·an·cho·li·ac** /mèllən kólee àk/ *n., adj.*

mel·an·chol·ic /mèllən kóllik/ *adj.* **1. PENSIVELY SAD** feeling or tending to feel a thoughtful or gentle sadness **2. DEPRESSED** experiencing psychiatric depression (*archaic*) ■ *n.* **DEPRESSED PERSON** somebody who has psychiatric depression (*archaic*) [14thC. Origin uncertain: either formed from MELANCHOLY, or via French *mélancolique* from, ultimately, Greek *melankholikhos,* from *melankholia* (see MELANCHOLY).] —**mel·an·chol·i·cal·ly** *adv.*

mel·an·chol·y /méllən kòllee/ *adj.* **FEELING OR CAUSING PENSIVE SADNESS** feeling or making somebody feel a thoughtful or gentle sadness ■ *n.* **1. PENSIVE SADNESS** thoughtful or gentle sadness **2. GLOOMY CHARACTER** the gloomy character of somebody said to have an excess of black bile, one of the four bodily humors that were once thought to determine people's health and emotional state (*archaic*) **3.** = **black bile** (*archaic*) [14thC. Directly or via French *mélancholie* from late Latin *melancholia,* from Greek *melankholia,* literally "black bile," from *melan-,* the stem of *melas* "black" + *kholē* "bile."] —**mel·an·chol·i·ly** *adv.* —**mel·an·chol·i·ness** *n.*

Me·lanch·thon, Philipp (1497–1560) German religious reformer. Working in association with Martin Luther, he produced some of the most important theological works of the Protestant Reformation, including *Commonplaces of Theology* (1521) and the Augsburg Confession (1530). Real name **Philipp Schwartzert**

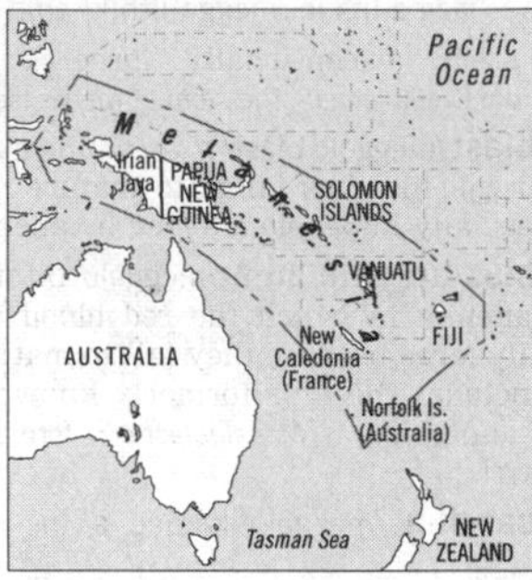

Melanesia

Mel·a·ne·sia /mèllə néezee ə, -néezhə/ ethnographic region in Oceania, encompassing a number of island groups in the western Pacific Ocean, south of the equator

Mel·a·ne·sian /mèllə néezh'n/ *adj.* **OF MELANESIA** relating to Melanesia, or its peoples, cultures, or languages ■ *n.* **1.** LANG **GROUP OF PACIFIC ISLAND LANGUAGES** a group of languages, including Fijian, spoken in Melanesia, a subgroup of the Eastern branch of the Austronesian family of languages. About 300,000 people speak a Melanesian language. **2.** PEOPLES **SOMEBODY FROM MELANESIA** a member of any of the peoples living on the islands of Melanesia

mé·lange /may láaNzh, may láanzh/, **me·lange** *n.* **1. MIXTURE OF THINGS** a collection of things of different kinds (*literary or formal*) **2.** GEOL **MIXTURE OF ROCKS** a region of rock that consists of a mixture of dissimilar rocky materials [Mid-17thC. From French *mêlange,* from *mêler* "mix," ultimately from Latin *miscere* (see MIXED).]

mel·a·nin /méllənin/ *n.* a dark brown or black pigment that is naturally present to varying degrees in the skin, hair, eyes, fur, or feathers of people and animals as well as in plants —**mel·a·noid** *adj.*

mel·a·nism /méllə nìzzəm/ *n.* **1.** BIOL **DARK PIGMENTATION** dark pigmentation of the skin, hair, fur, or feathers in a human being, animal, or plant, resulting from the presence of melanin **2.** MED = **melanosis** —**me·lan·ic** /mə lánnik/ *adj.* —**mel·a·nis·tic** /mèllə nístik/ *adj.*

mel·a·nite /méllə nīt/ *n.* a black form of andradite garnet containing titanium —**mel·a·nit·ic** /mèllə níttik/ *adj.*

melano- *prefix.* black, dark ○ *melanocyte* [From Greek *melan-,* the stem of *melas* "black" (source of English *melancholy*)]

mel·a·no·blast /méllə nō blàst, mə lánnə-/ *n.* a cell that gives rise to either a melanocyte or melanophore, which produces the black or dark brown pigment melanin —**mel·a·no·blas·tic** /mèllə nō blástik, mə lànnə-/ *adj.*

mel·a·no·cyte /méllə nō sīt, mə lánnə-/ *n.* a cell in the epidermal layer of the skin that produces the black or dark brown pigment melanin

mel·a·no·cyte-stim·u·lat·ing hor·mone *n.* either of two hormones in vertebrates produced in the pituitary gland that darken the skin by regulating melanin dispersal

mel·a·no·ma /mèllə nómə/ (*plural* **-mas** *or* **-ma·ta** /-nómətə/) *n.* a malignant tumor, most often on the skin, that contains dark pigment and develops from a melanin-producing cell (**melanocyte**)

mel·a·no·phore /méllə nō fàwr, mə lánnə-/ *n.* a cell in fishes, amphibians, and reptiles that contains the black to dark brown pigment melanin

mel·a·no·sis /mèllə nóssiss/ *n.* an unexpected presence of dark pigmentation in the tissues [Early 19thC. From modern Latin, from the Greek stem *melan-* (see MELANCHOLY).] —**me·lan·ic** /mə lánnik/ *adj.* —**mel·a·noid** /méllə nòyd/ *adj.* —**mel·a·not·ic** /mèllə nóttik/ *adj.*

mel·a·nous /méllənəss/ *adj.* having a dark complexion and dark hair [Mid-19thC. Formed from the Greek stem *melan-* (see MELANCHOLY).] —**mel·a·nos·i·ty** /mèllə nóssətee/ *n.*

mel·a·to·nin /mèlə tónin/ *n.* a hormone derived from serotonin and secreted by the pineal gland that produces changes in the skin color of vertebrates, reptiles, and amphibians and is important in regulating biorhythms [Mid-20thC. Blend of MELANO- + SEROTONIN.]

Library of Congress

Dame Nellie Melba

Mel·ba /mélbə/, **Dame Nellie** (1861–1931) Australian opera singer. She was a soprano who won international acclaim for her performances in roles such as Mimi in *La Bohème.* Real name **Helen Porter Mitchell**

Mel·ba sauce *n.* a sauce consisting of pureed sweetened raspberries, served especially with poached peaches and ice cream in peach Melba [Early 20thC. Named for Nellie MELBA, in whose honor peach Melba was created.]

Mel·ba toast *n.* very thin slices of bread toasted on both sides, sliced horizontally to expose two untoasted sides of bread that are then toasted too, causing the bread to curl [Early 20thC. Named for Nellie MELBA, because it was part of her diet during an illness in 1897.]

Mel·bourne /mélburn, -bawrn/ **1.** city in southeastern Australia, the capital of the state of Victoria. Population: 2,865,329 (1996). **2.** coastal city in eastern Florida. Population: 59,646 (1990).

Mel·chi·or /mélkee àwr/, **Lauritz** (1890–1973) Danish-born U.S. opera singer. He was a tenor known for his Wagnerian roles, especially at the Metropolitan Opera House (1929–50). Full name **Lauritz Lebrecht Hommel Melchior**

Mel·chite *n.* RELIG = **Melkite**

Mel·chiz·e·dek /mel kízzə dèk/ *n.* **1. BIBLICAL PRIEST AND KING** in the Bible, a priest and king of Salem who blessed Abraham **2. SENIOR MORMON PRIESTS** the senior order of priests in the Mormon Church

meld[1] /meld/ *vti.* (**meld·ed, meld·ing, melds**) **COMBINE** to cause various things to combine or blend and become one thing or substance, or be combined or blended in this way ■ *n.* **COMBINATION** a combination or blend of various things [Mid-20thC. Origin uncertain: perhaps from the past participle of a dialect word *mell* "to mix," from Old French *mesler* (see MELEE).]

meld[2] /meld/ *vti.* (**meld·ed, meld·ing, melds**) **SHOW A HAND OF CARDS** to show or declare some or all of a hand of cards in order to score points in games such as canasta or pinochle ■ *n.* **HAND OF SHOWN OR DECLARED CARDS** a hand of cards that are shown or declared in order to score points in games such as canasta or pinochle, or an act of showing or declaring these cards [Late 19thC. From German *melden* "to announce."]

Me·lea·ger /mélee áyər/ *n.* in Greek mythology, a prince who killed the Calydonian boar

me·lee /máy lày, may láy/, **mê·lée** /me láy/ *n.* **1. FIGHT** a noisy confused fight **2. CONFUSED MINGLING** a confused, often noisy mixing of people or things, usually in a public place [Mid-17thC. Via French *mêlée* from Old French *meslee,* the past participle of *mesler* "to mix," via assumed Vulgar Latin *misculare* from Latin *miscere.*]

me·le·na /mə léénə/ *n.* a condition characterized by the production of black stools that are caused by bleeding into the bowel and the subsequent chemical changes in the blood effected by the bowel fluids [Early 19thC. Via modern Latin from Greek *melaina*, feminine of *melas* "black" (source of English *melancholy* and *melano-*).]

mel·ic /méllik/ *adj.* used to describe an ancient Greek lyric poem that is meant to be sung rather than recited [Late 17thC. Via Latin from Greek *melikos*, from *melos* "song" (source of English *melody* and *melodrama*).]

Me·lil·la /mə léélə/ Spanish enclave and port on the Mediterranean coast of Morocco. Population: 64,727 (1995). Area: 5.5 sq. mi./14 sq. km.

mel·i·lot /méllə lòt/ *n.* a plant belonging to the pea family that has compound leaves consisting of three oval leaflets, and spikes of small flared yellow or white flowers. Genus: *Melilotus.* [14thC. Via French from, ultimately, Greek *melilōtos*, from *meli* "honey" + *lōtos* "lotus, clover."]

mel·i·nite /méllə nìt/ *n.* an explosive made from picric acid [Late 19thC. From French, formed from Greek *mēlinos* "quince-colored," from *mēlon* "apple, quince" (source of English *melon*); so called because of its yellow color.]

mel·io·rate /méelee ə ràyt/ (**-rat·ed, -rat·ing, -rates**) *vti.* to become better, or make something better [Mid-16thC. From late Latin *meliorare*, from Latin *melior* "better."] —**mel·io·ra·ble** *adj.* —**mel·io·ra·tion** /méelee ə ráysh'n/ *n.* —**mel·io·ra·tive** /méelee ə ràytiv/ *adj.* —**mel·io·ra·tor** /-ràytər/ *n.*

mel·io·rism /méelee ə rìzzəm/ *n.* the belief that human society has a natural tendency to improve and that people can consciously assist this process [Mid-19thC. Formed from Latin *melior* "better."] —**mel·io·rist** *n.* —**mel·io·ris·tic** /méelee ə rístik/ *adj.*

me·lis·ma /mə lízmə/ (*plural* **-ma·ta** /-mətə/ *or* **-mas**) *n.* **1. SEVERAL NOTES SUNG ON ONE SYLLABLE** a decorative phrase or passage in vocal music, especially one in which one syllable of a plainsong text is sung to a melodic sequence of several notes **2. EMBELLISHMENT OF MELODY** an embellishment or decoration of a melody **3.** = **cadenza** [Late 19thC. Via modern Latin from Greek, "tune," from *melizein* "to sing," from *melos* "song" (source of English *melody*).] —**mel·is·mat·ic** /mèlliz máttik/ *adj.*

Mel·kite /mél kìt/, **Mel·chite** *n.* a member of any of several Christian churches in the Middle East that use the Greek Orthodox liturgy but acknowledge the authority of the Roman Catholic Pope [Early 17thC. Via ecclesiastical Latin from Byzantine Greek *Melkhitai* "Melkites," from Syriac *malkāyē*, literally "royalists," from *malkā* "king."]

melli- *prefix.* honey ○ *melliphagous* [From Latin *mel* (source of English *molasses*). Ultimately from the Indo-European for "honey," which is also the ancestor of *marmalade* and *mildew*.]

mel·lif·er·ous /mə líffərəss/, **mel·lif·ic** /mə líffik/ *adj.* producing or bearing large quantities of honey [Mid-17thC. Formed from Latin *mellifer* "honey-bearing," from *mel* "honey."]

mel·lif·lu·ous /mə líffloo əss/, **mel·lif·lu·ent** /mə líffloo ənt/ *adj.* pleasant and soothing to listen to, and sweet or rich in tone [15thC. Formed from late Latin *mellifluus*, literally "flowing like honey," from Latin *mel* "honey" (see MELLI-) + *fluere* "to flow" (see FLUENT).] —**mel·lif·lu·ous·ly** *adv.* —**mel·lif·lu·ous·ness** *n.*

mel·liph·a·gous /mə líffəgəss/, **mel·liv·o·rous** /mə lívvərəss/ *adj.* feeding on honey

mel·lo·phone /méllə fòn/ *n.* a portable brass musical instrument similar in tone to a French horn, used mainly in brass bands and marching bands [Early 20thC. Coined from MELLOW + -PHONE.]

mel·low /méllō/ *adj.* **1. SOFT IN COLOR OR TONE** comfortingly soft, warm, and rich in color or tone and lacking any harsh, brash, or jarring quality **2. SMOOTH AND RICH IN TASTE** matured to a long-lasting smooth, rich taste **3. FULLY RIPE** soft, juicy, fully ripened and sweet **4. EASYGOING** good-humored, tolerant, and approachable, especially as a result of long experience or a relaxed atmosphere **5. MILDLY INTOXICATED** mildly intoxicated by drink or drugs **6.** AGRIC **MOIST AND RICH IN TEXTURE** having a moist, rich, loamy texture ■ *vti.* (**-lowed, -low·ing, -lows**) **1. BECOME MORE EASYGOING** to become or make somebody more good-humored, tolerant, and approachable, especially as a result of long experience or a relaxed atmosphere **2. BECOME OR MAKE RICHER IN QUALITY** to become or make something richer, smoother, or softer in taste, color, tone, or atmosphere [15thC. Origin uncertain: perhaps an adjectival use of Old English *melu* "meal, flour," the underlying sense being "soft and rich like flour."] —**mel·low·ly** *adv.* —**mel·low·ness** *n.*

mellow out *vti.* (*slang*) **1. RELAX** to become or make somebody more relaxed and friendly **2. CALM DOWN** to become calm, or make somebody calm

me·lo·de·on /mə lódee ən/ *n.* **1. SMALL REED ORGAN** a small reed organ, similar to a harmonium, that uses suction bellows to draw air through its reeds **2. SMALL ACCORDION** a small accordion, used especially by German folk musicians [Mid-19thC. Origin uncertain: probably an alteration of *melodium* "small reed organ," from MELODY on the model of HARMONIUM.]

me·lod·ic /mə lóddik/ *adj.* **1. CONSISTING OF MELODY** consisting of the melody of a piece of music ○ *the melodic line* **2. RELATING TO MELODY** relating to or characteristic of melody or the composition of melodies **3.** = **melodious** —**me·lod·i·cal·ly** *adv.*

me·lod·ic mi·nor scale *n.* a scale with the sixth and seventh notes raised a half step when played in ascending order but in the natural minor pitch when played in descending order

me·lo·di·ous /mə lódee əss/ *adj.* **1. PLEASING TO HEAR** tuneful or varied and interesting in tone **2. CHARACTERIZED BY MELODY** having the character of a melody —**me·lo·di·ous·ly** *adv.* —**me·lo·di·ous·ness** *n.*

mel·o·dist /méllə dist/ *n.* **1. COMPOSER OF MELODIES** somebody who composes melodies, especially beautiful or memorable melodies for song lyrics **2. SINGER** somebody who sings sweetly

mel·o·dize /méllə dìz/ (**-dized, -diz·ing, -diz·es**) *v.* **1.** *vti.* **COMPOSE MELODIES** to compose a melody or melodies, or compose a melody to which lyrics can be sung **2.** *vt.* **MAKE SOMETHING MELODIOUS** to make something tuneful and pleasing to hear —**mel·o·diz·er** *n.*

mel·o·dra·ma /méllə draamə, -drámmə/ *n.* **1. SENSATIONALIZED DRAMATIC OR LITERARY WORK** a dramatic or other literary work characterized by the use of stereotyped characters, exaggerated emotions and language, simplistic morality, and conflict **2. DRAMATIC OR LITERARY GENRE** melodramas collectively considered as a dramatic or literary genre **3. HISTRIONIC BEHAVIOR** exaggerated behavior or emotional displays, like those characteristic of a melodrama **4. DRAMA INTERSPERSED WITH MUSIC** formerly, a play with a sensational or romantic plot that is interspersed with musical numbers and often has music accompanying the action **5. SPOKEN WORDS WITH MUSICAL ACCOMPANIMENT** a piece of poetry or a scene in a dramatic or operatic work in which the text is recited to a musical accompaniment [Early 19thC. From French *mélodrame* "drama with songs," from Greek *melos* "song" + French *drame* (see DRAMA).]

mel·o·dra·mat·ic /mèllə drə máttik/ *adj.* **1. EXAGGERATEDLY THEATRICAL** behaving, speaking, done, or said in a way that is more dramatic, shocking, or highly emotional than the situation demands **2. RELATING TO MELODRAMA** relating to or typical of melodrama [Early 19thC. Formed from MELODRAMA, on the model of DRAMATIC.] —**mel·o·dra·mat·i·cal·ly** *adv.*

mel·o·dra·mat·ics /mèllə drə máttiks/ *npl.* exaggeratedly theatrical behavior, speech, or writing

melo·dra·ma·tize /mèllə draamə tìz, -drámmə tìz/ (**-tized, -tiz·ing, -tizes**) *vti.* to treat or react to something in an exaggeratedly theatrical way [Early 19thC. Formed from MELODRAMA, on the model of DRAMATIZE.] —**melo·dra·ma·ti·za·tion** /mèllə draaməti záysh'n, -drammәti-/ *n.*

mel·o·dy /méllədee/ (*plural* **-dies**) *n.* **1. TUNE** a series of musical notes that form a distinct unit, are recognizable as a phrase, and usually have a distinctive rhythm **2. LINEAR MUSICAL STRUCTURE** the linear structure of a piece of music in which single notes follow one another **3. MAIN TUNE** the primary and most recognizable part in a harmonic piece of music **4. MUSICALLY EXPRESSIVE QUALITY** the musically expressive quality of something, especially poetry **5. MUSICAL LYRIC** a poem that lends itself easily to being set to music or sung [12thC. Via French *mélodie* from, ultimately, Greek *melōidia* "choral song," from *melos* "tune" + *aoidē* "song" (see ODE).]

mel·oid /mé lòyd/ *n.* any beetle with a flexible body, e.g., the blister beetle or the oil beetle. Family: Meloidae. [Late 19thC. From modern Latin *Meloidae*, family name, from *Meloē*, genus name, of uncertain origin.]

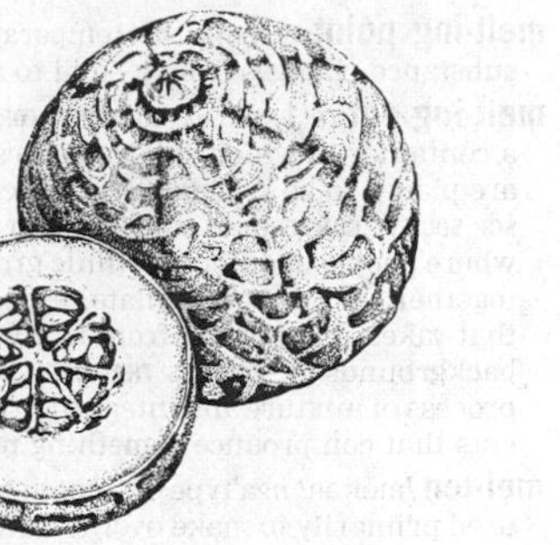

Melon

mel·on /méllən/ *n.* **1.** FOOD **ROUND JUICY GOURD FRUIT** the round edible fruit of vines belonging to the gourd family, with a tough rind and sweet juicy flesh ranging in color from pale yellow to deep orange **2.** PLANTS **PLANT THAT BEARS MELONS** a vine of the gourd family widely grown for its edible fruit. Latin name: *Cucumis melo* and *Citrullus lanatus.* **3.** ZOOL **IN SEA MAMMAL SOUND ORGAN'S HEAD** a rounded waxy mass found in the head of some dolphins and toothed whales that is thought to play a part in the focusing of sound signals **4.** FIN **SURPLUS PROFIT** a surplus of profit that can be distributed to stockholders (*informal*) **5.** FIN an unexpected financial gain (*informal*) **6. OFFENSIVE TERM** an offensive term for a woman's large breast (*offensive*) [14thC. Via French from, ultimately, Greek *mēlopepōn*, a kind of gourd, from *mēlon* "apple" + *pepōn* "gourd."]

Mel·pom·e·ne /mel pómmənee/ *n.* in Greek mythology, the muse of tragedy

Mel·rose /mél rōz/ city in northeastern Massachusetts, north of Malden, a northern suburb of Boston. Population: 27,426 (1996).

Mel·rose Park village in northeastern Illinois, west of Oak Park, a western suburb of Chicago. Population: 20,597 (1996).

melt[1] /melt/ *v.* **1.** *vti.* **CHANGE FROM A SOLID TO A LIQUID STATE** to change a substance from a solid to a liquid state by heating it, or be changed in this way **2.** *vti.* **DISSOLVE** to dissolve something, e.g., sugar, in a liquid or be dissolved in a liquid **3.** *vi.* **DISAPPEAR** to disappear gradually and inconspicuously **4.** *vi.* **MERGE INTO** to change into, or blend with, something in such a way that the actual point of change or blending is almost imperceptible **5.** *vti.* **BE MOVED EMOTIONALLY** to cause somebody to be moved emotionally so as to become gentler and more sympathetic, or be moved in this way **6.** *vi.* **FEEL HOT** to feel uncomfortably hot (*informal*) ■ *n.* **1. MASS OF MELTED MATERIAL** a mass or an amount of melted material, especially metal, produced in a single operation or during a specific period of time **2. MOLTEN MATERIAL** a material such as metal or glass in a molten state **3. MELTING OF SOMETHING** the process of melting something **4. LIQUEFACTION** the state or condition of being liquefied **5.** METEOROL **PERIOD OF THAW** the period of time during which snow and ice thaw **6.** FOOD **GRILLED SANDWICH** an open-faced hot sandwich with melted cheese on top —**melt·a·bil·i·ty** /mèltə bíllətee/ *n.* —**melt·a·ble** *adj.* —**melt·er** *n.*

melt down *vti.* to liquefy metal or glass by heating in order to reuse it, or to be liquefied in this way

melt[2] /melt/ *n.* the spleen of a slaughtered animal, used mainly for animal food (*often used in the plural*) [Late 16thC. Variant of MILT.]

melt·age /méltij/ *n.* **1. MELTING OF SOMETHING** the process of melting something **2. SUBSTANCE PRODUCED BY MELTING** a liquefied substance produced by a heating process, or an amount of such a substance

melt·down /mélt dòwn/ *n.* **1.** PHYS **MELTING OF NUCLEAR REACTOR FUEL RODS** the melting of fuel rods in a nuclear reactor because of overheating that results in the escape of radioactive materials or radiation **2. COMPLETE COLLAPSE OF AN ORGANIZATION** a situation of complete collapse of an organization or institution (*informal*) **3. EXTREMELY ANGRY STATE** a loss of composure, especially an extremely angry response to something (*informal*) **4. PERSONAL BREAKDOWN** a loss of coherence, rationality, or awareness of reality (*informal*)

melt·ing /mélting/ *adj.* full of or causing sweet and tender or sentimental emotion —**melt·ing·ly** *adv.* —**melt·ing·ness** *n.*

melt·ing point *n.* PHYS the temperature at which a substance changes from a solid to a liquid form

melt·ing pot *n.* **1.** METALL **CONTAINER FOR MELTING AND MIXING** a container in which substances, especially metals, are placed to be liquefied and mixed together **2.** SOC SCI **SOCIETY COMPOSED OF MANY DIFFERENT CULTURES** a place where people of different ethnic groups are brought together and can assimilate, especially a country that takes immigrants from many different ethnic backgrounds **3. PROCESS THAT CREATES SOMETHING NEW** a process of mixture and integration of different elements that can produce something new

mel·ton /méltən/ *n.* a type of smooth heavy wool cloth, used primarily to make overcoats [Mid-19thC. Named for the town of *Melton* Mowbray in Leicestershire, England, where it was made.]

melt·wa·ter /mélt wàwtər, -wòttər/ *n.* water formed by the melting of ice or snow, especially from a glacier

Mel·ville /mélvil/, **Herman** (1818–91) U.S. writer. His allegorical sea novel *Moby Dick* (1851) is sometimes held to be the greatest work of American fiction.

Mel·ville Is·land uninhabited island in northwestern Canada, divided between Nunavut and Northwest Territories, in the Arctic Ocean. Area: 16,274 sq. mi./42,149 sq. km.

mem /mem/ *n.* the 13th letter of the Hebrew alphabet, represented in the English alphabet as "m" [Early 19thC. From Hebrew *mēm*, literally "water."]

mem. *abbr.* **1.** member **2.** memoir **3.** memorandum **4.** memorial

mem·ber /mémbər/ *n.* **1. SOMEBODY BELONGING TO PARTICULAR GROUP** somebody who belongs to and participates in a particular group by birth, e.g., a family, species, or social class, or by choice, e.g., a club, church, or organization **2. mem·ber, Mem·ber** POL **POLITICAL REPRESENTATIVE** somebody elected to a legislative body such as the British Parliament or the U.S. Congress **3. LIMB** a part or organ of a plant or animal body, especially a limb **4. PENIS** a penis (*formal or humorous*) **5. INDIVIDUAL PART OF A WHOLE** a separate and distinct part of a whole, e.g., an object belonging to a mathematical set, a clause in a sentence, or a proposition in a syllogism **6.** CONSTR **STRUCTURAL UNIT IN BUILDING** a beam, wall, or similar structural unit in a building or other construction **7.** MATH **ELEMENT IN A MATHEMATICAL EQUATION** either of the expressions in a mathematical equation linked by an equal sign [14thC. Via French *membre* from Latin *membrum* "limb, part" (source also of English *membrane*).] —**mem·ber·less** *adj.*

mem·ber firm *n.* a company trading in securities that belongs to an organized exchange

Mem·ber of Con·gress *n.* somebody elected to the U.S. Congress, especially to the House of Representatives

Mem·ber of Par·lia·ment *n.* somebody who has been elected to a parliament

mem·ber·ship /mémbər shìp/ *n.* **1. BEING A MEMBER OF SOMETHING** the state or condition belonging to a particular group, e.g., a species, social class, team, club, or political party **2. MEMBERS OF AN ORGANIZATION** the members of a group, e.g., a species, social class, organization, or mathematical set, considered collectively

mem·brane /mém bràyn/ *n.* **1.** BIOL **THIN LAYER OF TISSUE** a thin flexible sheet of tissue connecting, covering, lining, or separating various parts or organs in animal and plant bodies, or forming the external wall of a cell **2.** CHEM **THIN POROUS SHEET** a thin, pliable, and often porous sheet of any natural or artificial material **3. PIECE OF PARCHMENT** a piece of parchment forming part of a roll [15thC. Directly or via French from Latin *membrana* "skin (covering part of the body)," from *membrum* "limb, part" (source of English *member*).] —**mem·bra·na·ceous** /mèmbrə náyshəss/ *adj.* —**mem·bra·nal** /mémbrən'l/ *adj.* —**mem·braned** *adj.*

mem·brane bone *n.* a bone that develops directly out of membranous connective tissue rather than from cartilage, e.g., the clavicle and some cranial bones

mem·brane trans·port *n.* the process by which substances in solution pass through a biological membrane

mem·bra·nous /mémbrənəss/ *adj.* **1.** BIOL **RELATING TO A MEMBRANE** relating to or similar to a membrane, especially in being thin, pliable, and often translucent **2.** PHYSIOL **RESULTING IN THE FORMATION OF A MEMBRANE** resulting in the formation of a membrane or of a thin layer similar to a membrane —**mem·bra·nous·ly** *adv.*

mem·bra·nous lab·y·rinth *n.* the structure of fluid-filled sacs in the inner ear that are vital to hearing and balance

me·men·to /mə mén tō/ (*plural* **-tos** *or* **-toes**) *n.* an object given or kept as a reminder of or in memory of somebody or something [Mid-18thC. From Latin, "remember" (originally the first word in prayers for the dead), from *meminisse* "to remember."]

me·men·to mo·ri /-máwree/ (*plural* **me·men·to mo·ri**) *n.* **1. REMINDER OF DEATH** an object, especially a skull, intended as a reminder of the fact that humans die **2. REMINDER OF HUMAN ERROR** a reminder of the fact that humans fail and make mistakes (*literary*) [From Latin, "remember (that you have) to die"]

Mem·non /mém nòn/ *n.* in Greek mythology, the Ethiopian king who fought for the Trojans in the siege of Troy and was killed by Achilles

mem·o /mémmō/ (*plural* **-os**) *n.* **1. WRITTEN COMMUNICATION** a written communication similar to a letter but without the formal address blocks at the beginning, especially one that is circulated to people within an office or organization **2.** U.K. = **memorandum** *n.* 2 [Early 18thC. Shortening of MEMORANDUM.]

mem·oir /mém waar/ *n.* **1. BIOGRAPHY OR HISTORICAL ACCOUNT** a biography or an account of historical events, especially one written from personal knowledge **2. ESSAY ON A SCHOLARLY SUBJECT** a short essay, article, or report on a scholarly subject, usually one in which the writer is a recognized specialist ■ **mem·oirs** *npl.* **1. AUTOBIOGRAPHY** somebody's written account of his or her own life, or of events in which he or she took part **2. PROCEEDINGS** the records of the business and discussions of a learned society [Mid-17thC. Via French *mémoire* "memory, recollection" from Old French *memorie* (see MEMORY).]

mem·o·ra·bil·i·a /mèmmərə bíllee ə/ *npl.* **1. OBJECTS CONNECTED WITH A FAMOUS PERSON** objects associated with a famous person or event, especially considered as collectors' items **2. PERSONAL SOUVENIRS** objects collected as souvenirs of important personal events or experiences [Late 18thC. From Latin, literally "memorable things," formed from *memorabilis* (see MEMORABLE).]

mem·o·ra·ble /mémmərəb'l/ *adj.* **1. WORTH REMEMBERING** sufficiently interesting, exciting, or unusual to be worth remembering or likely to be remembered **2. EASILY REMEMBERED** easy to remember [15thC. Via French from Latin *memorabilis*, from *memorare* "to bring to mind" (source of English *commemorate*), from *memor* "mindful" (see MEMORY).] —**mem·o·ra·bil·i·ty** /mèmmərə bíllətee/ *n.* —**mem·o·ra·ble·ness** /mémmərəb'lnəss/ *n.* —**mem·o·ra·bly** /mémmərəblee/ *adv.*

mem·o·ran·dum /mèmmə rándəm/ (*plural* **-dums** *or* **-da** /-rándə/) *n.* **1.** COMM = **memo** *n.* 1 **2. REMINDER** a note to serve as a reminder of something **3.** POL **BRIEF DIPLOMATIC COMMUNICATION** a brief, often unsigned communication circulated among diplomats, especially one that summarizes a country's position on a particular issue **4.** LAW **SUMMARY OF A LEGAL AGREEMENT** a written statement summarizing the terms of a contract or a similar legal transaction **5.** TRANSP **CONSIGNOR'S STATEMENT** a consignor's brief statement about a shipment of returnable goods [15thC. From Latin, literally "thing to be remembered," from *memorare* "to bring to mind," from *memor* "mindful" (see MEMORY).]

me·mo·ri·al /mə máwree əl/ *n.* **1. COMMEMORATIVE OBJECT** something that is intended to remind people of a person who has died or an event in which people died, e.g., a statue, speech, or special ceremony **2. STATEMENT OF FACTS ACCOMPANYING A PETITION** a written statement of facts accompanying a petition presented to somebody in authority ■ *adj.* **COMMEMORATIVE** intended as a reminder of a person or event or as a celebration of somebody's life and work [14thC. Via French from, ultimately, Latin *memoria* (see MEMORY).] —**me·mo·ri·al·ly** *adv.*

Me·mo·ri·al Day *n.* a public holiday to commemorate soldiers who died in war, now observed on the last Monday in May but originally celebrated on May 30

me·mo·ri·al·ist /mə máwree əlist/ *n.* **1. WRITER OF MEMOIRS** somebody who writes memoirs **2. WRITER OF A MEMORIAL ACCOMPANYING A PETITION** somebody who writes, signs, or presents a memorial accompanying a petition

me·mo·ri·al·ize /mə máwree ə lìz/ (**-ized, -iz·ing, -iz·es**) *vt.* **1. COMMEMORATE SOMETHING** to serve as a memorial to somebody or something, or provide somebody or something with a memorial **2. PRESENT SOMEBODY WITH A MEMORIAL ACCOMPANYING A PETITION** to present a written memorial accompanying a petition to somebody or a group in power —**me·mo·ri·al·i·za·tion** /mə màwree əli záysh'n/ *n.* —**me·mo·ri·al·iz·er** /-ə lìzər/ *n.*

me·mo·ri·al park *n.* a cemetery

mem·o·ri·a tech·ni·ca /mə màwree ə ték nikə/ (*plural* **mem·o·ri·a tech·ni·cas**) *n.* a means or device that aids the memory (*formal*) [From modern Latin, "artificial memory"]

mem·o·rize /mémmə rìz/ (**-rized, -riz·ing, -riz·es**) *vt.* to commit something to memory —**mem·o·riz·a·ble** *adj.* —**mem·o·ri·za·tion** /mèmməri záysh'n/ *n.* —**mem·o·riz·er** /mémmə-/ *n.*

mem·o·ry /mémməree/ (*plural* **-ries**) *n.* **1. ABILITY TO RETAIN KNOWLEDGE OF THE PAST** the ability of the mind or of an individual or organism to retain learned information and knowledge of past events and experiences and to retrieve it **2. SOMEBODY'S STOCK OF RETAINED KNOWLEDGE** an individual's stock of retained knowledge and experience ○ *has a good memory for faces* **3. RETAINED IMPRESSION OF PARTICULAR EVENT** the knowledge or impression that somebody retains of a particular person, event, period, or subject ○ *memories of a happy childhood* **4. RECOLLECTION** the act or a specific instance of remembering **5. PRESERVATION OF KNOWLEDGE** the preservation of knowledge of and, usually, celebration of a deceased person or past event ○ *a poem in memory of her father* **6. POSTHUMOUS IMPRESSION** the knowledge or impression of somebody retained by other people after that person's death **7. TEMPORAL EXTENT OF RECOLLECTION** the period of past time that a person or group is able to remember ○ *within living memory* **8.** COMPUT **DATA STORAGE UNIT IN COMPUTER** the part of a computer in which data is stored **9.** COMPUT **COMPUTER'S DATA STORAGE CAPACITY** the data storage capacity of a computer **10. ABILITY TO RETURN TO ORIGINAL SHAPE** the ability of some materials, e.g., plastics and metals, to return to their original shape after being subject to deformation [13thC. Via Old French *memorie* from Latin *memoria*, from *memor* "mindful." Ultimately from an Indo-European base meaning "to remember," which is also the ancestor of English *remember* and *mourn*.]

mem·o·ry bank *n.* COMPUT = **memory** *n.* 8

mem·o·ry en·gram *n.* PSYCHOL = **engram** (*technical or archaic*)

mem·o·ry lane *n.* the past, especially the past shared and remembered by a group of people, thought of as a path that can be traveled along to visit specific former times

mem·o·ry span *n.* a measure of somebody's memory, often for units of information such as nonsense syllables or sequences of random numbers, over a short period of time

mem·o·ry trace *n.* PSYCHOL = **engram**

Mem·phi·an /mémfee ən/ *n.* **1. SOMEBODY FROM MEMPHIS, TENNESSEE** somebody who was born in, or who lives in the city of Memphis, Tennessee **2. SOMEBODY FROM MEMPHIS, EGYPT** somebody who was born in or lived in the ancient Egyptian city of Memphis —**Mem·phi·an** *adj.*

Mem·phis /mém fiss/ **1.** ruined city and capital of ancient Egypt, located at the head of the Nile delta in the north of the country **2.** the largest city in Tennessee, located in the southwestern corner of the state. Population: 614,289 (1994).

Mem·phrem·a·gog, Lake /mèmfrə máygog/ lake in Quebec, Canada, and Vermont. It is the second largest lake in Vermont. Length: 27 mi./43 km.

mem·sa·hib /mem saab/ *n.* *S Asia* a respectful form of address formerly used by Indians to a European married woman [Mid-19thC. From MA'AM + SAHIB.]

men plural of **man**

men- *prefix.* = **meno-** (*used before vowels*)

men·ace /ménnəss/ *n.* **1. POSSIBLE SOURCE OF DANGER** somebody who or something that is a possible source of danger or harm to somebody or something else **2. NUISANCE** somebody who or something that is a constant source of trouble and annoyance (*informal*) **3. THREATENING QUALITY** a threatening quality, feeling, or tone **4. THREATENING ACT** a threatening act, gesture, or speech ○ *demanding money with menaces* ■ *v.* (**-aced, -ac·ing, -ac·es**) **1.** *vt.* **BE DANGEROUS TO SOMEBODY OR SOMETHING** to be a possible or actual source of danger or harm to somebody or something **2.** *vti.* **MAKE A**

THREAT AGAINST SOMEBODY to behave toward or speak to somebody in a way that threatens injury or harm (*often passive*) [14thC. Via French from, ultimately, Latin *minax* "threatening," from *minari* "to threaten," from *minae* "threats," literally "projecting points."] —**men·ac·er** *n.* —**men·ac·ing** *adj.* —**men·ac·ing·ly** *adv.*

men·a·di·one /mènnə dī ōn/ *n.* a yellow crystalline solid used as a fungicide and as a vitamin K supplement in medicines and animal feedstuffs. Formula: $C_{11}H_8O_2$. [Mid-20thC. Contraction of METHYL + NAPHTHALENE + DI- + -ONE.]

mén·age /may náazh/ *n.* (*formal*) **1.** HOUSEHOLD a group of people living together as a household **2.** MANAGEMENT OF A HOUSE the running of a household [Late 17thC. Via French from, ultimately, Latin *manere* "to dwell, stay" (see REMAIN).]

mén·age à trois /-aa trwáa/ (*plural* **mén·ages à trois** /mày naazh-/) *n.* a sexual relationship involving three people [From French, literally "household for three"]

me·nag·er·ie /mə nájjə ree/ *n.* **1.** WILD ANIMAL EXHIBIT a collection of wild animals kept in captivity for the curiosity and entertainment of the public, sometimes as part of a traveling show such as a circus **2.** WILD ANIMAL ENCLOSURE an enclosure in which wild animals are kept for public exhibition **3.** DIVERSE OR EXOTIC GROUP a diverse, exotic, or peculiar group of people or things

Men·ai Strait /mènnī stráyt/ narrow arm of the sea in northwestern Wales, separating the island of Anglesey from the mainland

men·a·quin·one /mènnə kwí nōn, -kwi nōn/ *n.* a form of vitamin K, produced by bacteria in the large intestine, that plays an essential part in the blood-clotting process [Mid-20thC. Contraction of METHYL + NAPHTHALENE + QUINONE.]

me·nar·che /mə náar kee/ *n.* the first time that a girl or young woman menstruates (*formal*) [Early 20thC. Coined from MENO- + Greek *arkhē* "beginning" (see ARCHAIC).] —**me·nar·che·al** *adj.*

Me·nash·a /mə náashə/ city in Wisconsin, in Winnebago County. Population: 15,557 (1994).

men·a·zon /ménnə zòn/ *n.* a colorless crystalline solid used to kill aphids. Formula: $C_6H_8N_5O_2PS_2$. [Mid-20thC. Contraction of METHYL + AMINO- + AZO- + THIONATE.]

Men·ci·us /ménshee əss/ (371?–289B.C.) Chinese philosopher. The successor of Confucius, he argued that humans are born good and are made better or worse by their environment. Born **Meng-tzu**

Menck·en /méngkən/, **H. L.** (1880–1956) U.S. journalist and critic. An authority on the American language, he was also an effective satirist. Full name **Henry Louis Mencken**

mend /mend/ *v.* (**mend·ed, mend·ing, mends**) **1.** *vti.* RESTORE SOMETHING TO SATISFACTORY CONDITION to work on something that is damaged or defective and return it to its original or a satisfactory condition **2.** *vt.* REMOVE A HOLE to fill, cover, or otherwise remove damage such as a hole or break **3.** *vti.* IMPROVE SOMETHING to improve something or make it more acceptable, or be improved or made more acceptable ○ *You'd better mend your ways.* **4.** *vi.* RECOVER OR HEAL to heal or return to a healthy state after illness or injury ■ *n.* REPAIR an instance of repair work or a repaired place on a damaged object, especially a darn on a piece of clothing [12thC. Partly a shortening of AMEND, and partly from Anglo-Norman *mender* (a shortening of *amender*; see AMEND).] —**mend·a·ble** *adj.* —**mend·er** *n.* ◇ **on the mend** recovering or healing after illness or injury

men·da·cious /men dáyshəss/ *adj.* **1.** TELLING LIES having lied in the past, or prone to lying at any time **2.** FALSE deliberately untrue [Early 17thC. Formed from Latin *mendac-*, the stem of *mendax* "lying."] —**men·da·cious·ly** *adv.* —**men·da·cious·ness** *n.*

men·dac·i·ty /men dássətee/ (*plural* **-ties**) *n.* **1.** TELLING OF LIES deliberate untruthfulness **2.** LIE a lie or falsehood [Mid-17thC. Via French *mendacité* from, ultimately, Latin *mendax* "lying."]

Men·de /méndee/ (*plural* **-de** *or* **-des**) *n.* **1.** PEOPLES MEMBER OF A SIERRA LEONE ETHNIC GROUP a member of one of several ethnic groups living in Sierra Leone **2.** LANGUAGE NIGER-CONGO LANGUAGE a language of the Niger-Congo language group, spoken by the Mende of Sierra Leone. Over one million people speak Mende. [Mid-18thC. From Mende.]

Men·del /ménd'l/, **Gregor Johann** (1822–84) Austrian monk and scientist. Through his experiments he developed the principles of heredity, and so laid the basis of modern genetics. —**Men·de·li·an** /mèn déelyən/ *adj.*

men·de·le·vi·um /mèndə léevee əm/ *n.* a synthetic short-lived radioactive chemical element produced by bombarding einsteinium atoms with helium particles. Symbol **Md** [Mid-20thC. Named in honor of the Russian chemist Dmitri Ivanovich MENDELEYEV.]

Men·de·le·yev /mèndə láyəf/, **Dmitri Ivanovich** (1834–1907) Russian chemist. He formulated the periodic law of elements and devised the periodic table (1869), using it to predict the existence of several then-unknown elements. He wrote a classic text, *Principles of Chemistry* (1868–70).

Men·del·ism /ménd'l ìzzəm/, **Men·de·li·an·ism** *n.* the theory of heredity formulated by Mendel, which explains how certain characteristics are passed on from one generation to the next through genes

Men·del's Laws *npl.* the laws of heredity formulated by Mendel to explain the transmission of characteristics from one generation to the next. There are two laws, the Law of Segregation and the Law of Independent Assortment.

Men·dels·sohn /ménd'lssən/, **Felix** (1809–47) German composer. His orchestral, choral, and keyboard music are key works of the romantic tradition. Full name **Jakob Ludwig Felix Mendelssohn-Bartholdy**

Men·de·res /men dérrəss/ river in southwestern Turkey, flowing west from the Anatolian Plateau into the Aegean Sea. Length: 363 mi./584 km.

men·di·cant /méndikənt/ *adj.* LIVING ON ALMS begging for and living on alms ■ *n.* **1.** BEGGAR somebody who begs for money, usually in the street (*formal*) **2.** FRIAR BEGGING FOR ALMS a member of a religious order, e.g., the Franciscans, Dominicans, Carmelites, or Augustinians, that forbids the ownership of property and encourages working or begging for a living [14thC. From Latin *mendicare* "to beg," from *mendicus* "beggar," from *mendum* "defect" (source of English *amend, mend*).]

mend·ing /ménding/ *n.* articles, especially clothes, to be mended

Men·do·za /men dṓzə/ city in western Argentina, the capital of Mendoza Province. Population: 121,696 (1991).

men·eer /mə néer/ *n. S Africa* a title in Afrikaans equivalent to "Mr." or a respectful form of address equivalent to "sir." [Mid-17thC. Via Afrikaans from Dutch *mijnheer*, literally "my lord."]

Men·e·la·us /mènnə láyəss/ *n.* in Greek mythology, the king of Sparta and husband of Helen of Troy. Her abduction by the Trojan prince Paris led to the Trojan War.

Men·em /mén em/, **Carlos Saúl** (*b.* 1930) Argentine political leader. A Peronist politician, he was twice elected president (1989 and 1995).

men·folk /mén fōk/, **men·folks** *npl.* (*takes a plural verb*) **1.** MEN ASSOCIATED WITH A FAMILY OR GROUP the men associated with a particular family or group **2.** MEN IN GENERAL men in general or considered collectively

M.Eng. *abbr.* Master of Engineering

men·ha·den /men háyd'n/ (*plural* **-dens** *or* **-den**) *n.* a North American marine fish belonging to the herring family, used mainly as a source of oil, fertilizer, and bait. Latin name: *Brevoortia tyrannus.* [Mid-17thC. Origin uncertain: possibly an alteration of Narragansett *munnawhattea*, literally "they fertilize" (from the fish's use as fertilizer by Native Americans), influenced by U.S. English dialect *poghaden* "menhaden" (of Algonquian origin).]

men·hir /mén heer/ *n.* a large single upright stone, erected by prehistoric people and thought to have been used for astronomical observations, found in the British Isles and northern France [Mid-19thC. Directly or via French from Breton *maen-hir*, literally "long stone," from *men* "stone" (source of English *dolmen*) + *hir* "long."]

me·ni·al /meenee əl/ *adj.* **1.** UNSKILLED relating to or involving work that requires little skill or training, is not interesting, and confers low social status on the person doing it **2.** RELATING TO SERVANTS suitable, typical of, or relating to a servant or servants ■ *n.* **1.** DOMESTIC SERVANT a domestic servant, especially one of low status **2.** SOMEBODY WHO DOES MENIAL WORK somebody employed to do work that requires no skill or training (*formal*) [14thC. Via Anglo-Norman, "of a household" from, ultimately, Latin *mansio* "house" (see MANSION).] —**me·ni·al·ly** *adv.*

Barnaby's

Menhir: Le Grand Menhir Dol, Brittany, France

Mé·ni·ère's dis·ease /màyn yáirz-/, **Mé·ni·ère's syn·drome** *n.* a disorder caused by an accumulation of fluid in the labyrinths of the inner ear. Symptoms include vertigo, persistent ringing in the ears, and some loss of hearing. [Late 19thC. Named for the French physician Prosper *Ménière* (1799–1862), who described it.]

me·ni·lite /ménnə lìt/ *n.* a liver opal, especially a brown or gray one [Early 19thC. From French, named for *Ménilmontant*, a quarter of Paris where such stones were found.]

mening- *prefix.* = **meningo-**

me·nin·ges /mə nínjeez/ *npl.* the three membranes that surround and protect the brain and the spinal cord, called the dura mater, the arachnoid mater, and the pia mater [Early 17thC. Via modern Latin from Greek *mēnigg-*, the stem of *mēnigx* "membrane."] —**me·nin·ge·al** /mə nínjee əl/ *adj.*

meningi- *prefix.* = **meningo-**

me·nin·gi·o·ma /mə nìnjee ṓmə/ (*plural* **-mas** *or* **-ma·ta** /-ṓmətə/) *n.* a slow-growing benign tumor that affects the meninges of the brain or spinal cord and may cause serious damage by compression [Early 20thC. Shortening of *meningothelioma*, from MENINGO- + ENDOTHELIOMA.]

men·in·gi·tis /mènnin jítiss/ *n.* a serious, sometimes fatal illness in which a viral or bacterial infection inflames the meninges, causing symptoms such as severe headaches, vomiting, stiff neck, and high fever —**men·in·git·ic** /mènnin jíttik/ *adj.*

meningo- *prefix.* meninges ○ *meningocele* [From Greek *mēnigg-*, the stem of *mēnigx* "membrane"]

men·in·go·cele /mə níng gə seel/ *n.* the protrusion of the meninges through a defect in the skull or backbone to form a cyst

me·nin·go·coc·cus /mə nìng gə kókəss/ (*plural* **-ci** /-kók sī, -kó kì/) *n.* a bacterium that causes cerebrospinal meningitis. Latin name: *Neisseria meningitidis.* —**me·nin·go·coc·cal** *adj.* —**me·nin·go·coc·cic** /-kóksik/ *adj.*

me·nin·go·en·ceph·a·li·tis /mə nìng gō en seffə lítiss/ *n.* an inflammation of the brain and the meninges —**me·nin·go·en·ceph·a·lit·ic** /-seffə líttik/ *adj.*

me·nis·cus /mə nískəss/ (*plural* **-ci** /-kì/ *or* **-cus·es**) *n.* **1.** PHYS UPPER SURFACE OF LIQUID the curved upper surface of a still liquid in a tube, concave if the liquid wets the walls of the container, convex if it does not, caused by surface tension **2.** ANAT CARTILAGE DISK a crescent-shaped cartilage disk cushioning the end of a bone where it meets another bone in a joint, especially in the knee **3.** OPTICS CONCAVO-CONVEX LENS a lens that is convex on one side and concave on the other **4.** CRESCENT SHAPE a crescent-shaped body or figure [Late 17thC. Via modern Latin from Greek *mēniskos*, literally "little moon," from *mēnē* "moon" (see MENO-).] —**me·nis·cal** *adj.* —**me·nis·cate** *adj.* —**me·nis·coid** *adj.* —**men·is·coi·dal** /mènniss kóyd'l/ *adj.*

Men·lo Park /mènlō-/ **1.** city in western California, in San Mateo County. Population: 29,755 (1994). **2.** town in central New Jersey, the location of Thomas Edison's laboratory

Men·non·ite /ménnə nìt/ *n.* a member of a Protestant denomination emphasizing adult baptism and pacifism and rejecting church organization and, in many cases, the holding of public office and the taking of oaths. There are many different bodies of

Mennonites throughout the world, with especially large communities in the United States and Canada. [Mid-16thC. From German *Mennonit*, from the name of *Menno* Simons (1496–1561), an early Frisian leader of the group.] —**Men·non·it·ism** *n.*

me·no /máynō, ménnō/ *adv.* used with a musical direction to mean less quickly or softly [Late 19thC. From Italian, "less."]

meno- *prefix.* menstruation ○ *menopause* [Formed from Greek *mēn(ē)* "month." Ultimately from an Indo-European word that is also the ancestor of English *moon, month,* and *menses,* from a base meaning "to measure."]

me·nol·o·gy /mə nólləjee/ (*plural* **-gies**) *n.* a church calendar of the months, especially in the Eastern Orthodox Church, that shows saints' days and gives biographies of the saints [Early 17thC. Via modern Latin from ecclesiastical Greek *mēnologion*, literally "month-reckoning," from *mēn* "month" + *logos* "account."]

Me·nom·i·nee[1] /mə nómmənee/ (*plural* **-nee** *or* **-nees**), **Me·no·mi·ni** (*plural* **-ni** *or* **-nis**) *n.* **1.** PEOPLES **MEMBER OF A NATIVE AMERICAN PEOPLE** a member of a Native American people who used to live along the shores of the Menominee River, some of whom now live in northeastern Wisconsin **2.** LANG **ALGONQUIAN LANGUAGE** an Algonquian language spoken in parts of Wisconsin, belonging to the Algonquian-Wakasan languages [Mid-18thC. From Ojibwa *manōmini*, literally "wild-rice person."] —**Me·nom·i·nee** *adj.*

Me·nom·i·nee[2] /mə nómənee/ river in Wisconsin, formed by the Brule and Michigamme rivers, and flowing into Lake Michigan. Length: 125 mi./201 km.

Me·nom·o·nee Falls /mənáamənee/ village in Wisconsin, in southeastern Waukesha County. Population: 28,448 (1994).

me·no mos·so /-máwsō/ *adv.* at a slower speed (*used as a musical direction*) [From Italian, literally "less agitated"]

men·o·pause /ménnə pàwz/ *n.* the time in a woman's life when menstruation diminishes and ceases, usually between the ages of 45 and 50 [Late 19thC. Coined from MENO- + Greek *pausis* (see PAUSE).] —**men·o·paus·al** /mènnə páwz'l/ *adj.* —**men·o·paus·ic** /-páwzik/ *adj.*

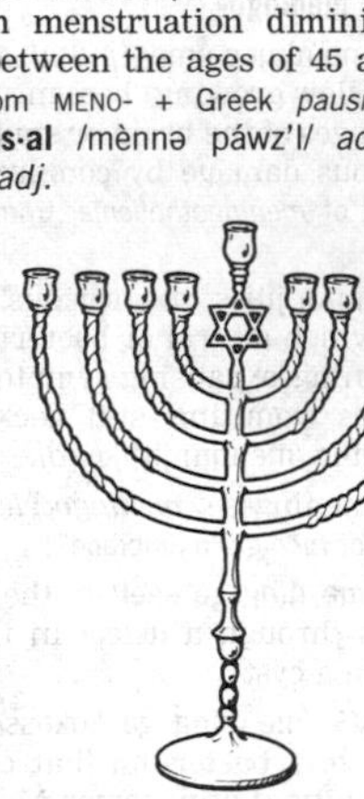

Menorah

me·no·rah /mə náwrə/ *n.* **1. 7-BRANCHED CEREMONIAL CANDLEHOLDER** a ceremonial candleholder consisting of a central stem surrounded by six curved branches, used in the Jewish Temple and as an emblem of Judaism and the state of Israel **2. 8-BRANCHED HANUKKAH CANDLEHOLDER** an eight-branched candleholder, lit during the festival of Hanukkah [Late 19thC. From Hebrew *mĕnōrāh*, literally "candlestick."]

men·or·rha·gi·a /mènnə ráyjee ə/ *n.* abnormally heavy or prolonged bleeding during menstruation —**men·or·rha·gic** *adj.*

men·or·rhea /mènnə reé ə/ *n.* normal bleeding during menstruation [Mid-19thC. Back-formation from AMENORRHEA.]

men·or·rhoea *n.* U.K. = **menorrhea**

Me·not·ti /mə nóttee/, **Gian-Carlo** (*b.* 1911) Italian-born U.S. composer. He is known for his operas including *The Consul* (1950) and *The Saint of Bleecker Street* (1954).

Men·sa /ménssə/ *n.* **1. CONSTELLATION IN THE SOUTHERN HEMISPHERE** a faint constellation, found between Hydrus and Volans in the southern hemisphere, that forms part of the Large Magellanic Cloud **2. HIGH-IQ ORGANIZATION** an international organization for people with a very high IQ. Members are admitted after passing an IQ test. [Mid-20thC. From Latin, "table."]

men·sal[1] /ménssəl/ *adj.* occurring monthly [Mid-19thC. Formed from Latin *mensis* "month." Ultimately from an Indo-European word that is also the ancestor of English *moon* and *month*, from a base meaning "to measure."]

men·sal[2] /ménssəl/ *adj.* used or done at the meal table, or connected with eating meals [15thC. From late Latin *mensalis*, from Latin *mensa* "table," of unknown origin.]

mensch /mensh/ (*plural* **mensch·en** /ménshən/ *or* **mensch·es**), **mensh** (*plural* **mensh·en** *or* **mensh·es**) *n.* somebody good, kind, decent, and honorable (*informal*) [Mid-20thC. Via Yiddish from, ultimately, Old High German *mennisco* "manly, human." Ultimately from an Indo-European word meaning "person, man" that is also the ancestor of English *man*.]

men·ses /mén seez/ *n.* (*technical*) (*takes a singular or plural verb*) **1. MENSTRUATION** menstruation, or the period of time that it lasts **2. MENSTRUAL DISCHARGE** the blood and other matter discharged from the womb during menstruation [Late 16thC. From Latin, plural of *mensis* "month" (see MENSAL[1]).]

Men·she·vik /ménshəvìk/ (*plural* **-viks** *or* **-vi·ki** /ménshə veekee/) *n.* a member of the moderate minority faction of the Marxist Social Democratic Party in pre-revolutionary Russia that advocated a gradual approach to social reform, in contrast to the Bolsheviks [Early 20thC. From Russian *men'shevik*, from *men'she* "less"; so called because they favored less extreme Socialist reform than the Bolsheviks.] —**Men·she·vism** /ménshə vìzzəm/ *n.* —**Men·she·vist** *n.*

mens re·a /mènz reé ə, -ráyə/ *n.* prior intention to commit a criminal act, without necessarily knowing that the act is a crime. For all but some minor statutory offenses, mens rea is basic to establishing the actual guilt of somebody alleged to have commited a crime. [From modern Latin, "guilty mind"]

men's room *n.* a public toilet for men

mens sa·na in cor·po·re sa·no /menz saánə in kawrpəray saánō/ *n.* a healthy mind in a healthy body, as an ideal in living (*formal*) [From Latin]

men·stru·al /ménstroo əl/ *adj.* occurring during or connected with menstruation

men·stru·ate /ménstroo àyt/ (**-at·ed, -at·ing, -ates**) *vi.* to discharge blood and other matter from the womb as part of the menstrual cycle [Early 19thC. Via late Latin *menstruare* from, ultimately, Latin *menstruus* "monthly, menstrual," from *mensis* "month" (see MENSAL[1]).]

men·stru·a·tion /mènstroo áysh'n/ *n.* the monthly process of discharging blood and other matter from the womb that occurs in women and female primates who are not pregnant between puberty and menopause

men·stru·ous *adj.* = **menstrual**

men·stru·um /ménstroo əm/ (*plural* **-ums** *or* **-a** /-ə/) *n.* a solvent, especially one used to extract compounds from plant or animal tissue or in the preparation of drugs [Early 17thC. Via medieval Latin, literally "menstruation," singular of Latin *menstrua* (see MENSTRUATE). By analogy between the alchemical use of solvents and the menses' supposed function in nurturing unborn babies.]

men·su·ra·ble /ménsərəb'l, ménshə-/ *adj.* **1.** MATH **ABLE TO BE MEASURED** capable of being measured **2.** MUSIC = **mensural** *adj.* 1 [Late 16thC. Via late Latin *mensurabilis* from, ultimately, Latin *mensura* "measure" (see MEASURE).] —**men·su·ra·bil·i·ty** /mènsərə bíllətee, mènshə-/ *n.* —**men·su·ra·ble·ness** /ménsərəb'lnəss, ménshə-/ *n.*

men·su·ral /ménsərəl, ménshə-/ *adj.* **1. RELATING TO MEASUREMENT** relating to or involving measurement or measurable values **2.** MUSIC **USING NOTES WITH FIXED VALUES** used to describe or relating to notes, particularly in medieval music, that have a fixed length or time value relative to one another [Late 16thC. From Latin *mensuralis*, from *mensura* (see MEASURE).]

men·su·ra·tion /mènsə ráysh'n, mènshə-/ *n.* **1.** MATH **WORKING OUT GEOMETRIC QUANTITIES** the calculation of geometric quantities such as length, area, and volume from dimensions and angles that are already known **2. MEASUREMENT** the act, process, or skill of measuring something (*formal*) [Late 16thC. Via late Latin from, ultimately, Latin *mensura* (see MEASURE).] —**men·su·ra·tion·al** *adj.* —**men·su·ra·tive** /ménsə ràytiv, ménshə-/ *adj.*

mens·wear /ménz wàir/, **men's wear** *n.* **1. MEN'S CLOTHING** clothing designed to be worn by men **2. MENSWEAR DEPARTMENT** the department in a store that sells menswear

-ment *suffix.* **1.** action, process ○ *arraignment* ○ *betterment* **2.** result of, or condition resulting from an action ○ *bewilderment* **3.** instrument or agent of an action ○ *refreshment* **4.** place ○ *emplacement* ○ *escarpment* [Directly and via French from Latin *-mentum*]

men·tal /mént'l/ *adj.* **1. RELATING TO THE MIND** relating to, found in, or occurring in the mind ○ *mental stimulation* **2. CARRIED OUT IN THE MIND** carried out in the mind without any physical action or the use of any physical aid ○ *mental arithmetic* **3. PRODUCED BY THE MIND** produced by the mind and visible only in the mind ○ *mental imagery* **4. EXPERIENCING EXTREME EMOTION** affected by extreme distress, anxiety, anger, or other emotional reaction to somebody or something (*informal offensive*) **5. OFFENSIVE TERM** an offensive term meaning having a psychiatric disorder (*offensive*) **6. UNINTELLIGENT** extremely unintelligent or silly (*informal insult*) [15thC. Via French from Latin *ment-*, the stem of *mens* "mind." Ultimately from an Indo-European word meaning "to think," also the ancestor of English *mind, mania, demented,* and *amnesia*.] —**men·tal·ly** *adv.*

men·tal age *n.* a measure of intellectual development developed by the French psychologist Binet, who devised norms against which children could be compared with other children of the same chronological age ○ *a four-year-old with a mental age of seven*

men·tal block *n.* an inability to carry out a mental task such as remembering something, especially when caused by subconscious emotional factors

men·tal cru·el·ty *n.* the infliction of psychological pain on somebody

men·tal hand·i·cap *n.* an offensive term for an intellectual impairment (*offensive*)

men·tal ill·ness *n.* any psychiatric disorder of the mind that causes untypical behavior

men·tal·ism /mént'l ìzzəm/ *n.* the belief that all objects of knowledge, including the physical universe, ultimately have no existence except as creations of the mind —**men·tal·ist** *n.* —**men·tal·is·tic** /mènt'l ístik/ *adj.* —**men·tal·is·ti·cal·ly** /-ístikalee/ *adv.*

men·tal·i·ty /men tállətee/ (*plural* **-ties**) *n.* **1. PERCEPTUAL FRAMEWORK** a habitual way of thinking or interpreting events peculiar to an individual or type of person, especially with reference to the behaviors that it produces **2. INTELLECTUAL ABILITY** somebody's intellectual ability

men·tal lex·i·con *n.* the words of a language that somebody knows the meanings of, can use, or uses habitually

men·tal·ly chal·lenged *adj.* affected by a condition that limits the ability to learn and to function independently, as a result of congenital causes, brain injury, or disease

men·tal re·tar·da·tion *n.* an offensive term for difficulty in learning or in daily functions (*dated offensive*)

men·ta·tion /men táysh'n/ *n.* (*formal*) **1. THINKING** mental activity, especially thinking **2. STATE OF MIND** somebody's state of mind or general attitude [Mid-19thC. Formed from Latin *ment-*, the stem of *mens* "mind" (see MENTAL).]

men·thol /mén thàwl/ *n.* an organic compound extracted from peppermint oil that has a cool minty taste and is used as a flavoring and as a mild anesthetic. Formula: $CH_3C_6H_9(C_3H_7)OH$. [Late 19thC. From German, literally "mint-oil," formed from Latin *mentha* (see MINT).]

men·tho·lat·ed /ménthə làytəd/ *adj.* flavored with or containing menthol

men·tion /ménshən/ *v.* (**-tioned, -tion·ing, -tions**) **1.** *vti.* **SAY A PARTICULAR WORD OR THING** to use a particular word or name when speaking or writing, often in a casual way ○ *I happened to mention your name to her.* **2.** *vt.* MIL **CITE SOMEBODY FOR BRAVERY** to refer to somebody by name in an official report as a way of acknowledging exceptional conduct, especially during a military action ■ *n.* **1. SPECIFIC REFERENCE** the use of a particular word or name, or a reference to a particular person or thing **2.** MIL **ACKNOWLEDGMENT OF SOMEBODY'S EXCEPTIONAL CONDUCT** an acknowledgment, especially in an official report, of somebody's exceptional conduct **3. HONORABLE MENTION** an honorable mention **4.** LOGIC **LINGUISTIC SELF-REFERENCE** the use of a word to refer to itself instead of to perform its usual linguistic function [14thC. Via French from Latin *mention-*, the stem of *mentio* "calling to mind."] —**men·tion·a·ble** *adj.* —**men·tion·er** *n.* ◇ **don't mention it** used in reply to an expression of thanks as a polite way of saying that none are necessary ◇ **not to mention** used to emphasize a point by introducing somebody who or something that needs to be taken into consideration and is even more significant than what has been spoken of before

men·tor /mén tàwr, méntər/ *n.* **EXPERIENCED ADVISER AND SUPPORTER** somebody, usually older and more experienced, who provides advice and support to, and watches over and fosters the progress of, a younger, less experienced person ■ *vt.* (**-tored, -tor·ing, -tors**) **BE A MENTOR TO SOMEBODY** to act as a mentor to somebody, especially a junior colleague [Mid-18thC. Via French from, ultimately, Greek *Mentōr* (see MENTOR).]

Men·tor *n.* in Homer's *Odyssey*, the friend whom Odysseus left in charge of the household while he was at Troy and who was the teacher and protector of Telemachus, Odysseus's son

men·tor·ing /méntəring/ *n.* the task of acting as a mentor to somebody, especially a junior colleague, or the system of appointing mentors

men·u /mén yoō/ *n.* **1. FOOD LIST OF DISHES AVAILABLE** a list of the dishes that can be ordered in a restaurant or that are to be served at a formal meal **2. COMPUT LIST OF PROGRAM OPTIONS** a list on a computer screen of the various options available to the user of a program or function **3. LIST OR COLLECTION** a list of things available, or a collection of things from which a selection can be made [Mid-19thC. Via French, "minute, detailed," from Latin *minutus* "small" (see MINUTE[2]); the underlying meaning is "detailed list."]

men·u-driv·en *adj.* COMPUT operated by selecting options from menus

Men·u·hin /ménnyoo in, ménnoō in/, **Yehudi, Baron Menuhin of Stoke d'Abernon** (1916–99) U.S.-born British violinist. He was known as much for mentoring younger players as for his own virtuoso performances.

MEP *abbr.* Master of Engineering Physics

me·per·i·dine /mə pérrə deèn/ *n.* a white crystalline compound used as a painkiller and sedative. Formula: $C_{15}H_{21}NO_2$. [Mid-20thC. Blend of METHYL and PIPERIDINE.]

Meph·i·stoph·e·les /mèffi stóffə leèez/, **Me·phis·to** /mə fístō/ *n.* in medieval mythology, a subordinate to the Devil, one of the seven archangels cast out of heaven, to whom Faust sold his soul —**Me·phis·to·phe·le·an** /mə fìstō feèlyən, mə fìstō feèlee ən/ *adj.*

me·phit·ic /mə fíttik/, **me·phit·i·cal** /mə fíttik'l/ *adj.* relating to or resembling a poisonous or foul smell (*literary*) [Early 17thC. From late Latin *mephiticus* "pestilential," from Latin *mephitis* (see MEPHITIS).] —**me·phit·i·cal·ly** *adv.*

me·phi·tis /mə fítiss/ *n.* **1.** GEOL **FOUL-SMELLING GAS** a foul-smelling or poisonous vapor coming out of the earth **2. STENCH** a foul smell (*literary*) [Early 18thC. From Latin, of unknown origin.]

mep·ro·bam·ate /mèpprō bá màyt, mə prṓbə-/ *n.* a bitter white powder used as a tranquilizer and muscle relaxant. Formula: $C_9H_{18}N_2O_4$. [Mid-20thC. Blend of METHYL, PROPYL, and CARBAMATE.]

mer. *abbr.* meridian

mer- *prefix.* = **mero-**

-mer *suffix.* polymer ○ *oligomer* [Back-formation from -MERISM]

Mer·a·no /me raànō/ city and health resort in Bolzano Province, Trentino-Alto Adige Region, northeastern Italy. Population: 33,638 (1993).

mer·an·ti /mə rántee/ *n.* a hardwood, white, yellow, or red in color, obtained from some Malaysian and Indonesian trees. Genus: *Shorea.* [Late 18thC. From Malay.]

mer·bro·min /mər brṓmin/ *n.* a green crystalline solid that forms a red solution when dissolved in water, mainly used as an antiseptic. Formula: $C_{20}H_8Br_2HgNa_2O_6$. [Mid-20thC. Coined from MERCURIC + BROM- + -IN.]

Mer·cal·li scale /mair kállee-/ *n.* a scale for measuring the intensity of earthquakes, ranging from 1 to 12, in which 1 denotes a weak earthquake and 12 one that causes complete destruction. ◊ **Richter scale** [Early 20thC. Named for Giuseppe *Mercalli* (1850–1914), the Italian geologist who devised it.]

mer·can·tile /múrkən tīl/ *adj.* **1. RELATING TO MERCHANTS OR TRADING** used for trade or by merchants, or characteristic of merchants or trading **2. RELATING TO MERCANTILISM** relating to or typical of mercantilism [Mid-17thC. Via French from, ultimately, Italian *mercante* "merchant," from Latin *mercari* "to trade" (see MERCHANT).]

mer·can·til·ism /múrkənti lìzzəm/ *n.* **1. ECONOMIC THEORY AND SYSTEM** an early modern European economic theory and system that actively supported the establishment of colonies that would supply materials and markets and relieve home nations of dependence on other nations **2. COMMERCIALISM** the principles and methods of commerce —**mer·can·til·ist** *n.* —**mer·can·til·is·tic** /mùrkənti lístik/ *adj.*

mer·cap·tan /mər káp tàn/ *n.* = **thiol** [Mid-19thC. Formed from modern Latin *(corpus) mercurium captans*, literally "(substance) that seizes mercury."]

mer·cap·to·pu·rine /mər kàptō pyoōrin/ *n.* a drug used in the treatment of leukemia. Formula: $C_5H_4N_4S$. [Mid-20thC. Coined from MERCAPTO- + PURINE.]

Mer·ca·tor /mur káytər/, **Gerardus** (1512–94) Flemish geographer, cartographer, and mathematician. His map projection allowed compass courses to be plotted as straight lines, and is widely used in navigation. Born **Gerhard Kremer**

Mer·ca·tor Pro·jec·tion *n.* a method of making a map of the globe on a flat surface in which the meridians and latitudes are shown as straight lines that cross at right angles [Mid-17thC. Named for Gerardus MERCATOR, who invented it.]

Mer·ced /mər séd/ city in central California, the administrative seat of Merced County. Population: 60,348 (1994).

mer·ce·nar·y /múrs'n èrree/ *n.* (*plural* **-ies**) **1.** MIL **PROFESSIONAL SOLDIER** a professional soldier paid to fight for an army other than that of his or her country **2. SOMEBODY INTERESTED ONLY IN PROFIT** somebody who works or serves only for personal profit ■ *adj.* **1. MOTIVATED ONLY BY MONEY** motivated solely by a desire for money **2. RELATING TO MERCENARIES** paid to serve in a foreign army, or consisting of mercenaries [14thC. Directly or via French *mercenaire* from Latin *mercen(n)arius* "hireling," from *merces* "wages" (source of English *mercy*).] —**mer·ce·nar·i·ly** *adv.* —**mer·ce·nar·i·ness** *n.*

Mer·cer Is·land /múrsər-/ island in Mississippi, in Adams County. Population: 21,522 (1995).

mer·cer·ize /múrsə rīz/ (**-ized, -iz·ing, -iz·es**) *vt.* to treat cotton fabric or thread with an alkali to strengthen it and make it more lustrous and more receptive to dyes [Mid-19thC. Named for John *Mercer* (1791–1866), the English calico printer who is said to have discovered the process.] —**mer·cer·i·za·tion** /mùrsəri záysh'n/ *n.*

mer·chan·dise /múrchən dīz/ *n.* **GOODS** goods bought and sold for profit ■ *v.* (**-dised** *or* **-dized, -dis·ing** *or* **-diz·ing, -dis·es** *or* **-dizes**) **1.** *vti.* **TRADE COMMERCIALLY** to trade in or buy and sell products for profit **2.** *vt.* **MARKET PRODUCTS** to promote a product by developing strategies for packaging, display, and publicity [13thC. From French *marchandise* "goods," from Old French *marchant* (see MERCHANT).] —**mer·chan·dis·able** *adj.* —**mer·chan·dis·er** *n.*

mer·chan·dis·ing /múrchən dīzing/, **mer·chan·diz·ing** *n.* **1. MARKETING** the promotion of a product by developing strategies for packaging, displaying, and publicizing it **2. SPIN-OFF PRODUCTS** commercial products that are developed as spin-offs from the success of a movie, TV program, sports team, or event

mer·chant /múrchənt/ *n.* **1. DEALER IN WHOLESALE GOODS** somebody who buys and sells goods, especially as a wholesaler or on the international market **2. RETAILER** somebody who sells products at retail, especially in a store or other outlet **3. SOMEBODY NOTED FOR SOME ACTIVITY** somebody who is noted for a particular activity or characteristic (*informal*) (*usually used in combination*) ○ *a speed merchant in a souped-up car* ■ *adj.* **1. RELATING TO TRADE OR MERCHANTS** used for or relating to commerce, wholesalers, or retailers **2.** SHIPPING **OF A MERCHANT MARINE** relating to, belonging to, or involving a merchant marine ■ *vt.* **DEAL IN SOMETHING** to trade or deal in products [12thC. Via Old French *marchant* from, ultimately, Latin *mercari* "to trade," from *merc-*, the stem of *merx* "merchandise" (source of English *merchandise* and *market*).]

WORD KEY: CULTURAL NOTE

The Merchant of Venice, a play by English dramatist William Shakespeare (1596–97). The story revolves around a loan made by usurer Shylock to Venetian merchant Antonio, and Shylock's subsequent attempts to claim the pound of flesh he has stipulated as security. Among the more serious issues raised in this blend of comedy, romance, and realism are the correct administration of justice and the power conferred by wealth. The well-known saying "It is a wise father that knows his own child" comes from Act II, scene ii, line 83 of this play.

Mer·chant /múrchənt/, **Ismail** (*b.* 1936) Indian movie producer and director. In partnership with James Ivory, he produced films set in India and created adaptations of European literary classics.

mer·chant·a·ble /múrchəntəb'l/ *adj.* suitable or of a sufficiently high quality for buying and selling —**mer·chant·a·bil·i·ty** /mùrchəntə bíllətee/ *n.*

mer·chant bank *n. U.K.* a bank that provides financial services mainly for companies and large-scale investors —**mer·chant bank·er** *n.* —**mer·chant bank·ing** *n.*

mer·chant·man /múrchənt mən/ (*plural* **-men** /-mən/) *n.* = **merchant ship**

mer·chant ma·rine *n.* a country's fleet of merchant ships, or the sailors who serve in them

mer·chant na·vy *n. U.K.* = **merchant marine**

mer·chant prince *n.* an extremely wealthy, powerful, and prestigious merchant, especially in Renaissance Italy

mer·chant ship *n.* a seagoing ship designed to carry goods, especially for international trade

Mer·ci·an /múrsh'n/ *n.* **DIALECT OF OLD ENGLISH** a dialect of Old English spoken in the Anglo-Saxon kingdom of Mercia, in central and southern England ■ *adj.* **OF MERCIA** relating to the Anglo-Saxon kingdom of Mercia, its people, its language, or its culture

mer·ci·ful /múrseef'l/ *adj.* **1. SHOWING MERCY** showing mercy or compassion to somebody **2. WELCOME** welcome because putting an end to something unpleasant or distressing —**mer·ci·ful·ness** *n.*

mer·ci·ful·ly /múrseefəlee/ *adv.* **1. SO AS TO SHOW MERCY** so as to show mercy or compassion **2. FORTUNATELY** fortunately or luckily

mer·ci·less /múrseeləss/ *adj.* **1. LACKING MERCY** showing no mercy or compassion toward somebody or something **2. STRICT AND INTOLERANT** very strict or harsh in the treatment of other people and extremely intolerant of their weaknesses or mistakes **3. RELENTLESS** continuing at a high level of violence or unpleasantness without pause or relief —**mer·ci·less·ly** *adv.* —**mer·ci·less·ness** *n.*

mercur- *prefix.* mercury ○ *mercurous* [From MERCURY]

mer·cu·rate /múrkyə ràyt/ (**-rat·ed, -rat·ing, -rates**) *vt.* to treat or combine something with mercury —**mer·cu·ra·tion** /mùrkyə ráysh'n/ *n.*

mer·cu·ri·al /mər kyoōree əl/ *adj.* **1. LIVELY AND UNPREDICTABLE** lively, witty, fast-talking, and likely to do the unexpected **2.** CHEM **CONTAINING MERCURY** containing or caused by mercury ■ *n.* MED **MEDICINE CONTAINING MERCURY** formerly, a drug or chemical preparation containing mercury [14thC. Directly and via French *mercuriel* from Latin *mercurialis*, from *Mercurius* "Mercury."] —**mer·cu·ri·al·i·ty** /mər kyoōree állətee/ *n.* —**mer·cu·ri·al·ly** /mər kyoōree əlee/ *adv.* —**mer·cu·ri·al·ness** /-kyoōreeəlnəss/ *n.*

Mer·cu·ri·al *adj.* **1.** MYTHOL **OF THE GOD MERCURY** relating to the Roman god Mercury **2.** ASTRON **OF THE PLANET MERCURY** relating to the planet Mercury

mer·cu·ri·al·ism /mər kyoōree ə lìzzəm/ *n.* poisoning caused by ingesting mercury

mer·cu·ri·al·ize /mər kyoōree ə līz/ (**-ized, -iz·ing, -izes**) *vt.* to treat somebody or something with mercury or with a compound containing mercury —**mer·cu·ri·al·i·za·tion** /mər kyoōree əli záysh'n/ *n.*

mer·cu·ric /mər kyoōrik/ *adj.* relating to or containing mercury with a valence of 2

mer·cu·ric chlo·ride *n.* a white crystalline solid that is poisonous, soluble, and used mainly as an insecticide, fungicide, or wood preservative or in photography. Formula: $HgCl_2$.

mer·cu·ric ox·ide *n.* a poisonous orange-yellow solid used as a pigment. Formula: HgO.

mer·cu·ric sul·fide *n.* a poisonous compound existing as a red or a black solid, both forms being used as pigments. Formula: HgS.

Mer·cu·ro·chrome /mər kyŏŏrə krōm/ *tdmk.* a trademark for a liquid antiseptic

mer·cu·rous /múrkyərəss/ *adj.* relating to or containing mercury with a valence of 1

mer·cu·ry /múrkyəree/ (*plural* **-ries**) *n.* **1.** CHEM ELEM **LIQUID METALLIC ELEMENT** a poisonous heavy silver-white metallic chemical element that is liquid at room temperature. It is obtained chiefly from the mineral cinnabar and is used in thermometers, barometers, pharmaceuticals, dental fillings, and lamps. Symbol **Hg 2.** METEOROL **TEMPERATURE OR PRESSURE** the mercury in a weather thermometer or barometer, or the air temperature or pressure it indicates ○ *The mercury rose steadily throughout the early part of the day.* **3.** PLANTS **WEEDY PLANT** any of various weedy plants. Genera: *Mercurialis* and *Acalypha.* [14thC. From Latin *Mercurius* (see MERCURY).]

Mer·cu·ry *n.* **1.** MYTHOL **ROMAN GOD** the Roman god of commerce and rhetoric, who also acted as a messenger between humans and gods. His symbol is the caduceus, a staff with two snakes entwined around it. **2.** ASTRON **PLANET NEAREST THE SUN** the smallest planet in the solar system and the one nearest the Sun [12thC. From Latin *Mercurius*, from *merc-*, the stem of *merx* "merchandise" (source of English *merchant*).]

mer·cu·ry chlo·ride *n.* CHEM = **mercuric chloride**

mer·cu·ry-va·por lamp *n.* an electric lamp whose light is generated when electricity is passed through a vapor of low-pressure mercury. Its bright bluish-green light has a strong ultraviolet component, and these rays are used for cosmetic and therapeutic treatment.

mer·cy /múrsee/ (*plural* **-cies**) *n.* **1. COMPASSION** kindness or forgiveness shown to an offender or to somebody a person has power over ○ *The judge showed mercy and imposed the shortest sentence he could.* **2. COMPASSIONATE DISPOSITION** a disposition to be compassionate or forgiving of others ○ *a killer completely without mercy* **3. SOMETHING TO BE THANKFUL FOR** a welcome event or situation that provides relief or prevents something unpleasant from happening ○ *It was a mercy that no one was hurt in the accident.* **4. EASING OF DISTRESS** the easing of distress or pain ○ *The supply convoy was on a mission of mercy.* [12thC. Via French *merci* "thank you", from Latin *merces* "reward, wages" (source of English *mercenary*).] ◇ **at the mercy of somebody** *or* **something** completely unprotected against whatever somebody or something does

mer·cy kill·ing *n.* **1. EUTHANASIA** euthanasia regarded as motivated by compassion **2. ACT OF EUTHANASIA** an act of killing somebody out of compassion, often at that person's request, in order to end his or her pain or distress

mer·cy seat *n.* **1.** JUDAISM **COVERING FOR THE ARK OF THE COVENANT** the gold covering on the Ark of the Covenant, regarded as God's resting place **2.** CHR **GOD'S THRONE** the throne of God in heaven [Modeled on late Latin *propitiatorium*, literally "something atoning," and German *Gnadenstuhle*, literally "mercy seat"]

mere[1] /meer/ (*superlative* **mer·est**) *adj.* **1. UTTER** just what is specified and nothing more ○ *She was no mere journalist.* **2. BY ITSELF** by itself and without anything more ○ *The mere mention of his ex-'s name would make him upset.* [14thC. Directly or via Anglo-Norman *meer*, Old French *mier*, from Latin *merus* "pure, unmixed" (especially of wine), the original meaning in English.]

mere[2] /meer/ *n.* a body of standing fresh water, especially a lake (*archaic or literary*) (*often used in place names*) [Old English, originally used for "sea" (source also of English *mermaid*). Ultimately from an Indo-European word that is also the ancestor of Latin *mare* (source of English *marine*).]

mere[3] /meer/ *n.* a boundary, or something that marks a boundary (*archaic*) [Old English *(ge)mǣre.* Ultimately from an Indo-European word meaning "to fix, build fences," which is also the ancestor of English *mural* and *ammunition.*]

-mere *suffix.* part, segment ○ *centromere* [Via French from Greek *meros* (see MERO-)]

Mer·e·dith /mérrə dith/, **George** (1828–1909) British novelist and poet. His novels are noted for their psychological analysis and distinctive style. They include *The Egoist* (1879) and *Diana of the Crossways* (1885).

mere·ly /meérlee/ *adv.* only as described and nothing more ○ *merely silly* ○ *merely a temporary setback*

me·ren·gue /mə réng gày/ *n.* **1.** BALLROOM **DANCE** a ballroom dance, originally from Dominica and Haiti, characterized by a shuffling step **2.** MUSIC **MUSIC FOR MERENGUE** a piece of music for the merengue [Mid-20thC. Via American Spanish from Haitian creole *méringue*, literally "meringue," from French (see MERINGUE).]

mer·e·tri·cious /mèrrə tríshəss/ *adj.* **1. SUPERFICIALLY ATTRACTIVE** attractive in a superficial or vulgar manner but without real value (*formal*) ○ *meretricious extras that don't really add to the car's value* **2. MISLEADINGLY PLAUSIBLE** seemingly plausible or significant, but actually insincere or false ○ *Don't be swayed by this meretricious argument in the project's favor.* **3. OF PROSTITUTES** relating to or like a prostitute (*archaic*) [Early 17thC. Formed from Latin *meretricius*, from, ultimately, *meretrix* "prostitute," from *mereri* (see MERIT).] —**mer·e·tri·cious·ly** *adv.* —**mer·e·tri·cious·ness** *n.*

Merganser

mer·gan·ser /mər gánsər/ *n.* a fish-eating diving duck with a crested head and a long bill notched like the blade of a saw. Genus: *Mergus.* [Mid-17thC. From modern Latin, literally "diver goose," from Latin *mergus* "diver" + *anser* "goose."]

merge /murj/ (**merged, merg·ing, merg·es**) *vti.* **1. COMBINE** to combine or unite with something to form a single entity, or make two or more things do this ○ *Two of the country's largest banks have decided to merge.* **2. BLEND** to blend or make two or more things blend together gradually ○ *The sky and sea seem to merge at the horizon.* [Mid-17thC. From Latin *mergere* "to plunge, dip" (source also of English *submerge* and *immerse*), the original sense in English.] —**mer·gence** *n.* —**merg·ing** *n.*

merg·er /múrjər/ *n.* **1.** BUSINESS **COMBINING OF COMPANIES** the joining together of two or more companies or organizations ○ *a merger between two of the country's leading manufacturers* **2. UNION** a blending, combining, or joining of something with something else, or the state of being blended, combined, or joined together [Early 18thC. From Anglo-Norman, literally "to drown," from, ultimately, Latin *mergere* (see MERGE).]

Mé·ri·da /mèrreedə/ **1.** city in southeastern Mexico, the capital of Yucatán State. It was founded by the Spanish on a Mayan site in 1542. Population: 523,422 (1990). **2.** city in western Spain, in Bajadoz Province. Population: 52,200 (1987).

Mer·i·den /mérridən/ city in southern Connecticut, on the Quinnipiac River. Population: 56,928 (1994).

me·rid·i·an /mə ríddee ən/ *n.* **1.** GEOG **LINE OF LONGITUDE** an imaginary line between the North and South poles that crosses the equator at right angles. A meridian is designated by the degrees of longitude that it is west or east of the prime meridian. **2.** GEOG **HALF OF A CIRCLE BETWEEN POLES** either half of the circle of the meridian, from pole to pole **3.** ASTRON **CELESTIAL GREAT CIRCLE** a great circle of the celestial sphere that passes through the celestial poles and the zenith of the observer **4. HIGHEST POINT** the peak or a high point, e.g., of development or success (*literary*) ○ *the decade when the empire's power reached its meridian* **5.** *Midwest* TRANSP = **median strip 6.** ALTERN MED **LINE OF ACUPUNCTURE POINTS** in acupuncture, one of the pathways in the body along which the body's energy is believed to flow and along which acupuncture points are located **7.** TIME **NOON** the hour of midday (*archaic*) [14thC. Via Old French from Latin *meridianus*, from *meridies* "midday," an alteration of *medidies*, literally "middle day" from *medius* "middle" + *dies* "day."]

Me·rid·i·an /mə ríddee ən/ city in eastern Mississippi. Population: 41,036 (1990).

me·rid·i·o·nal /mə ríddee ən'l/ *adj.* **1. OF A MERIDIAN** along, belonging to, relating to, or like a meridian **2.** GEOG **OF SOUTHERN REGIONS** typical of or located in the south, especially southern Europe **3. OF SOUTHERN PEOPLES** typical of people who live in the south, especially southern Europe ■ *n.* PEOPLES **SOUTHERN PERSON** somebody born or living in the south, especially the south of France [14thC. Via French from late Latin *meridionalis*, from Latin *meridies* (see MERIDIAN) on the model of *septentrionalis* "northern."] —**me·rid·i·on·al·ly** *adv.*

Mé·ri·mée /mèrri máy/, **Prosper** (1803–70) French writer. His works include the novella *Carmen* (1845), the basis of Bizet's opera. He was also a historian.

me·ringue /mə ráng/ *n.* **1. WHIPPED EGG WHITES** a mixture of egg whites and sugar beaten until stiff, cooked, and used as a topping for pies or to make cookies and shells **2. MERINGUE COOKIE OR SHELL** a cake, cookie, or shell made of meringue, often with a cream filling [Early 18thC. From French, of uncertain origin: perhaps via French dialect *maringue* "shepherd's loaf," from Latin *merenda* "snack," from a form of *merere* "to earn."]

me·ri·no /mə reénō/ *n.* (*plural* **-nos**) **1. me·ri·no, me·ri·no sheep** ZOOL **SHEEP BRED FOR WOOL** a sheep of a breed originally from Spain that is bred for its wool in many parts of the world, especially Australia **2. WOOL** the long fine white wool of the merino sheep **3.** TEXTILES **YARN OR FABRIC** a fine yarn or fabric made from the wool of the merino sheep, often mixed with cotton ■ *adj.* TEXTILES **OF MERINO WOOL** made of merino wool ○ *a merino shawl* [Late 18thC. Via Spanish from Arabic *(banū) marīn*, the name of a Berber people who raised the breed.]

-merism *suffix.* denoting a relationship between chemical constituents ○ *isomerism* [Coined from Greek *meros* "part" + -ISM]

mer·i·stem /mérri stèm/ *n.* embryonic plant tissue that is actively dividing, such as is found at the tip of stems and roots [Late 19thC. From Greek *meristos* "divided," from *merizein* "to divide," from *meros* "part" (see -MERE).] —**mer·i·ste·mat·ic** /mèrristə máttik/ *adj.* —**mer·is·te·mat·i·cal·ly** /-máttikəlee/ *adv.*

me·ris·tic /mə rístik/ *adj.* BIOL **1. SEGMENTED** divided into or having segments **2. WITH CHANGING BODY PARTS** involving a change in the number or arrangement of body parts or segments [Late 19thC. Formed from Greek *meris, meros* "part."] —**me·ris·ti·cal·ly** *adv.*

mer·it /mérrit/ *n.* **1. VALUE** value that deserves respect and acknowledgment ○ *The movie is a work of considerable technical as well as artistic merit.* **2. GOOD QUALITY** a good or praiseworthy characteristic that somebody or something has (*often used in the plural*) **3. ABILITY** proven ability or accomplishment ○ *She got her promotion based on merit.* **4.** RELIG **SPIRITUAL CREDIT** spiritual worthiness achieved by doing good works ■ **mer·its** *npl.* **FACTS OF A CASE** the facts of a matter considered without regard for emotional, procedural, or other issues ○ *to consider a proposal on its merits* ■ *vt.* (**-it·ed, -it·ing, -its**) **DESERVE** to be worthy of or earn something ○ *Some people feel the award wasn't merited.* [12thC. Via French *mérite* from Latin *meritum* "price, value," a form of the past participle of *merere* "to earn" (source of English *emeritus*), used as a noun.]

mer·i·toc·ra·cy /mèrri tókrəssee/ (*plural* **-cies**) *n.* **1. SYSTEM BASED ON ABILITY** a social system that gives opportunites and advantages to people on the basis of their ability rather than, e.g., wealth or seniority **2. ELITE GROUP** an elite group of people who achieved their positions on the basis of ability and accomplishment **3. LEADERSHIP BY ELITE** leadership by an elite group of people who are chosen on the basis of their abilities and accomplishments [Mid-20thC. Coined from MERIT + -CRACY.] —**mer·it·o·crat·ic** /mèrritə kráttik/ *adj.*

mer·i·to·ri·ous /mèrri táwree əss/ *adj.* deserving honor and recognition (*formal*) ○ *She was awarded a medal for meritorious service.* [15thC. Formed from Latin *meritorius*, from *merere* "to earn."] —**mer·i·to·ri·ous·ly** *adv.* —**mer·i·to·ri·ous·ness** *n.*

mer·it sys·tem *n.* a system of appointing and promoting civil servants on the basis of their ability rather than political connections

merle /murl/, **merl** *n.* a blackbird (*archaic or literary*) [15thC. Via French from Latin *merula*, of uncertain origin: probably ultimately from an Indo-European word that is also the ancestor of English *ouzel*.]

Merlin

mer·lin /múrlin/ *n.* a small dark falcon found throughout the northern hemisphere that has a broad black band on the end of its tail. Latin name: *Falco columbarius.* [14thC. Via Anglo-Norman *merilun*, an alteration of Old French *esmirillon*, literally "large merlin," from *esmiril* "merlin," of uncertain origin.]

Mer·lin *n.* a legendary magician and adviser to King Arthur

mer·lon /múrlən/ *n.* a solid part between two openings (**crenels**) in a battlement, e.g., on a castle [Early 18thC. Via French from Italian *merlone*, literally "large battlement," from *merlo* "battlement."]

mer·lot /mər lṓ, mair lṓ/, **Mer·lot** *n.* **1. WINE** a red wine made from a variety of black grape **2. WINE GRAPE** a variety of black grape used in winemaking, originally grown in France and now raised in many wine-growing regions worldwide [Early 19thC. From French, literally "small blackbird," from *merle* "blackbird" (source of English *merle*), probably from the color of the grape.]

mer·maid /múr màyd/ *n.* a mythical sea creature with the head and upper body of a woman and the tail of a fish instead of legs [14thC. From MERE[2] + MAID.]

mer·maid's purse *n.* MARINE BIOL = **sea purse**

mer·man /múr màn, -mən/ (*plural* **-men** /-mèn, -mən/) *n.* a mythical sea creature with the head and upper body of a man and the tail of a fish instead of legs [Early 17thC. Coined from MERE[2] + MAN.]

mero- *prefix.* part, partial ○ *merozoite* ○ *meroplankton* [From Greek *meros* "part"]

mer·o·blas·tic /mèrrə blástik/ *adj.* used to describe an egg undergoing only partial division after being fertilized, with the undivided cells becoming the yolk —**mer·o·blas·ti·cal·ly** *adv.*

mer·o·crine /mérrəkrin, mérrə krīn/ *adj.* relating to or produced by glands that make secretions without cell damage or disintegration [Early 20thC. Coined from MERO- + Greek *krinein* "to separate."]

Mer·o·ë /mérrō ee/ **1.** ruined city in northern Sudan, on the Nile River **2.** ancient kingdom ruled from the city of Meroë

mer·o·plank·ton /mèrrə plángktən/ (*plural* **-tons** *or* **-ton**) *n.* organisms that are plankton only for part of their life cycle, usually during the larval stage —**mer·o·plank·ton·ic** /-plangk tónnik/ *adj.*

-merous *suffix.* having a particular number or kind of parts ○ *tetramerous* ○ *heteromerous* [Formed from Greek *meros* "part"]

Mer·o·vin·gi·an /mèrrə vínjee ən, -vínjən/ *adj.* **OF A FRANKISH DYNASTY** belonging or relating to a dynasty of Frankish kings that was founded by Clovis I and reigned in Gaul and Germany from about A.D. 500 to 751 ■ *n.* **MEROVINGIAN KING** a member of the Merovingian dynasty [Late 17thC. Via French *mérovingien* from, ultimately, Latin *Meroveus* "Merowig" (d. 458), the grandfather of Clovis.]

mer·o·zo·ite /mèrrə zṓ ìt/ *n.* any of the protozoan cells produced by the fission of a schizont, e.g., that of the malaria protozoan

Mer·ri·am /mérree əm/ city in northeastern Kansas, a southwestern suburb of Kansas City. Population: 12,160 (1996).

Mer·ri·mack /mérri màk/, **Mer·ri·mac** river in the northeastern United States, flowing south through New Hampshire and Massachusetts. Length: 110 mi./177 km.

mer·ri·ment /mérrimənt/ *n.* fun and enjoyment marked by noise and laughter

Mer·ritt Is·land /mèrrit-/ island off the eastern coast of central Florida, lying between Cape Canaveral and the mainland. Area: 93 sq. mi./179 sq. km.

mer·ry /mérree/ (**-ri·er, -ri·est**) *adj.* **1. LIVELY AND CHEERFUL** full of or showing lively cheerfulness or enjoyment ○ *a merry laugh* **2. DELIGHTFUL** tending to produce cheerfulness or happiness in people (*archaic*) ○ *the merry month of May* **3. QUICK IN MOVEMENT** quick or fast in movement or manner ○ *The train moved at a merry clip.* [Old English *myrige* "pleasant." Ultimately from a prehistoric Germanic base meaning "short," which is also the ancestor of English *mirth*. The underlying idea is of making time seem short.] —**mer·ri·ly** *adv.* —**mer·ri·ness** *n.* ◇ **make merry** to be amused, or take part in a celebration or festivity

WORD KEY: CULTURAL NOTE

The Merry Wives of Windsor, a play by English dramatist William Shakespeare (1600–01). Shakespeare's only play in prose was written to exploit the popularity of Falstaff, a comic character in *Henry IV.* It tells of Falstaff's attempts to woo two married women in order to gain access to their wealth, the wives' discovery of his plan, and their imaginative revenge. The adjective *Falstaffian*, convivially jovial, derives from the character in both of the plays.

mer·ry·an·drew /mèrree ándroo/ *n.* a buffoon, clown, or jester (*archaic*) [*Andrew* the forename, used in the sense of "any man"]

mer·ry·bells (*plural* **mer·ry·bells**) *n.* BOT = **bellwort**

mer·ry-go-round *n.* **1. AMUSEMENT PARK RIDE** an amusement park or fairground ride with a rotating circular platform fitted with seats that are usually shaped like animals such as horses and move up and down to music **2. REVOLVING RIDE IN A PLAYGROUND** a piece of playground equipment in the form of a revolving structure for children to sit on and push, or be pushed, round and round **3. WHIRL OF ACTIVITY** a busy or continuous cycle of fast-paced activities or events ○ *a merry-go-round of press interviews and promotional events*

mer·ry·mak·ing /mérree màyking/ *n.* lively celebration, fun, or enjoyment —**mer·ry·mak·er** *n.*

mer·ry men *npl.* somebody's followers (*humorous*)

Mer·ton /múrt'n/, **Robert K.** (*b.* 1910) U.S. sociologist. He published important work on social deviance and mass persuasion, and helped to establish sociology as an academic discipline. Full name **Robert King Merton**

mes- *prefix.* = **meso-** (*used before vowels*)

Library of Congress/Corbis

Mesa: Devil's Tower, Wyoming

me·sa /máyssə/ *n.* a relatively flat elevated area with steep sides that is less extensive than a plateau, found especially in the southwestern United States. ◊ **butte** [Mid-18thC. From Spanish, literally "table," from Latin *mensa*.]

WORD KEY: REGIONAL NOTE

Mesa is most common in the southwestern states, including Colorado. The term contrasts with *butte*, which is used more frequently in the northwest, contrasting the place names *Mesa County*, Colorado, and *Mesa*, Arizona, with *Butte County*, South Dakota, and *Butte*, Montana.

Me·sa /máyssə/ city in south central Arizona, a southeastern suburb of Phoenix. It is a noted resort. Population: 344,764 (1996).

Me·sa·bi Range /mə saábee-/ narrow range of hills in northeastern Minnesota, parallel to Lake Superior, rich in iron ore. Length: 130 mi./210 km.

mé·sal·li·ance /may zállee əns, may zàl yaáNs/ *n.* a marriage with somebody of a lower social position, regarded as a bad match [Late 18thC. From French, literally "bad alliance," from *alliance* "alliance," from Old French *aliance*.]

me·sarch /mé zaàrk, meé zaàrk/ *adj.* ECOL used to describe a succession of plant or animal communities (**sere**) that originates in a moist habitat [Late 19thC. Coined from MESO- + Greek *arkhē* "beginning, origin."]

Me·sa Ver·de Na·tion·al Park /màyssə vúrd-/ national park in southwestern Colorado, established in 1906. It is noted for its well-preserved ancient cliff dwellings. Area: 52,122 acres/21,093 hectares.

mes·cal /mess kál/ (*plural* **-cals** *or* **-cal**) *n.* **1. ALCOHOLIC BEVERAGE** a colorless Mexican liquor distilled from the fermented sap of some species of agave plant. It is often sold with an agave worm in the bottle. ◊ **tequila 2.** = **peyote** [Early 18thC. Via Spanish *mezcal* from Nahuatl *mexcalli* "mescal liquor."]

Mes·ca·le·ro /mèsskə lérrō/ (*plural* **-ro** *or* **-ros**) *n.* a member of a Native American people who originally occupied lands in Mexico, New Mexico, and Texas, and whose members now live mainly in southern New Mexico [Mid-19thC. From Spanish, from *mezcal* (see MESCAL).]

mes·cla /méskla/ *n.* **1.** DRUGS a drug made from the residue of processing cocaine, which is mixed with marijuana and smoked **2. HALLUCINOGENIC DRUG** a hallucinogenic drug that is extracted from the button-shaped nodules on the stem of the peyote

Mes·dames /may daám/ **1.** plural of **Madame 2.** plural of **Madam 3.** plural of **Mrs.** [Late 16thC. From French, plural of *Madame*.]

mes·de·moi·selles plural of **mademoiselle**

me·seems /mi seémz/ (**-seemed**) *vi.* it seems to me (*archaic*) [14thC. From an earlier form of the phrase *it seems to me*.]

me·sem·bry·an·the·mum /mə zèmbree ánthəməm/ (*plural* **-mums** *or* **-mum**) *n.* a southern African succulent plant that has thick fleshy leaves and is widely grown for its colorful flowers. Genus: *Mesembryanthemum.* [Late 18thC. Via modern Latin, genus name, from, ultimately, Greek *mesēmbria* "noon" + *anthemon* "flower."]

mes·en·ceph·a·lon /mèz en séffə lòn, -lən/ *n.* the midbrain (*technical*) —**mes·en·ce·phal·ic** /mèz ensə fállik/ *adj.*

mes·en·chyme /mézzən kīm/ *n.* the cells within the embryo that develop into connective tissue, bone, cartilage, blood, and the lymphatic system [Late 19thC. Anglicization of *mesenchyma*, literally "middle infusion," from Greek *mesos* "middle" + *egkhuma* "infusion."] —**mes·en·chy·mal** /mə zéngkim'l/ *adj.* —**mes·en·chym·a·tous** /mèzz'n kímmətəss/ *adj.*

mes·en·ter·i·tis /mez èntə rītiss, mess-/ *n.* inflammation of the mesentery of the peritoneum

mes·en·ter·on /mez éntə ròn/ (*plural* **-a** /-tərə/) *n.* the middle section of the embryonic intestine, which develops into the stomach, small intestine, and most of the large intestine —**mes·en·ter·on·ic** /mez èntə rónnik, mess-/ *adj.*

mes·en·ter·y /mézz'n tèrree, méss'n-/ (*plural* **-ies**) *n.* **1.** ANAT **SUPPORTING MEMBRANE** a membrane that supports an organ or body part, especially the double-layered membrane of the peritoneum attached to the back wall of the abdominal cavity that supports the small intestine **2.** ZOOL **MEMBRANE IN INVERTEBRATES** a supportive membrane surrounding and giving structure to the inner organs of invertebrates [15thC. Via modern Latin *mesenterium* from Greek *mesenterion*, literally "middle intestine," from *enteron* "intestine" (source of English *enteron*).] —**mes·en·ter·ic** /mèzz'n térrik, mèss'n-/ *adj.*

mesh /mesh/ *n.* **1. NETLIKE MATERIAL** material or a piece of material made of plastic, thread, or wire woven together like a net ○ *wire mesh* **2. OPENING IN A NET** the open space between the threads or wires of a net **3. STRANDS OF NET** the threads or wires that make up a net **4. TRAP** something that holds or entangles like a net or a trap (*often used in the plural*) ○ *caught in the meshes of the criminal underworld* **5. SOMETHING INTERWOVEN** an interwoven or interlinked arrangement or construction ○ *the mesh of the girders against the sky* **6. INTERLOCKING METAL LINKS** a material consisting of interlocking metal links, used in jewelry **7.** MECH ENG **ENGAGEMENT OF GEARS** engagement of the teeth on gear wheels **8. OPENING IN A SCREEN** a measure of the number of openings in a screen for sorting things into different sizes, usually per inch. A 20-mesh screen has 20 openings per inch. ■ *vti.* **(meshed, mesh·ing, mesh·es) 1. FIT TOGETHER** to fit or work closely or well together, or make things work closely or well together ○ *Her vision of the company's future meshes perfectly with ours.* **2. CATCH OR ENTANGLE** to catch or entangle somebody or something, or become caught or entangled, in a mesh **3.** MECH ENG **ENGAGE GEARS** to make gear teeth engage together, or become engaged [14thC. Origin uncertain: probably from Middle Dutch *maesche,* and ultimately from an Indo-European word meaning "knot" or "to knit."] —**mesh·y** *adj.*

me·shu·ga /mə shŏŏgə/, **me·shu·gah** *adj.* totally unreasonable or thoughtless (*slang insult*) [Late 19thC. Via Yiddish *meshuge* from Hebrew *mĕshuggā.*]

me·shug·gen·er /mə shŏŏgənər/, **me·shu·ga·na** *n.* somebody who is totally unreasonable or thoughtless (*slang insult*) [Early 20thC. Variant of MESHUGA.]

me·si·al /meézee əl/ *adj.* DENT relating to or occurring along the dental arch near the middle of the front of the jaw [Early 19thC. Formed from Greek *mesos* "middle."] —**me·si·al·ly** *adv.*

mes·ic[1] /mézzik/ *adj.* ECOL growing in or characterized by moderate moisture [Early 20thC. Formed from Greek *mesos* "middle."] —**mes·i·cal·ly** *adv.*

mes·ic[2] /mézzik/ *adj.* PHYS relating to a meson [Mid-20thC. Formed from MESON.]

mes·mer·ic /mez mérrik/ *adj.* completely absorbing somebody's attention [Early 19thC. Formed from *Mesmer* (see MESMERIZE).] —**mes·mer·i·cal·ly** *adv.*

mes·mer·ism /mézzmə rìzzəm/ *n.* **1. FASCINATING POWER** the power to fascinate somebody in a way that is almost hypnotic **2.** HIST **HYPNOTISM** hypnotism, formerly believed to involve animal magnetism [Late 18thC. Formed from *Mesmer* (see MESMERIZE).] —**mes·mer·ist** *n.*

mes·mer·ize /mézzmə rīz/ **(-ized, -iz·ing, -iz·es)** *vt.* **1. ABSORB SOMEBODY'S ATTENTION** to fascinate somebody or absorb all of somebody's attention ○ *The speaker mesmerized the audience with his dramatic tale.* **2. HYPNOTIZE** to hypnotize somebody, especially formerly in a way believed to involve animal magnetism [Early 19thC. Formed from the name of F. A. *Mesmer* (1734–1815), an Austrian physician who conducted experiments in which he induced trancelike states in his subjects.] —**mes·mer·i·za·tion** /mèzzməri záysh'n/ *n.* —**mes·mer·iz·er** /mézzmə rīzər/ *n.*

mesne /meen/ *adj.* LAW happening or appearing between two other things, especially assignments of property [Mid-16thC. From legal French, a variant of Anglo-Norman *meen* "middle."]

meso- *prefix.* middle, intermediate ○ *mesopelagic* [From Greek *mesos.* Ultimately from an Indo-European word that is also the ancestor of English *middle* and *medial.*]

Mes·o·a·mer·i·ca /mèzzō ə mérrikə, mèssō-/ *n.* a region of Central America and southern North America that was occupied by several civilizations, especially the Mayan, in pre-Columbian times — **Mes·o·a·mer·i·can** *adj., n.*

mes·o·blast /mézzə blàst, méssə-/ *n.* CELL BIOL = **mesoderm**

mes·o·carp /mézzə kaàrp, méssə-/ *n.* the middle layer of a fruit wall **(pericarp)**, e.g., the fleshy part of some fruits

mes·o·crat·ic /mèzzə kráttik, mèssə-/ *adj.* used to describe igneous rock containing as much as 60 percent heavy dark ferromagnesium minerals in its composition

mes·o·derm /mézzə dùrm, méssə-/ *n.* the middle of the three cell layers in an embryo, from which connective tissue, muscle, blood, dermis, and bone develop —**mes·o·der·mal** /mèzzə dúrm'l, mèssə-/ *adj.* —**mes·o·der·mic** *adj.*

mes·o·gle·a /mézzə gleé ə, mèssə-/, **mes·o·gloe·a** *n.* a layer of gelatinous substance separating the inner and outer walls of a coelenterate such as a jellyfish [Late 19thC. From modern Latin, literally "middle glue," from Greek *glia* "glue" (source of English *glia*).] — **mes·o·gle·al** *adj.*

Mes·o·lith·ic /mèzzə líthik, mèssə-/, **mesolithic** *n.* the middle period of the Stone Age, between the Paleolithic and Neolithic —**Me·so·lithic** *adj.*

mes·o·morph /mézzə màwrf, méssə-/ *n.* a husky muscular body, or somebody who has such a body. ◊ **ectomorph, endomorph**

mes·on /meé zòn, mé-/ *n.* an elementary particle, e.g., a pion or kaon, that has a rest mass between that of an electron and proton and participates in the strong interaction. Mesons consist of a quark and antiquark, and have a spin that is zero or an integer. —**me·son·ic** /me zónnik, meé-/ *adj.*

mes·o·pause /mézzə pàwz, méssə-/ *n.* the upper boundary of the mesosphere, approximately 50 mi./80 km above the Earth's surface

mes·o·pe·lag·ic /mèzzə pə lájjik, mèssə-/ *adj.* found in or relating to the intermediate oceanic depths between approximately 300 and 3,300 ft./100 and 1,000 m

mes·o·phyll /mézzə fil, méssə-/ *n.* the soft tissue **(parenchyma)** containing chlorophyll between the epidermal layers of a plant leaf —**mes·o·phyl·lic** /mèzzə fíllik, mèssə-/ *adj.* —**mes·o·phyl·lous** /mèzzə fílləss, mèssə-/ *adj.*

mes·o·phyte /mézzə fīt, méssə-/ *n.* a land plant that needs moderate amounts of moisture for growth — **mes·o·phyt·ic** /mèzzə fíttik, mèssə-/ *adj.*

Mes·o·pot·am·i·a /mèssəpə táymee ə/ ancient region located between the Tigris and Euphrates rivers in modern Iraq and Syria. It was the site of several early urban civilizations, including Babylonia. — **Mes·o·pot·am·i·an** *n.*

mes·o·some /mézzə sòm, méssə-/ *n.* an indentation in the cell membrane of some bacteria

mes·o·sphere /mézzə sfeèr, méssə-/ *n.* the layer of the Earth's atmosphere in which temperature decreases rapidly, located between the stratosphere and thermosphere —**mes·o·spher·ic** /mèzzə sférrik, mèssə-, -sfeérik/ *adj.*

mes·o·the·li·um /mèzzə theélee əm, mèssə-/ (*plural* **-a** /-ə, -əl/) *n.* a cell layer derived from mesoderm that lines the body cavity of a vertebrate embryo and develops into epithelia and muscle tissue — **mes·o·the·li·al** *adj.*

mes·o·tho·rax /mèzzə tháw ràks, mèssə-/ (*plural* **-rax·es** *or* **-ra·ces** /mèzzə tháwrə seèz, -rə seèz/) *n.* the middle of the three segments of an insect's thorax, from which the middle pair of legs and first pair of wings grow —**mes·o·tho·rac·ic** /mèzzəthə rássik, mèssəthə-/ *adj.*

Mes·o·zo·ic /mèzzə zṓ ik, mèssə-/ *adj.* **BELONGING TO PREHISTORIC ERA** belonging to or dating from an era of geologi time 250 to 65 million years ago, between the Permian and Tertiary eras, when dinosaurs, birds, and flowering plants first appeared ■ *n.* **MESOZOIC ERA** the Mesozoic era

mes·quite /me skeét/ (*plural* **-quite** *or* **-quites**) *n.* **1.** TREES **SMALL SPINY TREE** a small spiny tree or shrub of the legume family that grows in the southwestern United States and has pods that are used as fodder. Genus: *Prosopis.* **2.** INDUST **MESQUITE WOOD** the wood of a mesquite tree or shrub, often burned in a barbecue to flavor food [Mid-18thC. Via Mexican Spanish *mezquite* from Nahuatl *mizquitl.*]

WORD KEY: REGIONAL NOTE

Mesquite is common in Upper Mexico and the lower Southwestern states, especially in Texas, where such growth is also called *chaparral* (a Spanish loanword), *mesquite flat(s), mesquite thicket,* and *mesquital.*

mess /mess/ *n.* **1. UNTIDY CONDITION** a dirty or untidy state ○ *The apartment was left in a terrible mess after the party.* **2. CHAOTIC STATE** a chaotic, confused, or troublesome state or situation ○ *Their business affairs were in a complete mess.* **3. UNTIDY PERSON OR THING** somebody or something in a confused, dirty, or untidy state (*informal insult*) **4. PLACE FOR COMMUNAL MEALS** a place where a group of people, especially members of the armed forces, have meals together **5. PEOPLE WHO EAT TOGETHER** a group of people, especially members of the armed forces, who have meals together **6. COMMUNAL MEAL** a meal eaten together by a group of people, especially members of the armed forces **7. QUANTITY OF FOOD** a serving or quantity of food, especially of soft or soggy food (*archaic*) ■ *v.* **(messed, mess·ing, mess·es) 1.** *vi.* **MEDDLE** to interfere or meddle in something ○ *Don't mess in their business.* **2.** *vi.* **USE SOMETHING CARELESSLY** to use something carelessly, causing a problem or damage as a result ○ *Who's been messing with my computer?* **3.** *vti.* **MAKE SOMETHING DIRTY** to make something dirty, muddled, or disordered ○ *She messed her jacket while checking the oil.* **4.** *vi.* **EAT TOGETHER** to take meals along with a particular group of people, especially members of the armed forces ○ *I used to mess with the three of them.* [13thC. From Old French, "portion of food," the original sense in English, from, ultimately, Latin *mittere* "to send, put," the underlying idea being "placing (as if on the table)."]

mess around *v.* **1.** *vi.* **WASTE TIME** to waste time in an unproductive or aimless manner (*informal*) **2.** *vi.* **RELAX** to spend time in a leisurely and pleasant manner (*informal*) **3.** *vti.* **INTERFERE** to interfere or meddle in something (*informal*) **4.** *vi.* **ASSOCIATE WITH SOMEBODY** to associate with somebody, especially somebody who is seen as undesirable (*informal*) ○ *She started messing around with that crowd last summer.* **5.** *vi.* **BEHAVE IN UNSERIOUS WAY** to joke or behave playfully (*informal*) ○ *I thought he was just messing around.* **6.** *vi.* **BE SEXUALLY UNFAITHFUL** to have sexual activity with somebody other than a spouse or regular partner (*slang*)

mess up *v.* (*informal*) **1.** *vti.* **RUIN SOMETHING** to spoil or bungle something, or make a mistake ○ *The rain messed up our plans for a picnic.* **2.** *vt.* **MAKE SOMETHING MESSY** to make something dirty or disordered **3.** *vt.* **UPSET SOMEBODY** to confuse or upset somebody

mes·sage /méssij/ *n.* **1. COMMUNICATION** a communication in speech, writing, or signals **2. MEANING** a lesson, moral, or important idea that somebody wants to communicate, e.g., in a work of art **3. ERRAND** the mission or errand of a messenger (*dated*) ○ *sent on a message to her grandmother's* **4. COMMERCIAL** a commercial, especially one on television, paid for by the sponsors of a program or event ○ *and now a message from our sponsor* ■ *vt.* **(-saged, -sag·ing, -sages) 1. COMMUNICATE WITH SOMEBODY** to send a message to somebody ○ *Can you message me about that?* **2. COMMUNICATE SOMETHING TO SOMEBODY** to send something as a message ○ *to message the news to your boss* [13thC. Via French from, ultimately, Latin *missus,* the past participle of *mittere* "to send" (source of English *mission, transmit,* and *promise*).] ◇ **get the message** to take something in and understand it (*informal*)

mes·sage board *n.* COMPUT = **bulletin board**

mes·sag·ing /méssijing/ *n.* **1. SYSTEM FOR MESSAGES** a system for sending messages to people, e.g., by computer, telephone, or pager **2. SENDING OF MESSAGES** the process of sending a message using a messaging system

mes·sa·line /mèssə leén/ *n.* a soft shiny lightweight silk fabric, used for making dresses [Early 20thC. From French, from the name of Valeria *Messalina,* adulterous wife of the Roman emperor Claudius; perhaps because the fabric was considered sensuous.]

Mes·sei·gneurs plural of **Monseigneur**

mes·sen·ger /méss'njər/ *n.* **1. SOMEBODY CARRYING MESSAGE** somebody who carries a message or messages between people **2. PAID COURIER** somebody who is employed to carry messages, especially an employee of a courier or telegram delivery service or a government courier **3. SOMEBODY RUNNING ERRAND** somebody who runs an errand **4. HERALD** a herald or forerunner of something (*archaic*) **5. mes·sen·ger, mes·sen·ger line** NAUT **LIGHT ROPE** a lightweight rope that is used to haul a heavier one, e.g., from one ship to another ■ *vt.* **(-gered, -ger·ing, -gers) SEND BY MESSENGER** to send something by messenger [12thC. From French *messager,* from *message* "a MESSAGE."]

mes·sen·ger RNA *n.* a form of RNA that is transcribed from a strand of DNA and translated into a protein sequence at a cell ribosome

Mes·ser·schmitt /méssər shmit/ *n.* a fighter airplane, especially the Me-109 or the Me-262, used by the German air force in World War II [Mid-20thC]

mess hall *n.* a building or room where a group of people, especially members of the armed forces, eat their meals together

mes·si·ah /mə sī ə/ *n.* somebody regarded as or claiming to be a savior or liberator of a country, people, or the world —**mes·si·ah·ship** *n.*

Mes·si·ah /mə sī ə/ *n.* **1.** CHR **JESUS CHRIST** in Christianity, Jesus Christ regarded as the Messiah prophesied in the Hebrew Bible **2.** JUDAISM **KING OF THE JEWS** in the Hebrew Bible, an anointed king who will lead the Jews back to the land of Israel and establish justice in the world [12thC. Via French *Messie* from, ultimately, Greek *Messias*, from Aramaic *mĕšīhā* and Hebrew *māšīăh*, literally "anointed," from *māšah* "to anoint."] —**Mes·si·ah·ship** *n.*

mes·si·an·ic /mèssee ánnik/ *adj.* **1. mes·si·an·ic, Mes·si·an·ic** JUD-CHR **RELATING TO THE MESSIAH** belonging or relating to the Messiah **2.** JUDAISM **OF JUDAIC GOLDEN AGE** relating to, belonging to, or constituting a Judaic golden age of peace, truth, and happiness **3. OF A LIBERATOR** relating or belonging to an inspirational leader, especially one claiming to be or regarded as a savior or liberator **4. INVOLVING GREAT ENTHUSIASM** done with or showing great enthusiasm or devotion ○ *preaching with messianic fervor* —**mes·si·an·i·cal·ly** *adv.*

mes·si·a·nism /mə sī́ ə nìzzəm, méssee-/, **Mes·si·a·nism** *n.* belief in the coming of the Messiah or a messiah or messianic age

Mes·si·dor /méssi dàwr/ *n.* the tenth month of the year in the French Revolutionary calendar, corresponding to June 20 to July 19 in the Gregorian calendar [Mid-19thC. From French, literally "harvest gift," from Latin *messis* "harvest" + Greek *dōron* "gift."]

Mes·sieurs plural of **Monsieur**

mess jacket *n.* a waist-length jacket, worn as part of a military uniform, especially on formal occasions

mess kit *n.* a compact set of cooking and eating utensils, usually made of metal, used especially by soldiers or campers

mess·mate /méss màyt/ *n.* somebody with whom somebody regularly eats, especially in a military mess

Messrs. plural of **Mr.**

mes·suage /mésswij/ *n.* a dwelling with its outbuildings and the surrounding land that is used by the dwelling's occupants [14thC. From Anglo-Norman, of uncertain origin: probably from a misreading of *mesnage*, from Old French (see MENAGE).]

mess·y /méssee/ (**-i·er, -i·est**) *adj.* **1. DIRTY OR DISORDERED** involving, producing, or marked by dirt or disorder ○ *Repairing a car can be a messy business.* **2. DIFFICULT TO SORT OUT** complicated and unpleasant to resolve or deal with **3. CARELESS** showing a lack of carefulness or precision ○ *an erroneous conclusion resulting from messy reasoning* —**mess·i·ly** *adv.* —**mess·i·ness** *n.*

mes·ti·za /mes teézə/ *n.* a woman who has parents or ancestors of different racial origins, especially a woman in Latin America of both Native American and European ancestry [Late 16thC. From Spanish, the feminine of MESTIZO.]

mes·ti·zo /mes teé zō/ (*plural* **-zos** *or* **-zoes**) *n.* somebody who has parents or ancestors of different racial origins, especially somebody in Latin America of both Native American and European ancestry. Mestizos form the largest population group in many Latin American countries. [Late 16thC. Via Spanish, from Latin *mixtus*, the past participle of *miscere* "to mix" (source of English *mix* and *meddle*).]

mes·tra·nol /méstrə nàwl/ *n.* a synthetic estrogen used in oral contraceptives. Formula: $C_{21}H_{26}O_2$. [Mid-20thC. Coined from METHYL + ESTRADIOL + -OL.]

Meš·tro·vić /mésh trovich/, **Ivan** (1883–1962) Croatian-born U.S. sculptor. His works have religious and folkloric subjects. He also sculpted portrait busts.

met past tense, past participle of **meet**

Met /met/ *abbr.* **1.** Metropolitan Museum of Art (in New York) **2.** Metropolitan Opera House (in New York)

met. *abbr.* **1.** metallurgy **2.** metaphor **3.** metaphysics **4.** meteorological **5.** meteorology **6.** metropolitan

meta- *prefix.* **1.** later, behind ○ *metaphase* ○ *metathorax* **2.** beyond, transcending, encompassing ○ *metagalaxy* ○ *metalanguage* **3.** change, transformation ○ *metaplasia* **4.** higher, more developed ○ *metaxylem* **5.** used in chemical names ○ *metaphosphate* [From Greek *meta* "beside, after." Ultimately from an Indo-European base meaning "between" that is also the ancestor of English *midwife*.]

met·a·bol·ic /mèttə bóllik/ *adj.* relating to or typical of metabolism [Mid-19thC. From Greek *metabolikos* "changeable," from *metabolē* (see METABOLISM).] —**met·a·bol·i·cal·ly** *adv.*

me·tab·o·lism /mə tábbə lìzzəm/ *n.* **1. LIFE-SUSTAINING CHEMICAL ACTIVITY** the ongoing interrelated series of chemical interactions taking place in living organisms that provide the energy and nutrients needed to sustain life **2. CHEMICAL ACTIVITY INVOLVING PARTICULAR SUBSTANCE** the chemical activity involving a particular substance in a living organism [Late 19thC. Formed from Greek *metabolē* "change," from *metaballein*, literally "to throw differently," from *ballein* "to throw" (source of English *ballistic*).]

me·tab·o·lite /mə tábbə lìt/ *n.* a substance that is involved in or is a byproduct of metabolism

me·tab·o·lize /mə tábbə lìz/ (**-lized, -liz·ing, -liz·es**) *vti.* to subject something to the biochemical processes of metabolism, or to undergo metabolism [Late 19thC. Formed from Greek *metabolē* (see METABOLISM).] —**me·tab·o·liz·a·ble** *adj.*

met·a·car·pal /mèttə kaárp'l/ *n.* **HAND OR FOREFOOT BONES** any of the bones in the human hand between the wrist and digits, or the similar bones in a vertebrate animal's forefoot ■ *adj.* **OF HAND OR FOREFOOT BONES** relating or belonging to the metacarpals —**met·a·car·pal·ly** *adv.*

met·a·car·pus /mèttə kaárpəss/ (*plural* **-pi** /-pī/) *n.* **1.** ANAT **BONES IN HUMAN HAND** the set of five long bones (**metacarpals**) in the human hand between the wrist and fingers **2.** ZOOL **FOREFOOT REGION** the region between the wrist and digits of the forefoot or hand of a vertebrate animal

met·a·cen·ter /méttə sèntər/ *n.* the intersection of the vertical line through the center of buoyancy of an object at equilibrium with the vertical line through the center of buoyancy when the object is tilted

met·a·cen·tric /mèttə séntrik/ *adj.* **1. OF METACENTER** relating or belonging to a metacenter **2.** GENETICS **HAVING CENTROMERE IN MIDDLE** used to describe a chromosome whose centromere is located at or near the middle. ◊ **acentric, telocentric**

met·a·chro·mat·ic /mèttə krō máttik/ *adj.* **1. TAKING ON DIFFERENT COLOR** taking on a color atypical of the staining solution **2. PRODUCING DIFFERENT SHADES** able to produce a color in different shades in tissue or cells [Late 19thC. Coined from META- + Greek *khrōmat-* (see CHROMAT-) + -IC.]

met·a·chro·ma·tism /mèttə krṓmə tìzzəm/ *n.* a change in color caused by a change in physical conditions such as temperature

met·a·cog·ni·tion /mèttə kog nísh'n/ *n.* knowledge about your own thoughts and the factors that influence your thinking —**met·a·cog·ni·tive** /mèttə kógnitiv/ *adj.*

met·a·eth·ics /mèttə éthiks/ *n.* the branch of linguistic philosophy that analyzes and seeks to clarify the meaning and use of ethical expressions such as "good" and "ought" (*takes a singular verb*) —**met·a·eth·i·cal** *adj.*

met·a·fe·male /mèttə feé màyl/ *n.* a female organism with an extra female chromosome

met·a·fic·tion /méttə fikshən/ *n.* **1. FICTION ABOUT NATURE OF LITERATURE** fiction that emphasizes the nature of fiction, the techniques and conventions used to write it, and the role of the author **2. PIECE OF METAFICTION** a work of metafiction —**met·a·fic·tion·al** *adj.* —**met·a·fic·tion·ist** *n.*

met·a·gal·ax·y /mèttə gálləksee/ *n.* the total of all galaxies making up the universe —**met·a·ga·lac·tic** /mèttə gə láktik/ *adj.*

met·age /meétij/ *n.* **1. OFFICIAL MEASUREMENT** the official measurement of the contents or weight of a load, e.g., of coal or grain **2. CHARGE** a charge for making an official measurement of the contents or weight of a load [Early 16thC. Formed from METE "to measure."]

me·tag·na·thous /mə tágnəthəss/ *adj.* used to describe a bird that has the tips of its bill crossed —**me·tag·na·thism** *n.*

Met·ai·rie /méttəree/ city in Louisiana, west of New Orleans. Population: 149,428 (1990).

met·al /mét'l/ *n.* **1.** METALL **TYPE OF CHEMICAL ELEMENT** a chemical element such as copper or iron that is usually solid in form, is usually a good conductor of heat and electricity, is malleable and ductile and has a characteristic luster **2.** METALL **MIXTURE OF METALS** a mixture (**alloy**) of one or more metals **3.** MUSIC **HEAVY METAL** heavy metal (*informal*) **4.** PRINTING **PRINTING TYPE** printer's type made of metal **5.** CRAFT **MOLTEN GLASS** molten glass for use in glassmaking **6.** HERALDRY **GOLD OR SILVER** gold or silver when used in heraldry **7.** NAVY **WEIGHT FIRED IN BROADSIDE** the collective weight of the projectiles a warship can fire in a broadside ■ *vt.* (**-aled** *or* **-alled, -al·ing** *or* **-al·ling, -als**) **FIT WITH METAL** to cover, fit, or provide something with metal [13thC. Directly or via French from Latin *metallum* "mine, metal," from Greek *metallon*, of unknown origin.]

metal. *abbr.* **1.** metallurgic **2.** metallurgy

met·a·lan·guage /méttə làng gwij/ *n.* a language or system of symbols used to describe or analyze another language or system of symbols

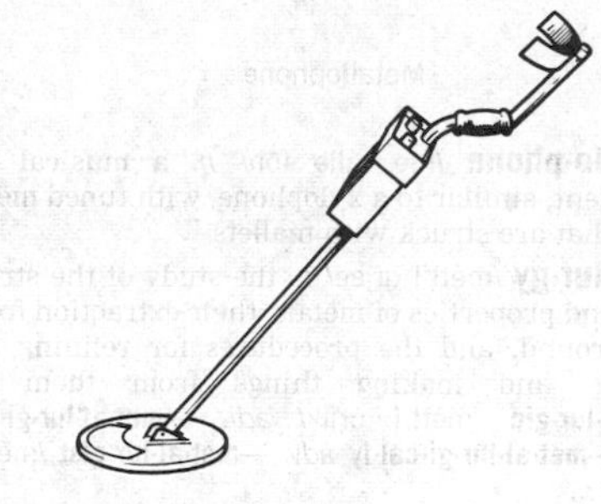

Metal detector

met·al de·tec·tor *n.* **1. DEVICE FOR DETECTING BURIED METAL** a portable electronic device with a search head that is swept over the ground and used to detect buried metal objects such as coins **2. DEVICE FOR DETECTING WEAPONS** an electronic device for detecting metal weapons, and e.g., to screen passengers at an airport **3.** FOOD TECH **DEVICE FOR DETECTING METAL IN FOOD** an electronic device used in the food industry to check for the presence of pieces of metal that might have accidentally gotten into food during processing

met·a·lin·guis·tic /mèttə ling gwístik/ *adj.* relating to a metalanguage or to metalinguistics

met·a·lin·guis·tics /mèttə ling gwístiks/ *n.* (*takes a singular verb*) **1. STUDY OF METALANGUAGES** the branch of linguistics that deals with the study of metalanguages **2. STUDY OF LANGUAGE AND CULTURE** the branch of linguistics that deals with the relation between a language and other aspects of a particular culture

met·al·ize /mét'l ìz/ *vt.* = **metallize**

metall. *abbr.* **1.** metallurgic **2.** metallurgy

me·tal·lic /mə tállik/ *adj.* **1. CONTAINING OR BEING METAL** made of, containing, or constituting metal or a metal **2. OF METAL** typical of a metal **3. SHINY** shiny and highly reflective ○ *a sports car with a metallic finish* **4. TASTING OF METAL** sharp and bitter to the taste ○ *This water has a slightly metallic taste.* **5. SOUNDING LIKE HIT METAL** like the sound of a metal object hitting or knocking against something **6. HARSH-SOUNDING** harsh and unpleasant in tone ○ *speaking with a metallic edge to her voice* —**me·tal·li·cal·ly** *adv.*

me·tal·lic bond *n.* a chemical bond characteristic of metals, in which electrons are shared between atoms and move about in the crystal

me·tal·lic lens *n.* a device consisting of louvers or slats, used to focus electromagnetic or sound waves

met·al·lif·er·ous /mètt'l íffərəss/ *adj.* containing or yielding metal

met·al·line /métt'lin, –n/ *adj.* **1. LIKE METAL** resembling a metal **2. WITH METAL IONS** containing metal ions

met·al·lize /métt'l ìz/ (**-lized, -liz·ing, -lizes**), **met·al·ize** *vt.* to coat or cover something with metal

metallo- *prefix.* metal ○ *metallophone* [From Latin *metallum* (see METAL)]

met·al·log·ra·phy /mètt'l óggrəfee/ *n.* the study of the composition and microscopic structure of metals —**met·al·log·ra·pher** *n.* —**me·tal·lo·graph·ic** /mə tàllə gráffik/ *adj.* —**me·tal·lo·graph·i·cal·ly** *adv.* —**met·al·lo·graph·ist** *n.*

met·al·loid /métt'l òyd/ *n.* **NONMETALLIC ELEMENT WITH METAL PROPERTIES** a nonmetallic element such as silicon that has properties between those of a metal and nonmetal ■ *adj.* **met·al·loid, met·al·loi·dal 1. OF METALLOID** relating to or having the characteristics of a metalloid **2. LIKE METAL** resembling a metal

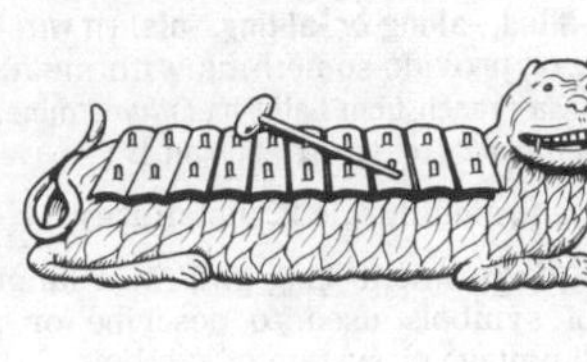

Metallophone

met·al·lo·phone /mə tállə fōn/ *n.* a musical instrument, similar to a xylophone, with tuned metal bars that are struck with mallets

met·al·lur·gy /mét'l ùrjee/ *n.* the study of the structure and properties of metals, their extraction from the ground, and the procedures for refining, alloying, and making things from them —**met·al·lur·gic** /mètt'l úrjik/ *adj.* —**met·al·lur·gi·cal** *adj.* —**met·al·lur·gi·cal·ly** *adv.* —**met·al·lur·gist** /métt'l ùrjist/ *n.*

met·al·work /métt'l wùrk/ *n.* **1. MAKING OF METAL OBJECTS** the craft of making objects out of metal **2. METAL THINGS** objects made of metal **3. METAL PART OF SOMETHING** the metal part of an object —**met·al·work·er** *n.*

met·al·work·ing /métt'l wùrking/ *n.* the process or technique of making or shaping objects out of metal

met·a·male /méttə màyl/ *n.* a male organism with an extra male chromosome

met·a·mere /méttə meer/ *n.* any of the series of similar segments into which the bodies of animals such as worms or lobsters are divided

met·a·mer·ic /mèttə mérrik/ *adj.* **1. HAVING METAMERES** with a body divided into a series of similar segments **(metameres) 2. OF METAMERISM** relating to or typical of metamerism —**met·a·mer·i·cal·ly** *adv.*

me·tam·er·ism /mə támmə rìzzəm/ *n.* the condition of having the body divided into a series of similar segments **(metameres)**, or an embryonic stage in which the body is divided in this way

met·a·mor·phic /mèttə máwrfik/, **met·a·mor·phous** /-əss/ *adj.* **1.** GEOL **BY OR FROM METAMORPHISM** relating to or having undergone metamorphism **2. OF METAMORPHOSIS** relating to or involving a change in physical form, appearance, or character —**met·a·mor·phi·cal·ly** *adv.*

met·a·mor·phism /mèttə máwr fìzzəm/ *n.* **1.** GEOL **CHANGE IN ROCK STRUCTURE** a change in the physical structure of rock that results from long-term heat and pressure, especially a change that increases the rock's hardness and crystalline structure **2. METAMORPHOSIS** metamorphosis (*archaic*)

met·a·mor·phose /mèttə máwr fōz, -fōss/ **(-phosed, -phos·ing, -phos·es)** *v.* **1.** *vti.* **CHANGE PHYSICAL FORM** to undergo or make somebody or something undergo a complete or marked change of physical form, structure, or substance ○ *The water had metamorphosed into ice.* **2.** *vti.* **CHANGE APPEARANCE OR CHARACTER** to undergo or make somebody or something undergo a complete or marked change in appearance, character, or condition **3.** *vti.* **CHANGE SUPPOSEDLY BY MAGIC** to undergo or make somebody or something undergo a transformation supposedly by magic **4.** *vi.* ZOOL **UNDERGO BODILY CHANGES DURING GROWTH** to undergo a complete or marked change of bodily form while developing into an adult animal ○ *The tadpole has metamorphosed into a frog.* **5.** *vti.* GEOL **CHANGE ROCK STRUCTURE** to undergo or make a rock undergo metamorphism [Late 16thC. From French *métamorphoser*, from *métamorphose* "metamorphosis," from Latin *metamorphosis* (see METAMORPHOSIS).]

met·a·mor·pho·sis /mèttə máwrfəssiss/ (*plural* **-ses** /-seez/) *n.* **1. CHANGE OF PHYSICAL FORM** a complete or marked change of physical form, structure, or substance ○ *the overnight metamorphosis of the pond water into ice* **2. CHANGE OF APPEARANCE OR CHARACTER** a complete or marked change in appearance, character, or condition **3. SUPPOSED SUPERNATURAL TRANSFORMATION** a transformation caused by supposed supernatural powers **4. TRANSFORMED PERSON OR THING** somebody or something that has gone through a complete or marked change **5.** ZOOL **CHANGE IN ANIMAL FORM** a complete or marked change in the form of an animal as it develops into an adult, e.g., the change from tadpole to frog or from caterpillar to butterfly [Mid-16thC. Via Latin from Greek *metamorphōsis*, from *metamorphoun* "to transform," literally "to form differently," from *morphē* "form" (see MORPH-).]

WORD KEY: CULTURAL NOTE

Metamorphoses, a poem by the Roman poet Ovid (AD 8). This long narrative work consists of a series of tales in which characters undergo some kind of transformation. The stories were based on Greek myths and legends and are presented in chronological order, but much of their liveliness derives from events, characters, and details invented by the poet.

WORD KEY: CULTURAL NOTE

The Metamorphosis, a short story by Czech writer Franz Kafka (1915). The protagonist of this bizarre tale, Gregor Samsa, awakens to find himself transformed into an insect, then dies as a result of his family's neglect and his own failure to act. Gregor's metamorphosis can be read as both a portrayal of the author's troubled family life and a metaphor for the artist's power to transform life into art.

met·a·neph·ros /mèttə né fròss/ (*plural* **-roi** /-fròy/) *n.* an embryonic organ of excretion in reptiles, birds, and mammals that develops into the kidney [Late 19thC. Coined from META- + Greek *nephros* "kidney" (see NEPHR-).]

met·a·phase /méttə fàyz/ *n.* the second stage of cell division, during which chromosomes line up in preparation for separation. ◊ **anaphase, prophase, telophase**

met·a·phase plate *n.* the equatorial plane along which chromosomes line up during the second stage of cell division in preparation for separation

met·a·phor /méttə fàwr/ *n.* **1. IMPLICIT COMPARISON** the application of a word or phrase to somebody or something that is not meant literally but to make a comparison, e.g., saying that somebody is a snake. ◊ **mixed metaphor, simile 2. FIGURATIVE LANGUAGE** all language that involves figures of speech or symbolism and does not literally represent real things **3. SYMBOL** one thing used or considered to represent another [15thC. From, ultimately, Greek *metaphora*, from *metapherein* "to transfer," literally "to carry between," from *pherein* "to carry" (see -PHORE).] —**met·a·phor·ic** /mèttə fáwrik/ *adj.* —**met·a·phor·i·cal** *adj.* —**met·a·phor·i·cal·ly** *adv.*

met·a·phos·phate /mèttə fós fàyt/ *n.* any salt or ester of metaphosphoric acid

met·a·phos·phor·ic ac·id /mettə fos fàwrik-/ *n.* a glassy solid containing linked phosphate groups and used as a drying agent and in dental cements. Formula: HPO_3.

met·a·phrase /méttə fràyz/ *n.* **LITERAL TRANSLATION** a word-for-word translation of something ■ *vt.* **(-phrased, -phras·ing, -phras·es) 1. TRANSLATE SOMETHING LITERALLY** to translate something, especially word for word **2. CHANGE WORDING OF** to change the wording of a text [Mid-16thC. From, ultimately, Greek *metaphrasis*, from *metaphrazein* "to translate," literally "to tell differently," from *phrazein* "to tell."]

met·a·phrast /méttə fràst/ *n.* somebody who changes the form of a text, e.g., from prose into verse [Early 17thC. From Greek *metaphrastēs*, from *metaphrazein* "to translate" (see METAPHRASE).] —**met·a·phras·tic** /mèttə frástik/ *adj.* —**met·a·phras·ti·cal** *adj.* —**met·a·phras·ti·cal·ly** *adv.*

met·a·phys·ic *n.* = **metaphysics**

met·a·phys·i·cal /mèttə fízzik'l/ *adj.* **1. RELATING TO METAPHYSICS** relating to the philosophical study of the nature of being and beings or a philosophical system resulting from such study **2. SPECULATIVE** based on speculative reasoning and unexamined assumptions that have not been logically examined or confirmed by observation ○ *a metaphysical system whose claim to truth is undermined by contradictions* **3. ABSTRACT** extremely abstract or theoretical ○ *metaphysical subjects removed from everyday life* **4. INCORPOREAL** without material form or substance ○ *the metaphysical realm of pure thought* **5. SUPERNATURAL** originating not in the physical world but somewhere outside it ○ *a metaphysical explanation of beauty and goodness* —**met·a·phys·i·cal·ly** *adv.*

Met·a·phys·i·cal, met·a·phys·i·cal *adj.* **OF EARLY 17C POETRY** relating to the poetic style of John Donne, George Herbert, and other early 17th-century English poets who used consciously intellectual language and elaborate metaphors that compared dissimilar things ■ *n.* **METAPHYSICAL POET** a poet of the Metaphysical group

met·a·phys·ics /mèttə fízziks/, **met·a·phys·ic** /-ik/ *n.* (*takes a singular verb*) **1. PHILOSOPHY OF BEING** the branch of philosophy concerned with the study of the nature of being and beings, existence, time and space, and causality **2. UNDERLYING PRINCIPLES** the ultimate underlying principles or theories that form the basis of a particular field of knowledge ○ *Symmetry is part of the metaphysics of quantum mechanics.* **3. ABSTRACT THINKING** abstract discussion or thinking [Mid-16thC. From medieval Latin *metaphysica* (plural), from medieval Greek *(ta) metaphusika* "(the) metaphysics," from *ta meta ta phusika* "the (works of Aristotle) after the 'Physics'" (see PHYSICS).]

met·a·pla·sia /mèttə pláyzhə, -zhee ə/ *n.* the transformation of one kind of tissue into another undesirable type, e.g., in tumor formation [Late 19thC. From Greek *metaplassein* "to mold into a new form," from *plassein* "to mold" (see -PLASIA).] —**met·a·plas·tic** /mèttə plástik/ *adj.*

met·a·psy·chol·o·gy /mèttə sī kólləjee/ *n.* the philosophical study of those aspects of psychology that cannot be examined experimentally —**met·a·psy·cho·log·i·cal** /mètə sīkə lójjik'l/ *adj.*

met·a·se·quo·ia /mèttə si kwóyə/ (*plural* **-ias** *or* **-ia**) *n.* = **dawn redwood**

met·a·so·ma·tism /mèttə sṓmə tìzzəm/, **met·a·so·ma·to·sis** /-tṓssiss/ *n.* the gradual change in rock structure caused by the natural replacement of chemicals through interaction with liquids or gases [Late 19thC. Coined from META- + the Greek stem *sōmat-* "body" (see SOMATIC) + -ISM.] —**met·a·so·mat·ic** /mèttə sō máttik/ *adj.* —**met·a·so·mat·i·cal·ly** *adv.*

met·a·sta·ble /mèttə stáyb'l/ *adj.* **1. IN APPARENT EQUILIBRIUM** in an apparent state of equilibrium, but likely to change to a more truly stable state if conditions change **2. IN EXCITED STATE** remaining in an excited physical state for a relatively long time —**met·a·sta·bil·i·ty** /mèttə stə bílləteel/ *n.*

me·tas·ta·sis /mə tástəssiss/ (*plural* **-ses** /-seez/) *n.* **1. SPREAD OF CANCER** the spread of a cancer from the original tumor to other parts of the body by means of tiny clumps of cells transported by the blood or lymph **2. MALIGNANT TUMOR** a malignant tumor that has developed in the body as a result of the spread of cancer cells from the original tumor [Late 16thC. From, ultimately, Greek, "removal, change," from *methistanai* "to remove," literally "to place differently," from *histanai* "to place" (see APOSTASY).] —**met·a·stat·ic** /mèttə státtik/ *adj.* —**met·a·stat·i·cal·ly** *adv.*

me·tas·ta·size /mə tástə sīz/ **(-sized, -siz·ing, -siz·es)** *vi.* to spread in the body from the site of the original tumor by means of tiny cells transported by the blood or lymph (*refers to a cancer*)

met·a·tar·sal /mèttə taárs'l/ *adj.* **OF FOOT BONES** belonging or relating to the bones between the toes and ankle ■ *n.* **FOOT BONE** any of the set of bones between the toes and ankle —**met·a·tar·sal·ly** *adv.*

met·a·tar·sus /mèttə taársiss/ (*plural* **-si** /-sī, -see/) *n.* **1.** ANAT **BONES OF HUMAN FOOT** the set of five long bones in the human foot between the toes and ankle **2.** ZOOL **PART OF VERTEBRATE HIND FOOT** the region between the ankle and toes of the hind foot in vertebrates

met·a·the·ri·an /mèttə theeree ən/ *adj.* **OF MARSUPIALS** relating or belonging to marsupials ■ *n.* **MARSUPIAL** a marsupial [Late 19thC. Formed from modern Latin *Metatheria*, group name, literally "wild animals between," from Greek *thēria* "wild animals," plural of *thērion* "wild animal."]

me·tath·e·sis /me táthəssiss/ (*plural* **-ses** /-seez/) *n.* **1.** LING **TRANSPOSITION OF SOUNDS** a reversal of the order of two sounds or letters in a word, either as a mispronunciation or as a historical development **2.** CHEM = **double decomposition** [Late 16thC. From, ultimately, Greek, from *metatithenai* "to transpose," literally "to place differently," from *tithenai* "to place" (see THESIS).] —**met·a·thet·ic** /mèttə théttik/ *adj.* —**met·a·thet·i·cal** *adj.* —**met·a·thet·i·cal·ly** *adv.*

me·tath·e·size /mə táthə sīz/ **(-sized, -siz·ing, -siz·es)** *vti.* LING to change or make a word change by metathesis

met·a·tho·rax /mèttə tháwraks/ (*plural* **-rax·es** *or* **-ra·ces** /-rə seez/) *n.* the last segment of an insect's thorax, where the hind legs and hind wings are located —**me·ta·tho·rac·ic** /mèttəthə rássik/ *adj.*

met·a·xy·lem /mèttə zīləm/ *n.* the rigid thick-walled tissue of plant parts that have matured

met·a·zo·an /mèttə zṓ ən/ *n.* an animal whose body consists of cells that are separated into different parts such as tissues and organs. All animals except for sponges and protozoans are classified as metazoans. Group: *Metazoa.* [Late 19thC. Formed from modern Latin *Metazoa,* division name, from Greek *meta-* "beside, after" + *zoion* "animal."] —**met·a·zo·an** *adj.*

mete out *vt.* to give out something such as punishment or justice, especially in a way that seems harsh or unfair [*Mete* from Old English *metan* "to measure." Ultimately from an Indo-European word that is also the ancestor of English *meet*[2], *moderate,* and *meditate.*]

me·tem·psy·cho·sis /mə tèmsə kṓssiss, mèttəm sī kṓssiss/ *n.* the passage of somebody's soul after death into the body of another person or an animal [Late 16thC. Via late Latin from Greek *metempsukhōsis,* from *meta* "after" + *empsukhos* "having a soul within."]

met·en·ceph·a·lon /mèt en séffə lòn/ (*plural* **-lons** *or* **-la** /-lə/) *n.* the part of an embryo's brain that develops into the cerebellum and the pons —**met·en·ce·phal·ic** /mèt en sə fállik/ *adj.*

me·te·or /meétee ər, -àwr/ *n.* **1. FIERY MASS OF ROCK FROM SPACE** a mass of rock from space that burns up after entering the Earth's atmosphere. ◆ **meteoroid, meteorite 2. LIGHT FROM METEOR** the brief streak of light that a meteor creates, visible in the night sky [Late 16thC. Via modern Latin *meteorum* "atmospheric phenomenon" from Greek *meteōron,* literally "something raised up," from *meta* "up" + *-aoros* "lifted."]

meteor. *abbr.* meteorology

me·te·or·ic /meètee áwrik/ *adj.* **1. RELATING TO METEORS** relating to or resembling meteors **2. VERY FAST OR BRILLIANT** characterized by great speed or brilliance —**me·te·or·i·cal·ly** *adv.*

me·te·or·ic wa·ter *n.* water in the ground that has recently come from the atmosphere, rather than forming chemically underground

me·te·or·ite /meétee ə rīt/ *n.* a piece of rock that has reached the Earth from outer space. ◆ **meteor, meteoroid** [Early 19thC. Formed from METEOR.]

me·te·or·it·ics /meètee ə ríttiks/ *n.* the scientific study of meteors and meteorites —**me·te·or·it·i·cist** /meètee ə ríttəsist/ *n.*

me·te·or·oid /meétee ə ròyd/ *n.* a mass of rock in space, often a remnant of a comet, that becomes a meteor when it enters the earth's atmosphere and a meteorite when it falls to earth. ◆ **meteor, meteorite** [Mid-19thC. Formed from METEOR.] —**me·te·or·oid·al** *adj.*

meteorol. *abbr.* meteorology

me·te·or·ol·o·gy /meètee ə róllәjee/ *n.* the scientific study of the Earth's atmosphere, especially its patterns of climate and weather [Early 17thC. From Greek *meteōrologia,* from *meteōron* (see METEOR).] —**me·te·or·o·log·i·cal** /meètee ərə lójjək'l/ *adj.* —**me·te·or·o·log·i·cal·ly** *adv.* —**me·te·or·ol·o·gist** /-róllәjist/ *n.*

me·te·or show·er *n.* a number of meteors seen at regular intervals in a particular area of the sky when a large group of meteors passes through the Earth's atmosphere

me·ter[1] /meétər/ *n.* **1. PATTERN IN VERSE** an arranged pattern of rhythm in a line of verse **2. PATTERN OF RHYTHM IN MUSIC** the pattern of beats that combines to form musical rhythm [Pre-12thC. Directly and via French *metre* from Latin *metrum,* from Greek *metron* "measure" (see METER[1]).]

me·ter[2] /meétər/ *n.* the basic SI unit of length, equivalent to approximately 1.094 yd. or 39.37 in. Originally based on a meter-long platinum-iridium bar kept in Paris, France, it is now defined as the distance traveled by light in vacuum in 1/299,792,458 seconds. Symbol **m** [Late 18thC. Via French *metre* from Greek *metron* (see METER[1]).]

me·ter[3] /meétər/ *n.* **1. DEVICE FOR MEASURING AMOUNT OR FLOW** a device that measures and records the quantity or flow of something such as electricity, gas, water, distance, or time **2.** = **parking meter** ■ *vt.* **(-tered, -ter·ing, -ters) MEASURE AMOUNT OR FLOW OF SOMETHING** to measure the amount or flow of something such as electricity or water, using a meter [Early 19thC. Origin uncertain: perhaps originally formed from METE "to measure out," later influenced by -METER.]

-meter *suffix.* measuring device ○ *heliometer* [Via French *-mètre* from Greek *metron* "measure" (see METER[1])]

me·tered mail *n.* mail that is postmarked privately by a postage meter

me·ter-kil·o·gram-sec·ond *adj.* using or based on the meter, kilogram, and second as the measuring units of length, mass, and time

me·ter maid *n.* a woman assigned by a police department to issue tickets for parking violations (*dated informal*)

Meth. *abbr.* Methodist

meth- *prefix.* methyl ○ *methicillin* [Shortening]

meth·ac·ry·late /meth ákrə làyt/ *n.* an ester derived from methacrylic acid

meth·a·cryl·ic ac·id /methə krillik-/ *n.* a synthetic, colorless liquid used to make plastic. Formula: $C_4H_6O_2$. [Coined from METH- + ACRYLIC]

meth·a·done /méthə dṑn/, **meth·a·don** /méthə dòn/ *n.* a synthetic narcotic drug similar in its painkilling effect to morphine and often prescribed as a substitute for heroin in the treatment of addiction. Formula: $C_{21}H_{27}NO$. [Mid-20thC. Coined from METH- + AMINO + DI- + -ONE.]

meth·aem·o·glo·bin /met heémə glṑbin/ *n.* U.K. = **methemoglobin**

meth·am·phet·a·mine /mèth am féttə meen, -min/ *n.* a form of the stimulant amphetamine. Formula: $C_{10}H_{15}N$.

meth·an·al /méthə nàl/ *n.* = **formaldehyde** [Late 19thC. Formed from METHANE.]

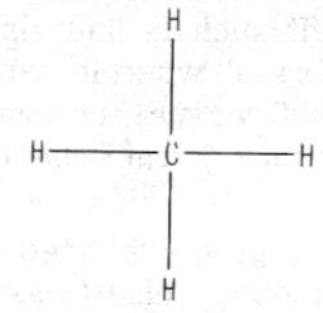

Methane

meth·ane /mé thàyn/ *n.* a colorless, odorless, flammable gas that is the main constituent of natural gas and is used as a fuel. Formula: CH_4. [Mid-19thC. Formed from METHYL.]

meth·a·no·ic ac·id /mèthə nṓ ik-/ *n.* = **formic acid** [Formed from METHANE]

meth·a·nol /méthə nàwl/ *n.* a colorless, volatile, poisonous, water-soluble liquid that is used as a solvent, a fuel, and in antifreeze for motor vehicles. Formula: CH_4O. [Late 19thC. Formed from METHANE.]

meth·a·qua·lone /mèthə kwáy lṑn/ *n.* a drug that is used to induce sleep and is also taken illegally. Formula: $C_{16}H_{14}N_2O$. [Mid-20thC. Coined from METH- + a contraction of *quinazolinon,* a derivative of quinoline.]

Meth·e·drine /méthə dreen, méthədrin/ *tdmk.* a trademark for a brand of methamphetamine

met·he·mo·glo·bin /met heémə glṑbin/ *n.* an abnormally altered form of hemoglobin that can occur as a result of poisoning with certain drugs or as a genetic disorder [Late 19thC. Coined from META- + HEMOGLOBIN.]

met·he·mo·glo·bi·ne·mi·a /met heémə glōbi neémee ə/ *n.* the presence in the blood of methemoglobin

me·the·na·mine /mə theénə meen, -min/ *n.* = **hexamethylenetetramine** [Early 20thC. Contraction of METHYLENE + AMINE.]

meth·i·cil·lin /mèthə sillin/ *n.* an antibiotic used against infections that are resistant to penicillin. Formula: $C_{17}H_{19}N_2NaO_6S$. [Mid-20thC. Coined from METH- + PENICILLIN.]

me·thinks /mi thíngks/ (**-thought** /mi tháwt/, **-thought**) *vi.* it seems to me (*humorous or archaic*) [Old English *mē þyncþ* "it seems to me," from *þyncan* "to seem." Ultimately from an Indo-European base that is also the ancestor of English *think, thought,* and *thank.*]

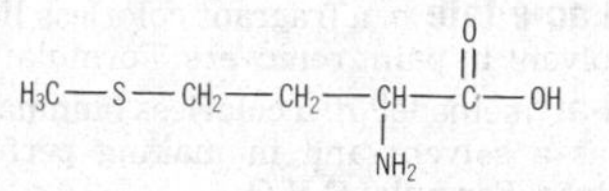

Methionine

me·thi·o·nine /mə thī́ ə neen/ *n.* a sulfur-containing amino acid that occurs in proteins or can be prepared synthetically [Early 20thC. Coined from METH- + THIO- + -INE.]

meth·od /méthəd/ *n.* **1. WAY OF DOING SOMETHING** a way of doing something or carrying something out, especially according to a plan **2. ORDERLINESS** orderly thought, action, or technique ○ *There is no method whatsoever in his approach to business.* **3. BODY OF SCIENTIFIC TECHNIQUES** the body of systematic techniques used by a particular discipline, especially a scientific one [15thC. Via Latin from Greek *methodos* "pursuit, way," from *meta-* "after" + *hodos* "journey."]

Meth·od *n.* a theory and system of acting that involves the actor identifying strongly with the internal motivation of the character being portrayed. It is based on the teachings of Konstantin Stanislavsky.

me·thod·i·cal /mə thóddik'l/, **me·thod·ic** /mə thóddik/ *adj.* systematic or painstaking —**me·thod·i·cal·ly** *adv.* —**me·thod·i·cal·ness** *n.*

Meth·od·ism /méthə dìzzəm/ *n.* the doctrines, principles, or organization of the Methodist church, or a specific feature of this Church

Meth·od·ist /méthədist/ *n.* **MEMBER OF METHODIST CHURCH** a member of the Methodist Church ■ *adj.* **RELATING TO THE METHODIST CHURCH** relating to Methodism or membership of the Methodist Church [Mid-18thC. Originally applied to members of a society founded at Oxford, from the methodical habits of life and worship it promoted.] —**Meth·od·is·tic** /mèthə dístik/ *adj.* —**Meth·od·is·ti·cal·ly** *adv.*

Meth·od·ist Church *n.* a group of evangelical Protestant denominations founded in 18th century England by John Wesley and his followers. The Methodist Church came out of the evangelical revivalist movement, and is rooted in personal faith, the singing of hymns, and praying.

meth·od·ize /méthə dīz/ **(-ized, -iz·ing, -iz·es)** *vt.* to reduce or arrange something according to a method —**meth·od·i·za·tion** /mèthədi záysh'n/ *n.* —**meth·od·iz·er** *n.*

meth·od·ol·o·gy /mèthə dóllәjee/ (*plural* **-gies**) *n.* **1. ORGANIZING SYSTEM** the methods or organizing principles underlying a particular art, science, or other area of study **2.** PHILOS **STUDY OF ORGANIZING PRINCIPLES** in philosophy, the study of organizing principles and underlying rules **3. STUDY OF RESEARCH METHODS** the study of methods of research —**meth·od·o·log·i·cal** /mèthədə lójjik'l/ *adj.* —**meth·od·o·log·i·cal·ly** *adv.* —**meth·od·ol·o·gist** /-dóllәjist/ *n.*

meth·o·trex·ate /mèthə trék sàyt/ *n.* a drug that inhibits cellular reproduction and is used to treat cancer. Formula: $C_{20}H_{22}N_8O_5$. [Mid-20thC. Coined from METH- + *-trex-,* of unknown origin.]

me·thought past participle, past tense of **methinks**

meth·ox·ide /meth ók sīd/ *n.* any chemical derivative of methanol that has some features of a salt, e.g., sodium methoxide. Formula: $NaOCH_3$. [Late 19thC. Coined from METH- + OXY- + -IDE.]

me·thox·y·chlor /mə thóksi klàwr/ *n.* a white crystalline compound used as an insecticide. Formula: $C_{16}H_{15}Cl_3O_2$. [Mid-20thC. Coined from METH- + OXY- + CHLORINE.]

Me·thu·se·lah /mə thoózələ/ *n.* **1. BIBLICAL FIGURE** a man in the Bible who was an ancestor of Noah and is said to have lived 969 years. (Gen 5: 21–27). **2. LARGE WINE BOTTLE** a wine or champagne bottle that holds the equivalent of eight normal bottles, approximately 208 fl oz/6 l

meth·yl /méthəl/ *adj.* containing the group of atoms CH_3 [Mid-19thC. From French *méthyl*, a back-formation from *méthylène* (see METHYLENE).] —**me·thyl·ic** /mə thíllik/ *adj.*

meth·yl ac·e·tate *n.* a fragrant colorless liquid used as a solvent in paint removers. Formula: $C_3H_6O_2$.

meth·yl·al /méthə làl/ *n.* a colorless flammable liquid used as a solvent and in making perfumes and adhesives. Formula: $C_3H_8O_2$.

meth·yl al·co·hol *n.* = **methanol**

meth·yl·a·mine /mèthələ meén, -lá meén, mə thíllə meén/ *n.* any of three colorless flammable derivatives of ammonia, epecially a gas used in dyes, drugs, and herbicides. Formula: CH_5N.

meth·yl·ate /méthə làyt/ *n.* = **methoxide** ■ *vt.* (**-at·ed, -at·ing, -ates**) **1.** **REPLACE HYDROGREN ATOM WITH METHYL GROUP** to replace one or more hydrogren atoms in a molecule with the methyl group **2.** **MIX WITH METHANOL** to mix something with methanol —**meth·yl·a·tion** /mèthə láysh'n/ *n.* —**meth·yl·a·tor** *n.*

meth·yl·at·ed spir·it, **meth·yl·at·ed spir·its** *n.* ethanol with methanol added, to make it undrinkable, and colored with a violet dye, used as a fuel and in solvents

meth·yl·ben·zene /mèthəl bén zeén, méthəl ben zeén/ *n.* = **toluene**

meth·yl bro·mide *n.* a poisonous colorless gas or liquid used as a solvent, fumigant, and refrigerant. Formula: CH_3Br.

meth·yl·cel·lu·lose /mèthəl séllyə lōss, -lōz/ *n.* a grayish-white powder derived from cellulose that swells up in water and is used as a food additive and in making paints and cosmetics

meth·yl chlo·ride *n.* a colorless poisonous gas used as a refrigerant and local anesthetic. Formula: CH_3Cl.

meth·yl·do·pa /mèthəl dṓpə/ *n.* a white powder used as a drug to treat hypertension. Formula: $C_{10}H_{13}NO_4$.

meth·yl·ene /méthə leén/ *n.* **METHANE DERIVATIVE** a bivalent group of atoms derived from methane. Formula: CH_2. ■ *adj.* **CONTAINING METHYLENE GROUP OF ATOMS** containing or relating to the group of atoms derived from methane containing one carbon atom and two hydrogen atoms. Formula: CH_2. [Mid-19thC. From French *méthylène*, from Greek *methu* "wine") + *hulē* "wood, substance."]

meth·yl·ene blue *n.* a crystalline compound that turns blue when dissolved in water and is used as a dye, an antiseptic, an antidote for cynanide poisoning, and a stain in laboratories. Formula: $C_{16}H_{18}ClN_3S$.

meth·yl i·so·cy·a·nate *n.* a flammable, colorless, extremely toxic liquid that is used in making herbicides. Formula: CH_3NCO.

meth·yl·mer·cu·ry /mèthəl múrkyəree/ *n.* an extremely toxic compound formed from metallic mercury by the action of microorganisms and used as a seed disinfectant. Mercury compounds such as this can enter the food chain and are toxic to living organisms.

meth·yl meth·ac·ry·late *n.* a colorless flammable liquid that can be converted into clear plastic resins

meth·yl·naph·tha·lene /mèthəl náfthə leén, -nápthə-/ *n.* either of two forms of naphthalene, a liquid used in making diesel fuels, or a solid used in making insecticides. Formula: $C_{11}H_{10}$.

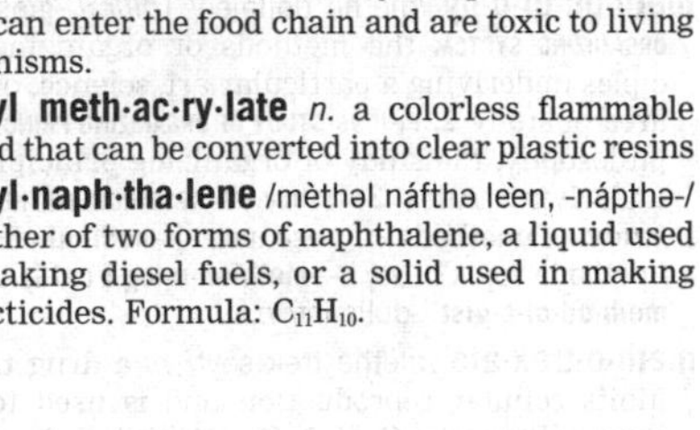

Methyl orange

meth·yl or·ange *n.* an alkaline dye that is used as a chemical indicator. It turns yellow when neutral and pink when acid.

meth·yl·phen·i·date /mèthəl fénni dàyt, -feéni-/ *n.* a stimulant of the central nervous system used to treat narcolepsy and attention deficit disorder. Formula: $C_{14}H_{19}NO_2$. [Mid-20thC. Contraction of METHYL + PHENYL + PIPERIDINE + ACETATE.]

met·i·cal /métti kàl, mètti kaál/ (*plural* **-cais** *or* **-cals**) *n.* **1.** **UNIT OF CURRENCY IN MOZAMBIQUE** the standard unit of currency in Mozambique, worth 100 centavos. See table at **currency** **2.** **BILL WORTH ONE METICAL** a bill worth one metical [Late 20thC. Via Portuguese *matical* from Arabic *mitkāl*, a unit of weight, from *ṯakala* "to weigh."]

me·tic·u·lous /mə tíkyələss/ *adj.* extremely careful and precise [Early 19thC. From Latin *meticulosus* "fearful, timid," from *metus* "fear," of unknown origin.] —**me·tic·u·lous·ly** *adv.* —**me·tic·u·lous·ness** *n.*

WORD KEY: SYNONYMS

See Synonyms at ***careful***.

mé·tier /me tyáy, may-/, **me·tier** *n.* **1.** **OCCUPATION** somebody's occupation or trade **2.** **FORTE** an activity that somebody is particularly good at [Late 18thC. Via French from assumed Vulgar Latin *misterium*, alteration of Latin *ministerium* (see MINISTRY).]

me·tol /meé tàwl/ *n.* a colorless soluble salt used in developing photographs. Formula: $C_{14}H_{20}N_2O_6S$. [Late 19thC. Arbitrarily coined by its inventor.]

Me·ton·ic cy·cle /mə tònnik-/ *n.* a cycle of 235 lunar months, after which the phases of the moon occur on the same days of the month as they did at the start of the cycle [Late 17thC. Named for the Athenian astronomer *Metōn* of the 5thC B.C., who discovered it.]

met·o·nym /méttə nìm/ *n.* a word or phrase used in a figure of speech in which an attribute of something is used to stand for the thing itself [Late 16thC. Back-formation from METONYMY.] —**met·o·nym·ic** /mèttə nímmik/ *adj.* —**met·o·nym·i·cal·ly** *adv.*

me·ton·y·my /mə tónnəmee/ *n.* a figure of speech in which an attribute of something is used to stand for the thing itself, such as "laurels" when it stands for "glory" or "brass" when it stands for "military officers" [Mid-16thC. Via late Latin from Greek *metōnumia*, literally "change of name," from *meta-* "beside, different" + *onuma* "name."]

me-too *adj.* using products, methods, or policies copied from somebody else (*informal*) —**me-too·er** *n.* —**me-too·ism** *n.*

met·o·pe /méttəpee/ *n.* in a Doric frieze, a square space between two sets of three vertical grooves (**triglyphs**) [Mid-16thC. From Greek *metopē*, from *meta-* "between" + *opē* "hole."]

me·top·ic /mə tóppik/ *adj.* relating to the forehead [Late 19thC. Formed from Greek *metōpon* "forehead," from *meta-* "between" + *ōps* "eye."]

me·tral·gi·a /mə tráljee ə/ *n.* pain in the womb

me·tre *n.* U.K. = **meter**[2]

met·ric /méttrik/ *adj.* **1.** MEASURE **RELATING TO METRIC SYSTEM** relating to or using the metric system of measurement **2.** = **metrical** ■ *n.* MATH **MATHEMATICAL FUNCTION** a mathematical function defined for a coordinates system that associates properties to each pair of elements that are analogous to distance between points on a line

met·ri·cal /méttrik'l/ *adj.* relating to or using poetic meter —**met·ri·cal·ly** *adv.*

met·ri·cate /méttri kàyt/ (**-cated, -cat·ing, -cates**) *vt.* to convert something from nonmetric to metric units of measurement —**met·ri·ca·tion** /mèttri káysh'n/ *n.*

metri·cize /méttri sīz/ (**-cized, -ciz·ing, -cizes**) *vt.* to express a measurement in metric units or change it into metric units

met·rics /méttriks/ *n.* the art of using meter in poetry (*takes a singular verb*)

met·ric sys·tem *n.* a decimal system of units of weights and measures based on the kilogram and meter

met·ric ton *n.* a unit of weight equal to 1000 kg

met·ri·fy /méttri fī/ (**-fied, -fy·ing, -fies**) *vt.* to put prose into verse or meter —**met·ri·fi·er** *n.*

met·rist /méttrist, meétrist/ *n.* somebody who is skilled in using poetic meter

me·tri·tis /mi trítiss/ *n.* inflammation of the womb

met·ro /méttrō/ *adj.* **METROPOLITAN** metropolitan (*informal*) ■ *n.* (*plural* **-ros**) **1.** **met·ro, Met·ro** **SUBWAY** an undergound railroad or subway system in a town or city **2.** **METROPOLIS** metropolis (*informal*) **3.** *Can* **LOCAL GOVERNMENT** the metropolitan area or government of a large city [Mid-20thC. Shortening of METROPOLITAN.]

metro- *prefix.* uterus ○ *metrorrhagia* [From Greek *mētra*, related to *mētēr* "mother." Ultimately from the Indo-European word for "mother," that is also the ancestor of English *mother* and *maternal*.]

me·trol·o·gy /mə tróllәjee/ (*plural* **-gies**) *n.* **1.** **STUDY OF MEASUREMENT** the scientific study of units of measurement **2.** **MEASUREMENT SYSTEM** a system of measurement [Early 19thC. Via French from Greek *metrologie*, from *metron* "measure" (see METER[1]).] —**met·ro·log·ic** /mèttrə lójjik/ *adj.* —**met·ro·log·i·cal·ly** *adv.* —**me·trol·o·gist** /mə tróllәjist/ *n.*

me·tron·i·da·zole /mèttrə nídə zōl/ *n.* a yellow crystalline compound used in treating infections, especially vaginal infections. Formula: $C_6H_9N_3O_3$. [Mid-20thC. Contraction of METHYL + NITRO- + IMIDAZOLE, elements of its chemical name.]

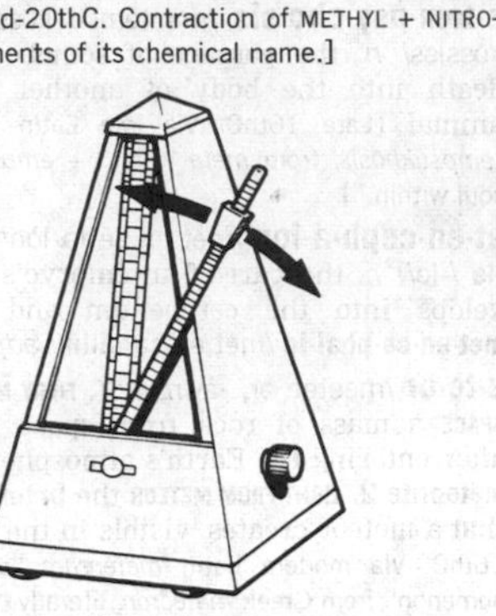

Metronome

met·ro·nome /méttrə nōm/ *n.* a device used to indicate a given tempo by means of an aural or visual signal produced electronically or by an adjustable pendulum [Early 19thC. From Greek *metron* "measure, meter" + *nomos* "rule, division."] —**met·ro·nom·ic** /mèttrə nómmik/ *adj.* —**met·ro·nom·i·cal·ly** *adv.*

me·tro·nym·ic *adj.* = **matronymic**

me·trop·o·lis /mə tróppəliss/ *n.* **1.** GEOG **LARGE CITY** a very large city, often the capital or chief urban center of a country, state, or region **2.** **CENTER OF AN ACTIVITY** the center or principal place for a particular activity **3.** CHR **MAIN DIOCESE** in Christianity, the principal diocese or see in an ecclesiastical province [Mid-16thC. Via late Latin from Greek *mētropolis*, literally "mother city," from *mētēr* "mother" + *polis* "city."]

WORD KEY: SYNONYMS

See Synonyms at ***city***.

met·ro·pol·i·tan /mèttrə póllit'n/ *adj.* **1.** GEOG **FORMING LARGE CITY** constituting a large urban area, usually including a city and its suburbs and outlying areas **2.** GEOG **TYPICAL OF A METROPOLIS** typical of a metropolis in scale, variety, or sophistication **3.** GEOG **DOMESTIC AND INTERNAL** relating to the home territory of a country rather than its territories elsewhere **4.** CHR **RELATING TO ECCLESIASTICAL METROPOLIS** relating to or constituting an ecclesiastical metropolis ■ *n.* **1.** GEOG **METROPOLIS INHABITANT** somebody who lives in a metropolis **2.** CHR **HIGH-RANKING CHURCH OFFICIAL** in Christianity, a high-ranking church dignitary such as an archbishop or head of an ecclesiastical province **3.** CHR **HEAD OF RUSSIAN ORTHODOX CHURCH** the head of the Russian Orthodox Church, based in Moscow

me·tror·rha·gi·a /meètrə ráyjə, -ráyjee ə, mèttrə-/ *n.* excessive discharge of blood from the womb —**me·tror·rha·gic** /meètrə ráyjik, mèttrə-/ *adj.*

-metry *suffix.* measuring ○ *cephalometry* [From Greek *-metria*, which was formed from *metron* "measure" (see METER[1])]

Met·ter·nich, Klemens, Prince of (1773–1859) German-born Austrian statesman. An Austrian diplomat and chancellor of the Hapsburg Empire (1821–48), he was the most powerful political figure in Europe between 1814 and 1848. He was driven from office in the Revolution of 1848. Full name **Klemens Wenzel Nepomuk Lothar Metternich**

met·tle /métt'l/ *n.* **1.** **STRENGTH OF CHARACTER** courage, spirit, or strength of character **2.** **INHERENT TEMPERAMENT** the particular mental and emotional character unique to an individual [Mid-16thC. Variant of METAL. The underlying meaning is "the substance somebody is made of."]

WORD KEY: SYNONYMS

See Synonyms at *courage.*

met·tle·some /méttˈlsəm/ *adj.* spirited and courageous

Me·tuch·en /mi túchən/ city in New Jersey, in Middlesex County. Population: 113,008 (1994).

Metz /mets/ capital of Moselle Department, Lorraine region, eastern France. Population: 119,594 (1990).

meu·nière /mən yáir/ *adj.* dredged in flour, fried in butter, and sprinkled with lemon juice and chopped parsley ○ *sole meunière* [Mid-19thC. From French *à la meunière*, literally "in the way of a miller's wife."]

Meur·sault /mər sṓ/ *n.* a dry white wine from the Burgundy region of northeastern France [Mid-19thC. From French, name of a commune in the Côte de Beaune.]

Meuse /mōz/ river that flows through northeastern France, Belgium, and the Netherlands. Length: 560 mi./900 km.

MeV, Mev, mev *symbol.* million electron volts

mew[1] /myoo/ *vi.* (**mewed, mew·ing, mews**) MAKE HIGH-PITCHED CRY to give out a high-pitched cry (*refers to cats and kittens*) ■ *n.* HIGH-PITCHED CRY the high-pitched sound a cat or kitten makes [14thC. An imitation of the sound.]

mew[2] /myoo/ *n.* any common seagull, especially the common gull [Old English *mǣw*]

mew[3] /myoo/ *n.* CAGE FOR KEEPING HAWKS a cage for keeping hawks in ■ *v.* (**mewed, mew·ing, mews**) **1.** *vt.* CONFINE HAWK OR FALCON to confine a hawk or falcon, especially by tying it to a perch **2.** *vi.* MOLT to shed feathers [14thC. From French *mue*, from *muer* "to molt," from Latin *mutare* "to change" (see MUTATION.)]

mewl /myool/ (**mewled, mewl·ing, mewls**) *vi.* to whimper or cry weakly [Early 17thC. Origin uncertain: possibly an imitation of the sound.] —**mewl·er** *n.*

mews /myooz/ *n. U.K.* a street that originally had stables built on it but has now been converted into housing, or the houses themselves (*takes a singular or plural verb*) [Early 19thC. From MEW[3].]

WORD KEY: ORIGIN

In the latter part of the 14th century the Royal Mews were built in London on the site of what is now Trafalgar Square, to house the royal hawks. By Henry VII's time they were being used as stables, and from at least the early 17th century the term ***mews*** was used for "stabling around an open yard." The modern application to a "street of former stables converted to human dwellings" dates from the early 19th century.

Mex. *abbr.* **1.** Mexican **2.** Mexico

Mex·i·cal·i /meksə káalee/ city in northwestern Mexico, on the border with the United States. Population: 601,938 (1990).

Mex·i·can /méksikən/ *adj.* PEOPLES relating to Mexico, or its people or culture

Mex·i·can bean bee·tle *n.* a North American ladybug that feeds on the leaves of bean plants. Latin name: *Epilachna varivestis.*

Mex·i·can hair·less *n.* a tiny, mainly hairless dog, belonging to a breed originating in Mexico

Mex·i·can i·vy vine *n.* = **cup-and-saucer plant**

Mex·i·can jump·ing bean *n.* = **jumping bean**

Mex·i·can Span·ish *n.* the form of the Spanish language used in Mexico —**Mex·i·can Span·ish** *adj.*

Mex·i·can stand·off *n.* a dispute or argument that cannot be won (*informal*)

Mex·i·can War *n.* a war between Mexico and the United States that lasted from 1846 to 1848, during which the United States won territory that now constitutes most of the states of the Southwest

Mex·i·can wave *n. U.K.* = **wave** [So called because it was first used at the World Cup soccer finals in Mexico in 1986]

Mex·i·co /méksik ō/ federal republic in North America, south of the United States. Language: Spanish. Currency: peso. Capital: Mexico City. Population: 96,807,451 (1997). Area: 758,452 sq. mi./1,964,382 sq. km. Official name **United Mexican States**

Mex·i·co, Gulf of arm of the Atlantic Ocean, bordered on the north by the United States, on the east by Cuba, and on the south and west by Mexico. Area: 700,000 sq. mi./1,812,990 sq. km.

Mexico

Mex·i·co City capital city of Mexico and of the Federal District, located in the south central part of the country. It the most populous urban area in the world. Population: 8,236,960 (1990).

Mey·nell /mə nél/, **Alice** (1847–1922) British poet and literary critic. Her essay collections include *The Colour of Life* (1896) and *Hearts of Controversy* (1917).

me·ze /mé zày, máy-/ (*plural* **-zes** *or* **-ze**) *n.* an assortment of snacks served with drinks as an appetizer or a light meal in Greece and the Near East and usually consisting of simple foods such as olives, cheese, cucumber, stuffed vine leaves, small pastries, or grilled sausages [Early 20thC. Via Turkish from Persian *maza* "to taste, relish."]

me·ze·re·on /mə zéeree ən/ *n.* a poisonous shrub of Europe and Asia that has clusters of fragrant purplish flowers and bark that was once used to treat blisters and arthritis. Latin name: *Daphne mezereum.* [15thC. Via medieval Latin from Arabic *māzaryūn.*]

me·zu·zah /mə zŏŏzzə/ (*plural* **me·zu·zahs** *or* **mezu·zot** /-zōt/) *n.* a scroll with biblical passages on one side and a name of God on the other, inserted in a small case attached by religious Jews to doorposts in the home [Mid-17thC. From Hebrew *mĕzūzāh*, literally "doorpost."]

mez·za·nine /mézz'n èen, mèzz'n éen/ *n.* **1. mez·za·nine, mez·za·nine floor** INTERMEDIATE STORY a low story, especially one between the first floor and the second floor in a building **2.** THEATER'S LOWEST BALCONY the lowest balcony in a theater ■ *adj.* FIN WITHIN INTERMEDIATE RANGE OF INVESTMENT constituting an intermediate range of funding or investment, such as certain unsecured high-yielding loans [Early 18thC. Via French from Italian *mezzanino*, literally "small one in the middle," from *mezzano* "middle," from Latin *medianus* (see MEDIAN).]

mez·za vo·ce /mètsə vṓ chày/ *adv.* with moderate volume from the voice or instrument (*used as a musical direction*) [From Italian, literally "half voice"] —**mez·za vo·ce** *adj.*

mez·zo /métsō, médzō/ *adv.* MODERATELY moderately (*used as a musical direction*) ■ *n.* (*plural* **-zos**) = **mezzo-soprano** [Mid-18thC. Via Italian, literally "middle, half," from Latin *medius* (see MEDIUM).]

mez·zo for·te *adv.* moderately loud (*used as a musical direction*) [From Italian] —**mez·zo for·te** *adj.*

mez·zo pi·a·no *adv.* moderately soft (*used as a musical direction*) [From Italian] —**mez·zo pi·a·no** *adj.*

mez·zo-re·lie·vo (*plural* **mez·zo-re·lie·vos**) *n.* a carving in which the depth of the relief is midway between high relief and bas relief [From Italian, literally "half-relief"]

mez·zo-so·pran·o *n.* a woman whose singing voice is between a soprano and a contralto in range [From Italian, literally "half soprano"]

mez·zo·tint /métsō tìnt, médzō-/ *n.* **1.** ENGRAVING PROCESS an engraving process that involves scraping and burnishing the roughened surface of a copper plate **2.** MEZZOTINT PRINT a print produced by the mezzotint process ■ *vt.* (**-zot·int·ed, -zot·int·ing, -zo·tints**) ENGRAVE PLATE USING MEZZOTINT to engrave a copper plate by using the mezzotint process [Mid-18thC. Anglicization of Italian *mezzotinto*, literally "half-tint."] —**mez·zot·in·ter** *n.*

mf *abbr.* **1.** medium frequency **2.** mezzo forte **3.** millifarad

mF *abbr.* millifarad

MF *abbr.* **1.** machine finished **2.** medium frequency **3.** Middle French

m.f. *abbr.* mezzo forte

M/F, m/f *abbr.* male or female (*in advertisements*)

M.F.A. *abbr.* Master of Fine Arts

mfd. *abbr.* manufactured

mfg. *abbr.* manufacturing

mfr. *abbr.* **1.** manufacture **2.** manufacturer

mg *symbol.* milligram

Mg *symbol.* magnesium

MG *abbr.* **1.** machine glazed **2.** machine gun **3.** Major General **4.** military government

MGB *n.* the secret police of the former Soviet Union from 1946 to 1954. Abbr of **Ministerstvo Gosudarstvennoi Bezopasnosti** [Mid-20th C. Shortening of Russian "Ministry of State Security."]

mgd *abbr.* million gallons per day

mgmt. *abbr.* management

mgr. *abbr.* manager

Mgr. *abbr.* **1.** Monseigneur **2.** Monsignor

mgt. *abbr.* management

mH *symbol.* millihenry

MH *abbr.* **1.** Medal of Honor **2.** mental health

MHA *abbr.* **1.** Master of Hospital Administration **2.** Member of the House of Assembly

MHC *n.* a group of genes in mammals located next or near to one another that serve to make cells separate and distinguishable from those of other organisms. Abbr of **major histocompatibility complex**

MHD *abbr.* magnetohydrodynamics

MHG *abbr.* Middle High German

M.H.L. *abbr.* Master of Hebrew Literature

M.H.R. *abbr.* Member of the House of Representatives

MHz *symbol.* megahertz

mi /mee/, **me** *n.* MUSIC a syllable that represents the third note in a scale, used for singing solfège. In fixed solfège it represents the note E, the third note in the scale of C, while in solfège with movable do, it is used to represent the third note of the key being sung. [15thC. From medieval Latin.]

MI *abbr.* **1.** Michigan **2.** Military Intelligence **3.** myocardial infarction

mi. *abbr.* **1.** mile **2.** mill

MI5 *n.* a former official and current popular name for Military Intelligence, section five, the British security and counterintelligence service

MI6 *n.* a former official and current popular name for Military Intelligence, section six, the British secret intelligence and espionage service

MIA *abbr.* Master of International Affairs ■ *n.* SOLDIER REPORTED MISSING IN ACTION a soldier who is reported missing during a military mission. Full form **missing in action**

Mi·am·i /mī ámee/ city and seaport in southeastern Florida. Population: 373,024 (1994).

Mi·am·i Beach /mī ámee-/ city and tourist resort in southeastern Florida. Population: 90,153 (1994).

Miao /myow/ *n., adj.* = **Hmong** [Early 20thC. From Chinese *Miáo*, literally "people."]

Miao-Yao /myŏw yów/ *n.* a group of languages, including Hmong and Yao, spoken in parts of the People's Republic of China, Vietnam, Laos, and Thailand. About six million people speak one of the Miao-Yao languages. —**Miao-Yao** *adj.*

mi·as·ma /mī ázmə, mee ázmə/ (*plural* **-mas** /-mətə/ *or* **-ma·ta**) *n.* **1.** HARMFUL FUMES a harmful or poisonous emanation, especially one caused by burning or decaying organic matter **2.** UNWHOLESOME ATMOSPHERE an unwholesome or menacing atmosphere [Mid-17thC. Directly or via French *miasme* from Greek *miasma* "defilement, pollution," from *miainein* "to pollute."] —**mi·as·mal** *adj.* —**mi·as·mat·ic** /mī əz máttik/ *adj.*

Mic. *abbr.* BIBLE Micah

mi·ca /mīkə/ *n.* any of several shiny silica minerals that occur in igneous and metamorphic rocks. They split easily and are used as electrical insulators and in heating elements because of their resistance to electricity and heat. [Early 18thC. From Latin, "grain, crumb." Ultimately from an Indo-European word that is also the ancestor of Greek *mikros* "small" (source of English *micro-*).]

Mi·cah[1] /mīkə/ *n.* in the Bible, a prophet who lived during the 8th century B.C. He was a contemporary of Isaiah.

Mi·cah[2] *n.* one of the 12 prophetic books of the Bible known as the Minor Prophets, containing both threats of doom and the prophecy of an age of universal peace. It is traditionally attributed to the prophet Micah. See table at **Bible**

Mi·caw·ber /mi káwbər/ *n.* somebody who is poor and idle but expects a better life to come along someday [Mid-19thC. Named for Wilkins *Micawber*, a character in *David Copperfield* (1850) by Charles Dickens.] —**Mi·caw·ber·ish** *adj.*

Mic·co·su·kee /mìkə sŏokee/ *n.* (*plural* **-kees** *or* **-kee**), *adj.* = **Mikasuki**

mice plural of **mouse**

WORD KEY: CULTURAL NOTE

Of Mice and Men, a novella by author John Steinbeck (1937). With great compassion and realism, Steinbeck recounts the tragic tale of two itinerant laborers, George Milton and Lennie Small. When Lennie, a mentally challenged giant, accidentally kills a girl, George shoots his friend rather than surrender him to a lynch mob. It was made into a film by Lewis Milestone in 1939.

mi·celle /mī sél, mi-/ *n.* an electrically charged particle formed by an aggregate of ions or molecules in soaps, detergents, and other suspensions [Late 19thC. From modern Latin *micella*, literally "small crumb," from Latin *mica* (see MICA).] —**mi·cel·lar** *adj.*

Mich. *abbr.* **1.** Michaelmas **2.** Michigan

Mi·chael /mík'l/, **King of Romania** (*b.* 1921). He held the throne from 1927 to 1930 and from 1940 to 1947, when he abdicated and went into exile.

Mich·ael·mas /mík'lməss/ *n.* a Christian holy day on September 29 celebrating the feast of St. Michael the Archangel. [Pre-12thC. Contraction of *Michael's mass*.]

Mich·ael·mas dai·sy *n.* a common aster that has small purple, pink, or white flowers and blooms in the fall

Michelangelo: Engraving after a 16th-century portrait by Giuliano Bugiardini

Mi·chel·an·ge·lo /mík'l ànjəlō/ (1475–1564) Italian sculptor, painter, architect, and poet. One of the great masters of the High Renaissance, his major works, such as the ceiling of the Sistine Chapel in the Vatican, were executed for patrons in Florence and Rome. Full name **Michelangelo di Lodovico Buonarroti Simoni**

Mi·chel·son /mík'lssən/, **Albert Abraham** (1852–1931) German-born U.S. physicist. He won a Nobel Prize in physics (1907) for his precise measurements of the velocity of light.

Mich·e·ner /míchənər/, **James Albert** (1907–97) U.S. writer. He wrote popular novels and short stories, such as the Pulitzer-prize-winning *Tales of the South Pacific* (1947), source of the musical *South Pacific* (1949).

Mich·i·gan[1] /míshigən/ state in the northern United States, consisting of two peninsulas situated among four of the Great Lakes. It has a border with Canada, and the states of Ohio, Indiana, Illinois, Wisconsin, and Minnesota. Capital: Lansing. Population: 9,773,892 (1997). Area: 58,513 sq. mi./151,549 sq. km. —**Mich·i·gan·der** /mìshi gándər/ *n.* —**Mich·i·gan·ite** /míshigə nīt/ *n., adj.*

Michigan

Mich·i·gan[2] /míshigən/ *n.* CARDS a gambling card game in which cards in the hand are played to match a sequence on the table [Early 20thC. Named for the state of MICHIGAN.]

Mich·i·gan, Lake lake in the northern United States. It is the only one of the Great Lakes that lies entirely in the United States. Area: 22,300 sq. mi./57,800 sq. km.

Mich·i·gan City /míshəgin sitee/ city in northern Indiana, on the southern shore of Lake Michigan just southwest of the Indiana-Michigan border. Population: 32,979 (1996).

Mick /mik/ *n.* a highly offensive term which deliberately insults somebody's Irish origin or Roman Catholic faith or an Irish person or a Roman Catholic (*offensive*) [Mid-19thC. From *Mick*, nickname for *Michael*.]

mick·ey /míkee/ (*plural* **-eys**) *n.* (*informal*) **1.** = **Mickey Finn 2.** *Can* **BOTTLE OF LIQUOR** a bottle of liquor, formerly a pint, now 375 ml, shaped to fit in a pocket [Early 20thC]

Mick·ey Finn *n.* an alcoholic drink to which a strong sedative has been added to make the drinker unconscious (*informal*) [Early 20thC. Origin uncertain: perhaps the name of an unidentified individual.]

mick·le /mík'l/ *adj.* *Scotland* **ABUNDANT** abundant or much ■ *adv.* *Scotland* **GREATLY** greatly or much [Old English *micel* (source also of *much*), later reinforced by Old Norse *mikill*, both ultimately from an Indo-European base that is also the ancestor of English *magnify*, *major*, *maximum*, and *mega-*]

Mic·mac /mík màk/ (*plural* **-mac** *or* **-macs**) *n.* a Native North American language belonging to the Algonquian branch of Algonquian-Wakashan languages, spoken in eastern parts of Canada. Micmac is spoken by about three thousand people. [Early 18thC. Via French from Micmac *migmac*, literally "allies."] —**Mic·mac** *adj.*

micr- *prefix.* = **micro-** (*sometimes used before vowels*)

mi·cro /míkrō/ *adj.* **SMALL** very small ■ *n.* (*plural* **-cros**) (*informal*) **1. MICROPROCESSOR** a microprocessor **2. MICROWAVE OVEN** a microwave oven **3. MICROCOMPUTER** a microcomputer [Mid-19thC. From MICRO-.]

micro-[1] symbol **small mu** [From Greek *mikros* "small" (source of English *micron* and *omicron*)]

micro-[2] *prefix.* **1.** small, minute ○ *microseism.* Symbol **small mu 2.** using a microscope or requiring magnification ○ *microanatomy* **3.** one millionth (10^{-6}) ○ *microcurie.* Symbol **small mu 4.** of a small area or on a small scale ○ *microhabitat* ○ *microteaching* **5.** microfilm, microphotography ○ *microform* **6.** abnormally small ○ *microdont* [From Greek *mikros* "small" (source of English *micron* and *omicron*)]

mi·cro·ae·ro·phile /mīkrō áirə fīl/ *n.* a tiny organism, e.g., a bacterium, that is capable of living in an environment where there is not much oxygen

mi·cro·am·pere /mīkrō ám peer/ *n.* one millionth part of an ampere

mi·cro·a·nal·y·sis /mīkrō ə nálləssiss/ (*plural* **-ses** /mīkrō ə nállə seez/) *n.* **1. ANALYSIS OF A TINY SAMPLE** the chemical analysis of tiny samples of a substance **2. DETAILED ANALYSIS** any extremely detailed analysis of something —**mi·cro·an·a·lyst** /mīkrō ánn'list/ *n.* —**mi·cro·an·a·lyt·i·cal** /mīkrō ann'l íttik'l/ *adj.*

mi·cro·bal·ance /míkrō bàlləns/ *n.* a balance for precisely weighing extremely small quantities up to 0.1 gm

mi·cro·bar /míkrō baar/ *n.* a unit of pressure equal to one millionth of a bar

mi·cro·bar·o·graph /mīkrō bérrə gràf/ *n.* a barograph that records tiny changes in atmospheric pressure

mi·crobe /mí krōb/ *n.* a microscopic organism, especially one that transmits a disease [Late 19thC. From French, from Greek *mikros* "small" + *bios* "life."] —**mi·cro·bi·al** /mī krōbee əl/ *adj.*

mi·cro·bi·ol·o·gy /mīkrō bī óllәjee/ *n.* the scientific study of microscopic organisms and their effects —**mi·cro·bi·o·log·i·cal** /mīkrō bī ə lójjik'l/ *adj.* —**mi·cro·bi·o·log·i·cal·ly** *adv.*

mi·cro·brew·e·ry /mīkrō brŏo əree/ (*plural* **-ries**) *n.* a small, usually independently owned brewery that produces limited quantities of specialized beers, often selling them on the premises —**mi·cro·brew·er** *n.* —**mi·cro·brew·ing** *n.*

mi·cro·burst /míkrō bùrst/ *n.* a strong localized air current that hits the ground and spreads, causing wind to rapidly change direction and speed

mi·cro·bus /míkrō bùss/ (*plural* **-bus·es** *or* **-bus·ses**) *n.* a vehicle resembling a small bus that has a passenger compartment with two or three rows of seats

mi·cro·cap·sule /míkrō kàpsəl, míkrō kàp sool/ *n.* a tiny capsule used to release a drug, flavor, or chemical

mi·cro·cas·sette /mīkrō kə sét/ *n.* a small audiotape cassette designed to fit into a pocket-size tape recorder or dictation machine

mi·cro·ceph·a·ly /mīkrō séffəlee/, **mi·cro·ceph·a·li·a** *n.* the condition of having a small head or having reduced space for the brain in the skull. This is often associated with learning difficulties. —**mi·cro·ce·phal·ic** /mīkrō sə fállik/ *adj.*

mi·cro·chem·is·try /mīkrō kémmistree/ *n.* the scientific study of extremely small quantities of substances —**mi·cro·chem·i·cal** *adj.* —**mi·cro·chem·ist** *n.*

mi·cro·chip /míkrə chìp/ *n.* = **chip**

mi·cro·cir·cuit /míkrō sùrkit/ *n.* = **integrated circuit** —**mi·cro·cir·cuit·ry** /míkrō sùrkitree/ *n.*

mi·cro·cli·mate /míkrō klīmət/ *n.* the climate of a confined space or small geographical area —**mi·cro·cli·mat·ic** /mīkrō klī máttik/ *adj.* —**mi·cro·cli·mat·i·cal·ly** /-kəlee/ *adv.*

mi·cro·cli·ma·tol·o·gy /mīkrō klīmə tóllәjee/ *n.* the scientific study of microclimates —**mi·cro·cli·ma·to·log·ic** /mīkrō klīmətə lójjik/ *adj.* —**mi·cro·cli·ma·tol·o·gist** /mīkrō klīmə tólləjist/ *n.*

mi·cro·cline /míkrō klīn/ *n.* a mineral of the feldspar group used in manufacturing glass and porcelain. Formula: $KAlSi_3O_8$. [Mid-19thC. From German *Mikroklin*, from Greek *mikros* "small" + *klinein* "to lean"; so called because its angle of cleavage differs only slightly from 90°.]

mi·cro·coc·cus /mīkrō kókəss/ (*plural* **-ci** /-kó kī, -kók sī/) *n.* any mainly harmless spherical bacterium, such as the one that ferments milk. Genus: *Micrococcus.* —**mi·cro·coc·cal** *adj.*

mi·cro·com·put·er /míkrō kəm pyōotər/ *n.* a small computer in which the central processing unit is a single silicon chip (**microprocessor**) [Late 20thC. Modeled on MINICOMPUTER.]

mi·cro·cop·y /míkrō kòppee/ (*plural* **-ies**) *n.* a photographic reproduction of something on microfilm or microfiche

mi·cro·cosm /míkrə kòzzəm/ *n.* a miniature copy of something, especially when it represents or stands for a larger whole ○ *Our classroom was a microcosm of the university.* [12thC. Via French *microcosme* from, ultimately, Greek *mikros kosmos* "little world."] —**mi·cro·cos·mic** /mīkrə kózmik/ *adj.* —**mi·cro·cos·mi·cal·ly** /-kəlee/ *adv.*

mi·cro·cos·mic salt *n.* a colorless odorless salt obtained from human urine and used to test metallic salts and oxides

mi·cro·cos·mos /mīkrō kòzməss, mīkrō kàz mōss/ *n.* = **microcosm**

mi·cro·crys·tal /míkrō krìst'l/ *n.* a crystal that can only be seen under a microscope —**mi·cro·crys·tal·line** /mīkrō krístəlin/ *adj.*

mi·cro·cur·ie /míkrō kyŏoree, mīkrō kyŏo rée/ *n.* a unit of radioactivity that is equal to a millionth of a curie

mi·cro·cyte /míkrə sīt/ *n.* an unusually small red blood cell —**mi·cro·cyt·ic** /mīkrə síttik/ *adj.*

mi·cro·dis·sec·tion /mīkrō di sékshən, -dī-/ *n.* dissection carried out using a microscope

mi·cro·dot /míkrə dòt/ *n.* **1.** TINY PHOTOGRAPH a tiny photographic reproduction of something, about the size of a dot or a pinhead **2.** DOSE OF LSD a dose of LSD in a tiny tablet (*informal*)

mi·cro·e·co·nom·ics /mìkrō eekə nómmiks, -ekə-/ *n.* the study of specific or localized aspects of an economy (*takes a singular verb*) —**mi·cro·e·co·nom·ic** *adj.*

mi·cro·e·lec·tron·ics /mìkrō i lek trónniks/ *n.* the technology and techniques involved in the design, development, and construction of extremely small electronic circuits, e.g., computers on a single silicon chip (*takes a singular verb*) —**mi·cro·e·lec·tron·ic** *adj.* —**mi·cro·e·lec·tron·i·cal·ly** *adv.*

mi·cro·el·e·ment /mìkrō èlləmənt/ *n.* = **trace element**

mi·cro·en·cap·su·late /mìkrō in kápsə lày t/ (**-lat·ed, -lat·ing, -lates**) *vt.* to enclose a substance in microcapsules —**mi·cro·en·cap·su·la·tion** /mìkrō in kapsə láysh'n/ *n.*

mi·cro·ev·o·lu·tion /mìkrō evvə lo͞osh'n, -eevə-/ *n.* minor change within a species or small group of organisms, usually within a short period of time —**mi·cro·ev·o·lu·tion·ar·y** /mìkrō evvə lo͞osh'n èrree, -eevə-/ *adj.*

mi·cro·far·ad /míkrō fè rad, -fèrrəd/ *n.* one millionth part of a farad

mi·cro·fau·na /mìkrō fáwnə/ *npl.* animals so small that they can only be seen under a microscope —**mi·cro·fau·nal** *adj.*

mi·cro·fib·ril /mìkrō fíbbrəl/ *n.* in cells, any extremely fine structure resembling a thread

mi·cro·fiche /míkrō feesh/ (*plural* **-fiche** *or* **-fich·es**) *n.* a sheet of microfilm containing information laid out in a grid pattern [Mid-20thC. From French, from Greek *mikros* "small" + French *fiche* "slip of paper."]

mi·cro·fil·a·ment /mìkrō fílləmənt/ *n.* a very thin cellular filament that contains protein, found in muscle and the cytoplasm of other cells —**mi·cro·fil·a·men·tous** /mìkrō fillə méntəss/ *adj.*

mi·cro·fi·lar·i·a /mìkrō fi láiree ə/ (*plural* **-as** *or* **-ae** /mìkrō fi láiree ee/) *n.* the early larval stage of a parasitic nematode worm (**filaria**), a cause of heartworm in dogs and elephantiasis in humans —**mi·cro·fi·lar·i·al** *adj.*

mi·cro·film /míkrə film/ *n.* TINY PHOTOGRAPHS a strip of photographic film on which highly miniaturized reproductions have been recorded ■ *vti.* (**-filmed, -film·ing, -films**) PHOTOGRAPH ON MICROFILM to photograph something on microfilm —**mi·cro·film·a·ble** *adj.*

mi·cro·flo·ra /mìkrō fláwrə/ *npl.* plants that can only be seen under a microscope —**mi·cro·flo·ral** *adj.*

mi·cro·form /míkrə fàwrm/ *n.* film or paper that contains miniature reproductions, as microfilm and microfiche do

mi·cro·fos·sil /míkrō fòss'l/ *n.* a fossil that can only be studied with a microscope, e.g., a bacterium fossil

mi·cro·fun·gus /míkrō fùng gəss/ (*plural* **-gi** /-fùn jī, -fùng gī/ *or* **-gus·es**) *n.* any fungus that has tiny or unobservable reproductive organs

mi·cro·gram /míkrə gràm/ *n.* one millionth part of a gram

mi·cro·graph /míkrə gràf/ *n.* **1.** PICTURE AS SEEN THROUGH MICROSCOPE a photograph or drawing of something as seen through a microscope **2.** DEVICE FOR PRODUCING FINE ENGRAVINGS a device that can produce engraving or writing using very fine lines —**mi·cro·graph·ic** /mìkrə gráffik/ *adj.* —**mi·cro·graph·i·cal·ly** /-kəlee/ *adv.*

mi·cro·grav·i·ty /mìkrō grávvitee/ *n.* a force of gravity so low that weightlessness occurs, e.g., during space travel

mi·cro·groove /míkrō gro͞ov/ *n.* the narrow spiral groove on a gramophone record

mi·cro·hab·i·tat /mìkrō hábbi tàt/ *n.* an environment that has a unique set of ecological conditions within a larger habitat and supports distinct flora and fauna. For example, wood lice are found beneath the bark of rotting wood in a deciduous woodland microhabitat.

mi·cro·inch /míkrō ìnch/ *n.* a unit of linear measurement equivalent to one millionth of an inch. Symbol **zzçin**

mi·cro·in·jec·tion /mìkrō in jékshən/ *n.* the injection of a very small amount of liquid into individual cells, using a specialized instrument and a microscope for observation —**mi·cro·in·ject** *vti.*

mi·cro·in·struc·tion /mìkrō in strúkshən/ *n.* a single instruction in a low-level computer program

mi·cro·lep·i·dop·ter·an /mìkrō lèppi dóptərən/ (*plural* **-a** /-dóptərə/) *n.* a small or medium-sized moth, e.g., a leaf miner, that is of little interest to a collector

mi·cro·lith /míkrə lìth/ *n.* a tiny flint tool, usually triangular, found in Mesolithic sites in Europe and dating from 12,000 to 3,000 B.C. —**mi·cro·lith·ic** /mìkrə líthik/ *adj.*

mi·cro·man·age /mìkrō mánnij/ (**-aged, -ag·ing, -ag·es**) *vt.* to manage a business or organization by paying extreme attention to small details —**mi·cro·man·age·ment** *n.* —**mi·cro·man·ag·er** *n.*

mi·cro·ma·nip·u·la·tor /mìkrō mə níppyə làytər/ *n.* a device consisting of geared controls for the manipulation of extremely small dissecting tools or miniature surgical instruments under a microscope —**mi·cro·ma·nip·u·la·tion** /mìkrō mə nippyə láysh'n/ *n.* —**mi·cro·ma·nip·u·la·tive** /-níppyə làytiv/ *adj.*

mi·cro·mere /míkrō meer/ *n.* either of the small cells (**blastomere**) formed by the division of a fertilized egg

mi·cro·me·te·or·ite /mìkrō meetee ə rīt/ *n.* a particle of cosmic dust that falls to Earth or onto the Moon's surface. Micrometeorites originate in space where they are called micrometeoroids. —**mi·cro·me·te·or·it·ic** /mìkrō meetee áwrik/ *adj.*

mi·cro·me·te·or·oid /mìkrō meetee ə ròyd/ *n.* an extremely small dust particle found in space that may land on Earth or the Moon as a micrometeorite

mi·cro·me·te·or·ol·o·gy /mìkrō meetee ə róllǝjee/ *n.* the study of weather conditions in the air immediately above ground level, especially in small areas such as the area around a tree trunk or above a puddle —**mi·cro·me·te·or·o·log·i·cal** /mìkrō meetee ərə lójjik'l/ *adj.* —**mi·cro·me·te·or·ol·o·gist** /-ə rólləjist/ *n.*

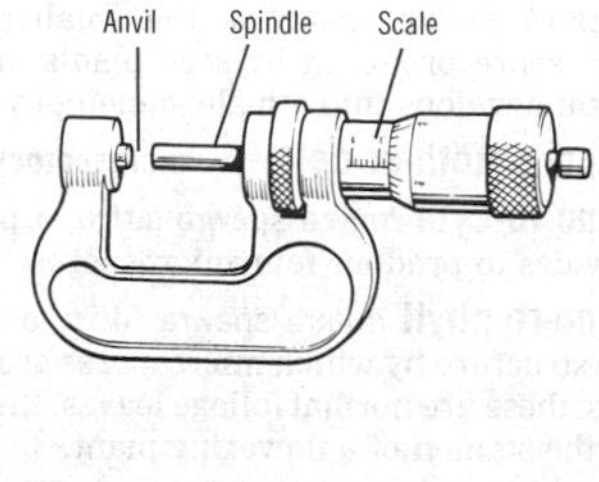

Micrometer

mi·cro·me·ter[1] /mī krómmətər/ *n.* a device for measuring small diameters, thicknesses, distances, or angles to a high degree of accuracy. The gap between the two measuring faces of the instrument is measured by the movement of one face that has a finely threaded screw marked with calibrated divisions. [Late 17thC. From French *micromètre*.] —**mi·cro·met·ric** /mìkrō méttrik/ *adj.* —**mi·cro·met·ri·cal·ly** /-kəlee/ *adv.* —**mi·crom·e·try** /mī krómmətree/ *n.*

mi·cro·me·ter[2] /míkrō meetər/ (*plural* **-ters**) *n.* a unit of linear measurement equivalent to one millionth of a meter. Symbol **zzçm**

mi·cro·me·tre *n.* U.K. = **micrometer**

mi·cro·min·i·a·tur·i·za·tion /mìkrō minnee əchəri záysh'n, mìkrō minnəchəri záysh'n/ *n.* the production and use of extremely small electronic components, especially semiconductors —**mi·cro·min·i·a·tur·ize** /mìkrō mínnee əchə rīz, mìkrō mínnəchə rīz/ *vt.* —**mi·cro·min·i·a·tur·ized** /mìkrō mínnee əchə rīzd, mìkrō mínnəchə rīzd/ *adj.*

mi·cro·mole /míkrə mòl/ *n.* a molecular weight expressed in grams that is equivalent to one millionth of a mole. Symbol **zzçmol** —**mi·cro·mo·lar** /mìkrə mólər/ *adj.*

mi·cro·mor·phol·o·gy /mìkrō mawr fólləjee/ *n.* the study of the fine detail in the external form and structure of organisms, or of other objects such as metal surfaces —**mi·cro·mor·pho·log·i·cal** /mìkrō màwrfə lójjik'l/ *adj.*

mi·cron /mí kròn/ *n.* a unit of linear measurement equivalent to one millionth of a meter [Late 19thC. Coined from Greek *mikros* "small" + -ON.]

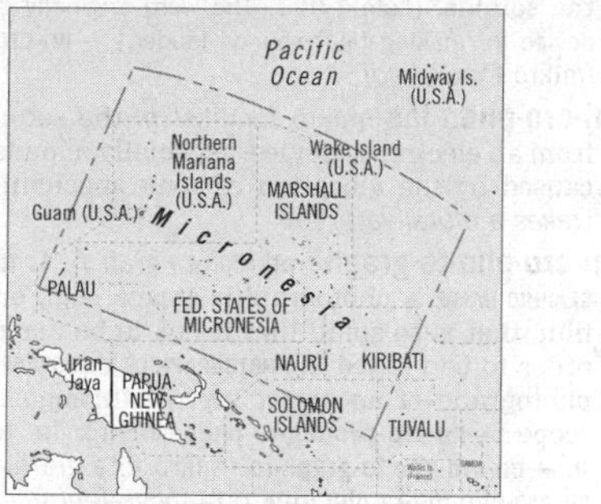

Micronesia

Mic·ro·nes·i·a[1] /mìkrə neé-ə, -neéshə/ one of the three major divisions of the Pacific Islands, comprising over 2,000 small islands in the western Pacific Ocean, mainly north of the equator

Mic·ro·nes·i·a[2] country in the western Pacific Ocean, comprising more than 600 islands, about 60 of which are inhabited. Language: English. Currency: U.S. dollar. Capital: Palikir. Population: 127,616 (1997). Area: 271 sq. mi./702 sq. km. Official name **Federated States of Micronesia**

Mi·cro·ne·sian /mìkrō neezh'n, mìkrō neesh'n/ *adj.* OF MICRONESIA relating to Micronesia or its people or culture ■ *n.* **1.** INHABITANT OF MICRONESIA a member of any of the groups of people native to Micronesia **2.** GROUP OF LANGUAGES SPOKEN IN MICRONESIA a group of languages, including Gilbertese and Marshallese, spoken in Micronesia. It forms a subgroup of the Eastern branch of Malayo-Polynesian languages. About 200,000 people speak a Micronesian language.

mi·cron·ize /míkrə nīz/ (**-ized, -iz·ing, -iz·es**) *vt.* to reduce the particle size of a powder down to a few millionths of a meter [Mid-20thC. Origin uncertain: perhaps formed from MICRON.]

mi·cro·nu·cle·us /mìkrō no͞oklee əss/ (*plural* **-i** /mìkrō no͞oklee ī/ *or* **-us·es**) *n.* the smaller of the two nuclei in the cells of ciliate protozoans. It contains genetic material and is involved in sexual reproduction. —**mi·cro·nu·cle·ar** *adj.*

mi·cro·nu·tri·ent /mìkrō no͞otree ənt/ *n.* a substance such as a vitamin or mineral that an organism requires for normal growth and development but only in very small quantities

mi·cro·or·gan·ism /mìkrō áwrgə nìzzəm/ *n.* a tiny organism, such as a virus, protozoan, or bacterium that can only be seen under a microscope

mi·cro·pa·le·on·tol·o·gy /mìkrō pallee on tólləjee/ *n.* a branch of paleontology that studies the microorganisms preserved as fossils in sedimentary rocks —**mi·cro·pa·le·on·to·log·ic** /mìkrō pallee əntə lójjik/ *adj.* —**mi·cro·pa·le·on·tol·o·gist** /mìkrō pallee on tólləjist/ *n.*

mi·cro·par·a·site /mìkrō pérrə sīt/ *n.* a microorganism that lives as a parasite on other organisms —**mi·cro·par·a·sit·ic** /mìkrō perrə síttik/ *adj.*

mi·cro·phage /míkrə fàyj/ *n.* a small white blood cell, part of the immune system, that removes bacteria and other foreign bodies from blood and tissue —**mi·cro·phag·ic** /mìkrə fáyjik/ *adj.*

mi·cro·phag·ous /mī króffəgəss/ *adj.* feeding on food in the form of microscopic particles, e.g., marine organisms

mi·cro·phone /míkrə fōn/ *n.* a device that converts

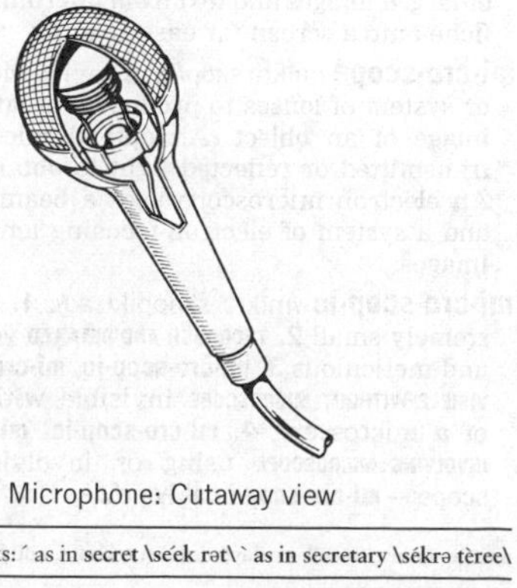
Microphone: Cutaway view

sounds to electrical signals by means of a vibrating diaphragm. The signals can then be amplified, transmitted for broadcasting, or used for recording the sounds. [Late 17thC. The word originally denoted a device for making faint sounds louder.] —**mi·cro·phon·ic** /mīkrō fónnik/ *adj.*

mi·cro·phon·ics /mīkrō fónniks/ *n.* the sound heard from an electronic device, especially a loudspeaker, caused by the vibration of some mechanical part (*takes a plural verb*)

mi·cro·pho·to·graph /mīkrō fṓtə gràf/ *n.* **1.** TINY PHOTOGRAPHIC IMAGE a photographic image, e.g., on microfilm, that is so small that it has to be magnified in order to be viewed **2.** PHOTOGRAPH OF MICROSCOPE IMAGE a photograph of an object viewed through a microscope —**mi·cro·pho·tog·ra·pher** /mīkrō fə tóggrəfər/ *n.* —**mi·cro·pho·to·graph·ic** /mīkrō fōtə gráffik/ *adj.* —**mi·cro·pho·tog·ra·phy** /mīkrō fə tóggrəfee/ *n.*

mi·cro·phys·ics /mīkrō fízziks/ *n.* the branch of physics that studies objects and systems such as molecules, atoms, and elementary particles that are observable only microscopically or indirectly (*takes a singular verb*) —**mi·cro·phys·i·cal** *adj.* —**mi·cro·phys·i·cal·ly** *adv.* —**mi·cro·phys·i·cist** *n.*

mi·cro·phyte /mīkrə fīt/ *n.* a plant observable only under a microscope, especially one that is parasitic —**mi·cro·phyt·ic** /mīkrə fíttik/ *adj.*

mi·cro·pi·pette /mīkrō pī pét/ *n.* a very slender graduated tube that is used to measure, transfer, or remove minute amounts of something

mi·cro·print /mīkrə prìnt/ *n.* printed text, e.g., on microfilm, that is so small that it has to be magnified in order to be viewed

mi·cro·prism /mīkrə prìzzəm/ *n.* a small prism that is part of the focusing screen of many single-lens reflex cameras. When the image is in focus, the prism prevents it from shimmering.

mi·cro·proc·es·sor /mīkrō pró sèssər/ *n.* the central processing unit that performs the basic operations in a microcomputer. It consists of an integrated circuit contained on a single chip.

mi·cro·pro·gram /mīkrə prṑgrəm/ *n.* a built-in program used within a microprocessor, consisting of a series of arithmetic and logic steps that enable basic instructions to be carried out

mi·cro·pro·gram·ming /mīkrə prṑgrəming/ *n.* a means of programming the central processing unit of a computer by breaking down instructions into a series of small steps

mi·crop·si·a /mī króppsee ə/ *n.* a vision defect in which the cones of the retina are abnormally separated by local swelling, making objects appear smaller than they really are [Mid-19thC. Coined from MICRO- + Greek *opsis* "sight" + -IA.]

mi·cro·pyle /mīkrə pīl/ *n.* **1.** SMALL OPENING IN PLANT OVULE a small opening in the covering of the ovule of a plant through which the pollen tube passes prior to fertilization. After fertilization, the ovule becomes a seed and water is absorbed through the opening. **2.** SMALL PORE OF INSECT EGG a small pore in the membrane of an insect egg that allows sperm to enter and fertilize the egg [Early 19thC. From French, from *micro-* "micro-" + Greek *pulē* "gate" (source of English *pylon*).] —**mi·cro·py·lar** /mīkrō pīlər/ *adj.*

mi·cro·ra·di·og·ra·phy /mīkrō raydee óggrəfee/ *n.* a technique that enlarges X-ray radiographs so that fine details can be examined —**mi·cro·ra·di·o·graph** /mīkrō ráydee ə gràf/ *n.* —**mi·cro·ra·di·o·graph·ic** /mīkrō raydee ə gráffik/ *adj.*

mi·cro·read·er /mīkrō reédər/ *n.* a device that projects enlarged images and text from microfilm and microfiche onto a screen for easy reading

mi·cro·scope /mīkrə skṓp/ *n.* a device that uses a lens or system of lenses to produce a greatly magnified image of an object. An optical microscope uses transmitted or reflected light to obtain the image. An electron microscope uses a beam of electrons and a system of electron-focusing lenses to obtain images.

mi·cro·scop·ic /mīkrə skóppik/ *adj.* **1.** VERY SMALL extremely small **2.** THOROUGH AND DETAILED very thorough and meticulous **3.** **mi·cro·scop·ic, mi·cro·scop·i·cal** INVISIBLE WITHOUT MICROSCOPE invisible without the use of a microscope **4.** **mi·cro·scop·ic, mi·cro·scop·i·cal** INVOLVING MICROSCOPE using or involving a microscope —**mi·cro·scop·i·cal·ly** *adv.*

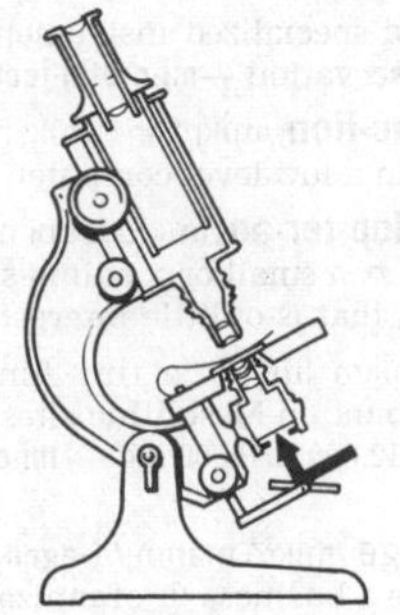

Microscope

Mi·cro·sco·pi·um /mīkrō skṓpee əm/ *n.* a small inconspicuous constellation in the skies of the southern hemisphere near Sagittarius

mi·cros·co·py /mī króskəpee/ (*plural* **-pies**) *n.* **1.** STUDY OF MICROSCOPES the study and design of microscopes **2.** EXPERIMENT USING MICROSCOPE an investigation, observation, or experiment that involves the use of a microscope —**mi·cros·co·pist** *n.*

mi·cro·sec·ond /mīkrō sékənd/ *n.* a measurement of time equivalent to one millionth of a second. Symbol μs

mi·cro·seism /mīkrə sīzzəm/ *n.* a recurrent low-level earth tremor caused by phenomena such as the force of crashing waves rather than by movement of rock masses —**mi·cro·seis·mic** /mīkrō sīzmik/ *adj.*

mi·cro·some /mīkrə sōm/ *n.* a small particle obtained after isolating a cell using centrifugal action, typically consisting of ribosomes associated with fragments of endoplasmic reticulum. Microsomes are filled with enzymes and may be involved in the synthesis of proteins. —**mi·cro·so·mal** /mīkrə sṓm'l/ *adj.*

mi·cro·spo·ran·gi·um /mīkrō spə ránjee əm/ (*plural* **-a** /-jee ə/) *n.* a part of the reproductive structure of certain plants, especially ferns, that produces microspores. ◊ **sporangium** —**mi·cro·spo·ran·gi·ate** /mīkrō spə ránjee ət/ *adj.*

mi·cro·spore /mīkrə spàwr/ *n.* the smaller of two kinds of spore produced by seed plants and some ferns that develops into a male gametophyte

mi·cro·spore moth·er cell *n.* = **microsporocyte**

mi·cro·spo·ro·cyte /mīkrə spáwrə sīt/ *n.* a plant cell that divides to produce four microspores

mi·cro·spo·ro·phyll /mīkrə spáwrə fil/ *n.* a leaf that bears a structure by which microspores are formed. In ferns, these are normal foliage leaves, the equivalent of the stamen of a flowering plant.

mi·cro·struc·ture /mīkrō strùkchər/ *n.* the fine structure of a material, usually only visible through a microscope and sometimes after some form of surface preparation, e.g., the etching of metal alloys —**mi·cro·struc·tur·al** /mīkrō strúkchərəl/ *adj.*

mi·cro·sur·ger·y /mīkrō súrjəree/ *n.* surgery performed with the aid of miniaturized precision instruments, including scalpels, needles, and a specially designed optical microscope. Microsurgery is used to perform almost all eye operations, in surgery on the middle and inner ear, and to reattach limbs. —**mi·cro·sur·gi·cal** *adj.*

mi·cro·switch /mīkrə swìch/ *n.* a very small sensitive switch that acts by the movement of a small lever and is used where rapid precise movements are required, especially in keyboards and automatic control devices

mi·cro·teach·ing /mīkrə teéching/ *n.* a training exercise used in teacher training in which a student or student teacher is videotaped during a class. The videotape is then played back for analysis and evaluation.

mi·cro·tome /mīkrə tòm/ *n.* an instrument that uses a steel blade to cut biological tissues into very thin transparent slices a few millionths of a meter thick for microscopic examination

mi·crot·o·my /mī króttəmee/ *n.* the process of preparing thin slices of biological tissues using a microtome, so that they can be observed under a microscope —**mi·cro·tom·ic** /mīkrə tómmik/ *adj.* —**mi·cro·tom·ist** /mī króttəmist/ *n.*

mi·cro·tone /mīkrə tòn/ *n.* a musical interval smaller than a semitone, especially a quartertone —**mi·cro·ton·al** /mīkrə tṓn'l/ *adj.* —**mi·cro·to·nal·i·ty** /mīkrə tō nállətee/ *n.* —**mi·cro·ton·al·ly** /mīkrə tṓnəlee/ *adv.*

mi·cro·tu·bule /mīkrō toō byool/ *n.* a hollow tubular structure composed of the protein tubulin that helps to maintain the shape and movement of a living cell and the transport of material within it. ◊ **tubule** —**mi·cro·tu·bu·lar** /mīkrō toōbyələr/ *adj.*

mi·cro·vas·cu·la·ture /mīkrō váskyələ choor, mīkrō váskyəlachər/ *n.* a part of the circulatory system made up of the smallest vessels such as capillaries, arterioles, and venules —**mi·cro·vas·cu·lar** *adj.*

mi·cro·vil·lus /mīkrō vílləss/ (*plural* **-li** /-lī/) *n.* a microscopic hair-shaped cell that projects from the surface of the lining of the small intestine, increasing the surface area available for the absorption of nutrients. ◊ **epithelium** —**mi·cro·vil·lar** *adj.*

mi·cro·volt /mīkrə vōlt/ *n.* a unit of electric potential or electromotive force equivalent to one millionth of a volt. Symbol μV

mi·cro·watt /mīkrə wòt/ *n.* a measurement of power equivalent to one millionth of a watt. Symbol μW

mi·cro·wave /mīkrə wàyv/ *n.* **1.** HIGH-FREQUENCY ELECTROMAGNETIC WAVE an extremely high-frequency electromagnetic wave whose wavelength ranges from 1.0 mm to 30 cm, used in radar, to carry radio transmissions, and in cooking or heating devices **2.** OVEN USING ELECTROMAGNETIC RADIATION an oven that cooks or heats food or beverages relatively quickly using high-frequency electromagnetic radiation ■ *vt.* (**-waved, -wav·ing, -waves**) HEAT OR COOK IN A MICROWAVE to heat or cook food or beverages using an oven that uses high-frequency electromagnetic radiation —**mi·cro·wav·a·ble** *adj.*

mi·cro·wave ov·en *n.* = **microwave** *n.* 2

mic·tu·rate /míkchə ràyt/ (**-rat·ed, -rat·ing, -rates**) *vi.* to urinate (*technical*) [Mid-19thC. Back-formation from *micturition* "urination," from Latin *micturire*, literally "to want to urinate," from *mict-*, the past participle stem of *meiere* "to urinate."] —**mic·tu·ra·tion** /mìkchə ráysh'n/ *n.*

mid /mid/ *adj.* **1.** OCCUPYING MIDDLE OR CENTRAL POSITION being in the center or halfway through something **2.** DONE WITH TONGUE IN MIDDLE POSITION produced as a vowel with the tongue halfway between the high and low positions, e.g., in the words "but" or "bet" [Old English *midd*. Ultimately from an Indo-European word that is also the ancestor of English *medium* and *meso-*.]

'mid /mid/, **mid** *prep.* among a group [15thC. Shortening of AMID.]

mid. *abbr.* middle

Mid. *abbr.* Midshipman

mid- *prefix.* middle ○ *midrange* ○ *midmost* [From MID]

mid·af·ter·noon /mìd aftər noōn/ *n.* the part of the afternoon midway between noon and sunset —**mid·af·ter·noon** *adj.*

mid·air /mid áir/ *n.* POINT IN AIR ABOVE SURFACE a point in the air above the ground or another surface ■ *adj.* OCCURING IN AIR ABOVE SURFACE occurring or located at a point in the air above the ground or another surface

Mi·das /mídəss/ *n.* in Greek mythology, a Phrygian king who had befriended Silenus, a follower of Dionysus, and was rewarded by Dionysus with the gift of making everything he touched turn into gold

Mi·das touch *n.* the ability to make large amounts of money, often with very little apparent effort

mid-At·lan·tic *adj.* influenced by both North America and Great Britain, especially in behavior or speech

Mid-At·lan·tic States *npl.* = **Middle Atlantic States**

mid·brain /míd bràyn/ *n.* the middle part of the three main divisions of either the embryonic or the adult brain in vertebrates. Technical name **mesencephalon**

mid·course /míd kàwrss/ *n.* MISSILE'S FLIGHT BETWEEN LAUNCH AND REENTRY the part of a missile's flight between the end of its launch and the beginning of its reentry ■ *adj.* HAPPENING PARTWAY THROUGH SOMETHING present or occurring partway through a course or course of action

mid·day /míd dày/ *n.* noon or the period around the middle of the day

mid·den /míddʼn/ *n.* **1.** DUNGHILL a pile of dung or refuse (*archaic*) **2.** = **kitchen midden** [14thC. Of Scandinavian origin.]

mid·dle /mídd'l/ *adj.* **1.** CENTRAL AND EQUIDISTANT FROM LIMITS equidistant from the sides, edges, or ends of something **2.** BEING HALFWAY BETWEEN BEGINNING AND END occurring or located halfway between the start and finish of a period of time, an event, or a series **3.** OCCUPYING INTERMEDIATE POSITION situated in an intermediate position, e.g., in age or status **4.** BEING MIDWAY BETWEEN EXTREMES lying between two extremes or opposites and, consequently, usually moderate **5.** GRAM CONCERNING VOICE EXPRESSING REFLEXIVE ACTION relating to the voice of verbs in some languages such as ancient Greek and Sanskrit that expresses the action of a subject on or for itself ■ *n.* **1.** MIDWAY PART OR POSITION the part or position farthest from the sides, edges, or ends of something ○ *sitting in the middle of the row* **2.** PART BETWEEN BEGINNING AND END the part between or halfway between the beginning and end of a period of time or an event ○ *in the middle of June* **3.** POSITION BETWEEN HIGHEST AND LOWEST the position or rank midway between the highest and lowest **4.** INSIDE PART the interior or central part of something **5.** CENTRAL PART OF BODY the waist, stomach, or central area of the human body (*informal*) **6.** SPORTS CENTER OF TEAM'S FORMATION the center of a team's formation or positioning, especially, in baseball, the area around second base **7.** GRAM VOICE EXPRESSING REFLEXIVE ACTION the voice of verbs in some languages such as ancient Greek and Sanskrit that expresses the action of a subject on or for itself ■ *vti.* (-dled, -dling, -dles) **1.** PUT SOMETHING IN MIDDLE to place something equidistant from the sides, edges, or ends of something **2.** SAILING FOLD SAIL IN HALF to fold a sail in half or to be folded in half [Old English *middel*]

Mid·dle *adj.* relating to a language or literature between its early and later stages of development

mid·dle age *n.* the period in somebody's life when that person is no longer considered young, usually between 40 and 60

mid·dle-aged *adj.* **1.** NO LONGER YOUNG no longer considered young, but not yet considered old **2.** TYPICAL OF SOMEBODY MIDDLE-AGED characterized by the behavior, attitudes, lifestyle, or interests considered typical of middle age, especially staidness, conventionality, or old-fashionedness

Mid·dle Ag·es *n.* the period in European history between antiquity and the Italian Renaissance, often considered to be between the end of the Roman Empire in the 5th century and the early15th century

Mid·dle A·mer·i·ca *n.* **1.** SOCIALLY TRADITIONAL U.S. MIDDLE CLASS a section of the middle class in the United States considered to be politically conservative and to hold traditional social and moral values **2.** = **Midwest** **3.** MEXICO AND CENTRAL AMERICA the area to the south of the United States and the north of South America that includes Mexico, Central America, and sometimes the West Indies —**Mid·dle A·mer·i·can** *adj., n.*

Mid·dle At·lan·tic States, **Mid·At·lan·tic States** *npl.* the states midway along the Atlantic coast of the United States, consisting of New York, New Jersey, and Pennsylvania, and usually Delaware and Maryland

mid·dle·break·er /mídd'l bràykər/, **mid·dle·bust·er** /mídd'l bùstər/ *n.* = **lister**

mid·dle·brow /mídd'l bròw/ *n.* somebody who is conventional and moderately inclined in cultural tastes and interests (*informal*) ◊ **highbrow, lowbrow** [Early 20thC. Modeled on HIGHBROW and LOWBROW.] —**mid·dle·brow** *adj.*

mid·dle C *n.* a note roughly in the middle of a piano keyboard, written in musical notation on the first ledger line below the treble staff or above the bass staff

mid·dle class *n.* the section of society between the poor and the wealthy, including many business and professional people and skilled workers —**mid·dle-class** *adj.*

mid·dle dis·tance *n.* **1.** AREA BETWEEN FOREGROUND AND BACKGROUND the portion of space that is further away from a viewer than the foreground but nearer than the background, especially in a landscape painting or photograph **2.** MEDIUM-LENGTH FOOT RACE a foot race that is between 440 yards/400 m and one mile/1500 m long

Mid·dle Dutch *n.* the form of the Dutch language spoken and written from about the 12th to the beginning of the 16th centuries A.D.

mid·dle ear *n.* the narrow air-filled space between the ear drum and the outer wall of the inner ear that contains the three tiny bones that transmit sound vibrations

Mid·dle Earth *n.* = **Midgard**

Mid·dle East *n.* **1.** REGION STRETCHING FROM EGYPT TO IRAN the region stretching from the eastern Mediterranean to the western side of the Indian subcontinent, including Egypt, the Arabian Peninsula, Israel, Jordan, Lebanon, Syria, Turkey, Iran, and Iraq **2.** HISTORICAL AREA FROM IRAN TO MYANMAR formerly, the area extending from Iran to Myanmar, including Afghanistan, India, and Tibet. Now called **West Asia** —**Mid·dle East·ern** *adj.* —**Mid·dle East·ern·er** *n.*

Mid·dle Eng·lish *n.* the form of the English language spoken and written from about the 12th to the beginning of the 16th centuries A.D. The leading dialects of this period were Kentish, West Saxon, West Midland, East Midland, and Northern. ◊ **Old English, Modern English**

Mid·dle French *n.* the form of the French language spoken and written from about the 14th to the beginning of the 17th centuries A.D. ◊ **Old French**

mid·dle game *n.* the middle part of a game of chess, after the opening moves and before the endgame

Mid·dle Greek *n., adj.* = **Medieval Greek**

mid·dle ground *n.* **1.** = **middle distance** **2.** POSITION BETWEEN EXTREMES an intermediate position between two opposing views or factions ○ *The two parties were unable to find any middle ground.*

Mid·dle High Ger·man *n.* the form of High German spoken and written from about the 12th to the beginning of the 16th centuries A.D.

mid·dle-in·come *adj.* earning a wage or salary that is roughly the same as the average for a population

Mid·dle I·rish *n.* the form of Irish Gaelic spoken and written from about the 11th to the beginning of the 15th centuries A.D.

Mid·dle King·dom *n.* **1.** PERIOD OF ANCIENT EGYPTIAN HISTORY a period of Egyptian history from the late 11th dynasty, approximately 2040 B.C., to the 13th dynasty, 1670 B.C. **2.** FORMER CHINESE EMPIRE the former Chinese Empire, so called because it was supposedly at the center of the earth **3.** CENTRAL TERRITORY OF CHINESE EMPIRE the central territory held by most Chinese Empires, including the Huang and Yangtze river valleys, and eventually the eighteen inner provinces of China

mid·dle la·mel·la (*plural* **mid·dle la·mel·lae**) *n.* a thin membrane, composed of pectin and other polysaccharides, that cements the walls of two adjacent plant cells together

Mid·dle Low Ger·man *n.* the form of Low German spoken and written from about the 12th to the beginning of the 16th centuries A.D.

mid·dle·man /mídd'l màn/ (*plural* **-men** /-mèn/) *n.* **1.** SOMEBODY WHO BUYS AND SELLS GOODS a trader who buys goods from a producer and then sells them to retailers or consumers **2.** GO-BETWEEN somebody who acts as a negotiator or intermediary

mid·dle man·age·ment *n.* managers who are responsible for relatively small numbers of staff and are involved in the details of running an organization rather than in making major decisions or setting policy —**mid·dle man·ag·er** *n.*

mid·dle·most /mídd'l mòst/ *adj.* = **midmost**

mid·dle name *n.* the name between a first name and a surname

mid·dle-of-the-road *adj.* **1.** OCCUPYING INTERMEDIATE POSITION taking a course of action or adopting a point of view that is midway between two extremes **2.** MUSIC INTENDED TO HAVE BROAD MUSIC APPEAL intended to be musically appealing to many people and avoiding stylistic extremes —**mid·dle-of-the-road·er** *n.*

Mid·dle Pa·le·o·lith·ic *n.* the period between the Lower and Upper Paleolithic ages, from about 70 000 B.C. to 32 000 B.C.

mid·dle pas·sage *n.* the journey from western Africa across the Atlantic to the West Indies or the Americas, undertaken by many slave ships

mid·dle school *n.* a school for children between the ages of about 11 and 14 years, depending on the school's location. ◊ **junior high**

Mid·dle Scots *n.* the form of the Scots language written and spoken between the late 15th and the early 17th centuries

mid·dle-sized *adj.* neither very big nor very small

mid·dle term *n.* LOGIC a term that appears in both premises of a syllogism but not in the conclusion

Mid·dle·ton /mídd'ltən/, **Arthur** (1742–87) U.S. statesman. He was a member of the Continental Congress (1776–77) and signed the Declaration of Independence (1776).

Mid·dle·town /mídd'l town/ **1.** city in central Connecticut, in Middlesex County, on the Connecticut River. Population: 42,615 (1994). **2.** city in southeastern New York, northwest of Spring Valley and southwest of Newburgh. Population: 24,192 (1996).

mid·dle·ware /mídd'l wàir/ *n.* COMPUT software that manages the connection between a client and a database

mid·dle watch *n.* NAUT the watch from midnight until 4:00 A.M. aboard a vessel

mid·dle·weight /mídd'l wàyt/ *n.* **1.** BOXING PROFESSIONAL BOXER LIGHTER THAN LIGHT HEAVYWEIGHT a professional boxer weighing between 147 and 160 lb./66.5 and 72.5 kg, heavier than a welterweight but lighter than a light heavyweight **2.** BOXING AMATEUR BOXER LIGHTER THAN LIGHT HEAVYWEIGHT an amateur boxer weighing between 157 and 165 lb./71 and 75 kg **3.** SPORTS, WRESTLING WRESTLER OF INTERMEDIATE WEIGHT a contestant in various sports, such as wrestling, of approximately the same weight as a middleweight boxer

Mid·dle Welsh *n.* the form of the Welsh language written and spoken from about the 12th to the beginning of the 15th centuries A.D.

Mid·dle West *n.* = **Midwest** —**Mid·dle West·ern** *adj.* —**Mid·dle West·ern·er** *n.*

mid·dling /míddling/ *adj.* **1.** MEDIUM, MODERATE, OR AVERAGE of average size, quantity, quality, or position **2.** ORDINARY AND UNEXCEPTIONAL neither good nor bad, especially in health or mood ■ **mid·dlings** *npl.* **1.** *Southern U.S.* FOOD CUT OF PORK a cut of pork taken from between the ham and the shoulder and often cured or salted **2.** COMM THINGS OF AVERAGE QUALITY commodities or resources, such as ore or petroleum, that are of average quality, grade, or price **3.** FOOD POOR-QUALITY FLOUR poor-quality flour made from coarsely ground wheat and bran (*takes a singular or plural verb*) [Late 16thC. Formed from MID + -LING.] —**mid·dling·ly** *adv.*

mid·dy /míddee/ (*plural* **-dies**) *n.* **1.** NAVY MIDSHIPMAN a midshipman (*informal*) **2.** **mid·dy, mid·dy blouse** CLOTHES BLOUSE WITH SAILOR COLLAR a loose blouse with a sailor collar worn by women and children

Mid·east /mid éest/ *n.* the Middle East —**Mid·east·ern** *adj.* —**Mid·east·ern·er** *n.*

mid·field /míd fèeld/ *n.* **1.** CENTRAL AREA OF FIELD the middle portion of a sports field, especially the area midway between the goals **2.** PLAYERS IN CENTRAL AREA OF FIELD the group of players who contest control of the central area of the field between the two penalty areas (*takes a singular or plural verb*) —**mid·field·er** *n.*

Mid·gard /míd gaard/, **Mid·garth** /míd gaarth/, **Mid·garthr** /míd gaarthər/ *n.* in Norse mythology, the home of humankind, midway between Asgard and the underworld, encircled by a huge serpent, and formed from the body of the giant Ymir

midge /mij/ *n.* **1.** INSECTS TINY SWARMING FLY a small slender flying insect that occurs globally, particularly in swarms near bodies of standing water, or a related biting insect that can transmit blood-borne diseases. Family: Chironomidae and Ceratopogonidae. **2.** PERSON OF SMALL STATURE a person or animal of small stature [Old English *mycg*. Ultimately from an Indo-European base, probably originally an imitation of the sound of humming, that is also the ancestor of English *mosquito*, *musket*, and *myiasis*.]

midg·et /míjjit/ *n.* **1.** OFFENSIVE TERM an offensive term for a very short person whose skeleton and features are of normal proportions (*offensive*) **2.** VERY SMALL VERSION OF SOMETHING a very small version of something, such as a car or boat ■ *adj.* MINIATURE OR SMALLER THAN USUAL miniaturized or belonging to a class smaller than the ordinary size [Mid-19thC. Formed from MIDGE, literally "little midge."]

mid·gut /míd gùt/ *n.* **1.** BIOL PART OF DIGESTIVE TRACT the central section of the digestive tract of a vertebrate, in which the processes of digestion and absorption take place **2.** BIOL PART OF INVERTEBRATE ALIMENTARY CANAL the middle section of the alimentary canal of an invertebrate **3.** EMBRYOL **PART OF EMBRYO** the middle portion of the gut of an embryo that develops into most of the small intestine and part of the large intestine

Mid·heav·en /mid hévv'n/ *n.* the point on the apparent annual path of the sun in the celestial sphere where the meridian is crossed, or the sign of the zodiac that contains it

mid·i /míddee/ (*plural* **-is**) *n.* a skirt or coat that comes down to just below the knee or halfway down the calf [Mid-20thC. From *midi-* "medium-sized," a combining form formed from MID on the model of MINI- and MAXI-.]

Mi·di /meédee/ name for the south of France

Mi·di, Canal du /mee deé/ canal that links the Bay of Biscay to the Mediterranean Sea

MIDI /míddee/ *n.* the interface between an electronic musical instrument and a computer, used in composing and editing music to allow the computer to control an instrument or one instrument to control others. Abbr of **musical instrument digital interface**

mid·i·ron /míd ìrn/ *n.* in golf, a number 5, 6, 7, or 8 iron, used to give the ball a medium amount of lift

mid·land /míddlənd/ *n.* **INTERIOR PART OF COUNTRY** the middle, inland, or interior part of a country ■ *adj.* **OF MIDDLE OF COUNTRY** relating to or being in the middle or interior of a country

Mid·land *n.* **1. FORM OF AMERICAN ENGLISH** a variety of American English spoken in parts of states south from New Jersey to Georgia, especially in the Appalachian and Piedmont mountains and in the Shenandoah Valley **2.** *U.K.* **FORM OF BRITISH ENGLISH** a variety of British English spoken in the Midlands of England, divided into East Midland and West Midland

Mid·lands /mídləndz/ central, largely industrialized part of England, centered on Birmingham (*takes a singular or plural verb*) —**Mid·land·er** *n.*

Mid·ler /míddlər/, **Bette** (*b.* 1945) U.S. singer and actress. Known for her lively stage act, she also played the Janis Joplin-like character in the movie *The Rose* (1979). Known as **The Divine Miss M**

mid·life /míd lìf/ *n.* = **middle age**

mid·most /míd mōst/ *adj.* **LOCATED AT OR NEAREST CENTER** situated at or nearest the center of something ■ *adv.* **IN MIDDLE** in the middle or midst of something [Old English *midmest*]

Midn. *abbr.* Midshipman

mid·night /míd nìt/ *n.* **1. MIDPOINT OF NIGHT** twelve o'clock at night or the period around the middle of the night **2. TIME OF GREAT DARKNESS** a period of intense darkness or gloom (*literary*) —**mid·night·ly** *adj., adv.*

mid·night blue *adj.* of a dark blue color verging on black, like the sky on a clear night —**mid·night blue** *n.*

mid·night sun *n.* the sun when it is visible from within the Arctic or Antarctic circles at midnight during their respcetive summer months

mid-o·cean ridge *n.* a long underwater mountain range of the Atlantic, Indian, or South Pacific Oceans formed from volcanic rock released during the movement of tectonic plates

mid·point /míd pòynt/ *n.* **1. POINT HALFWAY BETWEEN BEGINNING AND END** the point on a line, journey, or distance that is halfway between the beginning and end **2. POINT OF TIME HALFWAY THROUGH SOMETHING** the point of time halfway between the beginning and end of an event, course of action, or period of time

mid·range /míd ràynj/ *n.* **MIDDLE OF SERIES** the middle of a series, array, or range ■ *adj.* **COVERING MEDIUM DISTANCE** covering a distance midway between a short-range and long-range trajectory

mid·rash (*plural* **-rash·im**) *n.* the technique of interpreting or commenting on the Hebrew Scriptures

Mid·rash /mí draash/ (*plural* **-rash·im** /mi draáshim, mì draa sheém/) *n.* a body of Rabbinic literature consisting of commentary on and clarification of biblical texts, first compiled before 500 A.D. [Early 17thC. From Hebrew *midrāš*, from *dāraš* "to expound."]

mid·rib /míd rìb/ *n.* the thick central vein that runs from the base of a leaf to its apex

mid·riff /míddrif/ *n.* **1. MIDDLE FRONT AREA OF HUMAN BODY** the area of the human body between the chest and the waist **2.** ANAT **DIAPHRAGM** the diaphragm (*dated*) **3.** CLOTHES **PART OF CLOTHING OVER MIDDLE** the part of clothing that covers the area of the human body from the chest to the waist **4.** CLOTHES **CLOTHING EXPOSING STOMACH AREA** an article of clothing that exposes the stomach area [Old English *midhrif* "diaphragm," from *midd* (see MID) + *hrif* "belly" (ultimately from an Indo-European word meaning "body" that is also the ancestor of English *corpse*)]

mid·rise *adj.* **MODERATELY HIGH** relating to or consisting of buildings that are of moderate height, about five to ten stories ■ *n.* **MODERATELY HIGH BUILDING** a building of moderate height, about five to ten stories

mid·sag·it·tal /mid sájjit'l/ *adj.* relating to or situated along an imaginary plane that passes through the midline of the body or an organ

mid·sec·tion /míd sèkshən/ *n.* the middle part of something, especially the area of the human body between the chest and waist

mid·ship /míd shìp/ *adj.* relating to or located in the middle section of a ship or vessel

mid·ship·man /míd shìpmən/ (*plural* **-men**) *n.* **1. STUDENT TRAINING TO BE NAVAL OFFICER** a student who is training to be a naval officer, especially one at a naval academy. ◊ **cadet 2. NORTH AMERICAN TOADFISH** a toadfish of North America that has rows of light-producing organs along the underside of its body and produces a buzzing sound. Genus: *Porichthys.* [Late 17thC. Alteration of earlier *midshipsman*, so called because such officers were originally stationed amidships.]

mid·ships /míd ships/ *adv., adj.* = **amidships** [Mid-19thC. Shortening.]

mid·size /míd sìz/, **mid·sized** *adj.* with a size midway between large and small

midst /midst, mitst/ *n.* **CENTER** the middle or central part of something ■ *prep.* **AMID** amid somebody or something (*literary*) [15thC. Alteration of earlier *middes*, from MID.] ◇ **in the midst of** in the middle of a situation, place, event, or period of time ◇ **in our midst** among us

mid·stream /mid streém/ *n.* **1. MIDDLE PART OF RIVER** the middle part of a river or stream where the current is often very strong **2. POINT HALFWAY THROUGH SOMETHING** a point after the beginning and before the end of something such as a speech or course of action —**mid·stream** *adv.*

mid·sum·mer /míd sùmmər/ *n.* **1. MIDDLE OF SUMMER** the period of time in the middle of summer **2.** = **summer solstice**

Mid·sum·mer Day, **Mid·sum·mer's Day** *n.* the day of June 24, celebrated by Christians as the feast of St. John the Baptist.

mid·term /míd tùrm/ *n.* **1.** EDUC, POL **MIDPOINT OF TERM** the middle of an academic term or a term of office **2.** EDUC **EXAM HALFWAY THROUGH ACADEMIC TERM** an exam taken halfway through an academic term (*often used in the plural*) **3.** OBSTET **PERIOD MIDWAY THROUGH PREGNANCY** the period halfway through a pregnancy ■ *adj.* **IN MIDDLE OF TERM OF OFFICE** occurring in the middle of a term of office, especially the term of a president of the United States ○ *midterm elections*

mid·town /míd tòwn/ *n.* the central area of a city between the uptown and downtown areas especially in Manhattan

mid·way /míd wày/ *adv., adj.* **1. HALF OF THE WAY** halfway between two points, parts, or places **2. HALFWAY THROUGH SOMETHING** halfway through an event, course of action, or period of time ■ *n.* **AREA OF SIDESHOWS AT FAIR** an area in a fair, carnival, or circus for sideshows and other amusements [Old English *midweg*]

Mid·way Is·lands /míd way ílendz/ coral atoll consisting of two islets in the central Pacific Ocean, belonging to the United States. Area: 2 sq. mi./5 sq. km.

mid·week /míd weék/ *n.* **MIDDLE OF WEEK** the period of time in the middle of a week ■ *adj., adv.* **IN MIDDLE OF WEEK** on a day in the middle of the week —**mid·week·ly** /mid weéklee/ *adj., adv.*

Mid·week /míd weék/ *n.* the day of Wednesday, so called by members of the Society of Friends

Mid·west /mid wést/ *n.* the northern region of the central United States east of the Rocky Mountains, generally including the states of Illinois, Indiana, Iowa, Kansas, Michigan, Minnesota, Missouri, Nebraska, Ohio, and Wisconsin —**Mid·west·ern** *adj.* —**Mid·west·ern·er** *n.*

mid·wife /míd wìf/ *n.* **1.** MED **SOMEBODY TRAINED TO DELIVER BABIES** somebody trained to help deliver babies and offer support and advice to pregnant women **2. SOMEBODY HELPING TO CREATE SOMETHING** somebody who or something that helps create or produce something new ■ *vt.* (**-wifed** *or* **-wived**, **-wifed** *or* **-wived** /míd wìvd/, **-wif·ing** *or* **-wiv·ing** /míd wìving/, **-wifes**) **ASSIST IN BIRTH OF BABY** to assist in the delivery of a baby [13thC. Origin uncertain: probably from obsolete *mid* "with" + WIFE in the obsolete sense "woman."]

mid·wife·ry /míd wìferee, mid wíferee/ *n.* the technique or practice of helping to deliver babies and offering advice and support to pregnant women

mid·win·ter /mid wíntər/ *n.* **1. MIDDLE OF WINTER** the period in the middle of winter **2.** = **winter solstice**

mid·year /míd yeér/ *n.* **1. MIDDLE OF YEAR** the period in the middle of the academic, calendar, or fiscal year **2. EXAM HALFWAY THROUGH ACADEMIC YEAR** an exam taken halfway through the academic year (*informal*)

mien /meen/ *n.* somebody's appearance, bearing, or posture, especially facial expressions, as an indication of mood or character (*literary*) [Early 16thC. Origin uncertain: probably a shortening of obsolete *demeine* "demeanor" (from Old French, from *demener*; see DEMEAN); subsequently influenced by French *mine* "facial appearance."]

AKG London

Ludwig Mies van der Rohe

Mies van der Ro·he /meéz van dər rṓ ə/, **Ludwig** (1886–1969) German-born U.S. architect and designer. He was a pioneer in the design of glass-walled skyscrapers, in particular the Seagram Building, New York City (1958), on which he collaborated with Philip Johnson. His architecture and furniture are characterized by austere forms, elegant materials such as marble and chrome, and subtle proportion and detailing.

mi·fep·ri·stone /mi féppra stōn/ *n.* a drug used to abort a fetus in the first nine weeks following conception. It acts by blocking the hormone progesterone which is essential for maintaining a pregnancy. [Late 20thC. Contraction of *aminophenol* + *propyne* + *estradiol* (elements of the drug's chemical name) + -ONE.]

miff /mif/ *vt.* (**miffed, miff·ing, miffs**) **ANNOY OR OFFEND** to annoy or anger somebody (*informal*) (*often passive*) ■ *n.* **1. ILL HUMOR** an angry mood or sulk (*informal*) **2. PETTY QUARREL** a tiff or trivial quarrel [Early 17thC. Origin uncertain: perhaps an imitation of an exclamation of disgust.]

mif·fy /míffee/ (**-fi·er, -fi·est**) *adj.* **1. TOUCHY AND EASILY OFFENDED** easily upset or offended (*informal disapproving*) **2.** BOT **HARD TO GROW** difficult to propagate because very specific environmental conditions are required (refers to a plant) —**mif·fi·ly** *adv.* —**mif·fi·ness** *n.*

MiG /mig/ *n.* a type of high-speed high-altitude fighter aircraft built in Russia [Mid-20thC. Acronym formed from the names of A. I. *Mikoyan* and M. I. *Gurevich*, the aircraft's designers.]

might[1] /mīt/ CORE MEANING: a modal verb indicating the possibility that something is true or will happen in the future ○ *She said that John might be living abroad now.* ○ *The meeting might be next week.*

vi. **1. GIVING ADVICE** used as a polite way of making suggestions and giving advice ○ *I thought we might go out tonight.* ○ *You might want to give him a ring first.* **2. EXPRESSING OBLIGATION** used to indicate that somebody ought to do something, often when you are annoyed that the person has not done it ○ *You might at least have told me!* [Old English *mihte, meahte*, the past tense of *magan* (see MAY)]

might[2] /mīt/ *n.* **1. GREAT POWER** great power or influence ○ *up against the might of a huge organization* **2. PHYSICAL STRENGTH** physical strength and determination ○ *We must push with all our might.* [Old

English *miht.* Ultimately from an Indo-European base meaning "to be able" that is also the ancestor of English *may, main,* and *mechanism.*]

might-have-been *n.* an event or outcome that could have occurred but did not

might·i·ly /mítilee/ *adv.* **1. VERY** to a great extent or degree (*dated*) ○ *mightily relieved* **2. WITH MUCH PHYSICAL POWER** with considerable physical strength and effort

might·n't /mít'nt/ *contr.* a spoken form of "might not"

might·y /mítee/ (**-i·er, -i·est**) *adj.* **1. STRONG AND POWERFUL** of great strength and power **2. BIG AND IMPRESSIVE** very impressive in size, scope, or extent **3. VERY MUCH SO** extremely or to a great degree (*regional informal*) ○ *mighty fine* [Old English *mihtig,* from *miht* (see MIGHT[2])] **—might·i·ness** *n.*

mig·ma·tite /mígmə tìt/ (*plural* **-tites** *or* **-tite**) *n.* a coarsely crystalline rock composed of a mixture of bands of metamorphic and igneous rocks and found in areas where high-grade metamorphic rocks are partly melted to form igneous rock [Early 20thC. Coined from Greek *migmat-,* the stem of *migma* "mixture" + -ITE.]

mig·non (*dainty*) /mín yòn/; (*meat*) /meen yáwN, meén yàwN/ *adj.* **SMALL AND PRETTY** very delicate and pretty (*literary*) ■ *n.* **SMALL BEEF PORTION** a small portion of prime beef, especially filet mignon [Mid-16thC. From French, an alteration of Old French *mignot,* of uncertain origin.]

mi·gnon·ette /mìnnyə nét/ (*plural* **-ettes** *or* **-ette**) *n.* a Mediterranean plant with small fragrant greenish white flowers and spiky leaves. Genus: *Reseda.* [Early 18thC. From French, *mignon* "dainty" (see MIGNON).]

mi·graine /mí gràyn/ *n.* a recurrent, throbbing, very painful headache, often affecting one side of the head and sometimes accompanied by vomiting or by distinct warning signs including visual disturbances [14thC. Via French from, ultimately, Greek *hēmikrania* "half of the skull," from *hēmi-* "half" + *kranion* "skull" (see CRANIUM).] **—mi·grain·ous** /mí gráynəss/ *adj.*

mi·grant /mígrənt/ *n.* **1.** SOC SCI **SOMEBODY MOVING FROM PLACE TO PLACE** somebody who moves from one region or country to another, often in search of work or other economic opportunities **2.** ZOOL **MIGRATORY ANIMAL** an animal, especially a bird, that moves from one region to another, often at specific times of the year in order to breed or avoid unsuitable weather conditions ■ *adj.* **MOVING FROM PLACE TO PLACE** moving from one region or country to another [Late 17thC. From Latin *migrant-,* the present participle stem of *migrare* (see MIGRATE).]

mi·grate /mí gràyt/ (**-grat·ed, -grat·ing, -grates**) *vi.* **1.** SOC SCI **MOVE FROM PLACE TO PLACE** to move from one region or country to another, often to seek work or other economic opportunites **2.** ZOOL **MOVE BETWEEN HABITATS** to move from one habitat or environment to another in response to seasonal changes and variations in food supply **3. MOVE POSITION WITHIN ORGANISM** to move within an organism or substance as, e.g., cells do during the growth of an embryo [Early 17thC. From Latin *migrat-,* the past participle stem of *migrare.* Ultimately from an Indo-European base meaning "to move, change" that is also the ancestor of English *mutate* and *amoeba.*] **—mi·gra·tor** *n.*

mi·gra·tion /mī gráysh'n/ *n.* **1.** SOC SCI **MOVEMENT FROM ONE PLACE TO ANOTHER** the act or process of moving from one region or country to another **2.** SOC SCI **PEOPLE OR ANIMALS MIGRATING TOGETHER** a group of people or animals that are moving together from one region or country to another **3. SHIFT OF IONS** the movement of ions under the influence of an electric field **4.** CHEM **MOVEMENT OF ATOMS** the movement of an atom or a group of atoms or double bonds, from one part of a molecule to another **—mi·gra·tion·al** *adj.*

mi·gra·to·ry /mígrə tàwree/, **mi·gra·tive** /mígrətiv/ *adj.* **1.** ZOOL **MOVING TO ANOTHER REGION EVERY YEAR** moving as part of a bird, fish, or animal population from one region to another every year, usually at specific times in order to breed or avoid unsuitable weather conditions **2.** SOC SCI **RELATING TO MOVEMENT FROM PLACE TO PLACE** relating to the movement of people or animals from one place to another in order to achieve better living conditions **3. NOT SETTLING DOWN** tending to wander from one region or country to another without settling down in one place for any length of time

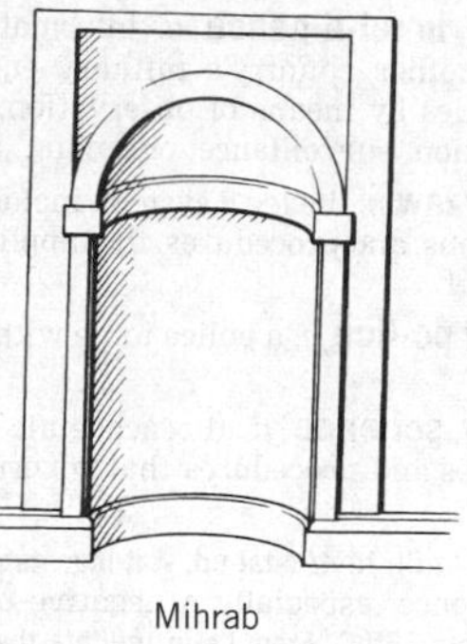

Mihrab

mih·rab /meérəb/ *n.* a small niche in a mosque that indicates the direction of Mecca [Early 19thC. From Arabic *miḥrāb.*]

mi·ka·do /mi kaá dō/ (*plural* **-dos**) *n.* formerly a title of the Japanese emperor [Early 18thC. From Japanese, literally "honorable gate."]

Mik·an /míkən/, **George Lawrence** (*b.* 1924) U.S. basketball player. A player in the Minneapolis Lakers (1947–56), he was one of the first very tall players in the professional sport.

Mik·a·su·ki /mìkə sóokee/ (*plural* **-ki** *or* **-kis**), **Mic·co·su·ki** (*plural* **-ki** *or* **-kis**), **Mic·co·su·kee** (*plural* **-kee** *or* **-kees**) *n.* **1. MEMBER OF NATIVE AMERICAN PEOPLE FROM FLORIDA** a member of a Native North American people that originally occupied lands in northern Florida and whose members now live mainly in southern Florida **2. MIKASUKI LANGUAGE** the language of the Mikasuki people. It belongs to the Muskogean branch of Hokan-Siouan languages. **3. MEMBER OF A FLORIDA PEOPLE** a member of a Native American people from Florida [Mid-20thC. From the Mikasuki language, the name of a lake in Northern Florida where they first settled.] **—Mik·a·su·ki** *adj.*

mike /mīk/ *n.* **MICROPHONE** a microphone (*informal*) ■ *vt.* (**miked, mik·ing, mikes**) **FIT WITH MICROPHONE** to supply somebody with or transmit something through a microphone (*informal*) [Early 20thC. Shortening.]

Mike, **mike** *n.* a code word used to represent the letter "m" in international radio communications

mik·vah /míkvə, meek vaá/, **mik·veh** /míkvə/, **mik·ve** *n.* among Orthodox Jews, a ritual bath for cleansing or purification, especially before the Sabbath or following menstruation, childbirth, or contact with a dead body [Mid-19thC. Via Yiddish *mikve* from Hebrew *miqweh,* literally "mass (of water)."]

mil /mil/ *n.* **1. ONE THOUSANDTH OF INCH** a unit of linear measurement equivalent to one thousandth of an inch/0.0254 mm, often used in measuring the diameter of wires **2. UNIT OF ANGULAR MEASUREMENT FOR ARTILLERY** a unit of measurement in the military that is the equivalent to the angle subtended by 1/6400th of a circumference. It is used in aiming artillery. **3. ONE MILLILITER** a unit of volume equivalent to one milliliter or a cubic centimeter **4. MILLION DOLLARS** a million dollars (*slang*) [Early 18thC. Shortening of Latin *millesimus* "thousandth," from *mille* thousand.]

mil. *abbr.* **1.** military **2.** militia

mi·la·dy /mi láydee/ (*plural* **-dies**) *n.* (*archaic*) **1. ARISTOCRATIC BRITISH WOMAN** a British gentlewoman or a woman member of the aristocracy **2. FORM OF ADDRESS FOR GENTLEWOMAN** a form of address for a gentlewoman or female member of the aristocracy [Late 18thC. Via French from English *my lady.*]

mil·age *n.* = **mileage**

Mi·lan /mi laán/ capital of Milan Province and Lombardy Region, northern Italy. Population: 1,334,171 (1993).

Mil·a·nese /mìllə neéz, mìllə neéss/ (*plural* **-nese**) *n.* **1. SOMEBODY FROM MILAN** somebody who was born in or is a resident of the Italian city of Milan **2. MILANESE DIALECT** the dialect of Italian spoken in and around Milan **3. KNITTED FABRIC USED FOR WOMEN'S CLOTHES** a knitted fabric of silk, rayon, or nylon, usually used in making women's clothing **—Mil·a·nese** *adj.*

milch cow /mílch-, mílk-/ *n.* = **milk cow** (*dated*) [*Milch* from Old English *-milce* "a milking," from the same prehistoric Germanic base as produced *milk*]

mild /mīld/ *adj.* **1. GENTLE AND AMIABLE** gentle, easy-going, and slow to get angry **2.** FOOD **LIGHTLY FLAVORED** lightly flavored and not strong, hot, spicy, or bitter in taste ○ *a mild sauce* **3.** METEOROL **PLEASANT AND TEMPERATE** pleasant and temperate and not excessively hot or cold ○ *one of the mildest winters on record* **4. SLIGHT OR NOT HARSH** not strict, severe, or strong ○ *a mild earth tremor* [Old English *milde.* Ultimately from an Indo-European base meaning "soft" that is also the ancestor of English *melt* and *mollify.*] **—mild·ly** *adv.* **—mild·ness** *n.*

mil·dew /míl doo/ *n.* **1. FUNGAL DISEASE OF PLANT** a plant disease in which the parasitic fungus is visible as white or gray powdery deposits on the leaves or fruit **2. PLANT FUNGUS** a fungus that forms a white or gray powdery growth on plants **3. GRAY OR WHITE FUNGUS** a gray or white fungus that grows on walls, paper, leather, and other similar materials in damp conditions ■ *vti.* (**-dewed, -dew·ing, -dews**) **AFFECT OR BE AFFECTED BY FUNGUS** to become affected or to affect something with a gray or white fungus [Old English *mildēaw* "honeydew, nectar." Ultimately from an Indo-European base meaning "honey" (source also of English *mellifluous* + an earlier form of DEW. The sense "kind of fungus" developed as a result of its appearance.] **—mil·dew·y** *adj.*

mild-man·nered *adj.* polite and of a gentle disposition

mild steel *n.* a strong steel containing a low proportion of carbon [From its being easily worked]

mile /mīl/ *n.* **1.** MEASURE **UNIT OF DISTANCE** a unit of linear measurement on land, used in English-speaking countries, equivalent to 5,280 ft. or 1,760 yd. or 1.6 km **2.** MEASURE = **nautical mile** **3.** MEASURE **UNIT OF MEASUREMENT COMPARABLE TO MILE** a unit of distance or length used in different historical periods or in non-English-speaking countries, e.g., the Roman mile **4.** SPORT **RACE OVER ONE MILE** a foot race that is a mile long ■ **miles** *npl.* **A LONG WAY** a considerable distance (*informal*) ○ *We're miles from anywhere.* [Old English *mīl,* from, ultimately, Latin *milia (passuum)* "a thousand (paces)"), from *mille* "thousand"]

mile·age /mílij/, **mil·age** *n.* **1. DISTANCE IN MILES** a distance or length measured in miles **2. NUMBER OF MILES VEHICLE HAS TRAVELED** the total number of miles a vehicle has traveled **3. MILES VEHICLE TRAVELS ON FUEL** the total number of miles a vehicle can travel on a specified amount of fuel, such as a gallon or a liter **4. TRAVEL ALLOWANCE AT FIXED RATE** a travel allowance, usually set and paid per mile by somebody's employer **5. ADVANTAGE OR USEFULNESS OF SOMETHING** the amount of use, advantage, profit, or service that may be obtained from something (*informal*)

mile·om·e·ter /mī lómmətər/, **mil·om·e·ter** *n. U.K.* = **odometer**

mile·post /míl pōst/ *n.* a post by the side of a road indicating the number of miles to a certain place, or placed a mile from a similar post

mil·er /mílər/ *n.* an athlete or horse that competes in a one-mile race

mi·les glo·ri·o·sus /meé layz glawree ṓsəss/ (*plural* **mi·li·tes glo·ri·o·si** /meélee tayz glawree ṓssee/) *n.* an arrogant, bragging, and often cowardly soldier, especially one who appears as a stock character in comedies (*literary*) [From Latin, literally "boastful soldier," the title of a comedy by Plautus]

Mi·le·sian[1] /mī leézh'n, mī leésh'n/ *n.* **SOMEBODY FROM MILETUS** somebody who was born in or was a citizen of the ancient Ionian city of Miletus ■ *adj.* **OF MILETUS** relating to the ancient Ionian city of Miletus, its people, or its culture [Mid-16thC. Formed from Latin *Milesius,* from Greek *Milēsios,* from *Milētos* "Miletus."]

Mi·le·sian[2] /mī leézh'n, mī leésh'n/ *n.* in Irish mythology, a member of a group of people from a royal Spanish family who invaded Ireland about 1300 B.C. and became the ancestors of the modern Irish [Late 16thC. Named for *Milesius,* the legendary head of the family.]

mile·stone /míl stōn/ *n.* **1. STONE SHOWING DISTANCE TO PLACE** a stone by the side of a road indicating the number of miles to a certain place **2. IMPORTANT EVENT** a significant or important event, e.g., in the history of a country or in somebody's life

mil·foil /míl fòyl/ (*plural* **-foils** *or* **-foil**) *n.* **1.** = **yarrow** **2.** = **water milfoil** [13thC. Via Old French from Latin *mil(l)efolium,* literally "thousand-leaf," a translation of Greek *muriophullon;* from the plant's feathery leaves.]

Mil·ford /mílfərd/ **1.** city in southwestern Connecticut, in New Haven County, on Long Island Sound. Population: 49,092 (1994). **2.** town in southern Massachusetts, south of Marlborough and southeast of Worcester. Population: 25,194 (1996).

Mil·ford Sound /mílfərd sównd/ deep coastal inlet in the southwestern part of the South Island, New Zealand

Mil·haud /meé ō/, **Darius** (1892–1974) French composer and teacher. A member of Les Six, his work was marked by polytonality and elements of jazz.

mil·i·ar·i·a /míllee áiree ə/ *n.* prickly heat (*technical*) [Early 19thC. Via modern Latin from, ultimately, Latin *miliarius* (see MILIARY).] —**mil·i·ar·i·al** *adj.*

mil·i·ar·y /míllee èrree/ *adj.* **1. LIKE MILLET SEEDS** resembling millet seeds **2.** DERMAT **HAVING SMALL NODULES OR LESIONS** consisting of or characterized by small nodules or lesions resembling millet seeds [Late 17thC. From Latin *miliarius*, from *milium* "millet" (source also of English *millet*).]

mil·i·ar·y tu·ber·cu·lo·sis *n.* an acute form of tuberculosis in which lesions resembling millet seeds occur in the affected organs after bacilli are spread by the blood from one point of infection

mi·lieu /mil yoō, mi lyṓ/ (*plural* **-lieus** *or* **-lieux**) *n.* the surroundings or environment that somebody lives in and is influenced by (*formal*) [Mid-19thC. From French, literally "middle-place," from *mi* "mid" (from Latin *medius*) + *lieu* "place."]

milit. *abbr.* military

mil·i·tant /míllit'nt/ *adj.* **1. AGGRESSIVE** extremely active in the defense or support of a cause, often in ways that other people find unacceptable **2. INVOLVED IN FIGHTING** engaged in fighting or warfare ■ *n.* **SOMEBODY AGGRESSIVELY SUPPORTING CAUSE** somebody who is active in the defense or support of a cause, often using methods that other people find unacceptable [15thC. Directly or via French from Latin *militant-*, the present participle stem of *militare* "to be a soldier," from the stem *milit-* (see MILITARY).] —**mil·i·tan·cy** *n.* —**mil·i·tant·ly** *adv.*

mil·i·tar·i·a /mìlli táiree ə/ *n.* military objects such as weapons, medals, and uniforms that are collected as a hobby or for historical interest [Mid-20thC. Formed from MILITARY.]

mil·i·ta·rism /míllitə rìzzəm/ *n.* **1. PURSUIT OF MILITARY AIMS** the pursuit or celebration of military ideals **2. STRONG INFLUENCE OF MILITARY ON GOVERNMENT** a high level of influence by military personnel and ideals in the government or policies of a country or state **3. GOVERNMENT POLICY OF INVESTING IN MILITARY** a government policy of investing heavily in and strengthening the armed forces

mil·i·ta·rist /míllitərist/ *n.* **1. SUPPORTER OF MILITARISM** somebody who zealously supports and promotes military ideals **2. STUDENT OF MILITARY HISTORY** a student of military history and strategy —**mil·i·ta·ris·tic** /mìllitə rístik/ *adj.* —**mil·i·ta·ris·ti·cal·ly** /-kəlee/ *adv.*

mil·i·ta·rize /míllitə rìz/ (**-rized, -rized, -riz·ing, -riz·es**) *vt.* **1. EQUIP OR TRAIN FOR WAR** to equip or train a person or group of people for war **2. CONVERT FOR MILITARY USE** to convert something such as a piece of land or a building for military use **3. PERSUADE TO SUPPORT MILITARISM** to persuade somebody to support a policy of aiding and promoting the military —**mil·i·ta·ri·za·tion** /mìllitəri záysh'n/ *n.*

mil·i·tar·y /mílli tèrree/ *adj.* **1. OF WAR OR ARMED FORCES** relating to matters of war or the armed forces **2. OF ARMY** relating to the army, especially as distinguished from the navy or air force **3. TYPICAL OF SOLDIER** characteristic of a soldier or the armed forces ■ *n.* **ARMED FORCES OR ITS HIGH-RANKING OFFICERS** the armed forces or high-ranking members of the armed forces [15thC. Directly or via French *militaire* from Latin *militaris*, from *milit-*, the stem of *miles* "soldier," of uncertain origin.] —**mil·i·tar·i·ly** /mìlli térrilee/ *adv.* —**mil·i·tar·i·ness** /mílli tèrreenəss/ *n.*

mil·i·tar·y a·cad·e·my *n.* **1. TRAINING SCHOOL FOR OFFICERS** a secondary school or college that prepares students to enter the military at officer level, and that typically emphasizes rigorous discipline **2. SCHOOL WITH MILITARY DISCIPLINE** a secondary school or college that follows military procedures and discipline and usually requires students to wear military uniforms but does not necessarily entitle them to become officers

mil·i·tar·y at·ta·ché *n.* an officer in the armed forces who has been assigned to the official staff of an ambassador in order to gather military intelligence

mil·i·tar·y-in·dus·tri·al com·plex *n.* the military and the defense industries considered as a combined influence on foreign and economic policy

mil·i·tar·y in·tel·li·gence *n.* information gathered about another country's military equipment and capabilities by means of observation, exchange of information, surveillance, or spying

mil·i·tar·y law *n.* the legal system, including statutes, regulations, and procedures, that applies to military personnel

mil·i·tar·y po·lice *n.* a police force within the armed forces

mil·i·tar·y sci·ence *n.* the academic study of the principles and procedures that govern the conduct of war

mil·i·tate /mílli tàyt/ (**-tat·ed, -tat·ing, -tates**) *vi.* to have an influence, especially a negative one, on something [Late 16thC. From Latin *militat-*, the past participle stem of *militare* "to be a soldier, wage war," from the stem *milit-* (see MILITARY).]

mi·li·tia /mə líshə/ *n.* **1. SOLDIERS WHO ARE ALSO CIVILIANS** an army of soldiers who are civilians but take military training and can serve full-time during emergencies **2. RESERVE MILITARY FORCE** a reserve army that is not part of the regular armed forces but that can be called up in an emergency **3. UNAUTHORIZED QUASI-MILITARY GROUP** an unauthorized group who arm themselves and conduct quasi-military training [Late 16thC. From Latin, "military service, body of soldiers," from the stem *milit-* (see MILITARY).]

mi·li·tia·man /mə líshəmən/ (*plural* **-men**) *n.* a man who serves in a militia

mili·tia·wom·an /mə líshə wŏŏmmən/ (*plural* **-en** /-wìmmin/) *n.* a woman who serves in a militia

mil·i·um /míllee əm/ (*plural* **-a** /míllee ə/) *n.* a whitehead (*technical*) [Mid-19thC. From Latin, "millet" (source of English *millet*); so called from the nodule's size and shape.]

milk /milk/ *n.* **1.** BIOL **NUTRITIOUS FLUID PRODUCED BY MAMMALS** a nutritious white fluid that women and other female mammals produce to feed their young immediately after birth. It is rich in protein, fats, lactose, and vitamins. **2.** FOOD **DAIRY PRODUCT** an opaque white fluid produced by mammals and used by human beings as a food and for other purposes. Milk, especially that produced by cows and goats, is widely used as a beverage, as a cooking ingredient, and to make other dairy products, e.g., butter, cheese, yogurt, and cream. **3.** BOT **PLANT SAP** a white or off-white liquid from a plant, such as the liquid inside a coconut or the sap of certain trees **4.** COSMETICS **COSMETIC OR PHARMACEUTICAL PRODUCT** a cosmetic or pharmaceutical product that is thick and white ○ *cleansing milk* ■ *v.* (**milked, milk·ing, milks**) **1.** *vti.* **TAKE MILK FROM COW** to draw milk for use as a dairy product from the udder of a cow, goat, sheep, or similar mammal manually or by using a special machine **2.** *vi.* **PRODUCE MILK** to yield or supply milk (*refers to a dairy animal*) **3.** *vt.* **REMOVE VENOM OR SAP FROM** to remove the venom from a snake or drain the sap from a tree **4.** *vt.* **STEAL MONEY IN SLOW STEADY AMOUNTS** to steal money from something such as a fund, in small quantities over a period of time (*informal*) **5.** *vt.* **EXPLOIT** to get as much money or benefit from something as possible, often in a dishonest or unscrupulous way (*informal disapproving*) [Old English *milc*. Ultimately from an Indo-European base meaning "to rub, milk" that is also the ancestor of English *emulsion*.]

WORD KEY: CULTURAL NOTE

Under Milk Wood, a play by Welsh poet Dylan Thomas (1953). This play for voices was originally written for radio but is occasionally presented as a stage play. It describes a day in the life of a Welsh fishing village and is noted for its poetic prose, rich humor, and vivid characterization.

Milk /milk/ river that originates in Montana and flows into Alberta, Canada, before joining the Missouri River. Length: 625 mi./1,006 km.

milk-and-wa·ter *adj.* weak or bland, especially in expression or sentiment [From the idea of dilution]

milk choc·o·late *n.* chocolate that has been made with milk and has a sweet creamy taste

milk cow *n.* **1. COW GIVING MILK** a cow that produces milk (*dated*) **2. SOURCE OF EASY INCOME** a source of easily gained income (*informal*)

milk·er /mílkər/ *n.* **1. MILK-YIELDING ANIMAL** an animal that produces milk used for human consumption, especially a cow **2. PERSON OR MACHINE THAT MILKS ANIMALS** a milking machine, or somebody who milks animals, especially cows

milk fe·ver *n.* **1. FEVER FOLLOWING CHILDBIRTH** mild fever that some new mothers have around the time that they begin to produce breast milk **2. ANIMAL DISEASE** a disease in cows, sheep, and goats that have recently given birth, caused by mineral depletion due to milk production. Symptoms include temporary loss of consciousness or ability to move.

milk·fish /mílk fìsh/ (*plural* **-fish·es** *or* **-fish**) *n.* a large toothless silver fish that lives in warm parts of the Pacific and Indian oceans and grows up to 5 ft./1.5 m long. It is related to the herring and the salmon. Latin name: *Chanos chanos*. [Early 20thC. *Milk* from its color.]

milk glass *n.* white or translucent whitish glass used in decorative glasswork

milk·ing /mílking/ *n.* the task of drawing milk from cows, goats, or sheep for human consumption, or a time when this is done (*often used before a noun*)

milk·ing stool *n.* a short simple three-legged stool of a style used in the past when milking cows

milk leg *n.* painful leg swelling that some women have following childbirth, caused by inflammation and clotting in the femoral vein

milk·maid /mílk màyd/ *n.* a woman or girl who milks cows or does other jobs in a dairy

milk·man /mílk màn, -mən/ (*plural* **-men** /-mèn, -mən/) *n.* a man who delivers or sells milk door to door

Milk of Mag·ne·sia *tdmk.* a trademark for a milky mixture of magnesium hydroxide and water, used as a laxative and antacid

milk punch *n.* a drink consisting of alcoholic liquor, milk, and sometimes sugar or spices

milk run *n.* a routine trip, especially an airline's regular flight or an uneventful sortie made by a military aircraft (*informal*) [From the routine early morning trips of milk trains]

milk shake, milk·shake *n.* **1. COLD MILK DRINK** a cold drink made by whisking or blending milk, flavoring, and usually ice cream **2. FLAVORED MILK** in New England, a drink made of milk and flavored syrup that is whipped until it is frothy (*regional*)

milk sick·ness *n.* MED a now uncommon disease caused by eating dairy products or meat from a cow that has eaten white snakeroot. The symptoms include shaking, weakness, vomiting, and constipation.

milk snake *n.* a white or tan nonpoisonous king snake of North America with red, yellow, brown, or black markings. Genus: *Lampropeltis*. [*Milk* from its color]

milk·sop /mílk sòp/ *n.* a weak-willed or ineffectual man (*dated insult*) [14thC. The original meaning was "bread soaked in milk."]

milk sug·ar *n.* = **lactose**

milk toast *n.* buttered toast served in warm milk, often with sugar and cinnamon

milk tooth *n.* a tooth in young mammals including humans that falls out in early life to be replaced by the adult tooth

milk vetch *n.* a plant with yellow, white, or purple flowers and seeds in pods. It is thought by some to increase milk production in goats. Genus: *Astragalus.*

milk·weed /mílk weèd/ *n.* a flowering plant that secretes a milky latex. The seed pods burst open to release seeds with a tuft of silky hair. Genus: *Asclepias.*

milk·weed bug *n.* a black crawling insect with red markings that feeds on the juice of the milkweed and is often used in scientific research. Latin name: *Oncopeltus fasciatus.*

milk·weed but·ter·fly *n.* any of a family of butterflies whose larvae feed on milkweed plants, such as the monarch butterfly. Family: Danaidae.

milk·wort /mílk wùrt, -wàwrt/ *n.* a plant with blue, pink, or white flowers with winged petals that in the past was believed to increase milk production in nursing mothers. Genus: *Polygala.*

milk·y /mílkee/ (**-i·er, -i·est**) *adj.* **1. MILK-COLORED** like milk in color or consistency **2. CONTAINING MILK** full of or containing milk **3. OPAQUE** cloudy or translucent, as if milk had been added **4. LACKING COURAGE** lacking

MILITARY RANKS

Military ranks of the United Kingdom, Australia, and New Zealand

Royal Navy	Royal Marines	British Army	Royal Air Force
Admiral of the Fleet	[1]	Field Marshal	Marshal of the Royal Air Force
Admiral	General	General	Air Chief Marshal
Vice Admiral	Lieutenant General	Lieutenant General	Air Marshal
Rear Admiral	Major General	Major General	Air Vice Marshal
Commodore	Brigadier	Brigadier	Air Commodore
Captain	Colonel	Colonel	Group Captain
Commander	Lieutenant Colonel	Lieutenant Colonel	Wing Commander
Lieutenant Commander	Major	Major	Squadron Leader
Lieutenant	Captain	Captain	Flight Lieutenant
Sub Lieutenant	Lieutenant	Lieutenant	Flying Officer
	Second Lieutenant	Second Lieutenant	Pilot Officer
Midshipman			
*			
Warrant Officer	Warrant Officer (1st, 2nd Class)	Warrant Officer (1st, 2nd Class)	Warrant Officer
Chief Petty Officer	Colour/Staff Sergeant	Colour/Staff Sergeant	Flight Sergeant
			Chief Technician
Petty Officer	Sergeant	Sergeant	Sergeant
Leading Rate[2]	Corporal	Corporal	Corporal
	Lance Corporal	Lance Corporal	
Able Rate[3]	Marine 1st Class	Private	Junior Technician/ Senior Aircraftman
Ordinary Rate[4]	Marine 2nd Class		Leading Aircraftman/ Aircraftman

Notes

NB Ranks shown are not comparative between United Kingdom, Australia, New Zealand and the United States and Canada

*** Indicates the end of officer rank**

1 Marine service not applicable for Australia and New Zealand.
2 Leading Rate: also called 'Leading Seaman' in some forces.
3 Able Rate: also called 'Able Seaman' in some forces.
4 Ordinary Rate: also called 'Seaman' in some forces.

Military ranks of the United States and Canada

United States Navy	United States Marine Corps	United States Army	United States Air Force
Fleet Admiral		General of the Army	General of the Air Force
Admiral	General	General	General
Vice Admiral	Lieutenant General	Lieutenant General	Lieutenant General
Rear Admiral Upper Half	Major General	Major General	Major General
Rear Admiral Lower Half	Brigadier General	Brigadier General	Brigadier General
Captain	Colonel	Colonel	Colonel
Commander	Lieutenant Colonel	Lieutenant Colonel	Lieutenant Colonel
Lieutenant Commander	Major	Major	Major
Lieutenant	Captain	Captain	Captain
Lieutenant Junior Grade	Lieutenant	Lieutenant	Lieutenant
Ensign	Second Lieutenant	Second Lieutenant	Second Lieutenant
*			
	Chief Warrant Officer 5	Chief Warrant Officer 5	
Warrant Officer 4	Chief Warrant Officer 4	Chief Warrant Officer 4	
Warrant Officer 3	Chief Warrant Officer 3	Chief Warrant Officer 3	
Warrant Officer 2	Chief Warrant Officer 2	Chief Warrant Officer 2	
	Warrant Officer 1	Warrant Officer 1	
Master Chief Petty Officer of the Navy	Sergeant Major of the Marine Corps	Sergeant Major of the Army	Chief Master Sergeant of the Air Force
Master Chief Petty Officer	Master Gunnery Sergeant	Command Sergeant Major	Chief First Sergeant
	Sergeant Major	Sergeant Major	Chief Master Sergeant
Senior Chief Petty Officer	First Sergeant	First Sergeant	Senior First Sergeant
	Master Sergeant	Master Sergeant	Senior Master Sergeant
Chief Petty Officer	Gunnery Sergeant	Sergeant First Class	First Sergeant
			Master Sergeant
Petty Officer 1st Class	Staff Sergeant	Staff Sergeant	Technical Sergeant
Petty Officer 2nd Class	Sergeant	Sergeant	Staff Sergeant
Petty Officer 3rd Class	Corporal	Corporal	Senior Airman
Seaman	Lance Corporal	Private First Class	Airman First Class
Apprentice	Private First Class	Private	Airman
Recruit	Private	Recruit	Airman Basic

Milkweed

courage, strength, or steadfastness (*dated*) —**milk·i·ly** *adv.* —**milk·i·ness** *n.*

milk·y dis·ease *n.* a disease in the larvae of Japanese beetles and other scarabs that is caused by bacteria and turns the larvae white

Milk·y Way *n.* the spiral galaxy to which the Earth and its solar system belong, some of which appears as a faint band of light in the night sky [14thC. A translation of Latin *via lactea* (compare GALAXY).]

mill[1] /mil/ *n.* **1.** INDUST **FLOUR-MAKING FACTORY** a building or group of buildings in which cereal grains are ground to make meal or flour. In previous times this place would have been a windmill or a water mill. **2.** INDUST **PROCESSING PLANT** a building or group of buildings used for processing raw materials and manufacturing a product such as paper, fabric, or steel **3. SMALL DEVICE FOR GRINDING GRAINS** a small device for grinding something such as coffee, pepper, or salt into granules **4.** INDUST **PROCESSING MACHINE** a machine that repeats a simple manufacturing procedure, e.g., one that stamps or cuts metal **5. JUICER** a machine that extracts juice from fruit or vegetables **6.** INDUST = **milling cutter 7.** = **milling machine 8. SOMETHING WORKING REPETITIVELY OR UNTHINKINGLY** an institution, person, or process that operates in the same automatic, repetitive, or productive manner as a factory (*disapproving*) ○ *Our family is a regular rumor mill.* **9. TEDIOUS PROCESS** a slow, unpleasant, or tedious process ○ *Getting the book through the editorial mill could take months.* **10.** BOXING **FIGHT** a boxing match or other fist fight (*archaic slang*) ■ *v.* (**milled, mill·ing, mills**) **1.** *vt.* **GRIND GRAIN BY MACHINE** to grind grain or seed by machine **2.** *vt.* INDUST **MANUFACTURE BY MACHINE** to manufacture a product such as paper or fabric from raw materials by machine **3.** *vt.* INDUST **PROCESS MATERIALS USING ROTARY MACHINERY** to process materials using machinery that grinds, presses, or pulverizes raw materials using a rotary motion **4.** *vt.* INDUST **SHAPE METAL BY MACHINE** to use a milling cutter or milling machine to cut, shape, or finish metals **5.** *vt.* INDUST **PUT RIDGES ON COIN EDGE** to cut ridges or grooves into something metal, especially the edge of a coin **6.** *vt.* INDUST **PROCESS RUBBER** to pass rubber through spinning rollers as part of the manufacturing process **7.** *vt.* **MAKE CREAM FROTHY** to whisk or shake something, e.g., cream or chocolate, until it is foamy **8.** *vt.* **HALT STAMPEDE** to stop a cattle stampede by turning the lead animals so that the cattle move in a circle, rather than forward (*regional*) **9.** *vi.* INDUST **UNDERGO CRUSHING PROCESS** to undergo the process of being crushed to make flour (*refers to grain*) **10.** *vi.* **FIGHT WITH FISTS** to fight using the fists (*archaic slang*) [Pre-12thC. From late Latin *molina*, from, ultimately, Latin *molere* "to grind" (source of English *molar*). Ultimately from an Indo-European base that is also the ancestor of English *meal*.] —**mill·a·ble** *adj.* ◇ **put somebody through the mill** to subject somebody to a difficult or unpleasant ordeal (*informal*)

WORD KEY: CULTURAL NOTE

The Mill on the Floss, a novel by English writer George Eliot (1860). Set in eastern England in the early 19th century, it describes the intellectual and emotional development of Maggie Tulliver, the daughter of a miller. By contrasting Maggie's inquisitiveness and independent spirit with the dreary conservatism of most of her family and acquaintances, Eliot highlights the obstacles faced by women in English society at the time.

mill about, mill a·round *vi.* to wander about aimlessly, restlessly, or in confusion

mill[2] /mil/ *n.* a monetary unit equal to one thousandth of a U.S. dollar, used in accounts and calculations but not in everyday currency [Late 18thC. Shortening of Latin *millesimum* "thousandth" (see MIL), on the model of CENT.]

Mill /mil/, **James** (1773–1836) British philosopher and economist. Father of John Stuart Mill and an associate of Jeremy Bentham, he was one of the founders of utilitarianism.

Mill, John Stuart (1806–73) British philosopher and economist. The son of James Mill, he was one of the leading intellectuals of his day, and a major proponent of utilitarianism. His most important works include *A System of Logic* (1843) and the essay "On Liberty" (1859).

mill·age /míllij/ *n.* a property tax rate stated in terms of tenths of cents in tax per dollar of property value

Mil·lais /míl ay, mi láy/, **Sir John Everett** (1829–96) British painter. A leading member of the Pre-Raphaelite movement, he painted many historical scenes and worked as a portraitist.

Mil·land /míllənd, mi lánd/, **Ray** (1905–86) British-born U.S. actor. He won an Academy Award as the alcoholic writer in *The Lost Weekend* (1945). Real name **Reginald Alfred Tuscott-Jones**

Mil·lay /mi láy/, **Edna St. Vincent** (1892–1950) U.S. poet and playwright. She is noted for her lyrical poetry of the 1920s and the satirical play *Aria da Capo* (1919).

mill·board /míl bàwrd/ *n.* thick paperboard used in binding books [Early 18thC. Alteration of *milled board*.]

mill·dam /míl dàm/ *n.* a dam built near a mill in order to raise the water level of a stream so that the flow is strong enough to turn a mill wheel

milled /mild/ *adj.* **1.** INDUST **PROCESSED OR GROUND IN MILL** processed or ground in a mill especially in an industrial context **2. RIDGED** with grooves or ridges cut by machine **3.** INDUST **PRESSED FLAT** pressed flat by rollers **4.** INDUST **POLISHED** polished by a machine (*archaic*)

Mil·ledge·ville /míllij vil/ city in central Georgia, the seat of Baldwin County. Population: 18,376 (1994).

mille·feuille /meel fōy/ (*plural* **-feuilles**) *n.* a dessert or pastry consisting of several layers of puff pastry with a filling of cream and fruit preserves, topped with confectioners' sugar or frosting [Late 19thC. From French, literally "a thousand leaves."]

mil·le·fi·o·ri /mìllə fee áwree/ *n.* decorative glassware made by cutting and arranging cross sections of fused glass rods of varied color and thickness [Mid-19thC. From Italian, literally "a thousand flowers."]

mille·fleurs /meel flúr, meel flóor, meel flör/ *adj.* covered with a design of small flowers or plants [Early 20thC. From French, literally "a thousand flowers."]

mil·le·nar·i·an /mìllə náiree ən/, **mil·le·nar·y** /míllə nèrree/ (*plural* **-ies**) *adj.* **1.** CHR **RELATING TO JESUS CHRIST'S SECOND COMING** relating to or believing in Jesus Christ's Second Coming, a final conflict between good and evil, the end of the world, or similar doctrines, especially based on the book of Revelation **2. RELATING TO FUTURE UTOPIA** relating to or expressing belief in the coming of some future utopian age **3. RELATING TO END OF WORLD** relating to or suggesting the end of the world **4. RELATING TO THOUSANDS** relating to units of one thousand, especially one thousand years [Mid-17thC. Formed from Latin *millenarius*, from, ultimately, *mille* "thousand."] —**mil·le·nar·i·an** *n.* —**mil·le·nar·i·an·ism** /mìllə náiree ə nìzzəm/ *n.*

mil·le·nar·i·an·ism /mìllə náiree ə nìzzəm/ *n.* **1.** CHR **BELIEF IN JESUS CHRIST'S SECOND COMING** belief in Jesus Christ's Second Coming, a final conflict between good and evil, the end of the world, or similar doctrines, especially based on the book of Revelation **2. BELIEF IN COMING UTOPIA** belief in a future utopian age, especially one created through revolution **3. BELIEF IN END OF WORLD** belief that the end of the world is near

mil·le·nar·y /míllə nèrree/ *adj.* = **millenarian** ■ *n.* **1.** (*plural* **-ies**) = **millennium** *n.* 1 **2.** = **millenarian** [Mid-16thC. From Latin *millenarius* (see MILLENARIAN).] —**mil·le·nar·ism** /míllənə rìzzəm/ *n.*

mill end *n.* either end of a roll of fabric or carpet that is finished, rather than cut

mil·len·ni·um /mi lénnee əm/ (*plural* **-ums** *or* **-a** /-lénnee ə/) *n.* **1. 1,000 YEARS** a period of 1,000 years, especially a period that begins or ends in a year that is a multiple of 1000 **2.** CHR **PROPHESIED RULE BY JESUS CHRIST** the thousand-year period of peace on earth that, according to one interpretation of prophecies in the book of Revelation, will follow the Second Coming of Jesus Christ **3. HOPED-FOR UTOPIAN AGE** an imagined future utopian period of joy, peace, and justice, especially one created through revolution **4. THOUSANDTH ANNIVERSARY** a thousand-year anniversary, especially the one in the year 2000 [Mid-17thC. From modern Latin, formed from Latin *mille* "thousand" + *annus* "year" (see ANNUAL).] —**mil·len·ni·al** *adj.* —**mil·len·ni·al·ism** *n.* —**mil·len·ni·al·ist** *n.* —**mil·len·ni·al·ly** *adv.*

WORD KEY: USAGE

See Usage note at ***century.***

mil·len·ni·um bug *n.* the problem posed by the year 2000 for computer software coding dates using only the last two digits of each year (*informal*)

The New Millennium Experience Company

Millennium Dome: Model by Richard Rogers Partnership

Mil·len·ni·um Dome *n.* a large structure by the Thames River in Greenwich, London, England, designed by Richard Rogers Partnership to celebrate the year 2000. The world's largest dome, more than half a mile/1 km in circumference, it houses commercial and educational facilities.

mil·le·pore /míllə pàwr/ *n.* a kind of coral that forms white or yellow reefs [Mid-18thC. From modern Latin *Millepora*, genus name, from Latin *mille* "thousand" + *porus* "pore" (see PORE).]

mill·er /míllər/ *n.* **1. MILL OPERATOR** somebody who owns, manages, or operates a mill **2. MACHINE THAT MILLS** a machine that mills materials **3. MOTH WITH POWDERY WINGS** any of various moths whose wings have a powdery appearance

AKG London

Arthur Miller

Mill·er /míllər/, **Arthur** (*b.* 1915) U.S. playwright. He won a Pulitzer Prize for his tragedy *Death of a Salesman* (1949). His play *The Crucible* (1953) was a veiled critique of the House Un-American Activities committee. His second wife was the movie actor Marilyn Monroe.

Mill·er, Glenn (1904–44) U.S. bandleader and composer. Leader of a big-band orchestra of the late 1930s and early1940s, he was noted for swing music such as "In the Mood" (1939). Full name **Alton Glenn Miller**

Mill·er, Henry (1891–1980) U.S. writer, His novels *Tropic of Cancer* (1934) and *Tropic of Capricorn* (1939) are sexually explicit and were banned in the United States. Full name **Henry Valentine Miller**

mil·ler·ite /míllə rìt/ *n.* nickel sulfide in the form of long wiry crystals. It is one of the sources of nickel. Formula: NiS. [Mid-19thC. Named for W. H. *Miller* (1801–80), English mineralogist.]

mill·er's thumb *n.* a small, flat, spiny fish found in European and North American fresh waters. Genus: *Cottus*. [From the shape of its body, alluding to the proverbial distrust of millers' methods of measurement]

mil·les·i·mal /mə léssim'l/ *adj.* **RELATING TO THOUSANDTHS** divided by one thousand or relating to thousandths

Henry Miller: Photographed in 1932 by Brassaï

■ *n.* **THOUSANDTH PART** a thousandth part of something [Early 18thC. Formed from Latin *millesimus* "thousandth," from *mille* "thousand."] —**mil·les·i·mal·ly** /mə léssimalee/ *adv.*

mil·let /míllit/ *n.* **1. CEREAL PLANT** a fast-growing annual cereal plant grown for its seed and used for hay. Latin name: *Panicum miliaceum.* **2. GRAIN** the pale shiny grain of the millet plant, used for food and as birdseed **3. GRASS PLANT** a grass that is similar or related to millet and is grown for its grain, e.g., pearl millet [15thC. Via Old French from, ultimately, Latin *milium.*]

mill fin·ish *n.* a particularly smooth surface on paper, made by a machine

milli-[1] symbol **m** [From Latin, formed from *mille* "thousand"]

milli-[2] *prefix.* one thousandth (10^{-3}) ○ *milliroentgen.* Symbol **m** [From Latin, formed from *mille* "thousand"]

mil·li·am·pere /míllee ám pèer/ *n.* a unit of electric current equal to one thousandth of an ampere

mil·li·ar·y /míllee èrree/ *adj.* indicating or marking a distance of one Roman mile, measured as one thousand paces [Mid-17thC. From Latin *milliarius*, from *mille* "thousand" (see MILE).]

mil·li·bar /míllə baar/ *n.* a unit of atmospheric pressure equal to one thousandth of a bar

mil·li·cur·ie /mílli kyòoree/ *n.* a unit of radioactivity equal to one thousandth of a curie

mil·lieme *n.* **1. MINOR UNIT OF EGYPTIAN AND SUDANESE CURRENCY** minor unit of currency in Egypt and Sudan equal to one thousandth of a pound. See table at **currency** **2.** = **millime** [Early 20thC. From French *millième* (see MILLIME).]

mil·li·far·ad /mílli fèrrəd, mílli fèr àd/ *n.* a unit of electrical capacitance equal to one thousandth of a farad

mil·li·gram /mílli gràm/ *n.* a unit of mass and weight equal to one thousandth of a gram

mil·li·hen·ry /míllə hènree/ (*plural* **-ries**) *n.* a unit of electrical inductance equal to one thousandth of a henry

Mil·li·kan /míllikən/, **Robert Andrews** (1868–1953) U.S. physicist. He received a Nobel Prize in physics (1923) for measuring the charge on the electron, and coined the term "cosmic rays."

mil·li·lam·bert /míllə làmbərt/ *n.* a unit of luminance equal to one thousandth of a lambert

mil·li·li·ter /míllə leetər/ *n.* a unit of volume equal to one thousandth of a liter

mil·li·li·tre /mìlli leetər, mílli leetər/ *n.* U.K. = **milliliter**

mil·lime /míllim, mí leem/, **mil·lieme** /mil yém/ *n.* a minor unit of currency in Tunisia equal to one thousandth of a dinar. See table at **currency** [Mid-20thC. Via French *millième* "thousandth" from Latin *millesimus*, from *mille* "thousand."]

mil·li·me·ter /míllə meetər/ *n.* a unit of length equal to one thousandth of a meter

mil·li·me·tre /mìlli meetər, mílli meetər/ *n.* U.K. = **millimeter**

mil·li·mi·cron /míllə mí kròn/ *n.* an obsolete name for a unit of length equal to one millionth of a millimeter, now called a nanometer (*dated*)

mil·li·mole /míllə mòl/ *n.* a unit used to measure the amount of a chemical substance, equal to one thousandth of a mole —**mil·li·mo·lar** /míllee mólər/ *adj.*

mil·line /mí lìn, mi lín/ *n.* **1. UNIT OF ADVERTISING COPY** a unit of advertising copy equal to one column line in agate type in one million copies of a newspaper or magazine **2.** = **milline rate** [Late 20thC. Blend of MILLION and LINE.]

mil·li·ner /míllənər/ *n.* somebody who designs, makes, or sells hats for women [Mid-16thC. Alteration of earlier *Milaner* "importer of fancy fabrics and wares from Milan, Italy."]

mil·line rate *n.* the cost per unit of advertising copy

mil·li·ner·y /míllə nèrree/ *n.* **1. WOMEN'S HATS** hats and other accessories for women, sold by a milliner **2. HAT BUSINESS** the design, manufacture, or sale of women's hats

mill·ing /milling/ *n.* the ridged edge of a coin

mill·ing cut·ter *n.* a rotary tool used for cutting, shaping, and finishing metal objects

mill·ing ma·chine *n.* a machine fitted with milling cutters to cut, shape, or finish metal objects

Mill·ing·ton /míllingtən/ city in New Jersey, in Morris County, on the Passaic River

mil·lion /míllyən/ *n.* **1. THOUSAND THOUSAND** a thousand thousand (10^6) **2. LARGE NUMBER** a very large number (*often used in the plural*) **3. MILLION UNITS OF A CURRENCY** a million units of a currency especially dollars or pounds **4. FIFTH DIGIT TO LEFT OF DECIMAL** the fifth digit to the left of the decimal point in the decimal number system ○ *In the number 54321, the 5 is in the millions place.* ■ **mil·lions** *npl.* **ORDINARY PEOPLE** ordinary people, considered collectively ○ *entertainment for the millions* [14thC. Via French from obsolete Italian *millione*, literally "great thousand," from Latin *mille* "thousand" (source of English *mile* and *milli-*).] —**million** *adj.*

mil·lion·aire /míllyə náir, míllyə nàir/ *n.* somebody whose net worth or income is more than one million dollars, or other unit of currency (*often used before a noun*) [Early 19thC. From French, where it was formed from *million* (see MILLION).]

mil·lion·air·ess /mìllyə náirəss/ *n.* a wealthy woman whose net worth or income is more than one million dollars or other unit of currency

mil·lionth /míllyənth/ *n.* one of a million equal parts of something —**millionth** *adj.*

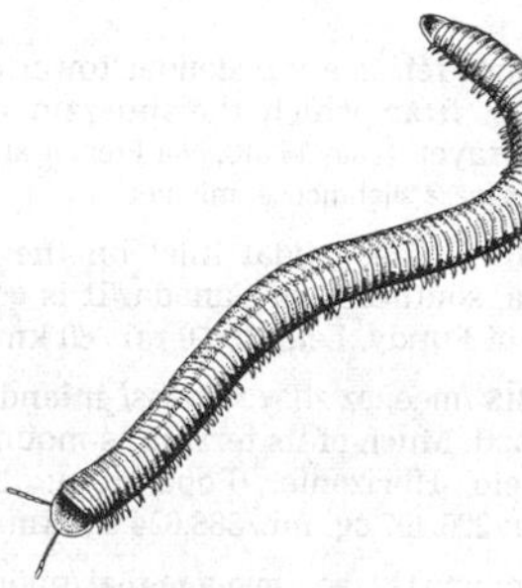
Millipede

mil·li·pede /míllə peed/, **mil·le·pede** *n.* a small plant-eating arthropod with a tubular body made up of segments. Most segments have two pairs of legs. Class: Diplopoda. [Early 17thC. From Latin *millipeda* "woodlouse," literally "with a thousand feet," from the stem *ped-* "foot" (see PEDAL).]

mil·li·sec·ond /míllə sèkənd/ *n.* a unit of time equal to one thousandth of a second

mil·li·volt /míllə vàwlt/ *n.* a unit of electrical voltage or potential difference equal to one thousandth of a volt. Symbol **mV**

mil·li·watt /míllə wòt/ *n.* a unit of electrical power equal to one thousandth of a watt. Symbol **mW**

mill·pond /míl pònd/ *n.* a pond created by damming a stream in order to create a flow of water to turn a mill wheel

mill·race /míll ràyss/ *n.* **1. WATER IN MILL WHEEL** the stream of water that flows through a mill wheel, making it turn **2. CHANNEL PROVIDING WATER FOR MILL WHEEL** a channel that directs water to and from a mill wheel

mill·run /míll rùn/ *n.* **1.** = **millrace** **2. MINERAL FROM TEST** a quantity or quality of mineral yielded by a millrun test **3. SAWMILL OUTPUT** the output of a sawmill **4. TEST OF MINERAL** a test to determine the quality of a mineral or the mineral content of an ore

mill·stone /míl stòn/ *n.* **1. GRAIN-GRINDING STONE** either of two large circular stones used to grind grain in a mill **2. BURDENSOME RESPONSIBILITY** a great burden or responsibility

mill·stream /míl streem/ *n.* **1. STREAM SUPPLYING MILL** a stream from which the water turns a mill wheel **2.** = **millrace** *n.* 1

Mill Val·ley /mil-/ city in California, in Marin County. Population: 13,190 (1994).

mill wheel *n.* a wheel that powers a mill, typically turned by a flow of water

mill·work /míl wùrk/ *n.* items of woodwork such as doors banisters and moldings made in a lumber mill

mill·wright /míl rìt/ *n.* somebody who designs, builds, or maintains mills or mill machinery

Milne /miln/, **A. A.** (1882–1956) British writer. He created the character Winnie the Pooh to amuse his son Christopher Robin, and wrote four much-loved collections of children's poems and stories, including *Now We Are Six* (1927) and *The House at Pooh Corner* (1928). Full name **Alan Alexander Milne**

mi·lo /mílō/ (*plural* **-los**) *n.* a variety of sorghum grain that resembles millet, known for growing early and resisting drought [Late 19thC. Origin uncertain: possibly from Sesotho *maili.*]

WORD KEY: REGIONAL NOTE

Milo is common in the Plains states from Iowa to Texas with scattered occurrences to the east and west.

mi·lord /mi láwrd/ *n.* **1. BRITISH ARISTOCRAT** a British gentleman or member of the aristocracy **2. FORM OF ADDRESS FOR A GENTLEMAN** a form of address for a gentleman or member of the aristocracy [Late 16thC. Via French, from English *my lord.*]

Mi·lo·še·vić /mi lóssə vich/, **Slobodan** (*b.* 1941) Yugoslavian national leader. After the breakup of the former Yugoslavia, he became president of Serbia (1989–97) and the Federal Republic of Yugoslavia (1997).

mil·pa /mílpə/ (*plural* **-pas**) *n.* an agricultural field that is made by clearing forest and then farmed for only a few seasons before being abandoned, especially such fields in Central America and Mexico [Mid-19thC. Via Mexican Spanish from Nahuatl.]

milque·toast /mílk tòst/, **Milque·toast** *n.* a timid or submissive person, especially a man (*dated*) [Mid-20thC. From Casper *Milquetoast*, a cartoon character created by Harold Tucker Webster (1885–1952).]

mil·reis /mill ráyss/ (*plural* **-reis** /mill ráyz/) *n.* an obsolete Portuguese and Brazilian unit of currency and coin equal to one thousand reis [Late 16thC. From Portuguese, formed from *mil* "thousand" + *real* "real" (a unit of currency).]

Mil·stein /míl stìn/, **Cesar** (*b.* 1927) Argentine-born British immunologist. He shared a Nobel Prize in physiology or medicine (1984) for his development of monoclonal antibody technology.

Mil·stein, Nathan (1904–92) Russian-born U.S. violinist. He studied at the St. Petersburg Conservatory and lived in the United States from 1929.

milt /milt/ *n.* the semen and seminal fluid of a fish [Old English *milte* "spleen," later reinforced by Middle Dutch *milte* "milt"]

milt·er /míltər/ *n.* a fertile male fish during the mating season

Mil·ton /míltən/ town in eastern Massachusetts, a southern suburb of Boston. Population: 25,794 (1996).

Mil·ton, John (1608–74) English poet. His poems rank among the greatest treasures of English literature, and include the epic narrative of Adam and Eve's banishment from Paradise, *Paradise Lost* (1667). During the English Civil Wars, he wrote powerful polemics that championed religious and civil liberty. —**Mil·to·ni·an** /mil tónee ən/ *adj.* —**Mil·ton·ic** /mil tónnik/ *adj.*

Mil·wau·kee /mil wáwkee/ the largest city in Wisconsin, located in the southeastern corner of the state. Population: 617,044 (1994).

Mi·mas /míməss, meeməss/ *n.* one of the satellites of Saturn, the nearest to the planet

Mim·bres /mímbrəss/ *n.* the last period of the Native American Mogollon culture, running from the 9th to the 13th century, noted for its distinctive black-

and-white pottery (*often used before a noun*) [From Spanish, "willows, withies," from Latin *vimen* "withy, wicker" (from the painted designs on pottery of the period)]

mime /mīm/ *n.* **1.** ACTING USING ONLY GESTURE AND ACTION a style of performance in which people act out situations or portray characters using only gesture and action (*often used before a noun*) **2.** PERFORMER WHO USES MIME a performer who relies on gesture, facial expression, and action rather than using the voice **3.** THEATRICAL PERFORMANCE IN MIME a theatrical piece performed with gesture, facial expression, and action rather than with words **4.** ANCIENT FARCE in ancient Greek and Roman theater, a lewd comedy including dialogue, dance, and gesture ■ *vti.* **(mimed, mim·ing, mimes) 1.** EXPRESS SOMETHING IN MIME to express something or act it out using gestures and facial expressions only **2.** = **mimic** *v.* 2 [Early 17thC. Via Latin *mimus* from Greek *mimos* "imitator, mimic" (source of English *mimic*).]

mim·e·o·graph /mímmee ə gràf/, **mim·e·o** /mímmee ò/ *n.* **1. mim·e·o·graph, Mim·e·o·graph** COPYING MACHINE a machine that prints copies onto paper from an inked stencil that is rotated on a cylinder across the pages **2. mim·e·o·graph, Mimeograph** MIMEOGRAPHED COPY a copy made on a mimeograph ■ *vt.* **(-graphed, -graph·ing, -graphs; -oed, -o·ing, -os)** MAKE COPIES USING MIMEOGRAPH to make a copy of a document using a mimeograph [Late 19thC. Originally a trademark, coined from Greek *mimeisthai* (see MIMESIS) + -GRAPH.]

mi·me·sis /mi méssiss, mī-/ *n.* **1.** BIOL = **mimicry** *n.* 2 **2.** MED DISEASE SYMPTOMS IN HEALTHY PERSON the occurrence of a disease's symptoms in somebody who does not have the disease, often psychosomatically caused **3.** ART'S IMITATION OF LIFE the imitation of life or nature in the techniques and subject matter of art and literature **4.** RHETORICAL DEVICE the rhetorical use of what somebody else might have said [Mid-16thC. From Greek *mimēsis*, from *mimeisthai* "to imitate," from *mimos* "mime."]

mi·met·ic /mi méttik, mī-/, **mi·met·i·cal** /-k'l/ *adj.* **1.** IMITATING SOMETHING imitating something, or relating to imitation, e.g., in artistic or literary mimesis **2.** BIOL, MED RELATING TO BIOLOGICAL MIMICRY relating to mimicry in animals and plants [Mid-17thC. From Greek *mimētikos*, from *mimēsis* (see MIMESIS).] —**mi·met·i·cal·ly** *adv.*

mim·ic /mímmik/ *vt.* **(-icked, -ick·ing, -ics) 1.** IMITATE SOMEBODY to imitate somebody, or copy somebody's voice, gestures, or appearance **2.** MOCK SOMEBODY THROUGH IMITATION to make fun of somebody by imitating him or her in an exaggerated way **3.** COPY SOMETHING to resemble something in a way that seems like a deliberate copy ○ *houses with facades that mimic the colonial style* **4.** BIOL RESEMBLE OTHER SPECIES to take on the appearance of another plant or animal, e.g., when a harmless animal evolves to look like a poisonous one to discourage predators ■ *n.* SOMEBODY WHO IMITATES OTHERS somebody who imitates others, especially for comic effect ■ *adj.* **1.** RELATING TO MIMICRY relating to mime, mimicry, or imitation **2.** SIMULATED simulated or pretend (*literary*) **3.** RESEMBLING SOMETHING imitating or resembling something (*literary*) [Late 16thC. Via Latin *mimicus* from Greek *mimikos*, from *mimos* (see MIME).] —**mim·ick·er** *n.*

WORD KEY: SYNONYMS

See Synonyms at *imitate*.

mim·icked *v.* past participle, past tense of **mimic**

mim·ick·ing *v.* present participle of **mimic**

mim·ic·ry /mímmikree/ *n.* **1.** ART OF IMITATION the imitating of other people's voices, gestures, or appearance, often for comic effect **2.** BIOL SIMILARITY OF APPEARANCE IN NATURE a plant's or animal's resemblance to another species or to a feature of its natural surroundings, evolved as protection from predators **3.** BIRDS BIRDS' IMITATION OF OTHERS' CALLS the ability of some birds to imitate the songs of other species and incorporate them into their own repertoire, especially developed in the mockingbird family

Mi·mir /mée meer/ *n.* in Norse mythology, the god of wisdom, a giant water demon who was said to reside at and drink from the well of wisdom at Yggdrasil

mi·mo·sa /mi móssə, mi mózə/ *n.* **1.** FLOWERING TREE WITH SENSITIVE LEAVES a tree or shrub that grows in warm climates and has round clusters of white, yellow, or pink flowers and leaves that are sensitive to touch. Genus: *Mimosa.* **2.** = **silk tree 3.** CHAMPAGNE COCKTAIL a cocktail of champagne and orange juice [Mid-18thC. From modern Latin, genus name, from Latin *mimus* "imitator" (see MIME), because its leaves seem to flinch when touched, mimicking a recoiling animal.]

mim·u·lus /mímmyələss/ (*plural* **-lus**) *n.* = **monkey flower** [Mid-18thC. From modern Latin, genus name, literally "little mime," from Latin *mimus* (see MIME); perhaps from its mask-like flowers.]

min. *abbr.* **1.** mineralogical **2.** mineralogy **3.** MEASURE minim **4.** minimum **5.** minister **6.** minor **7.** minute

mi·na /mínə/ (*plural* **-nae** /mí neè/ *or* **-nas**) *n.* a unit of weight and money used in ancient Greece and Asia, usually equal to one sixtieth of a talent [Late 16thC. Via Latin and Greek from Akkadian.]

mi·na·cious /mi náyshəss/ *adj.* menacing or threatening (*literary*) [Mid-17thC. Formed from the Latin stem *minac-*, from *minari* "to threaten" (see MENACE).] —**mi·na·cious·ly** *adv.* —**mi·na·cious·ness** *n.* —**mi·nac·i·ty** /mi nássətee/ *n.*

Min·a·ma·ta dis·ease /mìnnə maátə-/ *n.* a severe degenerative disease of the nervous system caused by mercury contamination, especially through eating mercury-tainted seafood [Mid-20thC. Named for *Minamata*, a town in Japan.]

Min·a·mo·to Yor·i·to·mo /mìnnəmōtō yórri tōmō/ (1147–99) Japanese leader. He founded the shogunate form of government, ruling most of medieval Japan (1192–99).

Minaret

min·a·ret /mìnnə rét/ *n.* a tall slender tower attached to a mosque, from which the muezzin calls the faithful to prayer [Late 17thC. Via French and Turkish from Arabic *manāra* "lighthouse, minaret."]

Mi·nas Ba·sin /mīnəs-/ tidal inlet on the coast of Nova Scotia, southeastern Canada. It is connected by the Bay of Fundy. Length: 50 mi./80 km.

Mi·nas Gerais /meènaz zhay ráyəss/ inland state in eastern Brazil. Much of its terrain is mountainous. Capital: Belo Horizonte. Population: 15,731,961 (1991). Area: 226,497 sq. mi./586,624 sq. km.

min·a·to·ry /mínnə tàwree/, **min·a·to·ri·al** /mìnnə táwree əl/ *adj.* menacing or threatening (*literary*) [Mid-16thC. From late Latin *minatorius*, from Latin *minari* "to threaten" (see MENACE).] —**min·a·to·ri·al·ly** *adv.* —**min·a·to·ri·ly** *adv.*

min·au·dière /meènō dyáir/ (*plural* **-dières**) *n.* a small decorative cosmetic or jewelry case that can be carried in a woman's purse (*archaic*) [Mid-20thC. From French, where it was formed from *minauder* "to flirt, be affected," from *mine* "mood, bearing."]

mince /minss/ **(minced, minc·ing, minc·es)** *v.* **1.** *vt.* = **grind 2.** *vt.* DIVIDE SOMETHING UP to divide land or property into very small portions, especially in a way regarded as detrimental **3.** *vt.* USE TACT to use words or deal with matters delicately, so as not to offend or upset others ○ *She did not mince her words.* **4.** *vti.* WALK DAINTILY to walk with small light steps in an affectedly dainty way **5.** *vti.* SPEAK DAINTILY to speak, or say something, in an affectedly dainty way [14thC. Via Old French *mincier* from assumed Vulgar Latin *minutiare*, from *minutus* "very small" (see MINUTE).] —**mincer** *n.*

mince·meat /minss meèt/ *n.* **1.** FRUIT AND SPICE MIXTURE a mixture of spiced and finely chopped fruits, such as apples and raisins, usually cooked in pies **2.** MINCED MEAT finely ground meat [Mid-17thC. Alteration of *minced meat.*] ◇ **make mincemeat of somebody** *or* **something** to defeat somebody or something thoroughly (*informal*)

Minch, The /minch/, **Minch·es, The** /mínchəz/ sea channel in northwestern Scotland, separating the Outer Hebrides from the Inner Hebrides and the mainland. It is divided into the North Minch and the Little Minch.

Min·cha /mínkhə, min khaá/, **Minchah** *n.* a daily Jewish prayer said in the afternoon [Early 19thC. From Hebrew *minḥāh*, literally "offering."]

Min·cho /mìn chō, mínchō/ (1352–1431) Japanese artist and Buddhist priest. He was noted for his Buddhist icons and ink paintings. Full name **Kichizan Mincho**

minc·ing /mínssing/ *adj.* affectedly dainty or prim —**minc·ing·ly** *adv.*

mind /mīnd/ *n.* **1.** SEAT OF THOUGHT AND MEMORY the center of consciousness that generates thoughts, feelings, ideas, and perceptions and stores knowledge and memories **2.** THINKING CAPACITY the capacity to think, understand, and reason (*often used in combination*) **3.** CONCENTRATION concentration, or the ability to concentrate ○ *My mind was wandering.* **4.** WAY OF THINKING an opinion or personal way of thinking about something ○ *I've changed my mind about going with you.* **5.** STATE OF THOUGHT OR FEELING the state of thought or feeling that is regarded as normal **6.** DESIRE the desire or intention to act or behave in a specified way ○ *After such insults, I had a mind to leave right then.* **7.** INTELLECTUAL PERSON somebody considered in terms of his or her intellect or intelligence ○ *Einstein was among the greatest minds of the modern era.* **8.** GENERAL TYPE OF PERSON a pattern of thinking or feeling that is typical of a particular group ○ *Who knows what goes through the criminal mind?* **9.** PHILOS NONMATERIAL THINGS in the philosophy of Descartes, all things that are not matter ■ *v.* **(mind·ed, mind·ing, minds) 1.** *vt.* PAY ATTENTION TO to pay attention to something, especially so as to avoid danger or an accident ○ *Mind your step!* **2.** *vt.* CONTROL to remain aware of the need to control something **3.** *vti.* OBJECT TO to object to somebody or something ○ *Do you mind if we leave early?* **4.** *vt.* TEMPORARILY WATCH OVER to watch over and look after somebody or something, usually for a short time ○ *Will you mind the dog over the weekend?* **5.** *vt.* OBEY to listen to and obey somebody ○ *Be sure to mind your father while I'm away.* **6.** *vt.* REMEMBER to remember something (*regional*) ○ *Mind what I told you.* **7.** *vi.* BE CAREFUL be careful or cautious ○ *Mind what you're doing, or you'll spill your milk.* **8.** *vi.* BE OBEDIENT to behave obediently ○ *Those twins don't mind very well, do they?* **9.** *vt.* REMIND to remind somebody of something (*regional*) **10.** *vt.* TAKE NOTE OF SOMETHING to notice or perceive something (*regional*) ○ *Mind the new detour signs or you'll get lost.* [Old English *gemynd.* Ultimately from an Indo-European base meaning "to think," which is also the ancestor of English *mental, amnesia, mania,* and *monitor.*] —**mind·er** *n.* ◇ **mind you** used to qualify something you have just said (*informal*)

mind-al·ter·ing *adj.* changing perceptions, moods, or thought patterns

Min·da·na·o /mində nów/ island in the southern Philippines, the largest after Luzon. Population: 14,536,000 (1990). Area: 36,537 sq. mi./94,630 sq. km.

mind-bend·ing *adj.* **1.** OVERWHELMING mentally overwhelming, e.g., because of great size or complexity (*informal*) **2.** ALTERING PERCEPTIONS changing perceptions, moods, or thought patterns (*dated informal*) —**mind-bend·ing·ly** *adv.*

mind-blow·ing *adj.* (*informal*) **1.** ALTERING PERCEPTIONS changing perceptions, moods, or thought patterns **2.** EXTREMELY EXCITING extremely exciting, surprising, or shocking —**mind-blow·er** *n.*

mind-bod·y prob·lem *n.* the philosophical question of whether the mind is part of the body or separate from it, first formulated as a problem by the French philosopher René Descartes

mind-bog·gling *adj.* mentally overwhelming, e.g., because of great size or complexity (*informal*) —**mind-bog·gling·ly** *adv.*

mind·ed /míndəd/ *adj.* inclined to do a particular thing or act in a particular way (*formal*)

mind-ex·pand·ing *adj.* **1.** ALTERING PERCEPTIONS changing perceptions, moods, or thought patterns **2.** EXPANDING KNOWLEDGE expanding knowledge and awareness

mind·fuck /mīnd fùk/ *n.* OFFENSIVE TERM an offensive term for an assault on somebody's mind, values, or thought processes, especially through the manipulation of perceptions or opinions (*slang* offensive) ■ vti. (-fucked, -fuck·ing, -fucks) **OFFENSIVE TERM** to attempt to manipulate the way somebody thinks, especially in order to lead him or her to adopt another perspective or system of beliefs (*slang offensive*) —**mind·fuck·er** *n.*

mind·ful /mī́ndfəl/ *adj.* paying attention or taking care —**mind·ful·ly** *adv.* —**mind·ful·ness** *n.*

WORD KEY: SYNONYMS

See Synonyms at *aware*.

mind game *n.* a psychologically manipulative and deceptive practice intended to deceive or confuse somebody (*informal*)

mind·less /mī́ndləss/ *adj.* 1. **UNINTELLIGENT** requiring or displaying very little intelligence 2. **PURPOSELESS** having no apparent purpose or rational cause 3. **UNCONCERNED** not careful or concerned —**mind·less·ly** *adv.* —**mind·less·ness** *n.*

mind-numb·ing *adj.* inspiring no interest or thought, especially because of dullness or repetitiveness —**mind-numb·ing·ly** *adv.*

Min·do·ro Is·land /min dáwrō ī́lənd/ island in the western Philippines. Area: 3,760 sq. mi./9,738 sq. km.

mind read·er *n.* somebody who can sense the thoughts of others without being told what they are

mind·scape /mī́nd skàyp/ *n.* 1. **IMAGINED SCENE** a mental scene constructed from memory or imagination 2. **PICTURE OF MIND'S CONTENTS** an artistic representation of a mental scene constructed from memory or imagination [Formed from MIND, modeled on LANDSCAPE]

mind·set /mī́nd sèt/ *n.* a set of beliefs or a way of thinking that determine somebody's behavior and outlook

mind's eye *n.* the mind as a place where visual images are conjured up from memory or imagination

mine[1] /mīn/ *n.* 1. **HOLE IN EARTH FOR EXTRACTING MINERALS** an excavated area from which minerals, often in the form of ore, are extracted 2. **MINERAL-EXCAVATING BUSINESS** the industrial and commercial buildings, machinery, and personnel used to work a mine 3. **MINERAL DEPOSIT** an area within or on the surface of the earth where there is a deposit of ore, minerals, or precious stones 4. **SOURCE** a rich source of something, especially information 5. ARMS **HIDDEN EXPLOSIVE** an explosive device that is concealed underground or underwater to be detonated by nearby people or vehicles 6. MIL **TUNNEL UNDER ENEMY TERRITORY** a tunnel dug under enemy territory in order to gain entry, undermine fortifications, or lay explosives 7. ZOOL **INSECT BURROW** a tunnel made by a burrowing insect or larva, especially in a plant leaf ■ *v.* (**mined, min·ing, mines**) 1. *vti.* MINING **REMOVE MINERALS** to extract minerals from the earth 2. *vt.* ARMS **LAY EXPLOSIVE MINES IN** to place mines throughout an area of ground or water 3. *vt.* **DIG TUNNEL BENEATH** to dig a tunnel under the surface of the earth 4. *vt.* **MAKE USE OF RESOURCE** to make use of a particular resource ○ *Generations of scholars mined the archives.* 5. *vt.* **UNDERMINE** to undermine (*archaic*) [14thC. Via Old French from assumed Vulgar Latin *mina*, of uncertain origin: probably from Celtic.] —**min·a·ble** *adj.*

mine[2] /mīn/ *pron.* **INDICATES POSSESSION** refers to something that belongs or relates to the speaker or writer ○ *He put on his coat, and told me to put mine on.* ○ *She was a friend of mine.* ■ *adj.* **MY** belonging to or associated with me (*archaic*) (*used before a vowel*) ○ *By mine eyes and by mine ears I swear.* [Old English *mīn*. Ultimately from an Indo-European word meaning "me," which is also the ancestor of English *me* and *my*.]

mine de·tec·tor *n.* an instrument used for finding explosive mines hidden under the ground or in water

mine·field /mī́n fèeld/ *n.* 1. **AREA CONTAINING EXPLOSIVE MINES** an area of land or sea in which explosive mines have been placed 2. **HAZARDOUS SITUATION** a situation in which great care is needed to avoid the many hazards that exist

mine·lay·er /mī́n làyr/ *n.* a ship fitted with equipment for laying explosive mines under water

Min·e·o·la /minə ṓlə/ village in New York, predominantly in North Hempstead town, Nassau County. Population: 18,629 (1994).

min·er /mī́nər/ *n.* 1. **SOMEBODY WORKING IN MINE** somebody who works in a mine digging for minerals, especially coal 2. **MINERAL-EXTRACTING MACHINE** a machine that extracts minerals, especially coal, from the ground 3. **SOMEBODY LAYING EXPLOSIVE MINES** somebody whose task is to place and set explosive mines 4. INSECTS = **leaf miner**

min·er·al /mínnərəl/ *n.* 1. **INORGANIC SUBSTANCE IN NATURE** an inorganic solid substance that occurs naturally in rocks and in the ground and has its own characteristic appearance and chemical composition 2. **MINED SUBSTANCE** any naturally occurring substance that is mined or extracted from the ground 3. **MATTER NOT ANIMAL OR VEGETABLE** non-technically anything that is not made of animal or vegetable matter 4. **INORGANIC NUTRITIVE SUBSTANCE** an inorganic substance that must be ingested by animals or plants in order to remain healthy ■ *adj.* **CONTAINING MINERALS** made of or containing minerals [15thC. Via medieval Latin *minerale* from, ultimately, Old French *miniere* "mine," from *mine* (see MINE[1]).]

min·er·al·ize /mínnərə lī̀z/ (**-ized, -iz·ing, -iz·es**) *v.* 1. *vt.* **IMPREGNATE SOMETHING WITH MINERALS** to impregnate something, e.g., water or organic matter, with minerals 2. *vti.* **MAKE OR BECOME MINERAL** to transform organic matter into a mineral, as happens in petrification, or to be transformed in this way —**min·er·al·iz·a·ble** *adj.* —**min·er·al·i·za·tion** *n.*

min·er·al·o·cor·ti·coid /mìnnərəlō káwrti kòyd/ *n.* a hormone (**corticosteroid**), e.g., aldosterone, that controls electrolyte and fluid balance in the body and is secreted by the adrenal cortex [Mid-20thC. Coined from MINERAL + CORTICOSTEROID.]

min·er·al·o·gy /mìnnə róllәjee/ (*plural* **-gies**) *n.* 1. **STUDY OF MINERALS** the scientific study of minerals and how to classify, distinguish, and locate them 2. **AREA'S MINERAL DEPOSITS** a profile of an area's mineral deposits —**min·er·a·log·i·cal** /mìnnərə lójjik'l/ *adj.* —**min·er·a·log·i·cal·ly** *adv.* —**min·er·al·o·gist** /mìnnə róllәjist/ *n.*

min·er·al oil *n.* 1. **LAXATIVE OIL** a clear oil distilled from petroleum and used as a laxative and skin softener 2. **OIL FROM MINERALS** any oil obtained from minerals, especially from petroleum

min·er·al spir·its *npl.* a liquid distilled from petroleum and used to thin paint and varnish (*takes a singular or plural verb*)

min·er·al spring *n.* a spring whose water has high mineral or gas content

min·er·al tar *n.* = **maltha**

min·er·al wa·ter *n.* drinkable water with a high mineral salt or gas content, either obtained from a mineral spring or with minerals added. It is usually sold in bottles.

min·er·al wax *n.* wax made from a mineral, especially a hydrocarbon wax (**ozocerite**) found in veins in sandstone

min·er·al wool *n.* a lightweight fibrous material made from slag or glass, used for insulation, packing material, and filters

min·er's let·tuce *n.* = **winter purslane** [*Miner's* because it grows commonly in the foothill country, where gold mines were active]

Mi·ner·va /mi núrvə/ *n.* in Roman mythology, the goddess of wisdom and patron of arts, trade, and art of war, who was born fully armed from the head of Jupiter

mine·shaft /mī́n shàft/ *n.* a nearly vertical passageway that provides access or ventilation to an underground mine

min·e·stro·ne /mìnnə strṓnee/ *n.* a thin Italian soup made with vegetables, pasta, beans, and herbs. It is often served sprinkled with Parmesan cheese. [Late 19thC. From Italian, from, ultimately, Latin *ministrare* "to serve," from *minister* "servant" (see MINISTER).]

mine·sweep·er /mī́n sweepər/ *n.* a ship fitted with equipment for detecting and clearing underwater explosive mines

mine·work·er /mī́n wùrkər/ *n.* somebody who works in a mine

Ming /ming/ *n.* the Chinese dynasty that ruled from 1364 to 1644, under which arts, trade, and scholarship were greatly developed (*often used before a noun*) [Late 18thC. From Chinese, literally "bright, clear."]

min·gle /míng g'l/ (**-gled, -gling, -gles**) *v.* 1. *vti.* **MIX GENTLY** to mix, or mix ingredients, together gently or gradually ○ *Heat gently to allow the flavors to mingle.* 2. *vi.* **SPEAK TO PEOPLE** to circulate among a group of people, e.g., guests at a party [15thC. Alteration of obsolete *menglen*, literally "to keep mixing," from Old English *mengan* "to mix."]

Min·grel /míng grəl/, **Min·grel·i·an** *n.* a language spoken in the mountainous region to the northeast of the Black Sea. It belongs to the Southern branch of Caucasian languages and is closely related to Georgian.

ming tree *n.* 1. **BONSAI TREE** an evergreen tree used for bonsai, usually in a flat-topped asymmetrical arrangement 2. **ARTIFICIAL BONSAI** an artificial bonsai tree [*Ming* of uncertain origin: perhaps from MING]

Min·gus /míng gəss/, **Charles** (1922–79) U.S. double bassist and composer. He played in various jazz bands, establishing the double bass as a principal jazz instrument.

min·gy /mínjee/ (**-gi·er, -gi·est**) *adj. U.K.* mean or stingy (*informal*) [Early 20thC. Origin uncertain; perhaps a blend of MEAN and STINGY.]

min·i /mínnee/ *n.* something that is small compared to other things of its type, especially a minicomputer or a miniskirt (*informal*) [Mid-20thC. From MINI-.]

mini- *prefix.* small, short, miniature ○ *ministroke* [Shortening of MINIATURE]

min·i·a·ture /mínnee ə chər, mínnee ə choor, mínnichər/ *n.* 1. **SMALLER VERSION** a smaller-than-usual version of something, e.g., a very small model or a smaller version of a particular breed of animal 2. ARTS **TINY PAINTING** a very small, detailed, and well-finished painting, especially a portrait made to fit inside a locket or other piece of jewelry 3. PAINTING **PAINTING OF MINIATURES** the art of painting miniatures 4. **ILLUMINATED MANUSCRIPT ILLUSTRATION** a small picture or decorative initial in an illuminated manuscript ■ *adj.* **SMALLER THAN USUAL** smaller in size or scale than others of its type [Late 16thC. Via Italian *miniatura* "illumination" from, ultimately, Latin *minium* "red lead."] ◇ **in miniature** on a small scale

WORD KEY: ORIGIN

Miniature Red lead was used in ancient and medieval times for making a sort of red ink with which manuscripts were decorated, and so the medieval Latin verb *miniare* was coined from *minium*, "red lead," meaning "to illuminate a manuscript." Italian took this over and derived *miniatura* "painting, illumination" from it. It referred particularly to the small paintings in manuscripts, and, after English acquired it, it was soon broadened out to refer to any "small image." Association with *minute*, *minimum*, etc. led by the early 18th century to its adjectival use for "small."

min·i·a·ture golf *n.* a novelty version of golf played with a putter on a very small course with obstacles such as tunnels and bridges for the ball to avoid or go through

min·i·a·tur·ize /mínnee əchə rī̀z, mínnichə rī̀z/ (**-ized, -iz·ing, -iz·es**) *vt.* to make a version of something in a much smaller size or on a greatly reduced scale —**min·i·a·tur·i·za·tion** /mìnnee əchəri záysh'n, minnichəri záysh'n/ *n.*

min·i·bar /mínnee baar/ *n.* a small refrigerator in a hotel room stocked with alcoholic beverages and often also with soft drinks and snacks

mi·ni·blind *n.* a venetian blind with narrow slits

mi·ni·break /mínnee bràyk/ *n.* a point won against the serve in a tie-break in a tennis match (*informal*)

min·i·bus /mínnee bùss/ *n.* a small bus for carrying around 10 to 15 passengers, usually on short journeys

Min·i·cam *tdmk.* a trademark for a portable, shoulder-mounted television camera used in outside broadcasts

min·i·car /mínnee kaar/ *n.* a very small automobile

mi·ni·com·pact /mìnnee kóm pàkt/ *n.* a passenger vehicle smaller than a subcompact in size

min·i·com·put·er /mínnee kəm pyootər/ *n.* a computer of a size, speed, and capacity intermediate between a standard personal computer and a mainframe

Min·i·con·jou /minni kón joo/ (*plural* **-jous** *or* **-jou**), **Min·ne·con·jou** *n.* a member of a Native North American people who originally occupied lands from the Black Hills to the Platte River, and whose members now live mainly in South Dakota

min·i·con·ven·tion /mínnee kən vènshən/ *n.* a small-scale convention, especially one that takes place before a larger political convention

min·i·course /mínnee kàwrs/ *n.* a short course of study, especially an intensive introductory course lasting less than a semester

Min·i·Disc *tdmk.* a trademark for a small recordable compact disc housed in a rectangular plastic case. It measures 2 in./5 cm in diameter.

min·i·dress /mínnee drèss/ *n.* a dress with a hemline above the knee

Min·ié ball /mínnee-, mínnee ày-/ *n.* a bullet with a cone-shaped head and a hollow base that expands when fired, used in muzzle-loading rifles of the 19th century [Mid-19thC. Named for the French army officer Claude-Étienne *Minié* (1804–79), who invented it.]

min·i·fy /mínnə fì/ (**-fied, -fy·ing, -fies**) *vt.* to understate or reduce the size or importance of something [Late 17thC. Formed from Latin *minimus* "least" (see MINIMUM), on the model of MAGNIFY.] —**min·i·fi·ca·tion** /mìnnəfi káysh'n/ *n.*

min·i·kin /mínnikin/ *n.* TINY CREATURE a tiny or dainty creature (*archaic*) ■ *adj.* DELICATE small and delicate (*archaic*) [Mid-16thC. From Dutch *minneken* "darling," from *minne* "love."]

min·i·lab /mínni làb/ *n.* a business that does basic photographic developing and printing on site, often within an hour

min·im /mínnəm/ *n.* **1.** MEASURE UNIT OF FLUID MEASURE a unit of fluid measure equal to one sixtieth of a fluid dram, 0.0616 milliliters, or approximately one drop **2.** MUSIC = **half note 3.** PEN STROKE a downward vertical stroke of the pen in handwriting [15thC. Via medieval Latin *minimus* "least" from Latin (see MINIMUM).]

min·i·ma *n.* plural of **minimum**

min·i·mal /mínnəm'l/ *adj.* **1.** VERY SMALL very small in amount or extent **2.** SMALLEST POSSIBLE smallest possible in amount or least possible in extent **3. min·i·mal, Min·i·mal** RELATING TO MINIMALISM relating to or displaying attributes associated with minimalism [Mid-17thC. Formed from Latin *minimus* "least" (see MINIMUM).] —**min·i·mal·i·ty** /mìnnə mállətee/ *n.* — **min·i·mal·ly** /mínnəm'lee/ *adv.*

WORD KEY: USAGE

Extensions of meaning Strictly speaking, ***minimal*** means "the least possible," just as *minimize* means "to reduce to a minimum; to reduce to the least possible amount." Often, however, these words are not used strictly: *a minimal amount of noise* is unlikely to mean none at all but may simply be the least amount of noise conveniently possible to make. If the word is to retain any sense of being a superlative (like *least*), it should not be used with modifiers such as *rather, somewhat,* and *slightly. Small, limited, reduced,* and *as little as possible* are all suitable alternatives to overextending ***minimal***; and *diminish, lessen,* and *reduce* do the job that *minimize* is sometimes improperly asked to do.

min·i·mal art, Min·i·mal Art *n.* **1.** = **minimalism** *n.* 1 **2.** MINIMALIST ART WORKS minimalist works of art — **min·i·mal art·ist** *n.*

min·i·mal·ism /mínnəm'lìzzəm/ *n.* **1. min·i·mal·ism, Min·i·mal·ism** ARTISTIC MOVEMENT a movement of abstract artists who produce uncluttered paintings and sculptures that make use of basic colors and geometric shapes in impersonal arrangements. The movement originated in New York in the 1960s. **2.** SIMPLICITY OF STYLE simplicity in artwork, design, interior design, or literature, achieved by using a few very simple elements to maximum effect **3.** MUSIC MOVEMENT FOR SIMPLICITY IN MUSIC a trend in music toward simplicity of rhythm and tone, including sustained or repeated rhythmic and melodic patterns resulting in a hypnotic effect

min·i·mal·ist /mínnəm'list/ *n.* **1. min·i·mal·ist, Min·i·mal·ist** PRACTITIONER OF ARTISTIC MINIMALISM somebody whose works of art, literature, or music display the simplicity associated with minimalism **2.** ADVOCATE OF SMALLER ROLE FOR GOVERNMENT somebody who advocates restricting the power and goals of an organization, especially somebody who wishes to restrict government involvement in nongovernmental matters ■ *adj.* PROVIDING MINIMUM AMOUNT providing only the least amount that is needed [Early 20thC. Translation of Russian *men'shevik*.]

Min·i·mal·ist /mínnəməlist/ *n.* = **Menshevik** [Early 20thC. Translation of Russian *men'shevik*.]

min·i·mal·ize /mínnəm'l ìz/ (**-iz·ed, -iz·ing, -iz·es**) *vt.* to reduce something to the minimum — **min·i·mal·i·za·tion** /mìnnəm'li záysh'n/ *n.*

min·i·mal pair *n.* in linguistics, a pair of words or other linguistic expressions that are the same except for one sound, e.g., "bit" and "pit"

min·i·max /mínnə màks/ *n.* MATH LOWEST MAXIMUM the lowest of a set of maximum values ■ *adj.* DESIGNED TO MINIMIZE LOSS used to describe options or strategies designed to minimize the risk of sustaining maximum loss in any situation that involves conflict or competition. ◊ **game theory** [Mid-20thC. Coined from MINIMUM + MAXIMUM.]

min·i·mill /mínnee mil/ *n.* a small mill, especially a steel mill that processes scrap metal

min·i·mize /mínnə mìz/ (**-mized, -miz·ing, -miz·es**) *vt.* **1.** REDUCE SOMETHING TO MINIMUM to reduce something to the lowest possible amount or degree **2.** UNDERRATE SOMETHING to play down the extent or seriousness of something —**min·i·mi·za·tion** /mìnnəmi záysh'n/ *n.* — **min·i·miz·er** *n.*

WORD KEY: USAGE

See Usage note at ***minimal.***

min·i·mum /mínnəməm/ *n.* (*plural* **-mums** *or* **-ma** /mínnəmə/) **1.** LOWEST POSSIBLE DEGREE the lowest possible amount or degree of something **2.** LOWEST RECORDED DEGREE the lowest recorded amount or degree of something **3.** LOWEST PERMISSIBLE DEGREE the lowest amount or degree of something permitted by law, e.g., the lowest speed on a highway or the youngest age at which something can be done legally **4.** SUM THAT PATRON MUST SPEND an minimum amount of money that a restaurant or nightclub requires each patron to spend **5.** MATH LOWEST NUMBER the lowest number in a finite set **6.** MATH FUNCTION'S LOWEST VALUE the smallest value of a continuous function over a specific interval ■ *adj.* LOWEST ALLOWED lowest possible, recorded, or allowed [Mid-17thC. From Latin, from *minimus* "least." Ultimately from an Indo-European base denoting "small," which is also the ancestor of English *minor, minute, diminish,* and *minister.*]

min·i·mum-se·cu·ri·ty *adj.* with security measures appropriate to inmates or patients who are not considered dangerous or who are not likely to try to escape

min·i·mum wage *n.* **1.** LOWEST LEGAL RATE OF PAY the lowest rate of pay allowed by law or contract, either in general or for a certain type of work **2.** = **living wage**

min·i·mus /mínnəməss/ (*plural* **-mi**) *n.* a very small or insignificant person (*literary*) [Late 16thC. From Latin, "least" (see MINIMUM).]

min·ing /míning/ *n.* **1.** REMOVING MINERALS FROM EARTH the process or business of removing minerals from the earth (*often used before a noun*) **2.** ARMS LAYING EXPLOSIVES the process of laying explosive mines

min·ion /mínnyən/ *n.* **1.** ASSISTANT a servile or slavish follower of somebody generally regarded as important **2.** SERVANT a servant or enslaved person (*archaic or literary*) **3.** FAVORITE a favored person (*archaic*) [Early 16thC. From French *mignon* "darling" (see MIGNON).]

min·i·park /mínnee paàrk/ *n.* a small maintained grassy area or playground in an urban area

min·i·pill /mínnee pil/ *n.* an oral contraceptive that contains progesterone but not estrogen

min·i·se·ries /mínnee seèriz/ (*plural* **-ries**) *n.* a short series of television programs, often a serialized fictional story, usually airing on consecutive nights

min·i·ski /mínnee skeè/ *n.* a short snow ski for beginners or one that attaches to a vehicle used to travel over snow (**skibob**)

min·i·skirt /mínnee skùrt/ *n.* a skirt with a hemline well above the knee

min·i·state /mínnee stàyt/ *n.* a nation that is very small in terms both of geographical area and population

min·is·ter /mínnistər/ *n.* **1.** CHR MEMBER OF CLERGY a member of the clergy of a Christian, especially Protestant, Church **2.** CHR HEAD OF ROMAN CATHOLIC ORDER the superior in some orders in the Roman Catholic Church **3.** POL SENIOR OFFICER OF STATE a senior officer of state in a government department, especially in the parliamentary system of government **4.** RELIG DIPLOMAT RANKED UNDER AMBASSADOR a diplomat representing a country, especially in the rank below ambassador **5.** BUSINESS REPRESENTATIVE somebody's agent or representative (*formal or literary*) ■ *v.* (**-tered, -ter·ing, -ters**) **1.** *vi.* GIVE HELP to give help to somebody in need (*formal*) **2.** *vi.* CHR DO RELIGIOUS MINISTER'S WORK to perform the duties of a member of the clergy **3.** *vt.* GIVE SOMETHING to administer something, e.g., aid, medicine, or a sacrament (*archaic*) [13thC. Via Old French from Latin, "servant."] —**min·is·ter·ship** *n.*

min·is·te·ri·al /mìnni steèree əl/ *adj.* **1.** RELATING TO CLERGY relating to a religious minister **2.** RELATING TO GOVERNMENT MINISTER relating to a government minister or the minister's department **3.** LAW REQUIRING FOLLOWING OF INSTRUCTIONS allowing no personal discretion, only the strict following of law **4.** INSTRUMENTAL playing an important part in achieving something (*formal*) — **min·is·te·ri·al·ly** *adv.*

min·is·ter plen·i·po·ten·ti·ar·y (*plural* **min·is·ters plen·i·po·ten·ti·ar·y**) *n.* a diplomat who ranks below an ambassador but who has full power and authority to represent a government

min·is·ter res·i·dent (*plural* **min·is·ters res·i·dent**) *n.* a diplomat who is ranked below a minister plenipotentiary

min·is·ter with·out port·fo·li·o *n.* a senior officer of state who has no direct responsibility for a government department

min·is·trant /mínnistrənt/ *n.* **1.** RELIGIOUS MINISTER somebody serving as a religious minister (*formal*) **2.** AID GIVER somebody who gives aid to others (*literary*) ■ *adj.* HELPING giving aid or serving others (*archaic*) [Mid-16thC. From Latin *ministrant-*, the present participle stem of *ministrare* "to serve," from *minister* "servant" (see MINISTER).]

min·is·tra·tion /mìnni stráysh'n/ *n.* **1.** TREATMENT help, treatment, or service (*formal*) (*often used in the plural*) **2.** RELIGIOUS MINISTER'S WORK the service provided by a religious minister **3.** ACT OF SUPPLYING the supplying or administering of something (*archaic*) [14thC. From the Latin stem *ministration-*, from *ministrare* (see MINISTRANT).]

min·i·stroke /mínnee stròk/ *n.* a temporary blockage of blood circulation in some part of the brain, causing short-term stroke symptoms, e.g., dizziness, inability to speak or move, or loss of senses

min·is·try /mínnistree/ (*plural* **-tries**) *n.* **1.** CHR WORK OF RELIGIOUS MINISTER the profession and services of a religious minister **2.** CHR PERIOD OF SERVICE a religious minister's career or period of service **3.** CHR MINISTERS ministers collectively, especially religious ministers (*takes a singular or plural verb*) **4. min·is·try, Min·is·try** POL GOVERNMENT DEPARTMENT a government department headed by a minister **5.** POL PRIME MINISTER'S SERVICE the period of government under a prime minister **6.** POL GOVERNMENT BUILDING the building in which a government department is housed [14thC. Via Old French from Latin *ministerium*, from *minister* "servant" (see MINISTER).]

Min·i·track *tdmk.* a trademark for an electronic system that tracks artificial satellites by sending and receiving radio signals from ground stations

min·i·um /mínnee əm/ *n.* = **red lead** [Mid-17thC. From Latin.]

min·i·van /mínni vàn/ *n.* a small passenger van, often with seats that can be removed or rearranged to accommodate cargo

min·i·ver /mínnivər/ *n.* white or light gray fur used as trim on ceremonial costumes [Late 16thC. From Old French *menu vair* "small vair."]

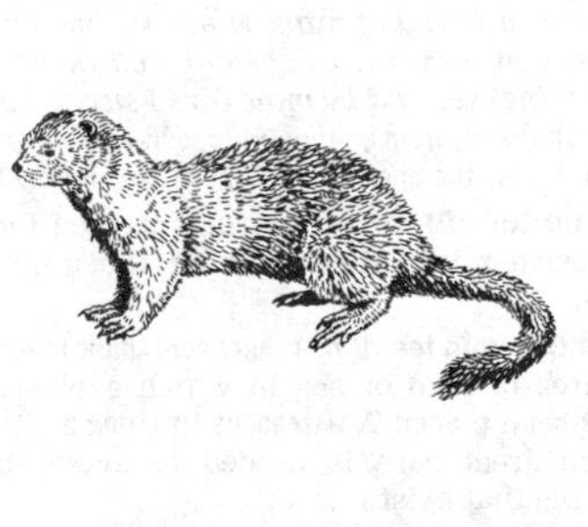

Mink

mink /mingk/ *n.* **1.** (*plural* **minks** *or* **mink**) WEB-TOED MEMBER OF WEASEL FAMILY either of two species of semiaquatic carnivorous members of the weasel family with webbed toes, a bushy tail, and thick dark brown fur. One is found in North America, the other in Europe. Genus: *Mustela.* **2.** MINK FUR the highly valued, thick, shiny brown fur of the mink (*often used before a noun*) **3. MINK FUR GARMENT** a coat, stole, or other garment made of mink fur [15thC. From Swedish.]

min·ke whale *n.* a small gray and white whale with a pointed snout. It is the smallest of the rorqual family, the family that includes the blue whale, and grows up to 30 ft./10 m long. Latin name: *Balaenoptera acutorostrata.* [Mid-20thC. *Minke* from Norwegian, of uncertain origin: possibly named for *Meincke*, a gunner on a 19th-century whaling crew.]

Minn. *abbr.* Minnesota

Min·na /mínnə/ city in west central Nigeria, the capital of Niger State, situated about 50 mi./80 km northwest of Abuja. Population: 134,000 (1995).

Min·ne·a·pol·is /minnee áppəliss/ the largest city in Minnesota, in the southeastern part of the state, close to St. Paul. Population: 368,383 (1990).

Min·ne·ha·ha Falls /minnə haáhaa-/ waterfall on Minnehaha Creek, southern Minnesota, celebrated in Henry Wadsworth Longfellow's *The Song of Hiawatha.* Height: 50 ft./15 m.

Min·nel·li /mi néllee/, **Liza** (*b.* 1946) U.S. stage and screen performer. Daughter of Judy Garland and Vincente Minnelli, she won an Academy Award for *Cabaret* (1972). Full name **Liza May Minnelli**

min·ne·o·la /minnee ṓlə/ *n.* an orange colored citrus fruit that is a cross between a tangerine and a grapefruit [Mid-20thC. Named for the town of *Minneola* in Florida, where it was developed.]

min·ne·sing·er /mínni singər, -zingər/ *n.* a German lyric poet and singer popular in the 12th to 14th centuries [Early 19thC. Via German from Middle High German, literally "love singer."]

Minnesota

Min·ne·so·ta[1] /minnə sṓtə/ state in the north central United States, bordered by Iowa, North Dakota, South Dakota, Wisconsin, the Manitoba and Ontario Provinces of Canada, and Lake Superior. Capital: St. Paul. Population: 4,685,549 (1997). Area: 84,397 sq. mi./218,588 sq. km. —**Min·ne·so·tan** /minni sṓt'n/ *adj., n.*

Min·ne·so·ta[2] river in southern Minnesota State, flowing from Big Stone Lake into the Mississippi River. Length: 332 mi./534 km.

Min·ne·so·ta Mul·ti·pha·sic Per·son·al·i·ty In·ven·to·ry *n.* a standardized test that uses true-false questions to assess somebody's psychological and social adjustment. It is widely used in recruitment and screening. [Named for the University of MINNESOTA, where it was developed]

min·now /mínnō/ *n.* **1. BAIT FISH** any small freshwater fish of the carp family, commonly used as fishing bait. Family: Cyprinidae. **2. SMALL FISH** any small silvery freshwater fish **3. INSIGNIFICANT PERSON OR THING** a person or organization of relatively low status or little importance [15thC. Origin uncertain: probably related to Old English *myne* "minnow" and perhaps influenced by French *menu* "small."]

Mi·no·an /mi nṓ ən/ *adj.* **RELATING TO ANCIENT CRETE** relating or belonging to the Bronze Age civilization that flourished on Crete from around 3000 to 1100 B.C. ■ *n.* **NATIVE OF ANCIENT CRETE** somebody who was born on or was a citizen of the island of Crete during ancient times, especially when the Minoan Bronze Age civilization flourished [Late 19thC. Named for *Minos*, legendary king of Crete associated with the great palace at Knossos.]

mi·nor /mínər/ *adj.* **1. SMALL** relatively small in quantity, size, or degree **2. LOW IN RANK** relatively low in rank or importance **3. LOW IN SEVERITY** relatively low in severity or danger **4.** MUSIC **DESCRIBING MUSICAL SCALE** used to describe a scale that has a semitone interval between the second and third, fifth and sixth, and sometimes seventh and eighth notes **5.** MUSIC **DESCRIBING MUSICAL INTERVAL** used to describe an interval that is a semitone less than a major interval **6.** MUSIC **DESCRIBING A KEY** used to describe a key that is based on a minor scale ○ *in B minor* **7.** LAW **NOT LEGALLY ADULT** younger than the legal age of adulthood **8.** EDUC **RELATING TO SECONDARY SPECIALIZATION** secondary to the major course of study ■ *n.* **1.** LAW **SOMEBODY NOT LEGALLY ADULT** somebody who has not reached the legal age of adulthood **2.** MUSIC **MUSICAL KEY OR HARMONY** a key or harmony based on a musical scale whose third and, usually, sixth and seventh notes are lower by a semitone than those in the major scale **3.** EDUC **SECONDARY SUBJECT** a second specialization in higher education that requires fewer courses than a major **4.** EDUC **SOMEBODY FOLLOWING MINOR COURSE** somebody who is following or has followed a particular course of study as a secondary specialization ■ *vi.* (**-nored, -nor·ing, -nors**) **STUDY AS SECONDARY SUBJECT** to have as a second specialization in higher education, in addition to a major specialization [13thC. From Latin, "lesser."]

mi·nor ax·is *n.* the shorter axis of an ellipse

Mi·nor·ca[1] /mi náwrkə/ Spanish island in the western Mediterranean Sea, the second largest of the Balearic Islands. Population: 66,900 (1989). Area: 271 sq. mi./702 sq. km. —**Mi·nor·can** /mi náwrkən/ *adj., n.*

Mi·nor·ca[2] /mi náwrkə/ *n.* a white and black domestic chicken from the Mediterranean region [Mid-19thC. Named for MINORCA.]

mi·nor el·e·ment *n.* = **trace element** *n.* 2

mi·nor·i·tar·i·an·ism /mi nàwrə táiree ə nìzzəm, mī-/ *n.* advocacy or political action on behalf of a minority

Mi·nor·ite /mínə rìt/ *n.* a friar of the Franciscan order [Mid-16thC. From *Minor Friars*, a translation of medieval Latin *Fratres Minores*, literally "lesser brethren," because the Franciscan order stressed the virtue of humility.]

mi·nor·i·ty /mi náwrətee, mī-/ *n.* (*plural* **-ties**) **1. SMALL GROUP** a group of people or things that is a small part of a much larger group **2. GROUP WITH INSUFFICIENT VOTES TO WIN** a group that has fewer votes in an organization than another group or groups **3. SMALLER SOCIALLY DEFINED GROUP** a group of people, within a society, whose members have different ethnic, racial, national, religious, sexual, political, linguistic, or other characteristics from the rest of society **4. OFFENSIVE TERM** offensive term for minority member, now avoided by careful speakers because it can cause offense (*offensive*) **5.** LAW **NONADULTHOOD** the state or period of being younger than the legal age of adulthood ■ *adj.* **OF A MINORITY** relating to or constituting a minority

mi·nor·i·ty lead·er *n.* the head of a minority party in a legislature

mi·nor key *n.* MUSIC a key based on a minor scale

mi·nor scale *n.* MUSIC a scale whose third and, usually, sixth and seventh notes are lower by a semitone than those in the major scale, giving it a less bright, more emotionally suggestive quality. ◊ **major scale**

mi·nor suit *n.* either clubs or diamonds, which in bridge and similar games are ranked below hearts and spades

Mi·nos /mín oss/ *n.* in Greek mythology, the son of Zeus and the king of Crete, who kept a monster (**Minotaur**) in a labyrinth

Mi·not /mí not/ city in northern North Dakota, west of Grand Forks and northwest of Bismarck. Population: 35,926 (1996).

Min·o·taur /mínnə tàwr, mínə-/ *n.* in Greek mythology, a monster with the body of a man and head of a bull that lived in the Cretan labyrinth and was fed human sacrifices until it was killed by Theseus

MINS /minz/ *abbr.* LAW minor in need of supervision

Minsk /minsk/ capital city of Belarus, situated in the north of the country. It is a major industrial city. Population: 1,700,000 (1996).

min·ster /mínstər/ *n.* a large or important cathedral or church, usually one originally connected with a monastery [Old English *mynster*, from, ultimately, late Latin *monasterium* (see MONASTERY)]

min·strel /mínstrəl/ *n.* **1. MEDIEVAL TRAVELING MUSICIAN** a medieval singer, musician, or reciter of poetry who traveled around from place to place giving performances **2. BLACKFACE ENTERTAINER IN VARIETY SHOW** one of a group of entertainers who wore blackface makeup and sang and performed in variety shows (*a form of entertainment now usually considered racist and highly offensive*) [13thC. Via Old French *menestral* "entertainer, handicraftsman" from, ultimately, late Latin *ministerialis* "official," from *ministerium* (see MINISTRY).]

min·strel·sy /mínstrəlsee/ (*plural* **-sies**) *n.* **1. MINSTREL'S ART** a minstrel's art or performance, or the profession of a minstrel **2. MINTSRELS' POEMS AND SONGS** the poems and songs written and performed by minstrels or by a particular minstrel **3. MINSTREL TROUPE** a troupe of medieval minstrels [14thC. From Old French *menestralsie*, from *menestrel* (see MINSTREL).]

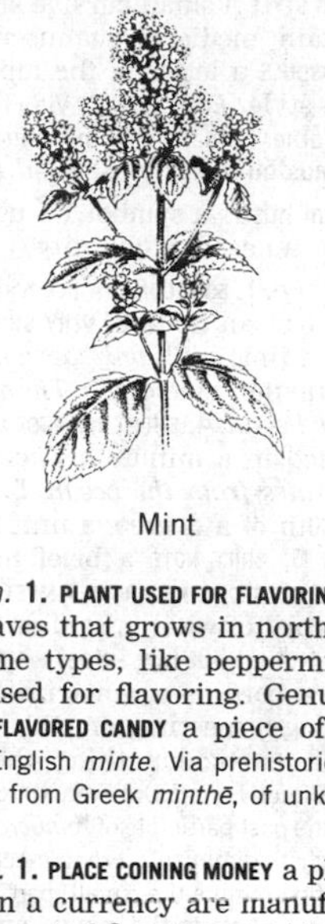
Mint

mint[1] /mint/ *n.* **1. PLANT USED FOR FLAVORING** a plant with aromatic leaves that grows in northern temperate regions. Some types, like peppermint and spearmint, are used for flavoring. Genus: *Mentha.* **2. PIECE OF MINT-FLAVORED CANDY** a piece of mint-flavored candy [Old English *minte*. Via prehistoric Germanic from Latin *mentha*, from Greek *minthē*, of unknown origin.] —**mint·y** *adj.*

mint[2] /mint/ *n.* **1. PLACE COINING MONEY** a place where the coins used in a currency are manufactured under government control **2. MUCH MONEY** a large amount of money (*informal*) ■ *vt.* (**mint·ed, mint·ing, mints**) **1. MAKE COINS** to make coins by stamping metal **2. INVENT** to create or invent something, especially a word or phrase, that is new ■ *adj.* **IN PERFECT CONDITION** in perfect condition as when first made [Old English *mynet*. Via prehistoric Germanic from Latin *moneta* "mint money" (see MONEY).] —**mint·er** *n.* ◇ **in mint condition** in perfect condition, as if brand-new

mint·age /míntij/ *n.* **1. MINTING COINS** the minting of coins **2. COINS FROM MINT** coins made in a mint, especially a quantity of coins minted at the same time **3. FEE FOR MINTING** a fee paid to a mint by a government for minting its coins

mint ju·lep *n.* a drink made by pouring liquor, usually bourbon, and sugar over crushed ice and flavoring or garnishing with mint

mint·mark /mínt maàrk/ *n.* a letter or symbol stamped on a coin that identifies the mint where it was made

min·u·end /mínnoo ènd/ *n.* the number from which another number (**subtrahend**) is to be subtracted [Early 18thC. From Latin *minuendus* "to be made smaller," from *minuere* "to diminish."]

min·u·et /minnoo ét/ *n.* **1. STATELY COURT DANCE** a slow stately court dance in triple time that originated in France in the 17th century **2. MUSIC FOR MINUET** a piece of music in slow triple time written for or in the style of a minuet, often forming part of a Baroque dance suite or classical sonata or symphony [Late 17thC. From French, noun use of *menuet* "small, dainty," from, ultimately, Latin *minutus* (source of English *minute*) from the steps taken in the dance.]

Min·u·it /mínnwit/, **Peter** (1580–1638) Dutch-born American colonial administrator. He founded the seaport of New Amsterdam on Manhattan Island, which eventually became New York City.

mi·nus /mínəss/ *prep.* **1.** MATH **LESS** reduced by the subtraction of a number ○ *Seven minus four is three.* **2. WITHOUT** lacking in or deprived of something ○ *Minus the tools, he cannot do the work required.* ■ *adj.* **1.** MATH **SHOWING SUBTRACTION** relating to or showing subtraction ○ *a minus sign* **2.** MATH **LESS THAN ZERO** relating to or showing a value less than zero ○ *Temperatures hovered near minus 20 degrees* ○ *a minus amount* **3. HAVING DETRIMENTAL EFFECT** having a negative or detrimental effect ○ *a minus factor in* *our assessment* **4.** SLIGHTLY BELOW STANDARD LEVEL used in grading or assessing something to show that it is slightly below the average standard indicated by a particular symbol ○ *a grade of C minus* ■ *n.* **1.** = **minus sign** ○ *The minus shows that it's a subtraction* **2.** NEGATIVE QUANTITY a quantity below zero ○ *If we take that away we're left with a minus.* **3.** DISADVANTAGE something that is detrimental or disadvantageous ○ *The power problem may prove to be a minus.* [15thC. From Latin, from *minor* "less" (source of English *minor*).]

min·us·cule /mínnə skyoōl/ *adj.* **1.** EXTREMELY SMALL extremely small or completely insignificant **2.** LOWERCASE lowercase, or printed in lowercase letters ■ *n.* **1.** PRINTING SMALL LETTER a lowercase letter **2.** PRINTING MEDIEVAL WRITING STYLE a small cursive style of writing used in certain medieval manuscripts **3.** LETTER WRITTEN IN MINUSCULE a letter of the alphabet written in minuscule style [Early 18thC. Via French from Latin *minusculus* "rather small," from *minus* "less" (see MINUS).] —**mi·nus·cu·lar** /mi núskyələr/ *adj.*

mi·nus sign, mi·nus *n.* a symbol, (-), used to indicate subtraction or a negative quantity

min·ute[1] /mínnit/ *n.* **1.** 60 SECONDS a period of 60 seconds, or a 60th part of an hour **2.** VERY SHORT TIME a very short period of time ○ *I'll only be gone a minute.* **3.** MOMENT a particular moment ○ *The minute we got there the show began.* **4.** SHORT DISTANCE a distance that can be traveled in a minute ○ *The villa is only a couple of minutes from the ocean.* **5.** UNIT OF ANGULAR MEASURE one 60th of a degree, a unit used in measuring angles **6.** BRIEF NOTE a brief note or memorandum ■ **min·utes** *npl.* RECORD OF A MEETING'S PROCEEDINGS an official record of what is said or done during a meeting ■ *vt.* **(-ut·ed, -ut·ing, -utes)** WRITE DOWN MEETING'S PROCEEDINGS to record or summarize officially what happens during a meeting, or make a note in the minutes of a particular thing that is said or done [14thC. Directly or via Old French from Latin *minuta*, from *minutus*, the past participle of *minuere* "to make small" (source of English diminish). From medieval Latin *pars minuta prima* "first minute (i.e. small) part," referring to one sixtieth of a unit.] ◇ **up to the minute** aware of, taking account of, or reporting the very latest developments

mi·nute[2] /mī noōt/ **(-nut·er, -nut·est)** *adj.* **1.** VERY SMALL extremely small in size or scope **2.** INSIGNIFICANT so very small as not to matter **3.** CONCERNED WITH EVERY DETAIL extremely or laboriously thorough and painstaking, and concerned with every detail [Early 17thC. From Latin *minutus* (see MINUTE[1]).] —**mi·nute·ness** *n.*

min·ute gun /mínnit-/ *n.* a gun fired every minute as a distress signal or sign of mourning

min·ute hand /mínnit-/ *n.* the longer pointer on a watch or clock that indicates the minutes

mi·nute·ly /mī noōtlee/ *adv.* **1.** IN GREAT DETAIL very thoroughly, carefully, and in great detail **2.** TO SMALL EXTENT to a very small extent **3.** INTO SOMETHING VERY SMALL into a very small shape or very small pieces

min·ute·man /mínnit màn/ (*plural* **-men** /-mèn/) *n.* an armed fighter in the Revolutionary War pledged to be ready to fight for the American Cause at a minute's notice

Min·ute·man (*plural* **-men**), **min·ute·man** (*plural* **-men**) *n.* an intercontinental ballistic missile of the United States armed forces

min·ute steak /mínnit stàyk/ *n.* a piece of steak sliced so thinly that it can be cooked very quickly

mi·nu·ti·ae /mī noōshee ee/ *npl.* small or trivial details [Mid-18thC. From Latin, literally "small things," from *minutus* (see MINUTE[1]).]

minx /mingks/ *n.* an offensive term that deliberately insults a woman's or girl's sense of propriety and decorous behavior (*offensive*) [Mid-16thC. Origin uncertain: perhaps from Middle Dutch *minnekijn* "darling."] —**minx·ish** *adj.*

Min·ya, Al- /mínyə/ city and trading center in the Nile valley, eastern Egypt. Population: 208,000 (1992).

min·yan /mínnyən, meen yaán/ (*plural* **-yan·im** /meen yaa neém, minnyə ním/ *or* **-yans**) *n.* the minimum number, ten, of adult Jewish men required to be present for an orthodox religious service [Mid-18thC. From Hebrew, "count, reckoning."]

Mi·o·cene /mí ə seèn/ *n.* the epoch of geologic time when the great mountain ranges of Europe, Asia, and the Americas were created and the mastodon first appeared, 23.3 to 5.2 million years ago. See table at **geology** [Mid-19thC. From Greek *meiōn* "less" + *kainos* "recent," from the remains of fewer modern species than in the PLIOCENE.] —**Mi·o·cene** *adj.*

mi·o·sis /mī óssiss/ (*plural* **-ses** /-ó seèz/), **my·o·sis** (*plural* **-ses**) *n.* a contraction of the pupil of the eye, caused e.g., by a reaction to a drug [Early 19thC. Coined from Greek *muein* "to shut the eyes" + -OSIS.] —**mi·ot·ic, my·ot·ic** /mī óttik/ *adj.*

Mi·łosz /meé losh, meé wosh/, **Czeslaw** (*b.* 1911) Lithuanian-born U.S. writer. He defected from communist Poland to the West in 1951, and wrote poetry, fiction, translations, and essays, often treating the relationship between culture, morality, and politics. He won the Nobel Prize in literature in 1980.

MIP *abbr.* **1.** marine insurance policy **2.** monthly investment plan

MIPS /mips/, **mips** *abbr.* COMPUT million instructions per second

Mi·que·lon Is·land ➧ **St Pierre and Miquelon**

mir /meer/ *n.* a peasant commune in czarist Russia [Late 19thC. From Russian.]

Popperfoto

Mir: Photographed from the space shuttle Atlantis (1997)

Mir *n.* a space station launched by the former Soviet Union in 1986, designed to be permanently crewed

mi·ra·bi·le dic·tu /mi raábilee dík toō/ *interj.* used to introduce the announcement of something the speaker, genuinely or ironically, considers to be amazing [From Latin, "amazing to relate," literally "amazing in the saying"]

mir·a·cid·i·um /mìrə síddee əm/ (*plural* **-a** /-síddee ə/) *n.* the free-swimming first-stage larva of a trematode worm that hatches from an egg and then reproduces asexually [Late 19thC. From modern Latin, from Greek *meirakidion* "little boy."] —**mir·a·cid·i·al** *adj.*

mir·a·cle /mírrək'l/ *n.* **1.** ACT OF GOD an event that appears to be contrary to the laws of nature and is regarded as an act of God **2.** AMAZING EVENT an event or action that is totally amazing, extraordinary, or unexpected ○ *It'll be a miracle if we get there on time.* **3.** MARVELOUS EXAMPLE OF SKILL something admired as a marvelous creation or example of a particular type of science or skill ○ *a miracle of modern engineering* [12thC. Via Old French from Latin *miraculum* "object of wonder," from *mirari* "to wonder at," from *mirus* "wonderful."]

mir·a·cle drug *n.* a drug, usually a new one, that is extraordinarily effective and seems to represent a breakthrough in the treatment of disease

mir·a·cle play *n.* a medieval play broadly depicting miracles taken from the life of a saint or a story from the Bible

mi·rac·u·lous /mi rákyələss/ *adj.* **1.** REGARDED AS CAUSED BY SUPERNATURAL INTERVENTION apparently contrary to the laws of nature and caused by a supernatural power **2.** EXTRAORDINARY totally unexpected, extraordinary, and marvellous **3.** ABLE TO PERFORM MIRACLES having the power to perform miracles [15thC. Directly or via French *miraculeux*, from, ultimately, medieval Latin *miraculum* (see MIRACLE).] —**mi·rac·u·lous·ly** *adv.* —**mi·rac·u·lous·ness** *n.*

mir·a·dor /meèrə dáwr/ *n.* a window, balcony, or turret designed to command a wide view [Late 17thC. From Spanish, from *mirar* "to look," from Latin *mirare* (see MIRAGE.]

Mi·ra·flo·res, Lake /meèrə fláwrayz/ lake in Panama, through which the Panama Canal passes

mi·rage /mi raázh/ *n.* **1.** OPTICAL ILLUSION an optical illusion of a sheet of water appearing in the desert or on a hot road, caused by light being distorted by alternate layers of hot and cool air **2.** SOMETHING ILLUSORY something that is unreal or merely imagined [Early 19thC. From French, from *mirer* "to look at," from Latin *mirare* "to wonder at," variant of *mirari* (see MIRACLE.]

Mir·a·mar /mírrə maàr/ city in southeastern Florida, in Broward County, near the Atlantic Ocean. Population: 47,985 (1994).

Mi·ran·da /mə ránndə/ *n.* one of the satellites of Uranus

Barnaby's

Carmen Miranda

Mi·ran·da /mi rándə/, **Carmen** (1909–55) Portuguese dancer and singer. Star of Brazilian and Hollywood musicals, she is remembered particularly for her elaborate costumes and head-dresses made from tropical fruit. Born **Carmo Miranda da Cunha**

Mi·ran·da rights *npl.* the rights of a person being arrested to remain silent, in order to avoid self-incrimination, and to have an attorney present during questioning [Late 20thC. Named for Ernesto A. *Miranda*, plaintiff in the case that led to the ruling.]

Mi·ran·dize /mə rán dìz/ **(-dized, -diz·ing, -diz·es)** *vt.* to inform formally a person being arrested of the rights to remain silent and to have an attorney (*informal*)

mire /mīr/ *n.* **1.** THICK MUD thick slimy mud **2.** BOG an area of very marshy ground or deep slushy mud **3.** DIFFICULT SITUATION a troublesome or oppressive situation or state that is very difficult to escape from ■ *v.* **(mired, mir·ing, mires) 1.** *vti.* GET SOMETHING STUCK IN MUD to sink into mud, or make something sink into mud, and become stuck **2.** *vt.* MAKE MUDDY to make something muddy or dirty **3.** *vt.* ENTANGLE to involve or entangle somebody or something in difficulties [13thC. From Old Norse *myrr* "bog."] —**mir·i·ness** *n.* —**mir·y** *adj.*

mi·rex /mī rèks/ *n.* an insecticide used especially to kill ants. Formula: $C_{10}Cl_{12}$. [Mid-20thC. Origin uncertain: perhaps a blend of PISMIRE and EXTERMINATE.]

Mi·ró /meérō, mee rṓ/, **Joan** (1893–1983) Spanish painter, sculptor, and printmaker. A leading surrealist, he developed a form of abstraction, that produced his dreamlike, ethereal compositions.

mir·ror /mírrər/ *n.* **1.** HIGHLY REFLECTIVE SURFACE a surface such as glass or polished metal that reflects light without diffusing it so that it will give back a clear image of anything placed in front of it **2.** GLASS FOR REFLECTING AN IMAGE a piece of reflective material, especially glass coated on one side with metal, mounted in a frame for use, e.g., in the home or a vehicle **3.** SOMETHING ACCURATELY REPRODUCING SOMETHING ELSE something that accurately reproduces, describes, or conveys something else **4.** EXAMPLE TO OTHERS something or somebody that serves as an example to others (*archaic*) ■ *vt.* **(-rored, -ror·ing, -rors) 1.** REFLECT IN SURFACE to reflect something clearly in a surface (*often passive*) ○ *The mountains were mirrored in the lake.* **2.** BE SIMILAR TO to be very similar to or correspond closely with something else, or to reproduce it accurately ○ *These developments are now mirrored on the other side of the world.* [13thC. From Old French *mirour*, from, ultimately, an assumed Vulgar Latin form of Latin *mirari* "to wonder at" (see MIRACLE.]

mir·ror carp *n.* a carp with very small scales that give its body a smooth shiny appearance. Latin name: *Cyprinus carpio*.

mir·ror im·age *n.* something that, like a reflection in a mirror, is identical to something else but reversed

mirth /murth/ *n.* happiness or enjoyment, especially accompanied by laughter [Old English *myrgzz*. Ultimately from a prehistoric Germanic word meaning "pleasant, joyful," which is also the ancestor of English *merry*.]

mirth·ful /múrthfəl/ *adj.* full of gaiety, laughter, or amusing things —**mirth·ful·ly** *adv.* —**mirth·ful·ness** *n.*

mirth·less /múrthləss/ *adj.* without, or not expressing, amusement, good humor, or gladness —**mirth·less·ly** *adv.* —**mirth·less·ness** *n.*

MIRV /murv/ *abbr.* multiple independently targeted re-entry vehicle

Mir·za /meerzə/ *n.* an Iranian title of respect signifying a learned man or official when placed before a name, or formerly a royal prince when placed after a name [Early 17thC. From Persian.]

MIS *abbr.* COMPUT management information system

mis- *prefix.* **1.** badly, wrongly ○ *mishandle* **2.** bad, wrong ○ *misdeed* **3.** opposite, lack, failure ○ *mislike* [Partly Old English, and partly via Old French *mes-* from a prehistoric Germanic word meaning "to go wrong," which is also the ancestor of English *miss* and *amiss*]

mis·ad·dress /missə dréss/ (**-dressed, -dress·ing, -dress·es**) *vt.* to put an incorrect address on an item of mail

mis·ad·ven·ture /missəd vénchər/ *n.* an unfortunate event, especially something untoward, unlucky, or amusing that happens to somebody [13thC. From Old French *mesaventure*, from *mesavenir* "to turn out badly," from *avenir* "to happen," from Latin *advenire* "to come to."]

mis·al·li·ance /missə lí əns/ *n.* an unsuitable alliance, especially a marriage between mismatched partners

mis·an·dry /mí sàndree/ *n.* hatred of men as a sexually defined group [Early 20thC. Coined from the Greek stem *andr-* "man" on the model of MISOGYNY.] —**mis·an·drist** *n.* —**mis·an·drous** *adj.*

mis·an·thrope /míss'n thrṑp/, **mis·an·thro·pist** /mi sánthrəpist/ *n.* somebody who hates humankind in general, or dislikes and distrusts other people and tends to avoid their company [Mid-16thC. Via French from Greek *misanthrōpos*, from MISEIN "to hate" + *anthrōpos* "man."] —**mis·an·throp·ic** /miss'n thróppik/ *adj.* —**mis·an·throp·i·cal·ly** /-klee/ *adv.* —**mis·an·thro·py** /mi sánthrəpee/ *n.*

mis·ap·pre·hend /miss àppri hénd/ (**-hend·ed, -hend·ing, -hends**) *vt.* to fail to understand (*formal*)

mis·ap·pre·hen·sion /miss àppri hénshən/ *n.* a false impression or incorrect understanding, especially of the nature of a situation or the intentions of somebody —**mis·ap·pre·hen·sive** *adj.* —**mis·ap·pre·hen·sive·ly** *adv.* —**mis·ap·pre·hen·sive·ness** *n.*

mis·ap·pro·pri·ate /missə prṓpree àyt/ (**-at·ed, -at·ing, -ates**) *vt.* to take something, especially money, dishonestly, or in order to use it for an improper or illegal purpose —**mis·ap·pro·pri·a·tion** /missə prṓpree áysh'n/ *n.*

WORD KEY: SYNONYMS

See Synonyms at ***steal***.

mis·be·come /missbi kúm/ (**-com·ing**) *vt.* to be unsuitable for or detrimental to somebody, or unfitting for an event or occasion (*formal*)

mis·be·got·ten /missbi gótt'n/ *adj.* **1.** ILL-CONCEIVED AND GENERALLY BAD from a bad source, badly planned, badly thought out, or generally deplorable from start to finish **2.** DISHONESTLY OBTAINED obtained by dishonest means **3.** ILLEGITIMATE born to parents who are not married to each other

mis·be·have /missbi háyv/ (**-haved, -hav·ing, -haves**) *vi.* **1.** BE NAUGHTY AND TROUBLESOME to be naughty and troublesome, or otherwise behave in an unacceptable way **2.** NOT FUNCTION PROPERLY to function badly or not at all, or to cause problems (*informal*) —**mis·be·hav·er** *n.*

mis·be·hav·ior /missbi háyvyər/ *n.* unacceptable behavior, especially naughtiness, disobedience, or troublesomeness on the part of children

mis·be·hav·iour *n. U.K.* = **misbehavior**

mis·be·lief /missbi léef/ *n.* a belief that is or is considered to be false or unorthodox

mis·be·lieve /missbi léev/ (**-lieved, -liev·ing, -lieves**) *vi.* to hold beliefs that are or are considered to be false or unorthodox, especially on religious matters (*disapproving*) —**mis·be·liev·er** *n.*

mis·brand /miss bránd/ (**-brand·ed, -brand·ing, -brands**) *vt.* to falsely label a product

misc. *abbr.* **1.** miscellaneous **2.** miscellany

mis·cal·cu·late /miss kálkyə làyt/ (**-lat·ed, -lat·ing, -lates**) *vti.* **1.** CALCULATE WRONGLY to calculate something incorrectly **2.** MAKE WRONG ASSESSMENT to judge or assess something incorrectly, or form false expectations as to the consequences of an action —**mis·cal·cu·la·tion** /miss kàlkyə láysh'n/ *n.* —**mis·cal·cu·la·tor** /miss kálkyə làytər/ *n.*

mis·call /miss kól/ (**-called, -call·ing, -calls**) *vt.* to use the wrong or an inappropriate name for somebody or something —**mis·call·er** *n.*

mis·car·riage /miss kérrij/ *n.* **1.** PREMATURE EXPULSION OF FETUS an involuntary ending of a pregnancy through the discharge of the fetus from the womb at too early a stage in its development for it to survive. Technical name **abortion 2.** FAILURE OF UNDERTAKING the mishandling or failure of something, such as a plan or project (*formal*)

mis·car·riage of jus·tice *n.* a failure of the legal system to come to a just decision

mis·car·ry /miss kérree/ (**-ried, -ry·ing, -ries**) *vi.* **1.** HAVE SPONTANEOUS ABORTION to lose a fetus, especially a human fetus, through a miscarriage **2.** BE SPONTANEOUSLY ABORTED to be expelled from the womb at too early a stage in development to be able to survive **3.** FAIL to result in failure (*formal*)

mis·cast /miss kást/ (**-cast, -cast·ing, -casts**) *vt.* (*often passive*) **1.** GIVE ACTOR UNSUITABLE PART to choose somebody to play a stage or movie part to which he or she is unsuited **2.** CHOOSE WRONG ACTORS FOR to choose unsuitable actors for the roles in a play or movie, or an unsuitable actor for a particular role

mis·ceg·e·na·tion /missijə náysh'n/ *n.* (*offensive when used disapprovingly, as often formerly*) **1.** SEXUAL RELATIONS BETWEEN RACES sexual relations between people of different races, especially of different skin colors, leading to the birth of children **2.** INTERMARRIAGE BETWEEN RACES marriage or cohabitation between people of different races [Mid-19thC. Coined from Latin *miscere* "to mix" + *genus* "race" + -ATION.] —**mis·ceg·e·na·tion·al** *adj.*

mis·cel·la·ne·a /missə láynee ə/ *npl.* miscellaneous things, especially pieces of writing, brought together as a collection [Late 16thC. From Latin, from *miscellaneus* (see MISCELLANEOUS).]

mis·cel·la·ne·ous /missə láynee əss/ *adj.* **1.** COMPOSED OF VARIED THINGS made up of many different things or kinds of things that have no necessary connection with each other **2.** EACH BEING DIFFERENT each being different or having different abilities or qualities from the others ○ *a taskforce of miscellaneous specialists* [Early 17thC. From Latin *miscellaneus*, from, ultimately, *miscere* "to mix" (source of English *mix*).] —**mis·cel·la·ne·ous·ly** *adv.* —**mis·cel·la·ne·ous·ness** *n.*

mis·cel·la·nist /missə láynist/ *n.* somebody who compiles or writes miscellanies

mis·cel·la·ny /míssə làynee/ (*plural* **-nies**) *n.* **1.** MISCELLANEOUS COLLECTION a miscellaneous collection of things **2.** COLLECTED MISCELLANEOUS WRITINGS a collection of miscellaneous pieces of writing in one volume, often by different authors on various subjects and in different genres [Late 16thC. Via French *miscellanées* from Latin *miscellanea* MISCELLANEA.]

mis·chance /miss chánss/ *n.* **1.** MISFORTUNE the occurrence of unfortunate events by chance **2.** PIECE OF BAD LUCK something that happens through bad luck [14thC. From Old French *mescheance* (see CHANCE).]

mis·chief /mísschif/ *n.* **1.** NAUGHTY BEHAVIOR behavior, especially by children, that is undesirable or troublesome without being malicious **2.** TENDENCY TO NAUGHTY BEHAVIOR a tendency to mildly troublesome or undesirable behavior such as teasing or practical jokes **3.** INJURY OR DAMAGE injury or damage caused by the actions of somebody or something **4.** HARMLESS TROUBLEMAKER somebody who causes or enjoys causing harmless trouble **5.** SOURCE OF HARM OR TROUBLE something or somebody that causes serious harm or trouble to somebody [13thC. From Old French *meschef*, from *meschever* "to meet with misfortune," from *chever* "to come to an end," from *chef* "head."]

mis·chief-mak·er *n.* somebody who deliberately causes trouble and sets people against each other, especially by spreading malicious gossip

mis·chie·vous /mísschivəss/ *adj.* **1.** PLAYFULLY NAUGHTY OR TROUBLESOME behaving or likely to behave in a naughty or troublesome way, but in fun and not meaning serious harm **2.** TROUBLESOME OR IRRITATING intended to tease or cause trouble, though usually in fun or without much malice **3.** FULL OF MISCHIEF expressing somebody's intention or inclination to have fun by teasing, playing tricks, or causing trouble **4.** DAMAGING causing or meant to cause serious trouble, damage, or hurt (*formal*) —**mis·chie·vous·ly** *adv.* —**mis·chie·vous·ness** *n.*

WORD KEY: SYNONYMS

See Synonyms at ***bad***.

misch met·al /mísh-/ *n.* an alloy of cerium and rare earth metals used, e.g.,, in the flints of cigarette lighters [Early 20thC. From German *Mischmetall*, literally "mix-metal."]

mis·ci·ble /míssəb'l/ *adj.* used to describe two or more liquids that can be mixed together [Late 16thC. From medieval Latin *miscibilis*, from Latin *miscere* "to mix" (source of English MIX).]

mis·com·mu·ni·ca·tion /misskə myoōni káysh'n/ *n.* **1.** FAILURE TO COMMUNICATE SOMETHING CLEARLY failure to communicate something clearly or correctly **2.** UNCLEAR COMMUNICATION a communication that is unclear or likely to be misinterpreted

mis·con·ceive /misskən séev/ (**-ceived, -ceiv·ing, -ceives**) *vt.* to fail to understand something correctly, or to form a false conception of something

mis·con·ceived /misskən séevd/ *adj.* resulting from a wrong or faulty understanding or idea of something and consequently doomed to failure

mis·con·cep·tion /misskən sépshən/ *n.* a mistaken idea or view resulting from a misunderstanding of something

mis·con·duct *n.* /miss kón dùkt/ **1.** IMMORAL, UNETHICAL, OR UNPROFESSIONAL BEHAVIOR behavior that is not in accordance with accepted moral or professional standards (*disapproving*) **2.** INCOMPETENCE incompetent or dishonest management of something, especially on behalf of others ■ *v.* /misskən dúkt/ (**-duct·ed, -duct·ing, -ducts**) **1.** *vr.* ACT IMMORALLY to act in an immoral or improper way **2.** *vt.* MANAGE INCOMPETENTLY to manage something in an incompetent or dishonest way ○ *guilty of misconducting the whole affair*

mis·con·struc·tion /misskən strúkshən/ *n.* GRAM **1.** FAULTY UNDERSTANDING a faulty understanding or interpretation of something **2.** FAULTY GRAMMAR a faulty grammatical construction

mis·con·strue /misskən stroō/ (**-strued, -stru·ing, -strues**) *vt.* to understand or interpret something incorrectly

mis·count /miss kównt/ *vti.* (**-count·ed, -count·ing, -counts**) COUNT INCORRECTLY to make a mistake when counting something ■ *n.* INCORRECT COUNT an incorrect count or calculation

mis·cre·ant /mísskree ənt/ *n.* **1.** SOMEBODY WHO DOES WRONG a villain, wrongdoer, or generally malicious and contemptible person (*literary*) **2.** INFIDEL an infidel or heretic (*archaic insult*) [13thC. From Old French, present participle of *mescroire* "to disbelieve," from, ultimately, Latin *credere* "to believe" (source of English *creed*).]

mis·cue /miss kyoō/ *n.* **1.** CUE GAMES **FAULTY SHOT IN BILLIARDS** in billiards, a shot that fails because the cue does not strike the cue ball properly **2.** MISTAKE a mistake, especially one that involves giving somebody the wrong cue to say or begin something or giving a cue at the wrong time (*informal*) ■ *v.* (**-cued, -cu·ing, -cues**) **1.** *vti.* CUE GAMES MAKE FAULTY SHOT in billiards, to fail to strike the cue ball properly, or to play a miscue **2.** *vti.* MISS A CUE to fail to respond to a cue, to give the wrong cue for something, or to give a cue at the wrong time **3.** *vi.* ERR to make a mistake (*informal*)

mis·deal /miss déel/ *vti.* (**-dealt, -deal·ing, -deals**) DEAL CARDS WRONGLY to deal playing cards incorrectly ■ *n.* MISTAKE IN DEALING CARDS a mistake in the way playing cards are dealt, or an incorrectly dealt hand —**mis·deal·er** *n.*

mis·deed /miss déed/ *n.* a wicked, blameworthy, or unlawful act (*formal*)

mis·de·mean·ant /missdi méenənt/ *n.* LAW somebody convicted of a misdemeanor

mis·de·mean·or /mìssdi meénər/ *n.* **1.** LESS SERIOUS CRIME a crime less serious than a felony and resulting in a less severe punishment **2.** MINOR MISDEED a relatively minor misdeed

mis·de·mean·our *n.* U.K. = **misdemeanor**

mis·di·al (**-aled, -al·ing, -als**) *vti.* /miss dí əl/ to dial a telephone number incorrectly —**mis·di·al** /míss dī əl/ *n.*

mis·di·rect /mìssdi rékt/ (**-rect·ed, -rect·ing, -rects**) *vt.* **1.** GIVE WRONG DIRECTIONS to give somebody wrong directions or instructions **2.** WRONGLY ADDRESS MAIL to put a wrong address on an item of mail **3.** AIM INACCURATELY to aim something, e.g., a punch or bullet, inaccurately, or direct something, e.g., a comment or insult, at the wrong person

mis·doubt /miss dówt/ (**-doubt·ed, -doubt·ing, -doubts**) *vt.* to doubt or suspect somebody or something (*archaic*)

mise en scène /meéz aaN sén/ (*plural* **mises en scène**) *n.* **1.** CINEMA, THEATER ARRANGEMENT OF ACTORS, SCENERY, ETC the positioning of actors, scenery, and properties on a stage or movie set for a particular scene or particular production **2.** SETTING FOR SOMETHING the physical environment in which an event takes place [From French, literally "putting on stage"]

mi·ser /mízər/ *n.* (*disapproving*) **1.** SOMEBODY WHO HOARDS MONEY somebody who hoards money, hates spending it, and as a result, though rich, lives as if he or she were poor **2.** UNGENEROUS OR SELFISH PERSON somebody who is mean and ungenerous, or selfish and greedy [Mid-16thC. From Latin, "unfortunate."]

mis·er·a·ble /mízzərəb'l/ *adj.* **1.** VERY UNHAPPY experiencing a serious lack of contentment or happiness ○ *feeling a bit miserable* **2.** VERY UNPLEASANT causing or accompanied by discomfort, unpleasantness, or unhappiness **3.** CONTEMPTIBLE deserving contempt or condemnation **4.** INADEQUATE inadequate, often insultingly or embarrassingly inadequate, in quantity or quality **5.** DIRTY OR SQUALID dirty, squalid, and lacking any comfort [15thC. Via Old French from Latin *miserabilis* "pitiable," from, ultimately, *miser* "unfortunate."] —**mis·er·a·ble·ness** *n.* —**mis·er·a·bly** *adv.*

WORD KEY: CULTURAL NOTE

Les Misérables, a novel by French writer Victor Hugo (1862). Set in mid-19th century France, it tells the story of Jean Valjean, whose attempts to lead escape his criminal past are dogged by guilt, fate, and persistent police inspector Javert. This epic tale is noted for its gripping plot and vivid descriptions of contemporary events such as the battle of Waterloo. The noun *javert*, meaning a persistent, bloodhound-like pursuing detective or prosecutor, derives directly from the name of the detective in this novel. The novel was successfully adapted as a stage musical.

mi·sère /mi záir/ *n.* **1.** CALL IN SOLO WHIST a call in certain card games, especially solo whist, indicating that a hand is expected to win no tricks **2.** HAND WINNING NO TRICKS a hand that is expected to win no tricks [Early 19thC. From French, literally "poverty, misery."]

mis·e·re·re /mìzzə ráiree, mìzzə reéree/ *n.* = **misericord** [Late 18thC. From Latin, "have mercy!", from *misereri* "to have mercy," from *miser* "unfortunate."]

Mis·e·re·re /mìzzə ráiree, mìzzə reéree/ *n.* **1.** BIBLE 50TH OR 51ST PSALM the 50th or 51st Psalm, depending on the version of the Bible **2.** MUSIC MUSICAL MISERERE a musical setting of the Miserere [13thC. From the first word of the Latin text, beginning MISERERE MEI, DEUS "have mercy on me, O God" (see MISERERE.]

mis·er·i·cord /mízzəri kàwrd, mi zérri kàwrd/ *n.* a projecting ledge often with elaborate carving on the underside of a seat in a church stall that, when the seat is turned up, gives a standing person something to rest against [14thC. Via Old French from, ultimately, Latin *misericors* "merciful, compassionate," from *miser* "unfortunate" + *cor* "heart."]

mi·ser·ly /mízərlee/ *adj.* **1.** AVARICIOUS greedy for money and unwilling to share or to spend it **2.** EXTREMELY SMALL so small as to be insufficient or inadequate —**mi·ser·li·ness** *n.*

mis·er·y /mízzəree/ (*plural* **-ies**) *n.* **1.** GREAT UNHAPPINESS a serious lack of contentment or happiness **2.** SOURCE OF GREAT UNHAPPINESS something that causes great unhappiness **3.** POVERTY a state of extreme poverty and squalor [14thC. Directly or via Anglo-Norman *miserie*, from Latin *miseria*, from Latin *miser* "unfortunate."] ◇ **put somebody out of his** *or* **her misery** to put an end to somebody's suspense or anxiety, especially by revealing something that he or she is desperate to know (*humorous*) ◇ **put something out of its misery** to kill an animal in order to prevent it suffering further pain

mis·fea·sance /miss feéz'ns/ *n.* LAW acting improperly or illegally in performing an action that is in itself lawful. ◊ **malfeasance, nonfeasance** [Early 17thC. From Anglo-Norman *mesfaisance*, from *mesfaire* "to misdo," from *mes-* "wrongly" + *faire* "to do," from Latin *facere.*] —**mis·fea·sor** *n.*

mis·fire *vi.* /miss fír/ (**-fired, -fir·ing, -fires**) **1.** NOT FIRE PROPERLY to fail to shoot a bullet or shell when fired **2.** FAIL TO OPERATE PROPERLY to fail to ignite the fuel mixture in the cylinder or to ignite it at the wrong time (*refers to an internal-combustion engine*) **3.** GO WRONG to fail to achieve a planned result ○ *the plot misfired* ■ *n.* /míss fìr, miss fír/ MALFUNCTION IN FIRING a failure to fire or function properly

mis·fit *n.* /míss fit/ **1.** SOMEBODY WHO DOES NOT BELONG somebody who is out of place in a particular situation or environment **2.** SOMETHING ILL-FITTING something that does not fit properly

mis·for·tune /miss fáwrchən/ *n.* **1.** ILL LUCK bad luck **2.** UNHAPPY EVENT an undesirable or unhappy event or circumstance

mis·give /miss gív/ (**-gave** /-gáyv/, **-giv·en** /miss gívvən/, **-giv·ing, -gives**) *vt.* to feel apprehensive, or to cause a feeling of apprehension or foreboding in somebody (*literary*) [Early 16thC. Formed from GIVE in the obsolete sense "to suggest."]

mis·giv·ing /miss gívving/ *n.* a feeling of doubt or apprehension, especially about undertaking a course of action (*often used in the plural*) ○ *I had misgivings about the plan from the beginning.*

mis·guide /miss gíd/ (**-guid·ed, -guid·ing, -guides**) *vt.* to lead somebody in a wrong direction or into making a mistake —**mis·guid·ance** *n.* —**mis·guid·er** *n.*

mis·guid·ed /miss gídəd/ *adj.* motivated by or based on ideas that are mistaken, heedless, or inappropriate (*disapproving*) —**mis·guid·ed·ly** *adv.* —**mis·guid·ed·ness** *n.*

mis·han·dle /miss hánd'l/ (**-dled, -dling, -dles**) *vt.* **1.** DEAL WITH INCOMPETENTLY to deal with something or somebody in an incompetent or ineffective way **2.** TREAT ROUGHLY to treat something or somebody roughly

mis·hap /míss hàp/ *n.* **1.** ACCIDENT an unfortunate accident or piece of bad luck **2.** BAD LUCK an unfortunate circumstance or set of circumstances (*formal*)

mis·hear /miss heér/ (**-heard** /-húrd/, **-hear·ing, -hears**) *vti.* to fail to hear somebody or something correctly

Mi·shi·ma /míshimə/, **Yukio** (1925–70) Japanese novelist. He celebrated Japan's nationalist and imperialist history, deploring the sterility of contemporary life, and committed ritual suicide. His novels include the tetralogy *The Sea of Fertility* (1965–70). Pseudonym of **Hiraoka Kimitake**

mis·hit (**-hit, -hit·ting, -hits**) *vt.* /miss hít/ to hit something badly, e.g., a ball or puck, so that it does not go in the desired direction or has insufficient force behind it —**mis·hit** *n.*

mish·mash /mísh màsh/ *n.* a disorderly collection or confused mixture of things [15thC. Formed from the repetition of MASH.]

Mish·mi /míshmee/ (*plural* **-mi** *or* **-mis**) *n.* **1.** MEMBER OF PEOPLE IN ASSAM a member of a people living in a mountainous region of Assam in northeast India **2.** MISHMI LANGUAGE the Tibeto-Burman language spoken by the Mishmi people —**Mish·mi** *adj.*

Mish·nah /míshnə/, **Mish·na** *n.* **1.** JEWISH LAW the primary body of Jewish civil and religious law, forming the first part of the Talmud. These laws were handed down orally until written down around A.D. 200. **2.** JEWISH ORAL LAW Jewish law from the oral tradition, as distinguished from law derived from the scriptures **3.** JEWISH LEGAL TEACHING the teaching of an authority on Jewish law [Early 17thC. From Hebrew *mišnāh* "repetition, teaching."] —**Mish·na·ic** *adj.*

mis·in·form /mìssin fáwrm/ (**-formed, -form·ing, -forms**) *vt.* to give incorrect information to somebody —**mis·in·form·ant** *n.* —**mis·in·form·er** *n.* —**mis·in·for·ma·tion** *n.*

mis·in·ter·pret /mìssin túrprət/ (**-pret·ed, -pret·ing, -prets**) *vt.* to understand or explain the meaning of something incorrectly —**mis·in·ter·pret·er** *n.*

mis·join·der /miss jóyndər/ *n.* an improper combining of plaintiffs, defendants, or causes of action in a single lawsuit

mis·judge /miss júj/ (**-judged, -judg·ing, -judg·es**) *v.* **1.** *vti.* MAKE A BAD JUDGMENT to make a mistake when judging or assessing something, or when attempting to do something that requires accurate judgment **2.** *vt.* FORM INCORRECT OPINION to form an incorrect opinion about somebody or something, especially to attribute bad qualities to somebody unjustly or mistakenly —**mis·judg·er** *n.* —**mis·judg·ment** *n.*

Mis·ki·to /mi skeétō/ (*plural* **-to** *or* **-tos**) *n.* **1.** MEMBER OF NATIVE CENTRAL AMERICAN PEOPLE a member of a Native Central American people living along the Caribbean coasts of Nicaragua and Honduras **2.** MISKITO LANGUAGE the language of the Miskito people [Late 18thC. From *miskito.*] —**Mis·ki·to** *adj.*

Mis·kolc /mísh koolts/ historic and industrial city in northeastern Hungary. Population: 182,000 (1995).

mis·lay /miss láy/ (**-laid, -laid** /-láyd/, **-lay·ing, -lays**) *vt.* to lose something temporarily, especially by forgetting where it was put —**mis·lay·er** *n.*

mis·lead /miss leéd/ (**-led** /miss léd/, **-lead·ing, -leads**) *vt.* **1.** INFORM FALSELY to cause somebody to make a mistake or form a false opinion or belief, either by employing deliberate deception or by supplying incorrect information ○ *The defendant is trying to mislead the jury.* **2.** LEAD INTO BAD ACTIONS to be responsible for making somebody, especially somebody younger, do wrong or adopt bad habits **3.** LEAD IN WRONG DIRECTION to lead somebody in a wrong direction —**mis·lead·er** *n.*

mis·lead·ing /miss leéding/ *adj.* likely or deliberately intended to confuse people or give them a false idea of something —**mis·lead·ing·ly** *adv.*

mis·led /miss léd/ past participle, past tense of **mislead**

mis·like /miss lík/ (**-liked, -lik·ing, -likes**) *vt.* (*archaic*) **1.** DISLIKE to dislike somebody or something **2.** DISPLEASE to displease somebody

mis·man·age /miss mánnij/ (**-aged, -ag·ing, -ag·es**) *vt.* to run, organize, or deal with something incompetently —**mis·man·age·ment** *n.*

mis·match *n.* /míss màch/ UNLIKELY OR ILL-SUITED PAIR a pairing or combination of people or things that are incompatible with or apparently ill-suited to each other ■ *vt.* /miss mách/ (**-matched, -match·ing, -match·es**) FAIL TO MATCH WELL to fail to match or pair suitably (*usually passive*) ○ *They'd been mismatched from the start.*

mis·no·mer /miss nōmər/ *n.* **1.** UNSUITABLE NAME a wrong or unsuitable name or term for something or somebody **2.** CALLING SOMETHING BY A WRONG NAME a use of a wrong or unsuitable name or term to describe something or somebody [15thC. From Old French, from *mes-* "wrongly" + *nommer* "to name," from Latin *nominare.*]

mi·so /meéssō/ *n.* Japanese fermented soy bean paste used mainly in vegetarian cooking [Early 18thC. From Japanese.]

mi·sog·a·my /mi sóggəmee/ *n.* an aversion to marriage and the married state [Mid-17thC. From modern Latin *misogamia*, which was coined from Greek *misein* "to hate" + *gamos* "marriage."] —**mis·o·gam·ic** /mìssə gámmik/ *adj.* —**mi·sog·a·mist** /mi sóggəmist/ *n.*

mi·sog·y·ny /mi sójjənee/ *n.* the hatred of women, as a sexually defined group [Mid-17thC. From Greek *misogunia*, from *misein* "to hate" + *gunē* "woman."] —**mis·o·gyn·ic** /mìssə jínnik/ *adj.* —**mi·sog·y·nist** /mi sójjənist/ *n.* —**mi·sog·y·nis·tic** /mi sòjjə nístik/ *adj.* —**mi·sog·y·nis·ti·cal·ly** *adv.*

mi·sol·o·gy /mi sólləjee/ *n.* the hatred of reason, logical argument, or enlightenment [Early 19thC. From Greek *misologia*, from *misein* "to hate" + *-logia* -LOGY.] —**mi·sol·o·gist** *n.*

mis·o·ne·ism /mìssə neé ìzzəm/ *n.* the hatred of new things or change [Late 19thC. From Italian *misoneismo*, which was coined from Greek *misein* "to hate" + *neos* "new" + Italian *-ismo* "-ism."] —**mis·o·ne·ist** *n.* —**mis·o·ne·is·tic** /mìssə nee ístik/ *adj.*

mis·pick·el /míss pìk'l/ *n.* = **arsenopyrite** [Late 17thC. From German, variant of earlier Mispūtl, of unknown origin.]

mis·place /miss pláyss/ (**-placed, -plac·ing, -plac·es**) *vt.* **1.** PUT IN WRONG PLACE to put something in a wrong place or position **2.** MISLAY to lose something, especially temporarily, through forgetting where it was put **3.** RELY ON SOMEBODY OR SOMETHING INAPPROPRIATE to put confidence, faith, or trust in somebody or something unsuitable or unworthy —**mis·place·ment** *n.*

mis·placed mod·i·fi·er *n.* a phrase positioned so that it is unclear what exactly it refers to, e.g., *lying in the gutter* in "Lying in the gutter, we saw a dead rat"

mis·play *vt.* /miss pláy/ (**-played, -play·ing, -plays**) **MAKE BAD MOVE** to play or move something such as a ball or game piece badly or carelessly ■ *n.* /míss plày, miss pláy/ **MISTAKE MADE IN GAME** a bad or unintended play in sports or a game

mis·plead /miss pléed/ (**-plead·ed, -plead** *or* **-pled** /-pléd/, **-plead·ing, -pleads**) *vti.* to make or answer an allegation in a lawsuit in a manner not in accordance with procedure or the law

mis·plead·ing /miss pléeding/ *n.* an error made or contained in the pleading in a lawsuit

mis·print *n.* /míss prìnt, miss prínt/ **MISTAKE IN PRINTED COPY OR PRINTING** an error in the printed copy of a text resulting from a mistake made when the text was being printed ■ *vt.* /miss prínt/ (**-print·ed, -print·ing, -prints**) **PRINT INCORRECTLY** to print something wrongly

mis·pri·sion[1] /miss prízh'n/ *n.* **1. HIDING A CRIME** the failure of somebody who knows of but is not involved in a felony or treason to report it to the authorities **2. WRONGDOING IN OFFICIAL DUTIES** neglect or wrong done by a public official in the performance of the duties of his or her office **3. SEDITION** sedition against a government or court [15thC. From Anglo-Norman *mesprisioun* "error," from Old French *mesprendre* "to make a mistake."]

mis·pri·sion[2] /miss prízh'n/ *n.* (*archaic*) **1. CONTEMPT** disdain for something or somebody considered of little value **2. FAILURE TO UNDERSTAND OR SEE VALUE** a misunderstanding of something, especially a failure to appreciate the true worth of somebody or something [Late 16thC. Formed from MISPRIZE + -ION on the model of MISPRISION[1].]

mis·prize /miss príz/ (**-prized, -priz·ing, -priz·es**) *vt.* (*formal*) **1. UNDERVALUE** to fail to appreciate the true worth of something or somebody **2. CONSIDER CONTEMPTIBLE** to consider somebody or something unworthy of respect or admiration [14thC. From Old French *mesprisier* literally "to misestimate value," from *prisier* (see PRIZE).] —**mis·priz·er** *n.*

mis·pro·nounce /mìssprə nówns/ (**-nounced, -nounc·ing, -nounc·es**) *vti.* to pronounce something incorrectly —**mis·pro·nun·ci·a·tion** *n.*

mis·quote /miss kwṓt/ (**-quot·ed, -quot·ing, -quotes**) *vti.* to quote somebody or something inaccurately —**mis·quot·er** *n.*

mis·read /miss réed/ (**-read, -read** /miss réd/, **-read·ing, -reads**) *vt.* **1. READ WRONGLY** to make a mistake in reading something, e.g., reading aloud inaccurately, mistaking one word for another, or misunderstanding the sense of what is written **2. MISINTERPRET** to fail to understand the true meaning or nature of something

mis·rep·re·sent /miss rèppri zént/ (**-sent·ed, -sent·ing, -sents**) *vt.* **1. GIVE FALSE ACCOUNT OF** to give an inaccurate or deliberately false account of the nature of somebody or something **2. NOT REPRESENT TRULY** not to be truly or typically representative of somebody or something —**mis·rep·re·sen·ta·tion** /miss rèppri zen táysh'n/ *n.* —**mis·rep·re·sen·ta·tive** /miss rèppri zéntətiv/ *adj.* —**mis·rep·re·sent·er** /-zéntər/ *n.*

mis·rule /miss róol/ *vti.* (**-ruled, -rul·ing, -rules**) **RULE BADLY** to govern a people or place unjustly or inefficiently ■ *n.* **1. BAD GOVERNMENT** unjust or inefficient government of a people or place **2. PUBLIC DISORDER** a state of public disorder or anarchy

miss[1] /miss/ *v.* (**missed, miss·ing, miss·es**) **1.** *vti.* **NOT HIT TARGET** to fail to hit, reach, or make contact with somebody or something that is being aimed at **2.** *vt.* **NOT ATTEND OR CATCH** to fail to be present or on time for something, or to fail to meet or be on time for somebody **3.** *vt.* **NOT HEAR, SEE, OR UNDERSTAND** to fail to hear, see, or understand something, e.g., through inattention or being distracted **4.** *vt.* **NOT TAKE ADVANTAGE OF CHANCE** to fail to take advantage of a chance or opportunity **5.** *vti.* **FAIL TO ACHIEVE** to fail to achieve a set target or goal **6.** *vt.* **AVOID** to escape or avoid somebody or something, especially being hurt or being involved in a dangerous or unpleasant situation **7.** *vt.* **OMIT** to leave something out **8.** *vt.* **DESIRE SOMEBODY'S PRESENCE** to feel sorry that somebody or something is absent ○ *missed her a lot while she was away* **9.** *vt.* **DISCOVER ABSENCE OF** to realize that somebody or something is not there, at a time when or in a place where somebody would expect him, her, or it to be present ○ *He was halfway home before he missed his wallet.* **10.** *vi.* **MISFIRE** to fail to ignite the fuel mixture in the cylinder (*refers to an internal-combustion engine*) ■ *n.* **1. FAILURE TO HIT** a failure to hit, reach, or make contact with somebody or something aimed at **2. A FAILURE** something that does not succeed or fails to impress [Old English *missan.* Ultimately from a prehistoric Germanic word meaning "to go wrong," which is also the ancestor of English *mis-*.] —**miss·a·ble** *adj.* ◇ **miss the boat** to fail to take advantage of an opportunity

miss out *vi.* to lose an opportunity of doing something

miss[2] /miss/ *n.* **1. WAY OF ADDRESSING A YOUNG WOMAN** a term of address for a girl or young woman, sometimes used in place of her name **2. YOUNG WOMAN** a girl or young woman [Mid-17thC. Shortening of MISTRESS.]

Miss *n.* **1. TITLE PRECEDING A NAME** a title placed before the name of a girl or unmarried woman **2. WINNER'S TITLE** used together with a place name or another word in the winner's title awarded in a beauty contest or similar event ○ *Miss Panama*

Miss. *abbr.* **1.** mission **2.** missionary **3.** Mississippi

mis·sal /míss'l/ *n.* a book that contains all the prayers, responses, and hymns used in Roman Catholic Mass [13thC. From medieval Latin *missale,* from, ultimately, late Latin *missa* (see MASS).]

mis·sel thrush /míss'l-/ *n.* = **mistle thrush**

mis·sense /míss sèns/ *n.* a genetic mutation in which a genetic coding sequence (**codon**) for one amino acid is changed to one that codes for another

mis·shap·en /miss sháypən/, **mis·shaped** /miss sháypt/ *adj.* having an undesirably unusual shape —**mis·shap·en·ly** *adv.* —**mis·shap·en·ness** *n.*

mis·sile /míss'l/ *n.* **1. ROCKET-PROPELLED WEAPON** a weapon consisting of a warhead propelled by a rocket **2. PROJECTILE** any object thrown or launched as a weapon, e.g., a rock or bullet [Early 17thC. From Latin *missilis,* from, ultimately, *mittere* "to send" (source of English *mission*).]

mis·sile·ry /míss'lree/, **mis·sil·ry** *n.* **1. MISSILES COLLECTIVELY** missiles, considered collectively **2. OPERATING OF MISSILES** the designing, building, or operating of missiles

miss·ing /míssing/ *adj.* **1. ABSENT** not present in an expected place, absent, or lost ○ *There's a page missing from the book.* **2. DISAPPEARED** not yet traced and not known for certain to be alive, but not confirmed as dead ○ *missing persons* ◇ **missing in action** absent after combat and not known to be captured, injured, or dead

miss·ing link *n.* **1. ANIMAL LINKING APES TO HUMANS** an animal theorized or sought as a transitional evolutionary stage between apes and humans **2. SOMETHING REQUIRED FOR COMPLETION** something that is absent from a sequence or series and is needed to connect up its various parts and complete it

mis·si·ol·o·gy /mìssee óllәjee/ *n.* the study of Christian missionary work [Mid-20thC. Coined from MISSION + -OLOGY.]

mis·sion /mísh'n/ *n.* **1. ASSIGNED TASK** a specific task given to a person or group to carry out **2. CALLING** an aim or task that somebody believes it is his or her duty to carry out or to which he or she attaches special importance and devotes special care **3.** AEROSP **SPACE VEHICLE'S TRIP** a single flight or voyage of a military aircraft or a spacecraft **4. GROUP OF REPRESENTATIVES** a group of people sent to a country to represent their government, a business, or other organization **5.** POL **REPRESENTATION ABROAD** a permanent diplomatic delegation in another country **6.** CHR **GROUP OF CHURCH WORKERS** a body of people sent by a church to another part of the country or to a foreign country to spread their faith or do medical and social work **7.** CHR **CHURCH WORK IN THE COMMUNITY** a campaign of religious work, often including community aid at home or abroad, carried out by a church **8.** CHR **COMMUNICATION OF BELIEFS** the vocation or work of a church or other religious organization or of individuals in communicating their faith in a variety of ways to the wider community **9.** CHR **HOUSING USED BY MISSIONARIES** a building or group of buildings belonging to a missionary organization **10.** CHR **MISSIONARY'S TERRITORY** an area assigned to a missionary or missionary group **11.** CHR **PLACE THAT HELPS THE NEEDY** a center run by a religious or charitable organization offering food, shelter, aid, and spiritual comfort to needy people **12.** CHR **MINOR CHURCH** a church that has no permanent clergy and is supported by a larger church ■ *adj.* **mis·sion, Mis·sion IN SPANISH MISSION STYLE** relating to or similar to a style of architecture or heavy dark oak furniture used in early Spanish missions in the southwestern United States ■ *vt.* (**-sioned, -sion·ing, -sions**) **1. SEND ON A MISSION** to send somebody on or give somebody a mission **2. OPERATE A MISSION** to establish or conduct a religious mission in a place or among a people [Late 16thC. Directly or via French from the Latin stem *mission-,* from, ultimately, *mittere* "to send off."]

WORD KEY: ORIGIN

The Latin word *mittere,* from which ***mission*** is derived, is also the source of English *admit, commit, mess, message, missile, missive, permit, promise, remit, submit,* and *transmit.*

mis·sion·ar·y /mísh'n èrry/ *n.* (*plural* **-ies**) **1. SOMEBODY WHO DOES A CHURCH'S WORK ABROAD** somebody sent to another country by a church to spread its faith or to do social and medical work **2. PERSUADER** somebody who tries to persuade others to accept or join something such as a belief, cause, or movement ■ *adj.* **OF OR LIKE A MISSIONARY** relating to or typical of a missionary

mis·sion·ar·y po·si·tion *n.* a position for sexual intercourse in which the woman lies on her back and the man lies on top of and facing her [Because missionaries held it to be least reprehensible]

Mis·sion·ar·y Ridge /mìshә neree ríj/ ridge in Georgia and Tennessee, southeastern United States, in the Appalachian mountains. Length: 10 mi./16 km.

Mis·sion Bend /mìshәn bénd/ park in Oklahoma, Mayes County

mis·sion·er /mísh'nər/ *n.* = **missionary**

mis·sion state·ment *n.* a formal document that states the aims of a company or organization

Mis·sion Vi·e·jo /mìsh'n veeáyhō/ city in California, in Orange County, near the Pacific Ocean coast. Population: 83,813 (1994).

mis·sis /míssiss/, **missus** *n.* (*informal*) **1. WAY OF ADDRESSING A WOMAN** used as a term of address for a woman, sometimes in place of her name **2. WIFE** used to refer to a man's wife or woman partner, usually either by the man himself or by another man (*sometimes considered offensive*) [Late 18thC. Alteration of MISTRESS.]

Mis·sis·sau·ga /mìssi sáwgə/ city in southern Ontario, Canada, on the shore of Lake Ontario. Population: 544,383 (1996).

Mississippi

Mis·sis·sip·pi /mìssi síppee/ **1.** state in the southeastern United States, bordered by Tennessee, Alabama, Louisiana, and Arkansas, and northwest of the Gulf of Mexico. Capital: Jackson. Population: 2,730,501 (1997). Area: 47,695 sq. mi./123,530 sq. km. **2.** largest river in the United States, flowing between Minnesota and Louisiana, with a basin of 1,200,000 sq. mi./3,100,000 sq. km. Length: 2,350 mi./3,782 km.

Mis·sis·sip·pi·an /mìssi síppee ən/ *n.* **1. SOMEBODY FROM MISSISSIPPI** somebody who lives in or was born or raised in the state of Mississippi **2.** GEOL **GEOLOGIC EPOCH** the epoch of geologic time in North America when large land masses were submerged underwater, 362.5 to 320 million years ago. It is the first of two epochs of the Carboniferous Period used by North American geologists. —**Mis·sis·sip·pi·an** *adj.*

Mis·sis·sip·pi·an cul·ture *n.* the last of the Native North American mound-building cultures, which flourished from about A.D. 800 to 1300. Its communities were characterized by large towns and ceremonial centers.

mis·sive /míssiv/ *n.* a letter or written communication [Early 16thC. Via medieval Latin *missivus* from, ultimately, Latin *mittere* "to send" (source of English *mission*).]

Missouri

Mis·sou·ri[1] /mi zóoree/ state in the north central United States, bordered by Iowa, Illinois, Kentucky, Tennessee, Arkansas, Oklahoma, Kansas, and Nebraska. Capital: Jefferson City. Population: 5,402,058 (1997). Area: 69,709 sq. mi./180,545 sq. km. —**Mis·sourian** *n., adj.*

Mis·sou·ri[2] the longest river in the United States, flowing from Montana into the Mississippi River in Missouri. Length: 2,565 mi./4,128 km.

mis·spell /miss spél/ (**-spelled, -spell·ing, -spells**) *vt.* to spell a word incorrectly

mis·spell·ing /miss spélling/ *n.* an incorrect spelling of a word

mis·spend /miss spénd/ (**-spent, -spent** /miss spént/, **-spend·ing, -spends**) *vt.* to spend money or time badly or wastefully —**mis·spend·er** *n.*

mis·state /miss stáyt/ (**-stat·ed, -stat·ing, -states**) *vt.* to state something incorrectly, e.g., by giving false information or mispronouncing something —**mis·state·ment** *n.*

mis·step /miss stép/ *n.* **1.** WRONG STEP a bad or awkward step, or a step in a wrong direction **2.** FAUX PAS an error in judgment or conduct

mis·sus /míssəz/ *n.* = **missis**

miss·y /míssee/ (*plural* **-ies**) *n.* used as a term of address for a girl or young woman, often expressing affection or reprimand (*informal*) (*sometimes considered offensive*)

mist /mist/ *n.* **1.** METEOROL THIN FOG a thin gray cloud of water droplets that condenses in the atmosphere just above the ground, limiting the view and making objects appear indistinct **2.** CONDENSED WATER VAPOR a film of water vapor that has condensed on a surface **3.** FINE SPRAY a fine spray of liquid, e.g., from an atomizer or aerosol **4.** LIQUID SUSPENSION IN GAS a suspension of liquid in a gas **5.** OBSCURING THING something that makes it difficult to see or understand something ■ *v.* (**mist·ed, mist·ing, mists**) **1.** *vti.* FILM OVER to cover or obscure something in a mist, or to become covered in or obscured by mist **2.** *vi.* BECOME BLURRED BY TEARS to become blurred by tears **3.** *vt.* SPRAY SOMETHING to apply a fine liquid spray to something [Old English. Ultimately from an Indo-European word meaning "urinate," which is also the ancestor of English *micturate*.]

mis·take /mi stáyk/ *n.* **1.** INCORRECT ACT OR DECISION an incorrect, unwise, or unfortunate act or decision caused by bad judgment or a lack of information or care ○ *It's an easy mistake to make.* **2.** ERROR something in a piece of work that is incorrect, e.g., a misspelling or a misprint **3.** MISUNDERSTANDING a misunderstanding of something ○ *There must be some mistake, I didn't order this.* ■ *vt.* (**-took** /-stóòk/, **-tak·en** /-stáykən/, **-tak·ing, -takes**) **1.** MISUNDERSTAND SOMETHING to misunderstand or misinterpret something ○ *I mistook the meaning of the phrase.* **2.** IDENTIFY SOMEBODY OR SOMETHING INCORRECTLY to identify somebody or something incorrectly or fail to recognize somebody or something ○ *We tend to mistake infatuation for real love.* **3.** CHOOSE SOMETHING INCORRECTLY to choose something incorrectly or injudiciously [14thC. From Old Norse *mistaka* "to take in error."] —**mis·tak·a·ble** *adj.* —**mis·tak·a·bly** *adv.* —**mis·tak·er** *n.* ◇ **by mistake** accidentally, without wishing or intending to do something

WORD KEY: SYNONYMS

mistake, error, inaccuracy, slip, blunder, faux pas

CORE MEANING: something incorrect or improper

mistake a general word used to talk about something incorrect, inappropriate, or unwise; **error** something that deviates from a recognized standard or guide. It is also used as a more formal word for *mistake*; **inaccuracy** something that is incorrect because it has been measured, calculated, or copied incorrectly; **slip** a fairly informal word for a minor mistake, especially one caused by carelessness; **blunder** an obvious and usually serious mistake, especially one that seems to be a result of ignorance or ineptitude; **faux pas** a fairly formal term for a mistake in behavior or speech that constitutes a breach of etiquette.

mis·tak·en /mi stáykən/ *adj.* **1.** WRONG IN YOUR OPINION wrong or incorrect in, e.g., an assumption, belief, or your understanding of something ○ *If you think that'll work, then you're sadly mistaken.* **2.** BASED ON INCORRECT INFORMATION based on incorrect information or values ○ *a mistaken sense of loyalty* —**mis·tak·en·ly** *adv.* —**mis·tak·en·ness** *n.*

mis·ter /místər/ *n.* **1.** WAY TO ADDRESS A MAN used as a term of address for a man, usually in place of his name **2.** HUSBAND used to refer to a woman's husband or man partner, either by the woman or by another woman (*informal*) (*sometimes considered offensive*) [Mid-16thC. Alteration of MASTER.]

Mis·ter *n.* used as the full form of the courtesy title "Mr" [Mid-18thC. From MISTER.]

mis·term /miss túrm/ (**-termed, -term·ing, -terms**) *vt.* to call something by a wrong or inappropriate name

Mis·ti, Volcán /méestə/ dormant volcano in southern Peru, in the Andes mountains, northeast of Arequipa city. Height: 19,101 ft./5,822 m.

mis·time /miss tím/ (**-timed, -tim·ing, -times**) *vt.* to time something wrongly, usually by missing the precise point of time at which something should be done to be successful [Old English *mistimian*, from *timian* "to time"]

mis·tle thrush /míss'l-/, **mis·sel thrush** *n.* a large European thrush with a spotted breast and grayish back that feeds on berries, especially those of mistletoe. Latin name: *Turdus viscivorus.*

mis·tle·toe /míss'l tō/ *n.* **1.** PARASITIC SHRUB an evergreen shrub of Europe and Asia that grows as a parasite on trees such as apple and oak, has leaves in horseshoe-shaped pairs, and bears white berries in winter. Latin name: *Viscum album.* **2.** PLANT RESEMBLING MISTLETOE a North American shrub that resembles the true mistletoe. Latin name: *Phoradendron flavescens.* **3.** CHRISTMAS DECORATION a sprig of mistletoe traditionally used as a decoration and for kissing under at Christmas [Old English *misteltan*. Ultimately from a prehistoric Germanic word meaning "urine" (because it is propagated by the droppings of the mistle thrush).]

mis·took past tense of **mistake**

mis·tral /místrəl, mi stráal/ *n.* a powerful cold dry northeasterly wind that blows in the south of France [Early 17thC. Via French from, ultimately, Latin *magistralis* "dominant," from its power.]

mis·treat /miss tréet/ (**-treat·ed, -treat·ing, -treats**) *vt.* to treat somebody or something badly or roughly

WORD KEY: SYNONYMS

See Synonyms at ***misuse***.

mis·tress /místrəss/ *n.* **1.** EXTRAMARITAL LOVER a woman with whom a man has a usually long-term extramarital sexual relationship and for whom he often provides financial support **2.** WOMAN OWNER OR CONTROLLER OF SOMETHING a woman who owns or controls something, e.g., a woman owner of an estate, head of a household, or employer of servants **3.** PERSONIFICATION AS WOMAN something that rules or controls, personified as a woman ○ *Venice, once mistress of the seas* **4.** ABLE WOMAN a woman who is highly skilled in a particular activity ○ *a mistress of the art of negotiation* **5.** WOMAN OWNER OF A PET the woman owner of a pet animal **6.** LOVED WOMAN a woman with whom a man is in love (*archaic*) [13thC. From Old French *maistresse*, feminine of *maistre* (see MASTER).]

Mis·tress /místrəss/ *n.* used as a courtesy title to address a married woman, usually in front of the surname (*archaic*)

mis·tress of cer·e·mo·nies *n.* a woman in charge of the proceedings at an event or entertainment

mis·tri·al /miss trí əl, miss tríl/ *n.* **1.** INVALID TRIAL a trial that is invalid because a mistake such as an error in procedure has been made **2.** INCONCLUSIVE TRIAL a trial that does not come to a proper conclusion, e.g., because the jury cannot agree on a verdict

mis·trust /miss trúst/ *n.* SUSPICION suspicion about or lack of confidence in somebody or something ■ *vt.* (**-trust·ed, -trust·ing, -trusts**) BE SUSPICIOUS OF SOMEBODY OR SOMETHING to be suspicious of and unable to trust or rely on somebody or something —**mis·trust·er** *n.* —**mis·trust·ful** *adj.* —**mis·trust·ful·ly** *adv.* —**mis·trust·ful·ness** *n.*

mist·y /místee/ (**-i·er, -i·est**) *adj.* **1.** METEOROL COVERED IN MIST with a lot of mist in the air or surrounded or covered by mist ○ *a misty mountain* ○ *a misty morning* **2.** LIKE MIST like mist, especially in being in a cloud or spray of fine drops **3.** DIM AND INDISTINCT dim and indistinct, as if veiled by mist **4.** SAD AND NOSTALGIC feeling sad or nostalgic [Old English *mistig*, from *mist* (see MIST)] —**mist·i·ly** *adv.* —**mist·i·ness** *n.*

mist·y-eyed *adj.* **1.** WITH TEARS IN THE EYES with a film of tears in the eyes **2.** SENTIMENTAL sentimental or dreamlike

mis·un·der·stand /mìss undər stánd/ (**-stood** /-stóòd/, **-stood, -stand·ing, -stands**) *vti.* to fail to realize the real or intended meaning of something, the true nature of something, or what somebody is really like

mis·un·der·stand·ing /miss undər stánding/ *n.* **1.** LACK OF COMPREHENSION a failure to understand or interpret something correctly **2.** MINOR DISPUTE a minor disagreement or dispute

mis·un·der·stood past participle, past tense of **misunderstand** ■ *adj.* not correctly understood, or not properly and sympathetically appreciated ○ *a misunderstood teenager*

mis·us·age /miss yóossij/ *n.* **1.** LANG INAPPROPRIATE USE OF LANGUAGE a wrong or inappropriate use of language **2.** = **misuse** *n.* **1**

mis·use *n.* /miss yóoss/ **1.** WRONG USE the incorrect or improper use of something **2.** CRUEL TREATMENT cruel treatment of a person or animal ■ *vt.* /miss yóoz/ (**-used, -us·ing, -us·es**) **1.** USE SOMETHING WRONGLY to use something in an incorrect or improper way or for a dishonest purpose **2.** TREAT SOMEBODY CRUELLY to treat a person or animal cruelly —**mis·used** *adj.*

WORD KEY: SYNONYMS

misuse, abuse, ill-treat, maltreat, mistreat

CORE MEANING: wrong or bad use or treatment of somebody or something

misuse a neutral word meaning to put something to an inappropriate use or purpose. It can be used in more formal contexts to talk about treating a person or animal badly or harshly; **abuse** a stronger word than *misuse*, used to emphasize that the way something is being used is wrong or inappropriate. It is also used to refer to cruel or violent treatment of a person or animal, especially on a regular basis; **ill-treat** treating a person or animal badly or wrongly. It suggests a more severe degree of bad treatment then *mistreat*; **maltreat** a more formal word meaning the same as *ill-treat*; **mistreat** to treat a person or animal badly, inconsiderately, or unfairly, not necessarily in a way that involves cruelty, physical abuse, or the desire to harm.

mis·us·er /miss yóozər/ *n.* the illegal use of a right, privilege, or position of authority [Mid-16thC]

MIT *abbr.* Massachusetts Institute of Technology

Mitch·ell /míchəl/ city in southeastern South Dakota, northwest of Sioux Falls and south of Huron. Population: 14,191 (1996).

Mitch·ell, Mount mountain in western North Carolina. It is the highest point in the United States east of the Mississippi River. Height: 6,684 ft./2,037 m.

Mitch·ell, Joni (*b.* 1943) Canadian singer and songwriter. Her albums include *Clouds* (1969), *Blue* (1971), and *Wild Things Run Fast* (1982). Real name **Roberta Joan Anderson**

Mitch·ell, Margaret (1900–49) U.S. writer. She wrote the enormously popular Civil War novel *Gone With the Wind* (1936), which won a Pulitzer Prize. Full name **Margaret Munnerlyn Mitchell**

Mitch·ell, Maria (1818–89) U.S. astronomer. She discovered a comet and tracked its orbit in 1847, and also researched sunspots.

Mitch·ell, William (1879–1936) U.S. army officer. He commanded U.S. air forces (1917–18) during World War I, subsequently becoming an advocate of air power.

Mitch·um /míchəm/, **Robert** (1917–86) U.S. movie actor. His many movies include *Night of the Hunter* (1955), *Farewell My Lovely* (1975), and *Cape Fear* (1961).

mite[1] /mīt/ *n.* a tiny eight-legged creature related to spiders and ticks. Some mites live freely and some as parasites that can carry disease, attack plants, and cause human allergies. Order: Acarina. [Old English *mīte*, from a prehistoric Germanic base meaning "cut" (which probably also produced English *mite*[2]), via the meaning "something cut up small"]

mite[2] /mīt/ *n.* **1. SMALL CHILD** a small child or animal, especially one that inspires pity (*informal*) **2. SMALL AMOUNT** a small piece or small amount (*dated*) **3. SMALL COIN** a small coin of little value (*archaic*) [14thC. From Middle Low German and Middle Dutch *mīte*, a small Flemish coin, also "tiny animal."]

mi·ter /mítər/ *n.* **1.** CHR **BISHOP'S HAT** the ceremonial headdress of a Christian bishop or abbot, consisting of a tall pointed hat creased across the top, with two ribbons hanging down the back **2.** WOODWORK = **miter joint 3.** WOODWORK **SURFACES OF A MITER JOINT** either of the surfaces that are joined together to form a miter joint **4.** SEW **DIAGONAL JOIN AT THE CORNER BETWEEN HEMS** in sewing, a diagonal join between the edges of two hems that meet at a corner of a piece of fabric ■ *vt.* (**-tered, -ter·ing, -ters**) **1.** WOODWORK **JOIN PIECES OF WOOD** to join pieces of wood using a miter joint **2.** WOODWORK **SHAPE WOOD FOR JOINT** to shape the end of a piece of wood, especially by cutting it off at an angle of 45° when making a corner or miter joint **3.** SEW **DIAGONALLY JOIN HEMS AT THE CORNER** in sewing, to make a diagonal join at a corner between two hems **4.** CHR **GIVE A MITER TO SOMEBODY** to confer a miter on somebody, indicating promotion to the rank of bishop [14thC. Via Old French from Latin *mitra*, from Greek, "belt, turban," of uncertain origin: perhaps from an Asian language.] —**mi·ter·er** *n.*

mi·ter block *n.* a block with slots cut in it to guide a handsaw at the appropriate angle when cutting a miter joint

mi·ter box *n.* a box with open ends that is used to hold wood and guide a handsaw at the appropriate angle when cutting a miter joint

mi·ter joint *n.* a corner joint in woodwork, usually made by cutting two ends to be joined at 45° angles and gluing or nailing them together into a right angle

mi·ter square *n.* a tool used in cutting wood at an angle that has a beveled arm either fixed at an angle of 45° or adjustable to any angle

mi·ter·wort /mítər wùrt, -wàwrt/ (*plural* **-worts** *or* **-wort**) *n.* an Asian and North American plant of the saxifrage family with clusters of small white flowers and seed pods that look a little like a bishop's miter. Genus: *Mitella*. [Mid-19thC. From the shape of its capsule.]

Mit·ford /mítfərd/, **Jessica** (1917–97) British-born U.S. writer. Her best-known book is *The American Way of Death* (1965).*Hons and Rebels* (1960) gives an account of her unconventional family, including her sister Nancy Mitford.

Mit·ford, Nancy (1904–73) British writer. Author of *Love in a Cold Climate* (1949) and *The Blessing* (1951), she was the sister of Jessica Mitford.

Mith·ra·ism /míthrə ìzzəm/ *n.* a religion originating in Persia and involving worship of the god Mithras. It became popular among the Roman military in the Late Roman Empire. [Early 19thC] —**Mith·ra·ic** /mi thráy ik/ *adj.* —**Mith·ra·ist** /míthrə ist/ *n.*

Mith·ras /míthrəss/ *n.* the god of light, truth, and goodness in the Zoroastrian tradition and Persian mythology. He is often shown with a bull, which he is said to have slain before fertilizing the world with its blood. [Mid-16thC. Via Latin *Mithras* from, ultimately, Old Persian and Avestan *Mithra*.]

mith·ri·date /míthrə dàyt/ *n.* a substance believed in ancient medicine and folklore to be an antidote to every poison and a cure for every disease [Early 16thC. Via medieval Latin *mithridatum* from, ultimately, late Latin *mithridatius* "relating to Mithridates." Named after Mithridates VI, king of Pontus (died 63 B.C.), who was reputedly immune to poisons.] —**mith·ri·dat·ic** /mìthrə dáttik/ *adj.* —**mith·ri·da·tism** /mìthrə dáy tìzzəm/ *n.*

mi·ti·cide /mítti sīd/ *n.* a substance that kills mites —**mi·ti·cid·al** /mítti sīd'l/ *adj.*

mit·i·gate /mítti gàyt/ (**-gat·ed, -gat·ing, -gates**) *vt.* **1. PARTLY EXCUSE A CRIME** to make an offense or crime less serious or more excusable **2. LESSEN SOMETHING** to make something less harsh, severe, or violent [15thC. From Latin *mitigatus*, past participle of *mitigare* "to make mild," from assumed *mitigus* "making mild," ultimately from *mitis* "gentle, soft" + *agere* "to make."] —**mit·i·ga·tion** /mìtti gáysh'n/ *n.* —**mit·i·ga·ble** /míttigəb'l/ *adj.*

mit·i·gat·ing /mítti gàyting/ *adj.* making an offense or a crime seem less serious, or partly excusing it ○ *mitigating circumstances*

mit·i·ga·tion spe·cial·ist *n.* a member of a criminal defense team who gathers detailed information about a defendant in order to persuade a jury not to impose the death penalty

mi·tis /mítiss, méetiss/, **mi·tis met·al** *n.* a form of iron made malleable by having a small amount of aluminum added to it [Late 19thC. Named by the inventor of the process, P. Östberg of Stockholm, apparently from Latin *mitis* "mild" used in the sense found in "mild steel."]

Mit·nag·ged /mìt naa géd/ (*plural* **-dim** /-déem/), **Mit·na·ged** (*plural* **-nag·dim**), **Mis·nag·ed** /mi snáagəd/ (*plural* **-dim** /-snáagədim/) *n.* in the 18th and 19th centuries, a Jew in central and eastern Europe who believed in rationalism and opposed Hassidism [Early 20thC. From Hebrew *mitnaggēd* "opponent."]

mi·to·chon·dri·on /mìtə kóndree ən/ (*plural* **-a** /-ə/) *n.* a small round or rod-shaped body that is found in the cytoplasm of most cells and produces enzymes for the metabolic conversion of food to energy [Early 20thC. From Greek *mitos* "thread" + *khondrion*, from *khondros* "granule, lump (of salt)."]

mi·to·gen /mítəjən/ *n.* PHYSIOL a substance or agent that induces mitosis [Mid-20thC. Formed from MITOSIS + -GEN.]

mi·to·my·cin /mìtə míss'n/ *n.* any of a group of antibiotics produced by a soil bacterium that inhibit DNA synthesis and are used against tumors [Mid-20thC. Coined from *mito-* (perhaps from Greek *mitos* "thread," MITOSIS, or MITOCHONDRION) + -MYCIN.]

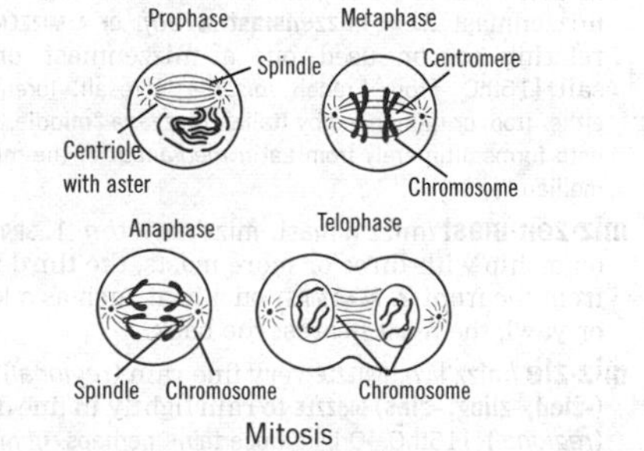

Mitosis

mi·to·sis /mī tóssiss/ *n.* the process by which a cell divides into two daughter cells, each of which has the same number of chromosomes as the original cell. ◊ **meiosis** [Late 19thC. Coined from Greek *mitos* "thread" + -OSIS. So named because in the first stage of the process the chromatin of the cell nucleus appears as long threads.]

mi·trail·leuse /mèetrə yṓz/ *n.* an early machine gun that had 35 barrels that could be fired simultaneously or in sequence and was mounted on a carriage drawn by four horses. The gun was developed in France and first used in the Franco-Prussian War of 1870. [Late 19thC. Ultimately from French *mitrailler* "to fire mitraille," from *mitraille* "small money, pieces of metal," alteration of Old French *mitaille*, from *mite*.]

mi·tral /mítrəl/ *adj.* relating to a bishop's miter or like it in shape, especially in having separate front and back sections [Early 17thC. Via modern Latin *mitralis* from Latin *mitra* (see MITER).]

mi·tral ste·no·sis *n.* the narrowing of the heart's mitral valve as the result of disease

mi·tral valve *n.* the one-way valve between the upper and lower chambers, or atrium and ventricle, on the left side of the heart [Named for its shape]

mi·tre /mítər/ *n.*, *vt.* U.K. = **miter**

Mi·tro·pou·los /mi tròppoo lóss/, **Dimitri** (1896–1960) Greek-born U.S. conductor and composer. Conductor of the New York Philharmonic Orchestra (1949–58) and the Metropolitan Opera orchestra (1954–60), he was known for championing modern music.

mitt /mit/ *n.* **1. MITTEN** a mitten, especially a child's mitten (*informal*) **2. HAND COVERING** a covering for the hand and fingers, especially one shaped like a mitten ○ *an oven mitt* **3. HAND** a hand, especially when large, clumsy, or dirty (*slang*) **4.** BASEBALL **BASEBALL PLAYER'S PADDED GLOVE** in baseball, a glove, especially a large fingerless padded glove worn by the catcher **5. GLOVE WITHOUT FINGERS** a woman's glove, popular in the 19th century, that left the fingers uncovered [Mid-18thC. Shortening of MITTEN.]

mit·ten /mítt'n/ *n.* a glove with one covering for the thumb and one covering for the four fingers [14thC. From French *mitaine*, of uncertain origin: perhaps originally denoting "glove cut off at the middle," ultimately from Latin *medietas* "half" (source of English *moiety*).]

Mit·ter·rand /méetə raáN/, **François** (1916–96) French statesman. A Socialist, as president (1981–95) he worked to strengthen France's position in the European Union.

mit·ti·mus /míttəməss/ (*plural* **-mus·es**) *n.* an official order to send somebody to prison [15thC. From Latin, literally "we send," the first word of this order in Latin.]

mitz·vah /mítsvə, míts vaá/ (*plural* **-voth** /-vōt, -vōth/ *or* **-vahs**) *n.* **1. RELIGIOUS DUTY** a Jewish religious duty or obligation, especially one of the commandments of Jewish religious law **2. GOOD DEED** an act of kindness performed by or to a Jewish person [Mid-17thC. From Hebrew *mi&sdotunder;wāh* "commandment."]

mix /miks/ *v.* (**mixed, mix·ing, mix·es**) **1.** *vt.* **COMBINE INGREDIENTS** to combine ingredients by putting them together or blending them to make a single new substance ○ *Mix the flour and dried fruit together.* **2.** *vi.* **BE COMBINED** to become combined, or be capable of becoming combined ○ *Oil and water don't mix.* **3.** *vti.* **MAKE SOMETHING BY COMBINING** to form or create something by combining separate ingredients ○ *Would you mix me a cocktail?* **4.** *vt.* **ADD SOMETHING EXTRA** to add something as an extra or later ingredient ○ *Mix the fruit into the batter.* **5.** *vt.* **COMBINE THINGS** to do something at the same time as something else, or to arrange things next to or alongside each other ○ *able to mix business with pleasure* **6.** *vi.* **GO TOGETHER** to go well together ○ *Reds and greens just don't mix.* **7.** *vi.* **MEET PEOPLE** to meet other people socially, or enjoy being with other people in social situations **8.** *vt.* **CONSUME THINGS TOGETHER** to consume different drinks or foods on a single occasion **9.** *vti.* RECORDING **BLEND MUSICAL SOUNDS** to adjust and blend sounds from prerecorded tracks or live performers to create the desired combination of musical sounds. The process is done either by using a mixing deck or a multitrack tape machine. **10.** *vt.* BIOL **CROSSBREED PLANTS OR ANIMALS** to breed one variety of a plant or animal with a different variety in order to create a new variety ■ *n.* **1. ACT OF MIXING SOMETHING** an act of mixing something, or an occasion on which it is done ○ *Give all the ingredients a good mix.* **2. COMBINATION** a combination or blend of things ○ *There's an intriguing mix of styles on her latest CD.* **3. SUBSTANCE USED TO PREPARE SOMETHING** a substance, especially a number of dried ingredients in powder form, from which something is prepared ○ *cake mix* **4.** RECORDING **MUSICAL BLEND** a balanced blend of live or prerecorded musical sound ○ *He thinks the drums are too low in the mix.* **5.** RECORDING **VERSION OF A RECORDING** a version of a musical recording that has been changed in some way to give it a different type of sound ○ *Their last hit has been rereleased in a disco mix.* **6.** BUILDING **RATIO OF MORTAR INGREDIENTS** the ratio of sand and cement in mortar, or of sand, cement, and gravel in concrete [15thC. Formed from MIXED.] —**mix·a·ble** *adj.*

mix down *vt.* to create a final finished sound recording by blending elements that have been recorded separately

mix up *v.* **1.** *vt.* **MISTAKE THE IDENTITY OF THINGS** to confuse things or people and mistakenly identify one as the other ○ *People always mix her up with her sister.* **2.** *vt.* **CHANGE THE ORDER OF THINGS** to change the usual or previous order of things, either deliberately or by accident ○ *The pages got mixed up on the way to the printer's.* **3.** *vti.* BECOME INVOLVED IN SOMETHING to involve yourself with a particular group of people or activity, especially something wrong or illegal **4.** *vt.* MAKE SOMETHING FROM INGREDIENTS to prepare or make something by mixing different ingredients

mix·down /míks dòwn/ *n.* the process of converting a multitrack recording, usually a master tape recorded in a studio, into a stereo recording, usually for public release

mixed /mikst/ *adj.* **1.** WITH DIFFERENT THINGS COMBINED consisting of different elements or different kinds of things combined **2.** INVOLVING BOTH SEXES intended for, used by, or done by people of both sexes together **3.** INVOLVING DIFFERENT RACES intended for, used by, or done by people of different races together **4.** WITH INCONSISTENT ELEMENTS consisting of inconsistent or conflicting elements ○ *The play has had mixed reviews.* [15thC. Ultimately via Old French from Latin *mixtus* (source of English *mustang*), past participle of *miscere* "to mix" (source of English *meddle, miscellaneous,* and *promiscuous*).] —**mix·ed·ly** *adv.* —**mixed·ness** *n.*

mixed bag *n.* a group of people or things of widely differing kinds

mixed bless·ing *n.* something that has both advantages and disadvantages or good points and bad points

mixed dou·bles *n.* a tennis, table tennis, or badminton match played by two pairs, each consisting of a man and a woman (*takes a singular verb*)

mixed drink *n.* a drink made by mixing two or more ingredients, at least one of which is alcoholic

mixed e·con·o·my *n.* an economy in which some industries and businesses are government-owned and some are privately owned

mixed farm·ing *n.* farming that combines growing crops and rearing livestock on the same farm

mixed mar·riage *n.* a marriage between people of different racial or religious backgrounds

mixed me·di·a *n.* **1.** USING DIFFERENT ARTISTIC MEDIA the use of different artistic media, e.g., painting combined with photography or collage, in a single composition or work **2.** USING DIFFERENT ADVERTISING METHODS the use of different advertising media together, e.g., billboards, TV, and radio

mixed met·a·phor *n.* a combination of two or more metaphors that together evoke a strange or incongruous image, e.g., "This thorn in my side has finally bitten the dust"

mixed nerve *n.* a nerve that has both motor and sensory fibers, and thus has nerve impulses passing in both directions

mixed num·ber *n.* a figure that consists of a whole number and a fraction, such as the figure $2\frac{3}{4}$

mixed-up *adj.* (*informal*) **1.** BADLY ORGANIZED in a disorganized state **2.** CONFUSED in a state of emotional or psychological confusion

mixed-use *adj.* combining commercial and residential elements in a single property, e.g. , an apartment building with offices or stores

mix·er /míksər/ *n.* **1.** MIXING DEVICE a machine or device for mixing food, cement, or some other substance **2.** NONALCOHOLIC DRINK OFTEN MIXED WITH ALCOHOL a nonalcoholic drink, e.g., fruit juice or soda water, that is often mixed with alcoholic drinks **3.** SOCIABLE PERSON a person considered in terms of whether he or she is good at socializing (*usually used in combination*) ○ *She's a good mixer.* **4.** GET-TOGETHER an informal party held as a way of allowing a group of people to get to know each other **5.** RECORDING ELECTRONIC DEVICE FOR MIXING SOUNDS an electronic device used to adjust and combine various inputs, e.g., performed or broadcast sounds, to create a single output **6.** BROADCAST, CINEMA SOMEBODY CREATING SOUND FOR FILM somebody who combines various sound recordings to create the final soundtrack of a motion picture

mix·ol·o·gy /mik sóllәjee/ *n.* the skill of preparing cocktails, especially cocktails containing alcohol (*informal*) —**mix·ol·o·gist** *n.*

Mix·tec /meéss tèk/ (*plural* **-tec** *or* **-tecs**), **Mix·tec·an** /meess ţékәn/ (*plural* **-ans** *or* **-an**) *n.* **1.** PEOPLES MEMBER OF A NATIVE MIDDLE AMERICAN PEOPLE a member of a Native Middle American people that originally lived in southern Mexico and are now spread throughout Mexico. The Mixtec are noted for their artistic and architectural skills. **2.** LANG NATIVE MIDDLE AMERICAN LANGUAGE a Native Middle American language spoken in parts of Mexico, belonging to the Oto-Manguean family of languages. Mixtec is spoken by about 400,000 people. [Late 18thC. Via Spanish from Nahuatl *mixtecah* "person from a cloudy place."] —**Mix·tec** *adj.*

mix·ture /míkschәr/ *n.* **1.** BLEND OF INGREDIENTS a substance containing several ingredients combined or blended together ○ *cough mixture* **2.** DIFFERENT THINGS COMBINED a number of different elements brought or existing together ○ *a mixture of old and new styles* **3.** CHEM SUBSTANCE FORMED WITHOUT CHEMICAL REACTION a substance consisting of two or more substances that have been combined without chemical bonding taking place **4.** ENG FUEL AND AIR MIX the combination of gasoline vapor and air in an internal-combustion engine **5.** ACT OF MIXING the combining or mixing of different ingredients or elements (*formal*) [15thC. Directly or via French from Latin *mixtura*, from *mixt-*, the past participle stem of *miscere* (see MIXED).]

WORD KEY: SYNONYMS

mixture, blend, combination, compound, alloy, amalgam

CORE MEANING: something formed by mixing materials

mixture a general word used to talk about something formed by mixing two or more things. It does not necessarily suggest that the materials involved have bonded together to form a new whole; **blend** something formed by putting together two or more things, especially in a skilled or scientific way, in order to form a new whole in which the original constituents are bonded irreversibly; **combination** something formed by mixing two or more things, usually in a skilled or careful way, especially when the result is pleasing or successful. It is usually used to describe a process in which the original constituents retain their separate identities; **compound** a technical word for a chemical formed from two or more elements. It is also used generally to describe a combination of two or more things and in particular a word that is made up of two or more existing words; **alloy** a technical word for a metal such as steel that is formed by combining two or more different metallic elements; **amalgam** a technical word for an alloy formed by combining mercury with another metal. It can also be used in a general context to describe something that is a mixture of two or more things.

mix-up *n.* a state of confusion, or an error resulting from confusion ○ *an administrative mix-up*

Mi·zar /mī́ zaàr/ *n.* a four-component multiple star in the constellation Ursa Major [From Arabic *Mi'zar* "cloak, Mizar"]

miz·zen /mízz'n/ *n.* **1.** SAIL ON A MIZZENMAST a sail on a mizzenmast **2.** = **mizzenmast** ■ *adj.* OF A MIZZENMAST relating to, or used on, a mizzenmast or its sail [15thC. From French *misaine* "foresail, foremast," either from or influenced by Italian *mezzana* "middle," with both forms ultimately from Latin *medianus* "of the middle, median."]

miz·zen·mast /mízz'n màst, mízz'nmәst/ *n.* **1.** 3RD MAST on a ship with three or more masts, the third mast from the front **2.** REAR MAST on a boat such as a ketch or yawl, the mast nearest the back

miz·zle /mízz'l/ *n.* DRIZZLE very fine rain (*regional*) ■ *vi.* (**-zled, -zling, -zles**) DRIZZLE to rain lightly in fine drops (*regional*) [15thC. Origin uncertain: perhaps from Low German *miseln*.] —**miz·zling** *adj.* —**miz·zly** *adj.*

Mk *abbr.* **1.** BIBLE Mark **2.** CARS mark

mk. *abbr.* FIN **1.** mark **2.** markka

mks, MKS *abbr.* **1.** FIN marks **2.** meter-kilogram-second

mksA *abbr.* meter-kilogram-second-ampere

mks u·nits *npl.* the metric system of measurement, which has the meter, the kilogram, and the second as its basic units of length, mass, and time

mkt. *abbr.* market

mktg. *abbr.* marketing

ml *abbr.* milliliter

mL *symbol.* millilambert

MLA, M.L.A. *abbr.* **1.** Master of Landscape Architecture **2.** Modern Language Association

MLD *n., abbr.* MED minimum lethal dose

MLF *abbr.* multilateral (nuclear) force

MLG *abbr.* Middle Low German

Mlle. *abbr.* Mademoiselle

Mlles. *abbr.* Mesdemoiselles

mm *abbr.* millimeter

MM. *abbr.* **1.** Messieurs **2.** Military Medal

m.m. *abbr.* mutatis mutandis

MMDS *abbr.* RADIO multipoint microwave distribution system

Mme. *abbr.* Madame

Mmes. *abbr.* Mesdames

mmf, m.m.f. *abbr.* PHYS magnetomotive force

mmHg *n.* a unit for measuring atmospheric pressure. Full form **millimeter of mercury**

MMPI *abbr.* PSYCHOL Minnesota Multiphasic Personality Inventory

MMR vac·cine *n.* a vaccine that is routinely given to small children to protect them against measles, mumps, and rubella

M.Mus. *abbr.* Master of Music

Mn *symbol.* manganese

MN *abbr.* **1.** Minnesota **2.** GEOG magnetic north

MNA *abbr.* Member of the National Assembly (of Quebec)

MNC *abbr.* multinational corporation

mne·mon·ic /ni mónnik/ *n.* MEMORY AID a short rhyme, phrase, or other mental technique for making information easier to memorize ■ *adj.* **1.** ACTING AS A MNEMONIC acting as a memory aid **2.** RELATING TO MNEMONICS relating to the practice of improving the memory, or to systems designed to improve the memory [Mid-18thC. Either formed from MNEMONICS or, perhaps via medieval Latin, from Greek *mnēmonikos* "relating to memory," from the stem *mnēmon-* "mindful."]

mne·mon·ics /ni mónniks/ *n.* the practice of improving or helping the memory, or the systems used to achieve this (*takes a singular verb*) [Early 18thC. From Greek *mnēmonika*, neuter plural of *mnēmonikos* (see MNEMONIC).]

Mne·mos·y·ne /ni móssәnee, -mózzәnee/ *n.* in Greek mythology, the goddess of memory and mother of the Muses [Via Latin from Greek *Mnēmosunē*]

mngr. *abbr.* manager

mo /mō/ (*plural* **mos**) *n. U.K.* a moment or short while (*informal*) ○ *I'll be there in half a mo.* [Late 19thC. Shortening, in the sense "short while," of MOMENT.]

Mo *symbol.* molybdenum

MO *abbr.* **1.** Missouri **2. m.o.** money order

mo. *abbr.* month

Mo. *abbr.* Missouri

m.o. = **MO**

M.O., m.o. *abbr.* **1.** mail order **2.** Medical Officer **3.** modus operandi

-mo *suffix.* used after numerals to indicate the number of pages made by folding a sheet of paper ○ *16mo* [From *12mo*, an abbreviation of Latin *(in) duodecimo* "(in) a twelfth"; *duodecimus* (see DUODECIMAL)]

mo·a /mṓ ә/ *n.* a large extinct flightless bird of New Zealand similar to the ostrich that existed in a number of varieties and died out at the end of the 18th century. Family: Dinornithidae. [Mid-19thC. From Maori.]

Mo·ab[1] /mṓ ab/ *n.* the son of Lot and his eldest daughter, whose descendants were the enemies of Israel

Mo·ab[2] /mṓ àb/ ancient kingdom situated on a plateau to the east of the Dead Sea in modern-day Jordan —**Mo·a·bite** /mṓ ә bī̀t/ *n., adj.*

moan /mōn/ *v.* (**moans, moaned, moaned, moan·ing**) **1.** *vi.* MAKE A LOW SOUND EXPRESSING PAIN to make a long low sound that expresses pain or misery **2.** *vti.* COMPLAIN to complain about something, especially unreasonably or needlessly (*informal*) ○ *What's he moaning on about?* **3.** *vt.* SAY SOMETHING IN A PAINED VOICE to say something in a voice that expresses pain or misery ○ *"Oh no!", she moaned* **4.** *vi.* MAKE A NOISE LIKE SOMEBODY IN PAIN to make a long low noise that sounds like somebody expressing pain ○ *the wind moaning in the trees* ■ *n.* **1.** SOUND OF PAIN a long, low sound made by somebody expressing pain or misery **2.** SOUND LIKE MOAN a long, low sound that resembles an expression of pain or misery, made by something such as the wind **3.** COMPLAINT a complaint, especially one that is unreasonable or trivial (*informal*) [12thC. Via assumed Old English *mān* "complaint" from a prehistoric Germanic base that is also the ancestor of English *bemoan* and *mean*[1].] —**moan·er** *n.* —**moan·ful** *adj.*

moat /mōt/ *n.* **1.** DITCH AROUND A CASTLE a wide water-filled ditch around a castle or fort, dug to give protection from invaders **2.** DITCH ACTING AS A BARRIER a water-filled ditch dug to prevent access or escape, e.g., to confine animals in a zoo ■ *vt.* **(moat·ed, moat·ing, moats)** PUT A MOAT AROUND A CASTLE to surround a castle or other fortified place with a moat [14thC. From Old French *mote* "mound" (source of English *motte*) or medieval Latin *mota*, perhaps of Gaulish origin. The sense "ditch around a castle" developed from "mound," which it surrounded.]

mob /mob/ *n.* **1.** NOISY CROWD a large and unruly crowd of people **2.** *U.K.* GROUP OF PEOPLE a particular group of people (*informal*) **3.** ORDINARY PEOPLE ordinary people, especially when thought of collectively as unintelligent or irrational (*informal*) ■ *vt.* **(mobbed, mob·bing, mobs) 1.** CROWD AROUND SOMEBODY to crowd around somebody or something noisily and excitedly **2.** CROWD INTO A PLACE to crowd into and fill a place **3.** ATTACK SOMEBODY to attack somebody in a large group **4.** ZOOL ATTACK A PREDATOR among animals that are preyed upon, to surround and harass a potential predator [Late 17thC. Shortening of archaic *mobile*, from Latin *mobile (vulgus)*, literally "excitable (crowd)," a form of *mobilis* (source of English *mobile*).] —**mob·ber** *n.* —**mob·bish** *adj.*

Mob *n.* a group of people who are involved in organized crime, or the world of organized crime (*informal*)

mobbed *adj. U.K.* crowded with people (*informal*)

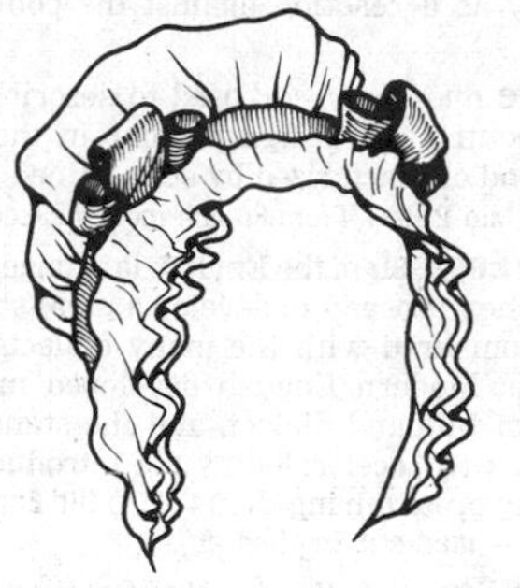

Mobcap

mob·cap /mób kàp/ *n.* **1.** WOMAN'S INDOOR CAP a loose-fitting frilly cap women often wore indoors in the 18th and early 19th centuries **2.** HAT SHAPED LIKE A MOBCAP a soft hat that is shaped like a mobcap and is worn especially by small children and babies [Mid-18thC. *Mob* from obsolete *mob* "prostitute, negligé," variant of *mab* "promiscuous woman," of unknown origin.]

mo·bile /mṓb'l, mṓ bèel, -bīl/ *adj.* **1.** EASY TO MOVE able to move freely or easily ○ *She's mobile again after her skiing accident.* **2.** OPERATING FROM A VEHICLE operating from or set up in a vehicle that travels from place to place **3.** CHANGING EXPRESSION changing expressions quickly and easily ○ *a mobile face* **4.** PREPARED FOR CHANGE able or willing to change job, move home, or alter other arrangements at short notice if necessary **5.** CHANGING SOCIALLY moving or able to move from one social or professional class or group to another, e.g., by changing jobs or moving to a new neighborhood ■ *n.* **1.** HANGING DECORATION a hanging sculpture or decoration whose parts are balanced to move in response to air currents **2.** *U.K.* MOBILE TELEPHONE a cellular telephone (*informal*) **3.** OUTSIDE EMPLOYEE somebody who works for a company outside its offices, especially using a computer link [15thC. Via French from Latin *mobilis* "movable," shortening of assumed *movibilis*, from *movere* "to move" (source of English *move*).]

Mo·bile /mō bèel/ **1.** river in southwestern Alabama, flowing into the Gulf of Mexico. Length: 38 mi./61 km. **2.** city and port in southwestern Alabama, on the northwestern shore of Mobile Bay. Population: 202,581 (1996).

-mobile *suffix.* automobile, vehicle ○ *bloodmobile* ○ *snowmobile* [From AUTOMOBILE]

mo·bile home *n.* a large trailer that can be transported on the back of a truck but is usually connected to utilities and left on a single site

mo·bile phone *n.* a portable telephone that works using a series of locally based cellular radio networks

mo·bil·i·ty /mō bíllətee/ *n.* **1.** ABILITY TO MOVE the ability to physically move about, especially to do work or take exercise **2.** MOVEMENT TO ANOTHER SOCIAL GROUP the ability of people to move from one social group or class to another [15thC]

mo·bi·lize /mṓbə līz/ **(-lized, -liz·ing, -liz·es)** *vti.* to organize people or resources to be ready for action, or to take action, especially in a military or civil emergency or to be the subject of such an organization [Mid-19thC. From French *mobiliser*, from *mobile* "movable," from Latin *mobilis* (see MOBILE).] —**mo·bi·liz·a·ble** *adj.* —**mo·bi·li·za·tion** /mòbəli záysh'n/ *n.*

Mö·bi·us strip /mṓbee əss-/ *n.* a continuous single-sided surface formed by rotating one end of a strip through 180° and joining it to the other end [Early 20thC. Named for the German mathematician August Ferdinand *Möbius* (1790–1868).]

mob·oc·ra·cy /mo bókrəssee/ (*plural* **-cies**) *n.* **1.** CONTROL BY A MOB political control exercised by a mob (*disapproving*) **2.** PLACE RUN BY A MOB a place where a mob has political control —**mob·o·crat** /móbbə kràt/ *n.* —**mob·o·crat·ic** /mòbbə kráttik/ *adj.* —**mob·o·crat·i·cal** *adj.*

mob·ster /móbstər/ *n.* somebody who is involved in organized crime (*informal*) [Early 20thC. Formed from MOB (sense 4) + *-ster*, on the model of GANGSTER.]

Mo·bu·tu, Lake /mə bṓotoo/ lake on the Zaire-Uganda border, in the north of the Rift Valley system. Area: 2,160 sq. mi./5,600 sq. km. Length: 100 mi./160 m.

Mo·bu·tu Se·se Se·ko /mə bṓotoo sayssay sáykō/ (1930–97) Zaïrean soldier and statesman. He was president of Zaïre (Democratic Republic of the Congo) from 1965 until he was forced into exile in 1997. Born **Joseph Désiré Mobutu**

moc /mok/ *n.* a moccasin shoe (*informal*) [Mid-20thC. Shortening.]

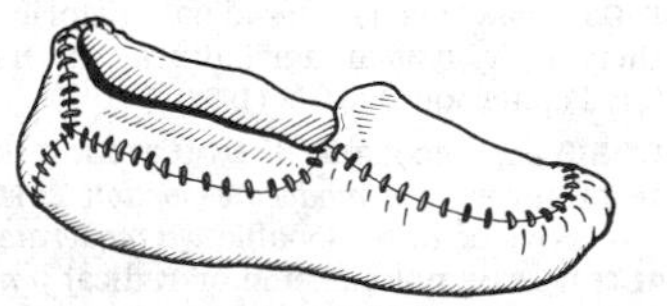

Moccasin

moc·ca·sin /mókəssin/ *n.* **1.** CLOTHES NATIVE AMERICAN SHOE a Native American heelless shoe made of deerskin or other soft leather wrapped around over the foot and stitched on top **2.** CLOTHES LEATHER SHOE a low-heeled leather shoe whose side panels are joined to the upper panel using prominent stitching to form a raised puckered seam **3.** ZOOL = **water moccasin** *n.* 1 [Early 17thC. From Virginia Algonquian *mockasin*; in sense 3 there may be a different, unknown, origin.]

moc·ca·sin flow·er *n.* = **lady's slipper** [From the shape]

mo·cha /mṓkə/ *n.* **1.** STRONG ARABIAN COFFEE a dark brown strong-tasting coffee from Yemen and some other countries on the Arabian peninsula **2.** FLAVORING a flavoring made by mixing coffee and cocoa, used in baking ■ *adj.* DARK BROWN of a dark brown color, like mocha coffee ■ *n.* INDUST LEATHER soft suede leather made from sheepskin or goatskin, originally from Africa [Late 18thC. Named for MOCHA, from where these goods were originally exported.]

Mo·cha /mṓkə, mókə/ town and seaport in southwestern Yemen, on the Red Sea, historically a coffee-exporting center. Population: 1,163 (1977 estimate).

Mo·che /mō chày, mō chè/ *adj.* OF THE MOCHICA PEOPLE relating to the Mochica people or their culture ■ *n.* = **Mochica** [From *Moche*, an archeological site and valley on the northwestern coast of Peru]

Mo·chi·ca /mō chéekə/ (*plural* **-cas** *or* **-ca**), **Mo·che** (*plural* **-ches** *or* **-che**) *n.* a member of an ancient Native South American people that lived along the northern coast of Peru, where their civilization flourished between the sixth century B.C. and the second century B.C. The Mochica are particularly noted for their pottery, which was decorated with realistic paintings of human and animal forms. [Mid-19thC. Via Spanish from a Native American word.]

mock /mok/ *v.* **(mocked, mock·ing, mocks) 1.** *vti.* TREAT SOMETHING WITH SCORN to treat somebody or something with scorn or contempt **2.** *vt.* MIMIC SOMEBODY to imitate people in a way that is intended to make them appear silly or ridiculous **3.** *vt.* PREVENT SOMETHING to prevent something from succeeding in a way that causes frustration or humiliation ○ *the wind mocking his efforts to light a fire* ■ *adj.* **1.** IMITATION made to appear like something else, usually something older or more expensive ○ *mock leather* **2.** PRETEND done as an act, especially in order to amuse people ○ *frowned in mock disapproval* **3.** PRACTICE done as practice for the real thing ○ *mock exams* ■ *n.* **1.** AN IMITATION something made as an imitation **2.** OBJECT OF SCORN something or somebody ridiculed by others (*dated*) [15thC. From Old French *mocquer*, perhaps from assumed Vulgar Latin *muccare* "to wipe the nose," and perhaps of imitative origin.] —**mock·a·ble** *adj.* —**mock·er** *n.* —**mock·ing** *adj.* —**mock·ing·ly** *adv.*

WORD KEY: SYNONYMS

See Synonyms at ***ridicule***.

mock up /mók ùp/, **mock·up** *vt.* to make a full-scale model of something, e.g., a working model of a machine to undergo testing

mock·er·nut /mókər nùt/ *n.* **1.** N AMERICAN HICKORY TREE a North American hickory tree with smooth bark and fragrant leaves that turn bright yellow in the fall. Latin name: *Carya tomentosa*. **2.** NUT OF THE MOCKERNUT TREE the large nut produced by the mockernut tree

mock·er·y /mókəree/ (*plural* **-ies**) *n.* **1.** SCORN words or behavior intended to make something or somebody look silly or ridiculous **2.** SOMETHING INADEQUATE something that is ridiculously inadequate or wholly unsuccessful ○ *the survey was a mockery from start to finish* [15thC]

mock-he·ro·ic *adj.* COMIC IN HEROIC STYLE used to describe poetry that satirizes the heroic style by using it to describe something trivial. Traditionally, heroic and mock-heroic poetry used classical forms such as the iambic pentameter (**heroic couplet**) or the hexameter (**alexandrine**). ■ *n.* MOCK-HEROIC VERSE verse written in the mock-heroic style

mock·ing·bird /móking bùrd/ *n.* a long-tailed grayish North American bird that incorporates the songs and calls of other birds into its own song. Latin name: *Mimus polyglottus*.

WORD KEY: CULTURAL NOTE

To Kill a Mockingbird, a novel by Harper Lee (1960). Set in the southern United States, it tells the story of a white lawyer who agrees to defend a black man wrongly accused of the rape of a white girl. The events are narrated from the point of view of the lawyer's six-year-old daughter, Scout. It was made into a movie by Robert Mulligan in 1962.

mock moon *n.* ASTRON = **paraselene**

mock or·ange *n.* **1.** TREE WITH FLOWERS LIKE THE ORANGE TREE a shrub or tree that bears fragrant white flowers like the flowers of an orange tree. Genus: *Philadelphus*. **2.** TREE SIMILAR TO THE MOCK ORANGE a shrub or tree that resembles the mock orange

mock sun *n.* ASTRON = **parhelion**

mock tur·tle soup *n.* an old-fashioned soup made in imitation of turtle soup, using meat from a calf's head to replace the flesh of the green turtle

mock-up *n.* **1.** FULL-SCALE MODEL a full-sized model of something, built to scale and with working parts, used especially for testing or research **2.** PUBL LAYOUT a preliminary layout of a newspaper, magazine, or other publication, showing the size and arrangement of material to be included

Mod /mod/, **mod** *n.* **mod, Mod** a member of a youth group in 1960s Britain remembered especially for their fashionable dress, motor scooters, and fights with motorcycle gangs (**rockers**) [Mid-20thC. Shortening of MODERN or MODERNISM.]

mod. *abbr.* **1.** moderate **2.** moderato **3.** modern

mo·dal /mṓd'l/ *adj.* **1.** GRAM EXPRESSING GRAMMATICAL MOOD used to describe verbs and auxiliary verbs expressing a grammatical mood, e.g., possibility or necessity. ◊ **modal auxiliary 2.** MUSIC RELATING TO MUSICAL

MODES relating to or using a mode, especially instead of a major or minor scale **3.** PHILOS **DESCRIBING LOGICAL MODALITIES** used to describe propositions involving necessity or probability, and those relating to knowledge, belief, and obligation [Mid-16thC. Directly or via French from medieval Latin *modalis*, from Latin *modus* (see MODE).] —**mo·dal·ly** *adv.*

mo·dal aux·il·ia·ry *n.* a verb used with other verbs to express such ideas as permission, possibility, and necessity. The modal auxiliaries in English grammar are "can," "could," "may," "might," "must," "ought to," "shall," "should," "will," and "would." Some classifications also include "dare," "need," and "used."

mo·dal·i·ty /mō dálləteé/ *n.* (*plural* **-ties**) **1.** GRAM **WHAT A MODAL VERB EXPRESSES** the idea or concept that a modal auxiliary verb expresses **2.** PHILOS **PROPOSITIONS OF NECESSITY OR POSSIBILITY** the purely logical classification of propositions that relate to necessity or possibility **3.** MED **TREATMENT** something used in the treatment of a disorder, e.g., surgery or chemotherapy ■ **mo·dal·i·ties** *npl.* POL **PROTOCOL** procedures that are followed in the course of political or diplomatic negotiations [Early 17thC. Directly or via French *modalité* from Medieval Latin *modalitas*, from *modalis* (source of English *modal*), in turn formed from Latin *modus* (see MODE).]

mo·dal log·ic *n.* the branch of logic that studies the relations between modal propositions

mode /mōd/ *n.* **1. MANNER OR FORM** a way, manner, or form, e.g., a way of doing something, or the form in which something exists **2. STYLE OR FASHION** a style or fashion, e.g., in art or in dress **3. MACHINE SETTING** a setting or function on a machine such as a computer **4. TYPE OF AUTOMATIC BEHAVIOR** a way of behaving, especially one that is instinctive, familiar, or habitual (*informal humorous*) **5.** MUSIC **MUSICAL SCALE** a musical scale that is one of the seven patterns of notes that can be played over an octave using only the white notes of the piano keyboard. Some modes were widely used in European religious, folk, and art music until around 1600, after which they were largely replaced by keys, while others were used in ancient Greece, although their exact nature remains unknown. **6.** MATH, STATS **MOST FREQUENT VALUE** the value that has the highest frequency within a statistical range **7.** LOGIC **MODAL STATUS OF A PROPOSITION** the modal status of a proposition, e.g., its being necessary or merely possible **8.** PHYS **RADIO FREQUENCY** one of the radio frequences characteristic of a given resonator or oscillator **9.** PHILOS **COMBINATION OF IDEAS** a combination of ideas that cannot be worked out merely by analysis of its components [14thC. From Latin *modus* "measure, rhythm, song, manner"; in the sense "fashion," from French *mode*.]

mod·el /mód'l/ *n.* **1. COPY OF AN OBJECT** a copy of an object, especially one made on a smaller scale than the original (*often used before a noun*) **2. PARTICULAR VERSION OF MANUFACTURED ARTICLE** a particular version of a manufactured article ○ *had traded in her car for the latest model* **3. SOMETHING COPIED** something that is copied or used as the basis for a related idea, process, or system **4. SOMEBODY PAID TO WEAR CLOTHES** somebody who is paid to wear clothes and demonstrate merchandise as a profession, e.g., in fashion shows and photographs for magazines and catalogues **5. SIMPLIFIED VERSION** a simplified version of something complex used, e.g., to analyze and solve problems or make predictions ○ *a financial model* **6. PERFECT EXAMPLE** an excellent example that deserves to be imitated **7. ARTIST'S SUBJECT** somebody who poses for a painter, sculptor, photographer, or other artist **8.** ZOOL **ANIMAL COPIED BY ANOTHER ANIMAL** an animal species repellent to predators which another animal mimics for protection **9.** LOGIC **INTERPRETATION** an interpretation of a theory arrived at by assigning referents in such a way as to make the theory true **10.** *U.K.* FASHION **EXCLUSIVE GARMENT** the first sewn example of a couturier's or clothing manufacturer's design, from which a new line of garments is produced ■ *v.* (**-eled, -el·ing, -els**) **1.** *vti.* **WORK AS FASHION MODEL** to work as a fashion model, wearing clothes, makeup, and other items in order to display them to others **2.** *vi.* **BE AN ARTIST'S MODEL** to sit as a model for somebody such as a painter or photographer **3.** *vt.* **BASE SOMETHING ON SOMETHING ELSE** to base something, especially somebody's appearance or behavior, on somebody or something else ○ *She modeled herself on her older sister.* **4.** *vt.* **SHAPE SOMETHING** to make something by shaping a substance or material, e.g., clay or wood [Late 16thC. Via French *modèle* from Italian *modello* "model," from, ultimately, Latin *modulus* "measure" (source of English *module*), from *modus* (see MODE).] —**mod·el·er** *n.*

mo·del home *n.* a house on a housing development that is decorated and furnished to show to prospective buyers [19thC]

mod·el·ing *n.* **1. FASHION MODEL'S WORK** the work of a fashion model **2. MAKING MODELS** the activity or hobby of making models **3.** PSYCHOL **DEMONSTRATION OF BEHAVIOR** the demonstration of a way of behaving to somebody, especially a child, in order for that behavior to be imitated

mod·el·ling *n.* U.K. = **modeling**

mod·el the·o·ry *n.* the branch of logic that deals with providing models for theories —**mod·el-the·o·ret·ic** *adj.*

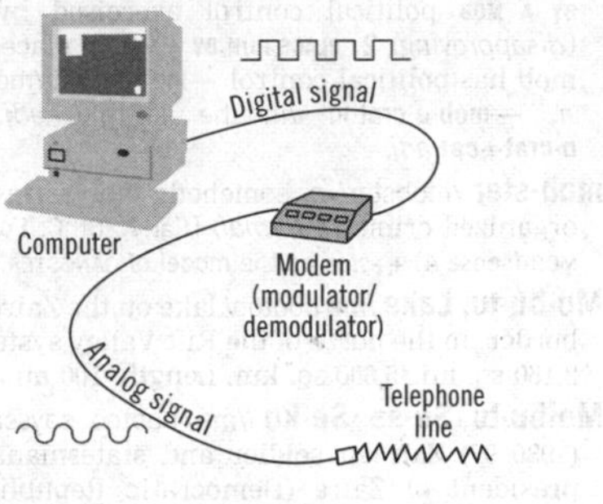

Modem

mo·dem /mṓ dèm/ *n.* an electronic device that connects computers via a telephone line, allowing the exchange of information. It consists of a modulator to convert computer information into a telephone signal and a demodulator to convert it back again. [Mid-20thC. Blend of MODULATE and DEMODULATE.]

Mo·de·na /maw dḗnə, mawd'nə/ historic city in northern Italy. It is an agricultural and industrial center. Population: 176,972 (1992).

mod·er·ate *adj.* /móddərət/ **1. SMALL OR SLIGHT** not large, great, or severe ○ *a moderate portion* **2. REASONABLE** not excessive or unreasonable ○ *a moderate eater* **3. MIDDLE-OF-THE-ROAD** not extreme or radical ○ *moderate views* **4. AVERAGE** neither particularly good nor particularly bad ○ *moderate results* ■ *n.* **SOMEBODY WITH MODERATE VIEWS** somebody who holds views, especially political views, that are not extreme ■ *vti.* /móddə ràyt/ (**-at·ed, -at·ing, -ates**) **1. MAKE OR BECOME LESS EXTREME** to become, or make something become, less great, extreme, violent, or severe **2. PRESIDE OVER SOMETHING** to chair or preside over something such as a meeting or discussion [14thC. From Latin *moderat-*, past participle stem of *moderari* "regulate," from a prehistoric pre-Latin stem that is also the source of English *modest*.] —**mod·er·ate·ly** *adv.* —**mod·er·ate·ness** *n.*

mod·er·ate breeze *n.* a wind that measures force four on the Beaufort scale, with a speed of between 13 and 18 mph or 20.9 and 29 kph

mod·er·ate gale *n.* a wind that measures force seven on the Beaufort scale, with a speed of between 32 and 38 mph or 51.5 and 61.2 kph

mod·er·ate-in·come *adj.* having an income close to the national average, and therefore neither poor nor rich

mod·er·a·tion /mòddə ráysh'n/ *n.* **1. BEING MODERATE** the state in which something remains moderate rather than becoming extreme or excessive ○ *moderation in all things* **2. MAKING SOMETHING MODERATE** the limiting, controlling, or restricting of something so that it becomes or remains moderate **3. ACTING AS MODERATOR** the position or function of moderating something [15thC] ◇ **in moderation** within reasonable limits, and never to excess

mod·e·ra·to /mòddə raátō/ *adv.* at a moderate tempo (*used as a musical direction*) [Early 18thC. Via Italian from Latin *moderat-* (see MODERATE).]

mod·er·a·tor /móddə ràytər/ *n.* **1. SOMEBODY IN CHARGE OF DISCUSSIONS** somebody who presides over an assembly, especially a legislative assembly, or who acts as a mediator in discussions or negotiations **2.** CHR **PRESIDING MINISTER** in the Presbyterian denominations of the Christian church, a minister presiding over a church court or other assembly **3.** NUCLEAR PHYS **NEUTRON ABSORBER** a substance, e.g., graphite or beryllium, that slows neutrons in a nuclear reactor so that they can bring about the fission of uranium —**mod·er·a·tor·ship** *n.*

mod·ern /móddərn/ *adj.* **1. BELONGING TO THE PRESENT DAY** relating or belonging to the present period in history **2. OF THE LATEST KIND** of the latest, most advanced kind, or using the most advanced equipment and techniques available ○ *modern medicine* **3. USING THE LATEST STYLES** relating to or using ideas and techniques that have only recently been developed or are still considered experimental. ◊ **modern dance, modern jazz** **4.** LING **OF A LANGUAGE'S LATEST STAGE** relating or belonging to the most recent stage in the development of a language. ◊ **modern English, modern Greek, modern Hebrew** ■ *n.* **1. MODERN PERSON** somebody living in the present period, especially somebody whose tastes and attitudes are regarded as nontraditional or strikingly new **2.** PRINTING **TYPEFACE** a typeface with heavy vertical strokes and straight serifs [Early 16thC. Directly or via French *moderne* from Latin *modernus*, from *modo* "just now, in a (certain) manner," from *modus* (see MODE).] —**mod·ern·ly** *adv.* —**mod·ern·ness** *n.*

WORD KEY: SYNONYMS

See Synonyms at ***new***.

mod·ern dance *n.* a free unrestricted style of theatrical dancing that developed in the early 20th century as a reaction against the conventions of ballet

mo·derne /mō dáirn/ *adj.* used to describe a style of architecture and design popular in the 1920s and 1930s and characterized by streamlined and curved forms [Mid-20thC. From French *moderne* (see MODERN).]

mod·ern Eng·lish *n.* the English language from about 1500, when it began to develop a more standardized form compared with the many dialects of Middle English. Modern English developed mainly from the East Midland dialect, and the standardization process was accelerated by the introduction of the printing press during the 1470s. ◊ **Old English, Middle English** —**mod·ern Eng·lish** *adj.*

mod·ern Greek *n.* the form of Greek spoken since around 1453, the year of the fall of Byzantium —**mod·ern Greek** *adj.*

mod·ern He·brew *n.* the form of the Hebrew language that is the official language of the state of Israel. It is a revival of the ancient form of the language. —**mod·ern He·brew** *adj.*

mod·ern his·to·ry *n.* the study of the period of European history after 1789. In the U.K. this term refers to the period from the end of the Middle Ages in Europe, around the middle of the 15th century, to the present day.

mod·ern·ism /móddər nìzzəm/ *n.* **1. LATEST THINGS** the latest styles, tastes, attitudes, or practices **2.** ARTS **MODERN STYLES IN ART** the revolutionary ideas and styles in art, architecture, and literature that developed in the early 20th century as a reaction to traditional forms **3.** CHR **MOVEMENT WITHIN ROMAN CATHOLICISM** a movement in European Roman Catholicism in which scholars and theologians attempt to accommodate the contemporary world view within Roman Catholic theology and doctrine —**mod·ern·ist** *n., adj.* —**mod·ern·is·tic** /mòddər nístik/ *adj.* —**mod·ern·is·ti·cal·ly** *adv.*

mo·der·n·i·ty /mo dúrnətee, mō-/ (*plural* **-ni·ties**) *n.* **1. QUALITY OF BEING MODERN** the quality of being modern or up-to-date **2. SOMETHING MODERN** a modern thing

mod·ern·ize /móddər nīz/ (**-ized, -iz·ing, -iz·es**) *vti.* to change something in order to make it conform to modern tastes, attitudes, or standards [Mid-18thC] —**mod·ern·iz·er** *n.* —**mod·ern·i·za·tion** /mòddərni záysh'n/ *n.*

mod·ern jazz *n.* a style of jazz that developed in the early 1940s, with rhythms and harmonies much more complex than those of traditional jazz

mod·ern pen·tath·lon *n.* an athletic competition consisting of the five events of swimming, horse riding and jumping, cross-country running, fencing, and pistol shooting

mod·est /móddəst/ *adj.* **1. HUMBLE** not having or expressing a high opinion of your own achievements or abilities **2. SHY** not confident or assertive, and tending to be easily embarrassed in company **3.**

REASONABLE not large, extreme, or excessive ○ *a modest income* 4. SIMPLE not showy, elaborate, or pretentious ○ *a modest dwelling* 5. NOT OVERTLY SEXUAL not drawing attention to or discussing sexuality, and so unlikely to offend or arouse others [Mid-16thC. Perhaps both a back-formation from MODESTY and via French *modeste* from Latin *modestus* "kept within due measure" (from the same source as English *moderate*).] —**mod·est·ly** *adv.*

Mo·des·to /mə déstō/ city in central California. It is the seat of Stanislaus County. Population: 176,357 (1994).

mod·es·ty /móddəstee/ *n.* 1. HUMILITY unwillingness to draw attention to your own achievements or abilities 2. SEXUAL RESERVE reserve about nudity or sexual matters, especially a preference for clothes that keep much of the body covered 3. SHYNESS lack of confidence when speaking to others or stating opinions, and the tendency to be uneasy or embarrassed in company 4. SIMPLICITY lack of grandeur or ostentation 5. MODERATION moderation in size, scale, or extent [Mid-16thC]

mod·i·cum /móddikəm/ *n.* a small amount, especially of something abstract, such as a particular quality ○ *It only requires a modicum of common sense.* [Late 15thC. From Latin, "little way, short time," a form of *modicus* "moderate," from *modus* (see MODE).]

modif. *abbr.* 1. modification 2. GRAM modifier

mod·i·fi·ca·tion /mòddəfi káysh'n/ *n.* 1. CHANGE a slight change or alteration made to improve something or make it more suitable ○ *made a few modifications to the original design* 2. ACT OF MODIFYING the act or process of modifying something, or the condition of having been modified ○ *in need of modification* 3. SOMETHING MODIFIED something that has been modified ○ *The new version is a modification and is based on existing software.* 4. GRAM GRAMMATICAL RELATIONSHIP WITH A MODIFIER in grammar, the relationship between a modifier and what it modifies [15thC. Directly or via French from Latin *modificatio(n)-*, past participle stem of *modificare* (see MODIFY).] —**mod·i·fi·ca·tive** /móddəfi kàytiv/ *adj.* —**mod·i·fi·ca·tor** *n.* —**mod·i·fi·ca·to·ry** *adj.*

mod·i·fi·er /móddə fīr/ *n.* GRAM 1. SOMEBODY OR SOMETHING THAT MODIFIES SOMETHING somebody or something that makes slight changes to something, especially to improve it 2. WORD QUALIFYING ANOTHER a word or phrase that affects the meaning of another, usually describing it or restricting its meaning. "Pink" in the phrase "the pink ribbon," "fire" in the compound "fire alarm," and "in the morning" in the sentence "She always goes jogging in the morning" are modifiers.

mod·i·fy /móddə fī/ (**-fied, -fy·ing, -fies**) *v.* 1. *vti.* MAKE CHANGES TO SOMETHING to make a slight change or alteration to something, or to change slightly 2. *vt.* LESSEN SOMETHING to make something less extensive, severe, or extreme 3. *vt.* GRAM AFFECT A WORD'S MEANING to affect the meaning of a word, usually by describing or limiting it, by adding an adjective, noun, or phrase 4. *vt.* LING CHANGE A VOWEL SOUND to change the sound of a vowel by adding an umlaut [14thC. Via French *modifier* from Latin *modificare* "to limit," ultimately from *modus* "measure" (source of English *mode*) + the base of *facere* "to make" (source of English *fact*).] —**mod·i·fi·a·bil·i·ty** /mòddə fī ə bíllətee/ *n.* —**mod·i·fi·a·ble·ness** /móddə fī əb'lnəss/ *n.* —**mod·i·fi·a·ble** /-fī əb'l/ *adj.*

WORD KEY: SYNONYMS

See Synonyms at ***change***.

Mo·di·glia·ni /mòddil yaánee/, **Amedeo** (1884–1920) Italian painter and sculptor. His distinctive style, seen to best effect in his portraits, is characterized by graceful, elongated proportions.

mo·dil·lion /mō díllyən/ *n.* ARCHIT a small curved ornamental bracket under the corona of a Corinthian or Composite column [Mid-16thC. Via French *modillion* from Italian *modiglione*, from, ultimately, Latin *mutulus* "mutule" (source of English *mutule*), perhaps of Etruscan origin.]

mo·di·o·lus /mō dī́ ələss/ (*plural* **-li** /-lī/) *n.* the bony central pillar of the cochlea in the inner ear [Late 17thC. From Latin "nave of a wheel," originally "small measure," from *modius* "a measure."]

mod·ish /mṓdish/ *adj.* in, or conforming to the very latest fashions or styles, especially those considered extreme or outrageous —**mod·ish·ly** *adv.* —**mod·ish·ness** *n.*

mo·diste /mō deést/ *n.* a designer, maker, or seller of fashionable women's clothes, especially in the late 18th and early 19th century (*dated*) [Mid-19thC. From French, from *mode* "fashion" (source of English *mode* in the sense "fashion").]

Mo·dred /máwdrəd, mṓ drèd/, **Mor·dred** /máwrdrəd/ *n.* in Arthurian legend, a knight of the Round Table who killed his uncle, King Arthur

mod·u·lar /mójjələr/ *adj.* 1. INVOLVING MODULES made up of separate modules that can be rearranged, replaced, or interchanged easily ○ *modular construction techniques* 2. INVOLVING MODULI relating to or resembling a modulus, or made up of moduli ○ *modular construction techniques* [Late 18thC. From modern Latin *modularis*, from Latin *modulus* (see MODULUS).] —**mod·u·lar·i·ty** /mòjjə lérratee/ *n.* —**mod·u·lar·ly** /mójjələrlee/ *adv.*

mod·u·lar a·rith·me·tic *n.* a branch of arithmetic that deals with the remainders of whole numbers after the numbers have been divided by a modulus

mod·u·lar·ized /mójjələ rīzd/ *adj.* made up of separate parts or modules that can be rearranged, replaced, or interchanged easily

mod·u·late /mójjə làyt/ (**-lat·ed, -lat·ing, -lates**) *v.* 1. *vt.* CHANGE SOUND to change the tone, pitch, or volume of sound or something that produces sound, e.g., a musical instrument or the human voice, usually by lowering or softening it 2. *vt.* ALTER SOMETHING to make alterations in something to make it less strong, forceful, or severe 3. *vti.* MUSIC CHANGE KEY in tonal music, to change from one key to another through a harmonic progression 4. *vt.* PHYS VARY WAVE CHARACTERISTICS to vary the frequency, amplitude, or other characteristic of a radio wave or some other carrier wave in order to transmit information [Mid-16thC. Perhaps both a back-formation from MODULATION and from Latin *modulat-*, past participle stem of *modulari* "to measure, adjust to rhythm," from *modulus* (see MODULUS).] —**mod·u·la·ble** *adj.* —**mod·u·la·bil·i·ty** /mòjjələ bíllətee/ *n.* —**mod·u·la·tive** /mójjə làytiv/ *adj.* —**mod·u·la·tor** /-lày tər/ *n.* —**mod·u·la·to·ry** /mójjələ tàwree/ *adj.*

mod·u·la·tion /mòjjə láysh'n/ *n.* 1. ADJUSTMENT OF SOUND adjustment of the tone, pitch, or volume of sound, or of something that produces sound, e.g., a musical instrument or the human voice 2. SLIGHT ALTERATION slight alteration that makes something less strong, forceful, or severe 3. PHYS PROCESS OF MODULATING CARRIER WAVE the process of changing the amplitude or frequency of a wave, used in radio broadcasting to superimpose a sound signal on a continuously transmitted carrier wave

mod·ule /mójjool/ *n.* 1. INDEPENDENT INTERCHANGEABLE UNIT a unit that is combined with others to form a larger structure or system and is self-contained enough to be easily rearranged, replaced, or interchanged to form different structures or systems 2. EDUC SHORT COURSE OF STUDY a short course of study that forms part of a larger academic course or training program, e.g., any of the elements that form part of a degree program 3. SPACE TECH PART OF A SPACE VEHICLE one of the self-contained units or craft that make up a space vehicle 4. ARCHIT UNIT OF MEASUREMENT a unit of measurement or a standard, used especially in measuring architectural elements [Late 16thC. Directly or via French from Latin *modulus* (see MODULUS). The current sense of "independent part" evolved from "allotted measure."]

mod·u·lo /mójjə lō/ *prep.* MATH with respect to a particular modulus ○ *9 and 30 are congruent modulo 7 because both leave the same remainder if they are divided by 7.* [Late 19thC. From Latin, ablative singular of *modulus* (see MODULUS).]

mod·u·lus /mójjələss/ (*plural* **-li** /-lī/) *n.* 1. PHYS COEFFICIENT a coefficient expressing the degree to which a substance exhibits a particular property 2. MATH DIVISION NUMBER a number by which two other numbers can be divided so that both give the same remainder 3. MATH ABSOLUTE VALUE the absolute value of a complex number 4. MATH LOGARITHM FACTOR the factor by which a logarithm of one base must be multiplied to become the logarithm of another base [Mid-16thC. From Latin, "small measure," from *modus* "measure" (source of English *mode*).]

mo·dus op·er·an·di /mṓdəss oppə rándee, -dī/ (*plural* **mo·di op·er·an·di** /mṓ dee oppə rándee, mṓ dī oppə rán dī/) *n.* a particular way of doing things [From Latin, "mode of operating"]

mo·dus vi·ven·di /mṓdəss vi véndee, -dī/ (*plural* **mo·di vi·ven·di** /mṓ dee vi véndee, mṓ dī vi vén dī/) *n.* 1. COMPROMISE a practical arrangement that allows conflicting people, groups, or ideas to coexist 2. WAY OF LIFE the way that a particular person or group of people lives [From Latin, "mode of living"]

mo·fette /mō fét/ *n.* a fumarole (*archaic*) [Early 19thC. Via French from Neapolitan Italian *mofetta*, from *muffa* "mold, moldy smell," probably of Germanic origin.]

Mog·a·dish·u /mògə díshoō/ capital city and chief port of Somalia, situated in the southeast of the country. Population: 1,200,000 (1990).

Mo·gen Da·vid /mòggən dáyvid/ *n.* = **Star of David** [From Hebrew, literally "shield of David"]

mog·gy /móggee/ (*plural* **-gies**) *n. U.K.* a cat (*slang*) [Late 17thC. Variant of *Maggie*, from *Mag*, shortening of *Margaret*.]

Mo·ghul *n.* = **Mogul**

Mo·gol·lon /mōgə yṓn/ (*plural* **-lons** *or* **-lon**) *n.* a member of a Native American people whose civilization flourished in parts of Arizona and New Mexico from around the 2nd century B.C. to the 13th century A.D. The Mogollon are particularly noted for their attractive pottery, traditionally decorated with black and white designs. [From the *Mogollon* Rim, Arizona, and the *Mogollon* Mountains, New Mexico, both named after Juan Ignacio Flores *Mogollon*, governor of New Mexico 1712–15]

mo·gul[1] /mṓg'l, mṓ gùl/ *n.* an important or powerful person, especially somebody working in the media [Late 17thC. From MOGUL.]

mogul[2] /mṓg'l, mṓ gùl/ *n.* a mound of hard compacted snow formed as an obstacle on a ski slope [Mid-20thC. Origin uncertain: perhaps from southern German dialect *Mugel* or a Scandinavian word.]

Mo·gul /mṓ gùl/, **Mo·ghul, Mu·ghal** /múgg'l/ MEMBER OF AN INDIAN MUSLIM DYNASTY a member of the Muslim dynasty of Mongol origin that ruled large parts of India from 1526 to 1857 ■ *n.* MOGUL EMPEROR the Mogul emperor of Delhi [Late 16thC. Via Urdu *muġal* from Persian and Urdu *muġul* "Mongol."]

mo·hair /mṓ hàir/ *n.* the soft silky wool of the Angora goat. ◊ **angora** [Late 16thC. By folk etymology (from HAIR) from earlier *mocayre*, ultimately from Arabic *mukayyar* "cloth of goat's hair," literally "select, choice," past participle of *kayyara* "to prefer."]

Mo·ham·med = **Muhammad**

Mo·har·ram /mō hérrəm/ *n.* = **Muharram**

Mo·ha·ve /mō haávee/ (*plural* **-ha·ve** *or* **-haves**), **Mo·ja·ve** (*plural* **-ve** *or* **-ves**) *n.* 1. PEOPLES MEMBER OF A NATIVE N AMERICAN PEOPLE a member of a Native North American people that originally occupied lands along the Colorado River valley on the border between California and Arizona 2. LANG NATIVE N AMERICAN LANGUAGE a Native North American language spoken along parts of the Colorado River valley. It belongs to the Yuman branch of Hokan-Siouan languages. [Mid-19thC. From Mohave *hàmakháv*.] —**Mo·ha·ve** *adj.*

mo·hawk /mṓ hàwk/ *n.* a hairstyle in which the sides of the head are shaved and the remaining hair is worn sticking up. It became associated with the punk movement and was often brightly colored. [Late 19thC. From Algonquian *Mohawk*, the name of a Native American people, because it resembles a hairstyle worn by them.]

Mo·hawk[1] (*plural* **-hawk** *or* **-hawks**) *n.* 1. PEOPLES MEMBER OF A NATIVE N AMERICAN PEOPLE a member of a Native North American people that originally occupied lands along the Mohawk and Hudson rivers, and whose members now live mainly in Ontario and New York State. The Mohawk were one of the five peoples who formed the Iroquois Confederacy, which later became known as the Six Nations. 2. LANG NATIVE N AMERICAN LANGUAGE a Native North American language spoken in Quebec, Ontario, and northern New York State, belonging to the Iroquoian language family. About 3,000 people speak Mohawk. [Mid-17thC. From Narragansett *mohowawog*, literally "man-eaters."]

Mo·hawk[2] /mṓ hàwk/ river in central New York. It is the largest tributary of the Hudson River. Length: 148 mi./238 km.

Mo·he·gan /mō heégən/ (*plural* **-gan** *or* **-gans**) *n.* 1. PEOPLES MEMBER OF A NATIVE N AMERICAN PEOPLE a member of a Native North American people that originally occupied lands in eastern Connecticut, and whose members now live mainly in southeastern Connecticut and Wisconsin **2.** LANG **NATIVE N AMERICAN LANGUAGE** an Algonquian language spoken in Connecticut and Wisconsin that belongs to the Algonquian-Wakashan languages. Mohegan is spoken by around one thousand people. [Variant of MOHICAN] —**Mo·he·gan** *adj.*

mo·hel /mō hèl, mṓ ĕl/ (*plural* **-he·lim**) *n.* somebody who is qualified under Jewish religious law to carry out circumcisions [Mid-17thC. From Hebrew *mōhēl.*]

Mo·hen·jo·da·ro /məhèn jō dáarō/ ruined Bronze Age city in southern Pakistan. It formed part of the Indus Valley civilization.

mo·hi·can /mō héekən, mə-/ *n.* = **mohawk** [Mid-20thC. From the deer-hair topknots worn by Native American men in *Last of the Mohicans* (1826), a novel by (1789–1851).]

Mo·hi·can (*plural* **-can** *or* **-cans**) *n.* a Mahican or the Mahican language (*archaic*) —**Mo·hi·can** *adj.*

Mo·ho /mṓ hṑ/ *n.* GEOG = **Mohorovicic discontinuity** [Mid-20thC. Shortening.]

Mo·hock /mṓ hòk/ *n.* a member of a gang of ruffians from the upper classes who terrorized people in the streets of London in the early 18th century [Mid-17thC. Originally a variant of MOHAWK.]

AKG London

László Moholy-Nagy

Mo·holy-Nag·y /mō hṑlee nóJ/, **László** (1895–1946) Hungarian-born U.S. artist. He was codirector, with Walter Gropius, of Chicago's American School of Design (1937–39), and was known for his artistic experiments involving modern technology.

Mo·ho·ro·vi·cic dis·con·ti·nu·i·ty /mōhə rṑvichich-/ *n.* the boundary between the Earth's crust and the mantle, occurring on average at 5 mi./8 km under the oceans to 22 mi./35 km under the continents [Mid-20thC. Named for A. *Mohorovičić* (1857–1936), Yugoslav seismologist.]

Mohs scale /mṓz-/ *n.* a scale ranging from zero to ten used to measure the hardness of minerals, with talc at the bottom end and diamond at the top end. Each mineral on the scale is hard enough to scratch the one below it in the scale. [Late 19thC. Named after Friedrich *Mohs* (1773–1839), German mineralogist.]

mo·hur /mṓ ər, mə hóor/ *n.* a gold coin worth 15 rupees used in British India in the 19th and early 20th centuries [Late 17thC. From Persian and Urdu *muhr* "seal."]

moi·dore /móy dàwr, moy dáwr/ *n.* an obsolete Portuguese or Brazilian gold coin [Early 18thC. From Portuguese *moeda d'ouro* "coin of gold."]

moi·e·ty /móy ətee/ (*plural* **-ties**) *n.* **1. ONE OF TWO PARTS** either of the two parts, not necessarily equal, into which something is divided (*formal*) **2.** ANTHROP **SOCIAL GROUP** among Native South Americans and Aboriginal Australians, one of two halves into which society is divided for ritual and marriage purposes. Marriages are forbidden within the same moiety. [15thC. Via French *moitié* "half" from late Latin *medietas*, from *medius* "middle."]

moil /moyl/ *n.* (*regional archaic*) **1. DRUDGERY** hard work **2.** *U.K.* **MUD** sticky, slimy dirt or mud **3.** *U.K.* **TURMOIL** a state of agitation or confusion ■ *v.* (**moiled, moil·ing, moils**) **1.** *vi.* **WORK HARD** to work very hard ○ *toiling and moiling* **2.** *vt. U.K.* **MAKE SOMETHING DIRTY** to dirty something, especially with soil or mud (*regional archaic*) [14thC. Via Old French *moillier* "to moisten, paddle in mud" from, ultimately, Latin *mollire* "to soften," from *mollis* "soft."] —**moil·er** *n.*

Moi·rai /móy rī/ *npl.* = **Fates** *npl.* 1 [From Greek]

moi·re /mwaar, mwaa ráy/, **moi·ré** /mwaa ráy/ *n.* a moiré fabric, especially silk but also in the past mohair [Mid-17thC. From French, a later form of *mouaire* "mohair."]

moi·ré /mwaa ráy/ *adj.* TEXTILES **WITH A WAVY PATTERN** used to describe fabric with a shiny or wavy pattern on the surface ■ *n.* **1.** TEXTILES **WAVY PATTERN ON FABRIC** a shiny finish and wavy pattern on fabric, especially silk, created by using engraved rollers **2. WAVY PATTERN** the wavy or blurred effect created by superimposing one geometric pattern on a similar or identical pattern that is slightly out of alignment with the first [Early 19thC. From French *moiré*, the past participle of *moirer* "to water," from *moire* "moiré fabric," probably an alteration of MOHAIR.]

moi·ré ef·fect *n.* = **moiré**

moi·ré pat·tern *n.* = **moiré** *n.* 2

moist /moyst/ *adj.* **1. DAMP** slightly wet or damp **2. FRESH** pleasantly fresh, rather than dry or stale ○ *a rich, moist fruitcake* **3. TEARFUL** full of tears ○ *moist eyes* **4. RAINY** humid or rainy, especially with light rain or drizzle [14thC. Via Old French *moiste* from, ultimately, Latin *mucidus* "moldy," from *mucus* "slime" (source of English *mucus*), apparently influenced by *musteus* "new."] —**moist·ly** *adv.* —**moist·ness** *n.*

WORD KEY: SYNONYMS

See Synonyms at ***wet***.

mois·ten /móyss'n/ (**-tened, -ten·ing, -tens**) *vti.* to make something moist or to become moist ○ *Moisten the mixture with a little beaten egg.* —**mois·ten·er** *n.*

mois·ture /móyschər/ *n.* wetness, especially droplets of condensed or absorbed liquid or in a vapor [14thC. From Old French *moistour*, from *moiste* (see MOIST).]

mois·tur·ize /móyschə rīz/ (**-ized, -iz·ing, -iz·es**) *v.* **1.** *vti.* **USE CREAM ON FACE** to apply a cosmetic cream or lotion to the skin, especially on the face, to help prevent the skin drying out **2.** *vt.* **MAKE SOMETHING MOIST** to make something moist or more moist

mois·tur·iz·er /móyschər īzər/ *n.* a cosmetic cream or lotion used to make the skin, especially on the face, feel less dry

mo·jar·ra /mō háarə/ (*plural* **-ras** *or* **-ra**) *n.* a small silvery sea fish found mainly in shallow tropical American waters, with mouthparts that can be thrust outward. Family: Gerridae. [Mid-19thC. From American Spanish.]

Mo·ja·ve *n., adj.* PEOPLES, LANG = **Mohave**

Mo·ja·ve Des·ert /mō haávee-/ arid region in southern California, part of the Great Basin region. Area: 15,000 sq. mi./39,000 sq. km.

mo·jo /mṓ jō/ (*plural* **-joes** *or* **-jos**) *n.* (*slang*) **1. MAGIC** witchcraft or magic, or some powerful influence **2. MAGIC CHARM** an object believed to have magical powers, especially the power to keep away evil spirits [Early 20thC. Probably of African origin.]

moke /mōk/ *n.* **1.** *U.K.* **DONKEY** a donkey (*slang*) **2. AN OFFENSIVE TERM** an offensive term for a Black person (*offensive*) [Mid-19thC. Probably from a personal name.]

mok·sha /mókshə/ *n.* in Hinduism, the spiritual goal of release from reincarnation [Late 18thC. From Sanskrit *mokṣa*, from *muc* "to set free, release."]

mol CHEM symbol **mole**

mol. *abbr.* **1.** molecular **2.** molecule

mo·la[1] /mṓlə/ (*plural* **-las** *or* **-la**) *n.* = **ocean sunfish** [Late 17thC. From French *mole.*]

mo·la[2] /mṓlə, mō laà/ *n.* a square of brightly colored cloth, woven or sewn with reverse appliqué in traditional Central American style and used on clothing, as a wall hanging, or draped over furniture [Mid-20thC. From Cuna.]

mo·lal /mṓləl/ *adj.* used to describe a solution consisting of one mole of dissolved substance (**solute**) per 1,000 grams of solution

mo·lal·i·ty /mō lállətee/ (*plural* **-ties**) *n.* the concentration of a solution, expressed as the number of moles of a dissolved substance (**solute**) that can be found in 1,000 grams of solvent

mo·lar[1] /mṓlər/ *n.* a large back tooth in humans and other mammals, used for chewing and grinding. Human beings have twelve molars. ◊ **incisor, canine, premolar** [14thC. From Latin *molaris* "of a mill; grindstone, molar tooth," from *mola* "mill."]

mo·lar[2] /mṓlər/ *adj.* **1.** CHEM **RELATING TO A MOLE** used to describe something that relates to or is a mole of a substance ○ *the molar volume of hydrogen* **2.** CHEM **CONTAINING ONE MOLE PER LITER** containing one mole of substance per liter of solution **3.** PHYS **RELATING TO A WHOLE RATHER THAN PARTS** relating to a body of matter rather than the properties of its molecules or atoms [In the chemical senses: Mid-19thC, formed from MOLE. In the sense "relating to a whole": Early 20thC, formed from Latin *moles* "mass."]

mo·las·ses /mə lássəz/ *n.* **1. SYRUP FROM SUGAR REFINING** the thick sticky sweet syrup produced during the refining of raw sugar, which ranges in color from dark brown to gold **2.** *U.K.* **RESIDUE OF SUGAR REFINING** the thick dark bitter residue produced at the end of the sugar refining process [Late 16thC. Via Portuguese *melaço* from late Latin *mellaceum* "new wine, must," from, ultimately, Latin *mel* "honey."]

mold[1] /mōld/ *n.* **1. CONTAINER FOR MAKING A SHAPE** a container that gives a shape to a molten or liquid substance poured into it to harden **2. FRAME** a frame on which something is formed or built **3. OBJECT MADE IN A MOLD** an object that was formed using a mold **4. SHAPE OF A MOLD** the shape or form of a mold **5. GENERAL SHAPE** the general shape or form of something **6. DISTINCTIVE TYPE** a particular type that has a distinctive character or nature ○ *a leader in the heroic mold* **7. SET OF ASSUMPTIONS** a fixed pattern or framework of assumptions, especially when regarded as restricting ○ *negotiators who break out of the traditional diplomatic mold* **8.** = **molding** *n.* 1 ■ *v.* (**mold·ed, mold·ing, molds**) **1.** *vt.* **MAKE SOMETHING IN MOLD** to shape or form something in a mold **2.** *vt.* **GIVE SOMETHING SHAPE** to shape or give form to something **3.** *vt.* **INFLUENCE SOMEBODY'S CHARACTER** to guide or influence the growth or development of somebody or something ○ *the childhood experience that helped mold her personality* **4.** *vti.* **FIT THE CONTOURS OF SOMETHING** to fit closely by following the contours or acquiring the shape of something **5.** *vt.* METALL **MAKE A MOLD FROM SOMETHING** to make a material into a mold to be used in casting metal **6.** *vt.* ARCHIT **PUT MOLDING ON SOMETHING** to decorate something with a molding [12thC. Via Old French *modle* from Latin *modulus*, literally "little measure," from *modus* "measure" (source of English *mode*).] —**mold·a·ble** *adj.*

mold[2] /mōld/ *n.* **1. FUNGUS** a fungus that causes organic matter to decay **2. GROWTH OF MOLD** a growth of mold on the surface of something, or the discoloration caused by the growth of mold ■ *vi.* (**mold·ed, mold·ing, molds**) **BECOME COVERED WITH MOLD** to become covered with or affected by mold [15thC. From earlier English *moul* "to go moldy," from assumed Old Norse *mugla.*]

mold[3] /mōld/ *n.* **1. SOIL RICH IN HUMUS** soil that is rich in humus and easily worked or crumbled **2.** *U.K.* **EARTH** the earth or ground (*literary*) [Old English. Ultimately from an Indo-European base meaning "to grind," which is also the ancestor of English *meal*[2] and *mill*[1].]

Mol·da·vi·a /mol dáyvee ə/ former principality, located in what is now Romania and Moldova —**Mol·da·vi·an** *n., adj.*

mold·board /mṓld bàwrd/ *n.* **1. BLADE OF A PLOW** the curved metal blade of a plow that turns over the soil **2. BLADE OF A BULLDOZER OR SNOWPLOW** the large curved blade on the front of a bulldozer or snowplow that pushes the soil or snow **3.** CONSTR **SIDE OF A CONCRETE MOLD** a board that forms one side or one surface of a concrete mold

mold·er[1] /mṓldər/ (**-ered, -er·ing, -ers**) *vti.* to crumble or decay because of natural processes, or to make something crumble or decay [Mid-16thC. From *mold* "loose soil," from, ultimately, a prehistoric Germanic word meaning "to grind."]

mold·er[2] /mṓldər/ *n.* somebody who makes molds or who molds things

mold·ing *n.* **1.** ARCHIT, WOODWORK **DECORATIVE STRIP** a strip of wood or some other material that is used to decorate or finish a surface of a wall or a piece of furniture **2. SOMETHING MADE IN A MOLD** something that is produced using a mold

Mol·do·va /mol dṓvə/ independent republic in south-

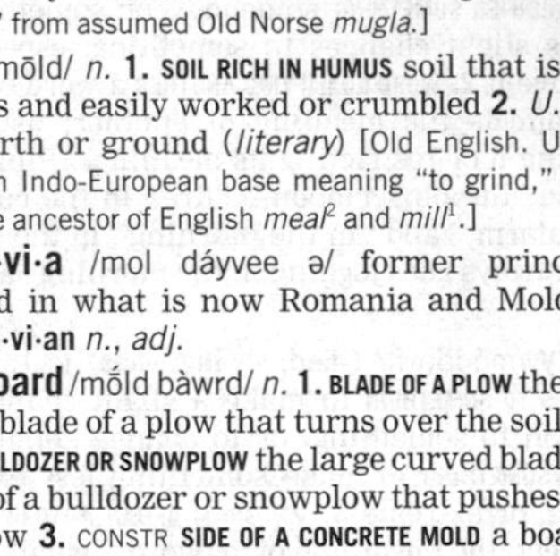

Moldova

eastern Europe. It was a republic of the Soviet Union until 1991. Language: Romanian. Currency: leu. Capital: Chisinau. Population: 4,372,000 (1996). Area: 13,012 sq. mi./33,008 sq. km. Official name **Republic of Modova** —**Mol·do·van** *n., adj.*

mold·y /mṓldee/ (**-i·er, -i·est**) *adj.* **1. WITH MOLD** with mold growing on or inside it **2. STALE FROM AGE OR ROT** stale and unpleasant from old age, neglect, or fungal growth **3. OLD** old-fashioned or out-of-date (*informal*) —**mold·i·ness** *n.*

mole[1] /mōl/ *n.* **1.** ZOOL **BURROWING MAMMAL** a small mammal that usually lives underground and has large forelimbs for digging, no external ears, minute eyes, and dense velvety fur. Family: Talpidae. **2.** CONSTR **TUNNELING MACHINE** a machine designed for boring through hard materials such as rock **3. SPY** somebody employed by a group or organization such as a government ministry who discloses sensitive information while keeping his or her own identity secret [14thC. Probably from Middle Dutch *mol*, of unknown origin.]

mole[2] /mōl/ *n.* a small dark, sometimes raised, growth on the human skin, sometimes with a hair or hairs growing from it [Old English *māl* "discolored mark." Ultimately from a prehistoric Germanic base meaning "spot, mark," which is also the ancestor of German *malen* "paint."]

mole[3] /mōl/ *n.* **1. SEA WALL** a massive wall, usually made of stone, that extends into the sea and encloses or protects a harbor **2. HARBOR** a harbor enclosed or protected by a mole [Mid-16thC. Via French *môle* and medieval Greek *molos* from Latin *moles* "mass, massive structure," the original sense in English.]

mole[4] /mōl/ *n.* an SI unit of measurement based on the amount of a substance that contains the same number of elementary units as the number of atoms in 12 grams of carbon-12. Symbol **mol** [Early 20thC. From German *Mol*, a shortening of *Molekul* "molecule."]

mo·le[5] /mṓlee/ *n.* a spicy Mexican sauce made with unsweetened chocolate and a variety of chilies and spices, used especially for cooking poultry [Mid-20thC. Via Mexican Spanish from Nahuatl *molli* "sauce, stew."]

Mo·lech *n.* BIBLE = **Moloch**

mole crab *n.* a small crustacean that has long eyestalks and hairy antennae and is often found burrowing in the sand on ocean beaches. Genus: *Emerita.*

mole crick·et *n.* a cricket with a heavy body and short wings that burrows in the ground using front legs that are adapted for digging. It feeds primarily on plant roots. Family: Gryllotalpidae.

mo·lec·u·lar /mə lékyələr/ *adj.* **1.** SCI **RELATING TO MOLECULES** relating to or made up of molecules **2.** LOGIC **MADE UP OF SIMPLER PARTS** relating to or organized from simpler parts —**mo·lec·u·lar·i·ty** /mə lèkyə lérrətee/ *n.* —**mo·lec·u·lar·ly** /mə lékyələrlee/ *adv.*

mo·lec·u·lar bi·ol·o·gy *n.* the branch of biology concerned with the nature and function, at the molecular level, of biological phenomena, such as RNA and DNA, proteins, and other macromolecules

mo·lec·u·lar film *n.* SCI = **monolayer**

mo·lec·u·lar for·mu·la *n.* a chemical formula that specifies which atoms and how many of each atom there are in a molecule of a compound

mo·lec·u·lar ge·net·ics *n.* the branch of genetics that studies genes, chromosomes, and the transmission of hereditary characteristics at the molecular level (*takes a singular verb*)

mo·lec·u·lar sieve *n.* a crystalline compound with molecule-sized pores that can be used in separating larger molecules from smaller ones

mo·lec·u·lar vol·ume *n.* the volume occupied by one mole of a substance when in the form of a gas

mo·lec·u·lar weight *n.* = **relative molecular mass**

mol·e·cule /mólla kyool/ *n.* **1.** CHEM **SMALLEST PART OF A CHEMICAL COMPOUND** the smallest physical unit of a substance that can exist independently, consisting of one or more atoms held together by chemical forces **2. TINY AMOUNT** a very small amount of something [Late 18thC. Via French *molécule* from modern Latin *molecula*, literally "small mass," from Latin *moles* "mass."]

mole·hill /mōl hìl/ *n.* a small mound of earth on the surface of the ground dug up by a burrowing mole

mole rat *n.* **1. EUROPEAN AND MIDDLE EASTERN RODENT** a tailless rodent found in eastern Europe and the Middle East that digs burrows with its enlarged incisors and powerful head. Genus: *Spalax.* **2. AFRICAN RODENT** a rodent found in Africa south of the Sahara that has large protruding incisors for digging burrows. Family: Bathyergidae.

mole·skin /mṓl skìn/ *n.* **1.** ZOOL **FUR OF THE MOLE** the short dense soft fur of a mole **2.** TEXTILES **CLOTHING FABRIC** a strong heavy cotton fabric used for clothing **3.** MED **PROTECTIVE PATCH** a soft fabric, usually with an adhesive backing, used to protect part of a foot from rubbing against a shoe ■ **mole·skins** *npl.* CLOTHES **MOLESKIN CLOTHING** clothing, especially trousers, made of moleskin fabric

mo·lest /mə lést/ (**-lest·ed, -lest·ing, -lests**) *vt.* **1.** LAW **ABUSE SOMEBODY SEXUALLY** to force unwanted sexual attentions on somebody, especially a child or physically weaker adult (*disapproving*) **2. ANNOY SOMEBODY** to pester, bother, or disturb a person or animal [14thC. Directly or via Old French *molester* from Latin *molestare*, from *molestus* "troublesome."] —**mo·les·ta·tion** /mō le stáysh'n/ *n.* —**mo·lest·er** /mə léstər/ *n.*

Mo·lière /mōl yáir/ (1622–73) French dramatist. He satirized contemporary society in a series of witty plays such as *Tartuffe* (1664). He also wrote *Le Bourgeois Gentilhomme* (1670) and *Le Malade imaginaire* (1673). Pseudonym of **Jean-Baptiste Poquelin**

mo·line /mō leén, mṓlin/ *adj.* HERALDRY used to describe a heraldic cross that has arms of equal length that broaden at the ends by forking and curving backward [Mid-16thC. Origin uncertain: probably via Anglo-Norman, from *molin* "mill," from late Latin *molinum.*]

Mo·line /mō leén/ city in northwestern Illinois, in Rock Island County, on the Mississippi River. Population: 43,472 (1994).

moll /mol/ *n.* (*slang*) **1. GANGSTER'S WOMAN COMPANION** the woman companion of a gangster **2. PROSTITUTE** a woman prostitute [Early 17thC. Shortening of the forename *Molly*, a petform of *Mary.*]

mol·lie *n.* ZOOL = **molly**

mol·li·fy /móllə fī/ (**-fied, -fy·ing, -fies**) *vt.* **1. PACIFY SOMEBODY** to calm or soothe somebody who is angry or upset **2. TEMPER SOMETHING** to make something less intense or severe **3. SOFTEN SOMETHING** to make something less hard, rigid, or stiff [15thC. Directly or via French *mollifier* "mollify."] —**mol·li·fi·a·ble** /móllə fī əb'l/ *adj.* —**mol·li·fi·ca·tion** /mòlləfi káysh'n/ *n.* —**mol·li·fi·er** /móllə fīr/ *n.* —**mol·li·fy·ing·ly** /-fī inglee/ *adv.*

mol·lusc *n.* = **mollusk**

mol·lus·ci·cide /mə lúski sīd/ *n.* a chemical that kills mollusks —**mol·lus·ci·cid·al** /mə lùski sīd'l/ *adj.*

mol·lus·cum con·ta·gi·o·sum /mə lùskəm kən tayjee ṓssəm/ *n.* a benign viral skin infection characterized by numerous small round dimpled pearly white nodules [Early 19thC. From modern Latin, literally "contagious fungus."]

Mollusk

mol·lusk /mólləsk/, **mol·lusc** *n.* an invertebrate with a soft unsegmented body, usually protected by a shell in one, two, or three pieces. The mollusks include clams, snails, slugs, squid, and octopuses. Most mollusks are aquatic. Phylum: Mollusca. [Late 18thC. Via French *mollusque* from, ultimately, Latin *molluscus* "thin-shelled nut," from *mollis* (see MOLLIFY).] —**mol·lus·kan** /mə lúskən/ *adj., n.*

mol·ly /móllee/ (*plural* **-lies**), **mol·lie** *n.* a tropical and subtropical fish native to Central and South America that bears live young and is popular as an aquarium fish. Genera: *Poecilia* and *Mollienesia.* [Mid-20thC. Shortening of modern Latin *Mollienisia*, the name of the genus, named for the French statesman Count F. N. *Mollien* (1758–1850).]

mol·ly·cod·dle /móllee kòdd'l/ *vt.* (**-dled, -dling, -dles**) **PAMPER AND SPOIL SOMEBODY** to treat somebody in an overprotective and overindulgent way ■ *n.* **OVERPROTECTED BOY** a child, especially a boy, who is spoiled and overprotected [Mid-19thC. From the name *Molly* (used for an effeminate boy or man) + CODDLE.] —**mol·ly·cod·dler** *n.*

Mol·ly Ma·guire /mòllee mə gwīr/ *n.* **1. IRISH FIGHTER AGAINST GOVERNMENT EVICTIONS** a member of a secret organization founded in Ireland in 1843 that used violent methods to stop evictions by the government **2. IRISH-AMERICAN MINER FIGHTING FOR BETTER CONDITIONS** a member of a secret Irish-American organization, active in the coalmining districts of Pennsylvania from about 1865 to 1877, that used violent methods to try to get improved working conditions [Mid-19thC. From the common Irish name, because members of the original society disguised themselves as women.]

Moloch

mo·loch /mṓ lòk, móllək/ (*plural* **-lochs**) *n.* a lizard found in the plains and deserts of central and southern Australia that has large spiny scales covering its head and back. Latin name: *Moloch horridus.* [Mid-19thC. Via Late Latin from Greek *Molokh* from Hebrew *Mōlek* "a Canaanite idol."]

Mo·loch /mṓ lèk/, **Mo·lech** *n.* **1.** BIBLE **BIBLICAL DEITY GIVEN CHILD SACRIFICES** in the Bible, a Semitic deity to whom children were sacrificed **2. SOMETHING REQUIRING COSTLY SACRIFICES** somebody or something that requires a costly and painful sacrifice [Early 17thC. Via late Latin from Greek *Molokh*, from Hebrew *mōlek.*]

Mo·lo·kai /mōlō kī́, mṓlə kī/ volcanic island in central Hawaii, between Oahu and Maui islands. Population: 6,717 (1990). Area: 260 sq. mi./673 sq. km.

Mo·lo·tov /mòllə táwf/, **Vyacheslav Mikhailovich** (1890–1986) Soviet statesman. He was a close associate and advisor of Joseph Stalin as premier (1930–41) and foreign minister (1939–49, 1953–56) of the Soviet Union. He negotiated the German-Soviet nonaggression pact in 1939. Born **Vyacheslav Mikhailovich Scriabin**

Mo·lo·tov cock·tail *n.* a crude bomb, usually made of a bottle filled with a flammable liquid such as gasoline and a wick that is set alight just before it is thrown [Mid-20thC. Named for Vyacheslav Mikhailovich MOLOTOV, who ordered their large-scale production after the Nazi invasion of Russia.]

Mol·son /mólssən/, **John** (1763–1836) British-born Canadian entrepreneur. He made his fortune as a brewer, banker, and steamship builder.

molt /mōlt/ *vti.* (**molt·ed, molt·ing, molts**) **LOSE FEATHERS, FUR, OR SKIN** to shed feathers, hair, or skin periodically, especially seasonally, to allow replacement of what is lost with new growth ■ *n.* **1. LOSS OF FEATHERS, FUR, OR SKIN** the process or time during which a bird or animal casts off all or part of its feathers, fur, or skin **2. SHED FEATHERS, FUR, OR SKIN** the material shed during molting [Pre-12thC. From Latin *mutare* "to change" (which also produced English *mutate*).] —**molt·er** *n.*

mol·ten /mṓlt'n/ *adj.* **1. MELTED** changed into liquid form by heat **2. MOLDED** produced by melting a material and then shaping it in a mold **3. GLOWING** glowing with great heat [13thC. Originally the past participle of MELT.]

mol·to /mṓltō/ *adv.* used for emphasis before or after a musical direction derived from Italian [Early 19thC. Via Italian from Latin *multus* "much" (source of English *multitude*).]

Mo·luc·cas /mə lúkəz/ group of islands in eastern Indonesia, part of the Malay Archipelago. Population: 1,741,800 (1998). Area: 28,800 sq. mi./74,500 sq. km. —**Mol·uc·can** *n., adj.*

mol wt *abbr.* molecular weight

mo·ly /mólee/ (*plural* **-lies**) *n.* **1.** MYTHOL **MAGIC HERB** in Homers' "Odyssey," a magic herb with milky white flowers and black roots that Hermes gave to Odysseus to protect him from Circe's spells **2.** PLANTS **EUROPEAN PLANT WITH YELLOW FLOWERS** a plant of the garlic family that has yellow flowers and is native to southern Europe. Latin name: *Allium moly.* [Mid-16thC. Via Latin from Greek *mōlu.*]

mo·lyb·date /mə líb dàyt/ *n.* any salt of molybdenum [Late 18thC. Formed from MOLYBDIC.]

mo·lyb·de·nite /mə líbdə nīt/ *n.* a grayish mineral, consisting of molybdenum sulfide, that is the main ore of molybdenum. Formula: MoS_2. [Late 18thC. Formed from modern Latin *molybdenum* (see MOLYBDENUM).]

mo·lyb·de·nous /mə líbdənəss/ *adj.* relating to or containing molybdenum, especially with a valence of 2 [Late 18thC. Formed from modern Latin *molybdenum* (see MOLYBDENUM).]

mo·lyb·de·num /mə líbdənəm/ *n.* a very hard, silver-colored metallic chemical element, used to strengthen steel alloys and found as a trace element in plants and animals. Symbol **Mo** [Early 19thC. Via modern Latin from, ultimately, Greek *molubdaina* "piece of lead," from *molubdos* "lead."]

mo·lyb·de·num sul·fide, mo·lyb·de·num di·sul·fide *n.* a black crystalline powder that is insoluble in water and is used as a lubricant. Formula: MoS_2.

mo·lyb·dic /mə líbdik/ *adj.* relating to or containing molybdenum, especially with a valence of 6 [Late 18thC. Formed from modern Latin *molybdenum* (see MOLYBDENUM).]

mo·lyb·dous /mə líbdəss/ *adj.* relating to or containing molybdenum, especially with a valence lower than 6 [Late 18thC. Formed from modern Latin *molybdenum* (see MOLYBDENUM).]

mom /mom/ *n.* somebody's mother (*informal*) [Late 19thC. Shortening of MOMMA.]

m.o.m. *abbr.* ACCT middle of month

MOMA /mṓmə/ *abbr.* Museum of Modern Art (New York)

mom-and-pop, ma-and-pa *adj.* **1.** **FAMILY-RUN** used to describe a business that is owned and operated by a family, especially by a husband and wife **2.** **FRIENDLY AND INFORMAL** friendly, relaxed, and pleasantly informal

Mom·ba·sa /mom bássə/ city and chief seaport of Kenya, in the southeast of the country on the Indian Ocean. It is also a tourist center. Population: 600,000 (1991).

mo·ment /mṓmənt/ *n.* **1.** **UNSPECIFIED SHORT TIME** a very short period of time ○ *Wait a moment.* **2.** **SPECIFIC INSTANT** a specific instant in time ○ *At that moment she walked in the door.* **3.** **PRESENT** the present time ○ *busy at the moment* **4.** **SIGNIFICANT PERIOD** an important or significant time or occasion ○ *great moments in world history* **5.** **SHORT PERIOD OF EXCELLENCE** a brief period of excellence or interest (*often used in the plural*) ○ *It's not a great opera, but it has its moments.* **6.** **IMPORTANCE** special importance or significance (*formal*) ○ *a decision of great moment* **7.** PHILOS **SPECIFIC STAGE** a specific stage or aspect of something **8.** PHILOS **MOMENTUM** a momentum (*dated*) **9.** PHYS **TENDENCY TO PRODUCE ROTATION** a tendency to cause motion, especially rotation **10.** PHYS **PRODUCT OF FORCE TIMES DISTANCE** the product of a quantity, e.g., force, multiplied by its perpendicular distance from a given point **11.** STATS **MEAN IN FREQUENCY DISTRIBUTION** the expected value of the deviations of a variable, compared to a fixed value, raised to a given power [14thC. Via French from Latin *momentum*, literally "movement," later "instant, moment" (from the notion of a tiny movement), hence "importance," from, ultimately, *movere* "to move" (source of English *move*).]

mo·men·tar·i·ly /mṑmən térrilee/ *adv.* **1.** **BRIEFLY** for a brief period of time **2.** **PROGRESSIVELY** with every passing moment **3.** **VERY SOON** within a very short period of time ○ *He'll be here momentarily.*

mo·men·tar·y /mṓmən tèrree/ *adj.* **1.** **VERY BRIEF** lasting for a very short time **2.** **CONSTANT** present or happening at every moment **3.** **WITH SHORT LIFE** living or continuing for only a relatively short time —**mo·men·tar·i·ness** *n.*

mo·ment·ly /mṓməntlee/ *adv.* **1.** **PROGRESSIVELY** with every passing moment ○ *to grow momently more uneasy* **2.** **VERY SOON** within a very short period of time **3.** **FOR AN INSTANT** for a very short period of time

mo·ment of in·er·tia *n.* PHYS a measure of resistance, calculated as the sum of the products of the component masses of an object multiplied by the square of its distance from an axis. Symbol *I*

mo·ment of truth *n.* **1.** **DECISIVE POINT** a point in time when a crucial decision has to be taken or when somebody or something is put to an important test **2.** **MOMENT OF BULLFIGHTER'S KILLING BLOW** in a bullfight, the point at which the bull is about to be killed with the final blow

mo·men·tous /mō méntəss/ *adj.* extremely important or crucial, especially in its effect on the future course of events —**mo·men·tous·ly** *adv.* —**mo·men·tous·ness** *n.*

mo·men·tum /mō méntəm/ (*plural* **-ta** /-méntə/ *or* **-tums**) *n.* **1.** **CAPACITY FOR PROGRESSIVE DEVELOPMENT** the power to increase or develop at an ever-growing pace ○ *The project was in danger of losing momentum.* **2.** **FORWARD MOVEMENT** the speed or force of forward movement of an object ○ *the momentum gained on the downhill stretches of the course* **3.** PHYS **MEASURE OF MOVEMENT** a quantity that expresses the motion of a body and its resistance to slowing down. It is equal to the product of the body's mass and velocity. Symbol *p* **4.** PHILOS **BASIC ELEMENT** an essential part of a whole [Early 17thC. From Latin *momentum* (see MOMENT).]

mom·ma /mómmə/ *n.* somebody's mother (*informal*) [Early 19thC. Alteration of MAMMA.]

mom·my /mómmee/ (*plural* **-mies**) *n.* somebody's mother (*informal*) [Early 20thC. Alteration of MAMMY.]

mom·my track *n.* a career route taken by a woman that may reduce her chances of career advancement by working flextime or fewer hours in order to look after a child or children (*informal*) ◊ **daddy track**

Mo·mus /mṓməss/ *n.* the god of fault-finding and mockery in Greek mythology. He is a son of Night. [Late 16thC. Via Latin from Greek *Mōmos.*]

Mon /mōn/ (*plural* **Mon** *or* **Mons**) *n.* **1.** PEOPLES **SOMEBODY FROM THE THAILAND AND MYANMAR BORDER** a member of a people that lives in adjacent parts of Thailand and Myanmar (Burma) **2.** LANG **LANGUAGE OF THE THAILAND AND MYANMAR BORDER** Mon-Khmer language belonging to the the Austro-Asiatic languages that is spoken in adjacent parts of Thailand and Myanmar (Burma). Mon is spoken by about 700,000 people. [Late 18thC. From Mon.] —**Mon** *adj.*

mon. *abbr.* **1.** monastery **2.** monetary

Mon. *abbr.* Monday

mon- *prefix.* = **mono-** (*used before vowels*)

Mon·a·can /mónnəkən/ *n.*, *adj.* = **Monegasque**

mon·a·chal /mónnik'l/ *adj.* relating to a monastery or monks, or resembling monastic life [Late 16thC. Directly or via French *monacal* from ecclesiastical Latin *monachalis*, from late Latin *monachus* (see MONK).] —**mon·a·chism** *n.* —**mon·a·chist** *adj.*, *n.*

mon·ac·id *n.* = **monoacid** ■ *adj.* = **monoacidic**

mon·a·cid·ic *adj.* = **monoacidic**

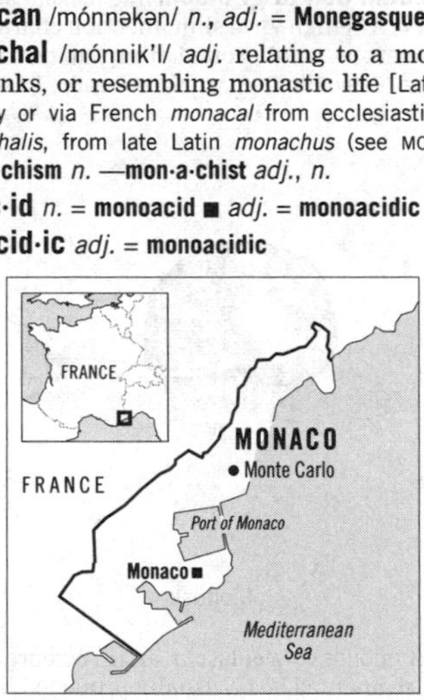

Monaco

Mon·a·co /mónnəkō/ small independent principality of Europe, bordered by France and the Mediterranean Sea. Language: French. Currency: French franc. Capital: Monaco. Population: 31,719 (1996). Area: 0.75 sq. mi./1.95 sq. km. Official name **Principality of Monaco** —**Mon·a·can** *n.*, *adj.*

mo·nad /mṓ nàd/ *n.* **1.** PHILOS **BASIC ENTITY IN THE METAPHYSICS OF LEIBNITZ** in the metaphysics of Leibnitz, an indivisible indestructible unit that is the basic element of reality and a microcosm of it **2.** BIOL **SINGLE-CELLED MICROORGANISM** a microorganism consisting of just one cell, especially a flagellate protozoan. Genus: *Monas.* **3.** CHEM **ATOM WITH A VALENCE OF 1** an atom or chemical group that has a valence of 1 [Mid-16thC. Directly or via French *monade* from the late Latin stem *monad-*, from, ultimately, Greek *monos* (see MONO-).] —**mo·nad·ic** /mō náddik/ *adj.* —**mo·nad·i·cal** /-náddə k'l/ *adj.* —**mo·nad·i·cal·ly** /-náddə kəlee/ *adv.* —**mo·nad·ism** /mṓnə dìzzəm/ *n.*

mon·a·del·phous /mònnə délfəss/ *adj.* **1.** **WITH FILAMENTS IN A TUBE SHAPE** used to describe stamens that have all the filaments united to form a single bundle in the shape of a tube **2.** **WITH MONADELPHOUS STAMENS** used to describe a flower that has monadelphous stamens [Early 19thC. Coined from MONO- + Greek *adelphos* "brother."]

mo·nad·nock /mə nád nòk/ *n.* an isolated mountain or rock that has resisted the process of erosion and stands alone in an otherwise flat area [Late 19thC. Named for such a peak in New Hampshire.]

mo·nan·drous /mə nándrəss/ *adj.* **1.** ANTHROP **WITH ONE HUSBAND** having only one husband at a time **2.** **WITH ONE MALE LOVER** having a sexual relationship with only one man during a period of time **3.** BOT **WITH ONE STAMEN** used to describe a flower that has a single stamen **4.** BOT **WITH MONANDROUS FLOWERS** used to describe a plant that has monandrous flowers

mo·nan·dry /mə nándree/ *n.* **1.** ANTHROP **MARRIAGE TO ONE HUSBAND** the practice of having only one husband at a time **2.** **TAKING OF ONE LOVER** the practice of having a sexual relationship with only one man during a period of time

Mo·na Pas·sage /mṓnə-/ area of sea separating the islands of Hispaniola and Puerto Rico, linking the Atlantic Ocean to the Caribbean Sea

mon·arch /mónnərk/ *n.* **1.** **SUPREME RULER** somebody, especially a king or queen, who rules a state or territory, usually for life and by hereditary right **2.** **EXCEPTIONALLY POWERFUL PERSON** somebody who possesses exceptional power or influence in a given sphere of activity (*literary*) **3.** **SOMETHING OUTSTANDING OR PREDOMINANT** something that occupies a preeminant or predominant position (*literary*) **4.** = **monarch butterfly** [15thC. Directly or via French *monarque* from late Latin *monarcha* from Greek *monarkhos*, literally "to rule alone," from MONO- "alone" + *arkhein* "to rule."] —**mo·nar·chal** /mə naárkəl/ *adj.* —**mo·nar·chal·ly** /-naárkəlee/ *adv.*

mon·arch but·ter·fly *n.* a large migrating orange and black North American butterfly whose caterpillars feed on milkweed plants. Latin name: *Danaus plexippus.*

mo·nar·chic /mə naárkik/, **mo·nar·chi·cal** /mə naárkik'l/ *adj.* relating to a monarch or monarchy —**mo·nar·chi·cal·ly** *adv.*

mon·ar·chism /mónnər kìzzəm/ *n.* **1.** **SUPPORT FOR MONARCHY** belief in or support for monarchy as a system of government **2.** **GOVERNMENT BY MONARCHY** the system of government in which a monarch rules —**mon·ar·chist** *n.*, *adj.* —**mon·ar·chis·tic** /mònnər kístik/ *adj.*

mon·ar·chy /mónnərkee/ (*plural* **-chies**) *n.* **1.** **SYSTEM OF RULE BY MONARCHS** a political system in which a state is ruled by a monarch **2.** **ROYAL FAMILY** a monarch and his or her family **3.** **STATE RULED BY A MONARCH** a country ruled by a monarch

mo·nar·da /mə naárdə/ *n.* a North American aromatic plant of the mint family. Bee balm and bergamot are monardas. Genus: *Monarda.* [Late 18thC. From modern Latin, the name of the genus. Named for the Spanish botanist Nicolas Monardes (1493–1588).]

mon·as·ter·y /mónnə stèrree/ (*plural* **-ies**) *n.* **1.** **MONKS' RESIDENCE** a building or buildings with grounds in which a group of people observing religious vows, especially monks, live together **2.** **COMMUNITY OF MONKS** a group of people, especially monks, living together and observing religious vows [14thC. Via ecclesiastical Latin *monasterium* from, ultimately, Greek *monazein* "to live alone," from *monos* (see MONO-).] —**mon·as·te·ri·al** /mònnə stéeree əl/ *adj.*

mo·nas·tic /mə nástik/ *adj.* **mo·nas·tic, mo·nas·ti·cal** **1.** RELIG **OF MONKS, NUNS, OR MONASTERIES** relating to monks, nuns, or their way of life or the buildings in which they live ○ *monastic rule* **2.** **RECLUSIVE OR AUSTERE** characteristic of the life of a monk, especially in being reclusive, self-denying, or austere ■ *n.* RELIG **MONK** somebody, especially a monk, who lives with others in a monastery and observes religious vows [15thC.

Directly or via French *monastique* from late Latin *monasticus* (source of English *minister*), from, ultimately, Greek *monazein* (see MONASTERY).] —**mo·nas·ti·cal·ly** *adv.*

mo·nas·ti·cism /mə násti sìzzəm/ *n.* the way of life typical of monks or nuns, in which they withdraw entirely or in part from society to devote themselves to prayer, solitude, and contemplation

mon·a·tom·ic /mònnə tómmik/, **mon·o·a·tom·ic** /mònnō-/ *adj.* **1.** WITH ONE ATOM having only one atom in the molecule **2.** WITH ONE REPLACEABLE ATOM OR GROUP with one atom or chemical group that can be replaced during a chemical reaction **3.** = **monovalent** —**mon·a·tom·ic·al·ly** *adv.*

mon·au·ral /mon áwrəl/ *adj.* **1.** MED HEARING WITH JUST ONE EAR relating to or involving the hearing of sound by one ear **2.** ELECTRON ENG = **monophonic** —**mon·au·ral·ly** *adv.*

mon·ax·i·al /mon áksee əl/ *adj.* CRYSTALS = **uniaxial**

mon·a·zite /mónnə zìt/ *n.* a reddish-brown mineral that is a phosphate of cerium and lanthanum and contains some thorium [Mid-19thC. Formed from Greek *monazein* "to be alone," from *monos* (see MONO-), because of its rare occurrence.]

Monc·ton /múngktən/ city in southeastern New Brunswick, Canada. It is a transportation center for the country's Maritime Provinces. Population: 159,313 (1996).

Mon·dale /món dàyl/, **Walter Frederick** (*b.* 1928) U.S. statesman. He was a U.S. senator (1965–77) and U.S. vice president under Jimmy Carter (1977–81).

Mon·day /mún dày, múndee/ *n.* the first day of the traditional working week, coming after Sunday and before Tuesday [Old English *mōnandæg*. Ultimately from a prehistoric Germanic translation of Latin *lunae dies* "day of the moon," which also produced German *montag*.]

Mon·day morn·ing quar·ter·back *n.* somebody who is critical of what somebody else has done or who claims to have the right answer after an event or situation has occurred (*informal*) [From the idea of someone knowing what the coach and team did wrong the day after a football game] —**Mon·day morn·ing quar·ter·back·ing** *n.*

Mon·days /mún dàyz, múndeez/ *adv.* every Monday

Mon·dri·an /móndree aàn, móndree aan/, **Piet** (1872–1944) Dutch painter. Founder of the magazine *De Stijl*, he formulated neoplasticism, a form of geometric abstraction with flat planes and straight lines. Born **Pieter Cornelis Mondriaan**

mo·ne·cious *adj.* BOT, ZOOL = **monoecious**

Mo·né·gasque /mònnə gáask/ *n.* SOMEBODY FROM MONACO somebody who was born in or who lives in Monaco ■ *adj.* RELATING TO MONACO relating to or typical of Monaco, or its people or culture [Late 19thC. Via French from, ultimately, *Mounegue* "Monaco."]

Mo·nel /mō nél/ *tdmk.* a trademark for a corrosion-resistant alloy of nickel and copper with some iron, manganese, and aluminum

mon·es·trous /mon éstrəss/ *adj.* used to describe mammals that have only one estrous cycle in a year or breeding season

Mon·et /món ay/, **Claude** (1840–1926) French painter. A leading figure of the impressionist movement, he is noted for his studies of the effects of light on scenes and subjects in nature. Full name **Claude Oscar Monet**

mon·e·ta·rism /mónnətə rìzzəm/ *n.* **1.** MONEY SUPPLY THEORY the theory that inflation and other economic variations are caused by changes in the money supply **2.** CONTROL OF THE MONEY SUPPLY the policy of controlling an economic system by increasing or decreasing the money supply, especially in a gradual manner —**mon·e·ta·rist** *n., adj.*

mon·e·tar·y /mónnə tèrree/ *adj.* **1.** RELATING TO MONEY relating to or involving money **2.** RELATING TO CURRENCY relating to a national currency ○ *The monetary unit of the U.S. is the dollar.* [Early 19thC. Directly or via French *monétaire* from late Latin *monetarius*, from Latin *moneta* (see MONEY).] —**mon·e·tar·i·ly** /mònnə térrilee/ *adv.*

mon·e·tize /mónnə tìz/ (**-tized, -tiz·ing, -tiz·es**) *vt.* **1.** MAKE SOMETHING LEGAL TENDER to make something the legal tender of a country **2.** COIN METAL to convert a metal into coins **3.** CONVERT DEBT INTO AVAILABLE MONEY to convert a government debt into available currency, especially by issuing securities [Late 19thC. Formed from Latin *moneta* (see MONEY).] —**mon·e·ti·za·tion** /mònnəti záysh'n/ *n.*

mon·ey /múnee/ *n.* **1.** SOMEBODY'S COINS AND BILLS the amount of coins and bills in somebody's possession at any one time **2.** SAVINGS OR CREDIT the amount of money held in a bank account or available on credit to somebody **3.** WAGES OR SALARY the amount somebody is paid for working **4.** CONVERTIBLE ASSETS assets or property that can be converted into cash **5.** NATIONAL CURRENCY the official currency of a country **6.** OFFICIAL MEDIUM OF EXCHANGE a commodity, usually gold, that is an official medium of exchange and a measure of value **7.** UNOFFICIAL MEDIUM OF EXCHANGE a medium of exchange that can be used to purchase goods and services **8.** RICH PEOPLE a rich individual, family, or class ○ *She married money.* ■ **mon·ey** (*plural* **monies**) *npl.* SUM OF MONEY a sum or amount of money, especially one that has a particular origin ○ *state education moneys* [13thC. Via Old French *monie* from Latin *moneta* "mint, money" (source also of English *mint*), from *Moneta* (epithet of the goddess Juno, in whose temple coins were minted).] ◇ **for somebody's money** in somebody's opinion ◇ **in the money** having a lot of money ◇ **on the money** correct or accurate ◇ **put your money where your mouth is** to take action to show that you truly mean what you have said (*informal*)

mon·ey-back *adj.* refunding money paid for something if the product or service is unsatisfactory ○ *It comes with a money-back guarantee.*

mon·ey·bags /múnnee bàgz/ (*plural* **-bags**) *n.* somebody who is rich, especially somebody who makes a show of being wealthy (*informal*) (*takes a singular verb*)

mon·ey·chang·er /múnnee chàynjər/ *n.* **1.** FOREIGN CURRENCY EXCHANGER somebody who exchanges currencies of different countries, usually for a fee **2.** MACHINE DISPENSING COINS a machine that dispenses coins in exchange for paper money

mon·eyed /múnneed/, **mon·ied** *adj.* **1.** RICH possessing a great deal of money **2.** CONSISTING OF MONEY consisting of or resulting from money

mon·ey·grub·ber /múnnee grùbbər/ *n.* somebody bent on making money at every possible opportunity (*disapproving*) —**mon·ey·grub·bing** *adj., n.*

mon·ey·lend·er /múnnee lèndər/ *n.* somebody whose business is lending money in exchange for interest on the amount borrowed

mon·ey·mak·er /múnnee màykər/ *n.* **1.** SOMEBODY GOOD AT MAKING MONEY somebody who is very good at making money **2.** SOMETHING THAT MAKES MUCH MONEY a business, product, or project that makes a lot of money —**mon·ey·mak·ing** *n., adj.*

mon·ey·man /múnnee màn/ (*plural* **-men** /-mèn/) *n.* (*informal*) **1.** FINANCE AND ECONOMICS EXPERT somebody who is an expert on finance and economics **2.** FINANCIAL MANAGER somebody who is the financial manager or accountant of a business or organization

mon·ey mar·ket *n.* **1.** SHORT-TERM TRADE IN LOW-RISK SECURITIES the trade in low-risk securities that have a life of one year or less **2. mon·ey mar·ket, mon·ey mar·ket fund** MUTUAL FUND a type of mutual fund that sells its shares to buy short-term securities and then converts the profits into additional shares for its shareholders

mon·ey of ac·count *n.* a monetary unit that is used to keep accounts. It does not necessarily correspond to an actual currency unit.

mon·ey or·der *n.* an order for a specific sum of money, usually purchased with cash at a bank or post office, that can be used to make payments

mon·ey plant *n.* BOT = **honesty** *n.* 3 [From its coin-like seedpods]

mon·ey shell *n.* the shell of the butter clam, formerly used as money by Native Americans on the western coast of North America

mon·ey sup·ply *n.* the total amount of money available in a given economy. The money supply may be measured in various ways, e.g., as the total amount of currency in circulation combined with the money available in bank deposits.

mon·ey·wort /múnnee wùrt, -wàwrt/ *n.* an evergreen creeping plant of Europe and eastern North America that has coin-shaped leaves and yellow flowers. Latin name: *Lysimachia nummularia.*

-monger *suffix.* seller, dealer, promoter ○ *fashionmonger* [Old English *mangere*, via prehistoric Germanic from, ultimately, Latin *mango* "peddler, swindler"]

mon·go /móng gō/ (*plural* **-go** *or* **-gos**) *n.* a Mongolian sub-unit of currency equal to one hundredth of a tugrik. See table at **currency** [Mid-20thC. From Mongolian *möngö* "silver."]

mon·gol /móng g'l, móng gōl/ *n.* a highly offensive term for somebody who is affected by Down syndrome (*dated offensive*)

Mon·gol *adj.* PEOPLES OF MONGOLIA OR MONGOLS relating to Mongolia, the Mongols, or their language or culture ■ *n.* **1.** PEOPLES SOMEBODY FROM MONGOLIA a member of the originally nomadic peoples who inhabit Mongolia and established the Mongol Empire in the 13th century **2.** LANG = **Mongolian** *n.* 2 [Late 17thC. From Mongolian.]

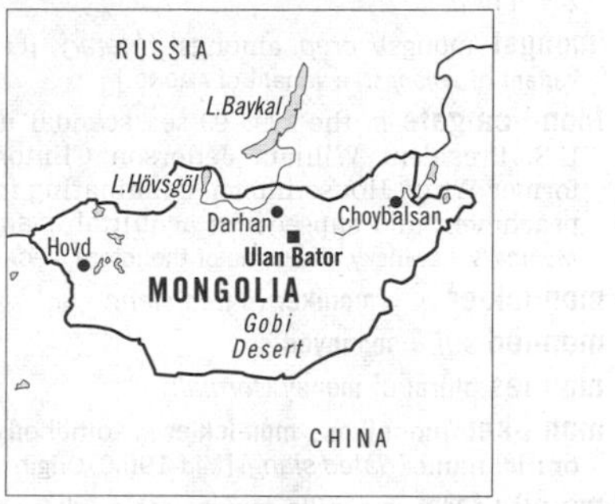

Mongolia

Mon·gol·i·a /mong gōlee ə/ nation in eastern Asia, bounded on the north by Russia and on the east, south, and west by China. Language: Mongolian. Currency: tughrik. Capital: Ulan Bator. Population: 2,538,211 (1997). Area: 604,830 sq. mi./1,566,500 sq. km.

Mon·go·li·an /mong gōlee ən, mon gōlee ən/ *n.* **1.** PEOPLES SOMEBODY FROM MONGOLIA somebody who was born in or lives in Mongolia **2.** LANG LANGUAGE OF MONGOLIA a group of languages or dialects of the Altaic family spoken in Mongolia, in the Chinese region of Inner Mongolia, in the Buryat Republic of Russia, and elsewhere in Central Asia. About 6 million people speak one of the varieties of Mongolian. —**Mon·go·li·an** *adj.*

Mon·gol·ic /mong góllik, mon góllik/ *n.* LANG GROUP OF ALTAIC LANGUAGES a group of languages belonging to the Altaic family that includes Mongolian, Buryat, and Santa ■ *adj.* **1.** ANTHROP RELATING TO MONGOLOID RACIAL GROUP belonging or relating to Mongoloid racial group (*dated*) **2.** LANG RELATING TO MONGOLIC LANGUAGE relating to the Mongolic languages

mon·gol·ism /móng gə lìzzəm/ *n.* a highly offensive term for Down syndrome (*dated offensive*)

mon·gol·oid /móng gə lòyd/ *adj.* a highly offensive term for Down syndrome (*dated offensive*)

Mon·gol·oid *adj.* relating to or belonging to the racial group that includes the peoples of eastern Asia, the Inuit, and the Native Americans (*no longer used technically*) —**Mon·gol·oid** *n.*

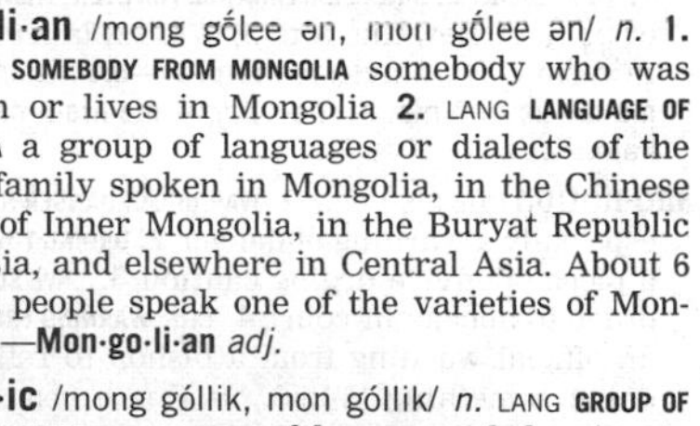

Mongoose

mon·goose /món gooss/ (*plural* **-goos·es**) *n.* a small short-legged carnivorous mammal that resembles a ferret and is native to India, noted for its ability to kill poisonous snakes. Genus: *Herpestes.* [Late 17thC. From Marathi *mangūs*.]

mon·grel /móng grəl/ *n.* **1.** ZOOL **DOG OF MIXED BREED** a dog that is a mixture of different breeds **2.** BIOL **ANIMAL OR PLANT OF MIXED BREED** an animal or plant that is a mixture of different breeds or strains **3.** **OFFENSIVE TERM** an offensive term for somebody who is of mixed racial ancestry (*offensive*) **4.** **STRANGE MIXTURE** a combination or mixture of different people or things, especially one that seems particularly strange ■ *adj.* **MIXED IN ORIGIN OR CHARACTER** of mixed breed, descent, type, or character [15thC. Origin uncertain: probably from, ultimately, a prehistoric Germanic base meaning "to mix" (source of English *among* and *mingle*), the underlying idea being "mixture."] —**mon·grel·ism** *n.* —**mon·grel·ly** *adj.*

mon·grel·ize /móng grə lìz/ (**-ized, -iz·ing, -iz·es**) *vt.* to make something or somebody become mongrel or mixed in character, type, or race (*offensive when used of a person*) —**mon·grel·i·za·tion** /mòng grəli záysh'n/ *n.*

'mongst /mungst/ *prep.* amongst (*literary*) [Late 16thC. Variant of *amongst*, a variant of AMONG.]

Mon·i·ca·gate *n.* the 1998–99 sex scandal involving U.S. President William Jefferson Clinton and a former White House intern, culminating in his impeachment and subsequent acquittal (*slang*) [From, *Monica* S. Lewinsky, the name of the intern + -GATE.]

mon·ick·er *n.* = **moniker** (*dated slang*)

mon·ied *adj.* = **moneyed**

mon·ies plural of **money** (*formal*)

mon·i·ker /mónnikər/, **mon·ick·er** *n.* somebody's name or nickname (*dated slang*) [Mid-19thC. Origin unknown.]

mo·nil·i·form /mə nílla fàwrm, mō-/ *adj.* used to describe a plant root or insect antenna that resembles a string of beads [Early 19thC. Directly or via French *moniliforme* from modern Latin *moniliformis*.] —**mo·nil·i·form·ly** *adv.*

mo·nism /mṓ nìzzəm, mó-/ *n.* **1.** PHILOS **THEORY OF REALITY AS A SINGLE ENTITY** the theory that reality is a unified whole and is grounded in a single basic substance or principle **2.** **SINGLE EXPLANATION FOR EVERYTHING** a theory or point of view that attempts to explain everything in terms of a single principle —**mo·nist** *n., adj.* —**mo·nis·tic** /mō nístik, mo-/ *adj.* —**mo·nis·ti·cal·ly** /-nísti kəlee/ *adv.*

mo·ni·tion /mə nísh'n/ *n.* **1.** **WARNING OF DANGER** a warning, especially a warning of danger **2.** **URGING TO BE CAUTIOUS** a piece of advice urging caution **3.** LAW **SUMMONS** an order to appear in court **4.** CHR **WARNING FROM A BISHOP** an official warning from a bishop to refrain from doing something [14thC. Via French from, ultimately, Latin *monit-*, the past participle stem of *monere* "to warn."]

mon·i·tor /mónnitər/ *n.* **1.** TV **CLOSED-CIRCUIT TELEVISION SET** a receiving device used in a closed-circuit television or video system **2.** COMPUT **COMPUTER VIDEO DISPLAY** a video device that displays data or images generated by a computer or terminal **3.** ARTS **STAGE LOUDSPEAKER** a loudspeaker on a stage during a concert used to let performers hear what they are playing ○ *playing a guitar solo with one foot up on the monitor* **4.** **SOMEBODY WHO CHECKS FOREIGN BROADCASTS** somebody who listens to and checks broadcasts from other countries for information useful to the government or organization he or she works for **5.** **SOMEBODY ENSURING PROPER CONDUCT** somebody who checks for incorrect or unfair conduct **6.** EDUC **SCHOOL STUDENT GIVEN SPECIAL DUTY** a school student who helps a teacher by being given a particular responsibility or special duty **7.** BROADCAST **VIEWING DEVICE IN A STUDIO** a receiver in a studio that enables the audience to watch the recorded portions of a show or performers to view parts of a program **8.** ZOOL = **monitor lizard** **9.** COMPUT **COMPUTER PROGRAM** a computer program that observes and controls other programs in a system **10.** **NOZZLE** a jointed device with a rotating nozzle that controls and aims a jet of water **11.** NAVY **WARSHIP** a warship used to bombard coastlines ■ *vt.* (**-tored, -tor·ing, -tors**) **WATCH OVER TO CHECK CONDUCT** to watch over somebody or something, especially in order to ensure that good order or proper conduct is maintained ■ *n.* HISTORY **19THC WARSHIP** a heavily armored warship with gun turrets used in the 19th century in coastal and inland waters ■ *vt.* (**-tored, -tor·ing, -tors**) **1.** **CHECK REGULARLY FOR DEVELOPMENTS** to check something at regular intervals in order to find out how it is progressing or developing **2.** **LISTEN TO BROADCASTS OR TELEPHONE CONVERSATIONS** to use an electronic receiver to listen in on broadcasts or telephone conversations, especially in order to discover secret or illegal plans and activities **3.** BROADCAST **CHECK THE QUALITY OF TRANSMITTED SIGNALS** to use an electronic receiver to check the quality of transmitted audio or visual signals [Early 16thC. From Latin, from *monit-*, the past participle stem of *monere* (see MONITION).] —**mon·i·to·ri·al** /mònni táwree əl/ *adj.* —**mon·i·to·ri·al·ly** /-táwree əlee/ *adv.* —**mon·i·tor·ship** /mónnətər shìp/ *n.*

WORD KEY: ORIGIN

The Latin word *monere*, from which ***monitor*** is derived, is also the source of English *admonish, demonstrate, monster, monument, muster, premonition, remonstrate,* and *summon*.

mon·i·tor lizard *n.* a large tropical carnivorous lizard found in Asia, Africa, and Australia. Family: Varanidae. [From the belief that they warn of the proximity of crocodiles]

mon·i·to·ry /mónni tàwree/ *adj.* **WARNING** communicating a warning ■ *n.* (*plural* **-ries**) CHR **WARNING LETTER** a letter, usually from a bishop, that warns somebody to refrain from doing something

monk /mungk/ *n.* a man who withdraws entirely or in part from society and goes to live in a religious community to devote himself to prayer, solitude, and contemplation [Old English *munuc*. Ultimately from a prehistoric Germanic word, from late Latin *monachus*, from, ultimately, Greek *monos* "alone" (source of English *mono-*).]

Thelonious Monk

Monk /mungk/, **Thelonious** (1917–82) U.S. pianist and composer. An influential modern jazz musician, he was known for his compositions in the bop style. Full name **Thelonious Sphere Monk**

monk·er·y /múngkəree/ (*plural* **-ies**) *n.* (*disapproving*) **1.** **MONASTIC WAY OF LIFE** the way of life led by monks in a monastery **2.** **MONKS** monks as a group

mon·key /múngkee/ *n.* (*plural* **-keys**) **1.** ZOOL **NONHUMAN PRIMATE** a medium-sized primate found mostly in tropical areas. Monkeys include baboons, marmosets, capuchins, macaques, guenons, and tamarins, but exclude apes, lemurs, and tarsiers. **2.** **MISCHIEVOUS CHILD** somebody, usually a child, who behaves badly, annoyingly, or high-spiritedly (*informal*) **3.** CONSTR **PILE DRIVER RAM** the ram of a pile driver **4.** DANCING **1960S DANCE** a dance popular in the 1960s in which the partners move their hands up and down, as if climbing a pole, and jerk their heads back and forth **5.** **DUPE** somebody who has been made to look foolish or ridiculous (*informal*) ○ *Nobody makes a monkey out of me.* ■ *vt.* (**-keyed, -key·ing, -keys**) **MIMIC** to copy or imitate somebody or something (*archaic*) [Mid-16thC. Origin uncertain: perhaps from, ultimately, Arabic *maimūn*, the probable source of Spanish *mono* and Old Italian *monno*.] ◇ **have a monkey on your back 1.** to have an addiction to drugs (*slang*) **2.** to have a serious problem or be in serious difficulties (*informal*) ◇ **I'll be a monkey's uncle** used to express surprise (*dated informal*)

monkey around *vi.* to behave in a silly, casual, or careless way

monkey with *vt.* to touch or move something casually or carelessly

mon·key bread *n.* **1.** **GOURD-SHAPED FRUIT** the gourd-shaped fruit of the baobab tree. Its pulp is eaten by monkeys. **2.** **mon·key bread, mon·key bread tree** = **baobab tree**

mon·key busi·ness *n.* (*informal*) **1.** **TRICKS** silly or mischievous behavior **2.** **DUBIOUS ACTIVITY** illegal, dishonest, or dubious activity

mon·key-faced owl *n.* = **barn owl**

mon·key flow·er *n.* a plant of the figwort family that has variously colored flowers with two lips. Genus: *Mimulus*. [Because spots on the flowers form a pattern that is reminiscent of a monkey's face]

mon·key in the mid·dle *n.* a game played by children in which two people throw a ball to each other and a third person stands in the middle and tries to intercept it

mon·key jack·et *n.* a tight-fitting waist-length jacket, especially one worn by a sailor or as part of a military dress uniform [Because it resembles the kind worn by an organ grinder's monkey]

mon·key pot *n.* **1.** TREES **TROPICAL AMERICAN TREE WITH LARGE PODS** a tropical American tree that bears large pods. Genus: *Lecythis*. **2.** TREES **POD OF THE MONKEY POT TREE** a large bulbous woody pod of the monkey pot tree **3.** CRAFT **GLASSMAKING POT** a melting pot used in the manufacture of flint glass

mon·key-puz·zle, **mon·key-puz·zle tree** *n.* a large, cone-bearing, evergreen Chilean tree with spreading branches, stiff sharp dark green leaves, and edible nuts. Latin name: *Araucaria araucana*. [Apparently because of its long intertwining limbs and leaves]

mon·key suit *n.* **1.** **TUXEDO** a suit worn by a man as part of formal evening wear (*slang*) **2.** **UNIFORM** a uniform, especially a military one (*dated slang*)

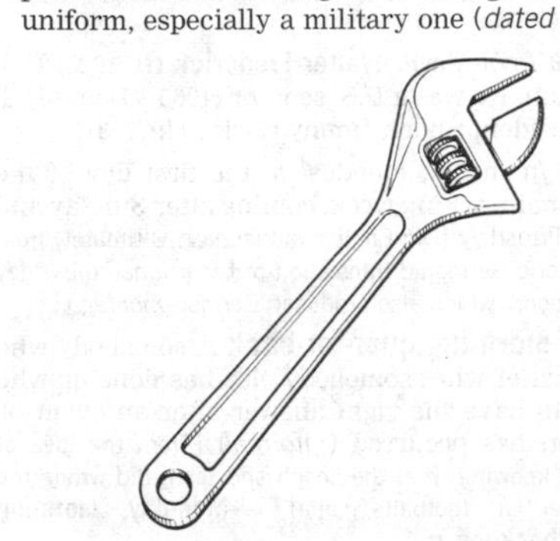

Monkey wrench

mon·key wrench *n.* **1.** **TYPE OF ADJUSTABLE WRENCH** a wrench with a jaw that can be adjusted so that it can be used to turn nuts of different sizes **2.** **PROBLEM** something that causes a problem for a plan or project (*informal*)

monk·fish /múngk fish/ (*plural* **-fish** *or* **-fish·es**) *n.* **1.** **LARGE EDIBLE ANGLERFISH** a large grotesque bottom-dwelling edible anglerfish of European and African Atlantic waters. Latin name: *Lophius piscatorius*. **2.** = **angel shark** [Early 17thC. *Monk* perhaps because its head slightly resembles a cowl.]

Mon-Khmer /mòn kmáir, -kə máir/ *n.* a group of languages of the Austro-Asiatic family that includes Mon and Khmer, spoken in parts of Southeast Asia —**Mon-Khmer** *adj.*

monk·ish /múngkish/ *adj.* **1.** RELIG **RELATING TO MONKS** relating to monks or their way of life **2.** **RECLUSIVE OR AUSTERE** characteristic of the life of a monk, especially in being reclusive, self-denying, or austere —**monk·ish·ly** *adv.* —**monk·ish·ness** *n.*

monk's cloth *n.* a heavy cotton fabric with a basket weave, used primarily to make drapes or bedcovers

monk seal *n.* a small dark brown subtropical seal that inhabits the waters of the Hawaiian Islands and the Mediterranean and is now endangered. Genus: *Monachus*. [Perhaps from the color of its coat, which is like that of a monk's robe]

monks·hood /múngks hòod/ (*plural* **-hood** *or* **-hoods**) *n.* **1.** **POISONOUS N EUROPEAN PLANT** a poisonous perennial plant native to northern Europe that has purplish flowers. Latin name: *Aconitum napellus*. **2.** = **aconite** [Late 16thC. From the hooded shape of its flowers.]

mon·o[1] /mónnō/ *n.* monophonic sound reproduction [Mid-20thC. Shortening.]

mon·o[2] /mónnō/ *n.* infectious mononucleosis (*informal*) [Mid-20thC. Shortening.]

mono- *prefix.* **1.** one, single, alone ○ *monoculture* **2.** containing a single atom, radical, or group ○ *monoxide* **3.** monomolecular ○ *monolayer* [Via Old French and Latin from Greek *monos* (source of English *monad* and *monk*)]

mon·o·ac·id /mònnō-/, **mon·ac·id** /mən-/ *n.* an acid that has only one replaceable hydrogen atom

mon·o·a·cid·ic /mònnō ə síddik/, **mon·a·cid·ic** /mòn ə síddik/, **mon·ac·id** *adj.* used to describe a chemical base or alcohol that has only one hydroxyl group that can react with an acid

mon·o·am·ine /mònnō áme̅en, -ə me̅en/ *n.* an amine compound that contains one amino group, especially a compound such as adrenaline or serotonin that transmits nerve impulses

mon·o·am·ine ox·i·dase *n.* an enzyme in cell tissue that breaks down monoamines

mon·o·am·ine ox·i·dase in·hib·i·tor *n.* an antidepressant drug that works by blocking the breakdown of monoamines by monoamine oxidase in the brain, thus allowing monoamines to build up

mon·o·a·tom·ic *adj.* = **monatomic**

mon·o·ba·sic /mònnə báyssik/ *adj.* used to describe an acid that has only one replaceable hydrogen atom in each molecule

mon·o·car·box·y·lic /mònnə kaar bok síllik/ *adj.* used to describe an acid that has only one carboxyl group

mon·o·carp /mónnə ka̅arp/ *n.* a plant that flowers and bears fruit only once before dying

mon·o·car·pel·lar·y /mònnə ka̅arpə lèrree/, **mon·o·car·pous** /mònnə ka̅arpəss/ *adj.* **1. WITH ONLY ONE CARPEL** used to describe a flower that has only one carpel **2. CONSISTING OF ONLY ONE CARPEL** used to describe a plant gynecium that consists of only one carpel

mon·o·car·pic /mònnə ka̅arpik/, **mon·o·car·pous** /mònnə ka̅arpəss/ *adj.* used to describe a plant that flowers and bears fruit only once before dying

mon·o·car·pous *adj.* BOT **1.** = **monocarpic 2.** = **monocarpellary**

mon·o·ce·phal·ic /mònnō sə fállik/, **mon·o·ceph·a·lous** /mònnō séffələss/ *adj.* used to describe a plant, e.g., a tulip or dandelion, with a stalk that bears a single flower head

Mo·noc·er·os /mə nóssərəss/ *n.* the Unicorn, a constellation lying across the celestial equator near Canis Major, Canis Minor, and Orion [Late 18thC. Via French from, ultimately, Greek *monokerōs* "having one horn."]

mon·o·cha·si·um /mònnə káyzhee əm, -zhəm/ (*plural* **-a** /-zhee ə, -zhə/) *n.* a flower cluster in which each branch bears one other branch and ends in a single flower [Late 19thC. Coined from MONO- + DICHASIUM.] —**mon·o·cha·si·al** *adj.*

mon·o·chord /mónnə kàwrd/ *n.* an ancient acoustical device consisting of a single string stretched over an oblong sounding box, used to determine mathematical intervals between musical tones

mon·o·chro·mat /mònnə krṓ màt/ *n.* somebody who is unable to perceive any colors and sees only shades of gray [Early 20thC. Back-formation from MONOCHROMATIC.]

mon·o·chro·mat·ic /mònnə krō máttik/ *adj.* **1.** COLORS **WITH ONLY ONE COLOR** having, or perceived as having, only one color **2.** PHYS **WITH ONLY ONE WAVELENGTH** consisting of radiation that has only one wavelength, like the light of a laser **3. IN ONE COLOR** painted, decorated, or printed in a single color **4.** MED **RELATING TO TOTAL COLORBLINDNESS** relating to or having total colorblindness (**monochromatism**) [Early 19thC] —**mon·o·chro·mat·i·cal·ly** *adv.* —**mon·o·chro·ma·tic·i·ty** /mònnə krōmə tíssətee/ *n.*

mon·o·chro·ma·tism /mònnə krṓmə tìzzəm/ *n.* a defect of vision in which the retina cannot distinguish any colors and a person sees only shades of gray

mon·o·chrome /mónnə krōm/ *adj.* **1.** COLORS **IN SHADES OF ONE COLOR** photographed in, using, or displaying only shades of one color or black and white **2.** COLORS **CONSISTING OF ONE COLOR** painted or drawn in different shades of a single color **3. DULL** dull, insipid, and lacking interest or distinctiveness ■ *n.* **1.** PHOTOGRAPHY **BLACK-AND-WHITE IMAGE** a black-and-white photograph or transparency **2.** ARTS **ARTWORK IN ONE COLOR** a painting, drawing, or print done in different shades of a single color **3.** COLORS **BLACK-AND-WHITE COLORATION** the condition of being only in black and white **4.** PAINTING, DRAWING **ART TECHNIQUE USING ONE COLOR** the art of painting or drawing using different shades of a single color **5.** ARTS **STATE OF HAVING ONE COLOR** the condition of being painted, drawn, or printed in shades of a single color [Mid-17thC. Via medieval Latin *monochroma* from Greek *monokhrōmatos* "of one color," from *khrōma* "color."] —**mon·o·chro·mic** /mònnə krṓmik/ *adj.* —**mon·o·chro·mist** /mónnə krṑmist/ *n.*

Monocle

mon·o·cle /mónnək'l/ *n.* an eyeglass for correcting the vision of one eye, held in position by the muscles around the eye socket [Mid-19thC. Via French from late Latin *monoculus* "single-eyed," from Greek *mono-* "single" + Latin *oculus* "eye."]

mon·o·cline /mónnə klīn/ *n.* GEOL a rock structure in which all the strata slope in one direction [Late 19thC. Coined from MONO- + Greek *klinein* "to lean." Ultimately from an Indo-European word that is also the ancestor of English *lean* and *lid*.] —**mon·o·cli·nal** /mònnə klīn'l/ *adj.* —**mon·o·cli·nal·ly** /-klīn'lee/ *adv.*

mon·o·clin·ic /mònnə klínnik/ *adj.* used to describe a type of crystal that has three unequal axes, with one pair not at right angles [Mid-19thC. Formed from Greek *klinein* (see MONOCLINE).]

mon·o·cli·nous /mònnə klīnəss/ *adj.* used to describe a flower that has both pistils and stamens [Early 19thC. Directly or via French *monocline* from modern Latin *monoclinus*, literally "in a single bed," from Greek *klinē* "bed" (source of English *clinic*).]

mon·o·clo·nal /mònnə klṓn'l/ *adj.* used to describe cells or products of cells that are formed or derived from a single clone

mon·o·clo·nal an·ti·bod·y *n.* a highly specific antibody produced in large quantities by clones of an artificially created cell

mon·o·coque /mónnə kṑk, -kòk/ *n.* **1. METAL OUTER SHELL** the metal outer shell of an aircraft, boat, or rocket that absorbs most of the stresses to which the craft is subjected **2. INTEGRATED CAR DESIGN** a type of motor vehicle design in which the body and frame are integrated [Early 20thC. From French, literally "having a single shell," from *coque* "shell."]

mon·o·cot /mónnə kòt/ *n.* a monocotyledon (*informal*)

mon·o·cot·y·le·don /mònnə kott'l e̅ed'n/ *n.* a flowering plant that has a single leaf in the seed and floral parts in multiples of three. Monocotyledons include grasses and lilies. Class: Monocotyledones. —**mon·o·cot·y·le·don·ous** /mònnə kott'l e̅ed'nəss/ *adj.*

mo·noc·ra·cy /mo nókrəssee, mə-/ (*plural* **-cies**) *n.* a form of government in which one person alone rules —**mon·o·crat** /mónnə kràt/ *n.* —**mon·o·crat·ic** /mònnə kráttik/ *adj.*

mo·noc·u·lar /mə nókyələr/ *n.* **OPTICAL DEVICE FOR ONE EYE** an optical device such as a field glass or a microscope designed for use with one eye only ■ *adj.* **RELATING TO ONE EYE** relating to, affecting, or having only one eye [Mid-17thC. Formed from late Latin *monoculus* (see MONOCLE).] —**mo·noc·u·lar·ly** *adv.*

mon·o·cul·ture /mónnə kùlchər/ *n.* **1. PRACTICE OF GROWING JUST ONE CROP** the practice of growing a single crop plant in a field or a larger area, e.g., a cereal crop such as wheat or corn **2. SINGLE CROP** a crop plant that is the only one grown in a field —**mon·o·cul·tur·al** /mònnə kúlchərəl/ *adj.*

mon·o·cy·cle /mónnə sīk'l/ *n.* = **unicycle**

mon·o·cy·clic /mònnə sīklik, -síklik/ *adj.* **1.** CHEM **WITH A SINGLE-RING MOLECULAR STRUCTURE** used to describe a chemical compound that has a molecular structure in which there is only one ring **2.** BIOL **FORMING ONE WHORL** forming a single whorl as, e.g., the petals of a flower do **3.** BOT **LIVING DURING ONE YEAR** used to describe a plant that completes its life cycle within a single year

mon·o·cyte /mónnə sīt/ *n.* a large circulating white blood cell, formed in the bone marrow and in the spleen, that has a single well-defined nucleus and consumes large foreign particles and cell debris —**mon·o·cyt·ic** /mònnə síttik/ *adj.* —**mon·o·cy·toid** /-sī tòyd/ *adj.*

mon·o·cy·to·sis /mònnə sī tṓssiss/ *n.* an abnormal increase in the numbers of a type of white blood cell (**monocyte**)

mon·o·dra·ma /mónnə draamə, mónnə drammə/ *n.* a dramatic piece written for one actor —**mon·o·dra·mat·ic** /mònnə drə máttik/ *adj.*

mon·o·dy /mónnədee/ (*plural* **-dies**) *n.* **1.** THEATER **ODE SUNG BY ONE ACTOR** in Greek tragedy, an ode for one actor to sing alone **2.** POETRY **ELEGY** a poem that mourns somebody's death **3.** MUSIC **17C ITALIAN VOCAL MUSIC** a type of Italian vocal music of the 17th century for solo voice with instrumental accompaniment **4.** MUSIC **MUSIC WITH A SINGLE MELODIC LINE** a piece of music that has a single melodic line [Early 17thC. Via late Latin *monodia* from, ultimately, Greek *monōdos* "singing alone," from *ōdē* "song" (source of English *ode*).] —**mo·nod·ic** /mə nóddik/ *adj.* —**mo·nod·i·cal·ly** /-nóddikəlee/ *adv.* —**mon·o·dist** /mónnədist/ *n.*

mo·noe·cious /mə ne̅eshəss/, **mo·ne·cious, mo·noi·cous** /mə nóykəss/ *adj.* used to describe a plant that has separate male and female flowers on the same plant [Mid-18thC. Formed from modern Latin *Monoecia*, the class name, literally "single house" (perhaps from the idea of males and females cohabiting), from Greek *oikos* "house."] —**mo·noe·cious·ly** *adv.*

mon·o·fil·a·ment /mònnə fílləmənt/ *n.* an untwisted and continuous single strand of natural or artificial fiber such as nylon, often used for fishing line

mo·nog·a·my /mə nóggəmee/ *n.* **1. PRACTICE OF HAVING ONE SEXUAL PARTNER** the practice of having a sexual relationship with only one partner during a period of time **2.** ANTHROP **MARRIAGE TO ONE PERSON** the practice of being married to only one person at a time. ◊ **monandry, monogyny 3.** ZOOL **PRACTICE OF HAVING ONE MATE** the practice of having only one mate at a time or during a lifetime [Early 17thC. Via French *monogamie* from, ultimately, Greek *monogamos*, literally "monogamous," which was coined from *mono-* "mono-" + *gamos* "marriage."] —**mo·nog·a·mist** *n.* —**mo·nog·a·mous** *adj.* —**mo·nog·a·mous·ly** *adv.*

mon·o·ge·ne·an /mònnə je̅enee ən/ *n.* a parasitic flatworm that spends its entire life cycle on the outside of the same fish. Order: Monogenea. [Mid-20thC. Formed from modern Latin *Monogenea*, the order name, literally "single generation," from Greek *genea* "generation" (source of English *genealogy*).]

mon·o·gen·e·sis /mònnə jénnəssiss/ *n.* BIOL **1. DESCENT FROM A SINGLE CELL** the theory that all living organisms are ultimately descended from a single cell **2. ASEXUAL REPRODUCTION** reproduction that does not involve the fusion of male and female gametes. = **asexual reproduction** —**mo·nog·e·nous** /mə nójjənəss/ *adj.*

mon·o·ge·net·ic /mònnəjə néttik/ *adj.* **1.** BIOL **RELATING TO MONOGENESIS** relating to or involving monogenesis **2.** MARINE BIOL **LIVING AS A PARASITE ON ONE FISH** used to describe a nematode that spends its entire life cycle as a parasite on the outside of the same fish

mon·o·gen·ic /mònnə jénnik/ *adj.* GENETICS **1. CONTROLLED BY ONE GENE** used to describe a characteristic that is controlled by one gene or one pair of genes **2. HAVING ONE SEX OF OFFSPRING** producing offspring that are all of the same sex —**mon·o·gen·i·cal·ly** *adv.*

mon·o·glot /mónnə glòt/ *n.* **SOMEBODY SPEAKING ONLY ONE LANGUAGE** somebody who is able to speak only one language ■ *adj.* **SPEAKING ONLY ONE LANGUAGE** able to speak only one language [Mid-19thC. From Greek *monoglōttos*, literally "one tongue," from *glōtta* "tongue."]

mon·o·glyc·er·ide /mònnə glíssə rīd/ *n.* any ester derived from glycerol in which only one hydroxyl group has combined with an acid

mon·o·gram /mónnə gràm/ *n.* **SET OF DECORATIVE INITIALS** a design of one or more letters, usually the initials of a name, used to decorate or identify an object ■ *vt.* (**-grammed** *or* **-gramed, -gram·ming** *or* **-gram·ing, -grams**) **PUT A MONOGRAM ON SOMETHING** to mark or decorate something with a monogram —**mon·o·gram·mat·ic** /mònnəgrə máttik/ *adj.*

mon·o·graph /mónnə gràf/ *n.* a scholarly article, paper, or book on a single topic —**mo·nog·ra·pher** /mə nóggrəfər/ *n.* —**mon·o·graph·ic** /mònnə gráffik/ *adj.* —**mon·o·graph·i·cal·ly** /-gráffikəlee/ *adv.*

mo·nog·y·ny /mə nójjənee/ *n.* **1.** ANTHROP **PRACTICE OF HAVING ONE WIFE** the practice of having only one wife at a time. ◊ **monogamy 2. PRACTICE OF HAVING ONE FEMALE**

LOVER the practice of having a sexual relationship with only one woman during a period of time. ◊ **monandry, monogamy** —**mo·nog·y·nist** *n.* —**mo·nog·y·nous** *adj.*

mon·o·hull /mónnō hùl/ *n.* a boat that has a single hull

mon·o·hy·brid /mònnō hī́brid/ *n.* a hybrid from parents that are different only with respect to a single gene pair

mon·o·hy·drate /mònnō hī́ drày̆t/ *n.* a salt that is combined with one molecule of water

mon·o·hy·dric /mònnō hī́drik/ *adj.* used to describe an alcohol that contains one replaceable atom of hydrogen

mon·o·hy·drox·y /mònnō hī dróksee/ *adj.* used to describe a compound that contains one hydroxyl group

mo·noi·cous *adj.* BOT = **monoecious**

mon·o·lay·er /mónnō làyr/ *n.* **1.** SCI **LAYER ONE MOLECULE IN THICKNESS** a film or or other coating of a compound that is one molecule thick **2.** BIOL **LAYER ONE CELL IN THICKNESS** a cultured layer of cells that is one cell thick

mon·o·lin·gual /mònnə líng gwəl/ *adj.* **1. SPEAKING ONLY ONE LANGUAGE** able to speak only one language **2. USING ONLY ONE LANGUAGE** written, spoken, or produced in only one language —**mon·o·lin·gual·ism** *n.*

mon·o·lith /mónnə lìth/ *n.* **1. PILLAR OF ROCK** a tall block of solid stone standing by itself, whether a natural rock feature or a stone column shaped and erected by people, e.g., as a monument **2.** CONSTR **LARGE BLOCK OF BUILDING MATERIAL** a large uniform block of a single building material such as concrete pieced together with others to form a building or other structure **3. SOMETHING LARGE AND IMMOVABLE** something massive and unchanging, especially a large and long-established organization that is slow to change, uniform in character, and difficult to deal with on a human level

mon·o·lith·ic /mònnə líthik/ *adj.* **1. IN THE FORM OF A LARGE STONE BLOCK** consisting of or formed into a tall column of solid stone **2. BUILT USING LARGE BLOCKS** constructed using massive stones or solid blocks of material **3. LARGE AND UNCHANGING** massive, uniform in character, and slow to change —**mon·o·lith·i·cal·ly** *adv.*

mon·o·lith·ic tech·nol·o·gy *n.* a technology in electronic manufacturing in which all circuit components, e.g., resistors, capacitors, and diodes, are mounted on a single uniform piece of material

mon·o·logue /mónnə lòg/, **mon·o·log** *n.* **1.** THEATER **ACTOR'S LONG SPEECH** a long passage in a play or motion picture spoken by one actor, or an entire play for one actor only **2. SOMEBODY'S LONG UNINTERRUPTED SPEECH** a long tedious uninterrupted speech during a conversation **3.** ARTS **PERFORMANCE BY COMEDIAN** a set of jokes or humorous stories following one another without a break, told by a solo entertainer —**mon·o·log·ic** /mònnə lójjik/ *adj.* —**mo·nol·o·gist** /mə nóllәjist, mónnə lòggist/ *n.* —**mo·nol·o·gize** /mə nóllə jīz, mónnələ gīz/ *vti.*

mon·o·ma·ni·a /mònnə máynee ə/ *n.* an obsessive interest in a single thing or a preoccupation with a single idea or thought —**mon·o·ma·ni·ac** *n.* —**mon·o·ma·ni·a·cal·ly** /mònnə mə nī́ əkalee/ *adv.*

mon·o·mer /mónnəmər/ *n.* a relatively light, simple organic molecule that can join in long chains with other molecules to form a more complex molecule or polymer —**mon·o·mer·ic** /mònnə mérrik/ *adj.*

mon·o·me·tal·lic /mònnō mə tállik/ *adj.* **1.** ECON **USING ONE METAL AS A MONETARY STANDARD** used to describe a currency or monetary system that uses one type of metal, especially gold or silver, as a monetary standard **2. MADE OF SINGLE METAL** made of one type of metal only

mon·o·met·al·lism /mònnō métt'l ìzzəm/ *n.* ECON the use of just one metal, especially gold or silver, as a basic monetary standard

mo·no·mi·al /mə nṓmee əl, mo-/ *n.* **1.** MATH **ALGEBRAIC EXPRESSION** an expression in algebra consisting of a single term, e.g., 3y, as distinct from one that contains two or more terms, e.g., 3x + 5y **2.** BIOL **SCIENTIFIC NAME WITH ONE ELEMENT** a scientific name that consists of one element only, as do the names of most families of plants and animals [Early 18thC. Formed from MONO- on the model of *binomial* (see BINOMIAL).] —**mo·no·mi·al** *adj.*

mon·o·mo·lec·u·lar /mònnō mə lékyələr/ *adj.* **1. RELATING TO A SINGLE MOLECULE** relating to or involving single molecules **2. WITH THE THICKNESS OF A SINGLE MOLECULE** used to describe a surface film that has a thickness of only one molecule. Monomolecular layers of alcohols or acids are used to retard water evaporation. —**mon·o·mo·lec·u·lar·ly** *adv.*

mon·o·mor·phic /mònnō máwrfik/, **mon·o·mor·phous** /mònnō máwrfəss/ *adj.* **1.** BIOL **WITH A SINGLE DISCRETE FORM** used to describe an organism or species that exists in a single discrete form, as distinct from one that changes form, as a caterpillar does when it becomes a butterfly **2.** CHEM **WITH ONE CRYSTALLINE FORM** exhibiting only a single crystalline form —**mon·o·mor·phism** *n.*

Mo·non·ga·he·la /mə nòng gə héelə/ river in the east central United States. It flows north through West Virginia and Pennsylvania. Length: 128 mi./206 km.

mon·o·nu·cle·ar /mònnō nóoklee ər/ *adj.* **1.** BIOL **WITH A SINGLE NUCLEUS** used to describe a cell that has a single nucleus **2.** CHEM **WITH ONE RING OF ATOMS** used to describe an organic compound with a molecular structure containing only one ring of atoms

mon·o·nu·cle·o·sis /mònnō nooklee ṓssiss/ *n.* **1. ABNORMAL PRESENCE OF LYMPHOCYTES** a significant rise in the number of atypical lymphocytes in the blood **2.** = **infectious mononucleosis**

mon·o·nu·cle·o·tide /mònnō nóoklee ə tīd/ *n.* a nucleotide that contains one molecule each of phosphoric acid, a sugar, and a nitrogenous base

mo·noph·a·gous /mo nóffəgəss/ *adj.* feeding on a single type of plant or animal —**mo·noph·a·gy** /mo nóffəjee/ *n.*

mon·o·phon·ic /mònnə fónnik/ *adj.* using only one channel to carry sound from the source to the loudspeaker, as distinct from, e.g., stereophonic sound that transmits across multiple channels to give some auditory perspective —**mon·o·phon·i·cal·ly** *adv.*

mon·oph·thong /mónnəf thàwng, -thòng/ *n.* a vowel sound that keeps the same quality for the whole syllable [Early 17thC. From Greek *monophthoggos*, from *phthoggos* "sound."] —**mon·oph·thon·gal** /mònnəf thàwng g'l, -thóng g'l/ *adj.*

mon·o·phy·let·ic /mònnō fī léttik/ *adj.* used to describe a group of plants or animals that are descended from a single stock or ancestral form —**mon·o·phy·let·i·cal·ly** *adv.* —**mon·o·phy·let·ism** /mònnō fī́lə tìzzəm/ *n.*

Mo·noph·y·site /mə nóffə sīt/ *n.* somebody who believes that Jesus Christ has a single inseparable nature that is both human and divine. This belief is held by the Coptic and Armenian churches among others. [Late 17thC. Via ecclesiastical Latin *Monophysita* from ecclesiastical Greek *monophusitēs*, from *phusis* "nature" (see PHYSIC).] —**Mo·noph·y·sit·ic** /mə nòffə síttik/ *adj.* —**Mo·noph·y·sit·ism** /mə nóffə sī tìzzəm/ *n.*

Monoplane

mon·o·plane /mónnə plàyn/ *n.* an airplane that has just one pair of wings

mon·o·ple·gi·a /mònnə pléejee ə, -pléejə/ *n.* inability to move a single limb or a single group of muscles —**mon·o·ple·gic** *adj.*

mon·o·pod /mónnə pòd/ *adj.* **CONSISTING OF ONE-LEGGED STRUCTURE** used to describe a structure whose only support is one central pillar. Such designs are used in drilling rigs in the Arctic where the shifting ice could damage conventional supports. ■ *n.* **ONE-LEGGED CAMERA SUPPORT** a single-legged adjustable support used to steady a camera

mon·o·pode /mónnə pōd/ *n.* **1.** BOT = **monopodium 2. ONE-FOOTED ANIMAL** a person or animal with a single foot, especially a member of a mythical African race of one-legged people [Early 19thC. From late Latin *monopodius* (see MONOPODIUM).] —**mon·o·po·di·al·ly** /mònnə pṓdee əlee/ *adv.*

mon·o·po·di·um /mònnə pṓdee əm/ (*plural* **-a** /-dee ə/) *n.* the main axis of some plants such as the pine tree that extends to the tip of the plant and produces lateral branches

mon·o·pole /mónnə pōl/ *n.* **1.** PHYS **SINGULAR MAGNETIC POLE OR ELECTRIC CHARGE** an electric charge or hypothetical magnetic pole isolated from its opposite charge or pole **2.** PHYS **HYPOTHETICAL MAGNETICALLY CHARGED ELEMENTARY PARTICLE** a theoretical elementary particle that has only one magnetic pole, instead of the two present in ordinary magnetic bodies **3.** RADIO **RADIO ANTENNA** a radio antenna made of an electrically charged conducting rod with an electrical connection at one end

mo·nop·o·list /mə nóppəlist/ *n.* **1. CONTROLLER OF A MONOPOLY** somebody who controls a monopoly **2. SUPPORTER OF MONOPOLY** a supporter of monopolistic policies —**mo·nop·o·lis·tic** /mə nòppə lístik/ *adj.* —**mo·nop·o·lis·ti·cal·ly** *adv.*

mo·nop·o·lize /mə nóppə līz/ (**-lized, -liz·ing, -liz·es**) *vt.* **1.** BUSINESS **HAVE EXCLUSIVE COMMERCIAL CONTROL OF** to have complete control of an industry or service and prevent other companies or people from participating or competing in it **2. DOMINATE SELFISHLY** to demand or take all of something such as somebody's time, attention, or affections, in a selfish way —**mo·nop·o·li·za·tion** /mə nòppəli záysh'n/ *n.* —**mo·nop·o·liz·er** *n.*

mo·nop·o·ly /mə nóppəlee/ (*plural* **-lies**) *n.* **1.** ECON **CONTROL OF MARKET SUPPLY** a situation in which one company controls an industry or is the only provider of a product or service **2.** COMM **BUSINESS CORPORATION WITH EXCLUSIVE CONTROL** a company with a commercial monopoly **3.** ECON **EXCLUSIVE COMMODITY OR AREA OF CONTROL** a product or service whose supply is controlled by only one company **4.** LAW **LEGAL RIGHT GRANTED TO SOMEBODY** a legal right to the exclusive control of an industry or service, as granted by a government **5. PERSONAL AND EXCLUSIVE POSSESSION** an exclusive right to have or do something ○ *He seems to think he has a monopoly on common sense.* [Mid-16thC. Via Latin *monopolium* from Greek *monopōlion*, from *pōlein* "to sell."] —**mo·nop·o·lism** *n.*

Mo·nop·o·ly /mə nóppəlee/ *tdmk.* a trademark for a real-estate trading board game

mo·nop·so·ny /mə nópsənee/ (*plural* **-nies**) *n.* a situation in which a particular type of product or service is only being bought or used by one customer [Mid-20thC. Coined from MONO + Greek *opsōnein* "to purchase provisions."] —**mo·nop·so·nist** *n.* —**mo·nop·so·nis·tic** /mə nòpsə nístik/ *adj.*

mo·nop·ter·os /mo nóptə ròss/ (*plural* **-oi** /-òyl/), **mo·nop·ter·on** /mo nóptə ròn/ (*plural* **-a** /-rə/) *n.* a circular classical temple surrounded by a single ring of columns [Late 17thC. Via Latin from Greek "having one wing," formed from *pteron* "wing."] —**mo·nop·ter·al** *adj.*

mon·o·rail /mónnə ràyl/ *n.* a passenger transport system in which the cars straddle or are suspended from a single beam

mon·o·sac·cha·ride /mònnə sákə rīd, -rid/ *n.* a simple sugar such as glucose or fructose that cannot be broken down into simpler sugars

mo·no·se·my /mo nóssəmee, mónnō séemee/ *n.* the linguistic feature or fact of having only one meaning [Mid-20thC. Formed from MONO-, on the model of POLYSEMY.]

mon·o·ski /mónnō skee/ *n.* a broad single ski on which a skier stands with both feet —**mon·o·ski·er** *n.* —**mon·o·ski·ing** *n.*

mon·o·so·di·um glu·ta·mate /monnə sṓdee əm-/ *n.* the crystalline sodium salt of glutamic acid, used in cooking primarily to enhance the flavor of food. Some people are sensitive to it and react with headaches or vomiting.

mon·o·some /mónnə sōm/ *n.* **1. UNPAIRED CHROMOSOME** a chromosome that abnormally exists on its own, without its usual pair, especially an unpaired X-chromosome **2. SINGLE RIBOSOME** a single protein-manufacturing particle (**ribosome**) combined with messenger RNA [Early 20thC. Formed from -SOME.] —**mon·o·so·mic** /mònnə sṓmik/ *adj.* —**mon·o·so·my** *n.*

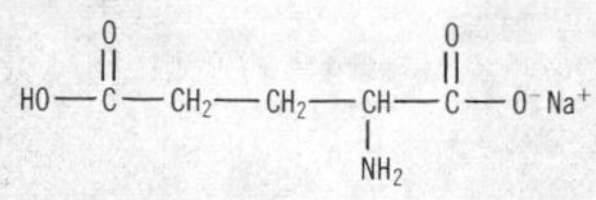

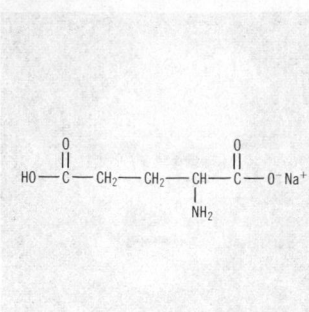

Monosodium glutamate

mon·o·sper·mous /mònnə spúrməss/ *adj.* used to describe a plant that produces only one seed

mon·o·sty·lous /mònnə stíləss/ *adj.* BOT used to describe a flower that has only one connecting stem (**style**) between the stigmas and the ovary

mon·o·syl·lab·ic /mònnə si lábbik/ *adj.* **1. BRIEF AND UNHELPFUL** saying very little, often in a way that gives an impression of unfriendliness or unintelligence **2. CONTAINING ONLY ONE SYLLABLE** consisting of one syllable only —**mon·o·syl·lab·i·cal·ly** *adv.* —**mon·o·syl·lab·i·ci·ty** /mònnə silə bíssətee/ *n.*

mon·o·syl·la·ble /mónnə sìlləb'l/ *n.* a word or sentence consisting of only one syllable, e.g., "Yes" or "me"

mon·o·the·ism /mónnə thee ìzzəm/ *n.* the belief that there is only one God. This belief is found, e.g., in Judaism, Christianity, and Islam. —**mon·o·the·ist** /mónnə thée ist/ *n., adj.* —**mon·o·the·is·tic** /mònnə thee ístik/ *adj.* —**mon·o·the·is·ti·cal·ly** *adv.*

mon·o·tint /mónnə tìnt/ *n.* DRAWING, PAINTING = **monochrome**

mon·o·tone /mónnə tōn/ *n.* **1. ONE UNCHANGING SOUND TONE** a sound, especially a speech sound, that does not rise and fall in pitch, but stays on the same tone all the time **2. SERIES OF IDENTICAL SOUNDS** a sequence of sounds, such as a piece of speech, singing, or music, that stays at exactly the same pitch throughout **3. UNVARYING QUALITY** complete lack of variety in color, expression, or style **4.** MUSIC **SINGER WITH NO SENSE OF PITCH** somebody who cannot produce, or distinguish between, sounds of varying pitches when singing ■ *adj.* **1. WITH UNVARYING QUALITY** lacking variety in pitch, color, or another quality **2. mon·o·tone, mon·o·ton·ic** MATH **ASCENDING OR DESCENDING IN SEQUENCE** used to describe a function or a sequence of real numbers that steadily increases or decreases —**mon·o·to·nic·i·ty** /mònnə tō níssətee/ *n.*

mo·not·o·nous /mə nótt'nəss/ *adj.* **1. REPETITIOUS AND UNINTERESTING** uninteresting or boring as a result of being repetitive and unvaried **2. UTTERED IN UNVARIED TONE** uttered or performed in one unvaried tone —**mo·not·o·nous·ly** *adv.* —**mo·not·o·nous·ness** *n.*

WORD KEY: SYNONYMS
See Synonyms at ***boring***.

mo·not·o·ny /mə nótt'nee/ *n.* **1. TEDIOUS LACK OF VARIETY** boredom or dullness arising from the fact that nothing different ever happens **2. UNVARYING CONDITION** repetitiousness or lack of variation in pitch or tone, especially in relation to music or speech

mon·o·type /mónnə tìp/ *n.* **1.** BIOL **SOLE MEMBER OF A BIOLOGICAL GROUP** a plant or animal that is the only member of the taxonomic category to which it belongs **2.** ART **UNIQUE PRINTED IMAGE** an artwork created by pressing on paper laid on an inked metal plate or sheet of glass. Although similar prints can be made, each one will be unique. —**mon·o·typ·ic** /mònnə típpik/ *adj.*

Mon·o·type *tdmk.* a trademark for a typesetting machine that is run from a keyboard activating a unit that sets type by individual characters

mon·o·un·sat·u·rat·ed /mònnō un sáchə ràytəd/ *adj.* used to describe vegetable oils and fatty acids whose molecular structure includes only one double carbon bond

mon·o·va·lent /mònnə váylənt/ *adj.* **1.** CHEM **WITH A VALENCE OF ONE** used to describe a chemical element or isotope that has a valence of one **2.** IMMUNOL **WITH ONE KIND OF ANTIBODY** containing only one type of antibody —**mon·o·va·lence** *n.* —**mon·o·va·len·cy** *n.*

mon·ox·ide /mə nók sìd/ *n.* a chemical compound with molecules that consist of one atom of oxygen and one or more atoms of another element

mon·o·zy·got·ic /mònnō zī góttik/ *adj.* used to describe twins that are derived from a single fertilized egg. In humans, identical twins are monozygotic.

Mon·roe /mən rṓ/ city in northeastern Louisiana, on the eastern bank of the Ouachita River, northeast of Alexandria and east of Shreveport. Population: 54,588 (1996).

James Monroe

Mon·roe, James (1758–1821) U.S. statesman and 5th President of the United States. He held numerous state and national offices in nearly fifty years of public service, and was a popular president (1817–25).

Marilyn Monroe

Mon·roe, Marilyn (1926–62) U.S. actor. She starred in movies such as *Bus Stop* (1956), *Some Like It Hot* (1959), and *The Misfits* (1961). She was married to the baseball player Joe DiMaggio and later the playwright Arthur Miller. Real name **Norma Jean Mortenson**

Mon·roe doc·trine *n.* the political principle, as stated by President James Monroe in 1823, that Europe should no longer involve itself in the American continent. The policy was part of the U.S. recognition of the independence of several Latin American countries. [Mid-19thC. Named for James MONROE, during whose presidency the principle was first advocated.]

Mon·ro·vi·a /mon rṓvee ə/ **1.** capital city and chief seaport of Liberia, situated in the west of the country. Population: 490,000 (1992). **2.** city in southwestern California, in Los Angeles County, below the San Gabriel Mountains. Population: 38,764 (1994).

mons /monz/ (*plural* **mon·tes** /món teez/) *n.* a fleshy body part that sticks out, especially the one formed by a pad of flesh at the juncture of the pubic bones. ◊ **mons pubis** [Mid-20thC. Shortening of MONS PUBIS.]

Mons /moNs/ historic city in southwestern Belgium, situated about 30 mi./48 km southwest of Brussels. Population: 92,260 (1996).

Mon·sei·gneur /mòn say nyúr, màwN say nyúr, màwN see nyúr/ (*plural* **Mes·sei·gneurs** /màyssə nyúr, mày say nyúr/) *n.* a title given to some dignitaries, especially bishops and princes, in France and French-speaking countries [Early 17thC. From French, from *mon* "my" + *seigneur* "lord" (see SEIGNEUR).]

Mon·sieur /mə syúr, -séer/ (*plural* **Mes·sieurs** /may syúr, -syúrz/), **mon·sieur** (*plural* **mes·sieurs**) *n.* **1. FRENCH FOR "MR."** a title for a man in France or a French-speaking country, if he has no other special title **2. FRENCH WORD USED TO ADDRESS MAN** a form of address used when speaking or referring to a French or French-speaking man whose name is not known [Early 16thC. From French, from *mon* "my" + *sieur* "lord," from, ultimately, Latin *senior* "older" (see SENIOR).]

Mon·si·gnor /mon séenyər/ (*plural* **-gnors** *or* **-gnor·i** /mòn seen yáwree/) *n.* a title used when speaking or referring to certain clerics of the Roman Catholic Church, especially bishops and officials of the papal court [Late 16thC. Via Italian from French *monseigneur* (see MONSEIGNEUR).] —**Mon·si·gnor·i·al** /mòn seen yáwree əl/ *adj.*

mon·soon /mon sóon/ *n.* **1. WINDS THAT REVERSE DIRECTION SEASONALLY** a large-scale wind system that seasonally blows in opposite directions and determines the climate of large regions. The reversal of wind direction is caused by the greater annual temperature differences over large land masses than over the adjacent waters. **2. RAINY SEASON, ESPECIALLY IN INDIA** any period of heavy rainfall, especially during the summer over Southeast Asia and India **3. HEAVY RAINFALL** a very heavy fall of rain (*informal*) [Late 16thC. Via obsolete Dutch *monssoen* from Portuguese *monção*, from Arabic *mawsim* "season."] —**mon·soon·al** *adj.*

mons pu·bis /-pyóobiss/ (*plural* **mon·tes pu·bis**) *n.* a prominence caused by the pad of fat that overlies the junction of the pubic bones in women and girls [Late 19thC. From Latin, literally "mount of the pubes."]

mon·ster /mónstər/ *n.* **1. UGLY TERRIFYING CREATURE** any large, ugly, terrifying animal or person found in mythology or created by the imagination, especially something fierce that kills people. Monsters often feature in folklore and fairytales as evil creatures resembling a mixture of different animals. **2. EVIL PERSON** somebody whose inhumanity or vicious behavior terrifies and disgusts people **3. HUGE THING** something extraordinarily or unusually large (*informal*) (*often used before a noun*) **4.** PATHOL **IMPROPERLY FORMED FETUS** a fetus that is markedly improperly formed, especially one that cannot live outside the uterus **5. SOMEBODY OR SOMETHING UNDESIRABLY FORMED** a person, animal, or plant that is undesirably formed (*archaic offensive*) [13thC. Via French *monstre* from Latin *monstrum* "monster, divine omen," from *monere* "to warn, remind" (source of English *muster* and *monument*).]

Monstrance

mon·strance /mónstrəns/ *n.* CHR a large gold or silver container in which the Host is placed and then shown to the congregation for adoration in a Roman Catholic Mass [13thC. Via medieval Latin *monstrantia* from, ultimately, Latin *monstrare* "to show," from *monstrum* (see MONSTER).]

mon·stros·i·ty /mon stróssətee/ (*plural* **-ties**) *n.* **1. VERY UGLY THING** an object, animal, or person that is very unpleasant or frightening to look at, often because it is large and strangely shaped **2. MONSTROUSNESS** frightening size, shape, and ugliness ○ ***a figure of overwhelming monstrosity*** [Mid-16thC. From late Latin *monstrositas*, from Latin *monstruosus* (see MONSTROUS).]

mon·strous /mónstrəss/ *adj.* **1. SHOCKING AND MORALLY UNACCEPTABLE** wicked, cruel, or unpleasant to an extent that is morally unacceptable **2. EXTREMELY LARGE** extremely large, often in a way that seems ugly and frightening **3. LIKE A MONSTER** resembling a monster of the type found in folklore and fairytales **4. EXTREMELY UNUSUAL** greatly different from the norm (*archaic*) [14thC. Via Old French *monstreux* from Latin *monstruosus*, from *monstrum* (see MONSTER).] —**mon·strous·ness** *n.*

mon·strous·ly /mónstrəsslee/ *adv.* in a way or to an extent that shocks or offends other people

mons ve·ne·ris /-vénnəriss/ (*plural* **mon·tes ve·ne·ris**) *n.* = **mons pubis** [Early 17thC. From Latin, literally "the mount of Venus," goddess of love.]

Mont. *abbr.* Montana

mon·ta·dale /móntə dàyl/ *n.* a white-faced sheep belonging to a U.S. breed that is raised for its wool or meat [Mid-20thC. Blend of MONTANA and DALE, on the model of names such as *Corriedale*.]

mon·tage /mon taázh/ *n.* **1.** ARTS **ARTWORK CREATED FROM MANY SMALL PIECES** a picture or other work of art composed by assembling, overlaying, and overlapping many different materials or pieces collected from different sources, e.g., photographs, magazines, and other pictures **2.** ARTS **CREATION OF IMAGE FROM COLLECTED PIECES** the technique of creating a montage **3.** CINEMA **SEQUENCE OF OVERLAPPING FILM CLIPS** a motion-picture sequence consisting of a series of dissolves, superimpositions, or cuts used to condense time or to suggest memories or hallucinations **4.** CINEMA **MOVIEMAKING STYLE** a style of moviemaking that makes extensive use of cuts, camera movements, and changes of camera position, particularly to set up new meanings not conveyed by the filmed action itself [Early 20thC. From French, formed from *monter* "to mount" (see MOUNT).]

Mon·tag·nais /mòntən yáy/ (*plural* **-nais**) *n.* **1.** PEOPLES **MEMBER OF NATIVE AMERICAN PEOPLE** a member of a Native American people who live in parts of Quebec and Labrador **2.** LANG **MONTAGNAIS LANGUAGE** the Algonquian language of the Montagnais people. Montagnais is spoken by about four thousand people. [Early 18thC. From French, formed from *montagne* "mountain."] —**Mon·tag·nais** *adj.*

Mon·ta·gnard /mòntən yaárd, -yaár/ (*plural* **-gnard** *or* **-gnards**) *n.* a member of a people who live in the mountainous border region between Vietnam, Laos, and Cambodia [Mid-19thC. From French, "mountaineer," from *montagne* "mountain."]

Mon·taigne, Michel de Eyquem (1533–92) French essayist. He invented the essay form in his *Essays* (1572–80,1588), original pieces on the ideas and personalities of his time.

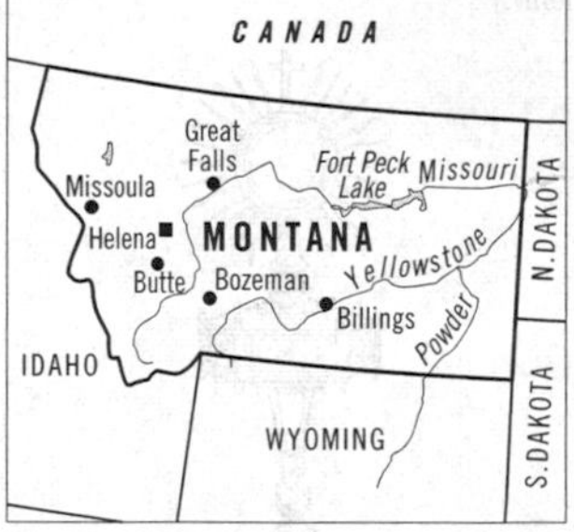

Montana

Mon·tan·a /mon taánə/ state in the northwestern United States, bordered by Canada, and the states of North Dakota, South Dakota, Wyoming, and Idaho. Capital: Helena. Population: 878,810 (1997). Area: 147,046 sq. mi./380,849 sq. km. —**Mon·tan·an** *n., adj.*

Mon·tan·a /mon tánnə/, **Joe** (*b.* 1956) U.S. football player. A quarterback, he led the San Francisco 49ers to four Super Bowl victories (1982, 1985, 1989, and 1990). Full name **Joseph Montana**

mon·tane /mon táyn, món tàyn/ *adj.* growing or living in mountainous regions [Mid-19thC. From Latin *montanus*, from the stem *mont-* "mountain" (see MOUNTAIN).]

mon·tan wax /móntən-, món tàn-/ *n.* a brittle, white to dark brown wax extracted from lignite and substituted in polishes and candles for carnauba and beeswax [Early 20thC. From Latin *montanus* "montane" (see MONTANE), because it is extracted from lignite, a mountain ore.]

Mon·tauk /món tàwk/ (*plural* **-tauk** *or* **-tauks**) *n.* a member of a Native American people that originally occupied lands in the eastern part of New York's Long Island [Mid-19thC. From *Montauk*, a local place name.]

Mont Blanc /mŏnt blángk, mŏN blaáN/ the highest mountain in western Europe, in the western Alps on the border of France and Italy. Height: 15,771 ft./4,807 m.

Mont·calm /mont kaám, moN kálm/, **Louis-Joseph de, Marquis de Montcalm** (1712–59) French soldier. He was commander of the French forces during the French and Indian War and he was mortally wounded fighting the British in the battle of the Plains of Abraham.

Mont·clair /mont klár/ **1.** city in southeastern California, in San Bernadino County. Population: 28,544 (1994). **2.** city in northeastern New Jersey, in Essex County. Population: 37,729 (1990).

mon·te /móntee/ *n.* CARDS a game in which a player chooses between two cards and bets on being dealt a card of that same suit before being dealt a card of the other suit [Early 19thC. Via Spanish from, ultimately, the Latin stem *mont-* "mountain" (see MOUNTAIN); from the mountain or heap of cards present on the table.]

Mon·te Car·lo /mònti kaárlō/ tourist resort with a famous casino in Monaco, on the Mediterranean Sea. Population: 13,154 (1982).

Mon·te·go Bay /mon teégō-/ **1.** inlet of the Caribbean Sea in northwestern Jamaica **2.** city, seaport and tourist resort in Jamaica, located on the bay of the same name. Population: 83,446 (1991).

mon·teith /mon teéth/ *n.* a silver or pewter basin with notches around the edge, made to hold punch, or to cool punch glasses by resting their bases over the scalloped edge [Late 17thC. Said to be named for a Scotsman *Monteith*, known for his capes with scalloped hems.]

Mon·té·li·mar /mòn tay lee maár/ town in Drôme Department, central France, situated about 80 mi./129 km south of Lyon. Population: 31,386 (1990).

Mon·te·ne·gro /mòntə négrō/ constituent republic of the Federal Republic of Yugoslavia, along with Serbia. Until 1991 it was part of the larger state of Yugoslavia. Capital: Podgorica. Population: 635,442 (1996). Area: 5,333 sq. mi./13,812 sq. km. —**Mon·te·ne·grin** *n., adj.*

Mon·te·rey /mòntə ráy/ city and port in western California, on Monterey Bay. Population: 29,812 (1994).

Mon·te·rey Jack *n.* a semihard cheese that is mild when young and becomes stronger and drier as it ages [Mid-20thC. Named for Monterey County, California, where it was first made.]

Mon·te·rey pine *n.* a pine tree that is native to the Monterey Peninsula of California and is now widely planted throughout the world for timber. Latin name: *Pinus radiata.*

Mon·te Ro·sa /mòntee rṓzə/ mountain in the Pennine Alps, on the Swiss-Italian border, south of Zermatt. Height: 15,200 ft./4,633 m.

Mon·ter·rey an industrial city in northeastern Mexico, capital of Nuevo Leon State. Population: 1,064,197 (1990).

Mon·tes Alp·es /mòn tayz ál pàyz/ extensive range of mountains on the moon arching around the north east of Mare Imbrium

Mon·tes Ap·en·ni·nus /mòn tayz àppa nīnəss/ extensive range of mountains on the moon surrounding the southeastern edge of Mare Imbrium

Mon·tes Ju·ra /mòn tayz jŏŏrə/ range of lunar mountains north of Mare Imbrium. Height: 15,000 ft./4,500 m.

Mon·tes·quieu /mòntə skyŏŏ/, **Charles Louis de Secondat, Baron de la Brède et de** (1689–1755) French jurist and writer. His works, including his seminal comparative political study *The Spirit of Laws* (1748), contributed to the European Enlightenment and helped to create the political climate that led to the French Revolution.

Mon·tes·so·ri /mòntə sáwree/, **Maria** (1870–1952) Italian physician and educationalist. She devised a system for educating young children.

Mon·tes·so·ri meth·od *n.* a system of educating young children that was initiated by Maria Montessori in 1952 and aims to develop the child's natural interests and activities rather than use formal teaching methods

Mon·te·ver·di /mònti váirdee/, **Claudio** (1567–1643) Italian composer. His secular and sacred choral works and his operas mark the transition from Renaissance to Baroque music. Full name **Claudio Giovanni Antonio Monteverdi**

AKG London

Maria Montessori

Mon·te·vi·de·o /mòntəvi dáyō/ capital city of Uruguay, located on the Atlantic Ocean in the south of the country. Population: 1,251,647 (1985).

Mon·te·zu·ma II /mònti zŏŏmə/ (1466–1520) Aztec emperor. His empire was brought down by Spanish invaders (1520).

Mon·te·zu·ma's re·venge /montə zŏŏməz-/ *n.* an offensive term for diarrhea and sickness experienced when visiting a foreign country, originally Mexico, and eating unfamiliar food (*informal offensive*) [Mid-20thC. Named for the last Aztec emperor of Mexico, MONTEZUMA II, as if the malady were his revenge for the loss of his empire to the Spanish.]

Mont·gom·er·y /mənt gəmməree/ capital city of Alabama, in the center of the state. It is a port on the Alabama River. Population: 196,363 (1996).

Mont·gom·er·y /mont gúmməree/, **Bernard Law, 1st Viscount Montgomery of Alamein** (1887–1976) British soldier. In World War II, he commanded the Eighth Army in northern Africa defeating Rommel, and became chief of the land forces in the Normandy invasion. After the war, he was deputy supreme commander of NATO forces (1951–58).

Mont·gom·er·y, L. M. (1874–1942) Canadian writer, known for her novel *Anne of Green Gables* (1908). Full name **Lucy Maud Montgomery**

month /munth/ *n.* **1.** CALENDAR **MAJOR DIVISION OF YEAR** any of the major named divisions of the year in various calendar systems. In the Gregorian calendar, there are 12 months, varying in length from 28 to 31 days. **2.** CALENDAR **FOUR WEEKS OR 30 DAYS** a period of time equivalent to about four weeks or 30 days **3.** **INTERVAL BETWEEN DATES IN CONSECUTIVE MONTHS** a time lasting from a specified date in one calendar month until the same date in the next calendar month **4.** ASTRON = **solar month 5.** ASTRON = **lunar month 6.** ASTRON = **sidereal month** ■ **months** *npl.* **LONG PERIOD OF TIME** a long time, often an excessively or unacceptably long time [Old English *mōnaþ*. Ultimately "something measured by the revolutions of the moon," from an Indo-European word meaning "to measure" that is also the ancestor of English *moon*.] ◇ **a month of Sundays** a long time, or one that is apparently unending (*informal*)

month·ly /múnthlee/ *adj.* **1.** **HAPPENING EACH MONTH** done, held, or arranged once every month ○ *a monthly meeting* **2.** **PRODUCED EVERY MONTH** published or issued once a month ○ *a monthly periodical* **3.** **LASTING A MONTH** valid for one month ○ *a monthly pass* ■ *adv.* **ONCE A MONTH** at intervals of one month ■ *n.* (*plural* **-lies**) **1.** PUBL **MAGAZINE ISSUED EVERY MONTH** a publication or periodical that is produced once a month **2.** **WOMAN'S MENSTRUAL PERIOD** a woman's monthly menstruation (*informal*) (*usually plural*)

mon·ti·cule /mónti kyool/ *n.* **1.** **SECONDARY VOLCANIC CONE** a subordinate volcanic cone **2.** **MOUND** any mound or small hill [Late 18thC. Via French from late Latin *monticulus*, a diminutive of the Latin stem *mont-* "mountain" (see MOUNTAIN).]

Mont·mo·ren·cy river in southern Quebec, Canada. It flows south to join the St. Lawrence River. Length: 60 mi./97 km.

Mont·mo·ren·cy Falls the highest falls in Quebec, Canada. They are located east of Quebec City where the Montmorency River empties into the St. Lawrence River. Height: 275 ft./84 m.

mont·mo·ril·lo·nite /mòntmə rillə nīt/ *n.* a soft clayey mineral that is composed of hydrous aluminum silicate. It is the major component of bentonite clay deposits. [Mid-19thC. Named for *Montmorillon*, the French town where it was discovered.] —**mont·mo·ril·lo·nit·ic** /mòntmə rillə níttik/ *adj.*

Mont·pel·lier /moN pə lyáy/ city in southern France, capital of the Hérault Department and administrative and commercial center of the Languedoc-Roussillon Region. Population: 207,996 (1990).

Mon·tre·al /mòntree áwl/ the second largest city in Canada, situated on Montreal Island in the St. Lawrence River, Quebec. Population: 3,326,510 (1996).

Mon·treux /mon trō/ major resort area in western Switzerland, on the northeastern shore of Lake Geneva. Population: 20,060 (1990).

Monts /monts/, **Pierre du Gua, Sieur de** (1560?–1630?) French explorer. He colonized what are now the Maritime Provinces of Canada for France and founded Port Royal, Nova Scotia (1604).

Mont-Saint-Mi·chel /moN saN mi shél/ steep granite hill off the Normandy coast in northern France that becomes an island when the tides are high

Mont·ser·rat /mòntsə rát/ island in the eastern Caribbean Sea, a dependency of the United Kingdom. It was economically devastated by volcanic eruptions in 1997. Population: 12,771 (1996). Area: 39 sq. mi./102 sq. mi.

mon·u·ment /mónnyəmənt/ *n.* **1. LARGE STONE STATUE OR CARVING** something designed and built as a lasting public tribute to a person, a group of people, or an event **2. FAMOUS PLACE OR BUILDING** a site or structure that is preserved because of its historical, cultural, or aesthetic importance **3. CARVED HEADSTONE** a tombstone, plaque, or ornamental stone structure placed on somebody's grave. A monument in a cemetery is usually inscribed with the name and dates of birth and death of the deceased person, and often a religious quotation or verse. **4. WORTHY REMINDER OF SOMETHING** something that remains as a reminder of something, especially something fine or distinguished **5. MEMORIAL TRIBUTE** a memorial to somebody in the form of a written or spoken tribute **6. BOUNDARY MARKER** an object such as a stone that marks a boundary [13thC. Via French from Latin *monumentum*, from *monere* "to remind."]

mon·u·men·tal /mònnyə mént'l/ *adj.* **1. LARGE** huge in size, importance, or intensity **2. DESERVING SPECIAL ADMIRATION** so important or enduring that people cannot fail to notice or be impressed **3. MAKING CARVED HEADSTONES** related to or involved in the making of tombstones and memorial items to go in cemeteries and churches **4. OF MONUMENTS** relating to monuments or taking the form of a monument —**mon·u·men·tal·i·ty** /mònnyə men tállətee/ *n.* —**mon·u·men·tal·ly** *adv.*

Monument Valley

Mon·u·ment Val·ley /mònnyəmənt-/ region in northeastern Arizona and southeastern Utah, notable for its scenic rock formations

mon·u·ron /mónnyə ròn/ *n.* a herbicide that is particularly effective against broad-leaved weeds, in the form of a white crystalline odorless solid [Mid-20thC. Blend of MONO- and UREA and -ON.]

Mon·za /móntsa, mónzə/ city in northern Italy, situated about 8 mi./13 km northeast of Milan. Population: 120,054 (1992).

mon·zo·nite /mon zṓ nìt, mónzə-/ *n.* a visibly crystalline, granular igneous rock composed chiefly of equal amounts of two feldspar minerals, plagioclase and orthoclase, and small amounts of a variety of colored minerals [Late 19thC. Named for Mount *Monzoni* in the Tyrol.] —**mon·zo·nit·ic** /mònzə níttik/ *adj.*

moo /moo/ *vi.* (**mooed, moo·ing, moos**) **MAKE NOISE LIKE COW** to produce the deep drawn-out sound that a cow makes ■ *n.* (*plural* **moos**) **NOISE THAT COW MAKES** a deep drawn-out sound made by a cow, or by somebody imitating this sound [Mid-16thC. An imitation of the sound.]

mooch /mooch/ (**mooched, mooch·ing, mooch·es**) *v.* **1.** *vti.* **GET THINGS FOR NOTHING FROM OTHERS** to get something for nothing from somebody by asking directly for it, without making any personal effort for it (*informal*) ○ *He's always mooching off friends.* **2.** *vt.* **STEAL** to steal something (*slang*) **3.** *vi.* **WANDER AIMLESSLY** to wander or linger in an aimless way (*slang*) ○ *just mooching about* **4.** *vi.* **SNEAK AROUND SUSPICIOUSLY** to move around or wait somewhere quietly and secretly, trying not to be noticed (*slang*) [15thC. From Old French *muchier* "to hide," of unknown origin.] —**mooch·er** *n.*

mood[1] /mood/ *n.* **1. STATE OF MIND** a state of mind that somebody experiences at a particular time ○ *a good mood* **2. GENERAL FEELING OF GROUP** the way a group of people think and feel about something at a particular time ○ *The mood of the country after the war was generally optimistic.* **3. BAD TEMPER** a feeling or display of sullen anger or irritability, especially one that begins suddenly or lasts a relatively short time ○ *He's in a mood.* [Old English *mōd* "mind, courage," from a prehistoric Germanic word] ◇ **in the mood** in the right or best state of mind for a particular activity or experience

mood[2] /mood/ *n.* **1.** GRAM **SET OF VERB FORMS** a group of verb forms expressing a particular attitude. English has the indicative mood, expressing factual statements, the imperative mood, expressing commands, and the subjunctive mood, expressing possibilities and wishes. **2.** LOGIC = **mode** *n.* 7 [Mid-16thC. Alteration of MODE.]

mood·y /mo͝odee/ (**-i·er, -i·est**) *adj.* **1. UNPREDICTABLY GRUMPY OR GLOOMY** tending to change mood unpredictably from cheerful to bad-tempered **2. CHANGEABLE** unusually changeable or difficult to predict **3. DISPLAYING PARTICULAR MOOD** displaying particular emotions, especially unhappiness or anger, clearly and intensely [Old English] —**mood·i·ly** *adv.* —**mood·i·ness** *n.*

Mood·y /mo͝odee/, **Dwight Lyman** (1837–99) U.S. evangelist. He founded Northfield Seminary girls' school (1879) and Mount Hermon School for boys (1881).

moo·la /mo͝o laa/, **moo·lah** *n.* money (*slang*) [Mid-20thC. Origin unknown.]

moo·li /mo͝olee/ (*plural* **-lis** *or* **-li**) *n. U.K.* = **daikon** [Mid-20thC. From Hindi *mūlī*.]

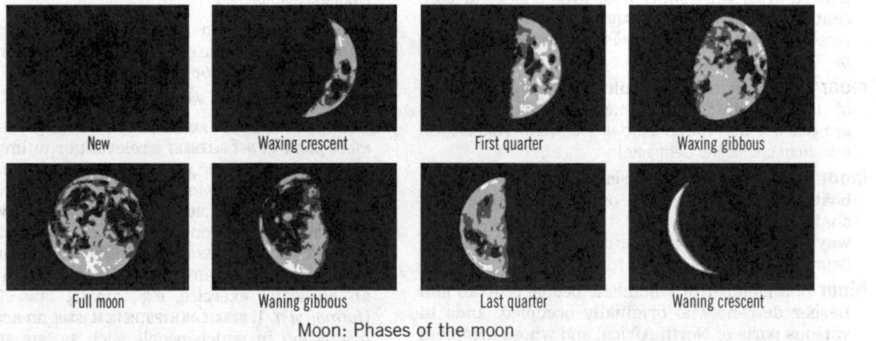

Moon: Phases of the moon

moon /moon/ *n.* **1. moon, Moon** ASTRON **ONLY NATURAL SATELLITE OF EARTH** the Earth's only natural satellite. It is the astronomical body nearest to the Earth, except for some artificial satellites and occasional meteors. **2.** ASTRON **PLANET'S NATURAL SATELLITE** any natural satellite revolving around a planet. Mars, Jupiter, Saturn, Uranus, and Neptune each have more than one moon. **3. MOON'S SHAPE AS SEEN FROM EARTH** a form or view of the Moon, called its phase, at a specific point in the lunar cycle. Since it shines only by reflected sunlight, the phases of the Moon depend on its position relative to the Earth and the Sun. **4. SYMBOLIC REPRESENTATION OF MOON** a simple or stylized representation of the Moon, usually in the form of a circle or crescent **5. PERIOD OF TIME** a month, either as a rough estimate of time or as the time it takes for the Moon to complete its cycle of the Earth (*archaic or literary*) **6. MOONLIGHT** light given out by the Moon ■ *v.* (**mooned, moon·ing, moons**) **1.** *vi.* **WANDER AIMLESSLY** to wander around in a dreamy or listless state, unable to concentrate on anything **2.** *vi.* **YEARN FOR LOVED ONE** to be stricken with longing for an absent loved one, and rendered listless and dreamy as a result (*literary or humorous*) **3.** *vti.* **BARE THE BUTTOCKS** to bend over and deliberately expose the bare buttocks to somebody, either as a rude joke or as an act of defiance and disrespect (*informal*) [Old English *mōna*, from a prehistoric Germanic word that is also the ancestor of English *month* (see MONTH)]

moon·beam /mo͝on be͞em/ *n.* a pale, milky, or iridescent beam of light reflected to the Earth by the Moon at night

moon blind·ness *n.* periodic episodes of impaired vision in horses that often lead to permanent loss of sight

moon·calf /mo͝on kàf/ (*plural* **-calves** /-kàvz/) *n.* **1. THOUGHTLESS PERSON** an unintelligent or thoughtless person (*archaic insult*) **2. SOMETHING BADLY FORMED** something that is badly formed, especially a stillborn human or animal baby (*archaic*) [Mid-16thC. From MOON + CALF; originally in the meaning of "shapeless fleshy mass in the womb," thought to be caused by the influence of the moon.]

moon dog *n.* ASTRON = **paraselene**

moon·eye /mo͝on ì/ *n.* a silvery freshwater fish found in North America that looks like a herring with very large eyes. Latin name: *Hiodon tergisus.*

moon-faced *adj.* with a large round face

moon·flow·er /mo͝on flòwr/ *n.* a name given to various plants whose flowers open at night, especially climbing plants related to the morning glories

Moon·ie /mo͝onee/ *n.* somebody who belongs to the Unification Church founded by Sun Myung Moon (*informal*) (*often considered offensive*)

moon·light /mo͝on lìt/ *n.* **LIGHT FROM THE MOON** the pale cool light that shines from the Moon on a clear night, often considered eerie or romantic. Moonlight is light from the Sun reflected from the Moon's surface. ■ *vi.* (**-light·ed, -light·ing, -lights**) **WORK AT SECOND JOB** to have a second job in addition to a main job (*informal*) —**moon·light·ing** *n.*

WORD KEY: CULTURAL NOTE

Moonlight Sonata, a piano sonata by the German composer Ludwig van Beethoven (1801). This nickname for Beethoven's somber piano sonata in C# minor, op. 27 no. 2, was coined by the poet Heinrich Renstab. In his review of the composition, he described how the first movement brought to his mind the image of moonlight on Lake Lucerne.

moon·lit /mo͝on lìt/ *adj.* brightened or illuminated by light from the Moon

moon pool *n.* INDUST an open shaft in a deep-sea drilling vessel, usually located in the center of the hull, through which the drilling takes place

moon·rak·er /mo͝on ràykər/ *n.* a small sail sometimes set above the skysail on a square-rigged ship [Early 19thC. Origin uncertain: probably from its great height (compare SKYSCRAPER).]

moon·rise /mo͝on rìz/ *n.* **1. MOMENT WHEN MOON APPEARS** the time of day when the Moon rises over the horizon **2. MOON'S APPEARANCE IN SKY** the Moon's rising in the sky over the horizon [Early 18thC. Formed from MOON on the model of *sunrise*.]

moon·scape /mo͝on skàyp/ *n.* **1. VIEW OF THE MOON'S SURFACE** the general appearance of the surface of the Moon as seen or portrayed **2. BARE DESERTED LANDSCAPE** a view or place that looks as rough, gray, and bleak as the surface of the Moon

moon·seed /mo͝on se͞ed/ *n.* a name given to various climbing plants that have tiny greenish flowers and red or black fruit with crescent-shaped seeds.

Genera: *Menispermum* and *Cocculus.* [Mid-18thC. From the crescent shape of their seeds.]

moon·set /mo͞on sèt/ *n.* **1.** MOMENT WHEN MOON GOES DOWN the time of day when the Moon disappears below the horizon **2.** MOON'S LEAVING THE SKY the disappearance of the Moon below the horizon [Mid-19thC. Formed from MOON on the model of *sunset.*]

moon shell *n.* a carnivorous marine mollusk with a smooth rounded shell. Family: Naticidae.

moon·shine /mo͞on shìn/ *n.* **1.** ILLEGALLY MADE ALCOHOL whiskey or other strong liquor produced and sold illegally (*informal*) **2.** NONSENSE talk, opinions, or ideas dismissed as senseless (*informal*) **3.** MOONLIGHT moonlight —**moon·shin·er** *n.*

moon·shot /mo͞on shòt/ *n.* the launch of a crewed or uncrewed spacecraft to orbit or land on the Moon

moon·stone /mo͞on stōn/ *n.* a translucent variety of the mineral feldspar that has a bluish-white luster and is used as a gemstone

WORD KEY: CULTURAL NOTE

The Moonstone, a novel by the English writer Wilkie Collins (1868). The first English detective novel, it involves the disappearance of a priceless Indian diamond and a subsequent puzzling murder. All the classic elements of the whodunit genre are present, including red herrings, alibis, and sufficient clues for the reader to solve the crime ahead of its hero, Sergeant Cuff of Scotland Yard.

moon·struck /mo͞on strùk/ *adj.* **1.** IN A DAZE acting in a rather irrational, dreamy, confused way, often out of love (*informal humorous*) **2.** WILDLY CONFUSED behaving in a wild or confused way (*dated literary*) [Late 17thC. The two senses of the word came from the romantic associations of moonlight and the popular belief that the Moon has an effect upon mental stability.]

moon·walk /mo͞on wàwk/ *n.* INSTANCE OF WALKING ON MOON an exploratory walk or expedition across part of the Moon's surface, carried out by an astronaut. The first person to walk on the Moon was Neil Armstrong on July 20, 1969. ■ *vi.* (**-walked, -walk·ing, -walks**) **1.** GO ON FOOT ACROSS MOON'S SURFACE to walk away from a spacecraft for some distance across the surface of the Moon **2.** DANCE PERFORM GLIDING DISCO DANCE to perform a disco dance with gliding movements of the feet and legs —**moon·walk·er** *n.*

moon·y /mo͞onee/ (**-i·er, -i·est**) *adj.* **1.** DREAMY in a distracted or dreamy state, with little energy or concentration (*informal*) **2.** RELATING TO MOON relating to or resembling the Moon —**moon·i·ly** *adv.* —**moon·i·ness** *n.*

moor[1] /moor/ *n.* a large uncultivated treeless stretch of land covered with bracken, heather, coarse grasses or moss (*often used in the plural*) [Old English *mōr*, from prehistoric Germanic]

moor[2] /moor/ (**moored, moor·ing, moors**) *vti.* to fix a boat, ship, or aircraft to one place with cables, chains, or an anchor, or to be secured in this way [15thC. Origin uncertain: probably from Middle Low German *mōren.*]

Moor *n.* a member of a nomadic people of Arab and Berber descent who originally occupied lands in various parts of North Africa, and whose members continue to live there. Their civilization flourished from the 8th to the 15th centuries, during which time they also settled in Spain. [14thC. Via Old French *More* from Latin *Maurus*, from Greek *Mauros* (source of English *morris dance*), of uncertain origin: probably from a North African language.]

moor·age /mo͝orij/ *n.* **1.** = **mooring** *n.* 1 **2.** MOORING FEE the fee charged for mooring somewhere

Moore /moor, mawr/ *n., adj.* LANG, PEOPLES = **Mossi**

Moore /moor, mawr/, **Clement Clarke** (1779–1863) U.S. scholar and writer. He is best known for the Christmas poem "A Visit from St. Nicholas" (1823).

Moore, Demi (*b.* 1962) U.S. actor. She first became well known for her role in *Ghost* (1990). Real name **Demi Guynes**

Moore, Dudley (*b.* 1935) British actor, comedian, and pianist. After working in partnership with comedian Peter Cook, he appeared in Hollywood movie comedies.

Moore, Henry (1898–1986) British sculptor, and printmaker. He is noted for his large-scale, stylized representations of the human body, many made for outdoor locations.

Moore, Marianne (1887–1972) U.S. poet. She is known for her witty ironic poetry, which covers a wide range of subjects. Her *Collected Poems* (1951) won a Pulitzer Prize. Full name **Marianne Craig Moore**

Moore, Mary Tyler (*b.* 1936) U.S. actor. She is best known for her television roles, as Laura Petrie on *The Dick Van Dyke Show* (1961–66) and Mary Richards on *The Mary Tyler Moore Show* (1970–77).

moor·hen /mo͝or hèn/ *n.* a medium-sized water bird found in marshy areas throughout the world. It has black plumage and a red bill. Latin name: *Gallinula chloropus.*

moor·ing /mo͝oring/ *n.* **1.** NAUT, AIR PLACE FOR SECURING WATERCRAFT OR AIRCRAFT a place where a boat, ship, or aircraft can be moored **2.** NAUT, AIR CABLE SECURING WATERCRAFT OR AIRCRAFT a rope, cable, or chain used to stop a watercraft or aircraft from drifting away **3.** PHYSICAL OR EMOTIONAL TIE something such as a family bond that gives a feeling of emotional or physical security (*usually used in the plural*)

moor·ing tow·er *n.* a permanent structure built as a place to moor airships. The structure provides facilities for transferring passengers, crew, and freight, for refueling, and for replenishing ballast and lifting gas.

Moor·ish /mo͝orish/ *adj.* **1.** OF MOORS relating to or typical of the Moors or their culture **2.** ARCHIT WITH ORNATE CURVED DECORATION built or designed in an architectural style popular in Spain between the 8th and the 16th century, noted for its use of ornate, curving decoration

Moor·ish i·dol *n.* a tropical marine fish that lives near Indo-Pacific reefs and has broad black and yellow stripes on its sides. Latin name: *Zanclus canescens.* [Because its markings resemble those found in Moorish art]

moor·land /mo͝or lànd, -lənd/ *n.* countryside, or a piece of countryside, consisting of a moor [Old English]

moose /mooss/ (*plural* **moose**) *n.* a large mammal of the deer family, with long legs and, in the male, large flat palmate antlers, found in North America, Europe, and Asia. Latin name: *Alces alces.* [Early 17thC. From Abenaki *mos.*]

Moose (*plural* **Moose**) *n.* a member of the Loyal Order of Moose, a fraternal organization [Late 19thC. From the tradition of naming such organisations after animals native to the area that are thought to have qualities such as strength and dignity.]

Moose Jaw city in southeastern Saskatchewan, Canada. It is the site of the nation's largest military jet-training base. Population: 32,973 (1996).

moose·wood /mo͞oss wo͝od/ *n.* = **striped maple**

moot /moot/ *adj.* **1.** ARGUABLE open to argument ○ *a moot point* **2.** NOT RELEVANT irrelevant or unimportant (*informal*) ○ *Whether you want to go or not is moot, because the performance has been cancelled.* ■ *v.* (**moot·ed, moot·ing, moots**) **1.** *vt.* SUGGEST FORMALLY to offer an idea for consideration or a topic for discussion (*usually passive*) **2.** *vi.* HAVE FORMAL ARGUMENT to take part in a debate, especially one organized as an academic exercise, e.g., among law students (*formal*) ■ *n.* **1.** DEBATE ON HYPOTHETICAL ISSUE an academic discussion in which people such as law students argue hypothetically or plead a hypothetical legal case **2.** HIST ANGLO-SAXON LOCAL COURT in Anglo-Saxon England, a formal gathering for settling legal and administrative matters [Old English *mōt* "assembly, meeting, litigation," from a prehistoric Germanic word meaning "meeting" that is also the ancestor of English *meet*]

moot court *n.* a court in which imaginary legal cases are conducted and tried by law students as part of their training

mop /mop/ *n.* **1.** FLOOR-WASHING TOOL a long-handled tool for washing floors, with a washing head consisting of a large sponge or a thick mass of absorbent threads or fabric strips **2.** DISHWASHING TOOL a short-handled dishwashing tool with a washing head consisting of a mass of twisted cotton threads **3.** UNTIDY MASS a thick or scruffy-looking tangle of hair ■ *vt.* (**mopped, mop·ping, mops**) **1.** WASH WITH A MOP to use a mop to wipe a floor surface clean, usually using warm, soapy water **2.** WIPE TO REMOVE PERSPIRATION to wipe perspiration from a part of the body, e.g., with a handkerchief [15thC. Origin uncertain: perhaps directly or via French dialect from Latin *mappa* "napkin, towel." Originally in the meaning of "bundle of cloth for caulking a ship."]

mop up *v.* **1.** *vti.* GET RID OF LIQUID WITH CLOTH to wipe or rub a piece of material over a liquid to soak it up **2.** *vt.* MIL DEAL WITH REMAINING ENEMY FORCES to capture or kill remaining enemy troops in order to secure an area after a decisive victory **3.** *vt.* FINISH OFF to complete or carry out the final details of a task (*informal*) [Early 18thC. From MOP.]

mop·board /móp bàwrd/ *n.* = **baseboard**

mope /mōp/ *vi.* (**moped, mop·ing, mopes**) **1.** BE MISERABLE to be full of self-pity or sulky unhappiness and lose interest in everything else **2.** WANDER ABOUT SADLY to show self-pity and sulky unhappiness, especially by listless or aimless lingering or with a self-consciously slumping gait ■ *n.* **mope** MISERABLE PERSON somebody who tends to mope and who depresses others as a result (*informal*) ■ **mopes** *npl.* GLOOMY MOOD a bout of melancholy or sulkiness (*informal*) [Mid-16thC. Origin uncertain: perhaps from a Scandinavian language.] —**mop·er** *n.* —**mop·ey** *adj.*

mo·ped /mō pèd/ *n.* a lightweight pedaled motorcycle with an engine of less than 50cc. Mopeds generally need pedals to start them up and to supply extra power, e.g., when going uphill. [Mid-20thC. Blend of MOTOR and PEDAL.]

mop·pet /móppət/ *n.* a small child, or a term of endearment for a child (*informal*) [Early 17thC. Literally "small 'mop'," formed from obsolete *mop* "baby, doll," earlier "fool," of uncertain origin.]

mo·quette /mō két/ *n.* thick fabric with a velvety texture, used as carpeting or for upholstery [Mid-19thC. From French, of unknown origin.]

MOR *abbr.* MUSIC middle-of-the-road (*used especially in radio programming*)

mor. *abbr.* morocco

Mor. *abbr.* **1.** Morocco **2.** Moroccan

mo·raine /mə ráyn/ *n.* a mass of earth and rock debris carried by an advancing glacier and left at its front and side edges as it retreats [Late 18thC. Via French from French dialect *morena* "mound," from, ultimately, an unassumed Vulgar Latin word.] —**mo·rain·al** *adj.* —**mo·rain·ic** *adj.*

mor·al /máwrəl/ *adj.* **1.** INVOLVING RIGHT AND WRONG relating to issues of right and wrong and to how individuals should behave **2.** DERIVED FROM PERSONAL CONSCIENCE based on what somebody's conscience suggests is right or wrong, rather than on what the law says should be done **3.** IN TERMS OF NATURAL JUSTICE regarded in terms of what is known to be right or just, as opposed to what is officially or outwardly declared to be right or just ○ *a moral victory.* **4.** ENCOURAGING GOODNESS AND RESPECTABILITY giving guidance on how to behave decently and honorably **5.** GOOD BY ACCEPTED STANDARDS good or right, when judged by the standards of the average person or society at large **6.** TELLING RIGHT FROM WRONG able to distinguish right from wrong and to make decisions based on that knowledge **7.** BASED ON CONVICTION based on an inner conviction, in the absence of physical proof ■ *n.* **1.** VALUABLE LESSON IN BEHAVIOR a conclusion about how to behave or proceed drawn from a story or event **2.** FINAL SENTENCE OF STORY GIVING ADVICE a short, precise rule, usually written in a rather literary style as the conclusion to a story, used to help people remember the best or most sensible way to behave ■ **mor·als** *npl.* STANDARDS OF BEHAVIOR principles of right and wrong as they govern standards of general or sexual behavior [14thC. From Latin *moralis*, from *mor-*, stem of *mos* "custom," in plural "morals" (source of English *morale* and *morose*).] —**morally** *adv.*

mo·rale /mə rál, maw-/ *n.* the general level of confidence or optimism felt by a person or group of people, especially as it affects discipline and willingness [Mid-18thC. Via French *moral* from Latin *moralis* (see MORAL). The spelling was altered in English to indicate stress.]

mor·al·ism /máwrə lìzzəm/ *n.* **1.** PIECE OF MORAL ADVICE a conventional moral maxim or saying **2.** MORAL BEHAVIOR behavior conforming to a system of moral standards that do not depend on religion **3.** MORALIZING criticism of other people's moral standards (*formal or dated*)

mor·al·ist /máwrəlist/ *n.* **1.** SOMEBODY GIVING ADVICE ON MORAL STANDARDS somebody who criticizes or lectures other people about their standards of morality, or who tries to teach them better moral standards **2.** SOMEBODY WITH HIGH MORAL STANDARDS somebody who follows a strict, personal, moral code **3.** SPECIALIST WHO STUDIES

MORALITY somebody who studies or teaches morals as an academic discipline —**mor·al·is·tic** /màwrə lístik/ *adj.* —**mor·al·is·ti·cal·ly** /-kəlee/ *adv.*

mo·ral·i·ty /mə rállətee, màw-/ (*plural* **-ties**) *n.* **1.** ACCEPTED MORAL STANDARDS standards of conduct that are accepted as right or proper **2.** HOW RIGHT OR WRONG SOMETHING IS the rightness or wrongness of something as judged by accepted moral standards **3.** MORAL LESSON a lesson in moral behavior

mo·ral·i·ty play *n.* a play intended to teach a moral lesson, in which the characters embody human virtues and vices, e.g., Mercy and Lust, especially a medieval play written in verse. Morality plays were popular in Europe from the 15th century to the 17th century, the later plays featuring some humor and satire.

mor·al·ize /máwrə lìz/ (**-ized, -iz·ing, -iz·es**) *v.* **1.** *vi.* CRITICIZE THE MORALS OF OTHERS to criticize other people's conduct or standards of behavior or give advice on how general moral standards should be improved **2.** *vt.* ANALYZE IN TERMS OF MORALITY to consider and explain something in terms of its moral significance **3.** *vt.* MAKE MORE MORAL to change something to make it conform, or conform better, with society's ideas of what is good, right, or decent —**mor·al·i·za·tion** /màwrəli záysh'n/ *n.* —**mor·al·iz·er** *n.*

mor·al·iz·ing /máwrə lìzing/ *n.* lecturing others on their low moral standards or pronouncing on how general standards of behavior should be improved

mor·al phi·los·o·phy *n.* = **ethics** *n.* 1

mor·al the·ol·o·gy *n.* the academic study of moral and ethical questions from a Christian viewpoint

mo·rass /mə ráss, màw-/ *n.* **1.** AREA OF SOGGY GROUND an area of low-lying ground that is soft and wet to a great depth and therefore difficult to walk on **2.** SOMETHING THAT OVERWHELMS, CONFUSES, OR IMPEDES a frustrating, confusing, or unmanageable situation that makes any kind of progress extremely slow [Mid-17thC. Via Dutch *moeras* from, ultimately, French *marais*, of uncertain origin: probably from a prehistoric Germanic word that is also the ancestor of English *marsh*.]

mor·a·to·ri·um /màwrə táwree əm/ (*plural* **-ums** *or* **-a** /-ə/) *n.* **1.** AGREED PERIOD OF DELAY a formally agreed period during which a specific activity is halted or a planned activity is postponed **2.** ALLOWED DELAY IN MEETING OBLIGATION a period during which a person, usually a debtor, has the right to postpone meeting an obligation [Late 19thC. From modern Latin, formed from late Latin *moratorius* "delaying" (see MORATORY).]

mor·a·to·ry /máwrə tàwree/ *adj.* giving somebody the right to delay making payments on a debt [Late 19thC. From late Latin *moratorius* "delaying," from Latin *morat-*, the past participle stem of *morari* "to delay," from *mora* "delay."]

Mo·ra·va /mə raávə/ river in Serbia, in the Federal Republic of Yugoslavia. It flows northward to join the Danube River. Length: 100 mi./160 km.

Mo·ra·vi·a /mə ráyvee ə/ region occupying the eastern part of the Czech Republic. Major cities include Brno and Ostrava.

Mo·ra·vi·an /mə ráyvee ən, maw-/ *n.* **1.** PEOPLES SOMEBODY FROM MORAVIA somebody who was born or raised in Moravia **2.** CHR MORAVIAN CHURCH MEMBER a member of the Moravian Church **3.** LANG DIALECT OF CZECH the dialect of the Czech language spoken in Moravia —**Mo·ra·vi·an** *adj.*

Mo·ra·vi·an Church *n.* a Protestant church founded in Moravia in 1722 whose members place a strong emphasis on evangelism, ecumenism, and the authority of the Bible

mo·ray /máw rày, mə ráy/, **mo·ray eel** *n.* a brightly colored sharp-toothed voracious eel that lives in rocky crevices of tropical coastal waters or reefs. Family: Muraenidae. [Early 17thC. Via Portuguese *moréia* from Latin *murena*, from, ultimately, Greek *muros* "sea eel."]

mor·bid /máwrbid/ *adj.* **1.** INTERESTED IN GRUESOME SUBJECTS showing a strong interest in unpleasant or gloomy subjects such as death, murder, or accidents **2.** GRISLY inspiring disgust or horror **3.** MED RELATING TO DISEASE relating to or resulting in illness [Early 17thC. From Latin *morbidus* "diseased," from *morbus* "sickness."] —**mor·bid·ly** *adv.* —**mor·bid·ness** *n.*

mor·bid·i·ty /mawr bíddətee/ *n.* **1.** DISEASED STATE the presence of illness or disease **2.** MED OCCURRENCE OF A DISEASE the relative frequency of occurrence of a particular disease in a particular area (*often used before a noun*)

mor·ceau /mawr sṓ/ (*plural* **-ceaux** /-sṓ, -sṓz/) *n.* **1.** SHORT COMPOSITION a short musical or literary composition **2.** SMALL PIECE a tiny piece, e.g., a small mouthful of food [Mid-18thC. Via French from Old French *morsel* MORSEL.]

mor·da·cious /mawr dáyshəss/ *adj.* **1.** SHARPLY SARCASTIC deliberately bitter or critical, and intended to hurt somebody's feelings **2.** BITING capable of biting or tending to bite (*archaic or literary*) [Mid-17thC. From the Latin stem *mordac-* "biting," from *mordere* "to bite."] —**mor·da·cious·ly** *adv.* —**mor·da·cious·ness** *n.* —**mor·dac·i·ty** /mawr dássətee/ *n.*

mor·dant /máwrd'nt/ *adj.* **1.** SARCASTIC sharply sarcastic or bitingly critical **2.** CORROSIVE having a corrosive effect ■ *n.* INDUST **1.** SUBSTANCE THAT FIXES DYES a substance that fixes a dye in and on textiles and leather by combining with the dye to form a stable insoluble compound (**lake**). Some dyes assume different colors depending on the mordant used. **2.** ACID USED IN ETCHING a corrosive substance used to etch treated areas on a metal plate ■ *vt.* (**-dant·ed, -dant·ing, -dants**) TEXTILES APPLY MORDANT TO to apply a mordant to fabric in order to fix a dye [15thC. Via French from, ultimately, a Vulgar Latin variant of Latin *mordere* "to bite" (source of English *morsel* and *remorse*).] —**mor·dan·cy** /máwrd'nsee/ *n.*

mor·dant·ly /máwrd'ntlee/ *adv.* in a cruelly sarcastic or bitingly critical way

mor·dent /máwrd'nt/ *n.* a musical embellishment, similar to a short trill, in which either the note above or the note below the written note is played as well as the principal note [Early 19thC. Via German from Italian *mordente*, from *mordere* "to bite," from, ultimately, Latin.]

Mord·vin /máwrdvin/ (*plural* **-vin** *or* **-vins**) *n.* **1.** PEOPLES MEMBER OF FINNISH PEOPLE a member of a Finnish people who live mainly in the middle of the Volga region of western Russia **2.** LANG MORDVIN LANGUAGE the Finno-Ugric language of the Mordvin people. Mordvin is spoken by about one million people. [Mid-18thC. From Russian.] —**Mord·vin** *adj.*

more /mawr/ CORE MEANING: a grammatical word, the comparative of "much" and "many," used to indicate a greater number of something, either a greater number than before, than average, or than something else ○ (adj) *a need for more adult education programs* ○ (pron) *As benefits go, this job offers me more.*

1. *adv.* TO A GREATER EXTENT having a larger amount or a greater extent of a particular quality (*forming the comparative of some adjectives and adverbs*) ○ (adv-attrib) *This problem is more complex than the other one.* **2.** *adv.* FOR A LONGER TIME doing something or happening for a longer time ○ *We chatted a bit more.* **3.** *adv., pron.* WITH GREATER FREQUENCY OR INTENSITY used as the comparative of "much" to mean "with greater frequency or intensity" ○ (adv-degree) *We go out more than we used to.* ○ (adv-degree) *It inspires me more now than ever.* ○ (pron) *The more you listen, the more you hear.* **4.** *adj., pron.* ADDITIONAL additional or further (*Pronoun takes a singular or plural verb*) ○ (adj) *I need more light.* ○ (pron) *There aren't any more of these.* ○ (pron) *No more is expected.* [Old English *māra*, from a prehistoric Germanic base that is also the ancestor of English *most*] ◇ **more or less 1.** approximately **2.** essentially or basically ◇ **more so, all the more so** to an even greater extent or degree ◇ **what is more** moreover or furthermore

More /mawr/, **Sir Thomas, St.** (1478–1535) English statesman and scholar. He resigned as Henry VIII's Lord Chancellor (1529–32) in protest against the King's break with the Roman Catholic Church, and was executed after refusing to recognize Henry as the head of the English Church. His literary works include *Utopia* (1516).

Mo·ree /maw rée/ town in northern New South Wales, a major cotton-growing center. Population: 9,270 (1996).

mo·reen /mə reén, maw-/ *n.* a thick, ribbed curtain material made of wool, cotton, or a mixture of both [Mid-17thC. Origin unknown.]

mo·rel /mə rél, maw-/ *n.* an edible mushroom with a brown pitted spongey cap. Genus: *Morchella.* [Late 17thC. From French *morille*, of uncertain origin: perhaps ultimately from Latin *Maurus* "Moor" (see MOOR).]

mo·rel·lo /mə réllō, maw-/ (*plural* **-los**) *n.* a small sour cultivated cherry with dark red skin [Mid-17thC. Origin uncertain: perhaps from Italian *amarello* "amarelle" (influenced by Italian *morello* "blackish"), from, ultimately, Latin *Maurus* "Moor" (see MOOR).]

mo·ren·do /mə réndō, maw-/ *adv.* growing continuously softer and sometimes slower (*used as a musical direction*) [Early 19thC. From Italian, literally "dying," a form of *morire* "to die."] —**mo·ren·do** *adj.*

more·o·ver /maw rṓvər/ *adv.* used to add a further piece of information that supports a previous statement

mo·res /máw ràyz, -reez/ *npl.* the customs and habitual practices, especially as they reflect moral standards, that a particular group of people accept and follow [Late 19thC. From Latin, plural of *mos* "manner, custom" (see MORAL).]

Mo·res·co /mə réskō/ *adj.* Moorish (*archaic*) [Mid-16thC. From Italian, formed from *Moro* "Moor," from Latin *Maurus* (see MOOR).]

Mo·resque /mə résk/ *adj.* ARCHIT Moorish (*dated*) [Early 17thC. Via French, from Italian *moresco* (see MORESCO).]

More·ton Bay /máwrt'n-/ bay in southeastern Queensland, Australia, bounded in the east by Moreton and North Stradbroke, two large islands. Area: 310 sq. mi./800 sq. km.

More·ton Bay chest·nut *n.* = **black bean** *n.* 3

More·ton Bay fig *n.* a large fig tree with glossy leaves that is native to eastern Australia. It has massive buttresses at the foot of its trunk and huge spreading roots. Latin name: *Ficus macrophylla.*

More·ton Is·land island in Moreton Bay, off the coast of Queensland, Australia. Population: 455 (1996). Area: 66 sq. mi./170 sq. km.

Mor·gan /máwrgən/ *n.* a black, bay, brown, or chestnut horse with a full mane and tail, short deep body, and slender legs, belonging to a U.S. breed popular for hunting, jumping, and recreation [Mid-19thC. Named for Justin *Morgan* (1747–98), U.S. schoolteacher and owner of a stallion from which the breed descends.]

Mor·gan /máwrgən/, **John Pierpoint** (1837–1913) U.S. financier. He was the founder of J. P. Morgan and Company (1895), and a noted art collector and philanthropist.

Mor·gan, Thomas Hunt (1866–1945) U.S. geneticist and biologist. He received a Nobel Prize in physiology or medicine (1933) for his discovery that chromosomes are the carriers of genetic information.

mor·ga·nat·ic /màwrgə náttik/ *adj.* used to describe a marriage in which neither the spouse of lower social rank nor any children of the marriage may inherit the title or possessions of the higher-ranking spouse [Late 16thC. Directly or via French or German from medieval Latin *(matrimonium ad) morganaticam* "(marriage for the) morning-gift" (the bridegroom's gift to the bride, which relieved him of further responsibility).] —**mor·ga·nat·i·cal·ly** *adv.*

Mor·gan City /màwrgən-/ city in southeastern Louisiana, on the Intracoastal Waterway, west of Houma and south of Baton Rouge. Population: 13,996 (1996).

mor·gan·ite /máwrgə nìt/ *n.* a pink gemstone that is a variety of beryl [Early 20thC. Named for John Pierpont MORGAN.]

Mor·gan le Fay /máwrgən lə fáy/ *n.* in Arthurian legend, an evil sorceress who was the half-sister and enemy of King Arthur

Mor·gan·ton /máwrgəntən/ city in western North Carolina. It is the seat of Burke County. Population: 17,370 (1994).

Mor·gan·town /máwrgən town/ city and port in northern West Virginia, on the Monongahela River, southeast of Wheeling. Population: 26,919 (1996).

mor·gen /máwrgən/ *n.* a unit of measurement for land area formerly used in various parts of the world and still in use in South Africa. It is equal in South Africa to just over 2 acres/0.85 hectare. [Early 17thC. From Dutch and German, with the sense "area of land that can be ploughed in a morning."]

Mor·gen·thau /máwrgən thaw/, **Henry, Jr.** (1891–1967) U.S. public official. He was secretary of the treasury (1934–45).

morgue /mawrg/ *n.* **1.** PLACE FOR DEAD BODIES a room or building usually run by a state or municipal government in which dead bodies are kept until they are autopsied or identified **2.** PRESS **COLLECTION OF INFORMATION** a room or file in a newspaper office containing miscellaneous pieces of information kept for future reference, e.g., for writing obituaries **3.** **DISMAL PLACE** a gloomy place that lacks warmth or cheer (*informal*) [Mid-19thC. From French *Morgue*, a building in Paris used as a morgue, perhaps from *morgue* "room in a prison where new prisoners were examined," perhaps ultimately from *morgue* "haughtiness."]

WORD KEY: CULTURAL NOTE

The Murders in the Rue Morgue, a novel by writer Edgar Allan Poe (1841). Regarded as the world's first detective story, it begins with the brutal murder of an old woman and her daughter, a crime that perplexes the police as the women's apartment is sealed from the inside. Amateur sleuth C. Auguste Dupin comes to their aid, providing an explanation based on a brilliant analysis of scattered clues.

mor·i·bund /máwrə bùnd/ *adj.* **1.** **DYING** nearly dead **2.** **STAGNANT** having lost all sense of purpose or vitality **3.** **OBSOLESCENT** becoming obsolete [Early 18thC. From Latin *moribundus*, from *mori* "to die" (source of English *mortuary*).] —**mor·i·bun·di·ty** /màwrə búndətee/ *n.* —**mor·i·bund·ly** *adv.*

Mor·i·or·i /màwree áwree/ (*plural* **-i** *or* **-is**) *n.* **1.** PEOPLES **MEMBER OF EXTINCT NEW ZEALAND PEOPLE** a member of a now extinct indigenous people that lived in New Zealand, especially on the Chatham Islands **2.** LANG **MORIORI LANGUAGE** the extinct language of the Moriori people. It belongs to the Eastern branch of Malayo-Polynesian languages. [Mid-19thC. From Polynesian.] —**Mor·i·or·i** *adj.*

Mo·ris·co /mə rískō/ (*plural* **-cos** *or* **-coes**), **Mo·res·co** /mə réskō/ (*plural* **-cos** *or* **-coes**) *n.* RELIG a Muslim of medieval Spain who was forcibly converted to Christianity and often continued the surreptitious practice of Islam, or a descendant of such a person [Mid-16thC. From Spanish, from *Moro* "Moor."] —**Mo·ris·co** *adj.*

Mor·i·son /mórrissən/, **Samuel Eliot** (1887–1976) U.S. historian. He wrote the Pulitzer-Prize-winning *Admiral of the Ocean Sea* (1942) and *John Paul Jones* (1959).

Berthe Morisot: Portrait by Marcellin Desboutin

Mo·ri·sot /mòrri sṓ/, **Berthe** (1841–95) French painter. Her paintings, in a subtle and delicate impressionistic style, often depict landscapes or women and children.

Mor·mon /máwrmən/ *adj.* relating to the Church of Jesus Christ of the Latter-day Saints, its members, or its doctrines and beliefs [Mid-19thC. Named for the prophet believed to be the author of the *Book of Mormon*, a sacred history of the Americas, translated by Joseph SMITH.] —**Mor·mon·ism** *n.*

Mor·mon crick·et *n.* a large wingless grasshopper of western parts of the United States that can be a serious crop-eating pest. Latin name: *Anabrus simplex.* [From their presence in areas settled by Mormons]

morn /mawrn/ *n.* a morning (*literary*) [Old English *morgen*, from prehistoric Germanic]

Mor·nay /mawr náy/ *adj.* served in a white sauce containing grated cheese ○ *eggs/ Mornay* [Early 20thC. Perhaps named for Philippe de *Mornay* (1549–1623), a French Huguenot writer.]

morn·ing /máwrning/ *n.* **1.** **EARLY PART OF DAY** the early part of the day, from dawn until noon or lunchtime **2.** **MIDNIGHT TO NOON** the part of the day between midnight and noon **3.** **DAWN** dawn or daybreak **4.** **EARLY PART** the beginning of something ■ *interj.* **GOOD MORNING** good morning (*informal*) [13thC. Coined from MORN + -ING, modeled on EVENING.]

morn·ing-af·ter pill *n.* a contraceptive pill designed to be taken after sexual intercourse

morn·ing dress *n.* a man's suit worn to formal daytime events such as weddings, consisting of a black cutaway, striped black pants, usually a vest, and sometimes a top hat

mor·ning glo·ry *n.* a climbing plant of the bindweed family, widely cultivated for its trumpet-shaped blue, purple, pink, or white flowers that close toward evening. Genus: *Ipomoea.*

morn·ing line *n.* a list of entrants and their odds for a race, estimated by a bookmaker and posted before betting begins, usually on the morning of the race

Morn·ing Prayer *n.* the morning service of worship in the Anglican Church

morn·ings /máwrningz/ *adv.* during the morning or every morning (*informal*)

morn·ing sick·ness *n.* nausea and vomiting experienced by many pregnant women, usually in the morning and during the early months of pregnancy

morn·ing star *n.* a planet, especially Venus, seen in the eastern sky around dawn

Morn·ing·ton Is·land /máwrningtən-/ island in the Gulf of Carpentaria, Australia, largest of the Wellesley group. Population: 1,114 (1996). Area: 387 sq. mi./1,002 sq. km.

Morn·ing·ton Pen·in·su·la peninsula in southern Victoria, Australia, near the city of Melbourne

Mo·ro /máwrō/, **Aldo** (1916–78) Italian statesman. He was prime minister of Italy twice (1963–68 and 1974–76). In 1978 he was kidnapped and murdered by the Red Brigades.

mo·roc·co /mə rókō/, **mo·roc·co leath·er** *n.* INDUST a soft leather made from goatskin, used especially for covering books and for shoes, or any similar leather made in imitation of it from sheepskin or calfskin [Mid-17thC. Named for MOROCCO, where it was first made.]

Morocco

Mo·roc·co /mə rókō/ monarchy in northwestern Africa. Formerly ruled by France and Spain, it became an independent kingdom in 1956. Language: Arabic. Currency: dirham. Capital: Rabat. Population: 27,020,000 (1996). Area: 172,414 sq. mi./446,550 sq. km. Official name **Kingdom of Morocco** —**Mo·roc·can** *n., adj.*

mo·ron /máw ròn/ *n.* **1.** **OFFENSIVE TERM** an offensive term that deliberately insults somebody's intelligence (*offensive insult*) **2.** PSYCHOL **OFFENSIVE TERM** an offensive term for somebody with very significant learning difficulties and difficulty in carrying out usual social functions (*offensive*) [Early 20thC. From Greek *mōron*, neuter of *mōros* "unintelligent, thoughtless."] —**mo·ron·ic** /mə rónnik, maw-/ *adj.* —**mo·ron·i·cal·ly** *adv.* —**mo·ron·ism** /máwrə nìzzəm, máw ro-/ *n.* —**mo·ron·i·ty** /mə rónnətee, maw-/ *n.*

mo·rose /mə rṓss, maw-/ *adj.* having a withdrawn gloomy personality [Mid-16thC. From Latin *morosus* "peevish," from, ultimately, *mos* "manner, disposition," which also produced English *moral*.] —**mo·rose·ly** *adv.* —**mo·rose·ness** *n.* —**mo·ros·i·ty** /mə róssətee, maw-/ *n.*

morph[1] /mawrf/ *n.* an element of speech or writing that represents and expresses one or more morphemes [Mid-20thC. Shortening of MORPHEME.]

morph[2] /mawrf/ *n.* one of two or more variant forms of an animal or plant [Mid-20thC. From Greek *morphē* "form."]

morph[3] /mawrf/ (**morphed, morph·ing, morphs**) *vti.* **1.** **TRANSFORM FROM ONE IMAGE TO ANOTHER** to transform one graphic image on screen into another or others, through the use of sophisticated computer software, or to be transformed in this way **2.** **TRANSFORM QUICKLY** to cause something to change its outward appearance completely and instantaneously, or to undergo this process [Late 20thC. From METAMORPHOSIS.]

morph. *abbr.* **1.** morphological **2.** morphology

-morph *suffix.* something that has a particular form, shape, or structure ○ *mesomorph* [From Greek *morphē* (see MORPHO-)] —**-morphic** *suffix.* —**-morphism** *suffix.* —**-morphous** *suffix.* —**-morphy** *suffix.*

mor·phac·tin /mawrf áktin/ *n.* a chemical that disrupts various aspects of plant development and induces dwarfing [Mid-20thC. Origin uncertain: probably coined from MORPH- + ACTIVE + -IN.]

mor·phal·lax·is /màwrfə láksiss/ *n.* the process whereby an organism regenerates body parts by the reorganization and transformation of existing tissue, rather than by the formation of new tissue [Late 19thC. Formed from Greek *morphē* "form" + *allaxis* "exchange."]

mor·pheme /máwr feem/ *n.* the smallest meaningful element of speech or writing [Late 19thC. Via French, from Greek *morphē* "form," modeled on English *phoneme*.] —**mor·phem·ic** /mawr féemik/ *adj.* —**mor·phem·i·cal·ly** *adv.*

mor·phem·ics /mawr féemiks/ *n.* (*takes a singular verb*) **1.** **MORPHEME COMBINATION PROCESS** the way in which morphemes combine to form words in a language **2.** **STUDY OF MORPHEME COMBINATION** the study and description of the ways in which morphemes combine in languages

Mor·phe·us /máwrfee əss, -fyooss/ *n.* in Greek mythology, the god of dreams and sleep, and son of Hypnos [14thC. From Latin.] —**Mor·phe·an** /máwrfee ən/ *adj.*

mor·phi·a /máwrfee ə/ *n.* morphine (*archaic*) [Early 19thC. Formed from MORPHEUS.]

mor·phine /máwr feen/ *n.* an alkaloid drug derived from opium and used in medicine to relieve severe pain. Prolonged non-medical use may lead to addiction. [Early 19thC. Via French, from *Morphée*, from Latin *Morpheus* (see MORPHEUS).]

mor·phin·ism /máwrfee nìzzəm, máwrfə-/ *n.* addiction to morphine and the related health problems of such addiction (*dated*) —**mor·phin·ist** *n.*

mor·pho /máwrfō/ (*plural* **-phos**) *n.* a large tropical American butterfly with iridescent blue wings. Genus: *Morpho.* [Mid-19thC. Via modern Latin, from Greek *Morphō*, an epithet of APHRODITE.]

morpho- *prefix.* form, shape, structure ○ *morphogenesis* [From Greek *morphē*, of unkown origin]

mor·pho·gen /máwrfəjən/ *n.* a substance produced in an embryo that influences the differentiation and development of the embryonic cells [Mid-20thC. Coined from MORPHO- + -GEN.]

mor·pho·gen·e·sis /màwrfō jénnəssiss/ *n.* **1.** **DEVELOPMENT OF INDIVIDUAL ORGANISM** the origin and development of an organism or of some part of one, as it grows from embryo to adult **2.** **DEVELOPMENT OF SPECIES OF ORGANISM** the development of an organism or of some part of one, as it changes as a species [Late 19thC. Coined from MORPHO- + -GENESIS.] —**mor·pho·ge·net·ic** /màwrfə jə néttik/ *adj.* —**mor·pho·ge·net·i·cal·ly** *adv.* —**mor·pho·gen·ic** *adj.*

morphol. *abbr.* **1.** morphological **2.** morphology

mor·phol·o·gy /mawr fólləjee/ (*plural* **-gies**) *n.* **1.** BIOL **STRUCTURE OF ORGANISM** the form and structure of an organism or of any part of an organism **2.** BIOL **STUDY OF STRUCTURE OF ORGANISMS** the study of the form and structure of organisms **3.** LING **STRUCTURE OF WORDS** the structure of words in a language, including patterns of inflections and derivation **4.** LING **STUDY OF WORD FORMATION** the study of the structure of words in a language **5.** **STRUCTURE OF SOMETHING** the structure of something, or the study of the structure of something [Mid-19thC. Coined from MORPHO- + -LOGY.] —**mor·pho·log·ic** /màwrfə lójjik/ *adj.* —**mor·pho·log·i·cal** *adj.* —**mor·pho·log·i·cal·ly** *adv.* —**mor·phol·o·gist** *n.*

mor·phom·e·try /mawr fómmətree/ *n.* the measurement of the outside of something [Mid-19thC. Coined from MORPHO- + -METRY.] —**mor·pho·met·ric**

/màwrfə méttrik/ *adj.* —**mor·pho·met·ri·cal·ly** /-méttrikəlee/ *adv.*

mor·pho·sis /mawr fṓssiss/ (*plural* **-ses** /-sèez/) *n.* a variation in the pattern of development (**morphogenesis**) of an organism as a result of changes in the external environment [Late 17thC. From Greek *morphōsis* "a shaping," from, ultimately, *morphē* "form."] —**mor·phot·ic** /mawr fóttik/ *adj.*

Mor·rill /mórril/, **Justin Smith** (1810–98) U.S. politician. He introduced the Tariff Act (1861) and the Land-Grant College Act (1862).

mor·ris /máwriss/ *n.* a lively English folk dance, traditionally performed by men, usually in white costumes and using small bells, sticks, and handkerchiefs [15thC. From Old French *morois* "Moorish," from *More* "Moor," because it is perhaps of Moorish origin.]

Mor·ris /mórriss/, **Gouverneur** (1752–1816) U.S. politician. He was a member of the Continental Congress and a senator (1800–03). He co-authored the Constitution (1787) and also spent many years in revolutionary France.

Mor·ris, Lewis (1726–98) American patriot. He was a signatory of the Declaration of Independence (1776) and the half-brother of Gouverneur Morris.

Mor·ris, Robert (1734–1806) American patriot and financier. He was a signatory of the Declaration of Independence (1776) and helped to finance the American Revolution.

Mor·ris, William (1834–96) British artist, poet, and social activist. His decorations and furnishings drew on medieval tradition and his love of craftsmanship, and laid the foundations for the Arts and Crafts movement and art nouveau. His poetry included classical translations, some published in fine editions by Kelmscott Press, which he founded in 1890.

Mor·ris chair *n.* a light carved wooden armchair with removable cushions and a reclining back that can be set at varying angles [Named for William MORRIS]

mor·ris dance *n.* = **morris** —**mor·ris danc·er** *n.* —**mor·ris danc·ing** *n.*

Mor·ris·on /mórriss'n/, **James** (*b.* 1962) Australian jazz musician. A performer on several instruments, he is known both for his solo and ensemble work.

Mor·ris·on, Jim (1943–71) U.S. rock singer and songwriter. He was the lead singer of the Doors and attracted a cult following after his death. Full name **James Douglas Morrison**

Toni Morrison

Mor·ris·on, Toni (*b.* 1931) U.S. writer. Her novels deal with the experience of being an African American. She received the Nobel Prize for literature in 1993. Pseudonym of **Chloe Anthony Wofford**

mor·ro /máwrō/ (*plural* **-ros**) *n.* a hill or headland with a rounded outline [From Spanish]

mor·row /máwrō/ *n.* **1.** NEXT DAY the day after today or after a particular day (*archaic or literary*) **2.** FOLLOWING PERIOD OF TIME the period of time following an event or occurrence (*literary*) [13thC. Variant of earlier form of MORN.]

Mors /mawrz/ *n.* in Roman mythology, the god of death. Greek equivalent **Thanatos** [From Latin, literally "death"]

Morse /mawrs/, **Morse code** *n.* a system for representing letters and numbers by signs consisting of one or more short or long signals of sound or light that are printed out as dots and dashes [Mid-19thC. Named for Samuel F. B. MORSE.]

Morse /mawrss/, **Samuel F. B.** (1791–1872) U.S. inventor and artist. He invented the electric telegraph (1837) and the Morse code. Full name **Samuel Finley Breese Morse**

mor·sel /máwrs'l/ *n.* **1.** SMALL PIECE OF FOOD a small piece of something, especially of food **2.** SMALL AMOUNT a small amount of something ■ *vt.* (**-seled** *or* **-selled, -sel·ing** *or* **-sel·ling, -sels**) DIVIDE UP to divide something into portions [13thC. From Old French, "little bite," from *mors* "bite," from, ultimately, the past participle of Latin *mordere* "to bite."]

mor·ta·del·la /màwrtə déllə/ *n.* a smoked, fried, or steamed Italian sausage consisting of pork and beef flavored with wine, garlic, and pepper [Early 17thC. Via Italian, from Latin *murtatum* "(sausage) seasoned with myrtle berries."]

mor·tal /máwrt'l/ *adj.* **1.** EVENTUALLY DYING certain to die eventually **2.** HUMAN relating to human beings **3.** FATAL causing death ○ *a mortal blow* **4.** CONTINUING UNTIL SOMEBODY DIES continuing, or intended to continue, until somebody dies ○ *mortal combat* **5.** OF DEATH relating to or accompanying death ○ *in mortal agony* **6.** SHOWING HATRED showing great and unrelenting hatred ○ *his mortal enemy* **7.** INTENSE intensely felt ○ *mortal fear* **8.** CONCEIVABLE being within the bounds of what is imaginable or possible ○ *What mortal reason could there be for him to leave like that?* ■ *adj., adv.* USED FOR EMPHASIS used for emphasis, and sometimes indicating that the speaker is frustrated or annoyed (*dated*) ■ *n.* HUMAN BEING a human being, who will eventually die [14thC. Directly or via Old French, from Latin *mortalis*, from, ultimately, *mors* "death" (which also produced English *mortify*).]

WORD KEY: SYNONYMS

See Synonyms at ***deadly***.

mor·tal·i·ty /mawr tállətee/ *n.* **1.** CERTAINTY TO DIE the state of being certain to die eventually **2.** NUMBER OF DEATHS the number of deaths that occur at a given time, in a given group, or from a given cause **3.** MANY DEATHS great loss of life **4.** RATE OF FAILURE the rate of failure of something, such as businesses or farms **5.** HUMAN BEINGS the human race **6.** DEATH death (*archaic*) [14thC]

mor·tal·i·ty rate *n.* the number of deaths in a particular place or group compared with the total number of residents in that place or members of that group

mor·tal·i·ty ta·ble *n.* a table listing the life expectancy and death rate for various ages or occupations and based on mortality statistics over the course of a number of years

mor·tal·ly /máwrtəlee/ *adv.* **1.** FATALLY so badly that death follows **2.** VERY in an extreme or intense way

mor·tal sin *n.* CHR in the Roman Catholic Church, a sin considered to be so evil that it causes a complete loss of grace and leads to damnation unless it is absolved. ◊ **venial sin**

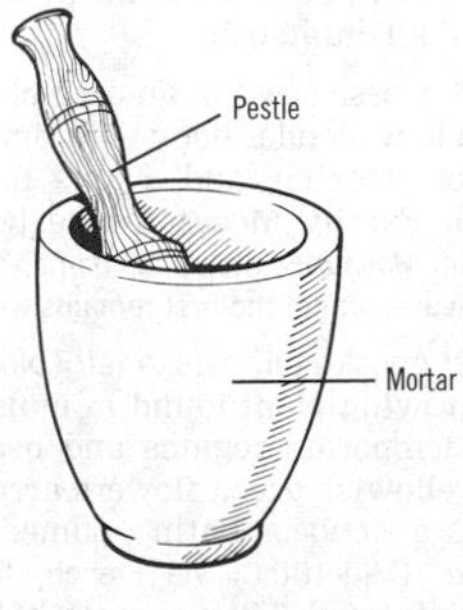

Mortar and pestle

mor·tar /máwrtər/ *n.* **1.** BUILDING CEMENT, SAND, AND WATER a mixture of sand, water, and cement or lime that becomes hard like stone and is used in building to join and hold bricks and stones together **2.** ARMS CANNON a cannon with a relatively short and wide barrel, used for firing shells at a high angle over a short distance. Formerly, mortars were heavy cannons operated by the artillery, but they are now light guns used by the infantry. **3.** GUN FIRING A LIFELINE a gun for firing something other than a bullet, e.g., a rope to somebody in need of rescue **4.** COOK BOWL USED FOR GRINDING a hard, heavy bowl in which substances are ground into small pieces or powder by means of a club-shaped tool (**pestle**) **5.** MINING BOWL FOR CRUSHING ORE a cast-iron bowl in which ore is crushed ■ *vt.* (**-tared, -tar·ing, -tars**) **1.** ARMS FIRE AT SOMEBODY OR SOMETHING to fire at somebody or something with a mortar **2.** BUILDING SECURE SOMETHING WITH MORTAR to hold stones and bricks together with mortar [Pre-12thC. Via Old English *mortere* and French *mortier*, "bowl for mixing," from Latin *mortarium* "bowl, substance prepared in it." In the sense "cannon," via French *mortier* in that sense.]

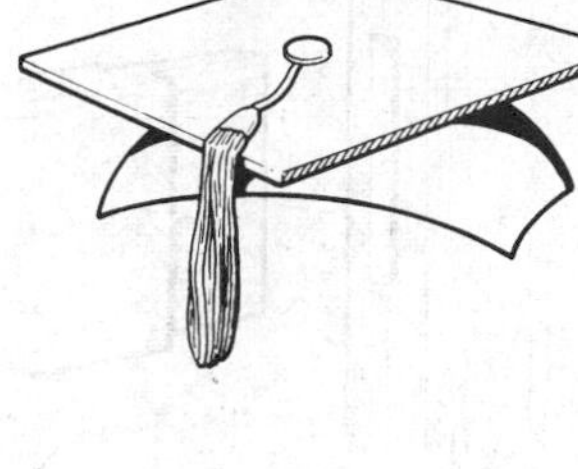
Mortarboard

mor·tar·board /máwrtər bàwrd/ *n.* **1.** BUILDING BOARD FOR CARRYING MORTAR a square board with a handle in the center of the underside, used by bricklayers for carrying mortar **2.** EDUC ACADEMIC HAT a hat often worn on formal academic occasions, consisting of a round cap with a hard, square, flat top and usually a tassel

mort·gage /máwrgij/ *n.* **1.** LOAN AGREEMENT FOR PROPERTY an agreement by which somebody borrows money from an organization and gives that organization the right to take possession of property given as security if the loan is not repaid. It is the main means by which people purchase homes. **2.** CONTRACT BETWEEN BORROWER AND LENDER a written contract describing the agreement between a borrower and a lender by which a loan is given against security **3.** TOTAL MONEY BORROWED the total amount of money lent to a borrower by a money-lending organization, with some of the borrower's property being given as security **4.** LOAN INSTALLMENT TO BE REPAID the money paid by a borrower, usually monthly, to a bank or savings-and-loan association until the entire sum borrowed by a mortgage agreement has been repaid ■ *vt.* (**-gaged, -gag·ing, -gag·es**) **1.** GRANT CLAIM TO OWNERSHIP OF PROPERTY to give a claim to legal possession of property to a money-lending organization such as a bank or savings-and-loan association as security for a loan **2.** PLEDGE RISKILY to pledge something when risk is involved (*informal*) [14thC. From Old French, from *mort* "dead" + *gage* "pledge," because property pledged as security is lost to a mortgagor who fails to repay the loan.] —**mort·gage·a·ble** *adj.*

mort·ga·gee /màwrgi jée/ *n.* an organization that lends money to a borrower by a mortgage agreement

mort·gag·er *n.* = **mortgagor**

mort·gage rate *n.* the interest rate charged by lenders on mortgage loans

mort·ga·gor /màwrgi jáwr, -jər/, **mort·gag·er** *n.* somebody who borrows money under a mortgage agreement [Late 16thC]

mor·tice *n.* = **mortise**

mor·ti·cian /mawr tísh'n/ *n.* = **undertaker** *n.* 1 [Late 19thC. Formed from the stem of Latin *mors* "death" + ENGLISH -ICIAN.]

mor·ti·fi·ca·tion /màwrtəfi káysh'n/ *n.* **1.** SHAME deep shame and humiliation **2.** SOMETHING CAUSING MORTIFICATION something that causes a feeling of shame and humiliation **3.** RELIG SELF-IMPOSED HARDSHIP the use of self-imposed discipline, hardship, abstinence from pleasure, and especially self-inflicted pain in an attempt to control or put an end to desires and passions, especially for religious purposes **4.** MED DEATH AND DECAY OF LIVING TISSUE the death and decaying of a part of a living body, e.g., because the blood supply to it has been cut off (*archaic*) [14thC. Directly and via Old French, from late Latin *mortificatio(n-)* "destruction," from the past participle stem of *mortificare* (see MORTIFY).]

mor·ti·fy /máwrtə fī/ (**-fied, -fy·ing, -fies**) *v.* **1.** *vt.* SHAME SOMEBODY to make somebody feel ashamed and humiliated **2.** *vt.* RELIG IMPOSE HARDSHIP ON to use self-imposed discipline, hardship, abstinence from pleasure, and especially self-inflicted pain in an attempt to control or put an end to desires and passions, especially for religious purposes **3.** *vi.* MED **DECAY** to decay and die (*archaic*) (*refers to living tissue*) [14thC. Via Old French *mortifier*, from Latin *mortificare* "kill," from the stem of *mors* "death." The main modern meaning developed via the sense "subdue by discipline."] —**mor·ti·fi·er** *n.* —**mor·ti·fy·ing** *adj.* —**mor·ti·fy·ing·ly** *adv.*

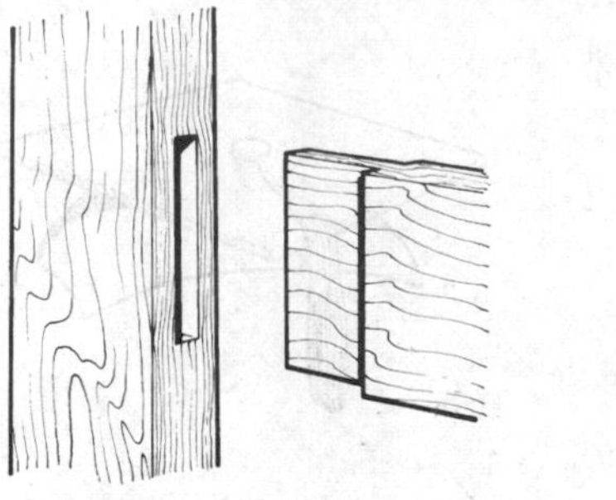

Mortise-and-tenon joint

mor·tise /máwrtiss/, **mor·tice** *n.* **1.** FURNITURE, BUILDING **HOLE CUT TO HOLD OTHER PART** a hole or slot cut into a piece of wood, stone, or other material, for a projecting part (**tenon**) to be inserted into it, in order to form a tight joint **2.** PRINTING **HOLE IN PRINTING PLATE** a hole cut in a printing plate to receive type or another plate ■ *vt.* (**-tised, -tis·ing, -tis·es; -ticed, -tic·ing, -tic·es**) **1.** FURNITURE, BUILDING **CUT MORTISE IN** to cut a mortise in something **2.** FURNITURE, BUILDING **JOIN BY MORTISE AND TENON** to join two things or parts by means of a mortise and tenon **3.** PRINTING **CUT HOLE IN PRINTING PLATE** to cut a hole in a printing plate [14thC. From Old French, probably from Arabic *murtaj* "locked."] —**mor·tis·er** *n.*

mort·main /máwrt màyn/ *n.* **1. PERPETUAL OWNERSHIP OF PROPERTY** the perpetual, nontransferable, and nonsalable ownership of property by organizations such as churches **2. INFLUENCE OF PAST ON PRESENT** the usually stultifying or stifling influence of the past on current events and living people [13thC. Via Anglo-Norman and Old French, from medieval Latin *mortua manus* "dead hand," from, ultimately, Latin *mortuus* "dead" + *manus* "hand," as a metaphor for impersonal ownership.]

Mor·ton /máwrt'n/, **Jelly Roll** (1885–1941) U.S. pianist and composer. He was a major figure in the development of jazz. Real name **Ferdinand Joseph La Menthe**

Mor·ton, John (1724–77) American patriot. He was one of the signatories of the Declaration of Independence (1776).

Mor·ton, Levi Parsons (1824–1920) U.S. banker and politician. He served as vice president of the United States under Benjamin Harrison (1889–95).

Mor·ton, William Thomas Green (1819–68) U.S. dentist. He claimed to be the first to have used ether as an anesthetic (1844).

Mor·ton Grove /màwrt'n-/ village in northeastern Illinois, west of Skokie, a northern suburb of Chicago. Population: 22,258 (1996).

mor·tu·ar·y /máwrchoo èrree/ *n.* (*plural* **-ies**) **PLACE FOR DEAD BODIES** a room or building in which dead bodies are kept until they are buried or cremated ■ *adj.* **RELATING TO DEATH** relating to death or funerals [14thC. Directly or via Anglo-Norman, from, ultimately, Latin *mortuus* "dead," the past participle of *mori* "to die" (source of English *moribund*).]

mor·tu·ar·y sci·ence *n.* the study and practice of embalming bodies and administering funerals

mor·u·la /máwryələ, máwrə-/ (*plural* **-las** *or* **-lae** /-lee/) *n.* an early stage in the development of an animal embryo, consisting of a solid ball of cells derived by cleavage of the fertilized egg (**zygote**). It precedes the blastocyst. [Mid-19thC. From an obsolete sense "growth (or disease causing growths) that resembles a berry," because of the segmentation, from modern Latin, "little mulberry," from *morum* "mulberry."] —**mor·u·lar** *adj.* —**mor·u·la·tion** /màwryə láysh'n, màwrə-/ *n.*

Mor·well /máwrwəl/ town in southeastern Victoria, Australia, a mining and dairy farming center. Population: 13,823 (1996).

MOS *abbr.* **1.** metal-oxide semiconductor **2.** military occupational specialty

mos. *abbr.* months

Mosaic: Detail of mosaic floor at the Roman settlement of Verulamium, St. Albans, England

mo·sa·ic /mō záy ik/ *n.* **1.** ARTS **PICTURE MADE WITH SMALL COLORED PIECES** a picture or design made with small pieces of colored material such as glass or tile stuck onto a surface **2.** ARTS **MAKING OF MOSAICS** the art of making mosaics **3. SOMETHING CONSISTING OF VARIETY OF ELEMENTS** something consisting of a number of things of different types, forms, or colors **4.** TV **LIGHT-SENSITIVE SURFACE IN TV CAMERA** a light-sensitive surface on a television camera tube, consisting of a thin sheet covered by particles that convert incoming light into an electric charge for scanning by an electron beam **5.** BOT **VIRAL PLANT DISEASE** a plant disease, often caused by a virus, in which the foliage develops irregular patches of discoloration. Tobacco, corn, and sugar cane are among the crops that can be seriously affected. **6.** BOT **PLANT DISCOLORATION** a pattern of light green or yellowish mottling on the foliage of a plant, usually caused by a viral infection **7.** GENETICS = **chimera** *n.* **2** ■ *vt.* (**-icked, -ick·ing, -ics**) **DECORATE WITH MOSAIC** to make something into, or decorate something with, a mosaic [14thC. Via Old French, from, ultimately, Latin *Musa* "Muse," from the decorations of medieval shrines dedicated to the Muses.]

Mo·sa·ic, Mo·sa·i·cal *adj.* relating to the biblical figure Moses [Mid-17thC. Directly or via French, from, ultimately, Latin *Moses* "Moses," from Hebrew *Mōšeh*.]

mo·sa·ic gold *n.* **1. TIN DISULFIDE** tin disulfide used in gilding **2. ALLOY RESEMBLING GOLD IN APPEARANCE** an alloy of copper and either zinc or tin that looks like gold and is used to decorate such things as furniture and jewelry

mo·sa·i·cism /mō záy ə sìzzəm/ *n.* the occurrence of genetically distinct cells within tissue or an individual organism

Mo·sa·ic Law *n.* the ancient code of law of the Hebrews, beginning with the Ten Commandments, believed to have been set down by Moses and contained in the Pentateuch

mo·sa·saur /mṓssə sàwr/ *n.* an extinct marine lizard that had a long slender body with limbs resembling paddles for steering, and a long flexible tail for propulsion. Family: Mosasauridae. [Mid-19thC. From modern Latin *Mosaurus*, the genus name, from Latin *Mosa*, the River Meuse, where the first remains were found.]

mos·cha·tel /mòskə tél, móskə tèl/ (*plural* **-tels** *or* **-tel**) *n.* a low-growing plant found in moist locations in northern temperate regions and bearing clusters of small yellowish-green flowers arranged like the faces of a cube. Latin name: *Adoxa moschatellina*. [Mid-18thC. Via French, from, ultimately, Italian *moscato* "musk," from the scent of the flowers.]

Mos·cow /móss kō/ **1.** capital city of Russia, located in the west central European part of the country. It was also the capital of the Soviet Union from 1922 to 1991. Population: 8,300,000 (1994). **2.** city in northwestern Idaho, on the border with Washington, north of Lewiston. Population: 20,101 (1996).

Mo·selle[1] /mō zél/ *n.* a light dry to sweet white wine from the Moselle valley in Germany

Mo·selle[2] /mō zél/ river in France and Germany. Length: 320 mi./515 km.

Mo·ses /mṓziz/ *n.* in the Bible, a Hebrew prophet and the brother of Aaron who led the Israelites from slavery in Egypt to the Promised Land. He is believed to have written down the Ten Commandments (Exodus 20).

Grandma Moses

Mos·es, Grandma (1860–1961) U.S. artist. She is known for her primitivist paintings of U.S. rural life, which she began in her late seventies. Real name **Anna Mary Robertson Moses**

Mos·es Lake city in Washington, in Grant County, on the northeastern shore of Moses Lake. Population: 11,235 (1990). Former name **Neppel**

mo·sey /mṓzee/ (**-seyed, -sey·ing, -seys**) *vi.* to walk somewhere at a leisurely unhurried pace (*informal*) [Early 19thC. Origin uncertain: perhaps a shortening and alteration of Spanish *vamos* "let's go," or an alteration of dialectal English *mose about* "to go about in a purposeless manner."]

mosh /mosh/ (**moshed, mosh·ing, mosh·es**) *vt.* to dance to rock music in a frenzied violent way (*informal*) [Late 20thC. Origin uncertain: probably thought to suggest the action.]

mo·shav /mō shaav/ (*plural* **-sha·vim** /mō shaa vém/) *n.* in Israel, a cooperative settlement consisting of independent small farms, or land farmed by the whole community with each family having its own house and garden [Mid-20thC. From modern Hebrew *mōšāḇ* "dwelling, colony."]

mosh pit *n.* an area in front of the stage at a rock concert where people dance in an unrestrained way (*informal*)

Mos·lem /mózləm, mósslәm/ *n.* (*plural* **-lems** *or* **-lem**), *adj.* a Muslim (*dated offensive*) [Variant]

Mos·ley /mṓzlee/, **Sir Oswald Ernald** (1896–1980) British politician. He founded the British Union of Fascists in 1932.

Mosque: Delhi, India

mosque /mosk/ *n.* a building in which Muslims worship [15thC. Via French, from, ultimately, Arabic *masjid* "place of worship," from *sajada* "bow down."]

mos·qui·to /mə skéetō/ (*plural* **-toes** *or* **-tos**) *n.* a small

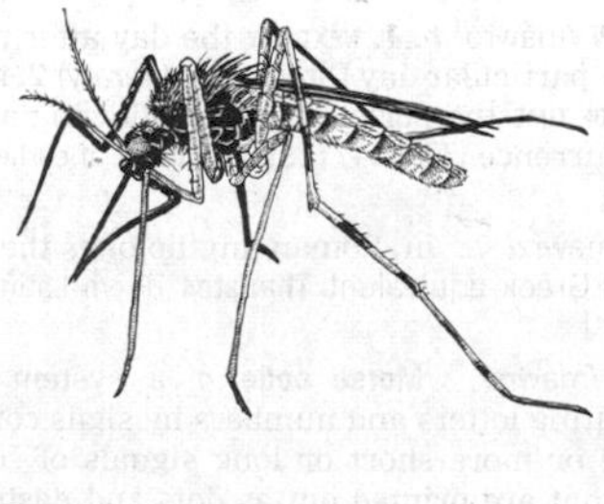

Mosquito

slender fly found worldwide, especially in the tropics, that feeds on the blood of mammals, including humans, and transmits diseases such as malaria, yellow fever, and dengue. Typically only females are blood-feeders, the males feeding on plant juices. Family: Culicidae. [Late 16thC. Via Spanish, "little fly," from *mosca* "fly," from Latin *musca.* Ultimately from an Indo-European base, imitative of humming, that is also the ancestor of English *midge.*]

mos·qui·to coil *n.* incense in the form of a coil that is lit at night to repel mosquitoes

mos·qui·to fern *n.* a small floating fern that has branched stems with small leaves resembling scales and is found on freshwater ponds and lakes, especially in warmer regions. The leaves harbor a nitrogen-fixing cyanobacterium and the fern is grown in rice paddies to enhance fertility. Genus: *Azolla.*

mos·qui·to fish *n.* a small, surface-feeding freshwater fish belonging to the guppy family and found in the southeastern United States that feeds on mosquito larvae and has been introduced widely to control mosquitoes. Latin name: *Gambusia affinis.*

mos·qui·to hawk *n.* 1. BIRDS = **nighthawk** *n.* 1 2. INSECTS **DRAGONFLY** a dragonfly (*regional*) ["Mosquito" probably because it feeds on mosquitoes]

mos·qui·to net *n.* a curtain of fine netting hung over a bed or across a window as a protection against mosquitoes

moss /mawss/ *n.* PLANTS **1. SIMPLE NONFLOWERING PLANT** a simple nonflowering plant (**bryophyte**) that has short stems bearing small spirally arranged leaves resembling scales and inhabits moist shady sites worldwide. Certain mosses, notably sphagnums, flourish in bogs, where their remains can accumulate to form peat. Class: Musci. **2. PLANT RESEMBLING MOSS** a plant that in some way resembles a true moss, e.g., a variety of seaweed known as Irish moss [Old English *mos* "swamp" (of which moss is the characteristic plant), from a prehistoric Germanic word that is also the ancestor of English *mire*]

Moss /moss/, **Stirling** (1929–98) British racing driver. He was winner of the British Grand Prix (1955, 1957) and the Mille Miglia (1955). An accident in 1962 ended his career. Full name **Stirling Crauford Moss**

Mos·sad /màw saad/ *n.* the intelligence service of Israel, established in 1951 [Mid-20thC. From Hebrew *mosad* "institution."]

moss ag·ate *n.* a whitish agate with dark green patterns resembling moss or ferns in it

moss an·i·mal *n.* = **bryozoan**

moss·back /máwss bàk/ (*plural* **-backs** *or* **-back**) *n.* **1. OLD TURTLE, SHELLFISH, OR FISH** an old turtle, shellfish, or fish with algae growing on its back **2. SOMEBODY CONSERVATIVE** somebody who is very old-fashioned or conservative (*insult*)

moss·bunk·er /móss bùngkər/ *n.* = **menhaden** [Late 18thC. From Dutch *marsbanker.*]

moss cam·pi·on *n.* a plant of the pink family found in cool alpine regions that forms tufts of leaves resembling moss and bears solitary pink flowers. Latin name: *Silene acaulis.*

moss green *adj.* of a dull green color tinged with yellow —**moss green** *n.*

moss·grown /máwss grōn/ *adj.* **1. MOSS-COVERED** covered with moss **2. OLD-FASHIONED** old-fashioned or out-of-date

Mos·si /máwssee/ (*plural* **-si** *or* **-sis**) *n.* **1.** PEOPLES **MEMBER OF W AFRICAN PEOPLE** a member of a people living in West Africa, especially in Burkina Faso **2.** LANG **MOSSI LANGUAGE** the language of the Mossi people. It belongs to the Gur branch of Niger-Congo languages. Mossi is spoken by about six million people. [Mid-19thC. An African name.]

mos·so /máwssō/ *adv.* in a quick and lively way (*used as a musical direction*) ◊ **meno mosso** [Late 19thC. From Italian, the past participle of *muovere* "move."]

moss pink *n.* a plant of the pink family native to eastern North America but widely grown ornamentally that produces spreading mats of tiny leaves and lavender, pink, or white flowers. Latin name: *Phlox subulata.*

moss rose *n.* a rose with a mossy surface to the calyx and flower stalk, and fragrant pink flowers. Latin name: *Rosa centifolia muscosa.*

moss stitch *n.* a basic knitting stitch consisting of alternating knit and purl stitches in one row, then alternating purl and knit stitches in the next row, producing a regular raised design

moss·y /máwssee/ (**-i·er, -i·est**) *adj.* **1. COVERED WITH MOSS** covered or overgrown with moss **2. RESEMBLING MOSS** similar to moss, e.g., in texture or color **3. OLD-FASHIONED** old-fashioned or out-of-date (*informal*) —**moss·i·ness** *n.*

moss·y zinc *n.* a form of zinc with a grainy texture made by pouring melted zinc into water

most /mōst/ CORE MEANING: a grammatical word indicating nearly all or the majority of the people or things mentioned ○ *Most people enjoy watching a good movie.* ○ *We'd finished off most of the work by lunchtime.*

1. *adj., pron.* **GREATEST** greatest in number, amount, extent, or degree ○ (adj) *He won the most seats in the election.* ○ (pron) *The most I can lend you is 50 dollars.* **2.** *adv.* **TO THE GREATEST EXTENT** in or to the greatest extent (*used to form the superlative of adjectives and adverbs*) ○ *the most expensive suit I'd ever bought* ○ *It works most effectively if you heat it gently first.* **3.** *adv.* **SUPERLATIVE OF "MUCH"** the superlative of "much" ○ *What I like most about him is his easygoing attitude.* **4.** *adv.* **VERY** in a high degree ○ *a most enjoyable day* **5.** *adv.* **ALMOST** nearly but not entirely ○ *Most everyone was invited.* [Old English *mæst.* Ultimately, from an Indo-European word meaning "big."] ◇ **at (the) most** at the maximum ○ *It'll take you two hours at the most.* ◇ **the most** the best of all (*slang*) ○ *That song is the most!* ◇ **for the most part** in the majority of cases ◇ **make the most of something** to take full advantage of something

-most *suffix.* **1.** nearest to or toward ○ *endmost* **2.** most ○ *nethermost* [Old English *-mest,* which was formed from *-mo, -ma*]

Mos·ta·ga·nem /mə stággə nèm/ fishing port on the Mediterranean Sea coast in northwestern Algeria. Population: 114,037 (1987).

Mos·tar /móss taar/ city in Herzegovina, southern Bosnia-Herzegovina. Population: 126,000 (1991).

most fa·vored na·tion *n.* a nation accorded the most favorable trading terms by another nation

most·ly /mốstlee/ *adv.* **1. MAINLY** almost entirely ○ *The audience was mostly made up of younger fans.* **2. USUALLY** on most occasions ○ *I swim mostly at weekends.*

Most Rev·er·end *adj.* a title given to to cardinals and archbishops in the Roman Catholic Church and to Anglican archbishops

mote /mōt/ *n.* a tiny speck or particle [Old English *mot,* of unknown origin]

mo·tel /mō tél/ *n.* a hotel intended to provide short-term lodging for traveling motorists, usually situated close to a highway and having rooms accessible from the parking area [Early 20thC. Blend of MOTOR and HOTEL.]

mo·tet /mō tét/ *n.* a vocal composition with parts for different voices, usually based on a sacred text [14thC. Via Old French "little word," from, ultimately, Latin *muttire* "to murmur."]

Moth

moth /mawth/ *n.* an insect resembling a butterfly but generally differing in having a duller color and differently shaped antennae, and in being active at night. Order: Lepidoptera. [Old English *moþþe,* of uncertain origin]

moth·ball /máwth bàwl/ *n.* **MOTH-REPELLENT CHEMICAL BALL** a small ball of a strong-smelling chemical such as camphor or naphthalene, used for keeping clothes moths away from clothing and other materials ■ *vt.* (**-balled, -ball·ing, -balls**) **1. PUT SOMETHING OFF INDEFINITELY** to postpone work or discussion on something for an indefinite time ○ *We'll mothball the expansion plans until we have the financing.* **2.** INDUST **TAKE A FACTORY OUT OF OPERATION** to take a factory out of operation but protect the equipment in it so that it can be used again at some time in the future **3.** INSUR, AEROSP **SEAL A CRAFT UP FOR STORAGE** to seal all the openings in a ship or aircraft in order to protect it from corrosion while it is not in use ◇ **in mothballs** put aside or stored and not in use

moth bean *n.* **1.** AGRIC **PLANT GROWN TO BOOST SOIL FERTILITY** a plant of the pea family grown in tropical regions, especially India, to provide forage, to boost soil fertility, and for its seeds. It has hairy foliage and small yellow flowers. Latin name: *Phaseolus aconitifolius.* **2.** FOOD **SEED OF THE MOTH BEAN PLANT** the yellowish-brown seed of the moth bean plant that is used for food

moth-eat·en *adj.* **1. EATEN BY MOTH LARVAE** damaged by clothes moth caterpillars **2. WORN-OUT** old and worn-out from use **3. OUTDATED** no longer usable or appropriate (*informal*)

moth·er[1] /mú*th*ər/ *n.* **1. FEMALE PARENT** a woman who has a child or a female animal that has produced young **2. WOMAN ACTING AS PARENT** a woman who acts as the parent of a child to whom she has not given birth **3. CHARACTERISTICS OF A MOTHER** the qualities or feelings that are traditionally associated with being a mother ○ *brought out the mother in her* **4. ORIGINATOR** a woman regarded as the creator, instigator, or founder of something **5. ORIGIN OF SOMETHING** the cause, source, or origin of something ○ *Necessity is the mother of invention* **6. PROTECTOR** something that protects and nourishes like a mother **7. Moth·er, moth·er TITLE OF RESPECT** used as a title of respect for a woman past middle age (*archaic*) (*sometimes considered as offensive*) **8. GOOD OR BAD EXAMPLE OF SOMETHING** something very big, good, bad, or extreme, or particularly noteworthy in some other way (*slang*) (*sometimes considered offensive*) ○ *a real mother of a headache* **9. OFFENSIVE TERM** a highly offensive term referring to somebody regarded as despicable or contemptible (*insult taboo*) ■ *vt.* (**-ered, -er·ing, -ers**) **1. LOOK AFTER SOMEBODY WITH CARE** to look after somebody with great care and affection, sometimes to an excessive degree **2. GIVE BIRTH TO A BABY** to give birth to and bring up a baby **3. BRING SOMETHING ABOUT** to give rise to something [Old English *modor.* Ultimately from an Indo-European word with descendants in most modern European languages, based on the baby-talk form *ma,* that also produced English *mammal.*] ◇ **at your mother's knee** in early childhood ◇ **every mother's son** every man or boy (*dated*)

moth·er[2] /mú*th*ər/ *n.* a slimy mass of bacteria and yeast cells that forms on the surface of alcohol being converted into acetic acid [Mid-16thC. Origin uncertain: probably by folk etymology from obsolete Dutch *moeder,* from Middle Dutch *moeder* "female parent," from its part in the production of vinegar.]

Moth·er *n.* used as a title or form of address for a senior nun in a religious community

moth·er·board /mú*th*ər bawrd/ *n.* a circuit board in a minicomputer or microcomputer through which all signals are directed

Moth·er Car·ey's chick·en *n.* a storm petrel (*dated*) [Probably a translation and alteration of medieval Latin *mater cara* "Virgin Mary"]

moth·er cell *n.* a cell that gives rise to other cells by cell division

moth·er church *n.* a church from which other churches derive their authority

moth·er coun·try *n.* **1. COUNTRY COLONISTS HAVE LEFT** the country of origin of people who have left to found a colony or colonies elsewhere **2. COUNTRY OF BIRTH** the country that somebody was born and grew up in

moth·er fig·ure *n.* a woman who embodies the qualities traditionally associated with a mother, especially support, advice, and affection

moth·er·fuck·er /mú*th*ər fùkər/ *n.* a highly offensive term referring to somebody regarded as despicable or contemptible (*insult*)

Moth·er Goose *n.* the supposed author of a collection of nursery rhymes first published in the 18th century

moth·er hen *n.* somebody who is too protective toward other people and who fusses over them

moth·er·hood /mú̱thər hòod/ *n.* **1.** STATE OF BEING A MOTHER the status of a mother or the state of being a mother **2.** QUALITIES TRADITIONALLY CHARACTERISTIC OF MOTHERS the qualities traditionally associated with mothers

moth·er·house /mú̱thər hòwss/ *n.* a monastery or convent from which monks or nuns have gone out to found new monasteries and convents

Moth·er Hub·bard /mù̱thər húbbərd/ *n.* a long loose-fitting shapeless dress [Late 16thC. Named for a nursery rhyme character who was depicted wearing such a dress.]

moth·er-in-law (*plural* **moth·ers-in-law**) *n.* the mother of your spouse

moth·er-in-law a·part·ment *n.* a small self-contained apartment that is in or attached to a house and is considered suitable for a parent in later years to live in independently of the rest of the family

moth·er-in-law's tongue *n.* PLANTS = **sansevieria** [From its long pointed leaves]

moth·er·land /mú̱thər lànd/ *n.* the country that somebody was born and grew up in

moth·er·less /mú̱thərləss/ *adj.* without a mother or having lost a mother through bereavement [Old English *modorleas*]

moth·er lode *n.* **1.** MINING MAIN VEIN OF ORE the main vein of ore in a mine **2.** GOOD SUPPLY a plentiful supply of something

moth·er·ly /mú̱thərlee/ *adj.* having or showing qualities traditionally considered to be typical of a mother, especially kindness and protectiveness [Old English] —**moth·er·li·ness** *n.*

moth·er-na·ked *adj.* completely naked

Moth·er Na·ture *n.* the forces of nature conceived of as a willful being

Moth·er of God *n., interj.* a title given to Mary, the mother of Jesus Christ, especially by Catholics

moth·er-of-pearl *n.* the hard pearly internal layer of the shells of some mollusks such as oysters and clams, used, e.g., as a gemstone and as a decorative inlay [Early 16thC. Translation of obsolete French *mère perle*.]

moth·er-of-thou·sands (*plural* **moth·ers-of-thous·ands** *or* **moth·er-of-thous·ands**) *n.* a creeping or trailing plant that produces masses of small flowers, especially the ivy-leaved toadflax or the strawberry geranium

moth·er of vin·e·gar *n.* = **mother**[2]

Moth·er's Day *n.* the second Sunday in May, when people traditionally give cards and presents to their mothers

moth·er ship *n.* a ship or spaceship that provides services and supplies for a number of other, usually smaller ships

moth·er su·pe·ri·or (*plural* **moth·er su·pe·ri·ors** *or* **moth·ers su·pe·ri·or**) *n.* the head of a convent or community of Christian nuns

moth·er-to-be (*plural* **moth·ers-to-be**) *n.* a woman who is expecting a baby

moth·er tongue *n.* **1.** FIRST LANGUAGE the first language somebody learns as a child at home **2.** ORIGINAL LANGUAGE a language from which other languages have developed

Moth·er·well /mú̱thərwəl, -wèl/, **Robert** (1915–91) U.S. artist. He is known for his brilliantly colored or black-and-white abstract expressionist paintings. Full name **Robert Burns Motherwell**

moth·er wit *n.* natural intelligence or good sense

moth·er·wort /mú̱thər wùrt, -wàwrt/ (*plural* **-worts** *or* **-wort**) *n.* a plant of Europe and Asia with deeply lobed leaves and white or pink purple-spotted flowers that was traditionally used as a medicinal herb during childbirth. Latin name: *Leonarus cardiaca*. [14thC. From obsolete sense of *mother* "womb."]

moth fly *n.* a tiny insect with wings covered with hairs that resembles an extremely small moth. Family: Psychodidae.

moth·proof /máwth pro͞of/ *adj.* PROTECTED AGAINST CLOTHES MOTHS treated with a substance designed to prevent damage by clothes moths ■ *vt.* (**-proofed, -proof·ing, -proofs**) PROTECT AGAINST CLOTHES MOTHS to treat something such as clothing with a substance designed to protect it from damage by clothes moths —**moth·proof·er** *n.*

moth·y /máwthee/ (**-i·er, -i·est**) *adj.* **1.** DAMAGED BY MOTHS damaged by the action of clothes moths **2.** FULL OF MOTHS full of or infested by moths

mo·tif /mō te͞ef/ *n.* **1.** ARCHIT, DESIGN REPEATED DESIGN a repeated design, shape, or pattern **2.** CRAFT SEWN OR PRINTED DECORATION a decorative repetitive design sewn into or printed on something such as a piece of clothing, or a single example of the pattern **3.** LITERAT THEME IN A WORK OF LITERATURE an important and sometimes recurring theme or idea in a work of literature **4.** MUSIC PROMINENT SEQUENCE OF NOTES a short prominent sequence of notes forming the basis for development in a piece of music [Mid-19thC. Via French, from Old French (see MOTIVE).]

mo·tile /mṓt'l, mṓ tīl/ *adj.* capable of or demonstrating movement by independent means [Mid-19thC. Formed from Latin *motus* "motion," from the past participle of *movere* "to move."] —**mo·til·i·ty** /mō tíllətee/ *n.*

mo·tion /mṓsh'n/ *n.* **1.** ACT OF MOVING the act or process of moving or the way in which somebody or something moves ○ *walked with a swaying motion* **2.** A MOVEMENT a movement, action, or gesture ○ *made a quick motion of the wrist* **3.** POWER OF MOVEMENT the power or ability to move something **4.** PROPOSAL a proposal put forward for discussion at a meeting **5.** LAW APPLICATION TO A JUDGE OR COURT an application made to a court or judge for an order or ruling in a legal proceeding **6.** MUSIC MOVEMENT FROM ONE NOTE TO ANOTHER the movement from one note to the next by a voice or instrument **7.** *U.K.* PHYSIOL PASSING OF SOLID WASTE FROM THE BODY the passing of solid waste matter out of the body through the anus **8.** *U.K.* PHYSIOL STOOL a piece of evacuated fecal matter (*dated*) (*often used in the plural*) ■ *vti.* (**-tioned, -tion·ing, -tions**) SIGNAL TO SOMEBODY to gesture or signal something such as a request or intention to somebody ○ *motioned me over and told me to sit down* [14thC. Via Old French, from, ultimately, the past participle of Latin *movere* "to move" (source of English *move*).] ◇ **go through the motions** to do something in a perfunctory or mechanical way, without enthusiasm or commitment ◇ **put** *or* **set something in motion** to cause something to start moving, functioning, or happening

mo·tion·less /mṓsh'nləss/ *adj.* not moving — **mo·tion·less·ly** *adv.* —**mo·tion·less·ness** *n.*

mo·tion pic·ture *n.* a movie (*formal or technical*)

mo·tion sick·ness *n.* a feeling of nausea resulting from overstimulation of the part of the ear that controls balance, caused especially by travel in a moving vehicle —**mo·tion sick** *adj.*

mo·tion stud·y *n.* = **time and motion study**

mo·ti·vate /mṓtə vàyt/ (**-vat·ed, -vat·ing, -vates**) *v.* **1.** *vt.* GIVE SOMEBODY AN INCENTIVE to give somebody a reason or incentive to do something **2.** MAKE SOMEBODY WILLING to make somebody feel enthusiastic, interested, and committed to something **3.** *vt.* CAUSE SOMEBODY'S BEHAVIOR to be the cause or driving force behind something that somebody does ○ *motivated purely by greed* [Mid-19thC. Formed from MOTIVE, modeled on French *motiver* "to motivate."] —**mo·ti·va·tor** *n.*

mo·ti·vat·ed /mṓtə vàytəd/ *adj.* **1.** INTERESTED OR ENTHUSIASTIC having enough interest or incentive to do something **2.** HAVING SOMETHING AS A MOTIVE having something such as an emotion or a belief as a motive

mo·ti·va·tion /mòtə váysh'n/ *n.* **1.** GIVING OF A REASON TO ACT the act of giving somebody a reason or incentive to do something **2.** ENTHUSIASM a feeling of interest or enthusiasm that makes somebody want to do something, or something that causes such a feeling **3.** REASON a reason for doing something or behaving in some way **4.** PSYCHOL FORCES DETERMINING BEHAVIOR the biological, emotional, cognitive, or social forces that activate and direct behavior —**mo·ti·va·tive** /mṓtə vàytiv/ *adj.* —**mo·ti·va·tion·al** /mòtə váyshən'l, -shnəl/ *adj.* —**mo·ti·va·tion·al·ly** /-váyshən'lee/ *adv.*

mo·ti·va·tion·al re·search, mo·ti·va·tion re·search *n.* the study of the motivation of consumers in their buying practices, used to plan marketing and sales

mo·tive /mṓtiv/ *n.* **1.** REASON the reason for doing something or behaving in a particular way **2.** ARTS = **motif** *n.* 1, **motif** *n.* 3 ■ *adj.* **1.** CAUSING MOTION causing or producing motion **2.** DRIVING SOMEBODY TO DO SOMETHING tending to make somebody want or be willing to do something ■ *vt.* (**-tived, -tiv·ing, -tives**) MOTIVATE SOMEBODY to make somebody want or be willing to do something [14thC. Via Old French *motif*, from, ultimately, the past participle of Latin *movere* "to move" (source of English *mobile*).]

WORD KEY: SYNONYMS

motive, incentive, inducement, spur, goad

CORE MEANING: something that prompts action

motive the emotion or intention that an action is driven by, e.g., love, revenge, or ambition; **incentive** something external that inspires extra enthusiasm or effort, often suggesting some kind of reward; **inducement** something external that persuades or attracts somebody to a course of action; **spur** something external or internal that increases effort or energy without necessarily involving reward; **goad** similar to *spur* but often used to suggest that force is used on an unwilling subject.

mo·tive pow·er *n.* **1.** ENG ENERGY OR A SOURCE OF ENERGY the power or energy that drives a piece of machinery, or the source of that power or energy **2.** MOTIVATING FORCE the driving force behind an action or activity

mo·tiv·ic /mō tívvik/ *adj.* relating to a musical motif or motifs

mo·ti·vi·ty /mō tívvətee/ *n.* the power to move or to make something move

mot juste /mṑ zho͞ost/ (*plural* **mots justes**) *n.* exactly the right word or words to express something [From French]

mot·ley /móttlee/ *adj.* (**-li·er, -li·est**) **1.** MADE UP OF DIFFERENT TYPES consisting of people or things that are very different from one another and do not seem to belong together **2.** OF VARIED COLORS made up of different colors ■ *n.* (*plural* **-lies**) **1.** CLOTHES JESTER'S COSTUME the multicolored clothing worn by medieval jesters **2.** VARIED GROUP a group of people or things that are very different from one another and do not seem to belong together [14thC. Origin uncertain: perhaps via Anglo-Norman, from earlier English *mot* "speck" (source of English *mote*).]

mot·mot /mót mòt/ *n.* a Central and South American bird with a broad downward-curved bill, long tail, and usually greenish plumage with a black patch on the chest. Family: Momotidae. [Mid-19thC. From American Spanish, of imitative origin.]

mo·to·cross /mṓtō kràwss/ *n.* a motorcycle race, or the sport of racing motorcycles, over a rough course with steep hills, wet or muddy areas, and turns of varying difficulty [Mid-20thC. From French, from *moto* "motorcycle" + English CROSS(-COUNTRY).]

mo·to·neu·ron /mṑtə no͝o ròn/ *n.* = **motor neuron** [Early 20thC. Coined from MOTOR + NEURON.] —**mo·to·neu·ron·al** /mṑtə no͝orən'l/ *adj.*

mo·tor /mṓtər/ *n.* **1.** ENG MACHINE THAT CREATES MOTION a machine that converts energy into motion and can be used as a power source, e.g., to drive another machine or to move a vehicle **2.** AUTOMOT ENGINE the engine of a car or other self-powered vehicle (*informal*) **3.** *U.K.* CAR a vehicle, especially a car, powered by a motor (*dated or slang*) ■ *adj.* **1.** AUTOMOT OF VEHICLES relating to vehicles, especially cars, powered by a motor **2.** AUTOMOT MOTOR-DRIVEN powered by a motor **3.** CAUSING MOTION causing or producing motion **4.** PHYSIOL OF MUSCLE ACTIVITY relating to muscle activity, especially voluntary muscle activity, and the consequent body movements ■ *vi.* (**-tored, -tor·ing, -tors**) **1.** DRIVE IN A CAR to travel by car or some other form of private vehicle, especially for pleasure (*dated*) **2.** PROCEED SMOOTHLY to be moving toward an objective, e.g., in work, with the desired degree of speed and momentum (*slang*) ○ *Now we're really motoring!* [15thC. From Latin, "mover," from *movere* "to move" (source of English *momentum*).]

mo·tor·bike /mṓtər bīk/ *n.* **1.** LIGHT MOTORCYCLE a light motorcycle **2.** BICYCLE WITH A MOTOR a bicycle powered by a small motor

mo·tor·boat /mṓtər bṓt/ *n.* a small boat powered by an engine —**mo·tor·boat·er** *n.* —**mo·tor·boat·ing** *n.*

mo·tor·bus /mṓtər bùss/ *n.* a passenger bus (*dated*)

mo·tor·cade /mṓtər kàyd/ *n.* a procession of cars or other vehicles, especially one forming an escort for somebody important [Early 20thC. Coined from MOTOR + CAVALCADE.]

mo·tor·car /mṓtər kaar/ *n.* a car (*dated or formal*)

mo·tor car·a·van *n. U.K.* = **motor home**

mo·tor cor·tex *n.* the region of the outer surface of the brain (**cortex**) where nervous impulses controlling voluntary muscle activity are initiated. The motor cortex in the right hemisphere of the brain is responsible for controlling muscles in the left side of the body, and vice versa for the left hemisphere.

mo·tor·cy·cle /mṓtər sìk'l/ *n.* **2-WHEELED MOTOR-POWERED**

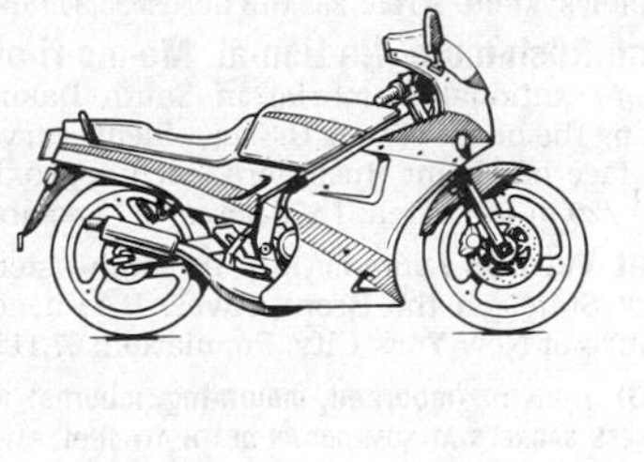

Motorcycle

VEHICLE a two-wheeled road vehicle powered by an engine ■ *vi.* **(-cled, -cling, -cles) RIDE ON A MOTORCYCLE** to ride or travel on a motorcycle —**mo·tor·cy·clist** *n.*

mo·tor drive *n.* a motorized mechanism to advance film in a camera

mo·tor home *n.* a motor vehicle that has facilities for cooking, living, and sleeping

mo·tor ho·tel *n.* = **motel**

mo·tor·ic /mō táwrik/ *adj.* relating to voluntary muscle movement —**mo·tor·i·cal·ly** *adv.*

mo·tor inn *n.* = **motel**

mo·tor·ist /mṓtərist/ *n.* a driver of a motor vehicle, especially a car

mo·tor·ize /mṓtə rìz/ **(-ized, -iz·ing, -iz·es)** *vt.* **1. FIT SOMETHING WITH A MOTOR** to fit something with a motor **2. GIVE TROOPS VEHICLES** to provide troops with motor vehicles —**mo·tor·i·za·tion** /mōtəri záysh'n/ *n.*

mo·tor·man /mṓtərmən/ (*plural* **-men** /-mən/) *n.* the driver of a streetcar, train locomotive, or subway train

mo·tor·mouth /mṓtər mòwth/ (*plural* **-mouths**) *n.* somebody who talks too much or too fast (*informal*)

mo·tor neu·ron *n.* a nerve cell (**neuron**) that conveys nerve impulses from the spinal cord or brainstem away from the central nervous system toward a muscle or gland

mo·tor neu·ron dis·ease *n.* a progressive degenerative disease involving the motor neurons and causing weakness and wasting of the muscles

mo·tor pool *n.* a number of motor vehicles kept by an organization for use as needed by its personnel

mo·tor rac·ing *n. U.K.* = **auto racing**

mo·tor rhythm *n.* a rhythmic motif in a piece of music maintaining a constant pulse, usually at a fast tempo, for an extended period

mo·tor sail·er *n.* a sailboat equipped with a motor

mo·tor scoot·er *n.* a light motorcycle with small wheels, an enclosed engine, and a framework that includes a protective front plate and support for the rider's feet

mo·tor ship *n.* a ship powered by an engine

mo·tor tor·pe·do boat *n. U.K.* = **PT boat**

mo·tor u·nit *n.* a motor neuron and the muscle fibers it acts on

mo·tor ve·hi·cle *n.* a car, truck, or other road vehicle powered by an engine

mo·tor vo·ter *n.* **1. VOTER REGISTRATION LEGISLATION** legislation that requires a state to allow citizens to register to vote when applying for or renewing a driver's license (*informal*) (*hyphenated when used before a noun*) ○ *motor voters increasing in number in rural areas* **2. VOTER REGISTERING WHEN GETTING A LICENSE** a citizen who registers to vote when applying for or renewing a driver's license

mo·tor·way /mṓtər wày/ *n. U.K.* in the U.K., a limited-access road usually consisting of three lanes for vehicles moving in both directions, intended for traveling relatively fast over long distances

Mo·town /mṓ tòwn/ *tdmk.* a trademark for a music company based in Detroit whose music, consisting of elements of pop, soul, and gospel, was especially popular during the 1960s and 1970s [From the nickname for Detroit, itself a shortening of *Motor Town*, from the association of the city with the auto industry]

Mott /mot/, **Lucretia** (1793–1880) U.S. feminist and abolitionist. She ran the American Antislavery Society (1833) and the Seneca Falls women's rights convention (1848). Born **Lucretia Coffin Mott**

motte /mot/ *n.* a mound on which a castle was built [Late 19thC. Via French, "mound," from Old French *mote* (source also of English *moat*).]

mot·tle /mótt'l/ *vt.* **(-tled, -tling, -tles) MARK SOMETHING WITH DIFFERENT COLORS** to mark something with an irregular pattern of patches or spots of different colors ■ *n.* **1. IRREGULAR PATTERN OF COLORS** an irregular pattern of patches or spots of different colors **2. PATCH OF COLOR** a patch or spot of color that forms part of an irregular pattern [Late 17thC. Probably a back-formation from MOTLEY.]

mot·tled e·nam·el *n.* tooth enamel that is mottled as a result of swallowing excessive amounts of fluoride at the age when teeth harden

mot·to /móttō/ (*plural* **-toes** *or* **-tos**) *n.* **1. RULE TO LIVE BY** a short saying that expresses a rule to live by ○ *"I heartily accept the motto, 'That government is best which governs least'; and I should like to see it acted up to more rapidly and systematically."* (Henry David Thoreau, *Civil Disobedience*; 1849) **2.** HERALDRY **SAYING ON A COAT OF ARMS** a short saying that forms part of a coat of arms and expresses something about the family or place whose coat of arms it is **3. QUOTATION AT BEGINNING OF WRITING** a short quotation at the beginning of a piece of writing, e.g., a book, a chapter of a book, or a poem, related in some way to its contents **4.** MUSIC = **motif** *n.* 4 [Late 16thC. From Italian, probably from an assumed Vulgar Latin word meaning "word."]

mo·tu pro·pri·o /mṓ too prṓpree ō/ (*plural* **mo·tu pro·pri·os**) *n.* a decree issued by a pope acting independently and on his own initiative [From Latin, literally "on your own initiative"]

moue /moo/ *n.* a look of discontent with the lips pressed together and forward [Mid-19thC. From French. Ultimately of Germanic origin.]

mou·flon /mo͞of lòN/ *n.* a reddish-brown wild sheep belonging to a Sardinian and Corsican breed. The males have prominent curved horns and a white patch on the back and on the rump. Latin name: *Ovis musimon.* [Late 18thC. Via French, from Italian *muflone.*]

mouil·lé /moo yáy/ *adj.* PHON used to describe a consonant pronounced with the tongue touching the palate [Mid-19thC. From French, the past participle of *mouiller* "to wet, moisten."]

mou·lage /moo laázh/ *n.* **1. MAKING OF A CAST OF SOMETHING AS EVIDENCE** the process of making of a mold or cast of something, e.g., a footprint, in the course of a criminal investigation **2. MOLD OR CAST** a mold or cast made in the course of a criminal investigation [Early 20thC. Via French, "molding, molded copy," from, ultimately, Old French *mouler* "to mold."]

mould /mōld/ *n., vti.* U.K. = **mold**

moul·der /mṓldər/ *vi., n.* U.K. = **molder**

mould·ing /mṓlding/ *n.* U.K. = **molding**

mould·y /mṓldee/ *adj.* U.K. = **moldy**

moules ma·ri·nières /mo͞ol marə nyáir/ *npl.* a dish of mussels cooked and served in their shells with a wine sauce [French]

mou·lin /moo láN/ *n.* an almost vertical shaft in a glacier, created by meltwater and debris boring into a crack in the surface of the ice [Mid-19thC. Via French "mill," from, ultimately, late Latin *molinum* (source of English *mill*).]

moult /mōlt/ *vti., n.* U.K. = **molt**

mound /mownd/ *n.* **1. SMALL HILL** a small hill **2. CONSTRUCTED PILE OF SOMETHING** a pile of earth, stones, or other material built up for some purpose, e.g., to provide shelter, defense, or concealment **3. PILE OF OBJECTS** a messy heap or pile of objects ○ *a mound of dirty laundry on the floor* **4. LARGE AMOUNT** a large amount of something ○ *a mound of mashed potato* **5.** BASEBALL **BASEBALL PITCHER'S PLACE** the slightly raised spot on a baseball diamond where the pitcher plays ■ *vt.* **(mound·ed, mound·ing, mounds) MAKE SOMETHING INTO A MOUND** to form something into a mound [Early 16thC. Origin uncertain.]

mound·bird /mównd bùrd/ *n.* = **megapode** [Mid-19thC. From its custom of depositing its eggs in a mound.]

Mound Build·er *n.* a member of an early Native North American people who built burial mounds and earthwork fortifications in what is now the Midwest and Southeast of the United States

mound-build·er *n.* = **megapode** [See MOUNDBIRD]

mount[1] /mownt/ *v.* **(mount·ed, mount·ing, mounts) 1.** *vt.* **BEGIN A COURSE OF ACTION** to put into operation a course of action such as a campaign, rescue, or attack **2.** *vt.* **ORGANIZE AN ARTS PRODUCTION** to organize something such as an exhibition or production of a play **3.** *vi.* **INCREASE** to become greater, stronger, or more intense ○ *tension was mounting* **4.** *vti.* **GET ONTO OR IN SOMETHING** to get onto an animal or a form of transportation such as a bicycle **5.** *vt.* **PUT SOMEBODY ON A FORM OF TRANSPORTATION** to put somebody onto an animal or a form of transportation such as a bicycle **6.** *vt.* **GET ONTO SOMETHING HIGHER** to get up onto a platform or other raised position **7.** *vti.* **CLIMB** to climb up something such as stairs or a hill **8.** *vi.* **GO UP INTO THE AIR** to move upward into the air **9.** *vt.* **SECURE SOMETHING TO SOMETHING ELSE** to attach something securely to something, e.g., a picture into a frame, a specimen onto a slide, a stamp into an album, or an exhibit onto a stand or support **10.** *vt.* **PUT SOMETHING SOMEWHERE FOR USE** to put something onto a support or into a particular position so that it is ready for use ○ *mount a camera* **11.** *vt.* **HAVE SEX WITH** to climb onto an animal or person, especially from behind, in order to copulate (*technical or offensive*) ■ *n.* **1. SOMETHING FOR FIXING SOMETHING IN PLACE** something such as a stand, support, frame, or backing on which or with which something can be mounted **2. ANIMAL FOR RIDING** an animal, e.g., a horse, used for riding **3.** STAMPS **SOMETHING FOR MOUNTING A STAMP** an envelope or card on which to mount a stamp [13thC. Via Old French *monter* "to go up," from, ultimately, Latin *mons* "mountain" (see MOUNTAIN).] —**mount·a·ble** *adj.* —**mount·er** *n.*

mount[2] /mownt/ *n.* = **mountain** (*often used in place names*) [Pre-12thC. Via Old English *mount* and Old French *mont* from Latin *mons* "mountain" (see MOUNTAIN).]

moun·tain /mównt'n/ *n.* **1. HIGH POINT OF LAND** a high and often rocky area of a land mass with steep or sloping sides ○ *a plateau surrounded by mountains* **2. LARGE PILE** a large pile or heap of something ○ *a mountain of books* **3. moun·tain, moun·tains LARGE AMOUNT** a large amount something (*informal*) ○ *a mountain of work* **4. SURPLUS** a large surplus of a particular commodity (*informal*) (*usually used in combination*) ○ *a butter mountain.* ◊ **lake**[1] [13thC. Via Old French *montaigne* from, ultimately, Latin *mont-*, stem of *mons.* Ultimately from an Indo-European word meaning "to project," which is also the ancestor of English *prominent.*] ◇ **make a mountain out of a molehill** treat something that is not important as if it were

moun·tain ash *n.* a shrub or bush of the rose family with small white flowers and red or orange berries that is common in the northern hemisphere. Genus: *Sorbus.*

moun·tain av·ens *n.* a small trailing plant of the rose family that grows in temperate mountainous and arctic areas and has white flowers. Latin name: *Dryas octopetala.*

moun·tain bea·ver *n.* a large thick-set rodent that lives in colonies made up of extensive burrows in northwestern North America. Latin name: *Aplodontia rufa.*

moun·tain bike *n.* a bicycle built for rough terrain with wide fat tires, straight handlebars, a strong frame, and more gears than a standard bicycle

moun·tain blue·bird *n.* a bluebird of western North America with a bright blue head, back, and wings and a pale blue breast. Latin name: *Sialia currocoides.*

moun·tain cat *n.* a mountain lion (*regional*)

moun·tain chain *n.* a range of mountains or a string of adjacent mountain peaks

moun·tain cran·ber·ry *n.* = **cowberry**

moun·tain dew *n.* = **moonshine** *n.* 1 (*informal*)

moun·tain·eer /mòwnt'n éer/ *n.* **1. MOUNTAIN CLIMBER** somebody who climbs mountains for sport **2. MOUNTAIN INHABITANT** somebody who lives in a mountainous area ■ *vi.* **(-eered, -eer·ing, -eers) CLIMB MOUNTAINS** to climb mountains for sport

moun·tain·eer·ing /mòwnt'n éering/ *n.* the sport or pastime of climbing mountains

WORLD'S HIGHEST MOUNTAINS

World order

1	Everest *Himalayas*	Height [29,028 ft / 8,848 m]
2	K2 *Himalayas*	Height [28,251 ft / 8,611 m]
3	Kanchenjunga *Himalayas*	Height [28,209 ft / 8,598 m]
4	Lhotse *Himalayas*	Height [27,940 ft / 8,516 m]
5	Makalu *Himalayas*	Height [27,824 ft / 8,481 m]
6	Cho Oyu *Himalayas*	Height [26,906 ft / 8,201 m]
7	Dhaulagiri *Himalayas*	Height [26,811 ft / 8,172 m]
8	Manaslu *Himalayas*	Height [26,781 ft / 8,163 m]
9	Nanga Parbat *Himalayas*	Height [26,657 ft / 8,125 m]
10	Annapurna *Himalayas*	Height [26,545 ft / 8,091 m]

Highest by continent

Europe	1 Mont Blanc	Location *Alps, France-Italy*	Height [15,771 ft / 4,807 m]
Africa	1 Kilimanjaro	Location *Kibo Peak, Tanzania*	Height [19,340 ft / 5,895 m]
North America	1 McKinley	Location *Alaska Range, United States*	Height [20,320 ft / 6,194 m]
South America	1 Aconcagua	Location *Andes, Argentina-Chile*	Height [22,834 ft / 6,960 m]
Oceania/Australasia	1 Puncak Jaya	Location *Sudirman Range, Indonesia*	Height [16,502 ft / 5,030 m]

moun·tain ev·er·last·ing *n.* PLANTS = **cat's-foot**

moun·tain goat *n.* a large white wild North American goat with a woolly coat that lives above the timberline in mountains from Alaska to Colorado. Latin name: *Oreamnus americanus.*

moun·tain go·ril·la *n.* a gorilla that lives in forests in the mountainous regions of east central Africa. Latin name: *Gorilla gorilla beringei.*

moun·tain lau·rel *n.* an evergreen shrub of the heath family that grows in eastern North America and has white or pink flowers and shiny poisonous leaves. It is the state flower of Pennsylvania and Connecticut. Latin name: *Kalmia latifolia.*

moun·tain lion *n.* a large wild cat with a light tan coat found in mountainous areas of the western hemisphere. Latin name: *Felis concolor.*

WORD KEY: REGIONAL NOTE

The Western term ***mountain lion*** goes by many other names, including *California cat, mountain cat,* and *mountain panther.* With scattered instances in the East, especially New York, Pennsylvania, and Georgia, the ***mountain lion*** is found most frequently in the Rocky Mountain and Pacific states.

moun·tain man (*plural* **moun·tian men**) *n.* a man who leads a solitary life in the mountains, especially an early North American pioneer

moun·tain·ous /mównt'nəss/ *adj.* **1.** HAVING MOUNTAINS characterized by many mountains **2.** VERY LARGE very large in height, shape, or size ○ *The ship was battered by mountainous waves.* —**moun·tain·ous·ness** *n.*

moun·tain pan·ther *n.* a mountain lion (*regional*)

moun·tain range *n.* a series of adjacent or interconnected mountains forming a distinct group and usually dating from the same geologic period

moun·tain res·cue *n.* an organization of experienced climbers who go to the aid of people who get into difficulties in a mountainous place

moun·tain sheep *n.* any of several kinds of wild sheep that live in mountainous areas, e.g., the bighorn

moun·tain sick·ness *n.* = **altitude sickness**

moun·tain·side /mównt'n sīd/ *n.* the sloping side of a mountain

Moun·tain Stan·dard Time, Moun·tain Time *n.* the standard time in the time zone centered on longitude 105° W, which includes the Rocky Mountains region of North America. It is seven hours earlier than Universal Coordinated Time.

moun·tain·top /mównt'n tòp/ *n.* the summit of a mountain

moun·tain·y /mównt'nee/ *adj.* having many mountains or forming part of a mountainous area

Mount·bat·ten /mownt bátt'n/, **Louis, 1st Earl Mountbatten of Burma** (1900–79) British naval officer and diplomat. After service in World War II he became the last viceroy of India in 1947. He was killed by an IRA bomb.

Mount Des·ert Is·land island in the Atlantic Ocean off southeastern Maine. Approximately half of the island is occupied by Acadia National Park. Area: 110 sq. mi./285 sq. km.

moun·te·bank /mówntə bàngk/ *n.* (*literary*) **1.** DECEIVER somebody who deceives other people **2.** FAKE HEALER in the past, somebody who sold ineffective medicines in public places [Late 16thC. From Italian *montambanco,* from *monta in banco* (command) "get up onto the bench," from the quack's practice of hocking goods from a platform.] —**moun·te·bank·er·y** *n.*

mount·ed /mówntəd/ *adj.* **1.** ON HORSEBACK riding on a horse ○ *mounted policemen* **2.** FIXED IN PLACE fixed onto something for use or display

Mount Gam·bier /-gámbee ər/ town in southeastern South Australia, built on the slopes of an extinct volcano. Population: 22,037 (1996).

Mount·ie /mówntee/, **Mount·y** (*plural* **-ies**) *n.* a member of the Royal Canadian Mounted Police (*informal*) [Early 20thC. Formed from MOUNTED.]

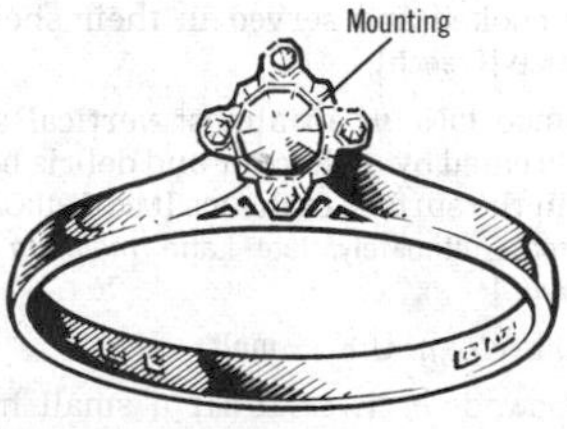

Mounting

mount·ing /mównting/ *n.* SUPPORTING DEVICE a support onto which another thing is fixed ■ *adj.* BECOMING GREATER becoming greater in size, number, or intensity ○ *We listened to the news with mounting alarm.*

mount·ing block *n.* a block of stone on which somebody stands to get onto a horse (*archaic*)

Mount I·sa /-ízə/ city in western Queensland, Australia. Population: 21,751 (1996).

Mount Loft·y Rang·es range of hills in South Australia, situated east of Adelaide. It forms part of the Flinders Range. Length: 200 mi./320 km.

Mount Rai·nier Na·tion·al Park /-ràynee ər-/ national park in western Washington State, established in 1899 and centered around Mount Rainier and its glacier system. Area: 235,613 acres/95,349 hectares.

Mount Rush·more Na·tion·al Me·mo·ri·al /-rùsh mawr-/ national memorial in South Dakota, featuring the heads of four U.S. presidents carved onto the face of Mount Rushmore, each approximately 60 ft./20 m tall. Area: 1,278 acres/517 hectares.

Mount Ver·non /-vúrnən/ city in southeastern New York State, on the Bronx River. It is a northern suburb of New York City. Population: 67,112 (1996).

mourn /mawrn/ (**mourned, mourn·ing, mourns**) *v.* **1.** *vti.* EXPRESS SADNESS AT SOMEBODY'S DEATH to feel and show sadness because somebody has died ○ *mourning the loss of his father* **2.** *vti.* WEAR MOURNING CLOTHES to wear mourning clothes or other things that indicate grief over a death **3.** *vi.* EXPRESS SADNESS AT SOMETHING LOST to feel and show sadness because something has been lost or no longer exists ○ *She mourned the loss of her independence.* [Old English *murnan.* Ultimately from an Indo-European base meaning "to remember," which is also the ancestor of English *remember* and *memory.*] —**mourn·er** *n.*

mourn·ful /máwrnfəl/ *adj.* **1.** FEELING SAD expressing or feeling deep sadness ○ *a youth with a mournful face* **2.** CAUSING SADNESS causing or suggesting deep sadness ○ *a mournful anniversary* —**mourn·ful·ly** *adv.* —**mourn·ful·ness** *n.*

mourn·ing /máwrning/ *n.* **1.** SHOW OF SADNESS the feeling or showing of deep sadness following the death of somebody ○ *was still in mourning over the death of her mother* **2.** CLOTHING FOR SOMEBODY WHO IS MOURNING clothing of a particular style, fabric, or color, e.g., black in Christian cultures, worn as a sign of sorrow following somebody's death ○ *wore mourning for a year* **3.** PERIOD OF SADNESS the period during which the death of somebody is mourned ○ *The family observed a period of 40 days' mourning.* [Old English] —**mourn·ing·ly** *adv.*

WORD KEY: CULTURAL NOTE

Mourning Becomes Electra, a play by dramatist Eugene O'Neill (1931). This 13-act drama, lasting six hours, is a somewhat Freudian reworking of the *Oresteia* trilogy by Greek author Aeschylus. Set in New England during the Civil War (O'Neill's equivalent of the Trojan Wars), it portrays Lavinia Brant's attempts to avenge her mother's infidelity by turning the rest of the family against her.

mourn·ing band *n.* a band of black cloth worn on the arm as a sign of mourning

mourn·ing cloak *n.* ZOOL a European and North American butterfly with purplish-brown wings that are spotted and rimmed with bright yellow. Latin name: *Nymphalis antiopa.*

mourn·ing dove *n.* a common North American dove with grayish-brown feathers, a long pointed tail, and a mournful call. Latin name: *Zenaida macroura.* [*Mourning* from the bird's mournful call]

mouse[1] /mowss/ *abbr.* MIL minimum orbital unmanned satellite of the earth

mouse[2] /mowss/ *n.* (*plural* **mice** /mīss/) **1.** SMALL RODENT a small rodent found all over the world that has a brown or grayish-brown coat and a long mostly hairless tail. Family: Muridae and Cricetidae. **2.** COWARD somebody who is thought to be timid or cowardly (*insult*) **3.** (*plural* **mous·es** *or* **mice**) COMPUTER CONTROLLING DEVICE a hand-held device for controlling a computer. A pointer on the screen (**cursor**) is controlled by moving the device, which has one or more pushbuttons that transmit instructions to the computer. **4.** BLACK EYE a dark swelling under the eye that is caused by a blow (*dated slang*) ■ *vi.* (**moused, mous·ing, mous·es**) HUNT MICE to hunt for and kill mice [Old English *mūs.* Ultimately from an Indo-European word meaning "mouse," which is also the ancestor of English *muscle* and *murine.*]

mouse·bird /mówss bùrd/ *n.* = **coly** [Early 19thC. *Mouse* from the bird's soft hairlike plumage.]

mouse but·ton *n.* a pushbutton, typically one of two or three, on a computer mouse that transmits instructions to the computer

mouse-col·ored *adj.* COLORS of a dull nondescript brown or gray color

mouse deer *n.* = **chevrotain** [From the animal's small size and its similarity in form to a deer]

mouse-ear, **mouse-ear chick·weed** *n.* a variety of chickweed or hawkweed with short hairy leaves resembling mouse ears. Genus: *Cerastium.*

mouse mat, **mouse pad** *n.* a piece of foam-backed material for a computer mouse to move on while being used

mouse po·ta·to *n.* somebody who spends a great deal of time sitting at a computer (*slang*) [Late 20thC. Modeled on COUCH POTATO.]

mous·er /mówssər/ *n.* a domestic animal such as a dog or cat that catches mice

mouse·tail /mówss tàyl/ *n.* a plant that grows in temperate regions and has long flower spikes resembling tails. Genus: *Myosurus.*

mouse·trap /mówss tràp/ *n.* **TRAP FOR CATCHING MICE** a trap for catching and often killing mice ■ *vt.* **(-trapped, -trap·ping, -traps) TO TRAP** to trap or ensnare somebody by clever deception

mous·ey (-i·er, -i·est) *adj.* = **mousy**

mous·ing /mówssing/ *n.* NAUT a cord or bar across the opening of a hook to prevent its load from slipping

mous·sa·ka /moo saákə, moòssə kaá/ *n.* a Greek casserole with alternating layers of eggplant and ground meat in a tomato sauce, topped with a savory white sauce [Mid-20thC. Via Turkish *musakka* from Arabic *musakkā.*]

mousse /mooss/ *n.* (*plural* **mouss·es**) **1. LIGHT FOOD** a light rich dish consisting mostly of whipped cream, eggs, or gelatin that is sweetened to serve as dessert, or flavored with vegetables, meat, or fish **2. FOAMY HAIR PRODUCT** a foamy substance used to set or style hair ■ *vt.* **(moussed, mouss·ing, mouss·es) STYLE HAIR** to apply mousse to hair in order to style it [Mid-19thC. From French, "moss, foam," of Germanic origin.]

mousse·line /moo sleén/ *n.* **1.** TEXTILES **LOOSELY WOVEN FABRIC** a loosely woven fine fabric of natural or synthetic fibers, resembling muslin **2.** CRAFT **GLASS** a type of delicate blown glass **3.** COOK = **mousseline sauce 4.** COOK **ASPIC** an aspic with whipped cream as one of its ingredients [Late 17thC. Via French from Italian *mussolina,* named for *Mosul,* a city of Iraq where the fabric was once manufactured.]

mousse·line de laine /moo sleén də láyn/ *n.* a thin lightweight woolen fabric, often with a printed pattern [From French, literally, "muslin of wool"]

mousse·line de soie /moo sleén də swaá/ *n.* a thin plain-woven fabric of rayon or silk [From French, literally, "muslin of silk"]

mousse·line sauce /moò sleen-/ *n.* hollandaise sauce to which whisked egg white or whipped cream has been added

mous·tache /mú stàsh, mə stásh/ *n.* U.K. = **mustache** [Late 16thC. Via French from Italian *mostaccio,* from, ultimately, Greek *mustax* "upper lip, moustache." Ultimately from an Indo-European base meaning "chew," which is also the ancestor of English *masticate.*]

Mous·te·ri·an /moo steéree ən/ *n.* a prehistoric culture of the Paleolithic period in Europe, North Africa, and the Middle East associated with the Neanderthals and marked by the use of flint tools [Late 19thC. From French *moustérien,* named for *Le Moustier,* a cave in southwestern France where remains from this period were discovered.]

mous·y /mówssee/ **(-i·er, -i·est), mous·ey (-i·er, -i·est)** *adj.* **1. DULL BROWN** dull brown in color **2. TIMID** shy or uncommunicative, especially boringly or irritatingly so **3. FULL OF MICE** overrun with mice **4. RESEMBLING MOUSE** having features that resemble a mouse, e.g., big front teeth or a pointed nose —**mous·i·ly** *adv.* —**mous·i·ness** *n.*

mouth *n.* /mowth/ (*plural* **mouths** /mowthz/) **1.** ANAT **FOOD AND VOICE ORGAN** in people and animals, the opening in the head and its surrounding lips, gums, tongue, and teeth, through which food is taken in and through which sounds come out **2.** ANAT **FACE FEATURE** the part of the mouth visible to others, including the lips and the opening between them ○ *She kissed him on the mouth.* **3. SPEECH ORGAN** the mouth regarded as the organ of speech ○ *You wouldn't believe some of the things that came out of his mouth.* **4. WAY OF SPEAKING** a particular way of using language that other people think is inappropriate or offensive (*disapproving*) ○ *a foul mouth* **5. BACK TALK** a response that refuses to respond to a question or an order and is impudent or sarcastic (*informal*) ○ *All I got from them was a lot of mouth.* **6. WATER JUNCTION** the place where a stream or river enters a sea or lake **7. OPENING IN THE EARTH** an opening to a cave, tunnel, mineshaft, or volcano **8. CONTAINER OPENING** the opening of a container such as a jar, tube, or bottle **9. OPENING BETWEEN PARTS OF A TOOL** the opening between the two sides of a device that can be closed to hold something, e.g., in a vice or clamp **10. GRIMACE** a facial expression that shows displeasure, distaste, or sulkiness (*dated*) ○ *She made a mouth at him and quickly turned away.* **11.** MUSIC **PIPE OPENING** the slit in the pipe of a pipe organ **12.** *vti.* MUSIC **FLUTE OPENING** the hole in a flute that the player blows into ■ *vt.* /mowth/ **(mouthed, mouth·ing, mouths) 1. SAY SOMETHING INSINCERELY** to speak or say something in a loud, affected, or insincere way ○ *How can you get up there and mouth such clichés?* **2. FORM WORDS** to form words with the tongue and lips without making a sound, usually in order to prevent being heard or to pretend to speak or sing something **3. MUMBLE SOMETHING** to say something in an indistinct way **4. PUT SOMETHING IN THE MOUTH** to put and hold something in the mouth as babies and young animals do **5. CARESS SOMETHING WITH THE MOUTH** to touch or caress something with the mouth **6.** *U.K.* **TRAIN A HORSE** to train a horse to get used to a bit and bridle [Old English *mūþ.* Ultimately from an Indo-European base meaning "to project," which is also the ancestor of English *eminent* and *mountain.*] ◇ **a mouth to feed** somebody who must be provided for, especially fed ◇ **be all mouth** to boast about doing something but never actually do it (*informal*) ◇ **down in the mouth** looking sad or gloomy (*informal*) ◇ **give mouth to** to express something in speech or writing

mouth off *vi.* (*informal*) **1. TALK BACK RUDELY** to reply rudely and impudently to somebody **2. EXPRESS FORCEFULLY** to express views loudly and forcefully in a way that annoys others ○ *They are always mouthing off about controversial issues.*

mouth·breed·er /mówth breédər/ *n.* a freshwater fish that carries its eggs and young in its mouth, especially an African fish of the cichlid family. Genus: *Haplochromis* and *Tilapia.*

-mouthed *suffix.* **1.** with a particular kind of mouth ○ *wide-mouthed* **2.** speaking in a particular way ○ *foul-mouthed*

mouth·ful /mówth fòòl/ (*plural* **-fuls**) *n.* **1. QUANTITY OF FOOD** the amount of food that can comfortably be chewed in the mouth at one time **2. SMALL AMOUNT OF FOOD** only a very little amount to eat ○ *You can't go all day on a mouthful of food like that.* **3. HARD-TO-PRONOUNCE WORD OR PHRASE** a word or phrase that is hard to pronounce because of its unfamiliar sound combinations ○ *Her last name's a mouthful!* ◇ **say a mouthful** to say something that is very meaningful or profound

mouth guard *n.* a hard plastic cover that fits inside somebody's mouth over the teeth and gums, worn as protection from injury by people involved in contact sports such as boxing and football

mouth·ing /mówthing/ *n.* something said that is hypocritical or meaningless

mouth or·gan *n.* = **harmonica**

mouth·part /mówth paàrt/ *n.* a body part near the mouth of an insect or arthropod that it uses to gather or chew food

mouth·piece /mówth peèss/ *n.* **1. PART HELD TO THE MOUTH** a part of a musical instrument, telephone, or other device that is held to or in the mouth **2. CONDUIT FOR VIEWS** a person or publication that expresses the views of an organization ○ *He is the mouthpiece for big business in this city.* **3. LAWYER** a criminal lawyer (*slang*) **4. DEVICE TO PROTECT AN ATHLETE'S TEETH** a rubber or plastic mold inserted between the teeth to protect them during a sport activity

mouth-to-mouth, **mouth-to-mouth re·sus·ci·ta·tion** *n.* a method of reviving somebody who is not breathing in which the rescuer places his or her mouth over the mouth of the person not breathing and inflates the lungs with air

mouth·wash /mówth wàwsh/ (*plural* **-wash·es**) *n.* a medicated liquid that is gargled and swished in the mouth to cleanse it and to freshen the breath

mouth·wa·ter·ing /mówth wàwtəring, -wòttəring/ *adj.* stimulating the appetite by having a delicious smell or appearance —**mouth·wa·ter·ing·ly** *adv.*

mouth·y /mówthee, mówthee/ **(-i·er, -i·est)** *adj.* tending to talk rudely, loudly, or too much (*informal*) —**mouth·i·ness** *n.*

mou·ton /moó tòn/ *n.* sheepskin processed to resemble a fur such as seal or beaver [Mid-20thC. From French (see MUTTON).]

mov·a·ble /moóvəb'l/, **move·a·ble** *adj.* **1. EASILY MOVED** able to move or be moved easily **2. CHANGING DATE FROM YEAR TO YEAR** falling on a different date from year to year ■ *n.* LAW **PROPERTY** something that can be easily moved from one place to another, especially personal property such as an item of furniture (*often used in the plural*) —**mov·a·bil·i·ty** /moòvə bíllətee/ *n.* —**mov·a·ble·ness** /moóvəb'lnəss/ *n.* —**mov·a·bly** /moóvəblee/ *adv.*

mov·a·ble feast *n.* a religious festival that is not fixed but falls on a different day from year to year, as does Easter in the Christian calendar

move /moov/ *v.* **(moved, mov·ing, moves) 1.** *vti.* **CHANGE POSITION** to change position or location, or to change the position or location of something ○ *Something moved behind that tree.* **2.** *vti.* **CHANGE YOUR RESIDENCE, JOB, OR SCHOOL** to change your place of residence, work, or study, or make somebody change ○ *move to the other side of town* **3.** *vti.* **TAKE ACTION** to take action, or make somebody act ○ *It's due next week so we need to move quickly.* **4.** *vti.* **CHANGE YOUR VIEW** to change a view or opinion or cause somebody to do so ○ *She has moved to a more moderate position.* **5.** *vti.* **IMPROVE OR PROGRESS** to make progress or start to go in the desired direction ○ *Finally things have started moving.* **6.** *vi.* **ASSOCIATE WITH A GROUP** to associate with a particular group ○ *She moves among the yachting set.* **7.** *vi.* **PROPOSE ACTION** to propose formally that something should happen or be done ○ *I move that the meeting be adjourned.* **8.** *vt.* **STIR SOMEBODY'S EMOTIONS** to make somebody feel something, especially tender feelings ○ *Her performance moved all of us.* **9.** *vti.* BOARD GAMES **TAKE A TURN IN A BOARD GAME** to take a turn in a board game ○ *Did you move yet?* **10.** *vti.* **SELL SOMETHING** to sell well or effectively, or sell something well or effectively ○ *The souvenir mugs aren't really moving.* **11.** *vti.* **EMPTY THE BOWELS** to empty the bowels, or be emptied ■ *n.* **1. ACT OF MOVING** an act or instance of moving ○ *One false move and we're done for.* **2. STEP IN SERIES** an action considered as one of a series ○ *Keep your rivals guessing what your next move will be.* **3.** BOARD GAMES **SOMEBODY'S TURN TO PLAY** somebody's turn in a board game ○ *It's your move.* **4. CHANGE OF LOCATION** a change of residence or location ○ *I'm considering a move across town.* **5. MANEUVER** a maneuver or particular way of doing something ○ *If you're interested in martial arts, I could show you a few moves.* [13thC. Via Anglo-Norman *mover* from Latin *movere.*] ◇ **get a move on** start doing something right away, or do something faster (*informal*) ◇ **make a move on somebody** to proposition somebody sexually (*slang*) ◇ **move it** to hurry, or do something quickly (*informal*) ◇ **on the move 1.** going from one place to another **2.** busy doing one thing after another **3.** going forward, or making progress

WORD KEY: ORIGIN

The Latin word *movere,* from which **move** is derived, is also the source of English *commotion, emotion, mobile, moment, motif, motive, motor, mutiny, promote,* and *remote.*

move in *v.* **1.** *vti.* **START LIVING OR WORKING SOMEWHERE** to begin living or doing business in a place **2.** *vi.* **GET CLOSER** to approach closer to somebody or something, especially to make an attack ○ *move in for the kill*

move in on *vt.* **1. INTRUDE ON SOMEBODY** to intrude on somebody **2. ATTEMPT TO TAKE CONTROL** to attempt to take control of somebody or something, or take over from somebody ○ *They're trying to move in on our station's share of prime time.* **3. APPROACH TO ATTACK** to approach closer to somebody or something, especially to make an attack ○ *The guards are moving in on the intruders.*

move into *vt.* **1. SET UP HOME** to begin living in a particular place ○ *move into a new apartment* **2. START DEALING WITH SOMETHING** to begin dealing with something or doing business in a particular field ○ *The company is set to move into home banking.*

move on *vi.* **1. LEAVE FOR ELSEWHERE** to leave a place and go somewhere else ○ *I think I'll be moving on.* **2. DO SOMETHING ELSE** to stop doing or dealing with something and start doing something else ○ *Let's move on to the next item in the agenda.*

move out *v.* **1.** *vi.* RELOCATE to leave a place of residence or business, or help somebody do this **2.** *vti.* GO ELSEWHERE to withdraw from a place, or make or help somebody do this ○ *Tell the platoon to move out, on the double.*

move over *vti.* to move to one side in order to make room, or to help or make somebody do this ○ *If you move over I'll be able to sit down.*

move·ment /mo͞ovmənt/ *n.* **1.** ACT OF MOVING an act of changing location or position ○ *an instrument to detect subtle movements* **2.** WAY OF MOVING the way in which somebody or something moves ○ *the awkward movement of an injured arm* **3.** EFFORT BY MANY TO ACHIEVE SOMETHING a collective effort by a large number of people to try to achieve something, especially a political or social reform ○ *the civil rights movement* **4.** PEOPLE ORGANIZED TO EFFECT CHANGE the people who organize themselves in order to achieve some political or social reform **5.** MOVING PARTS the parts of a clock or watch mechanism that drive and regulate it **6.** STOCK EXCH CHANGE IN PRICE a change in the prices of traded securities ○ *upward movement before the close of trading* **7.** LITERAT PLOT EVENTS developments in the plot of a literary work ○ *no movement in the plot for three chapters* **8.** ARTS SUGGESTED MOTION the illusion or suggestion of motion in a work of art, e.g., a sculpture or painting **9.** MUSIC SECTION OF MUSICAL WORK one of several self-contained sections that make up a large-scale musical work, often differentiated from one another by different tempos and characters ○ *the concerto's third movement* **10.** MIL TACTICAL CHANGE OF POSITION a tactical change in the position or location of a military unit **11.** POETRY RHYTHM the cadence or rhythm of a piece of poetry **12.** PHYSIOL ACT OF EMPTYING BOWELS an act of emptying of the bowels, or the matter emptied ■ **move·ments** *npl.* ACTIVITIES AND LOCATION what somebody does and where he or she goes, noted over a period of time ○ *The accused was asked to describe his movements on the day in question.*

mov·er /mo͞ovər/ *n.* **1.** SOMEBODY OR SOMETHING THAT CAUSES MOTION somebody or something that causes movement or accomplishes something ○ *She's the prime mover behind the project.* **2.** SOMEBODY WITH A PARTICULAR SOCIAL CIRCLE somebody who associates with a particular group of people socially ○ *a mover in high places* **3.** MOVING COMPANY a company or individual whose work is to transport the personal property of households or businesses from one location to another **4.** SOMEBODY WHO MAKES A MOTION somebody who formally proposes something during a meeting ○ *Does the mover of the motion consent to the amendment?*

mov·ers and shak·ers *npl.* people in society who are powerful or influential ○ *one of the industry's movers and shakers*

mov·ie /mo͞ovee/ *n.* SERIES OF MOVING PICTURES ON A SCREEN a series of real or fictional events recorded by a camera and projected onto a screen as a sequence of moving pictures, usually with an accompanying soundtrack ■ **mov·ies** *npl.* **1.** MOTION PICTURE INDUSTRY the motion picture industry, treated as a whole **2.** MOVIE SHOWING the showing of a movie in a theater [Early 20thC. Shortening and alteration of *moving picture.*]

mov·ie cam·er·a *n.* a camera that records live action on film

mov·ie film *n.* film for use in a movie camera

mov·ie·go·er /mo͞ovee gṑr/ *n.* somebody who goes to a theater to see movies

mov·ie·mak·er /mo͞ovi màykər/ *n.* = **filmmaker**

mov·ie star *n.* an extremely popular motion-picture actor or actress

Mov·ie·tone /mo͞ovee tṑn/ *tdmk.* a trademark for a technique of adding a soundtrack to a motion picture

mov·ing /mo͞oving/ *adj.* **1.** MAKING PEOPLE FEEL EMOTION making people feel deep emotions, especially sadness or compassion ○ *After such a moving speech we were all in tears.* **2.** MOVABLE able to move ○ *moving parts* **3.** IN MOTION in a state of movement (*usually used in combination*) ○ *slow-moving* **4.** CAUSED BY CHANGING PLACES involved in or caused by a change of residence or business location **5.** WHILE DRIVING happening while a vehicle is being driven ○ *a moving violation*

WORD KEY: SYNONYMS

moving, pathetic, pitiful, poignant, touching, heartwarming, heartrending

CORE MEANING: arousing emotion

moving causing feelings of deep sadness or compassion. It can also be used to describe something that arouses other strong emotions; **pathetic** likely to arouse feelings of compassion and pity, often centered on somebody who is vulnerable, helpless, or unfortunate; **pitiful** used in a similar way to *pathetic* but without necessarily suggesting vulnerability or helplessness on the part of the person pitied; **poignant** causing strong, often bittersweet feelings of sadness or regret; **touching** causing feelings of warmth and tenderness; **heartwarming** making people feel happy and more positive or optimistic because it involves people doing good things or behaving kindly to one another; **heartrending** arousing feelings of intense sadness or pity, especially because it involves suffering or tragic events.

mov·ing·ly /mo͞ovinglee/ *adv.* in a way that makes people feel deep emotions, especially tender ones ○ *She spoke movingly about their plight.*

mov·ing pave·ment *n. U.K.* = **moving sidewalk**

mov·ing pic·ture *n.* a motion picture (*dated*)

mov·ing side·walk *n.* an endless, moving belt on a long, flat, or inclined surface on which pedestrians are carried forward, typically found in airports

mov·ing spir·it *n.* somebody who works hard to bring something about and inspires others to do the same ○ *She was one of the moving spirits behind the campaign.*

Mov·i·o·la /mo͞ovee ṓlə/ *tdmk.* a trademark for a film editing machine

mow[1] /mō/ (**mowed, mown** /mōn/ *or* **mowed, mow·ing, mows**) *v.* **1.** *vti.* CUT DOWN TALL GROWTH to cut tall grass, hay, or grain with a scythe or machine **2.** *vt.* CUT GRASS to cut the grass, hay, or grain growing in a particular place ○ *Mow the front lawn today, please.* [Old English *māwan.* From a prehistoric Germanic base that is also the ancestor of English *meadow* and *aftermath.*]

mow down *vt.* **1.** KILL MANY PEOPLE QUICKLY to kill people quickly and in large numbers **2.** KNOCK SOMEBODY DOWN to knock somebody or something down by force **3.** OVERWHELM SOMEBODY to overwhelm somebody decisively

mow[2] /mō/ *n.* **1.** STORAGE PLACE FOR HAY the part of a barn where hay or grain is stored when it has been harvested **2.** STORED HAY a pile of hay or grain, especially in a barn [Old English *mūga*, of unknown origin]

Mow·at /mṓ ət, mów-/, **Sir Oliver** (1820–1903) Canadian statesman. He was prime minister of Ontario (1872–96).

mown past participle of **mow**

MOX /moks/ *n.* reactor fuel made from plutonium that has been separated from spent nuclear fuel by chemical reprocessing and mixed with natural or depleted uranium [Blend of MIXED and OXIDE]

mox·ie /móksee/ *n.* courage combined with inventiveness (*slang dated*) [Mid-20thC. Named for a brand of soft drink that was originally marketed as a "nerve tonic," said to restore virility and intelligence.]

Moy·ni·han /móynəe hàn/, **Daniel Patrick** (*b.* 1927) U.S. academic and politician. He was ambassador to India (1973–74), and won a seat in the Senate (1976).

Moz. *abbr.* Mozambique

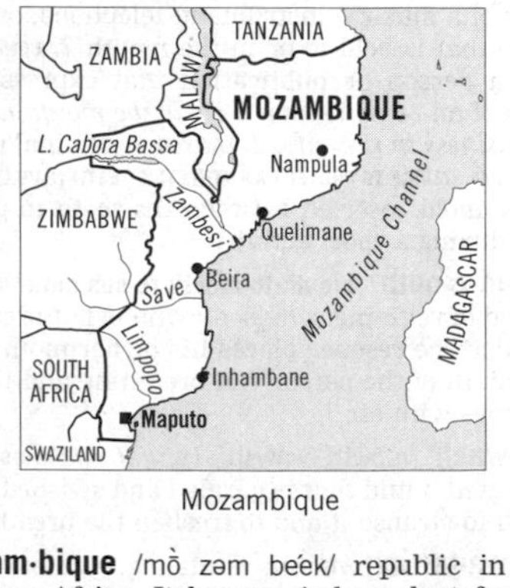

Mozambique

Mo·zam·bique /mṑ zəm be͞ek/ republic in southeastern Africa. It became independent from Portugal in 1975. Language: Portuguese. Currency: metical. Capital: Maputo. Population: 18,028,000 (1996). Area: 309,496 sq. mi./801,590 sq. km. Official name **Republic of Mozambique** —**Mo·zam·bi·can** *n., adj.*

Moz·ar·ab /mō zérrəb/ *n.* a Christian living in Moorish Spain who adopted some Arab customs without converting to Islam [Early 17thC. Via Spanish *mozárabe* from Arabic *musta'rib* "becoming an Arab."] —**Moz·ar·a·bic** *adj.*

Mo·zart /mṓts aart/, **Wolfgang Amadeus** (1756–91) Austrian composer. A figure of key importance in Western music, his compositions, in almost every musical genre, epitomize the classical style.

mo·zet·ta *n.* CHR = **mozzetta**

moz·za·rel·la /mòtsə réllə/ *n.* a rubbery white unsalted Italian cheese used in salads, cooking, and especially on pizza [Early 20thC. From Italian, literally "little mozza," from *mozza*, type of cheese (literally "a cut"), from *mozzare* "to cut off."]

moz·zet·ta /mō zéttə, mōt séttə/ (*plural* **-tas**), **mo·zet·ta** (*plural* **-tas**) *n.* a short hooded cape worn by the pope and other senior Roman Catholic clergymen [Late 18thC. Via Italian from, ultimately, medieval Latin *almutia* (also the source of English *amice*), of unknown origin.]

mp, **m.p.** *abbr.* **1.** melting point **2.** MUSIC mezzo piano

MP, **M.P.** *abbr.* **1.** Member of Parliament **2.** military police **3.** mounted police

M.P.A. *abbr.* **1.** Master of Professional Accounting **2.** Master of Public Administration **3.** Master of Public Accounting

M.P.E. *abbr.* Master of Public Education

mpg, **m.p.g.** *abbr.* miles per gallon

mph, **m.p.h.** *abbr.* miles per hour

M.Phil. *abbr.* Master of Philosophy

M.P.P. *abbr.* Member of the Provincial Parliament (of Ontario)

M·pu·ma·lang·a /əm po͝omə láng gə/ province in northeastern South Africa, bordering Swaziland and Mozambique. Capital: Nelspruit. Population: 3,007,100 (1995). Area: 30,259 mi./78,370 sq. km. Former name **Eastern Transvaal**

Mr. /místər/ *n.* **1.** MAN'S TITLE the customary title of courtesy used before the name or names of a man ○ *Mr. Smith* **2.** JOB OR FUNCTION TITLE a courtesy title used for a man before the name of his position or function ○ *Mr. President* **3.** DESCRIPTIVE TITLE a humorous title used for a man before a place, name, thing, or description that he is supposed to typify or represent ○ *He's not exactly Mr. Personality, is he?* **4.** JUNIOR OFFICER'S TITLE a title used in addressing an officer in the navy below the rank of commander, a warrant officer in the army, or a cadet in a service academy [15thC. Contraction of *maister*, an earlier form of MASTER.]

Mr. Big *n.* a powerful or important man, e.g., the chief of a criminal organization (*slang*)

MRBM *abbr.* medium-range ballistic missile

MRCA *abbr.* multirole combat aircraft

Mr. Clean *n.* somebody, especially a public figure, who is seen as being admirably upright, honest, and moral (*informal*) [Mid-20thC. Named for a cleaning solution trademark.]

M.R.E. *abbr.* MIL meal, ready to eat

MRI *abbr.* MED magnetic resonance imaging

mri·dan·ga /mri dúng gə/, **mri·dang** /mri dúng/, **mri·dan·gam** /-gəm/ *n.* an Indian drum that is shaped like a barrel and is made in various sizes [Late 19thC. From Tamil.]

mRNA *abbr.* messenger RNA

Mr. Right *n.* somebody seen as being a perfect partner for somebody else (*informal*) ○ *One day Mr. Right will come along.*

Mrs. /míssiz/ *n.* a customary title of courtesy for a married or widowed woman, used before her name or names or those of her husband ○ *Mrs. Wright* [Early 17thC. Contraction of MISTRESS.]

Mrs. Grun·dy /-grúndee/ *n.* an extremely conventional or rigid person, especially somebody who is about prescriptive grammatical rules (*informal disapproving*) [Late 18thC. Named for a character in the play *Speed the Plough*, by Thomas Morton (1764–1838).]

ms *abbr.* millisecond

MS *abbr.* 1. mail steamer 2. Master of Surgery 3. sacred to the memory of (*on gravestones*) 4. Mississippi 5. motor ship 6. multiple sclerosis

ms. *abbr.* manuscript

Ms. /məz, miz/ *n.* 1. WOMAN'S TITLE a customary title of courtesy used before the name or names of a woman without making a distinction between married and unmarried status ○ *Ms. Bennett* 2. WOMAN'S DESCRIPTIVE TITLE a title used for a woman before a place, name, thing, or description that she is supposed to typify or represent ○ *Ms. Efficiency* [Mid-20thC. Blend of MISS and MRS.]

MS. *abbr.* manuscript

M.S. *abbr.* Master of Science [From Latin *Magister Scientiae*]

MSB *abbr.* COMPUT most significant bit

M.Sc. *abbr.* Master of Science [From Latin *Magister Scientiae*]

MS-DOS /èm ess dáwss, èm ess dóss/ *tdmk.* a trademark for a widely used computer operating system

msec *abbr.* millisecond

Mses. plural of **Ms.**

MSG *abbr.* monosodium glutamate

msg. *abbr.* message

Msgr. *abbr.* 1. Monseigneur 2. Monsignor

MSGT *abbr.* Master Sergeant

M.Sgt. *abbr.* Master Sergeant

MSH *abbr.* melanocyte-stimulating hormone

MSI *abbr.* ELECTRON ENG medium scale integration

M.S.L., **m.s.l.** *abbr.* mean sea level

M.S.N. *abbr.* Master of Science in Nursing

Ms. Right *n.* somebody seen as being the perfect romantic partner for somebody else ○ *tired of waiting for Ms Right to come along*

mss., **MSS.** *abbr.* manuscripts

MST, **M.S.T.** *abbr.* Mountain Standard Time

MSTS *abbr.* Military Sea Transportation Service

M.S.W. *abbr.* Master in Social Work

mt *abbr.* 1. mount 2. mountain 3. Mountain Time

Mt *abbr.* 1. Mount 2. Mountain

MT *abbr.* 1. machine translation 2. megaton 3. Montana 4. Mountain Time

mt. *abbr.* 1. megaton 2. mount 3. mountain

Mt. *abbr.* 1. Mount 2. Mountain

m.t. *abbr.* metric ton

M·ta·ra·zi Wa·ter·fall falls in Zimbabwe, south eastern Africa, one of the highest in the world. Height: 2,500 ft./762 m.

MTBE *n.* a lead-free antiknock gasoline additive. Abbr of **methyl tertiary-butyl ethyl**

MTBF *abbr.* COMPUT mean time between failures

M.Tech. /èm ték/ *abbr.* Master of Technology

mtg. *abbr.* 1. meeting 2. mortgage

mtge. *abbr.* mortgage

mtn. *abbr.* mountain

Mtn. *abbr.* mountain

Mt. Rev. *abbr.* Most Reverend

mts., **Mts.** *abbr.* 1. mountains 2. mounts

MTTR *abbr.* MANUF mean time to repair

mu /myoo, moo/ *n.* the 12th letter of the Greek alphabet, represented in the English alphabet as "m" [Late 19thC. From Greek.]

Mu'aw·i·ya *n.* a leader of the Umayyad clan who became the first Umayyad caliph following civil war with Ali. He died in A.D. 680.

Mu·bar·ak, Hosni (*b.* 1928) Egyptian statesman. He succeeded Anwar Sadat as president of Egypt in 1981. He continued Sadat's foreign policy of peace with Israel while mending strained relations with the Arab League. Full name **Muhammad Hosni Said Mubarak**

muc- *prefix.* = **muco-** [See MUCO-]

much /much/ *adv.* 1. LARGELY used to indicate that something exists or is true to a great extent, intensity, or degree ○ *She hasn't changed much over the years.* ○ *It's a much more difficult game than the other.* 2. OFTEN happening often or frequently ○ *I don't get out much these days.* ○ *Do you see your children much over the holidays?* 3. NEARLY nearly or practically ○ *One day is much like the next when you're ill.* ○ *It's much the same problem all over again.* ■ *adj., pron.* LARGE AMOUNT a large amount or degree ○ (adj) *He doesn't have much free time due to the demands of work.* ○ (pron) *Much remains to be done.* ○ (pron) *She does much of her writing at home.* ■ *pron.* IMPRESSIVE something impressive, important, or unusual ○ *The house isn't much to look at, but it's very comfortable.* [13thC. Shortening of Old English *mycel.* Ultimately from an Indo-European base meaning "great," which is also the ancestor of English *major* and *mickle.*] ◇ **as much** precisely that ○ *I wasn't surprised when she said she'd taken the money, as I'd suspected as much from the start.* ◇ **(as) much as** although, or even though ○ *As much as I'd like to join you, I'm afraid I can't.* ◇ **much as** to almost the same degree, or in a similar manner ○ *You cook it much as you would a potato.* ◇ **not much of a** not particularly good at something or not a very good example of something ○ *It wasn't much of a celebration, was it?*

mu·cha·cha /moo chaá chaá/ *n.* a girl (*offensive in some contexts*) [Late 19thC. From Spanish, the feminine of MUCHACHO.]

mu·cha·cho /moo chaá chō/ (*plural* **-chos**) *n.* a boy (*offensive in some contexts*) [Late 16thC. From Spanish.]

much·ness /múchnəss/ *n.* greatness in quantity, extent, or degree (*archaic*) ◇ **much of a muchness** amounting to or being practically the same (*informal*)

muci- *prefix.* = **muco-** [Variant of MUCO-]

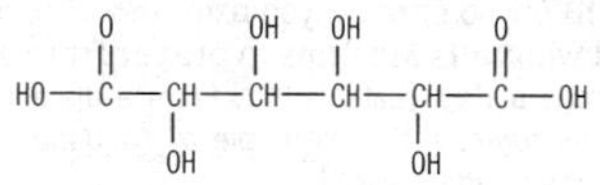

Mucic acid

mu·cic ac·id /myoóssik-/ *n.* a colorless crystalline solid obtained from lactose. It is used in the manufacture of other chemicals. Formula: $C_4H_4(OH)_4(COOH)_2$.

mu·cif·er·ous /myoo síffərəss/ *adj.* producing or containing a lot of mucus

mu·ci·gen /myoóssəjən/ *n.* a substance in mucous cells that is converted into mucin

mu·ci·lage /myoóssəlij/ *n.* 1. GLUE a thick water-based solution used as an adhesive 2. STICKY PLANT PRODUCT a gummy substance secreted by some plants such as seaweed that contains protein and carbohydrates [14thC. Via French from late Latin *mucillago* "moldy juice," from Latin *mucus* (see MUCUS).]

mu·ci·lag·i·nous /myoóssə lájjənəss/ *adj.* 1. PRODUCING MUCILAGE relating to or producing mucilage 2. MOIST AND STICKY moist and sticky like glue — **mu·ci·lag·i·nous·ly** *adv.* —**mu·ci·lag·i·nous·ness** *n.*

mu·cin /myoóssin/ *n.* a complex protein found in the substances secreted by mucous membranes — **mu·cin·ous** *adj.*

muck /muk/ *n.* 1. STICKY DIRT soft moist dirt or filth (*informal*) 2. MANURE moist manure or compost, especially when used to fertilize land 3. *U.K.* RUBBISH something that is distasteful, disgusting, or of very poor quality (*informal*) ○ *don't know how they can publish such muck* 4. MINE WASTE waste material from mining, e.g., earth or rubble ■ *vt.* (**mucked, muck·ing, mucks**) 1. FERTILIZE LAND to fertilize land with manure or compost (*informal*) 2. CLEAN OUT A PLACE to clean the muck out of a place such as a stable or barn 3. MAKE SOMETHING DIRTY to pollute something or make something dirty (*informal*) [13thC. From Scandinavian, ultimately from a prehistoric Germanic base meaning "soft." Originally "excrement"; the more general "dirt" is a 14thC development.]

muck around *vi. U.K.* to waste time instead of doing something useful or important (*informal*) ○ *We'd get this job finished sooner if you two stopped mucking around.*

muck up *vt.* to ruin or make a mess of something (*informal*) ○ *She's really mucked up her chances now.*

muck·a·muck *n.* = **high-muck-a-muck** (*informal*)

muck·er /múkər/ *n.* somebody whose job is to remove rocky mine waste

muck·luck *n.* CLOTHES = **mukluk**

muck·rake /múk ràyk/ *vi.* (**-raked, -rak·ing, -rakes**) EXPOSE SCANDAL to seek out and publicize misconduct by prominent people ■ *n.* RAKE FOR MANURE a rake used to spread manure or compost [Late 17thC. From MUCK + RAKE.] —**muck·rak·er** *n.* —**muck·rak·ing** *n.*

muck·worm /múk wùrm/ *n.* an insect larva that lives in mud or manure

muck·y /múkee/ (**-ier, -i·est**) *adj.* very dirty or covered with muck (*informal*) —**muck·i·ly** *adv.* —**muck·i·ness** *n.*

muco-, **muc-**, **muci-** *prefix.* mucus, mucous membrane ○ *mucocutaneous* [Formed from Latin *mucus* (see MUCUS)]

mu·co·cu·ta·ne·ous /myoòkō kyoo táynee əss/ *adj.* involving both skin and mucous membrane

mu·coid /myoó kòyd/, **mu·coid·al** /myoó kòyd'l/ *adj.* resembling mucus in appearance, consistency, or function

mu·co·lyt·ic /myoòkə líttik/ *adj.* able to break down substances that contain mucus

mu·co·pep·tide /myoòkō pép tīd/ *n.* = **peptidoglycan**

mu·co·pol·y·sac·cha·ride /myoòkō pollee sákə rīd/ *n.* a polysaccharide that forms complexes with proteins and contains an amino group

mu·co·pro·tein /myoòkō prō teen/ *n.* a complex protein that is found in body fluids and tissues

mu·co·pu·ru·lent /myoòkō pyoórələnt/ *adj.* containing both mucus and pus

mu·co·sa /myoo kóssə/ (*plural* **-sae** /-kóssee/) *n.* = **mucous membrane** [Late 19thC. From modern Latin *(membrana) mucosa* "mucous membrane," from the feminine of Latin *mucosus* (see MUCOUS).]

mu·cous /myoókəss/ *adj.* containing, secreting, resembling, or covered with mucus [Mid-17thC. From Latin *mucosus*, from *mucus* (see MUCUS).]

mu·cous mem·brane *n.* a moist lining in the body passages of all mammals that contains mucus-secreting cells and is open directly or indirectly to the external environment

mu·co·vis·ci·do·sis /myoòkō vissi dóssiss/ *n.* = **cystic fibrosis** [Mid-20thC. Formed from VISCID.]

mu·cro /myoó krō/ (*plural* **-cros**) *n.* a sharp point projecting from an organ or plant part [Mid-17thC. From Latin, "sharp point, sword."]

mu·cro·nate /myoókrə nàyt/, **mu·cro·nat·ed** /myoókrə nàytəd/ *adj.* BOT, ZOOL ending in a sharp point — **mu·cro·na·tion** /myoòkrə náysh'n/ *n.*

mu·cus /myoókəss/ *n.* the clear slimy lubricating substance consisting mostly of mucins and water that coats and protects mucous membranes [Mid-17thC. From Latin. Ultimately from an Indo-European word meaning "slimy," which is also the ancestor of English *meek* and *moist.*]

mud /mud/ *n.* 1. WET DIRT earth that is very wet, soft, and gummy 2. DEFAMATORY MATERIAL defamatory things said or written about somebody [14thC. Origin uncertain: probably from Middle Low German *mudde.*] ◇ **(as) clear as mud** not clear or understandable at all (*informal*) ◇ **sling** *or* **throw mud at** make defamatory statements about somebody or something (*informal*)

mud·bath /múd bàth/ (*plural* **-baths** /-bàths, -bàthz/) *n.* 1. BEAUTY TREATMENT a bath in heated mud, thought to tone the skin and organs 2. ACTIVITY IN A MUDDY PLACE something such as a football game that takes place outdoors in very muddy conditions (*informal*)

mud·cat /múd kàt/ *n. Southern U.S.* a catfish

mud daub·er *n.* = **mud wasp**

mud·dle /múdd'l/ *v.* (**-dled, -dling, -dles**) 1. *vt.* MIX THINGS TOGETHER IN DISORDER to mix things together in a confused or disordered way ○ *The disks have been carefully filed, so don't muddle them.* 2. *vt.* CONFUSE THINGS to confuse things in the mind (*often passive*) ○ *They look so much alike that it's easy to muddle them up.* 3. *vti.* CONFUSE OR BE CONFUSED to be confused or bemused or to cause somebody to be so ○ *Tell me again slowly – you're muddling me.* 4. *vt.* MAKE WATER MUDDY to make water muddy and unclear by stirring it 5. *vt.* STIR AN ALCOHOLIC BEVERAGE GENTLY to mix or stir an alcoholic drink ■ *n.* 1. CONFUSED STATE something that is in such a confused condition that it is hard to organize or understand ○ *How did our records get into such a muddle?* **2. MIXUP** a misunderstanding arising from or causing a confused situation or state ○ *There's been a muddle over the bookings.* [Mid-16thC. Origin uncertain: possibly from Middle Dutch *moddelen* "to make muddy," from *modde* "mud."] —**mud·dler** *n.* —**mud·dly** *adj.*

muddle through *vi.* to succeed or manage to keep going despite being disorganized ○ *I expect we'll muddle through somehow.*

mud·dled /múdd'ld/ *adj.* being in a condition of disorder or confusion

mud·dle·head·ed /mùdd'l héddəd/ *adj.* **1. CONFUSED** unable to think clearly **2. INEPT** not clearly thought out —**mud·dle·head·ed·ly** *adv.* —**mud·dle·head·ed·ness** *n.*

mud·dy /múddee/ *adj.* **(-di·er, -di·est) 1. MARKED WITH MUD** full of, covered in, or dirtied with mud **2. RESEMBLING MUD** like mud in being cloudy or thick **3. LACKING CLARITY** lacking clarity, brightness, or transparency ○ *a muddy color* **4. CONFUSED** hard to understand or lacking in logical reasoning ■ *vt.* **(-died, -dy·ing, -dies) 1. MAKE SOMETHING MUDDY** to make something muddy **2. MAKE SOMETHING UNCLEAR** to make something confused and unclear —**mud·di·ly** *adv.* —**mud·di·ness** *n.*

mud eel *n.* a salamander of the southeastern United States that has two short front legs, no hind legs, and external gills. Latin name: *Siren lacertina.* [*Mud* because the salamander lives in muddy water]

Mu·dé·jar /moo dé haar, -thé khaar/ *n.* (*plural* **-ja·res** /-haa rayss/) **SPANISH MOOR** a Moor who was allowed to stay in a part of Spain after it had been recaptured by the Christians ■ *adj.* **OF THE SPANISH MOORS** belonging to or typical of the Mudéjares, especially their style of architecture [Mid-19thC. From Spanish, from Arabic *mudajjan*, the past participle of *dajjana* "to permit to stay."]

mud·fish /múd fish/ (*plural* **-fish** *or* **-fish·es**) *n.* a fish that lives in muddy waters, especially the bowfin

mud flap *n. U.K.* = **splashguard**

mud·flat /múd flàt/, **mud flat** *n.* an area of low muddy land that is underwater only at high tide, especially one near an estuary

mud·flow /múd flō/ *n.* a fast-moving downhill flow of mud and soil loosened by rainfall or melting snow

mud·guard /múd gaard/ *n.* **1.** = **splashguard 2.** *U.K.* = **fender**

mud hen *n.* a bird that lives in marshes and low wetlands, e.g., the coot or rail

mud min·now *n.* a small North American freshwater fish that can survive in muddy oxygen-deficient water and is often used as bait. Family: Umbridae.

mud·pack /múd pàk/ *n.* a beauty treatment for the face made of fuller's earth and additives that is allowed to dry before being removed

mud pie *n.* a mass of mud shaped by children as a game

mud pup·py /múd pùppee/, **mud·pup·py** (*plural* **-pies**) *n.* an eastern North American salamander that lives on muddy banks and has dark red external gills. Genus: *Necturus.*

mu·dra /mə draa/ (*plural* **-dras**) *n.* any of the various symbolic positions in which the hands are held in Indian dancing and ritual [Early 19thC. From Sanskrit *mudrā* "seal, sign."]

mud·room /múd ròom, -ròom/ *n.* a small room near the entrance of a house where people remove muddy or wet shoes and clothing

mud·sill /múd sìl/ *n.* the lowest sill or horizontal support of a building, at or below ground level

mud·skip·per /múd skìppər/ *n.* an Asian or African tropical fish of the goby family that can maneuver on land or climb roots on its pectoral fins to feed. Genera: *Periophthalmus* and *Boleophthalmus.*

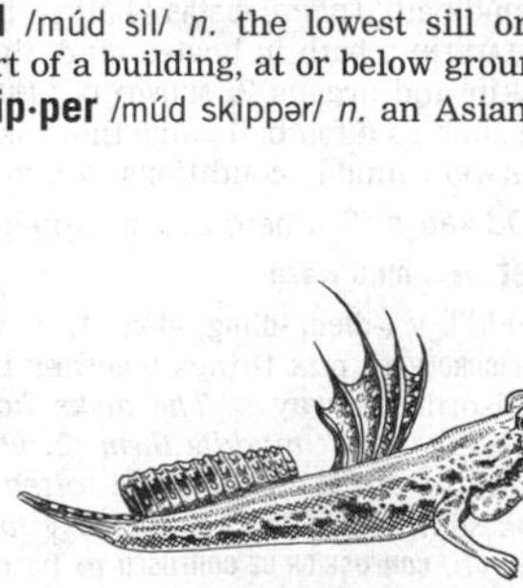

Mudskipper

mud·slide /múd slīd/ *n.* a slow-moving and often destructive mass of mud flowing down a slope

mud·sling·ing /múd slìnging/ *n.* the making of defamatory remarks about somebody, especially a political opponent or other competitor ○ *The level of debate in this election has seldom risen above petty mudslinging.* —**mud·sling·er** *n.*

mud snake *n.* a burrowing snake of the southeastern United States that is related to the grass snake and is dark blue and red in color. Latin name: *Farancia abacura.*

mud·stone /múd stōn/ *n.* a gray sedimentary rock formed from mud, similar to shale but with less developed lamination

mud tur·tle *n.* a small North and Central American freshwater turtle that lives at the bottom of muddy ponds and streams. Genus: *Kinosternon.*

mud vol·ca·no *n.* a conical mound of mud that forms around a hot spring or geyser

mud wasp *n.* a wasp that builds multicellular nests with mud. Family: Sphecidae.

Muen·ster /múnstər, mòonstər/, **muen·ster, Mun·ster, mun·ster** *n.* a white to yellow semisoft mildly flavored cheese that typically has an orange edible rind [Early 20thC. Named for the town of *Munster* in northeastern France, known for production of this cheese.]

mues·li /myòozlee/ *n.* an originally Swiss mixture of cereal flakes and rolled oats with dried fruit and nuts, eaten with milk for breakfast [Mid-20thC. From Swiss German, literally "little purée," from German *Mus* "purée."]

mu·ez·zin /myoo ézzin, myòo əzin, moo-/ *n.* a mosque official who calls Muslims to prayer from a minaret five times a day [Late 16thC. From a dialect variant of Arabic *mu'addin*, active participle of *"addana"* "to call to prayer," from *"udn"* "ear."]

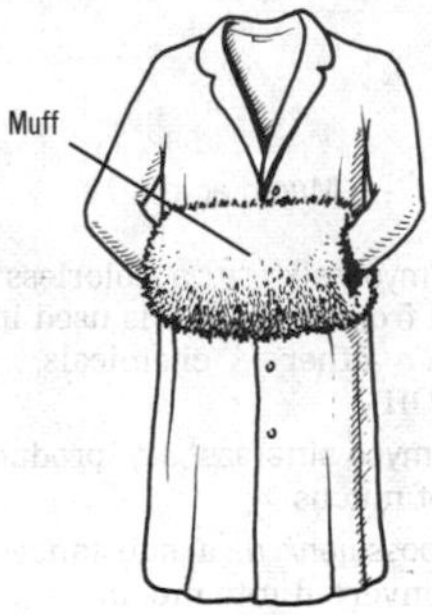

Muff

muff[1] /muf/ *n.* **1. CLOTHES FURRY CYLINDER** an open-ended cylinder of fur or cloth used for keeping hands warm, one hand going in at each end **2. BIRDS FOWL FEATHERS** either of the tufts of feathers on each side of the face of some fowl [Late 16thC. From Dutch *mof*, a shortening of Middle Dutch *moffel*, from medieval Latin *muffula* "glove," of unknown origin.]

muff[2] /muf/ *vt.* **(muffed, muff·ing, muffs) 1. FAIL TO CATCH SOMETHING** to fail to catch a ball or make a shot ○ *He got right under the ball and still muffed it.* **2. DO SOMETHING BADLY** to do something badly or awkwardly ○ *The play got off to a bad start when the actors muffed the opening lines.* ■ *n.* **FAILED ACTION** a badly performed catch, shot, or action [Mid-19thC. Origin unknown.]

muf·fin /múffin/ *n.* **1. SMALL CAKE** a small round cake for one person made from a thick batter and often containing fruit or nuts, eaten at breakfast or for a snack **2.** *U.K.* = **English muffin** [Early 18thC. Origin uncertain: perhaps from Low German *muffen*, plural of *muffe* "small cake."]

muf·fle[1] /múff'l/ *vt.* **(-fled, -fling, -fles) 1. WRAP SOMETHING TO STIFLE SOUND** to wrap or pad something with material in order to deaden the sound it makes **2. MAKE SOMETHING LESS LOUD** to make a sound less loud ○ *He put his hands over his ears to muffle the noise of the sirens.* **3. PREVENT SOMETHING BEING EXPRESSED** to prevent something from being said or written ○ *a government that sought to muffle all opposition* **4. KEEP SOMEBODY WARM** to wrap somebody or a part of somebody's body in a garment or cloth for warmth ○ *She muffled herself up in a thick shawl.* ■ *n.* **1. SOMETHING MUFFLING A SOUND** something used to muffle a sound **2. TYPE OF KILN** a kiln in which objects being fired are protected from direct contact with the flames [15thC. Origin uncertain: possibly via Old French *moufler* from, ultimately, medieval Latin *muffula* "glove," of unknown origin.]

muf·fle[2] /múff'l/ *n.* the moist fleshy hairless upper lip of some rodents and ruminants [Early 17thC. From French *mufle*, of unknown origin.]

muf·fled /múff'ld/ *adj.* **1. NOT HEARD CLEARLY** unable to be heard clearly because of being deadened or stifled ○ *There was a muffled cheer from the back of the audience.* **2. WRAPPED TO STIFLE SOUND** wrapped or padded with material in order to deaden the sound it is making ○ *The soldiers in the funeral procession marched to the beat of muffled drums.* [Late 16thC. Formed from MUFFLE[1].]

muf·fler /múfflər/ *n.* **1. SCARF** a scarf worn around the neck for warmth **2. CAR PART** a device attached to a car's exhaust pipe to reduce the amount of noise made by the engine **3.** = **muffle**[1] *n.* 1 [Mid-16thC. Formed from MUFFLE[1].]

muf·ti /múftee/ *n.* ordinary clothes when worn by somebody who is normally in uniform [Early 19thC. Origin uncertain: perhaps a humorous use of MUFTI "Muslim jurist."]

Muf·ti /múftee, mòoftee/ *n.* an expert on Islamic religious law [Late 16thC. From Arabic *muftī*, past participle of *aftā* "to decide a legal point."]

mug[1] /mug/ **(mugged, mug·ging, mugs)** *n.* **1. DRINKING CUP** a large round straight-sided cup typically made of earthenware and having a handle **2. CONTENTS OF A MUG** what a mug has in it, or the amount of liquid it can hold ○ *a mug of hot soup* [Early 16thC. Origin uncertain: possibly from Scandinavian.]

mug[2] /mug/ *n.* **1. SOMEBODY'S FACE** somebody's face or mouth (*informal*) **2.** *vt.* **VIOLENT MAN** a rough and violent man **3. MUG SHOT** a photograph of a suspected criminal's face (*informal*) **4.** *U.K.* **UNINTELLIGENT PERSON** somebody who is unintelligent or easily deceived (*slang*) ■ *v.* **(mugged, mug·ging, mug) 1.** *vt.* **ROB SOMEBODY** to attack and rob somebody, especially a pedestrian in a public place **2.** *vt.* **PHOTOGRAPH SUSPECTED CRIMINAL** to photograph a criminal or suspect in a crime **3.** *vi.* **MAKE FACES** to make exaggerated facial expressions when performing or posing for a camera ○ *The actors were playing it for laughs, mugging in every scene.*

Robert Mugabe

Mu·ga·be /mòo gaabee/, **Robert** (*b.* 1924) Zimbabwean politician. After leading the struggle against the white government of Rhodesia, he became the first prime minister of Zimbabwe (1980–87) and first president (1987-). Abandoning attempts to form a one-party state, he held multiparty elections in 1990. Full name **Robert Gabriel Mugabe**

mug·ful /múg fool/ *n.* = **mug**[1] *n.* **2**

mug·ger[1] /múggər/ *n.* **1. ATTACKER** somebody who attacks and robs another in a public place **2. SOMEBODY WHO OVERACTS** somebody who overacts, especially by making faces

mug·ger[2] /múggər/, **mug·gar, mug·gur** *n.* a freshwater crocodile of India and Sri Lanka. Latin name: *Crocodylus palustris.* [Mid-19thC. From Hindi *magar.*]

mug·ging /múgging/ *n.* the crime of attacking and robbing somebody

WORD KEY: SYNONYMS

See Synonyms at ***theft.***

mug·gy /múggee/ (**-gi·er, -gi·est**) *adj.* unpleasantly hot and humid [Mid-18thC. Ultimately from the obsolete and dialect form *mug* "to rain lightly," of Scandinavian origin.] —**mug·gi·ly** *adv.* —**mug·gi·ness** *n.*

Mu·ghal *n.* HIST = **Mogul**

mug shot /múg shòt/, **mug·shot** *n.* a photograph of somebody's face, especially one of a suspected criminal's face or profile taken by police

mug·wort /múg wùrt, -wàwrt/ *n.* an herbaceous perennial wormwood that grows in temperate regions in the northern hemisphere and has aromatic leaves and small pale green flowers. Latin name: *Artemisia vulgaris.* [Old English *mucgwyrt*, from earlier forms of MIDGE + WORT]

mug·wump /múg wùmp/ *n.* somebody who takes an independent or neutral stance, especially in politics [Mid-19thC. From Massachusett *mugquomp* "war leader."] —**mug·wump·er·y** *n.* —**mug·wump·ish** *adj.* —**mug·wump·ism** *n.*

Mug·wump *n.* a U. S. Republican who refused to support the party's candidates in the 1884 presidential election. [Late 19thC. From MUGWUMP.]

Mu·ham·mad /mə hámmid/, **Mo·ham·med** (570?–632) Arabian founder of Islam. According to Islamic tradition he received his first command from Allah in 1610. In 628 he made Mecca the religious capital of Islam. He recorded his visions and teachings in the Koran.

Mu·ham·mad, Elijah (1897–1975) U.S. political activist. He was leader of the Nation of Islam group (1934–75). Born **Elijah Poole**

Mu·har·ram /moo hérrəm/, **Mo·har·ram** *n.* the first month of the Islamic calendar, made up of 30 days and falling around the same time as September to October [Early 19thC. From Arabic *muḥarram* "inviolable," the past participle of *ḥarrama* "to forbid."]

Muir /myoor/, **John** (1838–1914) Scottish-born U.S. naturalist and explorer. He helped establish Yosemite, King's Canyon, and Sequoia national parks in the U.S.

Muir Gla·cier glacier in southeastern Alaska. It reaches the sea at Glacier Bay.

mu·ja·hed·din /mōō jaahə deen, mōōjəhə-/, **mu·ja·he·deen, mu·ja·hi·deen, mu·ja·hi·din** *npl.* Islamic guerrillas based in Iran and Pakistan who fought holy war (**jihad**) against the Soviet forces occupying Afghanistan in the late 1970s and the 1980s [Mid-20thC. From Persian or Arabic *mujāhidīn*, the plural of *mujāhid* "one who fights a jihad."]

muk·luk /múk lùk/, **muck·luck** *n.* **1. LARGE BOOT** a waterproof boot made of animal skin or canvas that is large enough to be worn over shoes or several pairs of socks **2. INUIT SEALSKIN BOOT** a sealskin boot originally worn by the Inuit [Mid-19thC. From Yupik *maklak* "bearded seal," misunderstood as meaning "sealskin" and then used as the name of the boot made of this material.]

mu·lat·to /mōō láttō, -laátō/ (*plural* **-tos** *or* **-toes**) *n.* (*dated offensive*) **1. OFFENSIVE TERM REFERRING TO PARENTS' RACES** an offensive term for somebody who has one Black and one Caucasian parent **2. REFERRING TO ANCESTORS' RACES** an offensive term for somebody who has both Black and Caucasian ancestors [Late 16thC. From Spanish *mulato* "young mule," from *mulo* "mule," from Latin *mulus* (source of English *mule*).]

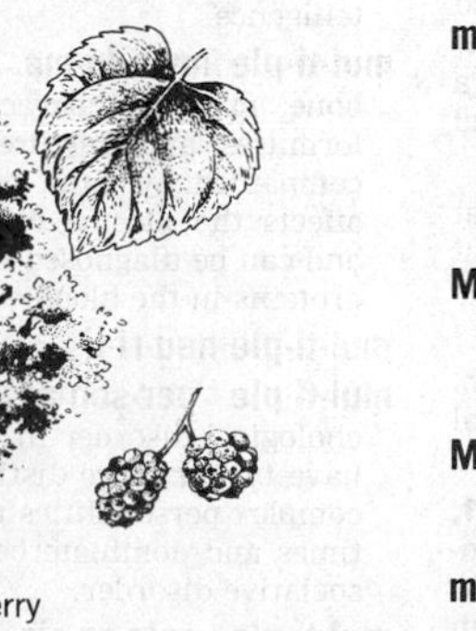

Mulberry

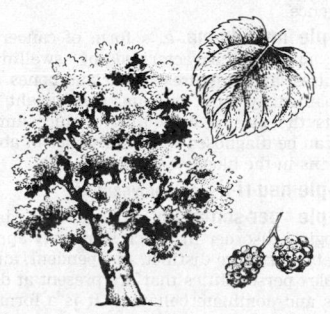

mul·ber·ry /múl bèrree/ *n.* (*plural* **-ries**) **1. TREES TREE WITH EDIBLE PURPLE FRUIT** a deciduous tree that grows in temperate regions with purplish edible fruit and leaves that are fed to silkworms. Genus: *Morus.* **2. PURPLE FRUIT** the fruit of the mulberry **3. COLORS PURPLE COLOR** a dark purple color with a tinge of red or gray ■ *adj.* COLORS **OF DARK PURPLE** of a dark purple color tinged with red or gray [Old English *mōrberie*, from *mōr-*, from Latin *morum* "mulberry," + BERRY]

mulch /múlch/ *n.* **SOIL COVERING** a protective covering of organic material laid over the soil around plants to prevent erosion, retain moisture, and sometimes enrich the soil ■ *vti.* (**mulched, mulch·ing, mulch·es**) **COVER SOIL WITH MULCH** to cover soil with mulch ○ *mulch with newspaper* [Mid-17thC. Origin uncertain: perhaps from Old English *melsc* "soft"; ultimately from an Indo-European base meaning "soft," which is also the ancestor of English *melt* and *mollify.*]

mulct /mulkt/ *vt.* (**mulct·ed, mulct·ing, mulcts**) (*archaic*) **1. FINE SOMEBODY** to fine somebody as a penalty **2. CHEAT SOMEBODY** to cheat somebody out of something ■ *n.* **PENALTY** a fine or penalty (*archaic*) [15thC. From Latin *mulctare*, from *mulcta* "fine."]

Mule

mule[1] /myool/ *n.* **1. CROSS BETWEEN A HORSE AND DONKEY** the offspring of a female horse and a male donkey **2. HYBRID PLANT OR ANIMAL** the sterile offspring of two closely related species of animal or plant **3. STUBBORN PERSON** somebody who is very stubborn (*informal*) **4. DRUG COURIER** somebody who transports illegal drugs for a dealer (*slang*) **5. SPINNING MACHINE** a machine that draws and spins cotton fibers into yarn and winds it onto spindles [Old English *mūl*, of uncertain origin: perhaps ultimately via Latin *mulus* from a pre-Latin language of the Mediterranean]

mule[2] /myool/ *n.* a backless slipper or shoe [Mid-16thC. Via French from Latin *mulleus (calceus)* "reddish-purple (shoe)." Ultimately from an Indo-European base meaning "having dark color," which is also the ancestor of English *mullet* and *melano-*.]

mule deer *n.* a large deer of western North America that has a grayish-brown coat, some white underparts, a black tail, and long ears. Latin name: *Odocoileus hemionus.*

mule·skin·ner /myōōl skìnnər/ *n.* a muleteer (*informal*)

mu·le·ta /moo láytə, -léttə/ (*plural* **-tas**) *n.* a short red cape attached to a stick that a matador uses instead of the full cape in the final stages of a bullfight [Mid-19thC. From Spanish, a diminutive of *mula* "female mule," from, ultimately, Latin *mulus* "mule" (see MULE[1]).]

mu·le·teer /myōōlə teer/ *n.* somebody whose occupation is driving mules [Mid-16thC. From French *muletier*, from *mulet*, a diminutive of Old French *mul* "mule," from Latin *mulus* (see MULE[1]).]

mu·ley /mōōllee, mōōlee, myōōlee/ *adj.* **HORNLESS** having no horns ■ *n.* (*plural* **-leys**) **HORNLESS ANIMAL** an animal that does not have horns [Late 16thC. Origin uncertain: probably from Irish *maol* or Welsh *moel* "bald"; ultimately from an Indo-European base meaning "to cut," which is also the ancestor of English *mite.*]

Mul·ha·cen /mōōla tháyn/ the highest peak on the Spanish mainland, situated in the Sierra Nevada, about 20 mi./32 km southeast of Granada. Height: 11,411 ft./3,478 m.

Mul·house /mə lōōz/ industrial city in Haut-Rhin Department, Alsace Region, northeastern France. Population: 108,357 (1990).

mu·li·eb·ri·ty /myōōlee ébbrətee/ *n.* (*literary*) **1. BEING A WOMAN** the condition of being a woman **2. CONVENTIONALLY WOMANLY QUALITIES** the qualities conventionally associated with women [Late 16thC. From Latin *muliebritas*, from, ultimately, *mulier* "woman."]

mul·ish /myōōlish/ *adj.* obstinate and unwilling to cooperate or listen to suggestions [Mid-18thC. Formed from MULE[1].] —**mul·ish·ly** *adv.* —**mul·ish·ness** *n.*

mull[1] /mul/ *n.* a period of deep thought [Mid-19thC. Origin uncertain: perhaps from obsolete and dialect *mull* "to pulverize"; ultimately from an Indo-European base meaning "to crush," which is also the ancestor of English *meal.*]

mull[2] /mul/ (**mulled, mull·ing, mulls**) *vt.* to heat, sweeten, and flavor wine, beer, or cider [Early 17thC. Origin unknown.]

mull[3] /mul/ *n.* soft cotton muslin used in dresses [Late 17thC. Shortening of Hindi *malmal.*]

mull[4] /mul/ *n.* nonacidic humus on a forest floor that eventually integrates into the soil beneath it [Early 20thC. From Danish *muld* "mold."]

mul·lah /múllə, mōōlə/ *n.* **1. MUSLIM SCHOLAR** in Iran and Central Asia, a Muslim cleric who specializes in the interpretation of Islamic religious law **2. MAN'S TITLE** used in Iran and Central Asia as a term of respect for a Muslim man who is thought to be very wise [Early 17thC. Via Persian or Urdu *mullā* from, ultimately, Arabic *mawlā.*]

mul·lein /múllin/ *n.* a tall plant that grows in Europe and Asia and has spikes of yellow, lavender, or white flowers and hairy leaves. Genus: *Verbascum.* [15thC. From Old French *moleine*, of uncertain origin: perhaps from a prehistoric Celtic word meaning "yellow."]

mul·ler /múllər/ *n.* a heavy smooth object made of stone, metal, wood, or glass, used for grinding paints or drugs on a flat surface [14thC. Origin uncertain: perhaps from Anglo-Norman *moldre* "to grind," from, ultimately, Latin *molere* (see MOLAR).]

Mül·ler /múllər, myōōlər/, **Paul Hermann** (1899–1965) Swiss chemist. He demonstrated the insecticidal properties of DDT, which was widely used from the 1940s to the 1970s.

Mül·le·ri·an mim·ic·ry /myoo leéree ən-/ *n.* mimicry in which two or more animals that are inedible or harmful assume one another's appearance so that predators will leave them alone [Late 19thC. Named for J. F. T. *Müller* (1821–97), the German-born Brazilian zoologist who described the phenomenon.]

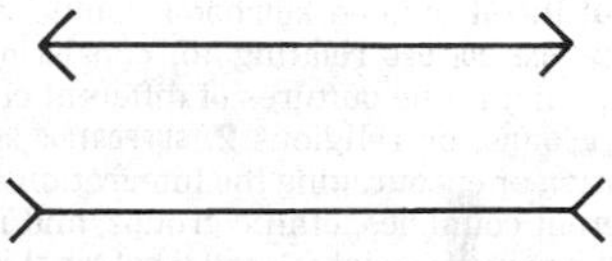

Müller-Lyer illusion

Mül·ler-Ly·er il·lu·sion /-līər-/ *n.* an optical illusion in which a line with inward-pointing arrows is seen as longer than one of equal length with outward-pointing arrows [Late 19thC. *Müller-Lyer* after Franz Carl Müller-Lyer, (1857–1916), German sociologist and philosopher.]

mul·let /múllət/ (*plural* **-lets** *or* **-let**) *n.* an edible spiny small-mouthed fish that lives in fresh water or salt water and is found all over the world. Family: Mugilidae and Mullidae. [15thC. From Old French *mulet*, from *mul*, from Latin *mullus* "red mullet," from Greek *mullos* "a sea-fish."]

mul·li·gan /múlligən/ *n.* a shot that, against the rules, a golfer allows an opponent to take again [Mid-20thC. Origin uncertain: probably from the name *Mulligan.*]

mul·li·gan stew *n.* a stew made from whatever suitable ingredients are at hand [*Mulligan* of uncertain origin: probably from the name *Mulligan*]

mul·li·ga·taw·ny /mùlligə táwnee/ (*plural* **-nies**) *n.* a spicy meat and vegetable soup originally from eastern India [Late 18thC. From Tamil *miḷaku-taṇṇi*, literally "pepper-water."]

Mul·li·ken /múllikən/, **Robert Sanderson** (1896–1986) U.S. chemist. He won a Nobel Prize in chemistry (1966) for his molecular studies. He helped develop the atomic bomb during World War II.

mul·lion /múllyən/ *n.* a vertical piece of stone, metal, or wood that divides the panes of a window or the panels of a screen [Mid-16thC. Variant (through the exchange of letters) of obsolete *monial* "mullion," from

Anglo-Norman *moinel*, literally "middle (part)," from *moien* "in the middle, median."] —**mul·lioned** *adj.*

Mul·lis /múlliss/, **Kary B.** (*b.* 1944) U.S. biochemist. He won a Nobel Prize in chemistry (1993) for developing a polymerase chain reaction.

mul·lite /mú lìt/ *n.* a colorless mineral consisting of crystalline aluminum silicate, able to withstand corrosion and very high temperatures [Early 20thC. Coined from *Mull*, name of an island in the Inner Hebrides, off the coast of Scotland, where the mineral was first identified + -ITE.]

mull o·ver *vti.* to consider something thoroughly

Mul·ro·ney /mul róonee/, **Brian** (*b.* 1939) Canadian statesman. As leader of the Progressive Party he was prime minister of Canada from 1984 to 1993. Full name **Martin Brian Mulroney**

mult- *prefix.* = **multi-**

Mul·tan /mòol taán/, **Multān** industrial town, district, and division of Punjab Province, eastern Pakistan. Population: 1,257,000 (1995).

multi- *prefix.* many, multiple, more than one or two ○ *multilevel* ○ *multiparous* [Via Old French from, ultimately, Latin *multus* "much, many" (source of English *multitude*)]

mul·ti·ac·cess /múltee áksess, mùltī-/ *adj.* relating to a computer system that allows several users to access it at the same time

mul·ti·cast·ing /múltee kàsting/ *n.* the process of sending out data across a network to a number of selected recipients at the same time —**mul·ti·cast** *vt.*

mul·ti·cel·lu·lar /mùltee séllyələr, mùltī-/, **mul·ti·celled** /mùltee séld, mùltī-/ *adj.* consisting of many cells —**mul·ti·cel·lu·lar·i·ty** /mùltee sellyə lérrətee, mùltī-/ *n.*

mul·ti·chan·nel com·mu·ni·ca·tion /mùltee chan nəl-, mùltī-/ *n.* the existence or use of two or more communication channels over the same path, e.g., in radio transmission or within a communication cable

mul·ti·col·or /múlti kùllər/, **mul·ti·col·ored** *adj.* **1.** OF DIFFERENT COLORS of many different colors **2.** PRINTING PRODUCING SEVERAL COLORS AT ONCE able to print more than one color at once

mul·ti·cul·tur·al /mùltee kúlchərəl, mùltī-/ *adj.* **1.** OF MORE THAN ONE CULTURE relating to, consisting of, or participating in the cultures of different countries, ethnic groups, or religions **2.** SUPPORTING INTEGRATION advocating or encouraging the integration of people of different countries, ethnic groups, and religions into all areas of society —**mul·ti·cul·tur·al·ism** *n.* —**mul·ti·cul·tur·al·ist** *n.*

mul·ti·di·men·sion·al /mùltee di ménshən'l, mùltī-/ *adj.* **1.** WITH MORE THAN THREE DIMENSIONS relating to or having more than three dimensions **2.** WITH MANY DIFFERENT ASPECTS having several different aims, qualities, or aspects —**mul·ti·di·men·sion·al·i·ty** /mùltee di mènshə nállətee, mùltī-/ *n.*

mul·ti·di·rec·tion·al /mùltee di rékshən'l, mùltī-/ *adj.* **1.** WITH SEVERAL AIMS OR CONCERNS having several aims or covering several aspects of a situation **2.** ELEC ENG COVERING SEVERAL DIFFERENT DIRECTIONS going, operating, or pointing in several different directions

mul·ti·dis·ci·pli·nar·y /mùltee díssipli nèrree, mùltī-/, **mul·ti·dis·ci·pline** /mùltee díssiplin, multi-/ *adj.* studying or using several specialized subjects or skills

mul·ti·eth·nic /mùltee éthnik, mùltī-/ *adj.* relating to or including several different ethnic groups

mul·ti·fac·et·ed /mùltee fássətəd, mùltī-/ *adj.* **1.** WITH DIVERSE QUALITIES with many different talents, qualities, or features **2.** WITH MANY FACETS having many facets or cut surfaces

mul·ti·fac·to·ri·al /mùltee fak táwree əl, mùltī-/, **mul·ti·fac·tor** /mùltee fáktər, mùltī-/ *adj.* **1.** WITH MULTIPLE FACTORS involving several different factors or elements **2.** DEPENDING ON MULTIPLE GENES relating to or used to describe inheritance depending on more than one gene. Height and weight are examples of characters determined by multifactorial inheritance. —**mul·ti·fac·to·ri·al·ly** *adv.*

mul·ti·fam·i·ly /mùltee fámmilee, mùltī-, -fámmlee/ *adj.* of or intended for use by several different families ○ *a multifamily house*

mul·ti·far·i·ous /mùltə fáiree əss/ *adj.* including parts, things, or people of many different kinds [Late 16thC. From Latin *multifarius* "varied, diverse," from *multi-* "many" + the suffix *-farius* "doing," a relative of *facere* "to do."] —**mul·ti·far·i·ous·ly** *adv.* —**mul·ti·far·i·ous·ness** *n.*

mul·ti·fid /múltə fìd/ *adj.* having many lobe-shaped segments

mul·ti·flo·ra rose /mùltə fláwrə-/ *n.* a wild climbing rose, native to Asia, that has clusters of small fragrant flowers. It is the origin of many cultivated roses. Latin name: *Rosa multiflora.*

mul·ti·flo·rous /mùltə fláwrəss/ *adj.* having many flowers [Mid-18thC. Formed from late Latin *multiflorus*, from Latin *multi-* "many" + the stem *flor-* "flower" (see FLORA).]

mul·ti·foil /múltə fòyl/ *n.* in architecture, a flat shape, opening, or decorative design with many lobes or scallops at its edges

mul·ti·form /múltə fàwrm/ *adj.* including or existing in many different shapes or kinds [Early 17thC. From French *multiforme* or Latin *multiformis.*] —**mul·ti·for·mi·ty** /mùltə fáwrmətee/ *n.*

mul·ti·gen·er·a·tion·al /mùltee jennə ráyshən'l, -ráyshnəl, mùltī-/ *adj.* including or affecting several generations

mul·ti·grade oil /mùltə grayd-/, **mul·ti·grade** *n.* engine oil that has a range of viscosities and is therefore effective over a range of temperatures

mul·ti·grav·i·da /mùlti grávvidə/ *n.* a pregnant woman who has had at least one previous pregnancy. ◊ **primigravida**

mul·ti·gym /múlti jìm/ *n.* an exercise apparatus with a range of weights, used for muscle toning [Late 20thC]

mul·ti·hull /múlti hùl/ *n.* a sailing vessel with two or more hulls

mul·ti·lat·er·al /mùltee láttərəl, mùltī-/ *adj.* **1.** INVOLVING SEVERAL PARTIES involving more than two parties or countries **2.** GEOM MANY-SIDED having many sides [Late 17thC. From medieval Latin *multilateralis*, from Latin *multi-* "many" + *lateralis* "belonging to the side" (see LATERAL).] —**mul·ti·lat·er·al·ly** *adv.*

mul·ti·lat·er·al·ism /mùltee láttərə lìzzəm, mùltī-/ *n.* the principle or belief that several nations should be cooperatively involved in the process of achieving something, especially nuclear disarmament [Early 20thC] —**mul·ti·lat·er·al·ist** *n., adj.*

mul·ti·lin·gual /mùltee líng gwəl, mùltī-/ *adj.* **1.** SPEAKING SEVERAL LANGUAGES able to speak more than two languages fluently **2.** INVOLVING SEVERAL LANGUAGES written in, expressed in, or using more than two languages —**mul·ti·lin·gual·ism** *n.* —**mul·ti·lin·gual·ly** *adv.*

mul·ti·loc·u·lar /mùltee lókyələr, mùltī-/ *adj.* BIOL consisting of or having several different chambers or cavities

mul·ti·me·di·a /mùltee meédee/ *n.* **1.** COMPUT SOUND AND VIDEO ON COMPUTERS programs, software, and hardware capable of using a wide variety of media such as film, video, and music as well as text and numbers **2.** EDUC USE OF MEDIA IN TEACHING the use of film, video, and music in addition to more traditional teaching materials and methods (*often used before a noun*) **3.** ARTS USE OF VARIOUS MATERIALS AND MEDIA the use in art, especially the plastic arts, of different kinds of materials and media such as television, sound, and text (*often used before a noun*) **4.** MARKETING USE OF ALL COMMUNICATIONS MEDIA the use in advertising of a combination of media such as television, radio, and the press (*often used before a noun*)

mul·ti·me·ter /múlti meétər/ *n.* an instrument that reads and measures the values of several different electrical parameters such as current, voltage, and resistance

mul·ti·mil·lion·aire /mùltee millyə náir, mùltī-/ *n.* somebody with money or assets worth several million dollars

mul·ti·na·tion·al /mùltee náshən'l, -náshnəl/ *adj.* **1.** OPERATING IN SEVERAL COUNTRIES operating or having investments in several countries **2.** INVOLVING PEOPLE FROM SEVERAL COUNTRIES relating to or including people from more than two countries ■ *n.* LARGE COMPANY OPERATING IN SEVERAL COUNTRIES a large company that operates or has investments in several different countries —**mul·ti·na·tion·al·ism** *n.*

mul·ti·no·mi·al /mùlti nṓmee əl, múlti-/ *n., adj.* MATH = **polynomial**

mul·ti·nu·cle·ar /mùltee nóoklee ər, mùltī-/, **mul·ti·nu·cle·ate** /mùltee nóoklee ət, mùltī-/, **mul·ti·nu·cle·at·ed** /mùltee nóoklee àytəd, mùltī-/ *adj.* having more than two nuclei

mul·ti·pack /múlti pàk/ *n.* a package that contains more than two of a particular item of consumer products e.g., batteries, and is sold at a reduced price

mul·tip·a·ra /mul típpərə/ (*plural* **-rae** /-típpəree/ *or* **-ras**) *n.* a woman who has borne a live child from each of two or more pregnancies [Mid-19thC. From the feminine form of modern Latin *multiparus* (see MULTIPAROUS).]

mul·tip·a·rous /mul típpərəss/ *adj.* **1.** BIOL PRODUCING SEVERAL YOUNG AT ONE TIME used to describe an animal, especially a mammal, that normally gives birth to two or more offspring at one time **2.** MED HAVING BORNE AT LEAST TWO CHILDREN used to describe a woman who has borne a child from each of two or more pregnancies, each pregnancy lasting for at least 20 weeks [Mid-17thC. From modern Latin *multiparus*, from Latin *multi-* "many" + *-parus* "-bearing" (see -PAROUS).] —**mul·ti·par·i·ty** /mùlti pérrətee/ *n.*

mul·ti·par·tite /mùlti paár tìt/, **mul·ti·par·ty** /múltə paártee/ *adj.* **1.** POL INVOLVING SEVERAL PARTIES involving more than two parties or countries **2.** WITH MANY SECTIONS divided into many sections

mul·ti·path /múlti pàth/ *adj.* relating to or used to describe television or radio signals that use more than one route from the transmitter to the receiver, causing picture or sound distortion

mul·ti·plane /múlti plàyn/ *n.* an aircraft with more than one pair of wings

mul·ti·ple /múltip'l/ *adj.* INVOLVING SEVERAL THINGS involving or including several things, people, or parts ■ *n.* **1.** MATH NUMBER DIVISIBLE BY ANOTHER a number that can be divided exactly by a particular smaller number **2.** TELECOM SYSTEM WITH MANY POSSIBLE ACCESS POINTS a system of wiring so arranged that a group of communication lines are accessible at a number of points [Mid-17thC. Via French from late Latin *multiplus*, an alteration of Latin *multiplex* (see MULTIPLEX).]

mul·ti·ple al·leles *npl.* three or more different forms of a gene. Any two of these forms can be present in a normal diploid cell or organism.

mul·ti·ple-choice *adj.* requiring the choice of the correct answer or answers out of several possible suggested answers ○ *a multiple-choice question*

mul·ti·ple fac·tor *n.* a polygene (*dated*)

mul·ti·ple fis·sion *n.* a form of asexual reproduction occurring in some single-celled organisms such as malaria parasites in which a single parent cell breaks up to yield numerous daughter cells. The nucleus of the parental cell divides to form many daughter nuclei, then the cytoplasm divides to form the daughter cells.

mul·ti·ple fruit *n.* a fruit such as a pineapple or fig that is produced from the ovaries of several flowers that merge to form a single structure

mul·ti·ple in·tel·li·genc·es *npl.* the several independent forms of human intelligence that exist, according to a recent psychological theory. They include verbal, quantitative, spatial, musical, kinesthetic, interpersonal, and intrapersonal intelligence.

mul·ti·ple my·e·lo·ma *n.* a form of cancer of the bone marrow characterized by swellings, deformities, and fractures of various bones and accompanied by pain, anemia, and weight loss. It affects the plasma cells that produce antibodies and can be diagnosed by the presence of abnormal proteins in the blood.

mul·ti·ple neu·ri·tis *n.* = **polyneuritis**

mul·ti·ple per·son·al·i·ty *n.* a very rare psychological disorder in which somebody appears to have two or more distinct, independent, and often complex personalities that are present at different times and dominate behavior. It is a form of dissociative disorder.

mul·ti·ple scle·ro·sis *n.* a serious progressive disease of the central nervous system, occurring mainly in young adults and thought to be caused by a malfunction of the immune system. It leads to the loss of myelin in the brain or spinal cord and causes muscle weakness, poor eyesight, slow speech, and some inability to move.

mul·ti·ple star *n.* a group of three or more stars, usually with the same gravitational center, that appears as one star to the naked eye

mul·ti·ple store *n. U.K.* = **chain store**

mul·ti·plet /múltiplət/ *n.* **1. SPECTRAL LINE** a line in a spectrum made up of two or more component lines, caused by slight variations in atomic or molecular energy levels **2. GROUP OF RELATED ELEMENTARY PARTICLES** a group of elementary particles such as nucleons that have a different electric charge but have otherwise similar properties [Early 20thC. Coined from MULTIPLE, on the model of "doublet," "triplet."]

mul·ti·plex /múlti plèks/ *n.* **1.** CINEMA **MOVIE THEATER COMPLEX** a large movie theater complex that has several separate units with screens **2.** ELECTRON ENG **MULTIPLE TRANSMISSION** the simultaneous transmission of two or more signals along one communications channel **3.** ELECTRON ENG **SYSTEM FOR SIMULTANEOUS TRANSMISSION** a transmission system that carries two or more individual channels over a single communication path ■ *adj.* **COMPLEX** involving or including several different things, parts, or factors ■ *vti.* **(-plexed, -plex·ing, -plex·es)** ELECTRON ENG **SEND BY MULTIPLEX** to send two or more messages or signals along one communications channel at the same time [Mid-16thC. From Latin, formed from *multi-* "many" + *-plex* "-fold" (see -PLEX).]

mul·ti·plex·er /múlti plèksər/, **mul·ti·plex·or** *n.* **1.** COMPUT **DEVICE FOR ROUTING DATA** a device for sending several different data streams down a single communications line and for splitting a received multiple stream into component parts **2.** VIDEO **FILM-TO-VIDEO SYSTEM** a device for transferring projected film to video

mul·ti·pli·cand /mùltəpli kánd/ *n.* a number that is multiplied by another number **(multiplier)**. The number 2 is the muliplicand in the statement 2 × 4 = 8. [Late 16thC. From medieval Latin *multiplicandus*, the gerundive of Latin *multiplicare* (see MULTIPLY).]

mul·tip·li·cate /múltipli kàyt/ *adj.* containing many elements or parts [15thC. From Latin *multiplicat-*, the past participle stem of *multiplicare* (see MULTIPLY).]

mul·ti·pli·ca·tion /mùltipli káysh'n/ *n.* **1.** MATH **ARITHMETIC OPERATION** a mathematical operation, symbolized by ×, that for integers is equivalent to adding a number to itself a specified number of times **2.** MATH **MATHEMATICAL OPERATION** a mathematical operation equivalent to multiplication extended to expressions that are not numbers, e.g., functions or matrices **3. INCREASE** a marked increase in the number or amount of something ○ *a multiplication of claims.* **4.** BIOL **REPRODUCTION** the act or process of reproduction in animals, plants, or people —**mul·ti·pli·ca·tion·al** *adj.*

mul·ti·pli·ca·tion sign *n.* the symbol × or ·, used to indicate that one number is to be multiplied by another

mul·ti·pli·ca·tive /mùltə plíkətiv, múltəpli kàytiv/ *adj.* **1. INCREASING** likely to increase, or capable of increasing **2.** MATH **INVOLVING MULTIPLICATION** involving or relating to multiplication —**mul·ti·pli·ca·tive·ly** *adv.*

mul·ti·plic·i·ty /mùltə plíssətee/ (*plural* **-ties**) *n.* **1. GREAT VARIETY** a considerable number or variety ○ *Her style was shaped by a multiplicity of influences.* **2. COMPLEXITY** the state of being multiple or varied **3.** PHYS **NUMBER OF MOLECULAR ENERGY LEVELS** the number of energy levels of a molecule, atom, or nucleus that result from interactions between angular momenta **4.** PHYS **PARTICLES IN A MULTIPLET** the number of elementary particles that form a multiplet [15thC. From late Latin *multiplicatus*, from Latin *multiplic-*, the stem of *multiplex* (see MULTIPLEX).]

mul·ti·pli·er /múltə plīr/ *n.* **1. SOMEBODY OR SOMETHING THAT MULTIPLIES** somebody who or something that multiplies or increases **2.** MATH **MULTIPLYING NUMBER** the number by which another number **(multiplicand)** is multiplied, e.g., the number 4 is the multiplier in the statement 2 × 4 = 8 **3.** PHYS = **photomultiplier**

mul·ti·ply[1] /múltə plī/ **(-plied, -ply·ing, -plies)** *v.* **1.** *vti.* MATH **PERFORM MULTIPLICATION** to perform the mathematical operation of multiplication **2.** *vti.* **INCREASE IN AMOUNT** to increase or make something increase by a considerable number, amount, or degree **3.** *vi.* BIOL **BREED** to increase in number by breeding [12thC. Via French *multiplier* from Latin *multiplicare*, from the stem *multiplic-* (see MULTIPLICITY).] —**mul·ti·pli·a·ble** *adj.* —**mul·ti·plic·a·ble** /mùltə plíkəb'l/ *adj.*

mul·ti·ply[2] /múltə plī/ *adv.* many times or in many different ways

mul·ti·ply *adj.* having more than one layer ○ *multiply tissues*

mul·ti·point /múlti pòynt/ *n.* = **multiple** *n.* 2

mul·ti·po·lar /mùltee pṓlər, mùltī-/ *adj.* **1. WITH MORE THAN TWO MAJOR POWERS** having several countries that are centers of power or influence **2.** ANAT **WITH MANY CONNECTIONS** used to describe a nerve cell with more than two of the connecting fibers that carry impulses into the cell body **3. WITH MULTIPLE POLES** having several poles —**mul·ti·po·lar·i·ty** /mùltee pō lérrətee, mùltī-/ *n.*

mul·ti·port /múlti pàwrt/ *adj.* used to describe a computer network with more than one point of access or connection

mul·ti·po·tent /mul típpətənt/, **mul·ti·po·ten·tial** /mùltee pə ténshəl, mùltī-/ *adj.* capable of developing into various types of cells, depending on the surrounding conditions

mul·ti·pro·cess·ing /mùltee pró sèssing, mùltī-/ *n.* the operation of a computer in which two or more processing units work on separate parts of the same program or set of instructions in order to reduce processing time

mul·ti·pro·ces·sor /mùlti pró sèssər/ *n.* a system of linked central processing units on which two or more programs can be run simultaneously by parallel processing

mul·ti·pronged /mùltee prόngd, mùltī-/ *adj.* **1. WITH MULTIPLE ELEMENTS** involving several different approaches or elements **2. WITH MULTIPLE PRONGS** having several prongs

mul·ti·pur·pose /mùltee púrpəss, mùltī-/ *adj.* designed or able to be used for several different purposes

mul·ti·ra·cial /mùltee ráysh'l, mùltī-/ *adj.* relating to, made up of, or involving people from several races ○ *a multiracial society* —**mul·ti·ra·cial·ly** *adv.*

mul·ti·ra·cial·ism /mùltee ráysh'l ìzzəm, mùltī-/ *n.* the principle or practice of ensuring that people of various races are fully integrated into a society —**mul·ti·ra·cial·ist** *adj.*

mul·ti·sense /múlti sèns/ *adj.* having many different meanings

mul·ti·sen·so·ry /mùlti sénsəree/ *adj.* relating to or involving two or more of the senses

mul·ti·serv·ice /mùlti súrviss/ *adj.* **1. WITH MULTIPLE SERVICES** offering more than one type of service **2.** MIL **OF MULTIPLE MILITARY FORCES** relating to or involving members of the different branches of the armed forces

mul·ti·sport /múlti spàwrt/, **mul·ti·sports** *adj.* **1. FOR MULTIPLE SPORTS** designed for or involving a variety of sports **2. SKILLED IN MULTIPLE SPORTS** trained, skilled, or competing in a variety of sporting disciplines

mul·ti·stage /múlti stàyj/ *adj.* **1. IN SEVERAL STAGES** divided into or taking place in several separate stages **2. WITH SEVERAL SOURCES OF MOTION** having several propulsion units, each of which operates sequentially ○ *a multistage rocket*

mul·ti·state /múlti stàyt/ *adj.* relating to or involving several states ○ *a multistate study of brain cancer rates*

mul·ti·sto·ry /múlti stàwree/, **mul·ti·sto·ried** /múlti stàwreed/ *adj.* having several stories

mul·ti·task·ing /múlti tàsking/ *n.* the simultaneous management of two or more distinct tasks by a computer

mul·ti·ton /múlti tùn/ *adj.* weighing or capable of carrying several tons [Mid-20thC]

mul·ti·track /múlti tràk/ *adj.* **1. RECORDING ON SEPARATE TRACKS** using, capable of, or produced by the separate recording of several different tracks **2. WITH MULTIPLE TOPICS** involving more than one topic or set of simultaneous discussions ○ *multitrack negotiations* **3.** EDUC **FOR STUDENTS OF VARYING ABILITY** having more than one set of courses for students according to their abilities or interests

mul·ti·tude /múlti tood/ *n.* **1. CROWD** a large crowd of people **2. LARGE NUMBER** a very large number of things or people (*often used in the plural*) **3. MAJORITY** the majority of ordinary people [14thC. Via French from Latin *multitudo*, from *multus* "much, many" (see MULTI-).]

mul·ti·tu·di·nous /mùlti tóod'nəss/ *adj.* **1. VERY NUMEROUS** very great in number **2. FULL OF VARIETY** with many parts, great in number, or existing in many varieties **3. CROWDED** crowded with people (*archaic*) [Early 17thC. Formed from Latin *multitudin-*, the stem of *multitudo* (see MULTITUDE).] —**mul·ti·tu·di·nous·ly** *adv.* —**mul·ti·tud·in·ous·ness** *n.*

mul·ti·us·er /mùlti yóozər/ *adj.* capable of being used by several people at the same time

mul·ti·va·lent /mùltee váylənt, mùltī-/ *adj.* **1.** = **polyvalent** *adj.* 1 **2. WITH MULTIPLE MEANINGS** with several meanings or values —**mul·ti·va·lence** *n.*

mul·ti·var·i·ate /mùltee váiree ət, mùltī-/, **mul·ti·var·i·a·ble** /mùltee váiree əb'l/ *adj.* used to describe or relating to a statistical distribution that involves a number of random but often related variables

mul·ti·ver·si·ty /mùlti vúrsətee/ (*plural* **-ties**) *n.* a university that has many affiliated or associated institutions such as research centers and colleges [Mid-20thC. Coined from MULTI- + UNIVERSITY.]

mul·ti·vi·bra·tor /mùlti vī bráytər/ *n.* an oscillating electronic circuit consisting of pairs of tubes, transistors, or other components, whose oscillation is sustained by coupling the output of one to the input of the other

mul·ti·vi·ta·min /mùlti vítəmin/ *n.* **PILL CONTAINING SEVERAL VITAMINS** a tablet or capsule containing a range of vitamins and sometimes minerals ■ *adj.* **CONTAINING SEVERAL VITAMINS** containing a range of vitamins and sometimes minerals [Mid-20thC]

mul·ti·vol·ume /mùltee vóllyəm, mùltī-/ *adj.* published in several volumes

mul·ti·year /múlti yeer/ *adj.* existing, valid, or taking place over several years ○ *a multiyear agreement* [Late 20thC]

Mult·no·mah Falls /mult nṓ maar fáwlz/ falls on Larch Mountain in northwestern Oregon, east of Portland on a Columbia River tributary. Height: 620 ft./189 m.

mul·tum in par·vo /mòol tòom in paár vṑ/ *n.* the quality or fact of containing, implying, or expressing much in a little space or time [From Latin, "much in little"]

mum[1] /mum/ *adj.* **SILENT** saying nothing, especially about a sensitive piece of information (*informal*) ■ *interj.* **KEEP QUIET** used to tell somebody to keep quiet [15thC. An imitation of the sound made when the lips are closed.]

mum[2] /mum/ **(mumming, mums)** *vi.* **1. ACT IN A PLAY** to act in a masked folk play or mime **2. CELEBRATE IN DISGUISE** to participate in festivities wearing a mask or disguise [Mid-16thC. From French *momer* "to act in a mime" (see MUMMER).]

mum[3] /mum/ *n.* PLANTS a chrysanthemum (*informal*) [Late 19thC. Shortening.]

mum[4] /mum/ *n. U.K.* = **mom** (*informal*)

mum[5] /mum/ *n.* a strong beer of German origin [Early 17thC. From German *Mumme*.]

Mum·bai /mòom bī/ capital of Maharashtra State and the largest city in India, situated on the Arabian Sea. Population: 9,925,891 (1991). Former name **Bombay**

mum·ble /múmb'l/ *vti.* **(-bled, -bling, -bles) 1. MUTTER** to speak or utter something quietly and unclearly without opening the mouth very much **2. CHEW WITH DIFFICULTY** to chew food with difficulty ■ *n.* **INDISTINCT SPEECH** an indistinct and quiet utterance [14thC. Formed from earlier English *mum* "to make an indistinct sound with closed lips." Also, probably thought to be imitative of the sound of mumbling.] —**mum·bler** *n.* —**mum·bling** *adj.* —**mum·bling·ly** *adv.* —**mum·bly** *adj.*

mum·ble·ty-peg /múmb'ltee-/, **mum·ble-the-peg** *n.* a game in which players flip a knife, trying to stick the blade into the ground, usually while standing in various prescribed positions [*Mumble* in the obsolete sense "to bite or chew (as if) toothlessly"; originally the unsuccessful player had to pull a peg out of the ground by biting it]

mum·bo jum·bo /mùmbō júmbō/ *n.* **1. CONFUSING LANGUAGE** complicated and confusing language, especially technical jargon, that is difficult to understand (*informal*) **2. WORTHLESS RELIGIOUS BELIEF OR RITUAL** religious beliefs, language, or rituals that appear pointless or meaningless to the speaker (*disapproving; offensive in some contexts*) **3. OBJECT BELIEVED SUPERNATURAL** an object or effigy that is believed to hold supernatural powers [Mid-18thC. Origin uncertain: perhaps from Mande *mama* "ancestor" + *dyumbo* "pompom-wearer"; originally applied to a masked figure worshipped by the Mande peoples of West Africa.]

mu mes·on *n.* = muon

mumm *vt.* = mum[2]

mum·mer /múmmər/ *n.* **1.** SOMEBODY WHO CELEBRATES IN DISGUISE somebody who participates in festivities wearing a mask or disguise **2.** ACTOR one of a group of actors in a folk play or mime show **3.** MIME ARTIST an artist who performs in mimes **4.** ACTOR an actor (*humorous*) [15thC. From Old French *momeur*, from *momer* "to act in a mime," perhaps ultimately of prehistoric Germanic origin.]

mum·mer·y /múmməree/ (*plural* **-ies**) *n.* **1.** PERFORMANCE BY MUMMERS a performance by a group of mummers **2.** SHOWY CEREMONY a showy or hypocritical ceremony (*disapproving*)

mum·mi·chog /múmmi chòg/ *n.* a North American fish in the killifish family that lives in salt marshes in Atlantic coastal regions and can bury itself in mud when the tide recedes. Latin name: *Fundulus heteroclitus*. [Late 18thC. From Narragansett *moamitteaug*.]

mum·mi·fy /múmmə fī/ (**-fied, -fy·ing, -fies**) *v.* **1.** *vt.* PRESERVE CORPSE FOR BURIAL to preserve the corpse of a person or animal for burial by embalming it and wrapping it in cloth **2.** *vti.* SHRIVEL to dry out and shrivel, or cause something to dry out and shrivel [Early 17thC. Formed from MUMMY[1] on the model of French *momifier*.] —**mum·mi·fi·ca·tion** /mùmməfi káysh'n/ *n.*

Mummy: Detail of wall painting in the tomb of Sennudjem, Deir-el-Medinah, near Luxor, Egypt (1295–1186B.C.)

mum·my[1] /múmmee/ (*plural* **-mies**) *n.* **1.** PRESERVED BODY the body of a person or animal that has been embalmed and wrapped in cloth, especially as was the custom in ancient Egypt **2.** NATURALLY PRESERVED BODY the body of an organism preserved by natural processes, e.g., by burial in peat or ice [Early 17thC. Via Old French *momie* from, ultimately, Arabic *mūmiyā* "embalmed body," perhaps formed from Persian *mūm* "wax."]

mum·my[2] /múmmee/ (*plural* **-mies**) *n. U.K.* = **mommy** (*usually used by or to children*) [Late 18thC. Dialectal variant of MAMMY.]

mumps /mumps/ *n.* an acute contagious disease, usually affecting children, that causes a fever with swelling of the salivary glands, sometimes also affecting the pancreas and ovaries or testes. It is caused by a virus and can be prevented through vaccination. It may cause sterility if contracted by a man. (*takes a singular or plural verb*) [Late 16thC. Plural of the obsolete noun *mump* "grimace," an imitation of the sounds made with a closed mouth.]

mu·mu *n.* = muumuu

munch /munch/ (**munched, munch·ing, munch·es**) *vti.* to chew food purposefully, usually with visible movements of the jaw and sometimes with a crunching sound [14thC. Origin uncertain: perhaps via Old French *mangier* "to eat" from Latin *manducare* "to chew."] —**munch·er** *n.*

Munch /mòóngk/, **Edvard** (1863–1944) Norwegian painter. His work, suffused with melancholy and anguish, most famously in *The Scream* (1893), anticipates expressionism.

Edvard Munch

Mün·chau·sen syn·drome /mún chowz'n-/ *n.* a psychological disorder in which somebody pretends to have a serious illness in order to undergo testing or treatment or be admitted to a hospital. In Münchausen syndrome by proxy, medical attention is sought for somebody else, who is sometimes harmed by attempts to create an illness to warrant such attention. [From Baron *Münchausen*, hero of exaggerated traveler's tales in a book (1785) by R. E. Raspe.]

munch·ies /múncheez/ *npl.* **1.** SNACK FOOD snack food, especially of the kind served with drinks at a party (*slang*) **2.** HUNGER FOR SNACKS a craving for snack food (*informal*)

munch·kin /múnchkin/ *n.* **1.** SMALL PERSON a small, sweet-natured, and harmless person **2.** CHILD a small child (*informal*) **3.** INSIGNIFICANT PERSON an insignificant person who keeps busy with trival matters (*informal*) [Late 20thC. From the name of creatures invented by L. Frank Baum in *The Wizard of Oz* (1900).]

Mun·cie /múnssee/ city in eastern Indiana, on the White River, southwest of Fort Wayne and northeast of Indianapolis. Population: 69,058 (1996).

Mun·da /mòóndə/ *n.* **1.** LANG INDIAN LANGUAGE GROUP one of the four major Indian language groups spoken thoughout the Indian subcontinent. Over 5 million people speak a Munda language. **2.** PEOPLES SPEAKER OF MUNDA somebody who speaks Munda as a native language [Mid-19thC. From Munda *Muṇḍā*.] —**Mun·da** *adj.*

mun·dane /mun dáyn/ *adj.* **1.** ORDINARY commonplace, not unusual, and often boring **2.** OF THIS WORLD relating to matters of this world [15thC. Via French *mondain* from late Latin *mundanus*, from Latin *mundus* "world."] —**mun·dane·ly** *adv.* —**mun·dane·ness** *n.*

Mun·de·lein /múndə lìn/ village in northeastern Illinois, southwest of North Chicago, a northwestern suburb of Chicago. Population: 27,043 (1996).

mung bean /múng-/ *n.* **1.** FOOD GREEN OR YELLOW BEAN a small green or yellow bean that is dried, sometimes split, and used in Indian cooking. It is also germinated to produce bean sprouts. **2.** PLANTS BEAN PLANT a bean plant native to eastern Asia that produces mung beans and is used as food for livestock. Latin name: *Vigna radiata*. [*Mung* from Hindi *mūng*]

mun·go /múng gō/ (*plural* **-gos**), **mon·go** /móng-/ (*plural* **-gos**), **mon·goe** *n.* a cheap fabric made from waste wool and rags [Mid-19thC. Origin uncertain: perhaps formed from dialectal *mong* "mixture," possibly on the model of the Scottish forename *Mungo*.]

Mun·go, Lake /múng gō/ dry lake in western New South Wales, Australia. It is part of Mungo National Park.

mu·ni /myòónee/ (*plural* **-nis**) *n.* a municipal bond (*informal*) [Late 20thC. Shortening.]

Mu·nich /myòónikh/ capital and largest city in the state of Bavaria, southeastern Germany. Population: 1,251,100 (1994).

Mu·nich Con·fer·ence *n.* a meeting concerning Germany's occupation of Czechoslovakia in 1938, at which Western leaders agreed to the division of Czechoslovakia after receiving Hitler's assurances that he would take no more land

mu·nic·i·pal /myoo níssəp'l/ *adj.* **1.** OF A MUNICIPALITY relating to a town, city, or region that has its own local government **2.** POL RELATING TO STATE'S INTERNAL AFFAIRS relating to a nation's or state's internal affairs (*archaic*) ■ *n.* FIN = **municipal bond** [Mid-16thC. Directly or via French from Latin *municipalis*, from the stem *municip-* "holder of a civic office," from *munus* "gift, service, duty" (see MUNIFICENT) + *capere* "to take" (see CAPABLE).] —**mu·nic·i·pal·ly** *adv.*

mu·nic·i·pal bond *n.* a bond or security issued by a city or other local government, usually to pay for public improvements

mu·nic·i·pal·i·ty /myoo nìssə pállətee/ (*plural* **-ties**) *n.* **1.** PLACE WITH OWN LOCAL GOVERNMENT a city, town, or other region that has its own local government **2.** MEMBERS OF LOCAL GOVERNMENT the appointed or elected members of a local government

WORD KEY: SYNONYMS

See Synonyms at ***city***.

mu·nic·i·pal·ize /myoo níssəp'l īz/ (**-ized, -iz·ing, -iz·es**) *vt.* **1.** BRING SOMETHING UNDER MUNICIPAL CONTROL to bring something such as a public service or area of land under the ownership or control of a city, town, or region with its own local government **2.** MAKE PLACE A MUNICIPALITY to grant a city, town, or region powers of government on local matters —**mu·nic·i·pal·i·za·tion** /myoo nìssəp'li záysh'n/ *n.*

mu·nif·i·cent /myoo nífiss'nt/ *adj.* **1.** VERY GENEROUS very generous in giving **2.** AMPLE characterized by generosity ○ ***a munificent award*** [Late 16thC. From Latin, formed from *munificus* "generous," from *munus* "gift, service, duty" (source also of English *municipal* and *remunerate*).] —**mu·nif·i·cence** *n.* —**mu·nif·i·cent·ly** *adv.*

WORD KEY: SYNONYMS

See Synonyms at ***generous***.

mu·ni·ment /myòóneemənt/ *n.* MIL PROTECTION something providing defense or protection (*archaic*) ■ **mu·ni·ments** *npl.* LAW DOCUMENTS THAT SUPPORT A CLAIM documents by which a claim to property or rights is supported, e.g., the title deeds to land [15thC. From Latin *munimentum* "fortification," from *munire* "to fortify" (see MUNITION). The meaning "title deeds" developed in medieval Latin.]

mu·ni·tion /myoo nísh'n/ *vt.* (**-tioned, -tion·ing, -tions**) SUPPLY WITH WEAPONS to supply somebody or a group with arms and ammunition ■ **mu·ni·tions** *npl.* MILITARY SUPPLIES military supplies such as weapons and ammunition [Early 16thC. Via French from the Latin stem *munition-*, from *munire* "to fortify," from *moenia* "defensive walls."] —**mu·ni·tion·er** *n.*

mun·nion /múnnyən/ *n.* a mullion between panes of glass in a window (*archaic*) [Late 16thC. Alteration of obsolete *monial* (see MULLION).]

Mu·ñoz Ma·rín /moo nŏz ma rín/, **Luis** (1898–1980) Puerto Rican statesman. He was the first elected governor (1949–65), after Puerto Rico's status changed to that of a commonwealth (1952).

Mun·ro /mən rṓ/, **Alice** (*b.* 1931) Canadian writer, known for her short stories of rural Ontario life. Pseudonym of **Alice Anne Laidlaw**

Mun·see /múnsee/ (*plural* **-see** *or* **-sees**), **Mun·si** (*plural* **-si** *or* **-sis**) *n.* **1.** LANG ALGONQUIAN LANGUAGE an Algonquian language spoken by the Delaware peoples in New Jersey and New York **2.** PEOPLES SPEAKER OF MUNSEE somebody who speaks Munsee as a native language —**Mun·see** *adj.*

Mun·ster[1] *n.* = **Muenster**

Mun·ster[2] /múnstər/ town in northwestern Indiana, near the border with Illinois, southwest of Gary, part of the suburban area of Chicago. Population: 20,438 (1996).

mun·tin /múnt'n/ *n.* a strip of wood or metal that separates and holds in place the panes of a window [Early 17thC. Alteration of Old French *montant* "upright," from the present participle of *monter* (see MOUNT).]

munt·jac /múnt jàk/ (*plural* **-jacs** *or* **-jac**), **munt·jak** (*plural* **-jaks** *or* **-jak**) *n.* a small deer, native to Southeast Asia, that has a reddish-brown coat, a cry like a dog's bark, and small antlers. Genus: *Muntiacus*. [Late 18thC. From Sundanese (an Austronesian language of western Java) *minchek* and Malay *menjangan* "deer."]

mu·on /myóò ón/ *n.* an elementary particle with a mass about 200 times that of an electron. It is a lepton with a negative charge and a half-life of two-millionths of a second. [Mid-20thC. Contraction of MU MESON.] —**mu·on·ic** /myoo ónnik/ *adj.*

mu·on neu·tri·no *n.* a lepton that exists in association with a muon. It has zero rest mass and no charge.

Mu·rad IV /myòór ad/ (1609–40) Arabian sultan. He succeeded Mustafa I as sultan of the Ottoman Empire (1623–40).

mu·ral /myòórəl/ *n.* PAINTING PAINTING ON WALL a usually large picture painted directly onto an interior or exterior wall ■ *adj.* OF WALLS applied to or relating to a wall [Mid-16thC. Via French from Latin *muralis*, from *murus* "wall" (source also of English *immure*).] —**mu·ral·ist** *n.*

mu·ram·ic ac·id /myoŏ rámmik-/ *n.* an amino sugar found in the cell walls of blue-green algae. Formula: $C_9H_{17}NO_7$. [*Muramic* coined from Latin *murus* "wall" + AMINE + -IC]

Mu·ra·sa·ki /moŏr aa saákee/, **Shikibu** (978?–1031?) Japanese court lady and writer. She is known for *The Tale of Genji* (?1010), considered one of the world's first novels.

Mur·cia /múrssee ə/ capital of Murcia Province and Murcia Region, southeastern Spain. Population: 344,904 (1995).

mur·der /múrdər/ *n.* LAW **CRIME OF KILLING SOMEBODY** the crime of killing another person deliberately and not in self-defense or with any other extenuating circumstance recognized by law ■ *v.* (**-dered, -der·ing, -ders**) **1.** *vti.* LAW **KILL SOMEBODY ILLEGALLY** to kill another person deliberately and not in self-defense or with any other extenuating circumstance recognized by law **2.** *vt.* **KILL SOMEBODY BRUTALLY** to kill somebody with great violence and brutality **3.** *vt.* **DESTROY** to put an end to or destroy something (*slang*) ○ *The fire murdered their chances of selling the house.* **4.** *vt.* **SPOIL** to spoil something such as a song or a piece of writing by performing it badly or changing it (*slang*) **5.** *vt.* SPORTS **DEFEAT COMPLETELY** to defeat a person or team completely, especially in a sporting contest (*slang*) [Old English *morþor*. Ultimately from an Indo-European word that is also the ancestor of English *mortal*, *moribund*, and *ambrosia*. Later reinforced by Old French *murdre*, from prehistoric Germanic.] —**mur·der·er** *n.* —**mur·der·ess** *n.* ◇ **get away with murder** to escape punishment for or detection of wrongdoing ◇ **something is murder** something is very difficult or unpleasant, requiring great effort or hardship (*slang*) ○ *Driving in this morning was murder.*

WORD KEY: SYNONYMS

See Synonyms at ***kill***.

mur·der·ee /mùrdə reé/ *n.* a victim of murder

mur·der·ous /múrdərəss/ *adj.* **1. LIKELY TO MURDER** capable of, guilty of, or likely to commit murder **2. LIKELY TO CAUSE DEATH** violent and likely to result in bloodshed or murder **3. DIFFICULT** very difficult, unpleasant, or dangerous (*informal*) —**mur·der·ous·ly** *adv.* —**mur·der·ous·ness** *n.*

Express Newspapers

Dame Iris Murdoch

Mur·doch /múr dok/, **Dame Iris** (1919–99) Irish-born British novelist and philosopher. Her novels are noted for their thoughtful exploration of moral and philosophical problems. She is author of *A Severed Head* (1961) and the Booker Prize-winning *The Sea, the Sea* (1978). Full name **Dame Jean Iris Murdoch**

Mur·doch, Rupert (*b.* 1931) Australian-born U.S. media proprietor. He extended his family newspaper empire to control a global network of media organizations. Full name **Keith Rupert Murdoch**

Popperfoto

Rupert Murdoch

mu·re·in /myoŏree in, -reen/ *n.* = **peptidoglycan** [Mid-20thC. Coined from Latin *murus* "wall" (see MURAL) on the model of PROTEIN; from its forming the walls of cells.]

mu·rex /myoŏ rèks/ (*plural* **-ri·ces** /-ri seez/ *or* **-rex·es**) *n.* a gastropod marine shellfish that lives mainly in tropical waters and typically has a spiny shell. One species yields a purple dye. Genus: *Murex*. [Late 16thC. From Latin.]

mu·ri·at·ic ac·id /myoŏree áttik-/ *n.* = **hydrochloric acid** [*Muriatic* from Latin *muriaticus* "pickled in brine," from *muria* "brine"]

mu·ri·cate /myoŏri kàyt, -kət/, **mu·ri·cat·ed** /-kàytəd/ *adj.* covered in short spines or points [Mid-17thC. From Latin *muricatus* "shaped like a murex," from *murex* (see MUREX).]

mu·rid /myoŏrid/ *n.* an animal such as a mouse or rat that belongs to the rodent family. Family: Muridae. [Early 20thC. Shortening of modern Latin *Muridae*, family name, from Latin *mur-*, the stem of *mus* (see MOUSE).]

mu·rine /myoŏrin, myoŏ reèn/ *adj.* **1. OF MOUSE AND RAT FAMILY** relating to or belonging to the family of long-tailed rodents that includes rats and mice. Family: Muridae. **2. LIKE A RODENT** like a mouse or a rat **3. SPREAD BY RODENTS** caused or transmitted by mice or rats [Early 17thC. From Latin *murinus*, from *mur-*, the stem of *mus* "mouse." Ultimately from the same Indo-European word as produced English *mouse*.]

mu·rine ty·phus *n.* a relatively mild form of typhus that is transmitted from rats to humans by fleas or lice. Symptoms include fever, headaches, and muscular pain, and recovery is usually rapid. It is caused by the microorganism *Rickettsia typhi*.

murk /murk/ *n.* **1. GLOOMY DARKNESS** gloomy darkness caused by mist, smoke, or cloud **2.** *N England* **MIST** a mist or thin fog (*informal*) ■ *adj.* **MURKY** murky (*archaic or literary*) [Old English *mirce*, *myrce*. Supplemented in Middle English by the related Old Norse *myrkr*.]

murk·y /múrkee/ (**-i·er, -i·est**) *adj.* **1. GLOOMY** dark and gloomy **2. HARD TO SEE THROUGH** thick with fog, cloud, smoke, or dirt, and difficult to see through **3. OBSCURE** unclear and difficult to understand ○ *offered several murky excuses* **4. DISHONEST** involving dishonesty or illegal activities —**murk·i·ly** *adv.* —**murk·i·ness** *n.*

Mur·mansk /mur mánsk/ city in northwestern Russia, on the Kola Inlet, an arm of the Barents Sea. Population: 472,000 (1990).

mur·mur /múrmər/ *n.* **1. CONTINUOUS HUM** a continuous low sound that often seems to be coming from some distance away **2. SOMETHING SAID QUIETLY** something said that is either very quiet or sounds indistinct **3. COMPLAINT** a complaint, especially one that is not made openly **4.** MED **SYMPTOMATIC SOUND IN THE CHEST** a soft blowing or fluttering sound, usually heard via a stethoscope, that originates from the heart, lungs, or arteries and may indicate disease or structural concerns. It is caused by turbulent blood flow. ■ *v.* (**-mured, -mur·ing, -murs**) **1.** *vti.* **SAY SOMETHING SOFTLY** to say something very softly so that it can hardly be heard **2.** *vi.* **COMPLAIN DISCREETLY** to complain in a discreet or secretive way **3.** *vi.* **MAKE A CONTINUOUS LOW SOUND** to make a continuous low sound, as if from a distance [14thC. Via French *murmurer* from Latin *murmurare*. Probably an imitation of the sound (compare Greek *mormurein* and German *murmeln*, which have a similar meaning).] —**mur·mur·er** *n.* —**mur·mur·ing·ly** *adv.* —**mur·mur·ous** *adj.* —**mur·mur·ous·ly** *adv.*

mur·mu·ra·tion /mùrmə ráysh'n/ *n.* **1. MURMURING** an act or sound of murmuring **2. STARLINGS** a flock of starlings [14thC. "Flock of starlings" because of the sound they make.]

mur·mur·ings /múrməringz/ *npl.* quiet and unforceful expressions of discontent

mur·phy /múrfee/ (*plural* **-phies**) *n.* a potato (*dated informal*) [Early 19thC. From the Irish surname *Murphy*; from the stereotypical prominence of the potato in the Irish diet.]

Mur·phy /múrfee/ (*plural* **-phies**), **mur·phy** (*plural* **-phies**) *n.* CRIMINOL = **Murphy game**

Mur·phy /múrfee/, **Eddie** (*b.* 1961) U.S. actor and comedian. He came to prominence in U.S. television's *Saturday Night Live* (1981–84) and has since appeared in numerous movies.

Mur·phy, Emily Gowan (1868–1933) Canadian writer and political and legal reformer. She was the first woman magistrate in the British Empire (1916) and an advocate of women's suffrage. Born **Ferguson, Emily Gowan**. Pseudonym **Janey Canuck**

Mur·phy, Frank (1890–1949) U.S. government official and jurist. He was appointed to the U.S. Supreme Court (1940) and consistently upheld civil liberties.

Mur·phy bed *n.* a bed that can be folded or swung into a closet or wall recess when not in use [Early 20thC. Named for the American inventor William L. *Murphy* (1876–1959), who developed it.]

Mur·phy game, mur·phy game *n.* a confidence game in which somebody is lured into handing over money for something that is promised but never given, sometimes receiving only paper when the money is apparently returned [Mid-20thC. Named for an imaginary prostitute, Miss *Murphy*, who was used as a lure.]

Mur·phy's Law *n.* the law or principle that if anything can go wrong, it will (*informal*) [Mid-20thC. Named for the American engineer Edward A. *Murphy* (b. 1917), who enunciated it.]

mur·rain /múrrən/ *n.* (*archaic*) **1. CATTLE DISEASE** an infectious disease such as anthrax that affects cattle **2. PLAGUE** an infectious and fast-spreading disease [14thC. From Anglo-Norman *moryn* and French *morine*, from *mourir* "to die," from, ultimately, Latin *mori* (source of English *mortgage* and *mortuary*).]

Mur·ray /múrree/ **1.** major river in southeastern Australia. Length: 1,566 mi./2,520 km. **2.** city in southwestern Kentucky, on the Clarke River, southwest of Hopkinsville and southeast of Paducah. Population: 15,316 (1996).

Mur·ray, James (1721?–94) British military officer and colonial administrator. He was the first British governor of Quebec (1760–66).

Mur·ray, John (1741–1815) British-born U.S. clergyman. He preached universal salvation and established the universalist church in North America (1779).

murre /mur/ *n.* an auk that has predominantly black plumage with white markings. Genus: *Uria*. [Late 16thC. Origin unknown.]

mur·re·let /múrlət/ (*plural* **-lets** *or* **-let**) *n.* a small diving bird that is related to and resembles an auk. Genera: *Brachyramphus* and *Synthliboramphus*.

mur·rey /múrree/ *adj.* of the purplish-red color mulberry (*archaic*) [15thC. Via Old French *moré* from medieval Latin *moratus*, from Latin *morum* "mulberry."]

mur·rhine /múrrin, mú rìn/, **mur·rine** *n.* a substance, possibly fluorite, that the ancient Romans used to make vases, cups, and other similar objects [Late 16thC. From Latin *murr(h)inus*, from *murra*, denoting this substance.]

Mur·row /múrrō/, **Edward Roscoe** (1908–65) U.S. journalist. His World War II radio broadcasts from London helped swing U.S. opinion behind the Allied cause. He went on to pioneer broadcast reportage in the early days of television.

Mur·rum·bidg·ee /mùrrəm bíjee/ river in southeastern Australia. Length: 1,050 mi./1,690 km.

mur·ther /múrthər/ *n.* murder, or a murder (*archaic*) [14thC. Variant of MURDER.]

mus. *abbr.* **1.** museum **2.** music **3.** musical **4.** musician

Mu·saf /moŏssəf/ *n.* in Judaism, a group of additional prayers that is included in morning services on Sabbaths, festivals, and Rosh Chodesh [From Hebrew, literally "addition"]

Mus.B., Mus.Bac. *abbr.* Bachelor of Music [Latin *Musicae Baccalaureus*]

Mus·ca /múskə/ *n.* a small constellation in the southern hemisphere between the Southern Cross and Chamaeleon

mus·ca·del, mus·ca·delle *n.* = **muscatel**

Mus·ca·det /mùskə dáy/ *n.* a dry white wine from the Loire Valley in France [Early 20thC. From French, name of the grape from which this wine is made, from *muscade* "nutmeg," from *musc* "musk" (see MUSK).]

mus·ca·dine /múskə dìn, -din/ *n.* **1. WILD GRAPEVINE** a grapevine, native to the southeastern United States, that is the ancestor of cultivated varieties used for winemaking. Latin name: *Vitis rotundifolia*. **2. PURPLE GRAPE** a purple grape from the muscadine vine with a thick skin and musky smell, used for making wine [Mid-16thC. Probably a variant of MUSCATEL.]

mus·cae vol·i·tant·es /moŏ skī vōlə taán tàyz/ *npl.* MED specks that appear to float before the eyes (*technical*) [Mid-18thC. From Latin, literally "flies flying about."]

mus·ca·rine /múskərin, -reen/ *n.* a toxic substance, found in fly agaric and certain other fungi, that when ingested affects the nervous system. Among other effects it dilates blood vessels, slows heart rate, constricts the airways, and stimulates the gut. [Late 19thC. Formed from modern Latin *Muscaria*, species name of the fly agaric, from Latin *musca* "fly."] —**mus·ca·rin·ic** /mùskə rínnik/ *adj.*

mus·cat /mú skàt, múskət/ *n.* **1.** PLANTS **WHITE GRAPEVINE** a grapevine with sweet white grapes that are used for winemaking and are dried as raisins **2.** FOOD **WHITE GRAPE** a sweet white grape from a muscat vine **3.** WINE = **muscatel** *n.* 1 [Mid-16thC. Via French from Provençal, formed from *musc* (see MUSK).]

Mus·cat /mús kàt/, **Mas·qat** /máss gàt/ capital city of Oman, on the northeastern coast of the country, on the Gulf of Oman. Population: 622,506 (1993).

mus·ca·tel /mùskə tél/, **mus·ca·del** /-déll/, **mus·ca·delle** *n.* **1.** **SWEET WHITE WINE** a sweet white wine made from muscat grapes **2.** **WHITE GRAPE OR RAISIN** a grape or raisin from the muscat vine [Mid-16thC. Via Old French from Provençal, literally "little muscat," formed from *muscat* (see MUSCAT).]

Mus·ca·tine /mùss kə teén/ city in southeastern Iowa, situated on the Mississippi River. Population: 23,096 (1996).

mus·cid /mússid/ *n.* any fly of the family that includes the housefly and the stable fly. Family: Muscidae. [Late 19thC. Back-formation from modern Latin *Muscidae*, family name, from Latin *musca* "fly."] —**mus·cid** *adj.*

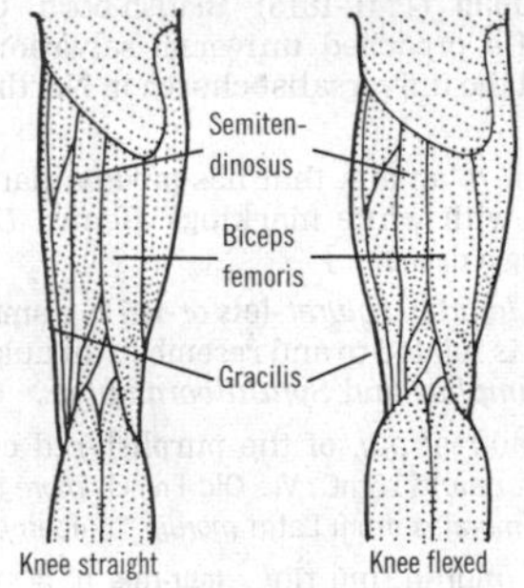

Muscle: Muscles of the human knee

mus·cle /múss'l/ *n.* **1.** **BODY TISSUE PRODUCING MOVEMENT** a tissue that is specialized to undergo repeated contraction and relaxation, thereby producing movement of body parts, maintaining tension, or pumping fluids within the body. There are three types: voluntary (**striped muscle**), involuntary (**smooth muscle**), and branched or heart muscle. **2.** **ORGAN COMPOSED OF MUSCLE TISSUE** an organ composed of bundles or sheets of muscle tissue, bound together with connective tissue and with tendons by which the contracting part is attached to the bones that it moves **3.** **INFLUENCE** power and influence, especially in the realm of politics, finance, or the military **4.** **STRENGTH** physical strength (*informal*) ○ *put some muscle into it* **5.** **HIRED THUGS** men who are employed to intimidate, harm, or menace people (*slang*) ■ *vti.* (**-cled, -cling, -cles**) **MOVE BY USING STRENGTH** to move, or make somebody or something move, using strength and force or effort (*informal*) [14thC. Via French from Latin *musculus*, literally "small mouse," from *mus* "mouse"; from the resemblance of certain muscles to mice moving under the skin.] —**mus·cly** *adj.*

muscle in *vi.* to become involved in or interfere in something by disregarding other people's wishes or by using strength, power, or influence (*informal*)

mus·cle-bound /múss'l bòwnd/, **mus·cle-bound** *adj.* **1.** **WITH OVERDEVELOPED MUSCLES** with muscles so bulky that they restrict movement **2.** **RIGID AND INFLEXIBLE** too large, powerful, or overdeveloped to be capable of flexibility or a swift response

mus·cle candy *n.* a dietary supplement used by athletes to enhance bursts of high performance (*slang*) [Late 20thC]

mus·cle car *n.* a flashy car with a big engine, designed to look like a sports car

mus·cle fi·ber *n.* a basic contracting unit of striated muscle, as found, e.g., in arm and leg muscles. Each is a microscopic threadlike structure, formed from several fused cells. It contains numerous cylindrical structures (**myofibrils**) that contract when stimulated.

mus·cle·man /múss'l màn/ (*plural* **-men** /-mèn/) *n.* **1.** **STRONG MAN** a man with highly developed muscles who is very strong **2.** **BODYGUARD** a strong man hired by a criminal or gangster for protection and to intimidate enemies

mus·cle mar·y (*plural* **mus·cle mar·ys**) *n.* a gay man with a very muscular physique (*slang*) (*offensive in some contexts*)

mus·cle sense *n.* = **kinesthesia**

mus·co·va·do /múskə váy dō, -vaá-/, **mus·ca·va·do** *n.* a raw or unrefined sugar made by evaporating the molasses from sugar-cane juice [Early 17thC. From Portuguese *mascabado* "made badly," referring to the quality of refinement.]

mus·co·vite /múskə vīt/ *n.* the most common of the mica group of minerals, consisting of potassium aluminum silicate and found in plutonic and sedimentary rocks [Mid-19thC. Coined from *Muscovy glass* "mica" (from its being obtained from Russia) + -ITE.]

Mus·co·vite /múskə vīt/ *n.* **SOMEBODY FROM MOSCOW** somebody who lives in or comes from Moscow, the capital of Russia ■ *adj.* **RUSSIAN** Russian (*archaic*) [Mid-16thC. Formed from modern Latin *Muscovia*, from Russian *Moskva* "Moscow."]

Mus·co·vy /múskəvee/ former principality in western Russia, centered on Moscow

Mus·co·vy duck /múskəvee-/ *n.* a large duck, native to Central America but widely domesticated, valued for its succulent flesh. It has greenish-black plumage with white markings and heavy red wattles. Latin name: *Cairina moschata.* [Alteration (by association with archaic *Muscovy* "of Moscow") of MUSK DUCK]

mus·cu·lar /múskyələr/ *adj.* **1.** **OF THE MUSCLES** consisting of, relating to, or affecting muscles **2.** **STRONG** physically strong and with well-developed muscles **3.** **VIGOROUS** having considerable power or strength but sometimes lacking subtlety [Late 17thC. Alteration of obsolete *musculous*, which came directly or via French *musculeaux* from Latin *musculosus*, from *musculus* (see MUSCLE).] —**mus·cu·lar·i·ty** /mùskyə lérrətee/ *n.* —**mus·cu·lar·ly** /múskyələrlee/ *adv.*

mus·cu·lar dys·tro·phy *n.* a medical condition in which there is gradual wasting and weakening of skeletal muscles. There are several forms in humans, generally linked to genetic defects and showing characteristic patterns of inheritance, the most common being Duchenne muscular dystrophy.

mus·cu·la·ture /múskyələchər, -choŏr/ *n.* **1.** **ARRANGEMENT OF MUSCLES** the way a person's or animal's muscles are arranged in a limb or organ **2.** **MUSCULAR SYSTEM** an organism's entire muscular system [Late 19thC. From French, formed from Latin *musculus* (see MUSCLE).]

musculo- *prefix.* muscle, muscular ○ *musculocutaneous* [From Latin *musculus* (see MUSCLE)]

mus·cu·lo·cu·ta·ne·ous /mùskyə lō kyoo táynee əss/ *adj.* relating to or supplying the muscles and skin

mus·cu·lo·skel·e·tal /mùskyə lō skéllət'l/ *adj.* relating to or involving the muscles and the skeleton

Mus.D., **Mus.Doc.** *abbr.* Doctor of Music [Latin *Musicae Doctor*]

muse[1] /myooz/ *v.* (**mused, mus·ing, mus·es**) **1.** *vti.* **THINK ABOUT SOMETHING** to think about something in a deep and serious or dreamy and abstracted way **2.** *vti.* **SAY SOMETHING THOUGHTFULLY** to say something in a thoughtful or questioning way (*literary*) **3.** *vi.* **GAZE THOUGHTFULLY** to gaze at somebody or something thoughtfully or abstractedly (*literary*) ■ *n.* **THOUGHTFUL STATE** a state of deep thought (*literary*) [14thC. From Old French *muser* "to meditate," perhaps literally "to go around with your nose in the air," from *muse* "muzzle, snout," from medieval Latin *musum* (source of English *muzzle*).] —**mus·er** *n.*

muse[2] /myooz/ *n.* **1.** **SOMEBODY WHO INSPIRES AN ARTIST** somebody who is a source of inspiration for an artist, especially a poet **2.** **ARTIST'S INSPIRATION** the inspiration that supposedly visits, leaves, and suggests things to an artist, especially a poet **3.** **ARTIST'S PARTICULAR TALENT** the particular gift or talent of an artist, especially a poet ○ *"With Donne, whose muse on dromedary trots, Wreathe iron pokers into true-love knots"* (Samuel Taylor Coleridge, *On Donne's Poetry*; 1818) [14thC. Directly or via French from Latin *musa*, from Greek *mousa*.]

Muse *n.* in Greek mythology, one of the nine daughters of Zeus and Mnemosyne, goddess of memory. The Muses inspired and presided over the different creative arts. They are Calliope (the muse of epic poetry), Clio (history), Erato (love poetry), Euterpe (lyric poetry), Melpomene (tragedy), Polyhymnia (sacred song), Terpsichore (dance), Thalia (comedy), and Urania (astronomy).

mu·se·ol·o·gy /myoŏzee óllәjee/ *n.* the study of how museums are designed, organized, and managed — **mu·se·o·log·i·cal** /myoŏzee ə lójjik'l/ *adj.* — **mu·se·o·log·i·cal·ly** *adv.* —**mu·se·ol·o·gist** /myoŏzee óllәjist/ *n.*

mu·sette /myoo zét/ *n.* MUSIC **1.** **FRENCH BAGPIPE** a French bagpipe that makes a relatively soft sound. It was popular in the 17th, 18th, and 19th centuries. **2.** **PASTORAL DANCE MUSIC** a piece of pastoral dance music that imitates the sound of a bagpipe or has a bagpipe playing the bass line [14thC. From French, literally "little bagpipe," formed from *muse* "bagpipe."]

mu·sette /myoo zét/, **mu·sette bag** *n.* a small leather or canvas knapsack with one shoulder strap, used by soldiers

mu·se·um /myoo zeé əm/ *n.* a building or institution where objects of artistic, historical, or scientific importance and value are kept, studied, and put on display [Early 17thC. Via Latin, "library, academy," from Greek *mouseion* "place of the Muses," from *mousa* "muse" (see MUSE[2]).]

mu·se·um piece *n.* **1.** **VALUABLE AND INTERESTING OBJECT** an object that is so valuable, interesting, or old that it could be in a museum **2.** **SOMEBODY OR SOMETHING OLD-FASHIONED** somebody or something considered very old-fashioned (*informal*)

Mus·grave Rang·es /mùss grayv-/ mountain range in central Australia, on the border between the Northern Territory and South Australia

mush[1] /mush/ *n.* **1.** **PULP** a soft pulpy mass **2.** **SENTIMENTAL STUFF** overly romantic and sentimental words or ideas, e.g., in a book or movie **3.** FOOD **COOKED CEREAL** a thick mixture made from cornmeal and milk or water ■ *vt.* (**mushed, mush·ing, mush·es**) **MASH SOMETHING** to mash something into a soft pulpy mass [Late 17thC. Origin uncertain: probably a variant of MASH.]

mush[2] /mush/ *interj.* **COMMAND TO SLED DOGS** used to make sled dogs start pulling or moving faster ■ *n.* **DOGSLED TRIP** a trip on a dogsled ■ *vti.* (**mushed, mush·ing, mush·es**) **TRAVEL BY DOGSLED** to travel on a dogsled, or drive a dogsled or team of dogs [Mid-19thC. From North American *Mush on!*, perhaps a variant of French *marchons* "let us march," from *marcher* "to march" (source of English *march*).] —**mush·er** *n.*

mush·room /músh roŏm/ *n.* **1.** **UMBRELLA-SHAPED FUNGUS** the typically umbrella-shaped spore-producing body of a fungus that consists of a usually fleshy cap on a stalk. Class: Basidiomycetes. **2.** **EDIBLE FUNGUS** an edible mushroom, especially the field mushroom **3.** **FAST-GROWING THING** something that grows very fast ■ *vi.* (**-roomed, -room·ing, -rooms**) **1.** **GROW QUICKLY** to grow or develop very rapidly **2.** **BECOME MUSHROOM-SHAPED** to swell into a shape like a mushroom **3.** **PICK MUSHROOMS** to go mushroom picking [15thC. Via French *mousseron* from the late Latin stem *mussirion-* "type of mushroom," of unknown origin.] —**mush·room·y** *adj.*

mush·room cloud *n.* the large mushroom-shaped cloud of dust and debris caused by an explosion, especially a nuclear explosion

mush·y /múshee/ (**-i·er, -i·est**) *adj.* **1.** **TOO SENTIMENTAL** overly romantic or sentimental **2.** **PULPY** forming a thick soft pulp —**mush·i·ly** *adv.* —**mush·i·ness** *n.*

mu·sic /myoŏzik/ *n.* **1.** **SOUNDS THAT PRODUCE EFFECT** sounds, usually produced by instruments or voices, that are arranged or played in order to create a pleasing or stimulating effect **2.** **ART OF ARRANGING SOUNDS** the art of arranging or making sounds, usually those of musical instruments or voices, in groups and patterns that create a pleasing or stimulating effect **3.** **TYPE OF MUSIC** music of a particular type, e.g., of a particular place or time, for a particular in-

AKG London

Mushroom cloud

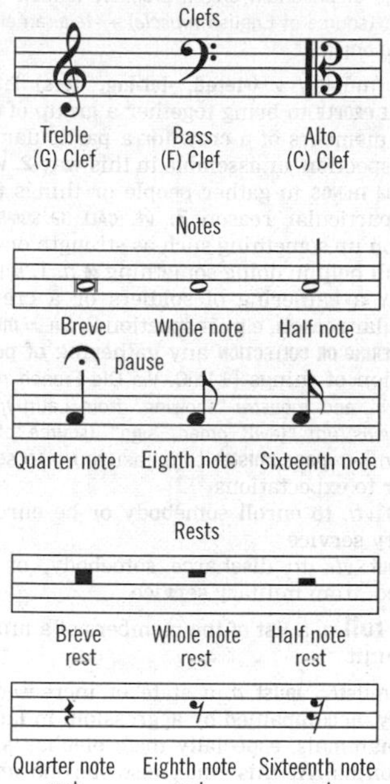

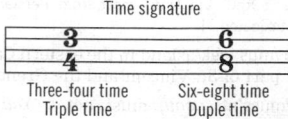

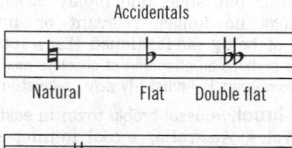

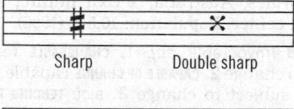

Music: Musical notation

strument, of a particular style, or appealing to a particular group ○ *rock-and-roll music* **4.** WRITTEN MUSIC written notation on paper indicating the pitch, duration, rhythm, and tone of notes to be played **5.** PLEASING SOUND any sound or group of sounds that is pleasing or stimulating ○ *the music of the wind in the trees* **6.** GROUP a group of musicians (*archaic*) [13thC. Via French *musique* from, ultimately, Greek *mousikē* "art of the Muse, music," from *mousikos* "of a Muse," from *mousa* "muse" (see MUSE[2]).] ◇ **face the music** to deal with a pressing and difficult situation arising from something done previously

mu·si·cal /myoózik'l/ *adj.* **1.** OF OR FOR MUSIC relating to or producing music **2.** PLEASANT-SOUNDING sounding pleasant and melodious **3.** GOOD AT MUSIC having a talent for or a strong interest in music **4.** WITH MUSIC set to, consisting of, or involving music ■ *n.* **1.** MOVIE OR PLAY WITH SONGS a lighthearted movie or play that has singing, music, and often dancing in it as important elements in developing the story and portraying the emotions of the characters **2.** MUSICALE a musicale (*archaic*) —**mu·si·cal·ly** *adv.* —**mu·si·cal·ness** *n.*

mu·si·cal box *n. U.K.* = **music box**

musicale /myoòzi kál/ *n.* a social occasion in which music is the featured entertainment

mu·sic box *n.* a box containing a mechanical device that plays music

mu·sic dra·ma *n.* a type of opera, first composed by Wagner in the late 19th century, in which the dramatic and musical content are intended to be of equal importance

mu·sic hall *n.* **1.** AUDITORIUM an auditorium for musical and theatrical productions **2.** *U.K.* = **vaudeville 3.** *U.K.* THEATER a vaudeville theater

mu·si·cian /myoo zísh'n/ *n.* somebody who plays, performs, conducts, or composes music, either as a hobby or a profession —**mu·si·cian·ly** *adj.*

mu·si·cian·ship /myoo zísh'n shìp/ *n.* skill in playing or performing music

mu·sic of the spheres *n.* the perfect but inaudible music that Pythagoras and other later philosophers believed was created by the movement of the celestial bodies

mu·si·col·o·gy /myoòzi kólləjee/ *n.* the academic study of music and its history —**mu·si·co·log·i·cal** /myoòzikə lójjik'l/ *adj.* —**mu·si·co·log·i·cal·ly** *adv.* —**mu·si·col·o·gist** /myoòzi kólləjist/ *n.*

mu·sic stand *n.* a height-adjustable frame for holding printed music that is being performed

mu·sic vid·e·o *n.* a short video or film made to accompany a song or piece of popular music, often as a cinematic or dramatic interpretation of it

mus·ings /myoózingz/ *npl.* thoughts, especially when aimless and unsystematic ○ *philosophical musings*

mu·sique con·crète /myoo zeék kong krét/ *n.* recorded music composed by electronically combining and enhancing natural and musical sounds [Mid-20thC. From French, literally "concrete music."]

musk /musk/ *n.* **1.** GLANDULAR SECRETION OF DEER a pungent and greasy secretion from a gland in the male musk deer, used in the manufacture of perfumes **2.** SUBSTANCE LIKE MUSK a secretion similar to musk from other animals such as the civet or otter, or a synthetic substance with similar properties **3.** PLANTS PLANT WITH MUSKY SCENT a plant that has a musky scent, especially the musk plant **4.** SMELL OF MUSK the smell of musk, or a similar smell **5.** = **musk deer** [14thC. Ultimately from Latin *muscus*, from Persian *mušk*, perhaps from Sanskrit *muṣka* "scrotum" (from the shape of the musk gland of the musk deer), literally "little mouse," from *mūṣ* "mouse."]

musk deer *n.* a small mountain-dwelling deer native to central and northeastern Asia. The males lack antlers but possess long canine teeth and secrete musk from an abdominal gland. Latin name: *Moschus moschiferus.*

musk duck *n.* = **Muscovy duck** [From its smell]

mus·keg /mú skèg/ *n.* **1.** BOGGY LAND an area of swamp or boggy land covered in sphagnum moss, leaves, and a mass of dead plant matter resembling peat **2.** DEAD PLANT MATTER the dead plant matter resembling peat that covers areas of muskeg [Early 19thC. From Cree *maske:k.*]

mus·kel·lunge /máskə lùnj/ (*plural* **-lung·es** *or* **-lunge**), **mus·ke·lunge** (*plural* **-lung·es** *or* **-lunge**), **mas·ki·nonge** /máskə nùnj/ (*plural* **-nong·es** *or* **-nonge**) *n.* a large freshwater fish of the pike family, native to the Great Lakes region of North America, that is a fierce predator and is caught for game and food. It is the largest member of the pike family, and can reach the weight of 100 lb./45.4 kg. Latin name: *Esox masquinongy.* [Late 18thC. From Ojibwa *muskinonje* "big fish."]

mus·ket /múskət/ *n.* a shoulder gun with a long barrel and a smooth bore. It was used between the 16th and 18th centuries, before rifling was invented. [Late 16thC. Via French *mousquet* from Italian *moschetto* "crossbow bolt," from *mosca* "fly," from Latin *musca.*]

WORD KEY: ORIGIN

Early ***muskets*** could fire crossbow bolts as well as bullets. The name was probably reinforced by Italian *moschetto* "sparrow hawk" (from its flylike markings), early guns being often named after birds of prey (e.g., "falconet," a type of small cannon).

mus·ket·eer /múskə teér, mùskə teér/ *n.* **1.** INFANTRYMAN an infantryman armed with a musket **2.** ROYAL BODYGUARD a member of a company of musketeers in the French royal household's personal troops in the 17th and 18th centuries

WORD KEY: CULTURAL NOTE

The Three Musketeers, a novel by French writer Alexandre Dumas (1844). Set in France during the reign of Louis XIII, this historical romance tells the story of a young adventurer, D'Artagnan, who is taken under the wing of three musketeers, Athos, Porthos, and Aramis. The four become embroiled in a series of adventures involving love, politics, swordsmanship, and the machinations of the evil Cardinal Richelieu.

mus·ket·ry /múskətree/ *n.* **1.** MUSKETS OR MUSKETEERS a group of muskets or musketeers **2.** FIRING OF SMALL GUNS the technique or practice of using small arms

mus·kie /múskee/, **mus·ky** (*plural* **-kies** *or* **-ky**) *n.* = **muskellunge** [Late 19thC. Shortening.]

musk mal·low *n.* **1.** MALLOW WITH PINK FLOWERS a plant of the mallow family, native to Europe and northern Africa, with a hairy and often purple-spotted stem, pink flowers, and a slight musky scent. Latin name: *Malva moschata.* **2.** = **abelmosk**

musk·mel·on /músk mèllən/ *n.* **1.** PLANTS MELON PLANT a trailing vine that bears melons with a ridged skin such as the cantaloupe. Latin name: *Cucumis melo.* **2.** FOOD MELON FRUIT the fruit of a muskmelon plant, having a ribbed or rough rind and white, yellow, or green flesh with a sweet full flavor and a pleasant slightly musky smell

Mus·ko·ge·an /mu skógee ən/, **Mus·kho·ge·an** *n.* a branch of Native American languages from the Hokan-Siouan family. It includes Chickasaw, Choctaw, and Creek. —**Mus·ko·ge·an** *adj.*

Mus·ko·gee /mu skógee/ (*plural* **-gee** *or* **-gees**) *n.* a member of a Native American people who inhabited the southeastern part of North America and formed part of the confederacy that included the Creek [Late 18thC. From Creek *ma:skó:ki.*]

musk ox /músk òks/ (*plural* **musk ox·en**), **musk·ox** (*plural* **-ox·en**) *n.* a large wild ox, native to the arctic tundra of northern Canada and Greenland, with a black or brown shaggy coat and flat downward-curving horns. Males emit a strong musky smell during the breeding season. Latin name: *Ovibos moschatus.*

musk plant *n.* a perennial North American plant of the figwort family with yellow tubular flowers that have a musky smell. Latin name: *Mimulus moschatus.*

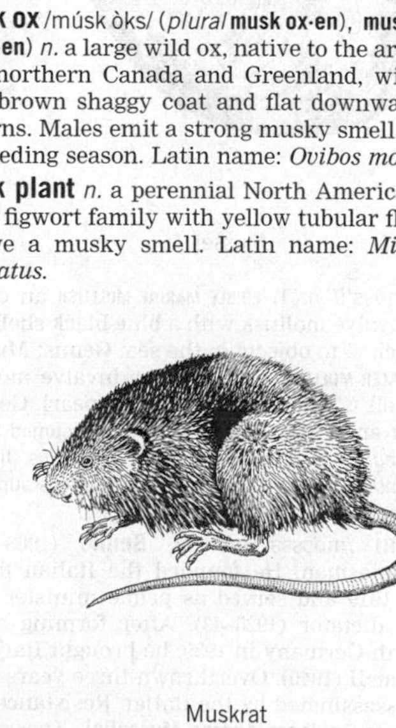

Muskrat

musk·rat /mú skràt/ (*plural* **-rat** *or* **-rats**) *n.* **1.** LARGE RODENT a large amphibious rodent, native to North America and widespread in Europe, with a thick brown coat and musk glands. Latin name: *Ondatra zibethica.* **2.** MUSKRAT FUR the fur of the muskrat [Early 17thC. By folk etymology from Algonquian *muscasus*, literally "it is red" (from the animal's color), by association with MUSK and RAT.]

folk etymology from Algonquian *muscascus,* literally "it is red" (from the animal's color), by association with MUSK and RAT.]

musk·root /músk ro͝ot/ *n.* = **moschatel**

musk rose *n.* a rose, native to the Mediterranean, that is widely cultivated for its musk-scented flowers. Latin name: *Rosa moschata.*

musk tur·tle *n.* a small freshwater turtle native to the eastern United States and Canada that gives off a pungent smell. Genus: *Sternotherus.*

musk·y /múskee/ (**-i·er, -i·est**) *adj.* with a sweet pungent smell similar to that of musk —**musk·i·ly** *adv.* —**musk·i·ness** *n.*

Mus·lim /múzzləm, mo͝oz-/ *n.* **FOLLOWER OF ISLAM** somebody who believes in and practices Islam ■ *adj.* **FOLLOWERS OF ISLAM** relating to the followers of Islam or to areas, cultures, or activities in which followers of Islam are especially numerous [Early 17thC. From Arabic, literally "somebody who surrenders (to God)," the active participle of *'aslama* (see ISLAM).]

Mus·lim Broth·er·hood *n.* an Egyptian nationalist movement founded by Hasan al-Bannah in 1928 that is committed to the Islamic fundamentalist cause and opposes Western influence. The Muslim Brotherhood is active in several other countries throughout the Middle East, North Africa, South Asia, and Southeast Asia.

Mus·lim League *n.* an organization founded in 1906 to support the demands of Muslims for separate electorates and legislative seats in Hindu-dominated India. It caused a division within the Indian nationalist movement.

mus·lin /múzzlin/ *n.* a thin plain-weave cotton cloth used for curtains, sheets, and dresses [Early 17thC. Via French *mousseline* MOUSSELINE and Italian *mussolina* from Arabic *mawsiliy* "of Mosul," the Iraqi city where the fabric was made.]

Mus.M. *abbr.* Master of Music [Latin *Musicae Magister*]

mus·quash /mú skwàwsh/ *n.* = **muskrat** [Early 17thC. From Western Abnaki *mòskwas.*]

muss /muss/ *vt.* (**mussed, muss·ing, muss·es**) **MESS UP** to make something, especially somebody's hair or clothes, messy or ruffled (*informal*) ■ *n.* **MESS** a state of messiness or disorder (*informal*) [Mid-19thC. Probably a variant of MESS.]

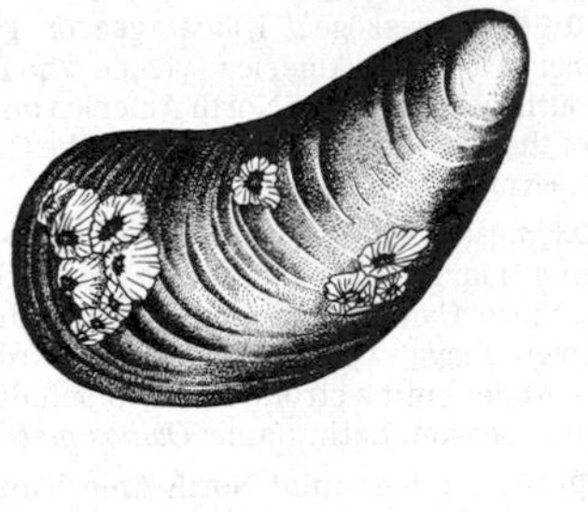

Mussel

mus·sel /múss'l/ *n.* **1. EDIBLE MARINE MOLLUSK** an edible marine bivalve mollusk with a blue-black shell that lives attached to objects in the sea. Genus: *Mytilus.* **2. FRESHWATER MOLLUSK** a freshwater bivalve mollusk whose shell is a source of mother-of-pearl. Genera: *Anodonta* and *Unio.* [Pre-12thC. From assumed Vulgar Latin *muscula,* an alteration of Latin *musculus,* literally "small mouse" (see MUSCLE); from the mussel's supposed resemblance in shape and color to a mouse.]

Mus·so·li·ni /mo͝ossə léenee/, **Benito** (1883–1945) Italian statesman. He founded the Italian fascist party in 1919 and served as prime minister from 1922 and dictator (1925–43). After forming an alliance with Germany in 1939, he brought Italy into World War II (1940). Overthrown three years later, he was assassinated by the Italian Resistance. Full name **Benito Anulcare Andrea Mussolini.** Known as **Il Duce**

Mus·sul·man /múss'lmən/ (*plural* **-men** /-mən/ *or* **-mans**) *n.* a Muslim (*archaic literary*) [Late 16thC. From Persian *musulmān* "Muslim" (adjective), from Arabic *muslim* "Muslim" (see MUSLIM).]

muss·y /mússee/ (**mus·si·er, mus·si·est**) *adj.* not neat or in an orderly state (*informal*) —**muss·i·ly** *adv.* —**muss·i·ness** *n.*

must[1] /must/ (**must**) CORE MEANING: a modal indicating that somebody is compelled to do something because of a rule or law, or that it is necessary or advisable to do something ○ *Accidents causing injury must be reported immediately.* ○ *Employment decisions must be based on ability.* ○ *We must improve our schools.* ○ *You must give him a chance to state his case.*

1. *v.* **BE COMPELLED** to be compelled to do something because of a rule or law ○ *You must stop when the light is red.* ○ *All guests must vacate their rooms by 12 noon.* **2.** *v.* **BE NECESSARY** to be important or necessary to do something ○ *Henceforth, he said, the central organizing principle of all governments must be the environment.* ○ *Health care insurance must be affordable.* **3.** *v.* **BE CERTAIN** indicates that somebody is sure that something is the case ○ *This must seem strange to you.* ○ *Those must be your footprints in the garden.* **4.** *v.* **INDICATES BELIEF** indicates that somebody concludes that something is the case, based on the available evidence ○ *Paleontologists know that primates must have immigrated to South America sometime before 28 million years ago.* **5.** *v.* **INTEND** to intend or be determined to do something ○ *I must be going.* ○ *I must telephone my brother.* **6.** *v.* **USED TO MAKE SUGGESTIONS** used to make suggestions or invitations, or to give advice ○ *You must see a doctor.* ○ *You must come around for dinner one evening.* **7.** *n.* **SOMETHING ESSENTIAL** something that is essential or obligatory ○ *Formal attire is a must at a state dinner.* **8.** *prefix.* **ABSOLUTELY NECESSARY** absolutely necessary for somebody or highly recommended for somebody (*informal*) (*added to a verb to form a noun or adjective*) ○ *a must-see movie* ○ *a must-have fashion* [Old English *mōste,* past tense of assumed *mōtan* "to have to, be able to"]

must[2] /must/ *n.* the juice from grapes or other fruit that is to be fermented into wine [Pre-12thC. From Latin *mustum,* a form of *mustus* "new, fresh" (source of English *mustard*).]

must[3] /must/ *n.* the condition of being musty or moldy [Early 17thC. Back-formation from MUSTY.]

must[4] *n.* = **musth**

mus·tache /mú stàsh, mə stásh/ *n.* **1. HAIR ON UPPER LIP** facial hair allowed to grow on somebody's upper lip and often down the sides of the mouth or onto the cheeks **2. HAIR ON ANIMAL'S FACE** hair, bristles, or feathers around the mouth or beak of an animal [Late 16thC. Via French from Italian *mostaccio,* ultimately from Greek *mustak-,* stem of *mustax* "upper lip, mustache."] —**mus·tached** *adj.*

mus·ta·chio /mə stáshee ō/ (*plural* **-chios**) *n.* a mustache that is thick or trimmed into a fancy shape (*archaic or humorous; often used in the plural*) [Mid-16thC. Blend of Spanish *mostacho* and its source Italian *mostaccio* (see MUSTACHE).] —**mus·ta·chioed** *adj.*

mus·tang /mú stàng/ *n.* a small hardy wild horse, living on the plains of North America, descended from Arabian horses brought to the continent by Spanish soldiers [Early 19thC. Via Mexican Spanish *mestengo* from Spanish, "ownerless," literally "mixed (with ranchers' herds)," from *mesta* "ranchers who appropriated wild cattle," from Latin *mixta,* a form of *mixtus* "mixed."]

mus·tard /mústərd/ *n.* **1.** PLANTS **PLANT WITH PUNGENT SEEDS** a plant with small yellow flowers and long thin seedpods containing small pungent seeds. Genus: *Brassica.* **2.** FOOD **SPICY CONDIMENT** powdered mustard seeds, or a hot spicy paste made from powdered, or sometimes whole, mustard seeds, water, and other ingredients, eaten in small quantities as a condiment **3. ENTHUSIASM** enthusiasm or zest (*informal*) **4.** COLORS **DARK YELLOW COLOR** a dark yellow color tinged with brown, like that of mustard ■ *adj.* COLORS **OF DARK YELLOW COLOR** of a dark yellow color tinged with brown, like that of mustard [12thC. Via Old French *mo(u)starde* from, ultimately, Latin *mustum* "must, new wine" (the condiment originally having been made by mixing crushed seeds with MUST[2].] —**mus·tard·y** *adj.* ◇ **cut the mustard** to be up to the desired standard of performance, ability, or quality (*informal*)

mus·tard gas *n.* an oily liquid, made from ethene and disulfur dichloride, that evaporates to a poison gas. Used in chemical warfare, it burns the skin and causes often fatal respiratory damage. Formula: $(ClCH_2CH_2)_2$. [*Mustard* from its smell, which resembles mustard]

mus·tard oil *n.* an oil obtained from mustard seeds that is used in making soap

mus·tard plas·ter *n.* a paste made from black mustard seeds, formerly applied to the skin to stimulate blood flow. It was a folk remedy used to aid healing and counter inflammation.

mus·tee /mu stée, mústee/ *n.* (*dated offensive*) **1. OFFENSIVE TERM REFERRING TO PARENTS' RACES** an offensive term referring to somebody with one Caucasian parent and one parent who has one Black grandparent **2. OFFENSIVE TERM REFERRING TO ANCESTORS' RACE** an offensive term referring to somebody of mixed racial descent [Late 17thC. Shortening and alteration of Spanish *mestizo* (see MESTIZO).]

mus·te·line /mústə līn, -lin/ *adj.* belonging to, relating to or typical of the group of mammals that includes weasels, otters, badgers, and skunks. Family: Mustelidae. [Mid-17thC. From Latin *mustelinus,* from *mustel* "weasel," of uncertain origin: probably formed from *mus* "mouse" (source of English *muscle*) + *-tela,* an element of unknown origin.]

mus·ter /mústər/ *v.* (**-tered, -ter·ing, -ters**) **1.** *vti.* MIL **ASSEMBLE PEOPLE** to bring together a group of soldiers or the members of a crew for a particular reason, e.g., inspection, or assemble in this way **2.** *vt.* **GATHER PEOPLE OR THINGS** to gather people or things together for a particular reason **3.** *vt.* **CALL UP SOMETHING** to summon up something such as strength or courage that will help in doing something ■ *n.* **1.** MIL **MILITARY ASSEMBLY** a gathering of soldiers or a crew for a particular reason, e.g., inspection **2.** MIL = **muster roll** **3. GATHERING OR COLLECTION** any gathering of people or collection of things [14thC. Via Old French *mo(u)strer* "to show" and *moustre* "showing" from Latin *monstrare,* from *monstrum* "(evil) omen, sign" (source of English *monster*).] ◇ **pass muster** to measure up to set standards or to expectations

muster in *vti.* to enroll somebody or be enrolled for military service

muster out *vti.* to discharge somebody, or be discharged, from military service

mus·ter roll *n.* a list of the members of a military or naval unit

musth /must/, **must** *n.* a state of increased sexual activity, accompanied by aggression, in large male land mammals, especially male elephants, lasting 2–3 months. At this time, testosterone levels are high, and an additional hormone, temporin, is excreted from a gland between the eye and the ear. [Late 19thC. Via Urdu *mast* from Persian, literally "drunk, intoxicated."]

Mus·tique /mus téek/ island in the eastern Caribbean Sea. It is part of St. Vincent and the Grenadines.

must·n't /múss'nt/ *contr.* must not ○ *You mustn't worry.*

must-see *n.* something such as a place, movie, or work of art that is so important, beautiful, or excellent that everyone should see it (*slang*)

must·y /mústee/ (**-i·er, -i·est**) *adj.* **1. WITH OLD DAMP SMELL** smelling old, damp, and stale because of not having been used or exposed to fresh air for a long time **2. STALE** tasting old, stale, and moldy **3. OUTDATED AND UNINTERESTING** no longer relevant or interesting because of being old-fashioned [Early 16thC. Origin uncertain: perhaps an alteration of obsolete *moisty* "moist, damp," from MOIST.] —**must·i·ly** *adv.* —**must·i·ness** *n.*

Mus·well·brook /mússəl bro͝ok/ town in eastern New South Wales, Australia, a coal mining and agricultural center. Population: 10,541 (1996).

mu·ta·ble /myo͞otəb'l/ *adj.* **1. CHANGEABLE** tending or likely to change **2. CAPABLE OF CHANGE** capable of changing, or subject to change **3.** BIOL **TENDING TO UNDERGO MUTATION** used to describe a gene or organism that has a tendency to undergo mutation **4.** ZODIAC **OF GEMINI, VIRGO, SAGITTARIUS, AND PISCES** used to describe the signs of the zodiac Gemini, Virgo, Sagittarius, and Pisces, thought to be characterized by adaptability. ◊ **cardinal, fixed** [14thC. From Latin *mutabilis,* from *mutare* "to change" (source of English *mew, molt,* and *mutant*).] —**mu·ta·bil·i·ty** /myo͞otə bíllətee/ *n.* —**mu·ta·ble·ness** /myo͞otəb'lnəss/ *n.* —**mu·ta·bly** *adv.*

mu·ta·gen /myo͞otəjən/ *n.* an external agent, e.g., radiation or some chemicals or viruses, that increases the rate of mutation of cells or organisms [Mid-20thC. Coined from MUTATION + -GEN.] —**mu·ta·gen·ic** /myo͞otə jénnik/ *adj.* —**mu·ta·gen·i·cal·ly** *adv.* —**mu·ta·ge·nic·i·ty** /myo͞otəjə nissétee/ *n.*

mu·ta·gen·e·sis /myo͞otə jénnəssiss/ *n.* the process of mutation in a cell or organism [Mid-20thC. Formed from MUTATION + -GENESIS.]

mu·tant /myoot'nt/ *n.* **1.** BIOL **SOMETHING THAT HAS MUTATED** an animal, organism, cell, or gene that has mutated **2. SOMETHING ODD-LOOKING** somebody who or something that has a strange appearance, unlike others of a similar type (*slang*) ■ *adj.* **1.** BIOL **RESULTING FROM MUTATION** undergoing or resulting from mutation **2. RESEMBLING GENETIC MUTANT** with an odd appearance or other qualities comparable to those of a genetic mutant (*slang*) [Early 20thC. From Latin *mutant-*, the present participle stem of *mutare* "to change" (see MUTABLE).]

Mu·tare /moo taaree/ resort town and capital of Manicaland Province in eastern Zimbabwe, close to the Mozambique border. Population: 131,808 (1992).

mu·tase /myoo tayss, -tayz/ *n.* an enzyme that promotes change in the arrangement of molecules in a substance, especially the movement of a phosphate group from one carbon to another [Early 20thC. Formed from Latin *mutare* "to change" (see MUTABLE) + -ASE.]

mu·tate /myoo tayt, myoo tayt/ (**-tat·ed, -tat·ing, -tates**) *vti.* to undergo or make something undergo mutation [Mid-18thC. Partly a back-formation from MUTATION; partly from Latin *mutatus*, the past participle of *mutare* "to change" (see MUTABLE).] —**mu·ta·tive** /myoo taytiv, -tətiv/ *adj.*

mu·ta·tion /myoo taysh'n/ *n.* **1.** BIOL **CHANGE IN GENETIC MATERIAL** a random change in a gene or chromosome resulting in a new trait or characteristic that can be inherited. Mutation can be a source of beneficial genetic variation, or it can be neutral or harmful in effect. **2.** BIOL = **mutant** *n.* 1 **3. ALTERATION** the action or process of changing something or of being changed **4.** PHON = **umlaut 5.** PHON **PHONETIC CHANGE** a phonetic change found in Celtic languages in which the initial consonant of a word changes according to the preceding word —**mu·ta·tion·al** *adj.* —**mu·ta·tion·al·ly** *adv.*

mu·ta·tion stop *n.* a stop that controls a set of organ pipes that do not play the tones of the written notes but usually a fifth or third above them

mu·ta·tis mu·tan·dis /moo taatiss moo taandiss, moo taatiss moo tandiss/ *adv.* with the necessary changes having been made (*formal*) [From Latin, literally "with things being changed that have to be changed"]

mute /myoot/ *adj.* **1. UNABLE TO SPEAK** unable or unwilling to speak **2. MAKING NO SOUND** saying nothing, or making no sound **3. NOT EXPRESSED IN WORDS** felt or expressed without speech **4.** LAW **REFUSING TO ANSWER CHARGE** refusing to answer a charge brought in a court of law **5.** PHON = **plosive** *adj.* **6.** PHON **NOT PRONOUNCED** not pronounced, like the final "e" in "cheese" ■ *n.* **1. OFFENSIVE TERM** an offensive term for somebody who is unable or unwilling to speak (*offensive*) **2.** LAW **SOMEBODY REFUSING TO ANSWER CHARGE** somebody who refuses to answer a charge in a court of law **3.** MUSIC **DEVICE TO ALTER INSTRUMENT'S TONE** a pad, clip, or other device used to reduce or alter in some way the tone of a brass or stringed instrument **4.** PHON **SILENT LETTER** a letter that is not pronounced **5.** PHON = **plosive 6.** HIST **HIRED MOURNER** somebody who is paid to act as a mourner at a funeral ■ *vt.* (**mut·ed, mut·ing, mutes**) **1. TURN DOWN SOUND** to moderate the volume of a sound **2. MAKE SOMETHING LESS BRIGHT** to make a color or light less bright or harsh **3.** MUSIC **ALTER INSTRUMENT'S TONE** to reduce or alter in some way the tone of a brass or stringed instrument using a pad, clip, or other device [14thC. From French *muet*, literally "slightly mute," from Old French *mu*, from Latin *mutus*.] —**mute·ly** *adv.* —**mute·ness** *n.*

WORD KEY: SYNONYMS

See Synonyms at ***silent***.

mut·ed /myootəd/ *adj.* **1. NOT BRIGHT OR INTENSE** not bright, intense, or harsh in color or tone **2. NOT LOUD** not loud or distinct enough to be heard clearly **3. UNDERSTATED** subdued and understated rather than forceful or enthusiastic **4.** MUSIC **MADE BY INSTRUMENT FITTED WITH MUTE** fitted with a mute, or produced by an instrument fitted with a mute

mute swan *n.* a large white swan with an orange bill, common in Europe and Asia and introduced to other regions. Latin name: *Cygnus olor.*

mu·ti·late /myoot'l ayt/ (**-lat·ed, -lat·ing, -lates**) *vt.* **1. REMOVE OR DESTROY BODY PART** to inflict serious injury on a person or animal or part of somebody or something's body by removing or destroying parts of it **2. RUIN SOMETHING BY REMOVING PARTS** to damage or spoil something such as a piece of writing or a movie by removing important parts of it **3. DAMAGE SOMETHING SERIOUSLY** to inflict serious damage on something [Mid-16thC. Partly from Latin *mutilat-*, the past participle stem of *mutilare* "to cut or lop off," from *mutilus* "maimed"; partly from earlier *mutilate* "mutilated," of the same origin.] —**mu·ti·la·tive** *adj.* —**mu·ti·la·tor** *n.*

mu·ti·la·tion /myoot'l aysh'n/ *n.* an act, the process, or the result of inflicting serious injury on a person or animal or part of somebody or something's body by removing or destroying parts of it

mu·ti·neer /myoot'n eer/ *n.* somebody who rebels against the legal authority of others, especially a soldier or sailor [Early 17thC. From French *mutinier*, from Old French *mutin* "rebellious" (see MUTINY).]

mu·ti·nous /myoot'nəss/ *adj.* **1. INVOLVING MUTINY** plotting, participating in, or typical of a mutiny **2. REFUSING TO OBEY** refusing to obey or submit to control, especially military control [Late 16thC. Either from Old French *mutineus*, from *mutin* "rebellious" (see MUTINY), or formed from English *mutine* "mutiny," ultimately of the same origin.] —**mu·ti·nous·ly** *adv.* —**mu·ti·nous·ness** *n.*

mu·ti·ny /myoot'nee/ *n.* (*plural* **-nies**) **REBELLION AGAINST LEGAL AUTHORITY** a rebellion against legal authority, especially by soldiers or sailors refusing to obey orders and, often, attacking their officers ■ *vi.* (**-nied, -ny·ing, -nies**) **PARTICIPATE IN MUTINY** to take part in a rebellion against legal authority [Mid-16thC. Via obsolete *mutine* "to revolt" from French *mutiner*, from Old French *mutin* "rebellious," from *muete* "revolt" (literally "movement"), via assumed Vulgar Latin *movitus* from Latin *motus* "moved" (see MOTION).]

mut·ism /myoo tizzəm/ *n.* **1. OFFENSIVE TERM** an offensive term for the inability to speak (*offensive*) **2. REFUSAL TO SPEAK** a refusal to speak either at all times or at some, which may indicate trauma or stress

mu·ton /myoo ton/ *n.* the smallest known unit of DNA in which mutation can take place, either spontaneously or caused by an external agent [Mid-20thC. Formed from MUTATION + -ON.]

mutt /mut/ *n.* **1. MONGREL DOG** a dog that is of mixed or unknown breed (*slang*) **2. OFFENSIVE TERM** an offensive term that deliberately insults somebody's intelligence or knowledge (*slang insult*) [Late 19thC. Shortening of MUTTONHEAD.]

mut·ter /müttər/ *v.* (**-tered, -ter·ing, -ters**) **1.** *vti.* **SAY SOMETHING QUIETLY** to speak or say something quietly and indistinctly **2.** *vi.* **GRUMBLE** to say something in a quiet voice, especially as a complaint or in annoyance ■ *n.* **SOMETHING SAID QUIETLY** an act of saying something quietly and indistinctly, or something said in this way [14thC. Origin uncertain: perhaps from Latin *muttire*.]

mut·ton /mútt'n/ *n.* the flesh of a fully grown sheep, eaten as food [13thC. Directly or via Old French *molton* "ram, wether, sheep" from medieval Latin *multon-*, the stem of *multo*, of uncertain origin: probably ultimately from assumed Gaulish *multo*.] —**mut·ton·y** *adj.*

mut·ton bird *n.* an Australasian sea bird of the shearwater family. Mutton birds are traditionally hunted by the Maori for food. [*Mutton* from the taste of its cooked flesh, which is said to resemble mutton]

mut·ton·chops /mútt'n chops/ *npl.* facial hair trimmed into a narrow strip beside each ear, broadening out along the lower cheek and stopping at the side of the chin, which is kept bare [From the shape]

mut·ton·fish /mútt'n fish/ (*plural* **-fish** *or* **-fish·es**) *n.* a bottom-dwelling sea fish with a large head and an elongated body that lives in the coastal waters of northeastern North America. Latin name: *Macrozoarces americanus.* [*Mutton* from the taste of its flesh, likened to mutton]

mut·ton·head /mútt'n hed/ *n.* an offensive term that deliberately insults somebody's intelligence or knowledge (*insult slang*) —**mut·ton·head·ed** /mutt'n héddəd/ *adj.*

mut·ton snap·per *n.* an olive-green fish in the snapper family that lives in tropical seas of the western Atlantic and is caught for food and sport. Latin name: *Lutjanus analis.*

mu·tu·al /myoochoo əl/ *adj.* **1. FELT AND EXPRESSED BY EACH** done, felt, or expressed by each toward or with regard to the other **2. WITH SAME FEELINGS OR RELATIONSHIP** with the same feelings, or in the same relationship to each other **3. SHARED BY TWO PEOPLE OR GROUPS** shared by or common to two or more people or groups **4.** INSUR **OF MUTUAL INSURANCE** relating to mutual insurance ■ *n.* BUSINESS = **mutual fund** [15thC. From French *mutuel*, from Latin *mutuus* "borrowed, reciprocal, done in exchange."] —**mu·tu·al·i·ty** /myoochoo állətee/ *n.* —**mu·tu·al·ly** /myoochoo əlee/ *adv.* —**mu·tu·al·ness** *n.*

mu·tu·al as·sured de·struc·tion *n.* the enormous reciprocal damage that the superpowers and their allies would inflict on each other in the event of a nuclear war

mu·tu·al fund *n.* an investment company that uses members' capital to buy a diverse group of stocks from other companies. It offers additional shares and buys back those shares as demand requires.

mu·tu·al in·duc·tance *n.* a measure of the change in the electromotive force of a circuit caused by a change in the current flowing through an associated circuit. It is given as the ratio of the electromotive force induced to the rate of current change producing it. Symbol *M*

mu·tu·al in·duc·tion *n.* the production of an electromotive force in a circuit resulting from a change in the current flowing through another circuit to which it is magnetically linked

mu·tu·al in·sur·ance *n.* a method of insurance in which the customers buying policies own the company, pay premiums into a common fund to cover claims, and share in the profits

mu·tu·al·ism /myoochoo ə lizzəm/ *n.* a relationship between two organisms of different species that benefits both and harms neither. For example, lichens are a fungus and an alga living in mutualism: The fungus provides a protective structure, and the alga produces a carbohydrate as food for the fungus. ◊ **symbiosis** —**mu·tu·al·ist** *n.* —**mu·tu·al·is·tic** /myoochoo ə lístik/ *adj.*

mu·tu·al·ize /myoochoo ə liz/ (**-ized, -iz·ing, -iz·es**) *v.* **1.** *vti.* **MAKE OR BECOME MUTUAL** to become mutual, or make something mutual **2.** *vt.* BUSINESS **ALTER ORGANIZATION OF COMPANY** to alter the organization of a company so that the majority of its shares become owned by the employees and customers —**mu·tu·al·i·za·tion** /myoochoo əli záysh'n/ *n.*

mu·tu·al sav·ings bank *n.* a bank without shareholders in which the depositors are technically the owners

mu·tu·el *n.* = **pari-mutuel**

mu·tule /myoo chool/ *n.* a projecting block that holds a gutta under a Doric cornice [Mid-17thC. Via French from Latin *mutulus*.]

muu·muu /moo moo/ (*plural* **-muus**), **mu·mu** (*plural* **-mus**) *n.* a loose shapeless dress made of brightly colored fabric worn especially by women in Hawaii [Early 20thC. From Hawaiian *mu'u mu'u*, literally "cut off" (from the fact that there was originally no yoke).]

mux /muks/ *n.* a multiplexer (*informal*) [Late 20thC. Shortening.]

Mu·zak /myoo zak/ *tdmk.* a trademark for recorded background music played in stores, restaurants, elevators, and other public places

mu·zhik /moozhik/ *n.* a Russian peasant, especially during the tsarist era [Mid-16thC. From Russian, literally "small man," from *muzh* "man, husband."]

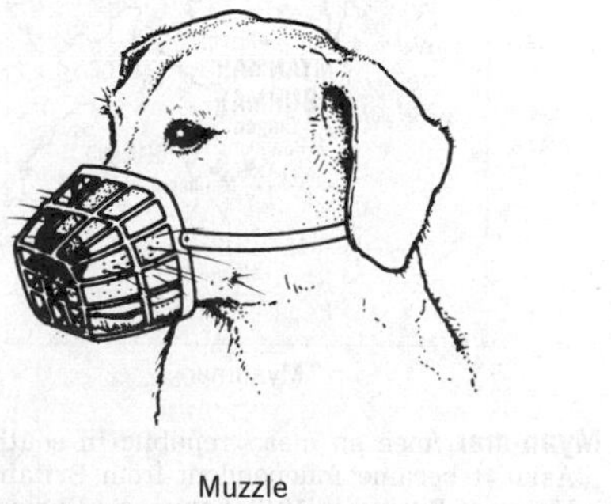

Muzzle

muz·zle /múzz'l/ *n.* **1.** ZOOL **ANIMAL'S NOSE AND JAWS** the projecting part of an animal's face, made up of its nose and jaws **2. RESTRAINING DEVICE FOR ANIMAL** a device that is strapped over the nose and jaws of an animal to prevent it from opening its mouth, e.g., to bite, bark, or eat **3.** ARMS **END OF GUN BARREL** the front open end of the barrel of a firearm **4.** SOMETHING THAT PREVENTS FREE EXPRESSION something that is meant to prevent free expression ■ *vt.* **(-zled, -zling, -zles) 1.** PUT MUZZLE ON ANIMAL to put a muzzle over the nose and jaws of an animal **2.** PREVENT SOMEBODY'S FREE EXPRESSION to prevent a person or group from publicly expressing particular views or opinions **3.** SAILING TAKE IN A SAIL to roll up and secure a sail [14thC. From Old French *musel*, literally "small muzzle," from *muse* "muzzle," from assumed Gallo-Romance *musa* "snout," of unknown origin.] —**muz·zler** *n.*

muz·zle·load·er /múzz'l lōdər/ *n.* a firearm that is loaded through its muzzle

muz·zle ve·loc·i·ty *n.* the speed of a bullet or other projectile as it leaves the muzzle of a firearm

muz·zy /múzzee/ **(-zi·er, -zi·est)** *adj.* **1.** NOT THINKING CLEARLY thinking in a confused way, especially as a result of illness or drinking alcohol **2.** VAGUE vague and confused [Early 18thC. Origin uncertain: perhaps a blend of MUDDLED and FUZZY.] —**muz·zi·ly** *adv.* —**muz·zi·ness** *n.*

mv *abbr.* mezza voce

mV *abbr.* millivolt

MV *abbr.* **1.** STATS mean variation **2.** MEASURE megavolt **3.** ARMS muzzle velocity

m.v. *abbr.* market value

MVD *n.* the Ministry for Internal Affairs in the former Soviet Union from 1946 to 1960, acting as secret police. Full form **Ministerstvo vnutrennikh del**

MVP *abbr.* Most Valuable Player (award)

mW *abbr.* milliwatt

MW *abbr.* **1.** RADIO medium wave **2.** CHEM molecular weight **3.** MEASURE megawatt **4.** Malawi (*international vehicle registration*)

Mx *abbr.* maxwell

MX *abbr.* **1.** MIL missile experimental **2.** MOTOR SPORTS motocross

mxd. *abbr.* mixed

my[1] /mī/ *adj.* BELONGING TO ME belonging or relating to the speaker (*first person possessive adjective*) ○ *You can borrow my car.* ○ *I always keep my promises.* ■ *interj.* USED TO EXPRESS SUDDEN EMOTION used to express sudden emotion such as surprise, fright, concern, or pleasure ○ *My! What a mess!* [12thC. Shortening of MINE originally found only before consonants other than "h."]

my[2] *abbr.* million years

MY *abbr.* motor yacht

my- *prefix.* = **myo-** (*used before vowels*)

my·al·gi·a /mī áljee ə, mī áljə/ *n.* pain or tenderness in a muscle or group of muscles [Mid-19thC. From modern Latin, from *my-* MY- + Greek *-algia* (see -ALGIA).] —**my·al·gic** *adj.*

my·al·ism /mī ə lìzzəm/ *n.* a type of witchcraft practiced in the West Indies [Mid-19thC. Formed from *myal*, of uncertain origin: perhaps from Hausa *maye* "sorcerer."] —**my·al·ist** *n.*

Myall Lake /mī awl-/ coastal lake in eastern New South Wales, north of Port Stephens. Area: 120 sq. mi./310 sq. km.

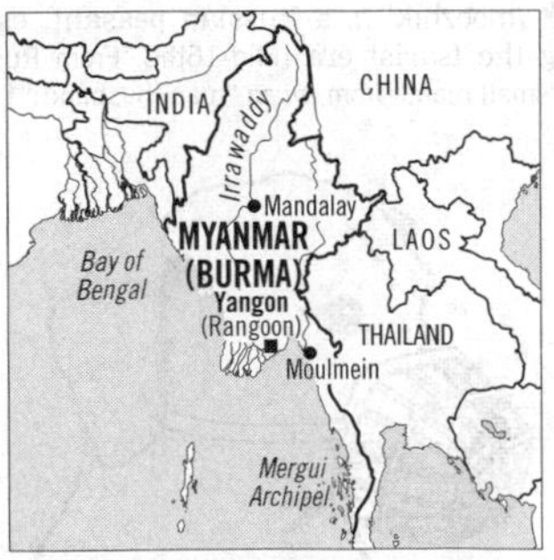

Myanmar

Myan·mar /mée ən maar/ republic in southeastern Asia. It became independent from Britain as the Union of Burma in 1948. Language: Burmese. Currency: kyat. Capital: Yangon. Population: 45,570,000 (1996). Area: 261,218 sq. mi./676,552 sq. km. Official name **Union of Myanmar**. Former name **Burma**

my·as·the·ni·a /mì əs théenee ə/ *n.* chronic condition of muscle weakness. Myasthenia is an autoimmune disease. [Mid-19thC. From modern Latin, from *my-* MY- + *asthenia* (see ASTHENIA).] —**my·as·then·ic** /mì əs thénnik/ *adj.*

my·ce·li·um /mī séelee əm/ (*plural* **-a** /-ə/) *n.* a loose network of the delicate filaments (**hyphae**) that form the body of a fungus, consisting of the feeding and reproducing hyphae [Mid-19thC. From modern Latin, from Greek *mukēs* "fungus" on the model of modern Latin *epithelium* (see EPITHELIUM).] —**my·ce·li·al** *adj.* —**my·ce·loid** /mísse lòyd/ *adj.*

My·ce·nae /mī sée nee/ *n.* an ancient Greek city in the Peloponnese that was a center of Bronze Age culture until its destruction around 1100 B.C. —**My·ce·nae·an** *n., adj.*

mycet- *prefix.* = **myceto-** (*used before vowels*)

-mycete *suffix.* a fungus [Via modern Latin *-mycetes* from Greek *mukētes*, the plural of *mukēs* "fungus" (source of English *mycelium*)]

myceto- *prefix.* fungus, fungi ○ *mycetophagous* [Via modern Latin from Greek *mukēt*, the stem of *mukēs* (see MYCO-)]

my·ce·to·ma /mìssə tṓmə/ (*plural* **-mas** *or* **-ma·ta** /-mətə/) *n.* an inflammation of tissues caused by a fungal or bacterial infection, usually of the feet or legs, which swell and develop pus-discharging nodules [Late 19thC. From modern Latin, from Greek *mukēt-*, the stem of *mukēs* "fungus."] —**my·ce·to·ma·tous** *adj.*

my·ce·to·phag·ous /mìssə tóffəgəss/ *adj.* feeding on fungi

-mycin *suffix.* a substance derived from a bacterium ○ *streptomycin* [Coined from MYCO- + -IN; so called because the bacteria were originally thought to be fungi]

myco- *prefix.* fungus, fungi ○ *mycotoxin* [From Greek *mukēs*. Ultimately from an Indo-European word meaning "slimy," which is also the ancestor of English *mucus*.]

my·co·bac·te·ri·um /mìkō bak téeree əm/ (*plural* **-a** /-ə/) *n.* a rodlike, Gram-positive, aerobic bacterium that can form branching structures resembling filaments. Some cause diseases in humans, e.g., tuberculosis or leprosy. Genus: *Mycobacterium.* —**my·co·bac·ter·i·al** *adj.*

my·col·o·gy /mī kólləjee/ *n.* **1.** BOT STUDY OF FUNGI a branch of botany that specializes in the scientific study of fungi **2.** FUNGI FUNGI OF PARTICULAR AREA the fungi that live in a particular area **3.** FUNGI CHARACTERISTICS OF INDIVIDUAL FUNGUS the characteristics of a particular fungus [Mid-19thC. From modern Latin *mycologia*, from *myco-* MYCO- + Latin *-logia* (see -LOGY).] —**my·co·log·ic** /mìkə lójjik/ *adj.* —**my·co·log·i·cal·ly** *adv.* —**my·col·o·gist** /mī kólləjist/ *n.*

my·co·phag·ist /mī kóffəjist/ *n.* an animal that eats fungi [Mid-19thC. Formed from *mycophagy*, from MYCO- + -PHAGY.]

my·coph·a·gous /mī kóffəgəss/ *adj.* feeding on fungi —**my·coph·a·gy** /-jee/ *n.*

my·co·plas·ma /mìkō plázmə/ *n.* a microorganism of a genus considered to be the smallest known living cells. Some species cause respiratory diseases in animals and human being. Regarded by some as primitive bacteria, they need sterols such as cholesterol for growth. Genus: *Mycoplasma.* —**my·co·plas·mal** *adj.*

my·cor·rhi·za /mìkə rízə/ (*plural* **-zas** *or* **-zae** /-zee/), **my·co·rhi·za** (*plural* **-zas** *or* **-zae**) *n.* a mutually beneficial association of a fungus and the roots of a plant such as a conifer or an orchid in which the plant's mineral absorption is enhanced and the fungus obtains nutrients [Late 19thC. From modern Latin, from *myco-* MYCO- + Greek *rhiza* "root."] —**my·cor·rhi·zal** *adj.*

my·co·sis /mī kóssiss/ (*plural* **-ses** /-seez/) *n.* any disease or infection of human beings or animals caused by a fungus

my·co·tox·in /mìkə tóksin/ *n.* a poisonous substance produced by a fungus. Mycotoxins may affect foods such as peanuts.

my·co·troph·ic /mìkō tróffik/ *adj.* used to describe a plant that lives in association with a fungus, as do various orchids in which the fungus lives on the roots

my·dri·a·sis /mi drī əssiss, mī-/ *n.* excessive dilation of the pupils of the eye, usually caused by prolonged drug therapy, coma, or injury to the eye [Early 19thC. Via Latin from Greek *mudriasis*.]

myel- *prefix.* = **myelo-** (*used before vowels*)

my·e·len·ceph·a·lon /mī ələn séffə lòn/ *n.* a part of the embryonic hindbrain formed by an extension of the spinal cord into the skull. It is the major pathway for nerve impulses leaving and entering the brain. [Mid-19thC. From modern Latin, from *myel-* MYEL- + *encephalon* (see ENCEPHALON).] —**my·e·len·ce·phal·ic** /mī ələnsə fállik/ *adj.*

my·e·lin /mī əlin/ *n.* a whitish material made up of protein and fats that surrounds some nerve cells in concentric sheaths, insulating adjacent nerve fibers and enabling transmission of nerve impulses [Late 19thC. Coined from MYEL- + -IN.]

my·e·li·nat·ed /mī əli nàytəd/ *adj.* used to describe nerve fibers that are surrounded by a sheath of myelin

my·e·lin sheath *n.* a layer of myelin that insulates some nerve cells. In multiple sclerosis, the myelin sheath is damaged and the nerve impulse is impaired.

my·e·li·tis /mī ə lítiss/ *n.* inflammation of the spinal cord or bone marrow

myelo- *prefix.* **1.** bone marrow ○ *myelofibrosis* **2.** spinal cord, spinal column ○ *myelencephalon* [Via modern Latin from Greek *muelos* "marrow," of uncertain origin: probably formed from *mus* "muscle" (see MYO-)]

my·e·lo·blast /mī ələ blàst/ *n.* a cell that develops into a type of white blood cell (**granulocyte**) and that is normally seen only in the bone marrow where blood is formed. In some diseases, e.g., leukemia, myeloblasts may appear in the blood. —**my·e·lo·blas·tic** /mī ələ blástik/ *adj.*

my·e·lo·cyte /mī ələ sīt/ *n.* an immature form of a type of white blood cell (**granulocyte**), normally found in the blood-forming tissue of the bone marrow —**my·e·lo·cy·tic** /mī ələ síttik/ *adj.*

my·e·lo·fi·bro·sis /mī ə lō fī brṓssiss/ *n.* a progressive disease in which the cells of the bone marrow that produce fiber rather than blood cells proliferate, leading to anemia and enlargement of the spleen and liver —**my·e·lo·fi·brot·ic** /mī ə lō fī bróttik/ *adj.*

my·e·log·e·nous /mī ə lójjənəss/, **my·e·lo·gen·ic** /mī ələ jénnik/ *adj.* originating in or produced by the bone marrow

my·e·log·e·nous leu·ke·mi·a *n.* = **myeloid leukemia**

my·el·o·gram /mī ələ gràm/ *n.* a radiographic image created by injecting an X ray-opaque liquid into the spinal cord, to diagnose disorders of the spine including slipped disks or tumors —**my·e·log·ra·phy** /mī ə lóggrəfee/ *n.*

my·e·loid /mī ə lòyd/ *adj.* relating to, involving, or derived from bone marrow or the spinal cord

my·e·loid leu·ke·mi·a *n.* a variety of leukemia in which some types of white blood cells, originating in the myeloid tissue of the bone marrow, proliferate abnormally, suppressing healthy red and white blood cells

my·e·lo·ma /mī ə lṓmə/ (*plural* **-mas** *or* **-ma·ta** /-mətə/) *n.* a malignant tumor that develops in the blood-cell-producing cells of the bone marrow —**my·e·lo·ma·toid** *adj.*

my·ia·sis /mī əssiss/ (*plural* **-ses** /-seez/) *n.* an infestation of living tissue or an organism by maggots such as fly larvae. It can affect the skin, eyes, digestive tract, or open wounds. [Mid-19thC. From modern Latin, from Greek *muia* "fly."]

My Lai /mī lī/ village in Vietnam that was the site of a massacre of civilians by U.S. troops during the Vietnam War (1968)

My·lar /mī laar/ *tdmk.* a trademark for a thin strong polyester film used in packaging, insulation, recording tapes, and photography

my·lo·nite /mīlə nīt/ *n.* a fine-grained layered metamorphic rock formed where the movement of rocks against each other causes crushing and grinding. It is found in fault zones. [Late 19thC. Formed from Greek *mulōn* "mill" (source of English *amyl*).]

my·nah /mīnə/, **my·nah bird, my·na** *n.* a medium-sized bird of the starling family, native to southeastern Asia and Australia. Some varieties are known for their ability to mimic human speech. Genera: *Acridotheres* and *Gracula.* [Mid-18thC. From Hindi *mainā*.]

Myn·heer /mə néer/ *n.* **1.** TITLE FOR DUTCH MAN a title used to address a Dutch man, equivalent to "Mr." when used before a surname and to "sir" when used alone. **2. Myn·heer, myn·heer** DUTCHMAN a Dutchman (*informal*) [Mid-17thC. From Dutch *mijnheer*, literally "my lord," from *heer* "lord, master."]

myo- *prefix.* muscle ○ *myofibril* [Via modern Latin from Greek *mus.* Ultimately from an Indo-European word meaning "mouse," which is also the ancestor of English *mouse* and *muscle.*]

MYOB *abbr.* mind your own business (*informal*)

my·o·car·di·al /mī ō kaárdee əl/ *adj.* relating to or affecting the thick muscular wall of the heart. ◆ **myocardium**

my·o·car·di·al in·farc·tion *n.* the death of a segment of heart muscle, caused by a blood clot in the coronary artery interrupting blood supply

my·o·car·di·tis /mī ō kaar dítiss/ *n.* acute or chronic inflammation of the heart muscle

my·o·car·di·um /mī ō kaárdee əm/ (*plural* **-a** /-ə/) *n.* the thick muscular wall of the heart. The myocardium is thickest around the left ventricle where the pressure generated by the heart is greatest. [Late 19thC. From modern Latin, from *myo-* MYO- + Greek *kardia* "heart."]

my·oc·lo·nus /mī óklənəss/ *n.* a sudden muscular contraction, or a series of these, which if persistent usually indicates a disorder of the nervous system. It is normal to experience these contractions when falling asleep. —**my·o·clon·ic** /mī ə klónnik/ *adj.*

my·o·e·lec·tric /mī ō i léktrik/, **my·o·e·lec·tri·cal** /-trik'l/ *adj.* **1. OF ELECTRICAL PROPERTIES OF MUSCLE** relating to or involving the electrical properties of muscle **2. USING ELECTRICAL PROPERTIES OF MUSCLE** using the detection of electrical impulses in muscle to activate a bionic part such as an artificial limb

my·o·fib·ril /mī ə fíbbril, -fībril/ *n.* structure resembling a thread running through a muscle cell that enables the muscle to contract

my·o·fil·a·ment /mī ō fílləmənt/ *n.* one of the filaments that make up a myofibril, either the thicker filaments composed of the protein myosin or the thinner filaments composed of the proteins actin or troponin

my·o·gen·ic /mī ə jénnik/ *adj.* originating in or able to form in muscle cells, as are the contractions of heart muscle fibers that are spontaneous and do not depend on nerve stimulation

my·o·glo·bin /mī ə glóbin/ *n.* an iron-containing protein resembling hemoglobin, found in muscle cells. It takes oxygen from the blood, releasing it to the muscles during strenuous exercise. The three-dimensional structure of myoglobin and the alpha and beta chains of hemoglobin are almost identical.

my·o·graph /mī ə gràf/ *n.* an instrument that produces a tracing corresponding to muscle contractions —**my·o·graph·ic** /mī ə gráffik/ *adj.* —**my·o·graph·i·cal·ly** *adv.*

my·ol·o·gy /mī óllәjee/ *n.* the study of the structure, function, and diseases of muscle [Mid-17thC. Directly or via French *myologie* from modern Latin *myologia*, from *myo-* MYO- + *-logia* (see -LOGY).] —**my·o·log·ic** /mī ə lójjik/ *adj.* —**my·ol·o·gist** /mī óllәjist/ *n.*

my·o·ma /mī ómə/ (*plural* **-mas** *or* **-ma·ta** /-mətə/) *n.* a benign tumor of the muscle tissue —**my·o·ma·tous** /mī ómətəss, -ómmə-/ *adj.*

my·o·neu·ral /mī ō noórəl/ *adj.* relating to or involving both muscles and nerves

my·op·a·thy /mī óppəthee/ (*plural* **-thies**) *n.* any disease of the muscles or muscle tissues, either inherited such as muscular dystrophy or acquired such as polio. All myopathies are characterized by muscle weakness and wasting with pain and tenderness. —**my·o·path·ic** /mī ə páthik/ *adj.*

my·ope /mī ōp/ *n.* somebody affected by myopia [Early 18thC. Via French from Latin *myop-*, the stem of *myops* "short-sighted," from Greek *muōps* (see MYOPIA).]

my·o·pi·a /mī ópee ə/ *n.* **1.** MED **SHORTNESS OF SIGHT** a common condition in which light entering the eye is focused in front of the retina and distant objects cannot be seen sharply. In high myopia the eyeball is unusually long, whereas in physiological myopia the eyeball length is normal but the power of the cornea is too great for the axial length. **2. LACK OF FORESIGHT** lack of foresight or long-term planning [Early 18thC. Via modern Latin from late Greek *muōpia*, from Greek *muōps* "short-sighted," from *muein* "to blink" (source of English *mystery*[1]).]

my·op·ic /mī óppik/ *adj.* **1.** MED **HAVING MYOPIA** affected by myopia **2. LACKING IN FORESIGHT** showing a lack of foresight or long-term planning —**my·op·i·cal·ly** *adv.*

my·o·sin /mī əssin/ *n.* a protein that is present in the filaments of muscles and is responsible for the contraction of muscle cells [Mid-19thC. Coined from MY- + -OSE + -IN.]

my·o·sis *n.* = **miosis**

my·o·si·tis /mī ō sítiss/ *n.* muscle inflammation and soreness [Early 19thC. From modern Latin, from Greek *muos* "of a muscle," a form of *mus* "mouse, muscle."]

my·o·so·tis /mī ə sótiss/ (*plural* **-tes** /mī ə sō teez/), **my·o·sote** /mī ə sōt/ *n.* a plant of the borage family with hairy leaves and stems and small flowers that may be pink at first and then blue. The forget-me-not is one variety of myosotis. Genus: *Myosotis.* [Early 17thC. Via modern Latin, genus name, from Latin, "mouse-ear (a plant)," from Greek *muosōtis*, from, ultimately, *mus* "mouse, muscle" + *ous* "ear" (source of English *otic*).]

my·o·tome /mī ə tōm/ *n.* **1.** BIOL **TYPE OF EMBRYONIC CELL** any of the cells in early embryos that give rise to all the muscles in the body **2.** ANAT **TYPE OF MUSCLE** a muscle that is supplied by a nerve of the spine

my·o·to·ni·a /mī ə tṓnee ə/ *n.* a muscle condition that results in the muscles maintaining contractions for much longer than normal and having difficulty in relaxing [Late 19thC. From modern Latin, from *myo-* MYO- + Greek *tonos* "tone."] —**my·o·ton·ic** /mī ə tónnik/ *adj.*

myr·i·ad /meéree əd/ *adj.* **1. TOO NUMEROUS TO COUNT** so many that they cannot be counted **2. OF MANY DIFFERENT ELEMENTS** made up of many different elements ■ *n.* **1. LARGE NUMBER** a huge number **2. TEN THOUSAND** ten thousand (*archaic*) [Mid-16thC. Directly or via Old French from the late Latin stem *myriad-*, from Greek *muriad-*, from, ultimately, *murios* "countless" (plural *murioi* "ten thousand").]

myr·i·a·pod /meéree ə pòd/ *n.* an arthropod such as a centipede or millipede with a head, a long segmented body, and at least nine pairs of legs. Class: Myriapoda. [Early 19thC. From modern Latin *Myriapoda*, class name, literally "with a myriad of feet," from, ultimately, Greek *murias* "myriad."]

my·ri·ca /mi ríkə/ *n.* a tonic and anti-diarrhea agent extracted from the root bark of the wax myrtle tree [Early 18thC. Via Latin, "tamarisk," from Greek *murikē.*]

my·ris·tic ac·id /mə rístik-, mī-/ *n.* an acid found in the fats of plants and animals and used in making soaps, flavorings, cosmetics, and perfumes. Formula: $C_{14}H_{28}O_2$. [*Myristic* from modern Latin *Myristica* (name of a genus of trees), from medieval Latin *(nux) myristica* "nutmeg," from Greek *murizein* "to anoint"]

myr·me·col·o·gy /mùrmə kólləjee/ *n.* the scientific study of ants [Late 19thC. Formed from Greek *murmēko-*, from *murmēx* "ant."] —**myr·me·co·log·ic** /mùrməkə lójjik/ *adj.* —**myr·me·col·o·gist** /mùrmə kólləjist/ *n.*

myr·mi·don /múrmi dòn, -d'n/ *n.* a faithful follower who obeys orders unquestioningly [Mid-17thC. See MYRMIDON.]

Myr·mi·don *n.* in Greek mythology, a member of a people who lived in Thessaly and were led by Achilles to the Trojan War [15thC. Via Latin *Myrmidones* (plural) from Greek *Murmidones* from *murmēkes* (according to legend , from "ants" (from which they were created according to legend).]

my·rob·a·lan /mī róbbələn, mee-/ *n.* **1. FRUIT USED IN DYEING** the dried fruit of a tropical shrub that resembles a plum and is used in dyeing and in making ink **2.** = **cherry plum** [Mid-16thC. Directly or via French from Latin *myrobalanum*, from Greek *murobalanon*, from *muron* "balsam, ointment" + *balanos* "acorn."]

myrrh /mur/ *n.* **1. AROMATIC RESIN** an aromatic resinous gum obtained from various trees and shrubs that are native to Africa and southern Asia, used in perfume, incense, and medicinal preparations **2.** BOT = **sweet cicely** [Pre-12thC. From Latin *myrrha*, from Greek *murra*, of Semitic origin (source of English *myrtle*).]

myr·tle /múrt'l/ *n.* **1.** TREES **EVERGREEN TREE** an evergreen tree or shrub, native to the Mediterranean region and western Asia, with white or pink flowers and edible blue-black fruit. Family: Myrtaceae. **2.** PLANTS = **periwinkle**[2] *n.* [14thC. Directly or via Old French from medieval Latin *myrtilla*, literally "small myrtle tree," from Latin *myrtus* "myrtle tree," from Greek *murtos*, of Semitic origin.]

Myrtle

Myr·tle Beach city and resort in eastern South Carolina, on the Atlantic Ocean, southeast of Florence. Population: 25,456 (1996).

my·self /mī sélf/ *pron.* **1. REFERS BACK TO SPEAKER** used to refer to the speaker or writer (*first person reflexive pronoun, used when the object of a verb or preposition refers to the same person as the subject of the verb*) ○ *I didn't enjoy myself very much.* ○ *Of all the people I am hard on, I am hardest on myself.* **2. REFERS EMPHATICALLY TO SPEAKER** refers emphatically to the speaker or writer ○ *I'm curious about that myself.* ○ *I can't expect you to be able to read my writing; I myself can't read it.* **3. MY NORMAL SELF** my normal or usual self ○ *I haven't been myself since the accident.* [Old English *mēseolf*, literally "me self" (*self* in the obsolete sense of "same")]

My·sore /mī sáwr/ city in the Mysore District, south central Karnataka State, southern India. Population: 480,006 (1991).

mys·ta·gogue /místə gòg/ *n.* **1. INSTRUCTOR OF INITIATES** somebody who instructs candidates for initiation into sacred mysteries **2. SOMEBODY SPREADING MYSTICAL DOCTRINES** somebody who believes in and disseminates mystical doctrines [Mid-16thC. Directly or via French from Latin *mystagogus*, from Greek *mustagōgos*, literally "leader of candidates for initiation," from *mustēs* "initiated person" (see MYSTERY[1]).] —**mys·ta·gog·ic** /mìstə gójjik/ *adj.* —**mys·ta·gog·i·cal·ly** *adv.* —**mys·ta·go·gy** /místə gòjee/ *n.*

mys·te·ri·ous /mi steéree əss/ *adj.* **1. ABOUT WHICH LITTLE IS KNOWN** about whom or which little is known or explained **2. DIFFICULT TO UNDERSTAND** difficult to understand or explain **3. FULL OF MYSTERY** full of or suggesting mystery [Late 16thC. Formed from French *mystérieux*, from *mystère* "mystery," via Old French from Latin *mysterium* (see MYSTERY[1]).] —**mys·te·ri·ous·ness** *n.*

mys·te·ri·ous·ly /mi steéree əsslee/ *adv.* **1. IN A PUZZLING WAY** in a way that is difficult to understand or explain **2. IN A WAY FULL OF MYSTERY** in a way that is full of or reminiscent of mystery

mys·ter·y[1] /místəree/ *n.* (*plural* **-ies**) **1. PUZZLING EVENT OR SITUATION** an event or situation that is difficult to understand or explain **2. SOMEBODY UNKNOWN** somebody who or something that is unknown, secret, or hidden **3. STRANGENESS** the quality of being strange, secret, or puzzling **4. STORY ABOUT PUZZLING EVENT** a book, play, or movie about a puzzling event, especially an unsolved crime, that makes great use of suspense **5.** CHR **SOMETHING KNOWN BY DIVINE REVELATION** a Christian belief or truth that is considered to be beyond human understanding and can be made known only by divine revelation **6.** CHR **INCIDENT FROM LIFE OF JESUS CHRIST** an incident in the life of Jesus Christ that Christians believe to have particular spiritual significance, especially, in Roman Catholicism, one of 15 events including the Annunciation and the Crucifixion **7.** CHR **CHRISTIAN SACRAMENT** one of the Christian sacraments, especially Communion **8.** RELIG **RELIGIOUS GROUP** a religious group having secret rites, especially one of the ancient Mediterranean religions, e.g., of the Romans **9.** RELIG **RELIGIOUS RITE** a secret rite or ceremony performed by a religious group, especially belonging to one of the ancient Mediterranean religions (*often used in the plural*) **10.** ARTS = **mystery play** ■ **mys·ter·ies** *npl.* **1. SECRET KNOWLEDGE** special knowledge known only to people skilled or involved in a particular activity, group, or subject **2.** CHR **CONSECRATED BREAD AND WINE** in Christianity, the consecrated bread and wine used in the sacrament of Communion [14thC. Directly or via assumed Anglo-Norman from Latin *mysterium*, from Greek *mustērion* "secret rite," from *mustēs* "initiated person," from *muein* "to close the eyes or lips, initiate."]

WORD KEY: SYNONYMS

See Synonyms at ***problem.***

mys·ter·y[2] /místəree/ (*plural* **-ies**) *n.* (*archaic*) **1. GUILD** a guild of merchants or craftsmen **2. CRAFT** a handicraft or trade [13thC. From medieval Latin *misterium* "service, office," a contraction (influenced by Latin *mysterium* "mystery") of Latin *ministerium,* from *minister* "servant" (see MINISTER).]

mys·ter·y play *n.* a medieval drama staged by a craft guild and often based on stories from the Bible such as the Flood or incidents from the life of Jesus Christ

mys·tic /místik/ *n.* RELIG **FOLLOWER OF MYSTICISM** somebody who practices or believes in mysticism ■ *adj.* = **mystical** [14thC. Directly or via French *mystique* (adjective) from Latin *mysticus,* from Greek *mustikos,* from *mustēs* "initiated person" (see MYSTERY[1]).]

mys·ti·cal /místik'l/ *adj.* **1.** RELIG **WITH DIVINE MEANING** with a divine meaning beyond human understanding **2.** RELIG **OF MYSTICISM** relating to, involving, or typical of mysticism or mystics **3.** PARANORMAL **WITH SUPERNATURAL SIGNIFICANCE** with supernatural or spiritual significance or power **4. MYSTERIOUS** mysterious or difficult to understand —**mys·ti·cal·ly** *adv.* —**mys·ti·cal·ness** *n.*

mys·ti·cism /místə sìzzəm/ *n.* **1.** RELIG **BELIEF IN INTUITIVE SPIRITUAL REVELATION** the belief that personal communication or union with the divine is achieved through intuition, faith, ecstasy, or sudden insight rather than through rational thought **2.** RELIG **SPIRITUAL SYSTEM** a system of religious belief or practice that people follow to achieve personal communication or union with the divine **3. CONFUSED AND VAGUE IDEAS** vague or unsubstantiated thought or speculation about something

mys·ti·fy /místə fì/ (**-fied, -fy·ing, -fies**) *vt.* **1. PUZZLE SOMEBODY** to put somebody in a position of being unable to understand or explain something **2. MAKE SOMETHING MYSTERIOUS** to make something mysterious or unclear [Early 19thC. From French *mystifier,* from *mystère* "mystery" (ultimately from Latin *mysterium;* see MYSTERY[1]) or *mystique* "mystic" (see MYSTIC).] —**mys·ti·fi·ca·tion** /mìstəfi káysh'n/ *n.* —**mys·ti·fi·er** /místə fìr/ *n.*

mys·ti·fy·ing /místi fì ing/ *adj.* difficult to understand or explain —**mys·ti·fy·ing·ly** *adv.*

mys·tique /mi stéek/ *n.* a special quality or air that makes somebody or something appear mysterious, powerful, or desirable [Late 19thC. Via French (source of English *mystic*) from, ultimately, Greek *mustikos,* from *mustēs* "initiated person" (see MYSTERY[1]).]

myth /mith/ *n.* **1.** MYTHOL **ANCIENT STORY** a traditional story about heroes or supernatural beings, often explaining the origins of natural phenomena or aspects of human behavior **2.** LITERAT, MYTHOL **MYTHS COLLECTIVELY** myths considered as a group or a type of story **3.** SOC SCI **SYMBOLIC CHARACTER OR STORY** a character, story, theme, or object that embodies a particular idea or aspect of a culture **4. SOMEBODY OR SOMETHING FICTITIOUS** somebody or something whose existence is or was widely believed in, but who is fictitious **5. ALLEGORY OR PARABLE** a story that has a hidden meaning, especially one that is meant to teach a lesson [Mid-19thC. Directly or via French *mythe* from modern Latin *mythus,* from Greek *muthos* "speech, myth" (source of English *mythos*).]

myth. *abbr.* **1.** mythological **2.** mythology

myth·i·cal /míthik'l/, **myth·ic** /míthik/ *adj.* **1. TYPICAL OF MYTH** relating to, appearing in, based on, or typical of myth **2. IMAGINARY** not true or real, but existing only in somebody's imagination **3. LIKE MYTH** like a myth, especially in being widely known or considered wonderful —**myth·i·cal·ly** *adv.*

myth·i·cize /míthi sìz/ (**-cized, -ciz·ing, -ciz·es**) *vt.* **1. MAKE INTO MYTH** to make somebody or something into a myth **2. TREAT AS MYTH** to see or explain an event or person as a myth —**myth·i·ci·za·tion** /mìthissi záysh'n/ *n.* —**myth·i·ciz·er** /míthi sìzər/ *n.*

myth·mak·er /míth màykər/ *n.* somebody who creates myths —**myth·mak·ing** *n.*

my·thog·ra·phy /mi thóggrəfee/ (*plural* **-phies**) *n.* **1.** LITERAT **VOLUME OF MYTHS** a collection of myths **2.** ARTS **ARTISTIC REPRESENTATION** the representation of a mythical subject in a work of art

my·thoi plural of **mythos**

mythol. *abbr.* **1.** mythological **2.** mythology

myth·o·log·i·cal /mìthə lójjik'l/, **myth·o·log·ic** /-ik/ *adj.* **1.** MYTHOL **IN MYTHS** relating to, typical of, or appearing in myth **2. IMAGINARY** not real, but existing only in the imagination —**myth·o·log·i·cal·ly** *adv.*

my·thol·o·gist /mi thóllәjist/ *n.* **1. WRITER OF MYTHS** somebody who writes or collects myths **2. STUDENT OF MYTHS** somebody who studies or is an expert on myths

my·thol·o·gize /mi thóllə jìz/ (**-gized, -giz·ing, -giz·es**) *v.* **1.** *vt.* **MAKE INTO MYTH** to make somebody or something into a myth **2.** *vti.* **EXPLAIN OR MAKE UP MYTHS** to explain or relate myths **3.** *vi.* **CREATE MYTHS** to create or make up myths —**myth·ol·o·gi·za·tion** /mi thòlləji záysh'n/ *n.* —**my·thol·o·giz·er** /mi thóllə jìzər/ *n.*

my·thol·o·gy /mi thólləjee/ (*plural* **-gies**) *n.* **1.** MYTHOL **BODY OF MYTHS** a group of myths that belong to a particular people or culture and tell about their ancestors, heroes, gods and other supernatural beings, and history **2. BODY OF STORIES** a body of stories, ideas, or beliefs that are not necessarily true about a particular place or individual **3.** MYTHOL **MYTHS COLLECTIVELY** myths considered as a group **4.** MYTHOL **STUDY OF MYTHS** the study of myths, or the branch of knowledge that deals with myths [15thC. Directly or via French from late Latin *mythologia,* from Greek *muthologia,* literally "science of myths," from *muthos* (see MYTH).] —**myth·o·log·er** *n.*

myth·o·ma·ni·a /mìthō máynee ə/ *n.* a very strong tendency to tell lies or exaggerate, which may be symptom of a disorder —**myth·o·ma·ni·ac** *n.*

myth·o·poe·ia /mìthō pée ə/, **myth·o·po·e·sis** /-pō éessiss/ *n.* the creating of myths [Mid-19thC. Directly or via late Latin from Greek *muthopoiia,* from *muthos* (see MYTH) + *poiein* "to make" (source of English *poem*).] —**myth·o·poe·ist** *n.*

myth·o·poe·ic /mìthō pée ik/ *adj.* relating to, involving, or engaged in the production of myths [Mid-19thC. Formed from Greek *muthopoios,* from *muthos* (see MYTH) + *poiein* "to make."]

my·thos /mí thòss, mí-/ (*plural* **-thoi** /-thoy/) *n.* **1. SET OF ATTITUDES** the interrelated set of beliefs, attitudes, and values held by a society or cultural group **2. MYTH OR MYTHOLOGY** a myth or mythology [Mid-18thC. From Greek *muthos* "speech, myth" (source of English *myth*).]

myx- *prefix.* = **myxo-** (*used before vowels*)

myx·e·de·ma /mìksi déemə/ *n.* **1. THYROID DISEASE** a disease caused by an underactive or atrophied thyroid gland, characterized by sluggishness and weight gain. It can be treated with artificial thyroid hormone. **2. SKIN SWELLING** dry swelling of the skin and subcutaneous tissues, associated with an underactive thyroid gland —**myx·e·dem·a·tous** /mìksi démmətəss, -déem-/ *adj.* —**myx·e·dem·ic** /mìksə démmik/ *adj.*

myxo- *prefix.* mucus ○ *myxomycete* [Via modern Latin from Greek *muxa* "slime, mucus" (source of English *match*)]

myx·o·ma /mik sṓmə/ (*plural* **-mas** *or* **-ma·ta** /-mətə/) *n.* a benign tumor composed of mucus and gelatinous material embedded in connective tissue, typically in the heart where it can obstruct blood flow and lead to sudden unconsciousness —**myx·o·ma·tous** /mik sómmətəss/ *adj.*

myx·o·ma·to·sis /mik sòmə tṓssiss/ *n.* a highly infectious disease of rabbits caused by a virus, leading to swelling of the mucous membranes and the formation of tumors similar to myxomas [Early 20thC. From modern Latin, from *myxomat-,* the stem of *myxoma* (see MYXOMA).]

myx·o·my·cete /mìksō mí seet/ *n.* = **slime mold** [Late 19thC. From modern Latin *Myxomycetes,* class name, from *myxo-* MYXO- + Greek *mukētes,* the plural of *mukēs* "fungus."]

myx·o·vir·us /míksə vìrəss/ *n.* any of a group of RNA-containing viruses, including those that cause diseases of the respiratory tract such as influenza, and those that cause measles and mumps (**paramyxoviruses**)

N n

n[1] /en/ (*plural* **n's**), **N** (*plural* **N's** *or* **Ns**) *n.* **1. LETTER OF ENGLISH ALPHABET** the 14th letter of the modern English alphabet **2. SPEECH SOUND CORRESPONDING TO LETTER "N"** the speech sound that corresponds to the letter "N" **3. LETTER "N" WRITTEN** a written representation of the letter "N"

n[2] *n.* an indefinite whole number

n[3], **n., N, N.** *abbr.* **1.** north **2.** northern

n[4] *symbol.* **1.** amount of substance **2. n, N** PRINTING en (dash) **3.** PHYS, OPTICS index of refraction **4.** MEASURE nano- **5.** PHYS neutron

n' /en/, **'n'** *conj.* and

N[1] *symbol.* **1.** PHYS Avogadro's number **2.** PHYS, MEASURE newton **3.** CHEM ELEM nitrogen

N[2] *abbr.* **1.** CHESS knight **2.** CARS neutral (*used on gearshifts*) **3.** November

n. *abbr.* **1.** natus **2.** COMM net **3.** GRAM neuter **4.** GRAM nominative **5.** noon **6.** note **7.** GRAM noun **8.** number

N. *abbr.* **1.** GEOG New (*in place names*) **2.** LANG Norse

n- *prefix.* normal

Na *symbol.* sodium [Shortening of modern Latin *natrium*, from, ultimately, Greek *nitron* "niter"]

N.A. *abbr.* **1.** DRUGS Narcotics Anonymous **2.** National Academy **3.** North America

n/a *abbr.* **1.** not applicable **2.** not available

NAACP, **N.A.A.C.P.** *abbr.* National Association for the Advancement of Colored People

nab /nab/ (**nabbed, nab·bing, nabs**) *vt.* **1. GRAB SOMETHING** to seize, snatch, or take something suddenly **2. CATCH SOMEBODY** to catch and arrest a criminal or fugitive (*informal*) [Late 17thC. Origin uncertain: probably a variant of earlier *nap*, from Scandinavian.]

WORD KEY: SYNONYMS

See Synonyms at ***catch***.

Nab·a·tae·an /nàbbə teé ən/, **Nab·a·te·an** *n.* **1.** PEOPLES **MEMBER OF AN ARAB PEOPLE** a member of an Arab people who in Roman times lived in part of modern Jordan, and whose capital city was Petra **2.** LANG **EXTINCT NABATAEAN LANGUAGE** the now extinct language spoken by the Nabataeans, a dialect of Aramaic [Early 17thC. Formed from Latin *Nabat(h)aeus*.] —**Nab·a·tae·an** *adj.*

nabe /nayb/ *n.* (*slang*) **1.** THEATER **MOVIE THEATER** a neighborhood movie theater (*often used in the plural*) **2. NEIGHBORHOOD** somebody's neighborhood [Mid-20thC. From the pronunciation of *neighb(orhood)*.]

Na·bis /naábee/ *npl.* a group of 19th-century French artists, including Bonnard, who embraced symbolism rather than the naturalism of the Impressionist painters [Mid-20thC. Plural of *nabi* "member of the Nabis," from Hebrew *nābī* "prophet."]

na·bob /náy bòb/ *n.* **1. SOMEBODY RICH** somebody who is very rich or powerful (*informal*) **2.** HIST = **nawab** *n.* [Early 17thC. Via Portuguese *nababo* or Spanish *nabab* from Urdu *nawwāb* "deputy governor."]

Na·bo·kov /nə bők of, -bók-, nábbə kof/, **Vladimir** (1899–1977) Russian-born U.S. writer. He is known for the stylish word-play of his novels, especially the controversial *Lolita* (1955). Full name **Vladimir Vladimirovich Nabokov**

Nab·u·lus /nábbəlòòss/, **Nāb·u·lus** city in the West Bank Region, 30 mi./48 km north of Jerusalem. Population: 106,944 (1987).

na·celle /nə sél/ *n.* a separate streamlined enclosure on an aircraft for crew, cargo, or engines [Early 20thC. Via French, "dinghy, gondola," from late Latin *navicella* "boat" (literally "small ship"), from Latin *navis* "ship" (source of English *navy*).]

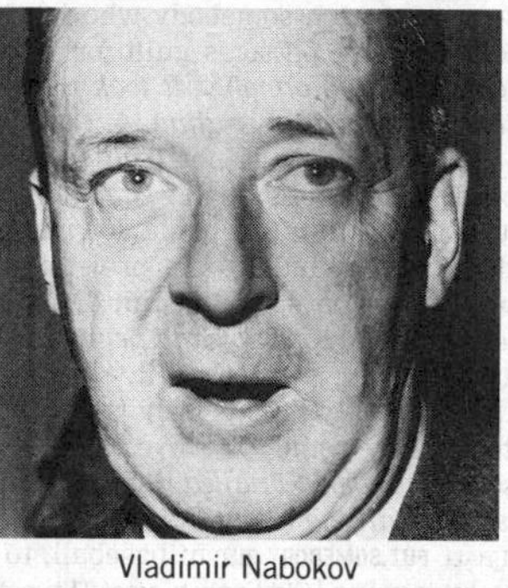

Hulton-Deutsch Collection/Corbis

Vladimir Nabokov

na·chos /naá chōz/ *npl.* a hot dish of tortilla chips covered with melted cheese, chili sauce, or another spicy topping, usually served as a snack or an appetizer [Mid-20thC. Plural of *nacho*, of uncertain origin: perhaps from Mexican Spanish, nickname for *Ignacio*, the name of the chef who is said to have created it.]

Nacimiento Peak /nàssimee èntō-/ mountain in southern Rio Arriba County, northern New Mexico. Height: 10,045 ft./3,060 m.

na·cre /náykər/ *n.* = **mother-of-pearl** [Late 16thC. Via French from Italian *naccaro*, from Arabic *nāqūr* "hunting horn," from the similarity in shape to a mollusk.]

na·cre·ous /náykree əss/ *adj.* **1. OF MOTHER-OF-PEARL** relating to, typical of, or made of mother-of-pearl **2. LIKE MOTHER-OF-PEARL** with the iridescent quality of mother-of-pearl

na·cre·ous cloud *n.* an iridescent cloud that looks like a cirrus and appears especially in the winter at high latitudes

NACU *abbr.* National Association of Colleges and Universities

NAD *n.* a coenzyme acting as a hydrogen acceptor in many biochemical reactions, e.g., in the electron transport chain, where it is vital in the production of energy. Full form **nicotinamide adenine dinucleotide**

Na-Den·e /naa dénnee/, **Na-Dén·é** *n.* a language group of over 30 Native American languages spoken in parts of Alaska, Canada, and the southwestern United States. About 200,000 people speak a Na-Dene language. [From Athapaskan *na* + North Athapaskan *dene* "people"] —**Na-Den·e** *adj.*

Na·der /náydər/, **Ralph** (*b.* 1934) U.S. consumer-protection advocate. He led several campaigns and wrote the controversial *Unsafe at Any Speed* (1965) on the automobile industry.

NADH *n.* the chemically reduced form of NAD that reverts to NAD in a process that initiates the generation of cellular energy [Mid-20thC. From NAD + *H* "hydrogen."]

na·dir /náydər, -deer/ *n.* **1. LOWEST POINT** the lowest possible point ○ *the nadir of despair* **2.** ASTRON **POINT ON CELESTIAL SPHERE** the point on the celestial sphere directly below the observer and opposite the zenith [14thC. Via French and medieval Latin from Arabic *nazīr (as-samt)*, literally "opposite (the zenith)."]

NADP *n.* a coenzyme in living cells that is similar to NAD but with an extra phosphate group. It tends to participate in biochemical syntheses rather than energy-yielding reactions. Formula: $C_{21}H_{28}N_7O_{17}P_3$. Full form **nicotinamide adenine dinucleotide phosphate**

nae /nay/ *adv. Scotland* **1. NO** no **2. NOT** not

nae·vus (*plural* **-vi**) *n. U.K.* = **nevus**

naff /naf/ *adj. U.K.* lacking real or fashionable stylishness and appearing boring, tasteless, or unattractive (*informal*)

naff off (**naffed off, naffing off, naffs off**) *vi. U.K.* used as a rude way of telling somebody to go away (*informal*)

NAFTA /naáftə/ *n.* a free trade agreement signed between the United States and Canada in 1989, and extended to include Mexico in 1994. Full form **North American Free Trade Agreement**

nag[1] /nag/ *v.* (**nagged, nag·ging, nags**) **1.** *vti.* **ASK REPEATEDLY** to ask or urge somebody persistently and annoyingly to do something ○ *He keeps nagging me to go and see the doctor.* **2.** *vti.* **KEEP CRITICIZING** to complain repeatedly to somebody in an irritating way, e.g., about some aspect of their behavior or appearance **3.** *vi.* **BE PERSISTENTLY PAINFUL OR BOTHERSOME** to be a persistent cause of discomfort, anxiety, or unease ○ *My conscience had been nagging me all week.* ○ *a nagging pain* ■ *n.* **SOMEBODY WHO NAGS** somebody, especially a woman, who tends to nag (*insult*) [Early 19thC. Originally "to gnaw, nibble," of uncertain origin: probably from Old Norse *gnaga* "to bite" or Low German *(g)naggen* "to irritate."] —**nag·ger** *n.* —**nag·ging** *n.* —**nag·ging·ly** *adv.*

WORD KEY: SYNONYMS

See Synonyms at ***complain***.

nag[2] /nag/ *n.* **1. OLD HORSE** an old horse, especially one that is worn out (*insult*) **2. RACEHORSE** a horse, especially a racehorse (*slang*) **3. SMALL HORSE** a small horse for riding (*archaic*) [15thC. Origin uncertain.]

Na·ga /naágə/ (*plural* **-ga** *or* **-gas**) *n.* **1.** PEOPLES **MEMBER OF SOUTH ASIAN PEOPLE** a member of a South Asian people who live in northeastern India and western Myanmar. They were headhunters until the 20th century and still maintain a very simple and traditional style of life. **2.** LANG **NAGA LANGUAGE** the Tibeto-Burman language of the Naga people. It is spoken by about 120,000 people. [Mid-19thC. Origin uncertain: perhaps from Sanskrit *nagna* "naked" or *naga* "mountain."] —**Naga** *adj.*

Na·ga·land /naágə land/ state in northeastern India, bordering Myanmar. Area: 6,400 sq. mi./16,579 sq. km. Population: 1,410,000 (1994).

Na·ga-Mi·kir /naága mi keér/ *n.* LANG = **Naga**

na·ga·na /nə gaánə/, **n'ga·na** /əng gaánə/ *n.* an often fatal disease caused by trypanosome protozoan parasites that affects hoofed animals such as cattle, horses, and goats in tropical Africa and is transmitted by the tsetse fly. It is related to sleeping sickness. [Late 19thC. From Zulu *nakane*.]

Na·ga·no /nə gaánō/ city and port in Japan, on Honshu Island. It is the commercial center and capital of Nagano Prefecture. Population: 347,036 (1990).

Na·ga·ri /naágəree/ *n.* **1. SET OF INDIAN ALPHABETS** a set of alphabets used for several languages of the Indian subcontinent, including Sanskrit and Hindi **2.** = **Devanagari** [Late 18thC. From Sanskrit *nagarī*, literally "script of the city."]

Na·ga·sa·ki /nàggə saákee/ city and port in southern Japan, on Kyushu Island, and capital of Nagasaki Prefecture. It was destroyed by an atomic bomb in 1945. Population: 445,000 (1990).

Na·go·ya /na góy yə/ city in Japan, on Honshu Island. It is the capital city and industrial center of Aichi Prefecture. Population: 2,091,000 (1994).

Nag·pur /nag po͝or/ city in central India, in Maharashtra State, on the Nag River. Population: 1,622,225 (1991).

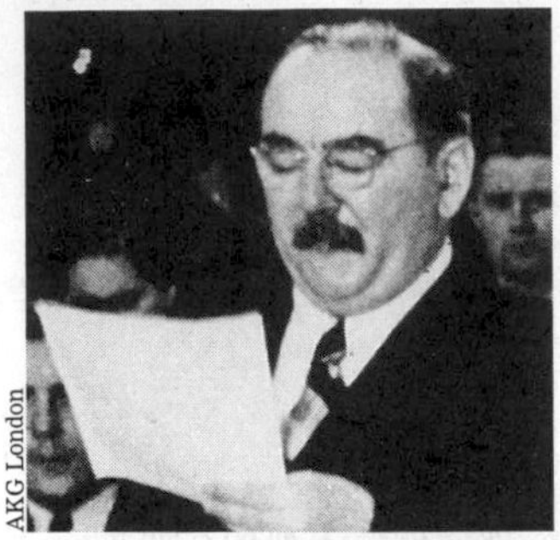

Imre Nagy

Nagy /nóddyə/, **Imre** (1896–1958) Hungarian statesman. Prime minister of communist Hungary (1953–55 and 1956), he led the Hungarian uprising (1956) and was later executed.

nah /na, naa/ *interj.* no (*nonstandard*) [Early 20thC. Alteration of NO.]

Nah. *abbr.* BIBLE Nahum

Na·han·ni Na·tion·al Park /nə haáni-/ national park and preserve in northern Canada, in southwestern Northwest Territories, on the South Nahanni River. It is a world heritage site. Area: 1,840 sq. mi./4,766 sq. km.

Ná·hua·tl /naá waát'l/ (*plural* **-tl** *or* **-tls**), **Na·hua** /naá waá/ (*plural* **-hua** *or* **-huas**) *n.* **1.** PEOPLES **MEMBER OF NATIVE CENTRAL AMERICAN PEOPLE** a member of a Native Central American people who live in southern Mexico and Central America. The Nahuatl include the ancient Aztecs. **2. Na·hua·tl, Na·hua, Na·huat·lan** /-waatlaán/ **NAHUATL LANGUAGE** the language of the Nahuatl people. It belongs to the Uto-Aztecan family of languages, and is spoken by over one million people. Also called **Aztec** [Early 19thC. Via Spanish from Nahuatl, singular of *Nahua* "the Nahuatl people." English words of Nahuatl origin include: avocado, Aztec, cacao, chili, chocolate, coyote, guacamole, mesquite, peyote, tamale, tomato.] —**Na·hua·tl** *adj.*

Na·hum /náyhəm, náyəm/ *n.* **1. BIBLICAL HEBREW PROPHET** a Hebrew prophet who lived in the 7th century B.C. He was one of the minor prophets. **2. BOOK OF THE BIBLE** a book of the Bible that records the prophecies of Nahum, including the prophecy foretelling the siege and sack of the Assyrian capital of Nineveh in 612 B.C. See table at **Bible**

NAIA *abbr.* National Association of Intercollegiate Athletes

nai·ad /náy ad, -àd, nī àd, náy-/ (*plural* **-ads** *or* **-a·des** /náyə deez, nī ə-/) *n.* **1.** MYTHOL **GREEK WATER NYMPH** in Greek mythology, a nymph of lakes, rivers, springs, and fountains. The naiads were skilled in music and dancing, and were supposed to have healing powers. **2.** INSECTS **AQUATIC LARVA** the immature water-dwelling form (**larva**) of a dragonfly, damselfly, mayfly, or stonefly **3.** BOT **AQUATIC PLANT** a plant that grows under water and has narrow leaves and small white flowers. Genus: *Najas.* [14thC. Via the Latin stem *naiad-* from the Greek stem *naiad-* "water nymph," from *naein* "to flow."]

Nai·ad /náy ad nī ad/ *n.* the innermost known natural satellite of Neptune, discovered in 1989 by Voyager 2. It is approximately 58 km (36 mi.) in diameter.

na·ïf /naa eéf/, **na·if** (*plural* **-ïfs** *or* **-ifs**) *n.* a naive person [Late 16thC. From French *naïf* (see NAIVE).]

nail /nayl/ *n.* **1. SHORT POINTED METAL PIN** a strong metal pin with a flat round head and a pointed end that is hammered into wood or masonry and used to fasten objects together or hang something on **2. SOMETHING LIKE NAIL** something that is like a nail in its shape, in being sharp, or in the way it is used **3.** ANAT, ZOOL **HARD AREA ON FINGER OR TOE** in humans and other primates, the thin horny covering that grows on the upper surface of the end of each finger and toe **4.** ZOOL **CLAW** the claw of a bird, mammal, or reptile **5.** MEASURE **UNIT OF MEASURE** an old unit of measure for cloth that was equal to $2\frac{1}{4}$ in./5.7 cm ■ *vt.* (**nailed, nail·ing, nails**) **1. ATTACH WITH NAILS** to fasten, attach, or secure something using nails **2. FIX STEADILY** to keep something fixed or focused on something ○ *His gaze was nailed to the astonishing scene.* **3. CATCH OR CONVICT GUILTY PERSON** to catch somebody who is guilty of an offense, prove the person's guilt, or have the person's convicted (*informal*) ○ *It took them five years to nail him for insider trading.* **4. EXPOSE UNTRUTH** to prove that something is not true or valid and so stop others from believing it (*informal*) **5. HIT WITH BULLET OR PROJECTILE** to hit or bring down somebody or something with a bullet or a projectile **6. STOP** to stop somebody and speak to him or her (*informal*) ○ *nailed me in the corridor and demanded a raise* **7. DO PRECISELY OR WELL** to catch, hit, seize, or execute something adroitly or precisely (*informal*) ○. **8. PIN DOWN** to identify somebody or establish something precisely (*informal*) ○ *I nailed him as a fraud as soon as he started talking about his wealthy background.* **9.** BASEBALL **PUT SOMEBODY OUT** in baseball, to put out a runner by tagging [Old English *nægl.* Ultimately from an Indo-European word denoting a fingernail or toenail that is also the ancestor of English *onyx* and *ungulate.* The meaning "fastener" evolved in prehistoric Germanic.] —**nail·a·ble** *adj.* —**nail·er** *n.* ◇ **hit the nail on the head** to be absolutely correct or accurate ◇ **a nail in somebody's coffin** an event or action that further weakens the position of somebody or something already in decline ◇ **on the nail** accurate or exact

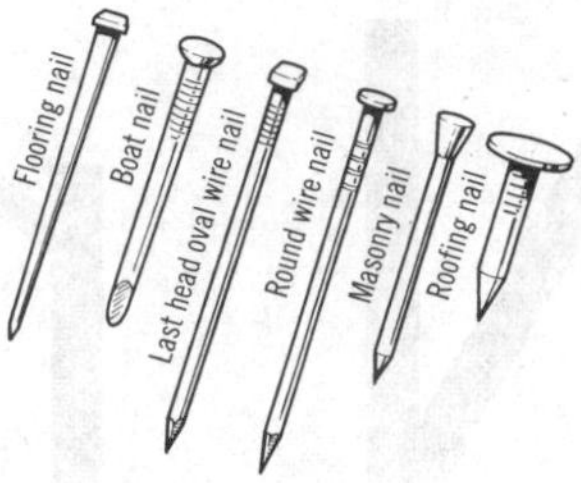

Nail

nail down *v.* **1.** *vt.* **PIN DOWN** to make somebody be definite about something **2.** *vt.* **SETTLE FINALLY** to settle something finally or come to a final decision about something **3. ESTABLISH DEFINITIVELY** to establish something clearly and conclusively ○ *an investigation that will attempt to nail down what really happened here* **4. BEAT SOMEBODY CONCLUSIVELY** to defeat an opponent decisively

nail bed *n.* the layer of tissue at the base of a fingernail or toenail from which new nail material develops

nail·bit·er *n.* a situation or contest that is extremely tense and exciting because its outcome remains uncertain until the end (*informal*) [From the stereotype of nail-biting as a sign of anxiety]

nail·bit·ing *n.* **HABIT OF BITING FINGERNAILS** the habit of biting off the ends of the fingernails, especially out of anxiety, tension, or boredom ■ *adj.* **TENSE** extremely tense and exciting because the outcome is uncertain [See NAIL-BITER]

nail bomb *n.* a bomb packed with nails to cause widespread injuries among people who are near it when it goes off

nail·brush /náyl brùsh/ *n.* a small brush used for cleaning the fingernails, with short stiff bristles on one or both sides

nail clip·pers *npl.* a small pair of clippers used for trimming fingernails and toenails

nail file *n.* a small file used for smoothing and shaping the ends of the fingernails

nail·head /náyl hèd/ *n.* a decorative design that resembles the round head of a nail, used on furniture and leather

nail pol·ish *n.* a fast-drying colored or transparent varnish, often worn by women on their fingernails or toenails

nail punch, **nail set** *n.* CONSTR a tool that pushes a nail level with or lower than the surrounding surface

nain·sook /náyn so͝ok/ *n.* a lightweight cotton fabric used for babywear and lingerie, originally from India [Late 18thC. From Hindi *nainsukh*, literally "pleasure to the eye."]

Nai·paul, V. S. (*b.* 1932) West-Indian born British novelist. His novels include *A House for Mr. Biswas* (1961) and the Booker Prize-winning *In a Free State* (1971). Full name **Sir Vidiadhar Surajprasad Naipaul**

nai·ra /nīrə/ *n.* **1. UNIT OF CURRENCY IN NIGERIA** the standard unit of currency in Nigeria, worth 100 kobo. See table at **currency 2. BILL WORTH ONE NAIRA** a bill worth one naira [Late 20thC. From Nigerian English, alteration of NIGERIA.]

Nairn·shire /náirn sheer, -shər/ former county of northern Scotland, abolished in 1975, and incorporated into Highland Region

Nai·ro·bi /nī róbee/ capital city of Kenya, situated in the south central part of the country. Population: 1,673,000 (1993).

Nai·ro·bi Na·tion·al Park national park in south central Kenya, near the capital city. It was established in 1946. Area: 44 sq. mi./115 sq. km.

Nai·smith /náy smith/, **James** (1861–1939) Canadian-born U.S. physical education teacher. He invented basketball (1891).

na·ive /naa eév/ (**-iv·er, -iv·est**), **na·ïve** (**-ïv·er, -ïv·est**), **na·ïf** /-eéf/ (**-ïf·er, -ïf·est**) *adj.* **1. EXTREMELY SIMPLE AND TRUSTING** having or showing an excessively simple and trusting view of the world and human nature, often as a result of youth and inexperience **2. NOT SHREWD OR SOPHISTICATED** showing a lack of sophistication and subtlety or of critical judgment and analysis ○ *a politically naive statement* **3. ARTLESS** admirably straightforward and uncomplicated or refreshingly innocent and unaffected **4.** ARTS **REJECTING SOPHISTICATED TECHNIQUES IN ART** not using the conventional styles and techniques of trained artists, e.g., in the treatment of perspective or light and shade **5.** SCI **NOT PREVIOUSLY EXPERIMENTED ON** not previously used in any scientific tests or experiments or not having previously used a particular drug ○ *naive laboratory mice* [Mid-17thC. From French *naïve*, feminine of *naïf*, from Latin *nativus* "born" (source of English *native*). The underlying idea is of the innocence or gullibility of the newborn.] —**na·ive·ly** *adv.* —**na·ive·ness** *n.*

na·ive re·al·ism *n.* the theory of perception that holds that when we look at an object what we see is the actual object, not a mental representation of it

na·ive·té /naá eevə táy, naa eévə tày/, **na·ïve·té** *n.* **1. NAIVENESS** a naive quality or naive behavior **2. NAIVE ACTION** a naive action or remark

Najd /najd, nejd/ region in central Saudi Arabia. Area: 447,000 sq. mi./1,158,000 sq. km.

NAK /nak/, **nak** *n.* TELECOM an ASCII control code used to indicate to the sender that a transmitted message has not been properly received. Full form **negative acknowledgment**

Na·ka·so·ne Ya·su·hi·ro /nàkə sóni yàssoo heérō/ (*b.* 1918) Japanese statesman. He was prime minister of Japan (1982–87).

na·ked /náykəd/ *adj.* **1. WITH NO CLOTHES ON** not covered by clothing, especially having no clothing on any part of the body **2. LACKING COVERING** without the usual covering or protection ○ *a naked lightbulb* **3. NOT CONCEALED** openly displayed or expressed and often threatening or disturbing ○ *naked aggression* **4. UNADORNED** plain and lacking any decoration or embellishment ○ *the naked truth* **5. UNARMED** unarmed and defenseless ○ *"If you carry this resolution you will send Britain's Foreign Secretary naked into the conference chamber."* (Aneurin Bevan1957) **6. DEVOID OF SOMETHING** without or unaccompanied by a particular quality or thing ○ *naked of all pretensions to grandeur* **7. WITHOUT NATURAL COVERING** without any natural covering in the form of earth, vegetation, or foliage **8.** ZOOL **WITHOUT HAIR, FUR, OR FEATHERS** without hair, fur, scales, shell, or feathers **9.** BOT **WITH NO GROWTH** without a covering of leaves or hairs ○ *naked stems* **10.** BOT **NOT ENCLOSED IN OVARY** used to describe conifer seeds that are not enclosed in an ovary **11.** BOT **WITHOUT SEPALS OR PETALS** used to describe flowers that have no sepals or petals [Old English *nacod.* Ultimately from an Indo-European word that is also the ancestor of English *nude.*] —**na·ked·ness** *n.*

WORD KEY: SYNONYMS

naked, bare, nude, undressed, unclothed

CORE MEANING: devoid of clothes or covering

naked the most general word used to describe somebody who is not wearing any clothes. It can also be used to describe an object that is uncovered or undecorated, especially when this is not what is usual or desirable; **bare** used to describe a part of somebody's body that is uncovered. It can also be used to describe objects or surfaces that are not decorated or covered; **nude** used to describe somebody who is not wearing any clothes at all, especially in an artistic context; **undressed** a general word used to describe somebody who is not wearing any clothes at all, especially in a situation where clothes have just been removed. It can also be used to describe somebody who has not finished putting on or taking off his or her clothes; **unclothed** a fairly formal word used to describe somebody who is not wearing any clothes.

WORD KEY: CULTURAL NOTE

The Naked and the Dead, a novel by Norman Mailer (1948). Set on a Pacific island during World War II, it is both a powerful account of the experience of war and, through its description of the conflicting political and philosophical views of the principal characters, a disturbing portrayal of the tensions in contemporary American society. It was made into a movie by Raoul Walsh in 1958.

na·ked eye *n.* human sight without the aid of a microscope, telescope, or other optical instrument

na·ked·ly /náykədlee/ *adv.* without any attempt at disguise or concealment ○ *a description of the state as a nakedly repressive machine*

na·ked op·tion *n.* a stock or commodity option sold by somebody who does not own the underlying asset, and who is exposed to considerable risk if the price of the underlying asset changes adversely

na·ked re·verse *n.* FOOTBALL a deceptive rushing play in football in which the ball carrier takes a handoff from a player going in the opposite direction and goes downfield with no blockers

Na·ku·ru /nə kóo roo/ city in west central Kenya. It is the capital of Rift Valley Province. Population: 124,200 (1994).

Na·ku·ru, Lake lake in west central Kenya, noted for its flamingos and other birds. Area: 24 sq. mi./62 sq. km.

nal·bu·phine /nal byóo feen/ *n.* a painkilling drug similar to morphine that is used for moderate to severe pain. Formula: $C_{21}H_{27}NO_4$. [Mid-20thC. Blend of NALORPHINE and BUTYL.]

na·led /náy lèd/ *n.* a short-lived insecticide used to control mosquitoes and crop pests. Formula: $C_4H_7Br_2Cl_2O_4P$. [Mid-20thC. Origin unknown.]

na·li·dix·ic ac·id /nàyli dìksik-/ *n.* an antibacterial drug used to treat bacterial infections of the urinary tract. Formula: $C_{12}H_{12}N_2O_3$. ["Nalidixic" coined from NAPHTHALENE + DI + *carboxylic*]

nal·or·phine /na láwr feen/ *n.* a drug resembling morphine used to diagnose narcotics addiction and to reverse the effects of narcotics poisoning by blocking morphine receptor cells, thereby preventing the morphine from acting. Formula: $C_{19}H_{21}NO_3$. [Mid-20thC. Contraction of *N-allylnormorphine*, coined from *N-* + ALLYL + NOR- + MORPHINE.]

nal·ox·one /na lók sōn/ *n.* a drug resembling morphine that is used to diagnose narcotics addiction and to reverse the effects of narcotics poisoning by blocking morphine receptor cells, thereby preventing the morphine from acting. Formula: $C_{19}H_{21}NO_4$. [Mid-20thC. Contraction of N-ALLYLNOROXYMORPHONE, coined from N- + ALLYL + NOR- + OXY- + MORPHINE + -ONE.]

Nam /naam, nam/ *n.* a name for Vietnam, used particularly by veterans of the war there during the 1960s and 1970s (*informal*) [Mid-20thC. Shortening.]

N. Am. *abbr.* 1. North America 2. North American

Na·ma /naámaa, -mə/ (*plural* **-ma** *or* **-mas**), **Na·ma·qua** /nə maákwə/ (*plural* **-qua** *or* **-quas**) *n.* 1. PEOPLES **MEMBER OF AFRICAN PEOPLE** a member of a Khoikhoi people who live in southwestern Africa 2. LANG **NAMA LANGUAGE** the language of the Nama people. It belongs to the San branch of Khoisan languages and features the use of click consonants. Nama is spoken by about 25,000 people. [Mid-19thC. From the Khoikhoin language.] — **Na·ma** *adj.*

nam·a·ble /náyməb'l/, **name·a·ble** *adj.* able to be identified by name

Na·ma·qua·land /nə maákwə land/ coastal region in southwestern Africa, in southern Namibia and South Africa. It is the homeland of the Nama people.

na·maste /nə mú stày/, **na·mas·kar** /nummə skaár/ *n.* a polite bow of greeting or farewell used by Hindus, made with the hands held at chest height and both palms pressed together [Mid-20thC. From Hindi, literally "bowing to you."]

Nam·bour /nám bòor/ town in southeastern Queensland, northeastern Australia. Population: 12,205 (1996).

nam·by-pam·by /nàmbee pámbee/ *adj.* (*informal*) 1. **WEAK** feeble, childish, and weak 2. **SILLY** silly, sentimental, or overly sensitive ■ *n.* (*plural* **nam·by-pam·bies**) **NAMBY-PAMBY PERSON** somebody who is considered weak or silly (*informal*) [Mid-16thC. Originally a mocking nickname for the English poet Ambrose Philips (1674–1749), who wrote feebly sentimental pastorals; based on *Amb(rose).*]

name /naym/ *n.* 1. **WHAT SOMEBODY OR SOMETHING IS CALLED** a word, term, or phrase by which somebody or something is known and distinguished from other people or things 2. **UNCOMPLIMENTARY WORD ABOUT SOMEBODY** a usually uncomplimentary or abusive word or phrase used to describe somebody's character ○ *called him names behind his back* 3. **REPUTATION** the reputation or standing of somebody or something ○ *She's made quite a name for herself in the music world.* 4. **FAMOUS PERSON** somebody who is famous ○ *All the big Hollywood names were there.* ■ *adj.* **RESPECTED** having an established and good reputation ○ *name brands at discount prices* ■ *vt.* (**named, nam·ing, names**) 1. **GIVE A NAME TO** to give somebody or something a name ○ *They named the dog Sport.* 2. **IDENTIFY BY NAME** to identify somebody or something by giving his, her, or its name ○ *He says he can name all fifty state capitals.* 3. **DECIDE ON SOMETHING** to decide upon or specify something, such as a date, time, or price ○ *would not name a figure* 4. **APPOINT TO OFFICE** to choose somebody for a particular office or honor ○ *They haven't yet named her successor.* [Old English *nama*. Ultimately from an Indo-European word.] — **nam·er** *n.* ◇ **in name only** supposedly or officially, but not in any real sense ◇ **in the name of** 1. by the authority of 2. for the sake of something ◇ **name names** to mention the names of specific people in order to blame or accuse them of something ◇ **somebody's name is mud** somebody is in trouble or the object of somebody else's disapproval ◇ **to somebody's name** belonging to somebody ○ *hasn't got a penny to his name* ◇ **the name of the game** what something is all about, its most important element or the kind of thing that most commonly happens in it ◇ **you name it** used to suggest that an enormous number of things are involved or an enormous number of options are possible (*informal*)

WORD KEY: ORIGIN

The Indo-European ancestor of ***name*** is also the ultimate source of English *anonymous, nomenclature, nominate, noun, renown, pseudonym,* and *synonym.*

name-call·ing *n.* verbal abuse, especially as a substitute for reasoned argument in a dispute

name day *n.* in the Roman Catholic and Eastern Orthodox Churches, the feast day of the saint that somebody is named for

name-drop·ping *n.* the practice of frequently mentioning the names of famous or influential people as friends or acquaintances in order to impress people —**name-drop·per** *n.*

name·less /náymləss/ *adj.* 1. **LACKING A NAME** not having a name 2. **ANONYMOUS** having a name that is unknown or not revealed 3. **INDESCRIBABLE** unable to be accurately described ○ *a nameless fear* 4. **DISTRESSING BEYOND WORDS** too unpleasant or disgusting to be described or mentioned 5. **ILLEGITIMATE** illegitimate or not legally entitled to a name

name·ly /náymlee/ *adv.* used to introduce a specific description or explanation of something just referred to in a more general way ○ *She was given a new post, namely, that of head of department.*

name·plate /náym plàyt/ *n.* a plate or plaque, e.g., on a door, bearing a name and associating the named person with the place or thing that the plate is attached to

name·sake /náym sàyk/ *n.* somebody or something with the same name as somebody or something else [Mid-17thC. Origin uncertain: probably ultimately from *for one's name's sake.*]

Na·mib Des·ert /nə mìb-/ desert in southwestern Africa, mostly in Namibia. Length: 1,200 mi./1,930 km.

Na·mibe /na meéb/ city and port in southwestern Angola. It is the capital of Namibe Province. Population: 77,000 (1987). Former name **Moçâmedes** (until 1982)

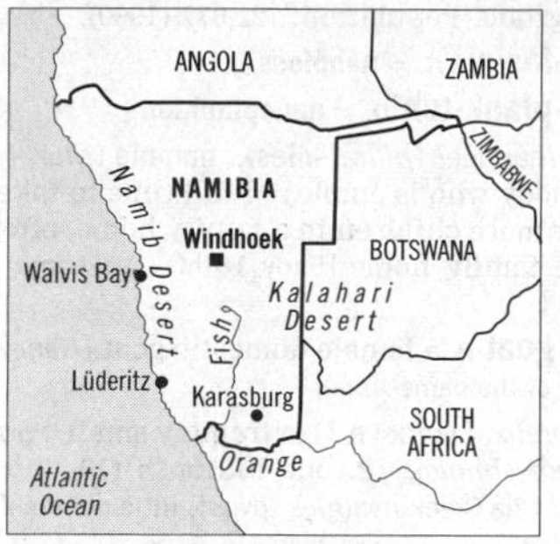

Namibia

Na·mib·i·a /nə míbbee ə/ republic in southwestern Africa, with its western coast on the Atlantic Ocean, directly north of South Africa. Language: English, German, Afrikaans. Currency: Namibian dollar. Capital: Windhoek. Population: 1,709,000 (1996). Area: 318,252 sq. mi./824,268 sq. km. Official name **Republic of Namibia** —**Na·mib·i·an** *n., adj.*

Nam·oi /nám oy/ river in northeastern New South Wales, southeastern Australia. Length: 525 mi./845 km.

Nam·pa /námpə/ city in southwestern Idaho, west of Boise and east of the Oregon border. Population: 37,558 (1996).

nam pla /nám plaa/ *n.* a thin sauce of fermented fish with a strong flavor and smell and a salty taste, widely used in Southeast Asian cookery [From Thai]

Na·mur /nə mòor-/ city in southeastern Belgium. It is the capital city of Namur Province. Population: 105,059 (1996).

nan /nan/ *n.* a flat round or oval bread served with Indian food [Early 20thC. From Persian and Urdu *nān*.]

nan·a /nánnə, naánə/, **nan·na** *n.* somebody's grandmother (*informal*)

Na·nai·mo /nə nīmō/ city in southwestern Canada, on Vancouver Island, on the Strait of Georgia. Population: 85,585 (1996).

Na·nai·mo bar *n.* in Canada, a layered confection consisting of a base of chocolate and coconut, a center of custard and a chocolate topping

Na·nak /naánək/ (1469–1539) Indian religious leader. He founded the Sikh religion, and his teachings were collected as the *Adi Granth*, the Sikh scriptures. Known as **Guru Nanak**

Nan·chang /nan chúng/ city in eastern China. It is the capital of Jiangxi Province. Population: 1,350,000 (1991).

nan·cy /nánsee/ (*plural* **nancies**), **nan·cy boy, nance** (*plural* **nan·ces**) *n.* a highly offensive term for an effeminate man or a homosexual man (*slang offensive*)

Nan·cy /noN seé/ city in northeastern France, in Lorraine Region. It is the capital of Meurthe-et-Moselle Department. Population: 102,410 (1990).

NAND /nand/ (*plural* **NANDs**), **NAND gate** *n.* a logic operator used in computing that produces an output signal only if at least one of its inputs has no signal, thus being the inverse of an AND operator [Mid-20thC. Blend of NOT and AND.]

Nan·da De·vi /nùndə deévee/ the second highest mountain in India after Kangchenjunga. It is in the extreme northwest of the country, in the Himalayas, near the Tibetan border. Height: 25,645 ft./7,817 m.

Nan·ga Par·bat /nùng gə paár baat/ mountain in northeastern Pakistan, in the Himalayas. Height: 26,660 ft./8,126 m.

Nan·jing /naán jíng/ city in eastern China, on the Yangtze River. It is the capital of Jiangsu Province. Population: 2,090,204 (1990). Former name **Nanking**

nan·keen /nan keén/ *n.* a durable yellowish-brown cotton fabric [Mid-18thC. Named for *Nanking* (Nanjing), city in China, because it was originally made there.]

Nan·king /nan kíng/ former name for **Nanjing**

nan·na *n.* = **nana** (*informal*)

Nan·ning /nan ning/ city and capital of Guangxi Zhuangzu Autonomous Region, southeastern China, situated approximately 330 mi./530 km west of Guangzhou. Population: 721,877 (1990).

nan·no·fos·sil *n.* = **nanofossil**

nan·no·plank·ton *n.* = **nanoplankton**

nan·ny /nánnee/ (*plural* **-nies**), **nan·nie** (*plural* **-nies**) *n.* somebody who is employed full-time to take care of one or more children in a family home, often living in the family home [Early 18thC. Nickname for name *Ann(e)*.]

nan·ny goat *n.* a female domestic goat [*Nanny* a former variant of the name *Anne*]

nano- *prefix.* Symbol **n 1.** extremely small ○ *nanofossil* ○ *nanotechnology* **2.** one billionth (10^{-9}) ○ *nanosecond* [Via Greek *nan(n)os* "dwarf, little old man"]

nan·o·bot /nánnō bòt/ *n.* a robot of microscopic proportions built using nanotechnology (*informal*) [Combination of prefix nano- + ROBOT]

nan·o·fos·sil /nánnō fòss'l/, **nan·no·fos·sil** *n.* a very small fossil, especially of nanoplankton

nan·o·gram /nánnə gràm/ *n.* one billionth of a gram

nan·o·me·ter /nánnə meetər/ *n.* one billionth of a meter

nan·o·plank·ton /nánnō plàngktən/, **nan·no·plank·ton** *n.* very small plankton including bacteria, algae, and protozoa. They are usually in the size range 5–60 micrometers.

nan·o·sec·ond /nánnə sèkənd/ *n.* one billionth of a second

nan·o·tech·nol·o·gy /nànnō tek nóllәjee/ (*plural* **-gies**) *n.* the art of manipulating materials on a very small scale in order to build microscopic machinery

Nan·sen /nánss'n/, **Fridtjof** (1861–1930) Norwegian explorer and statesman. He led several expeditions to the Arctic, and was also involved in humanitarian projects, for which he won the Nobel Peace Prize in 1922.

Nan·tong /nan tóong/ city and seaport in eastern China, in southeastern Jiangsu Province. Population: 343,341 (1990).

Nan·tuck·et /nan túkət/ island in southeastern Massachusetts, in the Atlantic Ocean, south of Cape Cod. Population: 6,012 (1990). Area: 57 sq. mi./148 sq. km.

Nant·wich /nántwich/ market town in northwestern England, in Cheshire. Population: 11,695 (1991).

Nan·u·et /nánnyoo ət/ city in New York, in Rockland County. Population: 14,065 (1990).

Na·o·mi /nay ómee/ *n.* in the Bible, the mother-in-law of Ruth (Ruth 1: 2)

na·os /náy òss/ (*plural* **-oi** /-òy/) *n.* ARCHIT = **cella** [Late 18thC. From Greek, "temple."]

nap[1] /nap/ *n.* **SHORT SLEEP** a period of short light sleep, especially during the day ■ *vi.* **(napped, nap·ping, naps) 1. SLEEP LIGHTLY** to have a short period of light sleep **2. BE OFF GUARD** to be inattentive or off guard [Old English *hnappian*]

nap[2] /nap/ *n.* **PILE** the small soft fibers that stick up slightly from the surface of a fabric such as velvet and that usually all lie in one direction only ■ *vt.* **(napped, nap·ping, naps) RAISE PILE OF FABRIC** to raise the nap of a fabric by brushing it [15thC. From Middle Low German and Middle Dutch *noppe*, from a prehistoric Germanic word perhaps meaning "to pluck," that may also be the ancestor of English *nip*.]

nap[3] /nap/ *n.* CARDS Full form **napoleon 1. CARD GAME** a card game similar to euchre, played with hands of five cards, in which players bid for the number of tricks they will take **2. BID IN NAP** a bid to win all five tricks in the game of nap [Early 19thC. Shortening of NAPOLEON.]

Nap·a /náppə/ city in west central Florida. It is the administrative seat of Napa County. Population: 61,842 (1990).

na·palm /náy paam, -paalm/ *n.* **1. JELLY USED FOR FIRE BOMBS** a highly flammable jelly, produced by mixing a thickening agent with gasoline and used in flamethrowers and fire bombs **2.** CHEM **THICKENING AGENT FOR JELLIED GASOLINE** a thickening agent, consisting of aluminum soap, that can be used for making jellied gasoline ■ *vt.* **(-palmed, -palm·ing, -palms) ATTACK WITH NAPALM** to attack or destroy something with napalm [Mid-20thC. Blend of NAPHTHENE and PALMITATE.]

nape /nayp/ *n.* the back part of the neck [13thC. Origin unknown.]

Na·per·ville /náypər vil/ city in northeastern Illinois, southeast of Aurora, and west of Chicago. Population: 85,351 (1990).

na·per·y /náypəree/ *n.* tablecloths and napkins, collectively (*archaic*) [14thC. From Old French *naperie*, from *nappe* "tablecloth" (see NAPKIN).]

Naph·ta·li /náftə lī/ *n.* in the Bible, the son of Jacob and Rachel's handmaid, Bilhah (Genesis 30: 7–8)

naph·tha /náfthə, nápthə/ *n.* a clear colorless flammable mixture of light hydrocarbons obtained from petroleum. It boils at between 45°C and 155°C and is used as a raw material for many petrochemicals and plastics. [Late 16thC. Via Latin from Greek, originally "inflammable liquid coming from the earth," from Iranian.]

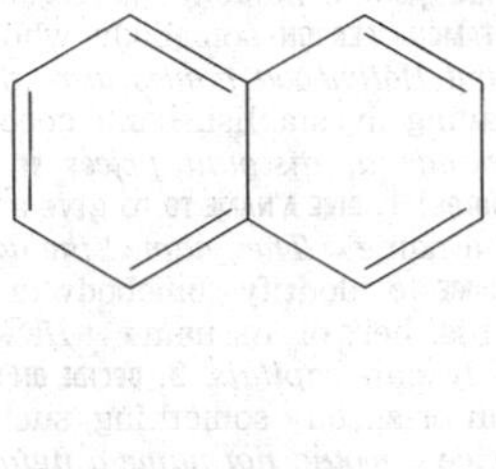

Naphthalene

naph·tha·lene /náfthə leen, nápthə-/ *n.* a white crystalline hydrocarbon derived from coal tar and used as a moth repellent, in solvents, and in the manufacture of dyes, resins, plasticizers, polyesters, and explosives. Formula: $C_{10}H_8$. [Early 19thC. Coined from NAPHTHA + AL + -ENE.] —**naph·tha·len·ic** /nàfthə lénnik, nàpthə-/ *adj.*

naph·thene /náf theen, náp-/ *n.* a cycloalkane obtained from petroleum [Late 19thC. Coined from NAPHTHA + -ENE.] —**naph·then·ic** /naf theénik, nap-, -thénnik/ *adj.*

naph·thol /náf thàwl, náp-/ *n.* either of two derivatives of naphthalene that are isomers, and are used as antiseptics and in manufacturing. Formula: $C_{10}H_7OH$. [Mid-19thC. Formed from NAPHTHA.]

Na·pi·er /náypee ər/ city in New Zealand, situated on the eastern coast of the North Island. Devastated by an earthquake in 1931, it was rebuilt in a distinctive art-deco style. Population: 55,044 (1996).

Na·pi·er, John (1550–1617) Scottish mathematician. He invented logarithms and a calculating device called Napier's bones.

Na·pier·i·an log·a·rithm /nay peeree ən-/ *n.* = **natural logarithm** [Early 19thC. Named for John NAPIER.]

Na·pi·er's bones /này peerz-/ *npl.* a set of graduated rods based upon the principles of logarithms, formerly used to perform multiplication and division but now used primarily for educational purposes [Mid-17thC. Named for John NAPIER.]

na·pi·form /náypə fàwrm/ *adj.* shaped like a turnip in being conical at one end and spherical at the other [Mid-19thC. Coined from Latin *napus* "turnip" + -FORM.]

nap·kin /nápkin/ *n.* **1. PIECE OF CLOTH FOR WIPING MOUTH** a usually square piece of cloth or tissue paper used at mealtimes to protect clothes and wipe the mouth **2.** = **sanitary pad** [14thC. Formed from French *nap(p)e* "tablecloth," from Latin *mappa* "napkin, cloth" (source of English *map*), from Carthaginian or Phoenician.]

Na·ples /náyp'lz/ **1.** city in southern Italy. It is the capital of Campania Region and of Napoli Province and an important seaport. Population: 1,061,583 (1993). **2.** city in southwestern Florida, in Collier County, on the Gulf of Mexico. Population: 19,505 (1990).

na·po·le·on /nə pōlee ən, -pōlyən/ *n.* **1.** FOOD **FLAKY PASTRY** a rectangular flaky pastry shape filled with custard cream **2.** MONEY **OLD FRENCH COIN** a gold coin formerly used in France, equivalent to 20 francs **3.** CARDS full form of **nap**[3] [Early 19thC. Named for NAPOLEON I; because the coin was issued in his reign.]

AKG London

Napoleon I, Emperor of the French: Portrait (1807) by Andrea Appiani

Na·po·le·on I /nə pōlee ən, nə pōlyən/, **Emperor of the French** (1769–1821). He made his name as a general, was appointed first consul of France in 1799, and took the title of emperor in 1804. After conquering most of Europe, he was exiled after defeat at the battle of Waterloo (1815). Real name **Napoleon Bonparte** —**Na·po·le·on·ic** /nə pōlee ónnik/ *adj.*

nappe /nap/ *n.* **1. SHEET OF WATER** a sheet of water flowing over a dam or a spillway **2.** GEOL **SHEET OF ROCK** a large arch-shaped sheet of rock that has been forced over underlying rocks by internal stresses **3.** GEOM **PART OF CONE** either of the two parts, or sheets, of a conical or pyramidal surface that are separated by a line through the vertex [Late 19thC. From French, literally "tablecloth" (see NAPKIN).]

nap·py /náppee/ (*plural* **-pies**) *n. U.K.* = **diaper** [Early 20thC. Shortening and alteration of NAPKIN.]

na·prox·en /nə próksən/ *n.* a drug used to treat pain, especially in arthritis and other diseases of the joints [Late 20thC. Shortening and alteration of *methoxynaphthylpropionic (acid)*, one of its chemical names.]

Na·ra /naárə/ city in Japan, on southern Honshu Island. It is the capital of Nara Prefecture. Population: 349,349 (1990).

Na·ra·coorte /nárrə kawrt/ agricultural town in southern South Australia. Population: 4,674 (1996).

Na·ra·yan /nə rīyən/, **Jayaprakash** (1902–79) Indian politician. He was the uniting force in the Janata Party, which defeated the government of Indira Gandhi in 1977.

Na·ra·yan, R. K. (*b.* 1906) Indian writer. Many of his gentle novels are set in the fictional southern Indian town of Malgudi. They include *The Vendor of Sweets* (1967) and *The World of Nagaraj* (1990). Full name **Rasipuram Krishnaswamy Narayan**

narc[1] /naark/, **nark** *n.* a government agent who investigates narcotics violations (*slang*) [Mid-20thC. Shortening of *narcotics agent*.]

narc[2] /naark/ **(narced, narc·ing, narcs), nark** *vi.* to act as an informer, especially for the police (*slang*) [Mid-19thC. From Romany *nāk* "nose."]

nar·cis·sism /naársə sìzzəm/ *n.* **1. SELF-ADMIRATION** excessive self-admiration and self-centeredness **2. PERSONALITY DISORDER** in psychiatry, a personality disorder characterized by the patient's overestimation of his or her own appearance and abilities and an excessive need for admiration. In psychoanalytic theory, emphasis is placed on the element of self-directed sexual desire in the condition. [Early 19thC. Named for NARCISSUS.] —**nar·cis·sist** *n.* —**nar·cis·sis·tic** /naarsə sístik/ *adj.*

nar·cis·sus /naar síssəss/ (*plural* **-si** /-sī/ *or* **-sus·es** *or* **-sus**) *n.* a spring-blooming plant that grows from a bulb and has narrow leaves and showy yellow or white flowers with a cup-shaped center. Genus: *Narcissus*. [Mid-16thC. Via Latin from Greek *narkissos*, from *narkē* "numbness" (source of English *narcotic*); in reference to its narcotic properties.]

Nar·cis·sus *n.* in Greek mythology, a youth who was punished for repulsing Echo's love by being made to fall in love with his own reflection in a pool. He died gazing at his own image, and was turned into a flower.

nar·co /naárkō/ *n.* a drug trafficker (*informal*)

narco-[1] *prefix.* sleep, stupor ○ *narcolepsy* [From Greek *narkoun* "to make numb,", from *narkē* "numbness"]

narco-[2] *prefix.* relating to illicit narcotics and the narcotics trade (*informal*)

nar·co·a·nal·y·sis /naàrkō ə nálləssiss/ *n.* psychoanalysis using drugs to induce a state akin to sleep [Mid-20thC. Coined from NARCO- + ANALYSIS.]

nar·co·lep·sy /naàrkə lèpsee/ *n.* a condition characterized by frequent, brief, and uncontrollable bouts of deep sleep, sometimes accompanied by hallucinations and inability to move [Late 19thC. Coined from NARCO- + -LEPSY, on the model of EPILEPSY.] —**nar·co·lep·tic** /naàrkə léptik/ *adj., n.*

nar·co·sis /naar kṓssiss/ *n.* a state of unconsciousness or stupor caused by a narcotic or other drug [Late 17thC. From Greek *narkōsis*, from *narkoun* (see NARCOTIC).]

nar·cot·ic /naar kóttik/ *n.* **1.** PHARM **DRUG** a drug, especially one derived from opium, that has effects ranging from mild dulling of the senses, pain relief, and sleep, to stupor, coma, and convulsions. Most narcotics are addictive. **2.** DRUGS **ILLEGAL DRUG** a drug whose use is illegal, whether or not it is an addictive narcotic **3. SOOTHING THING** something that soothes, induces sleep, relieves pain or stress, or causes a sensation of mental numbness ■ *adj.* **1. CAUSING SLEEP** able to induce drowsiness, sleep, or stupor, or alter mental states through its chemical properties **2. SOOTHING** having a generally soothing, numbing, or soporific effect **3.** PHARM **OF NARCOTICS** relating to narcotic drugs and their use **4.** DRUGS **OF ADDICTS** relating to people addicted to narcotics [14thC. Via French *narcotique* and medieval Latin from Greek *narkōtikos* "numbing," from *narkoun* "to make numb," from *narkē* "numbness."] —**nar·cot·i·cal·ly** *adv.*

nar·co·ti·za·tion /naàrkətə záysh'n/ *n.* the process by which a society falls under the control of drugs, drug traffickers, and the illegal drug business (*informal*)

nar·co·tize /naàrkə tīz/ (**-tized, -tiz·ing, -tiz·es**) *vt.* **1. TREAT WITH NARCOTIC** to treat somebody with a narcotic **2. PUT INTO STUPOR** to induce stupor in somebody, especially by administering a narcotic drug

nard /naard/ *n.* = **spikenard** [14thC. Via Latin *nardus* from Greek *nardos*, probably ultimately from Sanskrit *naladam* "Indian spikenard."]

nar·es /náireez/ *npl.* openings or passages leading out of the nose or naval cavity. Most vertebrate animals have paired external nares, the nostrils, and a pair of internal nares opening into the mouth. [Late 17thC. From Latin, plural of *naris* "nostril."]

nar·ghi·le /naàrgəlee/, **nar·gi·leh** *n.* = **hookah** [Mid-18thC. From (partly via French and Turkish) Persian *nārgīl* "coconut, hookah," from Sanskrit *nārikela* "coconut."]

Na·ri·ta /nə reétə/ city in Japan, on southeastern Honshu Island, in Chiba Prefecture. Population: 86,708 (1990).

nark[1] /naark/ (**narked, nark·ing, narks**) *v.* **1.** *vt. U.K.* **ANNOY** to irritate, offend, or annoy somebody (*informal*) **2.** *vi.* = **narc** (*slang*) [Mid-19thC. From Romany *nāk* "nose."]

nark[2] *n.* CRIMINOL, DRUGS = **narc** (*slang*)

Nar·ra·bri /nárrə brī/ town in northeastern New South Wales, southeastern Australia. Population: 14,653 (1991).

Nar·ra·gan·set /nèrrə gánsət/ (*plural* **-sets** *or* **-set**), **Nar·ra·gan·sett** (*plural* **-setts** *or* **-sett**) *n.* **1.** PEOPLES **MEMBER OF NATIVE AMERICAN PEOPLE** a member of a Native American people who originally lived in a broad territory centered on the western edge of present-day Rhode Island. The Narragansets were among the largest and strongest of the northeastern Native American peoples until large numbers of them were killed in a war against the New England colonists in the late 17th century. **2.** LANG **NARRAGANSET LANGUAGE** the now extinct Iroquoian language of the Narraganset people [Early 17thC. From Narraganset.] —**Nar·ra·gan·set** *adj.*

Nar·ra·gan·sett /nàrrə gánssət/ town and summer resort in southern Rhode Island, Washington County. Population: 14,985 (1990).

Nar·ra·gan·sett Bay inlet of the Atlantic Ocean in eastern Rhode Island. Length: 26 mi./42 km.

nar·rate /né ràyt/ (**-rat·ed, -rat·ing, -rates**) *vt.* **1. TELL THE STORY OF SOMETHING** to be the teller of a story, or to give an account of something in detail **2.** BROADCAST **SPEAK ON FILM** to provide the narration for a film or television program [Mid-17thC. From Latin, past participle stem of *narrare*, from *gnarus* "knowing."] —**nar·rat·a·ble** *adj.*

nar·ra·tion /ne ráysh'n/ *n.* **1. ACT OF NARRATING** the act of telling a story or giving an account of something **2. SOMETHING NARRATED** a narrative or story **3.** BROADCAST, CINEMA **SOUNDTRACK VOICED BY ACTOR** the voiced soundtrack of a broadcast or film when given by an actor or commentator who does not appear —**nar·ra·tion·al** *adj.*

nar·ra·tive /nérrətiv/ *n.* **1. STORY** a story or an account of a sequence of events in the order in which they happened **2. PROCESS OF NARRATING** the art or process of telling a story or giving an account of something **3.** LITERAT **STORY IN LITERARY WORK** the part of a literary work that is concerned with telling the story ■ *adj.* **1. TELLING A STORY** having the aim or purpose of telling a story ○ *narrative poetry* **2. RELATING TO NARRATION** relating to or involving the art of storytelling —**nar·ra·tive·ly** *adv.*

nar·ra·tor /né ràytər/ *n.* **1. STORYTELLER** somebody who tells a story or gives an account of something **2.** LITERAT **TALKING CHARACTER** a character in a work of fiction who is presented as telling the story and who refers to himself or herself as "I" **3.** CINEMA, BROADCAST **COMMENTATOR** somebody who provides the narration for a film or television program

nar·row /nérrō/ *adj.* **1. SMALL IN WIDTH** having a small width, especially in comparison to height or length ○ *a narrow gap* **2. LIMITED IN SIZE** limited or restricted in size or scope ○ *a narrow range of options* **3. NARROW-MINDED** limited and usually inflexible in outlook ○ *a narrow view of events* **4. JUST ENOUGH FOR SUCCESS** barely sufficient for success ○ *a narrow victory* ○ *a narrow escape* **5. NOT GENEROUS** mean and stingy **6. THOROUGH** close and thorough, leaving nothing uninvestigated **7.** PHON = **tense**[1] *adj.* 4 **8.** AGRIC **HIGH IN PROTEIN** used to describe animal feed that is very rich in protein ■ *n.* **A NARROW PASSAGE** a narrow place or passage. ◊ **narrows** ■ *vti.* (**-rowed, -row·ing, -rows**) **1. MAKE OR BECOME NARROW** to make something, or to become, narrow or narrower **2. CONTRACT OR BE CONTRACTED** to restrict or limit the scope or extent of something, or to become restricted or limited in scope or extent ○ *narrowed the focus of their investigation to two individuals* [Old English *nearu*, from prehistoric Germanic] —**nar·row·ness** *n.*

nar·row·band /nérrō bànd/ *adj.* functioning within a narrow band of broadcasting frequencies

nar·row·cast /nérrō kàst/ (**-cast** *or* **-cast·ed, -cast·ing, -casts**) *vt.* to aim a radio or television transmission at a limited group of people such as cable subscribers or a particular target audience

nar·row gauge *n.* **1. REDUCED DISTANCE BETWEEN RAILS** a distance between the two rails of a railroad track that is less than the 4 ft. $8\frac{1}{2}$ in./143.5 cm distance of the standard gauge railroads **2. TRACK OR VEHICLE WITH NARROW GAUGE** a railroad line with track of a narrow gauge, or a car or locomotive designed to run on one —**narrow-gauge** *adj.*

nar·row·ly /nérrōlee/ *adv.* **1. BY SMALL MARGIN** by a very small margin or distance ○ *narrowly avoided capture* **2. INTENTLY** in a very concentrated, searching, or detailed way ○ *eyed him narrowly* **3. WITHIN NARROW LIMITS** in a way that allows little freedom or scope ○ *narrowly circumscribed*

nar·row-mind·ed *adj.* having or showing a limited and often prejudiced or intolerant outlook —**nar·row-mind·ed·ly** *adv.* —**nar·row-mind·ed·ness** *n.*

narrows /nérrōz/ *n.* a narrow section of a river, or a narrow stretch of sea usually between two larger bodies of water (*takes a singular or plural verb*) ◊ **narrow**

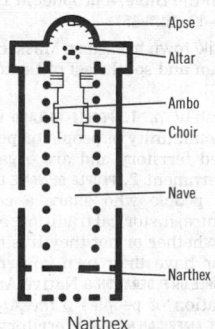

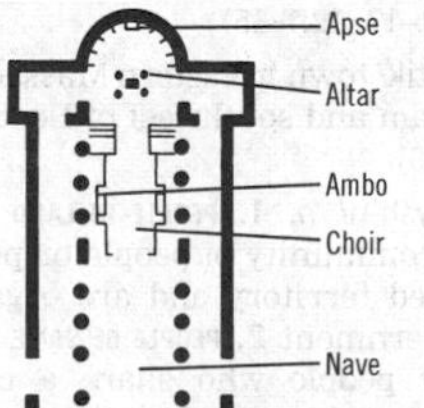

Narthex

nar·thex /naàr thèks/ *n.* **1. ENTRANCE HALL OF CHURCH** an entrance hall at the west end of a Christian church between the porch and the nave **2. SCREENED AREA AT END OF NAVE** an area at the west end of the nave of an early Christian church separated off by a screen or railing behind which women, catechumens, or penitents were admitted [Late 17thC. Via late Greek *narthēx* "giant fennel," later "casket" (because the plant was used to make boxes). The modern meaning evolved via the idea of an enclosed space.]

Nar·vá·ez /naar vī ez/, **Pánfilo de** (1470?–1528) Spanish explorer. His attempt to conquer Florida ended in disaster and his own death.

Narwhal

nar·whal /naàr waàl, -wəl, -hwaàl/ (*plural* **-whal** *or* **-whals**), **nar·wal** (*plural* **-wal** *or* **-wals**), **nar·whale** (*plural* **-whale** *or* **-whales**) *n.* a small arctic whale, about 20 ft./6 m long, with a spotted body, short flippers, and, in the male, a long twisted ivory tusk. It was formerly hunted for oil and ivory. Latin name: *Monodon monoceros.* [Mid-17thC. From Danish or Norwegian *narhval*, of uncertain origin: perhaps from Old Norse *náhvalr*, literally "corpse-whale," from *nár* "corpse" (in allusion to its pale skin).]

nar·y /náiree/ *adj.* not a single ○ *Nary a word was said.* [Mid-18thC. Alteration and contraction of NE'ER "a."]

NAS *abbr.* **1.** National Academy of Sciences **2.** naval air station

NASA /nássə/ *n.* the U.S. government agency responsible for nonmilitary programs in the exploration and scientific study of space. Full form **National Aeronautics and Space Administration**

na·sal /náyz'l/ *adj.* **1. OF THE NOSE** forming part of or relating to the nose **2.** PHON **PRONOUNCED THROUGH NOSE** pronounced with breath escaping mainly through the nose rather than the mouth **3. WITH NASAL SOUNDS** characterized by nasal sounds ○ *a nasal accent* ■ *n.* **1.** PHON **NASAL SOUND** a nasal sound or a letter that represents it **2. HELMET PART** the nosepiece of a helmet [Mid-17thC. Directly or via French from medieval Latin *nasalis*, from Latin *nasus* "nose."] —**na·sal·i·ty** /nay zállətee/ *n.* —**na·sal·ly** *adv.*

na·sal·ize /náyz'l īz/ (**-ized, -iz·ing, -iz·es**) *vti.* to make a sound nasal by lowering the soft palate so that air flows through the nose —**na·sal·i·za·tion** /nàyz'li záysh'n/ *n.*

NASCAR /nás kaàr/ *abbr.* National Association of Stock Car Auto Racing

nas·cence /náyss'ns, náss'ns/, **nas·cen·cy** /-see/ *n.* the beginning or coming into being of something (*literary*)

nas·cent /náyss'nt, náss'nt/ *adj.* **1. JUST BEGINNING TO DEVELOP** in the process of emerging, being born, or starting to develop **2.** CHEM **PRODUCED IN REACTION MEDIUM** in the process of being created in a reaction medium, often in a highly active form [Early 17thC. From Latin *nascent-*, present participle stem of *nasci* "to be born" (source of English *nation* and *nature*).]

NASD *abbr.* National Association of Securities Dealers

NASDAQ /náz dàk/ *n.* an electronic communications system that links all over-the-counter securities dealers to form a single market. Full form **National Association of Securities Dealers Automated Quotation System**

nase·ber·ry /náyz bèrree/ (*plural* **-ries**), **nees·ber·ry** /neéz-/ (*plural* **-ries**) *n.* TREES = **sapodilla** [Late 17thC. By folk etymology from Spanish *nispero* or Portuguese *nespera*, from Latin *mespilus* "medlar," by association with BERRY.]

Nash /nash/, **Ogden** (1902–71) U.S. writer and lyricist. He is known for his comic verse and the musical *One Touch of Venus* (1943). Full name **Frederic Ogden Nash**

Nash·u·a /náshoo͝ ə/ city in southern New Hampshire. It is the administrative seat of Hillsborough County. Population: 79,662 (1990).

Nash·ville /násh vìl/ capital city of Tennessee, situated in the north central part of the state. It is a major center for country-and-western music. Population: 504,505 (1994).

na·si go·reng /naàssi gə réng/ *n.* a Malaysian dish of fried rice with other ingredients, usually including meat or fish [From Malay, literally "fried rice"]

na·si·on /náyzee òn/ *n.* the point where the bridge of the nose meets the forehead [Late 19thC. From French, formed from *nasal* "nasal," on the model of INION.] — **na·si·al** *adj.*

naso- *prefix.* nose, nasal ○ *nasogastric* [From Latin *nasus* (source also of English *nasturtium.* Ultimately from the Indo-European word for "nose" that is also the ancestor of *nose* and *ness.*]

na·so·fron·tal /nàyzō frúnt'l/ *adj.* relating to the nasal and the frontal bones jointly

na·so·gas·tric /nàyzō gástrik/ *adj.* passing through the nose to the stomach

na·so·lac·ri·mal /nàyzō lákrəm'l/, **na·so·lach·ry·mal** *adj.* relating to or connecting the nose and the tear-producing sacs

na·so·pha·ryn·ge·al /nàyzō fərrín jee əl, -fə rínjəl, -fàrrən jée əl/ *adj.* relating to the nose and pharynx or to the nasopharynx

na·so·phar·ynx /nàyzō férringks/ (*plural* **-pha·ryn·ges** /-fə rín jeèz/ *or* **-phar·ynx·es**) *n.* the upper part of the pharynx, behind and above the soft palate, continuous with the nasal passages

Nas·rud·din /naàzroo͞ deén/ *n.* a trickster who appears in Muslim folklore. He first appeared in stories used by Sufis to teach their students. [Mid-20thC. From Turkish.]

Nas·sau /nássaw/ capital city and principal port of the Bahamas, situated on the northeastern coast of New Providence Island. Population: 171,542 (1990).

AKG London

Gamel Abdel Nasser

Nas·ser /nássèr, naàssər/, **Gamel Abdel** (1918–70) Egyptian statesman. Originally a soldier, he became prime minister in 1954 and president two years later.

Nast /nast/, **Thomas** (1840–1902) German-born U.S. satirical cartoonist. He is known for his attacks on the Tammany Ring (1869–72), and for creating the symbols of the Republican elephant and the Democratic donkey.

Na·sta·se /nə stássee/, **Ilie** (*b.* 1946) Romanian tennis player. He won the U.S. Open (1972) and French Open (1973), and many doubles titles.

nas·tic /nástik/ *adj.* BOT relating to the movement of the parts of a plant in response to external stimuli such as the opening of a crocus flower in response to temperature [Early 20thC. Formed from Greek *nastos* "pressed together," from *nassein* "to press."]

nas·tur·tium /nə stúrshəm, na-/ *n.* a plant with shield-shaped pungent leaves and showy long-spurred yellow, orange, or red irregular flowers. Its leaves, flowers, and seeds are edible. Genus: *Tropaeolum.* [12thC. From Latin, of uncertain origin: probably an alteration of assumed *nasitortium,* literally "nose-twister." From its pungent odor.]

nas·ty /nástee/ *adj.* (**-ti·er, -ti·est**) **1.** SPITEFUL showing spitefulness, malice, or ill-nature ○ *a nasty trick to play on someone* **2.** REPUGNANT TO SENSES repugnant or disgusting to the senses ○ *a nasty smell* **3.** UNPLEASANT generally disagreeable, unpleasant, or causing discomfort ○ *The weather turned nasty.* **4.** SERIOUS likely

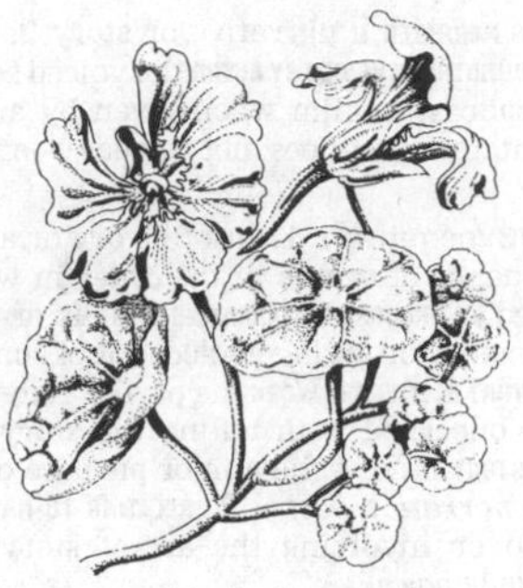

Nasturtium

to cause harm or to be painful ○ *a nasty accident* ○ *a nasty bump on the head* **5.** MORALLY OFFENSIVE morally offensive or obscene (*informal*) **6.** DIFFICULT difficult to solve or deal with (*informal*) ■ *n.* (*plural* **-ties**) UNPLEASANT PERSON OR THING somebody or something that is very disagreeable, harmful, or offensive (*informal*) [14thC. Origin uncertain: perhaps from a Scandinavian word meaning "dirty."] —**nas·ti·ly** *adv.* — **nas·ti·ness** *n.*

WORD KEY: SYNONYMS

See Synonyms at ***mean.***

-nasty *suffix.* nastic response ○ *thermonasty* [Formed from Greek *nastos* (see NASTIC)]

nat. *abbr.* **1.** national **2.** natural **3.** native

na·tal[1] /náyt'l/ *adj.* relating to birth or to the time and place of birth [14thC. Via Latin *natalis* (source of English *noel*) from, ultimately, *nasci* "to be born" (see NATION).]

na·tal[2] /náyt'l/ *adj.* relating to the buttocks [Late 19thC. Formed from Latin *natis* (see NATES).]

Na·tal /nə taál/ **1.** city and seaport in northeastern Brazil. It is the capital of Rio Grande do Norte State. Population: 606,541 (1991). **2.** former province of eastern South Africa, merged in 1994 with KwaZulu to form KwaZulu-Natal

na·tal·i·ty /nə tállətee, nay-/ *n.* = **birthrate**

na·tant /náyt'nt/ *adj.* ZOOL floating or swimming in water (*technical*) [15thC. From Latin *natant-*, the present participle stem of *natare* (see NATATORY).]

Nat·ar·a·ja /naàtə raájə/ *n.* the Hindu god Shiva when represented as a dancing figure with several arms and legs [Early 20thC. From Hindi, literally "prince of dancers."]

na·ta·tion /nə táysh'n, nay-/ *n.* the action or skill of swimming (*formal*) [Mid-16thC. From the Latin stem *natation-*, ultimately from *natare* (see NATATORY).] — **na·ta·tion·al** *adj.*

na·ta·to·ry /náytə tàwree/, **na·ta·to·ri·al** /nàytə táwree əl/ *adj.* relating to or adapted for swimming (*formal*) [Late 18thC. Via late Latin *natatorius* from Latin *natator* "swimmer," from *natare* "to keep on swimming," from *nare* "to swim, float."]

natch /nach/ *adv.* naturally or of course (*informal*) [Mid-20thC. Shortening of NATURALLY.]

Natch·i·toches /nákə tòsh/ city in western Louisiana, just west of the Red River. Population: 17,267 (1996).

na·tes /náy teèz/ *npl.* the buttocks [Late 17thC. From Latin, the plural of *natis* "buttock, rump."]

Na·than *n.* in the Bible, a prophet at David's court (2 Samuel 7:1–17, 12:1–15)

Na·tick /náttik/ town in eastern Massachusetts, east of Framingham and southwest of Boston. Population: 31,310 (1996).

na·tion /náysh'n/ *n.* **1.** PEOPLE IN LAND UNDER SINGLE GOVERNMENT a community of people or peoples who live in a defined territory and are organized under a single government **2.** PEOPLE OF SAME ETHNICITY a community of people who share a common ethnic origin, culture, historical tradition, and, frequently, language, whether or not they live together in one territory or have their own government **3.** NATIVE AMERICAN PEOPLE OR FEDERATION a Native American people or a federation of peoples ○ *the Apache nation* **4.** LAND OF NATIVE AMERICAN NATION **5.** a territory occupied by a Native American nation **5.** GROUP WITH COMMON INTEREST a group of people united by a common interest ○ *the hip-hop nation* [13thC. Via French from the Latin stem *nation-* "birth, race, nation," from *nat-*, past participle stem of *nasci* "to be born" (source of English *innate*).] — **na·tion·hood** *n.*

Nation /náysh'n/, **Carry** (1846–1911) U.S. temperance leader. She believed that she had a divine calling to carry out violent anti-alcohol attacks on saloons, armed with a hatchet. Full name **Carry Amelia Moore Nation**

na·tion·al /náshən'l, náshnəl/ *adj.* **1.** OF A NATION relating or belonging to, or representing a nation, especially a nation as a whole rather than any particular part of it or section of its territory ○ *the national team* **2.** CHARACTERISTIC OF PEOPLE OF PARTICULAR NATION relating to or characteristic of the people of a particular nation ○ *the British national character* **3.** OWNED OR CONTROLLED BY CENTRAL GOVERNMENT owned, maintained, or controlled by the central government of a nation ■ *n.* **1.** CITIZEN OF PARTICULAR NATION a citizen of a particular nation, especially when living in another country **2.** SPORTS COMPETITION INVOLVING CONTESTANTS FROM WHOLE COUNTRY a sports contest involving participants from every part of a country (*often used in the plural*)

na·tion·al an·them *n.* a nation's official hymn or song, expressing patriotic sentiments and played or sung on public occasions

na·tion·al as·sem·bly *n.* a legislative body consisting of the elected representatives of a particular nation or country

Na·tion·al As·sem·bly *n.* **1.** LEGISLATIVE ASSEMBLY OF FRENCH REVOLUTION the first legislative assembly set up during the French Revolution and ruling from 1789 to 1791 **2.** QUEBEC LEGISLATURE the legislative assembly in Quebec

na·tion·al bank *n.* **1.** PRIVATE BANK UNDER FEDERAL CHARTER a bank in a system of privately owned commercial banks in the United States, operating under federal charter and legally required to be a member of the Federal Reserve System **2.** BANK ACTING FOR GOVERNMENT a bank that acts as banker to a government and performs duties relating to national finances, especially the country's fiscal and monetary policy

Na·tion·al Cit·y city in southwestern California, in San Diego County, south of San Diego. Population: 54,249 (1990).

na·tion·al con·scious·ness *n.* the ideas, beliefs, and attitudes regarded as characteristic of a nation

na·tion·al cos·tume *n.* = **national dress**

na·tion·al debt *n.* the total amount of money owed by a nation's central government as a result of borrowing

na·tion·al dress *n.* clothes of a distinctive design that are, or were, typical of the people of a particular country

na·tion·al for·est *n.* a forested area that is owned and maintained by the federal government

Na·tion·al Gal·ler·y *n.* a museum in Trafalgar Square, London, that contains more than 2,000 paintings from the national collection. Founded in 1824, it opened in its present building in 1838.

Na·tion·al Gal·ler·y of Art *n.* a museum in Washington, D.C. that contains the national collection of paintings, prints, drawings, sculptures, photographs, and other works of art. It was founded in 1937 with the gift to the nation of the art collection of the financier Andrew W. Mellon.

Na·tion·al Gal·ler·y of Aus·tra·lia *n.* a museum in Canberra that contains the national collection of Aboriginal, modern Australian, and world art. The collection was begun in 1911, and is housed in a building dating from 1982. Formerly called **Australian National Gallery**

Na·tion·al Gal·ler·y of Can·a·da *n.* a museum in Ottawa that contains the national collection of Canadian and European art. It was created by an Act of Parliament in 1913.

na·tion·al guard *n.* a military organization that operates as a national defense or police force

Na·tion·al Guard *n.* in the United States, the military reserve units controlled by individual states and equipped by the federal government that can be called into service by either federal or state governments

Na·tion·al Health Ser·vice *n.* in the United Kingdom, the state system for providing free or subsidized medical care, established in 1948

Na·tion·al Hock·ey League *n.* the major league of professional ice hockey teams in Canada and the United States

na·tion·al in·come *n.* the total money earned or gained by all residents of a country over a particular period of time, including income from rent, profits, interest, government benefits, salaries, and wages

na·tion·al in·ter·est *n.* whatever will benefit a nation, or a nation's concern for its own survival and prosperity

na·tion·al·ism /náshən'l ìzzəm, náshnə-/ *n.* 1. DESIRE FOR POLITICAL INDEPENDENCE the desire to achieve political independence, especially by a country under foreign control or by a people with a separate identity and culture but no state of their own 2. PATRIOTISM proud loyalty and devotion to a nation 3. EXCESSIVE DEVOTION TO NATION excessive or fanatical devotion to a nation and its interests, often associated with a belief that one country is superior to all others —**nationalist** *n., adj.*

na·tion·al·is·tic /nàshən'l ístik, nàshnə-/ *adj.* relating to or supporting nationalism, especially the kind that emphasizes fervent devotion to one nation and its interests above all others —**na·tion·al·is·ti·cal·ly** *adv.*

na·tion·al·i·ty /nàshə nállətee/ (*plural* **-ties**) *n.* 1. CITIZENSHIP OF PARTICULAR NATION the status of belonging to a specific nation by origin, birth, or naturalization 2. PEOPLE FORMING NATION-STATE a people with a common origin, tradition, and often language, who form or are capable of forming a nation-state 3. ETHNIC GROUP WITHIN A LARGER ENTITY an ethnic group that is part of a larger entity such as a state 4. NATIONHOOD political independence as a separate nation 5. NATIONAL CHARACTER the character of a nation of people

na·tion·al·ize /náshən'l ìz, náshnə-/ (**-ized, -iz·ing, -iz·es**) *vt.* 1. TRANSFER BUSINESS TO STATE OWNERSHIP to transfer a business, property, or industry from private to governmental control or ownership 2. MAKE NATIONAL to make something national or to give a national character to something 3. = **naturalize** *v.* 1 —**na·tion·al·i·za·tion** /nàshən'li záysh'n, nàshnə-/ *n.* —**na·tion·al·ized** /náshnə-/ *adj.* —**na·tion·al·iz·er** *n.*

Na·tion·al Li·brar·y of Aus·tra·lia *n.* the national library of Australia, in Canberra, established as an independent institution by an Act of Parliament in 1960. It was founded in 1901 as part of the Commonwealth Parliamentary Library.

Na·tion·al Li·brar·y of Can·a·da *n.* the national library of Canada, founded in Ottawa in 1953

Na·tion·al Li·brar·y of New Zea·land *n.* the national library of New Zealand, in Wellington, created in 1966 by combining the collections of the General Assembly Library, the Alexander Turnbull Library, and the National Library Service

na·tion·al·ly /náshən'lee, náshnəlee/ *adv.* in, to, or throughout an entire nation

na·tion·al mon·u·ment *n.* a structure or site of scenic, historical, or scientific significance that is protected and maintained by a national government

na·tion·al park *n.* a large area of public land chosen by a government for its scenic, recreational, scientific, or historical importance and usually given special protection

Na·tion·al Par·ty *n.* in South Africa, a conservative political party that developed from the Afrikaaner nationalist movement, came to power in 1948, was largely responsible for instituting apartheid, and relinquished power in 1994

na·tion·al se·cu·ri·ty *n.* the protection of a nation from attack or other danger by maintaining adequate armed forces and guarding state secrets

Na·tion·al Se·cu·ri·ty Ad·vis·er *n.* a member of the White House staff who advises the President on security matters

Na·tion·al Se·cu·ri·ty Coun·cil *n.* a council consisting of the President, the secretary of state, and top military and intelligence officers that decides on policies and measures to maintain national security

na·tion·al ser·vice *n.* compulsory service in the armed forces or in a civilian role, as prescribed in some countries

na·tion·al so·cial·ism, Na·tion·al So·cial·ism *n.* the ideology and practices of the Nazi Party, in Germany's Third Reich, which included national expansion, state control of the economy, the totalitarian principle of government, and anti-semitism —**na·tion·al so·cial·ist** *n., adj.*

WORLD'S LARGEST NATIONAL PARKS

	Area	
Wood Buffalo *Canada*	17,298 sq. mi. / 44,802 sq. km	est. 1922
Ellesmere Island *Canada*	14,585 sq. mi. / 37,775 sq. km	est. 1988
Gates of the Arctic *United States*	11,756 sq. mi. / 30,448 sq. km	est. 1980
Death Valley *United States*	8,554 sq. mi. / 13,765 sq. km	est. 1994
Etosha *Namibia*	8,000 sq. mi. / 20,700 sq. km	est. 1958
Tsavo *Kenya*	8,000 sq. mi. / 20,700 sq. km	est. 1948
Kakadu *Australia*	7,770 sq. mi. / 20,000 sq. km	est. 1979
Kruger *South Africa*	7,523 sq. mi. / 19,485 sq. km	est. 1926
Serengeti *Tanzania*	5,700 sq. mi. / 14,760 sq. km	est. 1941
Hwange *Zimbabwe*	5,657 sq. mi. / 14,651 sq. km	est. 1929
Fiordland *New Zealand*	4,678 sq. mi. / 12,116 sq. km	est. 1952
Kalahari Gemsbok *Botswana/Namibia*	3,703 sq. mi. / 9,591 sq. km	est. 1933
Yellowstone *United States*	3,468 sq. mi. / 8,983 sq. km	est. 1872
Daintree *Australia*	2,734 sq. mi. / 7,000 sq. km	est. 1962
Everglades *United States*	2,354 sq. mi. / 6,096 sq. km	est. 1947
Grand Canyon *United States*	1,904 sq. mi. / 4,930 sq. km	est. 1919
Mount Aspiring *New Zealand*	1,109 sq. mi. / 2,873 sq. km	est. 1964
Lake District *England*	866 sq. mi. / 2,243 sq. km	est. 1951
Snowdonia *Wales*	840 sq. mi. / 2,171 sq. km	est. 1951
Dartmoor *England*	368 sq. mi. / 954 sq. km	est. 1951

Na·tion of Is·lam *n.* a movement of African Americans founded in 1930 whose members follow Islamic religious practice, because of a belief that Black Americans have Muslim origins. Malcolm X was a leading spokesman for the organization until he left it in 1964.

na·tion-state *n.* an independent state recognized by and able to interact with other states, especially one composed of people who are of one, as opposed to several, nationalities

na·tion·wide /náysh'n wìd/ *adj.* EVERYWHERE IN NATION applying to, happening in, or found in all parts of a nation ○ *a nationwide advertising campaign* ■ *adv.* THROUGHOUT NATION covering the whole nation or throughout the nation

na·tive /náytiv/ *adj.* 1. INBORN existing in or belonging to someone by nature ○ *her native intelligence* 2. BORN OR ORIGINATING SOMEWHERE born or originating in a particular place 3. RELATING TO SOMEBODY BECAUSE OF BIRTH relating or belonging to somebody or something because of the place or circumstances of birth 4. INDIGENOUS originating, produced, growing, or living naturally in a place 5. LOCAL, ESPECIALLY ABORIGINAL, INHABITANTS characteristic of, belonging to, or relating to, the indigenous inhabitants of a particular place, particularly those with an aboriginal culture 6. NOT EXTERNALLY AFFECTED unaffected by artificial or outside influences 7. CHEM ELEM OCCURRING NATURALLY found in nature, especially in a pure or unadulterated form ○ *native copper* 8. COMPUT FOR PARTICULAR COMPUTER SYSTEM designed exclusively for a particular computer operating system ■ *n.* 1. SOMEONE BORN IN PARTICULAR PLACE someone born or brought up in a particular place ○ *a native of Birmingham* 2. INDIGENOUS INHABITANT an original indigenous inhabitant of a place 3. OFFENSIVE TERM an offensive term for an original inhabitant of a place belonging to an indigenous non-white people with a traditional culture, as distinct from a colonial settler and immigrant (*dated offensive*) 4. BOT, ZOOL INDIGENOUS PLANT OR ANIMAL SPECIES a plant or animal species that originates from a particular area [14thC. Directly or via French *natif* from Latin *nativus* "born" (source of English *naive*), from, ultimately, *nasci* "to be born" (see NATION).] —**na·tive·ly** *adv.* —**na·tive·ness** *n.* ◇ **go native** to take up the customs and culture of the foreign place where you have settled (*humorous*)

WORD KEY: SYNONYMS

native, aboriginal, indigenous, autochthonous

CORE MEANING: originating in a particular place

native used to describe somebody or something born or originating in a particular place; **aboriginal** used to describe the people who are the earliest known inhabitants of a particular region; **indigenous** a fairly formal word used to describe species that occur naturally in a particular place and were not introduced from elsewhere; **autochthonous** a technical word used to refer to rocks and minerals that were formed in their present position.

WORD KEY: ORIGIN

The Latin word *nasci*, from which ***native*** is derived, and its past participle *natus* are also the source of English *cognate, impregnate, innate, naive, nascent, nation, nature, noel, pregnant, puny,* and *renaissance.*

Na·tive A·mer·i·can *n.* ABORIGINAL AMERICAN a member of any of the indigenous peoples of North, South, or Central America, belonging to the Mongoloid group of peoples ■ *adj.* RELATING TO INDIGENOUS AMERICAN PEOPLES relating to any of the indigenous American peoples, their languages, or their cultures

WORD KEY: USAGE

See Usage note at ***Indian.***

na·tive-born *adj.* belonging to a place by birth

na·tive land *n.* the land to which somebody belongs by birth

Na·tive Peo·ple *npl.* a term used in Canada to describe any one of the aboriginal peoples indigenous to Canada, or all these people collectively

na·tive son *n.* somebody born in a particular place and still associated with it ○ *Illinois is expected to support its native son in the presidential primary.*

na·tive speak·er *n.* somebody who has learned to speak a particular language as a first language

na·tive tongue *n.* the first language that somebody learns to speak

na·tiv·ism /náyti vìzzəm/ *n.* 1. POL POLICY OF FAVORING NATIVE INHABITANTS a policy, especially in the United States, of favoring the interests of the native inhabitants of a country over those of immigrants 2. ANTHROP POLICY OF REAFFIRMING INDIGENOUS CULTURE a policy of protecting and celebrating traditional cultures 3. PHILOS DOCTRINE OF INNATE IDEAS the belief that the mind possesses some ideas that are inborn and not derived from external sources 4. PSYCHOL THEORY CLAIMING PERSONALITY IS INNATELY DETERMINED a theory claiming that personality and behavior are determined from within, not externally —**na·tiv·ist** *n., adj.* —**na·tiv·is·tic** /nàyti vístik/ *adj.*

na·tiv·i·ty /nə tívvətee/ (*plural* **-ties**) *n.* 1. BIRTH OR ORIGIN birth or origin, especially the place, process, or circumstances of being born 2. HOROSCOPE a horoscope based on the time of somebody's birth [14thC. Via Old French from Latin *nativitas*, from *nativus* (see NATIVE).]

Na·tiv·i·ty (*plural* **-ties**) *n.* **1. BIRTH OF JESUS CHRIST** the birth of Jesus Christ, which is celebrated by Christians at Christmas **2. REPRESENTATION OF JESUS CHRIST'S BIRTH** an artistic representation, especially a painting, of the events surrounding the birth of Jesus Christ

natl. *abbr.* national

NATO /náytō/, **Nato** *n.* an international organization established in 1949 to promote mutual defense and collective security that was the primary Western alliance during the Cold War. Full form **North Atlantic Treaty Organization**

na·tri·um /náytree əm/ *n.* the Latin name for sodium, which gave it its chemical symbol of Na [Mid-19thC. Formed from NATRON.]

na·tri·u·re·sis /nàytree yoŏ réssiss/ *n.* the excretion of sodium in urine, especially in excessive amounts [Mid-20thC. Formed from NATRIUM + Greek *ourēsis* "urination."] —**na·tri·u·ret·ic** /-réttik/ *adj.*

na·tro·lite /náytrə līt, náttrə-/ *n.* a white hydrous silicate of sodium and aluminum related to zeolite [Early 19thC. Coined from NATRON + -LITE.]

na·tron /náy tròn, -trən/ *n.* a white, yellow, or gray mineral consisting of hydrous sodium carbonate, found in saline residues, and once used in embalming [Late 17thC. Via French, Spanish, and Arabic *natrūn* from Greek *nitron* (see NITER).]

nat·ter /náttər/ *vi.* **(-tered, -ter·ing, -ters) CHAT** to talk about not very serious matters, often rapidly and at length and sometimes in an irritating way (*informal*) ■ *n. U.K.* **NON-SERIOUS CONVERSATION** a trivial or gossipy conversation (*informal*) [Early 19thC. Variant of earlier *gnatter* "to chat, grumble, gnaw," of uncertain origin: probably an imitation of the sound made when talking rapidly.]

nat·ty /náttee/ **(-ti·er, -ti·est)** *adj.* neat and fashionable in appearance or dress [Late 18thC. Origin uncertain: perhaps a variant of earlier *netty* "neat," from *net* "clean, tidy" (see NEAT).] —**nat·ti·ly** *adv.* —**nat·ti·ness** *n.*

nat·u·ral /náchərəl, náchrəl/ *adj.* **1. OF NATURE** relating to nature **2. CONFORMING WITH NATURE** in accordance with the usual course of nature ○ *natural symptoms of aging* **3. PRODUCED BY NATURE** present in or produced by nature, rather than being artificial or created by people ○ *a natural sapphire* **4. OF PHYSICAL WORLD** relating to the physical rather than the spiritual world **5. LIKE HUMAN NATURE** in accordance with human nature ○ *It's only natural that they should want to be independent.* **6. INNATE** inborn, rather than acquired ○ *lots of natural charm* **7. BEING SOMETHING BY NATURE** having a particular character by nature ○ *a natural leader* **8. NOT AFFECTED** behaving in a sincere and unaffected way and not affected or adopted for a particular purpose **9. NOT ARTIFICIAL** not artificially colored or treated **10. LIKE REAL LIFE** representing something in a way that seems true to life **11. ILLEGITIMATE** illegitimate (*archaic*) ○ *a natural child* **12. BIOLOGICAL** related by blood, rather than adoption ○ *her natural mother* **13.** MUSIC **NOT SHARP OR FLAT** used to describe a note in music that is neither sharp nor flat **14.** MUSIC **WITHOUT SHARPS OR FLATS** used to describe a musical key or scale containing no sharps or flats **15.** CARDS **WITHOUT JOKER OR WILD CARD** not made using a joker or a wild card ○ *a natural flush* ■ *n.* **1. SOMEBODY WITH NATURAL SKILLS OR ABILITIES** somebody who has seemingly innate skills or abilities ○ *a natural at bowling* **2.** MUSIC **MUSICAL SIGN CANCELING SHARP OR FLAT** a sign placed before a musical note in order to cancel a previous sharp or flat **3.** MUSIC **NOTE AFFECTED BY NATURAL SIGN** a musical note affected by a natural sign **4.** CARDS, GAMBLING **STAKE-WINNING RESULT OR COMBINATION** a result or combination in certain card and dice games such as craps and blackjack that immediately wins the stake **5.** COLORS **LIGHT COLOR** a nearly white color with tints of gray, yellow, or brown, like that of undyed fibers or yarn [13thC. Via French from Latin *naturalis*, from *natura* (see NATURE).] —**nat·u·ral·ness** *n.*

nat·u·ral child·birth *n.* childbirth with little or no medication or medical intervention. The mother uses special techniques and exercises in order to minimize pain and assist in the delivery.

nat·u·ral death *n.* death caused by disease or old age rather than by an act of violence or an accident

nat·u·ral dis·as·ter *n.* a disaster such as an earthquake caused by natural forces rather than by human action

nat·u·ral fi·ber *n.* a fiber such as cotton, wool, or silk that forms naturally

nat·u·ral food *n.* food that has been minimally processed and does not contain any additives such as preservatives or artificial coloring

nat·u·ral gas *n.* a mixture of combustible hydrocarbon gases, mostly methane and ethane, found trapped in the pore spaces of certain sedimentary rocks, often along with petroleum deposits

nat·u·ral his·to·ry *n.* **1. STUDY AND DESCRIPTION OF NATURE** the study and description of living things, especially their behavior and how they relate to one another **2. NATURAL PHENOMENA OF TIME OR PLACE** the natural phenomena, especially plants and animals, of a particular time or place **3. NATURAL DEVELOPMENT OF SOMETHING** the natural development of something such as an organism or a disease over a period of time ○ *the natural history of the leech* **4. WRITTEN ACCOUNT OF ASPECT OF NATURE** a written account of a particular aspect of the natural world

nat·u·ral·ism /náchərə lìzzəm, náchrə-/ *n.* **1.** ARTS, LITERAT **MOVEMENT OR SCHOOL ADVOCATING REALISTIC DESCRIPTION** in art or literature, a movement or school advocating factual or realistic description of life including its less pleasant aspects. In literature, it is applied especially to Zola, Maupassant, and other 19th century French writers. In the visual arts, it refers to the practice of faithfully representing subjects. **2.** RELIG **BELIEF IN RELIGIOUS TRUTH FROM NATURE** a belief that all religious truth is derived from nature and natural causes, and not from revelation **3.** PHILOS **DOCTRINE REJECTING SPIRITUAL EXPLANATIONS OF WORLD** a system of thought that rejects all spiritual and supernatural explanations of the world and holds that science is the sole basis of what can be known

nat·u·ral·ist /náchərəlist, náchrə-/ *n.* **1.** BIOL **SOMEBODY STUDYING NATURAL HISTORY** somebody who studies or is interested in natural history, especially botany or zoology. The term is particularly used to describe a field biologist. **2.** ARTS, PHILOS **ADVOCATE OF NATURALISM** somebody who believes in or practices naturalism, especially in the arts ■ *adj.* **RELATING TO BELIEFS OF NATURALISM** relating to or in accordance with the beliefs of naturalism

nat·u·ral·is·tic /nàchərə lístik, nàchrə-/ *adj.* **1. REPRODUCING EFFECTS OF NATURE** imitating or reproducing nature or perceived reality in a very exact and faithful way **2. RELATING TO BELIEFS OF NATURALISM** relating to, characteristic of, or in accordance with the tenets of naturalism, especially in art or literature **3. OF NATURALISTS** relating to naturalists or natural history —**nat·u·ral·is·ti·cal·ly** *adv.*

nat·u·ral·ize /náchərə līz, náchrə-/ **(-ized, -iz·ing, -iz·es)** *v.* **1.** *vti.* **GRANT CITIZENSHIP TO** to grant citizenship to somebody of foreign birth, or to acquire citizenship in an adopted country. Also called **nationalize 2.** *vt.* **INTRODUCE SOMETHING FOREIGN INTO GENERAL USE** to introduce something foreign such as a word or custom into general use or into the language of a community **3.** *vti.* BOT, ZOOL **ACCLIMATE PLANT OR ANIMAL** to cause a plant or animal from another region to become established in a new environment or to adapt successfully to new environmental conditions **4.** *vt.* **EXPLAIN IN NATURAL TERMS** to explain a phenomenon in terms of natural as opposed to supernatural causes **5.** *vt.* **MAKE NATURAL** to make something natural or lifelike —**nat·u·ral·i·za·tion** /nàchərəli záysh'n, nàchrə-/ *n.* —**nat·u·ral·ized** /náchərə līzd, náchrə-/ *adj.* —**nat·u·ral·iz·er** /-līzər/ *n.*

nat·u·ral kill·er cell *n.* a white blood cell **(lymphocyte)** that can recognize microbes and tumor cells as "foreign," without requiring prior exposure to them, and destroy them

nat·u·ral lan·guage *n.* **1. NATURALLY EVOLVED HUMAN LANGUAGE** a naturally evolved human language as opposed to a created language such as a computer language **2. NATURALLY EVOLVED HUMAN LANGUAGES** naturally evolved human languages considered collectively

nat·u·ral lan·guage proc·ess·ing *n.* the branch of computational linguistics concerned with the use of artificial intelligence to process natural languages as, e.g., in machine translation

nat·u·ral law *n.* **1. LAW OF MORALITY** a law of morality believed to be derived from human beings' inherent sense of right and wrong, rather than from revelation or the legislation produced by society **2. LAW OF NATURE** a law that governs the behavior of natural phenomena **3.** PHILOS **BELIEF IN UNIVERSAL JUSTICE SYSTEM** the belief that general laws of nature can be applied as a system of justice for all societies, regardless of their individual culture or customs

nat·u·ral light *n.* light from a natural source, usually the sun, as opposed to artificial light

nat·u·ral log·a·rithm *n.* a logarithm with the irrational number *e* as a base

nat·u·ral·ly /náchərəlee, náchrəlee/ *adv.* **1. AS EXPECTED** as might be expected ○ *They naturally objected to being treated in this way.* **2. OF COURSE** without any question or doubt ○ *"You'll go then?" "Naturally."* **3. BY NATURE** as a result of a natural feature, talent, or quality that somebody possesses ○ *a naturally gifted player* **4. IN NORMAL WAY** in a normal and unaffected manner ○ *People seldom act naturally when being filmed.* **5. WITHOUT ARTIFICIAL AID OR TREATMENT** occurring as a natural feature or quality without artificial aid **6. REALISTICALLY** in a manner that faithfully represents nature

nat·u·ral med·i·cine *n.* = **naturopathy**

nat·u·ral num·ber *n.* any whole number greater than zero

nat·u·ral phi·los·o·phy *n.* the study of nature and natural phenomena (*archaic*)

nat·u·ral re·source *n.* a naturally occurring material such as coal or wood that can be exploited by people. Also called **resource**

nat·u·ral sci·ence *n.* any of the sciences such as biology, chemistry, and physics that deal with phenomena observable in nature —**nat·u·ral sci·en·tist** *n.*

nat·u·ral se·lec·tion *n.* the process, according to Darwin, by which organisms best suited to survival in a particular environment achieve greater reproductive success, thereby passing advantageous genetic characteristics on to future generations. ◊ **artificial selection**

nat·u·ral the·ol·o·gy *n.* a theology that holds that knowledge of God can be derived by human reason alone, not divine revelation

nat·u·ral vir·tue *n.* in theology, one of the four virtues of which people are capable without direct assistance from God, specifically fortitude, justice, prudence, and temperance

nat·u·ral world *n.* natural phenomena collectively, as opposed to supernatural or paranormal phenomena or those created by human activity

na·ture /náychər/ *n.* **1. PHYSICAL WORLD** the physical world including all natural phenomena and living things **2. na·ture, Na·ture FORCES CONTROLLING PHYSICAL WORLD** the forces and processes collectively that control the phenomena of the physical world independently of human volition or intervention, sometimes personified as a woman called "Mother Nature" **3. COUNTRYSIDE** the countryside or the environment in a condition relatively unaffected by human activity or as the home of living creatures other than human beings **4. TYPE** a type or sort of thing ○ *a detective novel or something of that nature* **5. INTRINSIC CHARACTER OF PERSON OR THING** the intrinsic or essential character of somebody or something **6. TEMPERAMENT** disposition or temperament in a person ○ *It's just not part of his nature to act unkindly.* **7. REAL APPEARANCE OR ASPECT** the appearance or aspect of a person, place, or thing that is considered to reflect reality ○ *The portrait was remarkably true to nature.* **8. PRIMITIVE EXISTENCE** a basic state of existence, untouched and uninfluenced by civilization **9.** RELIG **NATURAL STATE OF HUMANKIND** the natural and original condition of humankind, as distinguished from a state of grace **10. UNIVERSAL HUMAN BEHAVIOR** the patterns of behavior or the moral standards that are considered to be universally found and recognized among human beings **11. GENETIC MATERIAL AFFECTING ORGANISM** the inherited genetic material that partly determines the behavior, character, and structure of an organism, as opposed to what is learned from experience or the environment ○ *nature versus nurture* [13thC. Via Old French from Latin *natura* "birth, innate qualities, nature" from, ultimately, *nasci* "to be born" (see NATION).] ◇ **by nature** as a part of his, her, or its essential character ◇ **call of nature** the need to urinate or defecate (*humorous*) ◇ **in the nature of somebody** *or* **something 1.** characteristic of somebody *or* something **2.** in the category of something

-natured *adj.* having or showing a particular nature

or disposition (*often used in combination*) ○ *good-natured* [Formed from NATURE]

na·ture re·serve, **na·ture pre·serve** *n.* a managed and protected area of land usually containing rare or endangered plants or animals

na·ture trail *n.* a route through a natural area that is specially designed to draw attention to interesting natural features

na·tur·ism /náychə rìzzəm/ *n.* **1.** the practise of going without clothes, usually in a communal setting or in designated areas, in the belief that nudity is a healthy natural state. Also called **nudism** **2.** RELIG **NATURE WORSHIP** worship of nature in general, or of objects of nature such as trees and mountains

na·tur·ist /náychərist/ *n.* somebody who practices naturism —**na·tur·is·tic** /nàychə rístik/ *adj.* —**na·tur·is·ti·cal·ly** *adv.*

na·tur·op·a·thy /nàychə róppəthee/ *n.* a system of medicine founded on the belief that diet, mental state, exercise, breathing, and other natural factors are central to the origin and treatment of disease —**na·tur·o·path** /náychərə pàth/ *n.* —**na·tur·o·path·ic** /nàychərə páthik/ *adj.* —**na·tur·o·path·i·cal·ly** *adv.*

Nau·ga·hyde /náwgə hīd/ *tdmk.* a trademark for an imitation leather fabric

Nau·ga·tuck /náwgə tùk/ **1.** river in western Connecticut. Length: 65 mi./105 km. **2.** town in southern Connecticut, in New Haven County, south of Waterbury. Population: 30,625 (1990).

naught /nawt/, **nought** *n.* **1.** **ZERO** the number zero **2.** **NOTHING** nothing at all (*archaic or literary*) ○ *Their efforts were all for naught.* [Old English *nāwiht*. From *nā* NO + *wiht* "thing, being."]

naugh·ty /náwtee/ (**-ti·er**, **-ti·est**) *adj.* **1.** **BADLY BEHAVED** badly behaved, especially by being mischievous or disobedient **2.** **MILDLY INDECENT** mildly indecent or improper (*humorous*) ○ *a naughty smile* **3.** **SINFUL** mildly sinful (*humorous*) ○ *Would it be naughty of me to have another chocolate?* [14thC. The current meaning evolved from "having naught, poor" via "bad."] —**naugh·ti·ly** *adv.* —**naugh·ti·ness** *n.*

WORD KEY: SYNONYMS

See Synonyms at ***bad***.

nau·pli·us /náwplee əss/ (*plural* **-i** /náwplee ī/) *n.* a free-swimming larva that is produced by many different crustaceans, with an unsegmented body, three pairs of limbs, and a single eye [Mid-19thC. Via Latin, "kind of shellfish," from Greek *nauplios*.]

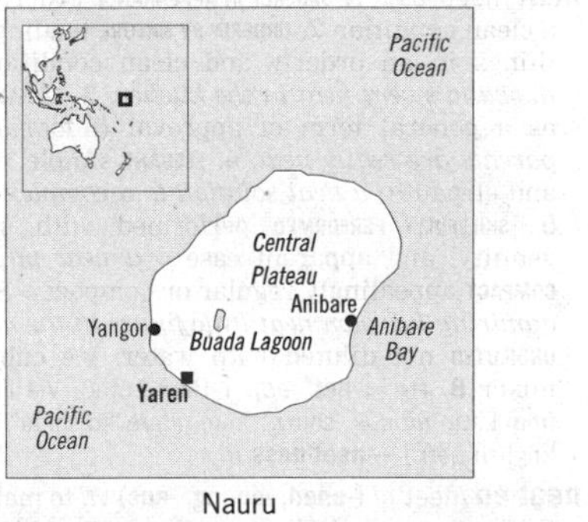

Nauru

Na·u·ru /nə róo/ island republic in Micronesia, in the central Pacific Ocean, northeast of Australia. Language: English, Nauruan, English. Currency: Australian dollar. Capital: Yaren. Population: 10,273 (1996). Area: 8.1 sq. mi./21 sq. km. Official name **Republic of Nauru**. Former name **Pleasant Island** —**Naur·u·an** *n., adj.*

nau·se·a /náwzee ə, náwshə/ *n.* **1.** **SICKNESS OF THE STOMACH** the unsettling feeling in the stomach that accompanies the urge to vomit **2.** **DISGUST** deep disgust (*literary*) [15thC. Via Latin and Greek *nausia* from, ultimately, *naus* (see NAUTICAL). The underlying idea is of seasickness.] —**nau·se·ant** /náwzee ənt, náwshee ənt/ *adj., n.*

nau·se·ate /náwzee àyt, náwshee-/ (**-at·ed**, **-at·ing**, **-ates**) *vti.* **1.** **MAKE OR BECOME SICK** to have, or make somebody have, the unsettling feeling in the stomach that accompanies the urge to vomit **2.** **DISGUST OR BECOME DISGUSTED** to feel, or make somebody feel, deep disgust

nau·se·at·ing /náwzee àyting, náwshee-/ *adj.* **1.** **CAUSING SICKNESS IN STOMACH** producing the unsettling feeling in the stomach that accompanies the urge to vomit **2.** **DISGUSTING** deeply disgusting —**nau·se·at·ing·ly** *adv.*

nau·seous /náwzee əss, náwshəss/ *adj.* **1.** **SICK IN THE STOMACH** suffering from the unsettling feeling in the stomach that accompanies the urge to vomit **2.** **CAUSING SICKNESS IN STOMACH** producing the unsettling feeling in the stomach that accompanies the urge to vomit —**nau·seous·ly** *adv.* —**nau·seous·ness** *n.*

naut. *abbr.* nautical

nautch /nawch/ *n.* a professional performance of traditional Indian dancing [Early 19thC. Via Hindi *nāc* from, ultimately, Sanskrit *nṛt* "to dance."]

nau·ti·cal /náwtik'l/ *adj.* relating to sailors, ships, or seafaring [Mid-16thC. Via Latin from Greek *nautikos*, from *nautēs* "sailor," from *naus* "ship" (source of English *astronaut*, *nausea*, and *noise*).] —**nau·ti·cal·ly** *adv.*

nau·ti·cal mile *n.* **1.** an international unit of measurement of distance at sea equal to 1.852 kilometers **2.** a measurement of distance at sea used in the U.K. and taken to be equal to 1.8532 kilometers or about 6076 ft. Also called **sea mile**

nau·ti·loid /náwt'l òyd/ *n.* a mollusk that belongs to the group that includes the nautiluses and many fossil species. The group includes species with chambered, straight, and coiled shells. Subclass: Nautiloidea. [Mid-19thC. Formed from NAUTILUS.]

nau·ti·lus /náwt'ləss/ (*plural* **-lus·es** *or* **-li** /-tī/) *n.* **1.** **SEA CREATURE WITH A COILED SHELL** a mollusk with numerous tentacles, a horny beak, and a spiral shell with gas-filled chambers for buoyancy. It is found in the South Pacific and Indian Oceans. Genus: *Nautilus.* **2.** = **paper nautilus** [Early 17thC. Via Latin from Greek *nautilos* "sailor, nautilus," from *nautēs* (see NAUTICAL).]

NAV *abbr.* FIN net asset value

nav. *abbr.* **1.** naval **2.** navigable **3.** navigation

Nav·a·jo /návvə hō, naávə-/, **Nav·a·ho** *n.* (*plural* **-jo** *or* **-jos**; *plural* **-ho** *or* **-hos**) **1.** PEOPLES **MEMBER OF A NATIVE AMERICAN PEOPLE** a member of a Native American people living mainly in northern New Mexico and Arizona. They are the most populous of all U.S. Native American peoples. **2.** LANG **LANGUAGE OF THE NAVAJO** a Native American language spoken in parts of Arizona, New Mexico, and Utah. It belongs to the Athabaskan branch of Na-Déné languages and is spoken by about 225,000 people. ■ *adj.* **OF THE NAVAJOS** produced by or belonging to the Navajo ○ *a Navajo rug* [Late 18thC. Via Spanish *(Apaches de) Navajó*, literally "(Apaches of) Navajó," from extinct Tewa (a Tanoan language) *navahū* "fields adjoining a ravine."]

na·val /náyv'l/ *adj.* relating or belonging to a navy or to warships —**na·val·ly** *adv.*

na·val ar·chi·tect *n.* somebody who designs ships —**na·val ar·chi·tec·ture** *n.*

na·val stores *npl.* products used in boatbuilding and shipbuilding, especially and originally turpentine and pitch

Na·varre /nə vaár/ autonomous region in northeastern Spain, between the Basque Country and Catalonia. Capital: Pamplona. Population: 519,227 (1991). Area: 4,024 sq. mi./10,421 sq. km.

nave[1] /nayv/ *n.* the long central hall of a cross-shaped church, often with pillars on each side, where the congregation sits [Late 17thC. Via medieval Latin from Latin *navis* (see NAVY). Perhaps from its resemblance in shape to or from the idea of the church as a ship.]

nave[2] /nayv/ *n.* the hub of a wheel [Old English *nafu*. Ultimately from a prehistoric Germanic word that is also the ancestor of English *navel*.]

na·vel /náyv'l/ *n.* a small rounded hollow on the surface of the human stomach, where the end of the umbilical cord was tied after being cut. Technical name **umbilicus** [Old English *nafela*. Ultimately from an Indo-European word that also produced English *nave* and Latin *umbilicus* (source of English *umbilical*).] ◇ **examine** *or* **contemplate your navel** to spend too much time in pointless self-analysis (*informal humorous*)

na·vel-gaz·ing *n.* pointless self-analysis as opposed to considering broader issues or making a decision

na·vel or·ange *n.* a sweet seedless orange with a small navel-shaped depression or bump at its blossom end enclosing a smaller secondary fruit. Latin name: *Citrus sinensis*.

na·vel·wort /náyv'l wùrt, -wàwrt/ *n.* = **pennywort** [15thC. From the navel-shaped indentation on its leaves.]

na·vic·u·lar /nə víkyələr/ *n.* ANAT = **navicular bone** ■ *adj.* **1.** **BOAT-SHAPED** shaped like a boat (*formal*) **2.** MED **OF THE NAVICULAR BONE** relating to a navicular bone [15thC. From late Latin *navicularis*, from Latin *navicula*, literally "a small ship," from *navis* (see NAVY).]

na·vic·u·lar bone *n.* **1.** ANAT **HUMAN BONE** a small boat-shaped bone in the human wrist or ankle **2.** VET **HORSE BONE** a small bone in a horse's hoof. It is prone to disease (**navicular disease**), causing lameness.

nav·i·ga·ble /návvigəb'l/ *adj.* **1.** **PASSABLE BY SHIP** passable by ship or boat, especially deep enough and wide enough to allow ships or boats to sail through **2.** **STEERABLE** able to be steered or otherwise controlled —**nav·i·ga·bil·i·ty** /nàvvigə bíllətee/ *n.* —**nav·i·ga·bly** /návvi gəblee/ *adv.*

nav·i·gate /návvi gàyt/ (**-gat·ed**, **-gat·ing**, **-gates**) *v.* **1.** *vti.* **FIND A ROUTE** to find a way through a place, or direct the course of something, especially a ship or aircraft, using a route-finding system ○ *navigating by the stars* **2.** *vt.* **PASS THROUGH A PLACE** to follow a correct or satisfactory course along a route ○ *Even a champion rafter would have difficulty navigating those rapids.* **3.** *vi.* **KEEP A CAR ON THE RIGHT ROUTE** to have responsibility for keeping a car on the right route, e.g., by following a map and giving the driver instructions **4.** *vt.* **FIND YOUR WAY** to find a way to a place, usually with difficulty (*informal*) ○ *managed to navigate his way to the bar* [Late 16thC. From the past participle stem of Latin *navigare* "to sail," from *navis* (see NAVY) + *agere* "to drive."]

nav·i·ga·tion /nàvvi gáysh'n/ *n.* **1.** **SCIENCE OF NAVIGATING** the science of plotting and following a course from one place to another and of determining the position of a moving ship, aircraft, or other vehicle **2.** **DIRECTING OF A VEHICLE'S COURSE** the plotting and directing of the course of a ship, aircraft, or other vehicle **3.** **MOVEMENT THROUGH A PLACE** the act or task of moving through a place or along a route, e.g., along a river or through a range of mountains —**nav·i·ga·tion·al** *adj.* —**nav·i·ga·tion·al·ly** *adv.*

nav·i·ga·tion light *n.* any one of a number of lights on the outside of a ship or aircraft that alert others to its position and direction

nav·i·ga·tion sat·el·lite *n.* an artificial satellite, used as an aid to navigation, that follows a fixed orbit made known to navigators on ships and aircraft

nav·i·ga·tor /návvi gàytər/ *n.* **1.** **SOMEBODY IN CHARGE OF NAVIGATION** somebody who is qualified in navigation, especially somebody responsible for navigating a ship or aircraft **2.** **DRIVER'S ROUTE INSTRUCTOR** somebody who gives information on the route ahead to the driver of a car

Popperfoto

Martina Navratilova

Nav·ra·ti·lo·va /nàvrə ti lṓvə/, **Martina** (*b.* 1956) Czech-born U.S. tennis player. She holds the women's record of 167 singles championships (1974–94), including nine Wimbledon titles.

NAVSAT /náv sàt/ *abbr.* navigation satellite (*informal*)

nav·vy /návvee/ (*plural* **-vies**) *n.* *U.K.* an unskilled laborer, especially somebody who does the heavy digging work involved in the building of roads, railroads, and canals (*dated*) [Early 19thC. Shortening of NAVIGATOR (in its earlier meaning "canal laborer").]

na·vy /náyvee/ *n.* (*plural* **-vies**) **1.** **SEAGOING MILITARY FORCE** the branch of a country's armed forces that crews, maintains, and fights on warships **2.** **FLEET OF SHIPS** a fleet of ships, especially one belonging to a country **3.** COLORS = **navy blue** ■ *adj.* COLORS = **navy blue** [14thC. Via Old French *navie* "fleet," from, ultimately, Latin *navis* "ship."]

na·vy bean *n.* a small white variety of kidney bean [From its former use as a food staple in the U.S. Navy]

na·vy blue, na·vy *n.* DARK BLUE a dark blue color ■ *adj.* COLORS DARK BLUE IN COLOR of a dark blue color (*hyphenated before a noun*) ○ *a navy-blue dress* [From the color of the British naval uniform]

Na·vy Cross *n.* a decoration awarded by the U.S. Navy for outstanding heroism in armed combat

na·vy yard *n.* a navy-owned shipyard where warships are built and repaired

na·wab /nə wób/ *n.* a title used for a local nobleman in India during the Mogul empire. Also called **nabob** [Mid-18thC. Via Urdu *nawāb* from, ultimately, Arabic *nā'ib* "deputy."]

nay /nay/ *n.* NO VOTE a vote of no or somebody who votes no ■ *adv.* INTRODUCING CORRECTION used to introduce a phrase that corrects something just said, often a phrase that states the truth in stronger terms (*archaic or literary*) ○ *It was a disappointing, nay, humiliating, outcome.* ■ *interj.* NO no (*archaic*) [12thC. From Old Norse *nei*, from *ne* "not" + *ei* "ever" (source of English *aye*).]

nay·say /náy sày/ (**-said** /-sèd/, **-say·ing, -says**) *vt.* to refuse, oppose, or criticize a proposal

nay·say·er /náy sàyər/ *n.* somebody who votes no or who speaks against something

Naz·a·rene /názzə reen, nàzzə reen/ *n.* **1.** SOMEBODY FROM NAZARETH somebody who was born or raised in Nazareth **2.** MEMBER OF PROTESTANT CHURCH a member of the Church of the Nazarene, a modern Protestant denomination **3.** JESUS CHRIST Jesus Christ, as connected with Nazareth (*literary*) [13thC. Via late Latin from Greek *Nazarēnos*, from *Nazaret* "Nazareth."]

Naz·a·reth /názzərəth/ town in northern Israel, in Galilee, situated southeast of Haifa. It is believed to be where Jesus Christ lived during his childhood. Population: 49,800 (1992).

Naz·a·rite /názzə rìt/, **Naz·i·rite** *n.* a member of a Jewish religious group in biblical times whose members made various vows of abstinence, including a vow not to drink wine or cut their hair [Mid-16thC. Formed from late Latin *Nazaraeus*, from Greek *Nazōraios*, from *Nazaret* "Nazareth."]

Naz·ca Lines /názkə/ *n.* a group of large-scale figures carved into the desert near Nazca, southern Peru, in pre-Inca times. They consist of long straight lines representing birds, fish, animals, or geometrical figures and are only visible from the air.

Na·zi /naatsee, nát-/ *n.* **1.** FOLLOWER OF HITLER a member of the German National Socialist Party that came to power under the leadership of Adolf Hitler in 1933 (*often used before a noun*) **2.** RACIST somebody with right-wing political views, especially somebody with right-wing views on race and immigration (*insult*) **3. Na·zi, na·zi** BOSSY PERSON somebody who behaves in an authoritarian or dictatorial manner (*insult*) (*offensive in some contexts*) [Mid-20thC. From German, a shortening of *Nationalsozialist* "national socialist" or *Nationalsozialismus* "national socialism."] —**Na·zi·fi·ca·tion** /naatsifi káysh'n, nàtsifi káysh'n/ *n.* —**Na·zi·fy** /naatsə fì, nát-/ *vt.*

Naz·i·rite *n.* = **Nazarite**

Na·zism /naat sìzzəm, nát-/ *n.* the philosophy of the German National Socialist Party under the leadership of Adolf Hitler. Central to it was a belief in the inherent superiority of a supposed Aryan race.

Nb *symbol.* niobium

NB, N.B. *abbr.* New Brunswick

n.b., nb used to draw somebody's attention to something particularly important, usually an addition to or qualification of a previous statement. Full form **nota bene** [Latin, *nota bene* "note well"]

NBA, N.B.A. *abbr.* **1.** National Boxing Association **2.** National Basketball Association

NBC *abbr.* National Broadcasting Company

NbE *abbr.* north by east

NBL *abbr.* National Book League

NbW *abbr.* north by west

NC *abbr.* **1.** no charge **2.** noncallable **3. NC, N.C.** North Carolina

n/c *abbr.* no charge

NC-17 *n.* a rating indicating that a movie cannot be seen by children under the age of 17 because of adult content

NCAA /èn see dùbb'l áy/, **N.C.A.A.** *abbr.* National Collegiate Athletic Association

NCO, N.C.O. *abbr.* noncommissioned officer

NCTE *abbr.* National Council of Teachers of English

NCTM *abbr.* National Council of Teachers of Mathematics

Nd *symbol.* neodymium

ND, N.D. *abbr.* North Dakota

n.d., N.D. *abbr.* no date

N. Dak. *abbr.* North Dakota

NDE *abbr.* near-death experience

NDEA *abbr.* National Defense Education Act

NDP *abbr. Can* New Democratic Party

né /nay/ *adj.* **1.** BORN AS used to introduce a man's former or original name **2.** FORMERLY KNOWN AS used to introduce the name that something was formerly known under [Mid-20thC. From French, the past participle of *naître* (see NEE).]

Ne *symbol.* neon

NE *abbr.* **1.** Nebraska **2. NE, N.E.** New England **3.** COMPASS northeast **4.** COMPASS northeastern

Ne. *abbr.* BIBLE Nehemiah

NEA *abbr.* **1.** National Education Association **2.** ARTS National Endowment for the Arts

Ne·an·der·tal /ni ándər taal/, **Ne·an·der·thal** /nee ándər thaal/ *adj.* **1.** RELATING TO NEANDERTAL MAN relating to Neandertal man or the culture **2. Ne·an·der·tal, ne·an·der·tal** OFFENSIVE TERM displaying the lack of intellect, lack of sensitivity, and boorishness traditionally associated with cavemen (*insult*) ○ *drinking with his neanderthal teammates* **3. Ne·an·der·tal, ne·an·der·tal** OLD-FASHIONED very old-fashioned or conservative (*insult*) ○ *neanderthal attitudes* ■ *n.* **Ne·an·der·tal, ne·an·der·tal** OFFENSIVE TERM an offensive term for somebody who is crude, primitive, or excessively old-fashioned (*insult*) [Mid-19thC. Named for a valley in western Germany where evidence of Neandertal man was first found.]

Ne·an·der·tal man *n.* an extinct subspecies of human beings that populated Europe, northern Africa, and western Asia in the early Stone Age. Physical characteristics include a sloping forehead and large brow ridges.

neap /neep/ *n.* = **neap tide** ■ *adj.* RELATING TO NEAP TIDE relating to or associated with a neap tide [15thC. From Old English *nēp-*, of uncertain origin.]

Ne·a·pol·i·tan /nee ə póllət'n/ *adj.* OF NAPLES relating to the Italian city of Naples, or its people or culture ■ *n.* SOMEBODY FROM NAPLES somebody who was born or raised or who lives in Naples [15thC. Via Latin *Neapolitanus* from, ultimately, Greek *Neapolis*, literally "new town," "Naples."]

Ne·a·pol·i·tan ice cream *n.* ice cream made in different colored and flavored layers

neap tide *n.* a tide that shows the least range between high and low and occurs twice a month between the first and third quarters of the moon

near /neer/ (**neared, near·ing, nears**) CORE MEANING: at or to a point that is not far away in space ○ (prep) *The art exhibit is near here.* ○ (adv) *He took a step nearer to the water.* ○ (adv) *as the car drew nearer* ○ (adj) *There must be a restaurant nearer than that.* ○ (adj) *Can you tell me where the nearest telephone is?*

1. *adv., prep., adj.* SHORT TIME AWAY at or to a time not far away ○ (adv) *as the time for her to leave drew near* ○ (prep) *He should arrive near the end of the week* ○ (adj) *We'll be moving in the very near future.* **2.** *adv., adj.* CLOSE at a point that is not far away in state, resemblance, or number ○ (adv) *He felt a sensation that was near to fear.* ○ (adj) *the nearest thing to a champion this county has ever had* **3.** *adv., adj.* ALMOST almost the state or situation mentioned ○ (adv) *I damn near fainted.* ○ (adv) *near total failure* ○ (adj) *living in near poverty* **4.** *adj., n.* ON THE LEFT on the left side, especially of an animal or a horse-drawn vehicle ○ *the near foreleg.* ◊ **nearside** **5.** *adj.* CLOSELY RELATED closely related to somebody **6.** *adj.* MISERLY reluctant to give or spend money (*archaic*) **7.** *v. vti.* APPROACH to approach, or approach a particular place, time, or state ○ *The project is nearing completion.* ○ *With the big event nearing, everyone was working hard.* [12thC. From Old Norse *nær* "nearer," from *nā* "near."] —**near·ness** *n.*

near a·bout, near hand *adj., adv.* close or almost (*informal regional*) ○ *Is it near about?* ○ *He's near hand 90.*

near beer *n.* a malt-based beverage that contains a negligible amount of alcohol, specifically below 0.5%

near·by /neer bí/ *adj., adv.* in, at, or to a place a short distance away ○ *a nearby grocer* ○ *His mother was waiting nearby.* ○ *The children's school is quite nearby.*

Ne·arc·tic /nee aarktik/ *adj.* related to or located in the region of plant and animal life in the Arctic and temperate areas of Greenland and North America [Mid-19thC. Coined from NEO- + ARCTIC.]

near-death ex·pe·ri·ence *n.* a sensation that people on the brink of death have described as leaving their own bodies and observing them as though they were bystanders

Near East *n.* **1.** = **Middle East** *n.* 1 **2.** THE BALKANS the countries on the Balkan peninsula, comprising Greece, Albania, Romania, Bulgaria, the states of the former Yugoslavia, and the European part of Turkey (*dated*)

near gale *n.* = **moderate gale**

near let·ter qual·i·ty *adj.* used to describe the printing quality of a computer printer that produces printed characters as clear as a typewriter's

near·ly /neerlee/ *adv.* **1.** ALMOST almost but not quite the case ○ *We waited for nearly an hour.* **2.** closely, in time, proximity, or relationship ○ *"Brennan described to the police the man he saw in the window and then identified Oswald as the person who most nearly resembled the man he saw ."* (Earl Warren et al, *The Report of the Warren Commission*; 1964) ◇ **not nearly** used to emphasize that something stated, implied, or assumed is very far from being the case ○ *not nearly enough time to answer all the questions*

near miss *n.* **1.** SHOT NEAR TARGET a shot or strike that comes very close to a target but does not quite hit it **2.** NEAR COLLISION a situation in which two vehicles only narrowly avoid colliding with each other **3.** BARELY AVERTED DISASTER something, especially something undesirable, that is only narrowly avoided or averted (*informal*)

near point *n.* the point nearest the eye at which an object remains in focus

near·sight·ed /neer sìtəd/ *adj.* unable to see clearly objects that are far away. U.K. = **shortsighted**

neat /neet/ *adj.* **1.** ORDERLY IN APPEARANCE orderly and in a clean condition **2.** ORDERLY BY NATURE tending to keep things in an orderly and clean condition ○ *My husband's very neat in the kitchen.* **3.** EXCELLENT used as a general term of approval (*informal*) ○ *Her parents are really neat.* **4.** ELEGANT simple, effective, and elegant ○ *a neat solution to a complex problem* **5.** SKILLFULLY PERFORMED performed with skill, ingenuity, and apparent ease ○ *a neat pirouette* **6.** COMPACT appealingly regular or compact ○ *She stood admiring her own neat little figure in the mirror.* **7.** UNDILUTED not diluted with water, ice cubes, or a mixer **8.** FIN = **net**[2] *adj.* 1 [Mid-16thC. Via French *net* from Latin *nitidus* "shiny," from *nitere* "to shine" (source of English *net*).] —**neat·ness** *n.*

neat·en /neet'n/ (**-ened, -en·ing, -ens**) *vt.* to make something neat or orderly

neath /neeth/, **'neath** *prep.* beneath (*literary*) [Late 18thC. Shortening of BENEATH.]

neat·ly /neetlee/ *adv.* **1.** CAREFULLY with care, order, and some precision ○ *a pile of clothes neatly folded* **2.** ELEGANTLY simply, effectively, and elegantly **3.** SKILLFULLY with skill, ingenuity, and apparent ease

neat's-foot oil *n.* a pale yellow oil made from the feet and shinbones of cattle, used to treat leather [From NEAT]

neb /neb/ *n.* **1.** POINT OR PROJECTION something that sticks out, e.g., an overhanging rock or peak (*archaic*) **2.** *N England* ANIMAL'S NOSE an animal's bill, beak, nose, or snout (*informal*) [Old English *nebb*]

NEB *abbr.* New English Bible

Neb. *abbr.* Nebraska

neb·bish /nébbish/ *n.* an offensive term that deliberately insults somebody's courage, personality, and initiative (*informal insult*) [Late 19thC. Via Yiddish *nebekh* "poor thing" from, ultimately, assumed Common Slavic *ne-bogŭ* "poor."]

NEbE *abbr.* northeast by east

NEbN *abbr.* northeast by north

Nebr. *abbr.* Nebraska

Nebraska

Ne·bras·ka /nè bráskə/ state in the central United States, bordered by South Dakota, Iowa, Missouri, Kansas, Colorado, and Wyoming. Capital: Lincoln. Population: 1,656,870 (1997). Area: 77,359 sq. mi./200,359 sq. km. —**Ne·bras·kan** *n., adj.*

Neb·u·chad·nez·zar II /nèbbyŏŏkəd nézzər/ (*fl.* 6th century B.C.) Babylonian king. He conquered and destroyed Jerusalem in 586 B.C., consigning its inhabitants to captivity. He is thought to have created the Hanging Gardens of Babylon.

Nebula: Eagle Nebula, photographed by the Hubble Space Telescope (1995)

neb·u·la /nébbyələ/ (*plural* **-lae** /-lee/ *or* **-las**) *n.* **1.** ASTRON **SPACE DUST** a region or cloud of interstellar dust and gas appearing variously as a hazy bright or dark patch **2.** MED **FLAW ON EYEBALL** a faint cloudy area or scar on the cornea **3.** MED **CLOUDY URINE** cloudiness in the urine **4.** MED **LIQUID FOR SPRAYING** liquid prepared for use in any kind of atomizing sprayer, especially a nebulizer [Mid-17thC. From Latin, "mist, vapor."] —**neb·u·lar** *adj.*

neb·u·lar hy·poth·e·sis *n.* a now largely rejected theory that the solar system evolved from a hot rotating flattened gaseous nebula. The theory states that as the nebula cooled, the Sun condensed at the center and planets and their moons formed from contracting concentric rings at the rim.

neb·u·lize /nébbyə līz/ (**-lized, -liz·ing, -liz·es**) *vt.* to reduce a liquid to a fine spray for medical use —**neb·u·li·za·tion** /nèbbyəli záysh'n/ *n.*

neb·u·liz·er /nébbyə līzər/ *n.* a device, with a face mask attached, for administering a medicinal liquid in the form of a fine spray that is breathed in through the mouth or nose

neb·u·los·i·ty /nèbbyə lóssətee/ (*plural* **-ties**) *n.* = **nebula** *n.* 1

neb·u·lous /nébbyələss/ *adj.* **1.** **UNCLEAR** not clear, distinct, or definite **2.** ASTRON **RELATING TO NEBULAS** relating to or resembling a nebula —**neb·u·lous·ly** *adv.* —**neb·u·lous·ness** *n.*

nec·es·sar·i·ly /nèssə sérrəlee/ *adv.* **1.** **INEVITABLY** inevitably, or in every case ○ *This route isn't necessarily the best one.* **2.** **UNAVOIDABLY** following as an unavoidable result or consequence ○ *Voting was a necessarily slow and complex process.*

nec·es·sar·y /néssə sèrree/ *adj.* **1.** **REQUIRED** needed, essential, or required by authority or convention ○ *Is it really necessary to contact the police?* **2.** **FOLLOWING INEVITABLY** inevitable given what has happened previously ○ *No doubt they will draw the necessary conclusion.* **3.** LOGIC **LOGICALLY TRUE** logically true because of being impossible to be false ■ *n.* (*informal*) **1.** (*plural* **-ies**) **SOMETHING ESSENTIAL** an essential item ○ *I've packed the necessaries.* **2.** *U.K.* **SOMETHING NEEDED** something that is needed, especially a sum of money or a particular action ○ *Tell him to do the necessary.* [14thC. Via Anglo-Norman from Latin *necessarius*, from *necesse*, literally "unyielding," from *cess-*, the stem of *cedere* (see CEDE).]

WORD KEY: SYNONYMS

necessary, essential, vital, indispensable, requisite, needed

CORE MEANING: used to describe something that is required

necessary used to describe something that must be done or provided, or to indicate that somebody's presence is required; **essential** used to emphasize that something is necessary, for example, because a process could not take place without it; **vital** a very emphatic word used to stress that something is urgently necessary; **indispensable** literally suggesting somebody who or something that cannot be done without, but also often used simply to indicate that something is desirable or useful; **requisite** a formal word used especially to suggest that something has been made necessary by a particular circumstance; **needed** used to describe something that is required or desired but implying less urgency than the other words in the group.

nec·es·sar·y con·di·tion *n.* something that must happen or exist in order for something else to happen or exist

nec·es·sar·y e·vil *n.* something that is unpleasant or undesirable but is needed to achieve a desired result

ne·ces·si·tar·i·an /nə sèssi táiree ən/ *n.* somebody who believes that there is no free will and that all events are determined by previous causes —**ne·ces·si·tar·i·an·ism** *n.*

ne·ces·si·tate /nə séssi tàyt/ (**-tat·ed, -tat·ing, -tates**) *v.* **1.** *vti.* **MAKE SOMETHING NECESSARY** to make something necessary or inescapable ○ *a dry climate that necessitates water conservation* **2.** *vt.* **OBLIGE SOMEBODY** to force or oblige somebody to do something (*formal*) —**ne·ces·si·ta·tion** /nə sèssi táysh'n/ *n.* —**ne·ces·si·ta·tive** /nə séssi tàytiv/ *adj.*

ne·ces·si·tous /nə séssitəss/ *adj.* **1.** **POOR** in a state of poverty (*literary*) ○ *"grew necessitous, pawn'd his cloaths, and wanted bread"* (Benjamin Franklin, *The Autobiography of Benjamin Franklin*; 1788) **2.** **NECESSARY** pressingly necessary (*formal*) —**ne·ces·si·tous·ly** *adv.* —**ne·ces·si·tous·ness** *n.*

ne·ces·si·ty /nə séssətee/ (*plural* **-ties**) *n.* **1.** **SOMETHING ESSENTIAL** something that is essential, especially a basic requirement ○ *food, shelter, and the other necessities of life* **2.** **COMPELLING CIRCUMSTANCES** circumstances that create a need or an obligation ○ *The decision was taken out of necessity.* **3.** **NEED** the condition of being needed or required ○ *We'll hire new staff when the necessity arises.* **4.** PHILOS **NECESSARY QUALITY** the quality of being necessary or of not being able to be otherwise [14thC. Via French *necessité* from Latin *necessitas*, from *necesse* (see NECESSARY).]

neck /nek/ *n.* **1.** ANAT **PART BETWEEN HEAD AND BODY** the part of the body that joins the head to the rest of the body **2.** CLOTHES **GARMENT PART AROUND NECK** the part of a garment that goes around or lies below the wearer's neck **3.** FOOD **CUT OF MEAT** a cut of meat from the neck of an animal **4.** **LONG OPENING** a long narrow opening ○ *a bottle with a long neck* **5.** GEOG **STRIP OF LAND OR WATER** a long narrow strip of land or stretch of water **6.** MUSIC **LONG NARROW FINGERBOARD** the long narrow fingerboard that projects out of the body or sound box of a hand-held string instrument such as a guitar or violin **7.** HORSERACING **WINNING MARGIN** in horseracing, a narrow winning margin equal to the distance between a horse's nose and its shoulder **8.** **SOMETHING IMPORTANT RISKED OR SAVED** somebody's life, job, reputation, or other important asset that has been placed at risk or saved from danger (*informal*) ○ *I'm not going to lie to save your neck again.* **9.** GEOL **SOLIDIFIED LAVA** a plug of solidified lava or igneous rock filling the vent of an extinct or dormant volcano **10.** MARINE BIOL = **siphon** *n.* 3 **11.** ARCHIT **BAND AROUND PILLAR** a narrow band around the top of a pillar ■ *v.* (**necked, neck·ing, necks**) (*informal*) **1.** *vi.* **KISS AND CUDDLE** to kiss and embrace sexually, usually sitting or lying with clothes on ○ *teenagers necking in the car* **2.** *vt.* COOK **KILL POULTRY** to kill a bird to be cooked by breaking its neck or chopping its head off [Old English *hnecca* "nape." Ultimately from an Indo-European word meaning "high point, ridge," which also produced German *Nacken* "nape."] ◇ **be breathing down somebody's neck 1.** to be close behind somebody **2.** to be putting pressure on somebody to do something more quickly ◇ **be in something up to your neck** to be very much involved in something, often something dishonest or illegal ◇ **break your neck** to try very hard to achieve something (*informal*) ◇ **get it in the neck** to be punished or scolded severely (*informal*) ◇ **neck and neck** level in a competition and with an equal chance of winning (*informal*) ◇ **neck of the woods** a particular area or part of the country (*informal*) ◇ **stick your neck out** to take a risk by saying or doing something that could bring blame or censure (*informal*)

neck·band /nék bànd/ *n.* the part of a garment that fits or wraps around the neck

necked *adj.* with a particular kind of neck (*used in combination*) ○ *long-necked*

neck·er·chief /nékər chìf, -chēef/ (*plural* **-chiefs** /-chìvz, -chēevz/ *or* **-chieves**) *n.* a square of cloth worn tied around the neck as a scarf [14thC. From NECK + KERCHIEF.]

neck·ing /néking/ *n.* **1.** **KISSING AND CUDDLING** kissing and embracing sexually while sitting or lying with clothes on (*informal*) **2.** ARCHIT **PART AT TOP OF PILLAR** a molding at the top of a pillar, below the capital

neck·lace /nékləss/ *n.* a decorative chain or string of jewels worn around the neck [From *lace*, "cord, string"]

neck·line /nék līn/ *n.* the line formed by the edge of a garment at or under the neck, especially at the front

neck ring *n.* a rigid necklace or ornamental band that fits snugly around the neck

neck·tie /nék tī/ *n.* **1.** **MAN'S NECK GARMENT** a shaped strip of cloth tied around the collar of a man's shirt, with the ends hanging down the front. It is usually worn as formal or professional wear. **2.** **NOOSE** a noose for hanging somebody (*slang*)

neck·wear /nék wàir/ *n.* garments or fashion accessories worn around the neck, e.g., ties, cravats, and scarves

necr- *prefix.* = **necro-** (*used before vowels*)

necro- *prefix.* death, the dead, dead body ○ *necrophobia* [From Greek *nekros* "corpse." Ultimately from an Indo-European base that is also the ancestor of English *pernicious, noxious, innocent*, and *nectar*.]

nec·ro·bi·o·sis /nèkrō bī óssiss/ *n.* the degeneration and death of the body's cells from natural processes. ◊ **necrosis** —**nec·ro·bi·ot·ic** /nèkrō bī óttik/ *adj.*

ne·crol·a·try /ne króllətree/ *n.* the worship of the dead —**ne·crol·a·trous** *adj.*

ne·crol·o·gy /ne królləjee/ (*plural* **-gies**) *n.* (*formal*) **1.** **LIST OF THE DEAD** a list of people who have died recently or during a particular period **2.** **OBITUARY** a notice of somebody's death —**nec·ro·log·i·cal** /nèkrə lójjik'l/ *adj.* —**ne·crol·o·gist** /ne królləjist/ *n.*

nec·ro·man·cy /nékrə mànsee/ *n.* **1.** **PREDICTION USING SPIRITS** the practice of attempting to communicate with the spirits of the dead in order to predict or influence the future **2.** **WITCHCRAFT** witchcraft or sorcery in general (*literary*) [13thC. Alteration of earlier *nigromancie*, via Old French, from medieval Latin *nigromantia* from late Latin *necromantia* (influenced by Latin *niger* "black") from Greek *nekromanteia*, from *nekros* "corpse" + *manteia* "divination."] —**nec·ro·man·cer** /nékrə mànsər/ *n.* —**nec·ro·man·tic** /nèkrə mántik/ *adj.* —**nec·ro·man·ti·cal·ly** /-kəlee/ *adv.*

ne·croph·a·gous /ne króffəgəss/ *adj.* feeding on the flesh of dead animals **(carrion)**

nec·ro·phil·i·a /nèkrə fíllee ə/ *n.* sexual feelings for or sexual acts with dead bodies —**nec·ro·phil·i·ac** /nèkrə fíllee àk/ *n.* —**nec·ro·phil·ic** /nèkrə fíllik/ *adj.*

nec·ro·pho·bi·a /nèkrə fóbee ə/ *n.* an irrational fear of death or of dead bodies —**nec·ro·pho·bic** /nèkrə fóbik/ *adj.*

ne·crop·o·lis /ne króppəliss/ (*plural* **-lis·es** *or* **-leis** /ne króppə làyss/) *n.* a cemetery, especially a large, elaborate, or ancient one [Early 19thC. From Greek, from *nekros* (see NECRO-) + *polis* "city."]

nec·rop·sy /né kròpsee/ (*plural* **-sies**) *n.* = **autopsy** [Mid-19thC. Coined from NECRO- + AUTOPSY.]

ne·cro·sis /ne krṓssiss/ (*plural* **-ses** /ne krṓ sēez/) *n.* the death of cells in a tissue or organ caused by disease or injury. ◊ **necrobiosis** [Mid-17thC. From modern Latin, formed from Greek *nekrōsis* "deadness," from, ultimately, *nekros* (see NECRO-).] —**ne·crot·ic** /ne króttik/ *adj.*

nec·ro·tiz·ing /nékrə tīzing/ *adj.* causing or undergoing the death of cells **(necrosis)** ○ *necrotizing bacteria* [Late 19thC. Formed from *necrotize* "to become affected with necrosis," from *necrotic* (formed from Greek *nekroun* "to kill").]

nec·ro·tiz·ing fa·ci·it·is /nèkrə t-zing fàshee ītiss/ *n.* a severe bacterial infection that causes cell tissue to decay rapidly. This is the "flesh-eating bacterium" sometimes referred to in the media.

nec·tar /néktər/ *n.* **1.** BOT **PLANT LIQUID** the sweet liquid that flowering plants produce as a way of attracting the insects and small birds that assist in pollination **2.** MYTHOL **DRINK OF THE GODS** in Greek and Roman mythology, the drink of the gods that sustained their beauty and immortality **3. ENJOYABLE DRINK** an enjoyable or much appreciated drink (*informal*) **4.** BEVERAGES **PULPY JUICE** a thick drink made from pureed fruit ○ *mango nectar* [Mid-16thC. Via Latin from Greek *nektar* "drink of the gods."] —**nec·tar·ous** *adj.*

nec·tar·ine /néktə rēen/ *n.* **1.** FOOD **SMOOTH-SKINNED PEACH** a variety of peach that has a smooth skin **2.** TREES **PEACH TREE** the tree that nectarines grow on. Latin name: *Prunus persica.*

nec·ta·ry /néktəree/ (*plural* **-ries**) *n.* the nectar-producing organ of a flowering plant —**nec·tar·i·al** /nek táiree əl/ *adj.* —**nec·tar·ied** /néktərid/ *adj.*

née /nay/, **nee** *adj.* **1. BORN AS** used to introduce a married woman's maiden name ○ *née Leppo* **2. FORMERLY KNOWN AS** used to introduce the name that something was formerly known under [Mid-18thC. From French, the feminine form of the past participle of *naître* "to be born," from Latin *nasci* (see NATURE).]

need /need/ *v.* (**need·ed, need·ing, needs**) **1.** *vti.* **REQUIRE** used to indicate that something is required in order to have success or achieve something ○ *Do you need any money?* ○ *He told me that I didn't need to know.* **2.** *vi.* **BE UNNECESSARY** used to indicate that a course of action is not desirable or not necessary (*used in negative statements*) ○ *You don't need to thank me; I'm happy to help whenever I can.* ○ *Studying medicine need not mean you can't study architecture later.* **3.** *vti.* **DESERVE** to deserve a particular, usually punishing treatment (*informal*) ○ *That little boy needs to be given a good talking to.* ○ *Those troops need to be shown who's boss.* **4.** *vi.* **TO BE ESSENTIAL** essential or necessary to something (*archaic*) ○ *"I think that we are all agreed in this matter, and therefore there needs no more words about it."* (John Bunyan, *Pilgrim's Progress*; 1678) ■ *n.* **REQUIREMENT** something that is a requirement or is wanted ○ *an economic system that recognizes the need for financial security* ○ *His needs are small.* [Old English *nē(o)d.* Ultimately from an Indo-European word that is also the ancestor of German *Not* "need, misery."] ◇ **in need 1.** not having enough of things essential for an adequate standard of living ○ *children in need* **2.** needing something ◇ **no need to** *or* **for** no reason or justification for something

WORD KEY: SYNONYMS

See Synonyms at ***necessary.***

need·ful /néedfəl/ *adj.* **1. REQUIRED** necessary or required (*formal or archaic*) ○ *"erection of forts, magazines, arsenals, dockyards, and other needful buildings"* (*Constitution of the Confederate States (1860–61)*) **2. REQUIRING** lacking or requiring (*formal*) ○ *a situation needful of common sense* **3. POOR** poverty-stricken (*archaic*) —**need·ful·ly** *adv.* —**need·ful·ness** *n.*

Need·ham /néedəm/ town in eastern Massachusetts, east of Natick and west of Boston. Population: 27,828 (1996).

nee·dle /néed'l/ *n.* **1.** SEW **SEWING TOOL** a small sharp metal pin used for sewing, with a hole at the blunt end for holding thread **2.** CRAFT **KNITTING TOOL** a rod with a dull point used in knitting **3.** HOUSEHOLD **STYLUS** the stylus on a record player **4.** MEASURE **POINTER** a pointed indicator on a dial, scale, or scientific instrument such as a compass or a car's speedometer **5.** MED **SYRINGE** a hypodermic syringe, or its hollow pointed end **6.** ALTERN MED **ACUPUNCTURE TOOL** a small sharp metal pin used in acupuncture to stimulate points on the body **7.** BOT **CONIFER LEAF** a small pointed leaf of a conifer tree ○ *pine needles* **8.** BIOL **POINTED PART** a long thin pointed part of an animal's body, e.g., a porcupine quill or a sea urchin spine **9.** CRYSTALS **POINTED CRYSTAL** a long thin pointed crystal **10.** ARCHIT **OBELISK** a tall stone pillar **11.** CRAFT **ENGRAVING TOOL** a sharp tool used in engraving **12.** BUILDING **SUPPORTING BEAM** a beam that passes through a wall as a temporary support **13. PROVOCATION** a remark or action intended to tease or provoke somebody (*informal*) ■ *vt.* (**-dled, -dling, -dles**) **1. PROVOKE** to tease or provoke somebody, especially repeatedly in an indirect way (*informal*) **2.** CRAFT **USE A NEEDLE ON SOMETHING** to sew, prick, or pierce something with a needle [Old English *n_ædl.* Ultimately from an Indo-European base meaning "to sew," which is also the ancestor of English *nerve* and *neural.*] —**nee·dler** *n.*

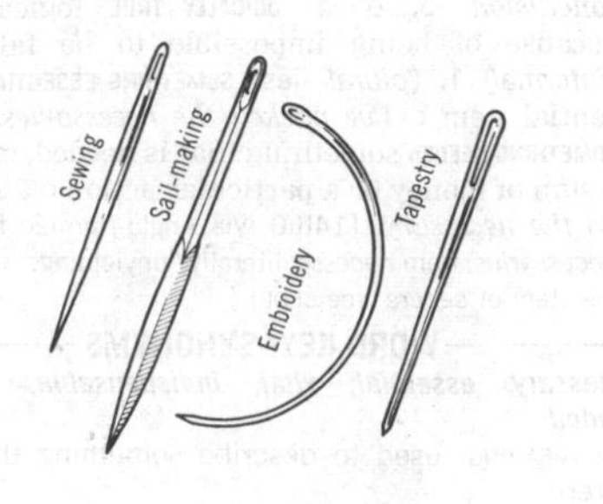

Needle

nee·dle·craft /néed'l kràft/ *n.* = **needlework**

nee·dle ex·change *n.* a public health program that allows drug addicts to exchange used hypodermic needles for new ones in an effort to stop the spread of disease and infection

nee·dle·fish /néed'l fish/ *n.* **1. LONG MARINE FISH** a carnivorous marine fish found in tropical and subtropical waters that has a very long slender body and long jaws with sharp teeth. Family: Belonidae. **2.** = **pipefish**

nee·dle·point /néed'l pòynt/ *n.* (*often used before a noun*) **1.** = **tapestry 2. LACE** a kind of lace made with a needle and a paper pattern

need·less /néedləss/ *adj.* without reason or justification —**need·less·ly** *adv.* —**need·less·ness** *n.*

nee·dle valve *n.* a valve in which the flow of a fluid or gas is precisely controlled by a needle-shaped insert in a conical seat

nee·dle·wom·an /néed'l wòomən/ (*plural* **-en** /-wìmmin/) *n.* = **seamstress**

nee·dle·work /néed'l wùrk/ *n.* **1. CRAFTS USING NEEDLES** a craft such as sewing, needlepoint, embroidery, quilting, crochet, or knitting, that involves the use of a needle **2. PIECE OF SEWING OR EMBROIDERY** an example or piece of work done with a needle in a craft such as sewing, needlepoint, embroidery, quilting, crochet, or knitting —**nee·dle·work·er** *n.*

need·n't /néed'nt/ *contr.* need not [Mid-19thC. Contraction.]

needs /needz/ *adv.* (*archaic*) **1. EMPHASIZING NECESSITY** used before or after "must" to reinforce necessity, urgency, or inevitability ○ *"any abstract ideas that are once true must needs be eternal"* (John Locke, *An Essay Concerning Human Understanding*; 1690) **2. EMPHASIZING DETERMINATION** used after "will" or "would" to emphasize determination or resolve ○ *"these men, who will needs have all knowledge"* (John Locke, *An Essay Concerning Human Understanding*; 1690)

need·y /néedee/ (**-i·er, -i·est**) *adj.* **1. POOR** living in poverty ○ *gifts for needy children* **2. NEEDING AFFECTION** feeling or showing a strong need for affection, love, or other emotional support —**need·i·ly** *adv.* —**need·i·ness** *n.*

neem /neem/ *n.* a tall evergreen tree native to India, grown for its bark, resin, and seed oil. Latin name: *Azadirachta indica.* [Early 19thC. Via Hindi *nīm* from Sanskrit *nimba.*]

ne'er /nair/ *adv.* never (*archaic or literary*) [13thC. Contraction.]

ne'er-do-well *n.* **LAZY PERSON** a lazy and irresponsible person ■ *adj.* **LAZY** lazy and irresponsible

ne·far·i·ous /nə féree əss/ *adj.* utterly immoral or wicked [Early 17thC. Formed from Latin *nefarius,* from *nefas* "sin," from *ne* "not" + *fas* "divine law."] —**ne·far·i·ous·ly** *adv.* —**ne·far·i·ous·ness** *n.*

Nef·er·ti·ti /nèffər tēetee/, **Queen of ancient Egypt** (*fl.* 14th century B.C.) As the chief wife of King Akhenaton, she supported his religious and cultural reforms. Her carved and painted image is a famous surviving Egyptian artwork.

neg. *abbr.* negative

ne·gate /nə gáyt/ (**-gat·ed, -gat·ing, -gates**) *vt.* (*formal*) **1. PROVE SOMETHING IS FALSE** to deny the truth of something, or prove something to be false ○ *a theory that negates all previous research* **2. INVALIDATE SOMETHING** to officially declare something to be invalid or render it invalid ○ *Failure to disclose such a change of circumstances would automatically negate the policy.* [Early 17thC. From the past participle stem of Latin *negare* "to deny."] —**ne·ga·tor** *n.*

WORD KEY: SYNONYMS

See Synonyms at ***nullify.***

ne·ga·tion /nə gáysh'n/ *n.* **1. DENIAL OR ANNULMENT** the denying, disproving, or nullifying of something **2.** LOGIC **LOGICAL DENIAL** a statement of denial or contradiction, especially an assertion that a particular proposition is false **3. NEGATIVE OF SOMETHING** the opposite of something regarded as positive, or the absence of such a thing ○ *The existence of happiness implies its negation.*

neg·a·tive /néggətiv/ *adj.* **1. MEANING "NO"** meaning "no," or refusing or denying something ○ *a negative response* **2. BAD** unhappy, discouraging, angry, or otherwise detracting from a happy situation ○ *You're having very negative feelings toward him.* **3. PESSIMISTIC** pessimistic, or tending to have a pessimistic outlook ○ *Don't be so negative, cheer up!* **4.** MED **SHOWING THAT SOMETHING IS NOT PRESENT** not showing the presence of a particular disease or condition that is being tested for ○ *The test came back negative.* **5.** MED = **Rh negative 6.** MATH **LESS THAN ZERO** indicating a quantity that is less than zero ○ *a negative number* **7.** MATH **OPPOSITE TO POSITIVE** used to describe something, e.g., a quantity or angle, of the same magnitude as, but opposite to, something considered positive **8.** PHYS **HAVING SAME CHARGE AS ELECTRON** with the same electric charge as that of an electron, shown by the symbol – **9.** PHOTOGRAPHY **WITH TONES AND COLORS REVERSED** used to describe photographic film that has been exposed to light, used as a basis for preparing final prints. Black and white tones are reversed and colors are complementary. **10.** LOGIC **OPPOSING** denying or contradicting a statement, proof, or argument **11.** BIOL **MOVING AWAY** moving or growing away from a source of stimulation, e.g., heat or light ○ *negative tropism* ■ *n.* **1.** PHOTOGRAPHY **PHOTOGRAPHIC IMAGE** a photographic image, or the film containing it, that shows black and white tones reversed and colors as complementary. It is used to make prints. **2. ANSWER OF "NO"** an answer meaning "no" ○ *The general answered in the negative.* **3.** GRAM **WORD IMPLYING "NO"** any word that expresses the idea "no," e.g., the words "not," "nothing," and "never" **4.** LOGIC **NEGATING PROPOSITION** a statement that contradicts, denies, or disproves something **5.** ELEC **DESTINATION OF ELECTRONS** the part of an electric circuit to which the electrons flow, e.g., a terminal or the cathode where negative ions are formed in electrolytic applications **6. SOMETHING OR SOMEBODY UNDESIRABLE** something that or somebody who is bad, undesirable, discouraging, or otherwise detracts from a pleasant situation (*informal*) ○ *The area's harsh winters will be a negative for anyone who doesn't like snow.* **7.** MATH **QUANTITY OPPOSITE TO POSITIVE** a number or quantity, e.g., speed, angle, or direction, that is less than zero or considered to be the opposite of positive ■ *interj.* **NO** used to say "no" to something or somebody (*formal*) ■ *vt.* (**-tived, -tiv·ing, -tives**) **1. SAY "NO"** to refuse, reject, deny, cancel, or forbid something (*formal*) ○ *"a polite request that Elizabeth would lead the way, which the other politely and more earnestly negatived"* (Jane Austen, *Pride And Prejudice*; 1813) **2.** LOGIC **DISPROVE PROPOSITION** to contradict or invalidate a proposition (*informal*) —**neg·a·tive·ness** *n.* —**neg·a·tiv·i·ty** /nèggə tívvətee/ *n.*

neg·a·tive eq·ui·ty *n.* a situation in which, as a result of falling prices, a piece of real estate is worth less than the amount of money that was borrowed to buy it

neg·a·tive feed·back *n.* in an electronic or mechanical system, the redirecting of part of the output back to the input as a way of improving the quality of the output

neg·a·tive·ly /néggətivlee/ *adv.* **1. SAYING "NO"** in a way that means "no" **2. ADVERSELY** in an adverse way ○ *patients reacting negatively to the medication* **3. PESSIMISTICALLY** in a pessimistic or defeatist way **4.** PHYS **WITH NEGATIVE ELECTRICAL CHARGE** with the same electric charge as that of one or more electrons, shown by the symbol –

neg·a·tive re·in·force·ment *n.* encouragement of a desired response by giving an unpleasant stimulus when the response is absent, or discouragement of an undesired response by an unpleasant stimulus when the response is present. An unpleasant stimulus is something such as pain or disapproval.

neg·a·tive stain·ing *n.* staining of an area around a biological subject, rather than the subject itself, so that the subject can be clearly seen against it

neg·a·tive trans·fer, **neg·a·tive trans·fer·ence** *n.* a stage in psychotherapy at which a patient relives hostile feelings toward parents by experiencing hostility to the therapist

neg·a·tiv·ism /néggəti vìzzəm/ *n.* **1. HABITUAL SKEPTICISM** a strong tendency to be pessimistic, to assess situations in the worst light, or to be unreasonably skeptical about generally accepted beliefs **2.** PSYCHOL **PERSISTENT UNREASONABLE DEFIANCE** persistent defiance of authority and refusal to obey instructions —**neg·a·tiv·ist** *n.*—**neg·a·tiv·is·tic** /nèggəti vístik/ *adj.*—**neg·a·tiv·is·ti·cal·ly** *adv.*

Ne·gev /né gev/, **Ne·geb** /né geb/ triangular desert region in southern Israel. Area: 5,000 sq. mi./12,950 sq. km.

ne·glect /nə glékt/ *vt.* (**-glect·ed, -glect·ing, -glects**) **1. NOT CARE FOR SOMETHING PROPERLY** to fail to give the proper or required care and attention to somebody or something **2. FAIL TO DO SOMETHING** to fail to do something, especially because of carelessness or forgetfulness ○ *I neglected to tell you that I won't be here next week.* ■ *n.* **1. WITHHOLDING OF PROPER CARE** the failure to give proper care or attention to somebody or something ○ *parents charged with criminal neglect* **2. LACK OF CARE** lack of proper care or attention ○ *Soon the business began to suffer from neglect.* [Early 16thC. From the past participle stem of Latin *neglegere*, from *legere* "to choose" (source of English *collect*, *legion*, and *lecture*).] —**ne·glect·er** *n.*

WORD KEY: SYNONYMS

neglect, forget, omit, overlook

CORE MEANING: to fail to do something

neglect to fail to act in a situation where it is obligatory or important to do so, especially as a result of carelessness or indifference; **forget** to fail to remember to do something; **omit** to fail to do something either deliberately or as a result of carelessness or haste; **overlook** to fail to notice or check something as a result of inattention, preoccupation, or haste.

ne·glect·ful /nə gléktf'l/ *adj.* tending to ignore or forget responsibilities —**ne·glect·ful·ly** *adv.*—**ne·glect·ful·ness** *n.*

neg·li·gee /nègli zháy, négli zhày/, **neg·li·gée, neg·li·gé** *n.* **1. LONG SILKY NIGHTGOWN** a woman's long nightgown made of thin silky often see-through fabric **2. CASUAL DRESS** informal dress (*dated formal*) [Mid-18thC. From French *négligé*, the past participle of *négliger* "to neglect," from Latin *neglegere* (see NEGLECT). The underlying idea is of having failed to get fully dressed.]

neg·li·gence /négglijəns/ *n.* **1. CONDITION OF BEING NEGLIGENT** the condition or quality of being negligent **2.** LAW **CIVIL WRONG CAUSING INJURY OR HARM** a civil wrong (**tort**) causing injury or harm to another person or to property as the result of doing something or failing to provide a proper or reasonable level of care. ◊ **contributory negligence 3. CASUALNESS** casualness in matters of dress or general appearance, whether regarded as stylish or slovenly (*dated formal*) ○ *"clad in an artist's velvet, but with none of an artist's negligence"* (G. K. Chesterton, *The Wisdom of Father Brown*; 1914)

neg·li·gent /négglijənt/ *adj.* **1. HABITUALLY CARELESS** habitually careless or irresponsible **2.** LAW **GUILTY OF NEGLIGENCE** guilty of failing to provide a proper or reasonable level of care **3. CASUAL IN APPEARANCE** casual in matters of dress or general apperance, whether considered stylish or slovenly (*dated formal*) [14thC. Via French from Latin *negligent-*, the present participle stem of *negligere*, a variant of *neglegere* (see NEGLECT).] —**neg·li·gent·ly** *adv.*

neg·li·gi·ble /négglijəb'l/ *adj.* too small or unimportant to be worth considering [Early 19thC. From obsolete French *négligible*, from *négliger* "to neglect," from Latin *neglegere* (see NEGLECT).] —**neg·li·gi·bil·i·ty** /nègglijə bíllətee/ *n.* —**neg·li·gi·ble·ness** /négglijəb'lnəss/ *n.* —**neg·li·gi·bly** *adv.*

ne·go·tia·ble /nə gṓshəb'l, -gṓshee-/ *adj.* **1. OPEN TO DISCUSSION** not fixed, but able to be established or changed through discussion and compromise ○ *Salary is negotiable, according to education and experience.* **2.** FIN **EXCHANGEABLE FOR MONEY** used to describe financial instruments, e.g., checks and securities, that can be transferred to another person in exchange for money **3. NAVIGABLE** able to be crossed, passed, or successfully dealt with —**ne·go·tia·bil·i·ty** /nə gṑshə bíllətee, -gṑshee ə-/ *n.* —**ne·go·tia·bly** /nə gṓshəblee, -gṓshee ə-/ *adv.*

ne·go·ti·ant /nə gṓshənt, -shee ənt/ *n.* = **negotiator** (*formal*)

ne·go·ti·ate /nə gṓshee àyt/ (**-at·ed, -at·ing, -ates**) *v.* **1.** *vti.* **DISCUSS TERMS OF AGREEMENT** to attempt to come to an agreement on something through discussion and compromise **2.** *vt.* FIN **SELL SOMETHING** to transfer ownership of a financial instrument, e.g., a check or security, to somebody else in exchange for money **3.** *vt.* **NAVIGATE SOMETHING SUCCESSFULLY** to manage to get past or deal with something that constitutes a hazard or obstacle ○ *A canoe can negotiate these waters when the wind is calm.* [Late 16thC. From the past participle stem of Latin *negotiari* "to do business," from *negotium* "business," from *neg-* "not" + *otium* "leisure" (source of English *otiose*).]

ne·go·ti·a·tion /nə gṑshee áysh'n/ *n.* **1. RESOLVING OF DISAGREEMENTS** the reaching of agreement through discussion and compromise **2. NAVIGATION** the tackling of a hazard or problem (*formal*) ■ **ne·go·ti·a·tions** *npl.* **DISCUSSION SESSIONS** one or more meetings at which attempts are made to reach agreement through discussion and compromise ○ *Negotiations are already under way between the opposing factions.*

ne·go·ti·a·tor /nə gṓshee àytər/ *n.* somebody who negotiates, especially in a political or diplomatic context

Ne·gress /néegrəss/ *n.* a highly offensive term for a Black woman (*offensive*)

Ne·gril·lo /nə gríllō/ (*plural* **-los** *or* **-loes**) *n.* a member of any of a number of peoples of central and southern Africa [Mid-19thC. From Spanish, literally "a small Negro," from *negro* (see NEGRO).]

Ne·gri·to /nə greétō/ (*plural* **-tos** *or* **-toes**) *n.* a member of any of a number of Asian peoples, including the Eta of the Philippines, the Semang of the Malay Peninsula, and the people of the Andaman Islands of India [Early 19thC. From Spanish, literally "a small Negro," from *negro* (see NEGRO).]

ne·gri·tude /néggri tōōd/ *n.* identity as a Black person, especially awareness of a distinct Black history and culture as something to be proud of (*dated*)

Ne·gro /nee grō/ (*plural* **-groes**) *n.* a highly offensive term for a Black person (*offensive*) [Mid-16thC. Via Spanish and Portuguese from the Latin stem *nigr-* "black" (source of English *denigrate* and *niello*).]

Ne·groid /née gròyd/ *adj.* an offensive term referring to a division of humankind that originated in Africa (*offensive*)

ne·gro·phile /néegrə fìl/ *n.* an offensive term for a person who favors the interests of Black people (*offensive*) —**ne·gro·phil·i·a** /nèegrə fíllee ə/ *n.* —**ne·gro·phil·ism** /ni gróffə lìzzəm/ *n.*

ne·gro·phobe /néegrə fōb/ *n.* somebody prejudiced against Black people or with an irrational fear of Black people (*dated*) —**ne·gro·pho·bi·a** /nèegrə fṓbee ə/ *n.*

ne·gus /néegəss/ *n.* a hot drink made of port or sherry with water, sugar, lemon juice, and spices [Mid-18thC. Named for the English colonel Francis *Negus* (died 1732), who reputedly invented the drink.]

Ne·gus /néegəss/ *n.* a title used in the past for the king or emperor of Ethiopia [Late 16thC. From Amharic *n'gus* "kinged, king."]

NEH *abbr.* National Endowment for the Humanities

Neh. *abbr.* BIBLE Nehemiah

Ne·he·mi·ah[1] /nee hə mí ə/ *n.* in the Bible, a Jewish leader and governor of Judea. He was responsible for rebuilding Jerusalem in 444 B.C.

Ne·he·mi·ah[2] *n.* a book of the Bible, recounting the rebuilding of Jerusalem in the 5th century B.C. and the reforms undertaken after its completion. It is traditionally attributed to Nehemiah. See table at **Bible**

Neh·ru /náy roo/, **Jawaharlal** (1889–1964). The first prime minister of independent India (1947–64). He abandoned his legal career to follow Gandhi in 1929 and was elected president of the Indian National Congress. He was the father of Indira Gandhi.

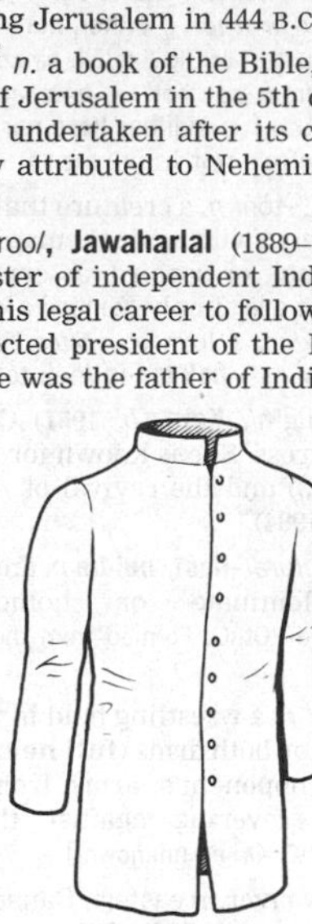

Nehru jacket

Neh·ru jack·et *n.* a long narrow jacket with a high stand-up collar [Mid-20thC. Named for Jawaharlal NEHRU, who often wore jackets of this style.]

neigh /nay/ *n.* **HORSE SOUND** the long high-pitched sound that a horse makes ■ *vi.* (**neighed, neigh·ing, neighs**) **MAKE SOUND OF HORSE** to make the high-pitched sound characteristic of a horse [Old English *hnǣgan*, of uncertain origin: probably an imitation of the sound]

neigh·bor /náybər/ *n.* **1. SOMEBODY LIVING NEARBY** somebody who lives or is located very close by, e.g., on the same street or in the same town **2. SOMETHING OR SOMEBODY NEARBY** a person, place, or thing located next to another or very nearby (*often used before a noun*) ○ *the Spanish and their Portuguese neighbors* **3. FELLOW HUMAN** a fellow human being (*archaic or literary*) ■ *vti.* (**-bored, -bor·ing, -bors**) **BE CLOSE TO SOMETHING OR SOMEBODY** to be very close to something or somebody [Old English *nēahgebūr*, from *nēah* "near" (source of English *nigh*) + *gebūr* "dweller"]

neigh·bor·hood /náybər hòòd/ *n.* **1. COMMUNITY** a local community with characteristics that distinguish it from the areas around it **2. APPROXIMATION OF AMOUNT** an approximate amount, size, or range (*informal*) ○ *expenses in the neighborhood of $175,000* **3.** MATH **SURROUNDING POINTS** the set of all points within a given distance from a specified point

neigh·bor·hood watch *n.* a program to raise awareness of crime and crime prevention within local communities, with members taking part in various initiatives, sometimes involving the patrolling of streets

neigh·bor·ing /náybəring/ *adj.* situated or located nearby

neigh·bor·ly /náybərlee/ *adj.* friendly, helpful, and kind, especially to a neighbor —**neigh·bor·li·ness** *n.*

neigh·bor note *n.* an auxiliary musical note a second away from its principal note

neigh·bour *n., vt.* U.K. = **neighbor**

neigh·bour·hood *n.* U.K. = **neighborhood**

neigh·bour·ing *adj.* U.K. = **neighboring**

neigh·bour·ly *adj.* U.K. = **neighborly**

Neill /neel/, **Sam** (*b.* 1948) New Zealand actor. His movies include *Jurassic Park* (1993) and *The Piano* (1993). Real name **Nigel Neill**

nei·ther /néethər/ *adj., pron.* **NOT ONE OR OTHER** used to indicate that each of two things or people is included when making a negative statement ○ (adj) *Neither shirt looks good on you.* ○ (pron) *Neither of the boys wants to go.* ○ (pron) *"Would you like pork or fish?" "Neither, thank you."* ■ *conj.* **NOT** used preceding two alternatives joined by "nor" to indicate that both did not happen or are not true ○ *Neither my boss nor his wife can cook.* ◊ **nor, either** ■ *adv.* **ALSO NOT** used to indicate people or things that can also be included in a statement just made (*used in response to no, not, or another negative*) ○ *"We've* *never been to Paris." "Neither have I."* ○ *She doesn't want to go? Me neither!* ○ *She can't play today, and neither can her brother.* ◊ **either, nor** [12thC. Alteration (influenced by EITHER) of Old English *nawzzer,* a contraction of *nāhwæzzer,* from *nā* "not" + *hwæþer* "which of two" (source of *whether*).] ◇ **neither here nor there** not relevant and therefore not important

nek·ton /néktən, -tòn/ *n.* a creature that lives in water and can actively swim against currents, e.g., a fish, reptile, mammal, or seabird, as opposed to microorganisms that are simply carried along [Late 19thC. From Greek *nēkton,* a form of *nēktos* "swimming," from *nēkhein* "to swim."] —**nek·ton·ic** /nek tónnik/ *adj.*

Nel·li·gan /néllig'n/, **Kate** (*b.* 1951) Canadian stage and movie actress. She is known for her stage roles in *Plenty* (1983) and the revival of *A Moon for the Misbegotten* (1984).

nel·ly /néllee/ (*plural* **-lies**), **nel·lie** *n.* an offensive term for an effeminate or homosexual man (*offensive*) [Mid-20thC. Formed from the name *Helen* or *Eleanor.*]

nel·son /nélsən/ *n.* a wrestling hold in which one arm (**half nelson**) or both arms (**full nelson**) are passed through the opponent's arms from behind and pulled back, levering against the opponent's back [Late 19thC. Origin unknown.]

Nel·son /nélsən/ river in eastern Canada, in northern Manitoba. It rises in Lake Winnipeg and empties into Hudson Bay. Length: 400 mi./644 km.

Nel·son /néls'n/, **Horatio, Viscount** (1758–1805) English admiral. He defeated the French at Trafalgar (1805), but was killed during the battle. His affair with Lady Hamilton caused a considerable scandal.

Nel·son, Thomas (1738–89) U.S. patriot. He signed the Declaration of Independence (1776) and commanded the Virginia state forces (1777–82) during the Revolution.

Nel·son, Willie (*b.* 1933) U.S. country-and-western singer and songwriter. His songs include "Georgia on My Mind."

nemat- *prefix.* = **nemato-** (*used before vowels*)

ne·mat·ic /nə máttik/ *adj.* used to describe a phase of liquid crystals in which the axes of the molecules become parallel in response to a magnetic field [Early 20thC. Formed from the Greek stem *nēmat-* (see NEMATO-).]

nemato- *prefix.* 1. thread, threadlike ○ *nematocyst* 2. nematode ○ *nematocide* [From Greek *nēmat-,* the stem of *nēma* "thread." Ultimately from an Indo-European base meaning "to spin," which is also the ancestor of English *needle.*]

nem·a·to·cide /némmətə sīd, nə máttə-/, **nem·a·ti·cide** *n.* a substance that destroys nematodes — **nem·a·to·ci·dal** /nèmmətə sīd'l, nə màttə-/ *adj.*

nem·a·to·cyst /némmətə sìst, nə máttə-/ *n.* a sting found in animals of the jellyfish family. It comprises a fluid-filled sac within which is a coiled hollow thread that is rapidly turned outward (**everted**) to capture food or for defense.

nem·a·tode /némmə tōd/ *n.* a worm, often microscopic, with a cylindrical unsegmented body protected by a tough outer skin (**cuticle**). Some nematodes are parasites of plants and animals, e.g., pinworms and hookworms. Phylum: Nematoda. [Mid-19thC. From modern Latin, coined from NEMATO- + modern Latin *-ōda* (an alteration of Greek *-oeidēs* (see -OID).]

nem·a·tol·o·gy /nèmmə tólləjee/ *n.* the branch of zoology that is concerned with the study of nematodes —**nem·a·to·log·i·cal** /nèmmətə lójjik'l/ *adj.* — **nem·a·to·log·i·cal·ly** /-lójjikəlee/ *adv.* —**nem·a·tol·o·gist** /-tólləjist/ *n.*

Nem·bu·tal /némbyə tàwl/ *tdmk.* a trademark for the sodium salt of pentobarbital, a barbiturate used as a sedative and an anticonvulsant

nem. con. /ném kón/ *adv.* without opposition ○ *The motion was carried nem. con.* [From Latin, shortening of *nemine contradicente* "with no one contradicting"]

Ne·me·an lion /néemee ən-, ni mée ən-/ *n.* in Greek mythology, the huge lion that Hercules killed as the first of his twelve labors [Late 16thC. Named for *Nemea,* a district in ancient Greece, where it was killed.]

ne·mer·te·an /ni múrtee ən/ *n.* a burrowing marine worm with a long flat unsegmented body. Phylum: Nemertia. [Mid-19thC. Formed from modern Latin *Nemertes,* genus name, from Greek *Nēmertēs* "Nereid."]

nem·e·sis /némməsssiss/ (*plural* **nemeses** /-seez/) *n.* (*literary*) 1. **UNBEATABLE OPPONENT** a bitter enemy, especially one who seems unbeatable 2. **SOURCE OF HARM** a source of harm or ruin ○ *Chocolate chip cookies have been the nemesis of my dieting plan.* 3. **DESERVED PUNISHMENT** punishment that is deserved, especially when it results in somebody's downfall 4. **nem·e·sis AVENGER** a person or force that inflicts punishment or revenge [Late 16thC. From Greek, "Nemesis, righteous indignation," from *nemein* "to distribute what is due."]

Nem·e·sis *n.* the ancient Greek goddess of just punishment or vengeance

ne·ne /náy nàỳ/ *n.* a rare wild goose with a grayish-brown body and a black face that is found in the Hawaiian Islands. Latin name: *Branta sandvicensis.* [Early 20thC. From Hawaiian.]

neo- *prefix.* new, recent ○ *neotype* ○ *neo-Darwinism* [From Greek *neos.* Ultimately from the Indo-European word for "new," which is also the ancestor of English *new* and *novel.*]

CORBIS/G. E. Kidder Smith

Neoclassical: Front porch of Monticello, Charlottesville, Virginia (begun 1770)

ne·o·clas·si·cal /nèe ō klássik'l/, **ne·o·clas·sic** /-sik/ *n.* ARTS **OF REVIVAL OF CLASSICISM IN ART** an 18th- and 19th-century revival in art and architecture of the simple symmetrical styles of ancient Greece and Rome, or created in this style ■ *adj.* 1. LITERAT **OF CLASSICAL REVIVAL** relating to or typical of the European revival of Greek and Roman literary form 2. MUSIC **OF PRE-ROMANTIC STYLE** relating to a movement in the late 19th and early 20th centuries that favored the more formal style of composers before the Romantic movement 3. ECON **OF MACROECONOMIC MONETARIST THEORY** related to macroecomomic monetarist theories that emphasize the need for the free operation of market forces —**ne·o·clas·si·cism** *n.* —**ne·o·clas·si·cist** *n.*

ne·o·co·lo·ni·al·ism /nèe ō kə lṓnee ə lìzzəm/ *n.* the domination by a powerful, usually Western nation of another nation that is politically independent but has a weak economy greatly dependent on trade with the powerful nation —**ne·o·co·lo·ni·al** *adj.* — **ne·o·co·lo·ni·al·ist** *n.*

ne·o·con /nèe ō kòn/ *n.* a neoconservative (*informal*) [Late 20thC. Shortening.]

ne·o·con·ser·va·tive /nèe ō kən súrvətiv/ *n.* **SUPPORTER OF RETURN TO CONSERVATIVE VALUES** somebody who, during the mid-1980s, began to support conservatism in society, and in politics in particular, as a reaction to the social freedoms sought throughout the 1960s and early 1970s ■ *adj.* **RELATING TO SHIFT TOWARD CONSERVATISM** relating to or forming part of the shift during the mid-1980s toward social and political conservatism that occurred after the freedom movement of the 1960s and early 1970s — **ne·o·con·ser·va·tism** *n.*

ne·o·cor·tex /nèe ō káwr tèks/ (*plural* **-ti·ces** /-tə sèez/ *or* **-tex·es**) *n.* the roof of the cerebral cortex that forms the part of the mammalian brain that has evolved most recently and makes possible higher brain functions such as learning —**ne·o·cor·ti·cal** /-káwrtik'l/ *adj.*

Ne·o-Dar·win·ism *n.* a theory of evolution that combines Darwin's theory and modern genetics, especially with regard to variations in populations as a result of genetic mutations —**ne·o-Dar·win·i·an** *adj.* —**ne·o-Dar·win·ist** *n., adj.*

ne·o·dym·i·um /nèe ō dímmee əm/ *n.* a silvery-white or yellowish metallic chemical element used in lasers and glass that is one of the lanthanide series or rare-earth elements. Symbol **Nd** [Late 19thC. Coined from NEO- + DIDYMIUM, because didymium was found to consist of two elements (neodymium and praesodymium).]

ne·o-Ex·pres·sion·ism, **ne·o·ex·pres·sion·ism** *n.* a 20th-century art movement, begun in Germany, Italy, and the United States, and based on expressionism, that focuses on the artist's inner experiences and often produces violent or erotic paintings —**ne·o-Ex·pres·sion·ist** *n., adj.*

ne·o·fas·cism /nèe ō fá shìzzəm/ *n.* 1. **MODERN SUPPORT FOR FASCISM** the modern-day revival of Fascist beliefs of the 1930s and 1940s, which assume that a supposed Aryan race is superior to all others and justify genocide 2. **RACIST BELIEFS** the views or actions of any modern-day Caucasian group or movement that holds racist views, especially anyone involved in the violent intimidation of people of color — **ne·o·fas·cist** *adj., n.*

ne·o-Freud·i·an·ism *n.* a theory of psychoanalysis that modifies Freudian theory by emphasizing social and cultural influences on personality development —**ne·o-Freud·i·an** *adj., n.*

ne·o·gen·e·sis /nèe ō jénnəssiss/ *n.* the regrowth of living tissue —**ne·o·ge·net·ic** /nèe ō jə néttik/ *adj.* — **ne·o·ge·net·i·cal·ly** *adv.*

ne·o-Goth·ic *adj.* **BASED ON THE GOTHIC REVIVAL** based on a reintroduction of the Gothic style of architecture, popular in the 18th and 19th centuries ■ *n.* **GOTHIC REVIVAL** the Gothic Revival style

ne·o·im·pres·sion·ism /nèe ō im présh'n ìzzəm/ *n.* the 19th-century movement in painting, led by the pointillist Georges Seurat, that favored stricter and more formal techniques of composition — **ne·o·im·pres·sion·ist** *adj., n.*

Ne·o-Lat·in *n., adj.* = **New Latin** ■ *adj.* **OF ROMANCE LANGUAGES** relating to a language that has developed from Latin

ne·o·lib·er·al·ism /nèe ō líbbərə lìzzəm, -líbbrə-/ *n.* the political view, arising in the 1960s, that emphasizes the importance of economic growth and asserts that social justice is best maintained by minimal government interference and free market forces —**ne·o·lib·er·al** *adj., n.*

ne·o·lith /nèe ə lìth/ *n.* a stone tool from the Neolithic period

Ne·o·lith·ic /nèe ə líthik/ *n.* **NEW STONE AGE** the latest period of the Stone Age, between about 8000 B.C. and 5000 B.C., characterized by the development of settled agriculture and the use of polished stone tools and weapons ■ *adj.* **RELATING TO NEOLITHIC** relating to or characteristic of the Neoloithic [Mid-19thC. Coined from NEO- + -LITH + -IC by Sir John Lubbock in his work *Prehistoric Times.*] —**Ne·o·lith·ic** *adj.*

ne·ol·o·gism /nee óllə jìzzəm/, **ne·ol·o·gy** /nee ólləjee/ (*plural* **-gies**) *n.* 1. **NEW WORD OR MEANING** a recently coined word or phrase, or a recently extended meaning of an existing word or phrase 2. **COINAGE OF NEW WORDS** the practice of coining new words or phrases, or of extending the meaning of existing words or phrases [Early 19thC. From French *néologisme,* from *néo-* NEO- + Greek *logos* "word."] —**ne·ol·o·gist** *n.* — **ne·ol·o·gis·tic** /nee òllə jístik/ *adj.* —**ne·ol·o·gis·ti·cal·ly** *adv.*

ne·ol·o·gize /nee óllə jīz/ (**-gized, -giz·ing, -giz·es**) *vi.* to coin new words or phrases, or extend the meaning of existing words or phrases

ne·ol·o·gy *n.* = **neologism**

ne·o-Mel·a·ne·sian *n.* a creole language based on English with borrowings from other languages that is widely used in the island groups of the southwestern Pacific

ne·o·my·cin /nèe ō míss'n/ *n.* an antibiotic used to treat a wide variety of bacterial infections, especially skin and eye infections, and obtained from the bacterium *Streptomyces fradiae*

ne·on /nèe òn/ (*plural* **-ons** *or* **-on**) *n.* 1. CHEM ELEM **GAS THAT GLOWS ORANGE** a colorless odorless gaseous chemical element that occurs in very small quantities in the air and glows orange when electricity is passed through it. Symbol **Ne** 2. ZOOL = **neon tetra** [Late 19thC. From Greek, a form of *neos* "new." Coined by the British chemists Sir William Ramsay and Morris W. Travers, who discovered the gas.]

ne·o·nate /nèe ə nàyt/ *n.* a newborn child, especially one less than one month old [Early 20thC. Coined from NEO- + Latin *natus* "born" (see NATAL).] —**ne·o·na·tal** /nèe ō náyt'l/ *adj.*

ne·o·na·tol·o·gy /nèe ō nay tóllәjee/ *n.* the branch of medicine that deals with the care and development of newborn babies and the treatment of their diseases —**ne·o·na·to·log·i·cal** /nèe ō nàytә lójjik'l/ *adj.* —**ne·o·na·tol·o·gist** /nèe ō nay tóllәjist/ *n.*

ne·o-Na·zi *n.* **1. MODERN-DAY ADVOCATE OF NAZISM** a member of a modern-day movement that promotes the idea that a supposed race of Aryans is superior to all others, and that genocide is justifiable **2. CAUCASIAN RACIST** a member of any modern-day group or movement of Caucasians who hold racist views, especially those involved in violent attacks on people of color —**ne·o-Na·zism** *n.*

ne·on tet·ra *n.* a small iridescent blue and red freshwater fish found in the Amazon river and often kept in aquariums. Latin name: *Hyphessobrycon innesi.* [From its bright colors like that of neon glowing]

ne·o·or·tho·dox·y /nèe ō áwrthә dòksee/ *n.* an early 20th-century Protestant movement connected with the theology of Karl Barth that emphasizes ethics and the teachings of the Bible —**ne·o·or·tho·dox** *adj.*

ne·o·phil·i·a /nèe ō fíllee ә/ *n.* a liking for new things, change for the sake of change, or novelty —**ne·o·phile** /nèe ә fìl/ *n.* —**ne·o·phil·i·ac** /nèe ō fíllee àk/ *n., adj.*

ne·o·phyte /née ә fìt/ *n.* **1. BEGINNER** a beginner or novice at some task, work, or endeavor **2. RECENT CONVERT** somebody who has recently converted to a particular religion **3. RELIGIOUS NOVICE** somebody who has recently joined a religious community but has not yet taken vows and is therefore not yet part of the order [14thC. Via late Latin *neophytus* from Greek *neophutos,* literally "newly planted," from, ultimately, *phuein* "to plant, cause to grow."] —**ne·o·phyt·ic** /nèe ә fíttik/ *adj.*

ne·o·pla·sia /nèe ō pláyzhә, -pláyzhee ә/ *n.* the formation or existence of tumors

ne·o·plasm /nèe ә plàzzәm/ *n.* a tumor or tissue containing an abnormal growth [Late 19thC. Coined from NEO- + Greek *plasma* "formation," from *plassein* "to form, mold."]

ne·o·plas·ti·cism /nèe ә plástә sìzzәm/ *n.* a style of abstract painting, as found in the work of Mondrian, using black, gray, white, and the primary colors and horizontal and vertical lines and planes —**ne·o·plas·tic** /nèe ә plástik/ *adj.*

ne·o·plas·ty /nèe ә plàstee/ *n.* the surgical construction of new tissue, or the repair of damaged tissue —**ne·o·plas·tic** /nèe ә plástik/ *adj.*

ne·o·Pla·to·nism /nèe ō pláyt'n ìzzәm/, **Ne·o·pla·to·nism** *n.* a philosophical system combining Platonism with mysticism and Judaic and Christian ideas and positing one source for all existence, developed by Plotinus and his followers in the 3rd century A.D. —**ne·o·Pla·ton·ic** /nèe ō plә tónnik/ *adj.* —**ne·o·Pla·to·nist** /nèe ō pláyt'nist/ *n.*

ne·o·prene /nèe ә prèen/ *n.* a synthetic material resembling rubber that does not deteriorate as quickly as rubber and is more resistant to oil, used in the manufacture of equipment for which waterproofing is important [Mid-20thC. Coined from NEO- + CHLOROPRENE.]

ne·o·re·al·ism /nèe ō rée ә lìzzәm/ *n.* a style of filmmaking developed in Italy in the 1940s by directors such as Rossellini, De Sica, and Visconti, dealing typically with the problems of ordinary working-class life —**ne·o·re·al·ist** *n., adj.* —**ne·o·re·al·is·tic** /nèe ō rèe ә lístik/ *adj.*

Ne·o·ri·can /nèe ō rèekәn/ *n.* a Puerto Rican who lives on the United States mainland, or who lived there for a time but has now returned to Puerto Rico [Mid-20thC. Origin uncertain: perhaps coined from NEO- + *Rican* (as in PUERTO RICAN), or perhaps from Spanish *Neorriqueño.*]

ne·o-Scho·las·ti·cism *n.* a late 19th-century Roman Catholic movement that used the writings of the early Scholasticists such as Albert the Great and Anselm as the basis for its teachings —**ne·o-Scho·las·tic** *adj.*

ne·o·stig·mine /nèe ō stíg mèen, -stígmin/ *n.* a white crystalline compound used in the treatment of myasthenia [Mid-20thC. Coined from NEO- + PHYSOSTIGMINE.]

ne·o·te·ny /nee óttәnee, -ótt'nee/ *n.* the existence of juvenile features in an adult animal, e.g., the retention of gills in certain salamanders [Late 19thC. Coined from NEO- + Greek *teinein* "to stretch, extend."]

ne·o·ter·ic /nèe ә térrik/ *adj.* having a contemporary origin [Late 16thC. Via Latin from Greek *neōterikos* "youthful."]

Ne·o·trop·i·cal /nèe ō tróppik'l/, **Ne·o·trop·ic** /-pik/ *adj.* relating to a geographic area of plant and animal distribution east, south, and west of Mexico's central plateau that includes Central and South America and the West Indies

ne·o·type /nèe ә tìp/ *n.* a specimen of a plant or animal selected to replace an original representative example used in classification (**holotype**) that has been lost or destroyed —**ne·o·typ·i·cal** /nèe ә típpik'l/ *adj.*

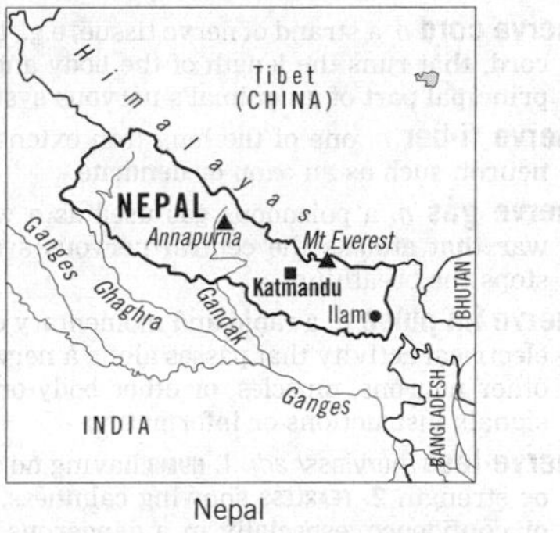

Nepal

Ne·pal /nә páal/ monarchy in southern Asia, northeast of India, in a mountainous region. Language: Nepali. Currency: rupee. Capital: Katmandu. Population: 22,090,000 (1996). Area: 54,362 sq. mi./140,797 sq. km. Official name **Kingdom of Nepal**

Nep·al·ese /nèpp léez, nèpp léess/ (*plural* **-ese**) *n.* **1.** LANG **DIALECT OF NEPALI** any of the several dialects, sometimes considered as separate languages, of Nepali spoken throughout Nepal and in some parts of adjacent countries **2.** PEOPLES = **Nepali** *n.* 2 —**Nep·al·ese** *adj.*

Ne·pal·i /nә páalee/ (*plural* **-i** *or* **-is**) *n.* **1.** LANG **LANGUAGE OF NEPAL** the official language of Nepal, also spoken in parts of Bhutan and northeastern India. It belongs to the Indic group of the Indo-Iranian branch of Indo-European languages. Nepali is spoken by about 16 million people. **2.** PEOPLES **SOMEBODY FROM NEPAL** somebody who was born raised or lives in Nepal —**Ne·pal·i** *adj.*

ne·pen·the /nә pénthee/ *n.* **1. ANCIENT DRUG INDUCING FORGETFULNESS** a supposed substance that people took in ancient times to forget their sadness or troubles, or the plant that produced the substance **2. DISTRACTION** something that eases pain or makes people forget their troubles (*literary*) ○ *"respite and nepenthe from thy memories of Lenore"* (Edgar Allan Poe, *The Raven*; 1845) [Late 16thC. Alteration (modeled on Italian *nepente*) of Greek *nēpenthēs,* literally "banishing pain," from *nē* "not" + *penthos* "grief."] —**ne·pen·the·an** /nә pénthee әn/ *adj.*

ne·per /náypәr, néepәr/ *n.* a unit for comparing two currents, voltages, or related quantities, equal to the natural logarithm of the ratio of the quantities. Symbol **Np**

neph·e·line /néffә lèen, néffәlin/, **neph·e·lite** /-lìt/ *n.* a white aluminosilicate of potassium and sodium found in igneous rock and used in the manufacture of glass and ceramics [Early 19thC. Via French from Greek *nephelē* "cloud." The underlying idea is that the crystals become cloudy when immersed in nitric acid.]

neph·e·lin·ite /néffәli nìt/ *n.* a fine-grained igneous rock that has nepheline and pyroxene as its main mineral ingredients

neph·e·lite *n.* = **nepheline**

neph·e·lom·e·ter /nèffә lómmәtәr/ *n.* **1.** CHEM **INSTRUMENT MEASURING PARTICLE SIZE OR DENSITY** an instrument that uses reflected light to measure the size or density of solid particles present in a liquid **2.** METEOROL **DEVICE MEASURING CLOUDINESS OF SKY** an instrument used to measure the degree of cloudiness in the sky [Late 19thC. Coined from Greek *nephelē* "cloud" + -METER.] —**neph·e·lo·met·ric** /nèffәlә méttrik/ *adj.* —**neph·e·lom·e·try** /nèffә lómmәtree/ *n.*

neph·ew /néffyoo/ *n.* the son of somebody's brother, sister, brother-in-law, or sister-in-law [13thC. Via French *neveu* from the Latin stem *nepot-* "sister's son, grandson, descendant" (source of English *nepotism*).]

neph·o·gram /néffә gràm/ *n.* a photograph of a cloud [Late 19thC. Coined from Greek *nephos* "cloud" + -GRAM.]

neph·o·graph /néffә gràf/ *n.* a device for taking photographs of clouds [Late 19thC. Coined from Greek *nephos* "cloud" + -GRAPH.]

ne·phol·o·gy /ne fóllәjee/ *n.* the branch of meteorology concerned with the study of clouds [Late 19thC. Coined from Greek *nephos* "cloud" + -LOGY.] —**neph·o·log·i·cal** /nèffә lójjik'l/ *adj.* —**ne·phol·o·gist** /ne fóllәjist/ *n.*

neph·o·scope /néffә skōp/ *n.* an instrument for measuring the altitude, speed, and direction of movement of clouds [Late 19thC. Coined from Greek *nephos* "cloud" + -SCOPE.]

nephr- *prefix.* = **nephro-** (*used before vowels*)

ne·phral·gia /nә frálјә/ *n.* pain in the kidneys

ne·phrec·to·my /nә fréktәmee/ (*plural* **-mies**) *n.* the surgical removal of a kidney

neph·ric /néffrik/ *adj.* relating to or affecting the kidneys

ne·phrid·i·um /nә fríddee әm/ (*plural* **-a** /-ә/) *n.* **1. EXCRETORY ORGAN** a simple tube-shaped organ in earthworms and many other invertebrate organisms for releasing waste matter into the gut or out of the body **2. EMBRYONIC KIDNEY** the organ that develops into the kidney in a vertebrate animal's embryo [Late 19thC. Coined from NEPHRO- "small kidney" + modern Latin *-idium* "small one" (from Greek *-idion*).] —**ne·phrid·i·al** *adj.*

neph·rite /né frìt/ *n.* a variety of jade that ranges in color from white to dark green and is made up primarily of iron, calcium, and magnesium in monoclinic crystalline form

ne·phrit·ic /nә fríttik/ *adj.* **1. RELATING TO NEPHRITIS** relating to or affected by nephritis **2. OF THE KIDNEYS** relating to or affecting the kidneys

ne·phri·tis /ni frítiss/ *n.* severe inflammation of the kidney, caused by infection, degenerative disease, or disease of the blood vessels

nephro- *prefix.* kidney ○ *nephrogenous* [From Greek *nephros*]

ne·phrog·e·nous /ni frójjәnәss/, **neph·ro·gen·ic** /nèffrә jénnik/ *adj.* **1. FOUND IN KIDNEY** located in or moving into a kidney **2. DEVELOPING INTO KIDNEY TISSUE** capable of developing into kidney tissue

ne·phrol·o·gy /nә fróllәjee/ *n.* the branch of medicine concerned with the study and treatment of diseases of the kidneys —**neph·ro·log·i·cal** /nèffrә lójjik'l/ *adj.* —**ne·phrol·o·gist** /nә fróllәjist/ *n.*

neph·ron /né fròn/ *n.* any of the numerous fine tubules in the kidneys of vertebrates that filter and excrete waste materials from the blood and produce urine

ne·phrop·a·thy /nә fróppәthee/ (*plural* **-thies**) *n.* a disease or medical disorder of the kidney —**neph·ro·path·ic** /nèffrә páthik/ *adj.*

neph·ro·scope /néffrә skōp/ *n.* a tube-shaped instrument inserted into an incision in the body wall in order to examine a patient's kidneys

ne·phro·sis /nә frṓssiss/ *n.* a disease that causes the kidneys to degenerate without inflaming them, especially one that affects the nephrons —**ne·phrot·ic** /nә fróttik/ *adj.*

neph·ro·stome /néffrә stōm/ *n.* the funnel-shaped inner opening of a nephridium that is lined with cilia and allows water and waste to enter from the body cavity [Late 19thC. Coined from NEPHRO- + Greek *stoma* "mouth."]

ne·phrot·o·my /nә fróttәmee/ (*plural* **-mies**) *n.* a surgical incision into a kidney

ne plus ul·tra /này plòoss òoltrә, nèe pluss últrә/ *n.* the highest level of excellence, or something that reaches it (*formal*) [Late 17thC. From Latin, literally "not farther beyond," supposed to have been inscribed on the Pillars of Hercules (the Strait of Gibraltar) as a warning to ships.]

nep·o·tism /néppә tìzzәm/ *n.* favoritism shown by somebody in power to relatives and friends, especially in appointing them to good positions [Mid-17thC. Via French *népotisme* from, ultimately, the Latin stem *nepot-* "grandson, descendant, sister's son" (source of English *nephew*).] —**nep·o·tist** *n.* —**nep·o·tis·tic** /nèppә tístik/ *adj.* —**nep·o·tis·ti·cal·ly** *adv.*

Nep·tune /nép to͞on/ *n.* **1.** ASTRON **EIGHTH PLANET** the eighth planet from the Sun in our solar system **2.** MYTHOL **ROMAN GOD OF SEA** in Roman mythology, the god of the sea, son of Saturn, brother of Jupiter and Pluto. Greek equivalent **Poseidon** [15thC. Directly or via French from Latin *Neptunus*.]

nep·tu·ni·um /nep to͞onee əm/ *n.* a silvery radioactive metallic chemical element found in small amounts in uranium ores. It is artificially produced in nuclear reactors as a by-product of plutonium production. Symbol **Np** [Late 19thC. Coined by R. Hermann as the next chemical element discovered after uranium; the sequence of names follows the order of the planets (Uranus, Neptune).]

nerd /nurd/ *n.* (*slang insult*) **1.** **OFFENSIVE TERM** an offensive term that deliberately insults somebody's, especially a man's or boy's, social skills or intelligence **2.** **SINGLE-MINDED ENTHUSIAST** an enthusiast whose interest is regarded as too technical or scientific and who seems obsessively wrapped up in it (*often used in combination*) ○ *a computer nerd* [Mid-20thC. Origin uncertain: perhaps created by children's author Dr. Seuss (Theodore Seuss *Geisel*, 1904–91) in *If I Ran the Zoo* (1950), referring to a small angry humanoid animal.] —**nerdish** *adj.* —**nerd·y** *adj.*

Ne·re·id[1] /neeree id/ (*plural* **-id·es**) *n.* in Greek mythology, a sea nymph, one of the 50 daughters of Nereus [Late 17thC. Via Latin from the Greek stem *Nērēid-*, from Greek *Nēreus*, name of a Greek sea god.]

Ne·re·id[2] /neeree id/ *n.* ASTRON the outermost known natural satellite of Neptune, discovered in 1949. It is 340 km (211 mi.) in diameter.

ne·re·is /neeree iss/ (*plural* **-i·des** /nə reé i deez/ *or* **-is·es**) *n.* a large segmented worm usually found living in saltwater, e.g., the clamworm. Genus: *Nereis.* [Mid-18thC. Via modern Latin, genus name, from Latin (see NEREID).]

ne·rit·ic /nə ríttik/ *adj.* relating to or found in shallow coastal waters [Late 19thC. Formed from Latin *nerita*, type of shellfish of shallow seas, from, ultimately, Greek *Nēreus* (see NEREID).]

Ne·ro /neérō/ (A.D. 37–68) Roman emperor. He succeeded Claudius (A.D. 54), but his tyrannical and neglectful rule led to his deposition, and he committed suicide. Born **Lucius Domitius Ahenobarbus**. Full name **Claudius Caesar Drusus Germanicus Nero**

ne·rol /neér àwl, né ràwl/ *n.* a colorless alcohol obtained from neroli and other essential oils, used in perfumes [Early 20thC. Coined from NEROLI + -OL.]

ner·o·li /nérrəlee/, **ner·o·li oil** *n.* an oil distilled from the flowers of orange trees, especially the Seville orange, used in aromatherapy, in perfumes, and as a flavoring in food [Late 17thC. Via French from Italian, from the name of an Italian princess who supposedly discovered the oil.]

nerts /nurts/ *interj.* a word used to express contempt, disgust, or unqualified refusal (*dated slang*) [Mid-20thC. Alteration of NUTS.]

Ne·ru·da /ne ro͞odə, -ro͞othə/, **Pablo** (1904–73) Chilean poet and diplomat. He is known for his socialist poetry and won the Nobel Prize in literature in 1971. Pseudonym of **Neftali y Ricardo Reyes Basoalto**

Ner·va /núrvə/, **Marcus Cocceius** (A.D. 35?–98) Roman emperor. He succeeded Domitian in 96, and introduced measures to help the poor. He was succeeded by his son Trajan.

nerve /nurv/ *n.* **1.** **FIBERS COMMUNICATING BETWEEN BRAIN AND BODY** a bundle of fibers forming a network that transmits messages, in the form of impulses, between the brain or spinal cord and the body's organs. Motor nerves carry impulses outward to the muscles and glands, while sensory nerves carry inbound information about the body's movements and sensations. Mixed nerves perform both functions. **2.** **SENSITIVE PULP IN TOOTH** the sensitive tissue inside the roots of a tooth **3.** **COURAGE** courage or self-assurance ○ *lost his nerve* **4.** **BOLDNESS** boldness or impudence ○ *You've got a nerve!* **5.** BOT **LEAF VEIN** a vein in a leaf **6.** INSECTS **VEIN IN INSECT'S WING** a thin rib visible inside an insect's wing ■ **nerves** *npl.* **1.** **STRESS THRESHOLD** somebody's ability to tolerate emotional stress or excitement ○ *My nerves are shattered.* **2.** **NERVOUSNESS** a state of emotional agitation (*informal*) ○ *He's a bundle of nerves before every performance.* ■ *vt.* (**nerved, nerv·ing, nerves**) **STEEL YOURSELF** to gather all your courage or self-control in preparation for dealing with something difficult, stressful, or frightening [14thC. Directly or via Old French *nerf* "sinew, tendon" from Latin *nervus* "nerve, sinew, tendon."]

WORD KEY: SYNONYMS

See Synonyms at ***courage***.

nerve block *n.* use of a local anesthetic to numb a part of the body, thereby preventing the transmission of pain messages to the brain

nerve cell *n.* = **neuron**

nerve cen·ter *n.* **1.** **CONTROL CENTER** a place from which a large organization, system, or network is controlled **2.** PHYSIOL **GROUP OF NEURONS** a cluster of interconnected nerve cells that performs a specific function in the body

nerve cord *n.* a strand of nerve tissue, e.g., the spinal cord, that runs the length of the body and forms a principal part of an animal's nervous system

nerve fi·ber *n.* one of the long thin extensions of a neuron such as an axon or dendrite

nerve gas *n.* a poisonous gas used as a weapon of war that attacks the central nervous system and stops the breathing

nerve im·pulse *n.* a rapid and momentary change in electrical activity that passes along a nerve fiber to other neurons, muscles, or other body organs and signals instructions or information

nerve·less /núrvləss/ *adj.* **1.** **NUMB** having no sensation or strength **2.** **FEARLESS** showing calmness, courage, or confidence, especially in a dangerous situation **3.** **COWARDLY** lacking courage or determination —**nerve·less·ly** *adv.* —**nerve·less·ness** *n.*

nerve net *n.* a simple nervous system, found in some invertebrates such as jellyfish, consisting of interconnecting nerve cells but lacking a control center such as a brain

nerve-rack·ing, **nerve-wrack·ing** *adj.* causing great anxiety or distress

nerve trunk *n.* a bundle of nerve fibers surrounded by a sheath of connective tissue that forms the main stem of a nerve

nerv·ous /núrvəss/ *adj.* **1.** **UNEASY** having a feeling of dread or apprehension ○ *feeling nervous about meeting his parents* **2.** **TIMID** easily worried or frightened ○ *people of a nervous disposition* **3.** **AFFECTING THE NERVES** relating to somebody's ability to tolerate anxiety and stress ○ *a nervous illness* **4.** **OF NERVES** relating to or located in nerves, or the nervous system ○ *nervous tissue* [14thC. Originally in the sense "sinewy"; its most important meanings today, of fear and worry, date from the 18thC.] —**ner·vos·i·ty** /nur vóssətee/ *n.* —**nerv·ous·ly** /núrvəsslee/ *adv.* —**nerv·ous·ness** *n.*

nerv·ous break·down *n.* a psychiatric disorder, usually caused by intense stress or anxiety, in which somebody becomes incapable of coping with daily life and exhibits low self-esteem or depression

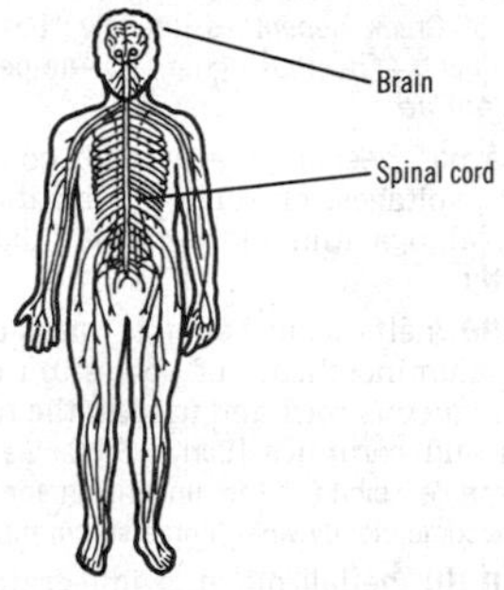

Nervous system

nerv·ous sys·tem *n.* the network of nerve cells and nerve fibers in most animals that conveys sensations to the brain and motor impulses to organs and muscles

nerv·ous tic *n.* an involuntary twitch of a muscle, especially of the face, that is sometimes a symptom of nervousness or a nervous disease

ner·vure /núrvyər, -vyo͝or/ *n.* **1.** INSECTS **STRUCTURE IN INSECT'S WING** a supporting structure resembling a rod that is visible inside an insect's wing **2.** BOT = **vein** *n.* **3** [Early 19thC. Via French, literally "strap," from, ultimately, Latin *nervus* (see NERVE).]

nerv·y /núrvee/ (**-i·er, -i·est**) *adj.* **1.** **FEARLESS** showing a lot of courage or foolhardiness (*informal*) **2.** **AGGRESSIVE** acting in ways that show lack of respect for the boundaries or feelings of other people (*informal*) **3.** **SINEWY** extremely strong (*archaic*) —**nerv·i·ly** *adv.* —**nerv·i·ness** *n.*

NES *abbr.* National Employment Service

nes·cience /nésh'ns, néshee əns, néssee əns/ *n.* lack of knowledge or experience (*formal*) [Early 17thC. From late Latin *nescientia*, from Latin *nescient-*, present participle stem of *nescire* "not to know," from *scire* "to know" (see SCIENCE).] —**nes·cient** *adj.* —**nes·cient·ly** *adv.*

ness /ness/ *n.* a section of coastline that projects into the sea (*often used in placenames*) [Old English *næs(s)*. Ultimately from an Indo-European word that is also the ancestor of *nose*. The underlying idea is of a nose-shaped projection from the mainland.]

Ness, Loch long narrow lake in northern Scotland, forming part of the Caledonian Canal. It is believed by some people to be the home of an ancient monster. Length: 24 mi./39 km.

-ness *suffix.* state, condition, quality ○ *callousness* [Old English *-nes*]

nes·sel·rode /néss'l rōd/, **Nes·sel·rode** *n.* a creamy frozen dessert containing puréed chestnuts, candied fruit, and usually a sweet wine or liqueur [Mid-19thC. Named for the Russian statesman Karl-Robert *Nesselrode* (1780–1862), whose chef invented it.]

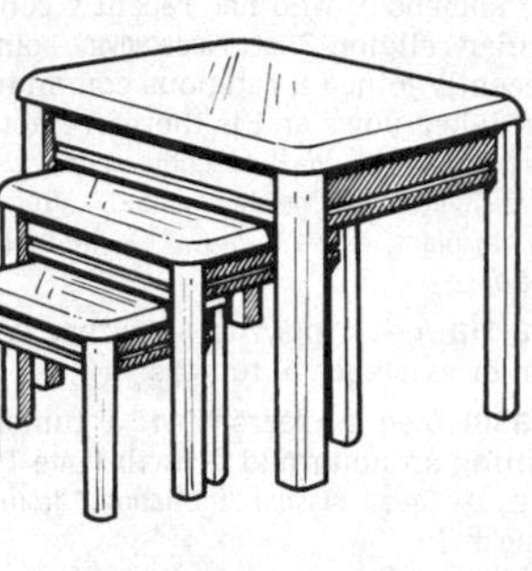

Nest: Nest of tables

nest /nest/ *n.* **1.** **BIRD OR ANIMAL'S DWELLING** a structure that birds and other animals, e.g., mice, build to shelter themselves and their young, using available natural materials such as grass, twigs, and mud **2.** **COMMUNITY OF ANIMALS** the community of animals living in a nest **3.** **SOMETHING SHAPED LIKE BIRD'S NEST** something shaped more or less like a bird's nest, especially something that encloses or contains things ○ *a meringue nest* **4.** **COZY PLACE** a cozy, protected, or secluded place **5.** **BAD PLACE** a place where something bad, such as crime or treason, flourishes ○ *a nest of vice* **6.** **CRIMINALS' SECRET PLACE** a hideaway for criminals, or a group of criminals hiding away there ○ *a nest of thieves* **7.** **SET OF THINGS** a set of things, e.g., tables or wooden eggs, that fit one inside the other **8.** **GUN EMPLACEMENT** a protected or camouflaged place from which a gun or other weapon is fired ■ *v.* (**nest·ed, nest·ing, nests**) **1.** *vi.* **BUILD NEST** to make or live in a nest, especially in preparation for giving birth to young **2.** *vi.* **MAKE PLACE MORE HOMELIKE** to make a place more comfortable and homelike (*informal*) **3.** *vt.* **PUT THINGS TOGETHER** to put one thing inside another, or group things together into a single unit, e.g., kitchen utensils of graduated size **4.** *vi.* **LOOK FOR BIRDS' NESTS** to go looking for birds' nests in order to take the eggs [Old English. Ultimately from an Indo-European word meaning "place where a bird sits down."]

nest-build·ing *n.* **1.** **BIRD'S BUILDING OF NEST** a bird's construction of a nest in preparation for having young **2.** **MAKING PLACE MORE HOMELIKE** the process of making a place more comfortable and homelike (*informal*)

nest egg *n.* **1.** **SAVINGS** a sum of money put aside for future expenses or emergencies **2.** **EGG TO ENCOURAGE LAYING** a real or artificial egg that is put in a hen's nest to encourage it to continue laying after the other eggs have been removed

nes·tle /néss'l/ (**nes·tled, nest·ling, nes·tles**) *v.* **1.** *vti.* **SETTLE INTO COMFORTABLE POSITION** to settle into a position that feels comfortable, warm, and safe, or lay a part of the body in such a position **2.** *vt.* **CUSHION SOMETHING WITH SOFT MATERIAL** to put something such as delicate china or glassware in a protected cushion of soft material **3.** *vi.* **BE SECLUDED** to be in a sheltered or secluded place [Old English *nestlian*. From a prehistoric

Germanic word that was formed from the ancestor of English *nest.*] —**nes·tler** *n.*

nest·ling /néstling, néss-/ *n.* a young bird that does not yet have its flight feathers, and is therefore not yet able to leave the nest [Late 14thC. Origin uncertain: formed from NEST or NESTLE, perhaps on the model of Dutch *nesteling.*]

Nes·to·ri·an /ne stáwree ən/ *adj.* **RELATING TO ASIAN CHRISTIAN GROUP** relating to an Asian Christian denomination that believes that two distinct persons, one divine and the other human, existed in Jesus Christ. This doctrine was declared heresy in A.D. 431. ■ *n.* **MEMBER OF NESTORIAN GROUP** a member of the Nestorian denomination [15thC. From late Latin *Nestorianus,* named for *Nestorius* (428–31), patriarch of Constantinople, who originated the doctrine.]

net[1] /net/ *n.* **1. MESH** material made from threads or wires knotted, twisted, or woven to form a regular pattern with spaces between the threads **2. MESHWORK BAG** a piece of meshwork fabric in a shape resembling a bag that is used for holding, carrying, trapping, or confining something ○ *a fishing net* **3. LIGHT MESHWORK FABRIC** a fine light fabric with an open weave, usually made of cotton or synthetic yarn **4. SELECTING OR RESTRICTING SYSTEM** a plan or system designed to select or restrict somebody or something ○ *those who slip through the net* **5.** SPORTS **STRIP OF MATERIAL ACROSS PLAYING AREA** a strip of meshwork material that divides a court into halves in some sports, e.g., tennis and volleyball, and over which the players must hit a ball or shuttlecock **6.** SPORTS **GOAL IN SOME SPORTS** a goal in some sports, e.g., soccer and water polo, with a backing made of meshwork material **7.** BASKETBALL **PART OF BASKETBALL NET** an open-bottomed piece of meshwork material attached to the hoop of the basket in basketball **8.** COMPUT, BROADCAST **NETWORK** telecommunications or computer network ■ *v.* **(net·ted, net·ting, nets) 1.** *vt.* **TRAP IN NET** to catch or snare something in a net **2.** *vt.* **GET SOMETHING** to manage to obtain or achieve something (*informal*) ○ *We may net ourselves several new clients this way.* **3.** *vt.* **PROTECT WITH NET** to cover something with a net in order to keep something out or away ○ *Net the cherry trees to keep birds out.* **4.** *vi.* **MAKE NET** to make a net by knotting, twisting, or weaving threads or wires together **5.** *vt.* SPORTS **HIT BALL INTO NET TO SCORE** to score by hitting the ball into the net in games such as soccer **6.** *vt.* SPORTS **SERVE BALL INTO NET** to lose a serve, and sometimes a point, by hitting the ball into the net in games such as tennis and volleyball [Old English. Ultimately from an Indo-European word meaning "to bind, tie," which is also the ancestor of English *nettle, node,* and *connect.*] —**net·less** *adj.* —**net·less·ly** *adv.*

net[2] /net/ *adj.* **1.** FIN **LEFT AFTER DEDUCTIONS** remaining from an amount, especially of money, after all necessary deductions have been made **2. RELATING TO CONTENTS** relating to contents only, excluding the container or the packaging **3. HAVING ALL THINGS CONSIDERED** general or overall when positive and negative features have been weighed against each other ■ *vt.* **(net·ted, net·ting, nets)** FIN **EARN PROFIT** to earn or provide a sum of money as pure profit after all necessary deductions have been made ■ *n.* **1. NET AMOUNT** a net profit or weight **2.** GOLF **GOLFER'S SCORE** a player's final score after his or her handicap has been deducted [15thC. Via Italian *netto* from Latin *nitidus* "gleaming, clean, elegant" (see NEAT).]

Net, net *n.* the Internet (*informal*) [Late 20thC. Shortening.]

NET *abbr.* National Educational Television

Net·an·ya·hu /nètt'n yaáhoo/, **Benjamin** (*b.* 1949) Israeli statesman. He was elected Likud prime minister in 1996. He was criticized for failing to press for the implementation of the peace agreements with the Palestinians.

net as·set val·ue *n.* the value of the securities owned by a mutual fund, calculated as the total value of assets minus the total amount of liabilities divided by the number of shares issued

net cord *n.* **1. TENNIS SHOT TOUCHING NET** a tennis shot, especially a serve, that touches the net before landing on the opponent's side. In the case of a serve, the server retakes the shot. **2. WIRE SUPPORTING TENNIS NET** the wire that holds up the net on a tennis court

net do·mes·tic prod·uct *n.* the gross sum of domestic production minus the cost of depreciation of capital goods

Neth. *abbr.* Netherlands

neth·er /néthər/ *adj.* located in a low or lower position or under something (*formal*) [Old English *neoþera.* Ultimately from an Indo-European word meaning "down," which is also one of the ancestors of English *nest.*]

Netherlands

Neth·er·lands monarchy in northwestern Europe, west of Germany, on the North Sea. Language: Dutch. Currency: guilder. Capital: Amsterdam. Population: 15,451,000 (1995). Area: 16,033 sq. mi./ 41,526 sq. km. Official name **Kingdom of the Netherlands.** Also called **Holland** —**Neth·er·land·er** *n.* —**Neth·er·land·ish** *adj.*

Neth·er·lands An·til·les two Dutch island groups in the western Caribbean Sea, part of the Lesser Antilles. Population: 202,244 (1994). Area: 390 sq. mi./996 sq. km.

Neth·er·lands Gui·an·a /nethərlənds geeaánə/ former name for **Suriname**

neth·er·most /néthər mōst/ *adj.* lowest or farthest down (*formal*)

neth·er·world /néthər wùrld/ *n.* **1.** RELIG **HELL** hell, or the place where evil spirits live in the belief system of some cultures (*formal*) **2.** MYTHOL **ABODE OF DEAD SOULS** in Greek and Roman mythology, the place below the earth's surface where the souls of the dead live **3. CRIMINAL UNDERWORLD** the world of organized crime, or the people involved in it (*literary*)

net·i·quette /nétti kèt/ *n.* a set of empirically derived rules for getting along harmoniously in the electronic communication environment (*informal*) [Late 20thC. Blend of NET and ETIQUETTE.]

Net·i·zen /néttiz'n/ *n.* somebody who has access to and uses the Internet frequently (*informal*) [Late 20thC. Blend of NET and CITIZEN.]

net na·tion·al prod·uct *n.* the amount left after subtracting a depreciation allowance for capital goods from the gross national product

net pres·ent val·ue *n.* the value of an investment project found by adding the present value of expected future cash flows and the cost of the initial investment

net prof·it *n.* gross profit minus all the costs incurred by a business

net re·al·iz·a·ble val·ue *n.* the value an asset would have if sold, allowing for the costs of bringing it to a condition for sale and making the sale

net·su·ke /nét sòokee, nétskee/ (*plural* **-ke** *or* **-kes**) *n.* a carved wooden or ivory ornamental toggle worn at the end of a cord that holds a kimono closed, originally used to fasten a purse or pouch [Late 19thC. From Japanese.]

Net surf·ing *n.* browsing through the information and sites available on the Internet, especially casually

net·ter /néttər/ *n.* somebody with an Internet address (*slang*)

net·ting /nétting/ *n.* fabric made from threads or wires knotted, twisted, or woven to form a regular pattern with spaces between the threads

net·tle /nétt'l/ *n.* **1. PLANT WITH STINGING LEAVES** a wild plant with serrated-edged leaves that are covered with fine hairs or spines that sting when touched. Genus: *Urtica.* **2. NONSTINGING PLANT RESEMBLING NETTLE** a wild plant with serrated leaves like a stinging nettle, but without the stinging hairs, especially a deadnettle. Genus: *Lamium.* ■ *vt.* **(-tled, -tling, -tles) 1. IRRITATE SOMEBODY** to irritate or annoy somebody (*informal*) **2. STING** to sting somebody [Old English *netele.* Ultimately from an Indo-European word meaning "to tie," which also produced English *net.* Nettles were often used as a source of fiber for making cords.]

net·tle rash *n.* = **urticaria**

net ton *n.* = **ton**[1] *n.* 1 [From NET[2]]

net weight *n.* the weight of the contents only, excluding the weight of the container or packaging [From NET[2]]

net-winged *adj.* used to describe the wings of beetles and midges that have a network of veins

net·work /nét wùrk/ *n.* **1. SYSTEM OF INTERCONNECTED LINES** a pattern or system that looks like a series of branching or interconnecting lines **2. COORDINATED SYSTEM OF PEOPLE OR THINGS** a large and widely distributed group of people or things such as shops, colleges, or churches, that communicate with one another and work together as a unit or system **3.** BROADCAST **GROUP OF BROADCASTING AFFILIATES** a group of radio or television station affiliates with a core of programs that they all broadcast at the same time, with local or regional variations at other times **4.** ELEC **SYSTEM OF ELECTRICAL CIRCUITS** a system of interconnected electrical circuits or components **5.** COMPUT **SYSTEM OF LINKED COMPUTERS** a system of two or more computers, terminals, and communications devices linked by wires, cables, or a telecommunications system in order to exchange information. The network may be limited to a group of users in a local area, (**local area network**), or be global in scope, as the Internet is. **6. NETTING** net or netting ■ *v.* **(-worked, -work·ing, -works) 1.** *vt.* BROADCAST **BROADCAST SOMETHING SIMULTANEOUSLY** to broadcast a program simultaneously on all the station affiliates that form a network **2.** *vt.* COMPUT **LINK COMPUTERS** to link a group of computers or their users so that information can be mutually accessed or exchanged **3.** *vi.* **MAINTAIN RELATIONSHIPS WITH PEOPLE** to build up or maintain informal relationships, especially with people whose friendship could bring advantages such as job or business opportunities

net·work·ing /nét wùrking/ *n.* **1.** COMPUT **LINKING OF COMPUTERS** the linking of computers so that users can exchange information or share access to a central store of information **2. GATHERING OF ACQUAINTANCES OR CONTACTS** the building up or maintaining of informal relationships, especially with people whose friendship could bring advantages such as job or business opportunities —**net·work·er** *n.*

neum *n.* = **neume**

Neu·mann /nyóomən/, **John von** (1903–57) Hungarian-born U.S. mathematician. He developed game theory and quantum mechanics, and was a pioneer in computer theory and design.

neume /noom/, **neum** *n.* during the Middle Ages in Europe, an early kind of musical notation that sometimes indicated only the approximate shape of a melody [15thC. Via French from, ultimately, Greek *pneuma* "breath." The modern usage is a 19thC revival.] —**neu·mat·ic** /noo máttik/ *adj.*

neur. *abbr.* **1.** neurological **2.** neurology

neur- *prefix.* = **neuro-** (*used before vowels*)

neu·ral /nóorəl/ *adj.* relating to or located in a nerve or the nervous system —**neu·ral·ly** *adv.*

neu·ral arch *n.* a bony or cartilaginous arch enclosing the spinal cord on the outward-facing side of a vertebra

neu·ral com·put·er *n.* = **neurocomputer**

neu·ral crest *n.* a ridge of cells in the ectoderm of the vertebrate embryo that develops into cranial, spinal, and autonomic ganglia

neu·ral·gia /noo ráljə/ *n.* intermittent and often severe pain in a part of the body that a particular nerve runs through, especially when there is no physical change in the nerve itself —**neu·ral·gic** *adj.*

neu·ral net *n.* a system of electrical circuits designed to perform like the human nervous system, especially a computer system mimicking the human brain

neu·ral net·work *n.* **1.** ANAT **SYSTEM OF NEURONS** an interconnecting system of nerve cells such as the system that makes the brain function **2.** COMPUT = **neural net**

neu·ral spine *n.* a projection that points backward from the neural arch of a vertebra

neu·ral tube *n.* the hollow tube of tissue in the embryo of humans and other vertebrates that develops into the spinal cord and brain

neu·ral tube de·fect *n.* a congenital disorder such as spina bifida caused by failure of the neural tube to close completely and resulting in loss of muscle function and various medical disorders

neu·ras·the·ni·a /nŏorəss theénee ə/ *n.* a condition marked by chronic mental and physical fatigue and depression (*dated*) —**neu·ras·then·ic** /-thénnik/ *adj.* —**neu·ras·then·i·cal·ly** *adv.*

neu·rec·to·my /noo réktəmee/ (*plural* **-mies**) *n.* the removal of part of a nerve using surgery, e.g., as a treatment for neuralgia

neu·ri·lem·ma /nŏorə lémmə/, **neu·ro·lem·ma** /nŏorə lémmə, nyŏorə lémmə/ *n.* the outermost layer of the myelin sheath that surrounds the axon of a myelinated nerve cell [Early 19thC. Coined from NEUR- + Greek *eilēma* "covering."] —**neu·ri·lem·mal** *adj.* —**neu·ri·lem·mal·ly** *adv.*

neu·ri·lem·mo·ma /nŏorələ mṓmə, nyŏorələ mṓmə/ (*plural* **-mas** *or* **-ma·ta** /-mətə/) *n.* = **neurofibroma** [Mid-20thC. Coined from NEURILEMMA + -OMA.]

neu·ri·no·ma /nŏorə nṓmə, nyŏorə-/ (*plural* **-mas** *or* **-ma·ta** /-mətə/) *n.* MED = **neurofibroma** [Early 20thC. Coined from NEURO- + INO- + -OMA.]

neu·ri·tis /noo rītiss/ *n.* inflammation of a nerve, accompanied by pain, loss of reflexes, and muscle shrinkage —**neu·rit·ic** /noo ríttik/ *adj.*

neuro- *prefix.* nerve, neural ○ *neurosurgery* [From Greek *neuron* (see NEURON)]

neu·ro·ac·tive /nŏorō áktiv/ *adj.* having an effect on neural tissue or the nervous system

neu·ro·a·nat·o·my /nŏorō ə náttəmee/ *n.* **1.** STRUCTURE OF NERVOUS SYSTEM the structure of the nervous system **2.** BRANCH OF ANATOMY the branch of anatomy that studies the structure of the nervous system —**neu·ro·an·a·tom·i·cal** /-ə ànnə tómmik'l/ *adj.* —**neu·ro·an·a·tom·i·cal·ly** *adv.* —**neu·ro·a·nat·o·mist** /-ə náttəmist/ *n.*

neu·ro·bi·ol·o·gy /nŏorō bī ólləjee, nyŏorō-/ *n.* = **neuroscience** —**neu·ro·bi·o·log·i·cal** /nŏorō bī́ ə lójjik'l, nyŏorō-/ *adj.* —**neu·ro·bi·o·log·i·cal·ly** *adv.* —**neu·ro·bi·ol·o·gist** /nŏorō bī óllәjist, nyŏorō bī óllәjist/ *n.*

neu·ro·blast /nŏorō blàst/ *n.* an embryonic cell that develops into a nerve cell

neu·ro·blas·to·ma /nŏorō bla stṓmə/ (*plural* **-mas** *or* **-ma·ta** /-mətə/) *n.* a malignant tumor of embryonic nerve cells (**neuroblasts**)

neu·ro·chem·is·try /nŏorō kémmistree/ *n.* the study of the chemical composition and reactions within the nervous system —**neu·ro·chem·i·cal** /-kémmik'l/ *adj.* —**neu·ro·chem·i·cal·ly** *adv.* —**neu·ro·chem·ist** /kémmist/ *n.*

neu·ro·com·put·er /nŏorō kəm pyootər/ *n.* a computer designed to imitate the human brain's ability to identify patterns, learn by trial and error, and find relationships in information. It is used in artificial intelligence research and to perform such tasks as machine translation, process control, handwriting recognition, and weather forecasting. —**neu·ro·com·put·ing** *n.* —**neu·ro·com·pu·ta·tion·al** /-kòmpyoo táyshən'l, -kòmpyoo táyshnəl/ *adj.*

neu·ro·en·do·crine /nŏorō éndəkrin, nŏorō éndə kreen/ *adj.* relating to or involving a nerve cell that releases a chemical messenger, especially a neurohormone, directly into the bloodstream

neu·ro·en·do·cri·nol·o·gy /nŏorō endəkrə nólləjee/ *n.* the study of the interrelationships between the nervous system, the endocrine system, and hormones —**neu·ro·en·do·cri·no·log·i·cal** /-krinnə lójjik'l/ *adj.* —**neu·ro·en·do·cri·no·log·i·cal·ly** *adv.* —**neu·ro·en·do·cri·nol·o·gist** /-krə nólləjist/ *n.*

neu·ro·fi·bril /nŏorə fíbrəl, -fíbbrəl/ *n.* a microscopic thin strand that occurs inside the cell body, axon, and dendrites of a nerve cell —**neu·ro·fi·bril·lar·y** /nŏorə fíbbrə lèrree/ *adj.*

neu·ro·fi·bro·ma /nŏorō fī brṓmə/ (*plural* **-mas** *or* **-ma·ta** /-mətə/) *n.* a usually benign tumor arising from the sheath of a nerve

neu·ro·fi·bro·ma·to·sis /nŏorō fī brōmə tṓssiss/ *n.* an inherited disorder marked by coffee-colored patches on the skin and neurofibromas formed along nerves, causing visual and hearing defects, other nervous disorders, and sometimes major deformities

neu·ro·gen·e·sis /nŏorō jénnəssiss/ *n.* the formation and development of nerve cells —**neu·ro·ge·net·ic** /-jə néttik/ *adj.* —**neu·ro·ge·net·i·cal·ly** /-kəlee/ *adv.*

neu·ro·ge·net·ics /nŏorō jə néttiks/ *n.* the branch of medicine that studies the genetic influences involved in neurological disorders (*takes a singular verb*) —**neu·ro·ge·net·i·cist** *n.*

neu·ro·gen·ic /nŏorō jénnik/ *adj.* **1.** CAUSING GROWTH OF NERVE TISSUE causing or relating to the growth of nerve tissue **2.** OF NERVOUS SYSTEM arising in or stimulated by nerve tissue or the nervous system —**neu·ro·gen·i·cal·ly** *adv.*

neu·rog·li·a /noo rógglee ə, nyə rógglee ə, nŏorə gleé ə/ *n.* the network of supporting tissue and fibers that nourishes nerve cells within the brain and spinal cord. It comprises several layers of cells and makes up about 40% of the total volume of nerve tissue. [Mid-19thC. Coined from NEURO- + Greek *glia* "glue."] —**neu·rog·li·al** *adj.*

neu·ro·hor·mone /nŏorō háwr mōn/ *n.* a hormone such as noradrenaline or vasopressin that acts on nerve cells or the nervous system —**neu·ro·hor·mo·nal** /-hawr mṓn'l/ *adj.* —**neu·ro·hor·mo·nal·ly** *adv.*

neu·ro·hy·poph·y·sis /nŏorō hī póffəssiss/ (*plural* **-ses** /-seez/ *or* **-sis·es**) *n.* the posterior lobe of the pituitary gland that secretes hormones such as vasopressin —**neu·ro·hy·po·phys·e·al** /-hīpə fízzee əl, -hi póffəsee əl/ *adj.*

neu·ro·lem·ma *n.* = **neurilemma**

neu·ro·lep·tic /nŏorō léptik/ *adj.* TRANQUILIZING reducing nerve activity and producing a tranquilizing effect ■ *n.* TRANQUILIZER a drug used in the treatment of conditions such as delirium and behavioral disturbances that has a tranquilizing effect by reducing nerve activity [Mid-20thC. Coined from NEURO- + Greek *lēptikos* "seizing," from, ultimately, *lambanein* "to seize, take."] —**neu·ro·lep·ti·cal·ly** *adv.*

neu·ro·lin·guis·tic pro·gram·ming *n.* **1.** RELATIONSHIP BETWEEN COMMUNICATION AND BEHAVIOR a theory and model of human behavior and communication based on linguistic insights into how people avoid change and how to assist them in changing **2.** GOAL-ORIENTED THERAPY a system of therapy in which the brain is viewed as a computer that can be reprogrammed to think and feel in a way that helps people achieve specific goals

neu·ro·lin·guis·tics /nŏorō ling gwístiks/ *n.* the branch of linguistics that explores how the brain encodes language (*takes a singular verb*) —**neu·ro·lin·guist** /nŏorō líng gwist/ *n.* —**neu·ro·lin·guis·tic** /-ling gwístik/ *adj.* —**neu·ro·lin·guis·ti·cal·ly** *adv.*

neu·rol·o·gy /noo rólləjee/ *n.* the branch of medicine that deals with the structure and function of the nervous system and the treatment of the diseases and disorders that affect it —**neu·ro·log·ic** /nŏorə lójjik/ *adj.* —**neu·ro·log·i·cal·ly** *adv.* —**neu·rol·o·gist** /noo rólləjist/ *n.*

neu·ro·ma /noo rṓmə/ (*plural* **-mas** *or* **-ma·ta** /-rṓmətə/) *n.* MED = **neurofibroma** [Mid-19thC. Coined from NEUR- + -OMA.]

neu·ro·mus·cu·lar /nŏorō múskyələr/ *adj.* **1.** OF NERVE AND MUSCLE TISSUE relating to or affecting both nerve and muscle tissue **2.** IN BOTH NERVE AND MUSCLE TISSUES having features common to both nerve and muscle tissue —**neu·ro·mus·cu·lar·ly** *adv.*

neu·ro·mus·cu·lar junc·tion *n.* the connection between a nerve cell and a muscle, where nerve impulses are transmitted to initiate contraction of the muscle

neu·ron /nŏŏ ròn/, **neu·rone** /nŏŏ rōn/ *n.* a cell, typically consisting of a cell body, axon, and dendrites, that transmits nerve impulses and is the basic functional unit of the nervous system [Late 19thC. Via German from Greek *neuron* "sinew, cord, nerve."] —**neu·ron·al** /nŏorənəl/ *adj.* —**neu·ron·al·ly** /nŏŏ rṓnəlee, nŏorənəlee/ *adv.*

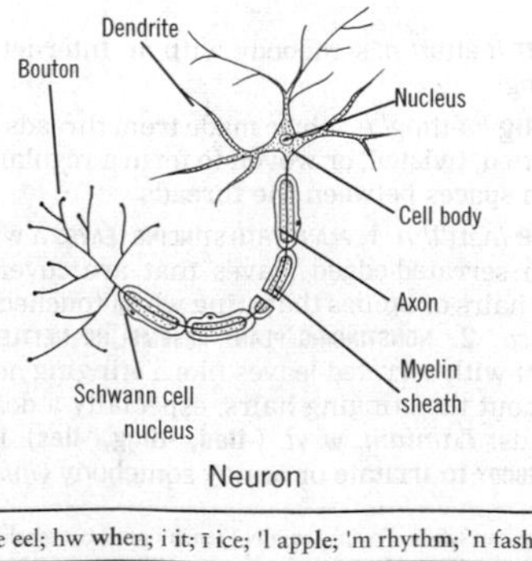

Neuron

neu·ro·path /nŏorə pàth/ *n.* somebody affected by a disorder of the nervous system

neu·ro·pa·thol·o·gy /nŏorōpə thólləjee/ *n.* the branch of medicine that studies diseases and disorders of the nervous system —**neu·ro·path·o·log·i·cal** /-pàthə lójjik'l/ *adj.* —**neu·ro·path·o·log·i·cal·ly** *adv.* —**neu·ro·pa·thol·o·gist** /-pə thólləjist/ *n.*

neu·rop·a·thy /noo róppəthee/ (*plural* **-thies**) *n.* a disease or disorder, especially a degenerative one, that affects the nervous system —**neu·ro·path·ic** /nŏorō páthik/ *adj.* —**neu·ro·path·i·cal·ly** *adv.*

neu·ro·pep·tide /nŏorō pép tīd/ *n.* a peptide that has the properties of a hormone or other neurotransmitter and is released into the blood stream by a nerve cell, not by endocrine tissue

neu·ro·phar·ma·col·o·gy /nŏorō faarmə kólləjee/ *n.* the branch of medicine that studies the effects of drugs on the nervous system —**neu·ro·phar·ma·co·log·i·cal** /-kə lójjik'l/ *adj.* —**neu·ro·phar·ma·co·log·i·cal·ly** *adv.* —**neu·ro·phar·ma·col·o·gist** /-mə kólləjist/ *n.*

neu·ro·phys·i·ol·o·gy /nŏorō fizzee ólləjee/ *n.* the branch of physiology that studies how the nervous system functions —**neu·ro·phys·i·o·log·i·cal** /-ə lójjik'l/ *adj.* —**neu·ro·phys·i·o·log·i·cal·ly** *adv.* —**neu·ro·phys·i·ol·o·gist** /-ólləjist/ *n.*

neu·ro·psy·chi·a·try /nŏorō si kī́ ətree, -sī-/ *n.* the study of the neurological aspects of psychiatric disorders —**neu·ro·psy·chi·at·ric** /nŏorō sī̀kee áttrik/ *adj.* —**neu·ro·psy·chi·at·ri·cal·ly** *adv.* —**neu·ro·psy·chi·a·trist** /-si kī́ ətrist, -sī-/ *n.*

neu·ro·psy·chol·o·gy /nŏorō sī kólləjee/ *n.* the branch of neurology that studies behavior, especially in disorders such as epilepsy, memory loss, or speech impairment —**neu·ro·psy·cho·log·i·cal** /-sīkə lójjik'l/ *adj.* —**neu·ro·psy·cho·log·i·cal·ly** *adv.* —**neu·ro·psy·chol·o·gist** /-sī kólləjist/ *n.*

neu·rop·ter·an /noo róptərən/ *n.* an insect such as the antlion or lacewing that has two large pairs of veined wings and mouthparts adapted for chewing. Order: Neuroptera. —**neu·rop·ter·ous** *adj.*

neu·ro·ra·di·ol·ogy /nŏorō raydee ólləjee/ *n.* the use of X-rays to diagnose and treat physiological disorders and diseases of the nervous system, or the branch of medicine that deals with their use in this way —**neu·ro·ra·di·o·log·i·cal** /-ə lójjik'l/ *adj.* —**neu·ro·ra·di·o·log·i·cal·ly** *adv.* —**neu·ro·ra·di·ol·o·gist** /-ólləjist/ *n.*

neu·ro·sci·ence /nŏorō sī́ əns/ *n.* **1.** SCIENTIFIC STUDY OF NERVOUS SYSTEM a scientific discipline such as neuroanatomy and neurophysiology that studies nerve cells or the nervous system or all such disciplines collectively **2.** MOLECULAR AND CELLULAR NEUROLOGY the scientific study of the molecular and cellular levels of the nervous system, of systems within the brain such as vision and hearing, and behavior produced by the brain —**neu·ro·sci·en·tif·ic** /-sī əntíffik/ *adj.* —**neu·ro·sci·en·tif·i·cal·ly** *adv.* —**neu·ro·sci·en·tist** /-sī́ əntist/ *n.*

neu·ro·sen·so·ry /nŏorō sénsəree/ *adj.* relating to the sensory activity of nerve cells or the nervous system —**neu·ro·sen·so·ri·ly** *adv.*

neu·ro·sis /noo rṓssiss/ (*plural* **-ses** /-seez/) *n.* a mild psychiatric disorder characterized by anxiety, depression, and hypochondria (*dated*)

neu·ro·sur·ger·y /nŏo rō súrjəree/ *n.* surgery on any part of the nervous system, including the brain —**neu·ro·sur·geon** *n.* —**neu·ro·sur·gi·cal** *adj.* —**neu·ro·sur·gi·cal·ly** *adv.*

neu·rot·ic /nŏo róttik/ *adj.* PSYCHIAT **1.** AFFECTED BY NEUROSIS relating to, involving, affected by, or typical of a mild mental disorder characterized by depression, anxiety, and hypochondria (*dated*) **2.** OVERANXIOUS OR OBSESSIVE overanxious, oversensitive, or obsessive about everyday things (*informal*) (*often considered offensive*) ■ *n.* **1.** PSYCHIAT SOMEBODY AFFECTED BY NEUROSIS somebody diagnosed as affected by neurosis (*dated*) **2.** SOMEBODY WHO IS EXTREMELY SENSITIVE somebody who is overanxious, oversensitive, or obsessive (*informal*) (*often considered offensive*) [Mid-17thC. Formed from

Greek *neuron* (see NEURO-).] —**neu·rot·i·cal·ly** *adv.* —**neu·rot·i·cism** *n.*

neu·rot·o·my /nŏŏ róttəmee/ (*plural* **-mies**) *n.* a surgical operation to cut a nerve, especially in order to relieve pain

neu·ro·tox·in /nóo rō tòksin/ *n.* a substance that damages, destroys, or impairs the functioning of nerve tissue —**neu·ro·tox·ic** /-tóksik/ *adj.* —**neu·ro·tox·i·cal·ly** *adv.* —**neu·ro·tox·ic·i·ty** /-tok síssətee/ *n.*

neu·ro·trans·mit·ter /nŏŏ rō transs míttər/ *n.* a chemical that carries messages between different nerve cells or between nerve cells and muscles, e.g., usually to trigger or prevent an impulse in the receiving cell. Excitatory neurotransmitters trigger a nerve impulse in the receiving cell while inhibitory neurotransmitters act to prevent further transmission of an impulse.

neu·ro·trop·ic /nŏŏrə tróppik/ *adj.* affecting or having an affinity with nerve tissue —**neu·ro·trop·i·cal·ly** *adv.* —**neu·rot·ro·pism** /nŏŏ róttrə pìzzəm/ *n.*

neu·ru·la /nŏŏrələ/ (*plural* **-ru·lae** /-lee/ *or* **-ra·las**) *n.* a vertebrate embryo in an early stage during which the nervous system begins to develop [Late 19thC. Coined from NEURO- + Latin *-ula* "small" on the model of BLASTULA and SCROFULA.] —**neu·ru·la·tion** /nŏŏrə láysh'n/ *n.*

neus·ton /nŏŏ stòn/ *n.* minute organisms that float or swim on the surface of water [Early 20thC. From German, from a form of Greek *neustos* "swimming," from *nein* "to swim."]

neut. *abbr.* **1.** neuter **2.** neutral

neu·ter /nóotər/ *vt.* (**-tered, -ter·ing, -ters**) VET **REMOVE TESTICLES OR OVARIES** to remove the testicles or ovaries of an animal ■ *adj.* **1.** PHYSIOL **WITHOUT SEX ORGANS** with undeveloped, nonfunctioning, or no sexual organs **2. NOT INDICATING SEX OR OTHER CHARACTERISTICS** not indicating the sex of a person, the qualities of a thing, or an attitude toward somebody or something **3.** GRAM **GRAMMATICALLY NEITHER MASCULINE NOR FEMININE** used to describe nouns and adjectives in languages such as Latin or German belonging to a separate gender that is neither masculine nor feminine **4.** GRAM **INTRANSITIVE** used to describe a verb that is neither active nor passive **5. NEUTRAL** supporting or belonging to neither side in a dispute (*archaic*) ■ *n.* **1.** VET **CASTRATED OR SPAYED ANIMAL** an animal that has been castrated or spayed **2.** GRAM **GRAMMATICALLY NEUTER WORD** a grammatically neuter noun, adjective, or verb **3.** INSECTS **INSECT WITH UNDEVELOPED SEXUAL ORGANS** an insect with undeveloped sexual organs, e.g., a worker bee **4.** BOT **FLOWER WITHOUT STAMEN OR PISTIL** an asexual flower without a stamen or pistil [14thC. From Latin *ne* "not" + *uter* "which of two," thus meaning "neither one thing nor the other" (compare English *neither*).]

neu·tral /nóotrəl/ *adj.* **1. NOT TAKING SIDES** not belonging to, favoring, or assisting any side in a war, dispute, contest, or controversy **2. WITHOUT DISTINCTIVE QUALITIES** not possessing any particular quality or revealing a particular attitude or feeling ○ *She was careful to explain the problem in neutral terms.* **3.** COLORS **WITHOUT HUE** used to describe a color such as white, black, or gray that does not belong in the spectrum **4.** COLORS **NOT STRONGLY COLORED AND BLENDABLE** not strongly or strikingly colored and thus relatively inconspicuous and able to blend easily with other colors **5.** PHYSIOL = **neuter** *adj.* 1 **6.** CHEM **NOT ACID OR ALKALINE** neither acidic nor alkaline **7.** PHYS **WITH ZERO ELECTRIC CHARGE** with zero electric charge or potential **8.** MECH ENG **WITH NO MOTION TRANSMITTED** in which no motion is transmitted **9.** PHON **PRONOUNCED WITH TONGUE MIDWAY** used to describe a vowel articulated with the tongue relaxed and in the mid-central position, as, e.g., in the first syllable of "away" ■ *n.* **1.** AUTOMOT **GEAR WITH NO MOTION TRANSMITTED** a gear in which no power is transmitted from the engine to the moving parts **2.** POL **SOMEBODY OR SOMETHING NONALIGNED** somebody who or a country that remains neutral in a war, dispute, contest, or controversy [15thC. From Latin *neutralis* "of neuter gender," from *neuter* (see NEUTER).] —**neu·tral·ly** *adv.*

neu·tral cor·ner *n.* either of the two corners of a boxing ring that are not used by boxers between rounds. If one boxer is knocked down during a round, the other must go to a neutral corner.

neu·tral ground *n.* *Southern U.S.* a paved or grassy strip of land between two lanes of a highway

neu·tral·ism /nóotrə lìzzəm/ *n.* the policy of remaining neutral in wars and other disputes, or support for this policy —**neu·tral·ist** *n., adj.* —**neu·tral·is·tic** /nyòotrə lístik/ *adj.* —**neu·tral·is·ti·cal·ly** *adv.*

neu·tral·i·ty /noo tráll ətee/ *n.* the state of being neutral, especially as regards noninvolvement in wars and disputes, not taking sides, and not joining alliances

neu·tral·ize /nóotrə lìz/ (**-ized, -iz·ing, -iz·es**) *vt.* **1. RENDER SOMETHING INEFFECTIVE** to make something ineffective, especially by removing its ability to act as a threat or obstacle **2.** POL **MAKE A PLACE NONALIGNED** to make or declare a country unaligned in an international dispute or war **3.** CHEM **MAKE SOMETHING NEITHER ACID NOR ALKALINE** to render a substance neither acid nor alkaline **4.** PHYS **GIVE ZERO CHARGE TO SOMETHING** to make the electric charge or potential of something zero —**neu·tral·i·za·tion** /nóotrəli záysh'n/ *n.* —**neu·tral·iz·er** /nóotrə lìzər/ *n.*

neu·tral spir·its *n.* alcohol distilled at or above 190 proof, often used in blending liquors (*takes a singular or plural verb*)

neu·tral zone *n.* the space between the areas of two competing teams, specifically the area between the linemen of football teams or the middle area of an ice hockey rink between the two blue lines

neu·tri·no /noo trée nō/ (*plural* **-nos**) *n.* any of three stable neutral elementary particles of the lepton family with a zero rest mass and no charge. Neutrinos have a spin of 1/2. [Mid-20thC. Coined from NEUTRAL + Italian *-ino* "small."]

neu·tron /nóo tròn/ *n.* a neutral elementary particle of the baryon family with a zero electrical charge and a mass approximately equal to that of a proton [Early 20thC. Coined from NEUTRAL + -ON.] —**neu·tron·ic** /noo trónnik/ *adj.*

neu·tron bomb *n.* a nuclear bomb designed to kill all life by a heavy bombardment with neutrons but to cause little blast damage and leave relatively low radioactive contamination

neu·tron star *n.* a celestial body consisting entirely of a very dense compact mass of neutrons, the remnant of a star that has collapsed under its own gravity

neu·tro·phil /nóotrə fil/ *adj.* **STAINABLE ONLY WITH NEUTRAL DYES** used to describe cells or tissues, e.g., white blood cells, that are readily stainable only with chemically neutral dyes ■ *n.* **neu·tro·phil, neu·tro·phile COMMON WHITE BLOOD CELL** the most common type of white blood cell in vertebrates, responsible for protecting the body against infection and stainable with neutral dyes [Late 19thC. Coined from Latin *neutr-*, stem of *neuter* (see NEUTER), + -PHIL.] —**neu·tro·phil·ic** /nóotrə fíllik/ *adj.*

Nev. *abbr.* Nevada

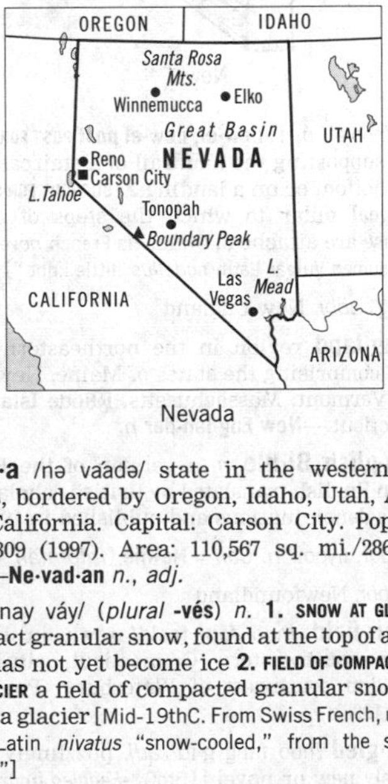

Nevada

Ne·vad·a /nə váadə/ state in the western United States, bordered by Oregon, Idaho, Utah, Arizona, and California. Capital: Carson City. Population: 1,676,809 (1997). Area: 110,567 sq. mi./286,367 sq. km. —**Ne·vad·an** *n., adj.*

né·vé /nay váy/ (*plural* **-vés**) *n.* **1. SNOW AT GLACIER TOP** compact granular snow, found at the top of a glacier, that has not yet become ice **2. FIELD OF COMPACTED SNOW ON GLACIER** a field of compacted granular snow at the top of a glacier [Mid-19thC. From Swiss French, ultimately from Latin *nivatus* "snow-cooled," from the stem *niv-* "snow."]

Nev·el·son /névv'lssən/, **Louise** (1900–88) Russian-born U.S. sculptor. She is best known for her 'sculptural walls' – arrangements of boxes filled with miscellaneous objects.

never /névvər/ CORE MEANING: an adverb indicating that something will not happen at any time, or that somebody will definitely not do something ○ *The details will never be known.* ○ *I would never do anything to harm or hurt her.*

1. *adv.* **AT NO TIME** at no time in the past or the future ○ *The bird has never been seen in Iceland before. It may never appear there again.* **2.** *adv.* **CERTAINLY NOT** not in any circumstances at all ○ *I would never turn my back on them.* **3.** *interj.* **EXCLAMATION OF SURPRISE** an exclamation indicating surprise or shock ○ *"He's won the election after all."* *"Never!"* ○ *"Never!"* [Old English, from *ne* "not" + an earlier form of EVER] ◇ **never ever** an emphatic expresion for "never" (*informal*) ◇ **something will** *or* **would never do** indicates that something is not appropriate or suitable in the circumstances ◇ **well I never!** an exclamation of surprise or shock ○ *Well I never! You've done it again!*

never-ending *adj.* continuing on and on and seeming unlikely ever to stop

nev·er·more /nèvvər máwr/ *adv.* never again (*literary*)

nev·er-nev·er *U.K.* the installment plan (*dated informal*) ○ *They bought a three-piece suite on the never-never.*

nev·er-nev·er land *n.* an unreal or imaginary place, especially one where wonderful things happen ○ *My opponent's budget proposals spring from the same never-never land as his job proposals.* [From *Never Never Land* in J. M. Barrie's *Peter Pan* (1904).]

nev·er·the·less /nèvvər thə léss/ *adv.* despite a situation or comment. Also called **nonetheless**

new /noo/ *adj.* **1. RECENTLY MADE** recently made, created, or invented ○ *a new drug* **2. FIRST-HAND** indicates that something has not been used by anyone else ○ *It's a totally new washing machine* **3. REPLACEMENT** replaced by something recent or innovative ○ *new rules to enhance security* **4. RECENTLY DISCOVERED** recently discovered or noticed ○ *The new comet will be visible at the beginning of July this year.* **5. AT START OF PERIOD** at the beginning of another day, month, or year ○ *I will come to visit you in the new year.* **6. RECENTLY ACQUIRED OR BECOME** having recently acquired a particular status or position ○ *a new mother* ○ *the new medical school graduates* **7. RECENTLY INTRODUCED** recently introduced and previously unfamiliar ○ *The city was completely new to me.* **8. RECENTLY INTRODUCED TO SOMETHING** recently introduced to a place or situation ○ *He's not new to this city.* **9. CHANGED** changed, especially for the better ○ *I felt as if I had slept, and had now just awakened – a new woman, with a new mind.* **10. EARLY** early in the season ○ *new potatoes* [Old English *nēowe*. Ultimately from an Indo-European word that is also the ancestor of English *novel*, *neon*, and *renovate*.]

WORD KEY: SYNONYMS

new, fresh, modern, newfangled, novel, original

CORE MEANING: never experienced before or having recently come into being

new a general word used to describe something that has just been invented, discovered, made, bought or experienced. It can also be used to describe somebody or something not previously known or encountered, for example, a new friend or a new doctor; **fresh** used to describe something new and different, especially when it involves a reexamination or reappraisal of somebody or something. It can also be used to describe something that seems interesting or exciting because it has not been tried or experienced before; **modern** used to describe something that is the result of or is characterized by up-to-date ideas, techniques, design, and equipment; **newfangled** used informally to show disapproval of something such as a machine or a system that is new or different, especially because it seems gimmicky or overcomplicated; **novel** used to describe something that is new and inventive; **original** used to describe something that is new and unique.

NEW[1] *abbr.* net economic welfare

NEW[2] *abbr.* nonexplosive warfare [This term was coined in 1988 by Richard Danzig who later became Secretary of the Navy in the Clinton Administration. It refers to two kinds of viruses—biological and and high-tech—that terrorists and rogue nations can use against a nation's military and civilian infastructure, creating illness, death, and communication chaos.]

New Age *adj.* **OF MODERN MOVEMENT EMPHASIZING SPIRITUALITY** relating to a cultural movement dating from the 1980s that emphasizes spiritual consciousness and often involves belief in reincarnation and astrology and the practice of meditation, vegetarianism, and holistic medicine ■ *n.* **New Age, New Age mu·sic MUSIC INDUCING SERENITY** a style of instrumental music with simple repetitive melodies, often synthesized or reproducing natural sounds, that is intended to promote mental tranquility —**New Ag·er** *n.*

New A·mer·i·can Bi·ble *n.* an English translation of the Bible produced by Roman Catholic scholars in the United States and first published in 1970

New·ark /nŏŏ ərk/ **1.** city in northeastern New Jersey. It is the county seat of Essex County, situated 9 mi./14 km west of New York. Population: 258,751 (1994). **2.** city in Alameda County, western California, east of San Francisco. Population: 37,861 (1990). **3.** city in northern Delaware, in New Castle County, situated 12 mi./19 km southwest of Wilmington. Population: 25,098 (1990).

new ar·ri·val *n.* **1. BABY** a recently-born baby (*informal*) ○ *I hear there's been a new arrival in the family.* **2. MOST RECENT ARRIVAL** somebody who or something that is the latest to arrive ○ *She's a new arrival at the company.*

New Bed·ford city and port in southeastern Massachusetts, on Buzzards Bay, southeast of Taunton. It was a major whaling center during the 1800s. Population: 96,903 (1996).

New Bern city, port, and county seat of Craven County, eastern North Carolina, situated 30 mi./48 km west of Pamlico Sound. Population: 17,363 (1990).

new·bie /nŏŏbee/, **New·bie** *n.* a new user of on-line computer services, especially the Internet ○ *most users welcome newbies*

new blood *n.* a person or group bringing fresh ideas and enthusiasm to a place, situation, or organization

new·born /nŏŏ bàwrn/ *adj.* **1. BORN RECENTLY** born very recently **2. NEWLY DISCOVERED OR RECOVERED** recently discovered or recovered afresh ○ *newborn faith* ■ *n.* **NEW BABY** a newborn child

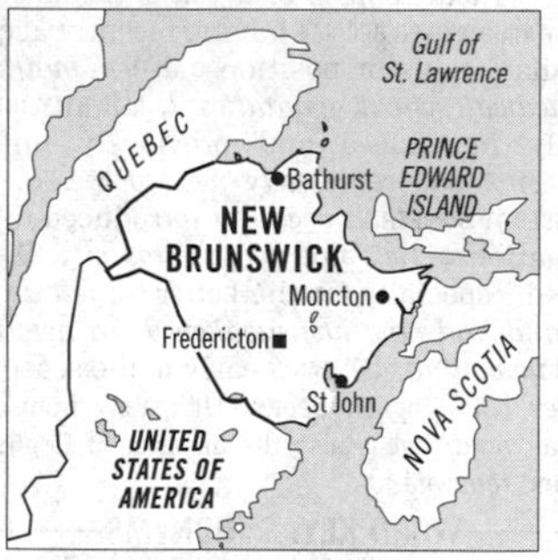

New Brunswick

New Bruns·wick /noo brúnz wik/ **1.** region in eastern Canada, the largest of the Maritime Provinces. Capital: Fredericton. Population: 738,133 (1996). Area: 28,355 sq. mi./73,440 sq. km. **2.** city in central New Jersey. It is the county seat of Middlesex County, situated 9 mi./14 km west of Perth Amboy. Population: 41,711 (1990).

New·burg /nŏŏ bùrg/ *adj.* cooked and served with a rich sauce of cream, butter, sherry, and egg yolks ○ *lobster Newburg* [Early 20thC. Origin unknown.]

New·burgh /nŏŏbərg/ city in southeastern New York State, on the Hudson River, northwest of New York City. Population: 26,248 (1996).

New·bur·y·port /nŏŏbəree pawrt/ town in northeastern Massachusetts, on the Atlantic coast, directly south of the New Hampshire border and northwest of Gloucester. Population: 16,558 (1996).

New Ca·naan town in southwestern Connecticut, in southwestern Fairfield County, situated on the New York State border. Population: 17,864 (1990).

New Car·roll·ton /-kárrəltən/ city in west central Maryland. It is a northeastern suburb of Washington, D.C. Population: 12,811 (1996).

New Cas·tle /nŏŏ kassəl/ city in western Pennsylvania on the Shenango River. Population: 28,334 (1990).

New·cas·tle dis·ease /nŏŏ kàss'l-/ *n.* a highly infectious viral disease that affects poultry and other birds, attacking the lungs and nervous system [Early 20thC. Named for NEWCASTLE UPON TYNE in England, where it was first recorded.]

New·cas·tle up·on Tyne /nŏŏ kassəl ə pon tīn/ city and port on the Tyne River, northeastern England. It is situated at one end of Hadrian's Wall, and the Romans built a bridge over the river there. Population: 283,600 (1994).

New·combe /nyŏŏkəm/, **John** (*b.* 1944) Australian tennis player. He was singles champion at Wimbledon in 1967, 1970, and 1971. Full name **John David Newcombe**

new·com·er /nŏŏ kùmmər/ *n.* somebody who has recently arrived in a place, situation, or organization, or something that has recently appeared or been introduced

New Coun·try *n.* a form of country-and-western music, originating in the 1980s, that typically features bland lyrics and smooth arrangements and is designed to appeal to an urban audience

New Deal *n.* **1. ROOSEVELT REFORM POLICIES** the policies of social and economic reform introduced in the United States in the 1930s under the presidency of Franklin D. Roosevelt. **2. PERIOD OF ROOSEVELT REFORMS** the period during which Franklin D. Roosevelt's policies of social and economic reform were implemented. [From the likening of the policies to a new deal in a card game] —**New Deal·er** *n.*

New Del·hi capital city of India, situated in the northern part of the country adjacent to Delhi. It was built between 1912 and 1929 and inaugurated as the capital in 1931. Population: 294,149 (1991).

New Dem·o·crat *n.* a moderate Democrat dedicated to economic reform and the concerns of the average voter rather than social issues of special interest groups

New Ec·o·nom·ic Pol·i·cy *n.* a program implemented in the Soviet Union between 1921 and 1928 that permitted some private enterprise although the state retained overall economic control

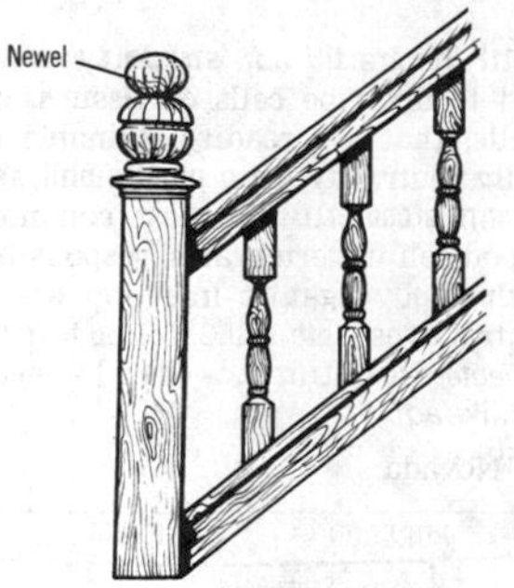

Newel

new·el /nŏŏ əl/ *n.* **1. new·el, new·el post POST FOR HANDRAIL** a post supporting the handrail of a staircase at the top or bottom or on a landing **2. SUPPORT FOR STAIRCASE** a vertical pillar to which the steps of a spiral staircase are attached [14thC. Via French *novel* "knob," from assumed Vulgar Latin *nodellus* "little knot."]

New Eng. *abbr.* New England

New Eng·land region in the northeastern United States, comprising the states of Maine, New Hampshire, Vermont, Massachusetts, Rhode Island, and Connecticut —**New Eng·land·er** *n.*

New En·glish Bi·ble *n.* a version of the Bible in modern English translated by British scholars from various denominations and published in 1970

Newf /noof, nyoof/ *n. Can* = **Newfie** (*informal*)

Newf. *abbr.* Newfoundland

New Fair·field /noo fáir feeld/ town in Fairfield County, southwestern Connecticut, situated 20 mi./32 km southwest of Waterbury. Population: 12,911 (1990).

new·fan·gled /noo fáng g'ld/ *adj.* puzzlingly or suspiciously new or novel [15thC. *-Fangled* from the past participle of Old English *fōn* "to capture."] —**new·fan·gled·ness** *n.*

WORD KEY: SYNONYMS

See Synonyms at ***new***.

new-fash·ioned *adj.* up-to-date or modern (*informal*) [Modeled on OLD-FASHIONED]

New·fie /nŏŏfee/ *n. Can* somebody who comes from Newfoundland (*informal*) [Mid-20thC. Shortening and alteration of *Newfoundland.*]

new·found /nŏŏ fòwnd/ *adj.* recently discovered or met

New·found·land /nŏŏfəndlənd, nŏŏfənd lànd/ *n.* a large sturdy dog with a long straight back and a dense, usually black, coat, belonging to a breed formerly used in water rescues

Newfoundland

New·found·land, Is·land of /noo fówndlənd, nŏŏ fəndlənd/ island in the Atlantic Ocean. Along with Labrador, it comprises the province of Newfoundland. Area: 36,900 sq. mi./93,830 sq. km. —**New·found·land·er** *n.*

New·found·land and Lab·ra·dor the easternmost province in Canada, comprising the island of Newfoundland and Labrador on the mainland. Capital: St. John's. Population: 551,792 (1996). Area: 156,649 sq. mi./405,720 sq. km. —**New·found·land·er** *n.*

New·found·land Stan·dard Time *n.* a time zone used in Newfoundland, Canada, that is 3 hours and 30 minutes behind Greenwich time and half an hour behind Atlantic Standard Time

new games *npl.* forms of play that attempt to minimize stress and anxiety by emphasizing participation, minimal equipment and expense, and cooperation over competition

New Guin·ea the second largest island in the world, in the western Pacific Ocean, off the northern coast of Australia. It is divided between the Indonesian province of Irian Jaya in the west and Papua New Guinea in the east. Area: 312,170 sq. mi./808,510 sq. km. —**New Guin·e·an** *n., adj.*

New Hampshire

New Hamp·shire state in the northeastern United States, bordered by Canada, Maine, the Atlantic Ocean, Massachusetts, and Vermont. Capital: Concord. Population: 1,172,709 (1997). Area: 9,283 sq. mi./24,043 sq. km. —**New Hamp·shir·ite** *n.*

New Har·mo·ny town in Posey County, southwestern Indiana, situated 23 mi./37 km northwest of Evansville. The Harmony Society and Robert Owen both established utopian communities here in the 19th century. Population: 846 (1990).

New Ha·ven /-hàyv'n/ city in New Haven County, southern Connecticut, situated 36 mi./58 km southwest of Hartford. Population: 119,604 (1994).

New Heb·ri·des former name for **Vanuatu** (until 1980)

New I·be·ri·a city in southern Louisiana, southwest of Baton Rouge and southeast of Lafayette. Population: 32,513 (1996).

Ne Win /này wín/ (*b.* 1911) Burmese statesman. Dictator (1962–74) and president (1974–81) of Burma (now Myanmar), he nationalized the economy and suppressed dissent. Real name **Maung Shu Maung**

New Jersey

New Jer·sey state on the eastern coast of the United States, bordered by New York, the Atlantic Ocean, Delaware, and Pennsylvania. Capital: Trenton. Population: 8,052,849 (1997). Area: 8,215 sq. mi./21,277 sq. km. —**New Jer·sey·an** *n., adj.* —**New Jer·sey·ite** *n.*

New Jour·nal·ism *n.* a style of journalism originating in the United States in the 1960s that emphasizes the subjective impressions of the reporter and uses techniques typically found in fiction writing

New King·dom *n.* a period in the history of ancient Egypt, from the 18th to the 20th dynasty (circa 1580 to 1090 B.C.)

New Lat·in *n.* the form of the Latin language used since about the beginning of the 16th century A.D. especially for scientific and taxonomic classification

New Left *n.* a political movement, chiefly among students and intellectuals in the United States and Europe during the 1960s and 1970s, that sought radical social and economic change —**New Left·ist** *n.*

New Lon·don city in New London County, southeastern Connecticut, situated on Long Island Sound, 43 mi./69 km east of New Haven. Population: 28,540 (1990).

new look *n.* a radical change in appearance, design, or style —**new-look** *adj.*

New Look *n.* a style in women's clothes introduced in 1947 by the designer Christian Dior that featured broad shoulders, narrow waists, and long full skirts

new·ly /nóolee/ *adv.* **1.** LATELY recently or lately **2.** AGAIN again or once more **3.** DIFFERENTLY in a different or novel way

new·ly·wed /nóolee wèd/ *n.* somebody who has recently been married —**new·ly·wed** *adj.*

New·man /nóomən/, **Barnett** (1905–70) U.S. painter. His abstract expressionist works feature a color field broken by one or more vertical lines.

New·man, John Henry, Cardinal (1801–90) English theologian. After converting in 1845, he became the leading British Roman Catholic, and was made a cardinal in 1879.

New·man, Paul (*b.* 1925) U.S. stage and movie actor. A popular leading man, he won an Academy Award for *The Color of Money* (1986).

New Man (*plural* **New Men**) *n.* a late-20th-century man characterized by emotional sensitivity, recognition of women as equals, and a desire to share in domestic chores and the work associated with child rearing

New·mar·ket[1] /nóo maarkət/ *n.* a long double-breasted close-fitting jacket with a full skirt worn in the 19th century as a riding coat or overcoat [Late 17thC. Named for NEWMARKET[2].]

New·mar·ket[2] /nóo maarkət/ market town in Suffolk, England, famous for its horseracing since the early 1600s. Population: 16,498 (1991).

new math *n.* a method of teaching mathematics, devised in the 1960s, in which children are introduced to elementary set theory at an early stage

New Mexico

New Mex·i·co state in the southwestern United States, bordered by Colorado, Oklahoma, Texas, Mexico, and Arizona. Capital: Santa Fe. Population: 1,729,751 (1997). Area: 121,598 sq. mi./314,937 sq. km. —**New Mex·i·can** *n., adj.*

New Mil·ford town in Litchfield County, northwestern Connecticut. Population: 23,629 (1990).

new mon·ey *n.* recently acquired wealth or people who have it ○ *It's largely new money that's buying this kind of property these days.*

new moon *n.* **1.** MOON AS NARROW CRESCENT the moon at the beginning of its cycle, when it is invisible from earth or when only a narrow crescent on the right-hand side of its surface is visible **2.** MOON PERIOD the period during which there is a new moon **3.** PHASE OF MOON one of the four phases of the moon, during which it is directly between Earth and the Sun and invisible or seen only as a narrow crescent

New Or·leans /noo áwrleenz, -áwrlinz/ city in southeastern Louisiana, on the eastern bank of the Mississippi River. The largest city in the state, it is known for its annual Mardi Gras festival. Population: 476,625 (1996). —**New Or·lea·ni·an** *n.*

New·port /nóo pawrt/ **1.** city in northern Kentucky, on the Ohio River, that borders Ohio, east of Covington. It is a southern suburb of Cincinnati. Population: 16,957 (1996). **2.** city in southeastern Rhode Island, on Rhode Island itself, connected to the mainland by bridges. Population: 24,295 (1996).

New·port Beach city in Orange County, southwestern California, situated on the Pacific Ocean coast, 18 mi./29 km southeast of Long Beach. Population: 66,643 (1990).

New Port Rich·ey /-ríchee/ city in Pasco County, central Florida, situated 20 mi./32 km northwest of Tampa. Population: 14,044 (1990).

New Right *n.* a conservative political movement that arose during the late 1960s and affirmed a commitment to established religion, patriotism and smaller, less interventionist government

New Riv·er river in the eastern United States that flows from North Carolina into West Virginia to form the Great Kanawha River. Length: 320 mi./515 km.

New Ro·chelle /-ro shél/ city in southeastern New York, on Long Island Sound. It is a northeastern suburb of New York City. Population: 67,369 (1996).

news /nooz/ *n.* **1.** RECENT INFORMATION information about recent events or developments ○ *I phoned the hospital, and the news is good.* **2.** CURRENT EVENTS information about current events printed in newspapers or broadcast by the media ○ *She has been in the news a lot lately.* **3.** PROGRAM a radio or television broadcast presenting the important events or developments that have taken place on a particular day ○ *I heard about it on the news.* **4.** SOMEBODY OR SOMETHING INTERESTING somebody or something considered as being of interest to people in general **5.** SOMETHING PREVIOUSLY UNKNOWN something previously unknown to somebody that he or she is surprised to hear about ○ *Their divorce was news to me.* [15thC. Plural of NEW.]

news a·gen·cy *n.* an organization that gathers information about current events and supplies it to the media

news·a·gent /nóoz ayjənt/ *n. U.K.* = **newsdealer**

news·boy /nóoz bòy/ *n.* a boy who sells newspapers in the street or delivers them to houses

news·break /nóoz bràyk/ *n.* **1.** NEWS DURING STATION BREAK a short station break during which two or three news items are broadcast **2.** NEWSWORTHY ITEM something that is newsworthy

news·cast /nóoz kàst/ *n.* a television or radio broadcast consisting of news

news·cast·er /nóoz kàstər/ *n.* somebody who reads or presents the news on a television or radio broadcast

news con·fer·ence *n.* = **press conference**

news·deal·er /nóoz deélər/ *n.* somebody who keeps a store or stall selling mainly newspapers, magazines, and often paperback books and candy

news desk *n.* an area of a newspaper office or a radio or television studio where news is prepared for publication or broadcasting

news flash *n.* a brief item of urgent news, often broadcast at short notice interrupting a scheduled program

news·gath·er·ing /nóoz gàthəring/ *n.* the collecting of news for possible use in a newspaper, news magazine, or broadcast —**news·gath·er·er** *n.*

news·girl /nóoz gùrl/ *n.* a girl who sells newspapers in the street or delivers them to houses

news·group /nóoz groop/ *n.* a discussion group maintained on a computer network such as the Internet in which people leave messages on topics of mutual interest for other participants to read

news·hawk /nóoz hàwk/, **news·hound** *n.* a newspaper reporter (*informal*)

news·let·ter /nóoz lèttər/ *n.* a printed report or letter containing news of interest to a particular group, e.g., the members of a society or employees of an organization, and circulated to them periodically

news mag·a·zine *n.* **1.** PRESS WEEKLY NEWS MAGAZINE a magazine, usually published weekly, containing news and news analysis from the preceding week **2.** BROADCAST NEWS-MAGAZINES WEEKLY RADIO OR TV PROGRAM a weekly radio or television program of interviews, investigative reportage, features, and commentary on the news

news·mak·er /nóoz màykər/ *n.* somebody whose activities are considered interesting enough to qualify as news for the general public

news·man /nóozmən, -màn/ (*plural* **-men** /-mən, -mèn/) *n.* a man journalist or broadcaster who reports news

news·mon·ger /nóoz mùng gər, nóoz mòng gər/ *n.* somebody who gathers and spreads gossip —**news·mon·ger·ing** *n.*

New South Wales state in southeastern Australia. Capital: Sydney. Population: 6,204,000 (1996). Area: 309,500 sq. mi./801,600 sq. km.

news·pa·per /nóoz pàypər, nóoss-/ *n.* **1.** PRINTED ACCOUNT OF NEWS a publication, usually appearing daily or weekly, containing news and comment on current events, together with features and advertisements, and printed on large sheets of paper that are folded together **2.** ORGANIZATION an organization that produces a newspaper **3.** PAPER FROM A NEWSPAPER a sheet or sheets of the printed paper from a newspaper when used for a purpose other than reading

news·pa·per·man /nóoz paypər màn, nóoss-/ (*plural* **-men** /-mèn/) *n.* **1.** MAN NEWS JOURNALIST a man who writes or edits for a newspaper **2.** NEWSPAPER OWNER a man who owns or publishes a newspaper

news·pa·per·wom·an /nóoz paypər wòommən, nóoss-/ (*plural* **-en** /-wìmmin/) *n.* **1.** WOMAN NEWS JOURNALIST a woman who writes or edits for a newspaper **2.** WOMAN NEWSPAPER OWNER a woman who owns or publishes a newspaper

new·speak /nóo speèk/ *n.* language that is ambiguous and designed to conceal the truth, especially that sometimes used by bureaucrats and propagandists [Named with reference to the propagandist language given official recognition in *Nineteen Eighty-Four*, by British novelist George Orwell, 1949]

news·per·son /nóoz pùrs'n/ (*plural* **-per·sons** *or* **-peo·ple** /-peèp'l/) *n.* a journalist or broadcaster who reports news

news·print /nóoz prìnt/ *n.* a relatively cheap and low-quality paper made from recycled materials or wood pulp and used for printing newspapers

news·read·er /nóoz reèdər/ *n. U.K.* = **anchor**

news·reel /nóoz reel/ *n.* a short film about recent news events, formerly often shown before a feature film

news re·lease *n.* = **press release**

news·room /nóoz ròom, -ròom/ *n.* a room in a radio or television studio or newspaper office where news is prepared for publication or broadcasting

news ser·vice *n.* = **news agency**

news·stand /nóoz stànd/ *n.* a stall or booth where newspapers and magazines are sold

New Style *n.* the reckoning of dates by the Gregorian calendar, in use since 1582

news·ven·dor /nóoz vèndər/ *n. U.K., Can* somebody who sells newspapers

news·week·ly /nóoz weeklee/ (*plural* **-lies**) *n.* a weekly newspaper or news magazine

news·wom·an /nóoz wòommən/ (*plural* **-en** /-wìmmin/) *n.* a woman journalist or broadcaster who reports news

news·wor·thy /nóoz wùrthee/ (**-thi·er, -thi·est**) *adj.* interesting or important enough to be reported in the media —**news·wor·thi·ly** *adv.* —**news·wor·thi·ness** *n.*

news·writ·ing /nóoz rìting/ *n.* the craft of writing news stories

news·y /nóozee/ (**-i·er, -i·est**) *adj.* filled with news and gossip —**news·i·ly** *adv.* —**news·i·ness** *n.*

Newt

newt /noot/ *n.* a small amphibian of the salamander family with short legs and a well-developed tail. Family: Salamandridae. [15thC. From the mistaken division of *an ewte, ewte* being a variant of Middle English *evete* "eft."]

New Ter·ri·to·ries /noo térritriz, -tə̀riz/ former region of Hong Kong that was leased to Great Britain by China

New Tes·ta·ment *n.* the second section of the Christian Bible dealing with the life and teachings of Jesus Christ, containing the Gospels, the Acts of the Apostles, the Epistles, and the Book of Revelations

new·ton /nóot'n/ *n.* an SI unit of force equivalent to the force that produces an acceleration of one meter per second on a mass of one kilogram. Symbol **N** [Early 20thC. Named for Sir Isaac NEWTON.]

New·ton /nóot'n/ city in eastern Massachusetts, composed of 14 villages, west of Boston and east of Marlborough. Population: 80,238 (1996).

New·ton /nóot'n/, **Sir Isaac** (1642–1727) English scientist. He discovered gravitation, invented calculus, and formulated the laws of motion. He recognized that white light is a mixture of colored lights, and wrote *Mathematical Principles of Natural Philosophy* (1687) and *Opticks* (1704).

New·to·ni·an /noo tṓnee ən, nyoo-/ *adj.* relating to, involving, derived from, or typical of the work and theories of Sir Isaac Newton ○ *Newtonian physics*

New·to·ni·an tel·e·scope *n.* a type of reflecting telescope in which mirrors transfer an image to an eyepiece in the side of the telescope's body

New·ton-John /nyòot'n jón/, **Olivia** (*b.* 1948) Australian singer and actor. She has starred in several movies including *Grease* (1978).

New·ton's cra·dle *n.* a toy consisting of five metal balls hanging side by side in a frame. Swinging one ball transmits force along the line so the other end ball swings away. [Named for Sir Isaac NEWTON]

New·ton's rings *n.* a pattern of light interference created by the contact of a convex lens with a glass plate, appearing as a series of alternating bright and dark rings [Named for Sir Isaac NEWTON, who discovered the pattern]

new town *n.* a complete self-contained town with all the usual facilities, created on an open site, usually to accommodate excess population from existing urban areas

New·town /nóo town/ town in Fairfield County, Connecticut. Population: 1,770 (1994).

new wave *n.* **1.** CINEMA **FORM OF FRENCH MOVIE-MAKING** a form of movie-making originating in France during the 1950s that emphasized spontaneity, unconventionality, and the individual styles of directors **2.** ARTS **INNOVATIVE ARTS MOVEMENT** any new and innovative movement in the arts **3.** MUSIC **POST-PUNK ROCK MUSIC** rock music made in the late 1970s after the punk rock era

New West·min·ster /nòo wéstminstər/ city in southwestern British Columbia, western Canada, situated on the Fraser River, 12 mi./18 km southeast of Vancouver. Population: 43,585 (1991).

New World *n.* North and South America as considered by Europeans following Columbus's discovery of the Americas (*dated*) ◊ **Old World**

new year *n.* the year following the current year, especially the early part of it ○ *We hoped that things would be better in the new year.*

New Year *n.* the first day or first few days of a calendar year

New Year's Day *n.* January 1, the first day of the year in the Gregorian calendar, widely celebrated as a public holiday

New Year's Eve *n.* December 31, the last day of the year in the Gregorian calendar, or the evening of December 31

New Year's res·o·lu·tion *n.* a decision to do or stop doing something, made or announced at the New Year, which is traditionally considered a time for a fresh start

New York

New York /nòo yáwrk/ **1. New York, New York City** city and major port in southeastern New York State. It is the most populous city in the United States. It is comprised of Manhattan, Bronx, Brooklyn, Queens, and Staten Island boroughs. Population: 7,380,906 (1996). **2.** state in the eastern United States, bordering the Atlantic Ocean, New Jersey, Pennsylvania, Ontario and Quebec in Canada, Vermont, Massachusetts, and Connecticut. Capital: Albany. Population: 18,137,226 (1997). Area: 53,989 sq. mi./139,831 sq. km. —**New York·er** *n.*

New York Eng·lish *n.* a variety of English spoken in New York

WORD KEY: WORLD ENGLISH

New York English is the English language as used in New York City, whose idiom has been influenced by waves of immigration, especially from Central Europe (notably Jewish and Italian immigrants) and from Latin America (notably Puerto Rican immigrants). Local pronunciation is largely "non-rhotic" (that is, "r" is not pronounced in such words as *art, door,* and *worker*). There is a distinctive "o"-sound in such words as *coffee* ("kawfee") and *ought* ("awght"). Although "broad New York" tends to have low prestige in the United States (including among its own speakers), its everyday usage has had a marked influence nationwide and abroad, notably in Yiddish-derived words like *bagel, chutzpah, klutz, maven, s(c)hmaltz,* and *s(c)hlock,* and the humorously or ironically dismissive repeated element *s(c)h-* as in "fancy-s(c)hmancy" (too fancy to be acceptable). New York English is also called New Yorkese.

New Zea·land /noo zéelənd/ country in the southwestern Pacific Ocean, consisting of two large islands, the North Island and the South Island, and numerous smaller islands. Its Maori name is Aotearoa, meaning "Land of the Long White Cloud." Language: English. Currency: New Zealand dollar. Capital: Wellington. Population: 3,681,546 (1996). Area: 104,454 sq. mi./270,534 sq. km. —**New Zea·lan·der** *n.*

New Zea·land Eng·lish *n.* a variety of English spoken in New Zealand

WORD KEY: WORLD ENGLISH

New Zealand English has been used in New Zealand for over 200 years. It has much in common with Australian English but differs from it in coexisting with, and influencing and being influenced by, Maori and other Polynesian languages. Some phoneticians identify three varieties of pronunciation: (1) Cultivated New Zealand, similar to Received Pronunciation in the U.K.; (2) Broad New Zealand, with low prestige; (3) General New Zealand, occupying the social middle ground. New Zealand English is predominantly "non-rhotic" (that is, "r" is not pronounced in words such as *art, door,* and *worker*). Distinctive pronunciations include the vowels in words like *ham* and *pen,* and a short *i* in a phrase like "fish and chips," these being heard by outsiders as "hem," "pin," and "fush and chups," respectively. In addition, final *y* as in *city* and *tidy,* may be lengthened, becoming "citee" and "tidee." There is little distinctiveness in grammar, but New Zealand English vocabulary has three special features, the first being adoptions from Maori—e.g., *Pakeha* (a European, also a common name for caucasian New Zealanders generally), *haere mai* a term of greeting, *hongi* (to press noses, the Maori greeting), *kiwi* (a flightless bird unique to New Zealand and by extension a New Zealander), and *rahui* (a sign warning against trespassing. The second major vocabulary feature involves words shared with and borrowed from Australia, such as *larrikin* for *hooligan, ocker* for *boor, shanghai* for *catapult,* and *truckie* for *truck driver.* Compare ***Australian English.***

NEX *abbr.* Navy exchange

next /nekst/ CORE MEANING: a grammatical word indicating that something is close to something else, e.g. in space or time ○ (adj) *He lives next door to me.* ○ (adj) *When I returned, my next patient was waiting.* ○ (adv) *Which patient do you want to see next?*

1. *adj., adv.* **IMMEDIATELY FOLLOWING** following immediately after the present or previous one ○ (adj) *Our next meeting is on April 2nd.* ○ (adv) *Are you wondering what to do next?* **2.** *adj.* **THE ONE AFTER THIS ONE** the day, month, or year following this one ○ *The case is scheduled for trial next month.* ○ *There is no way of predicting whether this might happen next year or in 300 years.* **3.** *adj.* **ADJOINING** the one that is nearest ○ *My colleague in the next office called.* **4.** *adj.* **CLOSEST TO** closest to in degree ○ *It's 40 times heavier than the next heaviest quark.* [Old English *nēhsta,* literally "most near," from a prehistoric Germanic word meaning "near," which is also the ancestor of English *nigh*] ◇ **next to 1.** adjacent to or beside something or somebody ○ *Come and sit next to me.* **2.** closest to, in comparison with something else ○ *Cleanliness, he said, was next to godliness.* **3.** almost, but not completely (*used with a negative*) ○ *I have spent many days trying to figure out a good alternative, and it's next to impossible.*

next door *adv.* **1. IN NEXT HOUSE OR ROOM** in or into the house or room next to the one somebody is in ○ *Go next door and see if their phone's working.* **2. VERY CLOSE** a very short distance away ■ *adj.* **IMMEDIATELY ADJACENT** situated immediately beside or very close to the one somebody is in or at, or living in the adjoining house or apartment (*hyphenated when used before a noun*)

next friend *n.* somebody who acts for a person who is not legally allowed to act independently, e.g., a child

next of kin *n.* somebody's nearest relative or relatives

nex·us /néksəss/ (*plural* **-us** *or* **-us·es**) *n.* **1. CONNECTION** a connection or link associating two or more people or things **2. CONNECTED GROUP** a group or series of connected individuals or things **3. CENTER** the center or focus of something **4.** BIOL **SPECIALIZED PART OF CELL MEMBRANE** a specialized area of the cellular membrane that helps cells to communicate or adhere [Mid-17thC. Formed from Latin *nex-,* past participle stem of *nectere* "to bind."]

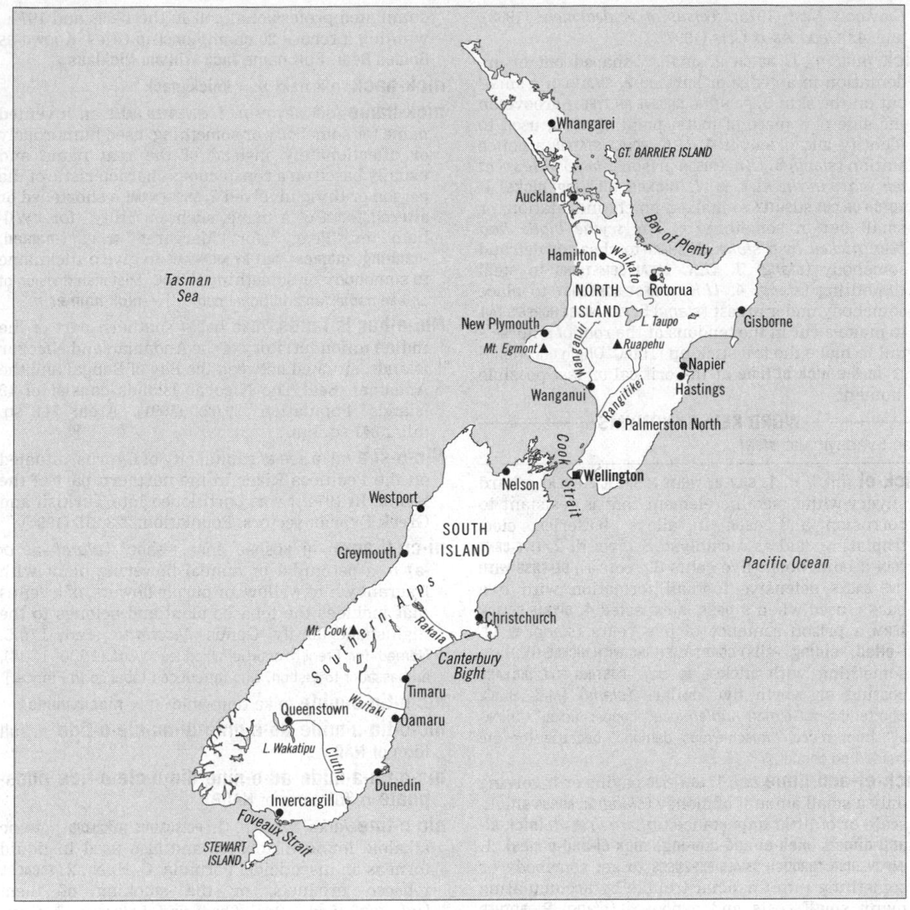

New Zealand

WORD KEY: ORIGIN

The Latin word *nectere*, from which ***nexus*** is derived, is also the source of English *connect*.

Nez Per·cé /nez púrss, ness-, -pur sáy/ (*plural* **Nez Per·cé** *or* **Nez Per·cés**), **Nez Per·ce** /nez púrss, ness-/ (*plural* **Nez Per·ce** *or* **Nez Per·ces**) *n.* **1.** PEOPLES **MEMBER OF NATIVE AMERICAN PEOPLE** a member of a Native American people that originally occupied lands along the Snake River, and whose members now live mainly in western Idaho and northeastern Washington state **2.** LANG **NATIVE AMERICAN LANGUAGE** a Native North American language, spoken in parts of Idaho and Washington, belonging to the Sahaptin-Chinook branch of Penutian languages. Nez Percé is spoken by about 5,000 people. [From French, literally "pierced nose"]

NF *abbr.* **1.** Newfoundland **2. NF, N/F, n/f** BANKING no funds **3.** LANG Norman French

n/f *abbr.* no funds

NFC *abbr.* National Football Conference

NFFE *abbr.* National Federation of Federal Employees

NFL *abbr.* National Football League

Nfld. *abbr.* Newfoundland

NFS *abbr.* **1.** network file service **2.** network file system **3.** not for sale

ng *abbr.* nanogram

NG, N.G., n.g. *abbr.* no good

N.G. *abbr.* National Guard

Ngo Dinh Diem /'ng gō din deém/ (1901–63) South Vietnamese statesman. During his presidency (1955–63), communist insurgence from North Vietnam became frequent and disruptive. He was assassinated in a coup.

ngul·trum /əng go͝oltrəm, əng go͝oltrəm/ *n.* **1. BHUTANESE CURRENCY UNIT** the main unit of currency in Bhutan. See table at **currency 2. COIN OR BILL WORTH A NGULTRUM** a coin or bill worth one ngultrum [Late 20thC. From Tibetan.]

ngwee /əng gwáy, əng gweé/ (*plural* **ngwee**) *n.* **1. MINOR UNIT OF ZAMBIAN CURRENCY** a minor currency unit of Zambia. See table at **currency 2. COIN WORTH A NGWEE** a coin worth one ngwee, 100 of which are worth one kwacha [Mid-20thC. From Bantu.]

NH, N.H. *abbr.* New Hampshire

NHL *abbr.* National Hockey League

Ni *symbol.* nickel

NI *abbr.* Northern Ireland

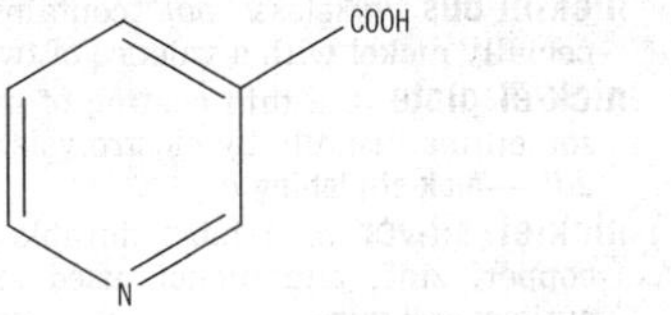

Niacin

ni·a·cin /nī́ əssin/ *n.* a vitamin of the B complex, found in wheat, meat, and dairy products, and used to prevent and treat pellagra. Formula: $C_6H_5NO_2$. [Mid-20thC. Coined from NICOTINE + ACID + -IN.]

ni·a·cin·a·mide /nī ə sínnə mīd/ *n.* a compound of the vitamin B complex that is an amide of niacin and is important in the human diet. Formula: $C_6H_6N_2O$.

Ni·ag·a·ra /nī ággərə/ river in east central North America, in New York State and Ontario, flowing between Lake Erie and Lake Ontario via the Niagara Falls. Length: 34 mi./55 km.

Ni·ag·a·ra Falls /nīgárə fawlz/ **1.** two waterfalls in North America, on the United States-Canada border, on the Niagara River. Height: 161 ft./49 m and 167 ft./51 m. **2.** city in Welland County, southeastern Ontario, Canada, situated on the Niagara River, directly below the falls. Population: 75,399 (1991). **3.** city in New York, on the Niagara

Niagara Falls

Falls, across the Niagara River from Ontario, Canada. Population: 58,357 (1996).

Nia·mey /nyaa máy/ capital city of Niger, situated on the Niger River in the southwestern part of the country. Population: 495,000 (1995).

nib /nib/ *n.* **1. METAL WRITING TIP OF PEN** a shaped detachable metal tip on the end of a pen such as fountain pen, by means of which the ink is transferred to the paper **2. SHARP POINT** a sharp point or tip, especially the sharpened end of a quill pen **3.** BIRDS **BEAK** a bird's beak [Late 16thC. Originally a Scottish variant of Old English *nebb* "beak, bill," from a prehistoric Germanic word meaning "beak."]

nib·ble /níbb'l/ *v.* **(-bled, -bling, -bles) 1.** *vti.* **TAKE SMALL QUICK BITES** to take a series of small quick bites at something, or eat something in a series of small quick bites ○ *She nibbled an apple while she read.* **2.** *vti.* **EAT SOMETHING DAINTILY OR CAUTIOUSLY** to take dainty, cautious, or reluctant little bites of something or eat something in this way taking a very small amount at a time ○ *The mouse had nibbled the cheese.* **3.** *vti.* **BITE PLAYFULLY AND CARESSINGLY** to take gentle playful little bites at part of somebody's body as a form of caress ○ *The lion cubs nibbled at each other playfully.* **4.** *vi.* **REDUCE GRADUALLY** to reduce or wear away something gradually by taking a small amount at a time ○ *These day-to-day expenses nibble away at our money.* **5.** *vi.* **SHOW MILD INTEREST** to show a tentative interest in something ○ *Lower the price a little and the buyers will start to nibble.* ■ *n.* **1. ACT OF NIBBLING** a series of small quick or gentle bites at something **2. TINY AMOUNT OF FOOD** a tiny amount of some type of food (*informal*) **3. EXPRESSION OF MILD INTEREST** an expression of tentative interest ○ *I've been trying to make a sale all day but not a nibble so far.* [Early 16thC. Origin uncertain: perhaps from Low German *nibbeln* "to nibble, gnaw."] —**nib·bler** *n.*

Ni·be·lung /neébə lo͝ong/ *n.* in German mythology, a member of a race of dwarfs who owned a hoard of treasure that was captured by the heroic prince Siegfried [Mid-19thC. From German.]

nib·lick /níbblik/ *n.* a golf club that has a short iron head with a steeply sloping face, used to give extra lift, e.g., when playing out of a sand trap (*dated*) [Mid-19thC. Origin unknown.]

nibs /nibz/ *n.* used as a kind of mock title when referring to an important or self-important person (*informal*) ○ *His nibs will doubtless be expecting the red carpet treatment.* [Early 19thC. Origin unknown.]

Nic. *abbr.* Nicaragua

ni·cad /nī́ kàd/, **ni·cad bat·ter·y** *n.* a dry cell battery with electrodes of nickel and cadmium in an alkaline electrolyte [Mid-20thC. From NICKEL + CADMIUM.]

Nic·a·ra·gua /nìkə raágwə/ republic and largest

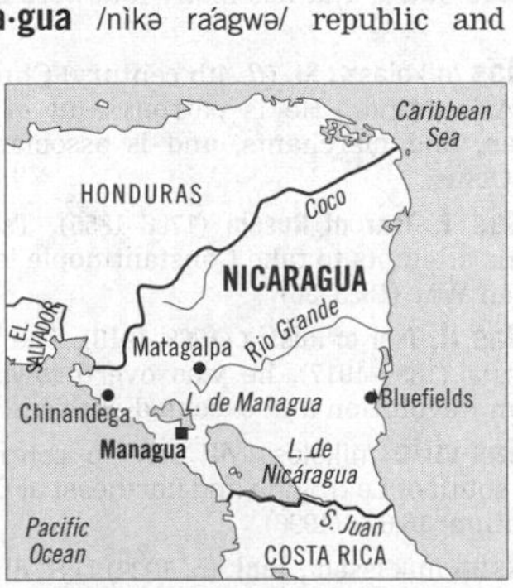

Nicaragua

nation in Central America, situated between the North Pacific Ocean and the Caribbean Sea. Language: Spanish. Currency: córdoba. Capital: Managua. Population: 4,272,000 (1996). Area: 50,893 sq. mi./131,812 sq. km. Official name **Republic of Nicaragua** —**Ni·ca·ra·guan** *n., adj.*

nic·co·lite /níkə lìt/ *n.* a copper-colored mineral that is a source of nickel. Formula: $NiAs$. [Mid-19thC. Formed from modern Latin *niccolum* "nickel."]

nice /nīss/ (**nic·er, nic·est**) *adj.* **1. PLEASANT** pleasant or enjoyable **2. KIND** kind, or showing courtesy, friendliness, or consideration ○ *It was a nice gesture to return the money.* **3. RESPECTABLE** respectable, or of an acceptable social or moral standard ○ *She's made some nice friends at work.* **4. GOOD-LOOKING** good-looking or pleasing to look at ○ *What a nice hat you're wearing!* **5. ACCOMPLISHED** skillful and accomplished ○ *That was a nice try.* **6. SUBTLE** subtle and involving delicacy or fine discrimination ○ *You may be correct technically, but that's a nice distinction you're making.* **7. FASTIDIOUS AND FUSSY** very concerned and careful about choosing, or being seen to do, the right thing ○ *You can't be too nice about your methods if you want to get the job done.* [13thC. Via Old French from, ultimately, Latin *nescius* "ignorant." The meanings "minutely discriminating" and "pleasant" developed by way of "shy," "fastidious," and "refined."] —**nice·ly** *adv.* —**nice·ness** *n.* ◇ **nice and** sufficiently or pleasingly ○ *It's nice and warm by the fire.*

Ni·cene creed /nī seen-, nī seén-/ *n.* a formal statement of Christian beliefs formulated at the first Nicene Council, held in Nicaea in A.D. 325, subsequently altered and expanded, and still in use in most Christian churches

nice-nel·ly /-néllee/ *adj.* **1. PRUDISH** prudish or excessively modest **2. FULL OF EUPHEMISMS** using or including a great many euphemisms (*disapproving*) ■ *n.* **nice-Nel·ly** (*plural* **nice-Nel·lies**) **PRUDE** somebody who is excessively prudish (*disapproving*) [From the name *Nelly*] —**nice-nel·ly·ism** *n.*

ni·ce·ty /nīssətee/ (*plural* **-ties**) *n.* **1. REFINEMENT OR DETAIL** a subtle distinction or point, or a small detail, especially of proper procedure or social etiquette (*often used in the plural*) **2. REFINED FEATURE** a feature that makes something particularly refined and pleasurable (*often used in the plural*) **3. SUBTLETY** a subtle, delicate, or fastidious quality, especially in somebody's feelings or taste **4. PRECISION** the ability to be precise and accurate and make fine distinctions ○ *the nicety of his powers of judgment* ◇ **to a nicety** with great precision or exactness

niche /nich/ *n.* **1. SUITABLE PLACE FOR SOMEBODY** a position or activity that particularly suits somebody's talents and personality or that somebody can make his or her own ○ *She carved out her own niche in the industry.* **2.** COMM **SPECIALIZED MARKET** an area of the market specializing in a particular type of product ○ *designed to undercut the competition in the same niche* **3.** ECOL **PLACE IN NATURE** the role of an organism within its natural environment that determines its relations with other organisms and ensures its survival **4.** ARCHIT **WALL RECESS** a recess in a wall, especially one made to hold a statue **5.** GEOL **RECESS IN ROCK** any recess or hollow, such as in a rock formation ■ *vt.* (**niched, nich·ing, nich·es**) **PUT SOMETHING IN NICHE** to place something in a niche [Early 17thC. Via Old French *nichier* "to build a nest, nestle," from Latin *nidus* "nest" (see NEST).]

Ni·chi·ren /neéch ee ren/ (1222–82) Japanese Buddhist monk. He established a form of Buddhism based on the Lotus Sutra, and has many followers in Japan today.

Nich·o·las /níkələss/, **St.** (*fl.* 4th century) Churchman from Asia Minor. He is patron saint of Russia, children, and merchants, and is associated with Santa Claus.

Nich·o·las I, Tsar of Russia (1796–1855). Tsar from 1825, his attempts to take Constantinople led to the Crimean War (1853–56).

Nich·o·las II, Tsar of Russia (1868–1918). The last tsar of Russia (1894–1917), he was overthrown in the Russian Revolution and executed with his family.

Nich·o·las·ville /níkələss vìl/ city in central Kentucky, south of Lexington and northeast of Danville. Population: 16,603 (1996).

Nich·o·lson /ník'lssən/, **Jack** (*b.* 1937) U.S. film actor. He won Academy Awards for *One Flew Over the Cuckoo's Nest* (1975), *Terms of Endearment* (1983), and *As Good As It Gets* (1997).

nick /nik/ *n.* **1. NOTCH** a small V-shaped cut or indentation in an edge or surface **2. SMALL CUT** a small cut on the skin **3.** PRINTING **GROOVE ON TYPE** a groove on the side of a piece of metal printing type, used to identify and orient it **4.** *U.K.* **POLICE STATION** a police station (*slang*) **5.** *U.K.* **PRISON** prison (*slang*) ○ *He spent ten years in the nick.* ■ *vt.* (**nicked, nick·ing, nicks**) **1. NOTCH OR CUT SLIGHTLY** to make a notch, indentation, or small cut in something ○ *The scythe blade had been nicked by a stone.* **2. CHEAT** to cheat or defraud somebody (*slang*) **3.** *U.K.* **STEAL SOMETHING** to steal something (*slang*) **4.** *U.K.* **ARREST SOMEBODY** to place somebody under arrest (*slang*) **5.** VET **INCISE HORSE'S TAIL** to make a cut in the tendons at the root of a horse's tail to make the tail stick up [15thC. Origin uncertain.] ◇ **in the nick of time** at the critical or last possible moment

WORD KEY: SYNONYMS

See Synonyms at ***steal***.

nick·el /ník'l/ *n.* **1. SILVERY WHITE METALLIC ELEMENT** a hard silvery-white metallic element that is resistant to corrosion and used in alloys, batteries, electroplating, and as a catalyst. Symbol **Ni** **2. FIVE-CENT COIN** a coin worth five cents **3.** FOOTBALL **DEFENSE WITH FIVE BACKS** defensive football formation with five backs, used when a pass is expected **4. 5-YEAR PRISON TERM** a prison sentence of five years (*slang*) ■ *vt.* (**-elled, -el·ling, -ells**) **COAT SOMETHING WITH NICKEL** to plate something with nickel ■ *adj.* **COSTING FIVE DOLLARS** costing or worth five dollars (*slang*) [Mid-18thC. Shortening of German *Kupfernickel* "copper nickel": "nickel" from *nickel* "mischievous demon," because the ore yielded no copper.]

nick·el-and-dime *adj.* **1. LOW-PAID** paying or involving only a small amount of money (*slang*) **2. MINOR** small-scale or of little importance (*informal*) ■ *vt.* (**nick·el-and-dimed, nick·el-and-dim·ing, nick·el-and-dimes**) **1. IMPOVERISH THROUGH SMALL EXPENSES** to get somebody or something into financial trouble by accumulating many small costs and expenses (*slang*) **2. BOTHER SOMEBODY IN MANY SMALL WAYS** to hinder or harass somebody with trivialities and insignificant matters

nick·el-cad·mi·um bat·ter·y *n.* = **nicad battery**

nick·el·ic /ni kéllik, níkəlik/ *adj.* containing nickel, especially nickel with a valence of three

nick·el·if·er·ous /nìkə líffərəss/ *adj.* containing or yielding nickel

nick·el·o·de·on /nìkə lṓdee ən/ *n.* **1. EARLY JUKEBOX** an early variety of coin-operated jukebox **2. FIVE-CENT MOVIE THEATER** an early 20th-century movie theater, charging five cents for admission **3. COIN-OPERATED PLAYER PIANO** an early variety of player piano operated by inserting coins [Early 20thC. From NICKEL + shortening of MELODEON.]

nick·el·ous /níkələss/ *adj.* containing nickel, especially nickel with a valence of two

nick·el plate *n.* a thin coating of nickel applied to something, usually by electrolysis —**nick·el-plat·ed** *adj.* —**nick·el-plat·ing** *n.*

nick·el sil·ver *n.* a hard durable white alloy of copper, zinc, and nickel, used, e.g., in making cutlery and wire

nick·er[1] /níkər/ (**-ered, -er·ing, -ers**) *vi.* to make a soft neighing sound ○ *The pony nickered and shook its head.* [Late 16thC. An imitation of the sound.] —**nick·er** *n.*

nick·er[2] /níkər/ (*plural* **-er**) *n. U.K.* a pound sterling (*slang*) [Early 20thC. Origin unknown.]

Nick·laus /ník lowss/, **Jack** (*b.* 1940) U.S. golfer. He dominated professional golf in the 1960s and 1970s, winning a record 20 championship titles. Known as **Golden Bear**. Full name **Jack William Nicklaus**

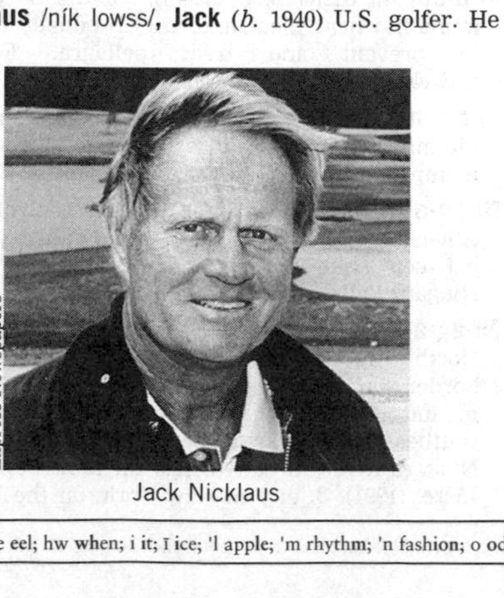

Jack Nicklaus

nick-nack /ník nak/ *n.* = **knickknack**

nick·name /ník nàym/ *n.* **1. INVENTED NAME** an invented name for somebody or something, used humorously or affectionately instead of the real name and usually based on a conspicuous characteristic of the person or thing involved **2. SHORT NAME** a shortened or altered form of a name, such as "Billy" for "William" or "Peggy" for "Margaret" ■ *vt.* (**-named, -nam·ing, -names**) **CALL BY NICKNAME** to give a nickname to somebody or something [15thC. Mistaken division of *an eke name* "an additional name."] —**nick·nam·er** *n.*

Nic·o·bar Is·lands /níkə baàr-/ southern part of the Indian union territory of the Andaman and Nicobar Islands, situated between the Bay of Bengal and the Andaman Sea. The Nicobar Islands consist of 19 islands. Population: 39,022 (1991). Area: 711 sq. mi./1,841 sq. km.

Nic·o·si·a /nìkə seé ə/ capital city of Cyprus, situated on the Pedhieos River in the northern part of the island. In 1974 it was partitioned into Turkish and Greek Cypriot sectors. Population: 228,215 (1994).

ni·co·ti·an·a /ni kṓshee ánnə, -aánə/ (*plural* **-as** *or* **-a**) *n.* a perennial or annual flowering plant with fragrant white, yellow, or purple flowers, of a genus that includes the tobacco plant and belongs to the nightshade family. Genus: *Nicotiana.* [Early 17thC. Named for French courtier Jacques *Nicot* (1530–1604), ambassador to Lisbon, who introduced tobacco to France.]

nic·o·tin·a·mide /nìkə tínnə mīd/ *n.* = **niacinamide**

nic·o·tin·a·mide ad·e·nine di·nu·cle·o·tide *n.* full form of **NAD**

nic·o·tin·a·mide ad·e·nine din·u·cle·o·tide phos·phate *n.* full form of **NADP**

nic·o·tine /níkə teén/ *n.* **1. POISONOUS ALKALOID** a toxic alkaloid found in tobacco and also used in liquid form as an insecticide. Formula: $C_{10}H_{14}N_2$. **2. TOBACCO** tobacco products, or the smoking of them (*informal*) [Early 19thC. Shortening of NICOTIANA + chemical suffix -INE.] —**nic·o·tin·ic** *adj.*

nic·o·tine gum *n.* chewing gum containing nicotine, used as a substitute for tobacco by people who are trying to give up smoking

nic·o·tine patch *n.* a small patch that when placed on the skin releases nicotine directly into the bloodstream, used by people who are trying to give up smoking

nic·o·tin·ic ac·id *n.* = **niacin**

nic·o·tin·ism /níkə tee nìzzəm/ *n.* poisoning caused by an excessive intake of nicotine through smoking

nic·ti·tate /níkti tàyt/ (**-tat·ed, -tat·ing, -tates**), **nic·tate** /ník tàyt/ (**-tat·ed, -tat·ing, -tates**) *vti.* to blink or wink (*technical*) [Early 19thC. Ultimately from medieval Latin *nictitat-*, past participle stem of *nictitare*, literally "to wink repeatedly," from Latin *nictare* "to wink."] —**nic·ta·tion** /nik táysh'n/ *n.* —**nic·ti·ta·tion** /nik táysh'n/ *n.*

nic·ti·tat·ing mem·brane *n.* a thin transparent layer of skin underneath the eyelid that can cover the eye surface of birds, reptiles, and some mammals to moisten and protect it

nide /nīd/ *n. U.K.* a brood of pheasants or a pheasant's nest [Late 17thC. Via French *nid*, from Latin *nidus* "nest."]

nidi plural of **nidus**

ni·dic·o·lous /nī díkələss/ *adj.* used to describe young birds that remain in the nest for some time after hatching [Early 20thC. Literally "frequenting a nest," formed from Latin *nidus* "nest."]

nid·i·fi·cate /nìddífə kayt, nī díffə kayt/ *vi.* = **nidify** [Early 19thC. From the Latin stem *nidificat-*, past participle stem of *nidificare* (see NIDIFY).]

ni·dif·u·gous /nī díffyəgəss/ *adj.* used to describe young birds that leave the nest a short time after hatching [Early 20thC. Formed from Latin *nidus* "nest" (see NEST) + *fugere* "to flee."]

nid·i·fy /níddə fī/ (**-fied, -fy·ing, -fies**), **nid·i·fi·cate** /níddəfi kàyt/ (**-cat·ed, -cat·ing, -cates**) *vi.* to build a nest [Mid-17thC. From Latin *nidificare* "to build a nest," from *nidus* "nest" (see NEST).] —**nid·i·fi·ca·tion** /nìddəfi káysh'n/ *n.*

ni·dus /nīdəss/ (*plural* **-dus·es** *or* **-di** /nī dī/) *n.* **1.** ZOOL **SPIDER OR INSECT NEST** a nest in which spiders or insects deposit eggs **2.** MED **FOCUS OF INFECTION** a site in the body at which an infection develops **3.** BOT **SPORE-DEVELOPING**

PLANT PART a place in a plant where its spores develop [Early 18thC. From Latin, "nest" (see NEST).]

niece /neess/ *n.* a daughter of somebody's brother, brother-in-law, sister, or sister-in-law [13thC. Via Old French, from Latin *neptis* "granddaughter, niece." Ultimately from an Indo-European base that is also the ancestor of English *nephew* and *nepotism*.]

ni·el·lo /nee éllō/ *n.* (*plural* **-li** /nee éllee/ *or* **-los**) **1. BLACK ALLOY USED AS INLAY** a deep black alloy of sulfur and silver, lead, or copper, used to fill lines inlaid as decoration on a metal surface **2. USE OF NIELLO** the process of using niello to decorate a metal surface **3. SOMETHING DECORATED WITH NIELLO** something decorated with niello as an inlay ■ *vt.* (**-loed, -lo·ing, -los**) **DECORATE SOMETHING WITH NIELLO** to decorate something using niello as an inlay [Early 19thC. Via Italian from Latin *nigellus* "blackish," diminutive of *niger* "black."] —**ni·el·list** *n.*

niels·bohr·i·um /neelz báwree əm/ *n.* an artificially produced radioactive chemical element with the atomic number 105 [Late 20thC. Named in honor of *Niels Bohr* (1885–1962), Danish physicist.]

Nie·mey·er /neé mī ər/, **Oscar** (*b.* 1907) Brazilian architect. He is best known for designing the major buildings in Brasília (1956–64), the new capital of Brazil. Full name **Oscar Niemeyer Soares Filho**

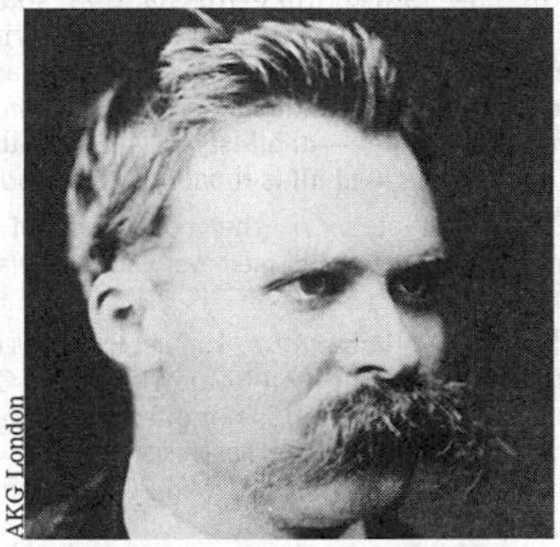

Friedrich Wilhelm Nietzsche

Nie·tzsche /neéchə, neéchee/, **Friedrich Wilhelm** (1844–1900) German philosopher. Author of *Thus Spake Zarathustra* (1883–85) and one of the most influential thinkers of the 19th century, he founded his philosophy on the will-to-power and rejected religion. —**Ni·et·zschean** *n.*, *adj.* —**Ni·et·zschean·ism** *n.*

ni·fed·i·pine /nə féddə peen, nī féddəpin/ *n.* a drug that stops the heart muscles from taking up calcium and is used to treat high blood pressure and angina pectoris. Formula: $C_{17}H_{18}N_2O_6$. [Late 20thC. Coined from NITRO- + *fe* (shortening and alteration of PHENYL) + DI- "twice" + *pine* (contraction of PYRIDINE).]

nif·ty /níftee/ *adj.* (**-ti·er, -ti·est**) (*informal*) **1. STYLISH AND GOOD-LOOKING** fashionable and good-looking **2. AGILE** good, quick, and clever at doing something or using something **3. VERY GOOD** very good or effective ■ *n.* (*plural* **-ties**) **SOMETHING CLEVER** something clever, neat, or excellent, especially a witticism (*informal*) [Mid-19thC. Origin unknown.] —**nif·ti·ly** *adv.* —**nif·ti·ness** *n.*

Nig. *abbr.* **1.** Nigeria **2.** Nigerian

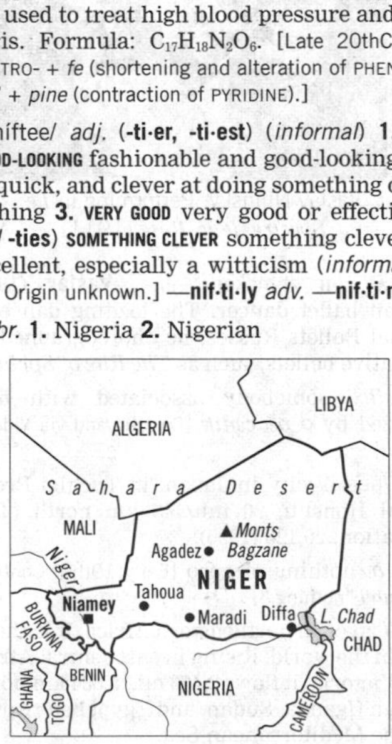

Niger

Ni·ger[1] /níjər/ republic in northwestern Africa, north of Nigeria and south of Libya. Language: French. Currency: CFA franc. Capital: Niamey. Population: 9,465,000 (1996). Area: 489,191 sq. mi./1,267,000 sq. km. Official name **Republic of Niger**

Ni·ger[2] /níjər/ river in northern West Africa. The third longest river in Africa, it rises in southern Guinea, and flows northward through Mali, then southwest into the Gulf of Guinea, through Niger and Nigeria. Length: 2,600 mi./4,180 km.

Ni·ger-Con·go *n.* a family of over one thousand languages spoken in central and southern parts of Africa, the major branches of which are Adamawa-Eastern, Benue-Congo, Gur, Kwa, Mande, and West Atlantic. Well over 200 million people speak one of the Niger-Congo languages. —**Ni·ger-Con·go** *adj.*

Ni·ge·ri·a /nī jeéree ə/ republic in western Africa, on the Gulf of Guinea, south of Niger. Language: English. Currency: kobo. Capital: Abuja. Population: 103,912,000 (1996). Area: 356,669 sq. mi./923,773 sq. km. Official name **Federal Republic of Nigeria** —**Ni·ge·ri·an** *n.*, *adj.*

Ni·ger·i·an Eng·lish *n.* a variety of English spoken in Nigeria

WORD KEY: WORLD ENGLISH

Nigerian English is the English language as used in the region of the Niger, West Africa, for purposes of trade since at least the 18th century, at missions since the 19th century, and increasingly in education, administration, the media, and the 20th-century workplace, especially since the formation by the British of a unified Nigeria in 1914. The existence of a single Nigerian English continues to be debated and disputed within the country, in which there is a spectrum of usage from West African Pidgin English through varieties influenced by local languages such as Hausa, Igbo, and Yoruba, to a standardizing general usage similar to other English-speaking West African countries. All varieties are "non-rhotic" (that is, "r" is not pronounced in such words as *art, door,* and *worker*). There is a tendency toward full vowels in all syllables (e.g., *7* pronounced *seh-ven,* not *sevn*). There is often no distinction between words like *chip* and *cheap* and ones like *caught, cot,* and *court.* In grammar, there is a tendency toward countability in nouns (as in *I gave them some advices*) and the reflexive pronoun *themselves* is often used instead of *one another* (as in *That couple really love themselves*). Distinctive vocabulary includes borrowings and loan translations from local languages, such as *danshiki* from *Hausa* ("a gown worn by men") and *to throw water* ("to offer a bribe"). See ***African English.***

nig·gard /níggərd/ *n.* somebody who is stingy or miserly [14thC. Alteration of *nigon,* of uncertain origin: possibly formed from *nig* "stingy," from Scandinavian.]

nig·gard·ly /níggərdlee/ *adj.* (**-li·er, -li·est**) **1. NOT GENEROUS** very reluctant to give or spend anything **2. SMALL OR INADEQUATE** very small or inadequate in quantity ■ *adv.* **IN A STINGY WAY** in a miserly or stingy way —**nig·gard·li·ness** *n.*

WORD KEY: USAGE

Although the etymology of ***niggardly*** and ***niggard*** remains subject to debate, these words probably have a Scandinavian origin not associated historically with the origin of the offensive word *Negro* and its related offensive racist slurs. These are derived ultimately from Latin. ***Niggardly,*** then, is in no way a racial slur. However, the fact that the word sounds as if it might be one is reason to consider context very carefully before using it.

nig·ger /níggər/ *n.* (*taboo*) **1. TABOO OFFENSIVE TERM** a highly offensive taboo term for a Black person **2. TABOO OFFENSIVE TERM** a highly offensive taboo term for a dark-skinned person [Late 17thC. Via Spanish *negro* from Latin *niger* "black."]

WORD KEY: USAGE

Racism trap: This term is arguably the single most offensive racist slur in the English language. The fact that African Americans and other people of color sometimes use this word in reference to themselves does not excuse its present-day use by members of other ethnic groups. Those who persist in using it should remember that their use of the word reflects directly upon them, the users. The terms of choice are *African American, Black* or *Black person,* and *person of color.*

nig·gle /nígg'l/ *v.* (**-gled, -gling, -gles**) **1.** *vi.* **CRITICIZE IN PETTY WAY** to criticize or find fault continually, especially about small matters **2.** *vi.* **BE PREOCCUPIED WITH DETAILS** to be preoccupied with petty details **3.** *vt.* **WORRY SOMEBODY** to be a source of worry and irritation to somebody, especially in a small way over a long period of time ■ *n.* *U.K., Can* **1. PETTY CRITICISM** a petty or carping criticism ○ *Once we have a broad agreement, we can sort out these niggles.* **2. NAGGING WORRY** a small but continuing source of annoyance or worry [Early 17thC. Origin uncertain: possibly from Scandinavian.] —**nig·gler** *n.*

nig·gling /níggling/ *adj.* **1. TOO PREOCCUPIED WITH DETAIL** petty or too preoccupied with details **2. IRRITATING** irritating, painful, or worrying, especially in a small but persistent way —**nig·gling** *n.* —**nig·gling·ly** *adv.*

nigh /nī/ *adv., adj.* **NEAR** near in place or time ○ (adv) *Daybreak drew nigh.* ○ (adj) *Morning was nigh.* ■ *adv.* **ALMOST** nearly ○ *We talked for nigh on to two hours.* [Old English *nēah,* from a prehistoric Germanic word that is also the ancestor of English *near* and *next*]

night /nīt/ *n.* **1. DAILY PERIOD OF DARKNESS** the period of darkness occurring each day in most parts of the world, or the entire period between sunset and sunrise **2. TIME BETWEEN BEDTIME AND WAKING** the time between somebody's going to sleep in the evening and waking the next morning **3. PERIOD OF EVENING ACTIVITIES** the period between sunset and bedtime, especially when spent in entertainment or some other activity ○ *We had a great night at her birthday party.* **4. night, Night EVENING DEVOTED TO SPECIAL ACTIVITY** any period after sunset devoted to a special activity, function, or observance ○ *Tomorrow night is Family Night at the ballpark.* **5. NIGHTFALL** the period of time just after the sun goes down, when it gets dark **6. DARK OR DARKENED STATE** a dark or darkened state, or an absence of light, consciousness, or enlightenment (*literary*) **7. SAD OR BAD PERIOD** a period marked by grief, gloom, ignorance, or obscurity ○ *Europe slipped into the long night of the Dark Ages.* ■ *adj.* **1. OCCURRING AT NIGHT** occurring, appearing, or visible at night ○ *night terrors* **2. USED AT NIGHT** used chiefly at night ○ *Use the night entrance.* **3. WORKING AT NIGHT** working at night in a job also done during the day ○ *the night porter* **4. ACTIVE AT NIGHT** awake or active at night ○ *night feeders* ■ *interj.* **GOODNIGHT** goodnight (*informal*) [Old English *niht.* Ultimately from an Indo-European word that is also the ancestor of English *nocturnal* and *equinox*.] ◇ **night and day** the entire time

night blind·ness *n.* an inability to see clearly in dim light while having normal vision in clear light. Technical name **nyctalopia** —**night-blind** *adj.*

night-bloom·ing ce·re·us *n.* a cactus whose large fragrant flowers open at night. Genera: *Hylocereus, Peniocereus, Nyctocereus, Selenicereus.*

night·cap /nít kàp/ *n.* **1.** BEVERAGES **DRINK BEFORE SLEEP** a drink, often alcoholic, taken before going to bed **2.** CLOTHES **CAP USED AS NIGHTWEAR** a soft cap worn in bed to keep the head warm, in use mainly until the late 19th century **3.** SPORTS **LAST EVENT** the last event of a day of sports, especially the second game of a baseball double-header

night·clothes /nít klōthz, -klōz/ *npl.* any clothes designed to be worn in bed

night·club /nít klùb/ *n.* a place of entertainment open late at night, offering music, dancing, and drinks, and sometimes serving food and providing a floor show

night·club·bing /nít klùbbing/ *n.* = **clubbing** *n.* 1

night court *n.* a court that sits at night, especially for routine matters like disposition of charges and granting of bail

night crawl·er *n.* a large earthworm found on the surface of the ground at night, often used as bait in fishing

WORD KEY: REGIONAL NOTE

Night crawler is a northern term that has spread across the country to become common everywhere except in the lower southern states.

night de·pos·i·to·ry *n.* a safe in the wall of a bank that can be opened from the outside to allow people to deposit money at times when the bank is closed

night·dress /nít drèss/ *n.* **1.** = **nightgown 2.** = **sleepwear**

night·fall /nít fàwl/ *n.* the time of evening at which it becomes dark and night begins ○ *Be home by nightfall.*

night fight·er *n.* a fighter aircraft designed to fly at night

night·glow /nít glò/ *n.* a dim light from the upper atmosphere seen at night

night·gown /nít gòwn/ *n.* a loose dress of light material worn in bed by women and girls

night·hawk /nít hàwk/ *n.* **1.** **INSECT-FEEDING NIGHTJAR** a North American nightjar, related to the whippoorwill, that feeds on flying insects after dark and has long pointed wings and black, white, and buff plumage. Genus: *Chordeiles.* **2.** = **night owl** (*informal*)

night her·on *n.* a stocky heron with short legs and a thick bill that is active at night or twilight. Genus: *Nycticorax.*

night·ie /nítee/, **night·y** (*plural* **-ies**) *n.* a nightgown (*informal*) [Late 19thC. Shortening and alteration.]

Nightingale

night·in·gale /nít'n gàyl, níting-/ *n.* **1.** **NIGHT-SINGING SONGBIRD OF THRUSH FAMILY** a migratory songbird of the thrush family with brownish plumage. The male is known for its melodious song, especially noticeable at night during the breeding season. Latin name: *Luscinia megarhynchos.* **2.** **WOMAN SINGER** a woman who sings sweetly (*dated*) [13thC. Alteration of Old English *nihtegala*, from a prehistoric Germanic compound meaning "night-singer," from the ancestors of English *night* and *yell*.]

WORD KEY: CULTURAL NOTE

Ode to a Nightingale, a poem (1819) by English writer John Keats. The poet recounts how on hearing the joyful song of the nightingale he is filled with an intense joy that provides an escape from his woes. But, as he considers the fact that the bird's song has been an inspiration throughout history, the sound fades and he is suddenly returned to reality.

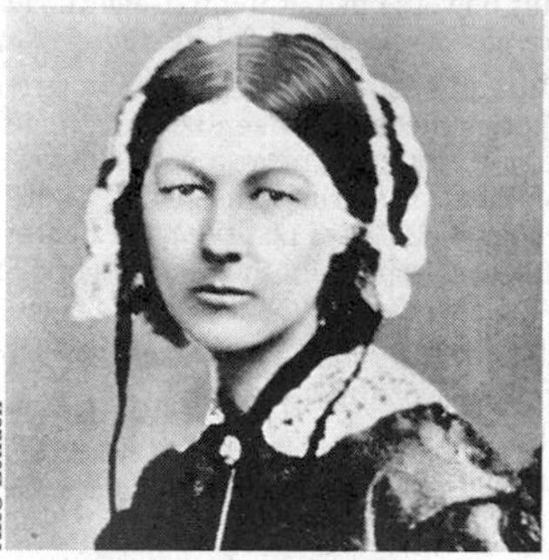

AKG London

Florence Nightingale

Night·in·gale /níting gàyl/, **Florence** (1820–1910) British nurse. She worked in the Crimean War, becoming known as "The Lady with the Lamp." Later she founded the Nightingale School of Nurses at St. Thomas's Hospital, London.

night·jar /nít jaar/ *n.* a bird with a short bill, large gaping mouth, and dark plumage that is active at night and twilight and feeds on insects caught in flight. Family: Caprimulgidae. [*Jar* from JAR with the sense "quivering sound"]

night jas·mine *n.* **1.** **ASIAN SHRUB** an Asian shrub with small fragrant orange-and-white flowers. Latin name: *Nyctanthes arbortristis.* **2.** **WEST INDIAN SHRUB** a West Indian shrub with small, greenish-white flowers that release fragrance at night. Latin name: *Cestrum nocturnum.*

night latch *n.* a door lock operated from inside by a knob and from outside by a key

night·life /nít lìf/ *n.* the entertainment or social life that goes on in a place in the evenings ○ *Let's go out and check out the local nightlife.*

night·light /nít lìt/ *n.* a small lamp or candle lit to give a dim light during the night, especially in a child's bedroom

night liz·ard *n.* any lizard of the southwest United States, Mexico, and Central America, typically found in arid regions and active only at night. Family: Xantusiidae.

night·long /nít làwng/ *adj.* lasting or occurring throughout the entire night —**night·long** *adv.*

night·ly /nítlee/ *adj.* **1.** **HAPPENING EVERY NIGHT** taking place every night **2.** **OCCURRING AT NIGHT** typically occurring at night ■ *adv.* **EVERY NIGHT** on or during each and every night ○ *The band is playing nightly this week.*

night·mare /nít m-r/ *n.* **1.** **BAD DREAM** a frightening or upsetting dream **2.** **TRAUMATIC EXPERIENCE** a traumatic, very upsetting, or extremely difficult and troublesome experience or situation **3.** **DREADED EVENT** a situation or event that somebody particularly fears **4.** PARANORMAL **EVIL SPIRIT** a malign spirit formerly believed to suffocate or haunt people during sleep ■ *adj.* **EXTREMELY FRIGHTENING OR DIFFICULT** extremely frightening, upsetting, or difficult to deal with [13thC. Literally "night goblin"; *mare* from Old English, from prehistoric Germanic.] —**night·mar·ish** *adj.* —**night·mar·ish·ly** *adv.*

night owl *n.* somebody who stays up late at night, especially to work or socialize (*informal*)

night rav·en *n.* any bird that cries at night (*literary*)

night·rid·er /nít rìdər/ *n.* a member of a group of masked horsemen who at night terrorized or intimidated African Americans and their sympathizers in the southern United States in the period after the Civil War

nights /níts/ *adv.* during the night or every night ○ *They work nights.*

night safe *n. U.K.* = **night depository**

night school *n.* a school or college that holds classes in the evening, especially for people who are at work during the day

night·scope /nít skòp/ *n.* an optical device, e.g., using infrared radiation, that gives better vision in the dark

night·shade /nít shàyd/ *n.* a plant with round stems, flowers that have five petals, a strong smell, and watery sap, many of which are poisonous, including deadly and woody nightshade, but some of which are not such as tobacco, pepper, tomato, potato, and eggplant. Family: Solanaceae. [Said to be so called with reference to its poisonous properties]

night shift *n.* **1.** **NIGHTTIME WORK PERIOD** a set period of work during the night ○ *The manager asked if anyone wanted to work a night shift.* **2.** **PEOPLE WORKING AT NIGHT** a group of people who work during a set period at night ○ *The night shift finishes up at seven in the morning.*

night·shirt /nít shùrt/ *n.* a long loose shirtlike garment worn in bed by men

night·side /nít sìd/ *n.* the side of a planet or moon that is not lit by the sun

night sight *n.* an infrared sight on a rifle used for taking aim in darkness

night soil *n.* human excrement collected at night from toilets or cesspools, especially for use as fertilizer

night·spot /nít spot/ *n.* = **nightclub**

night·stand /nít stand/ *n.* = **night table**

night·stick /nít stik/ *n.* a club carried by a police officer [*Night* because the club was traditionally carried especially at night]

night ta·ble *n.* a bedside table or stand. Also called **night stand**

night ter·ror *n.* a sudden awakening from sleep in a condition of extreme fear that is not associated with a dream or nightmare

night·time /nít tìm/ *n.* the period of each day when it is dark, or the time between sunset and sunrise

night vi·sion *n.* somebody's ability to see in the dark ○ *They say eating carrots improves your night vision.*

night watch *n.* **1.** **GUARD KEPT AT NIGHT** a guard or watch kept during the night ○ *I'm on night watch this week.* **2.** = **night watchman** *n.*

night watch·man *n.* somebody who keeps watch over or guards a building or a place such as a building site or factory at night

night·wear /nít wair/ *n.* = **sleepwear**

night·y *n.* = **nightie**

ni·gres·cence /nì gréss'nss/ *n.* the process of becoming black or dark (*formal*) [Mid-19thC. Formed from Latin *nigrescent-*, present participle stem of *nigrescere* "to grow black," from *niger* "black."] —**ni·gres·cent** *adj.* —**ni·gres·cent·ly** *adv.*

ni·gro·sine /níggrə seen, níggrəssin/, **ni·gro·sin** /níggrəssin/ *n.* a black aniline pigment or dye used in making ink and polish and in dyeing textiles [Late 19thC. Coined from Latin *niger* "black" (see NEGRO) + -OSE + -INE.]

NIH[1] *abbr.* National Institutes of Health

NIH[2] *adj., abbr.* not invented here (*informal*) ○ *They would have accepted the other department's suggestion if it hadn't been for the NIH factor.*

ni·hil·ism /nì ə lìzzəm, nee ə lìzzəm, níhi lìzzəm/ *n.* **1.** **TOTAL REJECTION OF SOCIAL MORES** the general rejection of established social conventions and beliefs, especially of morality and religion **2.** **BELIEF THAT NOTHING IS WORTHWHILE** a belief that life is pointless and human values are worthless **3.** **DISBELIEF IN OBJECTIVE TRUTH** the belief that there is no objective basis for truth **4.** **BELIEF IN DESTRUCTION OF AUTHORITY** the belief that all established authority is corrupt and must be destroyed in order to rebuild a just society **5.** **ni·hil·ism, Ni·hil·ism** **RUSSIAN POLITICAL MOVEMENT** a political movement in late 19th-century Russia that sought to bring about a just new society by destroying the existing one through acts of terrorism and assassination [Early 19thC. From German *Nihilismus*, from Latin *nihil* "nothing."] —**ni·hil·ist** *n.* —**ni·hil·is·tic** /nì ə lístik, nee ə-/ *adj.* —**ni·hil·is·ti·cal·ly** /-kəlee/ *adv.*

ni·hil·i·ty /nì híllətee/ *n.* the condition of being nothing [Late 17thC. From medieval Latin *nihilitas*, from Latin *nihil* "nothing."]

ni·hil ob·stat /nì hil ób stàt/ *n.* **1.** CHR **LACK OF OBJECTION TO PUBLICATION** a statement by a Roman Catholic Church official that a publication is not offensive to religion or morals **2.** **STATEMENT OF NONOPPOSITION** any offical statement of nonopposition [Mid-20thC. From Latin, literally "nothing hinders."]

Ni·i·ga·ta /nyee ə gaatə/ city and port in Japan, on northern Honshu. It is the capital city of Niigata Prefecture. Population: 486,097 (1990).

AKG London

Vaslav Nijinsky: Performing in *Le Spectre de la Rose* (1911)

Ni·jin·sky /ni zhínskee, -jín-/, **Vaslav** (1890–1950) Russian ballet dancer. The leading dancer of the original Ballets Russes, he choreographed several innovative ballets, such as *The Rite of Spring* (1913).

-nik *suffix.* somebody associated with or characterized by ○ *peacenik* [Directly and via Yiddish from Russian]

Nik·ko /neekō/ city in Japan, in Tochigi Prefecture, central Honshu, 90 mi./145 km north of Tokyo. Population: 20,128 (1990).

nil /nil/ *n.* nothing or zero [Early 19thC. Contraction of Latin *nihil* "nothing."]

Nile /nīl/ river in northeastern Africa. It is the longest river in the world. Rising in east central Africa near Lake Victoria, it flows 3,470 mi./5,584 km northward through Uganda, Sudan, and Egypt before emptying into the Mediterranean Sea.

Nile blue *adj.* of a pale greenish blue color —**Nile blue** *n.*

Nile green *adj.* of a yellowish green color —**Nile green** *n.*

Niles /nīlz/ city in northeastern Illinois, east of Park Ridge. It is a northwestern suburb of Chicago. Population: 29,081 (1996).

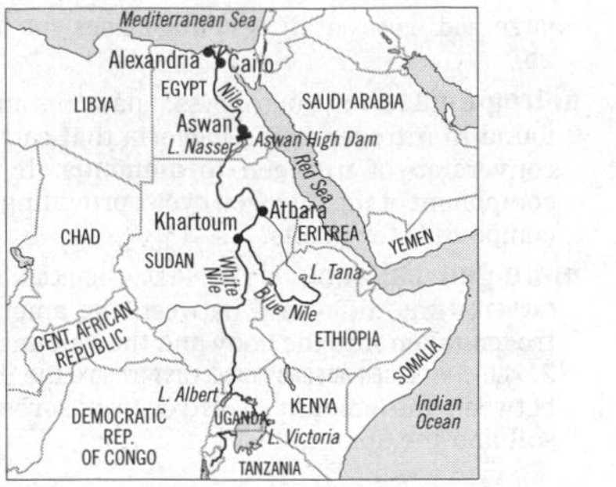

Nile

AKG London
Anaïs Nin

nil·gai /níl gī/ (*plural* **-gai** *or* **-gais**), **nil·gau** /níl gaw/ (*plural* **-gau** *or* **-gaus**), **nil·ghau** (*plural* **-ghau** *or* **-ghaus**) *n.* a large antelope of India, the male of which is bluish gray and horned, the female brown and hornless. Latin name: *Boselaphus tragocamelus.* [Late 18thC. From Hindi *nīlgāe*, from Sanskrit *nīla* "blue" + *-gāvī* "cow."]

Ni·lo-Sa·har·an /nílo sə hárrən, -sə haárrən/ *n.* a family of around 100 languages spoken in some central parts of Africa, the major branches of which are Chari-Nile, Nilotic, and Saharan. About 15 million people speak one of the Nilo-Saharan languages. —**Ni·lo-Sa·har·an** *adj.*

Ni·lot·ic /nī lóttik/ *adj.* **1.** RELATING TO THE NILE relating to, involving, or living beside the Nile River **2.** OF NILOTIC PEOPLE OR LANGUAGE relating to a Nilotic people or language ■ *n.* NILE VALLEY LANGUAGE GROUP a group of languages spoken in parts of the Nile valley, mainly in Uganda and Sudan and forming a branch of the Nilo-Saharan family of languages. About three million people speak a Nilotic language. [Mid-17thC. Formed from Greek *Neilos* "Nile."]

nim /nim/ *n.* a game in which players remove small, differently arranged items from piles, the winner being the player who takes, or sometimes does not take, the final item [Early 20thC. Origin uncertain, perhaps from German *nimm*, imperative form of *nehmen* "to take."]

nim·ble /nímb'l/ (**-bler, -blest**) *adj.* **1.** FAST AND AGILE agile, fast, and light in movement **2.** QUICK-THINKING able to think quickly and cleverly [Alteration (modeled on BRAMBLE and THIMBLE) of Old English *næmel* and *numol* "quick at grasping," from *niman* "to take"] —**nim·ble·ness** *n.* —**nim·bly** *adv.*

nim·bo·stra·tus /nìmbō stráytəss, nìmbō stráttəss/ (*plural* **-ti** /-tī/) *n.* a low dark layer of rain-bearing cloud covering all of the sky. ◊ **stratus** [Late 19thC. See NIMBUS.]

nim·bus /nímbəss/ (*plural* **-bus·es** *or* **-bi** /-bī/) *n.* **1.** METEOROL DARK RAIN-BEARING CLOUD a dense, dark rain-bearing cloud **2.** RELIG CLOUD OF LIGHT AROUND DEITY a cloud of light believed to surround a god or goddess while on earth or a saint or holy person **3.** PAINTING IMAGE OF HALO a bright halo or disk around the head of a deity, saint, or sovereign in a painting, icon, or medal **4.** AURA OF SPLENDOR an aura or atmosphere of splendor surrounding somebody or something [Early 17thC. From Latin, "cloud, rain, corona."] —**nim·bused** *adj.*

NIM·BY /nímbee/ (*plural* **-BYs**), **Nim·by** (*plural* **-bys**) *n.* **1.** SOMEBODY OBJECTING TO LOCATION OF SOMETHING somebody who objects to something unpleasant or dangerous being located near his or her home but is perfectly happy to see it located elsewhere (*informal*) **2.** NIMBY ATTITUDE the attitude of a NIMBY [Late 20thC. Acronym from *not in my backyard.*] —**nim·by·ism** *n.*

ni·mi·e·ty /ni mī ətee/ (*plural* **-ties**) *n.* an excess or overabundance of something (*formal*) [Mid-16thC. Formed from Latin *nimis* "too much."]

Nimitz /nímmits/, **Chester William** (1885–1966) U.S. naval officer. He was commander-in-chief of the U.S. Pacific Fleet during World War II.

nim·rod /ním ròd/ *n.* any skillful or enthusiastic hunter (*literary*) [Mid-16thC. From the tradition of *Nimrod* as a "mightly hunter" (Genesis 10:9).]

Nin /nin/, **Anaïs** (1903–77) French writer. She is best known for her passionate and self-revelatory *Journals* (1966–83).

nin·com·poop /nínkəm po͞op, níngkəm-/ *n.* an offensive term that deliberately insults somebody's intelligence or competence (*informal insult*) [Late 17thC. Alteration of *nicompoop*, of uncertain origin, possibly from French *nicodême* "simpleton" + *poop* with sense "clown."] —**nin·com·poop·er·y** *n.* —**nin·com·poop·ish** *adj.*

nine /nīn/ *n.* **1.** NUMBER 9 the cardinal number 9 **2.** SOMETHING WITH VALUE OF 9 something in a numbered series, e.g., a playing card, with a value of 9 ○ *a nine of clubs* ○ *to play the nine* **3.** BASEBALL BASEBALL TEAM a team of nine baseball players **4.** GOLF HALF OF GOLF COURSE half of the total number of holes on a golf course, usually specified as the front nine or the back nine **5.** GROUP OF NINE a group of nine objects or people [Old English *nigon*. Ultimately from an Indo-European word.] —**nine** *adj.* —**nine** *pron.* ◇ **dressed (up) to the nines** very elaborately or formally dressed

nine-band·ed ar·ma·dil·lo *n.* an armadillo with nine bands of hinged bony plates that is native to Central and South America and the southern United States. The female nine-banded armadillo usually gives birth to quadruplets that are always of the same sex. Latin name: *Dasypus novemcinctus.*

nine·bark /nín baárk/ *n.* a shrub of the rose family native to eastern North America with bark that separates into many layers. Genus: *Physocarpus.*

nine days' won·der, nine day won·der *n.* something that, or somebody who, briefly arouses great interest or excitement but is soon forgotten again [Named with reference to Lady Jane Grey (1537–54), who was proclaimed Queen of England in 1553 but was deposed after only nine days and subsequently beheaded]

nine·fold *adj.* /nín fòld/ **1.** BY NINE TIMES of nine times the original figure ○ *a ninefold rise* **2.** WITH NINE PARTS made up of nine parts ○ *The problem is ninefold.* ■ *adv.* /nīn fṓld, nín fṓld/ BY NINE TIMES AS MUCH by nine times as much or as many ○ *The numbers increased ninefold.*

nine·pin /nín pìn/ *n.* a pin in the game of ninepins

nine·pins /nín pìnz/ *n.* a game in which players try to knock over nine bottle-shaped pins by bowling a ball at them (*takes a singular verb*)

nine·teen /nīn teén/ *n.* **1.** NUMBER 19 the cardinal number 19 **2.** SOMETHING WITH VALUE OF 19 something in a numbered series with a value of 19 **3.** GROUP OF 19 a group of 19 objects or people [Old English *nigontȳne*, from a prehistoric Germanic compound meaning "nineteen"] —**nine·teen** *adj.* —**nine·teen** *pron.*

nine·teenth /nīn teénth/ *n.* one of 19 equal parts of something ○ *My share came to three-nineteenths.* —**nine·teenth** *adj.* —**nine·teenth** *pron.*

nine·teenth hole *n.* a place, especially the bar of a clubhouse, where players can drink and socialize after a round of golf (*slang*) [Named as the hole after the conventional 18 holes on a golf course]

nine·ti·eth /níntee əth/ *n.* one of 90 equal parts of something ○ *a ninetieth of the whole* —**nine·ti·eth** *adj.* —**nine·ti·eth** *pron.*

nine-to-five *adj.* requiring regular attendance, e.g., at an office job, especially between 9 A.M. and 5 P.M. (*informal*) ○ *without the self-discipline to hold down a nine-to-five job*

nine-to-fiv·er *n.* somebody who works regular hours, especially from 9 A.M. to 5 P.M. (*informal*) ○ *She took the morning train with the rest of the nine-to-fivers.*

nine·ty /níntee/ *n.* (*plural* **-ties**) NUMBER 90 the cardinal number 90 ■ *npl.* **1. nine·ties** NUMBERS BETWEEN 90 AND 99 the numbers between 90 and 99, particularly as a range of Fahrenheit temperature **2.** YEARS 90 TO 99 the years in a century from 90 to 99 **3.** PERIOD FROM AGE 90 TO 99 the period of somebody's life from the age of 90 to 99 —**nine·ty** *adj.* —**nine·ty** *pron.*

Nin·e·veh /nínnəvə/ ancient capital of the Assyrian Empire, situated on the Tigris River in northern Iraq. At the height of its importance from about 705 B.C., it was destroyed by the Babylonians and Medes in 612 B.C.

Ning·bo /ning bṓ/ city in northeastern Zhejiang Province, eastern China, situated approximately 90 mi./145 km southeast of Hangzhou. Population: 552,540 (1990).

nin·ja /nínjə/ (*plural* **-jas** *or* **-ja**) *n.* a member of a group of mercenaries in feudal Japan who were trained in stealth and the martial arts and employed as spies, saboteurs, or assassins [Mid-20thC. From Japanese, "spy."]

nin·jit·su /nin jút so͞o/ *n.* a Japanese martial art that emphasizes stealth in movement and camouflage [Mid-20thC. From Japanese, literally "stealth art."]

nin·ny /nínnee/ (*plural* **-nies**) *n.* an offensive term that deliberately insults somebody's intelligence, common sense, or effectiveness (*informal insult*) [Late 16thC. Origin uncertain, perhaps from a misdivision and shortening of *an inno(cent).*] —**nin·ny·ish** *adj.*

ni·non /neé nòn/ *n.* a sturdy sheer fabric made of silk or synthetic material [Early 20thC. From French.]

ninth /nīnth/ *n.* **1.** ONE OF 9 PARTS one of 9 equal parts of something ○ *A ninth of the total is still a lot of money.* **2.** MUSIC MUSICAL TONE OR INTERVAL a musical tone separated from another by an interval of an octave and a second, or the interval of this tone —**ninth** *adj.* —**ninth** *pron.*

ninth chord *n.* a musical chord containing four thirds, including the ninth, added above the root

ni·o·bic /nī ṓbik/ *adj.* concerning or containing niobium with a valence of five

ni·o·bite /nī ə bīt/ *n.* = **columbite**

ni·o·bi·um /nī ṓbee əm/ *n.* a lustrous light-gray ductile metallic chemical element, a superconductor that resembles tantalum chemically and is used in steel alloys. Symbol **Nb** [Mid-19thC. From the association of the element with tantalum, *Tantalus* being the father of *Niobe.*]

ni·o·bous /nī ṓbəss/ *adj.* concerning or containing niobium with a valence less than five

nip[1] /nip/ *v.* (**nipped, nip·ping, nips**) **1.** *vt.* PINCH SOMETHING to take hold of something and squeeze or compress it, often painfully, between two surfaces, e.g., to pinch skin between a forefinger and thumb **2.** *vti.* TAKE BRIEF BITE AT SOMETHING to bite something briefly, often painfully, but without doing much damage **3.** *vt.* SEVER SOMETHING to remove something by pinching, biting, or clipping ○ *She nipped off the growing point of the plant to encourage bushiness.* **4.** *vt.* AFFECT SOMEBODY WITH COLD to sting or chill a person or part of the body painfully with cold ○ *As she struggled with the car door the frost began to nip her fingers.* **5.** *vt.* INJURE GROWTH OF SOMETHING to halt or destroy the growth of something **6.** *vt.* MAKE SOMETHING NARROWER to make something narrower or tighter ○ *The dress is nipped in at the waist.* **7.** *vt.* STEAL SOMETHING to steal or snatch something (*informal*) **8.** *vi. U.K.* GO QUICKLY to go somewhere quickly or briefly (*informal*) ○ *She nipped down to the shop for bread.* ■ *n.* **1.** SHARP SQUEEZE a sharp or painful squeeze with the fingers or between two surfaces **2.** SMALL BRIEF BITE a small bite with the teeth that may be painful but does not do much damage ○ *The dog tried to give my ankle a nip as I passed.* **3.** SMALL CUT-OUT PIECE a small piece cut from something **4.** CHILL a chilly feeling caused by a marked drop in temperature ○ *There's a nip in the air tonight.* **5.** SHARP FLAVOR a sharp or pungent flavor [14thC. From Middle Low German *nipen* "to nip."] ◇ **nip and tuck** very closely and evenly contested so that the outcome remains in doubt

nip[2] /nip/ *n.* BEVERAGES SMALL DRINK OF SOMETHING a small portion or drink of something alcoholic ■ *vti.* (**nipped, nip·ping, nips**) SIP to drink an alcoholic beverage in small sips [Late 18thC. Origin uncertain: perhaps a shortening of archaic *nipperkin*, literally "small sip."]

ni·pa /neépə/ *n.* **1.** (*plural* **-pas** *or* **-pa**) TREES ASIAN PALM TREE a palm tree of southern Asia with long feathery leaves and edible fruit. Latin name: *Nipa fruticans.* **2.** FOOD FRUIT OF PALM TREE the edible fruit of the nipa palm **3.** LEAVES OF PALM TREE the long feathery leaves of the nipa palm, used in thatching and basketry **4.**

BEVERAGES **DRINK FROM PALM SAP** an alcoholic drink made from the sap of the nipa palm [Late 16thC. From Malay *nipah*.]

nip·per /níppər/ *n.* **1.** ZOOL **PINCER** a large claw of a crustacean, especially a lobster or crab **2.** *U.K.* **CHILD** a small child (*informal*) ■ **nip·pers** *npl.* **PLIERS** a tool, such as pliers, used to squeeze or clip something [Mid-16thC. "Small child" probably from an earlier sense of "costermonger's boy," because he nipped off to run errands.]

nip·ping /nípping/ *adj.* **1. SHARP AND COLD** very cold and biting **2. SARCASTIC** bitingly sarcastic —**nip·ping·ly** *adv.*

nip·ple /nípp'l/ *n.* **1.** ANAT **TIP OF MAMMARY GLAND** a small knob in the center of the breast that in females is the outlet for the ducts that provide young mammals with milk. In humans it is also an erogenous zone. **2. RUBBER BOTTLE TOP** the soft cap of a baby bottle, made of a synthetic material, through which a baby can suck milk **3.** = **pacifier 4. SMALL OUTLET** a small knob on a device that is the outlet for fluid such as oil or grease **5.** CONSTR **COUPLER FOR PIPES** a short piece of pipe threaded at both ends used for coupling other pipes [Mid-16thC. Origin uncertain: perhaps literally "little neb," formed from NEB.]

nip·ple·wort /nípp'l wùrt, -wàwrt/ (*plural* **-worts** *or* **-wort**) *n.* a European annual plant, now naturalized in eastern North America, that has small yellow flowers and a milky juice. It was once used as an herbal remedy for breast tumors. Latin name: *Lapsana communis.*

Nip·pon /ní pon/ the Japanese name for Japan —**Nip·pon·ese** /nìppə néez/ *adj.*

nip·py /níppee/ (**-pi·er, -pi·est**) *adj.* **1. CHILLY** rather chilly **2.** FOOD **SHARP-TASTING** slightly sharp in flavor **3. TENDING TO BITE** inclined to attempt to bite people or animals —**nip·pi·ly** *adv.* —**nip·pi·ness** *n.*

nip-up *n.* an acrobatic move in which a gymnast lying with the back flat on the floor or mat springs to an upright position

N.Ire. *abbr.* Northern Ireland

Nir·en·berg /nírən burg/, **Marshall Warren** (*b.* 1927) U.S. biochemist. He shared the 1968 Nobel Prize in physiology or medicine for research into how DNA determines the structure of proteins.

nir·va·na /neer váanə, nur-/ *n.* **1. nir·va·na, Nir·va·na** RELIG **SPIRITUAL ENLIGHTENMENT** in Hinduism, Buddhism, and Jainism, the attainment of enlightenment and freeing of the spiritual self from attachment to worldly things, ending the cycle of birth and rebirth **2. COMPLETELY ENJOYABLE EXPERIENCE** an ultimate experience of some pleasurable emotion such as harmony or joy [Mid-19thC. From Sanskrit, from *nirvā-* "to be extinguished," from *nis-* "out" + *vā-* "to blow."]

Ni·san /níss'n, nee sáan/, **Nis·san** *n.* in the Jewish calendar, the seventh month of the religious year and first of the civil year. It is 30 days long and occurs around March or April.

Ni·sei (*plural* **-sei** *or* **-seis**) *n.* somebody born or raised in the United States or Canada whose parents immigrated from Japan. ◊ **Issei, Sansei** [Mid-20thC. From Japanese, literally "second generation."]

ni·si /ní sī, néessee/ *adj.* scheduled to take effect on a specified date unless some cause can be shown for canceling or changing the date [Mid-19thC. From Latin, "unless."]

Nis·san *n.* = **Nisan**

Nis·sen hut /níss'n hùt/ *n.* a temporary shelter made of corrugated steel in the shape of a half cylinder that was first used by the British during World War I [Early 20thC. Named for its inventor Lt. Col. Peter Norman *Nissen* (1871–1930).]

NIST *abbr.* National Institute of Standards and Technology

ni·sus /nísssəs/ (*plural* **-sus**) *n.* an attempt or effort to accomplish an aim or goal (*formal*) [Late 17thC. From Latin, from *niti* "to strive."]

nit /nit/ *n.* the egg or larva of a parasitic insect, especially a louse [Old English *hnitu*, ultimately from Indo-European. Partly a shortening of NITWIT.] —**nit·ty** *adj.*

NIT *abbr.* **1.** National Intelligence Test **2.** SPORTS National Invitational Tournament

nite /nīt/ *n.* a slang spelling of the word "night," not appropriate for use in formal writing (*slang*)

Ni·ten /néet en, nee tén/ (1584–1645) Japanese artist and soldier. He is noted for his *sumi-e* ink paintings of birds, and was renowned for developing the technique of fencing with two swords. Real name **Miyamoto Musashi**

ni·ter /nítər/ *n.* **1.** = **potassium nitrate 2.** = **sodium nitrate** [14thC. Via Old French, from Latin *nitrum*, from Greek *nitron*, of uncertain origin: perhaps from Semitic, or Egyptian *ntrj*.]

nit·pick /nít pìk/ (**-picked, -pick·ing, -picks**) *vti.* to find fault, often unjustifiably, with insignificant details of something —**nit·pick·er** *n.* —**nit·pick·y** *adj.*

WORD KEY: SYNONYMS

See Synonyms at ***criticize***.

nit·pick·ing /nít pìking/ *n.* trivial, unnecessary, detailed, and often unjustified faultfinding

nitr- *prefix.* = **nitro-** (*used before vowels*)

ni·trate /nī tràyt/ *n.* **1.** CHEM **CHEMICAL RADICAL** a univalent radical or a compound such as a salt or an ester of nitric acid that contains the radical NO_3 **2.** AGRIC **FERTILIZER** a fertilizer that consists of sodium nitrate, potassium nitrate, or ammonium nitrate ■ *vt.* (**-trat·ed, -trat·ing, -trates**) CHEM, INDUST **USE NITRATE ON SOMETHING** to treat something with a nitrate or nitric acid, usually in order to change an organic compound into a nitrate [Late 18thC. From French, formed from *nitre* "niter."] —**ni·tra·tion** /nī tráysh'n/ *n.*

ni·tre /nítər/ *n.* U.K. = **niter**

ni·tric /nítrik/ *adj.* made from or containing nitrogen, especially in a high valence state

ni·tric ac·id *n.* a transparent fuming corrosive colorless or yellowish liquid that is a highly reactive oxidizing agent. It has many industrial uses, including the making of explosives, fertilizers, and rocket fuels, and is also used in various metallurgical processes. Formula: HNO_3.

ni·tric ox·ide *n.* a colorless poisonous gas that is a stage in the production of nitric acid from ammonia or atmospheric nitrogen. Formula: NO.

ni·tride /ní trīd/ *n.* a compound made up of nitrogen and another more electropositive element such as phosphorus or a metal [Mid-19thC. Coined from NITROGEN + -IDE.]

ni·tri·fy /nítrə fī/ (**-fied, -fy·ing, -fies**) *vt.* **1.** CHEM **TREAT WITH NITROGEN** to treat or combine something with nitrogen or nitrogen compounds **2.** BIOCHEM **OXIDIZE AMMONIA ION** to oxidize ammonia ions into nitrite or nitrate ions, as nitrobacteria do **3.** AGRIC **FERTILIZE SOIL** to introduce nitrogen or nitrogen compounds into the soil in order to increase fertility [Early 19thC. From French *nitrifier*, from *nitre* NITER.] —**ni·tri·fi·ca·tion** /nītrəfi káysh'n/ *n.* —**ni·tri·fi·er** /nítrə fīr/ *n.*

ni·trile /nítrəl/ *n.* an organic cyanide

ni·trite /ní trīt/ *n.* a salt or ester of nitrous acid

ni·trite bac·te·ri·um *n.* a nitrobacterium that converts ammonia to nitrites by oxidation

ni·tro /ní trō/ *n.* nitroglycerin (*informal*) [Early 20thC. Shortening.]

nitro- *prefix.* **1.** nitrogen ○ *nitrify* **2.** niter, nitrate ○ *nitrogen* **3.** containing a univalent NO_2 group ○ *nitroparaffin* [From Latin *nitrum* (see NITER)]

ni·tro·bac·te·ri·um /nītrō bak téeree əm/ (*plural* **-a** /-ə/) *n.* a type of bacterium, found in soil and water, that is involved in the nitrogen cycle and converts ammonium compounds into nitrites, or nitrites into nitrates

ni·tro·ben·zene /nītrō bén zeen/ *n.* a poisonous organic compound that occurs either as bright yellow crystals or an oily liquid that smells like almonds. It is used to make polishes and insulating compounds. Formula: $C_6H_5NO_2$.

ni·tro·cel·lu·lose /nītrō séllyə lòss, -lòz/ *n.* a chemical compound produced by the reaction of nitric and sulfuric acids on cellulose, used in the manufacture of plastics, explosives, and lacquers. ◊ **guncotton**

ni·tro·chlo·ro·form /nītrō kláwrə fàwrm/ *n.* =**chloropicrin**

ni·tro·gen /nítrəjən/ *n.* a nonmetallic chemical element that occurs as a colorless odorless almost inert gas and makes up four fifths of the Earth's atmosphere by volume. It is important in the making of ammonia, explosives, and fertilizers. Symbol **N** [Late 18thC. From French *nitrogène* from *nitre* NITER and *-gène* -GEN.] —**ni·trog·e·nous** /nī trójjənəss/ *adj.*

ni·trog·e·nase /nī trójjə nàyss, -nàyz/ *n.* an enzyme found in nitrogen-fixing bacteria that catalyzes the conversion of nitrogen to ammonia. It is a key component of the nitrogen cycle, providing nitrogen compounds for plants.

ni·tro·gen bal·ance *n.* **1.** PHYSIOL **NITROGEN INTAKE AND EXCRETION** the difference between the amount of nitrogen taken into the body and the amount excreted **2.** AGRIC **NITROGEN ABSORBED AND LOST BY SOIL** the difference between the amount of nitrogen absorbed by the soil and the amount lost

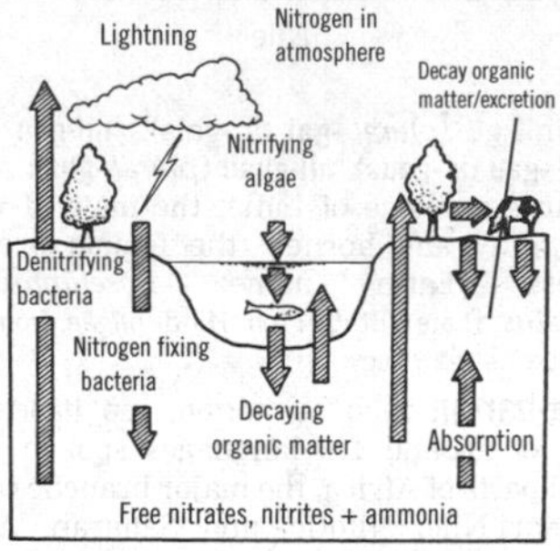

Nitrogen cycle

ni·tro·gen cy·cle *n.* the series of processes by which nitrogen is converted from a gas in the atmosphere to nitrogen-containing substances in soil and living organisms, then reconverted to a gas. The main chemical transformations are performed by microorganisms and include nitrogen fixation, nitrification, and denitrification.

ni·tro·gen di·ox·ide *n.* a highly poisonous brown gas used to make nitric and sulfuric acids. It is often found in smog and in the exhaust from vehicles that lack pollution control devices. Formula: NO_2.

ni·tro·gen fix·a·tion *n.* **1.** BIOL **NATURAL NITROGEN CONVERSION** the conversion of atmospheric nitrogen by certain bacteria found in the nodules of legumes into compounds in the soil that plants and other organisms can use **2.** INDUST **INDUSTRIAL NITROGEN CONVERSION** a process in which nitrogen from the atmosphere is changed into compounds such as ammonia by either chemical or bacterial agents —**ni·tro·gen-fix·er** *n.* —**ni·tro·gen-fix·ing** *adj.*

ni·trog·en·ize /nī trójjə nīz/ (**-ized, -iz·ing, -iz·es**) *vt.* to combine or treat something with nitrogen or one of its compounds —**ni·trog·en·i·za·tion** /nī tròjjəni záysh'n/ *n.*

ni·tro·gen mus·tard *n.* a poisonous substance similar to mustard gas but containing nitrogen instead of sulfur. Such compounds have been used to treat leukemia and other cancers.

ni·tro·gen nar·co·sis *n.* light-headedness, confusion, or exhilaration caused by increased nitrogen in the blood. This occurs in deep-sea divers exposed to pressures several times that of the atmosphere.

ni·tro·glyc·er·in /nītrō glíssərin, nītrə-/, **ni·tro·glyc·er·ine** *n.* a colorless thick oily flammable and explosive liquid used to manufacture explosives and in medicine to dilate veins in the treatment of angina pectoris. Formula: $C_3H_5N_3O_9$.

ni·tro·hy·dro·chlo·ric ac·id /nītrō hīdrō kláwrik-/ *n.* = **aqua regia**

ni·tro·meth·ane /nītrō mé thayn/ *n.* a poisonous col-

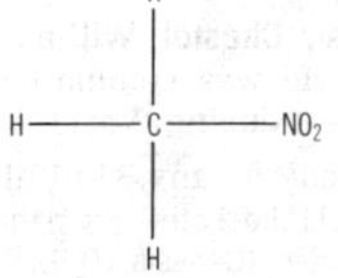

Nitromethane

orless oily slightly water-soluble liquid used to make dyes, resins, and rocket fuels, and as a solvent and gasoline additive. Formula: CH_3NO_2.

ni·tro·par·af·fin /nītrō pérrəfin/ *n.* a colorless simple hydrocarbon containing the chemical group NO_2

ni·tros·a·mine /nītrṓssə meén, -sá meén/ *n.* an organic carcinogenic compound found in various foods. Formula: R_2NNO. [Late 19thC. Coined from Latin *nitrosus* "nitrous" + AMINE.]

ni·trous /nítrəss/ *adj.* made from or containing nitrogen, especially in a low valence state

ni·trous ac·id *n.* a weak inorganic acid found only in solution or in the form of its salts. Formula: HNO_2.

ni·trous ox·ide *n.* a colorless nonflammable sweet-smelling, sweet-tasting gas used as an anesthetic in dentistry and surgery. Formula: N_2O.

nit·ty-grit·ty /nìttee gríttee/ *n.* **BASICS** the basic and most important details of something (*informal*) ■ *adj.* (*informal*) **1. BASIC AND IMPORTANT** concerning or involving the most important aspects of a subject **2. PRACTICAL** useful and direct in a practical down-to-earth way ○ *a nitty-gritty approach to teaching* [Mid-20thC. Origin unknown.]

nit·wit /nít wìt/ *n.* somebody thought to be silly or unintelligent (*insult*) [Early 20thC. Origin uncertain: perhaps from German dialect *nit* "not" + WIT.]

ni·val /nív'l/ *adj.* growing in or under the snow [Mid-17thC. From Latin *nivalis*, from *niv-*, stem of *nix* "snow."]

niv·e·ous /nívvee əss/ *adj.* resembling snow in color [Early 17thC. From Latin *niveus*, from *niv-*, stem of *nix* "snow."]

Niv·ôse *n.* the fourth month of the year in the French Revolutionary calendar, corresponding to December 22 to January 20 in the Gregorian calendar

nix[1] /niks/ *vt.* (**nixed, nix·ing, nix·es**) **SAY NO TO SOMETHING** to refuse, forbid, or veto something (*slang*) ■ *n.* **NOTHING** nothing (*dated slang*) ■ *interj.* **STOP!** used to warn somebody not to do something or stop doing something (*dated slang*) [Late 18thC. From German, dialectal and colloquial variant of *nichts* "nothing."] —**nixed** *adj.*

nix[2] /niks/ *n.* = **nixie**[1] [Mid-19thC. From German.]

nix·ie[1] /níksee/ *n.* in German mythology, a female water spirit that can appear in human form or as half-human, half-fish [Early 19thC. From German *Nixe*, feminine of *Nix* (see NIX[2]).]

nix·ie[2] /níksee/, **nix·y** (*plural* **-ies**) *n.* MAIL an item of mail that cannot be delivered because it has the wrong address or the address is unreadable (*slang*) [Late 19thC. Formed from NIX[1].]

Richard Milhous Nixon

Nix·on /níks'n/, **Richard Milhous** (1913–94) U.S. statesman and 37th president of the United States. President from 1969 until 1974, he was forced to resign after the Watergate scandal (1974). He was responsible for ending the U.S. commitment in Vietnam.

NJ, **N.J.** *abbr.* New Jersey

Nkru·mah /'n kroómə, 'ng kroómə/, **Kwame** (1909–72) Ghanaian statesman. He was the first prime minister (1957–60) and president (1960–66) of Ghana, and a strong supporter of pan-Africanism.

NKVD, **N.K.V.D.** *n.* the Soviet secret police from 1934 to 1946. Full form **Narodny Kommissariat Vnutrennikh Del** [Russian, "People's Commissariat of Internal Affairs"]

NL, **N.L.** *abbr.* **1.** BASEBALL National League **2.** New Latin

n.l. *abbr.* PRINTING new line

NLF *abbr.* National Liberation Front

NLP *abbr.* **1.** neurolinguistic programming **2.** natural language processing

NLRB, **N.L.R.B.** *abbr.* National Labor Relations Board

nm *abbr.* **1.** nanometer **2.** nautical mile **3.** nuclear magneton

NM *abbr.* **1.** New Mexico **2.** nautical mile

n.m. *abbr.* nautical mile

N.Mex., **N.M.** *abbr.* New Mexico

NMI *abbr.* no middle initial

NMR *abbr.* nuclear magnetic resonance

NNE *abbr.* north-northeast

NNW *abbr.* north-northwest

no[1] /nō/ *interj.* **1.** an interjection used to indicate a negative response in order to refuse, deny, or disagree with something ○ *"Will you be taking the car?" – "No, not today."* ○ *"Would you like coffee?" – "No, I'm fine, thanks."* **2. ACKNOWLEDGING A NEGATIVE STATEMENT** used to acknowledge a negative statement, by expressing acceptance or understanding of something ○ *"Nobody seems to have the time to really listen these days." – "No, they don't."* **3. INDICATING DISBELIEF** used to indicate shock, disbelief, or disappointment at something somebody has said ○ *"The car's going to be in the shop for another week." – "Oh no!"* ■ *n.* **1.** (*plural* **noes** *or* **nos**) **ANSWER OR VOTE** an answer or vote of "no" ○ *They all gave resounding noes to the proposition.* **2. SOMEBODY VOTING "NO"** somebody who answers "no" to a question or votes against something [Old English *nā*, from *ne* "not" + *ā* "ever" (see AYE)] ◇ **the noes have it** used to indicate that a majority has have voted against something

no[2] /nō/ CORE MEANING: an adjective used to indicate that there is not any or not one person or thing ○ *There is nothing in walking distance: no post office, no bank.* ○ *I had no choice in the matter.* ○ *They pay no attention to me.*

adj. **1. NOT AT ALL** used to indicate that somebody or something does not have any of the characteristic or identity mentioned ○ *She's no fool.* **2. NOT** not exceeding a particular amount or quality (*used with comparative adjectives and adverbs*) ○ *The issue was no less important to us than you.* [12thC. Shortening of NONE.]

No[1], **Noh** *n.* a form of Japanese drama that presents a story in a highly stylized fashion, using music, dance, and elaborate costumes. It flourished in the 14th and 15th centuries, and its development was influenced by Zen Buddhism. [Late 19thC. From Japanese *nō* "talent, ability."]

No[2] *symbol.* nobelium

no., **No.** *abbr.* **1.** north **2.** northern **3. no., No.** number

NOAA *abbr.* National Oceanic and Atmospheric Administration

no-ac·count, **no-count** *adj.* not have any redeeming or useful qualities (*informal*)

No·a·chi·an /nō áykee ən/, **No·ach·ic** /nō áykik/, **No·ach·i·cal** /-k'l/ *adj.* **1. OF NOAH** typical of or relating to Noah or his time **2. ANTIQUATED** long out-of-date [Late 19thC. Formed from *Noach*, a form of *Noah*.]

No·ah /nṓ ə/ *n.* in the Bible, at God's command, Noah built an ark and saved himself, his family, and a pair of every kind of animal from the Flood (Genesis 6–9)

No·ah's ark *n.* = **ark** *n.* **1**

nob[1] /nob/ *n. U.K.* somebody who is rich or socially powerful (*informal*) [Late 17thC. Origin unknown.]

nob[2] /nob/ *n.* **1. HEAD** the human head (*slang*) **2.** CARDS **JACK OF SUIT TURNED UP** in cribbage, the jack of the suit that the dealer turns up, which scores one point for the player who holds it [Late 17thC. Origin uncertain: perhaps from KNOB.]

nob·by /nóbbee/ *adj. U.K.* fashionable or elegant (*informal*) [Late 18thC. Formed from NOB[2].]

No·bel /nō bél/, **Alfred** (1833–96) Swedish chemist. His development of dynamite brought him great wealth, which was used after his death to set up the Nobel Prizes. Full name **Alfred Bernhard Nobel**

No·bel·ist /nō béllist/ *n.* somebody who has been awarded a Nobel Prize

no·bel·i·um /nō beélee əm/ *n.* an artificial chemical element produced from curium. Symbol **No** [Mid-20thC. Named for the *Nobel* Institute for Physics, and named for Alfred *Nobel* (see NOBEL PRIZE).]

No·bel Prize /nō bèl príz/ *n.* any of six international awards made annually for outstanding achievement in the fields of chemistry, literature, physics, physiology or medicine, economics, and for promoting world peace [Early 20thC. Named for the Swedish inventor of dynamite, Alfred *Nobel* who established the original five prizes.] —**No·bel prize·win·ner** *n.* —**No·bel-prize·win·ning** *adj.*

no·bil·i·ar·y /nō bíllee èrree, -yəree/ *adj.* relating to the nobility

no·bil·i·ar·y par·ti·cle *n.* a preposition, such as "de" in French or "von" in German, used before a title or surname as a mark of rank

no·bil·i·ty /nō bíllətee/ (*plural* **-ties**) *n.* **1. ARISTOCRATS** a noble class or people of noble rank in a country **2. NOBLE RANK** aristocratic social position or rank **3. NOBLE CHARACTER** high ideals or excellent moral character **4. MAGNIFICENCE** impressiveness or magnificence [14thC. Directly or via French *nobilité* from Latin *nobilis*, from *nobilis* (see NOBLE).]

no·ble /nṓb'l/ *adj.* (**-bler, -blest**) **1. HAVING EXCELLENT MORAL CHARACTER** possessing high ideals or excellent moral character **2. RELATING TO HIGH MORAL PRINCIPLES** based on high ideals or revealing excellent moral character **3. MAGNIFICENT** impressive in quality or appearance **4. ARISTOCRATIC** belonging or relating to an aristocratic social or political class **5.** CHEM **NONREACTIVE** chemically inactive or inert ■ *n.* **1. ARISTOCRAT** somebody who belongs to a titled aristocracy **2.** MONEY **FORMER ENGLISH COIN** a gold coin worth half a mark, formerly used in England [13thC. Via French, from Latin *(g)nobilis* (source of English *ignoble*). Ultimately from an Indo-European word that is also the ancestor of English *know*.] —**no·ble·ness** *n.* —**no·bly** *adv.*

no·ble gas *n.* a chemically inert rare gas belonging to group 18 of the periodic table, including helium, neon, argon, krypton, xenon, and radon

no·ble·man /nṓb'lmən/ (*plural* **-men**) *n.* a man who belongs to a titled aristocracy

no·ble met·al *n.* a metal, such as gold, silver, or platinum that is resistant to oxidation

no·ble rot *n.* a parasitic fungus that shrivels ripe grapes, increasing the proportion of sugar to liquid in them. It is desirable in the making of certain wines such as French Sauternes. Latin name: *Botrytis cinerea.*

no·ble sav·age *n.* somebody belonging to a non-technological culture whose life is, according to an idea popularized by *Rousseau*, purer because it is closer to nature (*offensive in some contexts*)

no·blesse /nō bléss/ *n.* **1. NOBLE RANK** aristocratic social position or rank **2. ARISTOCRATS** the members of an aristocracy, especially the French aristocracy [13thC. From French, "nobility," from *noble* (see NOBLE).]

no·blesse o·blige /nō blèss ə bleézh/ *n.* the idea that people born into the nobility or upper social classes must behave in an honorable generous way toward those less privileged [From French, literally "nobility obliges"]

no·ble·wom·an /nṓb'l wòomən/ (*plural* **-en** /nṓb'l wìmmin/) *n.* a woman who belongs to a titled aristocracy

no·bod·y /nṓbədee, -bòd-, -bùd-/ *pron.* **NOT ONE PERSON** not one single person ○ *Nobody can order the attack except the general.* ■ *n.* (*plural* **-ies**) **SOMEBODY UNIMPORTANT** somebody who feels or is regarded as unimportant or insignificant ○ *I felt like a nobody among so many important scientists*

no-brain·er *n.* something such as an idea or question that is so easily understood or done that it requires no thought (*slang*)

no·cent /nṓss'nt/ *adj.* causing harm, injury, or damage [15thC. From Latin *nocent-*, present participle stem of *nocere* "to hurt, harm" (source of English *noxious*).] —**no·cent·ly** *adv.*

no·ci·cep·tive /nòssi séptiv/ *adj.* **1. CAUSING PAIN** used to describe a stimulus that causes pain **2. IN RESPONSE TO PAIN** caused by or reacting to pain [Early 20thC. Coined from Latin *nocere* "to hurt, harm" (source of English *noxious*) + RECEPTIVE.] —**no·ci·cep·tive·ly** *adv.*

nock /nok/ *n.* **1. GROOVE ON BOW** one of the grooves at either end of a bow that holds the bowstring **2. NOTCH ON ARROW** the notch at the end of an arrow that holds it on the bowstring ■ *vt.* (**nocked, nock·ing, nocks**) **1. PREPARE TO FIRE ARROW** to place an arrow on a bowstring **2. NOTCH BOW OR ARROW** to put a notch in a bow or an arrow [14thC. Origin uncertain: probably from Middle Dutch *nocke* "projection, tip."]

no con·test *n.* = **nolo contendere**

no-'count *adj.* = **no-account** (*informal*)

noct- *prefix.* = **nocti-** (*used before vowels*)

nocti- *prefix.* night, at night ○ *noctilucent* [From Latin *noct-*, the stem of *nox* "night" (source of English *equinox*). Ultimately from an Indo-European word that is also the ancestor of *night*.]

noc·ti·lu·ca /nòktə lóokə/ (*plural* **-cae** /-lóo sèe/) *n.* a plankton that produces light. When present in large groups they make the sea appear to glow. Genus: *Noctiluca.* [Mid-19thC. From Latin, "moon, lantern."]

noc·ti·lu·cent /nòktə lóoss'nt/ *adj.* used to describe high clouds that are visible at night [Late 19thC. Coined from NOCTI- + Latin *lucere* "to shine."]

noc·tu·id /nókchoo id/ *n.* a dull-colored moth whose larvae, called army worms and cutworms, are destructive to young plants. Family: Noctuidae. [Late 19thC. Formed from Latin *noctua* "night-owl."] —**noc·tu·id** *adj.*

noc·tule /nók chòol/ *n.* a large reddish-brown bat, common in Europe and Asia, that eats insects. Latin name: *Nyctalus noctula.* [Late 18thC. Via French from Italian *nottola* "bat."]

noc·turn /nók tùrn/ *n.* one of the three divisions of the Roman Catholic service of matins, the first service of the day, previously held at midnight but now usually at daybreak [14thC. Directly or via French *nocturne*, from ecclesiastical Latin *nocturnus*, from Latin "of the night," from *noct-*, stem of *nox* "night."]

noc·tur·nal /nok túrn'l/ *adj.* ◊ **diurnal 1. AT NIGHT** occurring at night, as opposed to during the day **2.** ZOOL **ACTIVE AT NIGHT** used to describe animals that are active at night rather than during the day **3.** BOT **FLOWERING AT NIGHT** used to describe flowers that open at night and close during the day —**noc·tur·nal·ly** *adv.*

noc·turne /nók tùrn/ *n.* **1.** MUSIC **DREAMY MUSIC** a musical composition, especially for the piano, that suggests a tranquil, dreamy mood. It evolved during the early 19th century, and Chopin was the most famous composer of nocturnes. **2.** PAINTING **NIGHT SCENE** a painting of a night scene [Mid-19thC. From French (see NOCTURN).]

noc·u·ous /nókyoo əss/ *adj.* likely to cause injury or damage [Mid-17thC. From Latin *nocuus*, from *nocere* "to hurt."] —**noc·u·ous·ly** *adv.* —**noc·u·ous·ness** *n.*

nod /nod/ *v.* (**nod·ded, nod·ding, nods**) **1.** *vti.* **MOVE HEAD IN AGREEMENT** to lower and then raise the head quickly in order to show agreement or recognition **2.** *vi.* **DOZE** to let the head fall forward because of sleepiness **3.** *vi.* **LOSE CONCENTRATION** to be momentarily careless or negligent **4.** *vi.* **MOVE IN WIND** to droop, bend, or sway in a breeze ■ *n.* **1. MOVEMENT OF HEAD TO SHOW AGREEMENT** a quick lowering and raising of the head in order to show agreement or recognition **2. APPROVAL OF SOMETHING** an indication of approval or agreement [14thC. Origin uncertain: perhaps from Low German.] —**nod·der** *n.* ◇ **on the nod** *U.K.* agreed without formal discussion or procedures (*informal*)

nod off *vi.* to fall asleep unintentionally or go into a drug-induced state of semiconsciousness

nod·al /nód'l/ *adj.* resembling, constituting, or found at or near a node —**nod·al·ly** *adv.*

nod·ding ac·quain·tance *n.* **1. SLIGHT KNOWLEDGE OF SOMETHING** a slight familiarity with or knowledge of somebody or something **2. SLIGHT ACQUAINTANCE OF SOMEBODY** somebody whom somebody does not know very well

nod·dle /nódd'l/ *n.* the human head or brain (*dated slang*) [15thC. Origin unknown.]

nod·dy /nóddee/ (*plural* **-dies**) *n.* a dark-colored tern found on the coasts and islands of tropical waters in both hemispheres. Genera: *Anous* and *Micranous.* [Early 16thC. Origin uncertain: perhaps formed from NOD.]

nod·dy suit *n.* a protective suit worn by military personnel likely to be exposed to nuclear, biological, or chemical weapons (*slang*)

node /nōd/ *n.* **1. LUMP ON SOMETHING** a protruding knob, lump, or swelling on something **2.** ANAT **BULGE OR SWELLING** a knob, knot, or other kind of swelling that sticks out **3.** BOT **POINT ON PLANT STEM** the place on a plant stem where a leaf is attached or has been attached **4.** PHYS **POINT ON WAVE** in physics, a place in a standing wave that has little or no amplitude **5.** GEOM **POINT WHERE PARTS OF CURVE INTERSECT** in geometry, a place on a curve where it crosses itself **6.** MATH **POINT OF INTERSECTION** a point where lines meet or intersect in a diagram or graph **7.** ASTRON **POINT WHERE ORBIT INTERSECTS ECLIPTIC** either of the two points where an orbit, e.g., that of a planet, crosses the ecliptic plane **8.** COMPUT **TERMINAL OR POINT IN NETWORK** a terminal or other point in a computer network where a message can be created, received, or repeated **9.** LING **POINT IN SENTENCE STRUCTURE** in transformational grammars, a point in a sentence diagram where a category label, indicating the part of speech, appears and from which further branches may lead off [14thC. From Latin *nodus* "knot."]

node of Ran·vier /-raaN vyáy/ *n.* a short gap in the myelin sheath that occurs at intervals along the length of a nerve fiber [Named for the French histologist Louis Antoine *Ranvier* (1835–1922), who described them in 1878]

no·dose /nṑ dṓss, -dṓz/ *adj.* having many points at which leaves join the stem —**no·dos·i·ty** /nō dóssətee/ *n.*

nod·ule /nó jòol/ *n.* **1. SMALL LUMP** a small protruding knob, lump, or swelling on something **2.** BOT **ROOT PROTUBERANCE** a swelling or knob on the roots of legumes that contains bacteria **3.** ANAT **CELL OR TISSUE MASS** a small mass of cells or tissue, which may be a normal part of the body or a growth such as a tumor **4.** GEOL **LARGE ROUNDED MINERAL FORM** a form of a mineral that is massive with a rounded outer surface [15thC. From Latin *nodulus* "small knot," from *nodus* (see NODE).] —**nod·u·lar** /nójjələr/ *adj.* —**nod·u·lose** /-lṑss/ *adj.*

no·el /nō él/, **no·ël** *n.* a Christmas carol (*archaic or literary*) [12thC. From French, from *nael*, from Latin (*dies*) *natalis* "birth (day)," ultimately from *nasci* "to be born" (source of English *nascent*).]

No·el, No·ël *n.* Christmas, especially in carols or greetings

no·et·ic /nō éttik/ *adj.* typical of, coming from, or understood by the human mind [Mid-17thC. From Greek *noētikos*, ultimately from *noein* "to think," from *nous* "mind" (source of English *nous*).] —**no·et·i·cal·ly** *adv.*

no-fault *adj.* INSUR **COMPENSATING WITHOUT ASSIGNING BLAME FOR ACCIDENT** relating to a system of motor vehicle insurance in which insurance companies compensate accident victims without determining who is responsible for the accident ■ *n.* LAW **DIVORCING WITHOUT ASSIGNING BLAME** relating to a form of divorce in which no blame is placed on either party for the breakdown of the marriage

no-fly-zone *n.* **1.** an area over which aircraft, especially those of another country, are forbidden to fly, and in which they will be attacked if they enter it **2. FORBIDDEN TOPIC** a topic of questioning or conversation that is off-limits (*slang*) ○ *The press secretary declared that issue to be a no-fly-zone for reporters.*

no-frills *adj.* relating to a kind of service or establishment that does not offer extra or special treatment (*informal*)

nog[1] /nog/ *n.* **1.** BUILDING **WOODEN BLOCK FOR NAILING** a block of wood inserted into masonry or brickwork so that something can be nailed to it **2.** CONSTR **PEG** a wooden peg or pin ■ *vt.* (**nogged, nog·ging, nogs**) BUILDING **FILL WITH BRICKS** to fill a wall or partition with small stones or bricks [Early 17thC. Origin unknown.]

nog[2] /nog/ *n.* = **eggnog** [Early 17thC. Origin unknown.]

No·gal·es /no gáaləz/ **1.** city in Sonora State, northwestern Mexico, situated on the United States border. Population: 107,119 (1990). **2.** city in southeastern Arizona south of Tucson, on the Mexican border opposite Nogales, Mexico. Population: 22,087 (1996).

nog·gin /nóggin/ *n.* **1.** MEASURE **ONE FOURTH OF PINT** a measure for liquor equivalent to $\frac{1}{4}$ of a pint/0.148 liters (*dated*) **2. CUP** a small cup or mug (*dated*) **3. HEAD** the human head (*dated informal*) [Mid-17thC. Origin unknown.]

nog·ging /nógging/ *n.* **1. MASONRY BETWEEN STUDS** small stones, bricks, or bits of masonry used to fill the spaces between studs in a wall or partition **2. WOODEN PIECE BETWEEN TIMBERS** one of the pieces of wood that are inserted between the main timbers of a half-timbered wall

no-go *n.* **SOMETHING THAT WILL NOT HAPPEN** an event or situation that is not going to occur because of adverse conditions (*informal*) ■ *adj.* **CANCELED** no longer going to happen or scheduled to occur

no-go ar·e·a *n.* an area in which unauthorized people are forbidden to go

no-good *adj.* **GOOD-FOR-NOTHING** lacking merit, virtue, worth, or morals (*insult*) ■ *n.* **SOMEBODY OR SOMETHING WORTHLESS** somebody or something considered to lack merit, virtue, worth, or morals (*insult*)

No·gu·chi /naw gòochee/, **Hideyo** (1876–1928) Japanese bacteriologist. He helped discover the spirochete that causes syphilis, and devised a method to diagnose the disease.

CORBIS/Nathan Benn

Isamu Noguchi

No·gu·chi, Isamu (1904–88) U.S. sculptor. He is known for his abstract sculptures and his sculpture gardens.

Noh *n.* THEATER = **No**[1]

no-hit *adj.* relating to a baseball or softball game in which the opponents do not get a hit

no-hit·ter *n.* a baseball or softball game in which the pitcher does not allow opponents a hit

no-holds-barred *adj.* happening, or engaged in something, without restraint or control, like a wrestling match in which any hold is permitted (*informal*)

no·how /nṓ hòw/ *adv.* not in any way (*nonstandard*)

NoI *abbr.* Nation of Islam

noil /noyl/ *n.* short fibers separated during combing from the long fibers of cotton, wool, or another material [Early 17thC. Origin uncertain: probably from Old French *noel*, from medieval Latin *nodellus* "small knot," from Latin *nodus* "knot" (source of English *node*).]

noise /noyz/ *n.* **1. UNPLEASANT SOUND** a loud, surprising, irritating, or unwanted sound **2. ANY SOUND** any sound or combination of sounds **3. OUTCRY** a loud clamor or commotion concerning something **4. COMPLAINT** a complaint or protest about something (*informal*) **5. RUMOR** idle talk, rumor, or gossip (*informal*) **6.** PHYS **ELECTRIC DISTURBANCE** a random disturbance in an electric circuit that makes clear reception of a signal difficult **7.** COMPUT **MEANINGLESS DATA** unwanted or meaningless data intermixed with the relevant information in the output from a computer ■ *v.* (**noised, nois·ing, nois·es**) **1.** *vt.* **SPREAD GOSSIP** to spread a rumor or gossip ○ *an ugly story that was being noised about in newsrooms across the nation* **2.** *vi.* **TALK A LOT** to talk too much (*dated*) [13thC. Via French, "uproar, brawl," from assumed late Latin *nausea* "discomfort," from Latin, "seasickness," ultimately from Greek *naus* "ship" (source of English *nausea*).] ◇ **make noises** to do or say something intended to attract attention or indicate an intention ○ *He's making noises about a career change.*

noise a·bate·ment *n.* the reduction of noise pollution —**noise-a·bat·ing** *adj.*

noise·less /nóyzləss/ *adj.* not making any noise —**noise·less·ly** *adv.* —**noise·less·ness** *n.*

noise·mak·er /nóyz màykər/ *n.* **1. RATTLE OR HORN FOR CELEBRATING** a device such as a rattle or horn used to make noise at a party or a celebration **2. SOMEBODY MAKING NOISE** somebody who or something that makes noise or noises —**noise·mak·ing** *n.*

noise pol·lu·tion *n.* irritating, distracting, or physically dangerous noise to which people are exposed in their environment and over which they usually have no control. Also called **sound pollution**

noi·sette /nwaa zét/ *n.* a piece of boned and rolled meat, especially the neck or loin of lamb [Late 19thC. From French, literally "little nut," from its shape.]

noi·some /nóyssəm/ *adj.* **1.** FOUL so offensive, especially to the senses, as to arouse feelings of disgust or repulsion **2.** DANGEROUS extremely harmful [14thC. From obsolete *noy,* a shortening of ANNOY, + -SOME.] —**noi·some·ly** *adv.* —**noi·some·ness** *n.*

nois·y /nóyzee/ (**-i·er, -i·est**) *adj.* **1.** MAKING NOISE making a loud and annoying racket **2.** CONTAINING MUCH NOISE full of or characterized by loud sounds —**nois·i·ly** *adv.* —**nois·i·ness** *n.*

Nok /nók/ *n.* a civilization located in the forests of central Nigeria that flourished between 500 B.C. and A.D. 300. It is known for its highly developed art style.

no-kill *n.* TYPE OF ANIMAL SHELTER an animal shelter that does not euthanize the animals housed there, except under certain limited conditions ■ *adj.* NOT KILLING ANIMALS opposed to the euthanization of animals housed in an animal shelter, or not euthanizing animals, except under certain limited conditions

Sir Sidney Nolan

No·lan /nṓlən/, **Sir Sidney (Robert)** (1917–92) Australian painter. His colorful figurative works, often based on Australian folk history, include the *Ned Kelly* series.

No·land /nṓlənd/, **Kenneth** (*b.* 1924) U.S. painter. His abstract works feature various geometrical motifs, often on irregularly-shaped canvasses.

no·lens vo·lens /nṑlənz vṓlənz/ *adv.* whether willing or not willing [From Latin, literally "unwilling willing"]

noli me tan·ge·re /nṑlee may táng gə rày/ *n.* **1.** PROHIBITION AGAINST TOUCHING a warning not to touch or interfere with somebody or something **2.** SOMEBODY OR SOMETHING NOT FOR TOUCHING somebody who or something that must not be touched or interfered with **3.** PAINTING PAINTING OF JESUS CHRIST AND MARY MAGDALENE a depiction in art of Jesus Christ appearing to Mary Magdalene after his resurrection [From Latin, literally "do not touch me," from Jesus Christ's words to Mary Magdalene in the *Bible,* John 20:17]

nol·le pros·e·qui /nòlee próssə kwī/ *n.* an entry made in a court record when a plaintiff or a prosecutor decides not to proceed further with a case or action [From Latin, literally "to be unwilling to pursue"]

no·lo /nṑ lṓ/ (*plural* **-los**) *n.* = **nolo contendere** (*informal*) [Shortening]

no-load *adj.* sold directly to customers at net asset value without the addition of a sales commission or other fees ○ *a no-load mutual fund*

no·lo con·ten·de·re /nṑ lō kən téndəree/ *n.* in law, a plea entered by a defendant that does not explicitly admit guilt, but subjects the defendant to punishment, while allowing denial of the alleged facts in other proceedings. Also called **no contest, nolo** [From Latin, literally "I do not wish to contend"]

no-lose *adj.* certain to result in success or be beneficial, regardless of the outcome ○ *a no-lose proposition*

nol. pros. /nòl próss/ *abbr.* nolle prosequi

nol-pros /nàwl próss/ (**nol-prossed, nol-pros·sing, nol-pros·ses**) *vt.* to end the prosecution of a case by entering "nolle prosequi" in the court records [Shortening of Latin *nolle prosequi,* literally "to be unwilling to pursue"]

nom. *abbr.* nominative

no·ma /nṓmə/ *n.* a severe gangrenous inflammation of the mouth or genitals, usually occurring in children who are malnourished or otherwise debilitated [Mid-19thC. From a modern Latin alteration of Latin *nome,* ultimately from Greek *nom-,* stem of *nemein* "to feed."]

no·mad /nṓ màd/ *n.* **1.** ANTHROP MEMBER OF ITINERANT PEOPLE somebody who belongs to a group of people who move from place to place seasonally in search of pasture for their herds or food and water **2.** WANDERER somebody who wanders from one place to another [Late 16thC. From French *nomade,* ultimately from Greek *nomas* "wandering about to find pasture," from *nemein* "to pasture."] —**no·mad·ic** /nō máddik/ *adj.* —**no·mad·i·cal·ly** *adv.* —**no·mad·ism** /nṓ ma dìzzəm/ *n.*

no man's land *n.* **1.** MIL TERRITORY BETWEEN OPPOSING FORCES the area of land that lies between two opposing armies and is held by neither side **2.** UNCLAIMED TERRITORY any area of land that no one has established a claim to **3.** RACKET GAMES BAD POSITION ON TENNIS COURT in tennis and other court games, an area on a court in which a player is tactically at a disadvantage **4.** AMBIGUOUS AREA any indefinite or ambiguous situation in which boundaries, rules, or authority are unclear or unfamiliar

nom·ar·chy /nómmərkee/ (*plural* **-chies**) *n.* any of the administrative provinces into which modern Greece is divided [Mid-17thC. From Greek *nomarkhia,* from *nomos* "district" (see NOME) + *-arkhia* "government."]

nom·bril /nómbrəl/, **nom·bril point** *n.* in heraldry, the midpoint of the lower half of an escutcheon, halfway between the fess point and the base point [Mid-16thC. From French, literally "navel."]

nom de guerre /nòm də gáir/ (*plural* **noms de guerre** /nòm-/) *n.* an assumed name that somebody uses in certain situations, e.g., when fighting or writing [From French, literally "name of war"]

nom de plume /nòm də plóom/ (*plural* **noms de plume** /nóm-/) *n.* = **pen name** [From French, literally "name of pen"]

nome /nōm/ *n.* **1.** HIST EGYPTIAN PROVINCE a province of ancient Egypt **2.** = **nomarchy** [Early 18thC. From Greek *nomos,* from *nemein* "to divide."]

Nome /nōm/ city in western Alaska, on Seward Peninsula, on the northern shore of Norton Sound. Population: 3,792 (1996).

no·men /nṓmən/ (*plural* **nom·i·na** /nómmənə/) *n.* in ancient Rome, a citizen's second name, which indicated the clan to which he or she belonged [Early 18thC. From Latin, "name."]

no·men·cla·tor /nṑmən kláytər/ *n.* somebody who assigns names to objects or items in a scientific classification system **(taxonomy)** [Mid-16thC. From Latin, from *nomen* "name" + *calare* "to call."]

no·men·cla·ture /nṑmən kláychər/ *n.* **1.** ASSIGNING OF NAMES the assigning of names to organisms in a scientific classification system **(taxonomy) 2.** NAME SYSTEM a system of names assigned to objects or items in a particular science or art [Early 17thC. Via French from Latin *nomenclatura,* formed from *nomen* "name" + *calare* "to call."] —**no·men·cla·tur·al** *adj.*

no·men·kla·tu·ra /nṑmən klə tóorə, -klaa-/ *n.* **1.** ELITE COMMUNIST CLASS in Communist governments, the elite, privileged class consisting of the people holding positions of authority in the bureaucracy (*takes a singular or plural verb*) **2.** COMMUNIST PATRONAGE SYSTEM the system in the former Soviet Union and other Communist countries, controlled by committees in the Communist Party, for assigning senior positions in the bureaucracy (*takes a singular verb*) [Mid-20thC. From Russian, from Latin *nomenclatura* NOMENCLATURE.]

nom·i·na plural of **nomen**

nom·i·nal /nómmən'l/ *adj.* **1.** SO-CALLED acting or being something in name only, but not in reality **2.** VERY LOW IN COST representing very little cost when compared with the actual value received **3.** ACCT RELATING TO CURRENT PRICES considered in terms of the stated or original value only, and ignoring changes due to inflation and other factors **4.** GRAM OF NOUN relating to a noun or a group of words that functions as a noun **5.** BEARING SOMEBODY'S NAME assigned to a named person, and bearing that person's name **6.** OF NAMES relating to or consisting of a name or names ■ *n.* GRAM NOUN OR NOUN GROUP a word or group of words that functions as a noun [15thC. Either directly or via French from Latin *nominalis,* from *nomen* "name."] —**nom·i·nal·ly** *adv.*

nom·i·nal·ism /nómmən'l ìzzəm/ *n.* the philosophical doctrine that there are no realities other than concrete individual objects —**nom·i·nal·ist** *n., adj.* —**nom·i·nal·is·tic** /nòmmən'l ístik/ *adj.* —**nom·i·nal·is·ti·cal·ly** *adv.*

nom·i·nal·ize /nómmən'l īz/ (**-ized, -iz·ing, -iz·es**) *vt.* **1.** FORM NOUN FROM WORD to change a part of speech into a noun by the addition of a suffix **2.** FORM NOUN GROUP FROM CLAUSE to change an underlying clause by a syntactic process or series of rules so that it functions like a noun —**nom·i·nal·i·za·tion** /nòmmən'li záysh'n/ *n.*

nom·i·nal quote *n.* an approximate price given for a security when there is no firm bid or asking price

nom·i·nal val·ue *n.* = **par value**

nom·i·nal wag·es *npl.* wages expressed in terms of the money actually paid, rather than in terms of the purchasing power of the wages

nom·i·nate /nómmə nàyt/ (**-nat·ed, -nat·ing, -nates**) *vt.* **1.** PROPOSE SOMEBODY to suggest somebody for appointment or election to a position or for an honor or award **2.** APPOINT SOMEBODY to appoint somebody to a position, or make somebody responsible for a duty **3.** HORSERACING ENTER HORSE FOR RACE to enter a horse in a race [Mid-16thC. From Latin *nominat-,* past participle stem of *nominare* "to name," from *nomin-,* stem of *nomen* "name."] —**nom·i·na·tor** *n.*

nom·i·na·tion /nòmmə náysh'n/ *n.* **1.** PROPOSAL a suggestion of somebody for appointment or election to a position or for receiving an honor or award **2.** SOMEBODY OR SOMETHING PROPOSED somebody or something suggested for appointment or election to a position or for receiving an honor or award **3.** APPOINTMENT the appointment of somebody to a position, or assignment of somebody to a duty

nom·i·na·tive /nómmə nàytiv/; (*grammatical case*) /nómmənətiv/ *adj.* **1.** GRAM OF THE SUBJECT CASE relating or belonging to the case used in some languages to designate a noun or pronoun that is functioning as the subject of a clause or sentence. Other words such as adjectives may have a nominative form in agreement with a noun. **2.** APPOINTED TO OR PROPOSED FOR OFFICE appointed or suggested for election to an office or position **3.** WITH OWNER'S NAME having the name of the owner specified on it ■ *n.* GRAM **1.** SUBJECT NOUN CASE the grammatical case in some languages of a noun functioning as a subject of a sentence or clause, and of some other words agreeing with the noun **2.** NOUN IN SUBJECT CASE a form of a noun used in some languages when the noun functions as the subject of a sentence or clause, or when another word agrees with such a noun [14thC. Either directly or via French *nominatif* from Latin *nominativus (casus)* "nominative (case)," from *nominat-* (see NOMINATE).]

nom·i·nee /nòmmə née/ *n.* **1.** SOMEBODY PROPOSED somebody who has been suggested for a position, honor, or award, or as a candidate for office **2.** BUSINESS NOMINAL OWNER a person or group that holds title to a security or piece of real estate but is not actually the holder or owner [Mid-17thC. Formed from NOMINATE.]

nom·o·graph /nómmə gràf, nṓ-/, **nom·o·gram** /-gràm/ *n.* **1.** GRAPH WITH THREE SCALES a graph with three lines graduated so a straight line intersecting any two of the lines at their known values intersects the third at the value of the related variable. To show the relationship of the variables in more complicated expressions, nomographs often have to resort to nonuniform and even curved scales. **2.** GRAPH any graph that represents numerical relationships [Mid-18thC. Coined from Greek *nomos* "law, custom" + -GRAPH.] —**nom·o·graph·ic** /nòmmə gráffik, nṑ-/ *adj.* —**no·mog·ra·phy** /nō móggrəfee/ *n.*

nom·o·thet·ic /nòmmə théttik, nṑ-/, **nom·o·thet·i·cal** /-k'l/ *adj.* **1.** POL LEGISLATIVE relating to the enactment of laws **2.** PSYCHOL RELATING TO DISCOVERY OF GENERAL LAWS relating to the discovery of universal laws, e.g., those principles that explain how some aspects of personality affect behavior [Early 17thC. From Greek *nomothetikos,* from *nomothetēs* "lawgiver," from *nomos* "law."] —**nom·o·thet·i·cal·ly** *adv.*

-nomy *suffix.* system of rules, laws, or knowledge about a particular field ○ *gastronomy* [From Greek *-nomia,* from *nomos* "law, custom"] —**-nomic** *suffix.* —**-nomical** *suffix.* —**-nomically** *suffix.*

non *prefix.* = **nona-** (*used before vowels*)

-non *prefix.* not ○ *nonconducting* ○ *nondiscrimination* [Via Old French from Latin *non.* Ultimately from an Indo-

European base that is also the ancestor of English *no, un-,* and *in-*.]

non-A, non-B hep·a·ti·tis *n.* an acute chronic viral disease of the liver, similar to hepatitis B but caused by neither the hepatitis A nor the hepatitis B virus. Among the several new hepatitis viruses discovered relatively recently, non-A, non-B hepatitis, in most cases, is thought to be due to the hepatitis C virus.

nona- *prefix.* nine ○ nonagon [From Latin *nonus* "ninth" (source of English *noon*). Ultimately from the Indo-European word for "nine," which is also the ancestor of *nine, November,* and *ennead.*]

non·ac·a·dem·ic /non akə démmik/ *adj.* **1. NOT TEACHING** working at a university or college but not involved in teaching or research **2. NOT STUDIOUS** lacking an aptitude for studying **3. VOCATIONAL** practical or vocational in content

non·age /nónnij, nónij/ *n.* **1.** LAW **NOT BEING OF LEGAL AGE** the status of being under the requisite age for some legal entitlement (*formal*) **2. TIME BEFORE MATURITY** any time of immaturity [14thC. From Anglo-Norman *nounage*, a variant of Old French *nonage*, literally "not (the full) age," from *age* (see AGE).]

non·a·ge·nar·i·an /nònnəjə nérree ən, nò-/ *n.* **SOMEBODY 90 TO 99 YEARS OLD** somebody 90 years of age or between 90 and 100 years old ■ *adj.* **90 TO 99 YEARS OLD** 90 years of age or between 90 and 100 years old [Early 19thC. Formed from Latin *nonagenarius* "consisting of ninety," from, ultimately, *nonaginta* "ninety," from *nonus* (see NOON).]

non·ag·gres·sion /nònnə grésh'n/ *n.* a policy of not attacking other countries ○ *The two countries signed a nonaggression pact.*

non·a·gon /nónnə gòn, nónə-/ *n.* a plane geometric figure with nine angles and sides [Mid-17thC. Coined from NONA- + -GON.] —**non·ag·o·nal** /nō nággən'l/ *adj.*

non·al·co·hol·ic /non alkə hóllik/ *adj.* containing no alcohol, or an extremely low amount of alcohol

non·a·ligned /nònnə línd/ *adj.* not allied with any major world power —**non·a·lign·ment** *n.*

non·ap·pear·ance /nònnə peérənss/ *n.* failure to appear or attend, especially the failure of a defendant or witness to turn up for a court appearance

non·as·sess·a·ble /nònnə séssəb'l/ *adj.* **1. IMPOSSIBLE TO DETERMINE** impossible to estimate or determine ○ *nonassessable losses* **2.** STOCK EXCH **NOT LIABLE TO FINANCIAL PENALTY** used to describe stock for which an investor cannot be assessed or held liable for any financial loss beyond the amount of his or her investment

non·bank /non bángk/ *n.* a financial enterprise that is not a bank but performs a number of the functions of a bank —**non·bank·ing** *adj.*

non·be·liev·er /nònbi leévər/ *n.* somebody who has no religious faith or beliefs

non·book /nón bòòk/ *n.* **BOOK OF OTHER THAN LITERARY IMPORTANCE** a book meant primarily for practical use or visual enjoyment rather than literary merit ■ *adj.* **NOT IN BOOK FORM** kept in a permanent form other than as books, e.g., as videotapes ○ *the library's nonbook holdings*

non·break·ing /non bráyking/ *adj.* designed so as not to break ○ *a nonbreaking windshield*

non·breed·ing /non breéding/ *adj.* not kept for breeding purposes

non·busi·ness /non bíznəss/ *adj.* personal and not relating to business ○ *details of nonbusiness expenditure*

non·call·a·ble /non káwləb'l/ *adj.* used to describe a bond, stock, or security that is not subject to payment on demand or redemption prior to maturity

nonce /nonss/ *n.* the present time [12thC. Alteration resulting from misdivision of *for then anes* "for the one (occasion)," from *for* + *then*, a form of THE + *anes*, an obsolete form of ONE.] ◇ **for the nonce 1.** for the present occasion **2.** for the time being

nonce word *n.* a word that is coined for a single occasion

non·cha·lance /nònshə laáns, nónshə laàns/ *n.* the quality of appearing calm and unconcerned

non·cha·lant /nònshə laánt, nónshə laànt/ *adj.* calm and unconcerned about things [Mid-18thC. From French, literally "not being concerned," from *chalant*, present participle of *chaloir* "to be concerned," from, ultimately, Latin *calere* "to be hot or roused."] —**non·cha·lant·ly** *adv.*

non·cling /non klíng/ *adj.* made of a material that prevents the garment from clinging to the wearer's body

non·clin·i·cal /non klínnik'l/ *adj.* not relating to or involved in the medical care of patients

non·col·le·giate /nònkə leejee ət/ *adj.* **1. NOT CONSISTING OF COLLEGES** used to describe a university that does not consist of colleges **2. NOT BELONGING TO COLLEGE** not associated with or belonging to a particular college within a university

non·com /nón kòm/ *n.* a noncommissioned officer (*informal*) [Late 19thC. Shortening.]

non·com·bat·ant /nònkəm bátt'nt/ *n.* **1. CIVILIAN IN WARTIME** somebody who is not in the armed forces during a war **2. NONFIGHTING MEMBER OF ARMED FORCES** a chaplain, medical officer, or other member of the armed forces who does not take part in battle

non·com·mis·sioned of·fi·cer /nonkə mish'nd-/ *n.* an enlisted member of any of the armed forces who, without being given a commission, has been appointed to a position of authority over other enlisted members

non·com·mit·tal /nònkə mítt'l/ *adj.* not making clear any personal opinions or feelings about something —**non·com·mit·tal·ly** *adv.*

non·com·pet·i·tive /nònkəm péttitiv/ *adj.* **1.** COMM **WITHOUT BUSINESS RIVALRY** not characterized by competition between rival businesses or organizations **2.** COMM **UNABLE TO COMPETE COMMERCIALLY** unable to compete commercially against rival businesses or organizations **3.** COMM **NEITHER CHEAP NOR GOOD ENOUGH** neither low enough in price nor high enough in quality to compete in the marketplace **4. UNAMBITIOUS** not having the type of personality that makes somebody want to compete against and beat other people **5.** SPORTS **NOT INVOLVING COMPETING SPORTSPEOPLE** not involving competition between athletes, players, or teams

non·com·pet·i·tive bid *n.* a method of buying United States Treasury bills by which the purchaser commits to taking a specific amount of securities at the average weekly price

non·com·pli·ance /nònkəm plí əns/ *n.* a refusal or failure to obey a law, rule, contractual agreement, or a physician's order for medicine-taking —**non·com·pli·ant** *adj.*

non com·pos men·tis /non kòmpəss méntiss/ *adj.* in law, not mentally competent to understand what is happening and to make important decisions [From Latin, literally "not having control of (your) mind"]

non·con·duc·tor /nònkən dúktər/ *n.* a substance that does not conduct heat, electricity, or sound —**non·con·duct·ing** *adj.*

non·con·form·ist /nònkən fáwrmist/ *adj.* **UNCONVENTIONAL** not conforming to an established pattern of behavior ■ *n.* **1. UNCONVENTIONAL PERSON** somebody who does not conform to an accepted pattern of behavior **2. non·con·form·ist, Non·con·form·ist** CHR **MEMBER OF DISSENTING PROTESTANT CHURCH** a member of a Protestant church not adhering to the doctrines or usage of a national or established church, especially in Britain —**non·con·form·ism** *n.*

non·con·form·i·ty /nònkən fáwrmatee/ *n.* **1. UNCONVENTIONALITY** the practice of not conforming to an established pattern of behavior **2. LACK OF AGREEMENT** the state of being in disagreement with something

non·con·trib·u·to·ry /nònkən tríbbyə tàwree/ *adj.* **1. NOT REQUIRING CONTRIBUTIONS** used to describe a health insurance or pension plan that does not require contributions from an employee or member **2. NOT CONTRIBUTING** not contributing to a health insurance or pension plan

non·co·op·er·a·tion /nònkō oppə ráysh'n/ *n.* **1. REFUSAL TO COOPERATE** refusal or failure to cooperate **2.** POL **CIVIL DISOBEDIENCE** the practice of refusing to pay taxes or otherwise obey government decrees, as a means of protest —**non·co·op·er·a·tive** /nònkō óppərativ, -ràytiv/ *adj.*

non·cred·it /non kréddit/ *adj.* used to describe an educational course that contributes no official credit toward an academic degree

non·cus·to·di·al /nònkə stódee əl/ *adj.* **1.** LAW **NOT INVOLVING IMPRISONMENT** not involving imprisonment or detention in custody **2.** LAW, SOC SCI **NOT HAVING CUSTODY OF CHILD** not granted legal custody of a child

non·dair·y /non dáiree/ *adj.* used to describe ingredients or foods that contain no dairy products and can be substituted for them, e.g., some kinds of margarine ■ *n.* **PRODUCT WITH NO MILK CONTENT** a commercial product containing no ingredients such as milk, cream, or cheese

non·de·duct·i·ble /nòndi dúktəb'l/ *adj.* not allowed to be deducted, especially as an allowance against income taxes

non·de·grad·a·ble /nòndi gráydəb'l/ *adj.* not subject to decomposition by biological or chemical means

non·de·nom·i·na·tion·al /nòndi nommə náyshən'l, -náyshnəl/ *adj.* not associated with or restricted to a particular religious denomination

non·de·script /nòndi skrípt/ *adj.* **UNREMARKABLE** with no interesting or remarkable characteristics ■ *n.* **UNREMARKABLE PERSON** somebody with no interesting or remarkable characteristics [Late 17thC. Formed from Latin *descriptus*, past participle of *describere* (see DESCRIBE).]

non·de·struc·tive test·ing /nondi strùktiv-/ *n.* any technique used to test for flaws in materials, components, and joints without causing damage or destruction

non·di·rec·tive /nòndi réktiv/ *adj.* used to describe a form of psychotherapy or counseling in which the patient is encouraged to speak freely with minimal input from the therapist

non·dis·clo·sure a·gree·ment /nondi sklṓzhər-/ *n.* an agreement, often required of new or departing employees, not to disclose any proprietary or secret information relating to their new or previous employer

non·dis·crim·i·na·tion /nòndi skrimmi náysh'n/ *n.* **1. FAIR AND EQUAL TREATMENT FOR ALL** the practice of treating different people or groups fairly, equally, and without prejudice **2. NO DISCRIMINATION** the absence of discrimination —**non·dis·crim·i·na·to·ry** /nòndi skrímmənə tàwree/ *adj.*

non·dis·junc·tion /nòndiss júngkshən/ *n.* a failure of paired chromosomes or sister chromatids to separate during cell division —**non·dis·junc·tion·al** *adj.* —**non·dis·junc·tion·al·ly** *adv.*

non·dis·tinc·tive /nòndi stíngktiv/ *adj.* used to describe features of speech sounds that do not distinguish meanings

non dit /nòn deé/ *n.* a taboo subject or fact that remains unspoken or is not discussed ○ *His absence was a non dit.* [Late 20thC. From French *le non-dit*, "what is left unsaid."]

non·drink·er /non dríngkər/ *n.* somebody who does not drink alcohol —**non·drink·ing** *adj.*

non·drip /non dríp/ *adj.* not likely to drip while being applied

none /nun/ *pron.* **1. NOBODY** not one person ○ *Wealth that is free for all is valued by none.* ○ *None of us wanted the situation to continue.* **2. NOT ANY** not any of something, or any part of something ○ *None of it seemed to matter any more.* ○ *We wrote last week demanding some answers, but so far have received none.* ■ *adj.* **NOT ANY OF** not any of (*archaic*) (*used before vowels*) [Old English *nān*, literally "not one," from *ne* "not" + *ān*, an earlier form of ONE] ◇ **have none of something** to refuse to tolerate something ○ *We asked him to explain himself, but he would have none of it.* ◇ **none the** in no degree (*used in front of comparative adjectives*) ○ *I'm still none the wiser.* ◇ **none too** not very ○ *The room is none too pretty, painted like that.*

non·e·lect·ed /nònni léktəd/ *adj.* holding a position or office without having been elected to it

non·e·lec·tro·lyte /nònni léktrə lìt/ *n.* a substance that does not ionize readily in solution or in the molten state and is therefore a bad conductor of electricity

non·en·ti·ty /non éntitee/ (*plural* **-ties**) *n.* **1. INSIGNIFICANT PERSON** somebody who has no importance, influence, or significance **2. SOMETHING NONEXISTENT** something that does not exist in reality **3. NOT EXISTING** the state of being nonexistent [Late 16thC. From medieval Latin *nonentitas*, from *entitas* "existence" (see ENTITY).]

non·e·quiv·a·lence /nònni kwívvələnss/ *n.* **1. NOT BEING EQUAL** the state of not being equal or equivalent **2.** LOGIC **DIFFERENCE IN TRUTH VALUES** a situation in which two propositions can have different truth values —**non·e·quiv·a·lent** *adj.*

nones /nōnz/ *n.* (*takes a singular or plural verb*) **1.** CALENDAR, HIST **DAY IN ROMAN CALENDAR** the ninth day before the ides of each month in the ancient Roman calendar **2.** CHR **TIME FOR AFTERNOON PRAYER** the fifth canonical hour of prayer, originally held at the ninth hour after sunrise [15thC. "9th day" via French from Latin *nonas*, plural of *nonus* "ninth." "Prayer hour" plural of *none*, ultimately from Latin *nona*, feminine of *nonus* (see NOON).]

non·es·sen·tial /nònni sénshəl/ *adj.* **1. NOT NECESSARY** not absolutely necessary **2.** BIOCHEM **NOT NECESSARY TO THE DIET** manufactured by the body and therefore not essential in the diet ■ *n.* **NONESSENTIAL PERSON OR THING** somebody who or something that is not absolutely necessary

none·such /nún sùch/, **non·such** *n.* somebody who or something that has no equal (*archaic*) [Late 16thC. From NONE + SUCH.]

no·net /nō nét/ *n.* **1. COMPOSITION FOR NINE VOICES OR INSTRUMENTS** a piece of music composed for nine voices or instruments **2. GROUP OF NINE MUSICIANS** a group of nine singers or instrumentalists [Mid-19thC. From Italian *nonetto*, literally "small ninth," from *nono* "ninth," from Latin *nonus* (see NOON).]

none·the·less /nùn*th*ə léss/ *adv.* = **nevertheless**

non-Eu·clid·e·an *adj.* used to describe or relating to any branch of geometry not based on the postulates of Euclid

non·e·vent /nònni vént/ *n.* an occasion that is disappointingly unexciting

non·ex·ist·ent /nònnig zístənt/ *adj.* not in existence —**non·ex·ist·ence** *n.*

non·fat /non fát/ *adj.* without fat solids, or with the fat content removed

non·fea·sance /non féez'ns/ *n.* failure to do something that is legally obligatory. ◊ **malfeasance, misfeasance** [Early 17thC. Formed from obsolete *feasance* "doing," from Anglo-Norman *fesa(u)nce* and French *faisance*, from *fais-*, present stem of *faire* "to do," from Latin *facere*.]

non·fer·rous /non férrəss/ *adj.* **1. CONTAINING NO IRON** not composed of or containing iron **2. NOT IRON** being a metal other than iron

non·fic·tion /non fíkshən/ *n.* prose literature that consists of factual information rather than works of the imagination ○ *her first nonfiction work* —**non·fic·tion·al** *adj.*

non·fig·u·ra·tive /non fíggyərətiv/ *adj.* **1.** = **literal 2.** ARTS = **nonrepresentational**. Also called **nonobjective**

non·flam·ma·ble /non flámməb'l/ *adj.* difficult to burn or ignite. Also called **noninflammable**

non·food /non fóod/ *adj.* used to describe something that is sold in a supermarket that is not for eating or drinking

non·gon·o·coc·cal u·re·thri·tis /nòn gonnə kókəl-/ *n.* inflammation of the urethra not caused by any specific infection. It is sexually transmitted but is not caused by gonorrheal organisms.

non·grad·ed /non gráydəd/ *adj.* **1.** EDUC **NOT DIVIDED INTO CLASSES** used to describe an elementary school that is not divided into classes **2. NOT SORTED BY SIZE** not sorted into different sizes ○ *nongraded rocks*

non gra·ta /non gráatə, -gráttə/ *adj.* not welcome [Extracted from PERSONA NON GRATA]

non·he·ro /nòn héerō/ (*plural* **-roes**) *n.* = **antihero**

non·i·den·ti·cal /nòn ī déntik'l/ *adj.* **1. DIFFERENT** not the same **2.** BIOL = **fraternal** *adj.* 4 ○ *nonidentical twins*

no·nil·lion /nō níllyən/ *n.* **1. ONE FOLLOWED BY 30 ZEROS** the number equal to 10^{30}, written as 1 followed by 30 zeros **2.** *U.K.* **ONE FOLLOWED BY 54 ZEROS** the number equal to 10^{54}, written as 1 followed by 54 zeros [Late 17thC. From French, coined from Latin *nonus* "ninth" + *-illion* as in MILLION.] —**no·nil·lionth** *adj., n.*

non·im·mi·grant /non ímmigrənt/ *n.* **1. TEMPORARY NONCITIZEN RESIDENT** somebody who enters a country of which he or she is not a citizen for a temporary stay **2. RETURNING CITIZEN** somebody who returns to his or her own country after a period of time spent in another country

non·in·flam·ma·ble /nònnin flámməb'l/ *adj.* *U.K.* = **nonflammable**

non·in·su·lin-de·pend·ent di·a·be·tes *n.* a type of diabetes mellitus that does not require insulin for its treatment

non·in·ter·ven·tion /nòn intər vénshən/ *n.* the policy and practice of a nation's abstaining from involvement in the affairs of another state or population group —**non·in·ter·ven·tion·ist** *n., adj.*

non·in·va·sive /nònnin váyssiv/ *adj.* **1. NOT ENTERING INTO THE BODY** not involving cutting into the body or entry into a body cavity, e.g., the colon or stomach **2. LOCALLY CONFINED** not spreading or likely to spread to other parts of the body

non·in·volve·ment /nònnin vólvmənt/ *n.* the practice of not participating in something or not being associated with something

non·i·ron /non írn/ *adj.* *U.K.* not needing to be ironed because it is crease-resistant

non·is·sue /non íshoo/ *n.* something that is so unimportant that it is not worth considering or discussing

non·join·der /non jóyndər/ *n.* failure to include a party in a lawsuit who should have been included

non·judg·men·tal /nòn juj mént'l/ *adj.* not making or involving moral judgments —**non·judg·men·tal·ly** *adv.*

non·ju·ror /non jóorər, -ràwr/ *n.* somebody who refuses to take an oath, especially a member of the Church of England clergy who refused to take an oath of allegiance to William and Mary in 1689 —**nonjuring** *adj.*

non·ju·ry /non jóoree/ *adj.* used to describe a trial where the verdict is not the responsibility of a jury but of a judge

non·lin·e·ar /non línnee ər/ *adj.* **1. NOT IN A LINE** not lying on the same straight line **2. NOT PREDICTABLE FROM PAST** varying markedly as a result of individual factors or circumstances and so difficult to anticipate or likely to depart from previous patterns **3.** ALGEBRA **NOT IN DIRECT PROPORTION** used to describe a relationship or function that is not strictly proportional

non·mem·ber firm *n.* a company that is not a member of a stock exchange and thus requires an intermediary to operate on its behalf there

non·met·al /non métt'l/ *n.* a chemical element that does not have the chemical and physical properties of a metal, e.g., carbon or oxygen

non·mor·al /non máwrəl/ *adj.* **1. INDEPENDENT OF MORAL CONSIDERATIONS** neither immoral nor moral, but unrelated to moral or ethical considerations **2. WITHOUT MORALS** not having or showing moral principles

non·neg·a·tive /non néggətiv/ *adj.* in mathematics, relating to or being a real quantity that is positive or zero

non·ne·go·tia·ble /nònnə góshee əb'l, nòn nə-/ *adj.* **1. NOT OPEN TO NEGOTIATION** not open to negotiation or arbitration **2. NOT MARKETABLE** not legally transferable from one owner to another

non·nu·cle·ar /non nóoklee ər/ *adj.* not using nuclear power or weapons

no-no (*plural* **no-nos**) *n.* something that is not allowed or is disapproved of (*informal*)

non·ob·jec·tive /nònnəb jéktiv/ *adj.* **1. NOT IMPARTIAL** based on somebody's opinions or feelings, rather than on facts or evidence **2.** ARTS = **nonrepresentational**. also called **nonfigurative** —**non·ob·jec·tiv·i·ty** /nòn ob jek tívvətee/ *n.*

non·ob·ser·vance /nònnəb zúrvəns/ *n.* a failure to comply with something such as a law or practice, especially a religious practice —**non·ob·ser·vant** *adj.*

non ob·stan·te /non əb stántee, nōn-/ *prep.* notwithstanding (*formal*) [From medieval Latin, literally "not standing in the way"]

no-non·sense *adj.* **1. BUSINESSLIKE** direct and practical in dealing with things or people **2. BASIC AND UNADORNED** basic and offering no extras, frills, or luxuries

non·ox·y·nol-9 /no nóksi nawl-/ *n.* a type of spermicide used in contraceptive preparations [From *nonyl* + OXY- + PHENOL + 9 (from the fact that the compounds contained have an average of nine ethylene oxide groups per molecule)]

non·pa·reil /nònpə rél, nónpə rèl/ *n.* **1. SOMEBODY OR SOMETHING UNPARALLELED** somebody who or something that has no equal **2.** FOOD **CONFECTIONERY DECORATION** a small crisp bead of colored sugar used to decorate cookies and other confectionery **3.** FOOD **SUGAR-COVERED CHOCOLATE DISK** a small disk of chocolate covered in small beads of white nonpareils **4.** PRINTING **SIX-POINT TYPE** a size of printers' type equivalent to six point (*dated*) ■ *adj.* **PEERLESS** having no equal [15thC. From French, literally "not (having) equal," from *pareil* "equal," from popular Latin *pariculus*, diminutive of Latin *par* "equal" (see PAIR).]

non·par·ti·san /non páartizən/, **non·par·ti·zan** *adj.* **NOT SUPPORTING ANY POLITICAL PARTY** not belonging to, supporting, or biased in favor of any political party ■ *n.* **SOMEBODY NOT SUPPORTING ANY POLITICAL PARTY** somebody who does not belong to, support, or show bias in favor of any political party

non·pay·ment /non páymənt/ *n.* a refusal or failure to pay money owed

non·pen·e·tra·tive /non pénnə tràytiv/ *adj.* not involving penetration of the vagina or anus by the penis

non·per·for·mance /nònpər fáwrməns/ *adj.* used to describe a loan that is delinquent and making no progress toward becoming current

non·per·sis·tent /nònpər sístənt/ *adj.* used to describe chemicals, especially pesticides, that tend to decompose within a short time after application and are used with a view to limiting environmental damage

non·per·son /non púrs'n/ *n.* **1. SOMEBODY IGNORED BY A REGIME** somebody who is ignored by a government and the news media it controls, usually because the person's political or ideological views are disapproved of by the government **2. INSIGNIFICANT PERSON** somebody of no importance or significance

non pla·cet /non pláyssət, nōn-/ *n.* a negative vote in an ecclesiastical or academic assembly [From Latin, literally "it does not please"]

non·play·ing /non pláy ing/ *adj.* not playing in a game or competition, but usually having a coaching or advisory role

non·plus /non plúss/ *vt.* (**-plussed** *or* **-plused, -plus·sing** *or* **-plus·ing, -plus·ses** *or* **-plus·es**) **CONFUSE SOMEBODY** to make somebody feel confused and unable to decide what to do ■ *n.* **STATE OF CONFUSION** a state of confusion and nervousness (*dated*) [Late 16thC. From Latin *non plus* "no more"; from being a state in which "no more" can be done.] —**non·plussed** *adj.*

non·point source /non póynt-/ *n.* a large or dispersed land area, e.g., a farm or street, that discharges pollutants into the environment over a wide area

non·pre·scrip·tion /nònprə skrípsh'n/ *adj.* PHARM = **over-the-counter** *adj.* 3

non·pro·duc·tive /nònprə dúktiv/ *adj.* **1. NOT PRODUCING GOOD RESULTS** not producing adequate or satisfactory results **2.** ECON **NOT INVOLVED IN PRODUCING GOODS** not directly involved in producing goods **3. NOT YIELDING SOMETHING** not producing crops or a natural resource **4.** MED **NOT PRODUCTIVE OF PHLEGM** used to describe a cough that does not produce phlegm —**non·pro·duc·tive·ly** *adv.* —**non·pro·duc·tive·ness** *n.*

non·pro·fes·sion·al /nònprə féshən'l, -féshnəl/ *n.* **SOMEBODY WHO IS NOT PROFESSIONAL** somebody who does not have professional status ■ *adj.* **NOT PROFESSIONAL** not having professional status

non·prof·it /non próffit/ *adj.* not operated with the aim of making a profit

nonprof·it·mak·ing /non próffit màyking/ *adj.* *U.K.* = **nonprofit**

non·pro·lif·er·a·tion /nònprə liffə ráysh'n/ *n.* the practice of limiting the production or spread of something, especially nuclear weapons (*often used before a noun*) ○ *nonproliferation agreements*

non·pros /non próss/ *n.* (*plural* **-pros·ses**) = **non prosequitur** (*informal*) ■ *vt.* (**-prossed, -pros·sing, -pros·ses**) **JUDGE AGAINST PLAINTIFF IN DEFAULT** to enter a judgment against a plaintiff who fails to appear in court (*informal*) [Late 17thC. Shortening.]

non pro·se·qui·tur /non prə sékwitər/ *n.* a judgment in the defendant's favor when the plaintiff fails to appear in court [From Latin, "he or she does not prosecute"]

non·read·er /non réedər/ *n.* somebody who does not or is unable to read, especially a child who has difficulty in learning to read

non·re·com·bi·nant /nòn ree kómbinənt/ *adj.* not produced by artificially manipulating genetic material

non·rel·a·tiv·is·tic /nòn relləti vístik/ *adj.* not affected by the effects of relativity —**non·rel·a·tiv·is·ti·cal·ly** *adv.*

non·rep·re·sen·ta·tion·al /nòn repprə zen táyshən'l, -táyshnəl/ *adj.* not aiming to depict an object but composed with the focus on internal structure and form. Also called **nonfigurative, nonobjective** —**non·rep·re·sen·ta·tion·al·ism** *n.* —**non·rep·re·sen·ta·tion·al·ly** *adv.*

non·res·i·dent /non rézzidənt/ *adj.* **1.** NOT RESIDING IN PLACE not living or staying in a particular place **2.** NOT INVOLVING LIVING AT WORKPLACE not involving living at the place of work ■ *n.* SOMEBODY NOT RESIDING IN PLACE somebody who is not living or staying in a particular place or at a workplace —**non·res·i·dence** *n.* —**non·res·i·den·cy** *n.* —**non·res·i·den·tial** /nòn rezzi dénshəl/ *adj.*

non·re·sis·tant /nònri zístənt/ *adj.* **1.** SUSCEPTIBLE TO SOMETHING unable to withstand something, especially a disease **2.** PASSIVELY OBEDIENT exhibiting passive obedience to people in authority —**non·re·sis·tance** *n.*

non·re·stric·tive /nònri stríktiv/ *adj.* with few or no restrictions

non·re·stric·tive clause *n.* a relative clause that gives additional information about a noun or pronoun in the main clause but that is not essential to the understanding of the main clause. A nonrestrictive clause is usually separated from the rest of the sentence by commas, e.g., "My partner, who is an artist, comes from Chicago."

non·rig·id /non ríjjid/ *adj.* **1.** FLEXIBLE not stiff **2.** AIR WITH A FLEXIBLE GAS CONTAINER used to descibe airships such as balloons or dirigibles that have a flexible gas container held in shape by the internal gas pressure

non·run /non rún/ *adj.* designed not to develop runs easily ○ *nonrun pantyhose*

non·sched·uled /nonské jo͞old/ *adj.* **1.** UNPLANNED not planned to happen as part of a schedule **2.** TRANSP OPERATING WITHOUT PUBLISHED SCHEDULE operating according to demand, rather than on a published schedule

non·sec·tar·i·an /nònsek táiree ən/ *adj.* **1.** NOT RELATING TO RELIGIOUS SUBGROUP not relating to a group or denomination within a wider religion or disputes between such groups **2.** NOT RESTRICTED TO ONE DENOMINATION not restricted to members of one religious denomination, but open to all

non·self /non sélf/ *n.* any substance or tissue that is not recognized as part of the body by that body's immune system

non·sense /nónsəns/ *n.* **1.** MEANINGLESS LANGUAGE OR BEHAVIOR pointless or meaningless language or behavior **2.** POINTLESS ACT OR UTTERANCE an instance of pointless or meaningless language or behavior ○ *To pay more than the price would be a nonsense.* **3.** IRRITATING BEHAVIOR disrespectful, obnoxious, or irritating behavior ○ *the kind of judge who won't stand for any nonsense from lawyers* **4.** = **nonsense verse** **5.** GENETICS CODON THAT PRODUCES NO AMINO ACID a triple of nucleotides, or codon, in a DNA molecule that does not code for any amino acid. These codons are believed to signal the beginning and end of the synthesis of particular protein molecules. ■ *interj.* EXPRESSION OF CONTRADICTION used to contradict what somebody has said or written [Early 17thC. Coined from NON- + SENSE.]

non·sense verse *n.* poetry that is written in deliberately absurd language for humorous effect, mainly for children. Also called **nonsense**

non·sense word *n.* a word with no meaning, usually created for humorous effect

non·sen·si·cal /non sénsik'l/ *adj.* **1.** MEANINGLESS having no sense or meaning **2.** LAUGHABLE deserving ridicule —**non·sen·si·cal·ly** *adv.* —**non·sen·si·cal·ness** *n.*

non se·qui·tur /non sékwitər/ *n.* **1.** INCONGRUOUS STATEMENT a statement that appears unrelated to a statement that it follows **2.** UNWARRANTED CONCLUSION a conclusion that does not follow from its premises [From Latin, literally "it does not follow"]

non·sex·ist /non séksist/ *adj.* avoiding or not involving discrimination, limitation, or stereotypes based on gender

non·shrink /non shríngk/ *adj.* resistant to shrinking when washed

non·sked /non skéd/ (*plural* **-skeds** *informal*) *n.* a nonscheduled airline or plane (*informal*) [Mid-20thC. Shortening and alteration of NONSCHEDULED.]

non·skid /non skíd/ *adj.* designed to prevent or lessen skidding

non·slip /non slíp/ *adj.* designed to prevent people from slipping

non·smok·er /non smṓkər/ *n.* **1.** SOMEBODY WHO DOES NOT SMOKE somebody who does not smoke cigarettes, cigars, or a pipe **2.** RAIL COMPARTMENT WHERE NO SMOKING IS ALLOWED a car or compartment in a train in which smoking is not allowed

non·smok·ing /non smṓking/ *adj.* **1.** RESTRICTED TO NONSMOKERS reserved for people who do not want to smoke cigarettes, cigars, or pipes **2.** NOT SMOKING not smoking cigarettes, cigars, or a pipe ■ *n.* AREA WHERE SMOKING IS FORBIDDEN an area of, e.g., a restaurant or an aircraft, where smoking is not permitted ○ *Do you want smoking or nonsmoking?* Also called **no-smoking**

non·stan·dard /non stándərd/ *adj.* **1.** NOT OF ACCEPTED STANDARD not conforming to an accepted standard **2.** LANGUAGE NOT USED IN STANDARD LANGUAGE not conforming to a standard accepted as grammatically correct by educated native speakers, or not used by educated native speakers

non·start·er /non staártər/ *n.* **1.** SOMETHING OR SOMEBODY UNLIKELY TO SUCCEED something that or somebody who is obviously going to be unsuccessful right from the beginning (*informal*) **2.** SPORTS COMPETITOR WHO WITHDRAWS BEFORE START a competitor who does not start a race, event, or competition in which he or she has been entered **3.** *U.K.* HORSERACING HORSE THAT DOES NOT COMPETE a horse that does not run in a race in which it has been entered

non·ster·oid /non sté ròyd, -steér òyd/ *n.* DRUG WITHOUT STEROID a drug that does not contain a steroid ■ *adj.* **non·ste·roid, non·ste·roid·al** NOT STEROID not containing or being a steroid

non·stick /non stík/ *adj.* with a coating or surface that prevents food from sticking during cooking

non·stop /non stóp/ *adj., adv.* **1.** WITHOUT STOP continuing without a stop ○ *a nonstop flight* **2.** WITHOUT INTERRUPTION continuing without interruption or rest ○ *a weekend of nonstop partying*

non·such *n.* = **nonesuch**

non·suit /non so͞ot/ *n.* the dismissal of a suit by a judge when the plaintiff fails to make out a legal case or to produce adequate evidence

non·sup·port /nònsə páwrt/ *n.* failure or refusal to supply legally required financial support, usually for a child or ex-spouse

non·tar·get /non taárgət/ *adj.* used to describe cells, tissues, or organisms that are not intended for treatment, e.g., by drugs or radiation, but may be affected by such treatment aimed elsewhere

non·ten·ured /non ténnyərd/ *adj.* not having or conferring tenure

non trop·po /non tróppō/ *adv., adj.* not too much (*used as a musical direction*) [From Italian]

non-U *adj. U.K.* not belonging to or characteristic of the upper classes (*dated informal*) ○ *a non-U word for "napkin"* [*U* abbreviation of *upper (class)*]

non·un·ion /non yo͞onyən/ *adj.* **1.** NOT IN UNION not belonging to a labor union **2.** NOT USING UNION MEMBERS not employing labor union members **3.** NOT MADE BY UNION MEMBERS not produced by labor union members —**non·un·ion·ized** *adj.*

non·us·er /non yo͞ozər/ *n.* somebody who does not use something, especially somebody who does not take addictive drugs

non·ver·bal /non vúrb'l/ *adj.* not using or involving words

non·ver·bal com·mu·ni·ca·tion *n.* methods of communicating other than by using words, e.g., facial expressions, hand gestures, and tone of voice

non·vi·a·ble /non vī́ əb'l/ *adj.* **1.** BIOL NOT ABLE TO DEVELOP ALONE incapable of growing and developing independently **2.** NOT ABLE TO SUCCEED not capable of succeeding

non·vin·tage /non víntij/ *adj.* not belonging to an especially good year for a wine and not identified by year

non·vi·o·lence /non vī́ ələns, -vī́ləns/ *n.* **1.** PRINCIPLE OF REFRAINING FROM USING VIOLENCE the principle of refraining from using violence, especially as a means of protest **2.** ABSENCE OF VIOLENCE the absence of or freedom from violence —**non·vi·o·lent** *adj.* —**non·vi·o·lent·ly** *adv.*

non·vot·er /non vṓtər/ *n.* somebody who does not vote or is not entitled to vote

non·vot·ing /non vṓting/ *adj.* used to describe stock that does not give the holder the right to vote at company meetings

non·wo·ven /non wṓv'n/ *adj.* made of fibers that have been bonded or interlocked by mechanical, chemical, thermal, or solvent methods

non·ze·ro /non zeérō/ *adj.* greater or less than zero in value or quantity

noo·dle[1] /no͞od'l/ *n.* a long thin strip of pasta. Noodles are a staple of Italian and Chinese cooking. (*often used in the plural*) [Late 18thC. From German *Nudel*, of uncertain origin: perhaps a variant of *Knödel* "dumpling."]

noo·dle[2] /no͞od'l/ *n.* the head or mind (*slang*) [Mid-18thC. Origin uncertain: perhaps an alteration of NODDLE.]

noo·dle[3] /no͞od'l/ (**-dled, -dling, -dles**) *vti.* to improvise on a musical instrument in a random, meandering fashion, often for the purpose of warming up (*slang*) [Mid-19thC. Origin uncertain: probably from likening such playing to the disorganized, convoluted appearance of a dish of noodles.]

nook /no͝ok/ *n.* **1.** PRIVATE PLACE a quiet private place **2.** SMALL CORNER OR RECESS a corner or small recess in a room [13thC. Origin uncertain: probably from Old Norse.] ◇ **every nook and cranny** every tiny part of a place

nook·ie /no͝okee/, **nook·y** *n.* sexual intercourse (*slang*) (*sometimes considered offensive*) [Early 20thC. Origin uncertain: perhaps formed from NOOK (from sex taking place in a private place).]

noon /noon/ *n.* **1.** 12 O'CLOCK MIDDAY 12 o'clock in the middle of the day **2.** MOST IMPORTANT PERIOD the most important period of something (*literary*) [Pre-12thC. From Latin *nona (hora)* "ninth (hour) (of the Roman day, counted from sunrise)," feminine of *nonus* "ninth" (source of English *nonagenarian*). Originally about 3 p.m.]

noon·day /no͞on dày/ *adj.* RELATING TO MIDDAY relating to or happening at midday ■ *n.* MIDDAY the middle of the day (*dated or literary*)

no one *pron.* no person at all

noon·tide /no͞on tīd/ *n.* the middle of the day (*literary*)

noon·time /no͞on tīm/ *n.* the middle of the day, around 12 o'clock

noose /nooss/ *n.* **1.** LOOP IN ROPE a loop, tied with a knot, at the end of a rope that permits tightening and slackening, and is used for trapping animals or hanging people **2.** SOMETHING THAT TRAPS SOMEBODY something that traps somebody in an unpleasant or unwanted situation ■ *vt.* (**noosed, noos·ing, noos·es**) **1.** CATCH WITH A NOOSE to catch somebody or something with a noose **2.** TIE IN A NOOSE to tie a rope or cord in a noose [15thC. Origin uncertain: probably via Old French *nos* (singular) and *nous* (plural) from Latin *nodus* "knot" (source of English *denouement* and *node*).]

Noot·ka /no͞otkə/ (*plural* **-kas** *or* **-ka**) *n.* **1.** PEOPLES MEMBER OF NATIVE NORTH AMERICAN PEOPLE a member of Native North American people of the western coast of Vancouver Island, British Columbia, and Cape Flattery, on the Olympic Peninsula in Washington State **2.** LANGUAGE LANGUAGE OF NOOTKA the language of the Nootka, belonging to the Wakashan family of languages. Few people now speak Nootka. [Early 19thC. Named for *Nootka* Sound, an inlet on the coast of Vancouver Island, British Columbia, Canada.] —**Noot·ka** *adj.*

n.o.p. *abbr.* not otherwise provided (for)

no·pal /nṓp'l/ (*plural* **-pals** *or* **-pal**) *n.* **1.** PLANTS AMERICAN CACTUS an American cactus that has red flowers and long stamens and is a host plant to the cochineal insect. Latin name: *Nopalea cochinellifera*. **2.** FOOD FRUIT OF NOPAL the edible fruit of a nopal cactus, used in Mexican cookery [Mid-18thC. Via French from, ultimately, Nahuatl *nopalli*, literally "cactus."]

no-par, no-par-val·ue *adj.* used to describe a security without a par or face value

nope /nōp/ *interj.* used to indicate a negative response in order to refuse, deny, or disagree with something (*slang*) [Late 19thC. Alteration of NO[1] (probably reflecting the sound of the lips' closure after an emphatic pronunciation of the word).]

nor /nawr/ *conj.* **1.** AND NOT used to introduce an alternative, after a first alternative that is preceded by "neither" (*used in negative statements*) ○ *Neither he nor his wife had profited in any way from the crime.* **2.** AND NOT EITHER used to indicate that what has just been said also applies to somebody or something else, or to add extra information to what has just been said (*used after negative statements and followed by "have," "do," or "be"*) ○ *He doesn't* *want to move to another town, and nor do I.* ○ *No surrounding tissue was damaged, nor did the infection spread.* ■ *prep.* THAN than (*nonstandard*) ■ *conj.* NEITHER neither (*literary*) [13thC. Contraction of obsolete *nouther* "neither, nor" (see NEITHER).]

NOR /nawr/ *n.* a logical operator with two arguments that returns true if, and only if, both arguments are false [Mid-20thC. Blend of NOT and OR.]

Nor. *abbr.* 1. Norman 2. North 3. Norway 4. Norwegian

nor- *prefix.* an unaltered parent compound ○ *nornicotine* [Shortening of NORMAL]

NO·RAD /náwr àd/ *abbr.* North American Air Defense Command

nor·a·dren·a·line /nàwrə drénnəlin/, **nor·a·dren·a·lin** *n. U.K.* = **norepinephrine**

nor·ad·ren·er·gic /nàwr addrə núrjik/ *adj.* releasing or involving norepinephrine in the transmission of nerve impulses

NOR cir·cuit *n.* a computer circuit with two inputs and one output where the output is on only when both inputs are off

Nor·co /náwrcō/ city in Riverside County, southeastern California, situated 45 mi./72 km west of Palm Springs. Population: 23,302 (1990).

Nor·dic /náwrdik/ *adj.* 1. SCANDINAVIAN relating to the countries of northwestern Europe, especially the Scandinavian countries and Iceland 2. ANTHROP TALL, FAIR, AND BLUE-EYED tall, blond, fair-skinned and blue-eyed, in a way that is considered to be typical of people from Scandinavian countries 3. **Nor·dic, nor·dic** SKIING WITH CROSS-COUNTRY SKIING OR JUMPING used to describe or relating to ski events involving either cross-country racing or ski jumping or both ■ *n.* SOMEBODY NORDIC somebody from a Nordic country or of Nordic appearance [Late 19thC. From French *nordique*, from *nord* "north," ultimately from a prehistoric Germanic word that is also the ancestor of English *north*.]

Nor·dic Track *tdmk.* a trademark for a cross-country ski exercise machine

Nord-Ost·see-Ka·nal /nàwrt àwst zay kaa naál/ = **Kiel Canal**

nor'east·er /nawr éestər/ *n.* METEOROL = **northeaster** [Mid-19thC. Alteration.]

nor·ep·i·neph·rine /nàwr eppə néffrin/ *n.* a hormone, secreted by the adrenal gland and similar to epinephrine, that is also the principal neurotransmitter of sympathetic nerve endings supplying the major organs and skin. It increases blood pressure and rate and depth of breathing, raises the level of blood sugar, and decreases the activity of the intestines.

no·re·this·ter·one /nàwr e thístə rōn/ *n.* a progestogen drug used in oral contraceptives and hormone replacement therapy and to treat premenstrual syndrome, menstrual disorders, endometriosis, and cancer

Nor·folk Is·land pine *n.* a tall symmetrical pine tree, native to Norfolk Island off the eastern coast of Australia, but now found in many parts of Australia, especially lining the promenades of eastern coastal towns. Latin name: *Araucaria heterophylla.*

Nor·folk jack·et *n.* a loose jacket with a belt and box pleats, first worn by men and later adapted to women's fashions [Named for *Norfolk*, a county in the east of England]

Nor·folk ter·ri·er *n.* a small wirehaired breed of terrier with a short tail and drop ears [See NORFOLK JACKET]

NOR gate *n.* = **NOR circuit**

no·ri /náwree/ *n.* an edible preparation of dried pressed seaweed, often used to wrap sushi [Late 19thC. From Japanese.]

no·ri·a /náwree ə/ *n.* a series of buckets on a water wheel, used for raising water from a stream [Late 18thC. Via Spanish from Arabic *nāʿūra*.]

No·ri·e·ga /nòrree áygə/, **Manuel** (*b.* 1934) Panamanian dictator. He took power in 1983, but was seized by U.S. forces in 1989, and later jailed for drug trafficking and other offenses. Full name **Manuel Antonio Noriega Morena**

nor·ite /náw rīt/ *n.* a coarse-grained igneous rock containing mainly plagioclase and orthopyroxene [Late 19thC. Formed from NORWAY + -ITE.] —**nor·it·ic** /naw ríttik/ *adj.*

norm /nawrm/ *n.* 1. STANDARD PATTERN OF BEHAVIOR a standard pattern of behavior that is considered normal in a particular society 2. USUAL SITUATION the usual situation or circumstances 3. REQUIRED ACHIEVEMENT LEVEL a required level of achievement 4. PSYCHOL EXPECTED RANGE OF FUNCTIONING the range of functioning that can be expected of members of a particular population, e.g., babies of nine months or ten-year-old children. Psychologists use this to determine whether individuals functioning outside the expected range may need specialist help or support. 5. MATH REAL-VALUED FUNCTION the magnitude of a vector expressed as the square root of the sum of the squares of the absolute values of the components of the vector 6. MATH = **mode** *n.* 6 [Early 19thC. Anglicization of Latin *norma* "carpenter's square, rule," of uncertain origin; perhaps ultimately from Greek *gnōmōn*. Subsequently influenced by NORMAL.]

Norm /nawrm/ *n. Aus* an Australian man who enjoys watching sport on television while consuming large quantities of beer (*slang*) ○ *It's Grand Final week, so your average Norm will be glued to the box.* [From the first name *Norm*, short for *Norman*, influenced by NORM, NORMAL]

norm. *abbr.* GEOM normal

Norm. /nawrm/ *abbr.* Norman

Nor·ma /náwrmə/ *n.* a small faint constellation of the southern hemisphere lying in the Milky Way, located between Ara and Lupus

nor·mal /náwrm'l/ *adj.* 1. USUAL conforming to the usual standard, type, or custom 2. HEALTHY physically, mentally, and emotionally healthy 3. OCCURRING NATURALLY maintained or occurring in a natural state 4. MEASURE ONE GRAM EQUIVALENT WEIGHT PER LITER containing an equivalent weight of solute in grams per liter of solution 5. CHEM UNBRANCHED used to describe aliphatic hydrocarbons with unbranched chains of carbon atoms 6. GEOM = **perpendicular** *adj.* 1 ■ *n.* 1. USUAL STANDARD the usual standard, type, or custom 2. GEOM PERPENDICULAR LINE OR PLANE a line or plane that is perpendicular to another line or plane [15thC. Directly or via French from Latin *normalis* "made according to the square," from *norma* (see NORM).] —**nor·mal·ly** *adv.*

Nor·mal /náwrməl/ city in north central Illinois, southeast of Peoria and northeast of Bloomington. Population: 42,655 (1996).

nor·mal curve *n.* the symmetrical bell-shaped curve of a normal distribution

nor·mal·cy /náwrm'lsee/ *n.* = **normality**

nor·mal dis·tri·bu·tion *n.* a probability frequency distribution for a random variable that theoretically takes on a bell shape symmetrical about the mean

nor·mal·i·ty /nawr mállətee/ *n.* the way things are under normal circumstances

nor·mal·ize /náwrm'l ìz/ (**-ized, -iz·ing, -iz·es**) *v.* 1. *vti.* MAKE OR BECOME NORMAL to make something normal or return something to normal, or become or return to normal 2. *vt.* MAKE CONFORM to make something or somebody conform to a standard 3. *vt.* METALL HEAT STEEL to heat steel above a particular temperature and then cool it in order to reduce internal stress —**nor·mal·i·za·tion** /nàwrm'li záysh'n/ *n.*

nor·mal school *n.* a school or college for training teachers, especially in France and, in the past, in England, the United States, and Canada (*dated*) [Mid-19thC. Modeled on French *école normale*; from the first French school so named being considered a model for others.]

Nor·man /náwrmən/ *n.* 1. HIST MEDIEVAL INHABITANT OF NORMANDY OR ENGLAND a member of a Viking people who raided and then settled in the French province subsequently known as Normandy and who later successfully invaded England in 1066 2. PEOPLES SOMEBODY FROM NORMANDY a person who was born or raised in the French region of Normandy 3. LANG = **Norman French** *n.* 1 4. ARCHIT STYLE OF MEDIEVAL ARCHITECTURE in Europe, a style of Romanesque architecture developed by the Normans in the Middle Ages, characterized by groined vaults, heavy walls, and deeply recessed portals ■ *adj.* 1. HIST RELATING TO MEDIEVAL NORMAN PEOPLE relating to the medieval people of Normandy and, later, their descendants in England 2. GEOG RELATING TO NORMANDY relating to Normandy in France 3. ARCHIT RELATING TO ROMANESQUE ARCHITECTURAL STYLE belonging to the style of architecture known as Norman [13thC. From Old French *Normans*, plural of *Normant*, from Old Norse *Norðmaðr* (*Norðmenn* in plural), literally "northman," from *norð* "north."]

Nor·man /náwrmən/, **Greg** (*b.* 1955) Australian golfer. He was the winner of the British Open (1986, 1993), and the World Match Play Championship (1980, 1983, and 1986). Full name **Gregory John Norman.** Known as **Great White Shark**

Nor·man Con·quest *n.* the invasion and conquest of England by the Normans, led by William the Conqueror, in 1066

Nor·man·dy /náwrməndee/ region in northwestern France, on the English Channel. Capital: Rouen.

Nor·man·esque /nàwrmə nésk/ *adj.* resembling the Norman style of architecture

Nor·man French *n.* 1. FRENCH SPOKEN BY MEDIEVAL NORMANS a variety of French spoken by the Normans in the Middle Ages 2. FRENCH DIALECT OF MODERN NORMANDY the French dialect spoken in modern Normandy

nor·ma·tive /náwrmətiv/ *adj.* (*formal*) 1. OF STANDARDS relating to standards 2. CREATING STANDARDS tending to create or prescribe standards [Late 19thC. From French, from Latin *norma* (see NORM).] —**nor·ma·tive·ly** *adv.* —**nor·ma·tive·ness** *n.*

norm·ing /náwrming/ *n.* the practice of adjusting the scores on standardized tests in order to compensate for the possible effects that ethnic and cultural differences may have on the test results

nor·mo·ten·sive /nàwrmō ténsiv/ *adj.* WITH NORMAL BLOOD PRESSURE having or indicating normal blood pressure ■ *n.* SOMEBODY WITH NORMAL BLOOD PRESSURE somebody who has normal blood pressure [Mid-20thC. From NORM or NORMAL + TENSIVE.]

nor·mo·ther·mi·a /nàwrmō thúrmee ə/ *n.* the state of having a normal body temperature —**nor·mo·ther·mic** *adj.*

norm-ref·er·enced *adj.* using a comparison of a pupil's performance in a test with the performance of other children in the same test

Nor·ris /nórriss/, **Frank** (1870–1902) U.S. writer. He is known for his naturalistic novels, *McTeague* (1899) and *The Octopus* (1901). Full name **Frank Benjamin Franklin Norris**

Norse /nawrs/ *adj.* 1. HIST OF OLD SCANDINAVIA relating to ancient or medieval Scandinavia, or its people or culture 2. OF NORWAY relating to Norway, or its people or culture 3. LANG OF N GERMANIC LANGUAGES relating to the North Germanic languages ■ *npl.* 1. HIST VIKINGS the Viking people of medieval Scandinavia 2. PEOPLES NORWEGIANS the people of Norway 3. PEOPLES SCANDINAVIANS the people of Scandinavia 4. LANG, PEOPLES N GERMANIC NATIVE SPEAKERS the people who speak one of the North Germanic languages as their native language ■ *n.* LANG N GERMANIC LANGUAGE a language belonging to the North Germanic branch of Indo-European, especially Danish, Icelandic, or Norwegian in their earlier forms. ◊ **Old Norse, Proto-Norse** [Late 16thC. Via Dutch *Noorsch* from *noordsch* "northern."]

Norse·man /náwrsmən/ (*plural* **-men** /-mən/) *n.* a member of one of the medieval Scandinavian groups, especially a Viking

north /nawrth/ *n.* 1. DIRECTION the direction that lies directly to the left of somebody facing the rising sun or that is located toward the top of a conventional map of the world 2. COMPASS POINT one of the cardinal points on a compass. North is 90 degrees counterclockwise from east. 3. **north, North** AREA IN THE NORTH the part of an area, region, or country that is situated in or toward the north 4. CHR LEFT-HAND SIDE OF CHURCH the left-hand side of a church as you face the altar from the central section of the building 5. **north, North** POSITION EQUIVALENT TO NORTH the position equivalent to north in any diagram consisting of four points at 90-degree intervals ■ *adj.* 1. IN THE NORTH situated in, facing, or coming from the north of a place, region, or country 2. FROM THE NORTH blowing from the north ○ *a north wind* ■ *adv.* TOWARD THE NORTH in or toward the north [Old English *norþ*, of prehistoric Germanic origin]

North /nawrth/, **Frederick, 8th Baron North** (1732–92) British statesman. He was British prime minister from 1770 to 1782, and was widely held responsible for the American Revolution despite his opposition to the war. Known as **Lord North**

North Ad·ams town in northwestern Massachusetts, on the Hoosic River, northeast of Pittsfield. Population: 15,847 (1996).

North Af·ri·ca northern part of the African continent, comprising Morocco, Algeria, Tunisia, Libya, and northern Egypt —**North Af·ri·can** *adj., n.*

North A·mer·i·ca the third largest continent in the world, comprising Greenland, Canada, the United States, and Mexico —**North A·mer·i·can** *adj., n.*

North·amp·ton /nàwr thámptən/ city in west central Massachusetts, on the western bank of the Connecticut River, north of Holyoke. It is home to Smith College. Population: 28,838 (1996).

North An·do·ver town in northeastern Massachusetts, at the confluence of the Shawshine and Merrimack rivers, southeast of Lawrence. Population: 24,283 (1996).

North At·lan·ta city in Georgia, in DeKalb County, situated north of Atlanta. Population: 27,812 (1990).

North At·lan·tic drift *n.* the relatively warm current, originating in the Gulf of Mexico, that flows across the surface of the North Atlantic Ocean from Newfoundland to northwestern Europe, influencing the latter's climate

North At·lan·tic Trea·ty Or·ga·ni·za·tion *n.* full form of **NATO**

North At·tle·bor·o /-átt'lbərə/ town in southeastern Massachusetts, just east of the Rhode Island border, southwest of Brockton. Population: 25,550 (1996).

North Bat·tle·ford /-bátt'lfərd/ city in western Saskatchewan, Canada, on the North Saskatchewan River. Population: 17,987 (1996).

North Bay city on Lake Nipissing in southeastern Ontario, Canada. Population: 64,785 (1996).

North Bell·more /-bél mawr/ town in Nassau County, New York, situated on Long Island, east of New York City. Population: 19,707 (1990).

North Ber·gen city in New Jersey, Hudson County. Population: 48,414 (1990).

north·bound /náwrth bòwnd/ *adj.* leading, going, or traveling toward the north

North·brook /náwrth brŏŏk/ village in northeastern Illinois, northwest of Wilmette. It is a northern suburb of Chicago. Population: 32,943 (1996).

north by east *n.* the direction or compass point midway between north and north-northeast. See table at **compass** —**north by east** *adj., adv.*

north by west *n.* the direction or compass point midway between north and north-northwest. See table at **compass** —**north by west** *adj., adv.*

North Carolina

North Car·o·li·na state in the eastern United States, bordered by the Atlantic Ocean, South Carolina, Georgia, Tennessee, and Virginia. Capital: Raleigh. Population: 7,425,183 (1997). Area: 52,672 sq. mi./136,420 sq. km. —**North Car·o·lin·i·an** *adj., n.*

North Cas·cades Na·tion·al Park national park in northwestern Washington, established in 1968 and noted for its glaciers. Area: 789 sq. mi./2,043 sq. km.

North Charles·ton city in southeastern South Carolina between the Ashley and Cooper rivers, north of Charleston. Population: 59,923 (1996).

North Chi·ca·go city in northeastern Illinois, on Lake Michigan, south of Waukegan and north of Chicago. Population: 31,665 (1996).

North Dakota

North Da·ko·ta state in the north central United States, bordered by Minnesota, South Dakota, Montana, and Canada. Capital: Bismarck. Population: 640,883 (1997). Area: 70,704 sq. mi./183,123 sq. km. —**North Da·ko·tan** *adj., n.*

north·east /nawrth éest/; *nautical usage* /nawr éest/ *n.* **1. COMPASS POINT BETWEEN N AND E** the direction or compass point midway between north and east. See table at **compass 2. north·east, North·east AREA IN THE NORTHEAST** the part of an area, region, or country that is situated in or toward the northeast ■ *adj.* **1. north·east, North·east IN THE NORTHEAST** situated in, facing, or lying toward the northeast of a region, place, or country **2.** METEOROL **FROM NORTHEAST** blowing from the northeast ○ *a northeast wind* ■ *adv.* **TOWARD THE NORTHEAST** in or toward the northeast

North·east *n.* **1. NORTHEASTERN U.S. REGION** a region of the northeastern United States, usually thought of as consisting of the New England states, sometimes together with eastern New York, Pennsylvania, and New Jersey **2.** *U.K.* **NORTHEASTERN ENGLAND** northeastern England, especially the area from the Tees River northward including Tyneside, Northumberland, and Durham

north·east by east *n.* the direction or compass point midway between northeast and east-northeast. See table at **compass** —**north·east by east** *adj., adv.*

north·east by north *n.* the direction or compass point midway between northeast and north-northeast. See table at **compass** —**north·east by north** *adj., adv.*

north·east·er /nawrth éestər/; *nautical usage* /nawr éestər/ *n.* a storm or wind that blows from the northeast

WORD KEY: REGIONAL NOTE

This word is recurrent in Atlantic and Great Lakes states, from Pennsylvania to Minnesota. It is also gaining ground nationwide because of its use by television weathercasters.

north·east·er·ly /nawrth éestərlee/; *nautical usage* /nawr éestərlee/ *adj.* **1. IN THE NORTHEAST** situated in or toward the northeast **2.** METEOROL **FROM THE NORTHEAST** blowing from the northeast ○ *a northeasterly wind* ■ *n.* (*plural* **-lies**) METEOROL = **northeaster** —**north·east·er·ly** *adv.*

north·east·ern /nawrth éestərn/; *nautical usage* /nawr éestərn/ *adj.* **1. IN THE NORTHEAST** situated in the northeast of a region or country **2. COMING FROM OR FACING NORTHEAST** coming or blowing from, or facing toward the northeast **3. north·east·ern, North·east·ern OF THE NORTHEAST** relating or native to the northeast of a region or country —**north·east·ern·er** *n.* —**north·east·ern·most** *adj.*

North·east Pas·sage sea passage extending from the North Sea eastward along the northern coast of Europe and Asia to the Pacific Ocean. It was first successfully navigated by Adolf Erik Nordenskiöld in 1878–79.

north·east·ward /nawrth éestwərd/; *nautical usage* /nawr éestwərd/ *adj.* **IN THE NORTHEAST** toward or in the northeast ■ *n.* **POINT IN THE NORTHEAST** a direction toward or a point in the northeast ■ *adv.* **EAST OF NORTH** toward or from east of due north —**north·east·ward** *adv.* —**north·east·ward·ly** *adj., adv.*

north·er /náwrthər/ *n.* a very cold wind or storm that suddenly appears from the north

north·er·ly /náwrthərlee/ *adj.* **1. IN THE NORTH** situated in or toward the north **2. FROM THE NORTH** blowing from the north ○ *a northerly wind* ■ *n.* (*plural* **-lies**) METEOROL **WIND FROM THE NORTH** a wind blowing from the north [Mid-16thC. Ultimately from NORTH, on the model of *easterly.*] —**north·er·ly** *adv.*

north·ern /náwrthərn/ *adj.* **1. IN THE NORTH** situated in the north of a region or country **2. NORTH OF EQUATOR** lying north of the equator or north of the celestial equator **3. FACING NORTH** situated on the north side of something or facing north **4. north·ern, North·ern OF THE NORTH** relating or native to the north of a region or country **5.** METEOROL **FROM THE NORTH** blowing from the north ○ *a northern wind*

North·ern Cross *n.* a cross formed by six stars in the constellation Cygnus

North·ern Crown *n.* ASTRON = **Corona Borealis**

north·ern·er *n.* somebody who lives in or comes from the northern part of a country or region

north·ern har·ri·er *n.* a slim-bodied brown or grayish hawk that lives in marshy areas of North America, Europe, and Asia, and has a conspicuous white patch on its tail. Latin name: *Circus cyaneus.*

north·ern hem·i·sphere *n.* **1.** GEOG **HALF OF EARTH NORTH OF EQUATOR** the half of the Earth that lies to the north of the equator **2.** ASTRON **NORTHERN HALF OF CELESTIAL SPHERE** the half of the celestial sphere north of the celestial equator

North·ern·ism /náwrthər nìzzəm/ *n.* a pronunciation, word, or other linguistic construction typical of the northern region of a country

north·ern lights *npl.* = **aurora borealis**

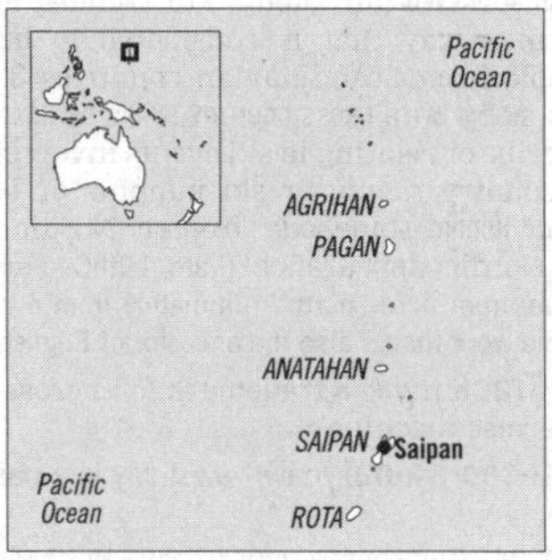

Northern Mariana Islands

North·ern Mar·i·an·a Is·lands /-màrri ánnə-/ self-governing commonwealth of the United States, situated in the western Pacific Ocean and comprising all of the Mariana Islands except Guam. Area: 184 sq. mi./477 sq. km.

north·ern·most /náwrthərn mōst/ *adj.* situated farthest north

north·ern o·ri·ole *n.* a North American oriole that has two subspecies, the Baltimore oriole and Bullock's oriole. The males have black and orange plumage. Latin name: *Icterus galbula.*

North·ern Pai·ute (*plural* **North·ern Pai·ute** *or* **North·ern Pai·utes**), **North·ern Pi·ute** (*plural* **North·ern Pi·ute** *or* **North·ern Pi·utes**) *n.* ◊ **Southern Paiute 1.** PEOPLES **MEMBER OF NATIVE N AMERICAN PEOPLE** a member of a Native North American people of Oregon, Nevada, and northeastern California **2.** LANG **NATIVE AMERICAN LANGUAGE** a Native American language spoken in Oregon, Nevada, and northeastern California, belonging to the Uto-Aztecan branch of Aztec-Tanoan languages. Northern Paiute is spoken by about 6,000 people. —**North·ern Pai·ute** *adj.*

north·ern pike *n.* ZOOL = **pike**[1] *n.* 1

WORD KEY: REGIONAL NOTE

With scattered instances in the East and South, the term, denoting the fish, recurs with high frequency in Michigan, Wisconsin, and Minnesota.

North·ern Pi·ute LANGUAGE a Native North American language spoken in Oregon, Nevada, and northeastern California. It belongs to the Uto-Aztecan branch of Aztec-Tanoan languages. Northern Piute is spoken by about six thousand people.

North·ern Ren·ais·sance *n.* a northern European cultural and intellectual movement of the 15th century in France, England, the Low Countries, and Germany that placed more emphasis on religion than the Italian Renaissance did

North·ern Yu·kon Na·tion·al Park national park in northwestern Canada, in the northwestern corner of Yukon Territory, on the Alaskan border. It is a sanctuary for Arctic wildlife and Inuit archeological sites. Area: 3,859 sq. mi./9,995 sq. km.

North Fort My·ers city in southwestern Florida, near Fort Myers, in Lee County. Population: 30,027 (1990).

North Ger·man·ic *n.* a group of languages that includes Danish, Faroese, Icelandic, Norwegian, and Swedish and forms a subgroup of the Germanic branch of Indo-European languages. About 20 million people speak one of the North Germanic languages. —**North Ger·man·ic** *adj.*

North Ha·ven town in southern Connecticut, in central New Haven County, northeast of New Haven. Population: 22,247 (1990).

North High·lands town in Sacramento County, north central California, northeast of Sacramento. Population: 42,105 (1990).

north·ing /náwrthing, -thing/ *n.* **1.** NAUT **MOVEMENT NORTH** distance covered or movement made in a northerly direction, especially as measured by the difference in latitude between two points **2.** NAUT **PROGRESS NORTH** progress made in a northern direction **3.** MAPS **LATITUDINAL GRID LINE ON MAP** a grid line on a map that runs from east to west. ◊ **easting 4.** MAPS **DISTANCE NORTHWARD** the distance northward from a specific east-west grid line shown in the second half of a map reference

North Is·land, the island in New Zealand, in the southwestern Pacific Ocean. It is the smaller and more northern of the country's two main islands. Population: 2,749,980 (1996). Area: 44,689 sq. mi./115,777 sq. km.

North Kings·town town in south central Rhode Island, on the western shore of Narragansett Bay, southwest of Warwick. Population: 25,594 (1996).

North Ko·re·a ♦ **Korea [North]**

north·land /náwrth lànd, -lənd/ *n.* the northern part of a country

North·land *n.* **1. SCANDINAVIAN PENINSULA** the Scandinavian peninsula containing Norway and Sweden **2.** *Can* **FAR NORTHERN CANADA** parts of Canada in the far north

North Lau·der·dale city in southeastern Florida in Broward County, situated northwest of Fort Lauderdale. Population: 26,506 (1990).

North Lit·tle Rock city in central Arkansas, across the Arkansas River from Little Rock. Population: 60,468 (1996).

north mag·net·ic pole *n.* the point on the Earth's surface to which the north-seeking pole of a compass needle is attracted

North·man /náwrthmən/ (*plural* **-men** /-mən/) *n.* = **Norseman**

North Mi·am·i city in southeastern Florida, in Miami-Dade County. It is a suburb of Miami. Population: 49,998 (1990).

North Mi·am·i Beach city in Dade County, southeastern Florida, situated north of Miami Beach. Population: 35,359 (1990).

north-north·east *n.* the direction or compass point midway between north and northeast. See table at **compass** —**north-north·east** *adj., adv.* —**north-north·east·er·ly** *adj., adv.*

north-north·west *n.* the direction or compass point midway between north and northwest. See table at **compass** —**north-north·west** *adj., adv.* —**north-north·west·er·ly** *adj., adv.*

north pole *n.* **1. north pole, North Pole NORTHERN END OF EARTH'S AXIS** the northern end of the Earth's axis at a latitude of 90° N **2.** = **north magnetic pole 3. POINT AT NORTHERN EXTENSION OF EARTH'S AXIS** the point at infinity along the northern extension of one end of the Earth's axis of rotation

North Prov·i·dence town in northeastern Rhode Island, southeast of Woonsocket. It is a northern suburb of Providence. Population: 31,194 (1996).

North Shore *n.* **1. CONNECTICUT SHORELINE** the Connecticut coast, which forms the northern side of Long Island Sound **2. SHORE NORTH OF BOSTON** the area of the Atlantic coastline immediately north of Boston **3.** *Can* **SHORE IN BRITISH COLUMBIA** the shore of the Burrard north of the city of Vancouver **4.** *Can* **SHORE IN EASTERN QUEBEC** the northern shore of the St. Lawrence River. **5.** *Can* **SHORE IN EASTERN NEW BRUNSWICK** the northern coast along the Northumberland Strait and the Gulf of St. Lawrence.

North Slope area of northern Alaska that holds the largest petroleum reserves in the United States

North Star *n.* ASTRON = **Polaris**

North Strad·broke Is·land /-strádbrok-/ island of northeastern Australia, in Moreton Bay, off the coast of southeastern Queensland. Population: 2,290 (1994). Area: 123 sq. mi./319 sq. km.

North Ton·a·wan·da /-tónnə wóndə/ city in western New York, southeast of Niagara Falls and north of Buffalo. Population: 33,773 (1996).

North Uist /-yoo ist/ island in northwestern Scotland, in the Outer Hebrides, situated off the northwestern coast of the mainland. Population: 1,404 (1991).

North·um·bri·an /nawr thúmbree ən/ *adj.* **1.** GEOG **OF NORTHUMBERLAND** relating to the English county of Northumberland, or its people or culture **2.** HIST **OF NORTHUMBRIA** relating to Northumbria, a region of Anglo-Saxon Britain, or its people or culture **3.** LANG **OF DIALECT OF OLD AND MIDDLE ENGLISH** relating to the dialect of Old and Middle English spoken in Northumbria ■ *n.* LANG **DIALECT OF OLD AND MIDDLE ENGLISH** a dialect of Old and Middle English spoken in an area roughly north of the Humber and Mersey rivers and into the Borders of Scotland

North Van·cou·ver city in southwestern Canada, in southern British Columbia, situated on Burrard Inlet across from Vancouver. Population: 38,436 (1991).

north·ward /náwrthwərd/; *nautical usage* /náwthərd/, **north·wards** *adv.* **TOWARD THE NORTH** in a northerly direction ■ *n.* **NORTHWARD POINT IN THE NORTH** a direction toward or a point in the north —**north·ward** *adj.* —**north·ward·ly** *adj., adv.*

north·west /nawrth wést/; *nautical usage* /nawr wést/ *n.* **1. COMPASS POINT BETWEEN N AND W** the direction or compass point midway between north and west. See table at **compass 2. north·west, North·west AREA IN THE NORTHWEST** the part of an area, region, or country that is situated in or toward the northwest ■ *adj.* **1. north·west, North·west IN THE NORTHWEST** situated in, facing, or lying toward the northwest of a region, place, or country **2.** METEOROL **FROM NORTHWEST** blowing from the northwest ○ *a northwest wind* ■ *adv.* **TOWARD THE NORTHWEST** in or toward the northwest

North·west *n.* **1. NORTHWESTERN UNITED STATES** the northwestern area of the United States, including the states of Washington, Oregon, and Idaho **2. FORMER AREA OF THE UNITED STATES** formerly, a region of the United States west of the Mississippi River and north of the Missouri River **3.** *Can* **CANADIAN REGION** the area of Canada north and west of the Great Lakes **4.** *U.K.* **AREA OF ENGLAND** the northwestern region of England, especially Cumbria and Lancashire and including the Lake District

north·west by north *n.* the direction or compass point midway between northwest and north-northwest. See table at **compass** —**north·west by north** *adj., adv.*

north·west by west *n.* the direction or compass point midway between northwest and west-northwest. See table at **compass** —**north·west by west** *adj., adv.*

north·west·er /nawrth wéstər/; *nautical usage* /nawr wéstər/ *n.* a wind blowing from the northwest

north·west·er·ly /nawrth wéstərlee/; *nautical usage* /nawr wéstərlee/ (*plural* **-lies**) *adj.* **1. IN THE NORTHWEST** situated in or toward the northwest **2.** METEOROL **FROM THE NORTHWEST** blowing from the northwest ○ *a northwesterly wind* —**north·west·er·ly** *adv.*

north·west·ern /nawrth wéstərn/; *nautical usage* /nawr wéstərn/ *adj.* **1. IN THE NORTHWEST** situated in the northwest of a region or country **2. FACING NORTHWEST** coming or blowing from, or facing toward the northwest **3. OF THE NORTHWEST** typical of or native to the northwest of a region or country —**north·west·ern·er** *n.* —**north·west·ern·most** *adj.*

North·west Pas·sage sea passage through the Arctic regions of North America, connecting the Pacific Ocean and the Atlantic Ocean

North·west Ter·ri·to·ries region in northern Canada, and its largest political subdivision, constituting a northern mainland region and numerous islands to the north. Capital: Yellowknife. Population: 64,402 (1996). Area: 1,322,904 sq. mi./3,426,320 sq. km.

north·west·ward /nawrth wéstwərd/; *nautical usage* /nawr wéstwərd/ *adj.* **IN THE NORTHWEST** toward or in

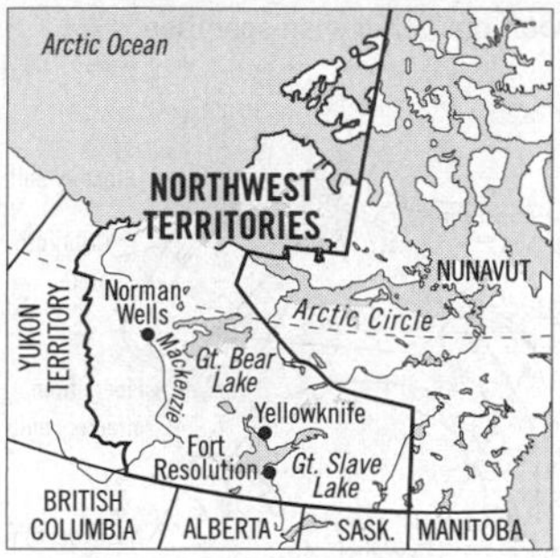

Northwest Territories

the northwest ■ *n.* **POINT IN THE NORTHWEST** a direction toward or a point in the northwest —**north·west·ward·ly** *adj., adv.* —**north·west·ward** *adv.*

Nor·ton /náwrt'n/, **Charles Eliot** (1827–1908) U.S. scholar and editor. He cofounded *The Nation* (1865) and pioneered the teaching of art history at Harvard (1873–97).

nor·trip·ty·line /nawr tríptə leen/ *n.* a compound used as an antidepressant, tranquilizer, and pain reliever. Formula: $C_{19}H_{21}N$. [Mid-20thC. Coined from NOR- + TRI + *ptyl* (a shortening of *heptyl*) + -INE.]

Norw. *abbr.* **1.** Norway **2.** Norwegian

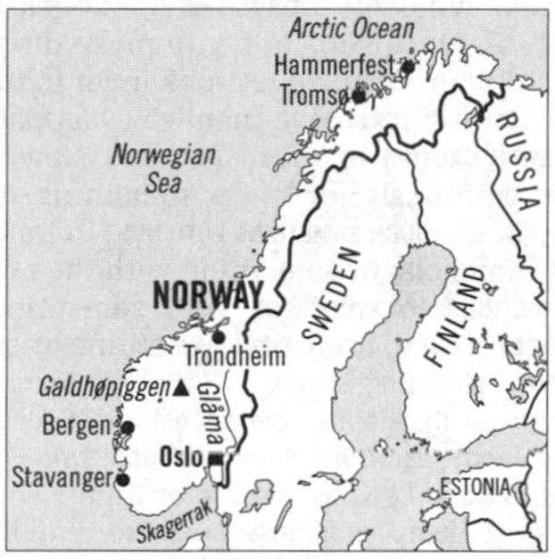

Norway

Nor·way /náwr way/ monarchy in northern Europe, occupying the western and northern portions of the Scandinavian Peninsula. Language: Norwegian. Currency: krone. Capital: Oslo. Population: 4,369,957 (1996). Area: 125,016 sq. mi./323,877 sq. km. Official name **Kingdom of Norway**

Nor·way ma·ple *n.* a tall Eurasian maple with broad five-lobed green or reddish leaves, widely grown as a shade tree in the United States. Latin name: *Acer plantanoides.*

Nor·way rat *n.* = **brown rat**

Nor·way spruce *n.* a European spruce tree with dark green needles, drooping branches, and long cones, widely grown for its timber and as an ornamental. Latin name: *Picea abies.*

Nor·we·gian /nawr weejən/ *n.* **1.** PEOPLES **SOMEBODY FROM NORWAY** somebody who was born or raised in Norway, or who has Norwegian citizenship **2.** LANG **OFFICIAL LANGUAGE OF NORWAY** the official language of Norway, belonging to the North Germanic group of Indo-European languages. Norwegian is spoken by about five million people. ◊ **Landsmål** ■ *adj.* **1.** PEOPLES **OF NORWAY** relating to Norway, or its people or culture **2.** LANG **OF NORWEGIAN** relating to the Norwegian language [Early 17thC. Formed from medieval Latin *Norvegia* "Norway," from Old Norse *Norvegr.*]

Nor·we·gian elk·hound *n.* a sturdy medium-sized dog with pointed ears, a broad head, and a thick gray coat, belonging to a breed developed in Norway to hunt elk and other game

nor'west·er /nawr wéstər/ *n.* **1.** METEOROL = **northwester 2.** *U.K.* BEVERAGES **ALCOHOLIC DRINK** a strong alcoholic drink (*slang*)

Nor·wich /nórrich/ city in southeastern Connecticut, in New London County. Population: 37,391 (1990).

Nor·wich ter·ri·er *n.* a small short-legged dog with wiry fur and erect ears, belonging to a breed that originated in East Anglia, England

nos., Nos. *abbr.* numbers

n.o.s. *abbr.* not otherwise specified

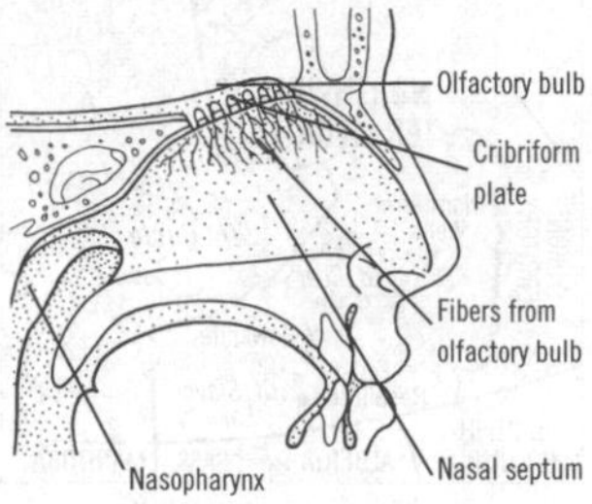

Nose: Cross section of the human nose

nose /nōz/ *n.* **1.** ANAT **ORGAN OF SMELL** the part of the face or head through which a person or animal breathes and smells **2. SENSE OF SMELL** the sense of smell, especially the ability to recognize things by smell or to follow a scent **3. TALENT FOR FINDING SOMETHING** an intuitive ability to discover, detect, or recognize something **4. PART RESEMBLING NOSE** a part that resembles the nose of a person or animal in appearance or function **5.** AUTOMOT, AIR **PROJECTING FRONT PART OF VEHICLE** the pointed or rounded front end of an aircraft, spacecraft, boat, car, or other vehicle **6. DISTINCTIVE SMELL** the characteristic aroma of something, e.g., wine or tobacco ■ *v.* **(nosed, nos·ing, nos·es) 1.** *vi.* **PRY OR SNOOP** to try to make discoveries by searching or asking questions in an inquisitive, impertinent, or intrusive manner (*informal*) **2.** *vti.* **ADVANCE WITH CAUTION** to move forward slowly, carefully, or cautiously, or make something move in this way **3.** *vt.* **TOUCH SOMETHING WITH NOSE** to touch, rub, or push somebody or something with the nose **4.** *vt.* **SMELL SOMETHING** to smell or sniff something **5.** *vi.* **SEARCH FOR BY SCENT** to try to find something by smelling or sniffing [Old English *nosu.* Ultimately from an Indo-European word that is also the ancestor of English *nasal, pince-nez,* and *nasturtium.*] —**nose·less** *adj.* ◇ **get up somebody's nose** *U.K.* to irritate or annoy somebody (*informal*) ◇ **keep your nose clean** to avoid getting into trouble (*informal*) ◇ **look down you nose at somebody** *or* **something** to regard somebody or something arrogantly or disdainfully as inferior or not worth your attention ◇ **nose to tail** so close together that the front of one vehicle almost touches the rear end of another ◇ **on the nose 1.** absolutely on target, with total accuracy, or completely correctly (*informal*) ○ *at 10 o'clock on the nose* **2.** in betting on horseraces, for a horse to win only, not to be placed second or third (*slang*) ◇ **put somebody's nose out of joint** to make somebody feel thwarted or offended because you do, obtain, or achieve something that he or she was intending or hoping for ◇ **turn up your nose at something** to refuse to accept something because you feel it is inferior or unworthy of you (*informal*) ◇ **under somebody's nose** in full view of or very close to somebody

nose around *vti.* to look or search through a place in an inquisitive and often intrusive way (*informal*)

nose out *v.* **1.** *vt.* **NARROWLY DEFEAT OPPONENT** to defeat an opponent by a very narrow margin **2.** *vi.* **DRIVE CAUTIOUSLY FORWARD** to move a vehicle very slowly and cautiously forward out of a place **3.** *vt.* **FIND SOMETHING OUT BY PRYING** to discover something by thorough and often cunning or intrusive searching or questioning **4.** *vt.* **FIND SOMETHING BY SCENT** to discover something by smelling or sniffing, or as if by following a scent

nose·bag /nṓz bàg/ *n.* = **feedbag**

nose·band /nṓz bànd/ *n.* the part of a horse's bridle that goes over its nose

nose·bleed /nṓz blēed/ *n.* a flow of blood from the nose. Technical name **epistaxis** ■ *adj.* **EXTREMELY HIGH** extremely high or excessive, e.g., in price or profit level (*informal*)

nose can·dy *n.* cocaine (*slang*)

nose cone *n.* the pointed front section of a missile, rocket, spacecraft, aircraft, or race car, designed for aerodynamic efficiency

nose·dive /nṓz dìv/ *n.* **1.** AIR **STEEP PLUNGE THROUGH AIR** an extremely steep sudden plunge by an aircraft toward the earth **2. SHARP DECREASE** a sudden very significant fall or decline in price, value, amount, or quality

nose-dive *vi.* **1.** AIR **PLUNGE VERY STEEPLY THROUGH AIR** to fall vertically or almost vertically with the front end pointing downward (*refers to aircraft*) **2. DECREASE SHARPLY** to experience a sudden very significant fall or decline in price, value, amount, or quality —**nose-div·er** *n.*

nose drops *npl.* liquid medication for the nose inserted in drops through the nostrils

no-see-um /nō sēe əm/ *n.* = **punkie** [From caricatured Native American English, "you can't see them," from its small size]

nose flute *n.* a wind instrument of the South Pacific Islands, usually played by being breathed into through one nostril while the other one is plugged

nose·gay /nṓz gày/ *n.* a small bouquet of flowers (*dated*) [*Gay* from GAY in the obsolete sense "ornament"]

nose·guard /nṓz gaàrd/ *n.* in football, a defensive lineman who plays opposite the center in the offensive line

nose job *n.* a surgical operation to improve the shape or size of the nose (*informal*)

nose or·na·ment *n.* a decorative ring or stud worn through the nostril or septum

nose·piece /nṓz pēess/ *n.* **1. PART OF EYEGLASSES** the part of a pair of eyeglasses that fits over the nose and connects the lenses **2. PART OF MICROSCOPE** the end piece of a microscope to which one or more objective lenses are attached **3. PROTECTION FOR NOSE** the part of a helmet or piece of armor that protects the nose **4.** = **noseband**

nose ring *n.* **1. RING FIXED THROUGH ANIMAL'S NOSE** a ring put through an animal's nose to lead or control it **2. RING WORN IN NOSE AS ORNAMENT** a ring worn for adornment through a hole pierced in the nostril or septum

nose stud *n.* a small stud worn for adornment in a hole pierced in the nostril or septum

nose tack·le *n.* FOOTBALL = **noseguard**

nose wheel *n.* a landing-gear wheel at the front end of an aircraft

nos·ey *adj.* = **nosy**

nosh /nosh/ *n.* **SNACK** a snack (*informal*) ■ *v.* **(noshed, nosh·ing, nosh·es)** (*informal*) **1.** *vt.* **EAT** to eat something **2.** *vi.* to eat a snack between meals [Early 20thC. From Yiddish *nashen* "to nibble," from Middle High German *naschen.*] —**nosh·er** *n.*

no-show *n.* somebody who makes a reservation or appointment, or buys a ticket, but fails to arrive, without cancellation or explanation

nos·ing /nṓzing/ *n.* **1. PROJECTING EDGE OF STAIR TREAD** the rounded edge of a stair tread that projects horizontally **2. PROTECTION FOR NOSING** a shield that protects a nosing on a staircase **3.** ARCHIT **PROJECTING EDGE OF MOLDING** the rounded projecting edge of a molding

no-smok·ing *adj.* **NOT ALLOWING SMOKING** where smoking is not allowed, or that prohibits smoking ■ *n.* = **nonsmoking**

noso- *prefix.* disease ○ *nosophobia* [From Greek *nosos,* of unknown origin]

nos·o·co·mi·al /nō zō kṓmee əl/ *adj.* originating or occurring in a hospital [Mid-19thC. Formed from Greek *nosokomos* "somebody who tends the sick."]

no·sog·ra·phy /nō sóggrəfee/ (*plural* **-phies**) *n.* a detailed classification and description of known diseases —**no·sog·ra·pher** *n.* —**no·so·graph·ic** /nòssə gráffik/ *adj.* —**no·so·graph·i·cal·ly** *adv.*

no·sol·o·gy /nō sólləjee/ (*plural* **-gies**) *n.* **1. CLASSIFYING OF DISEASES** the branch of medicine concerned with the classification and description of known diseases **2. CLASSIFIED LIST OF DISEASES** a completed classification of known diseases —**no·so·log·i·cal** /nòssə lójjik'l/ *adj.* —**no·so·log·i·cal·ly** *adv.* —**no·sol·o·gist** /nō sólləjist/ *n.*

nos·o·pho·bi·a /nòssə fṓbee ə/ *n.* an irrational fear of catching diseases

nos·tal·gi·a /no stáljə, nə-/ *n.* **1. SENTIMENTAL RECOLLECTION** a mixed feeling of happiness, sadness, and longing when recalling a person, place, or event from the past, or the past in general **2. THINGS THAT AROUSE NOSTALGIA** something, or things, intended to arouse a feeling of nostalgia or to evoke the past nostalgically **3. HOMESICKNESS** a longing for home or family when away from either (*dated*) [Late 18thC. From modern Latin, "homesickness," from Greek *nostos* "homecoming" + *algos* "pain."] —**nos·tal·gic** *adj.* —**nos·tal·gi·cal·ly** *adv.*

nos·toc /nó stòk/ *n.* a freshwater blue-green alga that lives in spherical colonies as coiled filaments and fixes atmospheric nitrogen. Genus: *Nostoc.* [Mid-17thC. From modern Latin; invented by Paracelsus (1493–1541), Swiss physician.]

nos·tol·o·gy /no stólləjee/ *n.* MED = **gerontology** [Mid-20thC. Coined from Greek *nostos* "return home" (from the former idea that later life is like a return to early years) + -OLOGY.] —**nos·to·log·ic** /nòstə lójjik/ *adj.* —**nos·to·log·i·cal·ly** *adv.* —**nos·tol·o·gist** /no stólləjist/ *n.*

Nostradamus

Nos·tra·da·mus /nòstrə dáyməss, -daáməss/ (1503–66) French astrologer and physician. His prophecies, composed in rhyming quatrains and first published as *Centuries* in 1555, were consulted for hundreds of years. Born **Michel de Notredame**

nos·tril /nóstrəl/ *n.* either of the two openings at the end of the nose of a person or animal [Old English *nospyrl,* from *nosu,* an earlier form of NOSE, + *þyrl* "hole," from *þurh,* an earlier form of THROUGH]

nos·trum /nóstrəm/ *n.* **1. INEFFECTIVE REMEDY** a remedy for a social, political, or economic problem, especially an idea or scheme that is often suggested but never proved to be successful **2. QUACK REMEDY** a medicine prepared or prescribed by an unqualified person whose claims for its effectiveness have no scientific basis [Early 17thC. From Latin *nostrum (remedium)* "our (remedy)," a form of *noster* "our."]

nos·y /nṓzee/ (**-i·er, -i·est**), **nos·ey (-i·er, -i·est)** *adj.* too curious about other people's business (*informal*) —**nos·i·ly** *adv.* —**nos·i·ness** *n.*

nos·y park·er /-paárkər/ *n. U.K.* somebody who pries into other people's affairs, especially somebody who asks impertinent or intrusive questions (*informal disapproving*) [Said to refer to Elizabeth I's Archbishop of Canterbury, Matthew *Parker,* who was noted for detailed inquiries concerning ecclesiastical affairs]

not /not/ *adv.* **1. FORMING NEGATIVES** a negative adverb used to form structures indicating that something is to no degree or in no way the case or conveying the general notion "no." It is often used to express refusal, denial, or the negation of a statement just made. (*often contracted in spoken and informal written English to "n't"*) ○ *Don't you think you've done enough?* ○ *Not every household has a dishwasher.* ○ *There's nothing in my account; not one cent.* ○ *Not only was the meal expensive, the service was bad too.* **2. SENTENCE SUBSTITUTE** used as a sentence substitute when indicating denial, refusal, or negation, in order to avoid repetition ○ *"Won't you come with us?" "Certainly not."* ○ *I don't think I'll be late, at least I hope not.* ■ *interj.* **USED TO CONTRADICT** used alone after somebody's statement to indicate decided opposition or contradiction (*slang*) ○ *"Of course the team will win the playoffs hands down." "Not!"* [14thC. Contraction of NOUGHT.] ◇ **not at all** used as a polite way of acknowledging somebody's thanks ◇ **not that** used to introduce a clause that explicitly denies something that the listener might infer from a previous or subsequent statement ○ *I'm actually seeing her tonight. Not that it's any of your business!*

NOT /not/ *n.* a NOT circuit (*technical*)

no·ta plural of **notum**

no·ta be·ne /nòtə bénnee/ *interj.* used to draw somebody's attention to something particularly important, usually an addition to or qualification of a previous statement (*formal*) Full form of **n.b., N.B.** [From Latin, from *nota,* imperative form of *notare* "to mark" + *bene* "well"]

no·ta·bil·i·ty /nōtə bíllətee/ (*plural* **-ties**) *n.* **1. SOMEBODY IMPORTANT** a particularly important or distinguished person **2. SIGNIFICANCE** the importance of somebody or something, or the quality that makes somebody or something worth paying attention to

no·ta·ble /nṓtəb'l/ *adj.* **1. WORTHY OF NOTE** significant or great enough to deserve attention or to be recorded ○ *a notable contribution to our understanding of this complex phenomenon* **2. INTERESTING** interesting, significant, and worth calling attention to ○ *more notable for what it leaves out than for what it includes* **3. DISTINGUISHED** particularly important, distinguished, or famous ■ *n.* **SOMEBODY IMPORTANT** a particularly important or distinguished person [14thC. From Old French *notable*, from Latin *notare* "to note."] —**no·ta·ble·ness** *n.*

no·ta·bly /nṓtəblee/ *adv.* **1. ESPECIALLY** especially, or in the most significant case ○ *There has been much opposition, notably from the farming community.* **2. EXTREMELY** extremely or remarkably ○ *She seems notably unimpressed by all their arguments.*

no·tar·i·al /nō táiree əl/ *adj.* relating to or done by a notary public —**no·tar·i·al·ly** *adv.*

no·ta·rize /nṓtə rīz/ (**-rized, -riz·ing, -riz·es**) *vt.* to certify something, e.g., a signature on a legal document, as authentic or legitimate by affixing a notary's stamp and signature —**no·ta·ri·za·tion** /nōtəri záysh'n/ *n.*

no·ta·ry /nṓtəree/ (*plural* **-ries**) *n.* **1.** = **notary public 2. CLERK** a secretary or clerk (*archaic*) [14thC. Via Old French *notarie*, from Latin *notarius* "shorthand writer, clerk."]

no·ta·ry pub·lic (*plural* **no·ta·ries pub·lic**) *n.* somebody who is legally authorized to certify the authenticity of signatures and documents

no·tate /nṓ tàyt/ (**-tat·ed, -tat·ing, -tates**) *vt.* to write something down using notation, especially musical notation [Early 20thC. Back-formation from NOTATION.]

no·ta·tion /nō táysh'n/ *n.* **1. SYMBOLIC REPRESENTATION** a set of written symbols used to represent something, e.g., the length and pitch of musical notes **2. USE OF NOTATION** the process of using a system of notation **3. NOTE** a note or annotation **4. NOTING** the act of making a note or writing something down [Late16thC. Via Old French or Latin from the Latin past participle stem *notat-*, from *notare* "to note."]

notch /noch/ *n.* **1. NICK OR INDENTATION** a small V-shaped cut in the edge or on the surface of something **2. NICK USED AS TALLY** any of a series of cuts made to record a score, a debt, or the number of times something has been done **3. DEGREE ON SCALE** a level or step on a scale, especially one measuring quality or achievement ○ *raise the tension on the wire another notch* **4.** GEOG **PASS OR GORGE** a narrow valley between hills or mountains ■ *vt.* (**notched, notch·ing, notch·es**) **1. MAKE V-SHAPED CUT IN** to make a notch in or on something **2. RECORD WITH NOTCHES** to record a score or debt by making a series of cuts in a surface **3. ACHIEVE OR SCORE** to achieve a victory or success, or score a point or goal (*slang*) ○ *notched up one more win* [Mid-16thC. Origin uncertain: perhaps from an Anglo-Norman word.] —**notch·y** *adj.*

notch·back /nóch bàk/ *n.* a car with a sloping roof that drops sharply to the beginning of the trunk. ◊ **hatchback**

NOT cir·cuit *n.* a logic circuit in a computer that produces a high-voltage output signal if the input signal is low, or a low-voltage output signal if the input signal is high

note /nōt/ *n.* **1. JOTTED RECORD OR SUMMARY** something written down, often in abbreviated form, as a record or reminder **2. INFORMAL LETTER** a short written message or informal letter **3.** MUSIC **MUSICAL OR VOCAL SOUND** a sound of a particular pitch, quality, or duration produced by a musical instrument or by the voice of a person or animal. Also called **tone 4.** MUSIC **SYMBOL IN MUSIC** in written or printed music, a symbol representing a sound of a particular duration and pitch **5.** MUSIC **KEY ON KEYBOARD** a black or white key of a piano or other keyboard instrument **6.** PRINTING, PUBL **ITEM OF SUPPLEMENTARY INFORMATION** a piece of additional information about something in a printed text, usually given at the bottom of the relevant page or at the end of the book or article **7. WRITTEN COMMENT** a short written comment or item of information, e.g., written in the margin of a book or piece of work **8. HINT** a hint or suggestion of something ○ *a note of dissatisfaction* **9.** LANG **INTONATION SHOWING EMOTION** a tone in the voice that indicates the speaker's feelings or adds to the meaning of what is said ○ *a note of urgency* **10. CHARACTERISTIC FEATURE** a distinctive element, feeling, quality, or atmosphere ○ *a note of caution* **11. DISTINCTION** distinction or excellence ○ *a writer of note* **12.** FIN = **promissory note 13.** FIN = **bill**[1] *n.* 6 **14.** POL **OFFICIAL LETTER** a formal communication in writing, especially between governments **15. DOCUMENT** a short official document **16.** MUSIC **TUNE** a tune (*archaic*) ■ **notes** *npl.* **SUMMARY FOR FUTURE REFERENCE** important facts written down by somebody listening to something, e.g., a student during a lesson ■ *vt.* (**not·ed, not·ing, notes**) **1. OBSERVE SOMETHING** to notice or remember something by paying particular attention to it **2. PERCEIVE SOMETHING** to notice or become aware of something **3. MENTION SOMETHING** to mention something important **4. WRITE SOMETHING DOWN** to write down something important as a record or reminder [13thC. Via Old French *note* "sign, characteristic, short letter" from Latin *nota* "sign, mark."] —**note·less** *adj.* —**not·er** *n.*

note·book /nṓt bòòk/ *n.* **1. SMALL WRITING BOOK** a small book in which to write, containing blank or lined pages **2.** COMPUT **SMALL PERSONAL COMPUTER** a small thin portable personal computer

note card *n.* a folded sheet of paper or thin card with a picture on the front, used for writing short informal letters

not·ed /nṓtəd/ *adj.* **1. WELL-KNOWN** well-known and especially distinguished by or admired for a particular thing or quality ○ *He is not noted for his generosity.* **2. MARKED OR SIGNIFICANT** significant or distinctive enough to be noticeable —**not·ed·ly** *adv.* —**not·ed·ness** *n.*

note·let /nṓtlət/ *n. U.K.* = **note card**

note of hand *n.* FIN = **promissory note**

note·pad /nṓt pàd/ *n.* a number of small sheets of blank or lined paper on which to write, fastened together in a way that makes it easy to detach a single page

note·pa·per /nṓt pàypər/ *n.* paper for writing letters or making notes on

note row *n.* MUSIC = **tone row**

note·wor·thy /nṓt wùrthee/ (**-thi·er, -thi·est**) *adj.* deserving notice or attention, usually because of particular significance, excellence, uniqueness, or interest —**note·wor·thi·ly** *adv.* —**note·wor·thi·ness** *n.*

NOT gate *n.* COMPUT = **NOT circuit**

noth·ing /núthing/ *pron.* **1. NOT ANYTHING** an indefinite pronoun indicating that there is not anything, not a single thing, or not a single part of a thing ○ *There is nothing more annoying than people who can't keep their personal lives private.* ○ *There's nothing else I can do for you.* ○ *There's nothing like a good soak in a hot bath to relieve backache.* **2. SOMETHING OF NO IMPORTANCE** a thing or matter of no importance or significance ○ *It's nothing to me whether they win or lose.* **3. NOT HAVING A QUALITY** used to indicate the complete lack of the quality mentioned in somebody or something ○ *He wore an ordinary dark blue jacket, with nothing special about it.* ○ *Nothing of any consequence was said.* **4. ZERO AMOUNT** a zero quantity or zero ○ *We won, three to nothing.* **5. STATE OF NONEXISTENCE** a state of nonexistence, or the absence of any perceptible qualities ○ *vanished into nothing* ■ *n.* **SOMEBODY OR SOMETHING COMPLETELY UNIMPORTANT** somebody who or something that is totally unimportant ■ *adj.* **COMPLETELY UNDISTINGUISHED** completely lacking in distinguishing qualities, interest, or significance (*informal*) ○ *a nothing product, despite all the hype* [Old English *nāðinc*, from earlier forms of NO + THING] ◇ **all or nothing** used to indicate that only complete success or obtaining everything counts and anything less than that has no value ◇ **not for nothing** for a very good reason ◇ **nothing but** only ◇ **nothing doing** used to indicate a complete refusal to do something or to cooperate (*informal*) ◇ **nothing for it** used to indicate that there is no other course of action open to somebody ○ *There was nothing for it but for us to admit our error.* ◇ **nothing if not** definitely, undoubtedly, or at the very least ○ *He's nothing if not fair.* ◇ **nothing less than, nothing short of** used to emphasize forcefully that something truly, definitely, or amazingly is as described ◇ **nothing like** having no resemblance to somebody or something else ◇ **nothing to it** used to indicate that something is very easy

noth·ing·ness /núthingnəss/ *n.* **1. ABSENCE OF EVERYTHING** the absence of life, existence, and all discernible qualities **2. VACUUM** space with nothing in it **3. COMPLETE WORTHLESSNESS** complete worthlessness or insignificance **4. SOMEBODY OR SOMETHING COMPLETELY WORTHLESS** somebody or something without any worth or significance **5.** PHILOSOPHY **LACK OF APPARENT MEANING** the condition of lacking any apparent meaning

WORD KEY: CULTURAL NOTE

Being and Nothingness, an extended essay by French philosopher Jean-Paul Sartre (1943). The fullest expression of Sartre's existential philosophy, it suggests that humans can be distinguished from the simple being or "thing-ness" of objects and other creatures by their consciousness or "no-thingness." This awareness provides humans with their freedom, but it also leaves them searching for meaning in life.

no·tice /nṓtiss/ *n.* **1. PUBLIC SIGN** a sign in a public place giving information, instructions, or a warning **2. WRITTEN ANNOUNCEMENT** a written or printed announcement or statement of information, often displayed on a board or wall or published in a newspaper or magazine **3. WARNING** advance warning or notification of something ○ *gave us notice that the system would be changed* **4. PERIOD OF WARNING** the period of time between the giving of a warning or notification and its taking effect ○ *a day's notice of repairs to the water mains* **5.** LAW **WARNING OF END OF EMPLOYMENT** official notification of the exercise of a right, especially the right to terminate employment, or the amount of time in advance that such notification is given **6. ATTENTION** somebody's attention, observation, or consideration ○ *How can such a glaring error possibly have escaped your notice?* **7. CRITICAL REVIEW** a written or published review of a book, play, or movie ■ *v.* (**-ticed, -tic·ing, -tic·es**) **1.** *vti.* **OBSERVE SOMETHING** to see or catch sight of somebody or something and register the fact in the mind ○ *Did you notice what he had in his hand?* **2.** *vti.* **PERCEIVE** to become aware of something or somebody and register the fact in the mind ○ *I noticed that he avoided mentioning her name.* **3.** *vt.* **MENTION SOMETHING** to mention or remark on something **4.** *vt.* **RECOGNIZE** to recognize somebody, or indicate that you recognize somebody **5.** *vt.* **TREAT POLITELY** to treat somebody with polite attention **6.** *vt.* **WRITE CRITICAL REVIEW OF** to write or publish a review of a book, play, or movie **7.** *vt.* **GIVE OFFICIAL NOTICE TO** to give official notice to somebody (*formal*) [15thC. Via Old French, from Latin *notitia* "being known, fame, knowledge," from *notus* "known."]

no·tice·a·ble /nṓtissəb'l/ *adj.* **1. EASILY SEEN** easy to see, hear, feel, or detect **2. NOTEWORTHY** important, distinctive, or worthy of comment —**no·tice·a·bil·i·ty** /nṓtissə bíllətee/ *n.* —**no·tice·a·ble·ness** /nṓtissəb'lnəss/ *n.* —**no·tice·a·bly** *adv.*

no·ticeboard *n. U.K.* = **bulletin board**

no·ti·fi·a·ble /nōtə fī́ əb'l/ *adj.* used to describe an infectious disease of people or animals that must be reported to the appropriate authorities when it occurs so that control or preventive measures can be taken

no·ti·fi·ca·tion /nōtəfi káysh'n/ *n.* **1. FORMAL ANNOUNCEMENT OR WARNING** official information about something that has happened or will happen, or a document containing such information **2. ACT OF INFORMING OFFICIALLY** the act of informing somebody officially about something

no·ti·fy /nṓtə fī/ (**-fied, -fy·ing, -fies**) *vt.* **1. TELL OFFICIALLY** to inform or warn somebody officially about somebody or something **2. MAKE SOMETHING KNOWN** to announce or report something officially, or make something officially known [14thC. Via Old French *notifier*, from Latin *notificare* "to make known," from *notus* "known."] —**no·ti·fi·er** *n.*

no-till·age *n.* a method of farming in which crops are planted in narrow slit trenches, without any plowing, and weeds are controlled with chemical weedkillers

no·tion /nṓsh'n/ *n.* **1. IDEA** an idea, opinion, or concept **2. IMPRESSION** a vague understanding or impression **3. DESIRE** a sudden desire or whim ■ **no·tions** *npl.* **ITEMS FOR NEEDLEWORK** small items used in sewing, e.g., needles, pins, thread, and buttons [14thC. From the Latin stem *notion-* "concept," from *not-*, past participle stem of *noscere* "to know."]

no·tion·al /nṓshən'l, nṓshnəl/ *adj.* **1.** IMAGINARY OR HYPOTHETICAL existing only as an idea or in theory, not in reality **2.** ABSTRACT OR SPECULATIVE relating to or characteristic of ideas or concepts **3.** LING USED WITH DEFINITE MEANING used in a specific, concrete sense, like, e.g., "did" in "We did the work," as opposed to expressing a grammatical relationship, like "did" in "Why didn't she come?" ◊ **relational** —**no·tion·al·ly** *adv.*

no·to·chord /nṓtə kàwrd/ *n.* a long flexible rod of cells that supports the body of chordates, e.g., the lamprey, and verterbate embryos and is in effect a primitive backbone [Mid-19thC. From Greek *nōtōn* "back" + CHORD, with the sense "line."] —**no·to·chord·al** /nṓtə káwrd'l/ *adj.*

no·to·ri·ous /nə táwree əss, nō-/ *adj.* **1.** FAMOUS FOR SOMETHING BAD well-known for some undesirable feature, quality, or act **2.** WELL-KNOWN widely known (*archaic*) [Mid-16thC. Formed from medieval Latin *notorius*, from the past participle of *noscere* "to know" (source of English *recognize*).] —**no·to·ri·e·ty** /nṓtə rī́ ətee/ *n.* —**no·to·ri·ous·ly** /nə táwree əsslee, nō-/ *adv.* —**no·to·ri·ous·ness** *n.*

no·tor·nis /nō táwrniss/ (*plural* **-nes** /-neez/) *n.* a rare flightless bird native to New Zealand, especially the takahe. Genus: *Notornis.* [Mid-19thC. From modern Latin, genus name, from Greek *notos* "south" + *ornis* "bird."]

no trump *n.* **1.** BID WITHOUT TRUMPS IN CARDS a bid or contract to play a hand of cards without a trump suit, especially in bridge **2.** HAND SUITABLE FOR NO TRUMP a hand of cards suitable for playing without a trump suit —**no-trump** *adj.*

Notts /nots/ *abbr.* Nottinghamshire

no·tum /nṓtəm/ (*plural* **-ta** /-tə/) *n.* a hard protective covering on an insect's thorax [Late 19thC. From Greek *nōton* "back."]

not·with·stand·ing /nòt with stánding, -with-/ *prep.* DESPITE in spite of (*formal*) (*often used after a noun*) ○ *Its democratic structures, notwithstanding inevitable flaws, are among the most solid on the continent.* ○ *The lack of a decent catalog notwithstanding, the exhibition contains much to marvel at.* ■ *adv.* NEVERTHELESS nevertheless, or in spite of this (*formal*) ○ *They, notwithstanding, persisted in their inquiries.* ■ *conj.* ALTHOUGH in spite of the fact that (*formal*) ○ *Notwithstanding they were provoked, they ought not to have reacted so violently.* [14thC. Modeled on Old French *non obstante* "being of no hindrance."]

not·work /nótwùrk/ *n.* a computer network that is nonfunctional (*slang humorous*) Also called **nyetwork** [Late 20thC. Blend of NOT + NETWORK.]

nou·gat /nóogət/ *n.* a chewy candy made with egg whites, honey, and usually chopped nuts or dried fruit that is wrapped in rice paper and cut into strips or pieces [Early 19thC. From Provençal *nogat*, from *noga* "nut," from Latin *nux*.]

nought /nawt/ *n.* **1.** *U.K.* = **naught** *n.* 1 **2.** NOTHING nothing (*archaic*) ◊ **naught** [Old English *nōwiht*, from *ne* "not" + *ōwiht* "anything," a variant of AUGHT]

noughts and cross·es *n. U.K.* = **tick-tack-toe**

nou·me·non /nóomə nòn/ (*plural* **-na** /-nə/) *n.* **1.** OBJECT OF INTELLECT something beyond the tangible world that can only be known or identified by the intellect, not by the senses **2.** INDEPENDENT OBJECT IN KANTIAN PHILOSOPHY in Kantian philosophy, something that exists independently of intellectual or sensory perception of it, e.g., the soul in some beliefs [Late 18thC. Via German from Greek, from the present participle of *noien* "to apprehend, conceive."] —**nou·men·al** *adj.* —**nou·men·al·ly** *adv.*

noun /nown/ *n.* a word or group of words used as the name of a class of people, places, or things, or of a specific person, place, or thing. For example, the words *bottle, spider, charity,* and *Africa* are nouns. [14thC. Via Anglo Norman, "name, noun," from Old French *nom*, from Latin *nomen* "name" (source of English *nominal*).]

noun phrase *n.* a word or group of words that functions syntactically as a noun, e.g., as the subject, object, or topic, in a clause or sentence

nour·ish /núr ish/ (**-ished, -ish·ing, -ish·es**) *vt.* **1.** GIVE FOOD TO to give people, animals, or plants the substances they require to live, grow, or remain fit and healthy **2.** SUPPORT OR FOSTER to encourage or strengthen a feeling or idea **3.** HELP TO DEVELOP to help something to grow or develop [13thC. From the Old French stem *norriss-*, from *norir*, from Latin *nutrire* "to suckle."] —**nour·ish·er** *n.*

nour·ish·ing /núr ishing/ *adj.* providing people, animals, or plants with a substantial quantity of the substances they require to live, grow, or remain fit and healthy —**nour·ish·ing·ly** *adv.*

nour·ish·ment /núr ishmənt/ *n.* **1.** FOOD OR FOOD VALUE food, or the valuable substances in food that a person, animal, or plant requires to live, grow, or remain fit and healthy **2.** SOMETHING ENCOURAGING GROWTH something that provides a stimulating and healthy emotional or intellectual environment for people or animals

nous /nooss, nowss/ *n.* **1.** INTELLECTUAL ABILITY in ancient Greek philosophy, the capacity to reason and acquire knowledge, as distinguished from sensation **2.** INTELLECT the part of the human spirit that is capable of rational thought **3.** COSMIC PRINCIPLE OF ORDER the principle of the cosmic mind that some believe to govern order in the physical universe **4.** RATIONAL COSMIC PRINCIPLE in Stoic philosophy, the active, material, rational principle of the cosmos **5.** IMAGE OF ABSOLUTE GOOD in Neo-Platonic philosophy, the reflection of the absolute good, which includes the universe of rational beings [Late 17thC. From Greek, "intelligence."]

nou·veau /noo vṓ/ *adj.* having recently appeared or become fashionable (*humorous*) [Early 20thC. From French.]

nou·veau riche /nòovō réesh/ (*plural* **nou·veaux rich·es** /nòovō réesh/) *n.* somebody who has recently become rich, especially a former member of the lower or middle classes who ostentatiously displays newly acquired wealth. ◊ **arriviste** [Early 19thC. From French, literally "new rich."] —**nou·veau riche** *adj.*

nou·veau ro·man /nòo vō rō maán/ (*plural* **nou·veaux ro·mans** /nòo vō rō maán/) *n.* LITERAT = **antinovel** [Mid-20thC. From French, literally "new novel."]

nou·velle cui·sine /noo vèl kwi zéen, -kwee-/ *n.* a style of French cooking consisting of tiny but beautifully presented dishes made from fresh lightly cooked ingredients in less rich sauces than in traditional French cooking [Late 20thC. From French, literally "new cooking."]

nou·velle vague /noo vél vaag/ *n.* CINEMA = **new wave** *n.* 1 [Mid-20thC. From French, literally "new wave."]

Nov., Nov *abbr.* November

no·va /nṓvə/ (*plural* **-vas** *or* **-vae** /-vee/) *n.* a star that suddenly increases dramatically in brightness and then fades to its original luminosity over a short period of months or years [Late 19thC. From Latin, a form of *novus* "new."]

No·va /nṓvə/ (*plural* **-vae**) *n.* = **Nova Scotia salmon**

no·vac·u·lite /nō vákyə lī̀t/ *n.* a hard dense fine-grained sedimentary rock containing quartz and feldspar and used as a whetstone [Late 18thC. Formed from Latin *novacula* "razor."]

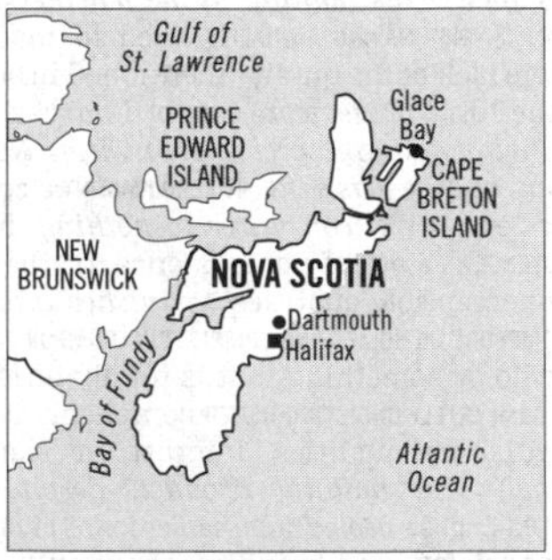

Nova Scotia

No·va Sco·tia /nòvə skóshə/ region of eastern Canada, and one of the three Maritime Provinces, consisting of a peninsula off New Brunswick and Cape Breton Island. Capital: Halifax. Population: 909,282 (1996). Area: 21,425 sq. mi./55,490 sq. km. —**No·va Sco·tian** *adj.*

No·va Sco·tia salm·on *n.* lox made from salmon caught near Nova Scotia. It is less salty than other lox.

no·va·tion /nō váysh'n/ *n.* the replacement of an old contract or obligation with a new one [Early 16thC. From the late Latin stem *novation-*, from, ultimately, *novare* "to make new," from *novus* "new."]

No·va·to /nō vaátō/ city in western California in Marin County, western California, situated north of San Francisco. Population: 47,585 (1990).

nov·el[1] /nóvv'l/ *n.* **1.** LONG STORY a fictional prose work with a relatively long and often complex plot, usually divided into chapters, in which the story traditionally develops through the thoughts and actions of its characters **2.** LITERARY GENRE novels considered collectively as a literary genre [15thC. Via Old French from Latin *novellus*, from *novus* "new." The meaning "prose narrative" came from Italian *storia novella* "short story" (literally "new story").]

WORD KEY: SYNONYMS

See Synonyms at ***new***.

nov·el[2] /nóvv'l/ *adj.* new, original, and different, and often particularly interesting or unusual as well [15thC. Via Old French from Latin *novellus*, literally "slightly new," from *novus* "new."]

nov·el[3] /nóvv'l/ *n.* in Roman law, a new decree or something that changes an existing statute [Early 17thC. From late Latin *novella (constitutio)*, literally "new (constitution)," a form of Latin *novellus* (see NOVEL).]

nov·el·ese /nòvv'l éez, -éess/ *n.* a type of language or style of writing that is typical of inferior novels (*disapproving*)

nov·el·ette /nòvv'l ét/ *n.* **1.** LITERAT SHORT NOVEL a long story or short novel. ◊ **novella 2.** LITERAT SENTIMENTAL NOVEL a light romantic novel, especially one that is considered trite or sentimental **3.** MUSIC SHORT LYRICAL MUSICAL COMPOSITION a short piece of music written in a free lyrical style, usually for the piano —**nov·el·et·tist** *n.*

nov·el·et·tish /nòvv'l éttish/ *adj.* having the qualities of an inferior piece of writing, especially triteness or sentimentality

nov·el·ist /nóvv'list/ *n.* somebody who writes novels

nov·el·is·tic /nòvv'l ístik/ *adj.* characteristic of a novel, especially in the treatment of real people or historical events —**nov·el·is·ti·cal·ly** *adv.*

nov·el·ize /nóvv'l īz/ (**-ized, -iz·ing, -iz·es**) *vt.* **1.** CONVERT MOVIE INTO NOVEL to write the story of a film, play, or television series in the form of a novel **2.** CONVERT FACT INTO FICTION to retell a true story in the form of a novel, sometimes adding fictional details —**nov·el·i·za·tion** /nòvv'li záysh'n/ *n.*

no·vel·la /nō véllə/ *n.* **1.** SHORT NOVEL a fictional prose work that is longer than a short story but shorter than a novel. ◊ **novelette 2.** MORAL TALE a moral or satirical tale (*archaic*) [Early 20thC. From Italian *(storia) novella* (see NOVEL[1]).]

nov·el·ty /nóvv'ltee/ (*plural* **-ties**) *n.* **1.** SMALL TOY OR TRINKET a small inexpensive toy, ornament, piece of jewelry, or trinket **2.** NEWNESS AND ORIGINALITY the quality of being new, original, and different **3.** NEW THING OR EXPERIENCE something new, original, and different that is interesting or exciting, though often for only a short time

No·vem·ber /no vémbər/ *n.* **1.** 11TH MONTH OF GREGORIAN CALENDAR in the Gregorian calendar, the 11th month of the year, made up of 30 days **2.** COMMUNICATION CODE WORD FOR LETTER "N" a code word for the letter "N," used in international radio communications [13thC. Via Old French *Novembre* from Latin *November*, the ninth month of the Roman calendar, from *novem* "nine."]

no·ve·na /nō véenə/ (*plural* **-nas** *or* **-nae** /-nee/) *n.* in the Roman Catholic Church, the recitation of prayers for nine consecutive days to achieve a specific purpose [Mid-19thC. From medieval Latin *novena*, a form of *novenus* "ninefold," from *novem* "nine."]

no·ver·cal /nō vúrk'l/ *adj.* relating to or said to be typical of a stepmother (*literary*) [Early 17thC. From Latin *novercalis*, from *noverca* "stepmother."]

nov·ice /nóvviss/ *n.* **1.** BEGINNER somebody who has just started learning or doing something new and has no previous experience in the skill or activity **2.** RELIG RELIGIOUS STUDENT somebody who has joined a religious order but has not yet taken the final vows of a monk or nun [14thC. Via Old French from late Latin *novicius* "newly enslaved person" or "inexperienced person in a new situation," from *novus* "new."]

WORD KEY: SYNONYMS

See Synonyms at ***beginner***.

novitiate /nō víshət, nō víshee ət/, **no·vi·ci·ate** *n.* **1.** PROBATIONARY PERIOD the period of time during which somebody is a novice, especially in a religious order

2. **NOVICES' LIVING QUARTERS** the part of a monastery or convent where novices live 3. = **novice** *n.* 2 [Early 17thC. From French *noviciat*, or medieval Latin *noviciatus*, formed from late Latin *novicius* (see NOVICE.]

No·vo·cain /nṓvə kàyn/ *tdmk.* a trademark for a synthetic anesthetic drug

now /now/ *adv.* 1. **AT PRESENT TIME** at the present time, often as opposed to in the past or in the future ○ *I've never done this before, and I'm not starting now.* 2. **IMMEDIATELY** at once or at this exact time ○ *We'll miss our train if we don't go now.* 3. **GIVEN THE CURRENT SITUATION** under the present circumstances ○ *She asked me not to tell anyone, but now I don't suppose she'll mind.* 4. **UP TO THE PRESENT TIME** used with statements of time to indicate that something has been happening for a specific length of time up to the present ○ *For six months now, I've been telling you to clean this room.* 5. **USED TO PREFACE OR CLARIFY REMARK** used to preface a remark, the second step in an argument, or a clarification of a statement, or to get somebody's attention, or for emphasis ○ *Now, what would you like to drink?* 6. **USED IN HESITATION** used in speech when hesitating, when thinking of what to say next (*informal*) ■ *conj.* **SINCE** since, or in view of the fact that this is the present situation ○ *She can afford a decent car now that she's working.* ■ *n.* **PRESENT TIME** the present time or moment ○ *Now would be a good time to tell her.* ■ *adj.* **FASHIONABLE** in the latest fashion (*informal*) ○ *the now look in menswear* [Old English *nu*, ultimately from Indo-European] ◇ **(every) now and then, (every) now and again** 1. occasionally 2. a short time ago 3. at the present moment ◇ **for now** for the time being, as a temporary measure ◇ **now now** 1. used as a friendly way of trying to comfort somebody 2. used to warn or reprimand somebody gently ◇ **now then** used to warn or reprimand somebody gently

NOW /now/ *abbr.* National Organization for Women

NOW ac·count /nów-/ *n.* a savings account that pays depositors interest and against which checks can be written [Late 20thC. *NOW* an acronym of *negotiable order of withdrawal*.]

now·a·days /nów ə dàyz/ *adv.* in the present, or in the times in which we are now living, usually in contrast to the past [14thC. Coined from NOW + *adayes* "during the day," from DAY.]

no·way /nṓ wày/ *adv.* **noway, noways NOT IN ANY WAY** in no way or not at all ■ *interj.* **no·way, no way CERTAINLY NOT** used to express emphatic refusal or denial (*informal*)

no·where /nṓ w-r, -hw-r/ *adv.* **IN OR TO NO PLACE** not in or to any place ○ *Nowhere does it mention any side-effects.* ■ *n.* **REMOTE PLACE** a remote or insignificant place ◇ **get nowhere, go nowhere** to fail to make any progress with something you are trying to do ◇ **nowhere near** not at all, or a long way from being as specified (*informal*)

no·wheres /nṓ w-rz, -hw-rz/ *adv.* nowhere (*regional*)

no-win /nṓ win, nō wín/ *adj.* in which there is no chance of a successful outcome for a participant (*informal*) ○ *a no-win situation*

no·wise /nṓ wīz/ *adv.* in no manner or by no means at all

nox·ious /nókshəss/ *adj.* 1. **PHYSICALLY HARMFUL** harmful to life or health, especially by being poisonous 2. **MORALLY HARMFUL** likely to cause moral, spiritual, or social harm or corruption 3. **DISGUSTING** very unpleasant ○ *a noxious smell* [15thC. Formed from Latin *noxius* "hurtful, damaging."] —**nox·ious·ly** *adv.* —**nox·ious·ness** *n.*

noz·zle /nózz'l/ *n.* 1. **PROJECTING SPOUT** a narrow or tapering part at the end of a tube or pipe, used to direct or control the flow of a liquid or gas 2. **SHORT TAPERED TUBE** a short tapered tube that directs or accelerates the flow of a fluid, e.g., in a jet engine 3. **NOSE** somebody's nose (*slang*) [Early 17thC. Literally "noselike appliance," coined from NOSE + *-le*.]

np, n.p. *abbr.* PRINTING new paragraph

Np *symbol.* 1. TELECOM neper 2. CHEM neptunium

NP *abbr.* 1. National Park 2. *ANZ, S Africa* National Party 3. neuropsychiatry 4. nurse practitioner 5. noun phrase

N.P. *abbr.* Notary Public

NPD *abbr.* new product development

NPN *abbr.* CHEM nonprotein nitrogen

NPR *abbr.* National Public Radio

NPV, n.p.v. *abbr.* 1. net present value 2. no par value

nr *abbr.* near

NRA *abbr.* 1. National Recovery Administration 2. National Rifle Association 3. Naval Reserve Association

NRC *abbr.* 1. National Research Council 2. Nuclear Regulatory Commission

NRDS *abbr.* neonatal respiratory distress syndrome

NREM *abbr.* nonrapid eye movement

NRV *abbr.* net realizable value

ns *abbr.* nanosecond

NS, N.S. *abbr.* 1. *U.K.* New Style 2. not sufficient (*funds*) 3. Nova Scotia 4. nuclear ship

n.s. *abbr.* 1. new series 2. not specified

n/s *abbr.* 1. nonsmoking 2. nonsmoker 3. BANKING not sufficient (funds)

N/S *abbr.* nonsmoker

NSA *abbr.* 1. National Security Agency 2. National Standards Association

NSAID *n.* a drug taken by mouth or applied externally and used to relieve pain and inflammation in a wide range of conditions, especially arthritic or muscular pain and menstrual period pain. Full form **nonsteroidal anti-inflammatory drug**

NSB *abbr.* 1. National Savings Bank 2. National Science Board

NSC *abbr.* National Security Council

NSE *abbr.* National Stock Exchange

nsec *abbr.* nanosecond

N.S.P.C.A. *abbr.* National Society for the Prevention of Cruelty to Animals

NST *abbr. Can* Newfoundland Standard Time

NSU *abbr.* nonspecific urethritis

NSW, N.S.W. *abbr. Aus* New South Wales

NT *abbr.* 1. **NT, N.T.** New Testament 2. **NT, N.T.** *Aus* Northern Territory 3. *Can* Northwest Territories 4. **NT, N.T.** CARDS no trump

nth /enth/ *adj.* 1. **LAST OR MOST RECENT** last or latest in a long and often tedious series of similar occurrences (*informal*) 2. MATH **INDEFINITELY LARGE NUMERICALLY** used to describe a very large but unspecified ordinal number, usually one that is the largest in a series of values [Mid-19thC. Formed from N "indefinitely large or small amount."]

NTI *abbr.* Nielsen Television Index

N.T.P., n.t.p. *abbr.* normal temperature and pressure

NTSB *abbr.* National Transportation Safety Board

nt. wt. *abbr.* net weight

nu /noo/ (*plural* **nus**) *n.* the 13th letter of the Greek alphabet, represented in the English alphabet as "n." See table at **alphabet** [Via Greek from a Semitic word]

Nu /nyoo/, **U** (1907–95) Burmese statesman. He was the first prime minister of independent Burma (1948–58 and 1960–62) and a leader of the prodemocracy movement from 1988.

nu·ance /nóo aàns/ *n.* 1. **SUBTLE DIFFERENCE** a very slight difference in meaning, feeling, tone, or color 2. **USE OF NUANCES** the use or awareness of subtle shades of meaning or feeling, especially in artistic expression or performance [Late 18thC. From French, "slight difference of tone," from *nuer* "to shade," ultimately from Latin *nubes* "cloud."] —**nu·anced** *adj.*

nub /nub/ *n.* 1. **HEART OF SOMETHING** the main point or core of something 2. **SMALL LUMP** a small lump or chunk 3. **SMALL PROJECTION** a small protuberance 4. TEXTILES **FIBER KNOT** a knot of fibers in yarn [Late 16thC. From Middle Low German *knubbe*, variant of *knobbe* "knob." Originallly "small lump or boil on the body."] —**nub·bi·ness** *n.* —**nub·by** *adj.*

Nu·ba /nóobə/ (*plural* **-ba** *or* **-bas**) *n.* 1. PEOPLES **MEMBER OF A SOUTHERN SUDANESE PEOPLE** a member of any of various peoples inhabiting the mountains of central Sudan 2. LANG = **Nubian** *n.* 2

nub·bin /núbbin/ *n.* a small undeveloped part of a fruit or vegetable, e.g., an ear of corn [Late 17thC. Literally "small nub," formed from NUB.]

nub·ble /núbb'l/ *n.* a small lump or knob —**nub·bli·ness** *n.* —**nub·bly** *adj.*

nu·bec·u·la /noo békyələ/ (*plural* **-lae** /-lee/) *n.* a Magellanic Cloud (*technical*) [Late 17thC. From Latin, literally "small cloud," from *nubes* "cloud."]

Nu·bi·a /nóobee ə, nyóo-/ region in the Nile River valley in northeastern Africa between Aswan in Egypt and Khartoum in Sudan

Nu·bi·an /nóobee ən, nyóo-/ *n.* 1. PEOPLES **INHABITANT OF NUBIA** somebody who lived in the ancient kingdom of Nubia 2. LANG **NILO-SAHARAN LANGUAGE** a Nilo-Saharan language spoken in Sudan. Nubian is spoken by about one million people. [15thC. From medieval Latin *Nubianus*, from *Nubia*.] —**Nu·bi·an** *adj.*

nu·bile /nóob'l, nóo bīl/ *adj.* 1. **READY FOR MARRIAGE** used to describe a young woman who is physically mature enough to have sexual intercourse and therefore suitable for marriage (*dated*) 2. **YOUNG AND DESIRABLE** young and sexually desirable (*informal*) [Mid-17thC. From Latin *nubilis*, from *nubere* "to take a husband" (source of English *nuptial* and *connubial*).] —**nu·bil·i·ty** /noo bíllətee/ *n.*

nu·cel·lus /noo séllәss/ (*plural* **-li** /-lī/) *n.* the central part of a plant ovule in which the embryo develops [Late 19thC. From modern Latin, of uncertain origin: probably literally "small kernel," formed from *nucleus* (see NUCLEUS).]

nucl- *prefix.* = **nucleo-** (*used before vowels*)

nu·cle·ar /nóoklee ər/ *adj.* 1. NUCLEAR PHYS **OF AN ATOM NUCLEUS** relating to the nucleus of an atom 2. ARMS, MIL **OF NUCLEAR WEAPONS** relating to or using weapons that produce a nuclear explosion 3. NUCLEAR PHYS **OF NUCLEAR ENERGY** relating to, using, or producing nuclear energy through fission or fusion 4. BIOL **OF A CELL NUCLEUS** relating to, involving, or contained in the nucleus of a cell 5. BIOL **FORMING A NUCLEUS** forming or resembling a nucleus [Mid-19thC. Formed from Latin *nucleus*, from *nux* "nut, kernel." Ultimately from an Indo-European word meaning "lump."]

nu·cle·ar bomb *n.* a bomb in which the explosive potential is controlled by nuclear fission or fusion. ◊ **atomic bomb, hydrogen bomb**

nu·cle·ar chem·is·try *n.* the branch of chemistry in which nuclear reactions are studied

nu·cle·ar de·ter·rent *n.* the nuclear weapons possessed by a country or an alliance thought of as a means of discouraging enemy attack

nu·cle·ar dis·ar·ma·ment *n.* the reduction or elimination of a nation's nuclear weapons or its capacity to manufacture them

nu·cle·ar e·mul·sion *n.* a photographic emulsion used to identify and show the paths of subatomic particles after development

nu·cle·ar en·er·gy *n.* the energy released by nuclear fission or fusion

nu·cle·ar en·ve·lope *n.* CELL BIOL = **nuclear membrane**

nu·cle·ar fam·i·ly *n.* a social unit that consists of a mother, a father, and their children

nu·cle·ar fis·sion *n.* = **fission** *n.* 1

nu·cle·ar-free zone *n.* an area, usually within a country, where all activities involving nuclear weapons or nuclear power are officially banned

nu·cle·ar fu·el *n.* a substance such as an isotope of uranium that undergoes fission in a nuclear reactor and is used to provide power for electricity and submarines

nu·cle·ar fu·sion *n.* the process in which light atoms such as those of hydrogen and deuterium combine and form heavier atoms, releasing a great amount of energy that primarily manifests itself in the form of heat

nu·cle·ar·ize /nóoklee ə rīz/ (**-ized, -iz·ing, -iz·es**) *vt.* to provide or equip a military force with nuclear weapons —**nu·cle·ar·i·za·tion** /nóoklee əri záysh'n/ *n.*

nu·cle·ar mag·net·ic res·o·nance *n.* the energy pulse released by an atomic nucleus exposed to high-frequency radiation in a magnetic field, which is used to provide data about the atom that can be transformed into an image by computer techniques. This phenomenon is the basis of devices used in medicine, where it is called magnetic resonance imaging, to produce images of tissues, and in physics and chemistry to study molecular structure.

nu·cle·ar med·i·cine *n.* the branch of medicine in which radioactive materials are used to diagnose and treat diseases

nu·cle·ar mem·brane *n.* a two-layered membrane surrounding the nucleus of a cell. Also called **nuclear envelope**

nu·cle·ar phys·ics *n.* the branch of physics in which the structure, forces, and behavior of the atomic nucleus are studied —**nu·cle·ar phys·i·cist** *n.*

nu·cle·ar pore *n.* any of thousands of complex openings in a nuclear membrane

nu·cle·ar pow·er *n.* the power, usually electrical or motive power, produced by nuclear fission or fusion —**nu·cle·ar-pow·ered** *adj.*

nu·cle·ar pow·er sta·tion, nu·cle·ar pow·er plant *n.* a power station in which the heat for producing steam to drive electric turbogenerators is derived from a nuclear reactor

nu·cle·ar re·ac·tion *n.* a process in which energy is produced by either the splitting of heavy atoms **(nuclear fission)** or the combining of light atoms **(nuclear fusion)**

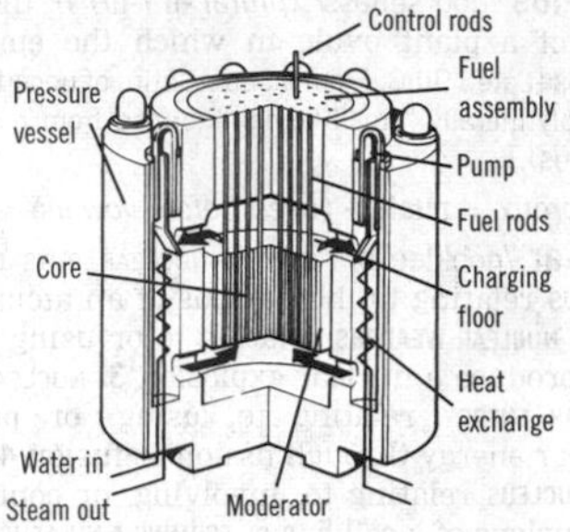

Nuclear reactor

nu·cle·ar re·ac·tor *n.* a device in which controlled nuclear fission takes place to produce heat energy

nu·cle·ar re·pro·cess·ing plant *n.* a facility in which various useful isotopes are removed from used rods of nuclear reactors

nu·cle·ar sap *n.* the colorless liquid in the nucleus of a cell

nu·cle·ar sub·ma·rine *n.* **1. SUBMARINE PROPELLED BY NUCLEAR ENERGY** a submarine in which a nuclear reactor produces steam to drive turbines for propulsion **2. SUBMARINE CARRYING NUCLEAR WEAPONS** a submarine that carries nuclear weapons

nu·cle·ar thresh·old *n.* the point in a war being fought with conventional weapons when one of the opposing forces decides to use nuclear weapons

nu·cle·ar war·head *n.* the forward part of a missile or other projectile whose explosive device derives its power from nuclear fission or fusion

nu·cle·ar waste *n.* unwanted, often radioactive, material that is produced by nuclear reactors and reprocessing plants

nu·cle·ar weap·on *n.* a military weapon that derives its explosive power from nuclear fission or fusion

nu·cle·ar win·ter *n.* a period of continual cold and darkness believed to follow a nuclear war, caused by the blocking of the sun's rays by high-altitude dust clouds, with disastrous environmental consequences

nu·cle·ase /nóoklee àyss, -àyz/ *n.* an enzyme that breaks down nucleic acids [Early 20thC. Coined from a shortening of NUCLEIC + -ASE.]

nu·cle·ate, nu·cle·at·ed /nóoklee àytəd/ *adj.* /nóoklee ət, -àyt/ BIOL **WITH A NUCLEUS** having a nucleus or nuclei. Also called **nucleated** ■ *vti.* /nóoklee àyt/ **(-at·ed, -at·ing, -ates) FORM A NUCLEUS** to come together as a nucleus, or to bring things together to form a nucleus [Mid-19thC. Coined from a shortening of NUCLEAR + -ATE.] —**nu·cle·a·tor** *n.*

nu·cle·a·tion /nóoklee áysh'n/ *n.* **1.** METEOROL **FORMATION PROCESS IN CLOUDS** the process by which ice crystals and rain drops form in clouds around a solid core **2.** GEOL **FORMATION OF CRYSTALS** the formation of crystals from a melt, often around a core of solid material

nu·cle·i plural of **nucleus**

nu·cle·ic ac·id /noo klee ik-, -kláy-/ *n.* any of various high-molecular-weight acids, e.g., DNA and RNA, consisting of nucleotide chains that convey genetic information and are found in all living cells and viruses

nu·cle·in /nóoklee in/ *n.* BIOCHEM = **nucleoprotein**

nucleo- *prefix.* **1.** nucleus, nuclear ○ *nucleoplasm* **2.** nucleic acid ○ *nucleocapsid* [From NUCLEUS]

nu·cle·o·cap·sid /nóoklee ə kápsid/ *n.* the basic viral structure consisting of a core of nucleic acid surrounded by a protein coat

nu·cle·o·late /nóoklee ə làyt/ *adj.* having a nucleolus or nucleoli

nu·cle·o·lus /nóoklee ələss/ (*plural* **-li** /-ə lī/) *n.* a small round body inside a cell nucleus, composed of protein and RNA and associated with the formation of ribosomes and ribosomal RNA [Mid-19thC. From late Latin, "little nucleus," from Latin *nucleus* (see NUCLEUS).] —**nu·cle·o·lar** *adj.*

nu·cle·on /nóoklee òn/ *n.* a proton or neutron, especially when part of an atomic nucleus

nu·cle·on·ics *n.* the branch of physics dealing with the properties of nucleons and the atomic nucleus (*takes a singular verb*)

nu·cle·on num·ber *n.* PHYS = **mass number**

nu·cle·o·phile /nóoklee ə fīl/ *n.* a substance that becomes an electron donor in bonding during a chemical reaction —**nu·cle·o·phil·ic** /nóoklee əfíllik/ *adj.*

nu·cle·o·plasm /nóoklee ə plàzzəm/ *n.* the liquid matter **(protoplasm)** of a cell nucleus

nu·cle·o·pro·tein /nóoklee ə prṓ tèen/ *n.* a protein in combination with a nucleic acid in cells that is the main constituent of genetic material in chromosomes

nu·cle·o·side /nóoklee ə sīd/ *n.* a type of organic compound, found especially in DNA and RNA in living organisms, consisting of a purine or pyrimidine base linked to a sugar, particularly ribose or deoxyribose [Early 20thC. Coined from NUCLEO- + GLYCOSIDE.]

nu·cle·o·some /nóoklee ə sòm/ *n.* a minute particle of DNA and protein that forms the basic packing unit of chromatin, the substance of chromosomes. Nucleosomes fit together like a tightly condensed string of beads.

nu·cle·o·syn·the·sis /nóoklee ō sínthəssiss/ *n.* the synthesis of heavier elements from lighter elements by fusion reactions within stars

nu·cle·o·tide /nóoklee ə tīd/ *n.* a type of chemical compound occurring most notably in nucleic acids such as RNA and DNA, consisting of a nucleoside linked to a phosphate group [Early 20thC. An alteration of NUCLEOSIDE.]

nu·cle·us /nóoklee əss/ (*plural* **-i** /-ī/ *or* **-us·es**) *n.* **1. IMPORTANT ELEMENT** a central or most important item or part that has others grouped or built around it **2.** PHYS **CENTRAL REGION OF AN ATOM** the positively charged central region of an atom, consisting of protons and neutrons and containing most of the mass **3.** BIOL **CENTRAL PART OF A LIVING CELL** the central body, usually spherical, within a eukaryotic cell, which is a membrane-encased mass of protoplasm containing the chromosomes and other genetic information necessary to control cell growth and reproduction **4.** ASTRON **CENTRAL PORTION OF A NEBULA OR GALAXY** the central brighter portion of a nebula or galaxy **5.** ASTRON **CORE OF A COMET'S HEAD** the central core in the head of a comet, consisting of ice, frozen gases, and dust **6.** CHEM **STABLE ATOMS IN A MOLECULE** a stable group of atoms in a molecule, e.g., a benzene ring, that forms the base structure of many compounds and remains unchanged in chemical reactions **7.** ANAT **GROUP OF NERVE CELLS** a group of nerve cells in the central nervous system or a small mass of gray matter in the brain that has a specialized function **8.** BOT **INNER KERNEL OF A NUT** the central kernel of a nut seed **9.** BOT **STARCH GRANULE'S CENTER** the central part of a starch granule **10.** PHON **MOST RESONANT PART OF A SYLLABLE** the most resonant part of a syllable, usually the vowel [Early 18thC. Via Latin *nuculeus* "kernel of a nut" from *nuculus* "little nut," from *nux* "nut" (source of English *nougat*).]

nu·clide /nóok līd/ *n.* one or more atomic nuclei identifiable as being of the same element by having the same number of protons and neutrons and the same energy content. Alternatively, the nuclide may be specified by its mass number, atomic number, and energy content. [Mid-20thC. Coined from NUCLEUS + -IDE.]

nude /nood/ *adj.* **(nud·er, nud·est) 1. UNCLOTHED** wearing no clothes ○ *the nude figure of a man* **2. FOR UNCLOTHED PEOPLE** intended for, or done by, people wearing no clothes ○ *a nude beach* **3. PLAIN** bare or plain, with no covering or decoration **4.** COLORS **LIGHT-COLORED** matching the skin color of a Caucasian person ○ *nude hose* **5.** LAW **LACKING A LEGAL REQUISITE** lacking a legal requisite such as supporting evidence or a contract ■ *n.* **UNCLOTHED FIGURE** an unclothed person, especially an unclothed figure in a painting or other artistic work [Mid-16thC. From Latin *nudus*.] —**nude·ly** *adv.* —**nude·ness** *n.* ◇ **in the nude** without clothes

WORD KEY: SYNONYMS

See Synonyms at ***naked***.

NUDETS *abbr.* nuclear detection system

nudge[1] /nuj/ *v.* **(nudged, nudg·ing, nudg·es) 1.** *vt.* **PUSH SOMEBODY OR SOMETHING GENTLY** to push or poke somebody gently, usually with a motion of the elbow **2.** *vt.* **MOVE SOMETHING GENTLY** to move something gently, especially by pushing it slowly and carefully **3.** *vt.* **APPROACH A LEVEL** to have very nearly reached a particular level or standard ○ *Their profits are nudging the 100 million mark.* **4.** *vi.* **MOVE SLOWLY** to move slowly or little by little **5.** *vt.* **GENTLY PERSUADE** to persuade somebody into an action, gently and delicately ■ *n.* **1. GENTLE PUSH** a gentle push to get somebody's attention **2. BIT OF PERSUASION** a gentle piece of persuasion [Late 17thC. Origin uncertain.]

nudge[2] /nuj/ *vt.* **(nudged, nudg·ing, nudg·es) PESTER SOMEBODY** to annoy somebody in a persistent and pestering way (*slang*) ○ *Can you stop always nudging me about money?* ■ *n.* = **nudnik** (*slang insult*) [Via Yiddish *nudyen* "to pester, bore" from Polish *nudzić*]

nud·ie /nóodee/ *adj.* **OF UNCLOTHED PEOPLE** relating to or involving people who are unclothed (*slang*) ■ *n.* **SOMETHING DEPICTING UNCLOTHED PEOPLE** something, e.g., a movie or a magazine, that depicts unclothed people (*slang*)

nud·ism /nóo dìzzəm/ *n.* = **naturism** *n.* 1

nud·ist /nóodist/ *n.* **SOMEBODY PREFERRING NUDITY** somebody who prefers to go without clothes, especially somebody who spends time in communes or designated areas with others who feel the same way ■ *adj.* **FOR NUDISTS** intended for people who prefer to go without clothes

nud·ist col·o·ny *n.* a place where the wearing of clothes is not allowed, intended for people who believe nudity is a healthy natural state

nu·di·ty /nóodətee/ *n.* **1. BEING UNCLOTHED** the state of having no clothes on **2. BARENESS** bareness or plainness, with no covering or decoration

nud·nik /nóodnik/ *n.* an offensive term for somebody considered to be annoying or boring (*slang insult*) Also called **nudge** [Mid-20thC. Formed from Yiddish *nudne* "boring" + -NIK.]

nu·ga·to·ry /nóogə tàwree/ *adj.* **1. TRIVIAL** of no importance whatsoever **2.** LAW **NOT VALID** with no legal force [Early 17thC. Via Latin *nugatorius* from, ultimately, *nugae* "trifling matters."] —**nu·ga·to·ri·ly** /nòo gə táwrəlee/ *adv.*

nug·get /núggət/ *n.* **1.** MINERALS **LUMP OF PRECIOUS METAL** a lump of gold or other precious metal in its natural state, dug up out of the ground **2. SMALL PRECIOUS THING** any small item or piece, especially of something abstract such as knowledge or information, regarded as very precious **3.** FOOD **A SMALL ROUND PIECE OF FOOD** a small piece of food, usually coated with breadcrumbs and fried or baked in an oven [Mid-19thC. Origin uncertain: probably from an English dialect word meaning "lump."]

nui·sance /nóoss'nss/ *n.* **1. SOMEBODY OR SOMETHING IRRITATING** an annoying or irritating person or thing **2.** LAW **ILLEGAL THING** something not allowed by law because it causes harm or offense, either to people in general **(public nuisance)** or to a private individual [15thC. Via Old French from, ultimately, Latin *nocere* "to harm, injure" (source of English *innocent* and *innocuous*).]

nui·sance call *n.* a usually anonymous telephone call made to annoy, harass, upset, or scare somebody

nui·sance tax *n.* a tax that is collected directly from the consumer on a wide variety of goods

nui·sance val·ue *n.* the relative usefulness of something based on its potential to cause problems or difficulties for somebody

nuke /nook/ *vt.* **(nuked, nuk·ing, nukes) 1.** MIL **ATTACK PEOPLE** to attack people or places with nuclear weapons (*slang*) **2.** FOOD **MICROWAVE SOMETHING** to cook something in a microwave oven (*informal*) ■ *n.* (*slang*) **1. NUCLEAR WEAPON** a nuclear weapon **2. NUCLEAR POWER PLANT** a nuclear power plant [Mid-20thC. Shortening of NUCLEAR.]

null /nul/ *adj.* **1.** LAW **INVALID** having no legal validity **2. VALUELESS** having no value or importance **3. AMOUNTING TO NOTHING** amounting to nothing in terms of context or character **4. AT ZERO LEVEL** at the level of zero or nothing **5.** MATH **RELATING TO ZERO** equal to or relating to zero **6.** MATH **EMPTY** containing no elements ○ *the null set* **7.** MATH **ENDING IN ZERO** converging to zero ○ *a null sequence* **8.** PHYS **INDICATING A READING OF ZERO** indicating a reading of zero when a measured quantity is undetectable or equal to another in comparison ■ *n.* **ZERO** a zero (*literary*) [Mid-16thC. Via Old French *nul* from Latin *nullus* "not any."] ◇ **null and void** not legally valid

nul·lah /núllə/ *n.* a ditch or ravine in India and other parts of Asia [Late 18thC. From Hindi *nālā*.]

nul·li·fi·ca·tion /nùlləfi káysh'n/ *n.* **1.** LAW **MAKING SOMETHING INVALID** the act of making something legally invalid **2. CANCELING OUT OF SOMETHING** the act of canceling something out **3.** LAW **STATE'S REJECTION OF A LAW** the refusal by a state government to allow application of a section of federal law —**nul·li·fi·ca·tion·ist** *n.*

nul·li·fy /núllə fī/ **(-fied, -fy·ing, -fies)** *vt.* **1.** LAW **MAKE SOMETHING INVALID** to make something legally invalid or ineffective **2. CANCEL SOMETHING OUT** to have the effect of canceling something out —**nul·li·fi·er** *n.*

WORD KEY: SYNONYMS

nullify, abrogate, annul, repeal, invalidate, negate

CORE MEANING: to put an end to the effective existence of something

nullify a fairly formal word meaning to end the effectiveness of something such as a contract, especially by doing something that counteracts its terms; **abrogate** a formal word used mainly in official or legal contexts to indicate the bringing to an end of a formal agreement, treaty, or contract; **annul** to declare something officially or legally invalid or ineffective in such a way as to indicate negation of its prior existence; **repeal** to end a law officially; **invalidate** to cause something to be considered illegal, unsound, or ineffective, e.g., by failing to comply with certain terms and conditions; **negate** to render something ineffective, for example, by doing something that counterbalances its force or effectiveness.

nul·lip·a·ra /nə líppərə/ (*plural* **-ras** *or* **-rae** /-rèe/) *n.* a woman who has never given birth to a child [Late 19thC. Formed from Latin *nullus* "none" + English *-para* "woman who has given birth," from Latin *parere* "to give birth."]

nul·li·ty /núllətee/ *n.* **1.** LAW **LEGAL INVALIDITY** the state of being legally invalid **2. NONEFFECTIVENESS** lack of effectiveness or usefulness

num., **num** *abbr.* **1.** number **2.** numeral

Num. *abbr.* BIBLE Numbers

numb /num/ *adj.* **1. WITH NO FEELING** unable to feel or have sensations, e.g., as a result of extreme cold or the application of a local anesthetic **2. EMOTIONLESS** unable to feel emotions ■ *vt.* **(numbed, numb·ing, numbs) 1. TAKE SENSATION AWAY FROM SOMETHING** to take away from a part of the body the power to feel or have sensations, or to take away the sensations themselves **2. TAKE AWAY SOMEBODY'S FEELINGS** to make somebody incapable of feeling emotion, or deaden somebody's emotions or feelings [15thC. Originally a past participle of Old English *niman* "to take." Ultimately from a prehistoric Germanic word meaning "to grasp," which is also the ancestor of English *nimble*.] —**num·bly** *adv.* —**numb·ness** *n.*

num·ber /númbər/ *n.* **1. IDENTIFYING FIGURE** any figure or group of figures identifying somebody or something, e.g., a set of figures identifying somebody as a telephone subscriber, or a figure identifying a sports player or competitor ○ *Let me have your fax number.* **2. QUANTITY** a quantity of people or things, especially a large quantity ○ *We have received a number of complaints.* **3. TOTAL** a total or sum ○ *The number of people treated has risen to over 3 million.* **4.** MUSIC **PIECE OF MUSIC** a self-contained piece of popular music, especially one of several that feature in a performance **5.** CLOTHES **GARMENT** an item of clothing, especially women's clothing (*informal*) ○ *a little silk number* **6. THING** a thing of any kind, especially something that gives pleasure or impresses (*informal*) **7.** GRAM **GRAMMATICAL QUANTITY** quantity expressed, in some languages, by the form of a word ○ *The qualifying adjective agrees with the noun in gender and number.* **8. SINGLE THING IN A SERIES** a single one of a series of things produced in sequence, especially a single issue of a magazine **9. PERSON** somebody regarded in sexual terms (*informal*) (*sometimes considered offensive*) **10. COUNTING, OR FIGURES USED TO COUNT** the concept of calculating quantities of individual things, or any of the words, figures, or symbols used in doing this ■ *v.* **(-bered, -ber·ing, -bers) 1.** *vt.* **ASSIGN A NUMBER TO SOMETHING** to give something or somebody an identifying number ○ *Don't forget to number the pages.* **2.** *vti.* **MAKE AS TOTAL** to reach a particular total amount ○ *Supporters numbered over 300, while there were only 15 dissenters.* **3.** *vt.* **INCLUDE SOMETHING** to include somebody or something as one of a group ○ *It is numbered among the world's most prestigious hotels.* [13thC. Via Anglo-Norman *numbre* from Latin *numerus* (source of English *numerous* and *enumerate*).] —**num·ber·er** *n.* ◇ **do a number on somebody** to treat somebody unfairly or harshly, e.g., by criticizing or ridiculing him or her in a deliberate and systematic way (*slang*) ◇ **get** *or* **have somebody's number** to understand somebody's true motives or character and so be well placed to deal with him or her ◇ **somebody's days are numbered** somebody's life or term of employment is about to come to an end

num·ber crunch·er *n.* (*slang*) **1.** COMPUTER a computer designed to perform large quantities of complex numerical calculations **2. SOMEBODY WHO DOES CALCULATIONS** somebody whose job consists of performing large quantities of arithmetic calculations —**num·ber crunch·ing** *n.*

num·bered ac·count *n.* a bank account identified by a number only, allowing the account holder to keep his or her identity secret

num·ber·less /númbərləss/ *adj.* **1. COUNTLESS** too numerous to be counted **2. NOT NUMBERED** not given a number or marked with a number

num·ber one *n.* **1. FIRST THING** the first one in a series of things or people ○ *She's number one among the top candidates.* **2.** MUSIC **BESTSELLING RECORD** a recording in a specific category that has sold the most copies in a given week **3. SELF** yourself and your own interests (*informal*) **4. IMPORTANT PERSON** the leader or the most important person in a group or organization (*informal*) **5. URINATION** the act or an instance of urinating, or urine (*babytalk*) ◊ **number two** *n.* 2 ■ *adj.* **1. MOST IMPORTANT** first, best, or most important **2. EXCELLENT** of a very high standard or quality (*informal*)

Num·ber One *n.* the first officer or first mate on a ship, next in rank after the captain (*informal*)

num·ber plate /númbər plàyt/ *n. U.K.* = **license plate**

num·bers /númbərz/ *n.* an illegal form of gambling in which people bet on an unpredictable number to be drawn or determined later (*takes a singular or plural verb*)

Num·bers *n.* the fourth book of the Bible

num·bers game *n.* GAMBLING = **numbers** *n.*

num·ber the·o·ry *n.* the branch of mathematics that deals with the properties of integers and relationships between integers

num·ber two *n.* **1. DEPUTY** somebody's deputy or second-in-command (*informal*) **2. DEFECATION** the act or an instance of defecating, or feces (*babytalk*) ◊ **number one** *n.* 5

numb·ing /númming/ *adj.* **1. CAUSING NUMBNESS** causing numbness in part of the body **2. DEADENING FEELINGS OR THOUGHTS** temporarily taking away somebody's ability to feel or think, e.g., as a result of shock ○ *a numbing experience*

numb·skull /núm skùl/ *n.* = **numskull**

nu·men /nóomən/ (*plural* **-mi·na** /nóomənə/) *n.* **1. SPIRIT INHABITING A PLACE** a god or spirit believed to inhabit a place or living object such as a tree **2. GUIDING FORCE** any guiding force or influence [Early 17thC. From Latin, "nod, command, divine power."]

nu·mer·a·ble /nóomərəb'l/ *adj.* able to be counted

nu·mer·a·cy /nóomərəssee/ *n.* competence in the mathematical skills needed to cope with everyday life and the understanding of information presented in mathematical terms like graphs, charts, or tables [Mid-20thC. Formed from NUMERATE, on the model of LITERACY.]

nu·mer·al /nóomərəl/ *n.* **SYMBOL REPRESENTING A NUMBER** a symbol or set of symbols used to represent a number, e.g., the Arabic numeral 5, the equivalent Roman numeral V, and the equivalent binary numeral 101 ■ *adj.* **OF NUMBERS** relating to numbers or representing a number or numbers [14thC. Via late Latin *numeralis* from Latin *numerus* (see NUMBER).] —**nu·mer·al·ly** *adv.*

nu·mer·ar·y /nóomərəree/ *adj.* relating to numbers [Early 18thC. Via medieval Latin *numerarius* from, ultimately, Latin *numerus* (see NUMBER).]

nu·mer·ate *adj.* /nóomərət/ **1. MATHEMATICALLY COMPETENT** able to do arithmetic calculations **2. WITH SOME MATH KNOWLEDGE** having a basic understanding of mathematics ■ *vt.* /nóomə ràyt/ **(-at·ed, -at·ing, -ates) ENUMERATE THINGS** to name a number of things in turn or in sequence (*archaic*) [Early 18thC. From Latin *numeratus*, the past participle stem of *numerare* "to count," from *numerus* (see NUMBER).]

nu·mer·a·tion /nóomə ráysh'n/ *n.* **1. GIVING OR NAMING OF NUMBERS** the naming of numbers, e.g., by schoolchildren, or the giving of numbers to items in a set or group **2. COUNTING SYSTEM** a system of symbols used for counting or numbering things

nu·mer·a·tor /nóomə ràytər/ *n.* the part of a common fraction appearing above the line, representing the number of parts of the whole that are being considered

nu·mer·i·cal /noo mérrik'l/, **nu·mer·ic** /noo mérrik/ *adj.* **1. CONSISTING OF NUMBERS** using numbers or consisting of numbers **2. OF NUMBERS OF THINGS** in terms of the number of people or things [Early 17thC. Formed from Latin *numerus* (see NUMBER).]

nu·mer·i·cal a·nal·y·sis *n.* a branch of mathematics dealing with the use of repeatedly used quantitative approximations to solve problems, and the measurement of the errors involved. Usually computers are used to execute the calculations. —**nu·mer·i·cal an·a·lyst** *n.*

nu·mer·i·cal con·trol *n.* an often computerized technique for controlling machine tools where the position or action of a tool, e.g., the depth of a drill, is determined by a numerical value. Also called **numeric control**

nu·mer·i·cal·ly /noo mérrikəlee/ *adv.* in terms of the numbers of people or things involved ○ *His forces were numerically superior to those of the enemy.*

nu·mer·i·cal or·der *n.* an ordering of people or things identified by number from the lowest to the highest

nu·mer·i·cal tax·on·o·my *n.* a procedure that involves comparing a large number of characteristics of one organism with the same characteristics of another

nu·mer·ic con·trol *n.* ENG = **numerical control**

nu·mer·ic key·pad *n.* a section of a computer keyboard, usually to the right of the main keypad, containing numbered keys in the same layout as the numbers on a calculator. The keys can be used in conjunction with other keys to perform special functions.

nu·mer·ol·o·gy /nóomə róllәjee/ *n.* the study of the occult use and supposed influence of numbers —**nu·mer·o·log·i·cal** /nóomərə lójjik'l/ *adj.* —**nu·mer·o·log·i·cal·ly** /-lójjikəlee/ *adv.* —**nu·mer·ol·o·gist** /nóomə róllәjist/ *n.*

nu·me·ro u·no /nóomərō óonō/ *n.* (*informal humorous*) **1.** = **number one** *n.* 3 **2. VIP** the leader or most important person in a group or organisation [Late 20thC. From Spanish or Italian, "number one."]

nu·mer·ous /nóomərəss/ *adj.* many in number [15thC. From Latin *numerosus*, from *numerus* (see NUMBER).] —**nu·mer·ous·ly** *adv.* —**nu·mer·ous·ness** *n.*

nu·mi·nous /nóomənəss/ *adj.* **1. MYSTERIOUSLY ASSOCIATED WITH A DEITY** having a mysterious power that suggests the presence of a spirit or god (*formal*) **2. HOLY** filled with inextricable associations with God (*formal*) **3. OF NUMINA** relating to numina, the spirits or gods believed in some cultures to inhabit places or things [Mid-17thC. From the stem of Latin *numen* (see NUMEN).] —**nu·mi·nous·ly** *adv.* —**nu·mi·nous·ness** *n.*

nu·mis·mat·ic /nóomiz máttik, -mis-/ *adj.* relating to the study or collecting of coins and medals [Late 18thC. Via French *numismatique* from, ultimately, Greek *nomisma* "coin, currency," from *nomizein* "to have in use," from *nomos* "custom."] —**nu·mis·mat·i·cal·ly** *adv.*

nu·mis·mat·ics /nòomiz máttiks, -mis-/ *n.* the study and collecting of coins and medals (*takes a singular verb*) —**nu·mis·ma·tist** /noo mízmətist/ *n.*

Num Lock /nùm-/ *n.* a toggle feature of computer keyboards that cancels the scrolling and cursor-moving abilities of keys on the numeric keypad so that it can be used to input numbers

num·ma·ry /númməree/ *adj.* relating to coins, or to coins and banknotes [Early 17thC. From Latin *nummarius*, from *nummus* "coin."]

num·mu·lar /númmyələr/ *adj.* shaped like a coin or disk (*formal*) [Mid-18thC. Formed from Latin *nummulus* "small coin," from *nummus* (see NUMMARY).]

num·mu·lite /númmyə lìt/ *n.* a type of fossil commonly found in limestone dating from between 56.5 million and 5.2 million years ago. It is common in the Mediterranean and is shaped like a flat disk. [Early 19thC. Formed from modern Latin *Nummulites*, former genus name, from Latin *nummulus* (see NUMMULAR), because of its shape.] —**num·mu·lit·ic** /-líttik/ *adj.*

num·nah /núm naà/ *n.* a pad placed under a saddle [Mid-19thC. From Urdu *namad_a* (see NUMDAH).]

num·skull /núm skùl/, **numb·skull** *n.* an offensive term that deliberately insults somebody's intelligence (*insult*) [Early 18thC. Formed from NUMB + SKULL.]

nun[1] /nun/ *n.* **1.** RELIG **RELIGIOUS WOMAN** a member of a religious community of women, e.g., any of various Christian orders of women who dedicate their lives to religious devotion and undertake not to marry **2.** BIRDS **KIND OF PIGEON** a variety of domestic pigeon with black-and-white feathers all over and a ring of white feathers around its neck and head that looks a little like a nun's headdress [Old English *nunne*. Via Old French *nonne* from ecclesiastical Latin *nonna*, from *nonnus* "old man, monk."]

nun[2] /nun/ *n.* the 14th letter of the Hebrew alphabet, represented in the English alphabet as "n" [Early 19thC. From Hebrew *nûn*.]

nun·a·tak /núnnə tàk/ *n.* a mountain peak surrounded by glacial ice, originally in Norway and Greenland [Late 19thC. From Inuit (Eskimo) *nunataq*.]

Nunavut

Nun·a·vut /nóonə vòot/ territory created at the end of the 20th century in northern Canada, replacing the central and eastern part of the Northwest Territories. It is a homeland for the Inuit people. The name means *our land* in Inuit. Capital: Iqaluit. Population: 22,000 (1997). Area: 770,000 sq. mi./2 million sq. km.

nun buoy *n.* a buoy with a rounded middle and tapering ends, used to mark the right-hand side of a channel that leads into a harbor [Early 18thC. From *nun* "child's top."]

Nunc Di·mit·tis /nùngk di míttiss, nóongk-/ *n.* a hymn or canticle with a text from Luke 2:29–32, starting in Latin with "Nunc dimittis servum tuum," in English meaning "Lord, now you are dismissing your servant in peace." The passage in the Bible describes Simeon being presented with the baby Jesus Christ.

nun·cha·ku /nùn chaá kòo/ *n.* a martial arts weapon consisting of two thick sticks joined at their ends by a rawhide band, a rope, or a chain [Late 20thC. From Japanese dialect.]

nun·ci·a·ture /núnsee ə choor/ *n.* the rank or position of a nuncio, or the period of time somebody spends as a nuncio [Early 17thC. From Italian *nunciatura*, from *nuncio* (see NUNCIO).]

nun·ci·o /núnsee ō, nóon-/ (*plural* **-os**) *n.* **1.** CHR **POPE'S REPRESENTATIVE** somebody appointed by the pope to represent him in a country, with the diplomatic status of an ambassador **2. REPRESENTATIVE OR INTERMEDIARY** somebody sent by a person to act on his or her behalf, especially a person regarded as self-important or authoritarian (*formal humorous*) [Early 16thC. Via Italian from Latin *nuntius* "messenger" (source of English *announce* and *enunciate*).]

nun·cu·pa·tive /núngkyə pàytiv/ *adj.* LAW given or declared orally by somebody making a will, and written down later by somebody else [Mid-16thC. Via late Latin *nuncupativus* from Latin *nuncupare* "to name, declare," from *nomen* "name" + *capere* "to take" (see CAPTIVE).]

nun·ner·y /núnnəree/ (*plural* **-ies**) *n.* a convent

Nu·pe /nóo pày/ (*plural* **-pe** *or* **-pes**) *n.* **1.** PEOPLES **MEMBER OF A NIGERIAN PEOPLE** a member of a Nigerian people who live between the rivers Benue and Niger **2.** LANG **LANGUAGE OF THE NUPE** the language spoken by the Nupe, belonging to the Benue-Congo branch of the Niger-Congo family of languages. Nupe is spoken by about one million people. [Early 19thC. Named for a former kingdom at the junction of the Niger and Benue.]

nup·tial /núpshəl, núpchəl/ *adj.* **1. OF MARRIAGE** relating to marriage or weddings. ◊ **nuptials 2. OF ANIMAL BREEDING** relating to mating or breeding in animals [15thC. Via Old French from Latin *nuptiae* "wedding," from *nubere* "to take a husband" (source of English *nubile*).] —**nup·tial·ly** *adv.*

nup·tial plum·age *n.* the distinctive feathers that some birds grow during their mating season

nup·tials /núpshəlz, núpchəlz/ *npl.* a wedding ceremony (*literary*)

Nu·rem·berg city in Bavaria, southern Germany. After 1933 the German Nazi Party held annual rallies in a stadium in the city, and between 1945 and 1946 it was the scene of Allied trials of German war criminals. Population: 497,496 (1992).

Rudolf Nureyev

Nu·re·yev /nyoóree ef, nyoo ráy-/, **Rudolf** (1938–93) Russian-born dancer and choreographer. He was connected from 1962 with Britain's Royal Ballet, where he often performed with Margot Fonteyn. Full name **Rudolf Hametovich Nureyev**

nurse /nurss/ *n.* **1.** MED **SOMEBODY CARING FOR PATIENTS** somebody trained to look after sick and injured people, especially somebody who works in a hospital or clinic, administering the care and treatment that a doctor prescribes **2. NANNY** a nanny or nursemaid (*dated*) **3.** = **wet nurse 4.** INSECTS **INSECT LOOKING AFTER YOUNG** an insect that looks after the young or the larvae in a colony of social insects such as ants or bees ■ *v.* (**nursed, nurs·ing, nurs·es**) **1.** *vti.* **BREASTFEED** to breastfeed a baby, or suckle at a mother's breast **2.** *vt.* MED **CARE FOR A SICK PERSON** to take care of somebody who is ill or injured **3.** *vt.* **CONSUME SOMETHING SLOWLY** to consume something, especially a drink, very slowly in order to make it last ○ *nursing her espresso* **4.** *vt.* **KEEP A FEELING** to keep a feeling in the mind for a long time and perhaps indulge in it, allowing it to grow or deepen ○ *nursing his resentment* **5.** *vt.* **MANAGE SOMEBODY OR SOMETHING CAREFULLY** to manage, guide, or supervise somebody or something with care and devotion **6.** *vt.* **TREAT A HEALTH PROBLEM** to take care of yourself while ill or injured ○ *I have been nursing a bad cold for three days.* **7.** *vi.* MED **WORK AS A NURSE** to do the work of a nurse, especially professionally in a hospital **8.** *vt.* **HOLD SOMETHING** to hold something precious with love or care [13thC. Via Old French *norrice* from, ultimately, Latin *nutricia* "wet nurse," from Latin *nutrix*.] —**nurs·er** *n.*

nurse·maid /núrss màyd/ *n.* a woman employed to look after somebody's children when they are young (*dated*)

nurse prac·ti·tion·er *n.* a registered nurse trained in primary health care to assume certain responsibilities once assumed only by a physician, such as the diagnosis and treatment of minor illnesses

nurs·er·y /núrssəree, núrssree/ (*plural* **-ies**) *n.* **1.** GARDENING **PLACE GROWING PLANTS COMMERCIALLY** a place where plants are grown commercially, either for sale direct to the public or to other retailers **2.** MED **HOSPITAL ROOM FOR NEWBORNS** a room in a hospital where newborns stay and are cared for by the nursing staff and pediatricians prior to going home **3.** EDUC = **nursery school 4. CHILD'S ROOM** a child's bedroom or playroom in a house **5. PLACE FOSTERING SOMETHING** a place where talents or abilities are allowed or encouraged to develop and flourish (*literary*) [14thC. Via Old French *norricerie* from *norrice* "wet nurse" (see NURSE). Originally in English, "attentive care."]

nurs·er·y·man /núrssəreemən, núrssreemən/ (*plural* **-men** /-mən/) *n.* a man who works in or owns a nursery where plants are grown commercially

nurs·er·y rhyme *n.* a short song or poem for young children, especially one that has become traditional

nurs·er·y school *n.* a prekindergarten school for children between the ages of three and five, staffed wholly or partly by qualified teachers who encourage and supervise educational play rather than simply providing childcare

nurs·er·y slopes *npl. U.K.* SKIING = **bunny slopes**

nurs·e's aide *n.* somebody with no specialized training employed in a hospital or other healthcare facility to perform basic nursing-support tasks such as bedmaking or giving patients baths

nurse shark *n.* a warm-water shark that has a bristle (**barbel**) hanging from its jaw and a deep groove on either side of its mouth. Family: Orectolobidae. [So called because it tends its eggs until they hatch]

nurs·ing /núrssing/ *n.* **1. CARING FOR SICK PEOPLE** the profession or task of looking after people who are sick or injured **2. BREASTFEEDING** breastfeeding, or the period of time that a mother spends breastfeeding her baby

nurs·ing bra *n.* a bra with removable or openable cups, worn by breastfeeding mothers

nurs·ing home *n.* a long-term healthcare facility that provides full-time care and medical treatment for people who are unable to take care of themselves

nurs·ling /núrssling/ *n.* (*literary*) **1. BREASTFED INFANT** a baby that is being breastfed **2. CHILD BEING CARED FOR** a baby or child that somebody is looking after or bringing up, especially somebody else's child **3. SOMETHING FOSTERED** something fostered or developed by a person, a place, or a set of circumstances

nur·ture /núrchər/ *vt.* (**-tured, -tur·ing, -tures**) **1. CARE FOR A YOUNG THING** to give tender care and protection to a child, a young animal, or a plant, helping it to grow and develop **2. ENCOURAGE TO FLOURISH** to encourage somebody or something to grow, develop, thrive, and be successful ○ *an agent who nurtured several budding young playwrights* **3. KEEP A FEELING** to keep a feeling in the mind for a long time, allowing it to grow or deepen ■ *n.* **1. CARE OR ENCOURAGEMENT** care and protection given to a young child, animal, or plant, or support and encouragement given to something to help it develop **2. ENVIRONMENTAL INFLUENCE** environmental influence on an organism, especially when contrasted with what is determined genetically. ◊ **nature** [14thC. Via Old French from late Latin *nutritura*, from Latin *nutrire* "to suckle" (see NOURISH).] —**nur·tur·er** *n.*

nut /nut/ *n.* **1.** BOT **PLANT'S SHELL-COVERED FRUIT** the fruit of a plant, especially a tree, with a hard outer shell and a fairly hard kernel or inner part that is the plant's seed **2.** FOOD **EDIBLE KERNEL** the kernel of a plant's shell-covered fruit, especially when it is edible **3.** BOT **HARD FRUIT OF SOME PLANTS** the hard dry one-seeded fruit of various plants, which does not split open to scatter its seed when it is mature **4. FASTENING SCREWED ONTO A BOLT** a piece of metal, usually square or hexagonal, with a hole in the middle, screwed on the end of a bolt as a fastening for it **5. ENTHUSIAST** somebody with a deep interest in something (*informal*) **6. HUMAN HEAD** a person's head (*informal*) **7. OFFENSIVE TERM** a highly offensive term for somebody

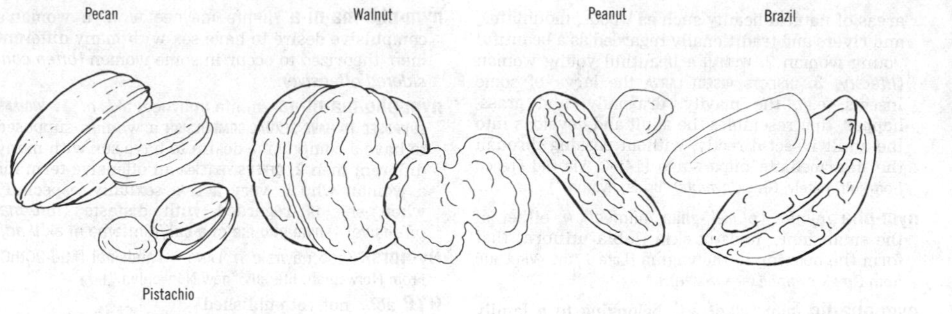

Nut

with a psychiatric disorder (*offensive*) **8.** **COSTS OF A BUSINESS** the amount of money needed to launch a business, particularly an entertainment business, or to keep it running (*slang*) ○ *The dance club's weekly nut is in the thousands.* **9.** MUSIC **PART OF A STRING INSTRUMENT** a ridge at the top end of the fingerboard of a violin, guitar, or other string instrument that the strings pass over just before they reach the tuning pegs **10.** MUSIC **PART OF AN INSTRUMENT'S BOW** a device like a screw at one end of a bow for a musical instrument that is turned to tighten the hairs of the bow ■ **nuts** *npl.* **TESTICLES** a man's testicles (*slang*) (*sometimes considered offensive*) ■ *n.* PRINTING = **en** ■ *vi.* (**nut·ted, nut·ting, nuts**) **GATHER NUTS** to gather edible nuts from trees [Old English *hnutu*. Ultimately from an Indo-European base that is also the ancestor of Latin *nux* (source of English *nucleus* and *nougat*).]

nu·ta·tion /noo táysh'n/ *n.* **1.** ASTRON **WOBBLY ROTATION** the wobbly rotation of a spinning object, especially a planet, caused by a temporary shift in the position of its axis **2.** BOT **PLANT'S IRREGULAR GROWTH** a spiral movement of a plant part caused by varying growth rates on each side **3.** **NODDING** the nodding of somebody's head (*formal*) [Early 17thC. From Latin *nutation-*, from the past participle stem of *nutare* "to nod."] — **nu·ta·tion·al** *adj.*

nut-brown *adj.* dark brown or reddish-brown in color

nut·case /nút kàyss/ *n.* a highly offensive term for somebody with a psychiatric disorder (*informal offensive*)

Nutcracker

nut·crack·er /nút kràkər/ *n.* **1.** **TOOL FOR CRACKING NUTS' SHELLS** a tool for cracking hard edible nutshells, usually consisting of two hinged metal arms between which the nut is squeezed **2.** BIRDS **BIRD THAT EATS PINE NUTS** a bird of the crow family that feeds mainly on nuts and the seeds of pines. Genus: *Nucifraga*.

WORD KEY: CULTURAL NOTE

The Nutcracker, a ballet by Russian composer Pyotr Ilyich Tchaikovsky (1892). Based on Hoffmann's *The Nutcracker and the King of the Mice*, it depicts the dream of a young girl during which her nutcracker turns into a handsome prince who leads her to the magical realm of the Sugar Plum Fairy. Though the story is particularly popular with children, the music and choreography have universal and lasting appeal.

nut·gall /nút gàwl/ *n.* a hollow nut-shaped growth on the trunks of oak and other trees caused by the gall wasp, which uses the growth as a shelter for its larvae

nut·hatch /nút hàch/ *n.* a small bird with a blue-gray back that usually hangs upside down on a tree trunk and works its way down, eating insects, seeds, and nuts. Family: Sittidae. [14thC. From NUT + *hache* "hatchet, ax," from Old French (see HATCHET), from its habit of hacking at nuts with its beak after wedging them into crevices.]

nut·house /nút hòwss/ *n.* **1.** **OFFENSIVE TERM** a highly offensive term for psychiatric hospital (*slang offensive*) **2.** **CHAOTIC PLACE** a place full of noisy, boisterous, chaotic activity (*slang*)

nut·let /nútlət/ *n.* **1.** **SMALL NUT** a small nut, especially a small hard dry one-seeded fruit of various plants **2.** **FRUIT'S STONE** the stone of fruits such as the cherry and the plum

nut·meat /nút mèet/ *n.* the edible inside part of a nut

Nutmeg

nut·meg /nút mèg/ *n.* **1.** COOK **SPICE** an aromatic spice made by grinding or grating the large hard seed of a nutmeg tree **2.** TREES **TROPICAL EVERGREEN TREE** an evergreen tree native to eastern India and widely grown in tropical regions for its seeds, which are the source of nutmeg and mace. Latin name: *Myristica fragrans.* ■ *adj.* COLORS **LIGHT BROWN** of a light brown color with a grayish tinge [13thC. Origin uncertain: probably ultimately from medieval Latin *nux muscata*, literally "nut smelling like musk," from *nux* "nut" + late Latin *muscus* (see MUSK).]

nut·pick /nút pìk/, **nut pick** *n.* a sharp metal tool for digging nutmeats out of their shells

nu·tri·a /nóotree ə/ *n.* **1.** **COYPU'S FUR** the light brown fur of the coypu **2.** ZOOL = **coypu** [Early 19thC. Via Spanish from, ultimately, Latin *lutra* "otter."]

nu·tri·ceu·ti·cal /nòotri sóotik'l/ *n.* = **medical food**

nu·tri·ent /nóotree ənt/ *n.* **NOURISHING SUBSTANCE** any substance that provides nourishment, e.g., the minerals that a plant takes from the soil or the constituents in food that keep a human body healthy and help it grow ■ *adj.* **NOURISHING** providing nourishment [Mid-17thC. From Latin *nutriens*, the present participle stem of *nutrire* (see NOURISH).]

nu·tri·ment /nóotrəmənt/ *n.* nourishment or nourishing substances [Mid-16thC. From Latin *nutrimentum*, from *nutrire* (see NOURISH).]

nu·tri·tion /noo trísh'n/ *n.* **1.** PHYSIOL **PROCESSING OF FOOD** the process of absorbing nutrients from food and processing them in the body in order to keep healthy or to grow **2.** SCI **SCIENCE OF FOOD** the science that deals with foods and their effects on health **3.** FOOD **FOODS** foods, or the minerals, vitamins, and other nourishing substances that they contain [Mid-16thC. Via Old French from the Latin stem *nutrition-*, from *nutrire* (see NOURISH).] —**nu·tri·tion·al** *adj.* — **nu·tri·tion·al·ly** *adv.*

nu·tri·tion·al ther·a·py *n.* the alleviation of symptoms by dietary changes, sometimes using vitamin and mineral pills

nu·tri·tion·ist /noo trísh'nist/ *n.* somebody who studies or is an expert on nutrition

nu·tri·tious /noo tríshəss/ *adj.* containing minerals, vitamins, and other substances that promote health —**nu·tri·tious·ly** *adv.* —**nu·tri·tious·ness** *n.*

nu·tri·tive /nóotrətiv/ *adj.* **1.** **NOURISHING** providing nutrients **2.** **OF NOURISHMENT** relating to or providing nutrition [15thC. Via Old French from medieval Latin *nutritivus*, from the past participle stem of *nutrire* (see NOURISH).] —**nu·tri·tive·ly** *adv.*

nuts /nuts/ *adj.* **1.** **OFFENSIVE TERM** a highly offensive term meaning having a psychiatric disorder (*slang offensive*) **2.** **ENTHUSIASTIC** wildly enthusiastic about something, or extremely fond of somebody (*slang*) ■ *interj.* **EXPRESSION OF ANNOYANCE** used to express annoyance, disbelief, or contempt (*slang*)

nuts and bolts *npl.* **BASICS** the most basic components, elements, or constituents of something (*informal*) ■ *adj.* **nuts-and-bolts** **BASIC** extremely basic, e.g., in attitude, approach, or strategy (*informal*) ○ *took a nuts-and-bolts approach to paring down the city's budget*

nut·shell /nút shèl/ *n.* the hard outer shell of a nut that surrounds the edible inner nut or kernel ◇ **in a nutshell** in very few words, getting right to the main point

nut·sy /nutsee/ (**-si·er, -si·est**) *adj.* an offensive term meaning having a psychiatric disorder (*slang offensive*) ○ *a nutsy racecar driver, willing to push the envelope of safety every time he competes*

nut·ty /núttee/ (**-ti·er, -ti·est**) *adj.* **1.** **OFFENSIVE TERM** an offensive term meaning having a psychiatric disorder (*slang offensive*) **2.** **WITH NUTS** containing a large amount of nuts **3.** **LIKE NUTS** like nuts in taste, appearance, texture, or smell —**nut·ti·ly** *adv.* — **nut·ti·ness** *n.*

nux vom·i·ca /nùks vómmikə/ (*plural* **nux vom·i·ca**) *n.* **1.** TREES **ASIAN TREE** an Asian tree that has narrow leaves and orange-red berries containing seeds from which a former cardiac medication was made. Latin name: *Strychnos nux-vomica.* **2.** BOT **SEEDS OF THE NUX VOMICA TREE** the highly poisonous seeds of the nux vomica tree which contain strychnine and other poisonous substances **3.** MED **MEDICINE** a medicine or homeopathic remedy made from the seeds of nux vomica [From medieval Latin, literally "emetic nut"]

nuz·zle /núzz'l/ *v.* (**-zled, -zling, -zles**) **1.** *vti.* **RUB SOMETHING WITH THE NOSE** to rub or push something gently with the nose, especially as a way of showing affection **2.** *vi.* **RUB SOMETHING WITH THE FACE** to make affectionate rubbing or stroking movements with the face ■ *n.* **RUBBING MOVEMENT** a rubbing or stroking movement with the nose or face [15thC. Origin uncertain: perhaps a back-formation from *noseling* "on your nose," from NOSE.] — **nuz·zler** *n.*

NV *abbr.* **1.** MAIL Nevada **2.** FIN nonvoting

NW *abbr.* **1.** northwest **2.** northwestern

NWbN *abbr.* northwest by north

NWbW *abbr.* northwest by west

Nwfld. *abbr.* Newfoundland

NWT *abbr. Can* Northwest Territories

n.wt. *abbr.* net weight

NY, **N.Y.** *abbr.* New York

nya·la /nyaalə/ (*plural* **-la** *or* **-las**) *n.* **1.** **CENTRAL AFRICAN ANTELOPE** an antelope found in central Africa, usually near water, that has vertical white stripes on its sides and, on the male, spiral horns. Latin name: *Tragelaphus angasi.* **2.** **NE AFRICAN MOUNTAIN ANTELOPE** an antelope with spiral horns on the male found in mountainous regions in northeastern Africa, above 9,000 ft./2,743. Latin name: *Tragelaphus buxtoni.* [Late 19thC. From Zulu *i-nyala*.]

Nyan·ja *n.* (*plural* **-ja** *or* **-jas**), *adj.* LANG = **Chewa** [Mid-19thC. From Bantu *nyanja* "lake."]

nyb·ble /níbb'l/ *n.* half of one byte, or four bits in size [Humorous play on the idea of a small bite]

NYC, **N.Y.C.** *abbr.* New York City

nyc·ta·lo·pi·a /niktə lópee ə/ *n.* the state of being unable to see well at night (*technical*) [Late 17thC. Via late Latin from Greek *nuktalōps* "sightless at night," from the stem of *nux* "night" + *alaos* "sightless" + *ōps* "eye" (source of English *myopia* and *triceratops*).] —**nyc·ta·lo·pic** /nìktə lóppik/ *adj.*

nyc·tit·ro·pism /nik títtrə pìzzəm/ *n.* the movement of parts of a plant in response to light and temperature differences between night and day, such as the opening and closing of flowers and the folding together of leaves at night. Also called **sleep** [Late 19thC. Formed from the stem of Greek *nux* "night" (see NYCTALOPIA) + TROPISM.] —**nyc·ti·tro·pic** /niktə tróppik/ *adj.*

nyc·to·pho·bi·a /niktə fóbee ə/ *n.* an irrational fear of the night, or of darkness in general [Early 20thC. Formed from the stem of Greek *nux* "night" (see NYCTALOPIA) + -PHOBIA.] —**nyc·to·pho·bic** *adj.* —**nyc·to·pho·bi·cal·ly** *adv.*

nyet·work /nyétwùrk/ *n.* = **notwork** (*slang humorous*) [Late 20thC. Blend of Russian *nyet* "no" + NETWORK.]

ny·lon /nī́ lòn/ *n.* TEXTILES **SYNTHETIC MATERIAL** a tough synthetic material widely used in different forms in manufactured articles, e.g., in food containers, in brush bristles, and in clothing ■ **ny·lons** *npl.* CLOTHES **WOMEN'S STOCKINGS** stockings made of a synthetic fiber such as nylon [Mid-20thC. Coined by its inventors, perhaps modelled on RAYON.]

NYMEX *abbr.* New York Mercantile Exchange

nymph /nimf/ *n.* **1.** MYTHOL **SPIRIT OF NATURE** a minor goddess or spirit of nature in mythology, inhabiting areas of natural beauty such as woods, mountains, and rivers and traditionally regarded as a beautiful young woman **2. WOMAN** a beautiful young woman (*literary*) **3.** INSECTS **INSECT LARVA** the larva of some insects, e.g., the mayfly, dragonfly, and grasshopper, that resembles the adult and develops into the adult insect directly, without passing through the intermediate pupa stage [14thC. Via Old French from, ultimately, Greek *numphē* "bride, nymph."]

nym·pha /nímfə/ (*plural* **-phae** /nímfee/) *n.* either of the small inner folds of skin (**labia minora**) that form the opening to the vagina [Late 17thC. Via Latin from Greek *numphē* (see NYMPH).]

nym·pha·lid /nim fállid/ *adj.* belonging to a family of butterflies that has brightly colored wings and includes the tortoiseshell butterfly and the red admiral. Family: Nymphalidae. [Late 19thC. Via modern Latin *Nymphalidae*, family name, from, ultimately, Latin *nympha* (see NYMPH).]

nym·phet /ním fèt, -fət/, **nym·phette** /nim fét/ *n.* a sexually aware and sexually desirable young woman, especially a woman in her early teens [Early 17thC. Originally, "a small or young nymph"; the modern sense appeared in the mid-20thC.]

nym·pho /ním fō/ (*plural* **-phos**) *n.* a nymphomaniac (*informal offensive*) [Mid-20thC. Shortening.]

nym·pho·ma·ni·a /nìmfə máynee ə/ *n.* a woman's compulsive desire to have sex with many different men, theorized to occur in some women (*often considered offensive*)

nym·pho·ma·ni·ac /nìmfə máynee àk/ *n.* **1. WOMAN SUPPOSED TO HAVE SEXUAL COMPULSION** a woman supposed to have a compulsive desire to have sex with many different men **2. OFFENSIVE TERM** an offensive term for a woman who is very active sexually, especially when she is regarded with distaste (*informal offensive*) —**nym·pho·ma·ni·a·cal** /nìmfəmə nī́ ək'l/ *adj.*

Ny·norsk /noo náwrsk/ *n.* LANG = **Landsmal** [Mid-20thC. From Norwegian, literally "new Norwegian."]

NYP *abbr.* not yet published

NYSE *abbr.* New York Stock Exchange

nys·tag·mus /ni stágməss/ *n.* an involuntary rhythmic movement of somebody's eyes, usually from side to side, caused by some illnesses that affect the nerves and muscle behind the eyeball [Early 19thC. Via modern Latin from Greek *nustagmos* "drowsiness," from *nustazein* "to nod, be sleepy."]

nys·ta·tin /nístətin/ *n.* an antibiotic drug used to treat fungal infections, especially thrush [Mid-20thC. Coined from *N(ew) Y(ork) Stat(e)*, where it was developed.]

NZ *abbr.* New Zealand

N Zeal. *abbr.* New Zealand

Oo

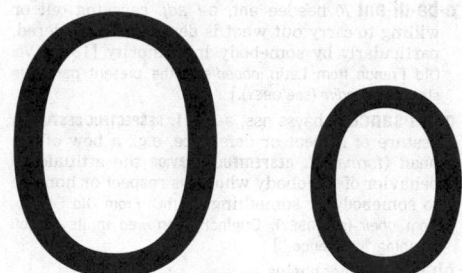

O /ō/ (*plural* **o's**), **O** (*plural* **O's** *or* **Os**) *n.* **1. 15TH LETTER OF ENGLISH ALPHABET** the 15th letter of the English alphabet **2. SPEECH SOUND CORRESPONDING TO LETTER "O"** the speech sound that corresponds to the letter "O" **3. LETTER "O" WRITTEN** a written representation of the letter "O"

O[1] *interj.* **1. USED TO ADDRESS SOMEBODY** used in addressing a person or topic or at the start of a plea or wish **2. EXPRESSION OF WONDER** used in expressing surprise or great wonderment (*literary*) [12thC. Representing a national exclamation.]

O[2] *symbol.* CHEM oxygen

O[3] *n.* MED a human blood type of the ABO group containing the O antigen. Somebody with type O blood can donate to all other types in the group but can receive only O blood.

o. *abbr.* **1. o., O, O.** GEOG ocean **2. o., O, O.** PRINTING octavo **3. o., O, O.** old **4. o., O.** MATH order **5. o., o, O** BASEBALL out **6. o., o, O** CRICKET over(s) **7.** PHARM pint [Shortening of modern Latin *octarius*]

-o *suffix.* **1.** used to form abbreviated words ○ *aggro* ○ *demo* ○ *hypo* **2.** somebody or something associated with or having the characteristics of something ○ *dumbo* [Origin uncertain: perhaps from OH]

OA *abbr.* MED osteoarthritis

o/a *abbr.* on or about

oaf /ōf/ *n.* (*insult*) **1. SOMEBODY UNINTELLIGENT** an unintelligent person **2. SOMEBODY CLUMSY** an awkward or clumsy person **3. SOMEBODY LOUTISH** a rough loutish person [Early 17thC. From Old Norse *álfr* "elf."]

oaf·ish /ṓfish/ *adj.* resembling an oaf, e.g., in clumsiness, unintelligence, or loutishness (*insult*) —**oaf·ish·ly** *adv.* —**oaf·ish·ness** *n.*

O·a·hu /ə wā́a hoo, ō ā́a-/ island in Hawaii, the most populous and third largest of the Hawaiian Islands. Area: 608 sq. mi./1,575 sq. km.

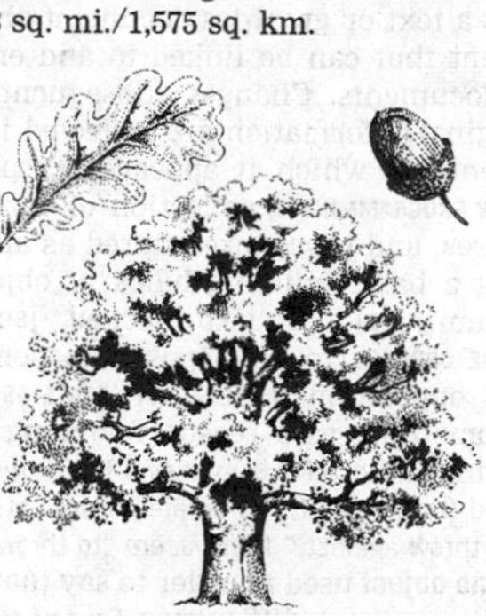

Oak

oak /ōk/ *n.* **1.** TREES **TREE BEARING ACORNS** a deciduous or evergreen tree or shrub that has acorns as fruit, and leaves with several rounded or pointed projections. Genus: *Quercus.* **2.** PLANTS **SHRUB WITH LOBED LEAVES** a shrub such as the Jerusalem oak or poison oak with lobed leaves like those of oak trees **3.** INDUST **HARD WOOD OF OAK TREE** the hard wood of the oak tree, highly valued by furniture makers and formerly widely used in construction and shipbuilding **4. OAK WREATH OR GARLAND** a decoration made from the leaves of an oak tree, especially a wreath or garland ■ *adj.* COLORS **OF RICH BROWN COLOR** of a rich brown color, similar to the color of oak wood [Old English *āc*]

oak ap·ple *n.* a rounded hollow growth on the trunk of an oak tree caused by infestation with gall wasps, which use the growths as shelters for their larvae

oak·en /ṓkən/ *adj.* made of oak wood (*literary*)

oak fern *n.* a light green woodland fern found in northern climates. Latin name: *Thelypteris dryopteris.*

Oak For·est city in northeastern Illinois, northeast of Joliet, a southern suburb of Chicago. Population: 27,461 (1996).

oak gall /-gawl, -gaal/ *n.* = **oak apple**

Oak·land /ṓk lənd/ city and county seat of Alameda County, western California, situated on the eastern side of San Francisco Bay. Population: 372,242 (1990).

Oak·land Park city in Broward County, southeastern Florida, situated north of Fort Lauderdale. Population: 26,326 (1990).

oak leaf clus·ter *n.* a small decoration shaped like a bunch of oak leaves and acorns, added to another military decoration to show that it has been awarded to the wearer more than once

Oak·ley /ṓklee/, **Annie** (1860–1926) U.S. sharpshooter. She performed with Buffalo Bill's Wild West Show, and inspired the musical *Annie Get Your Gun* (1946). Full name **Phoebe Anne Oakley Moses**

oak·moss /ṓk mòss/ *n.* any of various lichens that grow on oak trees and produce a resin used in the making of some perfumes. Latin name: *Evernia prunastri.*

Oak Park town in northeastern Illinois, on the western boundary of Chicago, north of Cicero. Population: 51,585 (1996).

oak prun·er *n.* a long-horned beetle that as a larva bores oak twigs until they are cut off. Latin name: *Hypermallus villosus.*

oa·kum /ṓkəm/ *n.* hemp or jute fibers, especially old ropes unraveled, soaked in tar, and used to seal the gaps between the planks forming a wooden ship's or boat's hull [Old English *ācumba* "broken fibers," literally "off-combing"]

Oak·ville /ṓk vil/ town in Halton Municipal Region, southeastern Ontario, Canada, situated 22 mi./35 km southwest of Toronto. Population: 114,670 (1991).

oak wilt *n.* a disease of oak trees caused by a fungus that kills their leaves

Oa·ma·ru /ómmə roo/ town and fishing port on the east coast of the South Island, New Zealand. Population: 13,695 (1996).

O & M *abbr.* organization and method

OAP *n. U.K.* somebody who is old enough to draw a pension from the state

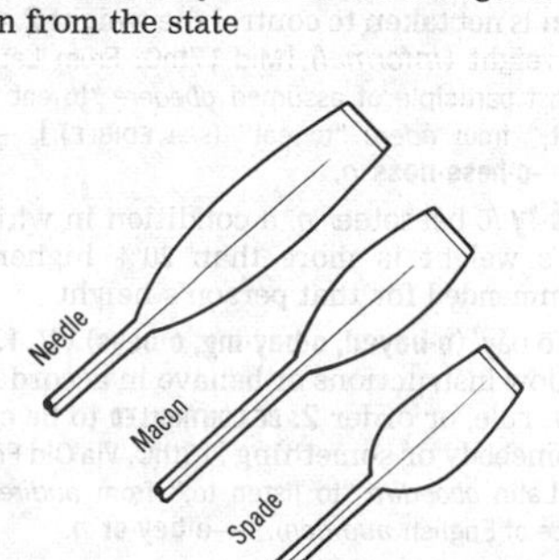

Oar

oar /awr/ *n.* **1. POLE USED TO PROPEL BOAT** a wooden pole with one broad flat end, used either singly or in pairs to propel a boat by dipping the broad end in the water **2. SOMEBODY ROWING** somebody who rows a boat, especially one of a team of rowers ■ *vti.* (**oared, oar·ing, oars**) **TO ROW** to row a boat [Old English *ār*]

oar·fish /áwr fish/ (*plural* **-fish** *or* **-fish·es**) *n.* a long marine fish shaped like an eel that grows up to 23 ft./7 m and has a dazzling red head fin and a red dorsal fin running the length of its body. It is found in tropical seas and warmer parts of the Atlantic. Latin name: *Regalecus glesne.* [Mid-19thC. From the shape of its body.]

oar·lock /áwr lòk/ *n.* a U-shaped pivoting metal rest attached to the side of a boat, in which an oar rests [Old English *ārloc, ār* "oar" + *loc* "lock"]

oars·man /áwrzmən/ (*plural* **-men** /-mən/) *n.* a man who rows a boat, especially as part of a team of rowers —**oars·man·ship** *n.*

oars·wom·an /áwrz wŏŏmmən/ (*plural* **-women** /-wìmmin/) *n.* a woman who rows a boat, especially as part of a team of rowers

OAS *abbr.* Organization of American States

OAS·DHI *abbr.* Old Age, Survivors, Disability, and Health Insurance

o·a·sis /ō áyssiss/ (*plural* **-ses** /-seez/) *n.* **1.** GEOG **FERTILE LAND IN DESERT** fertile ground in a desert where the level of underground water rises to or near ground level, where plants grow and travelers can replenish water supplies **2. PLACE OR TIME OF RELIEF** a place or period that gives relief from a troubling or chaotic situation [Early 17thC. Via late Latin from Greek. Probably ultimately of Egyptian origin.]

oast /ōst/ *n.* a kiln used for drying hops, especially hops used to flavor beer [Old English *āst* "kiln." Ultimately from an Indo-European base meaning "to be hot, burn" that is also the ancestor of English *estuary* and *edifice.*]

oast·house /ōst hòwss/ (*plural* **-hous·es** /-hòwzəz/) *n.* a building that contains, or formerly contained, hop-drying kilns and typically has conical or pyramid-shaped towers

Oat

oat /ōt/ *n.* **GRASS WITH EDIBLE SEED** a grass that has edible seeds and is grown in numerous northern countries as a cereal crop. Latin name: *Avena sativa.* ■ **oats** *npl.* **EDIBLE SEEDS OF THE OAT** the seeds of the oat grown as a cereal crop and used to make foods such as oatmeal and as a livestock feed [Old English *āte*]

oat·cake /ṓt kàyk/ *n.* a flat cake made of oatmeal

oat-cell *adj.* relating to a highly malignant form of lung cancer characterized by the rapid growth of undifferentiated small round cells. Oat-cell carcinoma is usually related to smoking. [Because the cells look like grains of oats]

oat·en /ṓt'n/ *adj.* made from oats, oatmeal, or oat straw

oat·er /ṓtər/ *n.* a movie about cowboys, Native Americans, and settlers in the Old West (*slang*) [Mid-20thC. From the staple food of the horses that were ubiquitous in them.]

Oates /ōts/, **Joyce Carol** (*b.* 1938) U.S. writer. Her naturalistic novels, often depicting violence in U.S. society, include *them* (1969), for which she won the National Book award.

oat grass *n.* a grass, especially in Africa and Asia, that looks like the oat. Genera: *Arrhenatherum* and *Danthonia.*

oath /ōth/ (*plural* **oaths** /ōthz/) *n.* **1.** SOLEMN PROMISE a formal or legally binding pledge to do something such as tell the truth in a court of law, made formally and often naming God or a loved one as a witness **2.** WORDS OF PROMISE the words said when making a formal pledge, especially when reciting a conventional formula such as that used in a court of law **3.** SWEARWORD a swearword, especially one that uses the name of God or another sacred name in a disrespectful way [Old English *āþ*]

oat·meal /ṓt mēel/ *n.* **1.** CRUSHED OATS oat grains ground or crushed into flakes or powder, used to make various foods such as cereal or oatcakes ○ *oatmeal cookies* **2.** BREAKFAST CEREAL a breakfast cereal made from rolled oats cooked in milk or water ■ *adj.* COLORS OF A LIGHT BROWN COLOR of a light grayish-brown color

OAU *abbr.* Organization of African Unity

Oa·xa·ca /waa khaá kaa, wə haá kə/ historic city in southern Mexico, the capital of Oaxaca State. It was founded by the Aztecs. Population: 212,818 (1990).

ob. *abbr.* **1. ob., Ob., OB** MED obstetric **2. ob., Ob., OB** MED obstetrics **3. ob., Ob., OB** MED obstetrician **4.** MUSIC oboe **5.** he or she died [Shortening of Latin [obiit] (see OBIT)]

Ob. *abbr.* BIBLE Obadiah

ob- *prefix.* inverse, inversely ○ *obvolute* [From Latin *ob* "in the way, against, toward"]

oba /ṓbə/ *n.* a ruler among the Yoruba people of West Africa [Early 20thC. From Yoruba.]

Obad. *abbr.* BIBLE Obadiah

O·ba·di·ah /ōbə dī́ ə/ *n.* **1.** BIBLICAL HEBREW PROPHET in the Bible, a minor Hebrew prophet of the 6th century B.C. **2.** BOOK OF THE BIBLE a book of the Bible containing the prophecies of Obadiah. Obadiah is the shortest book of the Bible. See table at **Bible**

obb. *abbr.* obbligato

ob·bli·ga·to /òbli gaá tō/, **ob·li·ga·to** *adj.* NOT TO BE LEFT OUT not to be omitted from a musical piece, either as an instrumental part in the piece or as an instrument accompanying a singer (*used as a musical direction*) ■ *n.* (*plural* **-tos** *or* **-ti** /-tee/) ESSENTIAL PART a musical part or accompaniment that is not to be left out [Early 18thC. Via Italian, literally "obliged," from Latin (see OBLIGATE).]

ob·com·pressed *adj.* BOT flattened from back to front, like the fruits of penny grass

ob·con·ic /ob kónnik/, **ob·con·i·cal** /ob kónnik'l/ *adj.* BOT cone-shaped and attached to a plant by the pointed end ○ *an obconic fruit*

ob·cor·date /ob káwr dàyt/ *adj.* BOT heart-shaped and attached to a plant by the pointed end

ob·du·ra·cy /ób doorəssee/ *n.* stubborn and total refusal to change an opinion or stance

ob·du·rate /ób doorət/ *adj.* **1.** STUBBORN not easily persuaded or influenced **2.** HARD-HEARTED not influenced by emotions, especially not inclined to feel sympathy or pity [15thC. From late Latin *obduratus*, the past participle of *obdurare* "to be hard," from *durus* "hard" (see ENDURE).] —**ob·du·rate·ly** *adv.* —**ob·du·rate·ness** *n.*

O.B.E. *abbr.* (Officer of the) Order of the British Empire

o·be·ah /ṓbee ə/, **o·bi** *n.* **1.** WEST INDIAN RELIGION a religion that involves witchcraft, originally practiced in Africa and surviving now in parts of the West Indies **2.** A CHARM an object believed to have magical powers, used in practicing obeah [Mid-18thC. From Twi *ɔ̄bayifo.*]

o·be·di·ence /ō beédee ənss, ə-/ *n.* **1.** ACT OF OBEYING the action or condition of obeying authority **2.** CHR CHURCH'S RULE the religious authority of a church or of a priest or other member of the clergy, or the people who are under this authority

o·be·di·ent /ō beédee ənt, ə-/ *adj.* carrying out or willing to carry out what is demanded or ordered, particularly by somebody in authority [13thC. Via Old French from Latin *oboediens*, the present participle stem of *oboedire* (see OBEY).]

o·bei·sance /ō báyss'nss, ə-/ *n.* **1.** RESPECTFUL GESTURE a gesture of respect or deference, e.g., a bow of the head (*formal*) **2.** RESPECTFUL BEHAVIOR the attitude or behavior of somebody who pays respect or homage to somebody or something [14thC. From Old French, from *obeir* (see OBEY). Originally borrowed in its French meaning "obedience."]

ob·e·li plural of **obelus**

o·be·lia /ō beélyə/ (*plural* **-lias**) *n.* a marine hydrozoan polyp that forms colonies that resemble moss on rocks, ships' hulls, and pilings. Genus: *Obelia.* [Late 19thC. Via modern Latin, genus name, from Greek *obelias* "leaf baked on a spit," from *obelos* (see OBELUS).]

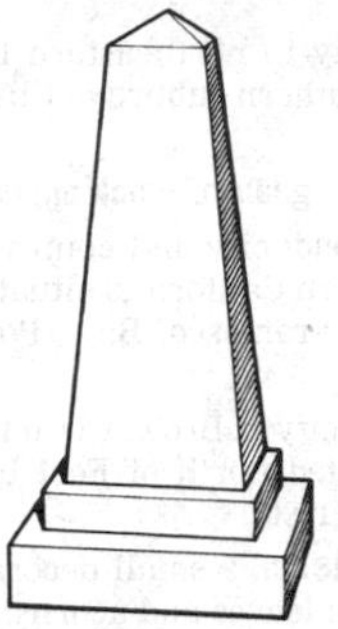

Obelisk

ob·e·lisk /óbbəlisk/ *n.* **1.** STONE PILLAR a pillar of stone, especially one built as a monument, that has a square base and sides that taper like a pyramid toward a pointed top **2.** PRINTING = **dagger** [Mid-16thC. Via Latin *obeliscus* from Greek *obeliskos*, from *obelos* (see OBELUS).] —**ob·e·lis·koid** /òbbə lís kòyd/ *adj.*

ob·e·lize /óbbə lī̀z/ (**-lized, -liz·ing, -liz·es**) *vt.* to mark a written or printed word or passage with a dagger or obelus [Mid-17thC. From Greek *obelizein*, from *obelos* (see OBELUS).]

ob·e·lus /óbbələss/ (*plural* **-li** /-lī/) *n.* **1.** = **dagger 2.** MARK IN ANCIENT MANUSCRIPTS a printed mark (†) used in modern editions of ancient manuscripts to indicate that the passage marked is thought not to be genuine [14thC. Via late Latin from Greek *obelos* "spit, obelisk."]

o·ben·to /ō béntō/ (*plural* **-tos**), **ben·to** (*plural* **-tos**) *n.* a Japanese meal that is packaged in a partitioned lacquer box [Late 20thC. From Japanese.]

O·ber·am·mer·gau /ṓbər aámər gòw/ town in Bavaria, southeastern Germany, famous for producing a Passion Play every ten years. Population: 5,425 (1991).

O·ber·on /ṓbə ron/ *n.* the second-largest natural satellite of Uranus, discovered in 1787. It is 945 mi./1,522 km in diameter and has a highly cratered surface.

o·bese /ō beéss/ *adj.* **1.** MED UNHEALTHILY OVERWEIGHT so overweight as to be at risk from several serious illnesses, including diabetes and heart disease, if action is not taken to control the weight **2.** OVERWEIGHT overweight (*informal*) [Mid-17thC. From Latin *obesus*, the past participle of assumed *obedere* "to eat until overweight," from *edere* "to eat" (see EDIBLE).] —**o·bese·ly** *adv.* —**o·bese·ness** *n.*

o·be·si·ty /ō beésətee/ *n.* a condition in which somebody's weight is more than 20% higher than is recommended for that person's height

o·bey /ō báy/ (**o·beyed, o·bey·ing, o·beys**) *vti.* **1.** DO AS TOLD to follow instructions or behave in accordance with a law, rule, or order **2.** BE CONTROLLED to be controlled by somebody or something [13thC. Via Old French *obeir* from Latin *oboedire* "to listen to," from *audire* "to hear" (source of English *audition*).] —**o·bey·er** *n.*

ob·fus·cate /óbfə skàyt/ (**-cat·ed, -cat·ing, -cates**) *v.* **1.** *vti.* MAKE SOMETHING OBSCURE to make something obscure or unclear, especially by making it unnecessarily complicated **2.** *vt.* MAKE DARK to make something dark or hard to see (*archaic*) **3.** *vt.* CONFUSE to make somebody confused (*archaic*) [Mid-16thC. From late Latin *obfuscat-*, the past participle stem of *obfuscare* "to darken," from *fuscus* "dark."] —**ob·fus·ca·tion** /òbfə skáysh'n/ *n.*

ob-gyn /ṓ bee jeé wī én/, **Ob-Gyn** *n.* (*informal*) **1.** OBSTETRICS AND GYNECOLOGY the branch of medicine that deals with obstetrics and gynecology **2.** MEDICAL SPECIALIST IN BABIES AND WOMEN a specialist in obstetrics and gynecology

o·bi[1] /ṓbee/ *n.* a silk sash worn by a Japanese person in traditional dress to fasten the kimono [Late 19thC. From Japanese, literally "belt, band, girdle."]

o·bi[2] *n.* = **obeah**

O·bie /ṓbee/ *n.* an annual award for achievement in off-Broadway theater [Mid-20thC. From the pronunciation of *OB* "off Broadway."]

Ob'-·Ir·tysh river system in southwestern Siberia, and the longest in Asia, incorporating the rivers Irtysh and Ob'. Length: 3,362 mi./5,410 km.

o·bit /ṓbit, ō bítt/ *n.* an obituary (*informal*) [14thC. Via French from Latin *obitus* "death," from (*mortem*) *obire* "to die," literally "to meet (death)," from *ire* "to go."]

o·bi·ter dic·tum /ōbitər díktəm/ (*plural* **o·bi·ter dic·ta** /-díktə/) *n.* **1.** JUDGE'S OBSERVATION an observation made by a judge that is incidental to the case being tried and, while being authoritative, is not binding on future courts under the doctrine of precedent **2.** PASSING COMMENT a comment made in passing [Early 19thC. From Latin, literally "said by the way, said in passing."]

o·bit·u·ar·y /ə bíchoo èrree, ō-/ *n.* (*plural* **-ies**) ANNOUNCEMENT OF DEATH an announcement, especially in a newspaper, of somebody's death, often with a short biography ■ *adj.* RECORDING A DEATH relating to or recording a death [Early 18thC. From medieval Latin *obituarius*, from Latin *obitus* "death" (see OBIT).]

obj. *abbr.* **1.** GRAM object **2.** objection **3.** GRAM objective

ob·ject *n.* /óbjəkt, ób jèkt/ **1.** SOMETHING VISIBLE OR TANGIBLE something that can be seen or touched **2.** FOCUS a focus of somebody's attention or emotion **3.** AIM an aim or purpose **4.** GRAM NOUN AFFECTED BY VERB a noun, pronoun, or noun phrase denoting somebody or something that is acted on by a verb or affected by the action of a verb **5.** GRAM NOUN GOVERNED BY PREPOSITION a noun, pronoun, or noun phrase that is governed by a preposition **6.** PHILOS SOMETHING PERCEIVED AND NAMED AS SEPARATE something that is perceived as an entity and referred to by a name ○ *mental objects* **7.** OPTICS SOURCE OF LIGHT RAYS the point or series of points that appear to be the source of light rays in an optical system. A point that is the source of the rays is called a (**real object**), while a point that only appears to be the source is called a (**virtual object**). **8.** COMPUT UNIT OF INFORMATION a block of information such as a text or graphics document or a part of a document that can be linked to and embedded in other documents. Changes subsequently made to the original information are reflected in the other documents in which it appears. **9.** COMPUT UNIT OF COMPUTER PROGRAMMING a collection of variables, data structures, and procedures stored as an entity and forming a basic building block of object-oriented programming ■ *v.* /əb jékt/ (**-ject·ed, -ject·ing, -jects**) **1.** *vi.* BE OPPOSED to be opposed to something, or express opposition to it **2.** *vt.* STATE AS OBJECTION to state something as a reason for being opposed to something [14thC. From medieval Latin *objectum* "thing presented (to the sight)," ultimately from Latin *obicere* "to present, throw against," from *jacere* "to throw."] ◇ **something is no object** used in order to say that something is not a concern or difficulty ○ *I want the best room you have – money's no object.*

WORD KEY: SYNONYMS

object, protest, demur, remonstrate, expostulate

CORE MEANING: to indicate opposition to something

object a general word used to talk about being opposed or averse to something, whether or not these feelings are expressed; **protest** to express strong feelings of objection in speech, writing, or actions; **demur** to raise objections in a hesitant or tentative way; **remonstrate** to indicate disagreement or objection by arguing with somebody and trying to dissuade him or her from a course of action; **expostulate** a formal word used to indicate that a disagreement or objection is expressed very vehemently.

ob·ject ball *n.* in pool or billiards, the ball that a player intends to hit with the cue ball in a particular shot

ob·ject code *n.* the binary version of a computer program that is used by the computer to run the program. ◊ **source code**

ob·ject com·ple·ment *n. U.K.* = **objective complement**

ob·ject glass *n.* OPTICS = **objective** *n.* 5

ob·jec·ti·fy /ob jéktə fī/ (**-fied, -fy·ing, -fies**) *vt.* **1. MAKE ACTUAL** to think of or represent an idea or emotion as if it were something that actually exists **2. REDUCE TO OBJECT** to reduce somebody, or something that is complex and multifaceted, to the status of a simple object

ob·jec·tion /ob jékshən/ *n.* **1. EXPRESSION OF OPPOSITION** a feeling or expression of opposition **2. CAUSE OF OPPOSITION** a reason for a feeling or expression of opposition

ob·jec·tion·a·ble /ob jékshənəb'l/ *adj.* causing disapproval, offense, or opposition ○ *an objectionable habit* —**ob·jec·tion·a·ble·ness** *n.* —**ob·jec·tion·a·bil·i·ty** /ob jèkshənə bíllətee/ *n.* —**ob·jec·tion·a·bly** /ob jékshənəblee/ *adv.*

ob·jec·tive /ob jéktiv/ *adj.* **1. FREE OF BIAS** free of any bias or prejudice caused by personal feelings **2. BASED ON FACTS** based on facts rather than thoughts or opinions **3.** MED **OBSERVABLE** used to describe disease symptoms that can be observed by somebody other than the person who is ill **4.** PHILOS **EXISTING INDEPENDENTLY OF MIND** existing independently of the individual mind or perception **5.** GRAM **BEING OBJECT OF VERB** in or constituting the grammatical case of a noun or pronoun that is the object of a verb ■ *n.* **1. AIM** an aim or goal **2. MILITARY TARGET** the target or goal of a military operation **3.** GRAM **OBJECTIVE CASE** the objective grammatical case **4.** GRAM **NOUN IN OBJECTIVE CASE** a noun or pronoun in the objective case **5.** OPTICS **LENS NEAREST OBJECT** the lens or combination of lenses in an optical instrument nearest to and facing the object being viewed —**ob·jec·tive·ness** *n.*

ob·jec·tive com·ple·ment *n.* GRAM a noun, pronoun, or adjective that is a complement of a verb and qualifies its direct object, e.g., "angry" in "He makes me angry"

ob·jec·tive cor·rel·a·tive *n.* LITERAT something in a written or performed work that is associated with a particular emotion and used to evoke it in the reader or audience

ob·jec·tive lens *n.* OPTICS = **objective** *n.* 5

ob·jec·tive·ly /ob jéktivlee/ *adv.* **1. WITHOUT BIAS** without being influenced by personal feelings **2. ACCURATELY** on the basis of fact, experience, or some measurable quality ○ *objectively derived measures such as test scores*

ob·jec·tiv·ism /ob jékti vìzzəm/ *n.* **1.** LITERAT **EMPHASIS ON THE ACTUAL** the emphasizing of external realities rather than beliefs or feelings in literature or art **2.** PHILOS **BELIEF IN INDEPENDENT TRUTHS** a philosophical belief that moral truths or external objects exist independently of the individual mind or perception —**ob·jec·tiv·ist** *n., adj.*

ob·jec·tiv·i·ty /òb jek tívvətee/ *n.* **1. ABILITY TO VIEW THINGS OBJECTIVELY** the ability to perceive or describe something without being influenced by personal emotions or prejudices **2.** PHILOS **ACTUAL EXISTENCE** the actual existence of something, without reference to people's impressions or ideas **3. ACCURACY** the quality of being accurate and independent of individual perceptions

ob·jec·ti·vize /ob jékti vìz/ (**-vized, -viz·ing, -viz·es**) *vt.* = **objectify** *v.* 1

ob·ject lan·guage *n.* COMPUT **1. LANGUAGE OF COMPUTER** the language that a computer interprets in running programs **2.** = **target language** *n.* 3

ob·ject lens *n.* OPTICS = **objective** *n.* 5

ob·ject les·son *n.* an incident that provides an opportunity for learning something, especially the best way to do something ○ *an object lesson in tact*

ob·ject-o·ri·ent·ed pro·gram·ming *n.* a form of computer programming based on objects arranged in a branching hierarchy

ob·ject re·la·tions *npl.* a psychoanalytic theory that sees an individual as motivated by a desire to form bonds with appropriate objects or people, rather than merely satisfying impulses in order to discharge tension

ob·jet d'art /àwb zhay daár/ (*plural* **ob·jets d'art** /òb zhay daár/) *n.* an object that has artistic value, especially a small piece [Mid-19thC. From French, literally "object of art."]

ob·jet trou·vé /àwb zhay troo váy/ (*plural* **ob·jets trou·vés** /òb zhay troo vay/) *n.* a natural or everyday object such as a pebble from a beach, treated as something of artistic value or incorporated into a work of art [Mid-20thC. From French, literally "found object."]

ob·jur·gate /óbjər gàyt/ (**-gat·ed, -gat·ing, -gates**) *vt.* to scold somebody angrily (*literary*) [Early 17thC. From Latin *objurgat-*, literally "to quarrel against," from *jurgium* "quarrel."] —**ob·jur·ga·tion** /òbjər gáysh'n/ *n.* —**ob·jur·ga·tor** *n.*

ob·jur·ga·to·ry /ob júrgə tàwree/ *adj.* angry and scolding (*literary*) —**ob·jur·ga·to·ri·ly** *adv.*

obl. *abbr.* oblique

o·blast /ó blàst, ő-/ *n.* a subdivision of a republic of the former Soviet Union [Late 19thC. From Russian *óblast*, literally "authority on," from *vlast* "authority, power."]

ob·late[1] /ó blàyt, o bláyt/ *adj.* GEOM shaped like a sphere but with the length of the diameter at the equator greater than the length from pole to pole [Early 18thC. From modern Latin *oblatus* "brought against or inversely," formed from Latin *latus* "brought," past participle of *ferre* "to bring," on the model of *prolatus* "lengthened."] —**ob·late·ly** *adv.* —**ob·late·ness** *n.*

ob·late[2] /ó blàyt/ *n.* CHR in the Roman Catholic Church, a lay person who is part of a religious community [Late 17thC. Via French from medieval Latin *oblatus*, literally "brought to," from the past participle of Latin *offerre* (see OFFER).]

ob·la·tion /ə bláysh'n, ō-/ *n.* **1.** RELIG **OFFERING OF GIFT TO DEITY** the offering of a gift or sacrifice to a deity **2.** CHR **COMMUNION OFFERING** the offering of bread and wine to God during the Christian service of Communion **3. RELIGIOUS OR CHARITABLE GIFT** something offered in a religious rite or as a charitable gift [15thC. Directly or via Old French from the late Latin stem *oblation-*, from Latin *offerre* (see OFFER).] —**ob·la·tion·al** *adj.*

ob·li·gate *vt.* /óbbli gàyt/ (**-gat·ed, -gat·ing, -gates**) **1. COMPEL LEGALLY OR MORALLY** to compel somebody to do something as a legal or moral duty **2.** FIN **COMMIT FUNDS AS SECURITY** to commit something, especially funds, to fulfil an obligation, e.g., as security ■ *adj.* /-gət, -gàyt/ BIOL **ONLY EXISTING IN ONE ENVIRONMENT** used to describe an organism that can exist only in a particular role or under particular environmental conditions. ◊ **facultative** [15thC. From Latin *obligatus*, past participle of *obligare* (see OBLIGE).] —**ob·li·ga·ble** /óbbligəb'l/ *adj.* —**ob·li·gate·ly** *adv.* —**ob·li·ga·tor** *n.*

ob·li·ga·tion /òbbli gáysh'n/ *n.* **1. STATE OF OWING** the state or condition of being obligated **2. DUTY** something that must be done because of legal or moral duty **3. SOMETHING OWED** something such as assistance or a debt that somebody owes in return for something given **4.** LAW **BINDING LEGAL AGREEMENT** a legal agreement by which somebody is bound to do something, especially pay money, or to refrain from doing something **5.** LAW **LEGAL CONTRACT** a legal contract that contains a penalty for non-fulfilment of it —**ob·li·ga·tion·al** *adj.*

o·blig·a·to·ry /ə blíggə tàwree/ *adj.* required by law or by a moral or religious rule —**o·blig·a·to·ri·ly** *adv.*

o·blige /ə blíj/ (**o·bliged, o·blig·ing, o·blig·es**) *v.* **1.** *vt.* **REQUIRE SOMEBODY TO DO SOMETHING** to bind somebody morally or legally to do something **2.** *vt.* **FORCE SOMEBODY TO DO SOMETHING** to make it necessary for somebody to do something **3.** *vt.* **CAUSE SOMEBODY TO FEEL INDEBTED** to cause somebody to feel indebted by doing something for that person **4.** *vt.* **DO FAVOR FOR SOMEBODY** to do a favor or service for somebody ○ *Would you oblige me by closing the door?* **5.** *vi.* **BE HELPFUL** to do something necessary or helpful ○ *was only too happy to oblige* [13thC. Via Old French *oblig(i)er* from Latin *obligare* "to tie to," from *ligare* "to tie, bind" (source of English *ligation*).] —**o·blig·er** *n.*

ob·li·gee /òbblə jée/ *n.* LAW somebody to whom another person is legally or morally bound, e.g. by a financial debt or obligation to do something

o·blig·ing /ə blíjing/ *adj.* willing to be helpful or do favors —**o·blig·ing·ly** *adv.* —**o·blig·ing·ness** *n.*

ob·li·gor /òbblə gáwr, óbblə gàwr/ *n.* LAW somebody who makes a legally binding agreement to do or pay something

o·blique /ō bléek, ə-/ *adj.* **1. SLOPING** sloping or joining something at an angle that is not a right angle **2. INDIRECT** not straightforward or direct ○ *an oblique reference to the lateness of the hour* **3.** GEOM **NOT PARALLEL OR PERPENDICULAR** neither perpendicular nor parallel to another line or plane **4.** GEOM **NOT RIGHT-ANGLED** not being or containing a right angle or a multiple of a right angle **5.** GRAM **NOT BEING SUBJECT** being a grammatical case other than the nominative or vocative **6.** BOT **WITH SIDES OF DIFFERENT LENGTHS** used to describe leaves that have sides of different length **7.** ANAT **NOT BEING ON ANATOMICAL PLANE** slanting away from any of the anatomical planes of the body, e.g., the horizontal or perpendicular plane **8.** GEOG **BEING AT TANGENT TO EARTH'S SURFACE** used to describe a map projection based on a plane of projection that is at a tangent to the Earth's surface at a point between the poles and the equator ■ *adv.* MIL **CHANGING DIRECTION AT 45°** changing direction to or at an angle of 45° ■ *n.* **1. SOMETHING SLANTING** something that is oblique, e.g., a slanting line **2.** NAVIG **COURSE CHANGE OF LESS THAN 90°** a change of course of less than 90° ■ *vi.* (**o·bliqued, o·bliqu·ing, o·bliques**) **1. TAKE OBLIQUE DIRECTION** to move or slant in an oblique direction **2.** MIL **ADVANCE IN OBLIQUE DIRECTION** to move forward at an angle in a military formation [15thC. From Latin *obliquus* "slanting, sidelong," of unknown origin.] —**o·blique·ness** *n.*

o·blique·ly /ō bleéklee, ə-/ *adv.* **1. INDIRECTLY** in a way that is not direct or straightforward **2. AT AN ANGLE** at an angle that is not a right angle

o·blique pro·jec·tion *n.* a map projection based on a plane of projection that is at a tangent to the Earth's surface at a point between the poles and the equator

o·blique-slip fault *n.* GEOL a fracture in a layer of rock in which the movement is both horizontal and vertical

o·bliq·ui·ty /ə blíkwətee, ō-/ (*plural* **-ties**) *n.* **1. STATE OF BEING OBLIQUE** the state or condition of being oblique **2. DEVIATION FROM PLANE** a deviation from the horizontal or perpendicular **3. CHARACTER FLOW** a departure from morality or reason **4. LACK OF DIRECTNESS** a lack of directness or straightforwardness in speech or conduct **5. obliquity, obliquity of the ecliptic** ASTRON **ANGLE BETWEEN EARTH'S ORBIT AND EQUATOR** the angle between the plane of the Earth's equator and the plane of the Earth's orbit around the sun, approximately 23.5°

o·bliq·ui·ty of the e·clip·tic *n.* ASTRON = **obliquity** *n.* 5

o·blit·er·ate /ə blíttə ràyt, ō-/ (**-at·ed, -at·ing, -ates**) *vt.* **1. DESTROY UTTERLY** to destroy something so utterly that nothing is left **2. ERASE OR OBSCURE** to erase or obscure something completely, leaving no trace [Late 16thC. From Latin *oblitterat-*, the past participle stem of *oblitterare* "to blot out, erase," from literally "to remove letters," OB- and *littera* "letter" (see LITERAL).] —**o·blit·er·a·tion** /ə blìttə ráysh'n, ō-/ *n.* —**o·blit·er·a·tive** /ə blíttə ràytiv, ō-/ *adj.* —**o·blit·er·a·tor** *n.*

o·bliv·i·on /ə blívvee ən/ *n.* **1. STATE OF BEING FORGOTTEN** a state of being utterly forgotten **2. STATE OF FORGETTING** a state of forgetting everything or of being unaware of surroundings **3.** LAW **OVERLOOKING OF PAST OFFENSES** the deliberate overlooking of past offenses [14thC. Via Old French from the Latin stem *oblivion-*, from *oblivisci* "to forget," of uncertain origin: perhaps literally "to smooth over," from *levis* "smooth."]

o·bliv·i·ous /ə blívvee əss/ *adj.* **1. UNAWARE** unaware of or paying no attention to somebody or something **2. FORGETTING** forgetting about somebody or something —**o·bliv·i·ous·ly** *adv.* —**o·bliv·i·ous·ness** *n.*

ob·long /ób lòng/ *adj.* **ELONGATED** having a shape that is considerably longer than it is wide, especially a rectangular or roughly circular shape ■ *n.* **ELONGATED SHAPE** something with a length greater than its width, especially a rectangle or distorted circle [15thC. From Latin *oblongus* "rather long," from *longus* "long."]

ob·lo·quy /óbbləkwee/ *n.* (*formal or literary*) **1. CENSURE** statements that severely criticize or defame somebody **2. DISGRACE** a state of disgrace brought about by being defamed [15thC. From late Latin *obloquium* "contradiction," literally "talking against," from *loqui* "to talk."]

ob·nox·ious /ob nókshəss, əb-/ *adj.* very offensive and unpleasant ○ *obnoxious stench* [Late 16thC. Formed from Latin *obnoxius* "vulnerable to harm" (its original English meaning), from *noxa* "harm" (source of English *noxious*).] —**ob·nox·ious·ly** *adv.* —**ob·nox·ious·ness** *n.*

o·boe /ő bō/ *n.* **1. WOODWIND INSTRUMENT** a woodwind instrument that produces a penetrating high sound and consists of a long slim tube enclosing a double reed with a conical bore and keys operated by the fingers 2. PLAYER OF OBOE somebody who plays an oboe [Late 17thC. Via Italian from French *hautbois* (see HAUTBOY).] —**o·bo·ist** *n.*

o·boe da cac·cia /ō bō də kaáchə/ *n.* an early form of oboe from which the cor anglais was developed [Late 19thC. From Italian, literally "hunting oboe."]

o·boe d'a·mo·re /ō bō daa máw rày/ *n.* an oboe used mainly in baroque music that has a lower pitch than the standard instrument [Late 19thC. From Italian, literally "oboe of love."]

ob·ol /óbbəl/, **ob·o·lus** /óbbələss/ (*plural* **-li** /-lī/) *n.* a coin or unit of weight used in ancient Greece, equal to one sixth of a drachma [Mid-17thC. Via Latin from Greek *obolos* "obol" (unit of weight and of money), variant of *obelos* "a spit."]

Ob·on /ō bón/ *n.* a Buddhist festival celebrating All Souls, held in Japan from July 13 to 31

ob·o·vate /o bṓ vàyt/ *adj.* BOT used to describe leaves that are oval with the narrow end at the base [Late 18thC. Coined from OB- + OVATE.]

ob·o·void /o bṓ vòyd/ *adj.* BOT used to describe fruits that are egg-shaped, with the narrow end at the base [Early 19thC. Coined from OB- + OVOID.]

ob·ruk /ób ro͝ok/ *n.* work obligations owed by Russian peasants to either their aristocratic landlords or the state during the 18th century

obs. *abbr.* 1. obscure 2. observation 3. **obs., Obs.** ASTRON observatory 4. obsolete 5. MED obstetrics

ob·scene /ob seén/ *adj.* 1. INDECENT offensive to conventional standards of decency, especially by being sexually explicit 2. DISGUSTING disgusting and morally offensive, especially because of showing total disregard for other people [Late 16thC. Via Old French from Latin *obscenus* "ill-omened, offensive, hateful," of unknown origin.] —**ob·scene·ly** *adv.*

ob·scen·i·ty /əb sénnətee, ob-/ (*plural* **-ties**) *n.* 1. INDECENCY offensiveness to conventional standards of decency, especially as a result of sexual explicitness 2. OBSCENE EXPRESSION a word, phrase, or statement that is offensive, especially because of being sexually explicit 3. SOMETHING OBSCENE something that is disgusting and morally offensive

ob·scur·ant /əb skyo͝orənt, ob-/ *n., adj.* = **obscurantist** ■ *adj.* CAUSING OBSCURITY concealing something or making it obscure (*literary*) [Late 18thC. Via German from Latin *obscurant-*, present participle stem of *obscurare* "to make dark," from *obscurus* (see OBSCURE).]

ob·scur·ant·ist /əb skyo͝orəntist, ob-/, **ob·scur·ant** *adj.* OPPOSED TO NEW IDEAS opposing or hindering the spread of new ideas and new social or political developments ■ *n.* OPPONENT OF NEW IDEAS somebody who opposes or hinders the spread of new ideas and new social or political developments —**ob·scur·ant·ism** *n.*

ob·scure /əb skyo͝or, ob-/ *adj.* 1. HARD TO UNDERSTAND difficult to understand because of not being fully or clearly expressed ○ *an obscure passage in the manuscript* 2. INDISTINCT not able to be seen or heard distinctly 3. UNIMPORTANT OR UNKNOWN not important or well-known ○ *an obscure portrait painter* 4. KNOWN TO FEW PEOPLE unknown to most people, e.g., because of being hidden or remote 5. DARK dark, shadowy, or clouded ○ *an obscure corner of the hall* 6. LING UNSTRESSED used to describe a vowel that has a neutral, unstressed pronunciation (*technical*) ■ *vt.* (**-scured, -scur·ing, -scures**) 1. MAKE UNCLEAR to make something unclear, indistinct, or hidden 2. DARKEN to make something dark or cover something with cloud [14thC. Via Old French from Latin *obscurus* "dark, unknown," literally "covered over," from the base *-scurus* "covered."] —**ob·scu·ra·tion** /òbskyə ráysh'n/ *n.* —**ob·scure·ness** *n.*

WORD KEY: SYNONYMS

obscure, abstruse, recondite, arcane, cryptic, enigmatic

CORE MEANING: difficult to comprehend

obscure a general word for something that is difficult to understand because it is expressed in a complicated way or because it involves areas of knowledge or study that are not known to most people; **abstruse** a formal word for something that is difficult to understand, often because it involves specialist knowledge or is expressed in specialist language; **recondite** a formal word for something that is difficult to understand without a high degree of scholarship or specialist knowledge; **arcane** a formal word for something secret known only to very few people; **cryptic** puzzling, often because it is expressed in code or in terms that only some people would understand; **enigmatic** having a quality of mystery and ambiguity that makes it difficult to understand or interpret.

ob·scure·ly /əb skyo͝orlee, ob-/ *adv.* 1. UNCLEARLY in a way that is not clear, definite, or easy to understand 2. DIMLY dimly or indistinctly 3. AWAY FROM PEOPLE'S ATTENTION in a place or position that is remote, secluded, or not prominent or well-known

ob·scu·ri·ty /əb skyo͝orətee, ob-/ (*plural* **-ties**) *n.* 1. STATE OF BEING UNKNOWN a state of being unknown or inconspicuous ○ *plucked from obscurity to star in a Broadway musical* 2. UNCLEARNESS difficulty in being understood or unclearness of meaning 3. SOMEBODY OR SOMETHING OBSCURE an obscure person or thing

ob·se·crate /óbsə kràyt/ (**-crat·ed, -crat·ing, -crates**) *vt.* to beseech a god or important person to give or do something (*archaic*) [Late 16thC. From Latin *obsecrat-*, the past participle stem of *obsecrare* "to beseech (in the name of something sacred)," ultimately from *sacer* (see SACRED).] —**ob·se·cra·tion** /òbsə kráysh'n/ *n.*

ob·se·quent /óbsəkwənt/ *adj.* GEOG used to describe a river, stream, or drainage system that flows into a subsidiary (**subsequent**) river in a direction contrary to that of the flow of the main (**consequent**) river [Late 19thC. From Latin *obsequent-*, present participle stem of *obsequi* "to comply," literally "to follow towards," from *sequi* "to follow" (see SEQUENCE).]

ob·se·quies /óbsəkweez/ *npl.* rites or ceremonies carried out at a funeral [14thC. Via Anglo-Norman from late Latin *obsequiae*, alteration (influenced by *obsequium* "compliance," see OBSEQUIOUS) of *exequiae*, literally "those following out (to the grave)," from *exsequi* (see EXECUTE).]

ob·se·qui·ous /əb seé kwee əss, ob-/ *adj.* excessively eager to please or to obey all instructions [15thC. From Latin *obsequiosus*, from *obsequium* "compliance," from *obsequi* (see OBSEQUENT).] —**ob·se·qui·ous·ly** *adv.* —**ob·se·qui·ous·ness** *n.*

ob·serv·a·ble /əb zúrvəb'l/ *adj.* 1. NOTICEABLE able to be seen or detected 2. WORTHY worthy of notice and attention (*archaic*) 3. REQUIRING RESPECT needing to be followed or respected (*archaic*) ■ *n.* SOMETHING DIRECTLY MEASURABLE something such as temperature that can be measured or observed directly —**ob·serv·a·bil·i·ty** /əb zùrvə bíllətee/ *n.*

ob·serv·a·bly /əb zúrvəblee/ *adv.* in a way or to an extent that can be seen or detected

ob·ser·vance /əb zúrvənss/ *n.* 1. COMPLIANCE the execution of or compliance with laws, instructions, or customs 2. RITUAL a custom, ritual, or ceremony, especially a religious one 3. PERFORMANCE OF RELIGIOUS CEREMONIES the celebration of a religious occasion, or the practice of a religious rite, ceremony, or action 4. RELIGIOUS RULE a rule of a religious order 5. OBSERVATION careful watching or close attention

ob·ser·vant /əb zúrvənt/ *adj.* 1. ATTENTIVE paying such careful attention that little or nothing is unnoticed 2. OBEDIENT carrying out rituals or obeying laws, especially religious ones —**ob·ser·vant·ly** *adv.*

ob·ser·va·tion /òbzər váysh'n/ *n.* 1. PAYING ATTENTION the attentive watching of somebody or something 2. OBSERVING OF DEVELOPMENTS IN SOMETHING the careful observing and recording of something that is happening, e.g., a natural phenomenon 3. REMARK OR COMMENT a remark or comment on something that has been noticed 4. RECORD OF SOMETHING SEEN OR NOTED the result or record of observing something such as a natural phenomenon and noting developments 5. ACT OF OBSERVING OR OBEYING the act of observing a religious occasion or ritual or of obeying a law or rule 6. NAVIG SIGHTING WITH NAVIGATIONAL INSTRUMENT a sighting with a navigational instrument to establish the observer's position in relation to a heavenly body such as the Sun 7. NAVIG NAVIGATIONAL INSTRUMENT READING the reading taken from a navigational instrument that has been used to find the observer's position in relation to a heavenly body —**ob·ser·va·tion·al** *adj.* —**ob·ser·va·tion·al·ly** *adv.*

ob·ser·va·tion car *n.* a railroad car fitted with extra or larger windows and often a partly transparent roof to allow passengers a better view of passing scenery

ob·ser·va·tion post *n.* a position from which soldiers can watch enemy movements and direct artillery fire

ob·ser·va·to·ry /əb zúrvə tàwree/ (*plural* **-ries**) *n.* 1. PLACE FOR SCIENTIFIC OBSERVATIONS a building, station, or artificial satellite used for scientific observation of natural phenomena such as astronomical objects, the weather, or earthquakes 2. PLACE FOR LOOKING AT VIEW a place or building that commands an expansive view

ob·serve /əb zúrv/ (**-served, -serv·ing, -serves**) *v.* 1. *vt.* NOTICE to see or notice something, especially while watching carefully 2. *vti.* WATCH ATTENTIVELY to watch somebody or something attentively, especially for scientific purposes 3. *vti.* BE FORMAL WITNESS to be a formal witness to something 4. *vi.* BE SPECTATOR to watch something without taking part 5. *vt.* COMMENT to make a comment or remark on something seen or noticed 6. *vt.* COMPLY WITH to carry out or comply with something such as a law or custom 7. *vt.* CELEBRATE FESTIVAL to celebrate or keep a religious or traditional festival [14thC. Via Old French *observer* from Latin *observare*, literally "to watch toward," from *servare* "to watch, pay attention."]

ob·serv·er /əb zúrvər/ *n.* 1. SOMEBODY WHO SEES OR WATCHES SOMETHING somebody who observes something that is happening 2. NONPARTICIPATING WITNESS somebody who attends something as a witness, often a formal one, without taking part 3. SOMEBODY OBSERVING CEREMONY OR OBEYING LAW somebody who observes a religious ceremony or ritual, or obeys a rule or law 4. AIRCRAFT IDENTIFIER somebody trained in identifying aircraft 5. WATCHER OF ENEMY MOVEMENTS a soldier who watches enemy movements or directs artillery fire

ob·sess /əb séss, ob-/ (**-sessed, -sess·ing, -sess·es**) *v.* 1. *vt.* PREOCCUPY to occupy somebody's thoughts constantly and exclusively ○ *The desire for vengeance obsesses him.* 2. *vi.* BE PREOCCUPIED WITH to think or worry about something constantly and compulsively ○ *You can't spend your vacation obsessing about money.* [Early 16thC. From Latin *obsess-*, past participle stem of *obsidere* "to besiege," literally "to sit opposite to," from *sedere* "to sit" (source of English *session*).]

ob·ses·sion /əb sésh'n, ob-/ *n.* 1. PREOCCUPATION an idea or feeling that completely occupies the mind 2. STATE OF BEING OBSESSED the state of being obsessed by somebody or something ○ *Their devotion to each other borders on obsession.* 3. PSYCHIAT UNCONTROLLABLE PERSISTENCE OF IDEA the uncontrollable persistence of an idea or emotion in the mind, sometimes associated with psychiatric disorder —**ob·ses·sion·al** *adj.* —**ob·ses·sion·al·ly** *adv.*

ob·ses·sive /əb séssiv, ob-/ *adj.* 1. RESEMBLING OBSESSION amounting to an obsession or as strong as an obsession 2. WORRYING UNCONTROLLABLY worrying compulsively about a particular thing, or things generally ■ *n.* PSYCHIAT SOMEBODY WITH AN OBSESSION somebody who has an obsession or a tendency to form obsessions —**ob·ses·sive·ly** *adv.* —**ob·ses·sive·ness** *n.*

ob·ses·sive-com·pul·sive *adj.* PSYCHIAT WITH OBSESSIVE-COMPULSIVE DISORDER with or characteristic of obsessive-compulsive disorder such as hand-washing ■ *n.* OBSESSIVE-COMPULSIVE PERSON somebody with obsessive-compulsive disorder

ob·ses·sive-com·pul·sive dis·or·der *n.* PSYCHOL a psychiatric disorder characterized by obsessive thoughts and compulsive behavior, e.g., continual washing of the hands prompted by a feeling of uncleanliness

ob·sid·i·an /əb síddee ən, ob-/ *n.* a jet-black volcanic glass, chemically similar to granite and formed by the rapid cooling of molten lava, that was used by early civilizations for manufacturing tools and ceremonial objects [14thC. From Latin *(lapis) Obsidianus*, a copyist's error for *Obsianus* "(stone) of Obsius," a Roman who according to Pliny the Elder discovered this or a similar stone in Ethiopia.]

ob·so·lesce /òbsə léss/ (**-lesced, -lesc·ing, -lesc·es**) *vi.* to become obsolete by being replaced by something new [Late 19thC. From Latin *obsolescere* (see OBSOLESCENT).]

ob·so·les·cence /òbsə léss'ns/ *n.* the state of becoming obsolete by being replaced by something new

ob·so·les·cent /òbsə léss'nt/ *adj.* becoming obsolete or disappearing from use or existence by being replaced by something new [Mid-18thC. From Latin *obsolescent-*, present participle stem of *obsolescere* "to wear out, decay," from *solere* "to be accustomed."] —**ob·so·les·cent·ly** *adv.*

ob·so·lete /òbsə leét/ *adj.* 1. NOT USED ANY MORE no longer in use because replaced by something new 2. OUT-OF-DATE superseded by something newer, though possibly still in use 3. BIOL UNDEVELOPED used to describe a part or organ of an animal or plant that is undeveloped or no longer functional [Late 16thC. From Latin *obsoletus*, past participle of *obsolescere* (see OBSOLESCENT).] —**ob·so·lete·ly** *adv.*

WORD KEY: SYNONYMS

See Synonyms at ***old-fashioned***.

ob·sta·cle /óbstək'l/ *n.* **1. HINDRANCE** somebody or something that hinders or prevents progress **2. SOMETHING IN WAY** something that blocks or impedes a road, passage, or somebody's way **3.** SPORTS **HURDLE** a fence or hedge set up for horses to jump over in show jumping [14thC. Via Old French from Latin *obstaculum*, from *obstare* "to stand in the way, block," from *stare* "to stand."]

ob·sta·cle course *n.* **1.** MIL **TRAINING AREA FOR SOLDIERS** a training area where soldiers have to get past various obstacles such as ditches or high walls as quickly as possible **2.** SPORTS **SPORTS COURSE** an area similar to a military obstacle course, used by competitors in an obstacle race

ob·sta·cle race *n.* a race in which competitors have to get past a range of obstacles

obstet. *abbr.* **1.** obstetric **2.** obstetrics

ob·stet·ric /ob stéttrik/ *adj.* relating to childbirth or obstetrics [Mid-18thC. From Latin *obstetricius* "of a midwife," from the stem *obstetric-* "midwife," literally "woman who is present, stands before," from, ultimately, *stare* "to stand."]

ob·ste·tri·cian /òbstə trísh'n/ *n.* a doctor who specializes in pregnancy, delivering babies, and the care of women after childbirth

ob·stet·rics /ob stéttriks/ *n.* the branch of medicine that deals with the care of women during pregnancy and childbirth, and for some six weeks following delivery (*takes a singular verb*)

ob·sti·na·cy /óbstinəssee/ (*plural* **-cies**) *n.* **1. STUBBORNNESS** the quality of being obstinate **2. OBSTINATE ACT** an example of obstinate behavior

ob·sti·nate /óbstinət/ *adj.* **1. STUBBORN** determined not to agree with other people's wishes or accept their suggestions **2. REFUSING TO CHANGE** unwilling to change or give up something such as an idea or attitude **3. DIFFICULT TO CONTROL** difficult to control, get rid of, solve, or cure ○ *an obstinate blockage in the pipe* [14thC. From Latin *obstinatus*, past participle of *obstinare* "to be resolved," literally "to stand by," from *stare* "to stand."] —**ob·sti·nate·ly** *adv.* —**ob·sti·nate·ness** *n.*

ob·sti·pa·tion /òbstə páysh'n/ *n.* severe constipation, often caused by a blockage in the intestines [Late 16thC. From the late Latin stem *obstipation-*, literally "pressing in the way of," from *stipare* "to press."]

ob·strep·er·ous /ob stréppərəss/ *adj.* **1. NOISY** noisily and aggressively boisterous **2. UNRULY** strongly objecting to something or noisily refusing to be controlled [Late 16thC. From Latin *obstreperus* "clamorous," literally "rattling against," from, ultimately, *strepere* "to rattle, rustle."] —**ob·strep·er·ous·ly** *adv.* —**ob·strep·er·ous·ness** *n.*

WORD KEY: SYNONYMS

See Synonyms at ***unruly***.

ob·struct /ob strúkt, əb-/ (**-struct·ed, -struct·ing, -structs**) *vt.* **1. BLOCK** to block a road, course, or passage **2. HINDER** to hinder or impede somebody or something **3. IMPEDE VIEW** to be in the way and prevent a clear view [Early 17thC. From Latin *obstructus*, past participle of *obstruere*, "to build up against," from *struere* "to heap up, pile."] —**ob·struc·tor** *n.*

WORD KEY: SYNONYMS

See Synonyms at ***hinder***.

ob·struc·tion /əb strúkshən, ob-/ *n.* **1. BLOCK OR HINDRANCE** somebody or something that causes or forms a blockage or hindrance **2. ACT OF BLOCKING** an act of blocking or hindering of somebody or something **3. STATE OF BEING BLOCKED** the state of being obstructed **4. DELAYING OF SOMETHING** the deliberate delaying of the business of something such as a legislative body **5.** SPORTS **UNFAIR IMPEDING OF OPPONENT** in soccer, the unfair impeding of an opposing player or competitor

ob·struc·tion·ist /əb strúkshənist, ob-/ *adj.* **USING DELAYING TACTICS** deliberately causing delay or impeding progress ■ *n.* **SOMEBODY WHO DELAYS SOMETHING** somebody who deliberately causes delay or impedes progress —**ob·struc·tion·is·tic** /əb strùkshə nístik, ob-/ *adj.* —**ob·struc·tion·ism** /əb strúkshə nìzzəm, ob-/ *n.*

ob·struc·tion of jus·tice *n.* the criminal offense of obstructing the administration and process of the law

ob·struc·tive /əb strúktiv, ob-/ *adj.* **1. UNCOOPERATIVE** hindering or preventing the progress of something **2.** MED **OF OR CAUSED BY OBSTRUCTION** relating to or caused by the obstruction of a passage in the body —**ob·struc·tive·ly** *adv.* —**ob·struc·tive·ness** *n.*

ob·struc·tive sleep ap·ne·a *n.* MED cessation or restriction of breathing during sleep that results in loud snoring

ob·stru·ent /ób stroo ənt/ *adj.* **1.** MED **OBSTRUCTING PASSAGE IN BODY** obstructing or closing a passage in the body, e.g., the intestinal tract **2.** PHON **PRODUCED BY CUTOFF OF AIR** used to describe a speech sound produced by a stoppage of air from the lungs ■ *n.* **1.** MED **OBSTRUCTION** something that obstructs or closes a passage in the body **2.** PHON **SOUND PRODUCED BY CUTOFF OF AIR** a speech sound produced by a stoppage of air from the lungs. ◊ **sonorant** [Mid-17thC. From Latin *obstruent-*, the present participle stem of *obstruere* (see OBSTRUCT).]

ob·tain /ob táyn/ (**-tained, -tain·ing, -tains**) *v.* **1.** *vt.* **GET** to get possession of something, especially by making an effort or having the necessary qualifications **2.** *vi.* **BE ESTABLISHED** to be established, valid, or current ○ *under the regulations that obtained at the time* **3.** *vi.* **RESULT** to follow as a result (*formal*) ○ *the unfortunate situation that obtains when such diverse elements are forced together* **4.** *vti.* **ARRIVE AT** to reach a place or goal (*archaic*) [15thC. Via Old French *obtenir* from Latin *obtinere* "to take hold of," literally "to hold to," from *tenere* "to hold" (source of English *tenant*).] —**ob·tain·er** *n.* —**ob·tain·ment** *n.*

WORD KEY: SYNONYMS

See Synonyms at ***get***.

ob·tain·a·ble /ob táynəb'l/ *adj.* able to be obtained or reached

ob·trude /ob tro͞od/ (**-trud·ed, -trud·ing, -trudes**) *v.* **1.** *vti.* **IMPOSE** to impose something such as opinions or yourself on other people **2.** *vt.* **PUSH OUT** to push something out or forward **3.** *vi.* **APPEAR UNWELCOME** to appear or be present in a way that is unwelcome but cannot be ignored ○ *"Not a leaf stirred; not a sound obtruded upon great Nature's meditation."* (Mark Twain, *The Adventures of Tom Sawyer*; 1875) [Mid-16thC. From Latin *obtrudere* "to thrust against," from *trudere* "to thrust."] —**ob·trud·er** *n.* —**ob·tru·sion** /ob tro͞ozh'n/ *n.*

ob·tru·sive /ob tro͞ossiv/ *adj.* **1. ANNOYING** tending to force your presence or opinions on other people ○ *plagued by an obtrusive photographer* **2. HIGHLY NOTICEABLE** highly noticeable, often with a bad or unwelcome effect **3. STICKING OUT** projecting or sticking out [Mid-17thC. Formed from Latin *obtrusus*, past participle of *obtrudere* (see OBTRUDE).] —**ob·tru·sive·ly** *adv.* —**ob·tru·sive·ness** *n.*

ob·tund /ob-/ (**-tund·ed, -tund·ing, -tunds**) *vt.* to blunt, dull, or deaden something (*formal*) [14thC. From Latin *obtundere* "to strike against, blunt," from *tundere* "to beat, strike."] —**ob·tund·ent** *adj.*

ob·tuse /əb to͞oss, ob-/ *adj.* **1. SLOW TO UNDERSTAND** slow to understand or perceive something **2.** MATH **BETWEEN 90° AND 180°** used to describe an angle greater than 90° and less than 180° **3.** MATH **WITH INTERNAL ANGLE GREATER THAN 90°** used to describe a triangle with one internal angle greater than 90° **4. BLUNT** not sharp or pointed **5.** BOT **WITH ROUNDED OR BLUNT TIP** used to describe a leaf that has a rounded or blunt tip [Early 16thC. From Latin *obtusus* "blunted," past participle of *obtundere* (see OBTUND).] —**ob·tuse·ly** *adv.* —**ob·tuse·ness** *n.*

ob·verse *n.* /ób vùrs, ob vúrs, əb-/ **1. MAIN SIDE OF COIN OR MEDAL** the side of a coin or medal that has the more important design on it, especially a head. ◊ **reverse 2. COUNTERPART** a counterpart, complement, or opposite **3.** LOGIC **EQUIVALENT CATEGORICAL PROPOSITION** a proposition derived from another proposition by denying it and then negating the predicate, e.g., "Everything is possible" becomes "Nothing is impossible" ■ *adj.* /ob vúrs, əb-, ób vùrs/ **1. VISIBLE** facing an observer **2. BEING A COUNTERPART** forming a counterpart to something else **3.** BOT **NARROWER AT BASE** used to describe a leaf that is narrower at the base than the tip [Mid-17thC. From Latin *obversus*, past participle of *obvertere* (see OBVERT).]

ob·ver·sion /ob vúrzh'n, əb-/ *n.* **1. PROCESS OF SHOWING OTHER SIDE** the process of turning something so that the other side is seen **2.** LOGIC **FORMING OF OBVERSE OF PROPOSITION** the process of forming the obverse of a proposition

ob·vert /ob vúrt/ (**-vert·ed, -vert·ing, -verts**) *vt.* **1. SHOW OTHER SIDE OF** to turn something such as a coin or medal so that the other side is seen **2.** LOGIC **FORM OBVERSE OF** to convert a proposition to its obverse [Early 17thC. From Latin *obvertere* "to turn toward," from *vertere* "to turn."]

ob·vi·ate /óbvee àyt/ (**-at·ed, -at·ing, -ates**) *vt.* **1. MAKE UNNECESSARY** to render something unnecessary (*formal*) **2. TO ANTICIPATE AND DISPOSE OF** to avoid an anticipated difficulty by doing something to prevent its arising [Late 16thC. From Latin *obviat-*, past participle stem of *obviare* "to withstand," literally "to stand in the way of," from *via* "way."] —**ob·vi·a·tion** /òbvee áysh'n/ *n.*

WORD KEY: USAGE

obviate the need for Because one of the meanings of ***obviate*** is "to make unnecessary," it is sometimes argued that *obviate the need* (or *necessity*) *for* is redundant. An older but still current meaning, however, is "to anticipate and dispose of" obstacles, that is, "to do away with" them. In a sentence like *Addressing these issues early can obviate any need for a joint resolution*, the need can be perceived as an obstacle — or early consideration can make the resolution unnecessary, in which case *any need for* is indeed redundant. There is little reason to prefer either interpretation to the other, except that the meaning "to make unnecessary" allows much the same thought to be expressed with fewer words.

ob·vi·ous /óbvee əss/ *adj.* **1. EASY TO SEE** easy to see or understand because not concealed, difficult, or ambiguous **2. UNSUBTLE** lacking subtlety or any attempt at concealment [Late 16thC. Formed from Latin *obvius* "in the way," hence "readily seen," from *via* "way" (source of English *voyage*).] —**ob·vi·ous·ness** *n.*

ob·vi·ous·ly /óbvee əsslee/ *adv.* **1. CLEARLY** in a way or to an extent that is obvious **2. UNDOUBTEDLY** used to suggest that there can be no doubt or uncertainty about something ○ *They want you to do it, obviously.*

ob·vo·lute /óbvə lo͞ot/ *adj.* BOT used to describe leaves or petals that are folded so as to overlap each other [Mid-18thC. From Latin *obvolutus*, past participle of *obvolvere* "to wrap around," from *volvere* "to roll."] —**ob·vo·lu·tion** /òbvə lo͞osh'n/ *n.* —**ob·vo·lu·tive** /óbvə lo͞otiv/ *adj.*

Oc., **oc.** *abbr.* GEOG Ocean

o.c. *abbr.* in the work cited [Shortening of Latin *opere citato*]

O.C. *abbr.* **1.** MIL Officer Commanding **2.** STAMPS original cover

o/c *abbr.* overcharge

oca /ókə/ *n.* **1.** PLANTS **S AMERICAN PLANT WITH EDIBLE TUBERS** a South American plant grown for its edible tubers. Genus: *Oxalis*. **2.** FOOD **EDIBLE OCA TUBER** the edible tuber of the oca plant [Early 17thC. Via Spanish from Quechua *ócca*.]

O·cal·a /ō kállə/ city and county seat of Marion County, northern Florida, situated 35 mi./56 km south of Gainesville. Population: 42,045 (1990).

O Can·a·da *n.* the title of the national anthem of Canada

oc·a·ri·na /òkə re͞enə/ *n.* a simple wind instrument related to the flute that has an oval body, finger holes, and a protruding mouthpiece [Late 19thC. From Italian, literally "little goose" (from its shape), from *oca* "goose," from assumed Vulgar Latin *avica*, ultimately from Latin *avis* "bird."]

OCAS *abbr.* Organization of Central American States

occ. *abbr.* **1.** GEOG occident **2.** occupation

Oc·cam's ra·zor *n.* = **Ockham's razor**

occas. *abbr.* **1.** occasional **2.** occasionally

oc·ca·sion /ə káyzh'n/ *n.* **1. PARTICULAR TIME** a particular time, especially a time when something happens **2. CHANCE OR OPPORTUNITY** a chance or opportunity to do something ○ *You might never have another occasion to do it.* **3. CAUSE OR REASON** a cause of or reason for something ○ *He has no occasion to criticize me.* **4. NEED** the need for something or to do something ○ *has never had occasion to use it* **5. IMPORTANT EVENT** an important or special event ■ **oc·ca·sions** *npl.* **SOMEBODY'S BUSINESS** somebody's business or needs (*archaic*) ■ *vt.* (**-sioned, -sion·ing, -sions**) **CAUSE** to cause or lead to something [14thC. Via Old French from the Latin stem *occasion-* "falling down, happening," ultimately from *cadere* "to fall."] ◇ **on occasion** from time to time

oc·ca·sion·al /ə káyzhən'l, ə káyzhnəl/ *adj.* **1.** **INFREQUENT** happening, seen, used, or doing something from time to time but not regularly or frequently **2.** **RELATING TO SPECIAL EVENT** done for or connected with a special event ○ *occasional verse* **3.** FURNITURE **DESIGNED FOR USE FROM TIME TO TIME** intended for use as needed, but not essential or in constant use ○ *an occasional table* **4.** **CAUSING** serving as the cause of something (*formal*)

WORD KEY: SYNONYMS

See Synonyms at ***periodic***.

oc·ca·sion·al·ly /ə káyzhən'lee, ə káyzhnəlee/ *adv.* from time to time, but not regularly or frequently

oc·ci·dent /óksidənt, óksi dènt/ *n.* the west (*literary or formal*) [14thC. Via Old French from Latin *occident-*, the present participle of *occidere* "to fall down, set (of the sun)," ultimately from *cadere* "to fall."]

Oc·ci·dent *n.* the western hemisphere, especially the countries in Europe and America. ◊ **Orient**

oc·ci·den·tal /òksi dénnt'l/ *adj.* western (*literary or formal*)

Oc·ci·den·tal *adj.* PEOPLES **OF OCCIDENT** relating to or typical of any of the countries of the Occident, or their peoples or cultures. ◊ **Oriental** ■ *n.* **WESTERNER** somebody who lives in or comes from the West. ◊ **Oriental**

oc·ci·den·tal·ize /òksi dént'l ìz/ (**-ized, -iz·ing, -iz·es**), **Oc·ci·den·tal·ize** *vt.* to make somebody or something conform to the culture of the West

oc·cip·i·ta plural of **occiput**

oc·cip·i·tal /ok síppət'l/ *adj.* **OF BACK OF HEAD** relating to or located at the back of the head or skull ■ *n.* = **occipital bone** [Mid-16thC. From medieval Latin *occipitalis*, from Latin *occiput* (see OCCIPUT).] —**oc·cip·i·tal·ly** *adv.*

oc·cip·i·tal bone *n.* the saucer-shaped bone at the rear of the skull that connects with the spinal column and has an opening at its base through which the spinal cord passes

oc·cip·i·tal lobe *n.* the pyramid-shaped area at the back of each hemisphere of the brain that deals with the interpretation of vision

oc·ci·put /óksi pùt/ (*plural* **-ci·puts** *or* **-cip·i·ta** /-síppətə/) *n.* ANAT the back part of the head or skull [14thC. From Latin, literally "back of the head," from *caput* "head."]

oc·clude /ə klóod/ (**-clud·ed, -clud·ing, -cludes**) *v.* **1.** *vt.* **STOP UP** to block or stop up something such as a passage **2.** *vt.* **CUT OFF FLOW OF** to cut off or prevent the flow or passage of something such as light or liquid **3.** *vti.* DENT **ALIGN TEETH PROPERLY** to align the upper and lower teeth in the proper position for chewing or for being in normal contact when the mouth is closed **4.** *vt.* CHEM **ABSORB OR ADSORB** to absorb or adsorb a liquid or gas on the surface of or within a solid **5.** *vti.* METEOROL **FORM OCCLUDED FRONT** to form an occluded front, or to undercut a mass of warm air so that it is no longer in contact with the earth's surface [Late 16thC. From Latin *occludere* "to close up," from *claudere* "to close" (see CLOSE).]

oc·clud·ed front *n.* METEOROL a composite front formed when a cold air mass meets and undercuts a warm air mass, and forces the warm air upwards and away from contact with the earth's surface

oc·clu·sal /ə klóoss'l/ *adj.* relating to the biting surface of a molar or pre-molar tooth

oc·clu·sion /ə klóozh'n/ *n.* **1.** **ACT OF OCCLUDING** an act of occluding or the state of being occluded **2.** **OBSTRUCTION** something that obstructs or occludes **3.** METEOROL = **occluded front** **4.** DENT **MEETING OF UPPER AND LOWER TEETH** the relation between the upper and lower teeth when the jaw is closed and their surfaces come in contact **5.** **CLOSURE OF HOLLOW ORGAN** the closure of a hollow organ such as the vocal tract in articulating a speech sound **6.** CHEM **ABSORPTION OR ADSORPTION OF LIQUID** the absorption or adsorption of a liquid or gas on or in a solid [Mid-17thC. Formed from Latin *occlus-*, past participle stem of *occludere* (see OCCLUDE).]

oc·clu·sive /ə klóossiv/ *adj.* **OF OCCLUSION** relating to, involving, or producing an occlusion ■ *n.* **CLOSED SPEECH SOUND** a speech sound that involves a closure of the vocal tract

oc·cult /ə kúlt/ *adj.* **1.** **SUPPOSEDLY SUPERNATURAL OR MAGIC** relating to, involving, or typical of the supposed supernatural, magic, or witchcraft **2.** **NOT UNDERSTANDABLE** not capable of being understood by ordinary human beings **3.** **SECRET** secret or known only to the initiated **4.** MED **HIDDEN** used to describe a diseased condition that is hidden or difficult to detect **5.** MED **DIFFICULT TO SEE** not visible to the naked eye, and only detectable by microscope or chemical testing ■ *n.* **THE SUPPOSED SUPERNATURAL** the realm of the supposed supernatural, magic, or witchcraft ■ *vti.* (**-cult·ed, -cult·ing, -cults**) **1.** ASTRON **TEMPORARILY HIDE CELESTIAL BODY** to hide a celestial body temporarily by moving between it and an observer, or to be hidden in this way **2.** **HIDE OR BE HIDDEN** to hide something from view or be hidden from view [Early 16thC. From Latin *occultus*, past participle of *occulere* "to conceal," of uncertain origin: probably literally "to conceal over," from *celare* "to hide."] —**oc·cult·ly** *adv.* —**oc·cult·ness** *n.*

oc·cul·ta·tion /ò kul táysh'n/ *n.* **1.** **TEMPORARY DISAPPEARANCE OF CELESTIAL BODY** the temporary complete or partial disappearance of a celestial body when another moves between it and an observer **2.** **ACT OF HIDING** an act of hiding something from view or the state of being hidden from view

oc·cult·ism /ə kúl tìzzəm/ *n.* the belief in and study of the supposed supernatural, magic, or witchcraft

oc·cu·pan·cy /ókyəpənsee/ (*plural* **-cies**) *n.* **1.** **ACT OF OCCUPYING** the act or state of occupying something such as a building or an official position **2.** **LEVEL OF OCCUPATION** the level of occupation of a place ○ *an apartment building with high occupancy* **3.** **DWELLING PLACE** a building or part of a building where people can live **4.** **TIME OF OCCUPYING** the period of time during which somebody occupies something such as a building or an official position **5.** LAW **POSSESSION OF UNOWNED PROPERTY** the act of taking possession of property, especially land, that has no owner, with the intention of becoming its owner **6.** LAW **LEGAL PREEMPTION** the presence of a higher level of government in an area of law that preempts the law of the lower level ○ *The federal government's occupancy of immigration law precludes state action.*

oc·cu·pant /ókyəpənt/ *n.* **1.** **HOLDER OR RESIDENT** somebody who lives or works in a place, or who holds a position of some sort **2.** LAW **SOMEBODY TAKING POSSESSION** somebody who takes possession of property, especially land, that has no owner, with the intention of becoming its owner

oc·cu·pa·tion /òkyə páysh'n/ *n.* **1.** **JOB** the job by which somebody earns a living **2.** **ACTIVITY** an activity on which time is spent **3.** **ACT OF OCCUPYING** an act of occupying or the state of being occupied **4.** MIL **INVASION** the invasion and control of a country or area by enemy forces **5.** **TIME OF OCCUPYING** the period of time during which something is occupied

oc·cu·pa·tion·al *adj.* relating to or caused by somebody's job —**oc·cu·pa·tion·al·ly** *adv.*

oc·cu·pa·tion·al dis·ease *n.* a disease that is directly caused by the conditions of somebody's work

oc·cu·pa·tion·al med·i·cine *n.* the branch of medicine that deals with work-related diseases and injuries incurred at work

oc·cu·pa·tion·al ther·a·py *n.* the use of regular periods of suitable productive activity as part of the treatment of illness or medical condition —**oc·cu·pa·tion·al ther·a·pist** *n.*

oc·cu·py /ókyə pì/ (**-pied, -py·ing, -pies**) *vt.* **1.** **LIVE IN PLACE** to live in or be the established user of a place such as a home or office **2.** **ENGAGE SOMEBODY'S ATTENTION** to take up somebody's time or attention (*often passive*) **3.** **FILL SPACE OR TIME** to take up a space or an amount of time (*often passive*) **4.** MIL **TAKE OVER PLACE** to invade and take control of a country, area, or building **5.** **HOLD POSITION** to hold a position or rank [14thC. Via Old French *occuper* from Latin *occupare* "to take hold of," literally "to take over," ultimately from *capere* "to take" (source of English *captive*).] —**oc·cu·pi·er** *n.*

oc·cur /ə kúr/ (**-curred, -cur·ring, -curs**) *vi.* **1.** **HAPPEN** to happen or come about **2.** **EXIST** to exist or be present **3.** **ENTER MIND** to come into somebody's mind ○ *It didn't occur to him to lock the door.* [Early 16thC. From Latin *occurrere* "to run to meet," literally "to run against," from *currere* "to run" (see COURSE).]

oc·cur·rence /ə kúrrəns/ *n.* **1.** **HAPPENING** something that happens **2.** **FACT OF OCCURRING** the fact or act of something happening —**oc·cur·rent** *adj.*

OCD *abbr.* obsessive-compulsive disorder

WORLD'S LARGEST OCEANS AND SEAS

1	Pacific Ocean	Area [64 million sq. mi. /165 million sq. km]
2	Atlantic Ocean	Area [31.7 million sq. mi. / 82 million sq. km]
3	Indian Ocean	Area [28.3 million sq. mi. / 73.4 million sq. km]
4	Arctic Ocean	Area [5.4 million sq. mi. / 14 million sq. km]
5	Mediterranean Sea	Area [0.97 million sq. mi. / 2.5 million sq. km]
6	Bering Sea	Area [0.87 million sq. mi. /2.26 million sq. km]
7	Caribbean Sea	Area [0.75 million sq. mi. / 1.94 million sq. km]
8	Sea of Okhotsk	Area [0.59 million sq. mi. / 1.53 million sq. km]
9	Sea of Japan	Area [0.39 million sq. mi. / 1 million sq. km]
10	Hudson Bay	Area [0.28 million sq. mi. /0.73 million sq. km]

o·cean /ósh'n/ *n.* **1.** GEOG **LARGE SEA** a large expanse of salt water, especially any of the Earth's five main such areas, the Atlantic, Pacific, Indian, Arctic, and Antarctic Oceans. The oceans occupy huge regions of the Earth's surface, and their boundaries are usually established by continental land masses and ridges in the ocean floor. **2.** GEOG **EARTH'S SEAS TOGETHER** the whole body of salt water on the Earth **3.** **LARGE AMOUNT** a vast amount or expanse of something [13thC. Via Old French from Latin *oceanus*, from Greek *ōkeanos*, the river surrounding the disk of the Earth, later applied to the Atlantic.]

o·cean·ar·i·um /ōshə náiree əm/ (*plural* **-ums** *or* **-a** /-ə/) *n.* a large saltwater aquarium for observing and exhibiting marine animals and plants [Mid-20thC. Blend of OCEAN and AQUARIUM.]

o·cea·naut /óshə nawt/ *n.* somebody who swims underwater in an ocean using an aqualung [Mid-20thC. Blend of OCEAN and AQUANAUT.]

O·cean Cit·y /ō shən-/ **1.** town and resort in Worcester County, southeastern Maryland, situated on a barrier island. Population: 5,146 (1990). **2.** city in Cape May County, southern New Jersey, situated on the Atlantic Ocean 10 mi./16 km southwest of Atlantic City. Population: 15,512 (1990).

o·cean·front /ósh'n frùnt/ *n.* **1.** **LAND BORDERING OCEAN** land next to the ocean (*often used before a noun*) ○ *oceanfront property* **2.** OCEANOG **DIVISION BETWEEN WARM AND COLD OCEAN** the point at which two oceanic water masses of different thermal characteristics meet

o·cean·go·ing /ósh'n gō ing/ *adj.* built, equipped, or used for travel on the ocean

o·cean grey·hound *n.* a fast ocean liner

O·ce·a·nia /ōshee ánnee ə/ geographical region consisting of most of the smaller islands of the Pacific Ocean, sometimes including Australia and New Zealand —**O·ce·an·i·an** *n., adj.*

o·ce·an·ic /ōshee ánnik/ *adj.* **1.** **IN OR FROM AN OCEAN** living, situated in, produced by, or taking place in an ocean, especially the depths of the open sea **2.** GEOL **VOLCANIC** resulting from volcanic activity in the ocean ○ *oceanic island* **3.** **IMMENSE** immense, vast, or overwhelming

O·ce·an·ic *n.* **LANGUAGE OF OCEANIA** a group of languages spoken mainly on the Pacific islands lying to the north and east of Australia. It forms a branch of the Malayo-Polynesian family of languages. About two million people speak one of the Oceanic languages. ■ *adj.* OF OCEANIA relating to or typical of any of the countries of Oceania, or their peoples or cultures

o·ce·an·ic ridge *n.* any section of a range of underwater mountains, found in all major oceans

o·ce·an·ic trench *n.* a long narrow deep furrow in the earth's crust at the bottom of an ocean

o·cean·og·ra·phy /ōshə nóggrəfee/ *n.* the scientific study of oceans, including their chemistry, biology, and geology —**o·cean·og·ra·pher** *n.* —**o·cean·o·graph·ic** /ōsh'nə gráffik/ *adj.* —**o·cean·o·graph·i·cal·ly** /-gráffikəlee/ *adv.*

o·cean·ol·o·gy /ōshə nóllәjee/ *n.* the branch of oceanography that studies how oceans may be used for economic or technological purposes —**o·cean·o·log·i·cal** /ōsh'nə lójjik'l/ *adj.* —**o·cean·o·log·i·cal·ly** /-lójjikəlee/ *adv.*

o·cean perch *n.* = **rosefish** *n.* 1

O·cean·side /ō shən sīd/ **1.** city in San Diego County, southwestern California, situated 45 mi./72 km north of San Diego. Population: 128,398 (1990). **2.** city in Nassau County, New York , situated on Long Island. Population: 32,423 (1990).

o·cean sun·fish *n.* a large brown and gray sunfish that lives in temperate or tropical seas and frequently lies on the surface of the water. Family: Molidae.

ocean tramp *n.* = **tramp steamer**

O·ce·a·nus Pro·cel·lar·um /ōssee áanəss prō se láаən/ *n.* a vast lunar lowland plain stretching between Mare Imbrium and Mare Humorum visible as a dark area in the west covering. Area: more than 775,000 sq. mi./2,000,000 sq. km.

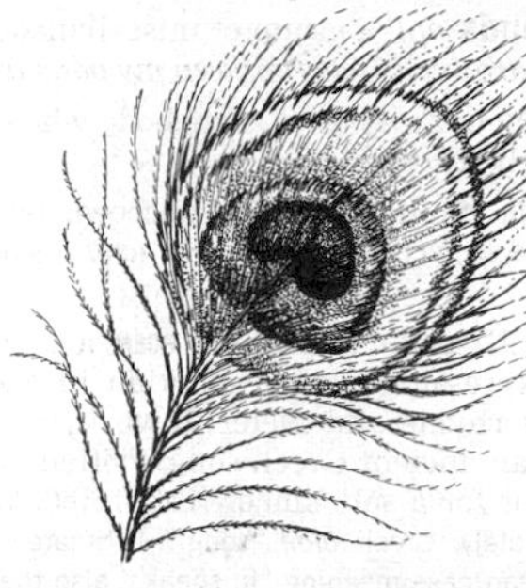

Ocellus: Peacock feather

o·cel·lus /ō sélləss/ (*plural* **-li** /-lī/) *n.* **1.** INSECTS **SIMPLE EYE IN INVERTEBRATES** a simple eye in some insects and other invertebrates that is sensitive to light but unable to focus clearly **2.** BIRDS **EYE-SHAPED SPOT ON FEATHERS** an eye-shaped spot on the feathers of some birds such as the peacock **3.** BOT **EYE-SHAPED SPOT ON LEAF** an enlarged discolored eye-shaped spot on a leaf **4.** ZOOL **EYE-SHAPED SPOT ON FISH** an eye-shaped spot on a fish, usually dark-ringed with a lighter color inside, believed to deceive predators [Early 19thC. From Latin, literally "small eye," from *oculus* "eye."]

Ocelot

oc·e·lot /óssə lòt, ṓss-/ (*plural* **-lots** *or* **-lot**) *n.* a small wild cat with dark spots on a light brownish coat that is found in small numbers from the southern United States to South America. Latin name: *Felis pardalis.* [Late 18thC. Via French from Nahuatl *tlatlocelotl*, literally "field jaguar."]

o·cher /ókər/, **o·chre** *n.* COLORS a brownish-yellow color [14thC. Via French *ocre* from Latin *ochra* from, ultimately, Greek *ōkhros* "pale, yellow."] —**o·cher** *adj.* —**o·cher·ous** *adj.* —**o·cher·y** *adj.*

och·loc·ra·cy /ok lókrəssee/ (*plural* **-cies**) *n.* = **mobocracy** [Late 16thC. Via French *ochlocratie* from Greek *okhlokratia* "mob rule," from *okhlos* "mob."] —**och·lo·crat** /óklə kràt/ *n.* —**och·lo·crat·ic** /óklə kráttik/ *adj.* —**och·lo·crat·i·cal·ly** *adv.*

Ochoa /ō chṓ ə, ō kṓ ə/, **Severo** (1905–93) Spanish-born U.S. biochemist. He shared a Nobel Prize for physiology or medicine (1959) for his work on synthesizing nucleic acids.

o·chre *n., adj.* = **ocher**

-ock *suffix.* something small or worthless ○ *hillock* ○ *mullock* [Old English *-oc, -uc*]

Ock·ham /ókəm/, **William of** (1285?–1349) English philosopher. He revived nominalism, and enunciated the principle known as Ockham's razor.

Ock·ham's ra·zor /ókəmz-/, **Occ·am's ra·zor** *n.* the philosophical and scientific rule that simple explanations should be preferred to more complicated ones, and that the explanation of a new phenomenon should be based on what is already known [Mid-19thC. Named for William of OCKHAM.]

o'clock /ə klók/ *adv.* **1. BEING A PARTICULAR HOUR IN TELLING THE TIME** in telling the time, used to indicate an exact hour of the day or night, rather than some minutes past or before the hour ○ *woke up at six o'clock in the morning* **2. INDICATING DIRECTION AS IF ON A CLOCKFACE** used to describe a position or direction of something by comparing it to the positions of numbers on a clockface, with the observer at the center of the clock ○ *Look at the man sitting to your right, at three o'clock.* [15thC. Contraction of *of the clock.*]

Oc·mul·gee /ōk mùl gee-/ river in Georgia, United States, flowing south and joining the Oconee River, to form the Altamaha River. Length: 255 mi./410 km.

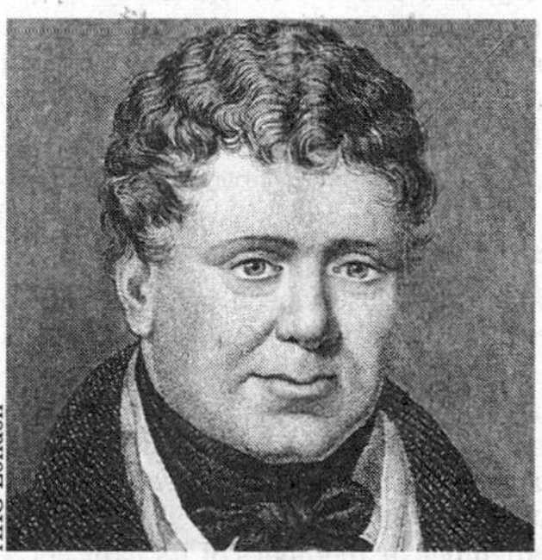

Daniel O'Connell

O'Con·nell /ō kónn'l/, **Daniel** (1775–1847) Irish politician and a Roman Catholic, he succeeded in obtaining Catholic emancipation, becoming a Member of Parliament at Westminster (1829). He agitated for repeal of the union of Ireland and Great Britain, and became Lord Mayor of Dublin (1841).

O'Con·nor /ō kónnər/, **Flannery** (1925–64) U.S. writer. She is known for her Southern Gothic novels, such as *Wise Blood* (1952). Full name **Mary Flannery O'Connor**

O'Con·nor, Sandra Day (*b.* 1930) U.S. jurist. She was the first woman to serve on the United States Supreme Court (from 1981).

o·co·til·lo /ōkə teéyō/ (*plural* **-los** *or* **-lo**) *n.* TREES a spiny shrub with red flowers at the tip of each branch, found in dry parts of the southwestern United States and in Mexico. Latin name: *Fouqueria splendens.* [Mid-19thC. Via American Spanish, literally "small ocote," from *ocote* "Mexican pine tree," from Nahuatl *ocotl* "torch."]

OCR *abbr.* **1.** optical character reader **2.** optical character recognition

oc·re·a /ókree ə/ (*plural* **-ae** /-ree ee/) *n.* BOT a cup-shaped sheath formed by appendages at the base of a leaf, as in rhubarb [Mid-19thC. From Latin, "soldier's leg-armor."]

OCS *abbr.* Officer Candidate School

oct. *abbr.* PRINTING octavo

Oct. *abbr.* October

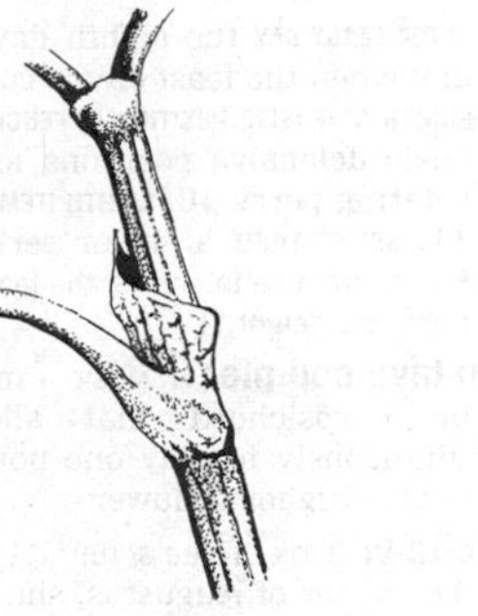

Ocrea

octa- *prefix.* = **octo-**

oc·tad /ók tàd/ *n.* **1. GROUP OF EIGHT** a group or series of eight **2.** CHEM **ELEMENT WITH VALENCE OF EIGHT** an element, atom, or group that has a valence of eight [Mid-19thC. From Greek *oktad-*, the stem of *oktas*, from *oktō* (see OCTO-).] —**oc·tad·ic** /ok táddik/ *adj.*

oc·ta·gon /óktə gòn/ *n.* a closed plane figure that has eight sides and eight angles

oc·tag·o·nal /ok tággən'l/ *adj.* having eight sides and eight angles

oc·ta·he·dral /òktə heédrəl/ *adj.* shaped like an octahedron —**oc·ta·he·dral·ly** *adv.*

oc·ta·he·dron /òktə heédrən/ (*plural* **-drons** *or* **-dra** /-drə/) *n.* a three-dimensional figure that has eight faces

oc·tal /ókt'l/ *adj.* MATH, COMPUT **HAVING NUMBER SYSTEM BASED ON EIGHT** using or having a number system based on eight instead of ten ■ *n.* COMPUT **1.** = **octal notation 2. OCTAL NUMBER** a number with eight as its base

oc·tal no·ta·tion *n.* COMPUT a number system used in writing computer programs that is based on eight and uses numerals 0 through 7, one octal unit equaling three bits

oc·tam·e·ter /ok támmətər/ *n.* a line of verse with eight metrical units or feet

oc·tane /ók tàyn/ *n.* **1. PETROLEUM COMPONENT** a liquid hydrocarbon found in petroleum that exists in 18 structurally different forms. Formula: C_8H_{18}. **2.** = **octane number** [Late 19thC. Coined from OCTO- + -ANE; from the number of carbon atoms in the hydrocarbon.]

oc·tane num·ber, **octane rating** *n.* a number that measures the ability of a liquid motor fuel such as gasoline to prevent preignition or knocking. Fuels with higher numbers are less likely to cause knocking.

Oc·tans /ók tànz/ *n.* a faint constellation of the southern hemisphere that contains the south celestial pole

oc·tant /óktənt/ *n.* **1.** ASTRON **EIGHTH OF A CELESTIAL CIRCLE** the position of one body in the sky one-eighth of a circle (45°) from another **2. EIGHTH OF A CIRCLE** one-eighth of a circle, with or without the enclosed area **3.** MATH **REGION OF SPACE IN CARTESIAN SYSTEM** any one of the eight regions into which space is divided by the three planes of the Cartesian coordinate system [Late 17thC. From Latin *octant-*, the stem of *octans* "half-quadrant", from *octo* (see OCTO-).] —**oc·tan·tal** /ok tánt'l/ *adj.*

oc·ta·pep·tide /òktə pép tīd/ *n.* a peptide consisting of eight amino acids

oc·ta·va·lent /òktə váylənt/ *adj.* used to describe an element, atom, or group that has a valence of eight

oc·tave /óktiv, ók tàyv/ *n.* **1.** MUSIC **INTERVAL ON MUSICAL SCALE** an interval between two notes consisting of eight notes inclusive or seven steps on the diatonic scale **2.** MUSIC **NOTE AT EACH END OF OCTAVE** the note at each end of an octave, especially the higher one, considered in relation to the note at the other end **3.** MUSIC **NOTES AT END OF OCTAVE TOGETHER** the two notes at each end of an octave played together **4.** MUSIC **ALL TONES INCLUDED WITHIN OCTAVE** the series of notes that fall within an octave, including the octave on each end, or the strings, keys, or other musical devices that produce these notes **5.** MUSIC **ORGAN STOP FOR PRODUCING HIGHER NOTES** an organ stop that causes tones to be produced an octave higher than the keys played alone **6.** POETRY **EIGHT LINES OF POETRY** a group of eight lines of verse, especially the first eight lines of a sonnet, or a poem that consists of eight lines **7.** CHR **CHRISTIAN FEAST DAY AND FOLLOWING WEEK** in Christianity, a feast day and the week following it **8.** CHR **EIGHTH DAY**

AFTER FEAST DAY the eighth day after an octave feast day when the feast day is counted as one **9.** FENCING **EIGHTH DEFENSIVE POSITION IN FENCING** the eighth of eight basic defensive positions in fencing, known as a rotating perry **10. EIGHTH ITEM** the eighth in a series **11. SET OF EIGHT** a set or series of eight [14thC. Via French from Latin *octava*, the feminine of *octavus* "eighth," from *octo* "eight."]

oc·tave cou·pler *n.* MUSIC a mechanism on an organ or harpsichord that allows somebody simultaneously to play one note and another one an octave higher or lower

Oc·ta·vi·a /ok táyvee ə/ (69?–11 B.C.) Roman aristocrat. The sister of Augustus, she married Mark Antony in a vain attempt to effect a reconciliation between the two men.

oc·ta·vo /ok táyvō, -taávō/ (*plural* **-vos**) *n.* a book size of about 6 by 9 in./16 by 23 cm, or a book of this size [Late 16thC. From Latin "in an eighth (of a sheet)," from *octavus* (see OCTAVE); from the folding of a sheet eight times.]

oc·tet /ok tét/ *n.* **1. GROUP OF EIGHT, ESPECIALLY MUSICIANS** a group of eight, especially eight singers or instrumentalists **2.** MUSIC **MUSICAL COMPOSITION FOR GROUP OF EIGHT** a musical composition for a group of eight voices or instruments **3.** POETRY = **octave** *n.* **6** [Mid-19thC. Alteration of Italian *otteto* (from, ultimately, Latin *octo* "eight"), influenced by OCTO-, on the model of words such as DUET.]

octo- *prefix.* eight ○ *octosyllable* [From Latin *octo* and Greek *oktō*. Ultimately from the Indo-European word for "eight" that is also the ancestor of English *eight*.]

Oc·to·ber /ok tṓbər/ *n.* in the Gregorian calendar, the tenth month of the year, made up of 31 days [Pre-12thC. From Latin, "eighth month," from *octo* "eight." The early Romans calculated the beginning of their year from March, and so October was the eighth month.]

oc·to·dec·i·mo /òktō déssəmō/ (*plural* **-mos**) *n.* a book size of about 4 by $4\frac{1}{2}$ in./10 by 16 cm, or a book of this size [Mid-19thC. From Latin, "in an eighteenth (of a sheet)," from, ultimately, *octodecim*, literally "eight and ten"; from the folding of a sheet 18 times.]

oc·to·ge·nar·i·an /òktə jə náiree ən/ *n.* somebody who is between 80 and 89 years old [Early 19thC. Formed from Latin *octogenarius*, from *octoginta* "eighty," literally "eight times ten."]

oc·to·nar·y /óktə nèrree/ *adj.* **1. BASED ON EIGHT** based on the number eight **2. CONSISTING OF EIGHT** consisting of eight things ■ *n.* (*plural* **-ies**) **1. GROUP OF EIGHT** a group or set of eight things **2.** COMPUT = **octal** *n.* **2** [Mid-16thC. From Latin *octonarius* "containing eight," from *octo* (see OCTO-).]

oc·to·ploid /óktə plòyd/ *n.* GENETICS a cell nucleus or an organism, especially a plant, containing eight haploid sets of chromosomes. ◊ **haploid, diploid, triploid, tetraploid**

oc·to·pod /óktə pòd/ *n.* a shell-less mollusk such as the octopus with a large head and eyes and eight tentacles. Order: Octopoda. [Early 20thC. From modern Latin *Octopoda*, order name, from Greek *oktōpod-*, the stem of *oktōpous* (see OCTOPUS).] —**oc·to·pod·ous** /ok tóppədəss/ *adj.*

oc·to·pus /óktəpəss/ (*plural* **-pus·es** *or* **-pi** /-pī/ *or* **-pus**) *n.* **1. SEA ANIMAL WITH EIGHT ARMS** a sea animal with a big head, a soft oval body, well-developed eyes, and eight arms containing rows of suckers. It usually lives on the ocean floor. Genus: *Octopus.* ◊ **squid 2. SOMETHING WITH FAR-REACHING INFLUENCE** something, especially an organization, that has many branches and forms of influence or control [Mid-18thC. From modern Latin, genus name, from Greek *oktōpous*, literally "eight feet," from *oktō* "eight" + *pous* "foot."]

oc·to·roon /òktə ro͞on/ *n.* an offensive term for somebody who has one Black grandparent and no other Black ancestors (*archaic offensive*) [Mid-19thC. Formed from OCTO- on the model of QUADROON.]

oc·to·syl·la·ble /óktə síllǝb'l/ *n.* POETRY a language unit of eight syllables, usually a complete line of verse but occasionally just a word —**oc·to·syl·lab·ic** /òktə si lábbik/ *adj.*

oc·tu·ple /ók to͞op'l, ok to͞op'l, óktəp'l/ *adj.* **1. EIGHT TIMES AS LARGE** eight times as large or effective **2. WITH EIGHT PARTS** consisting of eight parts ■ *vti.* **MULTIPLY BY EIGHT** to multiply something by eight or to be multiplied by eight ■ *n.* **QUANTITY EIGHT TIMES GREATER** an amount that is eight times more than another amount

ocul- *prefix.* = **oculo-** (*used before vowels*)

oc·u·lar /ókyələr/ *adj.* **RELATING TO EYES OR EYESIGHT** relating to, perceived by, or performed by the eye ■ *n.* **EYEPIECE** an eyepiece in an optical instrument [Late 16thC. Via French *oculaire* from late Latin *ocularis*, from Latin *oculus* "eye."]

WORD KEY: ORIGIN

The Indo-European ancestor of ***ocular*** is also the ultimate source of English *atrocious, eye, ferocious, inoculate,* and *optical.*

oc·u·list /ókyəlist/ *n.* an optometrist or opthalmologist (*dated*)

oculo- *prefix.* eye ○ *oculomotor* [From Latin *oculus* (see OCULAR)]

oc·u·lo·gy·ric /òkyəlō jīrik/ *adj.* relating to the movement of an eyeball in its socket

oc·u·lo·mo·tor /òkyəlō mṓtər/ *adj.* relating to or causing movement of the eyeball

oc·u·lo·mo·tor nerve *n.* either of the third pair of cranial nerves that carry nerve fibers from the brain to the eye muscles and eyelids

Od /od/ *interj.* used euphemistically as an oath to mean "God" (*archaic*) [Late 16thC. Alteration of GOD.]

O·D /ō deé/ *vi.* (**O·Ded, O·D·ing, O·Ds**) **TAKE DEADLY AMOUNT OF DRUG** to take a dangerous amount of a drug, often causing hospitalization or death (*slang*) ■ *n.* **OVERDOSE** an overdose (*slang*) = **overdose** [Mid-20thC. Shortening of OVERDOSE.]

o.d. *abbr.* **1.** outside diameter **2.** on demand **3.** MIL olive drab **4.** MED right eye [Shortening of Latin [oculus dexter]]

O.D. *abbr.* **1.** overdraft **2.** overdrawn **3.** Officer of the Day **4.** Doctor of Optometry **5.** LANG Old Dutch **6.** MIL olive drab

O/D, o/d *abbr.* **1.** overdraft **2.** overdrawn

o·da·lisque /ṓd'l ìsk/, **o·da·lisk** *n.* **1. ENSLAVED WOMAN IN HAREM** an enslaved woman or concubine, especially, formerly, in a Turkish harem **2.** PAINTING, SCULPTURE **ARTISTIC REPRESENTATION OF ODALISQUE** a representation of an odalisque in art [Late 17thC. Via French from Turkish *ōdalik*, literally "somebody who works in a chamber," from *ōda* "chamber."]

O·da No·bu·na·ga /ōdə nóbbyoo naágə/ (1534–82) Japanese feudal lord. He began the 16th-century reunification of Japan.

odd /od/ *adj.* **1. UNUSUAL** peculiar, unusual, or out of the ordinary ○ *There's something very odd about the letter.* **2.** MATH **NOT DIVISIBLE EXACTLY BY 2** being a number such as 1, 3, 5, 7, 9, or 11 that, when divided by 2, leaves a remainder of 1. ◊ **even 3. LEFTOVER** leftover, and usually few in number ○ *a few odd coins* **4. SEPARATED FROM PAIR OR SET** left on its own without the other member or members of its pair, set, or series ○ *a number of odd socks in the drawer* **5. IRREGULAR** irregular or occasional ○ *We get the odd day off here and there.* **6. SLIGHTLY GREATER THAN STATED NUMBER** used after a number to mean a little more than the number stated ○ *I figured on paying 50-odd dollars for it.* **7. REMOTE** not usually visited or reached by many people ○ *We found the papers lying about in odd corners of the house.* **8.** MATH **HAVING CHANGING MATHEMATICAL SIGNS** used to refer to a function that changes sign but not value when the sign of each independent variable is changed at the same time ■ *n.* **SOMETHING ODD IN NUMBER** something that is odd in number or numerical order [14thC. From Old Norse *oddi* "third or odd number." Ultimately from an Indo-European word meaning "pointed upward," the underlying idea being "triangular," hence "having one left over from two."] —**odd·ish** *adj.* —**odd·ly** *adv.* —**odd·ness** *n.*

odd·ball /ód bàwl/ *n.* somebody who is unconventional, unusual, or not typical, usually in a harmless way (*informal insult*) (*often used before a noun*)

Odd Fel·low *n.* a member of the Independent Order of Odd Fellows, a secret international social and charitable fraternity founded in England in the 18th century [From ODD "remote, out-of-the-way," with reference to the Order's mystic practices]

odd·i·ty /óddətee/ (*plural* **-ties**) *n.* somebody or something unique, unusual, or unconventional

odd job *n.* any of a series of unrelated unspecialized jobs such as household repairs, usually done casually and for low pay (*often used in the plural*) ○ *does odd jobs for a living*

odd lot *n.* a quantity or number of shares that is smaller than the usual trading unit, e.g., fewer than 100 shares when traded on a stock exchange, or less than one whole share when liquidated

odd man out (*plural* **odd men out**), **odd one out** (*plural* **odd ones out**) *n.* somebody in a group who differs from the rest of the group in some way, or who is not treated as part of the group

odd·ment /ódmənt/ *n.* **1. SOMETHING LEFT OVER** something left over when most of something has been used or disposed of (*usually used in the plural*) ○ *By the time she arrived there were only oddments left in the sale.* **2. ODDITY** an odd thing (*dated*) ■ **odd·ments** *npl.* **ODDS AND ENDS** odds and ends (*dated*) [Late 18thC. Formed from ODD on the model of FRAGMENT.]

odd-pin·nate *adj.* used to describe a plant leaf such as that of the rose that is pinnate with a single leaflet at the top —**odd-pin·nate·ly** *adv.*

odds /odz/ *npl.* **1. CHANCES OF SOMETHING HAPPENING** the likelihood or probability that something will occur, sometimes expressed as a ratio such as 10 to 1 ○ *The odds are that you'll never make it.* **2.** BETTING **PREDICTED CHANCES IN BETTING** a ratio of probability given to people placing a bet, usually the likelihood of a specific event happening, or of a competitor, team, or animal winning ○ *The horse was given odds of four to one.* **3.** SPORTS **HANDICAP OR ADVANTAGE USED IN COMPETITION** an advantage or handicap given to a person, animal, or team in a sporting contest, to equalize the chances of winning **4. PERCEIVED ADVANTAGE OR DISADVANTAGE** a perceived advantage or disadvantage, especially one that one person is believed to have over another in a competition [Early 16thC. Plural of ODD.] ◇ **at odds with somebody** *or* **something** in disagreement with somebody, or in conflict with something ◇ **over the odds** more than is usual or necessary ◇ **what's the odds?** used to indicate that something is of no importance

odds and ends *npl.* a group of miscellaneous items ○ *The top drawer is where I keep my odds and ends.*

odds·mak·er /ódz màykər/ *n.* somebody who officially calculates betting odds

odds-on *adj.* likeliest to win, succeed, or happen (*informal*) ○ *It was odds-on that he would succeed his father.*

ode /ōd/ *n.* **1.** POETRY **TYPE OF LYRIC POEM** a lyric poem, usually expressing exalted emotion in a complex scheme of rhyme and meter **2.** MUSIC, HIST **ANCIENT GREEK SONG** an ancient Greek song written either for a chorus or for a solo singer [Late 16thC. Via French from, ultimately, Greek *ōidē* "song." Ultimately from an Indo-European base meaning "to speak," also the ancestor of English *melody* and *comedy*.] —**od·ic** *adj.* —**od·ist** *n.*

-ode *suffix.* **1.** electrically conducting element ○ *electrode* **2.** electrode ○ *tetrode* [From Greek *hodos* "way, road, journey" (source of English *exodus, method, odometer,* and *period*)]

O·den·se /ṓd'n sə/; *locally* /ó͞o ənzə/ city and port in south central Denmark, on the island of Fyn. Population: 182,617 (1995).

O·der /ṓ dər/ river in north central Europe. Its northern course forms part of Poland's border with Germany. Length: 563 mi./906 km.

O·des·sa /ō déssə/, **O·desa** city and port in south central Ukraine, on the Black Sea. Population: 1,060,000 (1995).

O·dets /ō déts/, **Clifford** (1906–63) U.S. playwright. He is best known for his social-protest play *Waiting for Lefty* (1935) and the boxing drama *Golden Boy* (1937).

o·de·um /ṓdee əm/ (*plural* **-a** /-ə/), **o·de·on** /ṓdee ən/ (*plural* **-a**) *n.* an ancient Greek or Roman building in which musical performances were held [Early 17thC. Directly or via French from Latin *odeum*, from Greek *ōideion* (see ODE).]

o·di·ous /ṓdee əss/ *adj.* inspiring hatred, contempt, or disgust [14thC. Via Old French from Latin *odiosus*, from *odium* (see ODIUM).] —**o·di·ous·ly** *adv.* —**o·di·ous·ness** *n.*

o·di·um /ṓdee əm/ *n.* **1. HATRED** intense dislike, repugnance, or contempt for somebody or something ○ *incurred scorn and odium for his actions* **2. STATE OF BEING ODIOUS** the state of being hateful, contemptuous, or disgusting **3. DISREPUTE OR DISGRACE** a state of being considered odious by others [Early 17thC. From Latin (source also of English *annoy*).]

o·dom·e·ter /ō dómmətər/ *n.* a device built into the dashboard of a vehicle that records the distance traveled [Late 18thC. Via French *odomètre* or formed directly from Greek *hodos* "way."]

o·do·nate /ṓd'n àyt/ *n.* an insect belonging to the order of insects that includes the dragonfly and damselfly. Order: Odonata. [Early 20thC. From modern Latin *Odonata*, order name, from Greek *odōn*, a variant of *odous* "tooth."]

odont- *prefix.* = **odonto-** (*used before vowels*)

-odont *suffix.* having a particular kind of teeth ○ *acrodont* [From Greek *odont-*, the stem of *odous* (see ODONTO-)]

o·don·tal·gia /ṓd on táljee ə/ *n.* DENT toothache (*technical*)

-odontia *suffix.* condition or treatment of teeth ○ *anodontia* [Formed from Greek *odont-*, the stem of *odous* (see ODONTO-)]

odonto- *prefix.* tooth, teeth ○ *odontology* [From Greek *odont-*, the stem of *odous* "tooth." Ultimately from the Indo-European word for "tooth," which is also the ancestor of English *tooth* and *dental*.]

o·don·to·blast /ō dóntə blàst/ *n.* one of a layer of cells lining the pulp cavity of a tooth and taking part in the formation of dentin —**o·don·to·blas·tic** /ō dòntə blástik/ *adj.*

o·don·to·glos·sum /ō dòntə glóssəm/ *n.* a variety of orchid that grows on other plants in mountainous areas from Bolivia to Mexico and is widely cultivated for its clusters of brightly colored flowers. Genus: *Odontoglossum*. [Late 19thC. From modern Latin, genus name, literally "tooth tongue," from Greek *odont-* "tooth" + *glōssa* "tongue"; from the toothlike projection on the end of the flower.]

o·don·toid /ō dón tòyd/ *adj.* resembling a tooth, especially in shape

o·don·toid proc·ess *n.* a tooth-shaped peg that projects upward from the second neck vertebra to engage with the first, acting as a pivot for side-to-side movements of the head

o·don·tol·o·gy /ō don tóllajee/ *n.* the branch of science that studies the teeth and their anatomy, development, and diseases —**o·don·to·log·i·cal** /ō dòntə lójjik'l/ *adj.* —**o·don·to·log·i·cal·ly** /-lójjikəlee/ *adv.* —**o·don·tol·o·gist** /ō don tólləjist/ *n.*

o·dor /ṓdər/ *n.* **1. SMELL** smell or scent, whether pleasant or unpleasant ○ *the delicious odor of baking bread* **2. PERVASIVE QUALITY** a quality or attitude that suggests or resembles a particular thing ○ *odor of sanctity* [13thC. Via Anglo-Norman and Old French *odor, odur* from Latin *odor* "smell."]

o·dor·ant /ṓdərənt/ *n.* something that gives a characteristic smell to a product

o·dor·if·er·ous /ṑdə ríffərəss/ *adj.* having or diffusing a strong odor (*formal or technical*) —**o·dor·if·er·ous·ly** *adv.* —**o·dor·if·er·ous·ness** *n.*

o·dor·less /ṓdərləss/ *adj.* having no smell that is strong enough to be detected by the human nose —**o·dor·less·ness** *n.*

o·dor·ous *adj.* = **odoriferous** (*literary*) —**o·dor·ous·ly** *adv.* —**o·dor·ous·ness** *n.*

o·dour *n.* U.K. = **odor**

WORD KEY: SYNONYMS

See Synonyms at *smell*.

O·dys·seus /ō díss yoōss, ō díssee əss/ *n.* in Greek mythology, the King of Ithaca and one of the senior Greeks in the Trojan War. He is the main character in Homer's epic poem the *Odyssey*. ➧ **Ulysses**

od·ys·sey /óddəssee/ (*plural* **-seys**) *n.* a long series of travels and adventures [Late 19thC. From the *Odyssey*, from, ultimately, Greek *Odusseia*, from ODYSSEUS.]

WORD KEY: CULTURAL NOTE

The Odyssey, an epic poem by the Greek writer Homer (?8th century B.C.). The oldest surviving source of Greek mythology along with the *Iliad*, it describes Odysseus's ten-year journey home to Ithaca after the Trojan War. It provides both an insight into a long-lost civilization and a gripping narrative rich in evocative details, complex characters, and universal themes.

Oe *symbol.* oersted

OE, O.E. *abbr.* LANG Old English

OECD *abbr.* Organization for Economic Cooperation and Development

oe·de·ma[1] /i deémə, ə-/ *n.* MED U.K. = **edema**

oe·de·ma[2] *n.* **1. EXCESS FLUID** an abnormal buildup of excess serous fluid between tissue cells **2. EXCESS FLUID IN PLANT** an abnormal swelling in a plant, chiefly caused by a buildup of excess water [15thC. From Greek *oidēma* "swelling tumor," from *oidein* "to swell."]

Oed·i·pal /éddəp'l, eéd-/ *adj.* referring or relating to Oedipus or the Oedipus complex [Mid-20thC. Formed from OEDIPUS.]

Oed·i·pus /éddəpəss, eédəpəss/ *n.* in Greek mythology, a son of Jocasta and Laius, King of Thebes, who unwittingly killed his father and married his mother. He put out his own eyes when he discovered what he had done.

Oed·i·pus com·plex *n.* according to the controversial psychoanalytic theory of Sigmund Freud, feelings or desires originating when a child, especially a son, unconsciously seeks sexual fulfillment with the parent of the opposite sex. ◊ **Electra complex** [Early 20th C. Named for OEDIPUS.]

OEIC *abbr.* open-ended investment company

Ōe Ken·za·bu·rō /ō ay kènzə boórō/ (*b.* 1935) Japanese writer. Perhaps the greatest Japanese novelist since World War II, he won the Nobel Prize in literature in 1994.

OEM *abbr.* original equipment manufacturer

oe·nol·o·gy /i nólləjee/ *n.* U.K. = **enology**

oe·no·mel /eénə mèl/ *n.* a drink of wine and honey made in ancient Greece (*literary*) [Late 16thC. Via late Latin *oenomeli* from Greek *oinomeli*, literally "honey wine," from *oinos* "wine" + *meli* "honey."]

oe·no·phile /eénə fīl/ *n.* somebody who has a passionate interest in wine or is an expert on wines (*formal*) [Mid-20thC. From French, from *oeno-*, from Greek *oinos* "wine."]

OEO *abbr.* Office of Economic Opportunity

o'er /awr, ōr/ *prep., adv.* over (*literary*) ○ *The sun rose o'er the mountain.* [14thC. Contraction.]

oer·sted /úr stèd, -stəd/ *n.* the unit measure of magnetic field strength in the centimeter-gram-second system. It is equal to the magnetic field strength experienced by a magnetic pole when undergoing a force of one dyne in a free space. Symbol **Oe** [Late19thC. Named after H.C. *Oersted* (1777–1851), Danish physicist who discovered the magnetic effect of an electric current.]

oes·tra·di·ol *n.* U.K. = **estradiol**

oes·tri·ol *n.* U.K. = **estriol**

oes·tro·gen *n.* = **estrogen**

oes·trone *n.* U.K. = **estrone**

oes·trous *adj.* U.K. = **estrous**

oes·trus *n.* = **estrus**

oeu·vre /övrə, óovrə/ *n.* a work of art or literature, or such works considered as a unit, especially the complete work of a single artist (*formal*) [Late 19thC. Via French from Latin *opera*, the plural of *opus* "work" (source of English *opus*).]

of /uv, ov/; *unstressed form* /əv/ CORE MEANING: used between two nouns, the second providing more information about the first ○ *Most software has complex sets of commands and options.* ○ *She let out a little squeal of delight.*

prep. **1. AFFECTED BY ACTION** used to indicate the person or thing affected by or performing an action ○ *the promotion of junior staff* ○ *the death of her father* **2. USED IN MEASURING QUANTITIES** used after words or phrases expressing quantities to indicate the substance or thing being measured ○ *millions of dollars* ○ *a herd of cows* ○ *10 gallons of oil* **3. CONNECTED WITH** used to indicate the place that somebody or something belongs to or is connected with ○ *the president of France* **4. CONTAINING** containing the substance mentioned ○ *a mug of coffee* ○ *a busload of schoolchildren* **5. PART OF SOMETHING** used to indicate a part of something that is normally considered as a whole ○ *a slice of cake* ○ *a square of fabric* **6. MADE FROM** made from or used as a material to form something ○ *ruled with a rod of iron* ○ *a paste of flour and water* **7. INDICATING RELATIONSHIP OR ASSOCIATION** used to indicate a relationship, association, or cause ○ *I'll be thinking of you.* ○ *accused of negligence* **8. RELATING TO** used after words describing feelings and qualities to indicate the person or thing they relate to ○ *He's very sure of himself.* ○ *It's very kind of you to come.* **9. INDICATING A PARTICULAR TYPE** used to describe somebody or something in terms of a particular type or kind ○ *one heck of a gymnast* **10. HAVING A PARTICULAR QUALITY** used to indicate a quality that somebody or something has, or the person or thing having a particular quality ○ *announcements of a general nature* ○ *a musician of great talent* ○ *the gentleness of his manner* **11. INDICATING AMOUNT** used to indicate an amount, age, or value ○ *There is a limit of eight characters in a computer user name.* ○ *a young boy of 12* **12. EVERY** used to indicate a day or other period of time when an activity regularly occurs (*informal*) ○ *We usually go out for a meal of a Friday.* **13. BEFORE** before the hour of ○ *It was a quarter of ten before she returned.* **14. BY** used to indicate the agent of an action (*archaic*) (*used in the passive*) ○ *admired of everyone* [Old English. Ultimately from a prehistoric Germanic word that is also the source of English *off* and German *ab* "away."]

OF *abbr.* **1.** BASEBALL outfielder **2.** BASEBALL outfield **3.** LANG Old French

o·fay /ō fày/ *n.* a word used, especially by Black people, to refer to a Caucasian person disparagingly and sometimes offensively (*slang insult*) [Early 20thC. Origin unknown.]

off /awf, of/ CORE MEANING: a grammatical word used to indicate separation or distance between two points, especially movement away from the speaker ○ (adv) *He ran off before I could stop him.* ○ (prep) *The bottle rolled off the ledge and fell to the floor.*

1. *prep., adv.* **SO AS TO LEAVE** to come out of or leave a bus, train, or plane ○ *Check you have all your belongings before getting off the bus.* ○ *He got off at the next stop.* **2.** *prep., adv.* **SO AS TO KEEP AWAY FROM** so as to keep away from, avoid stepping on, or be at a distance from or to the side of ○ *The sign said "Please keep off the grass."* ○ *I stepped off the curb.* **3.** *prep., adv.* **AWAY FROM WORK** away from work or usual duties owing to illness, holidays, or normal nonwork time ○ *trying to get time off work to visit her in the hospital* ○ *I didn't see Jane – it must be her night off.* **4.** *prep., adv.* **REDUCED BY** so as to be reduced by the amount indicated ○ *10 percent off all swimwear this week* ○ *She knocked $10 off for the slight stain on the sleeve.* **5.** *prep., adv.* **IN THE FUTURE** a particular distance away in the future ○ *My fortieth birthday is only two years off!* **6.** *prep., adv.* **SO AS TO REMOVE** so as to eliminate or remove something from view ○ *The dirt should wash off easily.* ○ *He was rubbing something off the board when I came in.* **7.** *adv.* **TO A DISTANT PLACE** so as to be away from the present location ○ *He hopped in the car, started it up, and took off.* **8.** *adv.* **AWAY** at a particular physical distance away ○ *The nearest stop's about two miles off.* **9.** *adv.* **MEASURED** so as to be divided or measured ○ *Measure the gap, mark it off with a pencil, and cut the wood to size.* **10.** *adv.* **TO COMPLETION** to the point of completion ○ *We're trying to get our bills paid off.* **11.** *adv.* **INTO A PARTICULAR STATE** into a particular state, especially an unconscious state ○ *The baby dozed off on the way over here.* **12.** *prep.* **ABSTAINING FROM** no longer participating in or using ○ *stay off caffeine for a week* **13.** *prep.* **NOT LIKING** no longer inclined toward ○ *I'm really off horror movies at the moment.* **14.** *prep.* **ON A DIET OF** using as a means of subsistence ○ *living off vegetables from our garden* **15.** *prep.* **BRANCHING OUT FROM** near or next to, and leading or branching away from ○ *He lives in an apartment block just off the main street.* **16.** *prep.* **FROM** used to show the object of an action (*nonstandard*) ○ *I got these sunglasses off my sister for my birthday.* **17.** *adv., adj.* **NOT IN OPERATION** not functioning or in use ○ *Shall I switch the engine off?* ○ *He was always constantly checking to make sure the lights were off.* **18.** *adv., adj.* **CANCELED** so as to be no longer taking place ○ *The deal's off.* **19.** *adj.* **NO LONGER FRESH** smelling and tasting bad because of being no longer fresh ○ *We had to throw the fish away – it was going off.* **20.** *adj.* **IN A PARTICULAR CONDITION** in a particular condition with regard to something ○ *How are you off for cash?* **21.** *adj.* **NOT CORRECT** in error or out of alignment **22.** *adj.* **ON THE RIGHT OF** situated on the right side of a vehicle, farthest away from the curb **23.** *adj.* **UNACCEPTABLE** unacceptable or disappointing, not up to normal standards (informal) ○ *He was off his game today.* [Old English. Originally an emphatic variant of OF.] ◇ **off and on** occasionally

off. *abbr.* **1.** officer **2.** office **3.** official

off-air *adj.* spoken or occurring in broadcasting studios but not used during a broadcast —**off air** *adv.*

of·fal /áwf'l, óff'l/ *n.* **1. EDIBLE INTERNAL ORGANS** the edible, mainly internal organs of an animal, e.g., the heart, liver, brains, and tongue, sometimes regarded as unpalatable or even inedible **2. SOMETHING THROWN AWAY** something discarded as refuse [14thC. Formed from OFF + FALL; probably modeled on Dutch *afval*.]

off·beat /áwf beet, óf-/ *adj.* not conforming to convention or to expectations

off beat *n.* any unaccented beat in a bar of music

off-Broad·way *n.* professional productions of drama in New York City, sometimes experimental or innovative, that are staged outside the principal theater district, Broadway

off-cam·er·a *adj.* out of sight of the camera —**off cam·er·a** *adv.*

off-cam·pus *adj.* done, taking place, or existing outside the area of a university, college, or other campus —**off cam·pus** *adv.*

off-cen·ter *adj.* **1. NOT AT THE CENTER** not at the center and therefore sometimes causing a lack of symmetry, balance, or evenness of movement **2. ECCENTRIC** slightly unconventional or eccentric —**off cen·ter** *adv.*

off chance, off-chance *n.* a slight or remote possibility ◇ **on the off chance (that)** just in case something happens

off-col·or *adj.* **1. RUDE** rude, especially sexually indecent or suggestive (*informal disapproving*) **2.** *U.K.* **ILL** ill or not very well ○ *I'm feeling a bit off-color today.* **3. NOT COLORED NORMALLY** not having the usual or desired color

off-course *adj. U.K.* = **off-track**

off·cut /áwf kùt, óf-/ *n.* a remnant left after the main pieces of something such as fabric or paper have been cut

Of·fen·bach /áwf'n baakh, -baak/ city in Hesse State, west central Germany, on the Main River. Population: 116,700 (1994).

Of·fen·bach, Jacques (1819–80) French composer. He wrote witty satirical operettas, one of which includes the famous "Can-can," as well as the opera *The Tales of Hoffmann* (1880). Full name **Jacob Eberst Offenbach**

of·fence *n.* U.K. = **offense**

of·fend /ə fénd/ (**-fend·ed, -fend·ing, -fends**) *v.* **1.** *vti.* **CAUSE SOMEBODY ANGER, RESENTMENT, OR HURT** to hurt somebody's feelings, or cause resentment, irritation, anger, or displeasure ○ *The book offended too many people.* **2.** *vi.* **BREAK A LAW** to violate a law or code of conduct ○ *he offended against the club's rules of proper dress* [14thC. Directly or via Old French *offendre* from Latin *offendere* "to strike." Ultimately from an Indo-European base that is also the ancestor of English *gun*.] —**of·fend·er** *n.* —**of·fend·ing** *adj.*

of·fense /ə féns/ *n.* **1. LEGAL OR MORAL CRIME** an official crime, or a crime against moral, social, or other accepted standards ○ *mail fraud is a federal offense* **2.** /ó fènss/ MIL, SPORTS **ATTACK** an attack or assault, usually in the military or in sports ○ *The army launched its great offense that spring.* **3.** /ó fènss/ SPORTS **ATTACKING PLAYERS ON A TEAM** the players making up the part of a team that attempts to score in a game, as distinct from the defense that tries to stop the other team from scoring ○ *We lacked a good offense last spring.* ◊ **defense 4. ANGER OR RESENTMENT** anger, resentment, hurt, or displeasure ○ *"Please don't take offense."* ○ *His remarks caused great offense.* **5. CAUSE OF DISPLEASURE OR ANGER** something that causes displeasure, humiliation, anger, resentment, or hurt ○ *The request was an offense to their dignity.* [14thC. Via French from, ultimately, Latin *offens-*, the past participle stem of *offendere* (see OFFEND).]

of·fen·sive /ə fénssiv/ *adj.* **1. UPSETTING, INSULTING, OR IRRITATING** causing anger, resentment, or moral outrage ○ *removed the offensive material from the play* **2. UNPLEASANT TO THE SENSES** causing physical repugnance ○ *an offensive smell* **3. AGGRESSIVE** demonstrating aggression ○ *warned that this would be seen as an offensive action* **4. USED WHEN ATTACKING** used, or designed to be used, when attacking ○ *an offensive weapon* **5.** SPORTS **IN POSSESSION** relating to the team that has possession of the ball or puck in a game ■ *n.* MIL **ATTACK OR ASSAULT** an attack, assault, or siege ○ *The platoon braced itself for the dawn offensive.*

of·fer /áwfər, óf-/ *vt.* (**-fered, -fer·ing, -fers**) **1. PRESENT SOMETHING FOR ACCEPTANCE OR REJECTION** to attempt to give somebody something that may be taken or refused, usually something desirable ○ *They offered me the job.* **2. HAVE SOMETHING FOR THE USE OF OTHERS** to provide something, or make something available for those who want it ○ *The town offered many attractions.* **3. VOLUNTEER TO DO SOMETHING** to suggest doing something yourself as a favor for somebody else ○ *I offered to bring the salad.* **4.** COMM **HAVE SOMETHING FOR SALE OR RENT** to present or have something for sale or rental ○ *the first gym to offer professional trainers at a low cost* **5.** RELIG **GIVE AS WORSHIP** to present something to God, often as part of worship ○ *We offer hymns of praise to God.* **6. EXHIBIT A QUALITY** to exhibit or demonstrate a particular quality ○ *The city offered little resistance against the army.* ○ *a plan that offers hope to millions* **7.** COMM **MAKE A BID** to make a bid or financial proposal for something ○ *They offered 40 cents a share.* ■ *n.* **1. PROPOSAL OF A SUGGESTED GIFT OR ACTION** a suggestion from somebody to give something or do something for somebody else ○ *A home-cooked meal and a place to stay: that's the best offer I've had all day!* **2.** COMM **FINANCIAL PROPOSAL OR BID** a sum of money suggested as payment for something such as a house ○ *They made an offer for the house but we refused it.* **3.** COMM **REDUCED PRICE** a reduced price for something ○ *this week's special offer* **4.** LAW **PROPOSAL LEADING TO A BINDING CONTRACT** a proposal that, if accepted, creates a binding contract [Old English *offrian*. Via prehistoric Germanic from Latin *offerre*, literally "to bring to," formed from *ferre* "to bring." Ultimately from an Indo-European word (ancestor also of English *bear* "to carry").] —**of·fer·er** *n.*

offer up *vt.* RELIG = **offer** *v.* **5**

of·fer·ing /áwfəring, óf-/ *n.* **1. CONTRIBUTION** something that is offered, or the act of offering ○ *What are the bookstores latest offerings?* **2.** RELIG **GIFT FOR GOD** something offered as a sacrifice to a deity **3.** CHR **MONEY GIVEN DURING A CHURCH SERVICE** a financial contribution to a church, often made during a church service [Old English *offrung*]

of·fer price *n.* the price at which something, especially a share of a stock or mutual fund, is offered for sale

of·fer·to·ry /áwfərtàwree, óffər-/ (*plural* **-ries**) *n.* **1. OFFERING OF COMMUNION BREAD AND WINE** the offering of the bread and wine during the Christian service of Holy Communion **2. CHURCH COLLECTION** the offering of money or gifts made by a church congregation **3. PART OF A CHRISTIAN SERVICE** a part of a church service during which prayers are said or sung while offerings are received [14thC. Via ecclesiastical Latin *offertorium* "offering place," from, ultimately, Latin *offerre* (see OFFER).]

off-glide *n.* PHON a sound produced by the vocal organs prior to their making another sound or assuming a neutral position

off-guard *adj.* not paying attention or being prepared for possible attack (*not hyphenated after a verb*) ○ *caught the enemy off-guard*

off·hand /awf hánd, of-, áwf hànd, óf-/ *adv.* **1. CASUALLY** casually, thoughtlessly, or spontaneously **2. WITHOUT PREPARATION** without preparation or research ○ *Offhand, I'd say there must be 50 people in there.* ■ *adj.* **off·hand, off·hand·ed 1. UNCONCERNED AND UNCARING** so casual, uninterested, or blunt as to appear impolite or uncaring (*disapproving*) ○ *She was pretty offhand about the whole affair.* **2. CASUALLY DONE** taken or made casually or without planning, usually on the spur of the moment ○ *Only through her offhand comment did I realize who she was.*

off-hour *n.* (*informal*) **1. TIME OUTSIDE OF THE RUSH HOUR** a period of time that is not crowded with cars or people (*often used before a noun*) ○ *We try to visit the zoo during off-hours.* **2. TIME OUTSIDE OF WORKING HOURS** a period of time outside of normal business hours

of·fice /áwfiss, óf-/ *n.* **1. ROOM USED FOR BUSINESS ACTIVITY** a room in which business or professional activities take place, often occupied by a single person or a single section of the business **2. PLACE OF BUSINESS** the quarters in which a commercial, professional, or government organization carries out its activities **3. OFFICIAL ORGANIZATION** a commercial or professional organization **4. STAFF IN AN OFFICE** the people who work in an office ○ *get-well cards from the office* **5.** POL **LARGE DEPARTMENTS IN SOME GOVERNMENTS** a major executive branch in some national governments ○ *He works for the British Home Office.* **6.** POL **U.S. GOVERNMENT AGENCY OR DEPARTMENT** a U.S. government agency or subdivision, especially of the federal government **7. POSITION OF RESPONSIBILITY** an official post or position of duty, trust, or responsibility ○ *The mayor has been in office four years now.* **8. PLACE FOR TICKETS OR INFORMATION** a booth or other place where tickets or information may be obtained **9.** CHR **SET FORM OF A CHRISTIAN SERVICE** the prescribed order or form of a Christian church service, or of daily prayers **10. TASK OR ASSIGNMENT** a task, assignment, or chore (*formal*) (*usually used in the plural*) ■ **of·fic·es** *npl.* **1. SOMETHING DONE ON BEHALF OF ANOTHER** something said or done by somebody to or for another person (*formal*) ○ *I got the job through her kind offices.* **2.** *U.K.* **AREAS OR BUILDINGS WHERE SERVANTS WORK** the outbuildings or parts of a house in which the servants work (*dated*) [13thC. Via French from Latin *officium*, literally "doing work," from, ultimately, *opus* "work" + *facere* "to do."]

of·fice block *n.* = **office building**

of·fice boy *n.* a boy or man who does errands around an office (*dated*)

of·fice build·ing *n.* a large building holding offices

of·fice-free *adj.* relating to or involving a workforce that is not required to work from or at an office

of·fice hours *npl.* the regular times during which a business or profession, or business as a whole, is conducted

of·fi·cer /áwfissər, óf-/ *n.* **1.** MIL **SOMEBODY OF RANK IN THE ARMED FORCES** somebody in a military force who has rank or authority **2. ELECTED OR APPOINTED OFFICIAL** somebody who is elected or appointed to an administrative position in a society, corporation, or government department **3.** = **police officer 4.** SHIPPING **SOMEBODY IN AUTHORITY ON SHIP** somebody on a civilian ship who has a specialized or responsible post ■ *vt.* (**-cered, -cer·ing, -cers**) MIL, NAVY **SUPPLY SOMETHING WITH OFFICERS** to provide something such as a military unit or a ship with officers

of·fi·cer of arms *n.* HERALDRY a herald, especially one who devises, grants, or confirms coats of arms

of·fi·cial /ə físh'l/ *n.* **SOMEBODY HOLDING OFFICE** somebody who has a position of authority in an organization, corporation, or government department ■ *adj.* **1. OF A GOVERNMENTAL OR ORGANIZATIONAL OFFICE** relating to or concerned with a governmental or organizational office ○ *official rules and regulations* **2. AUTHORIZED BY SOME AUTHORITY** approved, recognized, or issued by some authority ○ *No official statement has been issued.* **3. FORMAL** formal or ceremonial ○ *invited to attend the official opening* —**of·fi·cial·ly** *adv.*

of·fi·cial·dom *n.* bureaucracy and those who work within it, especially when viewed as inefficient or pompous (*informal*) ○ *caught up in the red tape of officialdom*

of·fi·cial·ese /ə físh'l éez, -éess/ *n.* unclear, pedantic, and verbose language considered characteristic of official documents

of·fi·cial·ism /ə físh'l ìzzəm/ *n.* excessive respect or adherence to official routines and regulations, considered to be characteristic of officials (*informal*)

of·fi·ci·ant /ə físhee ənt/ *n.* somebody who conducts a religious ceremony

of·fi·ci·ar·y /ə físhee èrree/ *adj.* **DERIVED FROM HOLDING OF OFFICE** derived from the holding of an office, or having a title that is derived from an office held ○ *an officiary title* ■ *n.* (*plural* **-ies**) **OFFICIAL OR BODY OF OFFICIALS** an official or an organized group of officials [Early 17thC. Via medieval Latin *officiarius*, from Latin *officium* (see OFFICE).]

of·fi·ci·ate /ə físhee àyt/ (**-at·ed, -at·ing, -ates**) *vi.* to preside in an official capacity, especially at a religious ceremony [Mid-17thC. Via medieval Latin *officiat-*, the past participle stem of *officiare* "to conduct sacred service," from Latin *officium* (see OFFICE).]

of·fic·i·nal /ə físsən'l/ *n.* PHARM **MEDICINE KEPT IN STOCK** a medicine kept in stock in a pharmacy rather than specially prepared according to a prescription (*archaic*) ■ *adj.* BOT **MEDICINAL** having medicinal properties, especially those recognized by a pharmacopoeia (*archaic*) [Late 17thC. Via medieval Latin *officinalis*, from *officina*, literally "workshop" (later "storeroom for medicines"), from Latin *officium* (see OFFICE).] —**of·fic·i·nal·ly** *adv.*

of·fi·cious /ə físhəss/ *adj.* **1. MEDDLESOME AND INTERFERING** characteristic of somebody who is eager to give unwanted help or advice ○ *whisked away our unfinished meal in an officious manner* **2. UNOFFICIAL** unofficial or informal, especially in political or diplomatic dealings **3. HELPFUL** kind and helpful (*archaic*) [Late 15thC. Formed from Latin *officiosus*, from

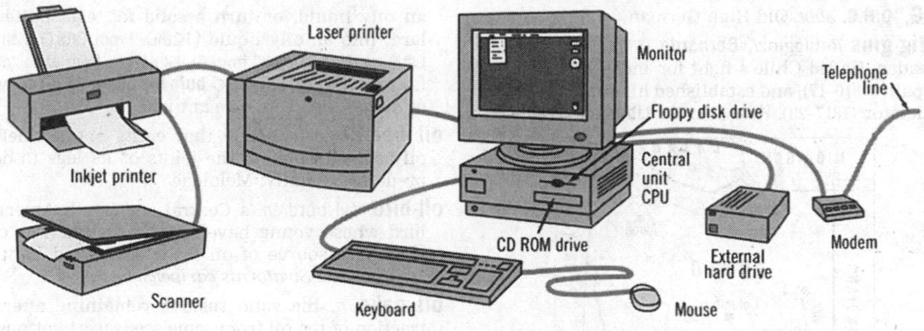

Office: Typical equipment used in an office

officium (see OFFICE). Originally in the sense "performing a function eagerly."] —**of·fi·cious·ly** *adv.* —**of·fi·cious·ness** *n.*

off·ing /áwfing, óf-/ *n.* NAUT the more distant part of the sea seen from the shore [Early 17thC. Origin uncertain: probably formed from OFF.] ◇ **in the offing** expected or likely in the future

off·ish /áwfish, óf-/ *adj.* standoffish (*informal*)

off-key *adj.* (*not hyphenated after a verb*) **1.** MUSIC **OUT OF TUNE** not having the correct pitch **2. INAPPROPRIATE** not usual, conventional, or appropriate ■ *adv.* **OUT OF TUNE** above or below the correct pitch

off-la·bel *adj.* using or involving the use of a prescription drug to treat a condition for which the drug has not been approved by the U.S. Food and Drug Administration

off-lim·its *adj.* to which entry is forbidden or barred ○ *That part of town was off-limits to us.*

off-line *adj.* **1.** COMPUT **DISCONNECTED FROM A COMPUTER NETWORK** used to describe a computer terminal or peripheral device that is disconnected or is functioning separately from an associated computer or computer network ○ *The printer was taken off-line for repairs.* ◊ **online 2.** COMMUNICATION **RELATING TO PREPARING BROADCAST MATERIAL** involved in preparing but not transmitting material for broadcasting ○ *off-line editing* —**off line** *adv.* ◇ **take something off-line** to remove something such as a discussion from a public forum to a more private one, e.g., from a chat room to personal e-mail

off-line news·read·er *n.* COMPUT software that allows a user to read newsgroup articles when the computer is not connected to the Internet

off·load /awf lőd, áwf lōd, of lőd, óf lōd/ (**-load·ed, -load·ing, -loads**) *v.* **1.** *vti.* **UNLOAD GOODS** to unload goods or a cargo from a vehicle or container ○ *ships waiting to offload* **2.** *vt.* **GET RID OF** to get rid of something unwanted by passing it on to somebody else ○ *managed to offload some of the work onto colleagues* **3.** *vti.* **UNBURDEN YOURSELF** to relieve yourself of a stressful emotion such as anxiety or frustration by talking to someone (*informal*) **4.** *vti.* COMPUT **TRANSFER DATA** to transfer data from one computer to another in order to create spare capacity in the original computer

off-off-Broad·way, **Off-Off-Broad·way** *n.* New York City theatrical productions that are considered to be fringe, experimental, or avant-garde. ◊ **off-Broadway**

off-peak *adj.* relating to the periods outside that of maximum use, frequency, or demand —**off peak** *adv.*

off-piste *adj.* relating to or taking place on fresh trackless snow that is away from the regular skiing runs —**off piste** *adv.*

off-price *adj.* offering goods at low prices, or being sold at a discount (*informal*)

off·print /áwf print, óf-/ *n.* a separate printing of a single article from a periodical, often given in small quantities to each individual contributor

off-put·ting *adj.* arousing irritation, repugnance, or mild unease —**off-put·ting·ly** *adv.*

off-ramp *n.* a one-way road serving as an exit from a main highway

off-rhyme *n.* POETRY a partial or near rhyme

off-road *adj.* designed, manufactured, or used for travel off public roads, especially over rough terrain

off-road ve·hi·cle *n.* any motorized vehicle designed or used for travel away from public roads or on rough terrain

off·scour·ings /áwf skòwringz, óf-/ *npl.* the leftover or discarded parts of something

off-screen *adj.* **1. NOT VISIBLE ON A SCREEN** not visible on a television or movie screen ○ *an off-screen commentator* **2. OCCURRING IN ORDINARY LIFE** occurring in ordinary life, not as fiction on television or in a movie ○ *Her off-screen life was just as exciting.* ■ *adv.* **IN ORDINARY LIFE** aside from television or movie performances ○ *Off-screen, he mostly played golf.*

off-sea·son *n.* **TIME OF LESS ACTIVITY** a time of year when activity or business is at a low level (*often used before a noun*) ○ *Hotel rooms were cheaper in the off-season.* ■ *adv.* **IN THE OFF-SEASON** during the off-season ○ *He liked to travel off-season.*

off·set /áwf sèt, óf sèt/ *n.* **1. SOMETHING COUNTERBALANCING SOMETHING ELSE** something that counterbalances or compensates, or an allowance made in order to counterbalance something (*often used before a noun*) **2.** CONSTR **ABRUPT BEND IN A STRAIGHT LINE** an abrupt bend put into an otherwise straight bar or pipe in order to avoid an obstruction **3.** PRINTING **PRINTING PROCESS USING INK TRANSFER** a method of printing in which inked impressions are transferred onto paper from another surface (*often used before a noun*) **4.** PRINTING **UNINTENTIONAL MARKING FROM WET INK** an accidental transfer of ink, usually from one piece of paper to another (*often used before a noun*) **5.** BOT **OFFSHOOT CAPABLE OF PROPAGATION** an offshoot or runner from the base of a plant that can propagate the plant **6.** GENETICS **OFFSHOOT OR DESCENDANT** something that has developed from something else, e.g., a collateral descendant or group of descendants of a family **7.** GEOL **SPUR IN A MOUNTAIN RANGE** a projecting spur or ridge in a mountain range (*often used before a noun*) **8.** GEOL **HORIZONTAL DISPLACEMENT OF ROCK** the horizontal displacement that occurs as a result of the movement of a rock mass along a fault **9. SOMETHING SET APART** anything set apart from something else (*often used before a noun*) **10. SURVEYING LINE** a short distance measured at right angles from a main survey line, used in finding the area of a piece of land **11. BEGINNING** the beginning of something (*dated*) **12.** ARCHIT = **setback** *n.* **2** ■ *v.* /awf sét, of-, áwf sèt, óf-/ (**-set, -set·ting, -sets**) **1.** *vt.* **COUNTERACT SOMETHING** to balance or make up for something (*often passive*) ○ *These improved sales were offset by last month's losses.* **2.** *vti.* PRINTING **PRINT SOMETHING BY TRANSFER** to print something by offset printing, or to accidentally transfer ink by an offset **3.** *vti.* CONSTR **FORM OR BE AN OFFSET IN SOMETHING** to make an offset in something such as a wall or pipe, or to be formed into an offset —**off·set** *adv.*

off·shoot /áwf shòot, óf-/ *n.* **1.** PLANTS **SHOOT FROM THE MAIN STEM OF PLANT** a branch or shoot growing from the main stem of a plant **2. SOMETHING THAT COMES FROM SOMETHING ELSE** something that springs or spreads from or that is a subsidiary of a main source or origin ○ *The company was an offshoot of their leisure empire.* **3. DESCENDANT OR BRANCH OF ANOTHER GROUP** an individual or group descending from specified ancestors, or branching off from a specified social group

off·shore /awf sháwr, of-/ *adv.* **1. FROM WATER TO LAND** on or over land that is near water, especially from a body of water ○ *An icy wind blew offshore.* **2. IN WATER SOME WAY FROM SHORE** in a body of water at some distance from the shore ○ *anchored offshore* ■ *adj.* **1. BLOWING FROM WATER TO LAND** blowing or moving from water to land ○ *offshore breezes* **2. AT SEA SOME WAY FROM SHORE** located at sea a considerable distance from shore **3.** FIN **IN FOREIGN COUNTRY** based in a foreign country, usually in order to avoid taxes

off·side (*adj-predicative*) /awf sīd, of-/; (*adj-attributive*) /áwf sīd, óf-/ *adj.* illegally beyond or in advance of a ball or puck during play —**off·side** *adv.*

off·site /áwf sīt, óf-/ *adj.* not based or occurring in an organization's principal place of activity

off-speed *adj.* used to describe a baseball pitch that is slower than is ordinary or expected

off·spring /áwf spring, óf-/ (*plural* **-spring** *or* **-springs**) *n.* **1. DESCENDANTS** the descendants of people, animals, or sometimes plants **2. RESULT OF SOMETHING** the product, consequence, or effect of something

off·stage /of stáyj/ *adv.* **1.** THEATER **OUTSIDE ACTING AREA** away from the area of the stage used for a performance, usually out of the view of the audience **2. IN PRIVATE LIFE** in private life, especially as opposed to the character an actor plays or the personality a performer projects **3. OUT OF PUBLIC VIEW** unseen by the public and media ■ *adj.* **1.** THEATER **HAPPENING OFFSTAGE** happening or situated outside the area of the stage visible to the audience **2. PRIVATE** occurring in or characteristic of somebody's private life **3. HAPPENING UNSEEN** occurring out of the gaze of the public and the media

off-street *adj.* not in the street but in a parking lot, garage, driveway, or another place ○ *off-street parking*

off-the-cuff *adj.* delivered spontaneously or without preparation or notes [From the custom of scribbling extempore remarks on a starched shirt cuff] —**off the cuff** *adv.*

off-the-peg *adj.* *U.K.* = **off-the-rack** —**off the peg** *adv.*

off-the-rack *adj.* ready-made and sold in standard sizes, not tailored for the individual customer ○ *off-the-rack evening wear* —**off the rack** *adv.*

off-the-rec·ord *adj.* not intended for publication or to be attributed by name to the person who said it —**off the rec·ord** *adv.*

off-the-shelf *adj.* readily obtainable or taken from an existing stock of merchandise or supplies ○ *a mix of components that were both cheap and off the shelf* —**off-the-shelf** *adv.*

off-the-wall *adj.* unusual or unconventional in a way that is particularly bizarre (*informal*) [Late 20thC. Perhaps from the expression *bouncing off the walls*, an allusion to the padded cells once used to contain people with psychiatric disorders.] —**off the wall** *adv.*

off-track *adj.* occurring somewhere other than a racetrack ○ *off-track betting*

off-white *adj.* of a very pale color, e.g., cream, that is a shade or two away from pure white —**off-white** *n.*

off year *n.* a year in which no major election, especially a presidential one, takes place —**off-year** *adj.*

oft /awft, oft/ *adv.* often (*archaic or literary*) (*now often used in combination*) ○ *oft-repeated phrase* [Old English. Related to German *oft* and Swedish *ofta*.]

of·ten /áwff'n, óff'n/ *adv.* at short intervals or repeatedly [13thC. An alteration of OFT, probably influenced by *selden* "seldom."] ◇ **every so often** regularly but with fairly long intervals between each occurrence ◇ **more often than not, as often as not** fairly frequently, or in a majority of instances

of·ten·times /áwff'n tīmz, óff'n-/, **oft·times** /áwft tīmz, óft-/ *adv.* frequently (*archaic or literary*)

OG, **o.g.** *abbr.* STAMPS original gum

og·am *n.* = **ogham**

Og·bo·mo·sho /aàgbə mő shō/ city in Oyo state, southwestern Nigeria, situated approximately 125 mi./201 km northeast of Lagos. Population: 660,600 (1992).

Og·dens·burg /ógdənz bùrg/ city in St. Lawrence County, northern New York. It was the site of the Ogdensburg Agreement between Canada and the United States (1940).

o·gee /ő jee/ *n.* ARCHIT **1. S-SHAPED MOLDING** a decorative molding with an ogee-shaped profile **2.** = **ogee arch** [Late 17thC. An alteration of OGIVE.]

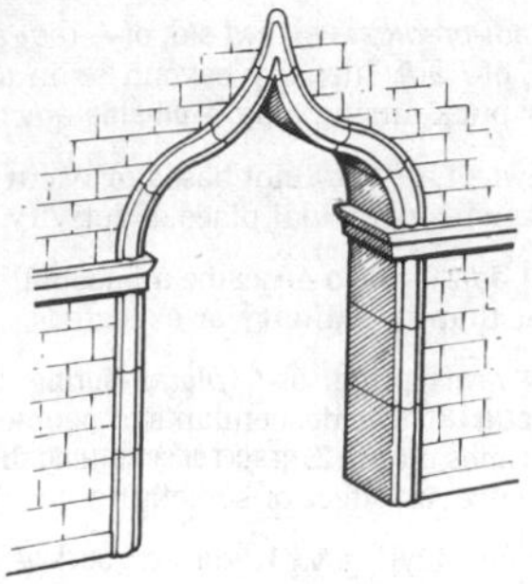

Ogee arch

o·gee arch *n.* an arch whose sides curve gently inward near the top and then curve upward steeply to meet in a point

og·ham /óggəm/, **og·am** *n.* **1.** ANCIENT CELTIC WRITING SYSTEM an ancient British and Irish Celtic alphabet consisting of twenty characters formed by inscribing lines on either side of or across a long straight baseline **2.** CELTIC LETTER any of the characters used in the ogham alphabet **3.** CELTIC INSCRIPTION an inscription written in ogham, or a stone bearing such an inscription [Early 18thC. Via modern Irish from Old Irish *ogam*, named for *Ogma*, the Celtic god who supposedly invented it.]

o·give /ṓ jìv/ *n.* **1.** ARCHIT RIB IN GOTHIC VAULT a diagonal rib in a Gothic vault **2.** ARCHIT POINTED ARCH an arch that rises to a sharp point **3.** STATS CUMULATIVE FREQUENCY GRAPH a graph or curve that represents the cumulative frequencies of a set of values [Origin uncertain; perhaps via Old French *augive* from, ultimately, late Latin *obviare* "to resist"]

o·gle /ṓg'l/ *vti.* (**o·gled, o·gling, o·gles**) STARE AT SOMEBODY DESIROUSLY to look at somebody for sexual enjoyment or as a way of showing sexual interest ■ *n.* DESIROUS LOOK a prolonged flirtatious or desirous look at somebody [Late 17thC. Origin uncertain: possibly from Low German *oegeln* "to keep eyeing," from *oege* "eye." Related to Old English *ēage* "eye."] —**o·gler** *n.*

WORD KEY: SYNONYMS

See Synonyms at *gaze*.

O·gle·thorpe /ṓg'l thawrp/, **James Edward** (1696–1785) British colonist. He founded Savannah, Georgia, and was the colony's governor (1733–43).

Og·oo·ué /ṑgə wáy/ river in Gabon, western central Africa. Length: 683 mi./970 km.

o·gre /ṓgər/ *n.* **1.** EVIL MONSTER an evil giant or monster in fairy tales, especially one who eats people **2.** FRIGHTENING PERSON a person who is particularly unpleasant and frightening —**o·gre·ish** /ṓgərish, ṓgrish/ *adj.*

o·gress /ṓgrəss/ *n.* **1.** MEAN FEMALE MONSTER an evil female giant or monster in fairy tales, especially one who eats people **2.** OFFENSIVE TERM an offensive term that deliberately insults a woman's appearance and temperament [Early 18thC]

O·gun /ō gŏŏn/ state in southwestern Nigeria, north of Lagos State. Capital: Abeokuta. Population: 2,338,570 (1991). Area: 6,472 sq. mi./16,762 sq. km.

oh /ō/ *interj.* **1.** USED TO EXPRESS STRONG EMOTION used to express a strong emotional reaction to something, e.g., surprise, shock, pain, or extreme pleasure ○ *Oh! That's wonderful news!* **2.** USED TO INTRODUCE STRONG REACTION used to introduce short phrases that express a strong emotion, e.g., anger, shock, delight, or triumph ○ *Oh what a fool I've been* **3.** USED TO INTRODUCE RESPONSE used to introduce a response to what somebody has just said or asked ○ *Oh, I'm fine. How are you?* **4.** USED TO SHOW THOUGHT used to indicate thought or hesitation concerning what will be said next ○ *We've got, oh, fifteen minutes before the bus is due.* **5.** USED TO ATTRACT ATTENTION used to attract somebody's attention or call attention to something ○ *Oh, John, can you come over here a minute?* [Mid-16thC. An alteration of O.]

OH *abbr.* Ohio

O'Ha·ra /ō háarə/, **John Henry** (1905–70) U.S. writer. His novels explore the themes of class conflict, status, and sexual mores. His works include the short-story collection *Pal Joey* (1940).

OHG, O.H.G. *abbr.* Old High German

O'Hig·gins /ō hígginz/, **Bernardo** (1778–1842) Chilean leader. He led Chile's fight for independence from Spain (1810–17), and established himself as a virtual dictator (1817–23). Known as **the Liberator of Chile**

Ohio

O·hi·o[1] /ō hī́ ō/ state of the United States bordered by Michigan, Lake Erie, Pennsylvania, West Virginia, Kentucky, and Indiana. Capital: Columbus. Population: 11,186,331 (1997). Area: 44,828 sq. mi./116,104 sq. km. —**O·hi·o·an** *adj., n.*

O·hi·o[2] major river of the eastern United States, originating from the confluence of two other rivers at Pittsburgh, Pennsylvania, and flowing southwards to join the Mississippi at Cairo, Illinois. Length: 981 mi./1,579 km.

ohm /ōm/ *n.* the SI unit of electrical resistance, equal to the resistance between two points on a conductor when a potential difference of 1 volt produces a current of 1 ampere. Symbol Ω [Mid-19thC. Named for Georg Simon OHM, who studied the measurement of electrical resistance.]

Ohm /ōm/, **Georg Simon** (1787–1854) German physicist. His research on electric currents led to the formulation of Ohm's law. The ohm is named for him.

ohm·age /ṓmij/ *n.* electrical resistance measured in ohms

ohm·me·ter /ṓm meètər/ *n.* an instrument that measures electrical resistance in ohms

Ohm's law *n.* the law of physics that states that electric current is directly proportional to the voltage applied to a conductor and inversely proportional to that conductor's resistance [Named for Georg Simon OHM, who formulated it]

o·ho /ō hṓ/ *interj.* used to express surprise or exultation, e.g., at making a discovery [14thC. Formed from O + HO.]

OHV *abbr.* **1.** off-highway vehicle **2. OHV, o.h.v.** MECH ENG overhead valve

-oid *suffix.* like, resembling, related to ○ *toxoid* ○ *cylindroid* [From Greek *-oeidēs*, from *eidos* "form, shape" (see IDOL)]

o·id·i·um /ō íddee əm/ (*plural* **-a** /-ə/) *n.* a thin-walled egg-shaped fungal spore produced by the fragmentation of a hypha [Mid-19thC. Via modern Latin, genus name, from Greek *ōion* "egg" (see OO-).]

oil /oyl/ *n.* **1.** THICK GREASY LIQUID a liquid fat obtained from plant seeds, animal fats, mineral deposits, and other sources that is thicker than and does not dissolve in water and will burn. Oils are used for a wide variety of purposes, most commonly as lubricants and fuels and in cooking. **2.** PETROLEUM petroleum, the crude product that is distilled and refined to produce a wide variety of industrial oils and oil-based products (*often used before a noun*) ○ *oil prices* **3.** PETROLEUM DERIVATIVE any of various liquids extracted from petroleum, e.g., heating oil and motor oil, that are used as domestic fuels or as machinery and engine lubricants (*often used before a noun*) **4.** PETROLEUM INDUSTRY the worldwide industry that is based on petroleum extraction and refining (*often used before a noun*) ○ *oil companies* **5.** THICK LIQUID CONTAINING OIL a thick liquid containing oil or with the consistency of oil, especially a cosmetic **6.** = **oil paint** (*usually used in the plural*) **7.** OIL PAINTING a painting done in oil paints **8.** FLATTERY insincere praise or flattery (*dated slang*) ■ *v.* (**oiled, oil·ing, oils**) **1.** *vt.* APPLY OIL TO SOMETHING to put oil into or onto something in order to lubricate, polish, preserve, or soften it **2.** *vti.* FUEL to take on oil as a fuel, or supply a ship with oil **3.** *vti.* TURN INTO OIL to become an oily liquid, or turn a solid fat, e.g., butter or lard, into an oily liquid [12thC. From Old French, via Latin *oleum* "olive oil" from Greek *elaion*, from *elaia* "olive" (source of English *olive*).] ◇ **burn the midnight oil** to work or study until very late at night

oil bee·tle *n.* a beetle that emits a foul-smelling oily substance from the joints of its legs to deter predators. Family: Meloidae.

oil·bird /óyl bùrd/ *n.* a Central and South American bird whose young have fatty flesh that was once used as a source of oil for cooking and lighting. Latin name: *Steatornis caripensis.*

oil cake *n.* the solid residue remaining after extraction of the oil from some seeds, e.g., cottonseed and linseed. It is used as livestock feed.

oil·can /óyl kàn/ *n.* a metal container with a long thin spout, used to squirt lubricating oil into machinery

oil·cloth /óyl klàwth/ *n.* cloth that has been treated with oil or a synthetic resin to make it waterproof, often used as a wipe-clean covering for tables (*often used before a noun*)

oil-cooled *adj.* with a cooling system that uses oil

Oil·dale /óyl dàyl/ city in Kern County, California. Population: 26,553 (1990).

oil drum *n.* a large metal cylinder designed for transporting and storing oil. Empty oil drums are often used as trash cans, flotation devices, and grills and to make instruments for steel bands.

oiled /oyld/ *adj.* **1.** TREATED WITH OIL treated with oil, usually for waterproofing or lubrication **2.** DRUNK drunk (*slang*)

oil·er /óylər/ *n.* **1.** REFUELING TANKER an oil tanker, especially one that refuels ships at sea **2.** OIL-FUELED SHIP a ship that uses oil as fuel **3.** OIL WELL an oil well (*informal*)

oil field *n.* an area of land or sea under which there are substantial reserves of petroleum, especially one that is being exploited

oil gland *n.* a gland at the base of a bird's tail that secretes an oily substance that the bird uses to preen and waterproof its feathers

oil·man /óyl màn, -mən/ (*plural* **-men** /-mèn, -mən/) *n.* **1.** OIL EXECUTIVE an executive in the petroleum industry **2.** OIL FIELD WORKER somebody who works in an oil field

oil of cloves *n.* an essential oil extracted from clove flowers, used to relieve toothache and used by dentists, mixed with zinc oxide, to form a pain-killing cement for use in temporary fillings

oil of win·ter·green *n.* an aromatic oil obtained from an evergreen North American shrub, used medicinally in liniments and also as a flavoring in food. It is the methyl ester of salicylic acid.

oil paint *n.* a paint that consists of pigment mixed with a drying oil

oil paint·ing *n.* **1.** PICTURE USING OIL PAINTS a picture painted with oil paints. Also called **oil 2.** USE OF OIL PAINTS the art of painting with oil paints

oil palm *n.* an African palm tree whose fruit and seeds are the source of palm oil. Latin name: *Elaeis guineensis.*

oil pan *n.* the lower section of the crankcase in an internal-combustion engine, which acts as a reservoir of motor oil

oil patch *n.* the region of the United States where there are substantial petroleum deposits, including the states of Oklahoma, Texas, and Louisiana (*informal*)

oil rig *n.* the equipment used for drilling for oil, including the platform that supports the drilling equipment

oil shale *n.* a black or dark brown type of shale from which petroleum can be extracted by distillation

oil·skin /óyl skìn/ *n.* **1.** WATERPROOF FABRIC cotton fabric that has been treated with oil to make it waterproof **2.** WATERPROOF GARMENT a garment, especially a coat, made of oilskin ■ **oil·skins** *npl.* WATERPROOF CLOTHING waterproof outerwear consisting of a coat and pants made of oilskin

oil slick *n.* a film of oil covering part of the surface of something, especially a large expanse of oil floating on the sea following a spillage of oil from an oil tanker

oil·stone /óyl stṑn/ *n.* a fine-grained stone that is lubricated with oil and used to sharpen cutting tools

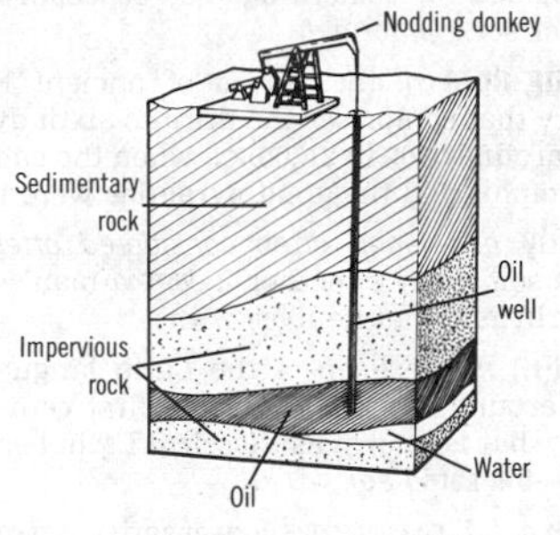

Oil well

oil well *n.* a shaft drilled into the earth or the bottom of the sea, through which petroleum is extracted

oil·y /óylee/ (**-i·er, -i·est**) *adj.* **1. DIRTY WITH OIL** covered, smeared, or dirtied with oil ○ *don't want to get my hands oily* **2. CONTAINING OIL** containing or producing a lot of oil **3. LIKE OIL** reminiscent of oil in texture, smell, or taste **4. INGRATIATING** unpleasantly eager to please or charm, or distressingly expert at doing this (*disapproving*) —**oil·i·ness** *n.*

oink /oyngk/ *interj., n.* **HOG SOUND** a word used for the nasal grunting sound made by a hog ■ *vi.* (**oinked, oink·ing, oinks**) **MAKE HOG SOUND** to make the nasal grunting sound of a hog [Mid-20thC. An imitation of the sound.]

oint·ment /óyntmənt/ *n.* a smooth greasy substance used on the skin to soothe soreness or itchiness, help wounds heal, or make the skin softer [13thC. Via Old French *oignement* from, ultimately, Latin *unguentum* (source of English *unguent, unctuous,* and *anoint*).]

Oise /waaz/ river in western Europe, flowing from southern Belgium through France and into the Seine. Length: 186 mi./299 km.

O·i·ta /ṓ i tàa/ city and seaport in Japan. It is the capital of Oita prefecture, on northeastern Kyushu Island. Population: 417,051 (1992).

OJ, oj *abbr.* orange juice

O·jib·wa /ō jíbbwə, ō jíb wày/ (*plural* **-was** *or* **-wa**), **O·jib·way** /ō jíb wày/ (*plural* **-ways** *or* **-way**) *n.* **1. NATIVE NORTH AMERICAN PEOPLE** a Native North American people who once lived north of Lake Huron but who later moved into territories ranging from Saskatchewan across to Michigan **2. NATIVE NORTH AMERICAN LANGUAGE** the Algonquian language spoken by the Ojibwa [Early 18thC. From Ojibwa *ojibwe*.] —**O·jib·wa** *adj.*

OJT *abbr.* on-the-job training

OK[1] /ō káy/, **o·kay** *interj.* (*informal*) **1. INDICATING AGREEMENT** used to indicate agreement to or approval of what somebody said or did ○ *"Can you help?" "OK. What do you want me to do?"* **2. USED TO CHECK FOR APPROVAL** used at the end of a statement to inquire whether somebody has understood and agrees with or approves of what was said ○ *It's your job to make the arrangements, OK?* **3. USED TO INDICATE FINISHING SOMETHING** used to indicate that something is finished and that something else will now be done or discussed ○ *OK, let's move to the next item on the agenda.* ■ *adj.* (*informal*) **1. PASSABLE** acceptable or tolerable but not exceptional ○ *It's OK for a first effort.* **2. PHYSICALLY WELL** in good health or condition ○ *I'll be OK if I can just sit down for a minute.* **3. ALLOWABLE** acceptable to somebody or permissible ○ *Is it OK for me to call home on the office phone?* **4. RATHER GOOD OR PLEASANT** better than just satisfactory or acceptable ○ *Her parents are OK; we get along really well.* ■ *adv.* **FAIRLY WELL** in an acceptable, tolerable, or satisfactory manner (*informal*) ○ *Everything's going OK, except that we're a little bit behind schedule.* ■ *vt.* (**OK'ed, OK'ing, OK's; o·kayed, o·kay·ing, o·kays**) (*informal*) **1. GIVE APPROVAL FOR SOMETHING** to approve of or consent to something ○ *I just need you to OK the agenda.* **2. OBTAIN SOMEBODY'S CONSENT** to obtain somebody's approval of or consent to something ○ *I'll need to OK that with my boss.* ■ *n.* (*plural* **OK's**) **APPROVAL** approval to do something or consent to something (*informal*) ○ *As soon as she gives the OK, we'll start work.* [Mid-19thC. Origin uncertain.]

WORD KEY: ORIGIN

Of the many competing theories about the origins of ***OK***, the one now most widely accepted is that the letters stand for *oll* or *orl korrect*, a facetious early 19th-century American phonetic spelling of *all correct*, and that this was reinforced by the fact that they were also coincidentally the initial letters of *Old Kinderhook*, the nickname of U.S. president Martin Van Buren (who was born in Kinderhook, New York State), which were used as a slogan in the presidential election of 1840 (a year after the first record of ***OK*** in print).

OK[2] *abbr.* Oklahoma

O·ka·na·gan /ṑkə naágən/ (*plural* **-gans** *or* **-gan**), **O·ka·nog·an** (*plural* **-ans** *or* **-an**) *n.* **1. NATIVE NORTH AMERICAN PEOPLE** a member of a Native North American people who live in and around the Okanagan river valley that runs from British Columbia down through Washington state **2.** LANG = **Okinagan** — **O·ka·na·gan** *adj.*

O·ka·na·gan, Lake lake in southern British Columbia, Canada. Area: 136 sq. mi./352 sq. km.

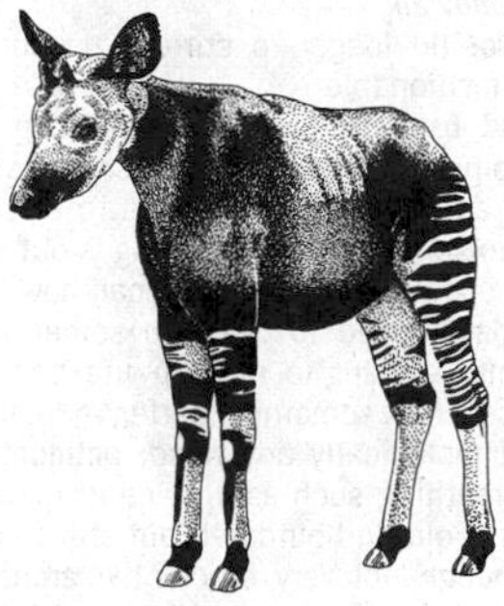
Okapi

o·ka·pi /ō kaápee/ (*plural* **-pis** *or* **-pi**) *n.* a plant-eating mammal of central Africa that looks rather like a small giraffe without the long neck. It is chestnut brown with white stripes on its hindquarters. Latin name: *Okapia johnstoni.* [Early 20thC. From an African language.]

O·ka·van·go /ṑkə vaáng gō/ river in south central Africa, rising in Angola, where it is called Cubango, and flowing through Namibia and Botswana into the Okavango Swamp. Length: 1000 mi./1600 km.

O·ka·van·go Swamp marsh region in northwestern Botswana, southern Africa, occupying an inland drainage basin. Area: 6,500 sq. mi./16,800 sq. km.

o·kay *interj., adj., adv., vt., n.* = **OK**[1]

O·ka·ya·ma /ṑkaa yaámaa/ city and port in Japan, on western Honshu Island, on the Inland Sea. Population: 593,730 (1990).

O·kee·cho·bee, Lake /ṑkə chṓbee/ lake in Florida, north of the Everglades, forming part of the Cross-Florida Waterway. Area: 663 sq. mi./1,717 sq. km.

Georgia O'Keeffe

O'Keeffe /ō keéf/, **Georgia** (1887–1986) U.S. artist. She is known for her stylized still lifes, notably of flowers and objects found in the desert.

O·ke·fe·no·kee Swamp /ṑkifə nṓki-/ marsh region in southeastern Georgia and northeastern Florida, It is noted for its rich wildlife. Area: 660 sq. mi./1,709 sq. km.

o·key-do·key /ṑki dṓk/, **o·key·doke** /-dṓkee/ *interj.* OK (*informal*) [Mid-20thC. An alteration of OK[1].]

Ok·hotsk, Sea of /ō kótsk, ə khótsk/ sea lying off the eastern coast of Siberia, part of the northwestern Pacific Ocean. Area: 590,000 sq. mi./1,530,000 sq. km.

O·kie /ṓkee/ *n.* **1. OFFENSIVE TERM** an offensive term for to a poor migrant farm laborer, especially one from Oklahoma or neighboring Dust Bowl states during the 1930s (*slang insult*) **2. OKLAHOMAN** somebody who was born or who lives in Oklahoma (*slang*)

Ok·i·na·gan /ṑki nóggən/ *n.* a Native North American language spoken by the Okanagan people. It belongs to the Salishan branch of Algonquian-Wakashan languages.

Okla. *abbr.* Oklahoma

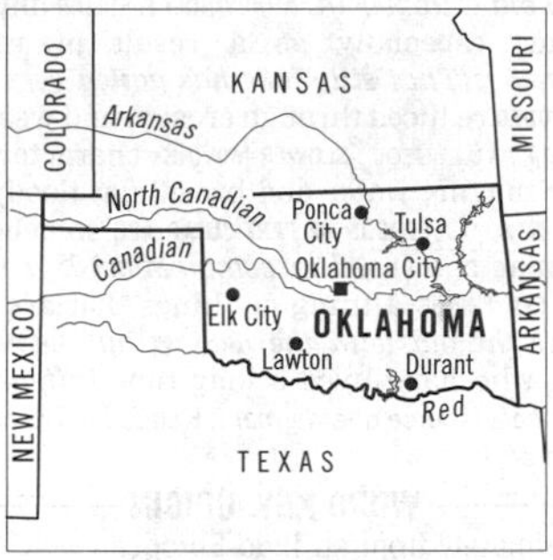

Oklahoma

O·kla·ho·ma /ṑklə hṓmə/ state of the United States bordered by Colorado, Kansas, Missouri, Arkansas, Texas, and New Mexico. Capital: Oklahoma City. Population: 3,317,091 (1997). Area: 69,903 sq. mi./181,048 sq. km. —**O·kla·ho·man** /ṑklə hṓmən/ *adj.*, *n.*

O·kla·ho·ma City capital city of Oklahoma, located in the central part of the state. Population: 463,201 (1994).

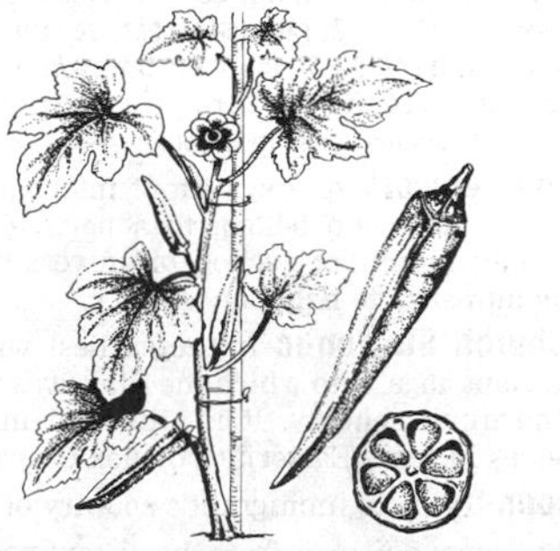
Okra

o·kra /ṓkrə/ (*plural* **o·kra** *or* **o·kras**) *n.* **1. POD USED AS VEGETABLE** a pod used as a vegetable and in soups and stews as a thickener **2. PLANT WITH FINGER-SHAPED PODS** a tall tropical Asian plant cultivated in warmer regions for its edible, usually green pods, that are about as long as a finger. Latin name: *Abelmoschus esculentus.* **3.** = **gumbo** *n.* 1 [Early 18thC. Of West African origin, related to Igbo *okuro*.]

ok·ta /óktə/ *n.* a unit of measure used to specify the amount of cloud cover, especially over an airfield, equivalent to enough clouds to cover one eighth of the sky [Mid-20thC. An alteration of OCTO-.]

-ol[1] *suffix.* compound containing hydroxyl, especially an alcohol or phenol ○ *glycerol* [From ALCOHOL]

-ol[2] *suffix.* = **-ole**

Ö·land /ö laand/ island of Sweden, located in the southwestern Baltic Sea. Population: 25,781 (1994). Area: 518 sq. mi./1,342 sq. km.

old /ōld/ *adj.* (**old·er, old·est**) **1. HAVING LIVED LONG** having lived for many years compared to others **2. ORIGINATING YEARS AGO** made, produced, or originating many years ago and still in existence **3. SENIOR** showing physical or mental characteristics sometimes associated with long life **4. WISE** showing the understanding, wisdom, or behavior that results from long experience of life ○ *She acts much older than she is.* **5. EXISTING FOR SPECIFIED TIME** having lived or existed for a specified amount of time (*usually used in combination*) ○ *The day was only a few hours old.* **6. ANCIENT** from the remote past ○ *the remains of an old civilization* **7. FORMER** from an earlier period of something, e.g., somebody's life ○ *We drove past my old school.* **8.** FAMILIAR familiar from past experience ○ *She always makes the same old excuses.* **9.** EXISTING OR USED OVER TIME having existed or been used for a long time, especially if showing wear or age ○ *Change into old clothes before gardening.* **10.** EXPERIENCED skilled or knowledgeable as a result of much experience over time ○ *Take advice from someone who's an old hand at this work.* **11. old, Old** EARLIER existing before one or all of the other stages, forms, or instances of something ○ *Old English words* **12.** USED FOR EMPHASIS used as an intensifer (*informal*) ○ *any old reason* **13.** EXPRESSING FAMILIARITY used to express affection or familiarity (*informal*) ○ *Good old Charlie!* **14.** ANNOYINGLY FAMILIAR annoyingly familiar, especially as a result of repetition (*informal*) ○ *That silly joke has gotten very old.* **15.** GEOL ERODED reduced through erosion and weathering. ◊ **young 16.** GEOL SLOWER-MOVING characterized by slower moving water and broad, flat floodplains. ◊ **young** ■ *n.* **1.** PERSON OF PARTICULAR AGE somebody of a particular age (*used in combination*) ○ *a two-year-old* **2.** OLD THINGS a thing or things that are old ○ *to balance the old with the new.* ■ *npl.* OFFENSIVE TERM people who have lived a long time (*offensive*) [Old English *eald* (source of *alderman*). Related to Dutch *oud* and German *alt.*]

WORD KEY: ORIGIN

Old is ultimately from an Indo-European word meaning "to grow, nourish," which is also the ancestor of English *adult, alumnus,* and *alimony.* In Latin the meaning evolved into "high," as seen in the English derivatives *altitude, exalt,* and *haughty,* whereas the Germanic languages preserved an old past participle meaning "grown, old," which is also the ancestor of English *elder, eldest,* and *world.*

old age *n.* the latter years of somebody's life lived out to its full term. ◊ **middle age**

old boy *n. U.K.* **1.** FORMER STUDENT a former student of a boys' or men's school, especially a British prep school or college **2.** FAMILIAR ADDRESS TO MAN a familiar way of addressing a man or boy (*dated informal*) ○ *See here, old boy, you can't enter this club uninvited.* [In school sense modeled on *new boy*]

old-boy net·work *n.* a system of informal contacts between men who belong to a particular group, especially alumni of a school or university, and use their influence to help one another

Old Church Sla·von·ic *n.* the earliest written Slavonic language, into which the Bible was translated in the ninth century. It is still used in religious services in some Eastern Orthodox Churches.

old coun·try *n.* an immigrant's country of origin

old·en /ṓldən/ *adj.* in or from the distant past (*archaic or literary*) [14thC. Formed from OLD + -EN.]

Oldenberg /ṓldən burg/**, Claes** (*b.* 1929) Swedish-born U.S. sculptor. A pioneer of pop art, he is known for his sagging "soft sculptures" of everyday objects. Full name **Claes Thure Oldenberg**

Ol·den·burg /ṓldən bŏŏrk, -bùrg/ city and river port in Lower Saxony State, northwestern Germany, situated approximately 25 mi./40 km west of Bremen. Population: 148,700 (1994).

Old Eng·lish *n.* **1.** LANG EARLIEST FORM OF ENGLISH the earliest form of the English language, used up to around A.D. 1150. Its three main dialects were West Saxon, Kentish, and Anglian. It was first written using the runic alphabet. ◊ **Middle English, Modern English 2.** PRINTING TYPEFACE a form of black letter typeface used by English printers until the 18th century —**Old Eng·lish** *adj.*

Old Eng·lish sheep·dog *n.* a large dog with a long shaggy coat and dark gray and white markings [Because they were originally bred in England]

old face *n. U.K.* = **old style**

old-fan·gled /ōld fáng g'ld/ *adj.* antiquated or out of date (*informal*) [Mid-19thC. Modeled on NEWFANGLED.]

old fart *n.* an offensive term referring to somebody, usually a person in authority, who is regarded as being set in his or her ways and as lacking a sense of humor or fun (*slang insult*)

old-fash·ioned *adj.* **1.** OUT OF DATE typical of or belonging to a time in the past and no longer considered fashionable or suitable for the present ○ *an old-fashioned car with a running board* **2.** MAINTAINING OLD-STYLE WAYS favoring or deliberately maintaining

Old English sheepdog

ideas, behavior, or ways of doing things from an earlier time ■ *n.* BEVERAGES WHISKEY COCKTAIL a cocktail made with whiskey, bitters, sugar, and lemon peel and garnished with fruit

WORD KEY: SYNONYMS

old-fashioned, outdated, antiquated, archaic, obsolete, passe, antediluvian

CORE MEANING: no longer in current use or no longer considered fashionable

old-fashioned used to describe something that is no longer in common use because of changes in taste or technology, although it may still be in existence. It is often used to suggest that something is out of date, but can also be used nostalgically to recall how things used to be; **out-dated** used to describe something that no longer seems relevant to modern life because it has been superseded by something better, more fashionable, or more technologically advanced; **antiquated** used to describe something such as a piece of machinery or a system that is old and outdated but still functioning or in use, although not very efficiently; **archaic** used to describe something that is so old-fashioned that it seems to have no relevance to modern life. It can also be used to describe things such as words that are no longer in common use but that could be used to create a particular effect; **obsolete** used to describe something that has passed totally out of use; **passe** a rather formal word used in a disapproving, sometimes even contemptuous, way to suggest that something is no longer current or fashionable; **antediluvian** a formal or literary word often used in a deliberately humorous way to suggest that something is extremely old-fashioned and outdated.

old-field *n.* a field lying fallow after being overcultivated (*regional archaic*)

old-field colt *n.* child born to parents who are not married (*regional archaic*) [From the unauthorized breeding of horses in fields that are not being watched]

Old French *n.* the earliest form of the French language, used until about A.D. 1400 or, in some analyses, A.D. 1600. ◊ **Middle French** —**Old French** *adj.*

old girl *n. U.K.* **1.** FORMER STUDENT a former student at a girls' or women's school, especially a British prep school or college **2.** FAMILIAR ADDRESS TO WOMAN a familiar way to address a woman or girl (*dated informal*) ○ *Sorry, old girl, didn't mean to lose my temper like that.*

old-girl net·work *n.* a system of informal contacts between women who belong to a particular group, especially alumnae of a school or university, and use their influence to help one another

Old Glo·ry *n.* a nickname for the flag of the United States

old gold *adj.* of a dark dull yellow color sometimes tinged with brown —**old gold** *n.*

old growth *n.* a long-established forest or woodland that contains some large old trees and has a relatively stable and diverse community of plants and animals (*hyphenated when used before a noun*)

old guard, Old Guard *n.* the members of a group or organization who have been in it the longest, are the staunchest defenders of its traditions, and are the least amenable to change (*takes a singular or plural verb*)

old hand *n.* somebody who has acquired skill and knowledge through long experience in a field of activity

old hat *adj.* boringly familiar or old-fashioned (*informal*)

Old High Ger·man *n.* the standard, literary form of German (**High German**) used in written documents up to around A.D. 1200 —**Old High Ger·man** *adj.*

old·ie /ṓldee/ *n.* something old, especially an old popular song (*informal*)

Old King·dom *n.* the period of ancient Egyptian history that comprises the third to sixth dynasties, from around 2700 to 2150 B.C., when the capital was at Memphis and the great pyramids were built

old la·dy *n.* (*slang*) (*often considered offensive*) **1.** MOTHER somebody's mother **2.** WIFE a man's wife, or his girlfriend that he lives with

Old Lat·in *n.* the form of the Latin language used until around the middle of the first century B.C., when what is known as Classical Latin began to be used —**Old Lat·in** *adj.*

old-line *adj.* **1.** CONSERVATIVE conservative or traditional in principles, policy, or outlook ○ *old-line fans praising players of 40 years ago* **2.** OLD AND ESTABLISHED in existence for a long time and having a high social status or good reputation that has endured ○ *an old-line publisher still proudly independent*

old maid *n.* **1.** OFFENSIVE TERM an offensive term for a woman in or past middle age who has never been married and seems unlikely ever to marry (*offensive*) **2.** OFFENSIVE TERM a man or woman insulted as being excessively prim and fussy (*offensive*) **3.** CARDS CARD GAME a card game played with a deck from which one card, usually a queen, has been removed, or the resulting unpaired card left at the end of the game. The players collect pairs of cards, and the player left with the unpaired card loses. **4.** CARDS LOSER IN OLD MAID the losing player in a game of old maid —**old-maid·ish** *adj.*

old maid flow·er *n. Southern U.S.* a zinnia

old man *n.* **1.** FATHER somebody's father (*slang*) **2.** HUSBAND a woman's husband, or the man that she lives with (*slang*) (*sometimes considered offensive*) **3.** COMMANDING OFFICER a man in a position of authority, especially a commanding officer (*slang*) ○ *The old man is on the bridge, mad as a hornet* **4.** *U.K.* FAMILIAR ADDRESS TO MAN a familiar way that one man addresses another (*informal dated*) ○ *Look here, old man, I'm in a spot of bother and wonder if you could help me out.*

old-man's-beard *n.* a popular name for several plants that have trailing or hanging whitish growths, especially traveler's-joy, Spanish moss, and the fringe tree

old mas·ter *n.* **1.** GREAT EUROPEAN PAINTER any of the great European painters of the period dating roughly from the late Middle Ages to the 18th century **2.** PAINTING BY OLD MASTER a picture painted by an old master

Old Nick *n.* a nickname for the Devil (*dated slang*)

Old Norse *n.* the old Germanic language from which the modern Scandinavian languages are derived, in use in Scandinavia from around A.D. 700 to 1350 —**Old Norse** *adj.*

Old Red Sand·stone *n.* a sedimentary rock, usually red in color, formed during the Devonian period and found in Britain and northwestern Europe

old rose *adj.* of a deep pink color tinged with gray —**old rose** *n.*

old salt *n.* a sailor who has years of experience at sea

Old Sax·on *n.* = **Saxon** *n.* 2

old school *n.* a group of people who adhere to traditional or old-fashioned values and practices ○ *As a disciplinarian of the old school, he was horrified at the laxity of the new regime.*

old school tie *n.* **1.** *U.K.* NECKTIE a necktie whose colors indicate which school, especially which British prep school, the wearer attended **2.** SCHOOL LOYALTY AND TRADITION the shared attitudes, traditions, and loyalties attributed to people who attended the same school, especially the same prep school or college **3.** CLANNISHNESS an attitude of smug self-sufficiency coupled with indifference or hostility to outsiders that is shown by members of a tight-knit group

old sol·dier *n.* **1.** VETERAN SOLDIER an experienced and long-serving soldier, or a former soldier **2.** VETERAN somebody with a great deal of experience

old·squaw /óld skwàw/, **old-squaw, old squaw** *n.* a long-tailed duck common in Arctic seas that has a black back and wings, a white breast, and a brown-and-white head. Latin name: *Clangula hyemalis.* [Mid-19thC. Probably from its gabbling voice.]

old·ster /óldstər/ *n.* somebody who has reached an advanced age (*offensive*) [Early 19thC. Modeled on YOUNGSTER. Originally it referred to a midshipman who had seen four years' service.]

old style *n.* a typeface that shows little difference between light and heavy strokes and has slanting serifs. It originated in the 18th century.

Old Style *adj.* used to indicate a date recorded according to the Julian calendar

old-style *adj.* typical of the past but now superseded by something else

Old Tes·ta·ment *n.* the first part of the Christian Bible, corresponding to the Hebrew Bible, that recounts the creation of the world and the history of ancient Israel and contains the Psalms and the prophetic books

old-time *adj.* **1. OLD-FASHIONED** typical of or dating from a time in the past ○ *old-time religion* **2. LONG-ESTABLISHED** in existence for a long time ○ *the old-time families of the town*

old-tim·er *n.* **1. SENIOR CITIZEN** a senior citizen, especially a man (*sometimes considered offensive*) **2. EXPERIENCED PERSON** somebody who has lived in or worked at a particular place for a long time

Ol·du·vai Gorge /óldoō vī, -vày, -wày/ ravine in northern Tanzania, where fossil remains of early humans and hominids have been found. It is the site of many important archeological discoveries.

old·wife /óld wīf/ (*plural* **-wives** /-wīvz/ *or* **-wife**) *n.* **1.** ZOOL **FISH** a popular name for several fishes, e.g., the alewife and the menhaden **2.** BIRDS = **oldsquaw**

old wives' tale *n.* a traditional belief or story, passed down by word of mouth, that is now considered untrue or superstitious [From *old wife*, an old woman]

old wom·an *n.* (*slang offensive*) **1. MOTHER** somebody's mother **2. WIFE** a man's wife, or the woman that he lives with (*sometimes considered offensive*) **3. OFFENSIVE TERM** an offensive term that deliberately insults a man's courage and decisiveness —**old-wom·an·ish** *adj.*

Old World *n.* the part of the world that was known to Europeans before Columbus's first voyage to the Americas, comprising Europe, Asia, and Africa. ◊ **New World**

old-world *adj.* considered to be typical of a former and more gracious age

Old World mon·key *n.* any of a family of monkeys closely related to the great apes, with close-set nostrils and nongrasping tails. The family includes baboons and mandrills. Family: Cercopithecidae.

o·lé /ō láy/ *interj.* **EXPRESSION OF TRIUMPH** used to express triumph, excited approval, or encouragement in Spanish. It is a customary cry at bullfights and during flamenco dancing. ■ *n.* **CRY OF OLÉ** a cry or shout of olé [Early 20thC. From Spanish.]

OLE /ólee/ *abbr.* object linking and embedding

ole- *prefix.* = **oleo-** (*used before vowels*)

-ole *suffix.* **1.** a chemical compound containing a five-membered, usually heterocyclic ring ○ *carbazole* **2.** a chemical compound, usually an ether, that does not contain hydroxyl ○ *anisole* [Via French from Latin *oleum* (see OIL)]

o·le·a plural of **oleum**

o·le·ag·i·nous /ōlee ájjənəss/ *adj.* **1. CONTAINING OIL** containing or producing oil **2. LIKE OIL** similar to oil in nature or consistency **3. INGRATIATING** unpleasantly eager to please, charm, or be of service to people ○ *An oleaginous embassy attaché showered me with obviously false compliments.* [Mid-17thC. Directly and via Old French *oleagineux* from Latin *oleaginus* "of an olive tree, oily," from *olea* "olive tree," an alteration of *oliva* (see OLIVE).] —**o·le·ag·i·nous·ly** *adv.* —**o·le·ag·i·nous·ness** *n.*

O·le·an /ōlee án/ city in Cattaraugus County, southwestern New York, situated on the Allegheny River. Population: 16,946 (1990).

o·le·an·der /ōlee ándər/ (*plural* **-ders** *or* **-der**) *n.* a poisonous evergreen shrub native to the Mediterranean region. It has leathery lance-shaped leaves, sweet-smelling white, pink, or purple flowers, and long seedpods. Latin name: *Nerium oleander.* [Mid-16thC. From medieval Latin.]

o·le·as·ter /ōlee ástər/ (*plural* **-ters** *or* **-ter**) *n.* **1. TREE WITH FRUITS LIKE OLIVES** a small tree that is similar to the olive tree. It has silvery leaves and branches, greenish yellow flowers, and fruits that resemble olives. Genus: *Elaeagnus.* **2. FRUIT OF OLEASTER** the fruit of the oleaster, which resembles an olive [14thC. Via Latin from *olea* "olive tree," an alteration of *oliva* (see OLIVE).]

o·lec·ra·non /ō lékrə nòn/ *n.* ANAT the upper end of the ulna bone that extends beyond the joint of the elbow to form the elbow's hard projecting point [Early 18thC. From Greek *ōlekranon*, from *ōlenē* "elbow" + *kranion* "head."]

o·le·fin /ólәfin/ *n.* **1. o·le·fin, o·le·fin fi·ber SYNTHETIC FIBER** any of a group of synthetic fibers that are long chains of polymers **2.** CHEM = **alkene** [Mid-19thC. From French *(gaz) oléfiant*, literally "oil-forming (gas)," from Latin *oleum* "oil" (see OIL).]

o·le·ic /ō leè ik/ *adj.* **1. RELATING TO OIL** derived from or relating to oil **2. RELATING TO OLEIC ACID** derived from or relating to oleic acid

o·le·ic ac·id *n.* a colorless oily liquid found in almost all animal and vegetable fats. An unsaturated fatty acid, it is used to make soap, ointments, cosmetics, and lubricating oils. Formula: $C_{18}H_{34}O_2$.

o·le·in /ólee in/, **o·le·ine** *n.* a yellow oily liquid that occurs naturally in most fats and is mainly used as a textile lubricant

o·le·o /ólee ò/ (*plural* **-os**) *n.* **1. MARGARINE** margarine (*dated*) **2. OLEOGRAPH** an oleograph (*informal*)

oleo- *prefix.* **1.** oil, oily ○ *oleograph* **2.** oleic acid ○ *oleate* [Via French *oléo-* from, ultimately, Latin *oleum* (see OIL)]

o·le·o·graph /ólee ə gràf/ *n.* a colored lithographic print made on canvas with oil colors in order to imitate an oil painting —**o·le·o·graph·ic** /ōlee ə gráffik/ *adj.*

o·le·o·mar·ga·rine /ōli ō márjərən/ *n.* = **margarine** *n.*

o·le·o oil *n.* a yellow fatty substance extracted from beef fat, used in the manufacture of margarine and soap

o·le·o·res·in /ólee ō rézz'n/ *n.* a mixture of a resin and an essential oil, either obtained naturally from plants or produced synthetically

o·le·um /ólee əm/ (*plural* **-a** /-ə/ *or* **-ums**) *n.* a solution of sulfur trioxide in sulfuric acid [Early 20thC. From Latin, "oil" (see OIL).]

ol·fac·tion /ol fákshən/ *n.* **1. SMELLING SENSE** the sense of smell **2. ACT OF SMELLING** the smelling of something [Mid-19thC. Formed from Latin *olfacere* "to smell."]

ol·fac·tom·e·ter /òl fak tómmətər/ *n.* an instrument for measuring the keenness of somebody's sense of smell [Late 19thC. Coined from OLFACTION + -METER.]

ol·fac·to·ry /ol fáktəree/ *adj.* used in smelling or relating to the sense of smell [Mid-17thC. Via assumed Latin *olfactorius* "used for smelling" from, ultimately, *olfacere* "to smell," from *olere* (source of English *redolent*) + *facere* "to do."]

Ol·gas, The /ólgəz/ group of monolithic rocks in southwestern Northern Territory, Australia, 16 mi./26 km west of Ayers Rock. Their highest point is Mount Olga, 1,072m/3,516ft.

ol·i·ba·num /o líbbə nəm/ *n.* = **frankincense** [14thC. Via medieval Latin *olibanum* and Greek *libanos* from Arabic *al-lubān* "storax."]

ol·i·garch /ólli gaàrk/ *n.* a ruler or leader in an oligarchy [Early 17thC. From Greek *oligarkhēs*, from *oligos* "few" + *-arkhēs* "-ARCH."]

ol·i·gar·chy /ólli gaàrkee/ (*plural* **-chies**) *n.* **1. SMALL GOVERNING GROUP** a small group of people who together govern a nation or control an organization, often for their own purposes **2. ENTITY RULED BY OLIGARCHY** a nation governed or an organization controlled by an oligarchy **3. GOVERNMENT BY SMALL GROUP** government or control by a small group of people [Late 15thC. From Greek *oligarkhia*, from *oligos* "few" + *-arkhia* "-archy" (see -ARCH).] —**ol·i·gar·chic** /òlli gaàrkik/ *adj.*

oligo- *prefix.* few ○ *oligophagous* [From Greek *oligos* "small, little, few"]

Ol·i·go·cene /ólli gō seèn, ə líggə-/ *n.* the third geologic period of the Tertiary Era, from 40 to 25 million years ago, when primates first appeared —**Ol·i·go·cene** *adj.*

ol·i·go·clase /ólli gō klàyss, ə líggə-/ *n.* a white, bluish, or reddish yellow feldspar mineral of the plagioclase series, found especially in more acidic igneous and metamorphic rock [Mid-19thC. Formed from OLIGO- + Greek *klasis* "breaking," from *klan* "to break" (see CLASTIC), from its imperfect cleavage.]

o·lig·o·mer /ólligəmər, ə líggə-/ *n.* a polymer consisting of less than five monomer units —**o·lig·o·mer·ic** /òlligə mérrik, ə lìggə-/ *adj.* —**o·lig·o·mer·i·za·tion** /òlligəməri záysh'n, ə lìggəməri-/ *n.*

ol·i·go·nu·cle·o·tide /òlli gō nóoklee ə tīd, ə lìggə-/ *n.* a polymeric chain containing ten nucleotides or fewer

ol·i·goph·a·gous /òlli góffəgəss/ *adj.* feeding on a restricted range of foodstuffs, usually a small number of different plants

ol·i·gop·o·ly /òlli góppəlee/ (*plural* **-lies**) *n.* an economic condition in which there are so few suppliers of a particular product that one supplier's actions can have a significant impact on prices and on its competitors [Late 19thC. Coined from OLIGO- + MONOPOLY.] —**ol·i·gop·o·lis·tic** /òlli góppə lístik/ *adj.*

ol·i·gop·so·ny /òlli gópsənee/ (*plural* **-nies**) *n.* an economic condition in which there are so few buyers for a particular product that one buyer's actions can have a significant impact on prices and the market in general [Mid-20thC. Coined from OLIGO- + MONOPSONY.] —**ol·i·gop·so·nis·tic** /òlli gopsə nístik/ *adj.*

ol·i·go·sac·cha·ride /òlli gō sákə rīd, ə lìggə-/ *n.* a carbohydrate made up of a relatively small number of linked monosaccharides. ◊ **polysaccharide**

ol·i·go·tro·phic /òlli gō tróffik, ə lìggə-/ *adj.* containing relatively little plant life and nutrients in its waters but rich in dissolved oxygen

o·lin·go /ō líng gō/ (*plural* **-gos**) *n.* a small tree-dwelling nocturnal mammal that is native to the tropical forests of South and Central America and looks a little like a slim sleek raccoon. Latin name: *Bassaricyon gabbii.* [Early 20thC. From American Spanish.]

o·li·o /ólee ò/ (*plural* **-os**) *n.* **1. SPICED STEW** a highly spiced stew made from a variety of meats and vegetables and usually including chickpeas **2. ASSORTMENT** a miscellaneous collection of things **3.** ARTS **MISCELLANY OR MEDLEY** something made up of works of various kinds or works by different people, e.g., a literary miscellany or a musical medley [Mid-17thC. An alteration of Spanish *olla* "pot, stew," see OLLA.]

Olive

ol·ive /ólliv/ *n.* **1.** FOOD **GREEN OR BLACK FRUIT** a small oval bitter-tasting fruit with a pit, green when unripe and black when ripe. It is the source of olive oil. **2.** TREES **OLIVE TREE** an evergreen tree native to the Mediterranean that produces the olive. Latin name: *Olea europaea.* (*often used before a noun*) **3.** INDUST **OLIVE WOOD** the wood of the olive tree, used in decorative work **4.** TREES **TREE RESEMBLING OLIVE** a tree or shrub that resembles the olive tree ■ *n., adj.* COLORS = **olive green** [12thC. Via Latin *oliva* from Greek *elaiwa*, a variant of *elaia* "olive, olive oil" (source of English *oil*).]

ol·ive branch *n.* **1. CONCILIATORY GESTURE** a gesture or offer intended to bring about a reconciliation **2. SYMBOL OF PEACE** a branch of an olive tree used as a symbol of peace [From Genesis 8:11]

ol·ive drab *n.* **1.** COLORS **GRAYISH GREEN** a grayish green color **2.** TEXTILES **GREEN CLOTH** cloth dyed in an olive drab color, used especially for military uniforms **3.** MIL **GREEN MILITARY UNIFORM** a military uniform made of olive drab cloth, especially one worn in the United States army —**ol·ive drab** *adj.*

ol·ive green *adj.* of a deep yellowish green color — **ol·ive green** *n.*

o·liv·e·nite /ō lívvə nìt, óllivə-/ *n.* a rare mineral that is often olive green in color. It is a hydrated arsenate of copper. Formula: $Cu_2(AsO_4)OH$. [Early 19thC. From German *Olivenit*, from *Olive* "olive," from its color.]

ol·ive oil *n.* monounsaturated oil with a distinctive flavor extracted from olives, extensively used in salad dressings and for cooking, and in the manufacture of soap and cosmetics. Extra virgin and virgin olive oil, pressed from olives without pits, are the best quality oils.

Ol·i·ver /óllivər/, **King** (1885–1938) U.S. musician. A cornet player, he was a pioneer of early New Orleans jazz, strongly influencing Louis Armstrong. Born **Joseph Oliver**

Ol·ives, Mount of /óllivz, -əvz/ ridge in central Israel, east of Jerusalem, with many biblical associations. It is separated from Jerusalem by the Valley of Kidron. Height: 2,700 ft./823 m.

Laurence Olivier

O·liv·i·er /ə lívvee ày/, **Laurence, 1st Baron Olivier of Brighton** (1907–89) British actor and director. An influential Shakespearean actor, he was a founding director of the British National Theatre (1961–73). Full name **Laurence Kerr Olivier**

ol·i·vine /ólli veen/ *n.* an olive-green form of magnesium-iron silicate that occurs naturally in igneous rocks. It is used in refractories and as a gemstone. Formula: $(MgFe)_2SiO_4$. —**ol·i·vin·ic** /òlli vínnik/ *adj.* —**ol·i·vi·nit·ic** /òllivə níttik/ *adj.*

ol·la /óllə/ *n.* **1.** HOUSEHOLD **EARTHENWARE POT** a large, usually unglazed pot with a spherical body and a wide mouth, used in Latin America and the southwestern United States for storing water and for cooking **2.** FOOD = **olla podrida** [Early 17thC. Via Spanish from, ultimately, Latin *aulla* "pot." Ultimately from an Indo-European word meaning "cooking pot" or "oven," which is also the ancestor of English *oven*.]

ol·la po·dri·da /òllə pə dreedə, àwlyə-, àwyə-/ (*plural* **ol·la po·dri·das** *or* **ol·las po·dri·das**) *n.* **1.** **TRADITIONAL SPANISH AND LATIN AMERICAN STEW** a traditional Spanish and Latin American stew of meat and vegetables, usually containing sausage and chickpeas, and highly seasoned **2.** **ASSORTMENT** a miscellaneous mixture or assortment of things [From Spanish, literally "rotten pot"]

Ol·mec /ól mèk/ (*plural* **-mecs** *or* **-mec**) *n.* **1.** **CENTRAL AMERICAN CIVILIZATION** a Central American civilization that arose around A.D. 1200, before the Mayan civilization. It featured irrigated agriculture, urbanism, and the beginnings of calendar and writing systems. (*often used before a noun*) **2.** **MEMBER OF OLMEC CIVILIZATION** a member of any of the peoples who made up the Olmec civilization [Late 18thC. From Nahuatl *olmecatl*, literally "somebody who lives in the rubber country."]

Olm·sted /ólmstəd/, **Frederick Law** (1822–1903) U.S. landscape architect. His naturalistic works, including New York's Central Park, greatly influenced park design throughout the United States and Canada.

ol·o·gy /óllәjee/ (*plural* **-gies**) *n.* any science or academic field, especially one whose name ends in "-ology" (*informal*) ○ *people studying ologies you've never heard of* [Early 19thC. From the suffix -OLOGY, as in "biology," "psychology," etc.]

o·lo·ro·so /òlə rṓssō/ (*plural* **-sos**) *n.* a golden-colored full-bodied sherry, typically medium-sweet [Late 19thC. Via Spanish, literally "fragrant," from Latin *olere* "to smell."]

O·lym·pi·a /ə límpee ə, ō lím-/ plain in southwestern Greece, in the western Peloponnese, near the Ionian Sea. It was an ancient religious site sacred to Zeus, and the first Olympic Games were held there in 776 B.C.

O·lym·pi·ad /ō límpee àd/ *n.* **1.** **SINGLE OLYMPIC GAMES** a holding of the modern Olympic Games **2.** **FOUR-YEAR PERIOD** a four-year interval between one holding of the Olympic Games and the next, used by the ancient Greeks as a way of calculating dates [14thC. Via Latin from, ultimately, Greek *Olumpia*, where the games were held.]

O·lym·pi·a Heights city in Dade County, Florida. Population: 37,792 (1990).

O·lym·pi·an /ō límpee ən/ *adj.* **1.** **ENORMOUS** extraordinarily great or demanding **2.** **LIKE GREEK DEITY** characteristic of a Greek god or goddess, or resembling one in power, majesty, or beauty (*literary*) **3.** MYTHOL **RELATING TO MOUNT OLYMPUS** relating to Mount Olympus, the home of the gods in Greek mythology **4.** **ALOOF OR SUPERIOR** so superior or grand as to be above everyday events and concerns ○ *his Olympian indifference to petty squabbles* **5.** GEOG **OF OLYMPIA** relating to ancient Olympia ■ *n.* **1.** SPORTS **OLYMPIC ATHLETE** a competitor in the Olympic Games **2.** **SUPERIOR PERSON** somebody who is so superior or grand as to be above everyday events and concerns **3.** MYTHOL **GREEK DEITY** any one of the twelve major Greek gods or goddesses who had their home on Mount Olympus **4.** PEOPLES **SOMEBODY FROM OLYMPIA** an inhabitant of ancient Olympia [15thC. Formed from Greek *olumpios*.]

O·lym·pic /ə límpik, ō-/ *adj.* relating to the Olympic Games

O·lym·pic Games, **O·lym·pic games** *npl.* **1.** **INTERNATIONAL SPORTS CONTEST** a large-scale international sports contest intended to promote international goodwill. It has been held every four years since 1896, except for 1940 and 1944, in different cities around the world. **2.** **ANCIENT GREEK FESTIVAL** an ancient Greek religious festival held every four years at Olympia in honor of Zeus, with athletic, literary, and musical contests involving participants from throughout Greece

O·lym·pic Moun·tains /ə lìmpik-, ō lìm-/ mountain range in northwestern Washington State, on the Olympic Peninsula, mainly in Jefferson and Clallam counties. The highest point is Mount Olympus, 2,428m/7,965.

O·lym·pic Na·tion·al Park national park in northwestern Washington State, in the Olympic Mountains, noted for its temperate rainforest and glaciers. It was established in 1938. Area: 373,387 hectares/ 922,626 acres.

O·lym·pics /ə límpiks, ō-/ *npl.* the modern Olympic Games

O·lym·pus, Mount /ə límpəss, ō lím-/ the highest mountain in Greece, located in the north of the country. In Greek mythology it was believed to be the home of the gods. Height: 9,570 ft./2,917 m.

O·lym·pus Mons /ə lìmpəss mónz/ *n.* large volcano in the northern hemisphere of Mars. It is three times as high as Mount Everest. Height: 88,000 ft./26,800 m.

Om /ōm/, **Aum** *n.* a sacred syllable that is chanted in Hindu and Buddhist prayers and mantras. It is symbolic of creation, destruction, and preservation or of the primary trinities of Hinduism or Buddhism.

O.M. /awm/ *abbr.* Order of Merit

-oma *suffix.* tumor ○ *encephaloma* [Directly and via modern Latin from Greek *-ōma*]

O·ma·ha[1] /ṓmə haa/ (*plural* **-has** *or* **-ha**) *n.* **1.** **MEMBER OF NATIVE NORTH AMERICAN PEOPLE** a member of a Native North American people who have lived in northeastern Nebraska since the 17th century **2.** **NATIVE NORTH AMERICAN LANGUAGE** the Siouan language spoken by the Omaha [Early 19thC. From Omaha *umonhon*, literally "upstream people."] —**O·ma·ha** *adj.*

O·ma·ha[2] /ṓmə haa/ city in eastern Nebraska, on the Missouri River. Population: 345,033 (1994).

O·man /ō maan/ independent state in southwestern Asia, on the southeastern coast of the Arabian Peninsula. Language: Arabic. Currency: Omani rial. Capital: Muscat. Population: 2,251,000 (1996). Area: 82,030 sq. mi./212,457 sq. km. Official name **Sultanate of Oman** —**O·man·i** *adj., n.*

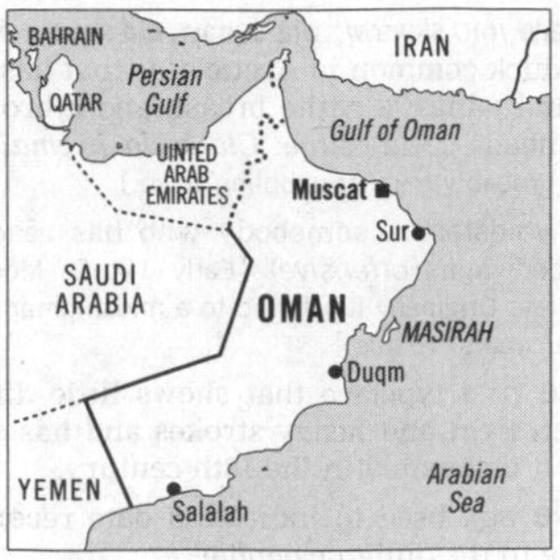

Oman

O·man, Gulf of arm of the Arabian Sea, situated between northern Oman and the southeastern coast of Iran

O·mar Khay·yam /ō maar kī aam/ (1050?–1122) Persian poet, mathematician, and astronomer. His *Rubáiyát* is an extensive collection of four-line stanzas, some of which were translated into English by Edward FitzGerald (1859). Full name **Abu ol-Fath Omar ebn Ebrahim ol-Khayyami**

o·ma·sum /ō máyssəm/ (*plural* **-sa** /-sə/) *n.* the third compartment of the stomach of a cow or other ruminant, situated between the abomasum and the reticulum. The inner surface has folds that break up food particles. [Early 18thC. From Latin, literally "bullock's tripe."]

OMB *abbr.* Office of Management and Budget

om·bre /ómbər/, **om·ber** *n.* a card game, popular in the 18th century, for three players using forty cards, with one player competing against the other two [Mid-17thC. From Spanish *hombre* "man, ombre," from Latin *homo* "man".]

ombro- *prefix.* rainfall, precipitation ○ *ombrogenous* [From Greek *ombros*]

om·buds·man /ómbədzmən, -bŏŏdz-, -bùdz-/ (*plural* **-men** /-mən/) *n.* somebody responsible for investigating and resolving complaints from consumers or other members of the public against a company, institution, or other organization [Mid-20thC. Via Swedish from Old Norse *umboðsmaðr* "manager, deputy," which was formed from *umboð* "commission" + *maðr* "man" (related to English *man*).] —**om·buds·man·ship** *n.*

om·buds·per·son /ómbədz pùrs'n, -bŏŏdz-, -budz-/ (*plural* **-sons**) *n.* somebody responsible for investigating or resolving complaints from consumers or other members of the public against a company, institution, or other organization [Modeled on OMBUDSMAN] —**om·buds·per·son·ship** *n.*

om·buds·wom·an /ómbədz wŏŏmmən, -bŏŏdz-, -budz-/ (*plural* **-en** /-wìmmin/) *n.* **1.** **NONGOVERNMENTAL INVESTIGATOR** a woman responsible for investigating and resolving complaints from consumers or other members of the public against a company, institution, or other organization **2.** **GOVERNMENT OFFICIAL** a woman government official responsible for impartially investigating citizens' complaints against a public authority or institution and trying to bring about a fair settlement [Mid-20thC. Modeled on OMBUDSMAN.] —**om·buds·wom·an·ship** *n.*

Om·dur·man /òmdŏŏr maan, -mán/ city in east central Sudan, on the west bank of the Nile River, opposite Khartoum. Population: 1,267,077 (1993).

-ome *suffix.* mass ○ *trichome* [Via modern Latin from Greek *-ōma*]

o·me·ga /ō máygə/ *n.* **1.** **LAST LETTER OF GREEK ALPHABET** the 24th and final letter of the Greek alphabet, represented in the English alphabet as "o." See table at **alphabet** **2.** **END** the end, or the last thing in a series (*literary*) [Early 16thC. From Greek *ō mega* "great (i.e., long) o," as opposed to "small (short) o," "o mikron."]

o·me·ga hy·per·on *n.* a negatively charged elementary particle with a rest mass 3,272 times that of an electron

o·me·ga mes·on *n.* an extremely short-lived neutral meson with a rest mass 1,532 times that of an electron

o·me·ga mi·nus *n.* = **omega hyperon** [From the symbol for the particle]

om·e·let /ómmlət/, **om·e·lette** *n.* a dish consisting of beaten eggs fried over high heat until set, often served folded in half over a savory filling such as cheese or mushrooms [Early 17thC. Via French from, ultimately, Latin *lamella* "small thin plate," from *lamina* "thin plate" (source of English *laminate*).]

o·men /ómən/ *n.* PROPHETIC SIGN a happening that is regarded as a sign of how somebody or something will fare in the future ■ *vti.* (**o·mened, o·men·ing, o·mens**) INDICATE SOMETHING'S FUTURE to indicate the future course of events relating to something [Late 16thC. From Latin (source of English *abominable*).]

o·men·tum /ō méntəm/ (*plural* **-ta** /-tə/ *or* **-tums**) *n.* any of the folds of the peritoneum, especially the fold that covers the intestines (**greater omentum**) or the fold that connects to the liver (**lesser omentum**) [Mid-16thC. From Latin.]

O·mer /ómər/ *n.* in Judaism, a seven-week period between the second day of Passover and the first day of Shavuoth, observed as a period of mourning, except on one day. Omer is named after the custom of offering an omer or sheaf of barley as a sacrifice in the Temple on the first day of this period.

o·mer·ta /ō mair taá/, **o·mer·tà** *n.* the code requirement alleged to apply to members of the Mafia, requiring that they remain silent about any crimes of which they have knowledge [Late 19thC. From Italian dialect, from Latin *humilitas* "humility," from *humilis*, "humble." The underlying meaning is "subjugation to the good of the society."]

om·i·cron /ómi kròn, ómmi-/ *n.* the fifteenth letter of the Greek alphabet, represented in the English alphabet as "o." See table at **alphabet** [Mid-17thC. From Greek *o mikron* "small (i.e., short) o," as opposed to "great (long) o," "ō mega."]

om·i·nous /ómminəss/ *adj.* suggesting or indicating that something bad is going to happen or be revealed ○ *I think it's rather ominous that they haven't replied to your letter.* [Late 16thC. From Latin *ominosus* "of an omen," from *omen* "omen."] —**om·i·nous·ly** *adv.* —**om·i·nous·ness** *n.*

o·mis·si·ble /ō míssəb'l/ *adj.* able to be left out or left undone

o·mis·sion /ō mísh'n/ *n.* **1.** SOMETHING LEFT OUT something that has been deliberately or accidentally left out or not done ○ *errors and omissions excepted* **2.** ACT OF OMITTING the omitting of something or the state of being omitted ○ *The omission of those three words changed the sense of the whole paragraph.* [14thC. Via Old French from the late Latin stem *omission-*, which was formed from *omittere* "to OMIT."]

o·mit /ō mít/ (**o·mit·ted, o·mit·ting, o·mits**) *vt.* **1.** LEAVE SOMEBODY OR SOMETHING OUT to fail to include or mention somebody or something, either deliberately or accidentally **2.** FAIL TO DO SOMETHING to fail or forget to do something, either deliberately or accidentally [15thC. From Latin *omittere*, which was formed from *ob-* "away" + *mittere* "to send" (source of English *mission*, *message*, and *promise*.]

WORD KEY: SYNONYMS

See Synonyms at ***neglect***.

OMM *abbr.* *Can* Officer of the Order of Military Merit

omni- *prefix.* all ○ *omnicompetent* [From Latin *omnis*. Ultimately from an Indo-European word meaning "abundance, to produce" that is also the ancestor of English *opulent*, *copy*, *optimum*, and *operate*.]

om·ni·bus /ómni bùss, ómnibəss/ *n.* **1.** BOOK COLLECTING SEPARATE WORKS a single book containing several works, usually by the same author, involving the same main character, or on the same subject, previously published separately **2. om·ni·bus, om·ni·bus e·di·tion** *U.K.* SINGLE BROADCAST OF PROGRAMS a single continuous broadcast consisting of several radio or television programs previously broadcast separately, e.g., installments of a serial or soap opera **3.** BUS a bus (*archaic or formal*) ■ *adj.* WITH MANY DIFFERENT THINGS bringing many different things together as a single unit ○ *an omnibus education bill* [Early 19thC. Via French and directly from Latin "for all," which was formed from *omnis* "all" (see OMNI-).]

om·ni·com·pe·tent /ómnee kómpətənt/ *adj.* **1.** WIDELY COMPETENT able to deal successfully with any task or situation **2.** LAW WITH FULL JURISDICTION competent to judge or try any kind of case

om·ni·di·rec·tion·al /ómnee di rékshən'l/ *adj.* able to transmit or receive radio or sound waves in or from any direction

om·ni·di·rec·tion·al ra·di·o range *n.* = **omnirange**

om·nif·i·cent /om níffiss'nt/, **om·nif·ic** /om níffik/ *adj.* with unlimited power to create (*literary*) [Late 17thC. Formed from Latin *omni-* (see OMNI-) + Latin *-ficus* "-fic" (see -FIC) + -ENT.] —**om·nif·i·cence** *n.*

om·nip·o·tence /om níppətəns/ *n.* the possession of complete, unlimited, or universal power and authority [15thC]

om·nip·o·tent /om níppətənt/ *adj.* possessing complete, unlimited, or universal power and authority [13thC. Via Old French from the Latin stem *omnipotent-*, which was formed from *omnis* "all" + *potens*, the present participle of *posse* "to be able."] —**om·nip·o·tent·ly** *adv.*

Om·nip·o·tent *n.* a word sometimes used to refer to God (*literary*) [Early 17thC]

om·ni·pres·ent /ómnee prézz'nt/ *adj.* **1.** ALWAYS PRESENT EVERYWHERE continuously and simultaneously present throughout the whole of creation **2.** FOUND EVERYWHERE present or seemingly present all the time or everywhere [Early 17thC. From medieval Latin *omnipraesent-*, which was formed from *omni-* "omni-" + *praesens* "present."] —**om·ni·pres·ence** *n.*

om·ni·range /ómnee ràynj/ *n.* a very-high-frequency radio navigation network that enables aircraft pilots to choose and fly any bearing relative to a transmitter on the ground

om·nis·ci·ence /om níssee əns/ *n.* knowledge of all things, whether real or apparent knowledge [Early 17thC. From medieval Latin *omniscientia*, literally "knowledge of all," from *scientia* "knowledge" (see SCIENCE).]

om·nis·cient /om níssee ənt/ *adj.* knowing or seeming to know everything [Early 17thC. From medieval Latin *omniscient-*, which was formed from Latin *omni-* "omni-" + *scire* "to know" (see SCIENCE).]

om·ni·um-gath·er·um /ómnee əm gáthərəm/ (*plural* **om·ni·um-gath·er·ums**) *n.* a collection of many different, often unsorted ideas or items (*humorous*) [From Latin *omnium* "of all" + pseudo-Latin *gatherum*, an alteration of "gathering"]

om·ni·vore /ómnə vàwr/ *n.* **1.** ANIMAL THAT EATS ANYTHING an animal that will feed on any kind or many different kinds of food, including both plants and animals **2.** SOMEBODY WITH WIDE INTERESTS somebody who has very wide interests and will read, study, or generally absorb anything that is available [Late 19thC. Via modern Latin *Omnivora* "omnivores," from Latin *omnivorus* (see OMNIVOROUS).]

om·niv·o·rous /om nívvərəss/ *adj.* **1.** EATING MANY FOODS eating any kind or many different kinds of food, including both plants and animals **2.** INTERESTED IN RANGE OF THINGS wide-ranging and often undiscriminating in interests and tastes [Mid-17thC. Formed from Latin *omnivorus*, which in turn was formed from *omni-* (see OMNI-) + *-vorus* "devouring."] —**om·niv·o·rous·ly** *adv.*

om·pha·los /ómfə lòss, ómfələss/ *n.* **1.** ANCIENT GREEK SACRED STONE a conical stone with sacred significance in ancient Greek religion, especially the one at Delphi that was believed to mark the center of the world **2.** FOCAL POINT the central or focal point, around which everything else revolves (*literary*) [Mid-19thC. From Greek, literally "navel."]

OMR *abbr.* optical mark reading

Omsk /áwmsk/ city and capital of Omsk Oblast, southwestern Russia, situated 480 mi./772 km east of Chelyabinsk. Population: 1,160,000 (1995).

on /on/ *prep.* **1.** INDICATES POSITION used to describe something in a position above and in contact with the surface of something else ○ *sitting on the bed* **2.** ATTACHED TO SOMETHING used to indicate attachment to or suspension from a surface or object ○ *a wooden wheel mounted on the wall* **3.** SUPPORTING WEIGHT used to indicate what part of the body is supporting somebody's weight ○ *They sat there leaning on their elbows.* **4.** CARRYING SOMETHING carrying something that is therefore readily accessible ○ *I didn't have any cash on me at the time.* **5.** IN THE VICINITY OF located in a place or situated close to or alongside a place ○ *driving around on dirt roads* ○ *a small town on the coast of Trinidad* **6.** TIME used to indicate when something happens ○ *just before noon on Tuesday* **7.** RELATING TO SOMETHING concerned with or relating to a particular subject, thing, or activity **8.** WHERE SOMETHING IS AVAILABLE used to indicate that specific information is currently available from a machine or instrument ○ *a comedy show on the radio* **9.** AS MEANS OF FUNCTIONING used to indicate the means by which somebody or something subsists or functions ○ *animals that feed on the leaves of the trees* **10.** BY MEANS OF using something as a means of transport ○ *They arrived on horseback.* **11.** DURING engaged in an activity ○ *My assistant is away on a course.* **12.** ACCORDING TO used to indicate that something is grounds for a statement, way of thinking, or action ○ *allowing them to compete on an equal basis* **13.** IN CURRENT RANK OR POSITION used to indicate somebody's current status or position in an organization or institution ○ *My sister in on the committee.* **14.** DIRECTED TOWARD used to indicate that something is directed toward somebody or something ○ *I shone my flashlight on the inscription.* **15.** CHARGED TO used to indicate that the cost of drinks or a meal is charged to a particular person ○ *The drinks are on me.* ■ *adv.* **1.** IN CONTACT WITH SOMETHING in contact with, attached to, or supported by something ○ *an envelope with a stamp on* **2.** INTO STATE OF ATTACHMENT OR SUSPENSION into a condition of being attached to or suspended from something ○ *sewing a button on* **3.** INTO OPERATION into the state of operating or functioning ○ *turned the television on* **4.** WITH CLOTHING wearing clothes or placing clothing over a part of the body ○ *I pulled my tee-shirt on.* **5.** PERSISTENTLY in a continuous or persistent way ○ *decided to stay on in Cambridge* **6.** IN PROGRESS in activity or performance at the present time or at some implied time ○ *putting a play on* **7.** BASEBALL INDICATING RUNNER'S POSITION in baseball, used to indicate whether an offensive player is on the bases ○ *left three runners on* **8.** BETTING WAGERED wagered as a bet ○ *put a bet on* ■ *adj.* **1.** TAKING PLACE happening or being performed at the present time ○ *There's nothing good on tonight.* ○ *I've got a lot on at the moment.* **2.** ARRANGED OR PLANNED indicating that an activity is arranged and will happen ○ *Are we still on for tomorrow?* **3.** FUNCTIONING indicating that a machine or device is functioning or in use ○ *Is the oven on?* [Old English. Ultimately from an Indo-European word that is also the ancestor of English *aloft*.] ◇ **be on** to be performing exceptionally well at something (*slang*) ◇ **be on to somebody** *or* **something** to have information on or be aware of the real nature of somebody or something (*informal*) ◇ **have something on somebody** have unfavorable information about somebody's activities ◇ **on and off** occasionally ◇ **on and on** in a continuous, persistent way ◇ **you're on** used to indicate that somebody is agreeing to do something proposed by somebody else (*informal*)

ON *abbr.* **ON, O.N. 1.** Old Norse **2.** Ontario

-on[1] *suffix.* **1.** subatomic particle ○ *fermion* **2.** fundamental hereditary unit ○ *muton* **3.** unit, quantum ○ *chronon* [From ION]

-on[2] *suffix.* = **-one** [Alteration of -ONE]

on-a·gain, off-a·gain, **on-a·gain-off-a·gain** *adj.* happening or continuing intermittently, and thus difficult to predict (*informal*)

on·a·ger /ónnəjər/ *n.* **1.** WILD ASIAN ASS a wild ass found in northern Iran and bordering areas that is dark yellow with a stripe along its back. Genus: *Equus hemionus.* **2.** ANCIENT WAR MACHINE in former times, a war machine used to throw stones [14thC. Via Latin, from Greek *onagros*, from *onos* "ass" + *agrios* "wild."]

o·nan·ism /ónə nìzzəm/ *n.* **1.** MASTURBATION masturbation (*literary*) **2.** COITUS INTERRUPTUS coitus interruptus [Early 18thC. Named for Onan, a character in the Bible (Genesis 38: 9), who spilled his semen onto the ground rather than impregnate his deceased brother's wife.] —**o·nan·ist** *n.* —**o·nan·is·tic** /ónə nístik/ *adj.*

O·ñat·e /ō naát ay/, **Juan de** (1550?–1630?) Spanish-American explorer. He founded New Mexico (1598) and explored territory in the present United States southwest.

on·board /on báwrd/, **on-board** *adj.* carried or available on an aircraft, ship, or other vehicle or vessel [Mid-20thC. *Board* from BOARD "side of a ship."]

once[1] *adv.* A TIME IN THE PAST used to indicate that something happened or was the case at some time in the past ○ *The place must have been nice once.* ○ *a once comfortable lifestyle* ■ *conj.* AS SOON AS happening when or whenever something else has happened ○ *Once he got started, it was clear we were dealing with an expert.* ■ *adv.* **1.** ARITH MULTIPLIED BY ONE indicating that a number is multiplied by one ○ *once* *three is three* **2.** BY ONE STEP distant by one place or degree ○ *a cousin once removed* ◇ **all at once 1.** happening suddenly, often unexpectedly ○ *I felt really sick all at once.* **2.** happening all at the same time ○ *She could not read the books all at once.* ◇ **at once 1.** immediately ○ *Tell him at once.* **2.** happening all at the same time ○ *It's a lot to take in at once.* ◇ **for once** happening on this particular ocassion, if or but at no other time ○ *For once my strategy worked.* ◇ **once and away 1.** conclusively **2.** occasionally ◇ **once and for all** completely or finally ◇ **once in a while** occasionally ○ *You ought to every once in a while sit back and relax.* ◇ **once or twice** *or* **once and again** a few times, but not often ○ *pausing once and again to listen* ◇ **once upon a time** used at the beginning of fairy tales and children's stories to indicate that something happened a long time ago or in an imaginary world

WORD KEY: CULTURAL NOTE

Once Upon a Time in the West, a spaghetti western directed by Sergio Leone (1968), is often considered the best of his movies and was reputedly Henry Fonda's favorite. He starts as a vicious gunman out to kill a feisty landowner, played by Claudia Cardinale, who is hoping to cash in on the Western expansion of the railroad. Charles Bronson, in the role of a mysterious character know as "Harmonica", is meanwhile hunting down Henry Fonda. Ennio Morricone, who wrote the music for many such movies, composed the atmospheric score.

once-o·ver *n.* a rapid inspection or examination of somebody or something (*informal*) ○ *I'll give the car a quick once-over.*

on·cho·cer·ci·a·sis /òngkō sur kī́ əssiss/ *n.* a disease caused by infestation with worms, especially a tropical disease of humans caused by a parasitic worm and transmitted by blackflies, causing skin nodules, lesions, and blindness [Early 20thC. Formed from modern Latin *Onchocerca*, a genus of worms, which was in turn formed from Greek *ogkos* "barb" + *kerkos* "tail," from their shape.]

onco- *prefix.* tumor ○ *oncolysis* [From Greek *onkos* "mass"]

on·co·gene /óngkə jeen/ *n.* a gene that can cause a cell to become malignant. Oncogenes are thought to be derived from normal cellular counterparts that have been taken up by certain viruses and altered so they malfunction when returned to the cell.

on·co·gen·e·sis /òngkō jénnəssiss/ *n.* the development of a tumor or tumors

on·co·gen·ic /òngkō jénnik/ *adj.* relating to or causing the formation and growth of tumors —**on·co·ge·nic·i·ty** /òngkō jə níssətee/ *n.*

on·col·o·gy /ong kóllajee/ *n.* the branch of medicine that deals with the study and treatment of malignant tumors —**on·co·log·i·cal** /òngkə lójjik'l/ *adj.* —**on·col·o·gist** *n.*

on·col·y·sis /ong kólləssiss/ *n.* the destruction of tumor cells, either spontaneously or, more usually, in response to drug or radiographic treatment

on·com·ing /ón kùmming/ *adj.* APPROACHING heading directly toward somebody or something ■ *n.* ONSET the approach of something that is soon to occur

on·cor·na·vi·rus /ong kàwrnə vīrəss/ *n.* a virus containing single-stranded RNA and capable of causing cancer [Late 20thC. Coined from ONCO- + RNA + VIRUS.]

Michael Ondaatje

On·daat·je /on dáatyə/, **Michael** (*b.* 1943) Sri Lankan-born Canadian writer. Among his many volumes of poetry and fiction is the British Booker Prize-winning *The English Patient* (1992) that was made into a successful movie.

On·des Mar·te·not /àwNd maartə nṓ/ *n.* an electronic musical instrument that can be played either on a keyboard or with a finger slider, producing a characteristic sliding sound. The instrument was favored by the composer Olivier Messiaen. [From French *Ondes (musicales)* "(musical) waves," original name of the instrument, + *(Maurice) Martenot*, 1898–1980, French inventor]

one /wun/ CORE MEANING: a grammatical word indicating a single thing or unit, and not two or more ○ (adj) *just one accident out of thousands* ○ (adj) *a one-legged man* ○ (pron) *Central Newark, once home to several bank branches, now has one.* ○ (pron+of) *Bill got one of his boxing gloves off.*

1. *adj., pron.* UNIQUE distinct from all others ○ *the one exception to this* **2.** *adj., pron.* USED TO DISTINGUISH SOMETHING distinct from all others of its kind in a comparison ○ *from one thought to the next* **3.** *adj.* A NONSPECIFIC TIME relating to an unspecified time in the past or future ○ *one August afternoon* **4.** *adj.* USED FOR EMPHASIS used instead of "a" and "an" to emphasize a following adjective or expression (*informal*) ○ *She's written one great novel!* **5.** *adj.* PARTICULAR introducing the name of somebody who may not be known ○ *This plan, one Whitman concedes, is the most helpful.* **6.** *pron.* TYPICAL INDIVIDUAL used to refer to people in general (*formal*) ○ *One can eat well here.* **7.** *pron.* SOMEBODY OR SOMETHING UNSPECIFIED used to indicate somebody or something not specifically identified (*dated*) ○ *the voice of one crying in the wilderness* **8.** *pron.* PREVIOUSLY MENTIONED used instead of a preceding noun to indicate somebody or something already mentioned ○ *nothing but an old vase, and a cracked one at that* **9.** *pron.* JOKE OR STORY used to refer to a question, joke, or remark ○ *That's a good one!* **10.** *n.* ARITH THE NUMBER 1 the number 1. It is the smallest whole number, designating a single unit, and the first cardinal number. **11.** *n.* SOMETHING WITH VALUE OF 1 something in a numbered series with a value of one ○ *to throw a one* **12.** *n.* DOLLAR BILL used to refer to a one dollar bill (*informal*) **13.** *n.* TIME MEASURE used to indicate the time as one hour after twelve midday or midnight ○ *We'll stop for lunch at one.* **14.** *n.* MUSIC MUSICAL NOTATION the numeral 1 used as the bottom figure in a time signature to indicate that the beat is measured in whole notes [Old English *ān*. Ultimately from an Indo-European word that is also the ancestor of English *union*.] ◇ **as one** doing something at the same time or in the same way ◇ **all one** not important enough to be of any consequence to somebody ◇ **at one** in harmony with somebody or something ◇ **one and all** everyone in a group ◇ **one by one** happening individually in sequence ◇ **one or two** a few people or things ◇ **one and only 1.** unique and without comparison (*often used to introduce a performer on a show*) **2.** the person that somebody loves

WORD KEY: USAGE

one of those people who is or *one of those people who are*? Sense determines whether the verb in a construction of this type should be singular or plural, and in any given case one choice is right and the other wrong. To decide which verb form to choose, start with the *of*. For example, *He is one of those people who is/are always trying to make a good impression* is not equivalent in meaning to *Of those people, he is one who is always trying to make a good impression.* Rather, the idea is *Of those people who are always trying to make a good impression, he is one.* Here the form of *to be* is not governed by *one* but by *people*, and therefore *one of those people who are* is right. In contrast, *He is the only one of those people who is/are worth talking to* surely does not mean *Of those people who are worth talking to, he is the only one.* Here the idea is *Of those people, he is the only one who is worth talking to*, so in this case *one of those people who is* is right.

-one *suffix.* ketone or related compound ○ *quinone* [Origin uncertain: possibly from Greek *-ōnē* "daughter of"]

one-act·er *n.* a play that consists of only one act

O'Neal /ō neél/, **Shaquille** (*b.* 1972) U.S. basketball player. He is considered one of the greatest players of the 1990s.

one an·oth·er *pron.* each of several members of a group to the others ○ *neighbors helping one another*

one-armed ban·dit *n.* a gambling machine that is operated by inserting a coin or token in a slot and pulling down a lever on one side (*informal*)

one-bag·ger *n.* BASEBALL a single (*informal*)

one-base hit *n.* BASEBALL = **single**

one-di·men·sion·al *adj.* **1.** IN ONE DIMENSION existing in or possessing only one dimension **2.** LACKING DEPTH presenting or perceiving only the most superficial aspects of something

O·ne·ga, Lake /ə nyéggə, ō néggə/ the largest lake in Europe, in northwestern Russia, east of Lake Ladoga, to which it is linked by the Svir River. Area: 3,745 sq. mi./9,700 sq. km.

one-horse *adj.* **1.** VERY SMALL AND BORING small, dull, and insignificant ○ *a one-horse town* **2.** HAVING ONE LIKELY WINNER fielding only one candidate or competitor who is likely to win ○ *a one-horse race* **3.** DRAWN BY SINGLE HORSE drawn by only one horse

O·nei·da[1] /ō nī́də/ (*plural* **-da** *or* **-das**) *n.* **1.** MEMBER OF NATIVE NORTH AMERICAN PEOPLE a member of a Native North American people who originally occupied lands in New York State and whose members now live mainly in Ontario, New York State, and Wisconsin. The Oneida were one of the five peoples who formed the Iroquois Confederacy, which later became known as the Six Nations. **2.** ONEIDA LANGUAGE the Iroquoian language of the Oneida people [Mid-17thC. From Oneida *onęyóte*, name of the main Oneida settlement.] —**O·nei·da** *adj.*

O·nei·da[2] /ō nī́də/ city in Madison County, central New York, situated 13 mi./21 km southwest of Rome. Population: 10,850 (1990).

Eugene O'Neill

O'Neill /ō neél/, **Eugene** (1888–1953) U.S. playwright. His realistic psychological dramas include *Mourning Becomes Electra* (1931), *The Iceman Cometh* (1946), and *Long Day's Journey into Night* (1956). He won the Nobel Prize for literature (1936). Full name **Eugene Gladstone O'Neill**

o·nei·ric /ō nī́rik/ *adj.* relating to, experienced in, or similar to a dream or dreams [Mid-19thC. Formed from Greek *oneiros* "dream."]

o·nei·ro·man·cy /ō nī́rə mànsee/ *n.* the practice of divining the future through the interpretation of dreams [Mid-17thC. Coined from Greek *oneiros* "dream" + -MANCY.] —**o·nei·ro·man·cer** *n.*

one-lin·er *n.* a short joke or funny remark in one sentence

one-man *adj.* consisting of, designed for, featuring, or performed by only one person

one-man band *n.* **1.** STREET MUSICIAN WITH SEVERAL INSTRUMENTS a street performer who plays several musical instruments at once usually having them strapped to his or her body **2.** ORGANIZATION OF ONE PERSON a business or organization in which one person does all or most of the work

one·ness /wún nəss/ *n.* **1.** SINGLENESS the quality of being one as opposed to many **2.** UNIQUENESS the quality of being unique **3.** AGREEMENT the state of being united or agreed **4.** SAMENESS the quality of being the same or monotonous [Old English]

one-night stand *n.* **1.** AFFAIR LASTING ONE NIGHT a sexual encounter that lasts for only one night (*informal*) **2.** ONE-NIGHT PERFORMANCE a single performance given at any one place for one night only

one-note *adj.* limited in ability, scope, or range (*informal*) ○ *a one-note writer*

one-off *adj. U.K.* OCCURRING ONCE happening only once, not as part of a series ■ *n. U.K.* SINGLE UNREPEATED EVENT a unique and unrepeatable or unrepeated thing or event

one-on-one *adj.* **1.** PERSONAL involving contact or communication between only two people **2.** SPORTS DIRECTLY AGAINST EACH OTHER playing directly against one other player ○ *a one-on-one drill* ■ *n.* SPORTS DRILL INVOLVING TWO PLAYERS a game or drill in which two players compete only against each other ○ *An hour of one-on-one exhausted me.* —**one-on-one** *adv.*

one-per·son *adj.* consisting of, designed for, featuring, or performed by only one person

one-piece *adj.* NOT SEPARATE consisting of a single, not two or more, components ■ *n.* ONE-PIECE SWIMSUIT a bathing suit consisting of a single piece

on·er /wúnnər/ *n.* a unique or extraordinary person or thing (*informal*)

on·er·ous /ónnərəss, ṓnərəss/ *adj.* **1.** DIFFICULT representing a great burden or much trouble **2.** LAW HAVING DISADVANTAGEOUS OBLIGATIONS involving obligations that are more disadvantageous than advantageous [14thC. Via Old French *onéreux*, from Latin *onerosus*, from *oner-*, stem of *onus* "burden."] —**on·er·ous·ly** *adv.* —**on·er·ous·ness** *n.*

one·self /wun sélf/ *pron.* REFERRING TO THE SUBJECT used as a pronoun, the reflexive form of "one," meaning a person's own self (*formal*) ○ *The aim is to improve oneself and one's ability* ■ (*formal*) **1.** WITHOUT HELP FROM OTHERS used to indicate that something is done without help or interference from others ○ *One should always try and manage things oneself* **2.** NORMAL SELF your usual or normal self ○ *In such situations one never feels oneself* [Mid-16thC. From *one's self*.]

one-shot *adj.* (*informal*) **1.** HAPPENING ONLY ONE TIME happening or doing something only once **2.** EFFECTIVE AT THE FIRST ATTEMPT taking effect after only one application or attempt ○ *a one-shot solution to financial problems* ■ *n.* SOMETHING TRIED ONCE something done or attempted only once (*informal*) ○ *It promised to be the start of a working relationship, but proved to be only a one-shot.*

one-sid·ed *adj.* **1.** UNFAIRLY WEIGHTED dominated by or favoring one side more than the other in a competition **2.** BIASED presenting or considering one side of a matter while ignoring other aspects of it **3.** BIGGER ON ONE SIDE larger, more prominent, or more developed on one side than the other **4.** BEING ON ONE SIDE having or occurring on only one side —**one-sid·ed·ly** *adv.* —**one-sid·ed·ness** *n.*

one-size-fits-all *adj.* **1.** FITTING PEOPLE OF MOST SIZES suitable to be worn by almost everyone **2.** MEDIOCRE suiting a wide variety of tastes, and offensive to none ○ *one-size-fits-all TV shows*

one-step *n.* **1.** DANCE BALLROOM DANCE a ballroom dance similar to the fox trot, in 2/4 time **2.** MUSIC DANCE MUSIC a piece of music written for the one-step ■ *vi.* (**one-stepped, one-step·ping, one-steps**) DANCE DANCE A ONE-STEP to perform the one-step

one-stop *adj. U.K.* offering a wide variety of services or goods in one location so that a customer has to go to only one place ○ *a one-stop home design center*

one-tailed, **one-tail** *adj.* used to describe a statistical test in which all values of the critical region either fall below or exceed a given value, but not both

one·time *adj.* **1.** FORMER having been something or played a particular role at a previous time ○ *the onetime world champion* **2. one·time, one-time** HAPPENING ONLY ONCE done or occurring only once and unlikely to happen again

one-to-one *adj., adv. U.K.* = **one-on-one** ■ *adj.* **1.** MATCHING with one part that corresponds to or matches another **2.** MATH WITH PAIRINGS THAT LEAVE NO REMAINDER used to describe a mathematical set with members such that each member can be paired with one of another set leaving no remainder —**one-to-one** *adv.*

one-track *adj.* focused on, obsessed with, or restricted to only one issue or subject ○ *a one-track mind*

one-two *n. U.K.* **1.** BOXING = **one-two punch 2.** SOCCER PASS TO ANOTHER PLAYER THEN BACK a pass made to another player on the same team who then immediately passes to a new position taken up by the original passer

one-two punch *n.* **1.** BOXING TWO SUCCESSIVE PUNCHES a punch with one hand followed by a punch from the side (**cross**) with the other hand ○ *I gave him a one-two punch.* **2.** QUICK SEQUENTIAL ACTIONS OR EVENTS two actions or events producing an effect because delivered or happening quickly and in sequence ○ *the one-two punch of a hurricane and then cholera*

one-up (**one-upped, one-up·ping, one-ups**) *vt.* to gain an advantage over an opponent (*informal*) ○ *Looks like I've been one-upped again.*

one-up·man·ship /wun úpmən shìp/ *n.* the practice of attempting to outdo or show yourself to be superior to a rival or opponent

one-way *adj.* **1.** TRANSP GOING IN ONE DIRECTION moving or allowing movement in one direction only ○ *a one-way street* **2.** TRANSP NOT ALLOWING A RETURN allowing somebody to travel to a destination but not to return ○ *a one-way ticket* **3.** INVOLVING ONLY ONE OF TWO PEOPLE agreed on, felt, or involving a contribution from one person or party only ○ *a one-way agreement* **4.** ALLOWING VIEWING FROM ONE SIDE made in such a way that it can be looked through from one side but not from the other ○ *one-way glass*

one-way mir·ror *n.* a sheet of glass that is a mirror on one side and can be seen through from the other. Such mirrors are used, e.g., by police to allow witnesses to identify suspects without themselves being seen.

one-wom·an *adj.* consisting of, designed for, featuring, or performed by one woman ○ *a one-woman show*

on·go·ing /ón gò ing/ *adj.* having existed or been in progress for some time and continuing to do so

ONI *abbr.* Office of Naval Intelligence

Onion

on·ion /únnyən/ *n.* **1.** EDIBLE BULB USED AS A VEGETABLE a vegetable in the form of a rounded edible bulb with hard pungent flesh in concentric layers beneath a flaky brown skin **2.** PLANT WITH PUNGENT BULBS an Asian plant of the lily family with greenish-white flowers whose bulb is the onion. Latin name: *Allium cepa.* **3.** PLANT RELATED TO THE ONION any plant related to the onion, e.g., the Welsh onion [12thC. From Latin *unio* "onion," of uncertain origin: perhaps directly or via *unio* "pearl" (from the color and shape), from *unus* "one" (from the "unity" formed by the layers).] —**on·ion·y** *adj.*

on·ion dome *n.* a rounded dome resembling an onion in shape, typical of Russian and Byzantine church architecture

on·ion·skin /únnyən skìn/ *n.* a type of smooth thin translucent paper formerly used especially for making carbon copies

O·nit·sha /ō nícha/ city in Anambra State, southeastern Nigeria, situated about 225 mi./362 km east of Lagos. Population: 336,600 (1992).

-onium *suffix.* a complex cation ○ *diazonium* [From AMMONIUM]

on·i·um i·on /ṓnee əm-/ *n.* CHEM a positively charged ion (**cation**) that is analogous to the ammonium ion. Formula: NH_4^+. ◊ **cation**

on·la·bel *adj.* using or involving the use of a prescription drug to treat a condition for which the drug is approved by the U.S. Food and Drug Administration

on·lay /ón lày/ *vt.* (**-laid, -lay·ing, -lays**) LAY SOMETHING ON A SURFACE to lay something on a surface, especially for decorative reasons, so that it stands in relief ■ *n.* **1.** MED SKIN GRAFT a skin graft surgically transferred to the surface of an organ or other part of the body **2.** DENT INLAY IN A TOOTH an inlay fixed to the biting surface of a tooth [15thC. From ON + LAY (verb).]

on·line, **on-line** *adj., adv.* COMPUT CONNECTED VIA A COMPUTER attached to or available through a central computer or computer network. ◊ **off-line** ■ *adj.* **1.** CHEM ENG DIRECTLY CONNECTED TO A MEASURABLE PROCESS used to describe an instrument or sensor that is connected directly to a process being measured, thus obviating the need to take samples for analysis in a laboratory or elsewhere **2.** ONGOING currently going on or being done ■ *adv.* WHILE CONNECTED TO A COMPUTER while under the control of a computer or connected to a computer network

on·lin·er /ón lìnər/ *n.* a user or a supplier of online computer services

on·load /ón lòd/ (**-load·ed, -load·ing, -loads**) *vti.* to load freight onto a vehicle

on·look·er /ón lòokər/ *n.* somebody who watches an event without participating in it —**on·look·ing** *adj.*

on·ly /ṓnlee/ CORE MEANING: an adverb used to indicate the one thing or person that solely or exclusively happens or is involved in a situation ○ *facilities for club members only* ○ *I will act only in the best interests of our country.* ○ *The regulations apply only to new firms.*

1. *adv.* INDICATING A CONDITION used to indicate the condition that exists for something to happen or be true ○ *I'll go to the party, but only if you come with me.* **2.** *adv.* MERELY merely the situation, level, or amount stated ○ *I could only stand and look.* ○ *That's only part of the picture.* **3.** *adv.* NO MORE AND NO LESS just the particular amount specified ○ *There are only 3.3 people at work for every person retired.* **4.** *adv.* AS RECENTLY AS considered as happening very recently ○ *only last March* **5.** *adv.* INDICATING AN EVENT HAPPENING IMMEDIATELY AFTER used to introduce a surprising or unpleasant event that happens immediately after the one mentioned ○ *We rushed the cat to the vet, only to find there was nothing wrong with it.* **6.** *adj.* THE SINGLE PERSON OR THING used to indicate the single person or thing involved in a situation ○ *the only Democratic candidate* ○ *the only barrier between himself and the job* **7.** *adj.* WITH NO SIBLINGS with no brothers or sisters ○ *an only child.* **8.** *adv. Ireland* EMPHASIZING used to emphasize a statement ○ *It was only terrible.* **9.** *conj.* BUT but or except ○ *It's the same product, only better.* [Old English *ānlic*, from *ān* "one" (see ONE)] ◇ **only too** used to emphasize the extent to which something is true ○ *Scenes like this are getting only too familiar.*

Yoko Ono and John Lennon

On·o, Yoko (*b.* 1933) Japanese-born U.S. artist. She was known for her avant-garde performance art, which after her marriage to John Lennon in 1969 included protests against the Vietnam War.

on·o·mas·i·ol·o·gy /ònnə mayssee óllәjee/ *n.* **1.** BRANCH OF SEMANTICS the branch of linguistics that studies how meaning is expressed **2.** = **onomastics** *n.* 1 [Early 20thC. Coined from Greek *onomasia* "name" + -LOGY.]

on·o·mas·tic /ònnə mástik/ *adj.* relating to, connected with, or explaining names [Late 16thC. Via French, from Greek *onomastikos*, from, ultimately, *onoma* "name" (source also of English *name*).]

on·o·mas·tics /ònnə mástiks/ *n.* (*takes a singular verb*) **1.** STUDY OF PROPER NAMES the study of proper names, their origins, and their formation **2.** SYSTEM OF NAMES IN A SPECIALIZED FIELD the system underlying the creation and use of proper names in a specialized field

on·o·mat·o·poe·ia /ònnə mattə péé ə/ *n.* the formation or use of words that imitate the sound associated with the thing or action in question e.g., "hiss" and "buzz" [Late 16thC. Via late Latin, from Greek *onomatopoiia* "making of words," from, ultimately, *onoma* "name" + *poiein* "to make" (see POEM).]

on·o·mat·o·poe·ic /ònnə mattə pée ik/ *adj.* imitative of the sound associated with the thing or action denoted by a particular word —**on·o·mat·o·poe·i·cal·ly** *adv.*

On·on·da·ga /ònnən dáwgə, -dáagə, -dáygə/ (*plural* **-ga** *or* **-gas**) *n.* **1.** PEOPLES **MEMBER OF A NATIVE AMERICAN PEOPLE** a member of a Native North American people that originally occupied lands in central New York State and whose members mainly continue to live there as well as in Ontario. The Onondaga were one of the five peoples who formed the Iroquois Confederacy, which later became known as the Six Nations. **2.** LANG **NATIVE AMERICAN LANGUAGE** an Iroquoian language spoken in central areas of New York State and in parts of Ontario, belonging to the Hokan-Siouan languages [Late 17thC. From Onondaga *onǫ́tą?ke*, the name of the main Onondaga settlement.] —**On·on·da·ga** *adj.*

On·on·da·ga, Lake lake in Onondaga County, central New York

on·rush /ón rùsh/ *n.* a forward rush or push ○ *the onrush of enemy soldiers* ○ *the onrush of events* —**on·rush·ing** *adj.*

on-screen *adj., adv.* appearing on the screen in a television program or film and therefore visible to the audience ○ *Their private life was very different from their on-screen relationship.*

on·set /ón sèt/ *n.* **1. START** the beginning of something, especially of something difficult or unpleasant ○ *the onset of winter* **2.** MIL **INITIAL MILITARY ATTACK** an initial attack or assault in battle [Early 16thC. Formed from SET (noun).]

on·shore /on sháwr/ *adj.* **ON LAND** on land as opposed to at sea ○ *onshore drilling* ■ *adj., adv.* METEOROL **IN THE DIRECTION OF LAND** toward land from the sea ○ *onshore breeze* —**on·shore** *adv.*

on·side /on sīd/ *adj., adv.* in a position that is allowed within the rules of the game, e.g., in soccer or hockey

on·side kick *n.* FOOTBALL a kickoff used when the kicking team wants to recover the ball and keep the other team from having possession of it. After the ball has traveled ten yards, either team may recover it.

on-site *adj., adv.* taking place or provided at the location where work or some other activity is being carried out

on·slaught /ón slàwt/ *n.* **1. OVERWHELMING ASSAULT OR FORCE** a powerful attack or force that overwhelms somebody or something **2. VERY LARGE AMOUNT OF SOMETHING** a very large quantity of people or things that is difficult to deal with or process ○ *faced with an onslaught of junk mail* [Early 17thC. Via Dutch *aanslag*, from Middle Dutch *aenslach*, literally "blow on," from *slach* "blow." Influenced by obsolete English *slaught* "slaughter."]

on·stage /on stáyj/ *adj., adv.* performing, happening, or existing on the stage as opposed to in the wings, backstage, or somewhere not visible to the audience

on-stream *adj., adv.* in or into production or operation ○ *when the new system comes on-stream*

Ont., **ON, O.N.** *abbr.* Ontario

ont- *prefix.* = **onto-** (*used before vowels*)

-ont *suffix.* cell, organism ○ *schizont* [From Greek *ont-*, literally "being" (see ONTO-)]

Ontario

On·tar·i·o Canadian province situated between the Great Lakes and Hudson Bay. Capital: Toronto. Population: 10,753,573 (1996). Area: 412,579 sq. mi./1,068,580 sq. km. —**On·tar·i·an** *n., adj.*

On·tar·i·o, Lake lake in North America, the easternmost and smallest of the Great Lakes, straddling the U.S.-Canadian border and bounded by New York and Ontario Province. Its outflow is the St. Lawrence River. Area: 7,340 sq. mi./19,011 sq. km.

on-the-job *adj.* provided or obtained while working at a job ○ *on-the-job training*

on·tic /óntik/ *adj.* relating to real existence [Mid-20thC. Formed from the Greek stem *ont-* "being" (see ONTO-).]

on·to /ón tòo, óntə/ CORE MEANING: a preposition indicating that somebody or something is located on something, or moves toward it so as to be on it ○ *I splashed water onto my face.* ○ *hop onto a bus* ○ *shine a flashlight onto the wall* ○ *loading the data onto a disk* ○ *come onto the market*

prep. **1. MAKING A DISCOVERY** making or about to make a discovery, often about something secret or illegal ○ *I'm really onto something big here.* ○ *The police were onto them.* **2. IN CONTACT** in contact with a person or organization ○ *Get onto the suppliers.* [Early 18thC. Formed from ON + TO.]

onto- *prefix.* **1.** being, existence ○ *ontology* **2.** organism ○ *ontogeny* [From Greek *ont-*, the present participle stem of *einai* "to be." Ultimately from an Indo-European base that is also the ancestor of English *am, is,* and *entity.*]

on·tog·e·ny /on tójjənee/, **on·to·gen·e·sis** /òntə jénnəsiss/ *n.* the development of an individual from a fertilized ovum to maturity, as contrasted with the development of a group or species (**phylogeny**) —**on·to·gen·ic** /òntə jénnik/ *adj.* —**on·to·gen·i·cal·ly** /-jénni kalee/ *adv.*

on·to·log·i·cal ar·gu·ment /òntə lójjik'l-/ *n.* an argument made by St. Anselm and others to prove the existence of God by pointing to God's essence as a perfect, necessary being.

on·tol·o·gy /on tólləjee/ (*plural* **-gies**) *n.* **1.** PHILOS **STUDY OF EXISTENCE** the most general branch of metaphysics, concerned with the nature of being **2. THEORY OF EXISTENCE** a particular theory of being [Early 18thC. From modern Latin, literally "study of being," from the Greek stem *ont-* "being" (see ONT-).] —**on·to·log·i·cal** /òntə lójjik'l/ *adj.* —**on·to·log·i·cal·ly** /-lójji kəlee/ *adv.* —**on·tol·o·gist** /on tólləjist/ *n.*

o·nus /ónəss/ *n.* **1. BURDEN** a duty or responsibility ○ *The onus is on her to make the first move.* **2. BLAME** the blame for something ○ *He'll always bear the onus of having caused the accident.* **3.** LAW **BURDEN OF PROOF OR PROCEEDING** the burden of proof or responsibility for acting in a legal proceeding [Mid-17thC. From Latin, "burden, load" (source of English *onerous*).]

on·ward /ónwərd/ *adj.* **MOVING FORWARD** directed or moving forward in space, time, or development ○ *the great onward march of organization and life* ■ *adv.* **on·ward, on·wards** moving toward a point or position ahead in space, time, or development. U.K. = **onwards**

on·y·chol·y·sis /ònni kóllississ/ *n.* the separation of all or part of a fingernail or thumbnail from its bed, associated with psoriasis or a fungal skin condition [From modern Latin, from Greek *onukh-*, stem of *onux* "nail, claw" (source of English *onyx*)]

on·y·choph·o·ran /ònni kóffərən/ *n.* a small invertebrate without jointed limbs, considered intermediate between annelid worms and arthropods. Order: Onychophora. [Late 19thC. Formed from modern Latin *Onychophora*, ultimately from the Greek stem *onukh-* "claw" + *-phoros* "bearing," from the curved claws.]

-onym *suffix.* name, word ○ *pseudonym* [From Greek *onuma* (see ONOMASTIC)]

on·yx /ónniks/ *n.* a fine-grained variety of the mineral chalcedony, used as a gemstone. It has alternating parallel layers of different colors, including white, brown, and black. Cameo brooches are sometimes carved from this stone with the white layer standing out in relief against a darker background. [13thC. Directly and via Old French and Latin from Greek *onux* "fingernail, claw." From the color of some types of the stone.]

oo- *prefix.* ovum, egg ○ *oospore* [From Greek *ōion*. Ultimately from the Indo-European word for "egg" that is also the ancestor of English *egg, oval, caviar,* and *cockney.*]

o·o·cyst /ó ə sìst/ *n.* ZOOL the fertilized gamete of certain parasitic organisms (**sporozoans**) that is enclosed in a thick wall

o·o·cyte /ó ə sìt/ *n.* BIOL a cell that develops into a female reproductive cell (**ovum**)

O.O.D. *abbr.* NAVY officer of the deck

O'O·dham /ó ə daam/ *n.* PEOPLES, LANG = **Papago**

oo·dles /óod'lz/ *npl.* a large amount or number of something (*informal*) ○ *She has oodles of friends.* [Mid-19thC. Origin uncertain: perhaps from HUDDLE "mass of things crowded together."]

o·o·ga·mete /ó ə gá meet, -gə méet/ *n.* BIOL a female reproductive cell (**ovum**)

o·o·gen·e·sis /ó ə jénnəsiss/ *n.* BIOL the formation and development of an ovum —**o·o·ge·net·ic** /ó əjə néttik/ *adj.*

o·o·go·ni·um /ó ə gónee əm/ (*plural* **-a** /-nee ə/ *or* **-ums**) *n.* **1. CELL IN AN OVARY** a cell in the ovary that develops into an an oocyte **2. ALGAL SEX ORGAN** the female sex organ of some algae and fungi that contains oospheres [Mid-19thC. Formed from OO- + Greek *gonos* "generation, seed."] —**o·o·go·ni·al** *adj.*

ooh /oo/ *interj.* **USED TO EXPRESS SURPRISE** used as an exclamation of surprise, excitement, pleasure, or pain (*informal*) ■ *vi.* (**oohed, ooh·ing, oohs**) **EXPRESS SURPRISE OR AWE** to exclaim in surprise, excitement, pleasure, or pain, especially on first encountering something ○ *When they went into the royal chambers, you could hear them oohing and aahing.* ■ *n.* **EXCLAMATION OF SURPRISE** an exclamation of surprise, excitement, pleasure, or pain [Early 20thC. Natural exclamation.] ◇ **ooh la la** used to show pleasant surprise or approval, or, humorously, to suggest that something is scandalous

o·o·lite /ó ə lìt/ *n.* **1. FORM OF SEDIMENTARY ROCK** a sedimentary rock, often shale, clay, or sandstone, that is made up of small spherical grains consisting of concentric layers **2. ROUND GRAIN OF ROCK** any of the small spherical grains that make up oolite [Early 19thC. Via French *oölithe*, from modern Latin *oolites*, from Greek *ōion* "egg" + *lithos* "stone."] —**o·o·lit·ic** /ó ə líttik/ *adj.*

oo·long /óo làwng/ *n.* a type of dark Chinese tea that is partly fermented before being dried (*often used before a noun*) ○ *oolong tea* [Mid-19thC. From Chinese (Mandarin) *wulong*, from *wu* "black" + *long* "dragon."]

oom·pah /óom paa, óom-/, **oom·pah-pah** /óom paa paa, óom-/ *n.* a representation of the sound made by a bass brass instrument, considered typical of some kinds of band music (*often used before a noun*) ○ *an oompah band* [Late 19thC. An imitation of the sound.]

oomph /óomf/ *n.* **1. ENERGY** energy or enthusiasm ○ *Put some oomph into it!* **2. SEXUAL ATTRACTIVENESS** strong or obvious sexual attractiveness (*slang*) [Mid-20thC. Origin uncertain: perhaps expressive of exertion.]

OOP *abbr.* COMPUT object-oriented programming

o·o·pho·rec·to·my /ó əfə réktəmee/ (*plural* **-mies**) *n.* = **ovariectomy** [Late 19thC. Formed from modern Latin *oophoron* "ovary," literally "egg-bearer," ultimately from Greek *ōion* "egg."]

o·o·pho·ri·tis /ó əfə rítiss/ *n.* ovary inflammation [Late 19thC. Formed from modern Latin *oophoron* "ovary" (see OOPHORECTOMY).]

oops /óops, oops/ *interj.* used as an exclamation when you drop something, bump into somebody, or do something in a clumsy or awkward manner (*informal*) ○ *She dropped the entire tray? Oops!* [Mid-20thC. Natural exclamation.]

Oort cloud /áwrt-/ *n.* a huge, roughly spherical, orbiting collection of comets thought to exist at the edge of the solar system [Late 20thC. Named for Jan Hendrix *Oort* (1900–92), the Dutch astronomer who postulated its existence.]

o·o·sphere /ó ə sfeer/ *n.* BIOL an unfertilized female reproductive cell in algae and fungi [Late 19thC. Coined from OO- + SPHERE.]

o·o·spore /ó ə spàwr/ *n.* BIOL a fertilized female reproductive cell in algae and fungi [Mid-19thC. Coined from OO- + SPORE.] —**o·o·spor·ic** /ó ə spáwrik/ *adj.* —**o·os·po·rous** /ō óspərəss, ó ə spáwrəss/ *adj.*

o·o·tid /ó ə tìd/ *n.* BIOL the stage in the development of an egg cell that becomes the mature ovum immediately prior to fertilization. It is a haploid cell formed by division of the secondary oocyte. [Early 20thC. Formed from OO-, modeled on SPERMATID.]

ooze[1] /ooz/ *v.* (**oozed, ooz·ing, ooz·es**) **1.** *vti.* **FLOW OR LEAK SLOWLY** to exude a liquid substance slowly and in small quantities, or to flow in this way ○ *Resin* *oozed from the trunk.* **2.** *vti.* **OVERFLOW WITH SOME QUALITY OR EMOTION** to possess a quality in abundance or express an emotion intensely, or to be expressed in an intense or overpowering way ○ *oozing charm and self-confidence* **3.** *vi.* **MOVE SLOWLY BUT STEADILY** to move slowly but steadily forward or outward ○ *The huge crowd oozed through the streets.* **4.** *vi.* **EBB** to disappear or decline slowly and gradually ■ *n.* **1. VERY SLOW FLOW** a slow and gradual leakage or flow **2. TANNING SOLUTION** an infusion used in tanning, made from oak bark and other plant materials [Old English *wōs* "juice, sap"]

ooze[2] /ooz/ *n.* **1. SLUDGE** thick mud or slime that is found at the bottom of a river or lake **2. SWAMP OR MARSH** a soft or muddy area such as a swamp or marsh **3.** MARINE BIOL **SEDIMENT ON THE OCEAN FLOOR** a layer of muddy sediment on the seafloor consisting mainly of the remains of microscopic organisms such as plankton [Old English *wāse*]

ooze leath·er *n.* a soft leather with a velvety finish [*Ooze* from OOZE[1] in the sense "tanning solution"]

ooz·y[1] /oózee/ **(-i·er, -i·est)** *adj.* leaking moisture [Old English; formed from OOZE[1]]

ooz·y[2] /oózee/ **(-i·er, -i·est)** *adj.* wet and muddy [Old English; formed from OOZE[2]]

op /op/ (*plural* **ops**) *n.* a surgical operation (*informal*)

OP *abbr.* **1.** observation post **2.** out of print

op. *abbr.* **1. op., Op.** opus **2. op., Op.** operation **3.** opposite **4.** optical **5.** opera

o·pac·i·fy /ō pássə fī/ **(-fies, -fied, -fy·ing, -fies)** *vti.* to become opaque or turn or make something opaque [Early 20thC. Formed from OPACITY.] —**o·pac·i·fi·er** *n.*

o·pac·i·ty /ō pássətee/ (*plural* **-ties**) *n.* **1. BEING OPAQUE** the quality, state, or degree of being opaque **2. OBSCURITY** the quality of being obscure in meaning **3.** PHOTOGRAPHY, PHYS **ABILITY OF MATERIAL TO STOP LIGHT** the capacity of a material such as photographic film to stop light, expressed as a comparison between light striking the material and light transmitted **4.** PHILOS **PROPOSITIONS NOT ADHERING TO LEIBNITZ'S LAW** propositions containing modal notions such as necessity or belief in which principles of logic such as Leibnitz's law do not obtain [Mid-16thC. Via French, from, ultimately, Latin *opacus* "shaded, dark" (which also produced English *opaque*).]

o·pah /ōpə/ *n.* a brightly colored marine fish that can be up to 6 ft./1.8 m long. Latin name: *Lampris regius.* [Mid-18thC. From a West African language.]

o·pal /ōpəl/ *n.* **1. NONCRYSTALLINE SILICA** a noncrystalline variety of silica that can be of almost any color and contains varying amounts of water **2. GEMSTONE** a piece of one of the non-crystalline varieties of opal, used as a gemstone [Late 16thC. From French *opale* or Latin *opalus*, of uncertain origin: probably ultimately from Sanskrit *upala* "precious stone," from, ultimately, *upa* "below" (source of English *Upanishad*.)]

o·pal·esce /ōpə léss/ **(-esced, -esc·ing, -esc·es)** *vi.* to display shimmering milky colors (*refers to opals*) [Early 19thC. Coined from OPAL + Latin *-esce* "assuming a certain state."]

o·pal·es·cent /ōpə léss'nt/ *adj.* showing or possessing shimmering milky colors —**o·pal·es·cence** *n.*

o·pal·eye /ōpəl ī/ (*plural* **-eyes** *or* **-eye**) *n.* a common greenish omnivorous marine fish of the Californian and Mexican coast that has two white spots on its back. Latin name: *Girella nigricans.* [From the opalescent appearence of its eyes]

o·pal·ine /ōpə līn, -leen/ *adj.* = **opalescent** ■ *n.* CRAFT **OPAL GLASS** a semitranslucent glass made by adding fluorides

o·paque /ō páyk/ *adj.* **1. NOT TRANSPARENT OR TRANSLUCENT** impervious to light, so that images cannot be seen through it **2. NOT SHINY** dull and without luster **3. HARD TO UNDERSTAND** obscure and unintelligible in meaning **4.** PHYS **IMPENETRABLE BY RADIATION** impenetrable by a specified form of radiation ■ *n.* **MATERIAL THROUGH WHICH LIGHT CANNOT PASS** something opaque, especially a photographic pigment [15thC. Directly or via French, from Latin *opacus* "shaded, dark."] —**o·paque·ly** *adv.* —**o·paque·ness** *n.*

o·paque pro·jec·tor *n.* an optical device that uses reflected light to project an enlarged image of an opaque object, e.g., a photograph or printed page, onto a screen

op art, Op Art, Op *n.* a 20th-century school of abstract art that uses geometric patterns and color to create the illusion of movement (*often used before a noun*) ○ *op art designs* [Shortening of OPTICAL ART, modeled on POP ART] —**op art·ist** *n.*

op. cit. *abbr.* in the text or texts quoted (*used in footnotes to refer to a source just mentioned*) [Shortening of Latin *opus citatum* or *opere citato*]

ope /ōp/ *adj.* **OPEN** open (*archaic or literary*) ■ *vti.* **(oped, op·ing, opes) TO OPEN** to open, or open something (*archaic or literary*) [From OPEN]

OPEC /ō pèk/ *n.* an organization of countries that share the same policies regarding the sale of petroleum. The members are Algeria, Gabon, Indonesia, Iran, Iraq, Kuwait, Libya, Nigeria, Qatar, Saudi Arabia, the United Arab Emirates, and Venezuela. Full form **Organization of Petroleum Exporting Countries**

op-ed /op éd/ *adj.* appearing on, writing for, or relating to the page opposite the editorial page of a newspaper ○ *the op-ed page* [Shortening of *opposite editorial (page)*]

Op·e·lou·sas /óppə lóossəss/ city in south central Louisiana, southeast of Alexandria and northeast of Lafayette. Population: 19,117 (1996).

o·pen /ōpən/ *adj.* **1. NOT CLOSED OR LOCKED** allowing people or things to pass through freely ○ *an open window* **2. ALLOWING ACCESS TO THE INSIDE** with the lid, cork, or other device removed or in a position that allows access to the inside ○ *an open box* **3. NOT SEALED** not sealed, fastened, or wrapped ○ *an open envelope* **4. APART OR WIDE** with a part of the body widened or apart ○ *The kitten's eyes were open.* **5. UNFOLDED OR APART** having been unfolded, extended, or left apart ○ *A newspaper lay open on the table.* **6. FRANK AND HONEST** not trying to hide anything or deceive anyone ○ *open hostility* **7. PUBLIC** conducted in a public manner ○ *open hearings* **8. RECEPTIVE** ready and willing to accept or listen to something, e.g., new ideas or suggestions ○ *I'm always open to suggestions.* **9. VULNERABLE** in a position where blame, criticism, or attack are likely ○ *That remark left him open to criticism.* **10. NOT ENCLOSED** having no boundaries or enclosures ○ *open countryside* **11. NOT COVERED** having no cover or roof ○ *an open fire* **12. AVAILABLE TO DO BUSINESS** ready for business and available for use by customers or clients ○ *The gas station is still open.* **13. FREELY ACCESSIBLE** accessible to all, with no restrictions on entry, membership, or acceptance ○ *an open meeting* **14.** POL **AVAILABLE TO ALL REGISTERED VOTERS** allowing all voters to participate, regardless of party affiliation ○ *an open primary* **15. ACCESSIBLE TO A PARTICULAR GROUP** accessible to a particular group of interested people ○ *This competition is open to all students under the age of 18.* **16. VACANT** ready for or available to applicants ○ *The vacancy is no longer open.* **17.** UTIL **TURNED ON** switched on and ready to use ○ *an open microphone* **18. NOT PREDETERMINED OR DECIDED** remaining undecided or unresolved ○ *I'm trying to keep my options open.* **19. ALERT** in a state of focused attention and alertness ○ *Keep your eyes and ears open.* **20. WITH NO TIME RESTRICTION** with no restrictions on the period of use ○ *an open ticket* **21. GENEROUS** very free or generous, especially with money ○ *She gave to charity with an open hand.* **22. NOT HAVING LEGAL RESTRICTIONS** not having restrictions that limit activities such as gambling or drinking ○ *an open town* **23.** SPORTS **UNGUARDED** unprotected by the assigned player ○ *He left the goal wide open.* **24. UNPROTECTED BY SKIN** unprotected and exposed, with the skin cut, torn, or missing ○ *an open wound* **25.** MED **NOT BLOCKED** free from blockage and therefore allowing unobstructed passage **26.** TEXTILES **HAVING GAPS** with small gaps or intervals between the stitches or threads ○ *an open weave* **27.** NAUT **FREE FROM ICE OR OTHER HAZARDS** not covered by ice or containing objects dangerous to shipping ○ *open water* **28.** MUSIC **NOT CLOSED OR MUTED** not closed off at the end, stopped by a finger, or covered with a mute ○ *an open organ pipe* **29.** METEOROL **FROSTLESS** mild and free of frost **30.** MIL **KNOWN TO BE UNDEFENDED** publicly declared not to be garrisoned or defended in wartime ○ *an open city* **31.** FIN **AVAILABLE WITHOUT LIMITATIONS** freely available without restrictions ○ *open credit* **32.** FIN **CURRENTLY ACTIVE** active and with transactions being made ○ *an open bank account* **33.** PRINTING **HAVING UNUSUALLY WIDE SPACES** with wide spacing between printed lines **34.** PHON **SAID WITH THE LIPS APART** pronounced with the tongue low in the mouth and the lips well apart ○ *an open vowel* **35.** PHON **ENDING IN A VOWEL** used to describe a syllable that ends in a vowel **36.** GRAM **HAVING SEPARATE ELEMENTS** formed by two or more words that are spelled separately and without hyphenation ○ *an open compound* **37.** CHESS **WITHOUT PAWNS** not having pawns as part of a file **38.** SPORTS **HAVING THE FRONT FOOT BACK** having the front foot farther from the line along which the ball is to be hit than the back foot ○ *Adopting an open stance, he began hitting the ball to the opposite field.* **39.** FOOTBALL **BEYOND THE LINE OF SCRIMMAGE** used to describe the part of the field beyond the line of scrimmage, where a ball carrier encounters fewer potential tacklers **40.** MATH **CONTAINING NO ENDPOINTS** used to describe a mathematical interval that contains neither of a set's endpoints **41.** MATH **REFERRING TO SET QUALITY** used to describe a mathematical set that has at least one neighborhood of every point within the set **42.** MATH **SERVING AS A COMPLEMENT TO A CLOSED SET** used to describe a mathematical set that is in a complementary relation to a closed set ■ *v.* **(o·pened, o·pen·ing, o·pens) 1.** *vti.* **UNFASTEN FROM A LOCKED OR CLOSED POSITION** to change position or move so as to allow access, or to change the position of or move something such as a door or window in order to allow access **2.** *vt.* **UNSEAL OR UNFASTEN SOMETHING** to remove or unseal the lid, cork, or other device that keeps something such as a container closed **3.** *vt.* **UNWRAP SOMETHING** to reveal the contents of something, e.g., by removing its wrapping ○ *I opened the package.* **4.** *vti.* **UNFOLD TO SHOW INSIDE** to unfold something or spread it apart so that the inner part is revealed ○ *Open your books at page 75.* **5.** *vti.* **PART THE LIPS OR EYELIDS** to move apart, or move the lips or eyelids apart **6.** *vti.* COMM **START TRADING** to start selling, trading, or doing business or to allow clients or customers access in order to buy, trade, or do business **7.** *vti.* **GET UNDER WAY** to start something formally ○ *She opened the meeting with a speech about the environment.* **8.** *vt.* BANKING **START AN ACCOUNT** to start an active banking or investment account **9.** *vt.* **DECLARE TO BE IN OPERATION OR SESSION** to make an official and usually public declaration that something is now ready for use or in session ○ *The sports center was officially opened by the mayor.* **10.** *vi.* **BEGIN SHOWING TO THE PUBLIC** to start being shown to or performed for the general public for the first time ○ *The show opens on Friday.* **11.** *vt.* **BECOME ACCESSIBLE TO THE PUBLIC** to be visited by the public, or become accessible to the public ○ *The house opens to the public in August.* **12.** *vt.* **REMOVE OBSTRUCTIONS** to allow people free access when formerly this was denied or obstructed ○ *The country had finally opened its borders to the West.* **13.** *vi.* **GIVE ACCESS TO A PLACE** to provide access directly to another place (*refers to part of a building*) ○ *The bedroom opened onto a large living room.* **14.** *vti.* **BE READY FOR NEW IDEAS** to become or make somebody ready to accept new ideas ○ *Try opening your mind a bit.* **15.** *vi.* **BEGIN TO RAIN** to produce a downpour ○ *The heavens opened.* **16.** *vi.* **UNFOLD** to open out fully (*refers to flowers or leaves*) ○ *The daffodils will open soon.* **17.** *vt.* MED **EMPTY BOWELS** to cause the bowels to evacuate **18.** *vi.* STOCK EXCH **START TRADING AT A PARTICULAR VALUE** to have a particular value at the start of a day's trading on a stock exchange ■ *n.* **1.** SPORTS **COMPETITION ANYONE CAN ENTER** a competition or championship in which anybody, amateur or professional, can compete **2. OUTSIDE** a large and unobstructed outdoor space ○ *in the open* **3. UNCONCEALED STATE** the state of being no longer hidden or held back ○ *It's good to get all the facts out in the open.* [Old English. Ultimately from an Indo-European word meaning "up from under, over" that is also the ancestor of English *up*.] —**o·pen·ness** *n.*

open up *v.* **1.** *vi.* **UNFOLD** to expand or unfold, e.g., before a viewer **2.** *vti.* **MAKE SOMETHING ACCESSIBLE** to make something more accessible or available to a wider range of people **3.** *vt.* **MAKE AN OPENING IN SOMETHING** to make an opening in something, especially in order to get access **4.** *vt.* **REMOVE A COVER OR OBSTRUCTION FROM** to remove the wrapping, restrictions, obstructions, or covering from something **5.** *vti.* = **open** *v.* 6 ○ *A new video store is opening up next week* **6.** *vi.* **SPEAK FREELY** to speak honestly, especially about personal feelings or experiences ○ *She opens up when she gets to know you.* **7.** *vi.* **TELL WHAT YOU KNOW** to confess to a crime or give information about a crime under coercion (*informal*) **8.** *vi.* **START SHOOTING A WEAPON** to start firing or cause a gun or other weapon to start firing **9.** *vti.* **OPEN BUSINESS FOR THE DAY** to unlock something, especially a store or business, and make it ready for the day **10.** *vi.* MAKE A VEHICLE GO FASTER to cause a motor vehicle to accelerate, or to travel at an accelerated speed (*informal*) **11.** *vti.* SPORTS BECOME OR MAKE SOMETHING MORE EXCITING to become, or cause something to become, more interesting or exciting ○ *After the first goal the game opened up.*

o·pen ad·mis·sions *n.* an educational policy in which students are admitted to college regardless of their academic qualifications or record (*takes a singular or plural verb*)

o·pen a·dop·tion *n.* an arrangement when a child has been adopted that maintains contact between the child's adoptive and biological parents

o·pen-air *adj.* situated or happening outside a building

o·pen-and-shut *adj.* simple and easily resolved ○ *an open-and-shut case*

o·pen bar *n.* a bar at a party, wedding, or other social function where the drinks are served free of charge

o·pen book *n.* somebody or something that is very easy to understand or about which everything is known

o·pen chain *adj.* an arrangement of atoms in a molecule in which the atoms are not joined at the ends to form a ring

o·pen class·room *n.* a classroom in which groups of pupils work in a flexible informal way on projects and have minimal supervision

o·pen court *n.* a trial or court that is open to members of the public, and whose proceedings are recorded

o·pen dat·ing *n.* the practice of providing information on food packaging that gives the date of packaging, the last day the food may be on sale, or the last day on which it should be consumed

o·pen day *n. U.K.* = **open house** *n.* **2**

o·pen door *n.* **1.** FREE TRADE POLICY a policy whereby a nation allows free and unrestricted trade with all other nations (*hyphenated before a noun*) **2.** UNRESTRICTED ACCESS free and unrestricted access at all times (*hyphenated when used before a noun*) ○ *open-door management*

o·pen-end *adj.* **1.** NOT HAVING LIMITS not having a limit in either time or amount ○ *an open-end contract* **2.** FIN ALLOWING INCREASED BORROWING allowing somebody to borrow an extra amount under the terms of a loan ○ *an open-end mortgage*

o·pen-end·ed *adj.* **1.** WITH NO PREARRANGED END with no planned or defined end **2.** EASILY MODIFIED not definite and easily changed ○ *We'd left everything pretty open-ended about the vacation.* **3.** NEEDING MORE THAN A ONE WORD ANSWER requiring or allowing an answer that is fuller than a simple yes or no ○ *an open-ended question* **4.** *U.K.* = **open-end** *adj.* **1**

o·pen-end in·vest·ment com·pa·ny *n.* FIN = **mutual fund**

o·pen en·roll·ment *n.* EDUC = **open admissions**

o·pen·er /ṓpənər/ *n.* **1.** OPENING DEVICE a device for opening containers such as cans or bottles **2.** INITIAL EVENT somebody or something that begins a discussion or event (*informal*) **3.** CARDS OPENING PLAYER somebody who opens the bidding, betting, or play in a card game **4.** FIRST ACT IN SHOW the first act in a variety show or musical concert **5.** SPORTS FIRST GAME the first game in a series or season ■ **o·pen·ers** *npl.* CARDS STARTING POINT a starting position or point, e.g., cards that allow somebody to begin the betting in some card games ◇ **for openers** used to open a statement or discussion (*informal*)

o·pen-eyed *adj.* **1.** WATCHFUL alert to all that is happening **2.** WITH EYES WIDE IN WONDER with the eyes wide open in wonder or surprise **3.** ASSESSING REALISTICALLY realistic in knowing and accepting all aspects of a situation

o·pen-faced *adj.* with a face that suggests an honest, straightforward, and sincere character

o·pen-faced sand·wich *n.* a sandwich consisting of a single slice of bread with filling on it but no second piece of bread on top, eaten with a knife and fork

o·pen-field *adj.* SPORTS able to run easily and quickly in the open field

o·pen·hand·ed /ṓpən hándəd/ *adj.* generous with money or other material things —**o·pen·hand·ed·ly** *adv.* —**o·pen·hand·ed·ness** *n.*

o·pen·heart·ed /ṓpən haártəd/ *adj.* sincere and generous in spirit toward other people — **o·pen·heart·ed·ly** *adv.* —**o·pen·heart·ed·ness** *n.*

o·pen-hearth *adj.* used to describe a steel-making process that uses a furnace with a shallow hearth and a low roof (**reverberatory furnace**) to produce high-quality steel

o·pen-heart sur·ger·y *n.* heart surgery during which the heart is exposed and blood is circulated outside the body by mechanical means

o·pen house *n.* **1.** READY HOSPITALITY a situation or occasion when visitors are welcome at any time ○ *It's open house here – come over whenever you like!* **2.** SCHOOL VISITING DAY a day on which an institution such as a school or college is open to the public for visitors to view aspects of its work and activities **3.** VIEWING PERIOD BEFORE A SALE a period of time during which a house or an apartment that is for sale is open to the public for viewing **4.** HOUSE OPEN TO VIEWING a house or apartment that is open to be viewed by the public before sale

o·pen·ing /ṓpəning/ *n.* **1.** GAP a gap or hole in something, especially one through which you can see or through which people or animals can pass ○ *We found an opening in the fence.* **2.** FIRST PART the first part of something ○ *The movie has a wonderful opening.* **3.** FIRST TIME SOMETHING IS USED OR DONE the often formal occasion when something new such as a building or road is used for the first time, or when something starts again after stopping for some time (*often used before a noun*) ○ *the opening ceremony* **4.** FIRST PERFORMANCE FOR THE GENERAL PUBLIC the first public performance or showing of a play, exhibition, or other production (*often used before a noun*) ○ *the opening night* **5.** CLEARING IN WOODS an area in a wood or forest in which trees do not grow **6.** OPPORTUNITY an opportunity to do something ○ *It gave her an opening to say how delighted she was.* **7.** VACANCY a job that is available ○ *We have an opening for a young person with drive and enthusiasm.* **8.** ACT OF OPENING the act of opening something **9.** CHESS BEGINNING OF A GAME the first moves of a game, especially in chess and checkers

o·pen in·ter·val *n.* in mathematics, a set of real numbers consisting of all numbers between but excluding its endpoints, usually written (a,b) or]a,b[

o·pen-jaw *adj.* AIR used to describe a flight or flight booking that goes to one destination and returns from another and is booked as a round-trip ticket

o·pen let·ter *n.* a letter that is addressed to an individual or organization but is intended for everybody to read and is published in a newspaper or magazine

o·pen·ly *adv.* without making any attempt at concealment ○ *Many members were openly hostile to the proposed plan.*

o·pen mar·ket *n.* a market with no commercial restrictions that allows free competition between buyers and sellers

o·pen mar·riage *n.* a marriage in which each partner agrees to allow the other to engage in sexual relationships with other people

o·pen-mind·ed *adj.* free from prejudice and receptive to new ideas —**o·pen-mind·ed·ly** *adv.* —**o·pen-mind·ed·ness** *n.*

o·pen-mouthed *adj.* **1.** WITH THE MOUTH OPEN with the mouth wide open in surprise or wonder **2.** VERY DEMANDING loudly and persistently demanding or complaining —**o·pen-mouth·ed·ly** *adv.* —**o·pen-mouth·ed·ness** *n.*

o·pen-necked *adj.* with the top button unfastened ○ *an open-necked shirt*

o·pen-plan *adj.* having a large space left open rather than divided up into smaller units, especially in a workplace

o·pen-pol·li·nat·ed *adj.* pollinated naturally, without human intervention

o·pen punc·tu·a·tion *n.* minimal punctuation, especially minimal use of commas

o·pen sand·wich *n. U.K.* = **open-faced sandwich**

o·pen sea·son *n.* **1.** HUNT FREE HUNTING PERIOD a period during the year when restrictions concerning the hunting and killing of game or the catching of fish are lifted **2.** TIME OF UNRESTRAINED CRITICISM a period of unrestrained attack or criticism (*informal*) ○ *It seems to be open season on lawyers at the moment.*

o·pen se·cret *n.* something that is supposed to be secret but in actual fact is widely known

o·pen sen·tence *n.* a formula containing a free variable, e.g. "X is human," that cannot be said to be true or false because the referent of the variable is not determined

o·pen ses·a·me *n.* a sure means of gaining access to or obtaining something [From the magical words used by Ali Baba, a character in the *Arabian Nights*, to open the door of the robbers' cave]

o·pen set *n.* MATH a mathematical set that is included within a particular topology

o·pen shop *n.* a workplace where being a member of a union, or of a specified union, is not a condition of employment. ◊ **closed shop, union shop**

o·pen-skies, o·pen-sky *adj.* allowing aircraft belonging to any nation the freedom to fly over an area, and therefore placing no restrictions on aerial surveillance of military installations

o·pen so·ci·e·ty *n.* a society in which there is freedom of thought, ideas, speech, and communication

o·pen stock *n.* merchandise that a store keeps on hand so that customers can replenish or replace individual items in sets, such as dishes and glasses

o·pen sys·tem *n.* COMPUT a computer design system that has uniform industry standards and is compatible with any similar type of system or part

o·pen-toe, o·pen-toed *adj.* used to describe a shoe, especially a sandal, that is not closed at the front, allowing the toes to be seen

o·pen·work /ṓpən wùrk/ *n.* **1.** DECORATIVE WORK USING PATTERNS OF HOLES decorative items that make use of patterns of holes, e.g. wrought-iron work, fretwork, or lace **2.** SEW EMBROIDERY WITH DECORATED HOLES an embroidery technique or the embroidery itself in which holes are formed in a fabric by either cutting or pulling threads and then embellishing with various stitches

op·er·a[1] /óppərə, ópprə/ *n.* **1.** MUSICAL DRAMA a dramatic work where music is a dominant part of the performance. It is usually highly stylized, with the actors often singing rather than reciting their lines, and typically has recurring themes intensified by musical repetitions developed as the piece progresses. **2.** OPERAS IN GENERAL operas thought of collectively or as an art form **3.** OPERATIC SCORE the musical score or libretto of an operatic work **4.** = **opera house** [Mid-17thC. Via Italian from Latin, "work," from *opus* (see OPUS).]

o·pe·ra[2] plural of **opus**

op·er·a·ble /óppərəb'l, ópprəb'l/ *adj.* **1.** MED SURGICALLY TREATABLE capable of being treated by surgery **2.** ABLE TO BE DONE capable of being done or put into practice — **op·er·a·bil·i·ty** /òppərə bíllətee, òpprə-/ *n.* —**op·er·a·bly** /óppərəblee, ópprə-/ *adv.*

o·pé·ra bouffe /òppərə bo͞of, òpprə-/ *n.* **1.** COMIC OPERA an opera with a comic or farcical theme **2.** OPÉRA BOUFFES AS A GROUP opéra bouffes thought of collectively or as an art form [From French, "comic opera"; translation of Italian *opera buffa*]

o·pe·ra buf·fa /-bo͞ofə/ *n.* a comic opera of the kind that originated in Italy in the 18th century, using themes or characters from everyday life and usually having a happy ending. Mozart's *The Marriage of Figaro* is an example. [From Italian, "comic opera"]

o·pé·ra co·mique /-kaw meék/ *n.* an opera on a lighthearted theme with spoken dialogue. This style of opera was especially popular in 19th-century France. [From French, "comic opera"]

op·er·a glass·es *npl.* small decorative low-powered binoculars for use by people in the audience at theatrical, operatic, or ballet performances

op·er·a·go·er /óppərə gō ər, ópprə gō ər/ *n.* somebody who attends opera performances regularly

op·er·a hat *n.* a man's collapsible top hat that is spring-operated

op·er·a house *n.* a theater that is designed for putting on operas. It is usually much more ornate and sumptuous than a theater designed for putting on plays.

op·er·and /óppə rànd/ *n.* **1.** MATH ENTITY WITH OPERATION PERFORMED ON IT a quantity, function, or other entity that is to have a mathematical operation performed on it **2.** COMPUT **PART OF A COMPUTER INSTRUCTION** the portion of a computer instruction that specifies the location in memory of the data to be manipulated [Late 19thC. From Latin *operandum*, literally "thing to be worked on," from *operari* (see OPERATE).]

op·er·ant /óppərənt/ *n.* **1. PERFORMER OF AN OPERATION** somebody or something that operates or that carries out some kind of operation **2.** PSYCHOL **VOLUNTARY ACTION** in learning theory, an action or other unit of behavior that does not appear to have a stimulus ■ *adj.* **HAVING EFFECT** producing a specified effect [Early 17thC. From Latin *operant-*, the present participle stem of *operari* (see OPERATE).] —**op·er·ant·ly** *adv.*

op·er·ant con·di·tion·ing *n.* PSYCHOL a form of learning that takes place when an instance of spontaneous behavior is either reinforced by a reward or discouraged by punishment. The principles involved have had a strong influence on behavior modification as well as on other kinds of therapy.

op·er·a se·ri·a /-séeree ə/ *n.* **1. TRAGIC OPERA WITH A MYTHOLOGICAL THEME** an opera that has a serious theme, often one taken from classical mythology, and usually a tragic ending. An example is Mozart's *The Clemency of Titus*. **2. OPERA SERIAS AS A GROUP** opera serias thought of collectively or as an art form [From Italian, "serious opera"]

op·er·ate /óppə ràyt/ (**-at·ed, -at·ing, -ates**) *v.* **1.** *vti.* **DO SOMETHING OR FUNCTION AS SOMETHING** to function or work, or make something function or work **2.** *vti.* BUSINESS **MANAGE OR BE MANAGED** to exist as a working business or organization, or to oversee the running of a working business or organization **3.** *vi.* MED **PERFORM SURGERY** to perform surgery on a person or animal **4.** *vi.* **EXERT AN EFFECT** to have an effect or influence on somebody or something **5.** *vi.* MIL **PERFORM MILITARY MANEUVERS** to carry out military maneuvers **6.** *vi.* FIN **TRADE IN THE FINANCIAL MARKET** to trade or deal in securities or commodities on the stock exchange **7.** *vi.* **ENGAGE IN ILLEGAL ACTIVITIES** to be active in some illegal or underhanded business [Early 17thC. From Latin *operat-*, the past participle of *operari* "to work," from *oper-*, the stem of *opus* "work."]

op·er·at·ic /òppə ráttik/ *adj.* **1. OF OPERA** belonging or relating to opera **2. FLAMBOYANT** overly or flamboyantly extravagant, especially in behavior [Mid-18thC. Formed from OPERA[1], on the model of DRAMATIC.] —**op·er·at·i·cal·ly** *adv.*

op·er·at·ics /òppə ráttiks/ *n.* flamboyantly exaggerated or extravagant behavior (*takes a singular or plural verb*)

op·er·at·ing room *n.* a room in a hospital where surgical operations are performed

op·er·at·ing suite *n.* a room or suite in a hospital or clinic equipped for doing procedures involving surgery

op·er·at·ing sys·tem *n.* the essential program in a computer that maintains disk files, runs applications, and handles devices such as the keyboard, mouse, monitor, and printer

op·er·at·ing ta·ble *n.* a table on which somebody undergoing a surgical operation lies

op·er·at·ing the·a·tre *n. U.K.* = **operating room**

op·er·a·tion /òppə ráysh'n/ *n.* **1. CONTROLLING OF SOMETHING** the controlling of something or the managing of the way it works **2. FUNCTIONING STATE** the state of functioning or of being in effect **3. SOMETHING DONE** something that is carried out, especially something difficult or complex ○ *the tricky operation of removing the sting* **4.** MED **SURGICAL INTERVENTION** any surgical procedure, e.g., one carried out to repair damage to a body part **5. ORGANIZED ACTION** an organized campaign, maneuver, or other form of action, especially one carried out by rescue personnel, the police, or diplomatic personnel **6. op·er·a·tion, Op·er·a·tion** MIL **MILITARY ACTION** an action conducted by military forces that can range in scope from a reconnaissance mission to an entire campaign (*often used before a noun*) ○ *Operation Desert Storm* **7.** MATH **MATHEMATICAL PROCESS** a mathematical process such as subtraction, multiplication, or differentiation in which certain entities are derived from others through the application of rules **8.** COMPUT **SINGLE PART OF A COMPUTER PROGRAM** a series of actions performed by a computer, defined by an instruction and forming part of a computer program **9. BUSINESS DEAL** a business deal or financial transaction **10. ILLEGAL BUSINESS** an illegal, dishonest, or underhanded business ○ *He got involved in a shady gambling operation.*

op·er·a·tion·al /òppə ráyshən'l, -shnəl/ *adj.* **1. ABLE TO BE USED** in proper working order and able to be used ○ *The new transportation link will be fully operational next month.* **2. OF THE OPERATION OF SOMETHING** relating to the operating of something or to the way it operates **3.** MIL **COMBAT-READY** ready for combat or maneuvers —**op·er·a·tion·al·ly** *adv.*

op·er·a·tion·al am·pli·fi·er *n.* an amplifier with high gain and high stability that is controlled by way of externally connected negative-feedback circuits

op·er·a·tion·al·ism /òppə ráyshən'l ìzzəm, -shnə lìzzəm/, **op·er·a·tion·ism** /òppə ráysh'n ìzzəm/ *n.* PHILOS the view that terms for scientific concepts should be defined in terms of the scientific operations, e.g., measuring or observing, performed to establish or disprove them —**op·er·a·tion·al·ist** *n., adj.* —**op·er·a·tion·al·is·tic** /òppə rayshən'l ístik, -shnə lístik/ *adj.*

op·er·a·tion·al re·search *n.* = **operations research**

op·er·a·tion·ism *n.* PHILOS = **operationalism**

op·er·a·tions /òppə ráysh'nz/ *npl.* the supervising, monitoring, and coordinating of the activities of a military or civilian organization or a complex machine (*often used before a noun*) ○ *the operations console of a computer*

op·er·a·tions re·search *n.* analysis of the problems that exist in complex systems such as those used to run a business or a military campaign, designed to give a scientific basis for decision-making

op·er·a·tive /óppərətiv, ópprətiv/ *adj.* **1. IN EFFECT** in place and having an effect, especially the right or desired effect **2. SIGNIFICANT** carrying a special meaning or significance **3.** MED **OF SURGERY** relating to or resulting from a surgical procedure ■ *n.* **1. SKILLED WORKER** a skilled worker, especially in a manufacturing industry **2. WORKER** somebody who performs a particular task or who works in a particular field (*formal or humorous*) ○ *a rodent operative* **3.** POL **POLITICAL WORKER** an employee of a political party who works in any behind-the-scenes capacity, e.g., political troubleshooting or manipulation of media stories **4. DETECTIVE** a private detective **5. SPY** a spy or secret agent —**op·er·a·tive·ly** *adv.* —**op·er·a·tive·ness** *n.* —**op·er·a·tiv·i·ty** /òppərə tívvətee, òpprə-/ *n.*

op·er·a·tor /óppə ràytər/ *n.* **1. SOMEBODY OPERATING SOMETHING** somebody who operates machinery, an instrument, or other equipment **2.** BUSINESS **BUSINESS OWNER OR MANAGER** somebody who owns or runs a business or other commercial enterprise **3.** FIN **STOCK EXCHANGE DEALER** somebody who deals on the stock exchange or in a money market, especially somebody who makes aggressive or highly speculative moves **4. MANIPULATIVE PERSON** somebody who behaves in a devious or manipulative way, especially in order to obtain some kind of self-advancement (*informal*) ○ *a smooth operator* **5.** MATH **DESCRIPTOR OR PERFORMER OF A MATHEMATICAL OPERATION** a mathematical symbol, term, or other entity that performs or describes an operation. Multiplication and subtraction signs are operators.

o·per·cu·lum /ō púrkyələm/ (*plural* **-la** /-kyələ/ *or* **-lums**) *n.* **1.** ANAT **MUCUS PLUG IN THE CERVIX** the plug of mucus that fills the opening of a woman's cervix while she is pregnant. It helps to prevent infection. **2. o·per·cu·lum** ZOOL **GILL-COVERING FLAP** the flexible bony flap covering the gills of bony fishes **3.** BOT **FLAP IN MOSSES AND FUNGI** a flap covering an aperture in the spore capsules of mosses and some fungi **4.** ZOOL **SEAL ON A MOLLUSK'S SHELL** a rounded plate that seals the mouth of the shell of some gastropod mollusks when the animal's body is inside [Early 18thC. From Latin, "lid," formed from *operire* "to cover."] —**o·per·cu·lar** *adj.* —**o·per·cu·lar·ly** *adv.* —**o·per·cu·late** *adj.* —**o·per·cu·lat·ed** *adj.*

op·e·ret·ta /òppə réttə/ *n.* a theatrical production, usually with a comic theme, similar to opera but with much spoken dialogue and usually some dancing. Gilbert and Sullivan wrote many operettas. [Late 18thC. From Italian, literally "small opera," formed from *opera* (see OPERA[1]).] —**op·e·ret·tist** *n.*

op·er·on /óppə ròn/ *n.* GENETICS a segment of a chromosome containing the genes that specify the structure of a given protein, alongside the genes that regulate its manufacture. Operons are relatively simple units of genetic control, found only in bacteria. [Mid-20thC. From French *opéron*, from *opérer* "to work," from Latin *operari* (see OPERATE).]

op·er·ose /óppə ròss/ *adj.* (*formal*) **1. TAXING** requiring a lot of effort **2. BUSY** busy, active, or hardworking [Late 17thC. From Latin *operosus*, from *oper-*, the stem of *opus* (see OPUS).] —**op·er·ose·ly** *adv.* —**op·er·ose·ness** *n.*

O·phe·li·a /ə féelee ə/ *n.* a very small inner natural satellite of Uranus, discovered in 1986 by the Voyager 2 planetary probe. Its gravitational influence seems to help stabilize the outer ring of Uranus.

oph·i·cleide /óffə klīd, ṓfə-/ *n.* an obsolete musical instrument similar to and superseded by the bass tuba [Mid-19thC. From French *ophicléide*, from Greek *ophis* "snake" + the stem *kleid-* "key"; from its resemblance to an earlier instrument called a "serpent," but with keys.]

o·phid·i·an /ō fíddee ən/ *adj.* **1. OF SNAKES** belonging or relating to snakes **2. LIKE A SNAKE** resembling a snake in appearance, habits, or movement [Early 19thC. Formed from modern Latin *Ophidia*, suborder name, from the Greek stem *ophid-* "snake."] —**o·phid·i·an** *n.*

oph·i·o·lite /óffee ə līt, ṓfee-/ *n.* any igneous and metamorphic rock that was formed from deep-sea sediment. Ophiolites are rich in iron and magnesium. [Mid-19thC. Coined from Greek *ophis* "snake" + -LITE; from its snaky texture.]

oph·i·ol·o·gy /òffee óllәjee, ṑfee-/ *n.* the branch of zoology that is concerned with snakes [Early 19thC. Coined from Greek *ophis* "snake" + -LOGY.] —**oph·i·o·log·i·cal** /òfee ə lójjik'l, ṑfee ə-/ *adj.* —**oph·i·ol·o·gist** /òffee óllәjist, ṓfee-/ *n.*

oph·ite /ṓ fīt/ *n.* any of several mottled green rocks, e.g., diabase or dolerite, that are made up of small long plagioclase crystals surrounded by larger pyroxene crystals [Mid-17thC. Via Latin from Greek *ophitēs* "serpentine stone," from *ophis* "snake"; from its markings, which are like a snake's.]

o·phit·ic /o fíttik, ō-/ *adj.* used to describe rocks consisting of small elongated plagioclase crystals completely enclosed by larger pyroxene crystals

Oph·i·u·chus /ò ffee óokəss/ *n.* a large constellation of the equatorial region located between Hercules and Scorpius

ophthal. *abbr.* **1.** ophthalmology **2.** ophthalmologist

ophthalm- *prefix.* = **ophthalmo-** (*used before vowels*)

oph·thal·mi·a /op thálmee ə, of-/ *n.* inflammation of the eye, especially of the conjunctiva and surrounding area [14thC. Via late Latin from Greek, from *ophthalmos* "eye" (see OPHTHALMO-).]

oph·thal·mic /op thálmik, of-/ *adj.* relating to the eyes, or located in the region of the eye

oph·thal·mi·tis /òpthəl mītiss, òf-/ *n.* inflammation of the eye

ophthalmo- *prefix.* eye, eyeball ○ *ophthalmoscope* [From Greek *ophthalmos*. Ultimately from an Indo-European word meaning "to see," which is also the ancestor of English *eye*, *ogle*, and *optic*.]

ophthalmol. *abbr.* **1.** ophthalmology **2.** ophthalmologist

oph·thal·mol·o·gist /òpthəl móllәjəst, òf-/ *n.* a physician qualified to diagnose and treat eye diseases and conditions with drugs, surgery, and corrective measures

oph·thal·mol·o·gy /òpthəl móllәjee, òfthəl-/ *n.* the branch of medicine that is concerned with the diagnosis and treatment of eye diseases and conditions —**oph·thal·mo·log·i·cal** /òpthəlmə lójjik'l, òfthəlmə-/ *adj.* —**oph·thal·mo·log·i·cal·ly** /òpthəlmə lójjikəlee, òfthəlmə-/ *adv.*

oph·thal·mo·scope /op thálmə skōp, of-/ *n.* a medical

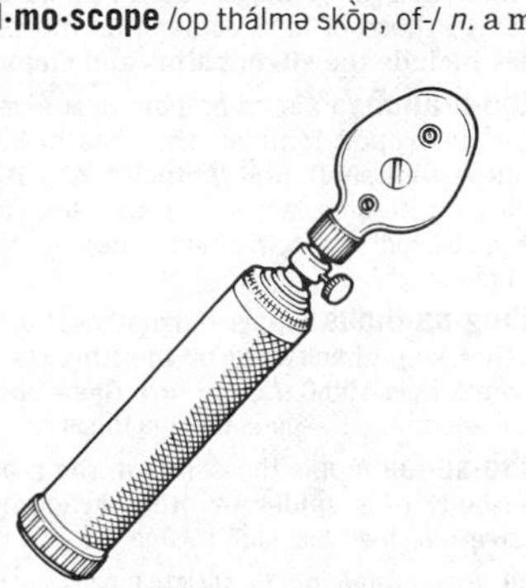

Ophthalmoscope

instrument used for examining the inside of the eye. A direct ophthalmoscope shines a fine beam of light into the eye and allows the examiner to see a magnified image of the spot where the beam falls. —**oph·thal·mo·scop·ic** /òpthəlmə skóppik, òfthəlmə-/ *adj.* —**oph·thal·mo·scop·i·cal·ly** /-kəlee/ *adv.*

oph·thal·mos·co·py /òpthəl móskəpee, òfthəl-/ (*plural* **-pies**) *n.* a medical examination of the inside of the eye using an ophthalmoscope to detect changes to the retina, such as those associated with diabetes and hypertension

-opia *suffix.* condition or defect of vision ○ *hyperopia* ○ *protanopia* [From Greek, formed from *ops* "eye, face." Ultimately from an Indo-European word meaning "to see," which is also the ancestor of English *eye, optic,* and *ocular.*]

o·pi·ate /ṓpee ət/ *n.* **1.** PHARM **OPIUM-CONTAINING DRUG** a drug such as morphine or heroin that contains opium or an opium derivative **2.** PHARM **SLEEP-INDUCING SUBSTANCE** a drug, hormone, or other substance that has sleep-inducing effects similar to those of opium or opium derivatives **3. SOMETHING WITH A SOOTHING OR DULLING EFFECT** something that has a relaxing, pacifying, or dulling effect ○ *TV, often described as the opiate of the masses* ■ *adj.* **1.** PHARM **CONTAINING OPIUM** containing opium or an opium derivative **2. BORING** mind-numbingly unexciting, especially because of being simplistic, cliché-ridden, or formulaic ■ *vt.* (**-at·ed, -at·ing, -ates**) **1.** PHARM **TREAT WITH AN OPIATE** to treat somebody, or somebody's symptoms, with an opiate **2. DEADEN OR DULL** to dull or deaden pain, anguish, or some other unwanted condition [15thC. From medieval Latin *opiatus*, from, ultimately, Latin *opium* (see OPIUM).]

o·pine /ō pīn/ (**o·pined, o·pin·ing, o·pines**) *vti.* to put forth an opinion (*formal*) [15thC. From Latin *opinari* "to suppose, believe."]

o·pin·ion /ə pínnyən/ *n.* **1. PERSONAL VIEW** the view somebody takes about a certain issue, especially when it is based solely on personal judgment ○ *In my opinion it's all a waste of time.* **2. ESTIMATION** a view regarding the worth of somebody or something ○ *They had a pretty low opinion of me.* **3. EXPERT VIEW** an expert assessment of something ○ *I told the doctor I wanted a second opinion.* **4. BODY OF GENERALLY HELD VIEWS** general assessment, judgment, or evaluation ○ *pundits and other opinion formers* **5.** LAW **CONCLUSION OF FACT** a conclusion drawn from observation of the facts [14thC. Via French from the Latin stem *opinion-* from *opinari* "to suppose."] ◇ **be a matter of opinion** to be open to dispute or debate ◇ **be of the opinion that** to think that something is the case

o·pin·ion·at·ed /ə pínnyə nàytəd/ *adj.* always ready to express opinions and tending to hold to them stubbornly, unreasonably dismissing other people's views —**o·pin·ion·at·ed·ly** *adv.* —**o·pin·ion·at·ed·ness** *n.*

o·pin·ion·a·tive /ə pínnyə nàytiv/ *adj.* (*formal*) **1. OF OPINIONS** relating to opinions or to the stating of them **2.** = **opinionated** —**o·pin·ion·a·tive·ly** *adv.* —**opin·ion·a·tive·ness** *n.*

o·pin·ion poll *n.* a survey that is carried out to discover what the general public or some smaller group of people thinks about something. ◊ **poll**

o·pi·oid /ṓpee òyd/ *n.* **NATURALLY OCCURRING OPIUM-CONTAINING SUBSTANCE** any of various opium-containing substances that are produced naturally in the brain ■ *adj.* **SIMILAR TO OPIUM** similar in effect or properties to opium but not derived from opium [Mid-20thC. Coined from OPIUM + -OID.]

o·pi·oid pep·tide *n.* a naturally occurring peptide that has pain-relieving, sedative, or other effects similar to those of opiates such as morphine. Examples include the eukaphalins and endorphins.

o·pis·tho·branch /ə písthə brangk/ *n.* MARINE BIOL any marine gastropod mollusk that has gills, a small or nonexistent shell, and tentacles [Mid-19thC. From modern Latin *Opisthobranchiata*, order name, from Greek *opisthen* "behind" + *bragkhia* "gills," because the gills are behind the heart.]

op·is·thog·na·thous /òppis thógnəthəss/ *adj.* having jaws that slope backward or mouthparts that face backward [Mid-19thC. Coined from Greek *opisthen* "behind" + -GNATHOUS.] —**op·is·thog·na·thism** *n.*

op·is·tho·so·ma /òppis thóssəmə/ *n.* the rear section of the body of a spider or other arachnid [Coined from Greek *opisthen* "behind" + *sōma* "body"]

o·pi·um /ṓpee əm/ *n.* **1. ADDICTIVE DRUG** a brownish gummy extract from the unripe seed pods of the opium poppy that contains several highly addictive narcotic alkaloid substances, e.g., morphine and codeine. Crude opium is no longer used in medicine, but its extracts, especially morphine, are widely used. **2. STUPEFYING THING** something that has a stupefying, numbing, or sleep-inducing effect ○ *soap operas dismissed as the opium of a bored populace* [14thC. Via Latin from Greek *opion* "poppy juice," from *opos* "vegetable juice."]

o·pi·um den *n.* a place where opium is sold and smoked, especially one that has facilities where people using the drug can stay while under its influence

o·pi·um pop·py *n.* a poppy of Europe and Asia with grayish-green leaves and attractive pink, red, or white flowers. It has long been grown as a source of opium. Latin name: *Papaver somniferum.*

OPM *abbr.* Office of Personnel Management

O·por·to /ō páwrtō/ city and port in northwestern Portugal, situated about 170 mi./274 km north of Lisbon. Population: 309,485 (1991).

Opossum

o·pos·sum /ə póssəm, póssəm/ (*plural* **-sums** *or* **-sum**) *n.* **1. AMERICAN MARSUPIAL** a small nocturnal tree-dwelling marsupial found in the United States and Central and South America. It has dense fur, a long snout, and a hairless prehensile tail. Latin name: *Didelphis marsupialis.* **2. AUSTRALIAN MARSUPIAL** any one of several similar marsupials found in Australia and New Zealand. They are mostly nocturnal plant-eating tree-dwellers, and some have prehensile tails. Family: Phalangeridae. [Early 17thC. From Virginia Algonquian *opassom*, from *op* "white" + *assom* "dog, doglike creature."]

o·pos·sum shrimp *n.* a crustacean that resembles a shrimp, the female of which carries the eggs and newly hatched young in a brood pouch just below the thorax. Order: Mysidacae.

opp. *abbr.* opposite

Op·pen·hei·mer /óppən hìmər/, **J. Robert** (1904–67) U.S. nuclear physicist. He was the director of the Los Alamos atomic bomb project (1943–45) and the United States Atomic Energy Commission (1946–53). In 1953 he was suspended from nuclear work because of his past Communist associations. He won the Enrico Fermi Award in 1963.

OPP film *n.* plastic film used for packaging

op·pi·dan /óppəd'n/ *adj.* **OF TOWNS** belonging to, relating to, or found in a town, often the town in which a university is sited as distinct from the university itself (*formal*) ■ *n.* **TOWN DWELLER** somebody who lives in a town (*formal*) [Mid-16thC. From Latin *oppidanus*, from *oppidum* "fort, town."]

op·pi·late /óppə làyt/ (**-lat·ed, -lat·ing, -lates**) *vt.* MED to block up a body passage such as a duct or a body opening such as a pore [15thC. From Latin *oppilat-* "to stop up," from *pilare*, literally "to heap up," from *pila* "heap of stones."] —**op·pi·la·tion** /òppə láysh'n/ *n.*

op·po·nent /ə pṓnənt/ *n.* **1. RIVAL IN A CONTEST** a person or team faced in a competition, debate, battle, or other contest **2. SOMEBODY OPPOSING SOMETHING** somebody who is against a particular course of action or who does not support a particular cause or belief ○ *a fierce opponent of reform of the voting system* **3.** ANAT **OPPOSING MUSCLE** any muscle that counteracts the motion of another ■ *adj.* **1. CONTRARY** working or arguing against something **2. CONTRADICTORY** serving to contradict something [Late 16thC. From Latin *opponent-*, the present participle stem of *opponere*, literally "to set against" (source of English *oppose*), from *ponere* "to place."] —**op·po·nen·cy** *n.*

op·por·tune /óppər tòon, òppər tòon/ *adj.* suitable for a purpose or occurring at just the right time [15thC. Via French from Latin *opportunus* "favorable" (used of the wind), from *ob portum veniens* "coming toward port."] —**op·por·tune·ly** *adv.* —**op·por·tune·ness** *n.*

op·por·tun·ist /óppər tòonist, òppər tòonist/ *n.* somebody who takes advantage of something, especially somebody who does so in a devious, unscrupulous, or unprincipled way —**op·por·tun·ism** *n.*

op·por·tun·is·tic /òppər too nístik/ *adj.* **1. TAKING ADVANTAGE OF OPPORTUNITIES** resourcefully taking advantage of all opportunities or situations, especially in a devious, unscrupulous, or unprincipled way **2.** MED **LIFE-THREATENING WHEN IMMUNITY IS LOW** used to describe a microorganism or relatively minor disease that is not normally serious but that can become pathogenic or life-threatening when the host has a low level of immunity ○ *opportunistic infections* —**op·por·tun·is·ti·cal·ly** *adv.*

op·por·tu·ni·ty /òppər tòonətee, óppər tòonətee/ (*plural* **-ties**) *n.* **1. ADVANTAGEOUS CHANCE** a chance, especially one that offers some kind of advantage **2. FAVORABLE CONDITIONS** a combination of favorable circumstances or situations

op·por·tu·ni·ty cost *n.* the cost of a commercial decision regarded as the value of the alternative that is forgone. For example, if the choice is between using a machine or scrapping it, the opportunity cost is the scrap value.

op·pos·a·ble /ə pṓzəb'l/ *adj.* **1. RESISTIBLE** capable of being opposed or resisted **2. ABLE TO BE PLACED OPPOSITE SOMETHING** capable of being put in a position that is opposite something else **3.** ANAT **TOUCHING THE END OF ANOTHER DIGIT** used to describe a thumb or big toe that can face and touch the end of one or more of the other digits of the same hand or foot —**op·pos·a·bil·i·ty** /ə pṓzə bíllətee/ *n.* —**op·pos·a·bly** /ə pṓzəblee/ *adv.*

op·pose /ə pṓz/ (**-posed, -pos·ing, -pos·es**) *v.* **1.** *vti.* **STAND IN OPPOSITION** to be against something or to take an active stance against something ○ *would not state openly that they oppose violence* **2.** *vt.* **SET IN CONTRAST TO** to set something up as a contrast to something else **3.** *vt.* **PUT OPPOSITE** to put one thing in a position directly facing another **4.** *vt.* **COMPETE WITH AS OPPONENTS** to be in competition, conflict, or battle with another person, team, or fighting force [14thC. From French *opposer*, an alteration (influenced by *poser* "to place") of Latin *opponere* (see OPPONENT).] —**op·pos·er** *n.* —**op·pos·ing** *adj.* ◇ **as opposed to** used to introduce something that is in contrast or is distinct

op·posed-cyl·in·der en·gine *n.* an engine in which cylinders or banks of cylinders are mounted on opposite sides of the crankcase in the same plane, with their connecting rods mounted on a common crankshaft. Piston strokes on each side of the camshaft work in a direction opposite to one another.

op·po·site /óppəzit/ *adj.* **1. ON THE FACING SIDE** on the side that faces something or at the farthest distance possible from something **2. FACING AWAY** pointing, facing, or moving away from each other ○ *went off in opposite directions* **3. TOTALLY DIFFERENT** of the same general class yet completely different **4.** BOT **LEVEL WITH ON THE OTHER SIDE** used to describe plant parts, especially pairs of leaves or flowers, that grow at the same level on a stem but on either side of it **5.** GEOM **FACING AN ACUTE ANGLE** used to describe the side of a right-angled triangle facing a specified acute angle **6.** GEOM **FACING EACH OTHER GEOMETRICALLY** used to describe sides or angles in an even-sided polygon that face each other ■ *n.* **1. SOMEBODY OR SOMETHING DIFFERENT FROM ANOTHER** somebody or something that is completely different from another or from what is expected **2. ANTONYM** a word that has an opposite meaning **3. OPPONENT** an opponent (*archaic or formal*) ■ *adv.* **IN THE OPPOSITE POSITION** in or into a position that is opposite ○ *They live directly opposite.* ■ *prep.* **1. ACROSS FROM** facing or across from something or somebody ○ *They moved to a house opposite the museum.* **2. IN A COMPLEMENTING ACTING ROLE TO** in an acting role that corresponds to or complements another, especially when the two roles are played by people of different genders ○ *excited to be playing opposite the great star* [14thC. Via French from Latin *oppositus*, the past participle of *opponere* (see OPPONENT).] —**op·po·site·ly** *adv.* —**op·po·site·ness** *n.*

op·po·site num·ber *n.* somebody who does a similar job or who holds a similar post to another person, especially in another department or organization

op·po·site prompt *n.* in a theater, the side of a stage that is to the actors' right when they face the audience. ◊ **stage right**

op·po·site sex *n.* women when thought of collectively as opposed to men, or men when thought of collectively as opposed to women

op·po·si·tion /òppə zísh'n/ *n.* **1.** ACTIVELY HOSTILE ATTITUDE an actively hostile attitude toward something, or a resistant stance against something ○ *public opposition to the plan was growing* **2.** SPORTS SPORTS OPPONENT a person or team that plays against another **3. op·po·si·tion, Op·po·si·tion** POL OUT-OF-POWER POLITICAL PARTY a political party that is not in power (*often used before a noun*) **4.** LING LINGUISTIC CONTRAST in linguistics, the contrast between two or more similar elements in a language **5.** PHON PHONETIC CONTRAST BETWEEN SOUNDS in phonetics, the contrast between two sounds that are articulated in a similar place in the mouth, e.g., between the voiced consonant /v/ and the voiceless consonant /f/ **6.** CHESS THE ADVANTAGE OF NOT HAVING TO MOVE a situation toward the end of a game of chess in which the two kings are in such a position that the opponent must make a king move and is therefore at a disadvantage **7.** LOGIC RELATIONS BETWEEN LOGICAL PROPOSITIONS the way in which logical propositions relate to each other **8.** ASTRON MOON OR PLANET POSITION the position of the Moon or one of the outer planets when it is on the opposite side of the Earth as seen from the Sun **9.** ASTRON CELESTIAL BODY ALIGNMENT the position of two celestial bodies when they are diametrically opposite on the celestial sphere **10.** ASTROLOGICALLY OPPOSING PLANETARY POSITION in astrology, a situation when two planets are 180 degrees from each other, believed to cause friction or symbolize confrontation —**op·po·si·tion·al** *adj.*

op·po·si·tion·ist /òppə zísh'nist/ *n.* somebody who supports a policy of political opposition —**op·po·si·tion·ism** *n.*

op·pos·i·tion re·search *n.* research done in order to discover damaging or detrimental information about somebody

op·press /ə préss/ (**-pressed, -press·ing, -press·es**) *vt.* **1.** DOMINATE HARSHLY to subject a person or a people to a harsh or cruel form of domination **2.** INFLICT STRESS ON to be a source of worry, stress, or trouble to somebody **3.** SUPPRESS to hold something in check or put an end to it (*archaic*) [14thC. From French *oppresser*, from Latin *oppress-*, the past participle stem of *opprimere*, literally "to press against," from *premere* "to press."] —**op·pres·sion** *n.* —**op·pres·sor** *n.*

op·pres·sive /ə préssiv/ *adj.* **1.** DOMINATING HARSHLY imposing a harsh or cruel form of domination ○ *an oppressive regime* **2.** HIGHLY STRESSFUL exerting a worrying, troubling, or burdensome pressure on somebody **3.** STIFLING so hot and humid as to make people feel tired, irritable, or sluggish (*refers to weather*) —**op·pres·sive·ly** *adv.* —**op·pres·sive·ness** *n.*

op·pro·bri·ous /ə próbree əss/ *adj.* **1.** SCORNFUL expressing scorn, contempt, or severe criticism **2.** SHAMEFUL bringing shame or disrepute [14thC. From late Latin *opprobriosus*, from Latin *opprobrium* (see OPPROBRIUM).] —**op·pro·bri·ous·ly** *adv.* —**op·pro·bri·ous·ness** *n.*

op·pro·bri·um /ə próbree əm/ (*plural* **-a** /-bree ə/) *n.* **1.** SCORN scorn, contempt, or severe criticism **2.** DISGRACE shame or disgrace that stems from disreputable behavior **3.** SOURCE OF SHAME something or somebody that brings shame or disgrace (*archaic*) ○ *"would render him an object of scorn and an opprobrium of the religion with which he had diligently associated himself"* (George Eliot, *Middlemarch*; 1872) [Mid-17thC. From Latin, "infamy, reproach," from *opprobare* "to reproach," from *probrum* "disgrace," literally "something brought before somebody."]

op·pugn /ə pyóon/ (**-pugned, -pugn·ing, -pugns**) *vt.* to question the validity or truthfulness of something (*formal*) [15thC. From Latin *oppugnare*, literally "to fight against," from *pugnare* "to fight."] —**op·pugn·er** *n.*

op·pug·nant /ə púgnənt/ *adj.* willfully hostile or opposed (*archaic or formal*) —**op·pug·nan·cy** *n.* —**op·pug·nant·ly** *adv.*

ops *npl.* the controlling of organized military or civilian activities (*informal*) (*often used before a noun*) ○ *Who's in the ops room tonight?* [Early 20th C. Shortening of OPERATIONS.]

op·sin /ópsin/ *n.* a component of the visual pigment found in the retina of the eye. It is a glycoprotein, and in the vertebrate eye it combines with retinal to form rhodopsin. [Mid-20thC. Back-formation from RHODOPSIN.]

op·son·ic /op sónnik/ *adj.* BIOL relating to or involving opsonins

op·son·ic in·dex *n.* MED a measure of the number of bacteria destroyed by certain blood cells, expressed as the ratio of opsonin in the infected patient's blood to the amount found in a healthy person's blood

op·so·nin /ópsənin/ *n.* BIOL a protein fragment in blood that binds to the surface of an invading antibody and promotes its destruction by white blood cells [Early 20thC. Coined from Latin *opsonare* "to cater, buy provisions" (from Greek *opsōnein* "condiment, delicacy," of unknown origin) + -IN.]

op·so·nize /ópsə nīz/ (**-nized, -niz·ing, -niz·es**), **op·son·i·fy** (**-fied, -fy·ing, -fies**) *vt.* BIOL to make foreign bodies such as bacteria susceptible to destruction by certain blood cells by coating them with opsonin —**op·so·ni·za·tion** /òpsəni záysh'n/ *n.*

-opsy *suffix.* examination ○ *biopsy* [From Greek *-opsia* "sight, seeing," from *opsis* "sight." Ultimately from an Indo-European word meaning "to see," which is also the ancestor of English *eye, optic,* and *ocular.*]

opt /opt/ (**opt·ed, opt·ing, opts**) *vi.* to choose something or choose to do something, usually in preference to other available alternatives [Late 19thC. Via French *opter* from Latin *optare* "to choose, desire" (source of English *optative* and *adopt*).]

opt out *vi.* to decide not to join in something or not to go along with something (*informal*)

opt. *abbr.* **1.** GRAM optative **2.** optical **3.** optician **4.** optics **5.** optimum **6.** optional

op·ta·tive /óptətiv/ *adj.* **1.** OF CHOICE-MAKING relating to the making of choices (*formal*) **2.** GRAM CONTAINING A VERB EXPRESSING A WISH containing a verb in the subjunctive mood that expresses a wish or desire, as does the independent clause "God save the queen" ■ *n.* GRAM **1.** OPTATIVE MOOD the optative mood of a verb **2.** VERB IN THE OPTATIVE MOOD a verb in the optative mood [Mid-16thC. Via French from Latin *optativus*, from *optare* "to choose, desire."] —**op·ta·tive·ly** *adv.*

op·tic[1] /óptik/ *adj.* OF THE EYES belonging or relating to the eyes, or situated in or near the eye ■ *n.* **1.** INSTRUMENT'S LENS any of the lenses or reflecting parts in an optical instrument **2.** EYE an eye (*archaic or humorous*) [14thC. Via French or medieval Latin from Greek *optikos*, from *optos* "seen, visible." Ultimately from an Indo-European word meaning "to see," which is also the ancestor of English *eye* and *ocular.*]

op·tic[2] *tdmk.* a trademark for a device that fits over the neck of a bottle and dispenses a measure of spirits, used in pubs

op·ti·cal /óptik'l/ *adj.* **1.** OF VISIBLE LIGHT relating to or producing light that can be seen **2.** OF VISION belonging or relating to the sense of sight **3.** OPTICS OF CORRECTIVE LENSES designed to correct or enhance faulty vision (*refers to a lens*) **4.** LIGHT-SENSITIVE sensitive to light (*refers to an instrument or device*) **5.** PHYS OF OPTICS belonging or relating to the science of optics —**op·ti·cal·ly** *adv.*

op·ti·cal ac·tiv·i·ty *n.* CHEM the property of a crystal or a chemical solution to rotate the plane of polarized light that passes through it. In the case of solutions, the rotation is caused by asymmetrical molecules and the angle of rotation depends on the thickness of the substance.

op·ti·cal art *n.* full form of **op art**

op·ti·cal char·ac·ter read·er *n.* a device for entering material into a computer by digitizing the image of a printed page, identifying the characters, and storing them as machine code for further processing. Initially such devices could recognize only a specially designed typeface, but more modern readers can recognize a wide variety of typefaces and even handwriting.

op·ti·cal char·ac·ter rec·og·ni·tion *n.* the use of light-sensing methods to identify printed and handwritten material and encode it in machine-readable form for inputting into a computer. ◊ **magnetic ink character recognition**

op·ti·cal com·put·er *n.* a proposed computer that uses optical switches, fibers, and laser light instead of wires, transistors, and printed circuits to achieve processing speeds far higher than those of conventional computers

op·ti·cal disk, op·ti·cal disc *n.* a rigid computer storage disk on which data is stored as tiny pits in the plastic coating and which is readable by laser beam, especially a recordable and erasable disk

op·ti·cal dou·ble star *n.* a pair of stars that appear to lie close together as viewed from the Earth. They are actually a long way apart, though lying along the same line of sight.

op·ti·cal fi·ber *n.* a fiber made of very pure glass or plastic that is used in modern communications systems to transmit information in the form of pulses of laser light. The core is usually of high refractive index and is enclosed in a sheath of lower refractive index, the light thus being transmitted by total internal reflection. ◊ **fiber optics**

op·ti·cal glass *n.* any high-quality glass used in lenses for its superior refractive quality

op·ti·cal il·lu·sion *n.* **1.** FALSE VISUAL PERCEPTION a visual experience in which there is some kind of false perception of what is actually there **2.** SOURCE OF OPTICAL ILLUSION something that causes an optical illusion, especially something drawn or designed deliberately to fool the eye

op·ti·cal i·som·er·ism *n.* the property exhibited by a pair of molecules that differ only in being mirror images of each other and that rotate plane-polarized light in opposite directions when in solution —**op·ti·cal i·so·mer** *n.*

op·ti·cal ro·ta·tion *n.* the rotation of plane-polarized light as it passes through an optically active medium

op·ti·cal scan·ner *n.* COMPUT = **scanner**

op·ti·cal sound *n.* a form of sound reproduction in motion pictures that employs a photographed pattern of light on the film that is read by a lamp in the projector. It has now largely been superseded by digital sound.

op·ti·cal tweez·ers *npl.* MICROBIOL a laser beam focused on a biological object of microscopic size that is used to trap it for study and manipulation. Optical tweezers are used to study molecules and could be used by surgeons to work on a single cell.

op·tic ax·is *n.* a line passing through a lens, a curved mirror, or a crystal along which light can travel without undergoing double refraction

op·tic chi·as·ma *n.* the X-shaped nerve tract beneath the brain where the optic nerves from each eye meet and that enables certain of their constituent nerve fibers to cross sides

op·tic cup *n.* a two-walled depression in a human embryo that develops into the retina

op·tic disk *n.* ANAT a small light-sensitive area of the retina marking the point where nerve fibers from the retinal cells converge to form the optic nerve

op·ti·cian /op tísh'n/ *n.* **1.** *U.K.* = **optometrist 2.** MAKER AND SELLER OF LENSES somebody who is qualified to fit and supply glasses and contact lenses, but not to examine eyes or prescribe corrective lenses

op·tic nerve *n.* either of the paired second cranial nerves whose nerve fibers transmit visual light signals from the eye to the brain

op·tics /óptiks/ *n.* STUDY OF LIGHT the study of light or electromagnetic radiation in the visible, infrared, and ultraviolet regions (*takes a singular verb*) ■ *npl.* LENS-EQUIPPED INSTRUMENTS instruments used for detecting electromagnetic radiation and for attaining highly accurate long-range vision (*takes a plural verb*)

op·tic ves·i·cle *n.* a fold of the embryonic forebrain that develops into the retina and optic nerve

op·ti·ma plural of **optimum**

op·ti·mal /óptəm'l/ *adj.* most desirable or favorable ○ *waited for optimal weather conditions* [Late 19thC. Formed from Latin *optimus* "best," literally "richest." Ultimately from an Indo-European word meaning "to produce," which is also the ancestor of English *opus* and *opulent.*] —**op·ti·mal·i·ty** /òptə mállətee/ *n.* —**op·ti·mal·ly** /óptəməlee/ *adv.*

op·ti·mism /óptə mìzzəm/ *n.* **1.** TENDENCY TO EXPECT THE BEST the tendency to believe, expect, or hope that things will turn out well **2.** CONFIDENCE the attitude of somebody who feels positive or confident **3.** PHILOS DOCTRINE THAT OUR WORLD IS BEST a philosophical doctrine, first proposed by Leibnitz, that ours is the best of all possible worlds **4.** PHILOS **BELIEF IN THE ULTIMATE POWER OF GOOD** the belief that things are continually getting better and that good will ultimately triumph over evil [Mid-18thC. From French *optimisme*, from, ultimately, Latin *optimum* (see OPTIMUM).]

op·ti·mist /óptəmist/ *n.* **1. SOMEBODY POSITIVE** somebody who tends to feel hopeful and positive about future outcomes **2.** PHILOS **FOLLOWER OF OPTIMISM** somebody who follows any philosophical doctrine of optimism

op·ti·mis·tic /òptə místik/ *adj.* tending to take a hopeful and positive view of future outcomes —**op·ti·mis·ti·cal·ly** *adv.*

op·ti·mize /óptə mīz/ (**-mized, -miz·ing, -miz·es**) *v.* **1.** *vt.* **ENHANCE THE EFFECTIVENESS OF** to make something function at its best or most effective, or to use something to its best advantage **2.** *vt.* **SOLVE IN THE BEST WAY POSSIBLE** to find the best possible solution to a technical problem in which there are a number of competing or conflicting considerations **3.** *vi.* **SHOW OPTIMISM** to feel and show optimism (*archaic or formal*) **4.** *vt.* COMPUT **WRITE CONCISELY** to write computer programming instructions for a task in as few lines as possible to maximize the speed and efficiency of program execution. This will have the effect of, e.g., reducing the time it takes to store or retrieve data from a computer's memory. [Early 19thC. Formed from Latin *optimus* (see OPTIMAL).] —**op·ti·mi·za·tion** /òptəmi záysh'n/ *n.*

op·ti·mum /óptəməm/ *n.* (*plural* **-ma** /óptəmə/ *or* **-mums**) **BEST OF SEVERAL OUTCOMES** the best out of a number of possible options or outcomes ■ *adj.* **BEST** most desirable or favorable ○ *optimum trading conditions* [Late 19thC. From Latin, "best thing," from *optimus* (see OPTIMAL).]

op·tion /ópshən/ *n.* **1. CHOICE** a choice that is or can be taken ○ *Several options were ruled out right away* **2. FREEDOM OF CHOICE** the right, power, or freedom to make a choice ○ *I'd no option but to refuse.* **3.** BUSINESS **OPPORTUNITY AVAILABLE FOR A LIMITED TIME** an opportunity, usually a commercial opportunity, that has been made available for a limited period only **4. FOOTBALL PLAY** a play in football where the quarterback starts running parallel to the line of scrimmage and either keeps the ball or laterals it to another back running in the same direction **5.** FIN **RIGHT TO BUY OR SELL** the right to buy or sell something, especially a stock-market commodity, at a specified price during a specified time period **6.** POL = **local option 7. PIECE OF NONSTANDARD EQUIPMENT** an item of nonstandard equipment that can be purchased separately, e.g., on a car ■ *vt.* (**-tioned, -tion·ing, -tions**) COMM **HAVE OR GIVE A RIGHT TO** to give or acquire an exclusive right to something [Mid-16thC. Via French from the Latin stem *option-*, from *optare* (see OPT).] ◇ **keep** *or* **leave your options open** to put off making a decision or selection until a later time

op·tion·al /ópshən'l/ *adj.* left to individual choice ○ *It comes with optional air conditioning.* —**op·tion·al·ly** *adv.*

opto- *prefix.* **1.** eye, vision ○ *optometry* **2.** optical ○ *optoelectronics* [From Greek *optos* "seen, visible" (see OPTIC)]

op·to·e·lec·tron·ics /òptō i lek trónniks/ *n.* the branch of electronics dealing with devices that generate, modulate, transmit, and sense electromagnetic radiation in the visible-light, infrared, and ultraviolet ranges (*takes a singular verb*) [Mid-20thC. Coined from Greek *optos* "seen, visible" (see OPTIC) + ELECTRONICS.] —**op·to·e·lec·tron·ic** *adj.*

op·tom·e·ter /op tómmətər/ *n.* an instrument used to examine the eye for defects in vision [Mid-18thC. Coined from Greek *optos* "seen, visible" (see OPTIC) + -METER.]

op·tom·e·trist /op tómmətrist/ *n.* somebody who is qualified to carry out eye examinations and to prescribe and supply glasses and contact lenses

op·tom·e·try /op tómmətree/ *n.* the practice of examining eyes in order to determine levels of vision and then prescribing and supplying any necessary corrective lenses [Late 19thC. Coined from Greek *optos* "seen, visible" (see OPTIC) + -METRY.] —**op·to·met·ric** /òptə méttrik/ *adj.*

op·to·phone /óptə fōn/ *n.* a device used especially by sightless or visually impaired people that can convert written text into sounds [Early 20thC. Coined from Greek *optos* "seen, visible" (see OPTIC) + -PHONE.]

op·u·lence /óppyələns/, **op·u·len·cy** /óppyələnsee/ *n.* **1. RICHES** great wealth or affluence **2. LUXURY** luxury, especially of an extravagant, showy, or vulgar nature

op·u·lent /óppyələnt/ *adj.* **1. LAVISH** characterized by an obvious or lavish display of wealth or affluence **2. AMPLE** in richly abundant supply [Mid-16thC. From Latin *opulentus*, literally "producing much." Ultimately from an Indo-European word meaning "to produce," which is also the ancestor of English *opus, copious*, and *optimum*.] —**op·u·lent·ly** *adv.*

o·pun·ti·a /ō púnshee ə, ō púnshə/ *n.* a prickly pear cactus with attractive brightly colored flowers and oval fruits. The fruits of some varieties are edible. Genus: *Opuntia*. [Early 17thC. From modern Latin, genus name, from *Opunt-*, the stem of *Opus*, a city in Greece. The word originally referred to a plant that grew there.]

o·pus /ṓpəss/ (*plural* **o·pe·ra** /ṓpərə, óppərə/ *or* **o·pus·es**) *n.* **1. ONE OF A SERIES OF MUSICAL WORKS** a musical work, especially one of a numbered series by the same composer arranged to show the order in which they were written or cataloged **2. CREATIVE WORK** a creative piece of work in any field of the arts. ◊ **magnum opus** [Early 18thC. From Latin, "work." Ultimately from an Indo-European word meaning "to produce," which is also the ancestor of English *opulent* and *optimum*.]

o·pus an·gli·ca·num /ṓpəss anglə káanəm/ *n.* a form of English embroidery that was popular in the Middle Ages, usually seen on ecclesiastical robes [Mid-19thC. From medieval Latin, literally "English work."]

o·pus·cule /ō pús kyool/, **o·pus·cu·lum** /ō púskyələm/ (*plural* **-la** /-kyələ/) *n.* a minor or insignificant creative work, especially a musical or literary work [Mid-17thC. Via French from Latin *opusculum*, literally "little work," from *opus* (see OPUS).]

or[1] /awr/; *unstressed* /ər/ CORE MEANING: a conjunction used to link two or more alternatives. In a series of alternatives, it is usually used only before the last alternative. ○ *Which do you prefer, butter or low-fat spread?* ○ *factors that may trigger or exacerbate the illness*

1. *conj.* **FOLLOWING "EITHER" OR "WHETHER"** used to join two alternatives when the first is introduced by "either" or "whether" ○ *Either you typed the wrong name, or something is wrong with the equipment.* **2.** *conj.* **INDICATING APPROXIMATION** used between two numbers to indicate an approximate quantity or to imply a few of something ○ *Hit the return key every three or four seconds until you get a greeting message* . **3.** *conj.* **REPHRASING A STATEMENT** used to introduce a rephrasing synonym or correction of a statement just made ○ *fetal oxygen deprivation, or hypoxia* **4.** *conj.* **OTHERWISE** used to give an explanation of a statement just made ○ *You'd better leave or you'll be late.* **5.** *conj.* **WHETHER OR EITHER** a poetic word for "either" or "whether," preceding the first of two alternatives, with "or" also preceding the second alternative (*archaic or literary*) **6.** *conj., prep.* **BEFORE** before (*archaic*)

or[2] *adj.* HERALDRY used to describe an element of a coat of arms or other heraldic insignia that is colored gold [15thC. Via French from Latin *aurum* "gold" (see AURUM).]

OR[1] /awr/ *n.* a computer circuit that reproduces the logical element represented by the word "or." It is one of the basic interconnected circuits that perform a computer's logical functions.

OR[2] *abbr.* **1. OR, O.R.** operating room **2.** INSUR owner's risk **3.** own recognizance **4.** operations research **5.** Oregon

-or[1] *suffix.* one that does or performs ○ *conductor* [Via Old French *-eor, -eur* and Anglo-Norman *-(o)ur* from Latin *-or* and *-ator*]

-or[2] *suffix.* condition, state, activity ○ *demeanor* [Via Old French *-eur* from Latin *-or*]

o·ra plural of **os**

or·ach /áwrəch/, **or·ache** *n.* a plant that has grayish-green edible leaves resembling spinach leaves and spikes of tiny green flowers. It grows wild throughout Europe. Genus: *Atriplex*. [13thC. Via Anglo-Norman *arasche* from, ultimately, Greek *atraphaxus*, of unknown origin.]

or·a·cle /áwrək'l/ *n.* **1. SOURCE OF WISDOM** somebody or something considered to be a source of knowledge, wisdom, or prophecy **2. WISE SAYING** a wise or prophetic statement **3. SHRINE OF AN ANCIENT GOD** in ancient Greece and Rome, a shrine dedicated to a particular god where people went to consult a priest or priestess in times of trouble or uncertainty. One of the most famous was the Delphic Oracle of Apollo, where Oedipus was given the prophetic warning that he would kill his father, Laius, and marry his mother, Jocasta. **4. GREEK OR ROMAN DEITY** an ancient Greek or Roman deity that a priest or priestess would consult for advice on behalf of troubled or uncertain people **5. ADVICE FROM GREEK OR ROMAN DEITY** a piece of advice, often in the form of a puzzle or an enigmatic statement, handed down by a Greek or Roman deity **6. GOD-GIVEN MESSAGE** a message believed to come from God in response to a request, plea, or petition **7.** BIBLE **AREA OF A BIBLICAL TEMPLE** the most sacred area in any of the biblical Temples, often referred to as the Holy of Holies [14thC. Via French from Latin *oraculum*, from *orare* "to speak" (see ORATE).]

or·a·cles /áwrək'lz/ *npl.* the books of the Bible

o·rac·u·lar /aw rákyələr, ə-/ *adj.* **1. OF OR AS AN ORACLE** relating to oracles or in the form of an oracle **2. WISE** knowing, wise, or prophetic **3. MYSTERIOUS** puzzling, ambiguous, or enigmatic [Mid-17thC. Formed from Latin *oraculum* (see ORACLE).] —**o·rac·u·lar·i·ty** /aw ràkyə lérrətee, ə-/ *n.* —**o·rac·u·lar·ly** /aw rákyələrlee, ə-/ *adv.*

o·ra·cy /áwrəsee/ *n.* the ability to speak fluently and articulately and to understand and respond to what other people say [Mid-20thC. Formed from ORAL, on the model of "literacy."]

o·ra et la·bo·ra /àw raa et lə báw ràa, àwrə et lə báwrə/ a Latin phrase meaning "pray and work"

o·ral /áwrəl/ *adj.* **1. OF THE MOUTH** relating to or belonging to the mouth ○ *oral hygiene* **2. FOR THE MOUTH** designed for use in the mouth **3. SPOKEN** existing in spoken form as distinct from written form **4. ADMINISTERED BY MOUTH** used to describe medicines that are taken by mouth. ◊ **parenteral 5.** PHON **WITH A RELEASE OF AIR THROUGH THE MOUTH** used to describe a speech sound that is produced by means of an airstream that escapes through the mouth only, with the nasal cavity sealed off by the velum. ◊ **nasal 6.** PSYCHOANAL **DERIVING PLEASURE VIA THE MOUTH** used in Freudian analysis to describe a stage in child development when erotic pleasure is derived from mouth-associated sensations, especially through feeding, thumb-sucking, and putting objects into the mouth. ◊ **phallic 7.** PSYCHOANAL **DEPENDENT AND AGGRESSIVE** used in Freudian analysis to describe a dependent, selfish and aggressive personality type with a tendency to derive pleasure from mouth-related activities such as eating, drinking, or smoking **8.** BIOL **WHERE THE MOUTH IS SITED** used to describe the surface of the body of an animal such as the underside of a starfish, on which the mouth is situated ■ *n.* **1.** EDUC **TEST REQUIRING SPOKEN ANSWERS** an examination or test that involves candidates giving spoken answers to spoken questions, as distinct from one where the questions and answers are in written form **2. ORAL SEX** oral sex, or an act of oral sex (*slang*) [Early 17thC. From late Latin *oralis*, from Latin *or-*, the stem of *os* "mouth" (source also of English *orifice, oscillate*, and *usher*).] —**o·ral·ly** *adv.*

WORD KEY: SYNONYMS

See Synonyms at ***verbal***.

o·ral con·tra·cep·tive *n.* a pill that is taken daily to prevent conception, especially one that combines an estrogen and a progestogen

o·ral his·to·ry *n.* **1. HISTORY RECORDED BY PARTICIPANTS IN EVENTS** the personal recollections of people who participated in historical events, recorded on audio or video tape or told to a younger generation **2. STUDY OF HISTORY RECORDED ORALLY** the branch of history that deals with personal accounts of historical events or periods recorded on audio or video tape —**o·ral his·to·ri·an** *n.*

o·ral hy·giene *n.* = **dental hygiene** —**o·ral hy·gien·ist** *n.*

O·ral Law, **Oral Torah** *n.* Jewish religious law that developed out of interpretations of the Torah and was originally passed on orally by rabbis and sages before being recorded in writing, principally in the Mishnah and Talmud

o·ral sex *n.* sexual activity that involves using the mouth and tongue to stimulate a partner's genitals

o·ral so·ci·e·ty *n.* a community in which people do not read or write

o·ral tra·di·tion *n.* a community's cultural and historical background preserved and passed on from one generation to the next in spoken stories and song, as distinct from being written down

O·ran /aw ráan/ city and port in Algeria, on the northwestern coast of the country. Population: 664,000 (1989).

o·rang /áw rang/ *n.* = **orangutan** [Late 18thC. Shortening.]

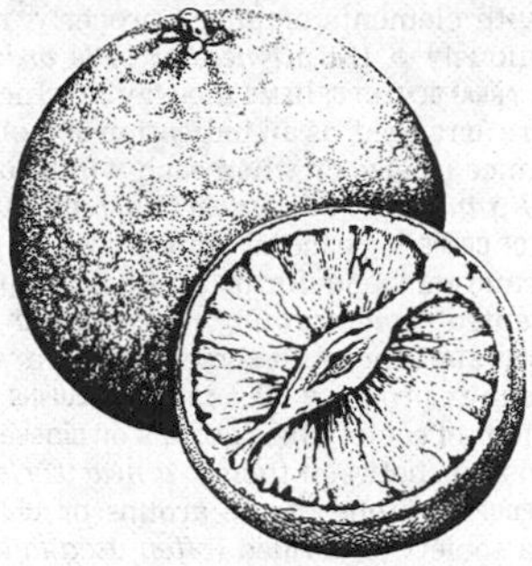

Orange

or·ange /áwrənj/ *n.* **1.** TREES **TREE YIELDING JUICY FRUIT** a tree that is widely grown throughout warmer regions for its edible juicy citrus fruit. It has sweet-smelling blossoms and fine-grained wood. Genus: *Citrus.* **2.** FOOD **CITRUS FRUIT** a round or oval fruit of the orange tree, with a thick skin and juicy flesh divided into segments. As well as being eaten fresh, it is often squeezed for its juice. (*often used before a noun*) **3.** COLORS **COLOR OF AN ORANGE** the bright color of the skin of an orange. It is a secondary color that is a mixture of red and yellow. **4.** INDUST = **orangewood 5.** TREES **TREE WITH FRUITS SIMILAR TO THE ORANGE** any tree or plant such as the mock orange and the Osage orange that produces fruits similar to the citrus orange **6.** ZOOL **ORANGE-COLORED BUTTERFLY** a butterfly with predominantly orange coloration such as the sulfur butterfly. Family: Pieridae. **7.** ARTS **PIGMENT MIXING YELLOW AND RED** a pigment or dye that is a mixture of red and yellow **8.** TEXTILES, CLOTHES **MATERIAL OF THE COLOR ORANGE** fabric or clothing that is orange in color **9. ORANGE-COLORED OBJECT** an object that is colored orange ■ *adj.* **OF REDDISH-YELLOW COLOR** having the bright reddish-yellow color of an orange [13thC. Via Old French *pomme d'orenge*, a translation (influenced by *Orange*, a town in France) of Italian *melarancia* "orange fruit," via Arabic *nāranj* and Persian *nārang* from Sanskrit *nāraṅgah*.] —**or·ang·ey** *adj.*

Or·ange /áwrənj/ *n.* **DUTCH ROYAL FAMILY** the royal house of the Netherlands from the accession of King William I in 1815. The family had earlier been Dutch princes and stadtholders, or magistrates. William of Orange became King William III of Great Britain and Ireland in 1689. ■ *adj.* **1. OF HOUSE OF ORANGE** relating to or belonging to the house of Orange **2. OF ORANGE ORDER** relating to or belonging to the Orange Order

Or·ange[1] **1.** river in southern Africa. Its lower course forms the boundary between South Africa and Namibia. Length: 1,300 mi./2,090 km. **2.** city in Orange County, southwestern California, situated 22 mi./35 km east of Long Beach. Population: 110,658 (1990). **3.** town in southwestern New Haven County, southern Connecticut, situated east of the Housatonic River. Population: 12,830 (1990). **4.** city in Essex County, northeastern New Jersey, situated 4 mi./6 km northwest of Newark. Population: 29,925 (1990). **5.** town in central New South Wales, Australia. It is a center for fruit and vegetable growing and light industry. Population: 34,980 (1996).

Or·ange[2] /aw ráaNzh/ town in Vaucluse Department, Provence-Alpes-Côte d'Azur Region, southeastern France. Population: 26,964 (1996).

or·ange·ade /áwrən jáyd/ *n.* a sometimes carbonated nonalcoholic drink flavored with orange or tasting like oranges [Early 18thC. Formed from ORANGE, on the model of "lemonade."]

Or·ange·burg /áwrinj bùrg, órrinj-/ city and county seat of Orangeburg County, central South Carolina, situated 35 mi./56 km southeast of Columbia. Population: 13,739 (1990).

or·ange chro·mide *n.* a freshwater tropical fish native to Asia with distinctive orange spotty markings that make it a popular aquarium fish. Latin name: *Etropus maculatus.*

or·ange hawk·weed *n.* a perennial European variety of the hawkweed plant that has clusters of orange-red flower heads. Latin name: *Hieracium aurantiacum.*

Or·ange·man /áwrənjmən/ (*plural* **-men** /-mən/) *n.* **1. ORANGE ORDER MEMBER** a member of the Orange Order **2. PROTESTANT IRISHMAN** an Irishman of the Protestant faith [Late 18thC. From the name of the ORANGE ORDER.]

or·ange milk·weed *n.* = **butterfly weed**

Or·ange Or·der *n.* a Protestant organization formed in 1795 with the aim of celebrating and defending Protestantism in Northern Ireland [So called because it was originally formed out of loyalty to William of *Orange* (WILLIAM III)]

or·ange peel *n.* the thick dimpled skin of an orange

or·ange-peel *adj.* having a dimpled surface caused, e.g., by open pores or cellulite ○ *orange-peel skin*

or·ange pe·koe *n.* a high-quality black tea grown in India and Sri Lanka and made using only the small, young, tender leaves growing at the tips of the stems

or·ange·root /áwrənj root/ *n.* BOT = **goldenseal**

or·ange·ry /áwrənjree/ (*plural* **-ries**) *n.* a building where orange trees are grown, especially a large greenhouse for use in cooler climates

or·ange stick *n.* a small stick used for manicuring the fingernails and cuticles that is usually wooden or plastic, with one pointed end and one rounded end [So called because it is usually made from orangewood]

or·ange·wood /áwrənj wòòd/ *n.* the yellowish hard fine-grained wood of the orange tree, used for making furniture and carved objects

Orangutan

o·rang·u·tan /ə rángə tán, aw-/, **o·rang·u·tang** *n.* a large tailless ape with reddish-brown coarse and shaggy hair and long powerful arms that is found only in the forests of Borneo and Sumatra. Latin name: *Pongo pygmaeus.* [Late 17thC. From Malay *orang hutan* "forest person."]

o·rate /aw ráyt, áw ràyt/ (**o·rat·ed, o·rat·ing, o·rates**) *vi.* **1. MAKE FORMAL PUBLIC SPEECH** to make a speech, especially a public, formal, or ceremonial speech (*formal*) **2. SPEAK POMPOUSLY** to speak in a pompous or boring way, or for an inappropriately long time [Early 17thC. From Latin *orare* "to speak, pray" (source of English *adore, oracle,* and *inexorable*).]

o·ra·tion /aw ráysh'n/ *n.* **1. FORMAL PUBLIC SPEECH** a speech, lecture, or other instance of formal or ceremonial public speaking **2. POMPOUS SPEECH** a speech that is considered pompous, boring, or inappropriately long **3. PUBLIC SPEECH SHOWING RHETORICAL SKILLS** an academic speech that is designed to show the speaker's rhetorical skills, especially a speech given as an exercise in public speaking, often in a public speaking contest

or·a·tor /áwrətər/ *n.* **1. GIVER OF SPEECHES** somebody who gives speeches, especially somebody practiced and skilled in giving formal, ceremonial, or persuasive public addresses **2. POMPOUS SPEAKER** somebody who has a tendency to speak in a pompous or boring way, or who speaks for an inappropriately long time **3.** LAW **PETITIONER** somebody who files a petition or a complaint in a court of law (*archaic*)

or·a·to·ri·o /áwrə táwree ō/ (*plural* **-os**) *n.* **1. PIECE OF RELIGIOUS CLASSICAL MUSIC** a musical composition for voices and instruments that has a religious theme, often telling a sacred story but not using costumes, scenery, or dramatic staging. Handel's *Messiah* is an example of this genre. **2. ORATORIOS IN GENERAL** oratorios as a musical genre [Mid-17thC. From Italian, named for the *Oratory* of Saint Philip Neri in Rome, where the form was used in musical services.]

or·a·to·ry[1] /áwrə tàwree/ *n.* **1. ART OF PUBLIC SPEAKING** the art of speaking in public with style, cogency, and grace **2. RHETORICAL SKILL AND ELOQUENCE** eloquence in public speaking, especially of the kind that shows the speaker's rhetorical skills **3. POMPOSITY IN SPEECH** pompous, boring, or inappropriately long speech [Early 16thC. From Latin *(ars) oratoria* "(art) of speaking," from *orator* (see ORATE).] —**or·a·tor·i·cal** /áwrə táwrik'l/ *adj.* —**or·a·tor·i·cal·ly** *adv.*

or·a·to·ry[2] /áwrə tàwree/ (*plural* **-ries**) *n.* a place for private prayer or worship such as a small secluded chapel, usually set aside in a church [14thC. Via Anglo-Norman *oratorie* from, ultimately, Latin *orare* "to speak, pray."]

Or·a·to·ry /áwrə tàwree/ *n.* a religious society that has secular priests and is a branch of the Roman Catholic Church. It was founded in 1575 by Saint Philip Neri.

Orb

orb /awrb/ *n.* **1. KING'S OR QUEEN'S JEWELED SPHERE** a small sphere usually made from a precious metal set with jewels and with a cross set onto the top of it that forms part of a sovereign's ceremonial regalia. ◊ **scepter 2. SPHERE** a sphere or spherical object **3. EYE** an eye (*literary*) **4. AREA OF INTEREST** a sphere of interest, influence, or activity (*literary*) **5.** ASTRON **CELESTIAL BODY** a planet or other celestial body, especially the Sun, the Moon, or the Earth (*archaic or literary*) **6. CELESTIAL BODY'S PATH** the orbiting path of a planet or other celestial body (*archaic or literary*) **7. CIRCLE** a circle (*archaic or literary*) **8.** ASTRON **CONCENTRIC PLANET-HOLDING SPHERE** any one of the concentric spheres that were formerly believed by astronomers to hold the planets in their orbital paths ■ *v.* (**orbed, orb·ing, orbs**) **1.** *vt.* **ENCIRCLE** to encircle something (*literary*) **2.** *vti.* **MAKE OR BECOME CIRCULAR** to become circular or make something circular (*archaic*) [14thC. From Latin *orbis* "wheel, circle," of unknown origin.]

or·bic·u·lar /awr bíkyələr/, **or·bic·u·late** /awr bíkyələt, -làyt/ *adj.* **1. ROUND** in the form of a circle or sphere (*formal*) **2.** BOT **FLAT AND ROUND** used to describe plant parts, especially leaves, that are flat and round or roundish [14thC. From late Latin *orbicularis*, from Latin *orbiculus*, literally "small globe," from *orbis* "globe."] —**or·bic·u·lar·i·ty** /awr bikyə lérrətee/ *n.* —**or·bic·u·lar·ly** *adv.* —**or·bic·u·late·ly** *adv.*

or·bit /áwrbit/ *n.* **1.** ASTRON, SPACE TECH **PATH OF A PLANET, SATELLITE, OR MOON** the path that a celestial body such as a planet, moon, or satellite follows around a larger celestial body such as the Sun **2.** ASTRON, SPACE TECH **CELESTIAL BODY'S REVOLUTION** a single revolution of a celestial body around a larger body **3. AREA OF INTEREST** a sphere of interest, influence, or activity **4.** ANAT, ZOOL **EYE SOCKET** a round cavity in which an eye is located in the skull of a vertebrate **5.** PHYS **ELECTRON'S PATH AROUND AN ATOM'S NUCLEUS** the path that an electron takes as it moves around the nucleus of an atom ■ *v.* (**-bit·ed, -bit·ing, -bits**) **1.** *vti.* ASTRON **MOVE AROUND A CELESTIAL BODY** to move around a celestial body in a path dictated by the force of gravity exerted by that body **2.** *vt.* SPACE TECH **PUT INTO CELESTIAL ORBIT** to send something, especially a spacecraft or an artificial satellite, into orbit **3.** *vi.* **FOLLOW A REGULAR PATH** to move regularly or repeatedly along the same path, especially a circular path [Mid-16thC. From Latin *orbita* "wheel-track," of uncertain origin: probably formed from *orbis* "wheel, circle."] ◇ **go into orbit** to become suddenly extremely angry and upset (*slang*) ◇ **put somebody into orbit** to make somebody suddenly extremely angry or upset (*slang*)

or·bit·al /áwrbit'l/ *adj.* OF ORBITS belonging to or relating to an orbit ■ *n.* PHYS SPACE IN AN ATOM OCCUPIED BY AN ELECTRON a subdivision of the available space within an atom for an electron to orbit the nucleus. An atom has many orbitals, each of which has a fixed size and shape and can hold up to two electrons. —**or·bit·al·ly** *adv.*

or·bit·al space ve·hi·cle *n.* a vehicle that transports payloads to and from points in space having different orbits such as a space station, a satellite, and the Moon

or·bit·al ve·loc·i·ty *n.* the speed an object must maintain in order to remain in a given orbit. If the speed slows, the orbit will decay and the orbiting object will be drawn to the larger body.

or·bi·teer /àwrbi tе́er/ (**-teered, -teer·ing, -teers**) *vti.* to go up a high mountain without using climbing gear and by walking in ever higher circles until reaching the summit [Back-formation from ORBITEERING]

or·bi·teer·ing /àwrbi tе́ering/ *n.* the sport or practice of going up high mountains without using climbing gear and by walking in circles of ever higher altitude until reaching the top [Coined from ORBIT, on the model of "mountaineering" or "orienteering"]

or·bit·er /áwrbitər/ *n.* a spacecraft or satellite that is designed to orbit a celestial body but not to land on it

orb weav·er *n.* a spider that weaves a broad intricate web of silk to entrap its prey

or·ca /áwrkə/ *n.* = **killer whale** [Mid-19thC. Via modern Latin, former genus name, from Latin *orca* "large sea creature."]

orch. *abbr.* MUSIC **1.** orchestra **2.** orchestrated by

or·chard /áwrchərd/ *n.* **1.** AREA OF FRUIT OR NUT TREES an area of land on which fruit or nut trees are grown, especially commercially **2.** FRUIT OR NUT TREES COMMERCIALLY PLANTED all the fruit or nut trees growing in a particular area, planted for commercial reasons [Old English *ortgeard*, from an uncertain first element + YARD]

WORD KEY: CULTURAL NOTE

The Cherry Orchard, a play by the Russian dramatist Anton Chekhov (1903–04). Chekhov described his last play as a comedy, but it is often played as tragedy. It depicts the decline of the Ranyevskayas, a family of upper-class landowners, who despite being faced with bankruptcy refuse to contemplate merchant Lopakhin's suggestion that they sell their beloved cherry orchard.

or·chard grass *n.* a tall grass grown in many countries for pasture and hay. Latin name: *Dactylis glomerata.*

or·char·dist /áwrchərdist/ *n.* somebody who owns or manages an orchard

or·ches·tra /áwrkəstrə/ *n.* **1.** MUSIC LARGE GROUP OF CLASSICAL MUSICIANS a large group of musicians playing classical music, consisting of sections of string, woodwind, brass, and percussion players, and directed by a conductor **2.** MUSIC GROUP OF MUSICIANS a group of musicians, especially a fairly large group usually but not always playing classical music **3.** THEATER PLACE FOR MUSICIANS IN THEATER the part of a theater where the musicians sit, immediately in front of the stage or under the front part of the stage **4.** THEATER MAIN FLOOR OF THEATER the main floor of a theater **5.** THEATER FRONT SEATS the front section of seats on the lower and main floor of a theater **6.** THEATER PLACE FOR THE CHORUS the semicircular area in front of the stage in ancient Greek theaters, reserved for the chorus [Early 17thC. Via Latin, "space in front of the stage where the chorus danced," from Greek *orkhēstra*, from *orkheisthai* "to dance."]

or·ches·tral /awr késtrəl/ *adj.* relating to orchestras or intended for an orchestra, especially a symphony orchestra —**or·ches·tral·ly** *adv.*

or·ches·tra pit *n. U.K.* = **orchestra**

or·ches·trate /áwrkə strayt/ (**-trat·ed, -trat·ing, -trates**) *vt.* **1.** MUSIC ARRANGE MUSIC FOR AN ORCHESTRA to arrange or compose music to be played by an orchestra **2.** ORGANIZE SOMETHING to organize a situation or event unobtrusively so that a desired effect or outcome is achieved ○ *The press conference had clearly been carefully orchestrated.* —**or·ches·tra·tor** *n.*

or·ches·tra·tion /àwrkə stráysh'n/ *n.* **1.** MUSIC MUSICAL ARRANGEMENT the arrangement of a piece of music to be played by an orchestra **2.** DISCREET ORGANIZING the unobtrusive organizing of a situation or event to produce a desired effect or outcome

or·ches·tri·on /awr késtree ən/, **or·ches·tri·na** /àwrkə stre̅e̅nə/ *n.* a mechanical musical instrument similar to a barrel organ, designed to imitate the sounds of an orchestra [Mid-19thC. Formed from ORCHESTRA on the model of *accordion*.]

Orchid

or·chid /áwrkid/ *n.* **1.** FLOWERING PLANT any one of a large family of perennial plants prized for their beautiful and fragrant flowers and found mostly in tropical climates. Family: Orchidaceae. **2.** ORCHID FLOWER a flower from an orchid plant, typically a delicate fragrant flower with three petals [Mid-19thC. From the Latin stem *orchid-*, which was mistakenly formed from *orchis* (see ORCHIS).]

or·chi·da·ceous /àwrki dáyshəss/ *adj.* relating to, belonging to, or characteristic of the orchid family [Mid-19thC. Formed from modern Latin *Orchidaceae*, family name of the orchid.]

or·chi·dec·to·my *n.* = **orchiectomy** [Late 19thC. Coined from Greek *orkhis* (see ORCHIS) + -ECTOMY.]

or·chid tree *n.* a Southeast Asian tree that belongs to the pea family and has purplish flowers and deeply lobed leaves. Latin name: *Bauhinia variegata.*

or·chi·ec·to·my /àwrkee éktəmee/ (*plural* **-mies**), **or·chi·dec·to·my** (*plural* **-mies**) *n.* surgical removal of one or both testicles [Late 19thC. Coined from Greek *orkhis* (see ORCHIS) + -ECTOMY.]

or·chil /áwrkil, -chil/ *n.* **1.** LICHEN a lichen that yields a reddish dye. Genera: *Roccella* and *Lecanora.* **2.** RED DYE a reddish dye derived from an orchil lichen, obtained by treating the lichen with aqueous ammonia [15thC. Via Spanish *orchilla* from Catalan *orxella* of, ultimately, Arabic origin.]

or·chis /áwrkiss/ *n.* an orchid with a fleshy tuber and spikes of small flowers with spurred lips. Genus: *Orchis.* [Mid-16thC. Via Latin from Greek *orkhis*, literally "testicle" (from the tuber's shape).]

or·chi·tis /awr kítiss/ *n.* inflammation of one or both testicles, usually caused by infection. It can also develop in mumps, and if both testicles are affected it may result in sterility. [Late 18thC. Via modern Latin, which was coined from Greek *orkhis* "testicle" + -ITIS.] —**or·chit·ic** /awr kíttik/ *adj.*

OR cir·cuit /áwr-/ *n.* a circuit with two or more inputs and one output, whose output is high if one input is high

ord. *abbr.* **1.** BIOL order **2.** ordinal **3.** BIOL ordinance **4.** ordinary **5.** MIL ordnance

or·dain /awr dáyn/ (**-dained, -dain·ing, -dains**) *vt.* **1.** RELIG MAKE A RELIGIOUS APPOINTMENT to appoint somebody officially as a priest, minister, or rabbi ○. **2.** COMMAND FORMALLY to order or establish something formally, especially by law or by another authority (*formal*) ○ *laws of commercial transactions that had long been ordained by the government* [13thC. Via Old French *ordener* from Latin *ordinare* "to set in order," from *ordo* (see ORDER).] —**or·dain·er** *n.*

or·deal /awr de̅e̅l/ *n.* **1.** DIFFICULT EXPERIENCE a very difficult or harrowing experience, especially one lasting a long time **2.** ANCIENT TRIAL a trial in the past that involved subjecting a defendant to life-threatening danger, e.g., from fire or water, with the outcome regarded as reflecting divine judgment [Old English *ordāl* "trial, judgment." Ultimately from a prehistoric Germanic base meaning "to share out" that is also the ancestor of English *deal*.]

or·deal bean *n.* = **Calabar bean** [From its use in witchcraft trials]

or·der /áwrdər/ *n.* **1.** INSTRUCTION an instruction to do something **2.** INSTRUCTION TO PROVIDE SOMETHING an instruction to bring or supply something, e.g., a spoken instruction to a waiter or waitress, or a written instruction to a manufacturer or supplier of goods ○ *Can I take your order now?* **3.** SOMETHING PROVIDED something provided in response to an instruction ○ *If you are not completely satisfied, you may return your order.* **4.** NEATNESS an organized state, with elements arranged properly, neatly, or harmoniously ○ *We all need a little order in our lives.* **5.** ARRANGEMENT OF ITEMS the way in which several items are arranged, as an indication of their relative importance or size or when each will be dealt with ○ *I will announce the winners in reverse order.* **6.** ABSENCE OF CRIME a peaceful state in which laws are obeyed and misbehavior or crime is not present or is prevented ○ *maintaining order on our streets* **7.** FUNCTIONING STATE the state something is in when it is functioning properly **8.** SOCIAL GROUPING the arrangement of society into groups or classes and the relationships between them ○ *a new world order* **9.** SOCIAL GROUP any one of the groups or classes into which a society is divided (*often used in the plural*) **10.** BIOL SET OF RELATED FAMILIES a taxonomic classification made up of related families of organisms ○ *the cat family, in the order Carnivora* **11.** TYPE a kind or type of something, often one judged on importance or worth ○ *Exactly what order of stupidity are we dealing with?* **12.** LAW COURT'S INSTRUCTION an instruction issued by a judge or a court of law **13.** FIN FINANCIAL INSTRUCTION a written instruction to pay money **14. or·der, Or·der** RELIG RELIGIOUS COMMUNITY a religious community in which members live according to principles that are often based on the writings of a particular saint ○ *the Order of Saint Francis* **15.** CHR RELIGIOUS RANK any one of the grades into which the ministry is divided in some Christian denominations, including deacons, priests, bishops, and archbishops **16.** CHR RELIGIOUS SERVICE a form of Christian religious service used on specific occasions **17. or·der, Or·der** GROUP OF HONORED PEOPLE a prestigious group consisting of people who have been awarded an honor for services to their country, or the decoration indicating such an honor ○ *the Order of the Garter* **18.** ARCHIT ARCHITECTURAL STYLE any one of the five major styles of classical architecture, namely the Doric, Ionic, Corinthian, Tuscan, and Composite. They differ in the shapes and styles of columns and entablatures. **19.** MATH NUMBER OF ROWS AND COLUMNS the number of rows and columns in a matrix **20.** MATH NUMBER OF DIFFERENTIATIONS the number of times differentiation must be applied to a mathematical expression to obtain a specified derivative **21.** MATH GROUP MEMBERS the number of elements in a finite group **22.** SCI = **order of magnitude** **23.** MATH ORDER OF HIGHEST ORDER DIFFERENTIAL in a differential equation, the order of the highest order differential **24.** CHEM CLASSIFICATION OF CHEMICAL REACTIONS a classification of chemical reactions based on the mathematical relationship between the rate of a given chemical reaction and the concentration of the reacting chemical compounds ■ **or·ders** *npl.* = **holy orders** ■ *v.* (**-dered, -der·ing, -ders**) **1.** *vt.* GIVE SOMEBODY INSTRUCTIONS to command somebody to do something ○ *The colonel ordered the troops to move out.* **2.** *vt.* PRESCRIBE SOMETHING to give an instruction for something to be done **3.** *vti.* REQUEST SOMETHING to give an instruction for something to be provided, e.g., food in a restaurant or merchandise from a manufacturer or supplier **4.** *vt.* ARRANGE ITEMS to arrange items in a particular way, especially in the sequence in which they are to be dealt with ○ *addresses ordered by zip code* **5.** *vt.* ARRANGE THINGS NEATLY to put things into a neat, well organized state or into the required state ○ *ordered her business affairs prior to leaving for the summer* ■ *interj.* CALL FOR CALM used to request calm or observance of correct procedure, e.g., by a person chairing a debate [13thC. Via French *ordre*, from, ultimately, Latin *ordin-*, the stem of *ordo* (source of English *ordinal, coordinate,* and *ordinary*). The underlying sense is "conforming to order."] —**or·der·er** *n.* ◇ **in order 1.** in a correct sequence or arrangement ○ *Put them in order alphabetically.* **2.** in a condition of being correct or appropriate ○ *The customs official was checking that the paperwork was in order.* ◇ **in order to** *or* **that** used to introduce the object or purpose of something ◇ **on order** requested but not yet supplied or delivered ◇ **out of order 1.** not working properly or at all **2.** not in the correct sequence or place within a sequence **3.** *U.K.* not following accepted rules of procedure or conduct (*regional informal*) ◇ **a tall order** a request that is very difficult to fulfill (*informal*)

order around *vt.* to subject somebody to domineering or bullying treatment ○ *Don't think you can order me around.*

or·der arms *n.* MILITARY DRILL MOVEMENT an act of bringing a weapon, usually a rifle, from the shoulder to a resting position on the ground alongside the right leg, performed as part of a military drill ■ *interj.* COMMAND TO ASSUME ORDER ARMS used as a command in a military drill to assume the order arms position

or·der·ly /áwrdərlee/ *adj.* **1.** WELL-BEHAVED well-behaved or peaceful ○ *The meeting passed off in an orderly fashion* **2.** NEATLY ARRANGED arranged or organized in a neat, sensible, or proper way ○ *orderly bookshelves* ■ *n.* (*plural* **-lies**) **1.** MED ASSISTANT WORKING IN A HOSPITAL a hospital worker with no medical training who is employed to do various ancillary jobs such as transporting patients **2.** MIL SOLDIER WITH MINOR DUTIES a soldier acting as a senior officer's personal assistant who carries out a variety of minor duties such as carrying messages —**or·der·li·ness** *n.*

or·der of bat·tle *n.* the way that military forces are organized in preparation for a battle

or·der of busi·ness *n.* **1.** ISSUE NEEDING ATTENTION an issue or problem that needs to be dealt with ○ *The first order of business was a budget vote.* **2.** ORDER FOR DEALING WITH THINGS the order in which a number of items are to be discussed or dealt with, e.g., at a meeting

Or·der of Can·a·da *n.* in Canada, an order awarded to persons who are seen to have made an outstanding contribution to society. Companion, Officer, and Member are the three possible awards.

or·der of mag·ni·tude *n.* MATH, SCI the difference in size, usually expressed in powers of 10, between two quantities. If a quantity were 10 times greater than another, it would be an order of magnitude greater; if 100 times greater, it would be two orders of magnitude greater. ○ *The mass of the Earth is an order of magnitude greater than that of Mars.*

or·der of the day (*plural* **or·ders of the day**) *n.* **1.** AGENDA a program of items to be discussed or dealt with on a particular day, e.g., by a legislative body **2.** TYPICAL THING something that is regularly done, offered, chosen, or experienced during a particular period ○ *Heroism was the order of the day during the last big battle of the war*

or·di·nal /áwrd'nəl/ *adj.* **1.** MATH SHOWING POSITION showing the relative position in a sequence of numbers **2.** BIOL RELATING TO BIOLOGICAL ORDERS relating to a biological order in the classification of plants and animals ■ *n.* **1.** = **ordinal number** *n.* 1 **2.** CHR CATHOLIC BOOKLET in the Roman Catholic Church, an instruction booklet that lists the order of services in church worship **3.** CHR CHRISTIAN BOOKLET an instruction booklet that outlines rules and ceremony for the ordination of Christian ministers [Late 16thC. From late Latin *ordinalis* "ordered," from the Latin stem *ordin-* (see ORDER).]

or·di·nal num·ber *n.* **1.** NUMBER SHOWING ORDER a number used to show the relative position of something or somebody in a sequence. "First" and "second" are ordinal numbers. **2.** MATH, LOGIC SIZE AND ORDER OF A SET a measure of the size of an ordered set in addition to the order of its elements

or·di·nal scale *n.* STATS a list that shows only the relative positions of items on a scale, giving no measure of the difference between them

or·di·nance /áwrd'nəns/ *n.* **1.** LAW a law or rule made by an authority, e.g., a city government **2.** SOMETHING PRESCRIBED something regularly done because it is formally prescribed, especially a religious ceremony, such as Holy Communion (*formal*) [14thC. Via Old French from, ultimately, Latin *ordinare* (see ORDAIN).]

or·di·nand /áwrd'n ànd/ *n.* somebody who is a candidate for ordination as a Christian minister [Mid-19thC. From Latin *ordinandus*, from *ordinare* (see ORDAIN).]

or·di·nar·i·ly /áwrd'n èrrilee, àwrd'n érrilee/ *adv.* usually or normally

or·di·nar·y /áwrd'n èrree/ *adj.* **1.** USUAL usual or customary **2.** UNREMARKABLE not remarkable or special in any way, and therefore uninteresting and unimpressive ○ *He's just a pretty ordinary kind of guy.* **3.** COMMON of a common everyday kind **4.** LAW WITH IMMEDIATE JURISDICTION with immediate jurisdiction, as opposed to jurisdiction by delegation or deputation **5.** MATH WITH TWO VARIABLES relating to a differential equation that has only two variables ■ *n.* (*plural* **-ies**) **1.** LAW JUDGE a judge who acts in his or her own right **2.** **or·di·nar·y, Or·di·nar·y** CHR CLERIC WITH JUDGE'S POWERS a member of the clergy, especially a bishop, whose position brings with it the power to act as a judge in some ecclesiastical matters **3.** **or·di·nar·y, Or·di·nar·y** CHR UNCHANGING PARTS OF THE RELIGIOUS MASS in the Roman Catholic Church, the parts of the daily Mass that do not change from day to day **4.** **or·di·nar·y, Or·di·nar·y** CHR FORM FOR A RELIGIOUS SERVICE in the Roman Catholic Church, the correct form that a religious service, especially Mass, should take, or a book that sets out the correct form **5.** HERALDRY SIMPLE DESIGN any one of the simpler shapes or designs used on coats of arms **6.** EATING HOUSE an eating establishment or a dining room in an old tavern (*archaic*) [14thC. Via Old French from medieval Latin *ordinarius* "following the usual course," from the Latin stem *ordin-* (see ORDER).] —**or·di·nar·i·ness** *n.* ◇ **out of the ordinary** unusual or extraordinary

or·di·nar·y sea·man *n.* the lowest rank of sailors in the navies of some countries, subordinate to the more experienced able seaman

or·di·nate /áwrd'nət/ *n.* MATH the vertical or y coordinate of a point on a two-dimensional graph or diagram in which pairs of numbers denote distances along fixed horizontal and vertical axes. ◊ **abscissa** [Late 17thC. From Latin *ordinare* (see ORDAIN).]

or·di·na·tion /àwrd'n áysh'n/ *n.* an official investiture as a Christian priest or minister, or as a rabbi, or a ceremony during which somebody is consecrated as a priest, minister, or rabbi [15thC. Directly or via French from the Latin stem *ordination-*, from *ordinare* (see ORDAIN).]

ordn. *abbr.* ordnance

ord·nance /áwrdnəns/ *n.* **1.** MILITARY WEAPONS SYSTEMS military weapons systems, including supplies for their use and equipment for their maintenance **2.** DEPARTMENT RESPONSIBLE FOR WEAPONS AND SUPPLIES the army or government department that has responsibility for military weapons and supplies [14thC. Variant of ORDINANCE.]

or·do /áwr dō/ (*plural* **-dos** *or* **-di·nes** /-də neez/) *n.* in the Roman Catholic Church, a calendar detailing the forms of Mass and other services to be followed for each day in the year [Mid-19thC. From Latin (see ORDER).]

or·don·nance /áwrd'nəns/ *n.* the general arrangement of elements in architecture and in works of art and literature (*formal*) [Mid-17thC. From French, an alteration of Old French *ordenance* "ordinance."]

Or·do·vi·cian /àwrdə víshʼn/ *adj.* GEOL belonging to or dating from the second oldest period of the Paleozoic era, approximately 500 to 440 million years ago. Primitive fish and other sea creatures appeared during this period. [Late 19thC. Formed from Latin *Ordovices*, the name of an ancient Celtic people of North Wales, where rocks from the period were first identified.]

or·dure /áwrjər/ *n.* **1.** EXCREMENT excrement or dung (*formal*) **2.** SOMETHING MORALLY CORRUPTING obscene or otherwise morally corrupting material or behavior, or an example of it (*literary*) [14thC. Via Old French from, ultimately, Latin *horridus* "frightful," from *horrere* (see HORROR).]

ore /awr/ *n.* a naturally occurring mineral from which particular constituents, especially metals, can be profitably extracted [Old English *ōra*, *ār* "brass, bronze" (later altered in form through confusion with Old English)]

ö·re /úr ə/ (*plural* **ö·re**) *n.* **1.** SWEDISH CURRENCY UNIT a subunit of currency in Sweden, worth one hundredth of a krona. See table at **currency** **2.** COIN WORTH ONE KRONA a coin worth one krona [Early 18thC. From Swedish, from Old Norse *aurar*, of uncertain origin: probably from Latin *aureus* "golden."]

øre /úrrə/ *n.* **1.** DANISH OR NORWEGIAN CURRENCY UNIT a subunit of currency in Denmark or Norway, worth one hundredth of a krone. See table at **currency** **2.** COIN WORTH ONE KRONE a coin worth one krone [Early 18thC. From Danish or Norwegian, from Old Norse *aurar* (see ÖRE).]

Ore. *abbr.* Oregon

o·re·ad /áwree àd/ *n.* in Greek mythology, a mountain nymph [14thC. Via the Latin stem *Oread-* from, ultimately, Greek *Oreias*, from *oros* "mountain."]

Ör·e·bro /örə bróo/ city and county seat of Örebro Province, central Sweden, situated 100 mi./160 km west of Stockholm. Population: 119,635 (1995).

ore dress·ing *n.* the separation of the mineral content of an ore from the unwanted rock or earth

Oreg. *abbr.* Oregon

o·reg·a·no /ə réggə nō/ *n.* **1.** AROMATIC PLANT a perennial plant of the mint family that is an aromatic Mediterranean variety of wild marjoram. Latin name: *Origanum vulgare*. **2.** OREGANO LEAVES the fresh or dried leaves of oregano, used to add flavor in cooking [Late 18thC. Via Spanish from, ultimately, Greek *origanon* "wild marjoram," of uncertain origin: perhaps from *oros* "mountain" + *ganos* "brightness, joy."]

Oregon

Or·e·gon /áwrəgən, órrə-/; *often by outsiders* /-gon/ state of the United States bordered by the Pacific Ocean, Washington, Idaho, Nevada, and California. Capital: Salem. Population: 3,243,487 (1997). Area: 97,093 sq. mi./251,470 sq. km. —**Or·e·go·ni·an** /àwrə gṓnee ən, òrrə-/ *n., adj.*

Or·e·gon Ci·ty historic city in northwestern Oregon. Population: 14,698 (1990).

Or·e·gon grape *n.* an evergreen shrub of the barberry family that is native to the U.S. Pacific coast and has yellow flowers and edible black berries. Latin name: *Mahonia aquifolium*.

Or·e·gon myr·tle *n.* = **California laurel**

Or·e·gon pine *n.* = **Douglas fir**

Or·e·gon Trail *n.* a 19th-century route to the western United States extending from western Missouri to northern Oregon that was used by pioneers and settlers

Or·el·la·na /ò re láanə/, **Francisco de** (1500?–45) Spanish explorer and soldier. He was the first European to navigate the Amazon from the Andes to the Atlantic.

Ore Moun·tains /awr-/ range of mountains along the Czech-German border. Height: 4080 ft./1244 m.

O·ren·burg /uryin bóork, áwrən bùrg/ city in southwestern Siberian Russia, the capital of Orenburg Oblast. Population: 557,000 (1992).

O·ren·se /aw rénse/ city in northwestern Spain and capital of Orense Province, in the autonomous region of Galicia. Population: 110,796 (1995).

O·re·o /áwree ō/ *tdmk.* a trademark for a cream-filled sandwich cookie

Ö·re·sund /őrə sùn, őrə sóond/, **Ø·re·send** channel in northern Europe, between the Kattigat Strait and the Baltic Sea. Length: about 65 mi./105 km.

O·re·ti /ō ráytee/ river in the south of the South Island, New Zealand. It rises in the Southern Alps and flows south to the Foveaux Strait. Length: 126 mi./203 km.

orf /awrf/ *n.* VET a pox caused by a virus, affecting sheep and goats, and also transmittable to humans, in which pus-filled blisters form on the animals' lips [Mid-19thC. Origin uncertain: probably from Old Norse *hrufa*.]

or·fray *n.* SEW = **orphrey**

org. *abbr.* **1.** organic **2.** organization **3.** organized

or·gan /áwrgən/ *n.* **1.** MUSIC MUSICAL KEYBOARD INSTRUMENT a large musical keyboard instrument that can produce a wide range of sounds at different volumes using compressed air passed through metal pipes **2.** MUSIC INSTRUMENT SIMILAR TO ORGAN any one of various musical instruments that make sounds similar to the organ without the use of pipes, e.g., electronically or using reeds **3.** BIOL BODY PART a complete and independent part of a plant or animal that has a specific function ○ *the organs of the digestive system* **4.** MEANS OF COMMUNICATION a newspaper or magazine regarded as a means of communication, especially one communicating the views of a

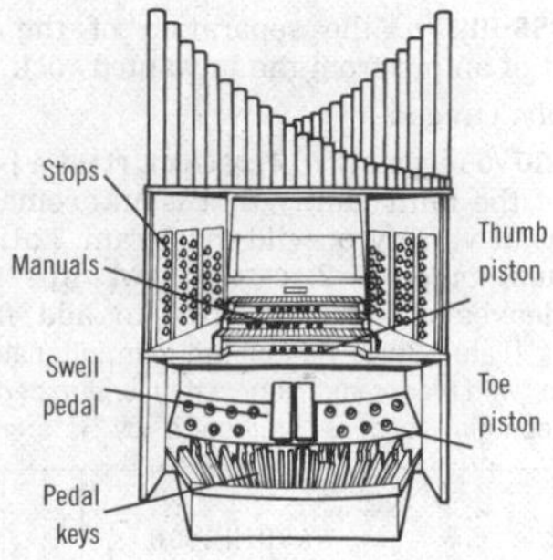

Organ

particular group such as a political party (*formal*) ○ *the daily organ of left-of-center politics* **5.** POL **AGENCY** an organization or body acting on behalf of a larger institution, especially a government (*formal*) ○ *There were no secrets about the institute's role as an organ of the business community* **6. PENIS** a penis (*used euphemistically*) [13thC. Via Old French *organe* and Latin *organum* from Greek *organon* "tool, instrument." Ultimately from an Indo-European word meaning "to do," ancestor also of English *work* and *orgy*.]

or·ga·na plural of **organon, organum**

or·gan·dy /áwrgəndee/ (*plural* **-dies**), **or·gan·die** *n.* a lightweight see-through stiff cotton fabric used especially in dressmaking [Early 19thC. From French *organdi*, of unknown origin.]

or·gan·elle /àwrgə nél/ *n.* CELL BIOL a specialized part of a cell, e.g., the nucleus or the mitochondrion, that has its own particular function [Early 20thC. From modern Latin *organella*, literally "small organ," from medieval Latin *organum* (see ORGAN).]

or·gan grind·er *n.* a street musician who plays a barrel organ, traditionally accompanied by a small monkey who circulates to collect money from bystanders [From the hand-cranked barrel organ]

or·gan·ic /awr gánnik/ *adj.* **1. OF LIVING THINGS** relating to, derived from, or characteristic of living things **2. DEVELOPING NATURALLY** occurring or developing gradually and naturally, without being forced or contrived **3. INTRINSIC** forming a basic and inherent part of something and largely responsible for its identity or makeup **4. WITH ELEMENTS EFFICIENTLY COMBINED** consisting of elements that exist together in a seemingly natural relationship that makes for organized efficiency **5.** AGRIC **AVOIDING SYNTHETIC CHEMICALS** relating to or employing agricultural practices that avoid the use of synthetic chemicals in favor of naturally occurring pesticides, fertilizers, and other growing aids **6.** FOOD **PRODUCED WITHOUT SYNTHETIC CHEMICALS** grown or reared without the use of synthetic chemicals ○ *a wide range of organic produce* **7.** MED **OF BODY'S ORGANS** relating to the organs of the body, specifically to basic changes in them brought about by physical disorders **8.** CHEM **BASED ON CARBON** belonging to a family of compounds characterized by chains or rings of carbon atoms that are linked to atoms of hydrogen and sometimes oxygen, nitrogen, and other elements ■ *n.* **ORGANIC SUBSTANCE** an organic substance, especially a fertilizer or pesticide —**or·gan·ic·i·ty** /àwrgə nissətee/ *n.*

or·gan·i·cal·ly /awr gánnikəlee/ *adv.* **1. NATURALLY** in a natural or seemingly natural way ○ *paintings with elements organically arranged* **2. WITHOUT CHEMICALS** without the use of synthetic chemicals, especially fertilizers and pesticides ○ *organically raised chickens*

or·gan·ic brain syn·drome *n.* a psychiatric disorder caused by a permanent or temporary physical change in the brain

or·gan·ic chem·is·try *n.* the scientific study of carbon-based compounds, originally limited to compounds that are the natural products of living things, now including the study of synthetic carbon compounds such as plastics. ◊ **inorganic chemistry**

or·gan·ic dis·ease *n.* MED a disorder associated with physical changes in one or more organs of the body

or·gan·i·cism /awr gánni sìzzəm/ *n.* **1.** BIOL = **holism** *n.* 1 **2.** MED **THEORY CONCERNING DISEASE** the theory that all diseases are due to structural changes in the body's organs **3.** SOC SCI **THEORY CONCERNING SOCIETY** the theory that society is analogous to, or shares characteristics with, living organisms —**or·gan·i·cist** *n.* —**or·gan·i·cis·tic** /àwrgənə sístik/ *adj.*

or·gan·ism /áwrgə nìzzəm/ *n.* **1.** BIOL **LIVING THING** a living thing such as a plant, animal, virus, or bacterium **2. SYSTEM OF INTERDEPENDENT PARTS** a functioning system of interdependent parts that resembles a living creature ○ *"Like any organism, public libraries and the people who run them must adapt and respond to change"* (Laurence Arnold, *Pulse of the People*; 1997) —**or·gan·is·mal** /àwrgə nízm'l/ *adj.* —**or·gan·is·mic** /-nízmik/ *adj.* —**or·gan·is·mi·cal·ly** /-níz mikəlee/ *adv.*

or·gan·ist /áwrgənist/ *n.* a musician who plays the organ

or·gan·i·za·tion /àwrgəni záysh'n/ *n.* **1. GROUP** a group of people identified by shared interests or purpose, e.g., a business ○ *Each news organization sent its own photographer.* **2. COORDINATION OF ELEMENTS** the coordinating of separate elements into a unit or structure ○ *in charge of the organization of international conferences* **3. RELATIONSHIP OF ELEMENTS** the relationships that exist between separate elements arranged into a coherent whole ○ *changes to the organization of the party* **4. EFFICIENCY IN ARRANGEMENT** efficiency in the way separate elements are arranged into a coherent whole ○ *Your working method lacks organization.*

or·gan·i·za·tion·al /àwrgəni záyshən'l, -záyshnəl/ *adj.* relating to the organizing of something or to the way in which it is organized ○ *Events like these are an organizational nightmare.* —**or·gan·i·za·tion·al·ly** *adv.*

or·gan·i·za·tion·al psy·chol·o·gy *n.* = **industrial psychology**

or·gan·i·za·tion the·o·ry *n.* the branch of sociology that deals with the structure of organizations and the systems and processes that operate within them

or·gan·ize /áwrgə nīz/ (**-ized, -iz·ing, -iz·es**) *v.* **1.** *vti.* **FORM SOMETHING** to form or establish something such as a club, by coming together or bringing people together into a structured group (*often passive*) **2.** *vt.* **COORDINATE** to oversee the coordination of the various elements of something **3.** *vt.* **ARRANGE ELEMENTS** to arrange the elements of something in a way that creates a particular structure ○ *a society organized along democratic lines* ○ *candidates organized into groups of three* **4.** *vt.* **MAKE MORE EFFECTIVE** to apply or impose efficient working methods in order to work effectively, or make somebody else work effectively ○ *Mature students are not necessarily better at organizing themselves.* **5.** *vti.* **FORM LABOR UNION** to recruit the workers in a place or industry into a labor union, or come together to form a labor union [15thC. Via French from medieval Latin *organizare*, literally "to provide with bodily organs," from Latin *organum* (see ORGAN). The underlying meaning is "having connecting parts like organisms."]

or·gan·ized /áwrgə nīzd/ *adj.* **1. LARGE-SCALE** existing on a large scale and involving the systematic coordination of many different elements ○ *organized religion* **2. EFFICIENT** working in a systematic and efficient way ○ *a motivated and organized self-starter*

or·gan·ized crime *n.* a powerful ruthless large-scale network of professional criminals, or such networks in general

or·gan·iz·er /áwrgə nīzər/ *n.* **1. SOMEBODY WHO ORGANIZES** somebody who is active in setting up or organizing projects and motivating others to take part **2. DATEBOOK** a small portable calendar and datebook used for planning, or a handheld computerized device with a simple database for managing appointments and other information **3. CONTAINER WITH COMPARTMENTS** a container with compartments for storing items in neat groups, e.g., a desktop container with compartments for pens, pencils, and other items of stationery **4.** EMBRYOL **EMBRYO PART** a part of an embryo that controls the differentiation of cells, eventually leading to the formation of organs and all the other specialized parts that make up an individual organism

organo- *prefix.* **1.** organ ○ *organography* **2.** organic ○ *organophosphate* [From Greek *organon* (see ORGAN)]

or·gan of Cor·ti /-káwrtee/ *n.* ANAT a part of the cochlea of the inner ear that transforms sound energy into nerve impulses and sends those impulses to the brain [Late 19thC. Named for the Italian anatomist Alfonso *Corti* (1822–88).]

or·gan·o·gen·e·sis /àwrgənō jénnəsiss, awr gànnə-/ *n.* the formation and development of animal or plant organs that takes place during the development of an embryo —**or·gan·o·ge·net·ic** /àwrgənō jə néttik, awr gànnə-/ *adj.* —**or·gan·o·ge·net·i·cal·ly** *adv.*

or·gan·og·ra·phy /àwrgə nóggrəfee/ *n.* the scientific description of the organs and other main structures of plants and animals —**or·gan·o·graph·ic** /àwrgənō gráffik, awr gànnə-/ *adj.* —**or·gan·o·graph·i·cal** *adj.* —**or·gan·o·graph·i·cal·ly** *adv.* —**or·gan·o·graph·ist** *n.*

or·gan·o·lep·tic /àwrgənō léptik, awr gànnə-/ *adj.* BIOL affecting an organ, especially a sense organ [Mid-19thC. From French *organoleptique*, from Greek *organon* "instrument" + *lēptikos* "receptive."] —**or·gan·o·lep·ti·cal·ly** *adv.*

or·gan·ol·o·gy /àwrgə nóllәjee/ *n.* the study of plant and animal organs —**or·gan·o·log·ic** /àwrgənō lójjik, awr gànnə-/ *adj.* —**or·gan·o·log·i·cal** *adj.* —**or·gan·ol·o·gist** *n.*

or·gan·o·me·tal·lic /àwrgənō mə tállik, awr gànnə-/ *adj.* CHEM relating to an organic compound containing one or more metal atoms, e.g., the gasoline additive tetraethyl lead

or·ga·non /áwrgə nòn/ (*plural* **-na** /-nə/ *or* **-nons**) *n.* a set of principles for use in philosophical or scientific investigation (*formal*) [Early 17thC. From Greek (see ORGAN).]

or·gan·o·phos·phate /àwrgənō fóss fàyt, awr gànnə-/ *n.* CHEM, AGRIC an organic compound containing phosphate groups. Organophosphates are widely used as pesticides and fertilizers, but there are medical concerns about their toxicity.

or·gan·o·ther·a·py /àwrgənō thérrəpee, awr gànnə-/ (*plural* **-pies**) *n.* MED treatment of diseases by administering substances derived from animal organs, e.g., bovine insulin, which is used to treat diabetes in humans —**or·gan·o·ther·a·peu·tic** /àwrgənō thèrrə pyóotik, awr gànnə-/ *adj.*

or·gan-pipe cac·tus *n.* a tall branched cactus native to the southwestern United States and northern Mexico. Latin name: *Lemaireocereus marginatus.* [From its tall pipe-shaped stems]

or·gan stop *n.* **1. SET OF ORGAN PIPES** a set of pipes on a musical organ, used to vary the tone and sometimes to imitate the sounds of other instruments **2. KNOB OPERATING PIPES** a knob or handle that controls the flow of air to an organ stop

or·ga·num /áwrgənəm/ (*plural* **-na** /-nə/ *or* **-nums**) *n.* **1. MUSICAL STYLE** a style of composition in western music of the late medieval period that combines plainsong melody with other melodies **2. MUSICAL PIECE** a piece of music in the organum style [Early 17thC. From Latin (see ORGAN).]

or·gan·za /awr gánzə/ *n.* a stiff see-through fabric, usually silk, rayon, or nylon, used for dressmaking [Early 19thC. Origin uncertain: probably an alteration of the U.S. trademark *organza*.]

or·gan·zine /áwrgən zeen/ *n.* yarn made from strands of silk twisted together, or fabric made from the yarn [Late 17thC. Via French *organsin* from Italian *organzino*, of uncertain origin: perhaps ultimately from *Organzi*, city in Uzbekistan (modern name Urgench).]

or·gasm /áwr gàzzəm/ *n.* **SEXUAL CLIMAX** the climax of sexual excitement, consisting of intense muscle tightening around the genital area experienced as a pleasurable wave of tingling sensations through parts of the body ■ *vi.* (**-gasmed, -gas·ming, -gasms**) **EXPERIENCE ORGASM** to experience sexual orgasm [Late 17thC. Via French or modern Latin from Greek *orgasmos*, from *organ* "to swell, be excited."] —**or·gas·mic** /awr gázzmik/ *adj.* —**or·gas·tic** /awr gástik/ *adj.* —**or·gas·mi·cal·ly** /awr gázzmikəlee/ *adv.* —**or·gas·ti·cal·ly** /awr gástikəlee/ *adv.*

OR gate *n.* ELECTRON ENG, COMPUT = **OR circuit**

or·gi·as·tic /àwrjee ástik/ *adj.* **1. MARKED BY WILD REVELRY** full of a spirit of wild revelry ○ *orgiastic gatherings* **2. LACKING RESTRAINT** showing extravagance or lack of restraint ○ *orgiastic shopping sprees* [Late 17thC. From Greek *orgiastikos*, from *orgiazein* "to celebrate secret rites," from *orgia* (see ORGY).] —**or·gi·as·ti·cal·ly** *adv.*

or·gone /áwr gōn/ *n.* a life force that is purported to exist in all living things. Some practitioners of alternative therapies claim it can be harnessed by patients sitting in specially designed booths. [Mid-20thC. Origin uncertain: probably formed from ORGANISM or ORGASM on the model of HORMONE.]

or·gu·lous /áwrgyələss/ *adj.* proud (*archaic*) ○ *"The princes orgulous, their high blood chafed, Have to the port of Athens sent their ships."* (William Shakespeare, *Troilus and Cressida*; 1601) [13thC. Anglicization of French *orgueilleux*, from *orgueil* "pride," of prehistoric Germanic origin.]

or·gy /áwrjee/ *n.* (*plural* **or·gies**) **1.** GROUP SEX PARTY a gathering at which a group of people indulge in promiscuous sexual activity **2.** DEBAUCHED PARTY a wild party or celebration characterized by excessive drinking and eating, with or without sexual promiscuity **3.** PERIOD OF INDULGENCE a period of indulgence in a particular activity or emotion, especially something that is disapproved of ○ *an orgy of self-pity* **4.** HIST WORSHIP OF ANCIENT GODS in ancient Greece and Rome, a secret worshiping of the gods of pleasure, especially Bacchus or Dionysus, that involved much dancing, drinking, and singing (*often used in the plural*) ■ *vi.* (**orgied, orgying, orgies**) OVERINDULGE to indulge in something without limit or restraint (*informal*) ○ *orgied on junk food* [Mid-16thC. Via French from, ultimately, Greek *orgia* "secret Dionysian rites." Ultimately from an Indo-European word meaning "to do" (ancestor also of English *work* and *organ*).]

or·i·bi /áwribee/ (*plural* **-bis** *or* **-bi**) *n.* a small tan antelope with long legs and, in the male, short horns, native to the plains of southern and eastern Africa. Latin name: *Ourebia ourebi.* [Late 18thC. Via Afrikaans from Khoikho.]

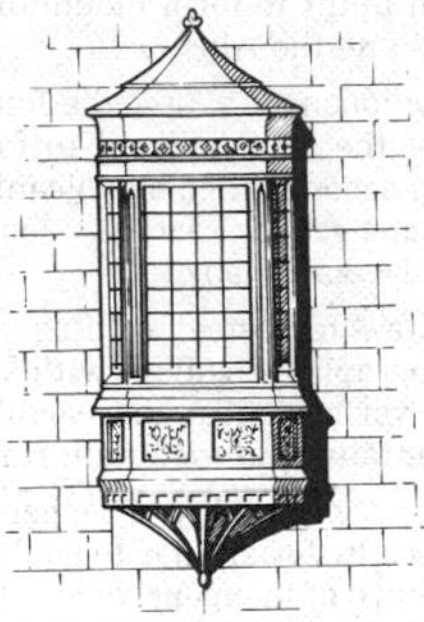

Oriel

o·ri·el /áwree əl/ *n.* **1.** **o·ri·el, o·ri·el win·dow** BAY WINDOW a bay window projecting from an outside wall and supported from beneath by a bracket **2.** RECESS a recess or small room formed by an oriel [15thC. Via Old French *oriol* "porch" from medieval Latin *oriolum* "upper chamber," of unknown origin.]

o·ri·ent *v.* /áwree ènt/ (**-ent·ed, -ent·ing, -ents**) **1.** *vt.* POSITION to position somebody or something so that the person or thing faces in a particular direction ○ *old stone buildings oriented north-south* **2.** *vr.* FIND YOUR POSITION to work out where you are and in which direction you need to travel ○ *the seaman's skill of orienting himself by the stars* **3.** *vt.* DIRECT to direct something in a particular way, e.g., toward a particular objective or audience ○ *advertising oriented toward teenage girls* **4.** *vt.* MAKE FAMILIAR to accustom somebody or yourself to a new situation or set of surroundings ○ *It might take you a few weeks to orient yourself.* **5.** *vt.* POSITION TOWARD EAST to position something so that it faces east, especially to build a church so that its length lies east to west, with the main altar at the eastern end ■ *n.* /áwree ənt/ **1.** EASTERN SKY the eastern part of the sky, where the sun rises (*archaic or literary*) **2.** DAWN the dawn (*archaic or literary*) **3.** PEARL'S LUSTER the luster of a pearl, especially a pearl of high quality (*archaic*) **4.** PEARL a pearl, especially one of high quality (*archaic*) ■ *adj.* /áwree ənt/ (*archaic*) **1.** EASTERN eastern **2.** WITH GOOD LUSTER having an exceptionally rich luster (*refers to pearls*) ○ *"These pearls are orient, but they yield in whiteness to your teeth."* (Walter Scott, *Ivanhoe*; 1819) **3.** GLOWING with a rich bright glow ○ *"her vanisht Night, Shot through with orient Beams"* (John Milton, *Paradise Lost*; 1667) [14thC. Via Old French from Latin *orient-*, the present participle stem of *oriri* "to rise" (source also of English *origin* and *abort*) because the sun rises in the east. The verb, borrowed from French *orienter* in the 18thC, originally meant "to position toward the east."]

O·ri·ent /áwree ənt/, **o·ri·ent** *n.* the countries of eastern Asia, especially China, Japan, and their neighbors (*dated*) ◊ **Occident**

O·ri·en·tal /àwree ént'l/, **o·ri·en·tal** *adj.* **1.** RELATING TO EASTERN ASIA relating to the countries and peoples of eastern Asia, especially to China, Japan, and their neighboring countries (*dated*) ◊ **Occidental** **2.** HIGH IN QUALITY of high quality and value (*refers to pearls and gems*) ○ *an oriental ruby* ■ *n.* ASIAN PERSON a word used in the past to refer to somebody from eastern Asia, now usually avoided because it generally causes offense (*dated offensive*)

O·ri·en·tal black mush·room *n.* = **shiitake**

O·ri·en·tal fruit moth *n.* a small moth that in the larval stage is a damaging pest to fruit trees. Native to Asia, it has been introduced to other parts of the world. Latin name: *Grapolitha molesta.*

O·ri·en·ta·li·a /àwree ən táylee ə/, **o·ri·en·ta·li·a** *n.* artifacts from countries in eastern Asia [Early 20thC. From Latin, literally "things from the Orient."]

o·ri·en·tal·ism /àwree ént'l ìzzəm/, **O·ri·en·tal·ism** *n.* **1.** ORIENTAL TRAIT a quality or characteristic typical of the countries, peoples, or cultures of eastern Asia **2.** STUDY OF EASTERN ASIA the study of the civilizations of eastern Asia —**o·ri·en·tal·ist** /àwree ént'list/ *n.* — **o·ri·en·tal·is·tic** /àwree ent'l ístik/ *adj.*

O·ri·en·tal pop·py (*plural* **O·ri·en·tal pop·pies**) *n.* a perennial poppy, native to Asia, grown for its large deep-red flowers. Latin name: *Papaver orientale.*

O·ri·en·tal rad·ish (*plural* **O·ri·en·tal rad·ish·es** *or* **O·ri·en·tal rad·ish**) *n.* = **daikon**

O·ri·en·tal rug *n.* a brightly colored and patterned carpet traditionally made by hand from high-quality wool in the Middle and Far East, now often factory-made from a variety of materials

or·i·en·tate /áwree ən tàyt/ (**-tat·ed, -tat·ing, -tates**) *vt.* to orient or be oriented [Mid-19thC. Back-formation from ORIENTATION.]

o·ri·en·ta·tion /àwree ən táysh'n/ *n.* **1.** POSITIONING the positioning of something, or the position or direction in which something lies ○ *slopes with a southerly orientation* **2.** DIRECTION OF DEVELOPMENT the direction in which something, e.g., a proposal, is developed or focused ○ *the program's clear orientation toward the white middle class* **3.** LEANING the direction in which somebody's thoughts, interests, or tendencies lie ○ *irrespective of sexual orientation* **4.** BECOMING ACCUSTOMED the process of becoming accustomed to a new situation or set of surroundings **5.** BRIEFING MEETING a meeting at which introductory information or training is provided to people embarking on something new, e.g., a course of study **6.** CHEM MOLECULE ARRANGEMENT the arrangement of atoms, ions, radicals, or groups relative to each other in crystals or molecules **7.** BIOL REACTION TO STIMULUS movement or direction of growth in response to a stimulus, e.g., the way a plant grows in response to light —**o·ri·en·ta·tion·al** *adj.*

o·ri·ent·ed /áwree èntəd/ *adj.* openly supporting or favoring a particular point of view or set of beliefs (*often used in combination*) ○ *a Marxist-oriented approach to economics*

or·i·en·teer /àwree ən téer/ *vi.* (**-teered, -teer·ing, -teers**) DO ORIENTEERING to take part in the sport of orienteering ■ *n.* PARTICIPANT IN ORIENTEERING somebody who takes part in orienteering [Mid-20thC. Back-formation from ORIENTEERING.]

or·i·en·teer·ing /àwree ən téering/ *n.* a sport that combines map-reading and cross-country running. Competitors make their way through unfamiliar terrain using a compass and a topographical map. [Mid-20thC. Anglicization of Swedish *orientering*, from *orientera* "to orient," from French *orienter* (see ORIENT).]

or·i·fice /áwrəfiss/ *n.* an opening, especially the mouth, anus, vagina, or other opening into a cavity or passage in the body (*literary*) [Mid-16thC. Via Old French from Latin *orificium*, literally "making a mouth" from the stem *or-* "mouth" + *-fic-*, the stem of *facere* "to make."]

or·i·flamme /áwrə flàm/ *n.* **1.** HIST MEDIEVAL FRENCH BANNER a red banner or flag that was adopted as the national flag of France in the Middle Ages **2.** SOURCE OF INSPIRATION something that inspires people or arouses support (*literary*) ○ *Her first collection became something of a literary oriflamme for the students of the day.* [15thC. From French *oriflambe*, of uncertain origin: perhaps from medieval Latin *auriflamma*, literally "golden flame."]

orig. *abbr.* **1.** original **2.** originally **3.** origin

Barnaby's

Origami: An origami paper pig

o·ri·ga·mi /àwri gaámee/ *n.* the Japanese art of paper folding [Mid-20thC. From Japanese, literally "fold paper."]

or·i·gin /áwrəjin/ *n.* **1.** STARTING POINT a starting point or first cause (*often used in the plural*) ○ *the origins of the universe* **2.** SOURCE the thing from which something develops or the place where it comes from (*often used in the plural*) ○ *the uncertain origin of the expression* **3.** ANCESTRY the race, social class, or country that somebody belongs to or that somebody's family comes from (*often used in the plural*) ○ *a great family whose origins stretch back to the Middle Ages* **4.** ANAT MUSCLE ATTACHMENT the place where a muscle is attached **5.** ANAT ANATOMICAL ROOT the root of a nerve or blood vessel **6.** MATH INTERSECTION OF AXES the point of intersection of all axes in a coordinate system. In a plane it has the coordinates (0,0), while in a three-dimensional space it has the coordinates (0,0,0). [Mid-16thC. Directly or via French from the Latin stem *origin-*, from *oriri* "to arise" (source of English *orient* and *abort*).]

WORD KEY: SYNONYMS

origin, source, derivation, provenance, root

CORE MEANING: the beginning of something

origin used to talk about the beginning of something in terms of the time, place, situation, or idea from which it arose. It can also be used to refer to somebody's ancestry or social background; **source** used to describe the place, person, or thing through which something has come into being or from which it has been obtained; **derivation** used to talk about the origin or source of something, especially a word or phrase; **provenance** a formal word used to talk about the origin or history of something, especially something such as a work of art or archaeological artefact; **root** used to describe the cause or origin of something, especially something such as a feeling or a problem.

o·rig·i·nal /ə ríjjən'l/ *adj.* **1.** FIRST existing first, from the beginning, or before other people or things ○ *The original plan was to turn the site into a shopping mall.* **2.** NEW completely new, and so not copied or derived from something else ○ *She doesn't have a single original idea in her head.* **3.** CREATIVE possessing or demonstrating the ability to think creatively ○ *blessed with an original mind* **4.** NOT TRADITIONAL representing a departure from traditional or previous practise ○ *a refreshingly original interpretation of the classics* **5.** SOURCE FOR COPIES relating to or being something from which a copy or alternative version has been made ○ *the original document* ■ *n.* **1.** FIRST VERSION the first or unique item from which copies or alternative versions are made ○ *The meaning of the original has been lost in translation.* **2.** AUTHENTIC PIECE OF ART a genuine work of art, and so not a copy or forgery ○ *verified as an original* **3.** ECCENTRIC PERSON an unusual or eccentric person **4.** CREATIVE PERSON a person of outstanding creativity or revolutionary thinking

WORD KEY: SYNONYMS

See Synonyms at ***new***.

o·rig·i·nal·i·ty /ə rìjjə nállətee/ *n.* **1.** NEWNESS the quality of newness that exists in something not done before or not derived from anything else ○ *Improvised music lives on the tension between tradition and originality.* **2.** CREATIVITY the ability to think creatively and depart from traditional or previous forms **3.** (*plural* **-ties**) ORIGINAL THING something original, e.g., a new idea or approach ○ *"That's always the case with my originalities – they are original to nobody but myself."* (Thomas Hardy, *A Pair of Blue Eyes*; 1889)

o·rig·i·nal·ly /ə ríjjən'lee/ *adv.* **1.** AT FIRST at first or from the beginning ○ *Originally a ballet dancer, she trained to become a circus acrobat.* **2.** INNOVATIVELY in a creative or innovative way ○ *thoughtfully assembled and originally presented*

o·rig·i·nal sin *n.* the sinful state, deriving from the disobedience of Adam and Eve, that Christians believe all people are born into

o·rig·i·nate /ə ríjjə nàyt/ (**-nat·ed, -nat·ing, -nates**) *v.* **1.** *vi.* HAVE ORIGIN to begin or develop somewhere or from something ○ *a custom that originated in the 19th century* **2.** *vt.* INVENT to invent something or bring something into being ○ *Einstein originated the theory of relativity.* —**o·rig·i·na·tion** /ə rìjjə náysh'n/ *n.*

o·rig·i·na·tion fee *n.* a charge made, e.g., by a bank, for setting up a loan

o·rig·i·na·tive /ə ríjjə nàytiv/ *adj.* with the ability to think of new ways of doing things —**o·rig·i·na·tive·ly** *adv.*

o·rig·i·na·tor /ə ríjjə nàytər/ *n.* **1.** CREATOR somebody who creates, invents, or instigates something **2.** FIN SOMEBODY STARTING TRANSACTION somebody who starts a financial transaction, especially somebody who writes a check

o·ri·na·sal /àwri náyz'l/ *adj.* WITH ORAL AND NASAL PASSAGES pronounced with both oral and nasal passages open, as the nasal vowels in French are ■ *n.* ORAL-NASAL SPEECH SOUND an orinasal speech sound [Mid-19thC. Coined from Latin *ori-*, from the stem *or-* "mouth" + NASAL.] —**o·ri·na·sal·ly** *adv.*

O-ring *n.* a plastic or rubber ring used in machinery as a seal against air, oil, or high pressure [Mid-20thC. From its shape.]

O·ri·no·co large river in Venezuela. Its main channel discharges into the Atlantic Ocean, but one branch flows into the Amazon river system. Length: 1,590 mi./2,560 km.

o·ri·ole /áwree ōl/ *n.* **1.** AMERICAN SONGBIRD a brightly colored North American songbird, especially an orange or yellow species called the Baltimore oriole. Family: Icteridae. **2.** SONGBIRD OF EUROPE, ASIA, AND AFRICA a forest-perching songbird, found throughout Europe, Asia, and Africa, with bold black and yellow markings and a loud melodious song. Family: Oriolidae. [Late 18thC. Via medival Latin *oriolus* from Latin *aureolus* from, ultimately, *aurum* "gold" (see AURIC).]

O·ri·on /ə rī́ ən, ō rī́ ən/ *n.* **1.** MYTHOL MYTHOLOGICAL GIANT in Greek mythology, a giant and hunter, the son of the sea god Poseidon, who was killed by the goddess Artemis and transformed into a constellation **2.** ASTRON EQUATORIAL CONSTELLATION an equatorial constellation near Gemini and Taurus, containing the Great Nebula and more than 200 stars visible to the naked eye

O·ris·sa /aw ríssə/ state in eastern India bordering Bihar, West Bengal, and the Bay of Bengal. Capital: Bhubaneswar. Population: 33,795,000 (1994). Area: 60,148 sq. mi./155,782 sq. km.

O·ri·ya /aw rée yə/ (*plural* **-ya**) *n.* **1.** PEOPLES INDIAN PEOPLE a member of a people who live mainly in Orissa and neighboring Indian states **2.** LANG LANGUAGE OF EASTERN INDIA a language spoken in eastern parts of India, especially in Orissa and neighboring states on the Bay of Bengal. Belonging to the Indo-Iranian branch of Indo-European languages, it is spoken by about 36 million people. [Early 19thC. Via *Oriya* from, ultimately, Sanskrit *Odra* "Orissa," a state in eastern India.]

Or·lan·do /awr lándō/ city and capital of Orange County, northern Florida, 78 mi./126 km northeast of Tampa. Population: 164,693 (1990).

orle /awrl/ *n.* a border that runs inside and parallel to the edge of the shield of a coat-of-arms [Late 16thC. From French, from, ultimately, Latin *ora* "border, edge."]

Or·le·an·ist /awr lée ənist/ *n.* a supporter of the family of the Duke of Orléans and of their claim to the French throne, especially a supporter of King Louis-Philippe, who reigned 1830 to 1848 [Mid-19thC. From French *Orléaniste*, from *Orléans*, a city in France.]

Or·lé·ans /awr lée ənz, awr lay aáN/ city in north central France, the capital of Loiret Department and Centre Region. Population: 107,965 (1990).

Or·lé·ans, Louis Philippe Joseph, Duc d' (1747–93) French nobleman. He supported the French Revolution but was executed during the Reign of Terror. He was father of the future king, Louis Philippe. Known as **Philippe Egalité**

Or·lon /áwr lòn/ *tdmk.* a trademark for an acrylic fiber or yarn

Or·ly /awr lée, áwrlee/ southern suburb of Paris, location of an international airport

Or·man·dy /áwrməndee/, **Eugene** (1899–1985) Hungarian-born U.S. conductor. He worked with the Minneapolis Symphony Orchestra (1931–36) and the Philadelphia Orchestra (1936–80). Real name **Eugene Blau**

or·mo·lu /áwrmə lòo/ *n.* a gold-colored alloy of copper, zinc, and sometimes tin, used for decorating furniture and making jewelry and moldings [Mid-18thC. From French *or moulu*, literally "ground gold."]

Or·mond Beach /áwrmənd-/ city in Volusia County, eastern Florida. Population: 29,721 (1990).

or·na·ment *(n)* /áwrnəmənt/; *(vb)* /áwrnə mènt/ *n.* **1.** DECORATIVE OBJECT a small decorative object displayed for its beauty **2.** DECORATION decoration or decorative quality ○ *manuscript pages entirely without ornament* **3.** SOMETHING THAT DECORATES a thing that decorates or adds beauty to something else **4.** MUSIC EMBELLISHING NOTE a note or set of notes added to embellish a melody or harmony **5.** VALUED PERSON somebody whose presence is a source of pride or honor (*archaic or literary*) ■ *vt.* (**-ment·ed, -ment·ing, -ments**) DECORATE to make something richer by adding decorative elements or items to it ○ *a stone facade ornamented with gargoyles* [14thC. Via Old French from Latin *ornamentum*, from *ornare* (see ORNATE).] —**or·na·ment·ed** *adj.*

or·na·men·tal /àwrnə mént'l/ *adj.* **1.** DECORATIVE serving as a decoration, as opposed to having any practical use ○ *The hitching post in the front yard was strictly ornamental.* **2.** GROWN FOR SHOW grown for beauty as distinct from food (*refers to plants*) ○ *an ornamental border* ■ *n.* ORNAMENTAL PLANT a plant that is grown for its beauty —**or·na·men·tal·ly** *adv.*

or·na·men·ta·tion /àwrnə men táysh'n, -mən-/ *n.* **1.** ADDITION OF DECORATIVE ELEMENTS the addition of elements that enhance beauty or visual appeal, especially in the arts **2.** DECORATIVE ELEMENT ADDED one or more elements added to enhance beauty or visual appeal, especially in the arts **3.** MUSIC ADDITION OF EMBELLISHING NOTES the addition of a note or set of notes that embellishes a melody or harmony

or·nate /awr náyt/ *adj.* **1.** EXCESSIVELY DECORATIVE with elaborate or excessive decoration **2.** USING ELABORATE LANGUAGE using or consisting of elaborate language, especially language that is designed to impress with its flair or literary quality ○ *expressions that are far too ornate for a TV soap opera* [Early 16thC. From Latin *ornatus*, the past participle of *ornare* "to equip," hence "to adorn."] —**or·nate·ly** *adv.* —**or·nate·ness** *n.*

or·ner·y /áwrnəree/ *adj.* **1.** IRRITABLE uncooperative and irritable (*informal*) ○ *"The Core States crowd became as ornery as Chewbacca with a toothache"* (Keith Gave *Game 1 Proves the Wings Have Nothing to Fear* (*Detroit Free Press*; *1997*) **2.** INSUFFICIENT meager, whether out of poverty or lack of generosity (*informal*) ○ *"how mean the preserves was, and how ornery and tough the fried chickens was"* (Mark Twain, *The Adventures of Huckleberry Finn*; 1884) **3.** COMMON ordinary (*regional*) ○ *"It was pretty ornery preaching – all about brotherly love, and such-like tiresomeness"* (Mark Twain, *The Adventures of Huckleberry Finn*; 1884) [Early 19thC. Dialectal variant of ORDINARY. The underlying meaning is "common, mean."] —**or·ner·i·ness** *n.*

ornith. *abbr.* **1.** ornithology **2.** ornithological

ornith- *prefix.* = **ornitho-** (*used before vowels*)

or·ni·thine /áwrnə thèen/ *n.* an amino acid formed in the liver as an intermediate in the manufacture of excretory urea. Formula: $C_5H_{12}O_2N_2$. [Late 19thC. Coined from ORNITH- + [-ine]; from its presence in birds' urine.]

or·nith·is·chi·an /àwrnə thískee ən/ *adj.* RELATING TO ORDER OF DINOSAURS belonging or relating to an order of dinosaurs that had a backward-rotating pelvis similar to that of birds. The order includes the triceratops and stegosaurus. Order: Ornithischia. ■ *n.* DINOSAUR an ornithischian dinosaur, e.g., an ankylosaur [Early 20thC. From modern Latin *Ornithischia*, order name, which was coined from the Greek stem *ornith-* + Greek *iskhion* "hip joint" (source of English *ischium*).]

ornitho- *prefix.* bird ○ *ornithophily* [From Greek *ornith-*, the stem of *ornis* "bird"]

or·ni·thol·o·gy /àwrnə thólləjee/ *n.* the branch of zoology that deals with the scientific study of birds —**or·ni·tho·log·i·cal** /àwrnəthə lójjik'l/ *adj.* —**or·ni·tho·log·i·cal·ly** /-kəlee/ *adv.* —**or·ni·thol·o·gist** /àwrnə thólləjist/ *n.*

or·nith·o·pod /awr níthə pòd/ *n.* a plant-eating dinosaur, e.g., the hadrosaur and the iguanadon, that had hind feet similar to those of birds. Suborder: Ornithopoda. [Late 19thC. From modern Latin *ornithopoda*, suborder name, from the Greek stem *ornitho-* "bird" + the stem *pod-* "foot."]

or·ni·thop·ter /àwrnə thóptər/ *n.* a flying machine that operates using flapping wings. Although the earliest aircraft designs imitated the flapping wings of birds and many prototypes have been flown in the past 100 years, no ornithopter has ever been commercially successful. [Early 20thC. From French *ornithoptère*, which was coined from the Greek stem *ornith-* "bird" + *pteron* "wing."]

or·ni·tho·sis /àwrnə thṓssiss/ *n.* the bacterial disease psittacosis, especially when contracted by humans from birds

oro- *prefix.* mountain ○ *orography* [From Greek *oros*, of unknown origin]

or·o·gen·e·sis /àw rō jénnəssiss/ *n.* GEOL = **orogeny** —**or·o·ge·net·ic** /àw rō jə néttik/ *adj.* —**or·o·ge·net·i·cal·ly** *adv.*

or·o·gen·ic belt *n.* a large linear feature on the earth's surface that has undergone tectonic compression and uplift to form mountain ranges such as the Andes and the Alps

o·rog·e·ny /aw rójjənee/ *n.* GEOL the folding, faulting, and uplift of the earth's crust to form mountain ranges, often accompanied by volcanic and seismic activity —**or·o·gen·ic** /àw rō jénnik/ *adj.* —**or·o·gen·i·cal·ly** /-kəlee/ *adv.*

o·rog·ra·phy /aw róggrəfee/ *n.* GEOG the branch of physical geography involved with the study and mapping of variations in the earth's surface, including mountains and mountain ranges

o·ro·ide /áw rō ìd/ *n.* an alloy of copper, zinc, tin, and iron that has a luster similar to gold and is used in the manufacture of inexpensive jewelry [Late 19thC. From French, literally "goldlike," from *or* "gold" (see OR).]

o·rol·o·gy /aw rólləjee/ *n.* GEOG = **orography** —**o·ro·log·i·cal** /àwrə"lójjik'l/ *adj.* —**o·ro·log·i·cal·ly** *adv.* —**o·rol·o·gist** /aw rólləjist/ *n.*

OROM *abbr.* COMPUT optical read-only memory

O·ro·mo /aw rṓ mō/ (*plural* **-mos** *or* **-mo**) *n.* **1.** PEOPLES AFRICAN PEOPLE a member of a people who originally occupied lands in Somalia, and whose members now live in parts of eastern Africa, especially in Ethopia and Kenya **2.** LANG LANGUAGE OF THE OROMO the Cushitic language of this people. Over 7 million people speak Oromo. [Late 19thC. From *Oromo*.] —**Oromo** *adj.*

O·ro·no /áwrə nō/ city in south central Maine, on the western bank of the Penobscot River. Northeast of Bangor, it is the site of the University of Maine. Population: 9,119 (1996).

O·ron·tes /aw raántiz/ **1.** mountain in Iran, just southwest of Hamadan. Height: 11,640 ft./3,548 m. **2.** river in southwestern Asia, flowing through Lebanon, Syria, and Turkey, and into the Mediterranean Sea. Length: 355 mi./571 km.

o·ro·pen·do·la *n.* any one of several Central and South American birds belonging to the family that includes the American blackbirds and orioles. They nest in colonies of long bag-shaped woven nests. Family: Icteridae.

o·ro·phar·ynx /àw rō férringks/ (*plural* **-phar·ynx·es** *or* **-pha·ryn·ges** /-fə rínjeez/) *n.* ANAT the part of the throat that is located below the soft palate and above the larynx [Late 19thC. Coined from the Latin stem *or-* "mouth" (see ORAL) + PHARYNX.] —**o·ro·pha·ryn·ge·al** /àw rō fə rínjee əl, àw rō ferrin jée əl/ *adj.*

o·ro·tund /áwrə tùnd/ *adj.* (*formal*) **1.** STRONGLY CLEAR loud, clear, and strong, as in tone or voice timbre **2.** POMPOUS pompous or bombastic in speech or prose [Late 18thC. From Latin *ore rotundo*, literally "with a round mouth."] —**o·ro·tun·di·ty** /àwrə túndətee/ *n.*

O·roz·co /o róthkō/, **José Clemente** (1883–1949) Mexican artist. His murals, using fresco technique, focus on Mexican history and the suffering of humanity.

or·phan /áwrfən/ *n.* **1. CHILD WITHOUT PARENTS** a child whose parents are both dead or who has been abandoned by his or her parents, especially a child not adopted by another family **2. ANIMAL WITHOUT MOTHER** a young animal whose mother is dead or has abandoned it **3.** PRINTING **STRANDED FIRST LINE** an opening line of a paragraph that is also the last line on a page, cut off from the rest of the paragraph by the page break. ◊ **widow** ■ *vt.* **(-phaned, -phan·ing, -phans) RENDER PARENTLESS** to make somebody an orphan ○ *a young boy orphaned by the war* [14thC. Via late Latin from Greek *orphanos* "orphaned." Ultimately from an Indo-European word that is also the ancestor of English *robot.*] —**or·phan·hood** *n.*

or·phan·age /áwrfənij/ *n.* a home or other institutional setting for orphans, often operated by a local government or charitable organization

or·phar·i·on /awr fáiree ən/ *n.* a large lute, popular during the Rennaissance, played by plucking or strumming the strings [Late 16thC. From the names of *Orpheus* and *Arion*, musicians in Greek mythology.]

Or·phe·an /áwrfee ən/ *adj.* **1. RELATING TO ORPHEUS** relating to Orpheus **2. BEAUTIFUL** hauntingly beautiful or enchanting (*literary*)

Or·phe·us /áwrfyooss, áwrfee əss/ *n.* in Greek mythology, a poet and musician. He descended to the underworld to seek his wife, Eurydice, after her death but failed to bring her back.

Or·phic /áwrfik/ *adj.* **1. RELATING TO POEMS OF ORPHEUS** relating to the poems and mystical writings associated with Orpheus **2. MYSTICAL** mystical or magical (*literary*)

Or·phism /áwr fìzzəm/ *n.* ARTS an artistic movement within Cubism that flourished briefly at the beginning of the 20th century, concentrating on achievement of harmony of color [Late 19thC. From ORPHEUS.] —**Or·phist** *n.* —**Or·phis·tic** /awr fístik/ *adj.*

or·phrey /áwrfree/ (*plural* **-phreys**), **or·fray** (*plural* **-frays**) *n.* SEW elaborate embroidery, often done in gold [13thC. Via Old French *orfreis* from, ultimately, medieval Latin *aurifrigium*, literally "Phrygian gold."]

or·pi·ment /áwrpimənt/ *n.* a crystalline bright yellow ore of arsenic, consisting of arsenic trisulfide, that is used in dyeing and tanning [14thC. Via French from Latin *auripigmentum*, literally "gold pigment."]

or·pine /áwrpin/, **or·pin** *n.* a low-growing succulent plant with pink or purple flowers. Latin name: *Sedum telephium.* [14thC. From French *orpin*, from *orpiment* (see ORPIMENT).]

Orr /awr/, **Bobby** (*b.* 1948) Canadian ice-hockey player. He played for the Boston Bruins and Chicago Blackhawks (1966–78) and was the leading NHL scorer in 1970 and 1975. Full name **Robert Gordon Orr**

or·re·ry /áwrəree/ (*plural* **-ries**) *n.* ASTRON a mechanical model of the solar system that shows the orbits of the planets around the sun at the correct relative velocities [Early 18thC. Named for Charles Boyle, fourth Earl of *Orrery* 1676–1731, who had one made for him.]

or·ris /áwriss/ (*plural* **-ris** *or* **-ris·es**) *n.* an iris with a fragrant root. Latin name: *Iris germanica.* [Mid-16thC. Origin uncertain: probably an alteration of IRIS.]

or·ris·root /áwriss ro͝ot, -ro͞ot/ (*plural* **-roots** *or* **-root**), **or·ris root, or·ris** *n.* the fragrant rootstock of the orris, often used in perfumes and cosmetics

ort /awrt/ *n.* a scrap or bit of food remaining after a meal is finished (*often used in the plural*) [15thC. Origin uncertain: probably from early Dutch *oorete*, "leftover" (literally "out-eat"), formed from *oor* "out" + *eten* "to eat."]

orth. *abbr.* **1.** orthopedic **2.** orthopedics

ortho- *prefix.* **1.** correct; correction, straightening ○ *orthography* ○ *orthodontia* **2.** straight, upright, vertical ○ *orthotropous* **3.** perpendicular ○ *orthorhombic* **4.** fully hydrated or hydroxylated ○ *orthophosphate* [Via Old French and Latin from Greek *orthos* "straight, right"]

or·tho·cen·ter /áwrthō sèntər/ *n.* the point at which the three altitudes of a triangle intersect

or·tho·chro·mat·ic /àwrthō krō máttik/ *adj.* **1. GIVING GOOD COLOR REPRODUCTION** reproducing accurately the colors found naturally in a subject **2. NOT SENSITIVE TO RED** sensitive to all the visible colors except red (*refers to film*)

or·tho·clase /áwrthə klàyss, -klàyz/ *n.* a type of feldspar of variable color that has monoclinic crystalline structure and is commonly found in igneous rock

or·tho·don·tics /àwrthə dóntiks/, **or·tho·don·tia** *n.* the area of dentistry concerned with the prevention and correction of irregularities of the teeth —**or·tho·don·tic** *adj.* —**or·tho·don·tist** *n.*

or·tho·dox /áwrthə dòks/ *adj.* **1. FOLLOWING TRADITIONAL DOCTRINE** following the established or traditional rules of social behavior, a philosophy, or a faith **2. OBSERVING CHRISTIAN CREEDS** following the teachings of Jesus Christ and the Christian faith as set down in the ecumenical creeds ■ *n.* **SOMEBODY WHO HAS TRADITIONAL BELIEFS** somebody who follows traditional or established beliefs or rules of behavior, or is a member of an orthodox religion [Late 16thC. Via French *orthodoxe* and late Latin from Greek *orthodoxos*, "having the correct opinion," from *doxa* "opinion."] —**or·tho·dox·ly** *adv.*

Or·tho·dox *adj.* **1. EASTERN ORTHODOX CHURCH** relating to the Eastern Orthodox Church **2. ORTHODOX JUDAISM** relating to Orthodox Judaism ■ *n.* **Or·tho·dox MEMBER OF EASTERN ORTHODOX CHURCH** a member of the Eastern Orthodox Church

Orthodox Church *n.* a Christian church that originated in the Byzantine Empire and recognizes the Patriarch of Constantinople as primate rather than the Pope. Orthodox Churches include the Eastern Orthodox Churches and the Coptic Church of Egypt.

Or·tho·dox Ju·da·ism *n.* the branch of Judaism that accepts without reservation that the Torah was directly handed down from God to Moses

or·tho·dox·y /áwrthə dòksee/ *n.* the practice of observing established social customs and definitions of appropriateness

Or·tho·dox·y *n.* **Or·tho·dox·y 1. PRACTICES OF EASTERN ORTHODOX CHURCH** the beliefs and practices of the Eastern Orthodox Church **2. ORTHODOX JUDAISM** the beliefs and practices of Orthodox Judaism

or·tho·e·py /awr thṓ əpee, áwrthō èppee/ *n.* **1. PRONUNCIATION** the study of the ways that words are pronounced **2. USUAL PRONUNCIATION** the usual pronunciation of words [Mid-17thC. Coined from ORTHO- + the Greek stem *epe-*, the stem of *épos* "word, tale, story," the source of English *epic.*] —**or·tho·ep·ic** /àwrthō éppik/ *adj.* —**or·tho·ep·i·cal·ly** /-éppikəlee/ *adv.* —**or·tho·e·pist** /awr thṓ əpist/ *n.*

or·tho·gen·e·sis /àwrthō jénnəsiss/ (*plural* **-ses** /àwrthō jénnə sèez/) *n.* an obsolete theory that evolution can proceed in a specific direction determined by internal genetic factors rather than the external forces of natural selection —**or·tho·ge·net·ic** /àwrthō jə néttik/ *adj.* —**or·tho·ge·net·i·cal·ly** /-kəlee/ *adv.*

or·thog·o·nal /awr thóggən'l/ *adj.* **1. RELATING TO RIGHT ANGLES** relating to or composed of right angles **2. DESCRIBING CRYSTAL STRUCTURE** all at right angles to each other in a crystal structure (*refers to a set of axes*) —**or·thog·o·nal·ly** *adv.*

or·thog·o·nal mat·rix *n.* a matrix in which two rows or two columns are vectors whose scalar product is zero

or·thog·o·nal pro·jec·tion *n.* a way of providing a two-dimensional graphic view of an object in which the projecting lines are drawn at right angles to the plane of projection. In so doing this type of presentation appears to give the feeling of three dimensions.

or·tho·grade /áwrthə gràyd/ *adj.* carrying the body upright (*refers to primates*) [Early 20thC. Coined from ORTHO- + Latin *gradus* "walking."]

or·tho·graph·ic /àwrthə gráffik/, **or·tho·graph·i·cal** /-gráffik'l/ *adj.* **1. RELATING TO SPELLING** relating to the study of spelling **2. SPELLED CORRECTLY** correctly spelled **3.** MATH **MADE UP OF VERTICAL LINES** composed of vertical lines —**or·tho·graph·i·cal·ly** *adv.*

or·tho·graph·ic pro·jec·tion *n.* = **orthogonal projection**

or·thog·ra·phy /awr thóggrəfee/ (*plural* **-phies**) *n.* **1. RELATIONSHIP BETWEEN SOUNDS AND LETTERS** the way letters and diacritic symbols represent the sounds of a language in a spelling system **2. STUDY OF CORRECT SPELLING** the study of correct spelling as it has come to be established by usage **3. STUDY OF HOW LETTERS ARE ARRANGED IN WORDS** the area of language study concerned with the letters of an alphabet and how those letters occur sequentially in words

or·tho·mor·phic *adj.* = **conformal**

or·tho·pae·dic *adj.* = **orthopedic**

or·tho·pae·dics *n.* = **orthopedics**

or·tho·pe·dic /àwrthə péedik/, **or·tho·pae·dic** *adj.* **1. RELATING TO ORTHOPEDICS** relating to or used in orthopedics **2. RELATING TO BONE DISORDERS** relating to or marked by disorders of the bones, joints, ligaments, or muscles [Mid-19thC. From French *orthopédique*, literally "of correct child-rearing," from, ultimately, Greek *paideia* "child-rearing," from the stem *paid-* "child"; originally applied specifically to childhood bone disorders.] —**or·tho·pe·di·cal·ly** *adv.* —**or·tho·pe·dist** *n.*

or·tho·pe·dics /àwrthō péediks/, **or·tho·pae·dics** *n.* the branch of medicine concerned with the nature and correction of disorders of the bones, joints, ligaments, or muscles (*takes a singular verb*)

or·tho·phos·phate /àwrthō fóss fàyt/ *n.* any salt or ester of phosphoric acid

or·tho·phos·phor·ic ac·id /àwrthə fosfáwrrik/ *n.* = **phosphoric acid**

or·tho·psy·chi·a·try /àwrthō si kī́ ətree, -sī-/ *n.* a cross-disciplinary method of diagnosing, preventing, and treating childhood psychological problems that involves psychiatrists, child psychologists, pediatricians, and social workers —**or·tho·psy·chi·at·ric** /àwrthə sī kee áttrik/ *adj.* —**or·tho·psy·chi·a·trist** /-kī́ ətrist/ *n.*

or·thop·ter·an /awr thóptərən/, **or·thop·ter·on** *n.* **PRIMITIVE INSECT** any member of the order Orthoptera of primitive winged insects, including cockroaches, mantises, locusts, and crickets ■ *adj.* = **orthopterous** [Late 19thC. Formed from modern Latin *Orthoptera* (plural), order name, literally "those with straight wings," ultimately from Greek *pteron* "wing."]

or·thop·ter·ous /awr thóptərəss/ *adj.* relating to the order Orthoptera of primitive winged insects, including cockroaches, mantises, locusts, and crickets

or·thop·tics /awr thóptiks/ *n.* the study of eye disorders and their detection and correction, especially using nonsurgical treatments, e.g., eye exercises (*takes a singular verb*) —**or·thop·tic** *adj.* —**or·thop·tist** *n.*

or·tho·rhom·bic /àwrthə rómbik/ *adj.* relating to a crystal system with three axes of different lengths that cross at right angles

or·tho·scop·ic /àwrthə skóppik/ *adj.* **1. ABLE TO SEE NORMALLY** able to see normally, without any visual distortion of images **2. GIVING NORMAL VISION** used to describe an optical instrument that gives normal vision

or·tho·stat·ic /àwrthə státtik/ *adj.* connected with or caused by standing upright

or·thot·ics /awr thóttiks/ *n.* the branch of medical engineering concerned with the design and fitting of devices, e.g., braces, in the treatment of orthopedic disorders (*takes a singular verb*) [Mid-20thC. Formed from *orthosis* "artificial external device," from Greek *orthōsis* "making straight," ultimately from *orthos* "straight."] —**or·thot·ic** *adj.* —**or·thot·ist** *n.*

or·tho·trop·ic /àwrthə tróppik/ *adj.* involving or characterized by vertical growth along a vertical axis —**or·tho·trop·i·cal·ly** *adv.* —**or·thot·ro·pism** /awr thóttrə pìzzəm/ *n.*

or·thot·ro·pous /awr thóttrəpəss/ *adj.* used to describe an ovule that grows straight

or·to·lan /áwrtələn/ (*plural* **-lan** *or* **-lans**) *n.* a small brownish bunting of Europe, Asia, and Africa that has a yellow throat and is known for its territorial display flight. It is sometimes eaten as a delicacy. Latin name: *Emberiza hortulana.* [Early 16thC. Via French from Provençal, literally "gardener," from Latin *hortulanus*, from *hortus* "garden," a source of English *horticulture.*]

ORV *abbr.* off-road vehicle

Or·vi·e·to /awr vyáytō/ (*plural* **-tos**) *n.* a light white wine produced in the region of Orvieto, Italy

Or·well /áwr wèl/, **George** (1903–50) British writer. A staunch critic of totalitarianism, he wrote political essays and fiction including the satirical political novels *Animal Farm* (1945) and *1984* (1949). Real name **Eric Arthur Blair** —**Or·well·i·an** *adj.*

-ory *suffix.* **1.** of or relating to ○ *conclusory* **2.** place or thing connected with or used for ○ *crematory* [Via Anglo-Norman and Old French dialect *-orie* from Latin *-orius* and *-orium*]

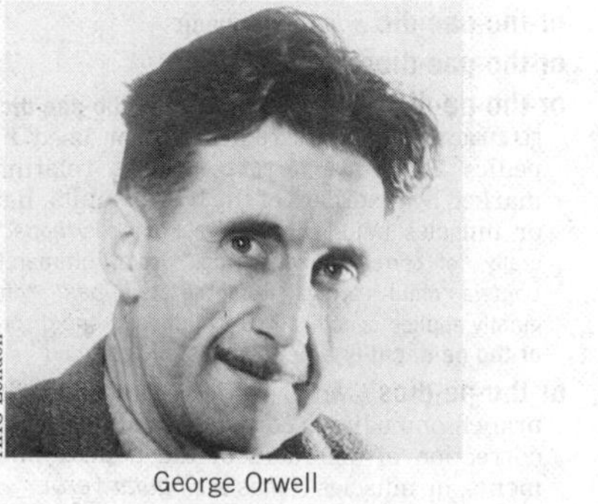
AKG London
George Orwell

o·ryx /áwriks/ (*plural* **o·ryx** *or* **o·ryx·es**) *n.* an antelope native to Africa and Arabia that has long horns, bold black and white markings on the face, and a hump above the shoulders. Genus: *Oryx.* [14thC. From Latin, from Greek *orux* "spike, pickaxe, oryx."]

or·zo /áwrzō/ (*plural* **-zos**) *n.* pasta that is the size and shape of rice grains, often served with lamb in Greek cooking [Early 20thC. From Italian, literally "barley," from Latin *hordeum.*]

os[1] /oss/ (*plural* **o·ra** /áwrə/) *n.* a mouth or mouthlike opening in an organism [Mid-18thC. From Latin, literally "mouth, face, head" (stem *or-*) (source of English *oral*).]

os[2] /oss/ (*plural* **os·sa** /óssə/) *n.* a bone (*technical*) [Mid-16thC. From Latin, literally "bone" (stem *oss-*) (source of English *ossify*).]

Os *symbol.* osmium

OS *abbr.* **1.** COMPUT operating system **2.** Old Saxon **3.** COMM out of stock

o.s. *abbr.* **1.** oculus sinistrus **2.** LAW old series **3.** COMM out of stock

O.S. *abbr.* **1.** ordinary seaman **2.** LAW old series **3.** Old Style

o/s *abbr.* **1.** COMM out of stock **2.** BANKING outstanding

OSA, O.S.A. *abbr.* Order of Saint Augustine

O·sage[1] /ō sáyj, ō̃ sàyj/ (*plural* **O·sage** *or* **O·sag·es**) *n.* **1. MEMBER OF NATIVE NORTH AMERICAN PEOPLE** a member of a Native North American people that originally occupied lands in Ohio, before settling in parts of Missouri and Kansas, and whose members now live mainly in Oklahoma **2. OSAGE LANGUAGE** the language of the Osage people. It belongs to the Siouan branch of Hokan-Siouan languages. Osage is spoken by about 1,000 people. [Late 17thC. Alteration of Osage *Wazhazhe*, one of the three Osage bands.] —**O·sage** *adj.*

O·sage[2] /ō sàyj-/ river in western Missouri, flowing northeast to join the Missouri River near Jefferson City. Length: 500 mi./805 km.

O·sage or·ange (*plural* **O·sage or·ange** *or* **O·sage or·ang·es**) *n.* **1. SPINY TREE OF SOUTHERN U.S.** a spiny tree native to the south-central United States that has a pulpy inedible fruit that resembles an orange. Latin name: *Maclura pomifera.* **2. FRUIT OF OSAGE ORANGE TREE** the pulpy inedible fruit of the Osage orange tree

O·sa·ka /ō saákə, ōsaakaá/ city and port in Japan, on southeastern Honshu Island. It is the capital of Osaka prefecture. Population: 2,481,000 (1994).

OSB, O.S.B. *abbr.* Order of Saint Benedict

Os·born /óz bawrn/, **Henry Fairfield** (1857–1935) U.S. paleontologist. While working for the American Museum of Natural History, he assembled one of the world's major collections of vertebrate fossils.

Os·can /óskən/ *n.* an extinct language spoken in southern parts of Italy during ancient times. It belongs to the Italic branch of Indo-European languages. [Late 16thC. Formed from Latin *Oscus* "Oscan."] —**Os·can** *adj.*

Os·car[1] /óskər/ *tdmk.* a trademark for the golden statuette awarded annually by the Academy of Motion Picture Arts and Sciences to people in the film industry for achievement in the making of movies

Os·car[2] *n.* a code word for the letter "O," used in international radio communications

OSCE *n., abbr.* Organization for Security and Cooperation in Europe

Os·ce·o·la /óski ólə/ (1800?–38) Seminole leader. He resisted government efforts to displace the Seminole people from Florida, and led them against federal troops during the Second Seminole War (1835–42).

os·cil·late /óssə làyt/ (**-lat·ed, -lat·ing, -lates**) *v.* **1.** *vi.* **MOVE BACKWARDS AND FORWARDS** to swing between two points with a rhythmic motion **2.** *vi.* **BE INDECISIVE** to keep changing your mind about which is better out of two positions, points of view, or courses of action **3.** *vti.* **CAUSE TO CHANGE PREDICTABLY** to cause or produce rhythmic, predictable variations between two extremes, usually within a set period of time [Early 18thC. From Latin *oscillat-*, the perfect participle stem of *oscillare* "to swing," from *oscillum* "swing, mask" (of Bacchus hung as a charm on a tree to swing), from OS[1].] —**os·cil·la·tor** *n.* —**os·cil·la·to·ry** /óssələ tàwree/ *adj.*

os·cil·la·tion /óssə láysh'n/ *n.* **1. PREDICTABLE VARIATION** an even, rhythmic change in value, position, or state around a mean value **2. ONE CYCLE OF VARIATION** a single cycle of variation between two values, positions, or states **3. MOTION BETWEEN EXTREMES** the act of moving backwards and forwards between two extreme points —**os·cil·la·tion·al** *adj.*

os·cil·lo·gram /ə síllə gràm/ *n.* the record produced by an oscillograph or oscilloscope [Early 20thC. Formed from a shortening of OSCILLOGRAPH + -GRAM.]

os·cil·lo·graph /ə síllə gràf/ *n.* a device that produces a visual record of variations between two points or states, e.g., of electric current [Late 19thC. From French *oscillographe*, literally "that which swings while writing," formed from Latin *oscillare* "to swing" (see OSCILLATE).] —**os·cil·lo·graph·ic** /ə sìllə gráffik/ *adj.* —**os·cil·lo·graph·i·cal·ly** /-kəlee/ *adv.* —**os·cil·log·ra·phy** /òssə lóggrəfee/ *n.*

os·cil·lo·scope /ə síllə skōp/ *n.* a device that uses a cathode ray tube to produce a visual record of an electrical current on a fluorescent screen. Uses include testing electronic equipment and measuring the electrical impulses of the heart or the brain. [Early 20thC. Formed from a shortening of OSCILLATION + -SCOPE.] —**os·cil·lo·scop·ic** /-skóppik/ *adj.*

os·cine /ó sìn/ *adj.* about, typical of, or belonging to the large suborder of passerine birds that includes most songbirds [Late 19thC. From modern Latin *Oscines*, suborder name, from Latin *oscen* "songbird, bird whose cry is used in augury," literally "singing towards," from *canere* "to sing" (source of English *chant, charm,* and *enchant*).]

os·ci·tan·cy /óssətənssee/ (*plural* **-cies**), **os·ci·tance** *n.* (*technical*) **1. YAWN** the act of yawning **2. DROWSINESS** a state of drowsiness or dullness [Early 17thC. From Latin *oscitant-*, the present participial stem of *oscitare* "to yawn, gape," formed from OS[1] + *citare* "to put in motion, move."] —**os·ci·tant** *adj.*

Os·co-Um·bri·an *n.* a group of extinct languages, including Oscan, Umbrian, and Faliscan, spoken in Italy during ancient times. It is a subgroup of the Italic branch of Indo-European languages. —**Os·co-Um·bri·an** *adj.*

os·cu·lant /óskyələnt/ *adj.* BIOL having some of the characteristics of two related or similar taxonomic groups [Early 19thC. From Latin *osculant-*, the present participial stem of *osculari* (see OSCULUM).]

os·cu·lar /óskyələr/ *adj.* **1. RELATING TO OSCULUM** relating to or characteristic of an osculum **2. RELATING TO THE MOUTH** relating to the mouth or activities of the mouth, e.g., kissing (*technical*) [Early 19thC. Formed from Latin *osculum* (see OSCULUM).]

os·cu·late /óskyə làyt/ (**-lat·ed, -lat·ing, -lates**) *v.* **1.** *vt.* **KISS** to kiss (*formal or humorous*) **2.** *vi.* MATH **TOUCH IN OSCULATION** to touch at a point of common tangency to a line passing between two branches of a curve, each branch continuing in both directions of the line (*refers to arcs*) **3.** *vi.* **MAKE CONTACT** to make contact or come together (*technical*) [Mid-17thC. From Latin *osculatus*, the perfect participle of *osculari* (see OSCULUM).]

os·cu·la·tion /òskyə láysh'n/ *n.* **1. KISSING** a kiss or the act of kissing (*formal or humorous*) **2.** MATH **POINT AT WHICH TWO SURFACES TOUCH** the point at which two surfaces touch, particularly the point at which two curves have a common tangent —**os·cu·la·to·ry** /óskyələ tàwree/ *adj.*

os·cu·lum /óskyələm/ (*plural* **-la** /-lə/) *n.* an opening like a mouth, through which a sponge expels water [Early 17thC. Via modern Latin from Latin, "little mouth, kiss," from *os* "mouth."]

OSD, O.S.D. *abbr.* Order of Saint Dominic

-ose[1] *suffix.* full of, having the qualities of, resembling ○ *frondose* [From Latin *-osus*]

-ose[2] *suffix.* **1.** carbohydrate, sugar ○ *maltose* **2.** product of primary hydrolysis ○ *proteose* [From GLUCOSE]

OSF, O.S.F. *abbr.* Order of Saint Francis

OSHA *abbr.* Occupational Safety and Health Administration

Osh·a·wa /óshəwə, -waà, -wàw/ city in southeastern Ontario, Canada, on Lake Ontario, northeast of Toronto. Population: 268,773 (1996).

O·shog·bo /ō shógbō/ capital city of Osun State, southwestern Nigeria, situated approximately 120 mi./190 km northwest of Lagos. Population: 441,600 (1992).

o·sier /ṓzhər, ṓzee ər/ *n.* **1. WILLOW TREE** a willow tree with long flexible twigs that are used to make baskets and furniture. Latin name: *Salix viminilis* and *Salix purpurea.* **2. WILLOW BRANCH** a branch or twig from a willow tree [14thC. From French, ultimately from medieval Latin *auseria*, of uncertain origin: perhaps from a Gaulish word meaning "riverbed."]

O·si·ris /ō sfriss/ *n.* MYTHOL in Egyptian mythology, the god of the underworld and the dead, husband of Isis and father of Horus

-osis *suffix.* **1.** abnormal or diseased condition ○ *chlorosis* **2.** condition, action, or process ○ *osmosis* **3.** formation of or increase in ○ *thrombosis* [Via Latin from Greek]

Os·lo /ózzlō, óss-/ capital city of Norway, situated in the southeast of the country, at the head of Oslo Fjord. Population: 483,401 (1995).

Os·man I /oz maán, ózmən/, **Othman, Ottoman** (1258–1324) Turkish warrior. He made himself ruler of a small state in northwestern Anatolia, from which grew the Ottoman Empire.

Os·man·li /oz mánlee, oss-/ *n.* (*plural* **-lis** *or* **-li**) **1. SUBJECT OF THE OTTOMAN EMPIRE** a subject of the Ottoman Empire **2. TURKISH LANGUAGE DURING THE OTTOMAN EMPIRE** the Turkish language during the Ottoman Empire, especially when it was written in Arabic script ■ *adj.* **RELATING TO THE OTTOMAN EMPIRE** relating to or typical of the Ottoman Empire [Late 18thC. From Turkish *Osmānli*, from *Osman.*]

os·me·te·ri·um /òzmə teéree əm/ (*plural* **-a** /òzmə teéree ə/) *n.* a gland found on many caterpillars that secretes an unpleasant smelling substance as a defense against predators [Early 19thC. From modern Latin, ultimately from Greek *osmē* "odor, smell."]

os·mic /ózmik/ *adj.* **1. CONTAINING OSMIUM** connected with or containing the element osmium, especially in a high valence state **2. RELATING TO ODORS OR SMELL** relating to odors or the sense of smell (*technical*)

os·mic ac·id *n.* = **osmium tetroxide**

os·mi·rid·i·um /òzzəmə ríddee əm/ *n.* a very hard white or gray naturally occurring alloy of osmium and iridium, which often contains platinum, rhodium, and other metals. Because it is resistant to corrosion, it is often used to make the nibs of pens. [Late 19thC. From German, a combination and shortening of OSMIUM + IRIDIUM.]

os·mi·um /ózmee əm/ *n.* a hard white crystalline metallic chemical element, the densest known, occurring naturally in association with platinum. It is used as a catalyst and alloyed with iridium to form an extremely hard alloy from which pen nibs are made. Symbol **Os** [Early 19thC. From modern Latin, from Greek *osmē* "smell, odor" + -IUM (from the pungent smell of osmium oxides).]

os·mi·um te·trox·ide *n.* a colorless or yellow crystalline solid with an unpleasant smelling, poisonous vapor. It is used in solution as a stain for cell components in electron microscopy. Formula: OsO_4.

os·mom·e·ter /oz mómmətər, oss-/ *n.* an instrument that measures osmotic pressure [Mid-19thC. A combination and shortening of OSMOSIS + -METER.] —**os·mo·met·ric** /òzzəmə méttrik, òssmə-/ *adj.* —**os·mom·e·try** /oz mómmətree, oss-/ *n.*

os·mo·reg·u·la·tion /òz mō reggyə láysh'n, òss-/ *n.* the control of the concentration of dissolved substances in the cells and body fluids of an animal [Mid-20thC. A combination and shortening of OSMOSIS + REGULATION.] —**os·mo·reg·u·la·to·ry** /-lə tàwree, òss mō-/ *adj.*

os·mose /óz mōss, óss mōss/ (**-mosed, -mos·ing, -mos·es**) *vti.* to cause or undergo diffusion by osmosis [Mid-19thC. Back-formation from OSMOSIS.]

os·mo·sis /oz mṓssiss, oss-/ *n.* **1.** SLOW CHANGE IN CONCENTRATION the flow of a solvent by diffusion through a semipermeable membrane from a more concentrated solution to a less concentrated one, until the concentrations are equalized. It is a major factor in regulating the movement of water into and out of tissues in living organisms. **2.** GRADUAL ABSORPTION the gradual, often unconscious, absorption of knowledge or ideas through continual exposure rather than deliberate learning ○ *She seemed to have picked up a working knowledge of Greek by osmosis.* [Mid-19thC. Latinization of OSMOSE.] —**os·mot·ic** /oz móttik/ *adj.*

os·mot·ic pres·sure *n.* the pressure that must be applied to a solution to stop the inward diffusion of a solvent by osmosis through a semipermeable membrane

os·mun·da /oz múndə/ (*plural* **-das** *or* **-da**) *n.* any of several ferns with large spreading fronds, including the royal and cinnamon ferns. The fibrous roots are sometimes used as a potting medium for orchids. Genus: *Osmunda.* [13thC. From modern Latin *Osmunda*, genus name, from Old French *osmunde*, of unknown origin.]

os·na·burg /óznə bùrg/ *n.* a heavy, coarse cotton cloth, used to make sacks for grain, upholstery, and draperies [Mid-16thC Named for *Osnaburg*, a variant of *Osnabrück*, a city in northwest Germany where the fabric was originally made]

Osprey

os·prey /óspree, óss pràỳ/ (*plural* **-preys** *or* **-prey**) *n.* a fish-eating hawk that is distributed worldwide and has long wings and a white head with a dark strip around the eyes. Latin name: *Pandion haliaetus.* [15thC. Origin uncertain: probably from assumed Old French *ospreit*, ultimately from Latin *avis predae*, literally "bird of prey."]

OSS *abbr.* Office of Strategic Services

Os·sa, Mount /óssə/ mountain in northern Tasmania, Australia. It is the highest mountain in Tasmania. Height: 5,305 ft./1,617 m.

os·sa·ture /óssə choor, óssəchər/ *n.* the underlying structure or framework that supports a building or sculpture [Late 19thC. From French, formed from *os* "bone" and modeled on MUSCULATURE.]

os·se·in /óssee in/ *n.* the organic component of bone, consisting mainly of collagen proteins [Mid-19thC. Formed from a contraction of OSSEOUS + -IN.]

os·se·ous /óssee əss/ *adj.* made of or resembling bone [Late 17thC. From Latin *osseus* "bony," from *os* "bone."]

Os·set /óssət, ó sèt/, **Os·sete** *n.* a member of a people that lives in parts of southern European Russia and Georgia, especially Ossetia [Early 19thC. From Russian *osetin*, from Georgian *osetci* "Ossetia."]

Os·set·ic /o séttik/, **Os·se·tian** *n.* LANGUAGE OF THE OSSETS the language spoken by the Ossets that belongs to the Iranian branch of Indo-European languages. Ossetic is spoken by about 300,000 people. ■ *adj.* RELATING TO OSSETIA OR OSSETS relating to or characteristic of Ossetia or the Ossets, their language, and culture

Os·sian /ósh'n, óssee ən/ *n.* a legendary Gaelic hero and poet supposed to have lived in the 3rd century A.D. —**Os·sian·ic** /òshee ánnik, òssee-/ *adj.*

os·si·cle /óssik'l/ *n.* a small bone, especially one of three bones of the middle ear in humans [Late 16thC. From Latin *ossiculum* "little bone, ossicle," from *os* "bone."] —**os·sic·u·lar** /o síkyələr/ *adj.* —**os·sic·u·late** /-lət/ *adj.*

os·si·fi·ca·tion /òssəfi káysh'n/ *n.* **1.** PROCESS OF BONE FORMATION the natural process of forming bone **2.** HARDENING OF SOFT TISSUE the hardening of soft tissue as a result of impregnation with calcium salts **3.** BONY MASS a mass or deposit of bony material in the human body **4.** PROCESS OF BECOMING INFLEXIBLE the process of becoming set and inflexible in behavior, attitudes, and actions **5.** INFLEXIBLE CONFORMITY rigid, unthinking acceptance of social conventions

os·si·frage /óssəfrij, óssə fràyj/ (*plural* **-frag·es** *or* **-frage**) *n.* (*archaic*) **1.** LAMMERGEIER a lammergeier **2.** OSPREY an osprey [Early 17thC. From Latin *(avis) ossifraga*, a bird of prey, literally "bone-breaking (bird)," formed from *frangere* "to break" (source of English *fragment* and *fraction*).]

os·si·fy /óssə fī/ (**-fied, -fy·ing, -fies**) *vti.* **1.** HARDEN INTO BONE to change or be changed from soft tissue, e.g., cartilage, into bone as a result of impregnation with calcium salts **2.** BECOME INFLEXIBLE to become or make somebody become rigidly set in a conventional pattern of behavior, beliefs, and attitudes [Early 18thC. From French *ossifier*, literally "to turn into bone," from Latin *os* "bone."]

Os·si·ning /óssə ning/ town in southeastern New York, on the Hudson River, southeast of Peekskill. Population: 22,788 (1996).

os·so bu·co /óssō bóokō, òssō bóokō/ (*plural* **os·so bu·cos** *or* **os·so bu·chi** /-bóokee/) *n.* an Italian casserole made with shin of veal cooked in white wine with tomatoes, traditionally served with risotto [From Italian, "bone marrow"]

os·su·ar·y /óshoo əree/ (*plural* **-ies**) *n.* an urn or a vault used to hold the bones of the dead (*formal*) [Mid-17thC. From late Latin *ossuarium*, ultimately from Latin *os* "bone."]

ost- *prefix.* = **osteo-**

os·te·al /óstee əl/ *adj.* **1.** BONY made of, containing, or resembling bone **2.** RELATING TO BONES OR SKELETONS relating to bones or the skeletons of mammals [Late 19thC. Ultimately from Greek *osteon* "bone."]

os·te·i·tis /òstee ítəss/ (*plural* **-tes** /òstee ī teez/) *n.* inflammation of a bone or bony tissue, caused by infection or injury

Ost·end /o sténd, ós tend/ town and seaport in West Flanders Province, western Belgium. Population: 68,635 (1996).

os·ten·si·ble /o sténsəb'l/ *adj.* presented as being true or appearing to be true, but usually hiding a different motive or meaning [Mid-18thC. Via French from medieval Latin *ostensibilis*, from Latin *ostensus*, perfect participle of *ostendere* "to show," literally "to stretch before," from *tendere* "stretch, spread" (source of English *tension*).] —**os·ten·si·bly** *adv.*

os·ten·sive /o sténssiv/ *adj.* ostensible (*formal*) [Early 17thC. From Late Latin *ostensivus*, a derivative of Latin *ostensus*, perfect participle of *ostendere* (see OSTENSIBLE).] —**os·ten·sive·ly** *adv.*

os·ten·so·ri·um /òss ten sáwree əm/ (*plural* **-a** /-ə/), **os·ten·so·ry** /os ténssəwree/ (*plural* **-ries**) *n.* CHR = **monstrance** [Late 18thC. From medieval Latin, formed from the past participle stem of Latin *ostendere* (see OSTENSIBLE).]

os·ten·ta·tion /òs ten táysh'n, òstən-/ *n.* a vulgar display of wealth and success designed to impress people (*disapproving*) [15thC. Via Old French from the Latin stem *ostentation-*, from *ostentare* "to display, exhibit," from *ostendere* (see OSTENSIBLE).]

os·ten·ta·tious *adj.* marked by a vulgar display of wealth and success designed to impress people (*disapproving*) [Mid-17thC. Formed from OSTENTATION.] —**os·ten·ta·tious·ly** *adv.*

osteo- *prefix.* bone ○ *osteotomy* [From Greek *osteon*. Ultimately from an Indo-European word that is also the ancestor of English *ossify, ostracize*, and *oyster*.]

os·te·o·ar·thri·tis /òsti ō aar thrítəss/ *n.* a form of arthritis characterized by gradual loss of cartilage of the joints, usually affecting people after middle age

os·te·o·blast /óstee ə blàst/ *n.* a cell from which bone develops —**os·te·o·blas·tic** /òstee ō blástik/ *adj.*

os·te·oc·la·sis /òstee ókləssiss/ (*plural* **-ses** /-seez/) *n.* **1.** **os·te·oc·la·sis** /òstee ō kláyzhə/, **os·teo·cla·sia** BONY TISSUE DISINTEGRATION the process of disintegration and assimilation of bony tissue that occurs during normal growth of bone, or as part of healing at a fracture site **2.** SURGICAL BREAKING OF BONE a surgical procedure in which a bone is broken in order to correct a natural deformity or a badly healed fracture [Early 20thC. Formed from OSTEO- + Greek *klasis* "breaking," from *klan* "to break."]

os·te·o·clast /óstee ə klàst/ *n.* **1.** BONE CELL a large cell with many nuclei, found in growing bone. It assimilates bony tissue and is active in the formation of canals and cavities. **2.** SURGICAL INSTRUMENT an instrument used to break bones during surgery to correct a deformity [Late 19thC. Formed from OSTEO- + Greek *klastas* "broken," from *klan* "to break."] —**os·te·o·clas·tic** /òsti ō klástik/ *adj.*

os·te·o·cyte /óstee ə sīt/ *n.* a branched cell within bone tissue

os·te·o·gen·e·sis /òstee ō jénnəssiss/ *n.* the formation of bone in the body

os·te·o·gen·e·sis im·per·fec·ta /-ìmpər féktə/ *n.* MED a rare hereditary disease in which abnormal connective tissue development causes fragile, brittle bones

os·te·o·gen·ic sar·co·ma *n.* = **osteosarcoma**

os·te·oid /óstee òyd/ *adj.* LIKE BONE resembling or having the characteristics of bone ■ *n.* BONE TISSUE the tissue from which bone develops (bone matrix), especially before it has hardened

os·te·ol·o·gy /òstee óllәjee/ (*plural* **-gies**) *n.* **1.** STUDY OF BONES the branch of anatomy concerned with the study of the structure and functions of bones **2.** SKELETON the bone structure or skeleton of an animal —**os·te·o·log·i·cal** /òstee ə lójjik'l/ *adj.* —**os·te·o·log·i·cal·ly** /-lójjikəli/ *adv.* —**os·te·ol·o·gist** /òstee óllәjist/ *n.*

os·te·o·ma /òstee ṓmə/ (*plural* **-ma·ta** /òstee ṓmətə/ *or* **-mas**) *n.* a benign tumor made of bone, usually on the skull

os·te·o·ma·la·cia /òstee ō mə láyshə, -shee ə/ *n.* a disease occurring mainly in women that results from a lack of vitamin D or calcium, causing softening of the bones and resulting pain and weakness

os·te·o·my·e·li·tis /òstee ō mí ə lítəss/ *n.* inflammation of bone and bone marrow, caused by infection

os·te·o·path /óstee ə pàth/ *n.* somebody who practices osteopathy

os·te·op·a·thy /òstee óppəthee/ *n.* a system of medicine based on the theory that many diseases are caused by misalignments of bones, ligaments, and muscles, and that correcting these through manipulation can cure the problems. It is often effective in treating joint and muscle disorders. —**os·te·o·path·ic** /òstee ə páthik/ *adj.* —**os·te·o·path·i·cal·ly** /-kəlee/ *adv.*

os·te·o·phyte /óstee ə fìt/ *n.* a small abnormal outgrowth of bone that occurs within joints or at other sites where there is degeneration of cartilage, e.g., due to osteoarthritis —**os·te·o·phyt·ic** /òstee ə fíttik/ *adj.*

os·te·o·plas·tic /òsti ō plástik/ *adj.* **1.** RELATING TO BONE SURGERY relating to or typical of bone surgery **2.** RELATING TO BONE DEVELOPMENT relating to or important in the process of bone development

os·te·o·plas·ty *n.* the surgical repair or correction of distortions of bones

os·te·o·po·ro·sis /òste ō pə róssiss/ (*plural* **-ses** /-seez/) *n.* a disease occurring among women after the menopause in which the bones become very porous, break easily, and heal slowly. It may lead to curvature of the spine after vertebrae collapse. [Mid-19thC. Formed from OSTEO- + Greek *poros* "passage" (see PORE) + -OSIS.]

os·te·o·sar·co·ma /òstee ō saar kṓmə/ (*plural* **-ma·ta** /-kṓmətə/ *or* **-mas**) *n.* a malignant bone tumor

os·te·o·tome /óstee ə tòm/ *n.* a surgical instrument used to cut or divide bone

os·te·ot·o·my /òstee óttəmee/ (*plural* **-mies**) *n.* a surgical procedure in which bone is divided or sectioned —**os·te·ot·o·mist** *n.*

Os·ti·a /áwstee ə, óstee ə/ ancient Roman port in Italy, at the mouth of the Tiber River, southwest of Rome

os·ti·ar·y /óstee èrree/ (*plural* **-ies**) *n.* a doorkeeper in a Roman Catholic church [15thC. From Latin *ostiarius* "doorkeeper," from *ostium* (see OSTIUM).]

os·ti·na·to /òstə naatō/ (*plural* **-tos**) *n.* a short musical phrase or melody that is repeated over and over, usually at the same pitch [Late 19thC. From Italian, literally "stubborn, obstinate."]

os·ti·ole /óstee ōl/ *n.* a small pore or opening in some algae or fungi, through which reproductive spores pass [Mid-19thC. From Latin *ostiolum* "little door," from *ostium* (see OSTIUM).]

os·ti·um /óstee əm/ (*plural* **-a**) *n.* **1.** ANAT **SMALL OPENING** a small pore or opening in a passage or organ of the body **2.** ZOOL **PORE IN SPONGE** a pore or small opening in a sponge through which water passes [Mid-17thC. From Latin, literally "mouth of a river, opening."]

os·tler *n.* = **hostler**

ost·mark /áwst maark/ *n.* the unit of currency that was formerly used in the German Democratic Republic, divided into 100 pfennig [Mid-20thC. From German, literally "east mark."]

os·to·mate /óstə màyt/ *n.* somebody who has had a stoma created, allowing the intestine to open at the body surface [Mid-20thC. Formed from OSTOMY.]

os·to·my /óstəmee/ (*plural* **-mies**) *n.* a surgical procedure such as a colostomy or ileostomy, in which an artificial opening for excreting waste matter is created [Mid-20thC. Extracted as a general term from terms like COLOSTOMY, ILEOSTOMY.]

-ostosis *suffix.* formation of bone ○ *hyperostosis* [Coined from Greek *osteon* "bone" (see OSTEO- + -OSIS]

os·tra·cize /óstrə sìz/ (**-cized, -ciz·ing, -ciz·es**) *vt.* **1.** **EXCLUDE FROM SOCIETY** to banish or exclude somebody from society or from a particular group, either formally or informally ○ *She was ostracized by all her former friends.* **2.** **BANISH** to banish somebody by a popular vote because that person is regarded as dangerous to society, as was the practice in ancient Greece [Mid-19thC. From Greek *ostrakizein*, a derivative of *ostrakon* "pottery fragment."] —**os·tra·cism** *n.*

WORD KEY: ORIGIN

Ostracize In ancient Athens, when it was proposed that a particular person should be sent into exile for a period because he was becoming a danger to the state, a democratic vote was taken on the matter. The method of registering one's vote was to inscribe the name of the prospective banishee on a piece of broken pottery (*ostrakon*). The pieces were counted, and if enough votes were cast against him, he was sent away for ten years.

os·tra·cod /óstrə kòd/ (*plural* **-cod** *or* **-cods**) *n.* a tiny crustacean that lives inside a hard outer shell made of two hinged halves. Subclass: Ostracoda. [Mid-19thC. From modern Latin *Ostracoda*, subclass name, from Greek *ostrakōdēs* "like a pottery fragment," from *ostrakon* "shell."]

Os·tra·va /áwstrəvə/ city in the northeastern Czech Republic, situated about 10 mi./16 km from the Polish border. Population: 325,827 (1994).

Ostrich

os·trich /óstrich, óstrij/ (*plural* **-trich·es** *or* **-trich**) *n.* **1.** **FLIGHTLESS BIRD** a two-toed African bird that runs very fast but cannot fly. It is the largest living bird and has a long bare neck, small head, and fluffy drooping feathers. Latin name: *Struthio camelus.* **2.** **SOMEBODY WHO IGNORES UNPLEASANT THINGS** somebody who tries to avoid unpleasant situations by refusing to acknowledge that they exist (*informal*) [13thC. Via Old French *ostrusce* from assumed Vulgar Latin *avistruthius*, ultimately from Latin *avis* "bird" + Greek *strouthiōn-*, from *strouthos* "sparrow."]

Os·tro·goth /óstrə gòth/ *n.* a member of the eastern branch of Gothic peoples that invaded Italy, where they ruled from the end of the 5th to the middle of the 6th centuries. ◊ **Visigoth** [14thC. From late Latin *Ostrogothi* (plural) "Ostrogoths," from a Germanic word that is also the ancestor of English *east* + Latin *Gothus* "Goth."] —**Os·tro·goth·ic** /òstrə góthik/ *adj.*

Os·ty·ak /óst yàk, óstee àk/ (*plural* **-aks** *or* **-ak**), **Os·ti·ak** (*plural* **-aks** *or* **-ak**) *n.* **1.** PEOPLES **MEMBER OF PEOPLE OF WESTERN SIBERIA** a member of a people that lives in parts of western Siberia **2.** LANG **OSTYAK LANGUAGE** the language of the Ostyak people. It belongs to the Finno-Ugric branch of Uralic languages. Ostyak is spoken by about 15,000 people. [Early 18thC. Via Russian from Tartar *ustyak* "one of another tribe."] —**Os·ty·ak** *adj.*

OSU, O.S.U. *abbr.* Order of Saint Ursula

Os·wald, Lee Harvey (1939–63) U.S. alleged assassin. Accused of assassinating President John F. Kennedy (November 22, 1963), Oswald was fatally shot two days later while in police custody.

Os·we·go /os weégō/ city and county seat of Oswego County, central New York, situated 33 mi./53 km northwest of Syracuse. Population: 19,195 (1990).

Os·we·go tea *n.* = **bee balm** [Mid-18thC. Named for the *Oswego* River, New York.]

OT *abbr.* **1. OT, O.T., o.t.** overtime **2. OT, O.T.** Old Testament **3.** occupational therapy

ot- *prefix.* = **oto-** (*used before vowels*)

O·ta·go /ō taágō/ administrative region of New Zealand, occupying the southeastern part of the South Island. Its principal city is Dunedin. Population: 193,132 (1996). Area: 14,918 sq. mi./38,638 sq. km.

O·ta·go Pen·in·su·la peninsula on the southeastern coast of the South Island, New Zealand. It extends 16 mi./25 km eastward from Dunedin to Cape Saunders.

O·ta·hei·te ap·ple *n.* = **ambarella** [Mid-19thC. "Otaheite" from Tahitian, "Tahiti."]

O·ta·hei·te or·ange /ōtə heétee-, ōtə háytee-/ *n.* a popular houseplant with fragrant blossoms and small orange fruit. Latin name: *Citrus otaitense.* ["Otaheite" from Tahitian, "Tahiti"]

o·tal·gi·a /ō táljee ə, ō táljə/ *n.* pain in the ear (*technical*) [Mid-17thC. From Greek *ōtalgia*, from *ōt-*, stem of *ous* "ear."]

OTB *abbr.* off-track betting

OTC, O.T.C. *abbr.* **1.** Officers' Training Corps **2.** over-the-counter

oth·er /úthər/ CORE MEANING: a grammatical word used to show that a thing, person, or situation is additional or different ○ (adj) *He does much to help the homeless and other people in need.* ○ (adj) *They met plenty of other children there.* ○ (adj) *I went on ahead, and the other climbers struggled on behind.* ○ (pron) *This is one problem, but there are many others.* ○ (pron) *As much as I demand of others, I am much more demanding of myself.*

1. *adj., pron.* **FURTHER** refers to an additional or further person or thing of the type already mentioned ○ (adj) *Let me make one other suggestion.* ○ (pron) *A couple of students failed the exam, but many others passed.* **2.** *adj., pron.* **DIFFERENT** refers to a different thing or things from that or those already specified ○ (adj) *Banks are unlike any other business in the United States.* ○ (adj) *Are there any other items you'd like to take home?* ○ (pron) *This problem, more than any other, has divided the critics.* **3.** *adj., pron.* **THE REMAINING** refers to the remaining people or things in a group, apart from the one specified ○ (adj) *She left earlier, with the other kids.* ○ (pron) *John and the others will be here soon.* **4.** *adj., pron.* **SECOND OF TWO THINGS** refers to the second of two things when the first is known or understood ○ (adj) *He threw his other glove out of the window.* ○ (pron) ○ *She had a cup in one hand and a glass in the other.* ○ (pron) *It goes in one ear and out the other.* [Old English *ōđer*] ◇ **every other** alternate ○ *They give us meat every other day.* ◇ **or other** used to show that the preceding words you use are not exact or definite ○ *For some reason or other, the house was crowded that night.* ◇ **other than** indicates an exception to a statement ○ *Was anyone there other than the two of you?* ◇ **other things being equal** In a situation in which there is little difference between two or more people, things ○ *Other things being equal, I would choose the cheaper holiday.* ◇ **the other day** *or* **night** a few days or nights ago ○ *A funny thing happened the other day.*

oth·er-di·rect·ed *adj.* more concerned with what other people think than with your own values and standards —**oth·er-di·rect·ed·ness** *n.*

oth·er·ness /úthərnəss/ *n.* the condition of being perceived as strange or different

oth·er·wise /úthər wìz/ *adv.* **1.** **OR ELSE** if things had been different ○ *"I overslept," said Joe, "otherwise you would have heard from me earlier."* **2.** **DIFFERENTLY** different from or opposite to something stated ○ *You may take your hand luggage with you unless otherwise requested.* **3.** **IN OTHER WAYS** in any other ways ○ *An otherwise dull day was enlivened by her arrival.* [Old English *(on) ōđre wīsan* "(in) (an)other wise, manner"]

oth·er·world /úthər wùrld/ *n.* a world or life that is beyond the conventional perception of reality —**oth·er·world·li·ness** *n.*

o·tic /ótik, óttik/ *adj.* relating to or located near the ear [Mid-17thC. From Greek *ōtikos*, from *ōt-*, the stem of *ous* "ear."]

-otic *suffix.* **1.** relating to a particular condition, action, or process ○ *hypnotic* **2.** having a particular abnormal or diseased condition ○ *psychotic* [Via French and Latin from, ultimately, Greek *-ōtikos*]

o·ti·ose /óshee òss, ótee òss/ *adj.* **1.** **NOT EFFECTIVE** with no useful result or practical purpose **2.** **WORTHLESS** with little or no value **3.** **LAZY** unwilling or uninterested in working or being active (*archaic*) [Late 18thC. From Latin *otiosus*, "at leisure, idle," from *otium* "leisure," of unknown origin.] —**o·ti·ose·ly** *adv.* —**o·ti·os·i·ty** /òshee óssətee, òtee óssətee/ *n.*

O·tis /ótiss/, **Elisha** (1811–61) U.S. inventor. He invented the elevator (1854) and founded the Otis Elevator Company (1861). Full name **Elisha Graves Otis**

o·ti·tis /ō títiss/ *n.* inflammation of the ear, caused by infection

o·ti·tis me·di·a *n.* a painful inflammation of the middle ear that can cause dizziness and temporary hearing loss

O·to /ótō/ (*plural* **O·tos** *or* **O·to**) *n.* **1.** **NATIVE NORTH AMERICAN PEOPLE** a member of a Native North American people that once lived in the Great Lakes region, later migrating to the Platte River in Nebraska and then to Oklahoma **2.** **OTO LANGUAGE** the language of the Otos, belonging to the Siouan branch of Hokan-Siouan languages

oto- *prefix.* ear ○ *otolith* [Via modern Latin from Greek *ōt-*, the stem of *ous* (see OTIC)]

o·to·cyst /ótə sìst/ *n.* **1.** **INNER EAR STRUCTURE** the structure from which the adult inner ear develops **2.** = **statocyst**

OTOH *abbr.* ONLINE on the other hand (*used in e-mail messages*)

otol. *abbr.* otology

o·to·lar·yn·gol·o·gy /òtō lerring góllәjee/ *n.* a branch of medicine concerned with the treatment and diagnosis of diseases of the ear, nose, and throat —**o·to·lar·yn·go·log·i·cal** /òtō lə ring gə lójjik'l/ *adj.* —**o·to·lar·yn·gol·o·gist** /òtō lerring góllәjist/ *n.*

o·to·lith /ótə lìth/ *n.* **1.** ANAT **GRANULE IN INNER EAR** a particle of calcium carbonate found in the inner ear of vertebrates and involved in sensory perception **2.** ZOOL = **statolith**

o·tol·o·gy /ō tóllәjee/ *n.* the branch of medicine concerned with the structure and function of the ear, its diseases, and their treatment —**o·to·log·i·cal** /òtə lójjik'l/ *adj.* —**o·tol·o·gist** /ō tóllәjist/ *n.*

O'Toole /ō tóol/, **Peter** (*b.* 1932) Irish-born British actor. He has starred in many films, notably *Lawrence of Arabia* (1964). Full name **Peter Seamus O'Toole**

o·to·rhi·no·lar·yn·gol·o·gy /òtō rínō lárring góllәjee/ *n.* = **otolaryngology** —**o·to·rhi·no·la·ryn·go·log·i·cal** /òtō rínō lə ríng gə lójjik'l/ *adj.* —**o·to·rhi·no·lar·yn·gol·o·gist** *n.*

o·to·scle·ro·sis /òtō sklə róssiss/ *n.* a hereditary disease of the inner ear in which spongy bone growth leads to progressive hearing impairment

o·to·scope /ótə skòp/ *n.* an instrument incorporating a light and a magnifying lens, used to examine the external canal of the ear and the eardrum —**o·to·scop·ic** /òtə skóppik/ *adj.*

o·to·tox·ic /òtə tóksik/ *adj.* toxic to the ear and hence impairing hearing or balance —**o·to·tox·ic·i·ty** /òtə tok síssətee/ *n.*

O·tran·to, Strait of sea passage between the Adriatic and Ionian seas. It separates the "heel" of Italy from Albania. Length: 43 mi./69 km.

OTS, **O.T.S.** *abbr.* Officers' Training School

ot·ta·va /ō taávə/ *adj.* sung or played at an octave higher or lower than the notes written on the staff, indicated by a sign placed above or below the staff [Early 19thC. From Italian, literally "octave, eighth," from *otto* "eight," from Latin *octo*.]

ot·ta·va ri·ma /-reémə/ *n.* a verse form made up of eight lines in iambic pentameter with the rhyme scheme abababcc [Early 19thC. From Italian, literally "eighth rhyme."]

Ot·ta·wa[1] /óttəwə, óttə waà/ (*plural* **-wa** *or* **-was**) *n.* **1.** NATIVE NORTH AMERICAN PEOPLE a member of a Native North American people that originally occupied lands along Lake Huron, and whose members now live mainly in Ontario, Michigan, Kansas, and Oklahoma **2.** OTTAWA LANGUAGE the language of the Ottawa. It belongs to the Algonquian branch of Algonquian-Wakasan languages. Ottawa is spoken by about 8,000 people. —**Ot·ta·wa** *adj.*

Ot·ta·wa[2] /óttəwə, óttə waà/ **1.** river in Canada. It is the chief tributary of the St. Lawrence River, forming part of the Ontario-Quebec border. Length: 789 mi./1,271 km. **2.** capital city of Canada, located in southeastern Ontario, on the Ontario-Quebec border. Population: 313,987 (1996).

Otter

ot·ter /óttər/ (*plural* **-ter** *or* **-ters**) *n.* **1.** WATER-LOVING ANIMAL an aquatic fish-eating mammal with smooth dark brown fur and webbed feet. It is distributed worldwide except in Australia, and is related to the weasels and minks. Family: Mustelidae. **2.** OTTER FUR the fur of the otter [Old English *ot(t)or.* Ultimately from an Indo-European word meaning "water," which is also the ancestor of English *water, hydrant*, and *whiskey*.]

ot·ter cat *n.* = **jaguarundi**

ot·ter hound *n.* any of an English breed of large dogs, used to hunt otters

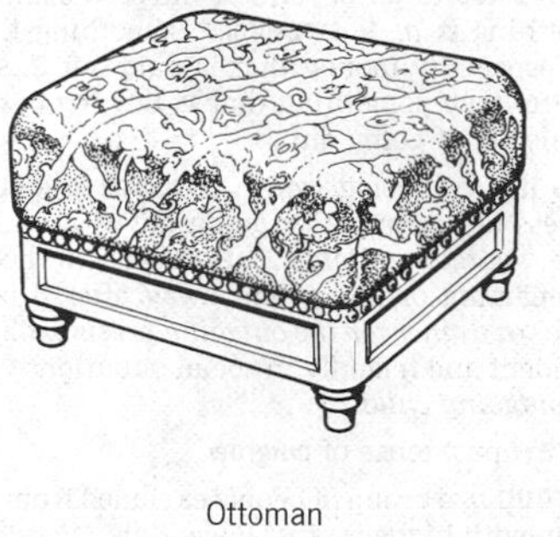

Ottoman

ot·to·man /óttəmən/ *n.* **1.** STOOL FOR FEET a low upholstered stool used for resting the feet or as a seat **2.** LONG SEAT an upholstered sofa that has no arms and is usually backless **3.** HEAVY FABRIC a heavy fabric made of silk or rayon that has a corded texture and is used to make coats and trimmings [Late 16thC. Via French or Italian from medieval Latin *ottomanus*, ultimately from Arabic *'Uṯmān Osman*.]

Ot·to·man *n.* a member of a Turkish people that conquered Asia Minor in the 13th century — **Ot·to·man** *adj.*

Ot·to·man Em·pire *n.* a Turkish empire established in in the late 13th century in Asia Minor, eventually extending thoughout the Middle East. It was responsible for the conquest of Constantinople and the end of the Byzantine Empire in 1453. It ended in 1922.

Ot·way Rang·es /òt wày-/ range of hills in southern Victoria, Australia, which extends from Anglesea to Cape Otway

oua·ba·in /waa báy in, waa báyn/ *n.* a poisonous chemical compound that is sometimes used as a heart stimulant. It is extracted from an African tree. Latin name: *Strophanthus gratis.* [Late 19thC. Via French *ouabaïo* from Somali *wabayo* "arrow poison."]

Ouach·i·ta /wòshi taw/ river flowing from Arkansas to Louisiana, known later on its course as the Black River. Length: 605 mi./975 km.

Ouach·i·ta Moun·tains /wòshi tàw-/ mountain range in central Arkansas and eastern Oklahoma. Highest Point:2,950 ft./899 m.

Oua·ga·dou·gou /waágə dóogoo/ capital city of Burkina Faso, located in the center of the country. Population: 690,000 (1993).

ou·bli·ette /òoblee ét/ *n.* a dungeon made so that the only way in or out is through a trap door at the top [Early 19thC. From French, from *oublier* "to forget," from assumed Vulgar Latin *oblitare*, from Latin *oblitus*, the perfect participle of *oblivisci*, the source of English *oblivion*.]

ouch /owch/ *interj.* an exclamation used to express sudden pain [Mid-19thC. Origin uncertain: possibly from German *autsch*, an exclamation of pain.]

oud /ood/ *n.* a stringed instrument of southwest Asia and northern Africa that resembles a lute or a mandolin [Mid-18thC. From Arabic *al-'ūd* "the wood" (see LUTE).]

ought[1] /awt/ CORE MEANING: a modal verb indicating what somebody should do ○ *It seems to me that we ought to support their initiative.* ○ *You ought to tell her how you feel.*

v. **1.** BE MORALLY RIGHT indicates that somebody has a duty or obligation to do something or that it is morally right to do something ○ *You ought to be ashamed of what you have done.* **2.** BE IMPORTANT indicates that something is important or a good idea ○ *You ought to see a doctor as soon as possible.* **3.** BE PROBABLE indicates probability or expectation ○ *We ought to be there by now.* **4.** BE WISHED FOR indicates a desire or wish ○ *You ought to come to dinner sometime.* **5.** BE THE CASE indicates that something should be the case but may not be ○ *That ought to be easy.* [Mid-18thC. From an erroneous division of "a nought."]

ought[2] *n.* MATH zero

ou·gui·ya /oo geé yə/ *n.* the unit of currency of Mauritania [Late 20thC. Via French from Mauritanian Arabic *ūgiyya*, ultimately from Greek *ougkia*, from Latin *uncia* (see OUNCE[1]).]

Oui·ja /weéjə, weéjee/, **Oui·ja board** *tdmk.* a trademark for a board with letters and a pointer or planchette by which answers to questions are spelled out, supposedly by spiritual forces

Ou·lu /ówloo, ő loo/ city and port on the Gulf of Bothnia, west central Finland. Population: 109,094 (1995).

ounce[1] /ownss/ *n.* **1.** UNIT OF WEIGHT a unit of weight equal to one-sixteenth of a pound in the avoirdupois system **2.** FLUID OUNCE a unit for measuring liquid, equal to 0.0284 of a litre **3.** SMALL AMOUNT a small amount of something ○ *Anyone with an ounce of common sense would take an umbrella on a day like this.* [14thC. Via Old French *unce* from Latin *uncia* "twelfth part, inch, ounce," from *unus* "one."]

ounce[2] (*plural* **ounce** *or* **ounc·es**) *n.* = **snow leopard** [14thC. From Old French *once*, variant of *lonce* (the "l" being mistaken for the definite article), from assumed Vulgar Latin *luncea*, from Latin *lync-* (see LYNX).]

our /owr/ *adj.* **1.** BELONGING TO US indicates that something belongs to or is associated with the speaker or writer and at least one other person (*first person plural possessive adjective*) ○ *Where are all our bags?* ○ *Today 80,000 new acres of our beautiful state are under Green Acres protection.* ○ *Our house is just a few hundred yards from yours.* **2.** BELONGING TO EVERYONE indicates that something belongs to or is associated with people in general ○ *the dreams that inspire us to do our best* **3.** REFERS TO MEMBER OF FAMILY refers to a member of the speaker's family (*informal*) ○ *Our John is an electrician now.* [Old English *ūre* "of us," the genitive plural of WE]

Our Fa·ther *n.* = **Lord's Prayer**

Our La·dy *n.* a title for the Virgin Mary

ours /owrz/ *pron.* refers to something or somebody that belongs to or is associated with the speaker and at least one other person (*first person plural possessive pronoun*) ○ *It's no surprise that their team is ahead of ours.* [13thC. Coined from OUR + -'s "belonging to."]

our·selves /owr sélvz/ *pron.* **1.** BELONGING TO US refers to the speaker or writer and at least one other person, sometimes emphatically (*used as the object of a verb or preposition when the subject refers to the same people*) ○ *We ourselves can't work it out, so we don't expect others to be able to.* **2.** REFERS TO PEOPLE IN GENERAL refers to people in general ○ *Many of us have secrets that we find difficult to admit even to ourselves.* **3.** REFERS EMPHATICALLY TO US refers emphatically to the speaker or writer and at least one other person ○ *These papers are of no interest to anyone but ourselves.* **4.** OUR USUAL SELVES our usual selves ○ *At home with the family, we can really be ourselves.*

-ous *suffix.* **1.** full of, having the qualities of ○ *virtuous* ○ *traitorous* **2.** having a lower valence than a corresponding compound or ion the name of which ends in -ic ○ *chromous* [Via Old French from Latin *-osus* and *-us*]

oust /owst/ *vt.* **1.** FORCE SOMEBODY OUT to use force to remove somebody from a place **2.** REMOVE SOMEBODY FROM OFFICE to remove or force somebody from an office or position [15thC. Via Old French *oster* from Latin *obstare* "to stand in the way, hinder," from *stare* "to stand," the source of English *obstetrics*.]

oust·er /ówstər/ *n.* **1.** REMOVAL the act of removing or forcing somebody out of a place or position **2.** WRONGFUL DISPOSSESSION the illegal removal or forceful dispossession of somebody's property

out /owt/ CORE MEANING: a grammatical word indicating that somebody or something is away from a place or removed from somewhere ○ (adv) *The child ran out and got back onto the bike.* ○ (adv) *She took out her laptop.* ○ (adj) *She's been out late every night.*

1. *adv.* OUTSIDE outside a place rather than inside ○ *It's cold out.* **2.** *adv.* IN ANOTHER PLACE in another place, usually far away ○ *She's out in Australia, I think.* **3.** *adv.* INDICATES END POINT indicates a goal or objective achieved in the action specified by the verb ○ *Stick it out – never give up.* **4.** *adv.* IN EXISTENCE that there is in existence ○ *It's one of the best albums out.* **5.** *adj., adv.* AWAY FROM HOME away from home or your place of work ○ (adj) *He's not answering the doorbell – he must be out.* ○ (adv) *She's not answering the phone – she must have gone out.* **6.** *adj., adv.* FURTHER AWAY refers to the tide when the sea moves away from the shore ○ (adj) *We can cross to the island when the tide is out.* ○ (adv) *The tide goes out at around five o'clock.* **7.** *adj., adv.* NO LONGER BURNING of a light or a fire, no longer alight or no longer burning ○ (adj) *The fire is out.* ○ (adv) *The fire has gone out.* **8.** *adj., adv.* IN FLOWER in flower ○ (adj) *The daffodils are out at last.* ○ (adv) *All the wild flowers are coming out.* **9.** *adj., adv.* AVAILABLE of a book, record, etc., available for people to buy. ○ (adj) *Her new book is out in paperback at last.* ○ (adv) *Their new album came out last week.* **10.** *adj., adv.* ON STRIKE on strike ○ (adj) *The miners have been out for a month now.* ○ (adv) *500 workers came out in protest over the benefit cuts.* **11.** *adj.* NO LONGER IN A GAME unable to take part any longer in a game or sport **12.** *adj.* CONSIDERING A VERDICT of a jury, considering its verdict **13.** *adj.* INCORRECT inaccurate or incorrect ○ *Look – the figures are way out.* **14.** *adj.* UNACCEPTABLE unacceptable or not worth considering ○ *That possibility is out, I'm afraid.* **15.** *adj.* UNFASHIONABLE no longer in fashion **16.** *adj.* INTENT ON determined or intent on ○ *He's just out for what he can get.* **17.** *adj.* UNCONSCIOUS unconscious ○ *She was out cold.* **18.** *adj.* USED UP used up or exhausted ○ *All our rations are out.* **19.** *adj.* NOT IN GOVERNMENT not in power or office **20.** *adj.* FINISHED completed or concluded ○ *before the year is out* **21.** *adj.* NOT WORKING not working ○ *All the phones are out.* **22.** *interj.* AWAY FROM HERE! a command for somebody to leave a place ○ *Out!* **23.** *vt.* TO EXPOSE SOMEBODY to expose somebody, especially a public figure or famous person, as a homosexual ○ *A gay action group outed a prominent celebrity.* **24.** *n.* WAY OF AVOIDING BAD CONSEQUENCE a way of escaping from a predicament or avoiding the undesirable consequences of something (*informal*) ○ *What's my out if things go wrong?* [Old English *ūt*] ◇ **out of 1.** indicates that somebody leaves a place ○ *Three men came out of the store.* **2.** indicates that somebody removes something from a place ○ *In her enthusiasm, she pulled the drawer right out of the desk.* **3.** toward the outside ○ *She looked longingly out of the window.* **4.** no longer available or in somebody's possession ○ *We're out of butter.* **5.** from ○ *Plastic products are made out of petroleum.* **6.** indicates proportion that something is true of ○ *This applies to one out of five adults.* **7.** indicates that somebody gains an advantage from something ○ *I think I got a lot out of the course.* **8.** indicates that somebody is sheltered from the weather ○ *Remember to keep out of the sun, or at least use sunblock.* **9.** beyond the range of a sound ○ *I called her, but she was out of earshot.* **10.** indicates the motivation behind an action ○ *He only did it out of spite.* **11.** indicates that somebody is not or is no longer in a situation ○ *A police officer warned them to stay out of trouble.* ◇ **out of it** very drunk or under the influence of drugs (*informal*) ○ *You were totally out of it last night!* ◇ **out with it** a command to somebody to let something be known immediately ○ *Come on, what's going on? Out with it!*

outa *prep.* = **outta**

out·age /ówtij/ *n.* **1.** TEMPORARY LOSS OF POWER a temporary loss of function or interruption of a power source, especially a loss of electric power **2.** AMOUNT MISSING an amount of something that is missing after delivery or storage

out-and-out *adj.* being a thorough, uncompromising, or unapologetic example of something

out·back *n.* /ówt bàk/ REMOTE AREA, ESPECIALLY IN AUSTRALIA a sparsely inhabited or wilderness region of a country, especially of Australia ■ *adj.* RELATING TO AUSTRALIAN OUTBACK relating to a remote, sparsely inhabited region of a country, especially the Australian interior ○ *an outback community*

out·bid /owt bíd/ (**-bid·ded, -bid·ding, -bids**) *vt.* to offer to pay more money for something than somebody else

out·board /ówt bàwrd/ *adj.* **1.** ON THE OUTSIDE OF A BOAT located on the outside of the hull of a ship or boat **2.** LOCATED TOWARD BOAT'S HULL positioned away from the center of a ship or boat **3.** AWAY FROM THE FUSELAGE away from the main body of an aircraft and toward the wingtips ■ *adv.* TOWARD OUTSIDE OF SHIP in a direction away from the center of a ship or aircraft ■ *n.* BOAT WITH OUTBOARD MOTOR a boat with an engine mounted outside the stern

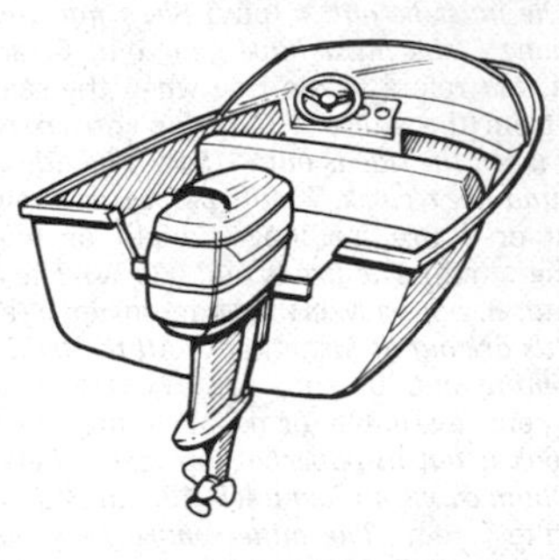

Outboard motor

out·board mo·tor, **out·board** *n.* a small or medium-sized engine with a propeller that can be mounted outside the stern of a boat

out·bound /ówt bòwnd/ *adj.* traveling away from rather than toward a particular place ○ *an outbound jurney*

out·brave /owt bráyv/ *vt.* (*archaic*) **1.** FACE SOMETHING DEFIANTLY to face a threat with defiance **2.** BE MORE COURAGEOUS THAN SOMEBODY to be braver than somebody else

out·break /ówt bràyk/ *n.* a sudden occurrence, usually of something unpleasant or dangerous such as illness or fighting ○ *the outbreak of war*

out·breed /owt bréed/ (**-bred** /owt bréd/, **-bred, -breed·ing, -breeds**) *vti.* to bring together distantly related members of a species in order to breed genetically varied offspring, or to reproduce in this way [Early 20thC. Modeled on "inbreed."]

out·build·ing /ówt bìlding/ *n.* a barn, shed, or other structure that is situated away from the main building on a property

out·burst /ówt bùrst/ *n.* **1.** SUDDEN DISPLAY OF EMOTION a sudden display of strong emotion ○ *an outburt of grief* **2.** INTENSE PERIOD OF ACTIVITY a sudden burst of energy or growth

out·call /ówt kàwl/ *n.* a visit made by a doctor or other professional to the home of a client or patient

out·cast /ówt kàst/ *n.* somebody who has been rejected by a particular group or by society as a whole ○ *a social outcast* [Late 16thC. Formed from OUT + CAST.] —**out·cast** *adj.*

out·caste /ówt kàst/ *n.* **1.** MEMBER EXPELLED FROM CASTE in India, somebody who has been expelled from a Hindu caste for violating its rules or customs **2.** INDIAN WITHOUT CASTE somebody in India who does not belong to a caste

out·class /owt kláss/ *vt.* to be so much better than others as to seem to be in a separate class altogether

out·come /ówt kùm/ *n.* the way that something turns out in the end

out·crop /ówt kròp/ *n.* ROCK PROJECTING FROM SOIL the part of a rock formation that is exposed on the surface of the ground ■ *vi.* (**-cropped, -crop·ping, -crops**) PROJECT FROM GROUND to stick out of the ground as an outcrop [Mid-18thC. From *crop out.*]

out·cross /owt kráwss/ *vt.* (**-crossed, -cross·ing, -cross·es**) BREED UNRELATED ANIMALS to mate two plants or animals not closely related but usually of the same breed in order to produce offspring ■ *n.* PRODUCT OF OUTCROSSING the process of outcrossing plants or animals, or the progeny produced as a result

out·cry /ówt krì/ (*plural* **-cries**) *n.* **1.** STRONG REACTION a strong and widespread public reaction against something **2.** CLAMOR a loud cry from a crowd of people

out·dat·ed /owt dáytəd/ *adj.* old-fashioned or out-of-date ○ *outdated notions about how to raise children*

WORD KEY: SYNONYMS

See Synonyms at ***old-fashioned.***

out·dis·tance /owt dístənss/ (**-tanced, -tanc·ing, -tanc·es**) *vt.* **1.** GO FASTER THAN OTHER COMPETITORS to be faster than others in a race and leave other competitors behind **2.** BE BETTER THAN OTHERS to be considerably more successful than others

out·do /owt dóo/ (**-did** /-díd/, **-done** /-dún/, **-do·ing, -does**) *vt.* to do more or better than other people, or better than previously

out·door /owt dáwr/ *adj.* **1.** CONCERNED WITH THE OPEN AIR located in, belonging in, or suited to the open air ○ *outdoor activities* **2.** ENJOYING BEING OUTSIDE enjoying activities that take place in the open air

out·doors /owt dáwrz/ *adv.* OUTSIDE outside or in the open air ■ *n.* AREA NOT IN OR NEAR BUILDINGS the open air, especially when away from populated areas [Early 19thC. From the phrase "out of doors."]

out·doors·man /owt dáwrzzəmən/ (*plural* **-men**) *n.* a man who spends a lot of time in outdoor activities such as camping, hunting, and fishing

out·doors·per·son /owt dáwrz pùrss'n/ *n.* somebody who spends a lot of time in outdoor activities such as camping, hunting, and fishing

out·doors·wom·an /owt dáwrz wòomman/ (*plural* **-en** /-wìmmən/) *n.* a woman who spends a lot of time in outdoor activities such as camping, hunting, and fishing

out·door·sy /owt dáwrzee/ *adj.* suited to or fond of the open air (*informal*)

out·draw /owt dráw/ (**-drew** /-dróo/, **-drawn** /-dráwn/, **-draw·ing, -draws**) *vt.* **1.** DRAW WEAPON QUICKER THAN SOMEBODY to draw a handgun faster than another person **2.** ATTRACT MORE PEOPLE to attract a larger audience than another performer or performance

out·er /ówtər/ *adj.* **1.** ON THE OUTSIDE on or around the outside of something ○ *the outer surface of the spacecraft* **2.** AWAY FROM THE CENTER on the edge or away from the center of something ○ *the outer islands* **3.** ABOUT BODY RATHER THAN SPIRIT concerning or belonging to external or worldly things rather than the life of the mind or spirit [14thC. Formed from OUT, replacing earlier "utter."]

out·er·most /ówtər mòst/ *adj.* farthest away from the center [14thC. Formed from OUTER, on the model of "innermost."]

out·er plan·et *n.* any of the five planets, Jupiter, Saturn, Uranus, Neptune, and Pluto, that have orbits lying beyond the asteroid belt

out·er space *n.* all space in the universe beyond the earth and its atmosphere, especially interplanetary and interstellar space, but including the region where astronauts walk and satellites orbit the earth

out·er·wear /ówtər wàir/ *n.* clothing that is designed to be worn outdoors over other clothing

out·face /owt fáyss/ (**-faced, -fac·ing, -fac·es**) *vt.* **1.** STARE SOMEBODY DOWN to win a confrontation, especially by staring at somebody or not looking away **2.** DEFY SOMEBODY to confront somebody boldly or confidently

out·fall /ówt fàwl/ *n.* the outlet of a sewer, drain, or stream, especially where it empties into a larger body of water

out·field /ówt fèeld/ *n.* **1.** BASEBALL AREA BEYOND THE INFIELD the part of a baseball or softball field beyond the diamond marked by the bases **2.** PLAYERS IN OUTFIELD the players in ball sports whose positions are in the outfield —**out·field·er** *n.*

outfielder /ówt feeldər/ *n.* BASEBALL a player who defends in the outfield

out·fit /ówt fìt/ *n.* **1.** SET OF CLOTHES a set of clothes worn together **2.** EQUIPMENT a set of tools or equipment for a particular task or occupation ○ *a diving outfit* **3.** SMALL ORGANIZATION a team or group of people who work closely together, e.g., a military unit (*informal*) ■ *vt.* (**-fit·ted, -fit·ting, -fits**) EQUIP SOMEBODY to provide somebody with all the equipment that is needed to do a particular job

out·fit·ter /ówt fìttər/ *n.* a store that sells equipment and supplies for outdoor leisure activities such as camping or hunting, and sometimes provides guides

out·flank /owt flángk/ (**-flanked, -flank·ing, -flanks**) *vt.* **1.** ATTACK THE ENEMY INDIRECTLY to go around the main body of an enemy force and attack it from the side or from behind **2.** WIN BY MANEUVERING to outwit or bypass an opponent or competitor

out·flow /ówt flò/ *n.* the flow, movement, or transfer of something such as gas, water, or money away from a place

out·fox /owt fóks/ (**-foxed, -fox·ing, -fox·es**) *vt.* to defeat somebody by being more cunning

out-front *adj.* frank and straightforward (*informal*) ○ *wasn't very out-front about her policies*

out·gas /owt gáss/ (**-gassed, -gas·sing, -gas·es**) *vti.* to remove or release trapped or absorbed gas, or to be released as gas

out·gen·er·al /owt jénnərəl/ (**-aled** *or* **-alled, -al·ing** *or* **-al·ling, -als**) *vt.* to defeat somebody in battle through better leadership

out·giv·ing /owt gívving/ *adj.* friendly and sociable

out·go /owt gṓ/ *vt.* (**-went** /-wént/, **-gone** /-gón/, **-go·ing, -goes**) OUTDO to go beyond or surpass somebody or something ■ *n.* **1.** EXPENDITURE something that goes out, especially money that is paid out **2.** SOMETHING THAT FLOWS OUT something that is flowing out **3.** GOING OUT the act of going out

out·go·ing /owt gṓing/ *adj.* **1.** LEAVING OR GOING OUT in the process of departing or going out of a building or place ○ *outgoing flights* **2.** LEAVING A JOB in the process of departing or being sent away after a period of office ○ *a dinner for the outgoing president* **3.** SOCIABLE confident and friendly in social situations ○ *a cheerful, outgoing child*

out·grew past tense of **outgrow**

out-group *n.* a group of people excluded from another group with higher status [Early 20thC. Modeled on "in-group."]

out·grow /owt grṓ/ (**-grew** /-gróo/, **-grown** /-grṓn/, **-grow·ing, -grows**) *vt.* **1.** GET TOO LARGE to grow too large for something **2.** MOVE BEYOND PREVIOUS INTERESTS to change so that old ideas, interests, or ways of behaving are lost in favor of new ones **3.** OUTSTRIP to grow larger or faster than other things or people

out·growth /ówt gròth/ *n.* **1.** EXTENSION a natural development or result of something else **2.** OFFSHOOT something that is growing out from the main part

out·guess /owt géss/ (**-guessed, -guess·ing, -guess·es**) *vt.* to get an advantage over somebody by anticipating what that person is thinking or planning to do

out·gun /owt gún/ (**-gunned, -gun·ning, -guns**) *vt.* **1.** HAVE BETTER WEAPONS to have more guns or firepower than somebody else **2.** OVERWHELM RIVAL to defeat a rival or competitor by being stronger or having better resources (*informal*)

out·haul /ówt hàwl/ *n.* a rope used to pull a sail taut along a spar or boom

out-Her·od (**out-Her·od·ded, out-Her·od·ded, out-Her·od·ding, out-Her·ods**) *vt.* to behave more excessively than somebody else ○ *out-Herod Herod* [From Shakespeare's *Hamlet* III.2, referring to the traditionally overdramatic character of Herod in the medieval mystery plays.]

out·house /ówt hòwss/ (*plural* **-hous·es** /-hòwzəz/) *n.* **1. OUTBUILDING** a small building situated near the main building on a property **2. OUTDOOR TOILET** an outdoor toilet consisting of a small building that encloses a seat with a hole in it built over a pit

out·ing /ówting/ *n.* **1. EXCURSION** a short pleasure trip usually lasting no more than a day **2. TAKING PART IN EVENT** an appearance at or participation in a public event, especially an athletic competition **3. WALK OUTDOORS** a walk or hike outdoors ○ *took the toddlers on a little outing around the block* **4. DECLARING SOMEBODY TO BE HOMOSEXUAL** the practice of making public the fact that somebody is homosexual when that person wants the information kept private

out·ing flan·nel *n.* a soft cotton fabric with a nap on both sides

out·jock·ey /owt jókee/ (**-eyed, -ey·ing, -eys**) *vt.* to get an advantage over somebody by cleverness or trickery

out·land /ówt lànd, ówtlənd/ *n.* **1. HINTERLAND** the remote or outlying areas of a country (*often used in the plural*) **2. DIFFERENT COUNTRY** a different country [Old English *ūtland*]

out·land·er /ówt làndər/ *n.* somebody from another country or from a different region, and thus a stranger [Late 16thC. Modeled on Dutch "uitlander" and German "Ausländer."]

out·land·ish /owt lándish/ *adj.* **1. VERY PECULIAR** extremely unusual or bizarre **2. ALIEN** alien or foreign (*archaic*) [Old English *ūtlandisc*] —**out·land·ish·ly** *adv.* —**out·land·ish·ness** *n.*

out·last /owt lást/ (**-last·ed, -last·ing, -lasts**) *vt.* to last or exist longer than somebody or something else

out·law /ówt làw/ *n.* **1. FUGITIVE** a notorious criminal, especially one on the run **2. SOMEBODY WITHOUT LEGAL RIGHTS** somebody, often a criminal, who has been officially deprived of legal rights and so is not protected by the law **3. REBEL** somebody who is rebellious or flouts the law **4. VICIOUS ANIMAL** a savage or uncontrollable animal ■ *vt.* (**-lawed, -law·ing, -laws**) **1. BAN SOMETHING** to make something illegal **2. TAKE AWAY SOMEBODY'S LEGAL RIGHTS** to deprive somebody officially of all their legal rights [12thC. Old English *ūtlaga*, from Old Norse *útlagi*, literally "person outside the law," from *útlagr* "outlawed, banished."]

out·law·ry /ówt làwree/ *n.* **1. DISREGARD FOR LAW** refusal to obey the law **2. STATE OF BEING LEGALLY OUTLAWED** a state in which somebody has been deprived of his or her legal rights and is no longer protected by the law, or the legal process by which this happens

out·lay /owt láy/ *n.* **1. SPENDING** the expending of resources or spending of money **2. MONEY SPENT** an amount of money spent ■ *vt.* (**-laid, -laid** /-láyd/, **-lay·ing, -lays**) **SPEND MONEY** to spend money on something

out·let /ówt lèt, ówtlət/ *n.* **1. VENT** a passage or opening for letting something out, e.g., water or steam **2. RELEASE FOR EMOTIONS** a way of releasing emotions or impulses **3. STORE** a place where something is sold, often a store that sells the products of a particular manufacturer **4. MARKET FOR GOODS** a market providing goods or services for purchasers **5. CONNECTION WITH ELECTRICITY SUPPLY** a receptacle, usually mounted on a wall, into which an electric plug is inserted to make a connection to a source of electric power **6. HOLE ON ELECTRICAL DEVICE FOR PLUG** a hole on a piece of electrical equipment into which a plug fits **7. MOUTH OF RIVER** the lower end of a river where it flows into a lake or the sea **8. STREAM DRAINING LAKE** a stream or channel flowing from a larger body of water

out·li·er /ówt lìr/ *n.* **1.** GEOL **ROCK FORMATION** an outcrop of rock that is separated from a main formation **2. OUTLYING PART OF SOMETHING** a separate part of a system, organization, or body that is at some distance from the main part **3. SOMEBODY LIVING AT DISTANCE FROM WORK** somebody who lives a long way from his or her place of work

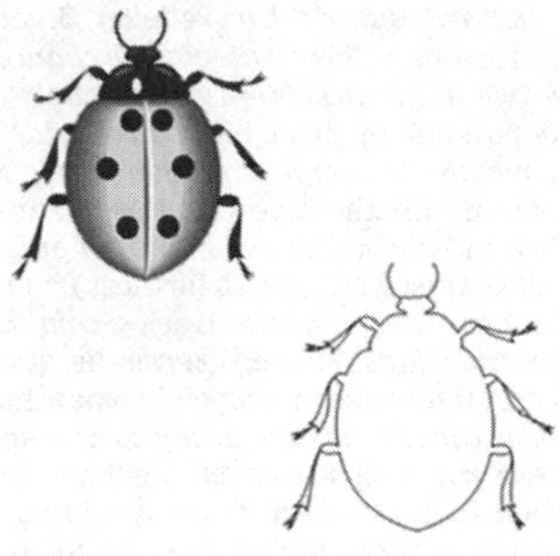

Outline

out·line /ówt lìn/ *n.* **1. LINE THAT SHOWS SHAPE** the edge or outer shape of something **2. LINE DRAWN AROUND SOMETHING** a line drawn around the outside edge of something **3. DRAWING WITHOUT SHADING** a style or example of drawing in which an object or figure is represented only by an outline **4. ROUGH PLAN** a list of the main points of a subject to be written about, or a rough idea of a proposed plan **5. SUMMARY** a short account of the main themes of a subject, or a list of the main points of an argument ○ *One of the books was an outline of European history.* ■ *vt.* (**-lined, -lin·ing, -lines**) **1. DRAW MAIN FEATURES** to draw a line showing or emphasizing the shape of something **2. GIVE ESSENTIAL ELEMENTS** to give the main points of an argument or plan

out·live /owt lív/ (**-lived, -liv·ing, -lives**) *vt.* **1. LIVE LONGER THAN** to live longer than somebody else **2. OUTLAST** to continue to exist beyond or last through something ○ *The policy has outlived its usefulness.*

out·look /ówt lo͝ok/ *n.* **1. ATTITUDE** an attitude or point of view **2. LIKELY FUTURE** expectations for the future, especially for the way a particular situation will develop **3. VIEW** a view seen from a particular place

out loud *adv.* aloud, rather than silently in somebody's head

out·ly·ing /ówt lì ing/ *adj.* far from the central part of a particular place or region

out·man /owt mán/ (**-manned, -man·ning, -mans**) *vt.* to have a larger force of people than an opponent has

out·ma·neu·ver /òwt mə no͞ovər/ (**-vered, -ver·ing, -vers**) *vt.* **1. OUTWIT** to get the better of somebody by using skill or cunning **2. SURPASS OTHER VEHICLES IN MANEUVERABILITY** to be easier to handle than other vehicles of a particular size or class

out·match /owt mách/ (**-matched, -match·ing, -match·es**) *vt.* to prove stronger or better than somebody else

out-mi·grant *n.* a person or animal that leaves one region or community in order to settle in another

out-mi·grate (**out-mi·grat·ed, out-mi·grat·ing, out-mi·grates**) *vi.* to leave one region or community in order to settle in another

out·mod·ed /owt mṓdəd/ *adj.* **1. OLD-FASHIONED** no longer fashionable or widely used **2. OBSOLETE** having been superseded by something newer or more efficient [Early 20thC. Translation of French *démodé*.]

out·most /ówt mṓst/ *adj.* farthest away from the center or main area [14thC. Alteration of UTMOST.]

out·num·ber /owt númbər/ (**-bered, -ber·ing, -bers**) *vt.* to be more numerous than another group or set of things

out-of-bod·y *adj.* undergoing an experience in which a person's consciousness appears to have an existence separate from the body, enabling the subject to see his or her own body from the outside

out-of-bounds *adj., adv.* in or indicating a place that is beyond the established or official boundaries

out-of-court *adj.* arranged without going to court or without completing a court case, usually in an effort to avoid a long court case or to minimize costs

out-of-date *adj.* old-fashioned or no longer current

out-of-door *adj.* = **outdoor**

out-of-doors *adj.* = **outdoors**

out-of-pock·et *adj.* **1. HAVING LOST MONEY** having no money, especially because of having spent it on something that did not produce good results ○ *I was seriously out-of-pocket.* **2. REQUIRING SOMEBODY TO SPEND CASH** relating to or being expenses paid for with cash ○ *out-of-pocket expenses*

out-of-state *adj.* coming from or relating to another state

out-of-stat·er *n.* somebody who is visiting or temporarily residing in one state but is a legal resident of another state

out-of-the-way *adj.* **1. REMOTE** far from a populated area or difficult to get to **2. UNUSUAL** uncommon or unconventional

out-of-town *adj.* coming from or happening in another town or city

out-of-town·er *n.* a person who comes from a different town or city

out·pace /owt páyss/ (**-paced, -pac·ing, -pac·es**) *vt.* to do better or go faster than something or somebody else

out·pa·tient /ówt pàysh'nt/ *n.* a patient who receives treatment at a hospital without staying overnight

out·per·form /òwt pər fáwrm/ (**-formed, -form·ing, -forms**) *vt.* to perform better than somebody or something else

out·place·ment /ówt plàyssmənt/ *n.* a service offered by a company to help employees who are being dismissed find new jobs

out·play /owt pláy/ (**-played, -play·ing, -plays**) *vt.* to play better than an opponent

out·point /owt póynt/ (**-point·ed, -point·ing, -points**) *vt.* **1. SAIL CLOSER TO WIND** to sail closer to the wind than another ship **2. SCORE MORE POINTS** to score more points than somebody else

outport /ówt pàwrt/ *n.* *Can* a small remote fishing village, especially one on the Newfoundland coast

out·post /ówt pṓst/ *n.* **1. TROOPS APART FROM MAIN FORCE** a small group of troops stationed at a distance from the main body of an army and assigned to guard a particular place or area **2. MILITARY BASE** a small military base in a remote area or different country **3. BASE** a settlement in unfamiliar territory or on a frontier

out·pour *vti.* /owt páwr/ (**-poured, -pour·ing, -pours**) **FLOW OUT** to flow out quickly or make something flow out quickly ■ *n.* /ówt pàwr/ **SOMETHING FLOWING** something that flows out freely or the act of flowing out

out·pour·ing /ówt pàwring/ *n.* something that pours or floods out, e.g., lava or a strong emotion

out·put /ówt po͝ot/ *n.* **1. PRODUCTION** the act of producing **2. YIELD** an amount of something produced or manufactured, especially during a fixed period of time **3. PRODUCTS PRODUCED** goods or services produced by an organization **4. CREATIVE OR ARTISTIC PRODUCTION** creative or intellectual work produced by somebody ○ *her literary output* **5. ENERGY PRODUCED** energy or power produced by a system **6.** ELEC ENG **ELECTRICAL POWER** the electrical energy, measured in watts, delivered by a generator or consumed by an electronic circuit **7.** COMPUT **INFORMATION FROM COMPUTER** information produced by a computer ■ *vt.* (**-put** *or* **-put·ted, -put·ting, -puts**) **PRODUCE COMPUTER INFORMATION** to display information from a computer on a monitor or direct it to a printer or other device

out·race /owt ráyss/ (**-raced, -rac·ing, -rac·es**) *vt.* to do something better or faster than others

out·rage /ówt ràyj/ *n.* **1. VIOLENT ACT** an extremely violent or cruel act **2. OFFENSIVE ACT** a very offensive or insulting act **3. FURY** intense anger and indignation aroused by a violent or offensive act ■ *vt.* (**-raged, -rag·ing, -rag·es**) **1. ATTACK OR VIOLATE** to commit a vicious crime against somebody **2. AROUSE ANGER IN SOMEBODY** to make somebody feel intense anger or indignation **3. RAPE** to rape somebody (*literary*) [13thC. Via French, "excess, atrocity," from Old French *outrer* "to exceed," ultimately from Latin *ultra* "beyond" (see ULTRA-). The meaning was later influenced by RAGE.]

out·ra·geous /owt ráyjəss/ *adj.* **1. EXTRAORDINARY AND UNCONVENTIONAL** extravagant or unconventional, and likely to shock people **2. MORALLY SHOCKING** violating accepted standards of decency or morality **3. EXCESSIVE** exceeding the bounds of what is reasonable or expected ○ *outrageous prices* **4. VIOLENT OR CRUEL** violent or unrestrained in mood or action —**out·ra·geous·ly** *adv.* —**out·ra·geous·ness** *n.*

out·range /owt ráynj/ (**-ranged, -rang·ing, -rang·es**) *vt.* to have a greater range than something else of the same class, e.g., a firearm or missile

out·rank /owt rángk/ (**-ranked, -rank·ing, -ranks**) *vt.* to have a higher rank or status than somebody else

ou·tré /oo tráy/ *adj.* passing well beyond what is usual, normal, or generally acceptable [Early 18thC. Via French from Old French, the past participle of *outrer* "to go too far" (see OUTRAGE).]

out·reach *vt.* /owt réech/ (**-reached, -reach·ing, -reach·es**) **1. REACH FARTHER** to reach or extend farther than somebody or something else **2. EXCEED** to exceed or go beyond a limit ■ *n.* /ówt reech/ **1. PROVISION OF COMMUNITY SERVICES** the provision of information or services to groups in society who might otherwise be neglected ○ *an outreach program for people who cannot read* **2. EXTENT OF REACH** the length or extent of the reach of somebody or something ○ *the outreach of a communications network*

out·ride /owt ríd/ (**-rode** /owt ród/, **-rid·den** /owt rídd'n/, **-rid·ing, -rides**) *vt.* **1. RIDE BETTER OR FASTER** to ride better, farther, or faster than somebody else **2.** SHIPPING **SURVIVE STORM** to survive the violence of the wind and waves during a storm

out·rid·er /ówt rìdər/ *n.* **1. ESCORT** somebody who rides in front of or at the side of a carriage, motor vehicle, or race horse and acts as an escort **2. MOUNTED RANGE HAND** a mounted cowboy or herdsman who rides the range watching over a herd or flock **3. FORERUNNER** somebody who goes ahead of a group and acts as a scout [Mid-16thC. The word originally denoted an officer of the sheriff's court who collected dues and issued summonses.]

out·rig·ger /ówt rìggər/ *n.* **1. PART OF A BOAT** a beam or framework sticking out from the side of a boat, used to extend a rope or sail or as a brace for an oarlock **2. FRAMEWORK ON CANOE** a long float attached to a framework that projects from the side of a seagoing canoe to prevent it from capsizing **3. KIND OF BOAT OR CANOE** a boat or canoe fitted with an outrigger **4.** AIR **STRUCTURE ON AIRCRAFT** a projection attached to an aircraft or other vehicle or machine to stabilize it or to support something [Mid-18thC. Origin uncertain: perhaps an alteration (influenced by RIG) of obsolete *outligger,* a type of spar for extending a sail, from Dutch *uitligger.*]

out·right *adv.* /owt rít/ **1. WHOLLY** wholly and completely ○ *He now owns the business outright.* **2. INSTANTLY** immediately or instantly ○ *They refused our offer outright.* **3. CANDIDLY** openly and without reservation ○ *I told him outright that he was making a big mistake.* ■ *adj.* /ówt rìt/ **1. ABSOLUTE** complete or total ○ *an outright lie* **2. WITHOUT QUALIFICATIONS** without restrictions or limitations ○ *The car was an outright gift from the corporation.* —**out·right·ly** *adv.*

out·run /owt rún/ (**-ran** /-rán/, **-run, -run·ning, -runs**) *vt.* **1. RUN FASTER** to run faster or farther than somebody else **2. RUN AWAY** to escape by or as if by running faster than a pursuer ○ *outrun the bill collectors* ○ *The hare outran the wolf.* **3. EXCEED** to develop faster or to exceed ○ *Demand for gasoline began to outrun supply.*

out·sell /owt sél/ (**-sold** /-sóld/, **-sold, -sell·ing, -sells**) *vt.* **1. SELL MORE** to be sold faster or in greater quantities than something else **2. BE BETTER AT SELLING** to sell more than another salesperson

out·set /ówt sèt/ *n.* the beginning or initial stage of an activity

out·shine /owt shín/ (**-shone** /-shón/ *or* **-shined, -shone** *or* **-shined, -shin·ing, -shines**) *v.* **1.** *vt.* **SHINE BRIGHTER** to shine brighter than something else **2.** *vt.* **SURPASS** to surpass somebody or something else, especially in terms of excellence or quality **3.** *vi.* **PRODUCE LIGHT** to give out light (*literary*)

out·shoot *vt.* /owt shóot/ (**-shot** /owt shót/, **-shot, -shoot·ing, -shoots**) **SHOOT BETTER** to shoot better than somebody else ■ *n.* /ówt shoot/ **PROJECTION** something that projects or shoots out

out·side /owt síd, ówt sìd/ CORE MEANING: a grammatical word indicating the outer surface or appearance of something ○ (noun) *Grill the chicken wings until the outsides are crisp.* ○ (adv) *The house still needs to be painted outside.*

1. *adv., prep., adj.* **OUT OF DOORS** in the open air rather than inside a building ○ (adv) *We should head outside soon if we're going to start the barbecue.* ○ (prep) *I'll meet you outside the post office.* ○ (adj) *an outside toilet* **2.** *adj., adv., prep.* **BEYOND IMMEDIATE ENVIRONMENT** happening, existing, or originating in places, people, or groups other than your own or what you are used to ○ (adj) *It was claimed that most of the substandard work had been done by outside contractors.* ○ (adv) *in the world outside* ○ (prep) *married outside her religion* **3.** *adj.* **SLIGHT** slight or remote ○ *There's an outside chance we may still be able to get tickets.* **4.** *adj.* **MAXIMUM** the most extreme possible or probable ○ *an outside estimate of three months to complete the job* **5.** *adj.* **AWAY FROM BATTER** passing on the side of home plate opposite the batter in baseball or softball ○ *an outside pitch* **6.** *adj.* **FARTHEST FROM SIDE OF ROAD** farthest from the side of a road or center of a race track ○ *coming up fast in the outside lane* **7.** *prep.* **BEYOND THE SCOPE OF** not included in the range or scope of something ○ *Such behavior is completely outside my comprehension.* **8.** *n.* **EXISTENCE NOT IN AN INSTITUTION** existence not in an institution such as prison or a psychiatric hospital ○ *We wondered what life was like on the outside.* **9.** *n.* **AREA FARTHEST FROM SIDE OF ROAD** the part farthest from the side of a road or center of a race track ○ *Large crowds of shoppers forced her to walk on the outside of the sidewalk.* **10.** *n.* **HEAVILY POPULATED AREA OF CANADA** the most populous areas of Canada and Alaska along the coasts or bordering the lower 48 states ◇ **at the outside** at the maximum amount or time that can be expected ◇ **outside of** other than the person or thing mentioned

out·side broad·cast *n. U.K.* = **remote**

out·sid·er /owt sídər/ *n.* **1. SOMEBODY WHO DOES NOT BELONG** somebody who is not part of a particular group or organization **2. COMPETITOR UNLIKELY TO WIN** a competitor or candidate who is considered unlikely to win

out·sight /ówt sìt/ *n.* the ability to take note of or judge external things [Early 17thC. Modeled on "insight."]

out·size /owt síz, ówt sìz/ *n.* **EXTRA LARGE SIZE** an unusual size, especially one that is larger than usual ■ *adj.* **out·size, out·sized EXTRA LARGE** much larger, heavier, or more extensive than is usual or expected ○ *an outsize ego*

out·skirts /ówt skùrts/ *npl.* the areas at the edge of a town or city, farthest from the center

out·smart /owt smaárt/ (**-smart·ed, -smart·ing, -smarts**) *vt.* to use cunning or cleverness to get an advantage over somebody

out·sold past participle, past tense of **outsell**

out·sole /ówt sòl/ *n.* the outer sole of a boot or shoe [Late 19thC. Modeled on "insole."]

out·source /ówt sàwrss/ (**-sourced, -sourc·ing, -sourc·es**) *vt.* to buy labor or parts from a source outside a company or business rather than using the company's staff or plant

out·spend /owt spénd/ (**-spent** /-spént/, **-spent, -spend·ing, -spends**) *vt.* **1. SPEND MORE THAN** to spend more than somebody else **2. EXCEED SPENDING LIMITS OF** to exceed fixed limits for something in spending ○ *outspent our budget*

out·spo·ken /owt spókən/ *adj.* expressing opinions directly, frankly, and fearlessly —**out·spo·ken·ly** *adv.* —**out·spo·ken·ness** *n.*

out·spread /owt spréd/ *adj.* **STRETCHED OUT** extended or spread out flat ■ *vt.* (**-spread, -spread·ing, -spreads**) **EXTEND** to stretch out or extend something ■ *n.* **ACT OF SPREADING OUT** the act or an example of extending outward

out·stand /owt stánd/ (**-stood** /-stóod/, **-stood, -stand·ing, -stands**) *vi.* to stand out or be prominent

out·stand·ing /owt stánding/ *adj.* **1. UNUSUALLY EXCELLENT** excellent, and superior to others in the same group or category ○ *outstanding work* **2. NOT YET RESOLVED** not yet paid, resolved, or dealt with ○ *outstanding debts* **3. JUTTING OUT** jutting outward or upward **4.** STOCK EXCH **PUBLICLY SOLD** publicly issued and sold as securities —**out·stand·ing·ly** *adv.*

out·stare /owt stáir/ (**-stared, -star·ing, -stares**) *vt.* to make somebody look away or submit by staring hard

out·sta·tion /ówt stàysh'n/ *n.* a post or station in a remote unsettled spot

out·stay /owt stáy/ (**-stayed, -stay·ing, -stays**) *vt.* **1. STAY LONGER THAN** to stay longer than other people, or longer than is appropriate ○ *outstayed their welcome* **2. SHOW GREATER ENDURANCE THAN** to show greater endurance than somebody ○ *outstayed their rivals*

out·stood past participle, past tense of **outstand**

out·stretch /owt stréch/ (**-stretched, -stretch·ing, -stretch·es**) *vt.* to hold out or extend something

out·strip /owt stríp/ (**-stripped, -strip·ping, -strips**) *vt.* **1. DO BETTER THAN** to achieve more or go faster than somebody, especially a competitor **2. EXCEED** to be greater than something ○ *Demand for their products has already outstripped supply.*

outta, outa *prep.* used as a written representation of "out of," reflecting popular pronunciation (*slang*) ○ *I'm outta here.* [From a pronunciation of *out of*]

out·take /ówt tàyk/ *n.* **1. EXCLUDED SECTION OF FILM** a recorded scene or sequence that is not included in the final version of a movie or television program, usually because it contains mistakes ○ *The outtakes were funnier than the movie itself.* **2. REJECTED RECORDING** a recording not used in the final version of an album

out·thrust /owt thrúst/ *adj.* **THRUST OUTWARD** extending out beyond something ○ *the dog's outthrust paw* ■ *n.* /ówt thrùst/ **OUTWARD PROJECTION** something that projects or extends outward

out·turn /ówt tùrn/ *n.* the amount produced during a specific period [Late 18thC. From *turn out.*]

out·vote /owt vót/ (**-vot·ed, -vot·ing, -votes**) *vt.* to defeat other candidates or a proposal by a majority of votes

out·ward /ówtwərd/ CORE MEANING: a grammatical word indicating that something is outside or on or toward the exterior of something, or relates to the exterior of something ○ *the rustic balustrading that bounded the arbor on the outward side*

1. *adj.* **VISIBLE** clearly observable ○ *She gave no outward indication that she was upset.* **2.** *adj.* **RELATING TO THE PHYSICAL BODY** relating to the physical body rather than the mind or spirit ○ *his outward appearance reflected his inner turmoil* **3.** *adj.* **APPARENT** apparent or superficial ○ *can't judge by outward appearances* **4.** *adj.* **OUTBOUND** heading away from a place **5.** *adv.* **out·ward, out·wards OUT** toward the outside and away from the inside or middle **6.** *n.* **MATERIAL WORLD** the reality of the external world (*literary*) [Old English *ūtanweard, ūteweard*] —**out·ward·ness** *n.*

out·ward-bound *adj.* making an outgoing journey or passage

out·ward·ly /ówtwərdlee/ *adv., adv.* **IN APPEARANCE** in appearance rather than in reality ■ *adv.* **TOWARD THE OUTSIDE** on or toward the outside

out·wards /ówtwərdz/ *adv.* = **outward 5**

out·wash /ówt wòsh/ *n.* sand and gravel deposited by streams that are flowing away from a glacier

out·wear /owt wáir/ (**-wore** /-wáwr/, **-worn** /-wáwrn/, **-wear·ing, -wears**) *vt.* to last longer or wear better than something else

out·weigh /owt wáy/ (**-weighed, -weigh·ing, -weighs**) *vt.* **1. BE MORE CRUCIAL THAN** to be more important or valuable than something else **2. WEIGH MORE THAN** to weigh more than somebody or something else

out·wit /owt wít/ (**-wit·ted, -wit·ting, -wits**) *vt.* **1. GAIN ADVANTAGE OVER SOMEBODY THROUGH CUNNING** to use cunning or trickery to get an advantage over somebody **2. BE SMARTER THAN SOMEBODY** to be more intelligent than somebody (*archaic*)

out·wore past tense of **outwear**

out·work *vt.* /owt wúrk/ (**-worked, -work·ing, -works**) **WORK HARDER THAN** to work harder or faster than somebody ■ *n.* /ówt wùrk/ **MILITARY OUTPOST** a trench or fortification built beyond the main line of defense

out·worn *adj.* outdated or no longer useful. Past participle of **outwear**

ou·zel /óoz'l/ *n.* a small European bird of the thrush family that has dark plumage with a white band across its throat. Latin name: *Turdus torquatus.* [Old English *ōsle* "blackbird." Ultimately from an Indo-European word that is also the ancestor of English *merle* and *merlon.*]

ou·zo /óozō/ (*plural* **-zos**) *n.* a colorless Greek alcoholic drink flavored with anise [Late 19thC. From modern Greek, of uncertain origin.]

o·va *npl.* plural of **ovum**

o·val /óvəl/ *adj.* **EGG-SHAPED** shaped like an egg ■ *n.* **1. TRACK** racetrack in the shape of an oval **2. EGG SHAPE** something shaped like an egg [Late 16thC. From medieval Latin *ovalis,* from Latin *ovum* "egg" (see OVUM).] —**o·val·ly** *adv.* —**o·val·ness** *n.*

ov·al·bu·min /òvvəl byóomən, óvəl-/ *n.* the main crystalline protein or albumin found in egg whites [Mid-19thC. From Latin *ovi albumen,* literally "white of egg," from *ovum* "egg" + *albumen* ALBUMEN.]

O·val Of·fice *n.* **1. U.S. PRESIDENT'S OFFICE** an oval-shaped room in the White House that is the private office used by the president of the United States **2.** U.S. **PRESIDENCY** the power and authority of the president of the United States

o·val win·dow *n.* a membranous opening between the middle ear and the inner ear that transmits sound vibrations [From its shape]

O·vam·bo /ō vaám bō/ (*plural* **-bo** *or* **-bos**) *n.* **1.** **MEMBER OF AFRICAN PEOPLE** a member of a Black people that lives in parts of southern Africa, especially in Angola and Namibia **2.** **OVAMBO LANGUAGE** the Bantu language of the Ovambo people. It belongs to the Benue-Congo branch of Niger-Congo languages. Ovambo is spoken by about 700,000 people. [Mid-19thC. Of Bantu origin, literally "people of leisure."] —**O·vam·bo** *adj.*

o·var·i·ec·to·my /ō vèrree éktə mee/ (*plural* **-mies**) *n.* the surgical removal of one or both ovaries

o·var·i·ot·o·my /ō vèrree óttəmee/ (*plural* **-mies**) *n.* **1.** **INCISION INTO OVARY** a surgical incision into an ovary **2.** = **ovariectomy**

o·va·ri·tis /ōvə rítiss/ *n.* = **oophoritis**

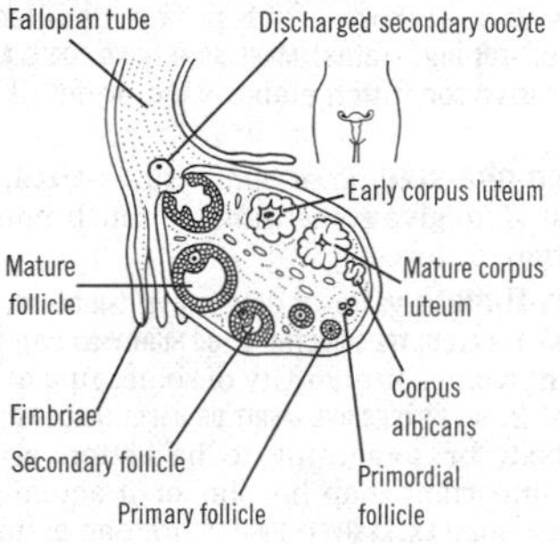

Ovary

o·va·ry /ṓvəree/ (*plural* **-ries**) *n.* **1.** **FEMALE REPRODUCTIVE ORGAN** either of the two female reproductive organs that produce eggs and, in vertebrates, also produce the sex hormones estrogen and progesterone **2.** **PART OF A FLOWER** the lower part of a pistil that bears ovules and ripens into a fruit [Mid-17thC. From modern Latin *ovarium*, from Latin *ovum* (see OVUM).] —**o·var·i·an** /ō váiree ən/ *adj.*

o·vate /ṓ vàyt/ *adj.* **1.** **EGG-SHAPED** shaped like an egg **2.** BOT **SHAPED LIKE A POINTED OVAL** used to describe a leaf or petal that is broad and rounded at the base and tapers towards the tip [Mid-18thC. From Latin *ovatus* "egg-shaped," from *ovum* (see OVUM).] —**o·vate·ly** *adv.*

o·va·tion /ō váysh'n/ *n.* **1.** **LOUD AND LONG APPLAUSE** enthusiastic applause or cheering, especially from a crowd or large group of people **2.** HIST **ROMAN VICTORY CELEBRATION** an ancient Roman victory ceremony for a returning military hero [Mid-16thC. Via the Latin stem *ovation-* from *ovare* "to rejoice," ultimately from an imitation of the sound of exulting.] —**o·va·tion·al** *adj.*

ov·en /úvv'n/ *n.* a compartment warmed by a heat source and used for baking, roasting, or drying [Old English *ofen.* Ultimately from an Indo-European word meaning "cooker" that is also the ancestor of English *olla.*]

ov·en·bird /úvv'n bùrd/ *n.* **1.** **NORTH AMERICAN BIRD** a North American warbler that has a shrill call and builds a dome-shaped nest on the ground. Latin name: *Seiurus aurocapillus.* **2.** **SOUTH AMERICAN BIRD** small brown South American bird that builds a dome-shaped nest from clay and dried leaves. Genus: *Furnarius.* [Early 19thC. From the ovenlike shape of the birds' nests.]

ov·en mitt *n.* a padded hand covering used as protection when putting hot dishes into and taking them out of an oven

ov·en·proof /úvv'n proof/ *adj.* capable of being used in an oven without being damaged by the heat

oven·ware /úvv'n wàir/ *n.* heat-resistant dishes that can be used for baking or roasting as well as for serving

o·ver /ṓvər/ (**o·vered, o·ver·ing, o·vers**) CORE MEANING: a grammatical word used to indicate a position directly above something, either resting on the top of something, or above the upper surface of something with a space in between ○ (prep) *a framed portrait over the fireplace* ○ (prep) *He wore a red flannel shirt over a T-shirt* . ○ (prep) *Julia was bent over the sink washing glasses.* ○ (adv) *flocks of geese flying over* ○ (adv) *Heat the milk and pour it over.*

1. *prep., adv.* **ON OR TO OTHER SIDE OF** positioned on or moving to the other side of something such as a barrier, obstacle, or area of land ○ (prep) *To see the cathedral you need to cross over the river.* ○ (adv) *He climbed over into the next field.* **2.** *prep., adv.* **THROUGHOUT** throughout the whole extent of ○ (prep) *traveling over Europe* ○ (prep) *In the past few years, fifties diners have sprung up all over town.* ○ (adv) *People are the same the world over.* **3.** *prep., adv.* **MORE THAN** more than a particular amount, measurement, or age ○ (prep) *go over your quota* ○ (adv) *people 30 and over* **4.** *adv.* **ACROSS INTERVENING SPACE** positioned in or moving to a point across intervening space ○ *She reached over and turned off the TV.* ○ *Jim sent a couple of guys over to help out.* **5.** *adv.* **SO AS TO FALL** so as to change position, especially from being upright ○ *knocked over a pile of books* ○ *He rolled over and turned out the light.* **6.** *adv.* **REMAINING** remaining or surplus after what was needed has been used ○ *There was plenty of food left over from the party.* **7.** *adv.* **AGAIN** doing something again, or again from the beginning ○ *If you make a mistake you'll just have to start over.* **8.** *prep.* **BY MEANS OF** by means of a device for communication such as a radio or telephone ○ *talk over the phone* **9.** *prep.* **ABOUT** on the subject of or related to ○ *grieving over the loss of her husband* **10.** *prep.* **AFFECTING** as an effect or influence upon somebody or something ○ *exercise more control over file access.* **11.** *prep.* **DURING** happening during or throughout a period of time or an occasion ○ *We can discuss this over lunch.* **12.** *prep.* **RECOVERED FROM** having recovered from the bad effects of something such as an illness ○ *get over a virus.* **13.** *prep.* **IN PREFERENCE TO** in preference to something else ○ *I'd choose steak over fish every time.* **14.** *adj.* **FINISHED** finished or no longer in progress ○ *When all this is over I'm going on vacation.* **15.** *interj.* RADIO **WORD SHOWING SOMEBODY'S TURN TO SPEAK** used when communicating via radio to indicate that somebody has finished talking and it is the other person's turn to speak **16.** *n.* **SHOT** shot that hits or explodes beyond its target **17.** *n.* CRICKET **BOWLING OF SIX BALLS** a series of six correctly bowled balls in cricket, or the play during this **18.** *n.* GAMBLING **SCORE ABOVE PARTICULAR NUMBER IN A WAGER** in a wager, the score abover a particular number of points or an amount above a particular total ○ *bet the over in the Super Bowl* **19.** *vt.* **PASS ABOVE** to pass above and across something [Old English *ofer.* Ultimately from an Indo-European word that is also the ancestor of English *super-* and *hyper-.*] ◇ **over again** once more ◇ **over against** in contrast with or in opposition to ◇ **over and above** in addition to or in excess of something ○ *benefits over and above the basic salary* ◇ **over and over** repeatedly or a great deal

o·ver·a·bun·dance /ṑvər ə búndənss/ *n.* an amount greater than what is needed or appropriate —**o·ver·a·bun·dant** *adj.*

o·ver·a·chieve /ṑvər ə cheev/ (**a·chieved, a·chiev·ing, a·chieves**) *vi.* to perform better or be more successful than expected —**o·ver·a·chiev·er** *n.* —**o·ver·a·chieve·ment** *n.*

o·ver·act /ṑvər ákt/ (**-act·ed, -act·ing, -acts**) *vti.* to exaggerate movements or emotions, especially when acting in a performance —**o·ver·ac·tion** *n.*

o·ver·ac·tive /ṑvər áktiv/ *adj.* excessively or abnormally active

o·ver·age[1] /ṑvər áyj/ *adj.* **1.** **TOO OLD FOR SOMETHING** older than the age fixed as a standard or considered appropriate for a particular activity **2.** **NO LONGER USEFUL** too old to be useful (*offensive if used of people*)

o·ver·age[2] /ṓvərij/ *n.* money, goods, or something else in excess of what is proper or shown in the records [Mid-20thC. Formed from OVER.]

o·ver·all /ṑvər áwl/ *adj., adv.* **1.** **END TO END** from one extremity to the other **2.** **TOTAL** including everything ■ *adj.* **GENERAL** considered as a whole ○ *an overall impression* ■ *adv.* **ON THE WHOLE** in general or as a whole ○ *Overall, we were disappointed with the results.* ■ **o·ver·alls** *npl.* **1.** **ONE-PIECE PROTECTIVE GARMENT** a one-piece garment with long sleeves and pants worn to protect a worker's clothes from dirt or wear **2.** **WORK PANTS WITH BIB** loose-fitting pants that have a bib and shoulder straps, originally worn over regular clothing as a protection from dirt and wear

o·ver·arch /ṑvər aárch/ (**-arched, -arch·ing, -arch·es**) *vt.* to form an arch over something or somewhere

o·ver·arch·ing /ṑvər aárching/ *adj.* embracing or overshadowing everything —**o·ver·arch·ing·ly** *adv.*

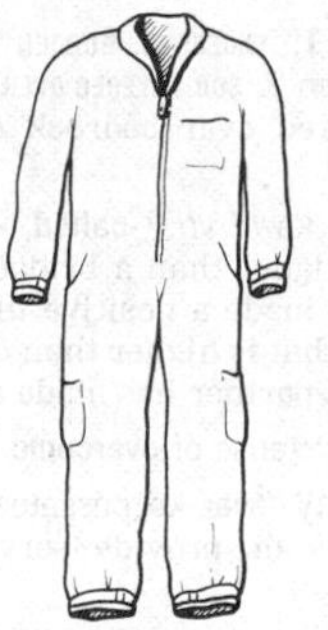
Overalls

o·ver·arm /ṓvər aárm/ *adj.* **1.** **WITH ARM ABOVE SHOULDER** thrown or done with the arm raised above the shoulder and rotating forward **2.** **WITH ARM RAISED** beginning a stroke in swimming with the arm raised above the shoulder and rotating forward ■ *adv. U.K.* SPORTS = **overhand**

o·ver·ate past tense of **overeat**

o·ver·awe /ṑvər áw/ (**-awed, -aw·ing, -awes**) *vt.* to make somebody feel subdued or inhibited by inspiring respect and some fear

o·ver·bal·ance /ṑvər bállənss/ *v.* (**-anced, -anc·ing, -anc·es**) **1.** *vti.* **LOSE BALANCE** to lose balance, or make somebody or something lose balance **2.** *vt.* **BE MORE IMPORTANT THAN** to have greater weight or importance than something else ■ *n.* **PREPONDERANCE** an excess of an amount, quantity, or weight

o·ver·bear /ṑvər báir/ (**o·ver·bore** /-báwr/, **o·ver·borne** /-báwrn/ *or* **over·born, o·ver·bear·ing, o·ver·bears**) *v.* **1.** *vt.* **OVERPOWER SOMEBODY** to defeat somebody by having superior weight or strength **2.** *vt.* **OUTWEIGH** to be more important than other considerations **3.** *vi.* **PRODUCE TOO MUCH** to produce too much fruit or too many offspring

o·ver·bear·ing /ṑvər báiring/ *adj.* arrogant and tending to order people around —**o·ver·bear·ing·ly** *adv.* —**o·ver·bear·ing·ness** *n.*

o·ver·bid /ṑvər bíd/ *v.* (**-bid, -bid·den** /ṑvər bídd'n/ *or* **-bid, -bid·ding, -bids**) **1.** *vti.* **BID MORE THAN WORTH OF SOMETHING** to bid more than something is worth **2.** *vi.* BRIDGE **BID FOR TOO MANY TRICKS** to bid for more tricks than can be won ■ *n.* **HIGHER BID** a bid that is higher than somebody else's bid —**over·bid·der** *n.*

o·ver·bite /ṓvər bīt/ *n.* a faulty alignment of the teeth in which the upper front teeth project too far over the lower teeth when the mouth is closed

o·ver·blouse /ṓvər blòwss, -blòwz/ *n.* a blouse designed to be worn outside the waistband of a skirt or slacks

o·ver·blow /ṑvər blṓ/ (**-blew** /-bloó/, **-blown** /-blṓn/, **-blow·ing, -blows**) *vti.* to blow a wind instrument with extra force so as to produce an overtone

o·ver·blown *adj.* **1.** **EXAGGERATED** done to excess and seeming exaggerated ○ *overblown stories that are barely credible* **2.** **PRETENTIOUS** showing pomposity or pretentiousness ○ *His style of writing is overblown and excessively wordy.* **3.** **PAST BEST** past full bloom and beginning to die ○ *an overblown rose*

o·ver·board /ṓvər bàwrd/ *adv.* over the side of a ship and into the water [Old English *ofer bord*, literally "over the side"]

o·ver·book /ṑvər boók/ (**-booked, -book·ing, -books**) *vti.* to take more reservations than there are seats or places available in a place

o·ver·bore past tense of **overbear**

o·ver·borne, o·ver·born past participle of **overbear**

o·ver·bought /ṑvər báwt/ *adj.* characterized by high prices on the stock exchange as the result of recent heavy trading, and so not likely to rise further in the near future

o·ver·build /ṑvər bíld/ (**-built** /-bílt/, **-built, -build·ing, -builds**) *v.* **1.** *vti.* **BUILD TOO MUCH** to construct more buildings than are necessary or desirable in an area **2.** *vti.* **BUILD OVERAMBITIOUSLY** to construct something that is too large or elaborate **3.** *vt.* **BUILD ON SOMETHING ELSE** to build something on top of a particular place or thing

o·ver·bur·den *vt.* /ṑvər búrd'n/ (**-dened, -den·ing, -dens**) **OVERLOAD** to place too much weight or worry on somebody or something ○ *overburdened with debt* ■ *n.*

/ṓvər bùrd'n/ **1.** EXCESSIVE BURDEN an excessive or onerous burden **2.** SOIL LAYERED OVER ROCK soil or other material layered over bedrock or over any geological deposit

o·ver·call /ṑvər káwl/ *vti.* (**-called, -call·ing, -calls**) BID HIGHER to bid higher than a bridge opponent before a partner has made a positive bid ■ *n.* HIGHER BID a bid in bridge that is higher than an opponent's bid, made before a partner has made a positive bid

o·ver·came past tense of **overcome**

o·ver·ca·pac·i·ty /ṑvər kə pássətee/ *n.* an ability to produce goods or provide services that exceed demand

o·ver·cap·i·tal·ize /ṑvər káppit'l ìz/ (**-ized, -iz·ing, -iz·es**) *vt.* **1.** SUPPLY TOO MUCH CAPITAL TO to provide a business with more capital than is justified by its condition or its ability to make profits **2.** OVERVALUE to give a corporation a nominal value that is higher than its fair market value

o·ver·cast *adj.* /ṓvər kaast/ **1.** METEOROL CLOUDY very cloudy, with no sun showing **2.** SEW SEWN WITH LONG STITCHES sewn along the edge with long loose stitches that prevent a piece of fabric from raveling ■ *n.* /ṓvər kaast/ **1.** METEOROL HEAVY CLOUD COVER a heavy covering of clouds in the sky **2.** MINING MINE ARCH an arch in a mine supporting a passage above it ■ *v.* /ṑvər kást/ (**-cast·ed, -cast·ing, -casts**) **1.** *vi.* METEOROL BECOME CLOUDY to become cloudy or dull **2.** *vt.* SEW SECURE WITH LOOSE STITCHES to sew the edge of a piece of fabric with an overcast stitch

o·ver·cast·ing /ṓvər kàsting/ *n.* long slanting stitches sewn loosely across the edge of a piece of fabric to prevent it from raveling

o·ver·cast stitch *n.* a stitch used to bind a raw edge or to form a smooth raised line, e.g., in working monograms

o·ver·charge *v.* /ṑvər chaarj/ (**-charged, -charg·ing, -charg·es**) **1.** *vti.* CHARGE TOO MUCH to charge somebody too much money for something **2.** *vt.* PUT EXCESSIVE POWER INTO to charge a battery or circuit with more electricity than it can safely hold **3.** *vt.* OVERFILL OR OVERLOAD SOMETHING to fill or load something with more than it can hold or bear **4.** *vt.* EXAGGERATE SOMETHING to make something seem greater or more important than it actually is (*literary*) ■ *n.* /ṓvər chaarj/ **1.** EXCESSIVE CHARGE an excessively high charge for something **2.** ACT OF CHARGING TOO MUCH an act of charging too much for something

o·ver·cloud /ṑvər klówd/ (**-cloud·ed, -cloud·ing, -clouds**) *vti.* **1.** CLOUD OVER to cover something, or become covered, with clouds **2.** MAKE OR BECOME DIM to become, or to make something become, dim and gloomy (*formal*)

o·ver·coat /ṓvər kòt/ *n.* **1.** THICK OUTER COAT a heavy coat worn over other outer clothes **2.** **o·ver·coat, o·ver·coat·ing** TOP LAYER OF PAINT an additional protective layer of something such as paint or varnish on top of a treated surface

o·ver·come /ṑvər kúm/ (**-came** /-káym/, **-come, -com·ing, -comes**) *v.* **1.** *vt.* MAKE SOMEBODY HELPLESS to make somebody incapacited or helpless, or to break down somebody's normal self-control (*usually passive*) ○ *completely overcome with emotion* **2.** *vt.* CONQUER PROBLEM to struggle successfully against a difficulty or disadvantage **3.** *vti.* DEFEAT SOMEBODY to defeat somebody or something, especially in a conflict or competition (*formal*) **4.** *vi.* WIN DESPITE OBSTACLES to win or be successful, especially in spite of obstacles [Old English; from OVER + COME]

WORD KEY: SYNONYMS

See Synonyms at ***defeat.***

o·ver·com·mit /ṑvər kə mít/ (**-mit·ted, -mit·ting, -mits**) *vti.* to undertake, or to make somebody or yourself undertake, more than can be accomplished (*often passive*)

o·ver·com·pen·sate /ṑvər kómpən sàyt/ (**-sat·ed, -sat·ing, -sates**) *vti.* **1.** TRY TOO HARD TO OVERCOME to try too hard to make up for a disadvantage or shortcoming and fall into a fault of another kind **2.** REWARD TOO MUCH to pay somebody too much in recompense or compensation for something done — **o·ver·com·pen·sa·tion** /ṑvər kómpən sáysh'n/ *n.* — **o·ver·com·pen·sa·to·ry** /ṑvər kəm pénsə tàwree/ *adj.*

o·ver·con·fi·dent /ṑvər kónfidənt/ *adj.* excessively confident or self-assured —**o·ver·con·fi·dent·ly** *adv.*

o·ver·cook /ṑvər kŏŏk/ (**-cooked, -cook·ing, -cooks**) *vt.* to cook something so long that it loses its flavor and texture

o·ver·cor·rect /ṑvər kə rékt/ *vti.* (**-rect·ed, -rect·ing, -rects**) CORRECT SOMETHING MORE THAN IS NECESSARY to do too much when trying to correct a mistake or fault, usually so that a further mistake is made ■ *adj.* TOO CORRECT excessively exact or proper

o·ver·cor·rec·tion /ṑvər kə rékshən/ *n.* **1.** LING = **hypercorrection** **2.** UNNECESSARY CORRECTING OF SOMETHING the fact of overcorrecting a mistake or fault

o·ver·crit·i·cal /ṑvər kríttik'l/ *adj.* judging or criticizing somebody or something too harshly or too fastidiously —**o·ver·crit·i·cal·ness** *n.*

o·ver·crop /ṑvər króp/ (**-cropped, -crop·ping, -crops**) *vt.* to make soil infertile by removing its nutrients through continuous cultivation

o·ver·crowd /ṑvər krówd/ (**-crowd·ed, -crowd·ing, -crowds**) *vt.* to put more people or things into an area than it is comfortably able to hold (*often passive*) — **o·ver·crowd·ed** *adj.* —**o·ver·crowd·ing** *n.*

o·ver·de·vel·op /ṑvər di vélləp/ (**-oped, -op·ing, -ops**) *vt.* **1.** DEVELOP SOMETHING EXCESSIVELY to develop something, e.g., muscles or previously open land, to excess **2.** DEVELOP FILM TOO MUCH to exceed the amount of time, temperature, or strength of solution required to develop a photographic film, thereby producing too much contrast —**o·ver·de·vel·op·ment** *n.*

o·ver·do /ṑvər dŏŏ/ (**-did** /-díd/, **-done, -do·ing, -does**) *vt.* **1.** OVERCOOK SOMETHING to cook food for too long **2.** SPOIL EFFECT BY EXAGGERATION to spoil the effect of something by exaggerating it ○ *You really overdid the sympathetic friend act on that occasion.* **3.** DO SOMETHING TO EXCESS to do something too much, often with a harmful effect [Old English] —**o·ver·do·er** *n.* ◇ **overdo it** **1.** to work too hard and tire yourself **2.** to do something to excess

o·ver·dog /ṓvər dòg/ *n.* somebody who is favored in a contest or powerful or in command (*humorous*) [Early 20thC. Formed from DOG, on the model of UNDERDOG.]

o·ver·done past participle of **overdo**

o·ver·dose *n.* /ṓvər dōss/ DANGEROUS AMOUNT OF DRUG dangerously large dose of a drug, especially a narcotic, causing hospitalization or death ■ *vti.* /ṑvər dṓss/ (**-dosed, -dos·ing, -dos·es**) TAKE OR GIVE OVERDOSE to take or give somebody an overdose

o·ver·draft /ṓvər dràft/ *n.* **1.** AMOUNT OWED TO BANK the amount that an account holder owes a bank because the balance in the account does not cover the amount that he or she has withdrawn from or debited to it **2.** BORROWING LIMIT a limit up to which an account holder may borrow from a bank when there are no funds in his or her checking account **3.** AIR CURRENT OVER FIRE a current of air passed over a fire, e.g., in a furnace or kiln

o·ver·dra·ma·tize /ṑvər drámmə tìz, -dráamə-/ (**-tized, -tiz·ing, -tiz·es**) *vti.* to behave, or to treat something, in an excessively dramatic way, e.g., by exaggerating the strength of your feelings or the gravity of a situation

o·ver·draught /ṓvər dràft/ *n.* = **overdraft**

o·ver·draw /ṑvər dráw/ (**-drew** /-drŏŏ/, **-drawn** /-dráwn/, **-draw·ing, -draws**) *v.* **1.** *vti.* FIN LACK ENOUGH FUNDS IN BANK ACCOUNT to withdraw or have debited more money from a bank account than it has credited to it, so that money is owed to the bank **2.** *vt.* EXAGGERATE SOMETHING to exaggerate in describing or telling about something **3.** *vti.* ARCHERY PULL BOW TOO TIGHT to pull a bow too tight

o·ver·drawn *adj.* **1.** HAVING WITHDRAWN MORE THAN ACCOUNT CONTAINS owing money to a bank because an account has had more money withdrawn or debited from it than credited to it **2.** EXAGGERATED showing exaggeration in the description of something

o·ver·dress /ṑvər dréss/ *vti.* (**-dressed, -dress·ing, -dress·es**) DRESS TOO ELABORATELY to dress, or to dress somebody, more formally or elaborately or in more clothes than the situation requires (*often passive*) ■ *n.* DRESS WORN OVER OUTER CLOTHING a dress that is intended to be worn over other outer clothing

overdrew *v.* past tense of **overdraw**

o·ver·drive *n.* /ṓvər drìv/ **1.** HIGHEST ENGINE GEAR the highest gear in the engine of a motor vehicle that is used at high speeds for fuel economy and to save engine wear **2.** EXTRA HARD LEVEL OF ACTIVITY a particularly intense and productive mode of activity, usually possible only for short periods (*informal*) ○ *Production has gone into overdrive.* ■ *vt.* /ṑvər drív/ (**-drove** /-drṓv/, **-driv·en** /-drívv'n/, **-driv·ing, -drives**) DRIVE TOO HARD to drive somebody, something, or yourself too hard

o·ver·dub /ṓvər dùb/ *vti.* (**-dubbed, -dub·bing, -dubs**) RECORD EXTRA SOUND OR MUSIC FOR to add supplementary sound or music to a recording ■ *n.* EXTRA LAYER OF RECORDED SOUND a supplementary layer of sound or music added onto a recording

o·ver·due /ṑvər dŏŏ/ *adj.* late or after the scheduled time, especially in arriving, occurring, or being paid ○ *The library said the books were overdue.*

o·ver·dye /ṑvər dí/ (**-dyed, -dy·ing, -dyes**) *vt.* **1.** DYE SOMETHING TOO MUCH to use too much dye on something **2.** DYE WITH ANOTHER COLOR to dye a fabric with another color over the original one

o·ver·eat /ṑvər éet/ (**-ate** /-áyt/, **-eat·en** /-éet'n/, **-eat·ing, -eats**) *vi.* to eat too much food, especially habitually —**o·ver·eat·er** *n.* —**o·ver·eat·ing** *n.*

o·ver·e·lab·o·rate /ṑvər i lábbə ràyt/ *adj.* TOO ELABORATE excessively elaborate, fussy, or detailed ■ *vti.* (**-rat·ed, -rat·ing, -rates**) MAKE SOMETHING TOO ELABORATE to add or give too much elaboration or detail to something

o·ver·em·pha·size /ṑvər émfə sìz/ (**-sized, -siz·ing, -siz·es**) *vt.* to give something too much importance, attention, or force

o·ver·es·ti·mate *vt.* /ṑvər éstə màyt/ (**-mat·ed, -mat·ing, -mates**) **1.** CALCULATE SOMETHING TOO HIGHLY to calculate the amount, value, or quantity of something at too high a level **2.** GIVE EXCESSIVE MERIT OR IMPORTANCE TO to judge somebody or something to be better, greater, or more important than he, she, or it actually is ■ *n.* /ṓvər éstəmət/ EXCESSIVELY HIGH ESTIMATE an estimate that is too high —**o·ver·es·ti·ma·tion** /ṑvər éstə máysh'n/ *n.*

o·ver·ex·pose /ṑvər ik spṓz/ (**-posed, -pos·ing, -pos·es**) *vt.* **1.** EXPOSE FILM TO TOO MUCH LIGHT to expose a photographic medium such as film to too much light or for too long a time, so that the colors or tones in the resulting photograph are too light **2.** ALLOW SOMEBODY TOO MUCH OF SOMETHING to allow somebody, or expose somebody to, too much of something, especially to allow somebody to appear in public or in the media too often

o·ver·ex·tend /ṑvər ik sténd/ (**-tend·ed, -tend·ing, -tends**) *v.* **1.** *vr.* RISK FINANCIAL RUIN to risk financial ruin by borrowing excessively, spending too much, or overcommitting resources **2.** *vt.* STRETCH LIMITS OF RESOURCES to force somebody, something, or yourself beyond a safe or reasonable limit **3.** *vt.* PROLONG SOMETHING BEYOND EXPECTED DURATION to prolong something beyond its normal or expected duration

o·ver·fa·mil·i·ar /ṑvər fə míllee ər/ *adj.* **1.** TOO FRIENDLY more friendly, informal, or intimate than is appropriate **2.** TOO WELL KNOWN used so much or so well known as to be boring or ineffective — **o·ver·fa·mil·iar·i·ty** /ṑvər fə míllee áirətee/ *n.*

o·ver·fill /ṑvər fíl/ (**-filled, -fill·ing, -fills**) *vti.* to become, or to make somebody or something become, too full

o·ver·fish /ṑvər físh/ (**-fished, -fish·ing, -fish·es**) *vti.* to take too many fish from a body of water and so deplete its population

overflew past tense of **overfly**

o·ver·flight /ṓvər flìt/ *n.* the flight of an aircraft or birds over an area

o·ver·flow *v.* /ṑvər flṓ/ (**-flowed, -flow·ing, -flows**) **1.** *vti.* FLOW OR POUR OVER to pour out over the limits or edge of a container because the container is too full of liquid **2.** *vt.* FLOOD SOMETHING to flood, cover, or flow over the surface of something **3.** *vt.* SPREAD BEYOND LIMITS OF SOMETHING to spread beyond the area intended to contain it ○ *The crowd overflowed the hall into the street outside.* **4.** *vi.* BE OVERWHELMED BY EMOTION to be so full of an emotion as to feel the need to express it ■ *n.* /ṓvər flṑ/ **1.** EXCESS LIQUID CONTENTS excess liquid that flows or pours over the edge of something **2.** EXCESS PEOPLE OR THINGS people or things that cannot be contained in the space originally set aside for them **3.** OUTLET THAT PREVENTS FLOODING an outlet that allows something, usually a liquid, to escape before it runs over the top of its container, e.g., water in a cistern **4.** AMOUNT IN EXCESS OF LIMIT the amount by which a limit is exceeded **5.** COMPUTER'S INABILITY TO HANDLE LARGE DATA the inability of a location in computer memory to handle data of an excessively large magnitude, or an instance of this ○ *an overflow error.* ◊ **underflow**

o·ver·fly /ṓvər flī́/ (**-flew** /-flo͞o/, **-flown** /-flṓn/, **-fly·ing**, **-flies**) *vti.* **1. FLY ABOVE AREA** to fly over an area **2. OVERSHOOT** to fly past a specific point ○ *The plane has overflown the runway.*

o·ver·fold /ṓvər fṑld/ *n.* a geological fold that has turned over on itself so that both sides dip in the same direction, causing the middle strata to be upside down

o·ver·gar·ment /ṓvər gaàrmənt/ *n.* an article of clothing such as an outer garment or protective wear worn on top of other clothes

o·ver·glaze *n.* /ṓvər glày̆z/ **1. EXTRA GLAZE ON POTTERY** an additional coat of glaze applied to pottery or porcelain **2. TOP LAYER OF DECORATION ON POTTERY** a decoration applied to pottery or porcelain on top of the glaze ■ *vt.* /ṑvər gláyz, ṓvər glày̆z/ (**-glazed, -glaz·ing, -glaz·es**) **APPLY GLAZE OR OVERGLAZE TO POTTERY** to apply a glaze or overglaze to pottery or porcelain ■ *adj.* **APPLIED ON TOP OF GLAZE** applied on top of a ceramic glaze ○ *overglaze colors*

o·ver·graze /ṑvər gráyz/ (**-grazed, -graz·ing, -graz·es**) *vt.* to graze land to the point that vegetation is harmed and as a consequence can no longer support stock (*often passive*)

o·ver·grow /ṑvər grṓ/ (**-grew** /-gro͞o/, **-grown** /-grṓn/, **-grow·ing, -grows**) *vti.* to grow so large, dense, or extensive as to cover the area of ground or container it is planted in and hinder the growth of other plants —**o·ver·growth** /ṓvər grṑth/ *n.*

o·ver·grown *adj.* **1. COVERED WITH VEGETATION GROWING WITHOUT CHECK** covered with plants or weeds that have been allowed to grow without check **2. GROWN TOO MUCH FOR ALLOTTED SPACE** grown too dense, large, or extensive for the area of ground or container in which it is planted **3. IMMATURE** grown to a large or adult size, but remaining immature ○ *behaving like an overgrown schoolboy*

o·ver·hand /ṓvər hànd/ *adj.* **1. MADE WITH HAND RAISED OVER SHOULDER** made with the hand coming forward in a semicircular motion from behind and above the shoulder **2. SEWN ON TOP OF SEAM** sewn with small vertical stitches passing over the two edges that are being joined together to make a seam ■ *adv.* **WITH HAND ABOVE SHOULDER** with the hand coming forward in a semicircular motion from behind and above the shoulder ■ *n.* **SOMETHING PERFORMED OVERHAND** a stroke, throw, or delivery of something made with an overhand motion

o·ver·hand knot *n.* a knot formed by passing one end of a cord or rope through a loop formed on another part of it, often used to prevent an end from fraying

o·ver·hang *v.* /ṑvər háng/ (**-hung** /-húng/, **-hung, -hang·ing, -hangs**) **1.** *vti.* **PROJECT OVER** to project or extend over something leaving a sheltered space beneath **2.** *vt.* **LOOM OVER SOMEBODY** to threaten or loom over somebody or something ■ *n.* /ṓvər hàng/ **1. PROJECTION** something, e.g., part of a rock face or the edge of a roof, that projects out over the space beneath **2. EXTENT OF PROJECTION** the degree or amount by which something projects or extends over something **3. HALF DIFFERENCE IN WINGSPAN** half the difference in the span of the two wings of a biplane **4. DISTANCE TO WING END ON MONOPLANE** the distance from the last outer strut to the end of a monoplane's wing

o·ver·haul *vt.* /ṑvər háwl, ṓvər hàwl/ (**-hauled, -haul·ing, -hauls**) **1. LOOK FOR MECHANICAL DEFECTS** to examine a piece of machinery thoroughly to identify defects **2. REPAIR MACHINE EXTENSIVELY** to carry out comprehensive repairs and adjustments to a piece of machinery **3. REVISE SOMETHING THOROUGHLY** to examine and revise something thoroughly **4. GRADUALLY OVERTAKE SOMEBODY** to catch up with and overtake somebody or something **5.** SAILING **SLACKEN OR RELEASE SOMETHING** to slacken or release something such as a rope or the blocks of a tackle ■ *n.* /ṓvər hàwl/ **COMPREHENSIVE REPAIR** a comprehensive examination and repair of something —**o·ver·haul·er** *n.*

o·ver·head *adv.* /ṑvər héd/ **DIRECTLY ABOVE** directly above somebody or something, especially up in the air ■ *adj.* /ṓvər hèd/ **1. POSITIONED DIRECTLY ABOVE** positioned directly above somebody or something **2. HIT WITH RACKET ABOVE HEAD** played hard and downward, with the racket held high above the head **3. RELATING TO ONGOING COSTS** relating to the general recurring costs of running a business, e.g., rent, maintenance, and utilities ■ *n.* /ṓvər hèd/ **1. ONGOING BUSINESS COSTS** the general recurring costs of running a business, excluding the costs of labor and materials, e.g., rent, maintenance, and utilities **2. SHOT IN RACKET GAMES** a shot played hard and downward, with the racket held above head height **3.** = **overhead projection 4.** = **overhead projector 5. SOMETHING LOCATED ABOVE** something such as a light that is mounted or located in an overhead position **6. EXTRA SPACE IN COMPUTER** excess capacity for support, checking, or memory to run programs in a computer operating system

o·ver·head cam·shaft, **o·ver·head cam** *n.* a camshaft in an internal-combustion engine that is mounted above the cylinder heads and controls the operation, opening, and closing of the cylinder's valves

o·ver·head com·part·ment *n.* a luggage compartment above the passenger seats for holding carry-on luggage in an airplane

o·ver·head pro·jec·tion *n.* **1. TRANSPARENCY FOR OVERHEAD PROJECTOR** a transparent sheet placed on an overhead projector so that its enlarged image can be projected on a screen or other surface **2. USE OR RESULT OF OVERHEAD PROJECTOR** the use or the image produced by the use of an overhead projector

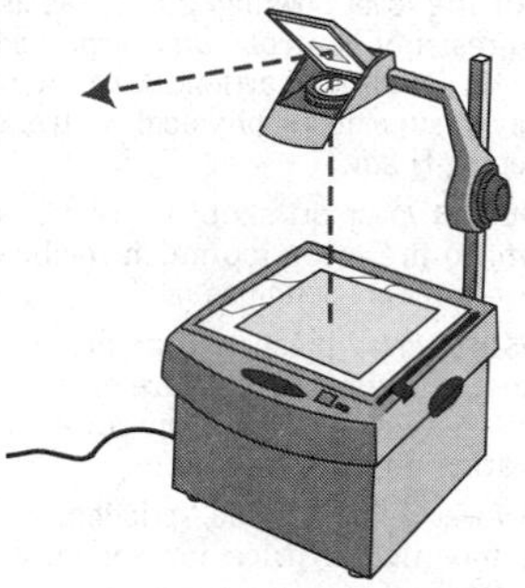

Overhead projector

o·ver·head pro·jec·tor *n.* a projector with a flat, transparent top on which a sheetlike transparency is placed, the enlarged image being projected on a screen or other surface

o·ver·head-valve en·gine *n. U.K.* = **valve-in-head engine**

o·ver·hear /ṑvər hée ər/ (**-heard** /-húrd/, **-heard, -hear·ing, -hears**) *vti.* to hear what somebody is saying only to others [Old English]

o·ver·heat /ṑvər héet/ (**-heat·ed, -heat·ing, -heats**) *vti.* **1. BECOME OR MAKE TOO HOT** to become, or to make somebody or something become, too hot **2.** ECON **GROW TOO QUICKLY** to experience too rapid growth in demand with a resultant increase in inflation, or to cause too rapid growth in an economy **3. MAKE OR BECOME TOO EXCITED** to become, or to make somebody become, too excited, agitated, or angry (*usually passive*)

o·ver·hit /ṑvər hít/ (**-hit, -hit·ting, -hits**) *vti.* to hit a ball too hard or put too much force into a stroke

o·ver·hung past tense, past participle of **overhang**

o·ver·hype /ṑvər hī́p/ (**-hyped, -hyp·ing, -hypes**) *vt.* to praise and publicize somebody or something excessively or misleadingly (*informal*)

o·ver·in·dulge /ṑvər in dúlj/ (**-dulged, -dulg·ing, -dulg·es**) *v.* **1.** *vti.* **PERMIT TOO MUCH** to give in to a desire for something too lavishly or too often, especially to eat or drink too much **2.** *vt.* **BE TOO INDULGENT WITH SOMEBODY** to allow somebody to do or have what he or she wants too much —**o·ver·in·dul·gence** *n.* —**o·ver·in·dul·gent** *adj.* —**o·ver·in·dul·gent·ly** *adv.*

o·ver·joyed /ṑvər jóyd/ *adj.* extremely delighted

o·ver·kill *n.* /ṓvər kìl/ **1. EXCESS** action that far exceeds what is needed in order to achieve a result **2. GREATER DESTRUCTIVE CAPACITY THAN NEEDED** the capacity of weaponry, especially nuclear weapons, to cause greater damage or destruction than is necessary to accomplish a mission ■ *vti.* /ṑvər kíl/ (**-killed, -kill·ing, -kills**) **DESTROY WITH EXCESS OF WEAPONS** to use excessive force, especially far more nuclear weapons than necessary, to destroy an enemy or place

o·ver·lad·en /ṑvər láyd'n/ *adj.* carrying too heavy a physical or emotional load

o·ver·land /ṓvər lànd/ *adv.* **BY LAND** by or across land ■ *adj.* **TAKING PLACE ON LAND** made by land, as a journey, or used for moving across land —**o·ver·land·er** /ṓvər làndər/ *n.*

O·ver·land Park /ṓvər lànd-/ city in northeastern Kansas. It is a southern suburb of Kansas City. Population: 131,053 (1996).

o·ver·lap *v.* /ṑvər láp/ (**-lapped, -lap·ping, -laps**) **1.** *vti.* **PLACE OR BE OVER** to position things in such a way that the edge of one thing is on top of and extending past the edge of another, or to be positioned in this way ○ *The roofers overlapped the shingles.* **2.** *vt.* **EXTEND BEYOND SOMETHING** to cover something such as a boundary or edge, and extend beyond it ○ *The tablecloth overlapped the table by several inches.* **3.** *vti.* **COINCIDE** to coincide or correspond in part with something in time, function, or purpose, or to make something coincide or correspond with something else ○ *Her area of responsibility to some extent overlaps mine.* ■ *n.* /ṓvər làp/ **1. PARTIAL OVERLAY** an edge that partly covers or is covered by something else **2. EXTENT OF OVERLAP** the amount by which something overlaps something else ○ *It needs an overlap of six inches.* **3. PARTIAL COINCIDENCE OR CORRESPONDENCE** a partial coincidence or correspondence of two things in time, function, or purpose **4.** GEOL **YOUNGER SEDIMENTARY ROCK OVER OLDER LAYER** a younger layer of sedimentary rock that extends over an older layer and conceals it completely [Early 18thC. Formed from LAP.]

o·ver·lay[1] *vt.* /ṑvər láy/ (**-laid** /-láyd/, **-laid, -lay·ing, -lays**) **1. PLACE SOMETHING AS COVERING** to place a covering or covering layer of something on top of something else **2. COVER SOMETHING** to cover the surface of something with something else **3. APPLY DECORATION TO SURFACE** to apply a decorative material to a surface (*often passive*) **4.** PRINTING **EQUALIZE PRESSURE OVER** to affix a piece of paper to the surface of a press to help make a uniform impression on a form or plate ■ *n.* /ṓvər lày/ **1. COVERING** a covering or covering layer laid on top of something else **2. EXTRA DECORATIVE LAYER** an layer of decorative material applied to a surface **3. ADDITIONAL TRANSPARENCY LAID ON TOP** a transparent sheet containing additional details, e.g., a chart or map, that is placed on top of another transparency in an overhead projector during a presentation or lecture **4.** PRINTING **PAPER TO EQUALIZE PRINTING PRESSURE** a piece of paper used to equalize the pressure on a form or printing plate before printing

o·ver·lay[2] past tense of **overlie**

o·ver·leaf /ṓvər lèef/ *adv.* on the other side of the page

o·ver·lie /ṑvər lī́/ (**-lay** /-láy/, **-lain** /-láyn/, **-ly·ing, -lies**) *vt.* **1. LIE ON TOP OF** to lie on top of somebody or something **2. SMOTHER OFFSPRING** to kill a newborn baby or animal by accidentally lying on and smothering it

o·ver·load *vt.* /ṑvər lṓd/ (**-load·ed, -load·ing, -loads**) **1. PUT EXCESSIVE LOAD ON SOMETHING** to put too large or heavy a load on somebody or something or in something **2.** ELEC **FUSE ELECTRICAL SYSTEM** to use more current than an electrical system can handle, e.g., by using too many electrical appliances simultaneously **3. OVERBURDEN SOMEBODY** to give somebody too much work, stress, or other difficulty ■ *n.* /ṓvər lṑd/ **1.** ELEC **EXCESSIVE ELECTRICAL LOAD** a greater amount of electrical current than an electrical system can handle **2. EXCESSIVE PHYSICAL WEIGHT** something that is physically too heavy or too much to carry **3. EXCESSIVE MENTAL OR EMOTIONAL BURDEN** something that is mentally or emotionally too difficult to cope with **4. MENTAL OR EMOTIONAL EXHAUSTION OR CONFUSION** the condition of having an excessive mental or emotional burden (*informal*) ○ *I'm in overload right now.*

o·ver·lock /ṓvər lòk/ *n.* a sewing technique using an invisible hem stitch made by a sewing machine or a special device

o·ver·long /ṑvər láwng/ *adj.* **TOO LONG** too long in extent or duration ■ *adv.* **FOR TOO LONG** for too long a time

o·ver·look *vt.* /ṑvər lo͝ok/ (**-looked, -look·ing, -looks**) **1. MISS SOMETHING** to miss or fail to notice something **2. IGNORE** to choose to disregard or ignore a shortcoming or fault **3. LOOK DOWN AT SOMETHING** to look at something from above **4. PROVIDE VIEW OF SOMETHING** to provide a view of something, especially from above **5. BE ABOVE SOMETHING** to be located high above something **6. EXAMINE SOMETHING** to look at something with care **7. SUPERVISE SOMEBODY** to observe somebody while he or she works ■ *n.* /ṓvər lo͝ok/ **VIEWING SPOT** a place that gives a view down over something ○ *We hiked up to the overlook for a great view of the wilderness area.*

WORD KEY: SYNONYMS
See Synonyms at ***neglect***.

o·ver·lord /ṓvər làwrd/ *n.* **1. PRINCIPAL RULER** a ruler with overall power, usually over several subservient rulers, and especially somebody who ruled over other lords in a feudal system **2. SOMEBODY POWERFUL** somebody of great power or influence —**o·ver·lord·ship** *n.*

o·ver·ly /ṓvərlee/ *adv.* to an extreme or excessive degree [Old English]

o·ver·man *vt.* /ṑvər mán/ (**-manned, -man·ning, -mans**) = **overstaff** ■ *n.* /ṓvər màn/ (*plural* **-men** /ṓvər mèn/) **1. SUPERVISOR** a man who supervises other workers (*archaic*) **2. SUPERMAN IN NIETZSCHEAN THOUGHT** in the thought of Friedrich Nietzsche, a man whose superior powers of creativity and insight enable him to live beyond standards of good and evil —**o·ver·man·ning** *n.*

o·ver·man·tel /ṓvər mànt'l/ *n.* an ornamental shelf above a mantelpiece

o·ver·mas·ter /ṑvər mástər/ (**-tered, -ter·ing, -ters**) *vt.* to conquer somebody's resistance or break down somebody's self-control and take control of him or her (*literary*) ○ *an overmastering urge to tell her precisely what I thought of her*

o·ver·match *vt.* /ṑvər mách, ṓvər màch/ (**-matched, -match·ing, -match·es**) **1. PROVIDE WITH SUPERIOR OPPONENT** to provide somebody with an opponent who is likely to defeat him or her easily **2. DEFEAT** to be superior enough to defeat or surpass somebody or something ■ *n.* /ṓvər màch/ **UNEQUAL CONTEST** a contest in which one competitor is far superior to another

o·ver·mat·ter *n.* copy typeset in excess of the space available for it

o·ver·med·i·cate /ṑvər méddi kàyt/ (**-cat·ed, -cat·ing, -cates**) *vt.* to give somebody or yourself too much medication —**o·ver·med·i·ca·tion** /ṑvər meddi káysh'n/ *n.*

o·ver·much /ṑvər múch/ *adv.* **TO EXCESS** to an excessive degree ■ *adj.* **EXCESSIVE** too much ■ *n.* **EXCESSIVE QUANTITY** an excessive quantity or amount

o·ver·night /ṑvər nī́t, ṓvər nī̀t/ *adv.* **1. THROUGHOUT THE NIGHT** for the duration of the entire night **2. DURING NIGHT** at some point in the course of the night **3. VERY QUICKLY** within a very short time ○ *It became a bestseller overnight.* ■ *adj.* **1. LASTING ONE NIGHT** lasting throughout a night **2. SPENDING NIGHT** resident for the night **3. OCCURRING AT NIGHT** taking place during the night **4. USED WHEN SPENDING A NIGHT** used when staying overnight somewhere **5. EXTREMELY SUDDEN** happening in a very short time ○ *an overnight success* **6. INTENDED FOR NEXT-DAY DELIVERY** guaranteed to get to the intended destination by the next day ■ *v.* (**-night·ed, -night·ing, -nights**) **1.** *vi.* **SPEND NIGHT** to stay somewhere for the night **2.** *vt.* **MAIL SOMETHING FOR NEXT-DAY DELIVERY** to send something by express mail for next-day delivery ■ *n.* **OVERNIGHT TRIP** an overnight stay or trip

o·ver·night bag, o·ver·night case *n.* a small piece of baggage used to carry necessities for a trip lasting one night

o·ver·night·er /ṑvər nī́tər/ *n.* **1. OVERNIGHT TRIP** an trip lasting one night (*informal*) **2. SOMEBODY ON AN OVERNIGHT STAY** somebody who takes an overnight trip or stays somewhere overnight

o·ver·op·ti·mis·tic /ṑvər opti místik/ *adj.* unrealistically hopeful about the future —**o·ver·op·ti·mism** /-ópti mìzzəm/ *n.* —**o·ver·op·ti·mis·ti·cal·ly** /-opti místikəlee/ *adv.*

o·ver·pass *n.* /ṓvər pàss/ *U.S., Can, ANZ* a road, bridge, or passage that crosses over another route

o·ver·pay /ṑvər páy/ (**-paid** /-páyd/, **-paid, -pay·ing, -pays**) *vti.* **1. PAY MORE THAN JOB WARRANTS** to pay somebody at a rate that is too high for the job **2. PAY TOO MUCH BY MISTAKE** to pay somebody too much for something as a result of an error

o·ver·per·suade /ṑvər pər swáyd/ (**-suad·ed, -suad·ing, -suades**) *vt.* to persuade somebody to act contrary to his or her inclination or judgment

o·ver·play /ṑvər pláy/ (**-played, -play·ing, -plays**) *v.* **1.** *vt.* **OVERSTATE SOMETHING** to exaggerate the importance or strength of something **2.** *vti.* **OVERDO** to play a part or role in an exaggeratedly dramatic or theatrical way **3.** *vt.* SPORTS **HIT SOMETHING TOO HARD OR FAR** to hit or kick a ball too hard or too far ◇ **overplay your hand** to make overconfident or heavy-handed use of an advantage or strong position and fail as a result

o·ver·plus /ṓvər plùss/ *n.* a larger amount than is needed or appropriate [14thC. Translation of French *surplus*.]

o·ver·pop·u·late /ṑvər póppyə làyt/ (**-lat·ed, -lat·ing, -lates**) *v.* **1.** *vt.* **INCREASE POPULATION OF PLACE TOO MUCH** to increase the population of a place so much that the amount of space, food, water, or other resources available to support it is insufficient (*often passive*) **2.** *vi.* **REPRODUCE TO EXCESS** to increase to unsustainable or undesirable numbers by excessive reproduction —**o·ver·pop·u·la·tion** /ṑvər poppyə láysh'n/ *n.*

o·ver·pow·er /ṑvər pówr/ (**-ered, -er·ing, -ers**) *vt.* **1. SUBDUE SOMEBODY PHYSICALLY** to use superior strength or force to defeat somebody, especially to make somebody physically helpless and unable to fight **2. OVERWHELM SOMEBODY MENTALLY** to have so strong an effect on somebody that he or she is unable to resist or control it **3. GIVE SOMETHING EXCESSIVE POWER** to supply something, especially a car, with more power than necessary

o·ver·pow·er·ing /ṑvər pówring/ *adj.* **1. IRRESISTIBLE** impossible to resist or control ○ *an overpowering urge to laugh* **2. PHYSICALLY OVERWHELMING** with overwhelmingly superior physical strength —**o·ver·pow·er·ing·ly** *adv.*

o·ver·pre·scribe /ṑvər pri skrī́b/ (**-scribed, -scrib·ing, -scribes**) *vti.* to prescribe too much medication for somebody —**o·ver·pre·scrip·tion** *n.*

o·ver·pres·sure /ṓvər prèshər, ṑvər préshər/ *n.* the amount that atmospheric pressure exceeds normal levels, e.g., in a shock wave from an explosion or an accelerating aircraft

o·ver·price /ṑvər prī́ss/ (**-priced, -pric·ing, -pric·es**) *vt.* to charge too high a price for something (*often passive*)

o·ver·print *vti.* /ṑvər prínt, ṓvər prìnt/ (**-print·ed, -print·ing, -prints**) **ADD PRINTING TO SOMETHING** to print something additional on an already printed surface, especially in order to add text, numbers, or another color ■ *n.* /ṓvər prínt/ **1. ADDITIONAL PRINTING** an additional printing on a surface, especially text, numbers, or another color **2. OVERPRINTED POSTAGE STAMP** a postage stamp with additional information printed on its surface

o·ver·priv·i·leged /ṑvər prívvəlijd, -prívvlijd/ *adj.* having too many advantages in life

o·ver·prize /ṑvər prī́z/ (**-prized, -priz·ing, -priz·es**) *vt.* to regard something as more valuable and important than it really is

o·ver·proof /ṑvər próof/ *adj.* higher in alcohol content than in proof spirit

o·ver·pro·por·tion /ṑvər prə páwrsh'n/ (**-tioned, -tion·ing, -tions**) *vt.* to make something larger than is usual or needed and out of proportion to other things —**o·ver·pro·por·tion·ate·ly** *adv.*

o·ver·pro·tect /ṑvər prə tékt/ (**-tect·ed, -tect·ing, -tects**) *vt.* to protect somebody or something more than is necessary or wise, especially to shield a child too much from the realities of life —**o·ver·pro·tec·tion** *n.* —**o·ver·pro·tec·tive** *adj.*

o·ver·qual·i·fied /ṑvər kwóllə fīd/ *adj.* with more academic or vocational qualifications or experience than is necessary or desirable for a job

o·ver·rate /ṑvər ráyt/ (**-rat·ed, -rat·ing, -rates**) *vt.* to regard somebody as better or more capable, or something as greater, than is in fact the case —**o·ver·rat·ed** *adj.*

o·ver·reach /ṑvər réech/ (**-reached, -reach·ing, -reach·es**) *v.* **1.** *vr.* **FAIL THROUGH OVERAMBITION** to fail through trying to do things that are beyond your abilities **2.** *vti.* **EXTEND TOO FAR OR BEYOND SOMETHING** to reach or extend too far or beyond something **3.** *vti.* **DEFEAT BY TRICKERY** to get the better of somebody by trickery or deception **4.** *vt.* **OVERTAKE SOMEBODY** to catch up with and pass somebody or something **5.** *vi.* **HURT ONE FOOT WITH ANOTHER** to strike and injure the forefoot with the hindfoot while walking or running (*refers to a horse*) **6.** *vi.* **SAIL ON TACK LONGER THAN NECESSARY** to sail on a tack longer than is wanted or needed

o·ver·re·act /ṑvər ree ákt/ (**-act·ed, -act·ing, -acts**) *vi.* to react to something with disproportionate action or excessive emotion —**o·ver·re·ac·tion** *n.* —**o·ver·re·ac·tive** *adj.*

o·ver·re·fine /ṑvər ri fī́n/ (**-fined, -fin·ing, -fines**) *vti.* to make something more refined, subtle, or fastidious than is desirable or appropriate, especially to make too many subtle points or distinctions in presenting an argument —**o·ver·re·fine·ment** *n.*

o·ver·reg·u·late /ṑvər réggyə làyt/ (**-lat·ed, -lat·ing, -lates**) *vt.* to impose too many regulations on somebody or something, especially a government on an industry

o·ver·rep·re·sent·ed /ṑvər répprə zéntəd/ *adj.* having too many representatives or represented by too many examples in proportion to the total ○ *His earlier work is rather overrepresented in this collection.* —**o·ver·rep·re·sen·ta·tion** /ṑvər repprə zen táysh'n, -repprəzən táysh'n/ *n.*

o·ver·ride *vt.* /ṑvər rī́d/ (**-rode** /-rṓd/, **-rid·den** /-rídd'n/, **-rid·ing, -rides**) **1. CANCEL SOMETHING** to cancel or change an action or decision taken by somebody else **2. OUTWEIGH SOMETHING** to be more important than and take priority over something else **3. TAKE MANUAL CONTROL OF** to take manual control of an automatic control system **4. RIDE HORSE OVER** to ride a horse over or across an area **5. RIDE HORSE TOO HARD** to tire a horse by riding it too hard **6. OVERLAP SOMETHING** to extend over something, especially by overlapping it ■ *n.* /ṓvər rīd/ **1. ASSUMPTION OF MANUAL CONTROL** the condition, process, or action of temporarily taking manual control of an automatic system **2. SWITCH FOR MANUAL CONTROL** a switch or some other manual control that temporarily cancels or reverses the effect of an automatic system **3.** FIN **COMMISSION PAID TO EXECUTIVE** a commission that is paid to an account executive on sales made by a representative [Old English from OVER + RIDE]

o·ver·rid·ing /ṑvər rī́ding/ *adj.* highest in priority —**o·ver·rid·ing·ly** *adv.*

o·ver·ripe /ṓvər rīp/ *adj.* too ripe, and past its best flavor and texture —**o·ver·ripe·ness** *n.*

o·ver·rode past tense of **override**

o·ver·ruff /ṓvər rùf, ṑvər rúf/ (**-ruffed, -ruff·ing, -ruffs**) *vti.* = **overtrump**

o·ver·rule /ṑvər róol/ (**-ruled, -rul·ing, -rules**) *vt.* **1. RULE AGAINST SOMEBODY'S ARGUMENT** to rule authoritatively that somebody's argument is unsound, especially in the case of a judge disallowing an attorney's objection ○ *Objection overruled!* **2. DECIDE AGAINST SOMEBODY** to decide against somebody or to overturn a decision made by somebody with lesser authority **3. EXERCISE CONTROL OVER SOMEBODY** to exercise dominion or control over somebody or something (*literary*)

o·ver·run /ṑvər rún/ *v.* (**-ran** /ṑvər rán/, **-run, -run·ning, -runs**) **1.** *vt.* **SPREAD RAPIDLY AND INFEST SOMETHING** to arrive in such large numbers or spread so rapidly in a place that it becomes infested or overcrowded (*often passive*) ○ *The cathedral square was overrun with tourists.* **2.** *vt.* **CONQUER ENEMY AND TERRITORY** to attack an enemy force, defeat it conclusively, and take over the territory occupied by it ○ *The rebels overran the government forces.* **3.** *vti.* **EXCEED LIMIT** to continue beyond a predetermined limit, especially a time limit or fixed budget **4.** *vt.* **OVERSHOOT SOMETHING** to go on beyond an intended stopping point such as a boundary line or the end of an airport runway **5.** *vti.* **OVERFLOW** to overflow or spill over something **6.** *vt.* PRINTING **PRINT MORE THAN PLANNED** to print extra copies of a publication **7.** *vt.* PRINTING **MOVE TYPESET MATERIAL** to transfer set type or illustrated material from one column, page, or line to another ■ *n.* **1. ACT OF OVERRUNNING** an instance of somebody or something overrunning, especially of going on beyond the intended stopping point **2. AMOUNT EXCEEDING ESTIMATE** the amount by which something exceeds a preset limit, an estimated cost, or a budget **3. EXTRA QUANTITY PRODUCED** an extra quantity of something produced, e.g., manufactured items or copies of printed matter **4. EXTRA AREA AT END OF RUNWAY** a cleared level area at the end of a runway, available in case a plane overshoots

o·ver·run brake *n.* a brake on a vehicle being towed, to prevent it from running into the back of the vehicle towing it

o·ver·saw past tense of **oversee**

over·scale /ṓvər skàyl/, **over·scaled** /-skàyld/ *adj.* larger than usual in size or scope ○ *an overscale portrait*

o·ver·score /ṑvər skáwr/ (**-scored, -scor·ing, -scores**) *vt.*

to draw a line over or through written text, usually so as to cancel or revise it (*formal*)

o·ver·seas /ṑvər seéz/ *adv.* **ACROSS THE SEA** across or beyond a sea, especially in another country ○ *They live overseas.* ■ *adj.* **1. RELATING TO PLACE ACROSS SEA** relating to, located in, or coming from, a place beyond a sea ○ *overseas visitors* **2. TRAVELING ACROSS SEA** involving travel across a sea ○ *an overseas assignment* ■ *n.* **SOMEWHERE BEYOND SEA** a place or places beyond a sea (*takes a singular verb*) ○ *come from overseas*

o·ver·seas cap *n.* a soft wedge-shaped military cap without a visor or brim

o·ver·see /ṑvər seé/ (**-saw** /-sáw/, **-seen** /-seén/, **-see·ing, -sees**) *vt.* **1. SUPERVISE SOMETHING** to watch over, manage, and direct somebody or a task done by somebody **2. OBSERVE SOMETHING** to observe something covertly or secretly while it is happening [Old English; from OVER + SEE]

o·ver·se·er /ṑvər seé ər/ *n.* somebody who supervises workers, especially those engaged in manual labor

o·ver·sell /ṑvər sél/ (**-sold, -sold** /ṑvər sṓld/, **-sell·ing, -sells**) *v.* **1.** *vt.* **PRAISE SOMETHING TOO HIGHLY** to exaggerate the value or worth of somebody, something, or yourself to an implausible extent **2.** *vti.* **SELL TOO AGGRESSIVELY** to use excessively aggressive sales techniques when selling a product **3.** *vti.* **SELL TOO MUCH OF** to sell too much of a product, especially more than can be produced or supplied

o·ver·set /ṑvər sét/ (**-set, -set·ting, -sets**) *v.* **1.** *vti.* PRINTING **TYPESET TOO MUCH COPY** to set too much type or copy for the available space **2.** *vt.* **TIP SOMETHING OVER** to tip or turn something over (*archaic*) **3.** *vt.* **DISTURB SOMEBODY** to disturb or upset somebody (*archaic*)

o·ver·sew /ṑvər sṓ/ (**-sewed, -sewn** /-sṓn/, **-sew·ing, -sews**) *vt.* to sew two edges together, with small stitches overlapping both edges

o·ver·sexed /ṑvər sékst/ *adj.* having an excessive preoccupation with or need for sex

o·ver·shad·ow /ṑvər sháddō/ (**-owed, -ow·ing, -ows**) *vt.* **1. TAKE ATTENTION AWAY FROM SOMEBODY** to take attention away from somebody or something by appearing more important or interesting **2. CAST SHADOW OVER SOMETHING** to cast a physical shadow over something, or make something become gloomy [Old English]

o·ver·shirt /ṑvər shùrt/ *n.* a loose shirt that is worn on top of another garment such as a sweater or another shirt

o·ver·shoe /ṑvər shoō/ *n.* a shoe, usually made of rubber or plastic, that is worn over an ordinary shoe to protect it from dampness or dirt

o·ver·shoot /ṑvər shoōt/ *v.* (**-shot, -shot** /-shót/, **-shoot·ing, -shoots**) **1.** *vti.* **SEND OR GO FARTHER THAN INTENDED** to shoot a projectile beyond the target that was being aimed at or be shot in this way **2.** *vti.* **MISS TARGET** to miss a target by missing or being shot too far **3.** *vti.* AIR **RUN OFF END OF RUNWAY** to fail to complete a take-off or landing before reaching the end of the runway and run off the end of it **4.** *vti.* **EXCEED LIMIT** to exceed a fixed or prearranged limit **5.** *vt.* **MOVE QUICKLY OVER SOMETHING** to move at a high speed over something ■ *n.* **1. ACT OF OVERSHOOTING** an instance of somebody or something overshooting an intended stopping point, especially the end of an airport runway **2. AMOUNT BY WHICH SOMETHING EXCEEDS** an instance of something exceeding a prearranged limit or the amount or extent by which it exceeds it

o·ver·shot *adj.* **1. WITH UPPER PART EXTENDING PAST LOWER** used to describe a jaw with an upper part that is longer than and sticks out over the lower part **2. DRIVEN BY WATER ON UPPER SURFACE** used to describe a waterwheel driven by water flowing onto it from above

o·ver·sight /ṑvər sìt/ *n.* **1. FAILURE BY OMISSION** a mistake, especially as a result of a failure to do or notice something **2. SUPERVISION** the responsibility of supervising something (*formal*)

o·ver·sim·pli·fy /ṑvər símplə fì/ (**-fied, -fy·ing, -fies**) *vt.* to reduce something to such a level of simplicity that it becomes distorted or falsified —**o·ver·sim·pli·fi·ca·tion** /ṑvər simpləfi káysh'n/ *n.*

o·ver·size /ṑvər sìz/ *adj.* **o·ver·size, o·ver·sized** /ṑvər sìzd/ **UNUSUALLY LARGE** larger than is usual or necessary ■ *n.* **1. UNUSUALLY LARGE SIZE** a size that is larger than usual **2. EXTRA-LARGE ARTICLE** an article that comes in a larger size than usual

o·ver·skirt /ṑvər skùrt/ *n.* a skirt that is worn on top of another garment, often revealing part of the lower one

o·ver·sleep /ṑvər sleép/ (**-slept** /-slépt/, **-slept, -sleep·ing, -sleeps**) *v.* **1.** *vi.* **SLEEP LONGER THAN WISHED** to continue sleeping for longer than desired or intended **2.** *vt.* **SLEEP TOO LATE FOR SOMETHING** to sleep beyond the time for something

o·ver·sold past participle, past tense of **oversell** ■ *adj.* STOCK EXCH **UNREASONABLY LOW IN PRICE** available at or characterized by prices that are excessively low as a result of previous heavy selling on the stock market. ◊ **overbought**

o·ver·spend (**-spent, -spent** /-spént/, **-spend·ing, -spends**) *v.* **1.** *vti.* **SPEND TOO MUCH** to spend more money than can be afforded or has been budgeted **2.** *vt.* **EXHAUST SOMETHING** to tire somebody or something out completely

o·ver·spill *n.* /ṑvər spìl/ **SOMETHING SPILLED** something that spills or has spilled over from something ■ *vti.* /ṑvər spíl/ (**-spilled** *or* **-spilt, -spilled** *or* **-spilt** /-spílt/, **-spill·ing, -spills**) **SPILL OVER** to spill over, or to make something spill over

o·ver·spread /ṑvər spréd/ (**-spread, -spread·ing, -spreads**) *vt.* to spread widely over or cover the surface of something ○ *Night overspread the land.* [Old English]

o·ver·staff /ṑvər stáf/ (**-staffed, -staff·ing, -staffs**) *vt.* to supply a workplace with too large a staff (*usually passive*)

o·ver·state /ṑvər stáyt/ (**-stat·ed, -stat·ing, -states**) *vt.* to exaggerate something in talking or writing about it —**o·ver·state·ment** *n.*

o·ver·stay /ṑvər stáy/ (**-stayed, -stay·ing, -stays**) *vti.* to remain beyond the expected, planned, or desired time

o·ver·steer /ṑvər steér/ *vi.* (**-steered, -steer·ing, -steers**) **MAKE SHARPER TURN THAN EXPECTED** to turn more sharply than expected, especially in a motor vehicle ○ *We oversteered and landed in a ditch.* ■ *n.* **TENDENCY TO TURN TOO SHARPLY** the tendency of a motor vehicle to turn more sharply than expected

o·ver·step /ṑvər stép/ (**-stepped, -step·ping, -steps**) *vt.* to go beyond the limit of something ○ *overstep the bounds of your authority* [Old English]

o·ver·stock /ṑvər stók/ *v.* (**-stocked, -stock·ing, -stocks**) **1.** *vti.* **STOCK IN EXCESS** to stock more of something than is necessary or desirable **2.** *vt.* **KEEP TOO MANY ANIMALS ON** to graze an area with more livestock than it can support ■ *n.* **EXCESS SUPPLY** an excessively large supply of something

o·ver·sto·ry /ṑvər stàwree/ (*plural* **-ries**) *n.* the top layer of foliage in a forest, forming the canopy

o·ver·strain /ṑvər stráyn/ (**-strained, -strain·ing, -strains**) *vti.* to try to force somebody, something, or yourself to perform beyond capacity, especially so that damage, injury, or breakdown results

o·ver·stress /ṑvər stréss/ *vt.* (**-stressed, -stress·ing, -stress·es**) **1. DEFORM AS RESULT OF EXCESSIVE FORCE** to deform material permanently by exerting too much force on it **2. PUT SOMEBODY UNDER TOO MUCH STRESS** to subject somebody to too much mental or emotional pressure **3. PUT EXCESSIVE EMPHASIS ON SOMETHING** to put too much emphasis on something ■ *n.* **EXCESSIVE EMPHASIZING OF SOMETHING** the putting of too much emphasis on something

o·ver·stretch /ṑvər stréch/ (**-stretched, -stretch·ing, -stretch·es**) *v.* **1.** *vti.* **STRETCH SOMETHING TOO FAR** to stretch something such as a muscle too much, so as to cause injury or damage **2.** *vt.* **STRETCH RESOURCES TOO FAR** to try to do too much with the resources available, with consequent strain on those resources and, usually, poor performance (*often passive*) ○ *Absenteeism is often a sign that employees are overstretched.* **3.** *vt.* **STRETCH OVER SOMETHING** to extend or stretch over something

o·ver·stride /ṑvər strìd/ (**-strode** /-strṓd/, **-strid·den** /-strídd'n/, **-strid·ing, -strides**) *vt.* **1. CROSS AREA BY STRIDING** to cross purposefully over or beyond an area **2. STAND OR SIT ASTRIDE** to stand or sit astride something **3. DOMINATE SOMEBODY** to have complete mastery or control of somebody or something **4. SURPASS SOMEBODY** to surpass or go beyond somebody or something

o·ver·strung *adj.* **1. TOO NERVOUS** excessively nervous and tense **2.** MUSIC **WITH DOUBLE SET OF STRINGS** used to describe a piano fitted with two sets of strings, one crossing the other at an angle **3.** ARCHERY **STRUNG TOO TIGHTLY** having the bowstring fixed too tightly

o·ver·stuff /ṑvər stúf/ (**-stuffed, -stuff·ing, -stuffs**) *vt.* to stuff a cavity or object with too much material

o·ver·sub·scribe /ṑvər səb skrìb/ (**-scribed, -scrib·ing, -scribes**) *vt.* to apply to participate in something in numbers in excess of the available number of places (*usually passive*) ○ *The course on modern poetry was heavily oversubscribed.* —**o·ver·sub·scrip·tion** /ṑvər səb skrípshən/ *n.*

o·ver·sup·ply /ṑvər sə plì/ *n.* (*plural* **-plies**) **EXCESSIVE SUPPLY** an excessive supply of something ■ *vti.* (**-plied, -ply·ing, -plies**) **SUPPLY TOO MUCH OF** to provide somebody or something with an excessive supply of something

o·vert /ō vúrt, ṓ vùrt/ *adj.* **1. UNCONCEALED** done openly and without any attempt at concealment **2.** LAW **OPEN AND INTENTIONAL** done openly and intentionally, and therefore able to be taken as a sign of criminal intent [14thC. From Old French, the past participle of *ovrir* "to open," from Latin *aperire* (see APERTURE).] —**o·vert·ly** *adv.* —**o·vert·ness** *n.*

o·ver·take /ṑvər táyk/ (**-took** /-tòok/, **-tak·en** /-táykən/, **-tak·ing, -takes**) *v.* **1.** *vti.* **GO PAST** to catch up with and pass a person or vehicle traveling in the same direction **2.** *vt.* **DO BETTER THAN SOMEBODY** to reach and then surpass a level achieved by somebody or something **3.** *vt.* **COME OVER SOMEBODY SUDDENLY** to come over somebody suddenly or catch somebody by surprise ○ *Sleep overtook them.* **4.** *vt.* **CATCH UP WITH SOMEBODY** to go after and catch up with somebody

o·ver·tax /ṑvər táks/ (**-taxed, -tax·ing, -tax·es**) *vt.* **1. EXHAUST SOMEBODY** to impose too great a strain on somebody, something, or yourself **2. LEVY EXCESSIVE TAX ON** to levy more tax on somebody or something than is justified or considered fair

o·ver-the-air *adj.* transmitted by radio or television —**o·ver the air** *adv.*

o·ver the count·er *adv.* directly to a customer, without requiring a doctor's prescription

o·ver-the-count·er *adj.* **1. BOUGHT AND SOLD ELECTRONICALLY** not quoted as a security on an exchange, but bought and sold electronically **2. DEALING IN OVER-THE-COUNTER SECURITIES** relating to or dealing in over-the-counter securities **3. BUYABLE WITHOUT PRESCRIPTION** sold directly to the public without a doctor's prescription [From the idea that anybody can buy such items directly from the seller, as in a store]

o·ver-the-hill *adj.* **1. PAST PRIME** past the point at which talent, energy, or physical performance is at its peak **2. MIDDLE-AGED OR PAST MIDDLE AGE** middle-aged or past middle age (*sometimes considered offensive*) [From the idea of being past your peak]

o·ver-the-shoul·der shot *n.* CINEMA a shot taken from over the shoulder of a character whose back can be seen at side of frame. It is frequently used for filming conversations.

o·ver-the-top *adj. U.K.* so exaggerated as to appear ridiculous or outrageous (*informal*)

o·ver-the-tran·som *adj.* submitted to a publisher for publication without prior contact [From the idea of delivering a manuscript to a publisher's office when the door is closed]

o·ver·throw *vt.* /ṑvər thrṓ/ (**-threw** /-thròo/, **-thrown** /-thrṓn/, **-throw·ing, -throws**) **1. REMOVE SOMEBODY FROM POWER BY FORCE** to remove a person or group of people from a position of power by force **2.** BASEBALL **PITCH BASEBALL TOO HARD** to pitch a baseball so hard that the pitcher's control is adversely affected **3.** SPORTS **THROW BALL TOO FAR OR HARD** to throw a ball too far so that it goes beyond the player it was intended to reach ■ *n.* /ṑvər thrṓ/ **1. REMOVAL FROM POWER BY FORCE** the removal of a person or group of people from a position of power by force **2.** SPORTS **THROW THAT GOES TOO FAR** a throw of a ball that goes beyond the player it was intended to reach [14thC. The underlying meaning is "to overturn, knock down."]

o·ver·thrust fault /ṑvər thrust-/, **o·ver·thrust** *n.* a rock fault produced by thrust action that causes older rocks to move long distances and eventually settle on top of younger rocks (**horizontal displacement**)

o·ver·time /ṑvər tìm/ *n.* **1. ADDITIONAL TIME WORKED** extra time worked beyond the normal hours of employment **2. PAY FOR ADDITIONAL TIME WORKED** payment, usually at a higher rate, for time worked beyond the normal hours of employment **3.** SPORTS **EXTRA TIME IN GAME** additional time added to the normal length of a game, often in order to break a tie ■ *adv.* **1.**

BEYOND NORMAL LENGTH OF TIME beyond the normal or contracted length of time 2. *U.K.* VERY HARD using a great deal of energy and effort (*informal*) ○ *been working overtime to try and make them see sense* ■ *vt.* (-timed, -tim·ing, -times) to exceed the proper time for a photographic exposure

o·ver·tone /ṓvər tṑn/ *n.* 1. SUPPLEMENTARY MEANING a subtle additional meaning, nuance, or quality 2. MUSIC HIGHER MUSICAL TONE a higher tone produced at the same time as the lowest tone that helps to determine the overall quality of the sound

o·ver·took past tense of **overtake**

o·ver·top /ṑvər tóp/ (-topped, -top·ping, -tops) *vt.* 1. RISE ABOVE SOMETHING to rise above somebody or something 2. SURPASS SOMEBODY to surpass somebody or something 3. OVERRIDE to be more important than somebody or something

o·ver·trade /ṑvər tráyd/ (-trad·ed, -trad·ing, -trades) *vi.* to trade beyond the level that can be supported by the trader's financial means or the market involved

o·ver·train /ṑvər tráyn/ (-trained, -train·ing, -trains) *vti.* to train or exercise, or make somebody train or exercise, excessively, especially before a competition, with a resulting decrease in effectiveness

o·ver·trick /ṓvər trìk/ *n.* a trick taken in bridge in addition to the number needed to make a contract

o·ver·trump /ṑvər trúmp, ṓvər trùmp/ (-trumped, -trump·ing, -trumps) *vti.* to play a higher trump card than one already played by another player in a trick

o·ver·ture /ṓvər choŏr/ *n.* 1. MUSIC MUSICAL INTRODUCTION a single orchestral movement that introduces an opera, play, ballet, or longer musical work, often including the work's themes 2. INTRODUCTORY PROPOSAL OR INITIATIVE an introductory proposal or initiative made to mark the beginning of a discussion, agreement, or relationship ○ *make overtures to someone* 3. PRELUDE something that is a first step toward something else 4. = **concert overture** 5. INTRODUCTION TO A POEM an introduction to a written work such as a poem or play [15thC. Via Old French, "opening," from, ultimately, Latin *apertura* (see APERTURE).]

o·ver·turn (-turned, -turn·ing, -turns) *v.* /ṑvər túrn/ 1. *vti.* TIP OVER to turn somebody or something upside down 2. *vt.* OVERTHROW SOMEBODY to remove a person or a group of people from a position of power 3. *vt.* REVERSE PREVIOUS DECISION to reverse a previous decision, ruling, or law by using legal or legislative procedures —**o·ver·turn** /ṓvər tùrn/ *n.*

o·ver-un·der *n.* a wager that the final score in a game will be above or below a particular number of points

o·ver·use *n.* /ṑvər yoṓss/ EXCESSIVE USE the excessive use of something ■ *vt.* /ṑvər yoṓz/ (-used, -us·ing, -us·es) USE SOMETHING TOO MUCH to use something excessively, often wearing it out or making it ineffective

o·ver·val·ue /ṑvər vállyoo/ (-ued, -u·ing, -ues) *vt.* to set too high a value or price on something —**o·ver·val·u·a·tion** /ṑvər vallyoo áysh'n/ *n.*

o·ver·view /ṓvər vyoō/ *n.* 1. BROAD SURVEY a general or comprehensive outline of something 2. SUMMARY a brief summary of something

o·ver·volt·age /ṓvər vṑltij, ṑvər vṓltij/ *n.* a voltage that is in excess of the normal voltage for which an electrical circuit or system was designed and may sometimes cause damage to components

o·ver·wear /ṑvər wáir/ (-wore /-wáwr/, -worn /-wáwrn/, -wear·ing, -wears) *vt.* to wear somebody or something out

o·ver·ween·ing /ṑvər wéening/ *adj.* 1. ARROGANT intolerably arrogant or conceited 2. EXCESSIVE excessive, especially in an arrogant and conceited way [14thC. Formed from WEEN "to think, believe."] —**o·ver·ween·ing·ly** *adv.*

o·ver·weigh /ṑvər wáy/ (-weighed, -weigh·ing, -weighs) *vt.* 1. = **outweigh** *v.* 2 2. WEIGH ON SOMEBODY to oppress or burden somebody heavily

o·ver·weight *adj.* /ṑvər wáyt/ 1. TOO HEAVY FOR GOOD HEALTH with more weight than is considered healthy for somebody of a specific height, build, or age 2. ABOVE WEIGHT LIMIT heavier than the allowed weight limit ○ *an overweight letter* ■ *vt.* /ṑvər wáyt/ (-weight·ed, -weight·ing, -weights) 1. OVEREMPHASIZE SOMETHING to give too much emphasis or consideration to something 2. OVERLOAD SOMETHING to weigh something down with an excessive load ■ *npl.* OVERWEIGHT PEOPLE people who weigh too much for their height, build, or age (*sometimes considered offensive*)

o·ver·whelm /ṑvər wélm, -hwélm/ (-whelmed, -whelm·ing, -whelms) *vt.* (*often passive*) 1. SURGE OVER AND COVER to flow over the top of and submerge or cover somebody or something 2. OVERCOME SOMEBODY PHYSICALLY to use superior strength, force, or numbers to defeat somebody, especially a military enemy, completely 3. OVERPOWER SOMEBODY EMOTIONALLY to affect somebody's emotions in a complete or irresistible way 4. PROVIDE WITH HUGE AMOUNT OF SOMETHING to supply somebody with a very large or excessive amount of something [14thC. Formed from OVER + WHELM.]

o·ver·whelm·ing /ṑvər wélming, -hwélming/ *adj.* 1. EMOTIONALLY OVERPOWERING having such a great effect as to be emotionally overpowering 2. PHYSICALLY OVERPOWERING overpowering in strength, force, or numbers 3. EXTREMELY LARGE extremely large in amount or proportion —**o·ver·whelm·ing·ly** *adv.*

o·ver·wind /ṑvər wī́nd/ (-wound /-wównd/, -wound, -wind·ing, -winds) *vt.* to wind up the spring of a clockwork device, especially a watch or clock, too tightly, so that it will not operate or the spring breaks

o·ver·win·ter /ṑvər wíntər/ (-tered, -ter·ing, -ters) *v.* 1. *vti.* KEEP OR STAY ALIVE THROUGHOUT WINTER to keep livestock or plants alive through the winter by sheltering them, or to be kept alive in this way 2. *vi.* SURVIVE THE WINTER SOMEWHERE to stay alive throughout the winter in a particular place 3. *vi.* STAY FOR WINTER to spend the winter by taking up residence in a particular place

o·ver·with·hold /ṑvər with hṓld, -wi*th* hṓld/ (-held /-with héld, -wi*th* héld/, -held, -hold·ing, -holds) *vti.* to deduct or have deducted an amount of tax from a salary or investment that is larger than the tax to be paid

o·ver·wore past tense of **overwear**

o·ver·work /ṑvər wúrk/ *v.* (-worked, -work·ing, -works) 1. *vti.* DO TOO MUCH WORK to work, or to make somebody, yourself, or an animal work, excessively 2. *vt.* OVERUSE SOMETHING to use something too often, especially a word or expression 3. *vt.* DECORATE SURFACE OF to apply decoration to the surface of something 4. *vt.* WORK TOO MUCH ON SOMETHING to expend too much effort on something, especially so as to reduce its quality or effectiveness ■ *n.* EXCESSIVE WORK too much work [Old English]

o·ver·worn past participle of **overwear**

o·ver·wound past participle, past tense of **overwind**

o·ver·write /ṑvər rī́t/ (-wrote /-rṓt/, -writ·ten /-rítt'n/, -writ·ing, -writes) *v.* 1. *vti.* REPLACE COMPUTER FILE to replace data or a program in memory or on a disk with a new file of the same name 2. *vti.* WRITE SOMETHING TOO ELABORATELY to make a piece of writing too elaborate, polished, or decorative 3. *vt.* COVER WRITING WITH MORE WRITING to cover a piece of writing by writing on top of it

o·ver·wrought /ṑvər ráwt/ *adj.* 1. VERY UPSET extremely upset, emotional, or agitated 2. TOO ELABORATE fashioned or decorated too elaborately 3. ORNAMENTED ON SURFACE ornamented on the surface with something

o·ver·zeal·ous /ṑvər zélləs/ *adj.* too enthusiastic or eager, especially in carrying out a duty, and usually causing trouble or annoyance as a result

ovi- *prefix.* egg, ovum ○ *oviform* [Formed from Latin *ovum* (see OVUM)]

Ov·id /óvvid/ (43 B.C.–A.D. 17) Roman poet. His works include *Amores* and *Metamorphoses*, a collection of mythical and historical tales. —**O·vid·i·an** /ō víddee ən/ *adj.*

o·vi·duct /ṓvi dùkt/ *n.* either of a pair of tubes in the body that transport eggs from the ovary to the uterus. ◊ **fallopian tube**

O·vie·do /ōv yé*th*ō/ city and capital of Oviedo Province, Asturias autonomous region, northern Spain. Population: 202,421 (1995).

o·vi·form /ṓvi fàwrm/ *adj.* shaped like an egg

o·vine /ṓ vīn/ *adj.* relating to or like a sheep [Early 19thC. Via late Latin *ovinus* from Latin *ovis* "sheep." Ultimately from the Indo-European word for "sheep" that is also the ancestor of English *ewe*.]

o·vip·a·rous /ō vípparəss/ *adj.* 1. PRODUCING EGGS THAT HATCH OUTSIDE BODY used to describe birds, fish, reptiles, and insects that reproduce by means of eggs that develop and hatch outside the mother's body. ◊ viviparous 2. RELATING TO EGG PRODUCTION OUTSIDE BODY relating to the production of eggs that develop and hatch outside the mother's body —**o·vip·a·rous·ly** *adv.*

o·vi·pos·it /ṑvi pózzit/ (-it·ed, -it·ing, -its) *vi.* to lay eggs (*refers usually to insects*) [Early 19thC. Coined from OVI- + Latin *posit-*, the past participle stem of *ponere* "to place" (see POSITION).]

o·vi·pos·i·tor /ṑvi pózzitər/ *n.* a tubular organ at the end of the abdomen of some female fish or animals, especially insects, that is used to deposit eggs

o·vi·sac /ṓvi sàk/ *n.* a sac or capsule in the ovary of a mammal that contains a mature ovum. When the ovisac is ruptured the ovum is released. ◊ **Graafian follicle**

ovo- *prefix.* = **ovi-**

o·void /ṓ vòyd/ *adj.* 1. WITH FORM OF EGG with the solid form of an egg 2. BOT SHAPED LIKE AN EGG used to describe a fruit or similar plant part that is shaped like an egg ■ *n.* SOMETHING EGG-SHAPED something with the shape or form of an egg [Early 19thC. Via French from, ultimately, Latin *ovum* "egg" (see OVUM).]

o·vo·lac·to·veg·e·tar·i·an /ṑvō laktō vejjə táiree ən/ *n.* a vegetarian who eats eggs and dairy products, but no products that involve the killing of animals. ◊ **vegan**

o·vo·lo /ṓvə lṑ, óvvə-/ (*plural* -li /-lī/) *n.* a convex molding that resembles a quarter-circle or ellipse when viewed in cross section [Mid-17thC. From Italian, literally "little egg," ultimately from Latin *ovum* "egg" (see OVUM).]

o·von·ic /ō vónnik/ *adj.* relating to, consisting of, or using glassy materials that can rapidly and reversibly become electrical conductors after a minimum voltage is applied [Mid-20thC. Coined from OVSHINSKY EFFECT + ELECTRONIC.]

o·von·ics /ō vónniks/, **O·von·ics** *n.* the study or use of glassy materials that can rapidly and reversibly become electrical conductors after a minimum voltage is applied (*takes a singular verb*)

o·vo·tes·tis /ṑvō téstiss/ (*plural* -tes /-teez/) *n.* the sexual organ of a hermaphroditic animal such as the garden snail that produces both sperm and eggs

o·vo·vi·vip·a·rous /ṑvō vī vípparəss/ *adj.* used to describe insects, fish, and reptiles that reproduce by means of eggs that develop within the female, deriving some nutrition from her but remaining encased within an egg membrane —**o·vo·vi·vip·a·rous·ly** *adv.*

Ov·shin·sky ef·fect /ov shínskee-/ *n.* an effect that occurs in thin films of glass containing selenium and tellurium in which the resistance of the material drops rapidly when a particular voltage is applied across it. Switches made from these materials will stay on after the voltage has been removed. [Mid-20thC. Named for the U.S. physicist Stanford R. *Ovshinsky* b. 1922.]

o·vu·late /ṓvyə lày t, óvvyə-/ (-lat·ed, -lat·ing, -lates) *vi.* to ripen and release an egg or eggs from the ovary for possible fertilization [Late 19thC. Formed from OVULE.] —**o·vu·la·to·ry** /ṓvyələ tàwree, óvvyələ-/ *adj.*

o·vu·la·tion /ṑvvyə láysh'n, òvvyə-/ *n.* the ripening and discharge of an egg or eggs from the ovary for possible fertilization

o·vule /ṓ vyoōl, ó-/ *n.* 1. BOT SMALL PLANT PART DEVELOPING INTO SEED a small structure in a seed plant that contains the embryo sac and develops into a seed after fertilization 2. BIOL IMMATURE EGG a small or immature egg [Early 19thC. Via French from modern Latin *ovulum*, literally "little egg," from Latin *ovum* "egg" (see OVUM).] —**o·vu·lar** /ṓvyələr, óvvyələr/ *adj.*

o·vum /ṓvəm/ (*plural* **o·va** /ṓvə/) *n.* a female reproductive cell [Early 18thC. From Latin, "egg" (source of English *oval* and *ovary*). Ultimately from an Indo-European word that is also the ancestor of English *egg*, *cockney*, and *caviar*.]

ow /ow/ *interj.* used to represent an involuntary expression of pain [Early 20thC. Natural exclamation.]

OW *abbr.* one-way

owe /ō/ (owed, ow·ing, owes) *v.* 1. *vt.* BE OBLIGATED TO PAY SOMEBODY MONEY to be under an obligation to pay or repay somebody an amount of money 2. *vti.* BE FINANCIALLY IN DEBT to be financially in debt to somebody or for something 3. *vt.* BE INDEBTED FOR SOMETHING to have something, usually some desirable thing, only because of something or somebody else ○ *I owe my* *success to my father.* **4.** *vt.* **FEEL THAT RESPONSE IS DESERVED** to feel that something should be given to or done for somebody in recompense for something ○ *She owes you an explanation.* ○ *I owe myself a night out.* **5.** *vt.* **BEAR GRUDGE TOWARD SOMEBODY** to feel a particular emotion, especially a grudge, toward somebody ○ *owe sb a grudge* [Old English *āgan* (source of English *ought*). Ultimately from an Indo-European word meaning "to own" that is also the ancestor of English *own*.]

O·wen /ō in/, **Wilfred** (1893–1918) British poet. Famous for his war poetry, he was killed in World War I a week before the armistice.

Barnaby's

Jesse Owens: Photographed in the long jump competition at the Berlin Olympics (1936)

O·wens /ō inz/, **Jesse** (1913–80) U.S. athlete. One of the greatest sprinters of all time, he won four gold medals at the 1936 Olympics, setting multiple Olympic and world records. Real name **James Cleveland Owens**

O·wens·bor·o /ōanz bùrō/ city in southwestern Kentucky, on the southern bank of the Ohio River, on the Kentucky-Indiana border. Population: 54,350 (1996).

O·wen Sound /ōən-/ city and seaport on the southwestern coast of Georgian Bay in Ontario, Canada. Population: 30,319 (1996).

Ow·er·ri /ō wérree/ capital city of Imo State, southern Nigeria. Population: 35,010 (1983).

ow·ing /ō ing/ *adj.* due to be given, especially in payment or repayment of a debt ○ *amounts still owing* ◇ **owing to** as a result or consequence of something

Owl

owl /owl/ *n.* **1. HOOTING BIRD OF PREY** a predatory, usually nocturnal bird with a large head, large front-facing eyes, hooked and feathered talons, a small beak, short neck, and a distinctive hooting call. The owl is traditionally described as wise, perhaps because of its fixed gaze, as if it were considering something carefully. Order: Strigiformes. **2. SOMEBODY RESEMBLING OWL** somebody who has habits or characteristics attributed to owls, e.g., wisdom, contemplativeness, solemnity, or staying up all night **3. FANCY PIGEON** a domestic pigeon belonging to a breed resembling the owl [Old English *ūle*, from a prehistoric Germanic word of uncertain origin: probably an imitation of an owl's call]

owl but·ter·fly *n.* a South American butterfly that has a spot like an owl's eye on the underside of each hind wing. Genus: *Caligo.*

owl·et /ówlət/ *n.* a young or baby owl

owl·et moth *n.* = **noctuid** ["Owlet" from the fact that its eyes shine in the dark when light strikes them]

owl·ish /ówlish/ *adj.* physically resembling an owl or displaying a characteristic attributed to owls, e.g., wisdom, contemplativeness, solemnity, or staying up all night —**owl·ish·ly** *adv.* —**owl·ish·ness** *n.*

owl par·rot *n.* = **kakapo**

owl's claws /ówlz clàwz/ *n.* a perennial plant that grows in western North America and has large yellow flowers. Latin name: *Helenium hoopesii.* (*regional*)

owl's clo·ver *n.* a plant of the figwort family found in western North and South America that has dense spikes of variously-colored flowers. Genus: *Orthocarpus.* [*Owl's* from the fact that its flowers look like owls' faces]

own /ōn/ *adj.* **EMPHASIZES POSSESSIVE** a grammatical word emphasizing that somebody or something belongs to a particular person or thing and not to somebody or something else ○ (adj) *I always wanted to have my own business.* ○ *Her own mother wouldn't have recognized her.* ○ (pron) ○ *At last he had a house of his own.* ■ *adj., pron.* **INDICATES THAT SOMEBODY DOES SOMETHING UNAIDED** used to indicate that somebody does something without help or interference ○ (adj) *She made her own dress.* ○ *I can make my own decisions.* ○ (pron) *I'd rather make my own than buy them ready-made.* ■ *v.* (**owned, own·ing, owns**) **1.** *vt.* **HAVE SOMETHING AS PROPERTY** to have something as your property ○ *He owns a chain of hotels.* **2.** *vti.* **ACKNOWLEDGE** to acknowledge or admit something (*archaic or formal*) ○ *He owned that the struggle had been hard.* [Old English *āgnian*, from *āgen* "one's own," past participle of *āgan*, an earlier form of OWE] ◇ **come into your own** to start to be really effective, useful, or successful ◇ **hold your own 1.** put up effective resistance in an argument or contest **2.** remain in a stable condition after an illness or injury, often when it might not be expected ◇ **on your own 1.** alone **2.** without help or interference

own up *vi.* to admit to having done something

own·er /ōnər/ *n.* somebody who owns something

own·er-oc·cu·pied *adj.* used as a residence by the person who owns it

own·er-oc·cu·pi·er *n.* somebody who owns or is in the process of buying the house or apartment he or she is living in

own·er·ship /ōnər shìp/ *n.* **1. RIGHT OF POSSESSION** the legal right of possessing something **2. FACT OR STATE OF OWNING SOMETHING** the fact or condition of being an owner of something

own goal *n. U.K.* a goal scored by mistake in a sport such as soccer or ice hockey for the opposing team, usually due to a miskick, mishit, or deflection off another player

own la·bel *n. U.K.* = **store brand**

Ox

ox /oks/ (*plural* **ox·en** /óksən/) *n.* **1. BOVINE DRAFT ANIMAL** an adult castrated bull, sometimes used for pulling heavy loads and plows. Genus: *Bos.* **2. COW OR BULL** a male or female bovine mammal, especially one belonging to a domestic breed **3. SOMEBODY UNINTELLIGENT AND CLUMSY** somebody who is unintelligent and clumsy, especially somebody with a large build (*insult*) [Old English *oxa*, from a prehistoric Germanic word that is also the ancestor of English *aurochs*]

ox- *prefix.* oxygen ○ *oxime* [From OXYGEN]

ox·a·cil·lin /óksə síllin/ *n.* an antibiotic used to treat bacterial infections that are resistant to penicillin [Mid-20thC. Coined from *isoxazole* + PENICILLIN.]

ox·a·late /óksə làyt/ *n.* a salt or ester of oxalic acid

of speaking that is considered to be refined and correct

Oxford English Dictionary *n.* the largest dictionary of the English language, first published in 10 volumes between 1884 and 1928, with supplements and a revised second edition

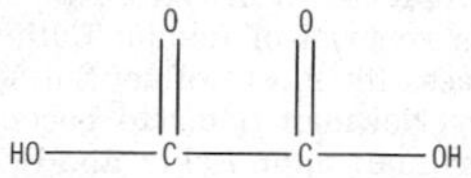

Oxalic acid

ox·al·ic ac·id /ok sàllik-/ *n.* a colorless poisonous acid found in plants as an oxalate and synthetically made for use in bleaching, dyeing, and cleaning. Formula: $H_2C_2O_4$. ["Oxalic" formed from Latin *oxalis* "wood sorrel" (see OXALIS), because it occurs naturally in the plant's leaves]

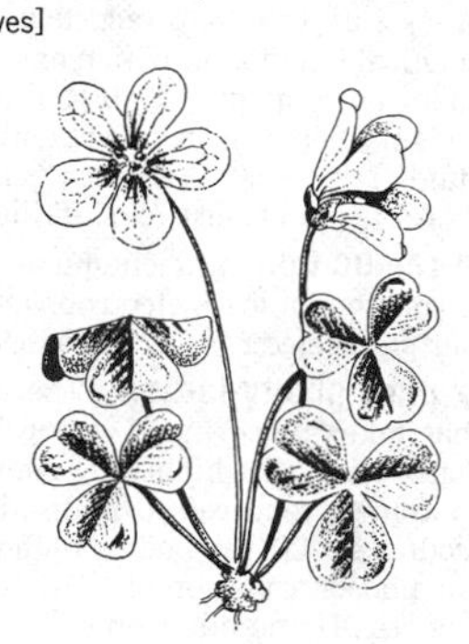

Oxalis

ox·a·lis /ok sálliss, óksəliss/ *n.* a plant such as wood sorrel with leaves similar to those of clover. Genus: *Oxalis.* [Early 17thC. Via Latin from Greek, "wood sorrel," from *oxus* "sour" (see OXYGEN), because of the taste of its leaves.]

ox·az·e·pam /ok sázzə pàm/ *n.* a tranquilizer used to manage anxiety, insomnia, and alcohol withdrawal. Formula: $C_{15}H_{11}ClN_2O_2$. [Mid-20thC. Coined from HYDROXY- + BENZODIAZEPINE + AMINE.]

ox·blood /óks blùd/, **ox·blood red** *adj.* of a dark brownish-red color —**ox·blood** *n.*

ox·bow /óks bō/ *n.* **1. U-SHAPED COLLAR FOR OX** a collar for an ox used as a draft animal, consisting of a U-shaped piece of wood attached to a yoke **2. BEND IN RIVER** a bend in a river shaped like an oxbow, or the land found in the bend of a river

ox·bow lake *n.* a small curved lake developed on a river floodplain by a river abandoning its original meandering course and cutting a new channel

Ox·bridge /óks brìj/ *n. U.K.* the universities of Oxford and Cambridge, seen as forming an institution distinct from all the other more recently established universities in England [Mid-19thC. Blend of *Oxford* and *Cambridge*.]

ox·cart /óks kaàrt/ *n.* a cart drawn by oxen, for transporting heavy goods

ox·en plural of **ox**

ox·eye /óks ì/ *n.* **1. PLANT WITH FLOWER HEADS LIKE A DAISY'S** a composite plant of Europe, Asia, and North America that has flower heads resembling a daisy's. Genus: *Buphthalum* and *Heliopsis.* **2.** = **daisy** *n.* 1

ox·eyed *adj.* with big round eyes like those of an ox

ox·eye dai·sy, **oxeye** *n.* = **daisy** *n.* 1

Ox·fam /óks fàm/ *n.* an international charity dedicated to providing poverty and disaster relief overseas. It was founded in Oxford, England, in 1942.

ox·ford /óksfərd/, **Ox·ford** *n.* a sturdy leather shoe that laces over the instep [Late 19thC. Named for *Oxford*, England.]

Ox·ford /óks fərd/ city in south central England, and administrative center of Oxfordshire. Its university is the oldest in England. Population: 118,795 (1991).

Ox·ford ac·cent *n.* a way of speaking using the pronunciation associated with Oxford English

Ox·ford En·glish *n. U.K.* a variety of English, associated with Oxford University, that uses a form of Received Pronunciation, the educated standard speech of southern England

Ox·ford Movement *n.* CHR a movement in the Church of England that began in Oxford in the 1830s and advocated a renewal of Roman Catholic doctrine and practices. Its most influential leaders were John Henry Newman (later to become a Roman Catholic cardinal), John Keble, and Edward Pusey.

ox·heart /óks haàrt/ *n.* a variety of cultivated cherry bearing large, sweet, heart-shaped fruits [Mid-19thC. From its shape and large size.]

ox·i·dant /óksidənt/ *n.* **1. OXIDIZING AGENT** a substance that oxidizes other substances **2. SUBSTANCE IN FUEL** a substance in a bipropellant rocket fuel that contains oxygen to support the combustion of another substance, usually liquid oxygen, hydrogen peroxide, or nitric acid [Late 19thC. Via French from, ultimately, *oxide* (see OXIDE).]

ox·i·dase /óksi dàyss, -dàyz/ *n.* an enzyme that catalyzes biological oxidation, especially in living organisms [Late 19thC. Formed from OXIDATION.]

ox·i·da·tion /òksi dáysh'n/ *n.* ◊ **reduction 1. ADDITION OF OXYGEN** a chemical reaction in which oxygen is added to an element or compound **2. LOSS OF ELECTRONS** the process of losing electrons from a chemical element or compound [Late 18thC. Via French from, ultimately, *oxide* (see OXIDE).] —**ox·i·da·tive** /óksi dàytiv/ *adj.*

ox·i·da·tion-re·duc·tion *n.* a chemical reaction in which one component loses electrons or is oxidized and another gains electrons or is reduced

ox·i·da·tive phos·pho·ry·la·tion /òksə daytiv-/ *n.* a process that takes place in all living cells in the presence of oxygen, in which they convert food to the energy that is required to maintain life. This process produces ATP, the body's high-energy fuel, through the phosphorylation of ADP driven by the oxidation of NADH and other donors of electrons.

ox·i·da·tive stress *n.* the impaired performance of cells, caused by the presence of too many oxygen molecules in them

ox·ide /ók sīd/ *n.* any compound containing oxygen, especially in combination with a metal [Late 18thC. From French, formed from *oxygène* "oxygen," on the model of *acide* "acid."]

ox·i·dize /óksi dīz/ (**-dized, -diz·ing, -diz·es**) *vti.* **1. REACT OR MAKE REACT WITH OXYGEN** to react or cause a chemical to react with oxygen, e.g. in forming an oxide. ◊ **reduce** *v.* 9 **2. LOSE OR MAKE LOSE ELECTRONS** to lose electrons, or to cause a chemical element or compound to lose electrons. ◊ **reduce** *v.* 10 **3. COVER WITH OXIDE COATING** to form an oxide coating or to cover something with an oxide coating —**ox·i·di·za·tion** /òksidi záysh'n/ *n.* —**ox·y·diz·a·ble** /óksi dīzəb'l/ *adj.*

ox·i·diz·er /óksi dīzər/ *n.* = **oxidant** *n.* 1

ox·i·diz·ing a·gent *n.* a substance that oxidizes other substances and undergoes reduction in the process

ox·i·do·re·duc·tase /òksidō ri dúk tàyss, -tàyz/ *n.* an enzyme that catalyzes a reaction involving oxidation and reduction

ox·ime /ók seèm, óksim/ *n.* an organic compound containing a hydroxile group bonded to a nitrogen atom [Late 19thC. Coined from OXY- + IMIDE.]

ox·im·e·ter /ok símmətər/ *n.* an instrument that measures the amount of oxygen in something, especially in blood [Mid-19thC. Coined from OXY- + -METER.] —**ox·i·met·ric** /òksi méttrik/ *adj.* —**ox·i·met·ri·cal·ly** /-méttriklee/ *adv.* —**ox·im·e·try** /ok símmətree/ *n.*

ox·lip /óks lìp/ *n.* a woodland plant of Europe and Asia that has clusters of small yellow flowers. Latin name: *Primula elatior*. [Old English *oxanslyppe*, literally "ox dung," from *oxa* "ox" + *slyppe* "slime" (see SLIP)]

Ox·o·ni·an /ok sṓnee ən/ *adj.* **1. RELATING TO OXFORD UNIVERSITY** relating to or typical of Oxford University, or its students and staff **2. RELATING TO BRITISH CITY OF OXFORD** relating to or typical of the British city of Oxford or its inhabitants [Mid-16thC. Formed from *Oxonia*, Latinized form of Old English *Ox(e)naford* "Oxford."] —**Ox·o·ni·an** *n.*

ox·peck·er /óks pèkər/ *n.* an African starling that climbs on the back of wild and domestic mammals and eats parasites from their skin. Genus: *Buphagus*. [Mid-19thC]

ox·tail /óks tàyl/ *n.* the tail of a beef animal, skinned and chopped into short lengths and simmered for a long time to make a rich soup or stew

oxy- *prefix.* oxygen ○ *oxyacid* [Shortening of OXYGEN]

ox·y·a·cet·y·lene /òksee ə sétt'l eèn, -sétt'lin/ *n.* a mixture of oxygen and acetylene that is used to produce an extremely hot flame for cutting, welding, or brazing metal

ox·y·ac·id /óksee àssid/ *n.* an acid that contains oxygen

ox·y·ceph·a·ly /òksee séffəlee/ *n.* a condition in which the skull becomes slightly pointed as a result of the premature closure of some connective bones (**sutures**) [Late 19thC. Formed from Greek *oxukephalos*, literally "pointed-headed," from *oxus* "sharp" (see OXYGEN) + *kephalē* "head."]

ox·y·gen /óksijən/ *n.* a colorless odorless gas that is the most abundant chemical element and forms compounds with most others. It is necessary for most combustion and essential for plant and animal respiration. Symbol **O** [Late 18thC. From French, literally "acid-former" (because it was thought to be a basic component of acids), formed from Greek *oxus* "sharp, sour."] —**ox·y·gen·ic** /òksi jénnik/ *adj.*

ox·y·gen·ase /óksijə nàyss, -nàyz/ *n.* an enzyme that catalyzes a reaction in which molecular oxygen is the oxidizing agent

ox·y·gen·ate /óksijə nàyt/ *vti.* (**-at·ed, -at·ing, -ates**) **COMBINE WITH OXYGEN** to combine something, or to be combined, with oxygen ■ *n.* **OXYGEN SUBSTANCE ADDED TO FUELS** a substance added to fuels, especially gasoline, to make them burn more efficiently

ox·y·gen debt *n.* the amount of oxygen needed to replenish the stores the body uses for its normal physiological processes after these have been depleted during strenuous physical exercise

ox·y·gen demand *n.* = **biochemical oxygen demand**

ox·y·gen mask *n.* a device fitting closely over the nose and mouth through which oxygen is supplied to assist breathing, e.g., at high altitudes

ox·y·gen tent *n.* a structure enclosing a patient in bed and resembling a transparent plastic tent, into which oxygen can be pumped to assist breathing

ox·y·he·mo·glo·bin /aàksi hímmə glō bən/ *n.* the bright red form of hemoglobin when it is combined with oxygen molecules, which it transports from the lungs to the tissues

ox·y·hy·dro·gen /aàksi hī́ drə gən/ *adj.* using a mixture of oxygen and hydrogen gases, thus allowing hydrogen to burn in an oxygen atmosphere and giving a flame temperature of 2,400°C degrees ○ *oxyhydrogen welding*

ox·y·me·taz·o·line /òksee mi tázzə leèn/ *n.* a vasoconstrictor used as a nasal decongestant and usually administered as a spray. Formula: $C_{16}H_{24}N_2O$.

ox·y·mo·ron /aàksi máwraan/ (*plural* **-ra**) *n.* a phrase in which two words of contradictory meaning are used together for special effect, e.g., "wise fool" or "legal murder" [Mid-17thC. From Greek *oxumōros*, a substantival use of the neuter singular of *oxumōros* "pointedly foolish," from *oxus* "sharp" (source of English *oxygen*) + *mōros* "foolish" (source of English *moron*).]

ox·yn·tic /ok síntik/ *adj.* producing or secreting acid ○ *oxyntic cells*

ox·y·sul·fide /òksi súl fīd/ *n.* any compound in which a chemical element is combined with sulfur and oxygen

ox·y·tet·ra·cy·cline /aàksi téttrə sī́ kleen/ *n.* a yellow crystalline antibiotic obtained from a soil bacterium and used to treat a wide variety of bacterial infections *Streptomyces rimosus*. Formula: $C_{22}H_{24}N_2O_9$.

ox·y·to·cic /aàksi tōssik/ *adj.* **SPEEDING UP CONTRACTIONS IN CHILDBIRTH** inducing or speeding up childbirth by stimulating the uterine muscles and causing contractions ■ *n.* **OXYTOCIC DRUG** a drug that induces or speeds up childbirth [Mid-19thC. Formed from Greek *oxutokia* "sudden delivery" (literally "sharp birth"), which in turn was formed from Greek *tokos* "birth" (related to English *thane*).]

ox·y·to·cin /aàksi tōssin/ *n.* a hormone released by the pituitary gland that stimulates contractions of the womb during childbirth and triggers the secretion of milk from the breast during nursing. It may be given to women during childbirth to assist labor. Formula: $C_{43}H_{66}N_{12}O_{12}S_2$.

ox·y·tone /aàksi tōn/ *adj.* **1. WITH ACUTE ACCENT ON LAST SYLLABLE** in classical Greek, having an acute accent on the final syllable **2. WITH STRESS ON FINAL SYLLABLE** with the stress on the final syllable ■ *n.* an oxytone word or syllable [Mid-18thC. From Greek *oxutonos*, literally "sharp pitch," which was formed from *tonos* "pitch, force" (see TONE).]

ox·y·u·ri·a·sis /aàksi yoŏ rī́əssiss/ *n.* infestation with pinworms [Early 20thC. From modern Latin, from *Oxyuris* "name of a genus of worms."]

oy·er and ter·mi·ner /òyər ənd túrminər/ *n.* **1. U.S. CRIMINAL COURT** a high court with general criminal jurisdiction in some states of the U.S. **2. BRITISH COMMISSION TO JUDGE ON ASSIZE** a commission from the British Crown empowering a judge to try cases in English courts of assize, abolished along with the assize system in 1972 [Partial translation of Anglo-Norman *oyer et terminer*, literally "to hear and determine" (*terminer* from Latin *terminare*, source of English *terminate*)]

o·yez /ō yéz, ō yéss, ō yáy/, **oyes** *interj.* **1. CALL FOR SILENCE** used, usually three times in succession, to call for silence and indicate that an official announcement is about to be made, e.g., in court or by a town-crier **2.** used to get somebody's attention (*informal*) ■ *n.* a cry of "oyez" [From Anglo-Norman, the imperative plural ("hear ye!") of *oyer* "to hear," from Latin *audire* "to hear"]

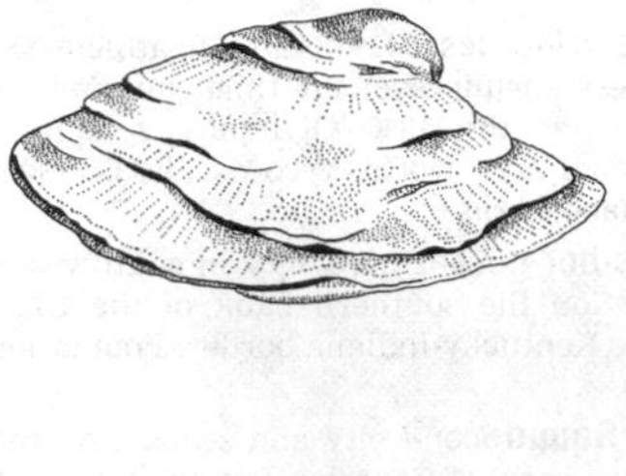

Oyster

oys·ter /óystər/ *n.* **1. EDIBLE SHELLFISH** an edible shellfish with a rough irregularly shaped shell that lives mainly on the sea bed in coastal waters. Oysters are generally eaten raw and considered a delicacy. Genera: *Ostrea* and *Crassostrea*. **2. SHELLFISH SIMILAR TO OYSTER** any of various types of shellfish similar to the edible oyster, e.g., the pearl oyster **3. SLIGHTLY GRAYISH OFF-WHITE** a pale beige or pink color with a grayish tinge **4. PIECE OF DARK MEAT IN FOWL** a small piece of dark meat found in a hollow on either side of the pelvic bone of a fowl such as a chicken or turkey **5. UNCOMMUNICATIVE PERSON** a person who does not say much or is secretive (*archaic slang*) ■ *vi.* (**oyster·ed, oyster·ing, oysters**) **GATHER OYSTERS** to grow or gather oysters [Via Old French *oistre* from Latin *ostrea*, *ostreum*, from Greek *ostreon*, etymologically an allusion to its shell, being related to *ostrakon* "shell" (source of English *ostracize*) and *osteon* "bone" (source of English *osteo-*)] ◇ **the world is your oyster** the world provides unlimited opportunities for you to be successful and prosper

oys·ter bed *n.* an area of seabed where oysters grow or are grown

Oystercatcher

oys·ter·catch·er /óystər katshər/ *n.* a common large shore bird, found worldwide, that has a long flat almost chisel-shaped red bill and black or black-and-white plumage, and lives on shellfish and worms. Genus: *Haematopus*.

oys·ter crab *n.* a small soft-bodied crab that lives inside the shell of a live oyster or other mollusk as a commensal. Latin name: *Pinnotheres ostreum.*

oys·ter crack·er *n.* FOOD a small round salty cracker

oys·ter·man /óystər mən/ (*plural* **oystermen**) *n.* **1.** SOMEBODY WHO GROWS OR GATHERS OYSTERS somebody who grows, collects, or sells oysters **2.** a boat used in gathering oysters

oys·ter mush·room *n.* an edible mushroom that grows on dead wood and has a soft flavorful gray cap. Latin name: *Pleurotus ostreatus.*

oys·ter plant *n.* **1.** = **salsify** *n.* 1 **2.** = **lungwort**

oys·ter sauce *n.* a salty bottled sauce flavored with oysters, used as a seasoning or flavoring in Chinese cooking

oys·ter shell scale *n.* an insect pest to shade trees and shrubs that in its wingless eyeless adult form lives under an impenetrable white shell and sucks the sap of its host. Latin name: *Lepidosaphes ulmi.*

oys·ters rock·e·fel·ler /óystərz ráaki felər/ *n.* oysters topped with chopped spinach, flavored with onion, celery, parsley, and a little aniseed liqueur, then baked [Mid-20thC. ROCKEFELLER of uncertain origin: probably named for John D. ROCKEFELLER.]

oz *abbr.* ounce [From Italian *ōz* being abbreviation of *onza* "ounce," from Latin *uncia* "twelfth part" (see OUNCE)]

Oz /oz/, **Amos** (*b.* 1939) Israeli writer. He is best known for his novels about life in Israel and Palestine. Full name **Amos Klausner Oz**

Ö·zal /ō zaál/, **Turgut** (1927–93) Turkish statesman. Founder of the Motherland Party, he was prime minister (1983–89) and president (1989–93) of Turkey.

oz ap *abbr.* apothecaries' ounce

O·zark Plat·eau /ō zaárk-/ mountainous region in the southern United States, predominantly in Arkansas, Missouri, and Oklahoma. Area: 50,000 sq. mi./130,000 sq. km.

oz av *abbr.* avoirdupois ounce

AKG London

Seiji Ozawa

O·za·wa /ō zaáwə/, **Seiji** (*b.* 1935) Japanese conductor. He has conducted the Boston Symphony Orchestra since 1973.

o·zo·ce·rite /ōzō sírrit/, **o·zo·ke·rite** /ōzō kírrit/ *n.* a waxy hydrocarbon substance occurring naturally in irregular veins in sandstone rock, ranging in color from brown to jet black, and used in making candles, wax paper, and polishes [Mid-19thC. From German *Ozokerit*, from Greek *ozein* "to smell" (source of English *ozone*) + *kēros* "beeswax."]

o·zone /ó zōn, ō zṓn/ *n.* **1.** FORM OF OXYGEN a form of oxygen gas with three oxygen atoms in its molecule, formed by electrical discharge in oxygen, acting as a strong oxidizing agent, and used in water purification. Although considered a pollutant in the lower atmosphere where it is present in very small quantities, it forms a protective ozone layer in the upper atmosphere. Formula: O_3. **2.** FRESH AIR fresh pure air (*informal*) [Mid-19thC. Via German *Ozon* from Greek *ozon*, the neuter present participle of *ozein* "to smell"; so called from its pungent smell.]

o·zone-friendly *adj.* causing no harm to the ozone layer

o·zone hole *n.* an area of the upper atmosphere where the ozone layer is absent or has become unusually thin

o·zone layer *n.* the layer of the upper atmosphere, from 10 to 30 miles/15 to 50 km above the Earth's surface, where most atmospheric ozone collects, absorbing harmful ultraviolet radiation from the Sun. In the 1980s it was realized that industrial pollutants such as chlorofluorocarbons were damaging the ozone layer and that holes had appeared in it, especially over the Antarctic.

o·zo·nide /ō zōnīd/ *n.* any of a group of explosive organic compounds formed by the addition of ozone to any organic compound with a double or triple carbon bond

o·zo·nize /ō zōnīz/ (**ozon·ized, ozon·izing, ozon·izes**) *vt.* **1.** CONVERT OXYGEN TO OZONE to convert oxygen into ozone **2.** TREAT WITH OZONE to treat something with ozone, or add ozone to an organic compound with a double or triple carbon bond

o·zo·niz·er /ṓzō nīzər/ *n.* a device that produces ozone from oxygen gas

o·zo·no·sphere /ō zṓnə sfeer, ō zónnə sfeer/ *n.* = **ozone layer**

oz t *abbr.* troy ounce

P p

p[1] /pee/ (*plural* **p's**), **P** (*plural* **P's**) *n.* **1. 16TH LETTER OF THE ALPHABET** the 16th letter of the modern English alphabet **2. SPEECH SOUND CORRESPONDING TO LETTER "P"** the sound made when speaking that corresponds to the letter "P" **3. LETTER "P" WRITTEN** a written representation of the letter "P"

p[2] *abbr.* **1.** MUSIC piano (*used as a direction*) **2.** pico- (*used in combinations*) **3.** PHYS momentum **4.** PHYS proton

p[3] *symbol.* CHEM ELEM phosphorus

P *abbr.* **1.** PHYS parity **2.** park (*used on gearshifts*) **3.** CHESS pawn **4.** played (*used in sports tables*) **5.** after noon **6.** PHYS power **7.** PHYS pressure

p. *abbr.* **1.** page **2.** part **3.** GRAM participle **4.** GRAM past **5.** pataca **6.** penny **7.** per **8.** peso **9.** pint **10.** pipe **11.** population **12.** pula **13.** KNITTING purl

P. *abbr.* **1.** Pastor **2.** President **3.** Priest **4.** Prince

pa /po/ (*plural* **pa's** *or* **pas**) *n.* father (*informal*) [Early 19thC. Shortening of PAPA.]

Pa *symbol.* **1.** PHYS pascal **2.** CHEM ELEM protactinium

PA[1] *abbr.* **1.** INSUR particular average **2.** MAIL Pennsylvania **3.** BANKING personal account **4.** MIL Post Adjutant **5.** press agent **6.** Press Association **7.** prosecuting attorney **8.** public accountant

PA[2] *n.* an electronic amplification system used to increase the sound level of speech or music in a large or open space such as a stadium or auditorium. Full form **public-address system**

Pa. *abbr.* Pennsylvania

p.a. *abbr.* yearly

P.A. *abbr.* **1.** physician's assistant **2.** power of attorney **3.** prosecuting attorney

P/A *abbr.* LAW power of attorney

pa'an·ga /paáang gə, paa áang gə/ *n.* **1. TONGAN UNIT OF CURRENCY** the main unit of currency of Tonga, worth 100 seniti. See table at **currency 2. BILL WORTH A PA'ANGA** a bill worth one pa'anga

PABA /pábbə, paábə/ *n.* a colorless form of aminobenzoic acid used in sunscreens to absorb ultraviolet light and in dyes and pharmaceuticals. It is part of the vitamin B complex and is found in yeast and liver. Full form **para-aminobenzoic**

pab·lum /pábbləm/ *n.* = **pabulum** *n.* 2 [Late 20thC. From PABULUM.]

pab·u·lum /pábbyələm/ *n.* **1. PLANT OR ANIMAL FOOD** a source of nourishment in an easily absorbable liquid, especially the nutrient intake of plants and lower animals **2. UNSATISFYING INTELLECTUAL MATERIAL** material whose intellectual content is thin, trite, bland, or generally unsatisfying (*literary*) [Mid-17thC. From Latin, where it was formed from the stem of *pascere* "to feed" (source of English *pasture*).]

PABX *abbr.* private automatic branch exchange

PAC /pak/ *abbr.* political action committee

Pac. *abbr.* Pacific

pa·ca /paákə, pákə/ *n.* a large burrowing plant-eating rodent with a large head and brown fur with white spots, found in the rainforests of South and Central America. Genus: *Cuniculus.* [Mid-17thC. Via Spanish and Portuguese from Tupi.]

Paca /paákə, pákə/, **William** (1740–99) U.S. statesman. He signed the Declaration of Independence (1776) and was governor of Maryland (1782–85).

Paca

pace[1] /payss/ *n.* **1. SPEED OF MOVEMENT** the particular speed at which somebody or something moves, especially when walking or running ○ *She quickened her pace.* **2. SPEED OF EVENTS** the rate or speed at which things happen or develop ○ *the pace of modern life* **3. SPEED IN PERFORMANCE** the degree of urgency, sharpness, or speed in the writing, composition, or performance of a dramatic or musical work **4. STEP** a step taken when walking or running **5. DISTANCE COVERED IN A STEP** the distance covered in a single step or stride **6. UNIT OF LENGTH** any of several units of distance ranging from 30 to 60 in./.76 to 1.52 m, based on the length of one or two human strides **7. WAY OF WALKING** a particular manner or style of walking **8.** EQU **GAIT OF HORSE** a distinctive way in which a four-legged animal walks or runs at different speeds, e.g., a walk, trot, or canter, especially as executed by a trained horse **9. 2-BEAT GAIT** a two-beat gait of a four-legged animal where both legs on one side of the body move and are put down together. It is natural in camels but the product of training in horses. ■ *v.* **(paced, pac·ing, pac·es) 1.** *vti.* **WALK BACK AND FORTH** to walk back and forth within a restricted area, especially in a state of nervous anxiety or deep thought ○ *paced up and down all night worrying* **2.** *vti.* **WALK ALONG SOMETHING** to walk along or through something with regular strides **3.** *vti.* **MEASURE BY COUNTING STEPS** to measure a distance by counting the paces taken to cover it ○ *I paced out the width of the room.* **4.** *vt.* **SET THE SPEED OF SOMETHING** to set the speed at which somebody runs, moves, or does something ○ *I helped her train for the marathon by pacing her on a bicycle.* **5.** *vr.* **DO SOMETHING AT CONTROLLED RATE** to run or work at an even controlled speed so as not to waste energy ○ *Learn to pace yourself.* **6.** *vi.* **MOVE AT A PACE** to move at a pace (*refers to horses*) [13thC. Directly or via French *pas* "step" from Latin *passus,* literally "stretch (of the leg)," ultimately from *pandere* "to stretch, extend" (source of English *expand*).] ◇ **at somebody's own pace** at the rate that is natural or comfortable for somebody ◇ **force the pace** to do something to force somebody to go faster or to make something happen more quickly ◇ **off the pace** SPORTS behind the leader or the score of the leading competitor ◇ **put somebody** *or* **something through his** *or* **her** *or* **its paces** to make somebody or something demonstrate his, her, or its capabilities, as a test or in order to impress other people ◇ **set the pace** to go at a speed or establish a standard that others have to keep up with ◇ **stand** *or* **stay the pace** to be able to keep up with other people, especially when the pace is fast, the standard high, or the competition fierce

pace[2] /páyssee, paá chày/ *prep.* used in front of a name or title as a gesture of real or ironic respect to somebody who is mistaken and about to be corrected ○ *Pace the critic of this newspaper, the character's name is Prospero, not Prosperus.* [Late 18thC. From Latin, literally "with peace, with permission," a form of *pax* "peace" (source of English *peace*).]

pace car *n.* a car that leads the competitors in a car race through a pace lap before the start of a race but does not participate in the race itself

pace lap *n.* a lap of the course driven by all the competitors in a motor race before the race begins, to warm up the engines

pace·mak·er /páyss màykər/ *n.* **1.** SPORTS **COMPETITOR WHO SETS THE PACE** a competitor in a race who sets the speed at which the whole or part of the race is run **2.** = **pacesetter** *n.* 1 **3.** MED **DEVICE THAT REGULATES THE HEARTBEAT** a battery-operated electrical device inserted into the body to deliver small regular shocks that stimulate the heart to beat in a normal rhythm **4.** ANAT **NATURAL HEARTBEAT REGULATOR** a small area of specialized heart-muscle tissue in the wall of the upper right chamber of the heart that sends out rhythmic electrical impulses to regulate the heartbeat

pac·er /páyssər/ *n.* **1.** SPORTS = **pacemaker** *n.* 1 **2.** EQU **HORSE TRAINED TO PACE** a horse trained to go at the pace in races

pace·set·ter /páyss sèttər/ *n.* **1. LEADER IN A FIELD OF ACTIVITY** a person or group regarded as being a leader in any field and one whom others may emulate **2.** SPORTS = **pacemaker** *n.* 1

pa·cha *n.* = **pasha**

pa·chi·si /pə cheézee/ *n.* an ancient Indian four-handed game similar to backgammon played on a cross-shaped board with six cowrie shells used as dice [Early 19thC. From Hindi *pac(c)īsī,* literally "(throw of) 25" (this being the highest in the game).]

pach·ou·li *n.* = **patchouli**

pach·y·derm /páki dùrm/ *n.* a large mammal with a thick skin, especially the elephant, rhinoceros, or hippopotamus [Mid-19thC. From French *pachyderme,* from Greek *pachydermos* "thick-skinned," from *pachys* "thick" + *derma* "skin."] —**pach·y·der·mal** /páki dúrm'l/ *adj.*

pach·y·der·ma·tous /pàki dúrmətəss/ *adj.* **1. RESEMBLING A PACHYDERM** having the thick skin or some other physical characteristic typical of a pachyderm **2. EMOTIONALLY THICK-SKINNED** insensitive to other people and unworried by criticism or attack (*literary or humorous*) [Early 19thC. Ultimately from Greek *pakhus* "thick" + *dermat-,* stem of *derma* "skin."]

pach·y·san·dra /pàki sándrə/ (*plural* **-dras** *or* **-dra**) *n.* a low-growing shrubby evergreen plant of the box family with toothed leaves and tiny white flowers, often used as ground cover. Genus: *Pachysandra.* [Early 19thC. From modern Latin (genus name), from Greek *pakhus* "thick" + *andr-* "man, male" (see ANDRO-); from the thick stamens.]

pach·y·tene /páki teen/ *n.* BIOL the third stage of cell division, during which the paired chromosomes become shorter and thicker and divide into four chromatids [Early 20thC. From French *pachytène,* from Greek *pakhus* "thick" + French *-tène* "ribbon" (from, ultimately, Greek *tainia*).]

Pacif. *abbr.* Pacific

pa·cif·ic /pə síffik/ *adj.* **1. BRINGING PEACE** leading to or promoting peace and an end to conflict **2. HAVING A**

PEACEFUL TEMPERAMENT calm and peaceful by nature **3. UNAGGRESSIVE** avoiding the use of force [Mid-16thC. Directly or via French *pacifique* from Latin *pacificus*, from *pac-*, stem of *pax* "peace" (see PEACE).]

Pa·cif·ic *n.* **PACIFIC OCEAN** the Pacific Ocean ■ *adj.* **RELATING TO THE PACIFIC OCEAN** relating to the Pacific Ocean, or to the territories that surround it or are surrounded by it

pac·i·fi·ca·tion /pàssifi káysh'n/ *n.* **1. PROCESS OF PACIFYING** the process of bringing about peace by calming somebody or putting an end to conflict **2.** MIL **ESTABLISHMENT OF AN ENFORCED PEACE** the use of military force or other measures to eradicate rebellion and restore an area to peace and government control

Pa·cif·ic North·west *n.* a region of the northwest United States on the Pacific coast that includes the states of Washington and Oregon and sometimes southwestern British Columbia, Canada

Pa·cif·ic O·cean the largest ocean in the world, stretching from the Arctic Ocean in the north to Antarctica in the south, and from North and South America in the east to eastern Asia, the Malay Archipelago, and Australia in the west. Its deepest point is the Mariana Trench, 35,840 ft./10,924 m. Area: 64,000,000 sq. mi./165,000,000 sq. km.

Pa·cif·ic Rim *n.* the countries that border the Pacific, especially the countries of East Asia, considered as a political or economic unit

Pa·cif·ic Rim Na·tion·al Park Re·serve national park in western Canada divided into three sections along the western coast of Vancouver Island, British Columbia. It also extends offshore to protect the marine environment. Area: 110 sq. mi./285 sq. km.

Pa·cif·ic Stan·dard Time, Pa·cif·ic Time *n.* the standard time for the western coastal regions of North America, one hour behind Mountain Time and eight hours behind Greenwich Mean Time

pac·i·fi·er /pássə fìr/ *n.* **1. SOMEBODY OR SOMETHING THAT PACIFIES** somebody or something that calms a person or situation **2.** BABYWARE **NIPPLE-SHAPED OBJECT THAT BABIES SUCK** an object made of rubber or plastic in the shape of a nipple or ring for a baby to suck on

pac·i·fism /pássə fìzzəm/ *n.* **1. BELIEF IN THE PEACEFUL RESOLUTION OF CONFLICTS** a belief that violence, war, and the taking of lives are unacceptable ways of resolving disputes **2. REFUSAL TO PARTICIPATE IN WAR** the refusal to take up arms or participate in war because of moral or religious beliefs **3.** POL **BELIEF IN DIPLOMACY OVER WAR** a belief that international conflicts should be settled by negotiation rather than war

pac·i·fist /pássəfist/ *n.* **1. BELIEVER IN PACIFISM** somebody who believes in, advocates, or practices pacifism **2. CONSCIENTIOUS OBJECTOR** somebody who refuses to perform military service or take part in a war ■ *adj.* **SUPPORTING PACIFISM** believing in, advocating, or practicing pacifism —**pac·i·fis·tic** /pàssə fístik/ *adj.* —**pac·i·fis·ti·cal·ly** /-fístikəlee/ *adv.*

pac·i·fy /pássə fì/ (**-fied, -fy·ing, -fies**) *vt.* **1. CALM** to calm somebody who is angry or agitated, or soothe violent or angry feelings **2.** MIL **BRING PEACE TO** to bring peace to an area, people, or situation, often by using military force to end conflict or unrest [15thC. Directly or via French *pacifier* from Latin *pacificare*, literally "to make peace," from *pac-*, stem of *pax* "peace" (see PEACE).] —**pac·i·fi·a·ble** /pássə fì əb'l, pàssə fí əb'l/ *adj.*

Pa·cin·i·an cor·pus·cle /pə sìnnee ən-/ *n.* a pressure-sensitive nerve ending resembling a tiny white onion that is connected to the end of nerve fibers in the skin, especially of the hands and feet, and in connective tissue [Mid-19thC. Named for Filippo *Pacini* 1812–83, an Italian anatomist.]

Pa·ci·no /pə cheénō/, **Al** (*b.* 1940) U.S. actor. He starred in *The Godfather* movies and won an Academy Award for *Scent of a Woman* (1992). Full name **Alfredo Pacino**

pack[1] /pak/ *n.* **1. COLLECTION OF THINGS IN A PACKAGE** a set of documents or other materials relating to a subject that are packaged together ○ *a free information pack* **2. COMMERCIAL CONTAINER** a container or piece of packaging holding several products or items of the same kind, or such a container and its contents ○ *a pack of matches* **3. AMOUNT CONTAINED IN A PACK** the contents of a pack, or the amount of something that can be contained in a pack **4. AMOUNT OF FOOD PRESERVED** an amount of food canned or preserved in a particular year or season **5. LARGE AMOUNT** a large amount of something ○ *a pack of lies* **6. GROUP OF ANIMALS** a group of animals that live and hunt together, especially wolves or dogs ○ *a pack of wolves* **7. LARGE GROUP OF PEOPLE ACTING TOGETHER** a group of people who behave in the same way, especially a group whose behavior appears to be threatening, predatory, or criminal ○ *always followed by a pack of photographers* **8. GROUP OF CUB SCOUTS** a local organized unit of Cub Scouts **9.** SPORTS **MAIN BODY OF COMPETITORS** the main body of competitors in a race or competition **10. SET OF CARDS** a set of 52 playing cards ○ *a pack of cards* **11. BAG CARRIED ON THE BACK** a bag or bundle, especially one designed to be carried on a person's or animal's back **12. PARACHUTE IN A CONTAINER** a parachute, rigged, folded, and in its container ready for use **13.** = **pack ice 14.** MED **COMPRESS USED IN SURGERY** a wad of soft absorbent material applied to a wound or temporarily inserted into a body cavity to control bleeding or keep tissues dry during surgery **15.** MED **MEDICINAL COMPRESS** a compress placed on the body for medicinal purposes **16. COSMETIC PASTE** a quantity of moist material applied to part of the body, especially the face, for cosmetic purposes ○ *a mud pack* **17.** MIL **GROUP OF SUBMARINES OR AIRCRAFT** a number of submarines, aircraft, or other military units who hunt and fight the enemy as a group **18. SOLDIER'S BAG FOR EQUIPMENT** a soldier's canvas or nylon bag with shoulder straps used to carry personal clothing and equipment in the field ■ *v.* (**packed, pack·ing, packs**) **1.** *vti.* **PUT BELONGINGS INTO A CONTAINER** to put personal belongings into a bag or other container for transportation **2.** *vti.* **PUT PRODUCTS IN CONTAINERS** to put something into a container or fill a container with something for sale, transport, or storage **3.** *vt.* **MAKE SOMETHING INTO A PACKAGE OR BUNDLE** to make up a package or bundle, or to wrap or roll something up in one **4.** *vt.* **FILL SOMETHING WITH A LARGE QUANTITY** to fill something, especially a limited space, tightly (*often passive*) ○ *a book packed with useful information* **5.** *vti.* **CROWD INTO OR FILL A PLACE** to crowd into a place so that it is full or overfull, or to fill a place with people **6.** *vt.* **FIT SOMETHING INTO A LIMITED TIME** to fit many different activities or events into a limited period of time ○ *packed a lot of sightseeing into one weekend* **7.** *vt.* COMPUT = **compress** *v.* 3 **8.** *vti.* **COMPACT SOMETHING OR BECOME COMPACTED** to compact a substance such as snow or soil into a dense mass, or to become densely compacted **9.** *vt.* **PRESS SOMETHING AROUND AN OBJECT** to wrap or press something in around an object to hold it firmly or protect it **10.** *vt.* MED **USE A PACK ON A WOUND** to apply a medical pack to a wound or insert one into a body cavity **11.** *vt.* MED **APPLY A COMPRESS TO A BODY PART** to apply cold compresses to part of a patient's body in order to control body temperature **12.** *vt.* MECH ENG **SEAL SOMETHING TO PREVENT LEAKAGE** to seal a mechanical joint by inserting a layer of compressible material between the moving parts to prevent leakage of fluid **13.** *vt.* MECH ENG **FILL A CAVITY WITH GREASE** to fill a cavity containing bearings with grease **14.** *vti.* **CARRY A GUN** to carry a weapon, especially a gun (*informal*) **15.** *vt.* **POSSESS SOMETHING AS A FORCEFUL CAPABILITY** to be capable of delivering something that has a powerful or devastating effect (*informal*) **16.** *vt.* **LOAD BAGGAGE ONTO AN ANIMAL** to put goods or belongings onto a horse, donkey, or other animal in order to transport them **17.** *vti.* **CARRY A LOAD** to carry a load [12thC. From Dutch or Low German *pakken* (noun of uncertain origin: probably from Flemish, Dutch, or Low German *pak*).] —**pack·a·ble** *adj.* ◇ **send somebody packing** to dismiss or send somebody away brusquely and unceremoniously (*informal*)

pack away *vt.* **1. STORE AWAY** to put things into storage containers after use or for reuse at a later time **2. EAT IN LARGE QUANTITIES** to eat food in large quantities (*informal*)

pack in *v.* **1.** *vt.* **ATTRACT IN LARGE NUMBERS** to attract very large audiences ○ *The show has been running three years and is still packing them in night after night.* **2.** *vti.* **STOP DOING SOMETHING** to stop or give up doing something (*informal*) ○ *She's packed in her job.* ◇ **pack it in** to stop doing something (*informal*)

pack off *v.* **1.** *vt.* **SEND UNCEREMONIOUSLY** to send somebody away unceremoniously to another place (*informal*) ○ *They traded him for a shortstop, and he was packed off to the Blue Sox.* **2.** *vi.* *U.K.* **GO SOMEWHERE UNCEREMONIOUSLY** to leave or to go somewhere hastily or unceremoniously ○ *They packed off home as soon as the work was done.*

pack up *v.* **1.** *vti.* **STOP DOING SOMETHING** to stop doing something **2.** *vi.* **FINISH WORK** to finish work for the day (*informal*) ○ *I'm packing up and going home.*

pack[2] /pak/ (**packed, pack·ing, packs**) *vt.* to ensure that a group such as a jury or committee is made up wholly or mainly of supporters of a particular side [Early 16thC. Origin uncertain: probably an alteration of PACT with the idea of private or secret dealings.]

pack·age /pákij/ *n.* **1. PARCEL** an object or set of objects, wrapped, boxed, or tied in a bundle for transportation or mailing **2. PACKAGING FOR GOODS** a container made of cardboard, plastic, foil, or other material in which goods are packed for sale, storage, or transportation, or a container of this type together with its contents ○ *a package of chewing gum* **3. DIFFERENT THINGS CONSTITUTING A SINGLE ITEM** a number of different components intended to constitute a single item **4.** COMPUT **PIECE OF GENERAL ADAPTABLE COMPUTER SOFTWARE** a piece of computer software that can be used for a range of related purposes, such as word-processing or financial analysis **5.** = **package tour** ■ *vt.* (**-aged, -ag·ing, -ages**) **1. PUT SOMETHING INTO PACKAGE** to put things into or wrap them up as a package **2. PRODUCE ATTRACTIVE PACKAGING FOR SOMETHING** to create suitable or attractive packaging in which a product is to be sold **3. PROMOTE OR PRESENT SOMETHING** to present somebody or something to others in a way intended to ensure appeal and acceptance ○ *It wasn't so much the policy that was wrong as the way it was packaged.* **4. GROUP SOMETHING AS A PACKAGE** to group or offer several different items together in a package **5.** PUBL, BROADCAST **PRODUCE SOMETHING FOR OTHERS TO MARKET** to produce a book or television program or series in finished form ready to be published or broadcast by another company

pack·age deal *n.* a proposal or agreement comprising a number of different items that must all be accepted together

pack·age hol·i·day *n.* *U.K.* = **package tour**

pack·ag·er /pákijər/ *n.* **1. SOMEBODY OR SOMETHING THAT PACKS GOODS** a person or machine that packs or wraps goods for sale, storage, or transport **2.** PUBL, BROADCAST **SUBCONTRACTED PRODUCER OF BOOKS OR PROGRAMS** a company that produces books or television programs in finished form for another company to publish or broadcast

pack·age store *n.* = **liquor store**

pack·age tour *n.* a tour organized in advance by a travel company to whom the vacationer or tourist pays a single fee covering transportation, accommodations, meals, and often entertainment

pack·ag·ing /pákijing/ *n.* **1. WRAPPING OR CONTAINER** the wrapping or container in which an item is presented for sale, or the materials used to make it **2. DESIGN OR STYLE OF WRAPPING** the design or style of the wrapping or container in which something is offered for sale, especially from the point of view of its appeal to buyers **3. PRESENTATION** the manner in which something or somebody is presented to the public in order to create a favorable image or impression

pack an·i·mal *n.* an animal that is used to carry goods or equipment, e.g., a horse, donkey, or mule

packed /pakt/ *adj.* **1. FULL OF PEOPLE** full of people and extremely crowded ○ *played to a packed house every night* **2. CONTAINING A LOT OF SOMETHING** containing or offering something in excitingly large quantities (*often used in combination*) ○ *a fun-packed adventure* **3. COMPRESSED** pressed together to form a compact mass ○ *packed snow*

packed lunch *n.* *U.K.* = **box lunch**

pack·er /pákər/ *n.* **1. SOMEBODY OR SOMETHING THAT PACKS GOODS** a person or machine that packs goods in containers or in packaging **2. WHOLESALE PROCESSOR OF MEAT** a person or company involved in the processing and packing of goods, especially meat or fresh produce, for the wholesale market

pack·et /pákət/ *n.* **1. SMALL CONTAINER FOR GOODS** a small box, envelope, or bag in which goods are sold or stored **2. CONTENTS OR QUANTITY IN PACKET** the contents of a packet, or the quantity of goods contained in a packet ○ *At least four packets of seeds never produced flowers.* **3. SMALL PARCEL** a small parcel or bundle or package **4.** COMPUT **MESSAGE FRAGMENT IN A COMPUTER NETWORK** a small piece of a message for transmission through a computer network **5. pack·et, pack·et boat BOAT ON A REGULAR SHORT RUN** a small ship that provides a regular service carrying passengers, freight, and mail over a fixed short route ■ *vt.* (**-et·ed, -et·ing, -ets**) PUT SOMETHING IN A PACKET to put something into a packet or wrap it up as a package [15thC. Origin uncertain: probably literally "small pack," formed from PACK[1] (perhaps on the model of Anglo-Norman *pacquet*).]

pack·et switch·ing *n.* the process of transmitting and routing data in the form of packet segments sent rapidly and sequentially over a channel that is occupied only during the actual transmission of data

pack·frame /pák fràym/ *n.* a lightweight frame with shoulder straps to which equipment or unwieldy loads can be strapped to be carried on a person's back

pack·horse /pák hàwrs/ *n.* a horse used for carrying goods or equipment

pack ice *n.* floating ice, especially in polar regions, that has formed itself into a solid mass covering a wide area

pack·ing /páking/ *n.* **1.** ACT OF PUTTING THINGS INTO CONTAINERS the task of putting things into containers, usually for storage or transport **2.** MATERIAL FOR PROTECTING A PACKED OBJECT material used to surround and protect something packed inside a container **3.** WATERTIGHT OR AIRTIGHT MATERIAL material used to fill or surround something such as a joint in a pipe in order to make it watertight or airtight **4.** FOOD TECH PROCESSING AND PACKAGING OF FOOD the processing and packaging of food such as meat or produce for sale **5.** MED ABSORBENT MATERIAL FOR MEDICAL PACKS absorbent material such as gauze for insertion in body cavities or wounds **6.** MECH ENG SPACERS BETWEEN CLAMPED SURFACES shims, washers, or other pieces of metal used to adjust the distance between component surfaces before they are secured

pack·ing frac·tion *n.* a measure of the stability of an atomic nucleus, arrived at by dividing the difference between its mass in atomic mass units and its mass number by that mass number

pack·ing·house (*plural* **-hous·es**) *n.* **1.** COMPANY THAT PROCESSES MEAT a company that slaughters, processes, and packages meat and meat products **2.** FOOD PROCESSING COMPANY a company that processes and packs food other than meat

pack·man /pák màn, pákmən/ (*plural* **-men** /-mèn, -mən/) *n.* = **peddler**

pack rat *n.* **1.** WOOD RAT THAT COLLECTS OBJECTS a North American rat that lives in woodlands and collects and carries away objects to its nest. The best-known species has a long bushy tail and cheek pouches. Latin name: *Neotoma cinerea.* **2.** SOMEBODY WHO HOARDS OBJECTS somebody who collects a large number of objects and never gets rid of any of them (*informal*)

pack·sack /pák sàk/ *n.* a bag with shoulder straps that can be carried on the back

pack·sad·dle /pák sàdd'l/ *n.* a saddle for carrying loads on a pack animal

pack·thread /pák thrèd/ *n.* strong twine used for sewing up packages wrapped in sacking or other fabric

pack train *n.* a line of pack animals carrying loads

pact /pakt/ *n.* an agreement made between two or more groups or individuals, either formally or informally, to do something together or for each other [15thC. Via French *pacte* from Latin *pactum*, a form of *pactus*, past participle of *pacisci* "to agree."]

pad[1] /pad/ *n.* **1.** PIECE OF SOFT MATERIAL a piece of soft material used to protect something or give it shape, to clean or polish articles, or to absorb moisture **2.** SPORTS PROTECTIVE MATERIAL WORN BY SPORTS PLAYERS a specially shaped covering of impact-absorbing material used to protect part of the body, especially when playing a sport **3.** BLOCK OF PAPER SHEETS a number of sheets of paper of the same size fastened together along one edge **4.** INK-FILLED MATERIAL a thick firm piece of material saturated with ink onto which a rubber stamp is pressed so that ink is transferred onto it **5.** AIR AREA FOR TAKING OFF AND LANDING a place where a helicopter can land and take off or from which a rocket is launched **6.** SANITARY NAPKIN a strip of absorbent material used externally during menstruation **7.** BACKING MATERIAL a firm backing or support for something that is laid on a surface **8.** ZOOL FLESHY CUSHION OF AN ANIMAL'S PAW a small rounded fleshy cushion on the underside of an animal's paw **9.** ANAT FLESHY TIP OF A FINGER OR TOE the rounded fleshy part at the end of a human finger or toe **10.** LIVING QUARTERS somebody's apartment or house (*slang dated*) **11.** BOT WATER LILY LEAF the broad leaf of an aquatic plant such as a water lily that floats on the surface of the water **12.** ELEC ENG SET OF RESISTORS a fixed configuration of resistors designed to reduce the strength of an electrical signal without distorting the signal itself ■ *vt.* (**pad·ded, pad·ding, pads**) **1.** LINE OR COVER SOMETHING WITH SOFT MATERIAL to use soft material to give something shape, to make it more comfortable, or to protect it **2.** ADD UNNECESSARY MATERIAL TO SOMETHING to add unnecessary material to something, especially a piece of writing or a speech, in order to lengthen it ○ *padded out the speech with anecdotes* **3.** INFLATE SOMETHING BY ADDING BOGUS EXPENSES to add extra charges to a bill or expense account to make it higher than it should be [Mid-16thC. Origin uncertain: perhaps from a Low Dutch word. Originally "bundle of straw."]

pad[2] /pad/ *vti.* (**pad·ded, pad·ding, pads**) WALK QUIETLY to walk, or to walk along or through somewhere, with soft or silent steps ○ *She padded along in her slippers.* ■ *n.* **1.** SOUND OF FOOTSTEPS the sound of soft steady footsteps **2.** FOOTPAD a footpad (*archaic*) **3.** EQU SLOW HORSE a horse that goes at a slow ambling gait [Mid-16thC. Origin uncertain: perhaps from Low German *padden* "to tread" (noun from Low German or Dutch *pad* "path").]

pad·ded cell *n.* formerly, a room in a psychiatric hospital with its walls and floor covered with padding to prevent a patient from doing himself or herself physical harm

pad·ding /pádding/ *n.* **1.** THICK SOFT MATERIAL thick soft material used as a protective lining or covering or to fill and give shape to things **2.** UNNECESSARY ADDITIONS TO SPEECH OR WRITING unnecessary or irrelevant material added to a piece of writing or speech to make it longer **3.** BOGUS ADDITIONS TO BILL extra charges added to a bill or expense account to make it higher than it should be

pad·dle[1] /pádd'l/ *n.* **1.** NAUT SHORT FLAT-BLADED OAR a short oar with a flat blade at one or both ends used to propel a canoe or small boat **2.** NAUT BLADE OF A PADDLE WHEEL a blade of a paddle wheel **3.** RACKET GAMES TABLE TENNIS RACKET a round wooden racket with a short handle used in table tennis **4.** PIECE OF WOOD FOR SPANKING a usually short piece of wood with a flattened end used for physical punishment **5.** ZOOL = **flipper** *n.* 1 **6.** FLAT-BLADED STIRRING TOOL a tool with a flat blade used for shaping, stirring, or beating **7.** VIDEO EARLY INPUT DEVICE FOR VIDEO GAMES an input device for early video games with a dial that allowed the user to move an on-screen object either up and down or from side to side ■ *v.* (**-dled, -dling, -dles**) **1.** *vti.* NAUT PROPEL A CANOE WITH A PADDLE to propel a canoe or small boat through water using a paddle **2.** *vt.* NAUT CARRY IN A CANOE to carry somebody or something somewhere in a canoe or paddleboat **3.** *vti.* ROW AT AN EASY PACE to row a boat at an easy pace **4.** *vt.* SPANK to spank somebody with a paddle or with the hand **5.** *vt.* STIR WITH PADDLE to stir, beat, or shape something using a paddle [15thC. Origin uncertain: perhaps via medieval Latin *padela* from Latin *patella* "small dish," from *patina* "shallow dish" (source of English *patina*).] —**pad·dler** *n.*

pad·dle[2] /pádd'l/ (**-dled, -dling, -dles**) *v.* **1.** *vti.* DABBLE IN WATER to move the hands or feet about gently in shallow water **2.** *vi.* WADDLE to walk along unsteadily like a very small child [Mid-16thC. Origin uncertain: perhaps from a Low Dutch word.] —**pad·dler** *n.*

pad·dle·ball /pádd'l bàwl/ *n.* a game for 2 to 4 players played by hitting a ball against a wall with small paddles, or the ball used in this game

pad·dle·board /pádd'l bàwrd/ *n.* a long narrow surfboard used especially in rescuing swimmers

pad·dle·boat /pádd'l bōt/ *n.* a boat propelled by one or more paddle wheels

pad·dle·fish /pádd'l fìsh/ (*plural* **-fish·es** *or* **-fish**) *n.* a large freshwater fish with a long flat snout and a cartilage skeleton, found in the Mississippi River and its tributaries and in the Yangtze River. Family: Polyodontidae.

pad·dle steam·er *n.* *U.K.* = **paddle wheeler**

pad·dle wheel *n.* a wheel with flat blades fixed all around its edge, attached to the hull of a ship and usually turned by an engine to propel the ship through water

pad·dle wheel·er *n.* a steamship that is moved through the water by a paddle wheel

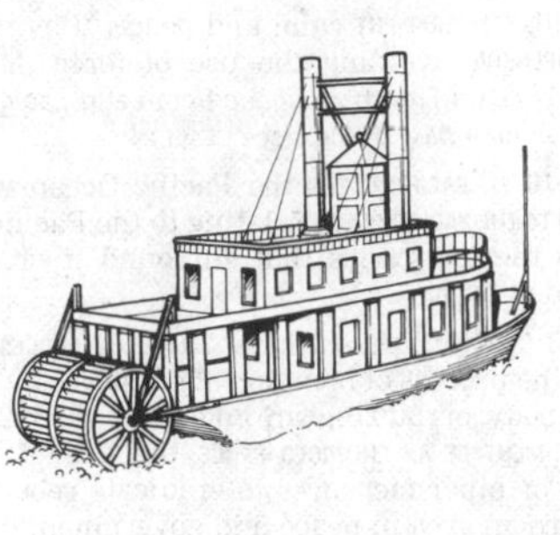

Paddle wheeler

pad·dock /páddək/ *n.* **1.** EQU ENCLOSED FIELD FOR HORSES a small field near a house or stable with grazing for horses **2.** EQU AREA FOR MOUNTING RACEHORSES an area on a racetrack where the racehorses are paraded before a race and the jockeys mount **3.** MOTOR SPORTS AREA FOR CARS BEFORE A RACE an area near the pits on a automobile racetrack where cars are worked on before a race ■ *vt.* (**-docked, -dock·ing, -docks**) EQU KEEP HORSES IN PADDOCK to keep animals, especially horses, in a paddock [Early 17thC. Alteration of *parro(c)k*, from Old English *pearroc* "fence, enclosed land," from a prehistoric Germanic word perhaps from assumed Vulgar Latin *parricus* (source of English *park*).]

pad·dy /páddee/ (*plural* **-dies**) *n.* **1.** RICE FIELD a field, usually kept covered with shallow water, in which rice is grown **2.** RICE rice as a crop in the field or when harvested but not yet processed [Early 17thC. From Malay *padi*.]

Pad·dy (*plural* **-dies**) *n.* an offensive term for an Irish person or somebody of Irish ancestry (*slang insult*) [Late 18thC. From the pet form of Irish *Pádraig* "Patrick."]

pad·dy wag·on *n.* *U.S., ANZ* a patrol wagon (*informal*) [Late 19thC. *Paddy* is said to have originally referred to Irish policemen in New York and New England.]

pad·lock /pád lòk/ *n.* SMALL DETACHABLE LOCK a detachable lock with a movable semicircular bar at the top, the free end of which is usually passed through a hasp and then locked shut ■ *vt.* (**-locked, -lock·ing, -locks**) LOCK SOMETHING WITH A PADLOCK to secure something using a padlock [15thC. *Pad-* is of unknown origin.]

pa·dre /paá drày, paádree/ *n.* **1.** USED TO ADDRESS A PRIEST used to address or refer to a Roman Catholic priest of a Spanish-speaking church in the United States, or in a country where Spanish, Italian, or Portuguese is spoken **2.** MIL CHRISTIAN CHAPLAIN IN THE ARMED FORCES a Christian cleric who ministers to the armed forces (*informal*) [Late 16thC. Via Italian, Spanish, or Portuguese from Latin *pater* "father" (source of English *patron*).]

pa·dro·ne /pə drṓ này, -drṓnee/ (*plural* **-nes** *or* **-ni** /-drṓnee/) *n.* **1.** ITALIAN OWNER OR MANAGER the owner or manager of an Italian business, especially a restaurant or café **2.** MAN WHO HIRES ITALIAN IMMIGRANTS a man who hires Italian immigrants to work for him, especially one who then exploits them [Late 17thC. Via Italian from Latin *patronus* "protector, patron," from *pater* (see PADRE).] —**pa·dro·nism** /pə drṓnee ìzzəm/ *n.*

pad·saw /pád sàw/ *n.* = **keyhole saw** [Late 19thC. *Pad* from PAD[1] in the sense "handle into which different tools can be fitted."]

Pad·u·a /pájjə wə/ city in northeastern Italy, and the capital of Padua Province, Veneto Region. Population: 213,656 (1992).

pad·u·a·soy /pájjoo ə sòy/ *n.* a rich heavy silk fabric [Late 16thC. Alteration (influenced by *Padua say* "cloth from *Padua*," Italian city known for textile manufacturing) of French *pou-de-soie* "pou of silk" (from Old French *pout*, of unknown origin).]

Pa·du·cah /pə dóokə/ city in western Kentucky, directly west of the confluence of the Tennessee and Ohio rivers. Population: 26,601 (1996).

pae·an /peé ən/, **pe·an** *n.* a written, spoken, or musical expression of enthusiastic praise or rapturous joy [Late 16thC. Via Latin, "religious hymn (originally in honor of Apollo)," from Greek *paian*, from *Paian* "name for Apollo."]

paed- *prefix.* *U.K.* = **paedo-** (*used before vowels*)

pae·di·at·rics *n.* U.K. = **pediatrics** —**pae·di·atric** *adj.* —**pae·di·a·tri·cian** *n.* —**pae·di·at·rist** *n.*

paedo- *prefix.* U.K. = **pedo-**

paed·o·phil·i·a *n.* U.K. = **pedophilia** —**paed·o·phile** *n.*

pa·el·la /paa áy àa, paa éllə/ *n.* a Spanish dish made of saffron-flavored rice with chicken, shellfish, and other ingredients that vary from region to region [Late 19thC. Via Catalan from, ultimately, Latin *patella* "small dish," from *patina* "shallow dish."]

pae·on /pée ən, pée òn/ *n.* a metrical foot consisting of one long and three short syllables arranged in any order [Early 17thC. Via Latin from Greek *paiōn*, variant of *paian* (see PAEAN).]

Paes·tum /péstəm, péestəm/ ancient city in southern Italy, noted for its Greek ruins

Pá·ez /páa ess/, **José Antonio** (1790–1873) Venezuelan revolutionary leader and statesman. He served as the first president of independent Venezuela (1831–35, 1838–43, 1846–47).

pa·gan /páygən/ *n.* **1.** FOLLOWER OF A LESS POPULAR RELIGION somebody who does not follow one of the world's main religions, especially somebody who is not a Christian, Muslim, or Jew, and whose religion is regarded as questionable (*sometimes considered offensive*) **2.** POLYTHEIST OR PANTHEIST a follower of an ancient polytheistic or pantheistic religion **3.** HEATHEN somebody who has no religion (*disapproving*) ■ *adj.* **1.** OF A LESS POPULAR RELIGION believing in or relating to a religion that is not one of the world's main religions and is regarded as questionable **2.** FOLLOWING POLYTHEISTIC OR PANTHEISTIC RELIGION believing in or relating to an ancient polytheistic or pantheistic religion **3.** NONRELIGIOUS having no religion (*sometimes considered offensive*) [14thC. Via late Latin *paganus* from Latin, "villager, civilian," from *pagus* "rural district" (source of English *peasant*).] —**pa·gan·ish** *adj.* —**pa·gan·ism** *n.* —**pa·gan·is·tic** /páygə nístik/ *adj.*

WORD KEY: ORIGIN

The Latin word *pagus*, from which ***pagan*** is derived, originally meant "something stuck in the ground as a landmark." It was extended metaphorically to "rural district, village," and the noun *paganus* was derived from it, denoting "country dweller, villager." This shifted in meaning, first to "civilian," and then (based on the early Christian notion that all members of the Church were "soldiers" of Christ) to "heathen."

Pa·ga·ni·ni /pàggə néenee/, **Niccolò** (1782–1840) Italian composer and violinist. Renowned as a virtuoso, his compositions include violin sonatas, caprices for solo violin, and concertos.

page[1] /payj/ *n.* **1.** ONE SIDE OF SHEET OF PAPER one side of a single sheet of paper, especially one bound into a book, newspaper, or magazine, or forming part of a piece of written work **2.** SINGLE SHEET IN A BOOK a single sheet of paper, especially one bound into a book, newspaper, or magazine ○ *a book with some pages missing* **3.** AMOUNT OF WRITING ON A PAGE the amount of writing or printed matter that can be contained on a page **4.** COMPUT COMPUTER DATA PRINTING OUT AS A PAGE the amount of text or graphics in a computer document that will print out as a single page **5.** COMPUT SCREENFUL OF COMPUTER DISPLAY the portion of text or graphics that can be seen on a computer screen at one time **6.** NOTEWORTHY PERIOD OR EVENT a period or event, especially a noteworthy one, in the history of something or somebody's life ○ *Antibiotics wrote an important page in the history of medical research.* ■ *v.* **(paged, pag·ing, pag·es) 1.** *vi.* LOOK THROUGH PAGES to turn and look over the pages of something **2.** *vt.* = **paginate** [Late 16thC. From French, shortening of *pagene*, from Latin *pagina*, literally "(strips of papyrus) fastened together."]

page[2] /payj/ *n.* **1.** BOY ATTENDANT a youth acting as an attendant to somebody on a ceremonial occasion, e.g., to a bride at her wedding **2.** BOY WHO RUNS ERRANDS a youth employed to run errands or carry messages for guests in a hotel or club **3.** POL ERRAND RUNNER IN U.S. CONGRESS somebody who is employed to run errands, carry messages, act as a guide, and perform other duties in the U.S. Congress **4.** HIST BOY SERVANT IN MEDIEVAL TIMES a youth who acted as a personal or household servant to somebody, especially a royal or noble person, in medieval times **5.** HIST BOY APPRENTICED TO KNIGHT a youth who acted as the personal servant to a knight in medieval times as the first stage of his training to become a knight ■ *vt.* **(paged, pag·ing, pag·es) 1.** SUMMON SOMEBODY BY NAME to summon somebody by calling out his or her name, e.g., over a loudspeaker system **2.** CONTACT SOMEBODY ON A BEEPER to try to contact somebody on his or her beeper or pager **3.** HIST SERVE SOMEBODY AS PAGE to serve somebody in the capacity of page [13thC. From French, of uncertain origin: perhaps ultimately from Greek *paidion* "little child, slave-boy," from *paid-* (see PEDO-).]

pag·eant /pájjənt/ *n.* **1.** LARGE-SCALE PLAY REPRESENTING A HISTORICAL EVENT a large-scale stage production representing historical or legendary events, especially local ones, in scenes or tableaux in which dramatic interest is less important than spectacle **2.** ELABORATE AND COLORFUL PROCESSION an elaborate and colorful procession, display, or ceremonial occasion [14thC. Alteration of earlier *pagyn* "scene, stage," from Anglo-Latin *pagina*, of uncertain origin: perhaps from Latin, "page, leaf" (see PAGE[1]).]

pag·eant·ry /pájjəntree/ *n.* **1.** MAGNIFICENT CEREMONIAL DISPLAY highly colorful, splendid, and stately display or ceremonies, usually with a historical or traditional flavor **2.** PAGEANTS pageants considered collectively (*archaic*)

page·boy /páyj bòy/ *n.* **1.** = **page**[2] *n.* 1 **2.** HAIR BOBBED HAIRSTYLE WITH BANGS a hairstyle in which the hair is cut to one length, usually jaw-length, and curls under slightly at the ends, with bangs at the front

page break *n.* a code or symbol on a computer screen that shows where a printer will start a new page, e.g., in a wordprocessing document

pag·er /páyjər/ *n.* a small electronic message-receiving device, often with a small screen, that beeps, flashes, or vibrates to let the user know that somebody is trying to contact him or her

Pag·et's dis·ease /pájjəts-/ *n.* **1.** BONE DISEASE a chronic disease in which the bones become enlarged and weakened and subject to fracture **2.** CANCEROUS CONDITION OF THE BREAST a cancerous inflammatory condition of the nipple and areola, associated with breast cancer [Late 19thC. Named for Sir James *Paget* (1814–99), English surgeon and pathologist who described these diseases.]

page-turn·er *n.* a book with a very gripping plot

pag·i·nal /pájjən'l/ *adj.* **1.** PUBL DUPLICATING PAGE FOR PAGE exactly duplicating a previous edition or version, so that the same text appears on the same page in both **2.** RELATING TO PAGES consisting of, relating to, or like a page or pages [Mid-17thC. From late Latin *paginalis*, from Latin *pagina* (see PAGE[1]).]

pag·i·nate /pájjə nàyt/ **(-nat·ed, -nat·ing, -nates)** *vt.* to number the pages of a book or computer document [Late 19thC. Origin uncertain: probably a back-formation from PAGINATION.]

pag·i·na·tion /pàjjə náysh'n/ *n.* **1.** PAGE NUMBERS the sequential numbers given to pages in a book or document **2.** ACT OF NUMBERING PAGES the process or work of numbering pages [Mid-19thC. From French, from Latin *pagina* (see PAGE[1]).]

pag·ing /páyjing/ *n.* the movement of a fixed-size block of data between faster main and slower auxiliary memories to optimize performance without the user being aware that the transfer has taken place

Pag·li·a /páylee ə/, **Camille** (*b.* 1947) U.S. writer. Her books, which mainly examine art and culture, take a controversial antifeminist position. Full name **Camille Anna Paglia**

Pagoda

pa·go·da /pə gṓdə/ *n.* **1.** EASTERN RELIG BUDDHIST TEMPLE WITH PROJECTING ROOFS a Buddhist temple building, especially one in the form of a tower with several stories, each with an upward curving roof that tapers slightly toward the top **2.** ARCHIT BUILDING DESIGNED LIKE A BUDDHIST PAGODA a building that is shaped like a Buddhist pagoda but has a decorative rather than a religious purpose [Late 16thC. From Portuguese *pagode*, of uncertain origin: perhaps ultimately from Persian *butkada*, literally "idol dwelling," but altered by association with Prakrit *bhagodī* "holy."]

pah /paa/ *interj.* used to show disgust, contempt, or annoyance [Late 16thC. Natural exclamation.]

Pah·la·vi /páala vee/, **Peh·le·vi** /páylə vee/ *n.* a literary form of classical Persian used especially in Zoroastrian and Manichean texts [Late 18thC. From Persian *pahlawī*, from *pahlav*, from *parthava* "Parthia (country of ancient Asia)."]

Pah·la·vi /páalə vee/, **Muhammad Reza Shah, Shah of Iran** (1919–80). During his reign (1941–79) he attempted to modernize and westernize Iran, but his dictatorial rule made him unpopular. He was overthrown in the 1979 Islamic revolution.

Pah·la·vi, Reza Shah, Shah of Iran (1877–1944). He seized power in a coup (1921) and became shah (1925). He initiated westernization, and abdicated in favor of his son (1941).

paid past participle, past tense of **pay** ■ *adj.* GIVEN MONEY OR EARNING MONEY given money in return for work, or done for the purpose of earning money

paid-up *adj.* **1.** NOT OWING ANYTHING having paid all the money owed to an organization or individual (*not hyphenated after a verb*) **2.** FULLY PAID FOR for which the full price or all installments have been paid (*not hyphenated when used after a verb*) ○ *a paid-up membership*

pail /payl/ *n.* a bucket [14thC. From Old French *paielle* "warming pan, liquid measure," of uncertain origin: perhaps from Latin *patella* "small dish" (see PAELLA).]

pail·lasse *n.* a thin straw-filled mattress [Early 16thC. Via French from Italian *pagliacchio*, from, ultimately, Latin *palea* "straw, chaff."]

pail·lette /pī yétt/ *n.* a sequin or spangle sewn onto a piece of clothing [Mid-19thC. From French, literally "small straw," from *paille* "straw, chaff," from Latin *palea* (see PAILLASSE).]

pain /páyn/ *n.* **1.** UNPLEASANT PHYSICAL SENSATION the acutely unpleasant physical discomfort experienced by somebody who is violently struck, injured, or ill in certain ways ○ *cried out in pain* **2.** FEELING OF DISCOMFORT a sensation of pain in a particular part of the body (*often used in the plural*) ○ *was complaining of pains in the lower abdomen* **3.** EMOTIONAL DISTRESS severe emotional or mental distress ○ *the pain of rejection* **4.** SOMEBODY OR SOMETHING TROUBLESOME somebody or something that is extremely annoying or causes many problems (*informal*) ■ **pains** *npl.* **1.** TROUBLE TAKEN TO DO SOMETHING conscientious effort or trouble taken, usually in tackling a piece of work **2.** LABOR PAINS the painful spasms experienced by a woman during childbirth, caused by the contraction of the womb ■ *v.* **(pained, pain·ing, pains) 1.** *vt.* SADDEN SOMEBODY to make somebody feel saddened or distressed ○ *It pains me to hear you speak like that.* **2.** *vti.* CAUSE OR FEEL PAIN to cause physical pain to somebody, or experience pain [13thC. Via French *peine* from Latin *poena* "penalty, punishment," from Greek *poinē* "penalty" (source of English *punish* and *subpoena*).] ◇ **a pain in the neck** somebody or something that is extremely annoying or troublesome or causes a great many problems (*informal*) ◇ **on** *or* **under pain of something** risking or threatened with something, e.g., death or instant dismissal, as punishment

Paine /payn/, **Robert Treat** (1731–1814) U.S. jurist and revolutionary leader. He was a delegate at the Continental Congress and signed the Declaration of Independence (1776).

Paine, Thomas (1737–1809) British writer and political

Library of Congress

Thomas Paine

philosopher. His pamphlet *Common Sense* (1776) influenced the move toward American independence.

pained /paynd/ *adj.* expressing wounded feelings or a sense of being disappointed or offended by something that somebody has done ○ *a pained expression*

pain·ful /páynfəl/ *adj.* **1. CAUSING PAIN** causing acute physical discomfort ○ *a painful cut* **2. HURTING** hurting as a result of an injury or disease ○ *My arm's still quite painful.* **3. CAUSING DISTRESS** causing emotional or mental distress ○ *painful memories* **4. DIFFICULT** accomplished with laborious effort ○ *making painful progress with the work* **5. VERY BAD** embarrassingly bad ○ *Her performance was painful to watch.* —**pain·ful·ly** *adv.* —**pain·ful·ness** *n.*

pain·kill·er /páyn kìllər/ *n.* something, especially a drug, that reduces pain —**pain·kill·ing** *adj.*

pain·less /páynləss/ *adj.* **1. CAUSING NO PAIN** not causing any pain **2. TROUBLE-FREE** involving little or no difficulty or effort ○ *a painless solution to our problem* —**pain·less·ly** *adv.* —**pain·less·ness** *n.*

pains·tak·ing /páynz tàyking/ *adj.* involving or showing great care and attention to detail [Late 17thC. From *pains taking.*] —**pains·tak·ing·ly** *adv.*

WORD KEY: SYNONYMS

See Synonyms at ***careful.***

paint /paynt/ *n.* **1. COLORED LIQUID APPLIED TO A SURFACE** a colored liquid applied to a surface in order to decorate or protect it, or in order to create a painting **2. DRIED PAINT ON A SURFACE** a film of dried paint on a surface (*often used before a noun*) ○ *paint remover* **3. SOLID PIGMENT** a solid block of pigment that forms liquid paint when moistened or dissolved **4. FACIAL MAKEUP** makeup for the face (*informal*) **5.** ZOOL, EQU = **pinto** ■ *adj.* ZOOL, EQU = **pinto** *n., adj.* ■ *v.* (**paint·ed, paint·ing, paints**) **1.** *vti.* **COVER SOMETHING WITH PAINT** to cover the surface of something with paint in order to decorate or protect it **2.** *vti.* **CREATE A PICTURE USING PAINT** to create a picture, or create a picture of something, by applying paint in different colors to paper, canvas, or some other surface **3.** *vt.* **ADD SOMETHING TO A SURFACE USING PAINT** to mark designs or words on a surface using paint ○ *The words "No Parking" were painted on the wall.* **4.** *vt.* **APPLY LIQUID WITH A BRUSH** to apply a liquid to a surface using a brush, e.g., to brush a medicated liquid onto the skin ○ *My father used to paint iodine onto our skinned knees.* **5.** *vt.* **APPLY COSMETICS TO THE FACE OR NAILS** to apply makeup to the face or lips, or polish to the nails **6.** *vi.* **USE COSMETICS** to use cosmetics, especially to cover blemishes or to lend a false attractiveness (*archaic*) **7.** *vt.* **DESCRIBE IN WORDS** to describe something in words, especially to give a vivid description of something ○ *In the book, he paints his uncle's home as a palace* [12thC. From French *peint*, past participle of *peindre*, from Latin *pingere* "to paint" (source of English *depict* and *picture*).]

paint·ball /páynt bàwl/ *n.* a team game in which each player has a gun that fires gelatin capsules filled with water-soluble marking dye, the object being to shoot members of the opposing team —**paint·ball·ing** *n.*

paint·brush /páynt brùsh/ *n.* a brush for putting paint onto surfaces or painting pictures

paint·ed bunt·ing *n.* a brightly colored bunting, native to the southern United States and Mexico. Latin name: *Passerina ciris.*

paint·ed cup *n.* BOT = **Indian paintbrush**

Paint·ed Des·ert /pàyntid-/ plateau region in Arizona noted for its vividly colored rocks. Parts of it lie within Native American reservations. Area: 7,500 sq. mi./19,425 sq. km.

paint·ed la·dy *n.* a widely distributed migratory butterfly with reddish-brown, black, and orange wings. Latin name: *Vanessa cardui.*

paint·ed tur·tle *n.* a North American turtle found near slow-moving water that has red or yellow stripes on its legs, head, and tail and red markings on the margins of its shell. Latin name: *Chrysemys picta.*

paint·er[1] /páyntər/ *n.* **1. SOMEBODY WHO PAINTS PICTURES** an artist who paints pictures ○ *a portrait painter* **2. SOMEBODY WHO PAINTS HOUSES** somebody whose job is to cover surfaces with paint, especially to paint the interiors of buildings

pain·ter[2] /páyntər/ *n.* NAUT a rope attached to the front of a boat that is used to tie it to something such as a mooring [14thC. Origin uncertain: probably from Old French *penteur* "rope running from masthead, cord for hanging," from *pendre* "to hang," from, ultimately, Latin *pendere* (source of English *suspend*).]

pain·ter[3] /páyntər/ *n. Southern U.S.* ZOOL = **mountain lion** [Mid-18thC. Alteration of PANTHER.]

paint·er·ly /páyntərlee/ *adj.* **1. USING COLOR RATHER THAN LINE** characterized by the use of color rather than line to represent shapes or to structure a composition **2. LIKE A PAINTER'S WORK** typical of a good painter and his or her work

paint·ing /páynting/ *n.* **1. PAINTED PICTURE** a picture made using paint **2. ACTIVITY OF APPLYING PAINT** the art or work of applying paint to surfaces

paint·work /páynt wùrk/ *n.* the painted surfaces of something, e.g., a vehicle's bodywork or the interior of a building

pair /pair/ *n.* **1. 2 SIMILAR THINGS USED TOGETHER** two matching objects that are designed to be used together ○ *a pair of socks* **2. THING WITH TWO JOINED PARTS** a garment or article consisting of two matching or identical parts joined together ○ *a pair of binoculars* **3. 2 PEOPLE TOGETHER** two people who are doing something together, or who are considered together because there is some connection between them **4. COUPLE** two people in a relationship such as a marriage **5.** ZOOL **2 MATING ANIMALS** a male and female animal of the same species who are together for mating **6. ONE OF TWO MATCHED ARTICLES** one of two matched articles such as shoes or gloves ○ *lost the pair to his cufflink* **7.** EQU **2 HORSES HARNESSED TOGETHER** two horses harnessed together to pull a carriage ○ *a coach and pair* **8.** CARDS **2 PLAYING CARDS** two playing cards that have the same value ○ *a pair of aces* **9.** POL **2 OPPOSING MEMBERS MAKING A VOTING AGREEMENT** two members from opposing sides in a legislative body who each agree not to vote on issues if the other is not present and able to vote. The arrangement covers occasions when members cannot vote because of illness or other commitments, the effect being to maintain the usual balance of numbers between the two opposing sides. **10.** POL **AGREEMENT TO FORM A PAIR** an arrangement between two members on opposing sides in a legislative body to form a pair **11.** ROWING = **pair-oar 12.** MATH, LOGIC **SET OF 2 ELEMENTS IN ORDER** a set consisting of two elements in order **13.** CHEM **ELECTRON BOND** two electrons forming a bond between atoms ■ *v.* (**paired, pair·ing, pairs**) **1.** *vti.* **PUT INTO GROUP OF 2** to form a pair with somebody, or to partner somebody with somebody else, for some shared activity or for romance or friendship **2.** *vt.* **MATCH 2 THINGS TOGETHER** to put two matching articles together **3.** *vt.* POL **FORM A LEGISLATIVE PAIR** to arrange a pair between two members of a voting assembly or to form a pair with another member **4.** *vi.* ZOOL **FORM A MATING PAIR** to form a mating pair [13thC. Directly or via French *paire* from Latin *paria* "equals," a plural form of *par* "equal, a pair" (source of English *compare* and *umpire*).]

pair bond *n.* ZOOL a relationship between a male and female animal, formed either during courtship and breeding or for life, that excludes others of the same species —**pair bond·ing** *n.*

pair-oar *n.* a racing shell in which two rowers with one oar each sit one behind the other

pair pro·duc·tion *n.* the creation of a negative particle (**electron**) and a positive particle (**positron**) when a fast particle (**photon**) passes through a strong electric field such as that surrounding an atomic nucleus

pair roy·al (*plural* **pairs roy·al**) *n.* in some card games, a set of three cards of the same value

pai·sa /pī saá/ (*plural* **-se** *or* **-sa**) *n.* **1. S ASIAN SUBUNIT OF CURRENCY** a subunit of currency in India, Pakistan, Bangladesh, and Nepal. See table at **currency 2. COIN WORTH A PAISA** a coin worth one paisa [Late 19thC. From Hindi *paisā.*]

pai·sa·no /pī zaá nō/ (*plural* **-nos**) *n.* a friend or countryman [Mid-19thC. Via Spanish, "peasant," from, ultimately, late Latin *pagensis* "inhabitant of a district," from Latin *pagus* (see PAGAN).]

pais·ley /páyzlee/ (*plural* **-leys**) *n.* **1. PATTERN WITH CURVING SHAPES** a distinctive bold design consisting of multicolored curving shapes, stylized cones, and feathers **2. GARMENT WITH A PAISLEY DESIGN** a fabric or piece of clothing with a paisley design, especially a type of woolen shawl popular in the 19th century [Early

Paisley

19thC. Named for *Paisley*, town in south-western Scotland where material with this pattern was first made.] —**pais·ley** *adj.*

Pai·ute /pī yoōt/ (*plural* **-utes** *or* **-ute**), **Pi·ute** (*plural* **-utes** *or* **-ute**) *n.* a Native North American language spoken in various parts of the United States, especially in California. It belongs to the Uto-Aztecan branch of Aztec-Tanoan languages and is spoken by about 12,000 people. [Early 19thC. From Spanish *payuchi*, of unknown origin.] —**Pai·ute** *adj.*

pa·ja·ma par·ty *n.* a party, especially for teenagers or children, at which the guests bring pajamas and spend the night

pa·ja·mas /pə jaáməz, pə jámməz/ *npl.* **1. SLEEPING CLOTHES** a light loose pair of pants and a matching loose-fitting shirt for wearing in bed or for lounging **2. LOOSE PANTS WORN IN EASTERN COUNTRIES** loose-fitting pants made of silk or lightweight cotton tied at the waist, worn by both men and women in India, Turkey, and other Eastern countries [Early 19thC. Plural of *pajama*, from Persian and Urdu *pāy-jāmah*, literally "leg garment."]

pak choi *n.* = **bok choy** [From Chinese (Cantonese) *paāk ts'oi*, literally "white vegetable"]

Pakistan

Pak·i·stan /páki stàn, paáki staán/ republic on the Arabian Sea in southern Asia. It occupies the northwestern corner of the Indian subcontinent. Language: Urdu. Currency: Pakistani rupee. Capital: Islamabad. Population: 132,185,388 (1997). Area: 307,293 sq. mi./796,095 sq. km. Official name **Islamic Republic of Pakistan** —**Pak·i·stan·i** *n., adj.*

pal /pal/ *n.* **AGGRESSIVE FORM OF ADDRESS** used to address somebody, often in an unfriendly or aggressive way (*informal*) ○ *Listen, pal, you'd better watch out!* ■ *vi.* (**palled, pal·ling, pals**) **BECOME FRIENDS WITH SOMEBODY** to become friends with and spend time with somebody [Late 17thC. Via English Romany, "pal, brother," from, ultimately, Sanskrit *bhrātṛ* "brother."]

pal around *vi.* to become friends with and spend time with somebody (*informal*)

Pal. *abbr.* Palestine

pal·ace /pálləss/ *n.* **1. OFFICIAL RESIDENCE OF A SOVEREIGN** a grand and imposing building that is the official residence of a king or queen, a head of state such as a president, or a high-ranking aristocrat or church dignitary **2. LARGE BUILDING FOR ENTERTAINMENT** a large public or private building with an imposing ornate style, used for entertainment or exhibitions ○ *an old movie palace fallen into disrepair* [13thC. Via Old French *palais* from Latin *palatium*, named for *Palatium* "Palatine Hill" where the emperor Augustus built a house.]

pal·ace rev·o·lu·tion *n.* the overthrow of a ruler by those who are already in the ruling group, often carried out with little violence

pa·la·di·a plural of **palladium**[2]

pal·a·din /pállәd'n, pállәdin/ *n.* **1. MEDIEVAL CHAMPION** a champion or hero, especially in medieval legend or history **2. CHAMPION OF A CAUSE** somebody known for championing a cause **3. ONE OF CHARLEMAGNE'S COMPANIONS** any one of the 12 legendary companions of Charlemagne [Late 16thC. Via French from, ultimately, Latin *palatinus* (see PALATINE).]

palaeo- *prefix.* = **paleo-**

pa·laes·tra *n.* = **palestra**

pal·an·quin /pàllәn kéen/ *n.* a covered seat carried on poles held parallel to the ground on the shoulders of two or four people. It was formerly used to transport an important person, especially in East Asia. [Late 16thC. Via Portuguese *palanquim* from, ultimately, Sanskrit *palyaṅka* "bed, litter."]

pal·at·a·ble /pállәtәb'l/ *adj.* **1. PLEASANT-TASTING** having a good enough taste to be eaten or drunk **2. ACCEPTABLE** acceptable to somebody's sensibilities [Mid-17thC. Formed from PALATE.]

pal·a·tal /pállәt'l/ *adj.* **1.** ANAT **FACING OR RELATING TO THE PALATE** occurring at, facing, or relating to the palate **2.** PHON **PRONOUNCED WITH THE TONGUE AT THE PALATE** used to describe a consonant sound that is produced by raising the tongue to or near the hard palate ○ *The "sh" sound is a palatal fricative.* **3.** PHON **PRONOUNCED WITH THE TONGUE FORWARD** used to describe a vowel sound that is produced with the tongue moved forward in the mouth ○ *The vowel in "meet" is palatal.* ■ *n.* PHON **PALATAL SPEECH SOUND** a speech sound pronounced with the tongue at or near the hard palate or with the tongue pushed forward, especially a palatal consonant —**pal·a·tal·ly** /pállәt'lee/ *adv.*

pal·a·tal·i·za·tion /pàllәt'li záysh'n/ *n.* the pronunciation of a speech sound by raising the tongue to or toward the hard palate

pal·a·tal·ize /pállәt'l īz/ (**-ized, -iz·ing, -iz·es**) *vt.* **1. PRODUCE AT THE HARD PALATE** to make a speech sound by raising the tongue to or toward the hard palate **2. MAKE MORE PALATAL** to alter a speech sound in pronunciation by placing the tongue closer to the hard palate, rather than to the teeth, alveolar ridge, or velum

pal·ate /pállәt/ *n.* **1.** ANAT **ROOF OF THE MOUTH** the roof of the mouth that separates it from the nasal cavity. It consists of a bony hard palate at the front and a muscular soft palate at the rear. **2. SENSE OF TASTE** a personal sense of taste and flavor **3. AESTHETIC TASTE** intellectual or aesthetic tastes or sensibilities **4.** BOT **PART OF A FLOWER** the lower projection of a flower such as the snapdragon, divided into two lips [14thC. From Latin *palatum*.]

pa·la·tial /pә láysh'l/ *adj.* **1. LUXURIOUS** grand or luxurious ○ *palatial mansions* **2. FIT FOR A PALACE** appropriate for a palace [Mid-18thC. From Latin *palatium* (see PALACE).] —**pa·la·tial·ness** *n.*

pa·lat·i·nate /pә látt'n àyt, pә látt'nәt/ *n.* the territory, office, or responsibilities of a feudal palatine

pal·a·tine[1] /pállә tīn/ *n.* **1. POWERFUL FEUDAL LORD** a feudal lord in central Europe with sovereign powers within his territory **2. IMPERIAL COURT OFFICIAL** a court official in the late Roman and Byzantine empires ■ *adj.* **1. FIT FOR A PALACE** relating to or suitable for a palace **2. HAVING POWER OVER TERRITORY** used to describe an official or feudal lord who had sovereign power over a territory **3. RULED BY LORD** used to describe a territory that is ruled by a sovereign feudal lord [15thC. Via French *palatine* from Latin *palatinus* "of the palace, palace official," from *palatium* (see PALACE).]

pal·a·tine[2] /pállә tīn/ *adj.* ANAT **OF THE PALATE** relating to the palate ■ *n.* ANAT **HARD PALATE BONE** either of the two bones that form the hard palate

Pal·a·tine[1] *adj.* relating to the German Palatinate, or its people or culture

Pal·a·tine[2] *n.* the central hill of the seven on which Rome was built, considered the oldest and the site of many of the imperial palaces

Pa·lau /paa lów/ republic in the western Pacific Ocean comprising a group of islands that are part of the Caroline Islands. Language: English, Palauan. Currency: U.S. dollar. Capital: Koror. Population: 17,000 (1996). Area: 191 sq. mi./495 sq. km. Official name **Republic of Palau**

pa·lav·er /pә lávvәr, pә laávәr/ *n.* **1. CONFERENCE BETWEEN DIFFERENT PARTIES** a conference or meeting between different parties (*humorous*) **2. EMPTY TALK** idle, flattering, or time-wasting talk **3. CONFERENCE BETWEEN DIFFERENT CULTURES** a conference between European explorers or colonialists and local African officials, usually requiring the use of a pidgin language (*archaic*) ■ *vi.* (**-ered, -er·ing, -ers**) **1. CONFER** to confer or hold a conference (*humorous*) **2. TALK IDLY** to talk idly, emptily, or with the intention of flattering (*archaic*) [Mid-18thC. Via Portuguese *palavra* "speech" from Latin *parabola* (see PARABLE). The word was adopted from Portuguese by British sailors visiting West Africa, where it was used to denote negotiations between Europeans and Africans.]

Palau

pa·laz·zo /pә laátsō/ (*plural* **-zos** *or* **-zi** /-tsee/) *n.* a large ornate building such as a museum or official residence, especially in Italy [Mid-17thC. Via Italian from Latin *palatium* (see PALACE).]

pa·laz·zo pants *npl.* women's loose-fitting lightweight pants with flared legs

pale[1] /payl/ *adj.* (**pal·er, pal·est**) **1. LACKING COLOR** lacking in color or intensity ○ *pale blue* **2. PALLID FROM ILLNESS** unusually light in skin complexion because of illness, shock, or worry **3. PRODUCING LITTLE LIGHT** producing or reflecting little light **4. INADEQUATE** inadequate or faint ○ *a pale version of his former flamboyant self* ■ *v.* (**paled, pal·ing, pales**) **1.** *vi.* **BECOME WHITER** to become whiter or lose brilliance **2.** *vi.* **BECOME LESS IMPORTANT** to be or become less important, remarkable, or intense, especially in comparison with something more important or serious **3.** *vt.* **CAUSE TO LOSE COLOR** to cause somebody or something to lose color or brilliance [14thC. Via Old French from Latin *pallidus* (see PALLID).]

pale[2] /payl/ *n.* **1. FENCE STAKE** a pointed slat of wood for a fence **2. FENCE** a fence marking a boundary **3. FENCED-IN AREA** an area fenced in or its boundary **4.** HERALDRY **VERTICAL STRIPE ON A SHIELD** a wide vertical band down the center of a shield ■ *vt.* (**paled, pal·ing, pales**) **FENCE IN** to fence in an area [12thC. Via French *pal* from Latin *palus* "stake."] ◇ **beyond the pale** outside the limits of what is considered to be acceptable

Pale *n.* formerly, a restricted area in Imperial Russia where Jews were allowed to settle

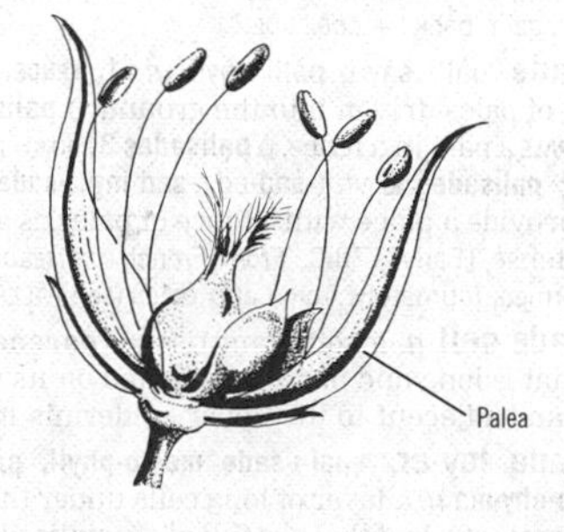

Palea

pa·le·a /páylee ә/ (*plural* **-ae** /-ee/) *n.* **1. LEAF ON FLOWERING GRASS** a dry membranous leaf with a single flower (**bract**) on a flowering grass **2. FLOWER SCALE** a dry membranous scale on the head of a composite flower such as a sunflower [Mid-18thC. From Latin "chaff."]

Pa·le·arc·tic /pàylee aárktik, pàylee aártik/ *adj.* relating to the biogeographic region of the Arctic and immediately adjacent temperate regions of Europe, Asia, and Africa, or to a species within that range such as the Eurasian sparrowhawk

pale-dry *adj.* used to describe beverages that are dry-flavored and light-colored

pa·le·eth·nol·o·gy /pàylee eth nóllәjee/ *n.* the study of prehistoric human beings —**pa·le·eth·no·log·i·cal** /pàylee ethnә lójjik'l/ *adj.* —**pa·le·eth·nol·o·gist** *n.*

pale·face /páyl fàyss/ *n.* an offensive term for a Caucasian person, allegedly used by Native Americans (*offensive*)

paleo- *prefix.* **1.** ancient, prehistoric ○ *paleozoology* **2.** primitive, early ○ *paleoethnology* [From Greek *palaios*, which was formed from *palai* "long ago." Ultimately related to *tēle* "far off," the source of English *tele-*.]

pa·le·o·an·throp·ic /pàylee ō an thróppik/ *adj.* relating to prehistoric human beings

pa·le·o·an·thro·pol·o·gy /pàylee ō ánthrә póllәjee/ *n.* the study of early human beings and related species through fossil evidence —**pa·le·o·an·thro·po·log·i·cal** /pàylee ō anthrәpә lójjik'l/ *adj.* —**pa·le·o·an·thro·pol·o·gist** /pàylee ō anthrә póllәjist/ *n.*

pa·le·o·bi·o·chem·is·try /pàylee ō bī ō kémmistree/ *n.* **1. STUDY OF THE EVOLUTION OF BIOCHEMISTRY** the study of the development and change in biochemical processes as indicated in fossils and other geologic evidence **2. FOSSIL CHEMICALS** the biological chemicals found in fossils of ancient organisms

pa·le·o·bi·o·ge·og·ra·phy /pàylee ō bī ō jee óggrәfee/ *n.* the study of the locations of prehistoric species on the basis of fossil evidence

pa·le·o·bot·a·ny /pàylee ō bótt'nee/ *n.* the study of prehistoric plants on the basis of fossil evidence —**pa·le·o·bo·tan·i·cal** /pàylee ō bә tánnik'l/ *adj.* —**pa·le·o·bot·a·nist** /pàylee ō bótt'nist/ *n.*

Pa·le·o·cene /páylee ә seen/ *n.* the epoch of geologic time when placental mammals first appeared, 65 to 55 million years ago. See table at **geology** [Late 19thC. Coined from PALEO- + Greek *kainos* "new."] —**Pa·le·o·cene** *adj.*

pa·le·o·cli·ma·tol·o·gy /pàylee ō klīmә tóllәjee/ *n.* the study of prehistoric climates on a global or regional scale from evidence preserved in glacial deposits, sedimentary structures, and fossils —**pa·le·o·cli·ma·tol·o·gist** *n.*

pa·le·o·cur·rent /páylee ō kùr әnt, -kùrrәnt/ *n.* a prehistoric current of water or wind, revealed by the study of the sedimentary structures and textures that it deposited

pa·le·o·e·col·o·gy /pàylee ō i kóllәjee/ *n.* the study of the interaction of prehistoric life forms and their environments —**pa·le·o·ec·o·log·i·cal** /pàylee ō ékә lójjik'l, -eekә-/ *adj.* —**pa·le·o·e·col·o·gist** /pàylee ō i kóllәjist/ *n.*

pa·le·o·eth·no·bot·a·ny /pàylee ō ethnō bótt'nee/ *n.* the study of fossilized seeds and grain in order to gain information about prehistoric patterns of cereal growth

Pa·le·o·gene /páylee ә jeen/ *n.* the early part of the Tertiary period of geologic time, comprising the Paleocene, Eocene, and Oligocene epochs. —**Pa·le·o·gene** *adj.*

pa·le·o·ge·og·ra·phy /pàylee ō jee óggrәfee/ *n.* the study of the geographic features of past epochs —**pa·le·o·ge·og·ra·pher** *n.* —**pa·le·o·ge·o·graph·ic** /pàylee ō jee ә gráffik/ *adj.* —**pa·le·o·ge·o·graph·i·cal** /-k'l/ *adj.* —**pa·le·o·ge·o·graph·i·cal·ly** /-kәlee/ *adv.*

pa·le·og·ra·phy /pàylee óggrәfee/ *n.* **1. STUDY OF ANCIENT WRITINGS** the study of ancient handwriting and manuscripts **2. OLD MANUSCRIPT** an ancient manuscript or piece of handwriting —**pa·le·o·graph·ic** /pàylee ә gráffik/ *adj.* —**pa·le·o·graph·i·cal** *adj.* —**pa·le·og·ra·pher** /pàylee óggrәfәr/ *n.*

Pa·le·o-In·di·an *adj.* relating to the earliest inhabitants of the Americas, who arrived from Asia by the Bering land bridge that connected Alaska and Siberia. By 12,000 to 10,000 years ago they were hunting game and living in small groups throughout North America. —**Pa·le·o-In·di·an** *n.*

pa·le·o·lith /páylee ә lìth/ *n.* a stone tool from the Paleolithic age

Pa·le·o·lith·ic /pàylee ә líthik/ *n.* the early part of the Stone Age, when early human beings made chipped-stone tools, from 750,000 to 15,000 years ago —**Pa·le·o·lith·ic** *adj.*

Pa·le·o·lith·ic man *n.* a member of any of the various peoples who lived in the Paleolithic period, such as Neanderthal, Cro-Magnon, or Java man

pa·le·o·mag·net·ism /pàylee ō mágnə tìzzəm/ *n.* **1.** MAGNETISM IN ANCIENT ROCK the polarity and intensity of residual magnetism in ancient rock **2.** STUDY OF THE EARTH'S PREHISTORIC MAGNETIC FIELD the study of changes in the intensity and direction of the Earth's magnetic field throughout geologic time. The recurring reversals of the Earth's magnetic field and the changing configurations of the continents have been established through such studies. —**pa·le·o·mag·net·ic** /pàylee ō màg néttik/ *adj.*

pa·le·on·tog·ra·phy /pàylee on tóggrəfee/ *n.* the branch of paleontology concerned with describing fossils —**pa·le·on·to·graph·ic** /pàylee óntə gráffik/ *adj.* —**pa·le·on·to·graph·i·cal** /-k'l/ *adj.*

paleontol. *abbr.* paleontology

pa·le·on·tol·o·gy /pàylee òn tóllәjee/ *n.* the study of life in prehistoric times by using fossil evidence —**pa·le·on·to·log·i·cal** /pàylee óntə lójjik'l/ *adj.* —**pa·le·on·to·log·i·cal·ly** /-kəlee/ *adv.* —**pa·le·on·tol·o·gist** /pàylee on tólləjist/ *n.*

pa·le·o·path·ol·o·gy /pàylee ō pə thólləjee/ *n.* the study of the evidence of disease processes in early human and animal remains, e.g., by using DNA analysis

Pa·le·o·zo·ic /pàylee ə zṓ ik/ *n.* the era of geologic time when fish, insects, amphibians, reptiles, and land plants first appeared, about 600 million to 230 million years ago —**Pa·le·o·zo·ic** *adj.*

pa·le·o·zo·ol·o·gy /pàylee ō zō óllәjee/ *n.* the study of ancient animals and animal life using fossils and other paleontological evidence —**pa·le·o·zo·o·log·i·cal** /pàylee ō zō ə lójjik'l/ *adj.*

Pa·ler·mo /pə lérmō, -láir-/ city and port in Sicily, Italy. It is the largest city on the island, and is situated on the northwestern coast. Population: 694,749 (1993).

Pal·es·tine /pállə stīn/ area in southwestern Asia between the Jordan River and the eastern coast of the Mediterranean Sea. During biblical times it was the Jewish homeland, comprising the kingdoms of Israel and Judah. The country was then successively occupied by the Romans, the Arabs, and the Ottoman Turks. In 1947 Palestine was partitioned between the new state of Israel and Jordan, which assumed control of the West Bank territories. Wars fought in 1948, 1967, and 1972 between Israel and the surrounding Arab states saw an increase in the land held by Israel. In 1993 an agreement was signed under which the Palestinian Arabs gained limited self-rule in territories in the Gaza Strip and on the West Bank of the Jordan River. —**Pal·es·tin·i·an** *n., adj.*

pa·les·tra /pə léstrə/ (*plural* **-trae** /-tree/ *or* **-tras**), **pa·laes·tra** (*plural* **-trae** *or* **-tras**) *n.* a public sports ground or gymnasium in ancient Greece [14thC. Via Latin from Greek *palaistra*, from *palaiein* "to wrestle."]

pale·tot /pállə tṑ, páltō/ *n.* a fitted coat worn by women in the 19th century, usually over a bustle or crinoline [Mid-19thC. From French, of unknown origin.]

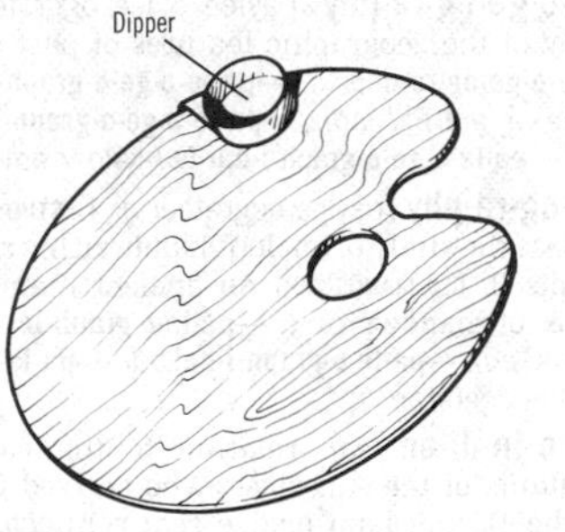

Palette

pal·ette /pállət/ *n.* **1.** PAINTING BOARD FOR ARTIST'S PAINTS a board or tray on which an artist arranges and mixes paints. A traditional style of palette is an oval board that curves in near a thumbhole, so that the artist can hold the board steadily from underneath. **2.** PAINTING RANGE OF COLORS USED BY AN ARTIST the assortment of colors on a palette, in a painting, or typical of an artist's work **3.** COMPUT COLOR RANGE OF A COMPUTER DISPLAY the range of colors that can be reproduced on a computer display **4.** ARTS QUALITIES IN NONGRAPHIC ART a range of qualities or elements in a nongraphic art such as music or literature [Late 18thC. Via French (see PALLET[1]).]

pal·ette knife *n.* a spatula-shaped implement with a slender flexible metal blade and a handle, used by an artist to mix and apply thick paints

pal·frey /páwlfree/ (*plural* **-freys**) *n.* a horse for everyday riding, especially one for a woman to ride (*archaic*) [12thC. Via Old French *palefrei* from, ultimately, late Latin *paraveredus*, literally "extra horse," from Latin *veredus* "light horse used by couriers," ultimately of Gaulish origin.]

Pa·li /paálee/ *n.* an ancient Indo-European language derived from Sanskrit and formerly spoken in various parts of India. It survives in the language of Hinayana Buddhist scriptures. [Late 18thC. From Pali *pāli*, denoting the canonical text, as opposed to the commentary, shortened from Sanskrit *pāli-bhāsā*, literally "language of the line."] —**Pa·li** *adj.*

pal·i·mo·ny /pállə mōnee/ (*plural* **-nies**) *n.* a maintenance allowance for an ex-lover or member of an unmarried couple, when required by a court of law [Late 20thC. A blend of PAL and ALIMONY.]

pal·imp·sest /pállimp sèst/ *n.* OVERWRITTEN MANUSCRIPT a manuscript written over a partly erased older manuscript in such a way that the old words can be read beneath the new ■ *adj.* OVERWRITTEN used to describe a document that has been overwritten [Mid-17thC. Via Latin *palimpsestus* from Greek *palimpsestos*, literally "something rubbed smooth again."]

pal·in·drome /pállin drōm/ *n.* **1.** TEXT READING THE SAME BACKWARD AS FORWARD a word, phrase, passage, or number that reads the same forward and backward, e.g., "Anna," "Draw, o coward," or "23832" **2.** GENETICS MIRROR-IMAGE DNA SEQUENCE a segment of DNA in which the nucleotide sequence in one strand read from one end is the same as the sequence in the complementary strand read from the opposite end. For example, the sequence GGTACC is a palindrome when the complementary strand is CCATGG. [Early 17thC. From Greek *palindromos*, literally "running back again."] —**pal·in·dro·mic** /pàllin drómmik, pàllin drṓmik/ *adj.*

pal·ing /páyling/ *n.* **1.** FENCE OF STAKES a fence formed by a line of pointed stakes planted in the ground **2.** = **pale**[2] *n.* 1 [14thC. Originally in the meaning "making of a fence with pales," hence, the fence itself.]

pal·in·gen·e·sis /pàllin jénnəsiss/ *n.* **1.** BIOL = **recapitulation** *n.* 2 **2.** CHR SPIRITUAL REGENERATION spiritual rebirth by means of baptism **3.** MIGRATION OF THE SOUL TO ANOTHER BODY the supposed transmigration of the soul of somebody who has died into the body of another person or animal [Early 19thC. Coined from Greek *palin* "again" + *genesis* "birth."] —**pal·in·ge·net·ic** /pàllin jə néttik/ *adj.* —**pal·in·ge·net·i·cal·ly** /-kəlee/ *adv.*

pal·i·node /pállə nōd/ *n.* **1.** POETRY POETIC RETRACTION a poem in which a poet retracts something written in a previous poem **2.** FORMAL RETRACTION a formal retraction of a statement [Late 16thC. Directly or via French from Latin *palinodia*, from Greek *palinōdia*, from *palin* "again, back" + *ōdē* "ODE."]

pal·i·sade /pàlli sáyd, pálli sàyd/ *n.* **1.** FENCE a fence made of pales driven into the ground. ◊ **palisades 2.** FENCE PALE a pale in a fence. ◊ **palisades 3.** BOT = **palisade cell.** ◊ **palisades** ■ *vt.* (**-sad·ed, -sad·ing, -sades**) FENCE IN to provide a place with a fence of pales as a means of defense [Early 17thC. From French *palissade*, which was formed, ultimately, from Latin *palus* (see PALE[2]).]

pal·i·sade cell *n.* a soft plant tissue (**parenchyma**) cell that is long and narrow, oriented on its vertical axis, and adjacent to the upper epidermis in a leaf

pal·i·sade lay·er, **pal·i·sade mes·o·phyll, pal·i·sade pa·ren·chy·ma** *n.* a layer of long cells under the upper epidermis of a leaf that are full of specialized chlorophyll-containing cell parts (**chloroplasts**)

pal·i·sades /pàlli sáydz, pálli sàydz/ *npl.* a row of high cliffs, usually rising sharply from the side of a river, stream, or lake [Mid-19thC. Originally the name of a line of cliffs along the Hudson River, above New York City.]

Palk Strait /pawk-, pawlk-/ inlet of the Bay of Bengal, separating southeastern India from northwestern Sri Lanka. Length: 85 mi./137 km.

pall[1] /pawl/ *n.* **1.** DARK COVERING a covering that makes a place dark and gloomy ○ *a pall of thick black smoke* **2.** GLOOMY ATMOSPHERE a prevailing gloomy mood or oppressive atmosphere ○ *Her departure cast a pall over the weekend.* **3.** CASKET COVERING a cloth covering for a casket, bier, hearse, or tomb **4.** CASKET a casket, especially when being carried in a funeral **5.** CHR CHALICE COVER a square cover for a communion chalice, especially a linen-covered board **6.** CHR PALLIUM a pallium (*archaic*) **7.** HERALDRY HERALDIC BEARING a heraldic bearing representing an archbishop's pallium in the form of three bands in a Y-shape, charged with crosses ■ *vt.* (**palled, pall·ing, palls**) COVER WITH A PALL to cover somebody or something with a pall or with something that resembles a pall [Pre-12thC. From Latin *pallium* "covering."]

pall[2] /pawl/ (**palled, pall·ing, palls**) *vi.* to be or become uninteresting, unsatisfying, or insipid ○ *The music soon began to pall on us.* [14thC. Alteration of APPALL.]

Pal·la·di·an[1] /pə láydee ən/ *adj.* ARCHIT typical of or similar to the classical architectural style developed by Andrea Palladio in the 16th century

Pal·la·di·an[2] /pə láydee ən/ *adj.* **1.** MYTHOL OF ATHENA relating to the goddess Pallas Athena **2.** RELATING TO WISDOM relating to wisdom or knowledge [Mid-16thC. From Latin *palladium* (see PALLADIUM[2]).]

Pal·la·di·o /pə láydee ō/, **Andrea** (1508–80) Italian architect. Working in the classical tradition of ancient Rome, he produced villa designs and wrote his *Four Books on Architecture* (1570), which influenced several generations of architects. Born **Andrea di Pietro della Gondola**

pal·la·di·um[1] /pə láydee əm/ *n.* a malleable silvery-white metallic chemical element that resembles platinum and is used as a chemical catalyst and in electrical contacts, jewelry, dental alloys, and medical instruments. Symbol **Pd** [Early 19thC. From *Pallas* (see PALLADIUM[2]), the name given to an asteroid discovered shortly before the metal.] —**pal·la·dic** /pə láydik, -lá-/ *adj.* —**pal·la·dous** /pə láydəss, pállədəss/ *adj.*

pal·la·di·um[2] /pə láydee əm/ (*plural* **-ums** *or* **-a**) *n.* **1.** SAFEGUARD a protection or safeguard, especially one protecting social and civic institutions **2.** **pal·la·di·um, Pal·la·di·um** PROTECTIVE CHARM an object believed to have the power to protect a city or nation, especially the statue of Pallas Athena that was believed to protect Troy [14thC. Via Latin from Greek *palladion*, from *Pallas*, epithet of Athena, goddess of wisdom.]

Pal·las /pálləss/ *n.* ASTRON SECOND LARGEST ASTEROID the second largest asteroid, discovered in 1802. It has an average diameter of approximately 530 km (330 mi.). ■ **Pal·las, Pal·las A·the·na** MYTHOL = **Athena**

pall·bear·er /páwl bàirər/ *n.* somebody who helps to carry or escort a casket at a funeral or burial

pal·let[1] /pállət/ *n.* **1.** PLATFORM FOR LOADS a standardized platform or open-ended box, usually made of wood, that allows mechanical handling of bulk goods during transport and storage **2.** CRAFT CLAY-WORKING TOOL a wooden tool similar to a knife, used to mix and shape ceramic clay **3.** CRAFT BOARD FOR DRYING CERAMICS a board on which ceramic pieces are dried **4.** REGULATING LEVER IN A TIMEPIECE a lever that regulates a ratchet wheel, especially one that regulates the movement of the balance wheel or pendulum in a timepiece by transmitting movements from the escape wheel. The pallet's function is to convert rotary to reciprocating motion, or vice versa. **5.** GILDING TOOL a tool for manipulating gold leaf in gilding **6.** MUSIC VALVE ON ORGAN a valve on an organ that opens in order to let air into a pipe **7.** PAINTING = **palette** *n.* 1 [15thC. Via French *palette*, literally "small blade or spade," from Latin *pala* "spade, shovel."]

pal·let[2] /pállət/ *n.* **1.** MAKESHIFT BED a temporary and usually uncomfortable bed, made from materials at hand **2.** STRAW MATTRESS a straw-filled mattress [14thC. From Anglo-Norman *paillete*, from *paille* "straw," from Latin *palea.*]

pal·le·tize /pállə tīz/ (**-tized, -tiz·ing, -tiz·es**) *vt.* to put, transport, or store a load of something on a standardized platform

pal·li·a plural of **pallium**

pal·liasse /pal yáss, pál yàss/ *n.* = **paillasse**

pal·li·ate /pállee àyt/ (**-at·ed, -at·ing, -ates**) *vt.* **1.** MITIGATE to reduce the intensity or severity of something **2.** PARTIALLY EXCUSE to make an offense seem less serious by providing excuses or mitigating evidence **3.** MED ALLEVIATE to alleviate a symptom without curing the underlying medical condition [15thC. From the past participle stem of *palliare* "to cover or hide," from *pallium* "a covering" (source of English *pallium*).] —**pal·li·a·tion** /pállee àysh'n/ *n.* —**pal·li·a·tor** /pállee àytər/ *n.*

pal·li·a·tive /pállee àytiv, pállee ətiv/ *adj.* **1. SOOTHING** soothing anxieties or other intense emotions **2. TREATING SYMPTOMS ONLY** alleviating symptoms without eliminating the cause ■ *n.* MED **SYMPTOM-TREATING MEDICINE** something that palliates, especially a medicine that treats symptoms only —**pal·li·a·tive·ly** *adv.*

pal·lid /pállid/ *adj.* **1. PALE** having an unhealthily pale complexion **2. LACKLUSTER** lacking color, spirit, or intensity [Late 16thC. From Latin *pallidus*, from *pallere* "to be pale."] —**pal·lid·i·ty** /pa líddətee, pə líddətee/ *n.* —**pal·lid·ly** *adv.*

Pal·lis·er /pállisər/ the southernmost point of the North Island, New Zealand, situated at the eastern end of the Cook Strait

pal·li·um /pállee əm/ (*plural* **-a** /pállee ə/ *or* **-ums**) *n.* **1.** CHR **VESTMENT WORN BY A POPE OR ARCHBISHOP** a white vestment that rests on the shoulders with pendants hanging at its front and back, worn by a pope, all Roman Catholic archbishops, and some bishops **2.** ZOOL = **mantle** *n.* 5 **3.** BIRDS = **mantle** *n.* 6 **4.** ANAT = **cerebral cortex 5.** ANAT **PART OF THE BRAIN** the layer of gray matter forming the surface of the cerebral cortex **6.** HIST **ANCIENT CLOAK** a man's rectangular cloak worn in ancient Rome [Late 16thC. From Latin, literally "covering."] —**pal·li·al** *adj.*

pall-mall /pel mél, pal mál, pawl máwl/ *n.* **1. OLD MALLET-AND-BALL GAME** a 17th-century game in which players used a mallet to hit a wooden ball through an iron hoop suspended at the end of a long alley **2. ALLEY FOR PLAYING PALL-MALL** an alley in which pall-mall is played [Mid-16thC. Via obsolete French *palle maille* from Italian *pallamaglio*, which was formed, ultimately, from *balla* "ball" + *maglio* "mallet."]

pal·lor /pállər/ *n.* an unhealthy-looking paleness of complexion [14thC. From Latin, from *pallere* "to be pale."]

pal·ly /pállee/ (**-li·er, -li·est**) *adj.* having a friendly relationship (*informal*) [Late 19thC. From PAL.]

palm[1] /paam/ *n.* **1.** ANAT **INNER SURFACE OF THE HAND** the inner surface of the hand, extending from the base of the fingers to the wrist **2.** ZOOL **UNDERSIDE OF A MAMMAL'S FOREFOOT** the part of a mammal's forefoot that is most often in contact with the ground **3.** MEASURE **HAND-SIZED MEASURE** a unit of length, based on the length or width of a hand **4. COVERING FOR THE PALM OF THE HAND** something that covers the palm of the hand, e.g., the inner hand surface of a glove **5. FLAT PART OF A BRANCHED STRUCTURE** the broad flat lobe of a branched structure such as the antler of a moose or deer, or of a cactus stalk **6.** ROWING **OAR BLADE** the blade of an oar **7.** NAUT **INNER FACE OF AN ANCHOR POINT** the inner face of an anchor's point ■ *vt.* (**palmed, palm·ing, palms**) **1. HIDE IN THE HAND** to hide something in the hand, especially as part of a trick **2. TAKE STEALTHILY** to take something secretly by hiding it in the hand **3. TOUCH WITH THE PALM** to touch something with the palm **4. SHAKE HANDS** to shake hands with somebody (*slang*) **5.** BASKETBALL **HOLD INSTEAD OF DRIBBLING** to let a basketball come to rest in the hands during a dribble, thereby committing a foul [Old English. Via a prehistoric Germanic word from Latin *palma* "palm of the hand, PALM[2]."] ◇ **grease somebody's palm** to bribe somebody (*slang*) ◇ **have somebody** *or* **something in the palm of your hand** to have complete power or influence over somebody or something

palm off *vt.* **1. GIVE IN A DECEITFUL WAY** to shift something into another's possession in a deceitful way ○ *The crooks needed a way to palm off the stolen CDs onto unsuspecting buyers.* **2. PASS ON SOMETHING UNWANTED** to give or pass on something unwanted to somebody else ○ *Don't try to palm off that old armchair on me!*

palm[2] /paam/ *n.* **1.** = **palm tree 2. PALM LEAF AS A VICTORY SIGN** a leaf from a palm tree, used as a symbol of victory or success **3.** MIL **MILITARY DECORATION INDICATING MULTIPLE AWARDS** a small decoration shaped like a palm leaf that is added to a military decoration to show that it has been awarded to the wearer more than once [12thC. Via French *paume* from Latin *palma* "palm of the hand, palm tree" (because a cluster of palm leaves was thought to look like a hand and fingers).]

Pal·ma /paálmaa/ port on Majorca. It is the capital city of the Spanish Balearic Islands. Population: 323,138 (1995).

pal·mar /paámər/ *adj.* relating to the palm of the hand or to the underside of an animal's forefoot

pal·mate /pál màyt, paál-, paá-/ *adj.* **1. pal·mate, pal·mat·ed** BOT, ZOOL **HAVING SEVERAL LOBES** forming a branching pattern that spreads like fingers from a hand **2.** BIRDS **HAVING WEBBED TOES** having three toes that are connected by webbing [Mid-18thC. From Latin *palmatus*, which was formed from *palma* (see PALM[1].] — **pal·mate·ly** *adv.*

pal·ma·tion /pal máysh'n, paal-, paa-/ *n.* **1.** BOT **LOBE OF A PALMATE STRUCTURE** any of the lobes of a palmate formation **2. BEING PALMATE** the state of having a palmate shape

Palm Beach /paàm-/ town in southeastern Florida on the Atlantic Ocean. It is a fashionable winter resort. Population: 9,814 (1990).

palm chat *n.* a gregarious bird of open woodlands and cultivated fields of the West Indies. It is olive-brown above and yellow with dark streaks below. Latin name: *Dulus dominicus.*

palm civ·et *n.* a tree-dwelling mammal of Africa and Asia, with short legs and sharp claws. Family: Viverridae.

Olof Palme

Palme /pálmə/, **Olof** (1927–86) Swedish statesman. He was Social Democratic prime minister of Sweden (1969–76, 1982–86) and was noted for his efforts to secure world peace. Full name **Sven Olof Joachim Palme**

palm·er /paámər/ *n.* **1. MEDIEVAL PILGRIM** a pilgrim, especially a medieval Christian pilgrim who carried or wore palm leaves as proof of a visit to the Holy Land **2.** ZOOL = **palmer worm** [14thC. Via Anglo-Norman *palmer* from medieval Latin *palmarius*, from *palma* (see PALM[2]).]

Arnold Palmer

Palm·er /paámər/, **Arnold** (*b.* 1929) U.S. golfer. He won the Masters (1958, 1960, 1962, and 1964), the U.S. Open (1960), and the British Open (1960, 1961) tournaments.

Palm·er·ston /paámərstən/, **Lord, Viscount** (1784–1865) British statesman. Changing from Tory to Whig (1830), he became prime minister (1855–58; 1859–65). His robust manner led to the nickname "Firebrand Palmerston".

Pal·mer·ston North city in the south of the North Island, New Zealand, situated 87 mi./140 km north of Wellington. Population: 73,862 (1996).

palm·er worm *n.* a destructive, swarming moth caterpillar

pal·mette /pal mét/ *n.* a stylized palm leaf used as an ornament or in a decoration [Mid-19thC. From French, literally "small palm," from, ultimately, Latin *palma* (see PALM[2]).]

pal·met·to /pal méttō/ (*plural* **-tos** *or* **-toes**) *n.* **1. LOW FANNING PALM PLANT** a low palm plant with fan-shaped leaves, especially the cabbage palmetto **2. BLADE USED FOR WEAVING** the blade of a palmetto leaf, used for weaving [Mid-16thC. From Spanish *palmito*, literally "small palm," from, ultimately, Latin *palma* (see PALM[2]). The ending was changed by association with Italian words ending in *-etto*.]

pal·met·to bug *n.* a cockroach

palm·ist /paámist/ *n.* somebody who practices palmistry

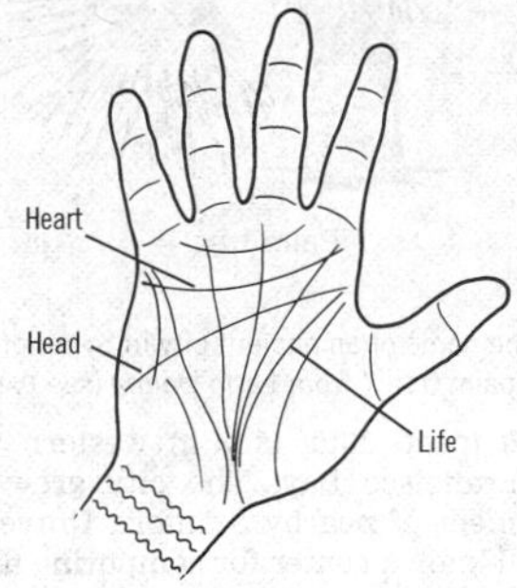

Palmistry

palm·is·try /paámistree/ *n.* the practice of examining the features of somebody's palms in order to predict that person's destiny

pal·mi·tate /pálmi tàyt, paálmi-, paámi-/ *n.* a salt or ester of palmitic acid

pal·mit·ic ac·id *n.* a waxy acid found in plant and animal fats and oils and used in making soap, candles, and food additives. Formula: $C_{16}H_{32}O_2$. [*Palmitic* from French *palmitique*, from *palme* (see PALMITIN)]

pal·mi·tin /pálmitin, paálmi-, paámi-/ *n.* an ester of palmitic acid and glycerol, found in animal fats and palm oil and used in soap-making [Mid-19thC. From French *palmitine*, from *palme* "palm tree," from Old French *paume* (see PALM[2]).]

palm oil *n.* a yellowish oil extracted from the fruit of oil palms and used as a lubricant and in soaps, foods, and cosmetics. Palm oil is high in saturated fats.

Palm Springs city in southern California, a resort and residential center. Population: 40,181 (1990).

palm sug·ar *n.* sugar made from palm tree sap

Palm Sun·day *n.* the Sunday before the Christian festival of Easter that commemorates Jesus Christ's triumphal entry into Jerusalem through a crowd waving palm branches, as narrated in the Bible. Palm fronds are distributed at some church services on this day.

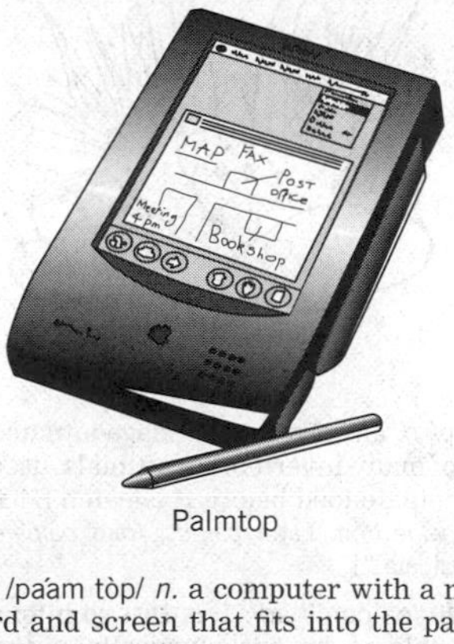

Palmtop

palm·top /paám tòp/ *n.* a computer with a miniature keyboard and screen that fits into the palm of the hand

palm tree *n.* a tree, shrub, or plant typically with a branchless trunk and a crown of pinnate or palmate leaves on top, found in tropical and subtropical regions. Family: Palmae.

palm vault·ing *n.* ARCHIT = **fan vaulting**

palm·y /paámee/ (**-i·er, -i·est**) *adj.* **1. OF PALM TREES** relating to, consisting of, or abundant in palm trees **2. FLOURISHING** prosperous or flourishing (*literary*) ○ *in her palmy days*

pal·my·ra /pal mírə/ (*plural* **-ras** *or* **-ra**) *n.* a tall Asian fan-leafed palm tree whose fronds, wood, and sap are harvested for various uses. Latin name: *Borassus flabellifer.* [Late 17thC. Alteration (influenced by

Palm tree

Palmyra, the name of an ancient city in Syria) of Portuguese *palmeira* "palm tree," from Latin *palma* (see PALM²).]

Pal·o Al·to /pàllō álltō/ city in western California on San Francisco Bay. The city grew after the establishment of nearby Stanford University, and it is a well-known center for computing technology. Population: 55,900 (1990).

Pal·o·mar, Mount /pállə maar/ mountain in southern California, northeast of San Diego. It is the site of an astronomical observatory. Height: 6,138 ft./1,871 m.

pal·o·mi·no /pàllə meenō/ (*plural* **-nos**) *n.* a golden-colored horse with a pale mane and tail, originally bred in the southwestern United States [Early 20thC. Via American Spanish from, ultimately, Latin *palumbinus* "like a dove."]

pa·loo·ka /pə lookə/ *n.* **1.** OAF somebody considered to be very clumsy and unintelligent (*slang insult*) **2.** POOR BOXER an easily beaten athlete, especially a boxer (*slang*) [Early 20thC. Origin unknown.]

Pa·louse /pə looss/ (*plural* **-louse** *or* **-lous·es**) *n.* a member of a Native North American people who originally occupied lands in southern Washington and northern Idaho, and who now live mainly in northern Washington

pa·lo·ver·de /pàllō vúrdee, -vúd/ (*plural* **-des** *or* **-de**) *n.* **1.** YELLOW-FLOWERED DESERT TREE a spiny tree or shrub of the southwestern United States and Mexico, with yellow flowers and blue-green bark. Latin name: *Cercidium floridium.* **2.** = **Jerusalem thorn** [Early 19thC. From American Spanish, literally "green tree."]

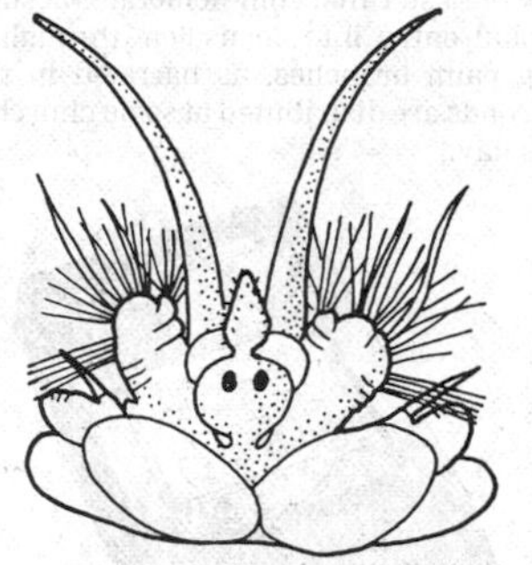

Palp

palp /palp/ *n.* a sensory appendage situated near the mouth of many invertebrate animals, used to assess or manipulate food before it is eaten [Mid-19thC. Via French *palpe* from Latin *palpus*, from *palpare* "to touch gently, palpate."]

pal·pa·ble /pálpəb'l/ *adj.* **1.** INTENSE so intense as to be almost able to be felt physically ○ *the palpable tension in the room* **2.** OBVIOUS obvious or easily observed ○ *a palpable need for change* **3.** MED FEELABLE able to be felt by the hands, especially in a medical examination ○ *a palpable lump in the abdomen* [14thC. From late Latin *palpabilis*, from Latin *palpare* "to touch gently, palpate."] —**pal·pa·bil·i·ty** /pàlpə bíllətee/ *n.* —**pal·pa·ble·ness** /pálpəb'lnəss/ *n.* —**pal·pa·bly** *adv.*

pal·pate¹ /pál pàyt/ (**-pat·ed, -pat·ing, -pates**) *vt.* to examine a part of the body by feeling with the hands and fingers, especially to distinguish between swellings that are solid and those that are filled with fluid [15thC. From Latin *palpatus*, from *palpare* "to touch gently."]

pal·pate² /pál pàyt/ *adj.* used to describe an invertebrate animal that is equipped with one or more palps [Mid-19thC. Coined from PALP + -ATE.]

pal·pe·bral /pálpəbrəl, pal peebrəl/ *adj.* relating to the eyelids [Mid-19thC. From Latin *palpebra* "eyelid."]

pal·pi plural of **palpus**

pal·pi·tate /pálpi tàyt/ (**-tat·ed, -tat·ing, -tates**) *vi.* to beat in an irregular or abnormally rapid way, either because of a medical condition or because of exertion, fear, or anxiety (*refers to the heart*) [15thC. From Latin *palpitatus*, past participle stem of *palpitare*, from *palpare* "to touch gently, palpate."] —**pal·pi·tant** *adj.*

pal·pi·ta·tion /pàlpi táysh'n/ *n.* an irregular or unusually rapid beating of the heart, either because of a medical condition or because of exertion, fear, or anxiety (*usually used in the plural*)

pal·pus /pálpəss/ (*plural* **-pi** /-pì/) *n.* = **palp** [Early 19thC. From Latin (see PALP).]

pals·grave /páwlz gràyv/ *n.* a count palatine, especially in Germany [Mid-16thC. From early Dutch *paltsgrave*, from *palts* "palatinate" + *grave* "count."]

pal·stave /páwl stàyv/ *n.* a metal ax that fits into a split handle, especially one of a distinctive bronze type found in ancient Europe [Mid-19thC. From Danish *paalstav.*]

pal·sy /páwlzee/ *n.* muscular inability to move part or all of the body (*archaic*) ◊ **Bell's palsy, cerebral palsy** [13thC. Via Old French *paralisie* from, ultimately, Latin *paralysis* (see PARALYSIS).]

pal·sy-wal·sy /pàlzi wálzee/, **pal·sy** /pálzee/ *adj.* very friendly, often in an insincere or unpleasant way (*slang*) [Mid-20thC. Humorous formation based on PAL.]

pal·ter /páwltər/ (**-tered, -ter·ing, -ters**) *vi.* (*archaic*) **1.** ACT OR TALK INSINCERELY to act or talk insincerely or deceitfully **2.** HAGGLE to haggle in bargaining [Mid-16thC. Origin unknown.] —**pal·ter·er** *n.*

pal·try /páwltree/ (**-tri·er, -tri·est**) *adj.* **1.** INSIGNIFICANT insignificant or unimportant ○ *a paltry sum of money* **2.** DESPICABLE low and contemptible [Mid-16thC. Origin uncertain: probably from Scots and northern English dialect *pelt* "coarse cloth, rubbish," of uncertain origin.] —**pal·tri·ly** *adv.* —**pal·tri·ness** *n.*

pa·lu·dal /pə lood'l, pállyəd'l/ *adj.* ECOL relating to or living in swamps or marshes [Early 19thC. From Latin *paludem*, stem of *palus* "marsh."]

pal·u·dism /pállyə dìzzəm/ *n.* malaria (*not in technical use*) [Late 19thC. From Latin *paludem* (see PALUDAL).]

pal·y /páylee/ *adj.* used to describe a heraldic shield that is divided into equal-sized sections by vertical lines [From French *palé*, from *pal* (see PALE²)]

pal·y·nol·o·gy /pàllə nóllәjee/ *n.* the study of spores and pollen, including the study of fossilized spores and pollen [Mid-20thC. Coined from Greek *palunein* "to sprinkle" + -LOGY.] —**pal·y·no·log·i·cal** /pàllənə lójjik'l/ *adj.* —**pal·y·nol·o·gist** /pàllə nóllәjist/ *n.*

pam /pam/ *n.* the jack of clubs in some card games such as loo, where it is the highest trump card [Late 17thC. Shortening of French *pamphile*, from the Greek name *Pamphilos*, literally "loved by all."]

pam. *abbr.* pamphlet

Pama-Nyun·gan *n.* a family of about 175 Native Australian languages, many of which are now extinct, spoken across most of the continent apart from some northwestern parts and Tasmania. About 100,000 people speak a Pama-Nyungan language.

Pa·mirs /pə meerz/ high plateau region in Central Asia, located mainly in Tajikistan. The highest point is Communism Peak, 24,590 ft./7,495 m.

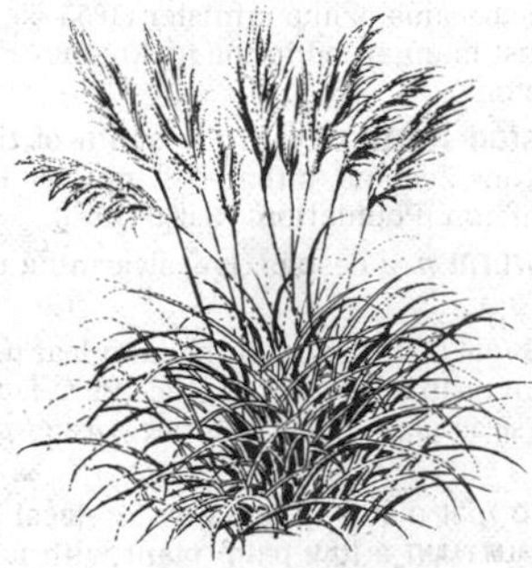

Pampas grass

pam·pas /pámpəz, pámpəss/ *n.* treeless grassy plains in temperate South America, especially Argentina (*takes a singular or plural verb*) [Early 18thC. Via Spanish *pampa* from Quechua, literally "plain."] —**pam·pe·an** /pámpee ən, pam pee ən/ *adj.*

pam·pas cat *n.* a small wild cat of South America, with long gray fur marked with dark spots and stripes. Latin name: *Felis colocolo.*

pam·pas grass *n.* a tall South American grass often grown in parks and gardens, naturalised in the southern United States. It has silky white plumes when flowering. Latin name: *Cortaderia selloana.*

pam·per /pámpər/ (**-pered, -per·ing, -pers**) *vt.* **1.** TREAT LAVISHLY to lavish attention on somebody, indulging his or her taste for luxury **2.** GRATIFY to indulge or gratify a desire or need **3.** FEED EXCESSIVELY to fill somebody with rich food (*archaic*) [14thC. Origin uncertain: probably from Low German or Dutch.] —**pam·per·er** *n.*

pam·pe·ro /pam pérrō, paam-/ (*plural* **-ros**) *n.* a strong, cold, dry wind that blows southwest from the Andes to the Atlantic, across the South American pampas [Late 18thC. From Spanish, formed from *pampa*, literally "plain."]

Pam·pers /pámpərz/ *tdmk.* a trademark for a brand of disposable diapers

pamph. *abbr.* pamphlet

pam·phlet /pámflət/ *n.* a small leaflet or paper booklet, usually unbound and coverless, that gives information or supports a position [14thC. From *Pamphilet* or *Pamflet*, popular names of *Pamphilus, seu de Amore*, a short anonymous 12thC Latin love poem, later used for any short text.]

pam·phlet·eer /pàmflə teer/ *n.* PAMPHLET WRITER somebody who writes pamphlets that contain opinionated essays, usually on a political topic ■ *vi.* (**-eered, -eer·ing, -eers**) WRITE PAMPHLETS to write material for pamphlets, especially political ones

Pam·plo·na /pam plṓnə/ city in northeastern Spain. It is the capital of the autonomous region of Navarre. Population: 181,776 (1995).

pam·pro·dac·ty·lous /pàmprō dákt'ləss/ *adj.* BIRDS used to describe a bird such as the swift that has all four toes facing forward [Late 19thC. Coined from PAN- + PRO- + DACTYL + -OUS.]

pan¹ /pan/ *n.* **1.** COOK COOKING POT a cooking pot, usually metal and with a handle, for use on the burner of a stove **2.** COOK SHALLOW COOKING DISH a shallow metal cooking dish used for baking food in an oven **3.** HOUSEHOLD CONTAINER FOR WASTE shallow container that household waste is put into for easy disposal **4.** SHALLOW, OPEN CONTAINER any shallow open container used to store, catch, or heat liquids or other substances **5.** MINING DISH FOR SORTING MINERALS a flat metal dish, shaped like a pie plate, used to separate precious minerals, especially gold, from loose soil, gravel, or sediment **6.** SCALE DISH either of the dishes suspended in a balance scale **7.** GEOL CONCAVITY IN EARTH a natural shallow sink or basin in the ground, usually filled with rainwater or mud **8.** SHALLOW AREA FOR EVAPORATING BRINE a natural or artificial concavity in the earth, in which brine is evaporated, leaving behind salt **9.** TRANSP = **hardpan 10.** THIN ICE FLOE a small, flat, thin ice floe of the type that forms near a shore or in a bay **11.** ARMS PRIMING CONTAINER IN GUN the hollow part of a flintlock gun, into which the gunpowder is loaded **12.** CRITICAL REVIEW a harshly critical review ■ *v.* (**panned, pan·ning, pans**) **1.** *vt.* CRITICIZE SEVERELY to criticize somebody or something severely, especially in a review (*informal*) **2.** *vi.* MINING SORT THROUGH DIRT FOR MINERALS to use a shallow dish to separate valuable minerals from loose soil, gravel, or sediment by washing or shaking **3.** *vi.* YIELD PRECIOUS METALS to yield valuable metals when separating minerals and leavings by means of washing or shaking using a shallow dish [Old English *panne*. From a prehistoric Germanic word that may derive, ultimately, from Latin *patina* (see PATEN).]

pan out *vi.* (*informal*) **1.** CONCLUDE to turn out or result ○ *After all our careful planning, it's a shame that things didn't pan out as we had hoped.* **2.** BE SUCCESSFUL to turn out well or successfully ○ *Her new career in moviemaking never panned out.* [From the practice by prospectors of washing gravel in a pan in order to separate the gold]

pan² /pan/ *vti.* (**panned, pan·ning, pans**) MOVE A CAMERA HORIZONTALLY FROM A FIXED POINT to move a camera horizontally from a stationary point in order to capture a broad view of a scene or to film or photograph a moving object ■ *n.* **HORIZONTAL CAMERA MOVEMENT FROM A FIXED POINT** a horizontal movement of a camera from a fixed point, or the resulting filmed shot [Early 20thC. Shortening of PANORAMA or PANORAMIC.]

pan³ /paan/ *n.* **1.** BOT **BETEL LEAF** a leaf of the betel plant **2. ROLLED BETEL LEAF WITH SPICES** a leaf of the betel plant rolled and filled with spices and lime, chewed for its flavor and as a stimulant in southwestern Asia [Early 17thC. From Hindi *pān*.]

Pan¹ /pan/ *n.* in Greek mythology, the god of nature, pastures, flocks, and forests, believed to have a human torso and head, and the hind legs, ears, and horns of a goat. Roman equivalent **Faunus**

Pan² *n.* the innermost known natural satellite of Saturn, discovered in 1990. It is approximately 20 km (12 mi.) in diameter.

Pan. *abbr.* Panama

pan- *prefix.* all, any, everyone ○ *panchromatic* ○ *Pan-Slavism* [From Greek, a form of *pas* "all" (source also of English *pancreas*)]

pan·a·ce·a /pànnə sée ə/ *n.* a supposed cure for all diseases or problems [Mid-16thC. Via Latin from Greek *panakeia*, from *panakēs* "all-healing," from *akos* "remedy."] —**pan·a·ce·an** *adj.*

pa·nache /pə násh, -naásh/ *n.* **1. DASHING STYLE** a sense or display of spirited style and self-confidence **2.** CLOTHES **HELMET PLUME** a plume or tuft of feathers, especially on a hat or helmet [Mid-16thC. Via French from Italian *pennacchio* "plume of feathers," from, ultimately, Latin *pinna* "feather" (source of English *pin*, *pinnacle*, and *pinion*).]

pa·na·da /pə naádə/ *n.* a very thick paste of flour or some other starchy ingredient and a liquid such as milk or stock that is used as a base for sauces or as binding for stuffing [Late 16thC. Via Spanish or Portuguese from, ultimately, Latin *panis* "bread."]

pan-Af·ri·can *adj.* relating to the nations of Africa, collectively or in cooperation with one another, or advocating freedom and independence for African people —**Pan-Af·ri·can·ism** *n.*

pan·a·ma /pánnə maa/, **Pan·a·ma** *n.* a Panama hat

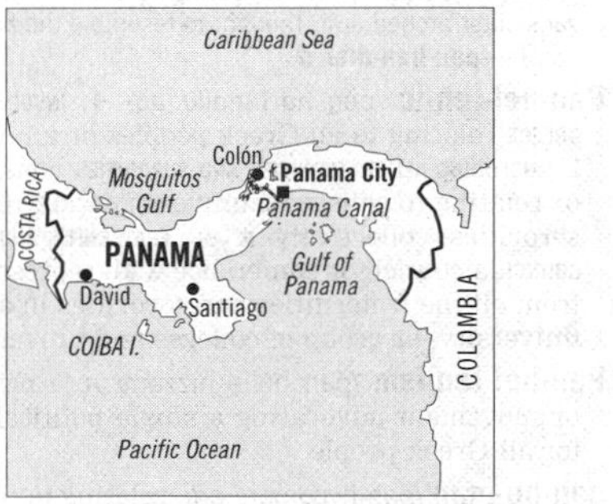

Panama

Pan·a·ma /pánnə maa/ republic in Central America. It has the Caribbean Sea to its north and the Pacific Ocean to its south, connected by the Panama Canal, and is situated between Costa Rica and Colombia. Language: Spanish. Currency: balboa. Capital: Panama City. Population: 2,674,490 (1996). Area: 29,157 sq. mi./75,517 sq. km. Official name **Republic of Panama** —**Pan·a·ma·ni·an** /pànnə máynee ən/ *n., adj.*

Pan·a·ma, Isth·mus of /pànnə maa/ narrow neck of land occupied by Panama, separating the Pacific Ocean and the Caribbean Sea

Pan·a·ma Canal canal across the Isthmus of Panama, completed in 1914. Length: 50 mi./82 km.

Pan·a·ma Cit·y capital city of Panama, located in the center of the country, on the Pacific Ocean. Population: 485,490 (1996).

Pan·a·ma hat, pan·a·ma hat, pan·a·ma *n.* a brimmed men's hat made from the plaited leaves of the jipijapa, or an imitation of such a hat

Pan·a·ma Red *n.* a very potent reddish strain of marijuana, originally from Panama

Pan-A·mer·i·can *adj.* relating to the nations of North, South, and Central America, collectively or in cooperation with one another —**Pan-A·mer·i·can·ism** *n.*

Pan-Ar·ab·ism *n.* a movement for greater cooperation among and self-reliance within Arab or Islamic nations —**Pan-Ar·ab** *n., adj.* —**Pan-Ar·a·bic** *adj.* —**Pan-Ar·ab·ist** *n., adj.*

pan·a·tel·la /pànnə téllə/, **pan·a·tel·a** *n.* a long thin cigar that does not bulge in the middle [Mid-19thC. Via American Spanish, denoting a long thin biscuit, from Italian *panatello* "small loaf," from, ultimately, Latin *panis* "bread" (source of English *pannier*).]

Pan·a·the·nae·a /pà nathə née ə/ *n.* a summer festival held annually in ancient Athens but with extra ceremony every fourth year. It involved games, sacrifices, and music and poetry contests. [Early 17thC. From Greek *panathēnaia hiera*, literally "festival of all Athenians."]

pan-broil (**pan-broiled, pan-broil·ing, pan-broils**) *vt.* to cook in an ungreased pan on a direct heat source

pan·cake /pán kàyk/ *n.* **1. THIN FRIED CAKE** a thin flat cake made by pouring batter onto a hot greased flat pan, and cooking it on both sides **2.** AIR = **pancake landing** ■ *v.* (**-caked, -cak·ing, -cakes**) **1.** *vti.* AIR **MAKE PANCAKE LANDING** to make a pancake landing or cause an aircraft to make such a landing **2.** *vt.* **FLATTEN** to turn parallel to the ground, especially a tennis racket in the course of a stroke

Pan-Cake *tdmk.* a trademark for a semisolid theatrical makeup, typically applied with a damp sponge

Pan·cake Day *n.* = **Shrove Tuesday** [So called because it is celebrated in the United Kingdom and Canada, for example, by eating pancakes, which were traditionally made to use up eggs and fat before the fast of Lent]

pan·cake ice *n.* a small flat thin piece of sea ice that drifts out into deeper water from near the shore or the bay in which it was formed

pan·cake land·ing *n.* an airplane landing in which the aircraft drops abruptly straight to the ground from a low altitude, usually due to engine failure

pan·cake tor·toise *n.* a Tanzanian turtle with a flattened flexible shell. It can slip between rocks and narrow crevices and then slightly inflate to resist being pulled out. Latin name: *Malachersus tornieri*.

Pan·cake Tues·day *n.* = **Shrove Tuesday**

pan·cet·ta /pan chéttə/ *n.* a salt-cured and spiced form of unsmoked belly of pork, used in Italian dishes [Mid-20thC. From Italian, literally "little belly," from, ultimately, Latin *pantix* "bowel, intestine" (source of English *paunch*).]

pan·chax /pán chàks/ *n.* a small tropical freshwater Southeast Asian fish that is olive, red, and yellow and is often kept as an aquarium fish. Latin name: *Aplocheilus panchax*. [Mid-20thC. From modern Latin, the former genus name.]

pan·chay·at /pən chaa yət, pən chí ət/ *n.* *S Asia* a village council in India [Early 19thC. Via Hindi *pañcāyat* from Sanskrit *pañcāyatta*, literally "depending on five" (the original number of members).]

Pan·chen La·ma /paanchən-/ *n.* the second highest ranking Lama in Tibetan Buddhism [From Tibetan, contraction of *pandi-tachen-po* "great learned one"]

pan·chro·mat·ic /pàn krō máttik/ *adj.* used to describe photographic film that is sensitive to all visible colors and some ultraviolet light

pan·cra·ti·um /pan kráyshee əm/ (*plural* **-a** /-shee ə/) *n.* an athletic event in ancient Greece, involving boxing and wrestling contests [Early 17thC. Via Latin from Greek *pagkration*, from *kratos* "strength."] —**pan·crat·ic** /pan kráttik/ *adj.*

pan·cre·as /pángkree əss, pánkree əss/ *n.* a large elongated glandular organ lying near the stomach. It secretes juices into the small intestine and the hormones insulin, glucagon, and somatostatin into the bloodstream. [Late 16thC. Via modern Latin from Greek *pagkreas*, from *kreas* "flesh."] —**pan·cre·at·ic** /pàngkree áttik, pànkree-/ *adj.*

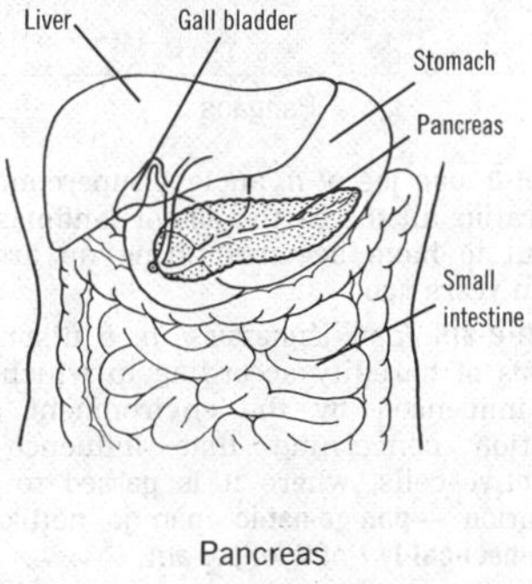

Pancreas

pancreat- *prefix.* pancreas ○ *pancreatitis* [From Greek *pankreat-*, the stem of *pankreas* (see PANCREAS)]

pan·cre·a·tec·to·my /pàngkree ə téktəmee, pànkree-/ (*plural* **-mies**) *n.* whole or partial removal of the pancreas by surgery

pan·cre·at·ic duct *n.* a duct that carries pancreatic juice and, in human beings, runs from the pancreas to join the common bile duct, which empties into the small intestine

pan·cre·at·ic juice *n.* a watery alkaline fluid secreted by the pancreas. It contains enzymes that break down partially digested food in the small intestine.

pan·cre·a·tin /pángkree ət'n, pan krée ət'n, -ətin/ *n.* **1. DIGESTIVE AID FROM PANCREATIC ENZYMES** a digestive aid made from a mixture of pancreatic enzymes extracted from domestic animals **2. MIXTURE OF PANCREATIC ENZYMES** the mixture of digestive enzymes produced by the pancreas, including amylase, lipase, and trypsin

pan·cre·a·ti·tis /pàngkree ə títiss, pànkree-/ *n.* inflammation of the pancreas

pan·cre·o·zy·min /pángkri ō zímin, pánkri ō zímin/ *n.* = **cholecystokinin** [Mid-20thC. From PANCREAS + *zymin*.]

Panda

pan·da /pándə/ *n.* **1. panda bear LARGE BLACK-AND-WHITE CHINESE MAMMAL** a large bamboo-eating mammal of central China, with bold black-and-white markings, including black patches over the eyes. Latin name: *Ailuropodia melanoleuca*. **2.** = **red panda** [Mid-19thC. Via French from the Nepalese name of the red panda.]

pan·da·nus /pan dáynəss, -dánnəss/ (*plural* **-nus·es** *or* **-nus**) *n.* a tropical plant resembling a palm, with prop roots and a crown of narrow leaves that are often used to make mats. Genus: *Pandanus*. [Mid-19thC. Via modern Latin from Malay *pandan*.]

Pan·de·an /pan dee ən/ *adj.* relating to the mythological Greek god Pan

Pan·de·an pipes *npl.* = **panpipes**

pan·dect /pán dèkt/ *n.* **1. BODY OF LAWS** a set of documents containing all the laws of a country or society **2. COMPREHENSIVE TREATISE** a comprehensive treatise on a subject [Mid-16thC. Directly or via French from Latin *pandecta*, from Greek *pandektēs* "all-receiving," from *dekhesthai* "to receive."]

Pan·dects /pán dèkts/ *n.* = **Digest** *n.*

pan·dem·ic /pan démmik/ *adj.* **HAVING WIDESPREAD EFFECT** existing in the form of a widespread epidemic that affects people in many different countries. AIDS is currently considered to be pandemic. ■ *n.* **VERY WIDESPREAD DISEASE** a disease or condition that is found in a large part of a population [Mid-17thC. From Greek *pandēmos* "public," literally "of all the people," from *dēmos* "people" (source of English *democracy*).]

pan·de·mo·ni·um /pàndə mónee əm/ *n.* **1. CHAOS** wild uproar and chaos **2. NOISY CONFUSED PLACE** a place or situation that is noisy and chaotic [Mid-17thC. From modern Latin *Pandaemonium*, from Greek *daimōn* (see DEMON).] —**pan·de·mo·ni·ac** *adj.* —**pan·de·mon·ic** /pàndə mónnik/ *adj.*

Pan·de·mo·ni·um *n.* Hell, or any place of chaos or torment (*literary*) [From the name of the capital of Hell in Milton's *Paradise Lost*]

pan·der /pándər/ *vi.* (**-dered, -der·ing, -ders**) **1. INDULGE WEAKNESSES** to indulge somebody's weaknesses or questionable wishes and tastes ○ *tired of pandering to their children's demands* **2. PROCURE SEXUAL FAVORS** to procure sexual favors for somebody (*disapproving*) ■ *n.* **1. pander, panderer SOMEBODY WHO INDULGES ANOTHER'S WEAKNESSES** somebody who indulges another's weaknesses or questionable wishes and tastes (*disapproving*) **2. pander, panderer ROMANTIC GO-BETWEEN** a go-between in an illicit or secret romantic or sexual relationship (*disapproving*) **3. PIMP** a pimp (*archaic*) [14thC. From *pandarus.*]

P and H, p. and h., p&h *abbr.* postage and handling

pan·dit /pándit/ *n.* a wise or learned man in India, especailly a Brahman who is an expert in Hindu culture, law, and philosophy

P & L *abbr.* profit and loss

Pan·do·ra[1] /pan dáwrə/ *n.* in Greek mythology, the first woman, who was sent by the gods with a jar full of evils in order to avenge Prometheus's theft of fire. She opened the jar out of curiosity, thus releasing the evils into the world.

Pan·do·ra[2] /pan dáwrə/ *n.* a small inner natural satellite of Saturn, discovered in 1980 by Voyager 2. It is irregular in shape having a maximum dimension of 110 km (68 mi.).

Pan·do·ra's box *n.* **1. OBJECT IN GREEK MYTHOLOGY** in Greek mythology, the jar, later referred to as a box, from which Pandora allowed all the world's evils to escape **2. SET OF ILLS** the source of a great collection of ills that need not be faced unless an unwise action is taken ○ *If you criticize her work, you'll be opening a real Pandora's box.*

pan·dore /pán dàwr/ *n.* = **bandore**

pan·dour /pán do͝or/ *n.* HIST, MIL **1. 18TH-CENTURY CROATIAN SOLDIER** a soldier in a notorious Croatian regiment in the 18th-century Austrian army **2. KHOIKHOI SOLDIER** a Khoikhoi soldier belonging to the Dutch East India Company's force in South Africa at the beginning of the 19th century [Mid-18thC. Via French *pandur* or German *Pandur* from Serbo-Croat *pandur* "constable, bailiff," of uncertain origin: probably from medieval Latin *banderius* "guard of vineyards or fields."]

pan·dow·dy /pan dówdee/ (*plural* **-dies**) *n.* a dish made of sliced apples and spices covered with a biscuit crust and baked in a deep pan [Mid-19thC. Origin uncertain: probably ultimately from PAN[1] + a variant of DOUGH.]

pan·du·rate /pan do͝orət/, **pan·du·ri·form** /pan do͝orə fàwrm/ *adj.* used to describe a leaf that is shaped like a violin, with rounded ends and a tapering middle [Late 18thC. From Latin *pandura*, from Greek *pandoura.*]

pan·du·ri·form /pan do͝orə fàwrm/ *adj.* = **pandurate**

pane /payn/ *n.* **1. GLAZED SECTION OF WINDOW** a glazed section of a window or door **2. PIECE OF GLASS IN WINDOW** a piece of plate glass in a window or door **3. SECTION OF SURFACE** a distinct section of a surface such as a door or wall **4. SURFACE OF FACETED OBJECT** a surface on a faceted object, e.g., a hardware nut or cut jewel **5. SECTION OF SHEET OF STAMPS** rectangular section into which a sheet of postage stamps is divided before being sold [13thC. Via French *pan* from Latin *pannus* "piece of cloth." Current senses evolved from "piece of cloth" via "distinct part or panel of a garment."]

pan·e·gyr·ic /pànnə jeérik, pànnə jírik/ *n.* extravagant praise delivered in formal speech or writing (*formal*) [Early 17thC. Via French *panégyrique* from Latin *panegyricus* "public eulogy" from, ultimately, Greek *paneguris* "public assembly," from *aguris* "assembly, marketplace."] —**pan·e·gyr·i·cal** *adj.* —**pan·e·gyr·i·cal·ly** *adv.* —**pan·e·gyr·ist** *n.*

pan·e·gy·rize /pánnəjə rìz/ (**-rized, -riz·ing, -riz·es**) *vti.* to praise somebody or something, especially extravagantly in formal speech or writing (*formal*)

pan·el /pánn'l/ *n.* **1.** BUILDING **FLAT RECTANGULAR PART** a flat rectangular piece of hard material that serves as a part of something such as a door or wall, often raised above or sunk in the surface **2.** BUILDING **FENCE SECTION** a section between two posts in a fence or gate **3.** SEW **STRIP OF FABRIC IN GARMENT** a vertical section of fabric sewn onto other such sections in a flowing garment or drapery **4.** PAINTING **WOODEN SURFACE FOR PAINTING** a thin piece of wood used as a surface for oil painting, or the painting on it **5.** DRAWING **COMIC STRIP FRAME** a section depicting a single scene in a comic strip **6.** AEROSP **PART OF AIRCRAFT WING** a section or surface of an airplane wing **7.** ENG **CLUSTER OF PERFORMANCE-MEASURING INSTRUMENTS** a surface on which performance-measuring instruments such as gauges, dials, lights, and digital displays are clustered **8.** COMPUT **CONTROL AREA OF COMPUTER** the collection of lights, digital displays, and switches used to monitor and control the operation of a computer **9.** COMPUT **DISPLAY ON COMPUTER SCREEN** a display of related information on a computer screen, often a list of options **10.** ARTS **GROUP OF JUDGES OR SPEAKERS** a group of people who publicly discuss or judge something, usually in a situation where they sit in a row to face an audience or a competition arena **11.** = **panel discussion 12.** LAW **LIST OF PEOPLE FOR JURY DUTY** a list of people summoned as potential jurors, or the people themselves **13.** LAW **JURY** a jury in a court proceeding ■ *vt.* (**-eled, -el·ing, -els**) **1.** BUILDING **SUPPLY WITH PANELS** to furnish, cover, or decorate something with panels, especially wooden paneling for walls **2.** LAW **IMPANEL** to impanel [14thC. Via Old French from *pan* "piece of cloth" (see PANE). The underlying sense is of a distinct part.]

pan·el dis·cus·sion *n.* a public discussion of an issue by a group of experts or other concerned people

pan·el heat·ing *n.* a domestic heating system in which heating elements are housed in panels attached to walls or floors

pan·el·ing /pánn'ling/ *n.* **1. WOODEN WALL COVERING** thin boards or sheets of wood for covering walls, especially as decoration **2. PANEL-COVERED WALL** a panel-covered wall or other surface

pan·el·ist /pánn'list/ *n.* somebody who is a member of a panel

pan·el·ling *n.* U.K. = **paneling**

pan·el·list *n.* U.K. = **panelist**

pan·el truck *n.* a small delivery truck or van that is entirely enclosed, with access to the storage area from the driver's seat

pan·et·to·ne /pànnə tónee/ (*plural* **-et·to·nes** *or* **-net·to·ni**) *n.* a tall Italian yeast cake flavored with vanilla and dried and candied fruits, traditionally eaten at Christmas [Early 20thC. From Italian, from *pane* "bread," from Latin *panis.*]

Pan-Eu·ro·pe·an *adj.* relating to all the nations of Europe, collectively or in cooperation with one another

pan fish *n.* a small freshwater food fish, considered too small to be classed as a game fish, that is the right size to fry whole in a skillet

pan-fry (**pan-fried, pan-fry·ing, pan-fries**) *vt.* to fry food, usually fish or meat, in a frying pan with a little fat

pang /pang/ *n.* **1. SHARP PAIN** a short sharp pain **2. INTENSE EMOTION** a sudden, intense, and usually distressing feeling [15thC. Origin uncertain: perhaps an alteration of PRONG.]

pan·ga /paáng gə/ *n.* an African knife with a long, broad, and heavy blade, often used for cutting down sugarcane [Mid-20thC. From Swahili.]

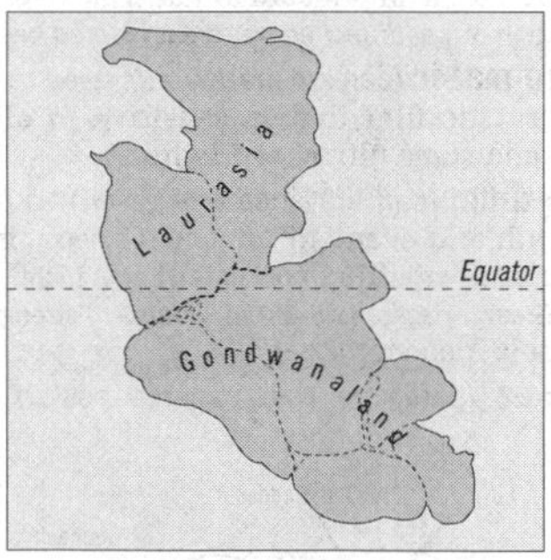

Pangaea

Pan·gae·a /pan jeé ə/ *n.* ancient supercontinent incorporating all the earth's major landmasses. It is thought to have begun splitting up around 200 million years ago.

pan·gen·e·sis /pan jénnəssiss/ *n.* a disproved hypothesis of heredity according to which somatic cells influenced by the environment send information concerning that influence to reproductive cells, where it is passed to the next generation —**pan·ge·net·ic** /pàn jə néttik/ *adj.* —**pan·ge·net·i·cal·ly** /-néttikəlee/ *adv.*

Pan·gloss·i·an /pan glóssee ən/ *adj.* excessively and inappropriately optimistic (*literary*) [Mid-19thC. From Dr *Pangloss*, a philosopher in Voltaire's *Candide* 1759, who always asserts that "all is for the best in the best of all possible worlds."]

pan·go·la grass /pan gólə-/ *n.* African grass of importance in the South [Mid-20thC. "Pangola" is a variant of *Pongola*; the grass was named for the *Pongola* river in South Africa.]

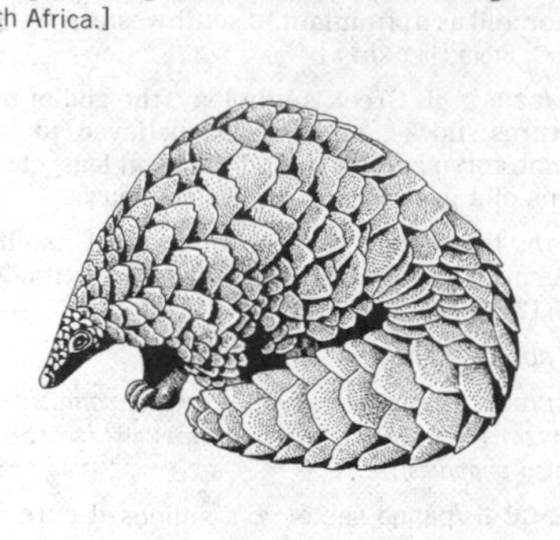

Pangolin

pan·go·lin /páng gəlin, pang gólin/ *n.* an African and Asian mammal with horny scales, a long tapering snout and tail, and a long sticky tongue for catching ants and termites. Order: Pholidota. [Late 18thC. From Malay *peng-guling*, literally "roller," because it rolls itself up when frightened.]

pan·han·dle[1] /pán hànd'l/ *n.* **1. HANDLE OF A PAN** the handle of a cooking pan **2. pan·han·dle, Pan·han·dle** GEOG **STRIP OF LAND EXTENDING FROM STATE** a narrow section of land shaped like the handle of a cooking pan that extends away from the body of the state or territory it belongs to ○ *the Texas Panhandle*

pan·han·dle[2] /pán hànd'l/ (**-dled, -dling, -dles**) *v.* **1.** *vi.* **BEG MONEY FROM STRANGERS** to beg for money on the street by approaching and talking to passers-by **2.** *vt.* **GET BY BEGGING** to get money from a stranger by approaching him or her in the street and begging **3.** *vt.* **BEG MONEY FROM** to approach and beg for money from somebody [Late 19thC. Probably so called from the beggar's outstretched arm, thought to resemble the handle of a pan.] —**pan·han·dler** *n.*

Pan·hel·len·ic /pàn hə lénnik/ *adj.* **1. INVOLVING ALL OF GREECE** relating to all Greek peoples or all of Greece **2. INCLUDING ALL FRATERNITIES AND SORORITIES** consisting of or relating to college or university fraternities and sororities collectively ■ *n.* **FRATERNITY AND SORORITY COUNCIL** a council or conference with representatives from all the fraternities and sororities in a college, university, or group of colleges and universities

Pan·hel·len·ism /pan héllə nìzzəm/ *n.* a philosophy or movement advocating a single political system for all Greek people

pan·hu·man /pan hyo͞omən/ *adj.* relating to the whole of the human race [Early 20thC. Coined from PAN- + HUMAN.]

pan·ic[1] /pánnik/ *n.* **1. OVERPOWERING FEAR OR ANXIETY** a sudden feeling of fear or anxiety, especially among many people, that comes on suddenly, is overwhelming, appears to be uncontrollable, and may seem to be unfounded **2. FUNNY PERSON OR THING** somebody or something extremely funny (*slang*) ○ *The comedian's monologue was a panic.* ■ *adj.* **ABOUT OR RESULTING FROM PANIC** relating to, responding to, or resulting from panic or possible panic ○ *panic selling on the stock market* ■ *vti.* (**-icked, -ick·ing, -ics**) **BE OR MAKE SOMEBODY EXTREMELY AFRAID** to feel panic, or make a person or animal feel panic [Early 17thC. Via French *panique* and modern Latin *panicus* "terrified," from, ultimately, Greek *Pan*, the Greek god of nature whose appearance was believed to induce irrational fear.] —**pan·ick·y** *adj.*

pan·ic[2] *n.* = **panic grass**

Pan·ic *adj.* referring or relating to Pan, a god in Greek mythology

pan·ic at·tack *n.* a sudden overpowering feeling of fear or anxiety that prevents somebody from functioning, often triggered by a past or present source of anxiety

pan·ic but·ton *n.* an alarm to call security staff or summon help in an emergency ◇ **hit** *or* **press** *or* **push the panic button** to react to a perceived emergency or crisis by panicking and responding too hastily (*informal*)

pan·ic buy·ing *n.* the buying of a particular product or products in quantity by a large number of people who fear a possible shortage

pan·ic dis·or·der *n.* a condition in which somebody has recurrent panic attacks

pan·ic grass, **pan·ic, pan·nick** *n.* a grass, e.g., millet, used for grain fodder and as a cereal. Genus: *Panicum.* [Panic from Latin *panicum* "foxtail millet," used as genus name]

pan·i·cle /pánnik'l/ *n.* **1. FLOWER CLUSTER ALONG STEM** a cluster of flowers on a plant consisting of a number of individual stalks (**racemes**) each of which has a series of single flowers along its length **2. PYRAMID-SHAPED FLOWER CLUSTER** a loose branching pyramid-shaped cluster of flowers [Late 16thC. From Latin *panicula*, literally "little ear of millet," from *panus* "swelling, ear of millet."]

pan·i·cled *adj.* = **paniculate**

pan·ic-strick·en, **pan·ic-struck** *adj.* suddenly affected by or characterized by panic

pa·nic·u·late /pə níkyələt, -làyt/, **pa·nic·u·lat·ed** /pə níkyə làytəd/, **pan·i·cled** /pánnik'ld/ *adj.* growing in, forming, or resembling a panicle

Pan·is·lam·ism /pàn iz laá mìzzəm, pan ízzlə-, pàn iss laá mìzzəm, pan ísslə-/ *n.* a movement that aims to unify Muslim countries and spread the Islamic religion [Late 19thC. Coined from PAN- + ISLAMISM.] —**Pan·is·lam·ic** /pàn iz laámik, pàn iss laámik/ *adj.* —**Pan·is·lam·ist** /pàn iz laámist, pan ízzlə-, pàn iss laámist, pan ísslə-/ *n., adj.*

Pan·ja·bi *n., adj.* = **Punjabi**

pan·jan·drum /pan jándrəm/ (*plural* **-drums** *or* **pan·jan·dra** /-drə/) *n.* somebody, especially an official, who is pompous or pretentious [Mid-18thC. Nonsense word.]

WORD KEY: ORIGIN

Panjandrum was coined in 1755 by the English actor and playwright Samuel Foote (1720–77) to test the memory of the actor Charles Macklin, who claimed to be able to memorize and repeat anything said to him (it was one of several inventions in the same vein that Foote put to him): "And there were present. . .the Joblillies, and the Garyulies, and the Grand Panjandrum himself, with the little round button at top." It did not spread into general use until the 19th century.

AKG London

Emmeline Pankhurst

Pank·hurst /pángk hùrst/, **Emmeline** (1858–1928) British campaigner for woman suffrage. She founded the Women's Social and Political Union (1903) in Manchester, England. She was frequently imprisoned for destroying property, but during World War I abandoned her campaign and encouraged women to do industrial war work.

pan·leu·ko·pe·ni·a /pàn lòokə peénee ə/, **pan·leu·co·pe·ni·a** *n.* feline distemper (*technical*) [Mid-20thC. Coined from PAN- + LEUKOPENIA.]

pan·mix·i·a /pan míksee ə/, **pan·mix·is** /pan míksiss/ *n.* random breeding and free interchange of genes within a population [Late 19thC. Via modern Latin from German *Panmixie*, literally "all mixing," from, ultimately, Greek *mixis* "mixing, mingling."] —**pan·mic·tic** *adj.*

panne /pan/ *n.* a lightweight silk or rayon fabric resembling velvet [Late 18thC. From French, of unknown origin.]

pan·nick *n.* = **panic grass**

pan·nier /pánnyər, pánnee ər/ *n.* **1. BASKET ON BACK OF ANIMAL** a large basket, often one of a pair, that is placed on the back of a horse, donkey, or other pack animal **2. BASKET CARRIED ON SOMEBODY'S BACK** a basket that can be carried on a person's back **3. BAG ON BACK OF BICYCLE** one of a pair of bags carried on either side of the back or front wheel of a bicycle or motorcycle **4.** CLOTHES, HIST **FRAMEWORK TO WIDEN SKIRT** a framework of cane worn by women in the 18th century at each side of the hips to widen a skirt **5.** CLOTHES, HIST **OVERSKIRT LOOPED UP AT HIPS** an overskirt looped up at the hips to show the underskirt and give the impression of fullness, worn in the second half of the 19th century [13thC. Via Old French *pannier* from Latin *panarium* "breadbasket," from *panis* "bread," earlier "food" (source also of English *pantry*).]

pan·ni·kin /pánnikin/ *n. U.K.* a small metal drinking cup [Early 19thC. Formed from PAN[1], on the model of CANNIKIN "cup."]

pa·no·cha /pə nṓchə/ *n.* **1. BROWN SUGAR** a coarse brown sugar produced in Mexico and usually sold in hard cone-shaped pieces **2.** = **penuche** [Mid-19thC. From American Spanish, of uncertain origin: probably from Spanish, "ear of grain," from Latin *panicula* (see PANICLE).]

pan·o·ply /pánnəplee/ (*plural* **-plies**) *n.* **1. FULL ARRAY** an impressive and magnificent display or array of something **2.** CLOTHES **FULL CEREMONIAL DRESS** ceremonial dress with all the necessary accessories **3.** MIL **FULL ARMOR** a full suit of armor and equipment for a warrior **4. PROTECTIVE COVERING** a covering that protects something [Late 16thC. Via French from Greek *panoplia*, literally "all weapons," from *hopla* "weapons."] —**pan·o·plied** *adj.*

pan·op·tic /pan óptik/, **pan·op·ti·cal** /-óptik'l/ *adj.* taking in or showing everything in a single view [Early 19thC. Formed from Greek *panoptos*, literally "seen by all," and *panoptēs*, literally "all-seeing," both formed in turn from *optos* "visible."] —**pan·op·ti·cal·ly** *adv.*

pan·o·ram·a /pànnə rámmə, pànnə raámə/ *n.* **1. 360° VIEW** an unobstructed view extending in all directions, especially of a landscape **2. COMPREHENSIVE SURVEY** an all-encompassing survey of a particular topic or issue **3.** ARTS, PHOTOGRAPHY **PICTURE WITH WIDE VIEW** a picture or photograph that has a wide view, especially one that is unrolled gradually in front of the spectator **4.** ARTS = **cyclorama** [Late 18thC. Coined from PAN- + Greek *horama* "view," from *horan* "to see."] —**pan·o·ram·ic** /pànnə rámmik/ *adj.* —**pan·o·ram·i·cal·ly** /-rámmikəlee/ *adv.*

WORD KEY: ORIGIN

Panorama was coined in the late 1780s by an Irish artist called Robert Barker for a method he had invented for painting a scene on the inside of a cylinder in such a way that its perspective would seem correct to someone viewing it from inside the cylinder. He put his invention into practice in 1793 when he opened his "Panorama," a large building in Leicester Square, London, where the public could come and gaze at such all-encompassing scenes. The modern abstract meaning was in use by the early 19th century.

pan·o·ram·ic sight *n.* a sight on a military weapon that gives the user a wide-angled view of the target area

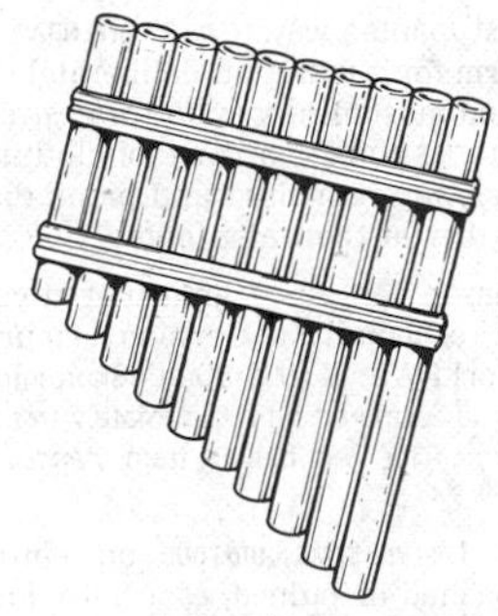

Panpipes

pan·pipes /pán pīps/ *npl.* a set of reeds of different lengths that are bound together in a row and played by blowing across the top of each pipe. Panpipes have been in use since ancient times and are today often associated with Peruvian music. [Early 19thC. *Pan* from the name of the mythological Greek god supposed to have invented them.]

pan·sex·ual /pan sékshoo əl/ *adj.* relating to a sexuality that expresses itself in many different forms [Early 20thC. Coined from PAN- + SEXUAL.] —**pan·sex·u·al·i·ty** /pan sèkshoo állətee/ *n.*

pan·sper·mi·a /pan spúrmee ə/ *n.* a theory of biogenetics that states that the universe is full of spores that germinate when they find a favorable environment [Mid-19thC. From Greek, "doctrine that the elements are made of all the seeds of things," from, ultimately, *sperma* "seed" (source also of English *sperm*).]

pan·sy /pánzee/ *n.* (*plural* **-sies**) **1.** PLANTS **FLOWER WITH BRIGHT VELVETY PETALS** a European plant with brightly colored velvety flowers that usually have black or dark centers. Genus: *Viola* and *Achimenes.* **2. OFFENSIVE TERM** a highly offensive term for a gay man or boy (*dated offensive*) **3. OFFENSIVE TERM** a highly offensive term for an effeminate man or boy (*dated offensive*) **4.** COLORS **DEEP VIOLET** a deep violet color ■ *adj.* COLORS **DEEP VIOLET IN COLOR** of a deep violet color [15thC. From French *pensée*, literally "thought" (from its lowered head), feminine past participle of *penser* "to think" (source also of English *pensive*).]

pant[1] /pant/ *v.* (**pant·ed, pant·ing, pants**) **1.** *vi.* **TAKE SHORT FAST SHALLOW BREATHS** to take short fast shallow breaths, especially when excited, hot, or after physical exertion **2.** *vt.* **SAY SOMETHING BREATHLESSLY** to say something while trying to catch your breath **3.** *vi.* **YEARN** to have a strong desire and yearning for somebody or something **4.** *vi.* **PULSATE QUICKLY** to throb at a fast rhythm ■ *n.* **SHALLOW BREATH** a short fast shallow breath [15thC. From assumed Anglo-Norman, "to gasp," ultimately from Vulgar Latin *phantasiare* "to gasp in horror," from Latin *phantasia* "apparition" (source also of English *fancy* and *fantasy*).]

pant[2] /pant/ *n.* a pair of trousers (*formal*) [Late 19thC. Back-formation.]

pant- *prefix.* = **panto-** (*used before vowels*)

pan·ta·lets /pàntə léts/, **pan·ta·lettes** *npl.* HIST **1. WOMEN'S LONG UNDERPANTS** long underpants extending below the skirt, usually with a frill around the bottom of each leg, worn by women in the first half of the 19th century **2. FRILLS ON PANTALETS** a pair of frills, one at the bottom of each leg, on a pair of pantalets [Mid-19thC. Formed from PANTALOON with the literal sense "little pantaloons."]

pan·ta·loon /pàntə lóon/ *n.* a character in pantomime who is the victim of the clown's jokes and tricks [Late 16thC. Via French *pantalon* from Italian *Pantalone* (see PANTALOON).]

Pan·ta·loon *n.* a character in Italian commedia dell'arte, a very thin man of advanced years who is easily tricked and who wears pantaloons and slippers [Late 16thC. Origin uncertain: probably named for *San Pantaleone* "Saint Pantaleon," patron saint of Venice.]

pan·ta·loons /pàntə lóonz/ *npl.* **1. WIDE PANTS GATHERED AT ANKLE** loose-fitting pants that are gathered at the ankle **2. BAGGY PANTS** pants that fit very loosely (*informal humorous*) **3.** HIST **TIGHT-FITTING MEN'S PANTS** tight-fitting men's pants fastened with buttons or ribbons at the ankle and sometimes held with a strap under the instep, worn in the early 19th century **4.** HIST **17C ENGLISH PANTS** men's wide ankle-length breeches, worn especially in England in the late 17th century [Mid-17thC. See PANTALOON.]

pant-dress *n.* a dress that has a divided skirt, consisting of a bodice with attached culottes (*dated*)

pan·tech·ni·con /pan téknikən, pan tékni kòn/ *n. U.K.* a large moving van [Mid-19thC. Coined from PAN- + Greek *tekhnikos* "artistic," because it originally denoted a building in London, England, used as a bazaar (and, later, as a furniture warehouse).]

WORD KEY: ORIGIN

The original ***Pantechnicon*** was a huge complex of warehouses, wine vaults, and other storage facilities in Motcomb Street, in London's Belgravia. Built in 1830 and supposed to be fireproof, it was almost totally destroyed by fire in 1874. It seems originally to have been intended to be a bazaar. Hence its name, literally "everything artistic," denoting that all sorts of manufactured wares were to be bought there. But it was its role as a furniture repository that brought it into the general language. Moving vans taking furniture there came to be known as "pantechnicon vans," and by the 1890s ***pantechnicon*** was a generic term for "moving van."

pan·the·ism /pánthee ìzzəm/ *n.* **1. BELIEF THAT GOD IS EVERYTHING** the belief that God and the material world are one and the same thing and that God is present in everything **2. BELIEF IN ALL DEITIES** the belief in and worship of all or many deities [Mid-18thC. Coined from PAN- + Greek *theos* "god" + -ISM.] —**pan·the·ist** *n.* —**pan·the·is·tic** /pànthee ístik/ *adj.* —**pan·the·is·ti·cal·ly** /-ístikəlee/ *adv.*

pan·the·on /pánthee ən, pánthee òn/ *n.* **1.** RELIG **TEMPLE** a temple dedicated to all deities **2.** RELIG **ALL DEITIES OF SPECIFIC RELIGION** all the deities of a particular religion considered collectively **3.** ARCHIT **MEMORIAL TO DEAD HEROES** a monument or public building commemorating the dead heroes of a nation **4. GROUP OF IMPORTANT PEOPLE** a group of people who are the most famous or respected in a particular field [15thC. Via Latin from Greek *pantheion*, literally "of all the gods," from, ultimately, *theos* "god."]

Pan·the·on *n.* a circular temple in Rome that was completed in 27 B.C. and dedicated to all the deities but which has been used as a Christian church since A.D. 609

pan·ther /pánthər/ (*plural* **-thers** *or* **pan·ther**) *n.* **1. BLACK LEOPARD** a leopard, especially in its black unspotted phase **2.** = **mountain lion** [13thC. Via Old French *pantere* from, ultimately, Greek *panthēr*.]

pant·ie gir·dle, **pant·y gir·dle** *n.* a woman's undergarment with a sewn-in crotch like underpants, but made of elasticized material in order to give the abdomen a flatter appearance

pant·ies /pánteez/ *npl.* short light fitted underpants for women or girls (*informal*) [Mid-19thC. Formed from PANTS.]

pan·ti·hose /pánti hōz/ *npl.* = **pantyhose**

pan·tile /pán tīl/ *n.* a roof tile made in an S shape so that the downcurving tail of the S overlaps the upcurving head of the S of the tile next to it [Mid-17thC. From PAN[1] + TILE, probably modeled on Dutch *dakpan* "roof pan."]

pan·ti·soc·ra·cy /pàntə sókrəssee/ (*plural* **-cies**) *n.* a planned Utopian community in which everyone shares power and is equal [Late 18thC. Coined from PANTO- + Greek *isokratia* "equality of power."]

panto- *prefix.* all ○ *pantograph* [From Greek *pant-*, the stem of *pas* (source also of English *pan* and *pancreas*)]

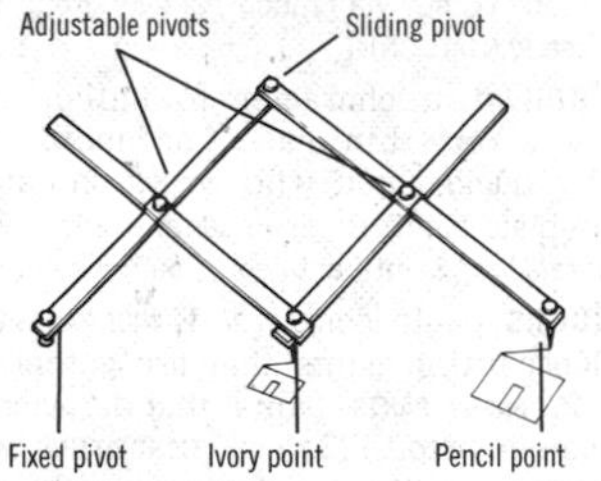

Pantograph

pan·to·graph /pántə gràf/ *n.* **1.** DRAWING **COPYING INSTRUMENT** an instrument that consists of a set of adjustable interconnected bars forming a parallelogram and is used to copy line drawings or maps to any scale **2.** TECH **FRAME OR BRACKET** a device shaped like a pantograph and used as a frame or bracket **3.** RAIL **CURRENT-SUPPLY DEVICE FOR ELECTRIC TRAIN** a device on the roof of electric trains and locomotives for picking up electric current from overhead wires [Early 18thC. Coined from PANTO- + -GRAPH.] —**pan·tog·ra·pher** /pan tóggrəfər/ *n.* —**pan·to·graph·ic** /pàntə gráffik/ *adj.* —**pan·to·graph·i·cal·ly** /-gráffikəlee/ *adv.*

pan·to·mime /pántə mīm/ *n.* **1.** THEATER **WORDLESS THEATRICAL PERFORMANCE** a style of theater or storytelling, or a performance in this style, that is acted without speaking and usually without any props, by using gesture and expression **2.** THEATER **MIME ARTIST** a person who acts without speaking, using gesture and expression **3. WORDLESS COMMUNICATION** communication using gesture and expression instead of words **4.** HIST, THEATER **ROMAN THEATRICAL PERFORMANCE** a theatrical performance in ancient Rome by one masked actor who played all the characters, using only dance, gesture, and expression, and no words, while a chorus narrated the story **5.** *U.K.* THEATER **HUMOROUS BRITISH THEATRICAL ENTERTAINMENT** a style of British theater, or a play in this style, traditionally performed at Christmas, in which a folktale or children's story is told with jokes, songs, and dancing **6.** HIST, THEATER **ROMAN ACTOR** an actor in a Roman pantomime ■ *vti.* (**mimed, mim·ing, -mimes**) THEATER **EXPRESS SOMETHING SILENTLY** to act out a story, event, or situation, or represent an object, without words by the use of hand and body movements and facial expressions [Late 16thC. Via Latin *pantomimus* "mime artist," from Greek *pantomōmos*, literally "complete imitator," from *mōmos* "imitator" (source of English *mime*).] —**pan·to·mim·ic** /pàntə mímmik/ *adj.* —**pan·to·mim·ist** /pántə mīmist, pántə mìmmist/ *n.*

pan·to·then·ate /pàntə thé nàyt, pan tóthə nàyt/ *n.* a salt or an ester of pantothenic acid [Mid-20thC. Coined from PANTOTHENIC ACID.]

pan·to·then·ic ac·id /pàntə thénnik-/ *n.* a thick oily acid that belongs to the vitamin B complex, is found in living tissue, and is essential for the growth of some animals. Formula: $C_9H_{17}NO_5$. [Formed from Greek *pantothen* "from every side," because it is widely found]

pan·toum /pan to͞om/ *n.* a form of verse in which the second and fourth lines of each four-line verse are repeated as the first and third lines of the following verse [Late 18thC. Via French from Malay *pantun*.]

pan·trop·ic /pan tróppik/, **pan·trop·i·cal** /-k'l/ *adj.* found throughout the tropics [Mid-20thC. Coined from PAN- + TROPIC.]

pan·try /pántree/ (*plural* **pan·tries**) *n.* **1. PLACE FOR STORING FOOD** a small closed space connected to a kitchen, often with a door, in which food and utensils for food preparation can be stored **2. SMALL ROOM FOR STORING FOOD** a highly ventilated cold small room or walk-in cupboard with shelves and a marble surface used for storing food [13thC. Via Old French *paneterie* "cupboard for bread," from, ultimately, late Latin *panarius* "breadseller," from Latin *panis* "bread" (source also of English *company*).]

pants /pants/ *npl.* **1.** *U.S., Can, Aus* **MEN'S OR WOMEN'S TROUSERS** an item of clothing that covers the part of the body from the waist to the ankles or, sometimes, the knees, each leg having a separate tubular piece **2. ITEM OF UNDERWEAR** an item of clothing worn next to the skin that covers the buttocks and genital area [Mid-19thC. Shortening of PANTALOONS.] ◇ **beat the pants off somebody** to defeat somebody decisively (*informal*) ◇ **bore** *or* **scare** *or* **charm the pants off somebody** to bore, scare, or charm somebody very much (*informal*) ◇ **caught with your pants down** to be caught in an unprepared or embarrassing position ◇ **wear the pants** *U.S., Can, ANZ* to be the boss

pant·suit /pánt so͞ot/, **pants suit** *n.* a woman's outfit consisting of a jacket and pants that are made of the same material

panty gir·dle *n.* = **pantie girdle**

pant·y·hose /pántee hōz/, **pant·y hose, pan·ti·hose** *npl.* a light tight-fitting sheer covering for a woman's legs that stretches from the toes up to an elastic waistband

pant·y·lin·er /pántee līnər/ *n.* a light, thin sanitary napkin

pant·y·waist /pántee wàyst/ *n.* **1. OFFENSIVE TERM** an offensive term for a man that deliberately insults his courage and masculinity (*slang offensive*) **2.** CLOTHES **ITEM OF CHILDREN'S CLOTHING** a piece of clothing for children, consisting of a shirt and pants that are buttoned together at the waist (*dated*)

pan·zer /pánzər, pántsər/ *n.* an armored vehicle such as a tank, especially a German armored vehicle used in World War II [Mid-20thC. Shortening of German *Panzerdivision* "armored unit," ultimately from Old French *pancier* "armor for the belly," from *pance* "belly" (see PAUNCH).]

pap[1] /pap/ *n.* **1.** FOOD **SEMILIQUID FOOD** soft semiliquid food, usually mashed or pulped, especially for babies or sick people **2. TRIVIAL OR WORTHLESS MATERIAL** something, especially a book, movie, television program, or idea, that is so lacking in depth and substance that it is considered worthless **3.** POL **POLITICAL PATRONAGE** political patronage in the form of money or favors (*slang*) [14thC. Via Old French *papa* (and probably also via medieval Latin), from Latin *pappa*, a children's word meaning "food."]

pap[2] /pap/ *n.* a teat or nipple (*regional informal*) [12thC. Origin uncertain: perhaps from Latin *papilla* (see PAPILLA), or perhaps an imitation of the sound of sucking.]

pa·pa[1] /paápə, pə paá/ *n.* **1. FATHER** a father (*informal dated*) **2.** CHR **POPE** a term used in the Roman Catholic Church to refer to the pope **3.** COMMUNICATION **CODE WORD FOR LETTER "P"** a code word for the letter "P," used in international radio communications [Late 17thC. Via French from Latin, from Greek *pappas* "father."]

pa·pa[2] /paápə/ *n.* a soft blue-gray clay of marine origin [Late 19thC. From Maori.]

pa·pa·cy /páypəssee/ (*plural* **-cies**) *n.* **1. PAPAL POWER OR STATUS** the power or position of the pope **2. POPE'S PERIOD IN POWER** the period of office of a pope **3. PAPAL GOVERNMENT** the system of government in the Roman Catholic church with the pope as the head [14thC. From medieval Latin *papatia*, from late Latin *papa* "pope."]

Pa·pa·go /páppə gò, paápə gò/ (*plural* **-go** *or* **Pa·pa·gos**) *n.* **1.** PEOPLES **MEMBER OF A NATIVE N AMERICAN PEOPLE** a member of a Native North American people that originally occupied lands in central Arizona, and whose members now live mainly in parts of northern Mexico and southern Arizona **2.** LANG **NATIVE AMERICAN LANGUAGE** a Native American language, spoken in parts of Arizona and northern Mexico, that belongs to the Uto-Aztecan branch of Aztec-Tanoan languages and is closely related to Pima. Papago is spoken by about 9,000 people. [Mid-19thC. Via Spanish *pápago* from, ultimately, a Pima-Papago word.] —**Pa·pa·go** *adj.*

pa·pa·in /pə páy in, pə pī in/ *n.* an enzyme found in the juice of papaya and used as a meat tenderizer and in medicine to promote digestion and healing of wounds [Late 19thC. Formed from PAPAYA.]

pa·pal /páyp'l/ *adj.* relating to the pope or the papacy [14thC. Via Old French from medieval Latin *papalis*, from late Latin *papa* "pope" (see POPE).] —**pa·pal·ly** *adv.*

Pa·pal States /pàyp'l-/ former territories in Italy over which the pope had sovereignty between 754 and 1870

Pap·an·dre·ou /pàppən dráy oo/, **Andreas** (1919–96) Greek statesman. He was the founder of the Pan-Hellenistic Socialist Movement (1974), and prime minister of Greece (1981–89 and 1993–96).

Pa·pa·ni·co·laou test /paápə neékə lòw tèst, páppə níkə lòw-/, **Pa·pa·ni·co·laou smear** *n.* a smear test [Mid-20thC. Named for G. N. *Papanicolaou*, 1883–1962, a Greek-born anatomist.]

pa·pa·raz·zo /paápə raát sō/ (*plural* **-zi** /-raát seé/) *n.* a freelance photographer who follows famous people hoping to get a newsworthy story, especially something shocking or scandalous (*often used in the plural*) [Mid-20thC. From Italian, with reference to the surname of a freelance photographer in the film *La Dolce Vita*, 1959, by Federico Fellini.]

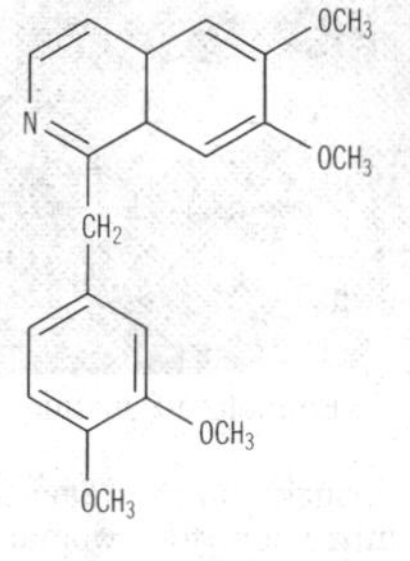

Papaverine

pa·pav·er·ine /pə pávvə reen, pə pávvərin/ *n.* a toxic white crystalline alkaloid, found in opium or derived synthetically, that is nonaddictive and is used as an antispasmodic to treat asthma and colic. Formula: $C_{20}H_{21}O_4N$. [Mid-19thC. Formed from Latin *papaver* "poppy" (see POPPY).]

pa·paw /páw paw/, **paw·paw** *n.* **1.** TREES **N AMERICAN TREE WITH EDIBLE FRUIT** a small North American deciduous tree or shrub of the custard apple family that has large oblong leaves, purple flowers, and small fleshy edible fruit. Latin name: *Asimina triloba*. **2.** FOOD **PAPAW FRUIT** the edible fruit of the papaw tree **3.** TREES, FOOD = **papaya** *n.* 2 [Early 17thC. Alteration of PAPAYA.]

pa·pa·ya /pə pī ə/ *n.* **1.** TREES **TROPICAL TREE WITH OBLONG FRUIT** a tropical evergreen tree that has a crown of broad leaves and large elongated or round yellow edible fruit. Latin name: *Carica papaya*. **2.** FOOD

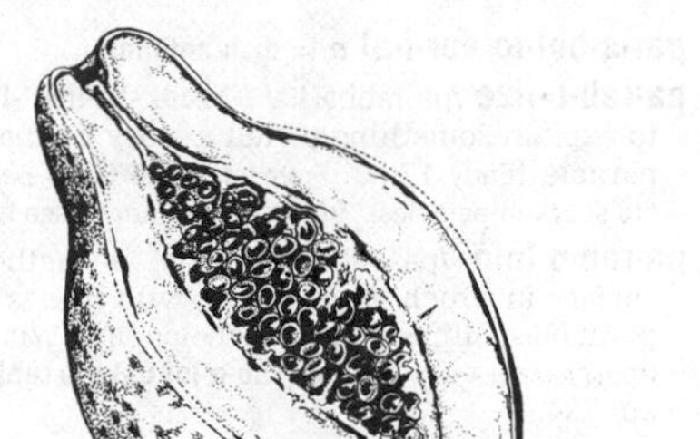

Papaya

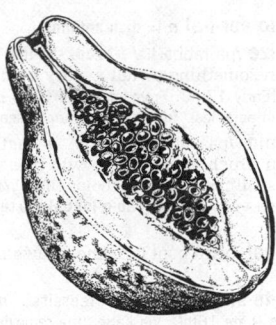

PAPAYA FRUIT the edible fruit of the papaya tree [Late 16thC. From Spanish *papaya*, from Carib or Arawak.]

pa·per /páypər/ *n.* **1.** INDUST **THIN FLAT MATERIAL FROM WOOD PULP** a thin material consisting of flat sheets, made from pulped wood, cloth, or fiber, used for various purposes, e.g., for writing and printing on, for wrapping things in, or for covering walls **2. SHEET OR SHEETS OF PAPER** one or more pieces or sheets of paper, especially for writing or drawing on **3.** PRESS = **newspaper 4.** EDUC **STUDENT'S ESSAY** an essay written by a student for a class **5.** EDUC **ACADEMIC ARTICLE OR TALK** an essay or article, particularly an academic one, read at a conference, or submitted for publication **6.** EDUC **SET OF EXAM ANSWERS** a written set of answers by a student to a set of examination questions **7.** *U.K.* EDUC **EXAMINATION** a set of examination questions prepared on paper **8.** = **wallpaper 9. WRAPPER** a piece of paper, especially one used to wrap a piece of candy or a cigarette (*often used in the plural*) **10.** FIN **COMMERCIAL NEGOTIABLE DOCUMENT** a negotiable instrument, e.g., a bill of exchange or promissory note **11.** THEATER **FREE THEATER TICKET** a free ticket that is given out in order to fill up a theater (*slang*) **12.** THEATER **THEATERGOERS WITH FREE TICKETS** members of the audience who have been given free tickets in order to fill up a theater (*slang*) ■ **pa·pers** *npl.* **1.** POL **PERSONAL IDENTITY DOCUMENTS** a document or documents, e.g., a passport, showing somebody's identity or status **2.** VET **ANIMAL'S PEDIGREE OR VACCINATION RECORDS** a document or documents showing an animal's pedigree or vaccination records **3. ASSORTMENT OF DOCUMENTS** a collection of documents relating to a particular issue or subject ○ *official papers in the archives* **4. SOMEBODY'S PERSONAL WRITINGS** somebody's diaries, letters, and other personal writings **5.** SHIPPING = **ship's papers** ■ *adj.* **1. MADE OF PAPER** consisting of or made of paper **2. RESEMBLING PAPER** similar to paper, e.g., in flimsiness **3. EXISTING IN DOCUMENTARY FORM** written in a document but not necessarily effective or useful in reality **4. IN WRITING** conducted in writing ■ *vt.* **(-pered, -per·ing, -pers) 1. WALLPAPER SOMETHING** to cover a wall or room with wallpaper **2. COVER SOMETHING WITH PAPER** to cover something with paper **3.** THEATER **FILL UP THEATER** to fill up a theater by giving out free tickets (*slang*) [14thC. Via Old French *papier* and Anglo-Norman *papir* from Latin *papyrus* (see PAPYRUS).] —**pa·per·er** *n.* ◇ **on paper 1.** in theory, but not in fact **2.** in writing ◇ **paper the walls with something** to disseminate or broadcast something (*slang*) ○ *They papered the walls with objections to the policy.*

paper over *vt.* **1. COVER SOMETHING WITH PAPER** to cover something up with paper, especially to cover a wall's imperfections or old paint with wallpaper **2. CONCEAL SOMETHING** to conceal something without resolving it, especially mistakes, disagreements, or faults

pa·per·back /páypər bàk/ *n.* **SOFTCOVER BOOK** a book that has a thin flexible cover instead of a hard cover ■ *adj.* **WITH FLEXIBLE COVER** with a thin flexible cover, instead of a hard cover

pa·per·bark /páypər baàrk/ *n.* an Australian species of tree with pale thin papery bark that peels off in large sheets. Genus: *Melaleuca.* [From the color and texture of the bark]

pa·per birch (*plural* **pa·per birch·es** *or* **pa·per birch**) *n.* a North American birch tree that has toothed oval leaves, valuable wood, and white peeling bark that is used to make baskets and other articles. Latin name: *Betula papyrifera.* [From the white color of the bark]

pa·per·board /páypər bàwrd/ *n.* a type of thick cardboard

pa·per·bound /páypər bòwnd/ *adj.* = **paperback**

pa·per·boy /páypər bòy/ *n.* a boy who delivers newspapers to people's homes, or who sells newspapers

pa·per chase *n.* an intense searching and collation of files, books, or documents

pa·per·clip /páypər klìp/, **pa·per clip** *n.* a clip designed to be slipped over two or more sheets of paper to hold them together, especially a piece of wire that is bent into a long flat oval spiral

pa·per cut·ter *n.* **1. MACHINE FOR CUTTING PAPER** a machine or device for cutting paper, especially a flat platform with a long arm containing a blade that can be raised and lowered in order to cut straight edges **2.** = **paperknife**

pa·per·girl /páypər gùrl/ *n.* a girl who delivers newspapers to people's homes, or who sells newspapers

pa·per·hang·er /páypər hàngər/ *n.* **1. SOMEBODY WHO HANGS WALLPAPER** somebody who puts up wallpaper, especially somebody who does this professionally **2.** CRIMINOL **PASSER OF BAD CHECKS** somebody who regularly passes bad checks in order to obtain money (*slang*) —**pa·per·hang·ing** *n.*

pa·per·knife /páypər nīf/ (*plural* **pa·per·knives** /-nīvz/) *n.* a blunt knife for slitting open envelopes, or for slitting folded paper, especially leaves of books

pa·per·less /páypərləss/ *adj.* using records or means of communication that are electronic rather than on paper ○ *the age of the paperless office*

pa·per mon·ey *n.* currency in the form of bills, as opposed to coins

pa·per mul·ber·ry (*plural* **pa·per mul·ber·ries**) *n.* a small Asian tree with an inner bark that was once used in Japan for making paper, now commonly grown as a shade tree. Latin name: *Broussonetia papyrifera.*

pa·per nau·ti·lus (*plural* **pa·per nau·ti·lus·es** *or* **pa·per nau·ti·li**) *n.* a cephalopod mollusk, the female of which has a thin delicate shell. Genus: *Argonauta.* ◊ **pearly nautilus** [From the delicacy and whiteness of its shell]

pa·per prof·it *n.* a profit that is not generated from the normal trading of a business and may or may not be realized (*often used in the plural*)

pa·per-push·er *n.* somebody with a routine clerical job involving much paperwork (*informal*)

pa·per round *n. U.K.* = **paper route**

pa·per route *n.* **1. NEWPAPER DELIVERY JOB** the job of delivering newpapers to people's homes **2. COURSE OF PAPER ROUTE** the course followed from house to house by somebody delivering newspapers

pa·per-thin *adj.* **THIN** extremely thin, like paper ■ *adv.* **THINLY** extremely thinly

pa·per ti·ger *n.* a person or thing, especially an organization or a nation, that appears to be very strong and powerful but is in fact weak and ineffectual

pa·per trail *n.* a sequence of documents that reflects the stages in the actions of a person or organization, especially as the object of an investigation (*informal*)

pa·per-train (**pa·per-trained, pa·per-train·ing, pa·per-trains**) *vt.* to train a house pet so that it urinates and defecates on paper when it is indoors

pa·per wasp *n.* a large slender wasp known for its elaborate nest that is made up of individual cells built of papery material. Genus: *Polistes.*

pa·per·weight /páypər wàyt/ *n.* a small heavy, usually ornamental object that is used to hold down papers and keep them in place

pa·per·work /páypər wùrk/ *n.* routine work that involves tasks such as filling in forms, keeping files up to date, or writing reports and letters

pa·per·y /páypəree/ *adj.* similar to paper in texture or thickness —**pa·per·i·ness** *n.*

pap·e·terie /páppə treè, pàppə treé/ *n.* **1. BOX FOR PAPER AND PENS** a box that holds paper and writing instruments **2. STATIONERY IN BOX** sheets of writing paper and matching envelopes sold in a box [Mid-19thC. From French "paper manufacture, writing-case," from, ultimately, *papier* (see PAPER).]

Pa·phi·an /páyfee ən/ *adj.* **1.** GEOG **RELATING TO PAPHOS** relating to the village of Paphos **2.** MYTHOL **RELATING TO APHRODITE** relating to the deity Aphrodite, who, in Greek mythology, rose fully formed from the sea at Paphos **3. CONCERNING SEXUAL ACTIVITY** relating to sexual love (*literary*) ■ *n.* **1.** PEOPLES, GEOG **SOMEBODY FROM PAPHOS** somebody who lives or was born in Paphos **2. Pa·phian, pa·phian PROSTITUTE** a prostitute (*literary*)

Pa·phos[1] /páy fòss/ *n.* a village in Cyprus that is the site of an ancient city near which, according to Greek mythology, Aphrodite was born, rising fully-formed from the sea

Pa·phos[2] /páy fòss/, **Pa·phus** /páyfəss/ *n.* in Greek mythology, a king of Cyprus who was the son of Pygmalion and Galatea

Pa·pia·men·tu /paàpee ə méntoo/, **Pa·pia·men·to** /paàpee ə méntō/ *n.* a Spanish-based creole spoken in the Netherlands Antilles, derived from a Portuguese pidgin and including many Dutch words. Papiamentu is spoken by about 200,000 people. [Mid-20thC. From Spanish *Papiamento*, from Papiamentu *papya* "talk" + *-mentu* "-ment."] —**Pa·pia·men·tu** *adj.*

pa·pier col·lé /pà pyay kaw láy/ *n.* scraps of paper and other objects that are glued onto a sheet as an abstract artistic composition [From French, literally "glued paper"]

pa·pier-mâ·ché /pàypər mə sháy, pà pyay maa sháy/ *n.* sheets of paper pulp and glue stuck together in layers, usually onto a frame or mold, used to make various objects such as figures, boxes, bowls, and masks [From French, literally "mashed paper"] —**pa·pier-mâ·ché** *adj.*

pa·pil·la /pə píllə/ (*plural* **pa·pil·lae** /-leè/) *n.* **1.** ANAT **NIPPLE** a nipple or teat (*technical*) **2.** ANAT, BIOL **SMALL LUMP OF TISSUE** a small nipple-shaped protuberance, e.g., on the tongue enclosing the taste buds, or at the root of a hair or feather **3.** BOT **SMALL PROJECTION ON PETAL OR LEAF** a small elevated pad on the surface of a stigma, petal, or leaf **4. SMALL PROJECTION RESEMBLING NIPPLE** a very small projection like a nipple on the surface of something [Late 17thC. From Latin, literally "a little swelling," from PAPULE "a swelling" (see PAPULE).] —**pap·il·lar·y** /páppə lèrree, pə pílləree/ *adj.* —**pap·il·late** /páppə làyt, pə píllət/ *adj.* —**pa·pil·lif·er·ous** /pàppə líffərəss/ *adj.* —**pa·pil·li·form** /pə píllə fàwrm/ *adj.*

pap·il·lo·ma /pàppə lṓmə/ (*plural* **-mas** *or* **-ma·ta** /-lṓmətə/) *n.* a benign tumor of the skin or mucous membrane projecting from a surface, e.g., a wart — **pap·il·lo·ma·tous** /pàppə lómmətəss, -lṓmə-/ *adj.*

pap·il·lon /páppə lòn, paàpee yáwN/ *n.* a small spaniel with a silky coat and heavily fringed tail and ears [Early 20thC. From French, literally "butterfly," because its pointed ears resemble the shape of a butterfly's wings.]

pap·il·lote /páppə lṑt, paàpee yṓt/ [Mid-18thC. Via French from Old French, "ornament for the hair," ultimately from *papillon* "butterfly."] ◇ **en papillote** baked in a wrapping of waxed paper, nonstick baking parchment, or foil

Pap·i·neau /páppinō/, **Louis Joseph** (1786–1871) Canadian politician. In 1837 he led the French-Canadian rebellion against British rule in Lower Canada (Quebec).

pa·pist /páypist/ *n.* an offensive term for a member of the Roman Catholic Church (*insult*) [Mid-16thC. Directly or via French from modern Latin *papista*, from ecclesiastical Latin *papa* "pope."] —**pa·pism** /páy pìzzəm/ *n.* —**pa·pis·tic** /pə pístik/ *adj.* —**pa·pist·ry** /páypistree/ *n.*

pa·poose /pa po͝oss, pə po͝oss/ *n.* **1. OFFENSIVE TERM** a Native North American baby or young child (*offensive*) **2. BAG FOR CARRYING BABY** a bag that fits over the shoulders, used for carrying a baby, especially in front of the body [Mid-17thC. From Algonquian, literally "very young."]

pa·po·va·vi·rus /pə pṓvə vīrəss/ *n.* any of a group of DNA-containing viruses, many of which can cause cancers in animals, including the papillomaviruses that are responsible for warts [Mid-20thC. Coined from PAPILLOMA + POLYOMA + VACUOLATION + VIRUS.]

pap·pus /páppəss/ (*plural* **-pi** /pá pī/) *n.* a covering of scales, bristles, and feathery hairs that surrounds the fruit of plants such as dandelions and thistles and helps to disperse the fruits [Early 18thC. Via Latin, from Greek *pappos*, literally "grandfather," hence "the down on seeds," from the idea of a gray-bearded man.] — **pap·pose** /pá pṑss/ *adj.*

pap·py[1] /páppee/ (**-pi·er, -pi·est**) *adj.* with a mushy consistency [Late 17thC. Formed from PAP[1].]

pap·py[2] /páppee/ (*plural* **-pies**) *n.* a father (*regional dated*) [Mid-18thC. Formed from PAPA.]

pa·pri·ka /pa préékə, pə préékə, pápprikə/ *n.* **1.** COOK **MILD RED SPICE FROM SWEET PEPPER** a mild red spice made from various sweet red peppers and used especially in Hungarian cooking **2.** PLANTS, FOOD **SWEET RED PEPPER** a sweet red pepper or the plant on which it grows. Genus: *Capsicum.* **3.** COLORS **REDDISH-ORANGE COLOR** a bright reddish-orange color, like that of paprika seasoning [Late 19thC. Via Hungarian from Serbian *pàpar* "pepper," from Latin *piper* (see PEPPER).]

Pap smear, Pap test *n.* a test to detect cancerous or precancerous cells of the cervix, allowing for early diagnosis of cancer [*Pap* a shortening of *Papanicolaou* (see PAPANICOLAOU TEST)]

Pap·u·an /páppyoo ən/ *n.* **1.** PEOPLES **SOMEBODY FROM PAPUA NEW GUINEA** somebody who was born in or is a citizen of Papua New Guinea **2. GROUP OF LANGUAGES OF NEW GUINEA** a group of languages spoken in much of New Guinea and nearby islands. They are not related to the Malayo-Polynesian languages, but exact classification has not yet proved possible. The Papuan languages are spoken by about two million people. —**Pap·u·an** *adj.*

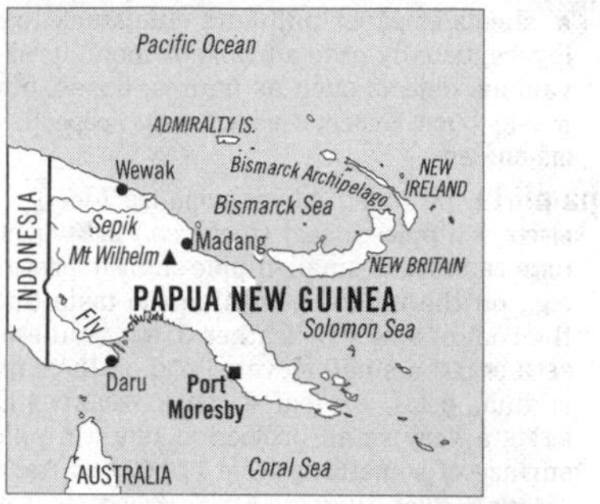

Papua New Guinea

Pap·u·a New Guin·ea /pàppyoo ə noo gínnee/ independent nation in Oceania, situated northeast of Australia, in the southwestern Pacific Ocean, consisting of the eastern half of the island of New Guinea together with many other islands. Language: English. Currency: kina. Capital: Port Moresby. Population: 4,394,537 (1996). Area: 178,704 sq. mi./462,840 sq. km. Official name **Independent State of Papua New Guinea** —**Pap·u·a New Guin·e·an** *n., adj.*

pap·ule /páp yool/ *n.* a small hard round protuberance on the skin [Early 18thC. From Latin *papula.*] —**pap·u·lar** /páppyələr/ *adj.* —**pap·u·lif·er·ous** /pàppyə líffərəss/ *adj.*

pa·py·ra·ceous /pàppə ráyshəss/ *adj.* made of or resembling paper [Mid-18thC. Formed from Latin *papyrus* (see PAPYRUS).]

pap·y·rol·o·gy /pàppə róllәjee/ *n.* the study of ancient papyrus manuscripts —**pap·y·ro·log·i·cal** /pàppərə lójjik'l/ *adj.* —**pap·y·rol·o·gist** /pàppə róllәjist/ *n.*

pa·py·rus /pə pírəss/ (*plural* **-ri** /-rī/ *or* **pa·py·rus·es**) *n.* **1.** PLANTS **TALL MARSH PLANT** a tall aquatic plant of the sedge family, native to southern Europe and the Nile valley, that has small flowers resembling umbrellas. Latin name: *Cyperus papyrus.* **2.** INDUST **MATERIAL RESEMBLING PAPER MADE FROM PAPYRUS** writing material made from the pith of the stem of the papyrus plant that was used by the ancient Egyptians, Greeks, and Romans **3. PAPYRUS DOCUMENT** an ancient manuscript written on material made from the papyrus plant [14thC. Via Latin from Greek *papuros* "papyrus plant."]

par /paar/ *n.* **1. AVERAGE LEVEL** a level or standard considered to be average or normal **2.** FIN **ACCEPTED VALUE OF CURRENCY** the accepted value of one country's currency in terms of the currency of another country that uses the same metal standard **3.** COMM = **par value 4.** GOLF **ALLOCATED STANDARD SCORE** the standard score assigned to each hole on a golf course, or to the sum total of these holes ■ *adj.* **AVERAGE** average or normal ■ *vt.* (**parred, par·ring, pars**) GOLF **SCORE PAR ON** to score the equivalent of the par on a hole or course [Late 16thC. From Latin, "equal," (source of English *pair* and *umpire*).] ◇ **be on (a) par (with somebody** *or* **something)** to be on the same level as somebody or something, or generally have the same status or value ◇ **be par for the course** to be usual or to be expected under the circumstances (*informal*)

par. *abbr.* **1.** paragraph **2.** parallel **3.** parenthesis **4.** parish

Par. *abbr.* Paraguay

par- *prefix.* = **para**

pa·ra /paárə/ (*plural* **-ras** *or* **-ra**) *n.* **1. A SUBUNIT OF YUGOSLAV CURRENCY** a subunit of currency in Yugoslavia, 100 of which are worth one new dinar. See table at **currency 2. COIN WORTH ONE PARA** a coin worth one para [Late 17thC. Via Turkish, from Persian *pāra* "piece, para."]

para-[1] *prefix.* **1.** beside, near, along with ○ *parataxis* **2.** beyond ○ *paranormal* **3.** isomeric or related compound ○ *paraldehyde* **4.** resembling ○ *paramyxovirus* **5.** faulty, undesirable ○ *paraphasia* **6.** assistant, auxiliary ○ *paralegal* **7.** occupying the para position in the benzene ring ○ *paradichlorobenzene* [From Greek *para* "beside." Ultimately from an Indo-European word meaning "next to, in front of" that is also the ancestor of English *fore* and *before.*]

para-[2] *prefix.* parachute ○ *paraskiing* [From PARACHUTE]

-para *suffix.* a woman who has given birth to a particular number of children ○ *nullipara* [From Latin, formed from *parere* "to give birth" (see PARENT)]

par·a-a·mi·no·ben·zo·ic ac·id /pèrrə ə meénō ben zṑ ik-, -ámmənō ben zṑ ik-/ *n.* full form of **PABA**

par·a-a·mi·no·sal·i·cylic ac·id /pèrrə ə meénō sàllə síllik-, -ámmənō sàllə síllik-/ *n.* a crystalline synthetic isomer of aminosalicylic acid that is effective against the bacteria that cause tuberculosis

par·a·ba·sis /pə rábbəsiss/ (*plural* **par·a·ba·ses** /-seez/) *n.* a speech to the audience that is made by the chorus in classical Greek comedy [Early 19thC. From Greek, where it was formed from *parabainein* "to go aside," from *bainein* "to step."]

par·a·bi·o·sis /pèrrə bī óssiss/ (*plural* **-ses** /-seez/) *n.* **1.** BIOL **ANATOMICAL UNION OF TWO INDIVIDUALS** the state in which two individuals are joined together and share the same circulation of blood. This is the case for conjoined twins, and it can also be induced experimentally or to establish a blood supply for some grafts. **2.** MED **TEMPORARY CESSATION OF NERVE ACTIVITY** the temporary suppression of nerve conduction [Early 20thC. Coined from PARA-[1] + Greek *biōsis* "way of life," from *bios* "life."] —**par·a·bi·ot·ic** /pèrrə bī óttik/ *adj.*

par·a·blast /pérrə blàst/ *n.* the yolk of a fertilized egg [Mid-19thC. Coined from PARA-[1] + Greek *blastos* "a bud, shoot."] —**par·a·blas·tic** /pèrrə blástik/ *adj.*

par·a·ble /pérrəb'l/ *n.* **1.** LITERAT **MORAL OR RELIGIOUS STORY** a short simple story intended to illustrate a moral or religious lesson **2.** BIBLE **STORY ASCRIBED TO JESUS CHRIST** a parable that appears in the Bible as told by Jesus Christ [14thC. Via Old French *parabole* and Latin *parabola* from, ultimately, Greek *paraballein,* literally "to put beside" (formed from *ballein* "to throw"), hence "to compare."]

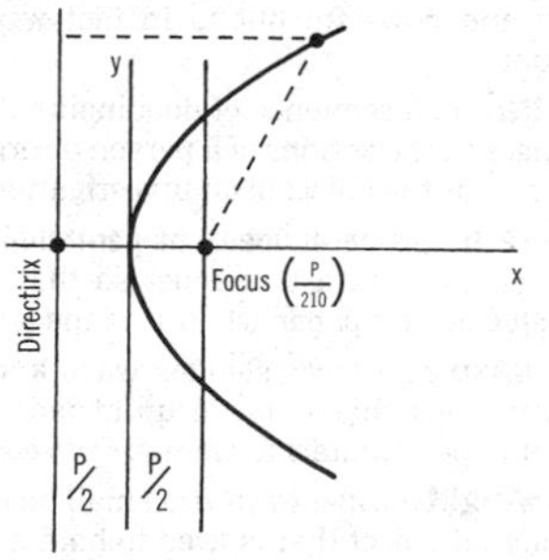

Parabola

pa·rab·o·la /pə rábbələ/ *n.* a curve formed by the intersection of a cone with a plane parallel to its side [Late 16thC. Via modern Latin, from Greek *parabolē* "application, comparison," from the relationship between the section of a cone that forms the parabola and part of the cone's surface.]

par·a·bol·ic[1] /pèrrə bóllik/ *adj.* **1. RELATING TO PARABOLA** relating to, resembling, or having the form of a parabola **2. WITH PARABOLOID SHAPE** with the form of a paraboloid

par·a·bol·ic[2] /pèrrə bóllik/, **par·a·bol·i·cal** /pèrrə bóllik'l/ *adj.* relating to or resembling a parable [15thC. Via late Latin *parabolicus* from late Greek *parabolikos* "figurative," from *parabolē* (see PARABLE).] —**pa·ra·bol·i·cal·ly** *adv.*

par·a·bol·ic aer·i·al *n.* = **dish antenna**

pa·rab·o·lize /pə rábbə līz/ (**-lized, -liz·ing, -liz·es**) *vt.* to explain something or tell a story by means of a parable [Early 17thC. From medieval Latin *parabolizare* "to speak in parables," from Latin *parabola* (see PARABLE).]

pa·rab·o·loid /pə rábbə lòyd/ *n.* a mathematical surface in which intersections with planes produce parabolas, ellipses, or hyperbolas [Mid-17thC. Coined from PARABOLA + -OID.] —**pa·rab·o·loi·dal** /pə ràbbə lóyd'l/ *adj.*

pa·ra·bun·tal /pèrrə búnt'l/ *n.* fine straw used in hat-making

par·a·cen·te·sis /pèrrə sen teéssiss/ *n.* = **thoracentesis** [Late 16thC. Via Latin "the removing of a cataract," from, ultimately, Greek *parakentein,* literally "to pierce at the side," from *kentein* "to prick, stab."]

par·a·cet·a·mol /pèrrə seétə màwl, -séttə-/ (*plural* **-mol** *or* **-mols**) *n. U.K.* = **acetaminophen** [Mid-20thC. From "par(a-)acet(yl)am(inophen)ol."]

pa·rach·ron·ism /pə rákrə nìzzəm/ *n.* an error in assigning a date to something, especially when the date given is later than it should be [Mid-17thC. Origin uncertain: either coined from PARA-[1] + Greek *khronos* "time" + -ISM, or an alteration of ANACHRONISM.]

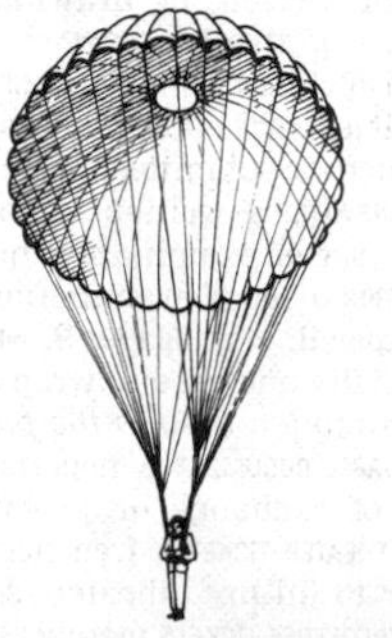
Parachute

par·a·chute /pérrə shoot/ *n.* **1. CANOPY FOR SLOWING FALL FROM AIRCRAFT** a device consisting of a canopy attached to a harness that is used to slow the speed at which a person or object drops from an aircraft **2.** ZOOL = **patagium** *n.* 1 ■ *vti.* (**-chut·ed, -chut·ing, -chutes**) **DROP BY PARACHUTE** to drop, or allow somebody or something to drop, from an aircraft by parachute [Late 18thC. From French, literally "protection against a fall," from *chute* "a fall."] —**par·a·chut·ist** *n.*

par·a·chute spin·na·ker *n.* a very large light triangular sail used on a racing yacht

Par·a·clete /pérrə kleet/ *n.* CHR in Christianity, the Holy Spirit [13thC. Via French *paraclet,* literally "someone called to assist," from, ultimately, Greek *parakalein,* literally "to call to your side," from *kalein* "to call."]

pa·rade /pə ráyd/ *n.* **1. CELEBRATORY PROCESSION OF PEOPLE** an organized procession of people celebrating a special occasion and often including decorated vehicles or floats, a marching band, people twirling batons, and people on horseback **2. DISPLAY OF PEOPLE OR THINGS** a long moving line of people or things intended to be publicly displayed **3. SUCCESSION OF PEOPLE OR THINGS** a large number of people or things in succession ○ *a parade of visitors to the palace* **4.** MIL **PROCESSION OF TROOPS** a march by troops along the streets or in a large area such as a square, usually as a celebration of an important event **5.** MIL **GATHERING OF TROOPS IN FORMATION** a formal gathering of a troop of soldiers in a regimented formation for a ceremonial march, inspection, or training **6.** MIL **PARADE GROUND** a parade ground **7. PEOPLE IN PARADE** people marching in a parade **8. FLAMBOYANT OR FLAUNTING EXHIBITION OF SOMETHING** a showy or ostentatious exhibition or display of something **9.** FENCING **PARRY** a type of parry in fencing ■ *v.* (**-rad·ed, -rad·ing, -rades**) **1.** *vti.* **GO ON FESTIVE PROCESSION** to march in a festive public parade **2.** *vti.* **USE IN FESTIVE PROCESSION** to use something or be used in a festive public parade **3.** *vti.* MIL **ASSEMBLE FOR MILITARY PARADE** to gather for and march in a military parade **4.** *vt.* **SHOW SOMEBODY OR SOMETHING OFF** to display or show somebody or something, especially proudly and ostentatiously **5.** *vi.* **WALK AROUND TO BE SEEN** to walk or stroll around in public, especially in order to be seen or admired **6.** *vti.* **CLAIM TO BE SOMETHING ELSE** to claim to be other than you really are, or claim that one person or thing is another person or thing ○ *parading old ideas as new reforms* [Mid-17thC. Via

French from Spanish *parada* "display," literally "stopping" (from the act of stopping a horse), ultimately from Latin *parare* "to prepare" (see PREPARE).] ◇ **rain on somebody's parade** to spoil things for somebody (*informal*)

pa·rade ground *n.* a place where troops regularly gather in formation for inspection or training

par·a·di·chlo·ro·ben·zene /pèrrə dī klawrə bén zeen/ *n.* a white crystalline compound used as a moth repellent. Formula: $C_6H_4Cl_2$. [Late 19thC. Coined from PARA-[1] + DI- + CHLORO- + BENZENE.]

par·a·did·dle /pérrə dìdd'l/ *n.* a drum roll in which left and right drumsticks alternate [Early 20thC. An imitation of the sound.]

par·a·digm /pérrə dīm/ *n.* **1. TYPICAL EXAMPLE** a typical example of something **2. MODEL THAT FORMS BASIS OF SOMETHING** an example that serves as a pattern or model for something, especially one that forms the basis of a methodology or theory **3.** GRAM **SET OF ALL FORMS OF WORD** a set of word forms giving all of the possible inflections of a word **4.** SCI, PHILOS **RELATIONSHIP OF IDEAS TO ONE ANOTHER** in the philosophy of science, a generally accepted model of how ideas relate to one another, forming a conceptual framework within which scientific research is carried out [15thC. Via late Latin from Greek *paradeigma* "example," from *paradeiknunai*, literally "to show beside," from *deiknunai* "to show."] —**par·a·dig·mat·ic** /pèrrə dig máttik/ *adj.* —**par·a·dig·mat·i·cal·ly** /-máttikəlee/ *adv.*

par·a·dise /pérrə dìss, -dīz/ *n.* **1. PLACE OR STATE OF PERFECT HAPPINESS** a place, situation, or condition in which somebody finds perfect happiness **2. PLACE IDEALLY SUITED TO SOMEBODY** a place where there is everything that a particular person needs for his or her interest (*informal*) ○ *a surfer's paradise* **3. par·a·dise, Par·a·dise** JUD-CHR **HEAVEN** in religions such as Christianity, Islam, and Judaism, the place where good people are believed to go or the state they are believed to attain after death **4. par·a·dise, Par·a·dise** BIBLE **GARDEN OF EDEN** according to the Bible, the perfect garden where Adam and Eve were placed at the Creation [12thC. Via Old French and late Latin *paradisus* from Greek *paradeisos* "enclosed place, park," from Avestan *pairidaeza*, literally "to form around," from *diz* "to form."] —**par·a·di·sa·ic** /pèrrədī sáy ik, -záy-/ *adj.* —**par·a·di·si·a·cal·ly** /-ākəlee, -zī-/ *adv.*

WORD KEY: CULTURAL NOTE

Paradise Lost, an epic poem by the English writer John Milton (1667). This monumental work describes Satan's rebellion against God, his corruption of Adam and Eve, and their subsequent expulsion from the Garden of Eden. The sustained brilliance of its language, structure, characterization, and imagery make it arguably the greatest epic poem in English literature. A sequel, ***Paradise Regained***, was published in 1671.

par·a·dise fly·catch·er *n.* a brightly-colored Asian and African flycatcher. The males have very long slender forked tails. Genus: *Terpsiphone.*

par·a·dor /pérrə dàwr/ *n.* **1. LATIN AMERICAN HOTEL** a privately owned and operated hotel or resort in Latin America **2. SPANISH TOURIST HOTEL** a tourist hotel in Spain, operated by the national government and located in a castle, monastery, convent, or other historic site [Mid-19thC. From Spanish, from *parar* "to stop, stay," from Latin *parare* "to prepare" (see PREPARE).]

par·a·dos /pérrə dòss/ *n.* a bank built up behind a trench or other fortification that gives protection from attack from the rear [Mid-19thC. From French, literally "defend the back," from *dos* "back."]

par·a·dox /pérrə dòks/ *n.* **1. SOMETHING ABSURD OR CONTRADICTORY** a statement, proposition, or situation that seems to be absurd or contradictory, but in fact is or may be true **2. SELF-CONTRADICTORY STATEMENT** a statement or proposition that contradicts itself **3. PERSON OF OPPOSITES** somebody who has qualities that seem to contradict each other **4. SOMETHING CONTRARY TO POPULAR BELIEFS** something that is contrary to or conflicts with conventional or common opinion (*archaic*) [Mid-16thC. Via Latin *paradoxum* from, ultimately, Greek *paradoxos*, literally "contrary to opinion," from *doxa* "opinion," from *dokein* "to think."] —**par·a·dox·i·cal** /pèrrə dóksik'l/ *adj.* —**par·a·dox·i·cal·ly** /pèrrə dóksikəlee/ *adv.* —**par·a·dox·i·cal·ness** /pèrrə dóksik'lnəss/ *n.*

par·a·dox·i·cal frog *n.* a frog of the Amazon forest and the island of Trinidad. The adult frog is less than a third the size of the tadpole. Latin name: *Pseudis paradoxa.*

par·a·dox·i·cal sleep *n.* = **REM sleep** [*Paradoxical* from the fact that the electrical brain patterns of this deep sleep more closely resemble those of the waking state]

par·a·drop /pérrə dròp/ *n.* **DELIVERY BY PARACHUTE** the delivery of personnel, materials, provisions, or other supplies to a place by attaching them to a parachute and dropping them from an aircraft ■ *vt.* (**par·a·dropped, par·a·drop·ping, -drops**) **PARACHUTE SOMEBODY OR SOMETHING** to deliver somebody or something to a place by paradrop

par·aes·the·sia *n.* U.K. = **paresthesia**

par·af·fin /pérrəfin/ *n.* **1.** = **paraffin wax 2.** CHEM = **alkane 3.** *U.K.* INDUST, DOMESTIC **FUEL OIL** a mixture of liquid hydrocarbons obtained from petroleum and used as a domestic heating fuel and as fuel for aircraft. ◊ **kerosene** ■ *vt.* (**-fined, -fin·ing, -fins**) INDUST **TREAT WITH KEROSENE** to treat something by saturating, impregnating, or coating it with kerosene or paraffin wax [Mid-19thC. Coined from Latin *parum* "little" + *affinis* "related" (source of English *affinity*), because it is not closely related to any other substance.] —**par·af·fin·ic** /pèrrə fínnik/ *adj.*

par·af·fin wax *n.* a white waxy solid mixture of hydrocarbons obtained from petroleum and used in making candles, pharmaceuticals, and cosmetics, and as a sealing agent

par·a·for·mal·de·hyde /pèrrə fawr máldə hīd/, **par·a·form** /pérrə fàwrm/ *n.* a white combustible polymer of formaldehyde used as a disinfectant and a fungicide, and as a component of contraceptive creams. Formula: $(HCHO)_n$, where n is greater than or equal to 6. [Late 19thC. Coined from PARA-[1] + FORMALDEHYDE.]

par·a·gen·e·sis /pèrrə jénnəssiss/, **par·a·ge·ne·sia** /-jə neezhə, -neezhee ə/, **par·a·form** *n.* the order in which the mineral constituents of a rock are formed [Mid-19thC. Coined from PARA-[1] + -GENESIS.] —**par·a·ge·net·ic** /pèrrə jə néttik/ *adj.* —**par·a·ge·net·i·cal·ly** /-néttikəlee/ *adv.*

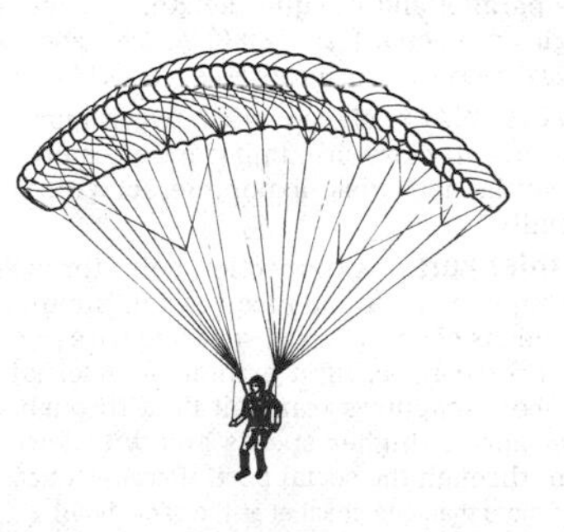

Paragliding

par·a·glid·ing /pérrə glīding/ *n.* a sport in which an individual jumps from an aircraft or an elevation wearing a rectangular parachute that allows control of direction in the descent to the ground [Coined from PARA + *gliding*] —**par·a·glid·er** *n.*

pa·rag·na·thous /pə rágnəthəss/ *adj.* with upper and lower jaws of the same length [Late 19thC. Coined from PARA-[1] + -GNATHOUS.]

par·a·goge /pérrə gōjee/ *n.* the addition of a letter, sound, or syllable at the end of a word as a word develops, e.g., the "s" in "towards" [Mid-16thC. Via late Latin from Greek *paragōgē*, literally "carrying beyond," from *agōgē* "carrying."] —**par·a·gog·ic** /pèrrə gójjik/ *adj.* —**par·a·gog·i·cal·ly** /-gójjikəlee/ *adv.*

par·a·gon /pérrə gòn, -gən/ *n.* **1. EXAMPLE OF EXCELLENCE** somebody or something that is the very best example of something **2.** MINERALS **LARGE UNFLAWED DIAMOND** a perfect diamond that weighs at least 100 carats **3. LARGE PERFECTLY SPHERICAL PEARL** an extremely large pearl that is a pefect sphere [Mid-16thC. Via archaic French from Italian *paragone*, originally "touchstone to test gold," ultimately from medieval Greek *parakonan*, literally "to sharpen against," hence "to compare."]

par·a·graph /pérrə gràf/ *n.* **1. SECTION OF WRITING** a piece of writing that consists of one or more sentences, begins on a new and often indented line, and contains a distinct idea or the words of one speaker **2.** PRESS **SHORT NEWS STORY** a short item of news or editorial comment in a newspaper ■ *vt.* (**-graphed, -graph·ing, -graphs**) **1. SET OUT IN PARAGRAPHS** to arrange something in a series of paragraphs **2.** PRESS **WRITE NEWS IN A PARAGRAPH** to report news or a story in a short paragraph [15thC. Via Old French from, ultimately, Greek *paragraphos* "stroke marking a line in which there is a break in sense," literally "writing beside," ultimately from *graphein* "to write."] —**par·a·graph·er** *n.*

par·a·graph·i·a /pèrrə gráffee ə/ *n.* the writing of words or letters different from the ones intended, as a result of a stroke or disease [Late 19thC. Coined from PARA-[1] + Greek *-graphia* "writing."]

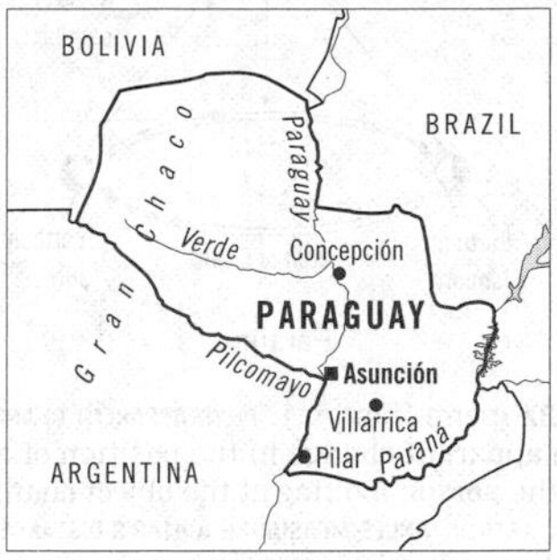

Paraguay

Par·a·guay[1] /párrə gwī, -gwày/ republic in South America, bordered by Bolivia, Brazil, and Argentina. Language: Spanish. Currency: kina. Capital: Asunción. Population: 5,504,146 (1996). Area: 157,048 sq. mi./406,752 sq. km. Official name **Republic of Paraguay** —**Par·a·guay·an** *n., adj.*

Par·a·guay[2] river of central South America, a tributary of the Paraná River. Length: 1,580 mi./2,550 km.

Par·a·guay tea *n.* = **maté** *n.* 2 [Late 18thC. Named for the country in which the tree proliferates.]

par·a·hy·dro·gen /pèrrə hīdrəjən/ *n.* a form of molecular hydrogen in which the two atomic nuclei spin in opposite directions. Parahydrogen makes up about 25 percent of hydrogen molecules. [Early 20thC. Coined from PARA-[1] + HYDROGEN.]

par·a·in·flu·en·za vi·rus /pèrrə infloo énzə-/ *n.* any of a group of four viruses, similar to the influenza virus, that cause respiratory illnesses, especially in children, with symptoms of severe sore throat, croup, and pneumonia

par·a·jour·nal·ism /pèrrə júrn'l ìzzəm/ *n.* = **new journalism** —**par·a·jour·nal·ist** *n.*

par·a·keet /pérrə keet/ *n.* a small tropical parrot that has a long tail and is usually very brightly colored [Mid-16thC. Anglicization of Old French *paraquet*, of uncertain origin: perhaps ultimately a form of *Pierre* "Peter," in the sense of "little Peter."]

par·a·lan·guage /pérrə làng gwij/ *n.* nonverbal vocal elements in communication that may add a nuance of meaning to language as it is used in context, e.g., tone of voice or whispering

par·al·de·hyde /pə ráldə hīd/ *n.* a colorless liquid polymer of acetaldehyde used as a sedative and as a solvent. Formula: $C_6H_{12}O_3$. [Mid-19thC. Coined from PARA-[1] + ALDEHYDE.]

par·a·le·gal /pèrrə leeg'l/ *n.* **LAWYER'S ASSISTANT** somebody with specialist legal training who assists a fully qualified lawyer ■ *adj.* **OF A PARALEGAL** relating to a paralegal or the work of a paralegal [Late 20thC. Coined from PARA-[1] + LEGAL.]

par·a·leip·sis *n.* = **paralipsis**

par·a·lin·guis·tics /pèrrə ling gwístiks/ *n.* the study of paralanguage (*takes a singular verb*) —**par·a·lin·guis·tic** *adj.*

par·a·lip·o·me·na /pèrrə lī pómmənə, -li-/ *npl.* material added to a literary work as a supplement [Late 17thC. Via late Latin (plural) from Greek *paraleipomena* "(things) left out," ultimately from *leipein* "to leave."]

Par·a·lip·o·me·na /pèrrə lī pómmənə, -li-/, **Par·a·lip·o·me·non** /pèrrə lī pómmə nòn, -li-/ *npl.* the title used for the Book of Chronicles in the Vulgate [14thC. Via ecclesiastical Latin from, ultimately, Greek *paraleipein*, literally "to leave to one side" (because it contains material omitted from the *Books of Kings*).]

par·a·lip·sis /pèrrə lípsiss/ (*plural* **par·a·lip·ses** /-seez/), **par·a·leip·sis** /-līpsiss/ (*plural* **par·a·leip·ses** /-seez/) *n.* a rhetorical technique of emphasizing a topic by saying in some way that you will not talk about it, e.g., by using the phrase "not to mention" [Mid-16thC. Via late Latin from Greek *paraleipsis* "omission," from *paraleipein*, literally "to leave on one side," from *leipein* "to leave."]

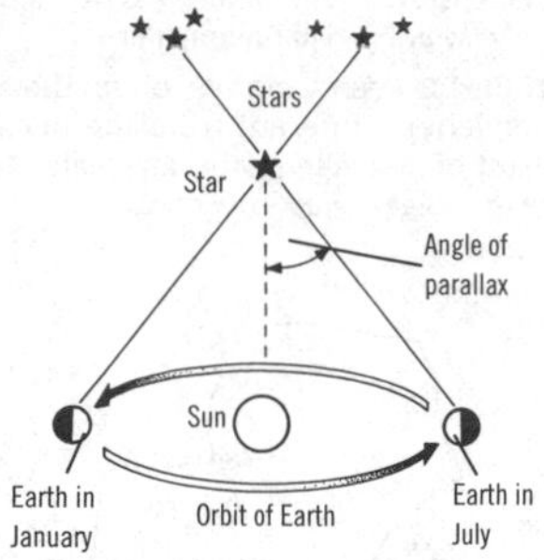

Parallax

par·al·lax /pérrə làks/ *n.* **1.** PHYS **APPARENT CHANGE OF POSITION** an apparent change in the position of an object when the person looking at the object changes position **2.** ASTRON **ANGLE MEASURING A STAR'S DISTANCE FROM THE EARTH** the angle between two imaginary lines from two different observation points meeting at a star or celestial body that is used to measure its distance from the Earth [Late 16thC. Via French from Greek *parallaxis* "alternation, angle between two lines," from *parallassein* "to alter," ultimately from *allos* "other."] — **par·al·lac·tic** /pèrrə láktik/ *adj.* —**par·al·lac·ti·cal·ly** /-láktikəlee/ *adv.*

par·al·lel /pérrə lèl/ *adj.* **1.** GEOM **ALWAYS SAME DISTANCE APART** relating to or being lines, planes, or curved surfaces that are always the same distance apart and therefore never meet **2. RESEMBLING EACH OTHER** relating to two things that are comparable because they are similar and share many characteristics **3.** GRAM **OF IDENTICAL SYNTACTIC CONSTRUCTIONS** used to describe two or more phrases or clauses in a single sentence that have identical syntactic constructions **4.** COMPUT **USING SEVERAL ITEMS OF INFORMATION SIMULTANEOUSLY** relating to a computer that processes several items of information at the same time. ◊ **serial 5.** MUSIC **KEEPING SAME MUSICAL INTERVAL THROUGHOUT** used to describe the movement of two voices or melodies that match each other exactly in pitch, while preserving the same interval between them ■ *n.* **1.** GEOM **PARALLEL LINE OR PLANE** any of a set of parallel geometric forms, especially lines or planes **2. SOMEBODY OR SOMETHING EQUIVALENT** somebody or something that is very similar to another, sharing many characteristics **3. COMPARISON** a comparison between two things that reveals their similarity ○ *It's easy to draw a parallel between their two careers* **4.** GEOG **LINE PARALLEL TO THE EQUATOR** an imaginary line around the Earth that lies parallel to the equator and represents a particular degree of latitude from the equator **5.** GEOG **LINE ON MAP** a line on a map representing a parallel of latitude **6.** ELEC ENG **CONFIGURATION OF ELECTRICAL COMPONENTS** the way in which electrical components or circuits are connected so that the same voltage is applied across each component or circuit ○ *connected in parallel* ■ *vt.* (**-leled, -lel·ing, -lels**) **1. BE PARALLEL** to be or run parallel to something **2. MAKE SOMETHING PARALLEL TO SOMETHING** to make something be or run parallel to something else **3. CORRESPOND TO SOMETHING** to be similar to something else, especially in following a similar course of events **4. COMPARE SOMETHING TO SOMETHING ELSE** to compare something with, or show something to be similar to, something else **5. MATCH SOMEBODY OR SOMETHING** to be equal to or as good as somebody or something else ■ *adv.* **ALONGSIDE** in a parallel manner so as to keep the same distance away from something and never meet it [Mid-16thC. Via French and Latin from Greek *parallēlos*, literally "beside each other," from *allēlōn* "each other," ultimately from *allos* "other."] ◇ **in parallel (with somebody** *or* **something)** in conjunction with and at the same time as somebody or something else

par·al·lel bars *npl.* GYMNASTICS **BARS FOR GYMNASTIC EXERCISES** a piece of gymnastic equipment consisting of two horizontal bars parallel to each other and supported on vertical posts. The bars may be at either the same or different heights. ■ *n.* GYMNASTICS **SPORTS EVENT USING PARALLEL BARS** an event in a gymnastics competition that uses the parallel bars (*takes a singular verb*)

par·al·lel cous·in *n.* a cousin who is the child of your mother's sister or your father's brother. ◊ **cross-cousin**

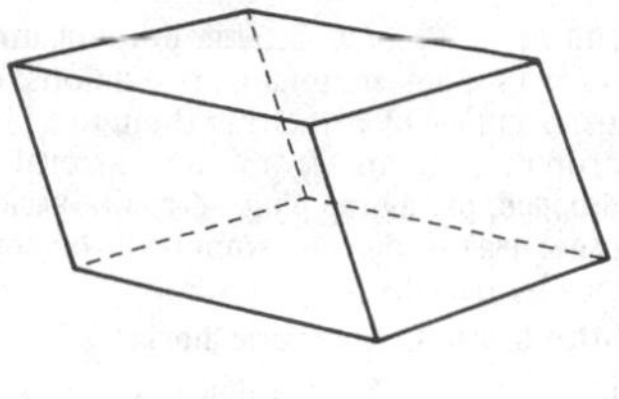

Parallelepiped

par·al·lel·e·pi·ped /pèrrə lellə pípəd, -píppəd/ *n.* a polyhedron consisting of six faces that are parallelograms [Late 16thC. From Greek *parallēlepipedon*, literally "parallel surface," from *epipedon* "surface," from, ultimately, *pedon* "ground."]

par·al·lel·ing /pérrə lèlling/ *n.* the exploitation of differences in commercial markets by buying an expensive product in a place where prices are relatively low and then selling it in a place where prices are higher

par·al·lel·ism /pérrə le lìzzəm/ *n.* **1. SIMILARITY** the condition of being parallel **2.** LITERAT **REPETITION FOR EFFECT** in writing, the deliberate repetition of particular words or sentence structures for effect **3.** PHILOSOPHY **THEORY OF MIND-BODY RELATIONSHIP** the philosophical theory that mind and body do not interact but follow separate parallel tracks, without any relationship of cause and effect existing between the two — **par·al·lel·ist** /pérrə lèllist/ *n.*

par·al·lel of lat·i·tude *n.* = **parallel** *n.* 4

par·al·lel·o·gram /pèrrə léllə gràm/ *n.* a four-sided plane figure in which both pairs of opposite sides are parallel and of equal length, and the opposite angles are equal [Late 16thC. Via late Latin from Greek *parallēlogrammon*, from *parallēlos* "parallel."]

par·al·lel play *n.* play in which two or more children who are in close proximity and possibly involved in similar activities, do not interact with each other socially

par·al·lel port *n.* a connection point through which a computer sends and receives data simultaneously by means of a number of separate wires, commonly used for connecting a printer or external storage device. Computers transmit data through the parallel port at higher speeds and with fewer errors than through the serial port. [Because it transfers data over more than one channel at the same time]

par·al·lel pro·cess·ing *n.* the use of two or more computer processors to run parts of the same program together and merge the results, with significantly faster program execution as a result. Parallel processing is used when many complex calculations are required, e.g., in weather modeling and digital special effects. [Because instructions are sent to multiple processors at the same time]

par·al·lel rul·er *n.* a ruler designed for drawing parallel lines, constructed with two linked straight edges that remain parallel although the distance between them may be varied

par·al·lel turn *n.* SKIING a turn executed by shifting the bodyweight and keeping the skis parallel, rather than by adjusting the line of the skis

pa·ral·o·gism /pə rállə jìzzəm/ *n.* in logic, an invalid argument that is unintentional or that has gone unnoticed [Mid-16thC. Via late Latin *paralogismus* from, ultimately, Greek *paralogos* "contrary to reason," from *logos* "reason" (see LOGIC).] —**pa·ral·o·gist** *n.* —**pa·ral·o·gis·tic** /pə ràllə jístik/ *adj.*

Par·a·lym·pic Games /perrə lìmpik-/, **Paralympics** /pèrrə límpiks/ *npl.* an international sports competition for physically challenged athletes — **Par·a·lym·pi·an** *n.*

pa·ral·y·sis /pə rálləssis/ *n.* **1.** MED **LOSS OF MOVEMENT** loss of voluntary movement as a result of damage to nerve or muscle function **2. INACTIVITY** failure to take action or make progress [Pre-12thC. Via Latin from Greek *paralusis*, from *paraluesthai* "to be unable to move," from *para-* "on one side" + *luein* "to release."]

pa·ral·y·sis ag·i·tans *n.* = **Parkinson's disease** [*Agitans* from Latin, the present participle of *agitare* "to shake"]

Paralympic Games

par·a·lyt·ic /pèrrə líttik/ *adj.* **OF PARALYSIS** relating to paralysis ■ *n.* **OFFENSIVE TERM** an offensive term for a physically challenged person (*offensive*) [14thC. Via Old French and Latin from Greek *paralutikos*, from *paralusis* (see PARALYSIS).] —**par·a·lyt·i·cal·ly** *adv.*

par·a·lyze /pérrə lìz/ (**-lyzed, -lyz·ing, -lyz·es**) *vt.* **1.** MED **DEPRIVE OF VOLUNTARY MOVEMENT** to cause somebody to lose the ability to move, either by damaging nerve or muscle function, or through the use of a paralyzing drug **2. MAKE TEMPORARILY UNABLE TO MOVE** to make somebody temporarily unable to move, e.g., with fear **3. BRING SYSTEM TO STANDSTILL** to bring a system or network to a stop or prevent it from functioning effectively [Late 18thC. Via French *paralyser* from, ultimately, Latin *paralysis* (see PARALYSIS).]

par·a·mag·net·ic /pèrrə mag néttik/ *adj.* used to describe a substance that is weakly magnetized so that it will lie parallel to a magnetic field. The phenomenon results from the presence of unpaired electrons in the atoms of the substance, which cause the atoms to act as tiny magnets when a magnetic field is applied. ◊ **diamagnetic, ferromagnetic**

Par·a·mar·i·bo /pàrrə márrə bō/ port and capital city of Suriname, located in the north of the country near the Atlantic Ocean. Population: 180,000 (1994).

par·a·mat·ta /pèrrə máttə/, **par·ra·mat·ta** *n.* a lightweight fabric made from wool blended with silk or cotton [Early 19thC. Named for the settlement of *Parramatta* in New South Wales, Australia, where a similar fabric was produced.]

par·a·me·ci·um /pèrrə méeshee əm, -méessee-/ (*plural* **par·a·me·ci·a** /-shee ə, -ssee ə/ *or* **-ums**) *n.* a single-celled microscopic aquatic organism **(protozoan)** with hairlike appendages **(cilia)** around its body that it uses to move around and to capture bacteria. Genus: *Paramecium*. [Mid-18thC. From modern Latin, genus name, from Greek *paramēkēs* "oval," from its shape.]

par·a·med·ic /pèrrə méddik/ *n.* somebody trained to perform emergency medical procedures in the absence of a doctor, especially a member of an ambulance crew —**par·a·med·i·cal** *adj.*

par·a·ment /pérrəmənt/ *n.* an object made of richly decorated fabric, especially a ceremonial robe, tapestry, or wall hanging (*archaic*) [14thC. From Old French, "ornament," from *parer* "to prepare, trim" (see PARE).]

pa·ram·e·ter /pə rámmətər/ *n.* **1. LIMITING FACTOR** a fact or circumstance that restricts how something is done or what can be done **2.** SCI **VARIABLE QUANTITY DETERMINING OUTCOME** a measurable quantity, e.g., temperature, that determines the result of a scientific experiment and can be altered to vary the result **3.** MATH **VARIABLE MATHEMATICAL VALUE** in a mathematical expression, a variable value that, when it changes, gives another different but related mathematical expression from a limited series of such expressions **4.** STATS **OVERALL QUANTITY** a general quantity that relates to an entire population, as distinct from an individual statistic that relates to a sample [Mid-17thC. From modern Latin *parametrum*, from PARA-[1] + Greek *metron* "measure."] —**par·a·met·ric** /pèrrə méttrik/ *adj.*

par·a·met·ric e·qua·tions *npl.* a set of mathematical equations in which coordinates of points are explicitly expressed in terms of independent parameters

par·a·mil·i·tar·y /pèrrə míllə tèrree/ *adj.* **1. MILITARY IN STYLE** similar to or modeled on the military but not belonging to it **2. ASSISTING OFFICIAL MILITARY FORCES** organized and staffed by civilians to provide support to the regular military services ○ *a paramilitary unit* **3. USING MILITARY TECHNIQUES** using military weapons and tactics to fight within a country against the official ruling power ■ *n.* (*plural* **-ies**) **UNOFFICIAL SOLDIER** a member of a paramilitary organization, especially one fighting against the official ruling power

par·am·ne·sia /pè ram neézhə/ *n.* **1. FALSE MEMORY** false memories of events that did not really take place **2. INABILITY TO RECALL MEANINGS OF WORDS** an inability to recall the meanings of common words

par·a·morph /pérrə màwrf/ *n.* a mineral that changes its crystalline structure without any change in its chemical composition. Aragonite changes to calcite in this way. —**par·a·mor·phism** /pèrrə máwr fìzzəm/ *n.*

par·a·mor·phine /pèrrə máwr feén/ *n.* = **thebaine**

par·a·mount /pérrə mòwnt/ *adj.* greatest in importance or significance [Mid-16thC. From Anglo-Norman *paramont,* from *par* "by" + *amont* "above."] —**par·a·mount·cy** *n.* —**par·a·mount·ly** *adv.*

par·a·mour /pérrə moòr/ *n.* a lover, especially one in a relationship with a married person (*literary*) ○ *"found thee out even in the arms of thy paramour"* (Sir Walter Scott, *Ivanhoe*; 1819) [14thC. From *par amur* "passionately," from Anglo-Norman *par amour* "by way of love."]

par·a·myx·o·vi·rus /pèrrə míksə vìrəss/ *n.* a virus belonging to the group that includes the mumps and measles viruses and the parainfluenza virus

pa·rang /paá ràng, pə raáng/ *n.* a large knife with a short straight-edged blade, used in Malaysia and Indonesia as a weapon and as a tool [Mid-19thC. From Malay.]

par·a·noi·a /pèrrə nóy ə/ *n.* **1. DISTRUST** extreme and unreasonable suspicion of other people and their motives **2.** PSYCHIAT **PSYCHIATRIC DISORDER** a psychiatric disorder involving systematized delusion, usually of persecution [Early 19thC. From Greek, "unreason," literally "out of one's mind," from *nous* "mind."]

par·a·noi·ac /pèrrə nóy àk/ *adj.* **RELATING TO PARANOIA** characteristic of or resembling paranoia ■ *n.* **SOMEBODY WITH PARANOIA** somebody who has paranoia

par·a·noid /pérrə nòyd/ *adj.* **1. DISTRUSTFUL** obsessively anxious about something, or unreasonably suspicious of other people and their thoughts or motives **2.** PSYCHIAT **SHOWING CHARACTERISTICS OF PARANOIA** relating to or showing the characteristics of paranoia ■ *n.* **PARANOID PERSON** somebody who is paranoid (*dated*)

par·a·nor·mal /pèrrə náwrm'l/ *adj.* **IMPOSSIBLE TO EXPLAIN SCIENTIFICALLY** unable to be explained or understood in terms of scientific knowledge ■ *n.* **PARANORMAL THINGS** paranormal events or phenomena

par·a·pa·re·sis /pèrrəpə reéssis, pèrrə pérrəssiss/ *n.* a medical condition in which both legs, and often the bladder, do not have much voluntary control but do have some voluntary control —**par·a·pa·re·tic** /pèrrəpə réttik/ *adj.*

par·a·pet /pérrəpət, pérrə pèt/ *n.* **1. LOW WALL** a low protective wall built where there is a sudden dangerous drop, e.g., along the edge of a balcony, roof, or bridge. Some parapets are battlemented, especially on castles, and many are built as ornamental features. **2.** MIL **PROTECTIVE WALL OF EARTH** a bank of earth, rubble, or sandbags piled up along the edge of a military trench for protection from enemy fire [Late 16thC. Via French from Italian *parapetto,* from *parare* "to shield" (see PARASOL) + *petto* "chest," from Latin *pectus* (see PECTORAL).]

par·aph /pérrəf, pə ráf/ *n.* a decorative flourish written under a signature to finish it off, or formerly to protect against forgery [Late 16thC. Via French from, ultimately, medieval Latin *paragraphus* "paragraph."]

par·a·pha·si·a /pèrrə fáyzhə/ *n.* a speech defect of neurological origin in which the speaker's words are jumbled unintelligibly. ◊ **aphasia**

par·a·pher·na·lia /pèrrəfər náylee ə/ *n.* **1. ASSORTED OBJECTS** assorted objects or items of equipment, often things that seem amusing, strange, or irritating **2.** LAW **WEDDING GIFTS TO WIFE** in former times, items of property given to a wife on her wedding by her new husband and regarded by law as belonging to her [Mid-17thC. Via medieval Latin from, ultimately, Greek *parapherna,* "married woman's own property," literally "beside the dowry," from *phernē* "dowry."]

par·a·phrase /pérrə fràyz/ *vt.* (**-phrased, -phras·ing, -phras·es**) **REPHRASE AND SIMPLIFY** to restate something using other words, especially in order to make it simpler or shorter ■ *n.* **REPHRASED VERSION** something that is rephrased and simplified through being made shorter [Mid-16thC. Via French from, ultimately, Greek *paraphrazein,* literally "to explain alongside," from *phrazein* "to explain."] —**par·a·phras·tic** /pèrrə frástik/ *adj.*

pa·raph·y·sis /pə ráffəssiss/ (*plural* **-ses** /-seez/) *n.* an erect sterile filament that grows among the reproductive organs of fungi, algae, and mosses [Mid-19thC. From modern Latin, literally "growth beside," from Greek *phusis* "growth."] —**par·a·phy·sate** /pə ráffəsət, pə ráffə sàyt/ *adj.*

par·a·ple·gi·a /pèrrə pleéjə, -pleéjee ə/ *n.* total inability to move both legs and usually the lower part of the trunk, often as a result of disease or injury of the spine [Mid-17thC. Via modern Latin from Greek *paraplēgiē* "stroke on one side," from *paraplēssein* "to strike on one side," from *plessein* "to strike."] —**par·a·ple·gic** *adj., n.*

par·a·po·di·um /pèrrə pōdee əm/ (*plural* **par·a·po·di·a** /-dee ə/) *n.* an appendage on the body of some marine worms, occuring in pairs on each segment of the worm's body, used for swimming, crawling, or holding onto things

par·a·pro·fes·sion·al /pèrrəprə féshən'l, -féshnəl/ *n.* somebody who is trained to give support to a professional person such as a teacher or a doctor

par·a·psy·chol·o·gy /pèrrə sī kólləjee/ *n.* the study of supposed mental phenomena that cannot be explained by known psychological or scientific principles, e.g., extrasensory perception and telepathy —**par·a·psy·cho·log·i·cal** /pèrrə sīkə lójjik'l/ *adj.* —**par·a·psy·chol·o·gist** /-sī kólləjist/ *n.*

Pa·rá rub·ber /pə raá-, paárə-/ *n.* rubber made from the latex of the Pará rubber tree [Mid-19thC. Named for the state of *Pará* in Brazil.]

Pa·rá rub·ber tree *n.* a tropical South American tree that yields latex used to make rubber. Latin name: *Hevea brasiliensis.*

Par·a·Sail *tdmk.* a trademark for a parachute

para·sail·ing /pérrə sàyling/ *n.* a sport in which a waterskier wearing a parachute or holding onto a type of hang-glider is towed along behind a motorboat and rises up into the air [Mid-20thC. Coined from PARA + SAIL.]

par·a·sang /pérrə sàng/ *n.* an old unit of measure for distance used in Persia, equal to about 31/2 mi./5.6 km [Late 16thC. Via Latin from Greek *parasaggēs,* of Persian origin.]

par·a·scend·ing /pérrə sènding/ *n.* a sport in which somebody wearing an open parachute is towed along by a speedboat or land vehicle, rises into the air, and descends independently using the parachute [Late 20thC. Coined from PARA + ASCEND.]

par·a·sci·ence /pérrə sī əns/ *n.* the study of phenomena that cannot be explained or tested by conventional scientific methods

par·a·se·le·ne /pèrrəsə leénee/ (*plural* **-nae**) *n.* an image of the moon seen within a lunar halo [Mid-17thC. Coined from PARA-[1] + Greek *selēnē* "moon."] —**par·a·se·le·nic** /pèrrəsə lénnik, -leénik/ *adj.*

par·a·sen·so·ry /pèrrə sénsəree/ *adj.* extrasensory (*technical*)

par·a·sex·u·al /pèrrə sékshoo əl/ *adj.* used to describe a type of reproduction, seen in certain fungi, in which the recombination of parental chromosomes takes place without the usual formation of sex cells by cell division (**meiosis**) —**par·a·sex·u·al·i·ty** /pèrrə sèkshoo állətee/ *n.*

Pa·ra·shah /paárə shaá/ (*plural* **Pa·ra·shoth** /paárə shōt, -shōth/) *n.* in Judaism, a passage from the Torah read during traditional weekly worship at the synagogue [Early 17thC. From Hebrew *pārāšāh* "division."]

par·a·site /pérrə sīt/ *n.* **1.** BIOL **ORGANISM LIVING ON ANOTHER** a plant or animal that lives on or in another, usually larger, host organism in a way that harms or is of no advantage to the host **2. SCROUNGER** somebody who lives off the generosity of others and does nothing in return [Mid-16thC. Via Latin from Greek *parasitos* "one who eats from another's table," from *sitos* "grain, food."]

par·a·sit·ic /pèrrə síttik/ *adj.* **1.** BIOL **LIVING IN OR ON ANOTHER ORGANISM** living in or on another host organism, usually causing it harm **2. LIVING OFF OTHER PEOPLE** living off the generosity of others without doing anything in return —**par·a·sit·i·cal·ly** *adv.*

par·a·sit·i·cide /pèrrə sítti sīd/ *n.* a substance that is used to destroy parasites —**par·a·sit·i·ci·dal** *adj.*

par·a·sit·ism /pérrəssi tìzzəm, -sī-/ *n.* **1.** BIOL **PARASITIC BEHAVIOR** a type of symbiosis in which one organism lives as a parasite in or on another organism **2.** VET = **parasitosis**

par·a·sit·ize /pérrəssi tīz, -sī-/ (**-ized, -iz·ing, -iz·es**) *vt.* to infest an animal or plant with a parasite, or to live on it as a parasite

par·a·sit·oid /pérrəssi tòyd, -sī-/ *adj.* **LAYING EGGS INSIDE HOST** used to describe an insect that lays its eggs inside the living body of another animal or insect. The hatched newborns feed off the body, eventually killing the host. ■ *n.* **PARASITOID INSECT** an insect that lays its eggs within a host, eventually causing the death of the host

par·a·si·tol·o·gy /pèrrəssi tólləjee, -sī-/ *n.* the scientific study of plants and animals that live as parasites —**par·a·si·to·log·i·cal** /pèrrə sītə lójjik'l/ *adj.*

par·a·si·to·sis /pèrrəssi tōsiss, -sī-/ (*plural* **par·a·si·tos·es** /pèrrəssi tō seez, -sī tō-/) *n.* VET a disease that develops as a result of infestation by parasites

par·a·ski·ing /pérrə skeè ing/ *n.* the sport of skiing off high mountains and descending using a light, steerable parachute composed of inflatable tubes of fabric [Mid-20thC. Coined from PARA + SKI.]

par·a·sol /pérrə sàwl/ *n.* an umbrella made to provide shade from the sun [Early 17thC. Via French from Italian *parasole,* from *parare* "to protect" + *sole* "sun."]

par·a·su·i·cide /pérrə soó i sīd/ *n.* **1. ACT BORDERING ON SUICIDE** a suicide attempt or act of self-injury that is motivated by a desire to draw attention to other personal problems rather than by a genuine wish to die **2. SOMEBODY CARRYING OUT PARASUICIDE** somebody who carries out a parasuicide

par·a·sym·pa·thet·ic /pèrrə símpə théttik/ *adj.* relating or belonging to the parasympathetic nervous system [Early 20thC. Because some of the nerves run beside sympathetic nerves.]

par·a·sym·pa·thet·ic nerv·ous sys·tem *n.* one of the two divisions in the part of the nervous system that controls involuntary and unconscious bodily functions (**autonomic nervous system**). Its actions include slowing the heart, constricting the pupils, and relaxing the bowels. ◊ **sympathetic nervous system**

par·a·syn·the·sis /pèrrə sínthəssiss/ (*plural* **-ses** /-seèz/) *n.* the formation of words by a combination of smaller words and additional elements. For example, "heavy-handed" combines the adjective "heavy" with "handed," which in turn is "hand" with "-ed" added. —**par·a·syn·thet·ic** /pèrrə sin théttik/ *adj.*

par·a·syn·the·ton /pèrrə sínthə tòn/ (*plural* **-ta** /-tə/) *n.* a word formed by the combination of smaller words and additional elements

par·a·tax·is /pèrrə táksiss/ *n.* the combination of clauses or phrases without the use of conjunctions such as "and" or "so," e.g., in "He saved my life – he deserves a medal." ◊ **asyndeton** [Mid-19thC. From Greek, from *paratassein* "to place side by side," from *tassein* "to arrange."] —**par·a·tac·tic** /pèrrə táktik/ *adj.* —**par·a·tac·ti·cal·ly** /-táktikəlee/ *adv.*

par·a·thi·on /pèrrə thī òn/ *n.* a colorless highly toxic oil that is used as an insecticide. Formula: $C_{10}H_{14}NO_5PS$. [Mid-20thC. Coined from PARA-[1] + *thiophosphate* + -ON.]

par·a·thy·roid /pèrrə thī ròyd/ *adj.* **1. OF PARATHYROID GLANDS** relating to or produced by the parathyroid glands **2. NEAR THYROID GLAND** in the area around the thyroid gland ■ *n.* = **parathyroid gland**

par·a·thy·roid·ec·to·my /pèrrə thī roy déktəmee/ (*plural* **-mies**) *n.* the surgical removal of one or more of the parathyroid glands

par·a·thy·roid gland *n.* any of four small glands that lie in or near the walls of the thyroid gland. They secrete a hormone that controls the depositing of calcium and phosphorus in bones.

par·a·thy·roid hor·mone *n.* a hormone secreted by the parathyroid glands that controls the depositing of calcium and phosphorus in bones

par·a·troop·er /pérrə troòpər/ *n.* a soldier trained to go into battle by parachute, especially one who is also a member of an airborne unit

par·a·troops /pérrə troòps/ *npl.* soldiers trained to parachute directly into action, or into enemy territory ○ *a paratroop regiment* —**par·a·troop** *adj.*

par·a·ty·phoid fe·ver *n.* an infectious bacterial disease similar to typhoid but with much less severe symptoms, usually limited to a pink rash, diarrhea, and some abdominal pain

par·a·vane /pérrə vàyn/ *n.* a torpedo-shaped device with sharp fins at the front, towed by a ship to cut the moorings of submerged mines [Early 20thC. Coined from PARA- "protector" (modeled on PARASOL) + VANE.]

par a·vi·on /paàr ə vyáwn, paàr aa vyáwN/ *adv.* by air mail [From French, literally "by airplane"]

par·a·zo·an /pèrrə zṓ ən/ (*plural* **-a** /-ə/) *n.* a member of the subkingdom of invertebrate animals that includes sponges. Subkingdom: *Parazoa.* [Early 20thC. From modern Latin, subkingdom name, from PARA-[1] on the model of PROTOZOAN and METAZOAN.]

par·boil /paàr bòyl/ (**-boiled, -boil·ing, -boils**) *vt.* to boil something, especially a vegetable, until it is partly cooked, usually before frying or roasting it [15thC. Via Old French *parboillir* "to boil thoroughly" from, ultimately, Latin *bullire* "to boil." Originally "boil thoroughly," later "boil partially" (influenced by PART).]

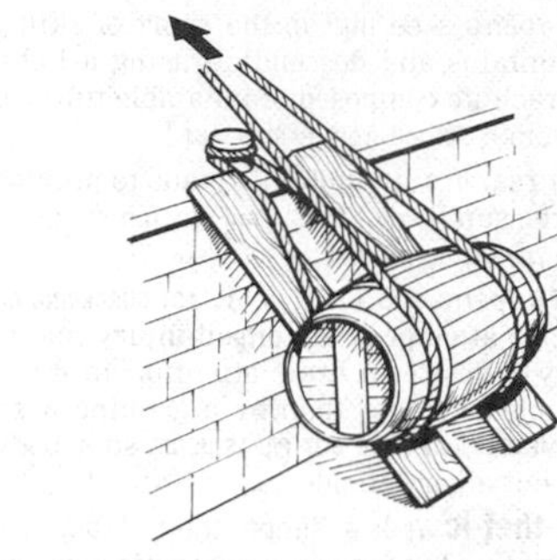

Parbuckle

par·buck·le /paàr bùk'l/ *n.* a rope sling for lifting or lowering barrels, logs, or similar objects [Early 17thC. Alteration (influenced by BUCKLE) of earlier *parbunkle*, of unknown origin.]

Par·cae /paàrsee/ *npl.* in Roman mythology, the Fates. Greek equivalent **Moirai** [Late 16thC. From Latin.]

par·cel /paàrs'l/ *n.* **1. SOMETHING WRAPPED UP** one or more things wrapped up together in paper or other packaging **2. PORTION** any of the portions into which something is divided, especially a piece of land that was originally part of a larger area **3.** COMM **BATCH OF COMMERCIAL GOODS** a specific quantity of wholesale merchandise, or a sales transaction involving such a batch **4. BUNCH** a collection of people or things (*archaic or literary*) ○ *"a parcel of rascals"* (Thomas Paine, *The Age of Reason*; 1794) ■ *vt.* (**-celed, -cel·ing, -cels**) **1. MAKE PARCEL OF SOMETHING** to wrap something or a group of things into a parcel **2.** NAUT **PROTECT ROPE** to bind canvas tightly around rope or cable to protect it [14thC. Via Old French from, ultimately, Latin *particula*, literally "small part." Originally "part, detail."]

parcel out *vt.* to divide and distribute something between a number of people

par·cel-gilt *adj.* partly gilded, often on the inside but not on the outside

par·cel post *n.* the postal service that collects, processes, and delivers packages

par·ce·nar·y /paàrs'n èrree/ *n.* LAW = **coparcenary** [15thC. From Anglo-Norman, from *parcen* "portion."]

parch /paarch/ (**parched, parch·ing, parch·es**) *vt.* to make somebody or something extremely dry through water deprivation or exposure to heat [14thC. Origin unknown.]

parched /paarcht/ *adj.* **1. THIRSTY** very thirsty (*informal*) **2. DRY** completely lacking in moisture because of hot conditions or lack of rainfall

WORD KEY: SYNONYMS

See Synonyms at ***dry***.

Par·chee·si /paar cheèzee/ *tdmk.* a trademark for a board game based on pachisi, an ancient game [Late 19thC]

parch·ment /paàrchmənt/ *n.* **1. FORMER WRITING MATERIAL** a creamy or yellowish material made from dried and treated sheepskin, goatskin, or other animal hide, used in former times for books and documents **2. DOCUMENT** a manuscript or other work written, drawn, or painted on a sheet of parchment **3.** PRINTING, PAPER **HIGH-QUALITY PAPER** strong, smooth or textured, usually off-white paper that is used for special documents, letters, or artwork [13thC. From Old French *parchemin*, via Latin *pergamena* from, ultimately, Greek *Pergamon*, the city of Pergamum in Asia Minor.]

par·close /paàr klṓz/ *n.* CHR a screen or railing that separates or encloses a side chapel, private tomb, or other special area within a large church [15thC. From Old French, the past participle of *parclore* "to close off, enclose," from Latin *claudere* "to close."]

par·course /paar kòor/ *n.* a training circuit in a park or other open space, where people can walk or run between stations equipped with equipment and instructions for specific fitness exercises [Partial translation of French *parcours* "course," a loan translation of medieval Latin *percursus*, literally "running through," from *percurrere*, literally "to run through"]

pard[1] /paard/ *n.* a large cat, especially a leopard or a panther (*archaic*) [13thC. Via Old French from, ultimately, Greek *pardos*, of Iranian origin.]

pard[2] /paard/ *n.* = **pardner** (*slang*) [Mid-19thC. Shortening.]

pard·ner /paàrdnər/ *n.* used to address a friend, in imitation of the cowboy's supposed pronunciation of the word "partner" (*slang*)

par·don /paàrd'n/ *vt.* (**-doned, -don·ing, -dons**) **1. FORGIVE SOMEBODY FOR WRONGDOING** to pronounce the official release of somebody who has committed a crime or other wrongdoing from punishment, or the official forgiving of a crime or wrongdoing **2. EXCUSE SOMEBODY FOR SOMETHING IMPOLITE** to excuse somebody for doing something impolite, or to excuse something impolite, e.g., interrupting or contradicting somebody ■ *n.* **1. RELEASE FROM PUNISHMENT** the act of officially releasing somebody guilty of a crime or wrongdoing from facing punishment **2. PAPER AUTHORIZING FREEDOM FROM PUNISHMENT** an official document stating that somebody may be released without receiving any or any further punishment **3. ACT OF EXCUSING SOMEBODY** the excusing of an impolite act or the forgiving of the person committing it **4.** CHR **INDULGENCE** an indulgence (*dated informal*) ■ *interj.* *U.K.* **1. WHAT DID YOU SAY?** used as a request to somebody to repeat something that has just been said **2.** used as an apology for doing something impolite or wrong [13thC. Via Old French *pardun* (noun) and *pardoner* (verb), literally "to grant thoroughly," from, ultimately, Latin *donare* "to give, grant."] —**par·don·a·ble** *adj.* —**par·don·a·bly** *adv.* ◇ **pardon me 1.** used as an apology for doing something impolite or wrong **2.** used as a request to somebody to repeat something that has just been said

par·don·er /paàrd'nər/ *n.* **1. SOMEBODY WHO PARDONS** somebody who gives a pardon **2.** CHR, HIST **SELLER OF RELIGIOUS PARDONS** somebody who, in medieval times, made a living by selling papal indulgences that were believed to free people from their sins

pare /pair/ (**pared, par·ing, pares**) *vt.* **1. REMOVE OUTER LAYER** to remove the skin or outer layer of something such as a vegetable or fruit thinly and neatly **2. TRIM NAILS** to trim something such as fingernails or toenails [13thC. Via Old French *parer* "to prepare, trim," from Latin *parare* (source of English *prepare, repair, rampart*, and *parade*).]

pare down *vt.* to reduce a total amount or number, usually an amount of money or a number of workers, slowly and steadily

par·e·gor·ic /pèrrə gáwrik/ *n.* **OPIUM-BASED PAINKILLER** a former painkilling medicine in the form of camphorated tincture of opium. Originally freely available without prescription, it was a major source of opium addiction. ■ *adj.* **SOOTHING** soothing or painkilling [Late 17thC. Via late Latin from Greek *parēgorikos* "soothing," from *para* "beside" + *agoreuein* "to speak."]

paren. *abbr.* parenthesis

pa·ren·chy·ma /pə réngkəmə/ *n.* **1.** BOT **PLANT TISSUE** soft plant tissue made up of thin-walled cells that forms the greater part of leaves, stem pith, roots, and fruit pulp **2.** ANAT **SPECIALIZED ORGAN TISSUE** the tissue that makes up the specialized parts of particular organs, rather than the blood vessels and connective or supporting tissue **3.** ZOOL **WORM TISSUE** the loose meshwork of cells that surrounds internal organs and fills spaces inside the body of animals such as flatworms [Mid-17thC. Via modern Latin from Greek *paregkhuma* "soft tissue," from *paregkhein* "to pour in beside," from *khein* "to pour."] —**par·en·chym·a·tous** /pèrrən kímmətəss/ *adj.*

par·ent /páirənt/ *n.* **1. MOTHER OR FATHER** somebody's mother, father, or legal guardian **2. ORIGIN OF SOMETHING ELSE** something from which one or more similar and separate things have developed, or to which they are attached (*often used before a noun*) ○ *money transferred from the parent fund* **3.** SCI **EARLIER ATOMIC FORM** an atom, molecule, or ion that undergoes change to become a new product. The starting components in a chemical reaction are the parent molecules. (*often used before a noun*) **4.** NUCLEAR PHYS **PARTICLE'S EARLIER FORM** a radioactive particle that disintegrates to give a new particle (**nuclide**) as a subsequent member of a radioactive decay series (*often used before a noun*) ■ *vt.* (**-ent·ed, -ent·ing, -ents**) **ACT AS PARENT TO** to be or act as a parent to somebody or something [15thC. Via Old French from Latin *parent-*, the present participle stem of *parere* "to give birth" (source of English *parturition, viper*, and *repertory*).]

par·ent·age /páirəntij/ *n.* **1. SOMEBODY'S PARENTS** the parents or ancestors of a particular person, especially when regarded in terms of social characteristics **2. DERIVATION** the particular origins or sources that something has developed from **3.** = **parenthood**

pa·ren·tal /pə rént'l/ *adj.* **1. OF PARENTS** relating to, belonging to, or provided by parents **2.** GENETICS **ORIGINAL** used to describe the original generation of individuals from which all subsequent generations have been bred —**pa·ren·tal·ly** *adv.*

pa·ren·tal leave *n.* time off from work, granted to a parent to care for a new child

par·en·ter·al /pə réntərəl/ *adj.* used to describe drug administration other than by the mouth or the rectum, e.g., by injection, infusion, or implantation [Early 20thC. Formed from PARA-[1] + Greek *enteron* "intestine" (source of English *dysentery*).] —**par·en·ter·al·ly** *adv.*

pa·ren·the·sis /pə rénthəsiss/ (*plural* **-ses** /-seèz/) *n.* **1. UPRIGHT CURVED MARK IN PUNCTUATION** one of a pair of shallow, curved signs (,) used to enclose an additional inserted word or comment and distinguish it from the sentence in which it is found **2. WORDS WITHIN PARENTHESES** a word or phrase that comments on or qualifies part of the sentence in which it is found and is isolated from it by parentheses or dashes **3. DEPARTURE FROM TOPIC** a piece of speech or writing that wanders off from the main topic **4. INTERVAL** something that acts as a pause or break in something (*formal*) [Mid-16thC. Via late Latin from Greek, formed from *parentithenai* "to insert," from *tithenai* "to place."] ◇ **in parenthesis** as an additional qualifying, explanatory, or otherwise separate comment

pa·ren·the·size /pə rénthə sīz/ (**-sized, -siz·ing, -siz·es**) *v.* **1.** *vt.* **PUT SOMETHING IN PARENTHESES** to enclose part of a written or printed passage in parentheses **2.** *vt.* **ADD SOMETHING AS EXTRA COMMENT** to add a word, phrase, or opinion as an extra comment that is not wholly related to what is being said **3.** *vti.* **INSERT EXTRA COMMENTS** to break up speech or writing with extra comments added throughout

par·en·thet·i·cal /pèrrən théttik'l/, **par·en·thet·ic** /-théttik/ *adj.* **1. ADDITIONAL** added as an extra comment or parenthesis **2. CONTAINING PARENTHESES** used to describe writing that uses or contains additional comments or notes added as parentheses [Early 17thC] —**par·en·thet·i·cal·ly** *adv.*

par·ent·hood /páirənt hòod/ *n.* the role or experience of being a parent, or the way of life that being a parent imposes

par·ent·ing /páirənting/ *n.* the experiences, skills, qualities, and responsibilities involved in being a parent and in teaching and caring for a child (*often used before a noun*) ○ *parenting skills*

par·ent met·al *n.* in welding, the metal of any of the components that are to be welded together

Par·ent-Teach·er As·so·ci·a·tion *n.* a school body run by teachers and parents to organize fundraising and social events and encourage cooperation and understanding

pa·re·sis /pə reèssiss, pérrəssiss/ *n.* muscular weakness or partial inability to move caused by diseases of the nervous system [Late 17thC. From Greek, literally "letting go," formed from *para* "aside" + *hienai* "to throw" (see CATHETER).]

par·es·the·si·a /pèrrəs théezhə, -zhee ə/ *n.* an abnormal or unexplained tingling, pricking, or burning sensation on the skin [Late 19thC. Coined from PARA-[1] + Greek *aisthēsis* "feeling."]

pa·re·u /paá ray oo/ *n.* a length of fabric worn wrapped around the hips by both men and women in Polynesian countries [Mid-19thC. From Tahitian.]

pa·rev /paárəvə/, **pa·re·ve, par·veh** /paárvə/, **par·ve** *adj.* used to classify a food that, under Jewish law, is neither a dairy nor a meat product and can therefore be eaten with either as part of the same meal. ◊ **fleishig, milchig** [Mid-20thC. From Yiddish.]

par ex·cel·lence /paar èksə laáNss/ *adj.* of the very best kind or highest quality [From French, literally "by virtue of preeminence"]

par·fait /paar fáy/ (*plural* **-faits** *or* **-fait**) *n.* **1. COLD FRUIT DESSERT** a sweet dish composed of various layers, including ice cream, fruit, syrup, and whipped cream **2. CREAMY FROZEN DESSERT** a rich dessert consisting of frozen whipped cream or rich ice cream flavored with fruit. It is sometimes lightened with egg whites to give it a texture similar to that of mousse. [Late 19thC. Via French, literally "perfect," from Latin *perfectus* "perfect."]

par·fait glass *n.* a short-stemmed glass with a tall, rather narrow body designed to show off the contrasting layers of a parfait

par·fleche /paár flèsh/ *n.* **1. DRIED ANIMAL SKIN** the hide of an animal, soaked and scraped to remove the hair, then stretched and dried, but not tanned **2. ANIMAL-SKIN ARTICLE** a shield, bag, or other item made of parfleche [Early 19thC. From Canadian French, formed from French *parer* "to defend" + *flèche* "arrow."]

par·get /paárjət/ *n.* **1. PLASTER FOR WALLS OR CHIMNEYS** plaster, whitewash, roughcast, or any similar material used to coat walls or line chimneys **2. PLASTERWORK** ornamental plasterwork on a wall ■ *vt.* (**-get·ed, -get·ing, -gets**) **COAT SOMETHING WITH PARGET** to cover walls, line chimneys, or decorate something with parget [14thC. Alteration (influenced by Old French *parjeter* "to throw about") of Old French *porgeter* "to plaster a wall," from *jeter* "to throw."] —**par·get·ing** *n.*

par·he·li·a plural of **parhelion**

par·he·lic cir·cle /paar heélik-/ *n.* a luminous horizontal band in the sky that passes through the sun and is caused by the sun's rays reflecting off ice crystals in the atmosphere

par·he·li·on /paar heélee ən, -heélyən/ (*plural* **-a** /-lee ə/) *n.* a bright colored spot on a parhelic circle, often seen in pairs and caused by ice crystals in the atmosphere diffracting light. ◊ **anthelion** [Mid-17thC. Via Latin from Greek *parēlion*, from *para* "beside" + *hēlios* "sun" (see HELIO-).] —**par·he·li·a·cal** /paárhi lí ək'l/ *adj.* —**par·he·lic** /paar heélik/ *adj.*

pari- *prefix.* equal ○ *parisyllabic* [From Latin, formed from *par* (see PAR)]

pa·ri·ah /pə rí ə/ *n.* **1. OUTCAST** somebody who is despised and avoided by other people **2. SOMEBODY OF LOW CASTE** in India and Myanmar, a member of a caste that is lower than the four main Hindu castes. A pariah usually does domestic or agricultural work. [Early 17thC. From Tamil *paraiyan*, literally "drummer," from *parai* "festival drum," because hereditary drummers belonged to this caste.]

pa·ri·ah dog *n.* = **pye-dog** [Because it is seen as belonging to the fringes of society, like the pariah caste]

Par·i·an /páiree ən/ *adj.* **1.** INDUST **OF MARBLE FROM PAROS** used to describe a fine white marble that was mined on the Greek island of Paros in ancient times **2.** CERAMICS **OF PORCELAIN FROM PAROS** used to describe a variety of fine porcelain used mainly to make figures and originally from the Greek island of Paros **3. OF PAROS** relating to or from the Greek island of Paros ■ *n.* PEOPLES **SOMEBODY FROM PAROS** somebody who was born in or is an inhabitant of the Greek island of Paros [Mid-16thC. Formed from Latin *Parius*.]

pa·ri·e·tal /pə rí ət'l/ *adj.* **1.** BIOL **OF WALLS OF HOLLOW PART** relating to the walls of any hollow part of a plant or animal such as a plant's ovary or an animal's skull **2.** EDUC **OF IN-COLLEGE RESIDENCE** relating to residence within a college ■ *n.* BIOL **PARIETAL PART** a parietal part of a plant or animal ■ **pa·ri·e·tals** *npl.* EDUC **COLLEGE VISITING RULES** the rules governing who can and cannot visit a college dormitory, especially in relation to members of the opposite sex [Early 16thC. Directly or via French from late Latin *parietalis*, from *paries* "wall."]

pa·ri·e·tal bone *n.* either of two bones, one on each side of the skull, that form a part of the sides and roof of the skull

pa·ri·e·tal cell *n.* any one of the cells that make up the peptic glands of the stomach and secrete hydrochloric acid

pa·ri·e·tal lobe *n.* the middle region of each of the two hemispheres of the brain, lying beneath the crown of the skull

par·i·mu·tu·el /pèrri myoóchoo əl/ (*plural* **par·i·mu·tu·els** /pèrri myoóchoo əl/ *or* **par·is·mu·tu·els** /pèrri myoóchoo əl/) *n.* **1. SYSTEM OF BETTING ON HORSERACES** a system of betting on horseraces using an electronic machine that totals all bets, deducts management charges and taxes, and determines the final odds and payouts **2. BETTING MACHINE** a machine that records bets and calculates winnings in the pari-mutuel betting system [From French, literally "mutual wager"]

par·ing /páiring/ *n.* something such as a thin slice of fruit or vegetable peel that has been pared or cut off something larger

par·ing knife *n.* a short tapered knife with a sharp blade designed for removing the outer skin of vegetables or fruit

pa·ri pas·su /pèrri pá soo, paári paá soo/ *adv.* **1.** LAW **FAIRLY** at an equal rate or in an otherwise fair way, with no one person or group taking precedence over another **2. AT SAME RATE** together, step for step (*literary*) [From Latin, literally "with equal step"]

par·i·pin·nate /pèrri pí nàyt, pérri pínnət/ *adj.* = **even-pinnate**

Par·is[1] /pérriss/ *n.* in Greek mythology, a Trojan prince whose abduction of Helen from her husband Menelaus started the Trojan War [Via Latin from Greek]

Par·is[2] /párriss/; *French* /pa reé/ **1.** capital city of France, situated in the north central part of the country. Population: 2,152,423 (1990). **2.** city in the Red River valley in northeastern Texas. Population: 24,699 (1990).

Par·is green *n.* a bright blue-green toxic powder used to add color to paint. It is also used as an insecticide and a wood preserver. It is a double salt of copper acetate and copper arsenate. Formula: $(CuO)_3As_2O_3.Cu(C_2H_3O_2)_2$. [Mid-19thC. Named for the city of PARIS, France.]

par·ish /pérrish/ *n.* **1.** CHR **DISTRICT WITH OWN CHURCH** in the Episcopal, Roman Catholic, and some other churches, a division of a diocese that has its own church and clergy member (*often used before a noun*) ○ *the parish priest* **2.** CHR **PEOPLE OF PARISH** the people who live in a particular parish **3.** POL **ADMINISTRATIVE AREA IN LOUISIANA** an administrative area in the state of Louisiana that corresponds to a county in other states [13thC. Via Old French *parroche* and ecclesiastical Latin *parochia* from, ultimately, Greek *paroikos* "neighbor," literally "dwelling nearby," from *oikos* "dwelling."]

pa·rish·ion·er /pə ríshənər/ *n.* somebody who lives in a particular religious or civil parish [15thC. Formed from earlier *parishon*, from Old French *parochien*, from *parroche* (see PARISH).]

Pa·ri·si·an /pə reézh'n/ *n.* **RESIDENT OF PARIS** somebody who was born in or who lives in the French city of Paris ■ *adj.* **OF PARIS** relating to Paris, its people, or its culture

par·i·syl·lab·ic /pèrri si lábbik/ *adj.* used to describe a noun or verb that contains the same number of syllables in all of its inflections

par·i·ty[1] /pérrətee/ *n.* **1. EQUALITY** equality of status or position, especially in terms of pay or rank **2. SIMILARITY BETWEEN THINGS** the quality of being similar or identical **3.** MATH **RELATIONSHIP BETWEEN NUMBERS** a relationship of oddness or evenness between two numbers (**integers**). If two numbers are both odd or both even, they are said to have the same parity. If one is odd and one is even, they have different parity. **4.** FIN **EQUALITY OF EXCHANGE RATE** equivalence in the rate of exchange between several currencies **5.** COMPUT **INTEGRITY OF TRANSMITTED DATA** equivalence between the data transmitted, e.g., by fax or e-mail, and the data received. Errors are checked by comparing the quantity of 1s in the message sent with the quantity in the message received. [Late 16thC. Directly or via Old French *parite* from late Latin *paritas*, from *par* "equal" (see PAR).]

par·i·ty[2] /pérrətee/ *n.* **1. CONDITION OF HAVING GIVEN BIRTH** the condition or fact of having given birth **2. NUMBER OF CHILDREN** the number of children that a particular woman has given birth to [Late 19thC. Coined from PAROUS + -ITY.]

park /paark/ *n.* **1.** LEISURE **AREA FOR PUBLIC RECREATION** a publicly owned area of land, usually with grass, trees, paths, sports fields, playgrounds, picnic areas, and other features for recreation and relaxation **2.** ENVIRON **PROTECTED AREA OF COUNTRYSIDE** an area of land reserved and managed so that it remains unspoiled, undeveloped, and as natural as possible **3.** LEISURE **PRIVATELY OWNED RECREATION FACILITY** an area of privately owned land, developed to offer recreation or amusements to paying customers **4.** BUSINESS **BUSINESS SITE** an area of land developed for a group of related commercial enterprises ○ *a high-technology park* **5.** SPORTS **STADIUM OR SPORTS FIELD** a sports stadium or sports field **6.** TRANSP **ROAD OR DISTRICT** a street or district, especially in a suburban area (*often used in place names*) **7.** CARS **POSITION ON AUTOMATIC GEARBOX** a position on the gear selector of an automatic gearbox that acts as a parking brake for a motor vehicle **8.** MIL **AREA HOUSING MILITARY VEHICLES** a designated area where military vehicles are kept, within a military base ■ *v.* (**parked, park·ing, parks**) **1.** *vti.* CARS **STOP AND LEAVE VEHICLE** to stop a motor vehicle beside or off the road and leave it there for some time **2.** *vti.* CARS **MANEUVER MOTOR VEHICLE INTO SPACE** to maneuver a motor vehicle into a space in order to park it **3.** *vt.* **SETTLE SOMEWHERE** to sit down somewhere, usually with the intention of staying there for some time (*slang*) ○ *Just park yourself over there.* **4.** *vt.* **LEAVE SOMETHING SOMEWHERE** to place or leave something somewhere temporarily, especially something heavy, bulky, or unwanted (*slang*) **5.** *vi.* **KISS IN PARKED CAR** to kiss and cuddle in a parked car in a quiet and secluded location (*slang*) **6.** *vt.* SPACE TECH **PLACE SPACECRAFT IN ORBIT** to place a spacecraft or satellite in orbit, usually temporarily [13thC. Via Old French *parc* from medieval Latin *parricus*, ultimately from a prehistoric Germanic word meaning "enclosure" that is also the ancestor of English *paddock*.]

WORD KEY: CULTURAL NOTE

Mansfield Park, a novel by the English writer Jane Austen (1814). It tells the story of young Fanny Price, who is sent to live with her wealthy relatives, the Bertrams. Fanny's warmth and moral strength, which are contrasted with her uncle's stern traditionalism and the irresponsible flirtations of her neighbors Mary and Henry Crawford, eventually win her the respect of the family and the hand of her cousin Edmund.

Park /paark/, **Mungo** (1771–1806) Scottish explorer. He explored the Niger River and wrote *Travels in the Interior Districts of Africa* (1799). In a subsequent expedition his party was attacked, and he drowned.

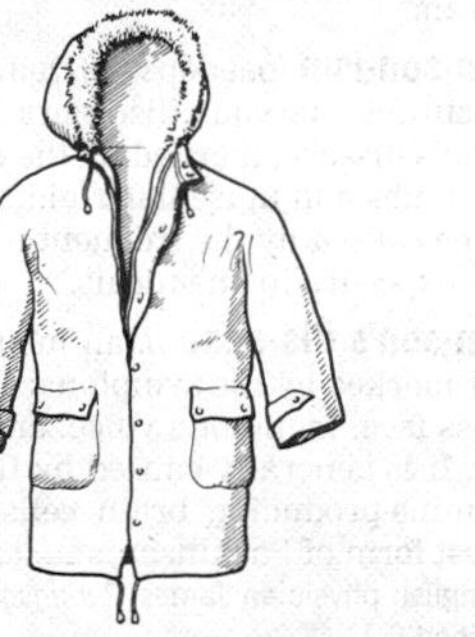

Parka

par·ka /paárkə/ *n.* **1. LONG, HOODED JACKET** a warm, knee- or thigh-length jacket with a hood that is often lined with fur or imitation fur **2. COAT OF ANIMAL SKIN** a thick, fur-lined, hooded outer garment for Arctic conditions, pulled on over the head. Traditionally, parkas are made of animal hide and worn by the Inuit and Aleut people. [Late 18thC. From Russian, "pelt, skin jacket," of Nenets origin.]

par·kade /paár kàyd/ *n.* a parking lot with several stories [Mid-20thC. Formed from PARK, probably on the model of ARCADE.]

Par·ker /paárkər/, **Bonnie** (1910–34) U.S. outlaw. With Clyde Barrow (1909–34) she robbed banks and killed 12 people. Both were killed in a police ambush.

Par·ker, Charlie (1920–55) U.S. musician and composer. He was an alto saxophonist and pioneer of the bebop movement in jazz. Known as **Yardbird** or **Bird**. Full name **Charles Parker, Jr.**

Dorothy Parker

Par·ker, Dorothy (1893–1967) U.S. writer and critic. She is known for her sardonic stories, poetry, and reviews for the *New Yorker* magazine. Full name **Dorothy Rothschild Parker**

Par·ker, Theodore (1810–60) U.S. clergyman and reformer. He supported prison reform and the abolitionist movement.

Par·kers·burg /páarkərz bùrg/ city and port in western West Virginia, at the confluence of the Little Kanawha and Ohio rivers. Population: 32,766 (1996).

Park For·est /paark-/ village in northeastern Illinois, near the Illinois-Indiana border. It is a southern suburb of Chicago. Population: 24,513 (1996).

park·ing /páarking/ *n.* **1. STOPPING AND LEAVING VEHICLE** the action of driving a road vehicle into a position beside or off the road and leaving it there **2. SPACE TO LEAVE VEHICLES** spaces in which vehicles may be parked **3. KISSING IN PARKED CAR** kissing and cuddling in a parked car in a quiet and secluded location (*slang*) **4.** *Midwest* **STRIP OF GRASS** the strip of grass, often planted with trees, between a sidewalk and a street

park·ing light *n.* either of the two small lights on a motor vehicle used in conditions of poor light but not poor enough to warrant the use of headlights

park·ing lot *n.* **1. PLACE WHERE MOTOR VEHICLES ARE PARKED** an open area of ground in which people can park their automobiles **2. TRAFFIC JAM** a traffic jam (*slang*)

park·ing me·ter *n.* a coin-operated roadside meter that displays the length of time for which a vehicle may remain legally parked in a parking space

park·ing or·bit *n.* a temporary orbit of a spacecraft while preparations are made for the next step in its program

Par·kin·son·ism /páarkinsə nìzzəm/ *n.* any of a group of incurable nervous disorders that includes Parkinson's disease, marked by the symptoms of trembling limbs and muscular rigidity. These disorders may be caused by the frequent use of certain drugs or by exposure to chemicals.

Par·kin·son's dis·ease *n.* an incurable nervous disorder marked by the symptoms of trembling hands, lifeless face, monotone voice, and a slow, shuffling walk. It is generally caused by the degeneration of dopamine-producing brain cells, and is the commonest form of Parkinsonism. [Late 19thC. Named for the English physician James *Parkinson* (1755–1824), who described it.]

Par·kin·son's law *n.* the observation that work always expands to fill the time set aside for it [Mid-20thC. Named for the English historian C. Northcote *Parkinson* (1909–93), who formulated it.]

Par·kin·son's syn·drome *n.* = **Parkinsonism**

park·land /páark lànd/ *n.* the land contained within a park, especially when the grassland contains shrubs and trees

Park Ridge /paark-/ city in northeastern Illinois, west of Niles. It is a northwestern suburb of Chicago. Population: 37,039 (1996).

Parks /paarks/, **Gordon** (*b.* 1912) U.S. writer, photographer, and movie director. His movies include *The Learning Tree* (1969), which was based on his own novel, and *Shaft* (1971).

Rosa Parks

Parks, Rosa (*b.* 1913) U.S. civil rights leader. Her arrest in Alabama for not relinquishing her bus seat to a white passenger (1955) led to Martin Luther King's boycott campaign of the bus company and gave impetus to the campaign for civil rights. Full name **Rosa Louise Parks**

park·way /páark wày/ *n. U.S., Aus* a wide stretch of public highway with grassy areas on both sides, often divided by a grassy median. Parkways are often designed to link separate areas on the outskirts of a city, with the design including trees, shrubs, and other landscaped features.

Parl. *abbr.* **1.** Parliament **2. Parl., parl.** parliamentary

par·lance /páarlənss/ *n.* **1. PARTICULAR WAY OF TALKING** the style of speech or writing used by people in a particular context or profession **2. SPEECH** speech, especially in a conversation [Late 16thC. Via Old French from *parler* "to speak."]

par·lan·do /paar laándō/ *adv.* sung in a style that suggests speech, usually without pitch or with less clear pitch (*used as a musical direction*) [Late 19thC. From Italian, literally "speaking."] —**par·lan·do** *adj.*

par·lay /páar lày, -lee/ *vt.* (**-layed, -lay·ing, -lays**) **1. BET WINNINGS ON** to stake an original bet and its winnings on a subsequent bet **2. USE ADVANTAGE** to make good use of an asset or advantage to obtain success ■ *n.* **INSTANCE OF BETTING WINNINGS** a bet in which winnings from a previous bet are gambled [Late 19thC. Alteration of obsolete *paroli*, via French and Italian from, ultimately, Italian *parare* "to place a bet," from Latin (see PREPARE).]

par·ley /páarlee/ *vi.* (**-leyed, -ley·ing, -leys**) **CONFER** to talk or negotiate, especially with an enemy ■ *n.* (*plural* **-leys**) **DISCUSSION** a talk or negotiation, especially between opposing military forces (*dated*) [Late 16thC. From Old French *parlee*, via *parler* "to speak" from late Latin *parabolare*, from *parabola* "talk."]

par·lia·ment /páarləmənt/ *n.* **1. LEGISLATIVE BODY** a nation's legislative body, made up of elected and sometimes nonelected representatives **2. ASSEMBLY OF PARLIAMENT** an assembly of a parliament, created following an election and dissolved before the next election [13thC. From Old French *parlement*, from *parler* "to speak." The underlying meaning is "discussion, consultation."]

Par·lia·ment *n.* the supreme legislative body in various countries. In the United Kingdom, Parliament consists of the House of Commons and the House of Lords.

par·lia·men·tar·i·an /paàrlə men táiree ən, -mən-/ *n.* **1. SOMEBODY IN PARLIAMENT** a member of a parliament **2. EXPERT IN HOW PARLIAMENTS WORK** an expert in parliamentary procedures and parliamentary history [Early 17thC]

Par·lia·men·tar·i·an *n.* during the English Civil War, a supporter or member of Oliver Cromwell's parliamentary army against King Charles I

par·lia·men·tar·i·an·ism /paàrlə men táiree ə nìzzəm, -mən-/ *n.* government of a country by a parliament, or support for this kind of government

par·lia·men·ta·ry /paàrlə méntəree, paàrlə méntree/ *adj.* **1. OF PARLIAMENTS** relating to parliaments, or in the form of a parliament ○ *parliamentary government* **2. FITTING FOR PARLIAMENT** used to describe language and behavior considered to conform to the standards that apply to a parliament

par·lor /páarlər/ *n.* **1. LIVING ROOM FOR ENTERTAINING GUESTS** a living room that is set aside for entertaining guests **2. WORK PREMISES** a room or set of rooms equipped and used for a specific line of business (*often used in combination*) ○ *a beauty parlor* [13thC. From Old French, formed from *parler* "to talk." The underlying meaning is "room for polite conversation."]

par·lor car *n.* a railroad passenger car containing individual reserved seats

par·lor grand *n.* a grand piano, intermediate in size between a baby grand and a concert grand

par·lour *n.* U.K. = **parlor**

par·lous /páarləss/ *adj.* **1. DANGEROUS** very unsafe, uncertain, or difficult (*archaic or humorous*) ○ *"Thou art in a parlous state, shepherd."* (William Shakespeare, *As You Like It*; 1599) **2. CRAFTY** mischievous, devious, or cunning (*archaic*) ■ *adv.* **VERY** used to emphasize the extreme or excessive nature of something (*archaic*) [14thC. Shortening and alteration of PERILOUS.] —**par·lous·ly** *adv.* —**par·lous·ness** *n.*

Par·ma /páarmə/ city in northern Italy. It is the capital of Parma Province, in Emilia-Romagna Region. Population: 170,555 (1992).

Par·me·san /páarmə zàn, páarmə zaán/ (*plural* **-sans** *or* **-san**) *n.* a pale yellow hard strong Italian cheese made with unpasteurized skim milk, often served grated as a garnish on pasta dishes. Parmesan is aged for at least two years before use. [Mid-16thC. Via French from Italian *parmigiano*, "from the city of Parma," where it is traditionally made.]

par·mi·gia·na /paàrmi zhaánə, paàrmi jaánə/ *adj.* used to describe a dish that has been prepared using Parmesan cheese ○ *veal parmigiana* [Late 19thC. From Italian, feminine of *parmigiano* "Parmesan" (see PARMESAN).]

Par·nas·si·an /paar nássee ən/ *adj.* **POETIC** found in poetry or associated with poetic works (*literary*) ■ *n.* **FRENCH 19THC POET** a poet of a late-19th-century French poetic school that advocated emotional detachment and purity of metrical form [Mid-17thC. Formed from Latin *Parnassius*, from Greek *Parnasos* "Parnassus." "Poet" from *Le Parnasse contemporain* (1866), a poetry anthology.]

Par·nas·sus /paar nássəss/ mountain in central Greece, directly north of Delphi. In ancient times it was sacred to Apollo and thought to be the home of the Muses. Height: 8,061 ft./2,457 m.

Par·nell /paar nél, páarn'l/, **Charles Stewart** (1846–91) Irish politician. In 1880 he became leader of the Home Rule Party. He lost support after being cited in the divorce case of Katherine O'Shea, whom he later married.

pa·ro·chi·al /pə rṓkee əl/ *adj.* **1. NARROW-MINDED** concerned only with narrow local concerns without any regard for more general or wider issues **2. CHR OF A PARISH** relating to or belonging to a parish, or to parishes [14thC. Via Old French from ecclesiastical Latin *parochia* "parish."] —**pa·ro·chi·al·ism** *n.* —**pa·ro·chi·al·ist** *n.* —**pa·ro·chi·al·ly** *adv.*

pa·ro·chi·al school *n.* a private school affiliated with a church that provides children with a general education as well as religious instruction

par·o·dy /pérrədee/ *n.* (*plural* **-dies**) **1. AMUSING IMITATION** a piece of writing or music that deliberately copies another work in a comic or satirical way **2. PARODIES IN GENERAL** parodies as a literary or musical style or type **3. POOR IMITATION** an attempt or imitation that is so poor that it seems ridiculous ■ *vt.* (**par·o·died, -died, -dy·ing, par·o·dies**) **IMITATE COMICALLY** to write or perform a parody of somebody or something [Late 16thC. Via late Latin from Greek *parōidia*, from *para* "secondary, indirect" + *ōidē* "song."] —**pa·rod·ic** /pə róddik/ *adj.* —**pa·rod·i·cal** /pə róddik'l/ *adj.* —**par·o·dist** /pérrədist/ *n.*

pa·rol /pə rṓl, pérrəl/ *adj.* **SPOKEN** used to describe a legal contract or lease that is made, done, or given by word of mouth only, rather than in writing ■ *n.* **ORAL CONTRACT** a legal contract or lease that is made, done, or given orally only [15thC. Via Anglo-Norman from, ultimately, Latin *parabola* "speech, talk" (see PARABLE).]

pa·role /pə rṓl/ *n.* **1. CONDITIONAL RELEASE OF PRISONER** the early release of a prisoner, with conditions such as good behavior and regular reporting to the authorities applying for a stated period of time ○ *on parole* **2. PRISONER'S PROMISE** the promise to fulfill set conditions, given by a prisoner released on parole **3. CONDITIONAL PERIOD** the period after a prisoner's release on parole during which the conditions of release continue to apply **4. PRISONER OF WAR'S PROMISE** a promise given by a prisoner of war, either not to escape, or not to take up arms again as a condition of release **5.** LING **REAL-WORLD LANGUAGE** language considered as the utterances of real people, as distinct from the system of language **(langue)** that governs how those utterances are constructed. ◊ **competence, performance** ■ *vt.* **(-roled, -rol·ing, -roles) GIVE PRISONER PAROLE** to release a prisoner on parole [15thC. Via French from, ultimately, Latin *parabola* "speech, talk" (see PARABLE).] —**pa·rol·a·ble** *adj.*

par·o·no·ma·sia /pèrrə nō máyzhə/ *n.* a play on words, especially a pun [Late 16thC. Via Latin from, ultimately, Greek *paronomazein*, literally "to name differently," from *onomazein* "to name."] —**par·o·no·mas·tic** /pèrrə nō mástik/ *adj.* —**par·o·no·mas·ti·cal·ly** /-mástikəlee/ *adv.*

par·o·nym /pérrənim/ *n.* a word that is derived from the same root as another word, e.g., "wise" is a paronym of "wisdom" [Mid-19thC. From Greek *parōnumon*, from *para-* "beside" + *onuma* "name."] —**par·o·nym·ic** *adj.* —**pa·ron·y·mous** /pə rónnəməss/ *adj.* —**pa·ron·o·mous·ly** /pə rónnəməsslee/ *adv.*

pa·rot·ic /pə róttik/ *adj.* situated close to or beside the ear [Mid-19thC. Formed from the Greek stem *ōt-* "ear" (see OTO-).]

pa·rot·id /pə róttid/ *adj.* **1. NEAR EAR** situated close to or beside the ear **2. RELATING TO PAROTID GLAND** relating to the parotid gland ■ *n.* = **parotid gland** [Late 17thC. Via French from, ultimately, the Greek stem *parōtid-*, literally "beside the ear," from the stem *ōt-* "ear" (see OTO-).]

pa·rot·i·dec·to·my /pə ròtti déktəmee/ (*plural* **-mies**) *n.* the surgical removal of a parotid gland

pa·rot·id gland, pa·rot·id *n.* a salivary gland located below the ear in humans

par·o·ti·tis /pèrrə títiss/, **pa·rot·i·di·tis** *n.* inflammation of a parotid gland or the parotid glands —**par·o·tit·ic** /pèrrə títtik/ *adj.*

par·ous /pérrəss/ *adj.* having given birth on at least one occasion [Late 19thC. From -PAROUS.]

-parous *suffix.* giving birth to, producing ○ *uniparous* [Formed from Latin *-parus*, from *parere* "to give birth" (see PARENT)]

Par·ou·si·a /paar óossee ə, pə róozee ə/ *n.* = **Second Coming** [Late 19thC. From Greek, literally "presence," from the present participle of *pareinai*, from *einai* "to be" (see ONTO-).]

par·ox·ysm /pérrək sìzzəm/ *n.* **1. SUDDEN OUTBURST OF EMOTION** a sudden and uncontrollable expression of emotion **2. OUTBURST OF SYMPTOM** a sudden onset or intensification of a pathological symptom or symptoms, especially when this is recurrent [Late 16thC. Via medieval Latin from, ultimately, Greek *paroxunein* "to irritate," literally "to sharpen beyond," from, ultimately, *oxus* "sharp" (see OXYGEN).] —**par·ox·ys·mal** /pèrrək sízməl/ *adj.* —**par·ox·ys·mal·ly** /-sízməlee/ *adv.* —**par·ox·ys·mic** /-sízmik/ *adj.*

par·ox·y·tone /pə róksi tōn/ *n.* **1. WORD WITH PENULTIMATE STRESS** a word in which the main stress is on the next to last syllable **2. GREEK WORD CATEGORY** in ancient Greek, a word with an acute accent on the next to last syllable ■ *adj.* **WITH STRESSED PENULTIMATE SYLLABLE** with the main stress on the next to last syllable [Mid-18thC. From Greek *paroxutonos*, from *para-* "beside" + *oxutonos* "oxytone."] —**par·ox·y·ton·ic** /pə ròksi tónnik/ *adj.*

par·pen /páarpən/, **par·pend** /-pənd/ *n.* *U.K.* = **perpend** [15thC. Via Old French from medieval Latin *parpannus*, of unknown origin.]

par·quet /paar káy/ *n.* **1. DECORATIVE WOODEN FLOORING** flooring consisting of blocks of wood laid in a decorative pattern **2.** THEATER = **orchestra** *n.* **4** ■ *vt.* **(-queted, -quet·ing, -quets) COVER FLOOR WITH PARQUET** to cover a floor in parquet [Early 19thC. From French, literally "small enclosed space," from *parc* "enclosure" (see PARK).]

par·quet cir·cle *n.* the rear section of the main floor of seating in a theater, below the balcony

par·quet·ry /páarkətree/ *n.* flooring or a decorative inlay for furniture made with blocks of wood

parr /paar/ (*plural* **parr** *or* **parrs**) *n.* **1. YOUNG SALMON** a young salmon up to two years old that has dark transverse bands **(parr marks)** and lives in freshwater **2. YOUNG FISH** the young of some fishes other than the salmon [Early 18thC. Origin unknown.]

par·rel /pérrəl/, **par·ral** *n.* a ring, loop, or band that secures a boom to a mast while allowing it to move up and down [15thC. Shortening and alteration of APPAREL, in the earlier sense of "rigging."]

Parquetry: Parquetry floor in an anonymous painting (1860?)

par·ri·cide /pérrə sīd/ *n.* **1. MURDER OF RELATIVE** the murder of a parent or close relative **2. MURDERER OF RELATIVE** somebody who murders a parent or close relative [Mid-16thC. From Latin *parricidium* "kin-slaying" and *parricida* "kin-slayer," which were both formed from assumed *parri-* "relative," of unknown origin.] —**par·ri·cid·al** /pèrrə sīd'l/ *adj.* —**par·ri·cid·al·ly** /-sīd'lee/ *adv.*

Par·ring·ton /párringtən/, **Vernon L.** (1871–1929) U.S. literary historian. He won a Pulitzer Prize for *Main Currents in American Thought* (1927–30).

Par·rish /párrish/, **Maxfield** (1870–1966) U.S. artist. He is best known for his illustrations, posters, and murals.

Parrot

par·rot /pérrət/ *n.* **1. BRIGHTLY COLORED TROPICAL BIRD** a tropical or subtropical bird with a stout hooked bill and variously colored, often brilliant plumage. Some species have the ability to mimic speech. Order: Psittaciformes. **2. SOMEBODY WHO COPIES OTHERS** somebody who simply repeats things that somebody else has said, without thought or understanding ■ *vt.* **(-rot·ed, -rot·ing, -rots) COPY OTHER PEOPLE** to repeat what somebody else says or writes without having thought about it or understood it [Early 16thC. Origin uncertain: probably from French dialect *Perrot* "little Pierre."] —**par·rot·er** *n.*

par·rot fe·ver *n.* = **psittacosis** [From the fact that humans can contract it from pet birds such as parrots]

par·rot·fish /pérrət fish/ (*plural* **-fish** *or* **-fish·es**) *n.* a brightly colored tropical marine fish with jaws shaped like a parrot's beak that it uses for scraping coral. Family: Scaridae. [Early 18thC. From its beak-shaped jaw and brilliant red, green, and blue coloring.]

par·ry /pérree/ *v.* **(-ried, -ry·ing, -ries) 1.** *vti.* **TURN BLOW ASIDE** to block or deflect the damaging effect of a blow or weapon **2.** *vt.* **AVOID ANSWERING** to evade a question by cleverly saying something that does not answer it ■ *n.* (*plural* **-ries**) **ACT OF EVADING** an act of evading a blow, criticism, or question [Late 17thC. Origin uncertain: probably via French *parez* "defend (yourself)!" from, ultimately, Latin *parare* "to prepare" (see PARE).]

Par·ry, Cape /párree/ headland in Canada, in the Northwest Territories, jutting into Amundsen Gulf between Franklin and Darnley bays

parse /paars/ **(parsed, pars·ing, pars·es)** *vti.* **1. DESCRIBE GRAMMATICAL ROLE OF WORD** to describe the grammatical role of a word in a sentence, or to be subject to this process **2. ANALYZE GRAMMATICAL STRUCTURE OF SENTENCE** to analyze and describe the grammatical structure of a sentence, or to be subject to this process of analysis and description [Mid-16thC. Origin uncertain; probably from earlier *pars* "part of speech," from Latin, part (see PART).] —**pars·a·ble** *adj.*

par·sec /páar sèk/ *n.* an astronomical unit of distance equal to 3.262 light years. A parsec is the distance from which the Earth's distance from the Sun would subtend one second of arc. [Early 20thC. Coined from PARALLAX + SECOND.]

Par·see /paar sée, páar sèe/, **Par·si** *n.* a member of a Zoroastrian group living mainly in western India, descended from Persian refugees of the 7th and 8th centuries [Early 17thC. From Persian *Pārsī*, from *Pārs* "Persia."] —**Par·see** *adj.* —**Par·see·ism** /páar see ìzzəm/ *n.*

pars·er /páarsər/ *n.* **1.** COMPUT **SOFTWARE FOR ANALYZING LANGUAGE** a computer program that breaks natural language or programming language statements or instructions into smaller more easily interpreted units understandable to the computer. The parser determines how a sentence can be constructed from the grammar of the language, producing a **(parse tree)** about the statement as the output. **2. ANALYZER** somebody or something that analyzes something into its component parts [Mid-19thC. Originally in the general sense "one who parses."]

Par·si *n., adj.* = **Parsee**

par·si·mo·ni·ous /pàarsə mṓnee əss/ *adj.* **1. FRUGAL** very frugal or ungenerous **2.** PHILOS **ECONOMICAL** requiring a minimum of detail as an explanation (*formal*) —**par·si·mo·ni·ous·ly** *adv.* —**par·si·mo·ni·ous·ness** *n.*

par·si·mo·ny /páarsə mṓnee/ *n.* **1. FRUGALITY** great frugality or unwillingness to spend money **2.** PHILOS **PRINCIPLE OF ECONOMY** economy in the use of means to achieve something, especially the principle of endorsing the simplest explanation that covers a case [15thC. From Latin *parsimonia*, from *pars-*, past participle stem of *parcere* "to spare."]

Parsley

pars·ley /páarslee/ *n.* a widely cultivated plant of the carrot family with small compound leaves that are used in cooking and as a garnish. Latin name: *Petroselinum crispum.* [Pre-12thC. From late Latin *petrosilium*, ultimately from Greek *petroselinon*, from *petra* "rock" + *selinon* "parsley."]

pars·ley fern *n.* a bright green European fern with leaves that look like parsley leaves. Latin name: *Cryptogramma crispa.*

pars·ley piert *n.* a small plant of the rose family with three-lobed leaves and tiny green flowers. Latin name: *Aphanes arvensis.* [Late 16thC. Alteration of French *perce-pierre*, literally "stone-piercer."]

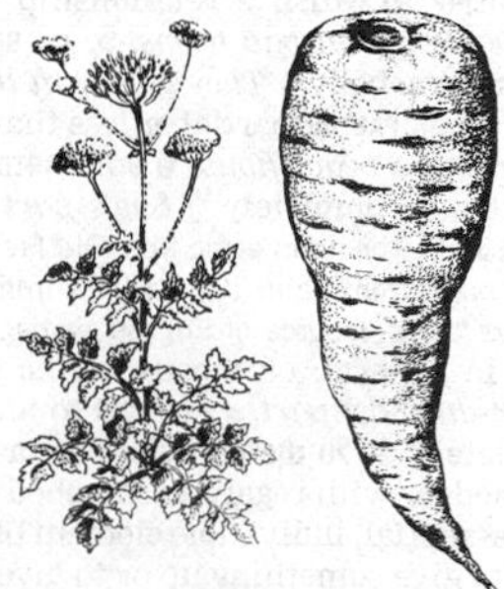

Parsnip

pars·nip /páarsnip/ *n.* **1. PLANT OF CARROT FAMILY** an aromatic plant of the carrot family cultivated for its edible root. Latin name: *Pastinaca sativa.* **2. ROOT**

VEGETABLE the long cone-shaped cream-colored root of the parsnip plant, cooked and eaten as a vegetable [14thC. Alteration (influenced by English *neep* "turnip") of Old French *pasnaie*, from Latin *pastinaca*, from *pastinum* "two-pronged gardening fork," probably because of its shape.]

par·son /paárs'n/ *n.* **1.** EPISCOPAL MINISTER an Episcopal parish minister **2.** CLERIC a member of the clergy, especially of the Protestant Church [13thC. From Old French *persone* "person" (see PERSON). The underlying meaning may be "important personage," or perhaps the "person" legally responsible for parish property.] —**par·son·ic** /paar sónnik/ *adj.* —**par·son·i·cal** /-sónnik'l/ *adj.*

par·son·age /paárs'nij/ *n.* the house, usually provided by the parish, where a parson lives

par·son bird *n. NZ* = **tui** [From resemblance of its markings to the dark suit and white preaching bands of a parson in church]

Par·sons /paárss'nz/, **Talcott** (1902–79) U.S. sociologist. He is known for functionalist theories about the mechanisms of society and the organizational principles behind societal structures.

par·son's nose *n.* = **pope's nose** [Variant of *Pope's nose*, an insulting term that originated during a period of anti-Catholicism during the reign of James II (1685–88)]

Par·sons ta·ble *n.* a square or rectangular table, the legs of which are flush with the tabletop at the four corners [Named for the *Parsons* School of Design in New York City]

part /paart/ *n.* **1.** PORTION OR DIVISION a portion or section of something ○ *the early part of the century* **2.** EQUAL PORTION any of several equal portions that make up something such as a mixture ○ *pastry that is one part fat to three parts flour* **3.** COMPONENT a separable piece or component of something such as a machine, system, or device ○ *a motor with only three moving parts* **4.** IMPORTANT ELEMENT OF SOMETHING an integral and essential feature or component of something ○ *She wants to be part of the community.* **5.** THEATER ACTOR'S ROLE a role in a dramatic performance ○ *played the part of Hamlet in the school play* **6.** INVOLVEMENT IN AN EVENT somebody's participation in or influence on something ○ *What part did he have to play in all this?* **7.** SIDE somebody's side or viewpoint ○ *You're always taking her part.* **8.** ORGANIC CONSTITUENT an organ, system, or other discrete element of an organism ○ *the part of the plant that carries out photosynthesis* **9.** MUSIC SEPARATE MUSICAL ROLE the score for a single voice or instrument in a symphonic, orchestral, or choral work **10.** LOGICAL DIVISION a logical division of something such as a report, book, or presentation ○ *Part three of the paper deals with environmental issues.* **11.** HAIR DIVIDING LINE IN HAIR the line in a hairstyle from which the hair is combed or brushed in different directions ■ **parts** *npl.* **1.** AREA a geographical region or local area (*informal*) ○ *That's unheard of in these parts.* **2.** ABILITIES intellectual abilities or talents (*literary*) ○ *a student of parts* ■ *v.* (**part·ed, part·ing, parts**) **1.** *vti.* SEPARATE to move or to move something in different directions so that there is a space between them ○ *They had to part the children to keep them from fighting.* ○ *The curtains parted.* **2.** *vti.* DIVIDE INTO PARTS to divide something into parts, or to undergo division into parts **3.** *vti.* HAIR DIVIDE HAIR to make a line in the hair by combing in opposite directions from it, or to separate naturally in this way **4.** *vi.* END RELATIONSHIP to finish a relationship with somebody ○ *We parted on bad terms.* **5.** *vi.* GO AWAY to go away from somebody ○ *They parted at the corner of the street.* ■ *adj.* PARTIAL partial or less than the whole ○ *part owner of a beach house* ■ *adv.* PARTIALLY to some extent but not completely ○ *She's part Irish, part French.* [13thC. The noun came from Old French; the verb via French *partir* from Latin *partire*; both from Latin *part-*, stem of *pars* "part" (source of English *parcel*).] ◇ **for the most part** in general, or mostly ○ *She does OK at school, for the most part.* ◇ **in part** to an extent but not completely ◇ **on the part of** as far as somebody is concerned, or with regard to somebody ◇ **part and parcel** an essential, indivisible element of something

part with *vt.* to give something up or to give something away, especially unwillingly

part. *abbr.* **1.** particle **2.** participle **3.** particular

par·take /paar táyk/ (**-took** /-tŏŏk/, **-tak·en** /paar táykən/, **-tak·ing, -takes**) *vi.* **1.** EAT OR DRINK SOMETHING to have something to eat or drink **2.** HAVE OR SEEM TO HAVE to have or appear to have a certain amount of some quality or characteristic (*formal*) **3.** PARTICIPATE to share in or take part in something ○ *How many students partake in sports activities?* [Mid-16thC. Back-formation from *partaker* "participator," from *part-taker*, a translation of Latin *particeps* (see PARTICIPATE).] —**par·tak·er** *n.*

part·ed /paártəd/ *adj.* **1.** IN PARTS divided into parts **2.** SEPARATED separated or kept separate **3.** DIVIDED BY A PART having a part ○ *a hairstyle parted on the left* **4.** BOT DIVIDED TO BASE used to describe a leaf or plant part that is separated or cleft nearly to the base

par·terre /paar táir/ *n.* **1.** GARDENING ORNAMENTAL GARDEN an ornamental garden laid out in a formal pattern that is usually marked out with low evergreen hedges and filled in with annual bedding plants **2.** THEATER = **parquet circle** [Early 17thC. From French, "ornamental garden," from *par terre* "on the ground."]

part ex·change *n. U.K.* the practice of paying part of the price of something by giving the seller something that the buyer owns

part-ex·change *vt. U.K.* to accept or give goods as part payment for something being bought

par·the·no·car·py /paárthə nō kaàrpee/ *n.* the production of fruits without fertilization or seeds [Early 20thC. From German *Parthenocarpie*, from Greek *parthenos* "virgin" + *karpos* "fruit."] —**par·the·no·car·pic** /paárthə nō kaàrpik/ *adj.* —**par·the·no·car·pous** /-pəss/ *adj.*

par·the·no·gen·e·sis /paárthə nō jénnəssiss/ *n.* a form of reproduction, especially in plants, insects, and arthropods, in which a female gamete develops into a new individual without fertilization by a male gamete [Mid-19thC. Coined from Greek *parthenos* "virgin" + GENESIS.] —**par·the·no·ge·net·ic** /paárthə nō jə néttik/ *adj.* —**par·the·no·ge·net·i·cal·ly** /-néttikəlee/ *adv.*

AKG London

Parthenon, Athens, Greece

Par·the·non /paáthə nòn/ *n.* a large temple to the goddess Athena on the Acropolis in Athens, Greece. Built in the 5th century B.C., it is considered the greatest example of Doric architecture.

Par·thi·an /paárthee ən/ *n.* somebody from Parthia, an ancient country in Asia that ruled an empire until the 3rd century —**Par·thi·an** *adj.*

Par·thi·an shot *n.* a final hostile remark or gesture made while leaving [From the Parthians' legendary tactic of firing arrows over their shoulders while retreating]

par·tial /paársh'l/ *adj.* **1.** INCOMPLETE not complete or total **2.** AFFECTING PARTS affecting a part or parts but not the whole **3.** LIKING SOMETHING having a particular liking for something ○ *partial to chocolate cake* **4.** BIASED showing an unfair preference for one person or thing over another ■ *n.* **1.** MATH = **partial derivative** **2.** MUSIC = **overtone** *n.* 2 **3.** BRIDGE = **part-score** [15thC. Via Old French *parcial* from late Latin *partialis*, from the stem *part-* (see PART).] —**par·tial·ness** *n.*

par·tial den·ture *n.* an artificial tooth or row of teeth that is usually removable

par·tial de·riv·a·tive, **par·tial** *n.* the derivative of a function of two or more variables calculated with respect to one of the variables and on the assumption that the others are fixed

par·tial dif·fer·en·tial e·qua·tion *n.* a differential equation that involves partial derivatives of more than one variable

par·tial e·clipse *n.* an eclipse in which only part of something such as the Sun or Moon is covered or darkened

par·tial frac·tion *n.* any one of a set of simpler fractions, the sum of which composes a more complex fraction

par·ti·al·i·ty /paàrshee álləteel/ (*plural* **-ties**) *n.* **1.** FONDNESS a liking for something **2.** BIASED ATTITUDE OR BEHAVIOR an unfair preference for one person or thing over another

par·tial·ly /paársh'lee/ *adv.* **1.** NOT COMPLETELY to a degree but not completely **2.** IN A BIASED WAY in a way that shows an unfair preference for one person or thing over another

par·tial·ly sight·ed *adj.* having a visual impairment that cannot be completely corrected by the use of glasses or contact lenses

par·tial pres·sure *n.* the pressure that one gas in a mixture of gases would exert if it were the only gas present

par·tial prod·uct *n.* the result when a quantity is multiplied by one digit of a number with two or more digits

par·ti·ble /paártəb'l/ *adj.* able to be divided [Mid-16thC. Via late Latin *partibilis* from Latin *partire* "to part" (see PART).]

par·tic·i·pant /paar tíssəpənt/ *n.* SOMEBODY TAKING PART somebody who takes part in something ■ *adj.* PARTICIPATING taking part in something [Mid-16thC. From French, present participle of *participier*, from Latin *participare* (see PARTICIPATE).]

par·tic·i·pate /paar tíssə pàyt/ (**-pat·ed, -pat·ing, -pates**) *v.* **1.** *vi.* TAKE PART to take part in an event or activity **2.** HAVE A QUALITY to have a particular quality (*archaic*) [15thC. From, ultimately, Latin *participare*, from *particeps* "sharing," literally "taking part," from the stem *part-* "part" (see PART).] —**par·tic·i·pa·tive** /paar tíssə pàytiv/ *adj.* —**par·tic·i·pa·to·ry** /-tíssəpə tàwree/ *adj.* —**par·tic·i·pa·tor** /-pàytər/ *n.*

par·tic·i·pa·tion /paar tissə páysh'n/ *n.* the act of taking part in an activity ○ *We would welcome your participation in any of the events.*

par·ti·cip·i·al /paàrti síppee əl/ *adj.* with the form or function of a verb that can be used as both adjective or verb [Late 16thC. From Latin *participialis*, from *participium* (see PARTICIPLE).] —**par·ti·cip·i·al·ly** *adv.*

par·ti·ci·ple /paàrti sipp'l/ *n.* a form of a verb that is used to form complex tenses, such as "was coming" and "has come" in English, and may also be used as an adjective [14thC. Via Old French from Latin *participium*, from *particeps* "sharing" (see PARTICIPATE), because it shares qualities of both adjectives and verbs.]

par·ti·cle /paártik'l/ *n.* **1.** TINY PIECE a very small piece of something ○ *airborne particles* **2.** TINY AMOUNT a very small amount of something ○ *There wasn't a particle of truth in anything he said.* **3.** PHYS BODY WITH FINITE MASS a minute body that is considered to have finite mass but negligible size **4.** PHYS BASIC UNIT OF MATTER any one of the basic units of matter, e.g., a molecule, atom, or electron **5.** PHYS SUBATOMIC UNIT a unit of matter smaller than the atom or its main components **6.** GRAM PART OF MULTI-WORD VERB an adverb or preposition that occurs as part of a multi-word verb, such as "up" in "blow up" **7.** CHR PIECE OF CONSECRATED BREAD OR WAFER in the Roman Catholic Mass, a small piece of consecrated bread or wafer [14thC. From Latin *particula* "small part," from the stem *part-* (see PART).]

par·ti·cle ac·cel·er·a·tor *n.* NUCLEAR PHYS = **accelerator** *n.* 2

par·ti·cle beam *n.* a very narrow concentrated stream of charged particles such as electrons or protons that is produced by a particle accelerator or a particle-beam weapon. Lenses are used to focus the beam and magnets change its direction.

par·ti·cle·board *n. U.S., NZ* a grainless wood board made from sawdust or wood particles and bonded with a resin binder. The particles of wood used in particle board tend to be smaller than those used in chipboard.

par·ti·cle phys·ics *n.* the branch of physics that deals with the study of subatomic particles, particularly the many unstable particles produced in particle accelerators and high-energy collisions (*takes a singular verb*)

par·ti-col·ored *adj.* with different parts in different colors ["Parti" from PARTY, in the sense "multi-colored"]

par·tic·u·lar /pər tíkyələr/ *adj.* **1.** ONE OUT OF SEVERAL relating to one person or thing out of several ○ *Which particular dress do you prefer?* **2.** PERSONAL belonging to one person and different from other people's **3.** EXCEPTIONAL great or more than usual **4.** SPECIAL special and worth mentioning **5.** FUSSY having or demanding high standards ○ *She's very particular about standards of hygiene.* **6.** CHOOSY taking great care when making a choice **7.** DETAILED going into great detail about something (*formal*) **8.** LOGIC NOT DEALING WITH ALL relating to or being a proposition that deals with some but not all members of a class ■ *n.* **1.** ITEM an individual fact, item, or detail (*often used in the plural*) **2.** SINGLE INSTANCE an individual case or instance, as opposed to a more general theory **3.** PHILOS REAL THING an entity with definite spatial and temporal properties [14thC. Via Old French from Latin *particularis* "concerned with small parts or details," from *particula* "small part" (see PARTICLE).] ◇ **in particular** specifically or especially

par·tic·u·lar·ism /pər tíkyələ rìzzəm/ *n.* **1.** COMMITMENT TO ONE GROUP undivided commitment to one particular group with exclusive concern for its interests, especially if this is detrimental to the interests or well-being of a larger group **2.** POL SELF-RULE PRINCIPLE a policy of allowing political divisions within a state or federation to be self-governing, without regard to what effect this may have on the larger body **3.** CHR BELIEF THAT GOD BESTOWS GRACE INDIVIDUALLY the belief that God chooses to bestow grace and salvation on particular individuals —**par·tic·u·lar·ist** *n.* —**par·tic·u·lar·is·tic** /pər tìkyələ rístik/ *adj.*

par·tic·u·lar·i·ty /pər tìkyə lérrətee/ (*plural* **-ties**) *n.* (*formal*) **1.** EXACTITUDE attention to detail and concern for accuracy **2.** FASTIDIOUSNESS the practice of taking great care when making a choice **3.** USE OF DETAIL the use of great detail in describing something **4.** = **particular 5.** SOMETHING CHARACTERISTIC a peculiarity or characteristic **6.** INDIVIDUALITY the condition of being peculiar to an individual rather than a group

par·tic·u·lar·ize /pər tíkyələ rìz/ (**-ized, -iz·ing, -iz·es**) *v.* **1.** *vt.* FOCUS ON INDIVIDUAL to make something become particular, e.g., by focusing on a particular person or thing **2.** *vt.* PROVIDE WITH SPECIFIC EXAMPLES to provide something with specific examples **3.** *vti.* GO INTO DETAIL to go into detail about something —**par·tic·u·lar·i·za·tion** /pər tìkyələri záysh'n/ *n.* —**par·tic·u·lar·iz·er** *n.*

par·tic·u·lar·ly /pər tíkyələrlee/ *adv.* **1.** VERY MUCH to a great degree **2.** MORE THAN USUAL more than usual or more than in other cases **3.** SPECIFICALLY as a specific example **4.** IN DETAIL with great attention to detail

par·tic·u·late /pər tíkyələt, -làyt/ *adj.* OF PARTICLES relating to or consisting of separate particles ■ *n.* SUBSTANCE CONSISTING OF PARTICLES a substance that consists of separate particles, especially airborne pollution [Late 19thC. Formed from Latin *particula* (see PARTICLE).]

par·tic·u·late in·her·i·tance *n.* a theory advanced by Gregor Mendel that parental genes do not blend in offspring but rather retain their characteristics from generation to generation

part·ing /paárting/ *n.* **1.** LEAVING the act of leaving somebody or something, especially if the separation is sad or upsetting **2.** SEPARATION the process or action of separating or dividing **3.** *U.K.* HAIR = **part 4.** CRYSTALS, MINERALS BREAKING OF CRYSTAL ALONG PLANE the tendency of some crystals to break along a plane of weakness through deformation ■ *adj.* **1.** DONE WHILE LEAVING done, made, or given when leaving ○ *a parting remark* **2.** DEPARTING leaving or coming to an end (*literary*) ○ *"The curfew tolls the knell of parting day..."* (Thomas Gray, *Elegy Written in a Country Churchyard*; 1751) **3.** DIVIDING used to divide or separate something

part·ing strip *n.* a thin strip of a material such as wood or metal used to keep two adjacent parts separate

par·ti pris /paártee preé/ (*plural* **par·tis pris**) *n.* a preconceived opinion or bias [From French, literally "side taken"]

Par·ti Qué·béc·ois /paárti kay be kwaá/ *n.* a Quebec provincial political party founded in 1968 that advocates sovereignty for Quebec

par·ti·san[1] /paártiz'n, -zàn/, **par·ti·zan** *n.* **1.** BIASED SUPPORTER a strong supporter of a person, group, or cause, especially one who does not listen to other people's opinions **2.** RESISTANCE FIGHTER a member of a group that has taken up armed resistance against occupying enemy forces ■ *adj.* SHOWING UNREASONING SUPPORT showing strong and usually biased support for a cause, especially a political one [Mid-16thC. Via French and Italian dialect *partisano* from Italian *parte* "part, side," from the Latin stem *part-* (see PART).] —**par·ti·san·ship** *n.*

par·ti·san[2] /paártiz'n, paárti zàn/, **par·ti·zan** *n.* ARMS, HIST a weapon with a long shaft and a blade, used in the 16th and 17th centuries [Mid-16thC. Via obsolete French from obsolete Italian *partesana*, variant of *partigiana (arma)*, literally "partisan (weapon)," feminine of *partigiano* (see PARTISAN[1]).]

par·ti·ta /paar teétə/ (*plural* **-te** *or* **-tas**) *n.* a suite or set of musical variations especially in Baroque music [Late 19thC. Via Italian, literally "composition divided into parts," from, ultimately, Latin *partire* "to divide" (see PART).]

par·tite /paár tìt/ *adj.* **1.** BOT DEEPLY SPLIT used to describe a plant part such as a leaf that is split almost to its base **2.** IN PARTS divided into or consisting of two or more parts (*usually used in combination*) [Late 16thC. From Latin *partitus*, the past participle of *partire* "to divide" (see PART).]

par·ti·tion /paar tísh'n/ *n.* **1.** SOMETHING THAT DIVIDES SPACE something that divides a space, e.g., a wall built to make two rooms out of one **2.** DIVIDED PART a section or part of something divided **3.** DIVISION OF COUNTRY the division of a country into two or more separate states or countries ○ *the partition of India* **4.** DIVIDING UP the division of something into parts, or the state of being divided into parts (*formal*) **5.** DIVISION OF PROPERTY the division of property among interested parties to settle a dispute ■ *v.* (**-tioned, -tion·ing, -tions**) **1.** *vt.* DIVIDE WITH A PARTITION to divide or separate something by means of a partition **2.** *vti.* SPLIT A COUNTRY to divide a country into two or more separate states **3.** *vt.* DIVIDE to divide something into separate parts [15thC. Via Old French from, ultimately, Latin *partire* "to divide" (see PART).] —**par·ti·tion·er** *n.* —**par·ti·tion·ist** *n.* —**par·ti·tion·ment** *n.*

par·ti·tive /paártətiv/ *adj.* **1.** SEPARATING separating or dividing something (*formal*) **2.** GRAM EXPRESSING PART OF SOMETHING used to describe a grammatical construction expressing a part of something, such as "of" in "a lump of coal" or the possessive form in "the dog's tail" ■ *n.* GRAM PARTITIVE CONSTRUCTION a partitive construction [14thC. Via Old French from, ultimately, Latin *partit-*, the past participle stem of *partire* "to divide" (see PART).] —**par·ti·tive·ly** *adv.*

part·ly /paártlee/ *adv.* to some extent, but not completely ○ *The road was partly blocked by a heavy snowfall.*

part·ner /paártnər/ *n.* **1.** SOMEBODY WHO SHARES ACTIVITY somebody who takes part in an activity or undertaking with somebody else **2.** MEMBER OF RELATIONSHIP either member of an established couple in a relationship **3.** FELLOW PARTICIPANT IN SEXUAL ACTIVITY either of two people who have or have had sex together **4.** ASSOCIATE IN DANCE OR GAME somebody who dances with another person or who plays on the same side as another person in a game **5.** COMM BUSINESS ASSOCIATE somebody who owns part of a company, usually a company he or she works in, and who shares both the financial risks and the profits of the business **6.** SOMETHING RELATED something that is related in some way to something else **7.** NAUT SUPPORTING TIMBER ON SHIP one of the timbers on a ship underneath the deck that is used to support the mast (*often used in the plural*) ■ *vt.* (**-nered, -ner·ing, -ners**) BE SOMEBODY'S PARTNER to be somebody's partner, e.g., in a game or dance [14thC. Alteration (influenced by PART) of *parcener*, via Anglo-Norman, literally "one who shares," from, ultimately, the Latin stem *partition-* "sharing" (see PARTITION).]

part·ner·ship /paártnər shìp/ *n.* **1.** RELATIONSHIP BETWEEN PARTNERS the relationship between two or more people or organizations that are involved in or share the same activity **2.** COOPERATION cooperation between people or groups working together **3.** GROUP OF PEOPLE WORKING TOGETHER an organization formed by two or more people or groups to work together for some purpose **4.** COMM, LAW COMPANY OWNED BY PARTNERS a company set up by two or more people who put money into the business and who share the financial risks and profits **5.** PARTNERS IN BUSINESS the people who make up a partnership, collectively

part of speech *n.* a grammatical category or word group in a language to which words may be assigned on the basis of how they are used in sentences. The traditional main parts of speech in English are noun, verb, adjective, adverb, pronoun, preposition, conjunction, and interjection. Others sometimes used are article and determiner. [Translation of Latin *pars orationis*]

par·ton /paár tòn/ *n.* a postulated elementary particle, proposed as a constituent of neutrons and protons [Mid-20thC. Formed from PARTICLE.]

Par·ton /paárt'n/, **Dolly** (*b.* 1946) U.S. singer, songwriter, and actor. She is known for her country-and-western songs, and for her appearances in several Hollywood movies.

par·took past tense of **partake**

Partridge

par·tridge /paártrij/ *n.* **1.** MEDIUM-SIZED GAME BIRD a medium-sized ground-nesting bird with variegated plumage, native to Europe and Asia and related to the pheasants and grouse. Genera: *Alectoris* and *Perdix*. **2.** BIRD LIKE A PARTRIDGE any of various North American game birds similar to the partridge, e.g., the ruffed grouse or bobwhite **3.** PARTRIDGE FLESH the flesh of the partridge served as food [13thC. Via Old French *perdriz* from, ultimately, Greek *perdix*, of uncertain origin: perhaps literally "farter."]

par·tridge·ber·ry /paártrij bèrree/ (*plural* **-ries**) *n.* **1.** N AMERICAN EVERGREEN PLANT a trailing evergreen plant of eastern North America that has rounded leaves, small white fragrant flowers, and scarlet berries. Latin name: *Mitchella repens*. **2.** BERRY OF PARTRIDGEBERRY PLANT the scarlet, relatively tasteless berry of the partridgeberry plant [Early 18thC. From the fact that partridges use it for food.]

part-score *n.* a score for tricks made in bridge that is not enough to win a game

part song, **part-song** *n.* a vocal musical composition with parts for different voices, usually performed without accompaniment

part-time *adj., adv.* for less than the usual amount of time associated with a particular activity ○ *a part-time job* —**part-tim·er** *n.*

par·tu·ri·ent /paar tóoree ənt/ *adj.* **1.** GIVING BIRTH about to give birth (*technical*) **2.** OF CHILDBIRTH relating to the process or time of childbirth **3.** ABOUT TO PRODUCE on the verge of producing something or coming forth (*literary*) [Late 16thC. From Latin *parturient-*, present participle stem of *parturire* (see PARTURITION).] —**par·tu·ri·en·cy** *n.*

par·tu·ri·fa·cient /paar tóoree fáysh'nt/ *adj.* INDUCING BIRTH inducing birth or making it easier to give birth ■ *n.* BIRTH-INDUCING DRUG a drug that induces birth or makes it easier to give birth [Mid-19thC. Coined from Latin *parturire* "to be in labor" (see PARTURITION) + -FACIENT.]

par·tu·ri·tion /paártə rísh'n, paárchə rísh'n/ *n.* the act of giving birth to offspring (*formal*) [Mid-17thC. Via the late Latin stem *parturition-* from, ultimately, Latin *parturire* "to be in labor," from *parere* "to give birth" (see PARENT).]

part·way /paárt wày/ *adv.* some but not all of the way through a process or distance

par·ty /paártee/ *n.* (*plural* **-ties**) **1.** SOCIAL GATHERING FOR FUN a social gathering to which people are invited in order to enjoy themselves and often to celebrate something ○ *Are you coming to my birthday party?* **2.** GROUP ACTING TOGETHER a group of people who are doing something together ○ *a search party* **3.** POL POLITICAL ORGANIZATION an organization of people who share the same broad political views and aims, usually attempting to elect members to government positions **4.** MIL GROUP OF SOLDIERS a detachment of soldiers given a particular task **5.** LAW ONE SIDE IN AGREEMENT OR DISPUTE a person or a group of people acting together and forming one side in an agreement, contract, dispute, or lawsuit **6.** PERSON an individual ■ *vi.* (**-tied, -ty·ing, -ties**) BE AT PARTY to socialize and have fun at a party or in a situation resembling a party (*informal*) ■ *adj.* HERALDRY OF TWO

COLORS divided into parts of two different colors [13thC. Via French *partie* "part, side," and Old French *parti* "political faction" from, ultimately, Latin *partitus*, the past participle of *partire* "to divide" (see PART).] ◇ **be (a) party to something** to participate or be involved in a particular activity

par·ty an·i·mal *n.* somebody who is a regular and enthusiastic participant at informal social occasions, especially parties (*informal*)

par·ty·go·er /paártee gō ər/ *n.* somebody who goes to a party or who goes to a lot of parties

par·ty line *n.* **1.** POL **POLITICAL POLICY** the official policy of a political party or other organization **2.** TELECOM **MULTIUSER TELEPHONE LINE** a telephone line shared by more than one subscriber —**par·ty·lin·er** *n.*

par·ty pol·i·tics *n.* political activity as carried on by political parties, especially if carried on by them more in their own interests than for the benefit of the people (*takes a singular or plural verb*) —**par·ty-po·lit·i·cal** *adj.*

par·ty poop·er *n.* somebody who spoils other people's fun or fails to join in the general enthusiasm for something (*informal*)

par·ty wall *n.* a wall separating adjoining homes, buildings, or pieces of land

pa·rure /pə rŏor/ *n.* a matching set of jewelry that includes earrings, a brooch, ring, necklace, and bracelet, and sometimes other items such as buckles [Early 19thC. From French, where it was formed from *parer* "to adorn" (see PARE).]

par val·ue *n.* the value printed on a security such as a share certificate or bond at the time of issue. It is used to calculate interest or dividend payments. ◊ **market value**

Par·va·ti /paar vaátee/ *n.* a Hindu mother and fertility goddess, the wife of Shiva. She is thought of as the model Hindu wife and is often depicted with a conch, mirror, and lotus.

par·ve *adj.* = **pareve**

par·ve·nu /paárvə nōo, paárvə nŏo/ (*plural* **-nus**) *n.* somebody who has recently become wealthy or risen to a higher position in society but who is still considered as inferior by established wealthy and powerful people [Early 19thC. Via French, literally "one who has arrived," from, ultimately, Latin *pervenire* "to arrive," from *venire* "to come" (see VENUE).]

par·vis /paárviss/, **par·vise** *n.* an enclosed area or portico at the front of a building, especially a church [14thC. Via Old French from, ultimately, late Latin *paradisus* "garden" (see PARADISE).]

par·vo /paár vō/ *n.* = **parvovirus** *n.* **2** [Shortening]

par·vo·vi·rus /paár vō vīrəss/ *n.* **1.** **SINGLE-STRANDED DNA VIRUS** any one of a group of viruses that have a single strand of DNA, especially those causing disease in mammals **2.** **VIRAL DISEASE OF DOGS** a contagious disease of dogs caused by a parvovirus and marked by fever, loss of appetite, and diarrhea [Mid-20thC. Coined from Latin *parvus* "small" + VIRUS.]

pas /paa/ (*plural* **pas**) *n.* a step in dancing, especially in classical ballet [Early 18thC. Via French from Latin *passus* "step" (see PACE).]

Pas·a·de·na /pàssə deénə/ **1.** city in southwestern California, home to the California Institute of Technology. Population: 134,170 (1994). **2.** city in southeastern Texas, a center of the oil industry. Population: 129,292 (1994).

pas·cal /pa skál, paa skaál/ *n.* a unit of pressure or stress equal to one newton per square meter. Symbol **Pa** [Mid-20thC. Named for Blaise PASCAL.]

Pas·cal /pa skál, paa skaál/ *n.* a high-level general-purpose computer language designed to encourage structured programming [Mid-20thC. Acronym for *programme appliqué à la sélection et la compilation automatique de la littérature*; also named for Blaise PASCAL.]

Pas·cal /pa skál, paa skaál/, **Blaise** (1623–62) French philosopher and mathematician. He is considered one of the great minds in Western intellectual history. Among his achievements are the invention of the first mechanical adding machine and the development of the modern theory of probablility.

Pas·cal's tri·an·gle *n.* a triangular arrangement of numbers with a 1 at the top and at the beginning and end of each row, with each of the other numbers being the sum of the two numbers above it [Named for Blaise PASCAL, who devised it]

Pasch /pask/ *n.* (*archaic*) **1.** **PASSOVER** the religious holiday of Passover **2.** **EASTER** the religious holiday of Easter [Pre-12thC. From Old French *pasches* (plural), from, ultimately, Greek *paskha*, via Aramaic from Hebrew *pesaḥ*.]

pas·chal /pásk'l/ *adj.* **1.** **OF EASTER** relating to Easter **2.** **OF PASSOVER** relating to Passover (*archaic*) [15thC. Via Old French *pascal* from, ultimately, ecclesiastical Latin *pascha*, from Greek *paskha* (see PASCH).]

pas·chal flow·er *n.* = **pasqueflower**

pas de deux /paà də dő/ (*plural* **pas de deux**) *n.* **1.** BALLET **DANCE FOR TWO** a dance or dance sequence for two dancers **2.** **CLOSE RELATIONSHIP** a close relationship between two people or things involved in a joint activity or venture [From French, "step for two"]

pa·se /paá sày/ *n.* a movement a matador makes with a cape to attract the bull's attention and make it charge [Mid-20thC. Via Spanish from, ultimately, assumed Vulgar Latin *passare* "to pass" (see PASS).]

pa·se·o /paa sáy ō/ (*plural* **-os**) *n.* **1.** **BULLFIGHTERS' PROCESSION** the procession of the matadors and other bullfighters into the arena before the bullfight begins **2.** *Southwest U.S.* **LEISURELY WALK** a stroll, especially in the evening **3.** *Southwest U.S.* **STREET** a street or boulevard (*used in place names*) [Mid-19thC. Via Spanish from, ultimately, assumed Vulgar Latin *passare* "to pass" (see PASS).]

pash /pash/ *n.* a brief infatuation for somebody (*dated slang*) [Early 20thC. Shortening of PASSION.]

pa·sha /paáshə, páshə/, **pa·cha** *n.* in the past in Turkey and other Middle Eastern countries, an official of high rank [Mid-17thC. From Turkish *paşa*.]

pashm /páshəm, púshəm/ *n.* the fine wool that grows beneath the outer wool of some goats, especially the soft, downy fiber from the undercoat of the Kashmir goat, used for cashmere shawls and other articles [Late 19thC. From Persian *pašm* "wool."]

Pash·to /púsh tō/ (*plural* **-to** *or* **-tos**), **Push·to** (*plural* **-to** *or* **-tos**), **Push·tu** /púsh tōo/ (*plural* **-tu** *or* **-tus**) *n.* **1.** **LANGUAGE OF AFGHANISTAN** one of the official languages of Afghanistan, also spoken in parts of northwestern Pakistan. It belongs to the Indo-Iranian branch of Indo-European languages and is spoken by about 21 million people. **2.** **PASHTO SPEAKER** somebody who speaks the Pashto language [Late 18thC. From Pashto *pəštō*.] —**Pash·to** *adj.*

Pa·siph·a·ë /pə síffə ee/ *n.* **1.** MYTHOL **MOTHER OF MINOTAUR** in Greek mythology, the wife of Minos, King of Crete, who fell in love with a bull and gave birth to the Minotaur **2.** ASTRON **MOON OF JUPITER** the eighth moon of Jupiter [Via Latin from Greek, literally "all-shining"]

pasque·flow·er /pásk flòwr/ *n.* a small perennial plant of the buttercup family with hairy compound leaves and large blue, purple, or white flowers that bloom in the spring. Genus: *Anemone.* [Late 16thC. Anglicization and alteration (influenced by French *pasque* "Easter," because it blooms in the spring) of French *passefleur*.]

pas·qui·nade /pàsskwə náyd/ *n.* **SATIRE** an often anonymous lampoon or satire that traditionally was left displayed in a public place (*archaic*) ■ *vt.* (**-nad·ed, -nad·ing, -nades**) **LAMPOON SOMEBODY OR SOMETHING** to ridicule somebody or something with a pasquinade (*archaic*) [Late 16thC. Via French from Italian *pasquinata*, from *Pasquino*, the name of a statue in Rome where lampoons were posted.] —**pas·qui·nad·er** *n.*

pass /pass/ *v.* (**passed, pass·ing, pass·es**) **1.** *vti.* **MOVE PAST** to move past or through a place, or past a person ○ *dark clouds passing overhead* **2.** *vti.* **OVERTAKE** to overtake and leave behind somebody or something **3.** *vti.* SPORTS **THROW OR KICK BALL TO PLAYER** to throw, kick, or hit a ball or other object to another player during a game **4.** *vt.* **HAND OVER** to hand something to somebody ○ *Could you pass me the salt, please?* **5.** *vti.* **TRANSFER OR BE TRANSFERRED** to transfer something such as property, authority, or responsibility to somebody, or to be transferred in this way ○ *The house will pass to his daughter when he dies.* **6.** *vti.* **MOVE INTO DIFFERENT PLACE OR CONDITION** to make somebody or something move, or to move from one place or condition to another **7.** *vti.* **MOVE IN A PARTICULAR WAY** to move something or move in a particular way in relation to something else ○ *He passed his hand along the banister.* **8.** *vt.* **GUIDE** to guide something into a particular position ○ *Pass the wire over that hook.* **9.** *vi.* **EXTEND PAST** to extend through, in front of, or along something such as a road or area ○ *The road passes by the cemetery.* **10.** *vi.* **CHANGE** to go from one condition, stage, or state to another ○ *It sheds its skin before it passes to the pupal stage.* **11.** *vt.* **SPEND TIME** to use up time doing something ○ *We passed the time playing cards.* **12.** *vi.* **ELAPSE** to elapse or go by ○ *Time passes quickly.* **13.** *vi.* **END** to come to an end ○ *The storm finally passed.* **14.** *vti.* **BE SUCCESSFUL IN AN EXAM** to be successful in a test or examination, or officially decide that somebody has been successful in a test or examination **15.** *vti.* **SUCCEED IN SUBJECT** to meet the requirements of a course of study **16.** *vi.* **BE ACCEPTABLE** to be of an acceptable standard ○ *It's not the best but it will pass.* **17.** *vti.* **APPROVE MEASURE OR BE APPROVED** to approve something such as a law, measure, or proposal, or to get official approval **18.** *vti.* **DIE** to stop living (*formal*) ○ *She passed from this life in 1967.* **19.** *vi.* **HAPPEN** to happen, especially without any intervention from anybody ○ *She could not let such rude behavior pass.* **20.** *vi.* **HAPPEN BETWEEN PEOPLE** to happen or be exchanged between two or more people ○ *A look passed between them.* **21.** *vi.* **NOT DO SOMETHING** to decide not to do something that is suggested or accept something that is offered **22.** *vi.* CARDS **NOT RAISE BID** to stop raising a bid in a card game **23.** *vt.* **EXCRETE** to process and excrete something from the body **24.** *vt.* **GIVE JUDGMENT** to give a judgment or opinion ○ *pass judgment* **25.** *vt.* **STATE** to say something or give an opinion ○ *She didn't pass any comment at all.* **26.** *vt.* **CIRCULATE FAKE MONEY** to use fake money to pay for something ○ *passing counterfeit bills* ■ *n.* **1.** **DOCUMENT GIVING PRIVILEGES** a document such as a ticket that entitles the holder to do something such as enter a place ○ *a press pass* **2.** SPORTS **ACT OF THROWING TO PLAYER** an act of throwing, kicking, or hitting a ball or other object to another player in a sport **3.** **SUCCESSFUL GRADE** a successful outcome in a test, examination, or course of study **4.** GEOG **WAY THROUGH MOUNTAINS** a way through or over mountains (*often used in place names*) **5.** **ATTEMPT TO KISS OR TOUCH SOMEBODY** an uninvited attempt to kiss or touch somebody in a sexual way **6.** **ACT OF GOING BY** an instance of something going past, through, over, or around a place **7.** **MOVEMENT** a particular movement of something such as the hand **8.** **OPERATION** a single cycle or complete operation of something such as machinery **9.** **DOCUMENT EXCUSING SOMEBODY FROM SOMETHING** a document that excuses the holder from normal activities **10.** **ACT OF NOT DOING SOMETHING** an instance of not doing something that is suggested or not accepting something that is offered **11.** CARDS **FAILURE TO BID** an instance of not bidding or raising the bid in a card game **12.** **STATE OF AFFAIRS** a particular and usually undesirable state of affairs ○ *How did we let things get to such a pass?* **13.** FENCING **SWORD THRUST** a thrust with a sword [13thC. Via Old French *passer* from assumed Vulgar Latin *passare*, from Latin *passus* "step" (source of English *passage* and *passenger*; see PACE).]

pass as *vt.* = **pass for**

pass away *vi.* **1.** **DIE** to stop living (*often used as a euphemism for "die"*) **2.** **COME TO END** to come to an end or no longer exist

pass by *vt.* to leave somebody or something unaffected or uninvolved ○ *The usual troubles of adolescence seemed to pass her by.*

pass for, pass as *vt.* to be so like somebody or something as to be easily mistaken for the real person or thing

pass off *vt.* to cause somebody or something to be accepted under a different, false identity

pass on *v.* **1.** *vi.* **DIE** to stop living (*often used as a euphemism for "die"*) **2.** *vt.* **CONVEY SOMETHING** to convey or transmit something that has been received to somebody else

pass out *v.* **1.** *vi.* **FAINT** to lose consciousness **2.** *vt.* **DISTRIBUTE** to distribute things among a number of people

pass over *vt.* **1.** **IGNORE** to ignore somebody's right to be considered for something, especially a job or a promotion **2.** **DISREGARD** to fail to consider or include somebody or something **3.** **DIE** to stop living (*dated*)

pass up *vt.* to decide not to take advantage of an opportunity

pass. *abbr.* **1.** passage **2.** passenger **3.** GRAM passive

pass·a·ble /pássəb'l/ *adj.* **1.** **ACCEPTABLE** adequate or good enough **2.** **ABLE TO BE CROSSED** capable of being crossed or traveled on **3.** POL **ABLE TO BE ENACTED** able to be passed or made law **4.** FIN **SUITABLE FOR CIRCULATION** suitable for circulation as legal and valid —**pass·a·bly** *adv.*

pas·sa·ca·glia /paàssə kaàlyə, pàssə kállyə/ *n.* a Baroque musical composition in slow triple time composed on a repeated bass line [Mid-17thC. Via Italian from Spanish *pasacalle*, from *pasar* "to pass" + *calle* "street," because it was often played in the streets.]

pas·sade /pə saàd/ *n.* a movement in dressage in which a horse is made to move forward and back again on the same spot [Mid-17thC. Via French from Italian *passata*, ultimately from assumed Vulgar Latin *passare* (see PASS).]

pas·sa·do /pə saà dō/ (*plural* **-dos** *or* **-does**) *n.* in fencing, a thrust made while stepping forward [Late 16thC. Alteration of Spanish *pasada* or French *passade*, ultimately from assumed Vulgar Latin *passare* (see PASS).]

pas·sage[1] /pássij/ *n.* **1.** CORRIDOR OR PATHWAY a corridor in an enclosed area or an outdoor path enclosed on both sides **2.** WAY THROUGH a path made for somebody through an obstruction such as a crowd of people **3.** ARTS PIECE OF WRITING OR MUSIC a section of a piece of writing, speech, or music, or a section of a painting or piece of artwork **4.** CHANGE OF PLACE OR CONDITION the act of going from one place to another or changing from one condition to another (*formal*) **5.** PROCESS OF TIME PASSING the process of time going by ○ *the passage of time* **6.** TRANSP TRIP a journey, especially one made by sea or air **7.** RIGHT TO TRAVEL the right to come and go, travel, or pass through somewhere ○ *The guides ensured our safe passage.* **8.** POL APPROVAL OF NEW LAW official approval of a new law or other proposal **9.** ANAT TUBE IN THE BODY a tube or channel in the body **10.** GEOG SEA CHANNEL a sea channel or strait (*often used in place names*) **11.** MED BOWEL MOVEMENT the act or process of expelling something from the body, e.g., emptying the bowels or the bladder **12.** INTERCHANGE an exchange of words, blows, or information between people or parties (*formal*) [13thC. Via Old French from, ultimately, assumed Vulgar Latin *passare* "to pass" (see PASS).]

WORD KEY: CULTURAL NOTE

A Passage to India, a novel by the English writer E.M. Forster (1924). In Forster's last and most highly regarded novel, an Englishwoman traveling in colonial India accuses a local doctor of assaulting her during a visit to the mysterious Marabar Caves. The conflicting responses of English expatriates and local Indians to the subsequent trial highlight the limitations of their belief systems and the problems of human understanding.

pas·sage[2] /pássij, pə saàzh/ *n.* MOVEMENT IN DRESSAGE either of two movements in dressage, one being a sideways walk and the other a slow deliberate trot ■ *vti.* **(-saged, -sag·ing, -sag·es)** PERFORM A PASSAGE to perform a passage or make a horse do this [Late 18thC. Via French *passager* from, ultimately, Latin *passus* "step" (see PACE).]

pas·sage hawk *n.* a hawk or falcon captured while in its first plumage

pas·sage·way /pássij way/ *n.* = **passage**[1] *n.* **1**

pas·sage·work /pássij wùrk/ *n.* **1.** NONTHEMATIC PASSAGES parts of a musical work that are thematically unrelated to the whole but enable a performer to display virtuosity **2.** PERFORMANCE OF PASSAGEWORK the performance or execution of passagework

Pas·sa·ic Falls /pə sày ik-/ falls on the Passaic River in northeastern New Jersey. Height: 70 ft./21 m.

pass-a·long *n.* something such as a tax that is passed along to the consumer, usually in the form of higher prices or rents, in order to prevent a loss of profit

pas·sant /páss'nt/ *adj.* HERALDRY used in heraldry to describe an animal shown walking to the left or right [15thC. From French, the present participle of *passer* (see PASS).]

pass·back /páss bàk/ *n.* SPORTS the act of passing the ball or puck to another player who is closer to the home goal

pass band *n.* RADIO the range of frequencies that an electronic filter will allow to pass without attenuation. A voice band filter in a telephone exchange will pass a frequency band of approximately 3,000 cycles.

pass·book /páss bòòk/ *n.* **1.** BANKING RECORD OF BANK TRANSACTIONS a book in which a record is kept of the money put into and taken out of a bank account **2.** COMM BOOK RECORDING CREDIT PURCHASES a book in which a merchant records the items a customer has bought on credit **3.** POL IDENTITY DOCUMENT a mandatory identification document issued to Black people in South Africa during apartheid that gave details of their ancestry and spelled out restrictions on their movements [Early 19thC. *Pass* of uncertain origin: possibly from the fact that it is handed back and forth between the bank and the customer.]

pas·sé /pa sáy/ *adj.* **1.** OUT OF DATE out of date or no longer fashionable **2.** PAST PRIME no longer in prime condition [Late 18thC. From French, the past participle of *passer* "to pass" (see PASS).]

WORD KEY: SYNONYMS

See Synonyms at ***old-fashioned***.

passed ball *n.* BASEBALL a ball that ought to have been caught by the catcher but is missed, thereby allowing a runner to advance. ◊ **wild pitch**

passed pawn *n.* CHESS a pawn with no opposing pawn in front of it on its own or on either adjacent file that could become a queen

pas·sel /páss'l/ *n.* a fairly large group or amount (*regional*) [Mid-19thC. Alteration of PARCEL.]

passe·men·terie /pass méntree/ *n.* **1.** DECORATIVE TRIMMING FOR CLOTHES a decorative trimming for clothing made, e.g., of beads, braid, or lace **2.** MAKING OF CLOTH DECORATIONS the craft of making fringes, tassels, and cords to embellish soft furnishings and upholstery [Early 17thC. From French, formed from *passement* "decorative lace or braid," literally "passing (over one another)," from *passer* (see PASS).]

pas·sen·ger /pássənjər/ *n.* **1.** SOMEBODY TRAVELING IN VEHICLE somebody who travels in a motor vehicle, train, aircraft, or ship, but is not a driver or crew member **2.** SOMEBODY NOT DOING SHARE OF WORK somebody in a team who does not do his or her fair share of the work [14thC. Alteration of Old French *passageor* "one who makes a passage," from *passage* (see PASSAGE).]

pas·sen·ger pi·geon *n.* an extinct migratory North American pigeon that was abundant until it was hunted to extinction in the 19th century. Latin name: *Ectopistes migratorius.* [*Passenger* in the earlier sense "migrating bird," because of its long migrations in huge flocks]

passe-par·tout /pàss paar tóò/ (*plural* **passe-par·touts** /pàss paar tóò/) *n.* **1.** MASTER KEY something such as a master key that gives unrestricted access to a building or area **2.** PICTURE FRAME a decorated mat around a framed picture **3.** ADHESIVE TAPE OR GUMMED PAPER adhesive tape or gummed paper used to fix pictures to mats before framing [From French, literally "pass everywhere"]

passe·pied /paàss pyáy/ *n.* a French court dance in triple time similar to the minuet, often part of instrumental dance suites [From French, literally "foot-pass"]

pas·ser-by (*plural* **pas·sers-by**) *n.* somebody who happens to be going past a place, especially on foot

pas·ser·ine /pássə rìn, -reen/ *adj.* RELATING TO PERCHING SONGBIRDS relating or belonging to an order of mainly perching songbirds. It is the largest order of birds and comprises more than half of all species. Order: Passeriformes. ■ *n.* PASSERINE BIRD any bird that belongs to the passerine order [Late 18thC. From late Latin *passerinus* "of sparrows," from *passer* "sparrow," of unknown origin.]

pas seul /paa sṓl/ (*plural* **pas seuls**) *n.* a dance or passage performed by a single dancer [From French, literally "solo step"]

pass-fail *adj.* GRADING ONLY AS A PASS OR FAIL used to describe, or relating to, a system of grading in which a student simply passes or fails, without a grade such as A, B, or C being awarded ■ *n.* SIMPLE GRADING SYSTEM a system of grading tests in which students simply pass or fail, without narrower grades such as A, B, and C being awarded

pas·si·ble /pássəb'l/ *adj.* sensitive to feeling emotions, especially when this causes pain (*formal*) [14thC. Via Old French from Latin *passibilis*, from *pass-*, the past participle stem of *pati* "to feel, suffer" (see PATIENT).] —**pas·si·bil·i·ty** /pàssə bíllətee/ *n.* —**pas·si·bly** /pássəblee/ *adv.*

pas·sim /pássim/ *adv.* used especially in footnotes to indicate that what is being referred to occurs in various places in a book or other text (*formal*) [Early 19thC. From Latin, literally "scatteredly," from *passus*, past participle of *pandere* "to spread out."]

pass·ing /pássing/ *adj.* **1.** GOING PAST moving past ○ *a passing car* **2.** TRANSITORY lasting only a short time **3.** BRIEF AND WITHOUT MUCH ATTENTION done briefly and without much attention being paid ○ *a passing interest* **4.** EXTREMELY very or extremely (*archaic*) ○ *She was passing fair.* ■ *n.* **1.** CEASING TO EXIST the fact or process of something becoming obsolete or ceasing to exist **2.** PLACE WHERE IT IS POSSIBLE TO PASS a place where it is possible to pass or cross something **3.** PROCESS OF TIME GOING BY the elapsing of time **4.** DEATH death ■ *adv.* VERY exceedingly (*archaic*)

pass·ing bell *n.* a bell rung to mark a death or a funeral

pass·ing lane *n.* a lane designated for passing slower traffic

pass·ing note *n.* MUSIC a note played between two chords or pitches to provide a melodic transition from one to the other

pass·ing shot *n.* in racket games such as tennis, a winning shot that passes beyond the reach of a player at the net

pass·ing tone *n.* MUSIC = **passing note**

pas·sion /pásh'n/ *n.* **1.** INTENSE EMOTION intense or overpowering emotion such as love, joy, hatred, or anger ○ *Try and play it with a little more passion.* **2.** STRONG SEXUAL DESIRE strong sexual desire and excitement **3.** OUTBURST OF EMOTION a sudden outburst of an emotion such as rage, hatred, or jealousy ○ *He flew into a passion.* **4.** INTENSE ENTHUSIASM FOR SOMETHING a keen interest in a particular subject or activity ○ *a passion for music* **5.** OBJECT OF ENTHUSIASM the object of somebody's intense interest or enthusiasm ○ *Orchids are my passion.* ■ **pas·sions** *npl.* EMOTIONS strong emotions, especially as distinct from reason or intellect ○ *a meeting at which passions were running high* [12thC. Via French from the ecclesiastical Latin stem *passion-* "suffering, affection," from, ultimately, *pati* "to suffer" (source of English *patient*, *passive*, and *compatible*).]

WORD KEY: SYNONYMS

See Synonyms at ***love***.

Pas·sion *n.* **1.** CHR SUFFERING OF JESUS CHRIST the sufferings of Jesus Christ from the Last Supper until his crucifixion **2.** BIBLE STORY OF JESUS CHRIST'S SUFFERING any of the accounts of the Passion in the Gospel, or a musical work based on one of these

pas·sion·al /páshən'l, páshnəl/ *adj.* OF PASSION relating to passion or arising from passion (*literary*) ■ *n.* CHR BOOK RECOUNTING MARTYRS' STORIES a book that tells of the sufferings of Christian saints and martyrs [15thC. From Latin *passionalis*, from *passion-* (see PASSION).]

pas·sion·ate /pásh'nət/ *adj.* **1.** SHOWING SEXUAL DESIRE expressing or showing strong sexual desire ○ *a passionate kiss* **2.** SHOWING INTENSE EMOTION expressing intense or overpowering emotion ○ *a passionate speech on human rights* **3.** ENTHUSIASTIC having a keen enthusiasm or intense desire for something ○ *a passionate golfer* **4.** HAVING STRONG EMOTIONS tending to have strong feelings, especially of love, desire, or enthusiasm ○ *a fiery, passionate personality* **5.** QUICK-TEMPERED easily made angry —**pas·sion·ate·ly** *adv.*

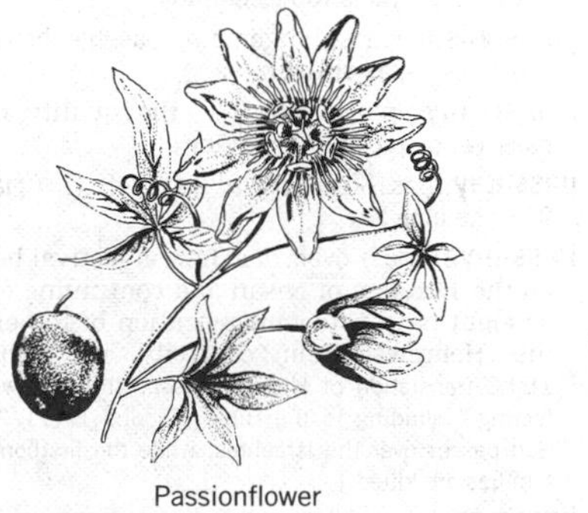

Passionflower

pas·sion·flow·er /pásh'n flòwr/ *n.* a chiefly tropical American climbing vine with large flowers. Some varieties have edible fruit. Genus: *Passiflora.* [Mid-17thC. Because parts of the flower are taken as symbols of Jesus Christ's Passion.]

pas·sion fruit *n.* the edible fruit of a passionflower, especially a granadilla

Pas·sion·ist /pásh'nist/ *n.* CHR a member of a Roman Catholic mendicant order devoted to commemorating the Passion of Jesus Christ by missionary work.

The order was founded in Italy in 1720 by St. Paul of the Cross.

pas·sion·less /páshən'ləss/ *adj.* **1.** LACKING LOVE empty of romantic or sexual love ○ *a passionless movie* **2.** EMOTIONALLY DETACHED feeling or expressing no emotion —**pas·sion·less·ness** *n.*

Pas·sion play *n.* a play that tells the story of the sufferings and crucifixion of Jesus Christ

Pas·sion Sun·day *n.* CHR **1.** 5TH SUNDAY IN LENT the fifth Sunday in Lent, or the second Sunday before Easter, when Passiontide begins **2.** = **Palm Sunday**

Pas·sion·tide /pásh'n tīd/ *n.* CHR the last two weeks of Lent, from Passion Sunday to Easter

Pas·sion Week *n.* CHR **1.** WEEK FOLLOWING PASSION SUNDAY the second week before Easter, from Passion Sunday to Palm Sunday (*archaic*) **2.** WEEK BEFORE EASTER Holy Week

pas·si·vate /pássə vàyt/ (**-vat·ed, -vat·ing, -vates**) *vt.* to coat the surface of a metal with a substance that protects it against corrosion

pas·sive /pássiv/ *adj.* **1.** NOT ACTIVELY TAKING PART tending not to participate actively, and usually letting others make decisions **2.** OBEYING READILY tending to submit or obey without arguing or resisting **3.** NOT OPERATIONAL not working or operating **4.** INFLUENCED BY SOMETHING EXTERNAL influenced, affected, or produced by something external **5.** GRAM EXPRESSING ACTION DONE TO THE SUBJECT indicating that the apparent subject of a verb is the person or thing undergoing, not performing, the action of the verb, as in "We were given work to do" **6.** CHEM UNREACTIVE chemically inactive or resistant to corrosion **7.** ELECTRON ENG LACKING A POWER SOURCE used to describe an electronic circuit or device that does not contain a source of energy **8.** FIN NOT MANAGED BY THE INVESTOR used to describe a form of investment that does not involve active management by the investor ■ *n.* GRAM PASSIVE VOICE the passive voice, or a verb in the passive voice [14thC. Directly or via French from Latin *passivus*, from, ultimately, *pati* (see PASSION).] —**pas·sive·ly** *adv.* —**pas·sive·ness** *n.*

pas·sive-ag·gres·sive *adj.* used to describe, or relating to, a personality type or way of behaving that seeks to manipulate others indirectly and resist their demands rather than confronting or opposing directly —**pas·sive aggres·sion** *n.*

pas·sive im·mu·ni·ty *n.* immunity from disease acquired by the transfer of antibodies from one person to another, e.g., through injections or between a mother and a fetus through the placenta

pas·sive re·sis·tance *n.* resistance to authority using only nonviolent methods such as peaceful demonstration or noncooperation —**pas·sive re·sist·er** *n.*

pas·sive re·straint *n.* an automatic safety device in an automobile that protects a driver or passenger in the event of an accident. Airbags and self-locking seat belts are passive restraints.

pas·sive smok·ing *n.* the involuntary breathing in of other people's tobacco smoke

pas·siv·ism /pássə vìzzəm/ *n.* passive behavior or attitudes —**pas·siv·ist** *n.*

pas·siv·i·ty /pa sívvətee/ *n.* the quality of being passive, or passive behavior

pass·key /páss kèe/ (*plural* **-keys**) *n.* **1.** = **master key 2.** = **skeleton key**

Pass·o·ver /páss ṑvər/ *n.* a Jewish festival beginning on the 14th day of Nisan and continuing for seven or eight days in commemoration of the exodus of the Hebrews from captivity in Egypt [Mid-16thC.Translation of Hebrew *pesah*, "to pass without affecting," alluding to the Bible (Exodus 12:11–27) where God passes over the Israelites, while the firstborn of other families are killed.]

pass·port /páss pàwrt/ *n.* **1.** OFFICIAL IDENTIFICATION DOCUMENT an official document issued by the government of a country to a citizen that identifies the bearer and gives permission to travel to and from that country **2.** ANY AUTHORIZATION TO TRAVEL any authorization or official permission to travel in or through a country **3.** MEANS OF ACCESS something that grants somebody access to something ○ *Education is the passport to a more fulfilling life.* [15thC. From French *passeport*, literally "to pass the seaport."]

pass-through /páss thro͞o/ *n.* **1.** OPENING IN A KITCHEN WALL an opening in a wall, often connecting a kitchen and dining area, through which food and dishes can be passed **2.** = **pass-along**

pass·word /páss wùrd/ *n.* **1.** WORD SECURING ACCESS a secret word or phrase that somebody must use to gain entry to a place **2.** COMPUT KEYED CHARACTERS GIVING COMPUTER ACCESS a sequence of characters that you have to key in to gain access to part of a computer system ○ *Don't let anyone know your password.*

past[1] /pást/ CORE MEANING: movement that involves passing or going beyond somebody or something ○ (prep) *Walk past the library and you'll arrive at the park.* ○ (adv) *She walked right past without saying a word to us.*
1. *prep., adv.* LATER later than a particular time ○ *It's twenty past seven.* ○ *It's past your bedtime.* ○ *It's half past.* **2.** *prep.* ON THE FARTHER SIDE OF SOMETHING on the farther side of or beyond something ○ *We prefer the bakery that's just past the school.* **3.** *prep.* BEYOND A NUMBER, AMOUNT, OR POINT beyond a particular number, amount, or point, especially a point at which something can be done ○ *Do what you like; I'm past caring.* **4.** *adv.* AGO before the present time (*archaic*) ○ *He left home six months past.* [13thC. Originally the past participle of PASS.] ◇ **not put something past somebody, not put it past somebody** to believe that somebody is quite capable of doing something, usually something disreputable or outrageous (*informal*)

past[2] /pást/ *adj.* **1.** ELAPSED gone by ○ *the past few days* **2.** RELATING TO AN EARLIER TIME having existed or occurred in a previous time ○ *in a past job* **3.** ONE-TIME having formerly occupied a particular position ○ *a gathering of past presidents* **4.** GRAM EXPRESSING ACTION THAT TOOK PLACE PREVIOUSLY used to describe or relating to the verb tense that is used for an action that took place previously ■ *n.* **1.** TIME BEFORE THE PRESENT the time before the present and the events that happened then **2.** SOMEBODY'S PREVIOUS HISTORY everything that has happened previously to somebody or something ○ *She has a mysterious past.* **3.** SHAMEFUL HISTORY a shameful or scandalous earlier period in somebody's life **4.** GRAM PAST TENSE the past tense of a language, or a verb form in the past tense [13thC. Originally the past participle of PASS.] —**past·ness** *n.*

pas·ta /paástə, pástə/ *n.* **1.** FOOD MADE FROM FLOUR a fresh or dried food that is usually made from flour, eggs, and water formed into a variety of shapes, e.g., macaroni or spaghetti **2.** PASTA DISH a dish made with cooked pasta [Late 19thC. Via Italian, from late Latin (see PASTE).]

paste[1] /payst/ *n.* **1.** ADHESIVE MIXTURE a soft mixture of flour and water or starch and water used as an adhesive, especially for sticking paper to something **2.** FOOD SEMISOLID MIXTURE a soft mass or mixture with a consistency between a liquid and a solid **3.** FOOD FOOD SPREAD a soft food product that can be spread on something such as bread ○ *anchovy paste* **4.** GLASS FOR IMITATION GEMS a hard, brilliant glass used to make imitation jewels **5.** COOK PASTRY DOUGH pastry dough usually made with shortening and used especially to make pie crusts **6.** PORCELAIN CLAY the clay mixture used to make porcelain ■ *vt.* (**past·ed, past·ing, pastes**) **1.** GLUE SOMETHING TO SOMETHING ELSE to stick things together using paste **2.** COVER A SURFACE WITH PASTE to cover a surface by sticking things to it with paste **3.** SPREAD SOMETHING THICKLY to spread a soft substance onto a surface in a thick layer **4.** COMPUT PLACE TEXT IN DOCUMENT ELECTRONICALLY to place text, data, or an image into a document electronically as an addition or alteration from another location [13thC. Via Old French from late Latin *pasta* from, ultimately, Greek *passein* "to sprinkle" (source of English *pastel*). Originally used for "dough," the underlying sense is "moist mixture."] —**past·er** *n.*

paste up *vt.* PRINTING to take printed pages or proofs and stick them onto separate sheets of paper so that they can be read and amended

paste[2] /payst/ (**past·ed, past·ing, pastes**) *vt.* to give somebody a severe beating or defeat somebody heavily (*informal*)

paste·board /páyst bàwrd/ *n.* **1.** CARD a ticket, card, or playing card (*informal*) **2.** THICK STIFF PAPER a stiff board made either of sheets of paper pasted together or of layers of paper pulp pressed together ■ *adj.* **1.** FLIMSY not of good quality, or not very substantial ○ *pasteboard houses* **2.** FAKE intended to pass for the genuine article

pas·tel /pa stél/ *adj.* PALE IN COLOR having a pale soft color ■ *n.* **1.** PALE COLOR a pale soft color **2.** PASTE USED FOR MAKING CRAYONS a paste of powdered pigment and gum, used for making crayons **3.** CRAYON a crayon for doing pastel drawings **4.** DRAWING something drawn using pastel crayons **5.** ART USING PASTELS the technique or process of drawing with pastels [Late 16thC. Directly or via French from Italian *pastello*, literally "small amount of paste," from *pasta* "paste," from late Latin (see PASTE).] —**pas·tel·ist** *n.*

pas·tern /pástərn/ *n.* **1.** PART OF A HORSE'S FOOT the part of a horse's foot between the fetlock and the top of the hoof **2.** BONE IN A HORSE'S FOOT either of two bones in a horse's foot that connect the hoof with the fetlock [13thC. Via Old French *pasturon*, from *pasture* "hobble for pastured animal" (the original sense in English), from, ultimately, Latin *pascere* "to feed" (source of English *pasture*).]

paste-up *n.* **1.** SHEETS WITH PAGES FOR CHECKING a number of sheets of paper onto which printed pages or proofs have been pasted for checking **2.** PREPARATION FOR PRINTING PLATES cards on which pieces of typesetting or artwork have been pasted to be photographed for making printing plates **3.** TECHNIQUE OF MAKING PASTE-UPS the technique or process of making paste-ups ○ *a paste-up artist*

Pas·teur /pas túr, paass-/, **Louis** (1822–95) French scientist. He developed the process of pasteurization and invented vaccinations to induce immunity against certain viral diseases. He founded, and was the first director of, the Pasteur Institute in Paris.

pas·teur·i·za·tion /pàschəri záysh'n, pàstəri-/ *n.* treatment of a liquid such as milk by heating it in order to destroy harmful bacteria

pas·teur·ize /páschə rīz, pástə-/ (**-ized, -iz·ing, -iz·es**) *vt.* to treat a liquid such as milk by heating it, in order to destroy harmful bacteria [Late 19thC. Named for Louis PASTEUR, who developed it.] —**pas·teur·iz·er** *n.*

Pas·teur treat·ment *n.* a treatment for somebody infected with rabies in which increasingly strong injections of a less infective form of the virus are given to produce antibodies against it [Late 19thC. Named for Louis PASTEUR, who devised the technique.]

pas·tic·cio /pa stéechō, pa stéechi ō, paa-/ (*plural* **-ci** /-chee/ *or* **pas·tic·cios**) *n.* a pastiche [Mid-18thC. Via Italian, literally "pie, pasty," from, ultimately, late Latin *pasta* (see PASTE).]

pas·tiche /pa stéesh, paa-/ *n.* **1.** MIXTURE a piece of creative work, e.g., in literature, drama, or art, that is a mixture of things borrowed from other works **2.** USE OF PASTICHE the creation or use of a pastiche **3.** IMITATIVE WORK a piece of creative work, e.g., in literature, drama, or art, that imitates and often satirizes another work or style [Late 19thC. Via French from Italian *pasticcio* (see PASTICCIO). The underlying sense is "mixture" or "medley."]

pas·tille /pa stéel/ *n.* **1.** LOZENGE a small flavored or medicated lozenge **2.** FUMIGATING SUBSTANCE a substance, usually in tablet or paste form, that is burned to scent or fumigate a room [Mid-17thC. Via French from Latin *pastillus*, literally "little loaf" (from the shape), from *panis* "loaf."]

pas·time /páss tīm/ *n.* an interest or activity that somebody pursues in his or her spare time [15thC. From PASS + TIME.]

pas·ti·na /pa stéenə/ *n.* tiny pieces of pasta often used in soup [Mid-20thC. From Italian, literally "little pasta," from *pasta* (see PASTA).]

past·ing /páysting/ *n.* a severe beating or a complete defeat (*informal*)

pas·tis /pa stéess/ *n.* a yellowish French liqueur flavored with aniseed, often drunk as an aperitif [Early 20thC. Via French, literally "muddle, mixture," from, ultimately, late Latin *pasta* (see PASTE).]

past mas·ter *n.* **1.** EXPERT somebody who has great experience and skill in doing something **2.** FORMER MASTER somebody who has held a position as master at one time, e.g., in the Freemasons

pas·tor /pástər/ *n.* **1.** MINISTER a Christian minister or priest in charge of a congregation **2.** SPIRITUAL ADVISOR somebody who is not a minister or priest but who gives spiritual advice to a group of people **3.** SHEPHERD a shepherd (*archaic*) ■ *vt.* ACT AS PASTOR to provide the services that a pastor performs for a church [14thC. Via Old French *pastre* from Latin *pastor* "herdsman, shepherd," from *past-*, the past participle stem of *pascere* "to feed or graze."] —**pas·tor·ship** *n.*

pas·tor·al /pástərəl/ *adj.* **1.** RURAL relating to the countryside or to rural life ○ *pastoral living* **2.** ARTS IDEALIZING RURAL LIFE presenting an idealized image of rural life and nature ○ *pastoral poetry* **3.** OF CLERGY relating to religious ministers or priests or their duties **4.** AGRIC **USED FOR PASTURE** used to describe land that is used as pasture **5.** **GIVING ADVICE TO STUDENTS** relating to the duties of a teacher who gives personal advice and support to students rather than just teaching them **6.** AGRIC **OF SHEEP OR CATTLE** relating to or keeping sheep or cattle ■ *n.* **1.** ARTS **DESCRIPTION OF RURAL LIFE** a literary work or painting that portrays rural life in an idealized way **2.** MUSIC = **pastorale 3.** CHR **LETTER FROM A RELIGIOUS MINISTER** a letter written by a religious minister to his or her congregation **4.** CHR **BISHOP'S STAFF** a staff carried by a bishop as a symbol of office [15thC. From Latin *pastoralis*, literally "to do with herdsmen or shepherds," from *pastor* (see PASTOR).] —**pas·tor·al·ly** *adv.*

WORD KEY: CULTURAL NOTE

Pastoral Symphony, a composition by German composer Ludwig van Beethoven (1808). Also known as Symphony No. 6 in F major, op. 68, this widely performed work was described by Beethoven as a "recollection of country life." It describes a day's outing to the Viennese countryside and features peasant dances, bird songs, and a storm.

pas·to·rale /pàstə raál, -rál/ (*plural* **-rales** *or* **-ra·li** /-raálee/), **pas·tor·al** /pástərəl/ *n.* **1.** **RUSTIC OPERA** an opera with a rural story and setting, popular in the 16th and 17th centuries **2.** **MUSIC WITH A PASTORAL THEME** a piece of music with a pastoral theme [Early 18thC. Via Italian, literally "pastoral," from, ultimately, Latin *pastor* (see PASTOR).]

Pas·tor·al E·pist·les *n.* in the Bible, the three Epistles, two to Timothy and one to Titus, traditionally attributed to St. Paul.

pas·tor·al·ism /pástərə lìzzəm/ *n.* **1.** **LIVESTOCK RAISING** the raising of livestock, especially by traditional methods, as the main economic activity of a society **2.** ARTS **ARTISTIC TREATMENT OF RURAL LIFE** the style in literary work or painting that portrays rural life, especially that of shepherds, in an idealized way **3.** **WAY OF LIFE DEPENDENT ON LIVESTOCK** a way of life that depends on raising livestock and living on its milk and meat

pas·tor·al·ist /pástərəlist/ *n.* somebody who has a pastoral way of life

pas·tor·ate /pástərət/ *n.* **1.** **OFFICE OF PASTOR** the office, term of office, or jurisdiction of a pastor **2.** **PASTORS COLLECTIVELY** pastors considered as a group

past par·ti·ci·ple *n.* a participle that expresses past time or a completed action. It is used with auxiliaries to form perfect tenses in the active voice and all tenses in the passive voice In the sentence "I waited until he had rung the bell," the past participle is "rung."

past per·fect *n.* **VERB TENSE WITH "HAD"** a verb tense that is formed with "had" and expresses an action that was completed at a time in the past ■ *adj.* **BEING IN PAST PERFECT TENSE** being in or relating to the past perfect tense

pas·tra·mi /pə straámee/ *n.* smoked and strongly seasoned beef, usually prepared from a shoulder cut, that is served cold or heated in thin slices [Mid-20thC. Via Yiddish from Romanian *pastramă*.]

pas·try /páystree/ (*plural* **-tries**) *n.* **1.** **DOUGH FOR PIES** a dough made with flour, water, and shortening, used to make crusts for pies **2.** **FOODS MADE FROM PASTRY** sweet baked food made from pastry **3.** **SOMETHING MADE WITH PASTRY** a pie or small cake made with pastry [15thC. Formed from PASTE on the model of Old French *pastaierie*.]

past tense *n.* a verb tense that expresses something that happened or was done in the past. In the sentence "I felt very proud of them," the verb "felt" is in the past tense.

pas·tur·age /páschərij/ *n.* **1.** = **pasture** *n.* 1 **2.** **GRAZING OF LIVESTOCK** the grazing of livestock, or the right to graze livestock on a particular area of land

pas·ture /páschər/ *n.* **1.** **LAND FOR GRAZING** grass-covered land used for grazing livestock **2.** **PLANTS FOR GRAZING** grass and other growing plants that are suitable food for livestock ■ *vti.* (**-tured, -tur·ing, -tures**) **GRAZE** to graze, or to put livestock somewhere to graze [13thC. Via Old French from late Latin *pastura*, from *past-*, the past participle stem of Latin *pascere* "to feed."] ◇ **put somebody out to pasture 1.** to impose retirement on somebody, usually on grounds of age (*informal or humorous*) **2.** to put a grazing animal into a field to graze

pas·ty[1] /pástee/ (*plural* **-ties**) *n. U.K.* a turnover made from a folded round of pastry with a filling in the middle [Via Old French *pasté(e)* from, ultimately, late Latin *pasta* (see PASTE)]

past·y[2] /páystee/ *adj.* (**-i·er, -i·est**) **1.** **UNHEALTHILY PALE** having a pale unhealthy appearance **2.** **RESEMBLING PASTE** resembling paste in consistency, color, or texture ■ *n.* (*plural* **-ies**) **NIPPLE COVERING** either of a pair of small adhesive coverings for a woman's nipples, worn usually by erotic dancers [Early 17thC. Formed from PASTE.] —**past·i·ly** *adv.* —**past·i·ness** *n.*

PA sys·tem *abbr.* public-address system. = **PA**

pat[1] /pat/ *vt.* (**pat·ted, pat·ting, pats**) **1.** **STRIKE LIGHTLY** to strike something lightly with the palm of the hand or something flat **2.** **LAY THE HAND ON SOMETHING REPEATEDLY** to touch somebody or something repeatedly with the palm of your hand, e.g., to show affection or to congratulate somebody ○ *I patted the child's curly head.* **3.** **SHAPE SOMETHING WITH THE HANDS** to shape or smooth something with the hands or with a flat object ■ *n.* **1.** **LIGHT BLOW** a light blow with the palm of the hand or with a flat object **2.** **LIGHT TOUCH** a light, usually repeated, touch with the hand to show affection or to congratulate somebody **3.** **SMALL PIECE** a small piece of something soft, especially butter **4.** **SOFT SOUND** the sound made by a light blow with the hand or with a flat object, or by a light footstep [14thC. Imitative of the sound of patting.] ◇ **a pat on the back** an expression of praise or congratulation (*informal*) ○ *You deserve a pat on the back for getting the work done so quickly.*

pat[2] /pat/ *adv.* **1.** **EXACTLY** in an exact, accurate, or fluent way ○ *He has his part down pat.* **2.** **OPPORTUNELY** at the most appropriate time or place ■ *adj.* **1.** **GLIB** so easily and readily produced as to suggest lack of proper thought ○ *pat answers* **2.** CARDS **NOT TO BE IMPROVED** used to describe a poker hand that is not likely to be improved by drawing additional cards [Late 16thC. Origin uncertain: probably from PAT[1], the underlying sense being "hitting the mark."]

Pat *n.* an offensive term for an Irishman (*offensive*) [Early 19thC. Pet-form of the name *Patrick*, common in Ireland.]

pat. *abbr.* **1.** patent **2.** patented

pa·ta·ca /pə taákə/ *n.* **1.** **UNIT OF CURRENCY** the basic unit of currency of Macao, worth 100 avos **2.** **COIN WORTH A PATACA** a coin worth one pataca [Mid-19thC. Via Portuguese from Arabic *abū ṭāqah*, a kind of coin.]

pa·ta·gi·um /pə táyjee əm/ (*plural* **-a** /-ə/) *n.* **1.** **FOLD OF MAMMAL SKIN** a loose fold of skin between the fore and hind limbs in some mammals, used as an aid to flying or gliding by, e.g., bats and flying lemurs **2.** **FOLD OF BIRD SKIN** a thin fold of skin between a bird's wing and its shoulder [Early 19thC. From Latin, literally "gold edging on a tunic."]

Pat·a·go·ni·a /pàttə gṓnee ə/ region of southern Argentina, between the Andes Mountains and the South Atlantic Ocean. Area: 300,000 sq. mi./777,000 sq. km. —**Patag·o·nian** *n., adj.*

pa·ta·phys·ics /pàatə fízziks/ *n.* an imaginary science invented by the French absurdist dramatist Alfred Jarry, supposedly investigating and explaining what is beyond metaphysics (*takes a singular verb*) [Mid-20thC. Via French *pataphysique*, an alteration of Greek *ta epi ta metaphusika*, "that which comes after the metaphysics."]

patch /pach/ *n.* **1.** **SOMETHING THAT COVERS OR MENDS** a piece of material used to cover, strengthen, or mend a hole in something ○ *an elbow patch* **2.** **SMALL AREA** a small area of something within a larger one ○ *a patch of ice* **3.** **SMALL GROWING AREA** a small area of land used for growing a particular crop ○ *a cabbage patch* **4.** **AREA OF CONTROL** an area under somebody's control or jurisdiction ○ *They warned him to stay off their patch.* ○ *Two vendors were arguing over whose patch it was.* **5.** **EYE SHIELD** a pad worn over an injured or missing eye ○ *an eye patch* **6.** MED **COVER FOR WOUND** a piece of material used to cover a wound **7.** **SEWN-ON BADGE** a cloth badge sewn onto clothing as identification, a sign of rank, or to commemorate something **8.** COMPUT **SOFTWARE BUG CORRECTOR OR UPDATE** a fragment of program code made available to fix a bug in a software application or to add a new feature before an updated version of the application is released ○ *a patch available on the Internet* **9.** PHARM **DRUG-IMPREGNATED MATERIAL** a piece of material impregnated with a drug and worn on the skin to allow the gradual absorption of the drug ○ *a nicotine patch* **10.** FASHION **ARTIFICIAL BEAUTY SPOT** a small piece of black silk or velvet, often in a distinct shape, worn on the face by men and women as an adornment in the 17th and 18th centuries ■ *vt.* (**patched, patch·ing, patch·es**) **1.** **REPAIR SOMETHING WITH MATERIAL** to cover or mend a hole in something or to strengthen a weak place using cloth or a pasty substance **2.** **MAKE SOMETHING FROM CLOTH PIECES** to make something by sewing together pieces of fabric **3.** COMPUT **AMEND A PROGRAM USING A PATCH** to fix or update software using a patch **4.** TELECOM **CONNECT A CALL** to connect one telephone or radio caller with another or transfer a call to somewhere else ○ *Patch me through to headquarters.* [14thC. Origin uncertain: perhaps ultimately from a dialect variant of Old French *piece* (see PIECE).]

patch up *vt.* **1.** **MEND SOMETHING HURRIEDLY** to mend or assemble something hurriedly or as a temporary measure **2.** **MAKE FRIENDS AGAIN** to become friends with somebody again after an argument **3.** **GIVE TREATMENT TO SOMEBODY** to give somebody medical treatment for an injury (*informal*)

patch board *n.* an electrical panel with numerous sockets into which electrical cords (**patch cords**) can be plugged to form temporary circuits. Telephone exchanges used to use patch boards before the advent of electronic switchboards.

patch·ou·li /pə chóolee, páchəlee/, **pach·ou·li** *n.* **1.** **TROPICAL ASIAN SHRUB** a tropical Asian shrub of the mint family whose leaves produce a fragrant oil. Latin name: *Pogostemon cablin.* **2.** **AROMATIC OIL** the aromatic oil obtained from the patchouli shrub, used in perfumes and in aromatherapy [Mid-19thC. From Tamil *paccuḷi*.]

patch pock·et *n.* a pocket made by sewing a patch of fabric on the outside of a garment

patch test *n.* a test for allergies in which small pads impregnated with allergens are applied to somebody's skin to check whether there is any negative reaction

patch·work /pách wùrk/ *n.* **1.** **PATCHES SEWN TOGETHER** needlework in which patches or scraps of fabric are sewn together to make a decorative cover ○ *a patchwork quilt* **2.** **MIXTURE** something made up of many different parts

patch·y /páchee/ (**-i·er, -i·est**) *adj.* **1.** **OCCURRING IN PATCHES** occurring only in patches, rather than throughout an area, or consisting only of patches, rather than a large expanse ○ *patchy fog* **2.** **OF VARYING QUALITY** good only at times or in places —**patch·i·ly** *adv.* —**patch·i·ness** *n.*

patd. *abbr.* patented

pate /payt/ *n.* the head, especially the top of the head (*archaic or humorous*) [14thC. Origin unknown.]

pâ·té /paa táy/ *n.* a paste made from meat, fish, or vegetables, often served as an appetizer [Mid-19thC. Via French from Old French *paste* (see PASTE).]

pâ·té de foie gras /paa tày də fwaa graá/ (*plural* **pâ·tés de foie gras**) *n.* a rich pâté made from the livers of geese that are fattened specifically for this purpose [From French, literally "pâté of fatty liver"]

pa·tel·la /pə téllə/ (*plural* **-lae** /-téllee/ *or* **-las**) *n.* a kneecap (*technical*) [15thC. From Latin, literally "small shallow dish" (from the shape), from *patina* (see PATEN).] —**pa·tel·lar** *adj.*

pa·tel·late /pə téllət, pə té làyt/, **pa·tel·li·form** /pə téllə fàwrm/ *adj.* BIOL shaped like a saucer or a shallow cup

pat·en /pátt'n/, **pat·in** *n.* a shallow metal plate, often made of gold or silver, used to carry the bread at the celebration of Communion [13thC. Directly or via French *patène* from Latin *patena, patina* "shallow dish or pan," from Greek *patanē* "plate."]

pa·ten·cy /páyt'nsee/ *n.* **1.** **OBVIOUSNESS** the obvious nature of something **2.** MED **UNBLOCKED CONDITION** the naturally open and unblocked state of an artery, duct, or other tube in the body

pat·ent *n.* /pátt'nt/ **1.** **EXCLUSIVE RIGHT TO MARKET AN INVENTION** an exclusive right officially granted by a government to an inventor to make or sell an invention **2.** **DOCUMENT GRANTING A PATENT** an official document setting out the terms of a patent **3.** **INVENTION PROTECTED BY PATENT** an invention for which a patent has been granted **4.** **DOCUMENT GRANTING A RIGHT** any official document that grants a right to somebody **5.** **GOVERNMENT GRANT** a government grant that gives an individual title to public lands **6.** **LAND** the land granted by a government in a patent ■ *adj.* /páyt'nt, pátt'nt/ **1.**

CLEAR OR OBVIOUS very obvious and not needing any further explanation or not being open to doubt ○ *his patent discomfiture* **2.** LAW OPEN FOR INSPECTION used to describe a legal document that is accessible to anyone for inspection **3.** OF PATENTS relating to or dealing in patents ○ *a patent lawyer* **4.** PROTECTED BY PATENT protected by a patent from being copied or sold by somebody else **5.** MED UNBLOCKED used to describe an artery, duct, or other tube in the body that is naturally open and unblocked **6.** BOT SPREADING used to describe plant parts that spread out widely from a center ■ *vt.* /pátt'nt/ (**-ent·ed, -ent·ing, -ents**) **1.** PROTECT RIGHTS TO SOMETHING BY PATENT to obtain a patent on or for something, especially an invention **2.** GRANT A PATENT TO SOMEBODY to grant a patent to somebody for something, especially for a piece of land [14thC. Directly or via French from Latin *patent-*, the present participle stem of *patere* "to lie open."]

pat·ent·ee /pàtt'n tée/ *n.* a person or group to whom a patent has been granted

pat·ent leath·er *n.* leather that has been treated with lacquer to give it a hard, glossy surface [From the idea of protection]

pat·ent log *n.* NAUT an instrument used to measure a ship's speed or the distance it has traveled by means of fins that rotate as the instrument is dragged through the water behind the vessel [Because it was patented]

pat·ent·ly /páyt'ntlee, pátt'ntlee/ *adv.* in a way that can easily be seen or understood ○ *He was patently ill at ease.*

pat·ent med·i·cine *n.* a medicine that can be bought without a prescription and is protected by a patent or trademark

pat·ent of·fice *n.* a government office that evaluates patent claims and grants patents

pat·en·tor /pátt'ntər, pàtt'n táwr/ *n.* a person or office that grants a patent

pat·ent right *n.* an exclusive right to make or sell something that is granted to somebody by a patent

pa·ter /páytər/ *n. U.K.* somebody's father (*dated slang or humorous*) [14thC. From Latin, "father."]

pa·ter·fa·mil·i·as /pàytər fə míllee əss, paátər-/ (*plural* **pa·tres·fa·mil·i·as** /páytreez fə míllee əss, paátreez-/) *n.* a man in the role of father and head of a household [15thC. From Latin, literally "father of a family."]

pa·ter·nal /pə túrn'l/ *adj.* **1.** FATHERS OR FATHERHOOD relating to fathers or typical of a father **2.** RELATED THROUGH A FATHER being on a father's side of a family ○ *her paternal grandfather* **3.** INHERITED FROM A FATHER inherited or deriving from a father [15thC. Via late Latin *paternalis*, from, ultimately, Latin *pater* "father."] —**pa·ter·nal·ly** *adv.*

pa·ter·nal·ism /pə túrn'l ìzzəm/ *n.* a style of government or management, or an approach to personal relationships, in which the desire to help, advise, and protect may neglect individual choice and personal responsibility —**pa·ter·nal·ist** *n.* —**pa·ter·nal·is·tic** /pə tùrn'l ístik/ *adj.* —**pa·ter·nal·is·ti·cal·ly** /-ístikəlee/ *adv.*

pa·ter·ni·ty /pə túrnətee/ *n.* **1.** FATHERHOOD a man's role or status as a father **2.** ANCESTRY descent from a father ○ *The court must first determine paternity before it can reach a verdict in the case.* **3.** ORIGIN the origin or authorship of something (*literary*) [15thC. Directly or via French *paternité* from late Latin *paternitas* from, ultimately, Latin *pater* "father."]

pa·ter·ni·ty leave *n.* time off work that an employer grants to a man whose partner has just had, or is about to have, a baby

pa·ter·ni·ty suit *n.* a lawsuit brought by a woman against a man whom she claims is the father of her child and therefore liable for contributing to the child's financial support

pa·ter·ni·ty test *n.* a medical test using DNA fingerprinting or other genetic information to determine whether or not a man is the father of a particular child

pa·ter·nos·ter /paátər nóstər, pàytər nóstər/ *n.* **1.** **pa·ter·nos·ter, Pa·ter·nos·ter** CHR LORD'S PRAYER in the Roman Catholic Church, the Lord's Prayer, or a recitation of it **2.** CHR LARGE BEAD IN A ROSARY in Roman Catholicism, a large bead in a rosary, used to indicate when the Lord's Prayer is to be recited **3.** WORDS IN PRAYER OR ATTEMPTED MAGIC a set form of words used in prayer or in attempting magic **4.** NONSTOP ELEVATOR a doorless elevator in which compartments move continuously and people step on and off as they wish [Pre-12thC. From Latin *pater noster* "our father," the first two words of the Lord's Prayer.]

path /path/ *n.* **1.** TRODDEN TRACK a track that has been made by people using it continuously **2.** SURFACED TRACK a surfaced track made for walking or cycling **3.** COURSE a route along which something moves ○ *the path of the Earth's orbit around the Sun* **4.** COURSE OF ACTION a course of action or a way of living **5.** COMPUT ROUTE TO A COMPUTER FILE the route that a computer operating system follows through the directories on a disk to locate a file, or the sequence of keyed characters that identifies this route [Old English *pæth.* Ultimately from an Indo-European word meaning "to tread," which is also the ancestor of English *find, pontiff*, and *sputnik.*] ◇ **the primrose path** an enjoyable, easy way of life considered to be the route to ruin or degeneration

path. *abbr.* pathology

-path *suffix.* **1.** somebody with a particular disorder ○ *neuropath* **2.** somebody who practices a particular type of treatment ○ *osteopath* **3.** somebody who possesses a particular ability ○ *telepath* [Back-formation from -PATHY]

Pa·than /pə taán/ (*plural* **-than** *or* **-thans**) *n.* a member of a people that lives in Afghanistan, where Pathans are the largest ethnic group, and in parts of Pakistan [Mid-17thC. From Hindi *Paṭhān.*]

pa·thet·ic /pə théttik/ *adj.* **1.** PITIFUL provoking or expressing feelings of pity **2.** CONTEMPTIBLY INADEQUATE so inadequate as to be laughable or contemptible (*informal*) [Late 16thC. Via French *pathétique* from, ultimately, Greek *pathētikos* "sensitive," which was formed, ultimately, from *pathos* "feeling" (source of English *pathos*). The underlying sense is "moving, arousing emotion."]

WORD KEY: SYNONYMS

See Synonyms at ***moving.***

pa·thet·ic fal·la·cy *n.* the attribution of human characteristics to nature or to inanimate objects, as in the phrase "the angry waves"

path·find·er /páth fìndər/ *n.* somebody who discovers a route, especially through unexplored territories or uncharted areas of knowledge —**path·find·ing** *n.*

patho- *prefix.* disease ○ *pathogen* [From Greek *pathos* (see PATHOS)]

path·o·gen /páthəjən/ *n.* something that can cause disease, such as a bacterium or a virus

path·o·gen·e·sis /pàthə jénnəssiss/, **pa·thog·e·ny** /pə thójjənee/ *n.* the cause, development, and effects of a disease —**path·o·ge·net·ic** /pàthə jə néttik/ *adj.*

path·o·gen·ic /pàthə jénnik/ *adj.* **1.** CAUSING DISEASE causing disease, or able to cause disease **2.** OF THE CAUSES OF DISEASE relating to the causes and development of diseases

pa·thog·no·mon·ic /pə thògnə mónnik, pàthəgnə-/ *adj.* MED used to describe a symptom or sign that indicates almost beyond doubt the correct diagnosis of a disease [Early 17thC. From Greek *pathognōmonikos*, literally "that is a judge of disease," from *pathos* "disease" + *gnōmōn* "judge."]

pathol. *abbr.* **1.** pathological **2.** pathology

path·o·log·i·cal /pàthə lójjik'l/ *adj.* **1.** EXTREME uncontrolled or unreasonable ○ *a pathological fear of heights* **2.** MED DISEASE relating to disease or arising from disease **3.** MED OF PATHOLOGY relating to pathology or used in pathology [Late 17thC. From Greek *pathologikos*, from *pathos* "disease."] —**path·o·log·i·cal·ly** *adv.*

pa·thol·o·gist /pə thólləjist/ *n.* a scientist who is skilled in identifying the nature, origin, progress, and cause of disease, especially one who determines the cause of somebody's death by an autopsy

pa·thol·o·gy /pə thólləjee/ (*plural* **-gies**) *n.* **1.** PROCESSES OF A PARTICULAR DISEASE the processes of a particular disease, observable either with the naked eye or by microscopy, or, at a molecular level, as inferred from biochemical tests **2.** CONDITION THAT IS NOT NORMAL any condition that is a deviation from the normal **3.** STUDY OF DISEASE the scientific study of the nature, origin, progress, and cause of disease [Late 16thC. Directly or via French *pathologie* from medieval Latin *pathologia*, from Greek *pathos* "disease."]

path·o·phys·i·ol·o·gy /pàthō fìzzee óllәjee/ *n.* the disturbance of function that a disease causes in an organ, as distinct from any changes in structure that might be caused

pa·thos /páy thàwss/ *n.* **1.** QUALITY THAT AROUSES PITY the quality in something that makes people feel pity or sadness **2.** EXPRESSION OF PITY feelings of pity, especially when they are expressed in some way [Late 16thC. From Greek, "feeling, disease" (source also of English *pathetic*).]

path·way /páth wày/ *n.* **1.** PATH a path or route **2.** MED SEQUENCE OF REACTIONS a sequence of biochemical reactions involved in a metabolic process

-pathy *suffix.* **1.** disorder, disease ○ *retinopathy* **2.** system of treating medical disorders ○ *hydropathy* **3.** feeling, perception ○ *telepathy* [From Greek *-patheia*, from *pathos* (see PATHOS)] —**-pathic** *suffix.*

pa·tience /páysh'ns/ *n.* **1.** CAPACITY FOR WAITING the ability to endure waiting or delay without becoming annoyed or upset, or to persevere calmly when faced with difficulties ○ *This job needs time and patience.* **2.** ABILITY TO TOLERATE TRYING CIRCUMSTANCES the ability to tolerate being hurt, provoked, or annoyed without complaint or loss of temper **3.** *U.K.* CARDS = **solitaire** [12thC. Via French from Latin *patientia*, from *patient-* (see PATIENT).]

pa·tient /páysh'nt/ *adj.* **1.** CAPABLE OF WAITING able to endure waiting or delay without becoming annoyed or upset or to persevere calmly when faced with difficulties **2.** ABLE TO TOLERATE DIFFICULT CIRCUMSTANCES able to tolerate being hurt, provoked, or annoyed without complaint or loss of temper ■ *n.* SOMEBODY GIVEN MEDICAL TREATMENT somebody who is being given medical treatment [14thC. Via French from Latin *patient-*, the present participle stem of *pati* "to suffer" (source of English *passion*).] —**pa·tient·ly** *adv.*

pat·in *n.* = **paten**

pat·i·na /pátt'nə, pə téenə/ (*plural* **-nas** *or* **-nae** /pátt'nee, pə téenee/) *n.* **1.** THIN GREEN LAYER ON COPPER a thin layer formed by corrosion on the surface of some metals and minerals, especially the green layer that covers copper and bronze and is valued for its color **2.** SURFACE SHEEN a pleasing surface sheen on something that develops with age or frequent handling **3.** SUPERFICIAL LAYER any thin or superficial layer on something [Mid-18thC. Via Italian from Latin (see PATEN).] —**pat·i·nat·ed** /pátt'n àytəd/ *adj.*

pat·i·o /páttee ō/ (*plural* **-os**) *n.* **1.** PAVED AREA OUTSIDE A HOUSE a paved area adjoining a house, used for outdoor dining, growing plants in containers, and recreation **2.** ROOFLESS COURTYARD a roofless inner courtyard typical of a Spanish-style house [Early 19thC. From Spanish, literally "courtyard of a house," of unknown origin.]

pat·i·o doors *npl.* a pair of glazed doors in an outside wall of a house that open onto a patio

pa·tis·se·rie /pə tíssəree/ *n.* **1.** BAKE SHOP a bakery that specializes in pastries and cakes **2.** CAKES sweet pastries or cakes collectively [Late 16thC. From French *pâtisserie*, from *patissier* "pastry chef," from, ultimately, late Latin *pasta* (see PASTE).]

Pát·mos /paát mawss, pát məss, -mos/ island in the Aegean Sea, one of the Greek Dodecanese island group. It is thought to be the place where John the Evangelist wrote the biblical book of Revelation. Population: 2,650 (1995). Area: 13 sq. mi./34 sq. km.

Pat·na /pútnə/ capital city of Bihar State, northern India. Population: 916,980 (1991).

Pat·na rice /pútnə-, pátnə-/ *n.* a variety of long-grained rice [Mid-19thC. Named for PATNA, where it is grown.]

pat. off. *abbr.* patent office

Pat. Off. *abbr.* Patent Office

pat·ois /pát waa, pa twaá/ (*plural* **pat·ois**) *n.* **1.** REGIONAL DIALECT a regional form of a language, used informally and usually containing elements regarded as nonstandard **2.** JARGON the jargon used by a particular group [Mid-17thC. From French "native speech," of uncertain origin: probably from *patoier*, literally "to paw roughly," from *patte* "paw" (probable source of English *patrol*).]

pat. pend. *abbr.* patent pending

patr- *prefix.* = **patri-** (*used before vowels*)

Pa·tras /pə tráss, páttrəss/ city in Greece, on the northwestern Peloponnesian Coast, facing the Ionian Sea. It is the country's main port. Population: 152,570 (1991).

pa·tres·fa·mil·i·as plural of **paterfamilias**

patri- *prefix.* father, paternal ○ *patrilineal* [From Latin *patr-*, the stem of *pater*, and Greek *patr-*, the stem of *patēr* (see PATER)]

pa·tri·arch /páytree aàrk/ (*plural* **-archs**) *n.* **1.** HEAD OF A FAMILY a man who is the head of a family or group **2.** RESPECTED SENIOR a respected and experienced senior man within a group or family **3.** BIBLE BIBLICAL ANCESTOR a figure mentioned in the Bible considered as the ancestor of the whole human race, e.g., Adam or Noah **4.** BIBLE HEBREW LEADER any of the ancestors and religious leaders of the Hebrew people in Hebrew Scriptures, especially in the book of Genesis, e.g., Abraham, Isaac, or Jacob **5.** OLDEST MEMBER the oldest male member of something, such as a community of people or a herd of livestock **6.** FOUNDER a man who is a founder of something **7.** CHR EASTERN ORTHODOX BISHOP in the Eastern Orthodox Church, a bishop of the sees of Constantinople, Alexandria, Antioch, or Jerusalem, and also of Russia, Romania, or Serbia **8.** CHR SENIOR ROMAN CATHOLIC BISHOP in the Roman Catholic Church, a bishop next in rank to the pope **9.** CHR DIGNITARY OF THE LATTER-DAY SAINTS a high dignitary of the Latter-Day Saints with the power to invoke blessings, especially one of the Melchizedek order of priests [12thC. Directly and via French from ecclesiastical Latin, from Greek *patriarkhēs*, literally "head of a family," from *patria* "family."]

pa·tri·ar·chal /pàytree aárk'l/, **pa·tri·ar·chic** *adj.* **1.** RELATING TO A PATRIARCH relating to or held to be typical of a patriarch **2.** TYPICAL OF A CULTURE RULED BY MEN relating to or typical of a culture in which men are the most powerful members **3.** CHR RULED BY A BISHOP in Roman Catholicism, governed by a bishop —**pa·tri·ar·chal·ly** *adv.*

pa·tri·ar·chal cross *n.* a Christian cross with a second and shorter horizontal bar above the main bar

pa·tri·ar·chal·ism /pàytree aárk'l ìzzəm/ *n.* institutionalized domination by men, with women being regarded as socially or constitutionally inferior

pa·tri·ar·chate /páytree aàrkət, -aàr kàyt/ *n.* **1.** CHR OFFICE OF A CHRISTIAN PATRIARCH the office, term of office, area of jurisdiction, or residence of a patriarch of a Christian church **2.** = **patriarchy** [Early 17thC. Via medieval Latin *patriarchatus*, from, ultimately, ecclesiastical Latin *patriarcha* (see PATRIARCH).]

pa·tri·ar·chy /páytree aàrkee/ (*plural* **-chies**) *n.* **1.** SOCIAL SYSTEM IN WHICH MEN DOMINATE a social system in which men are regarded as the authority within the family and society, and in which power and possessions are passed on from father to son **2.** PATRIARCHAL SOCIETY a form of society based on a system of patriarchy [Mid-16thC. Via medieval Latin *patriarchia* from, ultimately, Greek *patriarkhēs* (see PATRIARCH).]

pa·tri·cian /pə trísh'n/ *n.* **1.** ARISTOCRATIC ROMAN a member of an aristocratic family of ancient Rome, whose privileges included the exclusive right to hold certain offices **2.** ARISTOCRAT a member of the aristocracy in any country **3.** SOMEBODY TYPICAL OF THE UPPER CLASS somebody who has the qualities and manners typical of those of the upper class **4.** NONHEREDITARY BYZANTINE TITLE a nonhereditary honorary title bestowed by Byzantine emperors on people who had been of great service to the empire ■ *adj.* **1.** OF PATRICIANS relating to patricians, or belonging to a class of patricians **2.** ARISTOCRATIC typical of aristocrats or the upper class **3.** POL OPPOSED TO DEMOCRACY against the idea that people in all social classes should have voting rights [15thC. Via French *patricien* from Latin *patricius* "of a noble father," from *pater* "father."]

pa·tri·ci·ate /pə tríshee ət, -àyt/ *n.* **1.** RANK OF PATRICIAN the position or rank of a patrician **2.** PATRICIANS AS A GROUP the social class to which patricians belong [Mid-17thC. From Latin *patriciatus*, from *patricius* (see PATRICIAN).]

pat·ri·cide /páttri sìd/ *n.* **1.** MURDER OF OWN FATHER the murder of a father by his own child or children **2.** MURDERER OF OWN FATHER somebody who murders his or her own father [Late 16thC. From Late Latin *patricidium*, from Latin *pater* "father."] —**pat·ri·cid·al** /páttri sìd'l/ *adj.*

Pat·rick /páttrik/, **St.** (389?–461?) British-born Irish churchman. He spread Christianity throughout Ireland, and reorganized the church there. He is the patron saint of Ireland. Known as **the Apostle of Ireland**

pat·ri·cli·nous *adj.* = **patroclinous**

pa·tri·lin·e·age /pàttrə línnee ij/ *n.* **1.** DESCENT ON THE FATHER'S SIDE descent traced through the male line **2.** ANCESTRAL GROUP ON THE FATHER'S SIDE a group of people who are related to each other on the father's side of a family

pat·ri·lin·e·al /pàttrə línnee əl/, **pat·ri·lin·e·ar** /-ər/ *adj.* used to describe family relationships traced through the male line, or societies in which only such relationships are recognized —**pat·ri·lin·e·al·ly** *adv.*

pat·ri·lo·cal /pàttrə lṓk'l/ *adj.* used to describe a custom in which the wife goes to live with the husband's family or people after marriage, or a society in which this custom prevails — **pat·ri·lo·cal·ly** *adv.*

pat·ri·mo·ny /páttrə mōnee/ (*plural* **-nies**) *n.* **1.** INHERITANCE FROM A FATHER an inheritance from a father or man ancestor **2.** HERITAGE the things that one generation has inherited from its ancestors **3.** CHR ESTATE BELONGING TO A CHURCH an estate or endowment that belongs to a church [14thC. Via French from Latin *patrimonium*, from *pater* "father."] —**pat·ri·mo·ni·al** /pàttrə mṓnee əl/ *adj.* —**pat·ri·mo·ni·al·ly** / ɔlcc/ *adv.*

pa·tri·ot /páytree ət, -òt/ *n.* somebody who proudly supports or defends his or her country and its way of life [Late 16thC. Via French from late Latin *patriota* "fellow countryman," from, ultimately, Greek *patris* "fatherland."] —**pa·tri·ot·ic** /pàytree óttik/ *adj.* — **pa·tri·ot·i·cal·ly** /pàytree óttikəlee/ *adv.*

pa·tri·ot·ism /páytree ə tìzzəm/ *n.* pride in or devotion to the country somebody was born in or is a citizen of

pa·tris·tic /pə trístik/, **pa·tris·ti·cal** /pə trístik'l/ *adj.* CHR relating to the early Christian writers such as St. Augustine or St. Ambrose whose works have helped to shape the Christian church. [Mid-19thC. From German *Patristik*, from Latin *pater* "father."] — **pa·tris·ti·cal·ly** *adv.*

pa·tris·tics /pə trístiks/ *n.* the study of the writings and lives of the early Christian theologians (*takes a singular verb*) [Mid-19thC. Via German *Patristik* from Latin *pater.*]

patro- *prefix.* = **patri-**

pat·ro·cli·nous /pàttrə klínəss/, **pat·ri·cli·nous** *adj.* descended or inherited from the men's line [Early 20thC. Coined from PATRI- + Greek *klinein* "to lean."]

Pa·tro·clus /pə trṓkləss, pə trókləss/ *n.* in Greek mythology, a friend of Achilles and a warrior in the Trojan War. When Hector killed Patroclus, Achilles avenged his death by killing Hector.

pa·trol /pə trṓl/ *n.* **1.** REGULAR TOUR MADE BY A GUARD a regular tour made of a place in order to guard it or to maintain order **2.** SOMEBODY CARRYING OUT A PATROL a person or group that carries out a patrol **3.** MIL MILITARY UNIT ON A MISSION a military unit sent on a particular mission, e.g., to carry out an attack or reconnaissance **4.** SCOUTING SUBDIVISION OF A SCOUT TROOP a subdivision of a troop of Boy Scouts of America or Girl Scouts of America ■ *vti.* (**-trolled, -trol·ling, -trols**) GO ON PATROL to guard or protect a place ○ *the troops patrolling the border* [Mid-17thC. Directly or via German *Patrolle* from French *patroullier*, originally "to walk through mud in a military camp," from, ultimately, Old French *patte* "paw" (source of English *patois*).]

pa·trol car *n.* = **squad car**

pa·trol·man /pə trṓlmən/ (*plural* **pa·trol·men**) *n.* a police officer who patrols a beat

pa·trol·o·gy /pə tróllәjee/ *n.* CHR the study of the writings of the Fathers of the Christian church [Early 17thC. From Greek *patēr* "father."] — **pa·tro·log·i·cal** /pàttrə lójjik'l/ *adj.* —**pa·trol·o·gist** /pə tróllәjist/ *n.*

pa·trol tor·pe·do boat *n.* full form of **PT boat**

pa·trol wag·on *n. U.S., ANZ* an enclosed police vehicle for transporting prisoners

pa·trol·wom·an /pə trṓl wòommən/ (*plural* **pa·trol·wom·en** /-wìmmin/) *n.* a policewoman who patrols a beat

pa·tron /páytrən/ *n.* **1.** SPONSOR somebody who gives money or other support to somebody or something, especially in the arts **2.** REGULAR CUSTOMER a customer, especially a regular one, of a shop or business **3.** RELIG = **patron saint 4.** HIST ROMAN SLAVE MASTER a slave master in ancient Rome who freed a slave but retained some rights over him or her [14thC. Via French from Latin *patronus*, literally "one who protects, as a father does," from *pater* "father."] —**pa·tron·al** *adj.* — **pa·tron·ly** *adj.*

WORD KEY: SYNONYMS

See Synonyms at ***backer.***

pa·tron·age /páytrənij, páttrənij/ *n.* **1.** APPOINTMENTS ASSIGNED BY A POLITICIAN the appointments or privileges that a politician can give to loyal supporters **2.** POWER TO MAKE APPOINTMENTS the political power to grant privileges or appoint people to positions **3.** REGULAR PURCHASING FROM A STORE the regular purchasing of goods from a particular store or business **4.** SUPPORT OF A PATRON the encouragement, monetary support, or influence of a patron **5.** CONDESCENDING KINDNESS support or kindness offered in a condescending way [14thC. From French, from *patron* (see PATRON).]

pa·tron·ize /páytrə nìz, páttrə nìz/ (**-ized, -iz·ing, -iz·es**) *v.* **1.** *vti.* BE CONDESCENDING TO to treat somebody as if he or she were less intelligent or knowledgeable than yourself **2.** *vt.* BE A REGULAR CUSTOMER OF to be a regular customer of a particular store or business (*formal*) **3.** *vt.* SUPPORT SOMEBODY to give money or other material support to somebody or something, especially in the arts —**pa·tron·iz·er** *n.*

pa·tron·iz·ing /páytrə nìzing, páttrə nìzing/ *adj.* treating somebody as if he or she is less intelligent or knowledgeable than yourself —**pa·tron·iz·ing·ly** *adv.*

pa·tron saint *n.* a saint who is believed to be the special guardian of somebody or something, especially a country, trade, or group of people

pat·ro·nym·ic /pàttrə nímmik/ *adj.* DERIVED FROM A MAN ANCESTOR'S NAME used to describe a name derived from a man ancestor's name, especially one that adds a prefix, e.g., "Mac-," or a suffix, e.g., "-son," to the earlier name ■ *n.* PATRONYMIC NAME a patronymic name [Early 17thC. Via late Latin *patronymicus* from Greek *patrōnumikos*, from *patrōnumos* "father's name."]

pa·troon /pə tróon/ *n.* the owner of a manorial estate in New York or New Jersey granted under Dutch rule [Mid-18thC. Via Dutch from French *patron* (see PATRON).]

pat·sy /pátsee/ (*plural* **-sies**) *n.* somebody who is easily victimized, cheated, or manipulated (*insult*) [Late 19thC. Origin uncertain: perhaps from Italian *pazzo* "fool."]

pat·ten /pátt'n/ *n.* a clog, sandal, or overshoe with a raised wooden sole to raise the wearer's feet above mud [14thC. From French *patin*, from *patte* "paw" (source of English *patrol*).]

pat·ter[1] /páttər/ *vi.* (**-tered, -ter·ing, -ters**) **1.** MAKE A QUICK TAPPING SOUND to make a quick light tapping sound on something ○ *The rain pattered against the window.* **2.** STEP LIGHTLY to move or run with short quick light steps ○ *She pattered across the floor in her pajamas.* ■ *n.* TAPPING NOISE a quick light tapping sound [Early 17thC. Formed from PAT "to hit," with the literal sense "to keep on hitting," thought to suggest the action.]

pat·ter[2] /páttər/ *n.* **1.** GLIB AND RAPID TALK the fast well-prepared talk of someone such as a comedian or salesperson **2.** JARGON the language that belongs to a specific group or class of people **3.** SMALL TALK meaningless empty chatter ■ *v.* (**-tered, -ter·ing, -ters**) **1.** *vi.* TALK QUICKLY to speak rapidly and glibly **2.** *vt.* REPEAT SOMETHING RAPIDLY to repeat something quickly in a mechanical way [14thC. Shortening of PATERNOSTER. The modern meaning "fast speech" evolved from "to mumble prayers quickly" (the way the paternoster was said in church) via "to speak quickly and glibly."]

pat·tern /páttərn/ *n.* **1.** DESIGN a repeated decorative design, e.g., on fabric ○ *a zigzag pattern* **2.** PROTOTYPE an original design or model from which exact copies can be made **3.** PLAN FOR MAKING SOMETHING a plan or model used as a guide for making something ○ *a knitting pattern* **4.** REGULAR FORM a regular or repetitive form, order, or arrangement ○ *a predictable pattern of behavior* **5.** GOOD EXAMPLE a model that is considered to be worthy of imitation **6.** REGULAR WAY OF DOING SOMETHING a regular or standard way of moving or behaving ○ *the flight patterns of birds* **7.** METALL MODEL USED FOR MAKING A MOLD a wood, plaster, or metal shape used to make a mold for casting in a foundry. The original model is often slightly oversized to allow for the contraction on cooling. **8.** SEW LENGTH OF FABRIC a length of fabric that is enough to make a garment **9.** ARMS GUNSHOTS ON TARGET marks made by shots from a gun on a target **10.** ARMS SPREAD OF SPENT PROJECTILES the dispersal of projectiles such as artillery shells and shrapnel on the ground around a target ■ *vt.*

(**-terned, -tern·ing, -terns**) **1.** MIMIC to imitate the design of something **2.** PUT A PATTERN ON to make something into, or decorate something with, a repeated decorative design [14thC. Via Old French *patron* "pattern," also "patron," from Latin *patronus* "patron." The underlying meaning is of a patron commissioning work and providing a model or example to be copied.]

pat·tern·ing /páttərning/ *n.* a design or configuration that is in accordance with a pattern

USMA Archives, West Point

George S. Patton

Pat·ton /pátt'n/, **George S.** (1885–1945) U.S. general. In World War II he commanded the Third Army in France, successfully defeating the Germans.

pat·ty /páttee/ (*plural* **-ties**) *n.* **1.** FLAT PORTION OF FOOD a small flat individual cake made from ground or chopped meat, vegetables, or other food **2.** SMALL PIE a small pie or pasty **3.** = **patty shell** [Mid-17thC. Anglicization of French *pâté*, influenced by PASTY.]

pat·ty·pan squash *n.* a variety of wheel-shaped summer squash with a ribbed edge. Latin name: *Cucurbita pepo.* [*Pattypan* from PATTY + PAN]

pat·ty shell, pat·ty (*plural* **-ties**) *n.* a decorative edible shell of baked puff pastry that is filled with other food such as meat, fish, vegetables, or fruit

pat·u·lous /páchələss/ *adj.* BOT used to describe branches that spread or expand from a central point [Early 17thC. Formed from Latin *patulus*, "standing open," from *patere* "to be open."] —**pat·u·lous·ly** *adv.* —**pat·u·lous·ness** *n.*

pat·zer /pátsər, paátsər/ *n.* somebody who plays chess badly (*insult*) [Mid-20thC. Origin uncertain: perhaps from German *patzen* "to bungle."]

Pau /pō/ city in southwestern France. It is the capital of the Pyrénées-Atlantiques Department, in Aquitaine Region. Population: 83,928 (1990).

PAU, P.A.U. *abbr.* Pan American Union

pau·ci·ty /páwssətee/ *n.* **1.** DEARTH an inadequacy or lack of something **2.** FEWNESS a small number of something [14thC. Via Old French *paucité* from Latin *paucitas*, from *paucus* "few, little."]

Paul /páwl/, **St.** (3?–62?) Early Christian missionary. He became a Christian after having a vision of Jesus Christ on the road from Jerusalem to Damascus. A major missionary of Christianity, he was also its first theologian. His life and teachings are described in the Epistles and the Acts of the Apostles in the Bible. Known as **Saul of Tarsus, Paul the Apostle** —**Paul·ine** /páw līn, -leen/ *adj.*

Paul VI, Pope (1897–1978). He became pope in 1963, and presided over the Second Vatican Council. He traveled widely to extend the Vatican's influence. Real name **Giovanni Batista Montini**

Pauld·ing /páwlding/, **James Kirke** (1778–1860) U.S. writer. His novels and plays draw on Native American material.

Pau·li ex·clu·sion prin·ci·ple /pówlee-/ *n.* the law of quantum physics stating that no two identical particles of a particular type (**fermions**) may occupy the same quantum state at the same time [Early 20thC. Named for Wolfgang *Pauli*, the Austrian-born U.S. physicist who enunciated it.]

Pau·ling /páwling/, **Linus** (1901–94) U.S. chemist and peace activist. He won a Nobel Prize in chemistry (1954) and the Nobel Peace Prize (1962) for his efforts to end nuclear testing. Full name **Linus Carl Pauling**

pau·low·ni·a /paw lṓnee ə/ (*plural* **-as** *or* **-a**) *n.* a deciduous Chinese tree of the snapdragon family, especially one that has large heart-shaped leaves and pyramid-shaped clusters of purple or white flowers. Latin name: *Paulownia tomentosa.* [Mid-19thC. From modern Latin, named for Anna *Paulowna* (1795–1865), wife of William II of the Netherlands and daughter of Tsar Paul I of Russia.]

paunch /pawnch/ *n.* **1.** BIG STOMACH a large round stomach on somebody **2.** ZOOL = **rumen** [14thC. Via Old French *pance, panche*, from Latin *panticem* "belly, bowels."]

paunch·y /páwnchee/ (**-i·er, -i·est**) *adj.* having a large round stomach —**paunch·i·ness** *n.*

pau·per /páwpər/ *n.* **1.** VERY POOR PERSON somebody who is in extreme poverty **2.** RECIPIENT OF PUBLIC AID a needy person who is eligible to receive aid from public funds [15thC. From Latin, literally "getting little," from *paucus* "little" + *parare* "to get."] —**pau·per·ism** *n.*

pau·per·ize /páwpə rīz/ (**-ized, -iz·ing, -iz·es**) *vt.* to make somebody become extremeley poor

pau·piette /pō pyét/ *n.* a piece of meat or fish that is cut or rolled out very thin, topped with a stuffing, then rolled up into a neat shape and cooked [Early 18thC. Via French, and Italian *polpetta* from Latin *pulpa*, "pulp" (source also of English *pulp*).]

pau·ro·pod /páwrə pòd/ *n.* a small eyeless invertebrate with eleven segments and nine pairs of legs. Class: Pauropoda. [Late 19thC. From modern Latin *pauropoda*, literally "small-footed," from Greek *pauros* "small" + *podos* "-footed," from its tiny feet.]

pause /pawz/ *v.* (**paused, paus·ing, paus·es**) **1.** *vi.* STOP BRIEFLY to stop doing something before carrying on ○ *He paused for a moment and then continued eating.* **2.** *vi.* STAY BRIEFLY to stop somewhere for a short time ○ *I paused to glance into a shop window.* **3.** *vi.* HESITATE to hesitate before doing or saying something **4.** *vt.* CAUSE SOMETHING TO PAUSE to cause something such as a machine to stop temporarily, e.g., by pressing a pause button ○ *Can you pause the video for a moment?* ■ *n.* **1.** BRIEF STOP a temporary break in an activity **2.** SHORT SILENCE a brief moment of silence between words, sounds, or musical notes **3.** HESITATION a brief moment of hesitation or uncertainty before something happens or is done **4.** MUSIC MUSICAL SYMBOL FOR TIME EXTENSION a musical symbol indicating that a note, chord, or pause is to be held longer than the indicated time value. It is represented by a period with an upside-down "u" above it. **5.** POETRY = **caesura** *n.* 1 **6. pause, pause button** a control on an electronic or mechanical device such as a video machine that brings it temporarily to a halt [15thC. Via Middle French, and Latin *pausa* "stopping, cessation," from, ultimately, Greek *pauein* "to stop, cease."] —**paus·al** *adj.* —**paus·er** *n.* —**paus·ing** *n.* ◇ **to give somebody pause** to make somebody to hesitate or reconsider

WORD KEY: SYNONYMS

See Synonyms at ***hesitate***.

pa·vane /pə vaán, pə ván/ *n.* **1.** DANCE STATELY DANCE a slow stately court dance performed in the 16th and 17th centuries **2.** MUSIC MUSIC FOR A PAVANE a piece of music written for a pavane, usually in slow duple meter [Mid-16thC. Via French from Italian *pavana* "Paduan," from *Pavo*, a dialect name for the city of Padua.]

AKG London

Luciano Pavarotti

Pav·a·rot·ti /pàvvə róttee/, **Luciano** (*b.* 1935) Italian tenor. Known for his great vocal power and range, he is associated with 19th-century Italian opera.

pa·ve /payv/ (**paved, pav·ing, paves**) *vt.* **1.** PROVIDE WITH A SURFACE FOR WALKING ON to cover something with brick, concrete, or other hard materials in order to make it a suitable surface for walking or traveling on **2.** BE A SURFACE FOR WALKING ON to serve as the material that is used to cover the surface of something in order to make it suitable for walking or traveling on ○ *Large stone slabs paved the path.* **3.** COVER to cover a surface with a flat, uniform material, e.g., leaves or flowers [14thC. Via Old French *paver* from Latin *pavire* "to beat, tread down."] —**pav·er** *n.* ◇ **pave the way** to prepare for and facilitate the progress of somebody or something

pa·vé /pa váy, pə váy/ *n.* a jewel setting in which small stones are set very close together so as to cover the surface of the piece and obscure the metal base [Late 19thC. From French, "paved."]

pave·ment /páyvmənt/ *n.* **1.** TRANSP PAVED SURFACE a paved surface, especially of a road **2.** INDUST MATERIAL FOR PAVEMENTS material such as concrete or stone that is used to make a pavement **3.** CIV ENG LAYERED SURFACE OF A PATH the layered structure that forms the surface of a path, road, carriageway, or aircraft runway **4.** *U.K.* = **sidewalk 5.** GEOL LEVEL AREA OF ROCK a level area of bare rock that resembles a pavement [13thC. Via Old French from Latin *pavimentum* "beaten floor," from *pavire* "to beat, tread down."]

pav·id /pávvid/ *adj.* timid and fearful (*literary*) [Mid-17thC. From Latin *pavidus*, from *pavere* "to quake with fear."]

pa·vil·ion /pə víllyən/ *n.* **1.** BUILDING OUTDOOR STRUCTURE a summer house or other often ornamental building in a park, fair, or garden used for shelter and entertainment **2.** EXHIBITION TENT a large tent or other temporary structure used for displaying or exhibiting things **3.** BIG TENT a large and often extremely ornate tent **4.** BUILDING ANNEX a detached building that forms part of a complex for a hospital or other large public building **5.** MINERALS FACET OF A GEM a facet of a brilliant-cut gem that comes below the girdle ■ *vt.* (**-ioned, -ion·ing, -ions**) **1.** SET IN A PAVILION to enclose or house something inside a pavilion **2.** ENCLOSE SOMETHING to enclose or completely surround something (*literary*) ○ *"Pavilioned in splendour, And girded with praise"* (Sir Robert Grant, *O Worship the King*; 1833) **3.** CONSTRUCT A PAVILION FOR to construct a pavilion for something [Pre-12thC. Via Old French *pavilloun, paveillon, pavilun* from Latin *papilio* "butterfly, tent," because a tent was thought to resemble a butterfly's wings.]

pav·ing /páyving/ *n.* **1.** CONSTRUCTION OF PAVED SURFACE the act of making a paved surface **2.** PAVEMENT a surface of paved stone, brick, concrete, or other material **3.** MATERIAL FOR MAKING A HARD SURFACE material such as concrete or stones used for making a firm surface, e.g., for a path or road

pav·ior /páyvyər/ *n.* a person who lays paving [15thC. From Old French *paveur*, from *paver* "to pave" (see PAVE).]

pav·iour *n.* U.K. = **pavior**

pa·vis /pávviss/ *n.* a large heavy medieval shield used to protect the whole body [14thC. Via French and Italian *pavese* from medieval Latin *pavense* "from Pavia," a city in northern Italy where these shields were originally made.]

Pav·lov /páv lov, -làwf/, **Ivan Petrovich** (1849–1936) Russian physiologist. He became famous for his studies on conditioned reflexes with dogs. He won a Nobel prize in 1904.

AKG London

Anna Pavlova

Pav·lo·va /pav lṓvə, pávləvə/, **Anna** (1882–1931) Russian ballet dancer. Admired for the poetic quality of her movement, she performed many classic roles. The solo dance "The Dying Swan" was created for her.

Pav·lo·vi·an /pav lṓvee ən, pav láwvee ən/ *adj.* **1.** AUTOMATIC produced involuntarily in response to a stimulus **2.** RELATING TO PAVLOV relating to Ivan Pavlov and his work [Mid-20thC. Named for Ivan Petrovich PAVLOV.]

Pav·lo·vi·an con·di·tion·ing *n.* = **classical conditioning**

Pa·vo /páyvō/ *n.* a constellation of the southern hemisphere lying near to the pole between Indus and Ara. It contains the bright star Peacock.

pav·o·nine /pávvə nīn/ *adj.* resembling a peacock, especially the colors and design of its tail (*literary*) [Mid-17thC. From Latin *pavoninus* "peacock."]

paw /paw/ *n.* **1.** ZOOL **ANIMAL'S FOOT** the foot of a four-legged mammal, usually having claws or nails **2.** **HUMAN HAND** a human hand, especially one that is large or clumsy (*informal*) ■ *vti.* **(pawed, paw·ing, paws) 1.** **STRIKE REPEATEDLY WITH THE HOOF** to scrape or strike something repeatedly with a paw or hoof **2.** **TOUCH CLUMSILY** to touch or caress somebody roughly or rudely with the hands [13thC. Via Old French *powe, poue, poe* from, ultimately, the prehistoric Germanic language.]

pawk·y /páwkee/ **(-i·er, -i·est)** *adj. U.K.* witty or shrewd in a dry or sly manner (*regional*) [Mid-17thC. Formed from earlier *pawk* "trick, artifice, cunning plan."] — **pawk·i·ly** *adv.* —**pawk·i·ness** *n.*

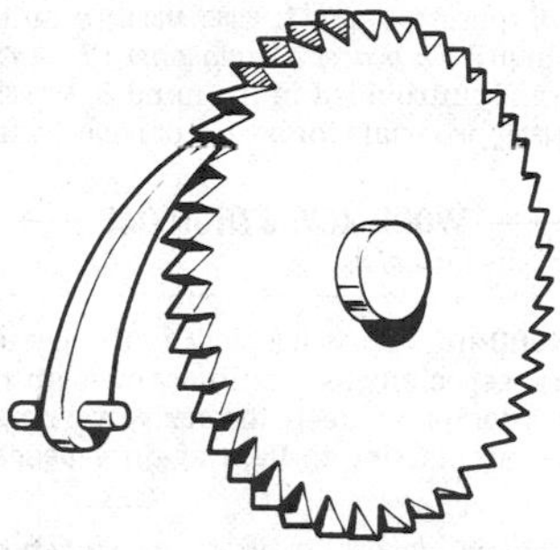

Pawl

pawl /pawl/ *n.* a hinged or pivoted catch, often spring-controlled, that is designed to catch in the teeth of a ratchet wheel to prevent reverse motion [Early 17thC. Origin uncertain: perhaps via French or Dutch *pal* "stake," from Latin *palus.*]

pawn[1] /pawn/ *vt.* **(pawned, pawn·ing, pawns) 1.** **DEPOSIT WITH A PAWNBROKER** to leave something with a pawnbroker as security against money borrowed **2.** **TO STAKE** to stake or pledge your honor, life, or word on something ■ *n.* **1.** **OBJECT DEPOSITED AS SECURITY** an object that is left as security with a pawnbroker in exchange for a loan of money **2.** **HOSTAGE** somebody who is held as security, usually as a hostage **3.** **ACT OF PAWNING** the act of pawning something [15thC. Via Old French *pan, pand, pant,* "pledge, security, plunder," from a Germanic word.] —**pawn·age** *n.* —**pawn·er** *n.*

pawn[2] /pawn/ *n.* **1.** CHESS **CHESS PIECE** a chess piece of the lowest value that can move one square forward at a time, with an optional first move of two squares. It can take other pieces by moving diagonally and can be exchanged for any other captured piece on reaching the farthest rank of the board. **2.** **MANIPULATED PERSON OR THING** somebody or something that is being used for the advantage of another person or thing [14thC. Via Anglo-Norman *poun* and Old French *peon* from medieval Latin *pedon-* "footsoldier," from Latin *ped-* "foot."]

pawn·bro·ker /páwn brōkər/ *n.* somebody who lends money at a fixed rate of interest in exchange for articles of personal property that are left as security

Paw·nee /páwnee/ (*plural* **-nee** *or* **-nees**) *n.* **1.** **MEMBER OF A NATIVE N AMERICAN PEOPLE** a member of a confederation of Native North American peoples who originally occupied lands in Nebraska and Kansas and who, apart from a small community in Oklahoma, are now mainly dispersed **2.** **PAWNEE LANGUAGE** the Caddoan language of the Pawnee people. Pawnee is spoken by about 3 thousand people. [Late 18thC. Via Canadian French *Pani* from a native North American language.]

pawn·shop /páwn shòp/ *n.* a shop where articles or personal property may be left as security in exchange for a loan of money

pawn tick·et *n.* a ticket that serves as a receipt for something that has been pawned

paw·paw /páw pàw/ *n.* BOT = **papaw, papaya**

Paw·tuck·et /paw túkət/ city in northeastern Rhode Island, at the confluence of the Blackstone and Seekonk rivers. Population: 72,644 (1990).

pax /paks, paaks/ *n.* **1.** **pax, Pax** POL **STABLE PERIOD UNDER A POWERFUL EMPIRE** a period of peace and stability under the influence of a powerful country or empire **2.** CHR **KISS IN THE CHURCH FOR PEACE** a kiss or other greeting given as a sign of peace during the Christian ceremony of Communion, especially in the Roman Catholic Mass **3.** CHR **TABLET KISSED AT CHRISTIAN COMMUNION** a tablet bearing a representation of the Crucifixion that is kissed by participants in the Christian ceremony of Communion, especially in the Roman Catholic Mass [Pre-12thC. From Latin, "peace."]

PAX *abbr.* UTIL private automatic exchange

Pax Ro·ma·na /-rō maánə/ *n.* the long period of peace and stability that existed under the Roman Empire, especially in the 2nd century A.D. [From Latin, literally "peace of the Romans"]

pax vo·bis·cum /-vō bískəm/ *interj.* peace be with you [From Latin]

pay[1] /pay/ *v.* **(paid, pay·ing, pays) 1.** *vti.* **GIVE MONEY FOR SOMETHING** to give somebody a particular amount of money for work done or for goods or services provided ○ *They were paid a small fortune for it.* **2.** *vti.* **SETTLE A DEBT** to settle a debt or other obligation **3.** *vti.* **BRING IN MONEY** to bring in a certain amount of money ○ *How much will the job pay?* **4.** *vti.* **BE PUNISHED** to be punished or suffer the bad consequences of something you have done ○ *He's paid the price for what he did.* **5.** *vt.* FIN **YIELD INTEREST** to yield a specific amount as a return on a sum of money invested ○ *The account pays 12% interest.* **6.** *vi.* **GIVE A POSITIVE RESULT** to be profitable or beneficial ○ *Crime doesn't pay.* **7.** *vt.* **BESTOW** to give something, e.g., attention or a compliment, to somebody or something ○ *pay a compliment* **8.** *vt.* **VISIT** to make a visit or call to see somebody **9.** *vt.* = **pay out 10.** *vt.* SAILING **LET GO LEEWARD** to allow a vessel to make leeway ■ *n.* **1.** **MONEY GIVEN IN RETURN FOR WORK** money that is given in return for work or services provided, especially in the form of a salary or wages **2.** **REWARD** reward, recompense, or recognition granted to somebody ■ *adj.* **1.** **NEEDING THE INSERTION OF A COIN TO FUNCTION** requiring the insertion of coins or a card in order to function ○ *pay TV* **2.** MINING **RICH IN METALS** yielding metal or minerals valuable enough to make mining them profitable [12thC. Via Old French *payer* "to satisfy, pacify" (the original sense in English, hence "to satisfy by handing over money"), from Latin *pacare,* from *pax* "peace."] ◇ **in the pay of somebody** employed by somebody, especially for a dishonest or criminal purpose ◇ **pay your dues** to gain a privilege or position through hard work or pain ◇ **pay your way** to pay your share of expenses ◇ **put paid to** to put an end to or ruin something (*informal*)

WORD KEY: SYNONYMS

See Synonyms at ***wage.***

pay back *vt.* **1.** **REPAY** to repay money that has been loaned ○ *I'll pay you back on Friday.* **2.** **TAKE REVENGE ON** to revenge yourself on somebody

pay for *vt.* to undergo the bad consequences of something you have done

pay in *vt.* to deposit money in a bank or other account

pay off *v.* **1.** *vt.* **REPAY IN FULL** to repay the full amount of a bill, debt, or other financial obligation, especially one that has been paid in installments **2.** *vt.* **BRIBE SOMEBODY** to give somebody money as a bribe, usually to prevent that person from causing trouble (*informal*) **3.** *vt.* **PAY AND LAY OFF WORKERS** to give employees or workers the money owing to them for work performed before dismissing them **4.** *vi.* **BE SUCCESSFUL** to be successful or profitable ○ *All that preparation paid off in the end.* **5.** *vt.* **TAKE REVENGE ON** to take revenge on somebody for something he or she has done to you **6.** *vi.* SAILING **MAKE LEEWAY** to make leeway

pay out *v.* **1.** *vti.* **PAY MONEY** to spend or pay money **2.** *vt.* **UNWIND** to release a rope or cable gradually by hand

pay over *vi.* to transfer money to somebody officially

pay up *vi.* to pay money that is due

pay[2] /pay/ **(payed, pay·ing, pays)** *vt.* to make a ship's hull waterproof with pitch or tar [Early 17thC. Via Old French *peier* from Latin *picare,* from *pix* "pitch."]

pay·a·ble /páy əb'l/ *adj.* **1.** **REQUIRING PAYMENT** due or needing to be paid **2.** BANKING **GRANTING PAYMENT TO SOMEBODY** requesting payment to be made to a particular person ○ *Shall I make the check payable to you or to Jean?* ■ **pay·a·bles** *npl.* FIN **LIABILITIES** money owed to a creditor or creditors

pay-as-you-go *n.* the practice or system of paying off debts as they arise

pay·back /páy bàk/ *n.* **1.** FIN **RETURN ON INVESTMENT** a financial return on an investment equaling the initial capital invested **2.** FIN **TIME REQUIRED TO RECOVER OUTLAY** the period of time required to recover the return on an initial investment **3.** **REQUITAL FOR SERVICE RENDERED** a benefit in exchange for an action or service performed (*informal*) **4.** **REVENGE** revenge or retaliation (*informal*)

pay ca·ble *n.* pay television that utilizes a cable system for transmission and reception

pay·check /páy chèk/ *n.* **1.** **SALARY CHECK** a check issued to an employee as payment for salary or wages **2.** **SALARY** wages or salary

pay·day /páy dày/ *n.* the day on which employees are paid their wages or salary

pay dirt *n.* **1.** **POTENTIALLY PROFITABLE DISCOVERY** a discovery or idea that is likely to be useful or profitable **2.** MINING **DEPOSIT WORTH MINING** gravel, sand, earth, or ore that is worth mining

pay·ee /pay eé/ *n.* a person to whom money is being paid or is due, especially in a transaction such as the payment of a check or money order

pay en·ve·lope *n.* **1.** **WAGE CONTAINER** an envelope containing an employee's wages **2.** **WAGES** wages received for a job or service

pay·er /páyr/ *n.* **1.** **SOMEBODY WHO PAYS** a person who pays somebody or something **2.** **SOMEBODY RESPONSIBLE FOR PAYMENT** the person named as responsible for the payment of a check, money order, or other financial paper when it is redeemed

pay·load /páy lōd/ *n.* **1.** FREIGHT **QUANTITY OF CARGO** the quantity of cargo or load that a plane, train, or other vehicle can carry, often expressed as weight or volume **2.** AIR **PLANE PASSENGERS AND EQUIPMENT** the passengers and instruments carried by an aircraft or spacecraft **3.** ARMS **EXPLOSIVE CHARGE** the explosive charge of a rocket or missile or the total explosive charge of the bomb load carried by an aircraft

Pay·load·er *tdmk.* a trademark for a machine with a large scoop that is used for lifting and moving earth and rubble

pay·mas·ter /páy màstər/ *n.* the person who is responsible for paying wages or salaries in a business or government organization

pay·ment /páymənt/ *n.* **1.** FIN **MONEY PAID** an amount of money that is paid or is due to be paid **2.** **REWARD** a reward or punishment given in return for something **3.** FIN **ACT OF PAYING** the act of paying money, or fact of being paid ○ *Payment will be made at the end of the month.* [14thC. From Old French *paiement,* from *payer* (see PAY).]

pay·nim /páynim/ *n.* (*archaic*) **1.** **PAGAN** a pagan **2.** **SOMEBODY NOT A CHRISTIAN** somebody who is not a Christian, especially a Muslim [13thC. Via Old French *pai(e)nime* from ecclesiastical Latin *paganismus* "paganism," from *paganus* "pagan." Originally meaning "all non-Christian countries."]

pay·off /páy àwf, páy òf/ *n.* **1.** FIN **FULL PAYMENT** full payment of a salary, wages, or a debt **2.** FIN **TIME FOR FULL PAYMENT** the time when full and final payment of a debt, salary, or wage is due **3.** **SETTLEMENT** a final settlement, reward, or reckoning **4.** **CLIMAX OF NARRATIVE** the final climax of a narrative, joke, or sequence of events **5.** **REVENGE** final retribution or revenge **6.** FIN **BRIBE** a payment made to someone as a bribe (*informal*) **7.** PSYCHOL **HIDDEN BENEFIT OF NEGATIVE BEHAVIOR** an often unconscious or hidden benefit of a negative thought pattern or action

pay·o·la /pay ṓlə/ (*plural* **-las** *informal*) *n.* a payment given in exchange for promoting a commercial product, or the system of making such payments, especially to disc jockeys [Mid-20thC. Coined from PAY + -OLA.]

pay·out /páy òwt/ *n.* the act of paying out money or the sum of money paid

pay pack·et *n. U.K.* = **pay envelope**

pay-per-view *n.* a cable or satellite television system in which individual programs can be watched for a fee

pay·phone /páy fōn/ *n.* a public telephone that operates only when coins or a card are used to pay for calls

pay·roll /páy rōl/ *n.* **1.** **LIST OF PAID EMPLOYEES** a list of employees and their salaries or wages **2.** **TOTAL PAID TO EMPLOYEES** the total sum of money to be paid to employees at a given time

pay·roll·er /páy rōllər/ *n.* an employee, often in a government department, who does little or no work, having acquired the job through connections or as reward for political favors

pay·slip /páy slìp/ *n. U.K.* = **paystub**

pay·stub /páy stùb/ *n.* a printed statement of the amount an employee is paid, showing deductions for tax, social security, and insurance

payt. *abbr.* payment

pay tel·e·vi·sion *n.* a system in which television programs are transmitted in a scrambled form that can be decoded by viewers who have paid for the appropriate equipment

pay TV *n.* = **pay television**

pay·ware /páy wàir/ *n.* commercial software as opposed to freeware or shareware

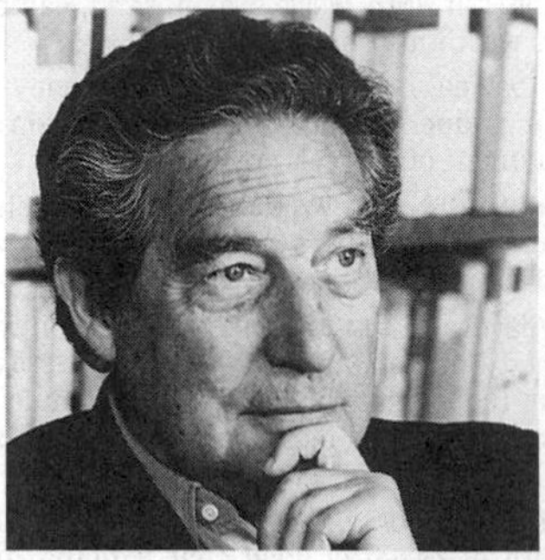

Octavio Paz

Paz /pass/**, Octavio** (1914–98) Mexican writer. Known for his poetry and essays, he won a Nobel Prize in literature in 1990.

Paz Es·tens·so·ro /pàss e sténss orō/**, Víctor** (*b.* 1907) Bolivian statesman. As president (1952–56, 1960–64, 1985–89) he instituted several reforms, including nationalization of foreign-owned tin companies.

Pb *symbol.* lead

PB, **P.B.** *abbr.* **1.** SPORTS personal best **2.** CHR prayer book

p.b. *abbr.* BASEBALL passed balls

PBB *abbr.* polybrominated biphenyl

PBJ *abbr.* peanut butter and jelly (sandwich)

PBS *abbr.* Public Broadcasting Service

PBX, **P.B.X.** *abbr.* UTIL private branch exchange

PC *abbr.* **1.** COMPUT personal computer **2.** politically correct **3.** *Can* POL Progressive Conservative **4.** Peace Corps **5.** BUSINESS professional corporation **6.** ELECTRON ENG printed circuit

pc. *abbr.* **1.** piece **2.** price

p.c.[1] *abbr.* **1.** percent **2.** postcard **3.** PHARM after meals (*used in prescriptions*)

p.c.[2], **p/c** *abbr.* **1.** petty cash **2.** price current

P.C. *abbr.* **1.** MIL Past Commander **2.** MIL Post Commander **3.** POL Privy Council

PCB *n.* a compound derived from biphenyl and containing chlorine that is used in electrical insulators, flame retardants, and plasticizers. PCB is a hazardous pollutant that is difficult to dispose of safely and has been banned in several countries. Full form **polychlorinated biphenyl**

PCI *n.* a specification for extending the internal circuitry, or bus, that transmits data from one part of a computer to another. The PCI bus allows the expansion of a computer by inserting printed circuit boards, or expansion boards, into sockets inside the computer called slots. Full form **peripheral component interconnect local bus**

p.c.m. *abbr.* UTIL pulse code modulation

PCMCIA *n.* a specification for extending the internal circuitry, or bus, that transmits data from one part of a computer to another. Originally designed for adding memory to portable computers, the PCMCIA bus is used to connect credit-card-sized peripheral devices as well. Full form **Personal Computer Memory Card Interface Adapter**

PCP *abbr.* **1.** CHEM phencyclidine **2.** MED pneumocystis carinii pneumonia **3.** *Can* POL Progressive Conservative Party

PCR *abbr.* polymerase chain reaction

pct. *abbr.* percent

Pd *symbol.* palladium

pd. *abbr.* paid

p.d., **P.D.** *abbr.* **1.** PHYS potential difference **2.** per diem

P.D. *abbr.* **1.** police department **2.** MAIL postal district

PDA *abbr.* Personal Digital Assistant

Pd.B. *abbr.* Bachelor of Pedagogy [Latin, *Pedagogiae Baccalaureus*]

Pd.D. *abbr.* Doctor of Pedagogy [Latin, *Pedagogiae Doctor*]

PDL *abbr.* page description language

Pd.M. *abbr.* Master of Pedagogy [Latin, *Pedagogiae Magister*]

pdq *adv.* at once or immediately (*informal*) Full form **pretty damn quick**

P-D ra·tio *abbr.* STOCK EXCH price-dividend ratio

PDT, **P.D.T.** *abbr.* Pacific Daylight Time

pe /pay/ *n.* the 17th letter of the Hebrew alphabet, represented in the English alphabet as "p" or "f." See table at **alphabet**

p.e. *abbr.* printer's error

P.E. *abbr.* **1.** EDUC physical education **2.** PHYS potential energy **3.** STATS probable error **4.** CHR Protestant Episcopal **5.** ENG professional engineer

P/E *abbr.* price-earnings

Pea

pea /pee/ *n.* **1.** FOOD **SEED AS A VEGETABLE** a round green seed that grows in a pod, eaten as a vegetable **2.** PLANTS **LEGUMINOUS PLANT WITH EDIBLE SEEDS** an annual vine of Europe and Asia of the legume family with compound leaves and small white flowers that is widely grown for its peas, contained in pods. Latin name: *Pisum sativum*. **3.** PLANTS **PLANT RELATED TO THE PEA** any of various plants related to or similar to the pea, such as the chickpea, sweetpea, or cowpea **4.** **SOMETHING RESEMBLING A PEA** something resembling a pea in form or size ■ **peas** *npl.* FOOD **PEA PODS** the unopened immature pods of the pea, containing the seeds and used as a vegetable [Mid-17thC. Back-formation from *pease* (originally the singular form, wrongly thought to be a plural), which came from Latin *pisa*.]

pea bean *n.* = **navy bean**

Pea·bod·y /pée bodee, -bədee/ city in northeastern Massachusetts, northeast of Boston and northwest of Marblehead. Population: 48,365 (1996).

Pea·bod·y /pée bodee/**, George** (1795–1869) U.S. businessman and philanthropist. He funded many educational institutions such as Baltimore's Peabody Institute and Yale's Peabody Museum, as well as new houses for workers in London.

peace /peess/ *n.* **1.** **FREEDOM FROM WAR** freedom from war, or the time when a war or conflict ends **2.** **MENTAL CALM** a state of mental calm and serenity, with no anxiety **3.** **PEACE TREATY** a treaty agreeing to an end of hostilities between two warring parties **4.** **LAW AND ORDER** the absence of violence or other disturbances within a state ○ *Peace reigned throughout the land.* **5.** **STATE OF HARMONY** freedom from conflict or disagreement among people or groups of people ■ *interj.* **BE CALM OR SILENT** used to tell somebody to be calm or silent or as a greeting or farewell (*archaic*) [12thC. Via Anglo-Norman *pes* from Latin *pax* "peace, peace treaty," which is also the source of English *appease, pacific*, and *pay*.] ◇ **at peace 1.** in a state of friendship and freedom from conflict **2.** dead (*used euphemistically*) **3.** in a state of calm and serenity ◇ **hold your peace** to refrain from speaking (*dated*) ◇ **keep the peace** to refrain from or prevent conflict or violence ◇ **make peace** to bring a disagreement or war to an end ◇ **make your peace with somebody** to become friends with somebody again after an argument

Peace /peess/ river in Canada, and an outlet of Lake Williston, British Columbia. It flows east into Alberta, joining the Slave River to discharge into Lake Athabasca. Length: 1,195 mi./1,923 km.

peace·a·ble /péessəb'l/ *adj.* **1.** **DISPOSED TOWARD PEACE** inclined toward peace and avoiding contentious situations **2.** **TRANQUIL** tranquil and free from strife and disorder [14thC. Formed from PEACE, or via French *peisible* and *plaisible* from late Latin *placibilis* "pleasing," from *placere* "to please."] —**peace·a·ble·ness** *n.* — **peace·a·bly** *adv.*

Peace Corps *n.* a United States government organization that trains volunteers to work in developing countries on educational and agricultural projects

peace·ful /péessfəl/ *adj.* **1.** **QUIET AND CALM** quiet, calm, and tranquil ○ *a peaceful atmosphere* **2.** **MENTALLY CALM** serene and untroubled in the mind **3.** **APPROPRIATE FOR PEACETIME** appropriate for a time of peace rather than war

WORD KEY: SYNONYMS

See Synonyms at ***calm***.

peace·keep·ing /péess kèeping/ *n.* the preservation of peace, especially as a military mission in which troops attempt to keep formerly warring armed forces from starting to fight again —**peace·keep·er** *n.*

peace·mak·er /péess màykər/ *n.* somebody who brings about peace and reconciliation between others —**peace·mak·ing** *n.*

peace·nik /péess nìk/ *n.* a pacifist, especially somebody who opposed the Vietnam War (*dated informal*) [Mid-20thC. Coined from PEACE + -NIK.]

peace of·fer·ing *n.* something done for or given to an enemy or somebody you have quarrelled with in the hope of bringing about a reconciliation

peace of·fi·cer *n.* a law enforcement officer such as a justice of the peace, police officer, or sheriff, whose main duty is to preserve public order

peace pipe *n.* a long-stemmed ceremonial pipe used by some Native North American peoples

peace sign *n.* a sign used to indicate peaceful intentions, made by holding the palm upright and outward and forming a V with the middle and index fingers

peace·time /péess tīm/ *n.* a time when there is no war

Peach

peach[1] /peech/ *n.* **1.** FOOD **SWEET ROUND FRUIT WITH STONE** sweet round juicy fruit with yellow flesh, a single stone, and a soft downy orange-yellow skin **2.** TREES **SMALL TREE WITH EDIBLE FRUIT** a small tree that originated in China and has pink flowers, is widely grown in temperate regions, and bears peaches as fruit. Latin name: *Prunus persica*. **3.** **SOMEBODY OR SOMETHING EXCELLENT** somebody or something that is particularly good or pleasing (*informal*) ○ *That was a peach of a throw!* **4.** COLORS **CREAMY ORANGE-YELLOW COLOR** a creamy orange color tinged with yellow, like a ripe peach ■ *adj.* **CREAMY ORANGE** of a creamy orange color tinged with yellow [13thC. Via Old French from medieval Latin *persica*, an alteration of earlier *persicum*, from *mālum Persicum*, literally "Persian apple," because it first became known in Europe through that country.]

peach[2] /peech/ (**peached, peach·ing, peach·es**) *vi.* to inform against somebody, especially an accomplice (*dated informal*) [15thC. Shortening of earlier *appeach*, via Anglo-Norman from late Latin *impedicare* (see IMPEACH).] —**peach·er** *n.*

peach mel·ba *n.* a dessert made with fresh or canned peaches, vanilla ice cream, and a raspberry sauce

peach palm *n.* a dense spiny Amazonian palm with an edible heart. Latin name: *Bactris gasipaes.*

peach·y /péechee/ (**-i·er, -i·est**) *adj.* **1. EXCELLENT** excellent or wonderful (*informal*) **2. RESEMBLING A PEACH** resembling a peach in color, taste, or texture [Late 16thC. Formed from PEACH[1].] —**peach·i·ly** *adv.* —**peach·i·ness** *n.*

pea coat *n.* = **pea jacket**

Peacock

pea·cock /pée kòk/ *n.* **1. MALE PEAFOWL** a male peafowl with a crested head and a large fan-shaped tail with brilliantly colored blue and green spots **2. PEAFOWL** a peafowl, either male or female **3. VAIN PERSON** somebody who is very vain, and who shows this especially in the way he or she behaves and dresses ■ *vi.* (**-cocked, -cock·ing, -cocks**) **SHOW OFF** to strut about in a vain and self-important way (*archaic*) [14thC. *Pea* originally an Old English word meaning "peacock," from Latin *pavo*.] —**pea·cock·ish** *adj.*

pea·cock blue *adj.* of a brilliant greenish-blue color, like the plumage on a peacock's breast and neck —**pea·cock blue** *n.*

pea·cock but·ter·fly *n.* a European butterfly with bold iridescent colors that makes communal nests. Latin name: *Nymphalis io.*

pea·cock ore *n.* a copper ore such as bornite or chalcopyrite that becomes iridescent as it tarnishes

pea·fowl /pée fòwl/ (*plural* **-fowl** *or* **-fowls**) *n.* either of two large pheasants native to India and Southeast Asia. The male holds up its brilliant iridescent tail like a fan in courtship displays. Latin name: *Pavo cristatus* and *Pavo muticus.* [Early 19thC. From "pea" (see PEACOCK).]

peag /peeg/ *n.* = **wampum** *n.* 1 [Early 17thC. Shortening of WAMPUMPEAG.]

pea green *adj.* of a medium yellowish-green color —**pea green** *n.*

pea·hen /pée hèn/ *n.* a female peafowl with much plainer plumage than the peacock [14thC. From "pea" (see PEACOCK).]

pea jack·et *n.* a heavy double-breasted jacket or short coat, made of mohair or thick wool and originally worn by sailors [By folk etymology from Dutch *pijjakker, pijjekker*, literally "coarse cloth jacket," from *pij* "coarse cloth" (by association with PEA) + *jekker* "jacket"]

peak[1] /peek/ *n.* **1. MOUNTAIN TOP** the pointed summit of a mountain **2. MOUNTAIN** a mountain with a pointed summit **3. HIGHEST POINT** the point of greatest success, development, or strength of a process or activity ○ *She's at the peak of her career.* **4. POINTED PART** a sharp projecting pointed part of something, e.g., the brim of a cap **5. TOP OF CURVE** the highest point in a curve, especially the curve of a wave **6.** HAIR = **widow's peak** ■ *n., n.* PHYS **MAXIMUM VALUE OF QUANTITY** a point at which a variable physical quantity such as temperature or voltage changes from rapidly increasing to rapidly decreasing, or the value of the quantity at such a point ■ *n.* **1.** NAUT **EXTREME END OF HULL** narrow part at the front or back end of a boat's hull **2.** SAILING **CORNER OF FORE-AND-AFT SAIL** the top rear corner of a fore-and-aft sail **3.** SAILING **GAFF END** the outermost end of a gaff sail ■ *v.* (**peaked, peak·ing, peaks**) **1.** *vi.* **REACH HIGHEST POINT** to reach the point of greatest success, development, intensity, or strength ○ *Sales peaked around July.* **2.** *vi.* **FORM PEAK** to form a peak or peaks ○ *The waves peaked as the storm grew.* **3.** *vt.* **CAUSE PEAK IN** to cause something to come to a high point or peak ■ *adj.* **1. HIGHEST** being at a maximum or highest point ○ *peak efficiency* **2. OF GREATEST USE** relating to the maximum use of something or the maximum demand on something ○ *peak viewing time* [Mid-16thC. Back-formation from PEAKED, a variant of PICKED "pointed."]

peak[2] /peek/ (**peaked, peak·ing, peaks**) *vi.* to become thin, pale, and sickly in appearance (*archaic*) [Early 16thC. Origin unknown.] —**peak·ish** *adj.*

peaked[1] /peekt, péekəd/ *adj.* having a peak or point —**peaked·ness** /péekədnəss/ *n.*

peaked[2] /peekt/ *adj.* thin, pale, and sickly in appearance

peak load *n.* the maximum instantaneous rate of power consumption in a load circuit

peak·y /péekee/ (**-i·er, -i·est**) *adj. U.K.* = **peaked** [Early 19thC. Formed from PEAK "to be sickly."]

peal /peel/ *n.* **1.** MUSIC **RINGING OF BELLS** a ringing of bells, especially a change or series of changes rung on bells **2.** MUSIC **GROUP OF BELLS** a set of tuned bells **3. NOISY OUTBURST** a loud repetitive sound, e.g., of thunder or laughter ■ *v.* (**pealed, peal·ing, peals**) **1.** *vti.* MUSIC **RING** to ring a bell loudly and sonorously, or to be rung in this way **2.** *vt.* **SAY LOUDLY** to say something loudly and sonorously [14thC. Variant of APPEAL "call, request."]

Peale /peel/, **Charles Willson** (1741–1827) U.S. artist. He was the most prominent U.S. portraitist of his time.

pe·an *n.* = **paean**

Peanut

pea·nut /pée nùt/ *n.* **1.** FOOD **OILY EDIBLE SEED** an oily edible seed with a thin shell that grows underground and is a source of vegetable oil **2.** PLANTS **PLANT PRODUCING PEANUTS** a low-growing annual plant of the legume family whose seeds are contained in pods that are forced underground as they grow. Latin name: *Arachis hypogaea.* **3. OFFENSIVE TERM** an offensive term for a short or insignificant person (*informal offensive*) **4. PIECE OF PACKING MATERIAL** a small piece of polystyrene or similar material used in quantity to protect items during packaging and shipment ■ **pea·nuts** *npl.* **SMALL AMOUNT OF MONEY** a very small amount of money, especially when smaller than would be expected (*informal*) ○ *They're paid peanuts!* ■ *adj.* **UNIMPORTANT** petty and insignificant (*informal*) [Early 19thC. From PEA (from the similarity of peanuts to peas, because peanuts also grow in a pod) + NUT.]

pea·nut brit·tle *n.* candy made of hard toffee and peanuts

pea·nut but·ter *n.* an oily paste made from ground roasted peanuts and usually spread on bread or used in cooking

pea·nut oil *n.* a combustible yellow oil extracted from peanuts, used in cooking, medicine, and in soaps

pear /pair/ *n.* **1.** FOOD **GREEN-SKINNED FRUIT** a sweet juicy fruit with firm white flesh, a usually green skin, and an approximately oval shape, larger and rounded at the base and tapering toward the stem **2.** TREES **TREE BEARING PEARS** a tree of the rose family that has shiny leaves and bears pears as fruit. Latin name: *Pyrus communis.* [Pre-12thC. Via assumed Vulgar Latin *pira* from, ultimately, Latin *pirum*.]

pearl[1] /purl/ *n.* **1. GEM FORMED IN MOLLUSK** a small lustrous sphere of calcium carbonate that forms around a grain of sand in a mollusk such as an oyster, and is valued as a gem **2.** = **mother-of-pearl 3. SOMEBODY OR SOMETHING MUCH VALUED** somebody or something highly esteemed or valued **4.** COLORS **PALE GRAYISH-WHITE COLOR** a pale grayish-white color tinged with blue ■ *adj.* COLORS **PALE GRAYISH-WHITE** of a pale grayish-white color tinged with blue ■ *v.* (**pearled, pearl·ing, pearls**) **1.** *vi.* **HARVEST PEARLS** to fish or dive for pearls **2.** *vi.* **MAKE BEADS** to form a pearl color or pearl-shaped drops **3.** *vt.* **DECORATE WITH PEARLS** to decorate something with pearls or with things that resemble pearls **4.** *vt.* **MAKE SOMETHING INTO SHAPE OF PEARLS** to make something into the shape or color of pearls [14thC. Via Old French from assumed Vulgar Latin *pernula*, literally "little mollusk whose feet resemble hams in shape," from Latin *perna*, "leg, ham, ham-shaped mollusk."]

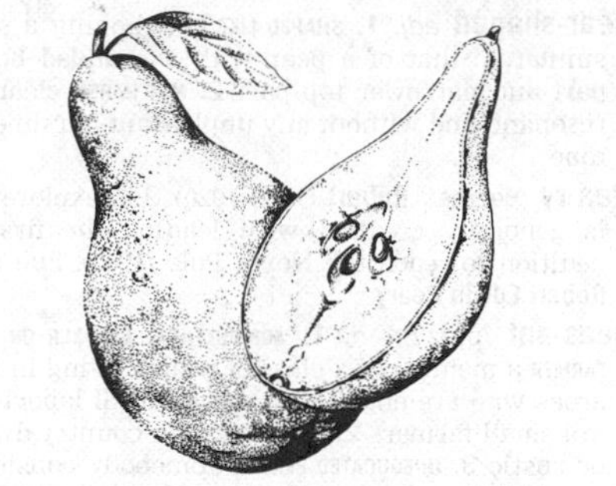

Pear

pearl[2] /purl/ (**pearled, pearl·ing, pearls**) *n.* = **purl**[1] *n.* 2, **purl**[1] *n.* 3

pearl ash *n.* the commercial form of potassium carbonate

pearl bar·ley *n.* grains of barley that have been polished and are used in soups and stews

pearl·er /púrrlər/ *n.* **1. PEARL DIVER OR TRADER** somebody who dives for pearls or trades in them **2. BOAT USED FOR PEARL DIVING** a boat used for pearl diving or for trading pearls

pearl·es·cent /pur léss'nt/ *adj.* with a lustrous surface like a pearl [Mid-20thC. Coined from PEARL and -ESCENT.]

pearl es·sence *n.* a silvery translucent substance extracted from the scales of fish such as herring, used to make artificial pearls, lacquers, and other products

pearl gray *adj.* of a pale blue-gray color —**pearl gray** *n.*

Pearl Har·bor /pùrl-/ inlet in Hawaii, on Oahu Island. The Japanese attack on it in 1941 prompted the United States' entry into World War II.

pearl·ite /púr lìt/ *n.* a microstructure of steel or cast iron made up of bands (**lamellae**) of pure iron (**ferrite**) and iron carbide (**cementite**) [Late 19thC. Coined from PEARL + -ITE.] —**pearl·it·ic** /pur líttik/ *adj.*

pearl·ized /púr lìzd/ *adj.* having a pearly iridescent luster

pearl mil·let *n.* a tall cereal grass widely grown for its whitish seeds. Latin name: *Pennisetum americanum.*

pearl on·ion *n.* a very small white onion that is often pickled

pearl oys·ter *n.* a tropical marine mollusk that is a source of pearls. Genus: *Pinctada.*

pearl·y /púrlee/ (**-i·er, -i·est**) *adj.* **1. RESEMBLING PEARL** resembling pearls or mother-of-pearl, particularly in having an iridescent luster **2. DECORATED WITH PEARLS** adorned or decorated with pearls or mother-of-pearl **3.** COLORS **PALE GRAYISH-WHITE** of a pale grayish-white color tinged with blue —**pearl·i·ness** *n.*

pearl·y ev·er·last·ing *n.* a plant with woolly leaves and white flower heads. Latin name: *Anaphalis margaritacea.*

Pearl·y Gates *npl.* in Christianity, the gates of Heaven (*informal*)

pearl·y nau·ti·lus *n.* a mollusk that has a spiral pearl-colored shell divided internally by cross walls into a series of chambers. Genus: *Nautilus.* ◊ **paper nautilus** [From the color of its shell]

pear psyl·la /-síllə/ (*plural* **pear psyl·las** *or* **pear psyl·la**) *n.* a jumping plant louse, originally from Europe but now a widespread pest in North America, that sucks the sap from pear trees. Latin name: *Psylla pyricola.*

pear-shaped *adj.* **1. SHAPED LIKE PEAR** having a shape similar to that of a pear with a rounded bottom part and narrower top part **2. NOT HARSH** clear and resonant, and without any unpleasant harshness of tone

Pea·ry /peeree/, **Robert** (1856–1920) U.S. explorer. He is generally credited with leading the first expedition to reach the North Pole (1909). Full name **Robert Edwin Peary**

peas·ant /pézz'nt/ *n.* **1. AGRICULTURAL LABORER OR SMALL FARMER** a member of a class of people living in rural areas who are engaged in agricultural laboring or are small farmers **2. RURAL PERSON** a country-dweller or rustic **3. UNEDUCATED PERSON** somebody considered to be ill-mannered or uneducated (*informal offensive*) [15thC. Via Anglo-Norman *paisant* and Old French *païsant, paisenc* "inhabitant of rural district," from, ultimately, Latin *pagus* "rural district."]

peas·ant·ry /pézz'ntree/ *n.* **1. PEASANTS** peasants as a class in society **2. RANK OR CHARACTERISTICS OF PEASANTS** the status or characteristic behavior of a peasant

pease·cod /peez kòd/ *n.* a pea pod (*archaic*) [14thC. From "pease," an earlier form of PEA + COD "pod, husk."]

pea·shoot·er /pee shootər/ *n.* a toy in the form of a pipe through which dried peas or similar small pellets can be blown

pea soup *n.* **1. SOUP WITH PEAS** soup made with fresh or dried peas **2. FOG** an extremely dense fog (*informal*)

pea·soup·er /pee soopər/ *n.* **1.** *U.K.* = **pea soup** (*informal*) **2.** *Can* **OFFENSIVE TERM** an offensive term for a French Canadian (*slang offensive*) [Late 19thC. Because the thick yellow fog resembles pea soup.]

peat /peet/ *n.* **1. DEPOSIT OF ORGANIC DEBRIS** a compacted deposit of partially decomposed organic debris, usually saturated with water **2. PIECE OF PEAT USED FOR FUEL** a cut and dried piece of peat used as fuel [14thC. Via Anglo-Latin from a Celtic word meaning "bit, part, piece."] —**peat·y** *adj.*

peat bog *n.* an area of land composed primarily of peat

peat moss *n.* a moss that grows in wet places, and whose partially decomposed remains form peat. Genus: *Sphagnum.*

peau de soie /pō də swaa/ *n.* a silk or artificial fabric such as rayon with a smooth texture and a fine grainy or ribbed surface [From French, literally "silk skin"]

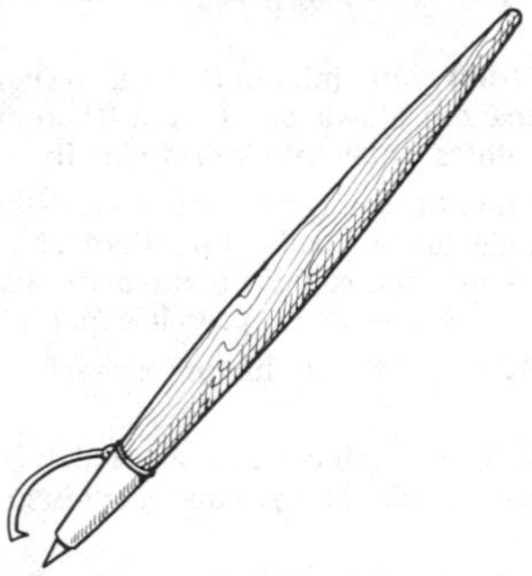

Peavey

pea·vey /peevee/ (*plural* **-veys**), **pea·vy** (*plural* **-vies**) *n.* a pointed lever with a hinged hook, used for handling logs [Late 19thC. Named for Joseph *Peavey*, its U.S. inventor.]

peb·ble /pébb'l/ *n.* **1. SMALL ROUND STONE** a small rounded stone that has been worn smooth by erosion **2.** GEOL **ROCK FRAGMENT** a rock fragment with a diameter between 0.16 in./4 mm and 2.51 in./64 mm **3.** GEOL **ROCK CRYSTAL USED FOR LENSES** a colorless form of quartz, or rock crystal, used for making lenses **4.** OPTICS **CRYSTAL LENS** a lens made from colorless rock crystal **5. IRREGULAR SURFACE** a rough grainy surface, especially of leather ■ *adj.* **THICK AND DISTORTING** being or containing lenses that make the eyes of the wearer seem very large and distorted (*informal*) ○ *wearing thick pebble glasses* ■ *vt.* (**-bled, -bling, -bles**) **1. COVER WITH PEBBLES** to cover or pave something with pebbles **2. GIVE IRREGULAR SURFACE TO** to give a rough grainy surface to something [Old English *papolstān, popelstān.* Ultimate origin unknown.]

pec /pek/ *n.* a pectoral muscle (*informal*) (*often used in the plural*) ○ *excercises to strengthen the pecs* [Mid-20thC. Shortening.]

pe·can /pi kaan, -kán, pee kàn/ *n.* **1.** FOOD **EDIBLE NUT** an edible nut with a thin dark red shell **2.** TREES **TREE WITH EDIBLE NUT** a large hickory tree with deeply furrowed bark and hard brittle wood, grown in the United States and Mexico for its nuts. Latin name: *Carya illinoensis.* [Late 18thC. Via French *pacane* from Algonquian *pakani.*]

pec·ca·ble /pékəb'l/ *adj.* open or prone to sin or temptation (*formal*) [Early 17thC. Via French from medieval Latin *peccabilis*, from Latin *peccare* "to sin."] —**pec·ca·bil·i·ty** /pèkə bíllətee/ *n.*

pec·ca·dil·lo /pèkə díllō/ (*plural* **-loes** *or* **-los**) *n.* a petty or unimportant offense or fault [Late 16thC. Via Spanish "little fault or sin," from *peccado* "sin," from, ultimately, Latin *peccare* "to sin."]

pec·cant /pékənt/ *adj.* (*formal*) **1. SINFUL** guilty of a sin **2. WILLFUL** violating a rule or practice [Late 16thC. From Latin *peccant-*, the present participle stem of *peccare* "to sin."] —**pec·can·cy** *n.* —**pec·cant·ly** *adv.*

pec·ca·ry /pékəree/ (*plural* **-ries**) *n.* a wild pig of Mexico and South America with a rudimentary tail and small tusks on the upper jaw that grow downward. Genus: *Tayassu.* [Early 17thC. From Carib *pakira.*]

pec·ca·vi /pə kaavee/ (*plural* **-vis**) *n.* an admission of sin or guilt (*literary*) [Early 16thC. From Latin, literally "I have sinned."]

Pe·cho·ra /pə káwrə/ river in northwestern European Russia, flowing northward to the Barents Sea. Length: 1,124 mi./1,809 km.

peck[1] /pek/ *v.* (**pecked, peck·ing, pecks**) **1.** *vt.* **PICK UP WITH BEAK** to take small bits of food using a beak **2.** *vti.* **STRIKE WITH BEAK** to strike somebody or something with a beak **3.** *vt.* **MAKE HOLE IN** to make a hole in something by repeatedly striking it with a beak **4.** *vi.* **NIBBLE** to eat small quantities of food with little interest ○ *She just pecked at her food.* **5.** *vt.* **KISS LIGHTLY** to kiss somebody lightly and briefly **6.** *vi.* **NAG** to nag or carp (*informal*) ■ *n.* **1. SWIFT BITE WITH BEAK** a quick light stroke, blow, or bite with a beak **2. HOLE MADE BY BEAK** a mark or hole made by a beak or pointed object **3. LIGHT KISS** a quick light kiss (*informal*) [14thC. Origin uncertain: probably originally a variant of PICK "to poke, pierce," perhaps influenced by Middle Low German *pekken* "to peck."]

peck[2] /pek/ *n.* **1. UNIT OF DRY MEASURE** a unit of dry measure equal to 8 quarts/7.57 liters **2. CONTAINER FOR PECK** a container that holds a peck of material **3. LARGE QUANTITY** a large amount or number of something (*informal*) [13thC. Origin unknown.]

peck·er /pékər/ *n.* **1. SOMETHING THAT PECKS** something that pecks, especially a woodpecker **2. PENIS** a penis (*slang*) (*sometimes considered offensive*) ◇ **keep your pecker up** *U.K.* used to tell somebody to keep his or her spirits up (*informal*)

peck·er·wood /pékər wòod/ *n. Southeast U.S.* **1. WOODPECKER** a woodpecker **2. OFFENSIVE TERM** an offensive term for a poor Caucasian person from a rural area (*slang offensive*) [Mid-19thC. Alteration of WOODPECKER.]

peck·ing or·der *n.* **1.** SOC SCI **SOCIAL HIERARCHY** a social hierarchy in which some members of a group are established as superior to others **2.** BIRDS **SOCIAL HIERARCHY AMONG FOWL** a social hierarchy among domestic fowl in which each member maintains its place by dominance over the lower members ["Pecking" formed from PECK "to strike with beak"]

peck·ish /pékish/ *adj.* (*informal*) **1. CRANKY** somewhat irritable or in a bad mood **2.** *U.K.* **HUNGRY** slightly hungry

Peck·sniff·i·an /pek sníffee ən/ *adj.* hypocritical and making a show of having high moral principles [Mid-19thC. Named for *Pecksniff*, a highly hypocritical character in *Martin Chuzzlewit* (1844) by Charles Dickens.]

pe·co·ri·no /pèkə reenō/ (*plural* **-nos**) *n.* a hard pungent Italian cheese made from ewe's milk [Mid-20thC. From Italian *pecora* "sheep."]

Pe·cos /páykəss/ river in the United States, flowing from New Mexico into Texas, where it joins the Rio Grande. Length: 926 mi./1,490 km.

Pécs /paych/ town and capital of Baranya County, southwestern Hungary, situated about 105 mi./170 km southwest of Budapest. Population: 172,177 (1994).

pec·tate /pék tàyt/ *n.* a salt or ester of pectic acid [Mid-19thC. Formed from PECTIC ACID.]

pec·tic ac·id *n.* a gelatinous acid that does not dissolve in water and is formed from certain esters of pectin. Formula: $C_{17}H_{24}O_{16}$. [*Pectic* from Greek *pēktikos*, from *pēktos* "curdled, congealed," which was formed in turn from *pēgnunai* "to make solid"]

pec·tin /péktin/ *n.* a soluble chemical substance found mainly in the rinds of citrus fruits that binds cells together and is used to gel foods and various commercial products [Mid-19thC. Via French from Greek *pektos* (see PECTIC ACID).] —**pec·tic** *adj.* —**pec·tin·ous** *adj.* —**pec·ti·na·ceous** /-náyshəss/ *adj.*

pec·ti·nate /pékti nàyt/, **pec·ti·nat·ed** /-təd/ *adj.* ZOOL having projections that resemble the teeth of a comb —**pec·ti·na·tion** /pèkti náysh'n/ *n.*

pec·tin·es·ter·ase /pèkti néstə ràyss, -ràyz/ *n.* an enzyme that catalyzes the hydrolytic breakdown of pectin into pectic acid and methanol [Mid-20thC. Coined from PECTIN + -ESTERASE.]

pec·tize /pék tìz/ (**-tized, -tiz·ing, -tiz·es**) *vt.* to change something into a gel —**pec·ti·za·ble** *adj.* —**pec·ti·za·tion** /pèkti záysh'n/ *n.*

pec·to·ral /péktərəl/ *adj.* **1.** ANAT **OF THE CHEST** relating to or located in or on the chest **2. WORN ON CHEST** worn on the chest ○ *a pectoral medal* ■ *n.* **1.** ANAT **CHEST MUSCLE** a chest muscle or organ ○ *an exercise for the pectorals* **2.** ZOOL = **pectoral fin 3. BREASTPLATE** something that is worn on the chest as a decoration or ornament **4.** MED **CHEST MEDICINE** a medicine for chest or respiratory disorders (*dated*) [15thC. Via French *pectorale* "something worn on the chest," from Latin *pectorale* "breastplate" and *pectoralis* "of the chest," which were formed from *pectus* "chest."] —**pec·tor·al·ly** *adv.*

pec·to·ral arch *n.* ZOOL = **pectoral girdle**

pec·to·ral fin *n.* either of a pair of fins of a fish located either directly behind the gill openings or below them

pec·to·ral gir·dle *n.* the part of the skeleton of a vertebrate animal that consists of bone or cartilage and provides attachment and support for the forelimbs

pec·to·ral mus·cle *n.* any of four flat muscles, two on each side of the front of the chest, that help to move the upper arm and shoulder. The large fan-shaped pectoralis major pulls the arm forward across the chest, while the pectoralis minor beneath it depresses the shoulder.

pec·to·ral sand·pi·per *n.* a rare North American shorebird with mottled brown markings that breeds only in the Arctic and migrates to Central and South America for the winter. Latin name: *Calidris melanotos.* [Because the male inflates its breast during courtship]

pec·u·late /pékyə làyt/ (**-lat·ed, -lat·ing, -lates**) *vt.* to appropriate money or property by embezzlement or theft (*formal*) [Mid-18thC. From Latin *peculari*, from *peculium* (see PECULIAR).] —**pec·u·la·tor** *n.* —**pec·u·la·tion** /pèkyə láysh'n/ *n.*

pe·cu·liar /pi kyoolyər/ *adj.* **1. UNUSUAL** unusual, strange, or unconventional ○ *The situation was very peculiar.* **2. UNIQUE** belonging exclusively to or identified distinctly with somebody or something ■ *n.* **SOMEBODY'S PROPERTY OR RIGHT** a privilege or property that belongs uniquely to somebody (*archaic*) [15thC. From Latin *peculiaris* "of private property" (later "individual," hence "strange"), from *peculium* "private property," from *pecus* "cattle," hence "wealth."] —**pe·cu·liar·ly** *adv.*

pe·cu·li·ar·i·ty /pi kyool yérrətee, -lee érrətee/ (*plural* **-ties**) *n.* **1. INDIVIDUAL CHARACTERISTIC** a characteristic or trait that belongs distinctively to a particular person, place, or thing **2. ODDNESS** the quality or state of being unusual or strange

pe·cu·li·um /pi kyoolyəm/ *n.* LAW, HIST in Roman law, property that a father allowed his child, or a master his enslaved person, to own independently [Late 17thC. From Latin (see PECULIAR).]

pe·cu·ni·ar·y /pi kyoonee èrree/ *adj.* **1. OF MONEY** relating to or involving money **2.** LAW **INVOLVING FINANCIAL PENALTY** involving a financial penalty such as a fine ○ *a pecuniary offense* [Early 16thC. From Latin *pecuniarius*, from *pecunia* "money, wealth in cattle," from *pecus* "cattle."] —**pe·cu·ni·ar·i·ly** /pi kyoonee èrrilee/ *adv.*

ped. *abbr.* pedal

ped- *prefix.* = **pedo** (*used before vowels*)

-ped *suffix.* foot ○ *Quadruped* [From Latin *ped-*, the stem of *pes* (see PEDAL)]

ped·a·gog·ics /pèddə gójjiks/ *n.* = **pedagogy** (*formal*) (*takes a singular verb*)

ped·a·gogue /péddə gòg/ *n.* **1.** TEACHER an educator or schoolteacher **2.** PEDANTIC TEACHER a teacher who teaches in a particularly pedantic or dogmatic manner [14thC. Via Latin *paedagogus* from Greek *paidagōgos* "slave who leads a child to school," from *pais* "child" + *agōgos* "leader."]

ped·a·go·gy /péddə gòjjee/ *n.* the science or profession of teaching [Mid-16thC. Via French *pédagogie* from Greek *paidagōgia* "duties of a pedagogue."] —**ped·a·gog·ic** /pèddə gójjik/ *adj.* —**ped·a·gog·i·cal** /-k'l/ *adj.* —**ped·a·gog·i·cal·ly** /-gójjiklee/ *adv.*

ped·al[1] /pédd'l/ *n.* **1.** FOOT-OPERATED LEVER FOR MACHINE a lever operated by the foot that powers a mechanism such as a bicycle, sewing machine, or the foot controls of a car **2.** MUSIC FOOT-OPERATED LEVER FOR MUSICAL INSTRUMENT a foot-operated lever used in playing the piano, organ, and other musical instruments **3.** MUSIC = **pedal point** ■ *vti.* (**-aled, -al·ing, -als**) **1.** TRANSP MAKE BICYCLE MOVE to use the pedals to make a bicycle or other vehicle move forward **2.** OPERATE OR PLAY INSTRUMENT USING FOOT MECHANISM to operate the pedals of something such as a piano, organ, or machine in order to make it work [Early 17thC. Via French from, ultimately, Latin *pedalis* "of the foot," from *ped-*, *pes* "foot" (source also of English *impede* and *pedigree*).] —**ped·al·er** *n.*

ped·al[2] /peéd'l/ *adj.* relating to the foot or feet [Early 17thC. From Latin *pedalis* "of the foot."]

pe·dal·fer /pi dálfər/ *n.* soil without a layer of accumulated calcium carbonate, but in which iron and aluminum have tended to accumulate [Early 20thC. Blend of PEDO- and ALUMINUM, and Latin *ferrum* "iron."]

ped·al point *n.* a note, usually in the bass, that is sustained while other musical parts and harmonies continue

ped·al push·ers *npl.* calf-length pants for women, originally designed for cycling

ped·al steel, ped·al steel gui·tar *n.* an electrically amplified floor-mounted guitar that is fretted with a steel bar and usually has ten strings, whose pitch can be varied by the use of pedals

ped·ant /pédd'nt/ *n.* **1.** SOMEBODY TOO CONCERNED WITH RULES AND DETAILS somebody who pays excessive attention to formal scholarship and to unimportant rules and details **2.** SOMEBODY WHO SHOWS OFF KNOWLEDGE somebody who makes an ostentatious display of learning **3.** TEACHER a schoolteacher (*archaic*) [Late 16thC. Via French *pédant* from Italian *pedante*, of uncertain origin: perhaps from, ultimately, Latin *paedagogus* (see PEDAGOGUE).]

pe·dan·tic /pə dántik/ *adj.* too concerned with what are thought to be correct rules and details, e.g. in language —**pe·dan·ti·cal·ly** *adv.*

ped·ant·ry /pédd'ntree/ (*plural* **-ries**) *n.* a pedantic attitude or an example of pedantic behavior

ped·ate /pé dàyt, péddət/ *adj.* possessing, used as, or resembling a foot or feet [Late 18thC. From Latin *pedatus* "having feet," from *pes* "foot."] —**pe·date·ly** *adv.*

ped·dle /pédd'l/ (**-dled, -dling, -dles**) *v.* **1.** *vti.* SELL GOODS to sell goods, especially while traveling from place to place **2.** *vt.* DRUGS SELL DRUGS to sell something illegal, especially drugs (*dated*) **3.** *vt.* PROMOTE IDEA to promote an idea or belief insistently [Mid-16thC. Back-formation from PEDDLER.]

ped·dler /péddlər/ *n.* **1.** SOMEBODY WHO PEDDLES GOODS somebody who travels from place to place selling goods **2.** DRUGS DRUG SELLER somebody who sells something, especially illegal drugs [14thC. Alteration of earlier *pedder*, of uncertain origin: perhaps from an obsolete word meaning "basket."]

ped·er·ast /péddə ràst/ *n.* a man who has sex with a boy (*formal*) [Mid-17thC. From Greek *paiderastēs*, literally "lover of boys."] —**ped·er·as·tic** /pèddə rástik/ *adj.* —**ped·er·as·ty** /péddə ràstee/ *n.*

pe·des plural of **pes**

ped·es·tal /péddəst'l/ *n.* **1.** ARCHIT BASE OF COLUMN a base or support for a column or statue **2.** FURNITURE SUPPORTING BASE the column-shaped base of a piece of furniture such as a table or washbasin **3.** POSITION OF BEING EXALTED OR ADMIRED a position in which somebody admires another person so much that he or she thinks that person is perfect ○ *I don't want to be put on a pedestal – I just want to be treated as a normal person!* ■ *vt.* (**-taled** *or* **-tal·led, -tal·ing** *or* **-tal·ling, -tals**) PUT SOMETHING ON PEDESTAL to provide somebody or something with a pedestal [Mid-16thC. Via French *piédestal* from Italian *piedestallo*, literally "foot of a stall."]

pe·des·tri·an /pə déstree ən/ *n.* SOMEBODY WALKING somebody who is traveling on foot, especially in an area also used by cars ■ *adj.* DULL ordinary, unimaginative, or uninspired [Early 18thC. Directly or via French *pédestre* from Latin *pedester* "going on foot," from *pes* "foot."] —**pe·des·tri·an·ism** *n.*

pe·des·tri·an·ize /pə déstree ə nìz/ (**-ized, -iz·ing, -iz·es**) *vt.* to change a street into an area for pedestrians only by banning motor vehicles —**pe·des·tri·an·i·za·tion** /pə dèstree ənə záysh'n/ *n.*

Pe·di /péddee/ (*plural* **-dis** *or* **-di**) *n.* **1.** PEOPLES SOUTH AFRICAN PEOPLE a member of a people that lives in parts of South Africa, mainly in Transvaal **2.** LANG LANGUAGE OF THE PEDI the Bantu language of the Pedi people, belonging to the Benue-Congo branch of Niger-Congo languages. Pedi is spoken by about three million people. —**Pe·di** *adj.*

pedi- *prefix.* foot, feet ○ *pedipalp* [From Latin *ped-*, the stem of *pes* (see PEDAL)]

pe·di·a·tri·cian /peèdee ə trísh'n/, **pe·di·at·rist** /peèdee áttrist/ *n.* a doctor who specializes in the care and development of children and in the prevention and treatment of children's diseases

pe·di·at·rics /peèdee áttriks/ *n.* the branch of medicine concerned with the care and development of children and with the prevention and treatment of children's diseases (*takes a singular verb*) —**pe·di·at·ric** *adj.*

pe·di·at·rist *n.* = **pediatrician**

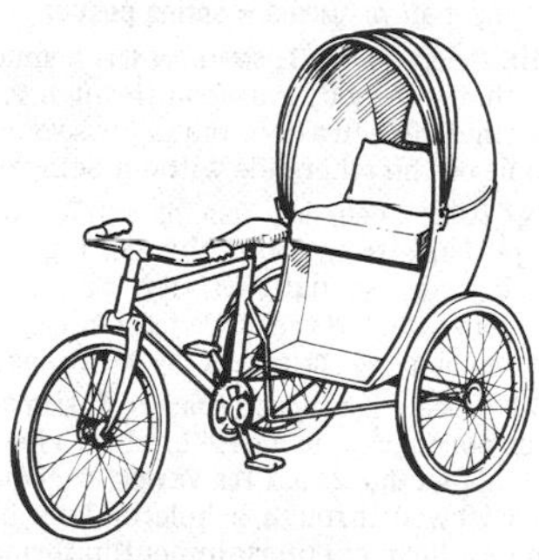

Pedicab

ped·i·cab /péddi kàb/ *n.* a pedal-operated tricycle with a seat in front for the driver and a passenger seat behind covered by a hood, available for hire in some Southeast Asian countries

ped·i·cel /péddis'l, -sèl/, **ped·i·cle** /péddik'l/ *n.* **1.** BOT STALK OF INDIVIDUAL FLOWER a stalk bearing a single flower or spore-producing body within a cluster **2.** ANAT STALK-SHAPED BODY PART an anatomical part that resembles a stem or stalk **3.** INSECTS NARROW SEGMENT a narrow anatomical part such as the waist between the thorax and abdomen of wasps and related insects [Late 17thC. From modern Latin *pedicellus*, from Latin *pediculus* "footstalk," from *pes* "foot."] —**ped·i·cel·lar** /pèddi séllər/ *adj.* —**ped·i·cel·late** /-séllət, -sé làyt/ *adj.*

pe·dic·u·late /pi díkyələt, -làyt/ *adj.* relating to the anglerfishes, which are characterized by a modified dorsal spine with an attachment for luring prey [Mid-19thC. From modern Latin *Pediculati*, order name, from Latin *pediculus* (see PEDICEL).] —**pe·dic·u·late** *n.*

pe·dic·u·lo·sis /pə dìkyə lóssiss/ *n.* infestation with lice, specifically the head and body louse *Pediculus humanus*. It can cause insomnia, irritability, and depression. [Early 19thC. Formed from Latin *pediculus* "louse."] —**pe·dic·u·lous** /pə díkyələss/ *adj.*

ped·i·cure /péddi kyòor/ *n.* **1.** MED MEDICAL CARE OF FEET medical treatment of the feet, e.g., the removal of corns **2.** COSMETICS COSMETIC TREATMENT OF FEET cosmetic treatment of the feet, e.g., the application of nail varnish **3.** COSMETICS, MED SESSION OF TREATMENT FOR FEET a session of cosmetic or medical treatment of the feet **4.** CHIROPODIST a chiropodist ■ *vt.* (**-cured, -cur·ing, -cures**) TREAT FEET OF SOMEBODY to give a pedicure to somebody [Mid-19thC. From French *pédicure*, from the Latin stem *ped-* "foot" + *cura* "care."] —**ped·i·cur·ist** *n.*

ped·i·form /péddi fàwrm/ *adj.* in the shape of a foot (*technical*)

ped·i·gree /péddi greè/ *n.* **1.** LINE OF ANCESTORS the line of ancestors of an individual animal or person, especially a pure-bred animal **2.** LIST OF ANIMAL'S ANCESTORS a document recording the line of ancestors of an animal, especially a pure-bred animal **3.** FAMILY TREE a table showing the line of ancestors of a person, especially an aristocratic or upper class person **4.** BACKGROUND the background, history, or origin of something, especially a group [15thC. From Anglo-Norman *pe de gru*, literally "crane's foot." From the resemblance of a family tree's branching lines to a bird's foot.] —**ped·i·greed** *adj.*

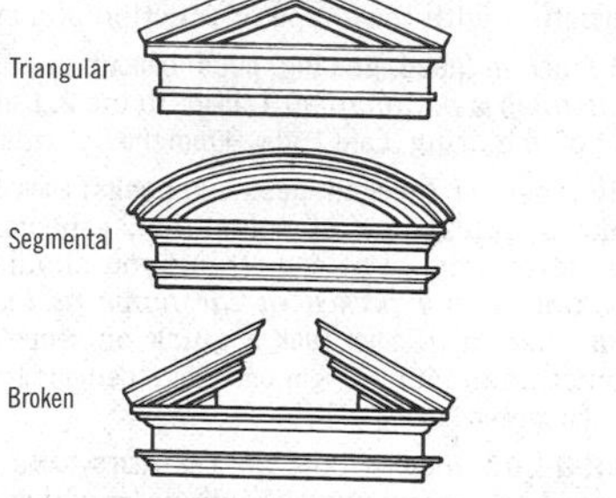

Pediment

ped·i·ment /péddimənt/ *n.* **1.** ARCHIT GABLE ON COLONNADE a broad triangular or segmental gable surmounting a colonnade as the major part of a facade **2.** GEOG BROAD ROCK AREA a broad flat rock surface of low relief adjacent to a steeper slope in an arid region, e.g., that of a mountain range, often covered with rock debris [Late 16thC. Origin uncertain: perhaps an alteration of PYRAMID.] —**ped·i·men·tal** /pèddi mént'l/ *adj.*

ped·i·palp /péddi pàlp/ *n.* either of a pair of appendages that are part of the mouths of spiders and other arachnids, used for various functions including manipulating food [Early 19thC. From modern Latin *pedipalpi*, from Latin *pes* "foot" and *palpus* "palp."]

ped·lar /péddlər/ *n. U.K.* = **peddler** [14thC. Alteration of *pedder*, of uncertain origin: perhaps from medieval Latin *pedarius* "one who goes on foot," from Latin *pes* "foot."]

pedo- *prefix.* soil ○ *pedology* [From Greek *pedon*. Ultimately from the Indo-European word for "foot" that is also the ancestor of English *foot* and *pedal*.]

pe·do·don·tics /peèdə dóntiks/, **pe·do·don·tia** /-shə, -shee ə/ *n.* the branch of dentistry concerned with dental care and treatment for children (*takes a singular verb*)

ped·o·gen·e·sis /peè dō jénnəssiss/ *n.* the natural process of soil formation, including erosion and leaching —**pe·do·ge·net·ic** /peè dō jə néttik/ *adj.* —**pe·do·gen·ic** /-jénnik/ *adj.*

pe·dol·o·gy[1] /pi dólləjee/ *n.* the scientific study of the physical and mental development of children —**ped·o·log·ic** /peèd'l ójjik/ *adj.* —**ped·o·log·i·cal** /-k'l/ *adj.* —**ped·o·log·i·cal·ly** /peèd'l ójjikəlee/ *adv.* —**pe·dol·o·gist** /pi dólləjist/ *n.*

pe·dol·o·gy[2] /pə dólləjee/ *n.* the scientific study of soil properties and the classification of soil types —**ped·o·log·ic** /pèdd'l ójjik/ *adj.* —**ped·o·log·i·cal** /-k'l/ *adj.* —**ped·o·log·i·cal·ly** /pèdd'l ójjikəlee/ *adv.* —**pe·dol·o·gist** /pə dólləjist/ *n.*

pe·dom·e·ter /pə dómmətər/ *n.* an instrument that measures the distance covered by a walker by recording the number of steps taken [Early 18thC. From French *pédomètre*, from the Latin stem *ped-* "foot" + French *-mètre* "-meter."]

ped·o·mor·pho·sis /pèddə máwrfəssiss, peèdə-/ *n.* = **neoteny**

ped·o·phile /péddə fìl, peèdə-/ *n.* an adult who has sexual desire for children or who has committed the crime of sex with a child —**ped·o·phil·ic** /pèddə fíllik, peèdə-/ *adj.*

ped·o·phi·li·a /pèddə fíllee ə, peèdə-/ *n.* sexual desire felt by an adult for children, or the crime of sex with a child —**ped·o·phil·i·ac** /pèddə fíllee àk, peèdə-/ *n.*, *adj.*

Pe·dro I /péddrō/, **Emperor of Brazil** (1798–1834). The son of the King of Portugal, he declared Brazil's independence in 1822, made himself emperor, and abdicated in 1831. He was also briefly king of Portugal (1826).

Pe·dro II, Emperor of Brazil (1825–91). He was emperor from his father's abdication (1831) until his own abdication (1889). He abolished slavery in Brazil.

pe·dun·cle /peé dùngkəl, pi-/ *n.* 1. BOT STALK the stalk of a plant 2. ZOOL PART RESEMBLING STALK a part resembling a stalk in shape or function, e.g., the base of a fish's tail or a structure attaching an invertebrate animal to the place where it lives [Mid-18thC. From modern Latin *pedunculus*, literally "a small foot," from Latin *pes* "foot."] —**pe·dun·cled** *adj.* —**pe·dun·cu·lar** /pi dúngkyələr/ *adj.*

pe·dun·cu·late /pi dúngkyələt, -làyt/, **pe·dun·cu·lat·ed** /-làytəd/ *adj.* having or resembling a stalk, or a structure with the shape or function of a stalk

pee /pee/ *vi.* (**peed, pee·ing, pees**) URINATE to pass urine (*informal*) ■ *n.* (*informal*) 1. URINE urine 2. URINATION an act of urinating [Late 18thC. From the first letter of PISS.]

peek /peek/ *vi.* (**peeked, peek·ing, peeks**) LOOK QUICKLY to take a quick look at something, especially in a secretive way or at something you should not be looking at ○ *I peeked at the name at the foot of the letter.* ■ *n.* QUICK LOOK a quick or secret look at something [14thC. Origin uncertain: perhaps from earlier Dutch *kieken* "to look."]

peek·a·boo /peékə boō/ *n.* CHILDREN'S GAME a game played to amuse small children, in which the face is hidden in the hands and then suddenly uncovered as "peekaboo!" is shouted ■ *interj.* WORD SAID IN GAME OF PEEKABOO the word used when playing a game of peekaboo ■ *adj.* CLOTHES HAVING HOLES having holes or gaps intended to reveal parts of the body [Late 16thC. Coined from PEEK + BOO.]

Peeks·kill /peék skil/ city in southeastern New York, on the Hudson River, southeast of Newburgh. Population: 20,805 (1996).

peel[1] /peel/ *v.* (**peeled, peel·ing, peels**) 1. *vt.* REMOVE OUTER LAYER OF SOMETHING to cut away or pull off the skin or outer layer of something, especially a fruit or vegetable 2. *vi.* HAVE REMOVABLE SKIN to have a skin that can be removed 3. *vt.* PULL SOMETHING OFF to pull or strip off something, especially something that is stuck to a surface 4. *vi.* LOSE OUTER LAYER to lose or shed an outer layer or covering, e.g., of paint or sunburned skin ○ *The skin on her nose was peeling.* 5. *vi.* COME OFF IN THIN PIECES to come off in flakes, small pieces, or thin strips 6. *vi.* UNDRESS to remove clothes (*informal*) 7. *vt.* SPORTS PUT BALL THROUGH CROQUET HOOP to make another player's ball go through a hoop in croquet ■ *n.* FOOD FRUIT OR VEGETABLE SKIN the rind or skin of a fruit or vegetable ○ *apple peel* [13thC. From Latin *pilare*, literally "to deprive of hair," from *pilus* "hair." Originally in the meaning "to plunder."]

peel[2] /peel/ *n.* COOK a large spatula with a long handle, used by bakers to move bread in and out of an oven [14thC. Via Old French *pele* from Latin *pala* "spade."]

peel[3] /peel/ *n.* ARCHIT a fortified tower of the type built in the border counties of Scotland and England in the 16th century to withstand raids [13thC. Via Anglo-Norman *pel* from, ultimately, Latin *palus* "stake."]

peel·a·ble /peéləb'l/ *adj.* 1. WITH A SKIN THAT PEELS with a skin that can be peeled off 2. REMOVABLE AND REUSABLE used to describe an adhesive label that can be removed and reused

peel·er /peélər/ *n.* 1. DEVICE FOR REMOVING SKIN FROM VEGETABLES a device for removing the skin from fruit or vegetables, usually a hand-held utensil with a blade 2. STRIPPER a striptease dancer (*slang*)

peel·ing /peéling/ *n.* a piece of something, especially fruit or vegetable skin, that has been peeled off (*often used in the plural*) ○ *potato peelings*

peen /peen/ *n.* END OF HAMMERHEAD OPPOSITE FACE the end of a hammerhead opposite the flat face, often rounded or wedge-shaped, and used for bending and shaping ■ *vt.* (**peened, peen·ing, peens**) SHAPE SOMETHING USING PEEN to bend or shape something by striking it with the peen of a hammer [Late 17thC. Origin uncertain: perhaps from a Scandinavian word.]

peep[1] /peep/ *v.* (**peeped, peep·ing, peeps**) 1. *vi.* LOOK QUICKLY OR SECRETLY to look quickly or secretly, e.g., through a small opening or from a hiding place 2. *vti.* EMERGE OR MAKE SOMETHING EMERGE to become or make something become partly visible or visible only for a short time ■ *n.* 1. QUICK LOOK a quick or secret look at something 2. THE FIRST SIGHT OF SOMETHING the first appearance or sight of something [15thC. Origin uncertain: perhaps an alteration of PEEK.]

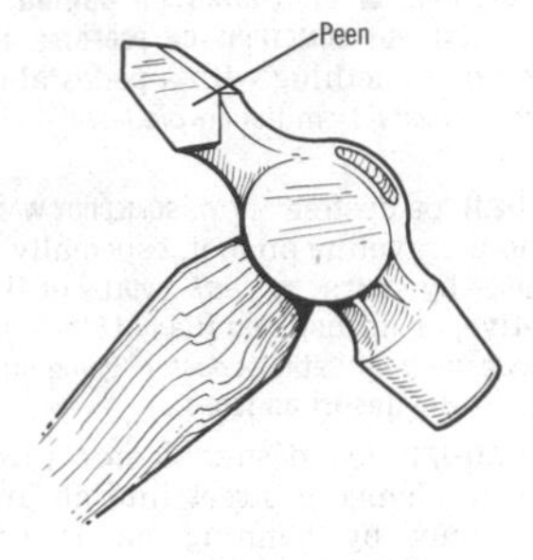

Peen

peep[2] /peep/ *vi.* (**peeped, peep·ing, peeps**) 1. MAKE A SHORT, HIGH-PITCHED NOISE to make a high-pitched little noise like a baby bird or a mouse 2. SPEAK IN HIGH OR QUIET VOICE to speak in a quiet, weak, or high-pitched voice 3. MAKE QUIET NOISE to make the quietest possible noise or remark ■ *n.* 1. SHORT HIGH-PITCHED SOUND a high-pitched sound like that of a baby bird or a mouse 2. SMALLEST SOUND a very quiet utterance ○ *I don't want to hear another peep out of any of you!* 3. SMALL SANDPIPER any of several smaller members of the sandpiper family of shorebirds [15thC. An imitation of the sound.]

peep·er[1] /peépər/ *n.* 1. SOMEBODY WHO PEEPS somebody who looks secretly at somebody or something 2. EYE somebody's eye (*dated slang*) (*often used in the plural*)

peep·er[2] /peépər/ *n.* AMPHIB = **spring peeper**

peep·hole /peép hōl/ *n.* 1. SMALL OPENING a small crack or hole that somebody can look through 2. SPY HOLE IN DOOR a small hole in a door that allows somebody to see people on the other side without being observed

Peep·ing Tom, **peep·ing Tom** *n.* a man who gets sexual pleasure from secretly watching somebody undressing or sexual activity between other people [Early 19thC. Named for a tailor in English legend who was the only person to look at Lady Godiva riding naked.]

peep·show /peép shō/, **peep show** *n.* 1. EROTIC SHOW an erotic or pornographic movie or show viewed from individual booths 2. BOX FOR VIEWING a sequence of pictures viewed through a hole or lens in a box, viewed as a form of entertainment in former times

peep sight *n.* a metal tab at the rear of a rifle barrel, containing a small circular opening through which the user looks to align the front sight with the target

pee·pul *n.* = **bo tree**

peer[1] /peer/ (**peered, peer·ing, peers**) *vi.* 1. LOOK CLOSELY to look very carefully or hard, especially at somebody or something that is difficult to see, often with narrowed eyes 2. BE PARTIALLY OR BRIEFLY VISIBLE to be partially visible or appear briefly [Late 16thC. Origin uncertain: perhaps from Low German *pīren* "to look."]

peer[2] /peer/ *n.* 1. PERSON OF EQUAL STANDING WITH ANOTHER somebody who is equal to another person or to other people in some respect such as age or social class 2. MEMBER OF BRITISH OR N IRISH NOBILITY member of the nobility in Great Britain and Northern Ireland 3. FRIEND a companion, fellow, or buddy (*archaic*) [13thC. Via Old French from Latin *par* "equal" (source of English *pair* and *par*).]

peer·age /peérij/ *n.* 1. NOBLES AS A GROUP noblemen and noblewomen considered as a class or group 2. NOBLE RANK the rank, status, or title of a nobleman or noblewoman 3. PUBL LIST OF NOBLES a book listing the members of the nobility and giving information about their families

peer·ess /peérəss/ *n.* 1. WOMAN PEER a woman who is a peer 2. WIFE OF PEER the wife or widow of a peer

peer group *n.* a social group consisting of people who are equal in such respects as age, education, or social class ○ *Teenagers usually prefer to spend time with their own peer group.*

peer·less /peérləss/ *adj.* incomparable, matchless, or without equal —**peer·less·ly** *adv.* —**peer·less·ness** *n.*

peer of the realm (*plural* **peers of the realm**) *n.* in Great Britain and Northern Ireland, a member of the nobility who has the right to sit in the House of Lords

peer pres·sure *n.* social pressure on somebody to adopt a particular type of behavior, dress, or attitude in order to be accepted as part of a group

peeve /peev/ *vt.* (**peeved, peev·ing, peeves**) ANNOY SOMEBODY to make somebody feel annoyed, irritated, or resentful (*informal*) ■ *n.* (*informal*) 1. SOMETHING THAT ANNOYS something that annoys or irritates somebody 2. BAD MOOD an irritated or resentful mood [Early 20thC. Back-formation from PEEVISH.]

pee·vish /peévish/ *adj.* bad-tempered, irritable, or tending to complain [14thC. Origin unknown.] —**pee·vish·ly** *adv.* —**pee·vish·ness** *n.*

pee·wee[1] /peé weè/ *n.* VERY SMALL PERSON OR THING somebody or something that is extremely or exceptionally small, especially a small child ■ *adj.* TINY very small [Late 19thC. Reduplication of WEE.]

pee·wee[2] /peé weè/ *n.* BIRDS = **pewee** [Late 19thC. An imitation of the sound made by the bird.]

pee·wit /peé wit/ *n.* = **lapwing** [Early 16thC. An imitation of the sound made by the bird.]

peg /peg/ *n.* 1. PIN FOR FASTENING OR MARKING SOMETHING a small piece of metal, plastic, or wood used to secure or mark something or to join two parts together 2. HOOK FOR HANGING THINGS a hook or projecting piece of wood or metal that is attached to a surface such as a door or wall and used to hang things, especially clothes 3. MUSIC PART FOR TUNING STRING a screw or pin around which a string is wound in the head (**pegbox**) of a stringed instrument. The string can be tightened or loosened to raise or lower its pitch by turning the peg. 4. REASON FOR DOING SOMETHING something used as an excuse or reason for doing something, or as a support for an argument 5. DEGREE OR STEP a degree, notch, or step, especially in somebody's opinion of a person or thing 6. *U.K.* SMALL DRINK OF LIQUOR a small drink of liquor such as brandy or whiskey (*dated informal*) 7. BASEBALL FAST THROW in baseball, a fast, low throw of the ball that puts a base runner out 8. SPORTS CROQUET PIN in croquet, a post that must be hit with a ball in order for a player to win the game ■ *vt.* (**pegged, peg·ging, pegs**) 1. SECURE SOMETHING WITH PEGS to fasten something with one or more pegs 2. PUT A PEG IN SOMETHING to insert a peg into something 3. MARK SOMETHING WITH PEG to mark something, such as the score in a game, with a peg or pegs 4. COMM FIX SOMETHING AT CERTAIN LEVEL to fix the cost or value of something at a certain level 5. CATEGORIZE SOMEBODY to classify somebody or something, especially as having a particular character 6. THROW A BASEBALL to throw something, especially a low and fast baseball (*informal*) [15thC. Origin uncertain: probably from obsolete Dutch *pegge*.] ◇ **bring** *or* **take somebody down a peg (or two)** to make somebody more humble ◇ **a square peg in a round hole** somebody who is completely unsuited to the situation he or she is in

Peg·a·sus /péggəsəss/ *n.* 1. MYTHOL HORSE WITH WINGS in Greek mythology, a horse with wings, born of the shed blood of Medusa 2. ASTRON LARGE NORTHERN CONSTELLATION NEAR AQUARIUS a large constellation of the northern hemisphere between Andromeda and Aquarius

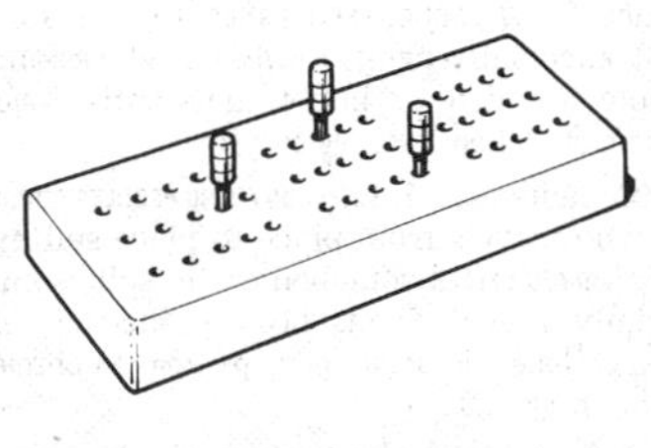

Pegboard

peg·board /pég bàwrd/ *n.* 1. BOARD WITH HOLES FOR PLAYING GAMES a board with a pattern of holes into which pegs are placed in certain games 2. BOARD WITH HOLES FOR KEEPING SCORE a board with a pattern of holes into which pegs are placed to keep the score in some games, especially card games such as cribbage

Peg-Board *tdmk.* a trademark for a thin board with evenly spaced holes into which pegs or hooks can be placed for displaying, hanging, or storing things

peg·box /pég bòks/ *n.* the portion of a stringed instrument that holds the tuning pegs

peg leg *n.* **1.** WOODEN LEG a prosthetic leg, especially a simple wooden one fitted at the knee (*informal*) (*often considered offensive*) **2.** OFFENSIVE TERM an offensive term for somebody who has a prosthetic leg

peg·ma·tite /pégmə tìt/ *n.* a coarse-grained igneous rock, usually granite, that is characterized by large well-formed crystals and often contains rare elements [Mid-19thC. Formed from the Greek stem *pēgmat-* "something joined together."] —**peg·ma·tit·ic** /pègmə títtik/ *adj.*

peg top *n.* SPINNING TOP a spinning top that is thrown from the hand and is caused to spin as a string quickly unwinds from around a central metal peg ■ **peg tops** *npl.* PANTS THAT NARROW TOWARD ANKLES pants that are full and gathered at the hips and narrow at the ankle (*dated*)

Pe·gu /pe góo/ city in Myanmar, formerly Burma. Between 1531 and 1635 it was the country's capital. Population: 150,447 (1983).

Peh·le·vi *n.*, *adj.* = **Pahlavi**

Popperfoto

I. M. Pei

Pei /pay/, **I. M.** (*b.* 1917) Chinese-born U.S. architect. His work combines elegance of form with functional efficiency. Full name **Ieoh Ming Pei**

P.E.I., **PEI** *abbr.* Prince Edward Island

pei·gnoir /payn wáar, pen-/ *n.* a woman's loose-fitting dressing gown, bathrobe, or negligee [Mid-19thC. From French, from *peigner* "to comb," from, ultimately, Latin *pecten* "comb."]

pej·o·ra·tion /pèjjə ráysh'n, peejə-/ *n.* **1.** WORSENING STATE a worsening, deterioration, or decline in quality, status, or value (*formal*) **2.** LING CHANGE TO NEGATIVE MEANING OF WORD a change over time in the meaning of a word so that it becomes less favorable or more negative. An example is the English word "cunning," formerly used to mean "learned" but now used to mean "cleverly deceitful." [Mid-17thC. From the medieval Latin stem *peioration-*, from late Latin *peiorare* "to worsen," from Latin *peior* "worse" (source of English *impair*).]

pe·jor·a·tive /pə jáwrətiv, péjjə ràytiv, peejə ràytiv/ *adj.* EXPRESSING DISAPPROVAL expressing criticism or disapproval (*formal*) ■ *n.* DISAPPROVING WORD a word, expression, or affix that expresses criticism or disapproval [Late 19thC. Via French *péjoratif* from, ultimately, late Latin *peiorare* (see PEJORATION).] —**pe·jor·a·tive·ly** *adv.*

pek·an /pékən/ *n.* ZOOL = **fisher** [Mid-18thC. Via Canadian French from Abnaki *pékané*.]

peke /peek/, **Peke** *n.* a Pekingese dog (*informal*) [Early 20thC. Shortening.]

pe·kin /pee kín/ *n.* **1.** TEXTILES SILK FABRIC WITH STRIPES silk fabric with broad stripes in various colors or patterns **2. pe·kin, Pe·kin** BIRDS LARGE WHITE DUCK a large white duck of a breed that originated in China [Late 18thC. From French. Named for *Pékin* "Beijing."]

Pe·kin /peekin/ city in north central Illinois, on the eastern bank of the Illinois River, south of Peoria. Population: 32,433 (1996).

Pe·kin·ese *n.*, *adj.* = **Pekingese**

Pe·king /pee kíng/ former name for **Beijing**

Pe·king duck *n.* Chinese dish in which small portions of duck meat, strips of crisp duck skin, cucumber, and scallions are rolled in thin pancakes

Pekingese

Pe·king·ese /pee king eez, -eess/, **Pe·kin·ese** /peekə neez, -neess/ *n.* (*plural* **-ese**) **1.** ZOOL SMALL CHINESE DOG a small pet dog of a Chinese breed with a short flat nose, a long straight silky coat, and a tail that curls over its back **2.** MANDARIN CHINESE Mandarin Chinese (*dated*) **3.** PEOPLES SOMEBODY FROM BEIJING somebody who was born or lives in Beijing ■ *adj.* OF BEIJING relating to Beijing, or its people or culture

Pe·king man *n.* the fossilized remains of an extinct human species that lived 400,000 to 500,000 years ago, originally classified as Pithecanthropus and now regarded as a subspecies of Homo erectus [Early 20thC. Named for PEKING because its remains were discovered in China.]

pe·koe /peekō/ *n.* a high-quality black tea [Early 18thC. From Chinese *pekho*, literally "white down." From the downy young leaves used.]

pel *n.*, *abbr.* pixel

pel·age /péllij/ *n.* a mammal's coat of fur, hair, or wool (*technical*) [Early 19thC. Via French from, ultimately, Latin *pilus* "hair."]

Pe·la·gi·an /pə láyjee ən/ *adj.* CHR OF PELAGIUS OR PELAGIANISM relating to Pelagius or his teachings ■ *n.* CHR BELIEVER IN PELAGIANISM a believer in the teachings of the Christian heretic Pelagius

Pe·la·gi·an·ism /pə láyjee ə nìzzəm/ *n.* CHR the belief of the heretical Christian Pelagius that people can earn salvation through their own efforts, without relying on the grace of God, and the rejection of the concept of original sin [Late 16thC. Named for PELAGIUS.]

pe·lag·ic /pə lájjik/ *adj.* living, occurring, or deposited in the deep waters of the ocean or the open sea as opposed to near the shore [Mid-17thC. Via Latin from Greek *pelagikos*, from *pelagos* "sea."]

Pe·lag·i·us /pi láyjee əss/ (360?–420?) Romano-British monk. His doctrine, known as Pelagianism, denies the existence of original sin and was condemned as heretical.

pelargonic ac·id *n.* a colorless to yellow oil obtained from beet and potatoes, used in plastics, pharmaceuticals, synthetic flavors and as an additive in gasoline. Formula: $CH_3(CH_2)_7COOH$.

pel·ar·go·ni·um /pè laar gṓnee əm/ (*plural* **-ums** *or* **-um**) *n.* a plant of South African origin with rounded or lobed leaves and clusters of red, pink, or white flowers. Many geraniums are cultivated forms of pelargoniums. Genus: *Pelargonium.* [Early 19thC. From modern Latin, genus name, from Greek *pelargos* "stork." From the resemblance of its capsules to a stork's bill.]

Pe·las·gi·an /pi lázjee ən, pi lázgee ən/ *n.* ANCIENT INHABITANT OF GREECE a member of any of the ancient peoples that lived in Greece and the Aegean Islands before the arrival of the Bronze Age Hellenic peoples ■ *adj.* **Pe·las·gi·an, Pe·las·gic** OF PELASGIANS OR THEIR CULTURES relating to the Pelasgian peoples or their cultures [15thC. Formed from Latin *Pelasgus*, from Greek *Pelasgos*, name of the Pelasgians' mythical founder.]

Pe·le /pél ay/ (*b.* 1940) Brazilian soccer player. He is considered one of the greatest players of all time. His Brazilian team won the World Cup in 1958, 1962, and 1970. He played for the New York Cosmos (1975–77) and then retired, having scored 1,281 goals during his career. Real name **Edson Arantes do Nascimento**

pe·lec·y·pod /pə léssə pòd/ *n.* = **bivalve** [Late 19thC. From modern Latin *Pelecypoda*, class name, from Greek *pelekus* "ax" + *-podos* "footed."]

Express Newspapers

Pele

pel·er·ine /pèllə reen, -rin/ *n.* a woman's short narrow cape with long pointed ends that meet at the front [Mid-18thC. Via French *pèlerine*, the feminine form of *pèlerin* "pilgrim" from late Latin *pelegrinus* (source of English *pilgrim*).]

Pe·le's hair /páy làyz-, peeliz-/ *n.* fine threads of volcanic glass formed by the action of the wind on jets of lava erupting into the air [Mid-19thC. Translation of Hawaiian *lauoho o Pele*. Named for *Pele*, the goddess of volcanoes in Hawaiian mythology.]

Pe·le·us /peelee əss, peel yooss/ *n.* in Greek mythology, the king of the Myrmidons in Thessaly. He and the sea nymph Thetis were the parents of Achilles.

pelf /pelf/ *n.* money, wealth, or riches, especially if obtained dishonestly (*dated*) [14thC. Via Anglo-Norman from Old French *pelfre* "booty," of unknown origin.]

pel·ham /pélləm/ *n.* a bit for a horse's bridle that is midway between the simple snaffle bit and the harsher curb bit [Mid-19thC. From the surname *Pelham*.]

Pelican

pel·i·can /péllikən/ *n.* a large web-footed bird found on warm-water coasts worldwide that has a large flat bill with a hanging pouch that can be expanded to catch and store fish. Family: Pelecanidae. [Pre-12thC. Via late Latin *pelicanus* from Greek *pelekan*, of uncertain origin: perhaps formed from *pelekus* "ax," in allusion to the shape of its bill.]

pe·lisse /pə leess/ *n.* **1.** MILITARY GARMENT WITH FUR a cloak, coat, or jacket lined or trimmed with fur, often worn as part of a military uniform, e.g., by members of the Hussar regiments **2.** WOMAN'S COAT a woman's long fitted coat or dress that opens at the front and is often trimmed with fur [Early 18thC. Via French and late Latin *pellicia* from, ultimately, Latin *pellis* "skin."]

pe·lite /pee lìt/, **pe·lyte** *n.* aluminum-rich metamorphic rock formed by the action of temperature and pressure on clay-rich sedimentary rocks [Late 19thC. Formed from Greek *pēlos* "clay."] —**pe·lit·ic** /pə líttik/ *adj.*

pel·lag·ra /pə láygrə, pə lággrə/ *n.* a disease caused by a dietary deficiency of niacin and marked by dermatitis, diarrhea, and disorder of the central nervous system [Early 19thC. From Italian, from pelle "skin" + *agra* "rough" or *-agra* "seizure."] —**pel·lag·rous** *adj.*

pel·lag·rin /pə láygrin, pə lággrin/ *n.* somebody who has the dietary deficiency disease pellagra

pel·let /péllət/ *n.* **1.** SMALL BALL OF COMPRESSED MATERIAL a small ball, or piece of material that has been pressed tightly together e.g. for animal feed or a medicine **2.** ARMS SMALL BULLET a small bullet or ball of metal fired from a gun **3.** IMITATION BULLET an imitation bullet for use in a toy gun **4.** ARMS, HIST STONE MISSILE FOR CANNON OR CATAPULT a ball, usually made of stone, formerly used as a cannonball or as a missile fired from a catapult **5.** BIRDS **UNDIGESTED MATTER REGURGITATED BY PREDATORY BIRDS** an undigested mass of food, mostly bone and hair, that is regurgitated by owls and other birds of prey **6. ANIMAL FECES** a small round piece of the feces of some animals such as sheep or rabbits ■ *vt.* **(-let·ed, -let·ing, -lets) 1. STRIKE SOMETHING WITH PELLETS** to bombard or hit somebody or something with pellets **2. MAKE PELLETS OF SOMETHING** to make or form something into pellets [14thC. Via French *pelote* from assumed Vulgar Latin *pilotta*, literally "a small ball," from Latin *pila* "ball" (source of English *pill*).] —**pel·leti·za·tion** /pèllәti záysh'n/ *n.* —**pel·let·ize** /péllә tīz/ *vt.* —**pel·let·iz·er** /-tīzәr/ *n.*

pel·li·cle /péllik'l/ *n.* **1. THIN FILM OR MEMBRANE** a thin film, membrane, or skin **2.** MICROBIOL **FLEXIBLE SHEATH BENEATH PROTOZOAN CELL MEMBRANE** a multilayered flexible sheath that lies immediately beneath the cell membrane of many protozoans [Mid-16thC. Via French *pellicule* from Latin *pellicula*, literally "a small skin," from *pellis* "skin."] —**pel·lic·u·lar** /pә líkyәlәr/ *adj.*

pel·li·to·ry /pélli tàwree/ (*plural* **-ries**) *n.* a Mediterranean plant whose oil was formerly used for the relief of toothache. Latin name: *Anacyclus pyrethrum.* [Mid-16thC. Via Old French *peletre* from Latin *pyrethrum* (see PYRETHRUM).]

pell-mell /pèl mél/ *adv.* **1. IN A DISORDERLY RUSH** in a disorderly frantic rush **2. MESSILY** in a confused, jumbled, or messy manner ■ *adj.* **DISORDERLY** confused, frantic, or disorderly ■ *n.* **CONFUSION OR DISORDER** a confused or disorderly condition or situation [Late 16thC. Via French *pêle-mêle* from Old French *pesle mesle*, a playful development of mesler "to mix."]

pel·lu·cid /pә lóossid/ *adj.* **1. TRANSPARENT** allowing all or most light to pass through (*literary*) **2. CLEAR IN MEANING** easy to understand or clear in meaning (*formal*) [Early 17thC. From Latin *pellucidus*, from *pellucere* "to shine through," from *lucere* "to shine."] —**pel·lu·cid·i·ty** /pèllyә síddәtee/ *n.* —**pel·lu·cid·ly** /pә lóossidlee/ *adv.* —**pel·lu·cid·ness** /-nәss/ *n.*

Pel·ly /péllee/ river in Canada. It is a tributary of the Yukon River in southeastern Yukon Territory and originates in the Mackenzie Mountains. Length: 330 mi./530 km.

pel·o·bat·id /pèllō báttid, peelō-/ *n.* a frog with the backbone development of more primitive frogs and the leg-muscle structure of more advanced ones. The European spadefoot toad is a pelobatid. Family: Pelobatidae. [Mid-20thC. Coined from Greek *pelos* "mud" + *bates* "walker" + -ID.]

Pel·o·pon·ne·sus /pèllәpә neéz, -neéss/, **Pel·o·pon·nese** /pèllәpә neéssees/ peninsula in southern Greece, linked to the rest of mainland Greece by the Isthmus of Corinth. Area: 8,278 sq. mi./21,439 sq. km. —**Pel·o·pon·ne·sian** /pèllәpә neézh'n, -neésh'n/ *n., adj.*

Pe·lops /peé lòps/ *n.* in Greek mythology, the son of Tantalus, killed by his father and served up as a meal to the gods. The gods punished Tantalus and restored Pelops to life.

pe·lo·ri·a /pә láwree ә/ *n.* unusual regularity of form in a flower that is commonly irregular [Mid-19thC. Via modern Latin from, ultimately, Greek *pelōr* "monster."] —**pe·lor·ic** /pә láwrik/ *adj.*

pe·lo·rus /pә láwrәss/ *n.* a device used to measure bearings relative to the direction in which a boat is traveling [Mid-19thC. Origin uncertain: perhaps named for *Pelorus*, Hannibal's alleged guide from Italy.]

pe·lo·ta /pә lṓtә/ *n.* **1. FAST COURT GAME OF BASQUE ORIGIN** a fast court game of Basque origin, in which two players use long wickerwork baskets strapped to their wrists to hurl a ball against a marked wall and catch it. ◊ **jai alai 2. BALL FOR PELOTA** the ball used in pelota [Early 19thC. Via Spanish, literally "ball," from, ultimately, Latin *pila* (see PELLET).]

pelt[1] /pelt/ *n.* INDUST **1. ANIMAL SKIN WITH FUR** the skin of an animal with the fur, hair, or wool still attached **2. ANIMAL SKIN READY FOR TANNING** the skin of an animal with the fur, hair, or wool removed so that it is ready for tanning into leather ■ *vt.* **(pelt·ed, pelt·ing, pelts) REMOVE ANIMAL'S SKIN** to remove the skin of an animal [15thC. Origin uncertain: perhaps from Old French *pelete*, literally "a small skin," from *pel* "skin," from Latin *pellis*.]

pelt[2] /pelt/ *v.* **(pelt·ed, pelt·ing, pelts) 1.** *vt.* **THROW THINGS AT SOMEBODY OR SOMETHING** to bombard somebody or something with many blows or missiles **2.** *vt.* **BEAT AGAINST SOMETHING** to beat against something continuously **3.** *vi.* **RAIN HEAVILY** to fall fast and hard as hail or rain **4.** *vi.* **TO MOVE QUICKLY** to hurry or move quickly ■ *n.* **A BLOW** a strong blow [15thC. Origin uncertain: perhaps a contraction of PELLET, or perhaps from Latin *pultare* "to hit."] —**pelt·er** *n.* ◇ **at full pelt** extremely fast

pel·tast /pél tàst/ *n.* a foot soldier of ancient Greece armed with a light shield and a javelin [Early 17thC. Via Latin *peltasta* from, ultimately, Greek *peltē* "a small light shield."]

pel·tate /pél tàyt/ *adj.* BOT used to describe a leaf that has its stalk attached to the lower surface in the center rather than at the edge [Mid-18thC. Via Latin, literally "armed with a light shield," from, ultimately, Greek *peltē* (see PELTAST).] —**pel·tate·ly** *adv.* —**pel·ta·tion** /pel táysh'n/ *n.*

Pel·ti·er ef·fect /pélt yay-/ *n.* the production or absorption of heat at the junction of two metals when an electric current is passed from one metal to another. Heat is produced or absorbed depending on the direction and amount of current flow. [Mid-19thC. Named for its discoverer, the French scientist J. C. A. *Peltier* (1785–1845).]

Pel·ton wheel /pélt'n-/ *n.* an impulse turbine in which cup-shaped buckets on the edge of a rotor are hit with a high-pressure jet of water, causing the rotor to turn [Late 19thC. Named for its inventor, the U.S. engineer L. A. *Pelton* (1829–1908).]

pel·try /péltree/ *n.* the skins of animals collectively, especially when the fur is still attached [15thC. Via Anglo-Norman *pelterie* from, ultimately, Old French *pel* (see PELT[1]).]

pel·ves *n.* plural of **pelvis**

pel·vic /pélvik/ *adj.* relating to, involving, or located in or near the pelvis

pel·vic fin *n.* either of a pair of fins on the lower surface of a fish that have skeletal support and are analogous to the hind limbs of land animals

pel·vic in·flam·ma·to·ry dis·ease *n.* an inflammation of a woman's reproductive organs in the pelvic area which can cause infertility

pel·vim·e·try /pel vímmәtree/ *n.* measurement of the inlet and outlet diameters of the pelvis, usually to assess whether there will be any difficulty during childbirth

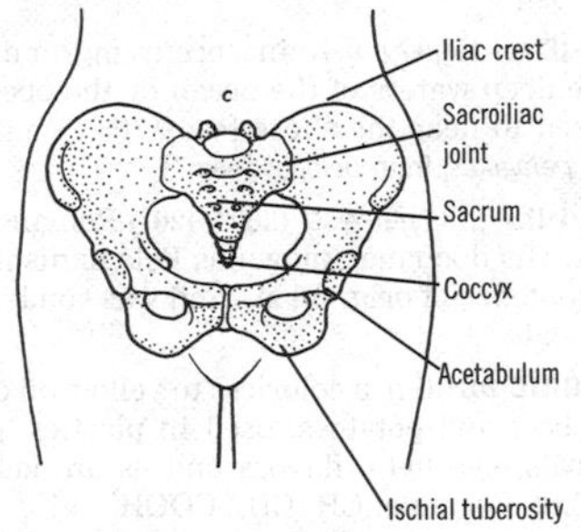

Pelvis

pel·vis /pélviss/ (*plural* **-vis·es** *or* **-ves** /pélveez/) *n.* **1. BASIN-SHAPED SKELETAL STRUCTURE IN VERTEBRATES** the strong basin-shaped ring of bone near the bottom of the spine formed by the hip bones on the front and sides, and the triangular sacrum on the back **2. BASIN-SHAPED CAVITY OR BODY PART** any basin- or cup-shaped anatomical cavity such as the region of the kidney into which urine is discharged before its passage into the ureter [Early 17thC. From Latin, literally "basin."]

pe·ly·co·saur /péllikә sàwr/ *n.* a large extinct reptile that was common in Europe and North America during the Permian period, 290 to 245 million years ago. Order: Pelycosauria. [Mid-20thC. Coined from the Greek stem *peluk-* "bowl" + -SAUR.]

Pem·ba /pémbә/ island in northeastern Tanzania, in the Indian Ocean. Its main towns are Wete and Chake Chake. Population: 265,039 (1988). Area: 380 sq. mi./984 sq. km.

Pem·broke /pém brŏok, pémbrәk/ **1.** town in southeastern Massachusetts, northwest of Plymouth and southwest of Scituate. Population: 16,010 (1996). **2.** city in Canada, in southeastern Ontario, on the Ottawa River. Population: 23,745 (1996). **3.** town in southwestern Wales, in Pembrokeshire. Population: 15,820 (1991).

Pem·broke ta·ble /pém brŏok-, pém brŏk-/, **pem·broke ta·ble** *n.* a small four-legged table with a top that folds down on two sides and one or two drawers [Late 18thC. Origin uncertain: perhaps named for PEMBROKE, Wales.]

pem·mi·can /pémmikәn/, **pem·i·can** *n.* **1. NATIVE NORTH AMERICAN FOOD OF DRIED MEAT** a traditional Native North American food made with strips of lean dried meat pounded into paste, mixed with melted fat and dried berries or fruits, and pressed into small cakes **2. FOOD USED AS EMERGENCY RATIONS** a nutritious food adapted from traditional Native North American pemmican and used as emergency rations, e.g., by explorers [Late 18thC. From Cree *pimihkan*, from *pimiy* "fat."]

pem·o·line /pémmә leen/ *n.* a synthetic stimulant of the central nervous system, used to treat depression and given to children who have attention deficit disorder. Formula: $C_9H_8N_2O_2$. [Mid-20thC. Coined from parts of *phenyliminooxoxazolidine*, its chemical name.]

pem·phi·gus /pémfigәss, pem fígәss/ *n.* a disease characterized by large blisters on the skin and mucous membranes, often accompanied by itching or burning sensations [Late 18thC. Via modern Latin from the Greek stem *pemphig-* "pustule."]

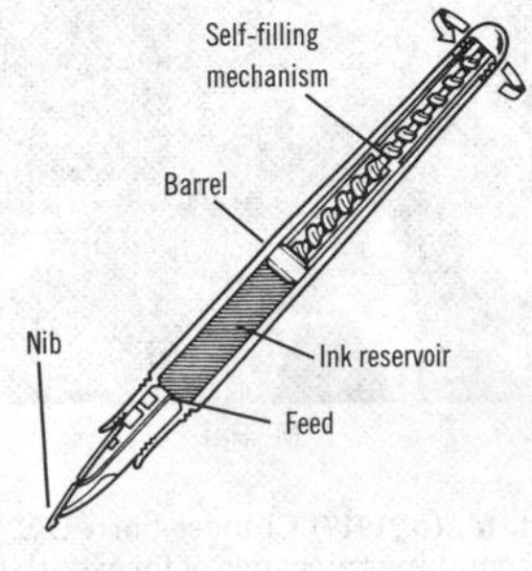

Pen

pen[1] /pen/ *n.* **1. INSTRUMENT FOR WRITING IN INK** a long thin instrument used for writing or drawing with ink. Early examples were made from sharpened quill feathers, but modern pens usually consist of a metal or plastic shaft with a nib, point, or revolving ball at one end. **2. WRITING** the written word considered as a means of expression ○ *They say the pen is mightier than the sword.* **3. STYLE OF WRITING** a particular style of writing **4. SOMETHING WRITTEN BY SOMEBODY** something written by a particular person **5.** ZOOL **SQUID'S INTERNAL SHELL** the internal feather-shaped horny shell of a squid ■ *vt.* **(penned, pen·ning, pens) WRITE SOMETHING** to write something, especially using a pen [13thC. Via French *penne* from Latin *penna* "feather."] —**pen·ner** *n.*

pen[2] /pen/ *n.* **1.** AGRIC **SMALL ENCLOSURE FOR ANIMALS** a small fenced area of land, or an enclosure within a building, used to keep farm animals **2.** AGRIC **ANIMALS KEPT IN PEN** the farm animals kept in a pen **3. AREA THAT CONFINES SOMEBODY OR SOMETHING** an enclosed area where somebody or something is confined or controlled **4.** NAVY **FORTIFIED DOCK FOR REPAIRING SUBMARINES** a heavily fortified dock for repairing or servicing submarines ■ *vt.* **(penned, pen·ning, pens) CONFINE SOMEBODY OR SOMETHING** to keep or shut somebody or something in a pen or other enclosed area [Old English *penn.* Origin unknown.]

pen[3] /pen/ *n.* CRIMINOL a state, provincial, or federal penitentiary (*slang*) [Late 19thC. Shortening.]

pen[4] /pen/ *n.* BIRDS a female swan [Mid-16thC. Origin unknown.]

PEN /pen/ *abbr.* International Association of Poets, Playwrights, Editors, Essayists, and Novelists

Pen. *abbr.* **1.** Peninsula (*used in place names*) **2.** Penitentiary (*used in names of prisons*)

pe·nal /peén'l/ *adj.* **1. OF PUNISHMENT** relating to, forming, or prescribing punishment, especially by law ○ *the penal system* **2. PUNISHABLE BY LAW** subject to punishment under the law **3. USED AS PLACE OF PUNISHMENT** used as a place of imprisonment and punishment ○ *a penal institution* [15thC. Via French *pénal* from, ultimately, Latin *poenalis*, from *poena* "penalty."]

pe·nal code *n.* a body or system of laws concerned with the punishment of crime

pe·nal col·o·ny *n.* a place of imprisonment and punishment at a remote location

pe·nal·ize /péen'l ìz/ (-ized, -iz·ing, -iz·es) *vt.* **1.** SUBJECT SOMEBODY OR SOMETHING TO PENALTY to impose a penalty on somebody or something for breaking a law or rule **2.** PUT SOMEBODY OR SOMETHING AT DISADVANTAGE to put somebody or something at a disadvantage or treat him or her unfairly **3.** SPORTS PUNISH PLAYER FOR BREAKING RULE to punish a team or player for breaking a rule by giving an advantage to the opposing team or player **4.** MAKE ACT PUNISHABLE to make something punishable by a law or rule —**pe·nal·i·za·tion** /pèen'li záysh'n/ *n.*

pen·al·ty /pénn'ltee/ (*plural* -ties) *n.* **1.** LEGAL PUNISHMENT FOR COMMITTING CRIME a legal or official punishment such as a fine or imprisonment for committing a crime or other offense **2.** LAW LEGAL PUNISHMENT FOR BREAKING CONTRACT a punishment such as a fine for failing to fulfill the terms of a legal agreement **3.** UNPLEASANT CONSEQUENCE something unpleasant suffered as the result of an unwise action **4.** SPORTS DISADVANTAGE FOR BREAKING RULE a disadvantage imposed on a player or team for breaking a rule in a sport or game, e.g., a free shot at the goal awarded to the opposing side **5.** SOCCER = **penalty kick 6.** SOCCER GOAL FROM PENALTY a goal scored from a penalty in soccer

pen·al·ty ar·e·a *n.* a rectangular area in front of a soccer goal within which the goalkeeper is allowed to handle the ball. A foul by the defending team within this area may result in a free shot at the goal awarded to the opposing side.

pen·al·ty box *n.* **1.** HOCKEY AREA WHERE PENALIZED PLAYERS MUST WAIT an area with a bench beside an ice-hockey rink where penalized players must stay during the period they have to serve as a time penalty **2.** SOCCER = **penalty area**

pen·al·ty kick *n.* **1.** SOCCER FREE KICK AT GOAL in soccer, a free kick from the penalty spot at the opposing team's goal, which is defended only by its goalkeeper. It is awarded for certain types of fouls within the penalty area. **2.** RUGBY KICK AWARDED AFTER FOUL a kick worth three points that can be aimed at the goal after a serious foul by a member of the opposing side

pen·al·ty shot *n.* in ice hockey and certain other games, a free shot at a goal awarded to a team if the opposing team commits any of various fouls

pen·al·ty spot *n.* **1.** SOCCER SPOT FOR PENALTY KICK a designated spot on a soccer field, 12 yd./11 m from the goal line, from which penalty kicks are taken **2.** HOCKEY CIRCLE ON HOCKEY FIELD in field hockey, a designated spot 23 ft./7 m from the goal line from which the shot is taken

pen·ance /pénnənss/ *n.* **1.** SELF-PUNISHMENT FOR COMMITTING SIN self-punishment or an act of religious devotion performed to show sorrow for having committed a sin **2.** CHRISTIAN SACRAMENT OF RECONCILIATION a sacrament in some Christian churches in which a person confesses sins to a priest and is forgiven after performing a religious devotion or duty such as praying or fasting **3.** DUTY IMPOSED BY PRIEST a duty or religious devotion imposed by a priest during the sacrament of confession in some Christian churches ■ *vt.* (-anced, -anc·ing, -anc·es) IMPOSE PENANCE ON SOMEBODY to make somebody do penance for a sin [13thC. Via Old French from Latin *paenitentia* "regret," from *paenitere* "to regret."]

Pe·nang /pə náng, -naáng/, **Pi·nang** state in northwestern Malaysia, comprising Penang Island and a small mainland area on the Malay Peninsula. Capital: George Town. Population: 1,065,075 (1990). Area: 398 sq. mi./1,031 sq. km.

pe·na·tes /pə náyteez, pə naáteez/, **Pe·na·tes** *npl.* in ancient Roman religious belief, the gods of a household or state [Early 16thC. From Latin, from *penus* "provisions."]

pence *U.K.* plural of **penny**

pen·cel /pénsəl/, **pen·sil** *n.* a small narrow flag (**pennon**) or streamer, especially one carried at the end of a lance [13thC. Via Anglo-Norman from Old French *penoncel*, literally "a small pennon."]

pen·chant /pénchənt/ *n.* a strong liking, taste, or tendency for something [Late 17thC. From French, the present participle of *pencher* "to incline," from, ultimately, Latin *pendere* (see PENDANT).]

pen·cil /pénsəl/ *n.* **1.** INSTRUMENT FOR DRAWING AND WRITING a thin cylindrical instrument used for drawing, or writing. It consists of a rod of graphite or some other erasable marking material inside a wooden or metal shaft. **2.** SOMETHING RESEMBLING PENCIL something that has a shape, structure, or function similar to a pencil, e.g., a stick for applying cosmetics ○ *an eyebrow pencil* **3.** OPTICS NARROW CYLINDER OF LIGHT a long narrow cylinder or cone of light with a small angle of convergence **4.** GEOM SET OF LINES THROUGH A POINT the set of all lines passing through a fixed point or of all lines parallel to a given line **5.** PAINTING ARTIST'S FINE BRUSH a fine brush used by an artist (*archaic*) **6.** DRAWING ARTIST'S INDIVIDUAL STYLE the individual drawing style or technique of an artist ■ *vt.* (-ciled, -cil·ing, -cils) DRAW OR WRITE SOMETHING WITH PENCIL to draw, mark, write, or color something with a pencil [14thC. Via Old French *pincel* from, ultimately, Latin *peniculus* "brush," literally "a small tail," from *penis* "tail."]

pencil in *vt.* to note or enter something provisionally, e.g., the time of a proposed engagement in an appointment book or on a calendar

pen·cil push·er *n.* somebody such as an office worker whose work involves much paperwork (*slang*)

pen com·put·er *n.* a computer that uses pattern-recognition circuitry or software to enable it to accept somebody's handwriting as a form of data input

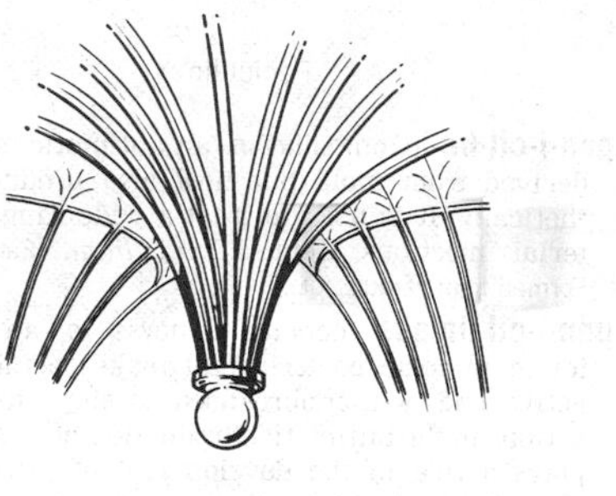

Pendant

pen·dant /péndənt/, **pen·dent** *n.* **1.** HANGING ORNAMENT OR JEWELRY an ornament or a piece of jewelry that hangs from a necklace, bracelet, or earring **2.** NECKLACE WITH HANGING ORNAMENT a necklace with a hanging ornament attached to it **3.** HANGING LIGHT a lamp, chandelier, or other lighting fixture that hangs from the ceiling **4.** ARCHIT ORNAMENT HANGING FROM CEILING an architectural ornament hanging from a vaulted ceiling or roof **5.** ONE OF MATCHING PAIR a piece of art that matches or goes with another piece **6.** NAUT LENGTH OF WIRE OR ROPE a length of wire or rope attached at the upper end to a spar or similar part and at the lower end to a block and tackle ■ *adj.* = **pendent** [14thC. From French, the present participle of *pendre* "to hang," from Latin *pendere*.]

pen·dent /péndənt/, **pen·dant** *adj.* **1.** HANGING OR SUSPENDED dangling, hanging, or suspended (*formal or literary*) **2.** OVERHANGING jutting, overhanging, or sticking out (*formal or literary*) **3.** GRAM GRAMMATICALLY INCOMPLETE used to describe an incomplete grammatical structure **4.** PENDING not yet dealt with, decided, or settled (*formal or literary*) ■ *n.* = **pendant** [13thC. Variant of PENDANT, influenced by Latin *pendent-*, the present participle stem of *pendere* "to hang."] —**pen·den·cy** *n.* —**pen·dent·ly** *adv.*

WORD KEY: ORIGIN

The Latin word *pendere*, from which ***pendent*** is derived, is also the source of English *append, appendix, compendium, depend, impend, penchant, pendulum, penthouse, perpendicular*, and *suspend*.

pen·den·tive /pen déntiv/ *n.* a sloping triangular piece of vaulting between the arches that support a dome and its rim [Early 18thC. Via French *pendentif* from, ultimately, Latin *pendere* "to hang."]

pend·ing /pénding/ *adj.* **1.** NOT YET TAKEN CARE OF not yet dealt with, decided, or settled **2.** ABOUT TO HAPPEN about to happen or come into effect ■ *prep.* **1.** UNTIL until or while waiting for ○ *pending further inquiries* **2.** DURING during something [Mid-17thC. Anglicization of French *pendant* (see PENDANT).]

pen·drag·on /pen drággən/, **Pen·drag·on** *n.* a supreme leader of the ancient Britons [15thC. From Welsh, from *pen* "head" + *dragon* "military standard" (from Latin *draco*).] —**pen·drag·on·ship** *n.*

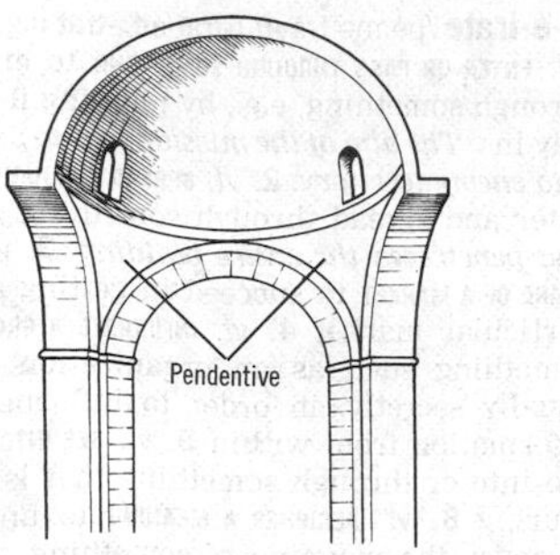

Pendentive

pen·du·lar /pénjələr, péndyələr/ *adj.* swinging back and forth with the motion of a pendulum

pen·du·lous /pénjələss, péndyələss/ *adj.* **1.** HANGING LOOSELY hanging loosely or swinging freely **2.** UNDECIDED undecided or wavering in making a decision [Early 17thC. Formed from Latin *pendulus* (see PENDULUM).] —**pen·du·lous·ly** *adv.* —**pen·du·lous·ness** *n.*

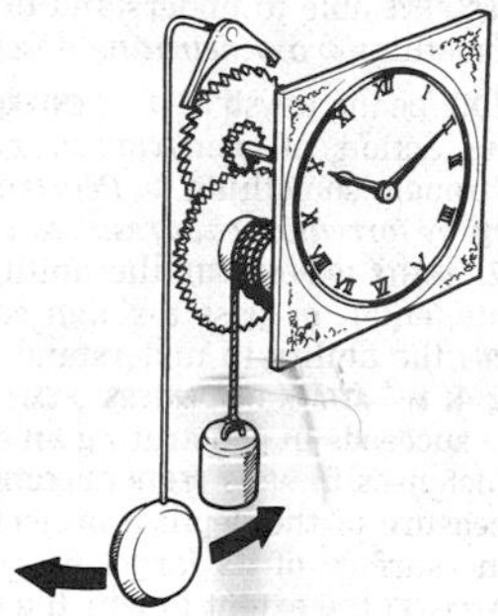

Pendulum

pen·du·lum /pénjələm, péndyələm/ *n.* **1.** WEIGHT SWINGING FREELY FROM A FIXED POINT a weight hung from a fixed point so that it can swing freely back and forth under the influence of gravity **2.** SWINGING ROD CONTROLLING A CLOCK MECHANISM a rod with a weight at its base that swings from side to side and controls the mechanism of a clock **3.** SOMETHING THAT CHANGES REGULARLY something that changes its direction or position regularly, often alternating between two extremes ○ *The pendulum has swung back to more traditional teaching methods.* [Mid-17thC. Via modern Latin from, ultimately, Latin *pendulus* "hanging," from *pendere* (see PENDANT).]

Pe·nel·o·pe /pə néllәpee/ *n.* in Greek mythology, the wife of Odysseus, who waited for his return from the Trojan War and was the mother of his son, Telemachus

pe·ne·plain /péenə plàyn/, **pe·ne·plane** *n.* an area of nearly flat featureless land that is the result of a prolonged period of erosion —**pe·ne·pla·na·tion** /pèenəplə náysh'n/ *n.*

pe·nes plural of **penis**

pen·e·tra·ble /pénnətrəb'l/ *adj.* capable of being penetrated —**pen·e·tra·bil·i·ty** /pènnətrə bíllətee/ *n.* —**pe·ne·tra·bly** /pénnətrəblee/ *adv.*

pen·e·tra·li·a /pènnə tráylee ə/ *npl.* the innermost parts of a place, especially a sanctuary within a temple (*formal*) [Mid-17thC. From Latin, from *penetralis* "innermost," from *penetrare* (see PENETRATE).] —**pen·e·tra·li·an** *adj.*

pen·e·tram·e·ter *n.* = **penetrometer**

pen·e·trance /pénnətrəns/ *n.* the frequency with which a particular hereditary characteristic, e.g., a genetic disease, occurs among individuals carrying the gene or genes for that characteristic [Mid-20thC. From German *Penetranz*.]

pen·e·trant /pénnətrənt/ *n.* **1.** CHEM SUBSTANCE THAT HELPS A LIQUID TO PENETRATE a substance that encourages a liquid to penetrate a porous material by lowering the surface tension of the liquid ○ *The aim of the mission was to penetrate deep into enemy territory.* **2.** SOMETHING THAT PENETRATES somebody or something that penetrates

of minerals, occurring in low-grade metamorphic rocks [Mid-19thC. Named for the *Pennine* Alps, on the Swiss-Italian border.]

pen·non /pénnən/ *n.* **1. LONG NARROW FLAG CARRIED ON A LANCE** a long narrow flag, usually triangular, tapering, or divided at the end, originally carried on a lance by a medieval knight **2.** NAUT = **pennant** *n.* 1 **3. BIRDS WING OR PINION** a bird's wing or the pinion of a wing (*literary*) [14thC. Via French *penon*, literally "a large feather," from, ultimately, Latin *penna* "feather."]

pen·non·cel /pènnən sél/, **pen·non·celle, pen·on·cel, pen·on·celle** *n.* a small narrow flag (**pennon**), usually triangular, tapering, or divided at the end, attached to the end of a lance [14thC. From Old French *penoncel*, literally "a small pennon" (see PENNON).]

Pennsylvania

Penn·syl·va·nia /pènsəl váynyə/ state in the eastern United States bordered by New York, New Jersey, Delaware, Maryland, West Virginia, and Ohio. Capital: Harrisburg. Population: 12,019,661 (1997). Area: 45,789 sq. mi./118,515 sq. km.

Penn·syl·va·nia Dutch *npl.* **GERMAN AND SWISS IMMIGRANTS IN PENNSYLVANIA** a group of people who emigrated from Germany and Switzerland to eastern Pennsylvania in the 17th and 18th centuries, or their descendants ■ *n.* **1. Penn·syl·va·nia Dutch, Penn·syl·va·nia Ger·man** LANG **GERMAN DIALECT SPOKEN IN PENNSYLVANIA** a dialect of German mixed with some English that is spoken in eastern parts of Pennsylvania by the Pennsylvania Dutch. Pennsylvania Dutch is spoken by about 70,000 people. **2. FOLK ART THAT USES STYLIZED FIGURES** a type of folk art developed by the Pennsylvania Dutch that uses stylized figures of people, plants, and animals, primarily in the decoration of household objects and in needlework [Mid-18thC. Alteration of German *Deutsch* "German."]

Penn·syl·va·nian /pènsəl váynyən, -váynee ən/ *n.* **1.** PEOPLES **SOMEBODY FROM PENNSYLVANIA** somebody who was born in or lives in Pennsylvania **2.** GEOL **GEOLOGIC PERIOD** the period of geologic time in North America when the climate was relatively warm and damp and the major coal beds were formed, 320 to 290 million years ago. It is the second of two epochs of the Carboniferous Period used by North American geologists. —**Penn·syl·va·nian** *adj.*

pen·ny /pénnee/ (*plural* **-nies**) *n.* **1. COIN IN UNITED STATES AND CANADA** a small coin worth one cent used in the United States and Canada **2. SMALL BRITISH COIN** a small bronze coin or unit of money used in Britain since 1971, worth one hundredth of a pound. Symbol **p 3. FORMER BRITISH COIN** a bronze coin or a unit of money used in Britain before 1971, worth one twelfth of a shilling, or one two-hundred-and-fortieth of a pound. Symbol **d 4. COIN WITH LOW VALUE** a coin or monetary unit with a low value or equal to one hundredth of a dollar or one hundredth of a pound in some countries **5. VERY SMALL AMOUNT OF MONEY** a very small amount of money ○ *It won't cost you a penny.* [Old English *penig*. Ultimately, from a prehistoric Germanic word that also produced German *Pfennig* "penny."] ◇ **a penny for your thoughts** used to ask somebody what he or she is thinking about ◇ **cost a pretty penny** to cost a great deal of money ◇ **the penny dropped** used to say that you suddenly understood or realized something ◇ **penny wise and pound foolish** economical with regard to small items of expenditure but extravagant with regard to large items ◇ **turn up like a bad penny** to keep making unwelcome appearances

pen·ny an·te *n.* **1.** CARDS **TYPE OF POKER** a game of poker in which the bets are limited to small sums of money **2.** COMM **BUSINESS TRANSACTION INVOLVING VERY LITTLE MONEY** any business arrangement that involves very little money or is inconsequential (*informal*) ○ *We're talking penny ante here.* —**pen·ny-an·te** *adj.*

pen·ny ar·cade *n.* a place or covered area that has coin-operated machines for the public to use

pen·ny can·dy *n.* small pieces of candy that cost about a penny, often purchased one or a few at a time through a machine

pen·ny·cress /pénnee krèss/ *n.* a plant with round flat seed pods, native to Europe and Asia but now naturalized throughout the United States. Genus: *Thlaspi.*

pen·ny pinch·er *n.* somebody who is extremely stingy or excessively careful with his or her money (*informal*)

pen·ny·roy·al /pènnee róyəl/ *n.* **1. MINT PLANT OF EUROPE AND ASIA** a plant of the mint family with clusters of small purple flowers that is native to Europe and Asia and is used in medicines and as an insect repellent. Latin name: *Mentha pulegium.* **2. N AMERICAN MINT PLANT** an aromatic plant of the mint family that grows in eastern North America, especially a variety with bluish flowers. Latin name: *Hedeoma pulegioides.* [Mid-16thC. Alteration of Anglo-Norman *puliol real*, literally "royal thyme."]

pen·ny stock *n.* securities that sell on a stock exchange, often at less than one dollar a share

pen·ny·weight /pénnee wàyt/ *n.* a unit of weight in the troy system, equal to 1/20 oz/1.555 g [Old English *penega gewiht*, the weight of a silver penny]

pen·ny whis·tle *n.* a small high-pitched flute with six finger holes, similar to a recorder but made of metal and very inexpensive to buy

pen·ny-wise *adj.* extremely careful about spending even small amounts of money

pen·ny·wort /pénnee wùrt, -wàwrt/ *n.* **1. ROCK PLANT** a plant that grows on rocks in Europe and Asia and has whitish-green tubular flowers and rounded leaves. Latin name: *Umbilicus rupestris.* **2. MARSH PLANT** a plant that grows in marshy areas in Europe and North Africa and has greenish-pink flowers and rounded leaves. Latin name: *Hydrocotyle vulgaris.* **3. PLANT WITH ROUNDED LEAVES** a North American plant of the gentian family with small white or purplish flowers and rounded leaves. Latin name: *Obolaria virginica.*

pen·ny·worth /pénni wùrth/ *n.* (*dated*) **1.** (*plural* **-worths** *or* **-worth**) **AMOUNT COSTING A PENNY** the amount of something that can be bought for a penny **2. SMALL AMOUNT** a small amount or the slightest amount **3. BARGAIN** something worth having at the price [Old English *penig weorð*]

pe·nol·o·gy /pee nóllәjee/ *n.* the theory, scientific study of, and practice of how crime is punished, how prisons are managed, and how rehabilitation is handled [Mid-19thC. Formed from Latin *poena* (see PENAL).] —**pe·no·log·i·cal** /pèenə lójjik'l/ *adj.* —**pe·no·log·i·cal·ly** *adv.* —**pe·nol·o·gist** /pee nóllәjist/ *n.*

pen pal *n.* either of two people usually in different countries, who become friends through an exchange of letters but who may never meet

pen point *n.* the tip, point, or nib of a pen

pen·push·er /pén pŏŏshər/ *n. U.K.* = **pencil pusher** (*informal*) —**pen·push·ing** *adj., n.*

Pen·sa·co·la /pènssə kṓlə/ city in northwestern Florida, on the Gulf of Mexico. Population: 58,165 (1990).

pen·sile /pénsəl/ *adj.* **1. HANGING** hanging or suspended ○ *a pensile nest* **2. BUILDING A HANGING NEST** used to describe a bird such as the Baltimore Oriole that builds a hanging nest [Early 17thC. Via Latin *pensilis*, from *pens-*, the past participle stem of *pendere* (see PENDANT).] —**pen·sile·ness** *n.* —**pen·sil·i·ty** /pen sílləte e/ *n.*

pen·sion[1] /pénshən/ *n.* **1. RETIREMENT PAY** a fixed amount of money paid regularly to somebody during retirement by the government, a former employer, or insurance company **2. REGULAR SUM PAID** a sum of money paid regularly as compensation, e.g., for an injury sustained on a job, or as a reward for service, e.g., to an ex-soldier ■ *vt.* (**-sioned, -sion·ing, -sions**) **PAY A PENSION** to pay a pension to somebody [14thC. Via French from Latin *pension-* "payment," from *pens-*, the past participle stem of *pendere* (see PENDANT).]

pension off *vt.* **1. FORCE SOMEBODY TO RETIRE** to force somebody into retirement with a pension, e.g. , as a cost-cutting measure or because of age **2. GET RID OF** to get rid of something because it is useless or no longer needed (*informal*)

pen·sion[2] /paan syáwn/ *n.* **1. SMALL HOTEL** a boarding house or small inexpensive hotel in continental Europe, especially in France **2. ACCOMMODATIONS** accommodations provided by a European pension **3.** = **room and board**

pen·sion·a·ble /pénshənəb'l/ *adj.* entitled to or relating to entitlement to receive a pension — **pen·sion·a·bil·i·ty** /pénshənə billətee/ *n.*

pen·sion·ar·y /pénshə nèrree/ *adj.* **OF A PENSION** relating to a pension or the paying of a pension ■ *n.* (*plural* **-ies**) = **pensioner** *n.* 2 (*archaic or literary*)

pen·sion·er /pénshənər/ *n.* **1. SOMEBODY RECEIVING PENSION** somebody who is paid a pension, especially somebody who has retired from work **2.** PENSIONS **HIRED PERSON** somebody whose services are bought, especially somebody paid to do menial or unpleasant work (*archaic or literary*)

pen·sive /pénsiv/ *adj.* thinking deeply about something, especially in a sad or serious manner [14thC. Via French, from *penser* "to think," from Latin *pensare*, literally "to keep on weighing," from *pendere* "to weigh" (source of English *poise*).] —**pen·sive·ly** *adv.* — **pen·sive·ness** *n.*

pen·ste·mon /pen stéemən, pénstəmən/ *n.* a North American plant belonging to the figwort family that has large brightly-colored flowers with five stamens, one of which is sterile. Genus: *Penstemon.* [Mid-18thC. From modern Latin, the genus name, literally "five stamens," from Greek *penta-* "five" + *stēmōn* "stamen."]

pen·stock /pén stòk/ *n.* a sluice, channel, or pipe used to control water flow or supply water to something such as a hydroelectric plant [Early 17thC. From PEN "enclosure."]

pent /pent/ *adj.* (*archaic*) **1. SHUT IN** shut in or confined **2. REPRESSED** stifled or repressed ■ past tense, past participle of **pen** (*archaic*) [Late 16thC. Originally, the past participle of PEN "to enclose."]

pent- *prefix.* = **penta-** (*used before vowels*)

penta- *prefix.* five ○ *pentaploid* [From Greek *pente* "five" (source of English *pentagon*). Ultimately from the Indo-European word for "five," which is also the ancestor of English *five, finger*, and *fist*, as well as Latin *quinque.*]

pen·ta·chlo·ro·phe·nol /pèntə klawrə fée nàwl/ *n.* a white chemical compound that is used in fungicides, disinfectants, and wood preservatives. Formula: C_6Cl_5OH.

pen·ta·cle /péntək'l/ *n.* MATH = **pentagram** [Late 16thC. From medieval Latin *pentaculum*, literally "little five," from Greek *penta-* (see PENTA-).]

pen·tad /pén tàd/ *n.* **1.** MATH **GROUP OF FIVE** any group or series of five **2.** CHEM **ATOM WITH VALENCE OF FIVE** an atom or chemical group with a valence of five **3.** METEOROL **5 DAYS** a period of five days [Mid-17thC. From Greek, from *pente* (see PENTA-).]

pen·ta·dac·tyl /pèntə dákt'l/ *adj.* ZOOL having five fingers on each hand or five toes on each foot — **pen·ta·dac·ty·late** /pèntə dákt'lət, -àyt/ *adj.* —**pen·ta·dac·tyl·ism** /pèntə dákt'l ìzzəm/ *n.*

pen·ta·gon /péntə gòn/ *n.* MATH a geometric figure that has five sides and five angles [Late 16thC. Via late Latin *pentagonum* from, ultimately, Greek *pentagōnos*, literally "five-angled," from *penta-* (see PENTA-).] — **pen·tag·o·nal** /pen tággən'l/ *adj.* —**pen·tag·o·nal·ly** *adv.*

Pen·ta·gon *n.* the U.S. Department of Defense, or the five-sided main building that houses it

Pen·ta·gon·ese /pèntəgə néez, -néess/ *n.* the euphemistic indirect jargon-ridden language considered by some to be characteristic of the U.S. military leadership

pen·ta·gram /péntə gràm/ *n.* MATH a star-shaped geometric figure with five points, especially one used as a magical or occult symbol [Mid-19thC. From Greek *pentagrammon*, a form of *pentagrammos* "of five lines."]

pen·ta·he·dron /pèntə héedrən/ (*plural* **-drons** *or* **-dra** /pèntə héedrə/) *n.* MATH a solid geometric figure that has five faces —**pen·ta·he·dral** *adj.*

pen·tam·er·ous /pen támmərəss/ *adj.* **1. WITH 5 SIMILAR PARTS** divided into or having five similar parts **2.** BOT **WITH 5 SIMILAR FLOWER PARTS** used to describe flowers that have petals or other parts such as sepals or stamens arranged in groups of five —**pen·tam·er·ism** *n.*

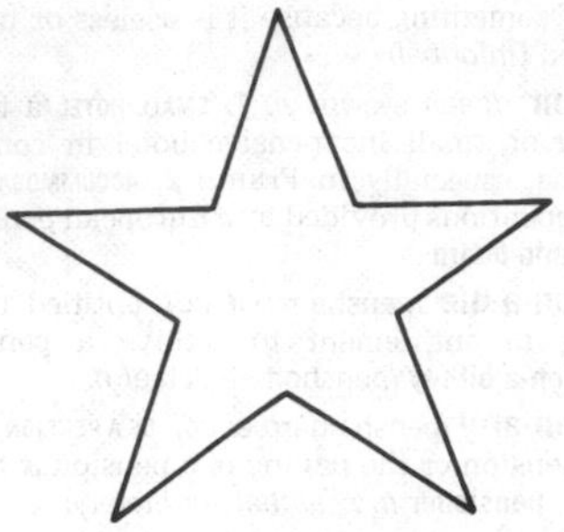

Pentagram

pen·tam·e·ter /pen támmətər/ *n.* a line of poetry that is made up of five units of rhythm, e.g., five pairs of stressed and unstressed syllables [Early 16thC. Via Latin from Greek *pentametros*, literally "having five measures," from *penta-* (see PENTA-) + *metron* (see METER).]

pen·tam·i·dine /pen támmə deen/ *n.* a drug used in treating protozoan infections, such as the African forms of sleeping sickness and the form of pneumonia often caught by AIDS patients. Formula: $C_{19}H_{24}N_4O_2$. [Mid-20thC. From PENTANE + *amidine*.]

pen·tane /pén tàyn/ *n.* an organic chemical belonging to the group containing only hydrogen and carbon (**hydrocarbons**). It has three isomers, one of which produces a colorless flammable liquid used as a solvent. Formula: C_5H_{12}. [Late 19thC. Formed from PENTA-.]

pen·tan·gle /pèn táng g'l/ *n.* MATH = **pentagram**

pen·tan·gu·lar /pen táng gyələr/ *adj.* MATH having five angles and five sides

pen·ta·pep·tide /pèntə pép tīd/ *n.* a peptide with five amino acids in its molecules

pen·ta·prism /péntə prìzzəm/ *n.* OPTICS a prism with five faces that deviates light at a 90-degree angle, making it useful in correctly presenting an image in the viewfinder of a single-lens reflex camera

pen·ta·quine /péntə kween/, **pen·ta·quin** /-kwin/ *n.* a synthetic drug used together with quinine in treating or preventing malaria. Formula: $C_{18}H_{27}N_3O$. [Coined from PENTA- + QUINOLINE]

pen·tar·chy /pén taarkee/ (*plural* **-chies**) *n.* **1. GOVERNMENT BY 5 RULERS** a system of government by five rulers **2. 5 POLITICAL UNITS** a federation of five political units **3. 5 RULERS** the group of five rulers who rule a pentarchy [Late 16thC. From Greek *pentarkhia* "rule of five," from *penta-* (see PENTA-) + *-arkhia* (see -ARCHY).] — **pen·tar·chi·cal** /pen taarkik'l/ *adj.*

pen·ta·stich /péntə stìk/ *n.* a poem or section of a poem consisting of five lines [Mid-17thC. Via modern Latin from Greek *pentastikhos*, literally "having five rows," from *penta-* (see PENTA-) + *stikhos* "row."]

pen·ta·stome /péntə stōm/ *n.* ZOOL = **tongue worm**

Pen·ta·teuch /péntə to͝ok/ *n.* the first five books of the Bible, traditionally regarded as having been written by Moses [15thC. Via ecclesiastical Latin from Greek *pentateukhos*, literally "having five books," from *penta-* (see PENTA-) + *teukhos* "book."] —**Pen·ta·teuch·al** /péntə to͝ok'l, pèntə to͝ok'l/ *adj.*

pen·tath·lete /pen táthleet/ *n.* an athlete who takes part in a pentathlon

pen·tath·lon /pen táthlən, -táth lòn/ *n.* **1.** = **modern pentathlon 2. OLYMPIC TRACK AND FIELD CONTEST** the Olympic competition consisting of five track and field events, usually sprinting, hurdling, long jumping, and discus and javelin throwing [Early 17thC. From Greek, literally "contest of five," from *penta-* (see PENTA-) + *athlon* "contest."]

pen·ta·tom·ic /pèntə tómmik/ *adj.* having five atoms in a molecule

pen·ta·ton·ic scale /pèntə tonnik-/ *n.* any musical scale that has five notes to an octave, especially a major scale in which the fourth and seventh tones are omitted [*Pentatonic* from PENTA- + TONIC]

pen·ta·va·lent /pèntə vàylənt/ *adj.* used to describe chemical elements that have a valence of five

pen·taz·o·cine /pen tázzə seen/ *n.* a synthetic narcotic drug used as a painkiller. Formula: $C_{19}H_{27}NO$. [Mid-20thC. Coined from PENTA- + AZO- + OCTA- + -INE.]

Pen·te·cost /péntə kòst/ *n.* **1.** CHR **CHRISTIAN CELEBRATION** a Christian festival celebrated on the seventh Sunday after Easter that commemorates the descent of the Holy Spirit upon the apostles **2.** JUDAISM = **Shavuoth** [Pre-12thC. Via late Latin from, ultimately, Greek *pentēkonta* "fifty" (because it falls fifty days after the second day of the Passover), from *pente* "five."]

Pen·te·cos·tal /pèntə kóst'l/ *adj.* **1. EMPHASIZING THE HOLY SPIRIT** belonging or relating to any Christian denomination that emphasizes the workings of the Holy Spirit, interprets the Bible literally, and adopts an informal demonstrative approach to religious worship **2. OF PENTECOST** relating to the Christian festival of Pentecost ■ *n.* **MEMBER OF A PENTECOSTAL DENOMINATION** a member of a Pentecostal denomination —**Pen·te·cos·tal·ism** *n.* —**Pen·te·cos·tal·ist** *n., adj.*

pen·tene /pén teen/ *n.* a colorless flammable liquid with several isomers that is used in making organic compounds. Formula: C_5H_{10}.

pent·house /pént hòwss/ (*plural* **-houses** /-hòwzəz/) *n.* **1. ROOFTOP DWELLING** an expensive and comfortable apartment on the top floor of a building or built on the roof (*often used before a noun*) ○ *a penthouse apartment* **2. HOUSING FOR SERVICE EQUIPMENT** a structure on the roof of a building to house elevator machinery, a water tank, or other service equipment **3. ADJOINING ROOF OR SHED** a sloping roof, or a shed with a sloping roof, built against the outer wall of a building **4.** SPORTS **ROOFED CORRIDOR** in court tennis, a roofed corridor that runs along three sides of a court [14thC. Alteration (influenced by HOUSE) of Anglo-Norman *pentiz* "lean-to," via Old French *apentis* from, ultimately, Latin *appendere*, literally "to hang onto," from *pendere* "to hang."]

pen·ti·men·to /pèntə méntō/ (*plural* **-ti** /-méntee/) *n.* **1. TECHNIQUE FOR RESTORING PAINTINGS** the technique of removing a top layer of paint to reveal a painting or part of a painting that has been painted over **2. REVEALED PAINTING** a painting or part of a painting that is revealed by pentimento [Early 20thC. Via Italian, "correction," literally "repentance," from Latin *paenitere* "to repent" (source also of English *penitent*).]

pent·land·ite /péntlən dīt/ *n.* a brownish-yellow mineral that is the principal ore and main source of nickel [Mid-19thC. Named for the Irish scientist Joseph B. *Pentland* (1797–1873), who discovered it.]

pen·to·bar·bi·tal so·di·um /pentə baarbət'l-/ *n.* a barbiturate used as a hypnotic and a sedative. Formula: $C_{11}H_{17}N_2O_3Na$. [*Pentobarbital* formed from *pentobarbitone* (see PENTOBARBITONE)]

pen·to·bar·bi·tone so·di·um /pentə baarbə tōn-/ *n. U.K.* = **pentobarbital sodium** [*Pentobarbitone* coined from PENTANE + BARBITONE]

pen·tode /pén tōd/ *n.* **ELECTRONIC DEVICE WITH 5 ELECTRODES** a vacuum tube that has five electrodes. They are a cathode, an anode, and three grids. ■ *adj.* **WITH 3 ELECTRODES** used to describe a transistor that has three electrodes at the base or gate [Early 20thC. Formed from PENTA-.]

pen·to·san /péntə sàn/ *n.* an organic compound found mainly in plants, whose polysaccharide carbohydrates break down to form pentoses

pen·tose /pén tōss/ *n.* a carbohydrate found in plants and nucleic acids that is a monosaccharide whose molecules each contain five carbon atoms

pen·tose phos·phate path·way *n.* BIOCHEM a cyclic sequence of chemical reactions in the cytoplasm of animal and plant cells in which glucose molecules are converted into biochemically useful smaller molecules. These smaller molecules include ribose molecules needed for nucleic acid synthesis.

Pen·to·thal /péntə thàwl/ *tdmk.* a trademark for thiopental sodium, also known as sodium pentothal, a barbiturate drug used in medicine

pent·ox·ide /pen tók sīd/ *n.* a chemical element whose oxides contain five atoms of oxygen in each molecule

pent-up *adj.* repressed or stifled rather than being released or freely expressed ○ *pent-up emotions*

pen·tyl /péntil/ *adj.* relating to a chemical group containing carbon and hydrogen, deriving from pentane. Formula: C_5H_{11}. [Late 19thC. Formed from PENTA-.]

pen·tyl ac·e·tate *n.* a colorless combustible liquid used as a solvent for paints, in extracting penicillin, in photographic film, and as a flavoring. Formula: $CH_3COOC_5H_{11}$.

pen·tyl·ene·tet·ra·zol /pèntəleen téttrə zòl/ *n.* a white crystalline powder used to stimulate the central nervous system. Formula: $C_6H_{10}N_4$. [Mid-20thC. Coined from PENTA- + METHYLENE + *tetrazole*.]

pe·nu·che /pə no͞ochee/, **pe·nu·chi** *n.* a fudge made from brown sugar, butter, milk, and nuts [Mid-19thC. Alteration of Mexican Spanish *panocha* "coarse brown sugar," via Spanish, "ear of maize," from, ultimately, Latin *panicula*, literally "little tuft," from *panus* "tuft."]

pe·nult /pee nùlt, pə núlt/ *n.* the second to last item in a series of things, especially the second to last syllable of a word [15thC. Shortening of Latin *penultima*, the feminine of *paenultimus* (see PENULTIMATE).]

pe·nul·ti·mate /pə núltimət/ *adj.* **1. SECOND TO LAST** second to last in a series or sequence ○ *the penultimate chapter* **2.** LING **OF A PENULT** relating to a penult [Late 17thC. From Latin *paenultimus*, from *paene* "almost" + *ultimus* "last" (see ULTIMATE).] — **pe·nul·ti·mate·ly** *adv.*

pe·num·bra /pə númbrə/ (*plural* **-brae** /-bree/ *or* **-bras**) *n.* **1.** ASTRON **PARTIAL SHADOW** a partial outer shadow that is lighter than the darker inner shadow (**umbra**), e.g., the area between complete darkness and complete light in an eclipse **2.** ASTRON **EDGE OF A SUNSPOT** a grayish area surrounding the dark center of a sunspot **3. INDETERMINATE AREA** an indistinct area, especially a state in which something is unclear or uncertain **4. PERIPHERY** the outer region or periphery of something [Mid-17thC. From modern Latin, literally "almost shadow," from Latin *paene* "almost" + *umbra* "shadow."] —**pe·num·bral** *adj.* —**pe·num·brous** *adj.*

pe·nu·ri·ous /pə no͝orree əss/ *adj.* (*literary*) **1. POOR** having very little money **2. NOT GENEROUS** not generous with money **3. BARREN** barren or yielding little — **pe·nu·ri·ous·ly** *adv.* —**pe·nu·ri·ous·ness** *n.*

pen·u·ry /pényəree/ *n.* extreme poverty [15thC. From Latin *penuria*, of uncertain origin.]

WORD KEY: SYNONYMS

See Synonyms at ***poverty***.

pe·on /pee òn, pee ən/ *n.* **1. LABORER** in Latin America and the southern United States, a farm laborer, especially in former times, who was forced to work for a creditor until a debt was paid off **2. DRUDGE** somebody who does boring menial work **3. LOW-PAID WORKER** formerly, in India and Sri Lanka, a low-paid office worker, soldier, or public servant [Early 17thC. Via Spanish *peón* and Portuguese *peão* "foot soldier," from the medieval Latin stem *pedon-*, from Latin *pes* "foot."]

pe·on·age /pee ənij/ *n.* **1. DEBT-REPAYMENT SYSTEM** a former system used in Latin America and the southern United States under which a debtor was forced to work for a creditor until a debt was paid **2. STATUS OF PEON** the status or condition of being a peon

pe·o·ny /pee ənee/ (*plural* **-nies**) *n.* **1. SHOWY FLOWERING PLANT** a shrub belonging to the buttercup family that has large globe-shaped red, white, or pink flowers and is native to Europe, Asia, and North America. Genus: *Paeonia*. **2. PEONY FLOWER** the flower of a peony [Old English *peonie*. Via medieval Latin from, ultimately, Greek *paiōnia*, from *Paiōn* "Paian," the physician of the deities.]

peo·ple /peep'l/ *n.* (*plural* **-ples**) **NATION** a nation, community, ethnic group or nationality ○ *a proud people* ■ *npl.* **1. HUMAN BEINGS COLLECTIVELY** human beings considered collectively or in general ○ *People tend not to mind if you ask them for help.* **2. SUBORDINATES** persons such as employees, subjects, or followers who are under the authority or leadership of somebody or something ○ *I'll get one of my people to phone them.* **3. FAMILY MEMBERS** the members of somebody's family, especially somebody's family (*informal*) ○ *My people were farmers.* **4. ORDINARY MEN AND WOMEN** the general population, as distinct from the government or higher social classes ○ *the will of the people* **5. POLITICAL UNIT** a group of persons comprising a political unit, electorate, or group ■ *vt.* (**-pled, -pling, -ples**) **POPULATE AREA** to populate an area (*usually passive*) ○ *mountain regions that are sparsely peopled* [13thC. Via Anglo-Norman from Latin *populus* (source of English *popular* and *public*), of Etruscan origin.]

peo·ple·hood /peep'l ho͝od/ *n.* identity as a member of a particular people, especially a nation or ethnic group

peo·ple mov·er *n.* any automated means of transporting large numbers of people over short distances

peo·ple skills *npl.* the ability to deal with people and get along with them, e.g., because of being sensitive or diplomatic

peo·ple's re·pub·lic *n.* a Socialist or Communist republic

pep /pep/ (**pepped, pep·ping, peps**) *n.* liveliness or vigor (*informal*) [Early 20thC. Shortening of PEPPER.]

pep up *vt.* to make somebody or something more lively, energetic, or interesting (*informal*)

pep·er·o·mi·a /pèppə rṓmee ə/ *n.* a tropical or subtropical plant belonging to the pepper family that is often cultivated as a house plant for its attractive heavily veined foliage. Genus: *Peperomia.* [Late 19thC. From modern Latin *Peperomia,* the genus name, from Greek *peperi* (see PEPPER).]

pe·pi·no /pə pée nō/ (*plural* **-nos**) *n.* **1.** PLANTS **SPINY PLANT** a Peruvian plant belonging to the nightshade family that has spiny foliage, bright blue flowers, and edible purple-streaked fruit. Latin name: *Solanum muricatum.* **2.** PLANTS **FRUIT OF PEPINO PLANT** the eggplant-shaped fruit of the pepino plant that has a flavor like that of a melon **3.** GEOG **CONE-SHAPED HILL** a steep conical hill, especially in Puerto Rico [Mid-19thC. Via American Spanish from, ultimately, Latin *pepo* (see PUMPKIN).]

pep·la plural of **peplum**

pep·los /pépplǝss/, **pep·lus** *n.* a loose-fitting garment worn by women in ancient Greece, draped in folds around the shoulders and reaching the waist [Late 18thC. From Greek.]

pep·lum /pépplǝm/ (*plural* **-lums** *or* **-la** /-plǝ/) *n.* a short flared ruffle attached to the waist of a jacket or blouse [Late 17thC. From Latin, from Greek *peplos* (see PEPLOS).]

pe·po /pée pō/ (*plural* **-pos**) *n.* a fruit of the gourd family such as a melon, squash, pumpkin, or cucumber that typically has a firm or hard rind, a large number of flat seeds, and soft watery flesh [Mid-19thC. From Latin (see PUMPKIN).]

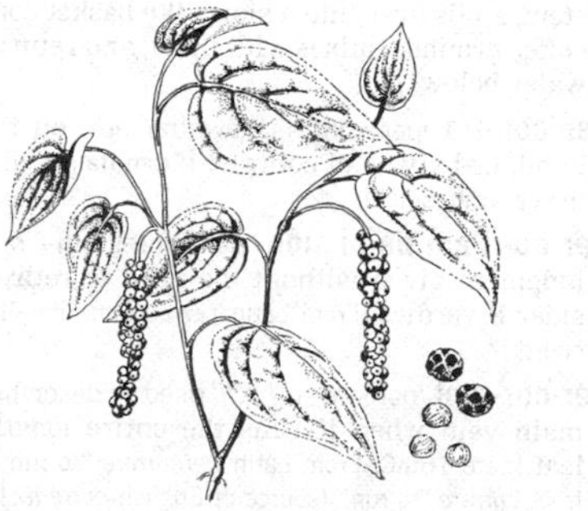

Pepper

pep·per /péppər/ *n.* **1.** FOOD **SEASONING** a hot condiment or seasoning made from the ground dried berries of a tropical climbing plant. Black pepper is made from berries that are dried before they ripen, and white pepper from berries that ripen before being dried. **2.** PLANTS **PLANT WITH BERRIES** a tropical climbing plant such as betel, cubeb, or kava whose berries are dried for use as pepper. Genus: *Piper.* **3.** FOOD **HOLLOW VEGETABLE** a green, red, or yellow vegetable that is hollow with firm walls containing seeds and has mild or pungent flesh that can be eaten either raw or cooked **4.** PLANTS **PLANT WITH EDIBLE PODS** a tropical plant of the nightshade family that bears mild or pungent peppers as fruit. Genus: *Capsicum.* **5.** FOOD **PUNGENT CONDIMENTS** condiments such as chili sauce or cayenne pepper made from the more strongly pungent peppers **6.** BASEBALL **BASEBALL WARMUP ROUTINE** a baseball warmup routine with fielders standing close to the batter and quickly tossing the ball to the batter, who in turn hits each toss back to the fielders ■ *v.* (**-pered, -per·ing, -pers**) **1.** *vt.* **SPRINKLE WITH PEPPER** to add or sprinkle pepper as a seasoning onto something **2.** *vt.* **ASSAIL SOMEBODY OR SOMETHING** to bombard somebody or something with something **3. SPRINKLE SOMETHING AROUND** to scatter things liberally on to or among something (*often passive*) ○ *manuscripts peppered with typing errors* **4.** *vt.* **MAKE SOMETHING LIVELY** to liven up something such as a speech with wit [Old English *piper.* Via the prehistoric West Germanic language from Latin *piper* (source of English *pimpernel*), from, ultimately, Sanskrit *pippalī* "berry, peppercorn."]

pep·per-and-salt *adj.* flecked with dark and light colors ○ *pepper-and-salt hair*

pep·per·box /péppər bòks/ *n.* **1.** = **peppershaker 2.** ARCHIT **CYLINDRICAL TURRET** a cylindrical turret or cupola **3.** ARMS **SMALL PISTOL** a small 18th-century pistol with several short revolving barrels

pep·per·corn /péppər kàwrn/ *n.* **1. PEPPER BERRY** a small dried tropical berry that is ground to make pepper. Black peppercorns are dried before they ripen, giving them a sweeter deeper flavor than white peppercorns. **2. SOMETHING INSIGNIFICANT** something that is very small or has little importance or value [Old English *piporcorn*]

pep·pered moth *n.* a moth that is gray and speckled when found in rural areas and black in smoke-darkened industrial regions. Latin name: *Biston betularia.*

Pep·per·ell /péppə rəl/, **Sir William** (1696–1759) colonial New England military officer. He commanded the forces that captured Louisbourg from the French in 1745.

pep·per game *n.* BASEBALL = **pepper** *n.* **6**

pep·per·grass /péppər gràss/ *n.* a plant of the mustard family whose pungent lower leaves are used in salads and to season dishes. Genus: *Lepidium.*

pep·per·idge /pépperij/ *n.* TREES = **sour gum** [Mid-16thC. Origin unknown.]

pep·per mill *n.* a kitchen utensil for storing and grinding peppercorns

Peppermint

pep·per·mint /péppər mìnt/ *n.* **1.** PLANTS **PUNGENT HERB** a plant of the mint family whose dark green downy leaves yield a pungent oil. Latin name: *Mentha piperita.* **2.** FOOD **FLAVORING** a flavoring prepared from the peppermint plant's aromatic oil, used in the food and pharmaceutical industries (*often used before a noun*) **3.** FOOD **PEPPERMINT CANDY** a candy flavored with peppermint

pep·per·o·ni /pèppə rṓnee/ *n.* a hard dry Italian sausage spiced with pepper, or a slice of this, often used on pizzas [Mid-20thC. Via Italian *peperone* "red pepper," from, ultimately, Latin *piper* (see PEPPER).]

pep·per pot *n.* **1.** FOOD **STEW** a Guyanese or West Indian stew made with meat, rice, and vegetables and seasoned with cassava syrup **2.** *U.K.* = **peppershaker 3.** FOOD **SOUP** a peppery Pennsylvania soup made with vegetables, tripe, or meat, and sometimes dumplings

pep·per·shak·er /péppər shàykər/ *n.* a small cylindrical container for ready-ground pepper with a perforated top for sprinkling

pep·per·shrike /péppər shrìk/ *n.* a small stocky North American bird of the vireo family with a thick hook-tipped bill. Genus: *Cyclarhis.*

pep·per spray *n.* an aerosol-deployed disabling agent with the active component oleoresin capsicum, used by law enforcement officers to disable somebody who is behaving in an aggressive or violent manner

pep·per steak *n.* a steak coated with crushed peppercorns before being fried or broiled

pep·per tree *n.* a subtropical South American tree belonging to the cashew family that is cultivated as an ornamental tree for its bright red fruits. Genus: *Schinus.*

pep·per·wort /péppər wùrt, -wàwrt/ *n.* **1. MARSH FERN** a freshwater fern with floating leaves and slender tangled stems that grows in marshes and ponds. Genus: *Marsilea.* **2.** = **peppergrass**

pep·per·y /pépparee/ *adj.* **1.** FOOD **CONTAINING PEPPER** strongly flavored with pepper or tasting of pepper **2. ANGRY** angry and critical **3. EASILY ANNOYED** easily annoyed

pep pill *n.* any pill that contains a stimulant drug, especially an amphetamine (*dated informal*)

pep·py /péppee/ (**-pier, -pi·est**) *adj.* lively and vigorous (*informal*) —**pep·pi·ly** *adv.* —**pep·pi·ness** *n.*

pep ral·ly *n.* a gathering designed to fire enthusiasm into those attending, especially in a school before a sporting event

pep·sin /pépsin/ *n.* an enzyme produced in the stomach that breaks down proteins into simpler compounds. It can be extracted from the stomachs of calves and hogs for use as a digestive aid and in the production of cheese. [Mid-19thC. Coined from Greek *pepsis* "digestion," from *peptein* (see PEPTIC).]

pep·sin·o·gen /pep sínnəjən/ *n.* a substance produced by stomach glands that is converted into pepsin after contact with hydrochloric acid during digestion

pep talk *n.* a short speech designed to give advice and generate enthusiasm, e.g., in a sports team or among a company's employees (*informal*)

pep·tic /péptik/ *adj.* **1. HELPING DIGESTION** relating to or helping digestion **2. INVOLVING PEPSIN** relating to, caused by, or producing pepsin **3. OF THE STOMACH** relating to or involving the stomach, especially any digestive actions or their results [Mid-17thC. Via Latin from Greek *peptikos* "capable of digesting," from *peptein* "to digest."]

pep·tic ul·cer *n.* erosion of the mucous membrane that lines the upper digestive tract, caused by excess secretion of acid in the stomach

pep·ti·dase /pépti dàyss, -dàyz/ *n.* an enzyme that breaks down peptides into amino acids

pep·tide /pép tīd/ *n.* **1. COMPOUND WITH AMINO BONDS** a chemical compound whose amino acids have chemical bonds between carboxyl and amino groups **2. LINEAR MOLECULE OF AMINO ACIDS** a linear molecule made up of two or more amino acids linked by peptide bonds [Early 20thC. From German *Peptid,* a back-formation from *Polypeptid* (see POLYPEPTIDE).] —**pep·tid·ic** /pep tíddik/ *adj.*

pep·tide bond *n.* a chemical bond formed when the amino group of one amino acid condenses with the carboxyl group of another

pep·ti·do·gly·can /pèptidō glīkən, -glī kàn/ *n.* a large molecule found in the cell walls of bacteria, giving the walls their strength and the cell its shape

pep·tize /pép tīz/ (**-tized, -tiz·ing, -tiz·es**) *vt.* to disperse fine particles of one substance evenly throughout another substance to create a state intermediate between a suspension and a solution (**colloid**) [Mid-19thC. Formed from PEPTONE.] —**pep·tiz·a·ble** *adj.* —**pep·ti·za·tion** /pèpti záysh'n/ *n.* —**pep·tiz·er** /pép tīzər/ *n.*

pep·tone /pép tōn/ *n.* a compound formed during the hydrolysis of proteins that does not dissolve in water and is used as a food source for microorganisms grown in laboratories [Mid-19thC. Via German from Greek *peptos* "digested," from *peptein* (see PEPTIC).]

pep·to·nize /péptə nīz/ (**-nized, -niz·ing, -niz·es**) *vt.* to digest food using an enzyme that breaks down protein —**pep·to·ni·za·tion** /pèptəni záysh'n/ *n.* —**pep·to·niz·er** /péptə nīzər/ *n.*

Pepys /peeps, péppiss/, **Samuel** (1633–1703) English diarist. His *Diary* (1660–69) includes detailed descriptions of the Plague and the Fire of London.

Pe·quot /pée kwòt/ (*plural* **-quot** *or* **-quots**) *n.* **1.** PEOPLES **MEMBER OF A NATIVE N AMERICAN PEOPLE** a member of a Native North American people who originally lived, and whose descendants still live, in eastern Connecticut **2.** LANG **PEQUOT LANGUAGE** an Algonquian language spoken in parts of New England, especially Connecticut. It is one of the Algonquian-Wakashan languages and is spoken by about seven thousand people. [Mid-17thC. From Narragansett *Pequtôog* "Pequot people."] —**Pe·quot** *adj.*

per /pər/ *prep.* **1. FOR EACH** for each or for every thing mentioned ○ *50 miles per hour* **2. ACCORDING TO SOMETHING** by, through, or according to something ○ *per instructions* ■ *adv.* **FOR EACH ONE** for each one (*informal*) [14thC. From Latin. Ultimately, from an Indo-European base meaning "through, forward," which is also the ancestor of English *for, pro,* and *pre-*.]

per. *abbr.* **1.** period **2.** person

per- *prefix.* **1.** through ○ *peroral* **2.** containing a large proportion of an element ○ *peroxide* **3.** containing an element in its highest oxidation state ○ *perchlorate* **4.** containing a peroxide group ○ *peracid* [From Latin *per* (see PER)]

per·ac·id /pə rássid/ *n.* an acid such as perchloric acid or permanganic acid in which one element is in its highest possible state of oxidation —**per·ac·id·i·ty** /pùrrə síddətee/ *n.*

per·ad·ven·ture /pùrrəd vénchər/ *adv.* PERHAPS possibly or perhaps (*archaic*) ■ *n.* CHANCE chance, doubt, or uncertainty (*literary*) [13thC. From Old French *per aventure* "by chance."]

per·am·bu·late /pə rámbyə làyt/ (**-lat·ed, -lat·ing, -lates**) *vti.* to walk about a place (*archaic or literary*) [Mid-16thC. From Latin *perambulare,* from *ambulare* "to walk" (source of English *amble*).] —**per·am·bu·la·to·ry** /pə rámbyələ tàwree/ *adj.* —**per·am·bu·la·tion** /pə ràmbyə láysh'n/ *n.*

per·am·bu·la·tor /pə rámbyə làytər/ *n.* **1.** BABY CARRIAGE a baby carriage (*archaic or formal*) **2.** TECH MEASURING DEVICE a device consisting of a wheel on a long handle, used to measure distance while walking [Early 17thC. Originally in the sense "somebody who walks."]

per an·num /pə ránnəm/ *adv.* in or for every year, or by the year [From modern Latin, literally "by the year"]

p/e ra·tio *abbr.* price-earnings ratio

per·bo·rate /pər báw ràyt/ *n.* a salt compound of borate used as a bleaching agent in washing powder

per·cale /pər káyl/ *n.* a smooth-textured closely woven cotton or polyester fabric used for bedsheets and clothing. It sometimes has a glazed finish. [Early 17thC. From French, of uncertain origin: possibly from Persian *pargālah* "rag."]

per·ca·line /pùrkə léen/ *n.* a glossy lightweight cotton fabric used for linings and book bindings [Mid-19thC. From French, from *percale* (see PERCALE).]

per cap·i·ta /pər káppitə/ *adv., adj.* by or for each person ○ *earnings per capita* [From modern Latin, literally "per head"]

per·ceive /pər séev/ (**-ceived, -ceiv·ing, -ceives**) *vt.* **1.** NOTICE USING THE SENSES to notice something, especially something that escapes the notice of others **2.** UNDERSTAND OR COMPREHEND to understand something in a particular way [13thC. Via Anglo-Norman and Old French variants of *perçoivre,* from Latin *percipere,* literally "to seize completely," from *capere* "to seize," (source of English *capture*).] —**per·ceiv·a·ble** *adj.* —**per·ceiv·a·bly** *adv.* —**per·ceiv·er** *n.*

per·cent *adv.* AS EXPRESSED IN HUNDREDTHS used to express a proportion of an amount in hundredths, represented by the symbol % ○ *a 10 percent rise* ■ *n.* (*plural* **-cent**) **1.** ONE HUNDREDTH one hundredth part of something **2.** PERCENTAGE a part or percentage [From Latin *per centum,* literally "by a hundred"]

per·cent·age /pər séntij/ *n.* **1.** PROPORTION IN ONE-HUNDREDTHS a proportion stated in terms of one-hundredths that is achieved by multiplying an amount by a percent **2.** PROPORTION a proportion of a larger group or set ○ *A larger percentage of students are choosing to go on to college* **3.** FIN COMMISSION OR CUT an amount charged that is based on the total amount involved, e.g., a commission charged on a sale, especially the commission that an agent charges a client (*informal*) **4.** ADVANTAGE advantage or benefit (*informal*) ○ *There's no percentage in accepting the proposal.*

per·cen·tile /pər sén tīl/ *n.* a value on a scale of one hundred that indicates whether a distribution is above or below it

per·cept /púr sèpt/ *n.* something that is perceived by the senses (*formal*) [Mid-19thC. From Latin *perceptum* "something perceived," the past participle of *percipere* (see PERCEIVE).]

per·cep·ti·ble /pər séptəb'l/ *adj.* large enough, great enough, or distinct enough to be noticed ○ *a perceptible difference* —**per·cep·ti·bil·i·ty** /pər sèptə bíllətee/ *n.* —**per·cep·ti·bly** *adv.*

per·cep·tion /pər sépshən/ *n.* **1.** PERCEIVING the process of using the senses to acquire information about the surrounding environment or situation ○ *the range of human perception* **2.** RESULT OF PERCEIVING the observation or result of the process of perception ○ *After watching the experiment closely, he noted his perceptions in his lab notebook.* **3.** IMPRESSION an attitude or understanding based on what is observed or thought ○ *a news report that altered the public's perception of the issue* **4.** POWERS OF OBSERVATION the ability to notice or discern things that escape the notice of most people **5.** PSYCHOL NEUROLOGICAL PROCESS OF OBSERVATION AND INTERPRETATION any of the neurological processes of acquiring and mentally interpreting information from the senses [14thC. Via Old French from the Latin stem *perception-,* from *percipere* (see PERCEIVE).] —**per·cep·tion·al** *adj.*

per·cep·tive /pər séptiv/ *adj.* **1.** QUICK TO UNDERSTAND quick to understand or discern things or showing understanding of a person or situation **2.** PERCEPTUAL relating to perception or capable of perceiving —**per·cep·tive·ly** *adv.* —**per·cep·tive·ness** *n.* —**per·cep·tiv·i·ty** /pùr sep tívvətee/ *n.*

per·cep·tu·al /pər sépchoo əl/ *adj.* relating to perception with the senses —**per·cep·tu·al·ly** *adv.*

per·cep·tu·al de·fense *n.* the process by which the mind may ignore or distort unwanted or threatening perceptions

perch[1] /purch/ *n.* **1.** PLACE FOR BIRD TO SIT a place for a bird to land or rest on, e.g., a branch or a pole in a cage **2.** RESTING PLACE any temporary resting place for a person or thing **3.** ADVANTAGEOUS POSITION a place or location that is secure, advantageous, or prominent **4.** MEASURE SOLID MEASURE FOR STONE a unit of measure for the volume of stone, equal to about 24 cu. ft./0.7 cu. m **5.** MEASURE UNIT OF LENGTH a unit of length equal to $5\frac{1}{2}$ yd./5.03 m **6.** MEASURE UNIT OF AREA a unit of area equal to $30\frac{1}{4}$ sq. yd./25.3 m^2 **7.** TEXTILES INSPECTION FRAME a frame that woven fabric is laid on to be inspected after weaving **8.** TRANSP = **pole 9.** PEG TO HANG THINGS a pole, bar, or peg on which to hang things ■ *v.* (**perched, perch·ing, perch·es**) **1.** *vt.* SIT PRECARIOUSLY to sit or stand somewhere awkwardly and precariously ○ *He was perched on a high stool.* **2.** *vt.* PUT IN A HIGH PLACE to situate something in a place high up ○ *the old fort perched on the clifftops* **3.** *vi.* BIRDS BE ON A PERCH to land or rest on a perch ○ *A pair of doves perched on the apple tree.* **4.** *vti.* TEXTILES LAY AN ITEM ON A PERCH to place something such as woven fabric on a perch to inspect after weaving [13thC. Via Old French from Latin *pertica* "pole, stick."] —**perch·er** *n.* ◇ **knock somebody off his** *or* **her perch** to make somebody feel less proud or superior

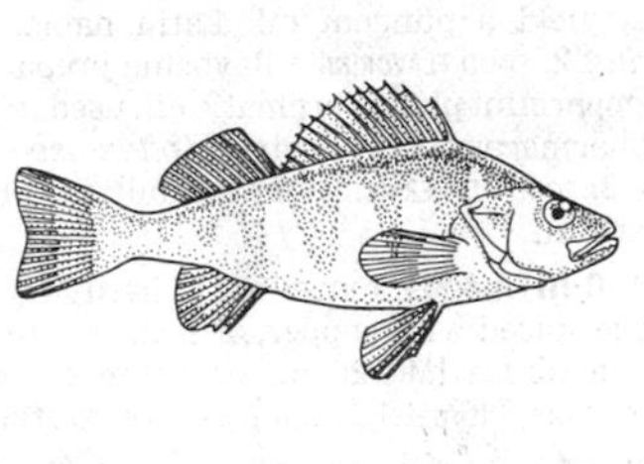

Perch

perch[2] /purch/ (*plural* **perch·es** *or* **perch**) *n.* an edible bony freshwater fish native to North America and Europe that has rough scales and two dorsal fins, one spiny and one soft. Genus: *Perca.* [14thC. Via Old French from, ultimately, Greek *perkē*.]

per·chance /pər chánss/ *adv.* (*archaic or literary*) **1.** PERHAPS possibly or perhaps **2.** BY CHANCE by chance [14thC. From Anglo-Norman *par chance,* literally "by chance."]

Per·che·ron /púrchə ròn, -ròn/ *n.* a large black or gray draft horse of a breed that originated in France [Late 19thC. From French, "of the Percheron breed," named for *le Perche,* a region of France where it was first bred.]

perch·ing bird *n.* a bird such as a lark, finch, or crow with feet adapted for clinging to horizontal branches

per·chlo·rate /pər kláw ràyt/ *n.* a salt or ester of perchloric acid

per·chlo·ric ac·id /pər klàwrik-/ *n.* a colorless acid of chlorine that is explosive under some conditions and that is used as a powerful oxidizing agent in laboratory work. Formula: $HClO_4$.

per·chlo·ride /pər kláw rīd/ *n.* a chloride of an element that contains more chlorine than all other chlorides of the same element

per·chlor·o·eth·yl·ene /pər klàwrō éthəleèn/ *n.* a colorless toxic organic solvent used in dry-cleaning fluid

per·cia·tel·li /pùrchə téllee/ *n.* pasta in the form of long thin tubes, thicker than spaghetti [From Italian dialect, literally "little pierced thing," from *perciato* "pierced," the past participle of *perciare* "to pierce," from Old French *percer* (see PIERCE)]

per·cip·i·ent /pər sippee ənt/ *adj.* INSIGHTFUL perceptive, observant, or discerning ■ *n.* SOMEBODY OR SOMETHING THAT PERCEIVES somebody or something capable of perceiving [Mid-17thC. From Latin *percipere* (see PERCEIVE).] —**per·cip·i·ent·ly** *adv.*

per·coid /púr kòyd/ *adj.* BONY AND SPINY-FINNED belonging or relating to a large suborder of bony spiny-finned fishes that includes the perch, sea bass, sunfishes, and red mullet. Suborder: Percoidea. ■ *n.* PERCOID FISH a fish belonging to the percoid suborder [Mid-19thC. From modern Latin *Percoidea,* the suborder name, from Latin *perca* (see PERCH).]

per·co·late /púrkə làyt/ *v.* (**-lat·ed, -lat·ing, -lates**) **1.** *vti.* PASS THROUGH A FILTER to make a liquid or gas pass through a filter or porous substance, or filter through in this way **2.** *vi.* PASS THROUGH SLOWLY to pass slowly through something or spread throughout a place ○ *I let the idea percolate through my mind.* **3.** *vti.* BEVERAGES MAKE COFFEE to prepare coffee in a percolator, or undergo preparation in a percolator **4.** *vi.* BE LIVELY to be lively, active, or energetic (*informal*) ■ *n.* SOMETHING PERCOLATED product of percolation or a liquid that has been percolated [Early 17thC. From Latin *percolare* "to sieve through," from *colare* "to sieve," from *colum* "sieve" (source of English *colander*).] —**per·co·la·ble** /púrkələb'l/ *adj.* —**per·co·la·tion** /pùrkə láysh'n/ *n.* —**per·co·la·tive** /púrkə làytiv/ *adj.*

per·co·la·tor /púrkə làytər/ *n.* a coffeepot in which boiling water rises repeatedly through a narrow stem, spills over into a sieve-like basket containing coffee grounds, mixes with them, and returns to the water below

per con·tra /pər kóntrə, -káwntrə/ *adv.* on the other hand, or by way of contrast [From Italian, literally "by the opposite side"]

per cu·ri·am de·ci·sion /pər kòoree əm-/ *n.* a court judgment given without the need to retire to consider a verdict [From Latin *per curiam,* literally "by the court"]

per·cur·rent /pər kúrrənt/ *adj.* used to describe a leaf's main vein when it runs the entire length of the leaf [Late 16thC. From Latin *percurrere* "to run through," from *currere* "to run" (source of English *current*).]

per·cuss /pər kúss/ (**-cussed, -cuss·ing, -cuss·es**) *vt.* MED to gently tap a part of a patient's body in order to diagnose an illness or condition [Mid-16thC. From Latin *percuss-,* the past participle stem of *percutere* "to strike hard," from *quatere* "to strike" (source of English *concuss*).] —**per·cus·sor** *n.*

per·cus·sion /pər kúsh'n/ *n.* **1.** MUSIC INSTRUMENTS THAT ARE HIT the group of instruments that produce sound by being struck, including drums and cymbals, or the section of the orchestra playing such instruments **2.** MED TAPPING OF THE BODY examination of part of a patient's body by tapping with the fingers to assess the presence of fluid, the enlargement of organs, or the solidification of normally hollow parts **3.** IMPACT the impact of one object striking another, or the noise or shock created when two objects hit each other (*formal*) **4.** ACT OF DETONATING A PERCUSSION CAP the striking or detonating of a percussion cap in a firearm [Mid-16thC. From the Latin stem *percussion-,* from *percussus,* the past participle of *percutere* (see PERCUSS).]

per·cus·sion cap *n.* a detonator consisting of a thin metal cap or strip of paper containing explosive powder, formerly used to fire some pistols

per·cus·sion in·stru·ment *n.* a musical instrument such as a drum, cymbal, or triangle that is hit to produce sound

per·cus·sion·ist /pər kúsh'nist/ *n.* a musician who plays a percussion instrument

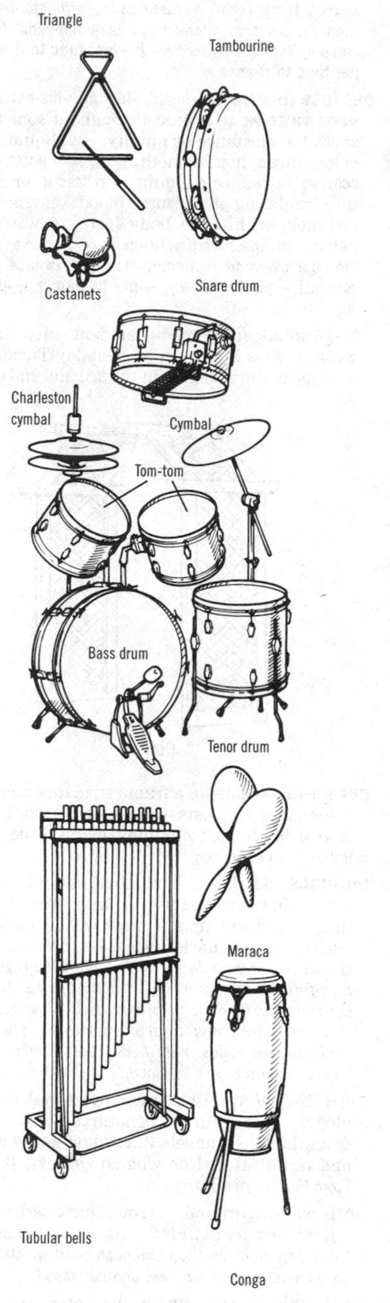

Percussion

per·cus·sion lock *n.* a mechanism on a gun that fires by striking a percussion cap

per·cus·sion tool *n.* any power tool that delivers repeated heavy blows e.g., a jackhammer

per·cus·sive /pər kússiv/ *adj.* having the effect of an impact or a blow —**per·cus·sive·ly** *adv.* —**per·cus·sive·ness** *n.*

per·cu·ta·ne·ous /pùrkyoo táynee əss/ *adj.* MED administered or absorbed through the skin, as an injection or, e.g., ointment —**per·cu·ta·ne·ous·ly** *adv.*

per di·em /pər dée əm/ *adv., adj.* **BY THE DAY** by the day or every day ■ *n.* **1. DAILY PAYMENT** a daily payment or allowance **2. WORKER PAID BY THE DAY** an individual who is hired to work as needed and is therefore paid by the day (*informal*) [From Latin, literally "by the day"]

per·di·tion /pər dísh'n/ *n.* **1.** CHR **PUNISHMENT IN HELL** in some religions, the state of everlasting punishment in Hell that sinners endure after death **2.** CHR **HELL** Hell itself as a location **3. COMPLETE DESTRUCTION** complete destruction or ruin (*archaic*) [14thC. Via Old French from, ultimately, Latin *perdere*, literally "to put to destruction," from *dare* "to put" (source of English *render*).]

per·du /pər dóo/, **per·due** *adj.* hidden or out of sight (*archaic or literary*) [Late 16thC. Via French, the past participle of *perdre* "to lose," from Latin *perdere* (see PERDITION).]

per·du·ra·ble /pər dóorəb'l/ *adj.* extremely durable or imperishable (*archaic*) [13thC. Via Old French from, ultimately, Latin *perdurare* (see PERDURE).] —**per·du·ra·bly** *adv.* —**per·du·ra·bil·i·ty** /pər dòorə bíllətee/ *n.*

per·dure /pər dóor/ (**-dured, -dur·ing, -dures**) *vi.* to last for a long time (*archaic*) [15thC. Via Old French from Latin *perdurare*, literally "to last through," from *durare* "to last" (source of English *duration, during,* and *endure*).]

père /pair/ *n.* **1. FRENCH PRIEST** the title given to Roman Catholic priests in France and French-speaking countries **2. SENIOR** in France and French-speaking countries, used after a man's surname to distinguish him from his son ○ *M. Doucet père.* ◊ **fils** [Early 17thC. Via French from, ultimately, Latin *pater* (see PATERNAL).]

Père Da·vid's deer *n.* a large reddish-gray deer that survives in captivity after having become extinct in China, its native habitat. Latin name: *Elaphurus davidianus.* [Late 19thC. Named for the French missionary and naturalist *Père* Armand *David* (1826–1900).]

per·e·gri·nate /pérrəgri nàyt/ (**-nat·ed, -nat·ing, -nates**) *vti.* to travel around a place or from place to place (*literary*) [Late 16thC. From Latin *peregrinari*, from *peregrinus* (see PEREGRINE).] —**per·e·gri·na·tor** *n.*

per·e·gri·na·tion /pèrrəgri náysh'n/ *n.* a journey or voyage (*literary*) [15thC. Directly or via French from Latin, from, ultimately, *peregrinari* "to travel," from *peregrinus* (see PEREGRINE).]

per·e·grine /pérrəgrin, -grèen/ *n.* BIRDS = **peregrine falcon** ■ *adj.* (*archaic*) **1. FROM A FARAWAY PLACE** coming from another region or country **2. WANDERING** wandering or traveling [14thC. Via French from Latin *peregrinus* "traveling," from *pereger*, literally "through fields," from *ager* "field" (source of English *agrarian*).]

per·emp·to·ry /pə rémptəree/ *adj.* **1. DICTATORIAL** expecting to be obeyed and unwilling to tolerate disobedience, **2.** LAW **CLOSED TO FURTHER CONSIDERATION OR ACTION** ending, or not open to, discussion, debate, or further action **3. EXPRESSING URGENCY** communicating urgency, command, or instruction [13thC. Via Anglo-Norman from, ultimately, Latin *perimere* "to take away completely," from *emere* "to buy, to take." The underlying meaning is "taking away possibility of debate."] —**per·emp·to·ri·ly** *adv.* —**per·emp·to·ri·ness** *n.*

per·en·nate /pérrə nàyt, pə ré-/ (**-nat·ed, -nat·ing, -nates**) *vi.* BOT to survive from one growing season to the next with reduced or arrested growth between seasons [Early 17thC. From Latin *perennare* "to last for years," from *perennis* (see PERENNIAL).] —**per·en·na·tion** /pèrrə náysh'n/ *n.*

per·en·ni·al /pə rénnee əl/ *adj.* **1.** BOT **LASTING OVER 2 YEARS** used to describe a plant that lasts for more than two growing seasons, either dying back after each season, as some herbaceous plants do, or growing continuously, as some shrubs do **2. RECURRING OR ENDURING** constantly recurring, or lasting for an indefinite time ○ *perennial problem of litter* ■ *n.* **1.** BOT **PERENNIAL PLANT** a plant that lasts for more than two growing seasons **2. SOMETHING HAPPENING AGAIN AND AGAIN** something that recurs or appears to recur yearly or on a continuing basis [Mid-17thC. Formed from Latin *perennis*, literally "through the year," from *annus* "year" (source of English *annual*).] —**per·en·ni·al·ly** *adv.*

pe·ren·tie /pə réntee/, **pe·ren·ty** (*plural* **-ties**) *n.* a large burrowing lizard that has brown skin with yellow patches and is found in the semiarid and desert regions of central and northern Australia. It can grow to 8 ft./2.5 m in length and is the largest Australian lizard, and the second-largest in the world. Latin name: *Varanus giganteus.* [Early 20thC. Of Aboriginal origin, probably from Diyari *pirindi*.]

per·e·stroi·ka /pèrrə stróykə/ *n.* **1. SOVIET REFORM POLICY** the political and economic restructuring in the former Soviet Union initiated by Mikhail Gorbachev from about 1986. The stated aims included decentralized control of industry and agriculture and some private ownership. **2. ANY POLITICAL RESTRUCTURING** any political, bureaucratic, or economic restructuring [Late 20thC. From Russian, literally "re-building, reconstruction."]

Pé·rez de Cuél·lar /pè ress də kwáy yaar/, **Javier** (*b.* 1920) Peruvian diplomat. He was the fifth secretary general of the United Nations (1982–91).

perf. *abbr.* **1.** STAMPS perforated **2.** GRAM perfect **3.** performance

per·fect *adj.* /púrfəkt/ **1. WITHOUT FAULTS** without errors, flaws, or faults ○ *in perfect condition* **2. COMPLETE AND WHOLE** complete and lacking nothing essential ○ *We had a perfect day together.* **3. EXCELLENT OR IDEAL** excellent or ideal in every way ○ *That's the perfect word to describe him.* **4. ESPECIALLY SUITABLE** having all the necessary or typical characteristics required for a given situation ○ *the perfect candidate for the job* **5. SKILLED** very proficient, skilled, or talented in a particular area ○ *a perfect host* **6. FLAWLESS** without any flaw or blemish ○ *perfect teeth* **7. UTTER, ABSOLUTE, COMPLETE** used to emphasize the extent or degree of something ○ *a perfect nuisance* **8. EXACTLY REPRODUCING SOMETHING** exactly reproducing an original ○ *a perfect likeness* **9.** BOT **WITH STAMENS AND PISTILS TOGETHER** used to describe a flower that has functional stamens and pistils in the same flower **10.** MATH **EXACTLY DIVISIBLE** exactly divisible into equal roots **11.** GRAM **WITH THE VERB ACTION FINISHED** used to describe a verb or verb tense for an action that is brought to a close **12.** MUSIC **OF MUSICAL INTERVALS** used collectively to describe the differences in pitch between the fourth, the fifth, and the octave, common to both major and minor scales **13.** FUNGI **WITH SEXUAL AND ASEXUAL REPRODUCTION** used to describe a fungus that reproduces both sexually and asexually during its life cycle **14.** INSECTS **SEXUALLY MATURE** sexually mature and completely differentiated ■ *vt.* /pər fékt/ (**-fect·ed, -fect·ing, -fects**) **1. COMPLETE SOMETHING** to make something as good as possible, or to bring something to completion ○ *They perfected the process last year.* **2.** PRINTING **PRINT THE REVERSE SIDE** to complete a printed page by printing its reverse side ■ *n.* GRAM **1. PERFECT TENSE OF VERB** the perfect tense of a verb. ◊ **future perfect** **2. VERB IN THE PERFECT TENSE** a verb that is in the perfect tense [13thC. Directly and via Old French *parfit* from, ultimately, Latin *perficere* "to make completely, finish," from *facere* "to make" (source of English *fact*).] —**per·fect·ness** *n.*

per·fec·ta /pər féktə/ *n.* GAMBLING = **exacta** [Late 20thC. From American Spanish *quiniela perfecta* "perfect quinella (a form of betting)."]

per·fect bind·ing *n.* a book binding in which the leaves of a book are cut into pages whose edges are bound with glue to the spine, as opposed to being stitched uncut —**per·fect bound** *adj.*

per·fect com·pe·ti·tion *n.* a market condition in which a product is traded freely by buyers and sellers in large numbers without any individual transaction affecting the price

per·fect game *n.* **1.** BASEBALL **FLAWLESSLY PITCHED BASEBALL GAME** a baseball game in which a pitcher plays a full game without allowing any player of the opposing team to reach a base **2.** BOWLING **12 STRIKES IN BOWLING** a game of bowling in which 12 consecutive strikes occur

per·fect gas *n.* PHYS, CHEM = **ideal gas**

per·fect·i·ble /pər féktəb'l/ *adj.* capable of being improved or made perfect —**per·fect·i·bil·i·ty** /pər fèktə bíllətee/ *n.*

per·fec·tion /pər fékshən/ *n.* **1. PERFECT NATURE** the quality of something that is as good or suitable as it can possibly be ○ *to strive for perfection as a goal* **2. PROCESS OF PERFECTING** the process of becoming or making something perfect ○ *The perfection of the technique, will require another two years research.* **3. EXAMPLE OR INSTANCE OF BEING PERFECT** somebody or something that reaches the highest attainable standard, or an instance of this ○ *His cooking that evening was sheer perfection* ◇ **to perfection** perfectly ○ *The piece showed off her talent as a pianist to perfection.*

per·fec·tion·ism /pər fékshə nìzzəm/ *n.* **1. DEMAND FOR PERFECTION** rigorous rejection of anything less than perfect **2.** PHILOSOPHY **BELIEF IN EXISTENCE OF PERFECTION** the doctrine that perfection is possible in human beings

per·fec·tion·ist /pər fékshənist/ *n.* **1. DEMANDING PERSON** somebody who demands perfection in all things, especially his or her own work **2.** PHILOSOPHY **BELIEVER IN PERFECTIONISM** somebody who believes in the doctrine of perfectionism

per·fec·tive /pər féktiv/ *adj.* **1. TOWARD PERFECTION** tending toward perfection **2.** GRAM **DESCRIBING COMPLETED ACTION** used to describe a verb that reports a completed action ■ *n.* GRAM **PERFECTIVE VERB OR ASPECT** a verb in the perfective aspect, or the aspect itself —**per·fec·tive·ly**

adv. —**per·fec·tive·ness** *n.* —**per·fec·tiv·i·ty** /pàrfek tívvitee/ *n.*

per·fec·tive as·pect *n.* the aspect that a verb is said to be in when it is in a perfect tense, reporting a completed action rather than an incomplete or continuing one

per·fect·ly /púrfəktlee/ *adv.* **1. IN A PERFECT WAY** in exactly the way desired or required ○ *That will suit her perfectly.* **2. USED FOR EMPHASIS** used to emphasize the degree or extent of something ○ *They're perfectly capable of managing on their own.*

per·fect num·ber *n.* a positive whole number that is equal to the sum of the numbers that can be multiplied to give it as a result, excluding itself

per·fec·to /pər fék tō/ (*plural* **-tos**) *n.* a medium-sized cigar with tapered ends and a thick center [Late 19thC. From Spanish, "perfect."]

per·fec·tor /pər féktər/, **per·fect·er** *n.* **1.** PRINTING **PRINTING MACHINE** a printing press that prints on both sides of a page simultaneously **2. SOMEBODY MAKING SOMETHING PERFECT** somebody who makes something perfect

per·fect par·ti·ci·ple *n.* GRAM = **past participle**

per·fect pitch *n.* MUSIC = **absolute pitch**

per·fect rhyme *n.* **1. RHYME OF DIFFERENTLY SPELLED WORDS** a rhyme of two words that are pronounced the same but spelled differently and have different meanings, e.g., "flew" and "flue" **2. RHYME WITH LAST PARTS THE SAME** a rhyme in which the stressed vowel and consonants following it are the same, e.g., "alive" and "contrive"

per·fect square *n.* a rational number equal to the square of another rational number

per·fer·vid /pər fúrvid/ *adj.* extremely passionate or enthusiastic (*literary*) [Mid-19thC. From modern Latin *perfervidus*, literally "extremely vehement," from Latin *fervidus* (see FERVID).] —**per·fer·vid·ly** *adv.* —**per·fer·vid·ness** *n.*

per·fid·i·ous /pər fíddee əss/ *adj.* guilty of treachery or deceit (*literary*) —**per·fid·i·ous·ly** *adv.* —**per·fid·i·ous·ness** *n.*

per·fi·dy /púrfidee/ *n.* treachery or deceit (*literary*) [Late 16thC. From Latin *perfidia*, from *perfidus*, literally "through faith" (found in *per fidem decipere* "to deceive through trustingness"), formed in turn from *fides* (see FAITH).]

per·fin /púrfin/ *n.* a postage stamp with initials perforated in it by a business or other organization to prevent misuse [Mid-20thC. Blend of PERFORATED + INITIAL.]

per·fo·li·ate /pər fólee ət/ *adj.* BOT used to describe a leaf that encloses a stem so that the stem seems to pass through it [Late 17thC. From modern Latin *perfoliatus*, literally "through a leaf," from Latin *folium* "leaf" (source of English *foliage*).] —**per·fo·li·a·tion** /pər fōlee áysh'n/ *n.*

per·fo·rate *v.* /púrfə ràyt/ (**-ra·ted, -rat·ing, -rates**) **1.** *vt.* **PUNCTURE SOMETHING** to make a hole or holes in something **2.** *vt.* **MAKE HOLES FOR TEARING** to make a line of small holes in paper to make tearing it easier **3.** *vi.* **PENETRATE SOMETHING** penetrate or pass through something ■ *adj.* /púrfərət, púrfə ràyt/ **1.** BIOL **WITH SMALL HOLES** dotted with small holes **2.** BIOL **WITH TRANSPARENT SPOTS** dotted with transparent spots **3.** STAMPS = **perforated** [Mid-16thC. From Latin *perforare* "to bore through," from *forare* "to bore."] —**per·fo·ra·ble** /púrfərəb'l/ *adj.* —**per·fo·ra·tive** /-rətiv, -ràytiv/ *adj.* —**per·fo·ra·tor** /-ràytər/ *n.* —**per·fo·ra·to·ry** /-rə tàwree/ *adj.*

per·fo·rat·ed /púrfə ràytəd/ *adj.* **1. WITH HOLES** pierced with a hole or holes, especially with a line of small holes designed to make tearing easy **2.** MED **WITH A HOLE** in which a hole has developed ○ *a perforated eardrum*

per·fo·ra·tion /pùrfə ráysh'n/ *n.* **1. HOLE** a hole made in something **2. MAKING HOLES OR HAVING THEM** the act of making a hole or holes in something or the state of being perforated **3. HOLES FOR TEARING** a small hole or series of holes punched into a piece of paper to make tearing easy **4.** MED **FORMATION OF A HOLE** the formation of a hole in an organ, tissue, or tube, usually as a consequence of disease

per·fo·ra·tion gauge *n.* STAMPS a small ruler used to measure the number of perforations along the borders of a postage stamp

per·force /pər fáwrs/ *adv.* unavoidably or as forced by circumstances (*archaic or literary*) [14thC. From Old French *par force* "by force."]

per·form /pər fáwrm/ (**-formed, -form·ing, -forms**) *v.* **1.** *vt.* **ACCOMPLISH** to carry out an action or accomplish a task ○ *the surgeon who performed the operation* **2.** *vt.* **FULFILL** to do what is stated or required **3.** *vti.* ARTS **PRESENT AN ARTISTIC WORK** to present or enact an artistic work such as a piece of music or a play to an audience **4.** *vi.* **FUNCTION OR BEHAVE** to function, operate, or behave in a particular way or to a particualr standard ○ *athletes who perform best under pressure* **5.** *vi.* **FULFILL AN OBLIGATION** to fulfill a promise or obligation [14thC. From Anglo-Norman *parformer*, an alteration of Old French *parfornir*, literally "to accomplish completely," from *fournir* "to accomplish" (source of English *furnish*).] —**per·form·a·ble** *adj.* —**per·form·er** *n.*

WORD KEY: SYNONYMS

perform, do, carry out, fulfill, discharge, execute

CORE MEANING: to complete a task or duty

perform a fairly formal word meaning to complete a task or duty, especially when this requires skill or care or when it forms part of a set procedure; **do** a general word meaning to complete a task or duty; **carry out** a general expression meaning to perform a task or procedure; **fulfill** to achieve the successful accomplishment or realization of something planned, promised, or anticipated, or the complete performance of a duty or obligation; **discharge** a fairly formal word meaning to fulfill duties or responsibilities successfully; **execute** a formal word meaning to complete an action or procedure that requires skill and expertise. It can also be used to refer to the accomplishment of a plan.

per·form·ance /pər fáwrməns/ *n.* **1.** ARTS **ARTISTIC PRESENTATION** a presentation of an artistic work to an audience e.g., a play or piece of music **2. MANNER OF FUNCTIONING** the manner in which something or somebody functions, operates, or behaves **3. WORKING EFFECTIVENESS** the effectiveness of the way somebody does his or her job (*often used before a noun*) **4. DISPLAY OF BEHAVIOR** a public display of behavior that others find distasteful, e.g., an angry outburst that causes embarrassment (*informal*) **5. THING ACCOMPLISHED** something that is carried out or accomplished **6. THE PERFORMING OF** the performing of something, e.g., a task or action **7.** LING **LANGUAGE PRODUCED** the language that a speaker or writer actually produces, as distinct from his or her understanding of the language. ◊ **competence, parole**

per·form·ance art *n.* art that combines two or more artistic media, a traditionally static medium, e.g., sculpture or photography, and a dramatic medium, e.g., recitation or improvisation —**per·form·ance art·ist** *n.*

per·form·ance en·hanc·er *n.* any one of various dietary supplements used by athletes to enhance bursts of high performance

per·form·a·tive /pər fáwrmətiv/ *adj.* **PERFORMING SPEECH ACT** used to describe speech that constitutes an act of some kind, e.g., the phrase "I promise I'll do my best," that constitutes a promise in itself ■ *n.* **SPEECH THAT CONSTITUTES AN ACT** a performative utterance [Mid-20thC. Formed from PERFORM, on the model of *declarative*.] —**per·form·a·tive·ly** *adv.*

per·form·ing arts *npl.* the forms of art that involve theatrical performance, especially drama, dance, and music

per·form·ing arts med·i·cine *n.* = **arts medicine**

per·fume /púr fyo͞om, pər fyo͞om/ *n.* **1. FRAGRANT LIQUID** a fragrant liquid that is sprayed or rubbed on the skin or clothes to give a pleasant smell **2. PLEASANT SCENT** a pleasant smell ■ *vt.* (**-fumed, -fum·ing, -fumes**) **GIVE SOMETHING PLEASANT SCENT** to give something a pleasant smell [Mid-16thC. Via French *parfum* from, ultimately, obsolete Italian *parfumare*, literally "to smoke through," from *fumare* "to smoke."] —**per·fumed** /pər fyo͞omd, púr fyo͞omd/ *adj.* —**per·fum·y** /púr fyo͞omee, pər fyo͞omee/ *adj.*

WORD KEY: SYNONYMS

See Synonyms at ***smell***.

per·fum·er /pər fyo͞omər/ *n.* somebody who manufactures or sells perfumes

per·fum·er·y /pər fyo͞oməree/ (*plural* **-ies**) *n.* **1. PERFUMES IN GENERAL** perfumes generally **2. PLACE MAKING OR SELLING PERFUMES** a place of business where perfumes are manufactured or sold **3. MAKING OF PERFUMES** the manufacture of perfumes, or the art of making perfumes

per·func·to·ry /pər fúngktəree/ *adj.* **1. DONE ROUTINELY** done as a matter of duty or custom, without thought, attention, or genuine feeling ○ *a perfunctory kiss* **2. HASTY** done hastily or superficially ○ *a perfunctory search* [Late 16thC. Via late Latin *perfunctorius* from, ultimately, *perfungi*, literally "to work through," from *fungi* (source of English *function*).] —**per·func·to·ri·ly** *adv.* —**per·func·to·ri·ness** *n.*

per·fuse /pər fyo͞oz/ (**-fused, -fus·ing, -fus·es**) *vt.* **1. PERMEATE SOMETHING** to spread throughout something, or spread a substance or quality, e.g., liquid, light, or color, throughout something **2.** MED **INJECT LIQUID INTO BODY** to introduce a liquid into tissue or an organ by circulating it through blood vessels or other channels within the body [Early 16thC. From Latin *perfus-*, the past participle stem of *perfundere*, literally "to pour over," from *fundere* "to pour" (source of English *found*).] —**per·fused** *adj.* —**per·fu·sion** *n.* —**per·fu·sive** *adj.*

Per·ga·mum /púrgəməm/ ancient city in northwestern Asia Minor, in present-day Turkey. It was a major cultural center in the 3rd and 2nd centuries B.C.

Pergola

per·go·la /púrgələ/ *n.* a frame structure consisting of colonnades or posts with a latticework roof, designed to support climbing plants [Late 17thC. Via Italian from Latin *pergula*.]

per·haps /pər háps, -áps/ CORE MEANING: an adverb expressing uncertainty, or indicating that something is possibly true or may possibly happen, often used to make remarks appear less definite ○ *Perhaps it will be warmer later.* ○ *He wondered if perhaps he had figured things wrong.* ○ *Perhaps his best-known ceramic work is his public mural "Voyage."*
adv. used to show approximation ○ *The house is perhaps five miles from here.* [15thC. From PER "by" + an earlier form of HAP "chance."]

per·i /péeree/ *n.* **1. MYTHOLOGICAL FIGURE** in Persian mythology, a beautiful supernatural being descended from the fallen angels **2. BEAUTIFUL WOMAN** a graceful and beautiful girl or woman (*literary*) [Late 18thC. From Persian *perī*.]

peri- *prefix.* **1.** around, surrounding ○ *pericarp* **2.** near ○ *perilune* ○ *perinatal* [From Greek *peri* "around, about." Ultimately from an Indo-European word which is also the ancestor of English *far*, *per-*, and *paradise*.]

per·i·anth /pérree ànth/ *n.* the outer structure of a flower, made up of the corolla, the calyx, or both [Early 19thC. Via French from modern Latin *perianthium*, literally "around a flower," from Greek *peri* "around" + *anthos* "flower."]

per·i·apt /pérree àpt/ *n.* a charm worn to protect the wearer from harm [Late 16thC. Via French from Greek *periapton*, literally "something fastened around," from *peri* "around" + *haptein* "to fasten."]

per·i·as·tron /pèrree ástrən, -á stròn/ *n.* the points in space and time in the orbits of two stars in a binary system at which they are closest together [Mid-19thC. Coined from PERI- + Greek *astron* "star," on the model of *perihelion*.]

per·i·car·di·tis /pèrrə kaar dítiss/ *n.* inflammation of the pericardium —**per·i·car·dit·ic** /pèrrə kaar díttik/ *adj.*

per·i·car·di·um /pèrrə ka͞ardee əm/ (*plural* **-a** /-dee ə/) *n.* a fibrous membrane that forms a sac surrounding the heart and attached portions of the main blood vessels [Late 16thC. Via medieval Latin from Greek *perikardion*, literally "around the heart," from *peri* "around" + *kardia* "heart."] —**per·i·car·di·al** *adj.* —**per·i·car·di·ac** *adj.*

per·i·carp /pérrə ka͞arp/ *n.* the part of a fruit that surrounds the seed or seeds, including the skin, flesh, and, e.g., in apples, the core —**per·i·car·pi·al** /pèrrə kaarpee əl/ *adj.* —**per·i·carp·ic** /pèrrə kaarpik/ *adj.*

per·i·chon·dri·um /pèrrə kóndree əm/ (*plural* **-a** /-dree ə/) *n.* the fibrous membrane that covers the surface of cartilage except at joints [Mid-18thC. Via modern Latin, literally "around the cartilage," from Greek *peri* "around" + *khondros* "cartilage."] —**per·i·chon·dri·al** *adj.*

per·i·clase /pérrə klàyss, -klàyz/ *n.* a colorless, gray, green, or yellow mineral consisting of magnesium oxide, often found in limestones [Mid-19thC. Directly or via German *Periklas* from modern Latin *periclasia*, literally "breaking around," from Greek *peri* "around" + *klasis* "breaking," from its perfect cleavage.] —**per·i·clas·tic** /pèrrə klástik/ *adj.*

Per·i·cles /pérrə kleez/ (495?–429? B.C.) Athenian statesman. He dominated Athens during its golden age by means of his oratory skills and honesty. He ordered the construction of the Parthenon and established Athens as a great center of art and literature. —**Per·i·cle·an** /pèrrə klee ən/ *adj.*

per·i·cli·nal /pèrrə klín'l/ *adj.* **1.** GEOL **DOME-SHAPED** used to describe a fold in sedimentary rocks that appears as a regular dome on the surface of the earth **2.** BOT **PARALLEL TO OUTSIDE WALL** used to describe cell walls that are parallel to the outer surface of a plant part [Late 19thC. Formed from Greek *periklinēs*, literally "sloping all around," from *peri* "all around" + *klinein* "to slope."]

per·i·cline /pérrə klìn/ *n.* **1.** GEOL **FOLD IN ROCK** a dome-shaped fold in sedimentary rock **2.** MINERALS **MINERAL WITH LONG WHITE CRYSTALS** a variety of the mineral albite, usually found in the form of long white crystals [Mid-19thC. From Greek *periklinēs*.]

per·i·cope /pə ríkəpee/ *n.* an extract from a book, especially a passage from the Bible selected for reading during a Roman Catholic Mass [Mid-17thC. Via late Latin from Greek *perikopē*, literally "cutting around," from *peri* "around" + *koptein* "to cut."] —**per·i·cop·ic** /pèrrə kóppik/ *adj.*

per·i·cra·ni·um /pèrrə kráynee əm/ (*plural* **-a** /-nee ə/) *n.* the membrane of connective tissue that surrounds the skull [Early 16thC. Via modern Latin from Greek *perikranion*, literally "round the skull," from *peri* "round" + *kranion* "skull."] —**per·i·cra·ni·al** *adj.*

per·i·cy·cle /pérrə sìk'l/ *n.* the outer layer of plant tissue surrounding the inner tissues in the roots and stems of plants (**stele**) that conducts moisture and nutrients around the plant [Late 19thC. Via French from Greek *perikuklos*, literally "circling around," from *peri* "around" + *kuklos* "circle."] —**per·i·cy·clic** /pèrrə sìklik, -síklik/ *adj.*

per·i·derm /pérrə dùrm/ *n.* the outer layer of plant tissue in woody roots and stems —**per·i·der·mal** /pèrrə dúrm'l/ *adj.* —**per·i·der·mic** *adj.*

pe·rid·i·um /pə ríddee əm/ (*plural* **-a** /-ə/) *n.* the covering of the spore-bearing organ in many kinds of fungi [Early 19thC. Via modern Latin from Greek *pēridion*, literally "small leather wallet," from *pēra* "wallet."]

per·i·dot /pérrə dòt, -dō/ *n.* a pale green or yellowish green transparent form of the mineral olivine, used as a gemstone [Early 18thC. From French, of unknown origin.]

per·i·do·tite /pèrrə dṓ tìt/ *n.* a coarse-grained igneous rock rich in iron and magnesium. It is found in meteorites and also on Earth, where it is thought to form much of the Earth's core. —**per·i·do·tit·ic** /pèrrə dō títtik/ *adj.*

per·i·gee /pérrəjee/ *n.* the point in the orbit of a satellite, moon, or planet at which it comes nearest to the object it is orbiting [Late 16thC. Via French from, ultimately, late Greek *perigeios* "close round the earth," from *peri* "close round" + *gaia* "earth."] —**per·i·ge·al** /pèrrə jée əl/ *adj.* —**per·i·ge·an** *adj.*

per·i·gla·cial /pèrrə gláyshəl/ *adj.* relating to or found in a region that borders on a glacier

Pé·ri·gueux /pày ree gṓ/ town in southwestern France, in Dordogne Department, Aquitaine Region. Population: 32,848 (1990).

pe·rig·y·nous /pə ríjjənəss/ *adj.* used to describe a flower that has petals, stamens, and sepals arranged around a cupshaped receptacle that contains the ovary, e.g., the flowers of cherries and roses —**pe·rig·y·ny** *n.*

per·i·he·li·on /pèrrə héelyən, -héelee ən/ (*plural* **-a** /-héelyə/) *n.* the point in the orbit of a planet or other astronomical body at which it comes closest to the Sun [Mid-17thC. Via modern Latin *perihelium*, literally "close round the sun," from Greek *peri* "close round" + *he_lios* "sun," on the model of *perigee*.] —**per·i·he·li·al** *adj.*

per·i·kar·y·on /pèrrə kérree òn, pèrrə kérree ən/ (*plural* **-a** /-kérree ə/) *n.* the part of a nerve cell that contains cytoplasm [Late 19thC. Coined from PERI- + KARYO- + -ON.] —**per·i·kar·y·al** *adj.*

per·il /pérrəl/ *n.* **1. EXPOSURE TO RISK** exposure to risk of harm **2. DANGER** a source of possible harm ■ *vt.* (**-iled, -il·ing, -ils**) **IMPERIL SOMEBODY OR SOMETHING** to expose somebody or something to the risk of harm (*archaic*) [13thC. Via French from Latin *periculum* "experiment, risk." Ultimately from an Indo-European base meaning "to try," which is also the ancestor of English *fear*, *experiment*, *expert*, and *empiric*.]

pe·ril·la /pə ríllə/ *n.* **1. FLOWERING PLANT** an annual plant native to Asia, especially a variety with white flowers and oil-rich seeds. Latin name: *Perilla frutescens.* **2. PLANT OIL** a pale yellow oil produced from the seeds of the perilla plant and used in varnishes and inks [Late 18thC. From modern Latin, the genus name.]

per·il·ous /pérrələss/ *adj.* involving exposure to very great danger —**per·il·ous·ly** *adv.* —**per·il·ous·ness** *n.*

per·i·lune /pérrə lo͞on/ *n.* the point at which a planet or other body orbiting the Moon comes closest to the Moon's surface [Mid-20thC. Coined from PERI- + Latin *luna* "moon," on the model of *apolune*.]

per·i·lymph /pérrə limf/ *n.* the fluid that fills the space between the membranous labyrinth and the bony labyrinth in the inner ear [Mid-19thC. Coined from PERI- + LYMPH.]

pe·rim·e·ter /pə rímmitər/ *n.* **1. BOUNDARY ENCLOSING AN AREA** a boundary that encloses an area **2.** GEOM **CURVE ENCLOSING AREA** a curve enclosing an area on a plane, or the length of such a curve **3. OUTER EDGE OF TERRITORY** the outer edge of an area of defended territory [Late 16thC. Via Latin from Greek *perimetros*, literally "measuring around," from *peri* "around" + *metron* "measure."] —**per·i·met·ric** /pèrrə méttrik/ *adj.* —**per·i·met·ri·cal** *adj.* —**per·i·met·ri·cal·ly** *adv.*

per·i·morph /pérrə màwrf/ *n.* a mineral that crystallizes around a grain of a different kind of mineral —**per·i·mor·phic** /pèrrə máwrfik/ *adj.* —**per·i·mor·phous** *adj.* —**per·i·mor·phism** *n.*

per·i·my·si·um /pèrrə mízzee əm, -mízhee-/ (*plural* **-a** /-mízzee ə/) *n.* the sheath of connective tissue that surrounds bundles of muscle fibers [Mid-19thC. Coined from PERI- + Greek *mus* "muscle."]

per·i·na·tal /pèrrə náyt'l/ *adj.* relating to or occurring during the period around childbirth, specifically from around week 28 of pregnancy to around one month after the birth —**per·i·na·tal·ly** *adv.*

per·i·na·tol·o·gy /pèrrə nay tólləjee/ *n.* a medical specialty concerned with the care and treatment of mother and infant immediately prior to, during, and following childbirth —**per·i·na·tol·o·gist** *n.*

per·i·neph·ri·um /pèrrə néffree əm/ (*plural* **-a** /-ree ə/) *n.* the fatty tissue that surrounds the kidney [Late 19thC. Coined from PERI- + Greek *nephros* "kidney."] —**per·i·neph·ric** *adj.*

per·i·ne·um /pèrrə née əm/ (*plural* **-a** /-née ə/) *n.* the region of the abdomen surrounding the urogenital and anal openings [Mid-17thC. Via late Latin from Greek *perinaion*, literally "near to where excretion takes place," from *peri* "near to" + *inan* "to excrete."] —**per·i·ne·al** *adj.*

per·i·neu·ri·tis /pèrrə no͝o rítiss/ *n.* inflammation of a perineurium —**per·i·neu·rit·ic** *adj.*

per·i·neu·ri·um /pèrri no͝oree əm/ (*plural* **-a** /-ree ə/) *n.* the sheath of connective tissue that surrounds a bundle of nerve fibers [Mid-19thC. Coined from PERI- + NEURO-.] —**per·i·neu·ri·al** *adj.*

pe·ri·od /péeree əd/ *n.* **1. INTERVAL OF TIME** an interval of time **2. IDENTIFIABLE TIME** an interval of time that is identified by what happens or exists during it **3. TIMETABLE SECTION** a division of a schedule or timetable, e.g., a portion of the school day **4. MENSTRUATION TIME** an occurrence of menstruation (*often used before a noun*) **5.** GEOL **UNIT OF GEOLOGIC TIME** a division of geologic time shorter than an era and longer than an epoch **6. PUNCTUATION MARK** the punctuation mark "." that is used at the end of a sentence or in abbreviations. **7. DIVISION OF GAME** a division of playing time in some sports **8.** PHYS **TIME FOR SINGLE CYCLE** the time required for one complete cycle of a repetitive system, e.g., the rotation of a star or the movement of an electromagnetic wave. Symbol *T* **9.** MATH **INTERVAL BETWEEN EQUAL VALUES** the interval between the points at which the values of a periodic function are equal **10.** CHEM **ROW IN PERIODIC TABLE** any of the horizontal rows of elements in the periodic table **11.** POETRY **UNIT OF POETIC RHYTHM** one of the longer units in the classical system of analyzing the rhythms of poetry **12.** MUSIC **MUSICAL PASSAGE** a long passage of music consisting of two or more contrasting musical phrases ■ *interj.* **SHOWING FINALITY** a word added to the end of a statement to emphasize that the speaker will not discuss it further (*informal*) ■ *adj.* **RELATING TO PARTICULAR HISTORICAL TIME** belonging to or intended to suggest a particular historical time ○ *actors in period costume* [14thC. Via French from, ultimately, Greek *periodos*, literally "way around," from *hodos* "way" (source of English *exodus* and *episode*), the underlying meaning being "circuit, cycle."]

pe·ri·od·ic /péeree óddik/ *adj.* **1. OCCASIONAL** recurring or reappearing from time to time **2. REGULAR** occurring or appearing at regular intervals or in regular cycles **3. INVOLVING PERIODS** associated with or occurring in periods [Mid-17thC. Via French and Latin from Greek *periodikos*, from *periodos* (see PERIOD).] —**pe·ri·od·i·cal·ly** *adv.*

WORD KEY: SYNONYMS

periodic, intermittent, occasional, sporadic

CORE MEANING: recurring over a period of time

periodic used to indicate that something occurs at intervals, suggesting a degree of regularity; **intermittent** used to indicate that something occurs at irregular intervals and emphasizing the absence of continuity or regularity; **occasional** used to indicate that something occurs infrequently and irregularly, often used to describe something fairly minor or unimportant; **sporadic** used to indicate that something occurs irregularly and unpredictably, often implying scattered instances.

pe·ri·od·ic ac·id *n.* any strongly oxidizing acid of iodine [Coined from PER- + IODIC]

pe·ri·od·i·cal /péeree óddik'l/ *n.* **MAGAZINE** a magazine or journal published at regular intervals such as weekly, monthly, or quarterly ■ *adj.* **1. PUBLISHED REGULARLY** published at regular intervals **2. OCCASIONAL** recurring or reappearing from time to time

pe·ri·od·i·cal ci·ca·da *n.* = **seventeen-year locust**

pe·ri·od·ic func·tion *n.* a mathematical function whose value is the same at regular intervals

pe·ri·o·dic·i·ty /péeree ə díssətee/ *n.* **1. REGULAR RECURRENCE** recurrence at regular intervals **2.** CHEM **CHEMICAL SIMILARITY** similarity between the properties of chemical elements that are close to each other in the periodic table

pe·ri·od·ic law *n.* the law stating that chemical elements fall into groups sharing similar properties when they are arranged according to atomic number

pe·ri·od·ic sen·tence *n.* in rhetoric, a complex sentence in which the main clause is left unfinished until the end in order to create the effect of anticipation or suspense

pe·ri·od·ic sys·tem *n.* the system of arranging chemical elements in a table according to the periodic law

pe·ri·od·ic ta·ble *n.* a table of the chemical elements arranged according to their atomic numbers

pe·ri·o·di·za·tion /péeree ədi záysh'n/ *n.* the dividing of history into distinct and identifiable periods

per·i·o·don·tal /pèrree ə dónt'l/ *adj.* relating to or affecting the tissues that surround the neck and root of a tooth [Mid-19thC. Coined from PERI- + Greek *odont* "tooth."] —**per·i·o·don·tal·ly** *adv.*

per·i·o·don·tics /pèrree ə dóntiks/, **per·i·o·don·tia** /-dónshə/, **per·i·o·don·tol·o·gy** /-don tólləjee/ *n.* the branch of dentistry concerned with the treatment of diseases of the gums and other periodontal tissues —**per·i·o·don·tic** *adj.* —**per·i·o·don·ti·cal** *adj.* —**per·i·o·don·ti·cal·ly** *adv.* —**per·i·o·don·tist** *n.*

pe·ri·od piece *n.* something, especially a curio or a work of art, that dates from or evokes a particular historical period, often something with no other value

per·i·o·nych·i·um /pèrree ō níkee əm/ (*plural* **-a** /-níkee ə/) *n.* the areas of skin that surround a fingernail or toenail [Early 20thC. From modern Latin, literally "round the nail," from Greek *onux* "nail."]

PERIODIC TABLE

Chemical elements are indicated by their symbols. The numbers above the elements are the atomic numbers, and those below are the atomic weights (those in parentheses are for the longest-lived isotopes, while those for Np, Pa, and Tc are for the most technologically important isotopes). The lanthanides and actinides do not fit easily into any group and are thus shown separate from the main table. Elements 113–118 are not known but are included in the table to show their expected positions.

Period \ Group	1	2		3	4	5	6	7	8	9	10	11	12	13	14	15	16	17	18
1	1 **H** 1.01																		2 **He** 4.00
2	3 **Li** 6.94	4 **Be** 9.01												5 **B** 10.81	6 **C** 12.01	7 **N** 14.01	8 **O** 16.00	9 **F** 19.00	10 **Ne** 20.18
3	11 **Na** 22.99	12 **Mg** 24.31												13 **Al** 26.98	14 **Si** 28.09	15 **P** 30.97	16 **S** 32.06	17 **Cl** 35.45	18 **Ar** 39.95
4	19 **K** 39.10	20 **Ca** 40.08		21 **Sc** 44.96	22 **Ti** 47.90	23 **V** 50.94	24 **Cr** 52.00	25 **Mn** 54.94	26 **Fe** 55.85	27 **Co** 58.93	28 **Ni** 58.71	29 **Cu** 63.55	30 **Zn** 65.38	31 **Ga** 69.72	32 **Ge** 72.59	33 **As** 74.92	34 **Se** 78.96	35 **Br** 79.90	36 **Kr** 83.80
5	37 **Rb** 85.47	38 **Sr** 87.62		39 **Y** 88.91	40 **Zr** 91.22	41 **Nb** 92.91	42 **Mo** 95.94	43 **Tc** 98.91	44 **Ru** 101.07	45 **Rh** 102.91	46 **Pd** 106.40	47 **Ag** 107.87	48 **Cd** 112.40	49 **In** 114.82	50 **Sn** 118.69	51 **Sb** 121.75	52 **Te** 127.60	53 **I** 126.90	54 **Xe** 131.30
6	55 **Cs** 132.91	56 **Ba** 137.34	*	71 **Lu** 174.97	72 **Hf** 178.49	73 **Ta** 180.95	74 **W** 183.85	75 **Re** 186.2	76 **Os** 190.2	77 **Ir** 192.22	78 **Pt** 195.09	79 **Au** 196.97	80 **Hg** 200.59	81 **Tl** 204.37	82 **Pb** 207.20	83 **Bi** 208.98	84 **Po** 209	85 **At** (210)	86 **Rn** (222)
7	87 **Fr** (223)	88 **Ra** (226)	**	103 **Lr** (256)	104 **Rf** (261)	105 **Db** (262)	106 **Sg** (266)	107 **Bh** (264)	108 **Hs** (269)	109 **Mt** (268)	110 **Uun** (269)	111 **Uuu** (272)	112 **Uub** (277)	113 **Uut**	114 **Uuq**	115 **Uup**	116 **Uuh**	117 **Uus**	118 **Uuo**

Lanthanides	*	57 **La** 138.91	58 **Ce** 140.12	59 **Pr** 140.91	60 **Nd** 144.24	61 **Pm** (145)	62 **Sm** 150.40	63 **Eu** 151.96	64 **Gd** 157.25	65 **Tb** 158.93	66 **Dy** 162.50	67 **Ho** 164.93	68 **Er** 167.26	69 **Tm** 168.93	70 **Yb** 173.04
Actinides	**	89 **Ac** (226)	90 **Th** 232.04	91 **Pa** 231.04	92 **U** 283.04	93 **Np** 237.05	94 **Pu** (244)	95 **Am** (243)	96 **Cm** (247)	97 **Bk** (247)	98 **Cf** (251)	99 **Es** (254)	100 **Fm** (257)	101 **Md** (258)	102 **No** (255)

per·i·os·te·um /pèrree óstee əm/ (*plural* **-a** /-tee ə/) *n.* the sheath of connective tissue that surrounds all bones except those at joints [Late 16thC. Via modern Latin from, Greek *periosteon*, literally "around the bone," from *osteon* "bone."] —**per·i·os·te·al** *adj.*

per·i·os·ti·tis /pèrree o stítiss, -ə-/ *n.* inflammation of the periosteum —**per·i·os·tit·ic** /pèrree o stíttik/ *adj.*

per·i·os·tra·cum /pèrree óstrəkəm/ (*plural* **-ca** /-kə/) *n.* the hard outer layer of the shell of some mollusks, especially freshwater mollusks [Mid-19thC. From modern Latin, literally "shell around," from Greek *ostrakon* "shell."]

per·i·o·tic /pèrree óttik/ *adj.* involving the area around the ear, especially the bones around the inner ear

per·i·pa·tet·ic /pèrrəpə téttik/ *adj.* GOING FROM PLACE TO PLACE traveling from place to place, especially working in several establishments and traveling between them ■ *n.* PERIPATETIC WORKER a peripatetic worker, especially a teacher who travels between schools [Early 17thC. Via French or Latin from Greek *peripatētikos*, from *peripatein* "to walk around," which in turn was formed form *patein* "to walk."] —**per·i·pa·tet·i·cal·ly** *adv.*

Per·i·pa·tet·ic /pèrrəpə téttik/ *adj.* RELATING TO ARISTOTLE'S PHILOSOPHY belonging or relating to the school of philosophy founded by Aristotle, who gave lectures while walking about the Lyceum in Athens ■ *n.* ARISTOTELIAN PHILOSOPHER a member of the Aristotelian school of philosophy

pe·rip·a·tus /pə ríppətəss/ *n.* = **onychophoran** [Mid-19thC. Via modern Latin, the genus name, from Greek *peripatos*, literally "way around," from *peripatos* "way."]

per·i·pe·te·ia /pèrrəpə tée ə, -tī ə/, **per·i·pe·ti·a** *n.* an abrupt change in events or circumstances, especially in drama (*formal*) [Late 16thC. From Greek, literally "falling down around," from *pet-*, the stem of *piptein* "to fall."] —**per·i·pe·tei·an** *adj.*

pe·riph·er·al /pə ríffərəl/ *adj.* **1.** AT THE EDGE at or relating to the edge of something, as opposed to its center **2.** NOT SIGNIFICANT minor or incidental in importance or relevance **3.** ANAT NEAR THE SURFACE near the surface of an organ or the body ■ *n.* COMPUT PERIPHERAL PIECE OF HARDWARE a piece of computer hardware such as a printer or a disk drive that is external to but connected with and controlled by a computer's central processing unit —**pe·riph·er·al·ly** *adv.*

pe·riph·er·al nerv·ous sys·tem *n.* the part of the nervous system that lies outside the brain and spinal cord

pe·riph·er·y /pə ríffəree/ (*plural* **-ies**) *n.* **1.** BOUNDARY the area around the edge of a place **2.** SURFACE the surface of an object **3.** POSITION OF LITTLE INVOLVEMENT the position or state of having only a minor involvement in something [Late 16thC. Via late Latin from, ultimately, Greek *peripherēs*, literally "carrying around," from *pherein* "to carry."]

pe·riph·ra·sis /pə ríffrəssiss/ (*plural* **-ses** /pə ríffrə seez/) *n.* **1.** INDIRECT SPEECH the use of overly long or indirect speech in order to say something **2.** INDIRECT STATEMENT an expression that states something indirectly [Mid-16thC. Via Latin from, ultimately, Greek *periphrazein*, literally "to explain around," from *phrazein* "to explain."]

per·i·phras·tic /pèrrə frástik/ *adj.* **1. USING PERIPHRASIS** concerning or using periphrasis **2.** GRAM **NOT FORMED WITH INFLECTIONS** formed using two or more words rather than an inflected form, especially used to describe a verb tense formed using an auxiliary verb rather than by inflecting the main verb [Early 19thC. From Greek *periphrastikos*, from *periphrazein* (see PERIPHRASIS).] —**per·i·phras·ti·cal·ly** *adv.*

pe·riph·y·ton /pə ríffə tòn/ *n.* aquatic plants and animals that live attached to rocks and other submerged objects [Mid-20thC. Origin uncertain: probably coined from PERI- + Greek *phuton* "plant," on the model of *plankton*.]

per·i·plasm /pérrə plàzzəm/ *n.* the area of a cell that lies immediately inside the cell wall but outside the plasma membrane

per·i·plast /pérrə plàst/ *n.* a cell wall or cell membrane

per·i·proct /pérrə pròkt/ *n.* the area surrounding the anus of some invertebrate animals such as sea urchins [Late 19thC. Coined from PERI- + Greek *prōktos* "anus."]

pe·rip·ter·al /pə ríptərəl/ *adj.* used to describe a classical building that has a single row of columns on all sides [Early 19thC. Formed from Greek *peripteros*, literally "with a wing around," from *pteron* "wing."]

pe·rique /pə réek/ *n.* a strongly-flavored tobacco grown in Lousiana. It is usually mixed with other tobaccos. [Late 19thC. From Louisiana French, of uncertain origin: possibly from *Périque*, the nickname of Pierre Chenet, the tobacco grower who developed it.]

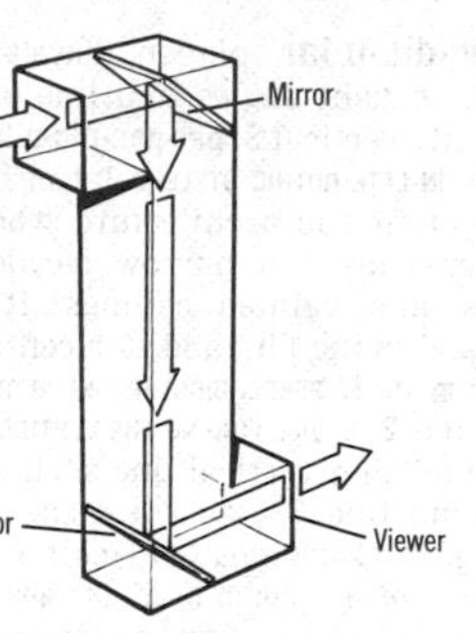

Periscope

per·i·scope /pérrə skōp/ *n.* a long tubular optical instrument, e.g., on a submarine, that uses lenses, prisms, and mirrors to allow a viewer to see objects not in a direct line of sight

per·i·scop·ic /pèrrə skóppik/ *adj.* **1. WITH WIDE FIELD OF VIEW** used to describe a lens that has a wide field of view **2. RELATING TO PERISCOPES** relating to or using a periscope —**per·i·scop·i·cal·ly** *adv.*

per·ish /pérrish/ (**-ished, -ish·ing, -ish·es**) *vi.* **1. DIE** to die, e.g., because of harsh conditions or accident (*literary*) **2. DISAPPEAR** to come to an end or cease to exist (*formal*) [13thC. Via French *périss-*, the stem of *périr*, from Latin *perire*, literally "to go completely," from *ire* "to go" (source of English *exit*).]

per·ish·a·ble /pérrishəb'l/ *adj.* **SPOILING EASILY** liable to decay, rot, or spoil ■ *n.* **PERISHABLE ITEM** something that is perishable, especially an item of food —**per·ish·a·bil·i·ty** /pèrrishə bílləte/ *n.* —**per·ish·a·ble·ness** /pérrəshəb'lnəss/ *n.* —**per·ish·a·bly** *adv.*

per·i·sperm /pérrə spùrm/ *n.* nutritive tissue from a plant nucleus that surrounds the seed embryo —**per·i·sperm·al** /pèrrə spúrməl/ *adj.*

pe·ris·so·dac·tyl /pə rìssə dákt'l/ *n.* a large mammal that belongs to the order of mammals with hooves and an odd number of toes, which includes horses, rhinoceroses, and tapirs. Order: Perissodactyla. [Mid-19thC. From modern Latin *Perissodactyla*, the order name, literally "uneven finger or toe," from Greek *perissos* "uneven" + *daktulos* "finger, toe."] —**pe·ris·so·dac·tyl** *adj.* —**pe·ris·so·dac·ty·lous** /pə rìssə dákt'ləss/ *adj.*

per·i·stal·sis /pèrrə stáwlsiss/ (*plural* **-ses**) *n.* the waves of involuntary muscle contractions that transport food, waste matter, or other contents through a tube-shaped organ such as the intestine [Mid-19thC. Via modern Latin from Greek *peristaltikos* "clasping, compressing," from *peristellein*, literally "to place around," from *stellein* "to place."] —**per·i·stal·tic** *adj.* —**per·i·stal·ti·cal·ly** /pèrrə stáwltikəlee/ *adv.*

per·i·stome /pérrə stōm/ *n.* the mouthparts of an invertebrate such as an earthworm or echinoderm —**per·i·sto·mal** /pèrrə stṓm'l/ *adj.*

per·i·style /pérrə stīl/ *n.* **1. ENCIRCLING COLUMNS** a line of columns (**colonnade**) that encircles a building or a courtyard **2. BUILDING WITH PERISTYLE** a building or courtyard that has a peristyle [Early 17thC. Via French from, ultimately, Greek *peristulos* "having columns around," from *stulos* "column."] —**per·i·sty·lar** /pèrrə stī́lər/ *adj.*

per·i·the·ci·um /pèrrə théessee əm, -théeshee-/ (*plural* **-a** /-théeshee ə/) *n.* in some kinds of fungus, a flask-shaped fruiting body that contains spores [Mid-19thC. From modern Latin, literally "case around," from Greek *peri* "around" + *thēkē* "case."]

per·i·to·ne·um /pèrrət'n ée əm/ (*plural* **-ums** *or* **-a** /-ée ə/) *n.* a smooth transparent membrane that lines the abdomen and doubles back over the surfaces of the internal organs to form a continuous sac [Mid-16thC. Via late Latin from, ultimately, Greek *peritonos* "stretched around," from *teinein* "to stretch."] —**per·i·to·ne·al** *adj.* —**per·i·to·ne·al·ly** *adv.*

per·i·to·ni·tis /pèrrət'n ī́tiss/ *n.* inflammation of the membrane that lines the abdomen (**peritoneum**). Symptoms can include swelling of the abdomen, severe pain, and weight loss. —**per·i·ton·it·ic** /pèrrət'n íttik/ *adj.*

per·i·track /pérrə trak/ *n.* = **taxiway** [Late 20thC. Coined from PERIMETER + TRACK.]

per·i·trich /pérrə trìk/ (*plural* **-tri·cha** /pə ríttrəkə/) *n.* a simple microscopic invertebrate (**protozoan**) covered in tiny filaments (**cilia**) that it uses to move around [Early 20thC. Shortening of modern Latin *peritricha*, literally "hair around," from Greek *peri* "around" + *trikh-*, the stem of *thrix* "hair."] —**pe·rit·ri·chous** /pə ríttrəkəss/ *adj.*

per·i·wig /pérrə wìg/ *n.* a wig, especially of the kind that men wore in the 17th and 18th centuries [Early 16thC. Alteration of an earlier form of PERUKE.]

per·i·win·kle[1] /pérrə wìngk'l/ *n.* MARINE BIOL = **winkle** [Mid-16thC. Origin uncertain: perhaps an alteration of Old English *pinewincle* "mussel shell."]

Periwinkle

per·i·win·kle[2] /pérrə wìngk'l/ *n.* PLANTS **TRAILING PLANT** a European or Asian trailing evergreen plant with blue or white flowers and dark green glossy leaves. Genus: *Vinca*. ■ *adj.* **PALE BLUISH PURPLE** of a pale bluish purple color [Pre-12thC. From late Latin *pervinca*, which evolved from Latin *vincapervinca*, of uncertain origin: perhaps formed from *pervincire*, literally "to wind around."]

per·jure /púrjər/ (**-jured, -jur·ing, -jures**) *vr.* to tell a lie in a court of law and therefore be guilty of perjury [15thC. Via French from Latin *perjurare* "to swear falsely," from *jurare* (see JURY).] —**per·jur·er** *n.*

per·jured /púrjərd/ *adj.* **1. GUILTY OF PERJURY** guilty of telling a lie in a court of law and therefore of committing perjury **2. CONTAINING PERJURY** containing lies and therefore breaking an oath to tell the truth in a court of law

per·ju·ry /púrjəree/ (*plural* **-ries**) *n.* **1. TELLING LIES UNDER OATH** the telling of a lie after having taken an oath to tell the truth, usually in a court of law **2. LIE UNDER OATH** a lie told in a court of law by somebody who has taken an oath to tell the truth [14thC. Via Anglo-Norman from Latin *perjurium*, from *perjurare* (see PERJURE).] —**per·ju·ri·ous** /pər jóoree əss/ *adj.* —**per·ju·ri·ous·ly** /-lee/ *adv.* —**per·ju·ri·ous·ness** /-nəss/ *n.*

perk[1] /purk/ *n.* a benefit given to an employee in addition to a salary, e.g., the use of a car or membership in a club [Early 19thC. Shortening of PERQUISITE.]

perk up *vti.* **1. MAKE OR BECOME LIVELY** to become or make somebody more cheerful, positive, or active **2. STICK UP** to stick up or make something stick up, especially quickly ○ *saw the dog's ears perk up* [*Perk* is of uncertain origin: perhaps from an obsolete word meaning "to perch," via medieval Latin *perca* "perch" from Latin *pertica* (see PERCH)]

perk[2] /purk/ (**perked, perk·ing, perks**) *vti.* to percolate, or to percolate coffee (*informal*) [Mid-20thC. Shortening.]

Per·kins /púrkinz/, **Maxwell** (1884–1947) U.S. book editor. He is known for his championing of writers such as F. Scott Fitzgerald and Ernest Hemingway. Full name **Maxwell Evarts Perkins**

perk·y /púrkee/ (**-i·er, -i·est**) *adj.* **1. LIVELY AND CHEERFUL** lively, cheerful, and energetic **2. OVERLY CONFIDENT** irritatingly self-confident —**perk·i·ly** *adv.* —**perk·i·ness** *n.*

Perl /purl/, **Martin L.** (*b.* 1927) U.S. physicist. He shared the Nobel Prize in physics (1995) for discovering the tau lepton, a fundamental atomic particle.

per·lite /púr līt/ *n.* a grayish volcanic glass in the form of grains that resemble pearls. It is often added to potting soil as a conditioner and is also used as a heat insulator. —**per·lit·ic** /pur líttik/ *adj.*

Perl·man /púrlmən/, **Itzhak** (*b.* 1945) Israeli-born U.S. violinist. He is considered one of the finest violinists of his generation.

per·lo·cu·tion /pùrlə kyóosh'n/ *n.* the effect that a speaker's words have on somebody. Their effect might be, e.g., to reassure or frighten. [Mid-20thC. Coined from PER + LOCUTION.]

perm /purm/ *n.* **HAIR TREATMENT** a hair treatment that uses chemicals to give hair long-lasting curliness or waviness ■ *vt.* (**permed, perm·ing, perms**) **GIVE HAIR A PERM** to treat hair chemically to give it long-lasting curliness or waviness [Early 20thC. Shortening of PERMANENT.]

Perm /purm, pairm/, **Perm'** city in eastern European Russia. Population: 1,098,600 (1992).

per·ma·frost /púrmə fràwst/ *n.* underlying soil or rock that remains permanently frozen, found mainly in the polar regions [Mid-20thC. Coined from PERMANENT + FROST.]

Perm·al·loy /púrmə lòy/ *tdmk.* a trademark for various nickel-iron alloys that are highly valued in the electronics industry because they allow magnetic fields to pass through them

per·ma·nence /púrmənəns/, **per·ma·nen·cy** *n.* existence in the same form forever or for a very long time [15thC. Directly or via French or medieval Latin *permanentia*, from the Latin stem *permanent-* (see PERMANENT).]

per·ma·nent /púrmənənt/ *adj.* **1. EVERLASTING** lasting forever or for a very long time, especially without undergoing significant change **2. UNCHANGING** never changing or not expected to change ■ *n.* HAIR **PERM** a perm (*formal*) [15thC. Directly or via French from Latin *permanere*, literally "to remain through," from *manere* "to remain" (source of English *remain*).] —**per·ma·nent·ly** *adv.* —**per·ma·nent·ness** *n.*

per·ma·nent mag·net *n.* a magnet that retains its properties after the magnetizing force has been removed from it. Permanent magnets are used in loudspeakers and small motors. —**per·ma·nent mag·net·ism** *n.*

per·ma·nent press *n.* any chemical process, e.g., the use of resin, used to give fabric shape and make it resistant to wrinkling (*hyphenated when used before a noun*)

per·ma·nent tooth *n.* any of the second and final set of teeth that grow to replace the milk teeth. A human adult has 32 permanent teeth.

per·ma·nent wave *n.* HAIR a perm (*formal*)

per·man·ga·nate /pur máng gə nàyt, -gənət/ *n.* a chemical compound that is a salt of permanganic acid [Mid-19thC. Formed from MANGANESE.]

per·man·gan·ic ac·id /pùr man gànnik-/ *n.* an unstable acid that exists only in dilute solution. Formula: $HMnO_4$. ["Permanganic" formed from PERMANGANATE]

per·me·a·bil·i·ty /pùr mee ə bíllətee/ (*plural* **-ties**) *n.* **1. PERMEABLE NATURE** the property of being permeable **2. RATE SUBSTANCE PASSES THROUGH POROUS MEDIUM** the rate at which something such as a liquid or a magnetic field passes through a membrane or other medium

3. **MAGNETIC PROPERTY** the property of a material to alter a magnetic field in which it is placed, or a measure of this property. Symbol μ

per·me·a·ble /púrmee əb'l/ *adj.* allowing liquids, gases, or magnetic fields to pass through — **per·me·a·bly** *adv.*

per·me·ance /púrmee əns/ *n.* **1. ACT OF PERMEATING** the act of passing through a porous substance or membrane **2. ABILITY TO BE MAGNETIZED** the ability of a magnetic component or assembly to be magnetized, measured in henries and calculated by dividing the magnetic flux by the magnetomotive force — **per·me·ant** *adj., n.*

per·me·ase /púrmee àyss, -àyz/ *n.* an enzyme that brings about a chemical reaction to carry a substance across a cell membrane [Mid-20thC. Formed from PERMEATE.]

per·me·ate /púrmee àyt/ (**-at·ed, -at·ing, -ates**) *vti.* **1. SPREAD THROUGH** to enter something and spread throughout it, so that every part or aspect of it is affected **2.** SCI **PASS THROUGH** to pass through the minute openings in a porous substance or membrane, or make something such as a liquid pass through [Mid-17thC. From Latin *permeare* "to pass through," from *meare* "to pass."] —**per·me·a·tion** /pùrmee áysh'n/ *n.* —**per·me·a·tive** /púrmee àytiv/ *adj.*

per men·sem /pur mén sèm/ *adv.* monthly or by the month (*formal*) [From modern Latin, literally "by the month"]

Per·mi·an /púrmee ən/ *n.* the period of geologic time when reptiles flourished, 290 million to 245 million years ago. [Late 16thC. Named for the province of *Perm* in eastern Russia, where strata from the period are easily visible.] —**Per·mi·an** *adj.*

per mill /pər míl/, **per mil** *adv.* in every thousand or by the thousand ["Mill" from Latin *mille* "thousand"]

per·mis·si·ble /pər míssəb'l/ *adj.* allowable or permitted [15thC. Via French from, ultimately, Latin *permiss-*, the past participle stem of *permittere* (see PERMIT).] — **per·mis·si·bil·i·ty** /pər missə bíllətee/ *n.* —**per·mis·si·bly** /pər míssəblee/ *adv.*

per·mis·sion /pər mísh'n/ *n.* agreement to allow something to happen or be done [15thC. Via French from, ultimately, Latin *permiss-*, the past participle stem of *permittere* (see PERMIT).]

per·mis·sive /pər míssiv/ *adj.* **1. ALLOWING FREEDOM OF BEHAVIOR** allowing or enjoying the freedom to behave in ways others might consider unacceptable, particularly in sexual matters **2. GIVING PERMISSION** granting permission **3. OPTIONAL** not required (*archaic*) [15thC. Via French from, ultimately, Latin *per.*] —**per·mis·sive·ly** *adv.* —**per·mis·sive·ness** *n.*

per·mit *v.* /pər mít/ (**-mit·ted, -mit·ting, -mits**) **1.** *vti.* **ALLOW SOMETHING** to allow something or give permission for it **2.** *vti.* **MAKE SOMETHING POSSIBLE** to allow somebody the possibility of doing something **3.** *vr.* **ALLOW YOURSELF SOMETHING** to allow yourself to have or do something, especially as a luxury or for a special occasion ■ *n.* /púrmit, pər mít/ **1. DOCUMENT GIVING PERMISSION** an official document or certificate giving permission for something **2. PERMISSION** permission granted, especially in written form (*formal*) [15thC. From Latin *permittere*, literally "to let go through," from *mittere* "to let go" (source of English *mission*).] —**per·mit·tee** /pùrmi tée/ *n.* —**per·mit·ter** /pər míttər/ *n.*

per·mit·tiv·i·ty /pùrmi tívvətee/ (*plural* **-ties**) *n.* the measure of the ability of a nonconducting material to retain electric energy when placed in an electric field. Symbol υ [Late 19thC. Formed from PERMIT, on the model of *conductivity*.]

per·mu·ta·tion /pùrmyə táysh'n, pùrmyoo-/ *n.* **1. ARRANGEMENT** an arrangement of items created by moving or reordering them **2. TRANSFORMATION** a change or transformation **3. REARRANGING** the reordering or rearranging of items in a group **4.** MATH **ORDER OF MATHEMATICAL ELEMENTS** an ordered arrangement of elements from a set —**per·mu·ta·tion·al** *adj.*

per·mute /pər myoót/ (**-mut·ed, -mut·ing, -mutes**) *vt.* **1. REARRANGE THINGS** to change the order of items in a group, especially to rearrange them in every possible way **2.** MATH **REARRANGE MATHEMATICAL ELEMENTS** to reorder the elements in a mathematical set [Late 19thC. From Latin *permutare*, literally "to change completely," from *mutare* "to change" (source of English *mutate*).] —**per·mut·a·bil·i·ty** /pər myoótə bíllətee/ *n.* — **per·mut·a·ble** /pər myoótəb'l/ *adj.* —**per·mut·a·bly** *adv.*

per·ni·cious /pər níshəss/ *adj.* **1. CAUSING SERIOUS HARM** causing great harm, destruction, or death **2. MALICIOUS** wicked or meaning to cause harm [Early 16thC. Via Old French from, ultimately, Latin *perniciés*, literally "complete destruction," from *nec-*, the stem of *nex* "destruction."] —**per·ni·cious·ly** *adv.* — **per·ni·cious·ness** *n.*

per·ni·cious a·ne·mi·a *n.* a severe form of anemia, found mostly in older adults, that results from the body's inability to absorb vitamin B_{12}. Symptoms include weakness, breathing difficulties, and weight loss.

per·nick·e·ty /pər níkətee/ *adj.* = **persnickety** (*informal*) [Early 19thC. Origin unknown: perhaps thought to suggest small pieces.] —**per·nick·e·ti·ness** *n.*

Per·nod /per nṓ/ *tdmk.* a trademark for an alcoholic liquor with the flavor of anise

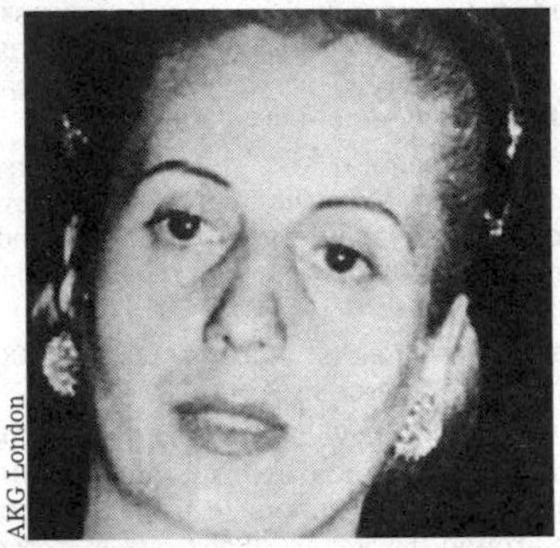

Eva de Perón

Pe·rón /pə rṓn/, **Eva de** (1919–52) Argentinian political figure. Married to President Juan Perón, she was adored by the Argentinian people for her charitable work. Born **María Eva Duarte**. Known as **Evita**

Pe·rón, Isabel de (*b.* 1931) Argentinian politician. She was the third wife of Juan Perón, and after his death succeeded him as president (1974–76). Born **María Estela Martínez Cartas**

Pe·rón, Juan (1895–1974) Argentinian statesman. He rose to power by a military coup (1943) and as president (1946–55 and 1973–74) enacted populist economic reforms. His wife Eva Perón was idolized by the poor, and, losing popularity after her death in 1952, he spent 18 years in exile. Full name **Juan Domingo Perón** —**Per·o·nist** /pə rṓnəst/ *n., adj.*

per·o·ne·al /pèrrə née əl/ *adj.* relating to the narrower of the two bones in the lower leg (**fibula**) [Mid-19thC. Formed from Greek *peronē* "pin of a brooch, fibula."]

per·o·ral /pər áwrəl/ *adj.* occurring by way of the mouth —**per·o·ral·ly** *adv.*

per·o·rate /pérrə ràyt/ (**-rat·ed, -rat·ing, -rates**) *vi.* (*formal*) **1. END SPEECH** to finish a speech by summarizing its main points **2. GIVE SPEECH** to speak at length, especially in a formal or pompous way [Early 17thC. From Latin *perorare*, literally "to speak all the way through," from *orare* "to speak" (source of English *oration*).] —**per·o·ra·tion** /pèrrə ráysh'n/ *n.* — **per·o·ra·tion·al** *adj.*

Pe·rot /pə rṓ/, **H. Ross** (*b.* 1930) U.S. business executive and politician. He ran unsuccessfully as an independent candidate for president (1992), and established the political movement "United We Stand America." Full name **Henry Ross Perot**

per·ov·skite /pə róv skìt, pə ráwf skìt/ *n.* a black, yellow, or brown mineral consisting of calcium titanate, with applications in superconductivity [Mid-19thC. Named for the Russian mineralogist L. A. *Perovski*, 1792–1856.]

per·ox·i·dase /pə róksə dàyz/ *n.* an enzyme found in plants that speeds up oxidation reactions involving hydrogen peroxide or other peroxides

per·ox·ide /pə rók sìd/ *n.* **1.** CHEM **CHEMICAL COMPOUND** a chemical compound such as hydrogen peroxide that contains oxygen atoms in the group $-O_2-$ **2. HAIR COLORING SUBSTANCE** a solution of hydrogen peroxide used as a hair lightener. It gives hair an unnaturally light blond tint that is almost white. (*often used before a noun*) ○ *a peroxide blonde* ■ *vt.* (**-id·ed, -id·ing, -ides**) **1. BLEACH HAIR WITH PEROXIDE** to bleach hair using peroxide **2.** CHEM **TREAT SOMETHING WITH PEROXIDE** to treat something with peroxide or hydrogen peroxide

per·ox·i·some /pə róksi sṑm/ *n.* a tiny part within a cell containing enzymes that oxidize toxic substances such as alcohol and prevent them from doing any harm. There are many peroxisomes in the cells of the liver and kidney. [Mid-20thC. Coined from PEROXIDE + -SOME.]

perp /purp/ *n.* somebody responsible for a crime (*slang*) [Late 20thC. Shortening of PERPETRATOR.]

per·pend[1] /pər pénd/ *n.* BUILDING a stone or brick built into a wall to go from one side of the wall to the other and act as a binder [15thC. Variant of PARPEN.]

per·pend[2] /pər pénd/ (**-pend·ed, -pend·ing, -pends**) *vti.* to ponder something (*archaic*) [Early 16thC. From Latin *perpendere*, literally "to weigh thoroughly," from *pendere* "to weigh" (source of English *pensive*).]

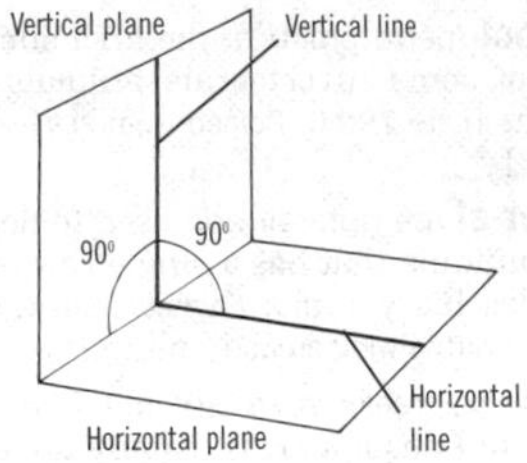

Perpendicular

per·pen·dic·u·lar /pùrpən díkyələr/ *adj.* **1. AT RIGHT ANGLES** at right angles to a line or plane **2. VERTICAL** perfectly vertical **3. per·pen·dic·u·lar, Per·pen·dic·u·lar** ARCHIT **IN LATE GOTHIC STYLE** relating to or typical of a style of Gothic architecture whose characteristic elements are tall narrow facades, windows, and doors, and vaulted ceilings. It was popular in England in the 14th and 15th centuries. **4. STEEP** very steep ■ *n.* **1. PERPENDICULAR LINE** a perpendicular line or plane **2. DEVICE FINDING THE VERTICAL** any device used to establish a vertical line such as a spirit level or a plumb line **3.** MOUNTAINEERING **SHEER ROCK** a sheer rock face [14thC. Via Old French from, ultimately, Latin *perpendiculum* "plumb line," literally "something weighed thoroughly," formed from *perpendere*, literally "to weigh thoroughly," formed in turn from *pendere* "to weigh."] — **per·pen·dic·u·lar·i·ty** /pùrpən dikyə lérrətee/ *n.* —**per·pen·dic·u·lar·ly** /pùrpən díkyələrlee/ *adv.*

per·pe·trate /púrpə tràyt/ (**-trat·ed, -trat·ing, -trates**) *vt.* to commit or be responsible for something, usually something criminal or morally wrong [Mid-16thC. From Latin *perpetrare*, literally "to completely bring about," from *patrare* "to bring about," literally "to father," from *pater* "father."] —**per·pe·tra·tion** /pùrpə tráysh'n/ *n.* — **per·pe·tra·tor** /púrpə tràytər/ *n.*

per·pet·u·al /pər péchoo əl/ *adj.* **1. LASTING FOR EVER** lasting for all time **2. LASTING INDEFINITELY** lasting for an indefinitely long time **3. OCCURRING REPEATEDLY** occurring over and over **4.** BOT **BLOOMING THROUGHOUT SEASON** used to describe flowers or flowering plants that bloom throughout the season [14thC. Via French from, ultimately, Latin *perpes* "continuous," literally "going towards throughout," from *petere* "to go toward" (source of English *petition*).]

per·pet·u·al cal·en·dar *n.* a calendar set out in such as way that it can be used for several years or for any year

per·pet·u·al check *n.* a situation in chess in which one player's king is placed in check with every move the other player makes, resulting in a draw

per·pet·u·al·ly /pər péchoo əlee/ *adv.* **1. FOREVER** forever or for a very long time **2. REPEATEDLY** repeatedly at very short intervals, and so appearing to be continuous

per·pet·u·al mo·tion *n.* **1. HYPOTHETICAL MOTION** the hypothetical continuous operation of a mechanism without the introduction of energy from an external source, known as perpetual motion of the first kind. A device demonstrating this would violate the first law of thermodynamics, which states that energy can neither be created nor destroyed. **2. HYPOTHETICAL CONVERSION OF HEAT** the hypothetical operation of a mechanism that would convert heat directly into work, known as perpetual motion of the second kind. A device demonstrating this would violate the second law of thermodynamics, which states that heat cannot be converted into work without producing some other effect.

per·pet·u·ate /pər péchoo àyt/ (**-at·ed, -at·ing, -ates**) *vt.* **1. MAKE SOMETHING LAST** to make something continue, usually for a very long time **2. MAKE SOMETHING BE REMEMBERED** to make something or somebody be remembered [Early 16thC. From Latin *perpetuare*, from *perpetuus* (see PERPETUAL).] —**per·pet·u·a·tion** /pər pèchoo áysh'n/ *n.* —**per·pet·u·a·tor** /pər péchoo àytər/ *n.*

per·pe·tu·i·ty /pùrpə tóo itee/ (*plural* **-ties**) *n.* **1. PERPETUAL CONDITION** the state of continuing for a long time or indefinitely **2. ETERNITY** eternity or the rest of time ○ *a sacrifice honored in perpetuity* **3.** LAW **TRANSFER OF REAL ESTATE FOR EVER** the transfer of real estate for an unlimited period of time, restricted in law by the rule against perpetuity. The maximum legal period of transferred ownership is based on the length of a life in existence at the time plus 21 years plus a nine month period of gestation. **4.** FIN **INVESTMENT** an investment designed to pay an annual return indefinitely, having no maturity date [15thC. Via French from, ultimately, Latin *perpetuus* (see PERPETUAL).]

per·phen·a·zine /pər fénnə zeèn/ *n.* a drug used to relieve anxiety, tension, and nausea. Formula: $C_{21}H_{26}ClN_3OS$. [Mid-20thC. Coined from PIPERIDINE + PHENYL + AZINE.]

Per·pi·gnan /pèrpeen yaáN/ city in southern France, near the Mediterranean Sea and the border with Spain. Population: 108,049 (1990).

per·plex /pər pléks/ (**-plexed, -plex·ing, -plex·es**) *vt.* **1. PUZZLE SOMEBODY** to puzzle or confuse somebody, especially causing doubt **2. COMPLICATE SOMETHING** to make something overly complicated or intricate [Late 16thC. Back-formation from PERPLEXED.]

per·plexed /pər plékst/ *adj.* **1. PUZZLED** puzzled, and usually troubled by doubt **2. OVERLY COMPLICATED OR INTRICATE** very complicated or intricate, especially in a way that causes difficulties [15thC. Via French from Latin *perplexus*, literally "completely woven together," from *plexus*, the past participle of *plectere* "to weave together" (source of English *plexus*).] —**per·plex·ed·ly** /pər pléksədlee/ *adv.*

per·plex·ing /pər pléksing/ *adj.* disconcertingly difficult to understand or come to terms with —**per·plex·ing·ly** *adv.*

per·plex·i·ty /pər pléksətee/ (*plural* **-ties**) *n.* **1. BEING PERPLEXED** the state of being perplexed **2. PERPLEXING THING** something that is difficult to understand, especially because it is complex or part of a complicated whole (*often used in the plural*) **3. COMPLEX NATURE** the nature of something that is disconcertingly complex

per pro·cu·ra·tion·em /pər pròkə rattee ő nèm/ *prep.* a fuller form of the abbreviation "pp" that is written in formal correspondence by somebody who is signing on behalf of another person [From Latin, literally "by proxy"]

per·qui·site /púrkwəzit/ *n.* **1. PERK** a perk (*formal*) **2. CUSTOMARY TIP** a tip that is customary on some occasions **3. A RIGHT** something considered to be an exclusive right [Early 18thC. From medieval Latin *perquisitum*, literally "something searched for," from *perquirere* "to seek for," from *quaerere* "to seek."]

Per·rault /pérrō/, **Charles** (1628–1703) French writer. In *Tales of Mother Goose* (1697) he set down from oral tradition such fairy tales as *Cinderella* and *Sleeping Beauty*.

Per·rier /pèrree áy, pérree ày/ *tdmk.* a trademark for a sparkling mineral water from France

per·ron /pérrən, pə rón/ *n.* **1. PLATFORM** a raised platform at an entrance that is not at ground level **2. STAIRWAY** an external stairway leading up to a perron [14thC. Via French from the assumed Vulgar Latin stem *petron-*, literally "large stone," from Latin *petra* "stone."]

per·ry /pérree/ (*plural* **-ries**) *n.* a drink made from fermented pear juice, similar to cider or wine [14thC. Via Old French *pere* from, ultimately, Latin *pirum* (see PEAR).]

Per·ry /pérree/, **Fred** (1909–95) British tennis player. He was winner of the U.S. Open (1933, 1934, 1936), Wimbledon (1934, 1935, 1936), Australian Open (1934), and French Open (1935) singles titles. Full name **Frederick John Perry**

Per·ry, Matthew Calbraith (1794–1858) U.S. naval officer. He negotiated the opening of Japan to United States ships and merchants (1853).

pers. *abbr.* **1.** personal **2.** person

perse /purs/ *adj.* COLORS of a dark bluish gray or purplish black color [14thC. Via French from medieval Latin *persus*.] —**perse** *n.*

per se /pər sáy/ *adv.* in itself, by itself, or intrinsically (*formal*) [From Latin, literally "by itself"]

per·se·cute /púrsə kyoot/ (**-cut·ed, -cut·ing, -cutes**) *vt.* **1. OPPRESS PEOPLE** to systematically subject a race or group of people to cruel or unfair treatment, e.g., because of their ethnic origin or religious beliefs **2. PESTER SOMEBODY** to make somebody the victim of continual pestering or harassment [15thC. Via French from, ultimately, Latin *persecut-*, the past participle stem of *persequi*, literally "to keep following," from *sequi* "to follow" (source of English *sequence*).] —**per·se·cu·tee** /pùrsə kyoo teé/ *n.* —**per·sec·u·tive** /púrsə kyootiv/ *adj.* —**per·se·cu·tor** /púrsə kyootər/ *n.* —**per·se·cu·to·ry** /púrsəkyə tàwree/ *adj.*

per·se·cu·tion /pùrsə kyoósh'n/ *n.* **1. THE PERSECUTING OF SOMEBODY** the subjecting of a group of people to cruel or unfair treatment, e.g., because of their ethnic origin or religious beliefs **2. SUFFERING OF PERSECUTED PEOPLE** the suffering felt by persecuted people

Per·se·id /púrsee id/ *n.* any meteor forming part of a meteor shower that appears around August 12 and seems to originate from the vicinity of the constellation Perseus

Per·seph·o·ne /pər séffənee/ *n.* in Greek mythology, the daughter of Demeter and Zeus who was abducted by Hades, king of the underworld. She spent half the year in the underworld and half the year on earth with her mother. Her return to earth symbolized the arrival of spring. Roman equivalent **Proserpina**

Per·sep·o·lis /pər séppəliss/ ruined city situated northeast of Shiraz in modern-day Iran. It was founded by Darius I in the 6th century B.C. as the Persian capital and destroyed by Alexander the Great.

Per·se·us[1] /púrsee əss/ *n.* a constellation in the northern hemisphere between Auriga and Andromeda

Per·se·us[2] /púrsee əss/ *n.* in Greek mythology, the son of Zeus and Danae. He killed the Gorgon Medusa and also rescued the princess Andromeda as she was about to be sacrificed to a sea monster.

per·se·ver·ance /pùrsə veérəns/ *n.* **1. DETERMINED CONTINUATION WITH SOMETHING** steady and continued action or belief, usually over a long period and especially despite difficulties or setbacks **2.** CHR **CALVINIST CONCEPT OF DIVINE GRACE** in Calvinism, the belief that God's grace brings selected people, the elect, to salvation **3.** CHR **ROMAN CATHOLIC BELIEF IN GOD'S GRACE** in the Roman Catholic Church, the belief that God's grace lasts to the end of somebody's life if that person has maintained his or her good works and faith —**per·se·ver·ant** *adj.*

per·sev·er·a·tion /pər sèvvə ráysh'n/ *n.* a tendency to repeat the response to an experience in later situations where it is not appropriate [Early 20thC. Formed from Latin *perseverare* (see PERSEVERE).]

per·se·vere /pùrsə veér/ (**-vered, -ver·ing, -veres**) *vi.* to persist steadily in an action or belief, usually over a long period and especially despite problems or difficulties [14thC. Via French *persévérer* from Latin *perseverare* "to follow strictly," from *perseverus* "very strict," from *severus* (see SEVERE).] —**per·se·ver·ing** *adj.* —**per·se·ver·ing·ly** *adv.*

Per·shing /púrshing/ *n.* a two-stage U.S. Army ballistic missile capable of delivering a nuclear warhead [Mid-20thC. Named in honor of General John J. PERSHING.]

Per·shing /púrshing/, **John J.** (1860–1948) U.S. general. He led the American Expeditionary Force in Europe during World War I. Full name **John Joseph Pershing**

Per·sia /púrzhə/ **1. IRAN** Iran (*archaic*) **2.** ancient empire in southwestern Asia that, at its height under Darius the Great in the 6th century B.C., stretched from the shores of the eastern Mediterranean to the Indus River in modern-day Tibet. It was conquered by Alexander the Great in 330 B.C.

Per·sian /púrzh'n/ *n.* **1.** PEOPLES **RESIDENT OR NATIVE OF IRAN** somebody who was born in or is a citizen of Iran **2.** LANG = **Farsi 3.** HIST **PEOPLE OF ANCIENT PERSIA** a member of a people who lived in ancient Persia and who founded an empire around 500 B.C. **4.** LANG **LANGUAGE OF ANCIENT PERSIANS** the language spoken by the ancient Persians **5.** = **Persian cat** ■ *adj.* PEOPLES **1. ABOUT ANCIENT PERSIA** relating to or typical of ancient Persia, or its people or culture **2. ABOUT MODERN IRAN** relating to modern Iran, or its people or culture

Per·sian blinds *npl.* outside louvered shutters for blocking sunlight while allowing ventilation [From their use and manufacture in that country]

Per·sian car·pet, Per·sian rug *n.* a carpet consisting of a woven backing to which wool or silk threads have been hand-knotted, made in the Middle East and typically having rich colors and strong designs

Persian cat

Per·sian cat *n.* a domestic cat with long silky hair belonging to a breed originally from the Middle East

Per·sian Gulf gulf of the Arabian Sea, with Iran to its northeast and the Arabian peninsula to its southwest. Area: 90,000 sq. mi./233,000 sq. km.

Per·sian lamb *n.* **1. SOFT CURLED FUR FROM KARAKUL LAMB** the soft curled usually black fur from the karakul lamb **2. KARAKUL LAMB** a lamb of the karakul sheep

Per·sian mel·on *n.* a melon that has musky orange flesh and a rind with a netted pattern. Latin name: *Cucumis melo*.

Per·sian wool *n.* a loosely twisted three-strand wool yarn used in needlepoint, each strand being two-ply

per·si·ennes /pùrzee én, -énz/ *npl. U.K.* = **Persian blinds** [Mid-19thC. From French, formed from *persian* "Persian."]

per·si·flage /púrsi flaàzh/ *n.* **1. LIGHT TEASING CHAT** light or teasing good-natured talk **2. LIGHT-HEARTED STYLE** light-heartedness or frivolity in the treatment of something [Mid-18thC. From French, formed from *persifler* "to banter," from *siffler* "to whistle," via Old French from, ultimately, Latin *sibilare* (see SIBILANT).]

Persimmon

per·sim·mon /pər símmən/ *n.* **1.** FOOD **TROPICAL FRUIT** a sweet juicy orange-red fruit with a slightly tough outer skin that is edible only when fully ripe **2.** TREES **TREE BEARING PERSIMMONS** a tropical tree that has hard wood and bears persimmons as fruit. Genus: *Diospyros*. [Early 17thC. Alteration of Virginia Algonquian *pessemmins*.]

per·sist /pər síst/ (**-sist·ed, -sist·ing, -sists**) *vi.* **1. KEEP CARRYING ON** to continue steadily or obstinately despite problems, difficulties, or obstacles **2. CONTINUE TO BE BELIEVED WRONGLY** to continue being widely believed or accepted despite evidence or proof to the contrary ○ *a view that persists to this day* **3. CONTINUE** to continue happening or existing [Mid-16thC. From Latin *persistere*, literally "to stand through," from *sistere* "to make stand," from *stare* (see STATION).] —**per·sis·ter** *n.*

per·sist·ence /pər sístəns/, **per·sist·en·cy** /-ənsee/ *n.* **1. THE QUALITY OF PERSISTING** the quality of continuing steadily despite problems or obstacles **2. ACT OF PER-**

SISTING the action of somebody who persists with something 3. LONG CONTINUANCE OF SOMETHING continuance of an effect after its cause has ceased or been removed 4. ZOOL RESILIENCE OF ORGANISM the ability of a living organism to resist being disturbed or altered

per·sist·ent /pər sístənt/ *adj.* 1. CONTINUING DESPITE PROBLEMS tenaciously or obstinately continuing despite problems or difficulties 2. INCESSANT OR UNRELENTING existing or continuing for a long time 3. BOT PERSISTING BEYOND MATURATION used to describe a plant part such as a scale on a pine cone that lasts beyond maturity without falling off 4. ZOOL SUSTAINING CONTINUAL GROWTH used to describe a body part such as a tooth that grows throughout life 5. ECOL ABLE TO REMAIN IN THE ENVIRONMENT used to describe a chemical that remains in the environment or a living organism for months or years, usually because of resistance to attack by oxygen, light, and microorganisms —**per·sist·ent·ly** *adv.*

per·sist·ent veg·e·ta·tive state *n.* a medical condition in which a patient has severe brain damage and as a result is unable to stay alive without the aid of a life-support system, showing no response to stimuli

per·snick·e·ty /pər sníkətee/ *adj.* 1. OBSESSED WITH DETAIL overly attentive to detail and trivia 2. SNOBBISH snobbish in terms of choice, and thus wanting or accepting only the finest things 3. REQUIRING A KEEN EYE TO DETAIL necessitating precise, keen attention to details [Early 20thC. Alteration of PERNICKETY.] —**per·snick·e·ti·ness** *n.*

per·son /púrs'n/ (*plural* **peo·ple** /péep'l/ *or* **per·sons** *formal*) *n.* 1. HUMAN BEING an individual human being 2. HUMAN'S BODY a human being's body, often including the clothing ○ *objects found on her person* 3. HUMAN'S APPEARANCE an individual human being's general appearance (*formal*) 4. A CHARACTER OR ROLE a character or role, e.g., in a play (*archaic*) 5. GRAM FORM OF VERB AND PRONOUN any one of three forms of verbs and pronouns used to denote the speaker, the person addressed, or somebody else being referred to 6. ETHICS OBJECT WITH SPECIAL MORAL VALUE an object with special moral value because of some spiritual status, or autonomous nature, or importance for other people 7. LAW INDIVIDUAL OR BODY OF INDIVIDUALS a living human being or a group, either or both having legal rights and responsibilities [12thC. Via Old French from Latin *persona* "mask worn by an actor, character," of uncertain origin: probably from Etruscan *phersu* "mask."] ◇ **in person** personally rather than being represented by somebody or something else

WORD KEY: USAGE

In combining forms terms that are not gender-specific have increasingly grown in prominence, and ones incorporating the combining form ***-person*** are now common (*chairperson, spokesperson*). The terms that have taken hold most strongly, however, tend to be those that do not simply replace *-man* (or *-woman*) with ***-person*** but are more subtly neutral with respect to sex: *chair* rather than *chairperson*, *representative* rather than *congressperson*, *angler* rather than *fisherperson*. Despite the powerful trend toward inclusive terms, however, it remains true that when the members of the group at issue are predominantly male, the traditional term incorporating *-man* tends to be used most frequently of all (*chairman, fisherman*). Forms with *-woman* are also seen, though in most cases these are now less common than the form incorporating ***-person.***

Per·son *n.* in Christianity, the Father, the Son, or the Holy Spirit, together being the Trinity

per·so·na /pər sṓnə/ (*plural* **-nas** *or* **-nae** /pər sṓnee/) *n.* 1. LITERAT CHARACTER IN LITERATURE a character in a literary work, especially a play (*often used in the plural*) 2. ASSUMED IDENTITY OR ROLE an identity or role that somebody assumes 3. PSYCHOL PERSONAL FACADE the image of character and personality that somebody wants to show the outside world. This concept originated in *Jungian* psychology. [Early 20thC. From Latin (see PERSON).]

per·son·a·ble /púrsənəb'l/ *adj.* having a pleasant personality and appearance —**per·son·a·ble·ness** *n.* —**per·son·a·bly** *adv.*

per·son·age /púrsənij/ (*plural* **-ag·es**) *n.* (*formal*) 1. IMPORTANT PERSON somebody who is distinguished, important, or famous 2. LITERAT, HIST HISTORICAL FIGURE OR FICTIONAL CHARACTER a historical figure or a character in a work of literature [15thC. From Old French, formed from *persone* (see PERSON).]

per·so·na gra·ta /pər sṓnə gráatə/ (*plural* **per·so·nae gra·tae** /pər sṓni gráatee, pər sṓ nī gráa tī/) *n.* somebody who is acceptable, especially as a diplomat, to the authorities of a country to which he or she is sent. ◊ **persona non grata** [From late Latin, "acceptable person"] —**per·so·na gra·ta** *adj.*

per·son·al /púrsən'l, púrsnəl/ *adj.* 1. RELATING TO SOMEBODY'S PRIVATE LIFE relating to the parts of somebody's life that are private 2. RELATING TO ONE PERSON relating to a particular individual 3. BELIEVED BY INDIVIDUAL PERSON believed by or originating from an individual person ○ *personal opinion* 4. DONE BY ONE INDIVIDUAL ONLY done by a particular individual rather than by that person's delegate ○ *that personal touch* 5. INTENDED FOR PARTICULAR INDIVIDUAL intended for or owned by a particular individual rather than anyone else 6. REFERRING OFFENSIVELY TO PARTICULAR PERSON referring, especially in an offensive way, to somebody's beliefs, actions, or physical characteristics ○ *That personal remark was definitely uncalled for.* 7. UNFAIRLY REMARKING OR QUESTIONING ABOUT OTHERS making unacceptable remarks or being too probing about other people ○ *There's no need to get personal.* 8. OF THE BODY relating to somebody's body 9. RELIG CONSCIOUS AND INDIVIDUAL having the character or nature of a conscious and individual entity 10. LAW OF MOVABLE PROPERTY relating to or consituting an individual's movable property ■ *n.* PRESS AD FOR FRIENDS OR ROMANCE a usually classified newspaper or magazine advertisement in which somebody expresses interest in meeting others or sends a message of a personal nature to somebody else (*often used in the plural*)

per·son·al ad *n. U.K.* = **personal**

per·son·al ap·pear·ance *n.* 1. VISUAL ASPECT OF PERSON the visual aspect of somebody, especially with regard to personal cleanness and neatness of clothing 2. PUBLIC PRESENCE OF NOTABLE PERSON the arrival or appearance, in a typically official capacity and in a formal setting, of a notable person

per·son·al as·sis·tant *n.* somebody employed to perform secretarial and administrative tasks for somebody such as an executive who has many responsibilities

per·son·al col·umn *n.* a section of a newspaper or magazine in which personals are printed

per·son·al com·put·er *n.* a computer with its own operating system and wide selection of software intended to be used by one person

Per·son·al Dig·i·tal As·sis·tant *n.* a small handheld computer with a built-in notebook, calendar, and fax capability, usually operated using a stylus rather than a keyboard

per·son·al ef·fects *npl.* possessions that somebody carries or wears either regularly or at a particular time

per·son·al flo·ta·tion de·vice *n.* a device such as a life jacket or lifebuoy for use by one person in a water emergency

per·son·al foul *n.* a foul, especially one committed in football or basketball, involving illegal physical contact with an opponent during a game and also sometimes involving unnecessary roughness

Per·son·al In·for·ma·tion Man·ag·er *n.* software that organizes random notes, contacts, and appointments for fast access

per·son·al in·ju·ry *n.* an actionable injury to an individual person, whether involving physical contact or not and whether fatal or not, but causing pain, discomfort, or injury

per·son·al·ism /púrsən'l ìzzəm, púrsnə lìzzəm/ *n.* a quirky or highly individualistic mode of expression or behavior —**per·son·al·ist** *n., adj.* —**per·son·al·is·tic** /pùrsən'l ístik, pùrsnə lístik/ *adj.*

per·son·al·i·ty /pùrs'n állətee/ (*plural* **-ties**) *n.* 1. SOMEBODY'S SET OF CHARACTERISTICS the totality of somebody's attitudes, interests, behavioral patterns, emotional responses, social roles, and other individual traits that endure over long periods of time 2. CHARACTERISTICS MAKING SOMEBODY APPEALING the distinctive or very noticeable characteristics that make somebody socially appealing ○ *a partner with real personality* 3. SOMEBODY REGARDED AS EPITOMIZING TRAITS an individual regarded as epitomizing particular character traits ○ *a difficult personality* 4. FAMOUS PERSON somebody who is famous, especially an entertainer or a sportsperson 5. UNUSUAL PERSON somebody who is very unusual and distinctive 6. QUALITY OF BEING A PERSON the quality of existing as a person ○ *Do you think that computers will ever achieve personality?* 7. PERSONAL COMMENT a personal comment or observation, especially one that might be considered offensive (*often used in the plural*) ○ *Let's not get into personalities.* 8. DISTINGUISHING CHARACTERISTICS the distinguishing characteristics of a place or situation

per·son·al·i·ty dis·or·der *n.* a psychiatric disorder in attitude or behavior that makes it difficult for somebody to get along with other people or to succeed at work or in social situations but that does not involve loss of touch with reality

per·son·al·i·ty in·ven·to·ry, **per·son·al·i·ty test** *n.* a standardized psychological test in which the subject is given questions about various aspects of personality, the answers supplying a character-trait profile unique to that individual

per·son·al·i·ty type *n.* a set of categories based on attitudes or behavioral tendencies into which people are grouped, e.g., introvert and extrovert

per·son·al·ize /púrsən'l ìz/ (**-ized, -iz·ing, -iz·es**) *vt.* 1. PUT INITIALS OR NAME ON SOMETHING to mark something such as a wallet, pen, or item of clothing with somebody's initials or name 2. CHANGE SOMETHING TO REFLECT OWNER'S PERSONALITY to change or modify something showing that it obviously originated from or belonged to a particular person 3. TAKE REMARK PERSONALLY to take a remark in a personal way 4. = **personify** *v.* 3 —**per·son·al·i·za·tion** /pùrsən'li záysh'n/ *n.*

per·son·al·ly /púrsən'lee/ *adv.* 1. AS OWN OPINION in one's own experience or showing one's own opinion ○ *Personally, I would have given it back.* 2. AS AN INDIVIDUAL as a particular individual ○ *Don't take it personally.* 3. WITHOUT OTHERS without intervention or assistance from others ○ *I'll handle it personally.* 4. AS PERSON IN SOCIAL CONTEXT as a person, considered in a social context ○ *personally likable but professionally inept* 5. OF SOMEBODY ONE HAS MET relating to somebody known by pesonal contact rather than by reputation ○ *I never knew your brother personally.*

per·son·al or·gan·iz·er *n.* 1. DATEBOOK WITH CHANGEABLE PAGES a datebook that also contains personal information and has replaceable pages so that it can be kept up to date 2. HAND-HELD MULTIFUNCTIONING COMPUTER a hand-held computer with a small keyboard and display that can function as a calendar, an address book, a scheduler, and a calculator

per·son·al pro·noun *n.* a pronoun such as "I," "you," or "she" that refers to a speaker, somebody being addressed, or another person

per·son·al prop·er·ty *n.* in law, the tangible, movable property of an individual, exclusive of land and including items such as automotive vehicles, boats, and money

per·son·al ster·e·o *n.* a small audio cassette or CD player used with earphones, designed to be carried in a pocket or worn attached to a belt

per·son·al·ty /púrsən'ltee, púrsnəltee/ (*plural* **-ties**) *n.* = **personal property** [Mid-16thC. Via Anglo-Norman from, ultimately, late Latin *personalitas* (see PERSONALITY).]

per·son·al un·con·scious *n.* in Jungian and related forms of psychotherapy, a section of an individual's unconscious mind that contains impulses, fears, and memories that have been repressed

per·so·na non gra·ta (*plural* **per·so·nae non gra·tae**) *n.* 1. UNWELCOME OR UNACCEPTABLE PERSON somebody who is unwelcome or unacceptable. ◊ **persona grata** 2. SOMEBODY UNACCEPTABLE AS DIPLOMAT somebody who is unacceptable as a diplomat to the authorities of a country to which he or she is sent [From late Latin, "unacceptable person"] —**per·so·na non gra·ta** *adj.*

per·son·ate[1] /púrs'n àyt/ (**-at·ed, -at·ing, -ates**) *vt.* 1. THEATER PLAY ROLE IN PLAY to play a dramatic role, especially in a play 2. CRIMINAL LAW IMPERSONATE SOMEBODY AS DECEPTION to impersonate somebody in order to deceive or defraud [Late 16thC. From late Latin *personare*, from Latin *persona* (see PERSON).] —**per·son·a·tion** /pùrs'n áysh'n/ *n.* —**per·son·a·tive** /púrs'n àytiv/ *adj.* —**per·son·a·tor** /púrs'n àytər/ *n.*

per·son·ate[2] /púrs'n àyt/ *adj.* used to describe a flower such as a snapdragon that has two lips with one lip curling over the other to close the opening between them [Late 16thC. From Latin *personatus* "masked," from *persona* (see PERSON).]

per·son·hood /púrs'n hòod/ *n.* the state of being human

per·son-hour *n.* a unit that measures the amount of work that can be done by one person in one hour and the cost of that hour's work

per·son·i·fi·ca·tion /pər sònnəfi káysh'n/ *n.* **1.** SOMEBODY WHO EMBODIES SOMETHING somebody who is an embodiment or perfect example of something **2.** REPRESENTION OF AN ABSTRACT QUALITY AS HUMAN a representation of an abstract quality or notion as a human being, especially in art or literature **3.** ATTRIBUTION OF HUMAN QUALITIES TO ABSTRACTS the attribution of human qualities to objects or abstract notions

per·son·i·fy /pər sónnə fì/ (**-fied, -fy·ing, -fies**) *vt.* **1.** BE PERFECT EXAMPLE OF SOMETHING to be an embodiment or perfect example of something **2.** REPRESENT SOMETHING ABSTRACT AS HUMAN to represent an abstract quality as a human being, especially in art or literature **3.** ASCRIBE HUMAN QUALITIES TO NONHUMAN to ascribe human qualities to an object or abstract notion —**per·son·i·fi·a·ble** /pər sònnə fí əb'l/ *adj.* —**per·son·i·fi·er** /pər sónnə fìr/ *n.*

per·son·nel /pùrsə nél/ *n.* DEPARTMENT OF ORGANIZATION DEALING WITH EMPLOYEES the department of an organization or business that deals with employees' hiring, records, and problems ■ *npl.* PEOPLE EMPLOYED IN ORGANIZATION the people employed in an organization, business, or armed force [Early 19thC. From French, formed from *personne* "person," on the model of "matériel."]

per·son-to-per·son *adj.* **1.** FACE-TO-FACE AND DIRECT referring to direct communication or contact between two or more people **2.** CHARGEABLE WHEN RECIPIENT IS REACHED relating to or being a telephone call chargeable only when a particular person is reached ■ *adv.* TO BE PAID IF RECIPIENT ANSWERS in such a way as to be chargeable or payable only if the person telephoned is reached

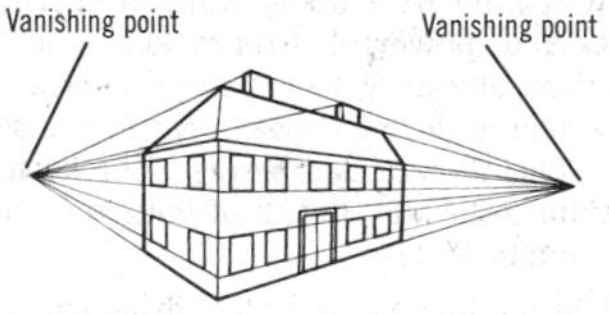

Perspective

per·spec·tive /pər spéktiv/ *n.* **1.** PARTICULAR EVALUATION OF SOMETHING a particular evaluation of a situation or facts, especially from one person's point of view **2.** MEASURED ASSESSMENT OF SITUATION a measured or objective assessment of a situation, giving all elements their comparative importance ○ *He's having trouble keeping things in perspective right now.* **3.** APPEARANCE OF DISTANT OBJECTS TO OBSERVER the appearance of objects to an observer allowing for the effect of their distance from the observer **4.** DRAWING, PAINTING ALLOWANCE FOR ARTISTIC PERSPECTIVE WHEN DRAWING the theory or practice of allowing for artistic perspective when drawing or painting **5.** VISTA a vista or view [14thC. Via Old French from, ultimately, late Latin *perspectivus* "optical," from Latin *perspicere* "to look closely," from *specere* (see SPECTACLE).] —**per·spec·tive·ly** *adv.*

per·spi·ca·cious /pùrspi káyshəss/ *adj.* penetratingly discerning, perceptive, or astute [Early 17thC. Formed from Latin *perspicac-*, the stem of *perspicax*, from *perspicere* (see PERSPECTIVE).] —**per·spi·ca·cious·ly** *adv.* —**per·spi·ca·cious·ness** *n.*

per·spi·cac·i·ty /pùrspi kássətee/ *n.* acuteness of discernment or perception

per·spi·cu·i·ty /pùrspi kyóo ətee/ *n.* **1.** = **perspicacity** **2.** BEING PERSPICUOUS the quality of being perspicuous

per·spic·u·ous /pər spíkyoo əss/ *adj.* clearly expressed and therefore easily understood [Late 16thC. Formed from Latin *perspicuus*, from *perspicere* (see PERSPECTIVE).] —**per·spic·u·ous·ly** *adv.* —**per·spic·u·ous·ness** *n.*

per·spi·ra·tion /pùrspə ráysh'n/ *n.* **1.** FLUID EXCRETED BY SWEAT GLANDS fluid lost from the body both in the form of sweat secreted by the sweat glands and as water that diffuses through the skin **2.** PROCESS OR ACT OF EXCRETING PERSPIRATION the process or act of excreting sweat secreted by the sweat glands or fluid that diffuses through the skin

per·spir·a·to·ry /pər spírə tàwree/ *adj.* relating to or causing perspiration

per·spire /pər spír/ (**-spired, -spir·ing, -spires**) *vti.* to secrete fluid from the sweat glands through the pores of the skin [Mid-17thC. Via obsolete French *perspirer*, from Latin *perspirare*, literally "to breathe through," from *spirare* "to breathe" (see SPIRIT).] —**per·spir·ing·ly** *adv.*

per·suade /pər swáyd/ (**-suad·ed, -suad·ing, -suades**) *vt.* **1.** GET SOMEBODY TO DO SOMETHING to successfully urge somebody to perform a particular action, especially by reasoning, pleading, or coaxing **2.** CONVINCE SOMEBODY OF SOMETHING to make somebody believe something, especially by giving good reasons for doing so [Early 16thC. From Latin *persuadere*, literally "to urge strongly," from *suadere* "to urge."] —**per·suad·a·ble** *adj.* —**per·suad·a·bil·i·ty** /pər swàydə bíllətee/ *n.*

WORD KEY: USAGE

See Usage note at ***convince.***

per·suad·er /pər swáydər/ *n.* **1.** SOMEBODY OR SOMETHING THAT PERSUADES somebody or something such as a situation that persuades or serves to persuade **2.** INTIMIDATING WEAPON a weapon such as a gun used to intimidate somebody (*slang*)

per·sua·sion /pər swáyzh'n/ *n.* **1.** ACT OF PERSUADING the act of persuading somebody to do something **2.** ABILITY TO PERSUADE the ability to persuade somebody **3.** SET OF BELIEFS a set of beliefs, e.g., a set of religious or political beliefs **4.** GROUP WITH PARTICULAR BELIEFS a group whose members share a particular set of beliefs or views or a particular lifestyle [14thC. Via Old French from, ultimately, Latin *persuas-*, the past participle stem of *persuadere* (see PERSUADE).]

per·sua·sive /pər swáyssiv/ *adj.* having the ability to persuade people or the effect of persuading them [Late 16thC. Via French or medieval Latin from Latin *persuas-*, the past participle stem of *persuadere* (see PERSUADE).] —**per·sua·sive·ly** *adv.* —**per·sua·sive·ness** *n.*

pert /purt/ *adj.* **1.** AMUSINGLY BOLD bold and lively in a pleasant or amusing way **2.** JAUNTY jaunty and stylish in design ○ *a pert hat* **3.** SMALL AND WELL-SHAPED small, well-shaped, and pretty ○ *a pert nose* [13thC. Via Old French *apert* "open, frank" from Latin *apertus* "open" (see APERTURE), influenced by Old French *espert* "clever" (from Latin *expertus*; see EXPERT).] —**pert·ly** *adv.* —**pert·ness** *n.*

PERT /purt/ *n.* a method of charting and scheduling a complex set of interrelated activities that identifies the most time-critical events in the process. Full form **program evaluation and review technique**

pert. *abbr.* pertaining

per·tain /pər táyn/ (**-tained, -tain·ing, -tains**) *vi.* **1.** HAVE RELEVANCE to relate to something or have relevance, reference, or a connection to it **2.** BE APPROPRIATE to be appropriate or suitable **3.** BE PART OR BELONG to be part of something or belong to something, especially as an attribute or accessory [14thC. Via Old French *partenir* from Latin *pertinere*, literally "to hold to," from *tenere* (see TENANT).]

Perth /perth/ capital city of Western Australia, located on the Swan River. Population: 1,096,829 (1996).

per·ti·na·cious /pùrti náyshəss/ *adj.* **1.** RESOLUTE determinedly resolute in purpose, belief, or action **2.** PERSISTENT highly persistent [Early 17thC. From Latin *pertinac-*, the stem of *pertinax*, literally "very tenacious," from *tenax* (see TENACIOUS).] —**per·ti·na·cious·ly** *adv.* —**per·ti·na·cious·ness** *n.* —**per·ti·nac·i·ty** /pùrti nássətee/ *n.*

per·ti·nent /púrt'nənt/ *adj.* relevant to the matter being considered [14thC. Via Old French from, ultimately, Latin *pertinere* (see PERTAIN).] —**per·ti·nence** *n.* —**per·ti·nent·ly** *adv.*

per·turb /pər túrb/ (**-turbed, -turb·ing, -turbs**) *vt.* **1.** DISTURB SOMEBODY to disturb and trouble or worry somebody **2.** RENDER SOMETHING INTO STATE OF DISORDER to render something into a state of confusion or disorder **3.** PHYS CAUSE SOMETHING TO UNDERGO A PERTURBATION to cause a small deviation in the behavior of a physical system, e.g., in the orbit of an electron or a planet [14thC. Via Old French from Latin *perturbare*, literally "to disturb thoroughly," from *turbare* "to disturb," from *turba* "turmoil" (see TURBID).] —**per·turb·a·ble** *adj.* —**per·turb·a·bly** *adv.* —**per·turb·ing** *adj.* —**per·turb·ing·ly** *adv.*

per·tur·ba·tion /pùrtər báysh'n/ *n.* **1.** BEING PERTURBED the act of being disturbed and troubled, or a disturbed and troubled state **2.** CAUSE OF TROUBLE something causing disruption, trouble, or disorder **3.** PHYS SECONDARY INFLUENCE ON A SYSTEM a slight disturbance of a system by a secondary influence within it **4.** ASTRON DEVIATION IN ORBIT CAUSED BY GRAVITY a deviation in an astronomical body's orbit or path caused by the gravitational attraction of another astronomical body —**per·tur·ba·tion·al** *adj.*

per·tus·sis /pər tússiss/ *n.* whooping cough (*technical*) [Late 18thC. From modern Latin, from *per-* "extreme" + *tussis* "cough" (see TUSSIS).] —**per·tus·sal** *adj.*

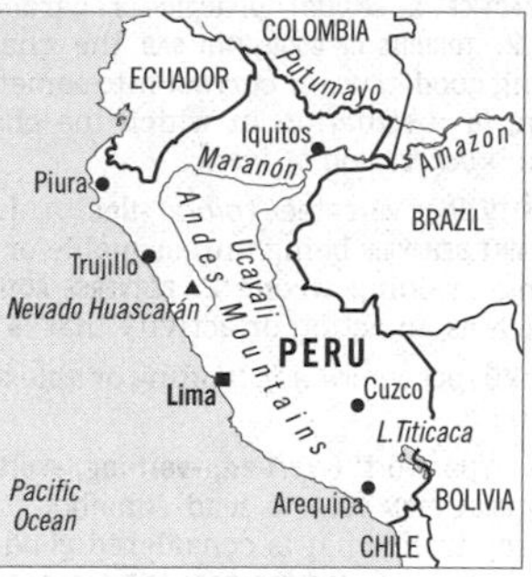

Peru

Pe·ru /pə róo, pe roo/ **1.** country in western South America, on the Pacific Ocean, bounded by Ecuador, Colombia, Brazil, Bolivia, and Chile. It is the third largest country in South America. Language: Spanish. Currency: nuevo sol. Capital: Lima. Population: 24,523,408 (1996). Area: 496,225 sq. mi./1,285,216 sq. km. Official name **Republic of Peru** **2.** city in north central Indiana, on the Wabash River, southwest of Fort Wayne and north of Kokomo. Population: 11,146 (1996).

Pe·ru Cur·rent *n.* = **Humboldt Current**

Pe·ru·gia /pə róojə/ city in central Italy. It is the capital of Perugia Province and Umbria Region. Population: 146,160 (1992).

Peruke: Samuel Pepys wearing a peruke

pe·ruke /pə róok/ *n.* a periwig (*archaic*) [Mid-16thC. Via French *perruque* (source of English *periwig*) from Italian *perrucca* "head of hair," of unknown origin.]

pe·ruse /pə róoz/ (**-rused, -rus·ing, -rus·es**) *vt.* to read or examine something in a leisurely or careful way [Mid-16thC. From PER- + USE; the word originally meant "to use thoroughly, use up."] —**pe·rus·a·ble** *adj.* —**pe·rus·al** *n.* —**pe·rus·er** *n.*

Pe·ru·vi·an /pə róovee ən/ *adj.* OF PERU relating to or typical of Peru, or its people or culture ■ *n.* SOMEBODY FROM PERU somebody who was born or raised in Peru, or who has Peruvian citizenship

Pe·ru·vi·an bal·sam *n.* = **balsam of Peru**

Pe·ru·vi·an bark *n.* the bark of the cinchona tree, formerly used to make quinine and other alkaloid drugs [So called because the trees originally grew in Peru]

perv /purv/, **perve** *n.* a pervert (*slang insult*) [Mid-20thC. Shortening of PERVERT.]

per·vade /pər váyd/ (**-vad·ed, -vad·ing, -vades**) *vt.* to spread through or be present throughout something [Mid-17thC. From Latin *pervadere*, literally "to go throughout," from *vadere* "to go" (see EVADE).] —**per·vad·er** *n.* —**per·va·sion** /-váyzh'n/ *n.*

per·va·sive /pər váyssiv/ *adj.* spreading widely and occupying a great area [Mid-18thC. Formed from Latin *pervas-*, the past participle stem of *pervadere* (see PERVADE).] —**per·va·sive·ly** *adv.* —**per·va·sive·ness** *n.*

per·verse /pər vúrss/ *adj.* 1. PURPOSELY BEING UNREASONABLE purposely deviating from what is accepted as good, proper, or reasonable 2. UNREASONABLY STUBBORN unreasonably stubborn, contrary, or awkward 3. WILLFULLY DOING WRONG willfully persisting in what is wrong 4. PERVERTED perverted (*archaic*) 5. CRANKY cranky or peevish [14thC. Via Old French from Latin *perversus*, the past participle of *pervertere* (see PERVERT).] —**per·verse·ly** *adv.* —**per·verse·ness** *n.*

per·ver·sion /pər vúrzh'n/ *n.* (*disapproving*) 1. UNUSUAL SEXUAL PRACTICE a sexual practice regarded as abnormal 2. TURNING OF GOOD INTO BAD the changing of something good, true, or correct into something bad or wrong or a situation in which the change has occurred ○ *perversion of justice*

per·ver·si·ty /pər vúrsətee/ (*plural* **-ties**) *n.* 1. STUBBORN UNREASONABLE BEHAVIOR being unreasonable or willfully persisting in doing wrong 2. PERVERSE ACTION something such as an action or activity that is perverse

per·ver·sive /pər vúrsiv/ *adj.* tending or able to pervert something

per·vert *vt.* /pər vúrt/ (**-vert·ed, -vert·ing, -verts**) 1. LEAD AWAY SOMEBODY FROM GOOD to lead somebody or something away from what is considered good, normal, moral, or proper 2. MISINTERPRET OR DISTORT SOMETHING to misinterpret or distort something such as a piece of text 3. USE SOMETHING IMPROPERLY to use something incorrectly or improperly 4. DEBASE SOMETHING to bring something into a state regarded as morally inferior or reprehensible ■ *n.* /púr vùrt/ SOMEBODY WITH UNUSUAL SEXUAL BEHAVIOR somebody whose sexual activities are considered abnormal (*disapproving*) [14thC. Via Old French *pervertir* from Latin *pervertere*, literally "to turn wrong," from *vertere* (see VERSE).] —**per·vert·er** *n.* —**per·vert·i·ble** *adj.*

per·vert·ed /pər vúrtəd/ *adj.* 1. DEVIATING FROM WHAT IS PROPER deviating greatly from what is accepted as right, normal, or proper 2. RELATING TO UNUSUAL SEXUAL ACTIVITIES relating to or practicing sexual activities considered abnormal (*disapproving*) 3. DISTORTED misinterpreted or distorted —**per·vert·ed·ly** *adv.* —**per·vert·ed·ness** *n.*

per·vi·ous /púrvee əss/ *adj.* 1. ABLE TO BE PERMEATED susceptible to permeation 2. OPEN TO NEW THINGS open to ideas, suggestions, and change [Early 17thC. Formed from Latin *pervius*, from *per-* "through" + *via* "way" (see VIA).] —**per·vi·ous·ly** *adv.* —**per·vi·ous·ness** *n.*

pes /peez/ (*plural* **pe·des** /pé dàyss/) *n.* 1. MED FOOT OR SIMILAR APPENDAGE the foot or a part resembling a foot 2. ZOOL FOUR-FOOTED ANIMAL'S HIND FOOT a hind foot of a four-footed vertebrate [Mid-19thC. From Latin, "foot" (source of English *pedal*). Ultimately from the Indo-European word for "foot," which is also the ancestor of *foot, fetter, impede*, and *podium*.]

Pe·sach /páy sa̋akh/ *n.* JUDAISM the Passover festival [Early 17thC. From Hebrew *pesaḥ*, from *pāsaḥ* "to pass over."]

pe·san·te /pay sa̋an tày/ *adv.* in a heavy or ponderous manner (*used as a musical direction*) [From Italian]

pe·se·ta /pə sáytə/ *n.* 1. UNIT OF SPANISH CURRENCY the unit of currency in Spain. See table at **currency** 2. COIN WORTH A PESETA a coin worth a peseta [Early 19thC. From Spanish, literally "small peso," formed from *peso* (see PESO).]

pe·se·wa /pay sáy wa̋a/ *n.* 1. MINOR UNIT OF GHANAIAN CURRENCY a minor unit of currency in Ghana, 100 of which are worth a new cedi 2. COIN WORTH A PESEWA a coin worth a pesewa, 100 of which are worth a new cedi [Mid-20thC. From Fante and Twi, "penny."]

Pe·sha·war /pe sha̋a wər/ city near the Khyber Pass in the North-West Frontier District, Pakistan. Population: 1,676,000 (1995).

Pe·shit·ta /pə shéetə/, **Pe·shit·to** /pə shéetō/ *n.* the Syriac version of the Bible, written around the 4th century [Late 18thC. From Syriac *pšīṭtā*, "the simple one."]

pes·ky /péskee/ (**-ki·er, -ki·est**) *adj.* troublesome or irritating (*informal*) [Late 18thC. Origin uncertain: probably from an alteration of PEST.] —**pes·ki·ly** *adv.* —**pes·ki·ness** *n.*

pe·so /páyssō/ (*plural* **-sos**) *n.* See table at **currency** 1. UNIT OF MEXICAN CURRENCY the unit of currency in Mexico 2. NOTE WORTH A PESO a note worth a peso [Mid-16thC. Via Spanish from Latin *pensum* "weight," from the past participle of *pendere* "to weigh" (see PENSIVE).]

pes·sa·ry /péssəree/ (*plural* **-ries**) *n.* 1. UTERINE SUPPORT a plastic device such as a ring placed in the vagina to keep the womb in position following a prolapse due to weakened ligaments 2. VAGINAL SUPPOSITORY a suppository containing medication for insertion into the vagina [14thC. Via late Latin *pessarium* from, ultimately, Greek *pessos*, originally an oval stone used in board games.]

pes·si·mism /péssə mìzzəm/ *n.* 1. TENDENCY TO EXPECT WORST a tendency to see only the negative or worst aspects of all things and to expect only bad or unpleasant things to happen 2. PHILOS DOCTRINE ABOUT EVIL a doctrine that all things become evil or that evil outweighs good in life [Late 18thC. From French *pessimisme*, from Latin *pessimus* "worst," on the model of "optimisme."]

pes·si·mist /péssəmist/ *n.* somebody who always expects the worst to happen in every situation —**pes·si·mis·tic** /pèssə místik/ *adj.* —**pes·si·mis·ti·cal·ly** *adv.*

pest /pest/ *n.* 1. DAMAGING ORGANISM an organism that is damaging to livestock, crops, humans, or land fertility 2. ANNOYING PERSON OR THING somebody or something that is a nuisance (*informal*) 3. OUTBREAK OF DISEASE an epidemic of infectious or contagious disease (*archaic*) [Mid-16thC. Via French, "pestilence," from Latin *pestis*, of unknown origin.]

pes·ter /péstər/ (**-tered, -ter·ing, -ters**) *vt.* to be a constant source of annoyance to somebody, e.g., by harassing him or her with demands [Mid-16thC. Via French *empestrer* "to embarrass" (influenced by PEST), of uncertain origin: perhaps via assumed Vulgar Latin *impastoriare* "to hobble" from, ultimately, Latin *pastor* "herdsman" (see PASTOR).] —**pes·ter·er** *n.* —**pes·ter·ing·ly** *adv.*

pest·hole /pést hōl/ *n.* a place where epidemic diseases are rife and from where they might spread (*dated*) [Early 20thC. Formed from PEST in the obsolete meaning "contagious disease."]

pest·house /pést hòwss/ (*plural* **-hous·es** /-zəz/) *n.* a hospital where patients suffering from infectious disease were once treated [Early 17thC. Formed from PEST in the obsolete meaning "contagious disease."]

pes·ti·cide /pésti sīd/ *n.* a chemical substance used to kill pests, especially insects [Mid-20thC. Coined from PEST + -CIDE.] —**pes·ti·cid·al** /pèsti sīd'l/ *adj.*

pes·tif·er·ous /pə stíffərəss/ *adj.* 1. ANNOYING troublesome or annoying 2. MED CAUSING INFECTIOUS DISEASE breeding or spreading a virulently infectious disease 3. CORRUPTING evil and corrupting (*formal*) [15thC. Formed from Latin *pestifer* "plague-carrying," from *pestis* "plague."] —**pes·tif·er·ous·ly** *adv.* —**pes·tif·er·ous·ness** *n.*

pes·ti·lence /péstiləns/ *n.* (*archaic*) 1. MED EPIDEMIC OF DISEASE an epidemic of a highly contagious or infectious disease such as bubonic plague 2. MED DISEASE a serious infectious disease 3. SOMETHING EVIL a malevolent belief, influence, or presence

pes·ti·lent /péstilənt/ *adj.* 1. CAUSING OR INFECTED WITH CONTAGIOUS DISEASE likely to cause a contagious disease or to be infected with one 2. DEADLY causing or tending to cause death 3. HARMFUL very harmful morally, socially, or physically (*archaic*) 4. ANNOYING annoying or infuriating (*dated*) [14thC. Via Old French from the Latin stem *pestilent-*, from *pestis* "plague."] —**pes·ti·len·tial** /pèsti lénshəl/ *adj.* —**pes·ti·len·tial·ly** *adv.* —**pes·ti·lent·ly** /péstiləntlee/ *adv.*

pes·tle /péss'l/ *n.* (*plural* **-tles**) OBJECT FOR CRUSHING OR GRINDING a rodshaped object made from hard material with a rounded end that is used for crushing or grinding substances in a mortar ■ *vti.* (**-tled, -tling, -tles**) CRUSH OR POUND SUBSTANCE USING PESTLE to crush, grind, or pound a substance or object using a pestle [14thC. Via Old French from Latin *pistillum* (source also of English *pistil*).]

pes·to /péstō/ *n.* 1. BASIL SAUCE a sauce or paste made by crushing together basil leaves, pine nuts, oil, Parmesan cheese, and garlic. It is traditionally served hot or cold with pasta or on meat. 2. FLAVORFUL PASTE a pureed or finely minced paste of herbs and vegetables, tomatoes, or olives, used as pasta sauce, bread spread, or in cooking [Mid-20thC. From Italian, from the past participle of *pestare* "to pound, crush," via late Latin *pistare* from Latin *pinsere* "to beat."]

pet[1] /pet/ *n.* 1. ANIMAL KEPT AT HOME an animal kept for companionship, interest, or amusement 2. FAVORITE PERSON somebody who is indulged, especially a favorite 3. LOVED PERSON somebody who is particularly loved by another, often used as a term of endearment in direct address ■ *adj.* 1. KEPT AS PET kept as a pet animal 2. SPECIAL OR FAVORITE TO SOMEBODY cherished by, special, or favorite to somebody ○ *a pet topic* ■ *v.* (**pet·ted, pet·ting, pets**) 1. *vt.* STROKE ANIMAL to pat or stroke an animal or to touch a child similarly 2. *vt.* TREAT SOMEBODY INDULGENTLY to treat a person or animal indulgently 3. *vi.* TOUCH FOR SEXUAL PLEASURE to touch each other in a way that causes sexual pleasure [Early 16thC. Origin uncertain: perhaps a back-formation from Middle English *pety* "small," an earlier form of PETTY.] —**pet·ter** *n.*

pet[2] /pet/ *n.* SULKY MOOD a fit of sulkiness or peevishness ■ *vi.* (**pet·ted, pet·ting, pets**) BE SULKY to be peevish or sulky [Mid-16thC. Origin unknown.]

PET /pet/ *abbr.* 1. positron emission tomography 2. polyethylene terephthalate

Pet. *abbr.* BIBLE Peter

peta- *prefix.* one million billion (10^{15}). Symbol **P** [Formed from PENTA-, on the model of "tera-" (as if from "tetra-"); so called because it represents 1,000 to the fifth power]

pet·al /pétt'l/ *n.* one of the showy colored parts that form the outer part of a flower that together are the corolla [Early 18thC. Via modern Latin *petalum* from Greek *petalon* "leaf." Ultimately from an Indo-European base meaning "to spread," which is also the ancestor of English *fathom* and *patent*.] —**pet·al·ine** /pétt'l īn, pétt'lin/ *adj.* —**pet·aled** /pétt'ld/ *adj.*

-petal *suffix.* moving toward ○ *centripetal* [Formed from modern Latin *-petus*, from Latin *petere* "to seek" (see PETITION)]

pet·al·if·er·ous /pètt'l íffərəss/, **pet·al·ous** /pétt'ləss/ *adj.* having petals

pet·al·oid /pétt'l òyd/ *adj.* resembling the petal of a flower

pet·al·ous *adj.* = **petaliferous**

pe·tard /pə ta̋ard/ *n.* 1. ARMS EXPLOSIVE CHARGE FOR BREACHING FORTIFICATION a small explosive charge or grenade used to blow a hole in a door, wall, or fortification 2. FIRECRACKER a powerful firecracker [Mid-16thC. Via French from, ultimately, Latin *pedere* "to break wind." Ultimately from an Indo-European word that is also the ancestor of English *fizzle* and *feisty*.] ◇ **be hoist with your own petard** to be the victim of your own attempt to harm somebody else

pet·au·rist /pə táwrəst/ *n.* ZOOL = **flying phalanger** [Mid-17thC. From Greek *petauristēs* "acrobat," from *petauron* "springboard."]

Pet·a·vi·us /pə táyvee əss/ *n.* a walled enclosure on the Moon with a prominent crack (**rille**) across the floor and a complex central peak, located south of Mare Fecundatis, 110 mi./177 km in diameter

pet·cock /pét kòk/ *n.* a small manually operated valve or faucet used to drain off waste material or excess fluid from the cylinder of an internal combustion engine [Mid-19thC. From *pet* (of uncertain origin: perhaps from PET[1] or obsolete *pet* "fart," via French from, ultimately, Latin *peditus*) + COCK[1] in the meaning of "spout."]

pe·te·chi·a /pe téekee ə/ (*plural* **-ae** /-ī/) *n.* a tiny purplish red spot on the skin caused by the release into the skin of a very small quantity of blood from a capillary [Late 18thC. Via modern Latin from Italian *petecchie* "spots on the skin," ultimately from Latin *impetigo* (see IMPETIGO).] —**pe·te·chi·al** *adj.*

pe·ter[1] /péetər/ (**-tered, -ter·ing, -ters**) *vi.* to become less [12thC. From the name *Peter*.]

peter out *vi.* to dwindle and finally stop or disappear [Early 19thC. Origin unknown.]

pe·ter[2] /péetər/ *n.* a penis (*slang*) (*considered offensive by some people*)

Pe·ter /péetər/, **St.** (*d.* A.D.64?). One of the 12 disciples of Jesus Christ, he was a leader and missionary in the early church, and traditionally the first bishop of Rome. Born **Simon**

Pe·ter·bor·ough /péetər bùrō, -bùrō, -bərə/ city in southeastern Ontario, Canada, approximately 25 miles/40 km north of Lake Ontario. Population: 100,193 (1996).

Pe·ter Pan *n.* a man who looks very young or behaves in a boyish way (*informal*) [Early 20thC. From the name of the hero of J. M. Barrie's play *Peter Pan, or The Boy Who Wouldn't Grow Up* (1904).]

Pe·ter Pan col·lar *n.* a flat collar attached to a round neck with rounded ends visible at the front

Pe·ter Prin·ci·ple *n.* the theory that all members of an organization will eventually be promoted to a level at which they are no longer competent to do their job [Mid-20thC. Named for the U.S. author Laurence Johnston *Peter* 1919–90, who propounded it.]

pe·ter·sham /péetər shàm/ *n.* TEXTILES a strong ribbed ribbon used to reinforce parts of garments such as waistbands [Early 19thC. Named for the English army officer Viscount *Petersham* 1790–1851, who wore such an overcoat.]

Pe·ter·son /péetərssən/, **Oscar** (*b.* 1925) Canadian pianist. He is known for his technical brilliance in jazz and ability to play. Full name **Oscar Emmanuel Peterson**

Pe·ter's pence *n.* **1.** ROMAN CATHOLIC DONATION a voluntary financial contribution made by some Roman Catholic dioceses to the Papal See **2.** HIST MEDIEVAL TAX TO PAPAL SEE a tax of one penny per household paid to the Papal See in medieval times until it was abolished by Henry VIII [From the tradition that the papacy was founded by Saint PETER]

Pe·ters' pro·jec·tion *n.* a form of map projection that represents the relative size of land masses more accurately than Mercator's projection [Late 20thC. Named for Arno *Peters*, who created it.]

Pe·ter the Great /pètər thə gráyt/, **Tzar** (1672–1725) Russian emperor. His victory over Sweden established Russia as a major European power.

pe·thi·dine /péthi deen/ *n.* = **meperidine** [Mid-20thC. A blend of P(IPER)IDINE and ETH(YL).]

pé·til·lant /pàytee yaaN/ *adj.* used to describe wine that is slightly sparkling [Late 19thC. From French, "effervescent," literally "passing gas."]

pet·i·o·lar /péttee ōlər, pèttee ólər/ *adj.* relating to the growth of petioles

pet·i·o·late /péttee ə làyt/ *adj.* having a petiole

pet·i·ole /péttee ōl/ *n.* a leafstalk (*technical*) [Mid-18thC. From modern Latin *petiolus*, a variant of Latin *peciolus*, literally "little foot" (see PEDICEL).]

pet·i·o·lule /péttee ə lool/ *n.* the stalk of a leaflet in a compound leaf [Mid-19thC. From modern Latin *petiolulus*, literally "little petiole," from *petiolus* (see PETIOLE).]

pet·it bour·geois /pètti boor zhwaá, pə tee-/ (*plural* **pe·tits bour·geois** /pètti-/) *n.* a member of the lower middle class [From French, literally "little citizen"]

pe·tite /pə téet/ *adj.* **1.** SMALL AND DELICATELY BUILT having a small and delicate build ○ *a petite woman* **2.** FOR SMALLER WOMEN designed to fit smaller women or girls [Mid-16thC. From French, feminine of *petit* "little."]

pe·tite bour·geoi·sie /pəteet boor zhwaa zée/ (*plural* **pe·tites bour·geoi·sies**) *n.* people in the lower middle class, a group traditionally including small business operators, craftspeople, and tradespeople

pet·it four /pétti fàwr, pə tee fáwr/ (*plural* **pe·tits fours**) *n.* any one of a mixture of bite-size sweet cakes served at the end of a meal with coffee [From French, literally "little oven"]

pe·ti·tion /pə tísh'n/ *n.* **1.** DEMAND FOR ACTION WITH SIGNATURES a written request signed by many people demanding a particular action from an authority or government **2.** APPEAL OR REQUEST TO HIGHER AUTHORITY an appeal or request to a higher authority or being **3.** SOMETHING REQUESTED something requested or appealed for **4.** ACT OF PETITIONING the act of making a petition **5.** PLEADING STATING CAUSE OF ACTION a pleading in a civil action by which the plaintiff sets down the cause of action and invokes the court's jurisdiction ■ *v.* (**-tioned, -tion·ing, -tions**) **1.** *vti.* GIVE PETITION TO SOMEBODY to give or address a petition to somebody, especially somebody in authority or a representative of an organization **2.** *vi.* MAKE DEMAND USING PETITION to urge for or against a course of action by presenting a petition **3.** *vi.* LAW MAKE FORMAL REQUEST to request formally, using a petition [14thC. Via Old French from, ultimately, Latin *petere* "to seek, go toward." Ultimately from an Indo-European base meaning "to fly," which is also the ancestor of English *feather* and *symptom*.] — **pe·ti·tion·ar·y** *adj.*

WORD KEY: ORIGIN

The Latin word *petere*, from which **petition** is derived, is also the source of English *appetite*, *compete*, *impetus*, *perpetual*, *petulant*, and *repeat*.

pe·ti·tion·er /pə tísh'nər/ *n.* **1.** SOMEBODY PETITIONING FOR SOMETHING somebody who requests or demands something using a petition **2.** LAW PLAINTIFF PETITIONING IN CIVIL ACTION the plaintiff in a civil action who presents a formal written pleading to a court

pe·ti·ti·o prin·ci·pi·i /pə tìshee ō prin síppee èe/ *n.* logically fallacious reasoning in which what has to be proved is already assumed [From Latin, literally "assuming the first thing"]

pet·it ju·ry /pètti jóoree/, **pet·ty ju·ry** *n.* = **trial jury**

pet·it lar·ce·ny, pet·ty lar·ce·ny *n.* the theft of something whose value lies below a particular standard in a particular jurisdiction

pet·it mal /pètti mál/ *n.* a form of epilepsy marked by episodes of brief loss of consciousness without convulsions or falling. It is found most frequently in children and adolescents. ◊ **grand mal** [From French, literally "small illness"]

pet·it point /pètti póynt/ (*plural* **pe·tits points**) *n.* **1.** SMALL STITCH IN NEEDLEPOINT FOR DETAILS a small stitch used in needlepoint when creating details **2.** EMBROIDERY WITH SMALL STITCHES work embroidered using small stitches [From French, "small stitch"]

pe·tits pois /pètti pwaá, pə tee-/ *npl.* small sweet green peas [From French, "small peas"]

pet name *n.* a name showing endearment used for a family member or special friend

pet·nap·ping /pét nàpping/ *n.* the stealing or kidnapping of a pet animal [Late 20thC. Modeled on "kidnapping."] —**pet·nap·per** *n.*

pet peeve *n.* somebody's constant issue or topic of complaint

Pet·ra /péetrə, péttrə/ ancient ruined city in southwestern Jordan, famous for its buildings and tombs that are carved out of solid rock

Pe·trarch /pée traark, pét raàrk/ (1304–74) Italian lyric poet and scholar. He is best remembered for his series of love poems addressed to Laura, the *Canzoniere* (1327). Born **Francesco Petrarca**

Pe·trarch·an son·net /pə traàrkən-/ *n.* a form of poetry that has an eight line stanza with the rhyme scheme abbaabba followed by six lines with various rhyme schemes, usually cdcdcd or cdecde [Early 19thC. Named for the Italian poet Francesco PETRARCH 1304–74, who developed the form.]

pet·rel /pétrəl/ *n.* a bird that lives on the sea such as the storm-petrel, the diving petrel, or the fulmar. Petrels are widespread in ocean environments and move awkwardly on land. Family: Hydrobatidae and Pelecanoididae and Procellariidae. [Early 17thC. Origin uncertain: perhaps formed from Saint *Peter*, who walked on water (Matthew 14:29), because the bird flies close to the surface.]

petri- *prefix.* = **petro-**

Petri dish

Pe·tri dish /péetree-/ *n.* a shallow flat-bottomed dish with a loose cover used especially to grow bacterial cultures in the laboratory [Named for Julius *Petri* (1852–92), the German bacteriologist who invented it]

pet·ri·fac·tion /pèttrə fákshən/, **pet·ri·fi·ca·tion** /pèttrəfi káysh'n/ *n.* **1.** CONVERSION OF SUBSTANCE TO STONE the process in which the porous structure of organic material such as bones, shell, and wood is infiltrated by salt-bearing groundwater, which preserves the structure when it solidifies. The Petrified Forest in Arizona contains whole tree trunks that have been turned into stone. **2.** CONDITION OF BEING PETRIFIED the condition of being turned into stone

Pet·ri·fied For·est Na·tion·al Park /pètrə fīd-/ national park in eastern Arizona, established as a national monument in 1906, and as a national park in 1962. It is noted for its petrified trees and Native American ruins. Area: 146 sq. mi./378 sq. km.

pet·ri·fy /péttrə fī/ (**-fied, -fy·ing, -fies**) *v.* **1.** *vt.* IMMOBILIZE SOMEBODY WITH FEAR to cause a person or animal to become immobile with terror **2.** *vti.* GEOL CAUSE PETRIFICATION to cause or bring about the process by which something organic is turned into stone **3.** *vti.* MAKE OR BECOME DEADENED OR STIFF to become or cause something to become dull, stiff, or deadened [15thC. From French *pétrifier* or medieval Latin *petrificare*, both formed from Latin *petra* "stone," from Greek *petra* (see PETRO-).] — **pet·ri·fi·er** *n.*

Pe·trine /pée trīn/ *adj.* **1.** OF THE APOSTLE PETER relating to or associated with St. Peter, the Apostle. **2.** OF CATHOLIC DISSOLUTION OF MARRIAGE in the Roman Catholic Church, associated with or used to describe a dissolved marriage between somebody who has been baptized and somebody who has not [Mid-19thC. Formed from ecclesiastical Latin *Petrus* "Peter."]

petro- *prefix.* **1.** rock, stone ○ *petrography* **2.** petroleum ○ *petrodollar* [From Greek *petros* "a stone" and *petra* "rock" (source also of English *petrify*, *parsley* and *saltpeter*)]

pet·ro·chem·i·cal /pèttrō kémmik'l/ *n.* DERIVATIVE OF PETROLEUM OR NATURAL GAS a substance derived from petroleum or natural gas, such as gasoline or paraffin ■ *adj.* RELATING TO PETROCHEMICALS relating to or derived from petrochemicals —**pet·ro·chem·i·cal·ly** *adv.*

pet·ro·chem·is·try /pèttrō kémmistree/ *n.* **1.** CHEMISTRY OF PETROLEUM the branch of chemistry that is concerned with petroleum and derivatives of petroleum **2.** GEOCHEMISTRY OF ROCKS the chemistry of rocks, especially with reference to their composition

pet·ro·dol·lar /péttrō dòllər/ *n.* dollars paid to global oil producers that are deposited in U.S. banks

petrog. *abbr.* petrography

pet·ro·gen·e·sis /pèttrō jénnəssiss/ *n.* the origin, formation, and history of rocks

pet·ro·glyph /péttrə glìf/ *n.* a prehistoric drawing done on rock [Late 19thC. From French, from Greek *petros* "stone" + *glyphē* "carving."]

pe·trog·ra·phy /pi tróggrəfee/ *n.* the systematic description of the texture of rocks and the minerals they contain, often using microscopy of thin slices of the rock to determine the mineral content —**pe·trog·ra·pher** *n.* —**pet·ro·graph·ic** /pèttrə gráffik/ *adj.* —**pet·ro·graph·i·cal·ly** /-kəlee/ *adv.*

pet·rol /péttrəl/ *n.* *U.K.* = **gasoline** [Mid-16thC. Via French *pétrole* from medieval Latin *petroleum* (see PETROLEUM).]

petrol. *abbr.* petrology

pet·rol bomb *n.* = **Molotov cocktail**

pe·tro·le·um /pə trṓlee əm/ *n.* crude oil that occurs naturally in sedimentary rocks and consists mainly of hydrocarbons. A wide variety of commercially important petrochemicals, such as gasoline and kerosene are derived from it. [Early 16thC. From medieval Latin, from Latin *petra* "rock" + *oleum* (see OIL).]

pe·tro·le·um jel·ly *n.* a greasy substance derived from petroleum and used as an ointment base, lubricant, and a protective covering

pe·trol·o·gy /pə tróləjee/ *n.* the study of sedimentary, igneous, and metamorphic rocks with respect to their occurrence, structure, origin, history, and mineral content —**pet·ro·log·i·cal** /pèttrə lójjik'l/ *adj.* —**pet·ro·log·i·cal·ly** /-kəlee/ *adv.* —**pe·trol·o·gist** /pə tróləjist/ *n.*

pet·rol sta·tion *n.* *U.K.* = **gas station**

pet·ro·nel /péttrənəl/ *n.* a short firearm with a curved butt whose length was between that of a long pistol and a short carbine, used mostly by cavalry in the 16th and 17th centuries [Late 16thC. Via French *petrinal* from, ultimately, Latin *pectus* "chest" (see PECTORAL), so called because the butt rested against the chest when the gun was fired.]

pe·tro·sal /pə tróss'l/ *adj.* affecting or belonging to the hard (**petrous**) portion of the temporal bone surrounding the inner ear [Mid-18thC. Formed from Latin *petrosus* (see PETROUS).]

pet·rous /péttrəss/ *adj.* **1.** GEOL OF ROCK relating to or resembling rock or stone **2.** ANAT OF HARD PART OF TEMPORAL LOBE used to describe the hard portion of the temporal bone surrounding the inner ear [Mid-16thC. Formed from Latin *petrosus* "rocky," from *petra* "rock" (see PETRIFY).]

PET scan /pét-/ *n.* an image of a bodily cross-section, usually of the brain, that reveals metabolic processes and that is obtained by means of positron emission tomography —**PET scan·ner** *n.* —**PET scan·ning** *n.*

pet·ti·coat /pétti kōt/ *n.* **1. WOMAN'S UNDERGARMENT** a woman's undergarment that is sometimes decorated and consists of an underskirt with or without a bodice **2. FORMERLY, ANY SKIRT** until the 20th century, any skirt whether worn on its own with a jacket or bodice, or underneath a gown **3. SOMETHING RESEMBLING SKIRT** something that resembles a petticoat, such as ruffles sewn on a skirt or a skirt-shaped covering for something **4. OFFENSIVE TERM** an offensive term for a woman or girl (*dated offensive*) ■ *adj.* **OFFENSIVE TERM** an offensive term referring to women or girls (*dated offensive*) [15thC. From PETTY "small" + COAT. The modern meaning evolved from "padded coat worn under armor" via "short coat worn by men."]

pet·ti·fog·ger /péttee fòggər/ *n.* **1. SOMEBODY WHO ARGUES OVER DETAILS** somebody who argues or fusses over trivia and details **2. INSIGNIFICANT LAWYER** a lawyer whose practice is small or insignificant [Mid-16thC. Origin uncertain: probably from PETTY + *fogger*, of unknown origin.] —**pet·ti·fog** *vi.* —**pet·ti·fog·ger·y** *n.*

pet·ti·fog·ging /péttee fògging/ *adj.* **1. TRIVIAL** petty or trivial ○ *pettifogging details* **2. QUIBBLING** quibbling or fussing over trivial matters (*insult*)

pet·ting /pétting/ *n.* touching between people that causes sexual pleasure but does not include sexual intercourse (*informal*)

pet·ting zoo *n.* a place where tame animals such as deer, goats, rabbits, and fowl are made available for small children to pet and feed

pet·tish /péttish/ *adj.* peevish, irritable, or sulky [Late 16thC. Formed from PET²] —**pet·tish·ly** *adv.* —**pet·tish·ness** *n.*

pet·ti·toes /péttee tōz/ *npl.* **1. PIG'S TROTTERS** pig's feet when used as food **2.** somebody's, especially children's, toes or feet (*informal*) [Mid-16thC. Origin uncertain: perhaps by folk-etymology from French *petite oie* "giblets of a goose," by association with PETTY and TOE.]

pet·ty /péttee/ (**-ti·er, -ti·est**) *adj.* **1. INSIGNIFICANT** of little importance **2. NARROW-MINDED** narrow-minded in nature **3. MEAN** spiteful in character **4. OF RELATIVELY LITTLE IMPORTANCE** subordinate in rank or importance [14thC. From Old French *peti*, a variant of *petit* "small," of unknown origin.] —**pet·ti·ly** /péttilee/ *adv.* —**pet·ti·ness** /pétteenəss/ *n.*

pet·ty cash *n.* a small amount of money kept, e.g., in an office, and used to cover minor everyday expenses

pet·ty ju·ry *n.* = **petit jury**

pet·ty lar·ce·ny *n.* = **petit larceny**

pet·ty of·fi·cer *n.* a noncommissioned naval officer ranking above enlisted sailors and below commissioned officers

pet·u·lant /péchələnt/ *adj.* ill-tempered or sulky in a peevish manner [Late 16thC. Via French from Latin *petulans* "insolent," from *petere* "to seek, assail" (see PETITION).] —**pet·u·lance** *n.* —**pet·u·lant·ly** *adv.*

Petunia

pe·tu·nia /pə tóonee ə/ *n.* **TROPICAL PLANT WITH BRIGHT FLOWERS** a flowering plant native to tropical America that has sticky stems and brightly colored funnel-shaped flowers. Genus: *Petunia.* ■ *adj.* **OF DARK PURPLE COLOR** of a dark purple or violet color [Early 19thC. Via modern Latin, genus name, from, ultimately, Portuguese *petum* "tobacco," from Tupi or Guarani; so called because it is related to tobacco.]

pe·tun·tze /pi tóontsə/, **pe·tun·tse** *n.* a variety of feldspar that can be melted and is used in the manufacture of Chinese porcelain [Early 18thC. From Chinese (Mandarin) *báidùnzi*, literally "white stone block."]

pew /pyoo/ *n.* a usually wooden bench with a straight back and often a kneeling bench attached to the one in front of it, used by worshipers in a church or synagogue [14thC. Via Old French *puie* "balcony" from, ultimately, Latin *podium* (see PODIUM). The word originally denoted a raised seating area in a church.]

pe·wee /pée wee/, **pee·wee** *n.* a drab medium-sized flycatcher with a plaintive song. Genus: *Contopus.* [Late 18thC. An imitation of its call.]

pe·wit /péewit, pyóo it/ *n.* BIRDS = **lapwing** [Early 16thC. An imitation of its call.]

pew·ter /pyóotər/ *n.* **1. TIN AND LEAD ALLOY** a silver-gray alloy of tin and lead sometimes containing antimony and copper **2. PEWTER OBJECTS COLLECTIVELY** articles made from pewter **3. DARK GRAYISH COLOR** a dark, dull gray color tinged with blue or purple ■ *adj.* **OF DARK DULL GRAY COLOR** of a dark dull gray color, with a tinge of blue or purple [14thC. Via Old French *peutre* from assumed Vulgar Latin *peltrum*, of unknown origin.]

pew·ter·er /pyóotərər/ *n.* a craftsperson who makes or repairs pewter articles

pe·yo·te /pay ṓtee/ *n.* **1.** PLANTS **GLOBESHAPED CACTUS** a spineless globeshaped cactus native to Mexico and the southwestern United States that has small rounded nodules containing mescaline. Latin name: *Lophophora williamsii.* **2. pe·yo·te, pe·yo·te but·ton** DRUGS **CACTUS USED AS DRUG** any one of the buttonshaped nodules on the stem of the peyote cactus that contains mescaline and is used as a hallucinogenic drug [Mid-19thC. Via American Spanish from Nahuatl *peyotl*.]

pF *symbol.* picofarad

pf. *abbr.* **1.** perfect **2.** pfennig

PFC, **Pfc** *abbr.* private first class

PFD *abbr.* personal flotation device

pfen·nig /fénnig/ (*plural* **-nigs** *or* **pfen·ni·ge**) *n.* **1. MINOR UNIT OF GERMAN CURRENCY** a minor unit of currency in Germany, 100 of which are worth a mark. See table at **currency 2. COIN WORTH A PFENNIG** a coin worth a pfennig [Mid-16thC. From German, ultimately related to English *penny*.]

pfft /ft/ *interj.* a sound indicating a sudden disappearance or failure of something, meaning "that's it" or "there it went" (*informal*) [Early 20thC. An imitation of the sound of a light or other device suddenly burning out.]

PG¹ *adj.* CINEMA used to describe a movie that would be inappropriate for children, unless accompanied by a parent. Full form **parental guidance** [Abbreviation of *parental guidance*]

PG² *abbr.* postgraduate

PG³ *abbr.* pregnant (*informal*)

pg. *abbr.* page

Pg. *abbr.* Portuguese

PG-13 *adj.* CINEMA used to describe a motion picture that is inappropriate for children under 13, unless accompanied by a parent, as judged by the Motion Picture Association of America

PGA *abbr.* Professional Golfers' Association

PGP *n.* a program to encrypt data for security purposes when the data is transmitted over public networks like the Internet. PGP uses public key encryption, a system that provides for privacy and authentication of both the sender and the receiver of the message. Abbr of **Pretty Good Privacy**

pH *n.* a measure of the acidity or alkalinity of a solution, such as vinegar, or a damp substance, such as soil. The pH of pure water is 7 with lower numbers indicating acidity and higher numbers indicating alkalinity. Full form **potential of hydrogen**

Ph *symbol.* phenyl group

PH, **P.H.** *abbr.* **1.** Purple Heart **2.** public health

ph. *abbr.* phase

PHA *abbr.* Public Housing Administration

phac·o·e·mul·si·fi·ca·tion /fà kō i múlsəfi káysh'n/ *n.* an ultrasonic technique using microsurgical instruments that allows a cataract-affected lens to be liquefied and removed by suction using a very small incision near the edge of the cornea. A foldable plastic lens is then inserted through the incision and unfolded. [Late 20thC. Coined from Greek *phakos* "lentil" (because of the shape of the lens) + *emulsification*.]

pha·e·ton /fáyət'n, fáyt'n/ *n.* **1. LIGHT FOUR-WHEELED HORSE-DRAWN CARRIAGE** a small light four-wheeled carriage, usually with two seats and usually drawn by two horses **2. ANTIQUE TOURING CAR** an old-fashioned touring car, now antique [Late 16thC. Via French from, ultimately, Greek *Phaethōn*, the son of Helios, who was killed by Zeus while trying to drive his father's chariot across the sky.]

phage /fayj/ (*plural* **phag·es**) *n.* = **bacteriophage** [Early 20thC. Shortening.]

-phage *suffix.* something that eats ○ *xylophage* [From Greek *-phagos* "-eating," which was formed from *phagein* "to eat" (see PHAGO-)]

phag·e·de·na /fàjjə déenə/, **phag·e·dae·na** *n.* an ulcer that spreads rapidly [Late 16thC. Via Latin from Greek *phagedaina*.]

-phagia *suffix.* eating ○ *aerophagia* ○ *hyperphagia* [From Greek, formed from *phagein* "to eat" (see PHAGO-)]

phago- *prefix.* eating, consuming ○ *phagocyte* [From Greek *phagein* "to eat." Ultimately from an Indo-European word meaning "to share out, distribute," which is also the ancestor of English *pagoda* and *nebbish*.]

phag·o·cyte /fággə sīt/ *n.* a cell in the body's bloodstream and tissues such as a white blood cell that engulfs and ingests foreign particles, cell waste material, and bacteria —**phag·o·cyt·ic** /fàggə síttik/ *adj.*

phag·o·cy·to·sis /fàggə sī tṓsiss/ *n.* BIOL the engulfing and ingesting of foreign particles or waste matter by phagocytes —**phag·o·cy·tot·ic** /fàggə sī tóttik/ *adj.*

-phagous *suffix.* eating ○ *polyphagous* [Formed from Latin *-phagus*, via Greek *-phagos* from *phagein* "to eat" (see PHAGO-)]

-phagy *suffix.* = **-phagia**

Pha·lange /fáy lànj, fə lánj/ *n.* a Lebanese Christian paramilitary group [Mid-20thC. Variant of *Falange*, from Spanish, literally "phalanx."] —**Pha·lang·ist** /fə lánjist, fállənjist/ *n., adj.*

pha·lan·ge·al /fə lánjee əl, fay-/ *adj.* relating to a phalanx or the phalanges

pha·lan·ger /fə lánjər/ *n.* a small tree-dwelling marsupial with dense woolly fur and a long tail, found in Australia and nearby islands. Family: Phalangeridae. [Late 18thC. Via modern Latin from the Greek stem *phalagg-* "toe bone," because of the webbed or fused toes on its hind feet.]

pha·lanx /fáy lànks, fá-/ (*plural* **-lanx·es** *or* **-lan·ges** /fə lánjeez, fay-/) *n.* **1. TIGHT GROUP** a group of people, animals, or objects that are moving or standing closely together **2.** ARMY, HIST **BODY OF TROOPS** especially in ancient Greece, a group of soldiers that attacks in close formation, protected by their overlapping shields and projecting spears **3.** (*plural* **-lan·ges**) ANAT **FINGER AND TOE BONE** a finger or toe bone of a human being or vertebrate animal [Mid-16thC. Via Latin (stem *phalang-*) from Greek *phalagx* "line of battle, finger, or toe bone."]

phal·a·rope /fállə rōp/ *n.* a small wading bird that is related to the sandpiper but has lobed toes adapted for swimming. Genus: *Phalaropus.* [Late 18thC. Via French from modern Latin *Phalaropus*, genus name, from Greek *phalaris* "coot" + *pous* "foot."]

Phal·gu·na /pál gŏŏnə, fál-/ *n.* in the Hindu calendar, the 12th month of the year, made up of 29 or 30 days and occurring about the same time as February or March

phal·li plural of **phallus**

phal·lic /fállik/ *adj.* **1. OF A PHALLUS** relating to or resembling a phallus **2.** PSYCHOANAL **RELATING TO THEORETICAL STAGE OF DEVELOPMENT** in psychoanalytic theory, relating to a stage of psychosexual development during which a young child's sexual feelings are concentrated on the genitals **3.** RELIG **OF PHALLICISM** relating to phallicism [Late 18thC. From Greek *phallikos*, from *phallos* (see PHALLUS).]

phal·li·cism /fálli sìzzəm/ *n.* the worshiping of the reproductive forces of life as symbolized by the penis —**phal·li·cist** /fállissist/ *n.*

phal·lo·cen·tric /fàllō séntrik/ *adj.* centered on men, or showing a preference for traditionally masculine qualities rather than traditionally feminine ones [Early 20thC. Coined from PHALLUS + -CENTRIC.]

phal·lus /fálləss/ (*plural* **-lus·es** *or* **-li** /fá lī/) *n.* **1. STYLIZED PENIS** a picture, sculpture, or other representation of a penis, especially one regarded as a symbol of the reproductive force of life **2. PENIS** the human penis, especially when erect [Early 17thC. Via late Latin from Greek *phallos*. Ultimately, from an Indo-European base denoting "to swell," which is also the ancestor of English *bowl*, *bull*, and *bold*.]

-phan *suffix.* = **-phane**

-phane *suffix.* a substance having the appearance or qualities of ○ *cymophane* [From Greek *-phanēs*, which was formed from *phainesthai* "to appear" (see PHENOMENON)]

phan·er·o·gam /fánnərō gàm/ *n.* a plant that produces seeds [Mid-19thC. Via French from modern Latin *phanerogamus*, from Greek *phaneros* "visible," which was formed from *phainein* (see PHENOMENON) + *gamos* "sexual union" (see -GAMOUS).] —**phan·er·o·gam·ic** /fànnərō gámmik/ *adj.*

phan·tasm /fán tàzzəm/ *n.* **1. SUPPOSED GHOST OR SPIRIT** a supposed being such as a ghost or a disembodied spirit that can be seen but does not have physical substance **2.** PHILOS **DELUSION OR ILLUSION** an understanding or perception that is not based on reality [13thC. Via Old French *fantasme* from, ultimately, Greek *phantasma*, from *phantazesthai* "to appear" (see FANTASTIC).] —**phan·tas·mal** /fan tázməl/ *adj.* —**phan·tas·mal·ly** /-məlee/ *adv.* —**phan·tas·mic** /-tázmik/ *adj.* —**phan·tas·mi·cal·ly** /-mikəlee/ *adv.*

phan·tas·ma·go·ri·a /fàntazmə gáwree ə/, **phan·tas·ma·go·ry** /fan tázmə gàwree/ (*plural* **-ries**) *n.* **1. BIZARRE IMAGES** a series or group of strange or bizarre images seen as if in a dream **2. EVER-CHANGING SCENE** a scene or view that encompasses many things and changes constantly [Early 19thC. From French *fantasmagorie* "art of making optical illusions," from *fantasme* (see PHANTASM), possibly on the model of *allégorie* "allegory."] —**phan·tas·ma·gor·ic** *adj.* —**phan·tas·ma·gor·i·cal** *adj.* —**phan·tas·ma·gor·i·cal·ly** *adv.*

phan·tom /fántəm/ *n.* **1. UNREAL BEING OR SENSATION** something that can be seen or heard or whose presence can be felt, but that is not physically present **2. ILLUSION** somebody or something that does not exist, or whose existence is difficult to prove **3. APPARENT POWER** somebody or something that appears to have power over somebody but has no reality ○ *The phantom of disaster seemed to threaten their success.* ■ *adj.* **NOT REAL** appearing to be real but not actually existing ○ *The local branch of the organization turned out to have a lot of phantom members.* [13thC. Via Old French *fantosme* from, ultimately, Greek *phantasma* (see PHANTASM).]

WORD KEY: CULTURAL NOTE

The Phantom of the Opera, a novel by French writer Gaston Leroux (1910). This romantic melodrama about a disfigured musical genius who dwells in the passageways of a Paris opera house was not widely known until the appearance of Rupert Julian's movie adaptation of 1925. This in turn inspired other film adaptations as well as Andrew Lloyd Webber's 1986 musical, one of the most successful musicals of all time.

phan·tom limb pain *n.* pain that appears to come from an amputated limb

phan·tom preg·nan·cy *n.* = **false pregnancy**

-phany *suffix.* a manifestation of something ○ *epiphany* [Formed from Greek *phan-*, the stem of *phainesthai* "to appear" (see PHENOMENON)]

Phar., **phar.** *abbr.* **1.** pharmacist **2.** pharmacopoeia **3.** pharmaceutical **4.** pharmacy

Phar·aoh /fáirō/, **phar·aoh** *n.* **1. ANCIENT EGYPTIAN RULER** the ancient Egyptian title for a ruler of Egypt **2. POWERFUL PERSON** somebody in a position of authority, especially somebody who is harsh, gives unreasonable orders, and expects unquestioning obedience [Pre-12thC. Via ecclesiastical Latin and Greek *Pharaō* and Hebrew *par'ōh* from Egyptian *pr-' o*, literally "great house."] —**Phar·a·on·ic** /fài ray ónnik/ *adj.*

Phar·aoh ant, **Phar·aoh's ant** *n.* a small yellowish-red ant that is a household pest in many tropical countries. Latin name: *Monomorium pharaonis*. [*Pharaoh* because it is common in warm parts of the world such as Egypt]

Phar·i·sa·ic /fèrri sáy ik/, **Pha·ri·sa·i·cal** /-ik'l/ *adj.* **1. ASSOCIATED WITH THE PHARISEES** relating to or characteristic of the Pharisees **2. Phar·i·sa·ic, phar·i·sa·ic, Phar·i·sa·i·cal, phar·i·sa·i·cal SELF-RIGHTEOUSLY OBSESSED WITH RULES** acting with hypocrisy, self-righteousness, or obsessiveness with regard to the strict adherence to rules and formalities (*disapproving*) [Early 17thC. Via ecclesiastical Latin *pharisaïcus* from, ultimately, Greek *pharisaios* (see PHARISEE).] —**Phar·i·sa·i·cal·ly** *adv.* —**Phar·i·sa·i·cal·ness** *n.*

Phar·i·sa·ism /férri say ìzzəm/, **Phar·i·see·ism** *n.* **1. PRACTICES OF PHARISEES** the beliefs and practices of the Pharisees, especially the great attention they paid to the detailed rules of everyday life **2. Phar·i·sa·ism, Phar·i·see·ism, phar·i·sa·ism, phar·i·see·ism SELF-RIGHTEOUSNESS ABOUT ADHERING TO RULES** hypocritical, self-righteous, or obsessive behavior or attitudes toward the observing of rules and formalities (*disapproving*) [Late 16thC. Via French from, ultimately, Greek *pharisaios* (see PHARISEE).]

Phar·i·see /férri see/ *n.* **1.** JUDAISM **MEMBER OF ANCIENT JEWISH RELIGIOUS GROUP** a member of an ancient Jewish religious group who followed the Oral Law in addition to the Torah and attempted to live in a constant state of purity **2. Phar·i·see, phar·i·see SELF-RIGHTEOUS OR HYPOCRITICAL PERSON** somebody who is self-righteous or hypocritical, especially with regard to adherence to rules and formalities (*disapproving*) [Pre-12thC. Via ecclesiastical Latin from Greek *pharisaios*, ultimately, from Aramaic *prīšayyā*, literally "those who are separate."]

Pharm., **pharm.** *abbr.* **1.** pharmacist **2.** pharmacopoeia **3.** pharmaceutical **4.** pharmacy

pharmac- *prefix.* = **pharmaco-** (*used before vowels*)

phar·ma·ceu·ti·cal /faarmə sóotik'l/ *adj.* involved in or associated with the manufacturing, preparation, dispensing, or sale of the drugs used in medicine [Mid-17thC. Formed from late Latin *pharmaceuticus* from, ultimately, Greek *pharmakeutēs* "one who prepares drugs," from *pharmakon* "drug."] —**phar·ma·ceu·ti·cal·ly** *adv.*

phar·ma·ceu·tics /faarmə sóotiks/ *n.* **SCIENCE OF DRUGS** the science of the preparation and dispensing of the drugs prescribed by doctors (*takes a singular verb*) ■ *npl.* **MEDICINAL DRUGS** drugs prescribed as medicines

phar·ma·cist /faarməsist/ *n.* somebody trained and licensed to dispense medicinal drugs and to advise on their use [Mid-19thC. Formed from PHARMACY.]

pharmaco- *prefix.* drugs, medicine ○ *pharmacodynamics* [From Greek *pharmakon* "drug, poison"]

phar·ma·co·dy·nam·ics /faarməkō dī námmiks/ *n.* the study of the effects of drugs on living organisms (*takes a singular verb*) —**phar·ma·co·dy·nam·ic** *adj.*

phar·ma·cog·no·sy /faarmə kógnəssee/ *n.* a branch of pharmacology dealing with active substances found in plants [Mid-19thC. Coined from PHARMACO- + Greek *gnōsis* "knowledge" (see GNOSIS).] —**phar·ma·cog·no·sist** *n.* —**phar·ma·cog·nos·tic** /faarmə kog nóstik/ *adj.*

phar·ma·co·ki·net·ics /faarməkō ki néttiks/ *npl.* **BODY'S REACTION TO DRUGS** the body's reaction to drugs, including their absorption, metabolism, and elimination (*takes a plural verb*) ■ *n.* **STUDY OF REACTION TO DRUGS** the study of the body's reaction to drugs (*takes a singular verb*)

pharmacol. *abbr.* pharmacology

phar·ma·col·o·gy /faarmə kólləjee/ (*plural* **-gies**) *n.* **1.** SCI **STUDY OF DRUGS** the science or study of drugs, including their sources, chemistry, production, use in treating diseases, and side effects **2.** MED, PHARM **DRUG'S EFFECTS** the effects that a drug has when taken by somebody, especially as a medical treatment —**phar·ma·co·log·i·cal** /faarməkə lójjik'l/ *adj.* —**phar·ma·co·log·i·cal·ly** /-kəlee/ *adv.* —**phar·ma·col·o·gist** /faarmə kólləjist/ *n.*

phar·ma·co·poe·ia /faarməkə pee ə/, **phar·ma·co·pe·ia** *n.* **1. BOOK DESCRIBING DRUGS AND THEIR USES** a book or database listing drugs used in medical practice and describing their composition, preparation, use, dosages, effects, and side effects, especially one published as an official guide for pharmacists **2. COLLECTION OF DRUGS** a stock or collection of drugs [Early 17thC. Via modern Latin from Greek *pharmakopoiia* "preparing of drugs," from *pharmakon* "drug."] —**phar·ma·co·poe·ial** *adj.* —**phar·ma·co·poe·ic** *adj.* —**phar·ma·co·poe·ist** *n.*

phar·ma·co·ther·a·py /faarməkō thérrəpee/ (*plural* **-pies**) *n.* the use of drugs to treat conditions, especially psychiatric disorders

phar·ma·cy /faarməsee/ (*plural* **-cies**) *n.* **1. DRUG DISPENSING** the science or profession of dispensing drugs used as medical treatments **2. SHOP SELLING OR DISPENSING MEDICINE** a place where the drugs used for treating diseases are dispensed or sold [14thC. Via Old French *farmacie* from, ultimately, Greek *pharmakeia* "use of drugs," from *pharmakon* "drug."]

pharyng- *prefix.* = **pharyngo-** (*used before vowels*)

pha·ryn·ge·al /fə rínjəl, fə rínjee əl, fèrrən jée əl/ *adj.* found in, affecting, or relating to the throat [Early 19thC. Formed from modern Latin *pharyngeus*, from the stem *pharyng-* (see PHARYNX).]

phar·yn·gi·tis /fèrrən jítiss/ *n.* MED inflammation of the pharynx, commonly known as a sore throat

pharyngo- *prefix.* pharynx ○ *pharyngoscope* [Via modern Latin from Greek, the stem of *pharugx* "throat" (see PHARYNX)]

phar·yn·gol·o·gy /fèrring gólləjee/ *n.* the branch of medicine concerned with the throat, its diseases, and their treatment —**phar·yn·go·log·i·cal** /fə ring gə lójjik'l/ *adj.* —**phar·yn·gol·o·gist** /fèrring gólləjist/ *n.*

pha·ryn·go·scope /fə ríng gə skōp/ *n.* a medical instrument for examining the throat —**phar·yn·go·scop·ic** /fə ring gə skóppik/ *adj.* —**phar·yn·gos·co·py** /fèrring góskəpee/ *n.*

phar·ynx /férringks/ (*plural* **pha·ryn·ges** /fə rínjeez/ *or* **phar·ynx·es**) *n.* **1.** ANAT **THROAT** the throat, the region of the alimentary canal in humans and in vertebrate animals that lies between the mouth and esophagus **2.** ZOOL **PART SIMILAR TO THROAT** a region between the mouth and the digestive system in sea anemones, worms, insects, and other invertebrate animals [Late 17thC. Via modern Latin (stem *pharyng-*) from Greek *pharugx* "throat." Ultimately, from an Indo-European word meaning "to pierce," which is also the ancestor of English *perforate*.]

phase /fayz/ *n.* **1. STAGE OF DEVELOPMENT** a clearly distinguishable period or stage in a process, in the development of something, or in a sequence of events **2. PATTERN OF BEHAVIOR** any period of time when a situation or particular pattern of behavior persists and is often annoying or worrying **3. PART OR ASPECT** one of the many parts or aspects of something ○ *We needed to restructure all phases of our business.* **4.** ASTRON **RECURRING SHAPE OF MOON** any of the recurring forms seen in the sky of the moon or a planet. The four principal phases of the moon are the first quarter, full moon, last quarter, and new moon. **5.** PHYS **PART OF REPEATING CYCLE** any part of a repeated uniform pattern of occurrence of a phenomenon or process, relative to a fixed starting point or time **6.** PHYS **STATE OF MATTER** any of the states in which matter can exist, depending on temperature and pressure, e.g., the solid, liquid, gaseous, and plasmic states **7.** ZOOL **VARIATION IN ANIMAL FORM** an alternate stage, appearance, or coloring that distinguishes a group of animals from most of their kind, or that a particular animal adopts under specific conditions **8.** BIOL **STAGE IN ORGANISM'S LIFE CYCLE** a stage in the life cycle of an organism ■ *vt.* (**phased, phas·ing, phas·es**) **1. DO SOMETHING IN STAGES** to plan or arrange something so that it is carried out in stages (*often passive*) ○ *a takeover that is being phased to minimize disruption* **2. SYNCHRONIZE THINGS** to cause two or more things to happen or operate simultaneously or in a coordinated way ○ *to phase the departure of one train with the arrival of another* [Early 19thC. Partly via French, partly a back-formation from modern Latin *phases* "moon phases," both, ultimately, from Greek *phasis* "appearance," from *phainein* "to show."] —**pha·sic** *adj.* ◇ **in phase** in the same phase at the same time, or operating in a synchronized or coordinated way ◇ **out of phase** not in the same phase, or not synchronized or coordinated with each other

phase in *vt.* to introduce something in stages over a period of time

phase out *vt.* to bring something to an end or remove it in stages over a period of time

phase-con·trast mi·cro·scope *n.* a microscope sensitive to small differences in the phase of light reflected by or passing through different parts of an object. By enhancing the differences, it provides a clearly contrasted image. Phase-contrast microscopes are particularly useful for examining colorless or transparent objects.

phase·down /fáyz down/ *n.* a gradual reduction in something [Mid-20thC. Modeled on PHASEOUT.]

phase mod·u·la·tion *n.* a method of transmitting a voice or other signal in which the phase of a radio carrier wave is varied in accordance with the signal

phase·out *n.* a gradual process of discontinuing something [Mid-20th C. From PHASE OUT.]

-phasia *suffix.* speech disorder ○ *aphasia* [Formed from Greek *phasis* "utterance," from *phanai* "to say". Ultimately from an Indo-European word meaning "to speak," which is also the ancestor of English *fable, fame,* and *boon.*]

phas·mid /fázmid/ *n.* **TROPICAL PLANT-EATING INSECT** a tropical plant-eating insect that has a body that looks like a twig with long legs and antennae. Walking stick insects and leaf insects are phasmids. Family: Phasmidae. ■ *adj.* **RELATING TO PHASMIDS** belonging or relating to the phasmids [Late 19thC. Via modern Latin *Phasmida,* order name, from, ultimately, Greek *phasma* "apparition," from *phainein* "to show" (see PHASE).]

phat·ic /fáttik/ *adj.* spoken in order to share feelings, create goodwill, or set a pleasant social mood, rather than to convey information. "Have a nice day!" is a phatic phrase. [Early 20thC. Formed from Greek *phatos* "spoken," from *phanai* "to say" (see -PHASIA).]

Ph.B. *abbr.* Bachelor of Philosophy [Latin, *Philosophiae Baccalaureus*]

Ph.C. *abbr.* Pharmaceutical Chemist

Ph.D. *abbr.* Doctor of Philosophy [Latin, *Philosophiae Doctor*]

Pheasant

pheas·ant /fézz'nt/ (*plural* **-ants** *or* **-ant**) *n.* **1.** BIRDS **LARGE LONG-TAILED BIRD** a large bird related to and resembling domestic poultry. Male pheasants have long curved tails, and are often brightly colored. Pheasants are frequently bred for shooting. Family: Phasianidae. **2.** FOOD **PHEASANT MEAT** the meat obtained from a pheasant [13thC. Via Old French *fesan* from, ultimately, Greek *phasianos (ornis),* "(bird) from the river Phasis" in western Georgia, where it was supposed to have originated.]

phel·lem /féllәm/ *n.* = **cork** *n.* 4 [Late 19thC. Formed from Greek *phellos* "cork," on the model of PHLOEM and XYLEM.]

phel·lo·derm /féllә dùrm/ *n.* a layer of plant cells produced by the inner surface of the cork cambium in woody plants, from which cork tissue develops [Late 19thC. Coined from Greek *phellos* "cork" + -DERM.] —**phel·lo·der·mal** /fèllә dúrm'l/ *adj.*

phel·lo·gen /féllәjәn/ *n.* = **cork cambium** [Late 19thC. Coined from Greek *phellos* "cork" + -GEN.] — **phel·lo·ge·net·ic** /fèllәjә néttik/ *adj.* —**phel·lo·gen·ic** /-jénnik/ *adj.*

phen- *prefix.* CHEM = **pheno-**

phe·na·caine /fénnә kàyn/ *n.* a white crystalline compound used as a local anesthetic in ophthalmology. Formula: $C_{18}H_{22}N_2O_2$. [Early 20thC. Coined from *phen-,* variant of PHENO-, + -CAINE.]

phe·nac·e·tin /fә nássәtin/ *n.* **1. DRUG USED TO TREAT PAIN** a white crystalline compound used in drugs to reduce fever or relieve pain. Formula: $C_{10}H_{13}NO_2$. **2. phe·nac·e·tin** (*plural* **-tins** *or* **-tins**) **PILL** a tablet containing phenacetin [Late 19thC. Alteration of acetophenetidin, its chemical name.]

phen·a·cite /fénnә sìt/, **phen·a·kite** /-kìt/ *n.* a colorless glassy mineral consisting of beryllium silicate that is sometimes used as a gemstone [Mid-19thC. Formed from Greek *phenak-,* stem of *phenax* "impostor," because it was mistaken for quartz.]

phe·nan·threne /fә nán thrèen/ *n.* a colorless crystalline aromatic hydrocarbon used in the manufacture of dyes, drugs, and explosives. Formula: $C_{14}H_{10}$. [Late 19thC. Contraction of PHENO- + ANTHRACENE.]

phen·cy·cli·dine /fen sìkli dèen, -sìkli-/ *n.* a drug used as an anesthetic in veterinary medicine and illegally as a hallucinogen. Formula: $C_{17}H_{25}N$. [Mid-20thC. Coined from *phen-* (variant of PHENO-) + CYCLO- + PIPERIDINE.]

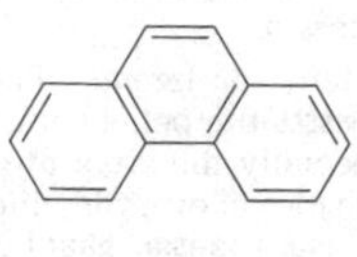

Phenanthrene

phe·net·ics /fә néttiks/ *n.* a system of biological classification based on overall similarities between organisms rather than on their genetic or developmental relationships (*takes a singular verb*) [Mid-20thC. Formed from Greek *phainesthai* "to appear" (see PHENOMENON + -ETIC.] —**phe·net·ic** *adj.* — **phe·net·i·cal·ly** *adv.* —**phe·net·i·cist** *n.*

phe·nix /fèeniks/ *n.* = **phoenix**

Phe·nix Cit·y /fèeniks-/ city in Alabama, situated east of Montgomery, on the Chattahoochee River, which separates Alabama from Georgia. Population: 28,000 (1996).

pheno- *prefix.* **1.** containing phenyl ○ *phenobarbitone* **2.** related to or derived from benzene ○ *phenol* **3.** appearing ○ *phenocryst* [From Greek *phainein* "to show" (see PHASE)]

phe·no·bar·bi·tal /fèenō baárbi tàwl/ *n.* a crystalline barbiturate used as a sedative, hypnotic, and anticonvulsant. Formula: $C_{12}H_{12}N_2O_3$.

phe·no·cop·y /fèenә kòppee/ (*plural* **-ies**) *n.* a noninheritable change in an organism induced by its response to its environment but resembling a genetic mutation [Mid-20thC. Blend of PHENOTYPE and COPY.]

phe·no·cryst /fèenә krìst/ *n.* any of the large embedded crystals in a porphyritic rock [Late 19thC. From French *phénocryste,* from *phéno-* "pheno-" (see PHENO-) + Greek *krustallos* "crystal" (see CRYSTAL).] — **phe·no·crys·tic** /fèenә krístik/ *adj.*

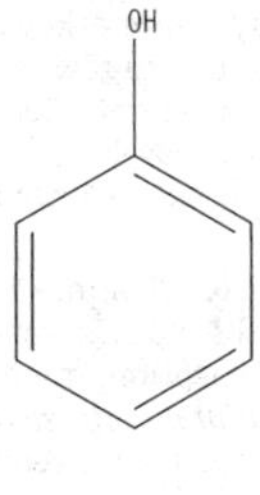

Phenol

phe·nol /fèe nàwl/ *n.* **1. POISONOUS CAUSTIC COMPOUND** a poisonous caustic crystalline compound obtained from coal, wood tar, or benzene, used in the manufacture of resins, dyes, and pharmaceuticals and as an antiseptic and disinfectant. Formula: C_6H_5OH. **2. COMPOUND BASED ON BENZENE RING** a chemical compound that has one or more hydroxyl groups attached to a benzene ring [Mid-19thC. Coined from *phen-,* variant of PHENO-, + -OL.]

phe·no·lic /fi nṓlik, -nóllik/ *n.* **phe·no·lic, phe·no·lic res·in RESIN USED IN PAINTS AND ADHESIVES** a type of thermosetting resin derived from phenol and used in plastics, paints, and adhesives ■ *adj.* CHEM **RELATING TO PHENOL** derived from or containing phenol

phe·nol·o·gy /fi nóllәjee/ (*plural* **-gies**) *n.* **1. STUDYING HOW CLIMATE AFFECTS BIOLOGICAL CYCLES** the study of regularly recurring biological phenomena such as animal migrations or plant budding, especially as influenced by climatic conditions **2. RELATIONSHIP BETWEEN RECURRING PHENOMENON AND CLIMATE** the relationship between a regularly recurring biological phenomenon and climatic or environmental factors that may influence it [Late 19thC. Coined from PHENOMENON + -LOGY.] —**phe·no·log·i·cal** /fèenә lójjik'l/ *adj.* —**phe·nol·o·gist** /fi nóllәjist/ *n.*

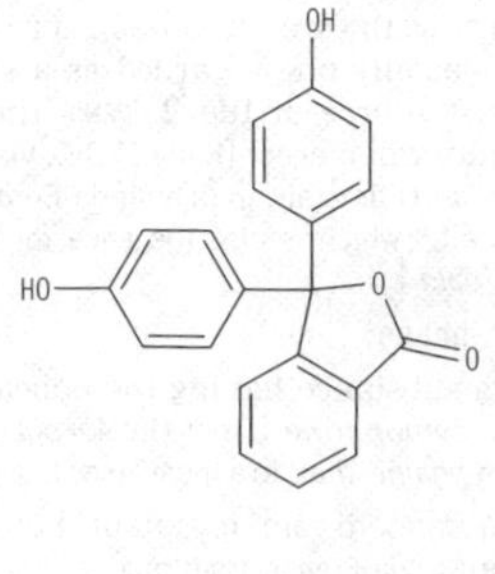

Phenolphthalein

phe·nol·phthal·ein /fèe nol tháy lèen, fèenәl tháy lèen/ *n.* a colorless or yellowish compound used as a chemical indicator and as a laxative. Alkalis turn a solution of phenolphthalein red. Formula: $C_{20}H_{14}O_4$.

phe·nol red *n.* a red dye used as an acid-base indicator and, in medicine, to test kidney function

phe·nom /fә nóm/ *n.* an outstanding or unusual person or thing (*slang*) [Late 19thC. Shortening of PHENOMENON.]

phe·nom·e·na plural of **phenomenon**

phe·nom·e·nal /fә nómmәn'l/ *adj.* **1. REMARKABLE** remarkable, especially if remarkably and impressively good or great ○ *a phenomenal talent* **2.** PHILOS **PERCEIVED BY SENSES** perceived by or perceptible to the senses, rather than the mind, and thus having at least an apparent external existence **3. OF A PHENOMENON** constituting or relating to a phenomenon — **phe·nom·en·al·ly** *adv.*

phe·nom·e·nal·ism /fә nómmәn'l ìzzәm/ *n.* a philosophical theory stating that knowledge of the external world is limited to appearances so that we know what our senses tell us about things (**sense-data**), not what they are in themselves — **phe·nom·e·nal·ist** /fә nómmәn'list/ *n., adj.* —**phe·nom·e·nal·is·ti·cal·ly** /-ístikәlee/ *adv.*

phe·nom·e·nol·o·gy /fә nòmmә nóllәjee/ *n.* **1. STUDY OF PHENOMENA** in philosophy, the science or study of phenomena, things as they are perceived, as opposed to the study of being, the nature of things as they are **2. PHILOSOPHICAL INVESTIGATION OF EXPERIENCE** the philosophical investigation and description of conscious experience in all its varieties without reference to the question of whether what is experienced is objectively real —**phe·nom·e·no·log·i·cal** /fә nòmmәnә lójjik'l/ *adj.* —**phe·nom·e·no·log·i·cal·ly** /-lójjikәlee/ *adv.* —**phe·nom·e·nol·o·gist** /-nóllәjist/ *n.*

phe·nom·e·non /fә nómmә nòn, fә nómmәnәn/ (*plural* **-na** /-nә/) *n.* **1. SOMETHING EXPERIENCED** a fact or occurrence that can be observed **2. SOMETHING NOTABLE** something that is out of the ordinary and excites people's interest and curiosity ○ *a strange phenomenon* **3. EXTRAORDINARY PERSON OR THING** somebody or something that is, or that is considered to be, truly extraordinary and marvelous **4.** PHILOS **OBJECT OF PERCEPTION** something perceived or experienced, especially an object as it is apprehended by the human senses as opposed to an object as it intrinsically is in itself [Late 16thC. Via late Latin from Greek *phainomenon* "that which appears," from the past participle of *phainein* "to bring to light" (source of English FANTASY), ultimately "to shine."]

phe·no·thi·a·zine /fèenō thí ә zèen, fèenә-/ *n.* **1.** VET **COMPOUND KILLING INTESTINAL WORMS AND INSECTS** a yellowish crystalline compound used in veterinary medicine to destroy intestinal worms and as an insecticide. Formula: $C_{12}H_9NS$. **2.** MED **DRUG USED TO TREAT SCHIZOPHRENIA** a derivative of phenothiazine used as a tranquilizer and in the treatment of schizophrenia

phe·no·type /fèenә tìp/ *n.* the visible characteristics of an organism resulting from the interaction between its genetic makeup and the environment [Early 20thC. From German *Phänotypus,* literally "type that shows," from Greek *phainein* (see PHENOMENON).] —**phe·no·typ·ic** /fèenә típpik/ *adj.* — **phe·no·typ·i·cal** /-k'l/ *adj.* —**phe·no·typ·i·cal·ly** /-kәlee/ *adv.*

phe·nox·ide /fi nók sìd/ *n.* any chemical compound that is a salt of phenol

phen·yl /fénn'l, fèen'l/ *n.* a chemical group derived from benzene by removing a hydrogen atom, thus having a valence of one. Formula: C_6H_5. [Mid-19thC.

From French *phényle*, from Greek *phainein* "to show" (see PHENOMENON), because it was first used to name compounds formed from lighting gas.]

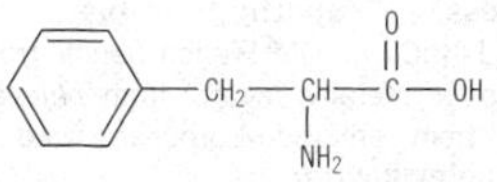

Phenylalanine

phen·yl·al·a·nine /fènn'l állə neen, feen'l-/ *n.* an essential amino acid found in many proteins and converted to a nonessential amino acid (**tyrosine**) by the body. Formula: $C_9H_{11}O_2N$.

phen·yl·bu·ta·zone /fènn'l byootə zōn, feen'l-/ *n.* an anti-inflammatory drug used to treat arthritis, bursitis, and gout. Formula: $C_{19}H_{20}N_2O_2$.

phen·yl·ke·to·nur·i·a /fènn'l keetə nooree ə, feen'l-/ *n.* a condition, resulting from a genetic mutation, in which the body lacks the enzyme to metabolize phenylalanine which, if untreated, results in developmental deficiency, seizures, and tumors

phen·yl·pro·pa·nol·a·mine /fènn'l prōpə nóllə meen, feen'l-/ *n.* a drug that constricts blood vessels and is used as a nasal and bronchial decongestant, and an appetite suppressant. Formula: $C_9H_{13}NO$.

phen·yl·thi·o·car·ba·mide /fènn'l thī ō kaarbə mīd, feen'l-/, **phen·yl·thi·o·u·rea** /fènn'l thī ō yooree ə, feen'l-/ *n.* a crystalline compound that tastes extremely bitter to people who possess a particular dominant gene, and is thus used to test for the presence of that gene

phen·y·to·in /fə níttō in/ *n.* an anticonvulsant drug used to treat epilepsy. Formula: $C_{15}H_{12}N_2O_2$. [Mid-20thC. Coined form DI- + PHENYL + HYDANTOIN.]

pher·o·mone /férrə mōn/ *n.* a chemical compound produced and secreted by an animal that influences the behavior and development of other members of the same species [Mid-20thC. Coined from Greek *pherein* "to carry" (see -PHORE) + HORMONE.] —**pher·o·mon·al** /fèrrə mṓn'l/ *adj.*

phew /fyoo/ *interj.* **1.** EXPRESSING TIREDNESS, RELIEF, OR DISGUST used to express tiredness, relief, surprise, or disgust **2.** EXPRESSING REPULSION used to express disgust at an unpleasant smell [Early 17thC. An imitation of the sound made by blowing through partly closed lips.]

Ph.G. *abbr.* Graduate in Pharmacy

phi /fī/ (*plural* **phis**) *n.* the 21st letter of the Greek alphabet, represented in the English alphabet as "ph." See table at **alphabet** [Mid-20thC. Via late Greek from Greek *phei.*]

phi·al /fī əl/ *n.* = **vial** [14thC. Via Old French *fiole* from, ultimately, Greek *phialē* "broad flat vessel."]

Phi Be·ta Kap·pa *n.* **1.** ACADEMIC HONOR SOCIETY an honor society of American college and university students showing high academic achievement. It was founded in 1776. **2.** HONOR SOCIETY MEMBER a member of Phi Beta Kappa

phi ef·fect *n.* = **phi phenomenon**

PHIGS /figz/ *abbr.* programmers' hierarchical interactive graphics standard

phil. *abbr.* **1.** philosophy **2.** philosopher **3.** philosophical **4.** philology **5.** philological

Phil. *abbr.* **1.** Philippines **2.** BIBLE Philippians **3.** MUSIC Philharmonic

phil- *prefix.* = **philo-** (*used before vowels or l*)

-phil *suffix.* = **-phile**

Phila. *abbr.* Philadelphia

Phil·a·del·phi·a /fillə délfee ə/ the largest city in Pennsylvania, situated on the Delaware River in the southeastern part of the state. It is known as the *Birthplace of the Nation* because both the Declaration of Independence and the Constitution of the United States were drawn up there. Population: 1,478,000 (1996).

Phil·a·del·phi·a law·yer *n.* a lawyer who has a detailed knowledge of legal technicalities and exploits them for a client's benefit [Named for PHILADELPHIA, because of the reputed shrewdness of lawyers from eastern cities]

Phil·a·del·phi·a pep·per pot *n.* = **pepper pot** [From *Philadelphia*, because this dish is common in Pennsylvania]

philadel·phus /fillə délfəss/ *n.* PLANTS = **mock orange** *n.* 1 [Late 18thC. Via modern Latin from Greek *philadelphos* "loving one's brother," from *philos* "loving" + *adelphos* "brother."]

Phi·lae /fī lee/ submerged island in southern Egypt, in the Nile River, south of Aswan. It was the site of ancient temples that were moved when the island was flooded after the building of the Aswan High Dam.

phi·lan·der /fi lándər/ (**-dered, -der·ing, -ders**) *vi.* to flirt with and have casual sexual affairs with women, especially when married to another woman (*dated disapproving*) [Late 17thC. From Greek *philandros* "loving men," from the stem *andr-* "man" (source of English *andro-*). Originally "lover."] —**phi·lan·der·er** *n.*

phil·an·throp·ic /fillən thróppik/, **phil·an·throp·i·cal** /-thróppik'l/ *adj.* **1.** CHARITABLE AND GENEROUS showing kindness, charitable concern, and generosity toward other people **2.** DEVOTED TO HELPING OTHER PEOPLE devoted to helping other people, especially through giving charitable aid —**phi·lan·throp·i·cal·ly** *adv.*

phi·lan·thro·py /fi lánthrəpee/ (*plural* **-pies**) *n.* **1.** DESIRE TO BENEFIT HUMANITY a desire to improve the material, social, and spiritual welfare of humanity, especially through charitable activities **2.** PHILANTHROPIC ACT OR GROUP a philanthropic action or organization **3.** LOVE FOR ALL HUMANITY general love for, or benevolence toward, the whole of humankind (*formal*) [Early 17thC. Via late Latin from, ultimately, Greek *philanthrōpos* "humane," from *philos* "loving" + *anthrōpos* "human being."] —**phi·lan·thro·pist** *n.*

phi·lat·e·ly /fi látt'lee/ *n.* the collection and study of postage stamps and related items [Mid-19thC. From French *philatélie*, from Greek *philos* "loving" + *ateleia* "exemption from tax," ultimately from *telos* "tax"; from the freedom from charges that a stamped letter provides.] —**phil·a·tel·ic** /fillə téllik/ *adj.* —**phil·a·tel·i·cal·ly** /-téllikəlee/ *adv.* —**phi·lat·e·list** /fi látt'list/ *n.*

WORD KEY: ORIGIN

When a Monsieur Herpin, a French stamp-collector, was looking for an impressive and learned-sounding term for his hobby, he was hampered by the fact that the Greeks and Romans did not have postage stamps, and therefore there was no classical term for them. So he decided to go back a stage beyond stamps, to the days of franking with a postmark. In France, such letters were marked with the words *franc de port* "carriage-free." The nearest he could get to this in Greek was *ateleia*, and from it he created *philatélie*, the English form of which made its first recorded appearance in 1865.

-phile *suffix.* **1.** one that loves or has an affinity for ○ *nucleophile* ○ *Europhile* **2.** loving or having an affinity for ○ *homophile* [Via Latin *-philus* from, ultimately, Greek *philos* "loving"] —**-philic** *suffix.* —**-philous** *suffix.* —**-phily** *suffix.*

Phi·le·mon *n.* BIBLE a book in the Bible, written by St. Paul, appealing to Philemon to take pity on his slave who had escaped and converted to Christianity. See table at **Bible**

phil·har·mon·ic /fil haar mónnik/, **Philharmonic** *adj.* PERFORMING OR PROMOTING MUSIC used to describe an orchestra or choir that performs music or a society that promotes the study, performance, and appreciation of music ■ *n.* PHILHARMONIC ORCHESTRA, CHOIR, OR SOCIETY a symphony orchestra, choir, or musical society that has the word "philharmonic" in its title [Mid-18thC. Via French *philharmonique* from, ultimately, Greek *philos* "loving" + *harmonia* "harmony" (see HARMONY).]

phil·hel·lene /fil hé leen/, **phil·hel·len·ist** /fil héllənist/ *n.* somebody who greatly admires ancient or modern Greece, the Greeks, and their culture [Early 19thC. From Greek *philellēn*, from *philos* "loving" + *Hellēn* "a Greek" (source of English *Hellene*).] —**phil·hel·len·ic** /fil he lénnik/ *adj.* —**phil·hel·len·ism** /fil héllə nìzzəm/ *n.* —**phil·hel·len·is·tic** /fil hèllə nístik/ *adj.*

Phil. I. *abbr.* Philippine Islands

-philia *suffix.* **1.** intense or abnormal attraction to ○ *neophilia* ○ *zoophilia* **2.** tendency toward ○ *basophilia* [Via modern Latin from Greek *philia* "fondness," from *philos* "loving"] —**-philiac** *suffix.*

Phil·ip /fílləp/ (*d.* 1676) Native American chief. He led the uprising known as King Philip's War against New England colonists (1675–76). Born **Metacomet**

Phil·ip, St. (*fl.* 1st century A.D.) New Testament apostle. One of the original 12 disciples of Jesus Christ, he was born in Bethsaida and was present at the miracle of the loaves and fishes.

Phil·ip I /fillip thə fúrst/, **Duke of Burgundy and King of Castile** (1478–1506). Father of Charles V and Ferdinand I, he founded the Hapsburg dynasty in Spain through his marriage to Joanna the Mad of Castile. Known as **Philip the Handsome**

Phil·ip II /fillip thə sékənd/, **King of Macedonia** (382–336 B.C.). After becoming king (359) he extended Macedonian power over the whole of Greece. He was the father of Alexander the Great.

Phil·ip IV /fillip thə fáwrth/, **King of France** (1268–1314). He succeeded to the throne in 1285. His conflict with Pope Boniface VII led to the residence of the popes in Avignon (1309–77). Known as **Philip the Fair**

Phil·ip V /fillip thə fífth/, **King of Spain** (1683–1746). The grandson of Louis XIV of France, he was the first of the Spanish Bourbons. His accession to the throne (1700) led to the War of the Spanish Succession.

Phil·ip /fílləp/, **Prince, Duke of Edinburgh** (*b.* 1921). The son of Prince Andrew of Greece and the great-great-grandson of Queen Victoria, he married Princess Elizabeth, later Queen Elizabeth II, in 1947.

Phi·lip·pi·ans /fi líppee ənz/ *n.* a book of the Bible consisting of a letter (**Epistle**) from St. Paul to the Christian church at Philippi. (*takes a singular verb*)

phi·lip·pic /fi líppik/ *n.* a verbal attack on somebody or something delivered in the most savage, bitter, and insulting terms, usually as a speech [Late 16thC. Via Latin *philippicus* from Greek *philippikos*, the speech of the fourth-century B.C. Greek orator *Demosthenes* urging the citizens of Athens to rise up against Philip of Macedon.]

Phil·ip·pine *adj.* **1.** OF PHILIPPINES relating to or typical of the Philippines, or its people or culture **2.** = **Filipino** *adj.*

Phil·ip·pine Eng·lish *n.* a variety of English spoken in the Philippines

WORD KEY: WORLD ENGLISH

Philippine English also Filipino English is the English language as used in the Philippines. It has some co-official status with Filipino. English is the second Western colonial language, after Spanish; the United States took the territory in 1898 from Spain, whose colony it had been since 1521. The nation is diverse, with a Malay majority, a Chinese minority, and many people of mixed Malay, Chinese, Spanish, and U.S. backgrounds. Because English is used in varying degrees by over half the population of about 60 million, the Philippines rightly claims to be a major English-speaking country. Like U.S. English, Philippine English is "rhotic" (that is, "r" is pronounced in words such as *art, door,* and *worker*). Also, *h* is pronounced as a retroflex "r" (that is, it is pronounced with the tip of the tongue curled back and raised). Vowels tend to be full in all syllables (e.g., seven being pronounced "'seh-ven," not "sevn"). An "s" or "sh" sound may serve instead of a "z" or "zh," as in "carss" (cars), "pleshure" (pleasure). In grammar, the present progressive is commonly used for habitual behavior, rather than the simple present ("We are doing this work all the time" for "We do this work all the time"), the present perfect may be used rather than the simple past ("We have done it yesterday" for "We did it yesterday") and the past perfect rather than the present perfect ("They had already been there" for "They have already been there"). Distinctive vocabulary includes: (1) Hispanicisms, unchanged or adapted, e.g., *asalto* (surprise party), *querida* (mistress), *aggrupation* (from *agrupación* meaning "group"); (2) words from Tagalog, e.g., *boondock* (mountain) – whence "the boondocks," *kundiman* (love song), *tao* (man) – as in "the common tao"); (3) local coinages, e.g., *carnap* (to steal a car), the formation by analogy with *kidnap* and *jeepney* (blending *Jeep* and *jitney,* "small bus," a Jeep adapted for passengers).

Phil·ip·pines /fílləpeenz/ republic in Asia, in the western Pacific Ocean, in the Malay Archipelago. It comprises over 7,000 islands. Language: Filipino. Currency: Philippine peso. Capital: Manila. Population: 68,614,612 (1995). Area: 115,830 sq. mi./300,000 sq. km. Official name **Republic of the Philippines**

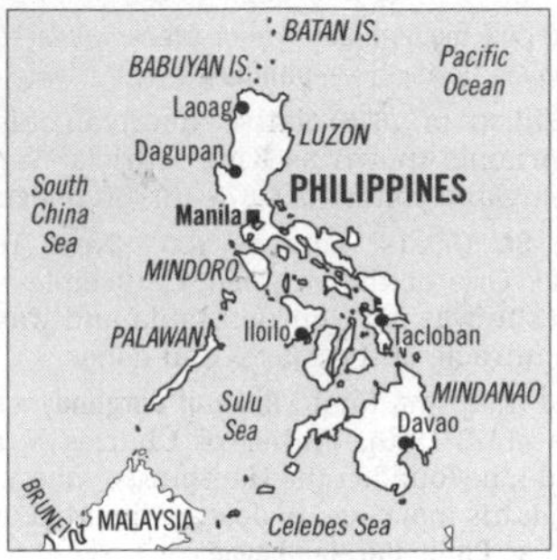

Philippines

Phil·is·tine /fílli steen, fílli stīn/ *n.* **1.** PEOPLES **SOMEBODY FROM ANCIENT PHILISTIA** a member of the Aegean people who settled in ancient Philistia around the 12th century B.C. **2. phil·is·tine, Phil·is·tine SOMEBODY WHO DOES NOT APPRECIATE ART** a materialistic person who is indifferent to artistic and intellectual achievements and values (*disapproving*) ■ *adj.* **1.** PEOPLES **RELATING TO PHILISTINES** relating to or typical of the ancient Philistines or their culture **2. phil·is·tine, Phil·is·tine UNCULTURED** ignorant, uncultured, and indifferent or hostile to artistic and intellectual achievement [14thC. Via late Latin and Greek from Hebrew *Pĕlištī* "people of Philistia" in Palestine. Derogatory sense from, ultimately, the hostility of the Philistines toward the ancient Israelites.] —**phi·lis·tin·ism** *n.*

Phil·lips screw /fíllips-/ *tdmk.* a trademark for a screw with a cross-shaped slot on its head

Phil·lips screw·driv·er /fíllips-/ *tdmk.* a trademark for a screwdriver that has a cross-shaped tip so that it can be used to turn a Phillips screw

phil·lu·men·ist /fi loománist/ *n.* somebody who collects matchboxes and matchbooks as a hobby [Mid-20thC. Coined from PHILO- + Latin *lumen* "light" (see LUMEN).] —**phil·lu·men·y** /fi loómanee/ *n.*

philo- *prefix.* loving, having an attraction to or affinity for ○ *philoprogenitive* [From Greek *philos* "loving"]

Phi·loc·te·tes /fíllak teéteez, fi lóktateez/ *n.* in Greek mythology, a friend of Achilles and the slayer of the Trojan prince Paris

phil·o·den·dron /fílla déndran/ (*plural* **-drons** *or* **-dra** /fílla déndra/) *n.* a tropical American climbing plant of the arum family, grown as a house plant for its evergreen leaves. Genus: *Philodendron.* [Late 19thC. Via modern Latin from, ultimately, Greek *philodendros* "loving trees" (because it climbs trees in its native habitat), from *dendron* "tree" (see DENDRON).]

phi·log·y·ny /fi lójjanee/ *n.* a positive and admiring attitude toward women in general (*literary*) — **phi·log·y·nist** *n.* —**phi·log·y·nous** *adj.*

philol. *abbr.* **1.** philology **2.** philological

phi·lol·o·gy /fi lóllajee/ *n.* **1.** LING **STUDY OF LANGUAGE IN TEXTS** the scientific study of the relationship of languages to one another, and their history, especially based on the analysis of texts **2.** HIST **STUDY OF ANCIENT TEXTS** the study and analysis of ancient texts, especially as an approach to the cultural history of a period or people **3.** LITERAT **STUDY OF LITERATURE** the study of literature in general (*archaic*) [14thC. Via Latin *philologia* from, ultimately, Greek *philologos* "fond of words," from *philos* "loving" + *logos* "word."] —**phil·o·log·i·cal** /fílla lójjik'l/ *adj.* —**phil·o·log·i·cal·ly** /-kalee/ *adv.* — **phi·lol·o·gist** /fi lóllajist/ *n.*

phil·o·pro·gen·i·tive /fíllō prō jénnitiv/ *adj.* **1. PRODUCING OFFSPRING** producing a large number of offspring (*formal*) **2. LOVING CHILDREN** loving children, especially your own offspring (*literary*)

philos. *abbr.* **1.** philosophical **2.** philosopher **3.** philosophy

phi·lo·sophe /fílla sôf, feéla zóf/ *n.* any of the leading writers and thinkers of the Enlightenment in 18th-century France, who advocated a rational approach to philosophy and government and criticized the French social and political system [Pre-12thC. From Latin *philosophus* "philosopher" (see PHILOSOPHER).]

phi·los·o·pher /fi lóssafar/ *n.* **1.** PHILOSOPHY **SOMEBODY WHO STUDIES LIFE AND REALITY** somebody who seeks to understand and explain the nature of life and reality, especially a scholar of philosophy or related fields **2. SOMEBODY HOLDING PARTICULAR BELIEFS** a person who believes in a particular philosophy and thinks and acts accordingly **3. THINKING PERSON** somebody who is given to thinking deeply and seriously about human affairs and life in general **4. CALM AND RATIONAL PERSON** somebody who responds calmly and rationally to events, especially adversity [14thC. Formed from Old French *philosophe* via Latin from Greek *philosophos,* literally "lover of knowledge," from *sophia* "learning, wisdom."]

phi·los·o·pher's stone, phi·los·o·phers' stone *n.* a substance that medieval alchemists believed could be used to convert other metals into gold

phil·o·soph·i·cal /fílla sóffik'l/, **phil·o·soph·ic** /-sóffik/ *adj.* **1.** PHILOSOPHY **RELATING TO STUDYING NATURE OF REALITY** concerned with the study of the nature of life and reality, or of related areas such as ethics, logic, or metaphysics **2. CONCERNED WITH DEEP QUESTIONS OF LIFE** concerned with or given to thinking about the larger issues and deeper meanings in life and events **3. SHOWING CALMNESS AND RESIGNATION** showing calmness, restraint, or resignation, especially reacting to adversity in a restrained or resigned way — **phil·o·soph·i·cal·ly** *adv.*

phi·los·o·phize /fi lóssa fīz/ (**-phized, -phiz·ing, -phiz·es**) *v.* **1.** *vi.* **DISCUSS NATURE OF REALITY** to comment on or attempt to explain the nature of life and reality, or some part of it such as logic, ethics, knowledge, or existence **2.** *vi.* **EXPLAIN OR MORALIZE IN SUPERFICIAL WAY** to express opinions of a supposedly philosophical nature in a superficial, tedious, or moralistic way **3.** *vt.* PHILOSOPHY **DEAL WITH SOMETHING FROM PHILOSOPHICAL STANDPOINT** to consider, explain, or deal with something from a philosophical standpoint —**phi·los·o·phi·za·tion** /fi lòssafi záysh'n/ *n.* —**phi·los·o·phiz·er** *n.*

phi·los·o·phy /fi lóssafee/ (*plural* **-phies**) *n.* **1.** PHILOSOPHY **EXAMINATION OF BASIC CONCEPTS** the branch of knowledge or academic study devoted to the systematic examination of basic concepts such as truth, existence, reality, causality, and freedom **2.** PHILOSOPHY **SYSTEM OF THOUGHT** a particular system of thought or doctrine **3.** PHILOSOPHY **GUIDING OR UNDERLYING PRINCIPLES** a set of basic principles or concepts underlying a particular sphere of knowledge **4. SET OF BELIEFS OR AIMS** a precept, or set of precepts, beliefs, principles, or aims, underlying somebody's practice or conduct **5. CALM RESIGNATION** restraint, resignation, or calmness and rationality in a person's behavior or response to events **6.** EDUC **THE LIBERAL ARTS** the branch of learning that includes the liberal arts and sciences and excludes medicine, law, and theology (*archaic*) [14thC. Via Old French *filosofie* from, ultimately, Greek *philosophia,* from *philosophos* "philosopher" (see PHILOSOPHER).]

phil·ter /fíltar/, **phil·tre** *n.* a magical potion or charm, especially one that causes somebody to fall in love (*literary*) [Late 16thC. Via French from, ultimately, Greek *philtron,* from *philein* "to love," from *philos* "loving."]

phil·tre *n.* = **philter**

phi·mo·sis /fī mṓssiss, fi-/ *n.* an abnormal narrowing of the opening in the foreskin to the extent that it cannot be drawn back over the penis. This precludes washing and often leads to irritation and infection. [Late 17thC. Via modern Latin from Greek *phimōsis* "muzzling."]

phi phe·nom·e·non, phi ef·fect *n.* an optical illusion in which the rapid appearance and disappearance of two stationary objects, e.g., flashing lights, is perceived as the movement back and forth of a single object

phleb- *prefix.* = **phlebo-** (*used before vowels*)

phle·bi·tis /fla bītiss/ *n.* inflammation of the wall of a vein

phlebo- *prefix.* vein ○ *phlebotomy* [From Greek *phleb-,* the stem of *phleps* "blood vessel"]

phle·bog·ra·phy /fla bóggrafee/ *n.* = **venography**

phle·bot·o·mize /fla bótta mīz/ (**-mized, -miz·ing, -miz·es**) *vt.* to make an incision into somebody's vein, formerly often done to release blood from a vein as a therapeutic treatment

phle·boto·mus fe·ver /fla bòttamass feévar/ *n.* = **sandfly fever** [From modern Latin, genus of sandfly]

phle·bot·o·my /fla bóttamee/ (*plural* **-mies**) *n.* a surgical incision made in a vein, or a puncture made by a needle to draw blood for testing — **phle·bot·o·mist** /fla bóttamist/ *n.*

phlegm /flem/ *n.* **1.** MED **THICK MUCUS** the thick mucus secreted by the walls of the respiratory passages, especially during a cold **2. UNFLAPPABILITY** calmness or composure that is not easily disturbed **3.** MED **BODILY FLUID DETERMINING HEALTH AND EMOTIONS** in medieval medicine, one of the four basic bodily fluids (**humors**). Phlegm was believed to be cold and moist in nature and to cause sluggishness and apathy. **4. INDIFFERENCE** sluggishness, apathy, or indifference (*archaic*) [14thC. Via Old French *fleume* from, ultimately, Greek *phlegma,* literally "heat," from *phlegein* "to burn." Ultimately, from an Indo-European word meaning "to shine."] —**phlegm·y** *adj.*

phleg·mat·ic /fleg máttik/, **pheg·mat·i·cal** /-máttik'l/ *adj.* characterized by a lack of emotion or emotional display, and not easily worried, excited, or annoyed [14thC. Via Old French *fleumatique* and Latin *phlegmaticus* from Greek *phlegmatikos,* from *phlegma* (see PHLEGM).] —**phleg·mat·i·cal·ly** *adv.*

WORD KEY: SYNONYMS

See Synonyms at ***impassive.***

phlo·em /flṓ èm/ *n.* one of the two main types of tissue in the more highly developed plants. Phloem conducts synthesized foodstuffs to all parts of the plant. [Late 19thC. From German, where it was formed from Greek *phloos* "bark."]

phlo·gis·ton /flō jístan/ *n.* HIST a hypothetical element that some early scientists, before the discovery of oxygen, believed to be present in all combustible substances to make them burn [Mid-18thC. From Greek, literally "inflammable thing," from *phlogizein* "to set on fire," from *phlox* "flame" (see PHLOX).] —**phlo·gis·tic** *adj.*

Phlox

phlox /floks/ (*plural* **phlox** *or* **phlox·es**) *n.* a common garden plant, originally native to North America, that has slim stems with oval narrow leaves and clusters of scented white, red, or purple flowers. Genus: *Phlox.* [Early 18thC. Via modern Latin, genus name, from Greek, "flame," from its brightly colored flowers. Ultimately from an Indo-European word that is also the ancestor of English *black.*]

Phnom Penh /pa nòm pén, nom-/ capital city of Cambodia, situated at the confluence of the Mekong and Tonle Sap rivers in the southern part of the country. Population: 900,000 (1991).

-phobe *suffix.* somebody who fears or dislikes something ○ *computerphobe* [Via French from, ultimately, Greek *phobos* "fear"]

pho·bi·a /fṓbee a/ *n.* an irrational or very powerful fear and dislike of something, e.g., spiders or confined spaces [Late 18thC. From -PHOBIA.]

-phobia *suffix.* an exaggerated or irrational fear ○ *claustrophobia* [Via Latin from, ultimately, Greek *phobos* "fear"]

pho·bic /fṓbik/ *adj.* **1. INTENSELY FEARFUL OF SOMETHING** having or showing an intense fear and dislike of something **2.** PSYCHIAT **RELATING TO PHOBIAS** affected with or arising out of a phobia ■ *n.* PSYCHIAT **SOMEBODY WITH A PHOBIA** somebody who has a strong or irrational fear and dislike of something

-phobic *suffix.* with a strong or irrational fear or dislike of somebody or something ○ *claustrophobic*

Pho·bos /fṓ bass, fóboss/ *n.* the innermost of the two natural satellites of Mars, both of which are small. It was discovered in 1877 and is ellipsoidal in shape.

phocine /fṓ sīn/ *adj.* relating to or resembling seals [Mid-19thC. From modern Latin *Phocinae,* subfamily name, from, ultimately, Greek *phōkē* "seal."]

pho·co·me·li·a /fōkə meélee ə/ *n.* a condition, present at birth, characterized by an absent or underdeveloped upper section of a limb, with a normal-sized hand or foot attached to the trunk by a short, broad, flat limb [Late 19thC. Formed from Greek *phōkē* "seal" + *melos* "limb"; from the short limbs of seals.]

phoe·be /feébee/ *n.* a bird of the flycatcher family, native to eastern North America, that has grayish-brown plumage and a yellowish-white breast and is noted for the flicking of its tail. Genus: *Sayornis.* [Early 18thC. An imitation of its song (influenced by the name PHOEBE).]

Phoe·be[1] *n.* **1.** MYTHOL **TITAN GODDESS** in Greek mythology, a Titan goddess who later became identified with the goddess of the moon, Artemis **2. MOON** a personification of the moon (*literary*) [14thC. Via Latin from Greek *Phoibē*, feminine of *phoibos* "bright, shining."]

Phoe·be[2] /feébee/ *n.* the outermost known natural satellite of Saturn, discovered in 1898. It is irregular in shape and has a maximum dimension of approximately 230 km (143 mi.).

Phoe·bus /feébəss/ *n.* **1.** = **Apollo 2. SUN** a personification of the sun (*literary*) [14thC. Via Latin from, ultimately, Greek *phoibos* "bright, shining."]

Phoe·ni·cian /fə nísh'n, fə neésh'n/ *n.* **1.** PEOPLES **SOMEBODY FROM ANCIENT PHOENICIA** a member of an ancient people that occupied Phoenicia, coastal lands in present-day Syria, where they established thriving trading ports. During pre-Christian times, their influence spread throughout the eastern Mediterranean. **2.** LANG **LANGUAGE OF ANCIENT PHOENICIA** an extinct language formerly spoken in ancient Phoenicia. It belongs to the Canaanitic group of the Semitic branch of Afro-Asiatic languages. —**Phoe·ni·cian** *adj.*

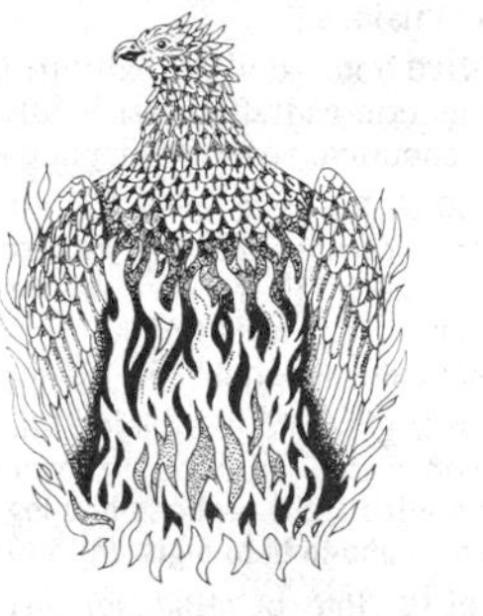

Phoenix

phoe·nix /feéniks/, **phe·nix** *n.* **1.** MYTHOL **MYTHOLOGICAL BIRD** in ancient mythology, a bird resembling an eagle that lived for 500 years and then burned itself to death on a pyre from whose ashes another phoenix arose. It commonly appears in literature as a symbol of death and resurrection. **2. SOMEBODY OR SOMETHING BEAUTIFUL OR UNIQUE** a supremely beautiful, rare, or unique person or thing (*literary*) ○ *a phoenix of princes* [Pre-12thC. Via Old French from, ultimately, Greek *phoinix.*]

Phoe·nix[1] /feéniks/ *n.* a constellation of the southern hemisphere situated between Sculptor and Eridanus

Phoe·nix[2] /feéniks/ capital of Arizona and its largest city, located in the southern part of the state. Population: 1,159,014 (1996).

phon /fon/ *n.* a unit of subjective measure of loudness level. The level in phons is equal in number to the sound intensity of a 1,000-hertz reference sound, measured in decibels, judged to be the same loudness as the measured sound.

phon. *abbr.* **1.** phonology **2.** phonetics

phon- *prefix.* = **phono-** (*used before vowels*)

pho·nate /fō nàyt/ (**-nat·ed, -nat·ing, -nates**) *vi.* to produce sounds, especially speech sounds, with the voice —**pho·na·tion** /fō náysh'n/ *n.* —**pho·na·to·ry** /fōnə tàwree/ *adj.*

phone[1] /fōn/ *n.* **TELEPHONE** a telephone ■ **phones** *npl.* **EARPHONES** a set of earphones (*informal*) ■ *v.* (**phoned, phon·ing, phones**) **1.** *vti.* **CALL SOMEBODY BY TELEPHONE** to call somebody on the telephone **2.** *vt.* **REPORT SOMETHING BY TELEPHONE** to report or communicate something using a telephone [Late 19thC. Shortening.]

phone[2] /fōn/ *n.* a single basic speech sound [Mid-19thC. See -PHONE.]

-phone *suffix.* **1.** device thats emits or receives sounds, musical instrument ○ *diaphone* ○ *hydrophone* ○ *sousaphone* **2.** telephone ○ *speakerphone* **3.** sound, speech sound ○ *isophone* **4.** speaker of a particular language ○ *Francophone* [From Greek *phōnē* (see PHONO-)] —**-phonic** *suffix.* —**-phony** *suffix.*

phone book *n.* a telephone book

phone booth *n.* a telephone booth

phone·card /fōn kaàrd/ *n.* a rectangular plastic card that can be used instead of money when making calls from some public telephones

phone-in *n. U.K.* BROADCAST = **call-in**

pho·neme /fō neém/ *n.* a speech sound that distinguishes one word from another, e.g., the sounds "d" and "t" in the words "bid" and "bit." A phoneme is the smallest phonetic unit. [Late 19thC. Via French from Greek *phōnēma* "sound produced," from *phōnein* "to produce a sound," from *phōnē* "sound, voice."]

pho·ne·mic /fə neémik, fō-/ *adj.* **1. OF PHONEMES** relating to a phoneme **2. OF DIFFERENT PHONEMES** relating to speech sounds that belong to different phonemes rather than being different ways of pronouncing the same phoneme **3. OF PHONEMICS** relating to the branch of linguistics that studies phonemes [Mid-20thC] —**pho·ne·mi·cal·ly** *adv.*

pho·ne·mics /fə neémiks, fō-/ *n.* the branch of linguistics involved in the classification and analysis of the phonemes of a language (*takes a singular verb*) [Mid-20thC] —**pho·ne·mi·cist** *n.*

phone phreak *n.* COMPUT somebody who breaks into telephone systems and other secure networks, often for the purpose of making free long-distance telephone calls (*slang*)

phonet. *abbr.* phonetics

pho·net·ic /fə néttik, fō-/ *adj.* **1. OF SPEECH SOUNDS** belonging to or associated with the sounds of human speech **2. SHOWING PRONUNCIATION** representing the sounds of human speech in writing, often with special symbols or unconventional spelling **3. OF PHONETICS** relating to the science of phonetics [Early 19thC. Via modern Latin from Greek *phōnētikos* "spoken," ultimately from *phōnein* (see PHONEME).] —**pho·net·i·cal·ly** *adv.*

pho·net·ic al·pha·bet *n.* **1.** PHON **SYMBOLS SHOWING PRONUNCIATION** a set of letters and symbols used to represent the sounds of human speech in writing **2.** TELECOM **WORDS REPRESENTING LETTERS** a set of words representing the letters of the alphabet, e.g., "Delta" for D and "Tango" for T, used in radio or telephone communications. The phonetic alphabet is used to distinguish between letters that sound similar, to spell out words, and in code names or call signs. U.K. = **NATO Phonetic Alphabet**

pho·ne·ti·cian /fōnə tísh'n/ *n.* somebody who specializes in the branch of linguistics involved in the study of speech sounds [Mid-19thC]

pho·net·ics /fə néttiks, fō-/ *n.* (*takes a singular verb*) **1. STUDY OF SPEECH SOUNDS** the scientific study of speech sounds and how they are produced **2. SOUND SYSTEM OF A LANGUAGE** the system or pattern of speech sounds used in a particular language [Mid-19thC]

pho·net·ist /fōnətist/ *n.* somebody who uses or favors the use of a particular phonetic spelling system [Mid-19thC. Shortening of *phoneticist.* (See PHONETICS).]

pho·ney *adj., n.* = **phony**

phon·ic /fónnik/ *adj.* **1. USING PHONICS** using or involving phonics as a method of teaching people to read **2. OF SOUND** associated with sound or the scientific study of sound **3. OF SPEECH SOUNDS** relating to the sounds used in speech [Early 19thC. Formed from Greek *phōnē* "sound, voice."] —**phon·i·cal·ly** *adv.*

phon·ics /fónniks/ *n.* (*takes a singular verb*) **1. READING METHOD INVOLVING LETTER RECOGNITION** a method of teaching reading in which people learn to associate letters with the speech sounds they represent, rather than learning to recognize the whole word as a unit **2. ACOUSTICS** acoustics (*archaic*) [Late 17thC. Formed from Greek *phōnē* "sound, voice."]

phono- *prefix.* **1.** sound, speech, voice ○ *phonogram* **2.** telephone ○ *phonecard* [From Greek *phōnē* "sound." Ultimately from an Indo-European base meaning "to speak," which is also the ancestor of English *fame, fable, fate,* and *ban.*]

pho·no·car·di·o·gram /fōnə kaàrdee ə gràm/ *n.* a visual record of heart sounds and murmurs made by a phonocardiograph

pho·no·car·di·o·graph /fōnə kaàrdee ə gràf/ *n.* an instrument that amplifies heart sounds and converts them into a visual display —**pho·no·car·di·o·graph·ic** /fōnə kaardee ə gráffik/ *adj.* —**pho·no·car·di·og·ra·phy** /fōnə kaardee óggrəfee/ *n.*

pho·no·chem·is·try /fōnō kémmistree/ *n.* a branch of science and technology dealing with the effect of sound and ultrasonic waves on chemical reactions

pho·no·gram /fōnə gràm/ *n.* **1. CHARACTER REPRESENTING A WORD OR SOUND** a symbol that represents a word, part of a word, or an individual speech sound **2. LETTER GROUP WITH A PARTICULAR SOUND** a sequence of letters that have the same pronunciation in several different words, e.g., "ear" in "earth," "heard," and "learn" [Mid-19thC] —**pho·no·gram·ic** /fōnə grámmik/ *adj.* —**pho·no·gram·i·cal·ly** *adv.*

pho·no·graph /fōnə gràf/ *n.* a record player [Late 19thC]

pho·nog·ra·phy /fə nóggrəfee, fō-/ *n.* **1. USE OF SYMBOLS FOR SOUNDS** the use of symbols to represent speech sounds in writing **2. SHORTHAND WITH SYMBOLS FOR SOUNDS** a method of writing in shorthand that uses symbols to represent speech sounds —**pho·nog·ra·pher** *n.* —**pho·no·graph·ic** /fōnə gráffik/ *adj.* —**pho·no·graph·i·cal·ly** *adv.* —**pho·nog·ra·phist** /fə nóggrəfist, fō-/ *n.*

phonol. *abbr.* phonology

pho·no·lite /fōnə līt/ *n.* a fine-grained light-colored volcanic rock characterized by the presence of alkali feldspar and nepheline [Early 19thC. Coined from PHONO- + -LITE; from the resonance of the rock when hit with a hammer.] —**pho·no·lit·ic** /fōnə líttik/ *adj.*

pho·nol·o·gy /fə nólləjee, fō-/ (*plural* **-gies**) *n.* **1. STUDY OF SPEECH SOUNDS** the scientific study of the system or pattern of speech sounds used in a particular language or in language in general **2. SOUND SYSTEM OF A LANGUAGE** the system or pattern of speech sounds used in a particular language —**pho·no·log·i·cal** /fōnə lójjik'l/ *adj.* —**pho·no·log·i·cal·ly** *adv.* —**pho·nol·o·gist** /fə nólləjist, fō-/ *n.*

pho·non /fō nòn/ *n.* PHYS a quantum of vibrational or acoustic energy in a crystal lattice [Mid-20thC]

pho·no·re·cep·tion /fōnō ri sépshən/ *n.* the perception of or response to high-frequency vibration, especially sound waves

pho·no·scope /fōnə skōp/ *n.* a device that produces a visual representation of the vibrations of sound waves, used especially with musical instruments [Mid-19thC. Originally the name of a device for testing the quality of musical strings.]

pho·no·tac·tics /fōnə táktiks/ *n.* the study of the sounds it is possible to put together to form words and parts of words in a language (*takes a singular verb*)

pho·no·typ·y /fōnə tīpee/ *n.* the representing of speech sounds with phonetic symbols in writing or print —**pho·no·typ·er** *n.* —**pho·no·typ·ist** *n.*

pho·ny /fōnee/, **pho·ney** *adj.* (**-ni·er, -ni·est**) **1. NOT GENUINE** not genuine and used to deceive **2. GIVING A FALSE IMPRESSION** putting on a false show of something such as sincerity or expertise ■ *n.* (*plural* **-nies** *or* **-neys**) **SOMEBODY OR SOMETHING PHONY** a phony person or thing ■ *vt.* (**-nied** *or* **-neyed, -ny·ing** *or* **-ney·ing, -nies**) **FALSIFY** to make something appear to be genuine when it is not [Late 19thC. Origin uncertain: possibly an alteration of slang *fawney* "gilt brass ring used by swindlers," from Irish Gaelic *fáinne* "ring."] —**pho·ni·ly** *adv.* —**pho·ni·ness** *n.*

phoo·ey /fóo ee/ *interj.* used to express contempt, disbelief, disgust, or disappointment (*informal*) [Early 20thC. Partly an alteration of *pfui.* Suggestive of the sound associated with spitting.]

pho·rate /fáw ràyt/ *n.* an organophosphorous compound used as an insecticide to control crop pests. Formula: $C_7H_{17}O_2PS_3$. [Mid-20thC. Shortening of *phosphorodithioate*, from PHOSPHORUS + DI- + THIO- + -ATE.]

-phore *suffix.* something that carries ○ *sporophore* [From Greek *-phoros* "bearing," from *pherein* "to carry." Ultimately from an Indo-European word that is also the ancestor of English *bear* and *transfer.*] —**-phorous** *suffix.*

-phoresis *suffix.* transmission ○ *diaphoresis* [From Greek *phorēsis*, which was formed from *phorein*, literally "to keep carrying," from *pherein* (see -PHORE)]

phos·gene /fóss jeèn, fóz-/ *n.* a highly toxic colorless gas used as a chemical weapon in World War I and in the manufacture of pesticides, plastics, and dyes. Formula: $COCl_2$. [Early 19thC]

phos·gen·ite /fósjə nìt, fózjə-/ *n.* a rare grayish fluorescent crystalline mineral consisting of a carbonate and chloride of lead. Formula: $Pb_2(Cl_2CO_3)$. [Mid-19thC. Formed from PHOSGENE, because the minerals are formed from the same substances as phosgene gas.]

phosph- *prefix.* = **phospho-** (*used before vowels*)

phos·pha·tase /fósfə tàyss, -tàyz/ *n.* an enzyme that catalyzes the breakdown and synthesis of phosphoric acid esters and the transfer of phosphate groups from these acids to other compounds [Early 20thC. Coined from PHOSPHATE + -ASE.]

phos·phate /fóss fàyt/ *n.* **1. SALT OF PHOSPHORIC ACID** any salt or ester formed by the reaction of a metal, alcohol, or other radical with phosphoric acid. A tribasic acid, phosphoric acid forms three series of phosphates by replacement of one, two, or all three of its hydrogen ions. **2. FIZZY DRINK** a soft drink made from carbonated water and flavored syrup [Late 18thC. From French *phosphate*, from *phosphore* "phosphorus."] —**phos·phat·ic** /foss fáttik/ *adj.*

phos·phate rock *n.* any of several sedimentary rocks that have a naturally high phosphate concentration and are used as fertilizers and in the manufacture of phosphorus compounds

phos·pha·tide /fósfə tìd/ *n.* BIOCHEM = **phospholipid** —**phos·pha·tid·ic** /fòsfə tíddik/ *adj.*

phos·pha·ti·dyl·cho·line /fòsfə tíd'l kṑ leèn, foss fáttəd'l kṑ leèn/ *n.* BIOCHEM = **lecithin** [Mid-20thC. Coined from PHOSPHATIDE + -YL + CHOLINE.]

phos·pha·ti·dyl·eth·a·no·la·mine /fòsfə tíd'l éthə nóllə meèn, foss fáttəd'l éthə nóllə meèn, fósfə tíd'l éthə n nōlə meèn, foss fáttəd'l éthə nōlə meèn/ *n.* BIOCHEM = **cephalin** [Mid-20thC. Coined from PHOSPHATIDE + -YL + ETHANOLAMINE.]

phos·pha·tize /fósfə tìz/ (**-tized, -tiz·ing, -tiz·es**) *v.* **1.** *vt.* **TREAT SOMETHING WITH PHOSPHATE** to treat something with phosphoric acid or with a phosphate, typically to protect ferrous metal against corrosion **2.** *vti.* **CHANGE INTO A PHOSPHATE** to convert something or be converted into a phosphate or phosphates —**phos·pha·ti·za·tion** /fòsfəti záysh'n/ *n.*

phos·pha·tu·ri·a /fòsfə tŏoree ə/ *n.* the presence in the urine of a high concentration of phosphate salts, giving it a cloudy appearance. It is associated with the formation of kidney stones. [Late 19thC. Coined from PHOSPHATE + -URIA.] —**phos·pha·tu·ric** *adj.*

phos·phene /fóss feèn/ *n.* a sensation of seeing light caused by pressure or electrical stimulation of the eye [Late 19thC. From modern French *phosphène*, from Greek *phōs* "light" + *phainein* "to show."]

phos·phide /fóss fìd/ *n.* any compound of phosphorus with a more electropositive element, e.g., a metal [Mid-19thC]

phos·phine /fóss feèn/ *n.* a colorless inflammable gas with a fishy smell, used as a pesticide. Formula: PH_3. [Late 19thC]

phos·phite /fóss fìt/ *n.* any salt or ester of phosphorous acid [Late 18thC]

phospho- *prefix.* **1.** phosphorus ○ *phosphate* **2.** phosphate ○ *phosphocreatine* [From PHOSPHORUS]

phos·pho·cre·a·tine /fòsfō kreé ə teèn/, **phos·pho·cre·a·tin** /-ətin/ *n.* an organic acid derived from creatine that is present in muscles and other tissue and is capable of storing and providing energy for muscle contraction. Formula: $C_4H_{10}N_3O_5P$.

phos·pho·fruc·to·ki·nase /fòsfō fruktō kí nàyss, -frŏoktō-, -nàyz/ *n.* an enzyme found in cytoplasm that catalyzes the transfer of a phosphate group to a fructose compound during the metabolism of glucose

phos·pho·glu·co·mu·tase /fòsfō glookō myŏo tàyss, -tàyz/ *n.* a reversible enzyme found in all living cells that catalyzes both the breakdown and the synthesis of glycogen, thus serving a cell's immediate need for energy storage or use

phos·pho·li·pase /fòsfō lí pàyss, -pàyz/ *n.* an enzyme often found in the membrane of a cell that catalyzes the hydrolysis of phospholipids

phos·pho·lip·id /fòsfō líppid/ *n.* a phosphorus-containing lipid that is soluble in organic solvents and is found in the cells of all living tissue, especially in the two-layered cellular membranes

phos·pho·nic ac·id *n.* CHEM = **phosphorous acid**

phos·pho·ni·um /foss fōnee əm/ *n.* a univalent radical derived from phosphene. Formula: PH_4. [Late 19thC. Coined from PHOSPHO- + ending of AMMONIUM.]

phos·phor /fósfər/ *n.* a substance that can emit light when irradiated with particles of electromagnetic radiation [Early 17thC. From Latin *phosphorus* (see PHOSPHORUS).]

phos·phor·ate /fósfə ràyt/ (**-at·ed, -at·ing, -ates**) *vt.* to treat, combine, or impregnate something with phosphorus

phos·phor bronze *n.* any one of several alloys containing copper, tin, and phosphorus that are resistant to wear and corrosion and are used in bearings, gears, and components exposed to sea water

phos·pho·resce /fòsfə réss/ (**-resced, -resc·ing, -resc·es**) *vi.* to continue to emit light without accompanying heat after exposure to and removal of a source of stimulating radiation

phos·pho·res·cence /fòsfə réss'ns/ *n.* the continued emission of light without heat after exposure to and removal of a source of electromagnetic radiation

phos·pho·res·cent /fòsfə réss'nt/ *adj.* continuing to emit light after the source of stimulating radiation has been removed —**phos·pho·res·cent·ly** *adv.*

phos·phor·ic /foss fáwrik/ *adj.* containing phosphorus with a valence state higher than that of the phosphorus ion or radical in an analogous phosphorous compound [Late 18thC]

phos·phor·ic ac·id *n.* **1. TRANSPARENT SOLID USED AS FERTILIZER** a water-soluble transparent solid acid used as a fertilizer, in soft drinks, pharmaceuticals, and animal feeds, and to rust-proof metals. It is formed by boiling a solution of phosphorus pentoxide in water. Formula: H_3PO_4. **2. ACID FORMED FROM PHOSPHORUS PENTOXIDE** any of the acids formed by the combination of phosphorus pentoxide with water, each having one more oxygen atom than the corresponding phosphorous acid

phos·pho·rism /fósfə rìzzəm/ *n.* poisoning caused by long-term exposure to phosphorus

phos·pho·rite /fósfə rìt/ *n.* **1. MINERAL DEPOSIT OF PHOSPHATES** a mineral deposit consisting of apatite and other phosphates **2.** = **phosphate rock** —**phos·pho·rit·ic** /fòsfə ríttik/ *adj.*

phos·pho·rol·y·sis /fòsfə róllәssiss/ *n.* a reversible reaction in which the covalent bonds of a molecule are broken by the addition of atoms of phosphoric acid, e.g., during the breakdown of glycogen [Mid-20thC. A blend of PHOSPHORUS or *phosphorylation* + HYDROLYSIS.]

phos·pho·rous /fósfərəss/ *adj.* relating to phosphorus with a valence state lower than that of the phosphorus ion or radical in an analogous phosphoric compound [Late 18thC. Coined from PHOSPHORUS + -OUS.]

phos·pho·rous ac·id *n.* **1. WHITE OR YELLOWISH CYSTALLINE SOLID** a white or yellowish cystalline solid that absorbs water from the atmosphere. It is used as a reducing agent and to produce phosphite salts, and is formed by reacting cold water with phosphorus pentoxide. Formula: H_3PO_3. **2. DIBASIC ACID FORMED FROM PHOSPHORUS PENTOXIDE** any of the acids formed by the combination of phosphorus pentoxide with water, each having one less oxygen atom than the corresponding phosphoric acid

phos·pho·rus /fósfərəss/ *n.* a phosphorescent substance or object [Early 17thC. Via modern Latin from Greek *phōsphoros* "morning star," literally "light-bringing," from *phōs* "light."]

phos·pho·rus pent·ox·ide, phos·pho·rus ox·ide *n.* a flammable hygroscopic white solid formed by burning phosphorus in air and used primarily to manufacture othophosphoric acid by reacting it with water. Formula: P_2O_5.

phos·pho·ryl /fósfəril/ *n.* a chemical group, usually with a valence of three, consisting of one phosphorus atom and one oxygen atom

phos·pho·ryl·ase /fósfərə làyss, -làyz/ *n.* an enzyme usually found in the cytoplasm of a cell that catalyzes the phosphorolysis of a molecule such as glycogen and the production of organic phosphates

phos·pho·ryl·ate /fósfərə làyt/ (**-at·ed, -at·ing, -ates**) *vt.* to add a phosphate group to an organic molecule to produce an organic phosphate —**phos·pho·ryl·a·tion** /fòssfərə láysh'n/ *n.* —**phos·pho·ryl·a·tive** /fóssfəri làytiv/ *adj.*

phot /fōt/ *n.* a unit of illumination in the centimeter-gram-second system equal to one lumen per square centimeter [Late 19thC. Via French from Greek *phōt-*, stem of *phōs* "light" (See PHOS-).]

phot. *abbr.* **1.** photograph **2.** photographer **3.** photographic **4.** photography

phot- *prefix.* = **photo-** (*used before vowels*)

pho·tic /fōtik/ *adj.* **1. OF LIGHT** relating to light, especially when produced by living organisms **2.** ECOL **OF THE OCEAN DEPTH WHERE PHOTOSYNTHESIS OCCURS** relating to or used to describe the area of the ocean where light penetrates and photosynthesis occurs [Mid-19thC. Formed from PHOT.]

Pho·ti·us /fōtee əss/ (820?–891?) Byzantine churchman and scholar. He was patriarch of Constantinople (858–67 and 877–86), initiating the spread of Orthodox Christianity in Eastern Europe.

pho·to /fōtō/ *n.* (*plural* **-tos**) = **photograph** ■ *vt.* (**-toed, -to·ing, -tos**) **PHOTOGRAPH SOMEBODY OR SOMETHING** to take a photograph or photographs of somebody or something [Mid-19thC. Shortening.]

photo- *prefix.* **1.** light, radiant energy ○ *photochemistry* **2.** photographic ○ *photodrama* **3.** photoelectric ○ *photocurrent* [From Greek *phōt-*, the stem of *phōs* "light." Ultimately from an Indo-European base meaning "to shine," which is also the ancestor of English *beacon*, *banner*, and *phenomenon*.]

pho·to·ac·tin·ic /fòtō ak tínnik/ *adj.* emitting radiation similar to visible and ultraviolet light in its chemical effects on such substances as photographic emulsions

pho·to·ac·tive /fòtō áktiv/ *adj.* exhibiting a reaction to electromagnetic radiation, especially visible light, either by chemical reaction or photoelectrically

pho·to·au·to·troph /fòtō áwtə tròf, -trōf/ *n.* an organism that derives its energy exclusively from light and uses it to synthesize food —**pho·to·au·to·troph·ic** /fòtō awtə tróffik, -trōfik/ *adj.* —**pho·to·au·to·troph·i·cal·ly** /-tróffək'lee, -trōfək'lee/ *adv.*

pho·to·bi·ol·o·gy /fòtō bī óllәjee/ *n.* a branch of biology concerned with the interaction of living organisms with light —**pho·to·bi·o·log·i·cal** /fòtō bī ə lójjik'l/ *adj.* —**pho·to·bi·ol·o·gist** /fòtō bī óllәjist/ *n.*

pho·to·bi·ot·ic /fòtō bī óttik/ *adj.* used to describe organisms that need light in order to live and grow

pho·to·ca·tal·y·sis /fòtō kə tállәssiss/ *n.* the acceleration or deceleration of the speed at which a chemical reaction occurs, caused by electromagnetic radiation and especially visible light

pho·to·cath·ode /fòtō ká thōd/ *n.* an electrode that emits electrons when exposed to electromagnetic radiation such as light. Photocathodes are used in television and digital cameras and photoelectric cells.

pho·to CD *n.* COMPUT a compact disc that stores images from photographs that can be displayed on a computer or television screen

pho·to·cell /fōtō sèl/ *n.* = **photoelectric cell**

pho·to·chem·i·cal smog *n.* air pollution caused by the effect of strong sunlight on nitrogen dioxide and hydrocarbons emitted by motor vehicles, creating a harmful haze of minute droplets in the air

pho·to·chem·is·try /fòtō kémmistree/ *n.* a branch of chemistry that studies the effect of radiation, especially of visible and ultraviolet light, on chemical reactions and of the emission of radiation by chemical reactions —**pho·to·chem·i·cal** *adj.* —**pho·to·chem·i·cal·ly** /-kémmik'lee/ *adv.* —**pho·to·chem·ist** /fòtō kémmist/ *n.*

pho·to·chrom·ic /fòtō krōmik/ *adj.* changing color or becoming darker or lighter in color as light increases or decreases in intensity

pho·to·co·ag·u·la·tion /fòtō kō ággyə láysh'n/ *n.* the use of a high-energy light source such as a laser to harden tissue for surgical repair, especially in eye injuries

pho·to·com·po·si·tion /fòtō kómpə zísh'n/ *n.* a typesetting process that involves projecting the characters that are to be printed onto photographic film and then making printing plates from the film —

pho·to·com·pose /fṓtō kəm pṓzər/ *vt.* —**pho·to·com·pos·er** /-pṓzər/ *n.*

pho·to·con·duc·tion /fṓtō kən dúkshən/ *n.* the conduction of electricity resulting from the absorption of electromagnetic radiation, especially visible light

pho·to·con·duc·tiv·i·ty /fṓtō kón duk tívvətee/ *n.* an increase in the electrical conductivity of a substance on exposure to electromagnetic radiation, especially visible light —**pho·to·con·duc·tive** /fṓtō kən dúktiv/ *adj.* —**pho·to·con·duc·tor** /-dúktər/ *n.*

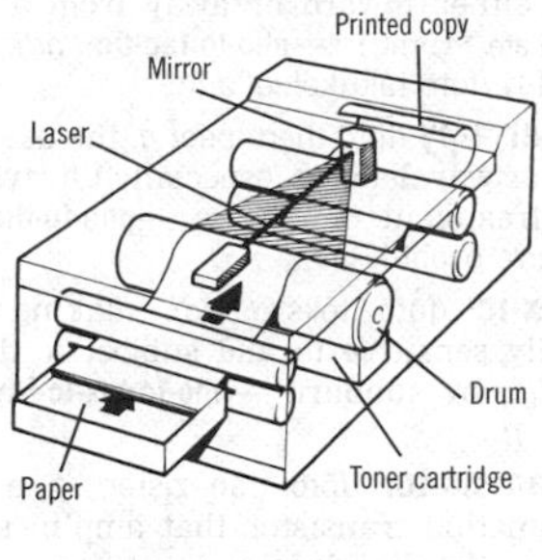

Photocopier

pho·to·cop·i·er /fṓtə kòppee ər/ *n.* a machine that uses a photographic process to produce an almost instant copy of something printed, written, or drawn

pho·to·cop·y /fṓtə kòppee/ *n.* (*plural* **-ies**) PHOTOGRAPHIC REPRODUCTION OF A TEXT OR PICTURE a copy of something printed, written, or drawn that is produced almost instantly by a photographic process in a machine designed for this purpose ■ *vti.* (**-ied, -y·ing, -ies**) MAKE PHOTOCOPY to make a photocopy of something, or be photocopied

pho·to·cur·rent /fṓtō kùr ənt, -kùrrənt/ *n.* an electric current that is produced by and varies with the intensity of illumination. The current is a result of photoconductivity or of the photoelectric or photovoltaic effect.

pho·to·de·com·po·si·tion /fṓtō dee kómpə zísh'n/ *n.* the breakdown of a chemical compound into simpler substances by means of incident electromagnetic energy, especially visible light

pho·to·de·grad·a·ble /fṓtō di gráydəb'l/ *adj.* able to be decomposed into simpler substances through prolonged exposure to incident electromagnetic energy, especially ultraviolet light

pho·to·di·ode /fṓtō dí ōd/ *n.* a semiconductor device in which the flow of current is controlled by the intensity of light and which can therefore be used to detect light

pho·to·dis·in·te·gra·tion /fṓtō diss íntə gráysh'n/ *n.* the ejection of a proton, neutron, or other elementary particle from an atomic nucleus as a result of its absorption of a photon, usually in the form of gamma radiation —**pho·to·dis·in·te·grate** /fṓtō diss íntə gràyt/ *vti.*

pho·to·du·pli·cate /fṓtō dóoplee kàyt/ *vt.* (**-cat·ed, -cat·ing, -cates**) MAKE A PHOTOCOPY OF SOMETHING to make a photocopy of something ■ *n.* PHOTOCOPY a copy of something made using a photocopier —**pho·to·du·pli·ca·tion** /fṓtō dóoplee káysh'n/ *n.*

pho·to·dy·nam·ic /fṓtō dī námmik/ *adj.* **1.** BIOL OF PHOTODYNAMICS relating to photodynamics or to the energy of light **2.** BIOL INVOLVING AN ADVERSE REACTION TO LIGHT bringing about or enhancing the toxic effects of some wavelengths of light, especially ultraviolet, on living tissue **3.** MED OF A LASER CANCER TREATMENT relating to or used to describe a cancer treatment in which the drug used is activated by a laser beam —**pho·to·dy·nam·i·cal·ly** *adv.*

pho·to·dy·nam·ics /fṓtō dī námmiks/ *n.* a branch of biology dealing with the effects of light on living organisms (*takes a singular verb*)

pho·to·e·lec·tric /fṓtō i léktrik/, **pho·to·e·lec·tri·cal** /-k'l/ *adj.* relating to any electrical effects that are due to the action of electromagnetic radiation, especially visible light —**pho·to·e·lec·tri·cal·ly** *adv.* —**pho·to·e·lec·tric·i·ty** /fṓtō i lek tríssətee, -ee lek-/ *n.*

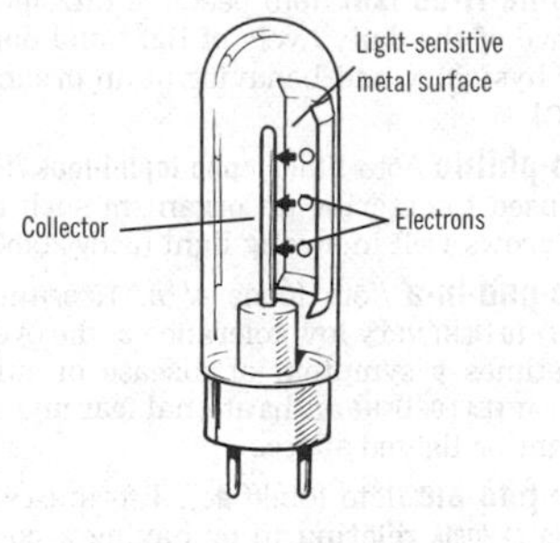

Photoelectric cell

pho·to·e·lec·tric cell *n.* a solid-state device sensitive to varying levels of light that is used to generate or control an electric current, e.g., in burglar alarms, smoke detectors, and exposure meters

pho·to·e·lec·tric ef·fect *n.* the emission of electrons from a substance exposed to electromagnetic radiation

pho·to·e·lec·tron /fṓtō i lék tròn/ *n.* an electron released from the surface of a substance that has been struck by a photon of electromagnetic radiation

pho·to·e·mis·sion /fṓtō i mísh'n/ *n.* the release of electrons from a substance by incident electromagnetic radiation —**pho·to·e·mis·sive** *adj.*

pho·to·en·grave /fṓtō in gráyv/ (**-graved, -grav·ing, -graves**) *vt.* to make a copy of something using photoengraving —**pho·to·en·grav·er** *n.*

pho·to·en·grav·ing /fṓtō in gráyving/ *n.* **1.** PROCESS OF ETCHING A PRINTING PLATE the process of making a printing plate by photographing an image onto a metal plate and then etching the image **2.** PRINTING PLATE MADE BY PHOTOENGRAVING a printing plate made by photographing an image onto a metal **3.** PRINT MADE BY PHOTOENGRAVING a print made using a photoengraved printing plate

pho·to·es·say /fṓtō èssay/, **pho·to es·say** *n.* = **photo story**

pho·to fin·ish *n.* **1.** RACE RESULT DETERMINED FROM A PHOTOGRAPH the end of a race in which two or more contestants are so close that the result must be determined from a photograph taken as they cross the finish line **2.** VERY CLOSE CONTEST a race or competition won by a very small margin

Pho·to·fit /fṓtō fìt/ *tdmk.* a trademark for a way of constructing a photograph of somebody using photographs of individual facial features arranged to fit a description closely. This method is often used to try to identify criminals.

pho·to·flash /fṓtō flàsh/ *n.* = **flashbulb**

pho·to·flood /fṓtō flùd/ *n.* a very bright incandescent lamp used in photography and filming

pho·to·fluor·o·gram /fṓtə flóorə gràm, -fláwrə-/ *n.* a photograph of an image produced using X-rays

pho·to·fluor·og·ra·phy /fṓtō floo róggrəfee, -flaw-/ *n.* a technique that photographs an X-ray image onto a fluorescent screen for diagnostic purposes [Mid-20thC] —**pho·to·fluor·o·graph·ic** /fṓtō floorə gráffik, -flawrə-/ *adj.*

pho·tog /fə tóg/ *n.* a photographer (*informal*)

photog. *abbr.* **1.** photograph **2.** photographic **3.** photography

pho·to·gel·a·tin proc·ess /fṓtō jéllət'n-/ *n.* = **collotype**

pho·to·gene /fṓtə jeen/ *n.* = **afterimage** [Mid-19thC]

pho·to·gen·ic /fṓtə jénnik/ *adj.* **1.** LOOKING ATTRACTIVE IN PHOTOGRAPHS tending to look good in photographs **2.** BIOL PRODUCING LIGHT used to describe an organism that produces its own light, especially by phosphorescence **3.** CAUSED BY LIGHT caused or aggravated by light, e.g., an epileptic episode brought about by blinking lights [Mid-19thC. Coined from PHOTO- + -GENIC.] —**pho·to·gen·i·cal·ly** *adv.*

pho·to·ge·ol·o·gy /fṓtō jee óllajee/ *n.* the study and identification of landforms and other geologic features by means of aerial and satellite photographs —**pho·to·ge·o·log·ic** /fṓtō jee ə lójjik/ *adj.* —**pho·to·ge·ol·o·gist** /fṓtō jee óllajist/ *n.*

pho·to·gram /fṓtə gràm/ *n.* **1.** PHOTOGRAPHIC IMAGE LIKE A SHADOW a photographic image produced without a camera, usually by placing an object on or near a piece of film or light-sensitive paper and exposing it to light **2.** ARTISTIC PHOTOGRAPH a photograph, especially an artistic one (*archaic*)

pho·to·gram·me·try /fṓtə grámmətree/ *n.* making measurements or scale drawings from photographs, especially using aerial photography in the construction of maps —**pho·to·gram·met·ric** /fṓtəgrə méttrik/ *adj.* —**pho·to·gram·me·trist** /fṓtə grámmətrist/ *n.*

pho·to·graph /fṓtə gràf/ *n.* PICTURE PRODUCED WITH A CAMERA an image produced on light-sensitive film or array inside a camera, especially a print or slide made from the developed film or from a digitized array image, or a reproduction in a newspaper, magazine, or book ■ *v.* (**-graphed, -graph·ing, -graphs**) **1.** *vti.* TAKE A PHOTOGRAPH OF SOMEBODY OR SOMETHING to produce an image of something by pointing a camera at it and allowing light briefly to fall on the film inside **2.** *vi.* BE PHOTOGRAPHED WITH A PARTICULAR RESULT to be able to be photographed, or to have a particular quality or appearance in a photograph ○ *Scenes like this photograph best in bright sunlight.* [Mid-19thC]

pho·tog·ra·pher /fə tóggrəfər/ *n.* somebody who takes photographs as a profession, hobby, or art form

pho·to·graph·ic /fṓtə gráffik/ *adj.* **1.** OF PHOTOGRAPHY relating to, used in, or produced by photography **2.** LIKE A PHOTOGRAPH as accurate and detailed as a photograph —**pho·to·graph·i·cal·ly** *adv.*

pho·to·graph·ic mag·ni·tude *n.* the magnitude of a star determined by measuring its size on a photographic plate. Depending on the color of the star, photographic magnitude and visual magnitude can differ because the eye and standard photographic plates have different color sensitivities.

pho·to·graph·ic mem·o·ry *n.* the ability to recall information, especially visual images, with great accuracy and clarity

pho·tog·ra·phy /fə tóggrəfee/ *n.* **1.** PRODUCING PICTURES WITH A CAMERA the art, hobby, or profession of taking photographs, and developing and printing the film or processing the digitized array image **2.** USING LIGHT TO MAKE PICTURES the process of recording images by exposing light-sensitive film or array to light or other forms of radiation

pho·to·gra·vure /fṓtə grə vyóor/ *n.* the process of using photography to make a printing plate with an image engraved into it [Late 19thC. From French, formed from *photo* + *gravure* "engraving," from *graver* "to engrave."]

pho·to·he·li·o·graph *n.* = **heliograph** *n.* 2

pho·to·in·duced /fṓtō in dóost/ *adj.* initiated through exposure to light —**pho·to·in·duc·tion** /-dúkshən/ *n.* —**pho·to·in·duc·tive** /-dúktiv/ *adj.*

pho·to·in·ter·pre·ta·tion /fṓtō in turprə táysh'n/ *n.* the science of identifying objects in photographs, especially in order to determine their potential military or topographic importance —**pho·to·in·ter·pret·er** /-túrprətər/ *n.*

pho·to·i·on·i·za·tion /fṓtō ī əni záysh'n/ *n.* the removal of one or more electrons from an atom or molecule by absorption of a photon of electromagnetic radiation, especially visible or ultraviolet light. The free electrons in the ionosphere are believed to be a product of molecular absorption of ultraviolet radiation from the Sun. —**pho·to·i·on·ize** /-ī́ ə nīz/ *vti.*

pho·to·jour·nal·ism /fṓtō júrn'l ìzzəm/ *n.* form of journalism in which photographs play a more important role than the accompanying text —**pho·to·jour·nal·ist** *n.* —**pho·to·jour·nal·is·tic** /-jurn'l ístik/ *adj.*

pho·to·ki·ne·sis /fṓtō ki néessiss, -kī-/ *n.* movement of an organism when stimulated by light [Early 20thC] —**pho·to·ki·net·ic** /fṓtō ki néttik, -kī-/ *adj.* —**pho·to·ki·net·i·cal·ly** /-kəlee/ *adv.*

pho·to·lith·o·graph /fṓtō líthə gràf/ *n.* a picture made by using photolithography

pho·to·li·thog·ra·phy /fṓtōli thóggrəfee/ *n.* **1.** LITHOGRAPHY USING PHOTOGRAPHY the process of creating lithographs using photographic methods **2.** PHOTOGRAPHIC TRANSFER OF PATTERNS FOR ETCHING a process of producing integrated circuits and printed circuit boards by photographing the circuit pattern on a photosensitive substrate and then chemically etching away the background —**pho·to·li·thog·ra·pher** *n.* —**pho·to·lith·o·graph·ic** /-lithə gráffik/ *adj.* —**pho·to·lith·o·graph·i·cal·ly** /-lithə gráffikəlee/ *adv.*

pho·to·lu·mi·nes·cence /fṓtō lóomə néss'ns/ *n.* the emission of light from a substance as a result of the absorption of electromagnetic radiation. The frequency of the light emitted is lower than that absorbed. [Late 19thC] —**pho·to·lu·mi·nes·cent** *adj.*

pho·tol·y·sis /fō tólləssiss/ *n.* the irreversible decomposition of a chemical compound as a result of the absorption of electromagnetic radiation, especially visible light [Late 20thC] —**pho·to·lyt·ic** /fōtə líttik/ *adj.* —**pho·to·lyt·i·cal·ly** /fōtə líttik'lee/ *adv.*

photom. *abbr.* photometry

pho·to·map /fótə màp/ *n.* MAP MADE FROM A PHOTOGRAPH a map produced by marking place names, grid lines, and other information on an aerial photograph ■ *vti.* **(-mapped, -map·ping, -maps)** MAKE A MAP FROM A PHOTOGRAPH to make a photomap of an area

pho·to·me·chan·i·cal /fòtō mə kánnik'l/ *adj.* relating to or used to describe a method of producing printed text or images that uses photographic methods —**pho·to·me·chan·i·cal·ly** *adv.*

pho·tom·e·ter /fō tómmətər/ *n.* an instrument for measuring the luminous intensity of light sources by comparison with a standard source [Late 18thC]

pho·tom·e·try /fō tómmətree/ *n.* **1.** MEASUREMENT OF LIGHT the measurement of the luminous intensities of visible light sources. This is sometimes expanded to include near-infrared and near-ultraviolet light. **2.** BRANCH OF PHYSICS the branch of physics concerned with the measurement of the intensity of light [Early 19thC] —**pho·to·met·ric** /fōtə méttrik/ *adj.* —**pho·to·met·ri·cal·ly** /-méttrikəlee/ *adv.* —**pho·tom·e·trist** /fō tómmətrist/ *n.*

pho·to·mi·cro·graph /fòtō mī́krə gràf/ *n.* a photograph made of something seen through a microscope —**pho·to·mi·cro·graph·ic** /fòtō mīkrə gráffik/ *adj.* —**pho·to·mi·crog·ra·phy** /fòtō mī króggrəfee/ *n.*

pho·to·mon·tage /fòtō mon taázh/ *n.* **1.** MAKING PICTURES FROM PARTS OF PHOTOGRAPHS the technique of combining a number of photographs or parts of photographs to form a composite picture, used especially in art and advertising **2.** PICTURE COMBINING PARTS OF PHOTOGRAPHS a composite picture made up of many photographs or parts of photographs, used especially in art and advertising

pho·to·mo·sa·ic /fòtō mō záy ik/ *n.* a large picture made up of many photographs, e.g., one combining aerial photographs to produce a detailed picture of an area

pho·to·mul·ti·pli·er /fòtō múlti plīr/, **pho·to·mul·ti·pli·er tube** *n.* an evacuated electronic device used to convert low-intensity electromagnetic radiation, especially visible light, into an electric current, and to amplify this current significantly

pho·to·mu·ral /fòtō myŏŏrəl/ *n.* a large picture decorating a wall, made up of one or more photographs or parts of photographs applied directly to the surface of the wall

pho·ton /fṓ tòn/ *n.* a quantum of visible light or other form of electromagnetic radiation demonstrating both particle and wave properties. A photon has neither mass nor electric charge but possesses energy and momentum. [Early 20thC] —**pho·ton·ic** /fō tónnik/ *adj.*

pho·to·neg·a·tive /fòtō néggətiv/ *adj.* **1.** PHYS SHOWING DECREASING CONDUCTIVITY AS LIGHT INCREASES used to describe a conductive material whose electrical conductivity decreases in response to increasing illumination **2.** BIOL MOVING AWAY FROM LIGHT used to describe organisms that move away from a source of light

pho·to·nu·cle·ar /fòtō nóoklee ər/ *adj.* relating to a nuclear reaction caused by the absorption of a photon, usually in the form of gamma radiation, by an atomic nucleus

pho·to-off·set *n.* a method of offset printing in which plates are created using photographic methods [Early 20thC]

pho·to op·por·tu·ni·ty, **pho·to op** *n.* an opportunity for the media to photograph a politician or other public figure doing something newsworthy, especially when this is deliberately staged to produce favorable publicity

pho·to·pe·ri·od /fòtō peéree əd/ *n.* the daily cycle of light and darkness that affects the behavior and physiological functions of organisms —**pho·to·pe·ri·od·ic** /fòtō peéree óddik/ *adj.* —**pho·to·pe·ri·od·i·cal·ly** /-óddikəlee/ *adv.*

pho·to·pe·ri·od·ism /fòtō peéree ə dìzzəm/ *n.* the influence of the daily cycle of light and darkness on the physiology and behavior of an organism [Early 20thC]

pho·to·phil·ic /fòtə fíllik/, **pho·toph·i·lous** /fō tóffiləss/ *adj.* used to describe an organism such as a plant that grows well in strong light [Early 20thC]

pho·to·pho·bi·a /fòtə fṓbee ə/ *n.* **1.** OPHTHALMOL SENSITIVITY TO LIGHT very low tolerance of the eye for light, sometimes a symptom of disease or migraine **2.** PSYCHIAT FEAR OF LIGHT an irrational fear and avoidance of light or lighted spaces

pho·to·pho·bic /fòtə fṓbik/ *adj.* **1.** OPHTHALMOL AFFECTED BY PHOTOPHOBIA relating to or having a condition in which the eye has very low tolerance to light **2.** PSYCHIAT HAVING A FEAR OF LIGHT being abnormally afraid of light **3.** BIOL GROWING WELL IN REDUCED LIGHT used to describe an organism such as a plant that grows well in reduced light

pho·to·phore /fṓtə fàwr/ *n.* a luminous light organ on many deep-sea and some nocturnal fish, squids, and shrimps [Late 19thC]

pho·to·phos·phor·y·la·tion /fòtō fosfəri láysh'n/ *n.* the process in photosynthesis that converts light energy to stored energy in plants and bacteria

pho·to·pi·a /fō tṓpee ə/ *n.* normal vision during daylight, when the activity of the cones in the retina enables the eye to perceive color [Early 20thC] —**pho·to·pic** /fō tṓpik, -tóppik/ *adj.*

pho·to·pol·y·mer /fòtō pólləmər/ *n.* a light-sensitive plastic whose physical properties change on exposure to visible or ultraviolet light

pho·to·pos·i·tive /fòtō pózzitiv/ *adj.* **1.** PHYS SHOWING INCREASING CONDUCTIVITY AS LIGHT INCREASES used to describe a conductive material whose electrical conductivity increases in response to increasing illumination **2.** BIOL MOVING TOWARD LIGHT used to describe organisms that move toward a light source

pho·to·re·al·ism /fòtō reé ə lìzzəm/ *n.* an artistic style, e.g., in painting or sculpture, that produces an accurate and detailed representation of the subject without attempting to conceal any unattractive aspects —**pho·to·re·al·ist** *adj.*, *n.* —**pho·to·re·al·is·tic** /fòtō reé ə lístik/ *adj.*

pho·to·re·cep·tion /fòtō rə sépshən/ *n.* BIOL the perception, absorption, and use of light, e.g., for vision in animals or photosynthesis in plants —**pho·to·re·cep·tive** /fòtō ri séptiv/ *adj.*

pho·to·re·cep·tor /fòtō rə séptər/ *n.* a cell or organ that responds to light. Simple ones may sense only changes in light intensity while more complex ones such as the eye may also form images of objects in the visual field.

pho·to·re·con·nais·sance /fòtō rə kónnəss'ns/ *n.* reconnaissance undertaken using cameras, usually from an aircraft or drone

pho·to·re·sist /fòtō rə zíst/ *n.* a photosensitive material that is applied to a surface, exposed to visible or ultraviolet light, and developed prior to chemical etching during the photolithographic process

pho·to·res·pi·ra·tion /fòtō respə ráysh'n/ *n.* the oxidation of carbohydrates in plants with the release of carbon dioxide during photosynthesis

pho·to·sen·si·tive /fòtō sénsitiv/ *adj.* reacting to incident electromagnetic radiation, especially visible, infrared, and ultraviolet light —**pho·to·sen·si·tiv·i·ty** /fòtō sensi tívvətee/ *n.*

pho·to·sen·si·tize /fòtō sénsi tīz/ **(-tized, -tiz·ing, -tiz·es)** *vt.* to increase the sensitivity of an organism or substance to electromagnetic radiation, especially visible light —**pho·to·sen·si·ti·za·tion** /fòtō sensiti záysh'n/ *n.* —**pho·to·sen·si·tiz·er** /fòtō sénsi tīzər/ *n.*

pho·to·sphere /fṓtə sfeer/ *n.* the intensely bright gaseous outer layer of a star, especially the Sun. Sunspots and faculae are both features of the photosphere. [Mid-17thC. The word originally meant "orb of light" and acquired its more technical meaning in the mid-19thC.] —**pho·to·spher·ic** /fòtə sféerik, -sférrik/ *adj.*

Pho·to·stat /fṓtə stàt/ *tdmk.* a trademark for a kind of photocopier [Early 20thC]

pho·to sto·ry *n.* a collection of photographs in a magazine or book, often accompanied by a short commentary, that tells a story

pho·to·syn·the·sis /fòtō sínthəssiss/ *n.* a process by which green plants and other organisms produce simple carbohydrates from carbon dioxide and hydrogen, using energy that chlorophyll or other organic cellular pigments absorb from radiant sources [Late 19thC] —**pho·to·syn·thet·ic** /fòtō sin théttik/ *adj.* —**pho·to·syn·thet·i·cal·ly** /-théttikəlee/ *adv.*

pho·to·syn·the·size /fòtō sínthə sīz/ **(-sized, -siz·ing, -siz·es)** *vti.* to produce carbohydrates and oxygen by photosynthesis [Early 20thC. Formed from PHOTOSYNTHESIS.]

pho·to·tax·is /fòtō táksiss/ *n.* movement of an organism either toward or away from a source of light [Late 19thC] —**pho·to·tac·tic** *adj.* —**pho·to·tac·ti·cal·ly** /fòtō táktikəlee/ *adv.*

pho·to·ther·a·py /fòtō thérrəpee/ *n.* the use of light of particular wavelengths, especially ultraviolet light, in the treatment of disease —**pho·to·ther·a·peu·tic** /fòtō therrə pyŏŏtik/ *adj.*

pho·to·tox·ic /fòtō tóksik/ *adj.* making the skin unusually sensitive to and subject to damage by light, e.g., by sunburn —**pho·to·tox·ic·i·ty** /fòtō tok síssətee/ *n.*

pho·to·tran·sis·tor /fòtō tran zístər/ *n.* a light-sensitive junction transistor that amplifies the base current as the illumination increases

pho·to·tro·pic /fòtə tróppik/ *adj.* used to describe organisms that can utilize light as a source of energy —**pho·to·troph** /fṓtə tròf, -trōf/ *n.*

pho·tot·ro·pism /fō tóttrə pìzzəm/ *n.* the tendency of an organism to grow toward or away from a source of light [Late 19thC. Coined from Greek *tropikos* "relating to turning," from *tropē* "turn."]

pho·tot·ro·py /fō tóttrəpee/ *n.* a property of some solids whereby they change color in relation to the wavelength of the incident electromagnetic radiation, especially visible light [Early 20thC]

pho·to·tube /fṓtō tŏŏb/ *n.* an electron tube that uses a cathode to convert visible light into electrical current at a rate proportional to the intensity of the illumination

pho·to·ty·pog·ra·phy /fòtō tī póggrəfee/ *n.* a printing process that uses photography —**pho·to·ty·po·graph·i·cal** /fòtō tīpə gráffik'l/ *adj.* —**pho·to·ty·po·graph·i·cal·ly** /-tīpə gráffikəlee/ *adv.*

pho·to·vol·ta·ic /fòtō vol táy ik, -vōl-/ *adj.* able to generate a current or voltage when exposed to visible light or other electromagnetic radiation

pho·to·vol·ta·ic cell *n.* a type of photoelectric cell that detects and measures light intensity using the potential difference that arises between unlike materials when they are exposed to electromagnetic radiation

pho·to·vol·ta·ic ef·fect *n.* the production of a potential difference across the junction of unlike materials or in a nonhomogeneous semiconductor material by the absorption of visible light or other electromagnetic radiation

phr. *abbr.* phrase

phras·al /fráyz'l/ *adj.* consisting of or belonging to a phrase [Late 19thC] —**phras·al·ly** *adv.*

phras·al verb *n.* a verb followed by an adverb, a preposition, or both, used with an idiomatic meaning that is often quite different from the literal meaning of the individual words. Examples include "put up with" meaning "tolerate" and "stand for" meaning "represent."

phrase /frayz/ *n.* **1.** GRAM GRAMMATICAL UNIT a string of words that form a grammatical unit, usually within a clause or sentence **2.** LANG FIXED EXPRESSION a string of words that are used together with an idiomatic meaning **3.** SHORT UTTERANCE a short expression **4.** LITERAT, POETRY WORDS SPOKEN AS GROUP a group of words that form a unit of meaning or rhythm in prose or poetry, often separated by punctuation in writing and by pauses in speech **5.** MUSIC MELODIC DIVISION a sequence of notes that form a unit of melody within a piece of music **6.** DANCE PART OF A CHOREOGRAPHIC PATTERN a short sequence of dance steps or movements ■ *v.* **(phrased, phras·ing, phras·es) 1.** *vt.* EXPRESS IN PARTICULAR WAY to express something with a particular pattern of words in speech or writing **2.** *vt.* SEPARATE TEXT INTO PHRASES to show clearly which groups of words belong together when reading something aloud or making a speech, usually by pausing in appropriate places or by stress and intonation **3.** *vti.* MUSIC SEP-

ARATE MUSIC INTO PHRASES to show clearly which sequences of notes belong together in a piece of music, especially when performing it [Mid-16thC. Via Latin from Greek *phrasis* "speech, way of speaking," from *phrazein* "to show, explain" (source of English *paraphrase* and *phraseology*).]

phrase book *n.* a book of useful words and phrases in a foreign language with translations for visitors to a country or region where that language is spoken

phrase·mak·er /fráyz màykər/ *n.* somebody who produces impressive phrases in speech or writing — **phrase·mak·ing** *n.*

phrase mark·er *n.* a representation of the structure of a sentence, usually in the form of a tree diagram

phra·se·o·gram /fráyzee ə gràm/ *n.* a symbol used to represent a particular phrase in shorthand

phra·se·o·graph /fráyzee ə gràf/ *n.* a phrase that is or can be represented by a symbol, usually in shorthand

phra·se·ol·o·gy /fràyzee óllәjee/ *n.* **1.** SET OF PHRASES the phrases used in a particular sphere of activity **2.** USE OF LANGUAGE the way words and phrases are chosen or used [Mid-17thC. From modern Latin *phraseologia* from, ultimately, Greek *phrasis* "speech" (see PHRASE).] —**phra·se·o·log·i·cal** /fràyzee ə lójjik'l/ *adj.* —**phra·se·ol·o·gist** /fràyzee óllәjist/ *n.*

phrase-struc·ture gram·mar *n.* a grammar that describes the structure and linear sequence of a sentence in terms of the phrases of which it is made up

phras·ing /fráyzing/ *n.* **1.** COMBINATION OF WORDS the way words are chosen and put together for a particular purpose, or the words themselves **2.** MUSIC GROUPING OF NOTES the way sequences of notes are grouped together to form units of melody in a piece of music, especially when it is played or sung

phra·try /fráytree/ (*plural* **-tries**) *n.* **1.** RELATED GROUP OF CLANS a group of clans claiming descent from a common ancestor **2.** KINSHIP GROUP a kinship group in ancient Greece [Mid-19thC. From Greek *phratria*, from *phratēr* "clansman, brother." Ultimately from an Indo-European word that is also the ancestor of English *brother*, *fraternal*, and *friar*.] —**phra·tric** *adj.*

phreak /freek/ (**phreaked, phreak·ing, phreaks**) *vi.* to use computer and telecommunications skills to illegally break into a telephone system in order to make free long-distance calls [Late 20thC. Alteration of FREAK on the model of PHONE.]

phre·at·ic /free áttik/ *adj.* **1.** OF SOIL BELOW WATER LEVEL relating to or used to describe the soil or rock below the water level, where all the pores and intergranular spaces are full of water **2.** CAUSED BY HEATED GROUNDWATER relating to an explosion caused by groundwater coming into contact with ascending magma, e.g., in a volcano [Late 19thC. Formed from Greek *phreat-*, stem of *phrear* "well, cistern." Ultimately from an Indo-European word meaning "to boil, bubble," which is also the source of English *brew* and *fervor*.]

phren. *abbr.* phrenology

phren·ic /frénnik, freénik/ *adj.* **1.** ANAT OF THE DIAPHRAGM belonging to or supplying the diaphragm **2.** OF THE MIND belonging to or associated with the mind [Early 18thC. From French *phrénique*, from Greek *phrēn* (see -PHRENIA).]

phrenol. *abbr.* phrenology

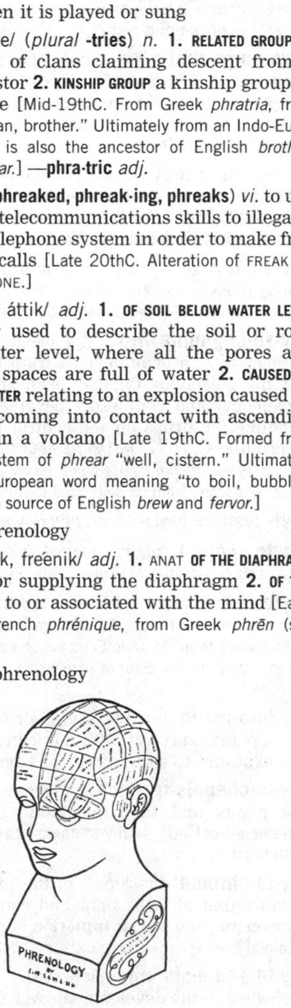

Phrenology

phre·nol·o·gy /frə nóllәjee/ *n.* the study of the bumps on the outside of the skull, based on the now discredited theory that these bumps reflect somebody's character [Early 19thC] —**phren·o·log·i·cal** /frènnə lójjik'l, freénə-/ *adj.* —**phre·nol·o·gist** /frə nóllәjist/ *n.*

Phryg·i·a /fríjjee ə/ ancient country in Asia Minor, in present-day west central Turkey. It reached the height of its importance in the 8th century B.C., and was conquered by Croesus, king of Lydia, in the 6th century B.C.

Phryg·i·an /fríjjee ən/ *n.* **1.** PEOPLES SOMEBODY FROM ANCIENT PHRYGIA somebody who was born in or was a citizen of ancient Phrygia **2.** LANG EXTINCT LANGUAGE OF ANCIENT PHRYGIA an extinct language spoken in ancient Phrygia, usually classified as belonging to the Anatolian branch of Indo-European languages — **Phryg·i·an** *adj.*

Phryg·i·an cap *n.* = **liberty cap** [*Phrygian* from the fact that the cap was worn by the ancient Phrygians]

PHS *abbr.* Public Health Service

phthal·ein /thá leèn, tháy leèn/ *n.* an organic dye obtained by reacting phthalic anhydride with a phenol [Late 19thC. Formed from PHTHALIC ACID.]

phthal·ic ac·id /thàllik-/ *n.* one of three isomers obtained by the oxidation of benzene derivatives and used in the manufacture of dyes, perfumes, pharmaceuticals, and synthetic fibers. Formula: $C_6H_4(CO_2H)_2$. [*Phthalic*, formed from a shortening of NAPHTHALENE]

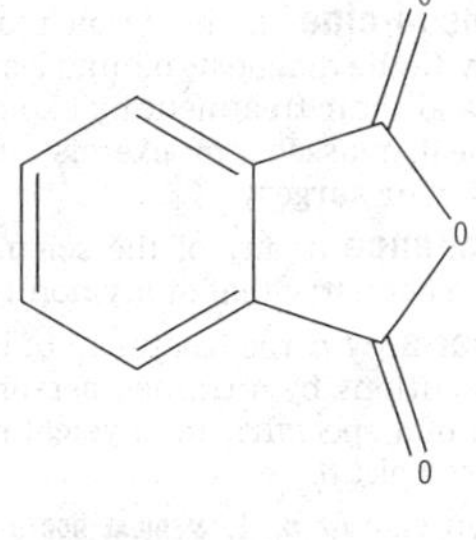
Phthalic anhydride

phthal·ic an·hy·dride *n.* a white crystalline organic compound derived from naphthalene and used in the manufacture of dyes, insecticides, and plastics. Formula: $C_6H_4(CO)_2O$.

phthal·o·cy·a·nine /thàllō sí ə neèn/ *n.* **1.** BRIGHT GREENISH-BLUE PIGMENT a bright greenish-blue crystalline compound derived from phthalic anhydride and used as a pigment, coating for CD-ROMs, and as an anti-cancer agent. Formula: $(C_6H_4C_2N)_4N_4H_2$. **2.** BLUE OR GREEN PIGMENTS a blue or green pigment developed as a metal-substituted form of phthalocyanine and used in enamels, plastics, printing inks, wallpaper, and linoleum

phthi·ri·a·sis /thi rí əssiss, thī-/ *n.* an infestation of the pubic hair of human beings with lice whose bite can irritate the skin [Late 16thC. Via Latin from Greek *phtheiriasis*, from *phtheirian* "to be infested with lice," from *phtheir* "louse."]

phthis·ic /tízzik, thízz-/ *n.* = **phthisis** ■ *adj.* **phthis·ic, phthis·i·cal** RELATING TO PHTHISIS relating to or having phthisis [14thC. Via Old French *tisike*, later *ptisique* from, ultimately, Greek *phthisikos* "consumptive," from *phthisis* (see PHTHISIS).]

phthi·sis /thíssiss, tíss-/ *n.* **1.** WASTING DISEASE any disease or condition marked by wasting of the body **2.** LUNG DISEASE any of several diseases of the respiratory system, especially asthma or tuberculosis (*archaic*) [Mid-16thC. Via Latin from Greek *phthisis* "consumption," from *phthinein* "to waste away."]

phyco- *prefix.* relating to seaweed or algae [From Greek *phukos* "seaweed"]

phy·co·cy·a·nin /fìkō sí ənin/ *n.* a protein pigment in blue-green algae

phy·co·er·y·thrin /fìkō érrithrin/ *n.* a red protein pigment in red algae

phy·col·o·gy /fī kóllәjee/ *n.* = **algology** — **phy·co·log·i·cal** /fìkə lójjik'l/ *adj.* —**phy·col·o·gist** /fī kóllәjist/ *n.*

phy·co·my·cete /fìkō mí seèt, -mī seèt/ *n.* a mold resembling algae. Class: Phycomycetes. [Mid-20thC. Ultimately from Greek *phukos* "seaweed" + *mukētes*, plural of *mukēs* "fungus," from its supposed resemblance to algae.] —**phy·co·my·ce·tous** /fìkō mī seètəss/ *adj.*

Phyfe /fīf/, **Duncan** (1768–1854) Scottish-born U.S. furniture designer. His neoclassical approach helped to define the federal style in the United States.

phyl- *prefix.* = **phylo-** (*used before vowels*)

phy·la plural of **phylum**

AKG London
Phylactery

phy·lac·ter·y /fi láktəree/ (*plural* **-ies**) *n.* **1.** JUDAISM JEWISH AID TO PRAYER either of two small leather boxes containing slips of paper with scriptures written on them, traditionally worn by Jewish men during morning weekday prayers as reminders of their religious duties (*often used in the plural*) ◊ **tefillin 2.** REMINDER a reminder of something important **3.** AMULET something worn because it is believed to have special powers, e.g., the power to keep away evil spirits (*archaic*) [14thC. Via Latin *phylacterium* from Greek *phulaktērion* "amulet," from *phulaktēr* "guard," from *phulassein* "to guard."]

phy·le /fīlee/ (*plural* **-lae** /-lee/) *n.* any one of a number of tribes or clans into which some peoples of ancient Greece were divided. The phylae formed political and administrative units within the large city-states. [Mid-19thC. From Greek *phulē* "tribe."] —**phy·lic** *adj.*

phy·let·ic /fī léttik/ *adj.* relating to the hereditary descent of a species or its development over time [Late 19thC. From Greek *phuletikos*, from *phulē* "tribe."] —**phy·let·i·cal·ly** *adv.*

phyll- *prefix.* = **phyllo-** (*used before vowels*)

-phyll *suffix.* leaf ○ *microphyll* [From Greek *phyllon* (see PHYLLO-)] —**-phyllous** *suffix.*

phyl·lid /fíllid/ *n.* a moss or liverwort leaf

phyl·lite /feè līt/ *n.* a fine-grained metamorphic rock with a distinctive shiny surface, containing large quantities of mica and resembling slate or schist [Early 19thC. Coined from Greek *phullon* "leaf" (see PHYLLO-) + -ITE.] —**phyl·lit·ic** /fi líttik/ *adj.*

phyl·lo /feèlō/, **phyl·lo pas·try** *n.* very thin sheets of pastry dough used to make papery, crisp small pastries or large dishes, used especially in Greek cooking [Mid-20thC. Via modern Greek, "leaf, sheet," from Greek *phullon* "leaf" (see PHYLLO-).]

phyllo- *prefix.* leaf ○ *phyllotaxis* [From Greek *phullon*. Ultimately from an Indo-European word that is also the ancestor of English *foliage*.]

phyl·lo·clade /fíllə klàyd/, **phyl·lo·clad** /fíllə klàd/ *n.* = **cladophyll** [Mid-19thC. From modern Latin, from Greek *phullon* "leaf" (see PHYLLO-) + *klados* "shoot."] — **phyl·lo·cla·dous** /fi lóklədəss/ *adj.*

phyl·lode /fí lōd/, **phyl·lo·di·um** /fi lōdee əm/ (*plural* **-a** /-ə/) *n.* a flat leaf stalk that functions as a leaf in certain plants, such as the acacia [Mid-19thC. From modern Latin *phyllodium*, from Greek *phullōdēs* "leaflike," from *phullon* (see PHYLLO-).] —**phyl·lo·di·al** *adj.*

phyl·loid /fí lòyd/ *adj.* like a leaf in shape or function [Mid-19thC. From modern Latin *phylloides*, from Greek *phullon* (see -PHYLL).]

phyl·loph·a·gous /fi lóffəgəss/ *adj.* used to describe an animal that eats leaves

phyl·lo·qui·none /fillō kwi nōn, -kwí nōn/ *n.* = **vitamin K**[1] [Mid-20thC. Coined from PHYLLO- + QUINONE, on the model of German *Phyllochinon*.]

phyl·lo·tax·y /fíllə tàksee/ (*plural* **-ies**), **phyl·lo·tax·is** /fìllə táksiss/ (*plural* **-es** /-seez/) *n.* **1.** POSITIONS OF PLANT'S LEAVES the way the leaves on a particular plant are arranged in relation to one another **2.** STUDY OF LEAF POSITIONING the study of the factors that determine the growth patterns and arrangement of plant leaves — **phyl·lo·tac·tic** *adj.*

phyl·lox·e·ra /fìlək séerə, fi lóksərə/ (*plural* **-ra** *or* **-ras** *or* **-rae** /-ree/) *n.* an aphid that is a major pest in wine-producing areas. Latin name: *Viteus vitifolii.* [Mid-19thC. From modern Latin, genus name, from PHYLLO- + Greek *xeros* "dry"; from the insect's effect on leaves.]

phylo- *prefix.* race, kind, tribe, phylum ○ *phylogeny* [From Greek *phulon* (see PHYLUM)]

phy·log·e·ny /fī lójjənee/ (*plural* **-nies**), **phy·lo·gen·e·sis** /fīlō jénnəsiss/ (*plural* **-ses** /-jénnə seez/) *n.* the development over time of a species, genus, or group, as contrasted with the development of an individual (**ontogeny**) —**phy·lo·ge·net·ic** /-jə néttik/ *adj.* —**phy·lo·ge·net·i·cal·ly** /-jə néttikəlee/ *adv.* —**phy·lo·ge·net·ics** /-jə néttiks/ *n.* —**phy·lo·gen·ic** /fīlō jénnik/ *adj.* —**phy·lo·gen·i·cal·ly** /-kəlee/ *adv.*

phy·lum /fīləm/ (*plural* **-la** /fīlə/) *n.* **1.** ZOOL MAJOR TAXONOMIC GROUP IN BIOLOGICAL CLASSIFICATION a major taxonomic group into which animals are divided, made up of several classes. The corresponding taxonomic group for plants and fungi is the division. **2.** LANG GROUP OF LANGUAGES a large group of languages or language stocks thought to be historically related, e.g., Afro-Asiatic or Indo-European [Late 19thC. Via modern Latin from Greek *phulon* "race."]

phys. *abbr.* **1.** physiological **2.** physiology **3.** physical **4.** physician **5.** physicist **6.** physics

phys·al·is /físsəliss, físsə-, fī sálliss/ (*plural* **-is·es** *or* **-es** /-eez/) *n.* = **Cape gooseberry** [Early 19thC. Via modern Latin, genus name, from Greek *phusallis* "bladder," with reference to the inflated calyx.]

phys. ed. *abbr.* physical education

physi- *prefix.* = **physio-** (*used before vowels*)

phys·i·at·rics /fìzzee áttriks/ *n.* MED (*takes a singular verb*) **1.** = **physical medicine 2.** = **physical therapy** [Mid-19thC. Coined from Greek *phusis* "nature" (see PHYSICS) + *iatrikos* "medical."] —**phys·i·at·ric** *adj.* —**phys·i·at·rist** /fìzzee áttrist/ *n.*

phys·ic /fízzik/ *n.* **1.** MED PROFESSION OF MEDICINE medicine or healing as an art or profession (*archaic*) **2.** MED A MEDICINE a medicine, especially one that purges the bowels (*archaic*) **3.** PICK-ME-UP something that lifts the spirits or energizes **4.** PHYS PHYSICS physics (*archaic*) ■ *vt.* (**-icked, -ick·ing, -ics**) (*archaic*) **1.** PURGE SOMETHING to purge something such as the bowels **2.** TREAT SOMEBODY OR SOMETHING to treat somebody or something with a medicine or cure [13thC. Directly or via Old French *fisique* from Latin *physica* (see PHYSICS). The original meaning was "knowledge of the natural world," which survives in PHYSICS.]

phys·i·cal /fízzik'l/ *adj.* **1.** OF THE BODY relating to the body, rather than with the mind, the soul, or the feelings **2.** REAL AND TOUCHABLE existing in the real material world, rather than as an idea or notion, and able to be touched and seen **3.** NEEDING BODILY STRENGTH involving or needing a lot of bodily strength or energy **4.** WITH BODILY CONTACT involving a lot of bodily contact or aggression ○ *Some of the players were a little too physical.* **5.** INVOLVING TOUCHING tending to touch people or involving touching, especially in an affectionate or sexual way (*informal*) **6.** SCI NOT SOCIAL OR BIOLOGICAL used to describe sciences such as physics and chemistry that deal with nonliving things such as energy and matter ○ *the physical sciences* ■ *n.* MED PHYSICAL EXAMINATION a physical examination (*informal*) —**phys·i·cal·i·ty** /fìzzi kálləṭee/ *n.* —**phys·i·cal·ness** /fízzik'lnəss/ *n.*

phys·i·cal an·thro·pol·o·gy *n.* the branch of anthropology that studies the development over time of human physical characteristics and the differences in appearance among the peoples of the world, as distinct from cultural differences

phys·i·cal chal·lenge *n.* **1.** RESTRICTED CAPABILITY TO PERFORM PARTICULAR ACTIVITIES an inability to perform some or all of the tasks of daily life **2.** MEDICAL CONDITION RESTRICTING ACTIVITIES a medically diagnosed condition that makes it difficult to engage in the activities of daily life

phys·i·cal chem·is·try *n.* the branch of chemistry that studies the physical and thermodynamic properties of substances in relation to their structures and chemical reactions

phys·i·cal ed·u·ca·tion *n.* gymnastics, athletics, team sports, and other forms of physical exercise taught to children in school

phys·i·cal ex·am·i·na·tion, **phys·i·cal** *n.* a doctor's general examination to determine somebody's state of physical health and fitness, sometimes as a requirement for a specific job or activity

phys·i·cal ge·og·ra·phy *n.* the branch of geography that studies the natural features of the Earth's surface as well as their formation

phys·i·cal·ism /fízzik'l ìzzəm/ *n.* in philosophy, a form of materialism that explains the phenomena of reality, including perceptual and intellectual processes, in terms of the physical —**phys·i·cal·ist** *n.*, *adj.* —**phys·i·cal·is·tic** /fìzzik'l ístik/ *adj.*

phys·i·cal·ize /fízzik'l ìz/ (**-ized, -iz·ing, -izes**) *vt.* **1.** SHOW EMOTION USING THE BODY to express or exhibit something such as emotion with the body **2.** REPRESENT SOMETHING ABSTRACT IN PHYSICAL TERMS to represent something abstract in the form of a physical or concrete thing

phys·i·cal·ly /fízzik'lee/ *adv.* **1.** IN THE REAL WORLD in terms of what is real or what exists in the material world, as opposed to what is theoretical or exists only in the mind ○ *physically impossible* **2.** OF THE BODY relating to somebody's body or appearance ○ *physically unattractive*

phys·i·cal·ly chal·lenged *adj.* UNABLE TO PERFOM PARTICULAR ACTIVITIES used to describe somebody with a condition that makes it difficult to perform some or all the basic tasks of daily life ■ *npl.* PHYSICALLY CHALLENGED PEOPLE people who are physically challenged

phys·i·cal med·i·cine *n.* the branch of medicine concerned with the diagnosis of injuries or physical conditions and their treatment by external means, including heat, massage, or exercise, rather than by medication or surgery

phys·i·cal sci·ence *n.* any of the sciences such as physics and chemistry that study nonliving things

phys·i·cal ther·a·py *n.* the treatment of injuries and physical conditions by a trained person under the supervision of a specialist in physical medicine —**phys·i·cal ther·a·pist** *n.*

phy·si·cian /fi zísh'n/ *n.* **1.** MEDICAL DOCTOR somebody qualified to practice medicine **2.** DOCTOR USING NONSURGICAL METHODS a doctor who diagnoses and treats diseases and injuries using methods other than surgery [13thC. From Old French *fisicien*, from *fisique* (see PHYSIC).]

phy·si·cian-as·sist·ed su·i·cide *n.* the act of somebody with an incurable disease committing suicide with the help of a physician. Physician-assisted suicide is illegal in most countries.

phy·si·cian's as·sis·tant, **phy·si·cian as·sis·tant** *n.* somebody trained and authorized to carry out some medical duties, under a doctor's supervision, e.g., taking a patient's medical history

phys·i·cist /fízzissist/ *n.* a scientist who specializes in physics [Mid-19thC. Coined from PHYSICS + -IST.]

phys·i·co·chem·i·cal /fìzzikō kémmik'l/ *adj.* **1.** OF PHYSICS AND CHEMISTRY relating to both physical and chemical characteristics **2.** OF PHYSICAL CHEMISTRY relating to physical chemistry [Mid-17thC. Coined from Greek *physikos* (see PHYSICS) + CHEMICAL.] —**phys·i·co·chem·i·cal·ly** *adv.*

phys·ics /fízziks/ *n.* PHYS STUDY OF PHYSICAL FORCES AND QUALITIES the scientific study of matter, energy, force, and motion, and the way they relate to each other. Physics traditionally incorporates mechanics, electromagnetism, optics, and thermodynamics and now includes modern disciplines such as quantum mechanics, relativity, and nuclear physics. (*takes a singular verb*) ■ *npl.* PHYSICAL ASPECTS the physical processes, interactions, qualities, properties or behavior of something [15thC. Formed from PHYSIC; translation of Latin *physica* (plural), from Greek *phusika*, plural of *phusikos* "of nature," from *phusis* "nature," from *phuein* "to make grow."]

phy·si·o /fízzee ō/ (*plural* **-os**) *n. U.K.* a physical therapist (*informal*) [Mid-20thC. Shortening of PHYSIOTHERAPY.]

physio- *prefix.* physical ○ *physiotherapy* [From Greek *phusis* "nature"; related to *phuein* "to make grow" (see PHYTO-)]

phys·i·og·no·my /fìzzee ógnəmee/ (*plural* **-mies**) *n.* **1.** FACIAL FEATURES the features of somebody's face, especially when they are used as indicators of that person's character or temperament **2.** JUDGMENT OF CHARACTER FROM FACIAL FEATURES the use of facial features to judge somebody's character or temperament **3.** CHARACTER OR APPEARANCE OF SOMETHING the character or outward appearance of something, e.g., the physical features of a landscape [13thC. Via Old French from, ultimately, Greek *phusiognōmonia* "judging of somebody's character by his or her features," from *phusis* "nature, character" (see PHYSICS) + *gnomon* "judge" (see GNOMON).] —**phys·i·og·nom·ic** /fìzzee ə nómmik/ *adj.* —**phys·i·og·nom·i·cal·ly** /-kəlee/ *adv.* —**phys·i·og·no·mist** /fìzzee ónnəmist, -ógnə-/ *n.*

phys·i·og·ra·phy /fìzzee óggrəfee/ *n.* physical geography (*dated*) —**phys·i·og·ra·pher** *n.* —**phys·i·o·graph·ic** /fìzzee ə gráffik/ *adj.* —**phys·i·o·graph·i·cal·ly** *adv.*

physiol. *abbr.* **1.** physiological **2.** physiology

phys·i·o·log·i·cal /fìzzee ə lójjik'l/, **phys·i·o·log·ic** *adj.* **1.** OF ORGANISM'S FUNCTION relating to the way that living things function, rather than to their shape or structure **2.** OF PHYSIOLOGY relating to physiology —**phys·i·o·log·i·cal·ly** *adv.*

phys·i·o·log·i·cal psy·chol·o·gy *n.* a branch of psychology that studies the interactions between physical or chemical processes in the body and mental states or behavior

phys·i·o·log·i·cal sa·line *n.* an aqueous salt solution used to keep cells alive and to administer medication intravenously. The solution is prepared so that it exerts the same osmotic pressure as that of fluids inside the cells.

phys·i·ol·o·gy /fìzzee óllәjee/ *n.* **1.** STUDY OF THE FUNCTIONING OF LIVING THINGS the branch of biology that deals with the internal workings of living things, including such functions as metabolism, respiration, and reproduction, rather than with their shape or structure **2.** BODY'S INTERNAL PROCESSES the way a particular body or organism works [Mid-16thC. Via French *physiologie* or Latin *physiologia* from Greek *phusiologia*, from *phusis* "nature" (see PHYSICS) + *-logia* "-logy."] —**phys·i·ol·o·gist** *n.*

phys·i·o·pa·thol·o·gy /fìzzee ōpə thóllәjee/ *n.* the branch of medicine that studies how disease disrupts normal body functions —**phys·i·o·path·o·log·ic** /fìzzee ō pathə lójjik/ *adj.* —**phys·i·o·pa·thol·o·gist** /fìzzee ōpə thóllәjist/ *n.*

phys·i·o·ther·a·py /fìzzee ō thérrəpee/ *n.* = **physical therapy** —**phys·i·o·ther·a·peu·tic** /fìzzee ō therrə pyóotik/ *adj.* —**phys·i·o·ther·a·peu·ti·cal·ly** /-kəlee/ *adv.* —**phys·i·o·ther·a·pist** /fìzzee ō thérrəpist/ *n.*

phy·sique /fi zeék/ *n.* the shape and size of somebody's body [Early 19thC. From French, from *physique* "physical," from, ultimately, Greek *phusikos* (see PHYSICS).]

phy·so·stig·mine /fìssō stíg meen/, **phy·so·stig·min** /-stígmin/ *n.* a drug derived from the dried leaves of the poisonous Calabar bean and used to treat glaucoma and counteract adverse effects of anticholinergic drugs on the central nervous system. Formula: $C_{15}H_{21}N_3O_2$. [Mid-19thC. Coined from modern Latin *Physostigma*, genus name (from Greek *phusa* "bladder" + STIGMA, from its distended form) + -INE.]

phyt- *prefix.* = **phyto-** (*used before vowels*)

-phyte *suffix.* **1.** plant ○ *saprophyte* **2.** pathological growth ○ *osteophyte* [From Greek *phuton* (see PHYTO-)]

phyto- *prefix.* plant ○ *phytohormone* [Via modern Latin from, ultimately, Greek *phuton*, from *phuein* "to make grow." Ultimately from an Indo-European base meaning "to be" that is also the ancestor of English *be*, *build*, *physical*, and *future*.]

phy·to·a·lex·in /fìtō ə léksin/ *n.* a chemical produced by a plant to protect it from infection by a pathogen or exposure to some agents of stress

phy·to·chem·is·try /fìtə kémmistree/ *n.* the chemistry of plants and their metabolic processes —**phy·to·chem·i·cal** *adj.* —**phy·to·chem·i·cal·ly** *adv.* —**phy·to·chem·ist** *n.*

phy·to·chrome /fìtə krōm/ *n.* the pigment in green plants that absorbs light and controls dormancy, flowering, and the germination of seeds [Late 19thC. Coined from PHYTO- + Greek *khrōma* "color."]

phy·to·gen·e·sis /fìtə jénnəsiss/, **phy·tog·e·ny** /fī tójjənee/ *n.* the development over time of plants —**phy·to·ge·net·ic** /fìtəjə néttik/ *adj.* —**phy·to·ge·net·i·cal·ly** /-kəlee/ *adv.*

phy·to·gen·ic /fìtə jénnik/, **phy·tog·e·nous** /fī tójjənəss/ *adj.* used to describe substances, such as coal, that are formed from plants

phy·to·ge·ny *n.* = **phytogenesis**

phy·to·ge·og·ra·phy /fìtəjee óggrəfee/ *n.* the study of the geographical distribution of plants —**phy·to·ge·og·ra·pher** *n.* —**phy·to·ge·o·graph·ic** /fìtəjee ə gráffik/ *adj.* —**phy·to·ge·o·graph·i·cal·ly** /-kəlee/ *adv.*

phy·tog·ra·phy /fī tóggrəfee/ *n.* the branch of botany concerned with the accurate description of plants —**phy·to·graph·ic** /fìtə gráffik/ *adj.*

phy·to·hor·mone /fítə háwr mōn/ *n.* = **plant hormone**

phy·tol /fī tàwl/ *n.* a liquid alcohol found in plants and used to synthesize vitamins E and K. Formula: $C_{20}H_{40}O$.

phy·tol·o·gy /fī tólləjee/ *n.* botany (*archaic*)

phy·ton /fī tòn/ *n.* the smallest part of a plant, usually a leaf and its stem, that can grow when it has been cut from the parent plant [Mid-19thC. From French, formed from Greek *phuton* (see -PHYTE) + *-on* "-on."]

phy·to·path·o·gen /fìtō páthəjən/ *n.* something that causes disease in plants

phy·to·pa·thol·o·gy /fìtōpə thólləjee/ *n.* the branch of botany that studies plant diseases —**phy·to·path·o·log·i·cal** /fìtō pathə lójjik/ *adj.* —**phy·to·path·o·log·i·cal·ly** /-kəlee/ *adv.* —**phy·to·pa·thol·o·gist** /fìtōpə thólləjist/ *n.*

phy·toph·a·gous /fī tóffəgəss/ *adj.* used to describe animals, especially insects, that feed on plants —**phy·to·pha·gy** /fī tóffəjee/ *n.*

phy·to·plank·ton /fìtō plánktən/ *n.* very small free-floating aquatic plants such as one-celled algae, found in plankton. ◊ **zooplankton** —**phy·to·plank·ton·ic** /fìtō plank tónnik/ *adj.*

phy·to·re·me·di·a·tion /fìtō ri méedee áysh'n/ *n.* the process of decontaminating soil by using plants to absorb heavy metals or other pollutants

phy·to·tox·ic /fìtō tóksik/ *adj.* poisonous to plants [Mid-20thC] —**phy·to·tox·ic·i·ty** /fìtō tok síssətee/ *n.*

phy·to·tox·in /fìtō tóksin/ *n.* **1. POISON MADE BY PLANTS** a poisonous substance obtained from plants such as the drug digitalis **2. SOMETHING POISONOUS TO PLANTS** something that is poisonous to plants

phy·to·tron /fítə tròn/ *n.* a place in which plants can be grown under controlled conditions, e.g., in a greenhouse

pi[1] /pī/ *n.* **1. 16TH LETTER OF THE GREEK ALPHABET** the 16th letter of the Greek alphabet, represented in the English alphabet as "p." ◆ **alphabet 2.** MATH **MATHEMATICAL CONSTANT** a number approximately equal to 3.14159 that is the ratio of the circumference of a circle divided by its diameter and is represented by the symbol π [Early 19thC. From Greek. In the sense "number," representing the first letter of Greek *periphereia* "circumference" or of its English equivalent *periphery*.]

pi[2] /pī/, **pie** *n.* **1.** PRINTING **JUMBLE OF PRINTER'S TYPE** a pile of printer's type that has been mixed up together **2. DISORDERED MIXTURE** a disorganized combination of things ■ *v.* (**pied, pi·ing, pies; pied, pie·ing, pies**) **1.** *vt.* PRINTING **JUMBLE TYPE** to mix printer's type up together **2.** *vti.* **MAKE OR BECOME JUMBLED** to mix things up in a confusing way or to become mixed up or confused [Mid-17thC. Origin uncertain: perhaps a translation of French *pâté* "pie, patty," with reference to the jumbled contents of a pie.]

PI *abbr.* **1.** personal injury **2.** politically incorrect **3.** private investigator

pi·a *n.* ANAT = **pia mater** —**pi·al** *adj.*

PIA *abbr.* COMPUT peripheral interface adaptor

Pia·cen·za /pyaa chént saa/ capital city of Piacenza Province, Emilia-Romagna Region, northern Italy. Population: 102,161 (1992).

pi·ac·u·lar /pī ákyələr/ *adj.* RELIG **1. ATONING FOR SIN** done or offered in order to make up for a sin or sacrilegious action **2. SINFUL** wicked or sinful and requiring the offender or sinner to atone [Early 17thC. From Latin *piacularis*, from *piaculum* "atonement," from *piare* "to appease."]

Pi·af /pée af/, **Édith** (1915–63) French singer. Her expressive performance of songs such as "Je ne regrette rien" and "La Vie en rose" led to international fame. Real name **Edith Giovanna Gassion**

piaffe /pee áf/ *n.* **TROTTING IN PLACE** a dressage movement performed by a horse in which it trots in one place and raises its legs very high ■ *vi.* (**piaffed, piaf·fing, piaffes**) **PERFORM A PIAFFE** to perform a piaffe [Mid-18thC. From French, formed from *piaffer* "to strut."]

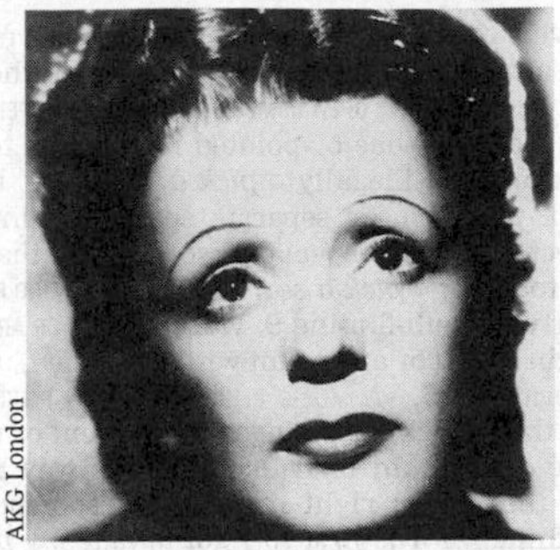

AKG London

Edith Piaf

Pia·get /pee ázh ay/, **Jean** (1896–1980) Swiss psychologist. His pioneering study of the intellectual development in children has had a major impact in psychology and education.

pi·a ma·ter /pì ə máytər/ *n.* the innermost and most delicate of the three membranes (**meninges**) that surround the brain and the spinal cord [14thC. From Latin, literally "tender mother," translated from Arabic *al-'umm ar-rakika*.]

pi·an·ism /peé ə nìzzəm/ *n.* piano-playing skill or technique —**pi·a·nis·tic** /pee ə nístik/ *adj.*

pi·a·nis·si·mo /pee ə níssi mò/ *adv.* **VERY SOFTLY** very softly and quietly (*used as a musical direction*) ■ *n.* (*plural* **-mos** *or* **-mi** /pee ə níssimee/) **SOFTLY PLAYED MUSICAL PART** a part of a musical composition that is played very softly [Early 18thC. From Italian, "very quiet," from *piano* (see PIANO[2]).] —**pi·a·nis·si·mo** *adj.*

pi·an·ist /peé ənist, pee ánnist/ *n.* somebody who plays the piano

pi·an·o[1] /pee ánnō/ *n.* (*plural* **-os**) **MUSICAL INSTRUMENT WITH KEYBOARD** a large musical instrument consisting of a wooden case with wires stretched inside it and a row of white and black keys. It is played by pressing the keys, each of which is attached to a small hammer that strikes one of the strings and makes a sound. ◊ **grand piano, upright piano** ■ *adj.* **1. OF OR FOR PIANO** relating to or played on a piano ○ *a piano sonata* **2. OF OR FOR ENSEMBLE CONTAINING PIANIST** used to describe a small musical ensemble that contains a pianist, and usually a violinist and cellist, or a piece of music written for such an ensemble ○ *a piano trio* [Early 19thC. From Italian, shortening of *pianoforte* PIANOFORTE.]

pi·a·no[2] /pee ánnō/ *adv.* **SOFTLY** softly and quietly (*used as a musical direction*) ■ *n.* (*plural* **-nos** *or* **-ni** /-nee/) **SOFTLY PLAYED MUSICAL PART** a part of a musical composition that is played softly [Late 17thC. Via Italian from Latin *planus* "soft, flat."] —**pi·a·no** *adj.*

pi·an·o ac·cor·di·on *n.* an accordion with a keyboard on one side to play the notes of the melody on —**pi·an·o ac·cor·di·on·ist** *n.*

pi·an·o bar *n.* a bar, or a lounge in a hotel, where a pianist plays to entertain customers or provide background music

pi·an·o·for·te /pee ànnō fáwr tày/ (*plural* **-tes**) *n.* a piano (*formal*) [Mid-18thC. From Italian, from *gravecembalo col piano e forte* "harpsichord with soft and loud," referring to the instrument's variation in tone compared with a standard harpsichord.]

pi·an·o hinge *n.* a long narrow hinge that has a pin running the length of its joint

Pi·an·o·la /peè ə nṓlə/ *tdmk.* a trademark for a type of player piano

pi·an·o no·bi·le /pyaánō nṓbi lày/ *n.* the second floor of a large residence or public building (*formal*) [From Italian, literally "noble floor," because it is high above the ground and provides a view]

pi·an·o play·er *n.* **1. SOMEBODY WHO PLAYS PIANO** somebody who plays the piano, especially somebody who plays popular or jazz music **2. MECHANICAL DEVICE** a mechanical device that plays a piano automatically

pi·an·o roll *n.* a roll of paper with patterns of perforations whose positions determine the sequence of notes played on a player piano

pi·an·o stool *n.* an adjustable stool for a pianist to sit on

pi·as·sa·va /pee ə saávə/, **pi·as·sa·ba** /pee ə saábə, pee ə saávə/ *n.* **1.** TREES **FIBER-PRODUCING PALM TREE** a Brazilian palm tree that produces a coarse fiber. Latin name: *Attalea funifera* and *Leopoldinia piassaba*. **2.** INDUST **COARSE FIBER** the coarse fiber obtained from the piassava tree, used to make rope, brooms, and brushes [Mid-19thC. Via Portuguese from Tupi *piaçába*.]

pi·as·tre /pee ástər/, **pi·as·ter** *n.* **1. SUBUNIT OF MIDDLE EASTERN CURRENCY** a subunit of currency in Egypt, Lebanon, Sudan, and Syria, 100 of which are worth one pound **2. COIN WORTH ONE PIASTRE** a coin worth one piastre [Late 16thC. Via French from Italian *piastra (d'argento)* "(silver) plate," from Latin *emplastrum* (see PLASTER).]

Pi·ave /pyaá ve/ river in northeastern Italy. Length: 137 mi./220 km.

pi·az·za /pee aátsə/ (*plural* **-zas**) *n.* **1.** (*plural* **-ze**) **ITALIAN PUBLIC SQUARE** a large open square, especially one in an Italian town **2. OPEN-SIDED PASSAGEWAY** a covered passageway that has arches on one or both sides and is usually attached to a building, e.g., along the inner walls of a courtyard or quadrangle **3. PORCH** a veranda or porch, especially one attached to a house (*regional dated*) [Late 16thC. Via Italian from Latin *platea* "open space" (see PLACE).]

WORD KEY: REGIONAL NOTE

Used of a porch, ***piazza*** is an old-fashioned term with currency in the Northeastern and Southeastern states, but not in the Midland territory. In the Carolinas, the incidence of this term with *earthworm* and *press peach* defines the northern limits of Southern speech.

pi·broch /peé bròk/ *n.* a piece of music written for the Scottish Highland bagpipes, consisting of a theme and variations, often with a mournful tone [Early 18thC. From Gaelic *piobaireachd* "the art of piping," from, ultimately, English *pipe*.]

pic /pik/ (*plural* **pics** *or* **pix** /piks/) *n.* a picture, especially a photograph, illustration, or movie (*informal*) [Late 19thC. Shortening of PICTURE.]

pi·ca[1] /píkə/ *n.* **1. MEASURE OF TYPE SIZE** a unit of measurement for printing type, equal to 12 points or 0.166 in./0.422 cm **2. TYPOGRAPHIC MEASURE** a linear measure used in typography, equal to about 0.166 in./0.422 cm [15thC. From Anglo-Latin, "church almanac"; from the resemblance to the handwriting in such books.]

pi·ca[2] /píkə/ *n.* indiscriminate craving for and eating of substances such as paint chips, clay, plaster, or dirt. It is found mostly among children and pregnant women and may result from mineral deficiencies. [Mid-16thC. From Latin, "magpie," as a literal translation of Greek *kissa, kitta* "magpie, false appetite"; from the magpie's indiscriminate feeding habits.]

pic·a·dor /píkə dàwr/ *n.* a bullfighter on horseback, who attacks the bull with a spear early in the fight, making it easier for the main bullfighter (**matador**) to kill with his sword [Late 18thC. From Spanish, formed from *picar* "to prick, pierce."]

pi·ca em *n.* = **pica**[1] *n.* 1

pi·can·te /pi kaán tày/ *adj.* spicy, especially in being served with a sauce that contains tomatoes, onions, peppers, vinegar, and spices [From Italian *piccante*, from the present participle of *piccare* "to sting"]

pi·ca·ra /píkərə/ *n.* (*archaic literary*) **1. DISHONEST WOMAN** a woman who is a cheat or swindler **2. WOMAN PIRATE** a woman pirate [Mid-20thC. From Spanish, feminine form of *picaro* PICARO.]

Pic·ar·dy third /píkərdee-/ *n.* a major third that appears in the final chord of some Baroque works that are predominantly in a minor key [Translation of *tierce de Picardy*; from its use in the church music of *Picardy*, France]

pic·a·resque /pìkə résk/ *adj.* **1. TYPICAL OF ROGUES** relating to or typical of rogues or scoundrels **2.** LITERAT **HAVING ROGUE AS HERO** belonging to or characteristic of a type of prose fiction that features the adventures of a roguish hero and usually has a simple plot divided into separate episodes ■ *n.* LITERAT **PICARESQUE FICTION** a type of prose fiction featuring the adventures of a roguish hero [Early 19thC. Via French from Spanish *picaresco*, from *picaro* "rogue," from, ultimately, assumed Vulgar Latin *piccare* "to prick, pierce," possible source of English *pick*.]

pi·ca·ro /píkərō/ (*plural* **-ros**) *n.* (*archaic literary*) **1. ROGUE** a cheat, swindler, or rogue **2. PIRATE** a pirate or adventurer [Early 17thC. From Spanish (see PICARESQUE).]

pic·a·roon /pìkə roón/ *n.* (*archaic literary*) **1. ROGUE** a rogue **2. PIRATE** a pirate **3. PIRATE SHIP** a pirate ship ■ *vi.* (**-rooned, -roon·ing, -roons**) **LIVE ADVENTUROUS LIFE** to live the adventurous life of a pirate, thief, swindler, or scoundrel (*archaic literary*) [Early 17thC. From Spanish *picaron*, literally "great rogue," from *picaro* (see PICARESQUE).]

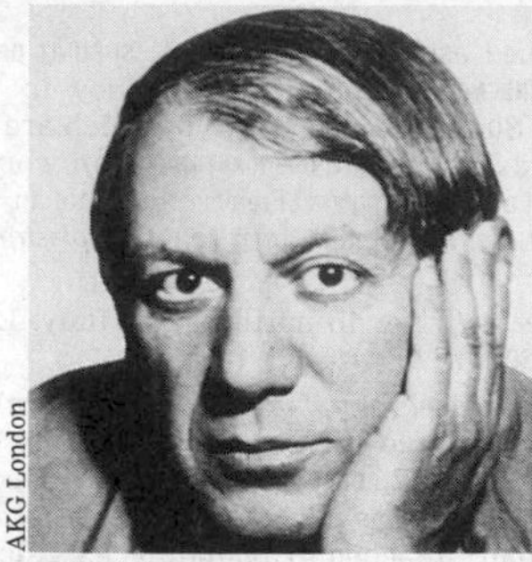

Pablo Picasso: Photographed in 1933 by Man Ray

Pi·cas·so /pi kaássō, -kaássō/, **Pablo** (1881–1973) Spanish painter and sculptor. An exceptionally versatile and prolific artist, he was the leading figure in the development of modern abstract art. Among his major works are the cubist masterpiece *Les Demoiselles d'Avignon* (1906–07) and *Guernica* (1937), which expresses his horror of war.

pic·a·yune /pìkə yoón/ *adj.* (*informal*) **1.** TRIFLING of very little importance **2.** SMALL-MINDED tending to fuss about unimportant things and to be childishly spiteful ■ *n.* **1.** TRIFLING THING something unimportant or of little value (*informal*) **2.** MONEY SPANISH-AMERICAN COIN a small silver coin formerly used in Spanish America, worth half of a real **3.** MONEY SMALL COIN a low-value coin, especially a five-cent piece (*archaic informal*) [Early 19thC. Via French *picaillon*, a Piedmontese coin, from Provençal *picaioun*, of unknown origin.]

pic·ca·lil·li /pìkə lìllee/ *n.* pickle relish consisting of chopped mixed vegetables with mustard, vinegar, and spices [Mid-18thC. Origin uncertain: probably from PICKLE + CHILLI.]

pic·ca·nin·ny (*plural* **-nies**) *n.* U.K. = **pickaninny** [Mid-17thC. Via Caribbean creole from, probably, Portuguese *pequenino* "very small, tiny," from *pequeno* "small."]

pic·ca·ta /pi kaátə/ *adj.* used to describe meats sautéed in slices and served in a spicy lemon and butter sauce ○ *veal piccata* [Via Italian from French *piqué*, past participle of *piquer* "to attach ingredients, to lard," literally "to prick"]

pic·co·lo /píkə lō/ (*plural* **-los**) *n.* a musical instrument that is the smallest member of the flute family, with a range one octave higher than the standard flute [Mid-19thC. From Italian, "small."]

pice /pīss/ (*plural* **pice**) *n.* MONEY a subunit of currency formerly used in the Indian subcontinent, 4 of which were worth an anna [Early 17thC. From Hindi *paisā* "paisa" (see PAISA).]

pi·ce·ous /píssee əss/ *adj.* thick and sticky or brownish-black in color, like pitch (*formal*) [Mid-17thC. Formed from Latin *piceus* "pitchy," from the stem *pic-* "pitch" (source of English *pitch*).]

pich·i·ci·e·go /pìchissee áygō/ (*plural* **-go** *or* **-gos**), **pich·i·ci·a·go** /-aágō/ (*plural* **-go** *or* **-gos**) *n.* **1.** SMALL ARMADILLO a very small silky-haired armadillo with pink armor found in Argentina. Latin name: *Chlamyphorus truncatus.* **2.** LARGE ARMADILLO a large armadillo found in South America that has yellowish-brown armor and coarse whitish hair. Latin name: *Burmeisteria retusa.* [Early 19thC. From Spanish *pichiego*, probably from Guarani *pichey*, name of a type of armadillo, literally "small" + Spanish *ciego* "sightless," from Latin *caecus*.]

pick[1] /pik/ *v.* (**picked, pick·ing, picks**) **1.** *vt.* REMOVE SOMETHING FROM PLANT to remove something, especially in quantity and by hand, from a plant on which it has grown ○ *picking strawberries* **2.** *vt.* STRIP SOMETHING OF FRUIT OR FLOWERS to strip a plant or all the plants in a particular place of fruit or flowers ○ *The bushes nearest the path had already been picked.* **3.** *vt.* CHOOSE to take or decide to take one or more things or people from a larger number ○ *Pick three people for your team.* **4.** *vt.* REMOVE SOMETHING IN SMALL PIECES to remove something part by part from the surface or middle of something using a sharp or pointed object such as a fingernail or a beak **5.** *vt.* SCRAPE BODY PART WITH FINGERNAIL to use a fingernail to loosen and remove something, or to loosen and remove something attached to the surface of a part of the body ○ *pick a scab* **6.** *vt.* OPEN SOMETHING WITHOUT PROPER KEY to use a special device or pointed instrument to open a lock, usually illegally ○ *pick a lock* **7.** *vt.* UNDO to loosen, unfasten, or separate something into disconnected parts, especially something that was sewn together ○ *pick a seam apart* **8.** *vi.* FIND FAULT to be petty or fault-finding **9.** *vt.* START FIGHT OR ARGUMENT to begin a fight or argument with somebody, usually deliberately **10.** *vt.* MUSIC PLUCK OR PLAY BY PLUCKING to pluck the strings of a stringed instrument or to play a tune on such an instrument in this way ■ *n.* **1.** CHOICE the act or right of choosing somebody or something ○ *I was first so I got to take my pick.* **2.** BEST the very best of a wide selection of people or things ○ *the pick of the bunch* **3.** CROP PORTION the amount of a crop gathered by hand at one time [13thC. Origin uncertain: probably from assumed Old English *pīcian* "to prick" and Old Icelandic *pikka* "to prick, peck"; later reinforced by French *piquer* "to prick, pick."] —**pick·a·ble** *adj.* ◇ **pick and choose** to take a lot of time or trouble when selecting something ◇ **pick holes in** *vt.* to look for and find mistakes or problems in something, especially somebody's argument ◇ **pick somebody's pocket** to steal something from somebody's pocket without the person feeling or noticing ◇ **pick your way** to step very carefully through a dirty, untidy, or dangerous area of ground

pick at *vt.* **1.** EAT LITTLE FOOD to eat very little of a meal ○ *He only picked at his breakfast.* **2.** SCRAPE SOMETHING WITH FINGERNAILS to scrape away surface pieces of something with the fingernails **3.** NAG SOMEBODY to nag or criticize somebody in a petty way (*informal*)

pick off *vt.* **1.** SHOOT THINGS ONE BY ONE to shoot a number of targets one by one, usually from a distance **2.** FOOTBALL INTERCEPT PASS in football, to intercept a pass **3.** BASEBALL PUT OUT BASE RUNNER in baseball, to put out a base runner caught off base, often when trying to steal the next base

pick on *vt.* **1.** PERSISTENTLY TREAT SOMEBODY UNFAIRLY to blame, criticize, or bully somebody repeatedly in a way that is considered unfair or unkind **2.** SELECT SOMEBODY OR SOMETHING to choose somebody or something from among others

pick out *vt.* **1.** CHOOSE SOMETHING to choose or select something from among others ○ *She picked out her favourite chocolate.* **2.** IDENTIFY SOMEBODY FROM CROWD OR BACKGROUND to recognize or distinguish somebody or something from among others or against a background that makes this difficult ○ *I couldn't pick him out in the crowd.* **3.** MUSIC PLAY SOMETHING NOTE BY NOTE to play a tune slowly, note by note

pick over *vt.* to go through something, selecting the best items or discarding unwanted items

pick up *v.* **1.** *vt.* LIFT SOMETHING to take hold of and raise or remove something or somebody **2.** *vti.* GATHER DROPPED THINGS to collect things that have been dropped or have fallen to the ground **3.** *vt.* CLEAN A PLACE to clean something, usually by gathering up things that have been carelessly left where they do not belong **4.** *vr.* REGAIN UPRIGHT OR STRONGER POSITION to stand up after falling down, or recover strength, courage, or sense of purpose after a setback ○ *She picked herself up.* **5.** *vti.* TAKE ON PASSENGERS to stop a vehicle and let a passenger or passengers in ○ *picked up a hitchhiker* **6.** *vt.* CLAIM SOMETHING to collect something such as items left for repair or merchandise ordered from a store ○ *pick up a library book* **7.** *vt.* PAY FOR SOMETHING to take on the responsibility for providing payment for something such as a bill **8.** *vt.* BUY SOMETHING ON IMPULSE to buy something in a casual or unplanned way **9.** *vt.* ACQUIRE SOMETHING CHEAPLY OR EASILY to get or buy something easily or cheaply **10.** *vt.* ACQUIRE SOMETHING CASUALLY to acquire something casually, without meaning to and without knowing it ○ *has picked up some bad habits* **11.** *vt.* MED CATCH A DISEASE to become infected with a disease **12.** *vt.* SPORTS GAIN POINTS in competitive sports, to gain something such as points or yards **13.** *vt.* NOTICE SOMETHING to notice something or become aware of it **14.** *vt.* FIND SOMETHING to find and follow something, such as a scent or trail ○ *pick up the scent* **15.** *vt.* UNDERSTAND SOMETHING to understand something that is communicated indirectly **16.** *vt.* LEARN SOMETHING to learn something in a casual or unsystematic way, e.g., by frequently hearing it, seeing it done, or trying to do it **17.** *vi.* BECOME BETTER to improve after being ill, injured, bad, or unsuccessful (*informal*) ○ *He picked up quickly* **18.** *vti.* ACCELERATE to increase in strength, speed, or intensity, or to cause something to increase ○ *Her speed picked up.* **19.** *vti.* RETURN TO SOMETHING AGAIN to continue something at a later time, usually after an interruption or break, or to be continued in this way ○ *She wanted to pick up her career.* **20.** *vt.* FIND SEXUAL PARTNER to make the acquaintance of a stranger, often in a public place, usually for sexual purposes (*informal*) ○ *picked him up in a bar* **21.** *vt.* ARREST to arrest somebody (*informal*) ○ *He was picked up on a burglary charge.* **22.** *vi.* PACK BELONGINGS to pack up belongings and leave without telling anyone why (*informal*) **23.** *vt.* RECEIVE SIGNAL to receive something such as a radio or television signal or a radar image on a piece of equipment

pick up on *vt.* **1.** LEARN QUICKLY to learn or understand something quickly **2.** NOTICE SOMETHING to notice something, and perhaps mention or question it (*informal*)

pick up with *vt.* to become acquainted and start associating with somebody (*informal*)

pick[2] /pik/ *n.* **1.** TOOL FOR BREAKING UP HARD SURFACES a tool used for breaking up hard surfaces, consisting of a long handle and a curved metal head that is pointed at one or both ends **2.** SMALL TOOL FOR BREAKING INTO PIECES a small tool used to break up something into smaller pieces (*often used in combination*) **3.** SHARP TOOL FOR PICKING a sharp tool for cleaning something for such as the teeth or for getting into small places, such as a lock (*often used in combination*) **4.** COMB FOR CURLY HAIR a comb having a handle and long teeth, used to comb curly hair **5.** MUSIC DEVICE FOR PLUCKING GUITAR STRINGS a device used to pluck the strings of a stringed instrument such as a guitar ■ *vi.* (**picked, pick·ing, picks**) WORK WITH PICK to use a pick or do work with a pick [14thC. Variant of PIKE.]

pick·a·nin·ny /píkə nìnnee/ (*plural* **-nies**), **pic·a·nin·ny** (*plural* **-nies**) *n.* highly offensive term for a small Black child (*offensive*) [See PICCANINNY]

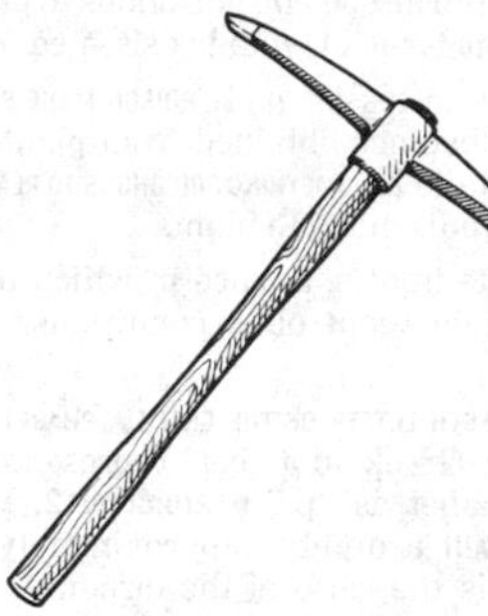

Pickax

pick·ax /pík àks/ *n.* a tool consisting of a long handle and a metal head that usually has one pointed end and one flattened end, used for breaking up something hard or cutting something [13thC. Middle English *pikois* from Old French *picois* (ultimately from Latin *picus* "woodpecker"), altered in the 15thC by association with AX.]

pick·er /píkər/ *n.* **1.** SOMEBODY OR SOMETHING THAT PICK SOMETHING a person or a machine that picks something, especially fruit or other crops (*often used in combination*) **2.** MUSIC PLAYER OF STRINGED INSTRUMENT somebody who plays a stringed instrument such as a banjo or guitar, usually performing country, folk, or bluegrass music (*informal*)

pick·er·el /píkərəl/ (*plural* **-el** *or* **-els**) *n.* a North American river fish of the pike family that is a fierce predator and is popular with anglers. Latin name: *Esox niger.* [14thC. Literally "small pike"; partly modeled on Anglo-Latin *picerellus*.]

pick·er·el·weed /píkərəl weèd/ *n.* a North American plant with heart-shaped leaves and purple flowers that grows in shallow water in rivers and lakes. Latin name: *Pontederia cordata.*

Pick·er·ing /píkəring/, **Edward Charles** (1846–1919) U.S. astronomer and physicist. He devised the meridian photometer with which he made more than 1,400,000 measurements of the magnitudes of stars.

pick·et /píkit/ *n.* **1.** POINTED POST STUCK IN THE GROUND a post or plank with a pointed end that is hammered into the ground, e.g., as a marker, as a support for a fence, or to tether an animal **2.** MIL SOLDIER OR SOLDIERS ON GUARD a soldier or small body of troops used to occupy ground of tactical importance **3.** PROTESTER OR PROTESTERS OUTSIDE BUILDING a person or group of people demonstrating or protesting outside a building, e.g., a striking worker who tries to persuade other people not to enter during a strike ■ *v.* **(-et·ed, -et·ing, -ets) 1.** *vt.* **ENCLOSE OR MARK SOMETHING WITH STAKES** to enclose or mark something with wooden stakes driven into the ground, or enclose it with a picket fence **2.** *vt.* MIL **POST GUARDS** to post troops as guards **3.** *vt.* MIL **GUARD** to patrol or guard a place, especially a military site or position **4.** *vti.* **HOLD PROTEST OUTSIDE PLACE** to hold a demonstration or protest outside a place, e.g., as part of a strike in order to persuade others not to enter a place of business **5.** *vt.* **TETHER ANIMAL** to tether a horse or other animal [Late 17thC. From French *piquet* "pointed stake," from *piquer* "to prick, pierce" (see PICK[1]). The meaning "guard" comes from the practice of soldiers tethering their horses to stakes.] —**pick·et·er** *n.*

pick·et fence *n.* a fence made of pointed stakes or posts driven into the ground and connected by one or more horizontal bars

pick·et line *n.* a line of people who are protesting outside a building, e.g., striking workers outside their workplace, who attempt to persuade other people not to enter

Pick·ett /píkit/, **George Edward** (1825–75) U.S. general. He led his Confederate troops in an unsuccessful charge at the Battle of Gettysburg (1863).

Mary Pickford

Pick·ford /píkfərd/, **Mary** (1893–1979) Canadian-born U.S. actor and producer. She starred in movies such as *Poor Little Rich Girl* (1917), and cofounded United Artists Studio (1919). Real name **Gladys Marie Smith**. Known as **America's Sweetheart**

pick·ings /píkingz/ *npl.* things available to be earned or taken in a particular place ○ *easy pickings*

pick·le /pík'l/ *n.* **1.** *U.K.* FOOD = **relish 2. PRESERVED VEGETABLE** a small cucumber or other vegetable that has acquired a sharp taste by being preserved in vinegar or brine ○ *okra pickles* **3.** FOOD **LIQUID FOR PRESERVING FOOD** liquid, usually brine or a vinegar solution, used to preserve cold foods such as vegetables or fish **4.** INDUST **CLEANING OR PROCESSING SOLUTION** an industrial or commercial solution used to clean or process something **5. AWKWARD SITUATION** a difficult or problematic situation (*informal*) ■ *vt.* **(-led, -ling, -les) 1.** FOOD **PRESERVE FOOD** to preserve food, especially vegetables or fish, in vinegar, brine, or another solution **2. DIP OR SOAK SOMETHING IN LIQUID** to clean or process something by dipping or soaking it in a liquid [14thC. From Middle Low German *pekel*, of unknown origin.] —**pick·ler** *n.*

pick·led /pík'ld/ *adj.* **1. PRESERVED** preserved in vinegar, brine, or another liquid **2. INEBRIATED** inebriated (*informal*)

pick·le·worm /pík'l wùrm/ *n.* the larva of a moth found in the southeastern United States that feeds on cucumbers, pumpkins, and other gourds. Latin name: *Diaphania nitidalis.*

pick·lock /pík lòk/ *n.* **1. LOCK-OPENING TOOL** a tool used to open locks without using the key **2. SOMEBODY WHO OPENS LOCKS UNLAWFULLY** somebody who opens locks without using a key, especially a burglar

pick-me-up *n.* something that lifts the spirits and energizes somebody, especially a stimulating drink (*informal*)

pick·off /pík àwf, -òf/ *n.* **1.** SPORTS **PASS INTERCEPTION** an interception of a pass, e.g., in football or basketball **2.** BASEBALL **BASEBALL PLAY** a play in which a runner who is off base is thrown out

pick·pock·et /pík pòkət/ *n.* somebody who steals from people's pockets and bags in public places, usually secretly and unnoticed

pick·up /pík ùp/ *n.* **1. LIFTING OR COLLECTING OF SOMETHING** the raising, gathering, collection, or removal of something to be taken somewhere else **2.** SPORTS **FIELDING BALL** the act of fielding a ball after it touches the ground **3. SOMEBODY OR SOMETHING TAKEN SOMEWHERE** somebody or something that is moved from one place to another **4. HITCHHIKER** a hitchhiker (*informal*) **5.** = **pickup truck 6. IMPROVEMENT OR INCREASE** an improvement or increase (*informal*) **7.** = **pick-me-up 8. PROSPECTIVE SEXUAL PARTNER** somebody met casually with the aim of developing a sexual relationship (*informal*) **9. ARREST** the taking of somebody into custody by a police officer (*informal*) **10. POWER TO ACCELERATE** the ability of a vehicle to accelerate quickly (*informal*) **11.** ACCT **BALANCE FORWARD** a balance carried forward in an accounting ledger **12.** PRESS **EARLIER WRITING** in journalism, the portion of a story written earlier to which additional copy is added later **13.** MUSIC **UNSTRESSED NOTE** an unstressed note or series of notes introducing a musical phrase or composition **14.** RECORDING **TONE ARM** the tone arm of a record player **15.** RECORDING **PART OF TONE ARM** a device inside the tone arm of a record player that converts the needle's vibrations into electrical signals that are converted into sound **16.** MUSIC **CONVERTER OF VIBRATIONS ON MUSICAL INSTRUMENT** an electromagnetic device that converts the vibrations from the strings of an electric guitar or other amplified instument into electrical signals that are amplified into sound **17.** PHYS **RECEIVING OF LIGHT OR SOUND WAVES** the receiving and gathering of light or sound waves that are to be converted into electrical impulses **18.** TECH **RECEIVER FOR LIGHT OR SOUND WAVES** a device used to receive light or sound waves **19. PART THAT LIFTS SOMETHING** a part of a machine or system that lifts or selects something, e.g., the rotating rake on a combine harvester that lifts and gathers straw or hay ■ *adj.* **INFORMAL AND IMPROMPTU** informally organized on the spot and made up of or involving people available at the time ○ *a pickup basketball game*

pick·up truck, pick·up *n.* a light truck with a low-sided open back and a tailgate that drops down for easy loading and unloading

Pick·wick·i·an /pik wíkee ən/ *adj.* **1. GENEROUS OR NAIVE** generous, naive, or benevolent **2. UNUSUAL** not literal or typical in usage or meaning [Mid-19thC. From the character of Mr. Pickwick in Charles Dickens' novel *The Pickwick Papers* (1837).]

pick·y /píkee/ **(-i·er, -i·est)** *adj.* having specific and inflexible likes and dislikes and, therefore, hard to please or satisfy [Mid-19thC. Formed from PICK[1].] —**pick·i·ly** *adv.* —**pick·i·ness** *n.*

pic·nic /pík nìk/ *n.* **1.** FOOD **MEAL TAKEN AND EATEN OUTDOORS** an informal meal prepared for eating in the open air or the food that makes up such a meal **2. EASY OR PLEASANT THING** something easy to do or pleasant to experience (*informal*) ○ *It was no picnic.* **3. CUT OF PORK** a cut of pork consisting of the shoulder with most of the butt removed ■ *vi.* **(-nicked, -nick·ing, -nics) HAVE A PICNIC** to eat an informal meal outdoors [Mid-18thC. From French *pique-nique*, of unknown origin.] —**pic·nick·er** *n.*

pic·nic ar·e·a *n.* = **rest area**

pico- *prefix.* **1. ONE TRILLIONTH** one trillionth (10^{-12}) ○ *picofarad.* Symbol **p 2.** very small ○ *picornavirus* [Via Spanish *pico* "beak, small amount" from Latin *beccus*; ultimately of Celtic origin]

pi·co·far·ad /péekə fèrrad, píkə-/ *n.* one trillionth of a farad. Symbol **pF**

pi·co·gram /péekə gràm, píkə-/ *n.* one trillionth of a gram

pic·o·line /-lèen, píkəlin/ *n.* a liquid found in coal tar and bone oil, used as a solvent and in organic synthesis. Formula: C_6H_7N. [Mid-19thC. Coined from the Latin stem *pic-* "pitch" (source of English *pitch*) + [oleum] "oil" (source of English *oil*) + -INE.] —**pic·o·lin·ic** /pìkə línnik/ *adj.*

pi·co·mole /péekə mòl, píkə-/ *n.* one trillionth of a mole

pi·cong /péekong/ *n.* *Carib* light-hearted teasing talk [Mid-20thC. From Spanish *picón*.]

pi·cor·na·vi·rus /pi káwrnə vìrəss/ *n.* a small infectious virus, such as the virus that causes polio or the common cold. Family: Picornaviridae. [Mid-20thC. Coined from PICO- + RNA + VIRUS.]

pi·co·sec·ond /péekə sèkənd, píkə-/ *n.* a trillionth of a second

pi·cot /péekō, pee kṓ/ *n.* **DECORATIVE LOOP** a loop that forms a pattern with others, e.g., in lace ■ *vt.* **(-cot·ed, -cot·ing, -cots) DECORATE WITH PICOTS** to embroider small loops on fabric [Early 17thC. From French, literally "small point," formed from *pic* "peak, point," from *piquer* "to prick" (see PICK[1]).]

pic·o·tee /pìkə tée/ *n.* a flower, especially a carnation or tulip, that has petals edged with a different, usually darker color [Early 18thC. From French *picotée*, feminine past participle of *picoter* "to prick," from *picot* (see PICOT).]

pi·co·wave /péekə wàyv, píkə-/ **(-waved, -wav·ing, -waves)** *vt.* to expose food to radiation in order to kill insects, worms, or bacteria

picr- *prefix.* = **picro-** (*used before vowels*)

pic·rate /pík ràyt/ *n.* a salt or ester of picric acid [Mid-19thC. Coined from Greek *pikros* "bitter" + -ATE.]

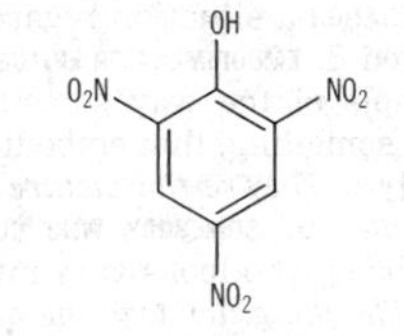

Picric acid

pic·ric ac·id /pìkrik-/ *n.* a strong toxic yellow crystalline acid used in dyes, antiseptics, and high explosives. Formula: $C_6H_3N_3O_7$. [From Greek *pikros* "bitter" + -IC]

pi·crite /pík rìt/ *n.* a dark-colored igneous rock made up primarily of coarse grains of olivine and other ferromagnesian minerals [Early 19thC. Coined from Greek *pikros* "bitter" + -ITE.]

picro- *prefix.* **1.** bitter ○ *picrotoxin* **2.** picric acid ○ *picrate* [From Greek *pikros* "sharp, bitter." Ultimately from an Indo-European base meaning "to cut, scratch" that is also the ancestor of English *paint* and *file*.]

pic·ro·tox·in /pìkrə tóksin/ *n.* a bitter crystalline compound derived from the seeds of an Indian vine and used as an antidote to barbiturate poisoning. Formula: $C_{30}H_{34}O_{13}$.

Pict /pikt/ *n.* a member of any of the ancient peoples that occupied lands north of the Forth and Clyde Rivers in Scotland from the 1st to the 4th centuries A.D. The Picts prevented the Romans from spreading into central and northern Scotland and later joined with the Scots to form the unified kingdom of Scotland. [Pre-12thC. From late Latin *Picti* (plural), of uncertain origin: perhaps from Latin *pictus* "painted" (see PICTURE), from the Picts' painted or tattooed skin.]

Pict·ish /píktish/ *adj.* **OF PICTS** relating to the Picts, their culture, or their language ■ *n.* **LANGUAGE FORMERLY USED IN SCOTLAND** an extinct language spoken in an area that is now part of Scotland to the north of the Forth and Clyde Rivers [Late 16thC]

pic·to·graph /píktə gràf/, **pic·to·gram** /-gràm/ *n.* **1.** LANG **PICTURE REPRESENTING WORD** a graphic symbol or picture representing a word or idea in some writing systems, as opposed to a symbol such as a letter of the alphabet representing an individual sound **2. CHART WITH PICTURES OR SYMBOLS** a chart or diagram that uses symbols or pictures to represent values [Mid-19thC. Coined from Latin *pictus* (see PICTURE) + -GRAPH.] —**pic·tog·ra·pher** /pik tóggrəfər/ *n.* —**pic·to·graph·ic** /pìktə gráffik/ *adj.* —**pic·to·graph·i·cal·ly** /-gráffikəlee/ *adv.* —**pic·tog·ra·phy** /pik tóggrəfee/ *n.*

Pic·ton /píktən/ town on the northeastern coast of the South Island, New Zealand. It is a ferry port and tourist center. Population: 3,061 (1996).

Pic·tor /píktər/ *n.* an inconspicuous constellation of the southern hemisphere between Dorado and Columba

pic·to·ri·al /pik táwree əl/ *adj.* **1. OF PICTURES** relating to, composed of, or shown by pictures **2. ILLUSTRATED** containing illustrations or photographs, as opposed to writing or text **3. DESCRIPTIVE** used to describe language that conjures up vivid images ■ *n.* HIGHLY ILLUSTRATED PERIODICAL a newspaper or magazine that has many pictures in it, especially one with far more pictures than text [Mid-17thC. Formed from late Latin *pictorius*, from Latin *pictor* "painter," from *pictus* (see PICTURE.] —**pic·to·ri·al·i·ty** /pik tàwree állətee/ *n.* —**pic·to·ri·al·ly** /pik táwree əlee/ *adv.* —**pic·to·ri·al·ness** *n.*

pic·to·ri·al·ize /pik táwree ə lìz/ (**-ized, -iz·ing, -iz·es**) *vt.* to represent something in drawings, paintings, or photographs, or illustrate something with them —**pic·to·ri·al·i·za·tion** /pik tàwree əli záysh'n/ *n.*

pic·ture /píkchər/ *n.* **1.** SOMETHING DRAWN OR PAINTED a shape or set of shapes and lines drawn, painted, or printed on paper, canvas, or some other flat surface, especially shapes that represent a recognizable form or object **2.** PHOTOGRAPHY PHOTO a photograph **3.** TV TV IMAGE the image on a television screen **4.** CINEMA MOVIE a motion picture **5.** MENTAL IMAGE a vivid image or impression in the mind of how somebody or something looks **6.** ARTISTIC DESCRIPTION OR REPRESENTATION a description or representation of something in writing, in a film, in music, or some other art form **7.** OBSERVED SITUATION a situation regarded as a scene being observed **8.** EMBODIMENT OR EPITOME a typical or perfect example of the way something looks, or somebody or something that embodies a quality or state perfectly ○ *They're the picture of the happily married couple.* **9.** SOMEBODY WHO CLOSELY RESEMBLES ANOTHER somebody who looks very much like somebody else ○ *The daughter was the absolute picture of the grandmother.* ■ **pic·tures** *npl.* CINEMA MOVIES movies as entertainment, rather than an industry (*informal dated*) ■ *vt.* (**-tured, -tur·ing, -tures**) **1.** IMAGINE SOMETHING to imagine or have an image of somebody or something in mind **2.** DESCRIBE SOMETHING to describe somebody or something in a particular way **3.** FEATURE PICTURE OF SOMEBODY to feature a picture, especially a photograph, of somebody or something in a newspaper, magazine, or book (*often passive*) [15thC. From Latin *pictura*, from *pictus*, the past participle of *pingere* "to paint" (source also of English *depict*, *paint*, and *pigment*).]

WORD KEY: CULTURAL NOTE

The Picture of Dorian Gray, a novel by the Irish writer Oscar Wilde (1890). In Wilde's update of the Faust legend, the decadent young gentleman Dorian Gray trades his soul for eternal youth and beauty, but is subsequently tormented by a portrait of himself that constantly changes to reflect the ravages of time and of his debauched lifestyle. It was made into a movie by Albert Lewin in 1945.

pic·ture book *n.* a highly illustrated book, especially one for children, written in a simple style

pic·ture card *n.* = **face card**

pic·ture hat *n.* a woman's elaborately decorated hat with a very broad brim, of the kind often featured in informal portraits of women painted in the 18th century

pic·ture li·brar·y *n.* a place where photographs and other images are stored, from which they may be borrowed for use in books, magazines, and newspapers

pic·ture mold·ing *n.* a strip of wood or plaster, usually a molding resembling a cornice, fixed high up around the walls of a room, from which pictures can be hung

pic·ture-per·fect *adj.* very clean, neat, ordered, and pleasing, as the subjects of paintings and photographs often are

pic·ture post·card *n.* a postcard with a picture, often a photograph of a landmark or landscape, on one side (*dated*)

pic·ture puz·zle *n.* GAME = **jigsaw puzzle**

pic·ture rail *n. U.K.* = **picture molding**

pic·tur·esque /pìkchə résk/ *adj.* **1.** VERY ATTRACTIVE visually pleasing enough to be the subject of a painting or photograph **2.** VIVID so accurate or detailed as to evoke a clear mental image of what has been described **3.** DISTINCTIVE having a pleasingly distinctive or unusual atmosphere ○ *We ate lunch in a picturesque fishing village.* ■ *n.* PLEASING OR DISTINCTIVE THINGS things that are unusually pleasing or distinctive, spoken of collectively [Early 18thC. Anglicization (modeled on PICTURE) of French *pittoresque*, from Italian *pittoresco*, from *pittore* "painter," from Latin *pictor* (see PICTORIAL).] —**pic·tur·esque·ly** *adv.* —**pic·tur·esque·ness** *n.*

pic·ture tube *n.* = **tube** *n.* 7

pic·ture win·dow *n.* a large window, usually with a single pane of glass, especially one that has a pleasant view

pic·ture writ·ing *n.* **1.** WRITING WITH SYMBOLS FOR WHOLE WORDS a writing system such as that of Chinese that uses symbols or pictures to represent whole words or ideas rather than individual sounds **2.** PICTURES RECOUNTING OR REPORTING SOMETHING the reporting of an event or telling of a story using pictures instead of words, e.g., in ancient cave paintings

pic·ul /pík'l/ *n.* any of various units of weight used in Southeast Asia, especially the Chinese unit, which is equal to 133 lb./60 kg [Late 16thC. From Malay and Javanese *pikul* "load."]

pic·u·let /píkyələt/ (*plural* **-let** *or* **-lets**) *n.* a very small tropical woodpecker. Genus: *Picumnus.* [Mid-19thC. Literally "small small woodpecker," formed from Latin *picus* "woodpecker."]

PID *n., abbr.* **1.** MED pelvic inflammatory disease **2.** COMPUT personal identification device

pid·dle /pídd'l/ *v.* (**-dled, -dling, -dles**) **1.** *vi.* URINATE to urinate (*informal*) (*usually used by or to children*) **2.** *vti.* DO THINGS HAPHAZARDLY to operate in a disorganized way, doing one thing and then another without a distinct purpose or method ■ *n.* (*plural* **-dles**) URINATION an act of urinating (*informal*) (*usually used by or to children*) [Late 18thC. Origin uncertain: perhaps a blend of PISS and PUDDLE.] —**pid·dler** *n.*

pid·dling /píddling/ *adj.* very small, insignificant, or trivial (*informal*) [Mid-16thC. Formed from PIDDLE.] —**pid·dling·ly** *adv.*

pid·dock /píddək/ *n.* MARINE BIOL a saltwater mollusk that has a hinged shell, like the mussel or clam, but with serrated edges that it uses to bore into rock and wood. Family: Pholadidae. [Mid-19thC. Origin unknown.]

pidg·in /píjjin/ *n.* a simplified language made up of elements of two or more languages, used as a communication tool between speakers whose native languages are different [Early 19thC. From Chinese, alteration of BUSINESS.] —**pidg·in·i·za·tion** /pìjjini záysh'n/ *n.* —**pidg·in·ize** /píjji nìz/ *vt.*

pidg·in Eng·lish *n.* a pidgin containing elements of English vocabulary, grammar, and pronunciation, especially one formerly used between Chinese people and Europeans, or one currently spoken in West Africa and some Pacific islands

pi-dog *n.* = **pye-dog**

PIDS *abbr.* primary immune deficiency syndrome

pie[1] /pì/ *n.* **1.** BAKED FOOD WITH PASTRY a baked dish consisting of a filling such as chopped meat or fruit enclosed in pastry and usually cooked in a container **2.** DIVISIBLE WHOLE something regarded as a resource to be shared or divided up ○ *Our competitors are always looking for a larger piece of the overseas pie.* [14thC. Origin uncertain: perhaps from PIE[4], since the assorted contents of a pie resemble items collected by a magpie.] ◇ **pie in the sky** something described very attractively that is not likely to happen or materialize

pie[2] /pì/ *n.* a very small coin formerly used in India, worth one third of a pice [Mid-19thC. Via Hindi *paī* from Sanskrit *pādikā*, from *pāda* "quarter."]

pie[3] *n.* PRINTING = **pi**[1] *n.* 2

pie[4] /pì/ (*plural* **pie** *or* **pies**) *n.* a magpie (*archaic*) [14thC. Via French from Latin *pica* "magpie."]

piece /peess/ *n.* **1.** PART DETACHED FROM LARGER WHOLE a part that has been broken, torn, or cut from a larger whole **2.** PORTION OR SERVING a portion or serving from a larger block or whole **3.** INDIVIDUAL ITEM OR ARTICLE an item or article of a particular kind or class ○ *an expensive piece of equipment* **4.** INTERCONNECTING PART any one of a set of parts that fit together to form a whole or unit **5.** EXAMPLE OF SOMETHING an instance or example of something, often something abstract such as luck **6.** DECLARATION OF OPINION a statement of opinion on a particular subject, event, or situation ○ *At least I said my piece.* **7.** ARTS ARTISTIC WORK a single artistic work, such as a musical composition, play, or painting **8.** PRESS PUBLISHED ARTICLE an article in a newspaper or magazine **9.** MONEY COIN a coin of a specified value ○ *a fifty-cent piece* **10.** BOARD GAMES OBJECT MOVED IN BOARD GAME any of a set of objects that players of board games move on the board **11.** FIREARM a gun, especially a handgun (*slang*) **12.** OFFENSIVE TERM an offensive term for a woman (*slang offensive*) **13.** OFFENSIVE TERM an offensive term for sexual intercourse (*slang offensive*) **14.** ESTIMATE OF DISTANCE an unspecified distance (*informal*) ○ *You go down the road a piece and then you come to the bridge.* ■ *vt.* (**pieced, piec·ing, piec·es**) **1.** WORK SOMETHING OUT to put something together gradually, part by part ○ *We finally managed to piece together the events of that night.* **2.** MEND to mend something by patching it [12thC. From Old French *piece*, probably of Gaulish origin.]

piece out *vt.* to bring all the fragments of something, such as a story, together gradually

pièce de ré·sis·tance /pee èss də rə zeéss taàns, pee èss də ray zeéss taàns/ (*plural* **pièces de ré·sis·tance**) *n.* **1.** MOST IMPRESSIVE THING the most impressive thing or something that brings the greatest pride or satisfaction **2.** MOST IMPORTANT DISH the most important dish served at a meal (*formal*) [Late 18thC. From French, literally "piece of resistance," originally applied to the most substantial dish in a meal.]

piece-dyed *adj.* dyed after being woven

piece goods *npl.* fabrics made and sold in standard lengths

piece·meal /peéss meèl/ *adv.* **1.** GRADUALLY little by little **2.** IN PARTS in separate parts or fragments ■ *adj.* DONE PART BY PART done in a disorganized or fragmentary way ○ *His novel is a ragtag, piecemeal work.* [13thC. From PIECE + obsolete *-meal* "measure," from Old English *mǣl* "measure, meal" (see MEAL).]

piece of cake *n.* something that is very easy to do (*informal*) [From the easiness of eating cake, a soft food]

piece of eight *n.* an old Spanish gold coin worth eight reals

piece of work *n.* somebody or something remarkable or outstanding

piecework /peéss wùrk/ *n.* work that is paid by the amount rather than by the time spent doing it

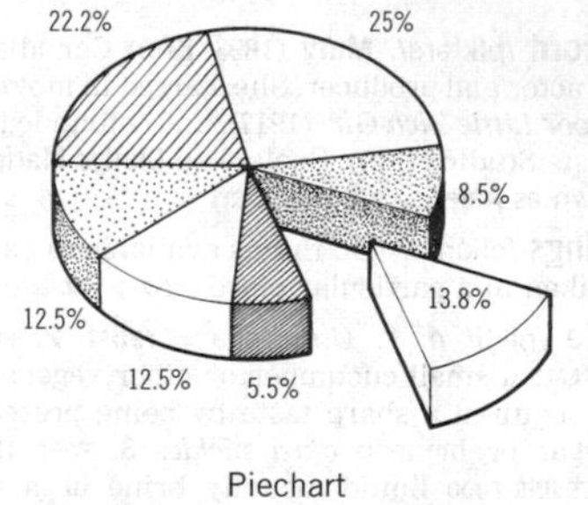

Piechart

piechart /pí chaàrt/ *n.* a diagrammatic representation of a group shown as a circle divided into sections by straight lines from its center with areas proportional to the relative size of the quantity represented

piec·ing /peéssing/ *n.* the sewing together of various pieces of cloth or leather to make a larger decorative fabric

pied-à-terre /pee àydə táir/ (*plural* **pieds-à-terre**) *n.* a small apartment or house used as a second home for vacations or business purposes [From French, literally "foot to earth"]

pied-billed grebe /pìd bild greéb/ *n.* a small brown waterbird with a stout striped bill, found on fresh water in North and South America. Latin name: *Podilymbus podiceps.*

pied·mont /peéd mònt/ *n.* AREA AT FOOT OF MOUNTAINS a region at the base of a mountain range ■ *adj.* AT FOOT OF MOUNTAINS lying or formed at the base of a mountain range [Mid-19thC. From *Piedmont*, hilly region of the eastern United States, named for *Piemonte*, a region of northwest Italy, literally in Italian "foot of the mountain."]

Pied·mont Pla·teau /peéd mont-/ region of the eastern United States between the Appalachian Mountains and the Atlantic Coastal Plain

Pied Pip·er /pìd pípər/ *n.* **1.** LEGENDARY PLAYER OF ENCHANTING MUSIC a visiting piper in German folklore whose entrancing music rid the town of Hamelin of its rats. He later lured away its children after town officials refused to pay him for his services. **2. Pied**

Pip·er, pied pip·er SOMEBODY OTHERS FOLLOW somebody who attracts supporters and followers, especially by making unrealistic promises

WORD KEY: CULTURAL NOTE

The Pied Piper of Hamelin, a poem by the English writer Robert Browning (1842). Based on a medieval legend, it tells the story of a piper who successfully rids a town of rats by luring the animals into a river with his music. When the citizens refuse to pay him for his services, he uses the same technique to abduct their children. The term *pied piper*, a charismatic leader who makes attractive but false promises, is taken from the title and main character of this poem.

pied wag·tail *n.* **1.** SMALL EUROPEAN BIRD a small European bird with black-and-white plumage and a long black tail. Latin name: *Motacilla alba yarrellii.* **2.** LONG-TAILED AFRICAN BIRD a long-tailed black-and-white bird found throughout Africa. Latin name: *Motacilla aguimp.*

pie-eyed *adj.* very drunk (*informal*) [Because vision is affected by the alcohol]

pie plant /pī plànt/, **pie·plant** *n.* = **rhubarb** *n.* 1 [Because it is used in pies]

pier /peer/ *n.* **1.** SEASIDE STRUCTURE a platform built on stilts jutting out into a body of water, used as a boat dock, a place from which to fish, or as an entertainment center **2.** VERTICAL STRUCTURAL SUPPORT a pillar, especially a rectangular one supporting the end of an arch, lintel, or vault **3.** BRIDGE SUPPORT a vertical structural support between two spans of a bridge **4.** WALL BETWEEN ADJACENT DOORS an area of wall between two adjacent doors, windows, or other openings **5.** COLUMN PROJECTING FROM WALL a column of masonry projecting from a wall **6.** WALL REINFORCEMENT a vertical structure, usually of masonry, built against a wall to support it **7.** BREAKWATER a barrier built out to sea to protect a harbor from heavy waves [12thC. From Anglo-Latin *pera.*]

WORD KEY: CULTURAL NOTE

The Road to Wigan Pier, a book by the British writer George Orwell (1937). It combines a first-hand account of the appalling living conditions endured by workers in northern England with a penetrating analysis of class interests and prejudices. Its graphic and moving descriptions, compelling arguments, and restrained anger make it a classic of literary journalism.

pierce /peers/ (**pierced, pierc·ing, pierc·es**) *v.* **1.** *vti.* BORE INTO SOMETHING to penetrate through or into something with a sharp pointed object **2.** *vt.* PUT HOLE IN to make a hole through something ○ *She had her ears pierced.* **3.** *vti.* PENETRATE A BARRIER to break through a barrier of some kind, e.g., a defensive line or security system **4.** *vti.* GAIN SIGHT OR KNOWLEDGE to perceive something with the eyes or the mind **5.** *vti.* PENETRATE SOMETHING WITH SOUND OR LIGHT to sound or shine suddenly and sharply through something, such as silence or darkness ○ *A dreadful scream pierced the silence.* **6.** *vt.* AFFECT DEEPLY to have a sudden intense, often painful effect on somebody ○ *A stab of fear pierced his heart.* [13thC. Via French *percer* from, ultimately, Latin *pertundere* "to bore through," from *tundere* "to bore."] —**pierc·er** *n.*

Franklin Pierce

Pierce /peerss/, **Franklin** (1804–69) U.S. statesman and 14th President of the United States (1853–57). A Democrat, he sided with the South on the slavery issue, yet was committed to the Union.

pierc·ing /peérsing/ *adj.* **1.** PENETRATING with an unpleasantly intense quality ○ *a piercing cry* **2.** PERCEPTIVE capable of perceiving acutely ○ *her piercing gaze* **3.** INTENSELY COLD with a sharp deeply chilling cold ○ *a piercing wind* ■ *n.* **1.** MAKING HOLES FOR RINGS IN BODY the practice of piercing holes in parts of the body so that rings or studs can be inserted ○ *body piercing* **2.** HOLE FOR RING IN BODY a hole pierced in a part of the body to take a ring or stud ○ *She had piercings on her eyebrow and nose.* —**pierc·ing·ly** *adv.*

Pi·e·ri·a /pī éeree ə/ region of ancient Macedonia where, according to Greek mythology, the Pierian Spring was located

Pi·e·ri·an /pī éeree ən/ *adj.* **1.** OF ANCIENT PIERIA relating to the region of Pieria in ancient Macedonia, to its spring, or to the Muses who lived there **2.** INSPIRING providing poetic inspiration (*literary*)

Pi·e·ri·an Spring *n.* in Greek mythology, the spring at Pieria in ancient Macedonia that was sacred to the Muses, who lived there, and gave poetic inspiration to anyone who drank from it

Pierre /peer/ capital city of South Dakota, on the Missouri River, west of Huron and northeast of Rapid City. Population: 13,422 (1996).

Pier·rot /peé ə rō, pye rṓ/ *n.* a character in traditional French pantomime. He is a white-faced clown with a white costume and pointed hat, and is often represented as sad or crying. [Mid-18thC. From French, literally "little Peter," from *Pierre* "Peter."]

Pie·tà /pee ay taá/, **pie·tà** *n.* a painting or sculpture of the Virgin Mary mourning over Jesus Christ's dead body [Mid-17thC. Via Italian from Latin *pietas* (see PIETY).]

Pie·ter·mar·itz·burg /peétər márrits bùrg/ capital city of Kwazulu-Natal Province, South Africa, situated 45 mi./72 km northwest of Durban. Population: 156,473 (1991).

pi·e·tism /pī́ ə tìzzəm/ *n.* **1.** PIOUSNESS devotion to a deity or deities and observance of religious principles in everyday life **2.** SANCTIMONIOUSNESS excessive or insincere religious devotion [Early 19thC. From PIETISM.] —**pi·e·tist** *n.* —**pi·e·tis·tic** /pī ə tístik/ *adj.* —**pi·e·tis·ti·cal·ly** /-tístikəlee/ *adv.*

Pi·e·tism /pī́ ə tìzzəm/ *n.* a German Protestant movement in the 17th and 18th centuries that changed the focus of Lutheranism from ritual and church government to personal piety. It was founded by Philipp Jakob Spener. [Late 17thC. Via German *Pietismus* from Latin *pietas* (see PIETY).]

pi·e·ty /pī́ atee/ (*plural* **-ties**) *n.* **1.** RELIGIOUS DEVOTION strong respectful belief in a deity or deities and strict observance of religious principles in everyday life **2.** DEVOUT ACT an action inspired by devout religious principles **3.** INSINCERE ATTITUDE a conventional or hypocritical statement or observance of a belief **4.** FAMILY LOYALTY loyalty to parents and family (*archaic*) [14thC. Via Old French *piete* from Latin *pietas*, from *pius* "devout," source of English *pious.*]

piezo- *prefix.* pressure ○ *piezoelectric crystal* [From Greek *piezein* "to press." Ultimately from an Indo-European base meaning "to sit" that is also the ancestor of English *sit* and Sanskrit *upaniṣad* (see UPANISHAD).]

pi·e·zo·e·lec·tric·i·ty /pee àyzō i lek tríssətee, -àytsō-/ *n.* PHYS the electric current produced by some crystals and ceramic materials when they are subjected to mechanical pressure —**pi·e·zo·e·lec·tric** /pee àyzō i léktrik, -àytsō-/ *adj.*

pi·e·zom·e·ter /pee ə zómmətər/ *n.* an instrument for measuring the compressibility of a material or fluid under pressure —**pi·e·zo·met·ric** /pee àyzō méttrik, -àytsō-/ *adj.* —**pi·e·zo·met·ri·cal·ly** /-méttrikəlee/ *adv.*

pif·fle /píff'l/ *n.* NONSENSE silly talk or ideas (*dated informal*) ■ *vi.* (**-fled, -fling, -fles**) BEHAVE THOUGHTLESSLY to behave in a silly or ineffective way (*dated informal*) [Mid-19thC. Origin uncertain: perhaps suggesting the sound of silly talk.]

pif·fling /píffling/ *adj.* of little use, value, or importance (*informal*)

pig /pig/ *n.* **1.** FARM ANIMAL WITH BROAD SNOUT a sturdy short-legged mammal with a broad snout, especially a young domesticated hog, commonly inept as a farm animal and traditionally represented as fat and pink with a curly tail. Latin name: *Sus scrofa.* **2.** PORK the meat of a pig **3.** GREEDY PERSON somebody who is slovenly, greedy, or gluttonous (*informal*) **4.** COARSE PERSON somebody who behaves in a coarse, discourteous, or brutal manner (*informal*) **5.** METALL BLOCK OF METAL a casting of metal in a basic shape suitable for storage or transportation **6.** METALL METAL MOLD a basic mold for casting metal, especially iron **7.** OFFENSIVE TERM an offensive term for a member of the police force (*slang offensive*) **8.** ESTABLISHMENT FIGURE a member of the established order of society, especially somebody in authority who is regarded by youth or a minority as having outdated, racist, or sexist views (*slang insult*) **9.** OFFENSIVE TERM an offensive term that deliberately insults a woman's morality (*slang offensive*) ■ *vi.* (**pigged, pig·ging, pigs**) GIVE BIRTH TO PIGS to give birth to a litter of pigs [Assumed Old English *picga.* Originally in the sense "young pig."] ◇ **a pig in a poke** something that is bought or obtained without being inspected to see if it is worth having

pig out *vi.* to eat greedily or gluttonously (*informal*)

pig·boat /píg bòt/ *n.* a submarine (*informal*)

pi·geon /píjjən/ *n.* **1.** BIRD COMMON IN CITIES a medium-sized bird with a stocky body and short legs, especially a domesticated variety of the rock dove, commonly seen in cities and throughout most of the world, or trained for racing and carrying messages. Latin name: *Columba livia.* **2.** GULLIBLE PERSON somebody who is easily swindled or deceived (*informal*) **3.** = **clay pigeon** *n.* 1 [14thC. Via Old French *pijon* "young bird" from a Vulgar Latin alteration of late Latin *pipio*, from an assumed base imitative of the sound of cheeping.]

pi·geon breast *n.* a condition in which the sides of the chest are flattened and the center protrudes like the keel of a boat —**pi·geon-breast·ed** *adj.*

pi·geon hawk *n.* a merlin (*dated*) [Because it preys on pigeons]

pi·geon·hole /píjjən hōl/ *n.* **1.** PLACE TO PUT MESSAGES any of a series of small compartments in a desk or wall unit into which papers or messages can be sorted or placed **2.** BROAD CATEGORY a category or label assigned to somebody or something without a great deal of thought ○ *the tendency to put writers into pigeonholes* **3.** PIGEON'S NESTING COMPARTMENT a small nesting hole in a shelter for domestic pigeons ■ *vt.* (**-holed, -hol·ing, -holes**) **1.** PUT IN BROAD CATEGORY to categorize somebody or something without a great deal of thought **2.** POSTPONE to put something off for a while

pi·geon pea *n.* **1.** AFRICAN PLANT WITH EDIBLE SEEDS a woody African plant of the pea family with three-lobed leaves and yellow or orange flowers, cultivated in tropical regions for its edible seeds. Latin name: *Cajanus cajan.* **2.** PIGEON PEA SEED the small edible nutritious seed of the pigeon pea plant that is a popular ingredient in West Indian cookery [From the use of its seeds as pigeon-feed]

pi·geon-toed *adj.* tending to walk or stand with the toes turned inward

pi·geon tre·mex *n.* a common black-and-yellow North American horntail, related to the sawfly, that lays its eggs in the wood of trees into which the larvae bore and grow. Latin name: *Tremex columba.*

pig·fish /píg fish/ *n.* a food fish of the grunt family found on the Atlantic coast of North America. Latin name: *Orthopristis chrysoptera.*

pig·ger·y /píggəree/ (*plural* **-ies**) *n.* **1.** PLACE FOR RAISING PIGS a farm or a building on a farm where pigs are bred and raised **2.** COARSE BEHAVIOR coarse, greedy, or otherwise distasteful behavior

pig·gish /píggish/ *adj.* **1.** GLUTTONOUS eating too much too fast **2.** OBSTINATE behaving in a stubborn, uncooperative, or obstructive way —**pig·gish·ly** *adv.* —**pig·gish·ness** *n.*

pig·gy /píggee/ *n.* (*plural* **-gies**) (*informal babytalk*) **1.** PIG a pig or piglet **2.** TOE a toe, especially a small child's toe ■ *adj.* (**-gier, -gi·est**) = **piggish**

pig·gy·back /píggee bàk/, **pick·a·back** /píkə bàk/ *n.* **1.** RIDE ON SOMEBODY'S BACK a ride on somebody's back or shoulders **2.** TRANSP HAULING OF ONE VEHICLE BY ANOTHER transportation of one vehicle by another, e.g., automobiles by truck or truck trailers by railroad car ■ *adj., adv.* **1.** ON SOMEBODY'S BACK carried on the back or shoulders of another person **2.** TRANSP ON OTHER VEHICLE transported on another vehicle **3.** AS AN ADDITION linked with or added onto something larger or more important ■ *v.* (**-backed, -back·ing, -backs**) **1.** *vt.* CARRY ON BACK to carry somebody on the back or shoulders **2.** *vt.* TRANSP TRANSPORT to transport one vehicle on another **3.** *vti.* ATTACH ONE THING TO ANOTHER to link or add something to a larger or more important item, or to become linked or added to something else [Mid-16thC. Origin uncertain: perhaps originally a dialect form of earlier English *pick back*, literally "to throw back" or "to throw a pack," which by folk etymology was associated with PIG.]

pig·gy bank *n.* a child's savings bank, especially but not necessarily one in the shape of a pig

pig·gy in the mid·dle *n. U.K.* = **monkey in the middle**

pig·head·ed /pig héddəd/ *adj.* stubbornly adhering to a belief, decision, or course of action —**pig·head·ed·ly** *adv.* —**pig·head·ed·ness** *n.*

pig i·ron *n.* a crude form of iron made in a blast furnace and shaped into rough blocks for storage or transportation. Pig iron is processed further to make steel, wrought iron, and other alloys. [From PIG]

pig Lat·in *n.* any joke dialect coined and used by children, especially one in which first consonants are moved to the end of the words and extra syllables added [From the perception of pigs as vulgar]

pig·let /pígglət/ *n.* a newborn or immature pig

pig·ment *n.* /pígmənt/ **1. COLORING SUBSTANCE** a substance that is added to give something, such as paint or ink its color. Pigments are often available in the form of dry powders to be added to liquids. **2. NATURAL PLANT COLORING** a natural substance in plant or animal tissue that gives it its color ■ *vt.* /pígmənt, pig mént/ (**-ment·ed, -ment·ing, -ments**) **GIVE COLOR TO** to impart color to something [Pre-12thC. From Latin *pigmentum*, from *pingere* "to paint" (source of English *picture*). Ultimately from an Indo-European base meaning "to cut" (ancestor also of English *file*).] —**pig·men·tar·y** /pígmən tèrree/ *adj.*

pig·men·ta·tion /pìgmən táysh'n/ *n.* **1. NATURAL COLOR** the natural color of plants and animals **2. DISCOLORATION** abnormal coloring in plant or animal tissue that occurs as a result of disease

Pig·my /pígmee/ *n.* = **Pygmy**

pig·my hip·po·pot·a·mus *n.* = **pygmy hippopotamus**

pig·nut /píg nùt/ *n.* **1. HICKORY TREE** a nut-bearing hickory tree native to the central and southern United States. Latin name: *Carya glabra* and *Carya cordiformis.* **2. NUT OF A PIG-NUT TREE** the bitter nut of a pignut hickory tree

pig·pen /píg pèn/ *n.* **1. PLACE FOR PIGS** a building or enclosure where pigs are kept **2. UNTIDY PLACE** a dirty or disorderly place

Pigs, Bay of /pigz/ ➧ **Bay of Pigs**

pig·skin /píg skìn/ *n.* **1. LEATHER FROM PIG** the skin of a pig, especially when made into leather **2. FOOTBALL** a football **3. SADDLE** a horse's saddle (*informal*) ■ *adj.* **MADE OF LEATHER FROM PIG** made of leather prepared from the skin of a pig

pig·sty /píg stì/ (*plural* **-sties**) *n.* = **pigpen**

pig·tail /píg tàyl/ *n.* **1.** HAIR **BRAID** a braid or bunch, often in pairs, into which the hair is either braided or gathered **2.** HAIR = **queue** *n.* 4 **3. TOBACCO STRAND** a thin twisted piece of tobacco **4.** ELEC **BRAIDED WIRE** a short length of flexible electrical cable or wire, usually braided, connecting two terminals —**pig·tailed** *adj.*

pig·weed /píg wèed/ *n.* **1. WEED WITH HAIRY LEAVES** a North American weed of the amaranth family with hairy leaves and green flowers growing in spikes. Latin name: *Amaranthus retroflexus.* **2. WEED WITH EDIBLE LEAVES** a common weed of the goosefoot family whose leaves have a grainy surface and are sometimes used as a vegetable or in salads. Latin name: *Chenopodium album.*

pi·ka /péekə, píkə/ (*plural* **-kas** *or* **-ka**) *n.* a small short-eared burrowing mammal that is related to the rabbit and lives in rocky mountainous regions of western North America and Asia. Family: Ochotonidae. [Early 19thC. From Tungus *piika*.]

pike[1] /pīk/ (*plural* **pikes** *or* **pike**) *n.* **1. LARGE SHARP-TOOTHED FRESHWATER FISH** a large predatory freshwater fish of northern waters with a long body, long broad snout, and sharp teeth. It is a popular food and game fish. Latin name: *Esox lucius.* **2. FISH RESEMBLING PIKE** a fish that resembles the pike or belongs to the same family, especially the muskellunge and the pickerel [14thC. From PIKE[3]; from its long pointed jaws.]

pike[2] /pīk/ *n.* **SPIKE ON POLE** a weapon, used in the past by foot soldiers, consisting of a very long pole with a pointed metal head ■ *vt.* (**piked, pik·ing, pikes**) **ATTACK WITH PIKE** to stab or kill somebody with a pike [Early 16thC. From French *pique*, from *piquer* (see PIQUE).]

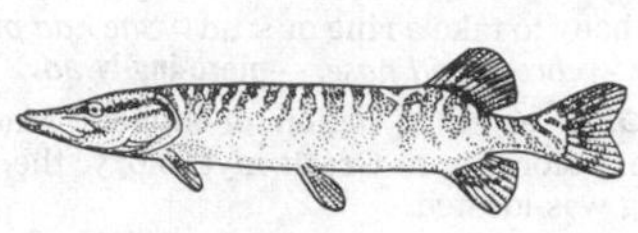

Pike

pike[3] /pīk/ *n.* a sharp pointed object of any kind [Old English *pīc*]

pike[4] /pīk/ *n.* a road on which a toll is paid [Early 19thC. Shortening of TURNPIKE.]

pike[5] /pīk/ *n.* a diving or gymnastic position in which the body is bent at the hips with the head tucked under and the hands touching the toes or behind the knees [Early 20thC. Origin unknown.] —**piked** *adj.*

Pike /pīk/, **Zebulon Montgomery** (1779–1813) U.S. explorer and soldier. He searched for the headwaters of the Mississippi River (1805–06) and explored Colorado and New Mexico.

pike·man /píkmən/ (*plural* **-men** /-mən/) *n.* a foot soldier armed with a pike

pike·perch /pík pùrch/ (*plural* **-perch·es** *or* **-perch**) *n.* = **walleye** *n.* 1

pik·er /píkər/ *n.* (*informal*) **1. STINGY PERSON** somebody who is stingy with money **2. PETTY PERSON** somebody who does things in a small-minded or petty way **3. CAUTIOUS GAMBLER** somebody who gambles cautiously with little money

Pikes Peak /pīks-/ mountain in Colorado, in the Rocky Mountains, west of Colorado Springs. It was named for the explorer Zebulon Pike. Height: 14,110 ft./4,301 m.

pike·staff /pík stàf/ *n.* **1. SHAFT OF PIKE** the wooden shaft of a pike, which forms the handle **2. POINTED WALKING STICK** a walking stick with a pointed metal end

pi·laf /pi láaf, pée làaf/, **pi·lau** /pi lów, pée lòw/ *n.* a Middle Eastern dish of spiced rice, often with chopped vegetables, fish, or meat added [Early 17thC. Directly or via Turkish *pilâv* "cooked rice," from Persian *pilaw* "cooked rice and meat."]

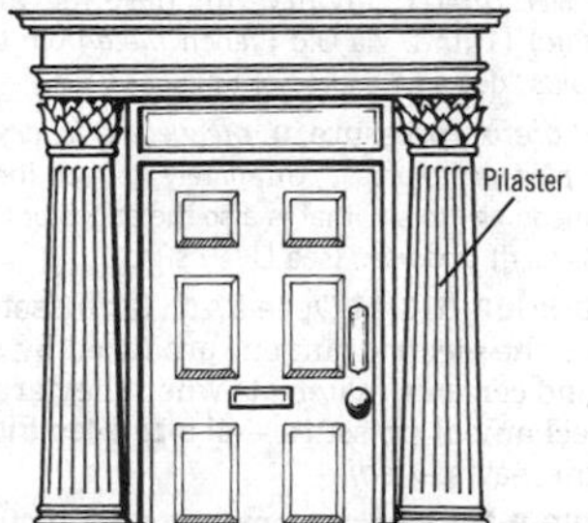

Pilaster

pi·las·ter /pi lástər/ *n.* a vertical structural part of a building that projects partway from a wall and is made to resemble an ornamental column by adding a base and capital [Late 16thC. Via French *pilastre* from Italian *pilastro* or medieval Latin *pilastrum*, from Latin *pila* "pillar."] —**pi·las·tered** *adj.*

Pi·late /pílət/, **Pontius** (*fl.* 1st century A.D.) Roman administrator. As procurator of Judaea (A.D. 26–36) he condemned Jesus Christ to death, albeit reluctantly, according to the Bible.

pi·lau *n.* = **pilaf**

Pil·ba·ra /píbrə/ region in northwestern Western Australia, located between the De Grey and Ashburton rivers

pil·chard /pílchərd/ (*plural* **-chards** *or* **-chard**) *n.* a small edible marine fish of the herring family that lives in European waters and has a rounded body and large scales. It is often sold in cans. Latin name: *Sardinia pilchardus.* [Mid-16thC. Origin unknown.]

pile[1] /pīl/ *n.* **1. MOUND OF THINGS** a number of things heaped or stacked one on top of another **2. LARGE QUANTITY** a very large amount of something (*informal*) (*often used in the plural*) ○ *I've got piles of work to do.* **3. FORTUNE** a very large amount of money, especially one large enough to retire on (*informal*) ○ *He'd already made his pile by the age of 30.* **4. BUILDING** a large impressive building **5. PYRE** a funeral pyre (*archaic*) **6.** ELEC = **voltaic pile 7.** NUCLEAR PHYS **NUCLEAR REACTOR** a nuclear reactor (*dated*) ■ *v.* (**piled, pil·ing, piles**) **1.** *vt.* **MAKE INTO A MOUND** to heap or stack things one on top of another **2.** *vt.* **PLACE LARGE AMOUNTS ON SOMETHING** to heap a large amount of something somewhere ○ *plates piled high with ribs* **3.** *vi.* **GO AS A CROWD** to move hurriedly in a large disorganized group ○ *We all piled into the car and headed for the diner.* [15thC. Via French, from Latin *pila* "pillar" (source also of English *pillar*).]

pile up *vti.* **1. AMASS** to accumulate, or accumulate something, rapidly, forming a large amount **2. CRASH** to crash a vehicle, or to collide with other vehicles, forming a chain of collisions

pile[2] /pīl/ *n.* **1.** CONSTR **SUNKEN SUPPORT FOR BUILDING** a vertical wood, metal, or concrete support for a building or other structure that is driven into the ground **2.** HERALDRY **HERALDIC SYMBOL** a heraldic figure in the shape of an arrowhead, usually displayed with the point downward **3.** ARMS **ARROWHEAD** the pointed head of an arrow (*technical*) **4.** ARMS **ANCIENT ROMAN JAVELIN** a javelin used by foot soldiers in ancient Rome ■ *vt.* (**piled, pil·ing, piles**) CONSTR **SUPPORT A STRUCTURE WITH PILES** to use piles as a support for a building or other structure [Pre-12thC. From Latin *pilum* "javelin."]

pile[3] /pīl/ *n.* **1. LOOPED FABRIC SURFACE** the surface of a carpet or of a fabric such as velvet that is formed of short, sometimes cut, loops of fiber **2. FUR** the fine soft fur or hair of an animal [Mid-16thC. Origin uncertain: probably via Anglo-Norman *peile* from, ultimately, Latin *pilus* "hair" (source of English *depilatory, pluck* and, perhaps, *pillage*).]

pi·le·a plural of **pileum**

pi·le·ate /pílee ət, píllee-/, **pi·le·at·ed** /pílee àytəd, píllee-/ *adj.* **1.** BIRDS **CRESTED** used to describe a bird that has a crest of feathers on its head **2.** FUNGI **WITH CAP-SHAPED PART** used to describe a fungus that has a cap-shaped upper part (**pileus**) [Early 18thC. From Latin *pileatus*, literally "wearing a felt cap," from *pileus* "felt cap."]

pi·le·at·ed wood·peck·er *n.* a large black-and-white woodpecker with a red crest, native to wooded areas of North America. Latin name: *Dryocopus pileatus.*

pile driv·er *n.* a large mechanical hammering device that uses steam, compressed air, or gravity to drive construction piles into the ground

pi·le·i plural of **pileus**

pil·e·ous /pílee əss, píllee-/ *adj.* BIOL covered with hair [Mid-18thC. From Latin *pileus*, literally "felt cap."]

piles /pīlz/ *npl.* hemorrhoids (*informal*) [15thC. Origin uncertain: probably from Latin *pila* "ball," from their shape.]

pi·le·um /pílee əm, píllee-/ (*plural* **-a** /-ə/) *n.* the top of a bird's head from the base of the bill to the nape of the neck [Late 19thC. Via modern Latin from Latin *pileus* "felt cap."]

pile-up /píl ùp/, **pile-up** *n.* **1. LARGE-SCALE COLLISION** a collision involving several vehicles (*informal*) **2. ACCUMULATION OF THINGS** an accumulated number or amount of things such as tasks

pi·le·us /pílee əss, píllee-/ (*plural* **-i** /-ì/) *n.* **1.** BOT **CAP OF MUSHROOM** the top cap-shaped part of a mushroom or other fungus **2.** MARINE BIOL **JELLYFISH'S BODY** the part of the body of a jellyfish that resembles an opened umbrella **3.** CLOTHES **ROMAN SKULLCAP** a close-fitting brimless cap worn by ancient Romans [Mid-18thC. From Latin *pileus* "felt cap."]

pile·wort /píl wùrt, -wàwrt/ (*plural* **-worts** *or* **-wort**) *n.* a flowering plant of the buttercup family such as the lesser celandine, sometimes used as a remedy for hemorrhoids [15thC. PILE the singular of PILES.]

pil·fer /pílfər/ (**-fered, -fer·ing, -fers**) *vti.* to steal small items of little value, especially habitually [14thC. From Anglo-Norman *pelfrer* "to rob," of uncertain origin.] —**pil·fer·age** *n.* —**pil·fer·er** *n.* —**pil·fer·ing** *n.*

WORD KEY: SYNONYMS

See Synonyms at ***steal.***

pil·grim /pílgrim/ *n.* **1. RELIGIOUS TRAVELER** somebody who goes on a journey to a holy place for religious reasons **2. TRAVELER** somebody who is making a journey of any kind (*literary*) [12thC. Via Provençal *pelegrin* from Latin *peregrinus* (see PEREGRINE).]

WORD KEY: CULTURAL NOTE

The Pilgrim's Progress, a story by the English writer John Bunyan (1678, 1684). An allegorical account of religious conversion, it describes the journey of a man called Christian from the City of Destruction (the contemporary, corrupt world) to the Celestial City (a state of religious grace). Much of its immense and lasting popularity can be attributed the author's skill in rendering complex abstract issues immediate, entertaining, and accessible. It is the source of three well-known expressions in use today – *muckraker* (an investigative journalist seeking sensational stories), *slough of despond* (a state of profoundly deep depression), and *vanity fair* (a place or situation of ostentatious, empty pride).

Pil·grim *n.* one of the English Puritans who founded Plymouth Colony in Massachusetts in 1620

pil·grim·age /pílgrimij/ *n.* **1. RELIGIOUS JOURNEY** a journey to a holy place, undertaken for religious reasons **2. TRIP TO SPECIAL PLACE** a journey to a place with special significance ○ *Thousands of fans make the pilgrimage to Elvis's birthplace every year.* [13thC. From Provençal *pelegrinatge*, from Latin *peregrinus* (see PEREGRINE).]

pi·li BIOL plural of **pilus**

pi·lif·er·ous /pī líffərəss/ *adj.* used to describe plant parts that are covered in fine hairs or have hairs growing at the tip [Mid-19thC. Coined from PILUS + -I- + -FEROUS.]

pil·i·form /pílee fàwrm/ *adj.* used to describe a plant part that takes the form of a hair [Early 19thC. Coined from PILUS + -I- + -FORM.]

Pil·i·pi·no /pìllə peénō/ *n., adj.* LANG = **Filipino**

pill /pil/ *n.* **1. ROUND TABLET OF MEDICINE** a round solid tablet of medicine to be taken orally **2. pill, Pill ORAL CONTRACEPTIVE** a contraceptive that is taken orally in pill form **3. SOMETHING ROUND** something round such as a baseball, bullet, or bomb (*informal*) **4. TIRESOME PERSON** somebody who is unpleasant or boring (*dated slang*) ■ *v.* **(pilled, pil·ling, pills) 1.** *vi.* **FORM LITTLE BALLS WHEN RUBBED** to become covered in small balls of matted fiber as a result of friction (*refers to fabrics*) **2.** *vt.* **EXCLUDE** to reject somebody either by vote or consensus (*dated slang*) [15thC. From Middle Low German or Middle Dutch *pille*, of uncertain origin: probably from Latin *pilula*, literally "little ball," from *pila* "ball."] ◇ **a bitter pill (to swallow)** something that it difficult or painful to accept

pil·lage /píllij/ *vti.* **(-laged, -lag·ing, -lag·es) 1. PLUNDER A PLACE** to rob a place using force, especially during a war **2. STEAL PEOPLE'S POSSESSIONS** to steal goods using force, especially during a war ■ *n.* **1. STEALING OF SOMEBODY'S POSSESSIONS** theft of goods from a place using force, especially during a war **2. STOLEN POSSESSIONS** goods that are stolen using force, especially during war [14thC. From French, from *piller* "to plunder," of uncertain origin: perhaps from Latin *pilare* "to remove hair," or from assumed Vulgar Latin *piliare*, from Latin *pilum* "javelin."] —**pil·lag·er** *n.*

pil·lar /píllər/ *n.* **1. COLUMN USED FOR SUPPORT OR DECORATION** a vertical column that is part of a building or other structure and can be either a support or decoration **2. SOMETHING TALL AND NARROW** something that is tall and slender like a pillar **3. CENTRAL FIGURE** somebody who is a mainstay of an organization or society ○ *She was a pillar of the community.* ■ *vt.* **(-lared, -lar·ing, -lars) SUPPORT WITH PILLARS** to support or strengthen something with pillars [13thC. Via Anglo-Norman *piler* from, ultimately, Latin *pila* "pillar" (source of English *compile* and *pile* "heap").] ◇ **from pillar to post** from one place to another

pil·lar·i·za·tion /pìllәri záysh'n/ *n.* the division of society into autonomous groups whose members share a common language or set of beliefs. Each group retains its own identity, while crossing lines of class and status. In Dutch society pillarization is based upon Calvinist, Roman Catholic, and Humanist social groupings. [Translation of Dutch *verzuiling*]

Pil·lars of Her·cu·les two promontories, the Rock of Gibraltar and Jebel Musa, on either side of the Strait of Gibraltar at the far western end of the Mediterranean. According to legend, the two rocks were separated by Hercules.

Pil·lars of Is·lam, Five Pil·lars of Is·lam *npl.* the basic tenets of Islam, which are a belief in Allah and in Muhammad as his prophet, in prayer, in charity, in fasting, and in making a pilgrimage to Mecca

pill·box /píl bòks/ *n.* **1. PILL-CONTAINER** a small container for pills **2. pill·box, pill·box hat WOMAN'S BRIMLESS HAT** a woman's shallow brimless hat with a flat top **3. GUN SHELTER** a small fortified shelter with a flat roof, in which a large gun is sited

pill bug *n.* = **wood louse** [Because it is able to roll itself into a ball]

pil·lion /píllyən/ *n.* **PASSENGER SEAT** a seat for a passenger behind the driver of a motorcycle or the rider of a horse ■ *adv.* **BEHIND THE RIDER** seated behind the driver of a motorcycle or the rider of a horse [15thC. From Gaelic *pillean* and Irish *pillín*, literally "little couch," from *pell* "couch," from Latin *pellis* "skin" (source of English *pelt* "skin").]

pil·lo·ry /pílləree/ *n.* (*plural* **-ries**) **OLD PUNISHMENT DEVICE** a device used in the past as a means of public punishment, in the form of a wooden frame with holes into which somebody's head and hands could be locked ■ *vt.* **(-ried, -ry·ing, -ries) 1. RIDICULE** to scorn or ridicule somebody or something openly, or expose somebody or something to scorn or ridicule **2. PUNISH IN PILLORY** to put somebody into a pillory as a public punishment [13thC. Via Anglo-Latin *pillorium* from Old French *pillorie*, of uncertain origin: perhaps from Provençal *espilori*.]

pil·low /píllō/ *n.* **1. CUSHION FOR HEAD** a soft support for the head in bed, in the form of a sealed fabric bag stuffed with feathers or a synthetic filling **2. SOMETHING LIKE A PILLOW** something that is similar to a pillow in appearance or use **3.** = **cushion** *n.* 6 ■ *vt.* **(-lowed, -low·ing, -lows) 1. CUSHION THE HEAD** to rest the head on a pillow or something else that is soft and comfortable **2. ACT AS PILLOW FOR** to provide a soft comfortable surface on which to rest something [Pre-12thC. Via a prehistoric West Germanic word (source also of German *pfühl* and Dutch *peluw*), from Latin *pulvinus*.]

pil·low block *n.* an enclosure and support for a shaft or axle of a machine

pil·low·case /píllō kàyss/ *n.* a fabric cover for a pillow

pil·low lace *n.* lace made using bobbins and a firm pad, or pillow as a base, as distinct from lace made with a needle and a paper pattern

pil·low la·va *n.* lava that has solidified into pillow-shaped masses, formed from underwater lava flows or from lava flowing into water from land. Each pillow can be up to 6 ft./2 m across and is surrounded by a fine-grained skin.

pil·low sham *n.* a decorative covering for a pillow on a bed

pil·low·slip /píllō slìp/ *n.* = **pillowcase**

pil·low talk *n.* the discussion of intimate or private matters in bed with a sexual partner

pi·lo·car·pine /pìlə kaár peèn, -kaárpin/ *n.* a poisonous colorless or yellow alkaloid obtained from the leaves of the jaborandi tree, used in the past to promote sweating and to treat glaucoma. Formula: $C_{11}H_{16}N_2O_2$. [Late 19thC. Coined from modern Latin *Pilocarpus*, genus name of the tree.]

pi·lose /pílōss/, **pi·lous** /píləss/ *adj.* used to describe plant parts that are covered with soft hair [Late 18thC. From Latin *pilosus* "hairy," from *pilus* "hair."] —**pi·los·i·ty** /pī lóssətee/ *n.*

pi·lot /pílət/ *n.* **1.** AIR **SOMEBODY WHO FLIES PLANE** somebody who is qualified to fly an aircraft or spacecraft **2.** NAVIG **SOMEBODY STEERING SHIPS THROUGH DIFFICULT AREA** somebody with local knowledge whose job is to navigate ships in and out of a harbor or through a particular stretch of water **3.** SHIPPING **STEERER OF SHIP** somebody who steers a ship or boat **4. LEADER** somebody who acts as a leader or guide **5.** BROADCAST **TELEVISION PROGRAM** a television or radio program made as a prototype for a projected series **6. TRIAL RUN** a test of something, e.g., a proposed manufacturing process, to discover and solve problems before full implementation **7.** = **pilot light** *n.* 1 **8.** ENG **MACHINE GUIDE** a guiding part of a tool or machine ■ *vt.* **(-lot·ed, -lot·ing, -lots) 1.** AIR **FLY AN AIRCRAFT** to fly an aircraft or spacecraft **2. NAVIGATE** to navigate a ship **3. BE IN CHARGE OF SOMETHING** to direct the course of something, e.g., a project or a program of research **4. RUN A TRIAL** to test something, such as a proposed manufacturing process, to discover and solve problems before full implementation [Early 16thC. Via French *pilote*, from medieval Latin *pilotus*, an alteration of *pedota*, from, ultimately, Greek *pēdon* "oar."]

pi·lot·age /pílətij/ *n.* **1.** NAVIG **PILOTING OF CRAFT** the controlling of a ship, aircraft, or spacecraft **2.** FIN **HARBOR OR RIVER PILOT'S FEE** the fee paid to a harbor or river pilot for steering a ship along a short difficult stretch **3.** NAVIG **MANUAL NAVIGATION** the navigation of an aircraft using landmarks and maps, rather than an aircraft's own navigation systems

pi·lot bal·loon *n.* a small balloon launched to study the speed and direction of winds at high altitudes. The balloon is visually tracked by a theodolite.

pi·lot bread, pi·lot bis·cuit *n.* = **hardtack**

pi·lot fish *n.* a small striped marine fish, often found swimming with sharks, mantas, and other large fishes, where it finds stray scraps of food. Latin name: *Naucrates ductor*.

pi·lot·house /pílət hòwss/ *n.* an enclosed control room on or near the bridge of a ship, containing the steering wheel and navigational and communication equipment

pi·lot lamp *n.* a small light in an electric circuit to show if the power is on or if an electrical device is operating

pi·lot light *n.* **1. pi·lot light, pi·lot FLAME USED FOR IGNITION** a small gas flame that remains lit in order to ignite a burner when it is turned on **2.** = **pilot lamp**

pi·lot whale *n.* a large black toothed whale with a bulbous head, found in warm seas. Genus: *Globicephala*.

pi·lous *adj.* = **pilose**

pil·sen·er *n.* = **pilsner**

pil·sner /pílznər, pílsnər/, **pil·sener** *n.* **1. LAGER BEER FLAVORED WITH HOPS** lager beer with a strong hops flavor, originally and especially made in Pilsen in the Czech Republic **2. pil·sner, pil·sner glass GLASS FOR DRINKING BEER** a tall, tapering, short-stemmed glass used for drinking beer [Late 19thC. From German, literally "of Pilsen," from *Pilsen* (Czech *Plzeň*), the name of a province in the Czech Republic.]

Pilt·down man /pílt dòwn-/ *n.* a supposed primitive form of human being represented by remains of bones found in Sussex, England in 1912, shown in 1953 to be a hoax [Early 20thC. Named for the village in Sussex, England, where the remains were found.]

pil·ule /píl yool/ *n.* a small pill [15thC. Via French from Latin *pilula*, literally "little ball," from *pila* "ball" (source of English *pill*.)]

pi·lus /píləss/ (*plural* **-li** /pí lì/) *n.* any part of a plant or animal organism that looks like a hair [Mid-20thC. From Latin, "hair."]

PIM /pim/ *n., abbr.* COMPUT Personal Information Manager

Pi·ma /peémə/ *n.* **1.** PEOPLES **NATIVE N AMERICAN PEOPLE** a member of a Native North American people that originally occupied lands in southern and central Arizona, and whose members now live mainly in central Arizona **2.** LANG **NATIVE N AMERICAN LANGUAGE** a Native American language spoken in parts of Arizona. It belongs to the Uto-Aztecan branch of Aztec-Tanoan languages and is closely related to Papago. Pima is spoken by about 15,000 people. [Early 19thC. From Spanish, a shortening of *Pimahito*, from Pima *pimahaitu* "nothing," perhaps because of a misunderstanding by missionaries.] —**Pima** *adj.*

pi·ma cot·ton *n.* a strong cotton with medium-length fibers that was bred in the southwestern United States from selected Egyptian cottons [Mid-20thC. Named for Pima County, Arizona.]

pi·men·to /pi méntō/ *n.* **1.** FOOD = **pimiento 2.** = **allspice** [Late 17thC. Via Spanish *pimiento*, from Latin *pigmentum* (see PIGMENT).]

pi mes·on *n.* = **pion**

pi·mien·to /pi méntō, pi myéntō/ (*plural* **-tos**), **pi·men·to** (*plural* **-tos**) *n.* **1.** FOOD **MILD RED PEPPER** a large sweet red pepper that is used especially to stuff olives, as a garnish, and to make paprika **2.** PLANTS **EUROPEAN PEPPER PLANT** a European plant that produces pimiento peppers. Latin name: *Capsicum annuum*. [Mid-17thC. From Spanish (see PIMENTO).]

pimp /pimp/ *n.* **MAN SOLICITING FOR PROSTITUTES** a man who finds customers for a prostitute in return for a portion of the prostitute's earnings ■ *vi.* **(pimped,**

pimp·ing, pimps) **BE A PIMP** to work as a pimp, finding customers for prostitutes [Late 16thC. Origin uncertain.]

pim·per·nel /pímpər nèl, pímpərnəl/ (*plural* **-nels** *or* **-nel**) *n.* a small plant with long trailing stems and small red, white, or purple flowers. Pimpernels belong to the primrose family. Genus: *Anagallis.* [15thC. Via Old French *pimpernelle* "burnet" (the plant), the original sense in English, from earlier *piprenelle*, from, ultimately, Latin *piper* "pepper," because its fruit resembles peppercorns.]

pimp·ing /pímping/ *adj.* **1. TRIFLING** of little significance **2. WEAK** appearing weak and unhealthy (*regional*) [Late 17thC. Origin unknown: perhaps thought to suggest smallness.]

pim·ple /pímp'l/ *n.* a small inflamed or pus-filled spot on the skin [14thC. From an alteration of the base that produced Old English *piplian* "to break out in spots."] — **pim·pled** *adj.* —**pim·ply** *adj.*

pimp·mo·bile /pímp mō bèel, -mə-/ *n.* a very showy large automobile, typical of one that might be used by a pimp (*disapproving*)

pin /pin/ *n.* **1. THIN POINTED METAL STICK** a small thin metal stick with a sharp point and a rounded head, used for holding pieces of fabric together **2. POINTED METAL FASTENER** any fastener that has a sharp metal point designed to pierce the things it is fastening **3.** = **safety pin** *n.* 1, **safety pin** *n.* 2 **4. SOMETHING DECORATIVE ATTACHED TO CLOTHING** a badge, piece of jewelry, or other decorative item that attaches to clothing by means of a sharp metal point or a clasp **5.** = **hairpin** *n.* 1 **6. BOBBY PIN** a bobby pin **7.** = **cotter pin 8.** = **rolling pin 9. LEAST BIT** the smallest amount (*dated informal*) ○ *not worth a pin* **10.** ELEC **PART OF ELECTRICAL CONNECTOR** a thin metal terminal extending from an electrical or electronic device such as a plug or a vacuum tube, used to connect the device by socket to other circuitry ○ *a three-pin plug* **11.** SURG **ROD TO JOIN BROKEN BONE** a thin metal rod used to hold the ends of a fractured bone together **12.** DENT **PEG USED IN DENTISTRY** a peg used to attach a crown to the root of a tooth **13.** TECH **KEY PART ENTERING LOCK** the part of a key that inserts into a lock **14.** MUSIC **PEG HOLDING INSTRUMENT STRING** any of the pegs on a stringed instrument such as a piano that hold the strings and can be turned to tighten or loosen them to tune the instrument **15.** ARMS **SAFETY CLIP ON GRENADE** the safety clip on a hand grenade that must be removed before the grenade can be detonated **16.** SPORTS **BOWLING PIN** any of the club-shaped targets used in various games of bowling **17.** GOLF **HOLE MARKER IN GOLF** a pole with a flag on it, used to mark each hole on a golf course **18.** WRESTLING **WRESTLING FALL** a fall in wrestling in which an opponent's shoulders are made to touch the mat **19.** COMPUT **GUIDE ON COMPUTER PRINTER** any of the rounded pegs that guide the paper through a computer printer **20.** COMPUT **PART OF PRINTHEAD THAT FORMS LETTERS** any of the tiny wires on the printhead of a dot matrix printer that form one dot of a letter or symbol **21.** NAUT = **belaying pin 22.** NAUT = **thole pin** ■ **pins** *npl.* **LEGS** somebody's legs (*informal*) ○ *He's a bit unsteady on his pins.* ■ *vt.* (**pinned, pin·ning, pins**) **1. FASTEN SOMETHING WITH PINS** to fasten, attach, or secure something with a pin **2. KEEP SOMEBODY OR SOMETHING FROM MOVING** to hold somebody or something immobile, e.g., on the ground ○ *The beam fell across his back, pinning him to the ground.* **3.** CHESS **RESTRICT OPPONENT'S CHESS PIECE** to make it impossible for a chess opponent to move a piece without exposing the king to check or a valuable piece to capture **4.** WRESTLING **HOLD WRESTLING OPPONENT DOWN** to hold a wrestling opponent's shoulders to the mat **5. GIVE A FRATERNITY PIN TO SOMEBODY** to give a young woman a fraternity pin as a sign of commitment to a relationship [12thC. From Latin *pinna* "feather, pointed peak." Ultimately from an Indo-European base meaning "to fly, rush" which is also the ancestor of English *feather.*] —**pin·ner** *n.*

WORD KEY: USAGE

See Usage note at ***ATM.***

pin down *vt.* **1. IDENTIFY PRECISELY** to determine something with certainty ○ *Can you pin down the time of death?* **2. FORCE TO DECIDE** to force somebody to keep a commitment or come to a decision ○ *I haven't managed to pin him down to a date for our meeting yet.* **3. PREVENT SOMEBODY FROM MOVING** to prevent somebody from going anywhere ○ *The platoon was pinned down by enemy fire.*

PIN /pin/ (*plural* **PINs**), **PIN num·ber** *n.* a multidigit number unique to an individual that is used, with a card, to get money from an ATM or to gain access to a computer or telephone system. Abbr of **personal identification number**

pi·ña cloth /peényə-/ *n.* a fine transparent fabric made of fiber from pineapple leaves [*Piña* via Spanish, "pineapple, pine cone," from Latin *pinea* "pine cone," from *pinus* (see PINE 1)]

pi·ña co·la·da /peényə kə laádə/ *n.* a cocktail made from pineapple juice, rum, and coconut [From Spanish, literally "strained pineapple"]

pin·a·fore /pínnə fàwr/ *n.* **1.** *U.K.* = **jumper 2. GIRL'S**

Pinafore

OVERGARMENT a sleeveless collarless garment worn by girls in the past over a dress and fastened at the top and back [Late 18thC. From PIN + AFORE, because it was originally used for a garment pinned to the front of a dress.]

Pi·nang = **Penang**

pi·nas·ter /pī nástər/ *n.* a pyramid-shaped Mediterranean pine tree with needles in pairs and clusters of long prickly cones. Latin name: *Pinus pinaster.* [Mid-16thC. From Latin, from *pinus* (see PINE).]

pi·ña·ta /pin yaátə, peen yaátə/ *n.* a decorated container of sweets or small gifts that is hung from the ceiling and is hit and broken by blindfolded people with sticks, traditionally during Latin American festivals [Late 19thC. From Spanish, literally "jug."]

pin·ball /pín bàwl/ *n.* a game played on an electronic table fitted with obstacles, targets, and pivoted flippers. The player controls the flippers to keep a ball in play, hitting targets to score points. (*often used before a noun*)

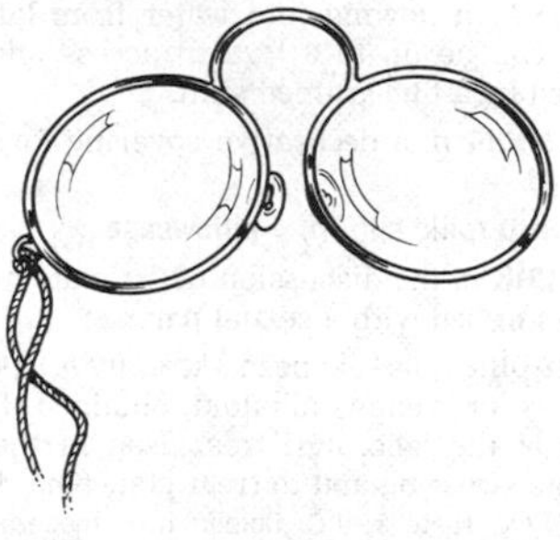

Pince-nez

pince-nez /pins náy/ (*plural* **pince-nez** /pìns náyz/) *n.* a pair of glasses without sidepieces, held in place by a clip that fits over the nose [From French, literally "to pinch the nose"]

pin·cer move·ment /pínsər moóvmənt/, **pin·cers move·ment** *n.* a military maneuver that attempts to surround an enemy by simultaneous attack from the front and two side columns that curve around the enemy and back toward each other

pin·cers /pínsərz/ *npl.* **1. LARGE CLAWS OF LOBSTER** the front claws of some crustaceans and arachnids, e.g., the lobster and scorpion, used for grasping things **2. TOOL FOR GRIPPING THINGS** a tool, resembling a pair of pliers or scissors, with curved pivoted jaws that are used to grip something, e.g., a nail, when they are closed [14thC. From Anglo-Norman, a variation of Old French *pincier* (see PINCH).]

pin·cers move·ment *n.* = **pincer movement**

pinch /pinch/ *v.* (**pinched, pinch·ing, pinch·es**) **1.** *vti.* **GRIP SOMETHING BETWEEN FINGER AND THUMB** to grip or squeeze

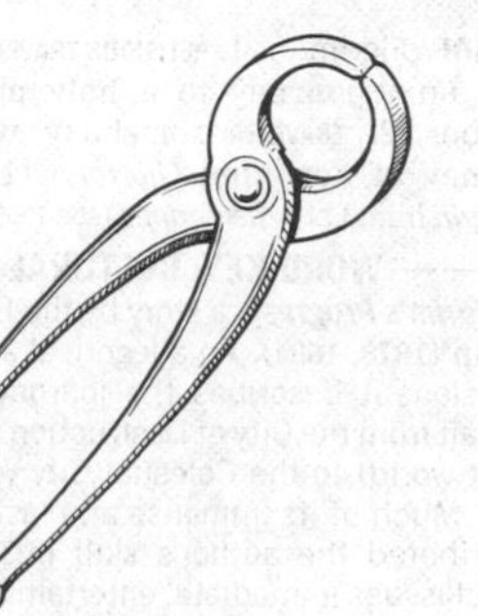

Pincers

something tightly between finger and thumb or between two hard objects or edges **2.** *vti.* **BE TOO TIGHT AND PAINFUL** to painfully constrict or squeeze a part of the body ○ *These shoes are pinching my feet.* **3.** *vt.* **WITHER SOMETHING** to make somebody or something become shrunken or withered, especially through harsh conditions like cold or hunger ○ *a face pinched with grief and pain* **4.** *vt.* **IMPOSE HARDSHIP ON** to put somebody in financial difficulty ○ *Unexpected expenses have really pinched me this month.* **5.** *vt.* GARDENING **REMOVE SHOOTS TO ENCOURAGE BUSHY GROWTH** to remove new shoots and buds from a plant to make it become more bushy **6.** *vti. U.K.* **STEAL SOMETHING** to steal something or take something without permission (*informal*) ○ *Who's pinched my pen?* **7.** *vt.* **ARREST SOMEBODY** to arrest somebody (*informal*) **8.** *vt.* SAILING **SAIL A VESSEL INTO THE WIND** to sail a sailing vessel too close to the wind, so that it loses wind from its sails **9.** *vi.* MINING **NARROW AND DISAPPEAR** to become gradually narrower, eventually disappearing entirely (*refers to a vein of ore*) ■ *n.* **1. PAINFUL SQUEEZE** a painful squeeze or nip, especially with the thumb and finger ○ *a pinch on the arm* **2. VERY LITTLE** a very small amount of a substance, especially the amount held between the thumb and first finger ○ *add a pinch of salt* **3. ROBBERY** a robbery (*informal*) **4. AN ARREST** an arrest made by the police (*informal*) **5. CRITICAL TIME** an emergency or critical situation ○ *If it comes to the pinch, we'll have to sell the house.* [13thC. Via assumed Anglo-Norman *pincher*, a variant of Old French *pincier*, from assumed Vulgar Latin *pinctiare* "to prick."] ◇ **feel the pinch** to have financial problems ◇ **in a pinch** if absolutely necessary, although preferably not

WORD KEY: SYNONYMS

See Synonyms at ***steal.***

pinch bar *n.* a crowbar with an attached projection that acts as a fulcrum

pinch·beck /pínch bèk/ *n.* **1. GOLD-COLORED METAL ALLOY** an alloy of copper and zinc used as imitation gold in inexpensive jewelry **2. CHEAP COPY** an inferior imitation ■ *adj.* **1. MADE OF PINCHBECK** made from pinchbeck alloy **2. IMITATION** made in imitation of something and usually of inferior quality [Mid-18thC. Named for Christopher *Pinchbeck*, died 1732, English watchmaker and inventor of the alloy.]

pinch·buck /pínch bùk/ *n.* a long-bodied beetle, native to Europe, with long curving antennae. Latin name: *Harpium sycophanta.*

pinch·cock /pínch kòk/ *n.* a clamp used to control the flow of fluid through a flexible tube

pinch ef·fect *n.* PHYS the narrowing of a beam of charged particles caused by the interaction of each particle with the magnetic field generated by the movement of the beam

pinch hit *n.* BASEBALL a hit made by a substitute hitter

pinch-hit (**pinch-hit, pinch-hit·ting, pinch-hits**) *vi.* **1.** BASEBALL **ACT AS SUBSTITUTE HITTER** to replace the scheduled batter at bat in baseball, especially when a hit is needed **2. SUBSTITUTE FOR** to take somebody else's place at something —**pinch hit·ter** *n.*

Pin·chot /pínch ot/, **Gifford** (1865–1946) U.S. conservationist. He advocated government protection of natural resources, and was chief of what is now the Forest Service (1898–1910).

pinch·pen·ny /pínch pènnee/ *adj.* **UNGENEROUS** unwilling to spend or give money ■ *n.* (*plural* **-nies**) **MISER** somebody who is unwilling to spend or give money

pinch run·ner *n.* BASEBALL a runner who replaces a batter who has successfully reached base, usually because the batter is slow or injured

Pinck·ney /píngknee/, **Charles Cotesworth** (1757–1824) U.S. statesman. He helped to draft the United States Constitution, and was four times governor of South Carolina.

pin curl *n.* a flat curl in hair, made by winding strands of hair into a circle and securing it with a clip or hairpin

pin·cush·ion /pín kòosh'n/ *n.* a small stuffed pad used for sticking dressmaking pins into when they are not being used

Pin·dar /píndər/ (*fl.* 522? B.C.-443 B.C.) Greek poet. He was the chief lyric poet of Greece, his *Triumphal Odes* surviving intact.

Pin·dar·ic /pin dérrik/ *adj.* **1. RELATING TO PINDAR** relating to the poet Pindar **2. IN STYLE OF PINDAR'S POETRY** relating to Pindaric odes or in the form of a Pindaric ode

Pin·dar·ic, Pin·dar·ic ode *n.* a form of ode with three-stanza sections, the first and second stanzas having one metrical form and the third having a different form

Pine

pine[1] /pīn/ *n.* **1.** TREES **EVERGREEN TREE** an evergreen coniferous tree with needle-shaped leaves and woody cones. The sticky sap of some species is used to make turpentine, and many species are planted as ornamentals. Genus: *Pinus.* (*often used before a noun*) **2.** INDUST **WOOD FROM PINE** the wood of any pine tree, varying from soft to hard. It is widely used for furniture and as a structural and finishing building material. **3.** TREES **TREE RESEMBLING THE PINE** a coniferous tree or shrub similar to the pine but unrelated, e.g., the Norfolk Island pine or ground pine [Pre-12thC. From Latin *pinus*, of uncertain origin: perhaps from, ultimately, an Indo-European base meaning "to swell" (ancestor also of English *fat*), the tree being "swollen" with resin.] —**pine·y** /pínee/ *adj.*

pine[2] /pīn/ (**pined, pin·ing, pines**) *vi.* **1. YEARN** to long for somebody or something, especially somebody or something unattainable **2. WASTE AWAY** to become weak and lose vitality as a result of grief or longing [Pre-12thC. Origin uncertain: probably from, ultimately, Latin *poena* "penalty" (source of English *pain* and *penal*), from Greek *poinē*. Originally in the sense "torture."]

pin·e·al /pínnee əl, pī nee əl/ *adj.* **1.** BIOL **RELATING TO PINEAL GLAND** relating to or secreted by the pineal gland **2.** BOT **CONE-SHAPED** shaped like a pine cone [Late 17thC. Via French *pinéal* from Latin *pinea* "pine cone," from its pine-cone-like shape, from *pinus* (see PINE[1]).]

pin·e·al gland, pin·e·al bod·y *n.* a small cone-shaped organ of the brain that secretes the hormone melatonin into the bloodstream. It is one of the endocrine glands and is situated beneath the back part of the corpus callosum.

pine·ap·ple /pí nàpp'l/ *n.* **1.** FOOD **JUICY YELLOW FRUIT** a large fruit with juicy yellow flesh, a thick lumpy yellowish brown skin, and a tuft of tough pointed leaves at the top **2.** (*plural* **-ples** *or* **-ple**) PLANTS **PLANT ON WHICH PINEAPPLES GROW** a tropical American plant that produces pineapples. It has a tall thick stem, tough sword-shaped leaves, and dense clusters of small flowers. Latin name: *Ananas comosus.* **3.** ARMS **GRENADE WITH PATTERNED SURFACE** a hand grenade with a surface of raised geometric shapes (*slang*) [14thC. Originally used for "pine cone"; the modern sense evolved because the fruit was thought to resemble a pine cone.]

Pineapple

pine·ap·ple weed *n.* a plant with greenish-yellow flower heads that smell like pineapple when crushed. It is native to Asia, but is naturalized in North America and Europe. Latin name: *Matricaria matri.*

Pine Bluff /pīn-/ city in southeastern Arkansas, on the Arkansas River, southeast of Little Rock. Population: 54,165 (1996).

pine cone *n.* a pine tree's seed case, usually woody, oval, and scaly [See PINEAPPLE]

pine·cone fish *n.* either of two marine fishes of the Indian and Pacific Oceans with heavy scales that resemble the scales of a pine cone. Family: Monocentridae.

pine·drops /pín dròps/ *npl.* a purplish brown North American plant of the wintergreen family. It is leafless, has drooping reddish or white flowers, and grows under pine trees as a parasite on the roots. Latin name: *Pterspora andromedea.* (*takes a singular or plural verb*)

pine·land /pín lànd/ *n.* an area forested mainly with pine trees (*often used in the plural*)

pine leaf scale *n.* an insect with a tough outer covering that attaches itself to pine needles and seriously inhibits their growth. Latin name: *Chionaspis pinifoliae.*

pi·nene /pí neen/ *n.* either of two colorless liquid compounds found in turpentine and eucalyptus. They have the same chemical formula and are used in manufacturing plastics and as a solvent. Formula: $C_{10}H_{16}$. [Late 19thC. Coined from Latin *pinus* "pine" + -ENE.]

pine nee·dle *n.* the needle-shaped leaf of a pine tree

pine nut *n.* a small sweet edible seed of some pine trees, especially a piñon

pin·er·y /pínəree/ (*plural* **-ies**) *n.* **1. PLACE WHERE PINEAPPLES ARE GROWN** a plantation or heated greenhouse where pineapples are grown commercially **2. PINE FOREST** a pine forest, especially one planted for timber production

pine·sap /pín sàp/ (*plural* **-saps** *or* **-sap**) *n.* a fleshy red or yellowish plant of the wintergreen family that resembles the Indian pipe and grows as a parasite on tree roots. Latin name: *Montropa hypopithys.*

pine sis·kin *n.* a small North American finch with brown plumage and yellow markings, that lives in coniferous forests and eats the seeds from cones. Latin name: *Carduelis pinus.*

pine snake *n.* a large bull snake with black and white markings that lives in pine forests in the eastern United States. Latin name: *Pituophis melanoleucus.*

pine straw *n. Southern U.S.* pine needles that have fallen to the ground

pine tar *n.* a thick sticky brown to black substance obtained by the destructive distillation of pine wood and used in making roofing materials, paints, medicines, and shampoos

pine war·bler *n.* a warbler with a yellow breast, native to pine forests of the eastern United States. Latin name: *Dendroica pinus.*

pine·wood /pín wòod/ *n.* **1. WOOD FROM PINE** the wood of a pine tree (*often used before a noun*) **2.** BOT **FOREST OF PINES** a small forest of pine trees (*often used in the plural*)

pin·feath·er /pín fèthər/ *n.* a feather only recently emerged from a bird's skin and still surrounded by a horny sheath

pin·fish /pín fish/ (*plural* **-fish·es** *or* **-fish**) *n.* a small marine fish of the porgy family with a thin dark green body and sharp dorsal spines, found along the southern Atlantic coast of the United States. Latin name: *Lagodon rhomboides.*

pin·fold /pín fòld/ *n.* **1. PLACE FOR STRAY ANIMALS** an enclosure for stray animals, especially farm animals **2. CONFINING PLACE** any place or situation that confines [Pre-12thC. From an alteration of earlier *pund-* "enclosure" (source also of *pound*) + FOLD.]

ping /ping/ *n.* **1. SOUND** a single short ringing sound **2.** AUTOMOT = **knock 3.** ACOUSTICS **SONAR PULSE** a brief sonic or ultrasonic pulse emitted by a sonar, the reflection or echo of which is used in detecting submarines or schools of fish ■ *v.* (**pinged, ping·ing, pings**) **1.** *vti.* ACOUSTICS **RING** to make a single short ringing sound, or to make something such as a bell produce a ringing sound **2.** *vi.* AUTOMOT = **knock 3.** *vi.* ACOUSTICS **DETECT UNDERWATER OBJECTS** to detect submarines or schools of fish by emitting and receiving the echo of a brief sonic or ultrasonic pulse [Mid-18thC. An imitation of the sound.]

ping·er /píngər/ *n.* a device that produces pinging noises, especially one used as part of underwater detection equipment (*informal*)

pin·go /píngō, píng gō/ (*plural* **-gos**) *n.* a large mound of soil-covered ice forced up by the pressure of water in permafrost [Mid-20thC. From Inuit (Eskimo) *pinguq.*]

Ping-Pong /píng pòng/ *tdmk.* a trademark for table tennis

pin·guid /píng gwid/ *adj.* containing a lot of fat, oil, or grease [Mid-17thC. From Latin *pinguis* "fat."] —**pin·guid·i·ty** /ping gwíddətee/ *n.*

pin·head /pínn hèd/ *n.* **1. BLUNT END OF PIN** the rounded head of a pin **2. SMALL THING** something that is very small or trivial **3. SOMEBODY VERY UNINTELLIGENT** somebody who is unintelligent or thoughtless (*informal insult*)

pin·head·ed /pín hèddəd/ *adj.* unintelligent or very thoughtless (*informal*)

pin·hole /pín hòl/ *n.* a tiny hole or puncture of the size made by a pin

pin·hole cam·er·a *n.* a basic form of camera with a tiny hole for the aperture, and no lens. Light passes through the hole to form an inverted image on the film emulsion.

pin·ion[1] /pínnyən/ *n.* ZOOL **BIRD'S WING** a bird's wing, especially the tip of the wing where the stiff flight feathers are found, containing the carpus, metacarpus, and phalanx bones ■ *vt.* (**-ioned, -ion·ing, -ions**) **1. RESTRAIN** to restrain or immobilize somebody, especially by tying his or her arms **2. KEEP FROM FLYING** to prevent a bird from flying by removing or binding its wing feathers [15thC. Via French *pignon* from, ultimately, Latin *pinna* (see PIN).]

pin·ion[2] /pínnyən/ *n.* a small gear wheel that engages with a larger gear or with a rack, e.g., in a vehicle steering system [Mid-17thC. Via French *pignon*, an alteration of earlier *pignol*, from, ultimately, Latin *pinea* "pine cone," from *pinus* (see PINE 1).]

pin·ite /pée nīt/ *n.* a gray-green mineral that is a mixture of mica and chlorite, formed by the alteration of the mineral cordierite [Early 19thC. From German *Pinit*, named for *Pini*, a mine in Saxony.]

pink[1] /pingk/ *n.* **1.** COLORS **PALE REDDISH COLOR** a pale reddish color that, as a pigment, is formed by mixing red and white **2.** PLANTS **PLANT WITH FRAGRANT FLOWERS** a plant with narrow grayish-green leaves and fragrant flowers in various colors, especially pink, white, or red. The carnation and sweet william are types of pink. Genus: *Dianthus.* **3.** PLANTS **FRAGRANT FLOWER** the fragrant pink, white, or red flower of a pink plant **4.** PLANTS **PLANT SIMILAR TO TRUE PINK** a plant that is similar but not related to the pink such as the wild pink or moss pink **5. HIGHEST FORM** the highest degree or perfect example of something ○ *the pink of perfection* **6.** CLOTHES **RED HUNTING JACKET** the scarlet riding coat traditionally worn by fox hunters **7.** = **pinko** (*slang disapproving*) ■ **pinks** *npl.* **U.S. OFFICERS' TROUSERS** light colored dress trousers formerly worn by United States Army officers ■ *adj.* **1.** COLORS **COLORED PINK** of the color pink **2.** POL **SLIGHTLY LEFT-WING** relating to or holding political views that tend toward the left (*informal disapproving*) [Late 16thC. Origin uncertain: probably from earlier Dutch *pinck* "small," from the phrase *pinck oogen*, literally "small eyes," translated in English as "pink eyes." Originally used for the plant.] ◇ **in the pink** in excellent physical health (*dated*)

WORD KEY: ORIGIN

The Dutch phrase *pinck oogen* meant literally "small eyes." It was adopted into English in the partially translated form *pink eyes*, and it is thought that this may have been used as the name of a plant of the genus *Dianthus*. The abbreviated form ***pink*** emerged as a plant name in the 16th century. Many of these plants have pale red flowers, and by the 18th century ***pink*** was being used as a color term.

pink[2] /pingk/ **(pinked, pink·ing, pinks)** *vt.* **1. CUT WITH PINKING SHEARS** to cut fabric with pinking shears to make a zigzag edge that will not easily fray **2. STAB** to prick somebody's skin with a sword or other pointed weapon **3. DECORATE WITH LITTLE HOLES** to make a pattern on leather or other material by punching little holes in the surface [14thC. Origin uncertain: perhaps from Low German.]

pink[3] /pingk/ *n.* a sailing ship with a narrow overhanging stern [Late 15thC. From Middle Dutch *pincke*.]

pink-col·lar *adj.* relating to jobs, especially clerical jobs, traditionally associated with women. ◊ **blue-collar, white-collar**

pink el·e·phants *npl.* hallucinations in any form that are sometimes experienced by somebody who has overindulged in alcohol or drugs (*informal humorous*)

Pin·ker·ton /píngkərtən/, **Allan** (1819–84) Scottish-born U.S. detective. He founded Pinkerton's National Detective Agency (1850), which later provided strikebreakers and ran the Union's secret service in the Civil War.

pink·eye /píngk ī/ *n.* **1. INFLAMMATION OF THE EYE** a contagious form of acute conjunctivitis in human beings and some domestic animals marked by inflammation of the eyelid and eyeball **2. CATTLE ILLNESS** an eye infection of cattle, caused by any of several different viruses or bacteria. It is characterized by redness of the eye, production of tears that attract flies, and sometimes blindness.

pink·ie /píngkee/, **pink·y** (*plural* **-ies**) *n. U.S., Can, Scotland* the little finger (*informal*) [Late 16thC. Origin uncertain: probably from Dutch *pinkje*, from *pink* "little finger."]

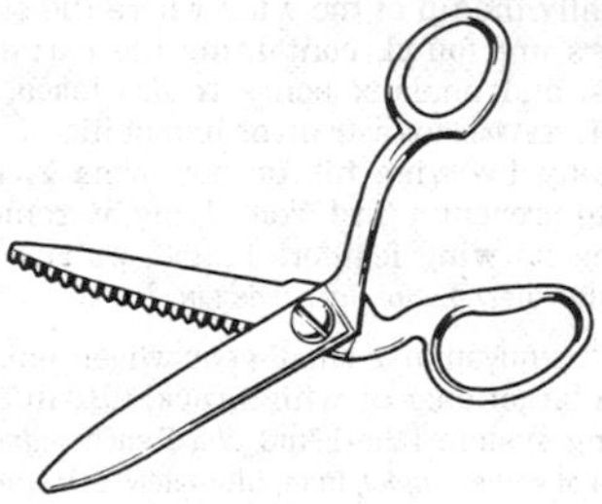

Pinking shears

pink·ing shears, pink·ing scis·sors *npl.* scissors for cutting cloth that have one blade or both blades serrated, so that whatever they cut has a zigzag edge, either for decoration or to prevent fraying [From PINK]

pink la·dy *n.* a cocktail that is made by mixing gin, brandy, lemon or lime juice, egg white, and grenadine

pink·o /píngkō/ (*plural* **-os** *or* **-oes**) *n.* somebody who leans toward the political left (*slang disapproving*) [Early 20thC. Formed from PINK, alluding to RED in the sense "communist."]

pink·root /píngk ro͞ot, -ro͝ot/ (*plural* **-roots** *or* **-root**) *n.* **1.** PLANTS **PLANT WITH RED AND YELLOW FLOWERS** a tropical or subtropical perennial plant with pinkish roots that grows in the southeastern United States and has red flowers tinged with yellow on the inside. Genus: *Spigella.* **2.** MED **POWDERED ROOT OF PINKROOT PLANT** the powdered root of the pinkroot plant, formerly used to treat intestinal worms **3.** BOT **PLANT DISEASE** a fungal plant disease that affects bulbous plants, especially onions, causing the roots to become pink and shriveled, and stunting root growth

pink salm·on *n.* **1.** ZOOL **SMALL PACIFIC SALMON** a small salmon of northern Pacific waters, the male of which has a pinkish body and a distinctive hump on the back at breeding times. Latin name: *Oncorhynchus gorbuscha.* **2.** FOOD **FLESH OF PINK SALMON** the edible pink flesh of the pink salmon, often canned

pink slip *n.* a termination of employment notice that an employer gives to an employee (*informal*) [From the traditional color of such notices]

Pink·ster /píngkstər/, **Pinx·ter** *n. Northeast U.S.* Whitsunday or Whitsuntide [Mid-18thC. Via Dutch from, ultimately, Greek *pentēkostē* (see PENTECOST).]

pink·y *n.* = **pinkie**

pin mon·ey *n.* **1. MONEY FOR BUYING PERSONAL THINGS** money that is earned, put aside, or used for buying personal, often nonessential, things **2. NOT MUCH MONEY** a small amount of money **3. MONEY THAT MAN GIVES TO WIFE** money that a man gives to his wife, woman partner, or daughter for personal use (*dated*)

pin·na /pínnə/ (*plural* **-nae** /-nee/ *or* **-nas**) *n.* **1.** ZOOL **FEATHER, WING, OR FIN** a feather, wing, fin, or other similarly shaped body part or appendage **2.** BOT **LEAFLET** any one of the several leaflets that make up a pinnate compound leaf **3.** ANAT = **auricle** *n.* 1 [Late 18thC. From Latin *penna* "feather" (source of English *pen*[1]). Ultimately from an Indo-European base meaning "to fly," which is also the ancestor of English *feather*.] —**pin·nal** *adj.*

pin·nace /pínnəss/ *n.* a small boat such as a sailboat carried by a larger vessel and used as a gig or a tender [Mid-16thC. Via French from, ultimately, Latin *pinus* "pine" (see PINE).]

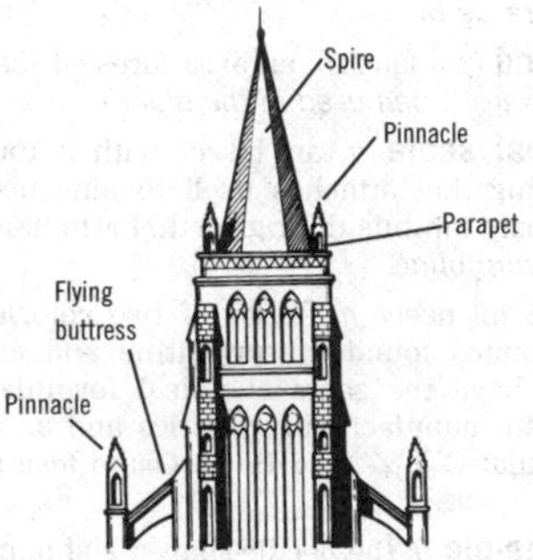

Pinnacle

pin·na·cle /pínnək'l/ *n.* **1. HIGHEST POINT** the highest or topmost point or level of something ○ *at the pinnacle of a career* **2.** GEOG **MOUNTAIN PEAK** a natural peak, especially a distinctively pointed one on a mountain or in a mountain range **3.** ARCHIT **POINTED ORNAMENT** a pointed ornament on top of a buttress or parapet ■ *vt.* **(-cled, -cling, -cles) 1.** ARCHIT **ADD PINNACLE TO SOMETHING** to provide something with a pinnacle **2. PUT SOMETHING ON PINNACLE** to put or set something on a pinnacle or on something resembling a top or peak [13thC. Via Old French from late Latin *pinnaculum* literally "little feather," from Latin *pinna* "feather" (see PINNA).]

pin·nae plural of **pinna**

pin·nate /pí nàyt/, **pin·nat·ed** /-təd/, **pen·nate** /pé nàyt/, **pen·nat·ed** /-təd/ *adj.* resembling a feather in appearance or structure, especially in having a central axis or stem with parts branching off it [Early 18thC. From Latin *pinnatus*, from *pinna* (see PINNA).] —**pin·nate·ly** *adv.* —**pin·na·tion** /pi náysh'n/ *n.*

pinnati- *prefix.* like a feather ○ *pinnatiped* [From Latin *pinnatus* (see PINNATE)]

pin·nat·i·fid /pi náttəfid/ *adj.* used to describe leaves that have a central axis with parts branching off it [Mid-18thC. Formed from PINNATI- + -FID.] —**pin·nat·i·fid·ly** *adv.*

pin·ni·ped /pínnə pèd/, **pin·ni·pe·di·an** /pinnə peédee ən/ *n.* any sea-dwelling mammal such as a walrus, sea lion, or seal that has a streamlined body and four flippers and eats fish and other meat. Suborder: Pinnipedia. [Mid-19thC. From modern Latin *Pinnipedia*, order name, from Latin *pinna* "wing, fin" + *pes* "foot."] —**pin·ni·ped** *adj.*

pin·nule /pínnyool/, **pin·nu·la** /pínnyələ/ (*plural* **-lae** /pínnyə leè/) *n.* **1.** ZOOL **FIN-SHAPED PART** a small fin or fin-shaped part of an organ or organism **2.** BOT **LOBES OF A LEAFLET** any of the small divisions or lobes of a leaf that has a central axis with parts branching off it [Late 16thC. From Latin *pinnula* "little feather" from PINNA.] —**pin·nu·lar** /pínnyələr/ *adj.*

PIN num·ber *n.* = **PIN**

pin oak *n.* an oak tree that grows in wet regions of the eastern United States and has a pyramidal shape, deeply lobed leaves, and small acorns. Latin name: *Quercus palustris.* [From the pinlike shape of some of the tree's branches]

Pi·no·chet /peénō shay/, **Augusto** (*b.* 1915) Chilean military dictator. Under his right-wing regime (1973–90) dissidence was suppressed. Full name **Augusto Pinochet Ugarte**

pi·noch·le /peé nùk'l, peé nòk'l/, **pi·noc·le, pe·nuch·le, pe·nuck·le** *n.* **1. CARD GAME WITH INCOMPLETE DECKS** a card game for two or four players using two decks of cards that do not include two to eight. Certain combinations of cards score points, as do tricks taken. **2. WINNING COMBINATION OF CARDS** a combination of the queen of spades and the jack of diamonds in the game of pinochle [Mid-19thC. Origin uncertain.]

pin·o·cy·to·sis /pìnnə si tṓsiss, pìnnə sī-/ *n.* the ingestion of fluid into a cell by turning a portion of the cell membrane inwards to form a sheath that is then pinched off to form an internal vesicle [Late 19thC. Formed from Greek *pinein* "to drink," on the model of "phagocytosis."] —**pin·o·cy·tot·ic** /pìnnə si tóttik, pìnnə sī-/ *adj.* —**pin·o·cy·tot·i·cal·ly** /-tóttikəlee/ *adv.*

pi·no·le /pi nṓlee/ *n.* flour that is made by mixing parched corn with ground mesquite beans and sometimes adding other ingredients such as sugar, spices, and vanilla [Mid-19thC. Via American Spanish from Aztec *pinolli*.]

pi·ñon /pín yòn, pínyən/ (*plural* **-ñons** *or* **-ño·nes** /pin yṓneez/), **pin·yon** *n.* **1.** TREES **U.S. PINE TREE** any of several low-growing pines of the southwestern United States that bear edible seeds. Latin name: *Pinus edulis* and *Pinus monophylla.* **2. pi·ñon, pi·ñon nut** FOOD **EDIBLE SEED OF PIÑON** the small sweet edible nut of the piñon [Mid-19thC. Via Spanish *piñón* from, ultimately, Latin *pineus* "of pines," from *pinus* (see PINE).]

pi·ñon jay, pin·yon jay *n.* BIRDS a short-tailed steel-blue jay of the arid western United States, often associated with piñon pines and junipers. Latin name: *Gymnorhinus cyanocephalus.*

Pi·not Gri·gio /peénō greéjō, pee nṑ-/ (*plural* **Pi·not Gri·gios**) *n.* **1. ITALIAN WINE GRAPE** a white grape grown in Italy, used for making wine **2. ITALIAN WHITE WINE** a crisp dry white wine made from the Pinot Grigio grape [From Italian, literally "gray Pinot," a grape variety (from French; see PINOT NOIR)]

Pi·not Noir /peénō nwaár, pee nṑ-/ *n.* **1. RED WINE GRAPE** a black grape grown in the Burgundy area of France and also in Australia, the United States, and elsewhere, used for making wine **2. RED WINE** red wine made from the Pinot Noir grape [From French, literally "black Pinot" (a grape variety), from, ultimately, *pin* "pine cone," from the resemblance of the grape bunch to a pine cone]

pin·point /pín pòynt/ *vt.* **(-point·ed, -point·ing, -points) IDENTIFY SOMETHING CORRECTLY** to identify or locate something accurately ■ *n.* **1. SOMETHING SMALL OR TRIVIAL** something small or trivial and with no value or consequence **2. PIN'S POINT** the sharp end of a pin or something that resembles it ■ *adj.* **PRECISELY EXACT** reflecting exact meticulous precision

pin·prick /pín prìk/ *n.* **1. SMALL HOLE MADE BY PIN** a small puncture, especially to the skin, made by a pin or something with a similarly sharp end **2. SLIGHT WOUND** a very minor wound **3. MINOR IRRITANT** a minor annoyance, nuisance, or distraction **4. SMALL MARK** a very small dot or mark of something ■ *vt.* **(-pricked, -prick·ing, -pricks) PUNCTURE SOMETHING WITH PIN** to puncture something, especially the skin, with a pin or something with a similarly sharp end

PINS *n., abbr.* LAW person in need of supervision

pins and need·les *n.* a tingling sensation, especially in the feet or hands, sometimes experienced when a temporarily restricted blood flow to the affected body parts returns to normal (*takes a singular or plural verb*)

pin·scher /pínshər/ *n.* = **Doberman pinscher** [Early 20thC. From German, of uncertain origin: probably from English *pinch*, because of the practice of clipping the dog's ears.]

pin·set·ter /pín sèttər/ *n.* a person or machine in a bowling alley that sets up and resets the pins

Pinsk /pinsk/ city in southwestern Belarus. Population: 130,000 (1996).

pin·stripe /pín strìp/ *n.* **1. NARROW LINE IN FABRIC** any one of many very narrow lines in a fabric **2. MATERIAL WITH VERY NARROW LINES** material that has very narrow lines in it, especially the kind of fabric used for making business suits (*often used before a noun*) **3. PINSTRIPE SUIT** a suit made of pinstripe fabric (*often used in the plural*) —**pin·striped** *adj.*

pint /pīnt/ *n.* **1.** MEASURE **UNIT OF LIQUID MEASURE** a unit of liquid measure equal to one half quart or 0.473 liter in the United States and 0.568 liter in the United Kingdom **2.** MEASURE **UNIT OF DRY MEASURE** a unit of dry measure equal to one half a quart or 0.551 liter in the United States and 0.568 liter in the United Kingdom **3. CONTAINER** a container or measure that has the capacity of a pint **4.** *U.K.* **PINT OF LIQUID** a pint of a liquid, especially of beer or milk (*informal*) [14thC. From French *pinte*, of uncertain origin: possibly via assumed Vulgar Latin *pincta* "painted (mark on a container)" from, ultimately, Latin *pingere* "to paint."]

pin·ta /píntə, peén taá/ *n.* an infectious bacterial skin disease of tropical America that is marked by the formation and eruption of papules, loss of pigmentation, and thickening of the skin [Early 19thC. Via Spanish, literally "painted spot," from assumed Vulgar Latin *pincta* (see PINT).]

pin·tail /pín tàyl/ (*plural* **-tail** *or* **-tails**) *n.* a slender duck of the northern hemisphere that has a long pointed tail and brown and white plumage. Latin name: *Anas acuta*. [From the pointed tip of the male bird's tail]

pin·tle /pínt'l/ *n.* a pin or bolt, especially one used as a vertical pivot or hinge, e.g., on a rudder [Old English *pintle* "peg, penis," of prehistoric Germanic origin]

pin·to /píntō/ *n.* (*plural* **-tos** *or* **-toes**), *adj.* used to describe a horse that has a coat marked with irregular patches of white and another color, usually brown, black, or gray [Mid-19thC. Via Spanish, literally "painted," from, ultimately, Latin *pingere* "to paint."]

pin·to bean *n.* **1.** PLANTS **BEAN PLANT** a variety of the kidney bean grown in the southwestern United States for food and fodder **2.** FOOD **EDIBLE SEED** a mottled brown and pink kidney-shaped bean of the pinto bean plant [*Pinto* from Spanish, "painted, mottled"]

pint-size, pint-sized *adj.* very small, especially smaller than usual or than expected (*informal*)

pin tuck *n.* a narrow vertical fold stitched in place and used for decoration, especially on the front of clothes —**pin-tucked** *adj.*

Pin·tu·pi /píntəpee/ (*plural* **-pi** *or* **-pis**), **Pin·tu·bi** /píntəbee/ (*plural* **-bi** *or* **-bis**) *n.* PEOPLES a member of a Native Australian people that lives in the border regions between Western Australia and Northern Territories [Mid-20thC. Of Australian Aboriginal origin.] —**Pin·tu·pi** *adj.*

pin·up /pín ùp/ *n.* **1. PICTURE OF SEXUALLY DESIRABLE PERSON** a photograph or poster of a person, especially one in which the person is posing in a suggestive way and scantily clothed or naked **2. SEXUALLY ATTRACTIVE PERSON** a person considered attractive enough to appear in a pinup picture ■ *adj.* **DESIGNED TO HANG ON WALL** relating to things that are designed for hanging on, or attaching to, a wall

pin·wale /pín wàyl/ *adj.* in textiles, made with narrow wales such as pinwale corduroy

pin·weed /pín weéd/ (*plural* **-weeds** *or* **-weed**) *n.* a North American herb of the rockrose family, having numerous narrow leaves and small flowers. Genus: *Lechea*.

pin·wheel /pín weél, -hweél/ *n.* **1. ROTATING TOY** a child's toy consisting of a stick with a set of plastic or paper blades fitted to it, which spin around when the wind blows them **2. FIREWORK** a firework that, when ignited, forms a multicolored wheel that spins

pin·work /pín wùrk/ *n.* the delicate stitches that are raised above the main design in the embroidery of needlepoint lace

pin·worm /pín wùrm/ *n.* **1.** ZOOL **PARASITIC NEMATODE WORM** a threadlike nematode worm that occurs as a parasite in the intestines of vertebrate animals, including human beings. Family: Oxyuridae. **2.** MED **PINWORM INFESTATION** an infestation of pinworms

pin wrench *n.* a specialized wrench containing a pin fitted for insertion into the head of a bolt so as to be able to drive the bolt

Pinx·ter /píngkstər/ *n.* = **Pinkster**

pinx·ter flow·er, pink·ster flow·er *n.* a deciduous woodland azalea of the southeastern United States that has funnel-shaped pink flowers. Latin name: *Rhododendron periclymenoides*. [*Pinxter* "Whitsuntide" (variant of *pinkster*, from Dutch, "Pentecost"), because it flowers around Whitsuntide]

pin·y /pīnee/ (**-i·er, -i·est**), **pine·y** (**pin·i·er, pin·i·est**) *adj.* relating to or resembling pine trees, e.g., in smell

Pin·yin /pìn yín/, **pin·yin** *n.* a system for transliterating written Chinese characters into the Roman alphabet for diplomatic, official, and media uses, introduced in 1959 and adopted by the People's Republic of China in 1979 [Mid-20thC. From Mandarin Chinese *pīnyīn*, literally "spell sound."]

pin·yon *n.* = **piñon**

pin·yon jay *n.* = **piñon jay**

PIO *n., abbr.* public information office

pi·o·let /pee ə láy/ *n.* a double-headed ice ax used by mountaineers [Mid-19thC. From French dialect, formed from *piola* "small ax"; ultimately of Germanic origin.]

pi·on /pī òn/ *n.* any of the group of three mesons that have either single positive, negative, or zero charge, a mass approximately 270 times that of the electron, and spin zero [Mid-20thC. Formed from *pi meson*.]

pi·o·neer /pī ə neér/ *n.* **1. INVENTOR OR INNOVATOR** a person or group that is the first to do something or that is a forerunner in creating or developing something new **2. FIRST PERSON TO EXPLORE TERRITORY** somebody who goes into previously uncharted or unclaimed territory with the purpose of exploring it and possibly colonizing or settling it **3.** ARMY **SOLDIER WHO BUILDS THINGS** a foot soldier whose duties include going ahead of the main company to pave the way for them by building roads, ditches, bridges, and other constructions **4.** ECOL **FIRST SPECIES TO GROW SOMEWHERE** the first species of plant or animal life to begin living in a previously unoccupied site, e.g., a moss beginning to grow on otherwise bare rock ■ *v.* (**-neered, -neer·ing, -neers**) **1.** *vt.* **INVENT OR DEVELOP NEW THING** to experiment with or develop something new **2.** *vt.* **GO INTO UNEXPLORED TERRITORY** to go into previously uncharted or unclaimed territory with the purpose of exploring it and possibly colonizing or settling it **3.** *vi.* **ACT AS PIONEER** to act as a pioneer in a specified field [Early 16thC. Via French *pionnier* from, ultimately, the medieval Latin stem *pedon-* "foot soldier," from Latin *ped-*, the stem of *pes* "foot."]

pi·ous /pī əss/ *adj.* **1.** RELIG **RELIGIOUS** devoutly religious **2.** RELIG **RELIGIOUSLY REVERENT** characterized by religious reverence **3. ACTING IN FALSELY MORALIZING WAY** talking or acting in a falsely, hypocritically, or affectedly moralizing way **4.** RELIG **HOLY OR SACRED** holy or sacred, especially as distinct from worldly **5. PRAISEWORTHY** deserving to be praised **6. SHOWING DUE RESPECT** showing appropriate respect, especially toward parents (*archaic*) **7. VIRTUOUS AND MORAL** professing or showing great virtue and morality in the strict, traditional sense of it [15thC. Formed from Latin *pius* "dutiful" (source of English *pity* and *expiate*).] —**pi·ous·ly** *adv.* —**pi·ous·ness** *n.*

pip[1] /pip/ *n.* **1. SEED OF FRUIT** a small hard seed of an edible fruit such as an apple, pear, or orange **2. SECTION OF PINEAPPLE SKIN** any one of the many irregular diamond-shaped sections on the outer skin of a pineapple **3. ROOTSTOCK OR FLOWER** a rootstock or flower of certain plants, especially the lily of the valley [Late 18thC. A shortening of PIPPIN.]

pip[2] /pip/ *n.* **1. SPOT ON DIE OR DOMINO** a single spot on a die or domino **2.** CARDS **MARK ON PLAYING CARD** a single symbol of a club, diamond, heart, or spade on a playing card. The type of symbol designates the suit and the number of them indicates the value of the card. **3.** *U.K.* MIL **SOMETHING INDICATING RANK** something such as a diamond-shaped insignia on the shoulder of a British Army officer's uniform that indicates rank (*informal*) **4. SPECK** a very small mark or piece of something ■ *v.* (**pipped, pip·ping, pips**) **1.** *vi.* BIRDS **CHEEP** to make a cheeping sound, especially when newly hatched (*refers to birds*) **2.** *vti.* BIRDS **USE BEAK TO BREAK SHELL** to use the beak to break through the shell during hatching (*refers to birds*) **3.** *vi.* **MAKE SHRILL NOISE** to make or emit a short shrill noise [Late 16thC. Origin unknown.]

pip[3] /pip/ *n.* **1.** VET **CONTAGIOUS POULTRY DISEASE** a contagious disease of birds, especially domestic ones, characterized by the presence of a thick crust in the mouth and throat, caused by an abnormal secretion of mucus **2.** MED **MINOR AILMENT** a slight ailment in humans (*informal dated*) [14thC. Via Middle Dutch *pippe* from, ultimately, Latin *pituita* "phlegm."]

pip[4] /pip/ (**pipped, pip·ping, pips**) *vt. U.K.* to wound or kill a person or animal with a bullet from a gun (*informal*) [Late 19thC. Origin uncertain: perhaps from PIP[1] or PIP[2].]

pi·pa[1] /peépə/ *n.* a completely aquatic American toad that has a flattened body, large webbed feet, and no eyelids or tongue. Genus: *Pipa*. [Early 18thC. Probably from Galibi.]

pi·pa[2] /peépə/ *n.* a plucked four-string Chinese instrument with a fretted fingerboard like a guitar's [Mid-19thC. From Chinese *píba*, literally "loquat"; so called from the instrument's shape.]

pi·page /pīpij/ *n.* **1. PIPES COLLECTIVELY** a number of pipes thought of collectively or as a functioning system **2. TRANSPORTATION USING PIPES** the transportation or delivery of something by means of pipes **3. COST OF TRANSPORTING SOMETHING BY PIPE** the cost of transporting or delivering something by means of pipes

pi·pal /peép'l/ *n.* = **bo tree**

pipe[1] /pīp/ *n.* **1. TUBE FOR TRANSPORTING LIQUID OR GAS** a long cylindrical tube that water, oil, gas, or other such material passes through **2. TUBE OF ANY KIND** an object in tubular form **3. DEVICE FOR SMOKING TOBACCO** a small bowl with a hollow stem coming from it, used for smoking tobacco or other substances. Pipes are usually made of wood or clay. The tobacco is burnt in the bowl and the smoke drawn into the mouth through the stem. **4. AMOUNT IN SMOKER'S PIPE** the amount of tobacco or other substance that the bowl of a smoker's pipe holds **5.** BIOL **HOLLOW BODY PART** a tubular part or organ in a plant or animal, especially one in an animal's respiratory system **6.** MUSIC **TUBULAR MUSICAL INSTRUMENT PLAYED BY BLOWING** any of several tubular musical instruments that are played by blowing air into them **7.** MUSIC **TUBULAR PART OF MUSICAL ORGAN** any of the upright tubular parts of a musical organ that produce sound when air is blown into them **8.** MUSIC, HIST **WIND INSTRUMENT OF MIDDLE AGES** a three-holed wind instrument, popular during the Middle Ages, played with one hand while the other hand beats on a small drum called a tabor **9.** NAUT **SAILOR'S WHISTLE** a small whistle used for signaling orders to a crew, usually by a boatswain **10.** GEOL **CYLINDER-SHAPED GEOLOGICAL FORMATION** a vertical cylinder-shaped geological formation such as a vein of ore **11.** GEOL **PASSAGE THROUGH WHICH LAVA FLOWS** a vertical passage through which molten lava flows **12.** METALL **HOLE IN CAST METAL** a conical cavity in the middle of a piece of metal, produced by gas escaping as the metal cools **13. HIGH-PITCHED NOISE** a high-pitched or shrill noise such as a birdcall ■ **pipes** *npl.* **1.** MUSIC **BAGPIPES** the bagpipes **2. HUMAN RESPIRATORY SYSTEM** the human respiratory system or vocal cords (*slang*) **3. HUMAN INTESTINAL SYSTEM** the human intestines and bowels (*slang*) ■ *v.* (**piped, pip·ing, pipes**) **1.** *vt.* **CARRY SOMETHING BY PIPE** to carry something, especially water, gas, or a semisolid, by means of a pipe, pipeline, or system of pipes ○ *The company pipes crude oil to the refinery.* **2.** *vti.* **INSTALL AND CONNECT PIPES** to equip something with pipes or install pipes and their connections in something **3.** *vt.* MUSIC **PLAY TUNE ON PIPE** to play a tune on a musical pipe **4.** *vt.* MUSIC **SEND PIPED MUSIC THROUGH PLACE** to send piped music through a public place or workplace **5.** *vt.* MUSIC **SIGNAL SOMETHING USING PIPE** to signal the arrival or departure of somebody or something using a pipe **6.** *vt.* NAUT **ORDER CREW USING BOATSWAIN'S PIPE** to give orders to a crew using a boatswain's pipe **7.** *vt.* SEW **DECORATE GARMENT WITH PIPING** to add decorative piping to a garment **8.** *vt.* FOOD **DECORATE FOOD WITH PIPING** to add decorative piping to food, especially by forcing it out of a bag that has a nozzle designed to create the various decorative forms **9.** *vti.* **MAKE HIGH-PITCHED NOISE** to make a high-pitched or shrill noise, or speak in a squeaky voice [Old English *pīpe*, via Vulgar Latin *pipa* from Latin *pipare* "to peep, cheep" (source of English *fife*), ultimately an imitation of the sound] —**pipe·ful** *n.*

pipe down *vi.* to stop talking or become less noisy or boisterous (*informal*) (*often used as a command*)

pipe up *vi.* **1. SAY SOMETHING** to say something, often as an interruption or a clarification **2.** MUSIC **BEGIN TO SING OR PLAY INSTRUMENT** to begin to sing or play a musical instrument

pipe[2] /pīp/ *n.* **1. LARGE CONTAINER FOR LIQUID** a large container for wine, oil, or some other liquid **2.** MEASURE **UNIT OF LIQUID CAPACITY** a unit of liquid measure for wine, equal to four barrels, two hogsheads, or 126 gallons **3.** MEASURE **CASK** a cask that has the capacity of four barrels, two hogsheads, or 126 gallons [14thC. Via Anglo-Norman from Vulgar Latin *pipa* (see PIPE[1]).]

pipe bomb *n.* a bomb made of a length of pipe that is filled with explosives and is capped at its ends

pipe clay *n.* a very fine white pure clay used in the manufacture of pottery and smokers' pipes, and for whitening leather and other materials

pipe clean·er *n.* a flexible wire covered with fluffy material that is used for cleaning the stems of smokers' pipes and other things that are difficult to access

piped mu·sic *n.* prerecorded, usually easy-listening music played through speakers in public places and some workplaces to create a soothing atmosphere

pipe dream *n.* a goal, hope, idea, or plan so fanciful that it is very unlikely to be realized [From the dreams caused by smoking opium]

pipe·fit·ter /pīp fìttər/ *n.* somebody whose job is to cut, fit, install, connect, and repair pipes

pipe·fit·ting /pīp fìtting/ *n.* **1. BRANCH OF PLUMBING INVOLVING PIPES** the branch of plumbing that involves measuring, cutting, bending, and joining lengths of pipe, either in installation or repairs **2. ACT OR PROCESS OF PIPE INSTALLATION** an act or process of installing or connecting pipes **3. SOMETHING USED IN CONNECTING PIPES** something that is used in the connection or joining of pipes

pipe·line /pīp līn/ *n.* **1. LONG PIPE SYSTEM FOR TRANSPORTING SOMETHING** a pipe or system of pipes designed to carry something such as oil, natural gas, or other petroleum-based products over long distances, often underground **2. CHANNEL OF COMMUNICATIONS** a channel of communications, especially a private one among several people within a single organization **3. SYSTEM FOR SUPPLYING SOMETHING** a system for the supply or transfer of something, especially goods or information ■ *vt.* **(-lined, -lin·ing, -lines) 1. SEND SOMETHING BY PIPE SYSTEM** to send, connect, or carry something by way of a long system of pipes **2.** TECH **EQUIP SOMETHING WITH LONG PIPE SYSTEM** to equip or supply something with a long system of pipes ◇ **in the pipeline** in preparation but not yet ready

pipe or·gan *n.* a musical organ that uses pipes to produce the sound, as opposed to a reed organ or an electric organ. Most church organs are pipe organs.

pip·er /pīpər/ *n.* **1. PLAYER ON PIPE** somebody who plays a pipe **2. BAGPIPER** somebody who plays the bagpipes ◇ **pay the piper** to take the consequences for something

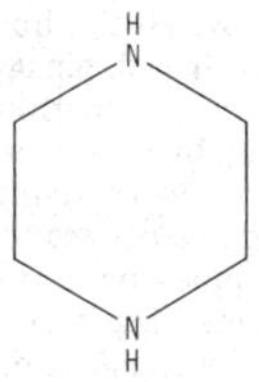

Piperazine

pi·per·a·zine /pī pérrə zeèn, pi p-/ *n.* a colorless crystalline compound used to kill or expel parasitic worms and as an insecticide. Formula: $C_4H_{10}N_2$. [Late 19thC. Blend of PIPERIDINE and AZINE.]

pi·per·i·dine /pī pérrə deèn, pi p-/ *n.* a colorless liquid compound that has a peppery odor resembling ammonia and is used in making rubber and epoxy resins. Formula: $C_5H_{11}N$. [Mid-19thC. Coined from PIPERINE + -IDINE.]

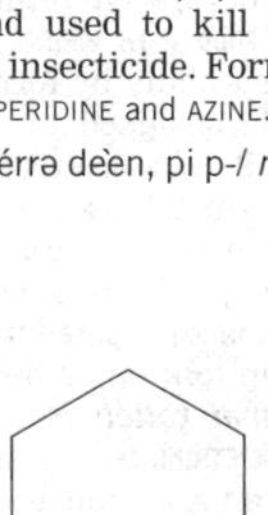

Piperidine

pip·er·ine /píppə reèn/ *n.* a white crystalline alkaloid compound that is the chief active component of pepper. Formula: $C_{17}H_{19}NO_3$. [Early 19thC. Formed from Latin *piper* (see PEPPER).]

pi·per·o·nal /pī pérrə nàl, pi p-/ *n.* a white crystalline compound that has an odor resembling heliotrope and is used in perfumes and flavorings. Formula: $C_{19}H_{63}$. [Mid-19thC. From German, formed from *Piperin* "piperine."]

pipe snake *n.* a snake found mostly in tropical areas that has a fused inflexible skull, vestiges of hind limbs, and two unequally-sized lungs. Family: Anilidae.

pipes of Pan *npl.* = **panpipes**

pipe·stem /pīp stèm/ *n.* **PIPE'S LONG STEM** the long, slender stem of a smoking pipe ■ *adj.* **SKINNY** long, narrow, and very skinny

pipe·stone /pīp stōn/ *n.* a reddish or pinkish stone resembling clay in consistency that some Native North Americans harden and use for decorative objects and long, often ornate pipes

pi·pette /pī pét/ *n.* **SMALL TUBE FOR SUCKING UP LIQUID** a small glass tube that liquid is drawn into so that it can be measured, often before delivering it to another container, e.g., in experiments or in medication doses ■ *vt.* **(-pet·ted, -pet·ting, -pettes) MEASURE OR TRANSFER LIQUID USING PIPETTE** to measure or deliver an accurate amount of liquid using a pipette [Mid-19thC. From French, literally "little pipe," from *pipe* "pipe," from Vulgar Latin *pipa* (see PIPE[1]).]

pipe wrench *n.* wrench with two adjustable, usually ridged jaws, one fixed and one moveable, used to grip and turn pipes and other tubular objects

pip·ing /pīping/ *n.* **1.** CONSTR **PIPES COLLECTIVELY** pipes thought of collectively, especially when they form a connected plumbing system in a house or other building **2.** SEW **DECORATIVE TWISTED CORD** a twisted cord covered with a folded strip of bias-cut fabric inserted into a seam as a decoration, e.g., on clothes and upholstery **3.** FOOD **DECORATIVE EFFECT ON FOOD** a decorative effect used on food, especially strands or swirls of icing in a contrasting color **4.** MUSIC **SKILL OF PLAYING MUSICAL PIPE** the art, technique, or skill of playing the bagpipes or another kind of musical pipe **5. SHRILL NOISE** a shrill, high-pitched, or whistling noise **6.** MUSIC **SOUND OF MUSICAL PIPE** the sound of bagpipes or some other musical pipe ■ *adj.* **SHRILLY PITCHED** shrill and very high in pitch, as some voices are

pip·i·strelle /pìppi strél, píppi strèl/, **pip·i·strel** *n.* a small brown insect-eating bat found throughout the world. Genus: *Pipistrellus.* [Late 18thC. Via French and Italian from, ultimately, Latin *vespertilio* "bat," from *vesper* "evening."]

pip·it /píppit/ *n.* a small songbird in the wagtail family, resembling the lark, with brown speckled plumage and a long tail. Family: Motacillidae. [Mid-18thC. An imitation of the bird's call.]

pip·kin /pípkin/ *n.* a small cooking pot, usually made of metal or earthenware and with a handle going across the top [Mid-16thC. Origin uncertain: possibly formed from PIPE[2].]

pip·pin /píppin/ *n.* **1.** FOOD **VARIETY OF APPLE** any of several varieties of cultivated eating or cooking apples **2.** BOT **PIP OR SEED** a pip or seed, especially an apple seed **3. DESIRABLE OR ADMIRABLE PERSON OR THING** somebody or something that is particularly desirable or admirable (*dated informal*) [14thC. From French *pepin.*]

pip·sis·se·wa /pip síssə wàw, -síssəwə/ (*plural* **-was** *or* **-wa**) *n.* an evergreen herb of the wintergreen family that has white or pinkish flowers and jagged astringent leaves that are used medicinally as a diuretic. Genus: *Chimaphila.* [Late 18thC. From Abnaki *kpi-pskwàhsawe* "flower of the woods."]

pip·squeak /píp skweèk/ *n.* somebody or something that is small or insignificant, but neverthless often annoying or troublesome (*informal*) [Early 20thC. Thought to suggest smallness and insignificance.]

pi·quant /peékənt, -kaànt, pee kaánt/ *adj.* **1. SPICY OR SAVORY** having a flavor, taste, or smell that is spicy or savory, often with a slightly tart or bitter edge to it **2. SHARPLY STIMULATING OR PROVOCATIVE** refreshingly interesting, stimulating, or provocative **3. SHARPLY CRITICAL AND BITING** excessively severe or hurtful, e.g., in tone or content [Early 16thC. From French, the present participle of *piquer* "to prick, sting" (see PIQUE[1]).] —**pi·quan·cy** *n.* —**pi·quant·ly** *adv.* —**pi·quant·ness** *n.*

pique[1] /peek/ *n.* **BAD MOOD** a bad mood or feeling of resentment, especially when brought on by an insult, hurt pride, or loss of face ■ *v.* **(piqued, piqu·ing, piques) 1.** *vt.* **PUT SOMEBODY IN BAD MOOD** to cause somebody to be in a bad mood or to feel resentful **2.** *vt.* **AROUSE SOMEBODY'S INTEREST** to cause a feeling of interest, curiosity, or excitement in somebody **3.** *vr.* **TAKE PRIDE IN SOMETHING** to take pride in something, especially a personal attribute or ability [Mid-16thC. Via French *piquer* "to prick, irritate" from assumed Vulgar Latin *piccare* (source of English *pick*[1] and *picket*).]

pique[2] /peek/ *n.* **WINNING SCORE IN PIQUET** in the game of piquet, a score of 30 points to an opponent's 0 from the hand as dealt ■ *vti.* **(piqued, piqu·ing, piques) SCORE A PIQUE AGAINST SOMEBODY** in the game of piquet, to score a pique against an opponent [Mid-17thC. From French *pic,* of uncertain origin.]

pi·qué /pi káy, pee-, peé kày/ *n.* a closely woven ribbed fabric produced from natural fibers, especially cotton or silk, and used mainly in making clothes [Mid-19thC. From French, the past participle of *piquer* "to prick, stitch" (see PIQUE[1]).]

pi·quet /pi káy/, **pic·quet** *n.* a card game for two players who use only 32 cards instead of the usual 52, all the twos, threes, fours, fives, and sixes having been left out. Scoring is by declaring and winning tricks. [Mid-17thC. From French, of uncertain origin: probably from Old French *pic* (see PIQUE[2]).]

pi·ra·cy /pírəssee/ *n.* **1.** SHIPPING **ROBBERY ON HIGH SEAS** robbery on the high seas, especially the stealing of a ship's cargo **2.** TRANSP **ROBBERY ON ANY FORM OF TRANSPORTATION** robbery committed on board any form of transportation, especially an aircraft **3.** TRANSP **HIJACKING** the hijacking of an aircraft or another form of transportation **4. USE OF COPYRIGHTED MATERIAL WITHOUT PERMISSION** the taking and using of copyrighted or patented material without authorization or without the legal right to do so **5.** BROADCAST **ILLEGAL BROADCASTING** the unauthorized or illegal broadcasting of TV or radio programs [Mid-16thC. From medieval Latin *piratia,* from Latin *pirata* (see PIRATE).]

pi·ra·gua /pi raágwə/ *n.* = **pirogue** [Early 17thC. Via American Spanish from Carib, "dugout."]

pi·ra·ña *n.* = **piranha**

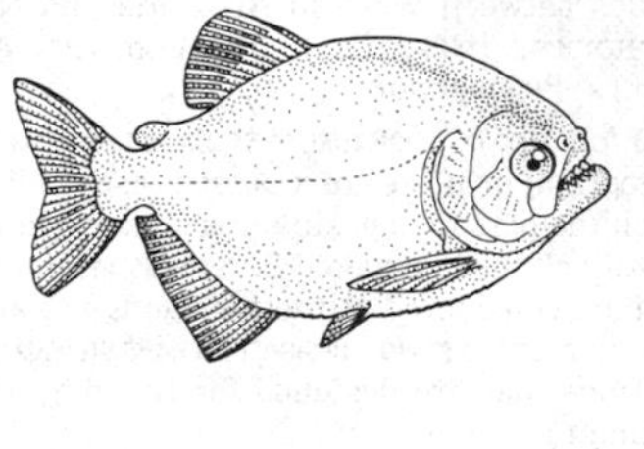

Piranha

pi·ra·nha /pi raányə, -rányə, -raánə, -ránnə/ (*plural* **-nhas** *or* **-nha**), **pi·ra·ña** (*plural* **-ñas** *or* **-ña**) *n.* a small South American freshwater fish that has sharp teeth, strong jaws, and is a dangerous predator when attacking in large numbers. Genus: *Serrasalmo.* [Mid-18thC. Via Portuguese from Tupi *piráya.*]

pi·rate /pírət/ *n.* **1.** SHIPPING **ROBBER AT SEA** somebody who commits robbery on the high seas, especially regularly **2.** SHIPPING **SHIP USED BY SEA ROBBERS** a ship used by people who rob or otherwise attack shipping on the high seas **3. SOMEBODY USING COPYRIGHTED MATERIAL WITHOUT PERMISSION** somebody who duplicates or uses copyrighted or patented material without authorization or without the legal right to do so **4.** BROADCAST **SOMEBODY INVOLVED IN ILLEGAL BROADCASTING** somebody who takes part in or manages the unauthorized or illegal broadcasting of TV or radio programs ■ *v.* **(-rat·ed, -rat·ing, -rates) 1.** *vti.* **ROB SOMETHING ON HIGH SEAS** to rob a vessel or commit robbery on the high seas **2.** *vt.* **USE COPYRIGHTED MATERIAL WITHOUT PERMISSION** to duplicate or use copyrighted or patented material without authorization or without the legal right to do so [13thC. Via Latin *pirata* from Greek *peiratēs,* from *peiran* "to attempt, attack." Ultimately from an Indo-European word that is also the ancestor of English *peril* and *empiric*.] —**pi·rat·ic** /pī ráttik/ *adj.* —**pi·rat·i·cal·ly** /-ráttikəlee/ *adv.*

pi·rog /pi rṓg/ (*plural* **-ro·gi** /-rṓgee/ *or* **-ro·ghi**) *n.* a large rectangular pie that has a pastry crust top and bottom, filled with chopped meat or cabbage, onions, and hard-boiled eggs [Mid-19thC. From Russian.]

pi·rogue /pi rṓg/ *n.* a canoe made from a hollowed-out tree trunk [Early 17thC. Via French from Carib *piragua* "dugout" (source of English *piragua*).]

WORD KEY: REGIONAL NOTE

Recurrent in neighboring Mississippi and East Texas, the term ***pirogue***, as well as the distinctive artifact itself, is a Louisiana marker. Although many occurrences appear across the state, north of the Atchafalaya River, nearly twice as many instances occur in the southern part of the state, the Cajun bayou country, west of New Orleans.

pir·ou·ette /peèroo ét/ *n.* BODY SPIN WHEN DANCING a fast complete spin of the body, especially one performed on the tip of the toe or the ball of one foot in ballet ■ *vi.* (**-et·ted, -et·ting, -ettes**) PERFORM A PIROUETTE to perform a fast body spin on one foot, especially in ballet [Mid-17thC. Via French from Old French, "spinning top," of unknown origin.]

pi·rozh·ki /pi ráwshkee, -róshkee/, **pi·rosh·ki** *npl.* very small fried or baked pastries, filled with finely chopped meat or cabbage and onions, sometimes also with chopped hard-boiled eggs, or with potato or some similar filling (*takes a singular or plural verb*) [Early 20thC. From Russian, literally "little pirog," from PIROG.]

Pi·sa /péezə/ capital of Pisa Province, Tuscany Region, central Italy. It is known for its leaning bell tower. Population: 97,872 (1993). ◊ **Leaning Tower of Pisa**

pis al·ler /péez a láy/ (*plural* **pis al·lers**) *n.* something that is done as a last resort or when no other option is available [From French, from *pis* "worse" + *aller* "to go"]

pis·ca·ry /pískəree/ (*plural* **-ries**) *n.* LAW the legal right to fish in a particular place even if it belongs to another person [15thC. Via medieval Latin *piscaria* from, ultimately, Latin *piscis* "fish" (see PISCI-).]

pis·ca·to·ri·al /pìskə táwree əl/, **pis·ca·to·ry** /pískətàwree/ *adj.* relating to fish, fishing, or fishers (*formal*) [Early 19thC. Via Latin *piscatorius* from, ultimately, *piscis* "fish" (see PISCI-).]

Pi·sce·an /píseeən/ *n.* = **Pisces** *n.* 2 —**Pi·sce·an** *adj.*

Pi·sces /pī séez/ (*plural* **-sces**) *n.* 1. ZODIAC 12TH SIGN OF ZODIAC the 12th sign of the zodiac, represented by two fishes and lasting from approximately February 19 to March 20. Pisces is classified as a water sign and its ruling planets are Jupiter and Neptune. 2. ZODIAC SOMEBODY BORN UNDER PISCES somebody whose birthday falls between February 19 and March 20 3. ASTRON ZODIACAL CONSTELLATION BETWEEN AQUARIUS AND PISCES a large faint zodiacal constellation between Aquarius and Pisces [Pre-12thC. From Latin, plural of *piscis* "fish" (source of English *porpoise*).] —**Pi·sces** *adj.*

pisci- *prefix.* fish ○ *pisciform* [From Latin *piscis*. Ultimately from the Indo-European word for "fish" that is also the ancestor of English *fish* and *porpoise*.]

pi·sci·cul·ture /písee kùlchər, píssee-/ *n.* the controlled breeding, hatching, and rearing of fish, especially for scientific or commercial purposes [Mid-19thC. Formed from Latin *piscis* "fish" (see PISCI-), on the model of "agriculture."] —**pi·sci·cul·tur·al** /pìsee kúlchərəl/ *adj.* —**pi·sci·cul·tur·al·ly** /-kúlchərəlee/ *adv.* —**pi·sci·cul·tur·ist** /-kúlchərist/ *n.*

pi·sci·form /písee fàwrm, píssee-/ *adj.* shaped like or otherwise resembling a fish (*formal*)

pi·sci·na /pi séenə, -sínə, -shéenə/ (*plural* **-nas** *or* **-nae** /-nee/) *n.* 1. SACRED CONTAINER FOR HOLY WATER in some Christian churches, a sacred container or basin that holds holy water, used to carry it away after ablutions have been completed 2. PLACE WHERE PRIEST WASHES SACRED CONTAINERS the place where a priest can wash his hands and the sacred containers used in Mass, located in the sacristy, especially in a Roman Catholic church [Late 16thC. Via medieval Latin, literally "fish pond," from *piscis* "fish" (see PISCI-).] —**pis·ci·nal** /píssən'l/ *adj.*

pi·scine /pī séen, pí sīn/ *adj.* relating to, characteristic of, or resembling fish (*formal*) [Late 18thC. Via medieval Latin *piscinus* from Latin *piscis* "fish" (see PISCI-).]

Pi·scis Aus·tri·nus /pìsiss o strínəss, pìsiss-/ *n.* a small constellation of the southern hemisphere between Grus and Aquarius

pi·sciv·o·rous /pi sívvərəss, pī-/ *adj.* feeding habitually or mainly on fish

pish /pish/ *interj.* used to express contempt, annoyance, or impatience [Late 16thC. Natural exclamation.]

pi·si·form /píssə fàwrm/ *adj.* LIKE A PEA resembling a pea in shape or size ■ *n.* = **pisiform bone** [Mid-18thC. Formed from Latin *pisum* "pea."]

pi·si·form bone *n.* the small knobbly bone at the place where the inner bone of the forearm (**ulna**) joins the wrist (**carpus**)

pis·mire /píss mīr, píz-/ *n.* an ant (*archaic*) [14thC. From PISS (from the smell of formic acid) + obsolete *mire* "ant."]

pis·mo clam /pízzəmō-/ *n.* a large edible thick-shelled marine clam native to the Pacific coast of North America. Latin name: *Tivela stultorum.* [Named for *Pismo* Beach in California, where the clams are found]

pi·so·lite /písə līt/ *n.* an inorganic limestone consisting of individual spherical concretions (**pisoliths**) [Early 18thC. Formed from Greek *pisos* "pea" + -LITE.] —**pi·so·lit·ic** /pìsə líttik/ *adj.*

pi·so·lith /písə lith, pízə-, píssə-, pízzə-/ *n.* a spherical concretion with concentric laminations that with others makes up an inorganic limestone. Pisoliths can be up to 4 in./10 cm in diameter. [Late 18thC. Formed from Greek *pisos* "pea" + -LITH.]

piss /piss/ *v.* (**pissed, piss·ing, piss·es**) (*slang offensive*) 1. *vi.* OFFENSIVE TERM an offensive term meaning to urinate 2. *vt.* OFFENSIVE TERM an offensive term meaning to discharge something, e.g., blood, when urinating 3. *vt.* OFFENSIVE TERM an offensive term meaning to urinate on or into something ■ *n.* (*slang offensive*) 1. OFFENSIVE TERM an offensive term for urine 2. OFFENSIVE TERM an offensive term for an act or instance of urinating [13thC. Via French *pisser* from assumed Vulgar Latin *pissiare*, ultimately an imitation of the sound.] ◇ **piss and vinegar** an offensive term for feisty strength of character and physical vigor (*slang offensive*)

piss away *vt.* an offensive term meaning to waste or squander something, e.g., money or time (*slang offensive*)

piss off *v.* (*slang offensive*) 1. *vt.* OFFENSIVE TERM an offensive term meaning to annoy, irritate, or upset somebody 2. *vi.* OFFENSIVE TERM an offensive term meaning to go away and stop being annoying (*often used as a command*)

piss·ant /píss ànt/, **piss-ant, piss ant** *n.* (*informal offensive*) 1. OFFENSIVE TERM an offensive term for somebody who pays too much attention to small details 2. OFFENSIVE TERM an offensive term for somebody of no importance or stature ■ *adj.* (*informal offensive*) 1. OFFENSIVE TERM an offensive term meaning paying too much attention to small details 2. OFFENSIVE TERM an offensive term meaning of no importance, significance, or consequence [Mid-17thC. From PISS + ANT; the underlying meaning is "insignificant person."]

Pis·sar·ro /pi saárō/, **Camille** (1830–1903) French painter. He was a major exponent of the impressionist style, and is known for his landscapes, river scenes, and street scenes. Full name **Camille Jacob Pissarro**

pissed /pist/ *adj.* (*slang offensive*) 1. OFFENSIVE TERM an offensive term meaning extremely angry or upset 2. OFFENSIVE TERM an offensive term meaning extremely drunk

pissed off *adj. U.K.* = **pissed** (*slang offensive*)

piss·er /píssər/ *n.* 1. OFFENSIVE TERM an offensive term for somebody or something regarded as extremely annoying, upsetting, or unpleasant (*slang offensive*) 2. SOMEBODY OR SOMETHING SURPRISINGLY GOOD somebody or something that is unexpectedly good or worthwhile (*offensive in some contexts*)

pis·soir /pee swaár/ *n.* a public urinal, especially one on the streets of some European cities, with a circular screen around it [Early 20thC. From French, formed from *pisser* (see PISS).]

piss·pot /píss pòt/ *n.* an offensive term for somebody regarded as ill-tempered and generally mean (*slang offensive*) [Originally in the literal meaning "chamber pot"]

pis·ta·chi·o /pi stáshe ō, -staáshee-/ *n.* 1. (*plural* **-os** *or* **-o**) TREES SMALL ASIAN TREE a small Mediterranean or Asian tree of the cashew family that yields hard-shelled nuts, the kernels of which are edible. Latin name: *Pistachia vera.* 2. **pis·ta·chi·o** (*plural* **-os**), **pis·ta·chi·o nut** NUT KERNEL OF PISTACHIO TREE the small edible green kernel of the nut of the pistachio tree [15thC. Via Old French *pistace* and Italian *pistacchio* from, ultimately, Greek *pistakion*, from *pistakē* "pistachio tree," possibly of Iranian origin.]

pis·ta·chi·o green *n.* of a pale yellowish-green color, like the kernel of a pistachio nut —**pis·ta·chi·o green** *n.*

piste /peest/ *n.* SKIING a downhill track or area of densely packed snow that provides good skiing conditions [Early 18thC. Via French, "track," from, ultimately, Latin *pinsere* "to beat"; the underlying meaning is "beaten track."]

pis·til /píst'l/ *n.* a carpel or group of fused carpels forming the female reproductive part of a flower and including the ovary, style, and stigma [Early 18thC. Directly or via French *pistile* from Latin *pistillum* "pestle," because of its shape.]

pis·til·late /píst'l àyt, -ət/ *adj.* having one or more pistils but usually without stamens

pis·tol /píst'l/ *n.* SMALL GUN a small short-barreled gun designed to be held in one hand ■ *vt.* (**-toled, -tol·ing, -tols**) SHOOT SOMEBODY OR SOMETHING WITH PISTOL to shoot somebody or something using a pistol [Mid-16thC. Via French *pistole* from, ultimately, Czech *pišt'ala*, literally "pipe," from *pištěti* "to whistle," ultimately an imitation of the sound.]

pis·tole /pi stṓl/ *n.* a gold coin used in some European countries during the 17th and 18th centuries [Late 16thC. From French, a shortening of *pistolet*, of unknown origin.]

pis·to·leer /pìstə léer/ *n.* somebody, especially a soldier, who carries or uses a pistol (*archaic*)

pis·tol grip *n.* a handle that resembles the butt of a pistol, especially in being shaped to fit the hand

pis·tol-whip *vt.* to hit or beat somebody or something with the butt or barrel of a pistol

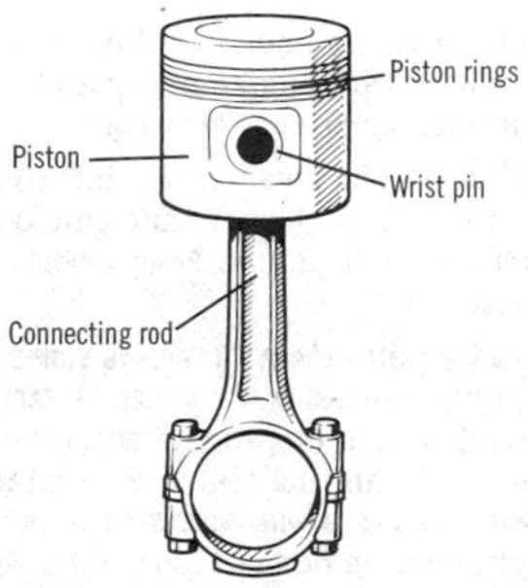

Piston

pis·ton /pístən/ *n.* 1. ENG METAL CYLINDER SLIDING WITHIN TUBE a metal cylinder that slides up and down inside a tubular housing, receiving pressure from or exerting pressure on a fluid, used e.g. in an internal-combustion engine 2. MUSIC VALVE IN BRASS INSTRUMENT the valve mechanism in a brass musical instrument that is used to alter its pitch [Early 18thC. Via French from Italian *pestone* "large pestle," from *pestare* "to crush."]

Pis·ton /pístən/, **Walter** (1894–1976) U.S. composer and teacher. Known for his orchestral and chamber works, he won Pulitzer Prizes for two of his symphonies.

pis·ton ring *n.* a metal ring or series of rings attached around a piston to ensure a tight seal with the cylinder wall and prevent gaseous leakage

pis·ton rod *n.* a rod connected to a piston that transmits the motion of the piston to a pump or an engine

pis·tou /pee stóō/ *n.* a sauce from Provence made of basil, garlic, and olive oil, similar to Italian pesto [Mid-20thC. Via French from Provençal, the past participle of pestar "to crush," from late Latin *pistare* (see PESTO).]

pit[1] /pit/ *n.* 1. BIG HOLE IN GROUND a large hole in the ground 2. MINING HOLE IN GROUND FOR MINING a deep hole in the ground that gives access to a mining resource, especially coal 3. MINING MINESHAFT a shaft that gives access to a mine 4. SMALL INDENTATION a small indentation that detracts from the appearance or functioning of something **5.** MED **SMALL INDENTATION LEFT BY ILLNESS** a small indentation in the skin, usually permanent, left by a disease such as chickenpox or by a skin disorder such as acne **6.** ANAT **NATURAL HOLLOW** a natural hollow, especially on the surface of a body part **7. LOWEST PART** the very bottom of something **8.** = **pitfall** *n.* 2 **9.** MOTOR SPORTS **SERVICING AREA FOR RACING CARS** an area, or section of an area, off the side of an auto racing track where vehicles can get fuel, fresh tires, and repairs (*often used in the plural*) **10.** AUTOMOT **SUNKEN AREA FOR EXAMINING CARS** a sunken area, especially in a garage, where the undercarriages of cars and other motor vehicles can be inspected and repaired **11.** SPORTS **ARENA FOR FIGHTING** an arena that is cordoned off for bouts of fighting, especially illegal fighting between cocks or dogs. ◊ **cockpit** **12.** GAMBLING **AREA IN CASINO** the area in a casino where the gambling takes place **13.** STOCK EXCH **AREA ON FLOOR OF EXCHANGE** the area of the floor of an exchange where commodities trading takes place **14.** SPORT **SANDY AREA WHERE JUMPERS LAND** a soft sandy area where a long jumper, triple jumper, or pole vaulter can land safely **15. AREA CONTAINING PARTICULAR SUBSTANCE** an area filled with a particular material or substance ○ *a tar pit* **16.** CHR **HELL** Hell (*archaic*) **17.** BOT **CONCAVE SPOT ON PLANT WALL** a tiny concavity or thin-walled area in the wall of a plant serving to help transport water and nutrients ■ *vt.* (**pit·ted, pit·ting, pits**) **1. SET UP IN OPPOSITION** to set somebody or something up in opposition to somebody or something else **2. MARK SURFACE WITH SMALL HOLES** to cause small holes or indentations to form in a surface **3. PUT SOMEBODY OR SOMETHING INTO DEEP HOLE** to put or bury somebody or something in a deep hole ■ **pits** *npl.* **WORST POSSIBLE THING, PERSON, OR PLACE** the worst or most unpleasant thing, person, or place it is possible to find (*informal*) [Old English *pytt*; ultimately from a prehistoric Germanic word that was borrowed from Latin *puteus* "pit, well"]

pit[2] /pit/ *n.* BOT **FRUIT KERNEL** the kernel or stone of a fruit ■ *vt.* (**pit·ted, pit·ting, pits**) **REMOVE KERNEL FROM FRUIT** to remove the kernel or stone from a fruit [Mid-19thC. Origin uncertain: probably from Dutch, from a prehistoric Germanic word that was also the ancestor of English *pith*.]

pi·ta[1] /péetə/ *n.* a plant such as the agave that yields a strong fiber used to make paper and cordage [Late 17thC. Via American Spanish from Taino.]

pi·ta[2] /péetə/, **pi·ta bread** *n.* a flat round Middle Eastern unleavened bread that can be opened to insert a filling [Mid-20thC. From modern Greek *pētta, pit(t)a* "bread, pie."]

pit·a·pat /pìttə pát/ *adv.* **WITH TAPPING SOUND** with quick light tapping noises ■ *n.* **SERIES OF TAPPING NOISES** a series of quick light tapping noises, especially those made by light, running feet ■ *vi.* (**-pat·ted, -pat·ting, -pats**) **MAKE SERIES OF TAPPING NOISES** to make a series of quick light tapping noises [Early 16thC. An imitation of the sound.]

pit boss *n.* the supervisor of all gambling-table operations in a casino

pit bull *n.* **1.** = **pit bull terrier** **2. AGGRESSOR** a highly aggressive or ruthless person (*slang*)

pit bull ter·ri·er *n.* a large bull terrier similar to the Staffordshire bull terrier but more muscular and powerful. The breed was first developed in the United States in dogfighting circles and remains unrecognized by the Kennel Clubs.

Pit·cairn Is·land /pít kairn-/ island in the central South Pacific Ocean. It is the main island of a group forming a dependency of the United Kingdom. It was first inhabited by mutineers from the HMS *Bounty* in 1790. Population: 61 (1991). Area: 2 sq. mi./5 sq. km.

pitch[1] /pich/ *v.* (**pitched, pitch·ing, pitch·es**) **1.** *vti.* **THROW SOMETHING** to throw or hurl something **2.** *vt.* **THROW SOMETHING AWAY** to get rid of or discard something by throwing it or by performing an action similar to throwing **3.** *vti.* BASEBALL **THROW BALL TO BATTER** to throw a ball from the mound to the batter **4.** *vt.* **SET UP TEMPORARY STRUCTURE** to set up a camp, tent, marquee, or other temporary structure **5.** *vt.* **SECURE SOMETHING IN GROUND** to secure, embed, or implant something in the ground **6.** *vti.* **FALL OR MAKE FALL DOWN** to fall or stumble, or cause somebody or something to fall or stumble, especially headfirst **7.** *vi.* **SLANT IN PARTICULAR WAY** to slant or slope in a particular way or to a particular level **8.** *vt.* **SET SOMETHING AT PARTICULAR INTELLECTUAL LEVEL** to put, set, or have something at a particular intellectual level **9.** *vi.* **WOBBLE UP AND DOWN** to move with the front and rear being alternately uppermost, e.g., in rough water or turbulent air currents (*refers especially to ships and aircraft*) **10.** *vt.* **TRY TO SELL OR PROMOTE SOMETHING** to try to sell or promote something such as a product, personal viewpoint, or potential business venture, often in an aggressive way **11.** *vti.* GOLF **HIT GOLF BALL HIGH** to hit a high ball, usually onto the green and often with some backspin so that it does not roll too much on landing **12.** *vt.* MUSIC **SET INSTRUMENT TO PARTICULAR KEY** to set a musical instrument to a particular key **13.** *vt.* CARDS **LEAD CARD TO ESTABLISH TRUMPS** to lead a card of a particular suit in order to establish that suit as trumps for the trick **14.** *vi.* **GIVE ENTHUSIASTIC SUPPORT** to provide enthusiastic support for somebody or something ■ *n.* **1. WAY OF THROWING SOMETHING** a particular way or manner of thowing something, especially a ball **2.** BASEBALL **THROW OF BALL TO BATTER** the act or an instance of the pitcher throwing a ball from the mound to the batter **3. PARTICULAR DEGREE OF SOMETHING** a particular degree or level of something ○ *What drove him to such a pitch of anxiety?* **4. DEGREE OF SLOPE OF SOMETHING** the degree, angle, or extent of the slope of something, especially a hill, road, or other feature **5.** BUILDING **DEGREE OF ELEVATION OF ROOF** the degree of elevation of a roof, usually expressed in terms of the ratio between its height and its span **6.** ARCHIT **HIGHEST OR LOWEST POINT ON FEATURE** the highest or lowest point on a feature such as an arch **7.** MUSIC **PARTICULAR FREQUENCY OF SINGLE NOTE** the level of a sound in the scale, defined by its frequency **8.** TECH **DISTANCE BETWEEN SIMILAR FORMS** the spacing between adjacent forms on an object that has repeated elements, e.g., the distance between threads on a screw thread **9.** AIR **ANGLE TO WHICH PROPELLER SET** the angle between the plane passing through a propeller blade and the plane of rotation of the propeller **10.** GOLF **HIGH GOLF SHOT** a golf shot, especially one from fairway to green, in which the ball lofts high in the air, often with some backspin, so that it does not roll too far on landing **11. AGGRESSIVE SPEECH AIMING TO PERSUADE SOMEBODY** an aggressive speech given, often more than once, in order to try to persuade somebody to accept or buy something (*informal*) **12. TOSSING MOTION** an act or instance of pitching up and down, e.g., in rough water or air turbulence **13.** *U.K.* SPORTS **FIELD FOR GAME** a playing area for a team ball game **14.** GEOL **TILT OF GEOLOGICAL FORMATION** the inclination from the horizontal of a geological formation or structure, e.g., a vein or stratum **15.** MOUNTAINEERING **DISTANCE SEPARATING CLIMBERS** the distance between climbers making an ascent or descent using the same ropes, equal to one rope length or less [12thC. Origin uncertain.]

pitch in *vi.* **1. HELP WILLINGLY** to help or cooperate, especially in a very willing way **2. BEGIN TO DO SOMETHING** to begin to do or participate in something, especially with great enthusiasm

pitch into *vt.* to begin to attack somebody, either verbally or physically (*informal*)

pitch[2] /pich/ *n.* **1. SUBSTANCE OBTAINED FROM TAR** a dark sticky substance obtained from tar and used in the building trades, especially for waterproofing roofs **2. NATURAL TARRY SUBSTANCE** a sticky dark substance such as asphalt, found naturally **3. RESIN** resin that is obtained from the sap of certain pine trees ■ *vt.* (**pitched, pitch·ing, pitch·es**) **SPREAD PITCH ON SURFACE** to coat a surface with pitch [Partly Old English *pic*, and partly from Anglo-Norman *piche*, both ultimately from Latin *pix* (source also of English *pay*)]

pitch-and-putt *n.* **1. SHORTENED VERSION OF GOLF** a game similar to regulation golf, but played on a much shorter course, in which players use only two clubs, an iron and a putter. The distance to each hole is around one third of the length of the average golf hole. **2. PITCH-AND-PUTT COURSE** a course for pitch-and-putt, with holes shorter than those for regulation golf

pitch-and-toss *n.* a game of skill and luck that involves each player throwing a coin toward a designated spot. The person whose coin lands closest to the mark then takes up all the coins and drops them, and any coins that land heads up are won by that player.

pitch bend *n.* an instrumental and vocal technique by which the pitch of a note is modified by raising or lowering it slightly

pitch-black *adj.* extremely dark, especially when dark enough to make seeing difficult or impossible

pitch·blende /pích blènd/ *n.* a dark-colored naturally occurring form of the mineral uraninite that is the principal source of uranium and radium [Late 18thC. From German *Pechblende*, from *Pech* "pitch" + *Blende* (see BLENDE).]

pitch-dark *adj.* = **pitch-black**

pitched bat·tle *n.* **1. FIERCE BATTLE AT PREARRANGED LOCATION** a fierce battle, usually involving a large number of people and fought between two sides who take up prearranged positions in close proximity to each other **2. FIERCE CONFLICT OR ARGUMENT** a large-scale, usually bitter conflict or confrontation, often including people who have no direct involvement with the matter

pitch·er[1] /píchər/ *n.* **1. LARGE SINGLE-HANDLED JUG** a large single-handled water jug, usually wide around the middle, gradually narrowing toward the neck, and flaring out at the lip or spout **2.** BOT **URN-SHAPED LEAF** any of the modified urn-shaped leaves of the pitcher plant [13thC. Via Old French *pichier* from, ultimately, medieval Latin *bicarium*, from an assumed Vulgar Latin word that is also the ancestor of English *beaker*.]

pitch·er[2] /píchər/ *n.* **1.** BASEBALL **PLAYER WHO THROWS BALL TO BATTER** the player on the fielding side who stands on the mound and throws the ball in the direction of the batter, attempting to cause the batter to make an out **2.** BUILDING **PAVING STONE** a paving stone, especially one made of granite [Early 18thC. Formed from PITCH[1].]

Pitch·er /píchər/, **Molly** (1754–1832) U.S. patriot. She carried pitchers of water to the soldiers at the Battle of Monmouth (1778), and may have fought in her fallen husband's place. Born **Mary Ludwig**. Real name **Mary Hays**

pitch·er plant *n.* a plant with leaves that are pitcher-shaped to attract, trap, and digest insects. Family: Sarraceniaceae.

pitch·er's mound *n.* = **mound** *n.* 5

pitch·fork /pích fàwrk/ *n.* **PRONGED FARMING TOOL** a farming implement, usually with a long handle and two or three widely spaced, slightly curved prongs, that is used for stacking, turning, and moving hay ■ *vt.* (**-forked, -fork·ing, -forks**) **USE PITCHFORK TO MOVE HAY** to use a pitchfork to lift, turn, or move hay [13thC. Alteration of earlier *pickfork* (influenced by PITCH[1]), of uncertain origin: perhaps "fork with pikes," from PICK[2]; or "fork for pitching (sheaves, etc.)," from, ultimately, PITCH[1].]

pitch·ing wedge *n.* an eight iron with a low-angled face used to hit pitches in golf

pitch·man /píchmən/ (*plural* **-men** /-mən/) *n.* **1. SELLER OF SMALL OR CHEAP THINGS** somebody who sells small or cheap things, especially on the streets or from a stall at markets, fairs, or carnivals **2. SALESPERSON** a very persuasive salesperson or advertiser **3. PRESENTER OF COMMERCIALS** somebody who presents commercials on TV or radio

pitch·out /pích òwt/ *n.* **1.** BASEBALL **PITCH OUT OF STRIKE ZONE** a throw by the pitcher that is high and outside the strike zone, allowing the catcher to throw out a runner attempting to steal a base **2.** FOOTBALL **LATERAL PASS BEHIND LINE OF SCRIMMAGE** a lateral pass after the snap by the back, usually the quarterback, to another back behind the line of scrimmage

pitch pine *n.* **1.** TREES **PINE TREE YIELDING PITCH** an eastern North American pine tree that yields pitch or turpentine. Latin name: *Pinus rigida.* **2. PITCH PINE WOOD** the wood of the pitch pine tree

pitch·stone /pích stòn/ *n.* a dark hydrated volcanic glass similar to obsidian

pitch·y /píchee/ (**-i·er, -i·est**) *adj.* **1. STICKY WITH PITCH** covered with or full of pitch **2. LIKE PITCH** resembling pitch, especially in color, smell, or consistency — **pitch·i·ness** *n.*

pit·e·ous /píttee əss/ *adj.* **1. DESERVING PITY** deserving pity or bringing out feelings of pity **2. FULL OF PITY** full of or expressing pity or compassion (*archaic*) [13thC. Via Old French *piteus*, literally "full of pity," from, ultimately, Latin *pietas* "compassion."] —**pit·e·ous·ly** *adv.* — **pit·e·ous·ness** *n.*

pit·fall /pít fàwl/ *n.* **1. POTENTIAL DISASTER** a potential disaster or difficulty, often one that is unexpected or cannot be anticipated **2. DISGUISED HOLE ACTING AS TRAP** a deep hole in the ground disguised in some way, often with a canopy of foliage covering its top opening and sides so steep that escape is impossible

pith /pith/ *n.* **1.** TISSUE UNDER RIND OF CITRUS FRUITS the soft whitish fibrous tissue that lies under the outer rind of citrus fruits **2.** TISSUE INSIDE STEM OF PLANT the central spongy tissue of the stem of a vascular plant **3.** SPONGY INTERIOR OF BODY PART the soft spongy inner material of a part of the body such as a hair shaft or bone **4.** CENTRAL PART OF SOMETHING the central or most important or significant part of something such as an argument or discussion **5.** VIGOR vigor, stamina, weight, or substance ■ *vt.* **(pithed, pith·ing, piths) 1.** CUT LABORATORY ANIMAL'S SPINAL CORD to cut or destroy the spinal cord of a vertebrate as part of a laboratory experiment **2.** KILL ANIMALS BY CUTTING SPINAL CORD to kill animals, especially cattle, by cutting through the spinal cord **3.** REMOVE PITH FROM PLANT STEM to remove the pith from the center of a plant stem [Old English *piþa*, from a prehistoric Germanic word that is also the ancestor of PIT[2]]

Pith·e·can·thro·pus /pìthə kánthrəpəss, -kan thrṓpəss/ (*plural* **-pi** /-pī/) *n.* the original genus name of Java Man, now classified as Homo erectus (*dated*) [Late 19thC. From modern Latin, former genus name, from Greek *pithēkos* "ape" + *anthrōpos* "human being."] —**pith·e·can·throp·ic** /pìthəkən thróppik/ *adj.*—**pith·e·can·thro·pine** /pìthə kánthrə pīn/ *adj.* —**pith·e·can·thro·poid** /pìthə kánthrə pòyd/ *adj.*

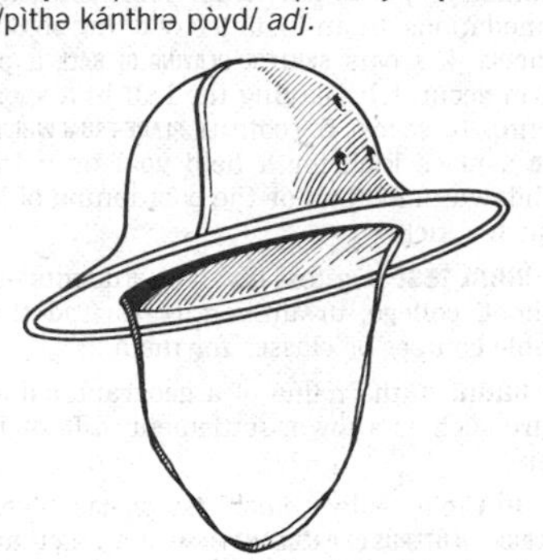

Pith helmet

pith hel·met *n.* a lightweight hat made from dried pith or some other material, worn in hot climates to protect the head, face, and the back of the neck from strong sunlight

pith·os /pí thòss, pī́-/ (*plural* **-oi** /-òy/) *n.* a large jar, usually made of pottery, used in ancient Greece for storing oil or grain [Late 19thC. From Greek.]

pith·y /píthee/ (**-i·er, -i·est**) *adj.* **1.** BRIEF AND TO THE POINT brief yet forceful and to the point, often with an element of wit **2.** OF PITH relating to, full of, or resembling pith —**pith·i·ly** *adv.* —**pith·i·ness** *n.*

pit·i·a·ble /píttee əb'l/ *adj.* **1.** EVOKING COMPASSION arousing or deserving pity or compassion **2.** EVOKING CONTEMPT arousing or deserving contempt or derision —**pit·i·a·ble·ness** *n.* —**pit·i·a·bly** *adv.*

pit·i·ful /píttif'l/ *adj.* **1.** AROUSING PITY arousing or deserving pity or compassion **2.** AROUSING CONTEMPT arousing or deserving contempt or derision —**pit·i·ful·ly** *adv.* —**pit·i·ful·ness** *n.*

pit·i·less /píttiləss/ *adj.* **1.** WITHOUT MERCY lacking in pity, mercy, or sympathy **2.** SEVERE severe to the highest degree possible ○ *the blazing, pitiless sun* —**pit·i·less·ly** *adv.* —**pit·i·less·ness** *n.*

Pit·jant·jat·ja·ra /pìchənchə chérrə/ (*plural* **-ra** *or* **-ras**), **Pit·jant·ja·ra** /pìchən chérrə/ (*plural* **-ra** *or* **-ras**) *n.* **1.** PEOPLES MEMBER OF ABORIGINAL PEOPLE a member of an Australian Aboriginal people who live in the desert regions in the south of the continent **2.** LANG PITJANTJATJARA LANGUAGE the language of the Pitjantjatjara people, which belongs to the Pama-Nyungan family. About 2,000 people speak Pitjantjatjara. [From Pitjantjatjara]

pi·ton /peé tòn/ *n.* a metal spike for driving into ice or a rock crevice, with an eye at the other end so that a rope can be passed through it and then secured [Late 19thC. From French, "eye-bolt."]

Pi·tot-stat·ic tube /peétō-, pee tṑ-/ *n.* a device consisting of a Pitot tube and a static tube, used to measure fluid velocity and especially as an air speed indicator in aircraft [Early 20thC. See PITOT TUBE.]

Pi·tot tube *n.* **1.** DEVICE FOR MEASURING FLUID VELOCITY an instrument placed in a moving fluid and used along with a manometer to measure fluid velocity **2.** = **Pitot-static tube** [Late 19thC. Named for the French physicist Henri *Pitot* 1695–1771, who invented it.]

pit stop *n.* **1.** MOTOR SPORTS REFUELING STOP FOR CAR DURING RACE a stop in the pits to allow a racing car to be refueled and serviced during a race **2.** BRIEF STOP DURING ROAD JOURNEY a brief stop during a journey by road to rest, refuel, use a rest room, or buy refreshments (*informal*) **3.** PLACE TO MAKE PIT STOP a place to make a pit stop during a road journey (*informal*)

William Pitt (the Younger)

Pitt /pít/, **William** (1759–1806) British statesman. Great Britain's youngest prime minister, at the age of 24 (1783–1801). He resigned following George III's refusal to accept Roman Catholic emancipation, but returned to office (1804–06) for a second administration. Known as **Pitt the Younger**

pit·ta *n.* U.K. = **pita**

pit·tance /pítt'nss/ *n.* a very small amount of something, especially a very small sum of money, wage, or allowance [13thC. Via Old French *pietance* from medieval Latin *pietantia* "pious or charitable gift," from Latin *pietas* "piety."]

pit·ter-pat·ter *n.* LIGHT CONTINUOUS TAPPING SOUND a light, rapid, and continuous tapping sound, similar to the sound of raindrops falling on something ■ *vi.* **(pit·ter-pat·tered, pit·ter-pat·ter·ing, pit·ter-pat·ters)** MAKE LIGHT CONTINUOUS TAPPING SOUND to make or move with a light, rapid, and continuous tapping sound ■ *adv.* WITH LIGHT CONTINUOUS TAPPING SOUND with a light, rapid, and continuous tapping sound [15thC. An imitation of the sound.]

pit·tos·po·rum /pi tóspərəm, píttə spàwrəm/ *n.* an evergreen shrub that has leathery leaves and small often sweet-smelling white, purple, or greenish-yellow flowers, and is often grown as an ornamental hedge in the southern United States. Genus: *Pittosporum.* [Late 18thC. From modern Latin, from Greek *pitta* "pitch" + *sporos* "seed"; from the resinous pulp around the seeds.]

Pitts·burg /píts bùrg/ city in southwestern Pennsylvania. It is the second-largest city in the state. Population: 369,879 (1990).

Pitts·field /píts feeld/ city in western Massachusetts, directly east of the New York border, on the eastern bank of the Housatonic River, northwest of Springfield. Population: 46,315 (1996).

pi·tu·i·tar·y /pi tóo i tèree/ *n.* (*plural* **-ies**) **1.** PHYSIOL = **pituitary gland 2.** PHARM = **pituitary extract** ■ *adj.* PHYSIOL OF PITUITARY GLAND relating to or produced by the pituitary gland [Early 17thC. From Latin *pituitarius* "of slime or mucus," from *pituita* "slime." From the fact that the pituitary gland was originally thought to secrete nasal mucus.]

pi·tu·i·tar·y ex·tract *n.* a pharmaceutical preparation made from substances obtained from the pituitary gland that is rich in beneficial hormones

pi·tu·i·tar·y gland *n.* a small oval gland at the base of the brain in vertebrates, producing hormones that control other glands and influence growth of the bone structure, sexual maturing, and general metabolism

pit vi·per *n.* a venomous American snake that has heat-sensitive pits below its eyes used to detect prey. Rattlesnakes and copperheads are pit vipers. Family: Crotalidae.

pit·y /píttee/ *n.* **1.** FEELING OF SYMPATHY a feeling of sadness because somebody else is in trouble or pain, or the capacity to feel this **2.** REGRETTABLE THING a sad or regrettable thing ○ *It's a pity you couldn't make it.* **3.** MERCY a willingness to help or to forgive somebody who is in pain or who has done wrong ■ *vt.* **(-ied, -y·ing, -ies)** FEEL PITY FOR SOMEBODY OR SOMETHING to feel pity for somebody or for somebody's pain or trouble ■ *interj.* EXPRESSION OF SYMPATHY OR REGRET used to express sympathy or regret about something (*informal*) [13thC. Via Old French *pité* from Latin *pietas* "piety, dutifulness, compassion" (see PIETY).] —**pit·y·ing** *adj.* —**pit·y·ing·ly** *adv.* ◇ **have** *or* **take pity on somebody** to feel pity for somebody or for somebody's pain or trouble, or show mercy to somebody ◇ **(the) more's the pity** used to express regret, disappointment, or annoyance that something is the case (*informal*)

pit·y·ri·a·sis /pìtti rī́ əssiss/ *n.* a skin disease affecting humans and animals in which the skin comes off in dry flakes [Late 17thC. Via modern Latin from Greek *pituriasis*, from *pituron* "corn husks."]

più /pyoo/ *adv.* more or increasingly (*used as a musical direction*) [Early 18thC. Via Italian from Latin *plus* (see PLUS).]

Pi·us IX /pī́ əss/, **Pope** (1792–1878). His pontificate (1846–78) was marked by the loss of the Papal States, the declaration of papal infallibility, and condemnation of all forms of liberalism. Real name **Giovanni Maria Mastai-Ferretti**

Pi·us X, St., Pope (1835–1914). During his pontificate (1903–14) he opposed modernism in the Roman Catholic Church, initiated changes to canon law, and introduced a new breviary. Real name **Giuseppe Melchiorre Sarto**

Pi·us XI, Pope (1857–1939). As pope (1922–34) he presided over the signing of the Lateran Treaty (1929), and spoke out against fascism, Nazism, and communism. Real name **Ambrogio Damiano Achille Ratti**

Pi·us XII, Pope (1876–1958). As pope (1939–58) he condemned modernism and communism. He sought to prevent World War II, although his role in the war is the subject of controversy. Real name **Eugenio Pacelli**

Pi·ute *n., adj.* = **Paiute**

piv·ot /pívvət/ *n.* **1.** TECH OBJECT ON WHICH LARGER OBJECT TURNS a small object such as a bar or pin that supports a larger object and lets it turn or swing **2.** CRUCIAL PERSON OR THING the one person or thing that is essential to the success or effectiveness of something **3.** TURNING MOVEMENT a turning movement carried out by pivoting on something **4.** MIL CENTER POINT OF WHEELING MOVEMENT a person, a group of people, or point that acts as the center around which a military formation carries out a wheeling movement **5.** BASKETBALL BASKETBALL POSITION OR PLAYER an offensive position in basketball in which a player faces away from the opposing basket, relays passes, and screens other members of the team, or a player in this position ■ *v.* **(-ot·ed, -ot·ing, -ots) 1.** *vi.* TURN ON PIVOT to turn or swing supported by a pivot **2.** *vi.* DEPEND ON SOMETHING to depend on somebody or something, usually a single person, thing, or factor **3.** *vt.* PROVIDE WITH PIVOT to provide something with a pivot on which it can turn or swing [From French, of unknown origin]

piv·ot·al /pívvət'l/ *adj.* **1.** VITALLY IMPORTANT vitally important, especially in determining the outcome, progress, or success of something **2.** TECH ACTING AS PIVOT relating to or functioning as a pivot

piv·ot man /pívvət màn/, **piv·ot·man** *n.* **1.** SOMEBODY ACTING AS PIVOT somebody who acts as the pivot for a military formation or who has a pivotal role in any organization or formation **2.** = **pivot** *n.* **5**

pix[1] plural of **pic**

pix[2] *n.* = **pyx**

pix·el /píks'l, -sèl/ *n.* an individual tiny dot of light that is the basic unit from which the images on a computer or television screen are made [Mid-20thC. Coined from PIX[1] + ELEMENT.]

pix·ie /píksee/, **pix·y** (*plural* **-ies**) *n.* a type of fairy or elf often depicted as having pointed ears, wearing a long pointed hat, and being cheerful and rather mischievous [Mid-17thC. Origin unknown.]

pix·ie cut *n.* a short tapered hairstyle for girls and women, first popular in the 1960s

pix·i·lat·ed[1] /píksə làytəd/, **pix·il·lat·ed** *adj.* **1.** BEHAVING ODDLY behaving in a strange or whimsical way **2.** BEWILDERED feeling bewildered because unable to understand what is happening **3.** DRUNK drunk (*slang*) [Mid-19thC. Coined humorously from PIXIE + *-lated* (as in English words such as "elated" and "titillated").] — **pix·i·la·tion** /pìksə láysh'n/ *n.*

pix·i·lat·ed[2] /píksə làytəd/ *adj.* used to describe an image on a computer or television screen that is made up of pixels, especially one that is unclear or distorted [Mid-20thC. Coined from PIXEL + *-ated.*]

pix·y *n.* = **pixie**

Pi·zar·ro /pi zaárō/, **Francisco** (1476?–1541) Spanish conquistador. He conquered the Inca Empire (1532), founded the city of Lima (1535), and was governor of Peru (1532–41).

pizz. *abbr.* pizzicato

piz·za /peétsə/ *n.* a flat round piece of bread dough topped with a tomato sauce and cheese, and often with other toppings such as sliced ham, sausage, or vegetables, then baked [Late 19thC. From Italian, "pie," of uncertain origin.]

piz·za par·lor *n.* = **pizzeria**

piz·zazz /pi záz/, **piz·azz, piz·zaz** *n.* an attractive and exciting vitality, especially when combined with style and glamor (*informal*) [Mid-20thC. The origin of this word is uncertain, but it may have been an invention of Diana Vreeland who was fashion editor for the publication *Harper's Bazaar* during the 1930s.]

piz·ze·ri·a /peètsə reé ə/ (*plural* **-as**) *n.* a restaurant that specializes in making and serving pizzas [Mid-20thC. From Italian *pizzeria*, from PIZZA.]

piz·zi·ca·to /pìtsee kaátō/ *adv.* BY PLUCKING STRINGS by using the fingers to pluck the strings of an instrument that is normally played with a bow, especially a violin (*used as a musical direction*) ■ *n.* (*plural* **-ti** /-tee/) PIZZICATO PIECE OF MUSIC a piece of music, or a section of a piece, played pizzicato [Mid-19thC. From Italian, from *pizzicare* "to pluck," from *pizzare* "to prick, sting," from *pizza* "point."] —**piz·zi·ca·to** *adj.*

piz·zle /pízz'l/ *n.* (*sometimes considered offensive*) **1.** ANIMAL'S PENIS the penis of an animal, especially a bull (*archaic*) **2.** WHIP a whip made out of a bull's penis [Late 15thC. From Low German *pēsel*, literally "little penis," from Middle Low German *pēse* "penis."]

PK *abbr.* **1.** PARANORMAL psychokinesis **2.** CARS Pakistan (*international vehicle registration*)

pk. *abbr.* **1.** pack **2.** park **3.** peak **4.** MEASURE peck

pkg. *abbr.* package

pkt. *abbr.* packet

PKU *abbr.* phenylketonuria

pkwy, pky *abbr.* parkway

PL *abbr.* **1. PL, pl.** GRAM plural **2.** LAW public law

pl. *abbr.* GRAM plural

Pl. *abbr.* Place (*used in addresses*)

PL/1 *n., abbr.* programming language 1

plac·a·ble /plákəb'l, pláy-/ *adj.* easily placated (*literary*) [14thC. Directly or via Old French from Latin *placabilis*, from *placare* "to calm" (see PLACATE).] — **plac·a·bil·i·ty** /plàkə bíllətee, plàykə-/ *n.* —**plac·a·bly** /plákəblee/ *adv.*

plac·ard /plá kaàrd, -kərd/ *n.* **1.** NOTICE DISPLAYED IN PUBLIC a large piece of card or board with something written or printed on it, displayed to be read by the public or carried by somebody such as a demonstrator **2.** SMALL CARD OR METAL PLAQUE a small card or metal plaque such as a doorplate, with a name or some other piece of writing on it ■ *vt.* (**-ard·ed, -ard·ing, -ards**) **1.** PUT PLACARDS ON SOMETHING to put up placards on or in something **2.** ADVERTISE OR ANNOUNCE WITH PLACARDS to display something on or advertise something with placards, or in a very conspicuous way [Late 15thC. From French, formed from Old French *plaquier* "to flatten, plaster," from Middle Dutch *placken* "to flatten, patch" (source also of English *plaque*).]

pla·cate /pláy kàyt, plá-/ (**-cat·ed, -cat·ing, -cates**) *vt.* to make somebody less angry, upset, or hostile, usually by doing or saying things to please him or her [Late 17thC. From Latin *placat-*, the past participle stem of *placare* "to calm." Ultimately from an Indo-European base that is also the ancestor of English *please, flake*, and *plank.*] —**pla·ca·tion** /play káysh'n/ *n.* —**pla·ca·to·ry** /pláykə tàwree, plákə-/ *adj.*

place /playss/ *n.* **1.** AREA OR PORTION OF SPACE an area, position, or portion of space that somebody or something can be in ○ *This is a good place to plant the sapling.* **2.** LOCALITY a particular geographical locality such as a town, country, or region ○ *People come here to work from lots of different places.* **3.** AREA IN TOWN a relatively open area in a town, e.g., a public square or a short street **4.** DWELLING the house or other type of accommodation where somebody lives ○ *a place of our own* **5.** AREA WHERE SOMETHING HAPPENS a building or area where something in particular happens or is located ○ *the firm's place of business* **6.** PARTICULAR POINT IN SOMETHING a particular point in something, e.g., a book, film, or story ○ *I lost my place when you interrupted me.* **7.** PROPER POSITION the position or location where somebody or something belongs ○ *A place for everything, and everything in its place.* **8.** OPPORTUNITY TO STUDY an opportunity to study at school or university ○ *hoping for a place at Oxford.* **9.** STATUS somebody's social position or rank in an organization ○ *know your place* **10.** RESPONSIBILITY somebody's responsibility or right, especially one arising from who the person is or the status he or she has ○ *It's not your place to tell me what to do.* **11.** JOB a job or position ○ *offered a place on the board* **12.** SOMEWHERE TO SIT somewhere for somebody to sit, e.g., at a table during a meal or in the audience of a theater ○ *I'll keep a place for you next to me.* **13.** POSITION IN RANK the position of somebody or something in a rank, sequence, or series ○ *She finished in second place.* **14.** HORSERACING SECOND POSITION second position in a race, especially a horse race **15.** MATH POSITION OF DIGIT IN NUMBER the relative position of a particular digit in a number ■ *v.* (**placed, plac·ing, plac·es**) **1.** *vt.* PUT SOMEWHERE to put something or somebody in a particular location or position ○ *placed the box on the table* **2.** *vt.* PUT IN PARTICULAR STATE to cause somebody or something to be in a particular state or condition ○ *Your actions placed all of us in danger.* **3.** *vt.* SEE SOMEBODY IN PARTICULAR WAY to see or treat somebody or something as having a particular value or character ○ *He placed his family above everything else in his life.* **4.** *vt.* REMEMBER SOMEBODY OR SOMETHING to be able to recognize or remember somebody or something ○ *I know the face but I can't place the name.* **5.** *vt.* ASSIGN SOMEBODY to assign somebody to a job, position, home, or the care of somebody else ○ *I'll see if I can place you with the sales team.* **6.** *vt.* AIM SOMETHING CAREFULLY to aim or calculate something carefully so that it lands in a particular spot or has a desired effect ○ *The champion's experience showed in the way he placed his punches.* **7.** *vt.* HAVE SOMETHING ACCEPTED to have something accepted and dealt with by somebody else ○ *placed an order for a new car* **8.** *vt.* SPORTS ALLOCATE FINISHING POSITION to assign a person or animal a particular finishing position in a contest ○ *placed fourth overall* **9.** *vi.* HORSERACING FINISH SECOND to finish in second position in a race, especially a horse race [Pre-12thC. Via French from, ultimately, Latin *platea* "broad way," from the Greek phrase *plateia hodos. Plateia* "broad" came from an Indo-European base meaning "to spread" that is also the ancestor of English *flat* and *plant.* The Latin word is the ultimate source also of English *plaza* and *piazza.*] ◇ **all over the place 1.** everywhere (*informal*) **2.** in a state of disorder or confusion (*informal*) ◇ **a place in the sun** a position of success, happiness, or prosperity ◇ **give place (to)** to make room for somebody or something or allow somebody or something to take precedence ◇ **go places** to be successful (*informal*) ◇ **in place 1.** where somebody or something belongs or ought to be **2.** in position or ready for use ◇ **in place of** instead of or as a replacement for somebody or something ◇ **out of place 1.** not where something or somebody should be **2.** inappropriate or incongruous ◇ **put somebody in his or her place** to humble somebody who is behaving in an arrogant, presumptuous, or insolent way (*informal*) ◇ **take place** to happen ◇ **take the place of** to be a substitute for or replace something or somebody

pla·ce·bo /plə seébō/ (*plural* **-bos** *or* **-boes**) *n.* **1.** MED DRUG WITH NO REAL EFFECT a drug containing no active ingredients given to a patient participating in a clinical trial in order to assess the performance of a new drug. It may also may be given to patients because it may benefit them psychologically to believe they are receiving treatment. **2.** SOMETHING DONE TO PLACATE SOMEBODY something done or said simply to placate or reassure somebody that has no actual effect on whatever is causing his or her problems or anxiety **3.** CHR VESPERS OF OFFICE FOR DEAD in the Roman Catholic Church, the vespers of the office for the dead [13thC. From Latin, "I shall please" (first word in the Vulgate text of Psalm 114:9, used in the Roman Catholic service for the dead), from *placere* "to please" (see PLEASE).]

pla·ce·bo ef·fect *n.* a sense of benefit felt by a patient that arises solely from the knowledge that treatment has been given

place card *n.* a small card with somebody's name on it, put on a table to show where that person is to sit, especially for a formal meal

place·hold·er /pláyss hōldər/ *n.* a symbol in a mathematical or logical expression used to show a pattern, e.g., by representing a term in an equation or a statement in an argument

place kick *n.* a kick , especially in football or rugby, for which the ball is propped or held up on the ground

place·kick (**-kicked, -kick·ing, -kicks**) *vt.* to kick the ball or to score a goal or points by kicking the ball while it is propped up on the ground —**place·kick·er** *n.*

place mat *n.* a protective mat set out for the plate of someone eating at a table

place·ment /pláyssmənt/ *n.* **1.** PLACING OR BEING PLACED the act of placing or arranging something in a particular place or position, or the fact of being placed or arranged in this way **2.** MATCHING SOMEBODY TO PARTICULAR SITUATION the task of finding something such as jobs or accommodations for people, or of assigning people to particular jobs, classes, or accommodations, or an instance of doing so **3.** *U.K.* = **practicum 4.** SPORTS SKILLFUL PLAYING OF BALL a player's skill in accurately playing the ball in a sport such as tennis or soccer **5.** FOOTBALL PLACE FROM WHICH BALL IS KICKED a place kick for a field goal or point after touchdown in football or the positioning of the ball for such a kick

place·ment test *n.* a test given to students entering a school, college, or university to find the most suitable courses or classes for them

place name *n.* the name of a geographical area or feature such as a town, settlement, hill, or body of water

pla·cen·ta /plə séntə/ (*plural* **-tas** *or* **-tae** /-tee/) *n.* **1.** BIOL ORGAN IN UTERUS OF PREGNANT MAMMAL a vascular organ that develops inside the uterus of most pregnant mammals to supply food and oxygen to the fetus through the umbilical cord. It is expelled after birth. **2.** BOT PART OF OVARY OF PLANT the part of the ovary in a flowering plant that bears ovules **3.** BOT SPORE-BEARING MASS OF TISSUE the tissue in a nonflowering plant where the sporangia or spores develop [Late 17thC. Via Latin, "cake," from, ultimately, Greek *plakous* "flat cake," from the stem *plak-* "flat surface." Ultimately from an Indo-European base meaning "to be flat."] — **pla·cen·ta·ry** *adj.*

pla·cen·tal *adj.* WITH PLACENTA having a placenta ■ *n.* ANIMAL WITH PLACENTA an animal that has a placenta, in contrast to marsupials or those that lay eggs

plac·en·ta·tion /plàss'n táysh'n/ *n.* **1.** BIOL FORMATION OR ATTACHMENT OF PLACENTA the process of forming a placenta during pregnancy, or the way in which the placenta is attached to the wall of the uterus **2.** BOT WAY OVULES ARE ATTACHED the way in which ovules are attached to the ovary of a plant **3.** BIOL PLACENTA TYPE the form, structure, or type of a placenta

plac·er /pláyssər/ *n.* a deposit of sand or gravel found, e.g., in the bed of a stream, containing particles of gold or some other valuable mineral [Early 19thC. From American Spanish, "shoal."]

plac·er min·ing *n.* the process of obtaining valuable minerals from placers by washing or dredging

place set·ting *n.* the set of items such as utensils, dishes, and glasses arranged on a table to be used by one person at a meal, or the utensils or dishes alone

place val·ue *n.* MATH the value of the place that a digit occupies in a numeral

plac·id /plássid/ *adj.* **1.** CALM IN NATURE OR APPEARANCE calm and tending not to become excited, upset, or disturbed, or appearing so **2.** COMPLACENT too easily satisfied [Early 17thC. Directly or via French *placide* from Latin *placidus* "gentle," from *placere* "to please" (see PLEASE).] —**pla·cid·i·ty** /plə síddətee/ *n.* —**plac·id·ly** /plássidlee/ *adv.*

WORD KEY: SYNONYMS

See Synonyms at ***calm.***

plac·ing /pláyssing/ *n.* the issuing of securities to the public through a stockbroker or another intermediary

plack·et /plákit/ *n.* **1.** OPENING IN WOMAN'S GARMENT an opening in a woman's garment such as a skirt or blouse, either where it fastens or at a pocket **2.** PIECE OF CLOTH BEHIND OPENING a piece of cloth sewn in behind an opening in a woman's garment [Early 17thC. Alteration of PLACARD.]

pla·co·derm /plákə dùrm/ *n.* an extinct creature resembling a fish that was covered with bony plates and lived in the Paleozoic era. Class: Placodermi. [Mid-19thC. Coined from the Greek stem *plak-* "flat stone" (see PLACENTA) + -DERM.]

plac·oid /plá kòyd/ *adj.* used to describe fish scales that have a flat base and a sharp projecting spine tipped with enamel. The subclass of fish that includes sharks, rays, and skates have placoid scales. [Mid-19thC. Coined from the Greek stem *plak-* "flat stone" (see PLACENTA) + -OID.]

pla·fond /plə fón, plaa fóN/ *n.* a ceiling, especially one that is highly ornamented [Mid-17thC. From French, literally "flat bottom."]

pla·gal /pláyg'l/ *adj.* MUSIC **1.** FROM SUBDOMINANT TO TONIC used to describe a musical cadence or harmonic progression in which the subdominant chord is immediately followed by the tonic chord **2.** RELATING TO MUSICAL MODE relating to or being a musical mode beginning on the note a fourth below the keynote of its equivalent authentic mode but ending on the same final note [Late 16thC. From medieval Latin *plagalis*, from, ultimately, medieval Greek *plagios ēkhos* "plagal mode." *Plagios* "oblique" was formed from *plagos* "side."]

plage /plaázh/ *n.* **1.** ASTRON MARK ON SUN'S SURFACE a mark on the Sun's surface often associated with sunspots **2.** LEISURE SANDY BEACH a beach, especially at a fashionable seaside resort [Via Old French, "region," from, ultimately, Greek *plagos* "side" (see PLAGAL)]

pla·gia·rism /pláyjə rìzzəm/ *n.* **1.** STEALING SOMEBODY'S WORK OR IDEA copying what somebody else has written or taking somebody's else's idea and trying to pass it off as original **2.** SOMETHING PLAGIARIZED something copied from somebody else's work, or somebody else's idea that somebody presents as his or her own —**pla·gia·rist** *n.* —**pla·gia·ris·tic** /plàyjə rístik/ *adj.*

pla·gia·rize /pláyjə rīz/ (**-rized, -riz·ing, -riz·es**) *vti.* to take something that somebody else has written or thought and try to pass it off as original —**pla·gia·riz·er** *n.*

plagio- *prefix.* **1.** oblique, offset ○ *plagiotropism* **2.** disturbance ○ *plagioclimax* [From Greek *plagios*, literally "sideways," from *plagos* "side." Ultimately from an Indo-European base meaning "to be flat," which is also the ancestor of English *flake, flag, plank*, and *placate*.]

pla·gi·o·clase /pláyjee ə klàyss, -klàyz/ *n.* a feldspar consisting of sodium and calcium aluminum silicates and belonging to a common series whose cleavages are not at right angles [Mid-19thC. Coined from PLAGIO- + Greek *klasis* "breaking."] —**pla·gi·o·clas·tic** /plàyjee ə klástik/ *adj.*

pla·gi·ot·ro·pism /plàyjee óttrə pìzzəm/ *n.* BOT the tendency of a plant's roots, stems, or branches to grow at an angle away from the vertical in response to a stimulus —**pla·gi·o·tro·pic** /plàyjee ə tróppik/ *adj.* —**pla·gi·o·tro·pi·cal·ly** /-tróppi kəlee/ *adv.*

plague /playg/ *n.* **1.** MED EPIDEMIC DISEASE a disease that spreads very rapidly, infecting very large numbers of people and killing a great many of them, or an outbreak of such a disease **2.** MED BUBONIC PLAGUE the bubonic plague **3.** APPEARANCE OF SOMETHING IN LARGE NUMBERS the appearance of something harmful or annoying such as vermin in abnormally large numbers, or with abnormal frequency **4.** SOMEBODY OR SOMETHING TROUBLESOME an affliction or extremely troublesome or annoying person or thing ■ *vt.* (**plagued, plagu·ing, plagues**) **1.** AFFLICT SOMEBODY OR SOMETHING to occur or recur frequently, causing a great deal of trouble, difficulty, or pain to somebody or something (*often passive*) **2.** ANNOY SOMEBODY CONSTANTLY to harass or annoy somebody constantly, usually by asking questions or making requests or demands [14thC. Via Latin *plaga* "blow, stroke, wound" from, possibly, Greek. Ultimately from an Indo-European word meaning "to strike" which is also the ancestor of English *complain* and *plankton*.]

pla·guy /pláygee/, **pla·guey** *adj.* (**-gui·er, -gui·est**) TROUBLESOME causing trouble or irritation ■ *adv.* ANNOYINGLY in a troublesome or annoying way or to a troublesome or annoying degree —**pla·gui·ly** *adv.*

plaice /playss/ (*plural* **plaice**) *n.* **1.** LARGE FLAT EDIBLE SEAFISH a large edible flat-bodied fish that lives in European seas and has brown skin with red or orange spots. Latin name: *Pleuronectes platessa.* **2.** FLATFISH OF NORTH AMERICAN ATLANTIC WATERS a fish similar and related to the European plaice, found in North American Atlantic waters. Latin name: *Hippoglossoides platessoides.* [13thC. Via Old French *plaïs* from late Latin *platessa* "flatfish," from Greek *platus* "broad."]

plaid /plad/ *n.* **1.** CLOTHES TARTAN CLOTH WORN OVER SHOULDER a long rectangular piece of tartan material worn draped over the shoulder as part of traditional Scottish Highland dress **2.** TEXTILES TARTAN FABRIC a fabric usually made of wool and woven in a tartan or checkered pattern **3.** TEXTILES TARTAN PATTERN a tartan or checked pattern [Early 16thC. Via Gaelic from Middle Irish, of unknown origin.] —**plaid·ed** *adj.*

plain /playn/ *adj.* **1.** SIMPLE AND ORDINARY simple and ordinary in nature or appearance and without additions or decorations ○ *plain, homely food* ○ *a plain brown envelope* **2.** CLEARLY VISIBLE not blocked or obscured by anything, so as to be clearly visible ○ *in plain view* **3.** CLEAR IN MEANING quite clear in meaning and easy to recognize or understand ○ *The plain fact is that they lied to us.* **4.** FRANK stating the truth clearly without concealing anything or sparing somebody's feelings ○ *The time has come for plain speaking.* **5.** PURE not combined with any other substances ○ *plain water* **6.** LACKING PATTERN OR COLORATION uncolored or unpatterned ○ *plain fabric* **7.** NOT PRETTY not pretty or striking in looks ○ *plain looks* **8.** KNITTING IN SIMPLEST KNITTING STYLE OR STITCH done in the simplest knitting style or stitch ■ *adv.* **1.** ABSOLUTELY used to emphasize an adjective or adverb ○ *just plain wrong* **2.** CLEARLY in a clear or distinct way ○ *I'll tell you plain, I've had enough of this.* ■ *n.* **1.** GEOG FLAT EXPANSE OF LAND a large expanse of fairly flat dry land, usually with few trees **2.** KNITTING KNITTING STYLE OR STITCH the simplest knitting style or stitch. The right needle goes into a loop of wool on the left needle and the wool is then passed around the right needle. ■ **plains** *npl.* GEOG TREELESS LEVEL EXPANSES large expanses of level, almost treeless country in some central states of the United States [13thC. Via Old French from Latin *planus* "flat" (also the source of English *plane* and *piano*).] —**plain·ly** *adv.* —**plain·ness** *n.*

plain·chant /pláyn chànt/ *n.* = **plainsong**

plain clothes /pláyn klōthz, pláyn klōz/, **plain·clothes** *npl.* ordinary civilian clothes when worn by a police officer on duty —**plain-clothes** *adj.*

plain deal·ing *n.* open and honest behavior or business

plain Jane *n.* a woman who is not pretty or striking in looks (*informal*) (*often considered offensive*)

Plain Peo·ple *npl.* members of Christian groups such as the Amish and the Mennonites who are noted for their simple lifestyle and plain way of dressing

plain sail·ing *n.* something that is straightforward and easy to do [Origin uncertain: perhaps an alteration of PLANE SAILING, from the comparative simplicity of this sort of navigation]

Plains In·di·an *n.* a member of any of the Native American peoples that in the past lived on the Great Plains of North America

plains·man /pláynzmən/ (*plural* **-men** /-mən/) *n.* a man who lives on a plain, especially somebody who settled or lives on the Great Plains of North America

plain·song /pláyn sàwng/ *n.* **1.** TYPE OF CHURCH MUSIC a type of church music intended to be sung in unison and unaccompanied by instruments that is particularly associated with services held in monasteries **2.** = **Gregorian chant** [15thC. Translation of Latin *cantus planus*.]

plain-spo·ken *adj.* saying or tending to say precisely what is thought without concealing anything or sparing other people's feelings —**plain-spo·ken·ness** *n.*

plains·wom·an /pláynz wŏŏmmən/ (*plural* **-en** /-wìmmin/) *n.* a woman who lives on a plain, especially one who settled or lives on the Great Plains of North America

plaint /playnt/ *n.* **1.** EXPRESSION OF GRIEF an expression of grief or sadness (*archaic literary*) **2.** COMPLAINT a complaint [12thC. Via French from Latin *planctus* "a beating of the breast," from *plangere* "to beat" (see PLANGENT).]

plain text, **plain·text** *n.* a form of a message that is in ordinary readable language rather than in code

plain·tiff /pláyntif/ *n.* somebody who begins a lawsuit against another person (**defendant**) in a civil court [14thC. From French (see PLAINTIVE).]

plain·tive /pláyntiv/ *adj.* expressing sadness or sounding sad [14thC. From French *plaintive, plaintif*, from *plaint* (see PLAINT).] —**plain·tive·ly** *adv.* —**plain·tive·ness** *n.*

plain weave *n.* a type of weave in which the weft passes alternately under and over the warp so that the threads form a simple criss-cross pattern

plain-wo·ven *adj.* woven in plain weave

plait /playt, plat/ *n.* **1.** WOVEN STRANDS something made by weaving strands together, especially a length of hair with strands woven together like rope **2.** SEW PLEAT a pleat ■ *vt.* (**plait·ed, plait·ing, plaits**) **1.** WEAVE STRANDS TOGETHER to weave three or more strands of something over and under each other, usually to form them either into something that looks like a rope or into a flat band **2.** MAKE SOMETHING BY PLAITING to make something by plaiting **3.** SEW PLEAT SOMETHING to pleat something [15thC. Via Old French *pleit* from, ultimately, Latin *plicit-*, the past participle stem of *plicare* "to fold" (source of English *pleat* and *plight*).]

plan /plan/ *n.* **1.** SCHEME FOR ACHIEVING OBJECTIVE a method of doing something that is worked out usually in some detail before it is begun and that may be written down in some form or simply retained in memory **2.** INTENTION something that somebody intends or has arranged to do (*often used in the plural*) **3.** DIAGRAM OF LAYOUT a drawing or diagram showing the layout, arrangement, or structure of something **4.** LIST OR OUTLINE a list, summary, or diagram that shows how the items that make up something such as a piece of writing or an organized meeting are to be arranged **5.** ARCHIT HORIZONTAL SECTION OF BUILDING a scale diagram showing a horizontal view of the arrangement of rooms and fixtures in a building on a particular level ■ *v.* (**planned, plan·ning, plans**) **1.** *vti.* WORK OUT HOW TO DO SOMETHING to work out in advance and in some detail how something is to be done or organized **2.** *vt.* INTEND TO DO SOMETHING to intend or to make arrangements to do something **3.** *vt.* ARCHIT MAKE A SCALE DRAWING to make a scale drawing of something, especially a building [Late 17thC. From French, "ground plan," an alteration (influenced by *plan* "flat") of *plant*, from, ultimately, Latin *plantare* "to push in with the sole of the foot" (see PLANT).]

plan ahead *vi.* to make preparations or arrangements for the future

plan for *vt.* to make preparations and arrangements for something based on what is expected to happen

plan on *vt.* to intend to do something (*informal*)

plan out *vt.* to make a detailed plan for something to be done or organized

plan- *prefix.* = **plano-**

pla·nar /pláynər, -naar/ *adj.* **1.** RELATING TO A GEOMETRIC PLANE about, involving, or typical of a geometric plane **2.** FLAT flat or lying in a single geometric plane **3.** TWO-DIMENSIONAL having only two dimensions —**pla·nar·i·ty** /play nérrətee/ *n.*

pla·nar·i·an /plə náiree ən/ *n.* a small flatworm that mainly lives in freshwater, is not a parasite, and has a three-branched intestine. Order: Tricladida. [Mid-19thC. Via modern Latin *Planaria*, the name of the genus, from Latin *planarius* "on level ground," from *planus* "flat" (see PLAIN).]

pla·na·tion /play náysh'n/ *n.* the leveling out of natural surfaces on land or under water by erosion or the depositing of new material [Late 19thC. Formed from PLANE[2].]

planch·et /plánchət/ *n.* **1.** BLANK DISK OF METAL FOR STAMPING a flat disk of metal ready to be stamped as a coin or medal **2.** CHEM SMALL METAL CUP a small metal container used to measure a radioactive substance [Early 17thC. Literally "little plank," formed from obsolete English *planch* "wooden plank, metal plate," from French *planche* (see PLANK).]

plan·chette /plan shét/ *n.* a small heart-shaped or triangular wooden board on two casters and with a pencil attached that spells out messages supposed to be from the spirit world when people touch it lightly [Mid-19thC. From French, literally "little plank," formed from *planche* "plank" (see PLANK).]

Planck /plängk/, **Max** (1858–1947) German physicist. The originator and developer of quantum theory, he won a Nobel Prize in physics (1918). Full name **Max Karl Ernst Ludwig Planck**

Planck's con·stant *n.* a basic physical constant that is equal to the energy of a photon divided by its frequency, with an approximate value of 6.6261 x 10^{-34} joule-seconds. Symbol *h* [Early 20thC. Named for Max PLANCK.]

plane[1] /playn/ *n.* **1.** AIR **AIRCRAFT** an airplane **2. FLAT SURFACE** a flat or level material surface **3. LEVEL OF REALITY** a level or category of existence, mental activity, or achievement **4.** MATH **TWO-DIMENSIONAL SURFACE OR SPACE** a two-dimensional surface in which a straight line between any two points will lie wholly on that surface **5.** AIR **WING OR HYDROFOIL** a flat surface such as a wing of a hydrofoil that provides lift for an aircraft or hydroplane ■ *adj.* **1. FLAT** completely flat and level **2.** MATH **TWO-DIMENSIONAL** lying within a particular plane ■ *vi.* **(planed, plan·ing, planes)** AIR **TRAVEL BY PLANE** to travel by airplane [Early 17thC. From Latin *planus* "flat" (see PLAIN).] —**plane·ness** *n.*

plane[2] /playn/ **(planed, plan·ing, planes)** *vi.* **1. SKIM OVER WATER'S SURFACE** to rise partly out of water and skim along the surface, in the way that a hydroplane does **2.** AIR **SOAR** to glide through the air without propulsion, in the way that a bird does without flapping its wings or an airplane does with its engine off

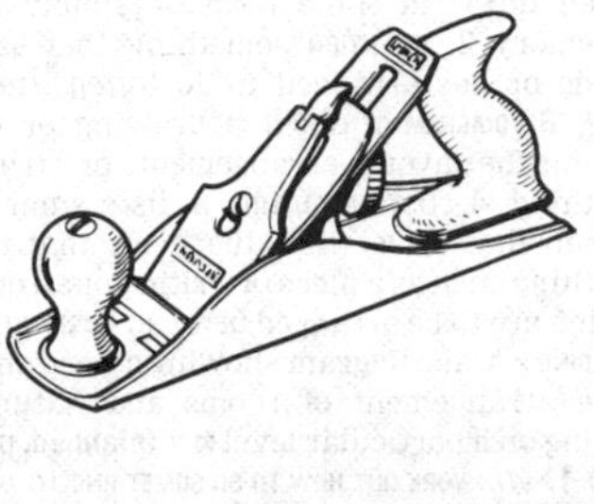

Plane

plane[3] /playn/ *n.* **1.** WOODWORK **TOOL FOR SMOOTHING WOOD** a hand tool for smoothing or shaping wood consisting of a wooden or metal body with a flat base in which an adjustable metal blade is held at an angle **2.** CERAMICS **SMOOTHING TROWEL** a hand tool with a flat metal blade used for smoothing the surface of clay or of plaster in a mold ■ *vt.* **(planed, plan·ing, planes)** WOODWORK **SMOOTH WOOD** to use a plane to smooth or shape the surface of wood, to reduce it to the required size, or to remove material from it [14thC. Via French from late Latin *plana*, from Latin *planare* "to make level," from *planus* "flat" (see PLANE[1]).]

plane[4] /playn/ *n.* = **plane tree**

plane an·gle *n.* an angle formed by two straight lines meeting in the same geometric plane

plane ge·om·e·try *n.* a branch of geometry dealing with the study of curves and figures

plane·load /pláyn lōd/ *n.* the number of passengers or the quantity of goods that can be carried in an aircraft

plan·er /pláynər/ *n.* **1.** WOODWORK **PLANING MACHINE** a person or machine that planes, especially a machine used to plane wood or to cut flat surfaces into metal **2.** PRINTING **WOODEN BLOCK TO KEEP TYPE LEVEL** a flat block of wood used to hold type level in a chase [15thC. Formed from PLANE[2].]

pla·ner tree *n.* a small deciduous tree similar to an elm that grows mainly in swamps in the southern United States and has a small oval ribbed fruit. Latin name: *Planera aquatica.* [Early 19thC. Named for the German botanist I. J. *Planer* (1743–89).]

plane sail·ing *n.* sailing using a form of navigation that treats the earth's surface as if it were flat for the purposes of calculating a ship's position and course

plan·et /plánnət/ *n.* **1.** ASTRON **ASTRONOMICAL BODY ORBITING STAR** an astronomical body that orbits a star and does not shine with its own light, especially one of the nine such bodies orbiting the Sun in the solar system **2.** ZODIAC **ASTROLOGICAL INFLUENCE** in astrology, any of the planets of the solar system, the Sun, the Moon, but not the Earth, that are considered to influence events on Earth and the fate or character of individuals **3. EARTH** the Earth ○ *save the planet* [12thC. Via French *planète* from Latin *planeta* "planet, wandering star," from Greek *planētēs* "wanderer."]

WORD KEY: CULTURAL NOTE

The Planets, an orchestral work by English composer Gustav Holst (1914–16). This suite for orchestra, organ, and chorus is divided into seven movements, each of which represents the astrological character of a planet with appropriate music. Thus, the section called "Mars, Bringer of War" consists of a brooding, sinister theme, while "Venus, Bringer of Peace" is calm and serene.

plane ta·ble *n.* a surveying instrument for use in the field, consisting of a drawing board mounted on adjustable legs with a sighting telescope and ruler

plan·e·tar·i·um /plànnə táiree əm/ (*plural* **-ums** *or* **-a** /-ə/) *n.* **1. BUILDING WITH IMAGE OF NIGHT SKY** a building with a domed ceiling onto which movable images of the stars, planets, and other objects seen in the night sky are projected for an audience **2. PROJECTOR USED IN PLANETARIUM** the special projector used to project images of the night sky for an audience in a planetarium **3. SOLAR SYSTEM MODEL** a model of the solar system, often a working model showing how the planets revolve around the Sun (*archaic*) [Mid-18thC. Via modern Latin from late Latin *planetarius* "astrologer," from *planeta* "planet" (see PLANET).]

plan·e·tar·y /plánnə tèree/ *adj.* **1.** ASTRON **INVOLVING PLANETS** relating to, belonging to, involving, or typical of planets **2. INVOLVING ALL OF EARTH** involving or relating to the whole earth, all the people or countries of the world, or a large proportion of them ■ *n.* (*plural* **-taries**) ENG = **planetary gear**

plan·e·tar·y gear, plan·e·tar·y (*plural* **-ies**) *n.* a gearwheel especially in an epicyclic train that travels around another usually central gearwheel

plan·e·tar·y neb·u·la *n.* a glowing ring-shaped nebula of expanding gases surrounding a small very hot white star

plan·e·tes·i·mal /plànnə téssəm'l/ *n.* a small rocky celestial object thought to have orbited the Sun in the early stages of the solar system before coalescing with others to form the planets [Early 20thC. Coined from PLANET + -esimal (as in "infinitesimal").]

plan·e·toid /plánnə tòyd/ *n.* **1.** = **asteroid 2.** a branch of astronomy that studies the origin and composition of the planets and other solid bodies in the solar system such as comets and meteors —**plan·e·toi·dal** /plànnə tóyd'l/ *adj.* —**plan·e·to·log·i·cal** /plànnətə lójjik'l/ *adj.* —**plan·e·tol·o·gist** /plànnə tóttəjist/ *n.*

plane tree, plane *n.* a tall deciduous tree that has leaves with pointed lobes, ball-shaped clusters of flowers and fruit, and bark that peels off in patches. Genus: *Platanus.* [14thC. "Plane" via French from, ultimately, Greek *platanos*, from *platus* "broad," from the shape of its leaf.]

plan·et wheel *n.* a wheel in an epicyclic gear system that rotates around the wheel with which it meshes

plan·gent /plánjənt/ *adj.* **1. EXPRESSING OR SUGGESTING SADNESS** expressing or suggesting grief or sadness, or resonating with a mournful sound (*literary*) **2. RESONANT** making a loud and resonant sound [Early 19thC. From Latin *plangent-*, the present participle stem of *plangere* "to beat" (source also of English *complain* and *plaint*).] —**plan·gen·cy** *n.* —**plan·gent·ly** *adv.*

plani- *prefix.* = **plano-**

pla·nim·e·ter /plə nímmətər/ *n.* a mechanical instrument that measures the area of a plane figure as a pointer is moved around the figure's edge [Mid-19thC. From French *planimètre.*] —**pla·ni·met·ric** /plàynə méttrik/ *adj.* —**pla·ni·met·ri·cal·ly** /-méttri kəlee/ *adv.*

plan·ish /plánnish/ **(-ished, -ish·ing, -ish·es)** *vt.* to toughen and smooth the surface of a metal by hammering or rolling it [Late 16thC. From Old French *planiss-*, the stem form of *planir* "to smooth," from *plain* "flat" (see PLAIN).] —**plan·ish·er** *n.*

pla·ni·sphere /pláyni sfeer/ *n.* a representation on a flat surface of all or part of a sphere, especially a map of the night sky as seen at a particular time and place [From medieval Latin *planisphaerium*, from Latin *planus* "flat, plane" (see PLAIN) + *sphaera* "sphere," from Greek *sphaira*] —**pla·ni·spher·ic** /plàyni sféerik, -sférrik/ *adj.*

plank /plangk/ *n.* **1.** WOODWORK, BUILDING **LONG FLAT PIECE OF WOOD** a piece of wood that has been sawn into a long flat fairly narrow rectangular shape, for use especially in building floors, shelves, and boats **2.** *vt.* WOODWORK, BUILDING **PLANKING** a number of planks especially when they are being used as building material **3.** POL **POLICY OF POLITICAL PARTY** a policy that is part of a political party's platform ■ *vt.* **(planked, plank·ing, planks)** BUILDING **COVER SOMETHING WITH PLANKS** to cover something with planks [13thC. Via Old Northern French *planke*, a variation of Old French *planche* (source of English *planchette*), from late Latin *planca* "slab," from the feminine of Latin *plancus* "flat."]

plank·ing /plángking/ *n.* **1.** WOODWORK, BUILDING **PLANKS** a number of planks especially when they are used as building material or as part of a boat **2.** BUILDING **COVERING SOMETHING WITH PLANKS** the work of covering something with planks or fixing planks to something

plank·ter /plángktər/ *n.* one of the tiny organisms that make up plankton [Mid-20thC. Via German from Greek *plagktēr* "wanderer," from *plazein* "to wander" (see PLANKTON).]

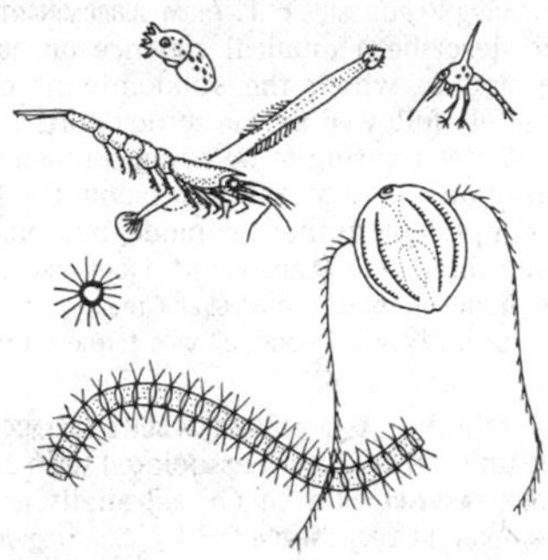

Plankton

plank·ton /plángktən/ *n.* a mass of tiny animals and plants floating in the sea or in lakes usually near the surface and eaten by fish and other aquatic animals [Late 19thC. Via German from Greek, "wandering thing," from *plazein* "to wander, lead astray."] —**plank·ton·ic** /plangk tónnik/ *adj.*

planned ob·so·les·cence *n.* a policy of designing and making products so that they will quickly become outdated or wear out, so that people will have to buy a replacement

Planned Par·ent·hood *tdmk.* an organization that researches family planning methods and gives advice

plan·ner /plánnər/ *n.* **1. SOMEBODY WHO PLANS SOMETHING** somebody who plans something, especially somebody whose job is to plan the development of an area **2. PLANNING AID** a chart or notebook in which future events can be indicated or noted

plano- *prefix.* flat ○ *planosol* ○ *plano-concave* [From Latin *planus* (see PLANE[1])]

pla·no-con·cave *adj.* flat on one side and concave on the other

pla·no-con·vex *adj.* flat on one side and convex on the other

plan·o·gam·ete /plànnō gá meet, -gə meet/ *n.* a gamete such as a spermotozoon that is capable of moving

pla·nog·ra·phy /plə nóggrəfee/ *n.* a printing process such as lithography in which the printing is done from a flat surface —**pla·no·graph·ic** /plàynə gráffik/ *adj.* —**pla·no·graph·i·cal·ly** /-gráffi kəlee/ *adv.*

pla·nom·e·ter /plə nómmətər/ *n.* a flat metal plate used to test the flatness of other surfaces in metalwork —**plan·o·met·ric** /plàynə méttrik/ *adj.* —**plan·o·met·ri·cal·ly** /-méttri kəlee/ *adv.* —**pla·nom·e·try** /plə nómmətree/ *n.*

plan·o·sol /plánnə sàwl/ *n.* a type of soil formation found on flat uplands that have high to moderate rainfall, in which a strongly leached upper layer overlies a layer of compacted clay or silt

plant /plant/ *n.* **1.** PLANTS **VEGETABLE ORGANISM** a photosynthetic organism that has cellulose cell walls, cannot move of its own accord, grows on the earth or in water, and usually has green leaves. Kingdom: *Plantae.* **2.** PLANTS **SMALLER VEGETABLE ORGANISM** a vegetable organism that does not have a permanent woody stem, e.g., a flower or herb rather than a bush or tree **3.** GARDENING **SEEDLING** a cutting or seedling that is ready to be planted **4.** INDUST **FACTORY** a factory, power station, or other large industrial complex where something is manufactured or produced **5.** INDUST **INDUSTRIAL EQUIPMENT** equipment together with the buildings and land necessary for carrying on an industrial process or running a business **6. SOMETHING DISHONESTLY HIDDEN TO INCRIMINATE** something secretly and dishonestly put somewhere it can be discovered later, e.g., by the police, in order to incriminate somebody (*informal*) **7. SOMEBODY SECRETLY INTRODUCED INTO GROUP** somebody who is secretly introduced into an organization in order to spy on it or to influence the behaviour of its members (*informal*) ■ *v.* (**plant·ed, plant·ing, plants**) **1.** *vti.* BOT, AGRIC **PUT SOMETHING INTO THE GROUND TO GROW** to put something such as a seed, plant, or tuber into the ground to enable it to grow, or to take part in this activity ○ *plant a tree* **2.** *vti.* AGRIC, GARDENING **PLACE PLANTS SOMEWHERE** to place young plants or sow seeds in an area of ground ○ *wanted to plant that bed with pansies* **3.** *vt.* **PUT SOMETHING DOWN FIRMLY** to put something down or take a position firmly or decisively ○ *planted the stakes about five feet apart* **4.** *vt.* **PUT AN IDEA IN SOMEBODY'S MIND** to introduce an idea into another person's mind ○ *She planted the notion in my head that we should move.* **5.** *vt.* **PLACE SOMETHING IN A CONCEALED POSITION** to place something such as an explosive or listening device where it will not be easily found by others **6.** *vt.* **HIDE SOMETHING TO INCRIMINATE SOMEBODY** to put something secretly where it can be discovered later, e.g., by the police, to incriminate somebody (*informal*) ○ *plant evidence* **7.** *vt.* **INTRODUCE A SPY INTO GROUP** to introduce somebody into an organization in order to spy on it or to influence the behaviour of its members (*informal*) ○ *planted an informer in the group* **8.** *vt.* **STRIKE SOMEBODY** to land a blow on somebody (*informal*) **9.** *vt.* AGRIC **STOCK WITH FISH** to place spawn, young fish, or shellfish into an area of water so that they will develop there ○ *plant oysters* **10.** *vt.* **ESTABLISH A COLONY** to establish a colony or settlement in a place, or send people to a place as colonists or settlers [Pre-12thC. From late Latin *plantare* "to plant." Latin *plantare* meant "to push in with the sole of the foot" and was formed from *planta* "sole of the foot."] —**plant·a·ble** *adj.* —**plant·like** *adj.*

WORD KEY: ORIGIN

There did exist a Latin noun *planta* which meant "shoot, cutting," of uncertain origin, but the meaning of the English noun ***plant*** is not found. It is likely that this sense developed after the classical Latin period and is linked with the action of pressing on a shovel, or some other tool, with the "sole of the foot" in order to work the soil for planting. Latin *planta* "sole of the foot" is ultimately from an Indo-European base meaning "to spread" which is also the ancestor of English *flat* and *place*.

Plan·tag·e·net /plan tájjənət/ *adj.* **OF ENGLISH ROYAL FAMILY OR REIGN** belonging or relating to the English royal family that ruled between 1154 and 1485, or to this period of English history. The period is spanned by the reigns of Kings Henry II, Richard I, John, Henry III, Edward I, Edward II, Edward III, Richard II, Henry IV, Henry V, Henry VI, Edward IV, Edward V and Richard III. ■ *n.* **MEMBER OF PLANTAGENET ROYAL FAMILY** a member of the Plantagenet royal family [From Latin *planta*"sprig" + Latin *genista* "broom," after the sprig of broom worn by Geoffrey IV, father of Henry II, in his cap]

plan·tain[1] /plántən/ *n.* a small plant mostly growing wild in northern temperate regions with leaves that grow mainly from the plant's base and spikes of tiny greenish flowers. Family: Plantaginaceae. [14thC. Via French from Latin *plantago*, from *planta* "sole of the foot" (see PLANT).]

plan·tain[2] /plántən/ *n.* **1.** FOOD **FRUIT LIKE BANANA** a green fruit resembling a banana, eaten cooked as a staple food in many tropical countries **2.** PLANTS **TROPICAL PLANT LIKE BANANA TREE** a large tropical plant of the banana family that produces clusters of green fruit that resemble bananas. Latin name: *Musa paradisiaca*. [16thC. Via Spanish *plátano* "plane tree" from Latin *platanus* (see PLANE TREE).]

plan·tain lil·y (*plural* **plan·tain lil·ies**) *n.* a perennial shade-loving plant with broad ribbed leaves and clusters of tubular white, blue, or lilac flowers. Genus: *Hosta*.

plan·tar /plántər, -taar/ *adj.* relating to, affecting, or occurring on the sole of the foot [Early 18thC. From Latin *plantaris*, from *planta* "sole of the foot" (see PLANT).]

plan·tar wart *n.* = **verruca**

plan·ta·tion /plan táysh'n/ *n.* **1.** AGRIC **LARGE ESTATE OR FARM** a large estate or farm especially in a hot country where crops such as cotton, coffee, tea, or rubber trees are grown, usually worked by resident laborers **2.** AGRIC **AREA OF PLANTED LAND** an area of land on which trees or crops are planted **3.** AGRIC **GROUP OF CULTIVATED PLANTS** a large group of plants, especially trees, that are being cultivated **4.** AGRIC **ESTATE IN SOUTHERN UNITED STATES** a large landed estate in the southern United States **5.** HIST **COLONY** a colony or settlement

plant·cut·ter *n.* a South American bird that has a short conical bill with a serrated edge. It eats fruit, leaves, and buds, often destroying crops. Family: Phytotomidae.

plant·er /plántər/ *n.* **1.** AGRIC **HEAD OF PLANTATION** somebody who owns or manages a plantation **2.** GARDENING **LARGE CONTAINER** a large decorative container for houseplants or small trees **3.** AGRIC **PLANTING MACHINE** a machine for planting seeds, tubers, or other plant parts **4.** HIST **SETTLER** a colonist (*archaic*)

plant·er's punch *n.* a drink made with rum, lime or lemon juice, sugar, water, or soda, and sometimes bitters

plant hor·mone *n.* a hormone produced naturally by plants that activates or regulates their growth, or a synthetic equivalent used to promote growth in cultivated plants

plan·ti·grade /plánti gràyd/ *adj.* **WALKING ON SOLES OF FEET** used to describe an animal such as a bear or a human being that walks on the soles of its feet with the heel touching the ground ■ *n.* **PLANTIGRADE ANIMAL** an animal that walks on the soles of its feet [Mid-19thC. Via French from modern Latin *plantigradus*, from Latin *planta* "sole of the foot" (see PLANT) + *-gradus* "stepping" (see GRADE).]

plant·let /plántlət/ *n.* a young or very small plant

plant louse *n.* = **aphid**

plan·toc·racy /plan tókrəssee/ (*plural* **-ra·cies**) *n.* a ruling class made up of the owners and managers of large plantations, or a society they rule

plants·man /plántsmən/ (*plural* **-men** /-mən/) *n.* a man who has expert knowledge of garden plants and gardening

plants·wo·man /plánts wòommən/ (*plural* **-men** /-wimmin/) *n.* a woman who has expert knowledge of garden plants and gardening

plan·u·la /plánnyələ/ (*plural* **-lae** /-lee/) *n.* a free-swimming larva of a coelenterate such as a hydra that has cilia and usually a flattened oval body [Late 19thC. From modern Latin, literally "little flat one," formed from Latin *planus* "flat" (see PLAIN).] —**plan·u·lar** *adj.*

plaque /plak/ *n.* **1. INSCRIBED METAL OR STONE** a small flat piece of metal, stone, or other hard material with an inscription or decoration on it that is fixed onto a surface, often to commemorate somebody or something **2.** DENT **DEPOSIT ON SURFACE OF TEETH** a film of saliva, mucus, bacteria, and food residues that builds up on the surface of teeth and can cause gum disease **3.** MED **SMALL PATCH** a small flattened patch or deposit, e.g., on the skin in psoriasis or on the inner wall of an artery in arteriosclerosis **4.** BIOL **CLEAR PATCH IN CULTURE** a clear patch in a bacterial or cell culture caused by a virus destroying the cells **5. SMALL PIN OR BROOCH** a small pin or brooch worn to show membership of or rank in an organization [Mid-19thC. Via French from Dutch *plak* "tablet," from *plakken*, from Middle Dutch *placken* "to flatten, patch" (source also of English *placard*).]

plash /plash/ *n.* **LIGHT SPLASH** a light splash or splashing sound (*literary*) ■ *v.* (**plashed, plash·ing, plash·es**) (*literary*) **1.** *vi.* **SPLASH IN OR THROUGH LIQUID** to move in or through something liquid, scattering drops of it and making a light splashing sound **2.** *vt.* **SPLASH SOMETHING** to splash or spatter something liquid [Early 16thC. An imitation of the sound.]

plash·y /pláshee/ (**-i·er, -i·est**) *adj.* wet and marshy (*literary*)

-plasia *suffix.* growth, formation ○ *hyperplasia* [Via modern Latin from, ultimately, Greek *plassein* "to form, mold" (source of English *plaster*)]

plasm /plázzəm/ *n.* **1.** = **plasma 2. PROTOPLASM** protoplasm of a specified type [Early 17thC. From late Latin *plasma* "image, creation" (see PLASMA).]

plasm- *prefix.* = **plasmo-** (*used before vowels*)

-plasm *suffix.* material that forms or is formed ○ *protoplasm* ○ *neoplasm* [Shortening of PROTOPLASM]

plas·ma /plázmə/, **plasm** *n.* **1.** MED **FLUID COMPONENT OF BLOOD** the clear yellowish fluid component of blood, lymph, or milk, excluding the suspended corpuscles and cells **2.** MED **BLOOD SUBSTITUTE** a blood substitute prepared by removing the cells and corpuscles from donated sterile blood and freezing the resulting fluid until it is needed **3.** PHYS **IONIZED GAS** a hot ionized gas made up of ions and electrons that is found in the Sun, stars, and fusion reactors. Plasma is a good conductor of electricity and reacts to a magnetic field but otherwise has properties similar to those of a gas. **4.** MINERALS **GREEN CHALCEDONY** a green variety of chalcedony used as a gemstone, in mosaics, and for other decorative purposes [Early 18thC. Via late Latin, "image, creation," from Greek, "something molded," from *plassein* "to mold" (see PLASTIC).] —**plas·mat·ic** /plaz máttik/ *adj.*

plas·ma cell, **plas·ma·cyte** /plázmə sīt/ *n.* a lymphocyte that produces antibodies and is derived from a B cell

plas·ma en·gine *n.* an engine used in space travel that generates thrust by using magnetic fields to emit a jet of plasma

plas·ma·gel /plázmə jèl/ *n.* a form of cytoplasm, often forming an outer layer in cells, that resembles jelly

plas·ma·gene /plázmə jeen/ *n.* a particle in the cytoplasm of organisms that can replicate itself and is thought to be able to pass on hereditary characteristics in the same way as a chromosomal gene —**plas·ma·gen·ic** /plàzmə jénnik/ *adj.*

plas·ma·lem·ma /plàzmə lémmə/ *n.* = **cell membrane**

plas·ma mem·brane *n.* = **cell membrane**

plas·ma·pher·e·sis /plàzmə férrə siss, -fə reéssiss/ *n.* a process in which blood taken from a patient is treated to extract the cells and corpuscles, which are then added to another fluid and returned to the patient's body. It is performed, e.g., to remove harmful antibodies or immune complexes from the blood, especially in autoimmune diseases such as myasthenia gravis.

plas·ma·sol /plázmə sàwl/ *n.* a form of cytoplasm that is more fluid than plasmagel, often forming an inner layer in cells

plas·ma torch *n.* a metal-cutting device in which a cutting flame is produced by the conversion of a gas into plasma

plas·mid /plázmid/ *n.* a small circle of DNA that replicates itself independently of chromosomal DNA, especially in the cells of bacteria. Plasmids often contain genes for drug resistance and are used in genetic engineering, since they can be transmitted between bacteria of the same and different species.

plas·min /plázmin/ *n.* an enzyme found in plasma that catalyzes the breakdown of blood-clotting agents such as fibrin [Mid-19thC. From French, coined from *plasma* "plasma."]

plas·min·o·gen /plaz mínnəjən/ *n.* a substance found in body fluids and blood plasma that when activated becomes plasmin

plasmo-[1], **plasm-** *prefix.* involving or like plasma [From late Latin *plasma* "image" (see PLASMA)]

plasmo-[2] *prefix.* plasma ○ *plasmogamy* [From PLASMA]

plas·mo·des·ma /plàzmə dézmə/ (*plural* **-ma·ta** /-mətə/) *n.* a very fine thread of cytoplasm that in some plants passes through openings in the walls of adjacent cells and forms a living bridge between them [Early 20thC. From German, coined from *Plasma* "plasma" + Greek *desma* "bond."]

plas·mo·di·um /plaz mōdee əm/ (*plural* **-a** /-dee ə/) *n.* **1. MASS OF PROTOPLASM** a mass of protoplasm containing many nuclei that is a stage in the life cycle of some organisms, especially slime molds **2. PARASITIC PROTOZOAN CAUSING MALARIA** a parasitic protozoan, especially one that causes malaria. Genus: *Plasmodium*. [Late 19thC. Coined from PLASMA + modern Latin *-odium* "resembling," from Greek *-ōdēs* (see -OID).] —**plas·mo·di·al** *adj.*

plas·mog·a·my /plaz móggəmee/ *n.* a type of fusion between cells in certain fungi in which the cytoplasm merges but the nuclei remain distinct

plas·mol·y·sis /plaz mólləssiss/ *n.* the shrinking of the protoplasm in a plant or bacterial cell away from the cell wall, caused by loss of water through osmosis —**plas·mo·lyt·ic** /plàzmə líttik/ *adj.* —**plas·mo·lyt·i·cal·ly** /-líttikəlee/ *adv.*

plas·mo·lyze /plázmə līz/ (**-lyzed, -lyz·ing, -lyz·es**) *vti.* to undergo plasmolysis, or make this happen in a cell

plas·mon /pláz mòn/ *n.* GENETICS the sum total of the genetic material in the cytoplasm, as opposed to the nucleus or nuclei, of a cell or an organism

-plast *suffix.* living cell, small body ○ *spheroplast* [From Greek *plastos*, a past participle of *plassein* (see -PLASIA)]

plas·ter /plástər/ *n.* **1.** LIME MIXTURE FOR WALLS a mixture of lime, sand, and water that is applied as a liquid paste to the ceilings and internal walls of a building and dries to a smooth hard surface **2.** PIECE OF IMPREGNATED MUSLIN a piece of muslin spread with a curative preparation formerly used for placing over a wound or sore. ◊ **mustard plaster 3.** = **plaster of Paris 4.** *U.K.* STICKY BANDAGE a strip of adhesive material, usually with a dressing attached, for sticking over a cut or wound ■ *vt.* (**-tered, -ter·ing, -ters**) **1.** COVER WALLS WITH PLASTER to apply plaster to the interior walls and ceilings of a building **2.** APPLY SOMETHING THICKLY to apply a thick layer of something to a surface (*informal*) **3.** STICK A MASS OF THINGS OVER A SURFACE to stick or spread objects in great profusion over a surface **4.** MAKE SOMETHING APPEAR IN MANY LOCATIONS to cause a name, story, or image to appear in many conspicuous places ○ *woke up to find her name plastered on every front page* **5.** BOMBARD to hit somebody or something repeatedly and effectively with blows or weapons (*informal*) **6.** DEFEAT SEVERELY to defeat an opponent severely, e.g., in a sports competition (*informal*) ○ *got plastered in the semifinals* **7.** APPLY MEDICINAL PLASTER to apply a medicinal plaster to a wound or sore [Old English *plaster* "medical dressing" and Old French *plastre* "wall plaster," both via medieval Latin *plastrum* from, ultimately, Greek *emplastron*, from *emplassein* "to plaster up," from *plassein* (see -PLASIA)] —**plas·ter·er** *n.* —**plas·ter·y** *adj.*

plas·ter·board /plástər bàwrd/ *n.* reinforced gypsum plaster sandwiched between two layers of strong paper in large sheets, used chiefly for interior walls

plas·ter cast *n.* **1.** RIGID COVERING FOR BROKEN LIMB a rigid covering of plaster of Paris molded around a broken limb to immobilize the fracture site during healing **2.** PLASTER COPY OF SOMETHING a copy or mold of an object, such as a statue or footprint in plaster of Paris

plas·tered /plástərd/ *adj.* very drunk (*informal*) [Early 20thC. From PLASTER in the sense "to hit hard."]

plas·ter·ing /plástəring/ *n.* **1.** APPLICATION OF PLASTER TO WALLS the application of a layer of plaster to walls **2.** PLASTER COVERING SURFACE the plaster that covers a surface **3.** SEVERE DEFEAT a severe beating or defeat (*informal*)

plas·ter of Par·is *n.* a white powder, calcium sulfate, mixed with water to form a quick-hardening paste, used in the arts for sculpting and making casts and used in medicine for molding casts around broken limbs [Named for PARIS, France, where it originated]

plas·ter·work /plástər wùrk/ *n.* objects in plaster, especially the layer of plaster applied to interior wall surfaces or decorative plaster moldings on ceilings or walls

plas·tic /plástik/ *n.* **1.** SYNTHETIC MATERIAL an extremely versatile synthetic material made from the polymerization of organic compounds. It can be molded into shapes or fabricated in many different forms for use in commerce and industry. **2.** CREDIT CARDS debit or credit cards as a form of payment as distinct from cash or a check (*informal*) ■ *adj.* **1.** MADE OF PLASTIC made of or consisting of plastic **2.** ARTIFICIAL seeming artificial and unnatural ○ *a plastic smile* **3.** ADAPTING EASILY adapting easily and readily to change **4.** ABLE TO BE MOLDED able to be shaped, molded, or modeled **5.** OF MOLDING, MODELING, OR SCULPTING relating to or involving molding, modeling, or sculpting **6.** PHYS ABLE TO HAVE SHAPE PERMANENTLY CHANGED able to be bent, stretched, squeezed, or pulled out so that the resulting change of shape is permanent **7.** BIOL ADAPTING TO CONDITIONS capable of adapting to conditions during growth or development **8.** OF PLASTIC SURGERY relating to or involving plastic surgery [16thC. Via French *plastique* and Latin *plasticus* from Greek *plastikos* "moldable," from *plastos*, the past participle of *plassein* "to form, mold" (see -PLASIA).] —**plas·ti·cal·ly** *adv.*

plas·tic art *n.* **1.** THREE-DIMENSIONAL ART a three-dimensional art such as sculpture, modeling or bas-relief work, pottery, or ceramics **2.** VISUAL ART an art that represents subjects for visual appreciation, such as painting, sculpture, or architecture

plas·tic bomb *n.* a bomb that employs a plastic explosive for its destructive force

plas·tic bul·let *n.* a large bullet made of PVC, sometimes used by the police for riot control in place of metal bullets

plas·tic ex·plo·sive *n.* an explosive with the consistency of putty that allows it to be easily molded

Plas·ti·cine /plásti seen/ *tdmk. U.K.* a trademark for a soft colored modeling material used especially by children

plas·tic·i·ty /pla stíssətee/ *n.* **1.** ABILITY TO BE MOLDED the condition of being soft and capable of being molded **2.** ABILITY TO KEEP SHAPE AFTER CHANGE the quality that will allow a substance to retain its change in shape after being bent, stretched, or squeezed **3.** THREE-DIMENSIONAL QUALITY the three-dimensional quality of an image

plas·ti·cize /plásti sīz/ (**-cized, -ciz·ing, -ciz·es**) *v.* **1.** *vti.* MAKE OR BECOME PLASTIC to give plastic or moldable qualities to something, or become plastic or moldable **2.** *vt.* TREAT WITH PLASTIC to impregnate or coat something with plastic, usually to make it waterproof —**plas·ti·ci·za·tion** /plàstiəssi záysh'n/ *n.*

plas·ti·ciz·er /plásti sīzər/ *n.* an industrial compound that affects the physical properties of a substance to which it is added

plas·tic mon·ey *n.* debit and credit cards as distinct from cash or checks

plas·tic sur·geon *n.* a physician who performs or specializes in plastic surgery

plas·tic sur·ger·y *n.* the branch of surgery that is concerned with repairing damage, relieving impairments, or improving appearance. Cosmetic surgery is a branch of plastic surgery.

plas·tic wrap *n.* a clear plastic film that sticks to itself and to surfaces, used to wrap food for storage

plas·tid /plástid/ *n.* a specialized organ or part (**organelle**) in a photosynthetic plant cell that contains pigment, ribosomes, and DNA, and serves particular physiological purposes such as food synthesis and storage [Late 19thC. Via the Greek stem *plastid-* from, ultimately, *plastos* "molded" (see PLASTIC).]

plas·tique /pla steek/ *n.* **1.** PLASTIC EXPLOSIVE plastic explosive **2.** GRACEFUL DANCE POSES graceful sustained movement or held poses in dance [Late 19thC. From French (see PLASTIC).]

plas·ti·sol /plásti sàwl/ *n.* a suspension of synthetic resin particles convertible by heat into solid plastic [Mid-20thC. Coined from PLASTIC + SOL.]

plas·tom·e·ter /pla stómmətər/, **plas·tim·e·ter** /-stímmətər/*n.* an instrument for measuring the plasticity of materials [Early 20thC. Coined from PLASTICITY + -METER.] —**plas·to·met·ric** /plàstə métrik/ *adj.* —**plas·tom·e·try** /pla stómmətree/ *n.*

plas·to·quin·one /plà stō kwi nṓn, -kwí nōn/ *n.* one of a series of compounds occurring in plants that has a quinone nucleus related to vitamin K and functions in photosynthesis [Mid-20thC. Coined from (CHLORO)PLAST + QUINONE.]

plas·tron /plástrən/ *n.* **1.** UNDER PART OF TORTOISE SHELL the under portion of the shell of a turtle or tortoise that is made up of several, often hinged bony plates joined to the carapace by bridges located between the animal's legs **2.** WATER-REPELLENT GILL IN AQUATIC INSECTS a tuft of water-repellent hairs on the bodies of some aquatic insects that traps air bubbles and acts as an external gill **3.** STEEL BREASTPLATE a steel breastplate worn as part of medieval armor beneath a chain-mail tunic (**hauberk**) **4.** CHEST PAD FOR FENCERS a leather-covered pad for protecting the chest, worn by professional fencers [Early 16thC. Via French from Italian *piastrone*, literally "large breastplate," from *piastra* "metal plate."] —**plas·tral** *adj.*

-plasty *suffix.* surgical repair, plastic surgery ○ *angioplasty* ○ *rhinoplasty* [Via modern Latin from, ultimately, Greek *plastos* (see PLASTIC)]

plat[1] /plat/ *n.* **1.** PLAN OR MAP a plan or map showing property boundaries and geographic features **2.** PLOT OF LAND a small plot or area of land ■ *vt.* (**plat·ted, plat·ting, plats**) MAP AREA OF LAND to map an area of land to show boundaries and features [Early 16thC. Origin uncertain: probably an alteration of PLOT.]

plat[2] /plat/ *n.* PLAIT a plait (*archaic*) ■ *vt.* (**plat·ted, plat·ting, plats**) PLAIT SOMETHING to plait something (*archaic*) [14thC. Alteration of PLAIT.]

plat. *abbr.* **1.** plateau **2.** platoon

Pla·ta, Río de la /plaátə/ large inlet on the eastern coast of South America, an estuary of the Paraná and Uruguay rivers, lying between Uruguay and Argentina. Length: 190 mi./300 km.

pla·tan /plát'n/, **pla·tane** *n.* = **plane tree** [14thC. Via modern Latin *Platanus*, genus name, from Greek *platanos* (see PLANE TREE).]

plat du jour /plaà də zhoor/ (*plural* **plats du jour** /plaà də zhoor/) *n.* the featured dish on the menu of a restaurant for a particular day [Early 20thC. From French, "dish of the day."]

plate /playt/ *n.* **1.** HOUSEHOLD DISH FROM WHICH FOOD IS EATEN a flat or shallow dish, usually round and made of earthenware, china, glass, or sometimes plastic or metal, from which food is eaten **2.** FOOD CONTENTS OF PLATE a portion of food consisting of the amount served on a plate **3.** FOOD SERVED FOOD a specified variety of prepared and served food ○ *a low-calorie plate* **4.** CHR COLLECTION DISH FOR MONEY a shallow metal or wooden container passed around a church for members of the congregation to put money in **5.** AUTOMOT LICENSE PLATE a vehicle's license plate **6.** BASEBALL = **home plate 7.** METALL COATING OF METAL a thin coating of metal, typically silver or gold, applied by electrolysis to copper or another base metal **8.** METALL THINLY BEATEN METAL metal produced in thin sheets of uniform thickness by beating, rolling, or casting **9.** ARMS SHEET OF ARMOR PLATING a sheet of metal used as part of the cladding of a warship or tank **10.** HIST SECTION OF SUIT OF ARMOR a thin piece of steel or iron used to make up a suit of armor (*often used in combination*) **11.** ENG FLAT CONSTITUENT PART OR FITTING a flat slab of metal or other material that constitutes part of a machine or mechanism **12.** DENT ARTIFICIAL PALATE FITTED WITH FALSE TEETH a piece of plastic molded to fit the mouth and holding false teeth or an orthodontic device such as a brace **13.** PHOTOGRAPHY SENSITIZED SHEET OF GLASS a sheet of glass or other material coated with a light-sensitive film to receive a photographic image **14.** ENGRAVED PLAQUE a metal plaque that bears an engraved or printed legend, name, number, or other inscription (*often used in combination*) **15.** THIN SHEET a thin flat rigid sheet or slice of some material, usually of uniform thickness and with a smooth surface **16.** ANAT FLAT ANATOMICAL STRUCTURE a thin flat bony or horny anatomical part or formation **17.** GEOL SECTION OF EARTH'S CRUST any of the segments of the earth's crust that move in relation to one another as defined by the theory of plate tectonics **18.** ELEC ELECTRODE a thin flat piece of metal acting as an electrode in a rechargeable battery **19.** HORSERACING PRIZE OF GOLD OR SILVER CUP a prize, especially in horseracing, consisting of a silver or gold cup **20.** HORSERACING RACE WITH CUP AS PRIZE a race, especially a horserace, in which the prize is a silver or gold cup **21.** PRINTING SURFACE FROM WHICH TO PRINT a template for printing, either an engraved metal sheet or a phototypeset page **22.** PRINTING ILLUSTRATION IN BOOK a full-page illustration or photograph in a book, especially on glossy or coated paper **23.** PRINTING PRINT TAKEN FROM ENGRAVED SURFACE a print made from a printing plate, especially one inserted into a book on paper different from that on which the text is printed **24.** SCI DISH FOR GROWING CULTURES a small flat glass or plastic dish with a vertical rim, used in laboratories for growing cultures of microorganisms **25.** HORSERACING SHOE WORN BY RACEHORSE a light shoe with which racehorses are shod in preparation for racing **26.** BUILDING HORIZONTAL SUPPORTING TIMBER a horizontal timber laid along the top of a wall of a building to support the ends of timbers laid at right angles to the wall **27.** FOOD CUT OF BEEF a thin cut of beef from the breast or ribs ■ *vt.* (**plat·ed, plat·ing, plates**) **1.** METALL COVER SOMETHING WITH GOLD OR SILVER to cover something with a thin coating or film of metal, especially to overlay something made of a baser metal with gold or silver **2.** ARMS COVER SOMETHING WITH METAL SHEETS to cover something, especially a ship or tank, with sheets of metal for protection and strength **3.** PRINTING SET UP TYPE IN PAGE FORM to set up movable type into page form ready for printing **4.** SURG STRENGTHEN BROKEN BONE WITH PLATE to hold a fractured bone in position once it has been set by screwing it, on either side of the fracture, to a metal plate [13thC. Via Old French from, ultimately, Greek *platus* "flat." Ultimately from an Indo-European base meaning "to spread flat" that is also the ancestor of English *flat, plan,* and *flounder*[2].] ◇ **have something handed to you on a plate** to obtain something without having to put any effort into obtaining it (*informal*) ◇ **have something on your plate** to have something that requires your attention

plate ar·mor *n.* body armor made up of metal plates, as distinct from the chain mail that it superseded

pla·teau /pla tṓ/ *n.* (*plural* **-teaus** *or* **-teaux** /pla tṓz/) **1. RAISED AREA WITH LEVEL TOP** a hill or mountain with a level top **2. STABLE PHASE** a period or phase in something when there is little increase or decrease **3. PHASE OF STAGNATION** a phase in mental or physical development during which little headway is made ■ *vi.* (**-teaued, -teau·ing, -teaus**) **LEVEL OUT** to reach a stable phase after a period of movement or development [Late 18thC. Via French from Old French *platel*, literally "small flat thing," from *plate* (see PLATE).]

plate bound·a·ry *n.* an area on the margins of tectonic plates where seismic, volcanic, and tectonic activity takes place as a consequence of the relative motion of the plates

plat·ed /pláytəd/ *adj.* **1. OVERLAID WITH GOLD OR SILVER** covered with a thin layer of gold or silver **2.** ENG **COVERED WITH PLATES** protected and strengthened by a covering of plates **3.** KNITTING **KNITTED WITH TWO YARNS** knitted with two kinds of yarn, one appearing on the front and one on the back of the fabric

plate·ful /pláyt fòol/ *n.* the amount of food that a plate will hold

plate glass *n.* strong thick glass in large sheets used for windows and as a construction material for larger buildings (*hyphenated when used before a noun*)

plate·lay·er /pláyt làyr/ *n. U.K.* = **trackman** ["Plate" from PLATE RAIL]

plate·let /pláytlət/ *n.* a tiny colorless disk-shaped particle found in large quantities in the blood that plays an important part in the clotting process

plate·mak·er /pláyt màykər/ *n.* a person or machine that prepares plates for printing

plate·mark /pláyt maark/ *n. U.K.* METALL = **hallmark** *n.* 3

plat·en /plátt'n/ *n.* **1. METAL PLATE IN PRINTING PRESS** a flat metal plate in a printing press that holds the paper against the inked type **2. TYPEWRITER ROLLER** the cylindrical roller against which the paper is held in a typewriter, and against which the type strikes **3. WORKTABLE** the movable worktable of a machine tool [Mid-16thC. From Old French *platine* "metal plate," from *plat* "flat," via assumed Vulgar Latin *plattus* from Greek *platus* (see PLATE).]

plat·er /pláytər/ *n.* **1. SOMEBODY OR SOMETHING THAT PLATES** a person or machine that plates things **2. RACEHORSE IN MINOR RACES** a racehorse of average quality that is entered in minor races **3. BLACKSMITH** a blacksmith who specializes in shoeing racehorses

plate rail *n.* an early type of rail with a flange along the outer edge to keep the unflanged wheels on the track

plat·er·esque /plàttə résk/ *adj.* relating to a heavily decorated architectural style fashionable in 16th-century Spain, reminiscent of elaborate silverware [Late 19thC. From Spanish *plateresco*, from *platero* "silversmith," from *plata* "silver" (see PLATINA).]

plate tec·ton·ics *n.* a theory that ascribes continental drift, volcanic and seismic activity, and the formation of mountain belts to moving plates of the earth's crust supported on less rigid mantle rocks (*takes a singular verb*)

plat·form /plát fàwrm/ *n.* **1. STAGE FOR PERFORMERS OR SPEAKERS** a raised level area of flooring for speakers, performers, or participants in a ceremony, making them easily visible to the audience **2. FLAT RAISED STRUCTURE** a simple structure, especially one composed of wooden planks, serving as base for keeping things clear of the ground **3.** RAIL **RAISED AREA PROVIDING ACCESS TO TRAINS** a raised structure beside the line at a rail station that makes it easier to get on or off and load or unload a train **4.** TRANSP **REAR STEP ON BUS OR TRAM** an open step at the rear of a bus or tram for passengers to stand on as they get into or out of the vehicle **5.** POL **STATED POLICY OF PARTY SEEKING ELECTION** the publicly announced policies and promises of a party seeking election, understood as the basis of its actions should it come to power **6. OPPORTUNITY FOR DOING SOMETHING** a position of authority or prominence that provides a good opportunity for doing something **7.** INDUST **OFFSHORE DRILLING STRUCTURE** an anchored offshore structure with living and working accommodations above water level, from which oil or gas wells can be drilled or maintained **8.** GEOG **RAISED AREA OF GROUND** a flat raised area of ground **9. THICKENED SOLE OF SHOE** a thick layer of leather or other material between the sole and upper of a shoe **10.** ACCESSORIES **SHOE WITH PLATFORM SOLE** a shoe or boot with a platform sole **11.** COMPUT **COMPUTER OPERATING SYSTEM** a computer operating system, often along with the associated equipment [Mid-16thC. From French *plateforme* "diagram," from *plat* "flat" + *forme* "form."]

plat·form bal·ance *n.* = **platform scale**

plat·form bed *n.* a bed consisting of a mattress lying on a platform raised on supports, the space under the platform being used for storage

plat·form rock·er *n.* a rocking chair with the rocker set into a stable base that lies flat on the floor

plat·form scale *n.* a scale with a flat surface that supports the object to be weighed

plat·form ten·nis *n.* a game similar to tennis played with table-tennis paddles and a rubber ball on a fenced wooden platform not quite as big as a tennis court

plat·form tick·et *n. U.K.* a ticket allowing access to a station platform, formerly purchased by nontravelers so that they could meet or see off passengers

CORBIS/Bettmann

Sylvia Plath

Plath /plath/, **Sylvia** (1932–63) U.S. poet. Her work is best known for its savage imagery and themes of self-destruction, anticipating her own suicide. She was married to the British poet Ted Hughes.

platin- *prefix.* platinum ○ *platinic* [From PLATINUM]

pla·ti·na /plə téenə, plátt'nə/ *n.* a naturally occurring platinum alloy [Mid-18thC. From Spanish, formed from *plata* "silver" (because of its silvery color), from assumed Vulgar Latin *plattus*.]

plat·ing /pláyting/ *n.* **1. THIN COVERING CONSISTING OF VALUABLE METAL** a thin covering of a valuable metal applied to a surface of base metal ○ *gold plating* **2. COVERING OF METAL PLATES** a covering or armor of metal plates applied to the surface of something, especially a ship or tank **3. APPLICATION OF A COVERING OF METAL** the process of applying a covering of metal or metal plates to the surface of something

pla·tin·ic /plə tínnik/ *adj.* relating to, containing, or consisting of platinum, especially in a valence state of four

pla·ti·nif·er·ous /plàtt'n íffərəss/ *adj.* containing or yielding platinum

plat·i·nize /plátt'n ìz/ (**-nized, -niz·ing, -niz·es**) *vt.* to coat, combine, or treat something with platinum or a platinum compound —**plat·i·ni·za·tion** /plàtt'ni záysh'n/ *n.*

plat·i·noid /plátt'n òyd/ *adj.* **RESEMBLING PLATINUM** resembling or containing platinum ■ *n.* **1. METAL CHEMICALLY SIMILAR TO PLATINUM** a metal that is chemically similar to platinum, specifically iridium, osmium, palladium, rhodium, or ruthenium **2. ALLOY SIMILAR TO PLATINUM** an alloy of copper, zinc, nickel, and tungsten that resembles platinum in not tarnishing readily and in having a strong resistance to the passage of an electric current

plat·i·nous /plátt'nəss/ *adj.* relating to, containing, or consisting of platinum, especially in a valence state of two

plat·i·num /plátt'nəm/ *n.* CHEM ELEM **PRECIOUS METALLIC ELEMENT** a precious silvery-white metallic element, highly malleable and ductile and highly resistant to chemicals and heat, used in jewelry and chemically as a catalyst and in electroplating. Symbol **Pt** ■ *adj.* MUSIC **TOP-SELLING** having sold one million as a single or two million as an LP or CD [Early 19thC. Formed from PLATINA, on the model of the names of other metals ending in *-um*.] ◇ **go platinum** to reach the level of sales designated for platinum status (*refers to musical recordings*)

plat·i·num black *n.* platinum in the form of a fine black powder, used as a catalyst in organic synthesis

plat·i·num blond, plat·i·num blonde *adj.* **SILVERY-BLOND** pale silvery-blond in color (*hyphenated before a noun*) ■ *n.* **SOMEBODY WITH PLATINUM-BLOND HAIR** somebody who has platinum-blond hair

plat·i·num met·al *n.* platinum or any of the metals in its group, specifically, iridium, osmium, palladium, rhodium, or ruthenium

plat·i·tude /pláttə tòod/ *n.* **1. BANAL STATEMENT** a pointless, unoriginal, or empty comment or statement made as though it was significant or helpful **2. USE OF PLATITUDES** the making of platitudes [Early 19thC. From French, literally "flatness," from *plat* "flat" (see PLATE).]

plat·i·tu·di·nar·i·an /plàttə tood'n érree ən/ *n.* **SOMEBODY WHO TALKS IN PLATITUDES** somebody whose speech or writing is full of platitudes ■ *adj.* **FULL OF PLATITUDES** using, containing, or resembling platitudes

plat·i·tu·di·nize /plàttə tóod'n ìz/ (**-nized, -niz·ing, -niz·es**) *vi.* to produce or talk in platitudes — **plat·i·tu·di·niz·er** *n.*

plat·i·tu·di·nous /plàttə tóod'nəss/, **plat·i·tu·di·nal** /plàttə tóodən'l/ *adj.* using, containing, or resembling platitudes

Pla·to /pláytō/ *n.* a distinctive dark-floored large crater on the Moon just north of Mare Imbrium, approximately 60 mi./100 km in diameter

Pla·to (428?–347 B.C.) Greek philosopher. A disciple of Socrates and teacher of Aristotle, he founded the Athenian Academy. His works, written in dialogue form, include *Phaedo, Symposium,* and *Republic.*

pla·ton·ic /plə tónnik/ *adj.* **1. NOT INVOLVING SEXUAL RELATIONS** involving friendship, affection, or love without sexual relations between people who might be expected to be sexually attracted to each other **2. PERFECT BUT UNREAL** perfect in form or conception but not found in reality [Mid-16thC. Via Latin from Greek *Platōnikos*, from *Platōn* (see PLATO).] —**pla·ton·i·cal·ly** *adv.*

Pla·ton·ic *adj.* relating to Plato or his philosophy

Pla·to·nism /pláytə nìzzəm/ *n.* the philosophy or teachings of Plato, especially the theory that both physical objects and instances of qualities are recognizable because of their common relationship to an abstract form or idea [Late 16thC. From modern Latin *Platonismus*, from Greek *Platōn* (see PLATO).] — **Pla·to·nist** *n.*

pla·toon /plə tóon/ *n.* **1. MILITARY SUBDIVISION** a subdivision of a company of soldiers, usually led by a lieutenant and consisting of two to three sections or squads of ten to twelve people **2. PEOPLE OR THINGS WORKING TOGETHER** a body of people or things with a common purpose or goal [Mid-17thC. From French *peloton*, literally "small ball," from *pelote* "ball" (see PELLET).]

pla·toon ser·geant *n.* a noncommissioned officer in the U.S. army who assists a lieutenant in leading a platoon

Platt·deutsch /plát dòych/ *n., adj.* LANG = **Low German** [Mid-19thC. Via German from Dutch *Platduitsch*, literally "low German," from the flat landscape of the North German lowlands where it is spoken.]

Plat·te /plat/ river in central Nebraska, flowing from near North Platte city into the Missouri River. Length: 310 mi./500 km.

plat·te·land /plát lànd/ *n.* remote rural areas in South Africa [Mid-20thC. Via Afrikaans from Middle Dutch, literally "flat country."]

plat·ter /pláttər/ *n.* **1.** HOUSEHOLD **LARGE FLAT DISH** a large flat dish for serving food **2.** FOOD **SERVED FOOD** a particular variety of prepared and served food (*often used in combination*) ○ *seafood platter* **3.** MUSIC **RECORD** a phonograph record (*dated informal*) **4.** COMP SCI **RECORDING SURFACE OF A HARD DISK** the recording surface of a hard disk [14thC. Via Anglo-Norman *plater* from Old French *plat* (see PLATE).]

plat·y[1] /pláytee/ (-i·er, -i·est) *adj.* used to describe minerals that crystallize in thin sheets and tend to flake along cleavage planes

plat·y[2] /pláytee/ (*plural* **-ys** *or* **-ies** *or* **-y**) *n.* a brightly colored Central American fish that bears live young, not eggs, and is popular as an aquarium fish. Genus: *Xiphophorus.* [Early 20thC. Shortening of modern Latin *Platypoecilus*, former genus name, from Greek *platus* "flat" + *poikilos* "spotted."]

plat·y·hel·minth /plàttee hélminth/ *n.* a flatworm (*technical*) [Late 19thC. From modern Latin *Platyhelminthes*, phylum name, from Greek *platus* "flat" + *helminth-* "worm."] —**plat·y·hel·min·thic** /plàttee hel mínthik/ *adj.*

plat·y·pus /pláttəpəss, plátta po͝oss/ (*plural* **-pus·es** *or* **-pi** /-pī/) *n.* = **duckbilled-platypus** [Late 18thC. Via modern Latin *Platypus*, genus name, from Greek *platupous* "flat-footed," from *platus* "flat" + *pous* "foot."]

plat·yr·rhine /plátta rīn/ *adj.* HAVING WIDELY SPACED NOSTRILS used to describe animals, especially New World monkeys, whose nostrils are well separated and point to either side ■ *n.* PLATYRRHINE MONKEY a platyrrhine animal, especially a monkey [Mid-19thC. Via modern Latin *Platyrrhini*, division name, from Greek *platurrhis* "broad-nosed."]

plau·dit /pláwdit/ *n.* an expression of praise or approval ○ *won plaudits for her skillful handling of the crisis* [Early 17thC. From Latin *plaudite* "applaud!", from *plaudere*; from the customary appeal made by Roman actors at the end of a play.]

WORD KEY: ORIGIN

The Latin word *plaudere* from which ***plaudit*** is derived is also the source of English *applaud* and *explode*.

plau·si·ble /pláwzəb'l/ *adj.* **1.** BELIEVABLE believable and appearing likely to be true, usually in the absence of proof **2.** PERSUASIVE having a persuasive manner in speech or writing, often combined with an intention to deceive [Mid-16thC. From Latin *plausibilis*, literally "deserving applause," from *plaus-*, the past participle stem of *plaudere*.] —**plau·si·bil·i·ty** /plàwzə bíllətee/ *n.* —**plau·si·ble·ness** /pláwzəb'lnəss/ *n.* —**plau·si·bly** /pláwzə blee/ *adv.*

plau·sive /pláwziv/ *adj.* (*archaic*) **1.** EXPRESSING PRAISE characterized by or expressing praise or approval **2.** PLAUSIBLE plausible [Early 17thC. Formed from Latin *plaus-*, the past participle stem of *plaudere* (source of English *applaud* and *explode*).]

Plau·tus /pláwtəss/, **Titus Maccius** (254?–184 B.C.) Roman comic dramatist. His 21 surviving plays, modeled on Greek New Comedy, influenced both Shakespeare and Molière.

play /play/ *v.* (**played, play·ing, plays**) **1.** *vi.* LEISURE ENGAGE IN ENJOYABLE ACTIVITY to take part in enjoyable activity for the sake of amusement **2.** *vti.* GAME, SPORT TAKE PART IN A GAME OR SPORT to take part in a game or a sporting activity ○ *likes to play football* **3.** *vt.* GAME, SPORT COMPETE AGAINST to compete against somebody in a game or sporting event ○ *They play their biggest rival tomorrow.* **4.** *vti.* SPORTS ASSIGN OR HAVE A POSITION ON FIELD to assign a player to a particular position on the field, or be assigned such a position **5.** *vt.* SPORTS HIT A SHOT to make a particular shot or stroke in a sporting event **6.** *vt.* SPORTS HIT BALL to hit or kick a ball, puck, or birdie in a particular direction, especially as a way of beating an opponent ○ *playing the ball straight down the line* **7.** *vt.* GAMES USE A PIECE OR CARD IN A GAME to use a card from a hand in a card game or a piece in a board game **8.** *vti.* MUSIC PERFORM ON A MUSICAL INSTRUMENT to use a musical instrument to produce music ○ *plays the trombone* **9.** *vt.* MUSIC PERFORM MUSIC to use an instrument or the voice to perform a piece of music ○ *play a sonata* **10.** *vt.* MUSIC PERFORM A COMPOSER to perform the music of a particular composer ○ *Chopin is notoriously difficult to play well.* **11.** *vti.* MUSIC REPRODUCE RECORDED MUSIC to reproduce recorded music for listening, or be reproduced in this way ○ *played my favorite CD* **12.** *vti.* ACT IN A PARTICULAR MANNER to deal with a situation in a particular way to achieve a desired result ○ *We decided to play it safe.* **13.** *vt.* PRETEND TO BE to pretend to be a particular type of person ○ *Don't play the innocent with me.* **14.** *vti.* ARTS ACT A PART IN A PLAY to portray a character in a theatrical or movie production ○ *played Macbeth on Broadway* **15.** *vt.* THEATER PERFORM IN PARTICULAR PLACES to perform in particular places or types of places ○ *plays the Catskills every summer* **16.** *vi.* ACT IN JEST to do something for fun, not in earnest **17.** *vti.* ARTS PERFORM OR BE PERFORMED SOMEWHERE to perform a play or show a movie at a particular theater, or be performed or shown there ○ *What's playing at the Roxy?* **18.** *vt.* THEATER PERFORM A DRAMATIC WORK BY to perform the work of a particular dramatist **19.** *vti.* GAMBLING GAMBLE to gamble on a game of chance such as roulette or on horse races **20.** *vt.* FIN SPECULATE IN A MARKET to speculate with securities or commodities in a market **21.** *vi.* MAKE A PARTICULAR IMPRESSION ON SOMEBODY to be received in a particular way by somebody or to make a particular impression on that person ○ *a policy that is likely to play well with middle-class voters* ○ *How will it play in Peoria?* **22.** *vti.* MOVE IRREGULARLY OVER A SURFACE to move or cause something to move unsteadily or irregularly over a surface, usually in a pleasing way ○ *sunlight playing on her brown hair* **23.** *vt.* LET A FISH PULL ON A LINE to tire an already hooked fish by letting it pull on the line as it tries to escape **24.** *vti.* DIRECT LIGHT OR WATER to direct light or water over a surface or in a particular way, or be directed in this manner ■ *n.* **1.** LEISURE ENJOYABLE ACTIVITIES activities bringing amusement or enjoyment, especially the spontaneous activity of young children or young animals ○ *young cubs at play* **2.** SPORTS ACTION OR MOVE IN A GAME a particular action or move in a game ○ *drilled the team in several new offensive plays* **3.** GAME, SPORT TURN IN A GAME somebody's turn to move in a game **4.** SPORTS ACTION DURING A GAME the action during a game or series of games ○ *The play was skilled during the first half but then the team began to tire.* **5.** GAME, SPORT HANDLING OF A SHOT OR MOVE a player's handling of a shot or move or use of a piece or card **6.** LOOSENESS the amount of looseness in something, such as a rope or between moving parts **7.** THEATER DRAMATIC COMPOSITION OR PRODUCTION a dramatic work written to be performed by actors on the stage, on television, or on the radio **8.** PLOY a ploy or deceptive act intended to achieve a particular end ○ *The defendant's tears were just a play for your sympathy.* **9.** GAMBLING GAMBLING participation in betting or gambling **10.** LANGUAGE PUN a pun on a word **11.** FLICKERING MOVEMENT flickering or shimmering movement, especially of light through or on something [Old English *pleg(i)an.* Ultimately from a prehistoric Germanic word meaning "to risk, exercise" that is also the ancestor of English *plight* and *pledge*.] —**play·a·bil·i·ty** /plàyə bíllətee/ *n.* —**play·a·ble** /pláyəb'l/ *adj.* ◇ **make a play for somebody** *or* **something** to try openly to gain something ◇ **play fair** to act in an honest and reasonable way ◇ **play fast and loose** to act irresponsibly or recklessly without regard to facts or others' feelings ◇ **play for time** to delay action or a decision in the hope that conditions will be more favorable later on ◇ **play hard to get** to avoid agreeing to a suggestion, invitation, or proposal, with the intention of appearing to be desirable or in demand ◇ **play it safe** to exercise caution and take few risks

play along *vi.* to pretend to agree with somebody or something in order to gain an advantage or avoid conflict

play around *vi.* **1.** SLEEP AROUND to engage in sexual activity with somebody other than a spouse or long-term partner **2.** WASTE TIME to behave in an irresponsible or childish way

play at *v.* **1.** *vt.* PRETEND to pretend to do or be something, usually without conviction or commitment ○ *I was tired of playing at being an entrepeneur.* **2.** *vi.* ENGAGE IN A ROLE-PLAY GAME to engage in a game that invoves role-playing (*refers typically to children*) ○ *playing at doctors and nurses*

play back *vti.* to reproduce recorded sound or video material

play down *vt.* to represent something as being less important or significant than it is ○ *The spin doctors are playing down the significance of the charge.*

play off *v.* **1.** TAKE PART IN DECIDING GAME to take part in a deciding game to find the winner of a tied contest **2.** *vt.* BRING INTO CONFLICT to set one person or group against another in order to gain an advantage ○ *children playing their parents off each other*

play on, play up·on *vt.* **1.** TAKE ADVANTAGE OF to use somebody's hope, fear, or insecurity as a way of manipulating that person **2.** MAKE A PUN to make a pun on a word

play out *vt.* **1.** FINISH PLAYING SOMETHING to continue to play something to the finish or end ○ *We'll play out this hand, then go home.* **2.** LET SOMETHING OUT GRADUALLY to release something such as a rope bit by bit **3.** ACT OUT SOMETHING to act out a scene or situation that has been rehearsed or envisaged previously

play up *vt.* to emphasize or exaggerate something ○ *She played up her commercial know-how for all she was worth.*

play up to *vt.* to attempt to please somebody by flattery and obsequiousness

play with *vt.* **1.** THINK ABOUT to consider a plan or idea without doing very much to make it happen **2.** TREAT CARELESSLY to treat somebody or somebody's feelings carelessly or irresponsibly **3.** DEAL WITH SOMETHING HALF-HEARTEDLY to deal with something unenthusiastically or haphazardly, e.g., by pushing food around a plate without eating **4.** MASTURBATE to masturbate

pla·ya /plaáyə/ *n.* the lower part of an inland desert drainage basin that is periodically filled with alkaline and briny salts washed down by rainwater from surrounding highlands [Mid-19thC. Via Spanish, "beach," from late Latin *plagia* "plain, shore," of uncertain origin: perhaps ultimately from Greek *plagos* "side."]

play-act (**play-act·ed, play-act·ing, play-acts**) *v.* **1.** *vi.* BEHAVE INSINCERELY to behave in an insincere and excessively dramatic fashion, usually in order to get attention (*informal*) **2.** *vti.* PRETEND TO BE ACTING to pretend to be acting a part, usually for fun **3.** *vi.* ACT IN A PLAY to take part in drama, especially as an amateur —**play·act·ing** *n.* —**play·act·or** *n.*

play-ac·tion pass *n.* in football, a play in which the quarterback fakes a handoff to a back before passing forward to a receiver

play·back /pláy bàk/ *n.* **1.** REPLAY OF A RECORDING the replay of a sound or video recording after it has been made, often as a check for quality or accuracy **2.** DEVICE FOR REPLAYING RECORDINGS the device or facility in a recording apparatus for replaying recordings

play·bill /pláy bìl/ *n.* **1.** THEATER PROGRAM the printed program accompanying a theatrical performance or concert, sold to theatergoers before the performance ○ *We had barely two minutes to study the playbill before the lights went down.* **2.** POSTER ADVERTISING A PLAY a poster advertising a play or other theatrical perfomance (*dated*)

play·book /pláy bo͝ok/ *n.* **1.** SPORTS BOOK DETAILING FOOTBALL MOVES a book in which football plays are explained and diagrammed **2.** THEATER BOOK OF PLAYS a book containing play scripts

play·boy /pláy bòy/ *n.* a rich man who does not work and devotes himself to a life of pleasure without commitments or responsibilities

play-by-play *adj.* LIVE AND DETAILED consisting of a description of each event as it happens, especially in a sports contest ■ *n.* SPOKEN DESCRIPTION OF AN EVENT a spoken description of an event as it happens, especially of a sporting event being broadcast on radio or television

Play-Doh *tdmk.* a trademark for a soft colored modeling material used especially by children

played out *adj.* **1.** EXHAUSTED drained of energy or inspiration as a result of excessive or prolonged effort or of being too long in the public eye ○ *After months of intensive but not very productive research I was feeling played out and in need of a vacation.* **2.** NO LONGER POPULAR OR FASHIONABLE having lost all usefulness or relevance through overuse or overexposure (*hyphenated before a noun*) [Originally describing a fish that has fought until it is exhausted]

play·er /pláyr/ *n.* **1.** SOMEBODY TAKING PART IN GAME somebody taking part in a sport or game, e.g., a member of a team (*often used in combination*) ○ *a hockey player* **2.** MUSICIAN somebody who plays a musical instrument (*usually used in combination*) ○ *a trumpet player* **3.** PARTICIPANT IN AN ACTIVITY a person, group, or business that has an influential role in a particular political or commercial activity ○ *a major player in the direct banking sector* **4.** STAGE ACTOR an actor, especially a member of a theatrical company **5.** DEVICE FOR PLAYING RECORDED SOUND a device for playing recorded sound (*usually used in combination*) ○ *a CD player* **6.** = **gambler**

play·er pi·an·o *n.* a piano with a mechanism for playing music automatically, usually by means of a perforated metal disk or roll of paper

play·fel·low /pláy fèlō/ *n.* a friend with whom a child plays (*dated*)

play·ful /pláyf'l/ *adj.* **1.** ENJOYING FUN AND GAMES fond of having fun and playing games with others **2.** SAID OR

DONE IN FUN said or done in a teasing way or in fun ○ *a playful poke in the ribs* —**play·ful·ly** *adv.* —**play·ful·ness** *n.*

play·girl /plày gúrl/ *n.* a rich woman who does not work and devotes herself to a life of pleasure without commitments or responsibilities

play·go·er /pláy gō ər/ *n.* somebody who frequents the theater as a spectator —**play·go·ing** *adj., n.*

play·ground /pláy gròwnd/ *n.* **1. PLAY AREA** an outdoor recreation area for children, usually equipped with swings, slides, seesaws, and other play equipment **2.** = **schoolyard 3. RESORT** a resort or other place used for a recreation by a particular group of people ○ *The coast has become a playground for millionaires.*

play·group /pláy gro͞op/ *n.* an organized meeting for preschool children to play together under supervision

play·house /pláy hòwss/ (*plural* **-houses** /-hòwzəz/) *n.* **1. THEATER** a theater, especially the main theater in a town or city **2. SMALL MODEL HOUSE FOR CHILDREN** a model house that is large enough for small children to go inside and play in **3. DOLLHOUSE** a dollhouse

play·ing card *n.* any of a set of cards printed with an identical design on the back and symbols on the face representing the numbers in different suits, used for playing various games. Playing cards were introduced to the West from Asia and were probably first used in China in the 10th century. The pack was standardized at 52 in the 15th century.

play·ing field *n.* an area of level ground used for organized sporting activities ◇ **a level playing field** a situation in which all those involved have an equal chance of being successful

play·land /pláy lànd/ *n.* an area designed and equipped for children to play in

play·let /pláylət/ *n.* a short play, often one with a rather slight plot

play·list /pláy lìst/ *n.* a list of musical recording that are to be played on a radio program or by a radio station —**play·list** *vt.*

play·mak·er /pláy màykər/ *n.* in team games, a player who initiates an offensive play designed to create a scoring opportunity

play·mate /pláy màyt/ *n.* somebody, especially a child, who plays with another

play·off /pláy àwf, -òf/ *n.* **1. TIEBREAKER** an additional match, game, or round to decide the winner in the case of a tie **2. ONE OF A SERIES OF GAMES** one of a series of games that decides a championship competition ○ *One more win should guarantee a spot in the playoffs.*

play on words *n.* a pun

play·pen /pláy pèn/ *n.* a portable structure that forms a small enclosure for a baby to play in safely

play·room /pláy ro͞om, -ro͝om/ *n.* a room reserved, designed, or equipped for children to play in

play·school /pláy sko͞ol/ *n. U.K.* a place where preschool children can be taken for supervised play and learning, usually for half-day sessions

play·suit /pláy so͞ot/ *n.* an outfit for a child or woman to wear when relaxing, either consisting of shorts and a top or made in one piece

play·thing /pláy thìng/ *n.* **1. TOY** a toy or other object with which to play **2. SOMEBODY OR SOMETHING TREATED AS A TOY** somebody or something used for amusement rather than being treated with respect or taken seriously

play·time /pláy tìm/ *n.* a time set aside for play, especially as a recess for children at school

play·wear /pláy wàir/ *n.* children's clothes suitable for playing in

play·wright /pláy rìt/ *n.* somebody who writes plays

pla·za /plaázə, plázzə/ *n.* **1. SPANISH SQUARE** an open square or marketplace in a Spanish-speaking country or somewhere influenced by Hispanic culture **2. SHOPPING CENTER** a mall or shopping center [Late 17thC. Via Spanish from Latin *platea* "broad street" (see PLACE).]

PLC *abbr.* **PLC, plc** *U.K.* public limited company ■ *n., abbr.* product life cycle

plea /plee/ *n.* **1. URGENT REQUEST** an urgent, often emotional, request ○ *a plea for understanding* **2. LAW DEFENDANT'S ANSWER TO CHARGE** the defendant's answer to a charge in a court of law, especially one stating that he or she is guilty or not guilty **3. LAW STATEMENT SUPPORTING DEFENDANT'S OR CLAIMANT'S CASE** a statement or argument made in a court of law in support of a defendant's or claimant's case **4. EXCUSE** an excuse or pretext [13thC. Via Anglo-Norman *plai* "lawsuit, agreement" from, ultimately, Latin *placitum* "decree," from the past participle of *placere* (see PLEASE).]

plea-bar·gain·ing *n.* the practice of arranging with the prosecution, and sometimes a judge, for a defendant to plead guilty to a less serious charge rather than be tried for a more serious one —**plea bar·gain** *n.* —**plea-bar·gain** *vi.*

pleach /pleech/ (**pleached, pleach·ing, pleach·es**) *vt.* to form or reinforce a hedge or arch by intertwining shoots or branches [14thC. From Old French dialect *plechier,* a variant of Old French *plassier* (source of English *plash*) from, ultimately, Latin *plectere* "to plait" (see PLEXUS).]

plead /pleed/ (**plead·ed** *or* **pled** /pled/, **plead·ed** *or* **pled, plead·ing, pleads**) *v.* **1.** *vi.* **BEG EARNESTLY** to make an earnest or urgent entreaty, often in emotional terms ○ *I pleaded with her to stay.* **2.** *vt.* **OFFER SOMETHING AS AN EXCUSE** to use a particular reason or circumstance to excuse or justify behavior ○ *It's no use pleading ignorance.* **3.** *vt.* **DECLARE GUILT OR INNOCENCE** to answer "guilty" or "not guilty" in response to a charge in a court of law **4.** *vti.* **OFFER AN ARGUMENT IN SUPPORT** to argue a case in support of somebody or something, especially in a court of law [13thC. Via Anglo-Norman *pleder* from, ultimately, medieval Latin *placitare* "to appeal," from *placitum* "decree" (see PLEA).] —**plead·a·ble** *adj.* —**plead·er** *n.*

plead·ings /pleédingz/ *npl.* the formal written statements made by the plaintiff and the defendant in a lawsuit

pleas·ance /plézz'ns/ *n.* **1. SECLUDED AREA OF A GARDEN** a quiet tree-planted area laid out with walks and often statues and fountains **2. PLEASURE** pleasure or delight (*archaic*) [14thC. From French *plaisance,* from *plaisant* (see PLEASANT).]

pleas·ant /plézz'nt/ *adj.* **1. ENJOYABLE** bringing feelings of pleasure, enjoyment, or satisfaction ○ *We spent a very pleasant evening together.* **2. GOOD-NATURED** friendly, kind, or good-natured **3. FULL OF JOKES** inclined to make jokes and be facetious (*archaic*) [14thC. From Old French *plaisant,* the present participle of Old French *plaisir* (see PLEASE).] —**pleas·ant·ly** *adv.* —**pleas·ant·ness** *n.*

pleas·ant·ry /plézz'ntree/ (*plural* **-ries**) *n.* **1. POLITE REMARK** a conventionally polite remark or enquiry **2. WITTY REMARK** a humorous or witty remark **3. AGREEABLE CONVERSATION** pleasing light conversation

please /pleez/ *adv., interj.* **USED IN REQUESTS** used to add politeness or urgency to requests, commands, and published rules and regulations ○ *Please be quiet.* ■ *interj.* **USED TO EXPRESS INDIGNATION** used to express astonishment or indignation, often facetiously ○ *Please! Do you expect me to believe that?* ■ *v.* (**pleased, pleas·ing, pleas·es**) **1.** *vti.* **GIVE PLEASURE** to give pleasure or satisfaction to somebody **2.** *vt.* **BE WHAT SOMEBODY WANTS** to be the wish or will of somebody (*formal or literary*) **3.** *vi.* **LIKE** to like or wish to do something ○ *He just does whatever he pleases.* [14thC. Via Old French *plaisir* from Latin *placere* (source of English *placid* and *complacent*).] —**pleas·er** *n.* ◇ **if you please 1.** used to make a polite request or command (*dated formal*) **2.** used to indicate mild annoyance, indignation, or amazement (*dated*)

pleased /pleezd/ *adj.* **1. HAPPY OR SATISFIED** feeling or expressing satisfaction or pleasure ○ *I'm really pleased with their progress.* ○ *Pleased to meet you.* **2. WILLING** willing to do something ○ *We would be pleased to answer any further requests you have.*

pleas·ing /pleézing/ *adj.* **1. PLEASANT** pleasant or gratifying ○ *a pleasing contrast* **2. SATISFYING** welcome or satisfying —**pleas·ing·ly** *adv.* —**pleas·ing·ness** *n.*

pleas·ur·a·ble /plézhərəb'l/ *adj.* giving pleasure or enjoyment —**pleas·ur·a·bil·i·ty** /plèzhərə bíllətee/ *n.* —**pleas·ur·a·bly** /plézhərəblee/ *adv.*

pleas·ure /plézhər/ *n.* **1. HAPPINESS OR SATISFACTION** a feeling of happiness, delight, or satisfaction ○ *I took great pleasure in pointing out his mistake to him.* **2. SENSUAL GRATIFICATION** gratification of the senses, especially sexual gratification **3. RECREATION** recreation, relaxation, or amusement, especially as distinct from work or everyday routine ○ *traveling for pleasure* **4. SOMETHING SATISFYING** a source of happiness, joy, or satisfaction **5. SOMEBODY'S DESIRE** somebody's desire, wish, or preference (*formal or literary*) ○ *serves at the President's pleasure* ■ *v.* (**-ured, -ur·ing, -ures**) **1.** *vt.* **GIVE SOMEBODY PLEASURE** to give somebody pleasure, especially through sensual or sexual stimulation or gratification **2.** *vi.* **ENJOY** to derive satisfaction or happiness from something (*archaic*) [14thC. From Old French *plaisir* "to please," used as a noun (see PLEASE).] —**pleas·ure·ful** *adj.* —**pleas·ure·less** *adj.*

pleas·ure prin·ci·ple *n.* in Freudian psychology, the principle that guides instinctive behavior, directing the subject toward gratifying immediate needs and avoiding pain

pleat /pleet/ *n.* **PRESSED FOLD** a vertical fold in cloth or other material, usually one of a number, sewn into position or pressed flat ■ *vt.* (**pleat·ed, pleat·ing, pleats**) **PUT PLEATS IN SOMETHING** to put pleats into cloth or a piece of clothing [14thC. From an early variant of PLAIT.] —**pleat·er** *n.*

pleb /pleb/ *n.* **1. HIST** = **plebeian** *n.* 1 **2.** *U.K.* **SOMEBODY REGARDED AS ILL-EDUCATED** somebody who is regarded ill-educated and unrefined and behaves in a coarse or crude manner, especially somebody from a lower social class (*insult*) **3. MIL** = **plebe** [Mid-17thC. Originally a back-formation from PLEBS, misunderstood as a plural, later also a shortening of PLEBEIAN.]

plebe /pleeb/ *n.* a first-year student at the U.S. Military Academy or the U.S. Naval Academy [Mid-19thC. Origin uncertain: probably a shortening of PLEBEIAN.]

ple·be·ian /plə beé ən/ *n.* **1. MEMBER OF THE ROMAN PLEBS** one of the ordinary citizens of ancient Rome as distinct from the patricians **2. SOMEBODY REGARDED AS ILL-EDUCATED** somebody who behaves in a coarse or crude manner, and has common or vulgar tastes, especially somebody from a lower social class (*insult*) ■ *adj.* **1. OF THE ROMAN PLEBS** relating or belonging to the ordinary people in a society, especially the plebs of ancient Rome **2. COMMON OR VULGAR** coarse, vulgar, or tasteless (*insult*) [Mid-16thC. Formed from Latin *plebeius,* from *plebs* (see PLEBS).] —**ple·be·ian·ism** *n.*

pleb·i·scite /plébbi sìt/ *n.* **1. VOTE OF ALL CITIZENS** a vote by a whole electorate to decide a question of importance. ◊ **referendum 2. EXPRESSION OF PUBLIC WILL** a public expression of the will or opinion of a whole community **3. HIST COMMON PEOPLE'S LAW** a law enacted by the plebs or ordinary citizens of ancient Rome gathered in assembly [Mid-16thC. Via French from Latin *plebiscitum,* literally "decree of the common people."] —**ple·bis·ci·tar·y** /plə bíssi tèree/ *adj.*

plebs /plebz/ *npl.* **HIST** the ordinary citizens of ancient Rome, as distinct from the patricians [Mid-19thC. From Latin.]

ple·cop·ter·an /plə kóptərən/ *n.* = **stonefly** ■ *adj.* **OF STONEFLIES** relating or belonging to the stoneflies. Order: Plecoptera. [Late 19thC. Formed from modern Latin *Plecoptera,* order name, from Greek *plekos* "wickerwork" + *pteron* "wing"; so called because of its netted wings.]

plec·tog·nath /plék tog nàth/ *n.* a bony strong-toothed marine fish with a small mouth and small gill openings, e.g., the triggerfish or the puffer. Order: Plectognathi. [Late 19thC. From modern Latin *Plectognathi,* order name, from Greek *plektos* "twisted" + *gnathos* "jaw."]

pled /pled/ *U.S., Can, Scotland* past participle, past tense of **plead**

pledge /plej/ *n.* **1. SOLEMN UNDERTAKING** a solemn promise or vow ○ *stood by her election pledges* **2. SOMETHING GIVEN AS SECURITY** something delivered as security for the keeping of a promise or the payment of a debt or as a guarantee of good faith **3.** a promise to donate money, e.g., to a charity or a political cause ○ *They have raised over $10,000 in donations and pledges.* **4. UNIV RECRUIT TO A UNIVERSITY SOCIETY** a student who has been invited, and has promised, to join a fraternity or sorority **5. LAW DEPOSIT OF PROPERTY** a handing over or deposit of property as security **6. BEING HELD AS SECURITY** the state of being held as security ○ *goods in pledge* **7. TOKEN OF SOMETHING** something given or received as a token of something such as love or friendship **8. TOAST** a toast drunk to somebody or something as a gesture of goodwill or support ■ *v.* (**pledged, pledg·ing, pledg·es**) **1.** *vt.* **PROMISE SOMETHING** to promise something solemnly, or promise solemnly to do something **2.** *vti.* **UNIV PROMISE TO JOIN A UNIVERSITY SOCIETY** to promise to join a society, fraternity, or sorority **3.** *vt.* **UNIV ENROLL STUDENT IN A SOCIETY**

to admit a student to a society as a new member **4.** *vt.* BIND to submit somebody to a binding pledge **5.** *vt.* GIVE SOMETHING AS SECURITY to hand over something as security for the payment of a debt, repayment of a loan, or the carrying out of some obligation (*dated*) **6.** *vti.* DRINK TO SOMEBODY to drink a toast to somebody (*archaic*) ○ *"Drink to me, only with thine eyes, And I will pledge with mine"* (Ben Jonson *"To Celia"*; 1616) [14thC. Via Old French *plege* from late Latin *plebium*, from *plebire* "to pledge," of Germanic origin.] —**pledg·a·ble** *adj.* ◇ **sign** *or* **take the pledge** to undertake solemnly to abstain forever from alcoholic drink (*dated*)

pledg·ee /ple jeé/ *n.* **1.** UNIV = **pledge** *n.* 4 **2.** SOMEBODY WHO RECEIVES PLEDGE somebody with whom a pledge or pawned object is deposited

Pledge of Al·le·giance *n.* a formula recited by citizens of the United States when saluting the U.S. flag as a promise of loyalty to the country

pledg·er /pléjjər/, **pledg·or** *n.* **1.** SOMEBODY WHO DEPOSITS A PLEDGE somebody who deposits a pledge or puts something in pawn **2.** SOMEBODY WHO MAKES A PLEDGE somebody who takes a pledge or vow

pled·get /pléjjət/ *n.* a small tuft of cotton or other material used on forceps to cleanse or apply medication to a confined space such as the ear passage [Mid-16thC. Origin unknown.]

pled·gor *n.* = **pledger**

-plegia *suffix.* inability to move ○ *quadriplegia* [Formed from *plēgē* "a blow, stroke," from *plēg-*, the stem of *plēssein* "to strike" (see PLECTRUM)]

Ple·iad /pleé əd/, **ple·iad** *n.* a brilliant group of seven people or things, specifically the group of poets of the French Renaissance, La Pléiade, which included Ronsard and Du Bellay, or seven Alexandrian Greek poets of the 3rd century B.C. [Early 17thC. Back-formation from PLEIADES.]

Ple·ia·des /pleé ə deéz/ *npl.* **1.** MYTHOL 7 DAUGHTERS OF ATLAS in Greek mythology, the seven daughters of Atlas and Pleione who were pursued by Orion and were turned into a constellation to escape him **2.** ASTRON CLUSTER OF STARS an open cluster of more than 300 stars in the constellation Taurus, six or seven of which are blue-white giants clearly visible to the naked eye [14thC. Via Latin from Greek (singular *Pleias*), related to *plein* "to sail."]

plein-air /plàyn áir/ *adj.* relating to or in the style of the French impressionist painters who sought to capture effects of light and atmosphere by completing their work out of doors [Late 19thC. From French *(en) plein air* "(in the) open air."] —**plein-air·ist** *n.*

pleio- *prefix.* = **pleo-**

Plei·o·cene *adj., n.* GEOL = **Pliocene**

plei·o·tax·y /pleé ō tàksee/ *n.* BOT the development of more petals or sepals than normal

plei·ot·ro·pism /plee óttrə pìzzəm/, **plei·ot·ro·py** /plee óttrəpee/ (*plural* **-pies**) *n.* the phenomenon in which a single gene determines two or more apparently unrelated characteristics of the same organism, or an instance of this —**ple·o·tro·pic** /pleé ə tróppik/ *adj.* —**plei·o·tro·pi·cal·ly** /-tróppiklee/ *adv.*

Pleis·to·cene /plístə seen/ *adj.* GEOLOGIC PERIOD relating to or used to describe the earlier epoch of the Quaternary Period in the Cenozoic Era, characterized by the disappearance of continental ice sheets and the appearance of humans ■ *n.* PLEISTOCENE EPOCH the Pleistocene epoch [Mid-19thC. Coined from Greek *pleistos* "most" + *kainos* "recent."]

ple·na·ry /plénnəree/ *adj.* **1.** FULL OR UNLIMITED full and complete and not limited in any respect (*formal*) **2.** ATTENDED BY EVERYONE attended or meant to be attended by every member or delegate ○ *a plenary session* ■ *n.* (*plural* **-ries**) PLENARY MEETING a plenary meeting, session, or lecture, e.g. at a conference [Early 16thC. From late Latin *plenarius*, from Latin *plenus* "full" (see PLENTY).] —**ple·na·ri·ly** /plénnərilee/ *adv.*

ple·na·ry in·dul·gence *n.* in the Roman Catholic Church, a complete remission of temporal punishment

plen·i·po·tent /plə nippət'nt/ *adj.* having complete authority [Mid-17thC. From late Latin (see PLENIPOTENTIARY).]

plen·i·po·ten·ti·ar·y /plènnəpə ténsheree/ *adj.* **1.** HAVING FULL POWER invested with complete authority to act independently **2.** CONFERRING FULL POWER giving the holder complete authority to act independently ■ *n.* (*plural* **-ies**) OFFICIAL WITH FULL POWERS an ambassador, envoy, or delegate invested with full authority to act or negotiate independently on behalf of a government or sovereign [Mid-17thC. Via medieval Latin *plenipotentiarius* from the late Latin stem *plenipotent-*, literally "having full power," from *plenus* "full" + *potens* "powerful."]

plen·i·tude /plénə toód/ *n.* (*literary*) **1.** ABUNDANCE an abundance or plentiful supply of something **2.** COMPLETENESS OR FULLNESS the state of being full or complete [15thC. Via Old French from late Latin *plenitudo*, from *plenus* "full" (see PLENTY).]

plen·te·ous /pléntee əss/ *adj.* (*literary*) **1.** ABUNDANT being in plentiful supply **2.** PRODUCTIVE giving an abundant yield [13thC. Via Old French *plentivous* from, ultimately, *plentet* (see PLENTY).] —**plen·te·ous·ly** *adv.* —**plen·te·ous·ness** *n.*

plen·ti·ful /plénteef'l/ *adj.* **1.** ABUNDANT present or existing in good supply ○ *Water is plentiful on the island.* **2.** PRODUCTIVE supplying a large amount or number —**plen·ti·ful·ly** *adv.* —**plen·ti·ful·ness** *n.*

plen·ty /pléntee/ *n.* **1.** LOTS an adequate or more than adequate amount or quantity ○ *There's plenty for the kids to do there.* ○ *Get plenty of rest.* **2.** PROSPERITY a situation in which there is a more than adequate supply of food, money, and other necessities ○ *had grown up in a time of plenty* ■ *adj.* AMPLY SUFFICIENT ample or more than sufficient (*informal*) ■ *adv.* SUFFICIENTLY used to emphasize the degree to which something is the case (*informal*) ○ *It should be plenty big enough.* [13thC. Via Old French *plentet* from Latin *plenitas*, from *plenus* "full." Ultimately, from an Indo-European word that is also the ancestor of English *full* and *folk*.]

ple·num /plénnəm, pleénəm/ (*plural* **-nums** *or* **-na** /-nə/) *n.* **1.** PHYS ENCLOSURE CONTAINING GAS AT A HIGHER PRESSURE an enclosure or chamber containing gas that is at a higher pressure than the surrounding atmosphere. Plenum systems may be used in air conditioning. **2.** GENERAL ATTENDANCE AT A MEETING a full or general assembly, e.g., of all the branches of a legislature **3.** PHILOS MATTER-FILLED SPACE space entirely filled with matter [Late 17thC. From Latin *plenum spatium*, literally "full space."]

pleo- *prefix.* more ○ *pleomorphism* [From Greek *pleīon*. Ultimately from an Indo-European base meaning "full, to fill," which is also the ancestor of English *complete*, *supply*, and *plethora*.]

ple·och·ro·ism /plee ókrō ìzzəm/ *n.* the property in some crystals of transmitting different colors when viewed along different axes [Mid-19thC. Coined from PLEO- + Greek *khrōs* "skin, color."] —**ple·o·chro·ic** /plee ə krṓ ik/ *adj.*

ple·o·mor·phism /plee ə máwr fìzzəm/, **ple·o·mor·phy** /pleé ə màwrfee/ *n.* BIOL the characteristic in some organisms of taking on at least two different forms during the life cycle, or the ability to do this under certain conditions —**ple·o·mor·phic** /plee ə máwrfik/ *adj.*

ple·o·nasm /pleé ə nàzzəm/ *n.* **1.** USE OF SUPERFLUOUS WORDS the use of more words than are necessary to express a meaning **2.** EXAMPLE OF USING SUPERFLUOUS WORDS an example of using more words than are necessary to express a meaning, such as "free gift" or "sufficient enough" [Mid-16thC. Via late Latin from Greek *pleonasmos*, from *pleonazein* "to be in excess," from *pleōn* "more" (see PLEO-).] —**ple·o·nas·tic** /plee ə nástik/ *adj.* —**ple·o·nas·ti·cal·ly** /-nástiklee/ *adv.*

ple·o·pod /pleé ə pòd/ *n.* ZOOL = **swimmeret**

ple·o·trop·ic /pleé ə tróppik/ *adj.* used to describe a gene that affects more than one characteristic of the phenotype

ple·si·o·saur /pleéssee ə sàwr, pleézee-/ *n.* an extinct marine reptile of the Mesozoic era with limbs like paddles, a large flattened body, and a short tail. Suborder: Sauropterygia. [Mid-19thC. From modern Latin *Plesiosaurus*, genus name, from Greek *plēsios* "near" + *sauros* "lizard," because it was similar to the saurians.]

pleth·o·ra /pléthərə/ *n.* **1.** LARGE OR EXCESSIVE AMOUNT OR NUMBER a very large amount or number of something, especially an excessive amount ○ *a plethora of new TV channels* **2.** EXCESS OF BLOOD an excess of blood in part of the body, especially in the facial veins, causing a ruddy complexion (*archaic*) [Mid-16thC. Via late Latin from Greek *plēthorē*, from *plēthein* "to be full."] —**ple·thor·ic** /pléthərik, plə tháwrik/ *adj.* —**ple·thor·i·cal·ly** /-tháwriklee/ *adv.*

pleur- *prefix.* = **pleuro-** (*used before vowels*)

pleu·ra /ploórə/ *n.* (*plural* **-rae** /-reé/ *or* **-ras**) ANAT MEMBRANE AROUND THE LUNGS the thin transparent membrane that lines the chest wall and doubles back to cover the lungs, thereby forming a continuous sac enclosing the narrow pleural cavity. The inner faces of the cavity are lubricated by fluid to ease breathing movements. ■ ZOOL plural of **pleuron** [15thC. Via medieval Latin from Greek, "side, rib" (source of English *pleurisy*).] —**pleu·ral** /ploórəl/ *adj.*

pleu·ral cav·i·ty *n.* the cavity formed between the pleural layer surrounding the lungs and the other layer lining the chest wall

pleu·ri·sy /ploórissee/ *n.* inflammation of the membrane (**pleura**) surrounding the lungs, usually involving painful breathing, coughing, and the buildup of fluid in the pleural cavity [14thC. Via Old French from, ultimately, Greek *pleuritis*, from *pleura* "side, rib."] —**pleu·rit·ic** /ploo ríttik/ *adj.*

pleuro- *prefix.* **1.** side, lateral ○ *pleurodont* **2.** pleura, pleural ○ *pleuropneumonia* [From Greek *pleura* "side, rib"]

pleu·ro·dont /ploórə dònt/ *adj.* **1.** FUSED RATHER THAN ROOTED used to describe teeth, e.g., those found in some reptiles, that are not rooted in the jawbone but fused to its inner side **2.** HAVING TEETH NOT ROOTED IN THE JAWBONE used to describe reptiles that have teeth not rooted in the jawbone but fused to its inner side

pleu·ro·dyn·i·a /ploórə dínnee ə/ *n.* **1.** PLEURITIC PAIN pain in the pleura, or between the ribs or in the chest wall area **2.** VIRAL ILLNESS WITH CHEST PAIN a Coxsackie viral illness resulting in pain in the muscles between the ribs or in other structures of the chest wall (*not used technically*) [Early 19thC. Coined from PLEURO- + Greek *odunē* "pain" (source of English *anodyne*).]

pleu·ron /ploó ròn/ (*plural* **-ra** /ploórə/) *n.* the part of the outer layer of the skin of an arthropod that covers the side of a body segment [Early 18thC. Via modern Latin from Greek, "rib, side."]

pleu·ro·pneu·mo·nia /ploórə noo mṓnee ə/ *n.* inflammation of the membrane (**pleura**) surrounding the lungs and of the lungs themselves at the same time

pleu·rot·o·my /ploo róttəmee/ (*plural* **-mies**) *n.* a surgical incision of the membrane (**pleura**) surrounding the lungs to permit drainage of fluid, especially in pleurisy

pleus·ton /ploóstən, ploó stòn/ *n.* small animals and plants such as algae that float on the surface of a pool of fresh water [Mid-20thC. Coined from Greek *pleusis* "sailing," on the model of PLANKTON. Ultimately, from an Indo-European base meaning "to flow," which is also the ancestor of English *float*.] —**pleus·ton·ic** /ploos tónnik/ *adj.*

Plev·en /plévv'n/ capital city of Pleven Province, northern Bulgaria, situated about 80 mi./129 km northeast of Sofia. Population: 125,000 (1996).

plex·i·form /pléksi fàwrm/ *adj.* resembling or in the form of a plexus or network [Early 19thC. Coined from PLEXUS + -FORM.]

Plex·i·glas /pléksi glàss/ *tdmk.* a trademark for a tough transparent acrylic plastic that can be used in place of glass

plex·or /pléksər/ *n.* MED a small rubber-headed hammer formerly used to tap the body in a medical examination by percussion and in testing reflexes, e.g., by tapping the knee [Mid-19thC. Formed from Greek *plēxis* "percussion," from *plēssein* "to strike."]

plex·us /pléksəss/ (*plural* **-us·es** *or* **-us**) *n.* **1.** ANAT NETWORK IN THE BODY a network of nerves, blood vessels, or other vessels in the body **2.** COMPLEX NETWORK any complex network or interwoven structure [Late 17thC. From Latin, past participle of *plectere* "to plait" (source of English *complex*). Ultimately, from an Indo-European word that is also the ancestor of English *flax*.]

plf, **plf., plff.** *abbr.* plaintiff

pli·a·ble /plí əb'l/ *adj.* **1.** FLEXIBLE flexible and easily bent **2.** EASILY INFLUENCED easily persuaded or influenced **3.** ADAPTABLE adaptable to change [15thC. From Old French, where it was formed from *plier* "to bend" (see PLY[2]).] —**pli·a·bil·i·ty** /plì ə billətee/ *n.* —**pli·a·ble·ness** /plí əb'lnəss/ *n.* —**pli·a·bly** /plí əblee/ *adv.*

WORD KEY: SYNONYMS

pliable, ductile, malleable, elastic, pliant

CORE MEANING: ready to be bent or molded

pliable used to refer to a substance or material that can be easily bent or molded; **ductile** a technical word used to describe metals that can be easily drawn out into a long continuous wire; **malleable** used to describe metals that can be worked and hammered or pressed into various shapes without breaking or cracking; **elastic** used to describe substances or materials that can be stretched without breaking and that return to their original shape after this; **pliant** used to describe something that is supple and springy and therefore easily bent or stretched.

pli·ant /plī́ ənt/ *adj.* **1.** SUPPLE supple and bending easily ○ *a pliant tree branch* **2.** ADAPTABLE easily adapted or modified **3.** EASILY INFLUENCED easily persuaded or influenced [14thC. From Old French, present participle of *plier* "to fold, bend" (see PLY[2]).] —**pli·an·cy** *n.* —**pli·ant·ly** *adv.* —**pli·ant·ness** *n.*

WORD KEY: SYNONYMS
See Synonyms at *pliable*.

pli·ca /plī́kə/ (*plural* **-cae** /-sēe, -kēe/) *n.* ANAT a fold or folded part, e.g., of skin [Early 18thC. Via medieval Latin, "fold," from Latin *plicare* "to fold" (see PLY[2]).] —**pli·cal** *adj.*

pli·cate /plī́ kàyt/, **pli·cat·ed** /plī́ kàytəd/ *adj.* **1.** BOT FOLDED LIKE A FAN arranged in folds like a fan **2.** GEOL WITH A PLEATED TEXTURE used to describe rock with a folded wrinkled texture [Late 17thC. From Latin *plicat-*, past participle stem of *plicare* "to fold" (see PLY[2]).] —**pli·cate·ly** *adv.* —**pli·cate·ness** *n.*

pli·ca·tion /plī kàysh'n/, **plic·a·ture** /plíkə chòor, plíkəchər/ *n.* **1.** SURG STITCHING THE SIDES OF A BODY ORGAN the pleating and stitching of the walls of a body organ in order to reduce its size **2.** FOLDING the action of folding or the condition of being folded **3.** A FOLD a fold in something

pli·é /plee áy/ *n.* a ballet movement in which the knees are bent and the back is kept straight [Late 19thC. From French, the past participle of *plier* "to bend" (see PLY[2]).]

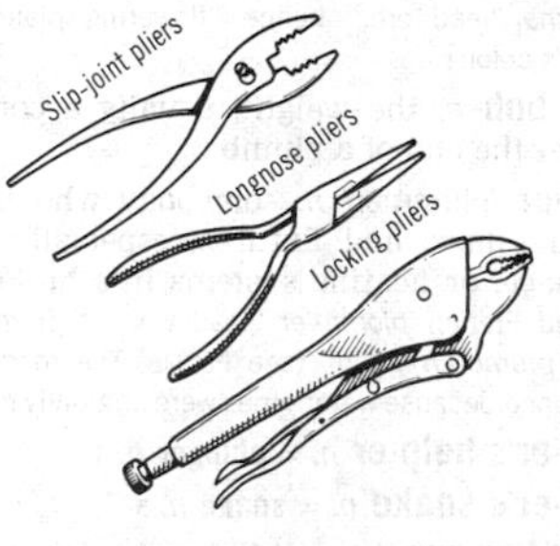

Pliers

pli·ers /plī́rz/ *npl.* a hand tool with two hinged arms ending in jaws that are closed by hand pressure to grip something [Mid-16thC. Formed from PLY[1].]

plight[1] /plīt/ *n.* a difficult or dangerous situation, especially a sad or desperate predicament [14thC. Via Anglo-Norman *plit* "wrinkle, situation" (influenced by PLIGHT[2]) from Latin *plicitum*, from the past participle of *plicare* "to fold" (see PLY[2]).]

plight[2] /plīt/ *vt.* (**plight·ed, plight·ed** *or* **plight, plight·ing, plights**) MAKE A VOW to make a formal pledge, especially when promising to marry ■ *n.* PLEDGE a formal promise or pledge (*archaic*) [Old English *plihtan* "to endanger," from *pliht* "risk, danger," from a prehistoric Germanic word meaning "to risk, pledge yourself," which is also the ancestor of English *pledge*] —**plight·er** *n.* ◇ **plight your troth** to solemnly promise something, especially to marry somebody (*dated*)

plim·soll /plímsəl, -sàwl/, **plim·sole** *n. U.K.* a light canvas shoe with a rubber sole [Late 19thC. Origin uncertain; probably from PLIMSOLL LINE, because the line around the shoe resembles it.]

Plim·soll line, **Plim·soll mark** *n.* any of several marks on the side of a merchant ship indicating the limit to which it can legally be submerged when loaded [Named for the British politician and reformer Samuel *Plimsoll* (1824–98), who introduced the Merchant Shipping Act of 1876 which advocated its use]

plink /plingk/ *n.* HIGH-PITCHED SOUND a short high-pitched metallic sound such as the sound made when the string of a musical instrument is plucked or a pebble is dropped into an empty glass bottle ■ *vti.* (**plinked, plink·ing, plinks**) **1.** MAKE HIGH-PITCHED SOUND to

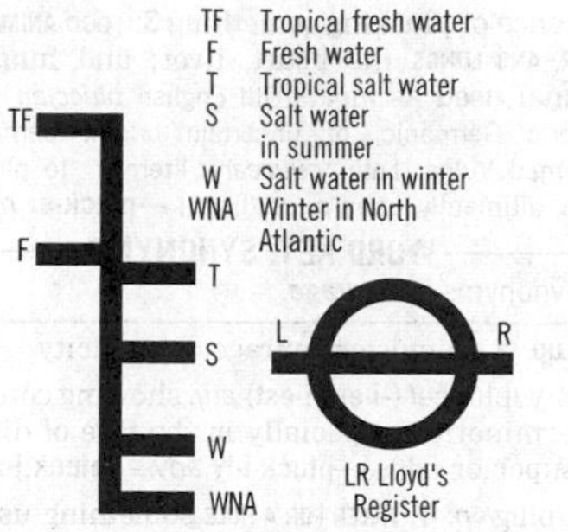

Plimsoll line

produce or make something produce a short high-pitched metallic sound **2.** SHOOT AT A TARGET to shoot at or hit targets for fun, especially targets that make a short high-pitched metallic sound when hit [Mid-20thC. An imitation of the sound.] —**plink·er** *n.*

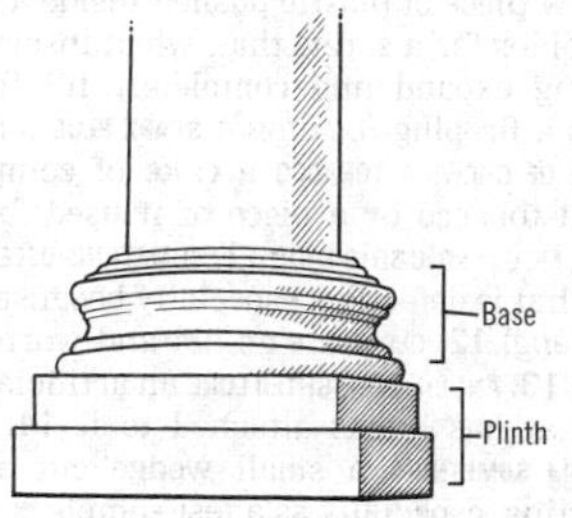

Plinth

plinth /plinth/ *n.* **1.** SUPPORTING BLOCK a square block beneath a column, pedestal, or statue **2.** ARCHIT SUPPORTING PART OF A WALL the part of the wall of a building immediately above the ground, usually a course of stones or bricks **3.** ARCHIT PART OF A DOORFRAME the square block at the base on each side of a doorframe **4.** FLAT BASE any flat block used as a base for something, e.g., underneath a heavy machine [Late 16thC. Via French from, ultimately, Greek *plinthos* "tile, squared building stone."]

Plin·y (the Elder) /plínnee-/ (23–79) Roman scholar. His *Natural History* (77 A.D.) was a major source of knowledge until the 17th century.

Plin·y (the Younger) (62–113) Roman politician and writer. He was the nephew of Pliny the Elder and author of nine books of Letters (100–109).

plio- *prefix.* = **pleo-**

Pli·o·cene /plī́ ə sēen/, **Plei·o·cene** *adj.* BELONGING TO THE TERTIARY PERIOD belonging to or typical of the last epoch of the Tertiary period, 5.4 to 1.6 million years ago, during which time a hominid species (**Homo erectus**) first appeared ■ *n.* PLIOCENE EPOCH OR ROCKS the Pliocene epoch, or rocks formed during that period [Mid-19thC. Coined from Greek *pleiōn* "more" (see PLEO-) + *kainos* "recent" (see -CENE), because it is later than the Miocene.]

Pli·o·film /plī́ ə film/ *tdmk.* a trademark for a type of plastic made of rubber hydrochloride that forms a clear flexible sheeting, used for packaging and raincoats

plis·sé /plee sáy/, **plis·se** *n.* **1.** WRINKLED FINISH a permanently wrinkled finish given to a fabric by treating it chemically **2.** FABRIC WITH A WRINKLED FINISH fabric with a plissé finish [Late 19thC. From French, past participle of *plisser* "to pleat," from *pli* "fold," from *plier* (see PLY[2]).]

PLO *abbr.* Palestine Liberation Organization

plod /plod/ *vi.* (**plod·ded, plod·ding, plods**) **1.** WALK HEAVILY to walk with a slow heavy tread **2.** WORK SLOWLY BUT STEADILY to work slowly but steadily, especially on something uninteresting or laborious ■ *n.* **1.** SLOW HEAVY STEPS a walk with slow heavy steps **2.** SOUND OF SOMEBODY PLODDING the sound of slow, heavy steps [Mid-16thC. Origin uncertain: thought to suggest the motion.] —**plod·der** *n.* —**plod·ding·ly** *adv.* —**plod·ding·ness** *n.*

-ploid *suffix.* having a chromosome number in a particular relationship to the basic number of chromosomes in a group ○ *tetraploid* [From DIPLOID and HAPLOID]

ploi·dy /plóydee/ *n.* the multiple of the number of chromosome sets in a cell [Mid-20thC. Formed from -PLOID.]

Ploi·eş·ti /plaw yésht, -yéshtee/ city in southeastern Romania. It is the capital of Prahova County and center of the national oil industry. Population: 254,408 (1994).

plonk[1] *vti., n., adv.* = **plunk** [Late 19thC. An imitation of the sound.]

plonk[2] /plongk/ *n. U.K.* cheap inferior wine (*informal*) [Mid-20thC. Shortening of *plink-plonk*, of uncertain origin: possibly an alteration of French *vin blanc* "white wine."]

plop /plop/ *n.* SOUND OF SOMETHING DROPPING INTO WATER the sound made by something dropping into water without making a large splash ■ *v.* (**plopped, plop·ping, plops**) **1.** *vti.* FALL WITH A PLOP to fall or drop something into water without making a large splash **2.** *vi.* DROP DOWN QUICKLY AND HEAVILY to drop or sit down quickly and heavily ○ *He plopped down on the nearest chair.* ■ *adv.* WITH A PLOP with a plopping sound or action ■ *interj.* IMITATION OF THE SOUND OF DROPPING INTO WATER used to imitate the sound of something dropping into water without splashing [Early 19thC. An imitation of the sound.]

plo·sion /plṓzh'n/ *n.* PHON the sound made by a sudden release of breath in pronouncing certain sounds, especially a stop consonant [Early 20thC. Back-formation from EXPLOSION.]

plo·sive /plṓziv, plṓssiv/ *adj.* PRONOUNCED WITH A SUDDENLY RELEASED BREATH used to describe a consonant such as the "p" in "pear" that is pronounced by completely closing the breath passage and then releasing air ■ *n.* CONSONANT PRONOUNCED WITH PLOSION a consonant pronounced with a sudden release of breath [Late 19thC. Back-formation from EXPLOSIVE.]

plot /plot/ *n.* **1.** SECRET HOSTILE PLAN a plan decided on in secret, especially to bring about an illegal or subversive act **2.** ARTS STORY LINE the story or sequence of events in a narrated or presented work such as a novel, play, or movie **3.** PIECE OF GROUND a small piece of ground **4.** BUILDING PLAN OF A BUILDING OR ESTATE an architectural plan of a building or estate **5.** A CHART a graph, chart, or diagram ■ *v.* (**plot·ted, plot·ting, plots**) **1.** *vti.* MAKE SECRET PLANS to make secret plans, especially to do something illegal or subversive with others **2.** *vt.* MARK SOMETHING ON A CHART to mark something on a chart, especially the course of a ship or aircraft **3.** *vt.* BUILDING MAKE A PLAN to make a plan or map of something, e.g., a building or estate **4.** *vti.* MARK ON A GRAPH to mark points on a graph or diagram using coordinates, or to be located on a graph by coordinates **5.** *vt.* DRAW ON A GRAPH to draw a line or curve through points marked on a graph or diagram **6.** *vt.* ARTS PLAN EPISODES OF A STORY to devise the sequence of events in a story or script [From Old English, "area of ground," and Old French *complot* "secret scheme," both of unknown origin] —**plot·less** /plóttləss/ *adj.*

plot·line /plót līn/, **plot line** *n.* the plot or storyline in a book or dramatic presentation, or the dialogue needed to develop the plot

plot·tage /plóttij/ *n.* the area of land that makes up a plot

plot·ter /plóttər/ *n.* **1.** SOMEBODY WHO SECRETLY PLANS somebody who makes secret plans, especially to do something illegal or subversive **2.** COMPUT COMPUTER DEVICE FOR DRAWING GRAPHS a computer output device that draws graphs and other pictorial images on paper, sometimes using attached pens. Large plotters are used in computer-aided design applications to produce more rapidly the engineering drawings and architectural plans once prepared by skilled draftspeople.

plough /plow/ *n., vti.* U.K. = **plow**

Plov·div /pláwv dìf/ city in southern Bulgaria, the administrative center of Plovdiv Region. Population: 344,000 (1996).

plov·er /plúvvər/ *n.* **1.** WADING BIRD a wading bird that lives on the shoreline and has a short bill and tail and long pointed wings. Family: Charadriidae. **2.** BIRD SIMILAR TO THE PLOVER a bird that resembles the plover but is in a different taxonomic family, e.g., the Egyptian plover or upland plover [14thC. Via Anglo-Norman from assumed Vulgar Latin *pluviarius*, from Latin *pluvia* "rain" (see PLUVIAL); from the fact that it lives near water.]

Plover

plow /plow/ *n.* **1.** AGRIC **FARM IMPLEMENT** a heavy farming tool with a sharp blade or series of blades for breaking up soil and making furrows, usually pulled by a tractor or draft animal **2. HEAVY TOOL** any of various heavy tools or machines used like a plow to cut a cleared route or channel, e.g., a snowplow ■ *v.* **(plowed, plow·ing, plows) 1.** *vti.* AGRIC **MAKE FURROWS IN THE EARTH** to break up earth and turn it over into furrows ○ *plowing a field* **2.** *vti.* **CUT THROUGH SOMETHING** to cut or force a way through something ○ *I plowed my way through the crowd.* **3.** *vt.* **MAKE A CLEARING IN SOMETHING** to make a channel or cleared route in something **4.** *vt.* AGRIC **PUT UNDER SOIL** to put something such as fertilizer or a crop under the surface of the soil, using a plow **5.** *vti.* **WORK METHODICALLY AT SOMETHING** to work at something and progress slowly and steadily ○ *We plowed through the backlog of applications.* ○ *plowing my way through pages of job ads* **6.** *vt.* **HAVE SEX** to have sexual intercourse with somebody (*slang*) [Old English *ploh,* via prehistoric Germanic from a northern Italic word] —**plow·er** /plówr/ *n.*

plow back *vt.* to invest profits from a business back into the business

plow in *vt.* to contribute or devote something, especially money, to a project or place

plow into *v.* **1.** *vt.* **CRASH INTO** to crash into or hit with a great deal of force ○ *We lost control and plowed into the car in front.* **2.** *vi.* **TO EAGERLY START SOMETHING** to start a job or undertaking, especially with energy and determination

plow under *vt.* **1. BURY** to bury something so that it disappears ○ *Large tracts of forest had been plowed under by the bulldozers.* **2. OVERWHELM SOMETHING OR SOMEBODY** to overwhelm somebody with too many responsibilities or jobs, or to overwhelm something with too heavy a burden ○ *I was plowed under for the whole weekend trying to fix the mess in the computer files.*

plow·boy /plów bòy/ *n.* **1. BOY LEADING PLOW ANIMALS** a boy who leads one or more animals while they pull a plow **2. COUNTRY BOY** any boy who lives in the country and may not be very sophisticated (*archaic*)

plow·man /plówmən/ (*plural* **-men** /-mən/) *n.* **1. OPERATING A PLOW** somebody who operates a plow, especially a plow drawn by animals **2. FARM LABORER** a farm laborer, especially somebody not very sophisticated —**plow·man·ship** *n.*

plow·share /plów shàir/ *n.* the part of a plow that cuts the soil for the furrow

plow steel *n.* a type of strong steel used mainly in making wire rope

ploy /ploy/ *n.* a tactic or maneuver, especially one calculated to deceive or frustrate an opponent [Late 17thC. Origin uncertain: possibly from EMPLOY.]

PLSS *abbr.* MED portable life-support system

plu. *abbr.* plural

pluck /pluk/ *v.* **(plucked, pluck·ing, plucks) 1.** *vt.* **TAKE SOMETHING AWAY QUICKLY** to take something away swiftly, often by means of skill or strength **2.** *vt.* **QUICKLY REMOVE SOMETHING ROOTED** to pull out by the roots some or all of the feathers or hair from something **3.** *vt.* **PULL OFF SOMETHING** to pull something off or out of something else, e.g., fruit from a tree **4.** *vt.* **TAKE SOMETHING CASUALLY** to select something randomly or with no obvious reason **5.** *vti.* **TUG AT SOMETHING** to tug quickly at something ○ *felt someone plucking at my sleeve* **6.** *vt.* MUSIC **PULL AND RELEASE STRINGS** to play a stringed musical instrument by quickly pulling and releasing strings with a finger or plectrum ■ *n.* **1. BRAVERY** courage and determination in meeting danger or difficulty **2. ACT OF PLUCKING** one act or instance of plucking something **3.** FOOD **ANIMAL'S HEART, LIVER, AND LUNGS** the heart, liver, and lungs of an animal used as meat [Old English *pluccian,* from prehistoric Germanic, of uncertain origin: perhaps from assumed Vulgar Latin *piluccare,* literally "to pluck hair," from, ultimately, Latin *pilus* "hair"] —**pluck·er** *n.*

WORD KEY: SYNONYMS

See Synonyms at ***courage***.

pluck up *vt.* to muster courage or audacity

pluck·y /plúkee/ **(-i·er, -i·est)** *adj.* showing courage and determination, especially in the face of difficulties or superior odds —**pluck·i·ly** *adv.* —**pluck·i·ness** *n.*

plug /plug/ *n.* **1. FILLER FOR A HOLE** something used to fill and tightly close up a hole **2. STOPPER FOR A SINK** a rubber or plastic stopper for the drainage hole in a sink or bath **3.** ELEC **ELECTRICAL CONNECTION** the connection at the end of the wire leading from an electrical device, with prongs or pins that allow it to fit into the socket of a power supply **4.** ELEC **SOCKET** an electrical socket, e.g., on a wall (*informal*) **5.** BROADCAST **PUBLICIZING MENTION** a favorable mention of something to publicize it, e.g., during a broadcast about something else (*informal*) **6. WEDGE FOR A SCREW** a hollow piece of plastic pushed inside a hole to act as a holder for a screw that, when inserted, makes the plug expand and completely fill the hole **7. FIREPLUG** a fireplug **8.** AUTOMOT **SPARK PLUG** a spark plug **9. CAKE OF CHEWING TOBACCO** a cake of compressed or twisted tobacco or a piece of it used for chewing **10.** SEISMOL = **volcanic plug 11. SOMETHING DEFECTIVE** something that is defective, especially because it is worn out (*slang*) **12. OLD HORSE** an old and worn-out horse (*slang*) **13.** ANGLING **WEIGHTED LURE** an artificial weighted lure that has hooks attached to it **14. SMALL PIECE CUT FROM SOMETHING** a small wedge cut away from something, especially as a test sample ■ *v.* **(plugged, plug·ging, plugs) 1.** *vt.* **CLOSE UP SOMETHING** to close up a hole or gap **2.** *vt.* **GIVE SOMETHING A FAVORABLE MENTION** to make a favorable mention of something to publicize it, e.g., during a broadcast about something else (*informal*) ○ *a chance to plug her latest novel* **3.** *vt.* **SHOOT SOMEBODY** to shoot somebody with a gun (*slang*) **4.** *vt.* **PUNCH SOMEBODY** to punch somebody (*slang*) **5.** *vi.* **WORK STEADILY** to work at something steadily and persistently (*informal*) ○ *He is still plugging away in the insurance business.* [Early 17thC. Via Dutch from Middle Dutch *plugge,* of unknown origin.] —**plug·ger** *n.* ◇ **pull the plug on something** to bring something abruptly to an end, especially by cutting off funds

plug in *v.* **1.** *vti.* **CONNECT SOMETHING TO A POWER SOURCE** to connect an electrical appliance to a power source or to another electrical appliance, or to function when connected in this way **2.** *vi.* to include or incorporate something (*informal*)

plug into *v.* **1.** *vti.* **CONNECT TO AN ELECTRICITY SUPPLY** to connect or become connected to an electrical power source by means of a plug **2.** *vi.* **BECOME INFORMED ABOUT SOMETHING** to become closely involved with or well-informed about something (*informal*)

plug and play *n.* a technical standard that allows a peripheral device such as a printer or DVD drive to be connected to a computer and to function immediately without the need for the user to alter the system's configuration files

plugged /plugd/ *adj.* **1. STOPPED UP** closed by or as if by a plug or an obstruction **2. MADE COUNTERFEIT** made counterfeit by adding base metal

plug-in *adj.* **CAPABLE OF CONNECTING TO A PLUG** capable of being connected by a plug to an electrical power source ○ *a plug-in hand drill* ■ *n.* **SOMETHING CONNECTED BY PLUG** a device or appliance that may be connected by a plug to an electrical power source

plug-ug·ly *adj.* **VERY UGLY** extremely unattractive (*insult*) ■ *n.* (*plural* **plug-ug·lies**) **TOUGH RUTHLESS PERSON** a tough and intimidating person, especially a gangster (*slang*) [From the *Plug Uglies,* a gang of hoodlums in several U.S. cities in the 1850s]

plum /plum/ *n.* **1.** TREES **SMALL FRUIT TREE** a small tree of the rose family that produces a round or oval smooth-skinned fruit. Genus: *Prunus.* **2.** FOOD **FRUIT OF THE PLUM TREE** the round or oval smooth-skinned edible fruit of a plum tree, containing a flattened pit **3.** COLORS **DARK REDDISH-PURPLE** a dark reddish-purple color **4. SOMETHING CHOICE** something that is highly desirable or enviable, especially a job or contract (*informal*) ■ *adj.* **1. DESIRABLE** highly desirable or profitable (*informal*) ○ *a plum job* **2.** COLORS **DARK REDDISH-PURPLE** of a dark reddish-purple color [12thC. Alteration of Middle Low German and Middle Dutch *prūme* and Old High German *pfrūma,* ultimately, from Latin *prunum* (see PRUNE).]

plum·age /plóomij/ *n.* the feathers that cover a bird's body, considered collectively [14thC. Via Old French from, ultimately, Latin *pluma* "feather, plume" (see PLUME).]

plu·mate /plóo màyt/ *adj.* resembling, having, or producing feathers [Early 19thC. From Latin *plumatus* "feathered," from *pluma* "feather" (see PLUME).]

plumb /plum/ *n.* **1. WEIGHT ATTACHED TO A LINE** a weight, usually made of lead, attached to a line and used to find the depth of water or to verify a true vertical alignment **2. TRUE VERTICAL POSITION** a true vertical position or alignment ■ *adv.* **1. IN TRUE VERTICAL OR PERPENDICULAR POSITION** in perfect alignment or a true vertical position **2. EXACTLY** precisely or exactly (*informal*) ○ *plumb in the middle* **3. COMPLETELY** utterly or totally (*informal*) ○ *plumb lazy* ■ *adj.* **1. VERTICAL** in a true vertical alignment ○ *Hanging the striped wallpaper he made sure the stripes were plumb.* **2. TOTAL** utter or total (*informal*) ■ *vt.* **(plumbed, plumb·ing, plumbs) 1. FULLY COMPREHEND** to succeed in fully understanding something, especially something mysterious **2.** to experience something, especially something unpleasant, to an extreme degree ○ *had plumbed the depths of despair* **3. FIND THE DEPTH OR VERTICAL ALIGNMENT OF** to find the depth of water or a vertical alignment with a plumb **4. MAKE VERTICAL** to make something properly vertical **5. TO INSTALL PLUMBING** to equip with plumbing, seal pipes with lead, or work as a plumber [13thC. Via Old French *plomb* "lead weight" from Latin *plumbum* "lead" (source of English *plumber* and *aplomb*).]

plumb in *vt.* to attach a device such as a washing machine to a system of inlet and drainage pipes

plum·ba·go /plum báygō/ (*plural* **-gos**) *n.* **1.** PLANTS **FLOWERING PLANT** an evergreen Mediterranean or tropical plant of the leadwort family that has clusters of blue, white, or red flowers. Genus: *Plumbago.* **2.** MINERALS = **graphite** [Early 17thC. From Latin, "lead ore, plumbago," from *plumbum* "lead," translation of Greek *molubdaina* "lead ore," hence "flowering plant," from the flower's color.]

plumb bob *n.* the weight, usually a conical metal one, at the end of a plumb

plumb·er /plúmmər/ *n.* somebody who installs and repairs pipes and fixtures, especially for water, drainage, or heating systems in a building [14thC. Via Old French *plommier* "lead worker" from, ultimately, Latin *plumbum* "lead" (see PLUMB).The modern meaning developed because water pipes were originally made of lead.]

plumb·er's help·er *n.* = **plunger** *n.* 1

plumb·er's snake *n.* = **snake** *n.* 3

plum·bif·er·ous /plum bíffərəss/ *adj.* containing or yielding lead [Late 18thC. Coined from Latin *plumbum* "lead" (see PLUMB) + -FEROUS.]

plumb·ing /plúmming/ *n.* **1.** CONSTR **PLUMBER'S WORK** the work that a plumber does **2.** CONSTR **PIPES AND FIXTURES** the pipes and fixtures that carry or use water or gas in a building **3. USE OF A PLUMB** the use of a plumb to test depth or show a vertical alignment **4. DIGESTIVE, URINARY, AND REPRODUCTIVE SYSTEMS** the digestive, urinary, and reproductive tracts and organs of the body (*humorous informal*)

plum·bism /plúm bìzzəm/ *n.* long-term lead poisoning (*technical*) [Late 19thC. Formed from Latin *plumbum* "lead" (see PLUMB).]

plumb line *n.* a line to which a weight is attached to find the depth of water or to verify a true vertical alignment

plumb rule *n.* a plumb attached to a board, used to check how vertical something such as a wall is

plume /ploom/ *n.* **1. FEATHER** a feather, especially a large or ornamental one **2. FEATHERS USED AS A CREST** a feather or bunch of feathers used as a decoration, especially on a hat or helmet **3. COLUMN OF SOMETHING** a rising column of something, e.g., smoke, dust, or water **4.** BIOL **PART RESEMBLING A FEATHER** any plant part or formation that looks like a feather, e.g., the part of some seeds that allows them to be blown about by the wind **5. TOKEN OF HONOR** a prize, award decoration, or token of honor ■ *v.* **(plumed, plum·ing, plumes) 1.** *vt.* BIRDS **PREEN FEATHERS** to preen, smooth, or clean the feathers **2.** *vr.* **BE PROUD OF SOMETHING** to take pride in or congratulate yourself on something **3.** *vt.* **DECORATE WITH FEATHERS** to decorate something with feathers [14thC. Via Old French from Latin *pluma* "down, feather." Ultimately from an Indo-European base denoting "fleece, feather," which is also the ancestor of English *fleece*.] —**plumed** *adj.*

plume·let /plóomlət/ *n.* a little plume or tuft

Plum·mer /plúmmər/, **Christopher** (*b.* 1927) Canadian stage and movie actor. He won Tony Awards for his roles in *Cyrano* (1973) and *Barrymore* (1997). Full name **Arthur Christopher Orme Plummer**

plum·met /plúmmət/ *vi.* (**-met·ed, -met·ing, -mets**) **1. DROP DOWNWARD** to drop steeply and suddenly downward ○ *temperatures have plummeted* **2.** FIN **SUDDENLY FALL IN VALUE** to take a sudden unexpected drop in value or price **3. SUDDENLY BECOME PESSIMISTIC** to decline or drop suddenly, particularly from a state of optimism to one of pessimism ■ *n.* **1. SUDDEN DECLINE** a sudden sharp fall in value or amount **2.** CONSTR = **plumb bob** [14thC. Via Old French *plomet* "small lead ball" from, ultimately, Latin *plumbum* "lead" (see PLUMB).]

plum·my /plúmmee/ (**-mi·er, -mi·est**) *adj.* **1. LIKE PLUMS** resembling, full of, or tasting like plums **2. RICH AND RESONANT** with a voice or tone that is rich, resonant, and mellow **3. DESIRABLE** highly desirable or of superior quality (*informal*)

plu·mose /plóo mòss/ *adj.* = **plumate** [Mid-18thC. From Latin *plumosus*, from *pluma* "feather" (see PLUME).] —**plu·mose·ly** *adv.* —**plu·mos·i·ty** /ploo móssitee/ *n.*

plump[1] /plump/ *adj.* **1. SLIGHTLY OVERWEIGHT** rounded and somewhat overweight (*sometimes considered offensive*) **2. WELL-FLESHED** having a pleasing amount of flesh ○ *a plump chicken* **3. FILLED WITH SOMETHING** rounded and filled with something ○ *a plump cushion* ■ *vti.* (**plumped, plump·ing, plumps**) **FATTEN OR ROUND** to become or make something fatter, rounder, or softer ○ *plump up the pillows* [15thC. From Middle Dutch or Middle Low German *plomp* "blunt, thick."] —**plump·ly** *adv.* —**plump·ness** *n.*

plump[2] /plump/ *vti.* (**plumped, plump·ing, plumps**) **DROP ABRUPTLY OR HEAVILY** to fall or come down heavily or suddenly, or to cause somebody or something to do so ○ *plumped down into an armchair* ■ *n.* **ABRUPT FALL OR ITS SOUND** a heavy or abrupt fall, or its sound ■ *adv.* **1. HEAVILY** in a sudden or heavy way **2. DIRECTLY** directly or in a direct line **3. BLUNTLY** in a blunt and direct way ■ *adj.* **DIRECT** blunt, direct, and forceful [13thC. Origin uncertain: probably from Dutch *plompen* or Low German *plumpen* "to fall into water," an imitation of the sound.]

plum peach *n. Southern U.S.* a clingstone peach

WORD KEY: REGIONAL NOTE

This type of peach is also called *Indian peach, pickle peach,* and *press peach.* ***Plum peach*** is a South Midland term that covers the same territory occupied by *open peach* ("freestone peach"). Usage is strongest in the Eastern Gulf states, the upper sectors of Georgia, Alabama, and Mississippi, with equally strong incidence in Tennessee and Arkansas.

plump·er /plúmpər/ *n.* a pad worn by an actor between the teeth and the inside of the cheeks to make the face seem fatter

plum pud·ding *n.* a rich steamed pudding made from flour, suet, dried fruit, and spices that is often flavored with brandy or rum [*Plum* from the use of PLUM to mean "raisin"]

plum to·ma·to *n.* an elongated firm-textured tomato that is often used in cooking and is the usual variety used for canned tomatoes [*Plum* from its shape]

plu·mule /plóom yòol/ *n.* **1.** BOT **RUDIMENTARY SHOOT** the rudimentary primary shoot of a plant embryo **2.** BIRDS **YOUNG BIRD'S DOWN FEATHER** one of a young bird's soft down feathers [Early 18thC. From Latin *plumula* "small feather," from *pluma* "feather" (see PLUME).]

plum·y /plóomee/ (**-i·er, -i·est**) *adj.* **1. LIKE FEATHERS** like a feather or plume **2. COVERED WITH PLUMES** made of, covered with, or decorated with feathers or plumes

plun·der /plúndər/ *v.* (**-dered, -der·ing, -ders**) **1.** *vti.* **ROB A PLACE OR STEAL GOODS** to rob a place or the people living there or steal goods using violence and often causing damage, especially in wartime or during civil unrest ○ *gangs of looters plundering the electrical stores* **2.** *vt.* **ROB OR STEAL BY FRAUD** to rob a place or steal goods or money by fraudulent means ○ *a military government that had steadily plundered the country's wealth* **3.** *vt.* **GET BY SUPERIOR STRENGTH** to gain or acquire by superior strength or skill ○ *They plundered five goals in a one-sided game.* ■ *n.* **1. STOLEN GOODS** something stolen by force, especially during wartime or civil unrest **2. ROBBERY** the theft of goods by force or fraud [Mid-17thC. Via German *plündern* or Low German *plünderen* from, ultimately, Middle Low German *plunder* "household goods," of unknown origin.] —**plun·der·a·ble** *adj.* —**plun·der·er** *n.* —**plun·der·ous** *adj.*

plunge /plunj/ *v.* (**plunged, plung·ing, plung·es**) **1.** *vti.* **MOVE OR BE THROWN SUDDENLY** to move, rush, dive, or be thrown suddenly downward or forward ○ *plunged into the undergrowth and disappeared* **2.** *vt.* **PUT SUDDENLY IN AN UNPLEASANT CONDITION** to bring or force somebody or something suddenly into an unpleasant or undesirable situation **3.** *vt.* **THRUST QUICKLY OR FIRMLY** to put or push something firmly into something such as a liquid or container ○ *Drain the beans and plunge them into cold water.* **4.** *vi.* **BECOME INVOLVED ENTHUSIASTICALLY** to become involved in something with great enthusiasm ○ *She plunged into student life.* **5. EMBARK ON RECKLESSLY** to begin a course of action suddenly and in a reckless or impetuous way ○ *warned against plunging into full monetary union* **6.** *vi.* **GO DOWN SUDDENLY** to go or drop downward suddenly or steeply **7.** *vi.* **DROP SUDDENLY IN VALUE** to drop suddenly and unexpectedly in value or price ○ *Prices plunged.* **8.** *vi.* GAMBLING **GAMBLE RECKLESSLY** to gamble, speculate, or take risks in a reckless way (*informal*) ■ *n.* **1. LEAP INTO WATER** a dive or leap into water ○ *a headlong plunge into the sea* **2. SUDDEN SHARP FALL** a sudden sharp fall in value or amount ○ *a 38% plunge in PC sales* **3. PLACE TO SWIM** a place for swimming or diving, e.g., a swimming pool **4. SUDDEN RUSH** a sudden or violent rush ○ *The dog made a plunge for the open door.* **5. GAMBLE** a reckless gamble or speculation (*informal*) [14thC. Via Old French *plongier* from assumed Vulgar Latin *plumbicare* "to heave a sounding lead," from Latin *plumbum* "lead" (see PLUMB).] ◇ **take the plunge 1.** to commit suddenly to doing something new, difficult, or irrevocable **2.** to get married or decide to get married (*informal humorous*)

plunge pool *n.* a small deep swimming pool used for cooling the body

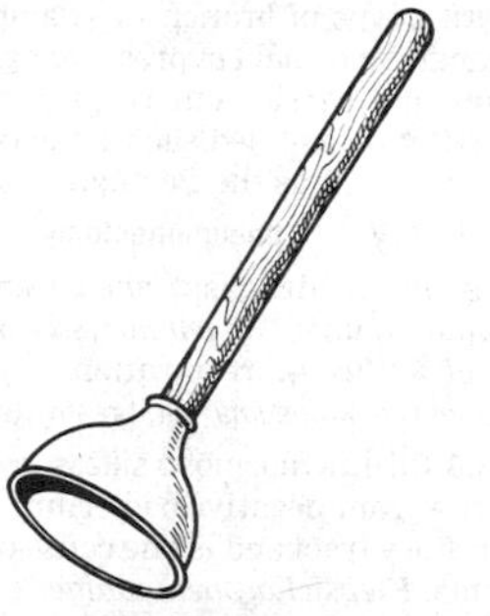

Plunger

plung·er /plúnjər/ *n.* **1.** CONSTR **TOOL FOR CLEARING DRAINS** a tool for clearing clogged drains consisting of a rubber suction cup attached to a long handle **2.** MECH ENG **THRUSTING MACHINE PART** a part of a machine that thrusts or drops downward, e.g., a piston **3. GAMBLER** somebody who gambles a lot (*informal*) [Early 17thC. The earliest meaning was "somebody who dives into water."]

plung·ing /plúnjing/ *adj.* in a direction or at an angle that plunges downward

plunk /plungk/, **plonk** /plongk/ *vti.* (**plunked, plunk·ing, plunks; plonked, plonking, plonks**) **1.** MUSIC **PLUCK STRINGS** to pluck the strings of a stringed instrument, especially in an inexpert or unexpressive way **2. DROP DOWN** to fall or cause something to drop heavily or suddenly ■ *n.* **1. TWANGING SOUND** a twanging sound, e.g., of a string on a stringed instrument being plucked **2. SUDDEN HEAVY FALL** the action or sound of a sudden heavy fall ○ *A stone hit the tin roof with a plunk.* **3. HARD BLOW** a hard blow (*informal*) ■ *adv.* **1. WITH A PLUNK** with a plunking sound or action **2. EXACTLY** precisely or exactly (*informal*) ○ *plunk in the middle* [Early 19thC. An imitation of the sound.]

plu·per·fect /ploo púrfəkt/ *adj., n.* GRAM = **past perfect** ■ *adj.* **UTTERLY PERFECT** even better than perfect ○ *a pluperfect talent* [15thC. From Latin *plus quam perfectum* "more than perfect."]

plu·ral /plóorəl/ *adj.* **1.** GRAM **REFERRING TO MORE THAN ONE** having a grammatical form that refers to more than one person or thing **2. CONCERNING MORE THAN ONE** concerning, involving, or made up of more than one, or more than one kind of, person or thing ■ *n.* GRAM **1. PLURAL CATEGORY** the plural number category **2. PLURAL FORM OF A WORD** the plural form of a word ○ *What's the plural of mouse in the computer sense?* [14thC. Via Old French from Latin *pluralis*, from *plus* "more."] —**plu·ral·ly** *adv.*

plu·ral·ism /plóorə lìzzəm/ *n.* **1. SOCIETY WITH DIFFERENT INTERNAL GROUPS** the existence of groups with different ethnic, religious, or political backgrounds within one society **2.** SOCIOL **SOCIAL POLICY AND THEORY** a policy or theory that minority groups within a society should maintain cultural differences but share overall political and economic power **3.** CHR **HOLDING OF MULTIPLE OFFICES** the holding of more than one office or position by an individual, especially in a church **4.** PHILOS **THEORY OF VARIED BEING OR SUBSTANCE** the philosophical theory that reality is made up of many kinds of being or substance **5. STATE OF BEING PLURAL** state or condition of being plural —**plu·ral·ist** *n.* —**plu·ral·is·tic** /plòorə lístik/ *adj.* —**plu·ral·is·ti·cal·ly** /-lístikəlee/ *adv.*

plu·ral·i·ty /ploo rállətee/ (*plural* **-ties**) *n.* **1.** GRAM **CONDITION OF BEING PLURAL** the condition of being plural or numerous **2. GREAT NUMBER OR PART OF SOMETHING** a great number or part of something, particularly when this represents more than half of the whole **3.** POL **MARGIN GAINED BY AN ELECTION CANDIDATE** the number of votes an election winner gets, or the number exceeding the nearest rival, when no one has more than fifty percent of the total votes cast **4.** CHR = **pluralism** *n.* **3**

plu·ral·ize /plóorə lìz/ (**-ized, -iz·ing, -iz·es**) *vti.* to make something plural or to become plural —**plu·ral·i·za·tion** /plòorəlizáysh'n/ *n.* —**plu·ral·iz·er** /plóorə lìzər/ *n.*

plu·ral mar·riage *n.* = **polygamy** *n.* **1**

plus /pluss/ *prep.* **1. USED FOR ADDING** used to show that one number or amount is added to another ○ *The flight cost $180, plus $20 airport tax.* **2. AND ALSO** together with (*informal*) ○ *Exports have been affected by transport problems plus the effect of a strong dollar.* ■ *adj.* **1.** ARITH **INVOLVING ADDITION** showing or involving addition **2.** MATH **ON POSITIVE SIDE** with a figure or value on the positive side of a scale or axis (*often written as "+"*) **3.** ELEC ENG **ON THE ELECTRICAL POSITIVE SIDE** on or involving the positive side of an electrical circuit **4. ADVANTAGEOUS** favorable, desirable, or advantageous ○ *one of its plus points* **5. SOMEWHAT MORE THAN STATED GRADE** somewhat higher than a stated grade for academic work (*often written as "+"*) **6.** FUNGI **REPRODUCING ONLY WITH OPPOSITE STRAIN** reproducing as an alga or fungus only with an opposite strain ■ *n.* (*plural* **plus·es** *or* **plus·ses**) **1.** MATH = **plus sign 2. POSITIVE QUANTITY** a positive quantity **3. ADVANTAGEOUS FACTOR** something beneficial or advantageous (*informal*) ○ *Having her in the team is a real plus.* **4. SURPLUS** a surplus ■ *conj.* **AND ALSO** and also or furthermore (*informal*) ○ *I'm too busy to come, plus I'm short of cash.* [Mid-16thC. From Latin *plus* "more."]

plus fours *npl.* baggy pants gathered and fastened just below the knee, worn mainly for sports or hunting ○ *golfers in their plus fours* [Because they were four inches longer in the leg than standard knickerbockers]

plush /plush/ *n.* TEXTILES **SOFT FABRIC** a rich smooth fabric with a long soft nap ■ *adj.* **plush, plush·y LUXURIOUS** luxurious, expensive, or lavish (*informal*) [Late 16thC. Via French *pluche* from, ultimately, assumed Vulgar Latin *piluccare* "to pluck" (see PLUCK); because loops of the woven fabric must be cut ("plucked") in making plush.]

plus sign *n.* the symbol "+," used to show addition or a positive quantity

Plu·tarch /ploo taark/ (46–120) Greek historian, biographer, and philosopher. His *Parallel Lives* (1st century) was used by Shakespeare as a source for his history plays.

Plu·to /plóotō/ *n.* **1. ROMAN GOD OF THE UNDERWORLD** in Roman mythology, the god of the underworld and husband of Proserpine. He was the god of the dead and also of riches, since precious metals and crops were believed to come from his underground realm. Greek equivalent **Hades 2.** ASTRON **SMALLEST, MOST DISTANT PLANET** the planet in the solar system that is the smallest in diameter and is, on average, the furthest away from the Sun. It was discovered in 1930, has one moon (**Charon**), and an equatorial radius 0.18 times that of the Earth. [Via Latin from Greek *Ploutōn*, from *ploutos* "wealth"] —**Plu·to·ni·an** /ploo tṓnee ən/ *adj.*

plu·toc·ra·cy /ploo tókrəssee/ (*plural* **-cies**) *n.* **1. RULE BY THE WEALTHY** the rule of a society by its wealthiest people **2. SOCIETY RULED BY THE WEALTHY** a society that is ruled by its wealthiest members **3. WEALTHY RULING CLASS** any wealthy social class that controls or greatly influences the government of a society [Mid-17thC. From Greek *ploutokratia*, from *ploutos* "wealth."] —**plu·to·crat** /plóotə kràt/ *adv.* —**plu·to·cra·tic** /plootə kráttik/ *adj.* —**plu·to·crat·i·cal·ly** /-kráttiklee/ *adv.*

plu·ton /ploo tòn/ *n.* a mass of intrusive igneous rock that solidified underground by the crystallization of magma [Mid-20thC. From German, back-formation from *plutonisch* "plutonic," from Latin *Pluto* (see PLUTO).] —**plu·ton·ic** /ploo tónnik/ *adj.*

plu·to·ni·um /ploo tónee əm/ *n.* a highly toxic silvery radioactive metallic chemical element, found in small amounts in uranium ores. The isotope plutonium-239 is used to produce atomic energy and in nuclear weapons. Symbol **Pu** [Mid-20thC. Named for the planet PLUTO, because it follows uranium and neptunium in the periodic table.]

plu·vi·al /plóovee əl/ *adj.* **1. RELATING TO RAIN** concerning, involving, or caused by rain **2. RAINY** involving a lot of rain ■ *n.* **WET PERIOD** a period of increased rainfall [Mid-17thC. From Latin *pluvialis*, from *pluvia* "rain," from *pluere* "to rain" (source of English *plover*).]

plu·vi·om·e·ter /plóovee ómmətər/ *n.* = **rain gauge** [Late 18thC. Coined from Latin *pluvia* "rain" (see PLUVIAL) + -METER.] —**plu·vi·o·met·ric** /plóovee ə méttrik/ *adj.* —**plu·vi·o·met·ri·cal·ly** /-méttrikəlee/ *adv.* —**plu·vi·om·e·try** /plóovee ómmətree/ *n.*

plu·vi·ous /plóovee əss/, **plu·vi·ose** /plóovee ōss/ *adj.* concerning, involving, or typical of rain, especially heavy rainfall [15thC. Via Old French from Latin *pluviosus*, from *pluvia* "rain" (see PLUVIAL).]

ply[1] /plī/ (**plied** /plīd/, **plied, ply·ing, plies** /plīz/) *v.* **1.** *vti.* **WORK HARD AT SOMETHING** to work at a trade or occupation, especially with diligence **2.** *vt.* **USE SOMETHING DILIGENTLY** to use something such as a tool or weapon in a diligent or skillful way ○ *the dexterity with which she plied her needle* **3.** *vt.* COMM **OFFER SOMETHING FOR SALE** to offer goods or services for sale, especially regularly or as an occupation **4.** *vt.* **SUPPLY SOMEBODY WITH SOMETHING** to keep supplying somebody with something, especially in an insistent way ○ *kept plying us with offers of food* **5.** *vt.* **SUBJECT TO URGENTLY AND INSISTENTLY** to keep subjecting somebody to something in an urgent and insistent way ○ *we were plied with questions* **6.** *vti.* **TRAVEL A ROUTE REGULARLY** to travel a route regularly, especially on water **7.** *vi.* SAILING **SAIL AGAINST THE WIND** to sail a boat on a zigzag course against the wind [14thC. Shortening of APPLY.]

ply[2] /plī/ *n.* (*plural* **plies**) (*often used in combination*) **1. TWISTED STRAND** a twisted single strand, especially in a yarn or rope **2. THIN LAYER OF SOMETHING** a layer, sheet, or thickness of something such as wood or a tire ■ *vti.* (**plied, ply·ing, plies**) **TWIST TOGETHER** to twist or fold things together [14thC. From Old French *pli*, from *plier* "to fold," from Latin *plicare*. Ultimately, from an Indo-European word that is also the ancestor of English *plait*.]

Plym·outh /plímməth/ town in southeastern Massachusetts, on Plymouth Bay, south of Duxbury. It was settled by the Pilgrims in 1620. Population: 48,329 (1996).

Plym·outh Rock *n.* a U.S. breed of domestic hen with white or gray barred plumage, raised for its eggs and meat

ply·wood /plī wòod/ *n.* a type of board made by gluing and compressing thin layers of wood together with the grain of each layer at right angles to the layer next to it [Early 20thC. *Ply* from PLY[2].]

pm, PM, p.m., P.M. **1.** between twelve noon and midnight. Abbr of **post meridiem** ■ *abbr.* **2.** phase modulation **3.** postmortem

Pm *symbol.* promethium

PM, P.M. *abbr.* **1.** Prime Minister **2.** Postmaster **3.** Provost Marshal **4.** Past Master (*of a fraternity*)

P.M.G. *abbr.* **1.** Postmaster General **2.** Provost Marshal General **3.** Paymaster General

PMS *abbr.* premenstrual syndrome

PMT *abbr. U.K.* premenstrual tension

PN, P/N, p.n. *abbr.* promissory note

PNdB *abbr.* perceived noise decibel

pneum- *prefix.* = **pneumo-** (*used before vowels*)

pneu·ma /nóomə/ *n.* in Stoicism, the vital spirit or soul [Late 19thC. From Greek, literally "breath, spirit," from *pnein* "to breathe." Ultimately, from an Indo-European word that is also the ancestor of English *sneeze* and *snort*.]

pneu·mat·ic /noo máttik/ *adj.* **1. USING COMPRESSED AIR** operated by compressed air in a tool or machine **2. FILLED WITH AIR** filled with air, especially compressed air **3.** PHYS **INVOLVING COMPRESSED GASES** relating to, involving, operated by, or typical of the pressure of compressed gases, especially air pressure or compressed air **4. OF GASES OR WIND** concerning, involving, or typical of air, gases, or wind **5.** RELIG **OF THE SOUL** concerning or involving the soul or spirit **6.** BIRDS **WITH AIR-FILLED CAVITIES IN THE BONES** used to describe birds that have air-filled cavities in the bones **7. FULL-BREASTED** having large breasts (*informal*) (*offensive in some contexts*) [Mid-17thC. Via French and Latin from Greek *pneumatikos*, from *pneuma* (see PNEUMA).] —**pneu·mat·i·cal·ly** *adv.*

pneu·mat·ics /noo máttiks/ *n.* PHYS the branch of physics dealing with the mechanical properties of air and other gases (*takes a singular verb*)

pneu·mat·ic tube *n.* a tube through which letters and packets are propelled by compressed air

pneumato- *prefix.* **1.** air, gas, vapor ○ *pneumatolysis* **2.** respiration, breathing ○ *pneumatometer* **3.** spirits, spiritual ○ *pneumatology* [Formed from Greek *pneumat-*, the stem of *pneuma* (see PNEUMA)]

pneu·ma·tol·o·gy /nòomə tólləjee/ *n.* **1. THEOLOGY OF THE HOLY SPIRIT** the branch of Christian theology that deals with the Holy Spirit **2. STUDY OF SPIRITS** the study of spirits or spiritual beings —**pneu·ma·to·log·i·cal** /nòomətə lójjik'l/ *adj.* —**pneu·ma·tol·o·gist** /nòomə tólləjist/ *n.*

pneu·ma·tol·y·sis /nòomə tólləssiss/ *n.* the alteration caused in rocks by hot gases escaping from solidifying magma —**pneu·ma·to·lyt·ic** /nòomətə líttik/ *adj.*

pneu·mat·o·phore /noo máttə fàwr/ *n.* **1.** BOT **SPECIALIZED PLANT BRANCH** a type of branch in swamp plants such as the mangrove or bald cypress that grows upward from roots and carries out respiration **2.** BIOL **SAC ACTING AS A FLOAT** a gas-filled sac that acts as a float in coelenterates such as the Portuguese man-of-war

pneu·mec·to·my *n.* = **pneumonectomy**

pneumo- *prefix.* **1.** air, gas ○ *pneumoencephalogram* **2.** lung, pulmonary ○ *pneumocystis* **3.** pneumonia ○ *pneumobacillus* **4.** respiration ○ *pneumograph* [Formed from Greek *pneuma* "air, breath" (see PNEUMA)]

pneu·mo·ba·cil·lus /nòomōbə sílləss, nyòo-/ (*plural* **-li** /-lī/) *n.* BIOL a gram-negative bacterium that occurs in the respiratory tract and is one cause of pneumonia. Latin name: *Klebsiella pneumoniae.*

pneu·mo·coc·cus /nòomə kókəss, nyòo-/ (*plural* **-ci** /-kók sī, -kó kī/) *n.* BIOL a gram-positive bacterium that occurs in the respiratory tract and is one cause of pneumonia. Latin name: *Streptococcus pneumoniae.* —**pneu·mo·coc·cal** /-kók'l/ *adj.*

pneu·mo·cys·tis /nòomə sístiss, nyòo-/ *n.* a form of pneumonia that mainly affects people with weakened immune systems. It is caused by the microorganism *Pneumocystis carinii.*

pneu·mo·nec·to·my /nòomə néktəmee, nyòo-/ (*plural* **-mies**), **pneu·mec·to·my** /noo méktəmee/ (*plural* **-mies**) *n.* the surgical removal of a lung [Late 19thC. Coined from Greek *pneumōn* "lung" (see PNEUMONIA) +-ECTOMY.]

pneu·mo·nia /noo mṓnee ə, nyoo-/ *n.* an inflammation of one or both lungs, usually caused by infection from a bacterium or virus or, less commonly, by a chemical or physical irritant [Early 17thC. Via modern Latin from, ultimately, Greek *pneumōn* "lung," alteration (influenced by *pneuma* "breath") of *pleumōn*.]

pneu·mon·ic /noo mónnik, nyoo-/ *adj.* **1. OF THE LUNGS** relating to or affecting the lungs **2. OF PNEUMONIA** relating to, involving, or affected by pneumonia [Late 17thC. Via French from, ultimately, Greek *pneumōn* "lung" (see PNEUMONIA).]

pneu·mo·ni·tis /nòomə nítiss, nyòo-/ *n.* any inflammation of the air sacs in the lungs, usually caused by a virus [Early 19thC. Via modern Latin from Greek *pneumōn* "lung" (see PNEUMONIA).]

pneu·mon·o·co·ni·o·sis /nòomənə kōni ṓssiss/ *n.* = **pneumoconiosis** [Mid-19thC. Formed from Greek *pneumōn* "lung" + *konis* "dust."]

pneu·mo·tho·rax /nòomə tháw ràks, nyòo-/ *n.* the presence of air or gas in a pleural cavity surrounding the lungs, causing pain and difficulty in breathing. Pneumothorax can occur spontaneously because of accidental rupture or perforation of the pleura, and in the past it was also a deliberate medical procedure in the treatment of tuberculosis.

PNG *abbr.* Papua New Guinea

po, p.o. *abbr.* BASEBALL putout

Po[1] *symbol.* polonium

Po[2] /pō/ the longest river in Italy. It rises in the Alps near Italy's northwestern border and flows into the Adriatic Sea. Length: 417 mi./670 km.

PO, P.O. *abbr.* **1.** Post Office **2. PO, P.O., p.o.** postal order **3.** purchase order **4.** Pilot Officer **5.** Petty Officer

p.o. *abbr.* **p.o., po** BASEBALL putout

poach[1] /pōch/ (**poached, poach·ing, poach·es**) *v.* **1.** *vti.* **CATCH GAME ILLEGALLY** to catch wild animals or fish illegally on public land or while trespassing on private land **2.** *vti.* **ENCROACH ON SOMETHING** to encroach on other people's rights, territory, or sphere of operation in order to appropriate or remove somebody or something ○ *The rival company's sales force was poaching on our turf.* **3.** *vti.* RACKET GAMES **PLAY SOMEBODY ELSE'S SHOT** to play a shot that properly should be handled by a partner in badminton, tennis, squash, or handball **4.** *vti.* **MAKE GROUND MUDDY** to become muddy or make ground muddy by trampling it **5.** *vi.* **SINK INTO MUD** to sink into soft earth or mud while walking across it [Early 17thC. From Old French *pocher* "to trample, trespass," origin uncertain: probably of Germanic origin.] —**poach·a·ble** *adj.*

poach[2] /pōch/ (**poached, poach·ing, poach·es**) *vt.* to cook something by simmering it in or over water or another liquid [15thC. From Old French *pochier*, originally "to enclose in a bag," from *poche* "bag" (see POCKET).]

poach·er[1] /pṓchər/ *n.* somebody who hunts or fishes illegally, usually while trespassing on other people's property

poach·er[2] /pṓchər/ *n.* a pan for poaching eggs that has a tightly fitting lid and small metal cups

POB *abbr.* Post Office Box

PO Box *abbr.* post office box

po'boy /pṓ bòy/ *n. Southern U.S.* FOOD a poor boy sandwich [Contraction]

Pocahontas: Posthumous portrait (1666)

Po·ca·hon·tas /pòkə hóntəss/ (1595?–1617?) Powhatan princess. According to legend she saved the life of colonist John Smith (1608). Born **Matoaka**

Po·ca·tel·lo /pṑkə téllō/ city in southeastern Idaho, east of American Falls Reservoir and southwest of Idaho Falls. Population: 51,344 (1996).

po·chard /pṓchərd/ *n.* a heavy-bodied diving duck of coastal waters of Europe and Asia that has a reddish head and a blue and black bill. Subfamily: Aythyini. [Mid-16thC. Origin unknown.]

pock /pok/ *n.* **1.** = **pockmark** *n.* 1 **2. SMALL HOLE** a small indentation, pit, or hole ■ *vt.* (**pocked, pock·ing, pocks**) **COVER WITH DISFIGURING MARKS** to cover with pockmarks or disfiguring marks (*often passive*) [Old English *poc*]

pock·et /pókət/ *n.* **1. SMALL POUCH IN CLOTHES** a shaped piece of material forming part of an item of clothing and used to hold small items, e.g., inside pants or on the outside of a shirt **2. SMALL FITTED POUCH** a small fitted pouch, e.g., a pouch-shaped compartment on the inside of a bag ○ *The suitcase has several inside pockets.* **3. SMALL POUCH** any small pouch, bag, or purse **4. PERSONAL MONEY** somebody's personal financial resources ○ *a vacation paid for out of his own pocket*

5. SMALL DIFFERENTIATED AREA a small area differentiated from neighboring areas by some feature ○ *pockets of wealth* **6. CAVITY** any type of cavity or opening **7.** GEOL **ORE IN A CAVITY** the quantity of petroleum, natural gas, or mineral found in an underground cavity, or the cavity that contains this substance **8.** SPORTS **POSITION IN A RACE** a position in a race in which a competitor is blocked by others **9.** CUE GAMES **POUCH ON A PLAYING TABLE** any of the pouches or nets at the corners and sides of a billiard or pool table ○ *He sank the red in the side pocket.* **10.** ZOOL **SAC ON AN ANIMAL** any pouch-shaped sac on an animal's body **11.** FOOTBALL **AREA FOR A QUARTERBACK TO THROW** in football, a defended area behind the offensive line in which a quarterback can stand to throw the ball **12.** BOWLING **SPACE SEPARATING 2 PINS** in bowling, a space between two pins, especially the head pin and one adjacent to it **13.** AIR **AIR POCKET** an air pocket **14. CENTER OF A BASEBALL GLOVE** depression in the center of a baseball glove where the ball is caught ■ *vt.* **(-et·ed, -et·ing, -ets) 1. PUT IN A POCKET** to put something into a pocket ○ *She pocketed the change.* **2. TAKE SOMETHING DISHONESTLY** to appropriate something, often dishonestly ○ *They buy tickets cheaply, sell them for high prices, and pocket the difference.* **3.** CUE GAMES **HIT A BALL INTO A POCKET** to hit a ball into one of the pockets on a billiard or pool table ○ *pocket the black* **4. PUT UP WITH SOMETHING** to tolerate something unpleasant, especially an insult, without protesting or retaliating **5. SUPPRESS FEELINGS** to hide or suppress feelings **6. ENCLOSE OR SURROUND** to enclose or hem in somebody or something **7.** POL **RETAIN A PIECE OF LEGISLATION** to retain a legislative bill without signing it, especially as a President, in order to stop it becoming approved by Congress ■ *adj.* **1. SMALL ENOUGH TO CARRY IN THE POCKET** designed for carrying in a pocket ○ *a pocket flashlight* **2. SMALL** small, especially smaller than something larger of the same type ○ *a pocket trumpet* **3. CONTAINED** isolated and contained in small areas [15thC. From Anglo-Norman *pokete*, literally "small bag," from *poke* "bag."] —**pock·et·a·bil·i·ty** /pòkətə bíllətee/ *n.* —**pock·et·a·ble** /pókətəb'l/ *adj.* ◇ **have deep pockets** to have large financial resources ○ *a price-cutting war which will be won by whoever has the deepest pockets* ◇ **in pocket** making a profit from something ◇ **in somebody's pocket 1.** fully under somebody's control **2.** almost certain to be won by somebody ○ *We thought she had the race in her pocket.* ◇ **line your pocket(s)** to profit at the expense of others ◇ **out of pocket** having lost money on something

pock·et bat·tle·ship *n.* a small but powerful and heavily armed battleship, especially one built by Germany in the 1930s to conform to limitations that were placed by treaty on size and armament

pock·et bil·liards *n.* a form of billiards played with a cue ball and 15 balls on a felt-covered table with six pockets (*used with a singular or plural verb*)

pock·et·book /pókət bòòk/ *n.* **1. SMALL CASE CARRIED IN THE POCKET** a small case or folder for money and documents, suitable for carrying in a pocket **2. PURSE** a purse or handbag **3. SOMEBODY'S FINANCES** somebody's financial resources **4. SMALL BOOK** a book small enough to be carried in a pocket

pock·et bor·ough *n.* POL a political constituency in Britain before the Reform Act of 1832, whose representative in Parliament was determined by one landowner or landowning family [*Pocket* from the idea that the landowner had the borough "in his pocket"]

pock·et cal·cu·la·tor *n.* a calculator small enough to be carried in a pocket

pock·et e·di·tion *n.* = **pocketbook** *n.* 4

pock·et·ful /pókət fòòl/ *n.* **1. AMOUNT IN A POCKET** the amount of something that would fit in a pocket **2. A LARGE AMOUNT** a large amount of something, especially money (*informal*)

pock·et go·pher *n.* = **gopher**

pock·et·knife /pókət nīf/ (*plural* **-knives** /-nīvz/) *n.* a small knife with one or more blades that fold away into the handle

pock·et mon·ey *n.* a small amount of money that somebody carries for making minor purchases or to cover incidental expenses

pock·et mouse *n.* a small nocturnal rodent of the deserts of the western United States and Mexico, with long hind legs, a long tail, and fur-lined cheek pouches for carrying food. Genus: *Perognathus.*

pock·et park *n.* a small park, usually located in an urban area

pock·et-sized, **pock·et-size** *adj.* **1. SMALL ENOUGH FOR THE POCKET** small enough or almost small enough to be carried in a pocket **2. SMALL** very small compared to things of the same type

pock·et ve·to *n.* **1. INDIRECT PRESIDENTIAL VETO** a U.S. presidential failure to return a bill passed by Congress during its last days in session, to prevent its being enacted **2. INDIRECT VETO BY A STATE GOVERNOR** the holding of a bill by a state governor or other executive toward the end of a legislative session to prevent its enactment [From the notion of the executive's holding the bill in a coat pocket]

pock·mark /pók maark/ *n.* (*often used in the plural*) **1.** MED **SCAR ON THE SKIN** a scar on the skin, especially one left by smallpox, chickenpox, or acne **2. SMALL HOLLOW MARK** a small hollow mark disfiguring a surface ■ *vt.* **(-marked, -mark·ing, -marks) 1.** MED **COVER THE SKIN WITH POCKMARKS** to disfigure the skin with pockmarks **2. MAKE POCKMARKS IN SOMETHING** to make many small indentations or marks in the surface of something

po·co /pṓkō/ *adv.* a little or slightly (*used in musical directions*) [Early 18thC. From Italian, "little."]

po·co a po·co *adv.* little by little (*used in musical directions*) [From Italian, "little by little"]

po·co·cu·ran·te /pṑkō kòò rántee, -raantee/ *adj.* **APATHETIC** uninterested, indifferent, or nonchalantly detached (*literary*) ■ *n.* **APATHETIC PERSON** somebody who does not care about something or remains unworried and indifferent (*literary*) [Mid-18thC. From Italian, from *poco* "little" + *curare* "to care."] —**po·co·cu·ran·te·ism** *n.* —**po·co·cu·ran·tism** *n.*

Po·co·no Moun·tains /pṓkə nō-/ range of forested mountains in northeastern Pennsylvania, reaching about 2,100 ft./640 m

po·co·sin /pə kṓssin/ *n.* *S Atlantic U.S.* a swamp in upland coastal regions of the southeastern United States, characterized by waterlogged soil and dense evergreen vegetation [Mid-17thC. Origin uncertain: probably from Virginia Algonquian *poquosin.*]

pod[1] /pod/ *n.* **1.** BOT **SEED CASE** the long narrow outer case holding the seeds of a plant such as the pea, bean, or vanilla **2.** SPACE TECH **DETACHABLE COMPARTMENT OF A SPACECRAFT** a specialized detachable compartment on a spacecraft, usually for carrying personnel or instruments **3.** AEROSP, NAVY **STREAMLINED HOUSING FOR EQUIPMENT** a streamlined housing attached to the wing or fuselage of an aircraft, or to the hull of a submarine, to carry fuel, an engine, weaponry, or other equipment **4.** ZOOL **PROTECTIVE EGG CASE** a protective case surrounding the eggs of some fishes and insects, e.g., the grasshopper ■ *v.* **(pod·ded, pod·ding, pods) 1.** *vt.* **SHELL PEAS** to strip peas out of their pod so that they can be eaten or cooked **2.** *vi.* **PRODUCE PODS** to produce fruit in the form of pods **3.** *vi.* **SWELL LIKE A POD** to swell out, as a pod does [Late 17thC. Origin unknown.]

pod[2] /pod/ *n.* ZOOL a small group of marine animals, especially seals, whales, or dolphins [Mid-19thC. Origin unknown.]

pod[3] /pod/ *n.* **1. SOCKET FOR A BORING-TOOL BIT** a socket holding the bit in a boring tool **2. CHANNEL IN THE BARREL OF A BORING TOOL** a lengthwise channel in the barrel of a boring tool [Late 16thC. Origin unknown.]

PO'd, **p.o.'d** *adj.* quite annoyed (*slang*) [Shortening of pissed off]

POD *abbr.* Post Office Department

-pod *suffix.* foot, part like a foot ○ *stomatopod* [From Greek *-pod*, the stem of *pous*. Ultimately from the Indo-European word for "foot," which is also the ancestor of English *foot, podium,* and *pedestrian.*] —**-podous** *suffix.*

po·dag·ra /pə dággrə/ *n.* gout in the foot or the big toe [13thC. Via Latin from Greek, literally "foot-trap," from *pod-* (the stem of *pous* "foot") + *agra* "trap."] —**po·dag·ral** *adj.* —**po·dag·ric** *adj.* —**po·dag·rous** *adj.*

Pod·bor·ski /pod báwrskee/, **Steve** (*b.* 1957) Canadian skier. He won seven World Cup events in downhill skiing between 1979 and 1982.

-pode *suffix.* = **-pod**

po·des·ta /pō déstə, pōdə staa/ *n.* HIST formerly, a chief magistrate or governor of an Italian town, especially during the Middle Ages and Renaissance [Mid-16thC. Via Italian from Latin *potestas* "power," from *potis* "powerful." Ultimately from an Indo-European word that is also the ancestor of English *potent* and *despot.*]

Popperfoto

Steve Podborski

Pod·gor·i·ca /pòdgo reétsə/ capital city of Montenegro, Federal Republic of Yugoslavia, situated about 12 mi./19 km north of Lake Shkoder. Population: 118,059 (1991).

po·di·a plural of **podium**

po·di·a·try /pə dī ətree/ *n.* the branch of medicine concerned with the treatment and care of the feet [Early 20thC. Coined from Greek *pod-*, the stem of *pous* "foot" + -IATRY.] —**po·di·at·ric** /pōdee áttrik/ *adj.* —**po·di·a·trist** /pə dī ətrist/ *n.*

po·di·um /pṓdee əm/ (*plural* **-ums** *or* **-a** /-ə/) *n.* **1. SMALL RAISED PLATFORM** a small raised platform that the conductor of an orchestra, a lecturer, or somebody giving a speech can stand on **2. SLOPING DESK ON A STAND** a sloping board on a stand for a speaker to rest his or her notes on **3.** ARCHIT **FOUNDATION WALL** a low wall forming a foundation or base, e.g., for a colonnade **4.** ARCHIT **WALL AROUND AN AMPHITHEATER'S ARENA** a low wall encircling the arena of an ancient amphitheater [Mid-18thC. Via Latin from Greek *podion*, literally "small foot," from *pous* "foot."]

-podium *suffix.* foot, part like a foot ○ *pseudopodium* [Via modern Latin from Greek *podion* (see PODIUM)]

pod·o·phyl·lin /pòddə fíllin/, **pod·o·phyl·lin res·in** *n.* a greenish or brownish bitter resin obtained from the root of the May apple, used medicinally to remove warts [Mid-19thC. Formed from modern Latin *Podophyllum*, genus name of the May apple, from the Greek stem *pod-* "foot" + *phullon* "leaf," so called because of the shape of its leaves.]

pod·sol *n.* = **podzol**

pod·sol·i·za·tion *n.* = **podzolization**

Po·dunk /pṓ dùngk/ *n.* a small, remote, and unimportant place (*informal*) ○ *She came from some podunk town in the Midwest.* [Mid-19thC. From a New England place name, originally the name of an Algonquian people that lived near the Podunk River.]

pod·zol /pód zàwl/, **pod·sol** /pód sàwl/ *n.* a basically infertile type of soil that forms in cool moist climates, usually under coniferous or mixed forests. The topsoil consists of leached clay under a layer of organic material. [Early 20thC. From Russian, from *pod-* "under" + *zol* "ash."] —**pod·zol·ic** /pod zóllik/ *adj.*

pod·zol·i·za·tion /pòd zolli záysh'n/, **pod·sol·i·za·tion** /-solli-/ *n.* the process whereby minerals are leached from the upper into the lower layers of a soil, leaving the topsoil acidic and infertile and forming a podzol —**pod·zol·ize** /pódzə līz/ *vti.*

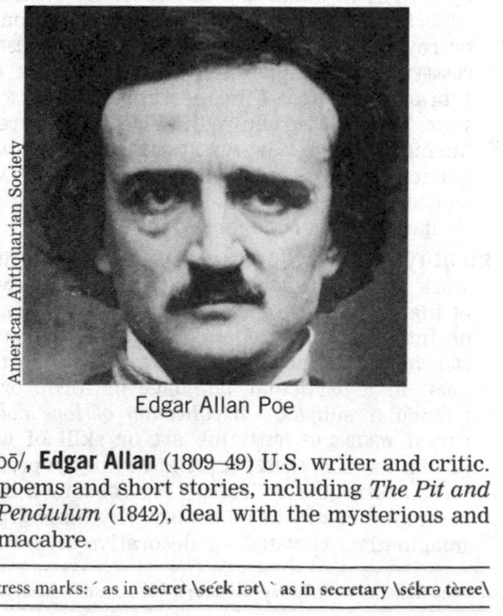

American Antiquarian Society

Edgar Allan Poe

Poe /pō/, **Edgar Allan** (1809–49) U.S. writer and critic. His poems and short stories, including *The Pit and the Pendulum* (1842), deal with the mysterious and the macabre.

POE, P.O.E. *abbr.* port of entry

po·em /pṓ əm/ *n.* **1.** POETRY **PIECE WRITTEN IN VERSE** a complete and self-contained piece of writing in verse that is set out in lines of a particular length and uses rhythm, imagery, and often rhyme to achieve its effect **2. WRITING WITH POETIC EFFECT** a piece of writing that is not in verse but that has the imaginative, rhythmic, or metaphorical qualities and the intensity usually associated with a poem **3. BEAUTIFUL OR DELIGHTFUL THING** something particularly lovely, beautiful, or delightful [15thC. Via French *poème* from, ultimately, Greek *poiēma*, literally "making," from *poiein* "to make."]

po·e·sy /pṓ əzee, pṓ əssee/ *n.* **1. POETRY** poetry or poetic compositions in general, or a particular piece of poetry (*archaic or literary*) **2. WRITING OF POETRY** the art or skill of writing poetry (*archaic*) [14thC. Via French *poésie*, from, ultimately, Greek *poiēsis*, literally "making" (see -POIESIS).]

po·et /pṓ ət/ *n.* **1.** POETRY **SOMEBODY WHO WRITES POEMS** somebody who writes poems, especially a regular and recognized writer of poems **2. SOMEBODY IMAGINATIVE OR CREATIVE** somebody who is very imaginative and creative or who possesses great skill and artistry and is able to produce beautiful things [13thC. Via French *poète* and Latin *poeta* from Greek *poiētēs* "maker, author," from *poiein* "to make."]

poet. *abbr.* **1.** poetic **2.** poetical **3.** poetry

po·et·as·ter /pṓ ə tàstər/ *n.* somebody who writes bad poetry [Late 16thC. From modern Latin, formed from Latin *poeta* (see POET).]

po·et·ic /pō éttik/, **po·et·i·cal** /-ik'l/ *adj.* **1.** POETRY **RELATING TO POETRY** relating to, typical of, or in the form of poetry **2. RESEMBLING POETRY** having qualities usually associated with poetry, especially in being gracefully expressive, romantically beautiful, or elevated and uplifting **3. SENSITIVE OR INSIGHTFUL** characteristic of a poet, especially in possessing unusual sensitivity or insight or in being able to express things in a beautiful or romantic way —**po·et·i·cal·ly** *adv.*

po·et·i·cal /pō éttik'l/ *adj.* **1.** = **poetic 2. EXCESSIVELY POETIC** inappropriately, exaggeratedly, or sentimentally poetic —**po·et·i·cal·i·ty** /pō ètti kállətee/ *n.* —**po·et·i·cal·ness** /pō éttik'lnəss/ *n.* —**po·et·i·cal·ly** /-éttikəlee/ *adv.*

po·et·i·cize /pō étti sīz/ (**-cized, -ciz·ing, -ciz·es**), **po·et·ize** /pṓ ə tīz/ (**-ized, -iz·ing, -iz·es**) *vti.* to express or describe something in a poetic style or in poetry

po·et·ic jus·tice *n.* a situation in which somebody meets a fate that seems a fitting punishment or, less often, a fitting reward for their past actions

po·et·ic li·cense *n.* liberties with the normal rules of fact, style, or grammar taken by a writer or speaker in order to achieve a particular effect

po·et·ics /pō éttiks/ *n.* **1. BASIC PRINCIPLES OF POETRY** the literary or philosophical study of the basic principles, forms, and techniques of poetry or of imaginative writing in general (*takes a singular verb*) **2. TREATISE ON POETRY** a treatise on the nature or principles of poetry **3. WAY OF COMPOSING A POEM** the art or technique of writing poetry (*takes a plural verb*)

po·et·ize *vti.* = **poeticize**

po·et lau·re·ate (*plural* **po·ets lau·re·ate** *or* **po·et lau·re·ates**) *n.* **1. BRITISH COURT POET** a poet who is appointed a member of the royal household for life by a British monarch and, especially formerly, is expected to write poems celebrating great national or royal events **2. POETRY CONSULTANT TO THE LIBRARY OF CONGRESS** a poet appointed as a consultant to the Library of Congress in the United States for one year. The poet is required to give a poetry reading during the year. **3. EMINENT POET** any poet who is particularly honored for his or her work, or who is considered to be the most eminent poet in a particular country, state, or group

po·et·ry /pṓ ətree/ *n.* **1.** LITERAT **LITERATURE IN VERSE** literary work written in verse, in particular verse writing of high quality, great beauty, emotional sincerity or intensity, or profound insight **2.** LITERAT **POEMS COLLECTIVELY** all the poems written by a particular poet, in a particular language or form, or on a particular subject ○ *a collection of love poetry* **3.** LITERAT **WRITING OF POEMS** the art or skill of writing poems **4.** LITERAT **PROSE LIKE POETRY** writing in prose that has a poetic quality **5. BEAUTY OR GRACE** something that resembles poetry in its beauty, rhythmic grace, or imaginative, elevated, or decorative style **6. POETIC QUALITY** a poetic or particularly beautiful or graceful quality in something [14thC. Via Old French from, ultimately, Latin *poeta* (see POET).]

po·gey /pṓgee/, **po·gy** *n. Can* in Canada, unemployment pay or other welfare benefits provided by the government for the unemployed (*slang*) [Late 19thC. Origin unknown.]

po·go·noph·o·ran /pṑgə nóffərən/ *n.* a marine animal found in deep water that resembles a worm. It has tentacles around the head area, lacks a digestive tract, and lives in vertical chitinous tubes. Phylum: Pogonophora. [Late 20thC. Formed from modern Latin *Pogonophora*, phylum name, from Greek *pōgōn* "beard" + *-phoros* "-bearing."] —**po·go·noph·o·ran** *adj.*

po·go stick /pṓgō-/ *n.* a strong metal pole with a spring at the bottom and two footrests to stand on, used to jump up and down or hop along on for play or exercise [Early 20thC. Formerly a trademark; of unknown origin.]

po·grom /pə gróm, pṓgrəm/ *n.* a planned campaign of persecution or extermination sanctioned by a government and directed against an ethnic group, especially against the Jewish people in tsarist Russia [Early 20thC. From Russian, "devastation," formed from *gromit* "to wreak havoc," from *grom* "thunder."]

po·gy /pṓgee/ *n.* **1.** (*plural* **-gies** *or* **-gy**) ZOOL = **menhaden 2.** *Can* = **pogey** (*slang*) [Mid-19thC. Origin uncertain: probably from Algonquian *pauhaugen*.]

poi /poy/ *n.* a dish made from the root of the taro, cooked, pounded to a paste, and fermented. It is eaten as a staple in Hawaii and other Pacific islands. [Early 19thC. From Hawaiian.]

-poiesis *suffix.* creation, formation, production ○ *erythropoiesis* [From Greek *poiēsis*, which was formed from *poiein* "to make" (source also of English *poem* and *onomatopoeia*)]

poign·ant /póynyənt/ *adj.* **1. CAUSING SADNESS OR PITY** causing a sharp sense of sadness, pity, or regret **2. SHARPLY PERCEPTIVE** particularly penetrating and effective or relevant (*literary*) **3. SHARPLY PAINFUL** causing acute physical pain (*literary*) **4. STRONG SMELLING OR TASTING** having an often pleasurably strong sharp smell or taste (*archaic*) [14thC. From French, the present participle of *poindre* "to prick," from Latin *pungere* "to prick, sting."] —**poign·ance** *n.* —**poign·ant·ly** *adv.*

poi·kil·o·cyte /poy kíllə sīt/ *n.* an abnormally shaped red blood cell [Late 19thC. Coined from Greek *poikilos* "spotted, irregular" + -CYTE.]

poi·kil·o·therm /poy kíllə thùrm/ *n.* an organism such as a reptile, amphibian, insect, or fish that has a body temperature that varies according to the temperature of the local atmosphere. ◊ **ectotherm**

poi·ki·lo·ther·mic /pòykilō thúrmik/, **poi·ki·lo·ther·mal** /-thúrm'l/, **poi·ki·lo·ther·mous** /-thúrməss/ *adj.* having a body temperature that varies according to the temperature of the local atmosphere. Reptiles, amphibians, insects, and fish are all poikilothermic. [Late 19thC. Coined from Greek *poikilos* "spotted, varied" + -THERMIC.] —**poi·ki·lo·ther·mism** /pòykilō thúr mìzzəm/ *n.* —**poi·ki·lo·therm·y** /pòykilō thúrmee/ *n.*

poi·lu /pwaa lóo/ *n.* a soldier in the French infantry, especially during World War I [Early 20thC. Via French, literally "hairy," from, ultimately, Latin *pilus* "hair" (see PILE[3]).]

poin·ci·an·a /pòynsee ánnə, -áanə/ (*plural* **-as** *or* **-a**) *n.* a tropical tree grown for its large reddish-orange flowers. Genera: *Caesalpinia* and *Delonix*. [Mid-18thC. From modern Latin, former genus name, named in honor of M. de *Poinci*, a 17th-century governor of the Antilles.]

poin·set·ti·a /poyn séttee ə, poyn séttə/ (*plural* **-as** *or* **-a**) *n.* a Central American shrub of the spurge family that has distinctive bright red bracts resembling petals surrounding a cluster of tiny yellow flowers. It is popular as a houseplant at Christmas. Latin name: *Euphorbia pulcherrima*. [Mid-19thC. Named for Joel R. *Poinsett* (1775–1851), U.S. botanist and ambassador to Mexico, who introduced the plant to the United States.]

Poinsettia

point /poynt/ *n.* **1. OPINION, IDEA, OR FACT** a particular opinion, idea, or fact put forward in the course of, or forming one of the main elements of, a discussion or argument ○ *She made several valid points in her report.* **2. UNDERLYING ESSENTIAL IDEA** the essential idea conveyed or intended in something that is said or written ○ *He seems to have missed the point entirely.* **3. PURPOSE** the purpose or usefulness of something ○ *Is there really any point in continuing?* **4. ITEM IN A LIST OR PLAN** one of several individual items or details in something such as a plan, a contract, or a list ○ *a four-point plan to revive the coal industry* ○ *a point-by-point examination of the contract* **5. CONVINCING ARGUMENT OR VIEWPOINT** a cogent or persuasive argument or observation ○ *You have to admit that she has a point there.* **6. QUALITY OR FEATURE** a distinguishing quality, feature, or item in the makeup of somebody or something ○ *Generosity is one of his strong points.* **7.** ZOOL **PHYSICAL FEATURE OF A LIVESTOCK ANIMAL** an external feature such as the face or fetlock that is assessed when judging the overall shape of a livestock animal **8. LOCATION** a particular place or position ○ *a point six miles east of here* **9. MOMENT** a particular moment in time ○ *At that point, the door opened and the teacher walked in.* **10. PARTICULAR STAGE IN A PROCESS** a particular moment or stage in a process, especially one at which a significant change or development occurs or a particular condition is reached ○ *we hvae reached the point at which a decision will have to be made* **11. LEVEL OR DEGREE** a particular level or degree of a quality ○ *He was confident to the point of almost being arrogant* **12. TIME JUST BEFORE SOMETHING HAPPENS** the moment or period of time just before something happens ○ *at the point of death* **13. SHARP END OF SOMETHING** the sharp narrowed end of something such as a needle, pencil, or weapon **14. END OR TIP** the end or tip of something such as a finger or the projecting angle of something such as the elbow or chin **15. SMALL PROJECTION** a small sharp or perceptible projection such as that in a piece of writing in Braille **16. OBJECT WITH A SHARP END** an object that has a sharp narrowed end or tip, e.g., a needle, pin, or sword (*archaic*) **17.** MUSIC **TIP OF A BOW** the tip of the bow of a string instrument. ◊ **heel 18.** ZOOL **ANTLER PRONG** one of the prongs on a deer's antlers **19.** GEOG **HEADLAND** a prominent headland on the coast that juts out into the sea, often the projecting tip of a peninsula (*often used in place names*) **20. ACT OF POINTING** the act of pointing, e.g., with a finger **21. DOT** a small dot or source of something such as color or light **22.** MATH **DECIMAL POINT** the dot separating the whole number and fraction in a decimal number. The term "point" is used particularly when such numbers are spoken aloud. ○ *five point nine* **23.** GEOM **DIMENSIONLESS GEOMETRIC ELEMENT** a dimensionless geometric element whose location in space is defined solely by its coordinates. Geometric figures such as circles, planes, or spheres can be treated as if they are sets of points. **24.** GRAM, PRINTING **PUNCTUATION MARK** in printing or writing, a punctuation mark, especially a period **25.** PHON = **vowel point 26.** SPORTS, LEISURE **UNIT USED IN SCORING** a unit used in scoring a sport, game, or competition, or as a means of making a quantitative evaluation of something ○ *Using a points system, each employee was rated on a scale from one to five.* **27. UNIT ON A SCALE** a single unit on a scale of measurement ○ *The earthquake measured 6 points on the Richter scale.* ○ *opened up a 10-point lead over her rivals in the polls* **28.** STOCK EXCH **INVESTMENT PRICE UNIT** a unit used to measure change in the value of an investment, e.g., on the Stock Exchange ○ *The market is up 5 points.* **29.** FIN **PERCENTAGE OF A LOAN** an amount equivalent to one percent of the value of a loan, used to calculate the sum the borrower pays up front to the lender as a service charge **30.** LAW **MOTORISTS' PENALTY UNIT** a penalty unit given for a driving offense recorded on a somebody's driving record. Receiving a certain number of points leads automatically to a penalty. **31.** EDUC **STUDENT'S UNIT OF CREDIT** a unit of academic credit for a student that is equivalent to one hour of class work per week over a period of one semester **32.** EDUC **GRADING UNIT** a unit, equivalent to a letter grade, that is used to assess a student's academic performance, with 4 being the highest grade **33.** BRIDGE **UNIT OF WINNING POTENTIAL** a unit used in assessing the strength of a hand in bridge **34.** PRINTING, MEASURE **PRINTING UNIT OF MEASUREMENT** a unit of measurement in printing equal to one twelfth of a pica, or approximately 0.01384 inch/0.03515 cm **35.** MEASURE **DIAMOND WEIGHT UNIT** a unit of weight for a diamond equivalent to one hundredth of a metric carat **36.** COMPASS **MARK ON A COMPASS** any of the 32 individual bearings or directions marked on a compass, e.g., west, west by north, west-northwest, or northwest **37.** COMPASS **ANGLE BETWEEN ADJACENT BEARINGS** the angle between any two adjacent bearings marked on a compass, measuring 11° 15' **38.** MIL **UNIT AHEAD OF A FORMATION** an individual or unit that moves ahead of a larger formation, acting as a scout and advance guard **39.** MIL **ADVANCE MILITARY POSITION** the position ahead of a larger formation taken by an individual or unit acting as point **40.** BASKETBALL **OFFENSIVE BASKETBALL POSITION** in basketball, the position in front court taken by the guard who directs the offensive **41.** HERALDRY **DIVISION OF A HERALDIC SHIELD** any of the positions on or divisions of a heraldic shield in which a charge can be placed ■ **points** *npl.* **1.** AUTOMOT **ELECTRICAL CONTACTS IN A DISTRIBUTOR** the two electrical contacts that act as circuit breakers in the distributor of an internal-combustion engine as current is passed in turn to the cylinders **2.** ZOOL **EXTREMITIES OF A DOMESTIC ANIMAL** the ears, feet, and tail of a domestic animal ■ *v.* (**point·ed, point·ing, points**) **1.** *vi.* **INDICATE WITH AN EXTENDED FINGER** to extend the finger or a long and thin object in the direction of something in order to draw attention to it ○ *I pointed at one of the shrubs and asked its cost.* **2.** *vt.* **AIM AT SOMETHING** to hold an object so that its end is aimed at somebody or something ○ *pointed the hose toward the flowers* **3.** *vi.* **BE TURNED IN A PARTICULAR DIRECTION** to be turned toward or aimed in a particular direction ○ *The arrow on the signpost was pointing to the right.* **4.** *vt.* **DIRECT SOMEBODY TOWARD** to indicate the direction in which somebody should go ○ *If you can just point me in the right direction I should be able to find it.* **5.** *vti.* COMPUT **AIM A MOUSE OR JOYSTICK** to move a mouse, joystick, or other device so that the cursor on a computer screen is positioned over or touching something ○ *Point at the icon, then double click on it.* **6.** *vi.* **SUGGEST SOMETHING IS THE CASE** to be strong evidence of something or lead the mind to believe or conclude something ○ *It all points to one conclusion.* **7.** *vi.* **CALL ATTENTION TO SOMETHING** to call attention to a particular fact or situation as being important **8.** *vt.* **GIVE FORCE TO A REMARK** to give additional force, emphasis, or incisiveness to something said or written **9.** *vt.* CONSTR **REPAIR WITH MORTAR** to repair or finish a wall, chimney, or other structural component by putting mortar or cement between the bricks or stones **10.** *vt.* **SHARPEN SOMETHING** to sharpen something so that it has a point at the end **11.** *vt.* **STRETCH THE FOOT DOWNWARD** to stretch out the foot or toes so that leg and foot make one comparatively straight line, especially in ballet **12.** *vti.* SAILING **SAIL CLOSE TO THE WIND** to sail a boat close to the wind **13.** *vti.* HUNT **POINT THE MUZZLE AT GAME** to stand still with muzzle and tail outstretched indicating the whereabouts of game (*refers to a hunting dog*) **14.** *vt.* MUSIC **MARK A PSALM FOR CHANTING** to mark a psalm to indicate how it is to be chanted **15.** *vt.* PHON **ADD MARKS OVER LETTERS** to place diacritics or vowel points over the relevant letters in a text **16.** *vt.* GRAM **PUNCTUATE** to put punctuation marks into a text **17.** *vi.* MED **COME TO A HEAD** to reach the stage of spontaneous rupture or surgical opening, allowing pus to drain (*refers to boils and abscesses*) [13thC. Via French from, ultimately, Latin *punctum* "prick-mark, dot, particle" (source of English *punctual* and *punctuation*), from the past participle of Latin *pungere* "to prick, pierce" (see PUNGENT).] ◇ **a sore point** a cause of annoyance ◇ **be on the point of doing something** to be just about to do something ○ *I was just on the point of leaving.* ◇ **beside the point** irrelevant or unimportant ◇ **in point of fact** ➧ **fact** ◇ **make a point of doing something** to be careful to do something and, often, to be seen by others to do it ◇ **stretch a point 1.** to allow something as an exception to the rule **2.** to exaggerate ◇ **stretch the point** to exaggerate ◇ **to the point** relevant or worth paying attention to ◇ **up to a point, to a point** to a certain extent, but not completely

point out *vt.* **1.** **SHOW SOMEBODY SOMETHING** to point at or otherwise indicate something so that somebody will look at it ○ *Our guide pointed out the most interesting architectural features of the building.* **2.** **TELL SOMEBODY SOMETHING** to tell somebody about or draw somebody's attention to something ○ *She did point out some of the difficulties we might expect to face.*

point up *vt.* to emphasize something or an aspect of something

point-and-shoot *adj.* used to describe cameras that require no adjustment by the user before taking a photograph because the focus and exposure are adjusted automatically or are fixed

point-blank *adv.* **1.** ARMS **AT CLOSE RANGE** at or from very close range **2.** **OUTRIGHT** directly or bluntly and without further explanation ○ *told them point-blank what I thought of them* ■ *adj.* **1.** ARMS **FIRED AT CLOSE RANGE** fired straight and from so close to the target ○ *point-blank shot* **2.** ARMS **CLOSE TO THE TARGET** very close to the target when shooting ○ *at point-blank range* **3.** **OUTRIGHT** direct and blunt ○ *a point-blank refusal* [Origin uncertain: possibly from French *point (de tir)* "firing point" + *blanc* "target"]

point de·fect *n.* an imperfection in the lattice structure of a crystal

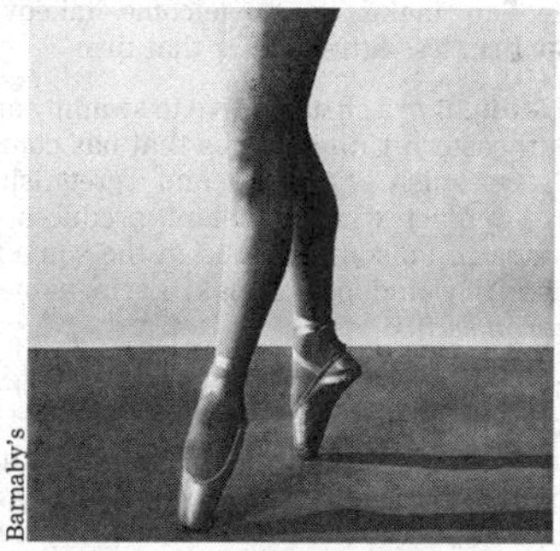

Pointe

pointe /pwaaNt/ *n.* the ends of the toes, a position on which a ballerina wearing special shoes raises herself up for certain moves and positions while performing [Mid-19thC. From French, "point."]

point·ed /póyntəd/ *adj.* **1.** **ENDING IN A POINT** ending in a point or sharp angle **2.** **MADE WITH EMPHASIS** made with emphasis and carrying an unmistakable message, often a criticism **3.** **CONSPICUOUS** made studiedly obvious or noticeable —**point·ed·ly** *adv.* —**point·ed·ness** *n.*

point·ed arch *n.* ARCHIT = **lancet arch**

point·ed·ly /póyntədlee/ *adv.* in a deliberate or emphatic way and with no attempt at tact or subtlety ○ *They pointedly ignored me.*

Pointe-Noire /pwaant nwaár/ city in the Republic of Congo, and the country's main port. Population: 576,206 (1992).

point·er /póyntər/ *n.* **1.** **CANE USED FOR POINTING** a stick or cane used, especially by a teacher or lecturer, to point something out, e.g. on a chart or large map **2.** **INDICATOR ON A MEASURING DEVICE** a needle that moves around on a measuring instrument to point to part of a dial **3.** **HELPFUL ADVICE OR INFORMATION** a piece of advice or information given to help somebody achieve something or do something the right way ○ *My coach gave me a few pointers on how to hold the racket.* **4.** **SIGN INDICATING A SITUATION** a sign of what is happening or what might happen in the future **5.** HUNT **HUNTING DOG THAT INDICATES THE POSITION OF GAME** a hunting dog, usually with a shorthaired white coat with colored patches, belonging to a breed trained to indicate the whereabouts of shot game by standing still with the muzzle and tail outstretched **6.** COMPUT **ARROW ON A COMPUTER SCREEN** an arrow or other symbol on a computer screen that shows the current position of the mouse or other pointing device. The symbol may change shape depending on the task being performed. **7.** COMPUT **COMPUTER MEMORY ADDRESS** an address, stored as data in a computer's memory, that is the location at which the desired data is stored ■ **point·ers, Point·ers** *npl.* ASTRON **GUIDE STARS IN THE BIG DIPPER CONSTELLATION** the two bright stars in the Big Dipper constellation forming the side of the quadrilateral furthest from the handle, and used as a guide to find the Polaris

point guard *n.* in basketball, the guard who is mainly reponsible for directing a team's offensive play

poin·til·lism /pwáantee ìzzəm, póynt'l ìzzəm/ *n.* **1.** PAINTING **STYLE OF 19C PAINTING** a late 19th-century style of painting in which a picture is constructed from dots of pure color that blend, at a distance, into recognizable shapes and various color tones. Pointillism developed out of impressionism and its best-known exponent is the French painter Georges Seurat. **2.** MUSIC **MUSICAL COMPOSITION TECHNIQUE** a technique of musical composition using sparse isolated notes in widely varying registers rather than traditional closely connected melodies [Early 20thC. From French *pointillisme*, via *pointiller* "to mark with dots" from, ultimately, Latin *punctum* "dot."] —**poin·til·list** *n., adj.* —**poin·til·lis·tic** /pwàantee ístik, pòynt'l ístik/ *adj.*

point·ing de·vice *n.* an input device such as a mouse, trackball, or joystick used to manipulate a cursor or pointer on a computer display

point lace *n.* lace made with a needle instead of bobbins [From POINT in the sense "to prick, stitch"]

point·less /póyntləss/ *adj.* **1.** **WITHOUT PURPOSE OR BENEFIT** having no purpose, use, or sense, or any positive or beneficial effect ○ *It's pointless even attempting to make sense of it.* **2.** SPORTS **SCORELESS** in sports, having or scoring no points —**point·less·ly** *adv.* —**point·less·ness** *n.*

point man *n.* **1.** MIL **LEAD SOLDIER IN A MILITARY FORMATION** the lead soldier in a military formation or patrol **2.** **SOMEBODY IN THE FOREFRONT** somebody who is in the forefront of an activity or endeavor and playing a crucial and possibly hazardous role in it

point mu·ta·tion *n.* a mutation that involves a change in a single base or base pair of the nucleotides in a gene, occurring as a result of addition, deletion, or substitution

point of ac·cu·mu·la·tion *n.* MATH = **limit point**

point of de·par·ture *n.* a starting point

point of hon·or *n.* something that a sense of honor, self-respect, or pride obliges somebody to do

point of no re·turn *n.* **1.** **CRITICAL STAGE IN A PROCESS** the time or stage in a process beyond which it becomes impossible to stop or discontinue it **2.** AIR **POINT ON A JOURNEY** the point in an aircraft's flight after which there will be insufficient fuel left to enable it to return to its starting point

point of or·der *n.* a question raised by one of the participants in a a formal debate or meeting that relates to the rules of procedure governing it, in particular as to whether those rules are being breached

point of pres·ence *n.* **1.** COMPUT full form of **POP** **2.** **PLACE TO CONNECT TO NETWORK** a location where a user can connect to a network, e.g., a place where subscribers can dial in to an Internet service provider

point of ref·er·ence *n.* something to which somebody can refer in order to check direction or progress, as a guide to action or conduct, or as an aid to understanding or communication

point-of-sale *adj.* located, used, or occurring at the place where a product is sold —**point of sale** *n.*

point of view *n.* **1.** **PERSPECTIVE SOMEBODY BRINGS** somebody's particular way of thinking about or approaching a subject, as shaped by his or her own character, experience, mindset, and history **2.** **OPINION** somebody's personal opinion on a subject **3.** **PARTICULAR ASPECT ON A SUBJECT** any of the various aspects from which a subject may be considered or judged **4.** LITERAT **ANGLE OF THE NARRATOR** the perspective on events of the narrator or a particular character in a story **5.** **POSITION OF AN OBSERVER** the position or angle from which somebody observes an event or a scene

point-of-view shot *n.* a movie or television shot that shows an event or scene as a particular character sees it

point source *n.* PHYS, ENVIRON a source of something such as radiant energy or pollution that is or appears to be very small

point-to-point *n.* **CROSS-COUNTRY STEEPLECHASE** a type of horse race in which horses regularly used in hunting are raced over a marked cross-country course that includes various jumps and obstacles ■ *adj.* **FROM PLACE TO PLACE** from one particular place to another —**point-to-point·er** *n.* —**point-to-point·ing** *n.*

Point-to-Point Pro·to·col *n.* a protocol for dial-up access to the Internet using a modem

point wom·an *n.* a woman who is in the forefront of any activity or endeavor, playing a crucial and possibly hazardous role in it

point·y /póyntee/ (**-i·er, -i·est**) *adj.* ending in a point

point·y-head·ed *adj.* intelligent or intellectual in an arrogant or impractical way (*slang*)

poise[1] /poyz/ *n.* **1.** COMPOSURE calm self-assured dignity, especially in dealing with social situations **2.** CONTROLLED GRACE IN MOVEMENT a graceful controlled way of standing, moving, or performing an action **3.** EQUILIBRIUM a stable state of balance **4.** SUSPENDED STATE a state of hovering or being in suspension (*literary*) ■ *v.* **(poised, pois·ing, pois·es) 1.** *vti.* BALANCE OR SUSPEND to be balanced or suspended, or to place or hold something in balance or suspension **2.** *vt.* WEIGH to weigh things, especially by holding them in the hands, or to weigh something up, especially alternatives (*archaic*) [14thC. The noun is via Old French *pois* "weight, balance"; the verb via *peser* "to weigh," both ultimately from Latin *pensare* (see PENSIVE).]

poise[2] /poyz/ *n.* the centimer-gram-second unit of viscosity equal to one dyne-second per square centimeter [Early 20thC. Shortening of *Poiseuille*, named for the French physiologist J. L. M. *Poiseuille* (1799–1868).]

poised /poyzd/ *adj.* **1.** READY TO ACT fully prepared or in position and about to do something ○ *We are now poised to take over the company.* **2.** READY TO MOVE motionless and balanced, or motionless and suspended in the air, often just before or in the midst of an action ○ *a bird poised on a branch* **3.** WITH COMPOSURE calm, self-assured, and dignified **4.** IN DANGER OF SOMETHING teetering on the edge of a sudden change ○ *stock prices seemingly poised to rise*

poi·son /póyz'n/ *n.* **1.** TOXIC SUBSTANCE a substance that causes illness, injury, or death if taken into the body or produced within the body **2.** SOMETHING EXERCISING AN INSIDIOUS INFLUENCE something that exercises a powerful destructive or corrupting force, especially in an insidious way **3.** CHEM REACTION-INHIBITING SUBSTANCE a substance that inhibits a chemical reaction or diminishes the activity of a catalyst **4.** NUCLEAR PHYS SUBSTANCE SLOWING A NUCLEAR REACTION any substance in a nuclear reactor that can absorb neutrons without undergoing fission and that therefore slows down the reaction ■ *vt.* **(-soned, -son·ing, -sons) 1.** GIVE POISON TO SOMEBODY to administer poison to a person or animal, especially with malicious intention **2.** HARM WITH A TOXIC SUBSTANCE to cause illness, injury, or death to somebody with a poison or other harmful chemical substance **3.** ADD POISON TO SOMETHING to put poison into or onto something so as to harm or kill somebody ○ *poisoned bait used to kill rats* **4.** POLLUTE THE ENVIRONMENT to pollute water, land, or air severely with harmful substances **5.** CORRUPT OR UNDERMINE SOMETHING to have an evil or corrupting influence on somebody or something, especially by planting hostility or suspicion in somebody's mind against another person **6.** SPOIL A SITUATION to have a harmful spoiling effect on something that should be pleasant, enjoyable, or friendly **7.** CHEM INHIBIT A CHEMICAL REACTION to inhibit a chemical reaction or activity **8.** NUCLEAR PHYS SLOW DOWN A NUCLEAR REACTION to slow down or stop a nuclear reaction by the addition of a substance that can absorb neutrons without undergoing fission [13thC. Via Old French from the Latin stem *potion-* from, ultimately, *potare* "to drink."] —**poi·son·er** *n.*
◇ **what's your poison?, name your poison** used to ask what somebody would like to drink (*informal*)

poi·son gas *n.* a lethal or incapacitating gas used as a weapon in warfare

poi·son hem·lock *n.* a highly poisonous plant found in Europe and North America that somewhat resembles parsley in appearance and has spotted stems, small delicately divided leaves, and flat-topped clusters of white flowers. Latin name: *Conium maculatum.*

poi·son i·vy *n.* **1.** VINE CAUSING AN ITCHING RASH a North American climbing vine of the cashew family that has three-part leaves, small green flowers, and white berries. Contact with the plant produces an itchy rash. Genus: *Rhus.* **2.** RELATED PLANT any plant related to poison ivy, such as poison oak **3.** MED RASH the rash produced by poison ivy

poi·son oak *n.* a plant similar or related to poison ivy that produces a skin rash as a result of being touched. Genus: *Rhus.*

poi·son·ous /póyz'nəss/ *adj.* **1.** CONTAINING OR PRODUCING POISON containing, producing, or acting as a poison **2.** MALICIOUS filled with or creating malice, distrust, or hostility —**poi·son·ous·ly** *adv.* —**poi·son·ous·ness** *n.*

poi·son-pen let·ter *n.* a letter sent anonymously

Poison ivy

to somebody that contains unpleasant or abusive comments

poi·son pill *n.* a strategic move adopted by a company designed to make an unwelcome takeover by another firm less attractive to that firm

poi·son su·mac *n.* a shrub native to swampy areas of the southeastern United States that has compound leaves, greenish flowers, and greenish-white berries. Contact with the plant produces an irritating rash. Poison sumac is in the same family as poison ivy and poison oak. Latin name: *Toxicodendron vernix.*

poi·son·wood /póyz'n wòod/ (*plural* **-woods** *or* **-wood**) *n.* a poisonous tree of the cashew family native to southern Florida and the West Indies that has compound leaves, yellowish-green flowers, and yellowish-orange fruits. Latin name: *Metopium toxiferum.*

Pois·son /pwáass on, pwa sáwn/, **Siméon-Denis** (1781–1840) French mathematician and physicist. He is noted for his work on electricity, magnetism, elasticity, and for the Poisson distribution in statistics.

Pois·son dis·tri·bu·tion *n.* a probability distribution that represents the number of random events occurring over a fixed period of time [Early 20thC. Named for Siméon POISSON, who first described it.]

Poi·tier /pwáatee ay/, **Sidney** (*b.* 1924) U.S. actor and director. He was the first African American Hollywood movie star. He won an academy award for his role in *Lilies of the Field* (1963).

Poi·tiers /pwaa tyáy/ city in west central France. It is the capital of Vienne Department in Poitou-Charente Region. Population: 78,894 (1990).

poke[1] /pōk/ *v.* **(poked, pok·ing, pokes) 1.** *vti.* PROD WITH SOMETHING to push the point of something such as an outstretched finger, elbow, or stick against somebody or something else **2.** *vt.* MAKE A HOLE IN SOMETHING to make a hole or opening in something by pushing at it with a finger or a sharp object **3.** *vt.* PUSH INTO A HOLE to push a finger or a long thin object into a hole, space, or opening **4.** *vti.* PROTRUDE FROM SOMETHING to stick, or stick something, out of or through an opening, surface, or covering in such a way that part of the object is visible ○ *One foot was poking out from under the covers.* **5.** *vi.* SEARCH HAPHAZARDLY to search or investigate in a haphazard or aimless manner ○ *poking around in a second-hand bookstore* **6.** *vi.* MEDDLE to pry or intrude into something, or meddle with something ○ *Stop poking around in my affairs.* **7.** *vt.* STIR A FIRE to stir a fire with a poker or similar object to make it burn better **8.** *vt.* PUNCH SOMEBODY to hit somebody with one of the fists (*informal*) **9.** *vi.* GO SLOWLY to move around or do things in a slow unhurried way ■ *n.* **1.** PROD a push or prod with a finger, elbow, stick, or similar pointed object **2.** LOOK OR SEARCH the activity of haphazard or casual browsing or investigating **3.** PROD a short prod with the fist (*informal*) **4.** = **slowpoke** (*informal*) [13thC. Origin uncertain.]

poke[2] /pōk/ *n.* a small bag or sack (*regional*) [13thC. From Old French dialect, a variant of *poche* (see POUCH).]

poke[3] *n.* = **pokeweed** [Mid-17thC. From Virginia Algonquian *poughkone* (source of English *puccoon*).]

poke·ber·ry /pōk bèrree/ *n.* **1.** (*plural* **-ries**) POKEWEED BERRY the berry that grows on a pokeweed plant **2.** (*plural* **-ry** *or* **-ries**) = **pokeweed**

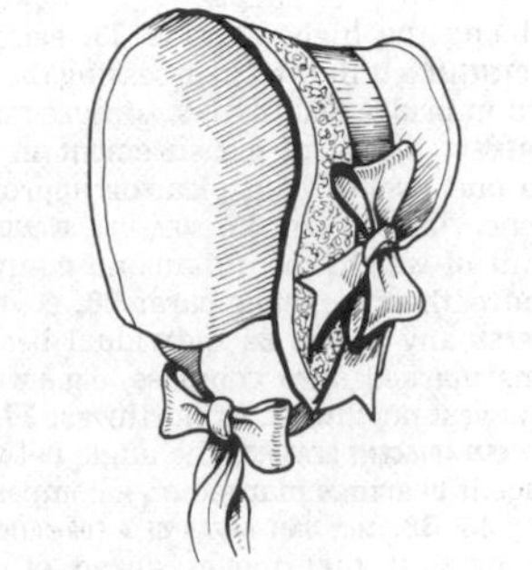

Poke bonnet

poke bon·net *n.* a woman's bonnet with a deep projecting rim, fashionable in the first half of the 19th century [From POKE[2]]

pok·er[1] /pókər/ *n.* CARDS a card game in which players attempt to acquire a winning combination of cards that involves betting at every deal [Mid-19thC. Origin uncertain: possibly from German *Pochspiel*, literally "bragging game," from *pochen* "to brag."]

pok·er[2] /pókər/ *n.* **1.** METAL ROD FOR STIRRING A FIRE a metal rod for stirring a fire to make it burn better **2.** SOMEBODY OR SOMETHING THAT POKES somebody or something that pokes, or something used for poking [Mid-16thC. Formed from POKE[1].]

pok·er face *n.* a face showing no expression and revealing nothing about what somebody is thinking or feeling [From POKER[1]] —**pok·er-faced** *adj.*

poke·weed /pók wèed/ (*plural* **-weed** *or* **-weeds**) *n.* a tall North American plant that has white flowers, juicy blackish berries in elongated clusters, edible shoots, and a poisonous root. Latin name: *Phytolacca americana.* [Mid-18thC. From POKE[3].]

poke·y[1] /pókee/ *adj.* = **poky**[1] (*informal*)

po·key[2] /pókee/ (*plural* **-keys** *or* **-kies**), **po·ky** (*plural* **-kies**) *n.* a jail (*dated slang*) [Early 20thC. Origin uncertain: possibly a variant of earlier *pogey* "hostel," of unknown origin.]

pok·y[1] /pókee/ (**-i·er, -i·est**), **pok·ey** (**-i·er, -i·est**) *adj.* (*informal*) **1.** SLOW annoyingly slow **2.** FRUMPY shabby and old-fashioned [Mid-19thC. From POKE[1]. The word originally meant "petty, pottering," and came from the idea of poking aimlessly at something.] —**pok·i·ly** *adv.* —**pok·i·ness** *n.*

pok·y[2] /pókee/ *n.* = **pokey**[2] (*dated slang*)

pol /pol/ *n.* a politician (*informal*) [Mid-20thC. Shortening.]

pol. *abbr.* **1.** political **2.** politics

Pol. *abbr.* **1.** Poland **2.** Polish

Po·lack /pó làk/ *n.* an offensive term referring to a Polish person (*slang offensive*) [Late 16thC. Directly or via French *Polaque* from Polish *Polak* (source of English *polka*).]

Poland

Po·land /pólənd/ republic in eastern Europe. Language: Polish. Currency: zloty. Capital: Warsaw. Population: 38,612,000 (1996). Area: 120,725 sq. mi./312,677 sq. km. Official name **Republic of Poland**

Po·land Chi·na *n.* a hog of a large American breed that is black with white markings

po·lar /pólər/ *adj.* **1.** GEOG OF OR NEAR THE EARTH'S POLES relating to, located at, or found in the regions surrounding the North or South Pole **2.** SCI OF A POLE OR POLES relating to a pole or poles of a rotating body, a magnet, or an electrically charged object **3.** ASTRON,

SPACE TECH **PASSING OVER A PLANET'S POLES** passing over, or traveling in an orbit that passes over, a planet's poles ○ *polar orbit* **4.** **UTTERLY OPPOSITE** completely opposite to each other, or at the other extreme from something else **5.** **PIVOTAL** of pivotal or central importance **6.** **GUIDING** serving as a guide or giving direction (*literary*) **7.** CHEM **HAVING A DIPOLE** having a permanent dipole, or having molecules with permanent dipoles ○ *polar molecule* **8.** CRYSTALS **HAVING AN IONIC BOND** having an ionic bond, or having crystals with ionic bonds ○ *polar crystal* **9.** MATH **IN A POLAR COORDINATE SYSTEM** relating to or measured with reference to a system of polar coordinates

po·lar ax·is *n.* MATH the fixed horizontal line in a system of polar coordinates from which the angle made by the radius vector is measured

Polar bear

po·lar bear *n.* a large white mainly meat-eating bear that lives in the Arctic on coasts and ice floes. It has wide front feet for swimming. Latin name: *Ursus maritimus.*

po·lar bod·y *n.* a cell with a nucleus but little cytoplasm that is produced along with an oocyte, and later discarded, in the process of cell division that leads to an ovum

po·lar cap *n.* **1.** GEOG **ICY AREA AROUND THE POLES** the area around either the North or South Pole that is permanently covered in ice **2.** ASTRON **POLAR ICECAP ON MARS** either of the two polar regions on Mars that are permanently covered with frozen carbon dioxide and water

po·lar cir·cle *n.* the lines of latitude that define the Arctic and Antarctic regions, 66°33′ N and 66°33′ S

po·lar co·or·di·nates *npl.* MATH the two coordinates that locate a point in a plane by specifying the length of a radius vector and the angle it makes with a horizontal line (**polar axis**)

po·lar front *n.* a weather front separating cold polar air and warmer air

po·lar·im·e·ter /pòlə rímmətər/ *n.* OPTICS an instrument used to measure the rotation of the plane of polarization of light as it passes through a substance, especially a liquid or solution. It is an important tool in the analysis of sugar solutions. [Mid-19thC. Coined from POLARIZATION + -METER.] —**po·lar·i·met·ric** /pōləri méttrik/ *adj.* —**po·lar·im·e·try** /pōlə rímmətree/ *n.*

Po·lar·is /pə lérriss/ *n.* **1.** ASTRON **BRIGHT STAR NEAR THE NORTH POLE** the brightest star in the Little Dipper formation in the constellation Ursa Minor, located very near the celestial North Pole. Because it always indicates due north from an observer anywhere on the Earth, Polaris is important for navigation. **2.** ARMS **MISSILE WITH A NUCLEAR WARHEAD** a U.S. intermediate-range ballistic missile that usually carries a nuclear warhead and is launched from a submarine

po·lar·i·scope /pō lérrə skōp/ *n.* an instrument used to study either a substance exposed to polarized light or the effects of a substance on polarized light [Early 19thC. Coined from POLARIZATION + SCOPE.]

po·lar·i·ty /pō lérrətee/ (*plural* **-ties**) *n.* **1.** **EXTREME DIFFERENCE** a situation in which two individuals or groups have qualities, ideas, or principles that are diametrically opposed to each other **2.** PHYS **OPPOSITE PHYSICAL CHARACTERISTICS IN A SYSTEM** the condition, in a system, of having opposite characteristics at different points, especially with respect to electric charge or magnetic properties

po·lar·i·za·tion /pōləri záysh'n/ *n.* **1.** **DIVISION INTO OPPOSITE VIEWS** a process in which the differences between groups or ideas become ever more clear-cut and extreme and the opposition between them hardens **2.** OPTICS **PROCESS LIMITING LIGHT VIBRATIONS** the process or property by which radiation, especially light, is restricted to vibrate in particular directions **3.** PHYS **POLARIZING OF CHARGES** the process in which the positive and negative charges in an atomic, molecular, or chemical system develop polarity

po·lar·ize /pṓlə rīz/ (**-ized, -iz·ing, -iz·es**) *vti.* **1.** **CAUSE A DIVISION OF OPINION** to make the differences between groups or ideas ever more clear-cut and extreme and harden the opposition between them, or to become ever more sharply divided and opposed **2.** PHYS **ACQUIRE POLARITY** to acquire, or cause something to acquire, polarity **3.** PHYS **RESTRICT LIGHT VIBRATION** to cause light to vibrate within certain planes, or to be restricted to vibration within certain planes — **po·lar·iz·a·ble** *adj.* —**po·lar·iz·er** *n.*

po·lar·iz·ing mi·cro·scope *n.* a microscope in which polarized light is used to examine specimens

po·lar nu·cle·us *n.* either of the two nuclei in the center of the sac of a seed plant embryo that eventually fuse into the endosperm

po·lar·og·ra·phy /pòlə róggrəfee/ *n.* an analytic technique used to study ions in a solution that compares the strength of electric currents passing through the solution during electrolysis and the voltages needed to produce them [Mid-20thC. Coined from POLARIZATION + -GRAPHY.] —**po·lar·o·graph·ic** /pōlərə gráffik/ *adj.*

Po·lar·oid /pṓlə ròyd/ *tdmk.* **1.** a trademark for a camera that produces pictures that develop within seconds of being taken, or the film used in such a camera **2.** a trademark for a specially treated transparent plastic that allows polarized light through and is used to reduce glare in sunglasses

po·lar star *n.* ASTRON = **Polaris**

pol·der /pṓldər/ *n.* an area of land reclaimed from the sea and protected by dikes, especially in the Netherlands [Early 17thC. From Dutch.]

pole[1] /pōl/ *n.* **1.** GEOG **NORTH OR SOUTH POLE** either of the two points on the Earth, the North and South Poles, that are the endpoints of its axis of rotation, are furthest from the equator, and are surrounded by icecaps **2.** ASTRON, GEOM **AXIS ENDPOINTS OF A SPHERE** either of the two endpoints of the axis of rotation of a sphere or a planet or other celestial body **3.** ASTRON = **celestial pole** **4.** **EITHER OF TWO OPPOSITES** one of two completely opposed or contrasted positions, states, or views ○ *They're at opposite poles as far as their taste in music is concerned.* **5.** PHYS **END OF A MAGNET** either of the two ends of a magnet or magnetized body where the lines of force are most concentrated **6.** ELEC **ELECTRIC TERMINAL** either of two terminals in something such as a battery, generator, or motor that have opposite electric charges **7.** BIOL **DISTINCT REGION IN A CELL** either of two opposite regions that are physiologically or functionally distinct in an organism, cell, or structure, e.g., the opposite ends of the spindle structure formed in the nucleus of a cell during cell division **8.** MATH **ORIGIN OF POLAR COORDINATES** the origin in a polar coordinate system **9.** **REFERENCE POINT** a fixed point of reference (*literary*) [14thC. Via Latin from Greek *polos* "axis" (source of English *pulley*). Ultimately from an Indo-European word meaning "to turn around," which is also the ancestor of *wheel* and *cycle.*] ◇ **be poles apart** to be as different or as opposed as it is possible to be

pole[2] /pōl/ *n.* **1.** **LONG STRAIGHT OBJECT** a long, straight, strong piece of wood, metal, or other material, usually with a round cross-section and thin enough to hold in the hands or arms **2.** SPORTS **POLE-VAULTER'S POLE** the long flexible shaft made of wood, metal, or fiberglass used by competitors in the pole vault **3.** HORSERACING, MOTOR SPORTS **RACETRACK STARTING POSITION OR LANE** the inside lane or the inside starting position on a racetrack **4.** MOTOR SPORTS = **pole position** **5.** TRANSP **SHAFT ON A HORSE-DRAWN VEHICLE** a single shaft projecting forward from the front of a vehicle between the animals that draw it and to which those animals are hitched **6.** MEASURE = **perch**[1] *n.* 5 **7.** MEASURE = **perch**[1] *n.* 6 ■ *v.* (**poled, pol·ing, poles**) **1.** *vti.* NAUT **PROPEL A BOAT WITH A POLE** to move a boat along by pushing with a pole against a firm surface **2.** *vt.* GARDENING **SUPPORT A PLANT WITH A POLE** to use a pole to provide support for a plant **3.** *vti.* SKIING **USE SKI POLES** to make forward progress on skis by pushing with ski poles [Old English *pāl.* From a prehistoric Germanic ancestor that was borrowed from Latin *palus* "stake."] ◇ **not touch somebody** *or* **something with a ten-foot pole** to avoid any contact or involvement with somebody or something

Pole *n.* **1.** **SOMEBODY FROM POLAND** somebody who was born or raised in Poland or who has Polish citizenship **2.** **SOMEBODY WITH A POLISH ANCESTOR** somebody who is of Polish descent [Late 16thC. Via German from, ultimately, Old Polish *Polanie,* literally "field-dwellers," from *pole* "field," from Slavic.]

pole·ax /pṓ làks/ *n.* **1.** **BUTCHER'S AX** a specialized ax with a hammer face opposite the blade, used, especially formerly, for slaughtering animals **2.** ARMS **BATTLE-AX** a battle-ax with a long or short handle, especially one with a hammer or spike opposite the ax blade **3.** NAVY **AX FOR CUTTING RIGGING** a short-handled ax used to cut rigging or ropes on sailing ships, especially during combat ■ *vt.* (**-axed** *or* **-axed, -axed, -ax·ing, -ax·es**) **1.** **AMAZE AND STUPEFY SOMEBODY** to leave somebody stupefied and speechless with astonishment **2.** **HIT SOMEBODY VERY HARD** to hit somebody hard enough to cause unconsciousness **3.** **HIT WITH A POLEAX** to hit somebody or something with a poleax [14thC. Alteration of *pollax,* literally "head-axe," from POLL, perhaps because it was for splitting heads or because it had a special kind of head.]

pole bean *n.* a climbing green bean that is grown supported on a pole

Polecat

pole·cat /pṓl kàt/ *n.* **1.** **SMALL ANIMAL RELATED TO THE WEASEL** an animal related to but larger than the weasel that lives in woodlands in Europe, Asia, and North Africa, has brown fur, and emits a foul smell when disturbed. Genus: *Mustela* and *Vormela.* ◊ **ferret** **2.** = **skunk** [14thC. Origin uncertain: perhaps from French *poule* "hen" (because it was known to take hens from farmyards) + CAT.]

pole horse *n.* a horse harnessed to the pole of a carriage or wagon

po·leis plural of **polis**

pole jump *n.* = **pole vault** —**pole-jump** *vti.* —**pole-jump·er** *n.*

po·lem·ic /pə lémmik/ *n.* **1.** **PASSIONATE ARGUMENT** a passionate, strongly worded, and often controversial argument against or, less often, in favor of something or somebody **2.** **PASSIONATE CRITIC** somebody who engages in a dispute or argues strongly or passionately against something or somebody (*literary*) ■ *adj.* **po·lem·ic, po·lem·i·cal** **CONTAINING PASSIONATE ARGUMENT** containing or expressing passionate and strongly worded argument against or in favor of something or somebody [Mid-17thC. Via medieval Latin from Greek *polemikos,* from *polemos* "war," of unknown origin.] —**po·lem·i·cal·ly** *adv.*

po·lem·i·cist /pə lémmissist/, **po·lem·ist** /pə lémmist, pólləmist/ *n.* somebody who writes or delivers a polemic or is skilled in polemical argument

po·lem·ics /pə lémmiks/ *n.* the art or practice of arguing powerfully and effectively for or against something and engaging in controversy (*takes a singular verb*)

po·lem·ist *n.* = **polemicist**

po·len·ta /pō léntə/ *n.* in Italian cooking, fine yellow cornmeal cooked to a mush with water or stock and served with meat, fish, or vegetables, or cooled, set, sliced, and baked or fried [Mid-16thC. Via Italian from Latin, "barley meal."]

pole po·si·tion *n.* **1.** HORSERACING = **pole**[2] *n.* 3 **2.** MOTOR SPORTS **BEST STARTING POSITION IN AN AUTO RACE** the best position on the starting grid of an automobile race, usually on the inside of the front row and taken by the driver with the fastest pre-race practice time **3. GOOD BEGINNING** a very good or advantageous position at the beginning of something

pol·er /pṓlər/ *n.* **1.** = **pole horse 2.** NAUT **SOMEBODY POLING A BOAT** somebody who uses a pole to move a boat along [Late 17thC. From POLE[2].]

pole·star /pṓl staar/ *n.* something considered as a guiding light and giver of direction (*literary*)

Pole Star *n.* ASTRON = **Polaris**

pole vault *n.* **1. HIGH JUMP WITH A POLE** a field event in which the competitors use a long flexible pole to swing themselves up and over a very high crossbar **2. JUMP IN THE POLE VAULT** a jump in the pole vault, or any jump made with the help of a pole —**pole-vault** *vti.* —**pole-vault·er** *n.*

po·lice /pə leéss/ *n.* **1. ORGANIZATION FOR MAINTAINING LAW AND ORDER** a civil organization whose members are given special legal powers by the government and whose task is to maintain public order and to solve and prevent crimes **2. POLICE OFFICERS** police officers considered as a group (*takes a plural verb*) **3. SPECIALIZED FORCE** an organized group of people whose job is maintaining order, ensuring that regulations are obeyed, and preventing crime within a particular area or sphere of activity **4.** MIL **CLEANLINESS AND ORDER IN THE MILITARY** the work of keeping a military base clean and orderly, or its state of cleanliness and order **5. ENFORCEMENT OF LAW** the enforcement of law and the prevention of crime in a community (*archaic*) ■ *vt.* (**-liced, -lic·ing, -lic·es**) **1. ENSURE LAW AND ORDER** to ensure that law and order is maintained in a particular area or at a particular event, using the police or a military force **2. ENSURE RULES ARE FOLLOWED** to ensure that rules and procedures are followed correctly in something or that something is implemented as agreed **3.** MIL **CLEAN A MILITARY BASE** to keep a military base clean and orderly [15thC. Via French from, ultimately, Greek *politeia* "civil organization, the state," from *politēs* "citizen"(see POLITIC).]

po·lice ac·tion *n.* a relatively small-scale military action undertaken without a declaration of war, e.g., to prevent violation of an international agreement. Soldiers used in police actions are usually deployed aiding the civil police.

po·lice dog *n.* **1. DOG WORKING WITH THE POLICE** a dog trained to work with the police in tracking or searching for people or in detecting illegal substances by smell **2.** = **German Shepherd**

po·lice force *n.* an organized body of police with jurisdiction within a particular geographic area or over a particular group of people

po·lice·man /pə leéssmən/ (*plural* **-men** /-mən/) *n.* a man who is a police officer

po·lice of·fi·cer *n.* somebody who belongs to a police force

po·lice pow·er *n.* the power of a government to impose what it considers reasonable restrictions on the liberties of its citizens for the maintenance of public order and safety

po·lice pro·ce·dur·al *n.* a crime novel or drama in which the crime is investigated by police officers

po·lice re·port·er *n.* a journalist who is assigned to cover news about crime and police work

po·lice state *n.* a country in which the government uses police, especially secret police, to exercise strict or repressive control over the population and deny them full civil liberties

po·lice sta·tion *n.* the local headquarters of a police force

po·lice·wom·an /pə leéss wŏŏmmən/ (*plural* **-en** /-wim min/) *n.* a woman who is a police officer

pol·i·cy[1] /póllәssee/ (*plural* **-cies**) *n.* **1. COURSE OF ACTION** a program of actions adopted by an individual, group, or government, or the set of principles on which they are based **2. PRUDENCE** shrewdness or prudence, especially in the pursuit of a particular course of action [14thC. From Old French *policie* "government, civil organization" (see POLICE). The underlying meaning is "an established system of government."]

pol·i·cy[2] /póllәssee/ (*plural* **-cies**) *n.* **1. CONTRACT** a contract that exists between an insurance company and an individual or organization buying insurance services, or the document that lists the contract terms **2. NUMBERS GAME** a game of chance such as a daily lottery where participants bet on what the number will be [Mid-16thC. From French *police*, of uncertain origin; probably via Latin *apodixis* from, ultimately, Greek *apodeiknunai* "to demonstrate, prove."]

pol·i·cy·hold·er /póllәssee hōldər/ *n.* a named person or organization responsible for an insurance policy

pol·i·cy·mak·ing /póllәssee mayking/ *n.* **DRAWING UP OF POLICY** the drawing up of policies, especially the formulating of political policies by members of a government ■ *adj.* **MAKING POLICIES** having the task of formulating policies, especially in a government —**pol·i·cy·mak·er** *n.*

pol·i·cy sci·ence *n.* the study of how policies are made and executed in governments and bureaucracies

po·li·o /pṓli ō/ *n.* = **poliomyelitis** [Mid-20thC. Shortening.]

po·li·o·my·e·li·tis /pōlee ō mī ə lítiss/ *n.* a severe infectious viral disease, usually affecting children or young adults, that inflames the brainstem and spinal cord, sometimes leading to paralysis and muscular wasting [Late 19thC. From modern Latin, from Greek *polios* "gray" (because the motor neurons it affects are known as "gray matter") + MYELITIS.] —**po·li·o·my·e·lit·ic** /pōlee ō mī ə líttik/ *adj.*

po·li·o·vi·rus /pólee ō vīrəss/ *n.* any of three forms of an enterovirus that causes poliomyelitis

po·lis /pṓliss/ (*plural* **-leis** /pṓ līss/) *n.* **1. ANCIENT GREEK CITY-STATE** a city-state in ancient Greece, typical of Greek political organization from 800 to 400 B.C. **2. GOVERNMENT USING CITY-STATES** the city-state form of government [Late 19thC. From Greek, "city" (source of English *metropolis, police,* and *politics*).]

pol·ish /póllish/ *v.* (**-ished, -ish·ing, -ish·es**) **1.** *vti.* **MAKE SMOOTH OR GLOSSY** to make something smooth or shiny, or become smooth or shiny, by rubbing with something **2.** *vt.* **REMOVE THE OUTER LAYER OF** to remove the outer layers of brown rice to make white rice by rotating the grain in a drum **3.** *vti.* **IMPROVE** to make something more refined, elegant, or complete, or to become so ■ *n.* **1. SUBSTANCE USED FOR POLISHING** a substance used to make something smooth or shiny ○ *furniture polish* **2. SMOOTHNESS** the smoothness or glossiness of something that has been polished ○ *car paintwork with a high polish* **3. RUB GIVEN TO SOMETHING** a rubbing of something designed to make it smooth or glossy **4. REFINEMENT** refinement, especially of style, that is the mark of expertise or experience [13thC. Via the Old French stem *poliss-* from Latin *polire* (source also of English *polite*). Ultimately from an Indo-European base meaning "to push," which also produced English *push*.] —**pol·ish·er** *n.*

polish off *vt.* **1. FINISH QUICKLY AND COMPLETELY** to finish something, especially food or a task, quickly and completely **2. KILL** to kill or eliminate somebody (*informal*) [From the idea of putting the finishing touches to something]

polish up *vt.* **1. MAKE SHINY** to make something smooth or shiny by rubbing it **2. IMPROVE** to improve or refine something, e.g., a prepared speech or knowledge of a foreign language

polish up on *vt.* to improve knowledge or skill in a particular area

Po·lish /pṓlish/ *npl.* PEOPLES **PEOPLE OF POLAND** the people of Poland ■ *n.* LANG **OFFICIAL LANGUAGE OF POLAND** the official language of Poland, also spoken in parts of the United States and Europe, especially Germany. It belongs to the Balto-Slavic branch of Indo-European languages and is spoken by about 44 million people. ■ *adj.* **1. OF POLAND** relating to Poland, its people, or culture **2. OF POLISH** relating to the Polish language

Po·lish no·ta·tion *n.* a notation for symbolic logic where the logical operators are placed as prefixes in front of formulas instead of between them, allowing parentheses to be dispensed with. For example, "p or (q and r)" becomes "or p and q r." [From the fact that it was developed by mathematicians in Poland]

polit. *abbr.* **1.** politics **2.** political

Pol·it·bu·ro /póllit byŏŏrō/ *n.* the executive and policymaking committee of a governing Communist Party, especially the committee consisting of twenty members in the former Soviet Union [Early 20thC. From Russian *politbyuro*, literally "political bureau."]

po·lite /pə līt/ (**-lit·er, -lit·est**) *adj.* **1. WELL-MANNERED** showing or possessing good manners or common courtesy **2. ELEGANT** socially superior to ordinary people and considered refined or cultivated [15thC. From Latin *politus*, the past participle of *polire* "to polish" (see POLISH).] —**po·lite·ly** *adv.* —**po·lite·ness** *n.*

pol·i·tesse /pòllee téss/ *n.* politeness of a very formal or genteel kind [Early 18thC. From French, literally "politeness."]

pol·i·tic /póllətik/ *adj.* possessing or displaying tact, shrewdness, or cunning [15thC. Via Old French from, ultimately, Greek *politēs* "citizen," from *polis* "city" (see POLIS).] —**pol·i·tic·ly** *adv.*

po·lit·i·cal /pə líttik'l/ *adj.* **1. CONCERNED WITH PARTY POLITICS** relating to politics, especially party politics **2. CONCERNED WITH GOVERNMENT** relating to civil administration or government **3. RESULTING FROM UNACCEPTABLE BELIEFS** arising from somebody's voiced opposition to a government or from voiced support for policies and principles regarded by authorities as unacceptable **4. PRAGMATIC** carried out for reasons that best serve a desired outcome rather than for reasons that are, e.g., morally justifiable ○ *denies that this was a political decision* —**po·lit·i·cal·ly** *adv.*

po·lit·i·cal ac·tion com·mit·tee *n.* a group that seeks to advance its interests by raising money to contribute to a political candidate or campaign

po·lit·i·cal e·con·o·my *n.* the study of ways in which economics and government policies interact (*dated*) —**po·lit·i·cal e·con·o·mist** *n.*

po·lit·i·cal·ly cor·rect *adj.* marked by language or conduct that deliberately avoids giving offense, e.g., on the basis of ethnic origin or sexual orientation —**po·lit·i·cal cor·rect·ness** *n.*

po·lit·i·cal par·ty *n.* an organization that collectively represents a political ideology, especially in a constitutional government or opposition

po·lit·i·cal pris·on·er *n.* somebody who is imprisoned because his or her political actions or beliefs are regarded as unacceptable or subversive

po·lit·i·cal sci·ence *n.* the study of political organizations and institutions, especially governments —**po·lit·i·cal sci·en·tist** *n.*

po·lit·i·cal ter·ror·ism *n.* the use of intimidating violence for political ends, or a specific instance of this —**po·lit·i·cal ter·ror·ist** *n.*

pol·i·ti·cian /pòllə tísh'n/ *n.* **1. SOMEBODY ACTIVE IN POLITICS** somebody who is actively or professionally engaged in politics **2. GOVERNMENT MEMBER** a member of a branch of government **3. SOMEBODY SEEKING PERSONAL POWER** somebody whose main political motive is self-advancement (*disapproving*) **4. SCHEMER** somebody who deviously manipulates interrelationships, especially in a workplace [Late 16thC. Formed from POLITIC.]

po·lit·i·cize /pə lítti sīz/ (**-cized, -ciz·ing, -ciz·es**) *v.* **1.** *vti.* **INTRODUCE INTO THE POLITICAL ARENA** to bring something such as an issue of public interest into the political arena **2.** *vt.* **GIVE A POLITICAL AWARENESS OR FLAVOR TO** to make somebody politically aware or active, or introduce a political element to something —**po·lit·i·ci·za·tion** /pə lìttissi záysh'n/ *n.*

pol·i·tick·ing /póllә tiking/ *n.* political activity, especially campaigning or speechmaking

po·lit·i·co /pə lítti kō/ (*plural* **-cos**) *n.* a politician, especially one whose words are dismissed as trite or whose motives are disapproved of as self-serving (*informal*) [Mid-17thC. From Italian or Spanish, "politician."]

pol·i·tics /póllətiks/ *n.* **1. THEORY AND PRACTICE OF GOVERNMENT** the theory and practice of forming and running organizations connected with government (*takes a singular verb*) **2. POLICYMAKING ACTIVITY** activity within a political party or organization that is concerned with debate and the creation and carrying out of distinctive policies rather than merely the administration of the state (*takes a singular or plural verb*) **3. INTERRELATIONSHIPS IN A SPECIFIC FIELD** the totality of interrelationships in a particular area of life involving power, authority, or influence, and capable of manipulation (*takes a singular or plural verb*) ○ *the politics of education* **4. CALCULATED ADVANCEMENT** the use of tactics and strategy to gain power in a group or organization (*takes a singular or plural verb*) **5. POLITICAL LIFE** political life as a profession (*takes a singular verb*) ■ *npl.* **1. POLITICAL ACTIVITY** political activity at any level **2. POLITICAL BELIEFS** political persuasions or beliefs

pol·i·ty /póllitee/ (*plural* **-ties**) *n.* **1. PARTICULAR FORM OF GOVERNMENT** a particular form of government that exists within a state or an institution **2. POLITICS AND GOVERNMENT WITHIN SOCIETY** that aspect of society that is oriented to politics and government **3. POLITICAL ENTITY**

a state, society, or institution regarded as a political entity [Mid-16thC. Via Latin from Greek *politeia* (see POLICE).]

Library of Congress

James Knox Polk

Polk /pōk/, **James Knox** (1795–1849) U.S. statesman and 11th president of the United States. Under his Democratic administration (1845–49), the United States expanded westward to the Pacific Ocean.

pol·ka /pṓlkə, pṓkə/ *n.* **1. LIVELY DANCE** a lively dance for couples consisting of three quick steps and a hop and originating in Central Europe **2. MUSIC FOR THE POLKA** a piece of music for the polka, in fast two-four time ■ *vi.* (**-kaed, -ka·ing, -kas**) **DANCE THE POLKA** to dance the polka [Mid-19thC. Origin uncertain: probably via Czech from Polish, the feminine form of *Polak* "Pole," which developed from a prehistoric Slavic word meaning "field."]

pol·ka dot *n.* a dot or round spot repeated to form a regular pattern in a contrasting color, especially on fabric

poll /pōl/ *n.* **1.** POL **ELECTION** a political election in its entirety, including the casting, recording, and counting of votes **2. SURVEY OF THE PUBLIC** a questioning of the population or of a representative sample to tally opinions or gather other information. ◊ **opinion poll 3.** POL **NUMBER OF VOTES** the total number of votes cast in an election **4. HEAD** the head, or the back part of the head (*archaic*) **5.** TECH **STRIKING SURFACE OF A HAMMER** the broad, hitting part of a hammer ■ **polls** *npl.* POL **PLACE FOR VOTING IN AN ELECTION** a place where votes are recorded during an election ■ *v.* (**polled, poll·ing, polls**) **1.** *vt.* **SAMPLE OPINION METHODICALLY** to sample the opinions or attitudes of a group of people systematically **2.** *vt.* POL **RECEIVE A CERTAIN NUMBER OF VOTES** to receive a particular number of votes in an election **3.** *vti.* **CAST A VOTE IN AN ELECTION** to cast a vote in an election **4.** *vt.* LAW **RECORD JURY VOTES** to take the vote of each member of a jury in turn **5.** *vt.* COMPUT **CHECK THE AVAILABILITY OF COMPUTER COMMUNICATION LINES** to check communication lines in a computer or computer network to determine if they can receive or transmit data **6.** *vt.* AGRIC **SHEAR AN ANIMAL** to clip or shear an animal **7.** *vt.* AGRIC **REMOVE AN ANIMAL'S HORNS** to cut an animal's horns short or cut them off [13thC. Origin uncertain: probably from Middle Dutch or Middle Low German. The original meaning underlying all its senses is "head"; the "voting" meaning comes from the idea of counting heads.]

pol·lack /póllək/ (*plural* **-lack**), **pol·lock** (*plural* **-lock**) *n.* a marine fish with a protruding lower jaw, found in North Atlantic waters. It belongs to the cod family and is an important food fish. Genus: *Pollachius.* [Early 16thC. Alteration of Scots *podlok*, of unknown origin.]

pol·lard /póllərd/ *n.* **1.** BOT **TREE WITH BRANCHES CUT** a tree whose branches are cut back extensively to encourage denser growth **2.** ZOOL **ANIMAL WITH HORNS REMOVED OR SHED** an animal that has shed its horns or antlers, or has had its horns removed ■ *vt.* (**-lard·ed, -lard·ing, -lards**) **CUT BRANCHES OR HORNS** to cut back the branches of a tree, or remove the horns of an animal [Mid-17thC. Formed from POLL. The underlying meaning is "having its head cut."]

pol·len /póllən/ *n.* a powdery substance produced by flowering plants that contains male reproductive cells. It is carried by wind and insects to other plants, which it fertilizes. [Mid-18thC. From Latin, "fine flour, dust."]

pol·len bas·ket *n.* the hollow part of a bee's hind leg, used to transport pollen

pol·len count *n.* a scientific measure of the amount of pollen in a specific volume of air during a 24-hour period

pol·len moth·er cell *n.* a cell in a flowering plant that produces four pollen grains after cell division

pol·len sac *n.* a cavity in the anther of a flower, where pollen is produced

pol·len tube *n.* a hollow tube that develops from a pollen grain and conveys male reproductive cells to the egg cell

pol·lex /pó lèks/ (*plural* **-li·ces** /-lə seez/) *n.* the first digit of the forelimb in birds and animals, or the thumb in humans (*technical*) [Mid-19thC. From Latin, of uncertain origin.]

pol·li·nate /póllə nàyt/ (**-nat·ed, -nat·ing, -nates**) *vt.* to transfer pollen from the anthers to the stigma, usually from one plant to another, and fertilize it [Late 19thC. Formed from Latin *pollin-*, the stem of *pollen* (see POLLEN).] —**pol·li·na·tion** /pòllə náysh'n/ *n.* —**pol·li·na·tor** /póllə nàytər/ *n.*

pol·lin·i·a plural of **pollinium**

pol·li·nif·er·ous /pòllə nífərəss/ *adj.* producing or carrying pollen [Mid-19thC. Coined from the Latin stem *pollin-* (see POLLINATE) + -FEROUS.]

pol·lin·ium /pə línnee əm/ (*plural* **-ia** /-iə/) *n.* a cohering mass of pollen grains transported as a whole during pollination, typical of orchids and milkweeds [Mid-19thC. From modern Latin, formed from the Latin stem *pollin-* (see POLLINATE).]

pol·li·no·sis /pòllə nóssiss/ *n.* hay fever (*technical*) [Early 20thC. Formed from the Latin stem *pollin-* (see POLLINATE).]

pol·li·wog /pólli wòg/, **pol·ly·wog** *n. U.K., U.S., Can* a tadpole (*regional*) [15thC. Alteration of earlier *polwygle*, from *poll* "head" (see POLL) + WIGGLE.]

pol·lock *n.* = **pollack**

Pol·lock /pólləck/, **Jackson** (1912–56) U.S. artist. A leading abstract expressionist, he used action-painting techniques to create intricate interlaced webs of paint. Full name **Paul Jackson Pollock**

poll·ster /pṓlstər/ *n.* somebody who conducts public opinion polls

poll tax *n.* any flat-rate tax levied on all the individuals in a population, often as a prerequisite to voting

pol·lut·ant /pə lóot'nt/ *n.* something that pollutes, e.g., chemicals or waste products that contaminate the air, soil, or water

pol·lute /pə lóot/ (**-lut·ed, -lut·ing, -lutes**) *vt.* **1. CONTAMINATE** to cause harm to an area of the natural environment, e.g., the air, soil, or water, usually by introducing damaging substances such as chemicals or waste products **2. CORRUPT OR DEFILE** to make somebody morally or spiritually impure **3. DESECRATE** to violate the sacred nature of a holy place [14thC. From Latin *pollut-*, the past participle stem of *polluere*. Ultimately from an Indo-European base meaning "dirt, to make dirty."] —**pol·lut·er** *n.*

pol·lut·ed /pə lóotəd/ *adj.* contaminated, tainted, corrupted, or desecrated

pol·lu·tion /pə lóosh'n/ *n.* **1. ACT OF POLLUTING** the act of polluting something, especially the natural environment **2. POLLUTED STATE** the state or condition of being polluted, or the presence of pollutants ○ *Pollution will destroy fish in the rivers.*

Pol·lux *n.* ◆ **Castor and Pollux**

Pol·ly·an·na /pòllee ánnə/ *n.* somebody who is invariably and unrealistically optimistic [Early 20thC. Named for the heroine of children's stories written by the U.S. author Eleanor Hodgman Porter (1868–1920).]

pol·ly·wog *n.* = **polliwog**

po·lo /pṓlō/ *n.* **1.** SPORTS **TEAM GAME PLAYED ON HORSEBACK** a game played by teams on horseback, with players using long-handled mallets to drive a wooden ball into a goal **2.** SPORTS **TEAM GAME PLAYED WITH BALL** any of several team games whose object is to drive a ball into a goal, e.g., water polo (*usually used in combination*) **3.** (*plural* **-los**) CLOTHES **POLO SHIRT** a polo shirt (*informal*) [Late 19thC. From Tibetan *pholo*, literally "ball game."]

Po·lo /pṓlō/, **Marco** (1254–1324) Venetian merchant and traveler. His accounts of his travels to China offered Europeans a firsthand view of Asian lands and stimulated interest in Asian trade.

po·lo coat *n.* a double-breasted overcoat, usually made of camel's hair

pol·o·naise /pòllə náyz, pòlə-/ *n.* **1.** DANCE **SLOW FORMAL DANCE FOR COUPLES** a slow and stately dance of Polish origin, for couples **2.** MUSIC **MUSIC FOR A POLONAISE** a piece of music for the polonaise, in $\frac{3}{4}$ time **3.** CLOTHES **CUTAWAY DRESS WITH UNDERSKIRT** a dress with a tight bodice, cut away at the waist to reveal an inner skirt [Mid-18thC. From French, "Polish."]

po·lo·ni·um /pə lṓnee əm/ *n.* a very rare naturally radioactive metallic element found in uranium ores, used to remove static electricity. Symbol **Po** [Late 19thC. Formed from medieval Latin *Polonia* "Poland," the home of Marie CURIE, one of the element's discoverers.]

po·lo po·ny *n.* a horse ridden in the game of polo

po·lo shirt *n.* a lightweight casual shirt, usually made of knitted cotton, with a small square collar and a buttoned opening at the neck [From the fact that it is traditionally worn by polo players]

Pol Pot /pòl pót/ (1928–98) Cambodian political leader. He led the communist Khmer Rouge to victory, and approximately 1.7 million people died under his rule (1975–79). Real name **Saloth Sar**

pol·ter·geist /pṓltər gìst/ *n.* a supposed supernatural spirit that reveals its presence by creating disturbances, e.g., by knocking over objects [Mid-19thC. From German, literally "noisy ghost."]

pol·troon /pol tróon/ *n.* an offensive term for a contemptible coward (*archaic*) [Early 16thC. Via French from Italian *poltrone* "coward, lazy person," of uncertain origin.]

pol·y /póllee/ (*plural* **-ys**) *n.* (*informal*) **1.** TEXTILES **POLYESTER** polyester **2.** MED **POLYMORPHONUCLEAR LEUKOCYTE** a polymorphonuclear leukocyte **3.** CHEM **POLYETHYLENE** polyethylene [Late 20thC. Shortening.]

poly- *prefix.* **1.** more than one ○ *polyandry* **2.** more than normal ○ *polyphagia* **3.** polymer ○ *polyethylene* [From Greek *polus* "much" (source of English *hoi polloi*). Ultimately from an Indo-European base meaning "to fill," which is also the ancestor of *full, plenty, plus,* and *plural*.]

pol·y·a·cryl·a·mide /pòllee akrə lá mìd, -ə kríllə-, -mid/ *n.* a white solid polymer of acrylamide, used as a thickening, clouding, and absorbent agent

pol·y·ad·e·nyl·ic ac·id /pollee add'n illik-/ *n.* a segment of RNA made up of multiple units of adenylic acid, found in messenger RNA molecules. It stabilizes RNA during protein synthesis.

pol·y·al·co·hol /pòllee álkə hòl/ *n.* = **polyol**

pol·y·am·ide /pòllee á mìd, -ámmid/ *n.* any synthetic polymer that has recurring amide groups. Nylon is a polyamide.

pol·y·a·mine /pòllee ə meén, -á meén/ *n.* any organic compound containing more than one amino group

pol·y·an·dry /pòllee àndree/ *n.* **1.** ANTHROP **HAVING MULTIPLE HUSBANDS** the custom of having more than one husband **2.** ZOOL **HAVING MULTIPLE MATES** animal mating in which a female mates with more than one male during any single breeding season **3.** BOT **HAVING MANY STAMENS** possession by a plant of a large number of stamens [Late 17thC. From Greek *poluandria*, literally "many husbands," from the stem *andr-* "man, husband."] —**pol·y·an·drous** /pòllee ándrəss/ *adj.*

pol·y·an·thus /pòllee ánthəss/ (*plural* **-thus·es** *or* **-thi** /-thì/) *n.* **1. HYBRID PRIMROSE** a hybrid primrose with bright flowers in a variety of colors. Latin name: *Primula polyantha.* **2.** = **polyanthus narcissus** [Early 18thC. Via modern Latin from Greek *poluanthos*, literally "having many flowers."]

pol·y·an·thus nar·cis·sus *n.* a narcissus with small white or yellow flowers, native to Europe and Asia. Latin name: *Narcissus tazetta.*

pol·y·a·tom·ic /pòllee ə tómmik/ *adj.* used to describe a molecule that has more than two atoms

pol·y·ba·sic /pòllee báyssik/ *adj.* used to describe a molecule or compound that has two or more atoms of replaceable hydrogen

pol·y·ba·site /pòllee báy sìt/ *n.* a rare gray to black crystalline mineral containing silver, found near silver ores [Mid-19thC. From German *Polybasit*, from Greek *polus* "much" + German *Basis* "base," from its chemical composition.]

pol·y·car·bon·ate /pòllee kaárbə nàyt, -kaárbənət/ *n.* a strong synthetic resin used in molded products, unbreakable windows, and optical components such as spectacle lenses

pol·y·cen·trism /pòllee sén trìzzəm/ *n.* the belief, formerly held, that national spheres of power not modeled on the Soviet Union were possible within Communism —**pol·y·cen·tric** *adj.* —**pol·y·cen·trist** *n., adj.*

pol·y·chete /póllee kèet/ *n.* a marine worm with a segmented body and bristled fleshy appendages used in swimming. Class: Polychaeta. [Late 19thC. From modern Latin *Polychaeta*, class name, from Greek *polukhaitēs* "having much hair," from *khaitē* "long hair."] —**pol·y·che·tous** /pòllee kèetəss/ *adj.*

pol·y·chlo·rin·at·ed bi·phen·yl /pòlli kláwri naytəd bī fénn'l, -fèen'l/ *n.* full form of **PCB**

pol·y·chro·mat·ic /pòllee krō máttik/ *adj.* **1. WITH MANY COLORS** having, showing, or consisting of many colors, either at the same time or in sequence **2. WITH MANY WAVELENGTHS** used to describe electromagnetic radiation that has multiple wavelengths

pol·y·chrome /póllee krōm/ *adj.* **1. WITH MULTI-COLORED DECORATION** decorated with many or varied colors **2.** PHYS = **polychromatic** *adj.* 1 ■ *n.* ARTS **MULITCOLORED OBJECT** a polychrome object or artifact

pol·y·clin·ic /pòllee klínnik/ *n.* a clinic, often independent of a hospital, in which medical care is provided by a range of specialists

pol·y·clone /póllee klōn/ *n.* a clone derived from groups of cells of different ancestry or genetic constitution —**pol·y·clo·nal** /pòllee klṓn'l/ *adj.* —**pol·y·clo·nal·ly** *adv.*

pol·y·con·ic pro·jec·tion /prə jékshən/ *n.* a conic map projection in which all meridians, except the central, are curved and the parallels are nonconcentric arcs

pol·y·cot·y·le·don /pòllee kótt'l èed'n/ *n.* a plant with more than two cotyledons —**pol·y·cot·y·le·don·ous** *adj.*

pol·y·cy·clic /pòllee sīklik, -síklik/ *adj.* **1.** BIOL **WITH SEVERAL WHORLS** used to describe a shell that has two or more whorls **2.** CHEM **WITH SEVERAL RINGS OF ATOMS** used to describe a compound having two or more closed rings of atoms —**pol·y·cy·clic** *n.*

pol·y·cys·tic /pòllee sístik/ *adj.* used to describe an organ, e.g., a kidney or ovary, that has developed multiple cysts

pol·y·cy·the·mi·a /pòllee sī thèemee ə/ *n.* an abnormal increase in red blood cells, occurring on its own or in conjunction with other diseases, especially of the respiratory or circulatory systems [Mid-19thC. Coined from POLY- + -CYTE + HEMO- + -IA, literally "many-blood-cell disease."]

pol·y·dac·tyl /pòllee dákt'l/ *adj.* used to describe vertebrates, including human beings, that have more than the normal number of fingers or toes —**pol·y·dac·tyl** *n.*

pol·y·dip·si·a /pòllee dípsee ə/ *n.* abnormally excessive thirst [Mid-17thC. Coined from POLY- + Greek *dipsa* "thirst" + -IA.] —**pol·y·dip·sic** *adj.*

pol·y·e·lec·tro·lyte /pòllee i léktrə līt/ *n.* an electrolyte that has a high molecular weight, e.g., a protein

pol·y·em·bry·o·ny /pòllee émbree ənee, -em brī-/ *n.* the production of more than one embryo from a single egg —**pol·y·em·bry·on·ic** /pòllee émbree ónnik/ *adj.*

pol·y·ene /póllee èen/ *n.* a hydrocarbon that has many alternating single and double carbon-carbon bonds

pol·y·es·ter /póllee èstər, pòllee éstər/ *n.* **1. SYNTHETIC POLYMER** a synthetic polymer used in making resins, plastics, and textile fibers. The monomer units of polyesters are linked together by the chemical group -COO-. **2. SYNTHETIC FABRIC** a strong hard-wearing synthetic fabric with low moisture absorbency, made from a polyester

pol·y·eth·yl·ene /pòllee éthə lèen/ *n.* a plastic polymer of ethylene used to make containers, packaging, and electrical insulation

pol·y·eth·yl·ene gly·col *n.* any of several polymers of ethylene compounds that are used as emulsifiers and lubricants in ointments and cosmetics

po·lyg·a·my /pə líggəmee/ *n.* **1.** ANTHROP **HAVING MULTIPLE SPOUSES** the custom of having more than one spouse at the same time **2.** ZOOL **HAVING MULTIPLE MATES** animal mating in which an individual mates with more than one animal during any single breeding season [Late 16thC. Via French from, ultimately, ecclesiastical Greek *polugamos* "often married," from Greek *gamos* "marriage."] —**po·lyg·a·mist** *n.* —**po·lyg·a·mous** *adj.* —**po·lyg·a·mous·ly** *adv.*

pol·y·gene /póllee jèen/ *n.* any in a group of genes where the number of those genes present collectively determines the extent of a characteristic, e.g., height —**pol·y·gen·ic** /pòllee jénnik/ *adj.* —**pol·y·gen·i·cal·ly** *adv.*

pol·y·gen·e·sis /pòllee jénnəssiss/ *n.* origin from more than one species, line of ancestors, or source —**pol·y·gen·et·ic** /pòllee jə néttik/ *adj.* —**pol·y·gen·et·i·cal·ly** *adv.*

pol·y·glot /póllee glòt/ *adj.* **1. COMPETENT IN MANY LANGUAGES** capable of reading, writing, or speaking many languages **2. IN MANY LANGUAGES** written or communicated in many languages ■ *n.* **1. MULTILINGUAL PERSON** somebody who has a command of many languages **2. BOOK CONTAINING TEXT IN MANY LANGUAGES** a book, especially a Bible, that gives the text in several languages **3. MIX OF LANGUAGES** a confused mixture of languages [Mid-17thC. Via French from Greek *poluglōttos*, from *glōtta* "tongue, language" (source of English *glottis* and *glossary*).] —**pol·y·glot·ism** *n.*

pol·y·gon /póllee gòn/ *n.* a geometrical plane figure with three or more straight sides [Late 16thC. Via late Latin from Greek *polugōnos* "many-angled," from *-gōnos* "-angled."] —**po·lyg·o·nal** /pə líggən'l/ *adj.* —**po·lyg·o·nal·ly** *adv.*

po·lyg·o·num /pə líggənəm/ *n.* a plant with bulbous stem joints and spikes of small flowers. Genus: *Polygonum*. [Early 18thC. Via modern Latin, genus name, from Greek *polugonon* "knotgrass," literally "many-jointed," from *gonu* "knee, joint."]

pol·y·graph /póllee gràf/ *n.* **1. DEVICE RECORDING INVOLUNTARY RESPONSES** an electrical device that registers several involuntary physical activities, including pulse rate and perspiration. It is often used as a lie detector. **2. TEST USING POLYGRAPH** a test using a polygraph, or a result of this test ■ *vt.* (**-graphed, -graph·ing, -graphs**) **TEST SOMEBODY USING POLYGRAPH** to test somebody, usually somebody suspected of committing a crime, using a polygraph [Mid-20thC. From the fact that it measures a number of physiological indicators at the same time.] —**pol·y·graph·ic** /pòllee gráffik/ *adj.* —**pol·y·graph·i·cal·ly** *adv.*

po·lyg·y·ny /pə líjjənee/ *n.* **1.** ANTHROP **HAVING MULTIPLE WIVES** the custom of being married to more than one wife at the same time. ◊ **polygamy 2.** ZOOL **HAVING MULTIPLE MATES** animal mating in which a male mates with more than one female during any single breeding season **3.** BOT **HAVING MANY PISTILS OR STYLES** the possession by a plant of many pistils or styles [Late 18thC. Formed from Greek *gunē* "woman" (source of English *gyneco-*).] —**po·lyg·y·nist** *n.* —**po·lyg·y·nous** *adj.*

pol·y·he·dra *n.* plural of **polyhedron**

pol·y·he·dral /pòllee hèedrəl/ *adj.* relating to or in the form of a polyhedron

pol·y·he·dral an·gle *n.* a geometric angle formed by the intersection of three or more planes meeting at a point, e.g., the peak of a pyramid

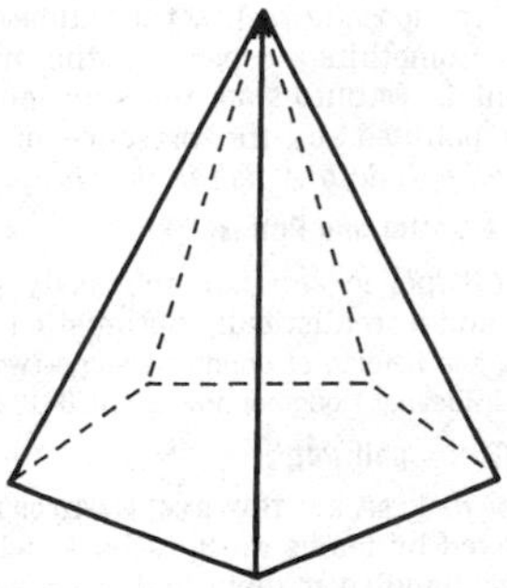

Polyhedron

pol·y·he·dron /pòllee hèedrən/ (*plural* **-drons** *or* **-dra** /-drə/) *n.* a solid geometric figure that has many faces. A regular polyhedron has its faces formed from identical regular polygons that make equal angles with each other. [Late 16thC. From Greek *poluedron* "many-based figure," from *hedra* "base."]

pol·y·hy·drox·y /pòllee hī dróksee/, **pol·y·hy·dric** /-hīdrik/ *adj.* used to describe a compound that has two or more hydroxyl groups in each molecule

Pol·y·hym·ni·a /pòllee hímnee ə/ *n.* in Greek mythology, the Muse responsible for songs and dances dedicated to the deities

pol·y·im·ide /pòllee í mīd, -ímmid/ *n.* any tough durable polymer that contains an imido group, chiefly used in heat-resistant coatings

pol·y·math /póllee màth/ *n.* somebody who is knowledgeable in a variety of subjects [Early 17thC. From Greek *polumathēs*, literally "somebody with much learning," from *manthanein* "to learn" (source of English *mathematics*).] —**pol·y·math·ic** /pòllee máthik/ *adj.* —**pol·y·ma·thy** /pə límməthee/ *n.*

pol·y·mer /pólləmər/ *n.* a natural or synthetic compound that consists of large molecules made of many chemically bonded smaller identical molecules. Starch and nylon are polymers. [Mid-19thC. From Greek *polumerēs* "having many parts," from *meros* "part."] —**pol·y·mer·ic** /pòllə mérrik/ *adj.*

pol·y·mer·ase /pə límmə ràyz, -ràyss/ *n.* any enzyme that catalyzes a polymer, especially in DNA or RNA

pol·y·mer·ase chain re·ac·tion *n.* a technique used to replicate a fragment of DNA in order to replicate the DNA sequence

po·lym·er·i·za·tion /pə lìmməri záysh'n, pòllimərì-/ *n.* the chemical reaction in which a compound is made into a polymer by the addition or condensation of smaller molecules —**pol·y·mer·ize** /póllәmə rīz, pə límmə-/ *vti.*

po·lym·er·ous /pə límmərəss/ *adj.* used to describe an organism that consists of many parts or segments

pol·y·morph /póllee màwrf/ *n.* **1.** BIOL **ANIMAL OR PLANT WITH MANY FORMS** an animal or plant that has several different adult forms **2.** CHEM **CHEMICAL COMPOUND WITH DIFFERENT FORMS** a chemical compound that has several crystalline forms —**pol·y·mor·phic** /pòllee máwrfik/ *adj.* —**pol·y·mor·phism** *n.*

pol·y·myx·in /pòllee míksin/ *n.* a peptide antibiotic that is derived from a soil bacterium [Mid-20thC. Formed from modern Latin *Polymyxa*, species name, from POLY- + Greek *muxa* "slime."]

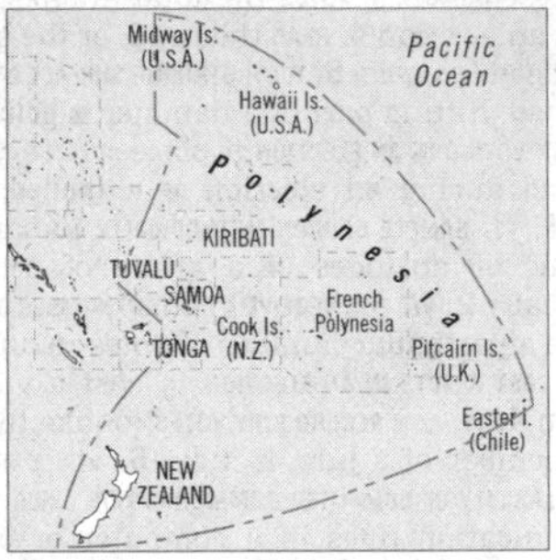

Polynesia

Pol·y·ne·sia /pòllə nèezhə/ one of three major divisions of the Pacific Islands, encompassing a number of island groups in the central and southern Pacific Ocean, including Hawaii, Samoa, and the Cook Islands

Pol·y·ne·sian /pòllee nèezh'n/ *n.* **1.** PEOPLES **SOMEBODY FROM POLYNESIA** somebody who was born or raised on any of the many islands of the central and southern Pacific **2.** LANG **LANGUAGE GROUP OF POLYNESIA** a group of languages, including Fijian, Hawaiian, and Maori, spoken on islands of the central and southern Pacific. They form a branch of the Austronesian family of languages. About 800,000 people speak a Polynesian language. ■ *adj.* **1. OF POLYNESIA** relating to any of the countries or islands of Polynesia, their people, or their cultures **2.** LANG **OF POLYNESIAN** relating to the group of languages called Polynesian

pol·y·neu·ri·tis /pòllee noo rítiss/ *n.* simultaneous inflammation of several nerves at once

Pol·y·ni·ces /pòllee nīseez/ *n.* in Greek mythology, one of the sons of Oedipus and Jocasta. He and his brother Eteocles killed each other in a struggle over the throne of Thebes.

pol·y·no·mi·al /pòllə nṓmee əl/ *adj.* SCI **WITH MORE THAN TWO TERMS** used to describe a mathematical expression that has more than two terms, or a system of taxonomic nomenclature that uses more than two names ■ *n.* **1.** MATH **MATHEMATICAL EXPRESSION** a mathematical expression consisting of the sum of a number of terms, each of which contains a constant and variables raised to a positive integral power **2.**

BIOL **MULTI-TERM TAXONOMIC NAME** a taxonomic name of a plant or animal that has more than two terms, e.g., one giving a genus, species, and subspecies [Late 17thC. Modeled on BINOMIAL.]

pol·y·nu·cle·o·tide /pòllee nóoklee ə tīd/ *n.* a chemical compound made up of many nucleotides linked to one another, forming a chain

pol·y·ol /póllee àwl/ *n.* any alcohol that contains more than two hydroxyl groups. Glycerol is a polyol.

poly·oma /pòlli ṓmə/, **poly·oma vi·rus** *n.* a virus in rodents that can produce tumors

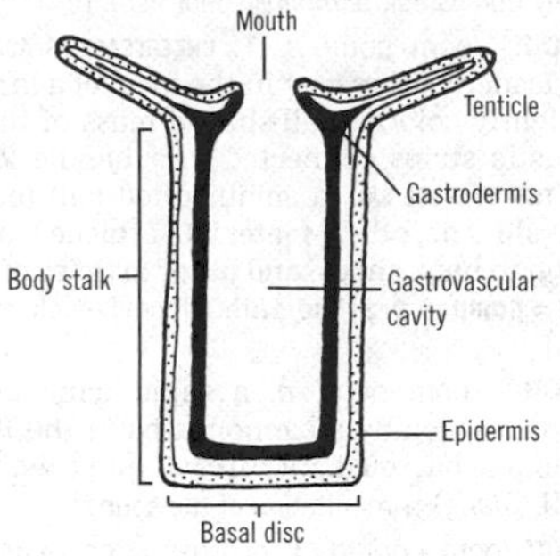

Polyp: Cross section of a polyp

pol·yp /póllip/ *n.* **1.** MARINE BIOL **SEDENTARY STAGE OF MARINE INVERTEBRATE** a single-cavity marine invertebrate (**coelenterate**) in its sedentary stage. It attaches to rock at one end of its cylindrical body and has a tentacled mouth at the other end. This stage usually alternates with a free-swimming form. **2.** MED **BENIGN GROWTH ON BODY** a small stalk-shaped growth sticking out from the skin or from a mucous membrane. Polyps are mostly benign, but some become malignant. [14thC. Via French *polipe* and Latin *polypus* from Greek *polupous* "octopus," literally "many-footed," from *pous* "foot" (source of English *podium*).] —**pol·yp·oid** *adj.* —**poly·pous** *adj.*

pol·y·pep·tide /pòllee pép tīd/ *n.* a natural or synthetic compound consisting of linked amino acids. Proteins are polypeptides.

pol·y·pet·al·ous /pòllee pétt'ləss/ *adj.* used to describe flowers with many separate petals, e.g., roses and carnations

pol·y·pha·gi·a /pòllee fáyjə, -jee ə/ *n.* **1.** MED **ABNORMALLY HUGE APPETITE** an abnormally insatiable appetite for food **2.** BIOL **DIET OF MANY FOODS** the habit on the part of certain animals of feeding on many different types of food —**po·lyph·a·gous** /pə líffəgəss/ *adj.*

pol·y·phase /póllee fàyz/ *adj.* producing two or more phases of alternating current, or two or more alternating voltages of the same frequency

Pol·y·phe·mus /pòllee féeməss/ *n.* in Greek mythology, a cyclops who imprisoned Odysseus, who put out Polyphemus's one eye

pol·y·phe·mus moth *n.* a large North American moth with a large transparent blue eyespot on each hind wing. Latin name: *Antheraea polyphemus.*

pol·y·phone /póllee fōn/ *n.* a letter or character that has more than one way of being pronounced

pol·y·phon·ic /pòllee fónnik/ *adj.* **1.** MUSIC **WITH SEVERAL MELODIES** consisting of two or more largely independent melodic lines, parts, or voices that sound simultaneously **2.** LING **WITH SEVERAL POSSIBLE PRONUNCIATIONS** used to describe a letter or character that may be pronounced in several different ways —**pol·y·phon·i·cal·ly** *adv.*

pol·y·phon·ic prose *n.* highly rhythmic prose that makes use of poetic devices such as alliteration and assonance

po·lyph·o·ny /pə líffənee/ *n.* **1.** MUSIC **MUSIC WITH SEVERAL MELODIES** musical composition that uses simultaneous, largely independent, melodic parts, lines, or voices **2.** LING **USE OF LETTER FOR DIFFERENT SOUNDS** the representation of different sounds by the same letter in a writing system [Early 19thC. From Greek *poluphōnia* "multiplicity of sounds," from, ultimately, *phōnē* "voice, sound" (see -PHONE).] —**po·lyph·o·nous** *adj.* —**po·lyph·o·nous·ly** *adv.*

pol·y·phy·let·ic /pòllee fī léttik/ *adj.* derived or descended from several groups of ancestors —**pol·y·phy·let·i·cal·ly** *adv.*

pol·y·ploid /póllee plòyd/ *adj.* having more than twice the basic number of chromosomes —**pol·y·ploid** *n.* —**pol·y·ploi·dy** *n.*

pol·y·pod /póllee pòd/ *adj.* used to describe an insect larva with a large number of legs and feet, or this larval stage in the development of some insects [Mid-18thC. Via French from the Greek stem *polupod-* "many-footed," from *pous* "foot" (source of English *podium*).] —**pol·y·pod** *n.*

pol·y·po·dy /póllee pōdee/ (*plural* **-dies**) *n.* a fern with evergreen pinnate leaves and a creeping rootstock. Genus: *Polypodium.* [15thC. Via Latin *polypodium* from Greek *polupodion*, literally "many-footed one."]

pol·yp·o·sis /pòllee pōssiss/ *n.* a condition in which numerous polyps develop in a hollow organ, e.g., the bowel

pol·y·pro·pyl·ene /pòllee prṓpə leen/, **pol·y·pro·pene** /-peen/ *n.* a thermoplastic substance that is a synthetic polymer of propylene, used in making pipes, industrial fibers, and molded objects

pol·yp·tych /póllip tìk/ *n.* an arrangement of three or more panels with a painting or carving on each, usually hinged together and used as an altarpiece in a church [Mid-19thC. Modeled on DIPTYCH.]

pol·y·rhythm /póllee rìthəm/ *n.* musical composition that employs several simultaneous, contrasting rhythms —**pol·y·rhyth·mic** /pòllee ríthmik/ *adj.* —**pol·y·rhyth·mi·cal·ly** *adv.*

pol·y·ri·bo·some /pòllee rībə sōm/ *n.* a cluster of ribosomes linked by a strand of messenger RNA and functioning as a site of protein synthesis

pol·y·sac·cha·ride /pòllee sákə rīd/, **pol·y·sac·cha·rose** *n.* a complex carbohydrate, e.g., starch or cellulose, made up of sugar molecules linked into a branched or chain structure

pol·y·semy /póllee seemee/ *n.* the existence of several meanings for a single word or phrase [Early 20thC. Via modern Latin *polysemia* from, ultimately, Greek *polusēmos* "having many meanings," from *sēma* "sign" (see SEMANTIC).] —**pol·y·se·mous** /pòllee seeməss/ *adj.*

pol·y·sep·al·ous /pòllee séppələss/ *adj.* used to describe flowers that have distinctly separate sepals

pol·y·some /pólli sōm/ *n.* = **polyribosome** [Mid-20thC. Contraction.]

pol·y·so·mic /pòllee sṓmik/ *adj.* used to describe a diploid cell or organism in which some of the chromosomes occur more than twice

pol·y·sor·bate /pòllee sáwr bàyt, -bət/ *n.* an emulsifier used in preparing some foods and drugs [Mid-20thC. Coined from POLY- + SORBITOL + -ATE.]

pol·y·sper·my /póllee spùrmee/ *n.* the fertilization of an egg by several spermatozoa

po·lys·ti·chous /pə lístikəss/ *adj.* used to describe parts of a plant that are arranged in two or more series of rows [Late 19thC. Modeled on DISTICHOUS.]

pol·y·sty·rene /pòllee stī reen/ *n.* a synthetic polymer of styrene that is stable in various physical forms. As a white rigid foam (**expanded polystyrene**) it is used for packing and insulation.

pol·y·sul·fide /pòllee súl fīd/ *n.* a sulfide whose molecules have two or more atoms of sulfur

pol·y·syl·lab·ic /pòllee si lábbik/ *adj.* **1.** **WITH SEVERAL SYLLABLES** having more than one or two syllables **2.** **WITH MANY LONG WORDS** using or containing very long words, often where shorter words would be adequate or better —**pol·y·syl·lab·i·cal·ly** *adv.*

pol·y·syl·la·ble /pòllee sílləb'l/ *n.* a word that has more than one or two syllables

pol·y·syn·ap·tic /pòllee si náptik/ *adj.* used to describe a reflex in the central nervous system that uses two or more synapses

pol·y·syn·de·ton /pòllee síndə tòn/ *n.* the use of multiple conjunctions or coordinate clauses in close succession, as, in "The bad news caused him to weep and cry and wail" [Late 16thC. Modeled on ASYNDETON.]

pol·y·syn·thet·ic /pòllee sin théttik/ *adj.* used to describe a language in which the syntax is conveyed by means of multiple affixes to single words —**pol·y·syn·the·sis** /pòllee sínthəssiss/ *n.* —**pol·y·syn·thet·i·cal·ly** /pòllee sin théttikəlee/ *adv.*

pol·y·tech·nic /pòllee téknik/ *n.* a college offering a range of courses, some of them vocational or technical, at or below the bachelor's degree level [Early 19thC. Via French from Greek *polutekhnos* "multi-skilled," from *tekhnē* "skill" (source of English *technical*).]

pol·y·tene /póllee teen/ *adj.* with multi-stranded chromosomes in contact with corresponding chromosomes —**pol·y·te·nic** /pòllee teenik/ *adj.* —**pol·y·ten·y** /póllee teenee/ *n.*

pol·y·tet·ra·fluor·o·eth·yl·ene /pòllee tettrə floorō éthə leen, -flawrō-/ *n.* a durable, chemically resistant, nonflammable thermoplastic substance widely used to coat metal surfaces, especially the surfaces of cooking pots to make them nonstick

pol·y·the·ism /póllee thee ìzzəm, pòllee thee-/ *n.* worshiping of or believing in more than one deity, especially several deities [Early 17thC. Via French from Greek *polutheos* "of many deities," from *theos* "deity" (see THEO-).] —**pol·y·the·ist** *n.* —**pol·y·the·is·tic** /pòllee thee ístik/ *adj.* —**pol·y·the·is·ti·cal·ly** *adv.*

pol·y·to·nal·i·ty /pòllee tō nállətee/ *n.* music composed in such a way that several keys are used at once —**pol·y·to·nal** /pòllee tṓn'l/ *adj.* —**pol·y·to·nal·ly** *adv.*

pol·y·tro·phic /pòllee tróffik/ *adj.* used to describe bacteria that derive food from several different sources

pol·y·typ·ic /pòllee típpik/, **pol·y·typ·i·cal** /-ik'l/ *adj.* used to describe a taxonomic subset, especially a species, that has many subdivisions

pol·y·un·sat·u·rat·ed /pòllee un sáchə ràytəd/ *adj.* belonging to a class of fats, especially plant oils, that are less likely to be converted into cholesterol in the body. Their molecules have long carbon chains with many double bonds unsaturated by hydrogen atoms.

pol·y·ur·e·thane /pòllee yóorə thàyn/ *n.* any of a group of thermoplastic polymers that are used in resins, coatings, insulation, adhesives, foams, and fibers. They contain the NHCOO chemical group.

pol·y·u·ri·a /pòllee yóoree ə/ *n.* the passing of abnormally large amounts of urine, e.g., in untreated diabetes

pol·y·va·lent /pòllee váylənt/ *adj.* **1.** CHEM **WITH MORE THAN ONE VALENCE** used to describe a chemical element that has more than one valence or a valence of more than two **2.** BIOL **EFFECTIVE AGAINST MULTIPLE AGENTS** used to describe a vaccine that is effective against more than one strain of microorganism, toxin, antigen, or antibody —**pol·y·va·len·cy** *n.*

pol·y·vi·nyl /pòllee vīn'l/ *adj.* used to describe plastics and resins produced by the polymerization of vinyls

pol·y·vi·nyl ac·e·tate *n.* full form of **PVA**

pol·y·vi·nyl chlo·ride *n.* full form of **PVC**

Pol·y·xe·na /pə líksənə/ *n.* in Greek mythology, one of the daughters of King Priam and Queen Hecuba of Troy, sacrificed at the command of the ghost of Achilles

pol·y·zo·an /pòlli zṓ ən/ *n.* BIOL = **bryozoan** [Mid-19thC. Formed from modern Latin *Polyzoa*, former phylum name, from POLY- + -ZOON.]

pom /pom/ *n.* *ANZ* a British person (*informal humorous or disapproving*) [Early 20thC. Shortening of POMMY.]

pom·ace /púmməss, póm-/ *n.* **1.** **REMAINS OF CRUSHED FRUIT** the pulpy mass that remains after apples or other fruits have been crushed and pressed to extract the juice, e.g., to make cider **2.** **FOOD REMAINS AFTER OIL EXTRACTION** the pulpy mass that remains after nuts, fish, or other foods have been crushed and pressed to extract oil or another liquid [Mid-16thC. Via medieval Latin *pomacium* "cider" from, ultimately, Latin *pomum* "apple, fruit."]

pom·ace fly *n.* a tiny fly that lives on decaying fruit, commonly found where cider or wine is being made. Family: Drosophilidae.

po·ma·ceous /pō máyshəss/ *adj.* used to describe a fruit in the form of a large fleshy receptacle with a central seed-bearing core (**pome**), e.g., the apple and the pear [Early 18thC. Formed from Latin *pomum* "apple."]

po·made /pō máyd, pə-, -maad/ *n.* **DRESSING FOR HAIR** a perfumed oil or ointment used to make hair look smooth and shiny ■ *vt.* (**-mad·ed, -mad·ing, -mades**) **PUT POMADE ON** to dress hair with pomade [Mid-16thC. Via French *pommade* from, ultimately, Latin *pomum* "apple," probably because it was originally made with apples.]

po·man·der /pṓ màndər, pō má-/ *n.* **1. AROMATIC MIXTURE** a mixture of aromatic substances enclosed in a sachet, ball, or other container, kept near stored clothes or in a room to impart a pleasant smell. In former times, a pomander was worn as a protection against disease. **2. POMANDER CONTAINER** a container for a pomander, usually a lidded pottery bowl with holes **3. CLOVE-STUDDED ORANGE** an orange or apple studded with cloves and used to scent clothes or a room [15thC. From Old French *pome d'embre*, literally "apple of amber."]

pome /pōm/ *n.* a fleshy fruit that has a central core typically containing five seeds, e.g., an apple or pear [14thC. Via Old French from, ultimately, Latin *pomum* "apple."]

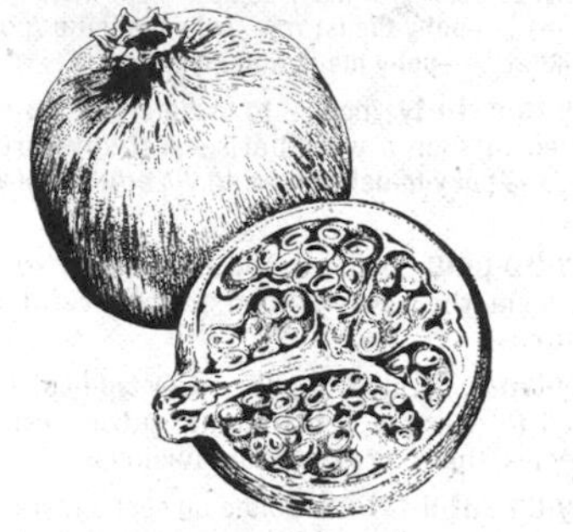
Pomegranate

pome·gran·ate /pómmə grànnət, póm gràn-, púmmə-, púm gràn-/ *n.* **1.** FOOD **ROUND RED FRUIT** a round reddish orange-sized fruit with a tough rind enclosing several chambers that are filled with numerous seeds surrounded by tart juicy red pulp **2.** TREES **ASIAN TREE** the tropical tree, native to Asia, that bears the pomegranate. Latin name: *Punica granatum.* [14thC. From Old French *pome grenate*, literally "seedy apple."]

pom·e·lo /pómmə lō/ (*plural* **-los**) *n.* **1.** FOOD **CITRUS FRUIT** a yellowy-orange citrus fruit similar to a large grapefruit **2.** (*plural* **-los** *or* **-lo**) TREES **CITRUS TREE** the citrus tree, native to Southeast Asia, that bears the pomelo. Latin name: *Citrus maxima.* **3.** FOOD = **grapefruit** [Mid-19thC. Origin uncertain: possibly an alteration of *pompelmous*, from Dutch *pompelmoes*.]

Pom·er·a·ni·an /pòmmə ráynee ən/ *n.* **1.** ZOOL **SMALL DOG** a breed of small dog with a long silky coat, pointed ears, a pointed muzzle, and a long curling tail **2.** PEOPLES **SOMEBODY FROM POMERANIA** somebody who was born in or is an inhabitant of the central European region of Pomerania, which lies mostly in modern Poland ■ *adj.* **OF POMERANIA** relating to the central European region of Pomerania, its people, or their culture [Mid-18thC. Formed from *Pomerania* in central Europe.]

po·mi·cul·ture /pṓmi kùlchər/ *n.* the cultivation of fruit [Late 19thC. Coined from Latin *pomum* "apple, fruit" + CULTURE.]

po·mif·er·ous /pō míffərəss/ *adj.* used to describe fruit plants that bear apples, pears, or any related fleshy fruit with five seeds (**pome**) [Mid-17thC. Formed from Latin *pomifer*, from *pomum* "apple, fruit."]

pom·mel /púmm'l, póm-/ *n.* **1.** EQU **FRONT OF SADDLE** the front part of a saddle that curves upward **2.** ARMS **PART OF SWORD HANDLE** the knob at the hilt of a sword **3.** GYMNASTICS **HANDLE ON POMMEL HORSE** either of the two curved handles on the top of a pommel horse ■ *vt.* = **pummel** [14thC. Via Old French *pomel*, literally "little fruit," from, ultimately, Latin *pomum* "fruit."]

pom·mel horse *n.* **1. GYMNASTICS APPARATUS** a padded oblong piece of gymnastics apparatus that is raised off the floor and has two curved handles on the top **2. GYMNASTICS EVENT** the men's gymnastics event that involves balancing and maneuvering on a pommel horse

pom·my /pómmee/ *adj. ANZ* **BRITISH** British (*informal humorous or disapproving*) ■ *n.* (*plural* **-mies**) *ANZ* = **pom** (*informal humorous or disapproving*) [Early 20thC. Origin uncertain: probably a shortening of *pomegranate*, alteration of *Jimmy Grant* or *Pummy Grant*, rhyming slang for *immigrant*.]

po·mo /pṓmō/, **po-mo** *adj.* postmodern (*informal*) ○ *"beat-generation, counterculture, and pomo literature"* (Hawkeye, *FutureCulture FAQ part 1 & 2*; 1992)

Po·mo (*plural* **-mo** *or* **-mos**) *n.* **1.** PEOPLES **MEMBER OF NATIVE N AMERICAN PEOPLE** a member of a group of Native North American peoples living in northern California **2.** LANG **NATIVE AMERICAN LANGUAGE** any of several closely related Native American languages spoken in parts of northern California. They belong to the Hokan branch of Hokan-Siouan languages. [Late 19thC. From northern Pomo *pʰó•mo•* "at the red earth hole."] —**Po·mo** *adj.*

po·mol·o·gy /pō móllәjee/ *n.* the study or practice of cultivating fruit [Early 19thC. Coined from Latin *pomum* "fruit" + -LOGY.] —**po·mo·log·i·cal** /pṑmə lójjik'l/ *adj.* —**po·mo·log·i·cal·ly** /-lójjikəlee/ *adv.* —**po·mol·o·gist** /pō móllәjist/ *n.*

Po·mo·na /pə mṓnə/ *n.* the Roman goddess of fruit [Mid-17thC. From Latin, from *pomum* "fruit."]

pomp /pomp/ *n.* **1. CEREMONIAL SPLENDOR** a display of great splendor and magnificence **2. SELF-IMPORTANCE** an ostentatious and vain display of importance [14thC. Via Old French from, ultimately, Greek *pompē* "solemn procession, sendoff, escort," from *pempein* "to send," of unknown origin.]

WORD KEY: CULTURAL NOTE

Pomp and Circumstance, an orchestral work by English composer Edward Elgar (parts 1 to 4: 1901–07; part 5: 1930). The title of this series of five military marches (op. 39) derives from the reference in Shakespeare's *Othello* (III iii) to the "pride, pomp, and circumstance of glorious war."

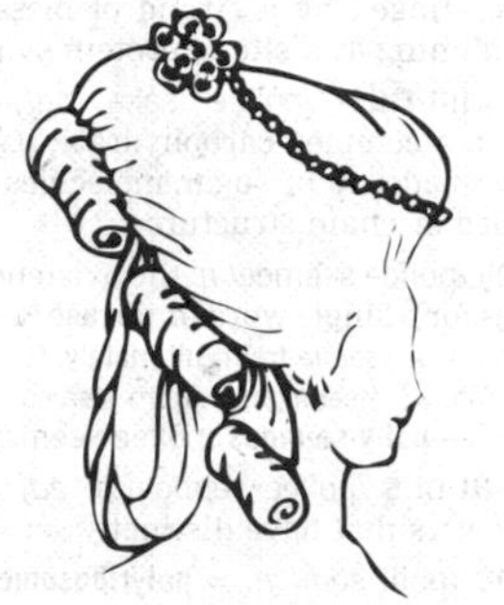
Pompadour

pom·pa·dour /pómpə dàwr, -dòor/ *n.* **1. WOMAN'S HAIRSTYLE** a woman's hairstyle, popular in the 18th century, in which the hair is swept back high off the face over a pad **2. MAN'S HAIRSTYLE** a man's hairstyle in which the hair is combed back off the face to form a mound above the forehead [Mid-18thC. Named for Jeanne-Antoinette Poisson, Marquise de *Pompadour* (1721–64), who popularized the style.]

pom·pa·no /pómpə nō/ (*plural* **-nos** *or* **-no**) *n.* **1. ATLANTIC FISH** a marine food fish with a deep flat body and forked tail, found off the southern Atlantic and Gulf coasts of North America. Latin name: *Trachinotus carolinus.* **2.** = **butterfish** [Late 18thC. From Spanish *pámpano*, of uncertain origin: possibly from *pámpana* "vine leaf" (from its shape) or Latin *pampinus* "tendril" (from its markings).]

Pom·pei·an red /pom pày ən-/ *adj.* of a red color that is tinged with orange, resembling the color of the walls of houses found in Pompeii —**Pom·pei·an red** *n.*

Barnaby's
Pompeii: View of the Forum, with Vesuvius in the background

Pom·pe·ii /pom páy, pom páy ee/ ancient Roman city in southern Italy. It was buried by volcanic ash during the eruption of Mount Vesuvius in A.D. 79, and has been partly excavated.

Pom·pey /pómpee/ (106–48 B.C.) Roman general and statesman. He formed the First Triumvirate with Caesar and Crassus. After quarreling with Caesar, he was defeated by him at Pharsalus (48 B.C.) and escaped to Egypt, where he was assassinated. Full name **Gnaeus Pompeius Magnus**. Known as **Pompey the Great**

Pom·pi·dou /pómpi dòo/, **Georges** (1911–74) French statesman. He was four times prime minister, and followed de Gaulle as president (1969–74).

pom·pil·id /pómpəlid/ *n.* = **spider hunting wasp** [Early 20thC. From modern Latin *Pompilidae*, family name, ultimately from Greek *pompilos* "pilot-fish."]

pom-pom[1] /póm pòm/ *n.* **1. CHEERLEADER'S ACCESSORY** a cheerleader's accessory in the form of a large white or brightly colored ball-shaped mass of thin paper or plastic strips connected to a handle **2.** CLOTHES **SMALL TUFTED WOOL BALL** a small tufted ball made from wool, silk, or other material, attached as a decoration to hats, shoes, and other articles of clothing **3.** BOT = **pompon** *n.* 2 [Mid-18thC. From French, of unknown origin.]

pom-pom[2] /póm pòm/ *n.* a rapid-firing automatic weapon, especially a cannon used in the Boer War or a double-barreled antiaircraft gun used in World War II (*slang*) [An imitation of the sound]

pom·pon /póm pòn/ *n.* **1.** CLOTHES = **pom-pom**[1] *n.* 2 **2.** BOT **SMALL ROUND FLOWER** a small round flower of some chrysanthemum or dahlia varieties, or a variety that has this kind of flower [Mid-18thC. From French, of unknown origin.]

pom·pos·i·ty /pom póssətee/ (*plural* **-ties**) *n.* **1. SELF-IMPORTANCE** an excessive sense of self-importance, usually displayed through exaggerated seriousness or stateliness in speech and manner **2. POMPOUS ACT** an act, remark, or gesture that is exaggerated in its seriousness or stateliness and conveys an excessive sense of self-importance

pom·pous /pómpəss/ *adj.* **1. SELF-IMPORTANT** having an excessive sense of self-importance, usually displayed through exaggerated seriousness or stateliness in speech or manner **2. REVEALING SELF-IMPORTANCE** displaying exaggerated seriousness or stateliness ○ *a pompous gesture* **3. CEREMONIALLY GRAND** full of splendor and magnificence [14thC. Via Old French *pompeux* from, ultimately, Greek *pompē* (see POMP).] —**pom·pous·ly** *adv.* —**pom·pous·ness** *n.*

'pon /pon/ *prep.* upon (*archaic or literary*) [Mid-16thC. Shortening.]

Pon·ca /póngkə/ (*plural* **-ca** *or* **-cas**) *n.* **1.** PEOPLES **MEMBER OF NATIVE N AMERICAN PEOPLE** a member of a Native North American people who formerly occupied lands around the Niobrara River in Nebraska and now live mainly in parts of Oklahoma and Nebraska **2.** LANG **NATIVE AMERICAN LANGUAGE** a Native American language spoken in parts of Oklahoma and Nebraska. It belongs to the Siouan branch of Hokan-Siouan languages and is closely related to Omaha. [Late 18thC. From Ponka *ppákka*.] —**Pon·ca** *adj.*

ponce /pons/ *n. U.K.* **1. OFFENSIVE TERM** an offensive term that deliberately insults a man's sexuality and appearance (*slang insult*) **2. PIMP** a pimp (*slang*) [Late 19thC. Origin unknown.] —**pon·cy** *adj.*

Pon·ce /páwnse/ city and port in southern Puerto Rico, on the Caribbean Sea. Population: 189,988 (1996).

Ponce (de León) /pònss də lée ən, pònth ay də lee ón/, **Juan** (1460–1521) Spanish explorer. He was the first European to reach Florida (1513), but failed in his attempt to set up a colony there (1521).

pon·cho /pónchō/ (*plural* **-chos**) *n.* **1. CLOAK** a simple

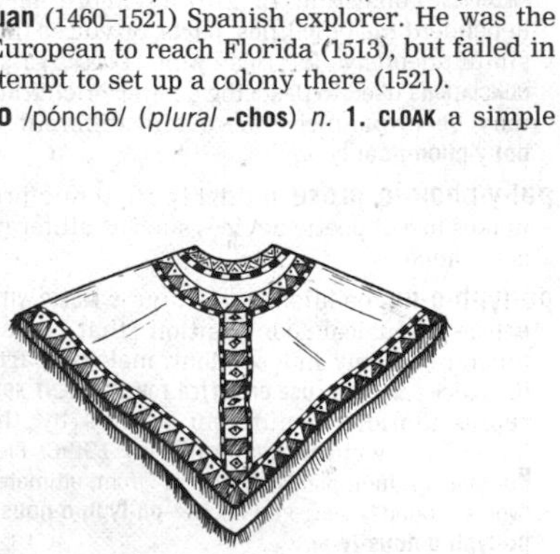
Poncho

outer garment for the upper body in the form of a single piece of heavy cloth, often wool, with a slit in it for the head. Ponchos were originally worn in South America. **2.** TYPE OF RAINCOAT a waterproof outer garment with a hood, made in the style of a poncho [Early 18thC. From American Spanish, of uncertain origin: perhaps from Spanish, variant of *pocho* "faded."]

pond /pond/ *n.* POOL a small still body of water formed naturally or created artificially, e.g., as a feature in a garden ■ *vi.* **(pond·ed, pond·ing, ponds)** FORM POOLS to collect into shallow pools (*refers to water*) [13thC. Alteration of POUND, in the sense "enclosure for fish."]

pond ap·ple *n.* an evergreen tree that has fragrant yellow flowers with red markings inside, found in southern Florida, the American tropics, and West Africa

pon·der /póndər/ **(-dered, -der·ing, -ders)** *vti.* to think about something carefully over a period of time [14thC. Via Old French *ponderer* from Latin *ponderare* "to weigh, consider," from *pondus* "weight" (see PONDEROUS).]

pon·der·a·ble /póndərəb'l/ *adj.* APPRECIABLE significant enough in size or extent to have an effect or be worth taking into consideration ■ *n.* a tall pine of western North America that has yellowish bark and long dark green needles grouped in twos or threes. It is valued for its timber. Latin name: *Pinus ponderosa*. ■ *adj.* MEASURABLE able to be measured, calculated, or predicted ■ *n.* PONDERABLE THING something that is ponderable —**pon·der·a·bil·i·ty** /pòndərə bíllətee/ *n.* —**pon·der·a·bly** /póndərəblee/ *adv.*

pon·der·ous /póndərəss/ *adj.* **1.** MOVING HEAVILY lumbering and laborious in movement **2.** DULL without liveliness or wit **3.** HEAVY-LOOKING disproportionately thick and heavy [14thC. Via Old French *pondereux* from Latin *ponderosus*, from *ponder-*, stem of *pondus* "weight."] —**pon·der·ous·ly** *adv.* —**pon·der·ous·ness** *n.*

pond lil·y *n.* = **water lily**

pond scum *n.* green freshwater algae that form a layer on the surface of stagnant water

pond·weed /pónd wèed/ (*plural* **-weed** *or* **-weeds**) *n.* an aquatic plant that has jointed stems, floating or submerged leaves, and greenish flowers. It grows in ponds and slow streams. Genus: *Potamogeton*.

pone[1] /pōn/ *n.* = **corn pone** [Early 17thC. From Virginia Algonquian *poan*.]

pone[2] /pṓnee, pōn/ *n.* in card games, the person who does not deal in two-handed games, or the person sitting to the right of the dealer [Early 19thC. From Latin *pone* "put," imperative of *ponere* "to place" (see POSITION).]

pon·gee /pon jée, pón jèe/ *n.* **1.** SILK a type of soft, usually unbleached, silk fabric from China or India **2.** IMITATION SILK an imitation of silk pongee, usually made of cotton or rayon [Early 18thC. Origin uncertain, probably from Chinese *běnjī*, literally "own loom," or *běnzhi*, literally "home-woven."]

pon·gid /pónjid/ *n.* any ape of the family that includes the gibbon and the great apes. Family: Pongidae. [Mid-20thC. Via modern Latin *Pongidae*, family name, from, ultimately, Congolese *mpongo* "ape."]

pon·iard /pónnyərd/ *n.* DAGGER a small dagger with a slim blade that is triangular or square in its cross section (*literary*) ■ *vt.* **(-iard·ed, -iard·ing, -iards)** STAB WITH PONIARD to stab somebody with a poniard (*literary*) [Mid-16thC. Via French *poignard* from, ultimately, Latin *pugnus* "fist" (see PUGNACIOUS). The underlying meaning is "weapon held in a clenched fist."]

pons /ponz/ (*plural* **pon·tes** /pón tèez/) *n.* a whitish band of nerve fibers on the surface of the brainstem between the medulla oblongata and midbrain [Late 17thC. From Latin, "bridge" (source of English *pontoon* and *pontiff*). Ultimately from an Indo-European word meaning "to pass over," which is also the ancestor of English *path*.]

pons as·i·no·rum /-assə náwrəm/ *n.* a proposition or problem that is especially difficult for an inexperienced person to understand [From Latin, literally "bridge of asses," originally applied to the proposition of Euclid that the base angles of an isosceles triangle are equal]

Pon·son·by /pónssənbee/, **Vere Brabazon, 9th Earl of Bessborough** (1880–1956) British Canadian administrator who was governor general of Canada (1931–35).

pons Va·ro·li·i /-və rṓli ī/ *n.* ANAT = **pons** [Late 17thC. From Latin, literally "bridge of Varolius," named for C. *Varoli* (1543–75), Italian anatomist.]

Pon·ta Del·ga·da /pòntə del gáadə/ city in Portugal, on São Miguel Island. It is the capital of the autonomous region of the Azores. Population: 21,091 (1991).

Pont·char·train, Lake /pónchər tràyn/ lake in southeastern Louisiana between the Gulf of Mexico and the Mississippi River. It is spanned by the world's longest causeway. Area: 630 sq. mi./1,632 sq. km.

pon·tes plural of **pons**

Pon·ti·ac /póntee àk/ city in southeastern Michigan, 25 mi./40 km northwest of Detroit. It is a car manufacturing center. Population: 71,166 (1990).

Pon·ti·ac /póntee ak/ (1720?–69) Ottawa chief. He led the Ottawa and other Native American peoples in Pontiac's Rebellion against the British (1763–65).

pon·ti·fex /póntə fèks/ (*plural* **-tif·i·ces** /-tíffi sèez/) *n.* a member of the highest council of priests in ancient Rome [Late 16thC. From Latin, literally "way-maker," formed from *pont-*, stem of *pons* "bridge, way" (see PONS).]

Pon·ti·fex Max·i·mus /pòntə feks máksiməss/ (*plural* **Pon·tif·i·ces Max·i·mi** /pon tiffə sèez máksə mī/) *n.* the chief priest who presided over the highest council of priests in ancient Rome

pon·tiff /póntif/ *n.* **1.** ROMAN CATHOLIC POPE the head of the Roman Catholic Church and bishop of Rome **2.** ROMAN CATHOLIC BISHOP a bishop in the Roman Catholic Church (*archaic*) **3.** HIST = **pontifex** [Late 16thC. Via Old French from Latin *pontifex* (see(PONTIFEX).]

pon·tif·i·cal /pon tíffik'l/ *adj.* **1.** OF A PONTIFF belonging to, befitting, or involving the Pope, a bishop, or a pontifex **2.** POMPOUS displaying an exaggerated sense of self-importance ■ *n.* CHR BISHOP'S BOOK a book containing the rites that may be performed only by a bishop ■ **pon·tif·i·cals** *npl.* PONTIFF'S VESTMENTS the vestments and insignia of a pope or bishop [15thC. From Latin *pontificalis*, from *pontifex* (see PONTIFEX).] —**pon·tif·i·cal·ly** *adv.*

Pon·tif·i·cal Mass *n.* a High Mass that is celebrated by a bishop, especially in the Roman Catholic Church

pon·tif·i·cate *vi.* /pon tíffi kàyt/ **(-cat·ed, -cat·ing, -cates)** **1.** SPEAK POMPOUSLY to speak about something in a knowing and self-important way, especially when not qualifed to do so **2.** SERVE AS A BISHOP to officiate as a bishop, especially in celebrating Mass ■ *n.* /pon tíffikət, -kàyt/ TERM OF OFFICE the office or term of office of a pope or bishop [Early 19thC. From medieval Latin *pontificat-*, the past participle stem of *pontificare*, from Latin *pontifex* (see PONTIFEX).] —**pon·tif·i·ca·tion** /pon tìffi káysh'n/ *n.* —**pon·tif·i·ca·tor** /pon tíffi kàytər/ *n.*

pon·til /pónt'l/ *n.* = **punty** [Mid-19thC. From French, of uncertain origin: probably from Italian *puntello*, literally "small point," from *punto* "point."]

pon·tine /pón tīn, -tèen/ *adj.* relating to or situated in the whitish band of nerve fibers (**pons**) on the surface of the brainstem between the medulla oblongata and midbrain [Late 19thC. Formed from Latin *pont-*, stem of *pons* "bridge, way" (see PONS).]

pon·toon[1] /pon tóon/ *n.* **1.** CIV ENG FLOATING SUPPORT FOR BRIDGE a floating structure used as a support for a bridge across a river, especially one put in place temporarily **2.** AIR FLOAT ON AN AIRCRAFT a float on an aircraft providing buoyancy or stability when on water **3.** SHIPPING FLOATING DOCK a floating structure used as a dock [Late 17thC. Via French *ponton* from the Latin stem *ponton-* "floating bridge," from *pont-*, stem of *pons* "bridge" (see PONS). Originally "flat-bottomed boat."]

pon·toon[2] /pon tóon/ *n. U.K.* = **blackjack** [Early 20thC. Origin uncertain: probably an alteration of French *vingt-et-un* "twenty-one."]

pon·toon bridge *n.* a temporary bridge built across a river, supported by floating structures

po·ny /pṓnee/ *n.* (*plural* **-nies**) **1.** SMALL HORSE any of several small horse breeds **2.** ANY HORSE a horse of any kind, especially a racehorse (*informal*) **3.** POLO HORSE a horse used in polo **4.** SMALL BOTTLE a small bottle of beer or another beverage, holding seven ounces/0.2 liter **5.** SMALL GLASS a small drinking glass, especially one used for liqueurs **6.** EDUC CRIB SHEET a literal translation of a text, used secretly by students during an exam or as an aid to studying a language (*informal*) **7.** *U.K.* £25 the sum of £25 (*slang*) ■ *vti.* **(-nied, -ny·ing, -nies)** *Northwest U.S., Rocky Mountains* PAY MONEY to pay out money that is due or owed (*informal*) ○ *They ordered some drinks, then ponied together the $5.50.* [Mid-17thC. Origin uncertain: possibly via French *poulenet*, literally "little foal," from, ultimately, Latin *pullus* "young animal" (see PULLET).]

po·ny ex·press *n.* a system of carrying mail using relays of horses and riders that operated from St. Joseph, Missouri, to Sacramento, California, from 1860 to 1861.

Ponytail

po·ny·tail /pṓni tàyl/ *n.* a hairstyle in which long hair is pulled back and tied behind the head so that it hangs down the back like a pony's tail —**po·ny·tail·ed** *adj.*

Pon·zi scheme /pónzee-/ *n.* an investment swindle in which high returns, allegedly profits, are made to early investors using funds from later investors. There may be no actual investing activity. [Early 20thC. Named for Charles *Ponzi* (died 1949), who perpetrated such a scheme in the United States in 1919.]

pooch /pooch/ *n.* a dog (*informal*) [Early 20thC. Origin unknown.]

Poodle

poo·dle /póod'l/ *n.* a dog with a thick curly coat usually clipped short, belonging either to a small breed (**toy poodle**), or a large breed (**standard poodle**) originally developed in Europe for hunting [Early 19thC. From German *Pudel*, shortening of *Pudelhund*, from Low German *pudeln* "to splash in water" + German *Hund* "dog."]

poo·dle cut *n.* a hairstyle in which the hair is cut short and curled

poof[1] /poof/, **pouf** *n. U.K.* an offensive term that deliberately insults a man for being homosexual or behaving in a way considered more characteristic of or suitable for a woman (*slang insult*) [Mid-19thC. Origin uncertain: probably an alteration (influenced by French *pouf* "women's hairstyle") of PUFF "powder-puff."] —**poof·y** *adj.*

poof[2] /pŏof, poof/ *interj.* (*informal*) **1.** INDICATING SUDDENNESS used to indicate that something happens suddenly **2.** EXPRESSING DISDAIN used to express disdain for or dismissal of something

pooh /poo/ *interj.* used to express disdain or dismissal (*informal*) [Late 16thC. An imitation of the sound made by blowing something away with the lips.]

Pooh-Bah /póo baa/, **pooh-bah** *n.* **1.** POMPOUS BUT USELESS OFFICIAL a pompous self-important official, especially one who holds more than one office but is ineffectual in all of them **2.** IMPORTANT PERSON a leader, high official, or important person [Late 19thC. Named for a character in *The Mikado*, an operetta by W. S. Gilbert and Arthur Sullivan.]

pooh-pooh **(pooh-poohed, pooh-pooh·ing, pooh-poohs)** *vt.* to dismiss or express disdain for something [Late 18thC. Doubled form of POOH.]

poo·ka /póokə/ *n. Ireland* a mischievous spirit in Irish folklore, especially one who takes on the form of an animal [Early 19thC. Via Irish *púca* from Old English *pūca* "puck" (see PUCK).]

pool[1] /pool/ *n.* **1.** LEISURE **SWIMMING POOL** a swimming pool or wading pool **2. PUDDLE** a small amount of any liquid lying on a surface **3. WATER** a small body of still water, usually one that occurs naturally **4. UNDERGROUND OIL OR GAS** an accumulation of oil or gas in a region of porous sedimentary rock **5.** CIV ENG **WATER BEHIND DAM** a body of water collected behind a dam **6. DEEP PART OF WATER** a deep place in a river or stream where the water runs more slowly **7. PATTERN RESEMBLING A POOL** a pattern or arrangement of something, e.g., light, that resembles a pool of liquid ■ *vi.* **(pooled, pool·ing, pools) 1. FORM A POOL** to collect in or form a pool **2.** PHYSIOL **ACCUMULATE IN A BODY PART** to collect in a body part or organ (*refers to blood*) [Old English *pōl*, from prehistoric Germanic]

pool[2] /pool/ *n.* **1.** CUE GAMES **FORM OF BILLIARDS** a form of billiards played with a cue ball and 15 balls on a felt-covered table with six pockets **2.** GAMBLING **FORM OF GAMBLING** a form of gambling in which the participants contribute an amount to a common fund that is divided among the winners **3.** GAMBLING **TOTAL AMOUNT STAKED** the collective amount that the players in a gambling game have staked **4. COLLECTIVE RESOURCE** a joint supply of vehicles, commodities, or workers that is shared and used by members of a group **5.** PRESS **GROUP OF REPORTERS** a selected group of reporters who cover an event and make their reports available to all participating news organizations **6.** FIN **INVESTMENT FUND** a collection of investments, e.g., stocks in a mutual fund, that are managed as a group for a common purpose or group of owners **7.** COMM **BUSINESS TRUST** an agreement between competing businesses to control production and sales in order to guarantee profits ■ *vt.* **(pooled, pool·ing, pools) SHARE RESOURCES** to combine something to form a supply that can be shared by a group of people or companies [Late 17thC. Via French *poule* "hen, gambling stakes" (hens were used as game prizes) from, ultimately, Latin *pullus* "young animal" (see PULLET). "Collective resource" arose via "players' collected bets."]

pool hall *n.* a commercial establishment where pool is played

pool·room /pòol ròom, -ròom/ *n.* a room or commercial establishment where pool or billiards is played

pool·side /pòol sīd/ *n.* the area around the sides of a swimming pool (*often used before a noun*)

pool ta·ble *n.* a felt-covered table used for playing pool. It is rectangular and has six pockets, one at each corner and one in the middle of each of the longer sides.

poon /poon/ (*plural* **poons** *or* **poon**) *n.* a southern Asian tree that has shiny leathery leaves and strong light wood that is used for masts and spars. Genus: *Calophyllum*. [Late 17thC. Via Singhalese *pūna* from Malayalam *punna* or Tamil *punnai*.]

poon·tang /pòon tàng/ *n.* a taboo offensive term for sexual relations (*dated taboo offensive*) [Early 20thC. Alteration of French *putain* "prostitute," from, ultimately, Latin *putida* "stinking, disgusting."]

poop[1] /poop/ **(pooped, poop·ing, poops)** *vt.* to make somebody feel exhausted (*informal*) (*usually passive*) ○ *pooped by the long hike* [Mid-20thC. Origin unknown.]

poop out *vi.* (*slang*) **1. QUIT DOING SOMETHING** to quit doing something, usually because of exhaustion or fear **2. STOP WORKING** to stop operating, e.g., because of mechanical failure

poop[2] /poop/ *n.* candid and accurate information about something (*slang*) [Mid-20thC. Origin unknown.]

poop[3] /poop/ *n.* **EXCREMENT** excrement, or a stool (*informal*) (*often used by or to children*) ■ *vi.* **(pooped, poop·ing, poops) DEFECATE** to defecate (*informal*) (*often used by or to children*) [Mid-16thC. Originally in the meaning of "to make a short blast of sound."]

poop[4] /poop/ *n.* **1. RAISED AREA AT SHIP'S REAR** the raised cabins at the stern of an old sailing ship, or the raised area at the stern of a modern ship, lying above the level of the main deck **2.** = **poop deck** ■ *v.* **(pooped, poop·ing, poops) 1.** *vt.* **BREAK OVER STERN** to break over a ship at the stern **2.** *vi.* **HAVE WAVES BREAKING OVER STERN** to have waves break over its stern, especially repeatedly (*refers to ships*) [15thC. Via Old French *pupe* from, ultimately, Latin *puppis*, of unknown origin.]

poop deck *n.* a raised open deck at the stern of a ship, with cabins below it

pooped /poopt/ *adj.* extremely tired (*informal*)

poop·er-scoop·er /pòopər skòopər/ *n.* a small shovel used to clean up dog excrement, used especially by a dog owner whose dog defecates in a public place (*informal*)

poo-poo *n.* **EXCREMENT** excrement, or the act of defecating (*babytalk*) ■ *vi.* **(poo-pooed, poo-poo·ing, poo-poos) DEFECATE** to defecate (*babytalk*) [Doubled form of POO]

poor /poor, pawr/ *adj.* **1. NOT RICH** lacking money or material possessions **2. AFFECTED BY POVERTY** where there is a lot of poverty, or where poverty is evident ○ *one of the poorest countries in the world* **3. INFERIOR** less than adequate, or below average in quality or condition **4. LACKING SKILL** below average in skill or ability **5. LOW OR INADEQUATE** lower than expected or needed in quantity, number, or amount ○ *Attendance at the concert was poor.* **6. WEAK** lacking strength, power, stamina, or resilience ○ *He has been in poor health recently.* **7. DEFICIENT** lacking or deficient in something (*often used in combination*) **8. LACKING PRODUCTIVE POTENTIAL** lacking fertility or nutrients **9. LOW IN VALUATION** low in a scale of value ○ *has a poor opinion of himself* **10. DESERVING PITY** deserving pity or compassion, especially because of something that has just happened ■ *npl.* **PEOPLE WHO ARE POOR** people who lack money or material possessions (*takes a plural verb*) ○ *The poor are always with us.* [12thC. Via Old French *povre* from Latin *pauper* (see PAUPER).] —**poor·ness** *n.* ◇ **a poor man's something** a cheaper or inferior version of something, especially one that is more widely available than the original

poor box *n.* a box, especially one kept in a church, that is used to collect money for the poor

poor boy *n.* a sandwich made with a long roll cut horizontally [So called because the sandwich was originally made from discarded scraps and ends and given to poor people]

poor farm *n.* a publicly funded farm that existed in former times to provide employment, housing, and support for poor workers

poor·house /pòor hòwss, pàwr-/ (*plural* **-hous·es** /-hòwzəz/) *n.* a publicly funded institution that existed in the past to house people who were too poor to provide for themselves

poo·ri /pòoree/ *n.* a thin flat unleavened Indian wheat bread, shaped into a small round and deep-fried, making it puff up and become crisp [Mid-20thC. From Hindi *pūrī*.]

Poor Knights Is·lands /pòor-/ group of uninhabited islands in the southwestern Pacific Ocean, 15 mi./24 km off the northeastern coast of the North Island, New Zealand. Area: 1 sq. mi./2.7 sq. km.

poor law *n.* a law or system of laws relating to the provision of support for poor people

poor·ly /pòorlee, pàwr-/ *adv.* **1. NOT WELL** in an inferior or inadequate way **2. UNFAVORABLY** with an unfavorable opinion or attitude ■ *adj.* *U.K.* **PHYSICALLY UNWELL** feeling physically unwell, or in poor physical health (*informal*)

poor mouth *n.* *U.S., Ireland* complaints about being poor, regarded as made to win sympathy, sometimes when the complainer is not truly poor (*disapproving*)

poor-mouth **(poor-mouthed, poor-mouth·ing, poor-mouths)** *vi.* to complain of a lack of money, especially when feigning or exaggerating poverty, often in order to win sympathy (*informal disapproving*)

poor re·la·tion *n.* somebody who or something that is inferior compared to another

poor white *n.* an offensive term for a poor and uneducated lower-class Caucasian person (*informal offensive*)

pop[1] /pop/ *n.* **1. SUDDEN BURSTING SOUND** a sudden explosive sound, like the sound produced when a balloon bursts or a cork comes out of a bottle **2.** *Midwest* **BUBBLY DRINK** a carbonated drink, usually sweet and flavored with fruit (*informal*) **3. GUNSHOT** a shot with a firearm **4.** BASEBALL = **pop fly 5. ATTEMPT** a try at doing something (*informal*) ■ *v.* **(popped, pop·ping, pops) 1.** *vti.* **MAKE A BURSTING SOUND** to make, or cause something to make, a sudden explosive sound, like the sound of a cork coming out of a bottle or a balloon bursting **2.** *vti.* **BURST** to burst, or make something burst, with a sudden explosive sound **3.** *vi.* **BULGE** to become wide open and seem to bulge out of the sockets (*refers to sb's eyes*) **4.** *vi.* **GO BRIEFLY** to go, come, or visit for a brief time (*informal*) **5.** *vt.* **OPEN OR CLOSE SOMETHING** to move something quickly and suddenly into an open or closed position (*informal*) **6.** *vt.* **PUT QUICKLY** to put or place something somewhere with a sudden rapid movement (*informal*) **7.** *vt.* **TAKE BY SWALLOWING** to take a drug orally (*informal*) **8.** *vti.* **FIRE SHOTS** to fire shots from a pistol or other firearm (*informal*) **9.** *vti.* BASEBALL **HIT POP FLY** to hit a baseball high into the air a short distance, especially where it can be caught by an infielder ■ *adv.* **1. WITH BURSTING NOISE** with a sudden bursting sound **2. UNEXPECTEDLY** suddenly or abruptly ■ *interj.* **INDICATING BURSTING NOISE** used to indicate a sudden bursting noise [14thC. An imitation of the sound.] ◇ **a pop** for each one (*slang*) ○ *It'll cost you $10 a pop.*

pop off *vi.* (*informal*) **1. SPEAK OUT** to speak out about something angrily or tactlessly **2. DIE** to die suddenly

pop[2] /pop/ *n.* **1. FATHER** a word used to refer to or address your father (*informal*) **2. OLDER MAN** a word used to address a much older man (*dated slang*) [Mid-19thC. Shortening of POPPA.]

pop[3] /pop/ *n.* **1.** MUSIC = **pop music** (*often used before a noun*) **2.** ARTS = **pop art** ■ *adj.* **POPULAR** intended for or appreciated by a wide public, and often regarded as oversimplified for the sake of greater accessibility (*informal*) ○ *magazines full of pop psychology* [Late 19thC. Shortening of POPULAR.]

POP *abbr.* **1.** COMM proof of purchase **2.** METEOROL probability of precipitation

pop. *abbr.* **1.** popular **2.** population

pop art *n.* an art movement in the 1960s and 1970s that incorporated elements of modern popular culture and the mass media. It included such artists as Andy Warhol and Roy Lichtenstein.

pop·corn /póp kàwrn/ *n.* **1. HEATED CORN KERNELS** the kernels of a variety of corn, heated until they become puffy, usually flavored with butter, caramelized sugar, or cheese and eaten as a snack **2. CORN** a variety of corn with hard kernels that pop open to form white puffs when heated. Latin name: *Zea mays praecox*. **3.** = **peanut** *n.* 4

pope /pōp/ *n.* **1. pope, Pope ROMAN CATHOLIC CHURCH HEAD** the head of the Roman Catholic Church and bishop of Rome **2. pope, Pope COPTIC CHURCH HEAD** the head of the Coptic Church **3. pope, Pope ORTHODOX PRIEST** a priest in the Eastern Orthodox Church **4. POWERFUL PERSON** somebody who has authority or status similar to that of a pope [Pre-12thC. Via Latin from, ultimately, Greek *pappas* "father."]

Pope /pōp/, **Alexander** (1688–1744) English poet. He wrote the mock-heroic poem *The Rape of the Lock* (1712) and *An Essay on Man* (1733–34).

pope·dom /pṓpdəm/ *n.* the office, tenure, or dominion of a pope

pop·er·y /pṓpəree/ *n.* an offensive term for the Roman Catholic Church, its doctrines, or its practices (*offensive*)

pope's nose *n.* the fatty piece of flesh at the rear end of a cooked chicken, turkey, or other bird, to which the tail feathers were attached (*offensive in some contexts*)

pop-eyed /póp īd/ *adj.* **1. WITH BULGING EYES** with the eyes bulging out **2. WIDE-EYED** with eyes wide open in surprise or disbelief

pop fly *n.* a high fly ball in baseball that travels a relatively short distance from home plate

pop·gun /póp gùn/ *n.* **1. TOY GUN** a toy gun that uses compressed air to shoot pellets, balls, or a cork tied to a string. It makes a popping sound. **2. USELESS GUN** a useless or unimpressive firearm (*informal*)

pop·in·jay /póppin jày/ *n.* a vain and conceited person (*dated*) [13thC. Via Old French *papegay* "parrot" from, ultimately, Arabic *babbaġā*. "Arrogant person" from the parrot's gaudy colors and meaningless chattering.]

pop·ish /pṓpish/ *adj.* an offensive term used to describe things associated with the Roman Catholic Church, its doctrines, or its practices (*offensive*) —**pop·ish·ly** *adv.*

pop·lar /pópplər/ *n.* **1.** TREES **SLENDER QUICK-GROWING TREE** a slender quick-growing tree of the willow family with triangular leaves, flowers in catkins, and light-colored soft wood. It is native to northern temperate regions. Genus: *Populus*. **2.** TREES = **tulip tree 3.** INDUST **POPLAR'S WOOD** the light-colored wood of a poplar (*often* *used before a noun*) [14thC. Via Anglo-Norman *popler* from, ultimately, Latin *populus*.]

pop·lin /pópplin/ *n.* a plain strong fabric with fine ribbing, usually made of cotton. It is used for making clothes and upholstery. (*often used before a noun*) [Early 18thC. Via obsolete French *papeline* from, ultimately, medieval Latin *papalis* "papal" (because it was made at the papal town of Avignon), from Latin *papa* (see POPE).]

pop·lit·e·al /pop líttee əl, pòpplə tée əl/ *adj.* relating to or located in the part of the leg behind the knee joint [Late 18thC. Formed from modern Latin *popliteus*, from Latin *poples* "ham, back of the knee."]

pop mu·sic *n.* modern commercial music, usually tuneful, uptempo and repetitive, that is aimed at the general public and the youth market in particular

Po·po·ca·te·petl /pòppə kéttə pètt'l, pàwpàw kaa té pètt'l/ volcano in southern central Mexico. Height: 17,887 ft./5,452 m.

pop·o·ver /póp ōvər/ *n.* a light hollow muffin-shaped quick bread made from eggs, flour, and milk

pop·pa /póppə/ *n.* = **papa** (*informal*) [Late 19thC. Alteration.]

pop·pa·dom /pópəpdəm/, **pop·pa·dum** *n.* a thin crisp circular Indian bread made from bean flour and flavored with spices. Poppadoms are dried and fried in hot fat. [Early 19thC. From Tamil *pappaṭam*, of uncertain origin: perhaps from *paruppa aṭam* "lentil cake."]

pop·per /póppər/ *n.* **1.** COOK **CORN-POPPING DEVICE** an appliance, container, or pan for popping popcorn **2.** DRUGS **AMYL NITRATE** a small capsule of amyl nitrate or butyl nitrate, prepared as an illicit drug (*slang*)

pop·pet /póppət/ *n.* **1.** ENG = **poppet valve 2.** NAUT **SUPPORT FOR SHIP** a steel beam or timber that is used to support the front and back ends of a ship when it is launched **3.** *U.K.* **USED AS TERM OF ENDEARMENT** used to address a sweet and dear person, especially a child (*informal*) [14thC. Origin uncertain: perhaps from French *poupette*, literally "small doll," from assumed *poupe* "doll," from Latin *pupa* "girl, doll."]

pop·pet valve *n.* a valve that is raised and lowered by a vertical guide, e.g., the intake and exhaust valves of the cylinders in an internal-combustion engine also called poppet

pop·ple[1] /pópp'l/ (**-pled, -pling, -ples**) *vi.* to move in an irregular tumbling or bubbling manner, like water does when it boils [14thC. Origin uncertain: probably from Middle Dutch *popelen* "to babble, murmur," originally an imitation of the sound.]

pop·ple[2] /pópp'l/ *n.* a poplar tree (*informal*) [14thC. From Latin *populus*.]

Poppy

pop·py /póppee/ (*plural* **-pies**) *n.* **1.** PLANTS **PLANT WITH RED FLOWERS** an annual or perennial plant that has large red, orange, or white flowers, cup-shaped seed pods, and milky sap. Genus: *Papaver*. **2.** PHARM, DRUGS **PLANT EXTRACT** an extract from the poppy that is used in drugs such as opium and medicine **3.** PLANTS **PLANT LIKE A TRUE POPPY** any of several flowering plants that are similar or related to the poppy, e.g., the California poppy and Welsh poppy **4.** COLORS **ORANGE-RED COLOR** a bright red color tinged with orange [Pre-12thC. Via assumed Vulgar Latin *papavum* from Latin *papaver*.]

pop·py·cock /póppee kòk/ *n.* absurd speech or writing (*dated informal*) [Mid-19thC. From Dutch dialect *pappekak*, from *pap* "soft, pap" + *kak* "dung."]

pop·py·head /póppee hèd/ *n.* an ornamental carved top on the end of a pew in a Gothic church

pop·py seed *n.* the small black seed of the poppy, used in cooking and in baking

pop quiz *n.* a quiz given without advance notice

pops[1] /pops/ *n.* a symphony orchestra that plays popular classical music and pop music (*often used before a noun*)

pops[2] /pops/ *n.* = **pop**[2] (*dated slang*) [Early 20thC. Extended form.]

Pop·si·cle /pópsik'l, póp sìk'l/ *tdmk.* a trademark for a colored fruit-flavored ice on one or two sticks

pop-top *n.* **1.** **CAN TOP** the top or portion of the top of a can that can be removed by pulling an attached ring **2.** **VAN ROOF** a van roof that can be raised to create extra headroom while the van is stationary **3.** **CAN** a can whose top can be opened by means of an attached ring or tab that is pulled **4.** **VAN** a van with a pop-top

pop·u·lace /póppyələss/ *n.* **1.** **INHABITANTS** the inhabitants of a town, region, or other area **2.** **GENERAL PUBLIC** ordinary people, as distinct from the political elite or the aristocracy [Late 16thC. Via French from Italian *popolaccio* "rabble," from *popolo* "people," from Latin *populus* (see POPULAR).]

pop·u·lar /póppyələr/ *adj.* **1.** **APPEALING TO THE GENERAL PUBLIC** appealing to or appreciated by a wide range of people ○ *the most popular name for babies this year* **2.** **WELL-LIKED** liked by a particular person or group of people ○ *popular with young audiences* **3.** **OF THE GENERAL PUBLIC** relating to the general public ○ *popular appeal* **4.** **AIMED AT NONSPECIALISTS** designed to appeal to or be comprehensible to the nonspecialist ○ *a popular gardening magazine* **5.** **BELIEVED BY PEOPLE IN GENERAL** believed, embraced, or perpetuated by ordinary people ○ *popular myths* **6.** **INEXPENSIVE** designed to be affordable to people on average incomes ○ *a new popular car* [15thC. Via Anglo-Norman *populer* from Latin *popularis* "of the people," from *populus* "people" (source of English *people* and *public*), of uncertain origin: probably from Etruscan.]

pop·u·lar front *n.* a broad-based coalition of left-wing political parties, formed to oppose fascism or institute social reforms, especially in Europe in the mid-1930s

pop·u·lar·i·ty /pòppyə lérrətee/ *n.* **1.** **FACT OF BEING WELL LIKED** admiration, approval, or acceptance of somebody or something by people in general or by a particular group of people **2.** **DEMAND FOR SOMETHING** desire or demand for something, e.g., a manufactured product

pop·u·lar·ize /póppyələ rīz/ (**-ized, -iz·ing, -iz·es**) *vt.* **1.** **MAKE POPULAR** to make something widely liked or appreciated **2.** **MAKE UNDERSTANDABLE** to make something accessible and comprehensible to a wide audience —**pop·u·lar·i·za·tion** /pòppyələri záysh'n/ *n.* —**pop·u·lar·iz·er** /póppyələ rīzər/ *n.*

pop·u·lar·ly /póppyələrlee/ *adv.* **1.** **GENERALLY** by most people or in most situations **2.** **BY NONSPECIALISTS** by the general public, as distinct from specialists

pop·u·lar sov·er·eign·ty *n.* **1.** **GOVERNMENT'S SUBJECTION TO PEOPLE** the doctrine that the people are sovereign and a government is subject to the will of the people **2.** HIST **DOCTRINE PERMITTING CHOICE ON SLAVERY** a pre-Civil War political doctrine that held that individual states should decide whether to permit slavery or not. It was espoused mainly by opponents of the abolition of slavery.

pop·u·late /póppyə làyt/ (**-lat·ed, -lat·ing, -lates**) *vt.* **1.** **INHABIT A PLACE** to live in an area, region, or country (*often passive*) **2.** **PEOPLE A PLACE** to supply an area with inhabitants [Late 16thC. From medieval Latin *populat-*, the past participle stem of *populare*, from Latin *populus* "people" (see POPULAR).] —**pop·u·lat·ed** *adj.*

pop·u·la·tion /pòppyə láysh'n/ *n.* **1.** **PEOPLE IN PLACE** all of the people who inhabit an area, region, or country **2.** **ALL PEOPLE OF GROUP** all of the people of a particular nationality, ethnic group, religion, or class who live in an area **3.** **NUMBER OF PEOPLE** the total number of people who inhabit an area, region, or country, or the number of people in a particular group who inhabit an area **4.** **SUPPLYING WITH INHABITANTS** the populating of an area with inhabitants **5.** STATS **GROUP STATISTICALLY SAMPLED** the entire group of individuals or items from which a sample may be selected for statistical measurement **6.** **INDIVIDUALS OF SAME SPECIES** all the plants or animals of a particular species present in a place

pop·u·la·tion con·trol *n.* the limiting of numbers of individuals living in an area. In humans it may be achieved through contraception while in animals it may occur through killing or the introduction of predators.

pop·u·la·tion ex·plo·sion *n.* a sudden and rapid increase in the number of individuals living in an area. In humans, this may be as a result of an increased birth rate or a decline in mortality, while in the case of animals it may be because of a lack of predators or altered environmental conditions.

pop·u·la·tion ge·net·ics *n.* the study of genetic variation in populations, particularly how and why the frequencies of different genes change over time or in different localities (*takes a singular verb*)

pop·u·la·tion rev·o·lu·tion *n.* the huge growth in population in western Europe that began about 1730. It was a prelude to the Industrial Revolution.

pop·u·lism /póppyə lìzzəm/ *n.* **1.** **ANTIELITE POLITICS** politics or political ideology based on the perceived interests of ordinary people, as opposed to those of a privileged elite **2.** **FOCUS ON ORDINARY PEOPLE** focus or emphasis on the lives of ordinary people, e.g., in the arts and in politics [Late 19thC. Formed from Latin *populus* "people" (see POPULAR).]

Pop·u·lism *n.* the political philosophy and program of the Populist Party

pop·u·list /póppyəlist/ *n.* **SUPPORTER OF ORDINARY PEOPLE** an advocate of the rights and interests of ordinary people, e.g., in politics or the arts ■ *adj.* **OF ORDINARY PEOPLE** emphasizing or promoting ordinary people, their lives, or their interests [Late 19thC. Formed from Latin *populus* "people" (see POPULAR).]

Pop·u·list *n.* **POPULIST PARTY SUPPORTER** a political supporter of the Populist Party ■ *adj.* **OF THE POPULIST PARTY** belonging or relating to the Populist Party

Pop·u·list Par·ty *n.* a U.S. political party formed in the 1890s to represent the interests of farmers and laborers. It favored free coinage of silver and other reforms, and was disbanded in 1904.

pop·u·lous /póppyələss/ *adj.* with a large number of inhabitants [15thC. From late Latin *populosus*, from Latin *populus* "people" (see POPULAR).] —**pop·u·lous·ly** *adv.* —**pop·u·lous·ness** *n.*

pop-up *adj.* **1.** **UPWARD-LIFTING** with a mechanism that makes it, or something in it move upward quickly ○ *pop-up headlights* **2.** COMP **PRESENTED ON SCREEN TEMPORARILY** appearing quickly and temporarily on a computer screen when a special key is pressed or a button is clicked with a mouse ○ *a pop-up menu* **3.** PUBL **WITH RISING CUT-OUT FIGURES** containing cut-out figures that rise up as a page is opened ○ *a pop-up book* ■ *n.* **1.** BASEBALL = **pop fly 2.** PUBL **ITEM WITH POP-UP FIGURES** a book or card that contains pop-up figures, or a pop-up figure

pop wine *n.* an inexpensive, sweet, usually fruit-flavored wine that has a low alcohol content

por. *abbr.* portrait

por·bea·gle /páwr beeg'l/ (*plural* **-gles** *or* **-gle**) *n.* a large and voracious shark with a crescent-shaped tail, found in North Atlantic waters. Latin name: *Lamna nasus*. [Mid-18thC. From Cornish *porbugel*.]

por·ce·lain /páwrsələn, páwrslən/ *n.* **1.** **CERAMIC MATERIAL** a hard translucent ceramic material used for making plates, cups, and other items (*often used before a noun*) **2.** **ITEMS MADE OF PORCELAIN** objects made of porcelain, e.g., expensive crockery or decorative figurines **3.** **DECORATIVE OBJECT** a single object made from porcelain, especially a decorative object [Mid-16thC. Via French from Italian *porcellana* "cowrie shell, porcelain" (from its texture), literally "like a young sow" (from its shape), via *porca* "sow" from, ultimately, Latin *porcus* "pig."]

por·ce·lain clay *n.* = **kaolin**

por·ce·lain e·nam·el *n.* a glass coating that is fused to a metal by firing

por·ce·lain flow·er *n.* = **wax plant**

por·ce·la·ne·ous /pàwrssə láynee əss/ *adj.* made of porcelain, or resembling porcelain in its translucence or whiteness [Late 18thC. Coined from Italian *porcellana* "porcelain" (see PORCELAIN) + -EOUS.]

porch /pawrch/ *n.* **1.** **COVERED ENTRANCE** a covered shelter at the entrance to a building **2.** **ROOFED EXTERIOR ROOM** a raised platform with a roof that runs along the side of a house, partly enclosed with low walls or fully enclosed with screens or windows [13thC. Via Old

French from Latin *porticus* "covered entry" (source of English *portico*), from *porta* "gate" (see PORT[2].)]

por·cine /páwr sīn, páwrs'n/ *adj.* relating to or resembling pigs [Mid-17thC. Via French from Latin *porcinus*, from *porcus* "pig" (see PORK).]

por·ci·no /pawr seénō/ (*plural* **-ni** /-seénee/), **por·ci·ni mush·room** *n.* = **cep** [Late 20thC. From Italian, shortening of *fungo porcino*, literally "porcine mushroom."]

Porcupine

por·cu·pine /páwrkyə pīn/ *n.* a large rodent whose body is covered with long protective quills that it can erect in defense against predators. Families: Hystricidae and Erethizontidae. [14thC. From Old French *porc espin*, literally "spiny pig."]

Por·cu·pine river in North America that originates in northern Yukon Territory, Canada, joining the Yukon River in northeastern Alaska. Length: 448 mi./721 km.

por·cu·pine fish *n.* a tropical marine fish that has strong sharp spines covering its body. It inflates the spines when attacked. Family: Diodontidae.

por·cu·pine grass *n.* = **spinifex** *n.*

pore[1] /pawr/ *n.* **1. TINY OPENING IN SKIN** a tiny opening in human skin, or in the skin or other outer covering of an animal, through which substances can pass. Perspiration is released through the pores. **2.** BOT **TINY OPENING IN PLANT** a tiny opening in a leaf or stem of a plant used to absorb or release substances, e.g., in photosynthesis or respiration **3.** GEOL **SMALL SPACE IN ROCK** a small space that is surrounded by rock or soil. It may be filled with water, crude oil, or natural gas. [14thC. Via Old French and Latin from Greek *poros* "passage" (source of English *emporium*). Ultimately from an Indo-European word that is also the ancestor of English *fare* and *ford*.]

WORD KEY: USAGE

See Usage note at ***pour***.

pore[2] /pawr/ (**pored, por·ing, pores**) *vi.* **1. LOOK CONCENTRATEDLY** to study something carefully and thoughtfully ○ *poring over a book* **2. REFLECT** to meditate on or think carefully about something [13thC. Origin uncertain: possibly related to PEER.]

pore fun·gus *n.* any fungus that has spores in tiny tubules that lead to outside pores. Families: Boletaceae and Polyporaceae.

por·gy /páwrgee/ (*plural* **-gies** *or* **-gy**) *n.* **1. MARINE FOOD FISH** a marine food fish that has a deep flat body with large scales, found in the Mediterranean Sea and Atlantic Ocean. Latin name: *Pagrus pagrus.* **2. FISH RELATED TO PORGY** any marine food fish related to the porgy, with a similarly deep flat body. Family: Sparidae. **3. UNRELATED FISH LIKE PORGY** any of various fishes that are similar to the porgy but unrelated, e.g., the menhaden [Mid-17thC. Via Spanish or Portuguese *pargo* from, ultimately, Greek *phagros* "sea bream."]

po·rif·er·an /paw ríffərən/ *n.* = **sponge** *n.* 1 (*technical*) ■ *adj.* **RELATING TO SPONGES** belonging or relating to the sponges [Mid-19thC. Formed from modern Latin *Porifera*, phylum name, literally "passage-bearing," ultimately from Latin *porus* (see PORE[1]).]

pork /pawrk/ *n.* **1.** FOOD **HOG MEAT** the flesh of a hog eaten as food, usually cooked fresh. Cured hog flesh is usually referred to as bacon or ham. (*often used before a noun*) **2.** POL **POLITICAL HANDOUTS** government money and jobs awarded by politicians to their supporters or constituents to win their favor, especially when awarded wastefully (*informal*) [13thC. Via Old French from Latin *porcus* "pig" (source of English *porcupine* and *porcelain*). Ultimately from an Indo-European word meaning "pig," which is also the ancestor of English *farrow*.]

pork bar·rel *n.* government-funded projects that bring jobs and other benefits to an area and give its political representative the opportunity to award favors and reap the ensuing prestige (*informal*) (*hyphenated when used before a noun*)

pork bel·ly *n.* a side of fresh pork, commonly traded on the commodities markets, or a cut of meat from this

pork·er /páwrkər/ *n.* **1.** AGRIC **FAT YOUNG HOG** a young fattened hog, especially one raised for its meat **2. OVERWEIGHT PERSON** an overweight person or animal (*informal insult*)

pork·pie hat /páwrk pī hat/, **pork·pie** *n.* **1. MAN'S HAT** a man's hat with a flat crown and small brim that can be turned up, first popular in the 1850s **2. WOMAN'S HAT** a woman's round hat without a brim, first popular in the 1860s [*Porkpie* from its shape]

pork rinds *npl.* small pieces of fried pork rind and fat that are eaten as a snack

por·ky[1] /páwrkee/ (**pork·i·er, pork·i·est**) *adj.* overweight (*informal insult*)

por·ky[2] /páwrkee/ (*plural* **-kies**) *n.* a porcupine (*informal*) [Mid-20thC. Shortening.]

porn /pawrn/, **por·no** /páwrnō/ *n.* pornography (*informal*) (*often used before a noun*) [Mid-20thC. Shortening.]

por·no·graph·ic /pàwrnə gráffik/ *adj.* **1. PORTRAYING SEX EXPLICITLY** sexually explicit and intended to cause sexual arousal **2. SELLING PORNOGRAPHY** producing or selling sexually explicit magazines, films, or other materials —**por·no·graph·i·cal·ly** *adv.*

por·nog·ra·phy /pawr nóggrəfee/ *n.* **1. SEXUALLY EXPLICIT MATERIAL** films, magazines, writings, photographs, or other materials that are sexually explicit and intended to cause sexual arousal **2. SEXUAL IMAGES INDUSTRY** the production or sale of sexually explicit films, magazines, or other materials [Mid-19thC. Via French from, ultimately, Greek *pornographos* "writing about prostitutes," from *pornē* "prostitute." Ultimately from an Indo-European word denoting "to sell."] —**por·nog·ra·pher** *n.*

po·ros·i·ty /paw róssətee/ (*plural* **-ties**) *n.* **1. POROUS QUALITY** the porous nature of something, or the extent to which something is porous **2.** GEOL **PERCENTAGE OF PORE SPACE** the ratio of the space taken up by the pores in a soil, rock, or other material to its total volume. It is expressed as a percentage. **3.** GEOL **PORE** a pore in soil, rock, or other material (*technical*) [14thC. Via French from, ultimately, medieval Latin *porosus* (see POROUS).]

po·rous /páwrəss/ *adj.* **1. PERMEABLE** permitting the movement of fluids or gases through it by way of pores or other passages **2. BREACHABLE** easy to cross, infiltrate, or penetrate **3. WITH PORES** with a surface that contains pores or a body that contains cavities [14thC. Via Old French *poreux* from medieval Latin *porosus*, from Latin *porus* "passage" (see PORE[1]).] —**po·rous·ly** *adv.* —**po·rous·ness** *n.*

por·phyr·i·a /pawr feéree ə/ *n.* a medical condition caused by the body's failure to metabolize porphyrins. Symptoms of the hereditary form include abdominal pain, sensitivity to sunlight, confusion, and excretion of porphyrins in the urine. [Early 20thC. Formed from PORPHYRIN.]

por·phy·rin /páwrfərin/ *n.* any of various organic compounds that are common in animal and plant tissue, e.g., as components of hemoglobin, chlorophyll, and some enzymes. They consist of four pyrrole rings linked by methylene groups. [Early 20thC. Formed from Greek *porphura* "purple" (source of English *purple*), from their color.]

por·phy·rit·ic /pàwrfə ríttik/ *adj.* **1. RELATING TO PORPHYRY** relating to or containing porphyry **2. WITH LARGE CRYSTALS** containing isolated large and distinct crystals in a mainly fine-grained rock

por·phy·ry /páwrfəree/ (*plural* **-ries**) *n.* **1. REDDISH-PURPLE ROCK** a reddish-purple rock containing large distinct feldspar crystals embedded in a fine-grained groundmass **2. ROCK WITH LARGE CRYSTALS** any predominantly fine-grained igneous rock that contains isolated large crystals [14thC. Via Old French *porfire* from, ultimately, Greek *porphuritēs*, from *porphura* "purple" (see PURPLE), from its color.]

por·poise /páwrpəss/ (*plural* **-pois·es** *or* **-poise**) *n.* **1. MARINE MAMMAL** a toothed marine mammal, related to the whales and dolphins, that has a blunt snout and a triangular dorsal fin. Family: Phocaenidae. **2. DOLPHIN** a popular but technically inaccurate term for a dolphin [14thC. From Old French *porpeis*, literally "pig-fish," ultimately from Latin *porcus* "pig" (see PORK) + *piscis* "fish"; perhaps from its snout or its curved back.]

por·rect /pə rékt/ *adj.* used to describe animal parts that extend forward [Early 19thC. From Latin *porrectus*, the past participle of *porrigere* "to stretch forward," from *regere* "to direct."]

por·rin·ger /páwrinjər/ *n.* a small bowl, usually with a handle, used for soup, stew, or oatmeal [Early 16thC. Alteration of *potinger*, via Old French *potager* from *potage* "pottage" (see POTTAGE).]

port[1] /pawrt/ *n.* **1. HARBOR** a place by the sea, or by a river or other waterway, where ships and boats can dock, load, and unload **2. TOWN WITH A HARBOR** a town or city built around a port **3. WATERFRONT** the waterfront area of a port **4. COVE** a sheltered place along a coast, where boats are protected from storms and rough seas **5.** = **port of entry** [Pre-12thC. From Latin *portus* (source of English *opportune*). Ultimately from an Indo-European word meaning "to go across," which is also the ancestor of English *pore*[1].]

port[2] /pawrt/ *n.* **1.** NAUT **OPENING IN BOAT** a watertight opening in the side of a boat, used for loading and unloading and as a means of general access to the holds **2.** NAUT = **porthole** *n.* 1 **3.** MIL **GUN HOLE** a small opening in an armored vehicle, military aircraft, naval vessel, or fortification through which a gun can be fired **4.** COMPUT **EXTERNAL COMPUTER CONNECTION** an external socket on a computer's main unit (**CPU**) where a peripheral device such as a printer, keyboard, or network cable is plugged in **5.** ENG **VALVE-OPERATED OPENING** an opening controlled by a valve, e.g., any of the openings in the cylinder of an internal combustion engine [13thC. Via Old French, "gate," from Latin *porta* (source of English *porch* and *portal*).]

port[3] /pawrt/ *n.* **LEFT SIDE ON SHIP OR PLANE** the left-hand side of a boat or airplane when facing forward ■ *adj., adv.* **ON LEFT** on or to the left-hand side of boat or airplane when facing forward. Also called **portside** ■ *vti.* (**port·ed, port·ing, ports**) **TURN TO PORT** to make a turn toward the port side, or make a ship do this [Mid-16thC. Shortening of *port side*, from PORT[1], because it was the side that faced the pier and over which cargo was loaded.]

port[4] /pawrt/ *n.* a strong sweet fortified wine usually drunk after dinner. It is usually a deep red color, but some kinds are brownish (**tawny port**) and some white. Originally from Portugal, port is now made in other countries. [Late 17thC. Named for the city of *Oporto* in Portugal, from where it was shipped.]

port[5] /pawrt/ *vt.* (**port·ed, port·ing, ports**) **CARRY ACROSS THE BODY** to carry a weapon positioned diagonally across the body with the muzzle or blade in front of the left shoulder ■ *n.* **DIAGONAL POSITION** the position of a rifle or sword when ported [Mid-16thC. Via French *porter* "to carry" from Latin *portare* (source of English *portable, transport, important*, and *portfolio*); see PORT[1].]

port[6] /pawrt/ (**port·ed, port·ing, ports**) *vt.* to convert software to run on different computer operating systems [Mid-20thC. From PORT[2].]

Port. *abbr.* **1.** Portugal **2.** Portuguese

por·ta /páwrtə/ (*plural* **-tas** *or* **-tae** /-tee/) *n.* an opening into an organ or other bodily part, especially the opening in the liver through which most of the blood vessels enter [14thC. Via modern Latin from Latin, "gate."]

port·a·ble /páwrtəb'l/ *adj.* **1. EASILY MOVED AROUND** designed to be light or compact enough to carry or move easily from place to place **2.** COMPUT **EASY TO CONVERT** easily converted to run on different computer operating systems ■ *n.* **EASILY TRANSPORTED OBJECT** a device or an appliance that is designed to be easily carried or moved from place to place [14thC. Via Old French from late Latin *portabilis*, from *portare* "to carry."] —**port·a·bil·i·ty** /pàwrtə bíllətee/ *n.* —**port·a·bly** /páwrtəblee/ *adv.*

por·tae plural of **porta**

port·age /páwrtij, pawr taázh/ *n.* **1. ACT OF CARRYING** the carrying or transporting of something **2. CHARGE FOR CARRYING** a charge made for carrying or transporting something **3. CARRYING OF BOATS OVERLAND** the carrying of boats or cargo across land from one waterway to another or around an unnavigable section of a waterway **4.** OVERLAND ROUTE TO WATERWAY an overland route used when transporting a boat or its cargo from one waterway to another ■ *vti.* **(-aged, -ag·ing, -ag·es)** CARRY SOMETHING OVERLAND TO WATERWAY to carry boats or cargo across land from one waterway to another or around an unnavigable portion of a waterway [13thC. Via Old French from, ultimately, Latin *portare* "to carry."]

Por·tage /páwrtij/ city in northwestern Indiana, directly south of Lake Michigan, southeast of Gary and southwest of South Bend. Population: 32,419 (1996).

Por·tage la Prai·rie /-lə práiree/ city in Manitoba, Canada, located on the Assiniboine River and the Trans-Canada Highway. Population: 20,385 (1996).

por·tal /páwrt'l/ *n.* **1.** LARGE GATE a large or elaborate gate or entrance (*literary*) **2.** ENTRANCE TO SOMETHING any entrance to a place, or any means of access to something (*literary*) **3.** COMPUT HOME SITE FOR WEB BROWSER on the Internet, a web site that provides links to information and other Web sites ■ *adj.* ANAT OF PORTAL VEIN OR SYSTEM relating to the portal vein, portal system, or the opening in the liver (**porta**) through which the portal vein passes [14thC. Via Old French from, ultimately, Latin *porta* "gate" (see PORT[1]).]

por·tal sys·tem *n.* a network of blood vessels that begin in the capillaries of one organ and end in the capillaries of another, especially the portal veins connecting the liver and intestines

por·tal vein *n.* a vein that carries blood from the digestive organs, gall bladder, and spleen to the liver, especially the vein from the intestines carrying nutrient-rich blood

por·ta·men·to /pàwrtə méntō/ (*plural* **-ti** /-tee/) *n.* a smooth glide from one note to another when singing or playing a stringed instrument [Late 18thC. From Italian, literally "carrying," because the player slides the same finger from one note to the next.]

Port Ar·thur city in southeastern Texas, the largest gasoline-refining center in the United States. Population: 58,724 (1990). ■ town in Australia, in southern Tasmania. It was the site of a major penal settlement between 1830 and 1837. Population: 190 (1994). ■ former name for **Lüshun**

por·ta·tive /páwrtətiv/ *adj.* (*formal*) **1.** portable **2.** RELATING TO OR FOR CARRYING relating to the carrying of things, or used for carrying things [14thC. Via Old French from, ultimately, Latin *portare* "to carry."]

por·ta·tive or·gan *n.* a small portable organ operated by bellows, used in medieval and Renaissance music

Port Au·gus·ta /-aw gústə/ city in South Australia, at the head of the Spencer Gulf. The city is a railway junction and industrial center. Population: 13,914 (1996).

Port-au-Prince /pàwrt ō prínss/ capital city and chief port of Haiti, on Gonâve Gulf. Population: 743,000 (1994).

Port Ches·ter village on Long Island Sound, in southeastern New York, on the Connecticut border. Population: 24,859 (1996).

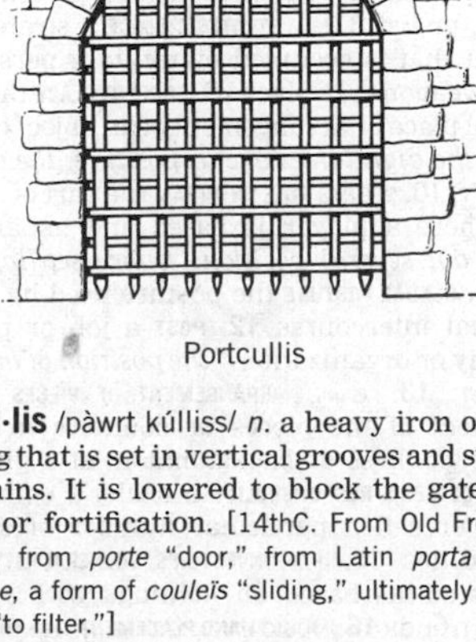

Portcullis

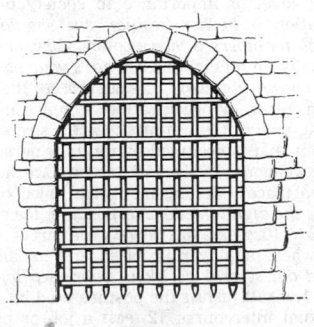

port·cul·lis /pàwrt kúlliss/ *n.* a heavy iron or wooden grating that is set in vertical grooves and suspended by chains. It is lowered to block the gateway to a castle or fortification. [14thC. From Old French *porte coleïce*, from *porte* "door," from Latin *porta* "gate," + *col(e)ïce*, a form of *couleïs* "sliding," ultimately from Latin *colare* "to filter."]

port de bras /pàwr də bráa/ *n.* the proper movement of the arms in ballet, or exercises for developing this [From French, literally "carriage of the arms"]

Port du Salut *n.* = **Port-Salut** *n.*

Porte /pawrt/ *n.* the court or government of the Ottoman Empire. It was situated in Constantinople. [Early 17thC. From French *(la Sublime) Porte* "(the exalted) Gate," translation of the Turkish title of the central office; from the palace gate where justice was administered.]

porte-co·chère /pàwrt kō sháir/, **porte-co·chere** *n.* **1.** EXTENDED ROOF a large roof or awning extending from the entrance of a building to the driveway **2.** COVERED ENTRANCE a large covered entrance for vehicles in a wall or building leading to a courtyard [Late 17thC. From French *porte cochère*, literally "door for coaches."]

Port E·liz·a·beth city in Eastern Cape Province, southeastern South Africa, situated on Algoa Bay, on the Indian Ocean. Population: 853,205 (1991).

por·tend /pawr ténd/ **(-tend·ed, -tend·ing, -tends)** *vt.* **1.** BE AN OMEN to be an indication that something, especially something unpleasant, is going to happen **2.** INDICATE to indicate or signify something [15thC. From Latin *portendere*, literally "to stretch forward," from *tendere* (see TENDER[2]).]

por·tent /páwr tènt/ *n.* **1.** OMEN an indication that something, often something unpleasant, is going to happen **2.** SIGNIFICANCE ominous or prophetic significance **3.** MARVEL a wonderful or marvelous thing (*formal*) [Late 16thC. From Latin *portentum*, from *portendere* (see PORTEND).]

por·ten·tous /pawr téntəss/ *adj.* **1.** SIGNIFICANT very serious and significant, especially in terms of future events **2.** POMPOUS excessively serious or pompous (*disapproving*) **3.** AMAZING inspiring wonder and amazement —**por·ten·tous·ly** *adv.* —**por·ten·tous·ness** *n.*

por·ter[1] /páwrtər/ *n.* **1.** LUGGAGE CARRIER somebody who is employed to carry people's luggage, e.g., at an airport, railroad station, or in a hotel **2.** RAILCAR ATTENDANT an attendant in a sleeping car or parlor car [14thC. Via French *porteur* from medieval Latin *portator*, literally "carrier," from *portare* (see PORT[1]).]

por·ter[2] /páwrtər/ *n.* a dark sweet beer, similar to light stout, made from malt that has been browned or charred [Early 18thC. Shortening of *porter's ale*, from PORTER[1]; probably because the beer was drunk mainly by porters.]

Por·ter /páwrtər/, **Cole** (1891–1964) U.S. composer and lyricist. He is known for his witty sophisticated songs, and for musicals such as *Kiss Me Kate* (1949). Full name **Cole Albert Porter**

Por·ter, Katherine Anne (1890–1980) U.S. writer. Regarded as one of the leading modern writers of short stories, she received the 1966 Pulitzer Prize for *Collected Short Stories* (1965).

por·ter·age /páwrtərij/ *n.* **1.** CARRYING WORK the work of carrying that is performed by porters **2.** FEE FOR CARRYING a fee charged by porters for carrying things

por·ter·house /páwrtər hòwss/ (*plural* **-hous·es** /-zəz/) *n.* **1.** FOOD = **porterhouse steak 2.** RESTAURANT an establishment that in the past sold porter and sometimes also served meals (*archaic*)

por·ter·house steak *n.* a beef steak from the thick end of the sirloin

port·fo·li·o /pawrt fṓlee ō/ (*plural* **-os**) *n.* **1.** FLAT CASE a large flat case for carrying documents, e.g., maps, photographs, or drawings **2.** PORTFOLIO CONTENTS the contents of a portfolio, especially as representing somebody's creative work **3.** FIN GROUP OF INVESTMENTS all the investments held by an individual or organization **4.** POL MINISTERIAL RESPONSIBILITIES the post or responsibilities of a cabinet minister, minister of state, or ambassador **5.** RANGE OF PRODUCTS the complete range of products or designs offered by a company (*formal*) [Early 18thC. From Italian *portafoglio*, from *portare* "to carry" + *foglio* "sheet, page."]

Port-Gen·til /pawr zhaan teé/ city and seaport in western Gabon. It is the capital of Ogooué-Maritime Province. Population: 97,900 (1993).

Port Har·court /-haar kawrt/ major port and capital city of Rivers State, southern Nigeria. Population: 400,000 (1995).

port·hole /páwrt hōl/ *n.* **1.** NAUT ROUND WINDOW a small round window with a metal frame in the side of a ship **2.** MIL OPENING FOR WEAPON a small opening in a fortified wall through which weapons can be fired

Por·tia /páwrshə/ *n.* a small inner natural satellite of Uranus, discovered in 1986 by the Voyager 2 planetary probe. It is approximately 68 mi./110 km in diameter.

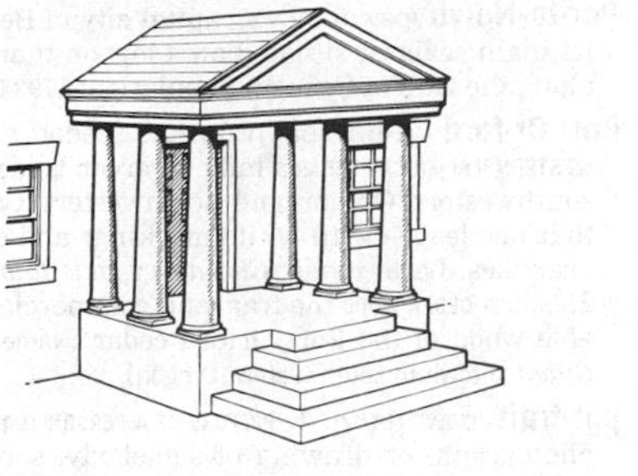

Portico

por·ti·co /páwrti kō/ (*plural* **-coes** *or* **-cos**) *n.* **1.** PORCH a covered entrance to a large building **2.** COVERED WALKWAY a covered walkway, often leading to the main entrance of a building, that consists of a roof supported by pillars [Early 17thC. Via Italian from Latin *porticus*, from *porta* "gate" (see PORT[2]).]

por·tière /pàwrtee áir/, **por·tiere** *n.* a heavy curtain hung across a doorway (*formal*) [Mid-19thC. From French, formed from *porte* "door," ultimately from Latin *porta* (see PORT[2]).]

por·tion /páwrsh'n/ *n.* **1.** HELPING OF FOOD an amount of food for one person **2.** FRACTION a part or section of a larger whole **3.** FATE an unavoidable event or part of somebody's life (*literary*) **4.** LAW INHERITANCE a part of an estate that has been bequeathed to an heir **5.** LAW = **dowry** *n.* **1** ■ *vt.* **(-tioned, -tion·ing, -tions) 1.** DIVIDE to divide something into parts for use **2.** LAW ENDOW to give a dowry to a woman (*archaic*) [14thC. Via French from the Latin stem *portion-*, of uncertain origin: possibly something related to *pars* "share" (source of English *part*).] —**por·tion·a·ble** *adj.* —**por·tion·er** *n.*

Port·land /páwrtlənd/ **1.** city in southwestern Maine, on the southern shore of Casco Bay, northeast of Saco. Population: 63,123 (1996). **2.** city in Oregon, situated in the northwestern part of the state on the Willamette River. It is the state's largest city, and its economic and cultural center. Population: 437,319 (1990).

Port·land ce·ment, port·land ce·ment *n.* a cement that hardens under water, made by burning limestone and clay [So called because its color resembles that of Portland stone, a limestone named for the Isle of Portland in southern England, where it was quarried]

Port Lou·is /-lo͞o is, -lo͞o ee/ capital city and chief port of Mauritius, on the northeastern coast of the island. Population: 142,850 (1992).

port·ly /páwrtlee/ **(-li·er, -li·est)** *adj.* **1.** SLIGHTLY OVERWEIGHT slightly overweight but dignfied **2.** STATELY having an air of grandeur (*archaic*) [15thC. Formed from PORT[5] in the sense "bearing, manner."] —**port·li·ness** *n.*

port·man·teau /pàwrt man tṓ, pawrt mántō/ (*plural* **-teaus** *or* **-teaux** /pàwrt man tōz/) *n.* an old type of large leather suitcase, especially one that opened out into two compartments [Mid-16thC. From French *portemanteau*, from *porter* "to carry" + *manteau* "cloak."]

port·man·teau word *n.* a word that combines the sound and meaning of two words, e.g., "smog," a combination of "smoke" and "fog" [From Humpty Dumpty's description (in Lewis Carroll's *Through the Looking Glass*) of the word "slithy" as a *portmanteau* because "there are two meanings packed up into one word"]

Port Mores·by /-máwrzbee/ capital city of Papua New Guinea, situated on the southern coast of the island of New Guinea. Population: 193,242 (1990).

Por·to A·le·gre /pàwr to͞o ə léggrə/ capital city of Rio Grande do Sul State, southeastern Brazil, and the country's leading river port. It lies at the junction of five rivers. Population: 1,286,251 (1996).

port of call *n.* **1.** NAUT PORT AWAY FROM HOME any port, other than the home port, that a vessel visits on a journey **2.** VISITED PLACE a place visited during a vacation, trip, or excursion (*informal*)

port of en·try *n.* a place, e.g., a port or an airport, where passengers and goods may enter a country under the supervision of customs officials

Port-of-Spain /pàwrt əv spáyn/, **Port of Spain** capital city and main port of Trinidad and Tobago. It is situated in the northwestern part of the island of Trinidad. Population: 59,200 (1988).

Por·to-No·vo /pàwrto nṓvō/ capital city of Benin, and its main seaport, situated on a lagoon that extends along the Gulf of Guinea. Population: 179,000 (1994).

Port Or·ford ce·dar /pawrt áwrfərd seédər/ *n.* **1.** TREES **WESTERN N AMERICAN CEDAR** a tall evergreen tree native to southwestern Oregon and northwestern California that has leaves with white markings and drooping branches. Latin name: *Chamaecyparis lawsoniana.* **2.** INDUST **CEDAR WOOD** the fragrant, commercially valuable wood of the Port Orford cedar [Named for *Port Orford*, a town in southwestern Oregon]

por·trait /páwrtrət/ *n.* **1. PICTURE OF A PERSON** a painting, photograph, or drawing of somebody, somebody's face, or a related group **2. DESCRIPTION** a description of something, e.g., a person, place, or period ■ *adj.* PRINTING **TALLER THAN WIDE** used to describe a piece of paper, illustration, book, or page that is taller than it is wide. ◊ **landscape** [Mid-16thC. From French, from the past participle of Old French *portraire* (see PORTRAY).]

WORD KEY: CULTURAL NOTE

Portrait of a Lady, a novel by Henry James (1881). Through the story of Isabel Archer, a young American woman who travels to Europe and is duped into marrying an urbane but materialistic fellow expatriate, the author explores the contrasting characteristics of the Old World (sophisticated but corrupt) and the New (idealistic but naive). It was made into a movie by Jane Campion in 1997.

por·trait·ist /páwrtrətist/ *n.* somebody such as a photographer or painter who specializes in portraits

por·trai·ture /páwrtrə chŏor, -trəchər/ *n.* **1. MAKING OF PORTRAITS** the art or practice of making portraits **2. PORTRAITS** portraits considered collectively **3. PORTRAIT** a portrait painting, drawing, or photography (*formal*)

por·tray /pawr tráy/ **(-trayed, -tray·ing, -trays)** *vt.* **1. DEPICT VISUALLY** to depict something, e.g., a person or a scene, in a painting, photograph, drawing, or sculpture **2. DEPICT VERBALLY** to represent somebody or something in words **3. PLAY A ROLE IN DRAMA** to play a character in drama [13thC. From Old French *portraire*, literally "to draw forth," from *traire* "to draw," from Latin *trahere* (see TRACTION.] —**por·tray·a·ble** *adj.* —**por·tray·er** *n.*

por·tray·al /pawrtráyəl/ *n.* **1. ACTING REPRESENTATION** the way an actor conveys the character of the role being played **2. ARTISTIC DEPICTION** an artist's depiction or representation of a subject **3. REPRESENTATION** a representation of somebody or something in words or images

Port Sa·id /-saa eéd/ city and port in northeastern Egypt, at the Mediterranean end of the Suez Canal. Population: 460,000 (1992).

Port-Sal·ut /pàwr sa lŏo/, **Port du Salut** /pàwr doo sa lŏo/ *n.* a flat round mild French cheese with an orange rind, made from whole milk [Late 19thC. Named for Notre Dame de *Port-du-Salut*, a Trappist monastery in northwestern France where the cheese was first produced.]

port·side /páwrt sīd/ *adj.* **BY A HARBOR** situated on or near the waterfront at a port ○ *a portside cafe* ■ *adj., adv.* NAUT = **port**[3] *adj., adv.*

Ports·mouth /páwrtsməth/ *n.* city in southeastern Virginia. It is a major seaport. Population: 103,907 (1990).

Port Su·dan city in northeastern Sudan, and the country's only seaport, situated on the Red Sea 200 mi./322 km northeast of Khartoum. Population: 305,385 (1993).

Port Tal·bot /-táwlbət, -tál-/ town in southern Wales. It is the administrative center of Neath and Port Talbot unitary authority, and was a major steel-making center. Population: 37,647 (1991).

Por·tu·gal /páwrchəgəl/ republic in southwestern Europe, in the southwestern part of the Iberian peninsula. Language: Portuguese. Currency: escudo. Capital: Lisbon. Population: 9,865,114 (1996). Area: 35,553 sq. mi./92,082 sq. km. Official name **Portuguese Republic**

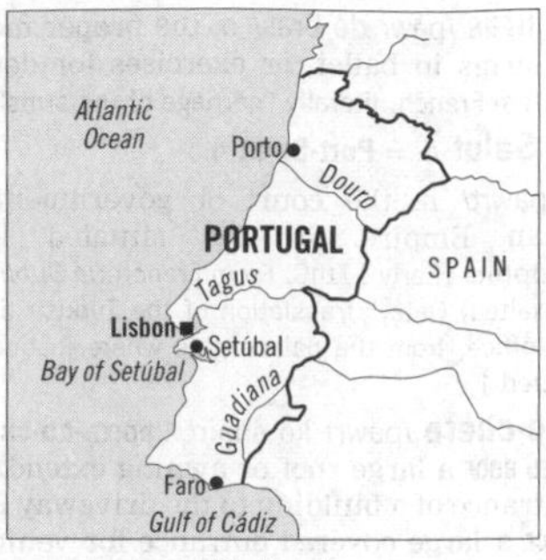

Portugal

Por·tu·guese /pàwrchə geéz, -geés/ *n.* **1.** LANG **LANGUAGE OF PORTUGAL AND BRAZIL** the official language of Portugal and Brazil, also an official language in some African countries, belonging to the Italic branch of Indo-European languages. Portuguese is spoken by about 150 million people, with a further approximately 30 million using it as a second language. **2.** PEOPLES **SOMEBODY FROM PORTUGAL** somebody who was born in or raised in Portugal, or who has Portuguese citizenship ■ *adj.* **1. OF PORTUGAL** relating to Portugal, or its people or culture **2.** LANG **RELATING TO PORTUGUESE** relating to the Portuguese language [Late 16thC. Via Portuguese *português* from, ultimately, medieval Latin *Portus Cale*, the port of Gaya (Oporto).]

Por·tu·guese In·di·a territories in India formerly ruled by Portugal, considered as a group. They included Goa, Daman, Diu, Dadra, and Nagar Haveli. They were taken over by India between 1954 and 1961.

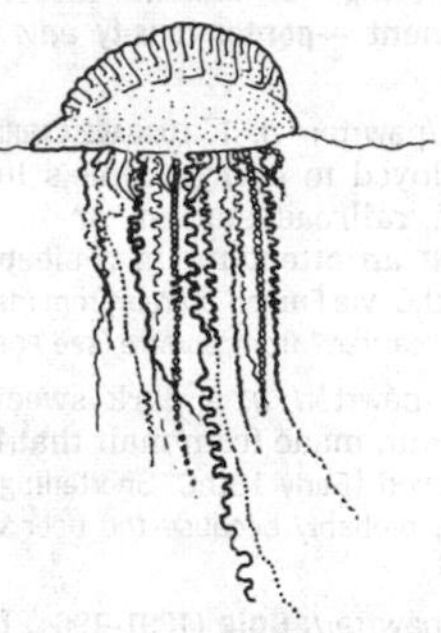
Portuguese man-of-war

Por·tu·guese man-of-war *n.* a sea organism **(hydrozoan)** resembling a jellyfish, that lives in warm waters, has a transparent gas-filled float, and long stinging often poisonous tentacles. Genus: *Physalia.* [From its crest, resembling a sail]

Por·tu·guese wa·ter dog *n.* a dog bred in Portugal to assist fishermen that has webbed feet and a dark coat with light markings and is an excellent swimmer

por·tu·lac·a /pàwrchə lákə/ *n.* a plant with fleshy leaves and brightly colored flowers, native to tropical and subtropical America but widely cultivated. Genus: *Portulaca.* [Mid-16thC. Via Latin, "purslane," from *portula*, literally "little gate," from *porta* (see PORT[2]); from the covering of the seed capsule, that resembles a gate.]

port-wine stain *n.* a conspicuous purplish birthmark, especially on the face or neck

POS *abbr.* point of sale

pos. *abbr.* **1.** position **2.** positive

po·sa·da /pō saádə, pə-/ *n.* a hotel, pension, or hostel in a Spanish-speaking country [Mid-18thC. From Spanish, formed from *posar* "to stay, lodge," via late Latin *pausare* from Latin *pausa* "rest" (see PAUSE).]

pose[1] /pōz/ *v.* **(posed, pos·ing, pos·es) 1.** *vti.* **ADOPT A POSTURE** to adopt a particular physical posture for a photograph or painting, or position somebody or something for this purpose **2.** *vi.* **IMPERSONATE** to pretend to be somebody or something else **3.** *vi.* **BE PRETENTIOUS** to behave, dress, or assume a mental attitude intended to impress others (*disapproving*) **4.** *vt.* **ASK** to ask a question, often one that requires some consideration **5.** *vt.* **PRESENT** to be the cause of something, e.g., a problem, threat, danger, or challenge ○ *a breakdown of negotiations that poses a threat to peace* ■ *n.* **1. POSTURE** a particular physical posture, e.g., one adopted for a painting or photograph **2. PRETENSE** a way of behaving or dressing calculated to impress others (*disapproving*) [14thC. Via Old French *poser* from, ultimately, late Latin *pausare* "to rest, cease," from *pausa* (see PAUSE).]

pose[2] /pōz/ **(posed, pos·ing, pos·es)** *vt.* to confuse or baffle somebody (*dated*) [Early 16thC. Partly a shortening of *appose* (variant of OPPOSE), and partly from Old French *poser* "to assume."]

Po·sei·don /pə sīd'n, pō-/ *n.* a U.S. ballistic missile capable of being launched from a submarine and carrying a nuclear warhead

pos·er[1] /pṓzər/ *n.* **1. SOMEBODY WHO POSES** somebody who adopts a particular posture for a photograph or painting **2. POSEUR** a poseur (*informal disapproving*) [Late 19thC. Formed from POSE[1].]

pos·er[2] /pṓzər/ *n.* a difficult question or problem [Late 16thC. Formed from POSE[2].]

po·seur /pō zúr/ *n.* somebody who behaves or dresses to impress others [Late 19thC. From French, formed from *poser* "to pose" (see POSE[1]).]

posh /posh/ *adj.* **FOR THE WELL-OFF** elegant, fashionable, and expensive (*informal*) ■ *adv. U.K.* **LIKE AN UPPER CLASS PERSON** like somebody from the upper classes (*informal*) ○ *She talks posh on the phone to try to impress people.* [Early 20thC. Origin uncertain.] —**posh·ly** *adv.* —**posh·ness** *n.*

WORD KEY: ORIGIN

The legend has become widely circulated that ***posh*** is an acronym formed from the initial letters of *port out, starboard home*, an allusion to the fact that wealthy passengers could afford the more expensive cabins on the port side of the ships going out to India, and on the starboard side returning to Britain, which kept them out of the heat of the sun. Pleasant as this story is, it has never been substantiated. Another possibility is that ***posh*** may be the same word as the now obsolete *posh* "dandy, swell," a slang term current around the end of the 19th century. This too is of unknown origin, but it has been linked with the still earlier 19th-century slang term *posh* "halfpenny," hence broadly "money," which may have come ultimately from Romany *posh* "half."

pos·it /pózzit/ *vt.* **(-it·ed, -it·ing, -its)** (*formal*) **1. PUT SOMETHING FORWARD** to put something forward for consideration, e.g., a suggestion, assumption, or fact **2. POSITION SOMETHING** to place something firmly in position ■ *n.* **SOMETHING PUT FORWARD** a fact, assumption, or suggestion for consideration (*formal*) [Mid-17thC. From Latin *posit-*, the past participle stem of *ponere* "to place" (see POSITION).]

pos·i·tif /pòzzə teéf/ *n.* a manual that controls the softer stops on a church organ [Via Old French, "positive organ," from Latin *positivus* (see POSITIVE)]

po·si·tion /pə zísh'n/ *n.* **1. LOCATION** the place where somebody or something is, especially in relation to other things **2. POSTURE** the posture that somebody's body is in ○ *the fetal position* **3. ARRANGEMENT** the way or direction in which an object is placed or arranged ○ *the position of the hour hand* **4. SITUATION** a particular set of circumstances ○ *I wouldn't sell just yet if I were in your position.* **5. RANK** somebody's standing or level of importance in society or an organization ○ *In her position she should set an example for others.* **6. VIEW** a policy, view, or opinion, especially an official one ○ *What's your position on the proposed highway?* **7. PLACE IN ORDER** the place a person, team, or organization occupies in a race, contest, or list **8.** MIL **STRATEGIC PLACE** a strategic area or point that is occupied by military personnel or where weapons are placed **9. CORRECT PLACE** the correct or usual place or arrangement of an object or person ○ *Once the dignitaries are in position, the ceremony can start.* **10.** SPORTS **ROLE ON A TEAM** the part of a playing area where a player is based and usually plays ○ *tried out several positions before settling on left field* **11. SEXUAL POSTURE** the posture used by a couple in sexual intercourse **12. POST** a job or post in a company or organization ○ *the position of marketing manager* **13.** GAME **ARRANGEMENT OF PIECES** the arrangement of the pieces or counters in a board game, e.g., chess or backgammon, at a given time **14.** FIN **DEALER'S RESPONSIBILITY** a dealer's commitment to buy or sell a particular number of stocks or commodities **15.** FIN **INVESTOR'S VULNERABILITY** an investor's status based on holdings with regard to market trends **16.** MUSIC **HAND PLACEMENT** the placement of the fingers on a keyboard or string instrument **17.** MUSIC **DEGREE OF EXTENSION OF TROMBONE SLIDE** the extent to which a trombone slide is pushed out **18.** MUSIC **ARRANGEMENT OF NOTES IN A CHORD** the arrangement of individual notes within a chord. Root position is the most fundamental position. **19.** POETRY **VOWEL TYPE IN CLASSICAL POETRY** a short vowel counting as a long vowel in classical poetry because it comes before two or more consonants ■ *vt.* **(-tioned, -tion·ing, -tions) 1. PUT SOMETHING IN PLACE** to put something in a particular or suitable place ○ *Position the two pieces so that they are at right angles.* **2. PLACE SOMEBODY** to place somebody or yourself in a particular or suitable area, place, or situation ○ *This strategy will position us advantageously in the market.* **3. LOCATE SOMETHING** to determine the site or location of something ○ *Air traffic controllers have positioned the unknown aircraft at 50 miles north of the airport.* [14thC. Via French from, ultimately, Latin *posit-*, the past participle stem of *ponere* "to place." Ultimately from an Indo-European word meaning "to drop off."] —**po·si·tion·al** *adj.* —**po·si·tion·al·ly** *adv.* —**po·si·tion·er** *n.*

WORD KEY: ORIGIN

The Latin word *ponere*, from which ***position*** is derived, is also the source of English *compose, compost, compound, deposit, dispose, expose, impose, oppose, positive, post, postpone, posture, repose, suppose,* and *transpose.*

po·si·tion·al no·ta·tion *n.* the method of denoting numbers by using digits in such a way that the value contributed by the digit depends on its position as well as its independent value. In the decimal system the value of the digits "37" is $(3 \times 10^1) + (7 \times 10^0)$, while in the octal system it is $(3 \times 8^1) + (7 \times 8^0)$, or 31 decimal.

po·si·tion au·dit *n.* an assessment of a company's or organization's commercial standing carried out to help future planning

po·si·tion ef·fect *n.* a change in a gene's expression depending on its location on the chromosome relative to other genes

po·si·tion pa·per *n.* an in-depth report on a particular matter that gives the official view and recommendations of a government or organization

pos·i·tive /pózzətiv/ *adj.* **1. SURE** certain and not in doubt **2.** LAW **IRREFUTABLE** conclusive and beyond doubt or question ○ *positive identification of the suspect* **3. OPTIMISTIC** confident, optimistic, and focusing on the good things rather than bad ○ *a positive attitude about work* **4. BENEFICIAL** producing good results because of having an innately beneficial character ○ *The workshop was a very positive experience.* **5. AFFIRMATIVE** indicating agreement or affirmation ○ *got some positive feedback from the survey* **6. QUANTIFIABLE** capable of being measured, detected, or perceived ○ *a positive correlation between investment in telecommunications and economic development* **7.** MED **INDICATING PRESENCE OF SOMETHING IN TEST** indicating the presence or existence of a particular organism, illness, especially HIV, or condition in the results of a test or examination ○ *a positive test for diabetes* **8.** MED = **Rh positive 9. ENCOURAGING GOOD BEHAVIOR** encouraging behavior, especially in the young, that is considered morally good ○ *a positive role model* **10. ADDING EMPHASIS** used to emphasize the degree to which something is true, striking, or impressive (*informal*) ○ *Hiring her is a positive triumph for the department.* **11.** MATH **MORE THAN ZERO** with a value higher than zero. Symbol **+ 12.** PHYS **WITH ELECTRICAL CHARGE LIKE A PROTON** with an electrical charge of an opposite polarity to an electron's and the same polarity as a proton's **13. NOT NEGATIVE** measured in a direction or designated as a quantity equal in magnitude but opposite to that regarded as negative **14.** ELEC **WITH POSITIVE CHARGE** with an overall positive electrical charge, sometimes caused by the loss of one or more electrons **15.** ELEC **WITH HIGHER ELECTRICAL POTENTIAL** with a higher electrical potential than the ground or the defined neutral point ○ *a positive electrode* **16.** ELEC = **electropositive** *adj.* 1 **17.** PHOTOGRAPHY **LIKE THE SUBJECT** used to describe photographic images that have colors or values of dark and light corresponding to the subject **18.** OPTICS **MAKING LIGHT CONVERGE** making a parallel beam of light converge **19.** GRAM **NOT COMPARATIVE OR SUPERLATIVE** relating to the basic form of an adjective or adverb, rather than its comparative or superlative forms **20.** PHILOS **EMPIRICAL** relating to the theory that knowledge can be acquired only through direct observation and experimentation rather than metaphysics and theology **21.** BIOL **SHOWING RESPONSE** indicating growth, response, or movement toward a stimulus, e.g., light **22.** ENG **MECHANICAL ACTION WITH NO SLACK** used to describe a mechanical action or device having little or no play **23.** ZODIAC **OF CERTAIN ZODIAC SIGNS** relating to the air and fire signs of the zodiac ■ *n.* **1.** ELEC **SOMETHING WITH POSITIVE CHARGE** something that carries a positive electrical charge **2.** ELEC **CELL PLATE OR TERMINAL** a positively charged plate or terminal in a cell **3.** PHOTOGRAPHY **IMAGE LIKE THE SUBJECT** a photographic image in which the light and dark tones and colors correspond to those of the original subject **4. POSITIVE THING** something that shows agreement, support, or affirmation (*informal*) ○ *Not a bad situation when we weigh all the positives.* **5.** MATH **SOMETHING GREATER THAN ZERO** a value or number higher than zero **6.** GRAM **BASIC FORM OF MODIFIER** an adjective or adverb in its basic form rather than the comparative or superlative **7.** MUSIC **MEDIEVAL ORGAN** a small medieval organ with just one manual and no pedals **8.** MUSIC = **positif** [14thC. Via French from Latin *positivus*, from *posit-*, the past participle stem of *ponere* (see POSITION); the underlying meaning is "firmly set down."] —**pos·i·tive·ness** *n.* —**pos·i·tiv·i·ty** /pòzzə tívvətee/ *n.*

pos·i·tive·ly /pózzətivlee/ *adv.* **1. DEFINITELY** used to emphasize the finality or extremity of a statement or response **2. FOR ADDING EMPHASIS** used to emphasize an often already emphatic quality, characteristic, or action ○ *looking positively radiant* **3. ENCOURAGINGLY** in an encouraging, supportive, or optimistic way

pos·i·tive pre·scrip·tion *n.* = **prescription** *n.* 7

pos·i·tiv·ism /pózzəti vìzzəm/ *n.* **1.** PHILOS **THEORY OF KNOWLEDGE** the theory that knowledge can be acquired only through direct observation and experimentation rather than through metaphysics and theology **2. POSITIVE STATE** the state or quality of being positive —**pos·i·tiv·ist** *n., adj.* —**pos·i·tiv·is·tic** /pòzzəti vístik/ *adj.* —**pos·i·ti·vis·ti·cal·ly** *adv.*

pos·i·tron /pózzə tròn/ *n.* an elementary particle of antimatter that has the same mass as an electron but the opposite electrical charge [Mid-20thC. Coined from POSITIVE + ELECTRON.]

pos·i·tron e·mis·sion to·mog·ra·phy *n.* a method of medical imaging capable of displaying the metabolic activity of organs in the body, and useful in diagnosing cancer, locating brain tumors, and investigating other brain disorders

pos·i·tro·ni·um /pòzzə trṓnee əm/ *n.* a combination of a positron and an electron that rapidly decays to produce two or three photons

po·so·le /pō sṓ lày/ *n.* a thick Mexican soup made with hominy, chicken or pork, chilies, and cilantro [Via Mexican Spanish from Nahuatl *pozolli*]

po·sol·o·gy /pə sólləjee/ *n.* the study of the dosage of medicines [Early 19thC. From French *posologie*, from Greek *posos* "how much."] —**po·so·log·i·cal** /pòssə lójjik'l/ *adj.*

poss. *abbr.* **1.** possession **2.** GRAMMAR possessive **3.** possible **4.** possibly

pos·se /póssee/ *n.* **1. SHERIFF'S HELPERS** a group of able-bodied citizens that a sheriff can call upon to assist in maintaining law and order. They are associated mainly with the 19th-century American South and West. **2. ASSEMBLED GROUP** a group of people assembled for a common purpose (*informal*) **3. SEARCHERS** a search party **4. STREET GANG** a group of youths who hang around together and have a leader (*slang*) [Mid-17thC. Shortening of POSSE COMITATUS.]

pos·se com·i·ta·tus /pòssi kómmə táatəss, pòssi kómmə táytəss/ *n.* a posse (*formal*) [From medieval Latin, literally "force of the county"]

pos·sess /pə zéss/ **(-sessed, -sess·ing, -sess·es)** *vt.* **1. OWN** to have or own something **2. HAVE AS AN ABILITY** to have a particular ability, quality, or characteristic **3. HAVE KNOWLEDGE OF SOMETHING** to have or acquire skill or knowledge of something **4. TAKE CONTROL** to take control of or influence somebody, affecting the person's behavior or thinking ○ *possessed by fear and unable to speak* **5. INFLUENCE** to cause somebody to be influenced or controlled by something, especially an emotion ○ *The news possessed us with foreboding.* **6. CONTROL FEELING** to control yourself or a feeling in a particular situation (*formal*) **7. HAVE SEX** to have sex with somebody (*dated*) (*sometimes considered offensive*) **8. SEIZE SOMETHING** to gain or seize something (*archaic*) [14thC. Via Old French *possesser* from Latin *possess-*, the past participle stem of *possidere*, literally "to sit on as head of," from *sedere*.] —**pos·ses·sor** *n.*

pos·sessed /pə zést/ *adj.* **1. CONTROLLED** controlled or strongly influenced, especially by a supposed evil supernatural force or a strong emotion ○ *screaming and shouting like a man possessed* **2. HAVING QUALITY** having as a quality, characteristic, or belief (*literary*) **3. OWNING** being the owner of something ○ *an only child possessed of a great fortune* **4.** = **self-possessed**

pos·ses·sion /pə zésh'n/ *n.* **1. OWNERSHIP** the act or state of owning or holding something **2. SOMETHING OWNED** something owned or held **3.** POL **COLONY** a country or region controlled or governed by another country (*often used in the plural*) **4. STATE OF BEING CONTROLLED** the condition of being controlled by or appearing to be controlled by a supernatural force or strong emotion **5.** SPORTS **CONTROL OF A BALL** control of the ball or puck in various sports **6.** CRIMINOL **HAVING SOMETHING ILLEGAL** the crime of having or owning something illegal, e.g., a weapon, contraband, stolen property, or illegal drugs **7.** LAW **OCCUPANCY** the physical occupancy of something, e.g., a house, whether or not accompanied by ownership ■ **pos·ses·sions** *npl.* **PERSONAL PROPERTY** personal property and wealth —**pos·ses·sional** *adj.*

pos·ses·sive /pə zéssiv/ *adj.* **1. EAGER TO DOMINATE** wishing to control somebody exclusively or to be the sole object of somebody's love (*disapproving*) **2. SELFISH** tending not to share possessions with others **3. OF OWNERSHIP** relating to ownership ○ *possessive pride* **4.** GRAM **SHOWING OWNERSHIP IN GRAMMATICAL TERMS** indicating grammatical ownership, e.g., in pronouns such as "his" or "her" ■ *n.* GRAM **1. WORD SHOWING OWNERSHIP** a noun, pronoun, adjective or form of a word that indicates ownership or association **2. POSSESSIVE CASE** the possessive or genitive case —**pos·ses·sive·ly** *adv.* —**pos·ses·sive·ness** *n.*

pos·ses·so·ry /pə zéssəree/ *adj.* **1. RELATING TO POSSESSION** relating to possession or a possessor (*formal*) **2.** LAW **DEPENDING ON POSSESSION** arising from or depending on possession

pos·si·bil·i·ty /pòssə bíllətee/ *n.* (*plural* **-ties**) **1. SOMETHING POSSIBLE** something that is possible **2. STATE OF BEING POSSIBLE** the condition or quality of being possible **3. CONTENDER** somebody who is considered a possible winner, choice, or candidate ■ **pos·si·bil·i·ties** *npl.* **POTENTIAL** the potential for successful future development ○ *The house needs a lot of work, but it's got possibilities.*

pos·si·ble /póssəb'l/ *adj.* **1. ABLE TO HAPPEN** capable of happening or likely to happen in the future **2. MAYBE REAL OR TRUE** capable of being real, present, or true **3. CAPABLE OF HAPPENING BUT UNLIKELY** theoretically capable of being done, of happening, or of existing, although difficult or unlikely in practice **4. POTENTIAL** having potential as a particular thing or for a particular purpose **5. PROPER** in keeping with convention, decorum, or tradition ■ *n.* **POSSIBILITY** somebody who or something that is a possibility [14thC. Via French from Latin *possibilis*, from *posse* "to be able" (see POTENT).]

pos·si·ble world *n.* a philosophical idea postulating an alternative world or situation in which a proposition's truth can be evaluated. A proposition is true if there is such a world in which it would be true and it is necessary if it is true in every such world.

pos·si·bly /póssəblee/ *adv.* **1. PERHAPS** likely, or maybe so, but not known for certain **2. AS A POSSIBILITY** as something that is possible or may be realized ○ *a new park to include a pond and possibly a playground* **3. ADDING EMPHASIS** used to express shock, disbelief, or amazement ○ *What could he possibly mean?* ○ *How could you possibly have believed that?* **4. SUGGESTING EFFORT** used to indicate the magnitude of effort or difficulty ○ *They've done everything they possibly could to help her.* **5. SUGGESTING IMPOSSIBILITY** used in negative sentences and phrases to emphasize that something cannot be done or cannot happen ○ *She can't possibly have known what I spent!* **6. USED AS REQUEST MODIFIER** used with requests to suggest the speaker's awareness of an imposition ○ *Could you possibly mail this letter for me on your way to work?*

POSSLQ *abbr.* person of the opposite sex sharing living quarters (*informal*)

pos·sum /póssəm/ *n.* = **opossum** (*informal*) [Early 17thC. Shortening.] ◇ **play possum** to feign death, illness, or sleep, or pretend to be uninvolved in something, in order to protect yourself

pos·sum·haw /póssəm hàw/ *n.* = **dockmackie** [From the plant's hairy leaves]

post[1] /pōst/ *n.* **1. UPRIGHT POLE** a pole of wood or metal fixed in the ground in an upright position, serving as a support, marker, or place for attaching things **2.** BUILDING **UPRIGHT FRAME PART** a vertical piece in a building frame that supports a beam **3.** HORSERACING **RACECOURSE INDICATOR** either of two upright poles marking the starting point and finishing line on a racecourse **4.** FURNITURE **FURNITURE SUPPORT** any one of the upright supports of a piece of furniture such as a chair or a four-poster bed **5.** SPORTS **GOALPOST** a goalpost (*informal*) **6. EARRING PART** a metal stem on a pierced earring that passes through the ear, and fits into a cap at the back **7.** COMPUT = **posting**[1] *n.* 1 ■ *vt.* (**post·ed, post·ing, posts**) **1. DISPLAY SOMETHING** to display something, e.g., an announcement, name, or result, in a public place **2. ERECT ANTITRESPASSING SIGNS** to put up signs around a property warning against trespassing or engaging in a forbidden activity **3.** GAME **SCORE** to score a point or points in a game **4.** ONLINE **PUBLISH ELECTRONICALLY** to make text appear online or at an Internet location **5. GIVE NOTICE OF MARRIAGE** to announce a forthcoming marriage in a church ○ *post the banns* **6.** NAUT **NAME A SHIP** to publish the name of a ship presumed lost or sunk **7. DENOUNCE PUBLICLY** to denounce somebody by displaying damaging information publicly (*dated*) [Pre-12thC. From Latin *postis*, literally "something that stands in front," ultimately from an Indo-European base meaning "to stand," which is also the ancestor of English *stud, stem*, and *station*.]

post[2] /pōst/ *n.* **1.** MIL **MILITARY BASE** a place where a military operation is carried out **2. WORKPLACE OR STATION** a place where somebody has particular responsibilities **3. EMPLOYMENT POSITION** a position of employment, especially one in another country **4.** MIL **VETERANS' ORGANIZATION** a local organization of military veterans ○ *a VFW post* **5.** COMM = **trading post** ■ *vt.* (**post·ed, post·ing, posts**) **1. SEND SOMEBODY TO WORK** to assign somebody to a particular position for a period of duty ○ *post a security guard at the exit* **2.** LAW **PAY TO SET FREE** to pay somebody's bond or bail **3. SEND SOMEBODY AWAY TO WORK** to send somebody somewhere, often overseas, to do a particular job for a specific period of time **4.** MIL **TRANSFER SOLDIER** to send somebody to a new military assignment or unit **5.** MIL **APPOINT TO COMMAND** to appoint somebody to a naval or military command [Mid-16thC. Via French *poste* from, ultimately, Latin *positum*, from the past participle of *ponere* "to place" (see POSITION).]

post[3] /pōst/ *n.* **1.** *U.K.* MAIL **POSTAL SERVICE** the official system for collecting, delivering, and sending letters and parcels from one place to another **2.** *U.K.* MAIL **LETTERS AND PARCELS** letters and parcels that have been sent or are to be sent through the postal system **3.** HIST **STATION ON A ROUTE** any one of a series of stations along a route where, in the past, mounted messengers or couriers rested and changed horses **4.** HIST **MAIL DELIVERER** a rider who, in the past, covered the distance from one post to the next in a delivery system ■ *v.* (**post·ed, post·ing, posts**) **1.** *vt.* COMPUT **UPDATE DATABASE** to update a database record by entering or transferring information **2.** *vti.* COMPUT **SEND MESSAGE ELECTRONICALLY** to place or send a message on the Internet or on some other electronic network **3.** *vi.* EQU **KEEP RHYTHM WITH HORSE** to bob up and down in the saddle in time with a horse's trot **4.** *vi.* HIST **TRAVEL BY POST** to travel using relays of horses **5.** *vi.* **TRAVEL FAST** to travel in haste (*archaic*) **6.** *vt. U.K., ANZ* MAIL **SEND A LETTER** to send a letter or parcel through the postal system. ◊ **mail 7.** *vt.* ACCT **WRITE IN LEDGER** to enter a transaction in a ledger ■ *adv.* (*archaic*) **1. QUICKLY** quickly **2. BY POST HORSE** by mounted messengers or couriers riding between posts [Early 16thC. Via French, "relay station," from, ultimately, Latin *posita*, the feminine past participle of *ponere* (see POSITION).] ◇ **keep somebody posted** to keep somebody informed by supplying new information regularly

post[4] /pōst/ *n.* a postmortem examination of a corpse (*informal*)

POST *abbr.* COMPUT Power On Self-Test

post- *prefix.* **1.** after, later ○ *postwar* **2.** behind ○ *postorbital* [From Latin *post*. Ultimately from an Indo-European word meaning "off, away," which is also the ancestor of English *off, after*, and *ebb*.]

post·age /pṓstij/ *n.* **1. PRICE FOR MAIL DELIVERY** the amount of money paid for the delivery of a piece of mail **2. MARKS SHOWING PAYMENT** the stamps, labels, or others marks on an item of mail showing that the charge has been paid

post·age me·ter *n.* an office machine that prints prepaid postage and a date stamp on items of mail

post·age stamp *n.* **1. GUMMED POSTAGE MARKER** an illustrated paper stamp affixed to mail to show payment of postage **2. PRINTED MARK** a printed mark or impression on an envelope indicating that the postage charge has been paid ■ *adj.* **TINY** unusually small (*hyphenated when used before a noun*)

post·al /pṓst'l/ *adj.* relating to a post office or a mail delivery service —**post·al·ly** *adv.*

post·al card *n.* a plain postcard with prepaid postage, sold by post offices

post·al code *n. Can* a sequence of letters and numbers assigned by the post office to addresses to facilitate mail delivery. ◊ **zip code**

post-bel·lum /pōst bélləm/, **post·bel·lum** *adj.* relating to or during the period after a war, especially the Civil War [From Latin *post bellum* "after the war"]

post-boost phase *n.* the last phase of a multistage missile's flight, when it releases its payload

post·box /pṓst bòks/ *n. U.K.* = **mailbox**

post·card /pṓst kaard/, **post card** *n.* **1. CARD FOR SHORT MESSAGE** a card used to carry a message, usually with a picture or a photograph on one side, that can be sent through the mail without an envelope. ◊ **picture postcard 2.** = **postal card**

post chaise *n.* a closed horse-drawn carriage with four wheels that was used in the 18th and 19th centuries as a fast means of transporting mail and passengers [From POST[3]]

post·code /pṓst kōd/ *n. U.K., Aus* = **zip code**

post·date /pōst dáyt/ (**-dat·ed, -dat·ing, -dates**) *vt.* **1.** FIN **DATE A CHECK LATER** to put a date on a check later than the current day's date in order to delay payment **2. HAPPEN LATER** to happen or be at a later date than something **3. ASSIGN LATER DATE** to assign a date to something, e.g., an event in history, that is later than the one previously assigned

post·di·lu·vi·an /pōst di lóovee ən/, **post·di·lu·vi·al** /-viəl/ *adj.* existing or occurring after the flood described in the book of Genesis in the Bible [Late 17thC. Modeled on ANTEDILUVIAN.]

post·doc /pōst dòk/ *n.* **POSTDOCTORAL STUDENT OR AWARD** a postdoctoral grant, fellowship, or scholar (*slang*) ■ *adj.* **POSTDOCTORAL** relating to postdoctoral work or students (*slang*) [Late 20thC. Shortening.]

post·doc·tor·al /pōst dóktərəl/ *adj.* relating to academic work or research done after a doctorate has been awarded

post·er[1] /pṓstər/ *n.* **1. PRINTED PICTURE** a printed picture, often a reproduction of a photograph or artwork, used for decoration or advertisement **2.** COMPUT **SENDER** somebody who posts a message to an online or Internet location, e.g., a newsgroup

post·er[2] /pṓstər/ *n.* somebody who is in a hurry or traveling quickly (*archaic*)

post·er child *n.* **1. REPRESENTATIVE PERSON** somebody, especially a child, chosen to represent a charitable or other cause by appearing in promotional material **2. PERFECT EXAMPLE** a perfect or quintessential example of something

poste res·tante /pōst re staant/ *n. U.K.* = **general delivery** [From French, "mail remaining" (at the post office)]

pos·te·ri·or /po steéree ər, pō-/ *adj.* **1. BEHIND** situated at the rear or behind something **2.** ZOOL, ANAT **NEAR THE BACK** situated near or toward the back of a human being's or animal's body **3.** BOT **NEAREST THE STEM** nearest the main stem or axis of a plant ○ *the posterior flower* **4. COMING AFTER** coming after something in an order or series (*formal*) **5. SUBSEQUENT** following something in time (*formal*) ■ *n.* **BUTTOCKS** the buttocks (*humorous*) [Early 16thC. From Latin, "coming farther after," from *posterus* "coming after," from *post* (see POST-).] —**pos·te·ri·or·ly** *adv.*

pos·ter·i·ty /po stérrətee/ *n.* (*formal*) **1. PEOPLE IN FUTURE** all future generations **2. ALL DESCENDANTS** all of somebody's descendants [14thC. Via French *postérité* from Latin *posteritas*, from *posterus* (see POSTERIOR).]

pos·tern /pṓstərn, póst-/ *n.* a small gate or entrance at the back of a building, especially a castle or a fort [13thC. Via Old French *pasterne* from, ultimately, late Latin *posterula* "small back door," from Latin *posterus* (see POSTERIOR).]

post ex·change *n.* a store on a military camp selling food, clothes, and other things

post·ex·il·i·an /pōst ig zíllee ən, -ik síllee ən/, **post·ex·il·ic** /-ig zíllik, -ig síllik/ *adj.* occurring or in existence after the period of Babylonian captivity of the Jewish people, 587–539 B.C.

post·fem·i·nist /pōst fémmənist/ *adj.* **1. AFTER FEMINISM** occurring or having developed after the feminist movement of the 1970s (*offensive in some contexts*) **2. GOING BEYOND FEMINISM** differing from or showing a reevaluation of the principles of feminism **3. REFLECTING FEMINISM** developing out of or including the principles of feminism ■ *n.* **SUPPORTER OF POSTFEMINIST IDEAS** a supporter of or believer in postfeminist ideas —**post·fem·i·nism** *n.*

post·gla·cial /pōst gláysh'l/ *adj.* occurring after a glacial period, especially one during the Quaternary Period

post·grad·u·ate /pōst grájjoo ət/, **post·grad** *informal* /pṓst gràd/ *adj.* = **graduate** *n.* 1 ■ *n.* **STUDENT WITH BACHELOR'S DEGREE** somebody who has graduated from a university or college with a bachelor's degree, especially one who is doing further study

post·haste /pōst háyst/ *adv.* **FAST** as quickly as possible ■ *n.* **SPEED** great speed (*archaic*) [Mid-16thC. From *haste, post, haste*, an instruction on letters.]

post hoc /pōst hók/ *n.* the fallacy of arguing that since one event happened before a second, the first caused the second [Mid-19thC. From Latin, "after this," referring to the fallacy *post hoc, ergo propter hoc* "after this, therefore because of this."]

post·hole /pṓst hōl/ *n.* a hole that has been dug in the ground for a post

post·hu·mous /póschəməss/ *adj.* **1. AFTER SOMEBODY'S DEATH** occurring after somebody's death **2.** PUBL **PUBLISHED AFTER DEATH** published or printed after the author's death **3. BORN AFTER FATHER'S DEATH** born after the death of the father ○ *a posthumous heir* [Early 17thC. Formed from late Latin *posthumus*, an alteration of Latin *postumus* "last" (from *posterus*; see POSTERIOR), under the influence of *humare* "to bury."] —**post·hu·mous·ly** *adv.* —**post·hu·mous·ness** *n.*

post·hyp·not·ic sug·ges·tion /pōst hip nòttik-/ *n.* a suggestion made to somebody under hypnosis that is to be acted upon at a later time after the period of hypnosis is over

pos·tiche /po steésh/ *n.* (*formal*) **1. FAKE COPY** an artificial or fake version or copy of something **2.** HAIR **HAIRPIECE** a small hairpiece or toupee [Early 18thC. Via French from Italian *posticcio*, of uncertain origin: perhaps ultimately from Latin *positus* "placed, added on," from *ponere* (see POSITION).]

pos·ti·cous /po stíkəss/ *adj.* situated behind another part of the same plant [Mid-19thC. Formed from Latin *posticus* "behind," from *post* (see POST-).]

pos·til·ion /pə stíllyən, pō-/, **pos·til·lion** *n.* somebody riding the left-hand front horse in a team of horses drawing a carriage [Early 17thC. Via French *postillon* "post rider" from Italian *postiglione*, from *posta*, from Latin *posita* (see POST[3]).]

post·im·pres·sion·ism /pōst im présh'n ìzzəm/ *n.* a school of painting in late 19th century France that rejected the naturalism of impressionism but adapted its use of color and form to a more subjective style —**post·im·pres·sion·ist** *n., adj.* —**post·im·pres·sion·is·tic** /pōst im presh'n ístik/ *adj.*

post·in·dus·tri·al /pōst in dústree əl/ *adj.* relating to or characteristic of the decline of heavy industry in the western nations as an economic base and the rise of service industries, information technology, and research

post·ing[1] /pṓsting/ *n.* **1.** COMPUT **MESSAGE** a message posted online, e.g., to an Internet newsgroup or forum **2.** ACCT **BOOKKEEPING ACTIVITY** the activity of making entries in a ledger **3.** ACCT **LEDGER ENTRY** an entry made in a ledger

post·ing[2] /pṓsting/ *n.* an appointment to a job, position, or unit, usually overseas

Post-it *tdmk.* a trademark for self-sticking slips of paper sold in pad form

post·lude /pṓst lood/ *n.* **1.** MUSIC **ORGAN COMPOSITION** a piece of organ music played at the end of a church service **2. FINAL PART** a final or concluding phase, chapter, or development (*literary*) [Mid-19thC. Modeled on PRELUDE.]

post·man /pṓstmən/ (*plural* **-men** /-mən/) *n. U.K.* = **mailman**

post·mark /pṓst maàrk/ *n.* **OFFICIAL STAMP** an official mark, usually covering a postage stamp, that indicates when and from where a piece of mail was sent ■ *vt.* (**-marked, -mark·ing, -marks**) **USE A POSTMARK** to stamp a postmark on an item of mail

post·mas·ter /pṓst màstər/ *n.* the person in charge of a post office or postal district

post·mas·ter gen·er·al (*plural* **post·mas·ters gen·er·al**) *n.* the executive head of the postal service in some countries

post·men·o·paus·al /pṑst mennə páwz'l/ *adj.* relating to or occurring in the time following the menopause

post·me·rid·i·an /pṑst mə ríddee ən/ *adj.* relating to or occurring in the afternoon (*formal*) [Early 17thC. From Latin *postmeridianus*, from *post* "after" + *meridiem* "midday."]

post me·rid·i·em /pṑst mə ríddee əm/ *adv.* full form of **p.m.** [From Latin, "after midday"]

post·mil·len·ni·al /pṑst mi lénnee əl/ *adj.* occurring or existing after the millennium

post·mil·len·ni·al·ism /pṑst mi lénnee ə lìzzəm/, **post·mil·len·na·ri·an·ism** /-millə náiree ə nìzzəm/ *n.* the belief that Jesus Christ will return to earth after, and not at, the millennium —**post·mil·len·ni·al·ist** *n.* —**post·mil·len·ni·an** *n., adj.*

post·mis·tress /pṓst mìstrəss/ *n.* a woman who has charge of a post office (*dated*)

post·mod·ern /pṑst móddərn/ *adj.* relating to art, architecture, literature, or thinking developed after and usually in reaction to modernism, returning to more classical or traditional elements and techniques —**post·mod·ern·ism** *n.* —**post·mod·ern·ist** *n.*

post·mo·der·ni·ty /pṑst mə dúrnitee, -mō-/ *n.* an intellectual movement against modernity and the certainty of universal rational scientific explanation

post·mor·tem /pṑst máwrtəm/ *adj.* **AFTER DEATH** occurring after death ■ *n.* **1.** *U.K.* full form. = **autopsy 2. RETROSPECTIVE ANALYSIS** an analysis carried out shortly after the conclusion of an event, especially an unsuccessful one ○ *the usual media postmortems the day after the election* [Mid-18thC. From Latin *post mortem* "after death."]

post·na·sal drip /pṑst náyz'l-/ *n.* a continual dripping of mucus from the rear of the nose into the throat, often caused by allergy or a cold

post·na·tal /pṑst náyt'l/ *adj.* occurring immediately or soon after childbirth —**post·na·tal·ly** *adv.*

post·nup·tial /pṑst núpshəl/ *adj.* occurring in the period after a marriage —**post·nup·tial·ly** *adv.*

post-o·bit *n.* **BOND PAYABLE AFTER SOMEBODY'S DEATH** a bond that pays after the death of a particular person (*dated*) ■ *adj.* **AFTER DEATH** coming into effect after somebody's death (*formal*) ○ *post-obit payments* [Mid-18thC. From Latin *post obitum* "after death."]

post of·fice *n.* **1. PLACE FOR MAILING AND STAMPS** an office or building where the public has access to services of the postal system **2. NATIONAL MAIL SYSTEM** the national organization or government department that is responsible for a country's mail service **3.** GAME **PARTY GAME** a children's game in which one player gives another a pretend letter and is given a kiss in return

post of·fice box *n.* a private numbered box in a post office where mail is held until collected by the addressee

post·op /pṓst òp/, **post-op** *adj.* postoperative (*informal*) [Late 20thC. Shortening.]

post·op·er·a·tive /pṑst óppərətiv/ *adj.* occurring after a surgical operation —**post·op·er·a·tive·ly** *adv.*

post·or·bi·tal /pṑst áwrbit'l/ *adj.* situated behind the eye or the eye socket

post·paid /pṑst páyd/ *adj.* with the postage paid in advance

post·par·tum /pṑst paártəm/ *adj.* occurring in or relating to the period immediately after childbirth [Mid-19thC. From Latin *post partum* "after childbirth."]

post·par·tum de·pres·sion *n.* a psychiatric disorder consisting of severe depression that can affect a woman soon after giving birth to a baby

post·pone /pṑst pṓn/ (**-poned, -pon·ing, -pones**) *vt.* **1. DELAY** to put something off until a later time or date **2. DEFER** to treat something with less importance (*formal*) [15thC. From Latin *postponere*, literally "to place later," from *ponere* (see POSITION).] —**post·pon·a·ble** *adj.* —**post·pone·ment** *n.* —**post·pon·er** *n.*

post·pose /pṑst pṓz/ (**-posed, -pos·ing, -poses**) *vti.* to place a word or phrase after another or at the end of a sentence or construction [Late 19thC. Back-formation from POSTPOSITION.]

post·po·si·tion /pṑstpə zísh'n/ *n.* **1. PLACEMENT AFTER HEAD OF PHRASE** the placing of a word or phrase after the word or phrase it qualifies, e.g., the placing of "bold and free" in the phrase "poets bold and free" **2.** = **postpositive** *n.* [Mid-17thC. Modeled on "preposition."] —**post·po·si·tion·al** *adj.* —**post·po·si·tion·al·ly** *adv.*

post·pos·i·tive /pṑst pózzətiv/ *adj.* **PLACED AFTER HEAD OF PHRASE** used to describe an adjective or modifier that is placed after the word or phrase it qualifies ■ *n.* **WORD PLACED AFTER** an adjective or modifier that is placed after the word it qualifies [Late 18thC. Via late Latin *postpositivus* from, ultimately, Latin *postponere* (see POSTPONE).] —**post·pos·i·tive·ly** *adv.*

post·pran·di·al /pṑst prándee əl/ *adj.* occurring after a meal, especially an evening meal (*formal or humorous*) —**post·pran·di·al·ly** *adv.*

post-print *adj.* belonging to the era of electronic communication rather than printing ○ *the post-print revolution*

post·pro·duc·tion /pṑst prə dúkshən/ *n.* the final stage of making a recording, film, or television program that includes editing, sound dubbing, and adding special effects

post rid·er *n.* somebody who delivered or relayed mail on horseback in the past

post road *n.* a road or route used regularly by the postal delivery service in the past

post·script /pṓst skrìpt/ *n.* **1. SHORT MESSAGE** a short message added onto the end of a letter, after the signature **2. ADDED-ON PART** an addition to the end of something such as a book, story, or document [Mid-16thC. From Latin *postscriptum*, from the past participle of *postscribere* "to write after," from *scribere* (see SCRIBE).]

Post·Script /pṓst skrìpt/ *tdmk.* a trademark for a page description language used in design, typesetting, and printing, usable on a variety of platforms

post-struc·tur·al·ism *n.* an intellectual movement derived from structuralism but questioning the basis upon which the structures of society, language, and mores have been conceptualized

post·syn·ap·tic /pṑst si náptik/ *adj.* used to describe a nerve cell, muscle cell, or a region of cell membrane that receives signals transmitted across a synapse from another nerve cell

post·synch /pṑst síngk/ (**-synched, -synch·ing, -synchs**) *vt.* to add sound or music to a film at a later time

post·test /pṓst tèst/ *n.* a test administered after a lesson or instruction to see what has been assimilated. ◊ **pretest**

post time *n.* the starting time of a horserace, after which no more bets can be accepted

post·tran·scrip·tion·al /pṑst tran skrípshən'l, -shnəl/ *adj.* used to describe processes or components involved in carrying out the genetic instructions of a living cell that participate only after the stage of transcription of a gene or genes

post·trans·fu·sion /pṑst trans fyóozh'n/ *adj.* occurring after or because of a blood transfusion

post·trans·la·tion·al /pṑst trans láyshən'l, -shnəl/ *adj.* used to describe processes or components involved in carrying out the genetic instructions of living cells that participate only after translation of RNA to protein

post-trau·mat·ic stress dis·or·der *n.* a psychological condition that may affect people who have suffered severe emotional trauma, e.g., combat, crime, or natural disaster, and may cause sleep disturbances, flashbacks, anxiety, tiredness, and depression

pos·tu·lant /póschələnt/ *n.* (*formal*) **1.** RELIG **RELIGIOUS ORDER APPLICANT** somebody who applies to join a religious order **2. PETITIONER** somebody who submits a request for something [Mid-18thC. Directly or via French from Latin *postulant-*, the present participle stem of *postulare* (see POSTULATE).] —**pos·tu·lan·cy** *n.*

pos·tu·late *vt.* /póschə làyt/ (**-lat·ed, -lat·ing, -lates**) **1. ASSUME** to assume or suggest that something is true or exists, especially as the basis of an argument **2. CLAIM SOMETHING** to demand or claim something ■ *n.* /póschələt, -làyt/ **1. SOMETHING ASSUMED TRUE** something that is assumed or believed to be true and that is used as the basis of an argument or theory **2. PRINCIPLE** a basic principle **3. PRECONDITION** an essential precondition or requirement **4.** MATH, LOGIC **STATEMENT UNDERPINNING A THEORY** a statement that is assumed to be true but has not been proven and that is taken as the basis for a theory, line of reasoning, or hypothesis [Mid-16thC. From medieval Latin *postulare* "to nominate," originally "to demand." Ultimately from an Indo-European base meaning "to ask," which is also the ancestor of English *pray* and *precarious*.] —**pos·tu·la·tion** /pòschə láysh'n/ *n.* —**pos·tu·la·tion·al** *adj.*

pos·tu·la·tor /póschə làytər/ *n.* **1.** CHR **ADVOCATE FOR SAINTHOOD** in the Roman Catholic Church, an official, usually a priest, who presents a request for a deceased person to be beatified or canonized **2. SOMEBODY WHO POSTULATES** somebody who postulates something

pos·ture /póschər/ *n.* **1. CARRIAGE** the way in which somebody carries his or her body, especially when standing **2. BODY POSITION** a position the body can assume, e.g., standing, sitting, kneeling, or lying down **3. ATTITUDE** a frame of mind or attitude toward a particular subject ○ *a conciliatory posture* **4. POSE CONVEYING ATTITUDE** a physical pose that conveys a mental or emotional attitude ○ *a posture of defiance* **5. DECEPTIVE STANCE** a position, attitude, or stance that is intended to deceive **6. CULTIVATED POSITION** a practiced or cultivated arrangement of the body, e.g., a position used in yoga **7. ARRANGEMENT OF PARTS** the way that components of an object or situation are arranged in relation to one another ■ *v.* (**-tured, -tur·ing, -tures**) **1.** *vi.* **ASSUME STANCE** to assume an affected or exaggerated pose or attitude **2.** *vti.* **MAKE A POSTURE** to arrange somebody in, or adopt, a particular posture [Late 16thC. Via French from, ultimately, Latin *positura*, from *posit-*, the past participle stem of *ponere* (see POSITION).] —**pos·tur·al** *adj.* —**pos·tur·er** *n.*

post·vo·cal·ic /pṑst vō kállik/ *adj.* coming after a vowel

post·war /pṑst wàwr, pṑst wáwr/ *adj.* occurring or existing after a war, especially World War II

po·sy /pṓzee/ (*plural* **-sies**) *n.* a blooming flower, or a bunch of blooming flowers [Mid-16thC. Alteration of POESY.]

pot[1] /pot/ *n.* **1. WATERTIGHT CONTAINER FOR COOKING OR STORAGE** a container made of metal, pottery, or glass that is usually cylindrical and watertight with an open top and sometimes a lid, used especially for cooking or storage **2. SOMETHING RESEMBLING POT IN SHAPE** something similar to a pot in shape or function e.g., a flowerpot, teapot, or chamber pot **3. CONTENTS OF POT** the contents of a pot, or the amount that it will hold ○ *made a pot of coffee* **4.** CERAMICS **OBJECT MADE FROM CLAY** a dish or container that is made from clay, especially one of artistic or historic interest **5.** = **potty**[2] (*informal*) **6. LARGE AMOUNT OF MONEY** a large amount of money (*informal*) **7.** CARDS **MONEY BET IN CARD GAME** all the money that is bet in a game of cards, especially poker, and that is taken by the winning player **8. COMMON FUND** a common fund of money that is contributed to by the members of a group, usually for a particular purpose, e.g., a party or trip (*informal*) **9.** CUE GAMES **HIT OF BALL INTO POCKET** in billiards or snooker, a hit of a ball that sends it into any of the pockets at the edge of the table **10.** AGRIC **FISH OR LOBSTER TRAP** a basket or cage used for catching lobsters, eels, or fish **11. POTBELLY** a round bulging stomach or abdomen (*informal*) **12.** = **potshot** *n.* 1 (*informal*) ■ *v.* (**pot·ted, pot·ting, pots**) **1.** *vt.* GARDENING **PUT PLANT IN POT** to put a plant into a pot with soil or compost **2.** *vti.* **SHOOT ANIMAL FOR FOOD** to shoot or shoot at a bird or animal, especially for food **3.** *vti.* **SHOOT AT SOMETHING WITHIN EASY REACH** to shoot or shoot at an easy target, especially casually **4.** *vt.* COOK **PRESERVE FOOD IN POT** to preserve food in a pot **5.** *vti.* CUE GAMES **HIT BALL INTO POCKET** in billiards or snooker, to hit a ball into any of the pockets at the edge of the table **6.** *vti.* CERAMICS **SHAPE SOMETHING WITH CLAY** to shape a pot or other item from clay **7.** *vt.* ELECTRON ENG to encapsulate electronic components in an insulating resin to protect them and hold them in place. The technique is used in high technology industries such as avionics as well as in automotive, medical, and consumer electronics. [Pre-12thC. From assumed Vulgar Latin *pottus* of unknown origin. Later also probably from French *pot*, of the same origin.] ◇ **go to pot** to get much worse or become useless, worthless, or extremely unsatisfactory (*informal*)

pot on *vt.* to transfer a growing plant from a smaller to a larger pot

pot[2] /pot/ *n.* the drug marijuana (*slang*) [Mid-20thC. Origin uncertain: probably a shortening of Mexican Spanish *potiguaya* "marijuana leaves."]

pot[3] /pot/ *n.* a potentiometer (*informal*) [Mid-20thC. Shortening.]

pot. *abbr.* potential

po·ta·ble /pṓtəb'l/ *adj.* **SUITABLE FOR DRINKING** suitable for drinking because it contains no harmful elements ■ *n.* **SOMETHING TO DRINK** a liquid that is suitable for drinking, especially an alcoholic drink [15thC. Directly or via French from late Latin *potabilis*, from Latin *potare* "to drink," from *potus* "drink" (source of English *potion*).] —**po·ta·bil·i·ty** /pṓtə bíllətee/ *n.* —**po·ta·ble·ness** /pṓtəb'lnəss/ *n.*

po·tage /pō taázh/ *n.* a thick soup [Mid-16thC. From French (see POTTAGE).]

po·ta·mic /pə támmik/ *adj.* relating to rivers or river navigation (*technical*) [Late 19thC. Formed from Greek *potamos* "river."]

pot·ash /pót àsh/ *n.* **1. POTASSIUM COMPOUND USED IN FERTILIZER** a potassium compound, especially potassium chloride, sulfate, or oxide, primarily used in fertilizers. The concentration of potassium in the fertilizer is usually expressed as a percentage. **2.** = **potassium carbonate 3.** = **potassium hydroxide** [Early 17thC. From obsolete Dutch *potasschen*, plural of *potasch*, literally "pot ash" (originally obtained by soaking wood ash in water and evaporating the resulting solution in iron pots).]

pot·ash al·um *n.* = **alum**

po·tas·si·um /pə tássee əm/ *n.* a soft silvery white very reactive element of the alkali metal group, commonly found combined in minerals. The metal has few uses other than being alloyed with sodium as a coolant in nuclear reactors, although its compounds are widely used, especially in fertilizers. Symbol **K** [Early 19thC. From modern Latin, from *potassa* "potash," from POTASH; from potassium being the basis of potash.]

po·tas·si·um-ar·gon dat·ing *n.* a technique for estimating the age of rocks older than 250,000 years, based on the time taken for the radioactive decay of the potassium-40 isotope into a stable argon isotope. The half-life of potassium-40 is about 1.28 x 10^9 years, and the ratio of potassium to argon in the specimen gives an indication of its age.

po·tas·si·um bi·tar·trate *n.* a white powder or crystalline compound used in baking powder, in medicine, and in food preparation. Formula: $KHC_4H_4O_6$.

po·tas·si·um bro·mide *n.* a white crystalline compound used in lithography, medicine, photography, and soaps. Formula: KBr.

po·tas·si·um car·bon·ate *n.* a white salt used in brewing, ceramics, explosives, fertilizers, glass, and soap. Formula: K_2CO_3.

po·tas·si·um chlo·rate *n.* a white salt that detonates with heat and is used in the manufacture of fireworks, matches, and explosives, in textile printing and paper manufacture, and as a bleach and disinfectant. It is also known to chemistry students for its use in the laboratory preparation of oxygen. Formula: $KClO_3$.

po·tas·si·um chlo·ride *n.* a colorless crystalline salt used as a fertilizer and in photography and medicine. Formula: KCl.

po·tas·si·um cy·a·nide *n.* a very poisonous white crystalline chemical salt used in the extraction of gold and silver from their ores, electroplating, photography, and as an insecticide. Formula: KCN.

po·tas·si·um di·chro·mate *n.* a yellow-red poisonous crystalline compound used in the manufacture of explosives, safety matches, and dyes. Formula: $K_2Cr_2O_7$.

po·tas·si·um fer·ri·cy·a·nide *n.* a bright red poisonous crystalline compound that decomposes when heated. It is used in textile printing, wool dyeing, blueprint paper, and as a fertilizer. Formula: $K_3Fe(CN)_6$.

po·tas·si·um fer·ro·cy·a·nide *n.* a yellow crystalline compound used in medicine and explosives. Formula: $K_4Fe(CN)_6$.

po·tas·si·um hy·dro·gen car·bon·ate *n.* a white powder or granular compound, used in baking powder and in medicine as an antacid. Formula: $KHCO_3$.

po·tas·si·um hy·dro·gen tar·trate *n.* = **potassium bitartrate**

po·tas·si·um hy·drox·ide *n.* a caustic toxic white solid used to make soap, detergents, liquid shampoos, and matches. Formula: KOH.

po·tas·si·um i·o·dide *n.* a white crystalline compound with a salty taste, used in medicine and photography and added to table salt to provide a source of iodine. Formula: KI.

po·tas·si·um ni·trate *n.* a white crystalline salt used in fireworks, explosives, and matches, as a fertilizer, and as a preservative for meats. Formula: KNO_3.

po·tas·si·um per·man·ga·nate *n.* a dark purple toxic odorless crystalline compound used as a bleach, disinfectant, and antiseptic, and in deodorizers and dyes. Formula: $KMnO_4$.

po·tas·si·um so·di·um tar·trate *n.* Rochelle salt (*technical*)

po·tas·si·um sul·fate *n.* a colorless crystalline compound used in aluminum, glass, and cement manufacture, in fertilizers, and in medicine. Formula: K_2SO_4.

po·ta·tion /pō táysh'n/ *n.* (*literary*) **1. DRINKING** the act or an instance of drinking **2. ALCOHOLIC DRINK** a drink, especially an alcoholic drink [15thC. Directly or via Old French from the Latin stem *potation-*, from, ultimately, *potare* "to drink" (see POTABLE).]

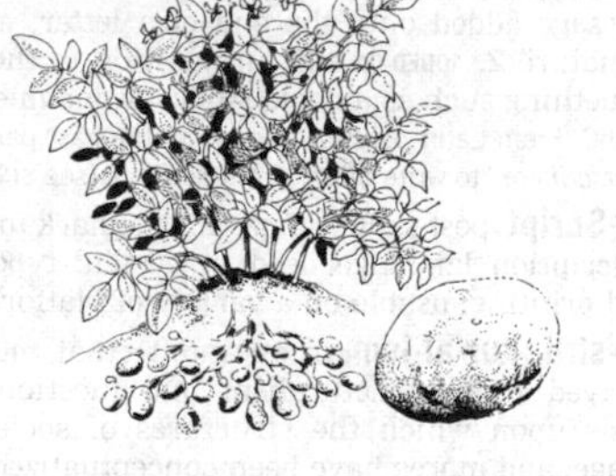

Potato

po·ta·to /pə táytō/ (*plural* **-toes**) *n.* **1.** FOOD **ROOT VEGETABLE** a rounded white tuber with a thin skin, cooked as a vegetable. It is an important source of starch, especially in Europe and North America. Potatoes can be boiled, baked, roasted, or fried, have many different varieties, and are used in many dishes. **2.** PLANTS **POTATO PLANT** a perennial plant, originally from South America and belonging to the nightshade family, that is widely cultivated for its fleshy underground tuber. Latin name: *Solanum tuberosum.* **3.** = **sweet potato** [Mid-16thC. From Spanish *patata*, an alteration of Taino *batata* "sweet potato."]

po·ta·to bee·tle *n.* = **Colorado potato beetle**

po·ta·to blight *n.* a highly destructive disease of the potato caused by the fungus *Phytophthora infestans.* It was the cause of the loss of the potato crop in Ireland in the 19th century.

po·ta·to chip *n. U.S., ANZ* a very thin slice of potato that has usually been deep-fried in oil, salted, sometimes flavored, and packaged and sold to be eaten cold as a snack

po·ta·to pan·cake *n.* a pancake made from a mixture of coarsely grated potato with egg, flour, and seasonings, and often eaten with applesauce

po·ta·to skin *n.* a piece of skin from a hollowed-out baked potato that is then baked further, or a piece of deep-fried skin of a raw potato, served as an appetizer (*often used in the plural*)

pot-au-feu /pàw tō fṓ/ (*plural* **pot-au-feu**) *n.* **1.** FOOD **DISH OF MEAT AND VEGETABLES** a French stew of slowly boiled meat and vegetables, the meat usually being eaten separately from the vegetables and stock, which are served first as a soup **2.** HOUSEHOLD **LARGE COOKING POT** a large earthenware pot in which pot-au-feu is traditionally cooked [From French, literally "pot on the fire"]

Pot·a·wat·o·mi /pòttə wóttəmee/ (*plural* **-mi** *or* **-mis**) *n.* **1.** PEOPLES **MEMBER OF NATIVE N AMERICAN PEOPLE** a member of a Native North American people who originally occupied lands in various northern central states, and whose members now live mainly in Kansas, Oklahoma, Michigan, and Ontario **2.** LANG **POTAWATOMI LANGUAGE** the Algonquian language of the Potawatomi people —**Pot·a·wat·o·mi** *adj.*

pot·bel·ly /pót bèllee/ (*plural* **-lies**) *n.* **1. BULGING STOMACH** a round bulging stomach or abdomen **2.** = **potbelly stove** —**pot·bel·lied** *adj.*

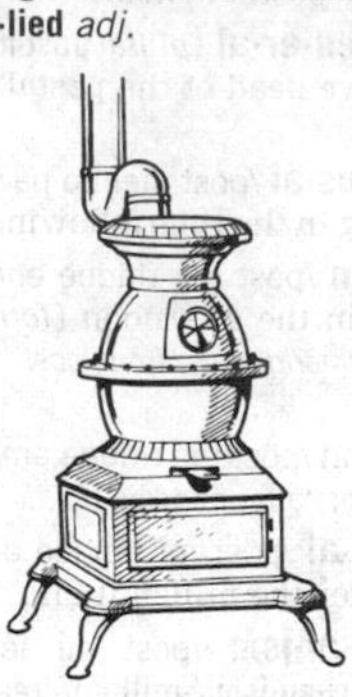

Potbelly stove

pot·bel·ly stove, pot·bel·lied stove *n.* a wood- or coal-burning stove that has a rounded bulbous body

pot·boil·er /pót bòylər/ *n.* a book, film, or other work that is produced quickly to make money and has little literary or artistic quality [From its exclusive purpose of "boiling the pot," that is, providing a livelihood so that somebody can eat]

pot·bound /pót bòwnd/ *adj.* used to describe a potted plant whose roots have grown very dense and have filled its pot so that its growth is restricted. Some plants grow well in this condition.

po·teen /pō téen/ *n.* in Ireland, liquor that has been distilled illegally, especially from potatoes [Early 19thC. From Irish *(fuisce) poitín*, literally "small pot (whiskey)," from *pota* "pot," from POT[1].]

Po·tem·kin vil·lage /pə témkin-/ *n.* something that is set up to produce a political advantage or effect, but is not really viable [Mid-20thC. Named for Grigoriĭ Aleksandrovich *Potëmkin* (1739–91), who reputedly ordered villages consisting of mere facades to be built along a route of a tour by Catherine the Great.]

po·ten·cy /pṓt'nsee/ (*plural* **-cies**) *n.* **1. STRENGTH OF MEDICINE** the strength of something such as a drug or alcoholic drink **2. STATE OF BEING POTENT** the state or quality of being potent **3. ABILITY TO DEVELOP** a capacity to grow or develop in the future

po·tent[1] /pṓt'nt/ *adj.* **1. STRONG AND EFFECTIVE** very strong, effective, or powerful **2. PERSUASIVE** exerting persuasion, influence, or force **3. WITH STRONG CHEMICAL EFFECT** with a strong or concentrated chemical or medicinal effect **4. HAVING POWER** having or using power, control, or authority **5. CAPABLE OF SEXUAL INTERCOURSE** capable of having an erection, sexual intercourse, or an ejaculation [15thC. From Latin *potent-*, present participle stem of *posse* "to be powerful" (source of English *posse*), contraction of *potis esse*, from *potis* "able" + *esse* "to be."] —**po·tent·ly** *adv.* —**po·tent·ness** *n.*

po·tent[2] /pṓt'nt/ *adj.* used to describe a heraldic cross that has four arms with a bar across the end of each arm [14thC. Alteration of obsolete English *potence* "crutch" or its Old French source, from Latin *potentia* "power," from the stem *potent-* (see POTENT[1]).]

po·ten·tate /pṓt'n tàyt/ *n.* somebody who has power, authority, and influence, especially a monarch or other leader who has the power to rule over others

po·ten·tial /pə ténshəl/ *adj.* **1. POSSIBLE BUT NOT YET REALIZED** with a possibility or likelihood of occurring, or of doing or becoming something in the future **2.** GRAM **EXPRESSING POSSIBILITY** used to describe a verb or verb form that expresses possibility, e.g., "may" or "might" in English ■ *n.* **1. CAPACITY TO DEVELOP** the capacity or ability for future development or achievement **2.** GRAM **POTENTIAL VERB FORM** a verb or verb form that expresses possibility, e.g., "may" or "might" in English **3.** PHYS = **electric potential** [14thC. Directly or via Old French *potenciel* from late Latin *potentialis*, ultimately from the Latin stem *potent-* (see POTENT[1]).] —**po·ten·tial·ly** *adv.*

po·ten·tial dif·fer·ence *n.* the work done in moving a unit electric charge between two points in an electric field. Symbol ΔV, ΔU

po·ten·tial en·er·gy *n.* the energy that a body or system has stored because of its position in an electric, magnetic, or gravitational field, or because of its configuration. Symbol *V*, E_p

po·ten·ti·al·i·ty /pə tènshee állətee/ (*plural* **-ties**) *n.* **1. CAPACITY FOR DEVELOPMENT** the capacity or ability for future development or for a future achievement or action **2. SOMEBODY OR SOMETHING WITH POTENTIAL** somebody who or something that has potentiality

po·ten·tial well *n.* a region in an electric, magnetic, or gravitational field in which an object has a lower potential energy than it would have in all adjacent regions

po·ten·ti·ate /pə ténshee àyt/ (**-at·ed, -at·ing, -ates**) *vt.* **1.** MED **INCREASE EFFECTIVENESS OF** to improve the effectiveness of a drug or treatment, especially by adding another drug or agent **2. MAKE SOMETHING POWERFUL** to make something potent or powerful —**po·ten·ti·a·tor** *n.*

po·ten·til·la /pōt'n tíllə/ (*plural* **-las** *or* **-la**) *n.* a flowering plant or small shrub cultivated for its small yellow, white, or red flowers that have five petals and many pistils. Genus: *Potentilla.* [Mid-16thC. From medieval Latin, literally "powerful little (plant)" (from its use in medicine), from the Latin stem *potent-* (see POTENT[1]).]

po·ten·ti·om·e·ter /pə tènshee ómmətər/ *n.* **1. INSTRUMENT FOR MEASURING ELECTROMOTIVE FORCE** a device for measuring an unknown potential difference or electromotive force by balancing part of it against a known standard **2. VOLUME OR BRIGHTNESS CONTROL** a three-terminal component, typically used as a volume or brightness control, that gives a variable electric potential by rotating a shaft or moving a slider [Late 19thC. Coined from POTENTIAL + -METER.] —**po·ten·ti·om·e·try** *n.*

po·ten·ti·o·met·ric /pə tènshee ə méttrik/ *adj.* indicating the completion of a chemical reaction by a change in potential at an electrode immersed in the solution where the reaction is taking place [Early 20thC. Coined from POTENTIAL + -METRIC.]

pot·ful /pót fòol/ *n.* the amount that a pot will hold

pot·head /pót hèd/ *n.* somebody who regularly smokes marijuana, especially in large amounts (*slang disapproving*)

poth·er /póthər/ *n.* **1. NERVOUS STATE** a state of emotional agitation, especially over something trivial **2. COMMOTION** a great deal of frenzied activity or conversation, especially over something trivial **3. CHOKING CLOUD** a cloud of smoke or dust that chokes ■ *vti.* (**-ered, -er·ing, -ers**) **CONFUSE SOMEBODY OR BE CONFUSED** to confuse or worry somebody or to become confused or worried [Late 16thC. Origin uncertain.]

pot·herb /pót hùrb/ *n.* an herb or vegetable used to add flavor in cooking

pot·hold·er /pót hòldər/ *n.* a pad of fabric used to protect the hands from hot pots and cooking utensils

pot·hole /pót hōl/ *n.* **1.** TRANSP **HOLE IN ROAD SURFACE** a hole that has formed in the surface of a road and that can be hazardous to motorists **2.** GEOL, GEOG **VERTICAL HOLE IN LIMESTONE AREA** a vertical deep hole or shaft formed naturally in limestone regions by the erosive action of running water **3.** GEOL, GEOG **HOLE IN RIVER BED** a bowl-shaped hole in the bed of a river or stream, formed by the abrasive action of stone, gravel, or ice being churned in an eddy **4.** AGRIC **PATCH OF MUD OR QUICKSAND** a patch of deep mud or quicksand where cattle might be bogged down or sink (*regional*)

pot·hook /pót hòok/ *n.* **1.** DOMESTIC **HOOK OVER FIRE** an S-shaped hook fixed above an open fire, from which a pot or kettle is hung **2. CURVED SHAPE MADE IN HANDWRITING** a handwriting mark beginning or ending in a curve

pot·hunt·er /pót hùntər/ *n.* **1.** HUNT **HUNTER OF GAME FOR PROFIT** somebody who hunts game for food or as a source of income, often indiscriminately and disregarding rules **2.** SPORTS, LEISURE **PRIZE-SEEKER** somebody who takes part in competitions and races with more interest in the prizes than the sport (*informal disapproving*) **3.** ARCHEOL **AMATEUR ARCHEOLOGIST** somebody who digs in search of ancient pots and other objects but is not a professional archaeologist

po·tion /pṓsh'n/ *n.* a liquid to be drunk that is medicinal, supposedly magical, or poisonous [13thC. Via Old French from the Latin stem *potion-*, from, ultimately, *potare* "to drink."]

pot·latch /pót làch/ *n.* among Native American peoples of the northwest coast of North America, a ceremony of feasting in which the host gains prestige by giving gifts or, sometimes, destroying wealth [Mid-19thC. From Chinook Jargon.]

pot liq·uor *n.* the liquid in a pot in which meat and vegetables have been boiled

pot·luck /pót lùk/ *n.* **1. WHATEVER IS AVAILABLE** whatever happens to be available to satisfy a need **2.** FOOD **FOOD AVAILABLE TO UNEXPECTED GUEST** whatever food happens to be available to give to an unexpected guest **3.** FOOD **MEAL TO WHICH EVERYONE BRINGS SOMETHING** a meal to which each participant brings one dish that is shared with everyone else [Late 16thC. From POT[1] + LUCK.]

pot mar·i·gold *n. U.K.* = **calendula** ["Pot" from its being grown for decoration]

Po·to·mac /pə tṓmək/ river of the eastern United States, formed by the confluence of its own north and south branches near Cumberland, Maryland, and emptying into Chesapeake Bay. It flows through Washington, D.C. Length: 285 mi./460 km.

po·to·roo /pōtə ròo/ (*plural* **-roos**) *n.* a rabbit-sized member of the kangaroo family that looks like a rat and has powerful hind legs that it uses for jumping. Latin name: *Potorous tridactylus.* [Late 18thC. From Aboriginal.]

pot·pie /pót pì/ *n.* a pie of meat and vegetables in a deep dish covered with a pastry crust

pot·pour·ri /pōpə reé/ (*plural* **-ris**) *n.* **1.** DOMESTIC **COLLECTION OF FRAGRANT DRIED FLOWERS** a collection of dried flower petals, leaves, herbs, and spices, sometimes colored and scented, that are used to scent the air **2. MISCELLANEOUS MIXTURE** a miscellaneous mixture of things [Early 17thC. From French, "mixed stew," literally "rotten pot" (translation of Spanish *olla podrida*); *pourri*, past participle of *pourrir* "to rot," from, ultimately, Latin *putris* "rotten."]

pot roast *n.* a dish consisting of a piece of beef cooked slowly in the oven in a closed pot in its own juices, often on a bed of vegetables —**pot-roast** *vti.*

POTS /pots/ *n.* a simple connection to the public telephone system with no special features, as distinguished from a private line or high-speed network connection. Abbr of **plain old telephone system**

Pots·dam /póts dam/ city in northeastern Germany, in Brandenburg State, approximately 18 mi./29 km southwest of Berlin. It was the site of the Potsdam Conference (July–August 1945), at which U.S., British, and Soviet leaders discussed the postwar administration of Germany. Population: 139,000 (1994).

pot·sherd /pót shùrd/, **pot·shard** /-shaard/ *n.* a fragment of pottery, especially one found at an archaeological site [14thC. From POT + SHERD.]

pot·shot /pót shòt/ *n.* **1. EASY SHOT** a shot taken quickly, carelessly, or on a chance opportunity at something such as game, especially when within easy reach **2. HASTY CRITICISM** a criticism made without careful consideration and aimed at an easy target ○ *journalists taking potshots at the government* [Mid-19thC. From the purpose of the shot originally being to get food for the cooking "pot" (not in accordance with the strict codes of shooting as a sport).]

pot still *n.* an apparatus for distilling whiskey that applies heat directly to the container holding the mash

pot·stone /pót stōn/ *n.* an impure variety of talc, used in the past to make cooking vessels

pot·tage /póttij/ *n.* a thick vegetable, or meat and vegetable, soup [12thC. Originally *potage*, from Old French, literally "what is put in a pot," from *pot* (see POT).]

pot·ted /póttəd/ *adj.* **1. GROWING IN POT** planted in a pot **2.** *U.K.* **PRESERVED IN POT** cooked or preserved in a vessel such as a pot or jar **3. DRUNK** drunk or intoxicated by a drug (*slang*) **4.** *U.K.* **SUPERFICIALLY SUMMARIZED** reproduced in a brief and often superficial form (*informal*)

pot·ted plant *n.* a plant that has been placed with soil in a flowerpot and is kept for display and decoration

pot·ter[1] /póttər/ *n.* somebody who makes pottery [Pre-12thC]

pot·ter[2] /póttər/ (**-tered, -ter·ing, -ters**) *vi. U.K.* = **putter** [Mid-16thC. Formed from obsolete *pote* "to push," from Old English *potian*, of uncertain origin.]

Popperfoto

Beatrix Potter

Pot·ter /póttər/, **Beatrix** (1866–1943) British children's writer and illustrator. Her illustrated animal stories, including *The Tale of Peter Rabbit* (1900) and *The Tailor of Gloucester* (1902), became children's classics. Full name **Helen Beatrix Potter**

Pot·ter·ies /póttəreez/ region in Staffordshire, west central England, famous for its ceramics factories

pot·ter's clay *n.* clay that does not contain any iron and is suitable for making pottery

pot·ter's field *n.* **1. BIBLICAL BURIAL GROUND FOR STRANGERS** in the Bible, an area of land near Jerusalem bought as a burial ground for strangers with the money that was given to Judas for betraying Jesus Christ **2. BURIAL GROUND FOR POOR** a public burial ground for poor or unidentified people

pot·ter's wheel *n.* a device for molding clay into pottery by hand, consisting of a horizontal disc that holds the clay and is rotated manually or by electricity. A technological advance in pottery-making, it was invented around 6000 B.C. and made faster and higher-quality ceramic pottery production possible.

pot·ter wasp *n.* a small solitary wasp that constructs elaborate clay pots in which it lays its eggs and puts caterpillars to serve as food for the young. Genus: *Eumenes.*

pot·ter·y /póttəree/ (*plural* **-ies**) *n.* **1. OBJECTS MADE OF BAKED CLAY** objects such as vases, pots, plates, or sculptured articles that are made by molding or shaping moist clay and hardening it by heating in a kiln **2. MAKING OF POTTERY** the art, craft, or occupation of making pottery **3. PLACE WHERE POTTERY IS MADE** a workshop, factory, or other place where pottery is made

pot·tle /pótt'l/ *n.* (*archaic*) **1. HALF A GALLON** a measure for liquids that is equal to half a gallon/1.9 liters **2. CONTAINER HOLDING POTTLE** a container, especially a drinking vessel, that can hold a pottle [14thC. From Old French *potel*, literally "small pot," from *pot* (see POT[1]).]

pot·to /póttō/ (*plural* **-tos**) *n.* a small primate of West and Central African rain forests that has small ears, large eyes, and a short bushy tail and lives in the lower branches of trees. Latin name: *Perodicticus potto.* [Early 18thC. Origin uncertain: probably from a West African source.]

Pott's dis·ease /póts-/ *n.* a tubercular disease of the spine, marked by the destruction of the bone and disks and curvature of the spine [Mid-19thC. Named for Sir Percivall *Pott* 1713–88, the English surgeon who described the disease.]

pot·ty[1] /póttee/ (**-ti·er, -ti·est**) *adj.* slightly irrational (*informal*) [Mid-19thC. Origin uncertain: perhaps formed from POT[1] in the sense of "container."] —**pot·ti·ness** *n.*

pot·ty[2] /póttee/ (*plural* **-ties**) *n.* (*informal*) **1. BOWL USED AS CHILD'S TOILET** a bowl, used especially by young children who cannot yet use a toilet, to eliminate body waste **2. TOILET** a toilet [Mid-20thC. Formed from POT[1].]

pot·ty-chair *n.* a small chair with a potty in the seat, used by young children who are being trained to use a toilet

pot·ty-train (**pot·ty-trained, pot·ty-train·ing, pot·ty-trains**) *vti.* to train a young child to use a potty instead of a diaper (*informal*)

pouch /powch/ *n.* **1.** SMALL SOFT BAG a small bag or container made of a soft material such as fabric or leather **2.** SOMETHING RESEMBLING POUCH something that looks like a pouch, especially a small baggy fold of skin **3.** ZOOL POCKET OF SKIN IN ANIMAL a structure in an animal resembling a pouch, especially one on the abdomen of a marsupial for carrying young, or in the cheek of a rodent for carrying food **4.** ANAT BODY CAVITY RESEMBLING POCKET a pocket-shaped space or structure in the body **5.** BOT PLANT CAVITY a cavity in a plant shaped like a pocket **6.** MAIL BAG FOR MAIL a lockable bag or sack for carrying mail, especially diplomatic correspondence **7.** *Scotland* POCKET a pocket ■ *v.* **(pouched, pouch·ing, pouch·es) 1.** *vt.* PUT IN POUCH to put something into a pouch **2.** *vti.* FORM POUCH to make something, or be made, into a shape resembling a pouch [13thC. Via Anglo-Norman *puche*, Old Northern French *pouche*, and Old French *poche*, from a prehistoric Germanic word meaning "bag" that is also the ancestor of English *pocket*.] —**pouch·y** *adj.*

pouf /poof/, **pouffe** *n.* **1.** HAIR PUFFED-OUT HAIRSTYLE a puffed-out hairstyle, similar to a bouffant, fashionable especially in the 18th century **2.** HAIR PAD IN HAIR a pad worn in the hair to help shape a pouf **3.** *U.K.* FURNITURE = **hassock 4.** CLOTHES BUNCHED-UP PART OF DRESS a part of a dress or skirt gathered up to form a soft projecting shape [Early 19thC. Via French from, ultimately, an imitation of the sound of a puff.]

Pough·keep·sie /pə kípsee/ city in southeastern New York, on the Hudson River, south of Albany. Population: 27,808 (1996).

Pouil·ly-Fuis·sé /poo yeè fwee sáy/ *n.* a dry white wine produced from the Chardonnay grape in the area around Pouilly and Fuissé in the Burgundy region of France

Pouil·ly-Fu·mé /-fyoo máy/ *n.* a dry white wine produced from the Sauvignon Blanc grape in the area around Pouilly-sur-Loire in the Loire valley of France [Mid-20thC. From French; *fumé* is the past participle of *fumer* "to smoke," from, ultimately, Latin *fumus* "smoke."]

pou·lard /poo laárd/, **pou·larde** *n.* a young domestic hen **(pullet)** that has been spayed to encourage fattening. Spaying of hens is rarely done in modern poultry production. [Mid-18thC. From French *poularde*, from *poule* "hen," from, ultimately, Latin *pulla*, feminine of *pullus* "chicken" (source of English *pony* and *poultry*).]

poult /pōlt/ *n.* a young fowl, especially a turkey [15thC. Contraction of PULLET.]

poul·ter·er /pṓltərər/ *n.* somebody who buys, prepares, and sells poultry [Late 16thC. Alteration of archaic *poulter*, from Old French *pouletier*, from *poulet* "young fowl."]

poul·tice /pṓltiss/ *n.* a warm moist preparation placed on an aching or inflamed part of the body to ease pain, improve circulation, or hasten the expression of pus. Poultices may be made from bread, clay, mustard, medicinal herbs, or other materials, but are now considered to have little medical benefit. [14thC. Originally *pultes*, from Latin, plural of *puls* "pottage, thick gruel" (source of English *pulse* "lentils").]

poul·try /pṓltree/ *n.* **1.** DOMESTIC FOWL domestic fowl in general, e.g., chickens, turkeys, ducks, or geese, raised for meat or eggs **2.** MEAT FROM POULTRY the meat of domestic fowl such as chickens and ducks [14thC. From Old French *pouletrie*, from *pouletier* "poulterer," from *poulet* "young fowl."]

pounce[1] /powns/ *v.* **(pounced, pounc·ing, pounc·es) 1.** *vi.* JUMP SUDDENLY ON to jump or swoop suddenly toward or onto somebody or something, especially onto prey **2.** *vi.* ATTACK OR TAKE QUICKLY to move very quickly and suddenly in attacking somebody or obtaining something ○ *He pounced on the book and carried it off to his room.* **3.** *vt.* REACT SWIFTLY TO to be quick to notice and make use of something ○ *She immediately pounced on his admission that he'd known all about it.* ■ *n.* ACT OF SUDDENLY JUMPING ON an act of suddenly jumping or swooping toward or onto somebody or something, especially onto prey [14thC. Origin uncertain: either a shortening of PUNCHEON, or from Old French *poinson* "pointed tool," via the assumed Vulgar Latin stem *punction-* from, ultimately, the Latin stem *punct-* (see PUNCTURE).] —**pounc·er** *n.*

pounce[2] /powns/ *n.* **1.** POWDER TO STOP INK RUNNING a very fine powder used in the past to stop ink from spreading on unglazed paper **2.** POWDER USED FOR PRODUCING IMAGE powdered charcoal or other fine powder sprinkled over a stencil to reproduce the main lines of a pattern or design on the surface beneath the stencil ■ *vt.* **(pounced, pounc·ing, pounc·es) 1.** SPRINKLE PAPER WITH POUNCE to sprinkle paper with pounce **2.** REPRODUCE SOMETHING WITH POUNCE to reproduce a pattern or design on something by sprinkling pounce over a stencil [Late 16thC. Via Old French *ponce* (noun) and *poncer* (verb) from, ultimately, Latin *pumic-*, stem of *pumex* "pumice" (source of English *pumice*).]

pound[1] /pownd/ *v.* **(pound·ed, pound·ing, pounds) 1.** *vti.* STRIKE HARD AND REPEATEDLY to strike somebody or something repeatedly and heavily **2.** *vt.* BEAT SOMETHING TO PULP OR POWDER to beat something into very fine pieces or to a mass, with repeated heavy blows **3.** *vi.* THROB to beat or throb heavily ○ *My heart was pounding.* **4.** *vt.* ATTACK CONTINUOUSLY to attack a place continuously with bombs or large guns ○ *pounding the city for a few weeks* **5.** *vi.* RUN HEAVILY to run with heavy steps **6.** *vt.* TEACH BY REPETITION to ensure that somebody learns or understands something by using constant repetition and drilling ■ *n.* ACT OF POUNDING the act or sound of pounding [15thC. Alteration of *pounen*, from Old English *pūnian*, from a prehistoric Germanic base that is also the ancestor of Dutch *puin* "rubbish, rubble."] —**pound·er** *n.*

pound out *vt.* **1.** PRODUCE SOMETHING WITH HARD WORK to produce something by working in a diligent continuous way ○ *pound out an essay* **2.** PRODUCE SOMETHING WITH HEAVY BLOWS to produce something with heavy blows or loud thumping noises ○ *pound out a tune on the piano*

pound[2] /pownd/ *n.* **1.** MEASURE AVOIRDUPOIS UNIT OF WEIGHT a unit of weight in the avoirdupois system, divided into 16 ounces and equivalent to 0.45 kg **2.** MEASURE TROY UNIT OF WEIGHT a unit of weight in the troy system that is divided into 12 ounces and is equivalent to 0.37 kg **3.** MONEY COMMON UNIT OF CURRENCY a unit of currency used in the United Kingdom, Cyprus and several Middle Eastern countries. See table at **currency 4.** MONEY COIN OR BILL WORTH A POUND a coin or bill worth a pound **5.** MEASURE BRITISH UNIT OF FORCE a British unit of force, equal to the gravitational force experienced by a pound mass accelerating at 32.174 ft./9.80665 m per second per second [Old English *pund* via prehistoric Germanic from Latin *pondo* "weight of a pound," from *(libra) pondo* "(pound) by weight," a form of assumed *pondos* "weight"]

pound[3] /powns/ *n.* **1.** ENCLOSURE FOR STRAY ANIMALS a fenced-off area or a building with cages where stray animals, especially dogs, are kept **2.** CRIMINOL ENCLOSURE FOR VEHICLES OR OTHER GOODS a fenced-off area where vehicles or other goods that have been taken by the police or another authority are kept until a debt or fine has been paid **3.** HUNT, AGRIC PLACE FOR ANIMALS OR FISH an area in which animals or fish are trapped or kept **4.** PRISON AREA a place where people are held prisoner ■ *vt.* **(pound·ed, pound·ing, pounds)** PUT SOMETHING IN POUND to confine somebody or something in a pound [From the Old English stem *pund-*]

Ezra Pound

Pound /pownd/, **Ezra** (1885–1972) U.S. writer. He was an influential poet, critic, translator, and mentor of other poets, and a founder of imagism. His major work is *Cantos* (1925–70). Full name **Ezra Loomis Pound**

pound·age[1] /pówndij/ *n.* **1.** COMM PAYMENT PER POUND OF WEIGHT a tax, charge, commission, or other payment for something calculated per pound of weight **2.** FIN PAYMENT PER POUND STERLING a tax, charge, commission, or other payment for something calculated per pound sterling **3.** MEASURE WEIGHT IN POUNDS the weight of somebody or something expressed in pounds

pound·age[2] /pówndij/ *n.* **1.** CONFINEMENT IN ENCLOSURE the confinement of animals in an enclosed area or pound **2.** FEE FOR RETURN OF SOMETHING the fee that must be paid for the return of an impounded vehicle, animal, or other goods

pound·al /pównd'l/ *n.* a British unit of force, equal to the force that will impart an acceleration of one foot per second per second to a mass of one pound [Late 19thC. Formed from POUND[2], perhaps on the model of QUINTAL.]

pound cake *n.* a rich dense yellow cake that is traditionally made with a pound each of butter, sugar, flour, and eggs, or with equal weights of each of these ingredients

pound-fool·ish *adj.* unwise when dealing with large amounts of money or important matters [From the phrase *penny-wise and pound-foolish*]

pound sign *n.* **1.** MONEY SYMBOL FOR MONEY the symbol (£), which indicates pound sterling **2.** UTIL, COMPUT THE SYMBOL # the symbol (#), especially on a telephone keypad or computer keyboard

pound ster·ling (*plural* **pounds ster·ling**) *n.* the official name for the unit of currency used in the United Kingdom

pour /pawr/ **(poured, pour·ing, pours)** *v.* **1.** *vt.* MAKE SOMETHING FLOW to make a fluid substance flow in a stream ○ *poured the sugar into the bowl* **2.** *vti.* SERVE DRINK to serve a drink from a container such as a pot or pitcher into a cup, mug, or glass ○ *Let me pour you some tea.* **3.** *vi.* FLOW IN LARGE QUANTITIES to flow down or out, especially in large quantities ○ *Smoke poured from the burning building.* **4.** *vi.* RAIN HEAVILY to rain very heavily ○ *It poured for hours.* **5.** *vi.* COME IN LARGE QUANTITIES to come or go quickly and in large quantities ○ *Letters of complaint came pouring in.* **6.** *vt.* EXPRESS FEELING to express a feeling at length and without restraint **7.** *vt.* GIVE LARGE AMOUNT OF to give a large amount of something such as effort or support to something ○ *poured a lot of blood, sweat, and tears into that project* [13thC. Origin uncertain: probably via Old French dialect *purer* "to sift, pour out" from Latin *purare* "to purify," from *purus* "pure" (source of English *pure*).]

WORD KEY: USAGE

pour or **pore**? "To gaze at or study intently" (***pore***) might seem to have more in common with "to drench" (***pour***) than with "a small opening in skin or a rock" (***pore***). Perhaps it has, but all three words have been derived separately, despite the fact that one of the verbs has the same spelling as the noun. You ***pour*** from the pot into a teacup, ***pore*** over a text, and have ***pores*** in your skin.

pour·boire /poor bwaár/ *n.* a sum of money given for services rendered or anticipated [Early 19thC. From French, literally "for drinking."]

pour·par·ler /pŏor paar láy/ *n.* an informal discussion or round of talks, often diplomatic, that precedes a larger and more important conference with official negotiations (*formal*) [Early 18thC. From French, literally "for talking."]

pour point *n.* the lowest temperature at which a liquid will continue to flow

pousse-ca·fé /pŏoss ka fáy/ *n.* **1.** LAYERED DRINK a drink consisting of different-colored liqueurs poured in one glass and forming layers because each liqueur has a different density **2.** AFTER-DINNER DRINK a liqueur served after dinner, with or after coffee [From French, literally "push coffee"]

pous·sette /poo sét/ *n.* MOVEMENT IN COUNTRY DANCING a movement in country dancing in which one or more couples hold hands and swing around the floor ■ *vi.* **(-set·ted, -set·ting, -settes)** DANCE POUSSETTE to perform a poussette in a dance [Early 19thC. From French, literally "small push," ultimately from *pousser* "to push," from Latin *pulsare*, literally "to push frequently," from *pellere* "to push."]

Pous·sin /poo sáN/, **Nicolas** (1594–1665) French-born Italian painter. He was a master of French classicism, and was influenced by Raphael.

pout[1] /powt/ *v.* **(pout·ed, pout·ing, pouts) 1.** *vti.* PUSH LIPS OUTWARDS to move the lower lip or both lips outwards to form an expression of bad temper or sulkiness, or in order to look sexually provoking **2.** *vi.* SULK to show disappointment, anger, or resentment, usually in silence ○ *still pouting because he missed the game* **3.** *vt.* SAY SOMETHING SULKILY to say something with a pout ○ *pouted that the whole thing wasn't fair* ■ *n.* **1.** EXPRESSION WITH LIPS PUSHED OUT an expression of the face with the lower lip or both lips pushed out **2.** SULKY MOOD a period or fit of sulking [14thC. Origin uncertain: perhaps from a Scandinavian source.] —**pout·y** *adj.*

pout[2] /powt/ (*plural* **pout** *or* **pouts**) *n.* **1.** = **eelpout 2.** = **hornpout** [Old English stem *-pūte*, of uncertain origin: perhaps from the same Scandinavian source as POUT[1]]

pout·er /pówtər/ *n.* **1.** POUTING PERSON somebody who pouts **2. pout·er, pout·er pi·geon** BIRDS DOMESTIC PIGEON WITH AN INFLATABLE CROP a domesticated pigeon belonging to a breed with a crop that can be greatly inflated [Early 18thC. Formed from POUT[1].]

pou·tine /poo téen/ *n.* a dish originating in Quebec that consists of french fries and curd cheese, covered with tomato sauce or gravy

pov·er·ty /póvvərtee/ *n.* **1.** STATE OF BEING POOR the state of not having enough money to take care of basic needs such as food, clothing, and housing **2.** LACK a deficiency or lack of something ○ *poverty of emotion* **3.** INFERTILITY OF SOIL lack of soil fertility or nutrients [12thC. Via Old French *poverte* from Latin *paupertas*, from *pauper* "poor" (source of English *pauper* and *poor*).]

WORD KEY: SYNONYMS

poverty, destitution, indigence, deprivation, penury, social exclusion, want

CORE MEANING: insufficiency of resources on which to live

poverty a general word used to describe the state of being without enough money or resources to live at a standard considered normal or basic by society. It can be used to describe varying states of need, from lack of material comfort to near-starvation; **destitution** used to describe poverty that is so extreme as to be life-threatening; **indigence** a formal word used to describe a state of very severe poverty; **deprivation** used to describe a state of severe poverty, emphasizing the fact that those affected have been denied the material benefits that others enjoy; **penury** used to describe a fairly severe state of economic need; **social exclusion** used in political or sociological contexts to suggest a lack of money or resources sufficient to sustain a basic standard of living, causing those affected to be disadvantaged; **want** a formal or literary word used to describe a situation where people do not have the money, food, or resources they need to have a basic standard of living.

pov·er·ty line, pov·er·ty lev·el *n.* a level of income below which somebody is considered to be living in poverty. It is based on the price of basic necessities and is usually determined by a government.

pov·er·ty-strick·en *adj.* extremely poor and with intense problems as a result

pow /pow/ *interj.* used to imitate the sound of an explosion or gun, or of a sudden impact, e.g., when somebody is hit (*informal*) [Late 19thC. An imitation of the sound.]

POW *abbr.* prisoner of war

pow·der /pówdər/ *n.* **1.** TINY LOOSE PARTICLES a substance in the form of a loose grouping of many tiny dry grains **2.** POWDER FOR PARTICULAR PURPOSE a substance in the form of powder that is produced for a particular purpose by crushing or drying a solid, or by mixing various powders ○ *face powder* **3.** ARMS GUNPOWDER gunpowder **4.** DRY SNOW light dry snow ■ *v.* (**-dered, -der·ing, -ders**) **1.** *vt.* PUT POWDER ON to cover something with powder, or to sprinkle powder on something **2.** *vti.* TURN INTO POWDER to turn a solid into powder or to become a powder [13thC. Via French *poudrer* (verb) and *poudre* (noun, alteration of *poldre*), from, ultimately, Latin *pulver-*, stem of *pulvis* "dust" (source of English *pulverize*).] —**pow·der·er** *n.* —**pow·der·y** *adj.*

Pow·der /pówdər/ **1.** river rising in Oregon's Blue Mountains and flowing into the Snake River, bordering with Idaho. Length: 110 mi./177 km. **2.** river forming in central Wyoming and flowing into the Yellowstone River in Montana. Length: 375 mi./603 km.

pow·der blue *adj.* of a very pale blue color with a slight tinge of purple (*hyphenated when used before a noun*) —**pow·der blue** *n.*

pow·der burn *n.* a minor skin burn caused by being very close to a brief intense explosion, especially gunfire, sometimes used as evidence in a court of law

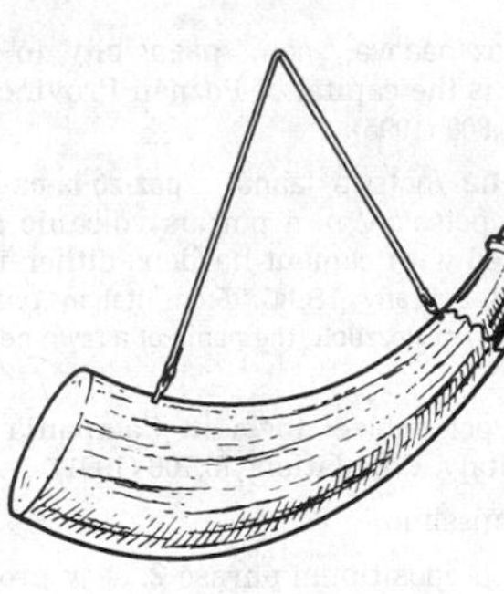

Powder horn

pow·der horn *n.* a small container to hold gunpowder

pow·der keg *n.* **1.** ARMS KEG FOR GUNPOWDER a small barrel used to hold gunpowder or blasting powder **2.** TENSE SITUATION a tense situation that may easily erupt into violence

pow·der met·al·lur·gy *n.* the technology of working powdered metals or some carbides by compressing or heating without melting, or by compressing and heating without melting, to produce solid objects such as self-lubricating bearings

pow·der mon·key *n.* (*informal*) **1.** NAVY BOY CARRYING GUNPOWDER ON SHIP a boy employed on a warship in the past to carry gunpowder from the store to the guns **2.** SOMEBODY WHO WORKS WITH EXPLOSIVES somebody who delivers, works with, or is in charge of explosives in fields such as mining or construction

pow·der puff *n.* a soft or fluffy pad used for putting powder on the face or skin

pow·der room *n.* **1.** LADIES' ROOM a public restroom for women **2.** BATHROOM FOR GUESTS a bathroom for use by guests, situated near the main living area of a house

pow·der·y mil·dew *n.* a fungal disease that produces a white powdery covering on plant leaves caused by various fungi

Pow·ell /pów əl/, **Adam Clayton, Jr.** (1908–72) U.S. politician and preacher. He was a Democratic congressman (1945–71), and campaigned against racial discrimination.

Department of Defense, Washington, D.C.

Colin Powell

Pow·ell, Colin (*b.* 1937) U.S. military leader. He was chairman of the Joint Chiefs of Staff during the Persian Gulf War (1991). Full name **Colin Luther Jr. Powell**

Pow·ell, John Wesley (1834–1902) U.S. ethnologist, explorer, and geologist. He classified Native American languages, and did pioneering survey work in the Rocky Mountains.

Pow·ell, Lewis Franklin, Jr. (*b.* 1907) U.S. jurist. He served on the United States Supreme Court (1972–87), where he was considered a moderate justice.

pow·er /pówr/ *n.* **1.** ABILITY OR CAPACITY TO DO SOMETHING the ability, skill, or capacity to do something **2.** STRENGTH physical force or strength **3.** CONTROL AND INFLUENCE control and influence over other people and their actions **4.** POLITICAL CONTROL the political control of a country, exercised by its government or leader **5.** AUTHORITY TO ACT the authority to act or do something according to a law or rule **6.** SOMEBODY WITH POWER somebody who has political or financial power **7.** IMPORTANT COUNTRY a country that has military or economic resources and is considered to have political influence over other countries **8.** PERSUASIVENESS the ability to influence people's judgment or emotions **9.** SKILL a faculty, skill, or ability ○ *musical powers* **10.** ENG, PHYS MEASURE OF RATE OF DOING WORK a measure of the rate of doing work or transferring energy, usually expressed in terms of wattage or horsepower. Symbol *P* **11.** ENERGY ENERGY TO DRIVE MACHINERY energy or force used to drive machinery or produce electricity **12.** ELECTRICITY electricity made available for use **13.** MATH NUMBER OF MULTIPLICATIONS the number of times a quantity is to be successively multiplied by itself, usually written as a small number to the right of and above the quantity **14.** OPTICS MAGNIFYING ABILITY a measure of the ability of a lens, mirror, or prism to magnify an image **15.** STATS PROBABILITY OF REJECTING NULL HYPOTHESIS the probability of rejecting the null hypothesis as false when a particular alternative hypothesis is true ■ *adj.* **1.** RUN BY ELECTRICITY OR FUEL receiving power from a motor using electrical energy or fuel such as gasoline, instead of relying on manual labor ○ *power tools* **2.** INTENDED FOR BUSINESS SUCCESS designed or believed to improve somebody's status, influence, or effectiveness in business ○ *power dressing* ■ *v.* (**-ered, -er·ing, -ers**) **1.** *vt.* PROVIDE ENERGY TO OPERATE SOMETHING to supply something such as a machine or tool with energy **2.** *vi.* MOVE ENERGETICALLY to move fast and with great power and energy (*informal*) [13thC. Via Anglo-Norman *poer* and Old French *poeir* from assumed Vulgar Latin *potere* "to be powerful," from *potis* "powerful" (source of English *potent*[1]).]

power down *vti.* to turn a computer off in the correct way, bringing an orderly end to system operation

power up *vti.* to turn on a computer, printer, or other peripheral device

pow·er base *n.* a position, area, or group of voters providing the foundation of somebody's political power or support

pow·er·boat /pówr bōt/ *n.* a small motorboat with a powerful outboard or inboard motor, used especially for racing —**pow·er·boat·ing** *n.*

pow·er brok·er *n.* a person or country that has great influence, especially in politics or commerce, and is able to use this influence to affect the policies and decisions of others

pow·er cut *n. U.K.* = **power outage**

pow·er dive *n.* a steep dive made by an aircraft with its engines at high power to increase the speed —**pow·er-dive** *vti.*

pow·er e·lite *n.* a small group with great power to influence the course of events in the society that it belongs to

pow·er·ful /pówrf'l/ *adj.* **1.** INFLUENTIAL able to exert a lot of influence and control over people and events ○ *a powerful nation* **2.** STRONG with great physical or mental strength or force **3.** EFFECTIVE with the strength or qualities to be effective in producing a result ○ *a powerful antibiotic* **4.** PERSUASIVE able to produce a strong effect on people's ideas or emotions ○ *a powerful movie* ■ *adv.* VERY extremely (*regional*) ○ *He was powerful thirsty.* —**pow·er·ful·ly** *adv.* —**pow·er·ful·ness** *n.*

pow·er·house /pówr hòwss/ (*plural* **-hous·es** /pówr hòwzəz/) *n.* **1.** SOMEBODY OR SOMETHING THAT IS PRODUCTIVE somebody or something that is full of energy and very productive, especially of new ideas (*informal*) **2.** ENERGY = **power plant**

pow·er·less /pówrləss/ *adj.* lacking power, strength, or effectiveness —**pow·er·less·ly** *adv.* —**pow·er·less·ness** *n.*

pow·er line *n.* a cable that carries electricity from a power station to the users of the electricity or between electric utilities in a network

pow·er lunch *n.* a meeting over lunch that gives somebody the opportunity to cultivate an important contact or discuss business matters at a high level

pow·er mow·er *n.* a lawn mower that is driven by a motor

pow·er of ap·point·ment *n.* the authority given to somebody to select beneficiaries and to allocate money and other property from a person's estate to those beneficiaries

pow·er of at·tor·ney *n.* the legal authority to act for another person in legal and business matters

pow·er out·age *n.* a temporary loss of electricity to a building or area

pow·er pack *n.* a device for converting electrical supply to direct or alternating current at the correct voltage for a piece of electrical or electronic equipment

pow·er plant *n.* **1.** ENERGY **PLANT FOR GENERATING ELECTRICITY** an industrial complex where power, especially electricity, is generated from another source of energy such as burning coal, nuclear reactions, or flowing water **2.** TRANSP **UNIT POWERING SELF-PROPELLED OBJECT** a unit that supplies the power to move a self-propelled object, e.g., a diesel-electric engine in a locomotive or an internal-combustion engine in an automobile

pow·er play *n.* **1. BID FOR ADVANTAGE** an attempt to gain an advantage by a display of strength or superiority, e.g., in a negotiation or relationship **2. TACTIC OF CONCENTRATING RESOURCES** a tactic in business, commerce, or politics of concentrating resources and effort on one particular area **3.** SPORTS **TACTIC OF CONCENTRATING PLAYERS** a tactic used in sports consisting of concentrating players in a particular area, especially an attack in football that involves extra blockers preceding the person carrying the ball **4.** HOCKEY **NUMERICAL ADVANTAGE IN ICE HOCKEY** a situation or period of time in ice hockey during which one team has a numerical advantage because the other team has one or more players in the penalty box

pow·er pol·i·tics *n.* political relations and actions based on an implied threat of use of political, economic, or military power by a participant (*takes a singular or plural verb*)

Pow·ers /pów ərz/, **Hiram** (1805–73) U.S. sculptor. He is known for the celebrated statue *The Greek Slave* (1843), depicting a female nude in chains.

pow·er se·ries *n.* an infinite series in which the terms contain regularly increasing integral powers of a variable. A typical series would be $Sn= 1+2x+3x^2+4x^3+\ldots+nx^{n-1}$.

pow·er shov·el *n.* a mobile machine for excavating and removing debris, with a movable lever arm ending in a hinged digging bucket

pow·er sta·tion *n.* = **power plant**

pow·er steer·ing *n.* a system of steering for a motor vehicle in which turning the steering wheel is made easier by supplementary power from the vehicle's engine

pow·er take·off *n.* a device for transferring power from a vehicle's engine to another piece of machinery

pow·er train *n.* the portion of a vehicle's drive mechanism that transmits power from the engine to the wheels, tracks, or propellers. An automobile's power train includes the clutch, transmission, driveshaft, and differential.

pow·er trip *n.* (*informal*) **1. ASSERTION OF CONTROL OVER OTHERS** an action designed to gain or keep control over other people in order to increase and enjoy a feeling of power **2. SITUATION GIVING CONTROL OVER OTHERS** a situation that increases somebody's feeling of being powerful or in control of others

pow·er us·er *n.* a computer user who is expert in one or more software applications (*informal*)

Pow·ha·tan /pów ə tan, pòwhə tán/ (1550?–1618) Native North American chief. He led the Powhatan confederacy of Algonquian tribes in Virginia, and was the father of Pocahontas. Real name **Wahunsonacook**

pow·wow /pów wòw/ *n.* **1. NATIVE AMERICAN CEREMONY** a traditional Native American ceremony featuring dance, feasting, and a blessing by a shaman for an event such as a marriage, a major hunt, or a gathering of nations **2. MEETING** a meeting or gathering to discuss something (*informal*) ■ *vi.* (**-wowed, -wow·ing, -wows**) **HAVE POWWOW** to hold a powwow (*informal*) [Early 19thC. From Narragansett *powah, powwaw,* literally "shaman."]

pox /poks/ *n.* MED **1. VENERAL DISEASE** a venereal disease, especially syphilis (*informal*) **2. DISEASE CAUSING SPOTS ON SKIN** a viral disease such as smallpox or chickenpox that causes pus-filled blisters (**pustules**) to form on the skin, and often leaves scars (**pockmarks**) [Alteration of the plural of POCK] ◇ **a pox on somebody** *or* **something** used to express a wish that misfortune will come to somebody or something (*archaic*)

pox·vi·rus /póks vìrəss/ *n.* an oval-shaped DNA-containing virus responsible for diseases that cause pus-filled blisters (**pustules**) to form on the skin

Poynt·ing the·o·rem /póynting-/ *n.* PHYS the theorem stating that the rate of flow of electromagnetic energy per unit area equals the cross product of the electric and magnetic vectors [Late 19thC. Named for J. H. *Poynting* (1852–1914), an English physicist.]

Poz·nán /pőz naanyə, -nan, -naan/ city in western Poland. It is the capital of Poznán Province. Population: 581,800 (1995).

poz·zuo·la·na /pòtswə laánə/, **poz·zo·la·na** /pòtsə-/, **poz·zo·lan** /pótsələn/ *n.* a porous volcanic ash that when mixed with cement hardens either in air or under water [Early 18thC. From Italian *pozz(u)olana (terra)* "(earth) of Pozzuoli (the name of a town near Naples in Italy)."]

Poz·zuo·li /pot swőlee/ town in Campania Region, southern Italy. Population: 75,706 (1991).

pp *abbr.* pianissimo

PP[1] *abbr.* **1.** prepositional phrase **2.** GRAM pronoun

p.p. *abbr.* **1.** by proxy (*used when signing documents on behalf of somebody else*) **2.** parcel post **3.** parish priest **4.** past participle

Pr. *abbr.* **1.** Priest **2.** Prince **3.** preferred (stock)

P.R. *abbr.* **1.** proportional representation **2.** public relations **3.** Puerto Rico

prac·ti·ca·ble /práktikəb'l/ *adj.* **1. CAPABLE OF BEING DONE** capable of being carried out or put into effect **2. USABLE** capable of being used [Mid-17thC. Via medieval Latin *practicabilis* from, ultimately, Greek *praktikē*, the feminine of *praktikos* "practical" (see PRACTICE).]

prac·ti·cal /práktik'l/ *adj.* **1. CONCERNED WITH MATTERS OF FACT** concerned with actual facts and experience, not theory ○ *the practical applications of this research* **2. USEFUL** sensible or useful, and likely to be effective ○ *practical advice* **3. GOOD AT SOLVING PROBLEMS** good at managing matters and dealing with problems and difficulties **4. PRACTICING** involved in the actual work of a profession or activity ○ *practical physician* **5. SUITABLE FOR EVERYDAY USE** plain, functional, and suitable for everyday use **6. VIRTUAL** resembling a particular thing in almost every way (*informal*) ○ *The campaign was a practical disaster.* ■ *n.* EDUC **CLASS WITH HANDS-ON ACTIVITIES** a class or examination that requires actually doing something such as an experiment or a medical procedure ○ *a physics practical* [Via medieval Latin *practicalis* from, ultimately, Greek *praktikos* (see PRACTICE)]

prac·ti·cal joke *n.* a trick that is carried out on somebody to make him or her look silly and to amuse others —**prac·ti·cal jok·er** *n.*

prac·ti·cal·ly /práktikəlee/ *adv.* **1. ALMOST** very nearly but not quite **2. IN PRACTICAL WAY** in a way that is useful, sensible, or practical

prac·ti·cal nurse *n.* **1. NURSE HOLDING BASIC QUALIFICATION** a nurse who has completed a certain level of training, lower than that of a registered nurse **2. NURSE WITH EXPERIENCE BUT NO QUALIFICATION** a nurse who has considerable experience of caring for people but who does not have a college degree in nursing

prac·tice /práktiss/ *v.* (**-ticed, -tic·ing, -tic·es**) **1.** *vti.* **REPEAT SOMETHING TO GET BETTER** to do something, especially exercises, repeatedly in order to improve performance in a sport, art, or hobby ○ *practices the piano daily* **2.** *vt.* **DO SOMETHING AS CUSTOM** to do something as an established custom or habit **3.** *vti.* **WORK IN LAW OR MEDICINE** to work in a particular job or profession, especially law or medicine ○ *She has been practicing law for 15 years now.* **4.** *vt.* RELIG **FOLLOW A RELIGION** to act according to the beliefs and customs of a religion ○ *We are proud to practice the religion of our ancestors.* **5.** *vt.* **PERPETRATE** to perpetrate something morally bad such as deceit or cruelty ■ *n.* **1. REPETITION IN ORDER TO IMPROVE** the process of repeating something such as an exercise many times in order to improve performance **2. PERFORMANCE OF RELIGION, PROFESSION, OR CUSTOMS** the performance of a religion, profession, set of customs, or established habit **3. PROCESS OF CARRYING OUT AN IDEA** the process of carrying out an idea, plan, or theory **4. WORK OF PROFESSIONAL PERSON** the business of a lawyer, doctor, dentist, or other professional **5. HABIT** a habit, custom, or usual way of doing something ○ *good business practices* [14thC. Directly or via obsolete French *practiser* from medieval Latin *practizare*, an alteration of *practicare*, from, ultimately, Greek *praktikos* "practical," from *prattein* "to do."]

WORD KEY: SYNONYMS

See Synonyms at ***habit***.

prac·ticed /práktist/ *adj.* expert in doing something because of long experience

prac·tic·ing /práktissing/ *adj.* actively involved in a particular activity, e.g., a profession, religion, or way of life

prac·ti·cum /práktikəm/ *n.* a period of work for practical experience as part of an academic course [Early 20thC. From late Latin, the neuter of *practicus* "active, practical," from Greek *praktikos* (see PRACTICE).]

prac·tise *vti.* U.K. = **practice**

prac·ti·tion·er /prak tísh'nər/ *n.* **1. SOMEBODY WHO PRACTICES A PROFESSION** somebody who practices a particular profession, especially medicine **2.** CHR **CHRISTIAN SCIENCE HEALER** in Christian Science, somebody who carries out ministry and spiritual healing [Mid-16thC. Formed from obsolete *practician*, from Old French *practicien*, from *practiser* "to practice" (see PRACTICE).]

Pra·do /praádō/ *n.* a museum in Madrid that contains the Spanish national collection of paintings, sculptures, and drawings. It was founded by Fernando VII in 1810.

prae·di·al /preédee əl/, **pre·di·al** *adj.* relating to land or farming [From medieval Latin *praedialis*, from Latin *praedium* "farm, estate"] —**prae·di·al·i·ty** /preédee állətee/ *n.*

prae·mu·ni·re /preémyə neéree/ *n.* the offense under English law of accepting the authority of some other power over that of the English crown, or an accusation to that effect [From medieval Latin *praemunire facias* "that you warn" (these words being part of the writ), the first word of which meant "to warn" (by association with Latin *praemonere* "to forewarn," source of English *premonition*) and came from Latin, "to fortify in front," from *munire* "to fortify, defend" (see MUNITION)]

prae·no·men /pree nṓmən/ (*plural* **-no·mens** *or* **-nom·i·na** /-nómmənə, -nṓmənə/) *n.* in ancient Rome, somebody's first name [Early 17thC. From Latin, "forename," from *nomen* "name" (source of English *nominal, noun,* and *renown*).] —**prae·nom·i·nal** /pree nómmən'l/ *adj.* —**prae·nom·i·nal·ly** /-nəlee/ *adv.*

prae·tor /preétər/, **pre·tor** *n.* in ancient Rome, any of several magistrates ranking immediately below the consuls and acting as the chief law officers of the state. At first there was only one praetor, but there were later as many as eight who were also responsible for organizing the public games. [15thC. From Latin, of uncertain origin: possibly formed from *praeire*, literally "to go in front."] —**prae·to·ri·al** /pree táwree əl/ *adj.* —**prae·tor·ship** /preétər ship/ *n.*

prae·to·ri·an /pree táwree ən/, **pre·to·ri·an** *adj.* **1. RELATING TO PRAETORS** relating to praetors or to the office of praetor **2. CORRUPT** corrupt and venal (*formal*) ■ *n.* **ANCIENT ROMAN OF PRAETOR RANK** in ancient Rome, a holder or former holder of the office of praetor, e.g., an ex-praetor who became governor of a province

Prae·to·ri·an, Pre·to·ri·an *adj.* **OF THE PRAETORIAN GUARD** belonging or relating to the Praetorian Guard ■ *n.* **MEMBER OF PRAETORIAN GUARD** a member of the Praetorian Guard

Prae·to·ri·an Guard *n.* **1. ANCIENT ROMAN EMPEROR'S BODYGUARD** the emperor's bodyguard in ancient Rome. The members of the Guard were reputed to be corrupt and often interfered with the selection of the emperor in later periods of the Roman Empire. **2. MEMBER OF PRAETORIAN GUARD** a soldier of the emperor's bodyguard in ancient Rome

prag·mat·ic /prag máttik/ *adj.* **1. CONCERNED WITH PRACTICAL RESULTS** more concerned with practical results than with theories and principles **2.** PHILOS **RELATING TO PHILOSOPHICAL PRAGMATISM** relating to or characteristic of philosophical pragmatism **3.** POL **POLITICAL** relating to the political affairs of a country (*formal*) **4. LEARNING LESSONS FROM HISTORY** dealing with or looking at the facts of history with particular regard to the lessons that can be learned from them **5.** LING **RELATING TO PRAGMATICS** relating or belonging to pragmatics [Late 16thC. Via late Latin *pragmaticus* from, ultimately, Greek *pragma* "deed, action."] —**prag·mat·i·cal·i·ty** /prag màttə kállətee/ *n.* —**prag·mat·i·cal·ly** /prag máttikəlee/ *adv.*

prag·mat·ics /prag máttiks/ *n.* the branch of linguistics that studies language use rather than language structure. Pragmatics studies how people choose what to say from the range of possibilities their language allows them, and the effect their choices have on those to whom they are speaking. (*takes a singular verb*)

prag·mat·ic sanc·tion *n.* a special decree issued by a sovereign that has the force of law

prag·ma·tism /prágmə tìzzəm/ *n.* **1. WAY OF THINKING ABOUT RESULTS** a straightforward practical way of thinking about things or dealing with problems, concerned with results rather than with theories and principles **2.** PHILOS **WAY OF EVALUATING THEORIES** a philosophical view that a theory or concept should be evaluated in terms of how it works and its consequences as the standard for action and thought. ◊ **instrumentalism** —**prag·ma·tist** *n.* —**prag·ma·tis·tic** /pràgmə tístik/ *adj.*

Prague /praag/ capital city of the Czech Republic, located in the west of the country. Population: 1,213,000 (1995).

pra·hu *n.* = **proa**

Prai·a /prí̄ ə/ capital city of the Republic of Cape Verde, in southeastern São Tiago Island. Population: 69,000 (1992).

Prair·i·al /práiree əl/ *n.* the ninth month of the year in the French Revolutionary calendar, corresponding to May 21 to June 19 in the Gregorian calendar [Late 18thC. From French *Prairial*, from *prairie* "meadow."]

prai·rie /práiree/ *n.* **N AMERICAN GRASSLAND** a treeless grass-covered plain in the United States and Canada, especially in the Midwest and the West ■ **prai·ries** *npl. Can* **PRAIRIE PROVINCES** the Prairie Provinces of Manitoba, Alberta, and Saskatchewan in Canada [Late 18thC. Via French from assumed Vulgar Latin *prataria*, from Latin *pratum* "meadow," of unknown origin.]

prai·rie chick·en *n.* a game bird belonging to the grouse family with mottled brownish plumage, native to grasslands of the United States. The male has inflatable air sacs on its throat, used in courtship. Latin name: *Tympanuchus cupido* and *Tympanuchus pallidicinctus.*

prai·rie dog *n.* a burrowing rodent of the squirrel family that lives in large underground colonies on the grasslands of North America. It has light-brown fur and a sharp barking or whistling warning call. Genus: *Cynomys.*

prai·rie dog town *n. Midwest, Rocky Mountains* a network of prairie dog burrows, especially within a large mound

WORD KEY: REGIONAL NOTE

These are familiar terms of the Great Plains, from Kansas and Nebraska through the Rocky Mountain states.

prai·rie fal·con *n.* a large falcon, native to the western United States, that has a squarish head, dark-brown back feathers with pale edges, and pale spotted underparts. Latin name: *Falco mexicanus.*

prai·rie oys·ter *n.* **1. RAW EGG DRINK** a drink consisting of a raw egg, Worcestershire sauce, salt, and pepper, taken as a cure for a hangover or hiccups **2. COOKED CALF OR PIG TESTICLE** the fried testicle of a calf or pig, eaten as a delicacy in the Midwest (*usually used in the plural*)

prai·rie schoo·ner *n.* a large covered wagon, pulled by horses or oxen that was used by pioneers crossing the prairies in the 19th century [From the imagined resemblance of their canvas tops, seen from a distance, to a ship's sails]

prai·rie soil *n.* a type of soil that typically forms under the grasses of the prairie. It is rich in plant nutrients and is nearly black in color.

Prai·rie Vil·lage /pràiri-/ city in northeastern Kansas, a southern suburb of Kansas City. Population: 23,545 (1996).

prai·rie wolf *n.* = **coyote**

praise /prayz/ *n.* **1. EXPRESSION OF ADMIRATION** words that express great approval or admiration, e.g., for somebody's ability or achievements or for something's good qualities **2. WORSHIP** worship and thanks to God or a deity (*often used in the plural*) ■ *vt.* **(praised, prais·ing, prais·es) 1. EXPRESS ADMIRATION FOR SOMEBODY OR SOMETHING** to express great approval or admiration, e.g., for somebody's ability or achievements or for something's good qualities **2. WORSHIP GOD** to give worship and thanks to God or a deity [13thC. Via Old French *preisier* from late Latin *pretiare* "to prize," from *pretium* "price."] —**prais·er** *n.* ◇ **sing somebody's or something's praises** to praise somebody or something enthusiastically

praise·wor·thy /práyz wùrthee/ *adj.* deserving praise —**praise·wor·thi·ly** *adv.* —**praise·wor·thi·ness** *n.*

pra·jna /prújnə/ *n.* in Buddhist teaching, direct awareness and understanding of truth not achieved by intellectual or rational means [Early 19thC. From Sanskrit *prajñā*, literally "to know directly."]

Pra·krit /praákrìt/ *n.* a language belonging to a group spoken in northern India from approximately 400 B.C. to A.D. 1000. Prakrits are Indic languages that developed form Sanskrit, the most well-known being Pali. [Mid-18thC. From Sanskrit *prākṛta* "natural, vernacular," from *pra-* "forward" + *kṛta-*, past participle stem of *karoti* "it makes" (see SANSKRIT).] —**Pra·krit** *adj.*

pra·line /práy leen/ *n.* **1. CHOCOLATE CANDY** a chocolate candy with a soft filling made from crushed caramelized nuts, usually almonds **2. NUTS BOILED IN SUGAR** a nut caramelized in boiling sugar syrup that hardens when cold, or a substance made from crushed caramelized nuts and used as a dessert topping or chocolate filling [Early 18thC. Named for the French officer Marshal de Plessis- *Praslin* (1598–1675), whose cook invented it.]

prall·tril·ler /praál trìllər/ *n.* a musical embellishment made by the quick alternation of a specific note with the note immediately above it [Mid-19thC. From German, literally "bouncing trill."]

pram[1] /pram/ *n. U.K.* = **baby carriage** [Late 19thC. Contraction of PERAMBULATOR.]

pram[2] /pram/, **praam** *n.* **1. FLAT-BOTTOMED FISHING BOAT** a small fishing boat boat with a flat bottom and a square front **2. FLAT-BOTTOMED BARGE** a flat-bottomed barge used in Baltic ports [Mid-16thC. Via Dutch *praam* from, ultimately, Czech *prám* "raft."]

pra·na /praánə/ *n.* **1. BREATH CONTROL IN YOGA** in yoga, the use of inhalation, holding the breath, and exhalation, according to particular patterns and time periods. It is designed to aid self-awareness, focus, and meditation. **2. BREATH OR BREATHING** in Hinduism, breath or breathing [Mid-19thC. From Sanskrit *prāṇa*, literally "breathing out."]

prance /prans/ *v.* **(pranced, pranc·ing, pranc·es) 1.** *vi.* **MOVE IN LIVELY WAY** to move around in a lively and carefree, but often silly or annoying, way **2.** *vi.* **SWAGGER** to walk in a way that displays excessive pride, arrogance, or a desire to be noticed and admired (*disapproving*) **3.** *vti.* EQU **JUMP FORWARD ON BACK LEGS** to raise the front legs and jump forward on the back legs, or to make a horse perform this step **4.** *vti.* EQU **WALK WITH LIVELY STEPS** to walk with lively springing steps, or to make a horse walk this way ■ *n.* **PRANCING MOVEMENT** a lively, springing, or carefree movement [14thC. Origin unknown.] —**pranc·er** *n.* —**pranc·ing** *adj.* —**pranc·ing·ly** *adv.*

pran·di·al /prándee əl/ *adj.* relating to a meal, especially lunch or dinner (*formal or humorous*) [Early 19thC. Formed from Latin *prandium* "late breakfast."] —**pran·di·al·ly** *adv.*

prang /prang/ *vt. U.K.* to crash or damage a vehicle or aircraft (*informal*) [Mid-20thC. Origin unknown.]

prank[1] /prangk/ *n.* a mischievous trick or silly stunt done for amusement [Late 16thC. Origin unknown.] —**prank·ish** *adj.*

prank[2] /prangk/ *vti.* to embellish or display something in an ostentatious manner ○ *Don't prank yourself up, it's only a family dinner.* [Mid-16thC. Origin uncertain: probably from Middle Dutch *pronken* or Middle Low German *prunken* 'to show off'.]

prank·ster /prángkstər/ *n.* somebody who enjoys playing mischievous tricks on people

Pra·sad /prə saád/, **Rajendra** (1884–1963) Indian statesman. A member of Indian National Congress, he presided over the Constituent Assembly (1946–49) and was the first president of India (1950–62).

prase /práyz/ *n.* a green form of quartz [Late 18thC. Via French from, ultimately, Greek *prasios* "leek-colored," from *prason* "leek."]

pra·se·o·dym·i·um /pràyzee ō dímmee əm/ *n.* a soft ductile silvery metallic chemical element belonging to the rare-earth group. It is characterized by a green tarnish and is used in alloys and to color glass. Symbol **Pr** [Late 19thC. Coined from Greek *prasios* "leek-colored" (see PRASE) + DIDYMIUM.]

prat /prat/ *n.* the buttocks (*slang*) [Mid-16thC. Origin unknown.]

prate /prayt/ *vi.* **(prat·ed, prat·ing, prates) CHATTER** to talk in a silly way and at length about nothing important ■ *n.* **PRATTLE** silly or idle talk [15thC. From Middle Dutch *praten.*] —**prat·er** *n.* —**prat·ing·ly** *adv.*

prat·fall /prát fàwl/ *n.* (*slang*) **1. COMIC FALL** a backward fall onto the buttocks, especially one executed deliberately for comic effect **2. EMBARRASSING MISTAKE** an embarrassing or humiliating mistake or failure

prat·in·cole /prátting kōl/ *n.* a brown or gray bird that is native to Europe and has long pointed wings, a forked tail, and a short bill. It lives on stony or grassy land, usually near water. Family: Glareolidae. [Late 18thC. From modern Latin *pratincola*, from Latin *pratum* "meadow" (source of English *prairie*) + *incola* "dweller."]

pra·tique /pra teék, prə-/ *n.* permission granted to a ship or boat to use a port on satisfying the local quarantine regulations or on producing a clean bill of health [Early 17thC. From French, literally "practice."]

prat·tle /prátt'l/ *vi.* **(-tled, -tling, -tles) TALK IDLY OR CHILDISHLY** to talk in a silly, idle, or childish way ■ *n.* **IDLE OR CHILDISH TALK** silly, idle, or childish talk [Mid-16thC. Origin uncertain: possibly formed from PRATE, or from Middle Low German *pratelen.*] —**prat·tler** *n.* —**prat·tling·ly** *adv.*

Pratt·ville /prát vil/ city in central Alabama, a northwest suburb of Montgomery. Population: 24,269 (1996).

prau *n.* = **proa**

prav·as·tat·in /pràvvə státt'n/ *n.* a drug used to reduce abnormally high levels of blood cholesterol

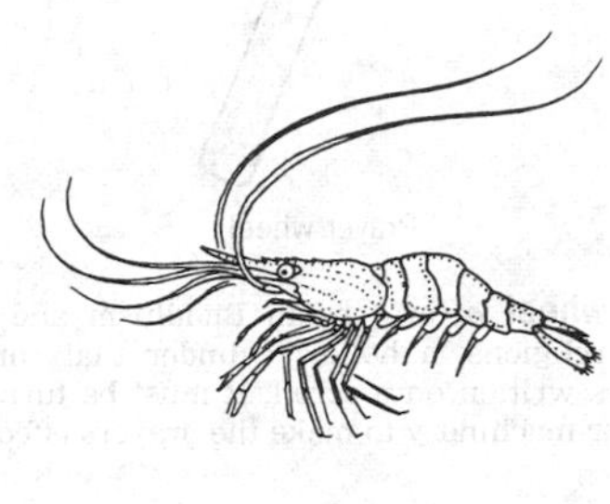

Prawn

prawn /prawn/ *n.* **EDIBLE CRUSTACEAN** an edible marine animal resembling a shrimp, with a slender body, a long tail, five pairs of legs, and two pairs of pincers. Genera: *Palaemon.* Latin name: *Penaeus.* ■ *vi.* **FISH FOR PRAWNS** to fish for prawns [15thC. Origin unknown.] —**prawn·er** *n.*

prax·e·ol·o·gy /pràksee óllәjee/, **prax·i·ol·o·gy** *n.* the study of human behavior [Early 20thC. Formed from Greek *praxis* "custom, behavior" (see PRAXIS).] —**prax·e·o·log·i·cal** /pràksee ə lójjik'l/ *adj.*

prax·is /práksiss/ *n.* (*formal*) **1. PERFORMANCE OR APPLICATION OF SKILL** the practical side and application of something such as a professional skill, as opposed to its theory **2. ESTABLISHED PRACTICE** an established custom or habitual practice [Late 16thC. Via medieval Latin from Greek, where it was formed from *prattein* "to do."]

pray /pray/ *v.* **(prayed, pray·ing, prays) 1.** *vti.* **SPEAK TO GOD OR OTHER BEING** to speak to God, a deity, or a saint, e.g., in order to give thanks, express regret, or ask for help **2.** *vti.* **HOPE STRONGLY** to hope strongly for something ○ *I'm just praying that it won't rain on Saturday.* **3.** *vti.* **MAKE AN EARNEST REQUEST** to ask somebody for something, especially earnestly or with passion ○ *He prayed to be allowed to go back home to his family.* **4.** *vt.* to achieve something by prayer ○ *The villagers tried to pray the drought away.* ■ *interj.* **EMPHASIZING A QUESTION OR COMMAND** used to emphasize a question or a command, either politely or sarcastically ○ *And what, pray, do you think you're doing?* [13thC. Via Old French *preier* from Latin *precari* "to entreat," from *prec-*, stem of prex "prayer" (source of English *deprecate* and *precarious*).]

prayer /práir/ *n.* **1. COMMUNICATION WITH GOD OR OTHER BEING** a spoken or unspoken communication with God, a deity, or a saint. It may express praise, thanksgiving, confession or a request for something such as help or somebody's wellbeing. **2. COMMUNICATING WITH GOD OR OTHER BEING** the act or practice of making spoken or unspoken communication with God, a deity, or a saint **3. RELIGIOUS SERVICE WITH PRAYERS** a religious service at which prayers are said (*often used in the plural*) **4. EARNEST REQUEST** an earnest request for something **5. SOMETHING WISHED FOR** something that is wanted or hoped for very much ○ *My only prayer is to see grandchildren before I die.* **6.**

SLIGHT CHANCE a slight chance or hope ○ *I don't have a prayer of getting the manager's job.* **7.** LAW **REQUEST IN PETITION** a request contained in a petition [13thC. Via Old French *preiere* from, ultimately, Latin *precarius* "obtained by entreaty," from *precari* "to entreat" (see PRAY).]

prayer beads *npl.* a string of beads such as a rosary used to keep count of prayers being recited

prayer book *n.* a book containing the prayers regularly used in religious services

prayer·ful /práirf'l/ *adj.* **1. PRAYING FREQUENTLY** liking to pray or praying frequently **2. INFLUENCED BY PRAYER** strongly influenced by prayer, or in which prayer plays an important part **3. EARNEST** earnest or sincere —**prayer·ful·ly** *adv.* —**prayer·ful·ness** *n.*

prayer rug, prayer mat *n.* a rug on which a Muslim kneels to pray

prayer shawl *n.* = **tallith**

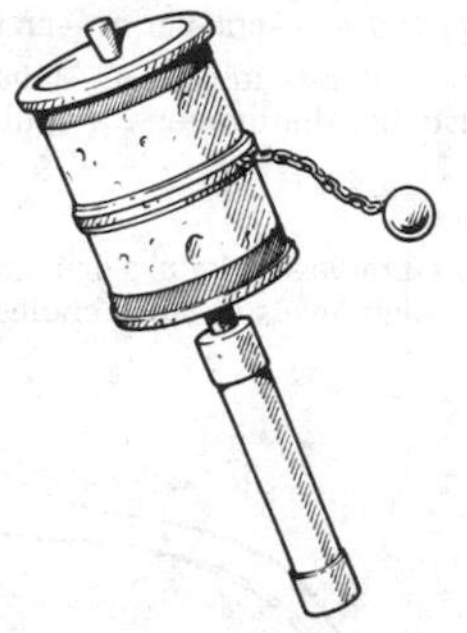

Prayer wheel

prayer wheel *n.* in Tibetan Buddhism and some other religions, a hollow cylinder that contains prayers written on a scroll. It must be turned by hand or machinery to make the prayers effective.

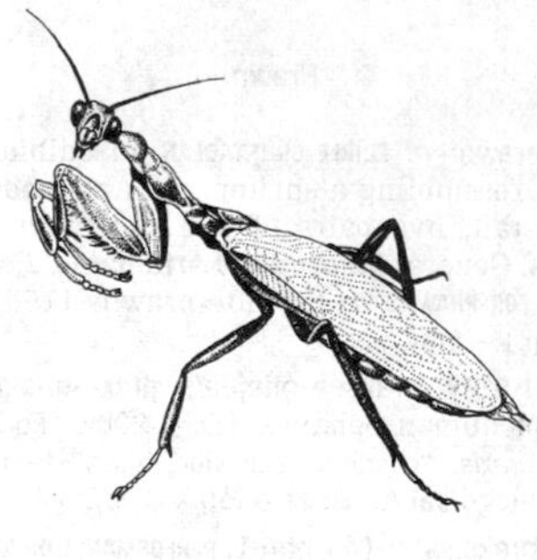

Praying mantis

pray·ing man·tis *n.* a large greenish brown predatory insect originating in Europe, with long forelegs that are raised and folded at rest, as if in prayer. Latin name: *Mantis religiosis.*

PRC *abbr.* People's Republic of China

pre- *prefix.* **1.** before, earlier ○ *preschool* **2.** in advance, preparatory ○ *presell* ○ *prerelease* **3.** in front of ○ *premolar* [From Latin *prae* "in front, before." Ultimately from an Indo-European word which is also the ancestor of English *prior, prime,* and *private.*]

preach /preech/ (**preached, preach·ing, preach·es**) *v.* **1.** *vti.* **GIVE SERMON** to give a talk on a religious or moral subject, especially in church **2.** *vi.* **GIVE ADVICE IN IRRITATING WAY** to give people advice on their morals or behavior in an irritatingly tedious or overbearing way **3.** *vt.* **URGE PEOPLE TO ACCEPT SOMETHING** to make an opinion or attitude known to others and urge others to share it [13thC. Via Old French *prechier* from, ultimately, Latin *praedicare* (see PREDICATE).] —**preach·a·ble** *adj.*

preach·er /préechər/ *n.* (*informal*) **1. MINISTER** somebody whose occupation is to give sermons, preach the gospel, or conduct religious services, especially a minister of a Protestant church **2. SOMEBODY WHO PREACHES** somebody who gives advice in an irritatingly tedious or overbearing way, or who urges others to share a belief or support a cause

preach·i·fy /préechə fī/ *vi.* to preach or give advice on morals or behavior in an irritatingly tedious or overbearing way (*informal*) —**preach·i·fy·ing** *n.*

preach·ment /préechmənt/ *n.* (*informal*) **1. SERMON** a sermon or talk on a moral or religious subject **2. OVERBEARING ADVICE** tedious or overbearing advice on morals or behavior

preach·y /préechee/ *adj.* giving, or in the habit of giving, advice on morals or behavior, especially in an irritatingly tedious or overbearing way (*informal*) —**preach·i·ness** *n.*

pre·ad·am·ite /pree áddə mīt/, **pre-Ad·am·ite** *n.* **1. BELIEVER IN PEOPLE BEFORE ADAM** somebody who believes that there were people living on earth before Adam **2. SOMEBODY LIVING BEFORE ADAM** any of the people believed to have been living on earth before Adam ■ *adj.* **RELATING TO PREADAMITES** relating to the belief or those who believe that people existed on earth before Adam

pre·ad·ap·ta·tion /prèe addap táysh'n/ *n.* anatomical or behavioral feature of an organism that is highly suited to an adjacent habitat, thus allowing for migration and increased survival rate in response to environmental change. The lungs that have developed in some fish were probably originally buoyancy aids, but were preadapted for breathing air. —**pre·a·dapt** /pree ə dápt/ *vti.* —**pre·ad·ap·tive** /-dáptiv/ *adj.* —**pre·a·dapt·ed** /-dáptəd/ *adj.*

pre·ad·o·les·cence /prèe addə léss'ns/ *n.* the period of two or three years before adolescence —**pre·ad·o·les·cent** *n., adj.*

pre·ag·ri·cul·tur·al /pree àggri kúlchərəl/ *adj.* having not yet developed agriculture as a means of providing food. ◊ **hunter-gatherer**

pre·am·ble /prée àmb'l, pree ámb'l/ *n.* **1. INTRODUCTORY EXPLANATION** a section at the beginning of a speech, report, or formal document that explains the purpose of what follows **2. SOMETHING THAT PRECEDES** something that precedes, introduces, or leads up to something else [14thC. Via French *préambule* from, ultimately, Latin *praeambulus,* literally "going in front," from *ambulare* "to walk."]

Pre·am·ble *n.* the introductory section of the United States Constitution, often cited as the best statement of the nation's self-understanding

pre·am·pli·fi·er /pree ámpli fīr/ *n.* an amplifying circuit, e.g., in a radio or television, that is designed to strengthen very weak signals and then transmit them to a more powerful amplifier

pre·ar·range /prèe ə ráynj/ (**-ranged, -rang·ing, -rang·es**) *vt.* to arrange, plan, or agree on something beforehand —**pre·ar·range·ment** *n.*

pre·a·tom·ic /prèe ə tómmik/ *adj.* relating or belonging to the time before atomic energy was developed or atomic weapons existed

preb·end /prébənd/ *n.* **1. PAYMENT TO CATHEDRAL CLERGY** an allowance paid by a cathedral or collegiate church to a member of its clergy, or the property or tithe that is the source of this allowance **2.** = **prebendary** [15thC. Via French from late Latin *praebenda,* literally "things to be supplied" (source of English *provender*), from Latin *praebere* "to offer," literally "to hold in front."] —**pre·ben·dal** *adj.*

preb·en·dar·y /prébbən dèree/ *n.* a member of the clergy of a cathedral or collegiate church, either one who receives an allowance from it or an honorary member who receives no payment —**preb·en·dar·y·ship** /prébbən derree shìp/ *n.*

pre·bi·o·log·i·cal /pree bī ə lójjik'l/ *adj.* relating or belonging to a time in geologic history before the appearance of living organisms

pre·built /pree bílt/ *adj.* made or put together before being taken to the location where it is to be set up ○ *a prebuilt structure*

prec. *abbr.* preceding

pre·cal·cu·lus /pree kálkyə ləss/, **pre·calc** /prée kàlk/ *n.* a course in mathematics taken in preparation for the study of calculus

Pre·cam·bri·an /pree kámbree ən/ *n.* the period of geologic time when the earth's crust consolidated and primitive life first appeared, 4,650 to 700 million years ago —**Pre·cam·bri·an** *adj.*

pre·can·cel /pree káns'l/ *vt.* (**-cel·ed, -cel·ing, -cels**) **CANCEL STAMP BEFORE MAILING** to cancel the postage stamp on an envelope, e.g., before mailing it ■ *n.* **PRECANCELED STAMP** a stamp that has been canceled before mailing, or an item bearing such a stamp —**pre·can·cel·la·tion** /prèe kans'l áysh'n/ *n.*

pre·can·cer·ous /pree kánsərəss/ *adj.* used to describe conditions or tissue abnormalities that are capable of becoming cancerous if left untreated

pre·car·i·ous /prə káiree əss/ *adj.* **1. UNSAFE** dangerously unstable, unsteady, uncertain, or insecure **2. NOT WELL FOUNDED** based on uncertain premises or unwarranted assumptions (*formal*) [Mid-17thC. Formed from Latin *precarius* "depending on entreaty, uncertain."] —**pre·car·i·ous·ly** *adv.* —**pre·car·i·ous·ness** *n.*

pre·cast /pree kást/ *adj.* poured into a cast of the required shape and allowed to harden before being taken out and put into position ○ *precast concrete* —**pre·cast** *vt.*

prec·a·to·ry /prékə tàwree/ *adj.* expressing a wish, a request, an entreaty, or a recommendation (*formal*) [Mid-17thC. From late Latin *precatorius,* from Latin *precari* "to entreat" (see PRAY).]

pre·cau·tion /prə káwsh'n/ *n.* **1. PROTECTION AGAINST POSSIBLE UNDESIRABLE EVENT** an action taken to protect against possible harm or trouble, or to limit the damage if something goes wrong **2. CAUTION TO FORESTALL FUTURE TROUBLE** the foresight to protect against possible harm or trouble [Late 16thC. Via French from, ultimately, Latin *precaut-,* past participle stem of *praecavere,* literally "to take care before," from *cavere* "to take heed" (see CAUTION).] —**pre·cau·tion·al** *adj.* —**pre·cau·tion·ar·y** *adj.* —**pre·cau·tious** *adj.*

pre·cede /prə séed/ (**-ced·ed, -ced·ing, -cedes**) *vt.* **1. COME OR GO BEFORE SOMETHING** to come, go, be, or happen before somebody or something else in time, position, or importance **2. INTRODUCE SOMETHING WITH SOMETHING** to say or do something before something else [14thC. Via French from Latin *praecedere,* literally "to go in front," from *cedere* "to give way."]

prec·e·dence /préssəd'ns/, **prec·e·den·cy** /-d'nsee/ *n.* **1. RELATIVE IMPORTANCE** relative importance in rank and status that determines something, e.g., the order in which participants are placed in a formal situation **2. PRIORITY** the right or need to be dealt with before somebody or something else or to be treated as more important than somebody or something else **3. GREATER IMPORTANCE** the fact of being more important than others (*formal*)

prec·e·dent /préssəd'nt/ *n.* **1. EXAMPLE FOR LATER ACTION OR DECISION** an action or decision that can be subsequently used as an example for a similar decision or to justify a similar action **2. ESTABLISHED PRACTICE** an established custom or practice **3.** LAW **REQUIREMENT TO FOLLOW EARLIER COURT DECISIONS** the doctrine that requires a court to follow decisions of superior or previous courts ■ *adj.* **PRECEDING** coming, going, existing, or happening before somebody or something else (*formal*) —**prec·e·dent·ly** *adv.*

prec·e·den·tial /prèssə dénshəl/ *adj.* (*formal*) **1. RELATING TO OR BEING PRECEDENT** relating to or serving as a precedent **2. MORE IMPORTANT** taking precedence over something or somebody else —**pre·ce·den·tial·ly** *adv.*

pre·ced·ing /prə séeding/ *adj.* coming, going, existing, or happening immediately before somebody or something else

pre·cen·sor /pree sénsər/ (**-sored, -sor·ing, -sors**) *vt.* to lay down rules in advance stating what will or will not be allowed in a publication, broadcast, or other item for public performance or release —**pre·cen·sor·ship** *n.*

pre·cen·tor /prə séntər/ *n.* **1. LEADER OF CHURCH SINGING** somebody who leads the singing of the congregation or choir in a church **2. SOMEBODY IN CHARGE OF CATHEDRAL MUSIC** a member of the clergy of a cathedral who is in charge of the music in the cathedral [Early 17thC. From Latin *praecentor,* from *praecinere,* literally "to sing before," from *canere* "to sing."] —**pre·cen·tor·ship** *n.*

pre·cept /prée sèpt/ *n.* **1. PRINCIPLE** a rule, instruction, or principle that guides somebody's actions, especially one that guides moral behavior (*formal*) **2.** LAW **WARRANT OR WRIT** a warrant or writ that is issued by a legal authority [14thC. From Latin *praeceptum,* literally "something taught," the past participle of *praecipere* "to teach," literally "to take before," from *capere* "to take."]

pre·cep·tive /prə séptiv/ *adj.* giving instructions or orders, or setting out principles (*formal*) —**pre·cep·tive·ly** *adv.*

pre·cep·tor /prə séptər, prée sèptər/ *n.* **1. TEACHER** a teacher or instructor (*formal*) **2. SPECIALIZED TUTOR** a specialist in a profession, especially medicine, who gives practical training to a student **3. HEAD OF PRECEPTORY** the head of a community of Knights Templars —**pre·cep·tor·al** *adj.* —**pre·cep·tor·ate** *n.* —**pre·cep·tor·ship** /prə séptər shìp, prée-/ *n.*

pre·cep·to·ri·al /prèe sep táwree əl, prə sèp-/ *n.* at some colleges, a class consisting of a small group of students who discuss a work of literature or other subject with a professor or instructor ○ *I'm taking a preceptorial on T.S. Eliot next quarter.*

pre·cep·to·ry /prə séptəree/ (*plural* **-ries**) *n.* a community of Knights Templars

pre·cess /prə séss/ (**-cessed, -cess·ing, -cess·es**) *vti.* to spin or make something spin with a motion in which the axis of rotation sweeps out a cone [Late 19thC. Back-formation from PRECESSION.]

pre·ces·sion /prə sésh'n/ *n.* the regular motion of a spinning body such as a spinning top or a planet, in which the axis of rotation sweeps out a cone [Late 16thC. From the late Latin stem *praecession-*, from *praecess-*, the past participle stem of *praecedere* "to go before" (see PRECEDE).] —**pre·ces·sion·al** *adj.*

pre·ces·sion of the e·qui·nox·es *n.* the slow westward movement of the equinoxes, resulting from the Earth's precessional motion, making them occur slightly earlier each year

pre-Chel·li·an /pree shéllee ən/ *adj.* relating to a culture of the Lower Paleolithic period in which crude stone hand axes were used [Early 20thC. Named for *Chelles*, a place in France.]

pre-Chris·tian *adj.* existing or occurring before Jesus Christ or Christianity

pré·cieux /pràv see yő/ *adj.* overly fastidious or affected in dress or manner [Early 18thC. From French, "precious."]

pre·cinct /prée sìngkt/ *n.* **1.** ELECTORAL DISTRICT a small electoral district of a city or town, part of a ward **2.** CITY AREA PATROLLED BY POLICE UNIT a district of a city or town under a particular unit of the police force **3.** POLICE UNIT OR STATION the police unit or police station of a city or town district **4.** *U.K.* SPECIAL PART OF TOWN a part of a town designated for a particular use, especially an area accessible only to pedestrians or a purpose-built area containing many stores ○ *a shopping precinct* **5.** BOUNDARY a boundary marking out an area ■ **pre·cincts** *npl.* AREA AROUND SOMETHING the area surrounding a building or institution such as a cathedral or college [15thC. From medieval Latin *praecinctum*, literally "something encircled," the past participle of Latin *praecingere*, literally "to gird about," from *cingere* "to gird."]

pre·ci·os·i·ty /prèshee áwssətee/ (*plural* **-ties**) *n.* ridiculous overrefinement in language and manners, or an example of this ○ *It might be a good poem if all the preciosities were removed.* [14thC. Via French from, ultimately, Latin *pretiosus* "precious" (see PRECIOUS).]

pre·cious /préshəss/ *adj.* **1.** VALUABLE worth a great deal of money **2.** VALUED highly valued, much loved, or considered to be of great importance ○ *Your friendship is very precious to me.* **3.** NOT TO BE WASTED rare or unique and therefore to be used wisely or sparingly or treated with care **4.** USED FOR EMPHASIS used for emphasis to express irritation, dislike, contempt, bemusement, or some other strong emotion (*informal*) ○ *I'm tempted to tell them what they can do with their precious training course!* **5.** FASTIDIOUS OR AFFECTED too carefully refined in language, dress, and manners ■ *adv.* VERY very, often by way of a complaint ○ *And precious little thanks I got!* ■ *n.* TERM OF ENDEARMENT used as term of affection in talking to somebody ○ *Good morning, my precious.* [13thC. Via Old French *precios* from Latin *pretiosus*, from *pretium* "price."] —**pre·cious·ly** *adv.* —**pre·cious·ness** *n.*

pre·cious cor·al *n.* = **red coral**

pre·cious met·al *n.* the metals gold, silver, or platinum

pre·cious stone *n.* any relatively rare and valuable mineral used in jewelry such as a diamond or ruby

prec·i·pice /préssəpiss/ *n.* **1.** HIGH CLIFF OR CRAG a high, vertical, or very steep rock face **2.** DANGEROUS STATE a very dangerous situation [Late 16thC. Directly or via French from Latin *praecipitium*, from the stem *praecipit-* "headlong" (see PRECIPITATE).] —**prec·i·piced** *adj.*

pre·cip·i·tan·cy /prə síppitənsee/ (*plural* **-cies**), **pre·cip·i·tance** /-təns/ *n.* **1.** RECKLESS HASTE reckless haste or suddenness **2.** HASTY ACTION a reckless, hasty, or impulsive action

pre·cip·i·tant /prə síppitənt/ *n.* CHEM SOMETHING CAUSING PRECIPITATION a substance that causes precipitation ■ *adj.* **1.** TOO HASTY done too quickly and impulsively, often resulting in mistakes **2.** SUDDEN OR UNEXPECTED happening suddenly or unexpectedly **3.** RUSHING acting too quickly [Early 17thC. From French *précipitant*, present participle of *précipiter* (see PRECIPITATE).] —**pre·cip·i·tant·ly** *adv.*

pre·cip·i·tate /prə síppi tàyt/ *v.* (**-tat·ed, -tat·ing, -tates**) **1.** *vt.* MAKE SOMETHING HAPPEN QUICKLY to make something happen suddenly and quickly **2.** *vt.* SEND SOMEBODY OR SOMETHING RAPIDLY to send somebody or something suddenly and rapidly into some state or condition ○ *A minor border skirmish precipitated the two countries into war.* **3.** *vti.* METEOROL MAKE RAIN OR SNOW FALL to cause liquid or solid forms of water, condensed in the atmosphere, to fall to the ground as rain, snow, or hail, or to fall in such a form **4.** *vti.* CHEM SEPARATE SOLID OUT OF SOLUTION to cause a solid to separate out from a solution as a result of a chemical reaction, or to separate out in this way **5.** *vti.* THROW OR FALL FROM ABOVE to throw somebody or something or fall from a great height (*formal*) ■ *adj.* **1.** DONE OR ACTING RASHLY done or acting too quickly and without enough thought ○ *I may have been precipitate in accepting their offer.* **2.** HURRIED very hurried **3.** SUDDEN sudden and unexpected ■ *n.* CHEM SUSPENSION OF SMALL PARTICLES a suspension of small solid particles that are formed in a solution as a result of a chemical reaction and usually settle out of the solution [Early 16thC. From Latin *praecipitat-*, past participle stem of *praecipitare* "to throw down," from *praeceps* "headlong," from *caput* "head."] —**pre·cip·i·ta·bil·i·ty** /prèssə pittə bíllətee/ *n.* —**pre·cip·i·ta·ble** /-síppitəb'l/ *adj.* —**pre·cip·i·tate·ly** /-tətlee/ *adv.* —**pre·cip·i·tate·ness** /-tətnəss/ *n.* —**pre·cip·i·ta·tive** /-tàytiv/ *adj.* —**pre·cip·i·ta·tor** /-tàytər/ *n.*

pre·cip·i·ta·tion /prə sìppi táysh'n/ *n.* **1.** RAIN OR SNOW OR HAIL rain, snow, or hail, all of which are formed by condensation of moisture in the atmosphere and fall to the ground **2.** FORMATION OF RAIN OR SNOW OR HAIL the formation of rain, snow, or hail from moisture in the air **3.** FORMATION OF SUSPENSION IN SOLUTION the formation of a suspension of an insoluble compound by mixing two solutions **4.** HASTE great or excessive haste (*formal*) ○ *He deeply regretted the precipitation of his elopement.* **5.** A QUICKENING OF SOMETHING a bringing about of something earlier or more suddenly than expected (*formal*) ○ *circumstances that led to the precipitation of my divorce* **6.** PROPULSION the propelling or throwing of somebody or something (*formal*)

pre·cip·i·tin /prə síppitin/ *n.* an antibody that, when combined with its antigen, forms a substance that separates out of solution and can be detected visually [Early 20thC. Coined from PRECIPITATE + -IN.]

pre·cip·i·tin·o·gen /prə síppitinəjən/ *n.* an antigen that causes the formation of a specific precipitin. This reaction can be used to identify an unknown antigen. [Early 20thC. Coined from PRECIPITIN + -GEN.]

pre·cip·i·tous /prə síppitəss/ *adj.* **1.** DONE RASHLY done or acting too quickly and without enough thought **2.** LIKE A PRECIPICE very high and steep **3.** WITH A PRECIPICE having several precipices [Mid-17thC. Via French *précipiteux* from, ultimately, Latin *praecipitium* (see PRECIPICE).] —**pre·cip·i·tous·ly** *adv.* —**pre·cip·i·tous·ness** *n.*

pré·cis /práy see, pray sée/ *n.* (*plural* **-cis**) SHORTENED VERSION a shortened version of a speech or written text, containing the main points and omitting minor details ■ *vt.* (**-cised, -cis·ing, -cis**) MAKE SHORTENED VERSION OF SOMETHING to make a précis of something [Mid-18thC. From French, literally "abridged."]

pre·cise /prə síss/ *adj.* **1.** EXACT OR DETAILED exact and accurate, or detailed and specific **2.** CAREFUL ABOUT DETAILS very careful about small details, especially of correct behavior **3.** INDICATING SOMETHING SPECIFIC indicating that something is the exact one that is being referred to ○ *At that precise moment, in he came.* **4.** HANDLING SMALL DETAILS able to assimilate details or wanting to be given details **5.** CLEAR distinct and correct [Early 16thC. Via French from Latin *praecisus*, the past participle of *praecidere*, literally "to cut off in front," from *caedere* "to cut."] —**pre·cise·ness** *n.*

pre·cise·ly /prə sísslee/ *adv.* **1.** EXACTLY exactly ○ *That is precisely what I mean.* **2.** ACCURATELY with absolute accuracy ○ *instruments that must be adjusted precisely before use* **3.** IN DETAIL in complete and accurate detail ○ *Tell me precisely what happened.* **4.** CLEARLY clearly and distinctly ○ *She speaks very precisely.* **5.** USED FOR EMPHASIS used to add emphasis when specifying something ○ *It was precisely because you didn't ask that she thought you didn't need her help.* **6.** EXPRESSING AGREEMENT used to indicate complete agreement with what has been said ○ *"But I don't think they can be relied on." "Precisely."*

pre·ci·sian /prə sízh'n/ *n.* somebody who is very concerned about the observance of rules and correct behavior, especially in matters of morality and religion —**pre·ci·sian·ism** *n.*

pre·ci·sion /prə sízh'n/ *n.* **1.** EXACTNESS exactness or accuracy **2.** MATH MATHEMATICAL ACCURACY the accuracy to which a calculation is performed, specifying the number of significant digits with which the result is expressed ■ *adj.* RELATING TO EXACTNESS OR ACCURACY allowing for, made with, or requiring great exactness or accuracy [Late 16thC. Via French from, ultimately, Latin *praecis-*, the past participle stem of *praecidere* (see PRECISE).]

pre·ci·sion·ist /prə sízh'nist/ *n.* somebody who insists on or strives for absolute precision —**pre·ci·sion·ism** /prə sízh'n ìzzəm/ *n.*

pre·clin·i·cal /pree klínnik'l/ *adj.* relating to or characteristic of a disease before the symptoms become evident —**pre·clin·i·cal·ly** *adv.*

pre·clude /prə klóod/ (**-clud·ed, -clud·ing, -cludes**) *vt.* **1.** PREVENT SOMETHING to prevent something or make it impossible, or to prevent somebody from doing something (*formal*) ○ *That shouldn't preclude a satisfactory outcome.* **2.** DEBAR SOMEBODY to exclude somebody or something, especially in advance ○ *Having a relative in the company precludes me from entering the contest.* [Early 17thC. From Latin *praecludere*, literally "to close off ahead," from *claudere* "to close."] —**pre·clu·sion** /-klóozh'n/ *n.* —**pre·clu·sive** /-klóossiv/ *adj.* —**pre·clu·sive·ly** /-klóossivlee/ *adv.*

pre·co·cial /prə kősh'l/ *adj.* used to describe some animals that display independent activity at birth, especially young birds that are hatched covered with down and with open eyes [Late 19thC. Formed from modern Latin *Praecoces* "the precocial birds," the plural of Latin *praecox* "precocious" (see PRECOCIOUS).]

pre·co·cious /prə kőshəss/ *adj.* **1.** MENTALLY ADVANCED FOR AGE more developed, especially mentally, than is usual or expected at a particular age, or showing such advanced development (*sometimes used disapprovingly*) **2.** BOT BLOSSOMING OR RIPENING EARLY used to describe a plant or tree that blossoms before its leaves appear, e.g., the magnolia, or one whose fruits ripen early [Mid-17thC. Formed from Latin *praecox* "ripening early," literally "cooked ahead," ultimately from *coquere* "to cook."] —**pre·co·cious·ly** *adv.* —**pre·co·cious·ness** /prə kőshəssnəss/ *n.* —**pre·coc·i·ty** /prə kóssətee/ *n.*

pre·cog·ni·tion /pree kog nísh'n/ *n.* the ability to know what is going to happen in the future, especially if based on extrasensory perception —**pre·cog·ni·tive** /pree kógnətiv/ *adj.*

pre-Co·lum·bi·an *adj.* relating to North, Central, or South America before the arrival of Christopher Columbus in 1492

pre·con·ceive /prèe kən sée v/ (**-ceived, -ceiving, -ceives**) *vt.* to form an opinion or idea about somebody or something before enough information or experience is available to make an educated or fair judgment

pre·con·ceived /prèe kən séevd/ *adj.* formed in the mind in advance, especially if based on little or no information or experience and reflecting personal prejudices

pre·con·cep·tion /prèe kən sépshən/ *n.* an idea or opinion formed in advance, especially if it is based on little or no information or experience and reflects personal prejudices

pre·con·cert /pree kónsərt/ (**-cert·ed, -cert·ing, -certs**) *vt.* to agree, arrange, or organize something beforehand (*formal*)

pre·con·di·tion /prèe kən dísh'n/ *n.* SOMETHING THAT MUST BE DONE FIRST something that must be done or agreed before something else will happen ○ *They made a total ceasefire a precondition of the talks.* ■ *vt.* (**-tioned, -tion·ing, -tions**) PREPARE SOMEBODY OR SOMETHING to prepare somebody or something for a process or put somebody into a desired mental state

pre·con·scious /pree kónshəss/ *n.* RECALLABLE THOUGHTS AND FEELINGS in Freudian theory, the part of the mind lying between the conscious and the unconscious. It contains information, thoughts, and feelings that are not present in conscious awareness but can readily be brought into the conscious mind. ■ *adj.* RELATING TO RECALLABLE PART OF MIND relating to or contained in the preconscious —**pre·con·scious·ly** *adv.* —**pre·con·scious·ness** *n.*

pre·cook /pree ko͝ok/ (**-cooked, -cook·ing, -cooks**) *vt.* to cook food completely or partially in advance, especially before it is sold, so that only minimal cooking or merely reheating is required —**pre·cooked** *adj.*

pre·crit·i·cal /pree kríttik'l/ *adj.* relating to the time or state before a crisis or before something such as a disease reaches a critical condition

pre·cur·sive *adj.* = **precursory**

pre·cur·sor /pree kùrsər/ *n.* **1.** SOMEBODY OR SOMETHING THAT COMES EARLIER somebody or something that comes before, and is often considered to lead to the development of, another person or thing **2.** PREVIOUS HOLDER OF JOB somebody who has held a particular position before somebody else **3.** CHEM CHEMICAL COMPOUND PRECEDING ANOTHER a chemical compound that leads to another, usually more stable, product in a series of connected reactions [Early 16thC. From Latin *praecursor*, from *praecurs-*, the stem of *praecurrere*, literally "to run before," from *currere* "to run."]

pre·cur·so·ry /prə kúrsəree, pree-/, **pre·cur·sive** /-kúrsiv/ *adj.* **1.** AT INITIAL STAGE at an initial or preparatory stage **2.** INDICATING SOMETHING TO COME serving as an indication of something to come (*formal*)

pred. *abbr.* LOGIC, GRAM predicate

pre·da·cious /prə dáyshəss/, **pre·da·ceous** *adj.* **1.** PREDATORY used to describe animals that hunt, kill, and eat other animals **2.** ATTACKING OTHERS attacking and stealing from other people (*formal*) [Early 18thC. Formed from Latin *praedari* "to seize as plunder" (see PREDATORY).] —**pre·da·cious·ness** *n.* —**pre·dac·i·ty** /prə dássətee/ *n.*

pre·date /pree dáyt/ (**-dat·ed, -dat·ing, -dates**) *vt.* **1.** PUT EARLY DATE ON SOMETHING to put a date on something, especially a check or a contract, that is earlier than the actual date, or to say that something occurred at an earlier date than it actually did **2.** EXIST EARLIER THAN SOMETHING OR SOMEBODY to come before something or somebody in time

pre·da·tion /prə dáysh'n/ *n.* **1.** PREYING OF ONE SPECIES ON ANOTHER the relationship between two groups of animals in which one species hunts, kills, and eats the other **2.** PLUNDERING the act of plundering, stealing, or destroying [15thC. From the Latin stem *praedation-*, from *praedari* "to seize as plunder" (see PREDATORY).]

pred·a·tor /préddətər/ *n.* **1.** CARNIVOROUS ANIMAL OR DESTRUCTIVE ORGANISM a carnivorous animal that hunts, kills, and eats other animals in order to survive, or any other organism that behaves in a similar manner **2.** SOMEBODY WHO PLUNDERS OR DESTROYS a person, group, company, or state that steals from others or destroys others for gain **3.** RUTHLESSLY AGGRESSIVE PERSON somebody who is extremely aggressive, determined, or persistent (*disapproving*) [Early 20thC. From Latin *praedator*, from *praedari* "to seize as plunder" (see PREDATORY).]

pred·a·to·ry /préddə tàwree/ *adj.* **1.** GREEDILY DESTRUCTIVE greedily eager to steal from or destroy others for gain **2.** RELATING TO PREDATORS relating to or characteristic of animals that survive by preying on others **3.** RUTHLESSLY AGGRESSIVE extremely aggressive, determined, or persistent (*disapproving*) [Late 16thC. From Latin *praedatorius*, from *praedari* "to seize as plunder," from *praeda* "booty" (source of English *prey, spree,* and *osprey*).] —**pred·a·to·ri·ly** /prèddə táwrilee/ *adv.* —**pred·a·to·ri·ness** /-táwreenəss/ *n.*

pred·a·to·ry pric·ing *n.* the act of setting prices at very low levels in order to force other companies out of the market

pre·de·cease /preè di seéss/ (**-ceased, -ceas·ing, -ceas·es**) *vt.* to die before somebody else (*formal*) ○ *His eldest son predeceased him.* —**pre·de·cease** *n.*

pred·e·ces·sor /préddə sèssər, preédə-/ *n.* **1.** PREVIOUS HOLDER OF JOB somebody who held a particular position or job before somebody else **2.** SOMETHING REPLACED BY SOMETHING ELSE something previously in use or existence that has been replaced or succeeded by something else **3.** ANCESTOR an ancestor (*old*) [14thC. Via French from late Latin *praedecessor*, literally "one who has departed before," from *decedere* "to depart."]

pre·del·la /prə déllə/ *n.* **1.** ALTAR PLATFORM the platform for an altar, or the step on which an altar rests **2.** DECORATED BASE OF ALTARPIECE the decorative base of an altarpiece, embellished with small paintings or sculptures [Mid-19thC. From Italian, "stool."]

pre·des·ti·nar·i·an /preè destə nérree ən/ *n.* BELIEVER IN PREDESTINATION somebody who believes in predestination ■ *adj.* RELATING TO PREDESTINATION relating to predestination or to people who believe in it —**pre·des·ti·nar·i·an·ism** *n.*

pre·des·ti·nate /pree déstə nàyt/ *vt.* (**-nat·ed, -nat·ing, -nates**) PREDESTINE to predestine something or somebody ■ *adj.* **1.** FOREORDAINED decided in advance **2.** FOREORDAINED BY GOD OR A DEITY decided and decreed by in advance by God, a deity, or fate [14thC. From ecclesiastical Latin *praedestinatus*, the past participle of *praedestinare* (see PREDESTINE).]

pre·des·ti·na·tion /preè destə náysh'n/ *n.* **1.** ADVANCE DECISION BY GOD ABOUT EVENTS the doctrine holding that God, a deity, or fate has established in advance everything that is going to happen and that nothing can change this course of events **2.** GOD'S DECISION WHO GOES TO HEAVEN the doctrine that God decided at the beginning of time who would go to Heaven after death and who would not **3.** FOREORDAINING the divine or human act of deciding the fate of people or things beforehand

pre·des·tine /pree déstin/ (**-tined, -tin·ing, -tines**) *vt.* **1.** FOREORDAIN EVENTS to decide in advance what is going to happen **2.** PRESELECT WHO WILL GO TO HEAVEN to select in advance who will go to Heaven after death and who will not [14thC. Directly or via French from ecclesiastical Latin *praedestinare*, literally "to foreordain," from Latin *destinare* "to decree."] —**pre·des·tin·able** *adj.*

pre·de·ter·mi·nate /preè də túrmənət/ *adj.* decided in advance (*formal*) —**pre·de·ter·mi·nate·ly** *adv.*

pre·de·ter·mine /preè də túrmən/ (**-mined, -min·ing, -mines**) *vt.* **1.** ARRANGE IN ADVANCE to decide, agree, or arrange something in advance **2.** INCLINE SOMEBODY TOWARD OPINION OR ACTION to make somebody inclined in advance toward a particular opinion or course of action —**pre·de·ter·mi·na·tion** /preèdə tùrmə náysh'n/ *n.* —**pre·de·ter·mi·na·tive** /preè də túrmə nàytiv/ *adj.*

pre·de·ter·min·er /preè də túrmənər/ *n.* a word that precedes and qualifies another determiner, as "both" does in "both my hands"

pre·di·al *adj.* = **praedial**

pred·i·ca·ble /préddikəb'l/ *adj.* ABLE TO BE ASSERTED able to be stated, or able to be said about somebody or something (*formal*) ■ *n.* QUALITY THAT DESCRIBES SOMETHING a quality or attribute by which somebody or something can be described (*formal*) [Mid-16thC. From medieval Latin *praedicabilis*, from Latin *praedicare* (see PREDICATE).] —**pred·i·ca·bil·i·ty** /prèddikə bíllətee/ *n.*— **pred·i·ca·ble·ness** *n.*

pre·dic·a·ment /prə díkəmənt/ *n.* **1.** DIFFICULT SITUATION a difficult, unpleasant, or embarrassing situation from which there is no clear or easy way out **2.** LOGIC CATEGORY any category or class that can be assigned to something [14thC. From late Latin *praedicamentum* "class, category" (translation of Greek *katēgoria*), from Latin *praedicare* "to proclaim" (see PREDICATE).]

pred·i·cant /préddikənt/ *adj.* RELATING TO PREACHING relating to or involved in preaching (*formal*) ■ *n.* PREACHING FRIAR a member of a religious order, especially the Dominicans, that has a particular commitment to preaching [Late 16thC. From Latin *praedicant-*, present participle stem of *praedicare* "to preach" (see PREDICATE).]

pred·i·cate *n.* /préddikət/ **1.** GRAM PART OF SENTENCE EXCLUDING SUBJECT a word or combination of words, including the verb, objects, or phrases governed by the verb that make up one of the two main parts of a sentence **2.** LOGIC EVERYTHING IN SENTENCE EXCLUDING NAMES everything in a simple sentence other than names, e.g., "runs" in "Fred runs" and "is taller than" in "Fred is taller than Ginger" **3.** LOGIC SOMETHING AFFIRMED OR DENIED that which is affirmed or denied about something ■ *vt.* /préddi kàyt/ (**-cat·ed, -cat·ing, -cates**) **1.** BASE SOMETHING ON SOMETHING to base an opinion, an action, or a result on something (*formal*) ○ *predicated on reason* **2.** STATE SOMETHING to state or assert something (*formal*) **3.** IMPLY SOMETHING to imply something (*formal*) **4.** LOGIC ASSERT SOMETHING ABOUT SUBJECT OF STATEMENT to assert or affirm something about the subject of a statement **5.** LOGIC MAKE EXPRESSION PREDICATE OF STATEMENT to make an expression or term the predicate of a statement [Mid-16thC. From late Latin *praedicatum*, from the past participle of Latin *praedicare* "to declare publicly," literally "to declare before," from *dicare* "to state."] —**pred·i·ca·tion** /prèddi káysh'n/ *n.* —**pred·i·ca·tive** /préddi kàytiv/ *adj.*

pred·i·cate cal·cu·lus *n.* the branch of symbolic logic that uses symbols to explore relationships between and within propositions

pred·i·cate nom·i·na·tive *n.* a noun or pronoun that completes the meaning of a sentence containing a linking verb, such as "you" in the sentence "Is that you?"

pred·i·ca·to·ry /préddikə tàwree/ *adj.* relating to or characteristic of a preacher or preaching (*formal*) [Early 17thC. From late Latin *praedicatorius*, from Latin *praedicare* "to proclaim, teach" (see PREDICATE).]

pre·dict /prə díkt/ (**-dict·ed, -dict·ing, -dicts**) *vti.* to say what is going to happen in the future, often on the basis of present indications or past experience [Mid-16thC. From Latin *praedict-*, the past participle stem of *praedicere*, literally "to say in advance," from *dicere* "to say."] —**pre·dic·tor** *n.*

pre·dict·a·ble /prə díktəb'l/ *adj.* **1.** HAPPENING AS EXPECTED happening or turning out in the way that might have been expected or predicted **2.** SELDOM UNEXPECTED rarely or never being or doing anything unusual or unexpected —**pre·dict·a·bil·i·ty** /prə diktə bíllətee/ *n.* —**pre·dict·a·ble·ness** /-díktəb'lnəss/ *n.* —**pre·dict·a·bly** /-díktəblee/ *adv.*

pre·dic·tion /prə díkshən/ *n.* **1.** STATEMENT ABOUT FUTURE a statement of what someone thinks will happen in the future **2.** ACT OF PREDICTING the making of a statement or forming of an opinion about what will happen in the future —**pre·dic·tive** *adj.* —**pre·dic·tive·ly** *adv.* —**pre·dic·tive·ness** *n.*

pre·di·gest /preè dī jést, -di-/ (**-gest·ed, -gest·ing, -gests**) *vt.* **1.** MAKE FOOD MORE DIGESTIBLE to treat food with chemicals or enzymes so that it is more easily digested, especially for people with digestion problems **2.** SIMPLIFY SOMETHING to produce information in a simplified form so that it is easy to understand —**pre·di·ges·tion** /preè dī jésch'n, -di-/ *n.*

pred·i·lec·tion /prèdd'l ékshən/ *n.* a particular liking or preference for something (*formal*) [Mid-18thC. Via French from, ultimately, medieval Latin *praediligere*, literally "to love first," from Latin *diligere* "to love."]

pre·dis·pose /preèdi spṓz/ (**-posed, -pos·ing, -pos·es**) *vt.* **1.** MAKE SOMEBODY FAVORABLE to make somebody feel favorably about somebody or something in advance (*formal*) **2.** MAKE SOMEBODY LIABLE TO SOMETHING to make somebody liable or inclined to do something, e.g., catch an illness or behave in a particular way (*formal*) ○ *Her fair skin predisposes her to sunburn.* **3.** LAW DISPOSE OF SOMETHING AHEAD OF TIME to dispose of something, e.g., property, in advance (*archaic*) —**pre·dis·pos·al** *n.*

pre·dis·po·si·tion /preè dispə zísh'n/ *n.* **1.** MED TENDENCY TO DEVELOP DISEASE a susceptibility to a disease, arising from a hereditary or another factor **2.** LIABILITY TO SOMETHING a liability or tendency to do something, e.g., behave in a particular way **3.** FAVORABLE ATTITUDE OR INCLINATION a favorable attitude toward somebody or something or an inclination to do something

pred·nis·o·lone /pred níssə lṑn/ *n.* a synthetic steroid hormone, similar to cortisone, used to treat allergies and suppress inflammatory diseases such as rheumatoid arthritis [Mid-20thC. Blend of PREDNISONE and -OL.]

pred·ni·sone /préddnə sṑn/ *n.* a synthetic steroid hormone produced from cortisone and used to treat allergies and autoimmune diseases [Mid-20thC. Coined from *pregnane* + DIENE + CORTISONE.]

pre·doc·tor·al /pree dóktərəl/ *adj.* **1.** OF NONDOCTORAL DEGREE relating to any degree other than a doctorate **2.** LEADING TO A PH.D. relating to or involving research or studies that will lead to a doctoral degree

pre·dom·i·nance /prə dómmənəns/, **pre·dom·i·nan·cy** /-nənsee/ *n.* **1.** SUPERIORITY greater or greatest importance, power, or influence **2.** MAJORITY the state of being the commonest or greatest in number or amount

pre·dom·i·nant /prə dómmənənt/ *adj.* **1.** MOST COMMON most common or greatest in number or amount **2.** MOST IMPORTANT most important, powerful, or influential

pre·dom·i·nant·ly /prə dómmənəntlee/ *adv.* in the greatest number or amount

pre·dom·i·nate (-nat·ed, -nat·ing) *v.* /prə dómmə nàyt/ 1. *vi.* BE IN MAJORITY to be the most common or greatest in number or amount 2. *vi.* BE MORE IMPORTANT to have greater importance, power, or influence than others 3. *vt.* DOMINATE SOMEBODY OR SOMETHING to dominate or control somebody or something [Late 16thC. From medieval Latin *predominat-*, the past participle stem of *predominari*, literally "to rule over," from Latin *dominari* "to rule."] —**pre·dom·i·nate·ly** /prə dómmənətlee/ *adv.* —**pre·dom·i·na·tion** /prə dòmmə náysh'n/ *n.* —**pre·dom·i·na·tor** /prə dómmə nàytər/ *n.*

pre·e·clamp·si·a /prèe i klámpsee ə, -klámsee ə/ *n.* a potentially dangerous condition that may develop in late pregnancy and may lead to convulsions if not treated. Symptoms are high blood pressure, fluid retention, abnormal weight gain, and the presence of protein in the urine. [Early 20thC. Coined from PRE- + ECLAMPSIA.]

pre·em·bry·o /pree émbree ò/ *n.* a fertilized ovum before implantation in the womb and before differentiation of embryonic tissue —**pre·em·bry·on·ic** /prèe embree ónnik/ *adj.*

pree·mie /préemee/, **pre·mie** *n.* a premature baby born before it is fully developed, usually before 35 weeks of gestation [Early 20thC. From shortening of PREMATURE.]

pre·em·i·nent /pree émminənt/ *adj.* standing out among all others because of superiority in a particular field or activity [15thC. From Latin *praeeminent-*, the present participle stem of *praeeminere*, literally "to stand out in front," from *eminere* "to stand out."] —**pre-·em·i·nence** *n.* —**pre-·em·i·nent·ly** *adv.*

pre·empt /pree émpt/ *v.* (-empt·ed, -empt·ing, -empts) 1. *vt.* ACT TO PREVENT SOMETHING to do something that makes it pointless or impossible for somebody else to do what he or she intended 2. *vt.* OCCUPY SOMETHING to occupy land in order to have the right to buy it later 3. *vt.* REPLACE SOMETHING to take the place of something, especially of something less important 4. *vi.* BRIDGE MAKE BRIDGE BID THAT BLOCKS OTHERS to make a bid so high that it discourages further bidding ■ *n.* BRIDGE PREEMPTIVE BID a preemptive bid in bridge [Mid-19thC. Back-formation from PREEMPTION.] —**pre·emp·tor** *n.* —**pre·emp·to·ry** *adj.*

pre·emp·tion /pree émpshən/ *n.* 1. ACTION PREVENTING SOMETHING action that makes it pointless or impossible for somebody else to do what he or she intended 2. OCCUPATION OF PUBLIC LAND the occupation of public land in order to have the right to buy it later, or the right to buy that is gained in this way 3. OPTION TO BUY PROPERTY an option to purchase property if and when it is put up for sale 4. STRATEGY OF FIRST ATTACK the strategy of attacking an enemy in order to prevent that enemy from attacking first 5. LAW EXCLUSION OF STATE ACTION the doctrine that prohibits a state from enacting laws in an area if the U.S. federal government has passed laws in that area (*formal*) [Early 17thC. From the medieval Latin stem *praeemption-*, ultimately from *praeemere*, literally "to buy first," from Latin *emere* "to buy."]

pre·emp·tive /pree émptiv/ *adj.* 1. DONE BEFORE OTHERS CAN ACT done before somebody else has had an opportunity to act so making his or her planned action pointless or impossible 2. MIL INTENDED TO PREVENT ATTACK intended to eliminate or lessen an enemy's capacity to attack ○ *a preemptive strike* 3. BRIDGE DISCOURAGING FURTHER BIDDING so high a bid that it discourages further bidding [Late 18thC] —**pre·emp·tive·ly** *adv.*

pre·emp·tive right *n.* a right to be offered first refusal in selling or buying an asset

preen[1] /preen/ (**preened, preen·ing, preens**) *vti.* 1. GROOM FEATHERS WITH BEAK to clean, smooth, or arrange the feathers with the beak ○ *swans preening their feathers* 2. GROOM FUR WITH TONGUE to clean and smooth the fur by licking it ○ *The cat was quietly preening on the windowsill.* 3. CARE FOR PERSONAL APPEARANCE to spend a long or excessive time attending to personal appearance, especially making small finishing touches to the hair, the face, or clothes ○ *busy preening in front of the mirror* 4. SHOW SELF-SATISFACTION to feel excessively self-satisfied and display that feeling by gloating (*disapproving*) ○ *He preens himself on his ability to deflect criticism.* [15thC. Origin uncertain: probably from Old French *proignier* "to prune."] —**preen·er** *n.*

preen[2] /preen/ *n.* a decorative pin or brooch [Old English *préon*, from a prehistoric Germanic word]

pre·en·gi·neered /prèe enji néerd/ *adj.* constructed using prefabricated parts

pre·es·tab·lish /prèe i stábblish/ (**-lished, -lish·ing, -lish·es**) *vt.* to set up, decide, or arrange something in advance

pre·ex·il·i·an /prèe ig zíllee ən/, **pre·ex·il·i·an** *adj.* relating to the Jewish people before their exile to Babylon in the sixth century B.C.

pre·ex·ist /prèe ig zíst/ (**-ist·ed, -ist·ing, -ists**) *vti.* to exist before another person, group, thing, or event

pre·ex·is·tence /prèe ig zístəns/ *n.* the existence of something at an earlier time and often in a different state —**pre·ex·is·tent** *adj.*

pref. *abbr.* 1. preface 2. prefatory 3. preference 4. preferred 5. prefix

pre·fab /prèe fàb/ *adj.* MANUFACTURED IN SECTIONS relating to or constructed from prefabricated parts (*informal*) ■ *n.* SOMETHING PREFABRICATED a prefabricated house or building (*informal*) [Mid-20thC. Shortening.]

pre·fab·ri·cate /pree fábbrə kàyt/ (**-cat·ed, -cat·ing, -cates**) *vt.* 1. PRODUCE IN SECTIONS to manufacture sections of something, especially a building, that can be transported to a site and assembled there easily 2. PRODUCE IN STANDARDIZED FORM to produce something in an unoriginal or standardized way —**pre·fab·ri·ca·tion** /pree fabbrə káysh'n/ *n.* —**pre·fab·ri·ca·tor** /pree fábbrə kàytər/ *n.*

pref·ace /préffəss/ *n.* 1. INTRODUCTORY PART OF TEXT an introductory section at the beginning of a book or speech that comments on aspects of the text such as the writer's intentions ○ *in the preface to the second edition* 2. PRELIMINARY ACTION an action or thing that precedes something more important 3. **pref·ace, Pref·ace** CHR PRAYER TO GOD a prayer said by a priest during Mass, especially the prayer that begins "Lift up your hearts" 4. **pref·ace, Pref·ace** CHR PRAYER FOR SPECIFIC PURPOSE in the Roman Catholic Church, any one of a number of prayers used for particular purposes ■ *vt.* (**-aced, -ac·ing, -ac·es**) 1. INTRODUCE WITH PREFACE to introduce an action, speech, or piece of writing with something ○ *He prefaced his remarks with an apology.* 2. SERVE AS INTRODUCTION TO to act as a preface to an action, speech, or piece of writing [14thC. Via French from, ultimately, Latin *praefatus*, the past participle of *praefari* "to say before," from *fari* "to speak."] —**pref·ac·er** *n.*

pre·fad·ed /pree fáydəd/ *adj.* given an artificially faded, worn, or old appearance ○ *prefaded denim*

pref·a·to·ry /préffə tàwree/ *adj.* serving to introduce something else such as a main body of text or a speech ○ *prefatory remarks introducing the Vice President* [Late 17thC. Formed from Latin *praefatus*, the past participle of *praefari* (see PREFACE).] —**pref·a·to·ri·ly** /prèffə táwrilee/ *adv.*

pre·fect /prée fèkt/ *n.* 1. EDUC STUDENT ASSISTING WITH DISCIPLINE a student who is given some authority over other pupils in matters of discipline in a private school 2. PUBLIC ADMIN HIGH-RANKING ADMINISTRATIVE OFFICIAL the highest official in an administrative district (**department**) or former territorial possession of France, or in an administrative region of Italy 3. FRENCH CHIEF OF POLICE the head of a French police force, especially in Paris 4. HIST ROMAN MAGISTRATE OR COMMANDER a senior administrative or military official in ancient Rome 5. CHR SENIOR MASTER AT JESUIT SCHOOL a senior master or administrator with special responsibilities at a Jesuit school or college [14thC. Via Old French from Latin *praefectus* "overseer," the past participle of *praeficere* "to set over," from *facere* "to make."] —**pre·fec·to·ri·al** /prèe fek táwree əl/ *adj.*

pre·fec·ture /prée fèkchər/ *n.* 1. PREFECT'S JURISDICTION the district over which a prefect has jurisdiction 2. OFFICE OF PREFECT the office or authority of a prefect —**pre·fec·tur·al** /pree fékchərəl/ *adj.*

pre·fer /pri fúr/ (**-ferred, -fer·ring, -fers**) *vt.* 1. LIKE BETTER THAN SOMETHING ELSE to like or want one thing more than another ○ *I prefer tea to coffee.* 2. LAW LAY BEFORE COURT to make a charge against somebody by submitting details of the alleged offense to a court, magistrate, or judge for examination, or to prosecute such a charge ○ *prefer charges* 3. LAW GIVE PRIORITY TO to give priority to one person, especially a creditor, over others 4. PROMOTE to promote somebody to a higher position or rank (*archaic*) [14thC. Via French *préferer* from Latin *praeferre*, from *prae-* "before, in front" (see PRE-) + *ferre* "to carry, bear."] —**pre·fer·rer** *n.*

pref·er·a·ble /préffərəb'l/ *adj.* more likely to be enjoyable, useful, or desired than something else —**pref·er·a·bil·i·ty** /prèffərə bíllətee/ *n.* —**pref·er·a·ble·ness** /préffərəb'lnəss/ *n.*

pref·er·a·bly /préffərəblee/ *adv.* used to specify more exactly what is required or desired ○ *Plan to arrive early, preferably before the rush hour.*

pref·er·ence /préffərəns/ *n.* 1. SELECTION OF SOMEBODY OR SOMETHING the view that a particular person, object, or course of action is more desirable than another, or a choice based on such a view ○ *The judges showed a marked preference for representational art* 2. RIGHT TO EXPRESS CHOICE the right or opportunity to choose a person, object, or course of action that is considered more desirable than another ○ *We exercised our preference.* 3. SOMEBODY OR SOMETHING PREFERRED a person, object, or course of action that is more desirable than another, or the state of being that desirable choice ○ *State your preferences clearly.* 4. LAW PRIORITY OF ONE CREDITOR OVER OTHERS priority given to a particular creditor, e.g., when a debtor goes bankrupt, or the right of a particular creditor to receive payment before others 5. COMM FAVORITISM IN INTERNATIONAL TRADE priority given to a particular country or group of countries in international trade

pref·er·ence shares *npl.* *U.K.* = **preferred stock**

pref·er·en·tial /prèffə rénshəl/ *adj.* 1. SHOWING FAVORITISM giving advantage or priority to a particular person or group ○ *preferential treatment* 2. COMM SHOWING FAVORITISM IN INTERNATIONAL TRADE giving advantage or priority to a particular country or group of countries in international trade —**pref·er·en·tial·ism** *n.* —**pref·er·en·tial·ist** *adj.* —**pref·er·en·tial·i·ty** /prèffə renshee állətee/ *n.* —**pref·er·en·tial·ly** /-rénshəlee/ *adv.*

pref·er·en·tial vot·ing *n.* an electoral system used in some countries, e.g., Australia, in which voters indicate their chosen candidates in order of preference

pre·fer·ment /pri fúrmənt/ *n.* (*formal*) 1. PROMOTION appointment to a higher position or rank 2. HIGH-RANKING POSITION an office, appointment, or position of high rank or honor, especially one that brings social advancement or financial reward

pre·ferred pro·vid·er or·gan·i·za·tion *n.* an organization providing approved health care under contract with an insurance agency

pre·ferred stock *n.* an equity stock that pays a fixed dividend and has no voting privileges

pre·fig·ur·a·tion /pri figgyə ráysh'n/ *n.* 1. INDICATION OF FUTURE PERSON OR THING a representation, often in form or likeness, of a person, thing, or event that is to come 2. SOMETHING REPRESENTING FUTURE PERSON OR THING somebody or something that represents, often in form or likeness, a person, thing, or event that is to come

pre·fig·ure /pree fíggyər/ (**-ured, -ur·ing, -ures**) *vt.* 1. INDICATE FUTURE EXISTENCE OF to represent or suggest, often in form or likeness, a person, thing, or event that will come later ○ *designs that prefigured modern architecture* 2. THINK ABOUT BEFOREHAND to think about or imagine a person, thing, or event in advance [15thC. From ecclesiastical Latin *praefigurare*, literally "to depict beforehand," from Latin *figura* "figure."] —**pre·fig·ur·a·tive** /pri fíggyərətiv/ *adj.* —**pre·fig·ur·a·tive·ly** *adv.* —**pre·fig·ur·a·tive·ness** *n.* —**pre·fig·ure·ment** /pree fíggyərmənt/ *n.*

pre·fix /prée fiks/ *n.* 1. GRAM WORD ELEMENT BEGINNING VARIOUS WORDS a linguistic element that is not an independent word but is attached to the beginning of words to modify their meaning. For example, "un-" is a prefix meaning "not." 2. TITLE a title before somebody's name ○ *the prefix "The Honorable" before a judge's full name* 3. SOMETHING PRECEDING SOMETHING ELSE something that comes before something else, e.g., a fixed group of digits at the beginning of a telephone number ■ *vt.* (**-fixed, -fix·ing, -fix·es**) 1. PUT BEFORE SOMETHING to place something in front of something else ○ *You must prefix the number with the area code.* 2. INTRODUCE WITH SOMETHING to say or do something by way of introduction ○ *His requests for money were usually prefixed by an apology.* 3. GRAM ADD PREFIX TO to attach a prefix at the beginning of a word to alter its meaning 4. ARRANGE IN ADVANCE to decide on something such as a price, date, or meeting place beforehand ○ *They duly arrived at the prefixed hour.* [15thC. Via French from Latin *praefixus*, *praefixum*, the past participle of Latin *praefigere* "to fix in front," from *figere* "to fasten."] —**pre·fix·al** /pree fíksəl/ *adj.* —**pre·fix·al·ly** *adv.* —**pre·fix·a·tion** /prèe fik sáysh'n/ *n.* —**pre·fix·ion** /pree fíkshən/ *n.*

pre·flight /pree flīt/ *adj.* **CARRIED OUT BEFORE TAKEOFF** occurring before an aircraft takes off ○ *The fault was discovered during a preflight check.* ■ *vt.* (**-flight·ed, -flight·ing, -flights**) **TO CHECK TO DETERMINE AIRWORTHINESS** to carry out a technical inspection of an aircraft before it takes off to ensure that it is airworthy ■ *n.* **PREFLIGHT CHECK** the set of procedures and checks that pilots and ground crew are required to carry out before an aircraft's takeoff ○ *During the preflight, the pilot discovered a problem in the landing gear.*

pre·form /pree fáwrm/ (**-formed, -form·ing, -forms**) *vt.* **1. FORM BEFOREHAND** to shape or form something beforehand **2. GIVE INITIAL SHAPE** to give something a preliminary shape [Early 17thC. From Latin *praeformare.*]

pre·for·ma·tion /prèe fawr máysh'n/ *n.* the preliminary shaping or forming of something beforehand

pre·for·ma·tion the·o·ry *n.* the obsolete theory that sperm and egg cells (**gametes**) contain miniature adults that grow during development

pre·fron·tal /pree frúnt'l/ *adj.* **1. AT VERY FRONT OF BRAIN** relating to or situated in the foremost part of the brain **2. ANTERIOR TO FRONTAL BONE** located in front of the frontal bone

pre·fron·tal lobe *n.* the area of the brain at the very front of each of the two cerebral hemispheres. The prefrontal lobes are concerned with the functions of learning, behavior, and the emotions.

pre·fron·tal lo·bot·o·my *n.* a surgical operation in which the nerves connecting the front part of the brain (**prefrontal lobe**) to the thalamus are severed. Prefrontal lobotomy was a method of reducing severe emotional disturbances, but the operation had serious side effects.

pre·gan·gli·on·ic /prèe gàng glee ónnik/ *adj.* used to describe fibers in a nerve pathway that end in a cluster of nerve cell bodies (**ganglion**), continuing on to muscles or organs

preg·gers /préggərz/ *adj. U.K.* pregnant (*informal*) [Mid-20thC. Alteration of PREGNANT.]

pre·gla·cial /pree gláysh'l/ *adj.* formed or occurring before a glacial period, especially the period that began about a million years ago (**Pleistocene epoch**), when the surface of the earth was covered with ice

preg·na·ble /prégnəb'l/ *adj.* able to be captured or attacked [15thC. Via Old French from, ultimately, Latin *prehendere* (see PREHENSION).] —**preg·na·bil·i·ty** /prègnə bíllətee/ *n.*

preg·nan·cy /prégnənsee/ (*plural* **-cies**) *n.* **1. CONDITION OF BEING PREGNANT** the physical condition of a woman or female animal carrying unborn offspring inside her body, from fertilization to birth. Technical name **cyesis 2. INSTANCE OF BEING PREGNANT** an individual occurrence or experience of being pregnant. Technical name **cyesis 3. TIME OF CARRYING UNBORN OFFSPRING** the period during which a woman or female animal carries an unborn offspring inside her body, from fertilization to birth. Technical name **cyesis 4. SIGNIFICANCE** importance or fullness of meaning ○ *the pregnancy of his words*

preg·nant /prégnənt/ *adj.* **1.** BIOL **CARRYING OFFSPRING WITHIN THE BODY** carrying unborn offspring inside the body **2. SIGNIFICANT** full of meaning or importance ○ *After a pregnant pause, the general began briefing the media on the surprise attack.* **3. FULL OF SOMETHING** pervaded by something, usually something intangible ○ *The tense, quiet operations center was pregnant with anxiety and dread.* **4. CREATIVE** full of creative power ○ *the child's pregnant imagination* **5. PRODUCTIVE** producing a lot of useful results ○ *It was a pregnant endeavor, yielding much experience, information, and help.* [15thC. Via Old French *preigne* from, ultimately, Latin *praegnas* "before birth," from *prae-* "before" + *gnatus* "born" (source of English *native*).] —**preg·nant·ly** *adv.*

pre·heat /pree hēet/ (**-heat·ed, -heat·ing, -heats**) *vt.* to heat an oven, dish, or other item before using it ○ *Preheat the oven to 350 degrees Fahrenheit.*

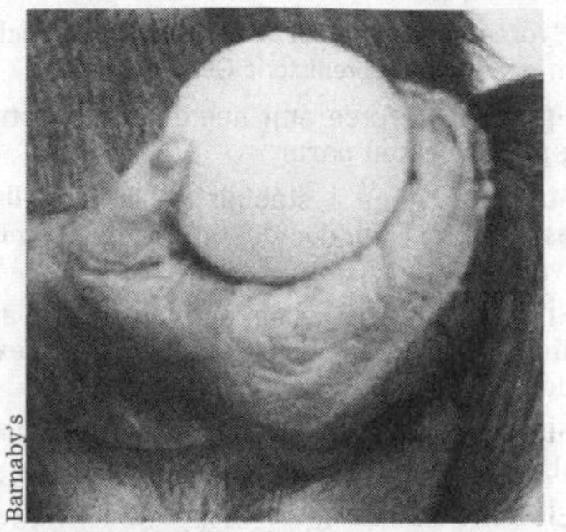

Prehensile: Chimpanzee grasping a ball

pre·hen·sile /pri héns'l/ *adj.* **1.** ZOOL **ABLE TO GRASP SOMETHING** able to take hold of things, especially by wrapping around them ○ *The monkey has a prehensile tail.* **2. QUICK TO UNDERSTAND** skilled at grasping ideas and concepts **3. AGGRESSIVELY EAGER** excessively eager for gain or profit [Late 18thC. Via French from, ultimately, Latin *prehendere* (see PREHENSION).] —**pre·hen·sil·i·ty** /prèe hen síllətee/ *n.*

WORD KEY: ORIGIN

The Latin word *prehendere*, from which ***prehensile*** is derived, is also the source of English *apprehend, apprentice, comprehend, comprise, depredation, impregnable, predator, prey, prison, reprehensible, reprieve,* and *surprise.*

pre·hen·sion /pri hénshən/ *n.* (*formal*) **1. ACT OF FIRMLY GRASPING** a taking hold of something firmly **2. PERCEIVING OF SOMETHING THROUGH SENSES** the perception by the senses of a sight, sound, smell, taste, or texture **3. COMPREHENSION** the process of understanding [Mid-16thC. From Latin *prehensionem*, from *prehendere* "to seize."]

pre·his·to·ri·an /prèe hi stáwree ən/ *n.* somebody who studies or specializes in the period before recorded history [Late 19thC. Formed from PREHISTORY on the model of HISTORIAN.]

pre·his·tor·ic /prèe his táwrik/ *adj.* **1. BEFORE RECORDED HISTORY** relating to the period before history was first recorded in writing **2. RELATING TO LANGUAGE BEFORE WRITING** relating or belonging to a language before it was recorded in writing **3. VERY OLD OR OLD-FASHIONED** relating to or being an object, idea, or attitude that is very old or out-of-date ○ *prehistoric views about nutrition* —**pre·his·tor·i·cal·ly** *adv.*

pre·his·to·ry /pri hístəree/ *n.* **1. HISTORY BEFORE WRITTEN WORD** the period before history was first recorded in writing **2. STUDY OF PREHISTORIC PERIOD** the study of the prehistoric period using archeological evidence **3. EVENTS LEADING UP TO SOMETHING** the events and circumstances preceding a current event or situation (*informal*)

pre·hom·i·nid /pri hómmənid/ *n.* any one of various animals believed to be early ancestors of the modern human race —**pre·hom·i·nid** *adj.*

pre·ig·ni·tion /prèe ig nísh'n/ *n.* ignition of fuel in an internal-combustion engine before the spark has been generated, causing inefficient operation. Preignition may be caused by a hot spot in the cylinder. —**pre·ig·nite** *vti.*

pre·in·dus·tri·al /prèe in dústree əl/ *adj.* relating to a society, country, or economic system in which industry has not yet developed on an extensive scale

pre·judge /pree júj/ (**-judged, -judg·ing, -judg·es**) *vt.* to judge a person, issue, or case before sufficient evidence is available [Late 16thC. Via French *préjuger* from Latin *praejudicare.*] —**pre·judg·er** *n.* —**pre·judg·ment** *n.*

prej·u·dice /préjjədiss/ *n.* **1. OPINION FORMED BEFOREHAND** a preformed opinion, usually an unfavorable one, based on insufficient knowledge, irrational feelings, or inaccurate stereotypes **2. THE HOLDING OF ILL-INFORMED OPINIONS** the holding of opinions that are formed beforehand on the basis of insufficient knowledge **3. IRRATIONAL DISLIKE OF SOMEBODY** an unfounded hatred, fear, or mistrust of a person or group, especially one of a particular religion, ethnicity, nationality, or social status **4.** LAW **DISADVANTAGE OR HARM** disadvantage or harm caused to somebody or something ■ *vt.* (**-diced, -dic·ing, -dic·es**) **1. CAUSE TO PREJUDGE SOMEBODY OR SOMETHING** to make somebody form an opinion about somebody or something in advance, especially an irrational one, based on insufficient knowledge **2. AFFECT ADVERSELY** to cause harm or disadvantage to somebody or something [13thC. Via French from Latin *praejudicium* "judgment in advance," from *judicium* "judgment."] ◇ **without prejudice** LAW without doing any harm to somebody's legal rights or any claim that somebody has (*formal*)

prej·u·diced /préjjədist/ *adj.* holding opinions, especially unfavorable ones, that are based on insufficient knowledge, irrational feelings, or inaccurate stereotypes

prej·u·di·cial /prèjjə dísh'l/ *adj.* **1. RESULTING IN HARM** causing disadvantage or harm to somebody or something **2. ENCOURAGING PREJUDICE** leading to the formation of prejudiced ideas or opinions —**prej·u·di·cial·ly** *adv.*

prel·a·cy /préllәssee/ (*plural* **-cies**) *n.* **1. POSITION OF PRELATE** the office or position of a prelate **2. PRELATES COLLECTIVELY** prelates considered as a group **3.** = **prelatism** [14thC. Via Anglo-Norman from medieval Latin *prelatia*, from *praelatus* (see PRELATE).]

pre·lap·sar·i·an /prèe lap sáiree ən/ *adj.* relating or belonging to the biblical time before Adam and Eve lost their innocence in the Garden of Eden [Late 19thC. Coined from PRE- + Latin *lapsus* "sin, fall."]

prel·ate /préllət/ *n.* a high-ranking member of the clergy, e.g., an abbot, bishop, or cardinal [13thC. Via Old French from medieval Latin *praelatus*, the past participle of Latin *praeferre* "to prefer."] —**pre·lat·ic** /prə láttik/ *adj.*

prel·at·ism /préllə tìzzəm/ *n.* government of a church by high-ranking members of the clergy (*disapproving*) —**prel·at·ist** *n.*

prel·a·ture /préllәchər/ *n.* = **prelacy** *n.* 2

pre·lect /pri lékt/ (**-lect·ed, -lect·ing, -lects**) *vi.* to give a lecture or speech in public (*formal*) [Late 18thC. From Latin *praelect-*, the past participle stem of *praelegere* "to read in front of," from *legere* "to read."] —**pre·lec·tion** *n.* —**pre·lec·tor** *n.*

pre·li·ba·tion /prèe lī báysh'n/ *n.* a sample or taste of something in advance (*formal*) [Early 16thC. From Latin *praelibationem*, from *praelibare* "to taste beforehand," from *libare* "to pour out."]

pre·lim /préelim/ *n.* SPORTS **PRELIMINARY CONTEST** a preliminary contest or event (*informal*) ■ *npl.* **BOOK FRONT MATTER** the initial pages of a book, including the title page and table of contents, that precede the main text (*informal*) ■ *n.* EDUC **PH.D. EXAM** an examination that a doctoral candidate must pass in order to be allowed to do dissertation research [Late 19thC. Contraction of PRELIMINARY.]

prelim. *abbr.* preliminary

pre·lim·i·nar·y /pri límmə nèrree/ *adj.* **COMING BEFORE SOMETHING** occurring before and leading up to something, especially an event of greater size and importance ■ *n.* (*plural* **-ies**) **1. INTRODUCTORY OR PREPARATORY ACTIVITY** something said or done before something else, often by way of introduction to or preparation for something of greater size and importance (*often used in the plural*) **2.** SPORTS **INTRODUCTORY CONTEST** a sporting contest held before the main event, especially in boxing and wrestling **3.** SPORTS **ELIMINATORY CONTEST** an eliminatory contest to select the finalists in a sports competition **4.** EDUC **PREPARATORY EXAMINATION** a test that prepares students for a subsequent examination of greater difficulty and importance [Mid-17thC. Directly or via French from modern Latin *praeliminaris*, from Latin *prae-* "before" + *limen* "threshold."] —**pre·lim·i·nar·i·ly** /pri lìmmə nérrilee/ *adv.*

pre·lit·er·ate /pree líttərət/ *adj.* **WITHOUT WRITTEN LANGUAGE** used to describe a society that has no written language ■ *n.* **MEMBER OF A PRELITERATE SOCIETY** a member of a society with no written language —**pre·lit·er·a·cy** *n.*

prel·ude /prél yo͞od, práy lo͞od/ *n.* **1.** MUSIC **INTRODUCTORY PIECE OF MUSIC** a piece of music that introduces or precedes another one **2.** MUSIC **FREE-STANDING PIECE OF MUSIC** a short musical composition, often one for piano, and often forming part of a set of such works **3. INTRODUCTORY EVENT OR OCCURRENCE** an event or action that introduces or precedes something else, especially something longer and more important ■ *v.* (**-ud·ed, -ud·ing, -udes**) **1.** *vti.* **ACT AS PRELUDE TO SOMETHING** to act as an introduction to something else, especially something that is longer and more important **2.** *vt.* **INTRODUCE WITH PRELUDE** to precede something, especially a piece of music, with a prelude [Mid-16thC. Via French from, ultimately, Latin *praeludere* "to play before," from *ludere* "to play."] —**prel·ud·er** *n.* —**pre·lu·di·al** /prə lóodee əl/ *adj.* —**pre·lu·sive** /prə lóossiv/ *adj.* —**pre·lu·sive·ly** /-lóoss ivlee/ *adv.* —**pre·lu·so·ri·ly** /-lóoss ərilee/ *adv.* —**pre·lu·so·ry** /-lóoss əree/ *adj.*

WORD KEY: CULTURAL NOTE

The Prelude, a poem by English writer William Wordsworth (1798–1850). Planned as a preface to a never-completed philosophical poem called *The Recluse*, this autobiographical account of the poet's intellectual and spiritual development was written over a period of more than 40 years and published posthumously. Rejecting contemporary rationalist philosophies, it proclaims Wordsworth's faith in the redeeming power of poetry and the imagination.

pre·lu·sion /pri lóozh'n/ *n.* = **prelude** *n.* 3

prem. *abbr.* premium

pre·ma·lig·nant /prèe mə lígnənt/ *adj.* = **precancerous**

pre·mar·i·tal /pri mérrət'l/ *adj.* occurring or existing before marriage

pre·ma·ture /prèemə chóor/ *adj.* **1. HAPPENING TOO SOON** occurring, existing, or developing earlier than is expected, normal, or advisable ○ *It would be premature to suggest that there is a link between these events.* **2.** MED **BORN TOO EARLY** born before completing the normal gestation period, or, for a human infant, weighing less than 5 lb. 8 oz/2.5 kg at birth [Early 16thC. From Latin *praematurus* "ripening too early," from *maturus* "ripe."] —**pre·ma·ture·ly** *adv.* —**pre·ma·ture·ness** *n.* —**pre·ma·tu·ri·ty** /prèemə chóorə tee/ *n.*

pre·max·il·la /prèe mak síllə/ (*plural* **-lae** /-lèe/) *n.* either of two bones that form the front part of the upper jaw in vertebrates and that bear the incisors. In humans, it merges with the rest of the maxilla during embryonic life. —**pre·max·il·lar·y** /pree máksi lèrree/ *adj.*

pre·med /pree méd/ *n.* (*informal*) **1. PREMEDICAL STUDENT** a student in a premedical program ○ *The premeds will be taking their exams soon.* **2. PREMEDICAL COURSEWORK** a premedical course of study ○ *majoring in premed* ■ *adj.* **PREMEDICAL** premedical (*informal*) [Mid-20thC. Shortening.]

pre·med·i·cal /pree méddik'l/ *adj.* relating to or engaged in the course of studies that somebody must complete before entering medical school —**pre·med·i·cal·ly** *adv.*

pre·med·i·ca·tion /prèe méddi káysh'n/ *n.* the practice of giving drugs to a patient before anesthesia, or the drugs given, to relieve anxiety, diminish body reactions to pain, or improve postoperative comfort

pre·med·i·tate /pri méddi tàyt/ (**-tat·ed, -tat·ing, -tates**) *v.* **1.** *vt.* **PLAN BEFOREHAND** to plan or devise something, especially a crime, in advance **2.** *vti.* **PONDER SOMETHING IN ADVANCE** to consider or think carefully about something beforehand [Mid-16thC. From Latin *praemeditatus*, the past participle of *praemeditari* "to think about beforehand," from *meditare* (see MEDITATE).] —**pre·med·i·ta·tive** *adj.* —**pre·med·i·ta·tor** *n.*

pre·med·i·tat·ed /pree méddi tàytəd/ *adj.* not committed in a moment of passion or mindlessness, e.g., intense rage or drunkeness, but thought out and decided on beforehand ○ *was charged with premeditated murder* —**pre·med·i·tat·ed·ly** *adv.*

pre·med·i·ta·tion /pree mèddi táysh'n/ *n.* **1.** LAW **CONTEMPLATION OF INTENDED CRIME** thinking about and planning a crime beforehand, rather than acting on impulse in a moment of passion or mindlessness **2. REFLECTION BEFORE ACTION** thinking about something before doing it [15thC. Directly or via French from Latin *praemeditationem*, from *praemeditari* (see PREMEDITATE).]

pre·me·no·paus·al /prèe mènnə páwz'l/ *adj.* used to describe the stage in a woman's life just before the onset of menopause, or a woman at this stage. Such a woman is still menstruating, but may show some signs of menopause, e.g., irregular menstrual periods.

pre·men·stru·al /pree ménstroo əl/ *adj.* relating to or occurring in the days immediately before the start of a woman's menstrual period

pre·men·stru·al syn·drome *n.* a group of symptoms, e.g., nervous tension, irritability, tenderness of the breasts, and headache, experienced by some women in the days preceding menstruation and caused by hormonal changes

pre·mie *n.* = **preemie**

pre·mier /pri méer/ *adj.* **BEST OR MOST IMPORTANT** first in importance, size, or quality ■ *n.* **1. PRIME MINISTER** a prime minister or head of government **2. LEADER OF CANADIAN PROVINCE** the governmental head of a Canadian province [15thC. Via French from Latin *primarius* "foremost."]

pre·mier dan·seur /pri méer daaN súr/ (*plural* **pre·miers dan·seurs** /pri méer daaN súr/) *n.* the principal man dancer in a ballet company [Early 19thC. From French, literally "first dancer."]

pre·miere /pri méer/ *n.* **1. FIRST PUBLIC PERFORMANCE** the first public performance or showing of something such as a play or movie **2. LEADING WOMAN ACTOR** the principal woman performer in a theatrical company ■ *v.* (**-miered, -mier·ing, -mieres**) **1.** *vti.* **PRESENT OR BE PRESENTED AS PREMIERE** to be publicly performed, shown, or broadcast for the first time, or present the first performance of something such as a play or movie ○ *The play premiered in New York.* **2.** *vi.* **GIVE FIRST PUBLIC PERFORMANCE** to appear on stage or screen for the first time, especially in a leading role ○ *Not many young performers get to premiere on Broadway.* ■ *adj.* **BEST OR MOST IMPORTANT** first in importance, quality, or size [Mid-20thC. From French, the feminine form of *premier* "first" (see PREMIER).]

pre·mière dan·seuse /pri méer daaN sóoz/ (*plural* **pre·mières dan·seuses**) *n.* the principal female dancer in a ballet company [Early 19thC. From French, literally "first (female) dancer."]

pre·mier·ship /pri méer shìp/ *n.* POL the office or position of premier

pre·mil·le·nar·i·an /pree mìllə náiree ən/ *adj.* **RELATING TO PREMILLENNIALISM** relating or belonging to premillennialism ■ *n.* **BELIEVER IN PREMILLENNIALISM** somebody who believes in premillennialism —**pre·mil·le·nar·i·an·ism** *n.*

pre·mil·len·ni·al /prèe mi lénnee əl/ *adj.* relating to or occurring in the period immediately before a millennium —**pre·mil·len·ni·al·ly** *adv.*

pre·mil·len·ni·al·ism /prèe mi lénnee ə lìzzəm/ *n.* the belief that Jesus Christ will return to earth for the Last Judgment just before the one-thousand-year reign of peace (**millennium**) mentioned in the Bible —**pre·mil·len·ni·al·ist** *n.*

Otto Preminger

Prem·in·ger /prémminjər/, **Otto** (1906–86) Austrian-born U.S. movie director, producer, and actor. His movies include *Laura* (1944), *Carmen Jones* (1954), and *Exodus* (1960). Full name **Otto Ludwig Preminger**

prem·ise /prémmiss/ *n.* **1. EVIDENCE FOR CONCLUSION** a statement given as the evidence for a conclusion **2. BASIS OF ARGUMENT** a proposition that forms the basis of an argument or from which a conclusion is drawn ○ *I question the premise on which your whole theory is based.* ■ *v.* (**-ised, -is·ing, -is·es**) **1.** *vt.* **SAY BY WAY OF INTRODUCTION** to state something in advance to introduce or explain what follows (*formal*) **2.** *vti.* **PROPOSE AS PREMISE** to put forward a proposition as a premise in an argument [14thC. Via French from medieval Latin *praemissa (propositio)* "(the proposition) set before," from the past participle of *praemittere* "to set in front," from *mittere* "to send."]

prem·is·es /prémmissəz/ *npl.* **1. LAND AND BUILDINGS** a piece of land and the buildings on it **2. PART OR ALL OF BUILDING** a building or part of a building, especially when used for commercial purposes **3.** LAW **MATTERS PREVIOUSLY MENTIONED** matters previously stated or referred to in a legal document such as a deed **4.** LAW **PRELIMINARY EXPLANATORY SECTION** the introductory part of a legal document, e.g., the part giving the names and other details of those concerned [15thC. From medieval Latin *praemissa* "things stated at the beginning" (see PREMISE).]

prem·iss /prémmiss/ *n.* = **premise** *n.* 1, **premise** *n.* 2

pre·mi·um /préemee əm/ *n.* **1. COST OF INSURANCE** the sum of money paid, usually at regular intervals, for an insurance policy ○ *My insurance premium went up as a result of the accident.* **2. ADDITIONAL SUM** a sum of money paid in addition to a normal wage, rate, price, or other amount **3. PRIZE** an award or prize given, e.g., to the winner of a competition **4. INDUCEMENT TO BUY** a gift or reduced price offered as an incentive to purchase another product or service ○ *The manufacturer offered premiums, in the form of free merchandise and trips, for every purchase of a new car.* **5. AMOUNT ABOVE PAR VALUE** the amount above its nominal value at which something such as a security sells **6. EXTRA CHARGE FOR BORROWING MONEY** an amount charged in addition to interest on a loan **7. COST OF SECURITIES OPTION** the sum or cost at which a securities option is bought or sold **8. FEE FOR INSTRUCTION** a fee paid for training or apprenticeship in a profession or trade ■ *adj.* **1. HIGH-QUALITY** of very high quality **2. UNUSUALLY HIGH** higher than normal, especially in price ○ *premium gasoline prices* [Early 17thC. From Latin *praemium* "reward," from *prae-* "pre-" + *emere* "to take, buy" (source of English *example*, *exempt*, and *redeem*).] ◇ **at a premium 1.** much in demand and therefore difficult to obtain **2.** selling for a high price, or for a higher price than usual, because of scarcity ◇ **put a premium on** to place a high value on somebody or something

pre·mix /pree míks/ *n.* **PREPARED MIXTURE** a product consisting of previously mixed ingredients or elements ■ *vt.* (**-mixed, -mix·ing, -mix·es**) **COMBINE AHEAD OF TIME** to mix something beforehand

pre·mo·lar /pree mṓlər/ *n.* **GRINDING TOOTH** either of two teeth on each side of both jaws that lie immediately behind the canines and in front of the molars and are used for grinding and chewing ■ *adj.* **OF GRINDING AND CHEWING TOOTH** relating to a grinding and chewing tooth —**pre·mo·lar** *adj.*

pre·mo·ni·tion /prèmmə nísh'n, prèemə nísh'n/ *n.* **1. INTUITION OF FUTURE EVENT** a strong feeling, without a rational basis, that a particular thing is going to happen **2. WARNING ABOUT FUTURE** an advance warning about a future event [Mid-16thC. Via French from, ultimately, Latin *praemonere* "to forewarn," from *monere* "to warn."] —**pre·mon·i·to·ri·ly** /pree mònni táwrilee/ *adv.* —**pre·mon·i·to·ry** /-mónni tàwree/ *adj.*

pre·na·tal /pree náyt'l/ *adj.* existing or happening during pregnancy but before childbirth —**pre·na·tal·ly** *adv.*

Pren·der·gast /préndər gaast/, **Maurice Brazil** (1859–1924) U.S. painter. He was a member of the Eight, a group of realist painters, and his subjects include landscapes with figures, painted in rich colors.

pre·no·tion /pree nṓsh'n/ *n.* **1. PRECONCEPTION** a preconceived idea about somebody or something **2. PREMONITION** a feeling that something is about to occur or may occur [Early 17thC. From Latin *praenotionem.*]

pre·nup·tial /pree núpshəl/ *adj.* occurring or existing before a marriage

pre·nup·tial a·gree·ment *n.* an agreement made between a couple before marriage relating to the arrangement of financial matters and division of property in the event of their divorce

pre·oc·cu·pan·cy /pree ókyəpənsee/ *n.* **1. PRIOR HABITATION** occupancy of a place in advance or before somebody else **2. PREOCCUPATION** the state of being interested in something, especially to the exclusion of other things

pre·oc·cu·pa·tion /prèe ókyə páysh'n/, **pre·oc·cu·pan·cy** (*plural* **-cies**) *n.* **1. CONSTANT THOUGHT ABOUT SOMETHING** constant thought about or persistent interest in something ○ *a preoccupation with fame and fortune* **2. FOCUS OF SOMEBODY'S ATTENTION** a particular subject or activity that constantly occupies somebody's thoughts ○ *His children are his main preoccupation at the moment.* **3.** = **preoccupancy** *n.* 1 [Early 17thC. Via Latin *praeoccupationem* "action" from *praeoccupare.*]

pre·oc·cu·pied /pree ókyə pīd/ *adj.* **1. HAVING ATTENTION TAKEN UP WITH SOMETHING** completely absorbed in doing or thinking about something else, sometimes excessively ○ *She was too preoccupied to notice what was going on.* **2.** OCCUPIED already occupied by somebody or something else ○ *a preoccupied airline seat* **3.** BIOL ALREADY IN USE used to describe a scientific name that has already been used to designate a species, genus, or other taxonomic group and therefore cannot be used again

pre·oc·cu·py /pree ókyə pī/ (**-pied, -py·ing, -pies**) *vt.* **1.** ABSORB SOMEBODY'S THOUGHTS to fill somebody's thoughts completely, sometimes excessively **2.** OCCUPY BEFOREHAND to occupy something in advance or before somebody else

pre·op /pree óp/ *adj.* preoperative (*informal*) [Mid-20thC. Shortening.]

pre·op·er·a·tive /pree ópparətiv, -ópprətiv/ *adj.* occurring or done before a surgical operation

pre·or·dain /prèe awr dáyn/ (**-dained, -dain·ing, -dains**) *vt.* **1.** PREDESTINE to decide in advance that something will happen, or determine somebody's future, usually by fate or divine decree **2.** ARRANGE IN ADVANCE to decide, determine, or arrange something beforehand —**pre·or·dain·ment** *n.* —**pre·or·di·na·tion** /prèe áwrd'n áysh'n/ *n.*

pre·o·vu·la·to·ry /pree ṓvyələ tàwree, pree óvyələ tàwree/ *adj.* relating to the stage of the menstrual cycle between menstruation and ovulation, lasting from 6 to 13 days

pre·owned /pree ṓnd/ *adj.* *U.S., ANZ* previously owned and now for sale

prep /prep/ *n.* (*informal*) **1.** PREPARATION preparation for activity **2.** PREPARATORY SCHOOL a preparatory school **3.** = **preppy** *n.* 2 **4.** *U.K.* HOMEWORK at a boarding school or private school in the United Kingdom, work to be done by students outside normal school hours **5.** *U.K.* STUDY TIME at a boarding school in the United Kingdom, the time during which students do homework or prepare for lessons ○ *No talking was allowed during prep.* ■ *v.* (**prepped, prep·ping, preps**) **1.** *vi.* PREPARE FOR SOMETHING to study or train for a particular examination, sporting event, or other activity (*informal*) **2.** *vt.* SURG PREPARE SOMEBODY FOR SURGERY to make a patient ready for an operation or other hospital procedure (*informal*) **3.** *vt.* PAINTING PREPARE SOMETHING FOR PAINTING to prime a surface for painting **4.** *vi.* EDUC ATTEND PRIVATE SECONDARY SCHOOL to attend a preparatory school ○ *prepped at Groton* ■ *adj.* PREPARATORY serving as preparation (*informal*) [Mid-19thC. Shortening of PREPARATION.]

prep. *abbr.* **1.** preparation **2.** preparatory **3.** GRAM preposition

pre·pack·age /pree pákij/ (**-aged, -ag·ing, -ag·es**) *vt.* **1.** PACKAGE BEFORE SALE to package a product before selling it **2.** ARRANGE COMPLETELY BEFOREHAND to arrange all the elements of something in advance, allowing no individual variation ○ *a prepackaged holiday*

prep·a·ra·tion /prèppə ráysh'n/ *n.* **1.** PREPARING SOMETHING OR SOMEBODY the work or planning involved in making something or somebody ready or in putting something together in advance (*often used before a noun*) ○ *a preparation time of about 45 minutes* **2.** READINESS a state of readiness ○ *Twenty place settings lay carefully arranged in preparation for the guests.* **3.** PREPARATORY MEASURE something done in advance in order to be ready for a future event (*often plural*) ○ *Preparations for the next Olympic Games are already under way.* **4.** MIXTURE a substance, e.g., a medicine, that is made for a specific purpose by combining various ingredients ○ *a cough preparation* **5.** *U.K.* EDUC HOMEWORK at a boarding school or private school in the United Kingdom, work to be done by students outside normal school hours **6.** *U.K.* EDUC STUDY TIME at a boarding school in the U.K., the time during which students do homework or prepare for lessons **7.** MUSIC SOFTENING APPROACH TO DISSONANCE in traditional composition, a lessening of the effect of a dissonant chord by using the discordant note harmonically in a preceding chord [14thC. Via French from Latin *praeparationem*, from *praeparare* "to prepare."]

pre·par·a·tive /pri pérrətiv/ *adj.* PREPARING OR INTRODUCING SOMETHING having the purpose of making something ready or of introducing something (*formal*) ○ *a series of preparative lectures* ■ *n.* PREPARATORY OR INTRODUCTORY MEASURE something that prepares for or introduces a more important event or action (*formal*) ○ *Her preparative was excellent and we felt ready to perform the procedure.* [15thC. Via French *préparatif* from medieval Latin *praeparativus*, from *praeparare* "to prepare."] —**pre·par·a·tive·ly** *adv.*

pre·par·a·to·ry /pri pérrə tàwree/ *adj.* **1.** MAKING SOMETHING READY serving to make something ready ○ *preparatory design work* **2.** INTRODUCTORY acting as an introduction to something **3.** EDUC PREPARING FOR COLLEGE relating to or engaged in a course of study that prepares students for advanced education, especially college ○ *Most of my classes this year are college preparatory.* [15thC. From medieval Latin *praeparatorius*, from *praeparator* "preparer" (see PREPARE).] —**pre·par·a·to·ri·ly** /pri pèrrə táwrilee/ *adv.* ◇ **preparatory to** before or in preparation for

pre·par·a·to·ry school *n.* **1.** PRIVATE SECONDARY SCHOOL in the United States, a private secondary school that prepares students for college, often with academic requirements for entry **2.** BRITISH PRIVATE ELEMENTARY SCHOOL in the United Kingdom, a private, usually single-sex school that prepares students between the ages of 6 and 13 for entrance into a private boarding school

pre·pare /pri páir/ (**-pared, -par·ing, -pares**) *v.* **1.** *vti.* MAKE READY to make something ready for use or action, or for a particular event or purpose ○ *preparing the aircraft for takeoff* **2.** *vti.* MAKE SOMEBODY READY to get ready or make somebody ready for something ○ *They prepared to go.* ○ *Prepare yourselves for a shock.* **3.** *vt.* MAKE BY PUTTING THINGS TOGETHER to make something by combining various elements or ingredients ○ *meals that can be prepared in less than half an hour* **4.** *vt.* PREPLAN to plan something in advance **5.** *vt.* EQUIP to provide a person or group with necessary equipment, e.g., for a ship or an expedition **6.** *vt.* MUSIC LESSEN EFFECT OF DISSONANCE to lessen the effect of a dissonant chord by using the discordant note harmonically in a preceding chord [15thC. Directly or via French from Latin *praeparare* "to make ready beforehand," from *parare* "to make ready."] —**pre·par·er** *n.*

pre·pared /pri páird/ *adj.* **1.** ABLE AND WILLING willing and able to do something ○ *Are you prepared to testify in court?* **2.** READY AND ABLE TO DEAL WITH SOMETHING ready and able to cope with something, often something hard or bad ○ *The flight was prepared for takeoff.* **3.** MADE, OR MADE READY, BEFOREHAND made ready or put together in advance ○ *a specially prepared surface* ○ *a prepared statement* —**pre·par·ed·ly** /pri páirədlee/ *adv.*

pre·par·ed·ness /pri páirədnəss/ *n.* readiness for action, especially military action

pre·pared pi·an·o *n.* a piano that has been modified to produce special effects, usually by placing objects on or between its strings

pre·pay /pree páy/ (**-paid, -pay·ing, -pays**) *vt.* to pay in advance for something —**pre·pay·a·ble** *adj.*

pre·pay·ment /pree páymənt/ *n.* **1.** ADVANCE PAYMENT a payment made in advance, usually for a service (*often used in the plural*) **2.** PAYING IN ADVANCE the act of paying for something in advance (*often used before a noun*)

pre·pense /pri péns/ *adj.* LAW planned or contemplated in advance (*formal*) ○ *acted with malice prepense* [Early 18thC. Alteration of *purpensed* "premeditated," via Anglo-Norman *purpenser* "to premeditate" from, ultimately, Latin *pensare* "to think."]

pre·pon·der·ance /pri póndərənss/, **pre·pon·der·an·cy** /-see/ *n.* (*formal*) **1.** MAJORITY a large number or the majority (*takes a singular or plural verb*) ○ *A preponderance of the settlers in this area were French.* **2.** DOMINANCE OR SUPERIORITY dominance or superiority in force, importance, or influence ○ *The preponderance of the evidence is in support of this theory.*

pre·pon·der·ant /pri póndərənt/ *adj.* greater in number, power, or importance than something else of the same nature or class [Mid-17thC. Via Latin *praeponderantem* from *praeponderare* "to outweigh."] —**pre·pon·der·ant·ly** *adv.*

pre·pon·der·ate *vi.* /pri póndə ràyt/ (**-at·ed, -at·ing, -ates**) BE GREATER OR DOMINANT to be greater in weight, strength, number, or importance than something else ■ *adj.* /pri póndərət/ = **preponderant** *adj.* [Early 17thC. From Latin *praeponderat-*, the past participle stem of *praeponderare* "to weigh more," from *ponderare* "to weigh."] —**pre·pon·der·ate·ly** /-póndərətlee/ *adv.* —**pre·pon·der·a·tion** /-pòndə ráysh'n/ *n.*

prep·o·si·tion /prèppə zísh'n/ *n.* a member of a set of words used in close connection with, and usually before, nouns and pronouns to show their relation to some other part of a clause. An example is "off" in "He fell off his bike" and "What did he fall off?" [14thC. From the Latin stem *praeposition-* "putting before," from *praeponere* "to put before," from *ponere* "to put" (see POSITION).]

pre·po·si·tion *vt.* to deploy ships and troops to an area of possible future conflict

prep·o·si·tion·al /prèppə zíshən'l, -zíshnəl/ *adj.* used as or belonging to a preposition —**prep·o·si·tion·al·ly** *adv.*

prep·o·si·tion·al phrase *n.* a phrase made up of a preposition followed by a noun or pronoun, e.g., "over the hill." Prepositional phrases can be used adverbially or adjectivally.

pre·pos·i·tive /pree pózzətiv/ *adj.* PLACED BEFORE WORD used to describe a word that is placed before the word it modifies ■ *n.* PREPOSITIVE TERM a prepositive word or element [Late 16thC. Formed from Latin *praepositivus*, the past participle of *praeponere* (see PREPOSITION).] —**pre·pos·i·tive·ly** *adv.*

pre·pos·sess /prèe pə zéss/ (**-sessed, -sess·ing, -sess·es**) *vt.* **1.** IMPRESS FAVORABLY IN ADVANCE to make a good impression on somebody before a more important moment **2.** INFLUENCE BEFOREHAND to cause somebody to form an opinion about somebody or something before it is necessary or appropriate to do so **3.** OCCUPY SOMEBODY'S MIND to occupy the thoughts of somebody to an excessive degree

pre·pos·sess·ing /prèe pə zéssing/ *adj.* creating a pleasing impression (*formal*) —**pre·pos·sess·ing·ly** *adv.* —**pre·pos·sess·ing·ness** *n.*

pre·pos·ses·sion /prèe pə zésh'n/ *n.* **1.** PREJUDICE prejudice or bias toward or against a particular person or thing **2.** ABSORPTION OF MIND the occupation of the mind by thoughts on a particular subject

pre·pos·ter·ous /pri póstərəss/ *adj.* going very much against what is thought to be sensible or reasonable [Mid-16thC. From Latin *praeposterus* "inverted," literally "having the first thing last." The underlying meaning is "unnatural, perverse."] —**pre·pos·ter·ous·ly** *adv.* —**pre·pos·ter·ous·ness** *n.*

pre·po·ten·cy /pri pṓt'nsee/ (*plural* **-cies**) *n.* **1.** GENETICS ABILITY TO TRANSMIT MORE GENETIC TRAITS the ability of one parent to confer more genetic traits on the offspring than the other parent **2.** BOT GREATER ABILITY TO FERTILIZE PLANT the dominance of pollen from one strain over pollen from others in its ability to fertilize a plant **3.** SUPERIORITY OF STRENGTH a superiority in power, force, authority, or influence

pre·po·tent /pri pṓt'nt/ *adj.* **1.** MORE POWERFUL AND INFLUENTIAL greater in power, force, or influence **2.** BOT, GENETICS EXHIBITING PREPOTENCY having or exhibiting prepotency in conferring genetic traits or in fertilization [15thC. Via Latin *praepotentem* from *praeposse* "to be more powerful," from *posse* "to be able."] —**pre·po·tent·ly** *adv.*

prep·py /préppee/, **prep·pie** *adj.* RELATING TO YOUNG WELL-EDUCATED AFFLUENT PEOPLE relating to or characteristic of well-educated, fairly affluent young people who are known for their neat, traditional, often expensive clothing style (*informal*) ■ *n.* (*plural* **-pies**) (*informal*) **1.** WELL-EDUCATED AFFLUENT YOUNG PERSON a young person who dresses with preppy style or behaves in a preppy manner **2.** PREPARATORY SCHOOL STUDENT a young person who is studying or has studied at a preparatory school —**prep·pi·ly** *adv.* —**prep·pi·ness** *n.*

pre·pran·di·al /pree prándee əl/ *adj.* taking place before a meal, especially an evening meal (*formal or humorous*)

pre·proc·ess /pree pró sèss/ (**-essed, -ess·ing, -ess·es**) *vt.* to analyze computer data, e.g., control statements embedded in a program, and take appropriate action before processing the data

pre·pro·duc·tion /prèe prə dúkshən/ *n.* PRELIMINARY WORK the plans and activities, e.g., those relating to finance, equipment, and personnel, that precede the production phase of a project, especially in the entertainment and manufacturing industries ■ *adj.* **1.** HAPPENING BEFORE PRODUCTION preceding a production phase **2.** PROTOTYPIC produced as a trial or prototype

pre·pro·fes·sion·al /prèe prə féshən'l, -féshnəl/ *adj.* undertaken in preparation for professional studies or practice

prep school *n.* a preparatory school (*informal*)

pre·pu·ber·ty /pree pyoobərtee/ *n.* the phase of physical and emotional development that immediately precedes puberty —**pre·pu·ber·tal** *adj.*

pre·pu·bes·cent /preepyoo béss'nt/ *adj.* RELATING TO PERIOD BEFORE PUBERTY at or characteristic of the stage of life just before puberty ■ *n.* PREPUBESCENT CHILD a child at the stage of development just before puberty

pre·puce /préé pyooss/ *n.* (*technical*) **1.** FORESKIN the foreskin **2.** SKIN COVERING CLITORIS the loose fold of skin that covers the tip of the clitoris [14thC. Via French from Latin *praeputium*.] —**pre·pu·tial** /pree pyoosh'l/ *adj.*

pre·quel /préekwəl/ *n.* a movie or novel set at a time preceding the action of an existing work, especially one that has achieved commercial success [Late 20thC. Blend of PRE- and SEQUEL.]

Pre-Raph·a·el·ite /pree ráafee ə līt, -ráffee ə-/ *n.* MEMBER OF 19C GROUP OF PAINTERS a member of a group of painters and writers **(the Pre-Raphaelite Brotherhood)** founded in 1848 with the aim of reviving the realistic style of Italian painting before Raphael. The group included Rossetti and Millais. ■ *adj.* RELATING TO PRE-RAPHAELITES relating or belonging to the Pre-Raphaelites, or characteristic of their style of painting or writing —**Pre-Raph·a·el·it·ism** *n.*

pre·re·cord /pree ri káwrd/ (**-cord·ed, -cord·ing, -cords**) *vt.* to record something such as a message or television or radio program for later use or broadcasting

pre·re·cord·ed /pree ri káwrdəd/ *adj.* **1.** RECORDED IN ADVANCE recorded in advance for later use or broadcasting **2.** WITH MUSIC OR MOVIE ALREADY RECORDED with sound or pictures already recorded on it, e.g., an audio cassette or CD

pre·reg·is·ter /pree réjjistər/ (**-tered, -ter·ing, -ters**) *vti.* to register for classes before the official registration period occurs, especially as a returning rather than a new college or university student —**pre·reg·is·tra·tion** /pree reji stráyshən/ *n.*

pre·re·lease /pree ri léess/ *n.* SOMETHING RELEASED EARLY a publication, recording, or product that is released before the appointed or official time ○ *The single is a prerelease from their upcoming album.* ■ *adj.* BEFORE AUTHORIZED RELEASE relating to or occurring during the period before the appointed or official time of release ○ *prerelease publicity*

pre·req·ui·site /pree rékwizit/ *n.* SOMETHING NEEDED AS PRIOR CONDITION an object, quality, or condition that is required in order for something else to happen ○ *A degree is a prerequisite for entry into this profession.* ■ *adj.* NEEDED AS PRIOR CONDITION required in order for something else to happen ○ *A good command of Spanish is prerequisite for the Spanish literature course.*

pre·re·tire·ment /pree ri tīrmənt/ *n.* the period of somebody's life just before retirement (*often used before a noun*) ○ *preretirement planning*

pre·rog·a·tive /pri róggətiv/ *n.* **1.** PRIVILEGE RESTRICTED TO PEOPLE OF RANK an exclusive privilege or right enjoyed by a person or group occupying a particular rank or position ○ *Being the leader, it was her prerogative to choose a successor.* **2.** INDIVIDUAL RIGHT OR PRIVILEGE a privilege or right that allows a particular person or group to give orders or make decisions or judgments ○ *It's not his prerogative to say who can come.* **3.** PRIVILEGE RESULTING FROM NATURAL ADVANTAGE the right conferred by a natural advantage that places somebody in a position of superiority ○ *the prerogatives conferred by age* **4.** SOVEREIGN POWER, PRIVILEGE, OR IMMUNITY the power or right of a monarch or government to do something or be exempt from something **5.** SUPERIORITY superiority in rank or nature [14thC. Via Old French from, ultimately, Latin *praerogare* "to ask first," from *rogare* "to ask."]

pres. *abbr.* **1.** GRAM present **2.** presidential

Pres. *abbr.* President

pres·age /préssij, pri sáyj/ *n.* **1.** PORTENT OR OMEN a sign or warning of a future event **2.** SENSE OF SOMETHING TO COME a feeling that a particular thing, often something unpleasant, is about to happen **3.** FUTURE IMPORT significance with regard to future events ○ *a moment of great presage* **4.** PREDICTION a prediction of a future event (*archaic*) ■ *v.* (**pre·saged, pre·sag·ing, pre·sag·es**) **1.** *vt.* FORETELL to be or give a sign or warning of a future event ○ *Clear skies that night presaged fine weather for the picnic.* **2.** *vt.* HAVE PRESENTIMENT OF SOMETHING to know intuitively that a particular thing is going to happen **3.** *vti.* PREDICT to predict a future event [14thC. Directly or via French from, ultimately, Latin *praesagire* "to forebode," from *sagire* "to perceive."] —**pre·sag·er** *n.*

pre·sale /pree sáyl/ *n.* **1.** PRIVATE SALE a private sale of products, objects, or works of art that takes place before a public sale **2.** PERIOD BEFORE SALE the period before something is sold to somebody, or the period before a product, object, or work of art is placed on sale to the general public

Presb., Presby. *abbr.* Presbyterian

pres·by·o·pi·a /prèzbee ópee ə/ *n.* MED progressive reduction in the eye's ability to focus, with consequent difficulty in reading at the normal distance, associated with aging. It typically starts at middle age, and is due to age-related loss of elasticity of the lens. [Late 18thC. Coined from Greek *presbus* "old man" (see PRESBYTER) + -OPIA.] —**pres·by·ope** /prézbee ōp/ *n.* —**pres·by·op·ic** /prèzbee óppik/ *adj.*

pres·by·ter /prézbitər/ *n.* **1.** MEMBER OF EARLY CHURCH ADMINISTRATION in early Christianity, an administrative official of a local church **2.** MEMBER OF CLERGY an ordained member of the clergy in many Christian churches **3.** LAY OFFICIAL IN PRESBYTERIAN CHURCH any of the laypeople chosen by the congregation to govern a Presbyterian or other Reformed church [Late 16thC. Via ecclesiastical Latin from Greek *presbuteros* "elder" (source of English *priest*), from *presbus* "old man."]

pres·byt·er·ate /prez bíttərət, -ràyt/ *n.* **1.** PRESBYTER'S POSITION the office or position of a presbyter **2.** GROUP OF PRESBYTERS an order or group of presbyters

pres·by·te·ri·al /prèzbi téeree əl/ *adj.* relating to a presbyter or presbytery

pres·by·te·ri·an /prèzbi téeree ən/ *adj.* RELATING TO ADMINISTRATION BY PRESBYTERS characterized by or relating to the government of a church by democratically elected lay officials ■ *n.* SUPPORTER OF ADMINISTRATION BY PRESBYTERS somebody who supports and advocates church government by democratically elected lay officials

Pres·by·te·ri·an /prèzbi téeree ən/ *adj.* RELATING TO PRESBYTERIAN CHURCH relating or belonging to the Presbyterian Church or any of the presbyterian churches ■ *n.* PRESBYTERIAN CHURCHMEMBER a member of a presbyterian church —**Pres·by·te·ri·an·ism** *n.*

pres·by·ter·y /prézbitəree/ (*plural* **-ies**) *n.* **1.** GROUP OF PRESBYTERS a group of presbyters in the early Christian church or in a modern Presbyterian church **2.** COURT OF PRESBYTERIAN CHURCH a court composed of ministers and lay officials in a Presbyterian Church, or the churches under the jurisdiction of such a court **3.** GOVERNMENT BY PRESBYTERS the government of a church by democratically elected lay officials **4.** PART OF CHURCH FOR CLERGY part of a church or cathedral, or a separate building, for the use of clergy only **5.** HOME OF ROMAN CATHOLIC PARISH PRIEST the home of a Roman Catholic parish priest

pre·school /pree skool/ *adj.* **1.** UNDER SCHOOL AGE below the age at which compulsory schooling begins **2.** FOR PRESCHOOL CHILDREN relating to or provided for children below the age at which compulsory schooling begins —**pre·school·er** *n.* —**pre·school·ing** *n.*

pre·sci·ence /préeshee əns, pré-, -sh'ns/ *n.* knowledge of actions or events before they happen [14thC. Via French from late Latin *praescientia* "foreknowledge" (see PRESCIENT).]

pre·sci·ent /préeshee ənt, pré-, -sh'nt/ *adj.* having or showing knowledge of actions or events before they take place [Early 17thC. Via Latin *praescientem* from *praescire* "to know beforehand," from *scire* "to know."] —**pre·sci·ent·ly** *adv.*

pre·sci·en·tif·ic /pree sī ən tíffik/ *adj.* relating to or happening during the time before the development of modern science and the application of modern scientific methods

pre·scind /pri sínd/ (**-scind·ed, -scind·ing, -scinds**) *vi.* to detach the mind from something, typically a concept, notion, or fixed idea (*formal*) ○ *if we can, for a moment, prescind from a focus on motive per se and consider instead opportunity and means* [Mid-17thC. From Latin *praescindere* "to cut off in front," from *scindere* "to cut off."]

Pres·cott /préskət, -kot/ city in central Arizona, near the source of the Hassayampa River, southwest of Flagstaff. Population: 32,841 (1996).

pre·scribe /pri skrīb/ (**-scribed, -scrib·ing, -scribes**) *v.* **1.** *vti.* MED ORDER USE OF MEDICATION to direct a patient to follow a particular course of treatment, specifically to use a particular drug at set times and in specified dosages **2.** *vt.* RECOMMEND SOMETHING AS REMEDY to recommend a particular course of action or treatment as a remedy for something ○ *I prescribe lots of tender loving care* **3.** *vt.* LAY SOMETHING DOWN AS RULE to say with authority that a certain course of action should be taken ○ *the penalties prescribed by law* **4.** *vi.* SET DOWN REGULATIONS to lay down rules or laws **5.** *vti.* LAW CLAIM PROPERTY AS RIGHT to claim a right to something on the grounds of possession over a long period of time [15thC. From Latin *praescribere* "to write before," from *scribere* "to write."] —**pre·scrib·a·ble** *adj.* —**pre·scrib·er** *n.*

pre·script /pree skript/ *n.* SOMETHING PRESCRIBED a rule or regulation that has been laid down (*formal*) ■ *adj.* PRESCRIBED laid down as a rule or regulation (*formal*) [Mid-16thC. From Latin *praescriptum* "something prescribed," the past participle of *praescribere* "to prescribe."]

pre·scrip·tion /pri skrípshən/ *n.* **1.** WRITTEN ORDER FOR MEDICINE a written order issued by a physician or other qualified practitioner that authorizes a pharmacist to supply a particular medication for a particular patient, with instructions on its use (*often used before a noun*) **2.** PRESCRIBED MEDICINE a drug or other medication prescribed by a physician or other qualified practitioner **3.** ORDER FOR LENS TO CORRECT EYESIGHT a written order from an optometrist or ophthalmologist for glasses or contact lenses of a particular type and strength to correct the eyesight of a particular person (*often used before a noun*) ○ *prescription sunglasses* **4.** PROVEN FORMULA FOR SOMETHING a proven formula for causing something else to happen ○ *Caring about others' feelings is a prescription for a fulfilling life.* **5.** ESTABLISHING OF REGULATIONS laying down of laws, rules, and regulations **6.** SOMETHING PRESCRIBED AS RULE a practice or course of action laid down as a regulation **7. pre·scrip·tion, pos·i·tive pre·scrip·tion** LAW PRESUMPTION OF RIGHT OF POSSESSION a presumption of the right of possession of property, based on long-term exercise of property rights [14thC. Via French from the Latin stem *praescription-*, from *praescribere* (see PRESCRIBE).]

pre·scrip·tion drug *n.* a drug that can be dispensed only upon presentation of a legally valid prescription

pre·scrip·tive /pri skríptiv/ *adj.* **1.** MAKING OR ADHERING TO REGULATIONS establishing or adhering to rules and regulations ○ *prescriptive grammarians* **2.** LAW GROUNDED IN LEGAL PRESCRIPTION based on legal prescription **3.** CUSTOMARY based on or authorized by long-standing custom (*dated*) —**pre·scrip·tive·ly** *adv.* —**pre·scrip·tive·ness** *n.*

pre·sea·son /pree séez'n/ *n.* the period just before the start of a new sports season, during which players train intensively and play games that are not part of a competition (*often used before a noun*) ○ *a preseason game*

pre·se·lect /pree sə lékt/ (**-lect·ed, -lect·ing, -lects**) *vt.* to select a person, object, place, or course of action in advance, usually on the basis of specific requirements

pre·sell /pree sél/ (**-sold, -sell·ing, -sells**) *vt.* **1.** MARKETING POPULARIZE SOMETHING BEFOREHAND to promote a product or entertainment before it is generally available to the public, by means of advertising and publicity **2.** PUBL SELL BOOK EARLY to sell a book before its official publication date **3.** COMM ARRANGE SALE OF SOMETHING BEFOREHAND to agree to sell a house, car, or other item before it is actually available

pres·ence /prézzəns/ *n.* **1.** BEING PRESENT the physical existence of somebody or something in a particular place ○ *Our presence is requested at the board meeting.* **2.** AREA WITHIN SIGHT OR EARSHOT the immediate vicinity of somebody or something ○ *How dare you use that kind of language in my presence!* **3.** PERSONAL DIGNITY dignified appearance and bearing ○ *has a certain presence about her that garners respect* **4.** IMPRESSIVE PERSON somebody who inspires awe and respect **5.** INVISIBLE SUPPOSED SUPERNATURAL BEING a supernatural spirit that is felt to be nearby ○ *a malevolent presence filled the room* **6.** PERSON PRESENT somebody who is present in a particular place ○ *the venerable scholar, a dignified presence in the academic procession* **7.** ARTS ABILITY TO CAPTIVATE AUDIENCE a quality of certain performers that enables them to achieve a rapport with and hold the attention of their audiences **8.** STATIONING OF PERSONNEL the existence of official personnel in a place, especially police, military, or diplomatic personnel ○ *maintained a heavy military, diplomatic, and intelligence presence in the capital* [14thC. Via French from Latin *praesentia*, from *praesent-* (see PRESENT[2]).]

pres·ence of mind *n.* the ability to remain calm and act decisively and effectively in a crisis ○ *At least she had the presence of mind to call the fire department.*

pre·sent[1] *v.* /pri zént/ (**-sent·ed, -sent·ing, -sents**) **1.** *vt.* GIVE SOMEBODY SOMETHING to give something to somebody, often in a formal manner ○ *Then she presented me with the bill!* **2.** *vt.* MAKE AWARD TO SOMEBODY to make a gift or award of something to somebody **3.** *vt.* OFFER SOMETHING FORMALLY to offer formally something such as compliments or apologies to somebody (*formal*) ○ *May I present my warmest congratulations?* **4.** *vt.* MAKE SOMETHING VISIBLE IN PARTICULAR WAY to show or display something in a particular way ○ *taking care to present his best side to the camera* **5.** *vt.* HAND SOMETHING OVER OFFICIALLY to put something forward for inspection or consideration, typically in a formal or official manner or capacity ○ *proposals to be presented at the next meeting* **6.** *vt.* CAUSE SOMETHING AS PROBLEM to pose a problem or difficulty to somebody ○ *presenting a direct threat to national security* **7.** *vt.* LAW BRING CHARGE to put a charge before a court of law so that it can be considered or tried **8.** *vt.* INTRODUCE WOMAN INTO SOCIETY to introduce a young woman formally into fashionable society ○ *Her family planned to present her at the Christmas debutante ball in New York.* **9.** *vt.* INTRODUCE SOMEBODY FORMALLY to introduce somebody formally, especially to somebody of higher rank ○ *They were presented to the Queen.* **10.** *vt.* BE HOST OF PROGRAM to introduce, or act as the host of, a television or radio program or an infomercial ○ *He used to present a game show.* **11.** *vt.* OFFER SOMETHING AS PUBLIC ENTERTAINMENT to bring a movie, play, or other form of entertainment to the public **12.** *vt.* PORTRAY SOMETHING ARTISTICALLY to represent something or somebody in a particular way in the arts ○ *In the film, Romeo and Juliet are presented as modern teenagers.* **13.** *vr.* BE IN APPOINTED PLACE to appear, especially at an appointed time and place ○ *Present yourselves at the gate at eight o'clock.* **14.** *vr.* ARISE to come into being or happen ○ *when an opportunity presents itself* **15.** *vi.* MED HAVE PARTICULAR SYMPTOMS to exhibit the specified symptom or symptoms on examination ○ *Monday, July 5th: The patient presents with arrhythmia and complains of arthralgia.* **16.** *vi.* MED EXIT BIRTH CANAL IN POSITION to appear during the process of being born (*refers to a fetus*) ○ *In most births, the first part to present is the back of the head.* **17.** *vi.* PRODUCE SPECIFIED IMPRESSION to produce a particular impression, especially a favorable one (*formal*) ○ *She presents as a pleasant young woman.* ■ *n.* /prézzənt/ GIFT something that is given to somebody out of kindness or to celebrate an occasion such as a birthday [13thC. Via French from Latin *praesentare* "to make present," from *praesent-* (see PRESENT[2]).]

WORD KEY: SYNONYMS

See Synonyms at ***give***.

pres·ent[2] /prézzənt/ *adj.* **1.** CURRENTLY HAPPENING taking place or existing now ○ *in our present circumstances* **2.** IN A PLACE in a particular place ○ *There were over a hundred people present at the reception* **3.** NOW UNDER DISCUSSION being considered or talked about at this time **4.** GRAM RELATING TO CURRENT TIME used to describe a verb form or tense that expresses the current time **5.** AT HAND readily available (*archaic*) **6.** ON HAND TO ACT ready to take action (*archaic*) ■ *n.* **1.** THE HERE AND NOW the current time or moment ○ *The story takes place in the present.* **2.** GRAM CURRENT-TIME VERB TENSE the verb tense that expresses current time **3.** GRAM CURRENT-TIME VERB a verb in the present tense, indicating that the action is happening now [13thC. Via French from Latin *praesent-*, the present participle stem of *praeesse* "to be in front of," from *esse* "to be."] ◇ **at present** just now ◇ **for the present** as far as the present time is concerned

pre·sent·a·ble /pri zéntəb'l/ *adj.* **1.** FIT TO APPEAR IN PUBLIC looking or being good enough to be introduced to other people ○ *Make sure you look presentable.* **2.** FIT TO BE DISPLAYED OR GIVEN good enough to be offered, shown, or given to other people ○ *still a presentable gift.* —**pre·sent·a·bil·i·ty** /pri zèntə bíllətee/ *n.* —**pre·sent·a·ble·ness** /-zéntəb'lnəss/ *n.* —**pre·sent·a·bly** /-zéntəblee/ *adv.*

pre·sent arms /pri zènt-/ *n.* a drill movement in which a salute is given by bringing a rifle vertically in front of the body, or the command to give such a salute —**pre·sent arms** *vi.*

pres·en·ta·tion /prèzz'n táysh'n/ *n.* **1.** ACT OF PRESENTING SOMETHING an act of presenting something or the state of being presented **2.** PREPARED PERFORMANCE FOR AUDIENCE a performance, exhibition, or demonstration put on before an audience **3.** FORMAL HANDING OVER OF GIFT the action of presenting somebody with an award or a token of appreciation in front of other people, or an occasion when this is done ○ *the presentation of the trophy* **4.** PREPARED REPORT READ BEFORE AUDIENCE a formal talk made to a group of people, e.g., on somebody's recent work or some aspect of business, often with handouts, diagrams, or other visual aids ○ *He gave a presentation on modern irrigation methods.* **5.** SOMEBODY'S INTRODUCTION INTO SPECIAL SOCIAL GROUP an occasion when somebody is first presented into society or at court, or the official or recognized process of first presenting somebody in this way **6.** WAY SOMETHING APPEARS WHEN OFFERED the manner in which something is shown, expressed, or laid out for other people to see ○ *Presentation is an important part of the chef's job.* **7.** MED PART OF BABY APPEARING FIRST the part of a baby that appears first at birth, normally the crown of the head ○ *a breech presentation* **8.** CHR ACT OF NOMINATING CLERGY MEMBER the act or power of nominating a member of the clergy to a particular paid office in a church **9.** OBJECT OF PERCEPTION something that is perceived, remembered, or acquired as knowledge **10.** = **presentment** *n.* 3 —**pres·en·ta·tion·al** *adj.*

Pres·en·ta·tion of the Vir·gin Mar·y *n.* the Roman Catholic festival that commemorates the Virgin Mary's presentation at the temple, held on November 21

pre·sent·a·tive /pri zéntətiv/ *adj.* able to be known directly without any reflective or cognitive process being necessary —**pre·sent·a·tive·ness** *n.*

pres·ent-day /prézz'nt dày/ *adj.* found or existing in modern times ○ *out of touch with present-day society and the TV culture*

pres·ent·ee /prèzz'n tée/ *n.* (*formal*) **1.** SOMEBODY WHO IS PRESENTED TO OTHERS somebody who is introduced in a formal or official way **2.** SOMEBODY WHO IS GIVEN SOMETHING somebody who is presented with something formally, e.g., an award or prize, or a gift from a large body of other people

pre·sent·er /pri zéntər/ *n.* **1.** SOMEBODY WHO PRESENTS SOMETHING somebody who presents something, e.g., an award or a gift ○ *The club president will be the presenter at the awards ceremony tonight.* **2.** INFOMERCIAL SALESPERSON somebody who presents and discusses a particular product during a television infomercial **3.** *U.K.* TV OR RADIO ANNOUNCER somebody who introduces a particular programme on television or radio and provides comments linking individual items or contributors during the programme

pre·sen·tient /pree sénshənt, -shee ənt/ *adj.* having a definite and usually uneasy sense that something is going to happen, or being aware of something before it occurs [Early 19thC. From, ultimately, Latin *praesentire* "to perceive beforehand," which was formed from *sentire* "to feel."]

pre·sen·ti·ment /pri zéntəmənt/ *n.* an awareness of some event, especially an unpleasant event, before it takes place and before there is any reason to suspect it or know about it ○ *She had a presentiment that something terrible would happen.* [Early 18thC. Via obsolete French *présentiment* from, ultimately, Latin *praesentire* (see PRESENTIENT).] —**pre·sen·ti·men·tal** /pri zèntə mént'l/ *adj.*

pres·ent·ly /prézz'ntlee/ *adv.* **1.** SOON not at this exact moment but in a short while (*formal or literary*) ○ *I'll be there presently.* **2.** AT THE PRESENT TIME now, or during the current period, especially if not at some other time (*some people object to this usage*) ○ *Yes, he's presently engaged in a research job for the company.* **3.** STRAIGHT AWAY immediately and without delay (*archaic*)

pre·sent·ment /pri zéntmənt/ *n.* **1.** PRESENTATION the act of presenting something or the way in which something is presented **2.** STATEMENT BY JURY in the past, a formal statement made on oath by a grand jury to a court concerning facts and matters within their own knowledge **3.** PRESENTING OF NEGOTIABLE INSTRUMENT the presenting of a negotiable instrument for payment

pres·ent par·ti·ci·ple *n.* the form of a verb that suggests a continuous or active sense and that ends in "-ing" in English, e.g., "flying"

pres·ent per·fect *n.* the form of a verb that suggests something completed, in English by preceding the verb with "have" or "has" and usually putting "-ed" after it, e.g., "have departed" —**pres·ent per·fect** *adj.*

pres·ent tense *n.* the tense of a verb that suggests actions or the situation at the time of speaking or writing

pres·ent val·ue *n.* the value now of a sum of money expected to be received in the future, calculated by subtracting the interest and other value that will accrue in the intervening period ○ *The judge reduced the jury's award of damages to present value, as required by law.*

pre·serv·a·ble /pri zúrvəb'l/ *adj.* able to be kept safe, unchanged, or unspoiled ○ *The east wing is preservable but the rest of the building will have to be demolished.* —**pre·serv·a·bil·i·ty** /pri zùrvə bíllətee/ *n.* —**pre·serv·a·bly** /pri zúrvəblee/ *adv.*

pres·er·va·tion /prèzzər váysh'n/ *n.* **1.** PROTECTION FROM HARM the guarding of something from danger, harm, or injury **2.** A KEEPING OF SOMETHING UNCHANGED maintenance of something, especially something of historic value, in an unchanged condition **3.** UPHOLDING OF SOMETHING the keeping of something intangible intact ○ *preservation of freedom of speech*

pres·er·va·tion·ist /prèzzər váysh'nist/ *n.* somebody who tries to prevent things from being damaged, destroyed, or altered from their current condition, particularly things of natural or historical interest —**pres·er·va·tion·ism** /prèzzər váysh'n ìzzəm/ *n.*

pre·ser·va·tive /pri zúrvətiv/ *adj.* ABLE TO KEEP FROM DECAY having the ability to protect something from decay or spoilage ■ *n.* SOMETHING THAT PREVENTS SPOILAGE something that provides protection from decay or spoilage, e.g., a food additive

pre·serve /pri zúrv/ *vt.* (**-served, -serv·ing, -serves**) **1.** MAKE SURE SOMETHING LASTS to keep something protected from anything that would cause its current quality or condition to change or deteriorate or fall out of use ○ *They are anxious to preserve the area's rural character.* ○ *We need to preserve professional standards of conduct.* **2.** MAINTAIN SOMETHING TO keep up or maintain something ○ *She preserved a cool and composed manner throughout the interrogation.* **3.** STOP FOOD FROM GOING BAD to treat or store food in such a way as to protect it from decay, e.g., by pickling, drying, salting, freezing, or canning **4.** MAKE JAM to make jelly, jam, or marmalade **5.** PROTECT SOMEBODY OR SOMETHING to protect somebody or something from danger, especially the danger of being killed or damaged (*formal or literary*) ○ *"The Lord shall preserve thee from all evil" (Psalm 121)* **6.** KEEP ANIMALS IN SECURE AREA to rear wild animals, especially fish and birds, in a protected area of water or land, so that they can be fished or shot for sport in the hunting season ■ *n.* **1.** EXCLUSIVE AREA OF ACTIVITY a type of work, sport, or interest that one particular person or group retains exclusive use of, or a place kept for one person or group to enjoy exclusively ○ *The children considered the treehouse their own preserve and resented adults intruding.* **2.** FOOD FRUIT JELLY OR JAM a sweet thick substance eaten on bread or in desserts and cakes, made by boiling fruit in sugar and water. Preserves can be kept for several years in airtight jars, bottles, or cans. (*often used in the plural*) **3.** AREA WHERE WILDLIFE IS PROTECTED a piece of water or land owned by the government or a conservation group, where wildlife, plants, or geographical features are protected or where fish or wild animals are bred [14thC. Via French *préserver* from medieval Latin *praeservare* "to guard beforehand," from Latin *servare* "to keep." Ultimately from an Indo-European word meaning "to protect."]

pre·serv·er /pri zúrvər/ *n.* something used to keep somebody or something safe, undamaged, or unchanged

pre·set *vt.* /pree sét/ (**-set, -set·ting, -sets**) SET MACHINE TO COME ON LATER to arrange the settings of a timing device controlling or built into an electrical appliance so that the appliance is automatically switched on at a specified time ○ *The bank's vault opens at a preset time every weekday morning.* ■ *n.* /prée sèt/ GADGET THAT TURNS MACHINE ON LATER an electronic timing

PRESIDENTS OF THE UNITED STATES

Term of office	President	Political party
1789–1797	George Washington	
1797–1801	John Adams	*Federalist*
1801–1809	Thomas Jefferson	*Democratic-Republican*
1809–1817	James Madison	*Democratic-Republican*
1817–1825	James Monroe	*Democratic-Republican*
1825–1829	John Quincy Adams	*Democratic-Republican*
1829–1837	Andrew Jackson	*Democrat*
1837–1841	Martin Van Buren	*Democrat*
1841	William Henry Harrison	*Whig*
1841–1845	John Tyler	*Whig*
1845–1849	James Polk	*Democrat*
1849–1850	Zachary Taylor	*Whig*
1850–1853	Millard Fillmore	*Whig*
1853–1857	Franklin Pierce	*Democrat*
1857–1861	James Buchanan	*Democrat*
1861–1865	Abraham Lincoln	*Republican*
1865–1869	Andrew Johnson	*Democrat*
1869–1877	Ulysses S. Grant	*Republican*
1877–1881	Rutherford B. Hayes	*Republican*
1881	James Garfield	*Republican*
1881–1885	Chester A. Arthur	*Republican*

Term of office	President	Political party
1885–1889	Grover Cleveland	*Democrat*
1889–1893	Benjamin Harrison	*Republican*
1893–1897	Grover Cleveland	*Democrat*
1897–1901	William McKinley	*Republican*
1901–1909	Theodore Roosevelt	*Republican*
1909–1913	William Howard Taft	*Republican*
1913–1921	Woodrow Wilson	*Democrat*
1921–1923	Warren G. Harding	*Republican*
1923–1929	Calvin Coolidge	*Republican*
1929–1933	Herbert Hoover	*Republican*
1933–1945	Franklin Delano Roosevelt	*Democrat*
1945–1953	Harry S. Truman	*Democrat*
1953–1961	Dwight D. Eisenhower	*Republican*
1961–1963	John F. Kennedy	*Democrat*
1963–1969	Lyndon Johnson	*Democrat*
1969–1974	Richard Nixon	*Republican*
1974–1977	Gerald Ford	*Republican*
1977–1981	Jimmy Carter	*Democrat*
1981–1989	Ronald Reagan	*Republican*
1989–1993	George Bush	*Republican*
1993–	Bill Clinton	*Democrat*

device or system that is used to make an appliance operate at a later time

pre·shrunk /pree shrúngk/ *adj.* with the fabric already shrunk before being sold, so that it will not shrink when the consumer washes it

pre·side /pri zíd/ (**-sid·ed, -sid·ing, -sides**) *vi.* **1. BE OFFICIALLY IN CHARGE** to be the chairperson or hold a similar position of authority at a formal gathering of people **2. HAVE CONTROL** to be the most powerful person or the one everyone else obeys, usually in a specified place or situation ○ *the question of who will preside over the business once their mother retires* **3.** MUSIC **PERFORM AS INSTRUMENTALIST** to be the featured instrumentalist in a performance ○ *preside at the organ* [Early 17thC. Via French *présider* from Latin *praesidere*, literally "to sit in front of," from *sedere* "to sit."] —**pre·sid·er** *n.*

pres·i·den·cy /prézzid'nsee/ (*plural* **-cies**) *n.* **1. POSITION OF PRESIDENT OF NATION** the job or function of president of a republic, or a president's term of office **2. JOB OF PRESIDENT** the status, post, or function of being president of a company, society, institution, or similar body ○ *The presidency of the club turned out to be a thankless task.* **3. LATTER-DAY SAINTS COUNCIL** a three-person executive council in the Church of Jesus Christ of Latter-day Saints **4. LATTER-DAY SAINTS GOVERNING COUNCIL** the governing body of the Church of Jesus Christ of Latter-day Saints

pres·i·dent /prézzid'nt/ *n.* **1. HEAD OF STATE OF A REPUBLIC** the chief politician of a republic, e.g., the United States of America ○ *President Kennedy was shot in 1963* **2. HIGHEST-RANKING MEMBER OF AN ASSOCIATION** somebody who holds the top official position in an organization, club, or society ○ *president of the Lawn Tennis Association* **3. HEAD OF A COMPANY** the highest-ranking executive officer of a business or corporation **4. HEAD OF EDUCATIONAL OR GOVERNMENTAL ESTABLISHMENT** the highest-ranking executive officer of certain universities, colleges, government departments, legal divisions, and other public offices **5. SOMEBODY IN CHARGE OF A MEETING** somebody who has been appointed or elected to take charge at a formal gathering of people **6. LATTER-DAY SAINTS LEADER** in the Church of Jesus Christ of Latter-day Saints, a man who is a member of the church's governing board. He, together with counselors and the Council of the Twelve Apostles, makes major church policy and decisions. [14thC. Via French *président* from, ultimately, Latin *praesidere* (see PRESIDE).] —**pres·i·dent·ship** *n.*

pres·i·dent-e·lect (*plural* **pres·i·dents-e·lect**) *n.* somebody who has been elected or appointed as president but who has not yet been officially installed into the job

pres·i·den·tial /prèzzə dénshəl/ *adj.* **1. RELATING TO PRESIDENT** concerning the post of president, or used or owned by a president ○ *The presidential elections dominated the news.* **2. LIKE A PRESIDENT** done in the manner of a president, or having the appearance of a president ○ *Pundits said that he was very presidential in refusing to trade insults with his political opponents.* **3. LED BY A PRESIDENT** presided over by a president, or presiding like one —**pres·i·den·tial·ly** *adv.*

Pres·i·den·tial Range chain of mountains in northern New Hampshire, in the White Mountains. The highest peak in the range is Mount Washington, 6,288 ft./1,917 m.

pre·si·di·o /prə síddee ō/ (*plural* **-os**) *n.* a fortified settlement, especially of the type established by Spanish colonizers in the southwestern part of what is now the United States [Mid-18thC. Via Spanish from Latin *praesidium* "garrison, fortification," from *praesidere* (see PRESIDE).]

Elvis Presley

pre·sid·i·um /prə síddee əm/ (*plural* **-a** /-ə/ *or* **-ums**) *n.* a permanent executive committee that acted for a larger legislature in the former Soviet Union and other Communist countries [Early 20thC. Via Russian from Latin *praesidium* (see PRESIDIO).]

pre·sig·ni·fy /pree sígnə fì/ (**-fied, -fy·ing, -fies**) *vt.* to indicate in advance something that is going to result or take place (*formal*)

Pres·ley /prézzlee/, **Elvis** (1935–77) U.S. singer and actor. Renowned as a pioneer of rock-and-roll, he also acted in several Hollywood movies. Full name **Elvis Aron Presley.** Known as **The King**

press[1] /press/ *v.* (**pressed, press·ing, press·es**) **1.** *vti.* **PUSH AGAINST SOMETHING** to use a steady and significant force to put weight on something, sometimes to make it move or start working ○ *I got into the elevator and pressed the down button but nothing happened.* **2.** *vt.* **SQUEEZE JUICE OUT OF SOMETHING** to squeeze the juice or oil out of something using force or weight to compress it ○ *pressing grapes* **3.** *vt.* **SMOOTH SOMETHING OUT** to push a flat object, especially a hot iron, onto a garment or piece of cloth so as to smooth out unwanted creases or make a crease where desired ○ *pressed a shirt and put it on* **4.** *vt.* **CHANGE SOMETHING'S SHAPE BY SQUEEZING** to change the shape of something by squeezing it or putting a steady weight on it, especially in order to make it more compact ○ *pressed the clay into a ball* **5.** *vt.* **HOLD SOMEBODY OR SOMETHING TIGHTLY** to grip or clasp somebody or something firmly but not roughly with the hands or arms, especially to show affection or moral support ○ *She pressed his hand in sympathy.* **6.** *vi.* **TRY TOO HARD** to exert great effort but not necessarily succeed, as an athlete under stress might ○ *Late in the crucial game, the players were obviously pressing and made one error after another.* **7.** *vt.* **FORCE SOMEBODY TO DO SOMETHING** to force somebody into doing something he or she did not want or intend to do ○ *They pressed her into accepting the nomination.* **8.** *vt.* **TRY TO OBTAIN SOMETHING FROM SOMEBODY** to ask somebody persistently or forcefully to supply, accept, or do a specific thing ○ *They pressed him for an immediate response.* **9.** *vt.* **EMPHASIZE SOMETHING** to make sure that something is fully recognized and understood, or stress its importance ○ *It is vital that you press the main items of the manifesto in your speech.* **10.** *vt.* **DEMAND SOMETHING** to plead or demand something insistently **11.** *vi.* **MOVE AS CROWD** to crowd around or together (*literary*) ○ *The crowd pressed forward as the gates opened.* **12.** *vi.* **REQUIRE ATTENTION** to need to be dealt with urgently (*dated or formal*) ○ *I'd like to help now, but business presses.* **13.** *vt.* **DRY SOMETHING OUT AND PRESERVE IT** to flatten and dry a natural object such as a flower so that it does not decompose and can be kept or used decoratively ○ *pressed flowers as a hobby* **14.** *vt.* **MAKE SOMETHING WITH A MOLD** to form something in a mold, especially to make phonograph records ○ *went down to the studio to press a record* **15.** *vti.* BASKETBALL **HARASS BASKETBALL OPPONENT AGGRESSIVELY** to use a harassing and aggressive defense against an opponent in basketball ■ *n.* **1.** an act of pressing something ○ *I gave the doorbell a few presses but nobody answered.* **2. CROWD** a tightly packed crowd of people **3. POWERFUL FORWARD OR COMBINED MOVEMENT** the crowding and pressing together of a lot of people or things at the same time (*literary*) ○ *He could not move because of the press of people.* **4. DEVICE FOR SQUEEZING SOMETHING** a piece of equipment designed to crush something to release the juices or create a pulp ○ *a garlic press* **5. DEVICE FOR FLATTENING SOMETHING** a piece of equipment used to keep or make something smooth and uncreased **6.** HOUSEHOLD **LINEN CLOSET** a shelved closet, usually of a large size, for storing bed or table linens or clothes **7.** MECH ENG **MACHINE THAT APPLIES MECHANICAL PRESSURE** a machine that, by applying pressure to a piece of metal or other material, can shape, form, cut, stamp, or otherwise cause a physical change to occur **8.** PRESS **NEWSPAPERS OR NEWS REPORTERS** the news-gathering business generally or all the people involved in gathering and reporting on the news, but in particular journalists working on newspapers ○ *She agreed to appear on television but refused to talk to the press.* **9.** PRESS **COMMENTS BY JOURNALISTS** the opinions expressed in articles or reviews in the newspapers or magazines ○ *His new musical had a lot of good press.* **10.** PRINTING = **printing press** **11.** PUBL **PUBLISHING COMPANY** a company that publishes books (*used especially in names*) **12.** PRINTING **BUSINESS OR SKILL OF PRINTING** the technical or physical process used by a printer and the skills a printer requires **13.** RACKET GAMES **CLAMP FOR RACKETS** a clamp for holding a tennis or other racket to prevent it from warping when it is not in use **14.** SPORTS **DEFENSE IN SPORTS** an aggressive defense, especially in basketball **15. LIFTING OF WEIGHT ABOVE HEAD** in weightlifting, a lift in which the weight is raised to shoulder height and then to above the head without moving the legs [14thC. Via French *presser* from Latin *pressare* "to keep on pressing," from *press-*, the past participle stem of *premere* "to press."] —**press·er** *n.* ◇ **be pressed for something** to be short of something, usually time ◇ **press your luck** to test how far you can go before running out of good fortune ○ *I forgive you this time but don't press your luck.*

WORD KEY: ORIGIN

The Latin word *pressare*, from which ***press*** is derived, is also the source of English *compress, depress, express, impress, oppress, repress,* and *suppress.*

press for *vt.* to seek or demand something with great urgency ○ *They pressed for an immediate review of the situation.*

press on *vi. U.K.* to continue in an urgent or persistent manner ○ *Night was falling but they pressed on despite their weariness.*

press[2] /press/ *vt.* (**pressed, press·ing, press·es**) **FORCE SOMEBODY INTO MILITARY SERVICE** to forcibly recruit somebody into military service ■ *n.* **FORCING OF SOMEBODY INTO MILITARY SERVICE** the act of recruiting people into military service by force [Late 16thC. Alteration (influenced by PRESS[1]) of obsolete *prest* "to enlist by paying in advance," via Old French *prester* from Latin *praestare*, literally "to stand before," from *stare* "to stand."]

press a·gen·cy *n.* = **news agency**

press a·gent *n.* somebody who is responsible for promoting clients by contacting and liaising with the press, and supplying the press with information, advertising material, photographs, and stories about them —**press a·gent·ry** *n.*

press as·so·ci·a·tion *n.* **1.** = **news agency 2. ORGANIZATION OF MEDIA PEOPLE** an organization, nationally, statewide, or locally, of media outlets and their representatives

press·board /préss bàwrd/ *n.* **1.** INDUST **CONSTRUCTION MATERIAL** a heavy glazed composition board **2.** HOUSEHOLD **SMALL IRONING BOARD** a small ironing board used particularly for pressing the sleeves of garments

press box *n.* a section in a sports stadium or similar venue kept exclusively for journalists to work in

press con·fer·ence *n.* an invited meeting for members of the press to enable them to hear a prepared statement by somebody in the news, and usually to ask questions about that statement

press gal·ler·y *n.* a raised gallery with seating at the back of a courtroom or legislative assembly room, where newspaper reporters and other members of the press can sit

press gang *n.* in former times, a group of military personnel whose job was to find people to force into military service

press-gang *vti.* to force people into military service or into doing anything that they are reluctant to do ○ *I never wanted to go to camp – my parents press-ganged me into it.*

press·ing /préssing/ *adj.* **1. URGENT** needing to be attended to without delay ○ *He had a pressing engagement and had to leave immediately.* **2. VERY PERSISTENT** persistent and demanding, and therefore difficult to ignore or refuse ○ *Her invitations were so pressing that we eventually had to accept.* ■ *n.* **PHONOGRAPH RECORDS MADE AT ONE TIME** all the phonograph records produced at one time from a master mold —**press·ing·ly** *adv.* —**press·ing·ness** *n.*

press kit *n.* a package of background and promotional material relating to a product, distributed to the media by a publicist or publicity department

press·man /présmən/ (*plural* **-men**) *n.* **1. OPERATOR OF PRINTING PRESS** somebody who operates a printing press **2.** *U.K.* **JOURNALIST** a man working as a newspaper reporter (*dated*)

press of sail /press əv sáyl/ *n.* the largest amount of sail that a ship can safely carry

pres·sor /préssər/ *adj.* relating to or bringing about an increase in blood pressure

press peach *n. Southern U.S.* a clingstone peach

WORD KEY: REGIONAL NOTE

This is the Lower Southern counterpart of *plum peach.* Most common in the lower sectors of Georgia, Alabama, Mississippi, and southwestern Louisiana, the term also recurs less frequently in Florida and eastern Louisiana.

press re·lease *n.* an official statement or account of a news story that is specially prepared and issued to newspapers and other news media for them to make known to the public

press·room /préss ro͝om, -ro͞om/ *n.* **1. ROOM CONTAINING PRINTING PRESSES** an enclosed area in a newspaper plant or printing establishment where the presses are located **2. PLACE FOR REPORTERS** a place where reporters work when not actually covering a newsworthy event, at a site, especially the White House, where such events often occur

press·run /préss rùn/ *n.* **1. CONTINUOUS RUNNING OF PRINTING PRESS** the continuous running of a printing press until a specified number of copies is printed **2. NUMBER OF COPIES RUN** the number of copies run off in a continuous printing operation

press sec·re·tar·y *n.* an employee responsible for managing the news media on behalf of an organization or a prominent individual

press stud *n. U.K.* = **snap**

press-up *n. U.K., NZ* any one of a series of identical exercise movements performed with the body straight and facing the floor. The arms are used to raise the body and then lower it again. ◊ **pushup**

pres·sure /préshər/ *n.* **1. PROCESS OF PRESSING STEADILY** the applying of a firm regular weight or force against something or somebody ○ *The pressure of her hand on his was comforting.* **2. CONSTANT STATE OF WORRY AND URGENCY** powerful and stressful demands on somebody's time, attention, and energy, or one of many demands of this sort **3. FORCE THAT PUSHES OR URGES** something that affects thoughts and behavior in a powerful way, usually in the form of several outside influences working together persuasively **4.** PHYS **FORCE PER UNIT AREA** the force acting on a surface divided by the area over which it acts. Symbol *p* **5.** = **compression 6. ATMOSPHERIC PRESSURE** atmospheric pressure ■ *vt.* (**-sured, -sur·ing, -sures**) **MAKE SOMEBODY DO SOMETHING** to apply great persuasion or a strong influence on somebody to force him or her to do something ○ *They were pressured into selling by the rest of the family.* [14thC. From Latin *pressura*, which was formed from the stem *press-* (see PRESS).] —**pres·sure·less** *adj.*

pres·sure cab·in *n.* an airtight cabin in an aircraft or spacecraft in which air pressure is maintained at a greater level than that of the outside atmospheric pressure for the comfort and safety of the occupants

pres·sure-cook *vt.* to cook something in a pressure cooker

pres·sure cook·er *n.* **1. HEAVY COOKING POT WITH AIRTIGHT LID** a specially designed pot used to steam food at high pressure, at a higher temperature and in a shorter time than by boiling **2. STRESSFUL PLACE** a place or situation in which people feel great stress ○ *The office of mayor of this city is a real pressure cooker.*

pres·sure gauge *n.* a device or instrument used to measure the pressure of a gas or liquid, e.g., a gauge that measures the air pressure in the tires of a car

pres·sure group *n.* a number of people who work together to make their particular concerns known to those in government, and to influence the passage of legislation

pres·sure point *n.* any point at which an artery can be compressed against a bone using a finger, stemming blood flow to the part of the body that the artery supplies. Compression of such a point can, at certain sites, reduce bleeding from a wound.

pres·sure sore *n.* = **bedsore**

pres·sure suit *n.* an inflatable airtight suit, similar to that worn by deep sea divers, used to protect against the effects of low pressure at very high altitude or in space

pres·sure ves·sel *n.* a cylindrical or spherically shaped container designed to withstand bursting pressures

pres·sur·ize /préshə rīz/ (**-ized, -iz·ing, -iz·es**) *vt.* **1. INCREASE AIR PRESSURE IN ENCLOSED SPACE** to increase the air pressure in an enclosed space, e.g., inside an aircraft, to maintain air at close to normal atmospheric pressure when the external pressure falls **2. INCREASE AIR PRESSURE IN CONTAINER** to increase the air pressure in a container beyond normal levels **3. PUT FLUID UNDER PRESSURE** to apply increased pressure to a fluid —**pres·sur·i·za·tion** /prèshəri záysh'n/ *n.* —**pres·sur·iz·er** *n.*

press·work /préss wùrk/ *n.* the operation, management, or work done by a printing press

Pres·ter John /prèstər jón/ *n.* a Christian priest who ruled in China according to medieval myth [From Old French *prestre Jehan* and medieval Latin *presbyter Johannes* "John the priest"]

pres·ti·dig·i·ta·tion /prèstə dijə táysh'n/ *n.* sleight of hand used in performing magic tricks (*dated or formal*) [Mid-19thC. From French, from *prestidigitateur* "person practicing sleight of hand," from *preste* "nimble" + Latin *digitus* "finger" (source of English *digit*).] —**pres·ti·dig·i·ta·tor** /prèstə díjjə taytər/ *n.*

pres·tige /pre stéezh, -stéej/ *n.* **1. RESPECT ASSOCIATED WITH HIGH QUALITY** the kind of honor, awe, or high opinion that is inspired by a high-ranking, influential, or successful person or product **2. GLAMOUR** the kind of attractiveness and importance that is very obvious or enviable, associated with wealthy and successful people ○ *It's a prestige car and its price reflects that.* [Mid-17thC. Via French from Latin *praestigiae* "illusions, juggler's tricks," of uncertain origin: probably ultimately from *praestringere* "to make dull, confuse," from *stringere* "to bind tight."]

pres·ti·gious /pre stéejəss, -stíjjəss/ *adj.* having a distinguished reputation or bringing prestige to the person who has it —**pres·ti·gious·ly** *adv.* —**pres·ti·gious·ness** *n.*

pres·tis·si·mo /pre stíssə mō/ *adv.* **EXTREMELY FAST** played or to be played as fast as possible (*used especially as a musical direction*) ■ *n.* (*plural* **-mos**) **EXTREMELY FAST MUSICAL PIECE** a musical composition or passage that is meant to be played as fast as possible [Early 18thC. From Italian, the superlative of *presto* "presto."] —**pre·stis·si·mo** *adj.*

pres·to /préstō/ *adv.* MUSIC **VERY FAST** played or to be played very fast (*used as a musical direction*) ■ *n.* (*plural* **-tos**) **VERY FAST MUSICAL PIECE** a musical composition or passage that is meant to be played very fast ■ *adv.* **SUDDENLY** instantly, as if magically (*informal*) ■ *interj.* **AT ONCE** used to indicate immediacy or quickness, often with an element of magic ○ *We turned the old key, and – presto! – the ancient gate creaked open.* [Late 16thC. Via Italian "quick," from, ultimately, Latin *praesto* "at hand."] —**pres·to** *adj.*

pre·stress /pree stréss/ (**-stressed, -stress·ing, -stress·es**) *vt.* to apply stress to something such as a cable or beam so that it will bear a load better when in use

pre·stressed con·crete /pree strést-/ *n.* concrete that is cast over cables that are under tension, so as to increase its strength

Prest·wick /prést wik/ town near Ayr, Scotland, on the Firth of Clyde. It is home to an international airport. Population: 13,705 (1991).

pre·sum·a·ble /pri zo͞oməb'l/ *adj.* probable, or capable of being assumed to be true

pre·sum·a·bly /pri zo͞oməblee/ *adv.* used to show that you expect that a specified thing is the case or will happen or has happened ○ *Presumably that man is her father.*

pre·sume /pri zo͞om/ (**-sumed, -sum·ing, -sumes**) *v.* **1.** *vti.* **BELIEVE SOMETHING TO BE TRUE** to accept that something is virtually certain to be correct even though there is no proof of it, on the grounds that it is extremely likely ○ *After several days of searching, they presumed that there were no survivors.* **2.** *vi.* **BEHAVE ARROGANTLY OR OVERCONFIDENTLY** to behave so inconsiderately, disrespectfully, or overconfidently as to do something without being entitled or qualified to do it (*usually used negatively*) ○ *I would never presume to tell you how to run your business.* **3.** *vt.* **REGARD SOMETHING AS TRUE WITHOUT PROOF** to assume that something is true in the absence of proof that will confirm or contradict it **4.** *vt.* **SEEM TO PROVE SOMETHING** to indicate the existence or truth of something (*formal*) ○ *Your line of reasoning presumes his being at home the whole evening.* **5.** *vi.* **TAKE ADVANTAGE** to exploit or take advantage of somebody unscrupulously ○ *would not want to presume on the generosity of a stranger* [14thC. Via French *présumer* from Latin *praesumere* "to take before, anticipate," which was formed from *sumere* "to take."] —**pre·sum·er** *n.* —**pre·sum·ing** *adj.* —**pre·sum·ing·ly** *adv.*

pre·sump·tion /pri zúmpshən/ *n.* **1.** SOMETHING BELIEVED WITHOUT ACTUAL EVIDENCE a belief based on the fact that something is considered to be extremely reasonable or likely ○ *I acted on the presumption that their IDs were genuine.* **2.** RUDENESS OR ARROGANCE behavior that is inconsiderate, disrespectful, or overconfident **3.** LAW LEGAL INFERENCE an inference that something is the case, in the absence of evidence rebutting that assumption and on the basis of other known facts ○ *a presumption of innocence* **4.** BELIEF IN SOMETHING THAT SEEMS REASONABLE the acceptance that something is correct, without having proof of it, on the grounds that it is extremely likely (*formal*) ○ *a decision based on presumption rather than on the facts* **5.** SOMETHING THAT COULD BE PROOF an indication that something exists or is true (*formal*) [12thC. Via Old French *presumpcion* from, ultimately, Latin *praesumere* (see PRESUME).]

pre·sump·tive /pri zúmptiv/ *adj.* **1.** PROBABLE based on what is thought most likely or reasonable (*formal*) **2.** CAUSING PEOPLE TO PRESUME SOMETHING forming a reasonable basis for the acceptance that something exists or is true (*formal*) **3.** EXPECTED TO BECOME expected or thought likely to become (*archaic or formal*) ○ *heir-presumptive* **4.** BIOL POTENTIALLY ABLE TO DIFFERENTIATE used to describe cells or tissue of an early embryo that, in the normal course of development, will differentiate to form a particular organ or tissue in the mature embryo [Mid-16thC. Via French *présomptif* from, ultimately, Latin *praesumere* (see PRESUME).] —**pre·sump·tive·ly** *adv.* —**pre·sump·tive·ness** *n.*

pre·sump·tu·ous /pri zúmpchoo əss/ *adj.* inconsiderate, disrespectful, or overconfident, especially in doing something when not entitled or qualified to do it [14thC. Via Old French *presumptueux* from, ultimately, Latin *praesumere* (see PRESUME).] —**pre·sump·tu·ous·ly** *adv.* —**pre·sump·tu·ous·ness** *n.*

pre·sup·pose /pree səpṓz/ (**-posed, -pos·ing, -pos·es**) *vt.* **1.** ASSUME SOMETHING IN ADVANCE to believe that a particular thing is true before there is any proof of it ○ *the tendency to presuppose that everybody will understand English* **2.** LOGIC REQUIRE SOMETHING AS PRIOR CONDITION to make something necessary if a particular thing is to be shown to be true or false. The sentence "Fred loves his daughter" presupposes that Fred has a daughter. —**pre·sup·po·si·tion** /prèe suppə zísh'n/ *n.*

pre·sys·to·lic /pree sis tóllik/ *adj.* used to describe the interval immediately before systole in the heart

pret. *abbr.* preterite

prêt-à-por·ter /prèt aa pawr táy/ *adj.* manufactured in standard sizes ready to be bought off the rack in stores [Mid-20thC. From French, literally "ready-to-wear."]

pre·tax /pree táks/ *adj.* before tax is or was deducted ○ *the company's pretax profits*

pre·teen /pree téen/, **pre·teen·ag·er** /pree téen ayjər/ *adj.* **1.** FOR CHILDREN BETWEEN 9 AND 12 relating to, made for, or directed at children in the few years immediately before they become teenagers, or referring to children of this age ○ *preteen clothing* **2.** BETWEEN 9 AND 12 YEARS OLD during the few years immediately before becoming a teenager ○ *her preteen years* ■ *n.* CHILD BETWEEN 9 AND 12 a girl or boy in the few years before becoming a teenager

pre·tence *n. U.K.* = **pretense**

pre·tend /pri ténd/ *v.* (**-tend·ed, -tend·ing, -tends**) **1.** *vti.* ACT AS IF SOMETHING WERE TRUE to make believe, e.g., by using the imagination or acting skills ○ *The little girl liked to pretend that she was an astronaut.* **2.** *vt.* MAKE INSINCERE CLAIM ABOUT SOMETHING to claim untruthfully or exaggeratedly to be or to have a particular thing, or to imply something in this way ○ *I won't pretend to be an expert on the subject, but I can't believe those figures are correct.* **3.** *vt.* MAKE SOMETHING SEEM TO BE TRUE to act in a way intended to make people believe something untrue or misleading about somebody or something ○ *She pretended to be an orphan just to get our sympathy.* **4.** *vi.* CLAIM TO OWN SOMETHING to make an untruthful or dubious claim of ownership or the right to something, especially something valuable, admirable, or prestigious (*formal*) ○ *pretends to the throne* ■ *adj.* IMAGINARY existing only in the imagination, not real (*informal*) (*usually used by or to children*) ○ *I made a pretend house where my pretend horse lives.* [14thC. Directly or via French *prétendre* from Latin *praetendere*, literally "to extend in front," from *tendere* "to stretch."]

pre·tend·ed /pri téndəd/ *adj.* appearing or claiming to be real, but in fact false or insincere ○ *I find her pretended concern quite offensive.*

pre·tend·er /pri téndər/ *n.* **1.** SOMEBODY GIVING FALSE IMPRESSION somebody who acts or speaks in a way that is designed to make people believe something that is untrue **2.** SOMEBODY CLAIMING THE RIGHT TO SOMETHING somebody who either sincerely or dishonestly claims the right to a special rank, title, or privilege, especially a royal title, although many people question or doubt the claim

pre·tense /prée tèns, pri téns/ *n.* **1.** INSINCERE OR FEIGNED BEHAVIOR something done or a way of behaving that is not genuine but is meant to deceive other people ○ *His display of affection was certainly a pretense.* **2.** UNWARRANTED CLAIM a claim, especially one with few facts to support it (*often used in the negative*) ○ *He makes no pretense of being an expert.* **3.** MAKE-BELIEVE make-believe or things imagined **4.** = **pretext 5.** = **pretension** *n.* 2 [14thC. Via Anglo-Norman from medieval Latin *pretensus* "alleged," from the past participle of Latin *praetendere* (see PRETEND).] ◇ **under false pretenses** in a way that is intended to deceive people ○ *She borrowed money from us under false pretenses.*

pre·ten·sion /pri ténshən/ *n.* **1.** QUESTIONABLE CLAIM TO SOMETHING an untruthful or dubious assertion of a right to something, especially something valuable, admirable, or prestigious (*often used in the plural and with negatives*) ○ *His pretensions to aristocratic birth were unconvincing.* **2.** AFFECTED BEHAVIOR behavior that is artificial, especially that which is given to display and grandeur **3.** MAKING OF CLAIM TO SOMETHING the formal act of putting forward a claim (*formal*) [15thC. From the medieval Latin stem *praetension-*, which was formed from the past participle stem of Latin *praetendere* (see PRETEND).]

pre·ten·tious /pri ténshəss/ *adj.* **1.** SELF-IMPORTANT AND AFFECTED acting as though more important, valuable, or special than is warranted, or appearing to have an unrealistically high self-image **2.** MADE TO LOOK OR SOUND IMPORTANT presenting itself unjustifiably as having a special quality or significance, and often seeming forced or overly clever ○ *dismissed it as yet another pretentious film* **3.** OSTENTATIOUS extravagantly and consciously showy or glamorous [Mid-19thC. Via French *prétentieux* from, ultimately, the medieval Latin stem *praetension-* (see PRETENSION).] —**pre·ten·tious·ness** *n.* —**pre·ten·tious·ly** *adv.*

preter- *prefix.* beyond ○ *preterhuman* [From Latin *praeter*, from *prae* "before" (see PRE-)]

pret·er·hu·man /prèetər hyóomən/ *adj.* more than human or beyond what is usually thought of as human (*literary*)

pret·er·it /préttərit/, **pret·er·ite** *n.* the past tense [Via Old French from Latin *(tempus) praeteritum* "past (tense)," from the past participle of *praeterire* (see PRETERITION)] —**pret·er·ite** *adj.*

pret·er·i·tion /prèttə rísh'n/ *n.* the act of passing over something or leaving something out (*formal*) [Late 16thC. From the late Latin stem *praeterition-* "a passing by," which was formed from Latin *praeterire* "to go by," which in turn was formed from *ire* "to go."]

pre·ter·i·tive /prə térrətiv/ *adj.* used to describe a verb that is in the past tense

pre·term /pree túrm/ *adj.* PREMATURE born before completion of a pregnancy of normal length ■ *adv.* PREMATURELY before completion of a pregnancy of normal length

pre·ter·mi·nal /pree túrmən'l/ *adj.* occurring at a time just before death

pre·ter·mit /pree túrmit/ (**-mit·ted, -mit·ting, -mits**) *vt.* (*formal*) **1.** OVERLOOK AN HEIR FROM A WILL to overlook or ignore something deliberately, especially a natural heir from a will **2.** LEAVE SOMETHING OUT to leave something out or undone [15thC. From Latin *praetermittere* "to let go by," which was formed from *mittere* "to let go."] —**pre·ter·mis·sion** /prèe tur mísh'n/ *n.* —**pre·ter·mit·ter** *n.*

pre·ter·nat·u·ral /prèetər náchərəl/ *adj.* **1.** GOING BEYOND NATURE exceeding what is normal in nature (*formal or literary*) **2.** SUPERNATURAL supernatural or uncanny (*literary*) [Late 16thC. From medieval Latin *praeternaturalis*, which was formed from the Latin phrase *praeter naturam* "beyond nature."] —**pre·ter·nat·u·ral·ism** *n.* —**pre·ter·nat·u·ral·i·ty** /prèetər nachə rállətee/ *n.* —**pre·ter·nat·u·ral·ly** *adv.* —**pre·ter·nat·u·ral·ness** *n.*

pre·test *n.* /prée tèst/ PRELIMINARY TEST a preliminary test carried out to evaluate the usefulness of further research ■ *vt.* /pree tést/ (**-test·ed, -test·ing, -tests**) SUBJECT SOMETHING TO PRELIMINARY TEST to run a preliminary test on something

pre·text /prée tèkst/ *n.* a misleading or untrue reason given for doing something in an attempt to conceal the real reason [Early 16thC. From Latin *praetextus* "show, display," from *praetext*, the past participle stem of *praetexere* "to weave before, adorn," from *texere* "to weave."]

pre·tick·et /pree tíkit/ (**-et·ed, -et·ing, -ets**) *vt.* to sell somebody a ticket in advance, especially before a flight

pre·tor *n.* = **praetor**

pre·to·ri·an *adj., n.* = **praetorian**

Pre·to·ri·us /pri táwree əss/, **Marthinus Wessels** (1819–1901) South African statesman. The son of Andries Pretorius, he was president of the South African Republic, which then comprised only the Transvaal (1857–71), and of the Orange Free State (1859–63).

pret·ti·fy /prítta fī/ (**-fied, -fy·ing, -fies**) *vt.* to give a person, place, or thing some added decoration, especially of a rather superficial or fussy kind —**pret·ti·fi·ca·tion** /prìttəfi káysh'n/ *n.* —**pret·ti·fi·er** *n.*

pret·ty /príttee/ *adj.* (**-ti·er, -ti·est**) **1.** HAVING A PLEASANT FACE with an attractive, pleasant face that is graceful and appealing rather than outstandingly beautiful **2.** NICE TO LOOK AT pleasing or charming in appearance in a delicate, gentle, or decorative way ○ *The garden looks so pretty at this time of year.* **3.** NICE TO LISTEN TO with a pleasant, gentle, or delicate sound quality ○ *operas with pretty music* **4.** LARGE large in size, extent or value (*dated informal*) ○ *a pretty sum* **5.** GRACEFUL AND EFFEMINATE having, as a boy or man, the pleasing looks and graceful manner often associated with a woman (*offensive in some contexts*) **6.** UNSATISFACTORY very bad or unsatisfactory (*dated informal*) ○ *That's a pretty mess you've gotten yourself into.* ■ *adv.* FAIRLY to quite a large, noticeable, or reasonable extent (*informal*) ○ *I'm pretty sure I left my keys on the kitchen table.* ■ *n.* (*plural* **-ties**) SOMEBODY WHO IS PRETTY a pretty person, thing, or animal (*archaic informal*) ■ **pret·ties** *npl.* delicate, feminine nightwear or underwear (*informal*) [Old English, *prættig*. Ultimately from a prehistoric Germanic base meaning "trick," of unknown origin. In Old English, "pretty" meant "clever" in a bad sense – "crafty, cunning." Not until the 15thC had it passed via "clever," "skillfully made," and "fine" to "beautiful."] ◇ **sitting pretty** in a good or favorable position (*informal*) ◇ **a pretty penny** a large amount of money (*informal*) ◇ **pretty well** nearly completely (*informal*)

WORD KEY: SYNONYMS

See Synonyms at ***goodlooking***.

Pret·ty Good Pri·va·cy full form of **PGP**

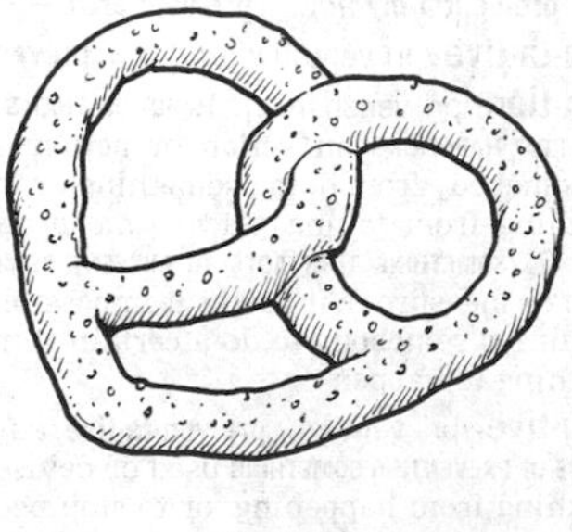

Pretzel

pret·zel /préts'l/ *n.* a usually small crisp knot-shaped or stick-shaped biscuit with a golden brown glaze [Mid-19thC. From German, of uncertain origin: perhaps ultimately from Latin *bracchiatus* "branched, wearing bracelets," which was formed from *brachium* "arm" (see BRACHIUM). According to tradition, the shape of the pretzel was devised by a Christian monk to represent arms and hands folded in prayer.]

pre·vail /pri váyl/ (**-vailed, -vail·ing, -vails**) *v.* **1.** *vi.* BE UNBEATEN AND IN CONTROL to prove to be stronger and in the position of greater influence and power ○ *He prevailed over his enemies* **2.** WIN THROUGH to prove to be effective ○ *Justice will prevail.* **3.** *vi.* **BE THE NORMAL THING** to predominate or be the most common or frequent ○ *Middle-class families prevail on this street.* **4.** *vi.* **BE CURRENT** to remain in general use or effect (*formal*) ○ *Witchcraft still prevails in some parts of the country.* [14thC. From Latin *praevalere* "to be stronger," which was formed from *valere* "to be strong."] —**pre·vail·er** *n.*

prevail on or upon *vt.* to persuade somebody to do something ○ *They prevailed on her to take part.*

pre·vail·ing /pri váyling/ *adj.* **1. USUAL** found most commonly or having the most power or effect in a particular area ○ *prevailing winds* **2.** found, existing, or in force currently ○ *the prevailing view among modern scientists* —**pre·vail·ing·ly** *adv.*

prev·a·lence /prévvələns/ *n.* **1. STATE OF BEING COMMON** the state of being frequent or widespread **2.** MED **NUMBER OF CASES OF DISEASE** the number of cases of an illness or condition that exists at a particular time in a defined population ○ *The prevalence of asthma in the country is increasing steadily.*

prev·a·lent /prévvələnt/ *adj.* occurring, or accepted and practiced, commonly or widely ○ *Roman Catholicism is the prevalent religion in most of southern Europe.* [Late 16thC. From Latin *praevalere* (see PREVAIL).] —**prev·a·lent·ly** *adv.*

WORD KEY: SYNONYMS

See Synonyms at ***widespread.***

pre·var·i·cate /pri vérrə kàyt/ (**-cat·ed, -cat·ing, -cates**) *vi.* to avoid giving a direct and honest answer or opinion, or a clear and truthful account of a situation, especially by quibbling or being deliberately ambiguous or misleading [Mid-16thC. From Latin *praevaricari* "to walk crookedly," from, ultimately, *varus* "crooked, knock-kneed."] —**pre·var·i·ca·tor** *n.*

pre·var·i·ca·tion /pri vèrrə káysh'n/ *n.* the attempt to avoid giving a direct and honest answer or opinion, or a clear and truthful account of a situation, often by telling a lie

pre·ven·ient /pri veényənt/ *adj.* (*formal*) **1. PRECEDING SOMETHING** coming or occurring in advance of another thing **2. CREATING ANTICIPATION** producing a sense of anticipation [Early 17thC. From Latin *praevenient-*, the present participle stem of *praevenire* "to come before" (see PREVENT).]

pre·vent /pri vént/ (**-vent·ed, -vent·ing, -vents**) *vt.* **1. STOP SOMETHING FROM TAKING PLACE** to cause something not to happen or not to be done ○ *Rain prevented them from playing the game.* **2. STOP SOMEBODY FROM DOING SOMETHING** to be the reason why somebody does not or cannot do a particular thing ○ *a sense of duty that prevented him from abandoning the project* [15thC. From Latin *prevent-*, the past participle stem of *praevenire* "to come before, prevent," which was formed from *venire* "to come." Ultimately from an Indo-European word meaning "to go, come" that is also the ancestor of English *come* and *basis.* The meaning "hinder" developed in Latin via "act in advance of, anticipate."] —**pre·vent·a·bil·i·ty** /pri vèntə bíllətee/ *n.* —**pre·vent·a·ble** *adj.* —**pre·vent·a·bly** *adv.* —**pre·vent·er** *n.*

pre·ven·ta·tive /pri véntətiv/ *adj., n.* = **preventive**

pre·ven·tion /pri vénshən/ *n.* **1. ACTION THAT STOPS SOMETHING FROM HAPPENING** an action or actions taken to stop somebody from doing something or to prevent something from taking place ○ *the prevention of crime* **2. SOMETHING THAT ACTS TO PREVENT SOMETHING** an action or measure that makes it impossible or very difficult for somebody to do a certain thing, or for something to happen

pre·ven·tive /pri véntiv/, **pre·ven·ta·tive** *adj.* **WITH THE PURPOSE OF PREVENTING SOMETHING** used or devised to stop something from happening, or to stop people from doing a particular thing ○ *preventive dentistry* ■ *n.* **SOMETHING THAT PREVENTS** something that stops something unwanted from happening, especially something that protects against illness ○ *The best preventive against heart disease is a healthy lifestyle.* —**pre·ven·tive·ly** *adv.* —**pre·ven·tive·ness** *n.*

pre·ven·tive de·ten·tion *n.* **1. PRETRIAL IMPRISONMENT** the pretrial jailing without bail of somebody accused of a crime who is thought likely to attempt to flee, commit additional crimes, or intimidate witnesses or prosecutors, or an instance of such jailing **2.** PSYCHOL **INSTITUTIONALIZATION OF DISTURBED PATIENTS** institutionalization of a psychologically disturbed patient in order to prevent him or her from committing a crime

pre·verb·al /pree vúrb'l/ *adj.* **1. NOT YET ABLE TO TALK** at the stage of development when a child is not yet able to use speech **2. PRECEDING VERB** coming before a verb

pre·view /preé vyoo/ *n.* **1. OPPORTUNITY TO SEE SOMETHING IN ADVANCE** a showing of something, especially a movie, play, exhibition, or work of art, to a select audience before the general public sees it **2. DESCRIPTION OF A FORTHCOMING SHOW** a piece printed in a paper or magazine or broadcast on radio or TV describing and commenting on something that is soon to be broadcast or presented to the public **3. pre·view, pre·vue PROMOTIONAL FILM** a short film shown on TV or at a movie theater promoting an upcoming movie or program ■ *vt.* (**-viewed, -view·ing, -views**) **1. SHOW SOMETHING IN ADVANCE** to put on a performance or showing of something for a select audience before the general public has the opportunity to see it **2. DESCRIBE A SHOW IN ADVANCE** to write, print, or broadcast a short piece that describes and comments on something that is soon to be broadcast or presented to the public

pre·vi·ous /preévee əss/ *adj.* **1. COMING BEFORE SOMETHING** occurring before something or somebody of the same kind ○ *his previous girlfriend* ○ *the previous edition* **2. ALREADY ARRANGED** existing, made, or settled before the one being referred to now ○ *She was unable to come because of a previous engagement.* **3. ACTING TOO HASTILY** saying or doing something earlier than is appropriate (*informal*) [Early 17thC. From Latin *praevius* "going before," from *prae* "before."] —**pre·vi·ous·ness** *n.* ◇ **previous to something** before a particular thing took place

pre·vi·ous·ly /preévee əsslee/ *adv.* at an earlier time or on an earlier occasion

pre·vi·ous ques·tion *n.* a motion to put a question that will end a debate so that a vote on a bill can be taken without delay

pre·vise /pri víz/ (**-vised, -vis·ing, -vis·es**) *vt.* (*formal or literary*) **1. PREDICT SOMETHING** to predict or foresee something **2. WARN SOMEBODY** to warn somebody about something [15thC. From Latin *praevis-*, the past participle stem of *praevidere* "to foresee," which was formed from *videre* "to see."]

pre·vi·sion /prə vízh'n/ (**-sioned, -sion·ing, -sions**) *n.* (*formal or literary*) **1. ABILITY TO PREDICT** the ability to predict or foresee things **2. PREDICTION** a prediction or premonition

pre·vo·cal·ic /pree vō kállik/ *adj.* used to describe a consonant that comes immediately before a vowel —**pre·vo·cal·i·cal·ly** *adv.*

Pre·vost /prév ost/, **Sir George** (1767–1816) British soldier and administrator. He was governor-in-chief of Canada (1811–12) and commander of British forces in North America during the War of 1812.

pre·vue *n.* = **preview**

pre·war /pree wáwr/ *adj.* **BEFORE THE WAR** dating from or belonging to the period before a particular war, especially World War II or World War I ○ *prewar buildings* ■ *adv.* **AT A TIME BEFORE THE WAR** during the period before a particular war took place, especially World War II or World War I

pre·washed /pree wáwsht/, **pre-washed** *adj.* washed before being packaged and sold in the store

pre·writ·ing /pree ríting/ *n.* the preparatory work needed before a piece of writing is begun, such as formation of ideas, organization of material, and discussion

prex·y /préksee/ (*plural* **-ies**), **prex** /preks/ *n.* a president, especially of a college or university (*slang*) [Early 19thC. Alteration of PREZ.]

prey /pray/ (**preyed, prey·ing, preys,** *plural* **prey** *or* **preys**) *n.* **1. ANIMALS HUNTED BY OTHER ANIMALS** an animal or animals that are caught, killed, and eaten by another animal as food ○ *The common shrew's prey consists largely of earthworms and woodlice.* **2. SOMEBODY TREATED UNKINDLY BY OTHERS** somebody who is attacked or receives cruel or unfair treatment from somebody else ○ *a young heiress who became prey to fortune hunters* **3. KILLING OF OTHER ANIMALS AS FOOD** the natural practice or habit of predatory animals to hunt, kill, and eat other animals ○ *a bird of prey* **4. PLUNDER** items stolen or plundered (*archaic or literary*) [13thC. Via Old French *preie* from Latin *praeda* "booty" (related to Latin *praehendere* "to seize," which is the source of English *apprehend* and *prison*). Ultimately from an Indo-European word meaning "to take" that is also the ancestor of English *get.*] —**prey·er** /práyr/ *n.* ◇ **prey on your mind** to cause you constant worry or distress ◇ **be prey to something** to experience something unpleasant regularly or be at risk of something

prey on or upon *vt.* **1. HUNT AND KILL OTHER ANIMALS** to hunt and kill other animals for food ○ *Owls prey on mice and rabbits.* **2. VICTIMIZE SOMEBODY** to victimize or exploit somebody **3. WORRY SOMEBODY** to cause somebody constant anxiety or distress ○ *an ever-increasing debt that preyed on his mind*

prez /prez/, **pres** *n.* a president (*slang*) [Late 19thC. Shortening.]

Pri·am /prí əm/ *n.* in Greek mythology, the king of Troy, husband of Hecuba, and father of Hector, Paris, and Cassandra. He was killed during the Trojan War.

pri·a·pic /prī áppik/ *adj.* **1. RELATING TO PHALLUS** relating to or resembling a phallus (*dated or literary*) **2.** MED **WITH PENIS PERMANENTLY ERECT** having a permanently erect penis **3. FASCINATED BY MALE SEXUAL ACTIVITY** showing a preoccupation with male sexual activity [Late 18thC. Formed from Latin *Priapus*, the god of procreation, symbolized by the erect phallus, from Greek *Priapos.*]

pri·a·pism /prí ə pìzzəm/ *n.* a medical disorder in which there is persistent, often painful erection of the penis in the absence of sexual interest [Early 17thC. Formed from Latin *Priapus* (see PRIAPIC).]

Pri·a·pus /prī áypəss/ *n.* in Greek mythology, the god of fertility. He was the son of Aphrodite and Dionysus.

Prib·i·lof Is·lands /príbbə làwf-/ group of islands off southwestern Alaska, in the southeastern Bering Sea, approximately 180 mi./290 km north of Unalaska Island. Population: 901 (1990). Area: 62 sq. mi./161 sq. km.

price /prīss/ *n.* **1. COST OF SOMETHING BOUGHT OR SOLD** the particular amount, usually of money, that is offered or asked for when something is bought or sold ○ *The price of food continued to soar.* **2. SOMETHING SACRIFICED TO GET SOMETHING ELSE** something lost or given in order to achieve a particular position or condition ○ *Unwanted media attention is the price of fame.* **3. SUFFICIENT BRIBE** the sum of money or other payment for which somebody is willing to do something or to refrain from doing something ○ *The price of her cooperation was an invitation to the gala dinner.* **4. REWARD MONEY** a sum of money offered as a reward for the capture or killing of a particular criminal or outlaw (*dated or literary*) ○ *an outlaw with a price on his head* **5. MEASURE OF SOMETHING'S VALUE** an estimate of what somebody or something is worth, e.g., how important, useful, or irreplaceable it is (*dated or literary*) **6.** BETTING **BETTING ODDS** betting or gambling odds ■ *vt.* (**priced, pric·ing, pric·es**) **1. DECIDE HOW MUCH SOMETHING COSTS** to state or fix the exact price that a customer or consumer must pay for something ○ *He priced the antique clock at $700.* **2. MARK SOMETHING WITH ITS PRICE** to show how much something costs, especially by writing on the article itself or by attaching a label or price tag ○ *spent the morning pricing merchandise* **3. FIND OUT WHAT SOMETHING COSTS** to check the price that has been set for a certain product, or compare the different prices charged at a variety of stores or from different companies ○ *priced a few computers before deciding which one to buy* [13thC. Via Old French *pris* from Latin *pretium* "price, money" (source of English *prize* and *praise*). Ultimately from an Indo-European base meaning "to sell" that is also the ancestor of English *pornography.*] —**pric·er** *n.* ◇ **at any price** no matter how much it costs (*often used with a negative*) ◇ **at a price** for a lot of money ◇ **be beyond price** to be priceless ◇ **have a price on your head** to have had a reward offered for your capture or death ◇ **price something out of the market** to charge so high a price for something as to make its sale very unlikely ◇ **what price something?** used to suggest that something such as an ideal or a promise has no value ○ *"What Price Glory?"* (Maxwell Anderson, *What Price Glory?*, 1924)

Price /prīss/, **Leontyne** (*b.* 1927) U.S. soprano. During a long career as a major international opera star (1952–85), she was especially associated with Italian opera. Full name **Mary Violet Leontyne Price**

price con·trol *n.* government control over prices of goods and services, usually introduced as an emergency measure

price-cut·ting *n.* the reduction of prices below their usual level in order to sell more than competitors

U.S. Information Agency

Leontyne Price

price-earn·ings ra·tio *n.* on the stock exchange, the ratio of a share's price to its earnings, providing an indication of its value

price fix·ing *n.* the setting of prices by government or following an agreement between producers, rather than by free market operation

price in·dex *n.* a mathematical quantity that is used to measure movements in price levels over different periods of time

price·less /prī́ssləss/ *adj.* **1. IMPOSSIBLE TO PUT A VALUE ON** worth more than can be calculated in terms of money ○ *the priceless treasures of the pharoahs' tombs* **2. HILARIOUS** extremely comic and amusing (*informal*) ○ *You should have seen his face when I walked in – it was priceless!* —**price·less·ness** *n.*

price sup·port *n.* government maintenance of prices levels by means such as subsidy

price tag *n.* **1. LABEL SAYING WHAT SOMETHING COSTS** a small label attached to an article that is for sale, with the price written or printed on it **2. PRICE THAT MUST BE PAID** the amount something costs, whether in money or in something else, e.g., emotional outlay or loss of life or health (*informal*) ○ *The price tag for involvement in the war was more than the country could stand.*

price war *n.* extreme competition within a market, characterized by price-cutting

pric·ey /prī́ssee/ (**-i·er, -i·est**), **pric·y** (**-i·er, -i·est**) *adj.* charging high prices or costing a great deal (*informal*) ○ *a pricey restaurant* —**pric·ey·ness** *n.*

Prich·ard /príchərd/ city in southwestern Alabama, a northern suburb of Mobile. Population: 32,887 (1996).

prick /prik/ *v.* (**pricked, prick·ing, pricks**) **1.** *vt.* **MAKE SMALL HOLE THROUGH SURFACE** to puncture the surface of something, especially the skin, by piercing it lightly with something sharp and finely pointed ○ *pricked her finger on a cactus needle* **2.** *vt.* **SUDDENLY DISTURB SOMEBODY EMOTIONALLY OR MENTALLY** to make somebody feel a sudden strong emotional twinge, e.g., of guilt or shame ○ *His conscience began to prick him.* **3.** *vt.* **MARK OUT SHAPE USING TINY HOLES** to make a number of small indentations in or through the surface of something such as a board or a piece of card or fabric so as to form the outline of something **4.** *vti.* **RAISE THE EARS** to stick up straight or cause an animal's ears to stick up straight ○ *The dog pricked its ears at the sound of its master's voice.* **5.** *vt.* **MAKE AN ANIMAL MOVE FASTER** to urge an animal, especially a horse, to gallop or move more quickly by digging the spurs or heels into its flank (*archaic or literary*) **6.** *vt.* **PUSH SOMEBODY INTO ACTIVITY** to force or encourage somebody to speed up with some task or project or to get started on some definite course of action ○ *If only we could prick him into action on this.* ■ *n.* **1. QUICK, SHARP PAIN** a sudden twinge of pain caused by a fine point being pushed into the skin **2. SMALL PUNCTURE** a small puncture hole or indented mark or an act of piercing that causes such a puncture **3. OFFENSIVE TERM** a penis (*taboo offensive*) **4. OFFENSIVE TERM** a highly offensive term for a man regarded as pathetically inadequate or unpleasant (*taboo insult*) **5. SOMETHING THAT ENTERS THE MIND PAINFULLY** a sudden, unpleasant thought or feeling, often one related to some past action or event **6. POINTED IMPLEMENT** any pointed implement or weapon such as a goad (*archaic*) **7. HARE'S FOOTPRINT** the footprint of a hare [Old English *prica*, of unknown origin. *Prick* is a word of the Low German area, which English shares with Dutch (*-prik*). The earliest record of its use for "penis" is from the late 16thC, and in the 16th and 17th centuries women used it as a term of endearment.] ◇ **prick up your ears** to begin to listen very carefully

prick out *vt.* to make a series of small holes in an area of earth and put young seedlings into these holes to grow

prick·er /príkər/ *n.* **1. GADGET FOR PRICKING** a tool used to prick or pierce small holes in something **2.** BOT = **prickle** *n.* 1

prick·et /príkət/ *n.* **1. YOUNG MALE DEER** a male deer in its second year, typically one with unbranched antlers **2. CANDLEHOLDER** a metal spike for sticking a candle on [14thC. Literally "small prick."]

prick·le /prík'l/ *n.* **1.** BOT **PROJECTION ON PLANT** a sharp pointed projection on the outer surface of a leaf or plant **2. TINGLING FEELING** a tingling or stinging sensation ■ *vti.* (**-led, -ling, -les**) **HURT IN A STINGING WAY** to feel a sharp, stinging pain or to cause something such as the eyes or the skin to hurt in this way [Old English *pricel*, literally "small prick," formed from the same prehistoric Germanic base that produced English *prick*]

prick·ly /príklee/ (**-li·er, -li·est**) *adj.* **1. WITH SMALL SHARP SPIKES** having a surface or skin with prickles on it **2. UNCOMFORTABLE** irritating to the skin, especially because of fibers or prickles that are rough to the touch **3. OVER-SENSITIVE** easily angered, offended, or upset (*informal*) ○ *He's very prickly on that subject.* **4. TRICKY TO HANDLE OR SOLVE** especially difficult and likely to upset people (*informal*) ○ *They tried to keep off prickly subjects like politics and religion.* —**prick·li·ness** *n.*

prick·ly ash *n.* **1. AROMATIC SHRUB OF EASTERN AMERICA** an aromatic shrub or small tree, native to eastern North America, that has prickly branches and bears clusters of small greenish flowers. Latin name: *Zanthoxylum americanum.* ◊ **toothache tree 2. PRICKLY SHRUB OF SOUTHERN UNITED STATES** a spiny shrub or tree of the southern United States with pinnately compound leaves. Latin name: *Zanthoxylum clava-herculis.* = **Hercules' club** *n.* 1

prick·ly heat /prìklee hḗt/ *n.* a rash of tiny raised spots, accompanied by redness and itching, appearing in hot or humid conditions. It is due to obstruction of the sweat gland ducts. Technical name **miliaria**

prick·ly pear *n.* any one of various tropical cacti that have flattened jointed spiny stems, large yellow or orange flowers, and pear-shaped fruits that are edible in some species. Native to North and South America, prickly pears have been introduced elsewhere, often becoming troublesome weeds. Genus: *Opuntia.*

prick·ly pop·py *n.* any of various plants of the poppy family that have bristly stems and leaves and bear yellow, lavender, or white flowers. Some are cultivated as ornamentals. They were traditionally used by herbalists as a source of medicines. Genus: *Argemone.*

prick-teas·er, **prick-tease** *n.* = **cock-teaser** (*taboo offensive*)

pride /prīd/ *n.* **1. FEELING OF SUPERIORITY** a haughty attitude shown by people who believe, often unjustifiably, that they are better than others ○ *Her pride prevented her from mixing with those she considered her social inferiors.* **2. PROPER SENSE OF OWN VALUE** the correct level of respect for the importance and value of your personal character, life, efforts, or achievements ○ *He had lost all his confidence and pride.* **3. SATISFACTION WITH SELF** the happy, satisfied feeling somebody experiences when having or achieving something special that other people admire ○ *She felt a sense of pride when she looked at her finished work.* **4. SOURCE OF PERSONAL SATISFACTION** something that somebody feels especially pleased and satisfied to own or to have achieved ○ *His grandchildren were his pride and joy.* **5. THE BEST TIME** the best condition or period of something (*literary*) **6. GROUP OF LIONS** a group of lions, consisting of typically comprises up to a dozen related adult females, their cubs and juveniles, plus from one to six adult males ■ *vr.* (**prid·ed, prid·ing, prides**) **BE PROUD OF SOMETHING** to obtain personal satisfaction and pleasure from a particular source, especially something accomplished or a quality possessed ○ *He prides himself on his meticulous timekeeping.* [Old English *prȳde*, a variant of *prȳte*, which was formed from *prūd* "proud". There is an isolated example of the use of the word for a "group of lions" from the 15thC, but the modern usage seems to be a 20th-century revival.] —**pride·ful** *adj.* —**pride·ful·ly** *adv.* ◇ **take pride in something** to have a sense of personal satisfaction because of a particular achievement or effort that you or somebody connected with you has made ◇ **pride of place** the most important or prominent position

WORD KEY: CULTURAL NOTE

Pride and Prejudice, a novel by the English writer Jane Austen (1813). Through the story of the relationship between Elizabeth Bennet, the fiercely independent daughter of minor gentry, and Mr. Darcy, a wealthy and haughty nobleman, Austen reveals how both pride and prejudices create barriers to mutual understanding. One of Austen's lighter social comedies, it was made into a movie by Robert Leonard in 1940.

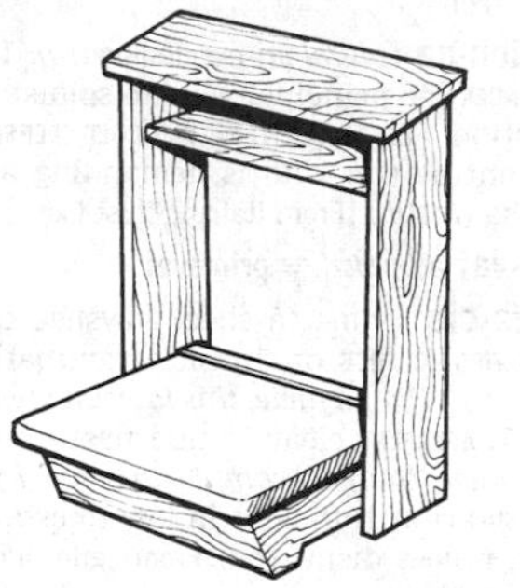

Prie-dieu

prie-dieu /prḗe dyṓ/ (*plural* **prie-dieux**) *n.* a shelved wooden desk for use when praying, usually with a low surface for kneeling on and a higher surface for resting the elbows or a book on [Mid-18thC. From French, literally "pray God."]

pri·er /prī́r/, **pry·er** *n.* somebody who pries

priest /preest/ *n.* **1. ORDAINED PERSON** an ordained minister, especially in the Roman Catholic, Anglican, and Eastern Orthodox churches, responsible for administering the sacraments, preaching, and ministering to the needs of the congregation **2. MINISTER OF NON-CHRISTIAN RELIGION** a spiritual leader or teacher of a non-Christian religion **3. DESCENDANT OF FAMILY OF AARON** somebody descended from the family of Aaron of the tribe of Levi, appointed as priests in the Hebrew Scriptures ■ *vt.* (**priest·ed, priest·ing, priests**) **ORDAIN SOMEBODY** to perform the necessary ceremonies to make somebody into a priest (*archaic*) [Old English *prēost* The word came into prehistoric Germanic from ecclesiastical Latin *presbyter* (see PRESBYTER)]

priest·ess /prḗestəss/ *n.* a woman who is a spiritual leader in a non-Christian religion

priest-hole /prḗest hōl/, **priest's hole** *n.* a small hidden room or space in an English house, created as a hiding place for Roman Catholic priests and others trying to escape persecution after the English Reformation

priest·hood /prḗest hŏŏd/ *n.* **1. PRIEST'S POSITION** the official role, position, or office of a priest **2. PRIESTS AS A GROUP** all Roman Catholic priests considered together, or all the priests of another religion [Old English *prēosthād*]

priest·ly /prḗestlee/ *adj.* used, worn, or performed exclusively by priests, or in some way typical of or suitable for a priest ○ *priestly garments* [Old English *prēostlic*] —**priest·li·ness** *n.*

priest-rid·den *adj.* influenced or controlled by priests or religious dogma to what the speaker or writer regards as an unacceptable degree (*dated or literary*)

prig /prig/ *n.* somebody who takes pride in behaving in a very correct and proper way, and who feels morally superior to people with more relaxed standards (*insult*) [Late 17thC. Origin uncertain: perhaps the same word as obsolete slang *prig* "tinker," of unknown origin. Its original meaning was "dandy."] —**prig·ger·y** *n.* —**prig·gish·ly** *adv.* —**prig·gish·ness** *n.* —**prig·gism** *n.*

prill /pril/ *vt.* (**prilled, pril·ling, prills**) **MAKE SOLID INTO GRANULES** to make a solid into granules or pellets that flow freely and do not clump together ■ *n.* **PRILLED GRANULE** a granule or pellet made by prilling [Late 18thC. Origin unknown.]

prim /prim/ *adj.* (**prim·mer, prim·mest**) **1. PRUDISH** easily shocked by vulgar or obscene language or behavior **2. FORMAL AND PROPER** excessively formal and proper in manner or appearance **3. VERY NEAT** excessively neat and tidy ■ *v.* (**primmed, prim·ming, prims**) **1.** *vti.* **ASSUME PROPER EXPRESSION** to take on an affectedly proper expression 2. *vt.* **MAKE SOMEBODY LOOK VERY PROPER** to make somebody look excessively proper [Early 18thC. Origin uncertain: perhaps via Old French *prin* "excellent, delicate" from Latin *primus* (see PRIME).] —**prim·ly** *adv.* —**prim·ness** *n.*

prim. *abbr.* 1. primary 2. primitive

pri·ma bal·le·ri·na *n.* the principal woman dancer in a ballet company [From Italian, "first ballerina"]

pri·ma·cy /prī́məssee/ (*plural* **-cies**) *n.* **1. PREEMINENCE** the state of being the first or most important part or aspect of something ○ *Speech is regarded as having primacy over writing.* **2. POSITION OF CHURCH PRIMATE** the position or office of a primate in a Christian church

pri·ma don·na (*plural* **pri·ma don·nas**) *n.* **1. LEAD WOMAN OPERA SINGER** the principal woman soloist in an opera production **2. CONCEITED, DIFFICULT PERSON** a self-important person who is demanding and difficult to please (*insult*) [From Italian, "first lady"]

pri·mae·val *adj. U.K.* = **primeval**

pri·ma fa·cie /prīmə fáyshee, -fáyshee ee, preemə-/ *adv.* **AT FIRST GLANCE** on initial examination or consideration ○ *Prima facie, this lawsuit seems spurious.* ■ *adj.* **1. APPARENT** clear from a first impression ○ *a prima facie counterexample to your hypothesis* **2. LEGALLY SUFFICIENT** sufficient in law to establish a case or fact, unless disproved [From Latin, literally "at first appearance"]

pri·ma fa·cie case *n.* a judicial case in which there is sufficient evidence for a judgment, unless the evidence is disproved

pri·ma fa·cie ev·i·dence *n.* evidence that, unless disproved, is sufficient to establish something as a fact (*technical*)

pri·mal /prī́m'l/ *adj.* **1. ORIGINAL** first or earliest, and often basic ○ *the primal instinct for survival* **2. BASIC** most significant and primary ○ *our primal need for a new fuel source* [Mid-16thC. From medieval Latin *primalis*, from Latin *primus* (see PRIME).] —**pri·mal·i·ty** /prī málləte e/ *n.*

pri·mal scream *n.* a cry of extreme anger that a client undergoing primal therapy is encouraged to use

pri·mal ther·a·py *n.* a style of psychotherapy in which clients relive past traumas and unleash repressed anger and frustration through screams, tantrums, or beating inanimate objects

pri·ma·quine /preemə kween, prī́mə-, -kwin/, **pri·ma·quine phos·phate** *n.* a synthetic drug used to treat malaria. Formula: $C_{15}H_{21}N_3O$. [Mid-20thC. Origin uncertain: possibly from Latin *primus* "first" + an alteration of QUINOLINE.]

pri·mar·i·ly /prī mérrilee/ *adv.* **1. CHIEFLY** mainly or mostly ○ *Baldness is primarily found among adult men.* **2. ORIGINALLY** originally or at first

pri·mar·y /prī́ mèrree, prī́məree/ *adj.* **1. FIRST IN SEQUENCE** first or earliest in a sequence ○ *the primary stage of development* **2. MOST IMPORTANT** ranked as most important **3. BASIC** essential or basic to something **4. ORIGINAL** being the first form of something ○ *Unlike musical chords, notes are primary.* **5. RELATING TO EARLY EDUCATION** relating to the early years of formal education, usually for children between the ages of 6 and 12 **6.** ELEC **PRODUCING ELECTRICITY** used to describe a cell that uses an irreversible chemical reaction to generate electricity and, as a result, cannot be recharged **7.** ELEC **RELATING TO CURRENT-INDUCING COMPONENT** used to describe a circuit component such as a coil that induces a current in a neighboring circuit **8.** CHEM **SUBSTITUTING ATOMS** relating to or resulting from the replacement of one or more atoms in a molecule **9.** CHEM **RELATING TO ATTACHED CARBON ATOM** having or used to describe a carbon atom in a molecule that is bonded to one other carbon atom only **10.** BIOCHEM **RELATING TO AMINO ACID SEQUENCE** relating to or used to describe the basic type, number, or sequence of component units in a polypeptide, especially a protein **11. RELATING TO NATURAL RESOURCE INDUSTRY** relating to or produced by an industry such as forestry, mining, or agriculture, that collects and processes a natural resource **12.** BIRDS **RELATING TO MAIN WING FEATHERS** relating to or used to describe any of the main flight feathers on the outer edge of a bird's wing **13.** BOT **GROWN FROM EMBRYONIC TISSUE** relating to or used to describe growth from embryonic tissue in the tip of a root or shoot ■ *n.* (*plural* **-ies**) **1. FIRST THING** something that is first in time or order **2. MOST IMPORTANT THING** a part or aspect of something that is the most important **3. BASIC PART OR ASPECT** something that is essential or basic to something **4. ORIGINAL FORM** something that is the earliest form of something **5.** POL **ELECTION OF CANDIDATES FOR GOVERNMENTAL POSITION** an election in which members of a party choose candidates for a governmental position **6.** POL **ELECTION OF DELEGATES TO CHOOSE CANDIDATES** an election to choose delegates who will choose the party's candidates at a political convention **7.** *U.K.* EDUC = **primary school** (*used in school names*) **8.** COLORS = **primary color 9.** ELEC = **primary coil 10.** ASTRON **BRIGHTER STAR OF DOUBLE STAR** the brighter or larger of two stars in a double star **11.** ASTRON = **primary planet 12.** BIRDS = **primary feather** [15thC. From Latin *primarius*, from *primus* (see PRIME).]

pri·mar·y ac·cent *n.* LING the strongest force used in pronouncing one of the syllables of a multisyllabic word or the mark, usually ('), used to indicate this. For example, in the word "secondary," the primary accent falls on the first syllable.

pri·mar·y a·typ·i·cal pneu·mo·nia *n.* an infectious but relatively mild form of pneumonia caused by the bacterium *Mycoplasma pneumoniae*. Its symptoms include malaise, fever, coughing, and a sore throat.

pri·mar·y care *n.* the level of health care at which a patient is assessed and treated by a general practitioner or nurse, or, if necessary, is referred to a specialist

pri·mar·y cell *n.* an electrical cell that uses an irreversible chemical reaction to generate electricity and, as a result, cannot be recharged

pri·mar·y coil *n.* a coil that forms part of a machine or circuit in which the current flow sets up the magnetic flux necessary for the operation of the machine or circuit

pri·mar·y col·or *n.* **1. RED, GREEN, OR BLUE** any one of the three basic colors of the spectrum, red, green, or blue, from which all other colors can be blended **2. CYAN, MAGENTA, OR YELLOW** any one of the three basic colors cyan, magenta, or yellow, which when subtracted from white can produce all other colors

pri·mar·y con·sum·er *n.* an animal that eats plants, in terms of its position in a food chain

pri·mar·y e·lec·tion *n.* = **primary** *n.* **5, primary** *n.* **6**

pri·mar·y feath·er *n.* any one of the main flight feathers on the outer edge of a bird's wing

pri·mar·y group *n.* the group of people that somebody regularly interacts with face-to-face

pri·mar·y growth *n.* a growth from the tips of roots and shoots of a plant that develops into the main part of the mature plant

pri·mar·y mer·i·stem *n.* a plant tissue derived from the tip of a root or shoot

pri·mar·y plan·et *n.* a planet in direct orbit around a sun

pri·mar·y proc·ess *n.* in Freudian terminology, a basic process that is involved in the functioning of the id and is ruled by the pleasure principle

pri·mar·y pro·duc·tion *n.* the total chemical energy produced by photosynthesis

pri·mar·y school *n.* **1. U.S. SCHOOL FOR YOUNGER STUDENTS** in the United States, a school in which the first three, or sometimes four, grades are taught, often including kindergarten as well **2. U.K. SCHOOL FOR YOUNGER CHILDREN** in the United Kingdom, a school in which children usually aged between 5 and 11 or 12 are taught

pri·mar·y stor·age *n.* the main memory in a computer, including the random-access memory, or RAM, and the read-only memory, or ROM, directly accessible by the processor

pri·mar·y stress *n.* = **primary accent**

pri·mar·y syph·i·lis *n.* the first of the three stages of syphilis, in which a painless growth (**chancre**) grows at the site of infection and the infecting bacterium (**spirochete**) spreads throughout the body

pri·mar·y tooth *n.* = **milk tooth**

pri·mar·y wave *n.* a seismic wave that creates vibrations parallel to its direction

pri·mar·y wind·ing *n.* ELECTRON ENG = **primary coil**

pri·mate *n.* /prī́ màyt/ **1. MEMBER OF MAMMAL ORDER** a member of an order of mammals with a large brain and complex hands and feet, including humans, apes, and monkeys. Order: Primates. **2. pri·mate, Pri·mate** /prī́ mət/ **ARCHBISHOP** an archbishop or high-ranking bishop **3. SOMEBODY OF HIGHEST RANK** somebody holding the highest rank (*archaic*) [12thC. From Latin *primat-*, the stem of *primas* "of the first rank," from *primus* (see PRIME).] —**pri·ma·tial** /prī máysh'l/ *adj.*

pri·ma·tol·o·gy /prīmə tólləjee/ *n.* the scientific study of primates, especially nonhuman primates —**pri·ma·to·log·i·cal** /prīmətə lójjik'l/ *adj.* —**pri·ma·tol·o·gist** /prīmə tólləjist/ *n.*

pri·ma·ve·ra[1] /preemə vérrə/ (*plural* **-ras** *or* **-ra**) *n.* **1. CENTRAL AMERICAN TREE** a Central American tree that has yellow flowers and palmate leaves. Latin name: *Cybistax donnellsmithii.* **2. LIGHT-COLORED WOOD** the light-colored wood of the primavera tree, used for making furniture [Late 19thC. Via Spanish, literally "springtime" (because the tree flowers in spring), from late Latin *prima vera* (see PRIMAVERA[2]).]

pri·ma·ve·ra[2] /preemə vérrə/ *adj.* made with an assortment of fresh spring vegetables, especially sliced as an accompaniment to pasta, meat, or seafood [Late 20thC. From Italian *(alla) primavera* "(in the) spring (style)," from late Latin *prima vera* "early spring," from Latin *primum ver*, literally "first spring."]

prime /prīm/ *adj.* **1. BEST** of the highest quality ○ *prime grade beef* **2. FIRST IN IMPORTANCE** of the greatest importance or the highest rank **3. EARLIEST** earliest in time or sequence **4.** MATH **NOT DIVISIBLE WITHOUT REMAINDER** used to describe a number that can be divided without a remainder only by one and itself **5.** MATH **BEING WITHOUT COMMON FACTORS** used to describe a number that has no common factors with another number ○ *15 is prime to 8.* ■ *n.* **1. BEST STAGE OF SOMETHING** the best state or stage of something, especially the most active and enjoyable period in adult life ○ *In his prime, he was one of the country's best tennis players.* **2. EARLIEST PERIOD OF SOMETHING** the earliest part of something, e.g., the early hours of daylight or the first season of the year **3. DISTINGUISHING MARK** a mark (′) added to a number, character, or expression in order to distinguish it from another, or as the symbol for measurement in feet **4.** FENCING **FIRST PARRYING POSITION** the first of the eight parrying positions in fencing **5.** MUSIC **FIRST NOTE IN MUSICAL SCALE** the first note of a musical scale **6.** MUSIC = **unison 7.** MATH = **prime number 8.** FIN = **prime rate** ■ *v.* (**primed, prim·ing, primes**) **1.** *vti.* **MAKE OR BECOME READY** to make something ready for use or become ready for use **2.** *vt.* **PREPARE SURFACE FOR PAINTING** to prepare a surface for painting or a similar process by treating it with a sealant or an undercoat of paint **3.** *vt.* **PUT CHARGE IN GUN** to make a firearm ready for use by putting a charge in it **4.** *vt.* **PROVIDE EXPLOSIVE WITH FUSE** to make an explosive ready for use by inserting a fuse **5.** *vt.* **PREPARE PUMP** to put liquid in a pump in order to get it started **6.** *vt.* **PUT FUEL INTO CARBURETOR** to put fuel into a carburetor in order to start an internal-combustion engine **7.** *vt.* **BRIEF SOMEBODY** to give somebody, especially a witness in a court case, information or instructions on how to behave or answer questions **8.** *vt.* **PLY SOMEBODY WITH DRINK** to provide somebody with large quantities of alcohol in order to prepare him or her for doing something [Pre-12thC. Via Old French from, ultimately, Latin *primus* "first." Ultimately from an Indo-European word that is also the ancestor of English *principal* and *pristine*.] —**prime·ly** *adv.* —**prime·ness** *n.*

WORD KEY: CULTURAL NOTE

The Prime of Miss Jean Brodie, a novel by the British writer Muriel Spark (1961). The best known of Spark's novels, it is set in an Edinburgh girls' school and describes the powerful and lasting influence of an unconventional schoolteacher, Miss Jean Brodie, on a group of promising but impressionable pupils. It was adapted for the theater in 1966 and made into a movie by Ronald Neame in 1968.

prime cost *n.* the cost of the material and labor necessary to make a product

prime in·ter·est rate *n.* = **prime rate**

prime me·rid·i·an *n.* the 0° longitude meridian, from which other longitudes are calculated. It passes through Greenwich, England.

prime min·is·ter *n.* **1. HEAD OF CABINET** in a par-

PRIME MINISTERS OF AUSTRALIA, CANADA, NEW ZEALAND, AND THE UNITED KINGDOM AFTER 1900

Prime Ministers of Australia

Term of Office	Prime Minister
1903–1904	John Christian Watson
1904–1905	George Houston Reid
1905–1908	Alfred Deakin
1908–1909	Andrew Fisher
1909–1910	Alfred Deakin
1910–1913	Andrew Fisher
1913–1914	Joseph Cook
1915–1923	Andrew Fisher
1914–1915	William Morris Hughes
1923–1929	Stanley Shelbourne Bruce
1929–1932	James Henry Scullin
1932–1939	Joseph Aloysius Lyons
1939	Earle Page
1939–1941	Robert Menzies
1941	Arthur William Fadden
1941–1945	John Curtin
1945	Francis Michael Forde
1945–1949	Joseph Benedict Chifley
1949–1966	Robert Menzies
1966–1967	Harold Holt
1967–1968	John McEwen
1968–1971	John Gorton
1971–1972	William McMahon
1972–1975	Gough Whitlam
1975–1983	Malcolm Fraser
1983–1991	Bob Hawke
1991–1996	Paul Keating
1996–	John Howard

Prime Ministers of Canada

Term of Office	Prime Minister
1896–1911	Wilfred Laurier
1911–1920	Robert Laird Borden
1920–1921	Arthur Meighen
1921–1926	W.L. Mackenzie King
1926	Arthur Meighen
1926–1930	W.L. Mackenzie King
1930–1935	Richard Bedford Bennett
1935–1948	W.L. Mackenzie King
1948–1957	Louis St. Laurent
1957–1963	John G. Diefenbaker
1963–1968	Lester B. Pearson
1968–1979	Pierre Trudeau
1979–1980	Joseph Clark
1980–1984	Pierre Trudeau
1984	John M. Turner
1984–1993	Brian Mulroney
1993	Kim Campbell
1993–	Jean Chrétien

Prime Ministers of New Zealand

Term of Office	Prime Minister
1893–1906	Richard John Seddon
1906	William Hall-Jones
1906–1912	Joseph George Ward
1912	Thomas Mackenzie
1912–1925	William Ferguson Masey
1925	Francis Henry Dillon Bell
1925–1928	Joseph Gordon Coates
1928–1930	Joseph George Ward
1930–1935	George William Forbes
1935–1940	Michael Joseph Savage
1940–1949	Peter Fraser
1949–1957	Sydney George Holland
1957	Keith Jacka Holyoake
1957–1960	Walter Nash
1960–1972	Keith Jacka Holyoake
1972	John Ross Marshall
1972–1974	Norman Eric Kirk
1974–1975	Wallace Edward Rowling
1975–1984	Robert David Muldoon
1984–1989	David Russell Lange
1989–1990	Geoffrey Palmer
1990	Michael Moore
1990–1997	James Bolger
1997–	Jenny Shipley

Prime Ministers of the United Kingdom

Term of Office	Prime Minister
1902–1905	Arthur James Balfour
1905–1908	Henry Campbell-Bannerman
1908–1916	Herbert Henry Asquith
1916–1922	David Lloyd George
1922–1923	Andrew Bonar Law
1923–1924	Stanley Baldwin
1924	Ramsay MacDonald
1924–1929	Stanley Baldwin
1929–1935	Ramsay MacDonald
1935–1937	Stanley Baldwin
1937–1940	Neville Chamberlain
1940–1945	Winston Churchill
1945–1951	Clement Attlee
1951–1955	Winston Churchill
1955–1957	Anthony Eden
1957–1963	Harold Macmillan
1963–1964	Alec Douglas-Home
1964–1970	Harold Wilson
1970–1974	Edward Heath
1974–1976	Harold Wilson
1976–1979	James Callaghan
1979–1990	Margaret Thatcher
1990–1997	John Major
1997–	Tony Blair

liamentary system, the head of the cabinet and, usually, chief executive **2. RULER'S CHIEF MINISTER** the chief minister appointed by the ruler of a country —**prime min·is·te·ri·al** *adj.* —**prime min·is·ter·ship** *n.*

prime mov·er *n.* **1. MOST IMPORTANT CAUSE OF SOMETHING** somebody or something that initiates a process or activity and is usually the most important factor in its continuation **2.** PHILOS **SOURCE OF ALL MOTION** in Aristotelian philosophy, the initial source of all movement **3. NATURAL OR PHYSICAL ENERGY SOURCE** a natural or physical source of energy such as wind or electricity that can be harnessed to power a machine **4. ENERGY CONVERTER** a machine that converts energy from a natural or physical source in order to power equipment such as a windmill or turbine **5. POWERFUL VEHICLE** a sturdy, powerful truck or tractor

prime num·ber *n.* a whole number that can only be divided without a remainder by itself and one

prim·er¹ /prī́mər/ *n.* **1. BASIC READING TEXTBOOK** a book used to teach young children to read, typically containing simple stories **2. INTRODUCTORY TEXT** a book that provides an introduction to a topic [14thC. Via Anglo-Norman from, ultimately, Latin *primarius* (see PRIMARY).]

prim·er² /prímmər/ *n.* **1. PRIMING AGENT** somebody or something that primes something **2. UNDERCOAT** a paint or sealant used to prepare a surface for painting or a similar process, or a coat of this material **3. EXPLOSIVE IGNITER** a small container or wafer of explosive material such as gunpowder, used to ignite the main explosive charge of a firearm or explosive **4.** BIOCHEM **GENETIC MATERIAL** a molecular substrate such as a DNA molecule needed in the polymerization reaction that produces another molecule structurally similar to the substrate [15thC. Formed from PRIME.]

prime rate, **prime in·ter·est rate** *n.* the lowest rate of interest on loans that is available from a bank at a given time

pri·me·ro /pri mérrō/ *n.* a card game played for money in the 16th and 17th centuries [Mid-16thC. Alteration of Spanish *primera*, literally "first," from Latin *primarius* (see PRIMARY).]

prime time *n.* **1. HOURS OF HIGHEST TV VIEWING** the hours when television audiences are usually largest, typically from 7:00 pm to 11:00 pm. Advertising rates are most expensive during these hours. **2. BUSIEST TIME** the busiest or most exciting period in some activity ○ *The department store needs more sales assistants to cope with shopping in prime time.* —**prime-time** *adj.*

pri·me·val /prī méev'l/ *adj.* **1. ANCIENT AND ORIGINAL** at or from the ancient, original stages in the development of something **2. PRIMITIVE** primitive, or arising from instinct rather than thought ○ *a primeval urge* [Mid-17thC. Formed from Latin *primaevus*, from *primus* "first" + *aevum* "age."] —**pri·me·val·ly** *adv.*

prime ver·ti·cal *n.* the imaginary circle around the Earth that goes through the highest point of the celestial sphere directly above an observer and meets the horizon at east and west

prim·i·grav·i·da /prìmi grávvidə/ (*plural* **-das** *or* **-dae** /-dèe/) *n.* a woman during her first pregnancy [Late 19thC. From modern Latin, formed from *gravida* "pregnant," on the model of PRIMIPARA.]

pri·mip·a·ra /prī míppərə/ (*plural* **-ras** *or* **-rae** /-rèe/) *n.* a woman who has given birth only once, whether it was a single or a multiple birth, and whether the baby was alive or stillborn [Mid-19thC. From modern Latin, from Latin *primus* "first" + *-para* "bearing," feminine form of *-parus* (see -PAROUS).] —**pri·mi·par·i·ty** /prìmi pérrətee/ *n.* —**pri·mip·a·rous** /prī míppərəss/ *adj.*

prim·i·tive /prímmitiv/ *adj.* **1.** FIRST at or relating to the first stages or form of something **2.** BIOL DEVELOPMENTALLY EARLY relating to or appearing in an earlier stage of biological development, particularly of an embryo or species **3.** VERY SIMPLE IN DESIGN crudely simple in design or construction (*offensive in some contexts*) **4.** ORIGINAL not derived from other things **5.** WITH SIMPLE TECHNOLOGICAL DEVELOPMENT not using or relying on complex modern technologies (*sometimes considered offensive*) **6.** MATH BEING BASIS acting as a basis from which something else is derived **7.** NATURAL arising from some inherent characteristic **8.** ARTS ARTISTICALLY UNTRAINED created by an artist with no formal training, especially using a simple style **9.** ARTS EARLY MEDIEVAL created by an early medieval European artist or a folk artist **10.** LING FROM WHICH OTHER FORM DERIVES used to describe a word form from which another word is derived ○ *The primitive root in "children" is "child."* **11.** LING EARLIER IN LINGUISTIC DEVELOPMENT being or belonging to an earlier form of a language ■ *n.* **1.** SOMEBODY OR SOMETHING FROM ORIGINAL STAGE somebody or something from the first stage or form of something **2.** SOMEBODY FROM A CULTURE WITH SIMPLE TECHNOLOGIES a member of a people who do not use or rely on complex modern technologies (*often considered offensive*) **3.** ARTS UNTRAINED ARTIST an artist without formal training, especially one using a simple style **4.** ARTS EARLY MEDIEVAL ARTIST an artist or folk artist, especially a painter, whose work was typical of the style of early medieval Europe **5.** ARTS EARLY MEDIEVAL WORK OF ART a painting or other work by an early medieval artist or a folk artist **6.** DERIVATION something such as a concept, feature, or formula from which something else is derived **7.** MATH BASIC GEOMETRIC FORM OR FUNCTION a geometric form or function from which another is derived **8.** LING WORD ROOT a word root (*dated technical*) **9.** COMPUT BASIC ELEMENT OF COMPUTER PROGRAM a simple element of a computer program or graphic design from which larger programs or images can be constructed [14thC. Via French from, ultimately, Latin *primitus* "in the first place," from *primus* (see PRIME).] —**prim·i·tive·ly** *adv.* —**prim·i·tive·ness** *n.*

prim·i·tiv·ism /prímmiti vìzzəm/ *n.* **1.** STATE OF BEING PRIMITIVE the state of being primitive or the qualities associated with being primitive **2.** ARTS SIMPLICITY OF STYLE simplicity or naivety of artistic style **3.** ANTIMODERNISM the belief that less technologically dependent cultures and ways of living are inherently better than more technologically dependent ones —**prim·i·tiv·ist** *n., adj.* —**prim·i·tiv·is·tic** /prìmmiti vístik/ *adj.*

pri·mo /preémō/ *n.* (*plural* **-mos** *or* **-mi** /-mee/) LEAD MUSICAL PART the lead musical part in a duet, trio, or ensemble composition ■ *adj.* **1.** FIRST first in a sequence or series (*formal*) **2.** EXCELLENT of the finest quality (*slang*) ○ *This pizza is primo!* **3.** VERY VALUABLE of great value (*slang*) ○ *She buys only primo stocks.* [Mid-18thC. Via Italian and Spanish, "first, prime," both from Latin *primus* (see PRIME).]

pri·mo·gen·i·tor /prìmō jénnitər/ *n.* **1.** ORIGINAL ANCESTOR the first ancestor of a people or other group **2.** ANCESTOR somebody who lived earlier in somebody's line of descent [Mid-17thC. Variant of PROGENITOR, on the model of *primogeniture*.]

pri·mo·gen·i·ture /prìmō jénni chòor/ *n.* **1.** FIRST-BORN STATUS the state of being the first-born child of a set of parents **2.** FIRST-BORN'S RIGHT OF INHERITANCE the right of the first-born child, usually the eldest son, to inherit the parents' entire estate [Early 17thC. From medieval Latin *primogenitura*, from Latin *primus* "first" + *genitura* "birth."] —**pri·mo·gen·i·tar·y** /-jénni tèrree/ *adj.*

pri·mor·di·al /prī máwrdee əl/ *adj.* **1.** EXISTING FIRST existing at the beginning of time or the development of something **2.** BASIC essential or basic to something **3.** BIOL OF EARLIEST STAGE OF DEVELOPMENT relating to cells, tissues, organs, or individuals at the earliest stage of development [14thC. From late Latin *primordialis*, from Latin *primordium* "origin," from *primus* "first" + *ordiri* "to begin."] —**pri·mor·di·al·i·ty** /prī màwrdee állətee/ *n.* —**pri·mor·di·al·ly** /prī máwrdee əlee/ *adv.*

pri·mor·di·um /prī máwrdee əm/ (*plural* **-a** /-dee ə/) *n.* a tissue or organ in the earliest stage of embryonic development, found when the dividing cells in the fertilized ovum first differentiate [Late 16thC. From Latin (see PRIMORDIAL).]

primp /primp/ (**primped, primp·ing, primps**) *vti.* to groom yourself, somebody, or something in a fussy way ○ *spending all day primping at the mirror* [Late 16thC. Origin uncertain.]

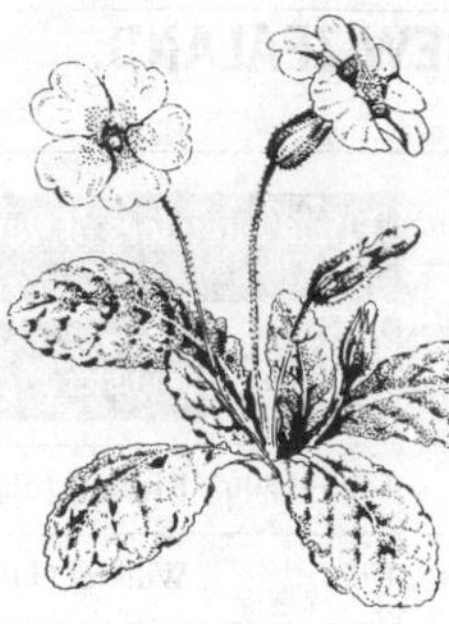

Primrose

prim·rose /prím rōz/ *n.* **1.** SMALL PLANT WITH COLORFUL FLOWERS a small perennial plant with colorful flowers. Genus: *Primula*. **2.** PRIMROSE FLOWER a flower of the primrose plant [14thC. Via Old French *primerose* from medieval Latin *prima rosa* "first rose," so called because of its early flowering.]

prim·rose path *n.* (*literary*) **1.** PLEASURABLE LIFESTYLE an easy or pleasurable way of life, especially one that leads to disaster **2.** EASY COURSE OF ACTION an easy way or option, especially one that leads to disaster [From the phrase "the primrose path of dalliance" in Shakespeare's *Hamlet*]

prim·u·la /prímmyələ/ (*plural* **-las** *or* **-la**) *n.* = **primrose** [Mid-18thC. Via modern Latin, genus name, from medieval Latin *primula (veris)*, literally "first fruit (of spring)," from Latin *primulus*, literally "small first," from *primus* (see PRIME).] —**prim·u·la·ceous** /prìmmyə láyshəss/ *adj.*

pri·mum mo·bi·le /prìməm mṓbə lee, preéməm mṓbə lày/ *n.* **1.** ASTRON OUTERMOST SPHERE OF UNIVERSE in Ptolemaic astronomy, the outermost sphere of the universe, thought to revolve every 24 hours, moving the inner spheres with it **2.** PHILOS = **prime mover** *n.* 2 [15thC. From medieval Latin, literally "first moving thing." Translation of Arabic *al-muḥarrik al-awwal*.]

pri·mus in·ter pa·res /prìməss intər pái reèz/ *n.* the representative or leader of a group of equals [From Latin, "first among equals"]

Pri·mus stove /príməss-/ *tdmk.* a trademark for a brand of portable kerosene cooking stove, used by campers

prin. *abbr.* **1.** principal **2.** principle

prince /prins/ *n.* **1.** SON OF MONARCH a man or boy in a royal family, especially the son of a reigning king or queen **2.** MAN RULER a man who rules a principality **3.** EUROPEAN NOBLEMAN a nobleman in some European countries, usually ranked below a duke **4.** HIGHLY REGARDED MAN a man or boy who is ranked highly in his field ○ *Robin Hood was the prince of thieves.* **5.** GENEROUS, KIND MAN a man who is extremely nice, especially in a generous or chivalrous way (*informal*) [12thC. Via French from Latin *princeps*, literally "one who takes first place" (source of English *principal*).]

WORD KEY: CULTURAL NOTE

The Prince, a political treatise by Italian writer Niccolò Machiavelli (1513). Machiavelli based this guide to gaining and maintaining political power on his study of history and his experience of politics. The first work of its kind to present a political philosophy derived from a study of human behavior rather than traditional ethics, it gained lasting notoriety by justifying the judicious use of ruthlessness and deceit.

Prince Al·bert[1] (*plural* **Prince Al·berts**) *n.* a men's double-breasted, knee-length coat with a fitted torso and sleeves and a flared skirt [Late 19thC. Named for Prince ALBERT.]

Prince Al·bert[2] city in central Saskatchewan, Canada, 83 mi./140 km north of Saskatoon. Population: 41,706 (1996).

Prince Al·bert Na·tion·al Park national park in central Saskatchewan, Canada. Area: 1,496 sq. mi./3,874 sq. km.

Prince Charles Is·land the largest island in Foxe Basin, west of Baffin Island, in Nunavut, Canada. Area: 3,676 sq. mi./9,521 sq. km.

prince charm·ing, **Prince Charm·ing** *n.* **1.** ROMANTICALLY IDEAL MAN a man who fulfills the romantic ideal of the perfect lover (*informal*) **2.** CHARMER a man who actively seeks to charm people, especially women, and gain their liking [Mid-19thC. From the name of the hero of the fairy tale *Cinderella*.]

prince con·sort *n.* a prince who is married to a reigning queen

prince·dom /prínsdəm/ *n.* PRINCE'S POSITION OR TERRITORY the position, territory, jurisdiction, or estate of a prince ■ **prince·doms** *npl.* = **principalities**

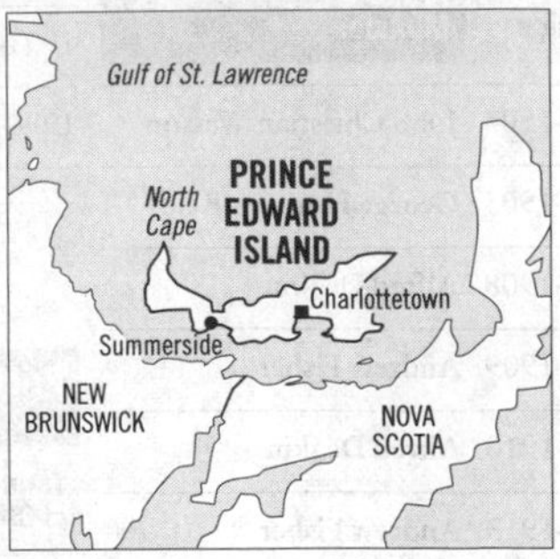

Prince Edward Island

Prince Ed·ward Is·land the smallest province in Canada, in the east of the country, in the Gulf of St. Lawrence, opposite New Brunswick and Nova Scotia. Capital: Charlottetown. Population: 134,557 (1996). Area: 2,185 sq. mi./5,660 sq. km. —**Prince Ed·ward Is·land·er** *n.*

Prince Ed·ward Is·land Na·tion·al Park national park in eastern Canada, on the northern shore of Prince Edward Island. Area: 9 sq. mi./22 sq. km.

Prince George city in central British Columbia, Canada, at the junction of the Nechako and Fraser rivers. Population: 75,150 (1996).

prince·ling /prínsling/, **prince·let** /prínslet/ *n.* a prince of low rank, age, or importance

prince·ly /prínslee/ (**-li·er, -li·est**) *adj.* **1.** RELATING TO PRINCE relating to, belonging to, or suitable for a prince **2.** VERY EXPENSIVE OR GENEROUS generous as an amount of money or requiring the expenditure of large sums of money ○ *a princely manor in the country* —**prince·li·ness** *n.*

Prince of Dark·ness *n.* Satan (*literary*) [Modeled on PRINCE OF PEACE]

Prince of Peace *n.* Jesus Christ (*literary*) [From the Christian interpretation of "and his name shall be called ... Prince of Peace" in the Bible, *Isaiah* 9:6]

Prince of Wales Is·land **1.** island in northern Canada, in Nunavut, between Victoria and Somerset islands. Area: 12,872 sq. mi./33,338 sq. km. **2.** island in northern Australia, in Queensland. Area: 70 sq. mi./180 sq. km.

prince re·gent (*plural* **prince re·gents** *or* **princes re·gent**) *n.* a prince who rules in the monarch's place, e.g., when the monarch is abroad, ill, or still a child

prince roy·al (*plural* **princ·es roy·al**) *n.* the eldest son of a reigning monarch

Prince Ru·pert city on the northwestern coast of British Columbia, Canada. Population: 17,414 (1996).

prince's-feath·er /prìnsəz féthər/ (*plural* **prince's-feath·ers** *or* **prince's-feath·er**) *n.* **1.** TALL RED-FLOWERED ANNUAL PLANT a tall annual plant with reddish leaves and spikes of red flowers. Family: Amaranthus. **2.** TALL PINK-FLOWERED PLANT a tall plant of Australia and Asia with oval leaves and drooping spikes of pink flowers. Latin name: *Polygonum orientale*.

prince's pine *n.* BOT = **pipsissewa**

prin·cess /prínsəss, -sèss, prin séss/ *n.* (*plural* **-cess·es**) **1.** MONARCH'S DAUGHTER a woman member of a royal family, other than the queen, especially a daughter of the reigning monarch **2.** PRINCE'S WIFE the wife of a prince **3.** WOMAN RULER a woman who rules a principality **4.** EUROPEAN NOBLEWOMAN a noblewoman in some European countries, usually ranked below a duchess **5.** HIGHLY REGARDED WOMAN a woman who is ranked highly in her field, or who has other qualities suitable for a princess (*dated*) **6.** SPOILED WOMAN a rich, spoiled young woman (*informal*) **7.** NAME FOR GIRL a pet name for a woman or girl, especially a daughter ■ *adj.* **prin·cess, prin·cess** FITTED AT TOP WITH FLARED SKIRT made with long triangular pieces of fabric that reach from neck to hem, fitted at the bodice with a flared skirt

prin·cesse /prin séss/ *adj.* = **princess** *adj.* [Mid-19thC. From French, "princess."]

prin·cess roy·al (*plural* **prin·cess·es roy·al**) *n.* the eldest daughter of a reigning monarch, especially of a British monarch, who confers the title on her as a special honor

prin·cess tree *n.* = **paulownia** [Mid-20thC. Named for Princess Anna Pavlovna, daughter of Tsar Paul I of Russia.]

Prince·ton /prínstən/ town in west central New Jersey. It is the site of Princeton University, founded in 1746. Population: 13,198 (1990).

prin·ci·pal /prínsəp'l/ *adj.* **1.** PRIMARY first or among the first in importance or rank **2.** FIN INITIALLY INVESTED relating to the initial amount of money that was invested or borrowed ■ *n.* **1.** MOST IMPORTANT PERSON somebody who is in charge or most highly ranked **2.** SIGNIFICANT PARTICIPANT any one of the most significant participants in an event or a situation ○ *the principals in the debate* **3.** EDUC HEAD OF SCHOOL the head administrator of a school, especially a grade school or high school **4.** ARTS LEAD PERFORMER a lead actor, singer, or dancer in a theatrical or musical performance **5.** MUSIC LEAD MUSICIAN the lead musician in a section of an orchestra, or the part played by that musician **6.** FIN ORIGINAL AMOUNT INVESTED the initial sum of money invested or borrowed, before interest or other revenue is added, or the remainder of that sum after payments have been made **7.** LAW REPRESENTED PERSON somebody for whom a representative or proxy acts in a legal matter **8.** LAW RESPONSIBLE PARTY somebody who has ultimate responsibility for something, rather than an accomplice or representative **9.** LAW CRIMINAL the perpetrator of a crime **10.** ARCHIT MAIN SUPPORT BEAM the main support beam, girder, or truss in a roof, bridge, or other construction [13thC. Via French from Latin *principalis*, from *princip-*, the stem of *princeps* (see PRINCE).] —**prin·ci·pal·ly** *adv.* —**prin·ci·pal·ship** *n.*

prin·ci·pal ax·is *n.* OPTICS the line that passes through the center of curvature of a lens

prin·ci·pal di·ag·o·nal *n.* in a square matrix, the diagonal line that extends from the upper left corner to the lower right corner

prin·ci·pal fo·cus *n.* OPTICS = **focal point** *n.* 1

prin·ci·pal·i·ty /prìnsə pállətee/ *n.* (*plural* **-ties**) **1.** PRINCE'S OR PRINCESS'S COUNTRY a territory ruled by a prince or princess **2.** POSITION OF PRINCE the position or jurisdiction of a prince ■ **prin·ci·pal·i·ties** *npl.* ORDER OF ANGELS one of the nine orders of angels in the traditional Christian hierarchy

prin·ci·pal parts *npl.* **1.** VERB FORMS OF INFLECTED LANGUAGE the basic forms of a verb, from which other forms are derived, in an inflected language such as Latin **2.** ENGLISH VERB FORMS the infinitive, past tense, and participial forms of an English verb

prin·ci·pal pho·tog·ra·phy *n.* the shooting of the main action and characters in a movie, as opposed to the shooting of backgrounds and crowd scenes by the second unit

prin·ci·pate /prínsə pàyt, -pət/ *n.* **1.** LAND RULED BY PRINCE a territory ruled by a prince **2. prin·ci·pate, Prin·ci·pate** PERIOD OF EARLY ROMAN EMPIRE a period of the early Roman empire in which some traditions and institutions of the Republic were preserved **3. prin·ci·pate, Prin·ci·pate** ROMAN POLITICAL SYSTEM the political system of the Roman principate [14thC. Directly or via French from Latin *principatus*, from *princeps* (see PRINCE).]

Prín·ci·pe /préeN səpə, prín-/ the second largest island in São Tomé and Príncipe. Population: 5,900 (1995). Area: 42 sq. mi./109 sq. km.

prin·cip·i·um /prin síppee əm/ (*plural* **-a** /-ee ə/) *n.* an essential or basic principle (*formal*) (*often used in the plural*) [Late 16thC. From Latin, formed from *princip-*, the stem of *princeps* (see PRINCE).]

prin·ci·ple /prínsəp'l/ *n.* **1.** BASIC ASSUMPTION an important underlying law or assumption required in a system of thought **2.** ETHICAL STANDARD a standard of moral or ethical decision-making ○ *I buy recyclable products as a matter of principle.* **3.** WAY OF WORKING the basic way in which something works **4.** SOURCE the primary source of something **5.** CHEM CHARACTERISTIC INGREDIENT an ingredient of a substance that gives the substance a particular quality [14thC. Alteration of French *principe*, from Latin *principium*, from *princip-*, the stem of *princeps* (see PRINCE).] ◇ **in principle** in theory or in the essentials ◇ **on principle** because of a particular ethical standard that somebody believes in

Prin·ci·ple *n.* a term used in Christian Science for God

prin·ci·pled /prínsəp'ld/ *adj.* based on or possessing moral principles, especially ones held in high regard

prink /pringk/ (**prinked, prink·ing, prinks**) *vti.* to dress or groom somebody or yourself in a fancy or fussy way [Late 16thC. Origin uncertain.] —**prink·er** *n.*

print /print/ *n.* **1.** MARK PRESSED INTO SOMETHING a mark made by pressing something onto a surface **2.** WRITING ON A SURFACE words, figures, or symbols on a surface, especially when produced by a machine ○ *books available in large print* **3.** PUBL PUBLISHED TEXT the state of being in a printed form or being published ○ *We don't want these typographical errors to make it into print.* **4.** ARTS ARTWORK MADE BY PRESSING DESIGN a work of art made by inking a surface with a raised design and pressing it onto paper or another surface **5.** ARTS FABRIC WITH INKED DESIGN a fabric with an ink or paint design on its surface, or the design itself (*often used before a noun*) ○ *She was wearing a new print dress.* **6.** PHOTOGRAPHY PHOTOGRAPH a photograph, usually on paper, made from a negative **7.** CINEMA MOTION PICTURE COPY a copy of a motion picture **8.** STAMP OR DIE a stamp or die used to make marks on a surface **9.** CRIMINOL FINGERPRINT a fingerprint (*informal*) ■ *v.* (**print·ed, print·ing, prints**) **1.** *vti.* PRINTING MAKE SOMETHING WITH PRINTING MACHINE to make a copy, document, or publication using a printing press or a computer printer ○ *These books were printed in Canada.* **2.** *vti.* PUBL PUBLISH SOMETHING to publish information or a publication ○ *The company prints several news magazines in addition to books.* **3.** *vti.* MARK SOMETHING USING PRESSURE to produce a mark, design, or lettering on a surface by pressing something on it ○ *A machine prints the corporate logo onto pencils.* **4.** *vti.* PRESS DESIGNS ONTO SOMETHING to press a mark, design, or lettering onto something ○ *We printed enough T-shirts for the whole team.* **5.** *vti.* WRITE SEPARATED LETTERS to write something by hand, using separated letters rather than script ○ *Print your name under your signature.* **6.** *vti.* PHOTOGRAPHY, CINEMA MAKE A COPY FROM A NEGATIVE to make a positive image or copy of a photograph or motion picture from a negative **7.** *vt.* MAKE IMPRESSION to make an impression on the mind of somebody **8.** *vi.* PRINTING WORK AS PRINTER to do the work of a printer ■ *adj.* PUBL RELATING TO PUBLISHED MEDIA produced by or relating to the published media [13thC. From Old French *preinte*, the feminine past participle of *preindre* "to press," from Latin *premere* (see PRESS).] ◇ **in print 1.** currently available from a publisher **2.** printed in a book, newspaper, or magazine ◇ **out of print** not currently available from a publisher

print out *vt.* COMPUT to produce a printed copy of data from a computer

print·a·ble /príntəb'l/ *adj.* **1.** ABLE TO BE PUBLISHED sufficiently inoffensive, correct, or well-written as to be fit to be printed in a publication ○ *Some of the player's comments weren't printable.* **2.** ABLE TO BE PRINTED capable of being printed or printed on ○ *This paper's too slick to be printable.* —**print·a·bil·i·ty** /prìntə bíllətee/ *n.*

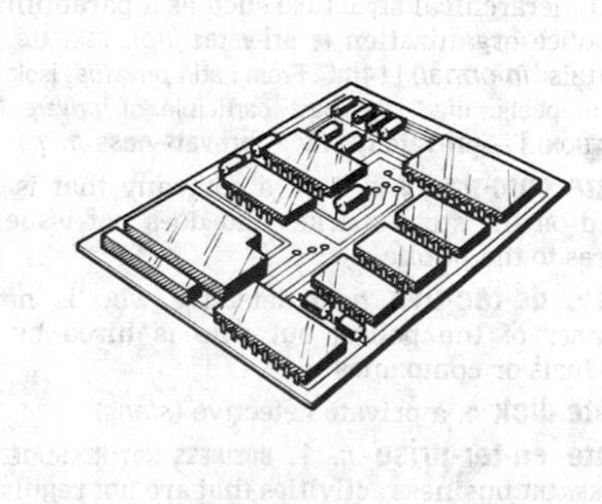

Printed circuit

print·ed cir·cuit *n.* an electronic circuit in which some components and the connections between them are formed by etching a metallic coating on one or both sides of an insulating board

print·ed mat·ter *n.* published material such as books, newspapers, magazines, or catalogs that qualifies for a special low postage rate

print·er /príntər/ *n.* **1.** PRINTING PERSON OR COMPANY IN PRINTING TRADE a person or company that prints books, newspapers, or magazines **2.** PRINTING, PUBL MACHINE FOR PRINTING BOOKS OR NEWSPAPERS a machine that prints books, newspapers, or magazines **3.** COMPUT MACHINE FOR PRINTING COMPUTER DATA a peripheral output device designed to produce computer-generated text or graphics on paper, transparencies, or similar media **4.** PHOTOGRAPHY MACHINE FOR MAKING COPIES OF FILM a machine that makes duplicates of film, normally a positive from a negative

print·er's dev·il *n.* an apprentice or young assistant to a printer (*dated*) [From DEVIL in the sense "apprentice"]

print·head /prínt hèd/ *n.* COMPUT a part of a computer printer that prints out the characters on paper

print·ing /prínting/ *n.* **1.** PRODUCTION OF COPIES the process or business of producing copies of documents, publications, or images **2.** PRINTED CHARACTERS typographical characters as they appear on paper or another surface ○ *The printing has washed off this bottle.* **3.** LETTERS WRITTEN SEPARATELY letters written separately or the act of writing letters separately, in contrast to script characters ○ *Her printing is easier to read than her handwriting.* **4.** PRINT RUN the process or output of one print run of a publication ○ *This book is in its eighth printing.*

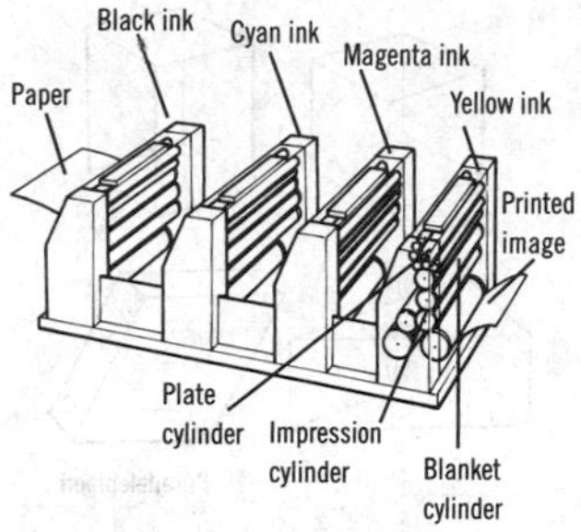

Printing press

print·ing press *n.* a machine that presses inked set type or etched plates onto paper or textiles that are fed through the machine

print·mak·er /prínt màykər/ *n.* an artist who designs and makes prints —**print·mak·ing** *n.*

print·out /prínt òwt/ *n.* a paper copy of data from a computer

print run *n.* the process or output of one printing of a publication, document, or artwork ○ *an initial print run of 30,000 copies*

print shop *n.* a small building, room, or business where documents, publications, or artworks are printed

pri·on[1] /prí òn/ *n.* BIOL an infectious particle of protein that, unlike a virus, contains no nucleic acid, does not trigger an immune response, and is not destroyed by extreme heat or cold. These particles are considered responsible for such diseases as scrapie, bovine spongiform encephalopathy, kuru and Creutzfeldt-Jakob disease. [Late 20thC. Coined from PROTEINACEOUS + INFECTIOUS + -ON.]

pri·on[2] /prí òn/ *n.* BIRDS a small seabird of the southern oceans with soft gray markings like a pigeon and a serrated bill. Genus: *Pachyptila.* [Mid-19thC. Via modern Latin from Greek *priōn* "saw."]

pri·or[1] /prír/ *adj.* **1.** EARLIER earlier in time or sequence ○ *a prior engagement* **2.** MORE IMPORTANT more important or basic ■ *n.* EARLIER CONVICTION an earlier conviction for a criminal act (*informal*) ○ *Check to see whether the suspect has any priors.* [Early 18thC. From Latin, "former, elder, superior," literally "more before."]

pri·or[2] /prír/ *n.* **1.** ABBOT'S DEPUTY an officer in a monastery who is ranked below an abbot **2.** MAN RELIGIOUS SUPERIOR a man superior in some religious communities **3.** SENIOR MEDIEVAL MAGISTRATE a senior magistrate in some medieval Italian republics, especially Florence [Pre-12thC. Via medieval Latin from Latin, "elder, superior" (see PRIOR[1]).]

pri·or·ate /prírət/ *n.* the position or term of office of a prior or prioress

pri·or·ess /prírəss/ *n.* **1.** ABBESS'S DEPUTY an officer in a convent who ranks below an abbess **2.** WOMAN RE-

LIGIOUS SUPERIOR a woman superior in some religious communities

pri·or·i·tize /prī áwrə tīz, prírə tīz/ (-tized, -tiz·ing, -tiz·es) *vti.* 1. RANK THINGS ACCORDING TO IMPORTANCE to order things according to their importance or urgency ○ *I must prioritize my list of things to do.* 2. RANK SOMETHING AS MOST IMPORTANT to regard something as most important or urgent ○ *I have to prioritize finding a job.*

pri·or·i·ty /prī áwrətee/ (*plural* -ties) *n.* 1. GREATEST IMPORTANCE the state of having most importance or urgency ○ *Give this case priority treatment.* 2. SOMEBODY OR SOMETHING IMPORTANT somebody or something that is ranked highly in terms of importance or urgency ○ *You've got to get your priorities right.* 3. EARLINESS the state of having preceded something else 4. RIGHT OF PRECEDENCE the right to be ranked above others

pri·o·ry /prīree/ (*plural* -ies) *n.* a religious community or home such as a monastery or convent, headed by a prior or prioress

Pri·pet Marsh·es /prìp ət-/, **Pri·pyat' Marsh·es** /preépyət-/ swamp region in southern Belarus and northwestern Ukraine, along the Pripet River

prise *vt., n.* = prize[3]

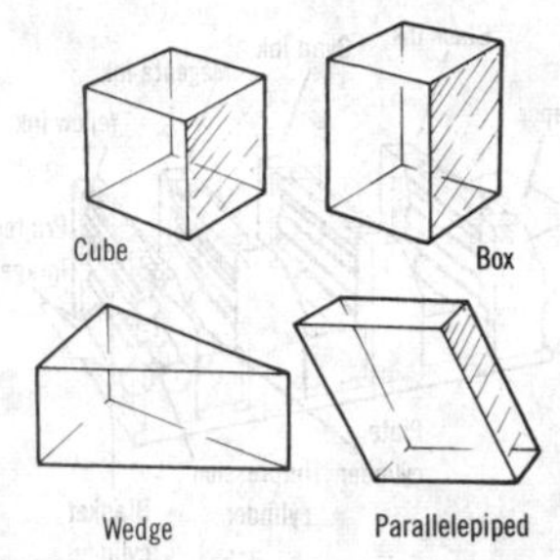

Prism

prism /prízzəm/ *n.* 1. OPTICS POLYGONAL SOLID FOR DISPERSING LIGHT a transparent polygonal solid object with flat faces and a usually triangular cross-section, used for separating white light into a spectrum of colors 2. SOMETHING MADE OF CUT GLASS a cut-glass object, especially one that can separate white light into a spectrum 3. CRYSTALS CRYSTAL TYPE a crystal form with faces that are parallel to a single axis 4. GEOM PARALLELOGRAM-SIDED SOLID a solid figure with ends that are identical polygons and with sides that are parallelograms [Late 16thC. Via late Latin from Greek *prisma*, literally "something sawn" (because of its shape), from *prizein* "to saw," of unknown origin.]

pris·mat·ic /priz máttik/, **pris·mat·i·cal** /priz máttik'l/ *adj.* 1. RELATING TO PRISM resembling or relating to a prism 2. SEPARATED BY PRISM used to describe light that shows the colors of the spectrum, as refracted by a prism 3. COLORFUL brightly colored, like a rainbow [Early 18thC. Via French *prismatique* from Greek *prismat-*, the stem of *prisma* (see PRISM).] —**pris·mat·i·cal·ly** *adv.*

pris·ma·toid /prízmə tòyd/ *n.* a polyhedron with all its vertices in one of two parallel planes [Mid-19thC. Formed from Greek *prismat-*, the stem of *prisma* (see PRISM).] —**pris·ma·toi·dal** /prìzmə tóyd'l/ *adj.*

pris·moid /príz mòyd/ *n.* a prismatoid with sides that are parallelograms or trapezoids and equal-sided polygons as bases [Early 18thC. Formed from PRISM, on the model of *rhomboid.*] —**pris·moi·dal** /prìz móyd'l/ *adj.*

pris·on /prízz'n/ *n.* 1. PLACE WHERE CRIMINALS ARE CONFINED a secure place where somebody is confined as punishment for a crime or while waiting to stand trial 2. CONFINEMENT a place or condition of captivity or unwanted restraint ○ *His fears are a prison that he cannot escape.* ■ *vt.* (-oned, -on·ing, -ons) IMPRISON to put somebody in prison (*archaic or literary*) [12thC. Via Old French from, ultimately, the Latin stem *prension-* "seizing," from *prehendere* "to seize."]

pris·on camp *n.* 1. CAMP FOR WAR PRISONERS a camp where prisoners of war are confined 2. MINIMUM SECURITY PRISON a minimum security prison, where prisoners have some freedom of movement

pris·on·er /prízz'nər/ *n.* 1. SOMEBODY HELD IN PRISON somebody confined in a prison as a punishment for a crime or while waiting to stand trial 2. SOMEBODY HELD AGAINST WILL somebody who has been captured and is held in confinement in a place 3. SOMEBODY WHO IS OR FEELS TRAPPED somebody who is unable to escape a situation or condition

pris·on·er of con·science *n.* somebody held in a prison by a state, especially an oppressive regime, because of his or her political or religious beliefs

pris·on·er of war *n.* somebody who has been captured and held captive by the enemy during a war

pris·on·er's base *n.* a children's game in which two teams try to tag each other's members, thereby adding them to their team at their base [Alteration of earlier *prison-bars*]

pris·on fe·ver *n.* typhus (*dated*)

priss /priss/ *n.* somebody who behaves in a prissy way (*informal*) [Early 20thC. Back-formation.]

priss around *vi.* to act in a fussily proper way

pris·sy /prissee/ (-si·er, -si·est) *adj.* behaving in a very prudish and proper way [Late 19thC. Origin uncertain: probably a blend of PRIM and SISSY.] —**pris·si·ly** *adv.* —**pris·si·ness** *n.*

Priš·tin·a /preéshtinə/ the largest city in the region of Kosovo in the Federal Republic of Yugoslavia. Population: 108,083 (1991).

pris·tine /prí steen, pri steén/ *adj.* 1. IMMACULATE so clean and neat as to look as good as new ○ *The house is in pristine condition.* 2. UNSPOILED not yet ruined by human encroachment ○ *acres of pristine forest* 3. IN OR OF ORIGINAL STATE in or belonging to an original state or condition [Mid-16thC. From Latin *pristinus* "former."]

prith·ee /príthee/ *interj.* used to introduce a request to somebody (*archaic*) [Late 16thC. Contraction of *(I) pray thee.*]

priv. *abbr.* 1. private 2. privative

pri·va·cy /prívəssee/ *n.* 1. SECLUSION the state of being apart from other people and not seen, heard, or disturbed by them ○ *Shut the door so we can have some privacy.* 2. FREEDOM FROM ATTENTION OF OTHERS freedom from the observation, intrusion, or attention of others ○ *If you seek celebrity, you must sacrifice privacy.* 3. HIDDEN CONDITION the state of being kept secret

pri·vate /prívət/ *adj.* 1. NOT FOR OTHERS concerning matters that are not for other people to see or know about 2. SECLUDED sufficiently secluded for it to be possible to be alone and not watched, heard, or disturbed by others ○ *Let's find a private corner where we can talk.* 3. PERSONAL belonging to, restricted to, or intended for an individual 4. NOT PUBLIC not open to the public 5. ACTING IN PERSONAL CAPACITY not holding an official position in government, or not relating to the official role of a government person ○ *a private citizen* 6. NONGOVERNMENTAL not supported by government funding 7. RESERVED AND SECRETIVE preferring not to disclose personal information or to discuss personal feelings with others ○ *She's a very private person.* 8. NOT UNDERSTANDABLE BY EVERYONE excluding other people who do not share the knowledge required to understand 9. MIL LOWEST-RANKING belonging to the lowest rank of soldier or marine ■ *n.* 1. MIL LOWEST-RANKING SOLDIER OR MARINE a soldier or marine of the lowest rank 2. SOMEBODY OF LOW RANK somebody of low rank in an organization with a rigid hierarchical structure such as a paramilitary or police organization ■ **pri·vates** *npl.* GENITALS the genitals (*informal*) [14thC. From Latin *privatus* "isolated, not in public life," the past participle of *privare* (see PRIVATION).] —**pri·vate·ly** *adv.* —**pri·vate·ness** *n.*

pri·vate com·pa·ny *n. U.K.* a company that is not listed on the stock market and does not issue its shares to the public

pri·vate de·tec·tive *n.* a detective who is not a member of the police, but who is hired by individuals or companies

pri·vate dick *n.* a private detective (*slang*)

pri·vate en·ter·prise *n.* 1. BUSINESS NOT REGULATED BY GOVERNMENT business activities that are not regulated or owned by the government 2. PRIVATELY OWNED COMPANY a company that is owned by a private individual or individuals and not by the government

pri·va·teer /prìvə teér/ *n.* 1. PRIVATE SHIP USED IN WAR a ship that belongs to and is run by a person or company but is authorized by the government to engage in battle during war 2. SOMEBODY SAILING ON PRIVATEER the commander or a crew member of a privateer [Mid-17thC. Modeled on *volunteer.*]

pri·vate eye *n.* a private detective (*informal*) [*Eye*, spelling of *I.*, a shortening of *investigator.*]

pri·vate first class (*plural* **pri·vates first class**) *n.* a soldier in the U.S. Army or Marine Corps who is ranked immediately above private

pri·vate in·come *n.* income from sources other than employment, e.g., from investments or allowances

pri·vate in·ves·ti·ga·tor *n.* = **private detective**

pri·vate lan·guage *n.* an exclusive language devised and spoken by a restricted group of people, especially twins

pri·vate law *n.* the branch of law concerned with the rights and responsibilities of individuals. ◊ **public law**

pri·vate life *n.* the part of somebody's life that relates to his or her personal activities and relationships and not to his or her job or public duties

pri·vate means *npl.* = **private income**

pri·vate parts *npl.* the genitals

pri·vate prac·tice *n.* a professional business owned and managed by an individual professional such as a lawyer, doctor or dentist, rather than by an organization

pri·vate prop·er·ty *n.* 1. SOMETHING OWNED BY INDIVIDUAL something, especially land or buildings, owned by an individual or a nongovernmental corporation 2. IDEA OF LAND OWNERSHIP the idea that land can be divided up, bought or claimed, and owned by an individual, company, or government

pri·vate school *n.* a school that is not run by the government and therefore charges fees for tuition, especially one below tertiary level

pri·vate sec·re·tar·y *n.* a secretary employed to manage somebody's personal or confidential affairs, especially those of a business executive or public figure

pri·vate sec·tor *n.* the part of a free market economy that is made up of companies and organizations that are not owned or controlled by the government

pri·vate view·ing *n.* a preview of a motion picture or an exhibition that is open only to invited guests

pri·va·tion /prī váysh'n/ *n.* 1. LACK OF LIFE'S NECESSITIES lack of the basic necessities of life such as food, housing, and heating 2. ACT OF DEPRIVING SOMEBODY the act of depriving somebody of something [14thC. From Latin *privare* "to deprive, isolate," from *privus* "single, isolated," literally "standing in front."]

pri·vat·ism /prívə tìzzəm/ *n.* an attitude or lifestyle in which somebody ignores all but his or her own interests —**pri·va·tist** *n., adj.* —**pri·va·tis·tic** /prìvə tístik/ *adj.*

priv·a·tive /prívətiv/ *adj.* 1. RELATING TO LACK OR NEGATION indicating the absence or negation of some quality ○ *a privative term* 2. CAUSING DEPRIVATION causing or experiencing deprivation ■ *n.* AFFIX DENOTING LACK OR NEGATION an affix, word, or expression that denotes the absence or negation of some quality, e.g., English "non-" or Greek "a-" [Late 16thC. Directly or via French from, ultimately, Latin *privare* (see PRIVATION).] —**priv·a·tive·ly** *adv.*

pri·va·ti·za·tion /prìvəti záysh'n/ *n.* the practice of transferring to private ownership an economic enterprise or public utility that has been under state ownership

pri·va·tize /prívə tīz/ (-tized, -tiz·ing, -tiz·es) *vt.* to transfer to private ownership an economic enterprise or public utility that has been under state ownership

priv·et /prívvət/ *n.* an evergreen shrub with small white flower clusters and black berries that is commonly used for hedges. Latin name: *Ligustrum vulgare* and *Ligustrum ovalifolium.* [Mid-16thC. Origin uncertain.]

priv·i·lege /prívvəlij, prívlij/ *n.* 1. RESTRICTED RIGHT OR BENEFIT an advantage, right, or benefit that is not available to everyone 2. RIGHTS AND ADVANTAGES ENJOYED BY ELITE the rights and advantages enjoyed by a relatively small group of people, usually as a result of wealth or social status ○ *a system founded on privilege* 3. SPECIAL HONOR a special treat or honor ○ *It was a privilege to work with you.* 4. CONFIDENTIALITY OF COMMUNICATION the special right to confidentiality of communication between two parties, such as a lawyer and client or doctor and patient 5. LAWMAKER'S RIGHT TO SPECIAL TREATMENT the right to, or granting of, special treatment or benefits to members of a lawmaking body, e.g., freedom from prosecution **6.** STOCK OPTION an option to buy or sell stocks over a period of time ■ *vt.* **(-leged, -leg·ing, -leg·es) 1.** GIVE SOMEBODY OR SOMETHING SPECIAL RIGHTS to grant special rights or benefits to somebody or something **2.** GRANT SOMEBODY OR SOMETHING EXEMPTION to exempt or release somebody or something from something [12thC. Via Old French from Latin *privilegium* "private law," from *privus* (see PRIVATION) + the stem *leg-* "law."]

priv·i·leged /prívvəlijd, prívvlijd/ *adj.* **1.** ENJOYING SPECIAL ADVANTAGES enjoying privileges, especially the resources and advantages associated with the upper classes or the rich **2.** HONORED OR FORTUNATE fortunate in having a special advantage or opportunity to do something ○ *I feel privileged to be here today.* **3.** AVAILABLE ONLY TO A SELECT GROUP restricted to a particular group of people ■ *npl.* PEOPLE ENJOYING SPECIAL ADVANTAGES a class of people, especially the rich or the upper classes, that benefits from special rights or resources (*takes a plural verb*)

priv·i·leged com·mu·ni·ca·tion *n.* LAW **1.** CONFIDENTIAL COMMUNICATION a confidential conversation or correspondence that does not have to be disclosed in a court of law **2.** COMMUNICATION EXEMPT FROM LIBEL OR SLANDER speech or writing that is not subject to libel or slander laws

priv·i·ly /prívvilee/ *adv.* in a secret or private way (*archaic*)

priv·i·ty /prívvətee/ (*plural* **-ties**) *n.* **1.** SHARED KNOWLEDGE OF SECRET the state of sharing knowledge of, or colluding in, something secret **2.** LAW LEGALLY RECOGNIZED RELATIONSHIP a legally recognized relationship between two parties, e.g., between members of a family, between an employer and employees, or between others who have entered into a contract together **3.** LAW RELATIONSHIP TO PROPERTY a successive or mutual relationship to some property [12thC. Via Old French from medieval Latin *privitas*, from Latin *privus* (see PRIVATION).]

priv·y /prívvee/ *adj.* **1.** SHARING SECRET KNOWLEDGE sharing knowledge of something secret or private ○ *I was privy to their plans to elope.* **2.** RELATING TO SOMEBODY IN PRIVATE CAPACITY relating to somebody, especially a British monarch, as a private individual, not as an official personage **3.** SECRET done or spoken secretly or privately (*archaic*) ■ *n.* (*plural* **-ies**) **1.** OUTSIDE TOILET an outhouse or latrine (*informal*) **2.** LAW SOMEBODY INVOLVED IN SOMETHING an individual who has an interest or agency in something that involves another party [12thC. Via French *privé* from Latin *privatus* (see PRIVATE).]

priv·y cham·ber *n.* an apartment reserved for private use in a royal residence

priv·y coun·cil *n.* **1.** RULER'S ADVISORS a committee that advises a ruler **2.** EXECUTIVE'S ADVISORS a group of people who advise an executive —**priv·y coun·cil·or** *n.*

Priv·y Coun·cil *n.* the committee that advises a British king or queen —**Priv·y Coun·cil·or** *n.*

prix fixe /pree fíks/ (*plural* **prix fixes** /-fíks/) *n.* **1.** RESTAURANT MEAL SERVED AT FIXED PRICE a meal with several courses that is offered by a restaurant at a set price **2.** SET PRICE FOR MEAL a set price for a restaurant meal with several courses [From French, "fixed price"]

prize[1] /prīz/ *n.* **1.** AWARD FOR WINNER something that is given to the winner of a contest or competition **2.** SOMETHING HIGHLY VALUED something that somebody values highly, especially because it takes great skill, effort, or luck to get ■ *vt.* **(prized, priz·ing, priz·es)** TREASURE SOMETHING to value something highly ○ *This award is something I'll always prize.* ■ *adj.* COMPLETE perfect as an example of something, especially something undesirable (*dated informal*) ○ *I made a prize fool of myself.* [Late 16thC. From earlier *prise* "value, reward."]

prize[2] /prīz/ *n.* something captured and kept, especially a ship or its contents taken by another ship in wartime [13thC. From Old French *prise*, literally "something seized," the feminine past participle of *prendre* "to take, seize," from Latin *prehendere* (see PREHENSION).]

prize[3] /prīz/, **prise** *vt.* **(prized, priz·ing, priz·es; prised, pris·ing, pris·es) 1.** LEVER SOMETHING to open or part something by levering ○ *I used a screwdriver to prize the lid off the paint.* **2.** EXTRACT INFORMATION to get something, especially information, from somebody or something with difficulty ■ *n.* LEVER something used as a lever [14thC. Origin uncertain: probably from French *prise* "seizing, capture" (see PRIZE[2]).]

prize·fight /príz fìt/ *n.* a boxing match in which the winner receives a cash prize —**prize·fight·er** *n.* —**prize·fight·ing** *n.*

prize ring *n.* **1.** BOXING RING a boxing ring where prizefights are held **2.** PROFESSIONAL BOXING the sport or business of professional boxing

prize·win·ner /príz wìnnər/ *n.* somebody or something that wins a prize in a competition, or that habitually wins prizes —**prize·win·ning** *adj.*

p.r.n. *abbr.* as required (*used on medical prescriptions*) [From Latin *pro re nata*]

pro[1] /prō/ *n.* (*plural* **pros**) **1.** ARGUMENT FOR SOMETHING an argument in favor of a proposal or position **2.** SIDE ARGUING FOR SOMETHING a person or side in a debate, argument, or campaign that is in favor of a proposal or proposition ■ *prep.* FOR in favor of ■ *adv.* IN SUPPORT OF SOMETHING on the side that favors one side of an issue [14thC. From Latin, "for" (see PRO-).]

pro[2] /prō/ *n.* (*plural* **pros**) **1.** PROFESSIONAL PERSON a professional, especially in sports (*informal*) **2.** SKILLED PERSON somebody who is very skilled at what he or she does **3.** PROSTITUTE a prostitute (*slang*) ■ *adj.* PROFESSIONAL relating to or typical of an activity, especially a sport, from which somebody earns a living ■ *adv.* PROFESSIONALLY as a professional [Mid-20thC. Shortening.]

PRO, P.R.O. *n., abbr.* public relations officer

pro-[1] *prefix.* **1.** substituting for, acting in place of ○ *proconsul* **2.** in favor of ○ *pronuclear* [Via Old French from, ultimately, Latin *pro* "for." Ultimately from an Indo-European word meaning "forward, before" that is also the ancestor of English *fro, from,* and *pro*[2].]

pro-[2] *prefix.* **1.** rudimentary, precursor ○ *promycelium* **2.** before, earlier than ○ *procambium* **3.** in front of ○ *procephalic* [Via Old French from, ultimately, Greek *pro* "in front, before." Ultimately from an Indo-European word meaning "forward, before" that is also the ancestor of English *fro, from,* and *pro*[1].]

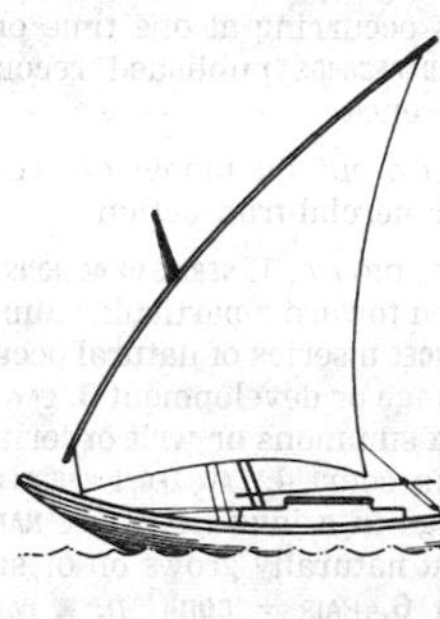

Proa

pro·a /prṓ ə/ (*plural* **-as**), **prau** /prow/ (*plural* **praus**), **prah·u** /praá hoo/ (*plural* **-us**) *n.* a Malayan boat with a triangular sail and a single outrigger [Late 16thC. From Malay *pārāhū* "boat."]

pro-a·bor·tion *adj.* in favor of open legal access to voluntary abortion

pro·ac·tive /prō áktiv/ *adj.* taking the initiative by acting rather than reacting to events [Mid-20thC. Modeled on *retroactive*.] —**pro·ac·tion** *n.* —**pro·ac·tive·ly** *adv.*

WORD KEY: USAGE

Jargon? When people name words they despise as jargon, ***proactive*** is often on the list. However, ***proactive*** does meet a need, serving as the opposite of *reactive* more naturally than, for example, *anticipatory* or *assertive* is able to. Nonetheless, it should be used sparingly.

pro-am /prō ám/ *adj.* COMBINING PROFESSIONALS AND AMATEURS involving or composed of professional and amateur sports players ■ *n.* PRO-AM COMPETITION a competition in which professional players compete against amateurs, or in which professionals and amateurs compete together [Mid-20thC. Contraction.]

prob. *abbr.* **1.** probable **2.** probably **3.** problem

prob·a·bi·lism /próbbəbə lìzzəm/ *n.* **1.** PHILOSOPHY RELIANCE ON PROBABILITIES the belief that certainty is impossible, and that therefore decisions must be based on probabilities **2.** PHILOSOPHY, CHR THE CHOOSING OF FAVORABLE PROBABILITY the principle whereby, in moral questions in which nothing is certain, somebody may follow the probability favorable to him or her rather than a more probable, but less favorable view —**prob·a·bi·list** *n., adj.* —**prob·a·bil·is·tic** *adj.* —**prob·a·bil·ist·i·cal·ly** *adv.*

prob·a·bil·i·ty /pròbbə bíllətee/ (*plural* **-ties**) *n.* **1.** STATE OF BEING PROBABLE the state of being probable or the extent to which something is probable ○ *We must take into account the probability of another earthquake.* **2.** SOMETHING LIKELY TO HAPPEN something that is likely to happen or exist ○ *We must prepare for all probabilities.* **3.** STATS MATHEMATICAL LIKELIHOOD OF EVENT the likelihood that an event will occur expressed as the ratio of the number of favorable outcomes in the set of outcomes divided by the total number of possible outcomes ◇ **in all probability** used to suggest that something is highly probable

prob·a·bil·i·ty den·si·ty func·tion *n.* **1.** = **probability function 2.** STATS FUNCTION OF CONTINUOUS VARIABLE a function of a continuous variable such that the integral of the function over a specific region yields the probability that its value will fall within the region

prob·a·bil·i·ty func·tion *n.* a function of a discrete random variable that yields the probability of occurrence of distinct outcomes

prob·a·bil·i·ty the·o·ry *n.* the branch of mathematics that deals with quantities having random distributions, with the aim of predicting how defined systems will behave

prob·a·ble /próbbəb'l/ *adj.* LIKELY likely to exist, occur, or be true, although evidence is insufficient to prove or predict it ■ *n.* LIKELY CHOICE somebody or something that is likely to be chosen for something or likely to do something ○ *a probable for the team* [14thC. Directly or via French from Latin *probabilis* "provable, plausible," from *probare* (see PROVE).]

prob·a·ble cause *n.* sufficient reason to believe that an arrest or search of a suspect is warranted

prob·a·ble er·ror *n.* the amount by which a statistic may vary from fact, based on chance factors

prob·a·bly /próbbəblee/ *adv.* as is likely or to be expected ○ *I'll probably come tonight.*

pro·band /prṓ bànd/ *n.* = **propositus** *n.* 2 [Early 20thC. From Latin *probandus*-, "for testing, to be tested," from *probare* (see PROVE).]

pro·bate /prṓ bàyt/ *n.* **1.** PROOF OF VALIDITY OF WILL the legal certification of the validity of a will **2.** VERIFIED COPY OF WILL an official copy of a will that is legally certified as genuine and given to the executors ■ *vt.* **(-bat·ed, -bat·ing, -bates)** VALIDATE WILL to certify legally that a will is valid [14thC. Via Middle English *probat* from Latin *probatum* "thing proved," ultimately from *probare* "to test."]

pro·bate court *n.* a court that deals with the legal certification of wills and the administration of estates of the deceased

pro·ba·tion /prō báysh'n/ *n.* **1.** SUPERVISION BY PROBATION OFFICER the supervision of the behavior of a young or first-time criminal offender by a probation officer. During the period of supervision, the offender must regularly report to the probation officer and must not commit any further offenses. **2.** PERIOD OF TESTING SOMEBODY'S SUITABILITY a period during which somebody's suitability for a job or other role is being tested **3.** EDUC PERIOD WHEN STUDENT MUST IMPROVE PERFORMANCE a period during which a student is given a chance to improve his or her academic grades or behavior **4.** TESTING OF SOMETHING the testing or proving of something (*formal*) —**pro·ba·tion·al** *adj.* —**pro·ba·tion·al·ly** *adv.* —**pro·ba·tion·ar·y** /prō báysh'n èrree/ *adj.*

pro·ba·tion·er /prō báysh'nər/ *n.* somebody who is on probation, especially a criminal offender who is under the supervision of a probation officer

pro·ba·tion of·fi·cer *n.* somebody who supervises the behavior of criminal offenders on probation

pro·ba·tion ser·vice *n.* the branch of the criminal justice system that deals with the supervision of criminal offenders after their release from prison or as an alternative to prison

pro·ba·tive /prṓbətiv/, **pro·ba·to·ry** /prṓbə tàwree/ *adj.* **1.** PROVIDING PROOF supplying proof or evidence **2.** TESTING designed to test or prove somebody or something [15thC. Via Old French *probatif* from, ultimately, Latin *probare* (see PROVE).]

probe /prōb/ *n.* **1.** INVESTIGATION a thorough investigation, often into illegal or suspicious activities **2.** ELEC ENG CIRCUIT-TESTING DEVICE a device with a metal tip used to test or the behavior of electrical circuits **3.** SURG, DENT **SURGICAL INSTRUMENT FOR EXPLORING** a long thin instrument used by doctors and dentists for exploring or examining **4.** SPACE TECH = **space probe** ■ *vti.* (**probed, prob·ing, probes**) **1. INVESTIGATE COMPLETELY** to conduct a thorough investigation of something **2. CHECK USING PROBE** to examine something with a probe **3. EXAMINE AREA** to search or explore a place [Mid-16thC. Via medieval latin *proba* "examination," from, ultimately, Latin *probare* "to test."] —**probe·a·ble** *adj.* —**prob·er** *n.*

pro·ben·e·cid /prō bénnəsid/ *n.* a drug that promotes the excretion of uric acid and is used to treat gout [Mid-20thC. From PROPYL + BENZENE + ACID.]

pro·bi·ty /próbətee/ *n.* absolute moral correctness (*formal*) [Early 16thC. Via Old French *probité* from , ultimately Latin *probus*-, "good, honest, upright."]

prob·lem /próbbləm/ *n.* **1. DIFFICULTY** a difficult situation, matter, or person **2. PUZZLE TO BE SOLVED** a question or puzzle that needs to be solved **3.** MATH **STATEMENT REQUIRING MATHEMATICAL SOLUTION** a statement or proposition requiring an algebraic, geometric, or other mathematical solution ■ *adj.* **HARD TO DEAL WITH** difficult to discipline or deal with [14thC. Via Old French from, ultimately, Greek *problēmat*-, "projection, obstacle," literally "thing thrown in front," from *ballein*, "to throw."] ◇ **no problem** used to indicate that something will not cause any difficulty or inconvenience (*informal*)

WORD KEY: SYNONYMS

problem, mystery, puzzle, riddle, conundrum, enigma

CORE MEANING: something difficult to solve or understand

problem a general word for a question or difficult situation in need of a solution; **mystery** something that has never been fully explained or understood and may never be so; **puzzle** a problem whose solution requires ingenuity as well as facts and skills and often involves the use of clues; **riddle** a problem or puzzling question deliberately devised to require a degree of skill and ingenuity in its solution. It can also be used to refer to something that has not yet been fully explained or understood; **conundrum** a problem that is so complicated or strange that it seems impossible to solve; **enigma** somebody or something that is mysterious and hard to understand.

prob·lem·at·ic /pròbblə máttik/, **prob·lem·at·i·cal** /-máttik'l/ *adj.* **1. DIFFICULT** involving difficulties or problems **2. UNCERTAIN** unsettled or posing an uncertain outcome ■ *n.* **SOMETHING PROBLEMATIC** a matter or issue that is problematic —**prob·lem·at·i·cal·ly** *adv.*

prob·lem play *n.* a dramatic work that deals with moral or social problems

pro bo·no /prō bō nō/ *adj., adv.* done or undertaken for the public good without any payment or compensation [Shortening of Latin *pro bono publico* "for the public good"]

pro·bos·ci·de·an /prŏbə síddee ən/, **pro·bos·cid·i·an** *n.* a very large mammal that has a trunk and tusks, e.g., the elephant or extinct mammoth or mastodon. Order: Proboscidea. [Mid-19thC. Formed from modern Latin *Proboscidea*, order name, from Latin *proboscid*-, the stem of *proboscis*.] —**pro·bos·ci·de·an** *adj.*

pro·bos·cis /prō bóssiss, -bóss kis/ (*plural* **-cis·es** *or* **-ci·des** /-dèez/) *n.* **1. ELEPHANT'S TRUNK** the trunk of an elephant or related extinct mammal **2. LONG FLEXIBLE SNOUT** the long flexible snout of some mammals such as the tapir, the elephant seal, and the proboscis monkey **3. LONG MOUTHPARTS OF INVERTEBRATE** the long or tubular mouthparts of certain insects, worms, and spiders, used for feeding, sucking, and other purposes **4. LARGE NOSE** a human nose, especially a large one (*humorous*) [Late 16thC. Via Latin from Greek *proboskis*, "elephant's trunk," from *boskein*, "to feed."]

pro·bos·cis mon·key *n.* a large monkey found on Borneo that has reddish fur and a protruding bulbous nose that in older males becomes pendulous. Latin name: *Nasalis larvatus*.

proc. *abbr.* **1.** procedure **2.** proceedings **3.** process

pro·caine /prṓ kàyn/ *n.* a white or colorless crystalline ester formerly used as a local anesthetic in medicine and dentistry in the form of its hydrochloride. Formula: $C_{13}H_{20}N_2O_2$.

pro·cam·bi·um /prō kámbee əm/ *n.* BOT undifferentiated plant tissue that develops into cambium and vascular tissue [Late 19thC. From PRO[2] + CAMBIUM.] —**pro·cam·bi·al** *adj.*

pro·carp /prṓ kaàrp/ *n.* BIOL the female sex organ of red algae

pro·car·y·ote *n.* = **prokaryote**

pro·ca·the·dral /prŏkə theédrəl/ *n.* a local or parish church that is temporarily being used as a cathedral

pro·ce·dur·al /prə seéjərəl/ *adj.* **RELATING TO PROCEDURE** involving a procedure, especially a legal procedure ■ *n.* = **police procedural** —**pro·ce·dur·al·ist** *n.* — **pro·ce·dur·al·ly** *adv.*

pro·ce·dur·al lan·guage *n.* a high-level programming language that requires the programmer to specify the sequence of operations that the computer must follow to accomplish a specific task. Pascal, BASIC, and COBOL are procedural languages.

pro·ce·dur·al mem·o·ry *n.* PSYCHOL knowledge in the long-term store of procedures that are unconscious

pro·ce·dure /prə seéjər/ *n.* **1. ESTABLISHED METHOD** an established or correct method of doing something **2. ANY METHOD** any means of doing or accomplishing something ○ *an extremely unorthodox procedure* **3.** COMPUT = **routine** *n.* 5 **4.** COMPUT = **subroutine** [Early 17thC. From French *procédure*, from *procéder* from Old French (see PROCEED).]

pro·ceed /prō seéd, prə-/ (**-ceed·ed, -ceed·ing, -ceeds**) *vi.* **1. BEGIN ACTION** to go on to do something **2. CONTINUE WITH ACTION** to continue with a course of action **3. PROGRESS** to progress in a steady or particular manner **4. GO IN SOME DIRECTION** to go in a particular direction, especially forward **5.** LAW **SUE** to bring legal action against somebody **6. DEVELOP** to come from or arise from something [14thC. Via Old French *proceder* from Latin *procedere*, "to go forward," from *cedere*, "to go."] —**pro·ceed·er** *n.*

pro·ceed·ing /prō seéding, prə-/ *n.* **1. PROCEDURE** an action or course of action **2.** LAW **LEGAL ACTION** legal action brought against somebody (*often used in the plural*) ■ **pro·ceed·ings** *npl.* **1. SERIES OF EVENTS** a series of related events occurring at one time or in one place **2. PUBLISHED RECORDS** published records of a meeting or conference

pro·ceeds /prṓ seèdz/ *npl.* the money derived from a sale or other commercial transaction

proc·ess[1] /pró sèss, prṓ-/ *n.* **1. SERIES OF ACTIONS** a series of actions directed toward a particular aim **2. SERIES OF NATURAL OCCURRENCES** a series of natural occurrences that produce change or development **3.** LAW **SUMMONS TO APPEAR IN COURT** a summons or writ ordering somebody to appear in court **4.** LAW **LEGAL PROCEEDINGS** the entire proceedings in a lawsuit **5.** BIOL **NATURAL OUTGROWTH** a part that naturally grows on or sticks out on an organism **6.** HAIR = **conk**[3] *n.* ■ *v.* (**-essed, -ess·ing, -ess·es**) **1.** *vt.* **PREPARE SOMETHING USING A PROCESS** to treat or prepare something in a series of steps or actions, e.g., using chemicals or industrial machinery **2.** *vt.* PHOTOGRAPHY **TREAT SOMETHING WITH PHOTOGRAPHIC CHEMICALS** to treat light-sensitive film or paper with chemicals in order to make a latent image visible **3.** *vt.* **USE PROCEDURES TO DO SOMETHING** to deal with somebody or something according to an established procedure **4.** *vti.* COOK **PREPARE FOOD IN FOOD PROCESSOR** to chop, mix, or otherwise prepare food in food processor or blender **5.** *vt.* COMPUT **USE PROGRAM ON DATA** to use a computer program to work on data in some way, e.g., to sort a database or recalculate a spreadsheet **6.** *vt.* LAW **SERVE SUMMONS ON SOMEBODY** to serve a summons or writ on somebody **7.** *vt.* LAW **BRING LEGAL ACTION** to bring a legal action against somebody **8.** *vt.* **STRAIGHTEN HAIR USING LYE** to straighten curly hair using lye **9.** *vt.* PSYCHOL **DISCUSS EMOTIONAL MEANING OF SOMETHING** to discuss the interpersonal dynamics and emotional content of an event or situation **10.** *vt.* HAIR = **conk**[3] *v.* ■ *adj.* **PREPARED IN A PROCESS** treated or prepared using a special process [14thC. Directly and via Old French *proces* from Latin *processus*, the past participle of *procedere* (see PROCEED).]

proc·ess[2] /prə séss/ (**-essed, -ess·ing, -ess·es**) *vi.* to move forward in a procession

proc·ess art *n.* art created primarily as a physical record of the creative process. Jackson Pollock's drip paintings are perhaps the most famous works of this kind.

proc·ess en·gi·neer·ing *n.* the branch of engineering that determines the sequence of operations and the selection of tools required to manufacture a product

proc·ess in·dus·try *n.* an industry in which raw materials are treated or prepared in a series of stages, e.g., using chemical processes. Process industries include oil refining, petrochemicals, water and sewage treatment, food processing, and pharmaceuticals.

pro·ces·sion /prə sésh'n/ *n.* **1. GROUP OF PEOPLE MOVING FORWARD** a group of people or vehicles moving forward in a line as part of a celebration, commemoration, or demonstration **2. FORWARD MOVEMENT** the movement forward of a group of people or vehicles as part of a celebration, commemoration, or demonstration **3. SUCCESSION** a series of people or things coming one after the other [12thC. Via Old French from ultimately Latin *process*, the past participle stem of *procedere* (see PROCEED).]

pro·ces·sion·al /prə séshən'l, -séshnəl/ *adj.* **1. FOR PROCESSION** used for or in a procession **2. FORMING PROCESSION** taking the form of a procession ■ *n.* **1.** MUSIC **MUSIC FOR PROCESSION** a piece of music suitable for accompanying a procession **2.** MUSIC, CHR **MUSIC FOR ENTRY OF CLERGY** a hymn or other piece of music that accompanies the entry of the clergy into a church **3.** CHR **BOOK OF HYMNS AND PRAYERS** a book of hymns and prayers for use during a religious procession —**pro·ces·sion·al·ly** *adv.*

pro·ces·sor /pró sèssər, prṓ sèssər/, **pro·ces·ser** *n.* **1. SOMETHING THAT PROCESSES** somebody or something that processes things **2. CENTRAL PROCESSING UNIT OF COMPUTER** the central processing unit of a computer **3.** COMPUT = **microprocessor 4.** HOUSEHOLD = **food processor**

proc·ess print·ing *n.* a method of full-color printing using multiple images from plates printed in yellow, magenta, blue, and cyan

proc·ess serv·er *n.* somebody who serves a writ or summons ordering somebody to appear in court

pro·cès-ver·bal /prō sày vər baál/ (*plural* **pro·cès-ver·baux** /-vər bṓ/) *n.* a written account of official proceedings [Mid-17thC. From French, literally "oral proceedings," originally with reference to the oral reports of evidence from police officers who could not write.]

pro-choice *adj.* advocating open legal access to voluntary abortion

pro·claim /prō kláym, prə-/ (**-claimed, -claim·ing, -claims**) *vt.* **1. DECLARE SOMETHING PUBLICLY** to announce something publicly or formally **2. DECLARE SOMEBODY TO BE SOMETHING** to declare publicly that somebody is something **3. SHOW WHAT SOMETHING IS** to show or reveal clearly what something is **4. MAKE SOMETHING CLEAR** to state something emphatically or openly [14thC. Via Old French *proclamer* from Latin *proclamare*, literally "to cry forth," from *clamare* "to cry."] —**pro·claim·er** *n.* — **pro·clam·a·to·ry** /prō klámmə tàwree, prə-/ *adj.*

proc·la·ma·tion /pròklə máysh'n/ *n.* **1. PUBLIC ANNOUNCEMENT** a public or formal announcement **2. MAKING OF PUBLIC ANNOUNCEMENT** the act of announcing something publicly or formally [14thC. Via Old French from, ultimately, Latin *proclaimare* (see PROCLAIM).]

pro·clit·ic /prō klíttik/ *adj.* used to describe a reduced form of a word that is closely attached in pronunciation to the word following it and has no accent of its own, e.g., "d' " in "d'you" [Mid-19thC. From modern Latin *procliticus*-, from PRO[2] on the model of ENCLITIC.] —**pro·clit·ic** *n.*

pro·cliv·i·ty /prō klívvətee/ (*plural* **-ties**) *n.* a natural tendency to behave in a particular way [Late 16thC. From Latin *proclivitas*, from *proclivis* "inclined," literally "leaning forward," from *clivus*, "slope."]

Proc·ne /próknee/ *n.* in Greek mythology, an Athenian princess whose husband, Tereus, raped her sister, Philomela. She avenged this act by killing their own son and feeding him to Tereus.

pro·con·sul /prō kónsəl/ *n.* **1.** HIST **GOVERNOR OF ANCIENT ROMAN PROVINCE** a governor of an ancient Roman province, usually a former consul **2. GOVERNOR OF COLONY** a governor or administrator of a colony or other dependency [14thC. From Latin "(person acting) for the consul," from *consul* (see CONSUL).] —**pro·con·su·lar** *adj.* —**pro·con·su·late** *n.* —**pro·con·sul·ship** *n.*

pro·cras·ti·nate /prō krásti nàyt, prə-/ (**-nat·ed, -nat·ing, -nates**) *vti.* to postpone doing something, especially as a regular practice [Late 16thC. From Latin *procrastinare*, "to put off until tomorrow," from *crastinus* "of tomorrow," from *cras*, "tomorrow."] —**pro·cras·ti·na·tion** /prō kràsti náysh'n, prə-/ *n.* —**pro·cras·ti·na·tor** /prō krásti nàytər, prə-/ *n.*

pro·cre·ate /prṓkree àyt/ (-**at·ed, -at·ing, -ates**) *v.* **1.** *vti.* HAVE OFFSPRING to produce offspring by reproduction **2.** *vt.* CREATE SOMETHING to create or produce something [Mid-16thC. From *procreare*, "to bring forth," from *creare* (see CREATE).] —**pro·cre·ant** /prṓkree ənt/ *adj.* —**pro·cre·a·tive** /prṓkree àytiv/ *adj.* —**pro·cre·a·tion** /-áysh'n/ *n.* —**pro·cre·a·tor** /-àytər/ *n.*

Pro·crus·te·an /prō krústee ən/, **pro·crus·te·an** *adj.* trying to establish conformity by using any and all means, including violence [Mid-19thC. Formed from PROCRUSTES.]

Pro·crus·tes /prō krústeez/ *n.* in Greek mythology, a robber who abducted strangers and forced them to fit perfectly into a bed by either cutting off or stretching their limbs

pro·cryp·tic /prō kríptik/ *adj.* used to describe an animal that has a coloration or pattern of shading that acts as camouflage [Late 19thC. Origin uncertain: probably from PROTECTIVE + CRYPTIC.] —**pro·cryp·ti·cal·ly** *adv.*

proct- *prefix.* = **procto-** (*used before vowels*)

proc·ti·tis /prok tī́tiss/ *n.* inflammation of the rectum [Early 19thC. Formed from Greek *prōktos* "anus."]

procto- *prefix.* anus, anal, rectum, rectal ○ *proctoscope* [From Greek *prōktos*]

proc·to·de·um /pròktə dée əm/ (*plural* **-a** /-ə/ *or* **-ums**), **proc·to·dae·um** (*plural* **-a** *or* **-ums**) *n.* the exterior section of an embryo that develops into part of the anal canal [Late 19thC. From modern Latin, from PROCTO- + Greek *hodaios*, "on the way," from *hodos* "way."]

proc·tol·o·gy /prok tólləjee/ *n.* the branch of medicine concerned with disorders of the colon, rectum, and anus —**proc·to·log·ic** /pròktə lójjik/ *adj.* —**proc·tol·o·gist** /prok tólləjist/ *n.*

proc·tor /próktər/ *n.* **1.** SUPERVISOR AT EXAMINATION somebody who supervises students at an examination **2.** DORMITORY SUPERVISOR at certain schools and universities, a supervisor in a dormitory ■ *vt.* (**-tored, -tor·ing, -tors**) SUPERVISE EXAM to supervise an examination, especially in order to prevent cheating [14thC. Contraction of PROCURATOR.] —**proc·to·ri·al** /prok táwree əl/ *adj.* —**proc·tor·ship** /próktər shìp/ *n.*

proc·to·scope /próktə skṑp/ *n.* a tubular medical instrument with an integral light source, used for examining the anal canal and rectum —**proc·to·scop·ic** /pròktə skóppik/ *adj.* —**proc·tos·co·py** /prok tóskəpee/ *n.*

pro·cum·bent /prō kúmbənt/ *adj.* **1.** LYING FACE DOWN lying down with the face to the ground **2.** BOT GROWING ALONG GROUND used to describe a plant stem that grows along the ground without taking root [Mid-17thC. From Latin *procumbent-*, the present participle of *procumbere*, "to fall forward," from *-cumbere* "to lie down."]

pro·cu·ra·tion /pròkyə ráysh'n/ *n.* **1.** ACQUIRING OF SOMETHING the obtaining of something, especially by effort (*formal*) **2.** CRIMINAL LAW PROVIDING OF PROSTITUTE the crime of providing somebody for prostitution **3.** LAW ENGAGING OF PROCURATOR the engaging of an agent to manage somebody's affairs **4.** LAW AUTHORIZING OF PROCURATOR the authorization given to somebody who acts as an agent to manage somebody else's affairs

proc·u·ra·tor /prókyə ràytər/ *n.* **1.** HIST ANCIENT ROMAN OFFICIAL in ancient Rome, an administrative official with legal or fiscal powers **2.** LAW AGENT MANAGING SOMEBODY'S AFFAIRS an agent engaged to manage somebody else's affairs —**proc·u·ra·to·ri·al** /pròkyərə táwree əl/ *adj.* —**proc·u·ra·tor·ship** /prókyə ràytər shìp/ *n.*

pro·cure /prō kyŏor, prə-/ (**-cured, -cur·ing, -cures**) *v.* **1.** *vt.* ACQUIRE SOMETHING to obtain something, especially by effort **2.** *vti.* CRIMINAL LAW PROVIDE PROSTITUTES to provide somebody for prostitution [13thC. Via Old French from Latin *procurare*, "to take care of, manage," from *curare* "to care for."] —**pro·cur·a·ble** *adj.* —**pro·cur·al** *n.* —**pro·cur·ance** *n.*

WORD KEY: SYNONYMS

See Synonyms at ***get***.

pro·cure·ment /prō kyŏormənt, prə-/ *n.* **1.** OBTAINING OF SOMETHING the obtaining of something, especially by effort **2.** PURCHASING OF SOMETHING the purchasing of something, especially for a company, government, or other organization

pro·cur·er /prō kyŏorər, prə-/ *n.* **1.** SOMEBODY GETTING SOMETHING somebody who obtains something **2.** CRIMINAL LAW SOMEBODY SUPPLYING PROSTITUTES somebody who provides people for prostitution

pro·cur·ess /prō kyŏorəss, prə-/ (*plural* **-ess·es**) *n.* a woman who provides people for prostitution (*dated*)

prod /prod/ *vti.* (**prod·ded, prod·ding, prods**) **1.** POKE SOMEBODY OR SOMETHING to poke somebody or something with a finger, elbow, or pointed object **2.** INCITE SOMEBODY TO ACTION to incite or encourage somebody to take action ■ *n.* **1.** A POKE a poke with a finger, elbow, or pointed object **2.** INCITEMENT TO ACTION an incitement or encouragement to do something **3.** POKING INSTRUMENT an instrument used for poking a person or animal [Mid-16thC. Origin uncertain: perhaps a variant of obsolete *brod* "goad," of uncertain origin: probably from Old Norse *broddr*.] —**prod·der** *n.*

prod. *abbr.* **1.** produce **2.** produced **3.** product **4.** production

prod·i·gal /próddig'l/ *adj.* **1.** EXTRAVAGANTLY WASTEFUL spendthrift or extravagant to a degree bordering on recklessness **2.** PRODUCING GENEROUS AMOUNTS giving or producing something in large amounts **3.** WASTING PARENTAL MONEY BUT STILL LOVED spending parental money wastefully, but returning home to a warm welcome (*literary*) ■ *n.* SPENDTHRIFT somebody who spends money, especially money from his or her parents, wastefully [Early 16thC. Via French from, ultimately, Latin *prodigus*, "wasteful," from *prodigere*, "to drive away, squander," from *agere*, "to drive."] —**prod·i·gal·i·ty** /pròddi gállətee/ *n.* —**prod·i·gal·ly** /próddigəlee/ *adv.*

pro·di·gious /prə díjjəss/ *adj.* **1.** SIZABLE great in amount, size, or extent **2.** MARVELOUS very impressive or amazing **3.** OMINOUS portentous or ominous (*archaic*) [Mid-16thC. From Latin *prodigiosus* "marvelous," from *prodigium* (see PRODIGY).] —**pro·di·gious·ly** *adv.* —**pro·di·gious·ness** *n.*

prod·i·gy /próddəjee/ (*plural* **-gies**) *n.* **1.** SOMEBODY WITH EXCEPTIONAL TALENT somebody who shows an exceptional natural talent for something from an early age **2.** SOMETHING MARVELOUS something very impressive or amazing **3.** WARNING SIGN a portent or omen (*archaic*) [15thC. From Latin *prodigium* "prophetic sign, portent," of uncertain origin: perhaps literally "something foretold," formed from *-igium*, from *aio* "I say."]

pro·drome /prṓ drṑm/ *n.* a symptom indicating the onset of a disease. ◊ **syndrome** [Mid-17thC. Via French from, ultimately, Greek *prodromos*, literally "a running before," from *dromos* "running" (see -DROME).] —**pro·dro·mal** /prō drṓm'l/ *adj.* —**pro·drom·ic** /-drómmik/ *adj.*

pro·duce *v.* /prə dŏoss/ (**-duced, -duc·ing, -duc·es**) **1.** *vti.* MAKE SOMETHING to make or create something **2.** *vti.* MANUFACTURE SOMETHING to manufacture goods for sale **3.** *vt.* CAUSE SOMETHING to cause something to happen or arise **4.** *vti.* YIELD SOMETHING to bring forth or bear something **5.** *vt.* OFFER SOMETHING to present or show something **6.** *vt.* ARTS ORGANIZE THE MAKING OF SOMETHING to organize and supervise the making of something **7.** *vt.* GEOM EXTEND SOMETHING IN SPACE to extend the length of a line, area of a plane figure, or volume of a solid ■ *n.* /prṓ dŏoss/ FARM OR GARDEN PRODUCTS products of farms or gardens, especially fruits and vegetables [15thC. From Latin *producere* "to lead or bring forth," from *ducere* "to lead."] —**pro·duc·i·bil·i·ty** /prə dŏossə bíllətee/ *n.* —**pro·duc·i·ble** /prə dŏossəb'l/ *adj.*

WORD KEY: SYNONYMS

See Synonyms at ***make***.

pro·duc·er /prə dŏossər/ *n.* **1.** SOMETHING THAT PRODUCES somebody or something that produces something **2.** SOMETHING GENERATING ITEMS FOR SALE a person, company, or country that produces goods or services for sale **3.** ARTS ORGANIZER OF MOVIE, RECORDING, ETC. somebody who organizes and supervises the making of a motion picture, play, broadcast, or recording **4.** INDUST APPARATUS FOR PRODUCER GAS a furnace used for making producer gas **5.** ECOL ORGANISM THAT MAKES ITS FOOD an organism such as a green plant, that manufactures its own food from simple inorganic substances. Producers are ultimately the sole source of food for all animals and other consumer organisms.

pro·duc·er gas *n.* a fuel consisting of carbon monoxide, nitrogen, and hydrogen, made by passing air and steam over hot coke in a furnace

prod·uct /pró dùkt/ *n.* **1.** SOMETHING MADE OR CREATED something that is made or created by a person, machine, or natural process, especially something that is offered for sale **2.** COMPANY'S GOODS OR SERVICES the goods or services produced by a company **3.** RESULT something that arises as a consequence of something else **4.** MATH RESULT OF MULTIPLYING the result of the multiplication of two or more quantities **5.** CHEM CHEMICAL SUBSTANCE a substance produced in a chemical reaction [15thC. From Latin *productus*, the past participle of *producere* (see PRODUCE).]

pro·duc·tion /prə dúkshən/ *n.* **1.** MAKING OF SOMETHING the making or creation of something **2.** SOMETHING PRODUCED something that has been made or created **3.** ECON PRODUCING OF GOODS the process of manufacturing a product for sale **4.** ECON COMPANY'S PRODUCT the goods or services produced by a company **5.** ARTS SUPERVISION OF MOVIE, RECORDING, ETC. the organization and supervision of the making of a movie, play, broadcast, or recording **6.** ARTS MOVIE, RECORDING, ETC. a motion picture, play, broadcast, or recording that has been produced for the public **7.** SHOWING OF SOMETHING the showing or presenting of something such as evidence ■ *adj.* MASS-PRODUCED mass-produced for sale to the general public —**pro·duc·tion·al** *adj.*

pro·duc·tion as·sis·tant *n.* an assistant to a movie producer who performs a variety of errands and tasks

pro·duc·tion com·pa·ny *n.* an organization that makes motion pictures

pro·duc·tion de·sign·er *n.* somebody who is responsible for the look of the physical world on screen in a movie, including sets and costumes

pro·duc·tion line *n.* a sequence of machines or processes in a factory through which the products pass until they are fully assembled

pro·duc·tion man·ag·er *n.* somebody who is in charge of arranging the shooting of a movie or the producing of a play, e.g., by planning schedules, ordering equipment, and hiring extras

pro·duc·tion num·ber *n.* a piece of music in a musical that is sung and danced by featured actors supported by the chorus

pro·duc·tive /prə dúktiv/ *adj.* **1.** PRODUCING SOMETHING producing or able to produce something **2.** PRODUCING MUCH producing something abundantly and efficiently **3.** WORTHWHILE producing satisfactory or useful results **4.** ECON PRODUCING GOODS producing goods and services of exchangeable value **5.** MED PRODUCING MUCUS used to describe a cough that produces mucus **6.** GRAM USED TO FORM WORDS used to describe a prefix or suffix that is used in forming new words —**pro·duc·tive·ly** *adv.* —**pro·duc·tive·ness** *n.*

pro·duc·tiv·i·ty /prō duk tívvətee/ *n.* **1.** ABILITY TO PRODUCE the ability to be productive **2.** ECON RATE OF PRODUCTION the rate at which a company produces goods or services, in relation to the amount of materials and number of employees needed

prod·uct li·a·bil·i·ty *n.* the liability of manufacturers and traders for damage or injury caused to purchasers or bystanders by their products

prod·uct line *n.* **1.** COMPANY'S WHOLE RANGE OF PRODUCTS the whole range of products marketed by a company **2.** COMPANY'S GROUP OF RELATED PRODUCTS a group of related products marketed by the same company that differ only in size or style

pro·em /prṓ èm/ *n.* an introduction to a literary work or a speech [14thC. Via Old French *pro(h)eme* from, ultimately, Greek *prooimion*, literally "song before," from *oimē* "song."] —**pro·e·mi·al** /prō émmee əl/ *adj.*

pro·en·zyme /prō én zīm/ *n.* the inactive precursor of an enzyme, especially one secreted by living cells and activated by an acid, another enzyme, or other catalytic means

pro·es·trus /prō éstrəss/ *n.* the period in the estrus cycle immediately preceding estrus

prof /prof/ *n.* a college or university professor (*informal*) [Mid-19thC. Shortening.]

Prof. *abbr.* professor

pro·fane /prō fáyn, prə-/ *adj.* **1.** IRREVERENT showing disrespect for God, any deity, or religion (*formal*) **2.** SECULAR not connected with or used for religious matters **3.** UNINITIATED not initiated into sacred or secret rites ■ *vt.* (**-faned, -fan·ing, -fanes**) TREAT SOMETHING IRREVENTLY to treat something sacred with disrespect [14thC. Via Old French *prophane* from Latin *profanus*, literally "outside the temple," hence "not sacred," from *fanum* "temple" (source of English *fanatic*).] —**prof·a·na·tion** /pròffə náysh'n/ *n.* —**pro·fan·a·to·ry** /prō fánnə tàwree, prə-/ *adj.* —**pro·fane·ly** /prō fáynlee, prə-/ *adv.* —**pro·fane·ness** /-fáyn nəss/ *n.* —**pro·fan·er** /-fáynər/ *n.*

pro·fan·i·ty /prō fánnətee, prə-/ (*plural* **-ties**) *n.* **1.** PROFANE LANGUAGE OR BEHAVIOR language or behavior that shows disrespect for God, any deity, or religion **2.** PROFANE WORD OR PHRASE a word or phrase that shows disrespect for God, any deity, or religion

pro·fess /prō féss, prə-/ (**-fessed, -fess·ing, -fess·es**) *v.* **1.** *vti.* DECLARE SOMETHING OPENLY to acknowledge something publicly **2.** *vt.* DECLARE SOMETHING FALSELY to make a false claim about something **3.** *vt.* RELIG BELIEVE A RELIGION to follow a particular religion **4.** *vti.* RELIG BECOME PRIEST, NUN, ETC. to admit somebody, or be admitted, into a religious order [15thC. From Old French *profes,* "having taken religious vows," ultimately from Latin *profess-,* the past participle of *profiteri* "to declare publicly," from *fateri* "to acknowledge."] —**pro·fessed** *adj.* —**pro·fess·ed·ly** /prō féssədlee, prə-/ *adv.*

pro·fes·sion /prō fésh'n, prə-/ *n.* **1.** OCCUPATION REQUIRING EXTENSIVE EDUCATION an occupation that requires extensive education or specialized training **2.** PEOPLE IN PROFESSION the members of a particular profession **3.** DECLARATION a public acknowledgment or declaration of something **4.** RELIG DECLARATION OF RELIGIOUS BELIEF a declaration of belief in a religion or faith

pro·fes·sion·al /prō féshən'l, -féshnəl, prə-/ *adj.* **1.** OF A PROFESSION relating to or belonging to a profession **2.** FOLLOWING OCCUPATION AS PAID JOB engaged in an occupation as a paid job rather than as a hobby **3.** VERY COMPETENT showing a high degree of skill or competence **4.** DOING SOMETHING HABITUALLY habitually, and usually annoyingly, indulging in a particular activity ○ *a professional complainer* ■ *n.* **1.** MEMBER OF PROFESSION somebody whose occupation requires extensive education or specialized training **2.** SOMEBODY DOING SOMETHING AS PAID JOB somebody who is engaged in an occupation as a paid job rather than as a hobby **3.** SOMEBODY VERY COMPETENT somebody who shows a high degree of skill or competence **4.** TEACHER AT SPORTS CLUB an expert player of a sport who is employed by a golf or other sports club to teach its members —**pro·fes·sion·al·ly** *adv.*

pro·fes·sion·al as·so·ci·a·tion *n.* a society of members of a profession that regulates entry to, and sets and maintains standards for, the profession

pro·fes·sion·al cor·po·ra·tion *n.* a business incorporated by licensed professionals such as doctors or lawyers

pro·fes·sion·al foul *n.* a deliberate foul in soccer, usually committed in order to prevent the opposing team gaining a potentially crucial advantage in field position or goal-scoring opportunity

pro·fes·sion·al·ism /prō féshən'l ìzzəm, -féshnə lìzzəm, prə-/ *n.* **1.** PROFESSIONAL STANDARDS the skill, competence, or character expected of a member of a highly trained profession **2.** USE OF PROFESSIONALS the use of professionals instead of amateurs

pro·fes·sion·al·ize /prō féshən'l ìz, -féshnə lìz, prə-/ (**-ized, -iz·ing, -iz·es**) *vt.* to make an occupation professional, especially by paying the people who engage in it or improving the conditions or standards of their work

pro·fes·sor /prə féssər/ *n.* **1.** EDUC COLLEGE TEACHER OF HIGHEST ACADEMIC RANK a teacher holding the highest academic rank in a college or university **2.** EDUC UNIVERSITY TEACHER a teacher in a university or college **3.** TEACHER OF A SKILL a senior teacher of a nonacademic discipline in an institution other than a university such as a music or drama school **4.** RELIG SOMEBODY PROFESSING BELIEF somebody who professes a religion or other belief (*formal*) —**pro·fes·so·ri·al** /pròffə sáwree əl/ *adj.* —**pro·fes·so·ri·al·ly** /-sáwree əlee/ *adv.* —**pro·fes·sor·ship** /prə féssər shìp/ *n.*

pro·fes·so·ri·ate /pròffə sáwree ət/, **pro·fes·so·ri·at, pro·fes·so·rate** *n.* **1.** PROFESSORS professors as a group **2.** PROFESSOR'S POSITION the status or position of professor

prof·fer /próffər/ *vt.* (**-fered, -fer·ing, -fers**) **1.** HOLD SOMETHING OUT to hold something out to somebody so that he or she can take or grasp it **2.** PROPOSE SOMETHING to offer something for consideration to somebody ■ *n.* PROPOSAL something offered for consideration ○ *proffer a suggestion* [13thC. From Old French *proffrir,* literally "to offer forth," from *offrir* "to offer."] —**prof·fer·er** *n.*

pro·fi·cien·cy /prə físh'nsee/ *n.* competence in something, or knowledge of it

pro·fi·cient /prə físh'nt/ *adj.* VERY SKILLED having a high degree of skill in something ■ *n.* SOMEBODY VERY SKILLED somebody with a high degree of skill in something (*archaic*) [Late 16thC. Via Old French from Latin *proficient-,* the present participle of *proficere* "to make progress," literally "to make forward," which was formed from *facere* "to make."] —**pro·fi·cient·ly** *adv.*

pro·file /prṓ fìl/ *n.* **1.** SIDE VIEW OF FACE the outline of somebody's face as seen from the side **2.** ARTS ARTWORK OF SOMEBODY'S PROFILE a visual representation of the outline of somebody's face as seen from the side **3.** COMMUNICATION SHORT BIOGRAPHY a short biographical account of somebody **4.** STATS DATA DESCRIBING SOMETHING a set of data, usually in graph or table form, that indicates the extent to which something matches tested or standard characteristics **5.** VISIBILITY a level or degree of noticeability ○ *Though he had become famous, he still tried to keep a low profile.* **6.** GEOG VERTICAL SECTION OF PHYSICAL FEATURE a vertical section through a physical feature, e.g., through soil, showing its development from bedrock, or through a river, showing its height above sea level along its course ■ *v.* (**-filed, -fil·ing, -files**) **1.** *vt.* COMMUNICATION DO SHORT BIOGRAPHY OF SOMEBODY to write or present a short biographical account of somebody **2.** *vt.* ARTS DRAW PROFILE OF SOMEBODY to draw or paint the outline of somebody's face as seen from the side **3.** *vi.* SHOW OFF to show off, strut, or otherwise try to attract attention (*slang*) [Mid-17thC. From Italian *profilo,* from *profilare* "to draw in outline," literally "to draw or spin forth," ultimately from *filo* "thread," from Latin *filum.*] —**pro·fil·er** *n.*

prof·it /próffit/ *n.* **1.** BUSINESS EXCESS OF INCOME OVER EXPENDITURE the excess of income over expenditure during a particular period of time **2.** FIN INCOME FROM SOMETHING income from an investment or transaction (*often used in the plural*) **3.** BUSINESS MONEY FROM BUSINESS ACTIVITY money made or to be made from business activity **4.** ADVANTAGE an advantage or benefit derived from an activity ■ *v.* (**-it·ed, -it·ing, -its**) **1.** *vi.* FIN MAKE MONEY ON SOMETHING to gain financial profit from something **2.** *vti.* BENEFIT FROM SOMETHING to gain an advantage or benefit from something, or to provide an advantage or benefit [13thC. Via Old French from Latin *profectus* "advance," the past participle of *proficere* (see PROFICIENT).] —**prof·it·er** *n.* —**prof·it·less** *adj.* —**prof·it·less·ly** *adv.*

prof·it·a·ble /próffitəb'l/ *adj.* **1.** FIN LUCRATIVE yielding a financial profit **2.** USEFUL of some use, benefit, or advantage to somebody —**prof·it·a·bil·i·ty** /pròffitə bíllətee/ *n.* —**prof·it·a·ble·ness** /próffitəb'lnəss/ *n.* —**prof·it·a·bly** /-əblee/ *adv.*

prof·it and loss *n.* an account showing income and expenditure over a given period and indicating net profit or loss

prof·it cen·ter *n.* **1.** PROFITABLE ACTIVITY OR SECTOR a section or activity of a company that is independently profitable **2.** SEPARATE SECTOR IN FINANCIAL ACCOUNTS an organizational unit or activity of a company for which income and expenses are reported independently

prof·it·eer /pròffi tee̍r/ *vi.* (**-eered, -eer·ing, -eers**) MAKE EXCESSIVE PROFITS to make excessive profits by charging high prices for scarce, necessary, or rationed goods ■ *n.* SOMEBODY MAKING EXCESSIVE PROFITS somebody who makes excessive profits by charging high prices for scarce, necessary, or rationed goods —**prof·it·eer·ing** *n.*

pro·fit·er·ole /prə fíttə rṑl/ *n.* a small ball of light pastry filled with cream and usually served with chocolate sauce [Early 16thC. From French, literally "small gain," from *profit* (see PROFIT).]

prof·it mar·gin *n.* the amount by which income exceeds the related expenditures

prof·it shar·ing *n.* a system by which the employees of a company receive a prearranged share of the company's profits (*hyphenated when used before a noun*)

prof·it tak·ing *n.* the selling of commodities, securities, or stocks at a time when their current market value is greater than the price at which they were purchased —**prof·it-tak·er** *n.*

prof·li·gate /prófflìgət, -gàyt/ *adj.* **1.** WASTEFUL extremely extravagant or wasteful **2.** WITH LOW MORALS having or showing extremely low moral standards ■ *n.* **1.** SOMEBODY WASTEFUL somebody who is extremely extravagant or wasteful **2.** SOMEBODY WITH LOW MORALS somebody with extremely low moral standards [Mid-16thC. From Latin *profligatus,* the past participle of *profligare* "to strike down, ruin," from *fligere* "to strike" (source of English *conflict*).] —**prof·li·ga·cy** *n.* —**prof·li·gate·ly** *adv.*

pro·flu·ent /pró flo͝o ənt/ *adj.* flowing smoothly or freely [15thC. From Latin *profluere* "to flow forth," from *fluere* "to flow."]

pro for·ma /prō fáwrmə/ *adj.* **1.** FORMAL OR CONVENTIONAL done or existing only as a formality **2.** PROVIDED IN ADVANCE provided in advance in order to supply descriptions of something or to serve as a model, e.g., of a later version of a document ○ *a pro forma invoice* ■ *adv.* FOR CONVENTION'S SAKE for the sake of or in accordance with convention [From Latin, literally "for form's sake"]

pro·found /prə fównd/ *adj.* **1.** GREAT very great, strong, or intense **2.** SHOWING GREAT UNDERSTANDING showing great perception, understanding, or knowledge **3.** REQUIRING GREAT UNDERSTANDING requiring great perception, understanding, or knowledge **4.** VERY DEEP extending to or situated at a great depth [13thC. Via Old French *profond* from Latin *profundus,* literally "bottom forward or downward," from *fundus* "bottom."] —**pro·found·ness** *n.* —**pro·found·ly** *adv.*

pro·fun·di·ty /prə fúndətee/ (*plural* **-ties**) *n.* **1.** GREAT UNDERSTANDING great perceptiveness, understanding, or knowledge **2.** SOMETHING REQUIRING GREAT UNDERSTANDING something requiring great understanding, perceptiveness, or knowledge **3.** INTELLECTUAL COMPLEXITY the intellectual complexity or abstruseness of something **4.** GREATNESS the greatness, strength, or intensity of something **5.** GREAT DEPTH extension to, or location at, a great depth [15thC. Via Old French *profundite* from late Latin *profunditas,* from *profundus* (see PROFOUND).]

pro·fuse /prə fyo͞oss/ *adj.* **1.** GENEROUSLY PROVIDED given freely and extravagantly ○ *profuse apologies* **2.** GENEROUS IN GIVING giving something freely and extravagantly **3.** COPIOUS being or appearing in large amounts [15thC. From Latin *profusus,* the past participle of *profundere* "to pour forth," from *fundere* "to pour."] —**pro·fuse·ly** *adv.* —**pro·fuse·ness** *n.*

pro·fu·sion /prə fyo͞ozh'n/ *n.* **1.** A GREAT DEAL a large quantity of something **2.** PROFUSE QUALITY the quality of being profuse

prog. *abbr.* **1.** program **2.** progress **3.** progressive

Prog. *abbr.* Progressive

pro·gen·i·tor /prō jénnitər/ *n.* **1.** ANCESTOR a direct ancestor of somebody or something **2.** ORIGINATOR the originator of, or original model for, something [14thC. From Latin, literally "begetter," from *progenit-,* the past participle stem of *progignere* "to beget," literally "to create forth," from *gignere* (see GENITAL).]

prog·e·ny /prójjənee/ (*plural* **-ny** *or* **-nies**) *n.* **1.** OFFSPRING OF ORGANISM an offspring of a person, animal, or plant **2.** SOMETHING RESULTING something that develops or results from something else [13thC. Via Old French *progenie* from Latin *progenies* "offspring," from *progignere* (see PROGENITOR).]

pro·ger·i·a /prō jeéree ə/ *n.* a rare condition of premature aging that begins in childhood or early adult life and leads to death within a few years [Early 20thC. Via modern Latin from Greek *progērōs,* literally "aged forward," from *gēras* "old age."]

pro·ges·ta·tion·al /prō je stáyshən'l, -stáyshnəl/ *adj.* **1.** PHYSIOL RELATING TO MENSTRUAL CYCLE PHASE relating to the stage of the menstrual cycle following ovulation during which progesterone is produced and the womb is prepared for pregnancy **2.** BIOCHEM, PHARM OF OR LIKE PROGESTERONE relating to or resembling progesterone or its effects

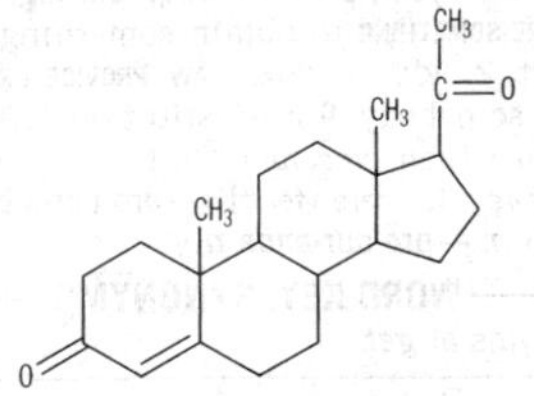

Progesterone

pro·ges·ter·one /prō jéstə rṑn/ *n.* a sex hormone produced in women first by the corpus luteum of the ovary to prepare the womb for the fertilized ovum and later by the placenta to maintain pregnancy. Formula: $C_{21}H_{30}O_2$. [Mid-20thC. Formed from PRO- + GESTATION + STEROL + -ONE.]

pro·ges·tin /prō jéstin/ *n.* any progestogen, usually progesterone [Early 20thC. Formed from PRO- + GESTATION + -IN.]

pro·ges·to·gen /prō jéstəjən/ *n.* a steroid hormone or agent having effects similar to those of progesterone [Mid-20thC. Formed from PRO- + GESTATION + -IN.]

pro·glot·tid /prō glóttid/, **pro·glot·tis** /-glóttiss/ (*plural* **-ti·des**) *n.* a segment of a tapeworm's body. Each segment contains a complete reproductive system. —**pro·glot·tic** *adj.*

prog·na·thous /prógnəthəss/, **prog·nath·ic** /prog náthik/ *adj.* used to describe an animal with a jaw that sticks out markedly [Mid-19thC. Coined from PRO- + Greek *gnathos* "jaw."] —**prog·na·thism** *n.*

prog·no·sis /prog nóssiss/ (*plural* **-ses** /-seez/) *n.* **1.** MED **OPINION ON COURSE OF DISEASE** a medical opinion as to the likely course and outcome of a disease **2. PREDICTION** a prediction about how a given situation will develop [Mid-17thC. Via late Latin from Greek *prognōsis*, literally "knowledge beforehand," ultimately from *gignōskein* "to know."]

prog·nos·tic /prog nóstik/ *adj.* **1.** MED **OF DISEASE PROGNOSIS** relating to or acting as a prognosis of a disease **2. OF PREDICTION** relating to or acting as a prediction ■ *n.* **1.** MED **INDICATION OF COURSE OF DISEASE** an indicator used in making a prognosis concerning a disease **2. PREDICTION** a prediction as to how a given situation will develop [15thC. Via Old French from, ultimately, Greek *prognōstikos* "of knowledge beforehand," from *prognœsis* (see PROGNOSIS).]

prog·nos·ti·cate /prog nósti kàyt/ (**-cat·ed, -cat·ing, -cates**) *v.* **1.** *vti.* **PREDICT THE FUTURE** to predict or foretell future events **2.** *vt.* **BE INDICATION OF SOMETHING** to be an indication of the likely future course of something —**prog·nos·ti·ca·tion** /prog nòsti káysh'n/ *n.* —**prog·nos·ti·ca·tive** /prog nósti kàytiv/ *adj.* —**prog·nos·ti·ca·tor** /-kàytər/ *n.*

pro·grade /prṓ gràyd/ *adj.* moving in the same orbital or rotational direction as another astronomical body

pro·gram /prṓ gràm/ *n.* **1. PLAN OF ACTION** a plan of action for achieving something **2.** BROADCAST **BROADCAST** a television or radio broadcast **3.** ARTS **BOOKLET GIVING DETAILS OF A PERFORMANCE** a booklet or leaflet giving details of a theatrical or musical performance or a ceremony **4.** EDUC **SET OF CLASSES** a series of classes or lectures on something **5. SYSTEM TO DEVELOP OR PROVIDE SOMETHING** a system of procedures or activities that has a specific purpose, e.g., to train an athletic team or provide certain social services **6. INSTRUCTIONS OBEYED BY COMPUTER** a list of instructions in a programming language that tells a computer to perform a certain task **7.** TECH **OPERATING INSTRUCTIONS FOR MACHINE** a set of coded operating instructions that is used to run a machine automatically **8. ROUTINE** the established routine (*slang*) ○ *I know you're new here, but try to get with the program!* ■ *v.* (**-grammed** *or* **-gramed, -gram·ming** *or* **-gram·ing, -grams**) **1.** *vt.* **SCHEDULE SOMETHING** to schedule something as part of a program **2.** *vti.* **WRITE COMPUTER PROGRAM** to write or load a program for a computer **3.** *vt.* TECH **INSERT OPERATING INSTRUCTIONS INTO MACHINE** to insert coded operating instructions into a machine **4.** *vt.* **TRAIN SOMEBODY TO DO SOMETHING AUTOMATICALLY** to train a person or an animal to do a particular thing automatically [Mid-17thC. Via French from, ultimately, Greek *programma* "public notice," literally "something written publicly," ultimately from *graphein* "to write."] —**pro·gram·ma·ble** /prō grámməb'l/ *adj.* —**pro·gram·ma·bil·i·ty** /prō gràmmə bíllətee/ *n.*

pro·gram di·rec·tor *n.* an executive who is responsible for the selection and scheduling of television or radio programs for broadcast

pro·gram·er *n.* = **programmer**

pro·gram e·val·u·a·tion and re·view tech·nique *n.* full form of **PERT**

pro·gram·ing *n.* = **programming**

pro·gram·mat·ic /prògrə máttik/ *adj.* **1. RELATING TO PROGRAM** relating to or consisting of a program **2. SYSTEMATIC** following a plan or program **3.** MUSIC **OF PROGRAM MUSIC** relating to or composed as program music —**pro·gram·mat·i·cal·ly** *adv.*

pro·grammed in·struc·tion *n.* a teaching method involving sequences of controlled steps in which a student has to learn thoroughly the material covered in one step before proceeding to the next

pro·gram·mer /prṓ gràmmər/, **pro·gram·er** *n.* somebody who writes computer programs

pro·gram·ming /prṓ gràmming/, **pro·gram·ing** *n.* **1. CREATING OF COMPUTER PROGRAMS** the designing or writing of computer programs **2.** BROADCAST **BROADCASTING OF PROGRAMS** the selection and scheduling of television or radio programs, or the programs themselves

pro·gram·ming lan·guage, pro·gram·ing lan·guage *n.* a unique vocabulary and set of rules for writing computer programs. This term is usually applied to high-level languages, e.g., C, C++, Java, Pascal, and BASIC.

pro·gram mu·sic *n.* music that depicts or is inspired by a specific story, object, or scene

pro·gram trad·ing *n.* the automatic buying and selling of large quantities of stock using computer programs that monitor price changes —**pro·gram trade** *n.* —**pro·gram trad·er** *n.*

pro·gress *n.* /pró grèss, prṓ-/ **1. IMPROVEMENT** gradual development or improvement of something **2. MOTION TOWARD SOMETHING** movement forward or onward **3.** (*plural* **-gress·es**) **ROYAL TOUR** an official royal tour (*archaic*) ■ *v.* /prə gréss, prō-/ (**-gressed, -gress·ing, -gress·es**) **1.** *vi.* **IMPROVE** to develop or advance continuously **2.** *vi.* **MOVE ALONG** to move forward or onward **3.** *vt.* **HELP COMPLETE SOMETHING** to bring something toward completion [15thC. From Latin *progressus*, the past participle of *progredi* "to go forward," from *gradi* "to walk."]

pro·gres·sion /prə grésh'n/ *n.* **1. GRADUAL ADVANCEMENT** a gradual change or advancement from one state to another **2. FORWARD MOVEMENT** movement forward or onward **3. SERIES OF RELATED THINGS** a series or succession of related things **4.** MATH **SEQUENCE OF RELATED NUMBERS** a sequence of numbers or terms in which each can be derived from its predecessor using a constant formula **5.** MUSIC **SERIES OF NOTES OR CHORDS** a movement from one note or chord to another —**pro·gres·sion·al** *adj.* —**pro·gres·sion·al·ly** *adv.*

pro·gres·sive /prə gréssiv/ *adj.* **1. PROGRESSING GRADUALLY** progressing gradually over a period of time **2.** MED **BECOMING MORE SEVERE** used to describe a disease that becomes more widespread or severe over time **3.** POL **FAVORING REFORM** advocating social, economic, or political reform **4.** EDUC **INFORMAL AND LESS STRUCTURED EDUCATIONALLY** relating to or using a more informal, less structured approach to the education of children **5.** FIN **WITH HIGHER RATES FOR HIGHER INCOMES** used to describe a form of taxation in which the tax rate increases in proportion to the taxable income **6.** CARDS, DANCING **HAVING CHANGES OF PARTNER** characterized by changes of partner at stages of a card game or dance **7.** GRAM **EXPRESSING CONTINUOUS ACTION** used to express continuous action ■ *n.* **1.** POL **ADVOCATE OF REFORM** somebody who advocates social, political, or economic reform **2.** GRAM **PROGRESSIVE FORM OF VERB** the progressive aspect of a verb, or a verb in the progressive aspect —**pro·gres·sive·ly** *adv.* —**pro·gres·sive·ness** *n.*

Pro·gres·sive *adj.* **1.** POL **OF PROGRESSIVE POLITICAL PARTY** belonging to or associated with a Progressive Party **2.** JUDAISM **OF NONORTHODOX JEWISH RELIGIOUS MOVEMENT** relating to a Jewish religious movement whose members do not believe that the Torah was given literally and directly by God to Moses ■ *n.* POL **MEMBER OF PROGRESSIVE PARTY** somebody who is a member of a Progressive Party

Pro·gres·sive Con·ser·va·tive *n.* **MEMBER OF CANADIAN PROGRESSIVE CONSERVATIVE PARTY** in Canada, a member or supporter of the Progressive Conservative Party ■ *adj.* **OF CANADIAN PROGRESSIVE CONSERVATIVE PARTY** in Canada, belonging to or supporting the Progressive Conservative Party

Pro·gres·sive Con·ser·va·tive Par·ty *n.* a Canadian federal and provincial political party founded in the 1850s as the Liberal-Conservative Party, becoming the Conservative Party after the 1870s and taking its present name in 1942

pro·gres·sive ed·u·ca·tion *n.* a 20th-century theory of education that stresses children's self-expression, an informal classroom atmosphere, and individual attention

Pro·gres·sive Fed·er·al Par·ty *n.* a South African political party formed in 1977 by a merger between the Progressive Party and members of the United Party

pro·gres·sive jazz *n.* a form of experimental, free-flowing, and improvisational jazz that uses dissonance and complex rhythms

Pro·gres·sive Par·ty *n.* **1.** U.S. **POLITICAL PARTY** in the United States, any of three related political parties that favored social reform and were active in the presidential elections of 1912, 1924, and 1948 **2. CANADIAN POLITICAL PARTY** a Canadian national political party formed in 1920 from members of farmers' movements and dissident Liberals that was dissolved in 1942

Pro·gres·sive Rock *n.* a type of rock music originating in the early 1970s and characterized by technically elaborate and sometimes experimental arrangements

pro·gres·siv·ism /prə gréssi vìzzəm/ *n.* **1. BELIEFS OF PROGRESSIVES** the beliefs and practices of progressives **2.** EDUC **BELIEFS AND PRACTICES OF PROGRESSIVE EDUCATION** the theories and practices of progressive education —**pro·ges·siv·ist** *n.*

pro·gress pay·ment *n.* a part of a larger payment made to a contractor when a stage of a job is completed

pro·hib·it /prō híbbit/ (**-it·ed, -it·ing, -its**) *vt.* **1. FORBID SOMEBODY** to forbid somebody from doing something by a law or rule **2. PREVENT SOMEBODY** to prevent somebody from doing something [15thC. Formed from Latin *prohibit-*, the past participle stem of *prohibere*, literally "to hold back," from *hibere* "to hold."] —**pro·hib·it·er** *n.*

pro·hi·bi·tion /prṑ ə bísh'n/ *n.* **1. FORBIDDING OF SOMETHING** the act or process of forbidding something **2. ORDER THAT FORBIDS** an act or order that forbids something **3.** LAW **COURT ORDER** an order from a superior court that forbids an inferior court from deciding on a matter beyond its jurisdiction **4. OUTLAWING OF TRADE IN ALCOHOLIC BEVERAGES** a policy that forbids by law the manufacture, sale, and transport of alcoholic beverages [14thC. Via French from, ultimately, Latin *prohibere* (see PROHIBIT).] —**pro·hi·bi·tion·ar·y** *adj.*

Pro·hi·bi·tion·ism /prṑ ə bísh'n ìzzəm/, **pro·hi·bi·tion·ism** *n.* the policy and principles of those who support a ban on alcoholic beverages —**Pro·hi·bi·tion·ist** *n.*

Pro·hi·bi·tion Par·ty *n.* a political party in the United States founded in 1869 that advocated the banning of alcoholic beverages

pro·hib·i·tive /prō híbbitiv/ *adj.* **1. TOO EXPENSIVE FOR MOST PEOPLE** too expensive or costly for most people to buy **2. FORBIDDING SOMETHING** prohibiting or forbidding something —**pro·hib·i·tive·ly** *adv.* —**pro·hib·i·tive·ness** *n.*

pro·hib·i·to·ry /prō híbbi tàwree/ *adj.* **1. LIKELY TO FORBID SOMETHING** likely to prevent or forbid something (*formal*) **2. FORBIDDING SOMETHING** preventing or forbidding something

pro·in·su·lin /prō ínsəlin/ *n.* the inactive precursor of insulin that is converted to the active substance by the action of enzymes in the pancreas

proj·ect *n.* /pró jèkt/ **1. TASK OR SCHEME** a task or scheme that requires a large amount of time, effort, and planning to complete **2. UNIT OF WORK** an organized unit of work ○ *a school project* **3. PUBLIC WORK** an extensive organized public undertaking ○ *a construction project* **4.** PUBLIC ADMIN = **housing project** (*often used in the plural*) ■ *v.* /prə jékt/ (**pro·ject·ed, pro·ject·ing, pro·jects**) **1.** *vt.* **ESTIMATE** to estimate something by extrapolating data ○ *They projected 3% annual growth.* **2.** *vti.* **STICK OUT** to jut out beyond or farther than something ○ *The balcony projected several feet.* **3.** *vt.* **COMMUNICATE SOMETHING** to communicate something effectively ○ *He projects himself as a confident man.* **4.** *vt.* PSYCHOL **BELIEVE OTHERS SHARE A MENTAL LIFE** to make a thought or feeling seem to have an external and objective reality, especially to ascribe something personal to others ○ *He had projected his fear of heights onto her.* **5.** *vt.* **THROW SOMETHING** to throw or cast something (*formal*) (*usually passive*) ○ *The ball was projected several feet upward.* **6.** *vt.* **PROPOSE A PLAN** to propose a plan of action (*often passive*) ○ *The tour was projected for the following summer.* **7.** *vt.* **DIRECT AN IMAGE ONTO SURFACE** to make an image appear on a surface ○ *projected the photograph onto the screen* **8.** *vt.* **IMAGINE SOMETHING** to use the imagination to see or remember something ○ *She projected herself back into the past.* **9.** *vti.* **MAKE THE VOICE AUDIBLE** to make the voice heard clearly and at a distance, or be effective in making the voice heard ○ *She projected her voice to the back of the auditorium.* **10.** *vt.* GEOM **DRAW A PROJECTION OF A FIGURE** to transform a geometric figure into another by drawing straight lines through every point of the figure to another plane. In this way, a circle may be projected as an ellipse and a square as a rectangle. [14thC. From Latin *projectum* "something thrown forward," from, ultimately, *proicere* "to throw forward," from *jacere* "to throw."]

pro·jec·tile /prə jékt'l/ *n.* **MISSILE OR SHELL** an object that can be fired or launched, e.g., an artillery shell or a rocket ■ *adj.* **1.** ZOOL **CAPABLE OF BEING THRUST FORWARD** used to describe a part of an animal's body that can be thrust forward such as the jaws in some types of fish **2. IMPELLED FORWARD** hurled or impelled forward

pro·jec·tion /prə jékshən/ *n.* **1. ESTIMATE** an estimate of the rate or amount of something **2. SOMETHING THAT STICKS OUT** something that juts out or overhangs **3. PROTRUSION** the act or process of protruding **4. CASTING OF SOMETHING ON SURFACE** the projecting of an image or picture on a surface **5. SOMETHING CAST ON SURFACE** an image or picture projected on a surface **6.** PSYCHOL **UNCONSCIOUS TRANSFER OF INNER MENTAL LIFE** the unconscious ascription of a personal thought, feeling, or impulse to somebody else, especially a thought or feeling considered undesirable **7.** MAPS **REPRESENTATION ON SURFACE** a means of representing lines, figures, or solids on a flat surface such as a map that conforms to the viewing direction or follows particular rules **8.** GEOM **DRAWN REPRESENTATION** the representation of a line, figure, or solid on a flat surface **9.** HIST **MIXING BY ALCHEMISTS** in alchemy, the mixing of powdered philosopher's stone with base metals in order to supposedly transmute them into gold or silver —**pro·jec·tion·al** *adj.*

pro·jec·tion booth *n.* an enclosed compartment in a theater from which films, slides, or lights are projected onto a screen or stage

pro·jec·tion·ist /prə jékshənist/ *n.* somebody whose job is to operate the projector and screen the film in a movie theater and take responsibility for the quality of the image and sound

pro·jec·tion room *n.* **1.** *U.K.* = **projection booth 2. PRIVATE SCREENING ROOM** a private room with a projector and screen in which movies are viewed

pro·jec·tion tel·e·vi·sion, **pro·jec·tion TV** *n.* a television picture display system in which an enlarged picture is projected onto a screen

pro·jec·tive /prə jéktiv/ *adj.* **1. MADE BY PROJECTION** relating to or made by projection **2.** PSYCHOL **OF A TYPE OF PSYCHOLOGICAL TEST** relating to or involving a psychological test in which something mentally hidden is revealed by a personal response to an image or group of images —**pro·jec·tive·ly** *adv.*

pro·jec·tive ge·om·e·try *n.* the study of those properties of plane geometric figures that do not vary when they are projected onto another plane and of the transformations of size and perspective that accompany this

pro·jec·tive test *n.* a psychological test that uses images in order to evoke responses from a subject and reveal hidden elements of the subject's mental life

pro·jec·tor /prə jéktər/ *n.* equipment for projecting the image from film onto a screen and for playing back recorded sound from tracks on the film

pro·jet /prō zhày/ *n.* a plan or outline, especially of a draft law or treaty [Early 19thC. Via French from Latin *projectum* (see PROJECT).]

pro·kar·y·on /prō kérree òn/ *n.* the nucleus of a cell or organism with no membrane separating the area containing DNA from the rest of it [Mid-20thC. Formed from Greek *pro-* "before" + *karuon* "nut."]

pro·kar·y·ote /prō kérree ōt/, **pro·car·y·ote** *n.* an organism whose DNA is not contained within a nucleus. Bacteria are prokaryotes. [Mid-20thC. Via French, literally "having nuts before," from Greek *karuōtos* "having nuts," from *karuon* "nut."] —**pro·kar·y·ot·ic** /prō kèrree óttik/ *adj.*

AKG London
Sergey Sergeyevich Prokofiev

Pro·ko·fi·ev /prə káwfee ef/, **Sergey Sergeyevich** (1891–1953) Russian composer. His symphonies, concertos, ballets, and operas include *The Love of Three Oranges* (1921), *Peter and the Wolf* (1934), and *Romeo and Juliet* (1936).

pro·lac·tin /prō láktin/ *n.* a hormone produced by the pituitary gland that stimulates lactation and the secretion of progesterone in mammals, as well as secretion by the crop gland in some birds [Mid-20thC. Coined from PRO- + LACTO- + -IN.]

pro·la·mine /prṓləmin, prṓlə meen/ *n.* a plant protein soluble in diluted alcohol that is found in rye, wheat, and other grains [Early 20thC. Coined from PROLINE + AMMONIA + -INE.]

pro·lapse /prō láps/, **pro·lap·sus** /prō lápsəss/ *n.* (*plural* **-sus·es**) **SLIPPAGE OF BODY PART** a slippage or sinking of a body organ or part such as a valve of the heart from its usual position ■ *vi.* (**-lapsed, -laps·ing, -lapses**) **BE DISPLACED IN BODY** to slip or fall out of its proper place in the body [Late 16thC. Formed from Latin *prolaps-*, the past participle stem of *prolabi* "to fall forward," from *labi* "to fall." Originally in English, "gliding forward."] —**pro·lapsed** *adj.*

pro·late /prṓ làyt/ *adj.* used to describe rock fragments that are elongated in the direction of the polar diameter [Late 17thC. From Latin *prolatus*, the past participle of *proferre*, literally "to carry forward," from *ferre* "to carry."] —**pro·late·ly** *adv.* —**pro·late·ness** *n.*

prole /prōl/ *n.* a proletarian (*informal*) [Late 19thC. Shortening.]

pro·leg /prṓ lèg/ *n.* a leg on the abdomen of a caterpillar or other insect larva

pro·le·gom·e·non /pròlə gómmə nòn, -nən/ (*plural* **-na** /-nə/) *n.* a preliminary discussion or introductory essay, especially to a book or treatise (*formal*) [Mid-17thC. From Greek, from, ultimately, *prolegein*, literally "to say before," from *legein* "to say."] —**pro·le·gom·e·nal** *adj.*

pro·lep·sis /prō lépsiss/ (*plural* **-ses** /-seez/) *n.* **1.** LOGIC **INTRODUCTORY ANTICIPATION OF OBJECTION** a preface intended to anticipate and answer an objection to an argument **2.** GRAM **ANTICIPATORY ADJECTIVE** the use after a verb of an adjective that anticipates the result of the verb's action, e.g., "to iron a shirt smooth" **3. ANACHRONISTIC ASSUMPTION** the anachronistic assumption that a future event or condition has already happened, e.g., in the phrase "precolonial United States" **4. ANTICIPATION OF SOMETHING** the assignment of something as existing or occurring before it could have done so, e.g., in the sentence "If you don't answer this letter you're a rat" [Late 16thC. Via Latin from, ultimately, Greek *prolambanein*, literally "to take before," from *lambanein* "to take."] —**pro·lep·tic** *adj.*

pro·le·tar·i·an /pròlə táiree ən/ *adj.* SOC SCI **OF WORKING CLASS** relating to the working class ■ *n.* **1.** SOC SCI **WORKER** a member pf the working class **2.** SOC SCI **INDUSTRIAL WAGE-EARNER** in Marxist theory, a member of the industrial working class whose only asset is labor sold to an employer **3.** HIST **IMPOVERISHED ANCIENT ROMAN** a member of an impoverished social class of ancient Rome that had the lowest status and possessed no property [Mid-17thC. Formed from Latin *proletarius* "low-status Roman who serves the state only by producing offspring," from *proles* "offspring."] —**pro·le·tar·i·an·ism** *n.*

pro·le·tar·i·at /prōlə táiree ət/ *n.* **1. WORKING CLASS** the class of wage-earning workers in society **2. CLASS OF INDUSTRIAL WAGE-EARNERS** in Marxist theory, the class of industrial workers whose only asset is the labor they sell to an employer **3.** HIST **ANCIENT ROMAN SOCIAL CLASS** social class of ancient Rome that had the lowest status and possessed no property [Mid-19thC. Via French *prolétariat* from, ultimately, Latin *proles* (see PROLETARIAN).]

pro-life *adj.* in favor of bringing the human fetus to full term, especially by campaigning against open access to abortion and against experimentation on embryos —**pro-lif·er** *n.*

pro·lif·er·ate /prə líffə ràyt/ (**-at·ed, -at·ing, -ates**) *v.* **1.** *vi.* **INCREASE GREATLY** to increase greatly in number **2.** *vti.* BIOL **REPRODUCE RAPIDLY** to multiply or be multiplied in the process of reproducing new cells, offspring, or parts, as in the budding of plants [Late 19thC. Back-formation from PROLIFERATION.] —**pro·lif·er·a·tive** *adj.*

pro·lif·er·a·tion /prə líffə ràysh'n/ *n.* **1. RAPID INCREASE** the rapid spread or increase of something **2.** BIOL **ORGANIC MULTIPLICATION** the multiplication of parts in an organism

pro·lif·er·ous /prə líffərəss/ *adj.* producing or growing many cells, buds, or shoots [Mid-17thC. Formed from medieval Latin *prolifer*, literally "bearing offspring," from *proles* "offspring."]

pro·lif·ic /prə líffik/ *adj.* **1. PRODUCTIVE** highly productive **2. FRUITFUL** abounding or fruitful **3.** BIOL **PRODUCING FRUIT OR OFFSPRING** producing a lot of fruit or many offspring [Mid-17thC. From medieval Latin *prolificus*, from *proles* "offspring."] —**pro·lif·i·ca·cy** *n.* —**pro·lif·i·cal·ly** *adv.*

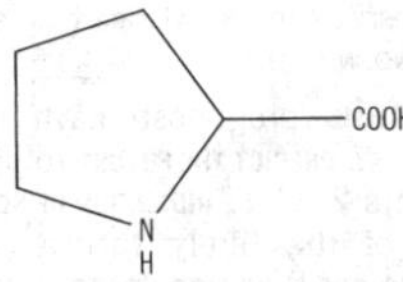

Proline

pro·line /prṓ leen/ *n.* an amino acid found in many proteins, particularly in collagen. Formula: $C_5H_9NO_2$. [Early 20thC. Contraction of *pyrrolidine*.]

pro·lix /prō líks, prṓ lìks/ *adj.* tiresomely wordy [15thC. Directly or via French from Latin *prolixus*, literally "that has flowed out," from the past participle of *liquere* "to flow" (source of English *liquid*).] —**pro·lix·i·ty** /prō líksətee/ *n.* —**pro·lix·ly** /-líks lee/ *adv.*

WORD KEY: SYNONYMS

See Synonyms at ***wordy***.

pro·loc·u·tor /prō lókyətər/ *n.* **1. SPOKESPERSON** a spokesperson (*formal*) **2. CHAIRPERSON** somebody who chairs a meeting (*formal*) **3.** CHR **SOMEBODY WHO CHAIRS ANGLICAN CONVOCATION** somebody who chairs an ecclesiastical convocation in the Anglican Church [15thC. Via Latin, "pleader, advocate," from, ultimately, *proloqui* "to speak out," from *loqui* "to speak" (source of English *locution*).] —**pro·lo·cu·tor·ship** *n.*

Pro·log /prṓ lòg/, **PRO·LOG** *n.* a high-level programming language based on logical rather than mathematical relationships

pro·logue /prṓ lòg/, **pro·log** *n.* **1. INTRODUCTORY STATEMENT** an introductory passage or speech before the main action of a novel, play, or long poem **2.** THEATER **ACTOR INTRODUCING ACTION OF PLAY** an actor who speaks introductory lines to a dramatic performance before the main action begins **3. PRELIMINARY EVENT** an event or act that leads to something more important ■ *vt.* (**-logued, -logu·ing, -logues; -loged, -log·ing, -logs**) **PREFACE WITH PROLOGUE** to preface something such as a novel or play with a prologue [14thC. Via French and Latin from Greek *prologos*, literally "speech before," from *logos* "speech."]

pro·log·u·ize /prṓlə gìz/ (**-ized, -iz·ing, -iz·es**) *vi.* to speak or write the prologue to a play, speech, or long poem

pro·long /prə láwng/ (**-longed, -long·ing, -longs**) *vt.* to make something go on longer [15thC. Directly or via French *prolonger* from late Latin *prolongare*, literally "to lengthen out," from Latin *longus* "long."] —**pro·lon·ga·tion**

/prō lawng gáysh'n/ *n.* —**pro·long·er** /prə láwngər/ *n.* —**pro·long·ment** /-láungmənt/ *n.*

pro·longe /prə lónj/ *n.* a rope with a hook and a toggle used to tow something heavy, especially a gun carriage [Mid-19thC. From French *prolonger* (see PROLONG).]

pro·lu·sion /prō lóozh'n/ *n.* a tentative, preliminary, or introductory essay (*formal*) [Early 17thC. Formed from Latin *prolusion-*, the stem of *prolusio* from, ultimately, *proludere*, literally "to play before," from *ludere* "to play."] —**pro·lu·so·ry** /prō lóosəree, -lóozəree/ *adj.*

prom /prom/ *n.* a formal high-school or college dance for students, usually held at the end of the school year [Late 19thC. Shortening.]

PROM /prom/ *abbr.* programmable read-only memory

prom. *abbr.* promontory

prom·e·nade /pròmmə náyd, pròmmə naád/ *n.* **1.** WALK FOR PLEASURE a leisurely walk or stroll, usually in a public place, that is taken for pleasure or to be seen (*formal*) **2.** DANCE MARCHING DANCE MOVEMENT a marching step or sequence in square or country dancing ■ *v.* (**-nad·ed, -nad·ing, -nades**) **1.** *vti.* TAKE A STROLL IN A PUBLIC PLACE to walk in a slow and leisurely way, especially up and down a street or in a public place (*formal*) **2.** *vi.* DANCE MARCH DURING A DANCE to perform a marching step or sequence in square or country dancing [Mid-16thC. Via French, *se promener* "to go for a walk" from, ultimately, late Latin *prominare* "to drive forward," formed from *minare* "to drive."]

prom·e·nade deck *n.* a covered upper deck on a passenger ship on which passengers can walk

pro·met·ha·zine /prō méthə zeen/ *n.* an antihistamine drug used to treat allergies and motion sickness. Formula: $C_{17}H_{20}N_2S$. [Mid-20thC. Coined from PROPYL + METHYL + AZINE.]

Pro·me·the·an /prə meéthee ən/ *adj.* **1.** MYTHOL OF PROMETHEUS relating to Prometheus **2.** BOLDLY CREATIVE creative and imaginatively original

Pro·me·the·us[1] /prə meéthee əss/ *n.* in Greek mythology, a Titan who became a hero to humankind because he stole fire from the gods and gave it to them. His eternal punishment was to be chained to a rock and have an eagle eat his liver, which would grow in the night only to be eaten again. [Late 16thC. Via Latin from Greek.]

Pro·me·the·us[2] /prə meéthee əss, prə meéthyooss/ *n.* a small inner natural satellite of Saturn, discovered in 1980 by Voyager 2. It is irregular in shape having a maximum dimension of 93 mi./150 km.

pro·me·thi·um /prə meéthee əm/ *n.* a radioactive metallic element produced by the fission of uranium, thorium, or plutonium. It is used in phosphorescent paints and as an X-ray source. Symbol **Pm** [Mid-20thC. Named for PROMETHEUS because it is the result of mankind's ability to utilize the energy of nuclear fission.]

prom·i·nence /prómminənss/, **prom·i·nen·cy** /prómminənsee/ (*plural* **-cies**) *n.* **1.** CONSPICUOUS IMPORTANCE the condition or quality of being significantly important or well-known **2.** SOMETHING THAT STICKS OUT something that projects or protrudes, especially a geographical feature or a body part **3.** ASTRON GAS STREAM FROM SUN a visible stream of glowing gas that shoots out from the Sun, seen in the upper chromosphere and lower corona. Prominences are best seen during an eclipse when they are visible at the rim of the Sun.

prom·i·nent /prómminənt/ *adj.* **1.** STICKING OUT large and projecting **2.** NOTICEABLE noticeable or conspicuous **3.** WELL-KNOWN distinguished, eminent, or well-known [15thC. From Latin *prominere*, literally "to project forward," from *-minere* "to project" (source of English *imminent*).] —**prom·i·nent·ly** *adv.* —**promi·nent·ness** *n.*

prom·is·cu·i·ty /pròmmi skyóo ətee/ *n.* **1.** UNDISCRIMINATING SEXUAL BEHAVIOR behavior characterized by casual and indiscriminate sexual intercourse, often with many people (*disapproving*) **2.** CONFUSED MIXING a confused or indiscriminate mixing of elements (*formal*)

pro·mis·cu·ous /prə mískyoo əss/ *adj.* **1.** SEXUALLY INDISCRIMINATE having many indiscriminate or casual sexual relationships (*disapproving*) **2.** CONFUSEDLY MIXED mixed in an indiscriminate or disorderly way (*formal*) **3.** CHOOSING WITHOUT DISCRIMINATING choosing carelessly or without discrimination (*disapproving*) **4.** CASUAL casual and unplanned [Early 17thC. Formed from Latin *promiscuus*, literally "mixed forward," from *miscere* "to mix" (source of English *mixed* and *miscellaneous*).] —**pro·mis·cu·ous·ly** *adv.* —**pro·mis·cu·ous·ness** *n.*

prom·ise /prómmiss/ *v.* (**-ised, -is·ing, -is·es**) **1.** *vti.* MAKE A VOW TO SOMEBODY to assure somebody that something will certainly happen or be done ○ *Promise that you'll be home on time.* **2.** *vt.* PLEDGE SOMETHING to pledge to somebody to provide or do something ○ *He promised the children a kitten.* **3.** *vti.* MAKE SOMEBODY EXPECT SOMETHING to cause somebody to expect something ○ *The overcast sky promised rain.* **4.** *vt.* ASSURE OR WARN to assure or warn somebody that something is true or inevitable ○ *Things will be fine, I promise you.* **5.** *vt.* AFFIANCE to engage somebody to be married (*dated*) ○ *She told him that she was promised to someone else.* ■ *n.* **1.** ASSURANCE OR UNDERTAKING an assurance that something will be done or not done ○ *He never keeps his promises.* **2.** GOOD INDICATION an indication that somebody or something will turn out well or successfully ○ *She showed great promise as an athlete.* [14thC. Directly or via French *promesse* from, ultimately, Latin *promittere*, literally "to send forward," from *mittere* "to send" (source of English *mission, missile,* and *transmit*).] —**prom·is·er** *n.*

prom·is·ee /pròmmi seé/ *n.* somebody to whom a promise is made (*formal*)

prom·is·ing /prómmissing/ *adj.* likely to be successful or to turn out well —**prom·is·ing·ly** *adv.*

prom·i·sor /prómmi sàwr/ *n.* somebody who undertakes to do something (*formal*)

prom·is·so·ry /prómmi sàwree/ *adj.* **1.** CONTAINING A PROMISE concerning, containing, or implying a promise **2.** INSUR SHOWING INSURANCE CONTRACT PROVISIONS stating how the terms of an insurance contract will be fulfilled [15thC. Via medieval Latin *promissorius* from, ultimately, Latin *promittere* (see PROMISE).]

prom·is·so·ry note *n.* a signed agreement promising payment of a sum of money on demand or at a particular time

pro·mo /prṓ mō/ *n.* (*plural* **-mos**) SOMETHING TO PROMOTE PRODUCT something that promotes or advertises a product, e.g., a recorded announcement, commercial, or video (*informal*) ■ *adj.* CONNECTED WITH PROMOTION OF SOMETHING involved or engaged in the promotion or advertising of something [Mid-20thC. Shortening of PROMOTION or PROMOTIONAL.]

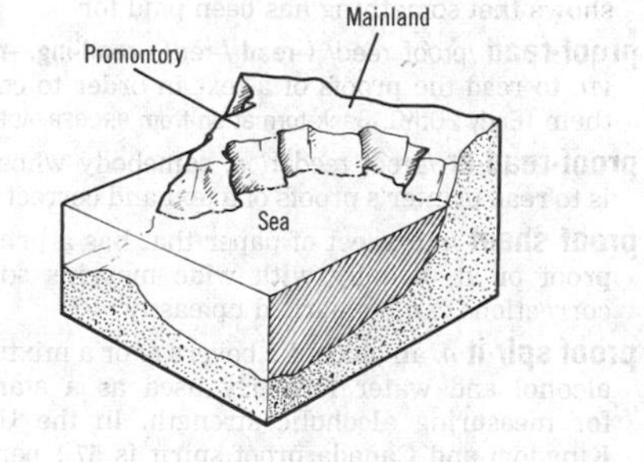

Promontory

prom·on·to·ry /prómmən tàwree/ (*plural* **-ries**) *n.* **1.** PROJECTING POINT OF LAND a point of land that juts out into the sea **2.** ANAT PROJECTING PART OF BODY a prominent or protruding part of the body [Mid-16thC. From medieval Latin *promontorium*, an alteration of Latin *promunturium*, of uncertain origin: perhaps formed from *mons* "mountain" (source of English *mountain*).]

pro·mote /prə mṓt/ (**-mot·ed, -mot·ing, -motes**) *vt.* **1.** HR ADVANCE IN RANK to raise somebody to a more senior job or a higher position or rank **2.** SUPPORT OR ENCOURAGE to encourage the growth and development of something **3.** BUSINESS ADVERTISE SOMETHING to publicize a product so that people will buy or rent it **4.** ADVANCE SOMETHING to further something by helping to arrange or introduce it **5.** CHESS EXCHANGE PAWN FOR MORE POWERFUL PIECE in chess, to exchange a pawn for a more powerful piece, usually a queen, when it reaches an opponent's end of the board [14thC. Formed from Latin *promot-*, the past participle stem of *promovere* "to move forward," from *movere* "to move" (source of English *move, motor,* and *moment*).] —**pro·mot·a·ble** *adj.*

pro·mot·er /prə mṓtər/ *n.* **1.** SOMEBODY OR SOMETHING ARRANGING PUBLIC EVENT a person or organization that stages an entertainment, sporting contest, or other public event **2.** FIN ACQUIRER OF CAPITAL FOR VENTURE somebody who secures capital for a financial or commercial undertaking such as a public company **3.** GENETICS BINDING SITE IN A DNA CHAIN in a DNA chain, a sequence to which the enzyme RNA polymerase binds so as to start transcription **4.** CHEM SUBSTANCE ADDED TO CATALYST a chemical additive that increases the efficiency of a catalyst **5.** MED SOMETHING THAT ENCOURAGES TUMOR CELLS a substance that when given after a carcinogen encourages tumor cells to form or grow

pro·mo·tion /prə mṓsh'n/ *n.* **1.** HR ADVANCEMENT IN POSITION an advancement to a more senior job or a higher rank, grade, or position **2.** BUSINESS SOMETHING THAT PROMOTES something that is designed to promote or advertise a product, cause, or organization **3.** ENCOURAGEMENT FOR ACTIVITY encouragement for the growth or development of something **4.** SPORTS ADVANCE INTO HIGHER DIVISION advance by a national sports team into a higher international group **5.** CHESS EXCHANGE OF PAWN FOR SUPERIOR PIECE in chess, the act of exchanging a pawn for a more powerful piece, usually a queen, when it reaches an opponent's end of the board

pro·mo·tion·al *adj.* relating to the promotion of a product or organization so that people become more aware of it

pro·mo·tive /prə mṓtiv/ *adj.* tending to further or encourage something —**pro·mo·tive·ness** *n.*

prompt /prompt/ *adj.* **1.** DONE IMMEDIATELY done at once and without delay **2.** QUICK TO ACT ready, punctual, or quick to act ■ *v.* (**prompt·ed, prompt·ing, prompts**) **1.** *vt.* URGE INTO ACTION to incite or urge somebody to do something **2.** *vt.* BRING ABOUT SOMETHING to give rise to something **3.** *vti.* THEATER PROVIDE ACTOR WITH LINES to provide actors or performers with the words or lines they have forgotten **4.** *vt.* REMIND OR SUGGEST to suggest something or give a reminder to a speaker ■ *n.* **1.** THEATER REMINDER OF WORDS TO PERFORMER a word or lines supplied to a performer who has forgotten them **2.** THEATER OCCURRENCE OF PROMPT the act or occasion of words being supplied to a performer who has forgotten them **3.** COMPUT SOMETHING CUING RESPONSE a symbol or message displayed on a computer monitor or an audio signal informing a computer user that some input is required **4.** COMM TIME LIMIT FOR PAYMENT the time limit of payment for goods or services, as stated on a prompt note [14thC. From Latin *promptus* "ready," past participle of *promere*, literally "to take forward," from *emere* "to take." The underlying idea is "bringing out," hence "making available."] —**prompt·ly** *adv.* —**prompt·ness** *n.*

prompt·book /prómpt bòok/ *n.* a copy of a script for a prompter to use

prompt box *n.* a box situated beneath the stage in a theater in which the prompter sits

prompt·er /prómptər/ *n.* somebody in a theater whose job is to prompt actors who have forgotten their words or lines

promp·ti·tude /prómpti tood/ *n.* punctuality or quickness to act (*formal*)

prompt note *n.* a written reminder sent to the purchaser of something, stating when payment is due

prompt side *n.* the side of the stage in a theater where the prompter sits. In Britain the prompt side is usually on the actor's left, and in the United States usually on the actor's right.

prom·ul·gate /prómm'l gàyt, prə múl gàyt/ (**-gat·ed, -gat·ing, -gates**) *vt.* (*formal*) **1.** DECLARE SOMETHING OFFICIALLY to proclaim or declare something officially, especially to publicize formally that a law or decree is in effect **2.** MAKE KNOWN to make something widely known [Mid-16thC. From Latin *promulgare*, literally "to milk forward," from *mulgere* "to milk." The underlying idea is of "bringing out into the light of day."] —**prom·ul·ga·tion** /pròmməl gáysh'n/ *n.* —**prom·ul·ga·tor** /prómm'l gàytər/ *n.*

pron. *abbr.* **1.** pronominal **2.** pronoun **3.** pronounced **4.** pronunciation

pro·nate /prṓ nàyt/ (**-nat·ed, -nat·ing, -nates**) *v.* **1.** *vt.* TURN HAND PALM DOWN to turn the hand or forearm so that the palm faces downward **2.** *vti.* ROTATE FOOT INWARD to rotate the bones of the foot so that the weight is borne mainly on the inside of the foot [Mid-19thC. Back-formation from PRONATE, from PRONE or Latin *pronus* (see PRONE).] —**pro·na·tion** /prō náysh'n/ *n.*

pro·na·tor /prṓ nàytər/ *n.* a muscle that turns a part of the body so that it faces downward, e.g., one of the muscles in the forearm that rotates the hand into the palm-down position [Early 18thC. From modern

Latin, from Latin *pronus* (see PRONE), on the model of SUPINATOR.]

prone /prōn/ *adj.* **1.** DISPOSED TO SOMETHING inclined to do or be affected by something **2.** FACE DOWN lying face down **3.** IN DOWNWARD DIRECTION sloping, leaning, or moving downward [15thC. From Latin *pronus* "bent forward," from *pro* "forward."] —**prone·ly** *adv.* —**prone·ness** *n.*

pro·neph·ros /prō néffrəss, -né fròss/ (*plural* **-roi** /-fròy/ *or* **-ra** /-rə/) *n.* the first of three segments of the kidney, functional in some vertebrate embryos but not in adults [Late 19thC. Formed from PRO[2] + Greek *nephros* "kidney."] —**pro·neph·ric** *adj.*

prong /prawng/ *n.* SHARP POINT a thin sharp point at the end of something ■ *vt.* (**pronged, prong·ing, prongs**) PIERCE WITH SOMETHING SHARP to prick or stab something with a sharp pointed end [15thC. From Anglo-Latin *pronga* of uncertain origin: perhaps from, ultimately, a prehistoric Germanic word meaning "pinching."]

pronged /prawngd/ *adj.* with a thin sharp point at the end (*often used in combination*)

prong·horn /práwng hàwrn/, **prong·horn an·te·lope** *n.* an animal similar to an antelope found in Mexico and the western United States that is the fastest North American mammal. The male has two horns, shed annually, each with a curved prong. Latin name: *Antilocapra americana.*

pro·no·grade /prṓnə gràyd/ *adj.* used to describe quadrupeds that walk with the body parallel to the ground [Early 20thC. Formed from Latin *pronus* "leaning forward" + *-gradus* "walking."]

pro·nom·i·nal /prō nómmən'l/ *adj.* ACTING AS PRONOUN like or functioning as a pronoun ■ *n.* WORD ACTING LIKE PRONOUN a word that functions like a pronoun [Late 17thC. From late Latin *pronominalis* "belonging to a pronoun," from Latin *pronomen* (see PRONOUN).] —**pro·nom·i·nal·ly** *adv.*

pro·nom·i·nal·ize /prō nómmən'l ìz/ (**-ized, -iz·ing, -iz·es**) *vt.* in transformational grammars, to replace a noun or noun phrase in a sentence with a pronoun —**pro·nom·i·nal·i·za·tion** /prō nòmmən'li záysh'n/ *n.*

pro·noun /prṓ nòwn/ *n.* a word that substitutes for a noun or a noun phrase, such as "I," "you," "them," "it," "ours," "who," "which," "myself," and "anybody." Pronouns are sometimes distinguished from nouns by having objective form, e.g., "her" for "she" and "me" for "I." [15thC. Formed from NOUN on the model of French *pronom* and its source Latin *pronomen*, literally "in place of a name," from *nomen* "name."]

pro·nounce /prə nówns/ (**-nounced, -nounc·ing, -nounc·es**) *v.* **1.** *vti.* UTTER SOUNDS OR WORDS to articulate sounds or words, especially in a way acceptable to the person to whom they are spoken or by most speakers of a language **2.** *vti.* FORMALLY DECLARE to declare something officially to be the case **3.** *vt.* GIVE JUDGMENT to render an opinion or judgment **4.** *vt.* PHON SYMBOLIZE SOUND OF WORD to indicate with symbols how a word should be spoken [14thC. Via Old French *pronuncier* from Latin *pronuntiare*, literally "to announce before," from *nuntiare* "to announce."] —**pro·nounce·a·ble** *adj.* —**pro·nounc·er** *n.*

pro·nounced /prə nównst/ *adj.* **1.** NOTICEABLE noticeable or obvious **2.** VOICED voiced or spoken —**pro·nounc·ed·ly** /prə nównsədlee/ *adv.*

pro·nounce·ment /prə nównsmənt/ *n.* **1.** OFFICIAL STATEMENT an official or formal statement **2.** AUTHORITATIVE STATEMENT a formal or authoritative statement

pron·to /prόntō/ *adv.* in a prompt or rapid way (*informal*) [Mid-19thC. Via Spanish from Latin *promptus* (see PROMPT).]

pro·nu·cle·ar /prō nóoklee ər/ *adj.* **1.** FAVORING NUCLEAR POWER in favor of using nuclear power in weapons or as a source of energy **2.** BIOL OF PRONUCLEUS relating to a pronucleus —**pro·nu·cle·ar·ist** *n., adj.*

pro·nu·cle·us /prō nóoklee əss/ (*plural* **-i** /-ì/ *or* **-us·es**) *n.* the nucleus of a fully matured ovum or spermatozoan before the nuclei are fused during fertilization

pro·nun·ci·a·men·to /prō nùnsee ə méntō/ (*plural* **-tos** *or* **-toes**) *n.* an announcement, proclamation, or manifesto, especially one issued by a revolutionary group [Mid-19thC. Via Spanish from, ultimately, Latin *pronuntiare* (see PRONOUNCE).]

pro·nun·ci·a·tion /prə nùnsee áysh'n/ *n.* **1.** MAKING SOUNDS OF SPEECH the way in which a sound, word, or language is articulated, especially in conforming to an accepted standard **2.** ACT OF SPEECH the act of articulating a sound or word **3.** PHON TRANSCRIPTION OF SOUNDS a phonetic transcription of sounds

proof /proof/ *n.* **1.** CONCLUSIVE EVIDENCE evidence or an argument that serves to establish a fact or the truth of something **2.** TEST OF SOMETHING a test or trial of something to establish whether it is true **3.** STATE OF HAVING BEEN PROVED the quality or condition of having been proved **4.** LAW TRIAL EVIDENCE the evidence in a trial that helps to determine the court's decision **5.** BEVERAGES STRENGTH OF ALCOHOLIC CONTENT the relative strength of an alcoholic beverage measured against a standard and expressed by a number that is twice the percentage of the alcohol present in the liquid **6.** PRINTING PRINTING IMPRESSION an impression used for checking corrections before the final printing of an image or text **7.** MATH, LOGIC SEQUENCE OF STEPS TO VALIDATE A SOLUTION the sequence of steps or stages used in establishing the validity of a mathematical or philosophical proposition. These steps are a logical derivation of the proposition from axioms, or explicit assumptions, and previously proved propositions. **8.** ARTS ARTIST'S IMPRESSION an impression taken from an engraved plate before it is printed **9.** PHOTOGRAPHY PRINT FROM A NEGATIVE a photographic print made from a negative and checked for quality prior to further reproduction **10.** COINS COIN IMPRESSION a preliminary impression of a coin, intended as a specimen for display ■ *adj.* **1.** IMPERVIOUS TO SOMETHING capable of resisting something that may have a harmful or unwanted effect **2.** BEVERAGES HAVING RELATIVE ALCOHOLIC STRENGTH having a specific alcoholic strength that is expressed by a number that is twice the percentage of alcohol present in the liquid (*often used in combination*) **3.** RESISTANT capable of resisting or withstanding something ■ *vt.* (**proofed, proof·ing, proofs**) **1.** MAKE RESISTANT to make something capable of resisting harm, injury, or damage **2.** PRINTING, ARTS MAKE A PROOF OF SOMETHING to make a trial impression of something printed or engraved **3.** PRINTING INSPECT FOR ERRORS to proofread a text, or inspect a printed impression for errors **4.** COOK ACTIVATE YEAST to cause yeast to become active by adding water and often sugar [13thC. Alteration of earlier *pref* (influenced by PROVE) via Old French *preve* from Latin *proba*, from *probare* "to prove, test" (source also of English *prove*).]

proof of pur·chase *n.* evidence such as a receipt that shows that something has been paid for

proof·read /próof rèed/ (**-read** /-rèd/, **-read·ing, -reads**) *vti.* to read the proofs of a text in order to correct them [Early 20thC. Back-formation from PROOFREADER.]

proof·read·er /próof rèedər/ *n.* somebody whose job is to read printer's proofs of a text and correct them

proof sheet *n.* a sheet of paper that has a printer's proof on it, usually with wide margins so that corrections can be marked up easily

proof spir·it *n.* an alcoholic beverage or a mixture of alcohol and water formerly used as a standard for measuring alcoholic strength. In the United Kingdom and Canada proof spirit is 57.1 per cent alcohol by volume at 10.6°C/51°F, in the United States, 50 per cent alcohol at 15.6°C/60°F.

proof the·o·ry *n.* the part of the theory of logic concerned with the exact nature of deriving propositions and conclusions

prop[1] /prop/ *n.* **1.** RIGID SUPPORT a rigid object such as a beam, stake, or pole that supports something or holds it in place **2.** COMFORTING PERSON OR THING somebody or something that provides comfort or assistance ■ *vt.* (**propped, prop·ping, props**) SUPPORT WITH PROP to use a rigid object to support something or hold it in place [15thC. From Middle Dutch *proppe* "vine prop, support."]

prop up *vt.* to give support or help to somebody or something

prop[2] /prop/ *n.* ARTS = **property** [Mid-19thC. Shortening.]

prop[3] /prop/ *n.* an aircraft propeller (*informal*) [Early 20thC. Shortening.]

Prop *n.* proposition placed before voters (*informal*) ○ *Prop 413 will provide money for a new library.*

prop. *abbr.* **1.** proper **2.** properly **3.** property **4.** PHILOS, MATH proposition **5.** proprietor

pro·pae·deu·tic /pròpi dóotik/ *adj.* GIVING PRELIMINARY TEACHING providing preparatory instruction (*formal*) ■ *n.* INTRODUCTORY STUDY a preliminary course of study that introduces more advanced instruction (*often used in plural*) [Late 18thC. Formed from PRO[2] + *paedeutics* "teaching" on the model of Greek *propaideuein* "to teach beforehand."]

prop·a·ga·ble /próppəgəb'l/ *adj.* **1.** BIOL, BOT CAPABLE OF BEING PROPAGATED capable of being grown or bred from a parent stock **2.** PHYS CAPABLE OF BEING IMPELLED FORWARD capable of being transmitted or impelled forward, especially in the form of light or sound waves —**prop·a·ga·bil·i·ty** /pròppəgə bíllətee/ *n.*

prop·a·gan·da /pròppə gándə/ *n.* **1.** PUBLICITY TO PROMOTE SOMETHING information or publicity put out by an organization or government to spread and promote a policy, idea, doctrine, or cause **2.** MISLEADING PUBLICITY deceptive or distorted information that is systematically spread [Early 18thC. From modern Latin *Propaganda Fide*, literally "propagating the faith" (see PROPAGANDA).] —**prop·a·gan·dism** *n.* —**prop·a·gan·dist** *n., adj.*

Pro·pa·ganda *n.* a committee of Roman Catholic cardinals, the Congregation for the Propagation of the Faith, in charge of supervising foreign missions and educating priests to serve in them

prop·a·gan·dize /pròppə gán dìz/ (**-dized, -diz·ing, -diz·es**) *vti.* to organize or spread propaganda

prop·a·gate /próppə gàyt/ (**-gat·ed, -gat·ing, -gates**) *v.* **1.** *vti.* BIOL REPRODUCE ORGANISM to reproduce a plant or animal or, cause one to reproduce **2.** *vti.* GARDENING CREATE NEW PLANTS to multiply plants by the use of seeds or cuttings **3.** *vt.* SPREAD SOMETHING WIDELY to spread ideas or customs to many people **4.** *vti.* PHYS IMPEL SOMETHING FORWARD to move or transmit something forward in space, especially as a light or sound wave [Late 16thC. From Latin *propagare* "to breed plants in layers (of vines)," from, ultimately, *propago* "layer," literally "planting out," from an assumed base meaning "to plant."] —**prop·a·ga·tion** /pròppə gáysh'n/ *n.* —**prop·a·ga·tion·al** /-gáyshən'l, -gáyshnəl/ *adj.* —**prop·a·ga·tive** /próppə gàytiv/ *adj.*

prop·a·ga·tor /próppə gàytər/ *n.* **1.** SPREADER OF IDEAS somebody who spreads ideas or beliefs widely **2.** GARDENING BOX FOR SEEDS OR CUTTINGS a shallow box with a transparent cover used for germinating seeds or allowing cuttings to take root, especially one that can be heated

prop·a·gule /próppə gyòol/, **pro·pag·u·lum** /prə póggyələm/ *n.* a part of a plant or fungus such as a bud or a spore that becomes detached from the rest and forms a new organism [Mid-19thC. From modern Latin *propagulum*, literally "little shoot," from *propago* (see PROPAGATE).]

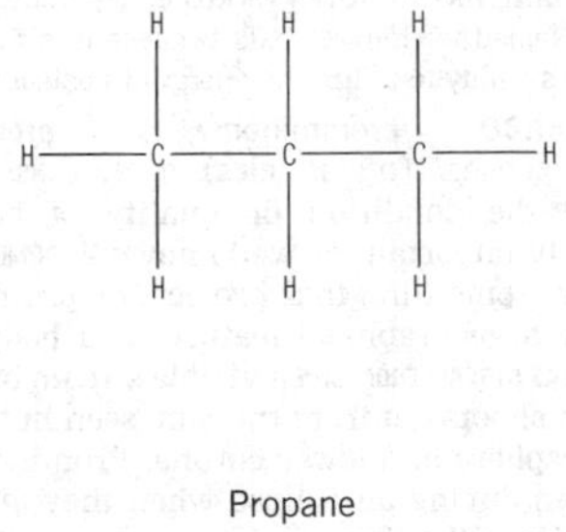

Propane

pro·pane /prṓ pàyn/ *n.* a flammable colorless hydrocarbon gas that is used as a fuel, propellant, and refrigerant. Formula: C_3H_8. [Mid-19thC. Formed from PROPIONIC.]

pro·pa·no·ic ac·id /prṑpə nṓ ik ássid/ *n.* = **propionic acid** [*Propanoic* was coined from PROPANE + -IC]

prop·a·none /prṓpə nṑn/ *n.* acetone (*technical*)

pro·par·ox·y·tone /prṑpə róksə tṑn/ *n.* ACCENTED WORD IN CLASSICAL GREEK in classical Greek grammar, a word that has an acute accent on the third syllable from the end, or a heavy stress on this syllable ■ *adj.* WITH PROPAROXYTONE with or using a proparoxytone [Mid-18thC. From Greek *proparoxutonos*, literally "having an accent before the last syllable," from, ultimately, *oxutonos* "having an accent accent."]

pro pa·tri·a /prō páttree ə/ *adv.* for somebody's own country (*formal*) [From Latin, literally "for the fatherland"]

pro·pel /prə pél/ (**-pelled, -pel·ling, -pels**) *vt.* **1.** PUSH FORWARD to move or push something or somebody forward **2.** CAUSE ACTION to impel or cause a course of

PROOFREADERS' MARKS

Mark in margin	Instruction	Textual mark	Corrected type
General			
	Delete	the new dictionary	the dictionary
	Delete and close up space	the dictionnary	the dictionary
new/	Insert indicated material	the / dictionary	the new dictionary
✓ or stet	Leave unchanged/ as before	the new dictionary	the new dictionary
?	Query	the newt dictionary	
sp	Spell out	3 dictionaries	three dictionaries

Mark in margin	Instruction	Textual mark	Corrected type
Paragraphing			
¶	New paragraph	It was a gift. The new dictionary was excellent.	It was a gift. The new dictionary was excellent.
¶	Flush paragraph	It was a gift. The new dictionary was excellent.	It was a gift. The new dictionary was excellent.
	Run on	It was a gift. The new dictionary was excellent.	It was a gift. The new dictionary was excellent.

Mark in margin	Instruction	Textual mark	Corrected type
Position and Spacing			
tr	Transpose	the dictionary new	the new dictionary
	Move left	the dictionary	the dictionary
	Move right	the dictionary	the dictionary
	Move down	the dictionary	the dictionary
	Move up	dictionary the	the dictionary
‖	Align	the dictionary the dictionary	the dictionary the dictionary
	Straighten line	the dictionary	the dictionary
#	Insert space	thedictionary	the dictionary
eq#	Equalize space	the new dictionary	the new dictionary
	Close up	the diction ary	the dictionary
1 2 3	Set characters/ words in order	the dictoinary	the dictionary

Mark in margin	Instruction	Textual mark	Corrected type
Punctuation			
⊙	Period/ Decimal point	The new dictionary is excellent	The new dictionary is excellent.
,	Comma	scribble scribble scribble	scribble, scribble, scribble
=	Hyphen	20th century dictionary	20th-century dictionary
:	Colon	The dictionary definition	The dictionary definition:
;	Semicolon	Look it up find it.	Look it up; find it.
'	Apostrophe	the worlds dictionary	the world's dictionary
" / "	Double quotation marks	the world dictionary	the "world" dictionary
' / '	Single quotation marks	the "world dictionary"	the "'world' dictionary"
[/]	Brackets	the world dictionary	the [world] dictionary
1/N	En dash/rule	1900 2000	1900–2000
1/M	Em dash/rule	the dictionary the world	the dictionary—the world
*	Asterisk	the dictionary	the dictionary*
§	Section symbol	World Dictionary	World Dictionary
/	Virgule/ Oblique/ slash	dictionary/world/English	dictionary/world/English
⊙/⊙/⊙/	Ellipsis	world dictionary a gift	world dictionary . . . a gift

Mark in margin	Instruction	Textual mark	Corrected type
Style of Type			
uc	Upper case/ capital letters	the dictionary	The Dictionary
lc	Lower case	The Dictionary	the dictionary
sc	Small capitals	the dictionary	THE DICTIONARY
ital	Italic	the world dictionary	the *world* dictionary
rom	Roman	*the world dictionary*	*the* world *dictionary*
bf	Bold face	the world dictionary	the **world** dictionary
lf	Light face	**the world dictionary**	**the** world **dictionary**
°	Superior/ superscript	85 F	85°F
2	Inferior/ subscript	HO	H_2O

action [15thC. From Latin *propellere* "to drive forward," from *pellere* "to drive" (source of English *pulse* and *repel*).]

pro·pel·lant /prə péllənt/, **pro·pel·lent** *n.* **1.** SPACE TECH **EXPLOSIVE SUBSTANCE** a substance that is burned to give upward thrust to a rocket **2.** ARMS **EXPLOSIVE CHARGE FOR GUN** an explosive charge that projects a bullet from a gun **3. GAS IN AEROSOLS** a compressed inert gas used to dispense the contents of an aerosol container when pressure is applied and released

pro·pel·lent /prə péllənt/ *adj.* tending to drive or move something forward

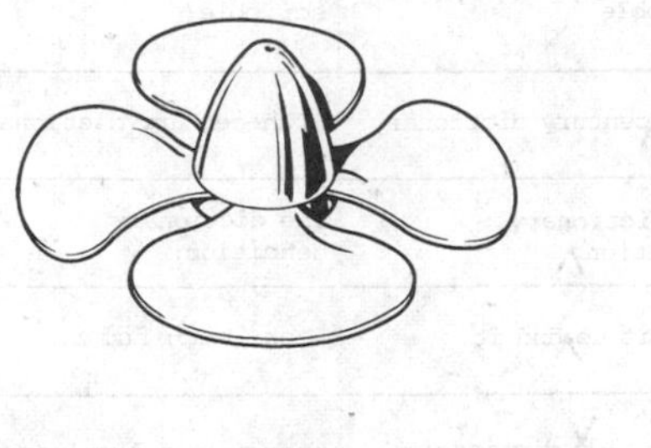

Propeller

pro·pel·ler /prə péllər/ *n.* a revolving shaft with spiral blades that causes a ship or an aircraft to move by the backward thrust of water or air

pro·pel·ler shaft *n.* **1. SHAFT TRANSMITTING POWER** the shaft in a ship or aircraft that transmits power from the engine to the propeller **2.** = **drive shaft** *n.* 1

pro·pel·ling pen·cil *n. U.K.* = **mechanical pencil**

pro·pend /prō pénd/ (**-pend·ed, -pend·ing, -pends**) *vi.* to incline to or toward something (*archaic*) [Mid-16thC. From Latin *propendere* "to hang forward," from *pendere* "to hang" (source of English *pendant*).]

pro·pene /prṓ peen/ *n.* = **propylene** [Mid-19thC. Coined from PROPYL + -ENE.]

pro·pen·o·ic ac·id /prṑpə nṓ ik-/ *n.* = **acrylic acid**

pro·pen·si·ty /prə pénsətee/ (*plural* **-ties**) *n.* a tendency to demonstrate particular behavior [Late 16thC. Formed from obsolete English *propense* "inclined, prone," from, ultimately, Latin *propendere* (see PROPEND).]

prop·er /próppər/ *adj.* **1. CORRECT** appropriate or correct ○ *proper winter clothing* **2. NEEDED AND APPROPRIATE** fulfilling all expectations or criteria ○ *proper equipment for the task* **3. WITH CORRECT MANNERS** behaving in a respectable or socially acceptable way **4. BELONGING EXCLUSIVELY TO SOMEBODY** characteristic of or belonging exclusively to somebody or something **5. NARROWLY IDENTIFIED** strictly identified and distinguished from something else **6.** HERALDRY **SHOWING NATURAL COLORS** showing the natural colors in the design or device of a heraldic object **7.** CHR **USED ON HOLY OCCASION** reserved as a prayer, lesson, or rite for a holy day or festival **8. GOODLOOKING** physically handsome and admirable (*archaic*) **9.** MATH **NONIDENTICAL SET WITHIN SECOND SET** included as a mathematical set in a second set but not being the same ■ *adv. U.K.* **TOTALLY** exceedingly or completely (*regional*) ■ *n.* **prop·er, Prop·er** CHR **SERVICE FOR HOLY OCCASION** a Christian church service that is used for a holy day or festival [13thC. Directly or via Old French *propre* from Latin *proprius* "one's own, particular, special," of uncertain origin: perhaps from *pro privo*, literally "for the individual."] —**prop·er·ness** *n.*

prop·er ad·jec·tive *n.* an adjective that is formed from a proper noun, as "Canadian" is from "Canada"

prop·er frac·tion *n.* a fraction in which the value of the numerator is less than the value of the denominator, e.g. $\frac{6}{8}$

prop·er·ly /próppərlee/ *adv.* **1. APPROPRIATELY** in a suitable or appropriate way ○ *properly dressed for the occasion* **2. CORRECTLY** in a correct or well-mannered way ○ *If you can't behave properly, we'll have to go home.* **3. IN REALITY** in a correct and appropriate situation ○ *The chair properly belongs in the corner.* **4.** *U.K.* **TOTALLY** to the fullest degree or extent ○ *By the end of the day she was properly tired.*

prop·er noun, **prop·er name** *n.* the name of something particular, normally beginning with a capital letter and not used with the indefinite article or a modifier, e.g., "York," "Sally," or "Henderson"

prop·er·tied /próppərteed/ *adj.* owning property, especially land

prop·er·ty /próppərtee/ (*plural* **-ties**) *n.* **1. SOMETHING OWNED** something of value such as land or a patent that is owned **2. OWNED LAND OR REAL ESTATE** a piece of land or real estate that is owned by somebody **3.** LAW **RIGHT TO OWN SOMETHING** the right to own, possess, or use something **4. TRAIT OR ATTRIBUTE** a characteristic quality or distinctive feature of something (*often used in the plural*) **5.** ARTS **PROP** a prop (*formal*) **6. SOMETHING AT SOMEBODY'S DISPOSAL** something at the disposal of a person, a group, or the public ○ *community property* **7.** PHILOS **DISTINCTIVE BUT NOT ESSENTIAL QUALITY** in the thought of Aristotle, an attribute or quality that is peculiar to a whole class or species but not essential to it [13thC. Via Anglo-Norman *proprete* and French *propriété* (source also of English *propriety*) from Latin *proprietas* "ownership," from *proprius* (see PROPER).]

prop·er·ty man *n.* = **propman** (*dated*)

prop·er·ty mis·tress *n.* a woman who looks after stage properties (*dated*)

prop·er·ty tax *n.* a tax that is based on the value of a house or other property

pro·phage /prṓ fàyj/ *n.* a stable form of virus that infects bacteria, with genetic material that is integrated into and replicated with that of its host without harming the host [Mid-20thC. Formed from PRO^2.]

pro·phase /prṓ fàyz/ *n.* the first phase in cell division, when chromosomes condense and can be seen as two chromatids. ◊ **anaphase, metaphase, telophase** [Late 19thC. Formed from PRO^2.]

proph·e·cy /próffəssee/ (*plural* **-cies**), **proph·e·sy** (*plural* **-sies**) *n.* **1.** RELIG **DIVINE PREDICTION** a prediction of a future event that reveals the will of a deity **2. PREDICTION** a prediction that something will occur in the future **3.** RELIG **ABILITY TO PREDICT THE FUTURE** the ability to predict the future when inspired by a deity

proph·e·sy /próffə sī/ *v.* **1.** *vti.* **PREDICT** to predict what is going to happen **2.** *vi.* RELIG **PREDICT WITH DIVINE AUTHORITY** to reveal the will of a deity in predicting a future event —**proph·e·si·able** *adj.* —**proph·e·si·er** *n.*

proph·et /próffət/ *n.* **1.** RELIG **SOMEBODY WHO INTERPRETS DIVINE WILL** somebody who interprets or passes on the will of a deity **2. SOMEBODY PREDICTING THE FUTURE** somebody who foretells the future **3. ADVOCATE OF SOMETHING** somebody who advocates a cause or idea **4. SOMEBODY WHO IS INSPIRED** somebody considered to be an inspired leader or teacher [12thC. Via French *prophète* and Latin *propheta* from Greek *prophētēs*, literally "someone who speaks beforehand," from *phētēs* "speaker."]

Proph·et *n.* **1. MUHAMMAD** Muhammad, the founder of Islam **2. FOUNDER OF LATTER DAY SAINTS** Joseph Smith, the founder of the Church of Jesus Christ of Latter-Day Saints. ■ **Proph·ets** *npl.* **PROPHETIC BOOKS OF BIBLE** the prophetic books of the Bible, comprising the second half of the Christian Old Testament, and the second of the three divisions of the Hebrew Bible. See table at **Bible**

proph·et·ess /próffətəss/ *n.* a woman prophet

pro·phet·ic /prə féttik/ *adj.* **1. CORRECTLY PREDICTING** predicting or foreshadowing something that does eventually happen **2. OF PROPHET** relating to a prophet —**pro·phet·i·cal** *adj.* —**pro·phet·i·cal·ly** *adv.*

Proph·et's Birth·day *n.* = **Mawlid al-Nabi**

pro·phy /prṓfee/ (*plural* **-phies**) *n.* a condom (*informal dated*) [Late 20thC. Shortening of PROPHYLACTIC.]

pro·phy·lac·tic /prṑfə láktik, prṑffə-/ *adj.* **GUARDING AGAINST DISEASE** guarding against infection or disease ■ *n.* **1. DRUG THAT GUARDS AGAINST DISEASE** a drug or agent such as anti-malarial pills that prevents the development of a disease **2. CONDOM** a condom (*regional formal*) [Late 16thC. Via French *prophylactique* from, ultimately, Greek *prophulassein* "to keep guard in front of," from *phulassein* "to guard."] —**pro·phy·lac·ti·cal·ly** *adv.*

pro·phy·lax·is /prṑfə láksiss, prṑffə-/ (*plural* **-es** /-seez/) *n.* **1.** MED **TREATMENT TO PREVENT DISEASE** treatment such as vaccination that prevents disease or stops it spreading **2.** DENT **REMOVAL OF PLAQUE AND TARTAR** a dental treatment to remove plaque and tartar from the teeth [Mid-19thC. From modern Latin, literally "guarding in front of," from Greek *pro* "in front of" + *phulaxis* "guarding," modeled on English *prophylactic*.]

pro·pin·qui·ty /prə píngkwətee/ *n.* nearness in space, time, or relationship (*formal*) [14thC. Directly or via Old French *propinquité* from Latin *propinquitas*, from, ultimately, *prope* "near" (source of English *approach*).]

pro·pi·o·nate /prṓpee ə nàyt/ *n.* a chemical compound that is a salt or ester of propionic acid [Late 19thC. Formed from PROPIONIC.]

pro·pi·on·ic /prṓpee ónnik/ *adj.* derived from propionic acid [Mid-19thC. Formed from Greek *pro* "in front" + *piōn* "fat," because it is first in order of the fatty acids.]

pro·pi·on·ic ac·id *n.* a colorless liquid fatty acid that is used in making artificial flavors, perfumes, and preservatives. Formula: $C_3H_6O_2$.

pro·pi·ti·ate /prō píshee àyt/ (**-at·ed, -at·ing, -ates**) *vt.* to appease or conciliate somebody or something (*formal*) [Late 16thC. From Latin *propitiare* "to make favorable," from *propitius* "favourable."] —**pro·pi·ti·a·ble** *adj.* —**pro·pi·ti·a·tion** /prō pìshee áysh'n/ *n.* —**pro·pi·ti·a·tive** /prō píshee àytiv/ *adj.* —**pro·pi·ti·a·tor** /-àytər/ *n.*

pro·pi·ti·a·to·ry /prō píshee ə tàwree, -píshə tàwree/ *adj.* designed to appease or win favor (*formal*) —**pro·pi·ti·a·to·ri·ly** *adv.*

pro·pi·tious /prō píshəss/ *adj.* **1. FAVORABLE** favorable and likely to lead to success **2. KINDLY** kindly disposed or gracious (*formal*) [15thC. Directly or via Old French *propicieus* from Latin *propitius* (see PROPITIATE).] —**pro·pi·tious·ly** *adv.* —**pro·pi·tious·ness** *n.*

prop·jet /próp jèt/ *n.* = **turboprop** *n.* 1, **turboprop** *n.* 2 [Mid-20thC. Coined from PROPELLER + JET.]

prop·man /próp màn/ (*plural* **-men** /-mèn/) *n.* a man who looks after stage properties

prop·o·lis /próppəliss/ *n.* a waxy resinous substance that comes from buds, used by bees as a cement and caulking in making their hives [Early 17thC. Via Latin from Greek, literally "before a city," from *polis* "city," because it originally referred to a structure around the opening of the hive.]

pro·po·nent /prə pṓnənt/ *n.* **1. ADVOCATE** somebody who advocates something **2.** LAW **PRESENTER OF WILL** somebody who presents a will for probate **3. PROPOSER** somebody who proposes something [Late 16thC. From Latin *proponent-*, present participle stem of *proponere* "to put forth," from *ponere* "to place."]

pro·por·tion /prə páwrsh'n/ *n.* **1. PART OF WHOLE** a quantity of something that is part of the whole amount or number ○ *What proportion of their time is spent on administration?* **2. RELATIONSHIP BETWEEN QUANTITIES** the relationship between two or more amounts or numbers, or between the parts of a whole ○ *The proportion of trucks to cars on the road has remained the same.* **3. RELATIVE SIZE OF THINGS** the correct or desirable relationship of size, quantity, or degree between two or more things or parts of something ○ *An understanding of proportion is essential for an architect.* **4. RELATIVE IMPORTANCE** the importance of different aspects of a situation when compared with each other ○ *The media blew the incident all out of proportion.* **5.** MATH **RATIO** a relationship or ratio between two variables that remains fixed **6.** MATH **EQUALITY OF TWO RATIOS** a relationship of equality between two ratios, in which the first term divided by the second equals the third divided by the fourth, as in $1/2 = 3/6$ ■ **pro·por·tions** *npl.* **1. SIZE OF SOMETHING** the size or shape of something **2. IMPORTANCE OF SOMETHING** the importance or seriousness of something ■ *vt.* (**-tioned, -tion·ing, -tions**) **1. KEEP THINGS IN SAME RELATIONSHIP** to create or maintain a relationship of size, quantity, or degree between two or more things ○ *The arms and body of the sweater had been badly proportioned.* **2. MAKE SOMETHING BALANCED IN APPEARANCE** to give something a pleasing shape, appropriate dimensions, or a harmonious arrangement of parts (*usually passive*) ○ *a beautifully proportioned design* [14thC. Directly or via Old French from the Latin stem *proportion-*, from the phrase *pro portione* "according to (each) part," from the stem *portion-* (see PORTION).] —**pro·por·tion·a·bil·i·ty** /prə pàwrsh'nə bílletee/ *n.* —**pro·por·tion·a·ble** /prə páwrsh'nəb'l/ *adj.* —**pro·por·tion·a·bly** /-páwrsh'nəblee/ *adv.* —**pro·por·tion·ment** /-mənt/ *n.*

pro·por·tion·al /prə páwrshən'l, -shnəl/ *adj.* **1. IN PROPORTION** in the correct relationship of size, quantity, or degree to something else, or remaining in the same relationship when things change ○ *The rate of pay is proportional to the complexity of the task.* **2.** MATH **RELATED BY A RATIO** related by or possessing a constant ratio ■ *n.* MATH **TERM IN PAIR OF EQUIVALENT RATIOS** any one of the four terms in a relationship of proportion between two ratios, where the first term divided by the second equals the third divided by the fourth —**pro·por·tion·al·i·ty** /prə pàwrsh'n állətee, -shə nállətee/ *n.* —**pro·por·tion·al·ly** /prə páwrshən'lee, -shnəlee/ *adv.*

pro·por·tion·al rep·re·sen·ta·tion *n.* an electoral system in which each party's share of the seats in government is the same as its share of all the votes cast

pro·por·tion·al tax *n.* a tax levied at the same rate on tax bases of different amounts

pro·por·tion·ate /prə páwrsh'nət/ *adj.* IN PROPORTION having the correct relationship of size, quantity, or degree to something else, or remaining in the same relationship when things change ○ *The fall in price led to a proportionate rise in sales.* ■ *vt.* (**-at·ed, -at·ing, -ates**) MAKE THINGS PROPORTIONAL to give two or more things the correct relationship of size, quantity, or degree —**pro·por·tion·ate·ly** *adv.* —**pro·por·tion·ate·ness** *n.*

pro·pos·al /prə pṓz'l/ *n.* **1.** IDEA OR PLAN a suggestion or intention, especially one put forward formally or officially **2.** ACT OF PROPOSING the act of making a suggestion or stating an intention **3.** REQUEST TO MARRY SOMEBODY a request for somebody to enter into marriage

pro·pose /prə pṓz/ (**-posed, -pos·ing, -pos·es**) *v.* **1.** *vt.* MAKE SUGGESTION to put something forward, often formally or officially, e.g., an idea or suggested course of action ○ *Harsher penalties have been proposed.* **2.** *vt.* STATE AN INTENTION to announce a plan or intended course of action (*formal*) ○ *What do you propose to do about it?* **3.** *vt.* NOMINATE SOMEBODY to put forward somebody's name for an elected position or a promotion ○ *propose her for the new position* **4.** *vti.* REQUEST MARRIAGE to ask somebody to marry ○ *He proposed while we were on vacation.* **5.** *vt.* SUGGEST TOAST OR VOTE OF THANKS to ask others to join in something such as a toast or a vote of thanks ○ *I propose a toast to Chris and Sarah.* [14thC. From Old French *proposer*, literally "to put forward," from *poser* (see POSE), modeled on Latin *proponere* "to put forward."] —**pro·pos·a·ble** *adj.* —**pro·pos·er** *n.*

pro·pos·i·ta /prō pózzitə/ (*plural* **-tae** /-tee/) *n.* a woman who is involved in legal poceedings [From Latin, feminine of *propositus* (see PROPOSITUS)]

pro·pos·i·ti plural of **propositus**

prop·o·si·tion /prŏppə zísh'n/ *n.* **1.** PROPOSAL an idea, offer, or plan put forward for consideration or discussion **2.** STATEMENT a statement of opinion or judgment **3.** SUGGESTION OF SEXUAL INTERCOURSE an invitation to have sexual intercourse **4.** PRIVATE AGREEMENT a private deal or agreement **5.** SOMETHING TO BE FACED something or somebody to be dealt with (*informal*) ○ *The news that he would be there certainly made the party a more attractive proposition.* **6.** MATH THEOREM a statement or theorem to be demonstrated **7.** PHILOSOPHY MEANING OF DECLARATIVE SENTENCE the meaning of a declarative sentence and what is said to be true or false **8. prop·o·si·tion, Prop·o·si·tion** LAW PROPOSAL FOR AMENDMENT TO LAW a proposal for an amendment to the law that is set forth to be voted on ○ *Propositions imposing term limits for politicians have been common recently.* ■ *vt.* (**-tioned, -tion·ing, -tions**) **1.** SUGGEST SEX to invite somebody to have sexual intercourse **2.** OFFER SOMEBODY A DEAL to offer to make a private deal or agreement with somebody [14thC. Directly or via French from the Latin stem *proposition-*, from *proposit-*, past participle stem of *proponere*, literally "to put forth," from *ponere* "to place."] —**prop·o·si·tion·al** *adj.* —**prop·o·si·tion·al·ly** *adv.*

prop·o·si·tion·al at·ti·tude *n.* in philosophy, an attitude taken by somebody towards a proposition, e.g., in believing it, knowing it, or desiring it

prop·o·si·tion·al cal·cu·lus *n.* the branch of deductive logic that deals with the relationships formed between propositions by connectives, e.g., "and," "but," "if," or "or"

prop·o·si·tion·al func·tion *n.* = **open sentence**

pro·pos·i·tus /prō pózzitəss/ (*plural* **-ti** /-tī/) *n.* **1.** MAN LITIGANT a man who is involved in legal proceedings **2.** MED FIRST PERSON INVESTIGATED IN FAMILY STUDY the first person to be investigated in the genetic study of a family [Mid-18thC. From Latin, past participle of *proponere* (see PROPONE).]

pro·pound /prə pównd/ (**-pound·ed, -pound·ing, -pounds**) *vt.* to put forward a suggestion or theory for others to consider [Mid-16thC. Alteration of PROPONE.] —**pro·pound·er** *n.*

propr. *abbr.* proprietor

pro·prae·tor /prō preétər/, **pro·pre·tor** *n.* an ancient Roman citizen sent to govern a province, usually after serving as a senior magistrate (**praetor**) in Rome [Late 16thC. From Latin, from earlier phrase *pro praetore* "(one acting) for the praetor."]

pro·pran·o·lol /prō práNnə làwl/ *n.* PHARM a drug used to treat angina pectoris, abnormal heart rhythms, migraine, and high blood pressure. Formula: $C_{16}H_{21}NO_2$. [Mid-20thC. Coined from PROPYL + PROPANOL with repetition of *-ol.*]

pro·pri·e·tar·y /prə príee ə tèrree/ *adj.* **1.** RELATING TO OWNERS OR OWNERSHIP relating to, involving, or associated with an owner, ownership, or something owned **2.** PRIVATELY OWNED privately owned and run **3.** EXHIBITING CHARACTERISTICS OF OWNERSHIP exhibiting characteristics that imply or assume ownership of somebody or something ○ *The child kept a proprietary hold on the toy.* **4.** USED WITH EXCLUSIVE LEGAL RIGHT used, manufactured, or sold by a person or company with an exclusive property right, e.g., a patent or trademark ○ *a proprietary drug* ■ *n.* (*plural* **-ies**) **1.** OWNER an owner or a group of owners **2.** PHARM PROPRIETARY AGENT a drug or other substance made and sold under the legal protection of a trademark or patent **3.** OWNERSHIP the right of ownership, or something exclusively owned **4.** HIST OWNER OF COLONY the owner of a proprietary colony [15thC. Directly or via French from medieval Latin *proprietarius*, both from late Latin, "of a property holder," from Latin *proprietas* (see PROPERTY).] —**pro·pri·e·tar·i·ly** /prə prī ə térrilee/ *adv.*

pro·pri·e·tar·y col·o·ny (*plural* **pro·pri·e·tar·y col·o·nies**) *n.* a North American colony granted to an individual or group by the British Crown with full ownership rights

pro·pri·e·tor /prə prī ətər/ *n.* **1.** OWNER OF A BUSINESS the owner of a commercial enterprise or business establishment such as a store, hotel, or restaurant **2.** LEGAL OWNER the legal owner of something **3.** SOMEBODY WITH PARTIAL RIGHTS OVER SOMETHING somebody who has rights, e.g., of management or use, but not full ownership of something **4.** HIST OWNER OF COLONY the owner of a proprietary colony. = **proprietary** *n.* 4 [15thC. Coined from PROPRIETARY + -OR.] —**pro·pri·e·to·ri·al** /prə prī ə táwree əl/ *adj.* —**pro·pri·e·to·ri·al·ly** /-táwree əlee/ *adv.* —**pro·pri·e·tor·ship** /prə prī ətər ṡhip/ *n.*

pro·pri·e·ty /prə prī ətee/ *n.* (*plural* **-ties**) **1.** SOCIALLY CORRECT OR APPROPRIATE BEHAVIOR conformity to the standards of politeness, respect, decency, or morality conventionally accepted by a society **2.** QUALITY OF BEING SOCIALLY APPROPRIATE quality of displaying behaviors thought to be correct or appropriate ■ **pro·pri·e·ties** *npl.* RULES OF ETIQUETTE the accepted standards of correct or appropriate social behavior [15thC. Via Old French from Latin *proprietas* "appropriateness, ownership," from *proprius* (see PROPER).]

pro·pri·o·cep·tor /prŏpree ə séptər/ *n.* a sensory nerve ending in muscles, tendons, and joints that provides a sense of the body's position by responding to stimuli from within the body [Early 20thC. Coined from Latin *proprius* "your own" + RECEPTOR.] —**pro·pri·o·cep·tion** *n.* —**pro·pri·o·cep·tive** *adj.*

prop root *n.* a root that grows from the stem of a plant above the ground and helps to support it. The mangrove and corn are examples of plants with prop roots.

props mas·ter *n.* somebody who looks after stage props

prop·to·sis /prop tóssiss/ *n.* the forward displacement or protrusion of an organ of the body, especially an eyeball [Late 17thC. Via late Latin from Greek *proptōsis* "a falling forward," from *propiptein* "to fall forward."]

pro·pul·sion /prə púlshən/ *n.* **1.** ACT OF DRIVING SOMETHING FORWARD the process by which an object such as an automobile, ship, aircraft, or missile is moved forward **2.** DRIVING FORCE the force by which something such as an automobile, rocket, or ship is moved forward [Early 17thC. Ultimately from Latin *propuls-*, past participle stem of *propellere* (see PROPEL).] —**pro·pul·sive** /prə púlsiv/ *adj.* —**pro·pul·so·ry** /prə púlsəree/ *adj.*

pro·pyl /prṓp'l/ *n.* either of two isomeric chemical groups or radicals derived from propane. Formula: C_3H_7. [Mid-19thC. Coined from PROPIONIC + -YL.]

prop·y·lae·um /pròppə leé əm/ (*plural* **-a** /-ə/) *n.* a colonnaded gate or entrance to a building, especially a temple, or to a group of buildings [Early 18thC. Via Latin from, ultimately, Greek *propulaios* "before the gate," from *pulē* "gate."]

pro·pyl al·co·hol *n.* a colorless alcohol used as a solvent and antiseptic. Formula: C_3H_8O.

pro·pyl·ene /prṓpə leèn/ *n.* a flammable gaseous hydrocarbon derived from petroleum and used in organic synthesis. Formula: C_3H_6.

pro·pyl·ene gly·col *n.* a colorless thick sweet-tasting liquid derived from propylene and used as an antifreeze in brake fluid, and as a solvent and lubricant. Formula: $C_3H_8O_2$.

prop·y·lon *n.* = **propylaeum** [Mid-19thC. Via Latin from Greek *propulon*, literally "before the gate," from *pulē* "gate."]

pro ra·ta /prō ráytə, -raátə/ *adv.*, *adj.* in accordance with a fixed proportion [From Latin, "according to the rate"]

pro·rate /prō ráyt/ (**-rat·ed, -rat·ing, -rates**) *vti.* to calculate, divide, or distribute something on a pro rata basis [Mid-19thC. Anglicization of PRO RATA.] —**pro·rat·a·ble** *adj.* —**pro·ra·tion** *n.*

pro·rogue /prō rṓg, prə-/ (**-rogued, -rogu·ing, -rogues**) *v.* **1.** *vti.* SUSPEND PARLIAMENTARY SESSION to discontinue the meetings of a parliament or other body without formally ending the session **2.** *vt.* POSTPONE SOMETHING to defer something to a later date or to a subsequent meeting [15thC. Via French *proroguer* from Latin *prorogare* "to prolong," literally "to ask the people (whether a term of office should be extended)," from *rogare* "to ask."] —**pro·ro·ga·tion** /prṑrə gáysh'n/ *n.*

pros. /práwssədee/ *abbr.* prosody

pro·sa·ic /prō záy ik/ *adj.* **1.** LACKING IMAGINATION not having any features that are interesting or imaginative **2.** RESEMBLING PROSE characteristic of, resembling, or consisting of prose **3.** STRAIGHTFORWARD lacking complications or subtleties [Late 16thC. Directly and via French from late Latin *prosaicus*, from Latin *prosa* (see PROSE).] —**pro·sa·i·cal·ly** *adv.* —**pro·sa·ic·ness** *n.*

pro·sa·ism /prṓ zay ìzzəm/, **pro·sa·i·cism** *n.* **1.** BORING WORD OR QUALITY a dull or unimaginative expression or style of writing **2.** SOMETHING CHARACTERISTIC OF PROSE a word, phrase, or style of writing used in prose —**pro·sa·ist** /prṓ zàyist/ *n.*

pros and cons *npl.* the arguments for and against something

Pros. Atty. *abbr.* prosecuting attorney

pro·sce·ni·um /prō seénee əm/ *n.* **1.** FRONT OF STAGE the part of a theater stage that is in front of the curtain **2.** STAGE IN ANCIENT GREECE OR ROME the stage of a theater in ancient Greece or Rome [Early 17thC. Via Latin from Greek *proskēnion* "forestage," from *skēnē* (see SCENE).]

pro·sciut·to /prō shoó tō/ *n.* a type of cured ham from Italy, usually served cold and uncooked in thin slices [Mid-20thC. Via Italian from, ultimately, Latin *exsuctus* "lacking juice," past participle of *exsugere* "to suck out," from *sugere* "to suck."]

pro·scribe /prō skríb/ (**-scribed, -scrib·ing, -scribes**) *vt.* **1.** CONDEMN OR BAN SOMETHING to prohibit something that is considered undesirable by those in authority **2.** CONDEMN SOMETHING to denounce or condemn something **3.** BANISH SOMEBODY to banish or exile somebody **4.** OUTLAW SOMEBODY PUBLICLY to state publicly that somebody is no longer protected by the law, especially in ancient Rome (*archaic*) [15thC. From Latin *proscribere* "to publish in writing, to publish somebody's name as outlawed," from *pro-* "in front of" + *scribere* (see SCRIBE).] —**pro·scrib·er** *n.*

pro·scrip·tion /prō skrípshən/ *n.* (*formal*) **1.** CONDEMNATION OF SOMETHING an act of condemning or forbidding something **2.** CONDITION OF BEING BANNED the condition of having been denounced or exiled —**pro·scrip·tive** /-skríptiv/ *adj.* —**pro·scrip·tive·ly** *adv.* —**pro·scrip·tive·ness** *n.*

prose /prōz/ *n.* **1.** LANGUAGE THAT IS NOT POETRY writing or speech in its normal continuous form, without the rhythmic or visual line structure of poetry **2.** ORDINARY STYLE OF EXPRESSION writing or speech that is ordinary or matter-of-fact, without embellishment **3.** CHR = **sequence** *n.* 6 ■ *v.* (**prosed, pros·ing, pros·es**) **1.** *vti.* WRITE IN PROSE to write something in prose, as opposed to poetry **2.** *vt.* REWRITE AS PROSE to turn poetry into prose **3.** *vi.* SPEAK OR WRITE PROSAICALLY to speak or write in an ordinary, matter-of-fact, or unimaginative style [13thC. Via Old French from Latin *prosa (oratio)* "straightforward (discourse)" from, ultimately, *provertere* "to turn forward," from *vertere* (see VERSE).]

pro·sec·tor /prō séktər/ *n.* somebody who prepares or dissects cadavers for anatomic demonstrations [Mid-19thC. Directly or via French from late Latin, literally "in place of the cutter," from Latin *sector* (see SECTOR).]

pros·e·cute /próssə kyo͝ot/ (**-cut·ed, -cut·ing, -cutes**) *v.* **1.** *vti.* TAKE LEGAL ACTION AGAINST SOMEBODY to have somebody tried in a court of law for a civil or criminal offense ○ *Trespassers will be prosecuted.* **2.** *vti.* TRY TO PROVE SOMEBODY IS GUILTY to represent the person or people who are taking legal action against somebody in a court of law **3.** *vt.* PERFORM ACTIVITY OR OCCUPATION to engage in or perform some activity or occupation (*formal*) ○ *prosecute a trade* **4.** *vt.* CONTINUE TO COMPLETION to continue doing something, usually until it is finished or accomplished (*formal*) ○ *prosecute an investigation* [15thC. From Latin *prosecut-*, the past participle stem of *prosequi* (see PURSUE).] —**pros·e·cut·a·ble** /próssə kyo͝otəb'l/ *adj.*

pros·e·cut·ing at·tor·ney *n.* a lawyer representing the state or the people in a criminal trial

pros·e·cu·tion /pròssə kyo͞osh'n/ *n.* **1.** PURSUIT OF LEGAL ACTION the trial of somebody in a court of law for a criminal offense **2.** LAWYERS TRYING TO PROVE SOMEBODY'S GUILT the lawyers representing the person or people who are taking legal action against somebody in a court of law, especially the state or the people in a criminal trial ○ *a witness for the prosecution* **3.** PERFORMANCE OF ACTIVITY OR OCCUPATION the carrying on of an activity or occupation (*formal*) ○ *the prosecution of your duty* **4.** CONTINUATION TO COMPLETION the continuation of or perseverance in some task or pursuit, usually until it is finished or accomplished (*formal*)

pros·e·cu·tor /próssə kyo͞otər/ *n.* **1.** = **prosecuting attorney** **2.** INITIATOR OF LEGAL PROCEEDINGS somebody who initiates a court prosecution

pros·e·lyte /pròssə līt/ *n.* SOMEBODY CONVERTED TO NEW BELIEF a new convert to a religious faith or political doctrine ■ *vti.* (**-lyt·ed, -lyt·ing, -lytes**) = **proselytize** [14thC. Via late Latin *proselytus* from Greek *prosēluthos* "person who comes to a place," from *proserkhesthai* "to come to."] —**pros·e·lyt·ic** /pròssə léttik/ *adj.* —**pros·e·ly·tism** /próssələ tìzzəm/ *n.*

pros·e·ly·tize /próssələ tīz/ (**-tized, -tiz·ing, -tiz·es**) *vti.* to try to convert somebody to a religious faith or political doctrine —**pros·e·ly·ti·za·tion** /pròssələti záysh'n/ *n.* —**pros·e·ly·tiz·er** /próssələ tīzər/ *n.*

pro·sem·i·nar /prō sémmi naar/ *n.* a course of study for graduates and advanced undergraduates, conducted in small groups under the supervision of a professor

prose po·em *n.* a piece of creative writing that has the structure of prose but the style and language of poetry —**prose po·et** *n.*

Pro·ser·pi·na /prō súrpənə/, **Pro·ser·pi·ne** /prō súrpīn/ *n.* the Roman goddess of the earth

pro·sim·i·an /prō símmee ən/ *n.* a nocturnal lower primate with large eyes and ears, e.g., a lemur, tarsier, or bush baby. Suborder: Prosimii.

pro·sit /prŏst, prṓzit/ *interj.* used as a drinking toast, to wish somebody good health or good fortune [Mid-19thC. Via German from Latin, "may it benefit," 3rd person present subjunctive singular of *prodesse* (see PROUD).]

pro·slav·er·y /prō sláyvəree/ *adj.* supporting or defending the principles and practice of slavery

pros·o·dy /próssədee/ (*plural* **-dies**) *n.* **1.** STUDY OF POETIC STRUCTURE the study of the structure of poetry and the conventions or techniques involved in writing it, including rhyme, meter, and the patterns of verse forms **2.** SYSTEM OR THEORY OF WRITING VERSE a particular system or theory of writing poetry **3.** RHYTHM OF SPEECH the rhythm of spoken language, including stress and intonation, or the study of these patterns [15thC. Via Latin *prosodia* from Greek *prosōidia* "song with an instrumental accompaniment," from *pros* "in addition to" + *ōidē* "song" (source of English *ode*).] —**pro·sod·ic** /prə sóddik/ *adj.* —**pro·sod·i·cal·ly** *adv.* —**pros·o·dist** /próssədist/ *n.*

pro·so·ma /prō sṓmə/ (*plural* **-mas** *or* **-ma·ta** /-sṓmətə/) *n.* the region near the head of spiders and some related arthropods, composed of fused segments of head and thorax [Late 19thC. Coined from PRO- "in front of" + Greek *sōma* "body."]

pros·o·pog·ra·phy /pròssə póggrəfee/ (*plural* **-phies**) *n.* a collection of biographical sketches used by social and political historians to convey larger patterns in a historical period [Mid-16thC. From modern Latin *prosopographia*, literally "writing about somebody," from Greek *prosōpon* "face, person."] —**pros·o·pog·ra·pher** *n.* —**pros·o·po·graph·i·cal** /pròssə pə gráffik'l/ *adj.*

pro·so·po·pe·ia /prə sòppə pée ə/, **pro·so·po·poe·ia** *n.* **1.** RHETORICAL FIGURE OF SPEECH a figure of speech in which an imaginary, dead, or absent person speaks **2.** = **personification** [Mid-16thC. Via Latin from Greek *prosōpopoiia* "representation in human form," from *prosōpon* "face, person" + *poiein* "to make."] —**pro·so·po·pe·ial** *adj.*

pros·pect /pró spèkt/ *n.* **1.** POSSIBILITY OF SOMETHING HAPPENING SOON a chance or the likelihood that something will happen in the near future, especially something desirable **2.** VISION OF FUTURE something that is expected or certain to happen in the future, or a mental picture of this ○ *I didn't relish the prospect of spending five months at sea.* **3.** EXTENSIVE OUTLOOK OR SCENE a view, especially one from a high position over a large expanse of land or water ○ *a pleasant prospect* **4.** DIRECTION FACED the direction in which something faces ○ *a northerly prospect* **5.** COMM LIKELY CUSTOMER somebody who is likely to be interested in buying a product or service **6.** SOMEBODY OR SOMETHING WITH POTENTIAL somebody or something that is likely to succeed ○ *She's our brightest prospect.* **7.** SURVEY an act of making a survey, examination, or observation **8.** MINING MINERAL LOCATION location of a mineral deposit, or an area believed to have mineral deposits **9.** MINING MINERAL DEPOSIT a probable mineral deposit or one that definitely exists **10.** MINING MINERAL YIELD the yield that can be obtained by mining a mineral ■ **pros·pects** *npl.* EXPECTATIONS OF SUCCESS the likelihood of being successful or prosperous in the future, especially in a job or career ○ *Young people who leave school early certainly narrow their prospects.* ■ *v.* (**-pect·ed, -pect·ing, -pects**) **1.** *vti.* MINING SEARCH FOR MINERAL DEPOSITS to explore an area in search of oil or valuable minerals, especially gold **2.** *vt.* MINING WORK A MINE to work a mine to see how profitable it is **3.** *vi.* LOOK FOR SOMETHING to search or watch for something ○ *prospect for business* [15thC. From Latin *prospectus* "view," from the past participle of *prospicere* "to look forward," from *specere* (see SPECTACLE).] —**pros·pect·less** *adj.*

pro·spec·tive /prə spéktiv/ *adj.* **1.** LIKELY TO BE SOMETHING expected or hoping to do or become something ○ *his prospective mother-in-law* **2.** LIKELY TO HAPPEN likely or expected to happen ○ *prospective changes* —**pro·spec·tive·ly** *adv.*

pros·pec·tor /pró spèktər/ *n.* somebody who explores an area in search of oil, gold, or other mineral deposits

pro·spec·tus /prə spéktəss/ *n.* **1.** *U.K.* = **catalog** *n.* 6 **2.** OFFICIAL ADVANCE INFORMATION ABOUT SOMETHING an official document giving details about something that is going to happen, e.g., a stock offering, a forthcoming publication, a new business, or a proposed project [Mid-18thC. From Latin (see PROSPECT).]

pros·per /próspər/ (**-pered, -per·ing, -pers**) *vi.* **1.** SUCCEED FINANCIALLY to be successful, especially in financial or economic terms, through effort or good fortune **2.** FLOURISH to flourish or thrive [14thC. Directly or via Old French from Latin *prosperare*, from *prosperus* "doing well."]

pros·per·i·ty /pro spérrətee/ *n.* the condition of enjoying great wealth, success, or good fortune

pros·per·i·ty gos·pel *n.* the doctrine taught in some Christian groups that through faith and prayer God will grant wishes to the faithful, especially those wishes involving material wealth

pros·per·ous /próspərəss/ *adj.* **1.** FINANCIALLY SUCCESSFUL successful and flourishing, especially earning or producing great wealth **2.** WEALTHY having great wealth, or associated with wealthy people **3.** FULL OF GOOD FORTUNE characterized by success or good fortune ○ *wishing you a prosperous New Year* **4.** PROMISING likely to be successful or bring a good result —**pros·per·ous·ly** *adv.* —**pros·per·ous·ness** *n.*

pross /pross/, **pross·ie** /próssee/ *n.* a prostitute (*slang*) [Early 20thC. Shortening.]

Pros·ser /próssər/, **Gabriel** (1776?–1800) U.S. slave and rebel. He led an unsuccessful slave uprising near Richmond, Virginia. He and some 35 other slaves were executed.

Alain Prost

pross·ie *n.* = **pross**

Prost /prost/, **Alain** (*b.* 1955) French racing driver and team owner. He was Formula One world champion (1985, 1986, 1989, and 1993) and four times runner-up.

pros·ta·cy·clin /pròstə sí kleen/ *n.* a type of unsaturated fatty acid (**prostaglandin**) that dilates blood vessels and inhibits the formation of blood clots [Late 20thC. Coined from PROSTATE + CYCLIC + -IN.]

pros·ta·glan·din /pròstə glánd'n/ *n.* an unsaturated fatty acid found in all mammals that resembles hormones in its activity, e.g., controlling smooth muscle contraction, blood pressure, inflammation, and body temperature [Mid-20thC. Coined from PROSTATE + GLAND + -IN.]

pros·tate /práws tàyt/ *n.* ANAT = **prostate gland** [Mid-17thC. Ultimately via modern Latin *prostata* from Greek *prostatēs* "guardian" (of the bladder), from *proïstanai* "to set before," from *histanai* "to cause to stand."] —**pros·tat·ic** /praw státtik/ *adj.*

pros·ta·tec·to·my /pròstə téktəmee/ (*plural* **-mies**) *n.* surgical removal of the whole or part of the prostate gland

pros·tate gland *n.* an O-shaped gland in males that surrounds the urethra below the bladder, secreting a fluid into the semen that acts to improve the movement and viability of sperm

pros·ta·tism /pròstə tìzzəm/ *n.* a disorder of the prostate gland, especially enlargement that blocks or inhibits urine flow

pros·ta·ti·tis /pròstə tī́tiss/ *n.* inflammation of the prostate gland

pros·the·sis /pros théessiss/ (*plural* **-ses** /-seez/) *n.* **1.** MED ARTIFICIAL BODY PART an artificial body part, e.g., an artificial limb or eye **2.** SURG REPLACEMENT OF BODY PART the branch of surgery concerned with replacing missing body parts with artificial devices **3.** LING = **prothesis** *n.* 1 [Mid-16thC. Via late Latin from Greek, "addition," from *prostithenai* "to add to," from *tithenai* "to place" (source of English *thesis*).] —**pros·thet·ic** /pros théttik/ *adj.* —**pros·thet·i·cal·ly** *adv.*

pros·thet·ic group *n.* the part of a conjugated protein that is not an amino acid, e.g., the lipid group in lipoprotein

pros·thet·ics /pros théttiks/ *n.* a branch of medicine dealing with the design, production, and use of artificial body parts (*takes a singular verb*) —**pros·the·tist** /prósthətist/ *n.*

pros·tho·don·tics /pròsthə dóntiks/ *n.* a branch of dentistry dealing with the replacement of teeth and parts of the jaw (*takes a singular verb*) [Mid-20thC. Coined from PROSTHESIS + -ODONTIA modeled on ORTHODONTICS.] —**pros·tho·don·tic** *adj.* —**pros·tho·don·tist** *n.*

pros·ti·tute /próstə to͞ot/ *n.* **1.** SOMEBODY PAID FOR SEXUAL INTERCOURSE somebody who receives money in return for sexual intercourse or other sex acts **2.** SOMEBODY WHO DEGRADES TALENT FOR MONEY somebody who uses a skill or ability in a way that is considered unworthy, usually for financial gain ■ *vt.* (**-tut·ed, -tut·ing, -tutes**) **1.** MISUSE SOMETHING FOR GAIN to use a skill or ability in a way that is considered unworthy, usually for financial gain ○ *He has been accused of prostituting his talent by appearing in TV commercials.* **2.** WORK OR OFFER SOMEBODY AS PROSTITUTE to work as a prostitute or offer somebody else for sexual intercourse or other sex acts in exchange for money [Mid-16thC. From the past participle of Latin *pro-*

stituere "to expose publicly, offer for sale," from *statuere* "to set, place" (source also of English *statute*).] —**pros·ti·tu·tor** *n.*

pros·ti·tu·tion /pròstə tóosh'n/ *n.* **1. WORK OF A PROSTITUTE** the act of engaging in sexual intercourse or performing other sex acts in exchange for money, or of offering another person for such purposes **2. MISUSE OF TALENT FOR GAIN** the use of a skill or ability in a way that is considered unworthy, usually for financial gain

pro·sto·mi·um /prō stṓmee əm/ (*plural* **-a** /-ə/) *n.* the part of the head of certain worms, including the earthworm, that is in front of the mouth [Late 19thC. Via modern Latin, from Greek *prostomion*, literally "something in front of the mouth," from *stoma* "mouth" (source also of English *stomach*).] —**pros·to·mi·al** *adj.*

pros·trate /pró stràyt/ *v.* (**-trat·ed, -trat·ing, -trates**) **1.** *vr.* **LIE FACE DOWNWARD** to lie flat on the face or bow very low, e.g., in worship or humility ○ *He prostrated himself before the soprano.* **2.** *vt.* **LAY SOMEBODY OR SOMETHING ON GROUND** to lay or throw somebody or something flat on the ground ○ *prostrated by a blow on the head* **3.** *vt.* **INCAPACITATE SOMEBODY** to make somebody physically or emotionally weak or helpless ○ *prostrated by illness* ■ *adj.* **1. LYING FLAT ON FACE** lying prone or stretched out with the face downward, e.g., in worship or submission **2. LYING DOWN** stretched out in a horizontal position, often because of illness or injury **3. DRAINED OF ENERGY** drained of physical strength or incapacitated by overexertion or powerful emotion ○ *prostrate with grief* **4.** BOT **GROWING ALONG THE GROUND** used to describe a plant that grows or trails along the ground ○ *a prostrate shrub* [14thC. From Latin *prostratus*, the past participle of *prosternere* "to throw in front of," from *sternere* "to spread out, lay down" (source also of English *strata*).] —**pros·tra·tion** /pro stráysh'n/ *n.*

pro·style /prṓ stìl/ *adj.* used to describe a building, e.g., a Greek temple, with a row of columns at the front [Late 17thC. From Latin *prostylos* "having pillars in front," from *stilus* "pointed writing instrument, stake" (source of English *style*).]

pros·y /prózee/ (**-i·er, -i·est**) *adj.* dull and commonplace, with no interesting, imaginative, or eloquent features —**pros·i·ly** *adv.* —**pros·i·ness** *n.*

Prot. *abbr.* Protestant

prot- *prefix.* = **proto-** (*used before vowels*)

pro·tac·tin·i·um /prō tak tínnee əm/ *n.* a toxic radioactive metallic chemical element found in uranium ores. Symbol **Pa** [Early 20thC. Coined from PROTO- + ACTINIUM, because the commonest isotope decays to give actinium.]

pro·tag·o·nist /prō tággənist/ *n.* **1.** LITERAT **MAIN CHARACTER** the most important character in a novel, play, story, or other literary work **2.** HIST **MAIN CHARACTER IN ANCIENT GREEK DRAMA** the first actor who interacted with the chorus in ancient Greek drama **3. LEADING FIGURE** a main participant in an event, e.g., a contest or dispute ○ *two protagonists in a long-running dispute* **4. SUPPORTER** an important or influential supporter or advocate of something such as a political or social issue ○ *an early protagonist of educational reform* [Late 17thC. From Greek *prōtagōnistēs* "actor who plays the chief part," from *agōnistes* "actor, competitor," from *agōn* "contest" (see AGONY).] —**pro·tag·o·nism** *n.*

pro·ta·mine /prṓtə meen, -min/ *n.* a water-soluble, strongly basic protein that has a low molecular weight, does not coagulate when heated, hydrolyzes to yield amino acids, in particular arginine, and is found in fish sperm. It is used therapeutically to control hemorrhage and diabetes.

pro·ta·no·pi·a /prōtə nṓpee ə/ *n.* a form of color blindness in which the retina fails to distinguish between red and green. ◊ **Daltonism** [Early 20thC. Coined from PROTO- (red being regarded as the first of the primary colors) + AN- + -OPIA.] —**pro·ta·nop·ic** /prōtə nóppik/ *adj.*

prot·a·sis /prótəssiss/ (*plural* **-ses** /-seez/) *n.* **1.** GRAM **CONDITIONAL CLAUSE** the part of a conditional sentence that contains the condition, e.g., "if he asks" in "if he asks, I'll tell him" **2.** LITERAT **FIRST PART OF POEM OR PLAY** the opening section of a narrative poem or play, especially a classical drama [Mid-16thC. Via Latin from Greek from *proteinein* "to put forward, propose," from *teinein* "to stretch."] —**pro·tat·ic** /prō táttik/ *adj.*

prote- *prefix.* = **proteo-**

pro·te·a /prṓtee ə/ (*plural* **-as** *or* **-a**) *n.* an evergreen shrub or tree of southern Africa, grown for its colorful bracts and dense flower heads. Genus: *Protea.* [Mid-18thC. From modern Latin, named for PROTEUS, from the variety of form in the genus.] —**pro·te·a·ceous** /prōtee áyshəss/ *adj.*

pro·te·an /prṓtee ən, prō tée ən/ *adj.* **1. ABLE TO CHANGE FORM** variable or continually changing in nature, appearance, or behavior **2. VERSATILE** showing great variety, diversity, or versatility

pro·te·ase /prṓtee àyz, -àyss/ *n.* an enzyme found in plant and animal cells that breaks down proteins or peptides by catalyzing the hydrolysis of peptide bonds

pro·te·ase in·hib·i·tor *n.* a compound, naturally occurring in plants, that breaks down the enzyme protease, inhibiting the replication and development of certain cells such as cancers and viruses, including the AIDS virus

pro·tect /prə tékt/ (**-tect·ed, -tect·ing, -tects**) *vt.* **1. KEEP SOMETHING OR SOMEBODY SAFE** to prevent somebody or something from being harmed or damaged **2.** ECON **HELP HOME INDUSTRIES BY TAXING IMPORTS** to help the industries in a country by imposing customs duties on imports from other countries [15thC. From Latin *protect-*, past participle stem of *protegere*, literally "to cover in front," from *tegere* "to cover" (source of English *integument*).]

WORD KEY: SYNONYMS

See Synonyms at ***safeguard***.

pro·tect·ant /prə téktənt/ *n.* a substance that prevents something from being damaged, e.g., a coating used to stop metal from rusting

pro·tect·ed /prə téktid/ *adj.* **1.** ECOL **ENDANGERED** legally classified as a species in danger of extinction **2. SHELTERED** sheltered from the elements **3.** COMPUT **LOCKED AGAINST UNAUTHORIZED CHANGES** locked against changes by unauthorized users of a computer program

pro·tec·tion /prə tékshən/ *n.* **1. SAFEGUARDING OF SOMEBODY OR SOMETHING** the act of preventing somebody or something from being harmed or damaged, or the state of being kept safe **2. SOMETHING THAT PROTECTS SOMEBODY OR SOMETHING** something that prevents somebody or something from being harmed or damaged **3.** INSUR **INSURANCE COVERAGE** an insurance company's agreement to pay compensation or costs if some specified undesirable event occurs **4.** CRIMINOL **PROMISE OF SAFETY FROM CRIMINAL ATTACK** a promise made by a gangster that somebody or something will not be harmed if money is paid, or the payment extorted in return for such a promise (*informal*) **5.** CRIMINOL **CRIMINALS' BRIBERY OF LAW ENFORCEMENT OFFICIALS** the bribery of law enforcement officials by criminals in an effort to escape prosecution, or the bribe paid (*informal*) **6. CONDOM** a form of contraception, usually a condom, used during sexual intercourse to prevent sperm or disease-causing organisms from entering the body **7. GUARANTEE OF FREEDOM AND SAFETY** a document that enables somebody to travel around in freedom and safety, especially in another country or in enemy territory **8.** ECON = **protectionism** **9.** MOUNTAINEERING **MOUNTAIN CLIMBERS' SAFETY EQUIPMENT** the safety equipment used by mountain climbers to keep them from falling, e.g., pitons, harnesses and ropes

pro·tec·tion·ism /prə tékshə nìzzəm/ *n.* the system of imposing duties on imports into a country in order to protect domestic industries —**pro·tec·tion·ist** *n., adj.*

pro·tec·tion mon·ey *n.* money paid to a gangster or other person who threatens to damage something or harm somebody unless the money is paid

pro·tec·tive /prə téktiv/ *adj.* **1. GIVING PROTECTION** preventing something or somebody from being harmed or damaged, or designed or intended for this purpose **2. TAKING GREAT CARE OF SOMEBODY** very anxious to protect or defend somebody or something, often excessively so ○ *She had always felt protective toward her younger brother.* **3.** ECON **INTENDED TO HELP DOMESTIC INDUSTRIES** intended to give an advantage to a country's domestic industries ○ *a protective tariff* ■ *n.* **SOMETHING THAT PROTECTS** something that prevents somebody or something from being harmed or damaged —**pro·tec·tive·ly** *adv.* —**pro·tec·tive·ness** *n.*

pro·tec·tive col·or·a·tion, pro·tec·tive col·or·ing *n.* the combination of surface colors and patterns of an animal that helps it blend into its surroundings and so evade predators

pro·tec·tive cus·to·dy *n.* detention in a particular place by the police in order to give protection from harm by other people

pro·tec·tor /prə téktər/ *n.* **1. SOMETHING THAT PROTECTS** something that prevents somebody or something from being harmed or damaged **2. SOMEBODY WHO PROTECTS** somebody who protects or defends somebody or something **3. pro·tec·tor, Pro·tec·tor SOMEBODY RULING IN PLACE OF MONARCH** somebody in charge of a country while the monarch is absent or too young or unfit to rule —**pro·tec·tor·al** *adj.* —**pro·tec·tor·ship** *n.*

Pro·tec·tor *n.* the title given to the head of the Commonwealth of England, Scotland, and Ireland during the period without a monarch that lasted from 1653 to 1659. The title was held by Oliver Cromwell (1653–58) and Richard Cromwell (1658–59).

pro·tec·tor·ate /prə téktərət/ *n.* **1. STATE DEPENDENT ON ANOTHER** a country or region that is defended and controlled by a more powerful state, or the relationship between the two **2. OFFICE OF PROTECTOR** the position or term of office of a protector

pro·té·gé /prṓtə zhày, prōtə zháy/ *n.* a young person who receives help, guidance, training, and support from somebody who is older and has more experience or influence [Late 18thC. From French, from the past participle of *protéger* "to protect," from Latin *protegere* (see PROTECT).]

pro·té·gée /prṓtə zhày, prōtə zháy/ *n.* a young woman who receives help, guidance, training, and support from somebody who is older and has more experience or influence [Late 18thC. From French, feminine of *protégé* (see PROTÉGÉ).]

pro·te·i plural of **proteus**

pro·te·id /prṓ tee id/ *n.* a salamander such as an olm or a mudpuppy that retains its larval form. Family: Proteidae. [Late 19thC. Formed from modern Latin *Proteus*, genus name, named for PROTEUS.]

pro·tein /prṓ teen/ *n.* **1.** BIOCHEM **COMPLEX NATURAL COMPOUND** a complex natural substance that has a high molecular weight and a globular or fibrous structure composed of amino acids linked by peptide bonds. Proteins are essential to the structure and function of all living cells and viruses. **2.** FOOD **FOOD RICH IN PROTEIN** a food source that is rich in protein molecules ○ *a protein-rich diet* [Mid-19thC. Via French from Greek *prōteios* "primary," from *prōtos* "first"; from its importance to the proper functioning of the body.] —**pro·tein·a·ceous** /prṑ tee náyshəss, prṓt'n-/ *adj.* —**pro·te·in·ic** /prṑ tee ínnik/ *adj.* —**pro·tein·ous** *adj.*

pro·tein·ase /prṓtee nàyss, -nàyz, prṓt'n àyss, -àyz/ *n.* an enzyme (**protease**) that catalyzes the hydrolysis of proteins into their component amino acids or simpler peptides

pro·tein·u·ri·a /prṑtee nóoree ə, prṑt'n-/ *n.* the presence of protein in the urine, usually indicating disease

pro tem /prō tém/ *adv., adj.* at the present time but not permanently [Shortening of PRO TEMPORE]

pro·te·ol·y·sis /prṑtee óllәssiss/ *n.* the breakdown of proteins or peptides into simpler molecules, e.g., in digestion —**pro·te·o·lyt·ic** /prṑtee ə líttik/ *adj.* —**pro·te·o·lyt·i·cal·ly** *adv.*

pro·te·ose /prṓtee ṑss/ *n.* a water-soluble protein derivative formed during hydrolytic processes such as digestion that does not coagulate when heated and precipitates if mixed with certain sulfur-containing compounds

Prot·er·o·zo·ic /prṑtərə zṓ ik/ *n.* the latter half of the Precambrian era, during which sea plants and animals first appeared [Early 20thC. Coined from PROTERO- + Greek *zōē* "life" + -IC.] —**Prot·er·o·zo·ic** *adj.*

pro·test *v.* /prə tést, pro-/ (**-test·ed, -test·ing, -tests**) **1.** *vti.* **COMPLAIN OR OBJECT STRONGLY** to express strong disapproval of or disagreement with something, or to refuse to obey or accept something, often by making a formal statement or taking action in public **2.** *vti.* **SAY FIRMLY THAT SOMETHING IS TRUE** to state or affirm something in strong or formal terms ○ *He continued to protest his innocence.* **3.** *vt.* **ANNOUNCE SOMETHING** to declare or proclaim something (*archaic*) ■ *n.* /prṓ tèst/ **1. STRONG COMPLAINT OR OBJECTION** an expression or display of strong disapproval of or disagreement with something, or a refusal to obey or accept something, often in the form of a public statement **2. DEMONSTRATION OF PUBLIC OPPOSITION OR DISAPPROVAL** an expression of strong opposition to or disapproval of something in the form of a public demonstration or other action ○ *student protests* **3.** LAW **CREDITOR'S FORMAL STATEMENT** a formal statement drawn up by a notary on behalf of a creditor, declaring that somebody has refused to honor a bill **4. TAXPAYER'S FORMAL DECLARATION** a taxpayer's formal declaration reserving the right to contest a given tax as either illegal or excessive (*formal*) [14thC. Via French from, ultimately, Latin *protestari* "to declare publicly," from *testari* "to declare" (source of English *testament*).] —**prot·es·tant** *n., adj.* —**pro·test·er** *n.* —**pro·test·ing·ly** *adv.*

WORD KEY: SYNONYMS

See Synonyms at ***complain*** and ***object***.

Prot·es·tant /próttəstənt/ *n.* a member or adherent of any denomination of the Western Christian church that rejects papal authority and some fundamental Roman Catholic doctrines, and believes in justification by faith. The formulation of Protestants' beliefs began with the Reformation in the 16th century. —**Prot·es·tant** *adj.*

Prot·es·tant E·pis·co·pal Church *n.* a Protestant church that began in the 18th century as an affiliated entity within the Church of England but later declared its independence

Prot·es·tant·ism /próttəstən tìzzəm/ *n.* **1. BELIEF IN PROTESTANT DOCTRINES** adherence to Protestant beliefs **2. RELIGIOUS MOVEMENT OPPOSING ROMAN CATHOLICISM** a Christian religious movement originating in the 16th century from Martin Luther's attack on Roman Catholic doctrine. It grew to encompass many churches and denominations denying papal authority and believing in justification by faith. **3. ALL PROTESTANT CHURCHES** the Protestant churches as a group

prot·es·ta·tion /pròttə stáysh'n/ *n.* **1. FORMAL AFFIRMATION** a strong or firm declaration that something is true or false (*often used in the plural*) ○ *protestations of loyalty* **2. ACT OF COMPLAINING OR OBJECTING** the expression of strong disapproval of or disagreement with something **3. COMPLAINT OR OBJECTION** an individual expression of strong disapproval of or disagreement with something

pro·test vote *n.* the casting of a vote for somebody who cannot win, done in order to register the voter's disgust with the candidates or parties standing for election

pro·te·us /prṓtee əss/ (*plural* **-i** /prṓtee ī/) *n.* a rod-shaped bacterium associated with enteritis and urinary tract infections. Genus: *Proteus.* [Early 19thC. From modern Latin, named for PROTEUS.]

Pro·te·us /prṓtee əss/ *n.* **1. GREEK SEA GOD** in Greek mythology, a prophetic sea god who could change his shape at will **2. SECOND-LARGEST MOON OF NEPTUNE** the second-largest natural satellite of Neptune, discovered in 1989 by Voyager 2. It is irregular in shape, having a maximum dimension of approximately 440 km (275 mi.).

pro·tha·la·mi·on /prṑthə láymee ən/ (*plural* **-a** /-ə/), **pro·tha·la·mi·um** /-mee əm/ (*plural* **-a**) *n.* a song or poem written or performed in celebration of a marriage (*formal*) [Late 16thC. From ***"Prothalamion"***, a poem by Spenser (1597), modeled on *epithalamion*, a variant of EPITHALAMIUM.]

pro·thal·lus /prō thálləss/ (*plural* **-li** /-lī/), **pro·thal·li·um** /prō thállee əm/ (*plural* **-a** /-ə/) *n.* a flat green organ bearing the reproductive organs (**gametophytes**) of ferns and related plants [Mid-19thC. From modern Latin, from *pro-* "before" + Greek *thallos* "green shoot."] —**pro·thal·li·al** *adj.* —**pro·thal·lic** *adj.*

proth·e·sis /próthəssiss/ (*plural* **-ses** /-seez/) *n.* **1.** LING **ADDITION OF SYLLABLE TO HELP PRONUNCIATION** the addition of a sound or sounds at the beginning of a word to make the word easier to pronounce **2.** CHR **PREPARATIONS FOR OFFERING EUCHARIST** the preparations for the offering of the Eucharist in the Eastern Orthodox Church [Late 16thC. From Greek, "a placing before or in public," from *thesis* "placing" (source of English *thesis*).] —**pro·thet·ic** /prə théttik/ *adj.* —**pro·thet·i·cal·ly** *adv.*

pro·thon·o·tar·y /prō thónnə tèrree, prṑthə nṓtəree/ (*plural* **-ies**), **pro·ton·o·tar·y** /-tónnə-, prṑtə-/ (*plural* **-ies**) *n.* **1.** LAW **CHIEF CLERK IN COURT** the chief clerk in some courts of law **2. pro·thon·o·tar·y, pro·thon·o·tar·y ap·os·tol·ic** (*plural* **pro·thon·o·tar·ies ap·os·tol·ic**) **ROMAN CATHOLIC CHURCH OFFICIAL** in the Roman Catholic Church, any one of twelve officials who can act as a notary to authenticate papal proceedings, documents, and acts [15thC. Via medieval Latin from Greek *prōto* + Latin *notarios* "first notary," from *notarios* (see NOTARY).] —**pro·thon·o·tar·i·al** /prō thònnə téree əl, prṑthənə térree əl/ *adj.*

pro·thon·o·tar·y war·bler *n.* a small songbird of eastern North America with blue-gray wings and a bright golden yellow body. Latin name: *Protonotaria citrea.*

pro·tho·ra·ces plural of **prothorax**

pro·tho·rac·ic /prṑthə rássik/ *adj.* relating to the front segment (**prothorax**) of the thorax of an insect

pro·tho·rac·ic gland *n.* a gland in insects that secretes the steroid hormone ecdysone, responsible for controlling molting and metamorphosis

pro·tho·rax /prō tháw ràks/ (*plural* **-rax·es** *or* **-ra·ces** /-rə sèez/) *n.* the front segment of the thorax of an insect, where the first pair of legs is located [Early 19thC. From modern Latin, literally "thorax in front," from *thorax* "thorax."]

pro·throm·bin /prō thrómbin/ *n.* a plasma protein produced in the liver and converted to thrombin during the clotting of blood

pro·tist /prṓtist/ *n.* an organism belonging to the kingdom that includes protozoans, bacteria, and single-celled algae and fungi. Kingdom: *Protista.* [Late 19thC. Formed from modern Latin *Protista*, former kingdom name, ultimately from Greek *prōtistos* "very first," from *prōtos* "first."] —**pro·tis·tan** /prṓtistən/ *adj.* —**pro·tis·tol·o·gy** /prṑtis tólləjee/ *n.*

pro·ti·um /prṓtee əm, prṓsh-/ *n.* the most common and lightest isotope of hydrogen, with atomic mass 1 [Mid-20thC. Coined from Greek *prōtos* "first" + -IUM.]

proto- *prefix.* **1.** first in time, earliest ○ *protolithic* ○ *protomartyr* **2.** original, ancestral ○ *protostar* ○ *Proto-Norse* **3.** first in a series, having the least amount of a particular element or radical ○ *protactinium* [From Greek *prōtos*; ultimately related to *pro* (see PRO[2])]

Pro·to-Al·gon·qui·an *n.* the reconstructed hypothetical language that is believed to be the ancestor of the Algonquian-Wakasan family of Native American languages —**Pro·to-Al·gon·qui·an** *adj.*

pro·to·col /prṓtə kàwl/ *n.* **1. ETIQUETTE OF STATE OCCASIONS** the rules or conventions of correct behavior on official or ceremonial occasions **2. CODE OF CONDUCT** the rules of correct or appropriate behavior for a particular group of people or in a particular situation **3.** INTERNAT REL **INTERNATIONAL AGREEMENT** a formal agreement between states or nations **4. RECORD OR DRAFT OF AGREEMENT** a written record or preliminary draft of a treaty or other agreement **5.** COMPUT **RULES FOR EXCHANGING INFORMATION BETWEEN COMPUTERS** a set of technical rules about how information should be transmitted and received using computers **6.** PHILOSOPHY = **protocol statement 7.** MED, SCI **RESEARCH PLAN** the detailed plan of a scientific experiment, medical trial, or other piece of research ■ *v.* (**-coled** *or* **-colled, -col·ing** *or* **-col·ling, -cols**) **1.** *vi.* **PREPARE OR ISSUE PROTOCOL** to draw up or issue a protocol or protocols **2.** *vt.* **RECORD SOMETHING IN PROTOCOL** to record something in a protocol [15thC. Directly and via Old French from medieval Latin from Greek *prōtokollon* "first leaf of a book." The modern meaning evolved via "draft of a diplomatic document."]

pro·to·col state·ment *n.* a statement that can be immediately verified by experience

pro·to·con·ti·nent /prṑtō kóntənənt/ *n.* **1. LANDMASS THAT COULD BECOME CONTINENT** a large, unbroken mass of land capable of becoming a major continent **2.** = **supercontinent**

pro·to·derm /prṓtə dùrm/ *n.* BOT = **dermatogen** —**pro·to·derm·al** /prṑtə dúrməl/ *adj.*

pro·to·gal·ax·y /prṑ tō gálləksee/ (*plural* **-ies**) *n.* a hypothetical cloud of gas believed to have been formed about 14 billion years ago from dark matter, neutral hydrogen, and helium, from which all the galaxies and stars evolved

Pro·to-Ger·man·ic *n.* the reconstructed hypothetical language that is believed to be the ancestor of the Germanic branch of the Indo-European family of languages —**Proto-Ger·man·ic** *adj.*

pro·to·his·to·ry /prṑ tō hístəree, -histree/ *n.* the archeological period of human development, before recorded history (*dated*) —**pro·to·his·tor·ic** /prṑ tō his táwrik/ *adj.*

pro·to·hu·man /prṑ tō hyóomən/ *n.* an extinct hominid or primate that has some of the characteristics of modern people —**pro·to·hu·man** *adj.*

Pro·to-In·do-Eur·o·pe·an *n.* the reconstructed hypothetical language that is believed to be the ancestor of all the Indo-European languages —**Pro·to-In·do-Eur·o·pe·an** *adj.*

pro·to·in·dus·tri·al·i·za·tion /prṑ tō in dustree əli zàysh'n/ *n.* the preliminary shift from an agricultural to an industrial economy, marked by the rapid spread of home-based manufacturing

pro·to·lan·guage /prṑ tō láng gwij/ *n.* a recorded or reconstructed language that is the ancestor of another language or family of languages

pro·to·lith·ic /prṑtə líthik/ *adj.* relating to the earliest part of the Stone Age [Late 19thC. Coined from PROTO- + -LITHIC on the model of NEOLITHIC.]

pro·to·mar·tyr /prṑ tō maártər/ *n.* **1. FIRST CHRISTIAN MARTYR** St. Stephen, the first Christian martyr. **2. FIRST MARTYR FOR CAUSE** the first person to die for a particular cause

pro·to·mor·phic /prṑtə máwrfik/ *adj.* having a primitive structure

pro·ton /prṓ tòn/ *n.* a stable elementary particle of the baryon family that is a component of all atomic nuclei and carries a positive charge equal to that of the electron's negative charge. Symbol **p** [Late 19thC. From Greek *prōton*, a form of *prōtos* "first, elementary."] —**pro·ton·ic** /prō tónnik/ *adj.*

pro·to·ne·ma /prṑtə néemə/ (*plural* **-ma·ta** /-mətə/) *n.* the primary thread-shaped structure of mosses and certain liverworts that results from the germination of a spore and gives rise to a new plant [Mid-19thC. Coined from PROTO- + Greek *nēma* "thread."] —**pro·to·ne·mal** *adj.*

pro·ton num·ber *n.* PHYS = **atomic number**

Pro·to-Norse *n.* the form of the North Germanic language used in parts of Scandinavia, especially Norway and Iceland, until about the 8th century A.D. —**Pro·to-Norse** *adj.*

pro·ton·o·tar·y *n.* = **prothonotary**

pro·ton syn·chro·tron *n.* a circular very high-energy particle accelerator that accelerates protons through the action of magnetic fields and a high-frequency electric field

pro·to·plan·et /prṓtə plànnət/ *n.* a theoretical mass of gas in the clouds of gas and dust around a star that is believed to develop into a planet

pro·to·plasm /prṓtə plàzzəm/ *n.* the colorless liquid or colloidal contents of a living cell, composed of proteins, fats, and other organic substances in water, and including the nucleus and cytoplasm [Mid-19thC. From German *Protoplasma*, literally "first created thing," from Greek *plasma* (see PLASMA).] —**pro·to·plas·mic** /prṑtə plázmik/ *adj.*

pro·to·plast /prṓtə plàst/ *n.* the living substance of a plant or bacterial cell, excluding the cell wall [Mid-16thC. Directly or via French from late Latin *protoplastus* "first created being," from Greek *prōtoplastos*, from *plastos* "formed," from *plassein* "to form."] —**pro·to·plas·tic** /prṑtə plástik/ *adj.*

pro·to·por·phy·rin /prṑ tō páwrfərin/ *n.* a purple porphyrin acid that combines with iron to form the deep red of iron-containing proteins, e.g., hemoglobin and cytochrome. Formula: $C_{34}H_{34}N_4O_4$.

Pro·to·se·mit·ic /prṑ tō sə míttik/ *n.* the hypothetical reconstructed language that is believed to be the ancestor of the Semitic branch of the Afro-Asiatic family of languages —**Pro·to·se·mit·ic** *adj.*

pro·to·star /prṓtə staàr/ *n.* an interstellar cloud of gas and dust thought to develop into a star when it has collapsed sufficiently for nuclear reactions to begin

pro·to·stele /prṓtə stèel, prṑtə steélee/ *n.* the conducting tissue (**stele**) of stems and roots, consisting of a core of xylem surrounded by phloem —**pro·to·ste·lic** /prṑtə steélik/ *adj.*

pro·to·stome /prṓtə stṑm/ *n.* an invertebrate animal such as a mollusk or arthropod in which the mouth forms directly from the blastopore

pro·to·the·ri·an /prṑtō théeree ən/ *n.* an echidna, platypus, or any of the many extinct related mammals. Subclass: Prototheria. [Late 19thC. Formed from PROTO- + Greek *therion* "wild animal."]

pro·to·troph /prṓtə tròf/ *n.* an organism such as a bacterium or fungus that can grow without having to find nutrients in its surrounding environment. ◊ **auxotroph**

pro·to·tro·phic /prṑtō trṓffik/ *adj.* having the same nutritional needs and metabolic characteristics as the wild parent strain

pro·to·type /prṓtə tīp/ *n.* **1. ORIGINAL USED AS MODEL** something having the essential features of a subsequent type, and on which later forms are modeled **2. STANDARD EXAMPLE** a standard example of a particular kind, class, or group **3. FULL-SIZE FUNCTIONAL MODEL** a first full-size functional model to be manufactured, e.g., of a car or a machine ○ *A prototype of the new convertible will be on display at the Motor Show.* **4.** BIOL **PRIMITIVE FORM** a primitive form believed to be the original type of a species or group, exhibiting the essential features of the later type ■ *vti.* **(-typed, -typ·ing, -types) CREATE A PROTOTYPE** to create a prototype of something [Early 17thC. Via French from late Latin *prototypus* "original, primitive" and Greek *prototypon* "primitive form," from *proto* "first" + *typos* "impression."] —**pro·to·typ·al** /prṓtə tīp'l/ *adj.* —**pro·to·typ·ic** /-típpik/ *adj.* —**pro·to·typ·i·cal** *adj.*

pro·tox·ide /prō tók sīd/ *n.* an oxide of an element that has the lowest proportion of oxygen of all the oxides of that element

pro·to·xy·lem /prṓtə zīləm/ *n.* the part of the water-carrying tissue **(xylem)** of a plant that develops first and has narrow thin-walled cells

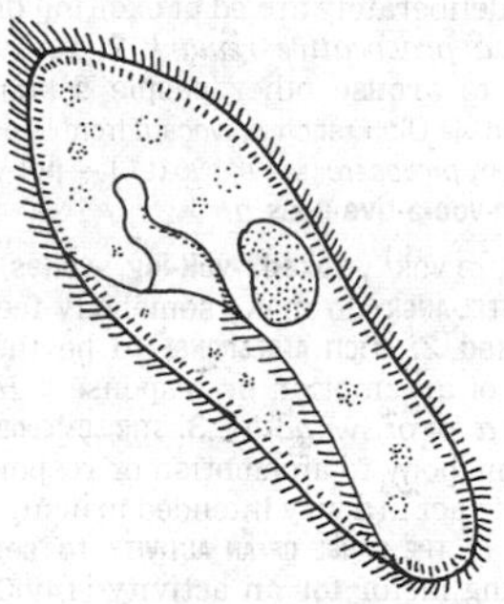

Protozoan

pro·to·zo·an /prṓtə zṓ ən/ (*plural* **-ans** *or* **-a** /-ə/), **pro·to·zo·on** /-òn/ (*plural* **-ons** *or* **-a**) *n.* a one-celled organism such as an amoeba, ciliate, or flagellate that can move and feeds on organic compounds of nitrogen and carbon. Phylum: Protozoa. [Mid-19thC. Formed from modern Latin *Protozoa*, literally "first animals," from Greek *zōia*, plural of *zōion* "animal."] —**pro·to·zo·an** *adj.* —**pro·to·zo·ic** *adj.*

pro·to·zo·ol·o·gy /prṓtə zō óllәjee/ *n.* the branch of zoology that studies protozoans [Early 20thC. Formed from modern Latin *Protozoa* (see PROTOZOAN).] —**pro·to·zo·o·log·i·cal** /prṓtə zṓ ə lójjik'l/ *adj.* —**pro·to·zo·ol·o·gist** /prṓtə zō óllәjist/ *n.*

pro·tract /prō trákt, prə-/ **(-tract·ed, -tract·ing, -tracts)** *vt.* **1. MAKE SOMETHING LAST** to make something last longer **2.** ANAT **EXTEND A BODY PART** to extend or lengthen a body part **3.** MATH **PLOT AND DRAW LINES** to plot lines and draw them using a scale and protractor [Mid-16thC. Back-formation from PROTRACTION.] —**pro·trac·tive** *adj.*

pro·tract·ed /prō tráktəd, prə-/ *adj.* lasting or drawn out for a long time —**pro·tract·ed·ly** *adv.* —**pro·tract·ed·ness** *n.*

pro·trac·tile /prō trákt'l, prə-/ *adj.* **1. THAT CAN BE PROTRUDED** capable of being thrust out **2.** ZOOL = **protrusile**

pro·trac·tion /prō trákshən, prə-/ *n.* **1. PROTRACTING OF SOMETHING** the act of protracting something **2. SCALE DRAWING OF BUILDING OR LAND** the act of drawing something such as a building or an area of land to scale, or a drawing of this kind

pro·trac·tor /prō tráktər, prə-/ *n.* **1.** GEOM **INSTRUMENT FOR MEASURING ANGLES** an instrument shaped like a semicircle marked with the degrees of a circle, used to measure or mark out angles **2. LENGTHENER** somebody or something that extends or lengthens something else **3.** ANAT **MUSCLE THAT EXTENDS BODY PART** a muscle with the function of extending a body part

pro·trude /prō trood/ **(-trud·ed, -trud·ing, -trudes)** *vti.* to stick out from the surroundings, or make something stick out [Early 17thC. From Latin *protrudere* "to thrust forward," from *trudere* "to thrust." Ultimately from an Indo-European word that is also the ancestor of English *thrust*.] —**pro·trud·a·ble** *adj.* —**pro·trud·ent** *adj.*

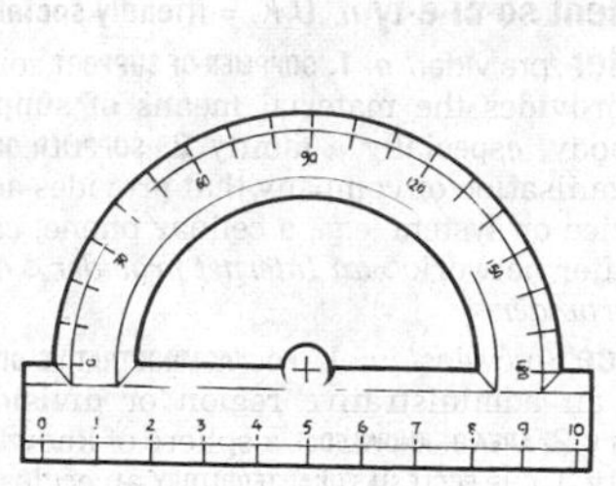

Protractor

pro·tru·sile /prō tróoss'l, prō tróo sīl/, **pro·tru·si·ble** /prō tróossib'l/ *adj.* used to describe an organ or appendage that can be quickly extended, as can the mouth of many fishes or the proboscis of nemertine worms [Mid-19thC. Formed from the Latin stem *protrus-* (see PROTRUSION).]

pro·tru·sion /prō tróozh'n/ *n.* **1. ACT OF PROTRUDING** the act of protruding, or the state of being protruded **2. SOMETHING THAT PROTRUDES** something that sticks out from its surroundings [Mid-17thC. From the medieval Latin stem *protrusion-*, from Latin *protrus-*, past participle stem of *protrudere* (see PROTRUDE).]

pro·tru·sive /prō tróossiv/ *adj.* **1. JUTTING OUT** jutting or sticking out **2. FORWARD IN MANNER** having a brash forward manner [Late 17thC. Formed from the Latin stem *protrus-* (see PROTRUSION).] —**pro·tru·sive·ly** *adv.* —**pro·tru·sive·ness** *n.*

pro·tu·ber·ance /prō tóobərəns/, **pro·tu·ber·an·cy** /-see/ (*plural* **-cies**) *n.* **1. SOMETHING THAT STICKS OUT** something, or a part of something, that sticks out from its surroundings ○ *the small fleshy protuberance that dangles down from the soft palate* **2. FACT OF STICKING OUT** the fact or condition of sticking out or being swollen or bulging [Mid-17thC. Formed from *protuberant* "bulging out," from, ultimately, late Latin *protuberare*, literally "to swell in front," from *tuber* "lump."]

pro·tu·ber·ant /prō tóobərənt/ *adj.* projecting out from the surroundings in a bulging, rounded manner [Mid-17thC. Formed from late Latin *protuberant-*, present participle stem of *protuberare*, literally "to swell forward," from *tuber* "lump."] —**pro·tu·ber·ant·ly** *adv.*

pro·tu·ber·ate /prō tóobə ràyt/ **(-at·ed, -at·ing, -ates)** *vi.* to swell out from surroundings [Late 16thC. From Latin *protuberat-*, past participle stem of *protuberare* (see PROTUBERANT).]

pro·tyle /prṓ tīl/ *n.* an imaginary substance from which the chemical elements were supposed to have been formed [Late 19thC. Formed from PROTO- + Greek *hulē* "matter, hyle."]

proud /prowd/ *adj.* **1. PLEASED AND SATISFIED** feeling pleased and satisfied, e.g., about having done something or about owning something ○ *I am very proud to be here today to give you this award.* **2. FOSTERING FEELINGS OF PRIDE** characterized by feelings of pride ○ *the proudest moment in your life* **3. HAVING SELF-RESPECT** having a proper amount of self-respect **4. ARROGANT** having an exaggerated opinion of personal worth or abilities **5. IMPRESSIVE** looking magnificent and impressive, or behaving in an impressive way ○ *the proud peaks of the Rockies* **6.** *Midwest, Southern U.S.* **FEELING PLEASED** feeling pleased, glad, or delighted **7. HIGH-SPIRITED** high-spirited and strong ○ *a proud horse* [12thC. Via Old French *prud*, from Latin *prodesse* "to be beneficial," literally "to be for," from *esse* "to be" (source of English *essence*).] —**proud·ly** *adv.* —**proud·ness** *n.* ◇ **do somebody proud 1.** to treat somebody well and generously **2.** to bring honor or distinction to somebody

WORD KEY: SYNONYMS

proud, arrogant, conceited, egotistical, vain

CORE MEANING: describing somebody who is pleased with himself or herself

proud can be used to describe somebody who is rightly self-satisfied. It can also be used disapprovingly to describe somebody who shows a lack of humility or who has an inordinately high opinion of himself or herself; **arrogant** used disapprovingly to describe somebody who seems inordinately self-confident or pleased with his or her achievements and who lacks humility; **conceited** used to describe somebody who displays excessive satisfaction and smugness with regard to his or her appearance or achievements, often combined with a rather superior attitude toward others; **egotistical** used to describe somebody who has an inflated sense of his or her own importance, especially when this is shown through constantly talking or thinking about himself or herself; **vain** used to describe somebody who shows an excessive concern with and admiration for his or her personal appearance.

AKG London

Marcel Proust

Proust /proost/, **Marcel** (1871–1922) French novelist. He is author of a 13-volume series of partly autobiographical novels, *À la recherche du temps perdu* (1913–27). —**Prous·ti·an** *adj.*

prous·tite /próo stīt/ *n.* a deep red mineral consisting of silver arsenic sulfide. It occurs in crystals or masses and is an ore of silver. Formula: Ag_3AsS_3. [Mid-19thC. Named for the French chemist, Joseph L. *Proust* (1754–1826).]

prov. *abbr.* **1.** province **2.** provincial **3.** provisional

Prov. *abbr.* **1.** Provost **2.** BIBLE Proverbs **3.** Provençal

prove /proov/ **(proved, proved** *or* **prov·en** /próovən/, **prov·ing, proves)** *v.* **1.** *vt.* **ESTABLISH TRUTH OF SOMETHING** to establish the truth or existence of something by providing evidence or argument **2.** *vt.* CHEM, MINERALS **TEST SOMETHING TO DETERMINE CHARACTERISTICS** to subject something to scientific analysis to determine its worth or characteristics **3.** *vr.* **DEMONSTRATE COMPETENCE** to show yourself to be competent and worthy **4.** *vt.* MATH **CHECK A MATHEMATICAL RESULT** to verify that a mathematical result is correct **5.** *vt.* MATH **DEMONSTRATE THE TRUTH OF A HYPOTHESIS** to demonstrate that a hypothesis or proposition is true **6.** *vt.* LAW **DEMONSTRATE THAT A WILL IS GENUINE** to establish that a will is genuine or valid **7.** *vt.* PRINTING, ARTS **MAKE AN IMPRESSION OF SOMETHING** to make a test impression of a negative, etching, or type **8.** *vi.* FOOD **RISE IN WARM PLACE** to rise in a warm place before being baked (*refers to dough*) **9.** *vti.* **TURN OUT TO BE** to turn out to be a particular thing or a thing of a particular character after time or testing [12thC. Via Old French *prover* from Latin *probare*, literally "to prove to be good," from *probus* "good."] —**prov·a·bil·i·ty** /próovə bíllətee/ *n.* —**prov·a·ble** /próovəb'l/ *adj.* —**prov·a·bly** *adv.*

WORD KEY: USAGE

Form of the past participle: The past participles ***proved*** and ***proven*** are both often used as verbs, with auxiliaries, and also as predicate adjectives: whether to say, for example, *We have proved our case* or *We have proven our case*, and *The case is proved* or *The case is proven* is a matter of choice. ***Proved*** is not, however, ordinarily employed as an adjective preceding a noun: *proven case* is the standard form.

WORD KEY: ORIGIN

The Latin word *probus*, from which ***prove*** is derived, is also the source of English *approve, probable, probe, probity, proof, reprobate*, and *reprove*.

prov·en /próovən/ *adj.* **1. TRIED AND TESTED** done or used before and known to work or be satisfactory **2.** LAW **PROVED TRUE** having been demonstrated beyond a doubt to be true —**prov·en·ly** *adv.*

prov·e·nance /próvvənəns, -naans/ *n.* **1. ORIGIN** the place of origin of something **2. SOURCE AND OWNERSHIP HISTORY** the source and ownership history of a work of art or literature, or of an archeological find [Late 18thC. Via French from Latin *provenire* "to arise," literally "to come forth," from *venire* "to come."]

WORD KEY: SYNONYMS

See Synonyms at ***origin***.

Pro·ven·çal /pròvən saál, pròvv-/ *adj.* **OF PROVENCE** relating to Provence, or its people or culture ■ *n.* **1. LANGUAGE OF SE FRANCE** a Romance language spoken in southeastern parts of France. It is closely related to French, Italian, and Catalan. Provençal is spoken by about four million people. **2. SOMEBODY FROM PROVENCE** somebody who was born, raised or who lives in, Provence [Late 16thC. Via French from Latin *provincialis* "provincial," from *provincia* "province," a colloquial name for southern Gaul during Roman rule.]

Pro·ven·çale /pròvən saál, pròvv-/ *adj.* prepared with olive oil, garlic, herbs, and tomatoes [Mid-19thC. From French *à la provençale* "in the Provençal manner."]

Pro·vence /prə vaánss/ region in southeastern France, bordering the Mediterranean Sea. It was an ancient Roman province.

prov·en·der /próvvəndər/ *n.* **1. FOOD FOR LIVESTOCK** food for livestock, especially hay or other dry fodder (*archaic*) **2. FOOD** food (*literary or humorous*) [14thC. From Old French *provendre*, variant of *provende*, alteration (influenced by Latin *providere* "to supply") of *praebenda* "things to be given."]

pro·ve·nience /prō veénee əns/ *n.* = **provenance** [Late 19thC. Formed from Latin *provenient-*, present participle stem of *provenire* (see PROVENANCE).]

pro·ven·tric·u·lus /prō ven tríkyələss/ (*plural* **-li** /-lī/) *n.* **1.** BIRDS **PART OF BIRD'S STOMACH** the first part of a bird's stomach, where digestive enzymes are mixed with food before it goes to the gizzard. It is analogous to the gizzard in insects and crustaceans. **2.** ZOOL **PART OF INVERTEBRATE'S STOMACH** the thin-walled section of the stomach of some invertebrates **3.** INSECTS **PART OF INSECT'S STOMACH** the part of the foregut in some insects that has teeth or plates for grinding food —**pro·ven·tric·u·lar** *adj.*

prov·erb /pró vùrb/ *n.* a short well-known saying that expresses an obvious truth and often offers advice [14thC. Via Old French *proverbe* from Latin *proverbium* "saying, saw," from *pro* "forth" + *verbum* "word."]

pro·ver·bi·al /prə vúrbee əl/ *adj.* **1. EXPRESSED AS A PROVERB** expressed as a proverb, or resembling a proverb either in form or because of being widely known or referred to **2. USED IN A PROVERB** often referred to metaphorically or as another descriptive device ○ *She was behaving like the proverbial cat on hot bricks.* —**pro·ver·bi·al·ly** *adv.*

Prov·erbs /pró vùrbz/ *n.* a book of the Bible made up of the proverbs of wise men, including Solomon

pro·vide /prə vīd/ (**-vid·ed, -vid·ing, -vides**) *v.* **1.** *vt.* **SUPPLY SOMEBODY WITH SOMETHING** to supply somebody with or be a source of something needed or wanted **2.** *vt.* **MAKE SOMETHING AVAILABLE** to make something available to somebody **3.** *vt.* LAW **REQUIRE SOMETHING AS A CONDITION** to require something in advance as a condition or as part of a contract **4.** *vi.* **TAKE PRECAUTIONS** to take precautions to prevent harm or bring about good **5.** *vi.* **SUPPLY MEANS OF SUPPORT** to supply the material means of support for somebody ○ *provides for his children* **6.** *vt.* **PREPARE SOMETHING IN ADVANCE** to get something ready in advance (*archaic*) [15thC. From Latin *providere* "to prepare in advance, supply," literally "to see ahead," from *videre* "to see."]

prov·i·dence /próvvid'ns, -dèns/ *n.* **1. prov·i·dence, Prov·i·dence GOD'S GUIDANCE** the wisdom, care, and guidance believed to be provided by God **2. prov·i·dence, Prov·i·dence GOD** God perceived as a caring force guiding humankind **3. GOOD JUDGMENT AND MANAGEMENT** good judgment and foresight in the management of affairs or resources [14thC. Directly and via Old French from Latin *providentia* "foresight," from *provident-*, the present participle stem of *providere* "to provide."]

Prov·i·dence /próvvidənss/ capital of Rhode Island and its largest city, located in the northeastern part of the state. Population: 152,558 (1996).

prov·i·dent /próvvid'nt, -dènt/ *adj.* **1. PREPARING FOR THE FUTURE** carefully preparing for future needs **2. FRUGAL** economical in the use of resources [15thC. From Latin *provident-*, the present participle stem of *providere* "to prepare in advance, supply."]

prov·i·den·tial /pròvvi dénshəl/ *adj.* **1. OF PROVIDENCE** relating to or believed to be determined by providence **2. VERY LUCKY** so lucky that it seems determined by providence

WORD KEY: SYNONYMS

See Synonyms at ***lucky***.

prov·i·dent so·ci·e·ty *n. U.K.* = **friendly society**

pro·vi·der /prə vīdər/ *n.* **1. SUPPLIER OF SUPPORT** somebody who provides the material means of support for somebody, especially a family **2. SUPPLIER OF SERVICE** an organisation or company that provides access to a service or system, e.g., a celluar phone, cable, or computer network ○ *an Internet provider* ○ *a health care provider*

prov·ince /próvvins/ *n.* **1.** POL **ADMINISTRATIVE DIVISION OF NATION** an administrative region or division of a country **2. AREA OF KNOWLEDGE** a sphere of knowledge or activity **3.** CHR **ECCLESIASTICAL TERRITORY** an ecclesiastical territory of more than two dioceses, under the jurisdiction of an archbishop or metropolitan **4.** HIST **REGION OF ROMAN EMPIRE** a country or region controlled by the ancient Roman Empire through an appointed governor **5.** ECOL **CATEGORY FOR RANKING VEGETATION** a category superior to a subregion and subordinate to a subkingdom, used in certain biogeographical systems for ranking global vegetation types ■ **prov·inc·es** *npl.* **NONMETROPOLITAN PARTS OF NATION** the parts of a country exclusive of the capital and larger cities [14thC. Directly and via Old French from Latin *provincia* "Roman territory," from *pro* "before" + *vincere* "to conquer."]

Prov·ince·town /próvvins town/ town in eastern Massachusetts, at the tip of Cape Cod, north of Dennis. It is an artists' colony, and the site of the Pilgrims' first landing in 1620. Population: 3,681 (1996).

pro·vin·cial /prə vínshəl/ *adj.* **1. OF A PROVINCE** belonging to or coming from a province **2. UNSOPHISTICATED AND NARROW-MINDED** unsophisticated and unwilling to accept new ideas or ways of thinking (*disapproving*) **3.** ARCHIT, FURNITURE **SIMPLE AND PLAIN** in a simple and plain decorative style ■ *n.* **1. SOMEBODY FROM PROVINCES** somebody from the provinces, as opposed to somebody from a city or the capital **2. UNSOPHISTICATED PERSON** an unsophisticated or narrow-minded person (*disapproving*) **3.** CHR **HEAD OF A PROVINCE** the head of an ecclesiastical province or of a religious order in a province [14thC. Directly and via Old French from Latin *provincialis*, from *provincia* (see PROVINCE).] —**pro·vin·ci·al·i·ty** /prə vìnshee álləteе/ *n.* —**pro·vin·cial·ly** /prə vínshəlee/ *adv.*

pro·vin·cial court *n.* a Canadian court that deals with less serious offenses and whose judges are appointed and paid by the province

pro·vin·cial·ism /prə vínshə lìzzəm/ *n.* **1. NARROW-MINDED AND UNSOPHISTICATED ATTITUDE** narrowness in outlook and lack of sophistication (*disapproving*) **2. SOMETHING FROM A PROVINCE** something, e.g., a word, phrase, trait, or custom, that originates in a province

pro·vin·cial po·lice *n.* a Canadian police force that has jurisdiction within a province but not in urban areas that have their own municipal police

prov·ing ground *n.* a place or situation in which somebody or something new is tried out or tested

pro·vi·rus /prō vīrəss, prō vīrəss/ *n.* a form of a virus that is integrated into the genetic material of the host and passed on from one cell generation to the next

pro·vi·sion /prə vízh'n/ *n.* **1. SUPPLYING OF SOMETHING** the act of providing or supplying something **2. ACTION TAKEN TO PREPARE** a preparatory step taken to meet a possible or expected need ○ *No provision has been made for people with disabilities.* **3.** LAW **LEGAL CLAUSE STATING CONDITION** a clause in a law or contract stating that a particular condition must be met **4. SOMETHING PROVIDED** something provided or supplied ■ **pro·vi·sions** *npl.* **FOOD AND OTHER SUPPLIES** supplies of food and other things required, especially for a journey ■ *vt.* (**-sioned, -sion·ing, -sions**) **PROVIDE SOMEBODY WITH SUPPLIES** to provide somebody with supplies, especially for a journey [14thC. Via French from the Latin stem *provision-* "foresight, preparation," from *provis-*, past participle stem of *providere* (see PROVIDE).] —**pro·vi·sion·er** *n.*

pro·vi·sion·al /prə vízhən'l, -vízhnəl/ *adj.* **TEMPORARY OR CONDITIONAL** temporary or conditional, pending confirmation or validation ○ *a provisional government* ■ *n.* **1.** HR **SOMEBODY HIRED TEMPORARILY** somebody hired temporarily for a job, especially before being qualified to do it permanently **2.** STAMPS **TEMPORARY POSTAGE STAMP** a postage stamp used temporarily until a regular stamp is issued —**pro·vi·sion·al·ly** *adv.*

Pro·vi·sion·al *n.* **MEMBER OF IRISH REPUBLICAN ARMY FACTION** a member of the faction of the Irish Republican Army that strives to achieve its goals through using force ■ *adj.* **RELATING TO IRISH REPUBLICAN ARMY FACTION** relating to the faction of the Irish Republican Army that strives to achieve its goals through using force

pro·vi·sion·al li·cence *n. U.K.* = **learner's permit**

pro·vi·so /prə vízō/ (*plural* **-sos** *or* **-soes**) *n.* **1.** LAW **CLAUSE ADDED TO CONTRACT** a clause introducing a condition in a contract **2. CONDITION WITHIN AGREEMENT** a condition asked as part of an agreement [15thC. From medieval Latin *proviso quod* "provided that," from Latin *proviso*, a form of *provisus*, past participle of *providere* "to prepare in advance, supply."]

pro·vi·so·ry /prə vízəree/ *adj.* **1.** LAW **CONDITIONAL** stating a condition **2.** = **provisional** *adj.* [Early 17thC. From medieval Latin *provisorius* "of papal provision," from *provisus* (see PROVISO).] —**pro·vi·so·ri·ly** *adv.*

pro·vi·ta·min /prō vítəmin/ *n.* a substance that is converted into an active vitamin as a result of the body's normal biochemical processes

prov·o·ca·tion /pròvvə káysh'n/ *n.* **1. ACT OF PROVOKING** the act of provoking somebody or something **2. CAUSE OF ANGER** something that makes somebody angry or indignant **3.** LAW **REASON FOR ATTACKING SOMEBODY** something that incites somebody to attack somebody else [14thC. Directly or via French from the Latin stem *provocation-*, ultimately from *provocare* (see PROVOKE).]

pro·voc·a·tive /prə vókətiv/ *adj.* **1. MAKING PEOPLE ANGRY OR EXCITED** deliberately aimed at exciting or annoying people ○ *a provocative remark* **2. SEXUALLY AROUSING** intended to arouse other people sexually [15thC. Directly and via Old French *provocatif* from late Latin *provocativus*, from *provocare* (see PROVOKE).] —**pro·voc·a·tive·ly** *adv.* —**pro·voc·a·tive·ness** *n.*

pro·voke /prə vṓk/ (**-voked, -vok·ing, -vokes**) *vt.* **1. MAKE SOMEBODY FEEL ANGRY** to make somebody feel angry or exasperated **2. ELICIT A RESPONSE** to be the cause or occasion of an emotion or response ○ *Her bravery provoked a lot of sympathy.* **3. STIR SOMEBODY TO EMOTION** to stir somebody to an emotion or response **4. INCITE SOMETHING** to act in a way intended to bring something about **5. BE THE CAUSE OF AN ACTIVITY** to serve as the stimulating factor for an activity [14thC. Directly or via Old French *provoker* from Latin *provocare* "to summon," from *vocare* "to call," from *vox* "voice."]

pro·vo·lo·ne /prōvə lṓnee/ *n.* a smoked cheese originally made in Italy that has a mild flavor and is light in color [Mid-20thC. From Italian, literally "large buffalo's milk cheese," from *provola*, of unknown origin.]

pro·vost /prṓ vōst, prṓvəst, próvvəst/ *n.* **1.** EDUC **IMPORTANT UNIVERSITY ADMINISTRATOR** a high-ranking administrative officer of a university **2.** CHR **SENIOR DIGNITARY OF CATHEDRAL** the senior dignitary of a cathedral or collegiate church **3. PRISON WARDEN** the keeper of a prison (*archaic*) [Pre-12thC. From medieval Latin *propositus*, alteration of Latin *praepositus*, literally "somebody placed in front," ultimately from *ponere* "to place" (source of English *preposition*).]

pro·vost court *n.* a military court set up in an occupied hostile territory for the trial of minor offenses

pro·vost guard *n.* a detail of soldiers having police duties under the authority of the provost marshal

pro·vost mar·shal *n.* the army officer in charge of a unit of military police

prow /prow/ *n.* **1. FRONT OF SHIP** the forward part of a ship **2. PROJECTING FRONT PART** the projecting front part of something other than a ship [Mid-16thC. Via French *proue* from Latin *prora*, from Greek *prōra* "front of a ship," from *pro* "forward."]

prow·ess /prówəss/ *n.* **1. SUPERIOR SKILL** exceptional ability or skill **2. VALOR IN COMBAT** extraordinary valor and ability in combat [13thC. From Old French *proesce* "bravery," from *prou* "brave," variant of *prud* (see PROUD).]

prowl /prowl/ *vti.* (**prowled, prowl·ing, prowls**) **ROAM AN AREA STEALTHILY FOR PREY** to roam around an area stealthily in search of prey, food, or opportunity ■ *n.* **ACT OF ROAMING** the act of roaming stealthily for prey [14thC. Origin unknown.] ◇ **on the prowl** moving around stealthily looking for something or somebody

prowl car *n.* a police patrol car (*dated*)

prowl·er /prówlər/ *n.* **1. SOMEBODY OR SOMETHING THAT PROWLS** an animal that or person who prowls **2. SOMEBODY PROWLING WITH UNLAWFUL INTENT** somebody who roams or looks around somewhere stealthily waiting for the opportunity to commit criminal acts

prox. *abbr.* proximo

prox·e·mics /prok seémiks/ *n.* the study of the distance individuals maintain between each other in social interaction and how this separation is significant [Mid-20thC. Formed from PROXIMITY on the model of PHONEMICS.]

prox·i·mal /próksəm'l/ *adj.* **1.** ANAT **NEARER CENTER OF BODY** nearer to the point of reference or to the center of the body. For example, the elbow is proximal to the hand. ◊ **distal 2.** DENT **NEAREST ANOTHER TOOTH** used to describe the surface of a tooth nearest to either the one behind it or the one in front of it [Early 18thC. Formed from Latin *proximus* (see PROXIMITY).] —**prox·i·mal·ly** *adv.*

prox·i·mate /próksəmət/ *adj.* **1. NEAREST** nearest in order, time, or place **2. VERY CLOSE** very close in space or time **3. ABOUT TO HAPPEN** soon to appear or take place **4. APPROXIMATE** almost accurate [Late 16thC. From Latin *proximat-*, past participle stem of *proximare* "to come near," from *proximus* (see PROXIMITY).] —**prox·i·mate·ly** *adv.* —**prox·i·mate·ness** *n.* —**prox·i·ma·tion** /pròksə máysh'n/ *n.*

prox·im·i·ty /prok símmətee/ *n.* closeness in space or time [15thC. From Latin *proximitas* "nearness," from *proximus* "nearest," the superlative form of *prope* "near" (source of English *approach*).]

prox·im·i·ty card *n.* a plastic card carrying electronically coded information accessed by holding the card near a reading device. Proximity cards are often used to open doors as part of a security system.

prox·im·i·ty fuze *n.* a fuze, typically part of a warhead, that will activate and cause detonation when the warhead is at a specified distance from the target

prox·i·mo /próksə mō/ *adv.* occurring during the next month (*formal*) ○ *propose a meeting for the fifth proximo* [Mid-19thC. From Latin *proximo (mense)* "in the next (month)."]

prox·y /próksee/ (*plural* **-ies**) *n.* **1. FUNCTION OR POWER OF SUBSTITUTE** the function, power, or capacity to act of a deputy authorized to substitute for another **2. SOMEBODY ACTING AS SUBSTITUTE** somebody authorized to substitute for somebody else **3. AUTHORIZATION DOCUMENT FOR STAND-IN** a document authorizing somebody to act for another person **4.** LAW, STOCK EXCH **DOCUMENT AUTHORIZING VOTE ON ANOTHER'S STOCK** a document authorizing somebody to vote on matters of corporate stock on behalf of somebody else [15thC. From medieval Latin *procuratia*, alteration of Latin *procuratio* "care, management," from *procurare* "to take care of."]

Pro·zac /prṓ zàk/ *tdmk.* a trademark for an antidepressant drug that slows down the uptake of serotonin by the central nervous system

prs. *abbr.* pairs

prude /prood/ *n.* somebody who is easily shocked by sex or nudity and who pays a great deal of attention to proper social behavior (*disapproving*) [Early 18thC. From French, back-formation from Old French *prudefemme* (misunderstood as "virtuous woman"), feminine of *prud'homme*, from assumed *pro de ome*, literally "fine (thing) of a man."] —**prud·er·y** *n.* —**prud·ish** *adj.* —**prud·ish·ly** *adv.* —**prud·ish·ness** *n.*

pru·dence /próod'ns/ *n.* **1. PRACTICALITY** good sense in managing practical matters **2. TENDENCY TO AVOID RISK** a tendency to evaluate situations carefully so as to avoid risk **3. FRUGALITY** careful management of resources [14thC. Directly or via French from Latin *prudentia*, contraction of *providentia* (see PROVIDENCE).]

pru·dent /próod'nt/ *adj.* **1. HAVING GOOD SENSE** having good sense in dealing with practical matters **2. CAREFULLY CONSIDERING CONSEQUENCES** using good judgment to consider consequences and to act accordingly **3. CAREFUL IN MANAGING RESOURCES** careful in managing resources so as to provide for the future [14thC. Directly or via French from Latin *prudent-*, contraction of the stem *provident-* (see PROVIDENT).] —**pru·dent·ly** *adv.*

WORD KEY: SYNONYMS

See Synonyms at ***cautious***.

pru·den·tial /proo dénshəl/ *adj.* **1. RESULTING FROM PRUDENCE** resulting from, depending on, or marked by prudence **2. USING PRUDENCE** using prudence, especially in business matters —**pru·den·tial·ly** *adv.*

Prud·hoe Bay /próodhō-, prùdhō-/ bay in the Beaufort Sea, northern Alaska. Vast petroleum reserves were discovered there in 1968.

pru·i·nose /próo ə nòss/ *adj.* having a white powdery coating, e.g., on a fruit or leaf [Early 19thC. From Latin *pruinosus*, from *pruina* "hoarfrost."]

prune[1] /proon/ *n.* **1. DRIED PLUM** a plum that has been preserved by drying **2. PLUM TO BE DRIED** a plum suitable for drying (*informal*) **3. OFFENSIVE TERM** an offensive term that deliberately insults somebody's intelligence, competence or ability to interest others (*informal insult*) [14thC. From French, ultimately from Latin *prunum*, from Greek *prounon*, variant of *proumnon* "plum."]

prune[2] /proon/ (**pruned, prun·ing, prunes**) *v.* **1.** *vti.* **CUT BRANCHES** to cut branches away from a plant to encourage fuller growth **2.** *vt.* **REDUCE SOMETHING BY REMOVING UNWANTED MATERIAL** to reduce something by removing whatever is unnecessary or unwanted **3.** *vt.* **REMOVE SOMETHING UNNECESSARY** to remove something considered unnecessary or unwanted [14thC. From Old French *proignier* "to cut in a rounded shape in front," from Latin *rotundus* "round" (source of English *rotund*).] —**prun·a·ble** *adj.* —**prun·er** *n.*

pru·nel·la /proo néllə/ *n.* a wool fabric with a twill weave, used for academic gowns, clerical robes, and shoe uppers [Mid-17thC. From French *prunelle* "sloe," a diminutive of *prune* "plum." Probably from its color.]

pru·nelle /proo nél/ *n.* **1.** BEVERAGES **SWEET LIQUEUR** a sweet French liqueur flavored with sloes **2.** TEXTILES = **prunella** [15thC. From French (see PRUNELLA).]

prun·ing hook *n.* a tool with a hooked blade and sometimes a long handle, used to prune trees and bushes

pru·ri·ent /próoree ənt/ *adj.* having or intended to arouse an unwholesome interest in sexual matters (*disapproving*) [Mid-17thC. From Latin *prurient-*, the present participle stem of *prurire* "to itch, long for," of uncertain origin: perhaps formed from *pruna* "burning coal."] —**pru·ri·ence** *n.* —**pru·ri·ent·ly** *adv.*

pru·ri·go /proo rī́gō/ *n.* a chronic inflammatory skin disease causing small itchy swellings [Mid-17thC. From Latin, "itching," from *prurire* (see PRURIENT).] —**pru·rig·i·nous** /proo ríjjənəss/ *adj.*

pru·ri·tus /proo rī́təss/ *n.* an intense feeling of itchiness [Mid-17thC. From Latin, past participle of *prurire* (see PRURIENT).]

Prus·sia /prúshə/ former state and kingdom in Germany. Its capital was Berlin. —**Prus·sian** *adj., n.*

Prus·sian blue *n.* **1. Prus·sian blue, prus·sian blue BLUE IRON PIGMENT** a water-insoluble blue iron pigment **2. DARK GREENISH BLUE** a rich dark blue color with a tinge of green ■ *adj.* **OF DEEP GREENISH BLUE** of a rich dark blue color with a tinge of green [*Prussian* because its discoverer, Diesbach, was Prussian]

prus·si·ate /prússee ət, -àyt, prúshee-/ *n.* **1. FERROCYANIDE OR FERRICYANIDE** a chemical compound that is ferrocyanide or ferricyanide **2. SALT OF HYDROCYANIC ACID** a chemical compound that is a salt of hydrocyanic acid [Late 18thC. Formed from *prussic* (see PRUSSIC ACID).]

prus·sic ac·id /prùssik ássid/ *n.* = **hydrocyanic acid** [*Prussic* formed from *Prussian*, because it was first obtained from Prussian blue]

pry[1] /prī/ *vi.* (**pried, pry·ing, pries**) **INQUIRE NOSILY** to look inquisitively or inquire nosily into somebody's private affairs ■ *n.* (*plural* **pries**) **1. ACT OF PRYING** the act of prying into somebody's private affairs **2. SOMEBODY WHO PRIES** somebody who engages in prying into other people's private affairs [14thC. Origin unknown.]

pry[2] /prī/ *vt.* (**pried, pry·ing, pries**) **1. OPEN USING LEVERAGE** to open or part something by using leverage **2. GET INFORMATION WITH DIFFICULTY** to get information from somebody with great difficulty ○ *pried the secret out of her* ■ *n.* (*plural* **pries**) **1. TOOL FOR APPLYING LEVERAGE** something such as a crowbar that is used to apply leverage **2. LEVERAGE** leverage exerted in order to open or lift something [Early 19thC. Back-formation from PRIZE, misunderstood as 3rd person present singular.]

pry·er *n.* = **prier**

pry·ta·ne·um /prìtt'n eé əm/ (*plural* **-a** /-ə/) *n.* a public building in ancient Greece used as a meeting place [Early 17thC. Via Latin from Greek *prutaneion*, from *prutanis* "prince, ruler."]

Prze·wal·ski's horse /shə vaálskiz-, pùrzhə-/ *n.* a wild Asian horse with a stocky body, a chestnut coat, and an erect dark mane. It is the only surviving wild horse, with just a tiny population found in the Gobi Desert on the border of China and Mongolia. Latin name: *Equus caballus przevalskii*. [Late 19thC. Translation of Latin *equus przewalskii*, named for the Russian explorer N. M. *Przheval'skiĭ* (1839–88), who was the first European to report seeing it.]

Ps. *abbr.* (Book of) Psalms

p.s. *abbr.* passenger steamer

P.S. *abbr.* **1.** GRAM phrase structure **2.** Police Sergeant **3. P.S., p.s.** postscript **4.** private secretary **5.** THEATER prompt side **6.** public school

Psa. *abbr.* (Book of) Psalms

psalm /saam, saalm/, **Psalm** *n.* a sacred song or poem of praise, especially one in the Book of Psalms in the Bible [12thC. Via late Latin *psalmus* from Greek *psalmos* "harpsong," from *psallein* "to pluck."] —**psalm·ic** *adj.*

psalm·ist /saámist, saálm-/ *n.* the author of a psalm

psalm·o·dy /saámədee, saálm-/ (*plural* **-dies**) *n.* **1.** RELIG **PSALM SINGING** the singing of psalms in divine worship **2.** MUSIC **MUSICAL ARRANGEMENTS FOR PSALMS** the prescribed arrangements for singing individual psalms from the Book of Psalms **3. SET OF PSALMS** a collection of psalms [14thC. Via late Latin *psalmodia* from Greek *psalmōidia*, ultimately from *psalmos* (see PSALM) + *ōidē* "song."] —**psalm·od·ic** /saa móddik, saal-/ *adj.* —**psalm·o·dist** /saámədist, saálm-/ *n.*

Psalms /saamz, saalmz/ *n.* a book of the Bible made up of 150 poems and hymns to God, traditionally believed to have been written by King David

Psal·ter /sáwltər/, **psal·ter** *n.* a book containing psalms, or the Book of Psalms, used in worship [Pre-12thC. From Latin *psalterium* "book of psalms" in ecclesiastical Latin (see PSALTERY); reinforced by Old French *sautier*.]

psal·te·ri·um /sawl teéree əm/ (*plural* **-a** /-ə/) *n.* ZOOL = **omasum** [Mid-19thC. Formed from Latin, "stringed instrument" (see PSALTERY).]

psal·ter·y /sáwltəree/ (*plural* **-ies**) *n.* an ancient musical instrument with numerous strings that can be plucked with the fingers or with a plectrum [13thC. Via Old French *sauterie* from Latin *psalterium* "stringed instrument," from Greek *psaltērion* "stringed instrument played by plucking," from *psallein* "to pluck."]

psam·mite /sá mīt/ *n.* **1. SANDSTONE** rock formed principally of sand **2. METAMORPHOSED SANDSTONE** a metamorphosed sandstone containing large amounts of quartz [Mid-19thC. Formed from Greek *psammos* "sand."] —**psam·mit·ic** /sa míttik/ *adj.*

p's and q's *npl.* the polite manners and behavior that somebody adopts, e.g., when eager to make a good impression ○ *We'd better mind our p's and q's.* [From *mind one's p's and q's*, of uncertain origin: perhaps a warning to children to distinguish the two letters when learning to write, or to printers' apprentices in handling type]

PSAT *abbr.* preliminary scholastic aptitude test

psec. *abbr.* picosecond

pse·phol·o·gy /si fólləjee/ *n.* the statistical study of elections [Mid-20thC. Formed from Greek *psephos* "pebble, vote"; from the Greek practice of using pebbles to vote.] —**pse·pho·log·i·cal** /seèfə lójjik'l/ *adj.* —**pse·pho·log·i·cal·ly** *adv.* —**pse·phol·o·gist** /see fólləjist/ *n.*

pseud. *abbr.* pseudonym

pseud- *prefix.* = **pseudo-** (*sometimes used before vowels*)

pseud·ax·is /soo dáksiss/ (*plural* **-es** /-ák seèz/) *n.* BOT = **sympodium**

pseud·e·pig·ra·pha /soodə píggrəfə/ *npl.* certain anonymous or pseudonymous writings professing to be biblical but not included in any biblical canon [Late 17thC. From Greek, a form of *pseudepigraphos* "with false title," from PSEUDO- + *epigraphein* "to write on" (see EPIGRAPH).] —**pseud·ep·i·graph·ic** /sood eppi gráffik/ *adj.* —**pseud·ep·i·graph·i·cal** *adj.* —**pseud·e·pig·ra·phous** /soodə píggrəfəss/ *adj.*

pseu·do /soódō/ *adj.* not authentic or sincere, in spite of appearances [14thC. From Greek *pseudo-*, from *pseudēs* (see PSEUDO-).]

pseudo- *prefix.* **1.** similar ○ *pseudobulb* **2.** false, spurious ○ *pseudoscience* [From Greek *pseudēs*, from *pseudein* "to lie," of unknown origin]

pseud·o·bulb /soódō bùlb/ *n.* a thickened part of a stem that lies above the ground, e.g., in many orchids

pseu·do·carp /soódō kaàrp/ *n.* a fruit formed by combining the ripened ovary with another structure, often the receptacle, as, e.g., in strawberries [Mid-

19thC. Formed from PSEUDO- + Greek *karpos* "fruit."] —**pseu·do·car·pous** /sòodō kaárpəss/ *adj.*

pseu·do·clas·sic /sòodō klássik/ *adj.* posing as or mistakenly believed to be classic

pseu·do·clas·si·cism /sòodō klássə sìzzəm/ *n.* the use in art and literature of ancient Greek and Roman styles —**pseu·do·clas·si·cal** *adj.*

pseu·do·coel /sóodə seèl/, **pseu·do·coe·lom** /sóodə seèləm/ *n.* a body cavity of some primitive invertebrates that has no mesodermal lining

pseu·do·coe·lo·mate /sòodō seèlə màyt/ *n.* an invertebrate that has a fluid-filled body cavity not lined with mesoderm tissue, e.g., a nematode or rotifer —**pseu·do·coe·lo·mate** *adj.*

pseu·do·cy·e·sis /sòodō sī eèssiss/ (*plural* **-ses** /-seèz/) *n.* a false pregnancy (*technical*) [Mid-19thC. Formed from Greek *kuesis* "conception."]

pseu·do·gene /sóodə jeen/ *n.* a nonfunctional DNA sequence that is very similar to the sequence of a functional gene

pseu·do·her·maph·ro·dit·ism /sòodō hər máffrə dī tìzzəm/ *n.* a condition in which somebody has either ovaries **(female pseudohermaphroditism)** or testes **(male pseudohermaphroditism)** but has external genitalia of ambiguous appearance

pseu·do·mo·nad /sóodə mṓ nàd/ *n.* a rod-shaped bacterium that lives in soil or decomposing organic material, some of which are pathogenic to plants and animals. Genus: *Pseudomonas.* [Early 20thC. From modern Latin *Pseudomonad-*, stem of *Pseudomonas*, literally "false monad," from the stem *monad-* "monad."]

pseu·do·morph /sóodə màwrf/ *n.* **1.** MINERAL WITH UNUSUAL CRYSTALLINE SHAPE a mineral that does not have its usual crystalline form as a result of having replaced another mineral in a rock and taken its shape **2.** IRREGULAR FORM an irregular or deceptive form —**pseu·do·mor·phic** /sòodə máwrfik/ *adj.* —**pseu·do·mor·phism** /-fìzzəm/ *n.* —**pseu·do·mor·phous** *adj.*

pseu·do·nym /sóodə nìm/ *n.* a name that is not somebody's correct name, especially one used by an author in publications [Mid-19thC. Via French *pseudonyme* from Greek *pseudōnumon*, literally "false name," ultimately from *onuma*, variant of *onoma* "name" (source of English *anonymous*).] —**pseu·do·nym·i·ty** /sòodə nímmətee/ *n.*

pseu·don·y·mous /soo dónnəməss/ *adj.* bearing or written under a name that is not the correct name of the person concerned —**pseu·don·y·mous·ly** *adv.* —**pseu·don·y·mous·ness** *n.*

pseu·do·po·di·um /sòodə pṓdee əm/ (*plural* **-a** /-ə/), **pseu·do·pod** /sóodə pòd/ *n.* a temporary cytoplasmic protrusion in amoeba and other protozoa used for locomotion and to take up food

pseu·do·preg·nan·cy /sòodə prégnənsee/ (*plural* **-cies**) *n.* = **false pregnancy**

pseu·do·ran·dom /sòodō rándəm/ *adj.* relating to random numbers generated by a computational process

pseu·do·sci·ence /sòodō sī əns/ *n.* a theory or method doubtfully or mistakenly held to be scientific

pseu·do·so·phis·ti·ca·tion /sòodō sə fisti káysh'n/ *n.* false or pretended sophistication

pseu·do·tu·ber·cu·lo·sis /sòodō too burkyə lṓssiss/ *n.* a disease marked by the formation of nodules of inflamed tissue similar to those in tuberculosis but not caused by the tubercle bacillus

psf, **p.s.f.** *abbr.* pounds per square foot

pshaw /shaw, pshaw/ *interj.* used to express disbelief, impatience, or contempt [Late 17thC. An imitation of the sound made.]

psi[1] /sī, psī/ *n.* the 23rd letter of the Greek alphabet, represented in the English alphabet as "ps." See table at **alphabet** [15thC. From Greek *psei.*]

psi[2], **p.s.i.** *abbr.* pounds per square inch

psia, **p.s.i.a.** *abbr.* pounds per square inch, absolute

psid, **p.s.i.d.** *abbr.* pounds per square inch, differential

psig, **p.s.i.g.** *abbr.* pounds per square inch, gauge

psil·o·cin /sílləsin, sīl-/ *n.* a hallucinogenic compound produced in the body after eating a particular mushroom. Formula: $C_{12}H_{16}N_2O$. [Mid-20thC. Formed from Greek *psilos* "smooth."]

psil·o·cy·bin /sìllə síbin, sīlə-/ *n.* a crystalline hallucinogen obtained from a particular mushroom. Formula: $C_{13}HN_2O_3P_2$. [Mid-20thC. Formed from Greek *psilos* "smooth" + *kubē* "head."]

psi·lom·e·lane /sī lómmə làyn/ *n.* a mixed hydrated manganese oxide ore, occurring in dark-colored rounded masses [Mid-19thC. Formed from Greek *psilos* "smooth" + *melas* "black."]

psi par·ti·cle *n.* = **J/psi particle**

psit·ta·cine /síttə sīn/ *adj.* OF PARROTS belonging to the parrot family, or affecting, resembling, or relating to parrots or related birds ■ *n.* MEMBER OF PARROT FAMILY a bird that belongs to the parrot family [Late 19thC. Via Latin *psittacinus* from *psittacus*, from Greek *psittakos* "parrot."]

psit·ta·co·sis /sìttə kṓssiss/ *n.* a contagious disease of parrots and related birds that can be transmitted to humans, sometimes causing serious lung infection. It is caused by the bacterium *Chlamydia psittaci.* [Late 19thC. Via Latin *psittacus* from Greek *psittakos* "parrot."]

pso·as /sṓ əss/ (*plural* **-ai** /-ī/ *or* **-ae** /-eè/) *n.* either of two pairs of muscles that are located in the groin and help to flex the hip joint. The psoas in oxen is the fillet steak muscle. [Late 17thC. From Greek, a plural form of *psoa* "muscle of the loins."]

pso·cid /sóssid, sóssid/ (*plural* **-cids** *or* **-cid**) *n.* tiny winged insect with reduced veins in the wings and unusual rasping mouthparts. Family: Psocidae. [Late 19thC. Via modern Latin *Psocus*, genus name, from Greek *psōkhein* "to grind."]

pso·ra·len /sáwrələn/ *n.* a toxic substance present in certain plants and used to treat severe acne and psoriasis [Mid-20thC. Via modern Latin *Psoralea*, genus name, from Greek *psōraleos* "itchy," from *psōra* "itch, mange."]

pso·ri·a·sis /sə rī əssiss/ *n.* a skin disease marked by red scaly patches [Late 17thC. Via Latin, "scurvy, mange," from Greek *psōriasis* "being itchy," ultimately from *psōra* "itch, mange."] —**pso·ri·at·ic** /sàwree áttik/ *adj.*

P.SS., **p.ss.** *abbr.* postscripts

psst /pst/ *interj.* used to get the attention of one person without alerting others [Early 20thC. An imitation of the sound.]

PST, **P.S.T.** *abbr.* **1.** Pacific Standard Time **2.** provincial sales tax

PSU *abbr.* COMPUT power supply unit

psych /sīk/ (**psyched, psych·ing, psychs**) *v.* **1.** *vt.* MAKE UNEASY to make somebody fearful, uneasy, or intimidated ○ *He really psyched me when he came out with all that scary stuff.* **2.** *vr.* PREPARE TO PERFORM WELL to prepare somebody psychologically to perform at peak levels ○ *The night before, she psyched herself for the job interview.* [Early 20thC. Origin uncertain: perhaps partly a shortening of PSYCHOANALYZE and partly from PSYCH-.]

psych out *vt.* (*informal*) **1.** *U.K.* = **psych 2.** PUZZLE SOMETHING OUT to analyze, solve, or understand something such as a problem **3.** GUESS SOMEBODY'S THOUGHT PROCESSES to guess or anticipate correctly the intentions or thoughts of another person

psych up *vr. U.K.* = **psych** *v.* 2 (*informal*)

psych. *abbr.* **1.** psychological **2.** psychology

psych- *prefix.* = **psycho-** (*used before vowels*)

psy·che /sīkee/ *n.* **1.** RELIG HUMAN SPIRIT the human spirit or soul **2.** PSYCHOL HUMAN MIND the human mind as the center of thought and behavior [Mid-17thC. Via Latin from Greek *psukhē* "breath, soul, mind," from *psukhein* "to breathe."]

Psy·che *n.* in Roman mythology, a beautiful young woman loved by Cupid. He visited her secretly at night, forbidding her ever to look at him. When she did, he abandoned her. They were eventually reunited and Jupiter made her immortal.

psy·che·de·li·a /sìkə deèlee ə/ *n.* the subculture of artifacts, phenomena, writings, or art associated with psychedelic drugs [Mid-20thC. Back-formation from PSYCHEDELIC.]

psy·che·del·ic /sìkə déllik/ *adj.* **1.** RELATING TO HALLUCINOGENIC DRUGS used to describe, or relating to or caused by, drugs that generate hallucinations, abnormal psychic states, or states that resemble psychiatric disorders **2.** OVERLOADING THE SENSES weird, distorted, wildly colorful, or otherwise resembling images or sounds experienced by somebody under the influence of a psychedelic drug ■ *n.* DRUG a psychedelic drug [Mid-20thC. From Greek *psukhē* "mind" + *dēloun* "to reveal, make visible," from *dēlos* "clear."] —**psy·che·del·i·cal·ly** *adv.*

psy·chi·at·ric /sìkee áttrik/ *adj.* relating to psychiatry or its patients

psy·chi·at·ric hos·pi·tal *n.* a hospital dedicated to the treatment, care, and protection of people with serious psychiatric disorders who are judged to be unfit or unsafe to be at large

psy·chi·a·trist /si kī ətrist, sī-/ *n.* a doctor trained in the treatment of people with psychiatric disorders

psy·chi·a·try /si kī ətree, sī-/ *n.* a medical specialty concerned with the diagnosis and treatment of disorders that have primarily mental or behavioral symptoms and with the care of people having such disorders [Mid-19thC. From French *psychiatrie*, from Greek *psukhē* (see PSYCHE) + *iatreia* "cure."]

psy·chic /sīkik/ *adj.* **1.** OF THE MIND relating to the human mind **2.** OUTSIDE SCIENTIFIC KNOWLEDGE outside the sphere of scientific knowledge **3.** SUPPOSEDLY SENSITIVE TO SUPERNATURAL FORCES claiming or believed to have extraordinary perception and sensitivity to nonphysical or supernatural forces ■ *n.* SOMEBODY SUPPOSEDLY SENSITIVE TO SUPERNATURAL somebody who claims or is believed to be sensitive to nonphysical or supernatural forces [Late 18thC. From Greek *psukhikos* "pertaining to the soul or spirit," from *psukhē* (see PSYCHE).] —**psy·chi·cal** *adj.* —**psy·chi·cal·ly** *adv.*

psy·cho /sīkō/ *n.* (*plural* **-chos**) OFFENSIVE TERM a highly offensive term for somebody who has a psychiatric or personality disorder (*slang*) ■ *adj.* OFFENSIVE TERM an offensive term used for somebody who behaves in an uncontrolled and unpredictable way (*slang offensive*) [Mid-20thC. Shortening of PSYCHOPATHIC.]

WORD KEY: CULTURAL NOTE

Psycho, a movie by English director Alfred Hitchcock (1960). A disturbing horror film with a rich vein of black comedy, it tells the story of a woman who flees her home after stealing money from her boss. Stopping at a motel run by the sinister Norman Bates and his apparently domineering mother, she is brutally murdered while taking a shower. Members of her family subsequently investigate the death. As a result of the impact of the movie, the term *Bates Motel* came to mean any rundown rooming house, motel, or structure redolent of oppressive fear and underlying horror.

psycho- *prefix.* **1.** mind, mental ○ *psychoactive* **2.** psychology, psychological ○ *psychobabble* [From Greek *psukhē* (see PSYCHE)]

psy·cho·a·cous·tics /sìkō ə kóostiks/ *n.* the scientific study of the psychological and physiological principles of sound perception (*takes a singular verb*)

psy·cho·ac·tive /sìkō áktiv/ *adj.* used to describe drugs or medication having a significant effect on mood or behavior

psychoanal. *abbr.* psychoanalysis

psy·cho·an·a·lyse *vt.* U.K. = **psychoanalyze**

psy·cho·a·nal·y·sis /sìkō ə nálləssiss/ *n.* **1.** METHOD OF UNDERSTANDING MENTAL LIFE a psychological theory and therapeutic method developed by Sigmund Freud, based on the ideas that mental life functions on both conscious and unconscious levels and that childhood events have a powerful psychological influence throughout life **2.** TREATMENT BY PSYCHOANALYSIS treatment by psychoanalysis, interpreting material presented by a patient in order to bring the processes of the unconscious into conscious awareness —**psy·cho·an·a·lyst** /sìkō ánnəlist/ *n.* —**psy·cho·an·a·lyt·ic** /sìkō annə líttik/ *adj.* —**psy·cho·an·a·lyt·i·cal** *adj.* —**psy·cho·an·a·lyt·i·cal·ly** *adv.*

psy·cho·an·a·lyze /sìkō ánnə līz/ (**-lyzed, -lyz·ing, -lyz·es**) *vt.* to apply the methods of psychoanalysis in a psychotherapeutic setting —**psy·cho·an·a·lyz·er** *n.*

psy·cho·bab·ble /sìkō bább'l/ *n.* psychological jargon used inaccurately to talk about personal problems

psy·cho·bi·og·ra·phy /sìkō bī óggrəfee/ (*plural* **-phies**) *n.* a biography that focuses on the psychological profile of the subject

psy·cho·bi·ol·o·gy /sìkō bī óllәjee/ *n.* the study of the biological bases of behavior. ◊ **sociobiology** —**psy·cho·bi·o·log·i·cal** /sìkō bī ə lójjik'l/ *adj.* —**psy·cho·bi·o·log·i·cal·ly** *adv.* —**psy·cho·bi·ol·o·gist** /sìkō bī óllәjist/ *n.*

psy·cho·chem·i·cal /sìkō kémmik'l/ *n.* PSYCHOACTIVE DRUG a drug that affects mood or behavior ■ *adj.* OF

PSYCHOACTIVE DRUGS relating to or acting like a psychoactive drug

psy·cho·dra·ma /sīkə draámə, -drámmə/ *n.* a form of psychotherapy pioneered by Jacob Moreno in which patients are required to perform roles in dramas illustrating their own particular problems before an audience of other patients —**psy·cho·dra·mat·ic** /sīkə drə máttik/ *adj.*

psy·cho·dy·nam·ics /sīkō dī námmiks/ *n.* **1.** INTERACTION OF EMOTIONAL FORCES the interaction of the emotional and motivational forces that affect behavior and mental states, especially on a subconscious level (*takes a singular or plural verb*) **2.** INNER FORCES AFFECTING BEHAVIOR the study of the emotional and motivational forces that affect behavior and mental states (*takes a singular verb*) —**psy·cho·dy·nam·ic** *adj.* —**psy·cho·dy·nam·i·cal·ly** *adv.*

psy·cho·gen·e·sis /sīkō jénnəsiss/ *n.* the psychological rather than physical cause of a psychological disorder —**psy·cho·ge·net·ic** /sīkō jə néttik/ *adj.* —**psy·cho·ge·net·i·cal·ly** *adv.*

psy·cho·gen·ic /sīkō jénnik/ *adj.* originating in mental or emotional rather than in physiological processes —**psy·cho·gen·i·cal·ly** *adv.*

psy·cho·his·to·ry /sīkō hìstəree, -hìstree, sīkō hístəree, -hístree/ (*plural* **-ries**) *n.* psychological analysis of somebody's life or of historical events —**psy·cho·his·tor·i·an** /sīkō his táwree ən/ *n.* —**psy·cho·his·tor·i·cal** /sīkō his táwrik'l/ *adj.*

psy·cho·ki·ne·sis /sīkō ki neéssiss, -kī-/ *n.* the supposed ability to use mental powers to make objects move or to otherwise affect them —**psy·cho·ki·net·ic** /sīkō ki néttik/ *adj.*

psychol. *abbr.* **1.** psychological **2.** psychologist **3.** psychology

psy·cho·lin·guis·tics /sīkō ling gwístiks/ *n.* the study of language acquisition and use in relation to the psychological factors controlling its use and recognition (*takes a singular verb*) —**psy·cho·lin·guist** /sīkō líng gwist/ *n.* —**psy·cho·lin·guis·tic** /-ling gwístik/ *adj.*

psy·cho·log·i·cal /sīkə lójjik'l/ *adj.* **1.** OF PSYCHOLOGY relating to psychology **2.** OF THE MIND relating to the mind or mental processes **3.** AFFECTING THE MIND affecting or intended to affect the mind or mental processes **4.** EXISTING ONLY IN THE MIND existing only in the mind, without having a physical basis ○ *His health problem is psychological.* —**psy·cho·log·i·cal·ly** *adv.*

psy·cho·log·i·cal de·pend·ence *n.* strong desire for something without being physically addicted to it

psy·cho·log·i·cal mo·ment *n.* the time at which the mental state of a person or group of people is most receptive or appropriate

psy·cho·log·i·cal war·fare *n.* **1.** MIL WARFARE BY PROPAGANDA tactics that use propaganda to try to demoralize an enemy in war, usually including the civilian population **2.** NONMILITARY PSYCHOLOGICAL UNDERMINING the use of psychological tactics to disconcert and disadvantage an opponent in an everyday or a business context, e.g., causing fear or anxiety

psy·chol·o·gism /sī kóllə jìzzəm/ *n.* a belief in or emphasis on the importance of psychology in other fields, e.g., history or philosophy —**psy·chol·o·gis·tic** /sī kòllə jístik/ *adj.*

psy·chol·o·gist /sī kólləjist/ *n.* **1.** PROFESSIONAL IN PSYCHOLOGY a professional who studies behavior and experience, usually either licensed to provide therapeutic services to the public or working in an academic setting **2.** STUDENT OF PSYCHOLOGY somebody who is studying or has studied psychology, especially as a main subject at college or university

psy·chol·o·gize /sī kóllə jīz/ (**-gized, -giz·ing, -giz·es**) *v.* **1.** *vt.* INTERPRET BEHAVIOR PSYCHOLOGICALLY to interpret behavior in psychological terms or concepts **2.** *vi.* ANALYZE PSYCHOLOGICALLY to think, analyze, or reason psychologically

psy·chol·o·gy /sī kólləjee/ (*plural* **-gies**) *n.* **1.** STUDY OF MIND the scientific study of the human mind and mental states, and of human and animal behavior **2.** CHARACTERISTIC MENTAL MAKEUP the characteristic temperament and associated behavior of an individual or group, or that exhibited by those engaged in a particular activity **3.** SUBTLE MANIPULATIVE BEHAVIOR subtle clever actions and words used to influence a person or group

psy·cho·met·rics /sīkə méttriks/ *n.* a branch of psychology dealing with the measurement of mental traits, capacities, and processes (*takes a singular verb*)

psy·chom·e·try /sī kómmətree/ *n.* **1.** PSYCHOL = **psychometrics 2.** PARAPSYCHOL DIVINATION BY TOUCHING OBJECT the alleged ability to obtain information about a person or event by touching an object related to that person or event —**psy·cho·met·ric** /sīkə méttrik/ *adj.* —**psy·cho·met·ri·cal** *adj.* —**psy·cho·met·ri·cal·ly** *adv.* —**psy·chom·e·tri·cian** /sī kòmmə trísh'n/ *n.* —**psy·chom·e·trist** /sī kómmətrist/ *n.*

psy·cho·mo·tor /sīkə mṓtər/ *adj.* relating to bodily movement triggered by mental activity, especially voluntary muscle action

psy·cho·neu·ro·im·mu·nol·o·gy /sīkō noo rō immyə nólləjee/ *n.* a branch of medicine concerned with how emotions affect the immune system

psy·cho·neu·ro·sis /sīkō noo rṓsiss, -nyoo-/ (*plural* **-ros·es** /-rō seez/) *n.* = **neurosis** —**psy·cho·neu·rot·ic** /sīkō noo róttik, -nyoo-/ *adj.*

psy·cho·path /síkə pàth/ *n.* an offensive term for somebody with a personality disorder marked by antisocial thought and behavior —**psy·cho·path·ic** /sīkə páthik/ *adj.* —**psy·cho·path·i·cal·ly** *adv.*

psy·cho·pa·thol·o·gy /sīkō pə thólləjee/ *n.* the study of the causes and development of psychiatric disorders —**psy·cho·path·o·log·i·cal** /sīkō pàthə lójjik'l/ *adj.* —**psy·cho·pa·thol·o·gist** /sīkō pə thólləjist/ *n.*

psy·chop·a·thy /sī kóppəthee/ (*plural* **-thies**) *n.* **1.** PERSONALITY DISORDER a severe personality disorder marked by antisocial thought and behavior (*informal*) **2.** PSYCHIATRIC DISORDER any psychiatric illness (*dated*)

psy·cho·phar·ma·col·o·gy /sīkō faarmə kólləjee/ *n.* the scientific study of the effects of drugs on thought and behavior —**psy·cho·phar·ma·co·log·i·cal** /sīkō faarməkə lójjik'l/ *adj.* —**psy·cho·phar·ma·col·o·gist** /-faarmə kólləjist/ *n.*

psy·cho·phys·ics /sīkō fízziks/ *n.* a branch of psychology dealing with the effects of physical stimuli on sensory perceptions and mental states (*takes a singular verb*) —**psy·cho·phys·i·cal** *adj.*

psy·cho·phys·i·ol·o·gy /sīkō fìzzee ólləjee/ *n.* = **physiological psychology** —**psy·cho·phys·i·o·log·i·cal** /sīkō fìzzee ə lójjik'l/ *adj.* —**psy·cho·phys·i·ol·o·gist** /-fìzzee ólləjist/ *n.*

psy·cho·sex·u·al /sīkō sékshoo əl/ *adj.* relating to the mental and emotional aspects of sexuality and sexual development —**psy·cho·sex·u·al·i·ty** /sīkō sékshoo állətee/ *n.* —**psy·cho·sex·u·al·ly** /-sékshoo əlee/ *adv.*

psy·cho·sis /sī kṓssiss/ (*plural* **-ses** /sī kō seez/) *n.* a psychiatric disorder such as schizophrenia or mania that is marked by delusions, hallucinations, incoherence, and distorted perceptions of reality —**psy·cho·tic** /sī kóttik/ *adj.* —**psy·chot·i·cal·ly** /-kóttikəlee/ *adv.*

psy·cho·so·cial /sīkō sṓsh'l/ *adj.* relating to both the psychological and the social aspects of something, or relating to something that has both of these aspects

psy·cho·so·mat·ic /sīkə sə máttik/ *adj.* **1.** MED MENTALLY INDUCED used to describe a physical illness that is caused by mental factors such as stress, or the effects related to such illnesses **2.** RELATING TO MIND AND BODY involving both the mind and body [Mid-19thC. Coined from PSYCHO- + SOMATIC.]

psy·cho·syn·the·sis /sīkō sínthəssiss/ *n.* **1.** PSYCHOTHERAPEUTIC MOVEMENT a psychotherapeutic movement, opposed to psychoanalysis, that attempts to restore useful inhibitions and control **2.** HOLISTIC FORM OF PSYCHOTHERAPY a holistic form of psychotherapy involving clients in an exploration of the emotional, intellectual, physical, and spiritual elements of the self

psy·cho·ther·a·py /sīkō thérrəpee/ *n.* the treatment of mental disorders by psychological methods —**psy·cho·ther·a·peu·tic** /sīkō thèrrə pyóotik/ *adj.* —**psy·cho·ther·a·peu·ti·cal·ly** /-pyóotikəlee/ *adv.* —**psy·cho·ther·a·pist** /sīkō thérrəpist/ *n.*

psy·chot·o·mi·met·ic /sī kòttō mi méttik/ *adj.* PRODUCING A REACTION LIKE PSYCHOSIS used to describe a drug or other factor that produces a condition resembling psychosis ■ *n.* PSYCHOTOMIMETIC DRUG a drug or other factor that produces a condition resembling psychosis [Mid-20thC. Coined from PSYCHOSIS + MIMETIC on the model of *psychotic*.]

psy·cho·tro·pic /sīkə tróppik/ *adj.* CAPABLE OF AFFECTING THE MIND used to describe drugs that are capable of affecting the mind, e.g., those used to treat psychiatric disorders ■ *n.* PSYCHOTROPIC DRUG a drug capable of affecting the mind, e.g., one used to treat psychiatric disorders

psychro- *prefix.* cold ○ *psychrophilic* [From Greek *psukhros*, of unknown origin]

psy·chrom·e·ter /sī krómmətər/ *n.* an instrument consisting of two thermometers, used to measure atmospheric humidity. The bulb of one thermometer is kept moist and the effect of evaporative cooling on it is compared to the other, which is kept dry.

psy·chro·phil·ic /sīkrō fíllik, sīkrə-/ *adj.* thriving at low temperatures ○ *psychrophillic bacteria* [Mid-20thC]

psyl·li·um /síllee əm/ *n.* **1.** PLANT WITH SPIKES OF SMALL FLOWERS an annual plant of the plantain family that is native to Europe and Asia and has dense spikes of small flowers. Latin name: *Plantago psyllium.* **2.** PHARM, FOOD SEEDS OF PSYLLIUM the seeds of psyllium, used as a mild laxative or as a dietary source of fiber [Mid-16thC. Via Latin from Greek *psullion*, literally "little flea," from *psulla* "flea"; because the seeds resemble fleas.]

Pt[1] *abbr.* (*used in place names*) **1.** Point **2.** Port

Pt[2] *symbol.* CHEM ELEM platinum

PT[1] *abbr.* **1.** Pacific Time **2.** part-time

PT[2] *abbr.* postal telegraph

pt. *abbr.* **1.** part **2.** FIN payment **3.** pint **4.** point **5.** port **6.** GRAM preterite

Pt. *abbr.* (*used in place names*) **1.** Point **2.** Port

p.t. *abbr.* **1.** past tense **2.** part-time **3.** pro tem

P.T. *abbr.* **1.** Pacific Time **2.** physical therapy

PTA, P.T.A. *abbr.* Parent Teacher Association

pta., pta *symbol.* MONEY peseta

Ptarmigan

ptar·mi·gan /taármigən/ (*plural* **-gan** *or* **-gans**) *n.* a wild grouse of cold or mountainous regions that has feet covered with feathers and white plumage in the winter. Genus: *Lagopus.* [Late 16thC. Alteration (influenced by Greek *pt-* as in *pteron* "wing") of Gaelic *tarmachan*, literally "little ptarmigan," from *tarmach* "ptarmigan."]

PT boat *n.* a highly maneuverable U.S. Navy vessel carrying light armament, 60 to 100 feet/18 to 31 meters in length, used especially in World War II to torpedo enemy shipping

PTC *abbr.* phenylthiocarbamide

-pteran *prefix.* = **-pterous**

pter·a·no·don /tə ránnə dòn/ *n.* an extinct toothless flying reptile with a bony crest. Genus: *Pteranodon.*

pter·i·dol·o·gy /tèrrə dólləjee/ *n.* a branch of botany dealing with ferns [Mid-19thC. Coined from Greek *pterid-*, the stem of *pteris* "fern" + -LOGY.] —**pter·i·do·log·i·cal** /tèrrədə lójjik'l/ *adj.* —**pter·i·dol·o·gist** /-dólləjist/ *n.*

pte·rid·o·phyte /tə ríddə fīt, térrədə-/ *n.* a plant that has no flowers or seeds and reproduces by means of spores. Ferns and some mosses are pteridophytes. Division: *Pteridophyta.* [Late 19thC. Coined from Greek *pterid-* (see PTERIDOLOGY) + -PHYTE.] —**pte·rid·o·phyt·ic** /tə rìddə fíttik, tèrrədə-/ *adj.* —**pter·i·doph·y·tous** /tèrrə dóffətəss/ *adj.*

pte·rid·o·sperm /tə ríddə spùrm, térrədə-/ *n.* an extinct plant resembling a fern that bore seeds [Early

20thC. Coined from Greek *pterid-* (see PTERIDOLOGY) + SPERM.]

pter·o·dac·tyl /tèrrə dákt'l/ *n.* an extinct flying reptile (**pterosaur**) of the Jurassic and Cretaceous periods with membranous wings and a rudimentary tail and beak. Genus: *Pterodactylus.* [Early 19thC. From modern Latin *Pterodactylus*, the genus name, literally "wing finger," from Greek *pteron* "wing" + *daktulos* "finger."]

pter·o·pod /térrə pòd/ *n.* a marine gastropod mollusk that has a foot with wingshaped lobes that are used as swimming organs. Group: *Pteropoda.* [Mid-19thC. Formed from modern Latin *Pteropoda*, the class name, which was coined from Greek *pteron* "wing" + modern Latin *-poda* "-pod."]

pter·o·saur /térrə sàwr/ *n.* an extinct flying reptile of the Triassic, Jurassic, and Cretaceous periods that had membranous featherless wings supported by an elongated fourth digit. Order: Pterosauria. [Mid-19thC. From modern Latin *Pterosauria*, the order name, literally "lizard with wings," from Greek *pteron* "wing" + *sauros* "lizard."]

-pterous *suffix.* having wings of a particular kind or number ○ *orthopterous* ○ *dipterous* [Formed from Greek *pteron* "wing, feather." Ultimately from an Indo-European base meaning "to fly, fall," which is also the ancestor of English *feather* and *pen.*]

pter·o·yl·glu·tam·ic ac·id /tèrrō il gloo tàmmik-/ *n.* folic acid (*technical*) [*Pteroylglutamic* coined from PTEROIC + -YL + GLUTAMIC]

pte·ryg·i·um /tə ríjjee əm/ (*plural* **-ums** *or* **-a** /-ə/) *n.* a triangular patch of tissue that obstructs vision by growing over usually the inner side of the eye. It results from degeneration of the cornea and is associated with prolonged exposure to sun and wind. [Mid-17thC. Via modern Latin from Greek *pterugion*, literally "little wing," from *pterux* "wing."]

pter·y·goid proc·ess /tèrrə goyd-/ *n.* either of two bony plates extending downward from the sphenoid bone of the skull [*Pterygoid* via modern Latin *pterygoides* "like a wing," from Greek *pterux* "wing"]

pter·y·la /térrələ/ (*plural* **-lae** /-lee, -lī/) *n.* a defined area on the skin of a bird from which feathers grow [Mid-19thC. From modern Latin, literally "feather forest," from Greek *pteron* "feather" + *hulē* "forest."]

PTFE *abbr.* polytetrafluoroethylene

ptg. *abbr.* printing

PTH *abbr.* parathyroid hormone

PTO *abbr.* **1.** Parent Teacher Organization **2.** please turn over

p.t.o. *abbr.* please turn over

Ptol·e·mae·us /tòllə máyəss/ *n.* a large walled plain on the Moon that is noticeably hexagonal in shape and has a highly cratered floor. Located northeast of Mare Imbrium, it is approximately 85 mi./140 km across.

Ptol·e·ma·ic /tòllə máy ik/ *adj.* **1.** ASTRON **OF THE ASTRONOMER PTOLEMY** relating to the geographer and astronomer Ptolemy or to his system of planetary motion **2.** HIST **OF THE EGYPTIAN PTOLEMIES** relating to the Ptolemies, Pharaohs of ancient Egypt, or to Egypt during their rule

Ptol·e·ma·ic sys·tem *n.* a theory of planetary motion developed by Ptolemy that held that the Earth was at the center of the universe with the Sun, Moon, and planets revolving around it. The most influential of the geocentric theories, it dominated thinking for 14 centuries until the Copernican system was accepted.

Ptol·e·ma·ist /tòllə máy ist/ *n.* a believer in the Ptolemaic system of planetary motion

Ptol·e·my /tólləmee/ (A.D. 100?–170) Greek astronomer, mathematician, and geographer. His Earth-centered model of the universe prevailed until the 16th century. His writings are collected in the *Almagest.* Full name **Claudius Ptolemaeus**

Pto·le·my I /tólləmee/ (367?–283? B.C.) Macedonian king of Egypt. A general in Alexander the Great's army, he became king of Egypt in 305 B.C., thereby founding the Ptolemaic dynasty. Known as **Ptolemy Soter**

pto·maine /tṓ màyn, tō máyn/ *n.* any one of a group of foul-smelling organic bases containing nitrogen, produced by bacteria during the decay of proteins [Late 19thC. Via French from Italian *ptomaina*, from Greek *ptōma*, "fallen body, corpse," from *piptein* "to fall" (source of English *symptom*).]

pto·maine poi·son·ing *n.* food poisoning caused by bacteria, but formerly believed to be caused by ptomaines

pto·sis /tṓssiss/ (*plural* **-ses** /-seez/) *n.* MED a drooping of the upper eyelid, resulting from muscle weakness or inability to move muscles [Mid-18thC. From Greek *ptōsis* "a falling," from *piptein* (see PTOMAINE).]

pts. *abbr.* **1.** parts **2.** payments **3.** pints **4.** points **5.** ports

PTSD *abbr.* posttraumatic stress disorder

PTV *abbr.* **1.** pay television **2.** public television

Pty. *abbr. U.K.* proprietary (*used in "Pty. Ltd." to indicate a private limited company*)

pty·a·lin /tī əlin/ *n.* an enzyme in saliva that catalyzes the conversion of starch into sugars [Mid-19thC. Coined from Greek *ptualon* "saliva" + -IN.]

pty·a·lism /tī ə lìzzəm/ *n.* excessive production of saliva [Late 17thC. From Greek *ptualismos* "salivation," from *ptualon* "spittle," from, ultimately, *ptuein* "to spit."]

Pu *symbol.* plutonium

pub /pub/ *n. U.K.* a bar that may also serve food [Mid-19thC. Shortening of PUBLIC HOUSE.]

pub. *abbr.* **1.** public **2.** publication **3.** published **4.** publisher **5.** publishing

pu·ber·ty /pyoóbərtee/ *n.* the stage of becoming physiologically capable of sexual reproduction, marked by genital maturation, development of secondary sex characteristics, and the first occurrence of menstruation [14thC. Directly or via French *puberté* from Latin *pubertas*, from, ultimately, *pubes* "adult."] — **pu·ber·tal** /pyoóbərtəl/ *adj.*

pu·ber·u·lent /pyoo bérryələnt, -bérrə-/ *adj.* BOT, ZOOL covered with fine down or hairs [Mid-19thC. Formed from *puber-*, the stem of *pubes* "adult."]

pu·bes[1] *n.* /pyoó beez/ (*plural* **-bes**) **AREA ABOVE THE EXTERNAL GENITALIA** the part of the abdomen immediately above the external genitalia that is covered with hair from puberty onward ■ *npl.* /pyoobz/ **PUBIC HAIR** the hair growing on the lower abdomen from puberty onward (*takes a plural verb*) [Late 16thC. From Latin *pubes* "adult males, genitals."]

pu·bes[2] plural of **pubis**

pu·bes·cent /pyoo béss'nt/ *adj.* **1. AT PUBERTY** reaching or having attained puberty **2.** BOT, ZOOL **HAIRY** covered with down or fine hair [Mid-17thC. Directly or via French from Latin *pubescent-*, the present participle stem of *pubescere* "to reach puberty," from *pubes* "adult."] — **pu·bes·cence** *n.*

pu·bic /pyoóbik/ *adj.* relating to or located near or on the pubes or pubis ○ *pubic hair*

pu·bic bone *n.* = **pubis**

pu·bic louse *n.* = **crab**[1] *n.* 4

pu·bis /pyoóbiss/ (*plural* **-bes** /-beez/) *n.* the joined pair of bones comprising the lower front of the hipbone in humans. Although a separate bone at birth, it later fuses with the ilium and the ischium. [Late 16thC. From the Latin phrase *os pubis*, literally "bone of the genital region."]

publ. *abbr.* **1.** publication **2.** published **3.** publisher

pub·lic /púbblik/ *adj.* **1. CONCERNING ALL MEMBERS OF THE COMMUNITY** relating to or concerning people as a whole or all members of a community ○ *public health* **2. FOR COMMUNITY USE** provided for the use of a community **3. OPEN TO ALL** open to everyone, and typically frequented by large numbers of people **4. OF THE STATE** relating to or involving government and governmental agencies rather than private corporations or industry ○ *working in the public sector* ○ *a public servant* **5. WELL KNOWN** known to large numbers of the community because of being involved in activities such as politics or entertainment ○ *a public figure* **6. DONE OPENLY** made, done, or happening openly, for all to see ○ *a public debate* **7. KNOWN BY ALL MEMBERS OF COMMUNITY** known or potentially known by all members of a community ○ *make the information public* **8.** POL **BELONGING TO THE COMMUNITY** belonging to the community as a whole and administered through its representatives in government ○ *public land* **9.** FIN **HAVING OPENLY PURCHASABLE SHARES** used to describe companies whose stock is available, or is made available, for anyone to buy ■ *n.* **1. EVERYONE** the community as a whole **2. PARTICULAR PART OF COMMUNITY** a part of a community sharing a particular interest ○ *the reading public* **3. FANS OR FOLLOWERS** the fans or followers of a performer or author [15thC. Directly or via French from Latin *publicus*, an alteration of *poplicus* (apparently under the influence of *pubes* "adult"), from *populus* "people."] — **pub·lic·ness** *n.*

pub·lic ac·cess *n.* in U.S. law, the availability of cable broadcasting facilities for the transmission of programs produced by members of the public

pub·lic-ad·dress sys·tem *n.* full form of **PA**

pub·lic af·fairs *npl.* issues that affect people generally, or issues arising from the relationship of the public to an organization such as a government body or a company

pub·li·can /púbblikən/ *n.* **1.** *U.K.* **PUB OWNER** the owner or manager of a pub **2.** HIST **TAX COLLECTOR IN ANCIENT ROME** a collector of taxes in ancient Rome [12thC. Via French *publicain* from, ultimately, Latin *publicus* (see PUBLIC). The modern meaning presumably arose from an association with PUBLIC HOUSE.]

pub·lic as·sis·tance *n.* aid given by government agencies to the poor, the homeless, dependent children, and others in financial distress. It can consist of money, food, food stamps, or other benefits.

pub·li·ca·tion /pùbbli káysh'n/ *n.* **1. PUBLISHING OF SOMETHING** the publishing of something, especially printed material for sale **2. PUBLISHED ITEM** an item that has been published, especially in printed form **3. PUBLIC COMMUNICATION OF SOMETHING** the communication of information to the public [14thC. Via French from, ultimately, *publicare* (see PUBLISH).]

pub·lic com·pa·ny *n. U.K.* = **public corporation**

pub·lic cor·po·ra·tion *n.* a company whose shares can be bought and sold on the stock market

pub·lic debt *n.* = **national debt**

pub·lic de·fend·er *n.* an attorney who represents defendants who cannot afford their own lawyer

pub·lic do·main *n.* **1. GOVERNMENT LAND** land that is owned and administered by a government **2. NOT IN COPYRIGHT** the condition of not being protected by patent or copyright and so freely available for use ○ *public domain software* **3. REVEALED CONDITION** the condition of being openly known or revealed as opposed to being kept a secret ○ *The information is now in the public domain.*

pub·lic en·e·my *n.* somebody who is thought to be a threat to the public, especially a violent criminal

pub·lic eye ◇ **in the public eye** regularly receiving attention from the media

pub·lic fig·ure *n.* somebody who is well known to people generally

pub·lic health *n.* the general health of a community and the practice and study of ways to preserve and improve this. It includes health education, sanitation, control of diseases, and regulation of pollution.

pub·lic house *n.* **1.** *U.K.* **PUB** a pub (*formal*) **2. HOTEL** an inn, tavern, or small hotel (*archaic*)

pub·lic hous·ing *n.* housing managed by the government and provided at a relatively low rent as a form of public assistance

pub·lic in·ter·est *n.* **1. COMMON BENEFIT** the general benefit of the public ○ *a law that would be contrary to the public interest* **2. GENERAL INTEREST IN ISSUE** the general level of interest shown by people toward an issue or event

pub·li·cist /púbblissist/ *n.* somebody who is responsible for obtaining media publicity for a client [Late 18thC. Via French *publiciste* (modeled on *canoniste* "canon lawyer"), from, ultimately, Latin *publicus* (see PUBLIC).]

pub·lic·i·ty /pu blíssətee/ *n.* **1. SOMETHING STIMULATING PUBLIC INTEREST** something such as advertising designed to increase public interest or awareness in something or somebody (*often used before a noun*) ○ *The event was dismissed as a mere publicity stunt.* **2. INTEREST CREATED BY PUBLICITY** public interest or awareness created by publicity **3. ATTENTION-GETTING INFORMATION** information used to attract public attention, or the business of disseminating this ○ *She works in publicity.* ○ *the company's publicity campaign for their new product* **4. CONDITION OF BEING PUBLIC** the condition of being known or available to the public [Late 18thC. From French *publicité*, from *public* (see PUBLIC).]

pub·li·cize /púbbli sīz/ (**-cized, -ciz·ing, -ciz·es**) *vt.* to make something generally known or known to members of a particular group, typically by advertising

pub·lic key en·cryp·tion *n.* in computing, a message encryption technique in which encoding is done using a generally available public key but decoding is done using a private key available only to the receiver

pub·lic law *n.* **1.** BRANCH OF LAW the branch of law that deals with a state and its relationships with its citizens. ◊ **private law** **2.** LAW APPLYING TO THE PUBLIC a law that applies to the public

pub·lic-li·a·bil·i·ty in·sur·ance *n.* insurance that compensates individuals if they experience injury or damage resulting from lack of reasonable care by an insured business or organization

pub·lic life *n.* public service, especially by a politician or any appointed or elected official

pub·lic lim·it·ed com·pa·ny *n.* a company in the United Kingdom whose shares can be bought and sold on the stock market and whose stockholders are subject to restricted liability for any debts or losses. Full form of **PLC**

pub·lic·ly /púbblikəlee/ *adv.* **1.** OPENLY in a public or open manner **2.** BY THE PUBLIC by or in the name of the public

pub·lic nui·sance *n.* **1.** UNACCEPTABLE PERSON somebody who is generally thought to be irritating or offensive (*insult*) **2.** LAW ILLEGAL ACTION HARMING THE COMMUNITY an illegal action that harms the members of a community in general

pub·lic o·pin·ion *n.* the general attitude or feeling of the public concerning an issue, especially when this has an effect on political decision-making

pub·lic pros·e·cu·tor *n.* a government law official prosecuting criminal offenses on behalf of the community or the state

pub·lic re·la·tions *n.* (*takes a singular or plural verb*) **1.** PROMOTION OF A FAVORABLE IMAGE the practice or profession of establishing, maintaining, or improving a favorable relationship between an institution, or person, and the public **2.** PUBLIC IMAGE how well or badly something such as an institution or person is regarded by the public ○ *Such projects provide good public relations for the government.* **3.** DEPARTMENT MANAGING PUBLIC RELATIONS the department in an organization that is responsible for public relations

pub·lic sale *n.* an auction of goods or property

pub·lic school *n.* **1.** STATE-FUNDED SCHOOL a state-funded elementary or secondary school providing education free for children in kindergarten through the twelfth grade **2.** INDEPENDENT FEE-CHARGING SECONDARY SCHOOL in England and Wales, an independent fee-charging secondary school, typically a single-sex boarding school

pub·lic sec·tor *n.* the portion of a nation's affairs, especially economic affairs, that is controlled by government agencies

pub·lic ser·vant *n.* an appointed or elected holder of a government position or office

pub·lic ser·vice *n.* **1.** GOVERNMENT EMPLOYMENT government employment, especially within the civil service **2.** PROVISION OF ESSENTIAL SERVICES the business or activity of providing the public with essential goods or services such as electric power **3.** SERVICE BENEFITING THE GENERAL PUBLIC a service that is run for the benefit of the general public, e.g., the utilities, the emergency services, and public transportation

pub·lic-ser·vice cor·po·ra·tion *n.* = **public utility**

pub·lic speak·ing *n.* the skill, practice, or process of making speeches to large groups of people — **pub·lic speak·er** *n.*

pub·lic spend·ing *n.* spending by government and government bodies

pub·lic-spir·it·ed *adj.* motivated by or showing genuine concern for others in the community

pub·lic tel·e·vi·sion *n.* noncommercial television that is supported by viewers and corporate sponsorship

pub·lic trans·por·ta·tion *n.* a network of passenger vehicles for use by the public running on set routes, usually at set times and charging set fares

pub·lic trus·tee *n. Can* in Canada, an official who manages the estates of those who are deemed not mentally competent in law or those who die without wills but have minor heirs

pub·lic u·til·i·ty *n.* ESSENTIAL PUBLIC SERVICE a government-regulated company that provides an essential public service such as water, gas, or electricity ■ **pub·lic u·til·i·ties** *npl.* STOCK EXCH PUBLIC UTILITY STOCK the stock of a public utility company

pub·lic works *npl.* civil-engineering projects that are government owned or financed, and undertaken specifically for the benefit of the public

pub·lish /púbblish/ (**-lished, -lish·ing, -lish·es**) *v.* **1.** *vti.* PREPARE AND PRODUCE TEXT OR SOFTWARE to prepare and produce material in printed or electronic form for distribution and, usually, sale **2.** *vt.* PUBLISH THE WORK OF AN AUTHOR to publish the work of a particular author **3.** *vt.* MAKE SOMETHING PUBLIC KNOWLEDGE to announce something publicly [14thC. Via Old French *publiss-*, the stem of *publier*, from, ultimately, Latin *publicus* "public" (source of English *public*).] —**pub·lish·a·ble** *adj.*

pub·lish·er /púbblishər/ *n.* **1.** PUBLISHING COMPANY OR PERSON a company or person that publishes products such as books, journals, or software **2.** OWNER OF A PUBLISHING BUSINESS the owner or representative of the owner of a newspaper, periodical, or publishing house

pub·lish·ing /púbblishing/ *n.* the trade, profession, or activity of preparing and producing material in printed or electronic form for distribution to the public

pub·lish·ing house *n.* an established publishing company that prepares and produces material in printed or electronic form for distribution and, usually, sale

PUC *abbr.* Public Utilities Commission

Puc·ci·ni /poō cheenee/, **Giacomo** (1858–1924) Italian composer. His lyrical, theatrical operas include *La Bohème* (1896), *Tosca* (1900), *Madame Butterfly* (1904), and *Turandot* (1926).

puc·coon /pə ko͞on/ (*plural* **-coons** *or* **-coon**) *n.* **1.** PLANTS PLANT YIELDING A RED DYE an American plant of the borage or poppy family such as gromwell or bloodroot whose roots yield a reddish dye. Latin name: *Lithospermum canescens* and *Sanguinaria canadensis.* **2.** INDUST DYE FROM PUCCOON a dye made from puccoon [Early 17thC. From Algonquian *poughkone.*]

puce /pyooss/ *adj.* of a brilliant purplish-red color [Late 18thC. Via French, "flea" (in the phrase *couleur puce* "flea-colored"), from Latin *pulex.* Ultimately from an Indo-European word meaning "flea," which is also the ancestor of English *flea.*] —**puce** *n.*

puck /puk/ *n.* **1.** HOCKEY DISK IN HOCKEY a small disk of hard rubber that the players hit in hockey **2.** SPORTS STROKE AT THE BALL a player's stroke at the ball in the Irish sport of hurling ■ *vt.* (**pucked, puck·ing, pucks**) SPORTS STRIKE A BALL to strike the ball in the Irish sport of hurling [Late 19thC. Origin uncertain: perhaps originally in dialect, "to strike."]

Puck[1], **puck** *n.* a mischievous or malevolent spirit in English folklore [Old English *pūca*]

Puck[2] *n.* a small natural satellite of Uranus, discovered in 1985 by the Voyager 2 planetary probe. It is approximately 154 km (96 mi.) in diameter.

puck·a *adj.* = **pukka**

puck·er /púkər/ *vti.* (**-ered, -er·ing, -ers**) GATHER INTO WRINKLES to gather something such as cloth or the skin around the lips in such a way that wrinkles or small creases are formed, or to become gathered in this way ■ *n.* SMALL WRINKLE a small wrinkle, fold, or crease [Late 16thC. Origin uncertain: probably from the stem of POCKET, in which case the underlying idea is of forming into pockets or small bag-shaped wrinkles.]

puck·ish /púkish/ *adj.* mischievous or naughty in a playful way [Late 19thC. Formed from PUCK[1].] —**puck·ish·ly** *adv.* —**puck·ish·ness** *n.*

PUD *abbr.* pickup and delivery

pud·ding /po͝odding/ *n.* **1.** SWEET COOKED DESSERT a sweet cooked dessert with a smooth creamy texture, typically consisting of flour, milk, eggs, and flavoring (*often used in combination*) **2.** *U.K.* DESSERT the dessert course of a meal [13thC. Via French *boudin* "black pudding," from, ultimately, Latin *botellus* "sausage," the original sense in English. The modern meaning evolved via "any food cooked in a bag or cloth."]

pud·ding stone *n.* a conglomerate rock in which the pebbles have a different color and texture from the material binding them together (**matrix**)

pud·dle /púdd'l/ *n.* **1.** SHALLOW POOL OF WATER a shallow pool of water, e.g., one formed by rainwater in a hollow on a road **2.** POOL OF LIQUID a small pool of liquid **3.** CIV ENG WATERPROOF LINING MATERIAL nonporous material made from thoroughly mixed wet clay and sand and used as a waterproof lining, e.g., in constructing a canal ■ *v.* (**-dled, -dling, -dles**) **1.** *vi.* SPLASH IN SHALLOW WATER to wade, dabble, or splash in shallow water or puddles **2.** *vt.* CIV ENG WATERPROOF SOMETHING WITH PUDDLE to make a canal or pool waterproof by lining it with puddle **3.** *vt.* CIV ENG MIX CLAY AND SAND to work clay and sand to make puddle **4.** *vt.* METALL PROCESS PIG IRON to convert pig iron to wrought iron by heating it in a furnace in the presence of an oxidizing agent such as ferric oxide to remove carbon [14thC. Formed from Old English *pudd* "ditch," with the literal sense "small ditch."] —**pud·dler** *n.* —**pud·dly** *adj.*

pud·dle jump·er *n.* a small light airplane that generally travels short distances (*informal*)

pu·den·dum /pyoo déndəm/ (*plural* **-da** /-déndə/) *n.* human external genital organs [Mid-17thC. From Latin, from, ultimately, *pudere* "to make or feel ashamed" (source of English impudent).] —**pu·den·dal** *adj.*

pudg·y /pújjee/ (**-i·er, -i·est**) *adj.* short and carrying more bodyweight than is desirable or advisable (*informal*) (*sometimes considered offensive*) — **pudg·i·ness** *n.*

pu·du /po͞o do͞o/ (*plural* **-dus** *or* **-du**) *n.* a very small deer with tiny straight antlers, found in the forests of Central and South America. Genus: *Pudu.* [Late 19thC. From Araucanian.]

Pueb·la /pwébblaa/ city in central Mexico, and the capital of Puebla State. It has one of the oldest cathedrals in Latin America. Population: 1,057,454 (1990).

pueb·lo /pwébblō/ (*plural* **-los**) *n.* **1.** NATIVE N OR CENTRAL AMERICAN VILLAGE a village built by Native North or Central Americans in the southwestern United States and Central America, containing at least one, but typically a cluster of multistory stone or adobe houses **2.** VILLAGE IN SPANISH-SPEAKING COUNTRIES a town or village in a Spanish-speaking country [Early 19thC. Via Spanish from Latin *populus* (see PUBLIC).]

Pueb·lo /pwébblō/ (*plural* **-lo** *or* **-los**) *n.* PEOPLES a member of any Native North or Central American people who live or lived in pueblos. The Hopi, Taos, and Zuñi are all Pueblo peoples. —**Pueb·lo** *adj.*

pu·er·ile /pyo͝orəl, pyo͝o rīl, pyoo ərəl/ *adj.* **1.** SILLY silly or immature, especially in a childish way **2.** RELATING TO CHILDHOOD relating to or characteristic of childhood [Late 16thC. Directly or via French *puéril* from Latin *puerilis*, from *puer* "child, boy." Ultimately from an Indo-European base meaning "little" (ancestor also of English *few*).] —**pu·er·ile·ly** *adv.* —**pu·er·il·i·ty** /pyoo ə ríll ətee/ *n.*

pu·er·il·ism /pyo͝orə lìzzəm, pyo͝o ərə-/ *n.* childish or immature behavior by an adult

pu·er·per·al /pyoo úrpərəl/ *adj.* relating to childbirth or the time immediately following childbirth [Mid-18thC. From Latin *puerperus* "bringing forth children," from *puer* "child" + *-parus* "bringing forth."]

pu·er·per·al fe·ver *n.* = **puerperal sepsis**

pu·er·per·al psy·cho·sis *n.* a psychiatric disorder that may affect women in the first two weeks after giving birth. It may be depressive or schizophrenic and may involve false ideas concerning the baby.

pu·er·per·al sep·sis *n.* blood poisoning following childbirth, caused by infection of the placental site

pu·er·pe·ri·um /pyo͝o ər peéree əm/ *n.* the period immediately after childbirth when the womb is returning to its normal size, lasting approximately six weeks [Early 17thC. From Latin, from Latin *puerperus* (see PUERPERAL).]

Puer·to Ri·co /pwèrtə reékō/ commonwealth of the United States, occupying one large island and several small ones in the northern Caribbean, east of the Dominican Republic. Language: Spanish, English. Currency: U.S. dollar. Capital: San Juan. Population: 3,522,037 (1990). Area: 3,427 sq. mi./8,876 sq. km. —**Puer·to Ri·can** *n., adj.*

puff /puf/ *n.* **1.** SHORT SUDDEN RUSH OF AIR a short sudden rush of air, wind, gas, or smoke **2.** SOUND OF PUFF the short sound made by a puff **3.** AMOUNT IN A PUFF the amount of substance contained in a puff **4.** SHORT EXHALATION a short blowing out of breath **5.** INHALING FOLLOWED BY EXHALING an inhalation followed by an

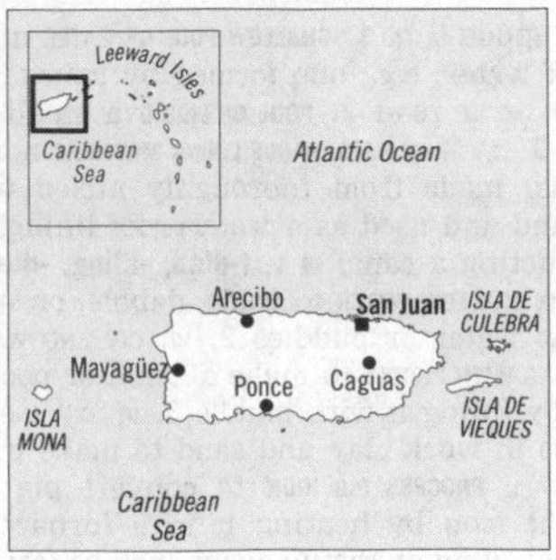

Puerto Rico

exhalation, especially when smoking **6.** FOOD = **puff pastry 7. EXAGGERATED PRAISE OR PUBLICITY** an exaggerated or flattering expression of praise, especially in publicizing something or somebody **8.** COSMETICS = **powder puff 9. SWELLING** a rounded swelling or projection on something **10.** CLOTHES **GATHERED SECTION OF FABRIC** a piece of fabric gathered around the edges and bulging in the middle **11. QUILTED BEDSPREAD** a quilted and padded covering for a bed (*dated*) **12.** HAIR **VOLUMINOUS HAIRSTYLE** hair arranged in an enlarged mass by combing, rolling, or padding it **13.** GENETICS **ENLARGED REGION ON A CHROMOSOME** an enlarged region on a chromosome resulting from active RNA synthesis ■ *v.* **(puffed, puff·ing, puffs) 1.** *vi.* **BREATHE QUICKLY** to breathe quickly in short blasts **2.** *vti.* **EMIT GAS IN SHORT BLASTS** to emit or blow steam, gas, or smoke in short blasts **3.** *vti.* **INHALE AND EXHALE SMOKE** to inhale and exhale smoke from a cigarette, cigar, or pipe **4.** *vi.* **MOVE EMITTING SMOKE PUFFS** to move in a particular direction or way emitting puffs of smoke or steam **5.** *vi.* **MOVE WHILE PANTING** to move in a particular direction or way while panting ○ *He puffed up the hill.* **6.** *vti.* **SWELL** to swell or make something swell, e.g., with air or pride **7.** *vt.* **SPEAK HIGHLY OF SOMEBODY OR SOMETHING** to praise somebody or something extravagantly, especially in publicity material [12thC. Origin uncertain: perhaps from Old English *pyf*, in which case an imitation of the sound.]

puff ad·der *n.* **1. AFRICAN INFLATING VIPER** an African viper that inflates its body and hisses when alarmed. Genus: *Bitis.* **2.** = **hognose snake**

puff·ball /púf bàwl/ *n.* a round fungus that produces a cloud of dark spores when disturbed. Many species are edible when immature. Genus: *Lycoperdon* and *Calvatia.*

puff·bird /púf bùrd/ *n.* a medium-sized bird with rounded wings and a large head, found in the forests of Central and South America. Family: Bucconidae. [Early 19thC. Because it puffs out its feathers.]

puffed-up *adj.* self-important or pompous

puff·er /púffər/ *n.* **1. PUFFING PERSON OR THING** something or somebody that puffs, especially a steam-driven train or cargo vessel **2.** ZOOL **INFLATING MARINE FISH** a marine fish of tropical waters that can inflate its body with water to appear larger to predators. Although poisonous, some varieties can be eaten as food after special preparation. Family: Tetraodontidae.

puff·er·y /púffəree/ *n.* exaggerated or overly flattering praise, especially in publicity (*informal*)

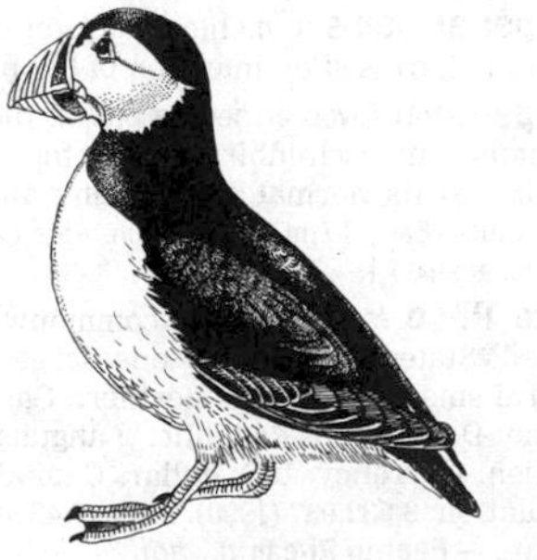
Puffin

puf·fin /púffin/ (*plural* **-fins** *or* **-fin**) *n.* a black-and-white diving bird of the auk family with a short neck and a triangular brightly colored bill. Genus: *Fratercula.* [14thC. Origin uncertain: perhaps by folk etymology from a Celtic word by association with PUFF because of its plump appearance.]

puff pas·try *n.* a light flaky multilayered pastry made by repeated rolling and folding of extremely rich buttery pastry dough, which then rises during baking

puff·y /púffee/ **(-i·er, -i·est)** *adj.* **1. SWOLLEN** swollen, especially because of tiredness, injury, crying, or poor health **2. SHORT OF BREATH** with a tendency to puff and pant **3. POMPOUS** pompous or self-important —**puff·i·ly** *adv.* —**puff·i·ness** *n.*

Pug

pug[1] /pug/ *n.* a short compact dog with a wrinkled face, short coat, and curled tail, belonging to a breed of Asian origin [Mid-18thC. Origin uncertain: perhaps from Dutch.]

pug[2] /pug/ *vt.* **(pugged, pug·ging, pugs) 1.** BUILDING, CERAMICS **KNEAD CLAY WITH WATER** to mix clay with water to make it pliable enough to form bricks or pottery **2.** BUILDING **FILL A GAP WITH CLAY** to fill in a gap with clay or mortar **3.** BUILDING **SOUNDPROOF SOMETHING** to make something soundproof with clay or some other material ■ *n.* BUILDING, CERAMICS **CLAY SUITABLE FOR MOLDING** clay mixed with water until it is pliable enough to form bricks or pottery [Early 19thC. Origin unknown.] —**pug·gy** *adj.*

pug[3] /pug/ *n.* the print of a foot or a trail of such prints, especially when made by an animal [Mid-19thC. From Hindi *pag* "footprint."]

pug[4] /pug/ *n.* a boxer (*slang*) [Mid-19thC. Shortening of PUGILISM.]

Pu·get Sound /pyóojət-/ deep inlet of the Pacific Ocean, in northwestern Washington State. Area: 561 sq. mi./1,453 sq. km.

pu·gi·lism /pyóojə lìzzəm/ *n.* the practice, sport, or profession of boxing [Late 18thC. Formed from Latin *pugil* "boxer." Ultimately from an Indo-European base meaning "to prick," which is also the ancestor of English *poignant.*] —**pu·gi·list** *n.* —**pu·gi·lis·tic** /pyóojə lístik/ *adj.* —**pu·gi·lis·ti·cal·ly** /-lístikəlee/ *adv.*

pu·gil·stick /pyóojəl-/ *n.* a long stick with padded ends used in the army to practice bayonet fighting, and in game shows involving mock combats [*Pugil* probably a shortening of PUGILISM]

pug mill *n.* a machine in which materials are ground and mixed, e.g., clay with water for building or pottery-making, or cement for building [From PUG[2]]

pug·na·cious /pug náyshəss/ *adj.* inclined to fight or be aggressive [Mid-17thC. Formed from Latin *pugnax*, from, ultimately, *pugnus* "fist."] —**pug·na·cious·ly** *adv.* —**pug·na·cious·ness** *n.* —**pug·nac·i·ty** /pug nássətee/ *n.*

pug nose *n.* a short stubby nose with a turned-up or flattened end [From PUG[1]] —**pug-nosed** *adj.*

puis·sant /pwíss'nt, pyoo əss'nt, pyoo íss'nt/ *adj.* powerful or mighty (*literary*) [15thC. Via French from, ultimately, Latin *potis* "able." Ultimately from an Indo-European base meaning "powerful," which is also the ancestor of English *despot.*] —**puis·sance** *n.* —**puis·sant·ly** *adv.*

pu·ja /póojə/ *n.* daily devotion in Hinduism, consisting of a ritual offering of food, drink, and ritual actions and prayers, most commonly to an image of a deity [Late 17thC. From Sanskrit *pūjā* "worship."]

Pu·kas·kwa Na·tion·al Park /pùkasso-/ nature preserve beside Lake Superior in Ontario, Canada. Area: 725 sq. mi./1,878 sq. km.

puke /pyook/ *vti.* **(puked, puk·ing, pukes) VOMIT** to vomit, or vomit something up (*slang*) ■ *n.* (*slang*) **1. SOMETHING VOMITED** vomited food or other matter **2. VOMITING** the vomiting up of something [Late 16thC. Origin uncertain: probably an imitation of the sound of vomiting.]

puk·ka /púkə/, **puck·a** *adj.* **1.** *S Asia* **WELL DONE OR MADE** properly done or made, or of superior quality **2.** *U.K.* **GENUINE** genuine or authentic (*informal*) **3.** *U.K.* **RESPECTABLE** of high social status (*informal*) **4. EXCELLENT** of the highest quality or standard [Late 17thC. From Hindi *pakkā* "cooked, ripe."]

pul /pool/ (*plural* **puls** *or* **pu·li** /póolee/) *n.* an Afghan monetary unit worth one hundredth of an afghani [Mid-19thC. From Pashto.]

Pu·las·ki /pə láskee/, **Casimir** (1747–79) Polish-born U.S. army officer. He organized and led the Pulaski Legion (1778), which fought for the colonists in the Revolution.

pul·chri·tude /púlkrə tòod/ *n.* physical beauty (*literary or humorous*) [14thC. From Latin *pulchritudo*, from *pulcher* "beautiful."] —**pul·chri·tu·di·nous** /pùlkrə tòod'nəss/ *adj.*

pule /pyool/ **(puled, pul·ing, pules)** *vi.* to whine, whimper, or cry plaintively (*archaic*) [Early 16thC. Origin uncertain: probably an imitation of the sound of whimpering.] —**pul·er** *n.* —**pul·ing·ly** *adv.*

pu·li /póolee, póolee, pyóolee/ (*plural* **-lis** *or* **-lik** /póolik, póolik, pyóolik/) *n.* a medium-sized Hungarian sheepdog with long hair that can be combed out or left corded [Mid-20thC. From Hungarian.]

Pu·lit·zer prize /póollitsər-/ *n.* any of several prizes awarded annually for excellence in American journalism, literature, and music [Early 20thC. Named for Joseph PULITZER.]

pull /pòol/ *v.* **(pulled, pull·ing, pulls) 1.** *vti.* **DRAW A PHYSICAL OBJECT NEARER** to apply force to a physical object so as to draw or tend to draw it toward the force's origin **2.** *vt.* **REMOVE SOMETHING FORCIBLY** to remove or extract something by exerting force **3.** *vt.* **DRAW A LOAD** to draw a load, e.g., a trailer or plow **4.** *vti.* **TUG** to tug at or jerk something or somebody **5.** *vt.* MED **STRAIN AND DAMAGE A MUSCLE** to strain and damage a muscle, ligament, or tendon **6.** *vt.* **ATTRACT CROWD** to draw a large number of people (*informal*) **7.** *vt.* **TAKE OUT A WEAPON** to take out a weapon in readiness to attack somebody (*informal*) **8.** *vt.* **APPLY FORCE TO A TRIGGER** to apply force to a trigger, lever, or switch so as to operate a weapon or machine **9.** *vt.* **OPEN OR CLOSE CURTAINS** to open or close curtains or window coverings **10.** *vti.* **TEAR** to tear or rip something **11.** *vt.* **STRETCH SOMETHING** to stretch something elastic **12.** *vt.* **DO SOMETHING UNDERHAND** to do something undesirable or despicable in an underhand way (*informal*) ○ *I just know they're trying to pull something, but I don't know what.* **13.** *vti.* CARS **MANEUVER A VEHICLE** to maneuver a vehicle in a particular direction **14.** *vi.* CARS **DRIFT TO ONE SIDE BECAUSE FAULTY** to drift to one side or the other, usually because of a fault (*refers to motor vehicles or their steering*) ○ *My car pulls to the left.* **15.** *vi.* CARS **PRODUCE SUFFICIENT DRIVING POWER** to produce sufficient driving power to move a vehicle **16.** *vi.* **INTAKE DEEPLY** to inhale deeply when smoking, or take a deep gulp at a drink **17.** *vt.* COMM, PUBL **REMOVE SOMETHING FROM CIRCULATION** to remove something from circulation, or prevent it from ever getting into circulation (*informal*) **18.** *vt.* PRINTING **MAKE A PRINTING PROOF** to make a proof from type **19.** *vt.* HORSERACING **REIN A HORSE BACK** to rein in a horse, especially so as to prevent it from winning a race **20.** *vt.* BASEBALL **HIT THE BALL WHERE THE PLAYER FACES** to hit a baseball toward the direction the batter is facing after completing a swing **21.** *vt.* SPORTS **HIT A BALL TOO FAR TO THE SIDE** to hit a ball farther left for a right-handed player or right for a left-handed player than intended ■ *n.* **1. PULLING OR BEING PULLED** the pulling of somebody or something, or an instance of being pulled **2. PULLING FORCE** the physical force involved in the action of pulling **3. SUSTAINED EFFORT** a sustained effort, especially under difficult circumstances **4. INFLUENCE** special influence, typically because of personal position within an organization or society, or personal connection with an individual (*informal*) **5. POWER TO ATTRACT** the ability or power to attract an audience or supporters (*informal*) **6. SOMETHING USED FOR PULLING** something such as a knob, handle, or tab used for pulling (*often used in combination*) **7. DEEP INHALING OR GULP** the inhaling or drinking of something deeply **8.** PRINTING **PRINTING PROOF** a proof made from type **9.** HORSERACING **RESTRAINT OF A HORSE** the restraining of a horse by its rider, especially to keep it from winning **10.** SPORTS **PULLING OF A BALL** the pulling of a ball, or a ball that is pulled **11.** ARMS **RESISTANCE IN A FIRING MECHANISM** the amount of resistance in a firing mechanism such as a trigger or bowstring [Old English *pullian*, originally "to pluck"] —**pull·er** *n.*

WORD KEY: SYNONYMS

pull., drag, draw, haul, tow, tug, yank

CORE MEANING: move something toward you or in the same direction as you

pull a general word meaning to move something toward you or in the same direction as you; **drag** to pull something with laborious effort, caused by the weight of the object or the type of surface it is being moved across; **draw** to pull something with a smooth movement; **haul** to pull something with a steady strong movement, often involving strenuous effort; **tow** to pull something along behind by means of a rope; **tug** to pull something with brief, energetic, or violent movements performed intermittently, without necessarily producing much movement in the object; **yank** an informal word meaning to pull something with a single strong movement.

pull ahead *vi.* to move in front of or gain a lead over somebody or something moving in the same direction

pull away *vi.* **1. MOVE AWAY** to move away from somebody or something **2. DRAW BACK** to draw back from somebody or something, either physically or emotionally

pull back *vti.* to withdraw, or make people, especially troops, withdraw

pull down *vt.* **1. DEMOLISH SOMETHING** to destroy or demolish something, especially a building **2. REDUCE SOMETHING TO A LOWER LEVEL** to reduce something such as a price to a lower level or value **3. DECREASE SOMEBODY'S WELL-BEING** to have a detrimental effect on somebody's health or mental well-being **4. EARN AN AMOUNT** to earn a particular amount of money (*slang*) **5.** COMPUT **MAKE A MENU APPEAR** to make a menu appear on a computer screen by clicking on its heading

pull for *vt.* to hope that somebody will succeed in an endeavor ○ *The whole town was pulling for him in the state spelling bee.*

pull in *v.* **1.** *vi.* TRANSP **ARRIVE** to arrive and stop at a place **2.** *vi.* **EARN AMOUNT** to earn a particular amount of money (*informal*) **3.** *vt.* **ARREST SOMEBODY** to arrest somebody, or take somebody in to the police station for questioning (*slang*)

pull off *vt.* to accomplish or arrange something despite difficulties (*informal*)

WORD KEY: SYNONYMS

See Synonyms at ***accomplish***.

pull on *vt.* to put on clothing or an item of clothing, especially in haste

pull out *v.* **1.** *vti.* TRANSP **MANEUVER INTO THE TRAFFIC FLOW** to drive a vehicle away from the side of a road, e.g., to join a flow of traffic **2.** *vi.* TRANSP **MANEUVER A VEHICLE BEFORE PASSING** to drive a vehicle out from behind another vehicle so as to pass **3.** *vi.* TRANSP **DEPART** to depart from a station or stopping place **4.** *vti.* **RETREAT** to retreat or cause somebody to retreat ○ *the army is pulling out* **5.** *vi.* **WITHDRAW** to withdraw from an obligation or commitment ○ *they are threatening to pull out of the deal* **6.** *vti.* AIR **LEVEL OUT AN AIRCRAFT** to level out or make an aircraft level out from a dive

pull over *v.* **1.** *vti.* **STOP A VEHICLE AT THE ROADSIDE** to drive a vehicle to the side of a road and stop, or force the driver of a vehicle to do this **2.** *vi.* **STOP AT A ROADSIDE FACILITY** to stop at a facility beside a road, e.g., a rest stop or restaurant

pull through *vti.* to recover or help somebody recover from a period of illness or difficulties

pull together *v.* **1.** *vi.* **WORK TOGETHER** to cooperate, collaborate, or otherwise work together **2.** *vr.* **RECOVER COMPOSURE** to recover your composure or self-control (*informal*)

pull up *v.* **1.** *vi.* TRANSP **STOP SOMEWHERE** to arrive and stop at a place **2.** *vi.* **CATCH UP IN A RACE** to move into a closer or level position with somebody, e.g., in a race **3.** *vti.* GARDENING **ROOT UP SOMETHING** to uproot something, e.g., in weeding, or be uprooted

pull·back /pŏŏl bàk/ *n.* **1. ACT OF PULLING BACK** an act or the process of pulling back, especially a withdrawal of troops **2. DEVICE FOR PULLING BACK** a device for holding, restraining, or drawing something back

pull-down *adj.* **MADE TO APPEAR ON A COMPUTER SCREEN** used to describe a menu or other screen item that can be made to appear on a computer screen by clicking on its heading ■ *n.* **PULL-DOWN ITEM** a pull-down feature on a computer screen

pulled thread·work *n.* an embroidery technique in which tight stitches are used to draw some threads together and separate others, thereby forming lacy patterns

pul·let /pŏŏllət/ *n.* a young female chicken, especially one that has not started to lay eggs [14thC. Via French *poulet*, literally "little hen," from *poule* "hen," from, ultimately, Latin *pullus* "young animal" (source of English *pony*).]

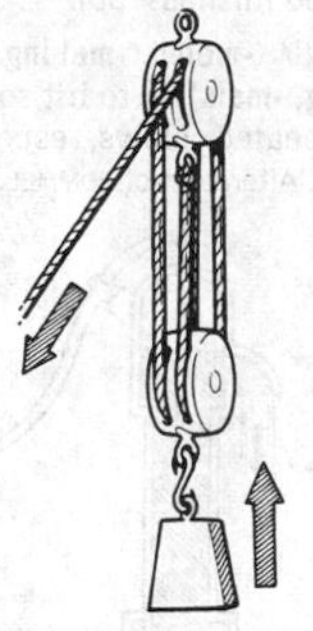

Pulley

pul·ley /pŏŏllee/ (*plural* **-leys**) *n.* **1. WHEEL WITH A GROOVED RIM** a mounted rotating wheel with a grooved rim over which a belt or chain can move to change the direction of a pulling force **2. SYSTEM OF PULLEYS** a system of pulleys along with a mounting block and tackle, used to improve leverage in lifting heavy weights [14thC. Via Old French *polie* from, ultimately, Greek *polos* "pole" (source of English *pole*). Ultimately from an Indo-European base meaning "to revolve" (ancestor also of English *wheel*).]

pul·ley bone *n.* *Southern U.S.* a wishbone

WORD KEY: REGIONAL NOTE

This is a general currency word throughout the South. Other names include *breastbone, good-luck bone, lucky bone*, and *pull bone*.

Pull·man /pŏŏlmən/ *n.* a comfortable train car for sitting or sleeping in [Mid-19thC. Named for George M. PULLMAN.]

Pull·man /pŏŏlmən/, **George Mortimer** (1831–97) U.S. inventor and manufacturer. He designed the first modern railroad sleeping car (1863).

pul·lo·rum dis·ease /pə láwrəm-/ *n.* a highly infectious disease of young poultry caused by the bacterium *Salmonella pullorum*, and marked by diarrhea. It is often fatal to chicks. [*Pullorum* from modern Latin, "of chickens"]

pull·out /pŏŏl òwt/ *n.* **1.** PUBL **OBJECT FOR PULLING OUT** an object intended to be pulled out of a publication, e.g., a removable section of a magazine or a part of a book that folds out **2. WITHDRAWAL** a withdrawal from an obligation or other demanding situation **3. RETREAT** a retreat from a place or military involvement **4.** AIR **LEVELING-OUT MANEUVER OF AIRCRAFT** an aircraft maneuver in which a dive changes to level flight

pull·o·ver /pŏŏl òvər/ *n.* a garment, especially a sweater, put on by being pulled over the head

pull-tab *n.* a ring or tab of metal on top of a drink can that is pulled in order to open it

pul·lu·late /púllyə làyt/ (**-lat·ed, -lat·ing, -lates**) *vi.* **1.** BOT **GERMINATE** to germinate or sprout (*technical*) **2.** ZOOL **BREED** to breed freely or rapidly (*technical*) **3. TEEM** to teem or swarm with something (*literary*) [Early 17thC. From Latin *pullulare*, from, ultimately, *pullus* (see PULLET).] —**pul·lu·la·tion** /pùllyə láysh'n/ *n.*

pull-up *n.* a physical exercise in which the hands are placed on an overhead horizontal bar, and the body is lifted by pulling upward with the arms

pul·mo·nar·y /pŏŏlmə nèrree, púlmə-/ *adj.* **1.** MED **RELATING TO LUNGS** concerning, affecting, or associated with the lungs **2.** ZOOL = **pulmonate** *adj.* 1 [Early 18thC. From Latin *pulmonarius*, from Latin *pulmo* "lung." Ultimately from an Indo-European base meaning "to flow," which is also the ancestor of English *flow* and *pneumonia*.]

pul·mo·nar·y ar·ter·y *n.* either of the two arteries that carry blood in need of oxygen from the right side of the heart to the lungs

pul·mo·nar·y vein *n.* any of the four veins that carry oxygen-rich blood from the lungs to the left side of the heart

pul·mo·nate /pŏŏlmə nàyt, púlmə-/ *adj.* ZOOL **1. WITH LUNGS** with lungs or organs that function as lungs **2. WITH SAC LIKE LUNG** used to describe a mollusk that has a sac functioning as a lung ■ *n.* ZOOL **MOLLUSK WITH LUNG SAC** a mollusk with a sac functioning as a lung. Examples include land snails, slugs, and many freshwater snails. Subclass: Pulmonata. [Mid-19thC. From modern Latin *pulmonatus*, from Latin *pulmo* (see PULMONARY).]

pul·mon·ic /pul mónnik/ *adj.* = **pulmonary** *adj.* 1 [Mid-17thC. Directly or via French from modern Latin *pulmonicus*, from Latin *pulmo* (see PULMONARY).]

pulp /pulp/ *n.* **1.** BOT **SOFT FLESHY PLANT TISSUE** soft or fleshy plant tissue such as the inner part of a fruit or vegetable **2.** BOT **STEM PITH** the pith inside a plant stem **3. SOFT MATERIAL** a soft or soggy mass **4.** PAPER **CRUSHED WOOD FOR PAPER** crushed wood or other materials that are used to make paper **5.** PUBL **CHEAP BOOKS AND MAGAZINES** thrilling novels and magazines produced on cheap paper, especially crime, horror, or science fiction stories (*often used before a noun*) ○ *a prize collection of classic pulp fiction* **6.** DENT **INSIDE OF TOOTH** the sensitive tissue at the center of a tooth, consisting of nerves and blood vessels **7.** MINING **PULVERIZED ORE** ore that has been mined and pulverized, especially when mixed with water ■ *v.* (**pulped, pulp·ing, pulps**) **1.** *vti.* COOK, INDUST **CRUSH SOMETHING** to crush something, or to be crushed, into pulp **2.** *vt.* COOK **REMOVE PULP FROM FRUIT** to remove the soft fleshy tissue from fruit or vegetables [14thC. From Latin *pulpa*, of unknown origin.]

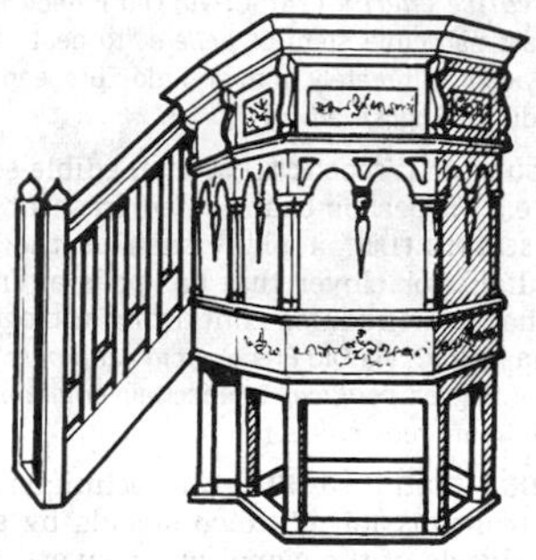

Pulpit

pul·pit /pŏŏl pìt, púl pìt/ *n.* **1. PLATFORM IN CHURCH** a raised platform or stand in a church that is used by the priest or minister for preaching or leading a service **2. CLERGY** the clergy considered as a group [14thC. Via late Latin from Latin *pulpitum* "platform, scaffold," of unknown origin.]

pulp·wood /púlp wŏŏd/ *n.* a soft wood such as aspen, pine, or spruce that is used to make paper

pulp·y /púlpee/ (**-i·er, -i·est**) *adj.* soft, moist, and smooth in consistency —**pulp·i·ness** *n.*

pul·que /pŏŏl kày, pŏŏlkee/ *n.* a thick alcoholic drink made in Mexico from the sap of the agave plant [Late 17thC. Via Mexican Spanish from Nahuatl *puliúhki*, literally "decomposed."]

pul·sar /púl saar/ *n.* a small dense star that emits brief, intense bursts of visible radiation, radio waves, and X-rays, and is generally believed to be a rapidly rotating neutron star [Mid-20thC. Contraction of *pulsating star*, on the model of "quasar."]

pul·sate /púl sàyt/ (**-sat·ed, -sat·ing, -sates**) *vi.* **1. THROB** to expand and contract with a strong regular beat **2. VIBRATE** to vibrate or quiver **3. BE FULL OF ENERGY** to be full of energy, bustling activity, and excitement ○ *The whole city is pulsating with excitement at this time of year.* **4.** PHYS **VARY REPEATEDLY IN INTENSITY OR MAGNITUDE** to vary in intensity or magnitude, especially in a repeated way [Late 18thC. From Latin *pulsare*, literally "to beat repeatedly," from *pellere* (see PULSE[1]).]

pul·sa·tile *adj.* = **pulsative** —**pul·sa·til·i·ty** /pùlsə tíllətee/ *n.*

pul·sa·tion /pul sáysh'n/ *n.* **1. PULSATING** the action of pulsating **2.** PHYSIOL **BEATING OF HEART** the rhythmic change in volume that takes place in the heart or an artery **3. ONE BEAT** a single beat or pulse

pul·sa·tive /púlsətiv/, **pul·sa·tile** /púlsət'l/ *adj.* pulsating, throbbing, or vibrating rhythmically —**pul·sa·tive·ly** *adv.*

pul·sa·tor /púl sàytər, pul sáytər/ *n.* **1. MACHINE THAT PULSATES** a device or machine that pulsates **2.** MED, PHYS **VIBRATING DEVICE** a device that stimulates or maintains a rhythmic motion

pul·sa·to·ry /púlsə tàwree/ *adj.* **1. VIBRATING RHYTHMICALLY** contracting and expanding or vibrating rhythmically **2. OF PULSATION** relating to or involving pulsation

pulse[1] /puls/ *n.* **1.** PHYSIOL **REGULAR BEAT OF BLOOD FLOW** the regular expansion and contraction of an artery, caused by the heart pumping blood through the body. It can be felt through an artery that is near the surface, e.g., the one in the wrist on the same side as the thumb. **2.** PHYSIOL **SINGLE BEAT OF BLOOD FLOW** a single expansion and contraction of an artery, caused by a beat of the heart **3. RHYTHMICAL BEAT** a beat or throb, e.g., of a drum, or a series of rhythmical beats or throbs **4.** PHYS **CHANGE OR REPEATING CHANGE IN MAGNITUDE** a brief temporary change in a normally constant quantity, e.g., in a voltage, or a series of intermittent disturbances that are regular in form and frequency of occurrence **5. CURRENT ATTITUDES** the sentiments, opinions, or attitudes current among the public or a particular group ○ *She really has the pulse of her audience.* **6. VITALITY** energy and excitement ○ *I love the pulse of city life.* ■ *vi.* **(pulsed, puls·ing, puls·es) 1. BEAT RHYTHMICALLY** to move or throb with a strong regular rhythm **2.** PHYS **UNDERGO BRIEF SUDDEN CHANGES** to undergo a series of brief sudden changes in quantity, e.g., in voltage **3. BE ENERGETIC** to be full of energy and excitement ○ *an area pulsing with creative energy* [14thC. Via Old French from Latin *puls-*, past participle stem of *pellere* "to beat" (source of English *push*). Ultimately from an Indo-European base that also produced English *anvil*.]

pulse[2] /puls/ *n.* **1.** FOOD **EDIBLE SEED** an edible seed from a pod, e.g., a pea or bean, eaten fresh or dried **2.** PLANTS **SEED-POD PLANT** a plant such as the pea, the bean, alfalfa, or clover that has pods as fruits and roots that bear nodules containing nitrogen-fixing bacteria [13thC. Via Old French from Latin *puls* "porridge" (source of English *poultice*), of uncertain origin: perhaps via Etruscan from Greek *poltos*.]

pulse code mod·u·la·tion *n.* a technique for electronic transmission of voice signals by sampling the amplitude of the signal and converting it to a coded digital form for transmission

pulse·jet /púls jèt/ *n.* a ramjet engine in which air, admitted through moveable vanes, mixes with fuel in the combustion chamber. The resulting explosion forces the vanes shut, causing a pulsating thrust.

pulse mod·u·la·tion *n.* a way of transmitting information using a series of electrical pulses, with the duration, amplitude, or frequency of the pulses modified to carry the information

pul·som·e·ter /pul sómmətər/ *n.* a lightweight pistonless pump that works using the partial vacuum created by pulses of condensing steam being forced between two chambers [Mid-19thC. Coined from PULSE[1] + -METER.]

pul·ver·a·ble /púlvərəb'l/ *adj.* capable of being pulverized [Early 17thC. Formed from Latin *pulverare* "to reduce to dust," from *pulvis* (see PULVERIZE).]

pul·ver·ize /púlvə rīz/ **(-ized, -iz·ing, -iz·es)** *v.* **1.** *vti.* **CRUSH SOMETHING TO POWDER** to crush or grind something, or become crushed or ground, into a powder or dust **2.** *vt.* **DEFEAT SOMEBODY** to subject an opponent to a crushing defeat (*informal*) ○ *We completely pulverized the opposition.* [15thC. From late Latin *pulverizare*, from Latin *pulver-*, the stem of *pulvis* "powder, dust" (source of English *powder*).] —**pul·ver·iz·a·ble** *adj.* —**pul·ver·i·za·tion** /pùlvəri záysh'n/ *n.* —**pul·ver·iz·er** /púlvə rīzər/ *n.*

pul·vil·lus /pul vílləss/ (*plural* **-li** /-lī/) *n.* a small cushion or pad between the claws at the tip of an insect's foot, used to cling to a surface [Early 18thC. From Latin, literally "small pad," from *pulvinus* "cushion," of unknown origin.]

pul·vi·nate /púlvə nàyt/ *adj.* **1. CUSHION-SHAPED** shaped like a cushion **2. SWELLING AT BASE** with a swelling at the base

pul·vi·nus /pul vīnəss/ (*plural* **-ni** /-nī/) *n.* a swelling at the base of a leafstalk. Changes in its rigidity cause changes in the position of the leaf. [Mid-19thC. From Latin, "cushion, pillow," of unknown origin.]

pu·ma /pōōmə, pyōōmə/ (*plural* **-mas** *or* **-ma**) *n.* = **mountain lion** [Late 18thC. Via Spanish from Quechua *púma*.]

pum·ice /púmmiss/ *n.* a very light porous rock formed from solidified lava, used in solid form as an abrasive and in powdered form as a polish [15thC. Via Old French from, ultimately, Latin *pumic-*, the stem of *pumex* "foam," because of the stone's spongy appearance.] —**pu·mi·ceous** /pyoo míshəss/ *adj.*

pum·mel /púmm'l/ **(-meled, -mel·ing, -mels)**, **pom·mel** **(-meled, -mel·ing, -mels)** *vt.* to hit somebody or something with repeated blows, especially using the fists [Mid-16thC. Alteration of POMMEL.]

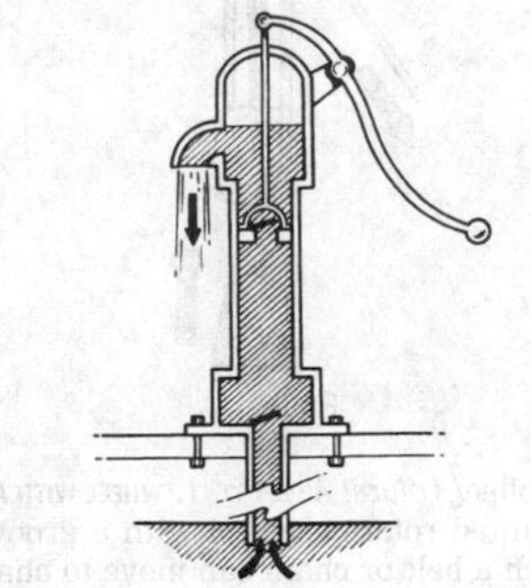

Pump: Cross section of a water pump

pump[1] /pump/ *v.* **(pumped, pump·ing, pumps) 1.** *vti.* **SHIFT LIQUID OR GAS** to force a liquid or gas to flow in a particular direction **2.** *vt.* **MAKE SOMETHING MOVE UP AND DOWN** to work a handle, lever, or other device energetically **3.** *vt.* **MAKE SOMEBODY EXCITED** to make somebody excited and enthusiastic about something (*informal*) ○ *The team was really pumped for the game.* **4.** *vt.* **ASK SOMEBODY QUESTIONS** to try to get information from somebody by asking questions repeatedly and forcefully **5.** *vt.* MED **FLUSH OUT SOMEBODY'S STOMACH** to flush out the contents of somebody's stomach, usually to remove poison, drugs, or alcohol. A tube and a funnel are used to pour in water and allow the diluted stomach contents to run out. ■ *n.* **1.** MECH ENG **DEVICE FOR SHIFTING LIQUID OR GAS** a device that is used to raise, compress, or transfer liquids or gases and is operated by a piston or similar mechanism **2.** PHYSIOL **WAY OF MOVING IONS OR MOLECULES** a mechanism for the active movement of ions or molecules across a cell membrane [15thC]

pump out *vt.* **1. PRODUCE A GREAT DEAL OF SOMETHING** to produce something continually and in large quantities ○ *a new radio station pumping out dance music 24 hours a day.* **2. REMOVE FLUID FROM SOMETHING** to remove fluid from something using a pump ○ *We had to pump out the boat again because it was leaking so badly.*

pump up *vt.* **1. INFLATE SOMETHING** to inflate something such as a tire or ball using a pump **2. TURN SOMETHING UP** to turn up the sound, especially of music, produced by amplifiers or speakers (*informal*) **3.** GYM **BUILD BODY MUSCLE** to increase the mass of a muscle by bodybuilding techniques (*informal*)

pump[2] /pump/ *n.* **1. WOMAN'S SHOE** a woman's shoe that is plain and cut low in front and has a moderately high heel **2. MAN'S FORMAL SHOE** a man's patent leather slip-on shoe worn with formal attire [Mid-16thC. Origin uncertain.]

pumped stor·age *n.* in hydroelectric systems, a way of generating power during peak periods that involves pumping water up to a reservoir during periods of low demand and releasing it during peak periods

pum·per·nick·el /púmpər nìk'l/ *n.* a dark, dense, slightly sour bread that originated in Germany and is made from coarse rye flour [Mid-18thC. From German dialect, earlier "lout," from *pumpern* "to break wind" + *Nickel* "goblin."]

pump·kin /púmpkin, púmkin/ *n.* **1.** FOOD **LARGE ORANGE FRUIT** a round large fruit with a thick orange-skinned rind, dry flesh, and many seeds **2.** PLANTS **PLANT THAT PUMPKINS GROW ON** a trailing or climbing plant with yellow flowers and large round orange edible fruit. Genus: *Cucurbita.* [Late 17thC. Alteration of earlier *pumpion*, via obsolete French *pompon* from, ultimately, Latin *pepo* (see PEPO).]

pump·kin·seed /púmpkin sèed, púmkin-/ *n.* a common North American freshwater sunfish that has an olive-colored upper body shading to yellow or orange on its belly, with one red spot on each gill

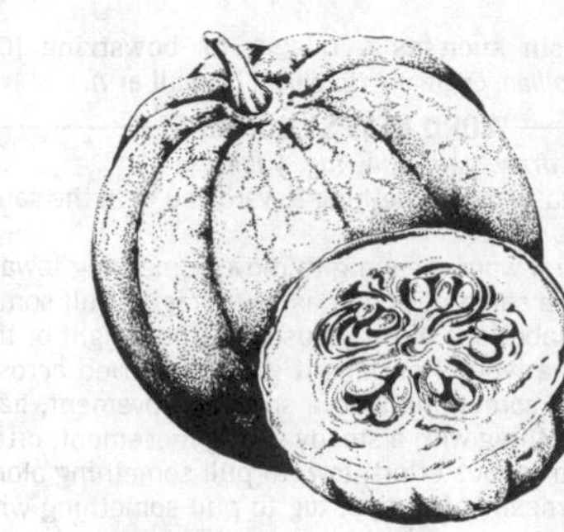

Pumpkin

cover. Latin name: *Lepomis gibbosus.* [Early 19thC. From its shape and its orange color.]

pump prim·ing *n.* **1.** ECON **INVESTMENT TO STIMULATE REGIONAL GROWTH** the use of investment to stimulate the economy in depressed regions and bring about self-sustaining growth **2. PROCESS TO GET PUMP WORKING** the process or act of making a pump work more effectively by pouring fluid into it as it starts up

pun /pun/ *n.* **PLAY ON WORDS** a humorous use of words that involves a word or phrase that has more than one possible meaning ■ *vi.* **(punned, pun·ning, puns) USE PLAY ON WORDS** to make a pun or use puns [Mid-17thC. Origin uncertain: perhaps a shortening of obsolete *pundigrion*, from Italian *puntiglio* (see PUNCTILIOUS).] —**pun·ner** *n.*

pu·na /pōōnə/ *n.* **1.** MED = **altitude sickness 2.** GEOG **PLATEAU IN ANDES** a cold dry flat treeless area at a high altitude in the Andes [Early 17thC. Via American Spanish from Quechua.]

Pun·cak Ja·ya /pōōn chaak jáa yaa/ the highest mountain in Indonesia, on the western half of the island of New Guinea, in the Surdiman Range. Height: 16,503 ft./5,030 m.

punch[1] /punch/ *vt.* **(punched, punch·ing, punch·es) 1. HIT SOMEBODY WITH FIST** to hit somebody or something with the fist **2. POKE SOMETHING** to poke or prod something ○ *He punched the pile of debris with a stick to see what was under it.* **3. PRESS BUTTON** to press a key or button on a computer keyboard or some other device with a quick thrusting movement of the finger ○ *Punch the return key.* **4.** AGRIC **HERD CATTLE** to herd cattle on horseback ■ *n.* **1. BLOW WITH FIST** a blow with the fist **2. VIGOR** drive, energy, or power that livens or invigorates something ○ *performance lacked that punch* [14thC. From Old French *poinsonner* "to prick," from *poinson, poinchon* (see PUNCHEON[2]).] ◇ **pack a punch** to be very powerful or strong (*informal*) ◇ **not pull your punches, pull no punches, not pull any punches** to use as much force and energy as necessary or possible to attain a goal or convey a message ◇ **roll with the punches** to adapt easily to a difficult situation (*informal*)

punch in *v.* **1.** *vi.* HR **REGISTER ARRIVAL FOR WORK** to arrive for work, or record the time of arrival by inserting a personalized card into a time clock **2.** *vt.* COMPUT **ENTER DATA USING KEYBOARD** to enter information into a computer using the keyboard

punch out *vi.* to leave work, or record the time of departure from work by inserting a personalized card into a time clock

punch up *vt.* to add force or liveliness to something (*informal*) ○ *That speech needs to be rewritten and really punched up.*

punch[2] /punch/ *n.* **1. TOOL FOR MAKING HOLES** a tool used to make holes in something **2. STAMPING TOOL** a tool that is hit to stamp a design on something or to cut something to a particular shape **3. STAMPING OR CUTTING PART OF PUNCH** the die or solid part of a punch, containing the stamping or cutting tool **4. TOOL FOR DRIVING BOLTS OUT** a tool used to knock a bolt or rivet out of a hole ■ *vt.* **(punched, punch·ing, punch·es) 1. MAKE HOLE USING PUNCH** to make a hole in something using a punch **2. STAMP SOMETHING USING PUNCH** to stamp or cut something using a punch [Early 16thC. Origin uncertain: possibly a shortening of PUNCHEON[1].]

punch[3] /punch/ *n.* BEVERAGES a drink made with a mixture of fruit juice and often spices and wine or liquor [Mid-17thC. Origin uncertain: perhaps via Hindi *pañc-* "five" from Sanskrit *pañca* (from the supposed five original ingredients of the drink); ultimately from the Indo-European word for "five."]

Punch /punch/ *n.* a character from traditional children's puppet shows. He is a red-cheeked, hook-nosed clown who behaves in a quarrelsome or aggressive manner. His wife is called Judy. ◊ **Punchinello** [Late 17thC. Shortening of PUNCHINELLO.] ◇ **pleased as Punch** extremely pleased (*informal*)

Punch and Ju·dy, Punch-and-Ju·dy, Punch-and-Ju·dy show *n.* a comic children's puppet show featuring Punch and Judy, a quarrelsome couple, together with a number of other standard characters. The show is often used as a belittling image of confrontation, e.g., when referring to politics.

punch·bag /púnch bàg/ *n. U.K.* = **punching bag**

punch·ball /púnch bàwl/ *n.* SPORTS a version of baseball played with a rubber ball that is struck with the player's fist instead of a bat

punch·board /púnch bàwrd/ *n.* a board with small holes, each containing a slip of paper. Players buy a chance to punch out a slip to see if they have won a prize.

punch·bowl /púnch bōl/ *n.* a large bowl for serving punch, often with a matching ladle and cups

punch card, punched card *n.* a card with patterns of holes punched in it, used to store information in early computers and telex machines

punch-drunk /púnch drùnk/ *adj.* **1.** BOXING **DISORIENTATED BY PUNCHES** showing signs of confusion and disorientation as a result of brain damage caused by blows to the head **2. DAZED BY EVENTS** dazed or confused by something such as a bad experience (*informal*)

punched card *n.* = **punch card**

pun·cheon[1] /púnchən/ *n.* **1. LARGE CASK** a large cask containing between 70 and 100 gallons **2.** MEASURE **UNIT OF CAPACITY** a unit of capacity, equal to between 70 and 100 gallons [15thC. From Old French *poinçon, poinchon*, of uncertain origin: possibly the same word as PUNCHEON[2].]

pun·cheon[2] /púnchən/ *n.* CONSTR **1. PART OF WOODEN FRAMING** a short upright piece of wood used for structural framing **2. WOODEN FLOORBOARD TIMBER** a large timber with one flattened side, usually used for flooring [15thC. Via Old French *poinchon* from, ultimately, Latin *punct-*, the past participle stem of *pungere* (see PUNGENT).]

Pun·chi·nel·lo /pùnchə néllō/ (*plural* **-los**) *n.* **1.** THEATER **ITALIAN PUPPET CHARACTER** a short character who appears in Italian puppet and clown shows and is probably the source of Punch **2. LUDICROUS PERSON** somebody who is considered a buffoon [Mid-17thC. From Italian dialect *Pollecinella*, of uncertain origin: perhaps via *pollecena* "turkey pullet," from, ultimately, Latin *pullus* (see PULLET); from the resemblance of his nose to a turkey's beak.]

punch·ing bag *n.* a large heavy bag, usually suspended from a rope, that boxers punch to improve their punching skills

punch line *n.* the last part of a joke or funny story that delivers the meaning and the bulk of the humor [From PUNCH[1]]

punch-up *n. U.K.* a fistfight or brawl (*informal*)

punch·y /púnchee/ (**-i·er, -i·est**) *adj.* (*informal*) **1. EFFECTIVE** forceful and concise ○ *What we need is a good punchy slogan.* **2. PUNCH-DRUNK** punch-drunk [Early 20thC. Formed from PUNCH[1].] —**punch·i·ly** *adv.* —**punch·i·ness** *n.*

punc·tate /púngk tàyt/ *adj.* with tiny spots, holes, or dents ○ *a punctate leaf* [Mid-17thC. Formed from Latin *punctum* (see POINT).] —**punc·ta·tion** /pungk táysh'n/ *n.*

punc·til·i·o /pungk tíllee ō/ (*plural* **-os**) *n.* (*formal*) **1. OBSERVANCE OF ETIQUETTE** strict adherence to even the finest points of etiquette **2. POINT OF ETIQUETTE** a very fine point of etiquette [Late 16thC. Via obsolete Italian *puntiglio* and Spanish *puntillo*, literally "small point," from, ultimately, Latin *punctum* (see POINT).]

punc·til·i·ous /pungk tíllee əss/ *adj.* **1. CAREFUL ABOUT CORRECT BEHAVIOR** very careful about the conventions of correct behavior and etiquette ○ *a courteous, punctilious manner* **2. FASTIDIOUS** showing great care in small details ○ *a punctilious execution of a complex design* [Mid-17thC. From French *pointilleux*, from *pointille* "small point," from *pointe*.] —**punc·til·i·ous·ly** *adv.* —**punc·til·i·ous·ness** *n.*

WORD KEY: SYNONYMS

See Synonyms at *careful*.

punc·tu·al /púngkchoo əl/ *adj.* **1. KEEPING TO ARRANGED TIME** arriving or taking place at the arranged time ○ *a punctual start to a meeting* **2.** MATH **OF POINT IN SPACE** relating to or with the properties of a point in space [14thC. From medieval Latin *punctualis*, from Latin *punctum* (see POINT).] —**punc·tu·al·i·ty** /pùngkchoo állətee/ *n.* —**punc·tu·al·ly** /púngkchoo əlee/ *adv.*

punc·tu·ate /púngkchoo àyt/ (**-at·ed, -at·ing, -ates**) *v.* **1.** *vti.* **ADD PUNCTUATION TO TEXT** to put punctuation marks in written work **2.** *vt.* **INTERRUPT SOMETHING OFTEN** to interrupt a situation or activity frequently (*often passive*) ○ *a meeting punctuated by humorous anecdotes* **3.** *vt.* **EMPHASIZE SOMETHING** to do or say something in order to add emphasis [Mid-17thC. From medieval Latin *punctuare* "to mark with points," from Latin *punctum* (see POINT).] —**punc·tu·a·tor** *n.*

punc·tu·a·tion /pùngkchoo áysh'n/ *n.* **1. MARKS USED TO ORGANIZE WRITING** the standardized nonalphabetical symbols or marks that are used to organize writing into clauses, phrases, and sentences, and in this way make its meaning clear **2. USE OF PUNCTUATION** the general use, or a particular use, of punctuation marks **3. ACT OF PUNCTUATING WRITING** the act of punctuating writing, or an occasion during which writing is punctuated

punc·tu·a·tion mark *n.* a symbol, e.g., a comma, period, or question mark, that is used to organize writing

punc·ture /púngkchər/ *n.* **SMALL HOLE** a small hole or wound made by a sharp object ■ *v.* (**-tured, -tur·ing, -tures**) **1.** *vti.* **MAKE OR GET HOLE** to sustain or cause a small hole or wound in something such as a tire or the skin **2.** *vt.* **RUIN SOMEBODY'S CONFIDENCE** to rapidly reduce or destroy somebody's confidence, arrogance, or conviction ○ *The interview punctured his self-esteem.* [14thC. From Latin *punctura*, from *punct-*, the past participle stem of *pungere* "to prick" (see PUNGENT).] —**punc·tur·a·ble** *adj.* —**punc·tur·er** *n.*

pun·dit /púndit/ *n.* **1. SOMEBODY WHO EXPRESSES OPINION** somebody who acts as a critic or authority on a particular subject, especially in the media ○ *The election results threw the political pundits into confusion.* **2.** = **pandit 3. SOMEBODY WISE** somebody with knowledge and wisdom [Late 17thC. Via Hindi *paṇḍit* from Sanskrit *paṇḍita-* "learned," of uncertain origin.]

Pune /pōōnə/ city in western India, in Maharashtra State. It is the administrative headquarters of Pune district. Population: 1,567,000 (1991).

pung /pung/ *n. Can, New England* a low one-horse sleigh shaped like a box [Early 19thC. Shortening of *tom pung*, from an Algonquian word.]

pun·gent /púnjənt/ *adj.* **1. STRONG-SMELLING OR STRONG-TASTING** with a strong smell or powerfully sharp or bitter taste **2. CAUSTIC AND POINTED** expressed in or showing a witty and biting manner ○ *pungent observations about government corruption* **3.** BIOL **SHARP AND POINTED** used to describe a plant or animal part that ends in a sharp point ○ *a plant with elongated pungent leaves* [Late 16thC. From Latin *pungent-*, the present participle stem of *pungere* "to prick, sting" (source of English *point, puncture*, and *poignant*).] —**pun·gen·cy** *n.* —**pun·gent·ly** *adv.*

Pu·nic /pyōōnik/ *adj.* **CARTHAGINIAN** relating to the ancient Carthaginians, Carthage, or the Carthaginian language. Carthage was eventually destroyed by the Roman Empire following the three Punic Wars, fought in 264–261 B.C., 218–201 B.C., and 149–146 B.C. ■ *n.* **CARTHAGINIAN LANGUAGE** the Semitic language of ancient Carthage, which was related to Phoenician [15thC. Via Latin *Punicus* from, ultimately, Greek *Phoinix* "Phoenician."]

pun·ish /púnnish/ (**-ished, -ish·ing, -ish·es**) *v.* **1.** *vti.* **MAKE SOMEBODY UNDERGO A PENALTY** to subject somebody to a penalty for doing something wrong **2.** *vt.* **IMPOSE CRIMINAL PENALTY** to respond to a crime or other wrong act by imposing a penalty (*often passive*) ○ *Any infringement of the rules will be punished by a fine.* **3.** *vt.* **TREAT SOMEBODY OR SOMETHING HARSHLY** to treat somebody or something harshly, causing damage or pain ○ *Lopez punished the champ with some powerful blows to the body.* **4.** *vt.* **TREAT SOMEBODY UNFAIRLY** to treat somebody unfairly or discriminate against somebody [14thC. Via Old French *puniss-*, the stem of *punir*, from Latin *punire*, from *poena* (see PENAL).] —**pun·ish·er** *n.*

pun·ish·a·ble /púnnishəb'l/ *adj.* leading to or liable to punishment ○ *a punishable offense* —**pun·ish·a·bil·i·ty** /pùnnishə bíllətee/ *n.*

pun·ish·ing /púnnishing/ *adj.* very demanding, either physically or mentally. ◊ **punitive** —**pun·ish·ing·ly** *adv.*

pun·ish·ment /púnnishmənt/ *n.* **1. ACT OF PUNISHING** the act or an instance of punishing **2. PENALTY FOR DOING SOMETHING WRONG** a penalty that is imposed on somebody for wrongdoing **3. ROUGH USE** rough treatment or heavy use ○ *a sturdy car that can take a lot of punishment*

pu·ni·tive /pyōōnətiv/, **pu·ni·to·ry** /-tàwree/ *adj.* **1. OF OR AS PUNISHMENT** relating to, done as, or imposed as a punishment ○ *punitive air strikes* **2. CREATING BURDEN** causing great difficulty or hardship [Early 17thC. From medieval Latin *punitivus*, from Latin *punit-*, the past participle stem of *punire* (see PUNISH).] —**pu·ni·tive·ly** *adv.* —**pu·ni·tive·ness** *n.*

pu·ni·tive dam·ag·es *npl.* damages that are awarded by a court to punish the defendant rather than to compensate the victim

pu·ni·to·ry *adj.* = **punitive**

Pun·ja·bi /pun jaábee, -jábbee/, **Pan·ja·bi** *n.* LANG the official language of Punjab. Punjabi is an Indo-European language belonging to the Indo-Iranian family. It is spoken by about 70 million people, and is the language in which the Sikh scriptures are written. [Early 19thC. From Urdu *Panjābī*, from *Panjāb* "Punjab," from Sanskrit *pañca āpas* "five rivers."]

punk /pungk/ *n.* **1. YOUTH MOVEMENT** a youth movement of the late 1970s, characterized by loud aggressive rock music, confrontational attitudes, body piercing, and unconventional hairstyles, makeup, and clothing **2. SOMEBODY BELONGING TO PUNK MOVEMENT** a member of the punk movement **3.** = **punk rock 4. OFFENSIVE TERM** an offensive term referring to a young man regarded as worthless, lazy, or arrogant (*insult*) **5. YOUNG HOMOSEXUAL PARTNER** a young homosexual partner of an older man (*archaic slang*) (*sometimes considered offensive*) **6. PROSTITUTE** a prostitute (*archaic*) **7. DRIED WOOD** dried or decayed wood used as tinder (*archaic*) ■ *adj.* **1. NOT FEELING GOOD** feeling bad, depressed, or ill **2. NO GOOD** inferior in quality or condition (*informal*) [Late 17thC. Originally "rotten wood used as tinder," of uncertain origin: perhaps from Algonquian (Delaware) *ponk*, literally "living ashes."]

pun·ka /púngkə/, **pun·kah** *n.* a large fan used in India, consisting of palm leaves or a large cloth-covered frame suspended from the ceiling and operated by a servant [Early 17thC. Via Hindi *paṅkhā* from Sanskrit *pakṣakaḥ*, from *pakṣaḥ* "wing."]

punk·ie /púngkee/, **punk·y** (*plural* **-ies**) *n.* a fly, virtually invisible to the naked eye, that sucks the blood of animals and other insects, leaving painful itching welts. Family: Ceratopogonidae. [Mid-18thC. Via assumed New York Dutch *punkje* from Delaware *pónkwas* "dust, ashes."]

punk rock *n.* fast loud rock music often with confrontational lyrics that characterized the punk movement —**punk rock·er** *n.*

punk·y *n.* = **punkie**

pun·ny /púnnee/ (**-ni·er, -ni·est**) *adj.* using or containing a pun ○ *a punny catch phrase*

pun·ster /púnstər/ *n.* somebody who frequently makes puns

punt[1] /punt/ *vti.* (**punt·ed, punt·ing, punts**) SPORTS **KICK BALL** to drop a ball and then kick it before it hits the ground ■ *n.* SPORTS **KICK** a kick in which somebody drops a ball and kicks it before it hits the ground [Mid-19thC. Origin uncertain: perhaps originally a variant of BUNT[1].] —**punt·er** *n.*

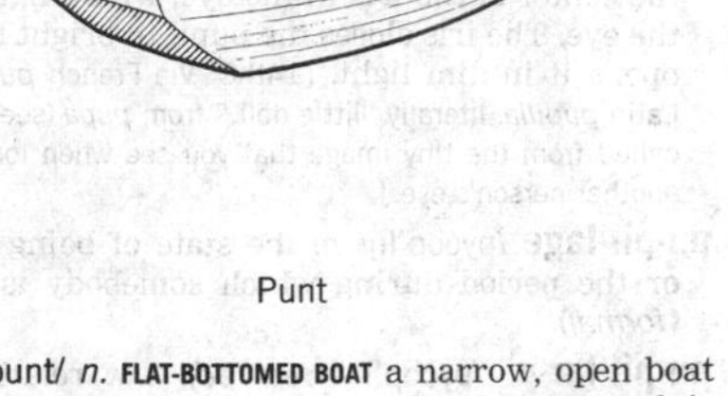

Punt

punt[2] /punt/ *n.* **FLAT-BOTTOMED BOAT** a narrow, open boat with square ends that has a flat bottom and is propelled using a long pole ■ *v.* **1.** *vi.* GO IN PUNT to travel in a punt **2.** *vti.* BOATS POLE PUNT to propel a punt using a long pole [Pre-12thC. From Latin *ponto* (see PONTOON).] —**punt·er** *n.*

punt^{3} /punt/ *n. U.K.* BET PLACED WITH A BOOKMAKER a bet, especially one placed with a bookmaker (*informal*) ■ *vti.* (**punt·ed, punt·ing, punts**) *U.K.* GAMBLE to bet or gamble, especially with a bookmaker [Early 18thC. From French *ponter,* of uncertain origin.] —**punt·er** *n.*

punt^{4} /poont/ *n.* MONEY **1.** IRISH UNIT OF CURRENCY unit of currency in the Republic of Ireland. See table at **currency 2.** COIN WORTH A PUNT a coin worth a punt [Late 20thC. From Irish *púnt.*]

punt^{5} /punt/ *n.* WINE the indentation in the bottom of a champagne or wine bottle [Mid-19thC. Origin uncertain: perhaps from PUNTY, or from French *pontil* (see PONTIL).]

Pun·ta A·re·nas /poontə ə rénnəss/ city on the Strait of Magellan in southern Chile. It is one of the southernmost cities in the world. Population: 109,110 (1992).

punt for·ma·tion *n.* in football, an offensive formation in which the back making the punt stands about ten yards behind the other backs, who are in a blocking position

pun·ty /púntee/ (*plural* **-ties**) *n.* a long metal rod on which molten glass is turned and worked during the glass blowing process [Mid-17thC. From French *pontil* (see PONTIL).]

Punx·su·taw·ney /pùngksə táwnee/ city in west central Pennsylvania, famous for its local groundhog, "Punxsutawney Phil," the emergence of which from its burrow every year on Groundhog Day, February 2, allegedly predicts the number of weeks of winter remaining. Population: 6,782 (1990).

pu·ny /pyóonee/ (**-ni·er, -ni·est**) *adj.* **1.** SMALL AND WEAK very small or thin and weak **2.** INADEQUATE less than is required to be effective ○ *a puny attempt at an apology* [Late 16thC. Anglicization of puisne.] —**pu·ni·ly** *adv.* —**pu·ni·ness** *n.*

pup /pup/ *n.* **1.** ZOOL YOUNG DOG a dog under a year old **2.** ZOOL YOUNG ANIMAL a young animal of various species including mice, rats, wolves, foxes, and seals **3.** CONCEITED YOUTH an inexperienced or arrogant young person, especially a boy or young man ■ *vi.* (**pupped, pup·ping, pups**) BEAR PUPS to give birth to pups [Late 16thC. Shortening of PUPPY.]

pu·pa /pyóopə/ (*plural* **-pae** /-pee/ *or* **-pas**) *n.* an insect at the stage between a larva and an adult in complete metamorphosis, during which the insect is in a cocoon or case, stops feeding, and undergoes internal changes [Late 18thC. From Latin, "girl, doll," feminine of *pupus* "boy" (source of English *pupil*^{1}).] —**pu·pal** *adj.*

pu·par·i·um /pyoo páiree əm/ (*plural* **-a** /-ə/) *n.* the hard case that encloses the pupa of the housefly and various other insects while they develop into adults [Early 19thC. From modern Latin, formed from Latin *pupa* (see PUPA).]

pu·pate /pyoo pàyt/ (**-pat·ed, -pat·ing, -pates**) *vi.* to develop from a larva into a pupa —**pu·pa·tion** /pyoo páysh'n/ *n.*

pup·fish /púp fish/ (*plural* **pup·fish** *or* **pup·fish·es**) *n.* a tiny killifish found in streams and springs in the southwestern United States and Mexico. Genus: *Cyprinodon.*

pu·pil^{1} /pyóop'l/ *n.* **1.** EDUC STUDENT a young student, taught at school or by a private teacher **2.** FOLLOWER OR STUDENT OF SOMEBODY somebody who is taught by or is influenced by the teachings of a particular person, usually an expert in a field ○ *a pupil of Jung* **3.** LAW TRAINEE BARRISTER somebody who is training to become a barrister [14thC. From Latin *pupillus,* literally "little boy," from *pupus* "boy."]

pu·pil^{2} /pyóop'l/ *n.* ANAT the dark circular opening at the center of the iris in the eye, where light enters the eye. The iris closes the pupil in bright light and opens it in dim light. [14thC. Via French *pupille* from Latin *pupilla,* literally "little doll," from *pupa* (see PUPA); so called from the tiny image that you see when looking into another person's eye.]

pu·pil·lage /pyóop'lij/ *n.* the state of being a pupil, or the period during which somebody is a pupil (*formal*)

pu·pil·lar·y^{1} /pyóop'l èrree/ *adj.* LAW relating to a minor child under the care of a guardian

pu·pil·lar·y^{2} /pyóop'l èrree/ *adj.* ANAT relating to or affecting the pupil of the eye

pup·pet /púppət/ *n.* **1.** ARTS MOVABLE DOLL a doll or figure representing a person or animal that is moved using the hands inside the figure or by moving rods, strings, or wires attached to it **2.** SOMEBODY WHO CAN BE MANIPULATED a person, government, or organization whose actions are controlled by others [Mid-16thC. Variant of earlier *poppet,* of uncertain origin: possibly via Anglo-Norman *poppe* "doll" from, ultimately, Latin *pupa* (source of English *pupa*).]

pup·pet·eer /pùppə téer/ *n.* somebody who operates puppets or who gives puppet shows

pup·pet·ry /púppətree/ *n.* the art of making or operating puppets

Pup·pis /púppiss/ *n.* a constellation of the southern hemisphere lying partly in the Milky Way, located between Vela and Canis Major

pup·py /púppee/ (*plural* **-pies**) *n.* **1.** YOUNG DOG a dog under a year old **2.** CONCEITED YOUTH an inexperienced or arrogant young person, especially a boy or young man (*informal*) [15thC. Origin uncertain: possibly via Old French *popée* "doll, toy" from, ultimately, Latin *pupa.*] —**pup·py·hood** *n.* —**pup·py·ish** *adj.*

pup·py dog *n.* a dog under a year old, especially one kept as a pet

pup·py love *n.* the love or infatuation felt by adolescents

pup tent *n.* = **shelter tent**

Pu·ra·na /poo raánə/ (*plural* **-nas**) *n.* one of a group of sacred Hindu texts written in Sanskrit that recount the lives of deities and the creation, destruction, and recreation of the universe [Late 17thC. From Sanskrit *purāṇaḥ,* from *purāṇa-* "belonging to former times," from *purā* "formerly."] —**Pu·ran·ic** /poo raánik/ *adj.*

Pur·bach /púr bàk/ *n.* a walled plain on the Moon having a noticeably hexagonal shape and ridges on the floor. Located east of Mare Nubium, it is approximately 75 mi./120 km across.

pur·blind /púr blìnd/ *adj.* **1.** OFFENSIVE TERM an offensive term meaning partly or completely unable to see (*offensive*) **2.** LACKING UNDERSTANDING slow or unwilling to understand (*formal*) [13thC. From PURE + BLIND.]

Pur·cell /pər sél/, **Henry** (1659–95) English composer. He wrote numerous instrumental and vocal pieces ranging from sacred to theatrical music. His works include the opera *Dido and Aeneas* (1689) and incidental music for *The Tempest* (1695).

pur·chas·a·ble /púrchəssəb'l/ *adj.* **1.** FOR SALE available to be bought **2.** CAPABLE OF BEING BRIBED willing to accept a bribe —**pur·chas·a·bil·i·ty** /pùrchəssə bíllətee/ *adj.*

pur·chase /púrchəss/ *v.* (**-chased, -chas·ing, -chas·es**) **1.** *vti.* GET SOMETHING BY PAYING MONEY to buy something using money or its equivalent **2.** *vt.* OBTAIN SOMETHING THROUGH EFFORT to obtain something by hard work or sacrifice ○ *a victory purchased with great effort* **3.** *vt.* MOVE SOMETHING USING A LEVER to move, lift, or hold on to something using a device such as a lever ■ *n.* **1.** ACT OF BUYING the act of buying something **2.** SOMETHING BOUGHT something that somebody has bought **3.** OBTAINING THROUGH EFFORT the acquisition of something through hard work or sacrifice ○ *a purchase achieved at great emotional cost* **4.** HOLD a firm grip or hold on something ○ *hands too slippery to get a purchase on the rock* **5.** ADVANTAGE influence, power, or another advantage that can be exercised ○ *an attempt to gain some purchase over his rivals* **6.** POWER GIVEN BY A LEVER a measure of the mechanical advantage given by a pulley or lever [13thC. From Anglo-Norman *purchacer* "to pursue," literally "to chase eagerly," from Old French *chacier* (see CHASE).] —**pur·chas·er** *n.*

pur·chas·ing pow·er *n.* **1.** ABILITY TO SPEND the ability to make purchases based on income and savings **2.** VALUE OF CURRENCY the value of a particular currency, measured in terms of the goods and services it can buy ○ *the purchasing power of the yen*

pur·dah /púrdə/ *n.* **1.** KEEPING WOMEN FROM PUBLIC VIEW the Hindu and Islamic custom of keeping women fully covered with clothing and apart from the rest of society **2.** SCREEN a screen or curtain used in Hindu communities to keep women out of view **3.** VEIL a veil worn by Hindu and Muslim women as part of purdah [Early 19thC. Via Urdu *pardah* "veil" from Middle Persian *pardak.*]

pure /pyoor/ (**pur·er, pur·est**) *adj.* **1.** WITHOUT ANOTHER SUBSTANCE not mixed with any other substance ○ *This jacket is pure wool.* **2.** FREE FROM CONTAMINATION clean and free from impurities ○ *The water from the spring is completely pure.* **3.** COMPLETE sheer or complete ○ *a look of pure terror* **4.** CHASTE virtuous and chaste (*literary*) **5.** CLEAR pleasingly clear and vivid (*refers to color, sound, or light*) **6.** RELATING TO THEORY relating to theory rather than practical applications ○ *Opportunities for pure research are increasingly rare nowadays.* ◊ **applied 7.** OF UNMIXED ANCESTRY with unmixed parentage or ancestry **8.** BIOL PRODUCED BY CONSTANT INBREEDING produced by continual inbreeding or self-fertilization and breeding true **9.** MUSIC, PHYS COMPOSED OF SINGLE FREQUENCY consisting of a single frequency without any overtones (*refers to sound*) ○ *a pure middle C* **10.** MUSIC WITHOUT DISCORD free of discord and in tune (*refers to a musical tone*) **11.** PHON PRONOUNCED WITH ONE UNCHANGING SOUND used to describe a vowel that is pronounced with a single unchanging sound **12.** PHON PRONOUNCED WITHOUT ANOTHER CONSONANT used to describe a consonant that is pronounced unaccompanied by any other consonant [13thC. Via French from Latin *purus* (source of English *purée, pour,* and *puritanical*).] —**pure·ness** *n.*

pure·blood /pyóor blùd/, **pure·blood·ed** /pyóor blùddəd, pyóor blúddəd/ *adj.* with an ancestry that is exclusively of a particular type —**pure·blood** *n.*

pure·bred /pyóor brèd/ *adj.* WITH ANCESTORS OF SAME BREED having ancestors that belong to the same breed or variety as a result of controlled breeding ○ *a purebred Arabian stallion* ■ *n.* SOMETHING PUREBRED a purebred plant or animal

pure de·moc·ra·cy *n.* a form of democracy in which the people exercise direct power rather than electing representatives to govern on their behalf

pu·rée /pyŏŏ ráy, pyə-/, **pu·ree** *n.* FOOD IN FORM OF PASTE food that has been made into a thick moist paste by rubbing it through a sieve, mashing it, or blending it ■ *vti.* (**-réed, -rée·ing, -rées; -reed, -ree·ing, -rees**) MAKE FOOD INTO PURÉE to become a purée, or sieve, mash, or blend food into a purée ○ *Purée the vegetables and add them to the stock.* [Early 18thC. From French *purée,* from the feminine past participle of *purer* "to squeeze out," literally "to make pure," from Latin *purare,* from *purus* "pure."]

Pure Land Bud·dhism *n.* groups of Mahayana Buddhism that venerate the Buddha Amitabha, or Amida, as a compassionate savior and promise rebirth in paradise, known as the Pure Land, as a reward for faith. These groups are commonest in East Asia, especially Japan and Korea. [*Pure Land* is a translation of Chinese *Qingtu*]

pure·ly /pyóorlee/ *adv.* **1.** ENTIRELY in a complete, entire, or total way ○ *It was a purely financial decision* **2.** MERELY for the sole reason of ○ *surgery for purely cosmetic purposes* **3.** WITH NOTHING ADDED in a way that is free of any added substances or elements or of contaminants ○ *sheep that have been purely bred from the original stock* **4.** INNOCENTLY in a way that is innocent, pure, or chaste

pur·fle /púrf'l/ *n.* ORNAMENTAL BORDER an ornamental border on clothes or furniture, consisting of a ruffled or curved band ■ *vt.* (**-fled, -fling, -fles**) DECORATE SOMETHING WITH PURFLE to decorate clothes or furniture with a purfle [14thC. Via Old French *porfil* from, ultimately, assumed Vulgar Latin *profilare,* literally "to spin forward," from Latin *filum* "thread" (see FILUM).]

pur·ga·tion /pur gáysh'n/ *n.* the act of purging or being purged (*literary*)

pur·ga·tive /púrgətiv/ *n.* SUBSTANCE FOR PURGING THE BOWELS a drug or other substance that causes evacuation of the bowels ■ *adj.* EMPTYING THE BOWELS acting as a purgative —**pur·ga·tive·ly** *adv.*

pur·ga·to·ri·al /pùrgə táwree əl/ *adj.* (*literary*) **1.** LIKE PURGATORY relating to or similar to purgatory **2.** PURGING SOMEBODY OF SIN serving to rid somebody of sin —**pur·ga·to·ri·al·ly** *adv.*

pur·ga·to·ry /púrgə tàwree/ *n.* **1. pur·ga·to·ry, Pur·ga·to·ry** PLACE OF SUFFERING in Roman Catholic doctrine, the place in which the souls remain until they have expiated their sins before they go to heaven **2.** MISERABLE SITUATION an extremely uncomfortable, painful, or unpleasant situation or experience ○ *the purgatory of lost love* [12thC. Via Old French *purgatoire* from, ultimately, Latin *purgare* "to purify" (see PURGE).]

purge /purj/ *v.* **(purged, purg·ing, purg·es) 1.** *vt.* GET RID OF OPPONENTS to remove opponents or people considered undesirable from a state or organization **2.** *vt.* REMOVE SOMETHING UNDESIRABLE to get rid of something undesirable, impure, or imperfect **3.** *vt.* RELIG FREE SOMEBODY FROM GUILT OR SIN to make somebody or something pure and free from guilt, sin, or defilement (*formal*) ○ *purge a soul of its sins* **4.** *vi.* PSYCHOL, MED VOMIT OR USE LAXATIVES to rid the body of food by using laxatives or inducing vomiting **5.** *vt.* COMPUT DELETE DATA to delete unwanted or unneeded data from disk storage in a systematic fashion so as to remove all references to the data **6.** *vti.* MED EMPTY THE BOWELS to empty the bowels or cause somebody to empty the bowels (*archaic*) ■ *n.* **1.** GETTING RID OF OPPONENTS the removal of opponents or people considered undesirable from a state or organization **2.** GETTING RID OF SOMETHING UNDESIRABLE the removal of something unwanted, unneeded, imperfect, or impure **3.** MED LAXATIVE SUBSTANCE something that acts as a laxative (*archaic*) [13thC. Via Old French *purgier* from Latin *purgare* "to purify."] —**purg·er** *n.*

pu·ri /pŏŏree/ (*plural* **-ri** *or* **-ris**), **poo·ri** (*plural* **-ri** *or* **-ris**) *n.* a small piece of light, flat, unleavened Indian bread that is fried and served hot [Mid-20thC. Via Hindi *pūrī* from Sanskrit *pūrikā*.]

pu·ri·fi·ca·tion /pyŏŏrəfi káysh'n/ *n.* **1.** PROCESS OF PURIFYING SOMETHING the process of ridding something of anything harmful, inferior, or unwanted **2.** RELIG RITUAL CLEANSING an act of purifying somebody as part of a religious ceremony or ritual to remove guilt, sin, or uncleanness ○ *a ritual of purification carried out by the priests*

pu·ri·fi·ca·tor /pyŏŏrəfi kàytər/ *n.* a linen cloth used in some Christian churches to wipe the chalice after the celebration of Communion —**pu·rif·i·ca·to·ry** /pyoo rífəkə tàwree/ *adj.*

pu·ri·fy /pyŏŏrə fī/ **(-fied, -fy·ing, -fies)** *v.* **1.** *vti.* MAKE SOMETHING PURE to rid something or become rid of something harmful, inferior, or unwanted ○ *We use special filters to purify the water.* **2.** *vt.* RELIG MAKE SOMEBODY SPIRITUALLY PURE to free somebody of sin, guilt, or uncleanness, e.g., in a ceremony or a ritual cleansing —**pu·ri·fi·er** *n.*

Pu·rim /pŏŏrim, poo rím/ *n.* a Jewish festival celebrated on the 14th day of Adar that commemorates the Jewish people's deliverance from Haman's plot to massacre them, as told in the Book of Esther. A lot was drawn, in Haman's presence, to decide the day and month of the massacre. [14thC. From Hebrew *pūrīm*, literally "lots," from *pūr* "lot."]

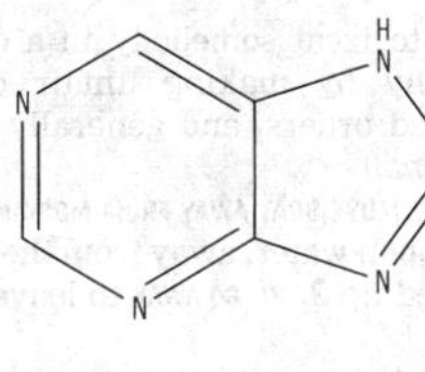

Purine

pu·rine /pyŏŏ reen, pyŏŏrin/ *n.* **1.** CRYSTALLINE SOLID a colorless crystalline solid that can be prepared from uric acid and is the parent compound of several biologically important substances. Formula: $C_5H_4N_4$. **2.** DERIVATIVE FOUND IN RNA AND DNA a biologically significant derivative of purine, especially either of the bases adenine and guanine, which are found in RNA and DNA [Late 19thC. From German *Purin*, formed from a blend of Latin *purus* "pure" and modern Latin *uricum* "uric acid."]

pur·ism /pyŏŏ rìzzəm/ *n.* insistence on the maintenance or observance of traditional standards in a field, especially in the use of language

pur·ist /pyŏŏrist/ *n.* somebody who insists on maintaining something in its traditional form —**pu·ris·tic** /pyŏŏ rístik/ *adj.* —**pu·ris·ti·cal·ly** /-rístikəlee/ *adv.*

pu·ri·tan /pyŏŏrət'n/ *n.* SOMEBODY WITH STRICT MORAL CODE somebody who lives according to strict moral or religious principles, especially somebody who regards pleasure as suspect ■ *adj.* = **puritanical** —**pu·ri·tan·ism** *n.*

Pu·ri·tan /pyŏŏrət'n/ *n.* PROTESTANT a member of a group of Protestants in 16th- and 17th-century England and 17th-century America who believed in strict religious discipline and called for the simplification of acts of worship. The movement was an attempt to remove Roman Catholic influences from the Church of England. ■ *adj.* OF PURITANS relating to Puritans, their beliefs, or movement ○ *a Puritan form of worship* [Late 16thC. Formed from Latin *puritas* "purity," from *purus* "pure."] —**Pu·ri·tan·ism** *n.*

pu·ri·tan·i·cal /pyŏŏrə tánnik'l/, **pu·ri·tan, pu·ri·tan·ic** *adj.* adhering to strict moral or religious principles —**pu·ri·tan·i·cal·ly** /-tánnikəlee/ *adv.* —**pu·ri·tan·i·cal·ness** /-tánnik'lnəss/ *n.*

pu·ri·ty /pyŏŏrətee/ (*plural* **-ties**) *n.* **1.** FREEDOM FROM ADDED ELEMENTS the absence, or degree of absence, of anything harmful, inferior, unwanted, or of a different type ○ *tests to establish the purity of the water in the river* **2.** INNOCENCE virtue and innocence ○ *the purity of young children* **3.** LING CORRECTNESS the observance of traditional standards of correctness in speech and writing **4.** COLOR SATURATION the degree of saturation or lack of white in a color **5.** CLARITY clarity of tone or sound

Pur·kin·je cell /pur kínjee-/ *n.* one of the many densely branching neurons found in the middle layer of the brain's cerebellar cortex [Late 19thC. Named for J. E. *Purkinje* (1787–1869), the Bohemian physiologist who originally described the structure.]

purl[1] /purl/ *n.* **1.** KNITTING STITCH IN KNITTING a reverse plain knitting stitch, often combined with a plain stitch to create a ribbed effect. ◊ **knit 2. purl, pearl** SEW GOLD OR SILVER THREAD sewing thread that is made from gold or silver wire **3. purl, pearl** SEW BORDER ON LACE OR BRAID a decorative looped border sewn on lace or braid ■ *vti.* **(purled, purl·ing, purls)** KNITTING KNIT WITH PURL to knit something using a purl stitch. ◊ **knit** [14thC. Origin unknown.]

purl[2] /purl/ *vi.* **(purled, purl·ing, purls)** FLOW GENTLY to flow with a soft murmuring sound, producing gentle ripples (*literary*) (*refers to rivers and streams*) ■ *n.* GENTLE FLOW the soft sound and gentle movement of a river or stream (*literary*) [15thC. Origin uncertain: probably from a Scandinavian source.]

pur·lieu /púrlyoo, púrloo/ *n.* **1.** OUTLYING DISTRICT a district on the outskirts of a city or town **2.** *U.K.* SHABBY AREA an area or district, especially one that is old and poor (*formal*) ○ *the lowest slums and purlieus of our great towns* **3.** FREQUENTED PLACE a place that somebody often visits (*formal*) ■ **pur·lieus** *npl.* ENVIRONS the outer regions or boundaries of a place (*formal*) ○ *the purlieus of the city* [15thC. Origin uncertain: probably an alteration (influenced by LIEU) of Anglo-Norman *puralee* "king's trip around the borders," from *pur-* "forth" + *aller* "to go."]

pur·lin /púrlin/ *n.* a horizontal roof beam that supports the rafters [15thC. Origin uncertain.]

pur·loin /pur lóyn/ **(-loined, -loin·ing, -loins)** *vt.* to steal something, especially when the theft breaks another's trust (*formal*) ○ *He purloined my watch when I visited him.* [14thC. From Anglo-Norman *purloigner*, literally "to move far away," from Old French *loing* "far," from Latin *longus* "long" (see LONGITUDE).] —**pur·loin·er** *n.*

WORD KEY: SYNONYMS

See Synonyms at ***steal***.

pur·ple /púrp'l/ *n.* **1.** COLORS COLOR COMBINING RED AND BLUE a dark color that reflects very little light and that is formed as a pigment by combining red and blue **2.** PURPLE OBJECT an object, substance, or fabric that is purple in color **3.** CLOTHES ROBE IN COLOR PURPLE a cloth or robe in the color purple that was formerly worn as a symbol of imperial, royal, or other high rank **4.** IMPERIAL RANK imperial power or high rank **5.** CHR RANK OF CARDINAL OR BISHOP the rank or office of a cardinal or a bishop **6.** CHR BISHOPS bishops regarded as a group ■ *adj.* **1.** COLORS OF A DARK RED-BLUE of a dark color that reflects very little light and that is formed as a pigment by combining red and blue **2.** LITERAT ELABORATE OR EXAGGERATED elaborate in style and containing too many literary effects ○ *purple prose* ■ *vti.* **(-pled, -pling, -ples)** TURN SOMETHING PURPLE to become or make something become purple ○ *His eyes narrowed and his cheeks purpled.* [Pre-12thC. Alteration of Latin *purpura*, from Greek *porphura* "shellfish yielding purple dye" (source of English *porphyry*).] —**pur·ple·ness** *n.* —**pur·plish** *adj.* —**pur·ply** *adj.*

pur·ple gal·li·nule *n.* a water-loving bird with dark bluish purple plumage and red legs. One species lives in the Mediterranean region, the other in North and South America. Genus: *Porphyrio.*

pur·ple grack·le *n.* the common grackle of eastern North America. It has deep purple iridescent plumage. Latin name: *Quiscalus quiscula.*

pur·ple·heart *n.* **1.** TREES TROPICAL S AMERICAN TREE a tropical tree of South America with hard brownish wood that turns purple when it is exposed to air. Genus: *Peltogyne.* **2.** INDUST, WOODWORK PURPLE WOOD the hard decorative purplish wood of the purpleheart

Pur·ple Heart *n.* a decoration awarded to members of the U.S. armed forces who have been wounded in action [From the silver heart and the purple ribbon from which it is suspended]

pur·ple loose·strife *n.* a marsh plant with lance-shaped leaves and spikes of purple flowers that has naturalized in North America, sometimes driving out native plants. Latin name: *Lystrum salicaria.*

pur·port *vti.* /pər páwrt/ **(-port·ed, -port·ing, -ports) 1.** CLAIM TO BE SOMETHING to claim, seem, or profess to be something specified ○ *The letter is purported to be by Napoleon.* **2.** INTEND SOMETHING to intend to do something (*formal*) ○ *While this new measure provided money for research, it also purported to cut spending overall.* ■ *n.* /púr pàwrt/ (*formal*) **1.** SENSE the meaning or significance of something ○ *The purport of the remarks was difficult to discern.* **2.** INTENT intention or purpose of something ○ *The principal purport of his letter was to inform them that he would soon be leaving the country.* [15thC. Via Anglo-Norman *purporter*, literally "to carry forward," from Latin *portare* "to carry" (see PORT[1]).]

pur·port·ed /pər páwrtəd/ *adj.* supposed or claimed to be, but without any evidence or proof of it (*formal*) —**pur·port·ed·ly** *adv.*

pur·pose /púrpəss/ *n.* **1.** REASON FOR EXISTENCE the reason for which something exists or for which it has been done or made ○ *the purpose of life* **2.** DESIRED EFFECT the goal or intended outcome of something ○ *The purpose of the law is to control pollution.* **3.** DETERMINATION the desire or the resolve necessary to accomplish a goal ○ *You need to act with purpose.* ■ *vt.* **(-posed, -pos·ing, -pos·es)** SET SOMETHING AS GOAL to intend or determine to do something [13thC. From Old French *purpos*, from *purposer* "to intend," literally "to put forth," an alteration (influenced by *poser* "to put") of Latin *proponere* (see PROPOSE).] ◇ **at cross purposes 1.** to be talking about different things and so be involved in a misunderstanding **2.** in conflict with somebody else or each other, when cooperation is needed ◇ **on purpose** deliberately ◇ **to good purpose** successfully, or with good results (*formal*) ◇ **to little** *or* **no purpose** without success or achieving useful results (*formal*)

pur·pose·ful /púrpəssfəl/ *adj.* **1.** DETERMINED showing a clear determination ○ *She set off with a purposeful stride.* **2.** HAVING A GOAL having a definite purpose or aim ○ *purposeful activity* —**pur·pose·ful·ly** *adv.* —**pur·pose·ful·ness** *n.*

pur·pose·less /púrpəssləss/ *adj.* **1.** WITHOUT REASON lacking a reason ○ *animal behavior that to human eyes seems entirely purposeless* **2.** WITHOUT PURPOSE lacking an aim or purpose ○ *walking about in a purposeless kind of way*

pur·pose·ly /púrpəsslee/ *adv.* deliberately or with an express purpose in mind ○ *They purposely humiliated me at the meeting.*

pur·po·sive /púrpəssiv/ *adj.* **1.** USEFUL having a use or purpose ○ *Most human activity is purposive.* **2.** DETERMINED showing determination ○ *She had a purposive air about her that morning.* —**pur·po·sive·ly** *adv.* —**pur·po·sive·ness** *n.*

pur·pu·ra /púrpyərə/ *n.* a condition in which bleeding under the skin causes purplish blotches to appear on the skin [Mid-18thC. From Latin, "purple" (see PURPLE).] —**pur·pu·ric** /pur pyŏŏrik/ *adj.*

pur·pure /púrpyər/ *n.* in heraldry, the color purple [Pre-12thC. From Latin *purpura* "purple," strengthened by Old French *purpre* (see PURPLE).]

pur·pu·rin /púrpyərin/ *n.* a reddish orange crystalline compound used in the manufacture of dyes, as a stain for biological specimens, and as a reagent for the detection of boron. Formula: $C_{14}H_8O_5$.

purr /purr/ *n.* **1.** CAT'S LOW MURMURING NOISE the characteristic soft low murmuring noise that a cat makes when it seems to be contented **2.** PURRING SOUND a sound similar to the purr of a cat ○ *the purr of the engine* ■ *v.* (**purred, purr·ing, purrs**) **1.** *vi.* EMIT PURR to emit a purr **2.** *vti.* SPEAK IN SOFT THROATY VOICE to speak, or say something, in a soft throaty voice that suggests pleasure, contentment, or sensuality **3.** *vi.* MAKE LOW REGULAR MECHANICAL SOUND to make the soft low vibrating noise that a machine, especially an engine, makes when it is perfectly tuned and is running well [Early 17thC. An imitation of the sound of a cat.] —**purr·ing·ly** *adv.*

purse /purss/ *n.* **1.** WOMAN'S BAG FOR CARRYING EVERYDAY BELONGINGS a bag that a woman or girl carries small personal day-to-day belongings in, such as keys, a wallet, a datebook, and pens **2.** SMALL BAG FOR CARRYING PERSONAL MONEY a small bag holding personal money carried in the pocket or kept inside a handbag or other bag **3.** PRIZE MONEY a sum of money collected as a gift or offered as a prize, especially the total sum of money offered in prizes ○ *with a purse of over $20,000* **4.** AVAILABLE FUNDS an amount of money available to spend ○ *The legislators overestimated the size of the public purse.* ■ *vt.* (**pursed, purs·ing, purs·es**) DRAW LIPS TOGETHER AT SIDES to draw the lips together at the sides so that they wrinkle and form a circle, usually when deep in thought or to express disapproval [13thC. Alteration of late Latin *bursa*, variant of *byrsa*, from Greek *bursa* "hide" (see BURSA).] ◇ **you can't make a silk purse out of a sow's ear** used to emphasize the impossibility of making something of superior quality from inferior materials or beginnings

purse crab *n.* a crab of the Gulf of Mexico and the Caribbean, the female of which carries its eggs in a sac. Latin name: *Persephona mediterranea* and *Persephona punctata.*

purs·er /púrsər/ *n.* the officer on a merchant ship or commercial aircraft who is responsible for managing the money and who, on a passenger ship, is responsible for the well-being of the passengers

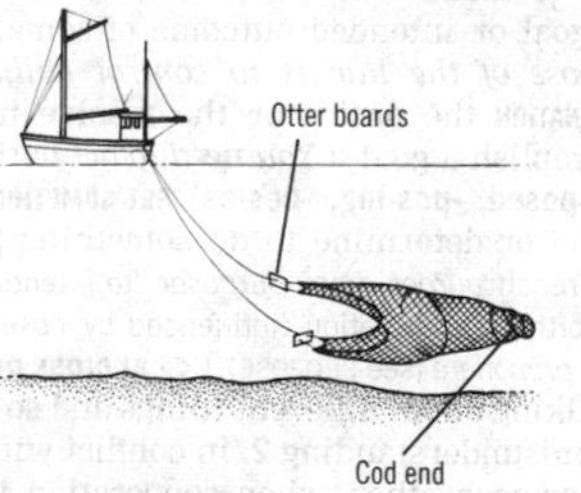

Purse seine

purse seine *n.* a large commercial fishing net pulled by two boats, with ends that are pulled together around a shoal of fish so that the net forms a pouch

purse strings *npl.* control over the money that is available to spend

purs·lane /púrslən, púr slàyn/ (*plural* **-lanes** *or* **-lane**) *n.* a trailing Asian weed sometimes used in salad or cooked and served as a vegetable. Genus: *Portulaca.* [14thC. From Old French *porcelaine*, which was formed (by confusion with *porcelaine*) (see PORCELAIN) from Latin *porcilaca*, from *portulaca*.]

pur·su·ance /pər sóo əns/ *n.* the process of doing something or carrying it out in the way that is expected or required (*formal*) ○ *in pursuance of our agreement*

pur·su·ant /pər sóo ənt/ *adj.* following in order to catch [Mid-16thC. From Old French *poursuiant*, present participle of *poursuir* (see PURSUE).] ◇ **pursuant to** in accordance with (*formal*)

pur·su·ant·ly /pər sóo əntlee/ *adv.* as a result (*formal*)

pur·sue /pər sóo/ (**-sued, -su·ing, -sues**) *v.* **1.** *vti.* CHASE SOMEBODY to follow or chase somebody in order to catch, overtake, or attack him or her **2.** *vt.* CARRY SOMETHING OUT to work at something or carry it out ○ *pursuing his studies* **3.** *vt.* CONTINUE WITH SOMETHING to continue with something or follow it up ○ *pursuing a number of lines of inquiry* **4.** *vt.* SEEK SOMEBODY PERSISTENTLY FOR SEXUAL PARTNER to make persistent attempts to start a sexual relationship with somebody **5.** *vt.* STRIVE FOR SOMETHING to try hard to achieve or obtain something over a period of time **6.** *vt.* BE EVER-PRESENT PROBLEM FOR SOMEBODY to be an ongoing, persistent problem for a person or organization ○ *Poor investment decisions pursued the company.* **7.** *vt.* FOLLOW ROUTE to go along a specified route or direction [14thC. Via Anglo-Norse *pursuer* and Old French *poursuir* from *pursivre*, ultimately from Latin *prosequi*, literally "to follow forward" (see PROSECUTE).] —**pur·su·a·ble** *adj.* —**pur·su·er** *n.*

WORD KEY: SYNONYMS

See Synonyms at ***follow.***

pur·suit /pər sóot/ *n.* **1.** ACT OF CHASING AFTER SOMETHING the act of chasing after somebody or something in order to catch, attack, or overtake that person or thing **2.** HOBBY a pastime, hobby, or leisure activity **3.** ACT OF STRIVING FOR SOMETHING the effort made to try to achieve or obtain something over a period of time ○ *the pursuit of happiness* **4.** *U.K.* CYCLE RACE WITH OBJECT OF OVERTAKING a cycle race in which the riders start from points on opposite sides of a ring-shaped track and race to overtake each other rather than reach a set finish line first [14thC. From Anglo-Norse *purseute* and Old French *poursuite*, formed from *poursuir* (see PURSUE).]

pur·suit plane *n.* a fighter plane before World War II

pur·sui·vant /púrswivənt, púrssivənt/ *n.* **1.** JUNIOR OFFICER IN COLLEGE OF ARMS an officer who ranks below a herald in a college of arms **2.** FOLLOWER a follower or attendant (*archaic*) [14thC. From Old French *pursivant*, present participle of *pursivre* "to pursue," ultimately from Latin *prosequi* (see PURSUE).]

pur·sy /púrssee/ (**-si·er, -si·est**) *adj.* (*archaic*) **1.** SHORT-WINDED getting out of breath easily **2.** OVERWEIGHT weighing more than is healthy [15thC. From Anglo-Norman *porsif*, variant of Old French *polsif*, from *polser* "to pant," from Latin *pulsare* "to agitate, drive" (see PUSH).] —**pur·si·ness** *n.*

pur·te·nance /púrt'nəns/ *n.* the inner organs of an animal (*archaic*) [14thC. From an Anglo-Norman variant of Old French *partinance*, from *partenir* (see PERTAIN).]

pur·ty /púrtee/ (**-ti·er, -ti·est**) *adj.* pretty (*regional nonstandard*) [Early 19thC. From a variant pronunciation of PRETTY.]

pu·ru·lent /pyóorələnt/ *adj.* relating to, containing, or consisting of pus [15thC. From French or Latin *purulentus* "full of pus," from the stem *pur-* "pus." Ultimately from an Indo-European word that is also the ancestor of English *foul*.] —**pu·ru·lence** /pyóorələns/ *n.* —**pu·ru·lent·ly** /pyóorələntlee/ *adv.*

pur·vey /pər váy/ (**-veyed, -vey·ing, -veys**) *vt.* **1.** SUPPLY GOODS to be a commercial supplier of goods, especially foods (*formal*) **2.** CIRCULATE GOSSIP to publish or pass on news or information, especially gossip, scandal, or other kinds of information that people generally feel should not be circulated [12thC. Via Anglo-Norman *purveier* from Latin *providere* "to provide" (see PROVIDE).]

pur·vey·ance /pər váy əns/ *n.* **1.** PROVISION OF FOOD the supplying of something, especially food **2.** PROVIDING OF SUPPLIES FOR MONARCH the task of providing, collecting, or requisitioning supplies for a king or queen (*archaic*)

pur·vey·or /pər váy ər/ *n.* **1.** COMMERCIAL SUPPLIER OF GOODS a person or company supplying goods, especially foods (*formal*) **2.** SOMEBODY CIRCULATING SOMETHING somebody who supplies, deals in, or circulates anything, especially something that is disapproved of or ridiculed **3.** OFFICER PROVIDING MONARCH'S SUPPLIES an officer employed to buy or commandeer supplies for a king or queen (*archaic*)

pur·view /púr vyòo/ *n.* **1.** SCOPE OR RANGE the scope or range of something, e.g., a court's jurisdiction or somebody's knowledge **2.** LAW MAIN ENACTING PART OF WRITTEN LEGISLATION the main body of a written piece of legislation that follows the introductory section or preamble and contains the clauses that state what the law requires [15thC. From Anglo-Norman *purveii* and Old French *porveii*, past participle of *porve(i)er* (see PURVEY).]

pus /puss/ *n.* the yellowish or greenish fluid that forms at sites of infection, consisting of dead white blood cells, dead tissue, bacteria, and blood serum [14thC. From Latin (stem *pur-*) "pus" (see PURULENT).]

Pu·san /poo saán/ city and port on Korea Strait in southeastern South Korea. It is the second largest city in the country. Population: 3,813,814 (1995).

Pu·sey·ism /pyóozee ìzzəm/ *n.* the teachings of Edward Bouverie Pusey, leader of the Oxford Movement, who advocated a renewal of Catholic practices in the Church of England [Mid-19thC. Named for Edward Pusey (1800–82), who advocated the observance of Catholic doctrine in the Church of England.]

push /pòosh/ *v.* (**pushed, push·ing, push·es**) **1.** *vti.* PRESS AGAINST TO MOVE to press against somebody or something in order to move that person or object **2.** *vti.* ADVANCE BY USING PRESSURE OR FORCE to advance or make somebody or something advance by using pressure or force ○ *She pushed to the front.* **3.** *vt.* ENCOURAGE SOMEBODY STRONGLY to urge somebody strongly to take some action or direction ○ *pushed their children to succeed* **4.** *vt.* DEPEND ON OR EXPLOIT SOMETHING to depend on or exploit something to the limits of what is wise or acceptable ○ *Don't push your luck, friend.* **5.** *vt.* USE ENERGY TO ACCOMPLISH SOMETHING to use effort or energy to promote or accomplish something ○ *push a bill through the legislative process* **6.** *vti.* EXTEND BEYOND LIMITS to extend something beyond the usual limits ○ *pushing the boundaries of knowledge in this field* **7.** *vt.* FORCE SOMETHING TO CHANGE to force something, especially a financial system, to change in a particular way ○ *a fear that increased competition will push prices down* **8.** *vt.* SELL DRUGS to engage in the sale of illegal drugs (*slang*) **9.** *vi.* MIL ADVANCE AGAINST ENEMY to make a sustained military advance **10.** *vt.* COMPUT ADD DATA TO PUSHDOWN LIST to add an item at the top of a pushdown list ■ *n.* **1.** APPLICATION OF PRESSURE the act of applying pressure to somebody or something in order to move that person or object **2.** ACT OF ADVANCING an act of advancing by using pressure or force **3.** ENERGETIC EFFORT an energetic effort used to promote or accomplish something ○ *make a push to reform the tax code* **4.** DETERMINATION vigorous energy or will to succeed ○ *dynamic graduates with plenty of push* **5.** MILITARY ADVANCE a sustained military advance ○ *a push into enemy territory* **6.** STIMULUS a stimulus or encouragement that helps the process of starting, finishing, or changing something **7.** HOCKEY CONTINUOUS NUDGING SHOT WITH STICK in field hockey, a shot in which the ball is moved forward along the ground by the application of continuous pressure with the stick, instead of being hit **8.** COMPUT NETWORK SERVICE TRANSMITTING DATA a network service in which the source of the data initiates the transmission. ◊ **pull** [14thC. Via French *pousser* from Latin *pulsare*, literally "to drive repeatedly," from *pellere* "to drive, thrust" (source of English *pulse* "beat").] ◇ **be pushing 40** to be approaching the age of 40 (*informal*) (*can be applied to other ages*) ◇ **when push comes to shove** at the point when something must be done or a decision must be made

push around *vt.* to treat somebody in a domineering way, especially by making unfair demands or giving repeated orders, and generally showing no respect (*informal*)

push off *v.* **1.** *vti.* MOVE BOAT AWAY FROM MOORING to move a boat out into open water, away from the place where it has been tied up **2.** *vi.* GO AWAY to leave or go away (*informal*)

push on *vi.* to continue on a journey, or carry on with an activity with renewed determination or effort

push through *vt.* to get something accepted or agreed quickly, especially by using persuasion or force

push·back /pòosh bàk/ *n.* a special stick stroke used in field hockey to start a game or to restart it after a goal has been scored

push broom *n.* a very wide brush designed to sweep large areas of flooring by pushing

push but·ton *n.* a button that, when pushed, mechanically opens or closes an electrical circuit, e.g., a doorbell

push-but·ton *adj.* **1.** OPERATED BY PUSHING BUTTON operated by pushing a button or buttons to open or close an electrical circuit **2.** EQUIPPED WITH AUTOMATIC DEVICES equipped with modern devices that perform tasks more or less automatically ○ *the push-button kitchen* **3.** INSTANTLY PROVIDED obtained, provided, or produced easily and instantly

push·cart /pòosh kaart/ *n.* a cart or barrow light enough to be pushed by hand, e.g., one from which goods are sold ○ *vendors selling their wares from pushcarts*

push·chair /pŏŏsh chàir/ *n. U.K.* a lightweight wheeled chair for pushing a baby or young child around in, especially one that can be folded or collapsed for easy storage. ◊ **stroller**

push·down /pŏŏsh dòwn/ *n.* a technique for organizing a list or storage of data in which the item most recently added to the list or storage becomes the next item to be retrieved. This is also called a last in, first out (or LIFO) algorithm. ○ *a pushdown stack*

pushed /pŏŏsht/ *adj.* (*informal*) **1.** SHORT OF SOMETHING lacking in something, usually time ○ *We're pushed for time now.* **2.** ALMOST UNABLE TO DO SOMETHING able to do something only with difficulty or effort

push·er /pŏŏshər/ *n.* **1.** SELLER OF ILLEGAL DRUGS somebody who sells illegal drugs, especially addictive drugs (*slang*) **2.** SOMEBODY FIERCELY COMPETITIVE OR AMBITIOUS somebody ambitious who is always trying aggressively to outdo others (*informal*)

push·ing /pŏŏshing/ *adj.* **1.** AMBITIOUS showing energy, initiative, and ambition **2.** ASSERTIVE aggressively self-confident or assertive —**push·ing·ly** *adv.* —**push·ing·ness** *n.*

Push·kin /pŏŏshkin/, **Aleksandr Sergeyevich** (1799–1837) Russian writer. He was an author of plays, novels, and short stories, and his best-known works include the verse novel *Eugene Onegin* (1831) and the tragic play *Boris Godunov* (1825).

push·o·ver /pŏŏsh ōvər/ *n.* (*informal*) **1.** EASY VICTIM somebody who is easily persuaded, deceived, or defeated **2.** SOMETHING EASY TO DO something that is very easy to do, deal with, or succeed at

push·pin /pŏŏsh pìn/ *n.* a tack with a cylindrical head, used to fix paper or other lightweight materials to a wall or bulletin board

push-pull *adj.* used to describe an electronic circuit in which two components are arranged so that an alternating input makes them transmit a current alternately. This type of circuit is commonly used in audio amplifiers to reduce harmonic distortion.

push rod *n.* a metal rod operated by a cam to open and close a valve in an internal combustion engine

push·up /pŏŏsh ùp/ *n.* **1.** *Aus, Can, U.S.* EXERCISE OF RAISING BODY FROM FLOOR a physical exercise in which, from a position of lying flat on the front with the hands under the shoulders, the body is pushed off the floor until the arms are straight **2.** COMPUT COMPUTER STORAGE TECHNIQUE a set of stored data in which the first item to be retrieved is the one stored earliest

push·y /pŏŏshee/ (**-i·er, -i·est**) *adj.* excessively aggressive or forceful in competing or dealing with others (*informal*) ○ *pushy sales techniques* —**push·i·ly** *adv.* —**push·i·ness** *n.*

pu·sil·lan·i·mous /pyŏŏssi lánniməss/ *adj.* showing a lack of courage or determination (*formal*) [15thC. Formed from late Latin *pusillanimis*, from *pusillis* "very small" + *animus* "mind."] —**pu·sil·la·nim·i·ty** /pyŏŏssilə nímmətee/ *n.* —**pu·sil·lan·i·mous·ly** /pyŏŏssi lánni məssle/ *adv.*

WORD KEY: SYNONYMS

See Synonyms at ***cowardly.***

puss[1] /pŏŏss/ *n.* (*informal*) **1.** CAT an affectionate word used for or to address a cat (*often used by or to children*) **2.** GIRL OR WOMAN an affectionately intended word for a girl or woman (*considered offensive by many people*) [Early 16thC. Origin uncertain: probably from Middle Low German *pūs*, of unknown origin.]

puss[2] /pŏŏss/ *n.* somebody's face or mouth (*slang*) ○ *a familiar puss* [Late 19thC. From Irish *pus* "lip, mouth."]

puss·ley /pússlee/ (*plural* **pus·s·leys** *or* **puss·ley**) *n.* = **purslane** [Early 19thC. Alteration.]

puss·y[1] /pŏŏssee/ (*plural* **-ies**) *n.* **1.** CAT an affectionate word used for or to address a cat (*informal*) (*often used by or to children*) **2.** CATKIN a furry hanging flower (**catkin**) that some trees produce, especially the catkin of the pussy willow tree [Late 16thC. Coined from PUSS[1] + -Y. Originally a term of endearment for a girl or woman.]

puss·y[2] /pŏŏssee/ (*plural* **-ies**) *n.* **1.** OFFENSIVE TERM an offensive term for the vulva (*taboo offensive*) **2.** OFFENSIVE TERM an offensive term for sexual intercourse with a woman (*slang offensive*) **3.** OFFENSIVE TERM a highly offensive term for women regarded as a source of sexual pleasure (*slang offensive*) [See PUSSY[1]]

pus·sy[3] /pússee/ (**-si·er, -si·est**) *adj.* resembling or full of pus [Late 19thC. Formed from PUS.]

puss·y·cat /pŏŏssee kàt/ *n.* **1.** CAT an affectionate word for a cat (*often used by or to children*) **2.** SOMEBODY GENTLE AND AMIABLE somebody who is gentle and easy-going (*informal*)

puss·y·foot /pŏŏssee fŏŏt/ (**-foot·ed, -foot·ing, -foots**) *vi.* (*informal*) **1.** BEHAVE HESITANTLY OR SPEAK VAGUELY to behave hesitantly or indecisively, or avoid speaking frankly or openly **2.** MOVE STEALTHILY to move quietly and usually secretively

puss·y·toes /pŏŏssee tōz/ (*plural* **-toes**) *n.* a low-growing perennial herb of the composite family with woolly leaves and clusters of small whitish flower heads resembling a cat's paws. Genus: *Antennaria.* [Late 19thC. So-called because the plant resembles a cat's paw.]

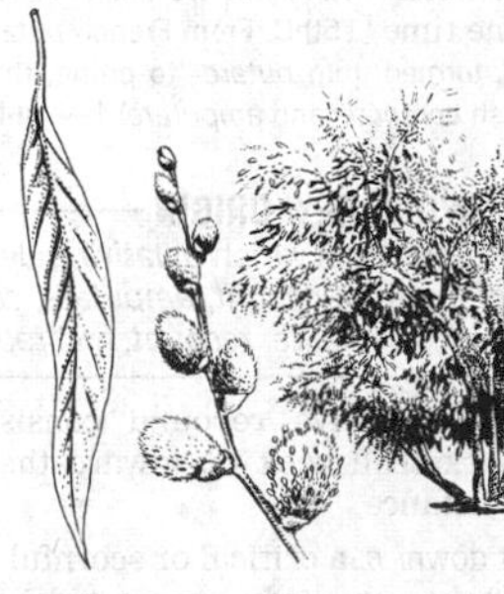

Pussy willow

puss·y wil·low *n.* **1.** N AMERICAN WILLOW TREE a North American willow shrub or small tree that has fluffy gray flowers (**catkins**) along its branches. Latin name: *Salix discolor.* **2.** WILLOW TREE a willow tree. Genus: *Salix.*

pus·tu·lant /púschələnt/ *adj.* CAUSING PUSTULES causing pustules to form on the skin ■ *n.* SUBSTANCE CAUSING PUSTULES a substance that causes pustules to form on the skin

pus·tu·late *vti.* /púschə làyt/ (**-lat·ed, -lat·ing, -lates**) CAUSE OR FORM PUSTULES to become covered with pustules, or cause pustules to form on the skin ■ *adj.* /púschə làyt, -lət/ HAVING PUSTULES covered with pustules —**pus·tu·la·tion** /púschə láysh'n/ *n.*

pus·tule /pús chŏŏl/ *n.* **1.** ANAT PIMPLE a small round raised area of inflamed skin filled with pus **2.** BIOL RAISED DISCOLORED SPOT a small raised discolored area, especially on a plant [14thC. From Latin *pustula*.] —**pus·tu·lar** /púschələr/ *adj.*

put /pŏŏt/ *vt.* (**put, put·ting, puts**) **1.** PLACE SOMETHING to move something into a particular place or position ○ *I put my arms around her.* ○ *They put the child's money into a trust fund.* **2.** CAUSE SOMEBODY TO GO to cause somebody to go to a place and stay there for a period of time **3.** PLACE SOMEBODY IN SITUATION to place somebody or something in a particular state or situation **4.** MAKE SOMEBODY DO SOMETHING to make somebody do something ○ *She was put to work in the garden.* **5.** MAKE SOMEBODY HAVE SOMETHING to make somebody or something have or be affected by something ○ *They put pressure on him to accept the offer.* **6.** EXPRESS JUDGMENT OF SOMETHING to express or experience a feeling about somebody or something ○ *put your trust in sb* **7.** USE SOMETHING to use or apply something for a particular purpose ○ *Put your mind to it.* **8.** INVEST SOMETHING to invest money, time, or effort in something ○ *We offered to put some money into the scheme.* **9.** EXPRESS SOMETHING to express or state something in a particular way ○ *put sth into words* **10.** CREATE SPECIFIED DISTANCE to create a distance of time or space between the self and something or somebody else **11.** BRING SOMETHING UP FOR SOMEBODY to bring something up as a question, vote, or proposal for somebody ○ *Feel free to put your questions to the president.* **12.** SET WORDS TO MUSIC to provide words with a musical form ○ *put the words to music* **13.** ESTIMATE SOMETHING to make an estimate of something, e.g., the time ○ *I put the time at about 11 o'clock.* **14.** SET RESTRICTION to set a limit or a restriction ○ *We must put a stop to this at once!* **15.** WRITE OR PRINT SOMETHING to change or translate information from one kind of language to another **16.** PLACE BET to bet an amount of money on a race or contest **17.** THROW HEAVY METAL BALL to throw the heavy metal ball in the shot put ■ *n.* **1.** THROW OF HEAVY METAL BALL in the shot put, a throw of the heavy metal ball **2. put, put op·tion** STOCK EXCH OPTION TO SELL a type of option giving the owner of an underlying asset the right to sell a set quantity at a set price during a specific time period [Assumed Old English *putian* "to urge"] ◇ **not know where to put yourself** to feel embarrassed (*informal*) ◇ **stay put 1.** remain in the same place **2.** of a mixture, to remain combined and mixed together

put about *v.* **1.** *vti.* NAUT CHANGE COURSE to make a ship change course, or to change course **2.** *vt.* CIRCULATE INFORMATION to circulate something such as news or gossip

put across *vt.* to make something understood or accepted by expressing it clearly ◇ **put one across somebody** to deceive or trick somebody (*informal*)

put aside *vt.* **1.** SEPARATE SOMETHING FOR DISCARDING OR SAVING to separate something from something else and discard it or save it for later use **2.** IGNORE SOMETHING to disregard something ○ *They agreed to put aside their differences.* **3.** SET SOMETHING DOWN to stop holding, looking at, or concentrating on something and set it to one side

put away *vt.* **1.** PUT SOMETHING IN USUAL STORAGE PLACE to put something in the place where it is normally stored or kept ready for use **2.** SAVE SOMETHING FOR THE FUTURE to save something, especially money, for future use **3.** EAT FOOD QUICKLY to eat food, especially quickly, greedily, or in large quantities (*informal*) **4.** CONFINE SOMEBODY to put somebody in prison or a psyhiatric (*informal*) **5.** KILL ANIMAL HUMANELY to kill an animal in a humane way, usually because it is old, injured, or terminally ill. = **put down** *v.* 6 **6.** BEAT OPPONENT DECISIVELY to beat an opponent decisively in a sporting event (*slang*)

put back *vt.* **1.** RETURN SOMETHING TO WHERE IT BELONGS to return something to the place it was taken from or to the place where it is normally kept **2.** PAY SOMETHING BACK to give something back to a person or group in exchange for help or benefits received **3.** RESTORE SOMETHING TO OPERATION to restore machine to operation **4.** RESTORE PIECES TO WHOLE to restore pieces or fragments to a unified whole **5.** DELAY OR POSTPONE SOMETHING to delay somebody or something, or postpone something **6.** MAKE CLOCK SHOW EARLIER TIME to change the time on a clock so that it shows an earlier time **7.** DRINK ALCOHOL QUICKLY to drink alcoholic drinks, especially quickly

put by *vt.* to save something, especially money, for future use

put down *v.* **1.** *vt.* WRITE SOMETHING to write something on paper **2.** *vt.* SUPPRESS REBELLION to use force to bring a rebellion to an end **3.** *vt.* DISPARAGE OR BELITTLE SOMEBODY to make somebody or something appear ridiculous or unimportant by being critical or scornful (*informal*) **4.** *vt.* PAY DEPOSIT ON SOMETHING to pay part of the cost of a purchase as a deposit **5.** *vt.* ATTRIBUTE SOMETHING TO SOMETHING to give something as or understand something to be a cause or reason for something else ○ *I put his unfriendliness down to shyness.* **6.** *vt.* KILL ANIMAL HUMANELY to kill an animal in a humane way **7.** *vti.* LAND AIRPLANE to land an aircraft somewhere **8.** *vt.* PUT CHILD TO BED to put a baby or small child to bed

WORD KEY: SYNONYMS

See Synonyms at ***kill.***

put forth *vt.* (*formal*) **1.** MAKE SOMETHING KNOWN to make something known, e.g., by stating it, publishing it, or formally submitting it for discussion **2.** GROW LEAVES OR OTHER PARTS to send out new leaves or new growth **3.** EXERT EFFORT to exert strength or make an effort in an attempt to accomplish something **4.** START TRIP to begin a trip or voyage

put forward *vt.* **1.** MAKE SOMETHING KNOWN to make something known, e.g., by stating it, publishing it, or formally submitting it for discussion **2.** OFFER SOMEBODY AS CANDIDATE to suggest somebody as a candidate for something **3.** ARRANGE FOR SOMETHING TO HAPPEN EARLIER to arrange for something to happen at a time earlier than originally planned

put in *v.* **1.** *vt.* GIVE TIME OR ENERGY to devote time or effort **2.** *vt.* MAKE CLAIM to make a claim or application for something **3.** *vt.* SAY SOMETHING to make a remark, especially to add something to a conversation **4.** *vt.* MAKE TELEPHONE CALL to make a telephone call to somebody and expect that it will be returned **5.** *vi.* BRING SHIP INTO PORT to bring a ship into a port, especially for a short stay

put off *vt.* **1.** POSTPONE SOMETHING to delay or postpone something **2.** DELAY OR HINDER SOMEBODY to delay somebody or stop somebody from acting or proceeding **3.** MAKE SOMEBODY DISGUSTED to disgust or repel somebody **4.** DISCOURAGE SOMEBODY to make somebody lose interest in or enthusiasm for, something **5.** TAKE CLOTHING OFF to remove clothes or an article of clothing (*archaic*) ○ *Put off that wet cloak.* ◇ **put somebody off his** *or* **her stride** to distract somebody from what he or she is doing and make that person do it less well

put on *vt.* **1.** START SOMETHING OPERATING to make something electrical or mechanical start operating, e.g., by turning a knob or pressing a switch **2.** COVER WITH CLOTHING to cover the body or a part of the body with clothing, headgear, footwear, or other accessories **3.** APPLY SOMETHING TO SKIN to apply something, e.g., makeup or lotion, to the skin **4.** ORGANIZE SOMETHING to organize and present an event, e.g., a theatrical entertainment **5.** GAIN OR ADD SOMETHING to gain something that is additional or extra ○ *He's been putting on weight.* **6.** PRESCRIBE SOMETHING FOR SOMEBODY to prescribe something for somebody, e.g., medication or a special diet **7.** ADOPT FALSE BEHAVIOR to adopt an attitude or way of behaving that is false or insincere **8.** PROVIDE SOMETHING to provide something as a service or facility **9.** MAKE SOMETHING SUBJECT TO IMPOSITION to impose something such as a tax or a restriction **10.** PLACE BET to make a bet, or offer money as a stake for a bet **11.** HAND TELEPHONE TO SOMEBODY to hand a telephone to somebody so that he or she can speak to somebody on the other end **12.** TEASE SOMEBODY to make fun of somebody, especially by pretending something (*informal*) ○ *You're putting me on.*

put out *v.* **1.** *vt.* EXTINGUISH LIGHT OR FIRE to switch off a light or extinguish a fire **2.** *vt.* ANNOY SOMEBODY to annoy, upset, or offend somebody ○ *He was very put out with me.* **3.** *vt.* MAKE SOMETHING KNOWN to make something widely known, e.g., by announcing or broadcasting it **4.** *vt.* CAUSE INCOVENIENCE to cause somebody inconvenience **5.** *vt.* TO CAUSE INJURY TO SOMETHING to cause injury to a part of the body ○ *I put my back out* **6.** *vt.* PRODUCE SOMETHING to manufacture or produce something **7.** *vi.* AGREE TO SEX of a woman, to agree to have sex (*slang*) (*often considered offensive*) **8.** *vt.* ELIMINATE PLAYER to eliminate a player from a game or competition ○ *The referee put the team's coach out of the game.* **9.** *vt.* BASEBALL RETIRE SOMEBODY to retire a batter or base runner **10.** *vi.* SET OFF IN BOAT to start sailing in a boat after a period spent at rest in harbor or on shore ◇ **put somebody out to pasture** to make somebody retire

put over *vt.* to make something understood by expressing it clearly ◇ **put one over (on somebody)** to make somebody believe or accept something by using deceit (*informal*)

put through *vt.* **1.** MAKE SOMEBODY UNDERGO SOMETHING to make somebody experience something difficult or unpleasant **2.** CARRY SOMETHING OUT to process something or take it to a successful conclusion **3.** CONNECT BY TELEPHONE to connect somebody by telephone to somebody else **4.** MAKE TELEPHONE CALL to make a telephone call to somebody

put to *v.* **1.** *vt.* SUBMIT TO SOMEBODY to submit a statement or question to somebody for a response ○ *I put it to you that you are not telling us the whole truth.* **2.** *vi.* BRING BOAT TO SHORE to tie up a boat in a sheltered spot or harbor **3.** *vi.* PUT HORSE BETWEEN SHAFTS to hitch a horse to a cart or other vehicle (*archaic*)

put up *v.* **1.** *vt.* PROVIDE MONEY to offer or provide something, especially money **2.** *vt.* BUILD SOMETHING to build or erect something **3.** *vt.* FASTEN SOMETHING TO WALL to fasten something to a wall, fence, or other upright surface **4.** *vti.* GIVE OR FIND SHELTER AND FOOD to give somebody accommodations, or find accommodations somewhere ○ *put us up for the night* **5.** *vt.* OFFER FOR SALE to offer something for sale ○ *The house contents were put up for sale at auction.* **6.** *vt.* PILE HAIR ON TOP OF HEAD to fix long hair in a style that is coiled or piled on the top of the head and then secured, usually with hairpins **7.** *vt.* ENGAGE IN SOMETHING to engage in or carry on something ○ *put up a fight* **8.** *vt.* ASSEMBLE AND PACKAGE SOMETHING to assemble something, especially according to particular instructions or specifications, and then package it appropriately for storage or transport **9.** *vti.* OFFER SOMEBODY AS CANDIDATE to offer somebody as a candidate **10.** *vt.* INCREASE SOMETHING to raise or increase something **11.** *vt.* RETURN SOMETHING TO STORAGE place something where it belongs for storage ○ *They'll put up their tools when the project is done.* **12.** *vt.* CAN FRUITS OR VEGETABLES to preserve fruits or vegetables ○ *We put up a dozen jars of apple jelly.* **13.** *vt.* RETURN WEAPON TO HOLDER to return a weapon taken out for use to its holder (*archaic*) ◇ **put up or shut up** used to indicate that somebody should either do something about something or else stop talking about it (*informal*)

WORD KEY: SYNONYMS

See Synonyms at ***build***.

put upon *vt.* to treat somebody badly or take advantage of somebody

put up to *vt.* to encourage or persuade somebody to do something unpleasant or destructive

put up with *vt.* to tolerate or accept somebody or something calmly

pu·ta·men /pyoo táymən/ (*plural* **-tam·i·na** /-támmənə/) *n.* the stone inside a peach, plum, apricot, or other similar fruit (*technical*) [Mid-19thC. From Latin, "shell, peel," from *putare* "to prune" (see PUTATIVE).]

pu·ta·tive /pyo͞otətiv/ *adj.* **1.** GENERALLY ACCEPTED generally believed to be or regarded as being something **2.** THOUGHT TO EXIST believed to exist now or to have existed at some time [15thC. From French *putatif* or late Latin *putativus*, formed from *putare* "to prune, think over" (source of English *computer* and *amputate*).] —**pu·ta·tive·ly** *adv.*

WORD KEY: ORIGIN

The Latin word *putare*, from which ***putative*** is derived, is also the source of English *account, amputate, compute, count, deputy, dispute, impute, recount*, and *reputation*.

put-back *n.* an offensive rebound consisting of tipping the basketball back up toward the basket from a short distance

put·down /po͝ot dòwn/ *n.* a critical or scornful remark intended to make somebody appear ridiculous or unimportant (*informal*)

put·log /po͝ot lòg/ *n.* CONSTR a short horizontal bar or beam that helps to support the planks forming the floor of a scaffold [Mid-17thC. Origin uncertain: perhaps from *put*, past participle of PUT + LOG.]

put-on *adj.* FALSE assumed or adopted for effect or in order to deceive ○ *a put-on accent* ■ *n.* (*informal*) **1.** FALSE OUTER APPEARANCE an exterior appearance intended to deceive or mislead somebody **2.** ACT OF TEASING SOMEBODY the act of intentionally deceiving or giving somebody the wrong impression, especially for humorous effect **3.** PRANK an instance of teasing somebody, especially as a joke

put out *adj.* having been inconvenienced, upset, annoyed, or offended by somebody or something ○ *I do feel a little put out that you didn't invite me.*

put·out /po͝ot òwt/ *n.* BASEBALL a play in which a batter or base runner is retired

put-put /pùt pút/, **putt-putt** *n.* (*informal*) **1.** SOUND OF SMALL ENGINE the sound made by a small gasoline engine, especially an old or broken one **2.** GASOLINE ENGINE a small gasoline engine **3.** VEHICLE WITH GASOLINE ENGINE a vehicle, especially a boat, fitted with a small gasoline engine ■ *vi.* (**put-put·ted, put-put·ting, put-puts; putt-put·ted, putt-put·ting, putt-putts**) MOVE SLOWLY UNDER LITTLE POWER to move slowly or hesistantly under the power of a small gasoline engine (*informal*) [An imitation of the sound]

pu·tre·fy /pyo͞otrə fì/ (**-fied, -fy·ing, -fies**) *vti.* to decay or make something decay with a foul smell [15thC. From Latin *putrefacere*, from *putr-*, the stem of *puter* "putrid" (see PUTRID) + *facere* "to make."] —**pu·tre·fi·a·ble** *adj.* —**pu·tre·fi·er** *n.* —**pu·tre·fac·tion** /pyo͞otrə fákshən/ *n.* —**pu·tri·fac·tive** /-fáktiv/ *adj.*

pu·tres·cent /pyoo tréss'nt/ *adj.* **1.** DECAYING decaying or rotting **2.** RELATING TO DECAY relating to the process of decay [Mid-18thC. From Latin *putrescent-*, present participle stem of *putrescere*, literally "to begin to rot," from, ultimately, *putr-*, the stem of *puter* "rotten."] —**pu·tres·cence** *n.*

pu·tres·ci·ble /pyoo tréssəb'l/ *adj.* capable of decaying or rotting [Late 18thC. Formed from Latin *putrescere* "to become rotten," ultimately from *putr* (see PUTRID).]

pu·tres·cine /pyoo tré seen, pyoo tréssin/ *n.* a colorless crystalline compound (**ptomaine**) formed during the decay of flesh. Formula: $C_4H_{12}N_2$. [Late 19thC. Formed from Latin *putrescere* "to become rotten," ultimately from *putr-* (see PUTRID).]

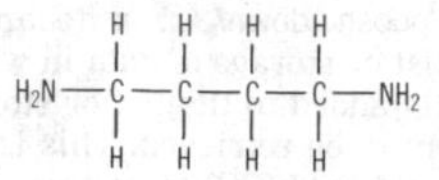

Putrescine

pu·trid /pyo͞otrid/ *adj.* **1.** DECAYING WITH DISGUSTING SMELL rotting and giving off a foul smell **2.** DISGUSTING physically or morally disgusting **3.** WORTHLESS worthless or contemptible (*informal*) [15thC. From Latin *putridus* "rotten," from, ultimately, *putr-*, stem of *puter*. Ultimately from an Indo-European word that is also the ancestor of English *filth* and *potpourri*.] —**pu·trid·i·ty** /pyoo tríddətee/ *n.* —**pu·trid·ly** /pyo͞otridlee/ *adv.* —**pu·trid·ness** /pyo͞o tridnəss/ *n.*

putsch /po͝och/ *n.* a sudden planned attempt to overthrow a government using military force [Early 20thC. From Swiss German, "thrust, blow."] —**putsch·ist** *n.*

putt /put/ *vti.* (**putt·ed, putt·ing, putts**) HIT GOLF BALL WITH TAPPING STROKE to hit a golf ball with a gentle tapping stroke along the ground on a green, aiming for the hole ■ *n.* TAPPING GOLF STROKE a gentle tapping stroke that hits a golf ball along the ground on a green, aiming for the hole [Mid-18thC. Variant of PUT.]

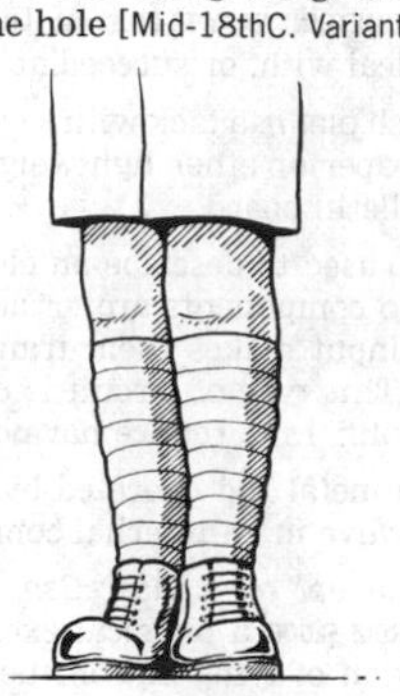

Puttee

put·tee /pu tée, púttee/ *n.* **1.** CLOTH STRIP WOUND AROUND LOWER LEG a strip of cloth wrapped around the lower leg from the ankle to the knee, especially one worn as part of a military uniform **2.** LEATHER COVERING FOR LOWER LEG a leather legging or gaiter that covers the lower leg [Late 19thC. From Hindi *patti*, from Sanskrit *pattika* "bandage, strip of cloth."]

put·ter[1] /púttər/ (**-tered, -ter·ing, -ters**) *vi.* to do trivial or unimportant tasks in a random, leisurely way ○ *just puttering in the garden* [Late 19thC. Variant of POTTER.] —**put·ter·er** *n.*

put·ter[2] /púttər/ *n.* **1.** GOLF CLUB FOR USE ON GREEN a golf club with a flat-faced metal head, for hitting a golf ball with a gentle tapping stroke on a green **2.** PUTTING GOLFER a golfer who is in the process of putting

putt·ing green *n.* **1.** = **green** *n.* 7 **2.** LAWN FOR PRACTICING PUTTING STROKES a lawn with holes for practicing putting strokes

put·to /po͞o tō/ (*plural* **-ti** /-tee/) *n.* in art especially of the baroque period, an infant boy or cherub, often portrayed with wings [Mid-17thC. Via Italian from Latin *putus* "boy."]

put·ty /púttee/ *n.* **1.** PASTE USED IN GLAZING WINDOWS a paste with the consistency of dough made from linseed oil and powdered chalk, used to fix glass into wooden window frames and to fill holes in wood **2.** PASTE FORMING TOP COAT ON PLASTER a thin paste of lime, water, and sand or plaster of Paris, used as a finishing coat on plaster **3.** COLORS LIGHT GRAY COLOR a light gray color tinged with yellow ■ *adj.* COLORS LIGHT GRAY of a light gray color with a tinge of yellow ■ *vt.* (**-tied, -ty·ing, -ties**) FIX OR REPAIR SOMETHING WITH PUTTY to fix windows into wooden frames, or fill holes in wood, using putty [Mid-17thC. From French *potée*, originally "potful," from *pot* "pot" (see POT[1]).] ◇ **be putty in somebody's hands** to be easily influenced and controlled by somebody

put·ty knife *n.* a tool similar to a knife with a blunt wide flexible blade, especially one used by glaziers to spread putty onto wooden window frames

put·ty pow·der *n.* a powder consisting of tin oxide or a mixture of tin and lead oxides that is used for polishing metal and glass

put·ty·root /pútti ro͝ot/ *n.* a North American orchid that has only one leaf and a brown or purplish brown flower. Latin name: *Aplectrum hyemale.* [Mid-19thC. So called because of the substance found in the plant's corm that resembles cement.]

put-up *adj.* fraudulently, dishonestly, or deviously planned or organized (*informal*) ○ *Was the fire a put-up job?*

put-up·on *adj.* treated badly, especially by being taken advantage of or being asked to do an excessive amount of work

putz /puts/ *n.* **1. UNINTELLIGENT PERSON** a very unintelligent and unpleasant person (*informal insult*) **2. OFFENSIVE TERM** an offensive term for a penis (*offensive slang*) [Early 20thC. From Yiddish *potz* "fool, penis."]

Puy de San·cy /pwee də saaN sée/ mountain in central France. It is the highest peak in the Massif Central. Height: 6,188 ft./1,886 m.

puz·zle /púzz'l/ *vt.* (**-zled, -zling, -zles**) **CONFUSE SOMEBODY** to confuse somebody by being difficult or impossible to understand ■ *n.* **1. DIFFICULT PROBLEM OR SITUATION** a problem that is difficult or impossible to solve or a situation that is difficult to resolve **2. SOMEBODY MYSTERIOUS** somebody whose behavior or motives are difficult to understand **3. GAME OF SKILL OR INTELLIGENCE** a game or toy designed to test skill or intelligence [Late 16thC. Origin uncertain.]

WORD KEY: SYNONYMS

See Synonyms at ***problem***.

puzzle out *vt.* to use logic or reasoning to reach an understanding of something confusing or complicated

puzzle over *vt.* to spend time thinking about and trying to understand something confusing or complicated

puz·zle·ment /púzz'lmənt/ *n.* a state of confusion resulting from an inability to understand or to deal with something

puz·zle pal·ace *n.* a place, especially a government department, where important decisions are made in great secrecy (*slang*)

puz·zler /púzzlər/ *n.* **1. SOMETHING CONFUSING OR CHALLENGING** something confusing, mystifying, or testing skill or intelligence **2. SOLVER OF PUZZLES** somebody who enjoys solving puzzles

PVA *n.* a colorless resin used in adhesives and paints. Full form **polyvinyl acetate**

PVC *n.* a hard-wearing synthetic resin made by polymerizing vinyl chloride, used for making flooring, piping, and clothing. Full form **polyvinyl chloride**

PVO *abbr.* private voluntary organization

PVS *abbr.* persistent vegetative state

Pvt. *abbr.* private

p.w. *abbr.* per week

PWA *abbr.* person with AIDS ■ *n., abbr.* **PWA, P.W.A.** Public Works Administration

PWR *abbr.* pressurized-water reactor

pwt. *abbr.* pennyweight

PX *n.* MIL a store in a military base selling goods to military personnel and their families, as well as to some authorized civilians. Full form **Post Exchange**

py- *prefix.* = **pyo-** (*used before vowels*)

py·a /pee áa, pyaa/ *n.* **1. MINOR UNIT OF MYANMAR CURRENCY** a minor unit of currency in Myanmar, 100 of which are worth a kyat. See table at **currency 2. COIN EQUIVALENT TO PYA** a coin worth a pya, 100 of which are worth a kyat [Mid-20thC. From Burmese.]

pyc·nid·i·um /pik níddee əm/ (*plural* **-a** /-ə/) *n.* an asexual flask-shaped structure in some fungi [Mid-19thC. From modern Latin, where it was formed from Greek *puknos* "dense."]

pycno- *prefix.* dense, density ○ *pycnometer* [From Greek *puknos* "strong, thick, dense"]

pyc·nog·o·nid /pik nóggənid, piknə gónnid/ *n.* = **sea spider** [Late 19thC. From modern Latin *Pycnogonida* from *pycnogonum* the genus name of these arthropods from *pycno-* + Greek *gonu* "knee."]

pyc·nom·e·ter /pik nómmətər/ *n.* a standard container of accurately defined volume used to determine the relative density of liquids and solids —**pyc·no·met·ric** /piknə méttrik/ *adj.*

pye-dog /pī-/ *n.* a stray, half-wild dog found in villages in Asia [Mid-19thC. "Pye" of uncertain origin: probably a contraction of *pariah(-dog)*, or from Hindi *pahi* "outsider."]

pyel- *prefix.* = **pyelo-** (*used before vowels*)

py·e·li·tis /pī ə lítiss/ *n.* inflammation of the part of the kidney **(pelvis)** from which urine drains into the tube leading to the bladder, sometimes caused by a bacterial infection that may occur during pregnancy —**py·e·lit·ic** /pī ə líttik/ *adj.*

pyelo- *prefix.* kidney, pelvis of the kidney ○ *pyelonephritis* [From Greek *puelos* "basin, trough"]

pye·lo·gram /pí ələ gràm/ *n.* an X-ray of the urine-collecting part of the kidney. The X-ray is taken following the introduction of a contrast medium, either into the bloodstream or directly into the kidney in order to highlight the internal structures.

pye·log·ra·phy /pī ə lóggrəfee/ *n.* the branch of radiography dealing with the kidneys and surrounding tissue, usually involving introduction of a contrast medium to highlight the internal structures —**pye·lo·graph·ic** /pī ələ gráffik/ *adj.*

py·e·lo·ne·phri·tis /pī ə lō nə frítiss/ *n.* inflammation of the kidney, including both the urine-forming and urine-collecting parts [Mid-19thC. From PYELITIS + NEPHRITIS.]

py·gid·i·um /pī jíddee əm/ (*plural* **-a** /-ə/) *n.* **1. HINDMOST PART OF INVERTEBRATE** the hindmost part of the body in some insects, worms, and other invertebrates **2. COVERING FOR PART OF INVERTEBRATE ABDOMEN** a protective covering of the anal portion of the abdomen of some invertebrates [Mid-19thC. Coined from Greek *puge* "rump" + -IDIUM.] —**py·gid·i·al** *adj.*

Pyg·ma·lion /pig máylee ən/ *n.* a king of Cyprus in Greek mythology who fell in love with the goddess Aphrodite and made a statue of her that she brought to life as Galatea

pyg·my /pígmee/, **pig·my** *n.* (*plural* **-mies**) **1. SOMEBODY SHORTER THAN AVERAGE** somebody who is of shorter than average height (*often considered offensive*) **2. OFFENSIVE TERM** an offensive term that insults somebody's importance, especially in a particular field (*offensive*) ■ *adj.* **OF SMALL BREED** belonging to a small breed (*offensive in some contexts*) ○ *a pygmy hippopotamus* [14thC. Via Latin *pygmaei* (plural) from, ultimately, Greek *pugmaios* (singular) "dwarfish," from *pugmē* "distance from the elbow to the knuckles."]

Pyg·my /pígmee/ (*plural* **-mies**), **Pig·my** (*plural* **-mies**) *n.* **1.** = **Negrillo 2.** = **Negrito**

pyg·my chim·pan·zee *n.* a species of chimpanzee from West Africa that is smaller than other chimpanzees, with a lighter build and darker color. Latin name: *Pan paniscus.*

py·ja·mas U.K. = **pajamas**

Pyle /pīl/, **Ernie** (1900–45) U.S. journalist. Known for his front-line reports during World War II, he was killed in fighting near Okinawa. Full name **Ernest Taylor Pyle**

Pyle, Howard (1853–1911) U.S. illustrator and writer. His work often deals with American history and medieval folklore.

Pylon

py·lon /pí lòn, pílən/ *n.* **1. METAL TOWER SUPPORTING HIGH-VOLTAGE CABLES** a tall metal tower typically made of crisscrossing steel bars that supports high-voltage cables across a long span **2. AIRFIELD TOWER TO GUIDE PILOT** a tower erected at an airfield to mark a course for pilots, e.g., in a race **3.** = **traffic cone 4. BRACKET FIXING SOMETHING TO AIRCRAFT BODY** a rigid metal bracket that attaches an external aircraft part such as an engine, fuel tank, or armament to the main body of the aircraft **5. TALL VERTICAL PART OF STRUCTURE** a tall vertical structure on or forming part of a building or other construction, especially an ancient structure, e.g., a decorative gateway or a monumental pillar [Mid-19thC. From Greek *pulōn* "gateway," from *pulē* "gate."]

py·lo·rec·to·my /pīlə réktəmee/ (*plural* **-mies**) *n.* the surgical removal of all or part of the pylorus, sometimes including the removal of part of the stomach [Late 19thC. Coined from PYLORUS + -ECTOMY.]

py·lo·rus /pī láwrəss/ (*plural* **-ri** /-rī/) *n.* the thick muscular ring **(sphincter)** surrounding the outlet of the stomach into the duodenum. It closes to prevent unduly large lumps of food from leaving, thus enabling stomach acid and enzymes to break them down further. [Early 17thC. Via late Latin from Greek *puloros* "gatekeeper," from *pulē* "gate."] —**py·lo·ric** *adj.*

Pyn·chon /pínchən/, **Thomas** (*b.* 1937) U.S. novelist. His works, known for their intricate plots and experimental techniques, include *V* (1963) and *Gravity's Rainbow* (1973).

PYO *abbr.* pick your own

pyo- *prefix.* pus ○ *pyoderma* [From Greek *puon.* Ultimately from an Indo-European word meaning "to rot," which is also the ancestor of English *foul, putrid,* and *purulent.*]

py·o·der·ma /pī ə dúrmə/ *n.* a skin infection causing the development of pus or pustules

py·o·gen·e·sis /pī ə jénnəsiss/ *n.* the formation or production of pus —**py·o·gen·ic** /pī ə jénnik/ *adj.*

Pyong·yang /pyáwng yàng/, **P'yŏng·yang** capital city of North Korea, situated on the Taedong River in the western part of the country. It is thought to be the oldest city on the Korean Peninsula. Population: 2,000,000 (1994).

py·or·rhe·a /pī ə reé ə/ *n.* inflammation of the gums with a loosening of the teeth and a discharge of pus from the tooth sockets [Early 19thC. From modern Latin, literally "flowing of pus," from Greek *puon* "pus" (see PYO-).] —**py·or·rhe·al** *adj.* —**py·or·rhe·ic** *adj.*

pyr- *prefix.* = **pyro-** (*used before vowels or h*)

py·ra·can·tha /pīrə kánthə/ *n.* U.K. = **firethorn** [Early 17thC. Via modern Latin from Greek *purakantha,* an unidentified plant, from *pur* "fire" + *akantha* "thorn."]

pyr·al·id /pírrəlid/ *n.* a small or medium-sized, slender, widely distributed moth with long triangular forewings. Family: Pyralidae. [Late 19thC. From modern Latin *Pyralidae,* from Greek *puralis* "mythical fly said to live in fire," from *pur* "fire."] —**py·ral·id** *adj.*

AKG London

Pyramid: Chephren Pyramid, Giza, Egypt

pyr·a·mid /pírrəmid/ *n.* **1. EGYPTIAN STONE TOMB** a huge stone tomb of ancient Egyptian royalty with a square base and triangular walls that slope to meet in a point at the top **2. SOLID SHAPE WITH SLOPING TRIANGULAR SIDES** a solid shape or structure that has triangular sides that slope to meet in a point and a base that is often, but not necessarily, a square. The volume of a pyramid is one-third of the product of the area of the base and the height of the vertex. **3. SYSTEM WITH GRADUALLY EXPANDING STRUCTURE** an arrangement or system that has a small number of elements at one point and expands gradually to have a large number of elements at the opposite point **4. POINTED BODY PART** a pointed or cone-shaped body part, e.g., either of two bundles of fibers located in the brain **5. INVESTMENT METHOD SPREADING RISK** a financial risk structure that spreads investments between high, medium, and low risk **6. CRYSTALLINE FORM WITH MULTIPLE**

NONPARALLEL FACES a crystalline form in which three or more nonparallel faces intersect all three axes of the crystal ■ *vi.* (-mid·ed, -mid·ing, -mids) TAKE ON PYRAMID SHAPE to take on the shape of a pyramid, with few elements at one point or level and gradually increasing numbers of elements toward the opposite point or level [Mid-16thC. Via the Latin stem *pyramid-* from Greek *puramis*, of uncertain origin: probably an alteration of Egyptian *pimar* through the exchange of the letters *m* and *r*.] —**py·ram·i·dal** /pi rámmidd'l/ *adj.* —**py·ram·i·dal·ly** /-rámmidd'lee/ *adv.* —**pyr·a·mid·ic** /pìrrə míddik/ *adj.* —**pyr·a·mid·i·cal** /-míddik'l/ *adj.* —**pyr·a·mid·i·cal·ly** /-míddikəlee/ *adv.*

py·ram·i·dal peak *n.* a high mountain peak formed by the walls of three or more adjacent steep-sided glacial basins, e.g., the Matterhorn in Switzerland

py·ram·i·dal tract *n.* either of two bundles of nerve fibers, shaped like inverted pyramids, running from either hemisphere of the cerebral cortex down the spinal cord to all voluntary muscles of the body. In the brain, they are susceptible to stroke damage that can lead to inability to move one side of the body.

pyr·a·mid sell·ing *n.* a method of distributing goods in bulk to a number of distributors, who in turn sell the goods in batches to a number of subdistributors, and so on

Pyr·a·mus and This·be /pìrrəməss ən thízbee/ *n.* two young Babylonian lovers in an ancient love story who were forbidden to marry. Pyramus, thinking Thisbe has been killed by a lion, kills himself, and Thisbe, on finding his body, kills herself.

py·ran /pī ràn/ *n.* either of two isomers of a crystalline cyclic compound with a ring consisting of five carbon atoms and an oxygen atom with two double bonds. It is best known for its benzene derivatives, which are naturally occurring dyes that produce the colors of flowers. Formula: C_5H_6O. [Early 20thC. Coined from *pyrone* + -AN.]

py·rar·gy·rite /pī raárjə rìt, pi-/ *n.* a deep-red to black mineral with a metallic luster consisting of silver antimony sulfide. An important source of silver, it is commonly found associated with other silver ores. [Mid-19thC. Coined from PYRO- + Greek *arguros* "silver" + -ITE.]

py·ra·zole /pírrə zòl/ *n.* a crystalline cyclic compound with a ring consisting of three carbon atoms and two nitrogen atoms with two double bonds. The ring system does not occur naturally, and pyrazole and its derivatives are exclusively synthetic compounds. Formula: $C_3H_4N_2$. [Late 19thC. Coined from PYRROLE + AZO-.]

pyre /pīr/ *n.* a pile of burning material, especially a pile of wood on which a dead body is ceremonially cremated [Mid-17thC. Via Latin *pyra* from Greek *pura*, from *pur* "fire." Ultimately from an Indo-European word that is also the ancestor of English *fire*.]

py·rene[1] /pī reen/ *n.* the stone inside some types of fruit, e.g., cherries (*technical*) [Mid-19thC. From modern Latin *pyrena*, from Greek *purēn*.]

py·rene[2] /pī reen/ *n.* a solid, colorless to yellow, crystalline, multiple-ringed hydrocarbon compound obtained from coal tar that has been shown to be carcinogenic. Formula: $C_{16}H_{10}$. [Mid-19thC. Coined from Greek *pur* "fire" + -ENE.]

Py·re·ne·an moun·tain dog *n. U.K.* a large bulky dog with a thick shaggy white coat, originally bred to protect sheep from wild animals in mountain areas [Named for the *Pyrenees*, the range of mountains separating France and Spain]

Pyr·e·nees /peérə neez/ mountain range in southwestern Europe, forming a natural boundary between France and Spain. Length: 270 mi./435 km. Area: 21,380 sq. mi./55,374 sq. km.

py·re·thrin /pī reéthrin, -réth-/ *n.* either of two oily liquid complex organic compounds obtained from pyrethrum flowers and used as a contact insecticide. Despite their quick lethal action on insects, pyrethrins are valued for their relative nontoxicity to humans and other animals, but they are highly allergenic. Formula: $C_{21}H_{28}O_3$ or $C_{22}H_{28}O_5$. [Early 20thC. Coined from PYRETHRUM + -IN.]

py·re·throid /pī reé thròyd/ *n.* COMPOUND WITH SIMILAR PROPERTIES TO PYRETHRIN a synthetic complex organic compound with insecticidal properties similar to those of pyrethrin ■ *adj.* WITH PROPERTIES SIMILAR TO PYRETHRIN belonging to the class of organic compounds with properties similar to those of pyrethrin [Mid-20thC. Coined from PYRETHRUM + -OID.]

py·re·thrum /pī reéthrəm, -réth-/ *n.* **1.** TYPE OF CHRYSANTHEMUM a chrysanthemum cultivated for its ornamental flowers. Genus: *Chrysanthemum.* **2.** INSECTICIDE IN POWDER FORM a mixture of pyrethrins extracted from the flowerheads of various chrysanthemums and used as an insecticide. It has low toxicity to warm-blooded animals and degrades rapidly in the environment, but has now been superseded by synthetic pyrethrins. [Mid-16thC. Via Latin from Greek *purethron* "feverfew," of uncertain origin: perhaps formed from *puretos* "fever."]

py·ret·ic /pī réttik/ *adj.* RELATING TO FEVER relating to, producing, or having a fever ■ *n.* FEVER-CAUSING AGENT an agent that causes fever [Mid-19thC. From modern Latin *pyreticos*, from Greek *puretos* "fever."]

Py·rex /pī rèks/ *tdmk.* a trademark for a type of borosilicate glass that is resistant to heat and chemicals and is used in household kitchenware and laboratory apparatus

py·rex·i·a /pī réksee ə/ *n.* fever (*technical*) [Mid-18thC. Via modern Latin from Greek *purexis*, from *puressein* "to be feverish," from *pur* "fire."] —**py·rex·i·al** *adj.* —**py·rex·ic** *adj.*

pyr·he·li·om·e·ter /pīr heelee ómmətər/ *n.* an instrument that measures the intensity of the sun's radiation received at the earth's surface [Mid-19thC. Coined from Greek *pur* "fire" + *helios* "sun" + -METER.] —**pyr·he·li·o·met·ric** /pīr heelee ə méttrik/ *adj.*

py·ric /pírik, pírrik/ *adj.* relating to burning, or produced as a result of burning [Mid-20thC. From French *pyrique*, from Greek *pur* "fire."]

Pyridine

pyr·i·dine /pírri deen/ *n.* a toxic, flammable, colorless to yellow liquid with a noxious smell, used in the manufacture of chemicals, pharmaceuticals, and paints, and in textile dyeing. It occurs naturally in bone oil and coal tar. Formula: C_5H_5N. [Mid-19thC. Coined from Greek *pur* "fire" + -IDINE.]

pyr·i·dox·al /pìrri dóksəl/ *n.* a crystalline aldehyde of the vitamin B_6 group that is a derivative of pyridoxine and acts as an active coenzyme in amino acid synthesis. Formula: $C_8H_9NO_3$. [Mid-20thC. Formed from PYRIDOXINE.]

pyr·i·dox·a·mine /pìrri dóksə meen/ *n.* a crystalline amine of the vitamin B_6 group that is a derivative of pyridoxine and acts as a coenzyme in protein metabolism. Formula: $C_8H_{12}N_2O_2$. [Mid-20thC. Coined from PYRIDINE + OXY- + -AMINE.]

pyr·i·dox·ine /pìrri dók seen, -dóksin/ *n.* a crystalline derivative of pyrimidine, found in cereals, yeast, liver, and fish. In an organism, pyridoxine is metabolically changed to pyridoxal and pyridoxamine. Formula: $C_{18}H_{11}NO_3$. [Mid-20thC. Coined from PYRIDINE + OXY-.]

pyr·i·form /pírrə fàwrm/ *adj.* shaped like a pear [Mid-18thC. From modern Latin *pyriformis*, from Latin *pyrum* "pear."]

py·ri·meth·a·mine /pìrə méthə meen/ *n.* a drug used as a preventive in the treatment of malaria [Mid-20thC. From *pyrimidine* + ETHYL-AMINE.]

py·rim·i·dine /pī rímmi deen, pi-/ *n.* **1.** CRYSTALLINE ORGANIC COMPOUND a strong smelling, weakly basic crystalline organic compound with a six-sided ring structure that includes two nitrogen atoms. Formula: $C_4H_4N_2$. **2.** PYRIMIDINE DERIVATIVE a biologically significant derivative of pyrimidine, especially the bases cytosine, thymine, and uracil found in RNA and DNA [Late 19thC. From PYRIDINE + IMIDE.]

py·rite /pī rìt/ *n.* a cubic iron sulfide mineral with a brassy metallic luster that is used as an iron ore, as a source of sulfur, and in the production of sulfuric acid. It is the commonest of the sulfide minerals and is widely distributed geographically. [Mid-19thC. From French or Latin (see PYRITES).] —**py·rit·ic** /pī ríttik/ *adj.*

py·ri·tes /pi rítiz, pī rítiz/ (*plural* -**tes**) *n.* = **pyrite** [Mid-16thC. Via Latin from Greek *purites (lithos)* "fire (stone), flint," from *pur* "fire."]

pyro- *prefix.* **1.** fire, heat ○ *pyromania* **2.** produced by fire or heat ○ *pyroligneous* **3.** fever ○ *pyrogenic* **4.** derived from an acid by loss of a molecule of water ○ *pyrophosphate* [From Greek *pur* "fire" (source also of English *pyre*). Ultimately from the Indo-European word that is also the the ancestor of English *fire*.]

py·ro·cat·e·chol /pìrō káttə chàwl/ *n.* = **catechol**

py·ro·cel·lu·lose /pìrō séllyə lòss, -lòz/ *n.* a highly nitrated cellulose used in the manufacture of explosives, particularly smokeless powder

py·ro·chem·i·cal /pìrō kémmik'l/ *adj.* relating to or resulting from chemical changes that take place at very high temperatures —**py·ro·chem·i·cal·ly** *adv.*

py·ro·clas·tic /pìrō klástik/ *adj.* used to describe sedimentary rock that is composed of fragments of volcanic rock produced by the explosion of a volcanic eruption

py·ro·con·duc·tiv·i·ty /pìrō kón duk tívvətee/ *n.* the capacity to conduct electricity created in a solid substance by heating it to a high temperature

py·ro·e·lec·tric·i·ty /pìrō i lék trísətee/ *n.* the production of electric charges on opposite faces of some crystals by a change in temperature —**py·ro·e·lec·tric** /pìrō i léktrik/ *adj.*

py·ro·gal·lol /pìrō gá làwl/ *n.* a toxic, bitter, lustrous, white crystalline organic compound used as a photographic developer, and as an absorbent for oxygen in gas analysis. Formula: $C_6H_6H_3$. [Late 19thC. Coined from PYROGALLATE + -OL.] —**py·ro·gal·lic** /pìrō gállik/ *adj.*

py·ro·gen /pírəjən/ *n.* MED a substance that causes fever, especially a substance introduced into somebody's bloodstream

py·ro·gen·ic /pìrō jénnik/ *adj.* **1.** MED CAUSING FEVER causing fever or produced as a result of fever **2.** GEOL IGNEOUS produced by igneous activity

py·rog·ra·phy /pī róggrəfee/ (*plural* -**phies**) *n.* **1.** BURNING DESIGNS INTO WOOD AND LEATHER the creation of designs on wood and leather using heated tools that burn away some of the surface **2.** DESIGN CREATED BY BURNING a design burned into wood or leather using a heated tool —**py·rog·ra·pher** *n.* —**py·ro·graph·ic** /pìrə gráffik/ *adj.*

py·ro·lig·ne·ous /pìrō lígnee əss/ *adj.* produced by the destructive distillation of wood

py·ro·lig·ne·ous ac·id *n.* a reddish-brown liquid, produced by the destructive distillation of wood, that was once a commercial source of acetic acid, which is its primary constituent. Among its impurities may be acetone, methanol, wood oils, and tars.

py·ro·lu·site /pìrə loó sìt/ *n.* a black or gray powdery mineral with high mass and a metallic sheen, that is an important source of manganese. It is found associated with other manganese ores, e.g., manganite, and as nodules on the seabed. Formula: MnO_2. [Early 19thC. Coined from PYRO- + Greek *lousis* "washing" (from its use in decolorizing glass) + -ITE.]

py·rol·y·sate /pī róllə sìt, pī róllәsәt/ *n.* a product of a chemical change caused by heating

py·rol·y·sis /pī róllassis/ *n.* the use of heat to break down complex chemical substances into simpler substances —**py·ro·lyt·ic** /pìrə líttik/ *adj.*

py·rol·yze /pírə lìz/ (-**yzed**, -**yz·ing**, -**yz·es**) *vt.* to make a complex chemical substance decompose into simpler substances by heating it [Early 20thC. From *pyrolysis* by analogy with *analyze*.] —**py·rol·yz·er** *n.*

py·ro·man·cy /pírə mànsee/ *n.* attempting to tell the future by using fire or flames [14thC. Via Old French *pyromancie* from late Latin *pyromantia*, from Greek *puromanteia*, from *pur* "fire."] —**py·ro·manc·er** *n.* —**py·ro·man·tic** /pìrə mántik/ *adj.*

py·ro·ma·ni·a /pìrō máynee ə, -máynyə/ *n.* the uncontrollable urge to set fire to things —**py·ro·ma·ni·ac** /pìrō máynee àk/ *n.* —**py·ro·ma·ni·a·cal** /pìrōmə nī ək'l/ *adj.*

py·ro·met·al·lur·gy /pìrō métt'l ùrjee/ *n.* the treatment of ores and metals using high-temperature processes, or the study of these processes, which include alloying, casting, distilling, roasting, refining, sintering, smelting, and heat treating

py·rom·e·ter /pī rómmətər/ *n.* an instrument that measures high temperatures, typically by converting brightness, radiation, or electric current measurements into temperature readings —**py·ro·met·ric** /pìrə méttrik/ *adj.* —**py·ro·met·ri·cal** /-méttrik'l/ *adj.* —**py·ro·met·ri·cal·ly** /-méttrikəlee/ *adv.* —**py·rom·e·try** /pī rómmətree/ *n.*

py·ro·mor·phite /pìrə máwr fìt/ *n.* a minor ore of lead found as brown, green, gray, white, and yellow crystals of lead chlorophosphate

py·rone /pī rōn/ *n.* either of two six-membered organic ring compounds containing five carbon atoms and an oxygen atom, with a second oxygen atom attached to one of the carbon atoms. The benzene derivative is used as a pharmaceutical. Formula: $C_5H_4O_2$.

py·ro·nine /pírə neen/ *n.* a red dye used in biological tests, especially a test to detect the presence of RNA [Late 19thC. From German, of uncertain origin: probably coined from PYRO- + -INE.]

py·rope /pī rōp/ *n.* a deep red garnet containing magnesium and aluminum, frequently used as a gemstone [Early 19thC. Via Old French *pirope* from Latin *pyropus*, from Greek *puropos* literally "fiery-eyed," from *pur* "fire."]

py·ro·pho·bi·a /pìrə fóbee ə/ *n.* an irrational fear of fire

py·ro·phor·ic /pìrə fáwrik/ *adj.* **1.** CHEM **IGNITING SPONTANEOUSLY** bursting into flames spontaneously when exposed to air **2.** METALL **PRODUCING SPARKS WHEN STRUCK** giving off sparks when struck or scraped [Mid-19thC. Formed from Greek *purophoros* "fire-bearing," from *pur* "fire."]

py·ro·phos·phate /pìrō fós fàyt/ *n.* a salt or ester produced when pyrophosphoric acid reacts with some metals or metallic compounds [Mid-19thC. Coined from *pyrophosphic* + -ATE.]

py·ro·phos·phor·ic ac·id /pìrō fos fàwrik-/ *n.* a viscous liquid, formed when orthophosphoric acid is heated and loses a water molecule, used as a catalyst. Formula: $H_4P_2O_7$.

py·ro·pho·tom·e·ter /pìrō fō tómmətər/ *n.* an instrument that determines the temperature of an incandescent body as a function of the light it emits

py·ro·phyl·lite /pìrō fí lìt, pī róffə lìt/ *n.* a silvery-white or greenish hydrous aluminum silicate mineral that resembles talc and is found in metamorphic rock [Early 19thC. From German *Pyrophyllit*, from Greek *pur* "fire" + *phullon* "leaf"; so called because it exfoliates when exposed to flame.]

py·ro·sis /pī róssiss/ *n.* heartburn (*technical*) [Late 18thC. Via Greek *purōsis* "burning" from, ultimately, *pur* "fire" (see PYRO-).]

py·ro·stat /pírə stàt/ *n.* a thermostat that is suitable for use at very high temperatures [Formed from PYRO- on the model of "thermostat"] —**py·ro·stat·ic** /pìrə státtik/ *adj.*

py·ro·tech·nic /pìrə téknik/, **py·ro·tech·ni·cal** /-téknik'l/ *adj.* **1. RELATING TO FIREWORKS** relating to, used in, or involving fireworks **2. BRILLIANT** showing brilliance, e.g., in style or technique ■ *n.* **FIREWORK** a firework or other explosive device [Early 19thC. Formed from modern Latin *pyrotechnia*, from Greek *pur* "fire" + *tekhnē* "craft."] —**py·ro·tech·ni·cal·ly** *adv.* —**py·ro·tech·nist** *n.*

py·ro·tech·nics /pìrə tékniks/ *n.* **CRAFT OF MAKING FIREWORKS** the craft or skill of making and using fireworks (*takes a singular verb*) ■ *npl.* (*takes a singular or plural verb*) **1. FIREWORKS DISPLAY** a display of fireworks **2. SHOWY DISPLAY** an extravagant display of brilliance, virtuosity, or strong emotion

py·rox·ene /pī rók seen/ *n.* a silicate mineral, usually dark green, brown, or black, that contains varying amounts of calcium, iron, magnesium, and sodium and is widely distributed in igneous and metamorphic rocks [Early 19thC. From French *pyroxène*, from Greek *pur* "fire" + *xenos* "stranger"; so called because it was originally thought to be a foreign substance in igneous rock.] —**py·rox·en·ic** /pì rok sénnik/ *adj.*

py·rox·e·nite /pī róksə nìt/ *n.* an igneous rock consisting mainly of pyroxene and olivine

py·rox·y·lin /pī róksəlin/ *n.* a highly flammable substance used to make plastics and lacquers. It is a form of cellulose nitrate. [Mid-19thC. Coined from PYRO- + XYLO- + -IN.]

pyr·rhic /pírrik/ *n.* **POETIC UNIT** a unit of poetic rhythm that has two short or unaccented syllables ■ *adj.* **1. IN PYRRHICS** relating to or written in pyrrhics **2.** HIST **RELATING TO WAR DANCE** relating to an ancient Greek war dance [Early 17thC. Via Latin from, ultimately, Greek *purríkhē*, named after the chorist *Pyrrhikhos*, who is supposed to have invented it.]

Pyr·rhic vic·to·ry *n.* a victory won at such great cost to the victor that it is tantamount to a defeat [Late 19thC. Named for PYRRHUS.]

Pyr·rho·nism /pírrə nìzzəm/ *n.* **1.** PHILOS **SKEPTICAL PHILOSOPHY OF PYRRHO** the doctrine of the ancient Greek philosopher Pyrrho, who believed that it was impossible to be certain about anything and therefore suspended judgment on everything **2. COMPLETE SKEPTICISM** skepticism to an extreme or excessive degree [Late 17thC. Formed from Greek *Purrhōn* "Pyrrho," (360?-272? B.C.), the Greek philosopher who founded philosophical skepticism.] —**Pyr·rhon·ist** *n.*, *adj.*

pyr·rho·tite /pírrə tìt/, **pyr·rho·tine** /pírrə teen/ *n.* a widely occurring yellow-brown lustrous iron sulfide mineral, found in igneous rocks and used as an iron ore. Formula: FeS. [Mid-19thC. Alteration of German *Pyrrhotin*, from Greek *purrotēs* "fiery redness," from *pur* "fire" (see PYRO-).]

pyr·rhu·lox·i·a /pìrrə lóksee ə/ (*plural* **-as** *or* **-a**) *n.* a bird of the southwestern United States, Mexico, and Central America that is related to and resembles the cardinal but with mostly gray plumage touched with red. Latin name: *Cardinalis sinuatus*.

Pyr·rhus /pírrəss/, **King of Epirus** (318?–272 B.C.). The king of a Greek province (307–272 B.C.), he invaded Italy and defeated the Roman army at Heraclea (280 B.C.) and Asculum (279 B.C.), but sustained huge losses to his troops.

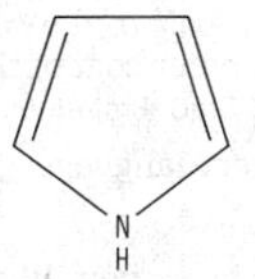

Pyrrole

pyr·role /pí rōl/ *n.* a colorless toxic liquid compound containing carbon, hydrogen, and nitrogen. It is found in many important biological substances, e.g., chlorophyll, hemoglobin, and bile pigments. Formula: C_4H_5N. [Mid-19thC. Coined from Greek *purros* "fiery red" (from *pur* "fire") + -OLE.] —**pyr·ro·lic** /pi róllik/ *adj.*

py·ru·vic ac·id /pī roōvik-/ *n.* a colorless acid that is formed as an intermediate compound during the metabolism of carbohydrates and proteins. Formula: $C_3H_4O_3$. [Mid-19thC. Coined from PYRO- + Latin *uva* "grape"; so called because it was obtained by dry distillation from racemic acid.]

Py·tha·gor·as /pī thággərəss/ (582?–500? B.C.) Greek philosopher and mathematician. He or his followers made important discoveries about number and proportion, which they believed underlay everything in the universe. They also proposed that the Earth is a globe, and that the planets orbit the Sun. Known as **Pythagoras of Samos**

Py·thag·o·re·an /pi thàggə reé ən, pī-/ *adj.* MATH, PHILOS **RELATING TO PYTHAGORAS** relating or belonging to the ancient Greek philosopher and mathematician Pythagoras, his theories, or his followers ■ *n.* **FOLLOWER OF PYTHAGORAS** a follower of Pythagoras and his theories

Py·thag·o·re·an·ism /pi thàggə reé ə nìzzəm, pī-/ *n.* the theories and teachings of Pythagoras, especially those that apply mathematics to the workings of the universe

Py·thag·o·re·an the·o·rem *n.* a proved geometric proposition stating that the square of the longest side (**hypotenuse**) of a right triangle is equal to the sum of the squares of the other two sides [Named for *Pythagoras*, who formulated it]

Pyth·i·an /píthee ən/, **Pyth·ic** /píthik/ *adj.* **1. OF DELPHI** relating to the ancient Greek city of Delphi, especially to Apollo's temple there, the site of Apollo's oracle **2. OF PYTHIAN GAMES** relating to the athletic games held in Delphi [Late 16thC. Via Latin from, ultimately, Greek *Puthō*, the ancient name of Delphi.]

Pyth·i·an Games *npl.* a series of athletic contests held every four years in Delphi in ancient Greece in honor of the god Apollo

Python

py·thon /pī thòn/ *n.* a nonvenomous constricting snake native to Asia, Africa, and Australia. Pythons kill their prey through suffocation and can reach lengths of over 19ft./6 m. Family: Pythonidae. [Mid-19thC. Directly or via French from Latin, name of a mythical serpent killed by Apollo, from Greek *Puthōn*.]

py·tho·ness /píthənəss/ *n.* in Greek mythology, a woman believed to be possessed by the spirit of an oracle, especially Apollo's priestess at Delphi [14thC. From late Latin *pythonissa*, feminine of *python*, from Greek *Puthōn*, named for the serpent that Apollo killed near Delphi.]

py·u·ri·a /pī yoōree ə/ *n.* the presence of pus in the urine [Early 19thC. Coined from PYO- + -URIA.]

pyx /piks/, **pix** *n.* **1.** CHR **BOX FOR COMMUNION WAFERS** a container in which the consecrated wafers for the Communion are placed so that they can be taken to those who cannot leave home **2. CONTAINER FOR COINS AT MINT** a chest in which newly minted coins are placed before being tested [14thC. Via Latin from Greek *puxis* "box" (see PYXIS).]

pyx·id·i·um /pik síddee əm/ (*plural* **-a** /-ə/) *n.* BOT = **pyxis** *n.* [Mid-19thC. Via modern Latin from Greek *puxídion*, "small box," from *puxis* (see PYXIS).]

pyx·ie /píksee/ (*plural* **-ies** *or* **-ie**) *n.* a low-growing evergreen shrub native to the eastern United States with small pink or white star-shaped flowers. Latin name: *Pyxidanthera barbulata*. [Late 19thC. Shortening of modern Latin *Pyxidanthera*, genus name, from *puxidium* "little box" + *anthera* "pollen."]

pyx·is /píksiss/ (*plural* **-i·des** /píksi deez/) *n.* BOT a seed capsule with a cap that falls off to release the seeds [Late 17thC. Via Latin from Greek *puxis* "box" (source of English *box*[1]), from *puxos* "boxwood" (source of *box*[3] and *bush*), of unknown origin.]

Pyx·is /píksiss/ *n.* a small inconspicuous constellation of the southern hemisphere lying partly in the Milky Way, located between Puppis and Antlia

Qq

q[1] /kyoo/ (*plural* **q's**), **Q** (*plural* **Q's** *or* **Qs**) *n.* **1.** LETTER OF ENGLISH ALPHABET the 17th letter of the modern English alphabet **2.** SPEECH SOUND CORRESPONDING TO LETTER "Q" the speech sound that corresponds to the letter "Q" **3.** LETTER "Q" WRITTEN a written representation of the letter "Q"

q[2] *symbol.* PHYS **1.** electric charge **2.** heat *n.* 1.

Q *abbr.* **1.** CHESS queen **2.** MONEY quetzal

q. *abbr.* **1.** quart **2.** quarter **3.** quarterly **4.** quarto **5.** question **6.** query **7.** quire **8.** MEASURE quintal

Q. *abbr.* **1.** quartermaster **2.** quarto **3.** Quebec **4.** queen

Qad·da·fi /gə dáafee, kə-/, **Gad·da·fi, Muammar al-** (*b.* 1942) Libyan military and political leader. He seized power in a coup against the monarchy (1969). He imposed Islamic and socialist policies, and supported revolutionary and terrorist movements abroad.

qadi *n.* = **cadi**

q & a *abbr.* question and answer

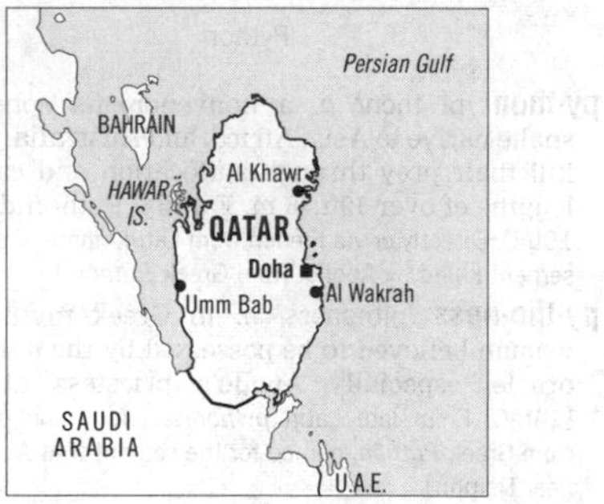

Qatar

Qa·tar /káa taar, kə táar/ independent state in the Middle East, on a peninsular in the Persian Gulf, north of Saudi Arabia and the United Arab Emirates. Language: Arabic. Currency: Qatar riyal. Capital: Doha. Population: 125,665 (1991). Area: 4,416 sq. mi./11,437 sq. km. Official name **State of Qatar** — **Qa·tar·i** *adj., n.*

Qat·ta·ra de·pres·sion /kə táarə-/ desert basin in northwestern Egypt. Its lowest point is 435 ft./133 m below sea level. Area: 7,500 sq. mi./19,400 sq. km.

Qayrawan, Al- /kírə waan/ city in northern Tunisia, capital of al-Qayrawan Governorate. Called the "City of 100 Mosques," it is one of the holiest Muslim cities. Population: 102,600 (1992).

qb *abbr.* FOOTBALL quarterback

QB *abbr.* LAW Queen's Bench

Q-boat *n.* = **Q-ship**

QC, Q.C. *abbr.* **1.** quality control **2.** Queen's Counsel

QCD *abbr.* quantum chromodynamics

q.e. *abbr.* which is (*used in doctors' prescriptions*) [Latin, *quod est*]

QED *abbr.* PHYS quantum electrodynamics

Q.E.D. *abbr.* quod erat demonstrandum [Latin, *quod erat demonstrandum*]

Q.E.F. *abbr.* which was to be done [Latin, *quod erat faciendum*]

QF *abbr.* ARMS quick-firing

Q fe·ver *n.* an infectious disease caused by rickettsial bacteria and characterized by fever, chills, and muscle pain [Mid-20thC. Origin uncertain: probably a shortening of QUEENSLAND, where the disease was first described.]

q.i.d. *abbr.* four times per day (*used in doctors' prescriptions*) [Latin, *quater in die*]

Qin /chin/, **Ch'in** *n.* a dynasty in ancient China that ruled from 221–206 B.C., during which the first unified Chinese empire emerged and much of the Great Wall of China was built [Late 18thC. From Chinese *Qín*.]

Qing /ching/, **Ch'ing** *n.* the last of the Chinese dynasties, founded by the conquering Manchu who ruled from 1644 until 1912, when the nationalist revolutionaries overthrew it [Late 18thC. From Chinese *Qīng*.]

Qing·dao /chìng dów/ city on the Yellow Sea, in Shandong Province, eastern China, between Beijing and Shanghai. Population: 2,060,000 (1991).

Qing·hai /ching hí/ province of western China bounded by Xinjiang Uygur, Gansu, Sichuan, and Tibet. Capital: Xining. Population: 4,740,000 (1994). Area: 278,378 sq. mi./720,999 sq. km.

Qing·hai Hu /chìng hí hoo/ lake in northeastern Qinghai Province, China

Qi·qi·ha'er /chée chee haár, chée chee haá ər/ city and port in the Heilongjiang Province, China, situated on the left bank of the Nen River 170 mi./274 km northwest of Harbin. Population: 1,260,000 (1986).

qi·vi·ut /keévee ət, -òot/ *n.* the soft wool that grows beneath the long outer coat of the musk ox, used to make yarn [Mid-20thC. From Inuit.]

QL *abbr.* COMPUT query language

ql. *abbr.* quintal

q.l. *abbr.* as much as you like (*used in doctors' prescriptions*) [Latin, *quantum libet*]

Qld. *abbr.* Queensland

qlty. *abbr.* quality

QM *abbr.* quartermaster

q.m. *abbr.* every morning (*used in doctors' prescriptions*) [Latin, *quaque mane*]

QMC *abbr.* quartermaster corps

QMG *abbr.* Quartermaster General

qn. *abbr.* question

q.n. *abbr.* every night (*used in doctors' prescriptions*) [Latin, *quaque nocte*]

Qom /kōm/ city in central Iran, on the Qom River. It is one of the sacred cities of Iran and a center of pilgrimage for Shiite Muslims. Population: 681,253 (1991).

qoph /kawf/ *n.* the 19th letter of the Hebrew alphabet, represented in the English alphabet as "q." See table at **alphabet** [From Hebrew *qōph*, from a Semitic word meaning "eye of a needle"]

qq. *abbr.* questions

qq.v. *abbr.* which (things) see (*used as a cross reference to more than one item*) [Latin, *quae vide*]

qr. *abbr.* **1.** quarter **2.** quarterly **3.** quire

qs *abbr.* quarter section (*used of land*)

q.s. *abbr.* as much as suffices (*used in doctors' prescriptions*) [Latin, *quantum sufficit*]

Q-ship *n.* an armed ship disguised as a merchant ship, used to decoy or destroy enemy vessels [From the naval designation for this type of vessel]

QSO *abbr.* ASTRON quasistellar object

qt. *abbr.* **1.** quantity **2.** quart

q.t. /kyoo teé/ *abbr.* quiet (*informal*) [Shortening of *quiet*] ◇ **on the q.t.** quietly and secretly (*informal*)

Q-Tips *tdmk.* a trademark for cotton-tipped swabs

qto. *abbr.* quarto

qty. *abbr.* quantity

qu. *abbr.* **1.** queen **2.** query **3.** question

qua /kway/ *prep.* in the capacity or function of ○ *"Restrictions on trade, or on production for purposes of trade, are indeed restraints; and all restraint, qua restraint, is an evil."* (John Stuart Mill, *On Liberty*; 1859) [Mid-17thC. From Latin *qua*, from *qui* "who" (source also of English *quorum* and *quibble*).]

quack[1] /kwak/ *n.* SOUND MADE BY A DUCK the harsh sound typically made by a duck ■ *vi.* (**quacked, quack·ing, quacks**) **1.** MAKE THE SOUND OF A DUCK to make the harsh sound that is characteristic of a duck **2.** SPEAK IRRITATINGLY to speak loudly and endlessly in an irritating manner (*slang*) [Early 17thC. An imitation of the sound.]

quack[2] /kwak/ *n.* **1.** FAKE DOCTOR somebody who practices medicine without training or a valid license **2.** SOMEBODY WHO IS A FRAUD somebody who makes false claims to skills and qualifications in fields other than medicine ■ *vi.* (**quacked, quack·ing, quacks**) BE A QUACK to practice medicine without training or a valid license, or to make false claims of expertise in any field [Early 17thC. Shortening of QUACKSALVER.] — **quack·ish** *adj.*

quack·er·y /kwákəree/ *n.* the practices or methods of somebody who makes false claims about medical or other skills or qualifications [Early 18thC. From QUACK[2].]

quack grass *n.* = **couch grass**

quack·sal·ver /kwák sàlvər/ *n.* somebody who falsely claims to have medical or other skills or qualifications (*archaic*) [Late 16thC. From obsolete Dutch, literally "salve-hawker," from Dutch *kwaken*, "to quack, prattle" + *zalf* "salve."]

quad[1] /kwod/ *n.* a quadruplet (*informal*) [Late 19thC. Shortening.]

quad[2] /kwod/ *n.* a quadrangle (*informal*) [Early 19thC. Shortening.]

quad[3] /kwod/ *adj.* quadraphonic (*informal*) [Late 20thC. Shortening.]

quad[4] /kwod/ *n.* PRINTING a piece of blank type metal used for spacing [Late 19thC. Shortening of QUADRAT.]

quad[5] /kwod/ *n.* a quadriceps (*informal*) [Mid-20thC. Shortening.]

quad[6], **quad.** *abbr.* **1.** quadrangle **2.** quadrant **3.** quadrilateral

quadr- *prefix.* = **quadri-** (*used before vowels*)

quadra- *prefix.* = **quadri-** (*used before vowels*)

Quad·ra·ges·i·ma /kwòddrə jéssimə/ *n.* in the Christian liturgical calendar, the first Sunday in Lent [14thC. Via late Latin *quadragesima (dies)*, "fortieth (day)" (before Easter), from *quadraginta* "forty."]

quad·ran·gle /kwód ràng g'l/ *n.* **1.** FOUR-SIDED SHAPE a two-dimensional figure that consists of four points connected by straight lines, especially a rectangle **2.** OPEN AREA SURROUNDED BY BUILDINGS an open rectangular yard that is surrounded on all four sides by buildings **3.** BUILDINGS SURROUNDING YARD the buildings that surround an open rectangular yard **4.** U.S. MAP UNIT ON SINGLE SHEET the area of land shown on any of the map sheets produced by the U.S. Geological Survey [15thC. Via Old French from, ultimately, Latin *quadrangulus*, "having four corners."] —**quad·ran·gu·lar** /kwod ráng gyələr/ *adj.*

quad·rant /kwóddrənt/ *n.* **1.** GEOM QUARTER OF CIRCUMFERENCE OF CIRCLE a 90-degree arc representing one fourth of the circumference of a circle **2.** GEOM QUARTER OF AREA OF CIRCLE the area bounded by a quadrant and the two perpendicular lines that connect it to the center of the circle **3.** GEOM QUARTER OF PLANE SURFACE any one of the four sections into which the perpendicular axes of a coordinate system divide a two-dimensional surface **4.** GEOM QUARTER OF AREA OR SURFACE any one of the four approximately equal parts into which an area or a surface is divided by two real or imaginary perpendicular lines **5.** ASTRON DEVICE FOR MEASURING ANGLE OF STAR an instrument with a movable sighting mechanism attached to a 90-degree arc, formerly used in astronomy and navigation to measure the angles and altitudes of stars **6.** DEVICE SHAPED LIKE QUARTER CIRCLE a mechanical device or machine part in the shape of a quarter of a circle [14thC. From Latin *quadrant-*, the stem of *quadrans* "fourth part, quarter."]

quad·ra·phon·ic /kwòddrə fónnik/, **quad·ri·phon·ic** *adj.* using a four-channel system to record and reproduce sound. The four separate signals may be fed to individual loudspeakers placed in the corners of a room. —**quad·ra·phon·ics** *n.* —**qua·draph·o·ny** /kwo dráffənee/ *n.*

quad·rat /kwóddrət/ *n.* **1.** PRINTING = **quad**[4] *n.* **2.** ECOL AREA OF LAND FOR ECOLOGICAL STUDY a small plot of land set aside for plant and animal population studies [Late 17thC. Variant of QUADRATE.]

quad·rate *n.* /kwód ràyt, kwóddrət/ **1.** SQUARE OR CUBE a square or cube or a square or cubic area, space, or thing **2.** ZOOL JAW JOINT OF SOME VERTEBRATES in birds, fish, reptiles, and amphibians, a bony or cartilaginous part of the upper jaw that articulates with the lower jaw at the side of the skull. In mammals, this structure has evolved into the incus, a small bone of the middle ear. ■ *adj.* **1.** ZOOL OF THE VERTEBRATE QUADRATE relating to the quadrate in vertebrates **2.** SQUARE OR RECTANGULAR with four sides and four right angles ■ *vti.* /kwód ràyt/ (**-rat·ed, -rat·ing, -rates**) CONFORM OR CORRESPOND WITH SOMETHING to conform or correspond with something or to make one thing conform or correspond with another [14thC. Via Latin *quadratum* from, ultimately, *quadrum* "square" (source of English *square* and *cadre*). Ultimately from an Indo-European word meaning "fourfold," which is also the ancestor of *quadrant*.]

quad·rat·ic /kwo dráttik/ *adj.* MATH relating to or containing terms with powers no higher than the power of two [Mid-17thC. Formed from QUADRATE.] —**quad·rat·i·cal·ly** *adv.*

quad·rat·ic e·qua·tion *n.* an equation containing one or more terms raised to the power of two but no higher

quad·rat·ics /kwo dráttiks/ *n.* the branch of algebra that deals with quadratic equations (*takes a singular verb*)

quad·ra·ture /kwóddrəchər, -chòor/ *n.* **1.** MAKING SOMETHING SQUARE making something square or dividing something into squares **2.** MATH MATHEMATICAL TECHNIQUE FOR EQUATING AREAS the construction of a square with an area equal to that of a specified surface **3.** ASTRON 90-DEGREE SEPARATION OF CELESTIAL BODIES the relative position of two celestial bodies with a separation of 90 degrees as seen from a third, especially the Sun and Moon as seen from the Earth

quad·ren·ni·a plural of **quadrennium**

quad·ren·ni·al /kwod rénnee əl/ *adj.* **1.** HAPPENING EVERY FOUR YEARS occurring every fourth year **2.** LASTING FOUR YEARS lasting for four years ■ *n.* FOUR-YEAR PERIOD a period of four years —**quad·ren·ni·al·ly** *adv.*

quad·ren·ni·um /kwod rénnee əm/ (*plural* **-ums** *or* **-a** /-nee ə/) *n.* a period of four years [Mid-19thC. From Latin, from *quadri-* "four" + *annus* "year."]

quadri- *prefix.* **1.** four, fourth ○ *quadripartite* ○ *quadricentennial* **2.** square ○ *quadric* [From Latin. Ultimately from the Indo-European word for "four," which is also the ancestor of English *quadrant, tetra-*, and *fourth*.]

quad·ric /kwóddrik/ *adj.* MATH = **quadratic** *adj.* ■ *n.* MATH SOMETHING DEFINED BY QUADRATIC EQUATION a surface or curve specified by a second degree equation [Mid-19thC. Formed from Latin *quadra*, feminine of *quadrum* "square" (see QUADRATE).]

quad·ri·cen·ten·ni·al /kwòddrə sen ténnee əl/ *n.* 400TH ANNIVERSARY a 400th anniversary or a celebration of it ■ *adj.* MARKING 400TH ANNIVERSARY marking or relating to a 400th anniversary

quad·ri·ceps /kwóddri sèps/ (*plural* **-ceps** *or* **-cep·ses** /-sèpseez/) *n.* ANAT a large four-part muscle at the front of the thigh that acts to extend the leg [Mid-19thC. From Latin, "four-headed."] —**quad·ri·cip·i·tal** /kwòddrə síppit'l/ *adj.*

quad·ri·ga /kwo drígə/ (*plural* **-gae** /-jee/) *n.* a two-wheeled chariot in ancient Greece or Rome that was drawn by four horses harnessed alongside each other [Early 18thC. Via Latin from, ultimately, *quadrijuga* "team of four," from *quadri-* "four" + *jugum* "yoke."]

quad·ri·lat·er·al /kwòddri láttərəl, -láttrəl/ *n.* FOUR-SIDED FIGURE a two-dimensional geometric figure with four sides ■ *adj.* FOUR-SIDED with four sides

qua·drille[1] /kwo dríl, kwə-, kə-/ *n.* **1.** SQUARE DANCE OF FRENCH ORIGIN a French square dance popular in the 18th and 19th centuries, danced by four or more couples together **2.** MUSIC MUSIC FOR QUADRILLE the music for a quadrille, often taken from a popular source and usually in a lively duple meter [Mid-18thC. Via French from Spanish *cuadrilla*, "troop, company," from *cuadro* "square," from Latin *quadrum* (see QUADRATE).]

qua·drille[2] /kwo dríl, kwə-, kə-/ *n.* a card game for four players that uses a deck of 40 cards. It was popular in the 18th century. [Early 18thC. From French, of uncertain origin: probably from Spanish *cuartillo*, from *cuarto* "fourth," from Latin *quartus* (see QUART).]

quad·ril·lion /kwo drīllyən/ (*plural* **-lions** *or* **-lion**) *n.* **1.** ONE FOLLOWED BY 15 ZEROS the number equal to 10^{15}, written as 1 followed by 15 zeros **2.** *U.K.* ONE FOLLOWED BY 24 ZEROS the number equal to 10^{24}, written as 1 followed by 24 zeros (*dated*) [Late 17thC. Formed from QUADRI-, on the model of "billion."] —**quad·ril·lion** *adj., pron.* —**quad·ril·lionth** *adj., n.*

quad·ri·par·tite /kwòddrə paar tīt/ *adj.* **1.** IN FOUR PARTS made up of four parts or divided into four **2.** INVOLVING FOUR PARTICIPANTS involving the participation of four individuals or groups

quad·ri·phon·ic /kwòddrə fónnik/ *adj.* = **quadraphonic**

quad·ri·ple·gi·a /kwòddrə pleejee ə, -pleejə/ *n.* the inability to move all four limbs or the entire body below the neck —**quad·ri·pleg·ic** *n., adj.*

quad·ri·va·lent /kwòddrə váylənt/ *adj.* **1.** = **tetravalent** **2.** WITH FOUR VALENCES with four different valences —**quad·ri·va·lence** *n.*

quad·riv·i·al /kwo drívvee əl/ *adj.* **1.** FOUR ROADS MEETING with four roads or ways going in different directions and meeting at the same point **2.** OF THE QUADRIVIUM relating to the quadrivium

quad·riv·i·um /kwo drívvee əm/ *n.* four of the seven liberal arts taught in medieval universities, consisting of arithmetic, geometry, music, and astronomy. The three lower arts (**trivium**) were grammar, rhetoric, and logic. [Early 19thC. Via late Latin from Latin, "crossroads," from *quadri-* "four" + *via* "road."]

quad·roon /kwo droon/ *n.* an offensive term for somebody with one Black and three Caucasian grandparents (*offensive*) [Mid-17thC. Via Spanish *cuarterón* from, ultimately, Latin *quartus* "quarter" (see QUART).]

quadru- *prefix.* = **quadri-** (*used before vowels*)

quad·ru·ma·nous /kwo droomənəss/ *adj.* with four feet that can also be used as hands, each having an opposable first digit. Most primates, apart from human beings, are quadrumanous. [Late 17thC. Formed from QUADRU- + Latin *manus* "hand."]

quad·rum·vi·rate /kwo drúmvərət/ *n.* a group of four people sharing power, especially forming a government [Mid-18thC. Formed from QUADRI-, on the model of "triumvirate."]

quad·ru·ped /kwóddrə pèd/ *n.* FOUR-FOOTED ANIMAL an animal such as a lion or lizard with four limbs and feet, all of which are used for walking ■ *adj.* FOUR-FOOTED with four feet —**quad·ru·pe·dal** /kwo droopəd'l/ *adj.*

quad·ru·ple /kwo droop'l/ *vti.* (**-pled, -pling, -ples**) INCREASE FOURFOLD to multiply something by four or become four times as great ■ *adj.* **1.** MULTIPLIED BY FOUR four times as great **2.** WITH FOUR PARTS made up of four parts **3.** MUSIC WITH FOUR BEATS PER MEASURE used to describe a time or meter consisting of four beats to a measure ■ *n.* QUANTITY FOUR TIMES AS GREAT a number or amount that is four times as great as another [14thC. Via French from Latin *quintuplus*, literally "fourfold," from *quadri-* "four" (see QUADRI-).] —**quad·ru·ply** *adv.*

quad·ru·plet /kwo drooplət/ *n.* **1.** ONE OF FOUR BABIES any one of four babies born to the same mother from one pregnancy **2.** FOUR SIMILAR THINGS a set of four identical or very similar things **3.** MUSIC FOUR NOTES PLAYED FASTER THAN NORMAL a group of four notes performed in the time usually occupied by three [Late 18thC. Formed from QUADRUPLE.]

quad·ru·pli·cate *vti.* /kwo drooplee kàyt/ (**-cat·ed, -cat·ing, -cates**) INCREASE FOURFOLD to multiply something by four or to be multiplied by four ■ *adj.* /kwo drooplikət/ WITH FOUR PARTS consisting of four identical or corresponding parts ■ *n.* /kwo drooplikət/ ONE OF FOUR any one of a set of four identical things or copies [Mid-17thC. Formed from Latin *quadri-* "four," on the model of "duplicate."] —**quad·ru·pli·ca·tion** /kwo droopli káysh'n/ *n.*

quaes·tor /kwéstər/ *n.* in ancient Rome, a magistrate responsible chiefly for financial administration [14thC. From Latin, formed from *quaest-*, the past participle stem of *quaerere* "to inquire" (see QUERY).] —**quaes·to·ri·al** /kwe stáwree əl/ *adj.* —**quaes·tor·ship** /kwéstər shìp/ *n.*

quaff /kwof/ *vti.* (**quaffed, quaff·ing, quaffs**) DRINK QUICKLY OR HEARTILY to drink something in large gulps or with great enjoyment (*literary or humorous*) ■ *n.* HEARTY DRINK a long deep drink (*literary or humorous*) [Early 16thC. Origin uncertain.] —**quaff·er** *n.*

quag /kwog/ *n.* = **quagmire** *n.* 1 [Late 16thC. Origin uncertain.]

quag·ga /kwóggə/ (*plural* **-gas** *or* **-ga**) *n.* an extinct mammal of the horse family, related to the zebra, with yellowish-brown coloring and stripes on the head, neck, and shoulders. It was found in southern Africa until the late 19th century. Latin name: *Equus quagga.* [Late 18thC. From Afrikaans, of Nguni origin, said to be an imitation of the animal's call.]

quag·gy /kwóggee/ (**-gi·er, -gi·est**) *adj.* soft and wet like a marsh or bog —**quag·gi·ness** *n.*

quag·mire /kwág mīr/ *n.* **1.** SWAMP a soft marshy area of land that gives way when walked on **2.** DIFFICULT SITUATION an awkward, complicated, or dangerous situation from which it is difficult to escape [Late 16thC. Formed from QUAG + MIRE.]

qua·hog /kwáw hàwg, kwó hòg/, **qua·haug** *n.* a thick-shelled edible clam of the North Atlantic coast of the United States. The shells were formerly used as money by Native North Americans. Latin name: *Mercenaria mercenaria.* [Mid-18thC. From Narragansett *poqua hock.*]

WORD KEY: REGIONAL NOTE

The ***quahog*** is also called *round clam* (especially in Connecticut) and *cohog.*

quaich /kwaykh/, **quaigh** *n. Scotland* a shallow drinking vessel with two handles, usually made from wood or metal [Mid-17thC. Via Scottish Gaelic from Old Irish *cúach*, which was borrowed from medieval Latin *caucus* "drinking cup" (possible source of English *caucus*).]

Quai d'Or·say /kee dawr sáy/ *n.* **1.** LOCATION OF FRENCH FOREIGN OFFICE the street along the south bank of the Seine River in Paris on which the French foreign office is located **2.** FRENCH FOREIGN OFFICE the French foreign office itself ○ *The Quai d'Orsay chose to make no immediate comment on the crisis.*

quail[1] /kwayl/ (*plural* **quail** *or* **quails**) *n.* **1.** BIRD WITH MOTTLED BROWN PLUMAGE a small game bird of Europe, Asia, and Africa with a rounded body, mottled brown plumage, and a short tail. Genus: *Coturnix.* **2.** NEW WORLD GAME BIRD any of several small New World game birds related to the quail, including the bobwhite [14thC. Via Old French from medieval Latin *coacula*, from a Germanic word that is ultimately an imitation of the bird's call.]

quail[2] /kwáyl/ (**quailed, quail·ing, quails**) *vi.* to tremble or shrink with fear or apprehension [Early 19thC. Of uncertain origin: possibly from Middle Dutch *qualen* "to suffer."]

Quail

WORD KEY: SYNONYMS

See Synonyms at ***recoil.***

quaint /kwaynt/ *adj.* **1. ATTRACTIVELY OLD-FASHIONED** with a charming old-fashioned quality ○ *a quaint little shop* **2. PLEASANTLY STRANGE** strange or unusual, especially in a pleasing or interesting way [12thC. Via Old French *cointe, queinte* "clever" from Latin *cognit-*, the past participle stem of *cognoscere* "to learn" (see COGNITION).] —**quaint·ly** *adv.* —**quaint·ness** *n.*

quake /kwayk/ *vi.* **(quaked, quak·ing, quakes) 1. TREMBLE WITH FEAR** to shake or tremble, especially with fear **2. SHAKE** to shake or rock, e.g., from instability or a geologic disturbance ■ *n.* **1. EARTHQUAKE** an earthquake (*informal*) **2. SHAKING** a tremor or shake [Old English *cwacian*, of unknown origin] —**quak·y** *adj.*

quak·er /kwáykər/ *n. Rocky Mountains* = **quaking aspen**

Quak·er /kwáykər/ *n.* a member of the Society of Friends, a Christian denomination founded in England in the 17th century that rejects formal sacraments, ministry, and creed, and is committed to pacifism. At meetings members are encouraged to speak when they feel moved to do so. [Late 17thC. Formed from QUAKE, probably because founder George Fox (1624–91) admonished that they should "tremble at the word of the Lord."] —**Quak·er·ism** *n.* —**Quak·er·ly** *adj.*

Quak·er gun *n.* a dummy gun or cannon, usually made of wood, used in military training or to deceive an enemy [From the Quakers' refusal to fight in wars]

quak·ing as·pen (*plural* **quak·ing as·pens** *or* **quak·ing as·pen**), **quaker** *n.* an aspen tree, native to the northern United States and Canada, with rounded flat leaves that tremble in the wind. Latin name: *Populus tremuloides.*

WORD KEY: REGIONAL NOTE

As a variant term for the tree name ***quaking aspen***, *quaker* or occasionally *quakie* is common in the Middle and Upper Rocky Mountain states, especially Colorado.

qual·i·fi·ca·tion /kwòlləfi káysh'n/ *n.* **1. ESSENTIAL ATTRIBUTE** a skill, quality, or attribute that makes somebody suitable for a particular job, activity, or task **2. OFFICIAL REQUIREMENT** a condition or requirement, e.g., passing an examination, that must be met to by somebody who is to be eligible for a position or privilege (*often used in the plural*) **3. MEETING OF REQUIREMENTS** the meeting of a condition or requirement to become eligible for a position or privilege **4. SOMETHING RESTRICTIVE** something that modifies, limits, or restricts **5. RESTRICTING OR CHANGING SOMETHING** the modification or limitation of something, e.g., in meaning, scope, or strength

qual·i·fied /kwóllə fìd/ *adj.* **1. OFFICIALLY ELIGIBLE** having met a condition or requirement to become legally eligible for or entitled to a position or privilege **2. SUITABLE OR ELIGIBLE TO DO SOMETHING** with the necessary skills, qualities, or attributes to do a particular thing ○ *She's well qualified to comment on international affairs.* **3. RESTRICTED OR CHANGED** modified or limited in some way —**qual·i·fied·ly** *adv.*

qual·i·fi·er /kwóllə fìr/ *n.* **1. QUALIFYING PERSON OR TEAM** an individual or team that is successful in the preliminary part of a competition and earns the right to take part in the next stage **2. EARLY ROUND** a preliminary round of a competition **3. SOMEBODY WITH A RIGHT OR SKILLS** somebody who meets the requirements of or has the qualifications for something **4.** GRAM **MODIFIER** a word or phrase that restricts or modifies the meaning of another word or phrase, e.g., the word "fairly"

qual·i·fy /kwóllə fì/ **(-fied, -fy·ing, -fies)** *v.* **1.** *vti.* **BE OR MAKE SOMEBODY SUITABLE** to have or give somebody a skill or attribute necessary for a particular activity **2.** *vti.* **HAVE OR GIVE SOMEBODY ELIGIBILITY** to become legally eligible or make somebody legally eligible for a position or privilege ○ *Did your exam results qualify you for the job?* **3.** *vi.* **WIN FIRST ROUND OF COMPETITION** to complete the preliminary part of a competition successfully and earn the right to go on to the next stage **4.** *vt.* **RESTRICT OR CHANGE** to modify or limit something in meaning, scope, or strength **5.** *vt.* **MODERATE** to make something less strong or extreme **6.** *vt.* **DESCRIBE AS SOMETHING** to attribute a particular quality or characteristic to something **7.** *vt.* GRAM **MODIFY OR RESTRICT MEANING** to modify or restrict the meaning of a word [Mid-16thC. Via French *qualifier* from medieval Latin *qualificare* "to attribute a quality to," from Latin *qualis* (see QUALITY).] —**qual·i·fi·a·ble** *adj.* —**qual·i·fi·ca·to·ry** /kwólləfikə tàwree/ *adj.*

qual·i·ta·tive /kwóllə tàytiv/ *adj.* relating to or based on the quality or character of something, often as opposed to its size or quantity [Early 17thC. Via late Latin *qualitativus* from Latin *qualitas* (see QUALITY).] —**qual·i·ta·tive·ly** *adv.*

qual·i·ta·tive a·nal·y·sis *n.* the identifying of the components in a mixture

qual·i·ty /kwóllətee/ (*plural* **-ties**) *n.* **1. DISTINGUISHING CHARACTERISTIC** a distinctive characteristic of somebody or something **2. ESSENTIAL PROPERTY** an essential identifying nature or character of somebody or something **3. STANDARD** the general standard or grade of something ○ *goods of a pretty dubious quality* **4. EXCELLENCE** the highest or finest standard (*often used before a noun*) ○ *quality products* **5. UPPER SOCIAL CLASS** high social position or aristocratic breeding (*dated informal*) **6. PEOPLE OF UPPER SOCIAL CLASS** people of high social position or aristocratic breeding (*dated informal*) ○ *quality manners* **7.** PHON **CHARACTER OF VOWEL SOUND** the character of a vowel sound that depends on such factors as the shape of the mouth and position of the tongue when it is uttered **8.** MUSIC **TONE OF NOTE** the distinctive tone of a musical note **9.** LOGIC **AFFIRMATIVE OR NEGATIVE CHARACTERISTIC** the positive or negative nature of a logical proposition [13thC. Via French *qualité* from the Latin stem *qualitat-*, from *qualis* "of what kind." Ultimately from an Indo-European word that is also the ancestor of English *what, how,* and *quantity.*]

qual·i·ty cir·cle *n.* COMM a group of employees from different levels of a company who meet regularly to discuss ways of improving quality and to resolve any problems related to production

qual·i·ty con·trol *n.* a system for achieving or maintaining the desired level of quality in a manufactured product by inspecting samples and assessing what changes may be needed in the manufacturing process

qual·i·ty fac·tor *n.* a number by which a given dose of absorbed radiation is multiplied to determine the radiation's biological effect

qual·i·ty of life *n.* the degree of enjoyment and satisfaction experienced in everyday life as opposed to financial or material well-being

qual·i·ty time *n.* time spent with loved ones in enjoyable activities that enhance the relationship ○ *working parents determined to spend quality time with their kids*

qualm /kwaam/ *n.* **1. DOUBT ABOUT PROPRIETY OF BEHAVIOR** an uneasy conscience about an action or conduct **2. SICK FEELING** a sudden pang of nausea **3. FEELING OF UNEASE** a sudden feeling of uncertainty or apprehension [Early 16thC. Of uncertain origin.] —**qualm·ish** *adj.* —**qualm·ish·ly** *adv.* —**qualm·ish·ness** *n.*

quam·ash /kwáamash/ (*plural* **-ash·es** *or* **-ash**) *n.* = **camas** *n.* 1

Qua·nah /kwáanə/ (1845?–1911) U.S. Native North American leader. He led the Comanche in raids against Caucasian settlers in the southwest during the early 1870s. Known as **Chief Quanah**. Full name **Parker Quanah**

quan·da·ry /kwóndəree, -dree/ (*plural* **-ries**) *n.* a state of uncertainty or indecision as to what to do in a particular situation [Late 16thC. Of uncertain origin.]

quan·dong /kwón dòng/ (*plural* **-dongs** *or* **-dong**) *n.* **1.** TREES **SMALL AUSTRALIAN TREE** a small Australian tree that bears a large edible red fruit with an edible kernel. Latin name: *Santalum acuminatum.* **2. FRUIT OF QUANDONG** the large red edible fruit of the quandong, or its edible kernel, used to make jam **3.** TREES **LARGE AUSTRALIAN TREE** a large Australian tree with a wide buttressed trunk that bears shiny blue fruits containing edible seeds and yields a light-colored wood used as lumber. Latin name: *Elaeocarpus grandis.* [Mid-19thC. From Wiradhuri *guwandhang.*]

quant /kwont/ *n.* somebody skilled in computing and the analysis of quantitative data, employed by a company to make financial predictions (*slang*) [Late 20thC. Shortening of QUANTITATIVE.]

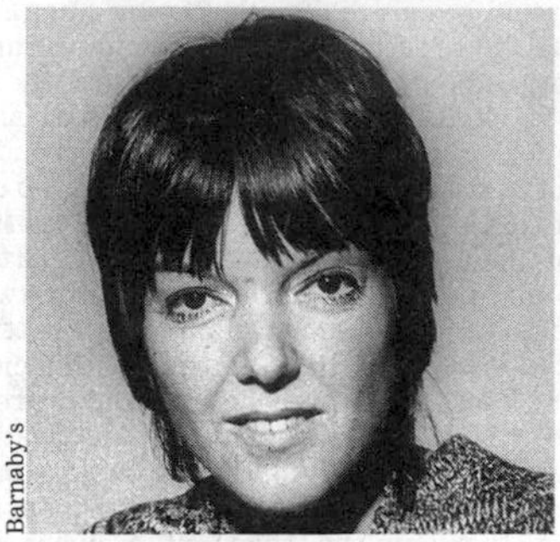

Barnaby's

Mary Quant

Quant /kwont/, **Mary** (*b.* 1934) British fashion designer. A leader of 1960s London style, she created the miniskirt and hotpants, and later expanded her business into cosmetics and textiles.

quant. /kwont/ *abbr.* quantitative

quan·ta plural of **quantum**

quan·tal /kwónt'l/ *adj.* **1.** PHYS **RELATING TO QUANTUM** relating to a quantum or to a system that has been quantized **2.** SCI **IN ONE OF TWO POSSIBLE STATES** used to describe something that at a given instant can be found in one of two possible states [Mid-20thC. Formed from QUANTUM.] —**quan·tal·ly** *adv.*

quan·tic /kwóntik/ *n.* a mathematical expression with more than one variable that contains terms raised to the same power with respect to all the variables [Mid-19thC. Formed from Latin *quantus* "how much" (see QUANTITY).]

quan·ti·fi·er /kwóntə fìr/ *n.* a word such as "all," "some," or "most," or a logical symbol with this meaning, that indicates the range of individuals or items referred to

quan·ti·fy /kwóntə fì/ **(-fied, -fy·ing, -fies)** *vt.* **1. DETERMINE NUMBER OR EXTENT OF SOMETHING** to calculate or express the number, degree, or amount of something **2.** LOGIC **SHOW RANGE OF REFERENCE OF SOMETHING** to use a quantifier to limit the range of individuals or items referred to in a sentence or proposition [Mid-19thC. From medieval Latin *quantificare*, from Latin *quantus* (see QUANTITY).] —**quan·ti·fi·a·ble** /kwòntə fí əb'l/ *adj.* —**quan·ti·fi·ca·tion** /-fi káysh'n/ *n.*

quan·ti·tate /kwóntə tàyt/ **(-tat·ed, -tat·ing, -tates)** *vt.* to estimate or determine precisely the number, degree, or amount of something [Mid-20thC. Back-formation from QUANTITATIVE.] —**quan·ti·ta·tion** /kwòntə táysh'n/ *n.*

quan·ti·ta·tive /kwóntə tàytiv/ *adj.* **1. RELATING TO QUANTITY** relating to, concerning, or based on the amount or number of something **2. MEASURABLE** capable of being measured or expressed in numerical terms **3.** POETRY **BASED ON LENGTH OF SYLLABLES** relating or belonging to a metrical system based on the length of syllables rather than on stress. Classical Latin and Greek verse uses a quantitative system. [Late 16thC. From medieval Latin *quantitativus*, from Latin *quantitas* (see QUANTITY).] —**quan·ti·ta·tive·ly** *adv.* —**quan·ti·ta·tive·ness** *n.*

quan·ti·ta·tive a·nal·y·sis *n.* the determining of the relative amounts of the components in a mixture

quan·ti·ta·tive dig·i·tal ra·di·og·ra·phy *n.* a method of detecting thinning of the bones (**osteoporosis**) by assessing the levels of calcium present, usually in the spine and hip

quan·ti·ty /kwóntətee/ (*plural* **-ties**) *n.* **1. AMOUNT** an amount or number of something **2. MEASURABLE PROPERTY** the measurable property of something **3. LARGE AMOUNTS** a large amount or number ○ *Foodstuffs were imported in quantity.* **4.** MATH **MATHEMATICAL ENTITY WITH NUMERICAL VALUE** a mathematical entity that has a numerical value or magnitude **5.** PHYS **SPECIFIED MAGNITUDE OF SOMETHING** the product of a measurable phenomenon such as electric current or radiation intensity and the time during which the phenomenon is measured **6.** LOGIC **UNIVERSAL OR PARTICULAR NATURE OF PROPOSITION** the characteristic of a logical proposition that distinguishes it as universal or particular **7.** PHON **RELATIVE DURATION OF SOUND** the length of a vowel sound or syllable [13thC. Via French *quantité* from the Latin stem *quantitat-*, from *quantus* "how much." Ultimately from an Indo-European word that is also the ancestor of English *what, how,* and *quality.*]

quan·ti·ty the·o·ry *n.* the theory that prices vary with the amount of money in circulation and the rate at which it circulates

quan·tize /kwón tīz/ (**-tized, -tiz·ing, -tiz·es**) *vt.* **1. EXPRESS IN QUANTUM NUMBERS** to express something in terms of quantum numbers **2. APPLY QUANTUM MECHANICS TO** to divide something into tiny discrete increments applying the rules of quantum mechanics [Early 20thC. Formed from QUANTUM.] —**quan·ti·za·tion** /kwòntə záysh'n/ *n.*

quant jock *n.* = **quant** *n.*

Quan·trill /kwóntril/, **William Clarke** (1837–65) U.S. military leader. He led a Confederate guerrilla band, many of them outlaws, against communities believed to be pro-Union.

quan·tum /kwóntəm/ *n.* (*plural* **-ta** /kwóntə/) **1.** PHYS **SMALLEST QUANTITY OF ENERGY** the smallest discrete quantity of a physical property, e.g., electromagnetic radiation or angular momentum **2.** PHYS **SMALLEST UNIT** the smallest unit used to measure a physical property. For example, the quantum of electromagnetic radiation is the photon. **3. QUANTITY** a quantity or amount of anything **4. SPECIFIC AMOUNT** a specific quantity or portion ■ *adj.* **MAJOR** sudden, dramatic, and significant [Early 17thC. From Latin, formed from *quantus* "how much" (see QUANTITY).]

quan·tum chro·mo·dy·nam·ics *n.* a quantum field theory of elementary particles that states that the color properties of quarks are bound together by gluons

quan·tum e·lec·tro·dy·nam·ics *n.* a quantum field theory that describes the properties of electromagnetic radiation and its interaction with electrically charged particles

quan·tum field the·o·ry *n.* a theory developed from quantum mechanics based on the assumption that elementary particles interact through the influence of fields around them and the exchange of energy

quan·tum jump *n.* **1.** PHYS **SUDDEN CHANGE OF ENERGY STATE** the sudden transition of an atom or particle from one energy state to another **2.** = **quantum leap**

quan·tum leap *n.* a sudden, dramatic, and significant change or advance ○ *a quantum leap in our understanding of molecular science*

quan·tum me·chan·ics *n.* the study and analysis of the interactions of atoms and elementary particles based on quantum theory. The study evolved in an effort to explain the behavior of atoms and subatomic particles, which do not obey the laws of classical Newtonian mechanics. (*takes a singular or plural verb*) —**quan·tum me·chan·i·cal** *adj.*

quan·tum num·ber *n.* any one of the set of integers or half integers that characterize the properties and energy states of an elementary particle or system

quan·tum the·o·ry *n.* a theory describing the behavior and interactions of elementary particles or energy states based on the assumptions that energy is subdivided into discrete amounts and that matter possesses wave properties

Qu'Ap·pelle /kwə pél/ river in southern Saskatchewan, which joins the Assiniboine River east of the Manitoba border. Length: 270 mi./435 km.

quar. *abbr.* 1. quarter 2. quarterly

quar·an·tine /kwáwrən teen/ *n.* **1. ISOLATION TO PREVENT SPREAD OF DISEASE** enforced isolation of people or animals that may have been exposed to a contagious or infectious disease, e.g., when entering a country **2. PLACE OF ISOLATION** a place in which people or animals spend a period of isolation to prevent the spread of disease **3. TIME OF ENFORCED ISOLATION** the period of time during which people or animals are kept in isolation to prevent the spread of disease **4. STATE OR PERIOD OF ISOLATION** enforced isolation, e.g., for social or political reasons, or a period of such isolation **5. 40 DAYS** a period of 40 days (*archaic*) ■ *vt.* (**-tined, -tin·ing, -tines**) **1. ISOLATE TO AVOID SPREAD OF DISEASE** to isolate a person or animal that may have been exposed to a contagious or infectious disease in order to prevent the possible spread of that disease **2. DETAIN** to isolate or detain somebody, e.g., for social or political reasons [Early 17thC. Via Italian *quarantina* from, ultimately, Latin *quadraginta* "forty"; so called because ships suspected of carrying disease were refused entrance to port for 40 days.] —**quar·an·tin·a·ble** /kwàwrən téenəb'l/ *adj.*

quark[1] /kwawrk/ *n.* any elementary particle with an electric charge equal to one-third or two-thirds that of the electron. Quarks are believed to be the constituents of baryons and mesons. There are six types (**flavors**) of quarks, each paired with an antiquark, and three properties (**colors**) that determine their role in interactions. [Mid-20thC. Coined by American physicist Murray Gell-Mann (b. 1929), alluding to the phrase "three quarks for Mr. Mark" in James Joyce's *Finnegans Wake*; because originally there were thought to be three quarks.]

quark[2] /kwawrk/ *n.* a type of soft cheese of German origin made from skim milk [Mid-20thC. From German, ultimately of Slavic origin.]

quar·rel[1] /kwáwrəl/ *n.* **1. ARGUMENT BETWEEN PEOPLE** an angry dispute between two or more people **2. REASON TO ARGUE** a reason for a disagreement or dispute between people ○ *I have no quarrel with their proposals.* ■ *vi.* (**-reled, -rel·ing, -rels**) **1. ARGUE VEHEMENTLY** to engage in an angry dispute **2. DISAGREE WITH SOMETHING** to dispute or disagree with something such as a decision **3. FIND FAULT** to complain about something [14thC. Via Old French from Latin *querela* "complaint," from *queri* "to complain" (source of English *querulous*).] —**quar·rel·er** *n.*

quar·rel[2] /kwáwrəl/ *n.* **1. CROSSBOW BOLT** a short square-headed bolt or arrow used in a crossbow **2. SQUARE GLASS PANE** any of several small square or diamond-shaped panes of glass in a window [12thC. Via Old French from assumed Vulgar Latin *quadrellus*, literally "small square," from Latin *quadrum* (see QUADRATE).]

quar·rel·some /kwáwrəlsəm/ *adj.* having a tendency to argue with people —**quar·rel·some·ly** *adv.* —**quar·rel·some·ness** *n.*

quar·ry[1] /kwáwree/ (*plural* **-ries**) *n.* **1. HUNTED ANIMAL OR BIRD** an animal or bird that is hunted by something or somebody **2. OBJECT OF PURSUIT** somebody or something that is chased or hunted by another [15thC. Via Anglo-Norman *coure* "entrails of an animal given to the hounds" from assumed Vulgar Latin *corata*, from Latin *cor* "heart" (see CORDATE).]

quar·ry[2] /kwáwree/ *n.* (*plural* **-ries**) **1. OPEN AREA FOR MINING** an open excavation from which stone or other material is extracted by blasting, cutting, or drilling **2. SOURCE** a rich source of something ■ *v.* (**-ried, -ry·ing, -ries**) **1.** *vti.* MINING **OBTAIN SOMETHING FROM QUARRY** to extract stone or other material from a quarry **2.** *vt.* **USE PLACE FOR EXTRACTING STONE** to make a quarry in a particular place such as a hillside and remove material from it ○ *The area was extensively quarried last century.* **3.** *vti.* **EXTRACT LABORIOUSLY** to obtain something, such as facts or information, by searching laboriously and carefully [14thC. Via medieval Latin *quarreia* from Old French *quarriere*, from assumed *quarre* "square-cut stone," from Latin *quadrum* "square" (see QUADRATE).]

quar·ry[3] /kwáwree/ (*plural* **-ries**) *n.* **1. SQUARE SHAPE** a square or diamond shape **2. SOMETHING SQUARE OR DIAMOND-SHAPED** something with a square or diamond shape, e.g., a pane of glass in a latticed window [Mid-16thC. Alteration of QUARREL[2].]

quar·ry tile *n.* a tile with a square or diamond shape, especially a hardwearing unglazed clay tile used for flooring [From QUARRY[3]]

quart /kwawrt/ *n.* **1. QUARTER OF GALLON** a unit of measurement for liquids equal to two pints **2. ONE-EIGHTH OF PECK** a unit of measurement for dry substances equal to two pints **3. CONTAINER OR CONTENTS** a container that holds one quart or its contents [13thC. Via Old French *quarte* from, ultimately, Latin *quartus* "fourth." Ultimately from an Indo-European word that is also the ancestor of English *fourth* and *farthing.*]

quar·tan /kwáwrt'n/ *adj.* used to describe a fever that recurs every fourth day, e.g., in some types of malaria [13thC. Via Old French *quartaine* from, ultimately, Latin *quartus* "fourth" (see QUART).]

quar·ter /kwáwrtər/ *n.* **1. ONE OF FOUR PARTS** any of four equal or approximately equal parts into which something is divided **2. ONE-FOURTH** a number that is equal to one divided by four, represented by the symbol $\frac{1}{4}$ **3. PERIOD OF THREE MONTHS** any of the three-month periods into which the year is divided, especially for accounting purposes **4. 25 CENTS** in the United States and Canada, the sum of 25 cents **5. COIN WORTH 25 CENTS** in the United States and Canada, a coin worth 25 cents or one quarter of a dollar **6. 15 MINUTES BEFORE OR AFTER HOUR** either of the points in time 15 minutes before or after the hour, marked on a traditional clock face at 3 and 9 **7.** MEASURE **25 LB. IN WEIGHT** in the United States, a unit of weight equal to 25 lb./11.35 kg or one quarter of a hundredweight **8.** MEASURE **28 LB. IN WEIGHT** in the U.K., a unit of weight equal to 28 lb./12.71 kg or one quarter of a hundredweight **9.** MEASURE **8 BUSHELS** a unit of capacity for grain and similar substances equal to approximately 8 bushels **10.** MEASURE **4 OZ. OF SOMETHING** an amount of something weighing 4 oz/113.4 g or a quarter of a pound (*informal*) **11. QUARTER OF STANDARD UNIT** an amount or length equal to one quarter of a standard unit, such as a yard or mile **12. QUARTER OF SQUARE MILE** one quarter of a square mile of rural land **13. quar·ter, Quar·ter DISTRICT OF TOWN** an area in a town of a particular type or inhabited by a particular group of people ○ *We visited the French Quarter while we were in New Orleans.* **14. UNSPECIFIED PERSON OR GROUP** an unspecified person or group of people ○ *They're looking for help from any quarter.* **15. MERCY** mercy offered to a defeated enemy **16.** ASTRON **MOON PHASE** either of the two phases of the Moon in which half of its illuminated surface can be seen from the Earth **17.** ASTRON **QUARTER OF MOON'S ORBIT** one fourth of the Moon's orbital period about the Earth **18.** EDUC **ACADEMIC TERM** an academic term at a college or university lasting 10 or 12 weeks **19.** SPORTS **PART OF SPORTS CONTEST** one of the four equal parts into which games are divided in some sports **20.** NAUT **SIDE OF REAR HALF OF VESSEL** either side of the rear half of a boat or ship, usually behind the rearmost mast **21.** GEOG **NORTHEAST, SOUTHEAST, SOUTHWEST, OR NORTHWEST** any one of the four compass points that lie midway between north, east, south, and west **22.** HERALDRY **ANY SECTION OF HERALDIC SHIELD** any one of the four sections into which a heraldic shield may be divided **23. PART OF ANIMAL OR BIRD** any one of the four parts into which the body of an animal or bird may be divided, with a leg or wing forming part of each quarter **24. SIDE OF HOOF** the side of a horse's hoof **25. SHOE PART** the part of a shoe between the heel and the front part of the upper ■ **quar·ters** *npl.* **ACCOMMODATIONS** living or sleeping accommodations provided for somebody, e.g., military personnel and their families, household employees, or members of a ship's crew ■ *adj.* **DIVIDED BY FOUR** used to describe one fourth part of something ■ *v.* (**-tered, -ter·ing, -ters**) **1.** *vt.* **DIVIDE SOMETHING INTO FOUR** to divide something into four equal or approximately equal parts **2.** *vt.* HIST **CUT BODY INTO FOUR** to cut a human body into four parts following an execution **3.** *vt.* **GIVE SOMEBODY LODGING** to assign accommodation to somebody ○ *The soldiers were quartered in an old barn.* **4.** *vt.* HERALDRY **DIVIDE SHIELD INTO FOUR SECTIONS** to divide a heraldic shield into four sections **5.** *vi.* **CROSS IN ZIGZAG COURSE** to cover all parts of an area of land, sea, or air by ranging from side to side while moving forward, e.g., while searching for somebody or something **6.** *vi.* NAUT **COME FROM REAR PART OF SIDE** to come from a direction at approximately 45 degrees to the stern of a boat or ship **7.** *vt.* **POSITION SOMETHING AT 90 DEGREES** to locate or position a machine part at right angles to another [13thC. Via Old French *quartier* from, ultimately, Latin *quartus* "fourth" (see QUART).]

WORD KEY: REGIONAL NOTE

Quarter can designate fifteen minutes to the hour with *of, till,* and *to.* Before World War II, the three prepositions outlined, respectively, the Northern, Midland, and Southern dialect areas, especially in the Eastern states. The pattern seems to endure, with *quarter to* gaining ground across the country.

quar·ter·age /kwáwrtərij/ *n.* a sum of money paid or received every three months

quar·ter·back /kwáwrtər bàk/ *n.* **PLAYER IN AMERICAN FOOTBALL** in football, a player positioned behind the center who directs the play by calling signals ■ *vt.* (**-backed, -back·ing, -backs**) **1. DIRECT TEAM** to direct the offensive play of a football team **2. BE IN CHARGE OF**

OPERATION to direct or mastermind an operation (*slang*)

quar·ter-bound *adj.* used to describe a book that is bound in one material, usually leather, on the spine and another on the covers

quar·ter·deck /kwáwrtər dèk/ *n.* NAUT the rear part of the upper deck of a ship, where official ceremonies traditionally take place on a vessel

quar·ter·fi·nal /kwàwrtər fín'l, kwáwrtər fìn'l/ *n.* any one of four contests in a tournament or competition, the winners of which go on to play each other in the semifinals [Early 20thC. Modeled on SEMIFINAL.] — **quar·ter·fi·nal·ist** *n.*

quar·ter horse *n.* a strong horse formerly bred to run short races in the United States [From "quarter-race," a race over a quarter mile]

quar·ter hour *n.* **1. 15 MINUTES** a period of 15 minutes **2. 15 MINUTES BEFORE OR AFTER HOUR** either of the points on a clock face that indicate a time 15 minutes before or after the hour ○ *The clock chimes on the quarter hour.*

quar·ter·ly /kwáwrtərlee/ *adj.* **1. HAPPENING EVERY THREE MONTHS** happening, produced, or published four times a year, at three-month intervals **2.** HERALDRY **DIVIDED INTO FOUR SECTIONS** used to describe a heraldic shield that is divided into four sections ■ *adv.* **EVERY THREE MONTHS** once every three months ■ *n.* (*plural* **-lies**) **JOURNAL PUBLISHED EVERY THREE MONTHS** a magazine or journal published four times a year, at three-month intervals

quar·ter·mas·ter /kwáwrtər màstər/ *n.* **1. ARMY OFFICER** an army officer responsible for providing soldiers with food, clothing, equipment, and living quarters **2. NAVAL OFFICER** in the navy, a petty officer or ship's mate with some responsibilities for navigation and signals

quar·tern /kwáwrtərn/ *n.* a fourth part of something, especially of some old weights and measures [13thC. From Anglo-Norman *quartrun*.]

quar·ter note *n.* a note with one fourth the time value of a whole note

quar·ter-phase *adj.* ELEC ENG = **two-phase** [So called because the two currents are 90 degrees out of phase]

quar·ter round *n.* a molding that, in cross-section, is the shape of a quarter of a circle

quar·ters /kwáwrtərz/ *npl.* a building or set of rooms where people live, especially military personnel or servants ◇ **at close quarters** from very near

quar·ter·sawn /kwáwrtər sàwn/, **quar·ter·sawed** /-sàwd/ *adj.* used to describe wooden boards sawed from a log cut into quarters lengthwise so as to show off the grain of the wood

quar·ter sec·tion *n.* a tract of land measuring half a mile/800 meters on each side, equal to 160 acres/65 hectares or one fourth of a section

quar·ter·staff /kwáwrtər stàf/ (*plural* **-staves** /-stàyvz/ *or* **-staffs**) *n.* a long heavy wooden stick tipped with iron, formerly used in hand-to-hand fighting [Mid-16thC. *Quarter* is of uncertain origin: possibly because it was made from a tree of a certain size cut into quarters.]

quar·ter tone *n.* a difference in pitch between two tones (**interval**) that is equal to half a semitone

quar·tet /kwawr tét/, **quar·tette** *n.* **1. MUSICAL GROUP** a group of four singers or musicians **2. PIECE OF MUSIC** a piece of music written for four voices or instruments **3. GROUP OF FOUR** a group or set of four people or things [Late 18thC. Via French *quartette* from Italian *quartetto*, from *quarto* "fourth," from Latin *quartus* (see QUART).]

quar·tic /kwáwrtik/ *adj.* MATH of or relating to the fourth degree. A quartic equation has the general form $ax^4 + bx^3 + cx^2 + dx + e = 0$. [Mid-19thC. Formed from Latin *quartus* (see QUART).]

quar·tile /kwáwr tìl, kwáwrt'l/ *n.* **1. STATISTICAL DIVISION** any one of the four equal groups into which a statistical sample can be divided **2. STATISTICAL VALUE** in statistics, any one of the three values that divide a frequency distribution into four parts, each containing a quarter of the sample population **3. DISTANCE BETWEEN PLANETS** the astrological aspect of planets that are distant from each other by 90 degrees, or one fourth of the zodiac [Early 16thC. Via Old French *quartil* from, ultimately, Latin *quartus* (see QUART).]

quar·to /kwáwrtō/ (*plural* **-tos**) *n.* **1. PAGE SIZE** the page size created by folding a single sheet of standard-sized printing paper in half twice to create four leaves or eight pages **2. BOOK WITH QUARTO PAGES** a book with quarto pages [Late 16thC. From Latin *(in) quarto*, "in a fourth," from *quartus* (see QUART).]

quartz /kwawrts/ *n.* a usually colorless transparent crystalline mineral widely distributed in rocks of all types. Colored varieties are used as gemstones. Its hardness makes it a valuable industrial component, e.g., as a frequency control in electronic communications and timing devices. [Mid-18thC. From German *Quarz*, ultimately from a western Slavic word meaning "hard."]

quartz clock *n.* a clock in which the time-keeping mechanism is accurately controlled by a quartz crystal that vibrates at a fixed frequency in an oscillating electric circuit

quartz crys·tal *n.* a small piece of quartz cut so that it vibrates at a known frequency. In an oscillating electric circuit, it produces a constant signal for accurate timekeeping.

quartz glass *n.* a clear glass made from melted silica. It can withstand high or rapidly changing temperatures and is unusually transparent to ultraviolet radiation. It is made in both transparent and translucent forms, the latter being clouded by minute gas bubbles trapped within it.

quartz heat·er *n.* a portable electric heater with heating elements sealed in quartz glass tubes

quartz·if·er·ous /kwart síffərəss/ *adj.* containing or consisting of quartz

quartz-i·o·dine lamp *n.* a very bright lamp with a bulb made of quartz glass that has a tungsten filament and usually contains iodine vapor. It is used in automobile headlights and movie projectors.

quartz·ite /kwáwrt sìt/ *n.* a pale metamorphic rock composed mainly of quartz, formed by the action of heat and pressure on a sandstone. It is an important construction material, used, e.g., for high-quality paving blocks and the facades of buildings. — **quartz·it·ic** /kwawrt síttik/ *adj.*

quartz lamp *n.* a mercury vapor lamp with a bulb made from quartz glass that produces light rich in ultraviolet radiation and is used for street lighting and sun lamps

quartz watch *n.* a watch in which the time-keeping mechanism is accurately controlled by a quartz crystal that vibrates at a fixed frequency in an oscillating electric circuit

qua·sar /kwáy zaar/ *n.* a remote compact object in space that usually has a large red shift and emits radio waves at high intensity [Mid-20thC. Contraction of *quasi-stellar object*.]

quash[1] /kwosh/ (**quashed, quash·ing, quash·es**) *vt.* to put a stop to something forcibly [14thC. Via Old French *quasser* from medieval Latin *quassare* "to shake to pieces," from *quatere* "to shake" (source of English *squash*[2] and *concussion*).]

quash[2] /kwosh/ (**quashed, quash·ing, quash·es**) *vt.* to declare formally that something such as an indictment or a subpoena is not valid [13thC. Via Old French *quasser* from, ultimately, Latin *cassare*, from *cassus* "empty, void."]

qua·si /kwáy zì, kwaazee/ *adj.* **1.** LAW **AS THOUGH** just as valid in law as if actual ○ *quasi contract* **2. ALMOST, BUT NOT QUITE** resembling somebody or something in some ways, but not exactly the same [15thC. Via Old French from Latin, "as if," from *quam* "as" + *si* "if."]

quasi- *prefix.* as if, resembling [Via Old French from Latin *quasi*, literally "as if," from *quam* "as" + *si* "if"]

qua·si-ju·di·cial /kwàyzì joo dísh'l, kwaazi joo dísh'l/ *adj.* used to describe decision-making powers that are similar to those of a court judge, or to describe any arbitrator or inquiry with such powers — **qua·si-ju·di·cial·ly** *adv.*

qua·si-leg·is·la·tive /kwayzì léjjə slàytiv, kwaazi-/ *adj.* used to describe regulations that are not regarded as laws proper but have the force of law, or to describe bodies that have the right to make such regulations

qua·si-stel·lar ob·ject /kwayzì stèllər óbjəkt, kwaazi stèllər óbjəkt/ *n.* = **quasar**

quas·sia /kwóshə/ *n.* **1. TREE YIELDING FINE-GRAINED TIMBER** a tropical American shrub or small tree with scarlet flowers that yields fine-grained timber from which an insecticide can be extracted. Genus: *Quassia*. **2. WOOD OF QUASSIA TREE** the fine-grained pale wood of the quassia tree, used for making furniture **3. INSECTICIDE DERIVED FROM QUASSIA WOOD** a bitter substance obtained from the bark and wood of the quassia tree, formerly used in medicine and now used as an insecticide [Origin uncertain]

qua·ter·cen·ten·a·ry /kwòttər sen ténnəree/ (*plural* **-ries**) *n.* a four hundredth anniversary [Late 19thC. "quater" from Latin, "four times" (see QUATERNARY).]

qua·ter·nar·y /kwóttər nèrree/ *adj.* **1. OCCURRING IN FOURS** consisting of four parts, or occurring in sets of four **2. HAVING FOUR-ATOM BONDS** bonded to four other nonhydrogen atoms or groups of atoms, or containing atoms bonded in this way ■ *n.* (*plural* **-ies**) **SET OF FOUR OR FOURTH MEMBER** a set of four, or the fourth member of a set [15thC. From Latin *quaternarius*, from *quaterni* "by fours," from *quater* "four times."]

Qua·ter·nar·y *adj.* **BELONGING TO PRESENT GEOLOGIC PERIOD** belonging to or dating from the most recent geologic period, spanning the last 2 million years ■ *n.* **MOST RECENT GEOLOGIC PERIOD** the current period of geologic time and the second period of the Cenozoic era. It is characterized by the appearance and dominance of humans.

qua·ter·nar·y am·mo·ni·um com·pound *n.* a nitrogen compound regarded as a derivative of ammonium. Some are used as solvents and disinfectants.

qua·ter·ni·on /kwə túrnee ən/ *n.* **1.** = **quaternary** *n.* **2. GENERALIZED COMPLEX NUMBER** a generalized complex number that contains four terms, one real and three imaginary, and is the sum of a real number and a vector [14thC. From the late Latin stem *quaternion-*, from Latin *quaterni* (see QUATERNARY).]

qua·ter·ni·ty /kwə túrnətee/ (*plural* **-ties**) *n.* a set of four, especially the four beings that, in some religions, are unified in God [Early 16thC. From late Latin *quaternitas*, from Latin *quaterni* (see QUATERNARY).]

quat·rain /kwó tràyn/ *n.* a verse of poetry consisting of four lines, especially one with lines that rhyme alternately [Late 16thC. From French, formed from *quatre* "four," from Latin *quattuor*. Ultimately from the Indo-European word for "four" that is also the ancestor of English *four*, *quarter*, and *tetra-*.]

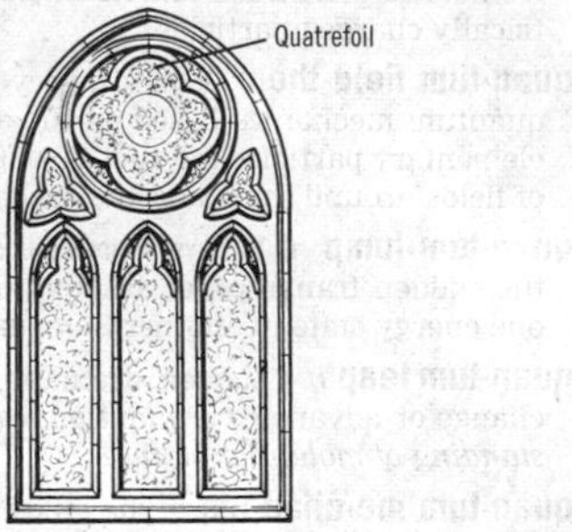

Quatrefoil

quat·re·foil /káttrə fòyl/ *n.* **1. FLOWER OR LEAF SYMBOL** a design or symbol in the shape of a flower with four petals, or a leaf with four parts. It is often used in heraldry. **2. ARCHITECTURAL ORNAMENT** an architectural decoration consisting of four arcs radiating from a center like flower petals [15thC. From Anglo-Norman, literally "four-leaf."]

quat·tro·cen·to /kwaatrō chén tō/ *n.* the 15th century in Italy, especially with reference to art and literature [Late 19thC. From Italian, shortening of *mil quattrocento* "one thousand four hundred."]

qua·ver /kwáyvər/ *v.* (**-vered, -ver·ing, -vers**) **1.** *vi.* **TREMBLE SLIGHTLY** to tremble because of nervousness or fear **2.** *vti.* **SAY TREMBLINGLY** to say something or speak in a trembling voice because of nervousness or fear **3.** *vi.* **SING WITH TRILL** to sing in a trilling voice ■ *n.* **1. TREMBLING SOUND** a tremble in the voice caused by nervousness or fear **2. TRILL** an alternation of a musical tone with the tone just above it **3.** *U.K.* = **eighth note** [15thC. Formed from earlier *quave* "to tremble," of prehistoric Germanic origin.] —**qua·ver·ing·ly** *adv.* — **qua·ver·y** *adj.*

qua·ver rest *n. U.K.* = **eighth rest**

quay /kee/ *n.* a platform that runs along the edge of a port or harbor, where boats are loaded and unloaded [14thC. Via Old North French *cai* from Gaulish *caio* "rampart." Ultimately from an Indo-European base denoting a fence that is also the ancestor of English *hedge*.]

quay·age /kée ij/ *n.* **1. FEE FOR USING QUAY** a charge that shipowners must pay to dock at a quay in order to load and unload there **2. QUAY SPACE** the space available on a quay for ships to load and unload **3. QUAY SYSTEM** a system of quays

quay·side /kée sīd/ *n.* the edge of a quay, where it meets the water

Que. *abbr.* Quebec

quean /kween/ *n.* an offensive term that deliberately insults a woman's morality (*archaic offensive*) [Old English *cwene* "woman" (see QUEEN)]

quea·sy /kweézee/ (**-si·er, -si·est**) *adj.* **1. NAUSEATED** feeling ill in the stomach, as if on the point of vomiting **2. EASILY NAUSEATED** easily nauseated **3. CAUSING UNEASINESS** causing a feeling of uneasiness **4. CAUSING NAUSEA** causing a feeling of nausea [15thC. Origin unknown.] —**quea·si·ly** *adv.* —**quea·si·ness** *n.*

Quebec

Que·bec[1] /kwi bék, ki-/ **1. Que·bec, Qué·bec** /kay bék/, **Que·bec City** capital city of the province of Quebec, Canada, situated on the St. Lawrence River. Population: 671,889 (1996). **2. Que·bec, Qué·bec** the largest province in Canada, situated between Ontario and Newfoundland, with French-based social institutions, language, and culture. Capital: Quebec. Population: 7,138,795 (1996). Area: 594,858 sq. mi./1,540,680 sq. km. —**Que·bec·er** /kwə békər/ *n.*

Que·bec[2] /kwə bék, kə-, kay-/ *n.* a code word for the letter "Q," used in international radio communications

que·bra·cho /kay braá chō/ (*plural* **-chos**) *n.* **1. TREE WITH MEDICINAL BARK** a tree native to Chile and Argentina whose bark yields a medicine used in treating respiratory ailments. Latin name: *Aspidosperma quebracho-blanco.* **2. TREE WITH TANNIN-RICH WOOD** a tree of southern South America whose hard tannin-rich wood is used in the leather industry. Genus: *Schinopsis.* **3. BARK OF QUEBRACHO TREE** the bark of the quebracho tree that yields a medicine utilized in treating respiratory ailments **4. WOOD OF QUEBRACHO TREE** the hard tannin-rich wood of the quebracho tree that is used in the leather industry [Late 19thC. From Spanish, an alteration of *quiebrahacha*, literally "axe-breaker," from *quebrar* "to break" + *hacha* "axe."]

Quech·ua /kéchwə/ (*plural* **-ua** *or* **-uas**), **Kech·ua** (*plural* **-ua** *or* **-uas**), **Quich·ua** /keéchwə/ (*plural* **-ua** *or* **-uas**) *n.* **1. MEMBER OF NATIVE SOUTH AMERICAN PEOPLE** a member of any of several Native South American peoples, including the Incas, living in the Andes **2. QUECHUA LANGUAGE** a Native South American language spoken in the Andes, from southern Colombia through Chile and Argentina. It belongs to the Andean branch of Andean-Equatorial languages. Quechua is spoken by about 10 million people. [Mid-19thC. From Spanish, of uncertain origin: probably from Quechua *kkechúwa* "plunderer."] —**Quech·ua** *adj.* —**Quech·uan** *adj., n.*

queen /kween/ *n.* **1. WOMAN RULER** a woman who rules over a country, usually by right of birth **2. KING'S WIFE** the wife of a king **3. FACE CARD** a playing card with a picture of a queen on it, ranking above a jack and below a king **4. ADMIRED WOMAN, PLACE, OR THING** a greatly admired woman who stands out above all others, or a place or thing considered the best of its kind and personified as a woman **5. EGG-LAYING BEE, ANT, OR TERMITE** a large, fully developed female that lays eggs in a colony of social insects, such as bees or ants. She is usually the only fertile female member of the colony. **6.** CHESS **MOST POWERFUL CHESS PIECE** the most powerful piece in chess, able to move forward, backward, sideways, and diagonally **7. OFFENSIVE TERM** an offensive term for a homosexual man (*offensive*) ■ *vti.* (**queened, queen·ing, queens**) **MAKE PAWN INTO QUEEN** to promote a pawn to the rank of queen by managing to take it to the opponent's end of the board, or to become promoted from pawn to queen [Old English *cwēn* "woman." Ultimately from an Indo-European word that is also the ancestor of English *gyno-* and *banshee.*]

Queen Anne *n.* a style of furniture popular in the early 18th century, characterized by the use of simple curves and cabriole legs [Early 19thC. Named for Queen ANNE.]

Queen Anne's lace *n.* the wild ancestor of the carrot, native to Europe and Asia but common elsewhere. It bears flat-topped clusters of white flowers and has a stout but inedible root. Latin name: *Daucus carota.* [Late 19thC. Named for Queen ANNE, perhaps from the resemblance of the plant's flowers to delicate embroidery.]

queen bee *n.* **1. FERTILE FEMALE BEE** a large, fully developed female bee that lays eggs continually. She is usually the only fertile female in the colony. **2. IMPORTANT WOMAN** a woman who is treated as the most important member of her group, or who behaves as if she is

Queen Char·lotte Is·lands /-shaárlət-/ group of 150 islands in Canada, off the western coast of British Columbia. Area: 3,705 sq. mi./9,596 sq. km. Population: 3,368 (1986).

queen con·sort (*plural* **queens con·sort**) *n.* a woman married to a reigning king

queen-cup *n.* a stemless plant of western North America that produces a single white flower and a blue berry. Latin name: *Clintonia uniflora.*

queen dow·a·ger *n.* a widow of a king

Queen E·liz·a·beth Is·lands /-i lízzəbèth-/ group of islands in northern Canada, in the Arctic Archipelago, shared between Nunavut and the Northwest Territories. Area: 164,000 sq. mi./425,000 sq. km.

queen·ly /kweénlee/ *adj.* **1. REGAL** having the qualities typical of a queen, especially grace and dignity **2. RELATING TO QUEEN** relating to a queen or suitable for a queen ■ *adv.* **REGALLY** in a way thought fitting for or typical of a queen, especially with grace and dignity —**queen·li·ness** *n.*

Queen Maud Gulf /-máwd/ gulf in the Arctic Ocean, between southeastern Victoria Island and the mainland of Nunavut, Canada

queen moth·er *n.* the mother of a reigning king or queen and the widow of a former king

Queen of the May (*plural* **Queens of the May**) *n.* = **May Queen**

queen of the prai·rie *n.* a plant that bears small pink flowers and grows in grasslands of the central and eastern United States. Latin name: *Filipendula rubra.*

queen ol·ive *n.* a large edible olive with a long flat pit

queen post *n.* either of two vertical posts forming part of the triangular framework that supports a roof. They support the rafters and the horizontal tie beam. Queen posts are used where the central support provided by a king post would be insufficient because of the width of the frame. ◊ **king post** [Modeled on "king post"]

queen re·gent (*plural* **queens re·gent**) *n.* a queen reigning on behalf of another person, especially one too young to take the throne

queen reg·nant (*plural* **queens reg·nant**) *n.* a queen who reigns in her own right, as distinct from the wife of a king

Queens /kweenz/ the largest borough in New York City, on western Long Island. Population: 1,951,598 (1990). Area: 109 sq. mi./282 sq. km.

Queen's Bench *n.* a division of High Court of Justice in England. It is called the King's Bench when the reigning British monarch is a king. ◊ **King's Bench**

Queens·ber·ry rules /kweénz bèrri-/ *npl.* accepted standards of fairness or courteousness in any situation (*informal*)

Queen's Coun·sel *n.* a senior barrister in England. The title is King's Counsel when the reigning British monarch is a king.

Queen's Eng·lish *n.* standard written or spoken British English, regarded as the most correct form of the language. It is called the King's English when the reigning British monarch is a king.

queen·ship /kweén shìp/ *n.* the rank or position of queen

queen·side /kweén sīd/ *n.* the side of a chessboard on which the queen is located at the beginning of a game

queen-size *adj.* **1. LARGE** extra large (*refers to women's clothes*) **2. LARGER THAN STANDARD** larger than the standard size but smaller than king-size (*refers to beds and bedclothes*) [Modeled on "king-size"]

Queens·land /kweénz lànd, -lənd/ state in northeastern Australia. Originally part of New South Wales, it became a separate colony in 1859. Capital: Brisbane. Population: 3,339,000 (1996). Area: 666,876 sq. mi./1,727,200 sq. km. —**Queens·land·er** *n.*

queen sub·stance *n.* a pheromone secreted by a queen bee and consumed by worker bees in the same hive that prevents the worker bees from becoming fully developed and reproducing

queer /kweer/ *adj.* **1. NOT USUAL** not usual or expected (*dated*) **2. ECCENTRIC** eccentric or unconventional (*dated*) **3. SUSPICIOUS** arousing suspicion (*dated*) **4. NAUSEATED** slightly unwell, especially nauseated or faint (*dated*) **5. OFFENSIVE TERM** an offensive term meaning homosexual (*offensive*) ■ *n.* **OFFENSIVE TERM** an offensive term for a homosexual person, especially a man (*offensive*) ■ *vt.* (**queered, queer·ing, queers**) **1. THWART** to spoil or thwart something, especially somebody's plans **2. COMPROMISE SOMEBODY** to put somebody in an awkward situation [Early 16thC. Origin uncertain: probably from Low German *quer* "oblique, crooked." Ultimately from an Indo-European base meaning "to twist" that is also the ancestor of English *thwart* and *contort.*] —**queer·ish** *adj.* —**queer·ly** *adv.* —**queer·ness** *n.*

queer·core /kweér kàwr/ *n.* (*slang*) **1. GAY YOUTH MOVEMENT** a gay youth movement that rejects the stereotype of the gay person as persecuted victim by confidently and assertively proclaiming homosexuality, especially in punk-style music **2. GAY YOUTH MUSIC** a style of music similar to punk rock with lyrics that proclaim homosexuality confidently and assertively [Late 20thC. Coined from QUEER + HARD-CORE.]

Queer Street [From an earlier thieves' cant use of QUEER in the sense "ill"] ◇ **be in Queer Street** *U.K.* to be in financial difficulties (*dated informal*)

quell /kwel/ (**quelled, quell·ing, quells**) *vt.* **1. PUT STOP TO** to bring something to an end, usually by means of force **2. SUPPRESS FEELING** to suppress or allay a feeling [Old English *cwellan* "to kill." Ultimately from an Indo-European word meaning "to stab, kill" that is also the ancestor of English *kill* and *quail*[2].]

quench /kwench/ (**quenched, quench·ing, quench·es**) *vt.* **1. SATISFY THIRST** to satisfy a thirst by drinking something **2. EXTINGUISH FIRE** to put out a fire or light **3. SUBDUE FEELING** to subdue a feeling, especially enthusiasm or desire **4. COOL METAL** to cool hot metal by plunging it into cold water or other liquid [Old English *ācwencan*] —**quench·a·ble** *adj.* —**quench·er** *n.* —**quench·less** *adj.*

que·nelle /kə nél/ *n.* a seasoned meat or fish dumpling poached in water and served with a sauce [Mid-19thC. Via French from German *Knödel* (dumpling).]

quer·ce·tin /kwúrsitin/ *n.* a yellow compound found in the rind and bark of many plants, especially the bark of the oak and Douglas fir, used medicinally to treat abnormally fragile capillaries. Formula: $C_{15}H_{10}O_7$. [Mid-19thC. Formed from Latin *quercetum* "oak-forest," from *quercus* "oak." Ultimately from an Indo-European word that also produced English *fir* and *cork.*]

quer·ci·tron /kwúrsitrən, -tròn, kwur síttrən/ *n.* **1. OAK BARK** the bright orange inner bark of the black oak tree, used in tanning and dyeing **2. YELLOW DYE** yellow dye made from quercitron [Late 18thC. Blend of Latin *quercus* "oak" and CITRON (from the color of its bark).]

que·rist /kweérist/ *n.* somebody who asks questions (*formal*) [Mid-17thC. Formed from an early variant of QUERY.]

quern /kwurn/ *n.* a simple stone mill used for grinding grain by hand [Old English *cweorn.* Ultimately from an Indo-European base meaning "heavy" that is also the ancestor of English *grave*[2], *baro-*, *brute*, and *guru.*]

quer·u·lous /kwérrələss/ *adj.* **1. TENDING TO COMPLAIN** inclined to complain or find fault **2. WHINING** whining or complaining in tone [15thC. Via late Latin *querulosus* from, ultimately, Latin *queri* "to complain" (source of English *quarrel*).] —**quer·u·lous·ly** *adv.* —**quer·u·lous·ness** *n.*

que·ry /kweeree/ *n.* (*plural* **-ries**) **1.** QUESTION a request for information **2.** DOUBT a doubt or criticism **3.** = **question mark** ■ *vt.* (**-ried, -ry·ing, -ries**) **1.** QUESTION SOMETHING to express doubts about, or objections to, something **2.** INQUIRE to ask a question [Mid-17thC. Anglicization of earlier *quere*, from Latin *quaere* "ask," from *quaerere* "to seek, ask" (source also of English *question, inquire*, and *conquer*.)] —**que·ri·er** *n.*

ques. *abbr.* question

quest /kwest/ *n.* **1.** SEARCH a search for something, especially a long or difficult one **2.** ADVENTUROUS EXPEDITION a journey in search of something, especially one made by knights in medieval tales **3.** SOMETHING SOUGHT the object or goal of a quest (*literary*) ■ *v.* (**quest·ed, quest·ing, quests**) **1.** *vti.* SEEK SOMETHING to seek or go in search of something (*literary*) **2.** *vi.* TRACK ANIMALS to follow the track of a bird or animal that is being hunted (*refers to hunting dogs*) [14thC. Via Old French *queste* from, ultimately, Latin *quaesta*, the feminine past participle of *quaerere* "to seek" (see QUERY).] —**quest·er** *n.* —**quest·ing·ly** *adv.*

ques·tion /kwéschən/ *n.* **1.** WRITTEN OR SPOKEN INQUIRY a request for information or for a reply, which usually ends with a question mark if written or on a rising intonation if spoken ○ *Does anyone have any questions?* **2.** DOUBT a doubt or uncertainty about somebody or something **3.** ISSUE a matter that is the subject of discussion, debate, or negotiation **4.** EXAMINATION PROBLEM a problem to be discussed or solved in an examination ■ *v.* (**-tioned, -tion·ing, -tions**) **1.** *vti.* INTERROGATE to ask somebody questions, especially formally or officially, about a particular topic **2.** *vi.* INQUIRE to ask questions **3.** *vt.* DOUBT SOMETHING to raise doubts about something, especially about its truth, genuineness, or usefulness [13thC. Via French from the Latin stem *quaestion-* "inquiry," from *quaest-*, the past participle stem of *quaerere* (see QUERY).] —**ques·tion·er** *n.* ◇ **beg the question 1.** to take for granted the very point that needs to be proved, and so fail to address an issue properly **2.** to give rise to something else that should be answered or explained ◇ **be out of the question** to be impossible or unacceptable ◇ **call something into question** to raise doubts about something ◇ **in question** used to indicate the person or thing under discussion ◇ **pop the question** to propose marriage to somebody (*informal*)

WORD KEY: SYNONYMS

question, quiz, interrogate, grill, give the third degree to

CORE MEANING: asking for information

question the process of asking somebody for information on a particular subject, for example, about something somebody has done or as part of a formal or official investigation; **quiz** persistent questioning in an ordinary situation; **interrogate** a formal or official systematic intensive questioning of a suspect or witness with a view to making him or her reveal information; **grill** an informal word similar in use to "interrogate" but suggesting an even greater degree of intensiveness or pressure; **give somebody the third degree to** an informal phrase for sustained intensive questioning, especially by police or the military in order to elicit a confession or information. It can also be used to suggest that somebody in an ordinary situation is questioning another person in an unnecessarily harsh or persistent manner.

ques·tion·a·ble /kwéschənəb'l/ *adj.* **1.** DUBIOUS open to doubt or disagreement **2.** IMMORAL not respectable or morally proper ○ *questionable motives* —**ques·tion·a·bil·i·ty** /kwèschənə bíllətee/ *n.* —**ques·tion·a·bly** /kwéschənəblee/ *adv.*

ques·tion·ing /kwéschəning/ *n.* INTERROGATION a situation in which somebody is asked a lot of questions, especially formally or officially, or an instance of this ■ *adj.* EXPRESSING QUESTION expressing a question without using words ○ *a questioning glance* —**ques·tion·ing·ly** *adv.*

ques·tion·less /kwéschənləss/ *adj.* **1.** = **unquestionable 2.** = **unquestioning**

ques·tion mark *n.* the punctuation mark (?) placed at the end of a sentence or phrase intended as a direct question ◇ **a question mark over** an area of doubt and uncertainty

ques·tion·naire /kwèschə náir/ *n.* a set of questions used to gather information in a survey, or the printed paper that contains the questions [Late 19thC. From French, formed from *questionner* "to ask," from *question* (see QUESTION).]

ques·tion time *n.* in the British Parliament, a period of time every day during which members of parliament may address questions to government ministers

Quet·ta /kwéttə/ capital city of Baluchistan Province, in west central Pakistan. Population: 285,719 (1981).

Quetzal

quet·zal /ket saál/ (*plural* **-zals** *or* **-za·les** /-saá làyz/) *n.* **1.** CENTRAL AMERICAN BIRD WITH BRIGHT PLUMAGE a Central American bird with brilliant green and red plumage and, in the male, long streaming tail feathers. Latin name: *Pharomachrus mocino.* **2.** UNIT OF GUATEMALAN CURRENCY the main unit of currency in Guatemala. See table at **currency 3.** BILL WORTH A QUETZAL a bill worth one quetzal [Early 19thC. Via American Spanish from, ultimately, Nahuatl *quetzalli* "brilliantly colored tail feather."]

Quet·zal·co·a·tl /kèts'l kō aát'l/ *n.* a Toltec and Aztec god and the legendary ruler of Mexico, represented as a feathered serpent. For the Toltecs, he was a god of soil fertility, while for the Aztecs, he was a sun god and also the god of death and resurrection. [Via Spanish from Nahuatl *Quetzalcōātl*, from *quetzal(li)* "brightly colored tail feather" + *cōātl* "snake"]

queue /kyoo/ *n.* **1.** *U.K.* = **line**[1] *n.* 3 **2.** COMPUT SET OF COMPUTER TASKS a series of messages or jobs waiting to be processed automatically one after the other by a computer system **3.** COMPUT LIST OF DATA ELEMENTS a list of computer data constructed and maintained so that the elements are inserted at one end and deleted from the other in first in, first out fashion **4.** HIST MAN'S PIGTAIL IN FORMER TIMES a short braid of hair worn at the back of the neck by soldiers and sailors in the late 18th and early 19th centuries ■ *v.* (**queued, queu·ing** *or* **queue·ing, queues**) **1.** *vt.* COMPUT ADD TO COMPUTER'S TASKS to add a job or message to the list of tasks being held in storage by a computer, awaiting automatic dispatching **2.** *vi.* FORM WAITING LINE to form a line while waiting for something [Late 16thC. Via French from Latin *cauda* "tail" (source also of English *coda*).] ◇ **jump the queue** *U.K.* to push in or move ahead of others unfairly in a queue

Quezón y Mo·li·na /kàyz on ee mo léenə, ke thòn-/, **Manuel Luis** (1878–1944) Philippine statesman. He worked for Philippine independence, and was the first president of the Commonwealth of the Philippines (1935–44).

quib·ble /kwíbb'l/ *vi.* (**-bled, -bling, -bles**) MAKE TRIVIAL OBJECTIONS to argue over unimportant things and make petty objections ■ *n.* **1.** PETTY OBJECTION an unimportant distinction or petty objection **2.** PUN a pun (*archaic*) [Early 17thC. Origin uncertain: probably formed from obsolete *quib* "pun, equivocation," from Latin *quibus* "to whom, for whom," often used in legal documents and thus associated with dubious legal proceedings and practices.] —**quib·bler** *n.* —**quib·bling·ly** *adv.*

quiche /keesh/ *n.* a savory pie filled with an egg-and-cream mixture and various meat or vegetable ingredients [Mid-20thC. Via French from German dialect *Küche* "small cake," from German *Kuchen* "cake" (see CAKE).]

quiche Lor·raine /-lə ráyn/ *n.* a quiche made with cheese and bacon [Mid-20thC. Named for its place of origin, the French region of *Lorraine*.]

Quich·ua /keéchoo ə/ *n., adj.* = **Quechua**

quick /kwik/ *adj.* **1.** DOING SOMETHING FAST moving or doing something fast **2.** ALERT demonstrating alertness or sharp perception ○ *She has a very quick mind.* **3.** NIMBLE moving swiftly and with skill ○ *quick fingers* **4.** DONE WITHOUT DELAY doing something without delay ○ *They promised a quick delivery.* **5.** EASILY ANGERED used to describe a temper that is easily aroused **6.** BRIEF taking or lasting only a short time ○ *We stopped to have a quick chat.* **7.** HASTY tending to be hasty ○ *Don't be too quick to blame others.* **8.** ALIVE living (*archaic*) ■ *n.* **1.** FLESH UNDER NAIL the sensitive flesh under a fingernail or toenail **2.** SENSITIVE AREA somebody's deepest feelings or most private emotions ○ *criticisms that cut him to the quick* **3.** THE LIVING the living (*archaic*) ○ *the quick and the dead* ■ *adv.* FAST in a speedy manner (*informal*) ○ *Come quick!* [Old English *cwic(u)* "alive, lively." Ultimately from an Indo-European base meaning "to live" that is also the ancestor of English *vital, bio-, zoo-*, and *whiskey*.] —**quick·ly** *adv.* —**quick·ness** *n.* ◇ **quick and dirty** produced to meet an immediate or pressing need, rather than in accordance with high standards of research or design

WORD KEY: SYNONYMS

See Synonyms at ***intelligent.***

quick as·sets *npl.* cash along with other assets that can readily be converted into cash

quick bread *n.* bread leavened with baking powder or soda, as opposed to yeast, and ready to bake as soon as it is mixed

quick·en /kwíkən/ (**-ened, -en·ing, -ens**) *v.* **1.** *vti.* BECOME OR MAKE SOMETHING FASTER to become faster or make something faster **2.** *vti.* STIMULATE OR BE STIMULATED to stimulate something, e.g., interest or enthusiasm, or to be stimulated **3.** *vi.* BEGIN TO COME TO LIFE to begin a period of development **4.** *vi.* MOVE IN WOMB to begin to move and be felt moving in the womb (*used to refer to a fetus*)

quick-fire /kwík fīr/ *adj. U.K.* = **rapid-fire**

quick fix *n.* a speedily or hastily contrived solution to a problem, often one that fails to resolve long-term issues (*informal*)

quick-freeze *vt.* to freeze food rapidly in an effort to keep its full flavor and nutritional value

quick·ie /kwíkee/ *n.* something that is done hurriedly, especially a hurried act of sex or a speedily consumed alcoholic drink (*informal*)

quick kick *n.* in football, a punt made on the first, second, or third down, intended to take the opposing team by surprise

quick·lime /kwík līm/ *n.* calcium oxide [14thC. Translation of Latin *calx viva*, literally "living lime."]

quick·sand /kwík sànd/ *n.* **1.** DANGEROUS SAND a deep mass of loose wet sand that sucks down any heavy object falling onto its surface **2.** DANGEROUS SITUATION a hidden trap from which escape is difficult or impossible [15thC. From QUICK.]

quick·sil·ver /kwík sìlvər/ *n.* MERCURY mercury (*archaic*) ■ *adj.* CHANGING UNPREDICTABLY tending to change rapidly and unpredictably [Pre-12thC. Translation of Latin *argentum vivum*, literally "living silver," from the way it moves when in its fluid state at room temperature.]

quick·step /kwík stèp/ *n.* **1.** FAST BALLROOM DANCE a ballroom dance with fast steps **2.** MUSIC DANCE MUSIC a piece of dance music in quadruple time for dancing the quickstep **3.** MIL MARCHING STEP the marching step used in the fastest marching pace (**quick time**)

quick stud·y *n.* somebody who is able to learn new things or pick up new skills quickly and easily ○ *She's a quick study.*

quick-tem·pered *adj.* having a short temper

quick time *n.* a fast military marching pace, approximately 120 paces per minute. It is the fastest of all marching paces.

quick-wit·ted *adj.* able to think quickly and inventively —**quick-wit·ted·ly** *adv.* —**quick-wit·ted·ness** *n.*

quid[1] /kwid/ (*plural* **quid**) *n. U.K.* a pound sterling (*informal*) [Late 17thC. Origin uncertain: perhaps from Latin *quid* "what, something," possibly inspired by the phrase *quid pro quo*.]

quid[2] /kwid/ *n.* a piece of chewing tobacco [Early 18thC. Alteration of CUD.]

quid·ditch /kwíddich/ *n.* fictional game [Late 20thC. Coined by J. K. Rowling in her novel, *Harry Potter and the Sorcerer's Stone* (1998).]

quid·di·ty /kwíddətee/ (*plural* **-ties**) *n.* **1.** ESSENCE the real nature or essential character of something **2.** TRIFLING DISTINCTION an unimportant or trifling distinction [Mid-16thC. From medieval Latin *quidditas*, from Latin *quid* "what." Ultimately from an Indo-European base that is also the ancestor of English *what* and *who*.]

quid·nunc /kwíd nùngk/ *n.* somebody who is nosy or gossipy (*literary*) [Early 18thC. From Latin, literally "what now."]

quid pro quo /kwìd prō kwṓ/ (*plural* **quid pro quos**) *n.* **1.** SOMETHING DONE IN EXCHANGE something given or done in exchange for something else **2.** RETURNING OF FAVOR the giving of something in return for something else, often in a spirit of cooperation [Mid-16thC. From Latin, literally "something for something."]

qui·es·cent /kwee éss'nt/ *adj.* inactive or at rest [Early 17thC. From Latin *quiescere* "to come to rest" (see QUIET).] —**qui·es·cence** *n.* —**qui·es·cent·ly** *adv.*

qui·et /kwī́ ət/ *adj.* **1.** MAKING LITTLE NOISE making little or no noise **2.** PEACEFUL free from noise or commotion ○ *in a quiet corner of the room* **3.** DONE IN PRIVATE carried out in private, with voices not raised, so as not to be overheard ○ *I'd like a quiet word with you.* **4.** FREE FROM TROUBLE free from trouble or disturbance ○ *a quiet life* **5.** RELAXING relaxing, peaceful, and free from excitement ○ *a quiet evening at home* **6.** NOT SHOWY not grand, showy, or pretentious ○ *a quiet wedding* **7.** DISPLAYING CALMNESS displaying calmness and self-control **8.** NOT EXPRESSED IN WORDS not expressed in words ○ *a sense of quiet optimism* **9.** NOT FLOURISHING not busy, active, or flourishing ○ *Business is a little too quiet.* **10.** CALM OR MOTIONLESS marked by very little motion ○ *a quiet sea* ■ *n.* ABSENCE OF NOISE the absence of noise or disturbance ○ *the quiet of the forest* ■ *v.* (**-et·ed, -et·ing, -ets**) **1.** *vti.* MAKE OR BECOME QUIET to become calm and quiet, or make somebody calm and quiet ○ *He sang lullabies to quiet the baby.* **2.** *vt.* ALLAY to calm somebody's feelings, such as doubts or fears ○ *We're looking for a way to quiet her doubts.* **3.** *vt.* LAW SECURE LEGAL CLAIM to make a legal claim secure by resolving all possible challenges to it [14thC. Via Old French from Latin *quietus*, the past participle of *quiescere* "to come to rest," from *quies* "rest, quiet" (source also of English *coy*).] —**qui·et·ly** *adv.* —**qui·et·ness** *n.* ◇ **on the quiet** secretly

WORD KEY: SYNONYMS

See Synonyms at ***silent***.

qui·et·ism /kwī́ ə tìzzəm/ *n.* **1.** CHRISTIAN MYSTICISM a system of Christian mysticism that requires a withdrawal from the world, a renunciation of the individual will, and passive contemplation of God and divine things **2.** CALMNESS a state of calmness, especially one arising from noninvolvement in something (*literary*) [Late 17thC. From Italian *quietismo*, from *quieto*, from Latin *quietus* (see QUIET).] —**qui·et·ist** *adj., n.* —**qui·et·is·tic** /kwī̀ ə tístik/ *adj.*

qui·e·tude /kwī́ ə tood/ *n.* the state of being quiet, peaceful, or tranquil (*literary*) [Late 16thC. Directly or via French *quiétude* from medieval Latin *quietudo*, from Latin *quietus* (see QUIET).]

qui·e·tus /kwī eétəss/ *n.* (*literary*) **1.** CHECK something that brings an activity to an end **2.** RELEASE a release from a debt or duty **3.** DEATH death, especially when viewed as a welcome release from life [Mid-16thC. From medieval Latin *quietus (est)* "(it is) at rest," a formula acknowledging receipt or discharge of an obligation.]

quill /kwil/ *n.* **1.** ZOOL LARGE FEATHER a large, stiff feather from a bird's wing or tail, or the hollow shaft of one of these feathers **2.** PEN MADE FROM FEATHER SHAFT an old-fashioned pen made from the shaft of a feather. The split and sharpened end was dipped in ink. **3.** ZOOL SPINE a sharp hollow spine on the body of a porcupine or hedgehog **4.** TEXTILES SPINDLE OR BOBBIN a spindle or bobbin onto which thread or yarn is wound **5.** HOLLOW SHAFT in a mechanical device, a hollow shaft in which a second independently rotating shaft is enclosed ■ *vt.* (**quilled, quill·ing, quills**) **1.** TEXTILES WIND THREAD to wind thread or yarn onto a spindle or bobbin **2.** SEW MAKE FOLDS IN to make small rounded ridges or folds in fabric, e.g., to make a ruff [15thC. Origin uncertain.]

quill·back /kwíl bàk/ (*plural* **-backs** *or* **-back**), **quill·back carp·suck·er** /kwìl bàk kaárp sukər/ *n.* a North American freshwater fish of the sucker family that has a long ray projecting from its dorsal fin. Latin name: *Carpiodes cyprinus.*

quill pen *n.* = **quill** *n.* 2

quill·work /kwíl wùrk/ *n.* handicrafts decorated with porcupine quills

quill·wort /kwíl wùrt, -wawrt/ *n.* a nonflowering water plant that produces a rosette of tubular leaves, at the bases of which are spore-forming organs. Genus: *Isoetes.*

quilt /kwilt/ *n.* **1.** BEDCOVER a bedcover made of two layers of fabric stitched together, with interior padding of cotton or feathers held in place by decorative intersecting seams **2.** SOMETHING SIMILAR TO QUILT something that resembles a quilt or is quilted ■ *vt.* (**quilt·ed, quilt·ing, quilts**) MAKE FABRIC ARTICLE to make a fabric article, especially a bedcover, by sewing two layers of fabric together with a filling, especially using decorative stitching [13thC. Via Anglo-Norman from Latin *culcita* "cushion, mattress" (source of English *counterpane* and *quoit*), of unknown origin.] —**quilt·er** *n.*

quilt·ing /kwílting/ *n.* **1.** MAKING QUILTS the sewing of quilted bedcovers or other quilted work **2.** QUILTED MATERIAL material that has been quilted or that is used to make quilts

Quim·per /kaN pér/ city and administrative center of Finistère Department, in Brittany Region, western France. Population: 62,540 (1990).

quin /kwin/ *n. U.K.* = **quint** *n.* 1 (*informal*) [Mid-20thC. Shortening.]

quin- *prefix.* = **quino-** (*used before vowels*)

quin·a·crine hy·dro·chlo·ride /kwìnnə kreen-/ *n.* a drug used to treat malaria [*Quinacrine* is a blend of QUININE and ACRIDINE]

quin·a·liz·a·rin /kwìnnə lízzərin/ *n.* a red crystalline organic compound with a green metallic luster, used especially to dye cotton. Formula: $C_{14}H_8O_6$. [Coined from QUINO- + ALIZARIN]

quin·ar·y /kwī́nəree/ *adj.* OCCURRING IN FIVES consisting of five parts, or occurring in sets of five (*formal*) ■ *n.* (*plural* **-ies**) SET OF FIVE OR FIFTH MEMBER a set of five, or the fifth member of a set (*formal*) [Early 17thC. From Latin *quinarius*, from *quini* "five each," from *quinque* "five" (see QUINQUE-).]

qui·nate /kwī́ nàyt/ *adj.* BOT used to describe leaves that occur in clusters of five [Early 19thC. From modern Latin *quinatus*, from Latin *quini* (see QUINARY).]

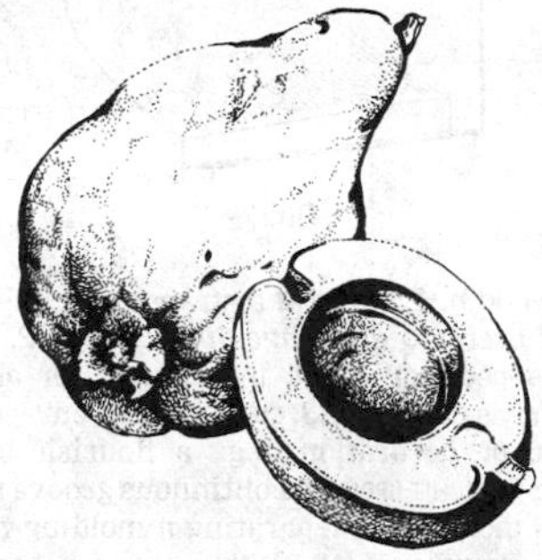

Quince

quince /kwins/ *n.* **1.** ASIAN FRUIT TREE a small tree native to western Asia but widely cultivated that bears white flowers and hard pear-shaped fruit. Latin name: *Cydonia oblonga.* **2.** FRUIT OF QUINCE TREE the fruit of the quince tree, edible only when cooked [14thC. Via Old French *cooin* from Latin *(malum) cotoneum*, from Greek *(mēlon) kudōnion*, literally "apple of Cydonia" (Canea), by folk etymology from a Lydian name for the fruit.]

quin·cen·ten·a·ry /kwìn sen ténnəree/ (*plural* **-ries**), **quin·cen·ten·ni·al** /-ténnee əl/ *n.* a 500th anniversary [Late 19thC. "quin" from Latin *quinque* (see QUINQUE-).] —**quin·cen·ta·ry** *adj.*

quin·cunx /kwín kùngks/ *n.* an arrangement of five objects in a square, with four at the corners and one in the center [Mid-17thC. From Latin, literally "five-twelfths" (from the use of this pattern on a Roman coin worth five-twelfths of an as), from *quinque* "five" + *uncia* "a twelfth" (see OUNCE[1]).] —**quin·cun·cial** /kwin kúngshəl/ *adj.*

Quin·cy /kwínzee, -see/ **1.** city and port in western Illinois, on the eastern bank of the Mississippi River on the Illinois-Missouri border. Population: 40,545 (1996). **2.** city in eastern Massachusetts, on Massachusetts Bay. It is a southeastern suburb of Boston and the birthplace of U.S. presidents John Adams and John Quincy Adams. Population: 85,532 (1996).

quin·de·cen·ni·al /kwìndə sénnee əl/ *adj.* **1.** HAPPENING EVERY 15 YEARS happening once every 15 years **2.** LASTING 15 YEARS lasting for 15 years ■ *n.* 15TH ANNIVERSARY a 15th anniversary [20thC. Formed from Latin *quindecim* "fifteen," on the model of CENTENNIAL.]

Quine /kwīn/, **W. V.** (*b.* 1908) U.S. philosopher. He contributed to the theory of pragmatism and mathematical set theory. Full name **Willard Van Orman Quine**

qui·nel·la /kwi néllə, kee néllə/, **qui·nie·la** /keen yéllə/ *n.* a bet in which the bettor picks the first two finishers in a race or other sporting event without specifying their order of finish [Early 20thC. From American Spanish *quiniela*, from Spanish *quina* "keno," from French *quine* (see KENO).]

qui·nic ac·id /kwìnnik-, kwīnik-/ *n.* a white crystalline organic compound found in cinchona bark, coffee beans, and the leaves of many plants. It is used in medicine. Formula: $C_6H_7(OH)_4COOH$. [From Spanish *quina* "cinchona bark" (see QUINO-)]

quin·i·dine /kwínni deen/ *n.* a colorless crystalline organic compound related to quinine that is used in medicine to treat malaria and heart disorders. It is found in cinchona bark. Formula: $C_{20}H_{24}N_2O_2$. [Mid-19thC. Coined from QUINO- + -IDINE.]

qui·nie·la ex·act·a *n.* = **exacta**

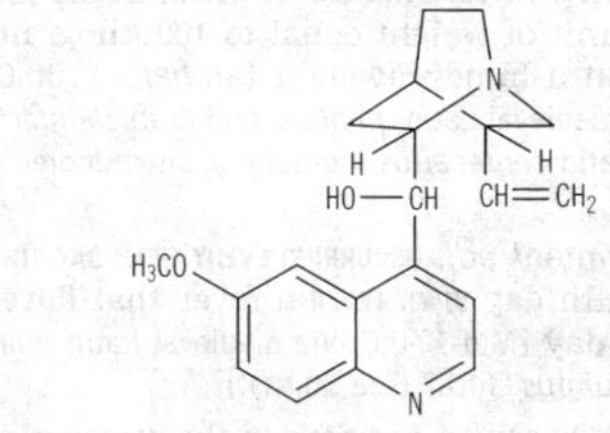

Quinine

qui·nine /kwī́ nīn/ *n.* a bitter-tasting drug made from cinchona bark, used to treat forms of malaria resistant to chloroquine [Early 19thC. Formed from Spanish *quina* "cinchona bark" (see QUINO-).]

qui·nine wa·ter *n.* a carbonated drink flavored with quinine, usually used as a mixer with liquor

Quinn /kwin/, **Anthony** (*b.* 1916) Mexican-born U.S. movie actor. His movies include *Viva Zapata!* (1952), *Lust for Life* (1956), and *Zorba the Greek* (1964).

quin·nat salm·on /kwínnat-/ *n.* = **Chinook salmon** [From Chinook *ikwanat*]

quino- *prefix.* **1.** cinchona, cinchona bark ○ *quinone* **2.** quinone ○ *quinoid* [Via Spanish *quina* "cinchona bark" from Quechua *kina*]

qui·no·a /kee nṓ ə, keen waá/ *n.* a plant of the goosefoot family that is native to the Andes and cultivated for its seeds, which are ground and eaten. Latin name: *Chenopodium quinoa.* [Early 17thC. Via Spanish from Quechua *kinoa.*]

quin·o·line /kwínnə leen, kwínnəlin/ *n.* an oily colorless substance obtained from coal tar and used in making antiseptics and dyes. Formula: C_9H_7N. [Mid-19thC. Formed from QUINOL.]

qui·none /kwi nṓn, kwí nōn/ *n.* **1.** = **benzoquinone 2.** PLANT PIGMENT OR ANIMAL VITAMIN an organic compound found as a yellow, orange, or red pigment in plants, fungi, and bacteria and also as vitamins in animals. Vitamin A is a quinone.

quin·o·noid /kwínnə nòyd/ *n.* SOMETHING RESEMBLING QUINONE a substance that contains quinone or resembles it in chemical structure or physical properties ■ *adj.* RESEMBLING QUINONE resembling quinone in chemical structure or physical properties [Late 19thC. Formed from QUINONE.]

quin·qua·ge·nar·i·an /kwìngkwəjə náiree ən/ *adj.* 50 YEARS OLD 50 years old, or between the ages of 50 and 59 (*formal*) ■ *n.* SOMEBODY 50 YEARS OLD somebody who is 50 years old or between the ages of 50 and 59 (*formal*) [Early 19thC. Via Latin *quinquagenarius*, from, ultimately, *quinquaginta* "fifty."]

Quin·qua·ges·i·ma /kwìngkwə jéssimə/ *n.* in the Christian liturgical calendar, the Sunday before Lent, seven weeks or the fiftieth day before Easter [14thC. From medieval Latin, literally "fiftieth (day)," from Latin *quinquagesimus, quinquaginta* "fifty."]

quinque- *prefix.* five ○ *quinquepartite* [From Latin *quinque* "five." Ultimately from the Indo-European word for "five," which is also the ancestor of English *five, pentad, finger*, and *fist*.]

quin·quen·ni·um /kwing kwénnee əm/ (*plural* **-ums** *or* **-a** /-ə/) *n.* a period of five years [Early 17thC. From Latin, from *quinque* "five" + *annus* "year."] — **quin·quen·ni·al** *adj.* —**quin·quen·ni·al·ly** *adv.*

quin·que·va·lent /kwìngkwə váylənt/ *adj.* = **pentavalent**

quin·sy /kwínzee/ *n.* a severe inflammation of the throat near a tonsil that sometimes leads to the formation of an abcess that may require surgery [14thC. Via Old French *quinencie* and medieval Latin *quinancia* from Greek *kunagkhē*, literally "dog-strangling," from *kuōn* "dog" + *ankhein* "to squeeze."]

quint /kwint/ *n.* **1.** QUINTUPLET a quintuplet (*informal*) **2.** SET OF FIVE CARDS in the card game piquet, a sequence of five cards of the same suit [Late 17thC. Via French, literally "fifth," from Latin *quintus*. Ultimately from an Indo-European word that is also the ancestor of English *fifth*.]

quin·tain /kwíntən/ *n.* a medieval knight's target for jousting practice [15thC. Via Old French from Latin *quintana (via)*, "fifth (street)" (in a Roman camp), possibly so called because this street was used for military exercises.]

quin·tal /kwínt'l/ *n.* **1.** METRIC UNIT OF WEIGHT in the metric system, a unit of weight equal to 100 kilograms **2.** HUNDREDWEIGHT a hundredweight (*archaic*) [15thC. Via Old French, medieval Latin *quintale*, and Arabic *kinṭār* from, ultimately, Latin *centenarius* "containing one hundred" (see CENTENARY).]

quin·tan /kwíntən/ *adj.* OCCURRING EVERY FIFTH DAY flaring up every fifth day ■ *n.* FEVER a fever that flares up every fifth day [Mid-17thC. Via medieval Latin *quintana* from Latin *quintus* "fifth" (see QUINT).]

quinte /kwīnt, kaaNt/ *n.* the fifth in the series of eight standard positions used to teach fencing [Early 18thC. From French, feminine of *quint* (see QUINT).]

quin·tes·sence /kwin téss'ns/ *n.* **1.** EMBODIMENT the purest or most perfect example of something **2.** CHEM EXTRACT the purest extract or essence of a substance. It contains the substance's properties in their most concentrated form. **3.** PHILOS FIFTH ELEMENT in ancient and medieval philosophy, the fifth element after earth, air, fire, and water. Heavenly bodies were said to be made of it. [15thC. Via French from medieval Latin *quinta essentia*, literally "fifth essence," a translation of Greek *pemptē ousiā*.] —**quin·tes·sen·tial** /kwintə sénshəl/ *adj.* —**quin·tes·sen·tial·ly** /-shəlee/ *adv.*

quin·tet /kwin tét/, **quin·tette** *n.* **1.** MUSICIANS a group of five singers or musicians **2.** MUSIC a piece of music written for five voices or instruments **3.** GROUP OF FIVE a group or set of five people or things [Late 18thC. Via French *quintette* from Italian *quintetto*, from *quinto* "fifth," from Latin *quintus* (see QUINT).]

quin·tic /kwíntik/ *adj.* relating to the fifth power in a mathematical expression or equation [Mid-19thC. Formed from Latin *quintus* (see QUINT).]

quin·tile /kwín tìl, kwínt'l/ *n.* **1.** STATISTICAL DIVISION any one of the five equal populations into which a statistical sample can be divided **2.** STATISTICAL VALUE in statistics, any one of the values that divide a frequency distribution into five parts, each containing a fifth of the sample population **3.** DISTANCE BETWEEN PLANETS the astrological aspect of planets that are distant from each other by 72 degrees, or one fifth of the zodiac [Early 17thC. From Latin *quintilis*, from *quintus* "fifth" (see QUINT).]

quin·til·lion /kwin tíllyən/ *n.* the number equal to 10^{18}, written as 1 followed by18 zeros —**quin·til·lion** *adj., pron.* —**quin·til·lionth** *adj., n., pron.*

quin·tu·ple /kwin to͞op'l, -túpp'l/ *adj.* **1.** BEING FIVE TIMES AS MUCH being five times as much or as many **2.** CONSISTING OF FIVE PARTS made up of five parts **3.** MUSIC HAVING FIVE BEATS TO MEASURE having five musical beats to the measure ■ *vti.* (**-pled, -pling, -ples**) MULTIPLY BY FIVE to multiply something by five or to be multiplied by five [Late 16thC. Via French from medieval Latin *quintuplus*, literally "fivefold," from *quintus* "fifth" (see QUINT).]

quin·tu·plet /kwin túpplət, -to͞op-/ *n.* **1.** ONE OF FIVE OFFSPRING one of five offspring born to one mother from a single pregnancy **2.** GROUP OF FIVE a group of five things, especially five of the same kind **3.** MUSIC GROUP OF FIVE MUSICAL NOTES a group of five musical notes to be played in the time usually occupied by three or four notes [Late 19thC. Formed from QUINTUPLE.]

quin·tu·pli·cate *adj.* /kwin to͞oplikət, -túppli-/ MULTIPLIED BY FIVE multiplied by five ■ *n.* /kwin to͞oplikət, -túppli-/ **1.** ONE OF FIVE one of a set of five identical things **2.** GROUP OF FIVE a group of five usually identical things ■ *vt.* /kwin to͞opli kàyt, -túppli-/ (**-cat·ed, -cat·ing, -cates**) MAKE FIVE COPIES to make five copies of something [Mid-17thC. Formed from Latin *quintus* "fifth" (see QUINT) on the model of "duplicate."] —**quin·tu·pli·ca·tion** /kwin tùppli káysh'n, kwin to͞opli-/ *n.*

quip /kwip/ *n.* **1.** WITTICISM a witty remark, especially one made on the spur of the moment **2.** PETTY DISTINCTION a small and unimportant distinction (*archaic*) **3.** SOMETHING STRANGE something odd or strange (*archaic*) ■ *vti.* (**quipped, quip·ping, quips**) SAY SOMETHING WITTILY to make a witty remark [Mid-16thC. Origin uncertain: perhaps from Latin *quippe* "indeed, really" (used sarcastically), from *quid* "something, what."]

quip·ster /kwípstər/ *n.* somebody who makes witty remarks

qui·pu /kée po͞o/ (*plural* **-pus**) *n.* a device consisting of a set of colored and knotted cords used by the Incas for conveying messages and for record-keeping [Early 18thC. Via Spanish from Quechua *kipu*, literally "knot."]

quire /kwīr/ *n.* **1.** PAPER MEASURE a set of 24 or 25 sheets of paper of the same size and quality, equaling one twentieth of a ream **2.** PAPER FOLDED FOR BINDING a bundle of sheets of paper folded together for binding into a book, especially a four-sheet bundle, folded once to make eight leaves or sixteen pages [15thC. Via Old French *qua(i)er* "copybook," literally "set of four (sheets)," from Latin *quaterni* (see QUATERNARY).]

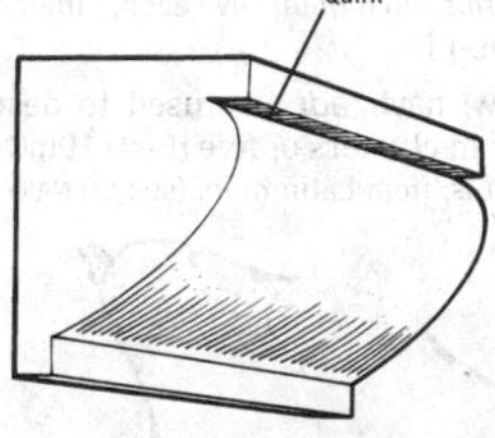

Quirk

quirk /kwurk/ *n.* **1.** ODD EVENT a strange and unexpected turn of events ○ *a strange quirk of fate* **2.** ODD MANNERISM a peculiar habit, mannerism, or aspect of somebody's character **3.** CURVED SHAPE a curved shape, pattern, or decoration, e.g., a flourish in handwriting **4.** ARCHIT GROOVE a continuous groove running along a molding or separating a molding from adjoining members [Mid-16thC. Origin unknown.] — **quirk·i·ly** *adv.* —**quirk·i·ness** *n.* —**quirk·y** *adj.*

quirt /kwúrt/ (**quirt·ed, quirt·ing, quirts**) *n.* a riding whip with a short handle and a braided leather lash [Mid-19thC. From Mexican Spanish *cuarta* "whip."]

quis·ling /kwízzling/ *n.* a traitor, especially somebody who collaborates with an occupying force (*dated*) [Mid-20thC. Named for Vidkun *Quisling*.] — **quis·ling·ism** *n.*

WORD KEY: ORIGIN

Vidkun ***Quisling*** was a Norwegian politician who from 1933 led the National Union Party, the Norwegian fascist party. (***Quisling*** was not his real name – he was originally Abraham Lauritz Jonsson.) When the Germans invaded Norway in 1940 he gave them active support, urging his fellow Norwegians not to resist them, and in 1942 he was installed by Hitler as a puppet premier. In 1945 he was shot for treason.

quit /kwit/ *v.* (**quit** *or* **quit·ted, quit·ting, quits**) **1.** *vti.* RESIGN to give up, leave, or resign from a position or organization **2.** *vti.* STOP DOING SOMETHING to stop doing something, especially something bad or irritating ○ *Quit complaining.* **3.** *vt.* LEAVE to depart from a place (*archaic*) **4.** *vti.* COMPUT EXIT FROM PROGRAM to exit from a computer program using the required exit procedure, so that the data and program configuration are saved **5.** *vti.* LAW MOVE OUT to move out of rented property ○ *He gave his tenants notice to quit.* **6.** *vt.* PAY OFF to settle a debt (*archaic*) **7.** *vt.* = **acquit 8.** *vt.* UNBURDEN to free somebody from something burdensome (*archaic*) ■ *adj.* FREE OF SOMETHING no longer troubled with a problem or difficult situation (*formal*) [13thC. Via Old French *quiter* "to release, set free" from, ultimately, Latin *quietus* (see QUIET).]

quitch grass /kwich-/, **quitch** *n.* = **couch grass** [Old English *cwice*]

quit·claim /kwít klàym/ *n.* RENUNCIATION OF CLAIM a formal statement renouncing a legal claim previously made ■ *vt.* (**-claimed, -claim·ing, -claims**) **1.** RENOUNCE CLAIM to formally withdraw a legal claim previously made **2.** FREE SOMEBODY OF LIABILITY to formally declare somebody to be no longer legally liable for something [13thC. From Anglo-Norman *quiteclamer* "to proclaim (someone) free," from *quite* "free" + *clamer* "to proclaim."]

quite /kwīt/ *adv.* **1.** ENTIRELY in the highest degree, or to the fullest extent ○ *I was quite sure I'd met him before.* **2.** RATHER to a considerable or great degree ○ *quite small* **3.** NEARLY used with a negative to indicate that something is almost in a particular state or condition ○ *The dress is not quite finished.* **4.** EMPHASIZING EXTENT used with expressions of quantity to emphasize the great extent of something ○ *They spent quite some time considering the problem.* **5.** EMPHASIZING EXCEPTIONAL QUALITY used to emphasize the exceptional or impressive nature of somebody or something ○ *That was quite a celebration we had yesterday.* **6.** *U.K.* EXPRESSING AGREEMENT used on its own or with "so" to express agreement or understanding ○ *"I didn't want to mention it until I was sure." "Quite."* [14thC. Originally a variant of QUIT "unburdened, free," the modern meaning evolved via the sense "clearly, thoroughly."] ◇ **be quite something** to be remarkably good, fine, attractive, or otherwise admirable or impressive (*informal*)

Qui·to /kéetō/ capital city of Ecuador, situated in the north of the country. Population: 1,100,847 (1990).

quit·rent /kwít rènt/ *n.* in the feudal system, a rent paid by a tenant to a feudal lord in exchange for being released from certain feudal obligations [15thC. From QUIT "unburdened."]

quits /kwits/ *adj.* on even terms, especially following the repayment of a debt (*informal*) [Mid-17thC. Origin uncertain: probably formed from QUIT "unburdened," influenced by medieval Latin *quittus* "freed."] ◇ **call it quits 1.** to agree or decide to stop doing work or an activity (*informal*) **2.** to agree that an argument or dispute is over and that both parties are equal (*informal*)

quit·tance /kwítt'ns/ *n.* **1.** EXEMPTION release from a debt or obligation **2.** EXEMPTING DOCUMENT a document or statement that releases somebody from a debt or obligation [13thC. Via Old French from *quiter* (see QUIT).]

quit·ter /kwíttər/ *n.* somebody who gives up easily (*informal*)

quit·tor /kwíttər/ *n.* an infectious disease that affects the feet of horses and donkeys, causing inflammation [13thC. Origin uncertain: possibly via Old French *quiture* "boiling" from, ultimately, Latin *coquere* "to cook."]

quiv·er[1] /kwívvər/ *vi.* (**-ered, -er·ing, -ers**) TREMBLE to shake rapidly with small movements ■ *n.* TREMBLING MOVEMENT a repeated light and fast shaking movement [15thC. Origin uncertain: probably from assumed Old English *cwifer* "active, nimble," thought to suggest rapid movement, in which case related to English *quick*.] — **quiv·er·er** *n.* —**quiv·er·y** *adj.*

quiv·er[2] /kwívvər/ *n.* **1.** ARROW CASE a long narrow case for holding arrows **2.** ARROWS the arrows contained in a quiver [14thC. Via Anglo-Norman *quiveir* from, ultimately, medieval Latin *cucurum*, possibly of Hunnish origin.]

qui vive /kee véev/ ["Qui vive" from French, literally "long live who?", a phrase used by sentries to challenge someone approaching their post] ◇ **on the qui vive** alert and vigilant (*literary*)

quix·ot·ic /kwik sóttik/ *adj.* **1.** ROMANTIC tending to take a romanticized view of life **2.** IMPRACTICAL motivated by an idealism that overlooks practical considerations **3.** IMPULSIVE tending to act on whims or impulses [Late 18thC. Formed from the name Don Quixote, the hero of the novel of the same name, written by Miguel de Cervantes.] —**quix·ot·i·cal·ly** *adv.* —**quix·o·tism** /kwíksə tìzzəm/ *n.*

quiz /kwiz/ *n.* (*plural* **quiz·zes**) **1.** EDUC STUDENTS' TEST a short test given by a teacher to a class **2.** TEST OF KNOWLEDGE a test of knowledge in the form of a short or rapid series of questions **3.** TRICK a hoax, joke, or other trick (*archaic*) ■ *vt.* (**quizzed, quiz·zing, quiz·zes**) **1.** EDUC TEST STUDENT OR CLASS to give a short test to a class of pupils or students **2.** INTERROGATE SOMEBODY to subject somebody to a round of sustained close questioning ○ *She was again called in and quizzed about the disappearance of the money.* **3.** PEER AT SOMEBODY to look quizzically at somebody (*archaic*) [Late 18thC. Origin unknown: originally in the sense "odd person," the main modern meaning evolved via "to ridicule."] —**quiz·zer** *n.*

WORD KEY: SYNONYMS

See Synonyms at ***question***.

quiz·mas·ter /kwíz màstər/ *n.* the emcee of a quiz show, who puts the questions to the contestants

quiz show *n.* a television or radio program in the form of a game in which contestants compete against each other for prizes by answering questions that test their general or specialist knowledge

quiz·zi·cal /kwízzik'l/ *adj.* **1.** QUESTIONING expressing a question or expressing puzzlement or doubt ○ *a quizzical glance* **2.** KNOWING communicating, in an amused or mocking way, the possession of secret knowledge about a speaker or about what is being said, e.g., that it is not true —**quiz·zi·cal·i·ty** /kwìzzi kállətee/ *n.* —**quiz·zi·cal·ly** /kwízzikəlee/ *adv.*

quod e·rat de·mon·stran·dum /kwàwd érraat dày mawn straán dóom/ *adv.* used in a formal conclusion to indicate that a particular fact is proof of the theory that has just been been advanced. Full form of **Q.E.D.** [From Latin, literally "which was to be shown"]

quod·li·bet /kwóddli bèt/ *n.* **1.** PHILOSOPHY THEOLOGICAL DISCUSSION POINT a theological question put forth as an exercise for discussion **2.** MUSIC MEDLEY OF TUNES a musical performance composed largely of familiar tunes [14thC. Via medieval Latin *quodlibetum* from Latin *quodlibet*, literally "whatever pleases."]

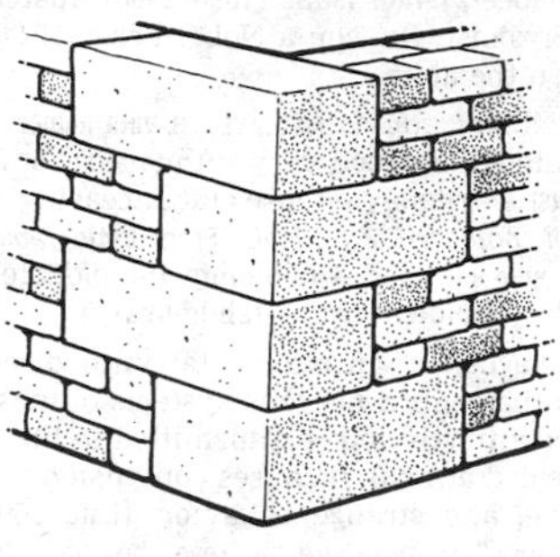

Quoin

quoin /kwoyn, koyn/, **coign** /koyn/ *n.* **1.** OUTER CORNER the outer corner of a wall **2.** BLOCK FORMING CORNER a stone block used to form a quoin, especially when it is different, e.g., in size or material, from the other blocks or bricks in the wall **3.** = **keystone** *n.* 1 ■ *vt.* (**quoined, quoin·ing, quoins; coigns**) BUILD CORNER WITH DISTINCTIVE BLOCKS to build an outer corner of a wall using blocks that are different, e.g., in size or texture, from the other blocks or bricks used to build the wall [Mid-16thC. Variant of COIN.]

quoit /kwoyt, koyt/ *n.* a ring used in the game of quoits [14thC. Origin uncertain: probably via Old French *coite* "flat stone, quoit" from Latin *culcita* "cushion" (source of English *quilt*).]

Quoit

quoits /kwoyts, koyts/ *n.* a game in which players attempt to throw rings over or near a small post (*takes a singular verb*) [14thC. Plural of *quoit*, originally "flat disc," of uncertain origin: perhaps from Old French.]

quok·ka /kwókə/ *n.* a small short-tailed wallaby that lives in large colonies. It is now found mainly on islands off the coast of Western Australia. Latin name: *Setonix brachyurus.* [Mid-19thC. From Australian Aboriginal Nyungar *kwaka.*]

quon·dam /kwóndəm, -dàm/ *adj.* of an earlier time (*archaic or literary*) ○ *"... now torn and rent by their quondam allies"* (Jack London, *The Iron Heel*; 1907) [Mid-16thC. From Latin, from *quom* "when."]

Quon·set /kwónsət/ *tdmk.* a trademark for a prefabricated structure that has a semicircular roof curving downward to form walls, often used to house military personnel

quo·rum /kwáwrəm/ *n.* a fixed minimum percentage or number of members of a legislative assembly, a committee, or other organization who must be present before the members can conduct valid business [15thC. From Latin, literally "of whom," from the words used in requests for people to serve on committees.]

quot. *abbr.* quotation

quo·ta /kwṓtə/ *n.* **1.** PROPORTIONAL SHARE a proportional share of something that somebody should contribute or receive **2.** MAXIMUM PERMITTED NUMBER OR AMOUNT a maximum number or quantity that is permitted or needed [Early 17thC. Via medieval Latin *quota (pars)*, literally "how large (a part)?", the feminine of *quotus* (see QUOTE).]

quot·a·ble /kwṓtəb'l/ *adj.* **1.** WORTH QUOTING worthy of being quoted **2.** ON THE RECORD able to be quoted in a publication such as a newspaper because the person speaking or writing has given permission —**quot·a·bil·i·ty** /kwṑtə bíllətee/ *n.*

quo·ta·tion /kwō táysh'n/ *n.* **1.** SOMETHING QUOTED a piece of speech or writing quoted somewhere, e.g., in a book or magazine ○ *a quotation from Henry James* **2.** QUOTING OF WHAT SOMEBODY HAS SAID the quoting of what somebody else has said or written **3.** BUSINESS = **quote** *n.* 3 **4.** STOCK EXCH STOCK PRICE the prevailing price at which a stock, bond, or commodity may be purchased or sold **5.** STOCK EXCH QUOTING OF PRICES the quoting of prevailing stock, bond, or commodity market prices **6.** ARTS REUSE OF ARTISTIC MATERIAL the use in an artistic work, especially music, of material taken from or alluding to somebody else's work —**quo·ta·tion·al** *adj.* —**quo·ta·tion·al·ly** *adv.*

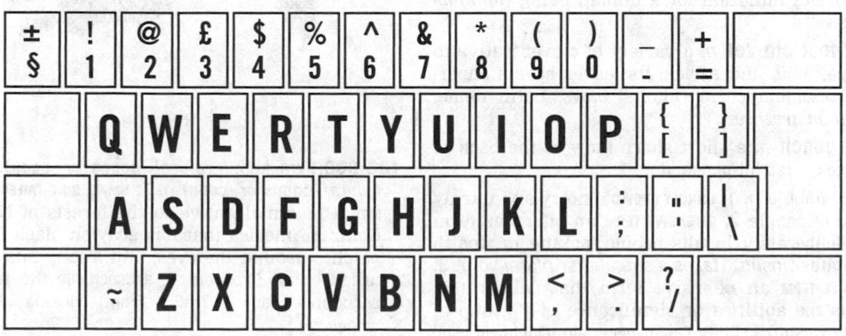

Qwerty keyboard

quo·ta·tion mark *n.* either of a pair of punctuation marks, either in double ("") or single ('') form, used in printed or written English to mark the beginning and end of a quotation

quote /kwōt/ *v.* (**quot·ed, quot·ing, quotes**) **1.** *vti.* REPEAT SOMEBODY'S EXACT WORDS to repeat or copy the exact words spoken or written by somebody **2.** *vti.* REFER TO SOMETHING FOR PROOF to refer to something as an example in support of an argument ○ *He quoted some recently published statistics.* **3.** *vti.* BUSINESS GIVE ESTIMATE FOR COST to give an estimate of the price of providing somebody with a product or service **4.** *vt.* STOCK EXCH GIVE CURRENT MARKET PRICE to state the current market price of a stock, bond, or commodity **5.** *vt.* BETTING GIVE BETTING ODDS to give somebody or something, e.g., a racehorse, specified betting odds (*usually passive*) **6.** *vti.* PRINTING PUT PUNCTUATION AROUND QUOTATION to place quotation marks around a passage of speech or writing that is being quoted **7.** *vt.* ARTS REPEAT FROM ARTISTIC WORK to repeat an excerpt from an artistic work created by somebody else, especially a piece of music ■ *n.* **1.** QUOTATION something that is repeated exactly (*informal*) **2.** PRINTING QUOTATION MARK one of a pair of quotation marks (*often used in the plural*) **3.** BUSINESS ESTIMATE FOR WORK an estimated price for a job or service ■ *interj.* INTRODUCING QUOTATION used to show that the following words are a quotation (*often used with "unquote"*) ○ *She told me she is, quote, "too good for him," unquote.* [14thC. Via medieval Latin *quotare* "to number chapters" from, ultimately, Latin *quot* "how many?" (source of English *quotient*).] —**quot·er** *n.*

quoth /kwōth/ *vt.* said, when used with direct speech (*archaic or literary*) ○ *quoth he* [Old English *cwæð*, the past tense of *cweþan* "to say" (source of English *bequeath*)]

quo·tha /kwṓthə/ *interj.* used after quoting another person to express contempt, sarcasm, or surprise (*archaic*) ○ *Love, quotha; what manner of love is this?* [Early 16thC. Shortening and alteration of "quoth he."]

quo·tid·i·an /kwō tíddee ən/ *adj.* **1.** COMMONPLACE of the most ordinary everyday kind (*formal*) **2.** DAILY done or experienced on a daily basis (*formal*) **3.** MED RECURRING DAILY recurring or flaring up every day ■ *n.* MED FEVER RECURRING DAILY a fever, especially malaria, in which attacks of the illness recur daily [14thC. Via Old French *cotidien* from Latin *quotidianus*, from *cotidie* "every day."]

quo·tient /kwṓsh'nt/ *n.* **1.** MATH RESULT OF DIVISION the number that results from the division of one number by another **2.** MATH WHOLE NUMBER RESULT OF DIVISION the whole number element of the result of dividing one number by another. ◊ **remainder 3.** AMOUNT OF SPECIFIED QUALITY a scale, or a point on a scale indicating the amount, degree, or level of something (*informal*) [15thC. From Latin *quotiens* "how many times?", from *quot* (see QUOTE).]

quo war·ran·to /kwō wə ráantō, -ràntō/ (*plural* **quo war·ran·tos**) *n.* a document issued by a court of law formally requiring somebody to state by what authority he or she has acted or has held a position [From Law Latin, literally "by what warrant?", words in the writ]

Qŭ·qon city in eastern Uzbekistan, in the Fergana Province. Population: 175,000 (1991).

Qur·'an, Qur·an *n.* = **Koran**

q.v. *abbr.* which see (*used to indicate a cross reference to sth within the same book or article*) [Latin, quod vide]

Qwa·qwa /kwáa kwáa/ former homeland in South Africa. It was abolished in 1994 and incorporated into Free State Province.

qwer·ty key·board /kwúrtee-/, **QWER·TY key·board** *n.* a typewriter or computer keyboard with the standard arrangement of keys for the alphabet, with the top row of alphabetic characters beginning with the letters q,w, e, r, t, and y

qy. *abbr.* query

Rr

r[1] /aar/ (*plural* **r's**), **R** (*plural* **R's** *or* **Rs**) *n.* **1. 18TH LETTER OF ENGLISH ALPHABET** the 18th letter of the modern English alphabet **2. SOUND CORRESPONDING TO LETTER "R"** the speech sound that corresponds to the letter "R" **3. LETTER "R" WRITTEN** a written representation of the letter "R" ◇ **the three R's** the basic skills of reading, writing, and arithmetic

r[2] *symbol.* **1. r, r.** MATH radius *n.* **1. 2. r, R** ELEC ENG resistance

r[3] *abbr.* recto

R[1] *symbol.* **1.** PHYS gas constant **2.** CHEM radical **3.** Réaumur scale **4.** ELEC ENG resistance

R[2] *n.* CINEMA a movie rating indicating that a movie can be seen by children under the age of 17 only if accompanied by an adult

R[3] *abbr.* **1.** MATH radius **2.** MONEY rand **3.** Regina (*used after the name of a queen*) **4.** CHR response (*in Christian liturgy*) **5.** Rex (*used after the name of a king*) **6.** CARS Romania (*international vehicle registration*)

r. *abbr.* **1. r., R.** railroad **2.** rare **3.** COMM received **4.** retired **5. r., R.** right **6. r., R.** river **7. r., R.** road **8.** MEASURE rod **9.** CARDS rubber **10. r., R.** MONEY ruble **11.** BASEBALL run **12. r., R.** MONEY rupee

R. *abbr.* **1.** JUDAISM rabbi **2.** GEOG range **3.** CHR rector **4.** POL republican **5.** royal

Ra[1] /raa/, **Re** /ray/ *n.* in ancient Egyptian mythology, the sun god, creator and controller of the universe, represented as having a human body and a hawk's head. ◊ **Osiris, Isis** [From Egyptian *rʿ*]

Ra[2] *symbol.* CHEM ELEM radium

RA *abbr.* **1.** NAVY Rear Admiral **2. RA, R.A.** ARMY Regular Army **3.** CARS Argentina (*international vehicle registration*) **4.** ASTRON right ascension

R.A. *abbr.* **1.** NAVY Rear Admiral **2.** Research Assistant **3.** UNIV Resident Advisor **4.** ASTRON right ascension

Ra·bat /rə baát/ capital city of Morocco, situated in the northwest of the country, at the mouth of the Bou Regreg River, on the Atlantic coast. Population: 1,386,000 (1994).

rab·bet /rábbət/ *n.* **GROOVE CUT FOR WOOD JOINT** a groove or step cut along the length of the edge of a piece of wood that is to be joined to another with a corresponding tongue or ledge cut into it (*often used before a noun*) ■ *vt.* (**-bet·ed, -bet·ing, -bets**) **1. CUT RABBET IN** to cut a rabbet in a piece of wood **2. JOIN WITH RABBET** to join two pieces of wood at their edges by means of a rabbet [15thC. From Old French *rab(b)at* "recess," from *rabattre* (see REBATE).]

rab·bi /rá bī/, **Rabbi** *n.* **1. JEWISH RELIGIOUS LEADER** the leader of a Jewish congregation, or the chief religious official of a synagogue **2. JEWISH SCHOLAR** a scholar qualified to teach or interpret Jewish law [Pre-12thC. Via late Latin and Greek from Hebrew *rabbī*, literally "my master."]

rab·bin·ate /rábbə nàyt, -nət/ *n.* **1. RABBI'S POSITION** the post or term of office of a rabbi **2. RABBIS COLLECTIVELY** rabbis considered as a group

rab·bin·i·cal /rə bínnik'l/, **rab·bin·ic** /rə bínnik/ *adj.* relating to rabbis or to their beliefs, language, teachings, or writings —**rab·bin·i·cal·ly** *adv.*

Rab·bin·ic He·brew *n.* the form of Hebrew used by rabbis between the 5th and 16th centuries. It contains much of the Aramaic language and was influenced by the language of the Talmud.

rab·bin·ism /rábbə nìzzəm/ *n.* the teachings of Jewish scholars, especially the scholars of the Talmudic period —**rab·bin·ist** *n.*, *adj.* —**rab·bin·is·tic** /ràbbə nístik/ *adj.*

Rabbit

rab·bit /rábbit/ *n.* (*plural* **-bits** *or* **-bit**) **1.** ZOOL **SMALL FURRY MAMMAL** a small burrowing mammal with long ears, soft fur, and a short tail. Rabbits are commonly kept as pets. Family: Leporidae. **2.** ZOOL **HARE** a word used inaccurately to refer to a hare (*informal*) **3.** INDUST **RABBIT'S FUR** the fur of a rabbit, used to make hats and other accessories **4.** FOOD **RABBIT'S FLESH** the meat of a rabbit **5.** SPORTS **PACESETTER IN RACE** a long-distance runner who sets a fast pace for a stronger teammate in the early part of a race **6.** SPORTS **DEVICE THAT RACING GREYHOUNDS CHASE** a mechanical device that greyhounds chase at a racetrack ■ *vi.* (**-bit·ed, -bit·ing, -bits**) **HUNT RABBITS** to go hunting for wild rabbits [14thC. Origin uncertain: probably via Old French from, ultimately, Middle Dutch or Low German *robbe*.] —**rab·bit·er** *n.*

WORD KEY: CULTURAL NOTE

Rabbit, Run, a novel by John Updike (1960). It depicts the disastrous attempts of Harry Rabbit Angstrom to flee an unhappy marriage and the responsibilites of adulthood. Updike continued Harry's story in three subsequent novels, *Rabbit Redux* (1971), *Rabbit is Rich* (1981), and *Rabbit at Rest* (1990), creating a tetralogy that highlights sexual and moral confusion in late 20th century American society.

rab·bit ears *npl.* a V-shaped antenna made up of two metal rods on a base, designed to sit on top of a television set

rab·bit fe·ver *n.* = **tularemia**

rab·bit food *n.* an offensive term that deliberately dismisses a vegetarian diet, especially as providing insufficient nutrition for a human being (*informal offensive*)

rab·bit-foot clo·ver *n.* a variety of clover native to Europe, Asia, and Africa. Its leaves bear a superficial resemblance to rabbits' paws. Latin name: *Trifolium arvense.*

rab·bit punch *n.* a short sharp blow to the back of the neck —**rab·bit-punch** *vt.*

rab·ble[1] /rább'l/ *n.* **1. UNRULY CROWD** a noisy and unruly crowd of people **2. OFFENSIVE TERM** an offensive term that deliberately insults people lacking in wealth and status (*insult*) (*takes a singular or plural verb*) **3. OFFENSIVE TERM** an offensive term that deliberately insults the abilities or significance of a group of people (*insult*) [14thC. Origin uncertain. Originally used for "pack of dogs."]

rab·ble[2] /rább'l/ *n.* **FURNACE TOOL** a device for stirring or skimming molten metal in a furnace ■ *vt.* (**-bled, -bling, -bles**) **STIR WITH RABBLE** to stir or skim molten metal with a rabble [Mid-19thC. Via French *râble* "fire rake," from, ultimately, Latin *rutabulum*, from *ruere* "to rake up."] —**rab·bler** /rábblər/ *n.*

rab·ble-rous·er *n.* somebody who stirs up anger, violence, or other strong feelings in a crowd, especially for political reasons (*disapproving*) —**rab·ble-rous·ing** *n.*, *adj.*

Ra·be·lais /rábbə láy/, **François** (1493?–1553) French humanist and writer. His greatest works, *Pantagruel* (1532) and *Gargantua* (1534), satirized medieval scholasticism and are notable for their exuberance and earthy humor. —**Rab·e·lai·si·an** /ràbbə láyzee ən, -láyzh'n/ *adj.*, *n.*

Ra·bi /raábee/, **Ra·bia** /rə beé ə/ *n.* **1. Ra·bi, Ra·bi·a, Ra·bi I, Ra·bi·a I 3RD MONTH OF ISLAMIC CALENDAR** in the Islamic calendar, the third month of the year, made up of 30 days **2. Ra·bi, Ra·bi·a, Ra·bi II, Ra·bi·a II 4TH MONTH OF ISLAMIC CALENDAR** in the Islamic calendar, the fourth month of the year, made up of 29 days [Mid-18thC. From Arabic *rabīʿ*.]

Ra·bi /raábee/, **Isidor Isaac** (1898–1988) Austrian-born U.S. physicist. He won a Nobel Prize (1944) for his work on the atom.

rab·id /rábbid/ *adj.* **1.** MED, VET **HAVING RABIES** infected with rabies **2. FANATICAL** very enthusiastic or fanatical **3. INTENSE** extremely intense and unceasing ○ *a rabid lust for power* [Early 17thC. From Latin *rabidus*, from *rabere* (see RABIES).] —**ra·bid·i·ty** /rə bíddətee/ *n.* —**rab·id·ly** /rábbidlee/ *adv.* —**rab·id·ness** *n.*

ra·bies /ráybiz/ *n.* an often fatal viral disease that affects the central nervous systems of most warm-blooded animals and is transmitted in the saliva of an infected animal. It causes convulsions, inability to move, and strange behavior. [Late 16thC. From Latin, "fury," from *rabere* "to rave, be mad" (source of English *rage*).] —**ra·bic** *adj.* —**ra·bi·et·ic** /ràybee éttik/ *adj.*

Ra·bin /raa beén/, **Yitzhak** (1922–95) Israeli statesman. He served as prime minister from 1974 to 1977 and from 1992 until he was assassinated in 1995. He received the Nobel Peace Prize (1994).

Raccoon

rac·coon /ra kóon/ (*plural* **-coons** *or* **-coon**), **racoon** (*plural* **-coons** *or* **-coon**) *n.* **1. SMALL RING-TAILED MAMMAL** a small mammal native to the forests of North and Central America that has grayish black fur, black patches around the eyes, and a long bushy ringed tail. Genus: *Procyon.* **2. RACCOON FUR** the fur of the raccoon [Early 17thC. From Virginia Algonquian *aroughcun*.]

rac·coon dog *n.* a small wild dog, native to woodland areas of eastern Asia, with facial markings similar to a raccoon's and a thick yellow-brown coat. Latin name: *Nyctereutes procyonoides.*

race[1] /rayss/ *n.* **1.** SPORTS **CONTEST OF SPEED** a contest, e.g., between or among runners or horseback riders, to decide who is the fastest **2. CONTEST BETWEEN RIVALS** a contest between two or more people seeking to do or reach the same thing, or do or reach it first **3.** OCEANOG, GEOG **WATER CURRENT** a strong localized current in the sea or a river **4.** CIV ENG **WATER CHANNEL** a channel that carries water from one place to another, especially from a stream to a waterwheel **5.** TECH **GROOVE GUIDING SLIDING OBJECT** a groove along which something, e.g., a ballbearing, slides **6. NARROW PASSAGE** any narrow path or passage, e.g., one leading sheep from their enclosure to a dip **7. REGULAR COURSE** the fixed course regularly followed or traveled by something, especially the Sun or the Moon (*archaic or literary*) **8. JOURNEY** a single passage along a fixed course, especially the course that somebody's life follows (*archaic or literary*) ■ **rac·es** *npl.* HORSERACING **HORSERACES OR HORSERACING** horseraces, the racetrack at which they are run, or horseracing as a spectator sport ○ *We spent the day at the races.* ■ *v.* **(raced, rac·ing, rac·es) 1.** *vti.* SPORTS **COMPETE AGAINST IN RACE** to compete with somebody in a contest of speed **2.** *vt.* **ENTER SOMETHING IN RACE** to enter, ride, or drive something, e.g., a horse or car, in a race **3.** *vti.* **MOVE VERY FAST** to move somewhere with great speed or haste, or make somebody or something move or be transported in this way **4.** *vi.* **BEAT FAST** to beat much faster than usual, e.g., out of nervousness or excitement (*refers to the heart*) **5.** *vti.* AUTOMOT **IDLE FAST** to run or make an engine or motor run at a high speed [13thC. From Old Norse *rás* "rush, running." Ultimately from an Indo-European word meaning "to be in motion," which is also the ancestor of English *err* and *error*.]

race[2] /rayss/ *n.* **1. GROUP OF HUMANS** any one of the groups into which the world's population can be divided on the basis of physical characteristics such as skin or hair color **2. FACT OF BELONGING TO A GROUP** the fact of belonging to a group of humans who share the same physical features such as skin color ○ *an attempt to end discrimination on grounds of race* **3. HUMANKIND** humanity considered as a whole ○ *the fate of the race* **4.** BIOL **STRAIN OF ORGANISM** a breed, strain, or subspecies of an organism **5.** WINE **WINE'S DISTINCTIVE TASTE** the distinctive taste of a particular wine, by which its grape variety or region of origin can be identified [Early 16thC. Via French from Italian *razza*, of unknown origin.]

race·car /ráyss kaar/ *n.* a car used, designed, or adapted for the sport of automobile racing

race·course /ráyss kàwrs/ *n.* **1. TRACK FOR CARS OR RUNNERS** a track around which cars or runners race, or the grounds in which the track is sited **2.** *U.K.* = **race-track** *n.* 1

race·horse /ráyss hàwrs/ *n.* a horse bred and trained to run in races

race·mate /rássə màyt/ *n.* a chemical compound that does not deflect or absorb any of the light passing through it [Mid-19thC. Formed from RACEMIC.]

ra·ceme /ray séem, rə séem/ *n.* a flower cluster **(inflorescence)** in which the flowers are borne on short stalks along an elongated main stem, as they are in the lily of the valley [Late 18thC. From Latin *racemus* "bunch of grapes" (source of English *raisin*).]

ra·ce·mic /ray séemik, rə-, ray sémmik, rə-/ *adj.* used to describe a chemical compound that does not deflect or absorb any of the light passing through it. This is due to its consisting of a precise mixture of dextrorotatory and levorotatory isomers. [Late 19thC. Formed from Latin *racemus* "bunch of grapes," because the compound was originally derived from grapes.]

ra·ce·mic ac·id *n.* a form of tartaric acid that does not deflect or absorb any of the light passing through it. It is found in grape juice.

ra·ce·mi·form /ray séemə fàwrm/ *adj.* having the form of a raceme

rac·e·mi·za·tion /ràyssəmə záysh'n/ *n.* the process of converting from an optically active compound or mixture to one that is racemic —**ra·ce·mize** /ráyssə mìz, ray sée-, rə sée-/ *vt.*

rac·e·mose /ráyssə mòss/ *adj.* **1.** BOT **WITH FLOWERS CLUSTERED ALONG STEM** used to describe a flower cluster **(inflorescence)** in which the flowers are borne on short stalks along an elongated main stem, as they are in the lily of the valley **2.** BOT **WITH YOUNGEST FLOWERS AT TIP** used to describe any pyramidal or flat-topped flower cluster in which the youngest flowers develop nearest the tip of the main stem or main side branches. Examples include the panicle, corymb, umbel, and capitulum, as well as the raceme. **3.** ANAT **CLUSTERED LIKE BUNCH OF GRAPES** used to describe glands that resemble a bunch of grapes in their structure —**rac·e·mose·ly** /ráyssə mòsslee/ *adv.* —**rac·e·mous·ly** /ráyssəməsslee/ *adv.*

rac·er /ráyssər/ *n.* **1. SOMEBODY OR SOMETHING THAT RACES** a person, animal, or vehicle competing in a race **2. THIN FAST-MOVING SNAKE** a slender fast-moving nonvenomous North American snake. Genus: *Coluber.*

race·run·ner /ráyss rùnnər/ *n.* a fast-moving lizard found in North and Central America. Genus: *Cnemidophurus.*

race·track /ráyss tràk/ *n.* **1.** *U.K.* = **racecourse** *n.* 1 **2. TRACK FOR HOLDING RACES** a track around which horses race, or the grounds in which the track is sited

race-walk *vi.* to compete in the sport of race walking

race walk·ing *n.* the sport of racing at a fast walking pace, with rules that require walkers to keep at least one foot on the ground at all times —**race walk·er** *n.*

race·way /ráyss wày/ *n.* **1.** CIV ENG = **race**[1] *n.* 4 **2.** SPORTS **RACETRACK** a track on which races, especially harness races, are held, or the grounds in which the track is sited **3.** MECH ENG **PIPE FOR HYDRAULICS** a pipe, channel, or other means by which water is conveyed to or from hydraulic machinery **4.** ELEC ENG **PROTECTIVE TUBE FOR WIRES** a tube or channel that holds, guides, and protects electric wires

Ra·chel /ráchəl/ *n.* in the Bible, the daughter of Laban, wife of Jacob, and mother of Joseph and Benjamin (Genesis 29–35)

rachio- *prefix.* spine ○ *rachiotomy* [Via modern Latin from Greek *rhakhis* "spine"]

ra·chis /ráykiss/ (*plural* **ra·chis·es** *or* **rach·i·des** /ráki dèez, ráyki-/) *n.* **1.** BOT **PLANT STEM** the main stem of a flower cluster or a compound leaf **2.** BIRDS **FEATHER SHAFT** the main shaft of a feather **3.** ANAT **SPINE** the spine of a vertebrate animal (*technical*) [Late 18thC. Via modern Latin from Greek *rhakhis* "spine, ridge."] —**ra·chi·al** /ráykee əl/ *adj.* —**ra·chid·i·al** /rə kíddee əl/ *adj.*

ra·chi·tis /rə kítiss/ *n.* the disease rickets (*technical*) [Early 18thC. From Greek *rhakhitis* "disease of the spine," from *rhakhis* "spine."] —**ra·chit·ic** /rə kíttik/ *adj.*

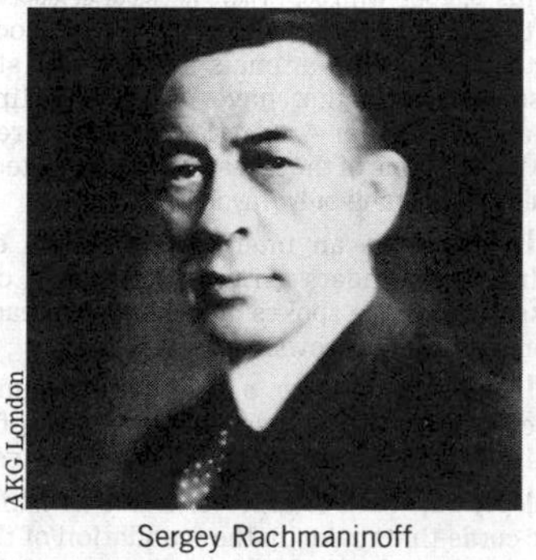

Sergey Rachmaninoff

Rach·ma·ni·noff /raak maánnə nàwf/, **Sergey** (1873–1943) Russian-born composer and pianist. His symphonies and compositions for piano are considered the last major musical expression of the Romantic era. Full name **Sergey Vasilyevich Rachmaninoff**

ra·cial /ráysh'l/ *adj.* **1. EXISTING BETWEEN RACES** existing or taking place between different races ○ *racial harmony* **2. RELATING TO RACE** relating to or characteristic of races or a particular race of people —**ra·cial·ly** /ráysh'lee/ *adv.*

ra·cial·ism /ráysh'l ìzzəm/ *n.* *U.K.* **RACISM** racism (*dated*) —**ra·cial·ist** *n., adj.* —**ra·cial·is·tic** /ràysh'l ístik/ *adj.*

ra·cial·ly-cor·rect·ed *adj.* adjusted to eliminate cultural bias or racial prejudice from something, especially a standardized test

Ra·cine /rə séen/, **Jean Baptiste** (1639–99) French playwright. Considered to be the greatest French classical tragedian, he adapted Greek and Roman plays in works such as *Bajazet* (1672) and *Phèdre* (1677).

rac·ing car *n.* *U.K.* = **racecar**

rac·ing form *n.* a sheet giving details of the previous performances of competitors in a race, especially a horserace, for use by people wishing to place bets

ra·cism /ráy sìzzəm/ *n.* (*disapproving*) **1. ANIMOSITY TOWARD OTHER RACES** prejudice or animosity against people who belong to other races ○ *"I am a Muslim and ... my religion makes me against all forms of racism."* (Malcolm X, *Speech, Prospects for Freedom*; 1965) **2. BELIEF IN RACIAL SUPERIORITY** the belief that people of different races have different qualities and abilities, and that some races are inherently superior or inferior

rac·ist /ráyssist/ *adj.* (*disapproving*) **1. BASED ON RACISM** based on notions and stereotypes related to race **2. PREJUDICED AGAINST OTHER RACES** prejudiced against all people who belong to other races ○ *"Black power ... a call to reject the racist institutions and values of this society"* (Stokley Carmichael [Kwame Toure] and Charles Vernon Hamilton, *Black Power!*; 1967) ■ *n.* **RACIST PERSON** somebody who is racist (*disapproving*)

rack[1] /rak/ *n.* **1. FRAMEWORK FOR HOLDING THINGS** a framework or stand for carrying, holding, or storing things ○ *a wine rack* **2.** AGRIC **FEED-HOLDING FRAMEWORK** a framework containing hay or other fodder for livestock **3.** AIR FORCE **BOMB-HOLDING FRAMEWORK** a bomb- or rocket-carrying framework attached to an aircraft **4.** MECH ENG **TOOTHED BAR** a bar with notches, designed to engage the teeth of a pinion or worm gear and convert rotary motion to linear motion, e.g., in a vehicle's steering system **5. INSTRUMENTS OF TORTURE** a torture device used to stretch the body of a victim strapped horizontally onto it **6.** ZOOL **ANTLERS** a pair of antlers **7.** CUE GAMES **BALL-PLACING FRAME** a triangular frame for grouping the balls at the beginning of a game of pool, billiards, or snooker **8. BED** a bed or a bunk (*slang*) **9. SLEEP** sleep (*slang*) ○ *Time to get some rack.* ■ *vt.* **(racked, rack·ing, racks) 1. CAUSE PAIN** to cause somebody great pain or stress ○ *the coughing spasms that racked his body* **2. SHAKE SOMETHING** to shake or strain something with violent force ○ *The high winds racked villages all along the coast.* **3. STRAIN SOMETHING** to stretch something with extreme force or mental effort ○ *I racked my brain trying to think where I'd seen him before.* **4. TORTURE SOMEBODY ON RACK** to torture somebody on a rack **5. PUT SOMETHING IN RACK** to place something in or on a rack **6.** MECH ENG **MOVE SOMETHING WITH RACK** to move a device or part using a rack-and-pinion system **7.** CUE GAMES **POSITION BALLS** to set up the balls for a game of billiards, pool, or snooker using a rack [14thC. From Dutch *rak*, which evolved from Middle Dutch *rec* "framework."] —**rack·er** *n.* —**rack·ful** *n.* ◇ **off the rack** ready to wear, not tailor-made ◇ **on the rack** experiencing great mental anguish (*informal*)

rack out *vi.* to go to bed or get some sleep (*slang*)

rack up *vt.* (*informal*) **1. AMASS THINGS** to accumulate something, usually points **2.** = **wrack up**

rack[2] /rak/ *n.* a joint of meat, usually lamb, consisting of one or both sides of the front ribs prepared for roasting, often joined end to end in a circle [Late 16thC. Origin uncertain: possibly from RACK[1].]

rack[3] /rak/ **(racked, rack·ing, racks)** *vt.* to siphon clear wine or beer out of a barrel, leaving the sediment behind [15thC. From Provençal *arracar*, from *raca* "dregs," of unknown origin.]

rack[4] /rak/ *n.* **SHOWY WALKING PACE FOR HORSE** in dressage, a fast walking pace for a horse in which each foot is lifted off the ground in turn ■ *vi.* **(racked, rack·ing, racks) WALK AT RACK** to walk at a fast pace, lifting each foot off the ground in turn (*refers to horses*) [Late 16thC. Origin unknown.]

rack[5] /rak/ *n.* **MOVING CLOUD MASS** a mass of broken cloud blown fast by the wind ■ *vi.* **(racked, rack·ing, racks) RACE ACROSS SKY** to be blown fast by the wind (*refers to clouds*) [14thC. Origin uncertain: possibly from Old Norse.]

rack[6] /rak/ *n.* = **wrack** (*archaic*) [Late 16thC. Variant of WRACK.] ◇ **go to rack and ruin** to deteriorate into a state of neglect or ruin

rack-and-pin·ion *adj.* using or relating to a mechanical system in which a toothed wheel **(pinion)** engages a notched bar **(rack)** to convert rotary motion into linear motion

racket[1] /rákət/, **rac·quet** *n.* **1.** SPORTS **SPORTS BAT** a lightweight bat with a network of strings, used in tennis, racquetball, badminton, squash, and similar games. The frame is usually made of a substance such as wood, aluminum, or graphite, and the strings of gut or nylon. **2. SNOWSHOE** a snowshoe in the shape of a racket [Early 16thC. Via French *raquette* from, ultimately, Arabic *rāḥat* "palm of the hand."]

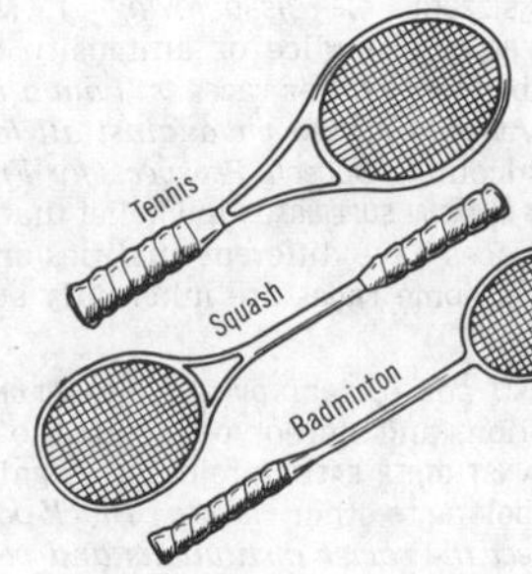

Racket

rack·et[2] /rákət/ (**-et·ed, -et·ing, -ets**) *n.* **1.** **NOISE** a loud noise, especially when it disturbs people **2.** CRIMINOL **ILLEGAL SCHEME** an illegal or dishonest money-making scheme, involving, e.g., bribery, fraud, or intimidation **3.** **BUSINESS** a business, job, or activity of any kind (*informal*) ○ *He's in the advertising racket.* **4.** **EASY LIVING** an easy and very profitable way of earning a living (*informal*) [Mid-16thC. Origin unknown: perhaps thought to suggest loud noise.]

rack·et·eer /ràkə tée̍r/ *n.* **CRIMINAL PLOTTER** somebody who makes money from illegal activities, involving, e.g., bribery, fraud, or intimidation ■ *vi.* (**-eered, -eer·ing, -eers**) **RUN CRIMINAL RACKET** to make money from illegal activities, or operate a racket —**rack·et·eer·ing** *n.*

rack·ets *n.* = **racquets**

rack·et·y /rákətee/ *adj.* noisy and boisterous (*dated*)

rack rail·way *n.* = **cog railway**

rack-rent *n.* **EXCESSIVE RENT** an unreasonably high rent ■ *vti.* (**rack-rent·ed, rack-rent·ing, rack-rents**) **CHARGE TENANT EXCESSIVE RENT** to charge tenants an unreasonably high rent [From RACK[1], in the sense "to torture"] —**rack-rent·er** *n.*

ra·clette /raa klét, ra klét/ *n.* **1.** **DISH OF MELTED CHEESE WITH POTATOES** a Swiss dish consisting of slices of melted cheese served on boiled potatoes or bread. The cheese is traditionally melted over a fire but electric raclette machines are now available. **2.** **CHEESE USED FOR RACLETTE** a hard-crusted type of Swiss cheese that melts easily, traditionally used for raclette [Mid-20thC. From French, from *racler* "to scrape," because the cheese is melted and scraped onto a plate.]

ra·con /ráy kòn/ *n.* = **radar beacon** [Mid-20thC. Blend of RADAR and BEACON.]

rac·on·teur /ra kon túr/ *n.* somebody who tells stories or anecdotes in an interesting or entertaining way [Early 19thC. Via French from, ultimately, Old French *raconter* "to recount, retell."]

ra·coon *n.* = **raccoon**

rac·quet *n.* = **racket**[1]

rac·quet·ball /rákət bàwl/ *n.* a game played on a four-walled indoor court by two, three, or four players using short-handled rackets and a ball larger than the ball used in squash or racquets

rac·quets /rákəts/, **rack·ets** *n.* a fast game similar to squash played by two to four people on a four-walled indoor court using long-handled rackets and a small hard ball. It is derived from the old game of court tennis. [Mid-18thC. From French *raquette* (see RACKET).]

rac·y /ráyssee/ (**-i·er, -i·est**) *adj.* **1.** **MILDLY INDECENT** mildly shocking because of references to or descriptions of sex **2.** **LIVELY** full of energy or spirit **3.** **DISTINCTIVE** with a distinctive quality or flavor **4.** **PUNGENT** sharp or piquant in taste or smell [Mid-17thC. Formed from RACE[1]. Originally in the sense "having a distinctive flavor."] —**rac·i·ly** *adv.* —**rac·i·ness** *n.*

rad[1] /rad/ *n.* the unit formerly used to measure the level of ionizing radiation absorbed by something, equal to 0.01 joule per kilogram of irradiated material [Early 20thC. Acronym of "radiation absorbed dose."]

rad[2] /rad/ (**rad·der, rad·dest**) *adj.* very good, desirable, admirable, or fashionable (*slang*) ○ *a totally rad idea* [Early 19thC. Shortening of RADICAL.]

rad[3] *symbol.* MATH radian

rad. *abbr.* **1.** MATH radical **2.** radio **3.** MATH radius **4.** MATH radix

ra·dar /ráy daar/ *n.* **1.** **OBJECT-LOCATING SYSTEM** the use of reflected radio waves to determine the presence, location, and speed of distant objects. The system has military, law-enforcement, and navigational applications. It is used, e.g., to locate enemy aircraft or ships and to monitor vehicle speeds. **2.** **OBJECT-LOCATING EQUIPMENT** the electronic equipment that transmits and receives high-frequency radio waves to detect, locate, and track distant objects [Mid-20thC. Acronym formed from "radio detection and ranging."] ◇ **be on somebody's radar screen** to be a focal point of interest to somebody (*informal*) ○ *This issue of bank fraud has been on the district attorney's radar screen for at least six months.*

ra·dar as·tron·o·my *n.* the use of radar techniques to study and map celestial bodies in the solar system

ra·dar bea·con *n.* a ground-based fixed position radar receiver-transmitter whose signals can be received by an aircraft or ship's navigator to determine bearing and range

ra·dar gun *n.* a small handheld radar device used to determine the speed of nearby objects

ra·dar·scope /ráy daar skòp/ *n.* the display screen on radar equipment, displaying the reflected radio signal as a dot of light. In sophisticated screens, textual data such as speed, direction, and altitude are also shown.

ra·dar trap *n.* = **speed trap**

Rad·cliff /ràd klíf/ city in north central Kentucky, southwest of Louisville and northeast of Elizabethtown. Population: 19,411 (1996).

rad·dle[1] (**-dled, -dling, -dles**) *vt.* to twist or weave things together [Late 17thC. Via Anglo-Norman *reidele* "wooden pole" from Old French *reddalle*, perhaps of Middle High German origin. Originally used for "strip of wood twisted between stakes to make a fence."]

rad·dle[2] *n., vt.* = **ruddle**

rad·dled /rádd'ld/ *adj.* with a worn-out appearance that suggests long life or a life of indulgence [Late 17thC. Origin uncertain.]

ra·di·al /ráydee əl/ *adj.* **1.** **RUNNING FROM CENTER OUTWARD** spreading out from a common center like the spokes of a wheel ○ *petals in a radial arrangement* **2.** **OF RADIUS** relating to a radius, especially moving along a radius **3.** ZOOL **WITH BODY PARTS IN CIRCULAR ARRANGEMENT** used to describe the arrangement of the bodies of invertebrate marine animals such as the starfish and sea anemone that have parts spreading out from a single center **4.** ANAT **OF FOREARM BONE** relating to the radius bone of the forearm ■ *n.* CARS alternative for **radial tire** —**ra·di·al·ly** /ráydee əlee/ *adv.*

ra·di·al en·gine *n.* an internal-combustion engine that has its cylinders arranged around a central crankshaft like the spokes of a wheel, instead of in one or two straight rows. ◊ **rotary engine**

ra·di·al ker·a·tot·o·my *n.* a surgical procedure for correcting nearsightedness, using a series of small radial incisions to change the shape of the cornea

ra·di·al-ply *adj.* used to describe a tire in which the fabric cords that make up the foundation of the tire run at right angles to the circumference of the tire

ra·di·al sym·me·try *n.* symmetry in which something can be divided into two identical halves by a line or plane passing through a central point or axis at any angle —**ra·di·al·ly sym·met·ri·cal** *adj.*

ra·di·al tire *n.* a tire in which the fabric cords that make up the foundation of the tire run at right angles to the circumference of the tire

ra·di·al ve·loc·i·ty *n.* the velocity of a star or other celestial body measured along the observer's line of sight

ra·di·an /ráydee ən/ *n.* a unit of angular measurement equivalent to the angle between two radii that enclose a section of a circle's circumference (**arc**) equal in length to the length of a radius. There are 2π radians in a circle. Symbol **rad** [Late 19thC. Formed from RADIUS.]

ra·di·ance /ráydee əns/ *n.* **1.** **HAPPINESS OR ENERGY** joy, energy, or good health discernible in somebody's face or demeanor **2.** **LIGHT** bright or glowing light **3.** PHYS **MEASURE OF RADIANT ENERGY** a measure of the amount of radiant energy emitted or received per unit area of a surface over a specified time. Symbol L_e

ra·di·ant /ráydee ənt/ *adj.* **1.** **SHOWING HAPPINESS** expressing joy, energy, or good health in a pleasing way **2.** **SHINING** lit with a bright or glowing light **3.** PHYS **EMITTED AS WAVES** used to describe light, heat, or other energy emitted in the form of waves or rays ○ *radiant heat* **4.** PHYS **EMITTING RADIANT ENERGY** emitting light, heat, or other energy in the form of waves or rays ■ *n.* **1.** **HEATING ELEMENT** an element in a heater that gives out radiant heat **2.** ASTRON **METEOR SHOWER'S POINT OF ORIGIN** a point in space from which a meteor shower appears to originate [15thC. From Latin *radiant-*, the present participle stem of *radiare* "to RADIATE."] —**ra·di·ant·ly** *adv.*

ra·di·ant en·er·gy *n.* energy emitted as waves, usually electromagnetic waves, through space or some other medium. Symbol Q_e

ra·di·ant flux *n.* the rate of flow of radiant energy. Symbol Φ_e

ra·di·ant heat *n.* heat transmitted by infrared radiation from a heat source, as distinct from heat transmitted by conduction or convection

ra·di·ant heat·ing *n.* heating by means of heaters such as radiators, baseboard heaters, and electric coils rather than by forced hot air

ra·di·ate *v.* /ráydee àyt/ (**-at·ed, -at·ing, -ates**) **1.** *vti.* PHYS **SEND OR BE SENT IN RAYS** to send out energy, e.g., heat or light, in the form of rays or waves, or be sent out in this form **2.** *vti.* **SHOW A FEELING OR QUALITY** to clearly show a feeling or quality through looks, speech, behavior, or content ○ *a popular speech that radiated goodwill and commitment* **3.** *vti.* **SPREAD FROM CENTER** to spread out, or cause something to spread out, from a central point like rays **4.** *vi.* BIOL **DEVELOP AND SPREAD** to develop into several different forms capable of exploiting different resources or of living in different environments (*refers to animal and plant species*) ■ *adj.* /ráydee ət/ **1.** **WITH RADIATING PARTS** with, or in the form of, parts spreading out from a common center **2.** BOT **WITH PETALS RADIATING FROM CENTER** used to describe a flower head that has petals radiating from a center, e.g., a daisy **3.** ZOOL **WITH RADIALLY SYMMETRICAL BODY** used to describe the bodies of starfish and other vertebrate marine organisms with body parts radiating from a common center **4.** **WITH RAYS** surrounded or decorated with rays [Early 17thC. From Latin *radiat-*, the past participle stem of *radiare* "to emit rays," from *radius* "ray" (source of English *ray*[1]).] —**ra·di·ate·ly** /ráydee ətlee/ *adv.* —**ra·di·a·tive** /ráydee aytiv/ *adj.*

ra·di·a·tion /ràydee áysh'n/ *n.* **1.** PHYS **PARTICLES EMITTED BY RADIOACTIVE SUBSTANCES** energy emitted in the form of particles by substances, e.g., uranium and plutonium, whose atoms are not stable and are spontaneously decaying. This energy can be converted into electric power, but it also causes severe or fatal health problems to people who are exposed to it. **2.** PHYS **ENERGY EMITTED IN RAYS OR WAVES** any kind of energy that is emitted from a source in the form of rays or waves, e.g., heat, light, or sound **3.** PHYS **RADIATING OF ENERGY** the emission of energy in the form of waves **4.** **EFFECT OF RADIATING** the feeling of something being radiated, e.g., heat from a hot oven **5.** MED = **radiotherapy** **6.** BIOL **ADAPTIVE RADIATION** adaptive radiation —**ra·di·a·tion·al** *adj.*

ra·di·a·tion·al cool·ing *n.* loss of heat from the Earth's surface and from air near the Earth's surface, occurring mainly at night

ra·di·a·tion bi·ol·o·gy *n.* = **radiobiology**

ra·di·a·tion chem·is·try *n.* the branch of chemistry concerned with chemical changes caused by the impact of radiation

ra·di·a·tion phys·ics *n.* the branch of physics that is concerned with the interaction between radiation and matter (*takes a singular verb*)

ra·di·a·tion sick·ness *n.* a medical condition caused by overexposure to X-rays or to emissions from radioactive material. Symptoms include fatigue, headache, vomiting, diarrhea, loss of hair and teeth, and in severe cases, hemorrhaging.

ra·di·a·tion ther·a·py *n.* = **radiotherapy**

ra·di·a·tor /ráydee àytər/ *n.* **1.** **ROOM HEATER WITH PIPES** a room-heating device that emits heat from pipes through which hot water, steam, or hot oil circulates, especially one connected to a central boiler-fed system **2.** CARS **ENGINE-COOLING DEVICE** a device that prevents a vehicle's engine from overheating, consisting of tubes through which heated water from the engine circulates to be cooled. Cool air is usually circulated around the tubes by means of a fan. **3.** TECH **DEVICE EMITTING RADIANT ENERGY** a device that emits radiant energy, e.g., a light bulb or a television transmitter

rad·i·cal /ráddik'l/ *adj.* **1.** BASIC relating to or affecting the basic nature or most important features of something ○ *a radical difference between the two* **2.** PERVASIVE far-reaching, searching, or thoroughgoing ○ *a radical reorganization of the company* **3.** FAVORING MAJOR CHANGES favoring or making economic, political, or social changes of a sweeping or extreme nature ○ *radical policies* **4.** EXCELLENT excellent, admirable, or awe-inspiring (*slang*) **5.** MED REMOVING DISEASE'S SOURCE used to describe medical treatment that is intended to remove the source of a disease, rather than simply treat the symptoms **6.** BOT GROWING FROM ROOT growing from a root of a plant or from the base of a stem **7.** MATH OF A MATHEMATICAL ROOT relating to the roots of numbers **8.** LING OF WORD ROOTS relating to the roots of words ■ *n.* **1.** POL, SOC SCI, ECON SOMEBODY WITH RADICAL VIEWS somebody with radical views on political, economic, or social issues ○ *left-wing radicals* **2.** MATH MATHEMATICAL ROOT a mathematical root of another number or quantity **3.** CHEM FREE RADICAL a free radical **4.** CHEM CHEMICAL GROUP a chemical group that behaves as a single entity in reactions **5.** LING = **root**[1] *n.* 7 [14thC. From late Latin *radicalis* "of roots" (the original sense in English), from *radix* "root" (source of English *radish*).] —**rad·i·cal·ly** *adv.* —**rad·i·cal·ness** *n.*

rad·i·cal chic *n.* the fashionable adoption of radical left-wing views by rich or famous people (*disapproving*) ○ *"Radical chic invariably favors radicals who seem primitive, exotic, and romantic."* (Tom Wolfe, *Radical Chic*; 1970)

rad·i·cal·ism /ráddik'l ìzzəm/ *n.* **1.** POLITICS ADVOCATING MAJOR CHANGES political policies that advocate more sweeping political, economic, or social change than that traditionally supported by the mainstream political parties **2.** POLITICALLY RADICAL ATTITUDES support for radical political policies **3.** SIGNIFICANT CHANGE sweeping change in any context, or the attitudes of people who favor sweeping change

rad·i·cal·ize /ráddik'l ìz/ (**-ized, -iz·ing, -iz·es**) *vti.* **1.** CHANGE FUNDAMENTALLY to undergo fundamental change, or introduce sweeping change in something **2.** MAKE OR BECOME POLITICALLY RADICAL to adopt, or cause somebody to adopt, politically radical views ○ *The experience of war radicalized the younger generation.* —**rad·i·cal·i·za·tion** /ràddik'lə záysh'n/ *n.*

rad·i·cal sign *n.* the sign √ placed before a mathematical expression to denote the extraction of a square root or higher root. Roots higher than a square root are indicated by a superscript number preceding the sign.

rad·i·cand /ráddi kànd/ *n.* a mathematical quantity from which a square root or higher root is to be extracted [Late 19thC. Formed from Latin *radicandus*, from *radicare* "to take root."]

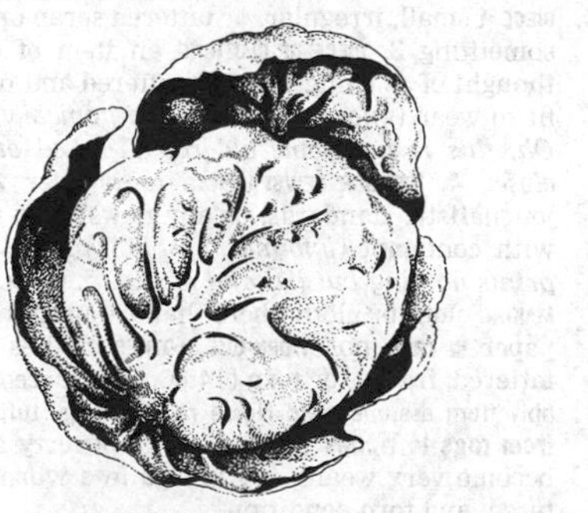
Radicchio

ra·dic·chi·o /rə déeki ō, raa-/ (*plural* **-os**) *n.* an Italian variety of chicory with reddish purple and white leaves, usually eaten raw in salads [Late 20thC. Via Italian, "chicory," from, ultimately, Latin *radicula* (see RADICLE).]

rad·i·ces plural of **radix**

rad·i·cle /ráddik'l/ *n.* **1.** BOT EMBRYONIC ROOT the part of a plant embryo that forms the root of the young plant **2.** ANAT BODY PART LIKE ROOT a small body part such as a branch of a nerve that superficially resembles the root of a plant [Late 17thC. From Latin *radicula*, literally "little root," from *radix* "root" (source of English *radish*).] —**ra·dic·u·lar** /rə díkyələr/ *adj.*

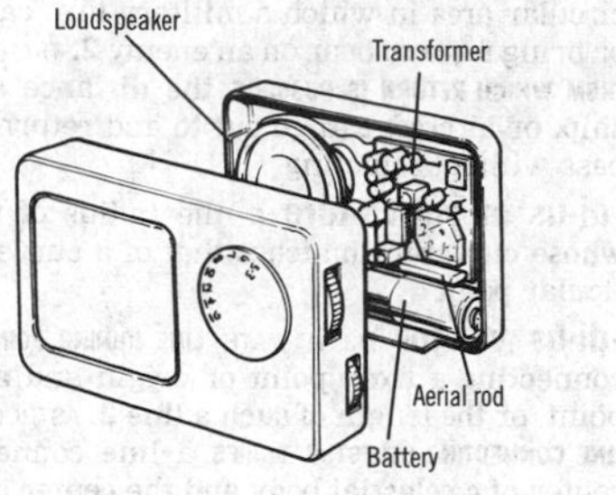

Radio

ra·di·o /r'aydi ō/ *n.* (*plural* **-os**) **1.** USE OF ELECTROMAGNETIC WAVES FOR COMMUNICATION the use of electromagnetic waves to transmit and receive information, as in sound broadcasts or two-way communication, without the need for connecting wires **2.** COMMUNICATION USING RADIO WAVES communication that takes place by means of radio waves **3.** DEVICE RECEIVING SOUND BROADCASTS an electronic device for receiving sound broadcasts transmitted via radio signals **4.** TWO-WAY COMMUNICATION DEVICE an electronic device used to send and receive radio signals, used for two-way communication **5.** RADIO BROADCASTS sound broadcasts transmitted by means of radio waves **6.** BROADCASTING OF PROGRAMS BY RADIO the broadcasting by radio of programs for the public **7.** SOUND BROADCASTING radio broadcasting as an industry or profession ○ *She works in radio.* ■ *vti.* (**-oed, -o·ing, -os**) COMMUNICATE BY RADIO to communicate or send somebody a message by radio ■ *adj.* PHYS OF ELECTROMAGNETIC WAVES relating to electromagnetic waves or electromagnetic phenomena with frequencies between 10 kHz and 300,000 MHz [Early 20thC. Shortening of *radiotelegraph*.]

radio- *prefix.* **1.** radiation ○ *radiocarbon* **2.** radio ○ *radiolocation* [Shortening of words such as RADIATION and RADIOACTIVE]

ra·di·o·ac·tive /ràydi ō áktiv/ *adj.* **1.** EMITTING RADIATION used to describe a substance such as uranium or plutonium that emits energy in the form of streams of particles, owing to the decaying of its unstable atoms. This energy can be damaging or fatal to the health of people exposed to it. **2.** OF OR USING RADIOACTIVE SUBSTANCES relating to or making use of radioactive substances or the radiation they emit —**ra·di·o·ac·tive·ly** *adv.*

ra·di·o·ac·tive de·cay *n.* = **decay** *n.* 4

ra·di·o·ac·tive se·ries *n.* a series of related atom types (**nuclides**) of radioactive isotopes, each of which is transformed into the next by the emission of an elementary particle until a stable nuclide results. There are three such sequences, the thorium, the uranium-radium, and the actinium, and almost all naturally occurring radioactive isotopes belong to one of them.

ra·di·o·ac·tive trac·er *n.* a chemical substance that has a radioactive isotope attached, making it detectable when introduced into the body. Such tracers are used medically to diagnose diseases and biologically to study biochemical processes.

ra·di·o·ac·tive waste *n.* waste material that is radioactive, particularly the waste from nuclear reactors and medical treatment and research

ra·di·o·ac·tiv·i·ty /ràydi ō ak tívvətee/ *n.* **1.** RADIOACTIVE NATURE the radioactive nature of a substance such as uranium or plutonium **2.** RADIATION the high-energy particles emitted by radioactive substances

ra·di·o as·tron·o·my *n.* a branch of astronomy that deals with the detection and analysis of radio waves received from space —**ra·di·o as·tron·o·mer** *n.*

ra·di·o bea·con *n.* a fixed ground-based radio transmitter that sends out a distinctive signal to help aircraft and ships to identify their position

ra·di·o beam *n.* a beam of radio signals transmitted by a radio beacon for navigation purposes

ra·di·o·bi·ol·o·gy /ràydi ō bī óllәjee/ *n.* a branch of biology that deals with the effects of radiation on living tissues and organisms —**ra·di·o·bi·o·log·ic** /ràydi ō bī́ ə lójjik/ *adj.* —**ra·di·o·bi·o·log·i·cal** /-lójjik'l/ *adj.* —**ra·di·o·bi·o·log·i·cal·ly** /-ikəlee/ *adv.* —**ra·di·o·bi·ol·o·gist** /ràydi ō bī óllәjist/ *n.*

ra·di·o but·ton *n.* in a computer dialogue box, one of several circles or rectangles, each with text next to it, representing a fixed set of choices, one of which must be selected

ra·di·o car *n.* **1.** CAR WITH A TWO-WAY RADIO a car, especially a police car, equipped with a two-way radio **2.** VEHICLE FOR RADIO INTERVIEWS a vehicle from which radio broadcasts are made, especially interviews

ra·di·o·car·bon /ràydi ō kaárbən/ *n.* a radioactive form of carbon, especially the isotope of carbon that has a mass number of 14

ra·di·o·car·bon dat·ing *n.* = **carbon dating**

ra·di·o cas·sette, ra·di·o·cas·sette play·er *n.* a radio and a cassette player combined in a single, usually portable, machine

ra·di·o·chem·is·try /ràydi ō kémmistree/ *n.* a branch of chemistry that deals with radioactive elements and their applications —**ra·di·o·chem·i·cal** *adj.* —**ra·di·o·chem·i·cal·ly** *adv.* —**ra·di·o·chem·ist** *n.*

ra·di·o com·pass *n.* a navigation device that uses incoming radio signals from radio beacons to determine a ship's or aircraft's position

ra·di·o·con·trolled *adj.* used to describe a device whose operation or movement is controlled from a distance using a transmitter, often handheld, that sends radio signals to the device

ra·di·o·el·e·ment /ràydi ō élləmənt/ *n.* a chemical element that is radioactive

ra·di·o fre·quen·cy *n.* **1.** PHYS FREQUENCY USED FOR RADIO TRANSMISSIONS any one of the frequencies of electromagnetic radiation in the range between 10 Khz and 300 MHz, including those used for radio and television transmission **2.** BROADCAST RADIO STATION'S FREQUENCY a frequency on which a radio station broadcasts its programs

ra·di·o gal·ax·y *n.* a galaxy that is a strong source of radio waves

ra·di·o·ge·nic /ràydi ō jénnik/ *adj.* **1.** CREATED BY RADIOACTIVE DECAY used to describe a substance created as a result of the spontaneous decaying of the unstable atoms of another substance ○ *a radiogenic isotope* **2.** FROM RADIOACTIVE DECAY emitted as a result of radioactive decay ○ *radiogenic heat*

ra·di·o·gram /ráydi ō gràm/ *n.* **1.** TELECOM TELEGRAM a telegram sent by radio **2.** MED = **radiograph** *n.*

ra·di·o·graph /ráydi ō gràf/ *n.* X-RAY PHOTOGRAPH an image produced on film or another sensitive surface by radiation, e.g., X-rays or gamma rays, passing through an object ■ *vt.* (**-graphed, -graph·ing, -graphs**) TAKE X-RAY OF SOMETHING to make a radiograph of something, especially a part of the body —**ra·di·og·ra·pher** /ràydee óggrəfər/ *n.* —**ra·di·o·graph·ic** /raydiō gráfik/ *adj.* —**ra·di·o·graph·i·cal·ly** /-gráfiklee/ *adv.* —**ra·di·og·ra·phy** /raydee aágrəfee/ *n.*

ra·di·o·im·mu·no·as·say /ràydi ō ímmyənō á sày/ *n.* the technique of measuring the levels of antibodies in the blood by introducing into the bloodstream a substance that has a radioactive tracer attached to it —**ra·di·o·im·mu·no·as·say·a·ble** /ràydi ō ímmyənō á sày əb'l/ *adj.*

ra·di·o·i·o·dine /ráydi ō í ə dìn/ *n.* a radioactive form of iodine, often used in medicine as a tracer

ra·di·o·i·so·tope /ráydi ō íssə tōp/ *n.* a particular form of a chemical element (**isotope**) that is radioactive —**ra·di·o·i·so·top·ic** /ràydi ō íssə tóppik/ *adj.*

ra·di·o·la·bel /ràydi ō láyb'l/ *n.* RADIOACTIVE SUBSTANCE ATTACHED TO ANOTHER a radioactive substance attached to another substance as a means of tracing the location or tracking the movement of that substance. The technique is used in medicine, e.g., to monitor the distribution of a drug throughout the body. ■ *vt.* (**-labeled** *or* **-labelled, -labeling** *or* **-labelling, -labels**) TAG SUBSTANCE WITH A RADIOLABEL to attach a radiolabel to a substance —**ra·di·o·la·beled** *adj.* —**ra·di·o·la·bel·ing** *n.*

ra·di·o·lar·i·an /ràydi ō láiree ən/ *n.* a single-celled marine organism with a round silica-containing shell that has the organs of movement radiating around it. Amoebas are radiolarians. [Late 19thC. Formed from modern Latin *Radiolaria*, the class name, from *radiolus*, literally "little staff, stick," from *radius* (see RADIUS).]

ra·di·o·lo·ca·tion /ràydi ō lō káysh'n/ *n.* the use of radar to detect distant objects

ra·di·o spec·trum *n.* the range of radio frequencies used for radio, television, and other electromagnetic communications, between 10 Khz and 300 Mhz

ra·di·o tel·e·scope *n.* an astronomical instrument used to detect and analyze radio waves from celestial objects. It consists of an antenna, often in the form of a large dish, a detector, and an amplifier.

ra·di·o·tel·e·type /ràydi ō téllə tīp/ *n.* **1.** RADIO TELEPRINTER a teleprinter that transmits and receives by radio rather than along a cable **2.** RADIOTELETYPE SYSTEM a receiving and transmitting system that uses radioteletypes

ra·di·o·ther·a·py /ràydi ō thérrəpee/ *n.* the treatment of disease using radiation X-rays or beta rays directed at the body from an external source or emitted by radioactive materials placed within the body —**ra·di·o·ther·a·peu·tic** /ràydee ō thérə pyóotik/ *adj.* —**ra·di·o·ther·a·pist** /ràyddee ō thérrəpist/ *n.*

ra·di·o·tho·ri·um /ràydi ō tháwree əm/ *n.* a radioactive isotope of the element thorium, with a mass number of 228

ra·di·o·tox·ic /ràydi ō táwksik/ *adj.* relating to the toxic effects of radiation or radioactive substances

ra·di·o·trac·er /ràydi ō tráyssər/ *n.* a radioactive substance introduced into the body as a tracer, e.g., to observe the steps in a chemical or biochemical process or locate diseased cells or tissue

ra·di·o wave *n.* an electromagnetic wave whose frequency falls within the radio spectrum

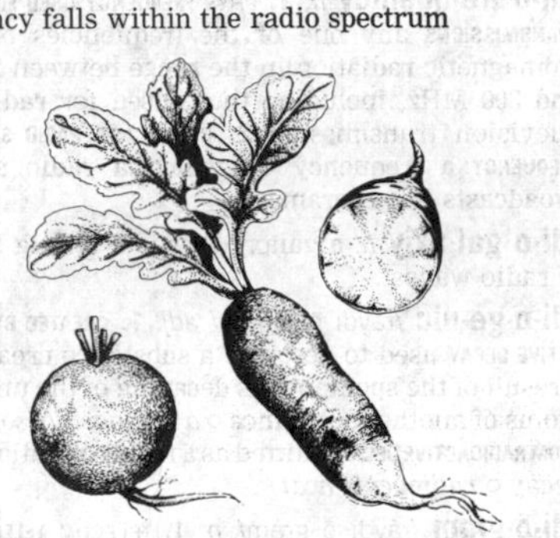

Radish

rad·ish /ráddish/ *n.* **1.** FOOD EDIBLE ROOT a crisp pungent root, usually white with a red skin, eaten raw **2.** PLANTS PLANT ON WHICH RADISHES GROW a Eurasian plant of the mustard family that has white to purple flowers and whose root is a radish. Latin name: *Raphanus sativus.* [Pre-12thC. Formed from Latin *radic-*, the stem of *radix* "root" (see RADIX), perhaps modeled on French *radis* "radish."]

Rad·is·son /ràddee sóN/, **Pierre Esprit** (1636?–1710?) French-born Canadian explorer and fur trader. He is noted for his knowledge of Native North American life and Canadian geography.

ra·di·um /ráydee əm/ *n.* a white highly radioactive metallic element found in minerals such as pitchblende and carnotite. It emits alpha particles as it decays to radon and is used in luminous coatings and the treatment of cancer. Symbol **Ra** [Late 19thC. Formed from Latin *radius* (see RADIUS), from the rays emitted by radium, which penetrate certain opaque materials.]

ra·di·um ther·a·py *n.* the medical use of radium to treat cancer and other diseases with radiation

ra·di·us /ráydee əss/ (*plural* **-i** /-dee ī/ *or* **-us·es**) *n.* **1.** GEOM LINE FROM CENTER a straight line extending from the center of a circle to its edge or from the center of a sphere to its surface. Symbol **r 2.** GEOM LENGTH OF RADIUS the length of a radius. Symbol **r 3.** CIRCULAR AREA an area enclosed by a circle that has a radius of a specified length ○ *all the houses within a radius of 2 miles of the explosion* **4.** RANGE OF EFFECTIVENESS OR INFLUENCE the area or range within which somebody or something can act, work, or exert influence effectively ○ *beyond the radius of the governor's influence* **5.** ANAT BONE IN ARM OR FORELIMB the shorter and thicker of the two bones in the human forearm, the one on the thumb side, or the equivalent bone in the lower forelimbs of animals **6.** RADIATING PART a radiating line, part, or structure [Late 16thC. From Latin, "staff, spoke, ray, beam of light" (source also of English *ray*[1]).]

ra·di·us of ac·tion *n.* **1.** MIL AREA OF OPERATION a broadly circular area in which a military unit can operate or bring force to bear on an enemy **2.** TRANSP DISTANCE FROM WHICH RETURN IS POSSIBLE the distance a vehicle, ship, or aircraft can go out to and return safely to base without refueling

ra·di·us of cur·va·ture *n.* the radius of the circle whose curvature matches that of a curve at a particular point

ra·di·us vec·tor *n.* **1.** MATH LINE JOINING POINTS a line connecting a fixed point or origin and a variable point, or the length of such a line **2.** ASTRON IMAGINARY LINE CONNECTING CELESTIAL BODIES a line connecting the center of a celestial body and the center of another in orbit around it

ra·dix /ráydiks, ráddiks/ (*plural* **rad·i·ces** /ràddi seéz, ràydi-/ *or* **ra·dix·es**) *n.* **1.** MATH BASE NUMBER the base of a number system or system of logarithms **2.** BIOL ROOT a root part or point where a plant or animal part begins [Late 16thC. From Latin, literally "root, radish, foundation." Ultimately from an Indo-European base that is also the ancestor of English *root* and *wort*.]

RADM, R.Adm. *abbr.* rear admiral

ra·dome /ráy dōm/ *n.* a dome-shaped protective enclosure for a radar antenna, made from materials that do not interfere with the transmission and reception of radio waves [Mid-20thC. Blend of RADAR and DOME.]

ra·don /ráy dawn/ *n.* a heavy gaseous radioactive chemical element formed from the decay of radium that is used in radiotherapy and found in small quantities in rock and soil. The radon in rock and soil accounts for most of normal background radiation. In heavier concentrations, however, sometimes detected inside homes, it is thought to pose a risk of cancer. Symbol **Rn** [Early 20thC. Coined from RADIUM + -ON.]

rad·u·la /rájjələ/ (*plural* **-lae** /rájjəlee/ *or* **-las**) *n.* a band of tissue in the mouth of some mollusks (**gastropods**) containing rows of small teeth, used in scraping off particles of food and bringing them into the mouth [Mid-18thC. From Latin, "scraper," from *radere* "to scrape" (source of English *abrade, erase, rail*, and *rash*).] —**rad·u·lar** *adj.*

rad·waste /rád wàyst/ *n.* radioactive waste (*informal*) [Late 20thC. Contraction of RADIOACTIVE WASTE.]

RAF, R.A.F. *abbr.* Royal Air Force

raf·fi·a /ráffiə/, **raphia** *n.* **1.** INDUST FIBER OF PALM TREE fiber in the form of flexible straw-colored ribbons obtained from the leaves of the raffia palm, used in making mats, baskets, and other products **2.** TREES = **raffia palm** [Late 19thC. From Malagasy *rafia*.]

raf·fi·a palm *n.* a palm tree that grows in Madagascar and has large leaves that yield a strong fiber used to make mats and baskets and other products. Latin name: *Raphia ruffia*.

raf·fi·nate /ráffə nayt/ *n.* the remaining or refined part of a liquid mixture, left after other substances dissolved in it have been extracted [Early 20thC. From French *raffinat*, from *raffiner* "to refine."]

raf·fi·nose /ráffə nōss, -nōz/ *n.* a white crystalline slightly sweet sugar present in many plant products and obtained commercially from cottonseed meal, sugar beet, and molasses. Formula: $C_{18}H_{32}O_{16}$. [Late 19thC. Coined from French *raffiner* (see RAFFINATE) + -OSE.]

raff·ish /ráffish/ *adj.* **1.** CHARMINGLY UNCONVENTIONAL OR DISREPUTABLE displaying a charming, free-spirited disregard for the conventions of society or for approved behavior ○ *a raffish politician whose engaging antics never alienated the voters* **2.** SHOWY displaying an exaggerated or obtrusive showiness ○ *a raffish hotel* [Early 19thC. Formed from earlier *raff* "common people," of unknown origin.] —**raff·ish·ly** *adv.* —**raff·ish·ness** *n.*

raf·fle[1] /ráff'l/ *n.* LOTTERY WITH OBJECTS AS PRIZES an event, usually held in order to raise money, in which numbered tickets are sold, some of which are drawn at random to win prizes. The prizes in a raffle are usually objects rather than money and raffles are usually held in order to raise money for some cause or organization. ■ *vt.* (**-fled, -fling, -fles**) AWARD SOMETHING IN RAFFLE to offer or give away something as a prize in a raffle [14thC. Via Old French, "act of plundering," of uncertain origin: perhaps from Middle Dutch *raffel* "game of dice," the original meaning in English.] —**raf·fler** /ráff'lər/ *n.*

raf·fle[2] /ráff'l/ *n.* **1.** TRASH unwanted items or debris **2.** NAUT TANGLE tangled ropes or other bits and pieces on a ship [Late 18thC. Origin uncertain: perhaps from Old French *ne rafle* "nothing at all."]

raf·fle·sia /rə fleézhee ə, ra-, rə fleézhə, ra-/ *n.* a leafless tropical Asian plant that is a parasite of other plants and has large foul-smelling flowers pollinated by carrion flies. One species has the largest flower of all plants, measuring up to 40 in./1 m across. Genus: *Rafflesia*. [Early 19thC. From modern Latin, genus name, named for Sir Stamford *Raffles*, (1781–1826), British colonial administrator in Southeast Asia, who obtained the type specimen.]

raft[1] /raft/ *n.* **1.** NAUT FLAT BOAT a flat floating structure made of wooden planks, logs, barrels, or similar materials, used as a boat or anchored in the water as a dock or diving platform **2.** LEISURE INFLATABLE BOAT OR MAT an inflatable flat-bottomed rubber or plastic boat used for drifting along on a river, or an inflatable rectangular mat used for surfing or lounging in the water **3.** COLLECTION OF FLOATING OBJECTS a group of animals, especially wildfowl, or a mass of things floating or traveling together on water ○ *a raft of ducks* ■ *v.* (**raft·ed, raft·ing, rafts**) **1.** *vt.* MOVE BY RAFT to transport something by raft **2.** *vi.* NAUT SAIL ON A RAFT to travel on a raft **3.** *vt.* FORM A RAFT to form something into a raft, or make something gather together into a raft ○ *The lumberjacks rafted the logs together before sending them downstream.* [13thC. From Old Norse *raptr* "log, beam."]

WORD KEY: CULTURAL NOTE

The Raft of the Medusa, a painting by French artist Théodore Géricault (1819). This monumental work is a harrowing depiction of the suffering of the survivors of an infamous 1816 shipwreck. Géricault's treatment of a contemporary subject in an epic style more traditionally associated with classical or historical themes was seen as a significant development in European art.

raft[2] /raft/ *n.* a very large number or amount of something (*informal*) ○ *a whole raft of proposals* [Mid-19thC. Alteration of earlier *raff*, probably modeled on RAFT[1].]

raf·ter[1] /ráftər/ *n.* any of the sloping supporting timbers, beams, or boards that run from the ridge beam of a roof to its edge [Old English *ræfter*, of prehistoric Germanic origin] —**raf·tered** *adj.* —**raf·ter·ing** *n.*

raft·er[2] /ráftər/ *n.* **1.** SOMEBODY WHO SAILS ON A RAFT somebody who travels on a raft **2.** MAKER OF A LOG RAFT a lumberjack who ties logs into a raft to transport them downstream

raft·ing /ráfting/ *n.* the outdoor leisure pursuit of floating on a lake or sailing on a river in a raft

rag[1] /rag/ *n.* **1.** SMALL PIECE OF CLOTH a small piece or scrap of usually old or unwanted cloth taken, e.g., from torn-up old clothing, often used for cleaning, polishing, or applying liquid substances **2.** SMALL TATTERED PIECE a small, irregular, or tattered scrap or piece of something **3.** PIECE OF CLOTHING an item of clothing, thought of as being worn or tattered and not really fit to wear (*informal*) (*often used ironically*) ○ *This? Oh, this is just some old rag I pulled out of the closet.* **4.** INFERIOR NEWSPAPER a newspaper with low journalistic standards, or any newspaper regarded with contempt (*informal, disapproving*) ○ *That rag prints nothing but lies and gossip.* **5.** CLOTH FOR PAPERMAKING cloth or cloth fibers that are used in making paper ■ **rags** *npl.* WORN-OUT CLOTHES clothes that are tattered, frayed, or torn [14thC. Origin uncertain: probably from assumed Old Norse *rogg* "shaggy tuft."] ◇ **go from rags to riches** to start off in poverty and then become very wealthy ◇ **in rags** in a worn-out, tattered, and torn condition

rag[2] /rag/ (**rag·ged, rag·ging, rags**) *v.* **1.** *vti.* TEASE OR TAUNT SOMEBODY to subject somebody to persistent teasing or taunting (*dated*) **2.** *vt.* SCOLD SOMEBODY to scold somebody persistently or vehemently [Mid-18thC. Origin unknown.] —**rag·ging** *n.*

rag[3] /rag/ (**ragged, ragging, rags**) *vt.* to compose or perform ragtime music [Late 19thC. Origin uncertain: perhaps a shortening of RAGGED, from the syncopation of the music.]

rag[4] /rag/ *n.* a roofing slate that has a rough surface on one side [13thC. Origin unknown.]

ra·ga /raágə/ *n.* any of a body of scales, melodies, or rhythmic patterns that form the basis of the classical music of the Indian subcontinent. Particular ragas are associated with different times of the day, and are intended to create different moods. Performances may be partly or completely improvised. [Late 18thC. From Sanskrit *rāga* "color, musical color, harmony."]

rag·a·muf·fin /rággə mùfən/ *n.* a child dressed in worn or tattered clothes, often one allowed to roam the streets (*dated*) [14thC. Origin uncertain: perhaps from RAG[1] + Middle Dutch *muffe*, *moffe* "mitten" (source of English *muff*).]

rag·bag /rág bàg/ *n.* **1.** MISCELLANY a collection of miscellaneous things (*informal*) **2.** BAG OF RAGS a bag in which unwanted clothes and bits of cloth are kept for use as rags

rag doll *n.* a floppy stuffed cloth doll

rage /rayj/ *n.* **1.** EXTREME ANGER sudden and extreme anger, or an outburst of strong anger **2.** OBJECT OF FAD something that is the object of a short-lived fascination, fashion, or enthusiasm shared by many people ○ *Those toys are all the rage for kids at the moment.* **3.** FORCE OR INTENSITY extreme or unrelenting intensity **4.** STRONG PASSION OR ENTHUSIASM a strong and sometimes overpowering desire or enthusiasm ■ *vi.* (**raged, rag·ing, rag·es**) **1.** ACT WITH OR FEEL RAGE to speak or do something with sudden, extreme anger, or feel such strong anger **2.** OCCUR WITH VIOLENCE to occur, continue, move, or spread with great force and violence ○ *The battle raged for three days.* [13thC. Via Old French, from Vulgar Latin *rabia*, an alteration of Latin *rabies* "fury" (see RABIES).]

WORD KEY: SYNONYMS

See Synonyms at ***anger***.

rag·fish (*plural* **-fish·es** *or* **-fish**) *n.* a scaleless deep-sea fish with a cartilaginous skeleton that makes it so flexible it flops like a rag when taken out of the water. Latin name: *Icosteus aenigmaticus.*

rag·ged /rággəd/ *adj.* **1.** TATTERED frayed or torn into irregular shapes or pieces, especially along the edge **2.** WITH UNEVEN EDGE OR SURFACE with a surface, edge, or outline that is rough, uneven, or jagged **3.** OF VARYING QUALITY of unequal quality, some parts being less good than others ○ *The acting in the play was rather ragged.* **4.** WEARING RAGS dressed in torn, tattered, or frayed clothes **5.** UNKEMPT rough and irregular in appearance and suggesting neglect and a lack of grooming ○ *a ragged beard* **6.** NOT FIRM OR REGULAR done in an uncoordinated, hesitant, or irregular way, especially by a group who do not manage to do something all together or in unison **7.** EXHAUSTED extremely tired or anxious [13thC. Formed from RAG[1].] —**rag·ged·ly** *adv.* —**rag·ged·ness** *n.*

rag·ged rob·in *n.* a perennial plant of the pink family that has narrow leaves and pink or, less commonly, white flowers with ragged lobed petals. Latin name: *Lychnis floscuculi.*

rag·ged·y /rággədee/ *adj.* (*informal*) **1.** TATTERED having been torn and worn excessively **2.** BADLY DRESSED wearing worn-out torn clothes **3.** ROUGH OR UNEVEN having rough untidy ends or edges

rag·gee *n.* = **ragi**

rag·gle-tag·gle /ràgg'l tágg'l, rágg'l tàg'l/ *adj.* consisting of a mixture of strange or very different kinds, often with an element of messiness or scruffiness [Early 20thC. Alteration of RAGTAG.]

ra·gi /rággee/, **rag·gee** *n.* **1.** CEREAL GRASS a cereal grass cultivated for its edible grain in southern Asia and parts of Africa. Latin name: *Eleusine coracana.* **2.** GRAIN USED AS FOOD the grain of ragi used as food [Late 18thC. From Hindi *rāgī*.]

rag·ing /rájing/ *adj.* **1.** VERY ANGRY out of control or angry **2.** VERY STRONG done or happening with great force or intensity **3.** VERY SEVERE OR PAINFUL very severe and causing great pain or distress ○ *a raging toothache* **4.** VERY GOOD very good or great ○ *The play was a raging success.*

rag·lan /rágglən/ *adj.* **1.** OF SLEEVE EXTENDING TO COLLAR used to describe a sleeve extending to the collar of a garment instead of ending at the shoulder, attached with slanting seams running from under the arm to the neck **2.** HAVING RAGLAN SLEEVES raglan sleeves ■ *n.* GARMENT WITH RAGLAN SLEEVES an overcoat, sweater, or other garment that has raglan sleeves [Mid-19thC. Named for Field Marshal Lord *Raglan* (1788–1855), British soldier, who favored overcoats in this style.]

Rag·na·rök /raágnə ràwk/ *n.* in Norse mythology, the final destruction of the gods in a great battle against the forces of evil, after which a new world will arise [Mid-18thC. From Old Norse *ragnarök*, literally "fate of the gods," from *regin* "gods" + *rok* "fate."]

ra·gout /ra gōo/ *n.* a rich slow-cooked stew of meat and vegetables [Mid-17thC. From French, from *ragoûter* "to renew the appetite," from *goût* "taste," from Latin *gustus* (source of English *disgust* and *gusto*).]

rag·pick·er /rág pìkər/ *n.* somebody who makes money by collecting old clothes and other discarded items and selling them

rag rug *n.* a rug made by knotting or hooking short strips of waste fabric through an openweave base to form a shaggy pile

rag·stone /rág stōn/ *n.* a hard sandstone or limestone that tends to break up into slabs and is used as a building material

rag·tag /rág tàg/ *adj.* **1.** MIXED AND QUESTIONABLE made up of a wide-ranging mix of people or things, often ones that are of questionable quality (*disapproving*) ○ *a ragtag team of strangers who felt like playing* **2.** MESSY messy, unkempt, or ragged in appearance [Late 19thC. From RAG[1].]

rag·tag and bob·tail *n.* people who are members of the lowest social classes, especially when considered as dissatisfied with their lives and likely to be disorderly or rebellious (*dated insult*)

rag·time /rág tīm/ *n.* a style of U.S. popular music of the late 19th and early 20th centuries characterized by distinctive syncopated right-hand rhythms against a regularly accented left-hand beat. Ragtime was widely popularized by the pianist and composer Scott Joplin.

rag·top /ràg táwp/ *n.* a car with a retractable fabric roof (*slang*)

rag trade *n.* the clothing industry and the various professions involved in the design, manufacture, and sale of clothing (*slang*)

rag·weed /rág weed/ *n.* **1.** PLANT CAUSING HAY FEVER a weedy, chiefly North American plant that has small green flower heads and large amounts of pollen that is a cause of hay fever in many people. Genus: *Ambrosia.* **2.** *U.K.* = **ragwort** [From the raggedness of the leaves]

rag·worm /rág wùrm/ *n. U.K.* = **clamworm** [From the ragged appearance of its appendages]

rag·wort /rág wùrt, -wàwrt/ *n.* a plant with clusters of small yellow flowers with radiating petals like daisies. Genus: *Senecio.* [From the raggedness of the leaves]

rah /raa/ *interj.* used to express approval or encouragement (*informal*) [Mid-19thC. Shortening of HURRAH.]

Rah·man /rəmaán/, **Sheikh Mujibur** (1920–75) Bangladesh statesman. The founding father of Bangladesh, he served as the country's first prime minister (1972–75). Soon after becoming president (1975), he was assassinated.

Rah·man, Ziaur (1935–81) Bangladesh statesman. As president of Bangladesh (1977–81), he ended martial law but was assassinated in an attempted military coup.

rah-rah /raá raa/ *adj.* spiritedly and often unthinkingly enthusiastic (*slang*) ○ *the rah-rah attitude of the project's supporters*

raid /rayd/ *n.* **1.** SUDDEN ATTACK a sudden attack made by soldiers, aircraft, police, bandits, or any other force in an attempt to seize or destroy something **2.** BUSINESS LURING PEOPLE AWAY in the business world, an attempt by an organization to hire or lure away a competitor's employees, members, or clients ○ *a raid by one advertising agency on another's clients* **3.** STOCK EXCH ATTEMPT TO BUY CONTROL the buying of shares of a company's stock in an attempt to gain control of the company ○ *The company beat off the raid but took on debt to buy its own stock.* **4.** STOCK EXCH ILLEGAL ATTEMPT TO LOWER STOCK PRICE the illegal coordinated selling of shares in a company's stock by a group of speculators in an attempt to make the stock price fall ■ *v.* (**raid·ed, raid·ing, raids**) **1.** *vti.* MAKE SURPRISE ATTACK to make or participate in a raid on somebody or something **2.** *vt.* STEAL SOMETHING FROM SOMEWHERE to take something secretly or stealthily because it is illegal or forbidden ○ *The bank's funds had been raided by its former president.* **3.** *vt.* BUSINESS LURE SOMEBODY AWAY to lure somebody away from another organization, usually from a competitor ○ *The new league began to raid players from its rival.* [15thC. Scots dialect form of Old English *rād* "expedition, riding, road" (source of English *road*).] —**raid·er** *n.*

rail[1] /rayl/ *n.* **1.** LONG PIECE OF WOOD OR METAL a long horizontal or sloping piece of wood, metal, or other material that is used as a barrier, support, or place to hang things **2.** FENCE OR RAILING a structure made of a rail or rails and their supports, e.g., a fence or railing (*often used in the plural*) **3.** STEEL BAR OF RAILROAD TRACK a narrow steel bar, or a series of connected bars laid in two parallel lines, supporting and guiding the wheels of railroad locomotives and cars or anything similar. ◊ **third rail 4.** TRANSP RAILROAD the railroad as a means or form of transportation ○ *We'll ship the goods by rail.* ○ *rail travel* ■ *vt.* (**railed, rail·ing, rails**) PUT RAIL ON OR AROUND SOMETHING to put a rail or railing on or around something to provide a guard, barrier, or support ○ *They ought to rail off the playground.* [13thC. Via Old French *reille* "bar" from Latin *regula* "straight stick, rod" (source also of English *rule*). Ultimately from a Latin base that also produced English *regal* and *royal*.] —**rail·less** /ráyl liss/ *adj.* ◇ **go off the rails 1.** to begin to go wrong and lose direction **2.** to begin to behave in an unacceptable, irresponsible, or illegal way

rail[2] /rayl/ (**railed, rail·ing, rails**) *vi.* to denounce, protest against, or attack somebody or something in bitter or harsh language ○ *Some people rail against the injustice of the system.* [15thC. Via French *railler* "to mock, tease" from Old Provençal *ralhar* "to chat, joke," from, ultimately, late Latin *ragere* "to neigh, roar."] —**rail·er** *n.*

rail[3] /rayl/ (*plural* **rails** *or* **rail**) *n.* a small or medium-sized bird with a short tail, short wings, long legs, and long toes. Rails are usually found near water or marshy ground. Family: Rallidae. [15thC. Via Old French *raale* from, ultimately, assumed Vulgar Latin *rasclare*, *rasiculare* "to scrape" (from the bird's harsh-sounding call), from Latin *ras-*, the past participle stem of *radere* (see RADULA).]

rail·bird /ráyl bùrd/ *n.* an enthusiastic fan of a sport, especially a horseracing fan who stands at the fence bordering the track in order to get close to the action (*slang*) [Late 19thC. Humorously from RAIL[1] "fence bounding a racetrack," modeled on JAILBIRD.]

rail·car /ráyl kaar/ *n.* a railroad car

rail fence *n.* a fence made of split logs, either fastened to upright poles or else laid across each other

rail·head /ráyl hèd/ *n.* **1.** END OF RAILROAD LINE the farthest point to which the track of a railroad line runs **2.** DISTRIBUTION POINT FOR RAILROAD a place where supplies, often military materials, are unloaded from railcars for distribution to other points

rail·ing /ráyling/ *n.* **1.** STRUCTURE WITH RAILS AND POSTS a structure consisting of one or more rails and their supports, used to provide a barrier or support in walking or climbing, or the upper rail of such a structure **2.** RAILS rails for making a railing

rail·ler·y /ráyləree/ (*plural* **-ies**) *n.* **1.** GOOD-HUMORED TEASING humorous, playful, or friendly ridiculing of somebody or something **2.** JOKING REMARK a remark that ridicules somebody or something jokingly and with good humor

rail·link /ráyl lingk/ *n.* a short connecting rail line, usually between a city center and an airport

rail·road /ráyl rōd/ *n.* **1.** TRACK MADE OF RAILS a track consisting of steel rails usually fastened to wood or concrete ties, designed to carry a locomotive and its cars or anything similar **2.** RAIL SYSTEM a network of railroad lines, together with the trains, buildings, equipment, and staff needed to operate a rail transport system, or the organization or company that owns or runs this ■ *v.* (**-road·ed, -road·ing, -roads**) **1.** *vt.* FORCE SOMETHING THROUGH QUICKLY WITHOUT DISCUSSION to push something through a legislature, committee, or other decision-making body quickly so that there is not enough time for objections to be considered **2.** *vt.* FORCE SOMEBODY TO ACT HASTILY to force a person or group to make a decision or take action quickly, without time for consideration or discussion (*informal*) **3.** *vt.* CONVICT SOMEBODY TOO QUICKLY to convict somebody on the basis of flimsy or false evidence (*informal*) **4.** *vt.* TRANSP SHIP SOMETHING BY RAIL to transport or send something by rail **5.** *vi.* WORK ON RAILROAD to work on a railroad ○ *She used to railroad for the Southern Pacific.* —**rail·road·er** *n.*

rail·road flat *n.* an apartment that has its rooms arranged in a straight line, often also lacking a hallway, so that one room can only be entered through another

rail·road·ing /ráyl rōding/ *n.* constructing a railroad line, or operating or managing it

rail·split·ter *n.* a person who or device that splits logs to make rails and posts for use in fences

rail·way /ráyl wày/ *n.* **1.** *U.K.* = **railroad 2.** LIGHT RAIL SYSTEM a railroad system, especially one that uses lighter-weight equipment and operates in a limited area

rai·ment /ráymənt/ *n.* clothing (*formal*) [14thC. Shortening of *arrayment*.]

rain /rayn/ *n.* **1.** WATER FALLING FROM CLOUDS water condensed from vapor in the atmosphere and falling in drops from clouds **2.** PERIOD OF WET WEATHER any storm, shower, or other quantity of water falling from the sky **3.** RAINY WEATHER weather marked by heavy or persistent rainfall **4.** GREAT NUMBER OR FLOW a great number of small individual things coming in a steady flow or anything else flowing or falling like rain ○ *A rain of dust fell from the crumbling ceiling.* ■ **rains** *npl.* RAINY SEASON in some countries, a season of the year when a lot of rain falls ■ *v.* **(rained, rain·ing, rains) 1.** *vi.* DROP RAIN to fall from the sky or release water in the form of rain ○ *It's raining again.* **2.** *vti.* COME IN A GREAT NUMBER to come or fall, or drop or deliver something, in the form of a great number of units arriving separately but in very quick succession, or in a continuous stream ○ *They rained blows on the poor man's head.* ○ *Missiles rained down on us from the defenders on the battlements.* **3.** *vt.* GIVE GENEROUSLY to give somebody something in large quantities, continuously, and over a considerable period of time ○ *Generous to a fault, they positively rained gifts on all their friends.* [Old English *regn, rēn*, of prehistoric Germanic origin] —**rain·less** *adj.* ◇ **rain or shine, come rain or shine, come rain or come shine** whatever the weather or the circumstances ○ *The picnic will be held, rain or shine.* ◇ **(as) right as rain** perfectly all right (*informal*)

rain out *vt.* to cause something such as a game to be canceled or postponed because of rain

rain·bird /ráyn bùrd/ *n.* a bird, e.g., the green woodpecker or certain members of the cuckoo family, thought to call before rainstorms

rain·bow /ráyn bō/ *n.* **1.** MULTICOLORED ARC IN SKY an arc of light separated into bands of color that appears when the sun's rays are refracted and reflected by drops of mist or rain. The colors of the rainbow are conventionally said to be red, orange, yellow, green, blue, indigo, and violet. **2.** ARC OF BANDS OF COLOR a multicolored arc similar to a rainbow **3.** BRIGHT MULTICOLORED SIGHT an arrangement, display, or sight containing many bright colors or bright multicolored objects ○ *the rainbow of colors on an artist's palette* **4.** FALSE HOPE a goal, hope, or ideal that is unlikely to be achieved or realized **5.** VARIED ASSORTMENT a wide range or varied assortment of things, usually coexisting without clashing ■ *adj.* **1.** WITH VARIED COLORS having the colors of the rainbow or colors as varied as those of a rainbow **2.** WITH MANY DIFFERENT THINGS comprising a wide variety of types or elements, especially made up of people of different ethnic groups or from a variety of minority groups ○ *a rainbow coalition*

WORD KEY: CULTURAL NOTE

The Rainbow, a novel by English writer D. H. Lawrence (1915). Set in the English Midlands between 1840 and 1905, it describes the impact of contemporary social developments on the lifestyles and attitudes of succeeding generations of a provincial family, the Brangwens. The latter part of the book focuses on Ursula, the family's first independent woman, whose story is continued in a subsequent novel *Women in Love* (1920).

rain·bow cac·tus *n.* either of two varieties of cactus found in the southwestern United States and Mexico, with yellow or magenta flowers. Latin name: *Echinocereus pectinatus.*

rain·bow curve *n.* a curveball with an exceptionally great arc

rain·bow fish *n.* a brightly colored fish such as the guppy or parrot fish

rain·bow run·ner *n.* a large colorful fish found in tropical Indian and Pacific waters. Latin name: *Elagatis bipinnulatus.*

rain·bow trout *n.* a freshwater food and game fish, originally from North America, with a reddish or pinkish band along either side of its body and numerous black spots. Latin name: *Salmo gairdneri.*

rain check *n.* **1.** TICKET FOR RESCHEDULED EVENT a ticket or ticket stub entitling somebody to attend an event canceled because of rain at a later rescheduled time **2.** GUARANTEE OF OFFER a promise or coupon guaranteeing that an offer that cannot be fulfilled or accepted at present will be fulfilled or accepted at a later time ◇ **take a rain check (on something)** to delay doing something until a later date or time (*informal*)

rain·coat /ráyn kōt/ *n.* a coat designed to keep the wearer dry when worn in the rain, with a water-resistant or waterproof surface or coating

rain date *n.* a date that an event will be rescheduled to if rainy weather forces cancellation on the intended date

rain·fall /ràyn fáwl/ *n.* **1.** AMOUNT OF RAIN FALLEN OVER TIME the amount of rain that falls in a particular location over a particular period of time ○ *the annual rainfall in a city* **2.** OCCURRENCE OF RAIN a rain shower or rainstorm

rain for·est *n.* a thick evergreen tropical forest found in areas of heavy rainfall and containing trees with broad leaves that form a continuous canopy

rain gauge *n.* a device used to measure the amount of rain that falls in a particular location

Rai·ni·er III /ráynee āy/, **Prince of Monaco** (*b.* 1923). He acceded to the throne in 1949, and in 1962 agreed to a new constitution reducing the power of the monarchy.

Rai·nier, Mount /rə néer, ray néer, ráy nir/ the highest peak in Washington State. It is a dormant volcano, with a permanently snow-covered summit. Height: 14,410 ft./4,393 m.

rain lil·y *n.* = **zephyr lily**

rain·mak·er /ráyn màykər/ *n.* **1.** ACHIEVER somebody who achieves outstanding results in business or politics (*informal*) **2.** SOMEBODY WHO CAUSES RAIN somebody who causes rain to fall, e.g., by seeding clouds with chemicals such as silver iodide, or who is believed to do so by magic —**rain·mak·ing** *n.*

rain·out /ráyn òwt/ *n.* an event that is canceled or postponed because of rainy weather, or the cancellation or postponement of an event because of rain ○ *The second game of today's doubleheader is a makeup for a March rainout.*

rain·proof /ráyn proof/ *adj.* IMPERVIOUS TO RAIN designed or treated to prevent rain from soaking into it or passing through it ■ *vt.* **(-proofed, -proof·ing, -proofs)** MAKE SOMETHING IMPERVIOUS TO RAIN to treat something such as an item of clothing so that it becomes rainproof

rain shad·ow *n.* an area on the side of a mountain barrier that is sheltered from prevailing winds and rain-bearing clouds, resulting in relatively dry conditions

rain·spout /ráyn spòwt/ *n.* *Northeast U.S.* a roof gutter or downspout

rain·squall /ráyn skwàwl/ *n.* a sudden, brief storm of strong winds and heavy rain

rain·storm /ráyn stàwrm/ *n.* a storm with heavy or steady rain

rain·wash /ráyn wàwsh/ *n.* rock and soil washed away and deposited elsewhere by rainwater, or the process of erosion by rainwater

rain·wa·ter /ráyn wàwtər/ *n.* water that has fallen as rain, which usually has relatively small amounts of minerals dissolved in it

rain·wear /ráyn wàir/ *n.* clothing, mainly outerwear, that is waterproof and is designed to keep the wearer dry in rainy weather

rain·y /ráynee/ **(-i·er, -i·est)** *adj.* characterized by or bringing rain, especially long or frequently recurring periods of rainfall —**rain·i·ly** *adv.* —**rain·i·ness** *n.*

rain·y day *n.* a possible time of need in the future

raise /rayz/ *v.* **(raised, rais·ing, rais·es) 1.** *vt.* MOVE SOMETHING HIGHER to cause somebody or something to move upward or to a higher level or position ○ *She was too weak to raise her head from the pillow.* **2.** *vt.* ACT AS PARENT OR GUARDIAN TO to look after somebody as or like a parent, while he or she is growing up (*often passive*) ○ *After my parents died, I was raised by my grandfather.* **3.** *vt.* MAKE LARGER OR MORE to increase something in size, amount, value, or scope ○ *They've raised the ticket prices yet again.* **4.** *vt.* AGRIC, GARDENING GROW OR BREED to grow vegetables or breed and care for animals, usually for profit or personal satisfaction **5.** *vt.* CONSTR PUT SOMETHING UP to set up, erect, or build something **6.** *vt.* CAUSE TO SWELL UP to make something rise up or swell up, e.g., on somebody's skin **7.** *vt.* INCREASE SOMETHING to increase something in degree, strength, or pitch ○ *raised voices* **8.** *vt.* OFFER SOMETHING FOR CONSIDERATION to put something forward for consideration or discussion ○ *I'd like to raise a number of points that I think need clarification.* **9.** *vt.* START SOMETHING NOISY to start something that involves a lot of loud noise or boisterous activity ○ *Raise the alarm!* **10.** *vt.* DIRECT AT HIGHER ANGLE to direct something upward, or make something point at a higher angle ○ *She answered without raising her eyes from the book.* **11.** *vt.* STAND OR SIT UP to move yourself or somebody else to a standing or sitting position **12.** *vt.* COLLECT TOGETHER to gather something together, collect something, or ask for something and be given it ○ *raising money for the local orphanage* **13.** *vt.* MATH MULTIPLY NUMBER to multiply a term or number by itself a specified number of times ○ *2 raised by the power of 4 is 16.* **14.** *vti.* CARDS INCREASE BET OR BID in poker and other games, to increase a bet or bet more than another player, often specifying the amount of the increase, or, in bridge, to increase a partner's bid **15.** *vt.* INCREASE PARTNER'S BID in bridge, to make a higher bid in the suit bid by your partner **16.** *vt.* COMMUNICATION CONTACT SOMEBODY BY RADIO to get into contact with somebody by radio ○ *The carrier tried to raise the overdue plane.* **17.** *vt.* ROUSE SOMEBODY to rouse somebody from sleep, or bring a dead person back to life ○ *They were shouting loud enough to raise the dead.* **18.** *vt.* MIL END SIEGE to end a siege by withdrawing the besieging force or forcing it to withdraw **19.** *vt.* END SOMETHING to bring a ban or restriction imposed on somebody to an end ○ *finally raised the arms embargo* **20.** *vt.* IMPROVE to make something better in some way ○ *Their visit raised his spirits.* **21.** *vt.* IMPROVE CONDITION to improve somebody's situation or condition, or move somebody to a higher rank or status ○ *After three years, he was raised to the rank of sergeant.* **22.** *vt.* CAUSE to cause something to appear, arise, form, or occur ○ *The strict new rules raised a storm of protest.* **23.** *vt.* GIVE SIGN OF FEELING to produce a response such as a smile or cheer, or cause somebody else to produce one ○ *She obviously felt awful, but still managed to raise a faint smile.* **24.** *vt.* PARANORMAL CALL SOMETHING UP to attempt to cause a supernatural being to appear, e.g., by special ceremonies or magic **25.** *vt.* PUT SOMEBODY IN AUTHORITY to place somebody in a position of power or authority (*literary*) **26.** *vt.* STRETCH SOMETHING OUT to make something such as a crest or frill stretch out and become more visible **27.** *vt.* NAUT SEE LAND APPEAR ON HORIZON to have approached near enough to land after a sea voyage for it to make its first appearance on the horizon ○ *The ship raised Bermuda two days after leaving New York.* **28.** *vt.* FIN FRAUDULENTLY INCREASE VALUE to increase the face value of something, especially a check, in an attempt to defraud somebody ○ *The embezzler was caught raising checks.* **29.** *vt.* COOK MAKE DOUGH RISE to make dough rise and swell by using yeast or a similar agent **30.** *vt.* PHON REPLACE BY HIGHER VOWEL to replace a vowel by one formed with the tongue higher in the mouth **31.** *vi.* RISE to rise (*nonstandard*) ○ *"Jimmy gazed at her in such consternation that he felt his hair begin to raise!"* (George Randolph Chester, *The Jingo*; 1912) ■ *n.* **1.** *Aus, Can, U.S.* PAY INCREASE a pay increase **2.** ACT OF INCREASING the raising of somebody or something, or the amount by which somebody or something is raised, e.g., in cards [12thC. From Old Norse *reisa*. Ultimately from a prehistoric Germanic base that also produced English *rise* and the verb *rear*.] —**rais·a·ble** *adj.* —**rais·er** *n.*

WORD KEY: SYNONYMS

raise, elevate, lift, hoist

CORE MEANING: to place something in a higher position

raise to move something to a higher position, usually by means of physical effort. It does not suggest great physical effort; **elevate** a formal word meaning the same as "raise"; **lift** to raise something either by means of physical effort or using a mechanism; **hoist** to raise something by mechanical means, sometimes by heavy manual effort.

---

raised /rayzd/ *adj.* made so that its surface is higher than its background or what surrounds it ○ *raised lettering on an envelope*

raised beach *n.* a former beach found above the present shoreline of a sea or lake following a fall in water level or a rise in land level. Raised beaches are common in areas once glaciated, which rise as the land surface readjusts to the removal of the weight of a former icecap.

raised point *n.* **1.** EMBROIDERY STITCH a large half cross-stitch used in embroidery **2.** EMBROIDERY embroidery done with gros point

raised work *n.* embroidery stitches that produce a raised surface on the fabric or that are worked over a piece of padding

rai·sin /ráyz'n/ *n.* a sweet grape that has been dried in the sun or by being processed with heat, usually to prevent spoiling and permit long-term storage [14thC. Via French, "grape," from Latin *racemus* "bunch, cluster" (source also of English *raceme*).]

rai·son d'é·tat /rà zawn dat táa/ (*plural* **rai·sons d'é·tat**) *n.* an overriding concern, usually the interests of the country concerned, that justifies political or diplomatic action that might otherwise be considered reprehensible [From French, literally "reason of state"]

rai·son d'ê·tre /rà zawn déttrə/ (*plural* **rai·sons d'ê·tre**) *n.* something that gives meaning or purpose to somebody's life, or the justification for something's existence [From French, literally "reason for being"]

Raj /raaj/ *n.* the British rule of the Indian subcontinent, now the countries of India, Pakistan, and Bangladesh, from 1757 to 1947 [Late 18thC. Via Hindi *rāj* from Sanskrit *rājya* "kingdom, rule." Ultimately from an Indo-European base that is also the ancestor of English *regal*, *rich*, and *rule* and German *Reich* "empire."]

Raj·ab /rújjəb/ *n.* in the Islamic calendar, the seventh month of the year, made up of 30 days [Late 18thC. From Arabic.]

ra·jah /ráajə/, **ra·ja** *n.* a king, prince, or chief in India or among the Malays, Javanese, and other peoples of Southeast Asia [Mid-16thC. Via Hindi *rājā* from Sanskrit *rājan* "king," from the same base as produced English *Raj*.]

Ra·ja·sthan /ráajə staán/, **Rā·ja·sthān** state in northwestern India, bordering Pakistan. Capital: Jaipur. Population: 48,040,000 (1994). Area: 132,139 sq. mi./342,239 sq. km.

Ra·jas·tha·ni /ráajə staánee/ *n.* **1.** INDIAN LANGUAGE a group of Indic languages spoken in northwestern India and neighboring parts of Pakistan that form a subgroup of the Indo-Iranian branch of Indo-European languages. About 25 million people speak one of the Rajasthani languages. **2.** SOMEBODY FROM RAJASTHAN somebody who lives in or was born or raised in Rajasthan [Early 20thC. From Hindi, from *Rajasthan*, state in northwestern India.] —**Ra·jas·tha·ni** *adj.*

Raj·kot /ráaj kōt/ city and administrative headquarters of Rajkot District, in Gujarat State, west central India. Population: 556,137 (1991).

Raj·neesh /ráaj néesh/, **Bhaghwan Shree** (1931–90) Indian spiritual teacher. As founder of the Neo-Sannyas Movement in the late 1960s, he established meditation centers in India, Europe, and the United States. Real name **Rajneesh Chandra Mohan**

Raj·put /ráaj pōot/ *n.* a Hindu belonging to a fierce warrior caste, the second-highest caste after the Brahmins. Many kings and princes were Rajputs. [Late 16thC. From Hindi *rājpūt*, literally "king's son," from Sanskrit *rājan* "king" + *putra* "son."]

Ra·kai·a /rə kī́ ə/ river in the South Island, New Zealand. It rises in the Southern Alps and flows into the Pacific Ocean west of the Banks Peninsula. Length: 90 mi./145 km.

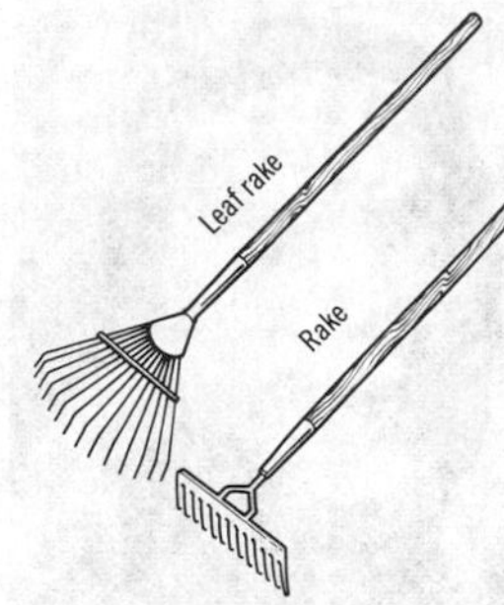

Rake

rake[1] /rayk/ *n.* **1.** GARDENING LONG-HANDLED TOOTHED GARDENING TOOL a tool with a long handle and a head with long teeth, used for gathering leaves or cut grass or for smoothing or loosening the surface of the soil **2.** TOOL RESEMBLING A GARDEN RAKE any tool that is broadly similar to a garden rake but is used for a different purpose, e.g., digging clams or gathering money at a gambling table ■ *v.* (**raked, rak·ing, rakes**) **1.** *vti.* MOVE WITH A RAKE to gather something together, remove, or clear something using a rake or similar implement ○ *raked up the dead leaves* **2.** *vti.* GARDENING WORK WITH A RAKE to make something neat, smooth it out, or loosen it using a rake or similar tool **3.** *vti.* SEARCH to search through or examine something thoroughly, or to make a search for something **4.** *vt.* USE SOMETHING LIKE A RAKE to draw or move something through or across something else like a rake ○ *She raked her fingers through her hair.* **5.** *vti.* SCRAPE OR SCRATCH SOMETHING to claw, scrape, or scratch somebody or something with a dragging movement like a rake ○ *The cat raked his arm with her claws.* **6.** *vti.* PASS ACROSS SOMETHING to pass across the whole length or extent of something in a continuous sweeping movement, or cause something to do this ○ *The spotlight raked around the perimeter fence.* **7.** *vti.* SHOOT ALONG THE LENGTH OF SOMETHING to aim shots from a gun or guns in quick succession over the whole length or extent of something ○ *The ship's cannon raked the land battery.* [Old English *raca*, racu. Perhaps ultimately from an Indo-European base meaning "to direct" (ancestor of English *regal*, *rich*, and *rule*), in which case the underlying idea is "stretching out, collecting."] ◇ **rake somebody over the coals** to reprimand somebody severely

rake in *vt.* to take in large quantities of something, especially money gained or earned with relatively little effort (*informal*)

rake together *vt.* to gather people or things together with difficulty (*informal*)

rake up *vt.* (*informal*) **1.** BRING SOMETHING TO MIND to mention or bring up for discussion something unfortunate or undesirable that happened in the past **2.** = **rake together**

rake[2] /rayk/ *n.* somebody who indulges without restraint in physical pleasures and vices such as drinking and gambling [Mid-17thC. Shortening of RAKEHELL.]

WORD KEY: CULTURAL NOTE

The Rake's Progress, a series of paintings by English artist William Hogarth (1735?). These eight satirical scenes, which were much influenced by contemporary theater, depict the moral decline of a young city gentleman who inherits a fortune and squanders it on vice. Hogarth created engravings of the same images, which were immensely popular. In 1951, Stravinsky turned the story into an opera with a libretto by W.H. Auden.

---

rake[3] /rayk/ *n.* **1.** NAUT SLANT OR SLOPE a slant away from an upright or perpendicular position, or an incline upward from a flat or horizontal position such as that on a ship or a stage **2.** AEROSP ANGLE OF A WING OR PROPELLER the angle that a wing or propeller blade of an aircraft makes with a perpendicular or line of symmetry ■ *vti.* (**raked, raked, rak·ing, rakes**) ANGLE to design or build something, or be designed or built, with a slant or slope away from the vertical or horizontal ○ *a jet with wings that rake sharply back* [Early 17thC. Origin unknown.]

rake·hell /rák hèl/ *n.* somebody who indulges without restraint in physical pleasures and vices such as drinking and gambling (*archaic*) [Mid-16thC. By folk etymology from Middle English *rakel* "hasty, rash" (of unknown origin), by association with RAKE[1] and HELL.]

rake-off *n.* a portion or share of a profit, fee, or something similar, especially as a bribe or other illegal or morally dubious payment (*informal*)

rak·i /raákee, ráykee/ *n.* any of various alcoholic drinks from the eastern Mediterranean, especially a brandy made in Turkey and the Balkans from grapes, plums, or grain and flavored with anise [Late 17thC. Via Turkish *rāqī* from Arabic *araḳī*.]

rak·ish[1] /ráykish/ *adj.* **1.** DASHINGLY STYLISH stylish in a dashing or sporty way ○ *a hat worn at a rakish angle* **2.** NAUT MAKING A BOAT LOOK FAST having a streamlined look that suggests rapid movement through the water ○ *a rakish yacht* [Early 19thC. Formed from RAKE[3].] —**rak·ish·ly** *adv.* —**rak·ish·ness** *n.*

rak·ish[2] /ráykish/ *adj.* having or showing a strong concern for presenting a stylish self-confident appearance [Early 18thC. Formed from RAKE[2].] —**rak·ish·ly** *adv.* —**rak·ish·ness** *adv.*

ra·ku *n.* a pottery technique in which pots are raw-glazed at a low temperature then taken red-hot from the kiln and plunged in water or sawdust for reduction or carbonizing [Late 19thC. From Japanese, literally "ease, enjoyment."]

rale /raal, ral/, **râle** *n.* a symptomatic intermittent crackling or bubbling sound produced by the lungs and heard via a stethoscope. It indicates fluid in the air passages and air sacs. [Early 19thC. From French *râle*, from *râler* "to make a rattling sound in the throat," of uncertain origin: probably from assumed Vulgar Latin *rasclare* "to scrape" (see RAIL[3]).]

Ra·leigh /ráwlee, raá-/ capital city of North Carolina, located in the center of the state. Population: 236,707 (1994).

Ra·leigh, Sir Walter (1554–1618) English navigator and writer. A favorite of Queen Elizabeth I, he led three expeditions to the Americas, founding the first English settlement in North America at Jamestown, Virginia (1585). He wrote his *History of the World* (1614) while imprisoned for treason (1603–13).

rall. *abbr.* MUSIC rallentando

ral·len·tan·do /ràllən tán dō, raàlən taán dō/ *adv.* MUSIC with a gradual slowing of pace (*used as a musical direction*) [Early 19thC. From Italian, the present participle of *rallentare* "to slow down."]

ral·ly[1] /rállee/ *n.* (*plural* **-lies**) **1.** RECOVERY OR IMPROVEMENT a sudden recovery or improvement after a setback, crisis, or period of illness, inactivity, or deterioration **2.** GATHERING a large meeting or gathering of people, usually organized by a movement or political party and intended to inspire and generate enthusiasm among those present **3.** STOCK EXCH RENEWED BUYING OF STOCKS a renewed buying of stocks after a period of selling, leading to a rise in stock prices ○ *a rally in the industrial sector of the stock market* **4.** MOTOR SPORTS AUTOMOBILE RACE an automobile race that is held on public roads using a route not known in advance by the drivers and having special rules for speed or time **5.** RACKET GAMES EXCHANGE OF SHOTS in tennis and other racket sports, an exchange of several shots between two opponents or sides before a point is scored **6.** MIL REASSEMBLY OF TROOPS a regrouping of a disorganized military force and the reestablishment of command over it, or the signal calling for this ○ *The retreating hussars made a rally and drove the attackers back.* ■ *v.* (**-lied, -ly·ing, -lies**) **1.** *vti.* GATHER TOGETHER FOR SOMETHING to come together, uniting for a common purpose or in a common cause, or to call on people to come together and unite **2.** *vti.* REVIVE OR RECOVER to recover or improve after a setback, crisis, or period of illness, inactivity, or deterioration, or to bring about a recovery or improvement in something ○ *Our spirits rallied once we had our first success.* **3.** *vi.* STOCK EXCH INCREASE IN VALUE to increase sharply in value or price owing to renewed buying by investors **4.** *vi.* STOCK EXCH EXPERIENCE RENEWED BUYING OF STOCKS to be involved in renewed buying of stocks after a period of selling **5.** *vi.* RACKET GAMES EXCHANGE SHOTS to exchange a series of shots before scoring a point in tennis and other racket sports **6.** *vti.* MIL FORM TOGETHER AGAIN to reorganize, or reorganize forces, after a setback and restore order and morale, especially to stop troops retreating further ○ *The captain rallied his retreating troops and formed a defensive line.* [Late 16thC. From French *rallier* "to reunite," from *alier* "to unite" (see ALLY).] —**ral·li·er** *n.*

rally round *vi.* to come to the aid of somebody in

difficulty or need, offering either practical or moral support

ral·ly^{2} /rállee/ (**-lied, -ly·ing, -lies**) *vt.* to tease or ridicule somebody in a friendly or good-humored way [Mid-17thC. From French *railler* "to mock, scoff" (see RAIL^{2}).]

ral·ly·ing /rállee ing/ *n.* automobile racing on public roads using a route not known in advance by the drivers and with special rules for speed or time

ralph /ralf/ (**ralphed, ralph·ing, ralphs**) *vi.* to vomit (*slang*) [Late 20thC. Origin uncertain: probably from the male first name *Ralph*, chosen for a supposed resemblance to the sound of vomiting.]

Ralph *n.* a right turn (*informal*) ○ *At the next corner, hang a Ralph.* [Late 20thC. From the male first name, used as an easily understood substitute for the first sound in the word RIGHT.]

ram /ram/ *n.* **1.** AGRIC **MALE SHEEP** a male sheep **2.** TECH **BATTERING OR CRUSHING DEVICE** a device designed to batter, crush, press, or push something, e.g., a projecting underwater part of a boat's prow or the weight dropped by a pile driver **3.** TECH **HYDRAULIC RAM** a hydraulic ram **4.** NAUT **WARSHIP WITH A RAM** a former type of warship equipped with a projecting underwater part on the prow that was designed to make a hole in the hull of an enemy warship ■ *v.* (**rammed, ram·ming, rams**) **1.** *vti.* **STRIKE SOMETHING WITH GREAT FORCE** to hit or collide with something, or make something hit something else, with great force or violence ○ *I rammed my fist down on the table.* **2.** *vt.* **COLLIDE WITH SOMETHING DELIBERATELY** to collide with another ship or vehicle deliberately in order to sink, disable, or damage it ○ *The police car rammed the getaway vehicle and pushed it off the road.* **3.** *vt.* **FORCE SOMETHING INTO PLACE** to press, force, or push something into place ○ *He quickly rammed another charge down the barrel and took aim.* **4.** *vt.* POL **FORCE ACCEPTANCE OF** to force the passage of a bill or acceptance of a suggestion, usually despite strong objection ○ *rammed the legislation through Congress.* [Old English *ram(m)*] —**ram·mer** *n.*

Ram /ram/ *n.* ZODIAC = **Aries**

RAM *abbr.* **1.** COMPUT random-access memory **2.** FIN reverse annuity mortgage ■ *n., abbr.* **1.** ENG rocket-assisted motor **2. RAM, R.A.M.** MUSIC Royal Academy of Music

r.a.m. *abbr.* relative atomic mass

Ra·ma /raámə/ *n.* an incarnation (**avatar**) of the god Vishnu

Ra·ma IX /raámə/, **King of Thailand** (*b.* 1927). He ascended the throne in 1950.

ra·ma·da /rə maádə/ *n. Southwest U.S.* an open porch or trellis supporting plants [Mid-19thC. Via Spanish from, ultimately, Latin *ramus* "branch" (see RAMIFY).]

Ram·a·dan /raámə daán/ *n.* in the Islamic calendar, the ninth month of the year, made up of 30 days. During Ramadan Muslims fast between dawn and dusk. [Late 16thC. From Arabic, literally "the hot month," from *ramad* "dryness."]

Ra·ma·krish·na /raámə kríshnə/, **Sri** (1834–86) Indian religious teacher. He taught that all mystical religious experiences are equally valid, and was instrumental in bringing about the 19th-century Hindu revival in India. His followers founded the Ramakrishna Mission. Real name **Gadadhar Chatterji**

Ra·man /raámən/, **Sir Chandrasekhara Venkata** (1888–1970) Indian physicist. His work on molecular diffraction of light won him a Nobel Prize in physics (1930).

Ra·man ef·fect *n.* PHYS the change in wavelength and phase exhibited by monochromatic light passing through a transparent medium. The scattering that results is used in Raman spectroscopy to obtain information about the structure of molecules. [Early 20thC. Named for Sir Chandrasekhara Venkata RAMAN, who discovered it.]

ra·mate *adj.* BIOL = **ramose**

Ra·ma·ya·na /raáma yaánə/ *n.* a great epic of the Hindu religion and of classical Sanskrit literature that tells of the adventures of Rama, an incarnation (**avatar**) of the god Vishnu

Barnaby's

Dame Marie Rambert

Ram·bert /raam báir/, **Dame Marie** (1888–1982) Polish-born British ballet dancer and teacher. She founded the Ballet Rambert (1926), later called the Rambert Dance Company, which promoted the work of British choreographers. Real name **Miriam Rambach**

ram·ble /rámb'l/ *vi.* (**-bled, -bling, -bles**) **1. TALK OR WRITE AIMLESSLY** to talk, write, or continue for a long time, not always keeping to the intended subject or tending to change the subject ○ *The speaker rambled on for over an hour.* **2. WALK FOR PLEASURE** to go for a walk for pleasure, usually in the countryside and sometimes without a fixed route in mind ○ *He had spent a week rambling through the villages of the Apennines.* **3. FOLLOW A CHANGING COURSE** to have, follow, or proceed along a winding or often changing course ○ *The path rambled though the fields down to the river.* **4.** BOT **GROW IN RANDOM WAY** to grow in random directions, usually covering a sizable area in the process ○ *Vines rambled all over the low stone wall.* ■ *n.* **WALK** a walk for pleasure, usually in the countryside and less strenuous than a hike ○ *a ramble through the woods on a spring vacation* [15thC. Origin uncertain.]

ram·bler /rámb'lər/ *n.* **1. SOMEBODY WHO TALKS TOO MUCH** somebody who talks or writes for too long and does not keep to the subject **2. WALKER** somebody who goes walking in the countryside for pleasure **3.** PLANTS **CLIMBING ROSE** a hybrid climbing rose with long flexible canes and clusters of small double flowers **4.** = **ranch house** *n.* 2

ram·bling /rámb'ling/ *adj.* **1. NOT TO THE POINT** continuing for too long and with many changes of subject ○ *a long, rambling story* **2. SPREAD OUT** built or spread over a large area and not clearly organized or regular in shape ○ *a rambling old house* **3.** BOT **GROWING AS RAMBLER** growing with long straggling shoots **4. MEANDERING** not following a direct course ○ *a narrow rambling path through the hills* **5. PREFERRING TO ROAM** preferring to move from place to place rather than stay in one place or settle down —**ram·bling·ly** *adv.*

WORD KEY: SYNONYMS

See Synonyms at ***wordy***.

Ram·bo /rám bō/ (*plural* **-bos**) *n.* somebody who is extremely aggressive or readily resorts to violence, willingly breaking rules, laws, or other generally accepted regulations to achieve what he or she believes to be right (*slang*) [Late 20thC. Named for John *Rambo*, the aggressive protagonist in the motion picture *First Blood* (1982).] —**Ram·bo·esque** /ràm bō ésk/ *adj.* —**Ram·bo·ism** /rám bō izzəm/ *n.*

WORD KEY: CULTURAL NOTE

Rambo is a character who appeared in a series of movies including *First Blood* by director Ted Kotcheff (1982), *Rambo: First Blood, part II* by director George Pan Cosmatos (1985), and *Rambo III* by director Peter MacDonald (1988). Played by Sylvester Stallone, Rambo is a vengeful Vietnam Vet, hired by the authorities to rescue fellow fighters still trapped in Southeast Asia, and, subsequently, to fight Communist oppression in Afghanistan. The terms *Rambo, Ramboism, Rambo cop,* and *Rambo driver/motorist* have entered the general language, meaning respectively "an overly aggressive person," "great aggressiveness in actions," "an overly zealous police officer prone to unnecessary force," and "a motorist who engages in acts of aggression and road rage while behind the wheel.".

Ram·bouil·let^{1} /rámbə lay, ràmbə láy, raaN boo yáy/ *n.* a large sturdy sheep belonging to a breed developed in France from the merino and bred for wool and meat [Early 20thC. Named for *Rambouillet*, a town in northern France where the breed was developed.]

Ram·bouil·let^{2} /rámbə lay, ràmbə láy, raaN boo yáy/ town in Yvelines Department, north central France, southwest of Paris. The town's chateau is the French president's summer residence and is used for international conferences, e.g., the talks that tried to find a peaceful settlement to the Balkan crisis in Kosovo in spring 1999. Population: 24,343 (1990).

ram·bunc·tious /ram búngkshəss/ *adj.* noisy, very active, and hard to control, usually as a result of excitement or youthful energy [Mid-9thC. Origin uncertain: perhaps an alteration of RUMBUSTIOUS.] —**ram·bunc·tious·ly** *adv.* —**ram·bunc·tious·ness** *n.*

ram·bu·tan /ram bŏŏt'n/ *n.* **1. MALAYSIAN TREE** a Malaysian tree with red spiny edible fruit. Latin name: *Nephelium lappaceum.* **2. FRUIT OF THE RAMBUTAN TREE** the oval fruit of the rambutan tree [Early 18thC. From Malay, from *rambut* "hair," from the hairy skin of the fruit.]

ram·e·kin /rámməkin/, **ram·e·quin** *n.* **1. SMALL BAKING DISH** a small ovenproof dish with vertical fluted sides designed to hold a single serving of a prepared food, especially one that is baked **2. FOOD SERVED IN A RAMEKIN** a portion of food cooked and served in a ramekin [Early 18thC. Via French *ramequin* from Middle Dutch *rameken*, literally "little cream," from *ram* "cream."]

ra·men /ráymən/ *n.* a Japanese dish of thin white noodles in small dried cakes, served in a thin well-flavored soup or stock [Late 20thC. Via Japanese *rāmen* from Chinese *lāmiàn*, literally "pulled noodles."]

ram·e·quin *n.* = **ramekin**

Ram·e·ses II /rámmə seez/, **Ram·ses II** (*fl.* 13th century B.C.) Egyptian pharaoh. His long and prosperous reign (1279–12 B.C.), which marked the pinnacle of Egypt's power, saw the building of numerous monuments including the sandstone temples at Abu Simbel. The Jewish exodus from Egypt is thought to have occurred during his rule. Known as **Rameses the Great**

Ram·e·ses III, Ram·ses III (*fl.* 12th century B.C.) Egyptian pharaoh. As pharoah (1182–51 B.C.) he was a great military leader who repeatedly saved the country from invasion, notably by the Libyans.

ra·met /ráymət/ *n.* BIOL any individual in a clone [Early 20thC. Formed from Latin *ramus* "branch" (see RAMUS).]

ra·mi plural of **ramus**

ram·ie /rámmee, ráymee/ *n.* **1.** BOT **ASIAN SHRUB** a perennial Asian shrub of the nettle family that has broad leaves and small flowers. It yields a tough fiber resembling flax. Latin name: *Boehmeria nivea.* **2.** INDUST **STRONG FIBER** a strong lustrous fiber obtained from the stem of the ramie shrub, used in fabric and rope **3.** TEXTILES **CLOTH** cloth made from ramie fiber [Early 19thC. From Malay *rami.*]

ram·i·fi·ca·tion /ràmməfə káysh'n/ *n.* **1. COMPLICATING RESULT** a usually unintended consequence of an action, decision, or judgment that may complicate the situation or make the intended result more difficult to achieve ○ *an unexpected ramification of the new law* **2. BRANCHING DIVISION** the process of dividing or spreading out into branches **3. BRANCH** a branch or arrangement of branches

ram·i·form /rámmə fawrm/ *adj.* spreading out like branches or having the form of a branch or branches [Mid-19thC. Coined from Latin *ramus* "branch" (see RAMUS) + *-iform* (see -FORM).]

ram·i·fy /rámmə fī/ (**-fied, -fy·ing, -fies**) *vi.* **1.** BIOL **BRANCH** to divide into branches or similar parts **2. HAVE COMPLICATING RESULTS** to have unforeseen results or effects that will cause complications or interfere with the purpose intended [Mid-16thC. Via Old French *ramifier* from medieval Latin *ramificare*, from Latin *ramus* "branch" (see RAMUS).]

ram·jet /rám jèt/ *n.* a jet engine in which fuel is burned in a duct with air compressed by the forward motion of the aircraft

Ra·mos /rámōss/, **Fidel Valdez** (*b.* 1928) Filipino statesman. He was instrumental in overthrowing President Ferdinand Marcos (1986) and himself became president of the Philippines (1992).

ra·mose /ráy mōss, rə mōss/, **ra·mous, ra·mate** /ráy màyt/ *adj.* BIOL having many branches or divided into many branches [Late 17thC. From Latin *ramosus* "having many branches," from *ramus* "branch" (see RAMUS).] —**ra·mose·ly** *adv.*

ramp[1] /ramp/ *n.* **1. SLOPING PATH OR ACCESS** a sloping surface used, e.g., to allow access from one level to a higher or lower level or to raise something up above floor or ground level ○ *The ship slid slowly down the ramp into the water.* **2. MOVABLE STAIRS** a movable set of stairs used for boarding or disembarking from an aircraft **3. CURVED BEND IN A HANDRAIL** a curved bend or slope in a handrail or coping where it changes direction, e.g., on a stair landing ■ *vt.* **(ramped, ramp·ing, ramps) 1. INCREMENT SOMETHING GRADUALLY** to increase something gradually ○ *had to ramp up production to meet increasing demand* **2. BUILD SOMETHING WITH A SLOPE** to build something with a sloped surface, or provide something with a ramp ○ *The entrance must be ramped for wheelchair access.* [Late 18thC. From French *rampe*, from *ramper* (see RAMP[2]).] —**ramped** *adj.*

ramp[2] /ramp/ **(ramped, ramp·ing, ramps)** *vi.* **1. ACT THREATENINGLY** to act in a threatening manner or assume a threatening stance, e.g., rearing with the forelegs ready to strike **2. MOVE VIOLENTLY OR THREATENINGLY** to move or rush violently, threateningly, or furiously **3.** HERALDRY **BE SHOWN REARED UP IN PROFILE** to be in the rampant position ○ *an old seal marked with a ramping lion on a shield* [14thC. From French *ramper* "to crawl, creep, rear up."]

ram·page /ram páyj, rám pàyj/ *n.* **VIOLENT BEHAVIOR** an outburst of uncontrolled violent or riotous behavior or a series of violent or riotous actions ■ *vi.* **(-paged, -pag·ing, -pag·es) ACT VIOLENTLY OR RIOTOUSLY** to engage in uncontrolled violent or riotous behavior, or to commit a series of violent or riotous acts ○ *This weather system has rampaged up the coast, with blizzards and howling winds causing severe damage.* [Early 18thC. Origin uncertain: probably formed from RAMP[2].] —**ram·pa·geous** *adj.* —**ram·pa·geous·ly** *adv.* —**ram·pa·geous·ness** *n.* —**ram·pag·er** *n.* —**ram·pag·ing** *adj.* ◇ **on the rampage** behaving in a wild and uncontrolled manner

ram·pant /rámpənt/ *adj.* **1. OCCURRING UNCHECKED** happening in an unrestrained manner, usually so as to be regarded as a menace ○ *rampant inflation* **2.** BOT **GROWING WILDLY** growing strongly and to a very large size, or spreading uncontrollably **3. FIERCE** exhibiting ferocious behavior or fierceness of spirit **4.** HERALDRY **ON HIND LEGS** used to describe a heraldic beast depicted reared up, in profile, and with its forelegs raised, the right one above the left **5.** BUILDING **WITH UNEQUAL SUPPORTS** having a support or an abutment that is higher on one side than the other [14thC. From French, the present participle of *ramper* (see RAMP[2]).] —**ram·pan·cy** *n.* —**ram·pant·ly** *adv.*

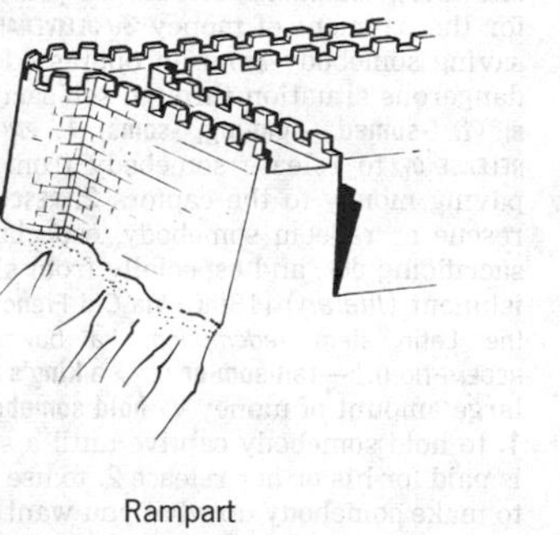

Rampart

ram·part /rám paart/ *n.* **FORTIFIED EMBANKMENT** a defensive fortification made of an earthen embankment, often topped by a low protective wall ■ *vt.* **(-part·ed, -part·ing, -parts) FORTIFY OR PROTECT SOMETHING** to protect somebody or something with ramparts or something similar [Late 16thC. From French *rempart*, from *remparer*, literally "to defend again," from Old French *emparer* "to defend," from, ultimately, assumed Vulgar Latin *parare* "to prepare" (source of English *prepare*).]

ram·pike /rám pīk/ *n.* a dead tree that is still standing, especially one reduced by fire to little more than a trunk [Late 16thC. Origin unknown.]

ram·pi·on /rámpee ən/ *n.* **1. EURASIAN PLANT WITH BLUISH FLOWERS** a plant of Europe and Asia with clusters of bluish flowers and a white edible root used in salads. Latin name: *Campanula rapunculus.* **2. BLUE-FLOWERED PLANT** any plant related to the rampion, typically with blue flowers. Genus: *Phyteuma.* [Late 16thC. Origin uncertain: probably an alteration of Old French *raiponce*, from Old Italian *raponzo*, from Latin *rapum* "turnip" (source of English *rape* "plant").]

Ram·pur /rám pòor/ city and administrative headquarters of Rampur District, Uttar Pradesh State, northern India. Population: 243,000 (1991).

ram·rod /rám ràwd/ *n.* **1.** ARMS **ROD FOR LOADING GUNS** a rod for loading a charge into a muzzle-loading musket, cannon, or other gun **2.** ARMS **CLEANING ROD** a rod for cleaning the barrel of a firearm **3. STERN OR STRICT OVERSEER** a stern or strict boss, commander, or other person in a position of authority ■ *vt.* **(-rod·ded, -rod·ding, -rods) 1. PUSH SOMETHING THROUGH BY FORCE** to push through or achieve something by force or threat ○ *tried to ramrod the bill through the legislature* **2. CONTROL SOMEBODY STRICTLY** to exert strict control over somebody or enforce strict discipline on somebody

Ram·ses II ◆ **Rameses II**

Ram·ses III ◆ **Rameses III**

ram·shack·le /rám shàk'l/ *adj.* poorly maintained or constructed and seeming likely to fall apart or collapse [Mid-19thC. Back-formation from earlier *ramshackled*, from, ultimately, RANSACK.]

ram's horn *n.* JUDAISM = **shofar**

ram·sons /rámz'nz, ráms'nz/ *n.* a wild garlic of Europe and Asia with a bulbous root eaten in salads. Latin name: *Allium ursinum.* (*takes a singular verb*) [Mid-16thC. Formed from Old English *hram(e)san*, plural of *hramsa*, later erroneously regarded as singular.]

ram·til /rámtil/ *n.* an Ethiopian plant with yellow flowers, grown for its oil-rich seeds. Latin name: *Guizotia abyssinica.* [Mid-19thC. From Bengali *rāmtil*, literally "pleasing sesame."]

ram·u·lose /rámmyə lōss/ *adj.* BIOL having many small branches [Mid-18thC. From Latin *ramulosus* "full of branching veins," from, ultimately, *ramus* (see RAMUS).]

ra·mus /ráyməss/ (*plural* **-mi** /ráy mī/) *n.* a small branching part, such as a stem, bone, or nerve [Early 18thC. From Latin, "branch."]

ran past tense of **run**

Ran /ran/ *n.* in Norse mythology, the goddess of the sea

Rance /raaNss/ river in Brittany, in northwestern France. Length: 60 mi./100 km.

ranch /ranch/ *n.* **1. LIVESTOCK FARM ON RANGELAND** a farm where cattle, sheep, horses, or other livestock are raised on large tracts of open land, especially in North and South America and Australia **2. FARM FOR RAISING A PARTICULAR SPECIES** a large farm devoted to keeping a single species of animal or growing a single type of crop **3.** = **ranch house** *n.* 1, **ranch house** *n.* 2 **1.** FOOD = **ranchdressing** ■ *v.* **(ranched, ranch·ing, ranch·es) 1.** *vi.* **WORK ON A RANCH** to own, manage, or work on a ranch **2.** *vt.* **RAISE ON A RANCH** to breed, raise, or tend animals on a ranch ■ FOOD = **ranch dressing** [Early 19thC. Via American Spanish *rancho* from Spanish, "group of people who eat together," from, ultimately, French *ranger* "to arrange in position," from *rang* "row, line" (source of English *rank*).] —**ranch·ing** *n.* ◇ **meanwhile, back at the ranch** used to draw listeners' attention back to the main theme or point of the conversation or the scene of the main action (*informal*)

ranch dress·ing *n.* a creamy salad dressing that has a mixture of mayonnaise and buttermilk or milk as its base

ranch·er /ránchər/ *n.* somebody who owns or manages a ranch

ran·che·ro /ran chérrō/ (*plural* **-ros**) *n. Southwest U.S.* AGRIC somebody who owns or manages a ranch, particularly a rancher in the southwestern United States and Spanish-speaking countries of Latin America [Early 19thC. From American Spanish, formed from *rancho* (see RANCH).]

ranch house *n.* **1. HOUSE ON A RANCH** the building on a ranch where the owner or manager lives, typically having one story, a spread-out floor plan, and a roof that is not steeply pitched **2. SINGLE-STORY HOUSE** a single-story house built in a style similar to a traditional ranch house, especially one located in a suburban housing development

Ran·chi /ránchee/ city and administrative headquarters of Ranchi District, in Bihar State, northeastern India. Population: 599,000 (1991).

ran·cho /rán chō/ (*plural* **-chos**) *n. Southwest U.S.* **1. RANCH** a ranch **2. RANCH WORKER'S HUT** a hut where a ranch worker lives, or a group of such huts [Early 19thC. From American Spanish (see RANCH).]

ran·cid /ránsəd/ *adj.* **1. WITH A DISAGREEABLE TASTE** having the strong disagreeable smell or taste of decomposing fats or oils **2. CAUSING DISGUST** causing disgust or greatly offensive [Mid-17thC. From Latin *rancidus* "stinking, rank," from *rancere* "to stink."] —**ran·cid·i·ty** /ran síddətee/ *n.* —**ran·cid·ness** /ránsədnəss/ *n.*

ran·cor /rángkər/ *n.* bitter, deeply held, and long-lasting ill will or resentment [12thC. Via Old French from Latin *rancor* "stinking smell or offensive flavor, bitterness," from *rancere* "to stink."] —**ran·cor·ous** *adj.* —**ran·cor·ous·ly** *adv.* —**ran·cor·ous·ness** *n.*

ran·cour *n.* U.K. = **rancor**

rand /rand/ (*plural* **rand**) *n.* **1. UNIT OF S AFRICAN CURRENCY** the standard unit of currency in the Republic of South Africa, worth 100 cents. See table at **currency** **2. COIN WORTH A RAND** a coin worth one rand [Mid-20thC. Named for the *Rand*, a gold-mining district in the Transvaal, from Afrikaans *rand* "ridge of ground," from Dutch, "edge."]

ran·dan /ran dán, rán dan/ *n.* **1. ROWBOAT** a type of boat designed to be rowed by three people **2. METHOD OF ROWING** the method of rowing a randan, with one person using two oars and the other two one oar each [Early 19thC. Origin unknown.]

r & b, **R & B** *abbr.* rhythm and blues

R & D *abbr.* research and development

Ran·dolph /rándolf/ town in eastern Massachusetts, northeast of Stoughton. It is a southern suburb of Boston. Population: 30,554 (1996).

Ran·dolph, A. Philip (1889–1979) U.S. labor leader. The founding president of the Brotherhood of Sleeping Car Porters and Maids (1925–68), he unionized African American workers, campaigned for civil rights, and was a principal organizer of the great 1963 civil rights march in Washington, D.C. Full name **Asa Philip Randolph**

Ran·dolph, Edmund Jennings (1753–1813) U.S. statesman. He was a Virginia delegate to the Constitutional Convention (1787), and served as U.S. secretary of state (1794–95).

Ran·dolph, John (1773–1833) U.S. statesman. He served in the U.S. House of Representatives and Senate (1799–1829), and helped draft a new constitution for Virginia. Known as **John Randolph of Roanoke**

ran·dom /rándəm/ *adj.* **1. WITHOUT A PATTERN** done, chosen, or occurring without a specific pattern, plan, or connection ○ *random testing for drugs* **2. LACKING REGULARITY** with a pattern or in sizes that are not uniform or regular ○ *a wall constructed of random stones* **3.** STATS **EQUALLY LIKELY** relating or belonging to a set in which all the members have the same probability of occurrence ○ *a random sampling* **4.** STATS **HAVING DEFINITE PROBABILITY** relating to or involving variables that have undetermined value but definite probability [Mid-17thC. From Old French *randon* "impetuosity, rush" (the original sense in English), from *randir* "to run." Ultimately from a prehistoric Germanic base (probably also the ancestor of English *run*).] —**ran·dom·ly** *adv.* —**ran·dom·ness** *n.* ◇ **at random** with no set plan, system, or connection

ran·dom-ac·cess *adj.* COMPUT relating to the capability of a computer to obtain information from any memory location without having to begin its search at the memory's starting point and work through it in sequence ○ *random-access input/output*

ran·dom-ac·cess mem·o·ry *n.* **1.** COMPUT **COMPUTER STORAGE MEDIUM** a computer storage medium on which data items are stored in an arbitrary fashion but can be accessed directly because each has a unique address. Because each data item can be addressed independent of any other item, the time it takes to access any memory location on a given medium is the same. **2. PRIMARY WORKING MEMORY OF A COMPUTER** the primary working memory in a computer used for the temporary storage of programs and data and in which the data can be accessed directly and modified

ran·dom·ize /rándə mīz/ (**-ized, -iz·ing, -iz·es** *or* **-is·es**) *vti.* to arrange or select items so that no specific pattern or order determines the selection process —**ran·dom·i·za·tion** /rànda mə záysh'n/ *n.* —**ran·dom·iz·er** /rándə mīzər/ *n.*

ran·dom num·ber *n.* any of a series of numbers that have no pattern in their progression

ran·dom sam·ple *n.* a sample of subjects that is randomly selected from a group and is therefore assumed to be representative of that group

ran·dom var·i·a·ble *n.* STATS a variable that can have any of a range of values that occur randomly but can be described probabilistically

ran·dom walk *n.* MATH a model applicable to various processes such as diffusion in which the direction and sometimes the magnitude of successive steps are determined by chance

R and R, **R & R** *abbr.* MIL rest and recreation ■ *n., abbr.* rest and relaxation

R & R /aar ən aar/, **R and R** *abbr.* rest and recreation

ran·dy /rándee/ (**-di·er, -di·est**) *adj.* having a strong desire for sex (*informal*) [Late 17thC. Formed from *rand* "to rant," an earlier Scots variant of RANT. Originally in the sense "aggressive, rude."] —**ran·di·ly** *adv.* —**ran·di·ness** *n.*

rang past tense of **ring**[2]

range /raynj/ *n.* **1.** VARIEDNESS the number and variety of different things that something includes or can deal with ○ *The range of her interests is extraordinary.* **2.** NUMBER OF SIMILAR THINGS a number or set of different things belonging to the same general category ○ *available in a range of styles and colors* **3.** CATEGORY DEFINED BY LIMITS a category defined by an upper and a lower limit ○ *the age range 25 to 45* **4.** AREA OF EFFECTIVE OPERATION the area within which, or the distance over which, something can operate effectively ○ *out of range of the radar* **5.** MIL FARTHEST DISTANCE FOR AN EFFECTIVE OPERATION the farthest distance at which something can operate effectively, e.g., the farthest distance to which a gun can shoot a bullet or shell **6.** ARMS DISTANCE BETWEEN A WEAPON AND A TARGET the distance between something, especially a gun or a tracking device, and the object it is aimed at **7.** SPORTS PRACTICE AREA a place where an activity is practiced or performed **8.** TRANSP DISTANCE TRAVELED WITHOUT REFUELING the farthest distance that a vehicle or aircraft can travel without refueling **9.** AGRIC OPEN LAND FOR GRAZING FARM ANIMALS a large area of open land on which farm animals can graze **10.** MUSIC PRODUCIBLE NOTES the notes, from the highest to the lowest, that somebody's voice or a musical instrument is capable of producing **11.** MUSIC REGISTER OF A MUSICAL PASSAGE the register of a musical passage, from the highest to the lowest note it contains **12.** GEOG ROW OF MOUNTAINS a number of mountains or hills forming a connected row or group **13.** MOVEMENT OVER AN AREA movement over or within an area **14.** MATH SET OF VALUES the set of values that can be taken by a function or a variable **15.** HOUSEHOLD STOVE a cooking stove with one or more ovens and with hotplates or burners on top **16.** ECOL AREA WHERE AN ORGANISM IS NORMALLY FOUND a geographical area in which a species of organism normally lives or grows **17.** STATS EXTENT OF FREQUENCY DISTRIBUTION the difference between the smallest and the largest value in a frequency distribution **18.** CONSTR NORTH-SOUTH STRIP OF TOWNSHIPS a north-south strip of townships six miles square and numbered east and west from a meridian in a U.S. public land survey ■ *v.* (**ranged, rang·ing, rang·es**) **1.** *vi.* VARY BETWEEN LIMITS to vary between a particular upper and lower limit ○ *prices ranging from $3.95 to $15.00* **2.** *vt.* ARMS TRAVEL CERTAIN DISTANCE to be able to travel a particular distance (*refers to bullets or missiles*) **3.** *vti.* TRAVEL FREELY AND EXTENSIVELY to move freely across, through, or back and forth within a particular area ○ *She allowed her thoughts to range freely over the events of the previous week.* **4.** *vi.* ECOL LIVE OR GROW to live or grow in a particular geographical area (*refers to animals or plants*) ○ *Buffalo once ranged over the plains.* **5.** *vt.* AGRIC PUT LIVESTOCK OUT TO GRAZE to put livestock out to graze on a large open area **6.** *vt.* ALIGN OR CLASSIFY to put something or somebody into a particular group or category **7.** *vt.* ARRANGE IN LINE to arrange things in a particular way, especially in a line or row (*usually passive*) ○ *Jars of pickles were ranged along the kitchen shelf.* **8.** *vti.* POINT OR AIM SOMETHING AT SOMETHING to point or aim something such as a gun, missile or telescope at a specific object, or to be pointed at a specific object **9.** *vi.* DEAL WITH A NUMBER OF THINGS to include, cover, or deal with a number of different things, usually within a particular context ○ *Her interests range from parapsychology to parachuting.* **10.** *vr.* GIVE PERSONAL SUPPORT to support or side with somebody [13thC. From Old French *rangier* "to put in order," from *ranc* "row" (see RANK[1]).]

range find·er, **range·find·er** *n.* **1.** DISTANCE-FINDING INSTRUMENT an instrument used to estimate the distance between the user and an object, especially one that is to be shot at or photographed **2.** = **transit** *n.* 8

range·land /ráynj lànd/ *n.* = **range** *n.* 9

range pole *n.* CONSTR = **ranging pole**

rang·er /ráynjər/ *n.* **1.** OFFICIAL OVERSEEING A FOREST OR NATIONAL PARK somebody whose job is to oversee, protect, and patrol a forest or an area of natural beauty such as a national park. ◊ **game warden** **2.** MEMBER OF A RURAL POLICE UNIT a member of an armed law-enforcement unit in certain parts of the United States, especially Texas **3.** WANDERER somebody who wanders

Rang·er /ráynjər/ *n.* a member of a military unit of the United States army specially trained for commando raids

rang·ing pole, **rang·ing rod, range pole** *n.* a pole, usually held vertically, used to mark a specific position when surveying a plot of land

Ran·goon /rang go͞on/ former name for **Yangon** (until 1989)

rang·y /ráynjee/ (**-i·er, -i·est**) *adj.* tall and lean with long legs —**rang·i·ness** *n.*

ra·ni /raanee, raanée/, **ra·nee** *n.* a queen or princess, or the wife or widow of a rajah in India or a neighboring country [Late 17thC. Via Hindi from, ultimately, Sanskrit *rājñī*, from *rājan* "king" (see RAJAH).]

rank[1] /rangk/ *n.* **1.** MIL OFFICIAL STATUS WITHIN AN ORGANIZATION an official title or category that shows the holder's relative importance or seniority within an organization, especially a military force **2.** STATUS RELATIVE TO OTHERS the degree of importance or excellence of somebody or something relative to other members of a group ○ *a political journalist of the first rank* **3.** HIGH STATUS high status or importance, especially in the military or among the wealthy **4.** LINE OF PEOPLE OR THINGS a line of people, especially soldiers, or things standing side by side **5.** CHESS HORIZONTAL LINE OF SQUARES ON A CHESSBOARD any of the horizontal lines of squares on a chessboard **6.** MATH LINEARLY INDEPENDENT ROWS the largest number of linearly independent rows in a matrix **7.** MUSIC SET OF ORGAN PIPES a set of organ pipes linked to a particular stop ■ **ranks** *npl.* **1.** ORDINARY PEOPLE members of the armed forces who are not officers, or the ordinary members or personnel of any organization who do not hold high office **2.** PEOPLE OF A PARTICULAR GROUP OR CATEGORY the people belonging to a specified group or category, considered collectively and usually with the understanding that there are large numbers of them ○ *among the ranks of her supporters* ■ *v.* (**ranked, rank·ing, ranks**) **1.** *vti.* HAVE OR GIVE SOMETHING A SPECIFIC RATING to have, or to give somebody or something, a particular rating, position, or importance relative to other people or things in a group ○ *This ranks fairly high on my list of desirable improvements.* **2.** *vt.* OUTRANK to have a higher rank than and take precedence over somebody or something else in a group, especially in a hierarchy ○ *A colonel ranks a major.* **3.** *vti.* POSITION OR STAND IN ROWS to place people or things in a row or rows or to stand or form in rows (*usually passive*) **4.** *vi.* SEEM MOST IMPORTANT to have the greatest importance or receive the best treatment among the members of a particular group ○ *You got the best seat in the house. You must really rank with the producer.* **5.** *vi.* INSULT SOMEBODY to insult somebody in a childish way (*slang*) ○ *Quit ranking on me!* [14thC. From Old French *ranc* "row," from a prehistoric Germanic word that is also the ancestor of English *range* and *ring*.] ◇ **break ranks 1.** to fall out of an ordered line of soldiers, especially when being attacked **2.** to stop supporting the policy of a group which you are a member ◇ **close ranks 1.** to unite closely, especially when taking some kind of defensive action **2.** to form in tight disciplined lines in preparation for an expected attack (*refers to soldiers*) ◇ **pull rank (on somebody)** to assert authority over other people in a hierarchy, especially in order to obtain personal advantage ◇ **rise (up) through the ranks** to reach a senior position in an organization by gradual promotions from an originally low position

rank[2] *adj.* **1.** UTTER of the most extreme and obvious kind ○ *a rank amateur* **2.** FOUL foul-smelling or foul-tasting (*literary*) ○ *"O, my offense is rank! It smells to heaven."* (Shakespeare, *Hamlet 3.ii*; 1604) **3.** SHOWING VIGOROUS GROWTH growing and spreading in a particularly vigorous way (*refers to vegetation*) ○ *"the rank ailanthus of the April dooryard"* (T.S. Eliot, *The Dry Salvages*; 1941) [Old English *ranc* "haughty, full-grown," of uncertain origin: perhaps ultimately from an Indo-European word meaning "to move straight ahead," which is also the ancestor of English *right*] —**rank·ly** *adv.* —**rank·ness** *n.*

rank and file *n.* **1.** ORDINARY MEMBERS the majority of a group or organization, often a labor union, especially all of the members who have no power or influence **2.** MIL ENLISTED TROOPS enlisted troops in a military organization, excluding officers —**rank-and-file** *adj.* —**rank and fil·er** *n.*

Ran·kine scale *n.* an absolute temperature scale in which each degree equals one degree on the Fahrenheit scale, with the freezing point of water being 491.67°, and its boiling point 671.67° [Mid-19thC. Named for the British physicist and engineer W. J. M. *Rankine* (1820–72).]

rank·ing /rángking/ *adj.* **1.** HOLDING HIGH RANK holding a high rank in military or other organization ○ *the ranking diplomat at the reception* **2.** FOREMOST considered to be the most eminent or important of the members of a particular group ■ *n.* **1.** POSITION RELATIVE TO OTHERS the position or status held by or allocated to somebody or something relative to others in a particular group **2.** WORKING OUT RANKING ORDER the work of establishing the order in which people or things should be ranked, usually according to their importance or ability ○ *Are we prepared to do a preliminary ranking of the candidates?*

ran·kle /rángk'l/ (**-kled, -kling, -kles**) *vi.* to cause persistent feelings of bitterness, resentment, or anger [14thC. From Old French *raoncler*, from *raoncle* "festering sore," literally "little snake (bite)," from, ultimately, Latin *dracunculus*, from *draco* "serpent" (see DRAGON).]

ran·sack /ránsak/ (**-sacked, -sack·ing, -sacks**) *vt.* **1.** ROB AND DESPOIL SOMETHING to go through a place stealing some things and usually destroying or spoiling everything else **2.** SEARCH VERY THOROUGHLY to search something very thoroughly but handling things carelessly ○ *I ransacked the drawers but couldn't find my keys.* [13thC. From Old Norse *rannsaka*, from *rann* "house" + *-saka* (related to English *seek*) "to search."] —**ran·sack·er** *n.*

ran·som /ráns'm/ *n.* **1.** MONEY DEMANDED FOR RELEASING A CAPTIVE a sum of money demanded or paid for the release of somebody who is being held prisoner **2.** RELEASE OF A PRISONER the release of a prisoner in return for the payment of money **3.** DELIVERANCE the act of saving somebody from an oppressed condition or dangerous situation through self-sacrifice (*literary*) ■ *vt.* (**-somed, -som·ing, -soms**) **1.** PAY MONEY FOR THE RELEASE OF to release somebody from captivity by paying money to the captors **2.** RESCUE OR REDEEM to rescue or redeem somebody, especially by a self-sacrificing act, and especially from sin or its punishment (*literary*) [13thC. Via Old French *ransoun* from the Latin stem *redemption-* "a buying back" (see REDEMPTION).] —**ran·som·er** *n.* ◇ **a king's ransom** a very large amount of money ◇ **hold somebody for ransom 1.** to hold somebody captive until a sum of money is paid for his or her release **2.** to use threats to try to make somebody do what you want

Ran·som /ráns'm/, **John Crowe** (1888–1974) U.S. poet and critic. He was a leader of the Southern literary renaissance in the 1920s, and helped found the *Kenyon Review*.

rant /rant/ *vti.* (**rant·ed, rant·ing, rants**) SPEAK IN A LOUD EXAGGERATED MANNER to speak in a very loud, aggressive, or bombastic way, usually at length and repetitively ■ *n.* LOUD AND THREATENING SPEECH speech or language that is very loud and threatening but also monotonous or unconvincing [Late 16thC. From Dutch *ranten*.] —**rant·er** *n.* —**rant·ing** *adj.* —**rant·ing** *n.* —**rant·ing·ly** *adv.*

ran·u·la /rányələ/ *n.* a cyst that forms on the underside of the tongue when the duct of a salivary or mucous gland is blocked [Mid-17thC. From Latin, literally "little frog," from *rana* "frog."]

ra·nun·cu·lus /rə núngkyələss/ (*plural* **-lus·es** *or* **-li** /-ī/) *n.* a plant that has divided leaves and flowers with five petals such as the buttercup, clematis, and columbine. Genus: *Ranunculus*. [Late 16thC. From modern Latin, genus name, from Latin, literally "little frog," from *rana* "frog."] —**ra·nun·cu·la·ceous** /rə nùngkyə láyshəss/ *adj.*

rap[1] *v.* **(rapped, rap·ping, raps) 1.** *vti.* **HIT SOMETHING SHARPLY** to strike something with a quick sharp blow ○ *The teacher rapped on the desk to get the students' attention.* **2.** *vt.* **REBUKE SOMEBODY** to criticize or reproach somebody harshly **3.** *vt.* **SAY SOMETHING QUICKLY** to say something in a quick sharp way ○ *The sergeant rapped out an order.* ■ *n.* **1. SOUND OF KNOCKING** a quick sharp knocking sound **2. SOMEBODY OR SOMETHING NEGATIVE** somebody or something thought of as negative or unfortunate (*slang*) ○ *You got a bum rap this time.* **3. SHARP BLOW** a sharp quick blow **4. REBUKE** a harsh rebuke or criticism (*slang*) **5. JAIL SENTENCE** a jail sentence given to somebody found guilty of a crime (*slang*) [13thC. Origin uncertain: perhaps an imitation of the sound.] —**rap·per** *n.* ◇ **beat the rap** to avoid conviction on a charge (*informal*) ◇ **take the rap (for something)** to take the blame or punishment for something, whether or not it was your fault (*slang*) ◇ **not give a rap** to not care at all

rap[2] *n.* **1.** MUSIC **POPULAR MUSIC WITH RHYMING VERSES** popular music characterized by spoken rhyming vocals and often featuring a looped electronic beat in the background **2. INFORMAL TALK** an informal talk or discussion (*slang*) **3. SCRIPTED SPEECH OR ACTION** the structured form or substance of something that somebody knows well and can perform at will (*slang*) ○ *You've really got the whole rap down on making quick money!* ■ *v.* **(rapped, rap·ping, raps) 1.** *vi.* MUSIC **PERFORM RAP** to perform rap music **2.** *vt.* **TALK INFORMALLY** to talk or discuss something informally (*slang*) ○ *We rapped till dawn.* [13thC. Origin uncertain: perhaps an imitation of the sound.] —**rap·per** *n.*

ra·pa·cious /rə páyshəss/ *adj.* **1. GRASPING** greedy and grasping, especially for money, and sometimes willing to use unscrupulous means to obtain what is desired **2. DESTRUCTIVE AND VICIOUS** engaging in violent pillaging and likely to harm or destroy things **3.** ZOOL **PREDATORY** living by eating live prey [Mid-17thC. From Latin *rapac-*, stem of *rapax* "tearing, grasping," from *rapere* (see RAPE[1]).] —**ra·pa·cious·ly** *adv.* —**ra·pa·cious·ness** *n.*

rape[1] /rayp/ *n.* **1.** CRIMINOL **FORCING OF SOMEBODY INTO SEX** the crime of forcing somebody to have sex **2.** CRIMINOL **INSTANCE OF RAPE** an instance of the crime of rape **3. VIOLENT DESTRUCTIVE TREATMENT** violent, destructive, or abusive treatment of something ○ *the rape of a beautiful stretch of countryside* **4. ABDUCTION** an act of seizing somebody and carrying him or her away by force (*archaic*) ■ *vt.* **(raped, rap·ing, rapes) 1. FORCE TO HAVE SEX** to force somebody to have sex **2. VIOLATE SOMETHING** to treat something in a violent, destructive, or abusive way ○ *rape the land for its resources* **3. ABDUCT SOMEBODY** to seize and carry off somebody or something by force (*archaic*) [14thC. Via Anglo-Norman *raper* from Latin *rapere* "to seize."]

WORD KEY: ORIGIN

The Latin word *rapere* from which ***rape*** is derived is also the source of English *rapacious, rapine, rapid, rapture, ravage, ravenous, ravine, ravish, surreptitious,* and *usurp.*

rape[2] /rayp/ *n.* PLANTS an annual plant of the cabbage family that has bright yellow flowers and is grown commercially for its oil-bearing seeds and as a fodder crop. Latin name: *Brassica napus.* [14thC. From Latin *rapa* "turnip."]

rape[3] /rayp/ *n.* WINE the skins and stalks of grapes after their juice has been extracted for use in winemaking [Early 17thC. From French *râpe* "grape stalk," from Old French, from *rasper* "to scratch" (see RASP).]

rape oil *n.* oil extracted from the seeds of the rape plant, used as a lubricant, in making soap, and in cooking

rape·seed /ráyp seed/ *n.* the seeds of the rape plant

rape·seed oil *n.* = **rape oil**

rape shield law *n.* a law that prohibits the defense in a rape trial from questioning the victim about her or his previous sexual experiences

Raph·a·el /ráffee əl/ *n.* in Hebrew tradition, one of the seven archangels, and the angel of healing

Raph·a·el /ráffee əl/ (1483–1520) Italian artist. A master of the Italian High Renaissance, he is best known for his religious paintings. Real name **Raffaello Sanzio**

ra·phe /ráyfee/ *n.* **1.** ANAT **CONNECTING RIDGE** a connecting ridge or seam between two similar parts of an organ of the body, e.g., between the two halves of the medulla oblongata or along the scrotum **2.** BOT **RIDGE ALONG SOME SEEDCOATS** a ridge along the coat of some seeds formed by fusion of the connecting stalk **(funiculus)** with the outer layer of the developing ovule **3.** BOT **LONGITUDINAL GROOVE** a longitudinal groove on the valve of a diatom [Mid-18thC. Via modern Latin from Greek *rhaphē* "seam," from *rhaptein* "to sew."]

ra·phide /ráyfəd/, **ra·phis** /ráyfiss/ (*plural* **raph·i·des** /-də̀ez/) *n.* any one of a bundle of needle-shaped crystals, usually of calcium oxalate, that develop in some plant cells as a byproduct of their metabolism [Mid-19thC. Via French from the Greek stem *raphid-* "needle," from *rhaptein* "to sew."]

rap·id /ráppid/ *adj.* **SWIFT** acting, moving, or happening very quickly ○ *a rapid increase in turnover* ■ **rap·ids** *npl.* **TURBULENT PART OF A RIVERBED** a part of a riverbed where the water moves very fast, usually over rocks or around boulders [Mid-17thC. From Latin *rapidus* "seizing," from *rapere* (see RAPE[1]).] —**rap·id·ly** *adv.* —**rap·id·ness** *n.*

Rap·id Cit·y /ràppid-/ city in western South Dakota, in the Black Hills, northwest of Pierre. Population: 57,642 (1996).

rap·id eye move·ment *n.* jerky movements of the eyeballs while the eyes are closed that are characteristic of somebody who is dreaming while asleep, especially during REM sleep

rap·id eye move·ment sleep *n.* = **REM sleep**

rap·id-fire *adj.* **1. COMING IN VERY QUICK SUCCESSION** delivered or happening in very quick succession ○ *The salesman had an incredible rapid-fire delivery.* **2.** ARMS **DESIGNED TO FIRE VERY QUICKLY** designed to fire bullets or shells in very quick succession or at a faster rate than a standard gun

rap·id pro·to·typ·ing *n.* a method of quickly creating mechanical components, especially those with complex shapes, from a computer-based drawing that can be used to check the validity of a design

rap·id tran·sit *n.* a high-speed urban public transportation system, using underground or elevated trains or a combination of both

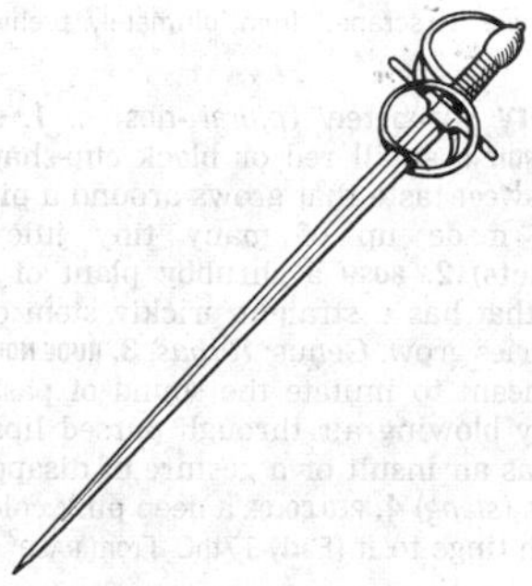

Rapier

ra·pi·er /ráypeer/ *n.* a sword with a cup-shaped hilt and a long slender blade that can have two cutting edges or only a sharply pointed tip for thrusting [Early 16thC. Origin uncertain: probably via Dutch or Low German *rappir* from French *(espee) rapière* "rapier (sword)," of unknown origin.]

rap·ine /ráppən, ráppīn, ráypīn/ *n.* the use of force to seize somebody else's property (*archaic or formal*) [14thC. Directly or via French from Latin *rapina*, from *rapere* (see RAPE[1]).]

rap·ist *n.* somebody who uses force to have sex with somebody else

Rapp /rap, raap/, **George** (1757–1847) German-born U.S. religious reformer. He founded the Harmony Society, a separatist Protestant community, in Pennsylvania in 1803.

Rap·pa·han·nock /ràppə hánnək-/ river in Virginia, rising in the Blue Ridge Mountains and flowing southeast into Chesapeake Bay. Length: 212 mi./341 km.

rap·pee /ra pée/ *n.* a moist, strongly flavored snuff made from dark coarse tobacco (*archaic*) [Mid-18thC. From French *tabac râpé*, literally "rasped tobacco," from *râper* "to rasp," from Old French *rasper* "to scrape" from, ultimately, prehistoric Germanic.]

rap·pel /rə pél/ *vi.* **(-pelled, -pel·ling, -pels) DESCEND BY ROPE** to descend a steep slope or vertical face using a rope that is secured at the top and passed through a series of coils or a harness around the body ■ *n.* **DESCENT BY RAPPELLING** a descent made by rappelling [Mid-20thC. From French, from Old French *rapeler* "to recall," from *apeler* "to call."]

rap·pen /rápp'n/ (*plural* **-pen**) *n.* a Swiss centime [Mid-19thC. From German, from Middle High German *rappe* "raven," referring to the depiction of a bird on a coin of the Middle Ages.]

rap·port /ra páwr, rə páwr/ *n.* an emotional bond or friendly relationship between people based on mutual liking, trust, and a sense that they understand and share each other's concerns [Mid-17thC. From French, from Old French *raporter*, literally "to bring back," from *aporter* "to bring," ultimately from Latin *portare* "to bear" (see PORT[5]).]

rap·por·teur /ra pàwr túr/ *n.* (*formal*) **1. SCRIBE** somebody who records and reports to a higher body the results of the deliberations of a subordinate body such as a committee **2. SOMEBODY WHO REPORTS SOMETHING** somebody who is appointed to investigate a subject and deliver a report on it [Late 15thC. From French, from, ultimately, Old French *raporter* (see RAPPORT).]

rap·proche·ment /ra práwshmaaN, raa práwshmaaN/ *n.* the establishment or renewal of friendly relations between people or nations that were previously hostile or unsympathetic toward each other (*formal*) [Early 19thC. From French, from *rapprocher*, literally "to bring together," from *approcher* "to approach" (see APPROACH).]

rap·scal·lion /rap skállyən/ *n.* a mischievous and annoying child or disreputable and dishonest person (*archaic or humorous*) [Late 17thC. Alteration of earlier *rascallion*, of uncertain origin: probably formed from RASCAL.]

rap ses·sion *n.* an informal discussion, especially between people in the same line of business or with shared concerns (*informal*)

rap sheet *n.* a list of somebody's past arrests and the disposition of charges (*slang*)

rapt /rapt/ *adj.* **1. COMPLETELY ENGROSSED** involved in, fascinated by, or concentrating on something to the exclusion of anything else ○ *staring with rapt attention at the speaker* **2. BLISSFULLY HAPPY** showing or suggesting deep emotions of joy or ecstasy [14thC. From Latin *raptus* "seized," past participle of *rapere* (see RAPE[1]).] —**rapt·ly** *adv.* —**rapt·ness** *n.*

rap·tor /ráptər/ *n.* a bird of prey [14thC. From Latin, "robber," from *rapere* (see RAPE[1]).]

rap·to·ri·al /rap táwree əl/ *adj.* **1. LIVING BY PREDATION** able to live by catching prey **2. ADAPTED FOR CATCHING PREY** specially adapted for seizing prey, as are the feet of birds of prey with their sharp talons **3. OF PREDATORY BIRDS** typical of or relating to birds of prey

rap·ture /rápchər/ *n.* **1. OVERWHELMING HAPPINESS** a euphoric transcendent state in which somebody is overwhelmed by happiness or delight and unaware of anything else **2.** CHR **MYSTICAL TRANSPORTATION** a mystical experience of being transported into the spiritual realm, sometimes applied to the second coming of Jesus Christ when true believers are expected to rise up to join him in heaven ■ **rap·tures** *npl.* **STATE OF GREAT HAPPINESS OR ENTHUSIASM** a state of great happiness or enthusiasm about something, or words and gestures that express this ○ *went into raptures about the meal they'd had* [Late 16thC. Directly or via French from medieval Latin *raptura* "seizure," from Latin *raptus* "seized" (see RAPT).]

rap·ture of the deep *n.* MED = **nitrogen narcosis**

rap·tur·ous /rápchərəss/ *adj.* expressing great enthusiasm, happiness, or pleasure ○ *a rapturous welcome* —**rap·tur·ous·ly** *adv.* —**rap·tur·ous·ness** *n.*

ra·ra a·vis /ràirə áyviss, ràirə ávvəss/ (*plural* **ra·rae a·ves** /ràir áy vée z/ *or* **ra·ra a·vis·es**) *n.* somebody or something that is rarely encountered (*literary*) [From Latin, literally "rare bird"]

rare[1] /rair/ **(rar·er, rar·est)** *adj.* **1. NOT OFTEN HAPPENING** not often happening or found ○ *It's rare for them to miss a meeting.* **2. VALUABLE** particularly interesting or valuable, especially to collectors or scholars, because only a few exist **3. GREAT** unusually great or excellent ○ *a rare gift for languages* **4. CONTAINING LITTLE OXYGEN** thin in density and containing so little oxygen that breathing is difficult (*refers to a gas, especially the atmosphere at high altitudes*) [15thC.

From Latin *rarus* "having a loose texture, scarce."] — **rare·ness** *n.*

rare² /rair/ (**rar·er, rar·est**) *adj.* cooked quickly and lightly so as to remain raw and juicy inside (*refers to meat*) [Mid-17thC. Alteration of dialect *rear* "underdone" (of eggs), from Old English *hrēr*, of uncertain origin: possibly originally "lightly stirred."]

rare·bit /ráir bit/ *n.* = **Welsh rarebit** [Late 19thC. Alteration of *rabbit* in *Welsh rabbit* (see WELSH RAREBIT).]

rare earth *n.* an oxide of a rare-earth element

rare-earth el·e·ment *n.* a member of the lanthanide series, which contains 15 elements that have atomic numbers from 57 to 71 and share closely related chemical properties

rar·ee show *n.* (*archaic*) **1. PEEPSHOW** a peepshow **2. CARNIVAL** a street show or spectacle with unusual or outlandish items on view [Alteration of *rare show*]

rar·e·fac·tion /rèrrə fáksh'n, rérrə faksh'n/, **rar·e·fi·ca·tion** /rèrrəfə káysh'n/ *n.* the process of becoming or of making something such as a gas less dense [Early 17thC. From the medieval Latin stem *rarefaction-*, from Latin *rarefacere* (see RAREFY).] — **rar·e·fac·tion·al** *adj.*

rar·e·fied /rérrə fīd/, **rar·i·fied** *adj.* **1. PHYS WITH LOW DENSITY** having a low density (*refers especially to an atmosphere containing little oxygen*) **2. ESOTERIC OR ELITE** seemingly distinct or remote from ordinary reality and common people, and often purged of elements perceived as coarse or tasteless **3. ABOVE THE ORDINARY** existing or showing very high quality in character or style (*literary*) ○ *Milton's rarefied prose*

rar·e·fy /rérrə fī/ (**-fied, -fy·ing, -fies**), **rar·i·fy** (**-fied, -fy·ing, -fies**) *v.* **1.** *vti.* **BECOME OR MAKE SOMETHING LESS DENSE** to make something, especially a gas, less dense, or to become less dense **2.** *vt.* **MAKE MORE REFINED** to make something less connected with or typical of the ordinary [14thC. Directly or via French *raréfier* from medieval Latin *rareficare*, from Latin *rarefacere*, literally "to make rare," from *rarus* "rare" (see RARE¹) + *facere* "to make" (see FACT).] —**rar·e·fi·a·ble** /rérrə fī əb'l/ *adj.*

rare gas *n.* CHEM = **noble gas**

rare·ly /ráirlee/ *adv.* **1. ALMOST NEVER** almost never or not very often **2. THOROUGHLY** in a thorough way or to an unusual extent (*archaic*) **3. WELL** exceptionally well (*regional*) ○ *wrote rarely on the final essay*

rare·ripe /ráir rīp/ *adj.* **RIPENING EARLY** that ripens early ■ *n.* **SOMETHING THAT RIPENS EARLY** a fruit or vegetable that ripens early [Early 18thC. *Rare* "early" is a variant of RATHE.]

rar·i·fied *adj.* = **rarefied**

rar·i·fy *v.* ➧ **rarefy**

rar·ing /ráiring/ *adj.* very enthusiastic and eager to start doing something ○ *They were raring to go.* [Early 20thC. Present participle of *rare*, variant of REAR¹.]

rar·i·ty /rérrətee/ (*plural* **-ties**) *n.* **1. RARE OBJECT OR EVENT** something that happens rarely or that is particularly interesting or valuable because it is so unusual **2. INFREQUENCY** the fact of happening very seldom or of being very unusual

ras·bo·ra /raz báwrə, rázbərə/ *n.* a tropical freshwater fish found in East Africa and Asia, several species of which are brightly colored and often kept in home aquariums. Genus: *Rasbora.* [Mid-20thC. From modern Latin, of unknown origin.]

ras·cal /rásk'l/ *n.* **1. SOMEBODY WHO BEHAVES MISCHIEVOUSLY** somebody who behaves in a teasing mischievous way, especially a child (*humorous*) **2. DISHONEST PERSON** somebody, especially a man, who is dishonest or otherwise unethical [14thC. From Old French *rascaille* "mob, rabble," of uncertain origin: probably ultimately via *rasche* "scurf, scab" from Latin *radere* "to scrape" (see RAZE).] —**ras·cal·ly** *adj.*

rase *vt.* = **raze** (*dated*)

rash¹ *adj.* acting with, resulting from, or typical of thoughtless impetuous behavior [14thC. Origin uncertain: probably via assumed Old English *ræsc* from a prehistoric Germanic word meaning "quick," that is also the ancestor of English *rathe.*] —**rash·ly** *adv.* —**rash·ness** *n.*

rash² *n.* **1.** MED **SKIN ERUPTION** an outbreak on the skin's surface that is often reddish and itchy **2. SEVERAL INSTANCES** a series of events that happen in a brief period and are considered to be unusual or rare ○ *a rash of burglaries* [Early 18thC. Origin uncertain: perhaps from obsolete French *rache* "a sore," from, ultimately, Latin *rasus*, past participle of *radere* "to scrape" (see RAZE).]

rash·er /ráshər/ *n.* **1. PORTION OF BACON OR HAM** an order or portion of slices of cooked bacon or ham **2. SLICE OF BACON** a slice of bacon or ham, broiled or fried [Late 16thC. Origin unknown.]

ra·so·ri·al /rə sáwree əl/ *adj.* capable of or adapted for scratching the ground to look for food (*refers to a bird, especially a chicken*) [Mid-19thC. Formed from late Latin *rasor* "scraper," from Latin *rasus* (see RASH²).]

Rasp

rasp¹ /rasp/ *n.* **1. TYPE OF FILE** a tool used for scraping or smoothing wood or metal, similar to a file but with larger teeth on its cutting surface **2. HARSH GRATING SOUND** a harsh grating sound, similar to that of a rasp or saw cutting into wood **3. ACT OF SMOOTHING SOMETHING** the act of smoothing the surface of something such as wood or metal with a rasp ■ *v.* (**rasped, rasp·ing, rasps**) **1.** *vt.* **SAY SOMETHING IN HARSH VOICE** to say something, especially to give an order, in a harsh voice **2.** *vti.* **FILE OR SCRAPE SOMETHING** to use a rasp to file or scrape a surface in order to remove unevenness **3.** *vt.* **IRRITATE SOMEBODY** to irritate or annoy somebody [13thC. From Old French *rasper* "to scrape," from, ultimately, prehistoric Germanic.] —**rasp·er** *n.* — **rasp·ing** *adj.* —**rasp·ing·ly** *adv.* —**rasp·y** *adj.*

rasp² *n.* *Scotland* a raspberry [Mid-16thC. Shortening of obsolete *raspis* "raspberry," of unknown origin.]

ras·pa·to·ry /ráspə tàwree/ (*plural* **-ries**) *n.* a surgical instrument similar to a rasp, used to smooth the ends of a bone [15thC. From medieval Latin *raspatorium*, from *raspare* "to scrape," from, ultimately, prehistoric Germanic.]

rasp·ber·ry /ráz bèree/ (*plural* **-ries**) *n.* **1. SMALL CUP-SHAPED FRUIT** a small red or black cup-shaped fruit with a sweet taste that grows around a pithy stalk and is made up of many tiny juicy globes (**drupelets**) **2. BUSH** a shrubby plant of the rose family that has a straight prickly stem on which raspberries grow. Genus: *Rubus.* **3. RUDE NOISE** a rude noise meant to imitate the sound of passing gas, made by blowing air through pursed lips and intended as an insult or a gesture of disapproval or defiance (*slang*) **4. RED COLOR** a deep pink color with a purplish tinge to it [Early 17thC. From RASP² + BERRY.]

AKG London

Grigory Yefimovich Rasputin

Ras·pu·tin /rass pyōōtin/, **Grigory Yefimovich** (1872–1916) Russian peasant and self-proclaimed holy man. His friendship with Russia's last emperor and empress wrecked the Romanov dynasty's prestige and contributed to the coming of the Russian Revolution (1917).

rasse /rássə,ráss/ *n.* a small carnivorous mammal that is similar to a cat in appearance. It has anal scent glands and is native to South and Southeast Asia. Latin name: *Viverricula indica.* [Early 19thC. From Javanese.]

Ras·ta /rástə/ *n.* **RASTAFARIAN** a Rastafarian (*informal*) ■ *adj.* **OF RASTAFARIANS** relating to Rastafarians or Rastafarianism (*informal*) [Mid-20thC. Shortening.]

Ras·ta·far·i·an /ràstə férree ən/ *n.* a member of an Afro-Caribbean religious group that venerates the former emperor of Ethiopia, Haile Selassie, forbids the cutting of hair, and stresses Black culture and identity [Mid-20thC. Formed from Amharic *Ras Tafari*, the name by which Haile Selassie was known prior to his coming to power, literally "prince to be feared."] — **Ras·ta·far·i·an·ism** *n.*

rast·er /rástər/ *n.* the pattern of horizontal scanning lines made by an electron beam on the surface of a cathode-ray tube that create the image that appears on a television or computer screen [Mid-20thC. Via German, "screen," from Latin *rastrum* "rake," from *radere* "to scrape" (see RAZE.]

ras·ter·ize /rástə rīz/ (**-ized, -iz·ing, -iz·es**) *vt.* to convert digitized image into a format suitable for display on a computer monitor or printout

Rat

rat *n.* **1.** ZOOL **LONG-TAILED RODENT** a long-tailed rodent, larger than a mouse. Genus: *Rattus.* **2. ANIMAL LIKE A RAT** an animal that resembles a rat **3. SOMEBODY UNTRUSTWORTHY** a mean sneaky deceitful person, especially somebody who betrays friends or confidences (*slang*) **4. ARTIFICIAL HAIR** a pad with tapered ends used in hairdressing to add height to the hair (*dated*) ■ *vt.* (**rat·ted, rat·ting, rats**) **1.** HUNT **HUNT RATS** to hunt and kill rats **2. MAKE THE HAIR STAND HIGH ON THE HEAD** to use a comb to tease hair into knots with quick repeated movements, which makes it stand up high from the scalp [Old English *ræt*] ◇ **smell a rat** be suspicious that something is not right (*informal*)

rat on *vt.* to betray somebody's trust, especially by revealing something told in confidence (*informal*)

rat·a·ble /ráytəb'l/, **rate·a·ble** *adj.* **ABLE TO BE RATED** able to be estimated or have a value placed on it ■ **rat·a·bles, rate·a·bles** *npl.* **1. PROPERTY TAX INCOME** for a government, income from taxes on property **2. TAXABLE BUILDINGS OR OTHER PROPERTY** buildings or other property, especially those in commercial use, that supply local government with tax income — **rat·a·bil·i·ty** /ràytə bíllətee/ *n.* —**rat·a·bly** /ráytəblee/ *adv.*

rat·a·fi·a /ràttə féē ə/ *n.* **1. LIQUEUR** a liqueur made from fruit juices or softened fruit in liquor, especially brandy, and often flavored with almonds or with peach or apricot kernels **2. rat·a·fi·a, rat·a·fi·a bis·cuit BISCUIT** a small biscuit similar to a macaroon, flavored with almond or ratafia. ◊ **macaroon** [Late 17thC. Via French from Caribbean Creole.]

rat·a·plan /ráttə plàn/ *n.* a noise like the rapid beating of a drum, the sound of horses' hooves striking the ground, or machine-gun fire, made up of a series of short repeated sounds [Mid-19thC. From French, an imitation of the sound.]

rat-a-tat-tat, **rat-tat-tat, rat-tat** *n.* **SOUND OF KNOCKING AT A DOOR** the distinctive rhythmic pattern of short loud sounds made by somebody knocking at a door ■ *interj.* **IMITATION OF A KNOCKING SOUND** an imitation of the sound of somebody knocking on a door [Late 17thC. An imitation of the sound.]

rat·a·tou·ille /ràttə tōōy/ *n.* a dish of stewed vegetables, originally from southern France, usually consisting of tomatoes, onions, peppers, eggplant, and zucchini cooked slowly in olive oil [Late 19thC. From French, an alteration of *touiller* "to stir," from Old French *tooiller* (see TOIL).]

rat-bite fe·ver *n.* an infectious disease in humans caused by the bite of a rat infected with either of two bacteria, *Streptobacillus moniliformis* or *Spirillum minus*

rat·catch·er *n.* somebody whose job is to rid buildings of rats and other vermin

rat cheese *n.* Cheddar cheese (*informal humorous*)

ratch·et /ráchət/ *n.* **1.** TURNING DEVICE MOVING IN ONE DIRECTION a mechanism, used especially in lifting devices and some hand tools, consisting of a metal wheel operating with a catch that permits motion in only one direction **2.** RATCHET WHEEL OR PAWL either of the main parts of a ratchet device, the toothed wheel or bar, or the pawl ■ *v.* (**-et·ed** *or* **-et·ted, -et·ing** *or* **-et·ting, -ets**) **1.** *vt.* FORCE UP OR DOWN to force something such as prices or political rhetoric to rise or fall in level or intensity by deliberately applying pressure in successive and irreversible stages **2.** *vti.* MOVE WITH A RATCHET to move, or to move something gradually up or down by means of a ratchet [Mid-17thC. Via French *rochet* "spool" from, ultimately, a prehistoric Germanic word that is also the ancestor of English *rocket*.]

ratch·et ef·fect *n.* the failure of wages or prices that have risen or fallen because of temporary market pressure to return to their previous level once that pressure is removed

ratch·et wheel *n.* a toothed wheel in a ratchet mechanism

rate /rayt/ *n.* **1.** SPEED the speed at which one measured quantity happens, runs, moves, or changes compared to another measured amount such as time **2.** AMOUNT IN RELATION TO A STANDARD FIGURE the amount, frequency, or speed of something expressed as a proportion of a larger figure or in relation to a whole ○ *The dropout rate at the end of the first year is around one in three.* **3.** COMM CHARGE the amount of money charged per unit, e.g., per hour, per page, or per thousand, for a particular job, service, or commodity ○ *I'm charging you the going rate for the job.* ■ *v.* (**rat·ed, rat·ing, rates**) **1.** *vt.* SET A VALUE ON to calculate or appraise the value of something ○ *How would you rate this gem collection?* **2.** *vti.* ASSESS to have or to be regarded as having a particular value, position, or importance relative to other people or things ○ *This rates as undoubtedly the worst movie I have ever seen.* **3.** *vt.* DESERVE to deserve or be worthy of something ○ *Her latest book didn't even rate a review.* **4.** *vt.* CLASSIFY to give a particular classification or rating to something such as a machine, that identifies its performance capabilities and limits **5.** *vt.* FIN VALUE FOR TAX PURPOSES to value something, especially a property, for tax purposes [15thC. Via Old French from medieval Latin *(pro) rata (parte)*, literally "(according to a) fixed (part)," from Latin *ratus*, past participle of *reri* "to calculate."] ◇ **at any rate** used to indicate that an important point is true, whatever other considerations there may be

WORD KEY: ORIGIN

The Latin word *reri* from which *rate* is derived is also the source of English *ratify, ration*, and *reason*.

rate·a·ble *adj., n.* = **ratable**

rate cap *n.* a maximum interest charge permitted during the life of an adjustable-rate mortgage

ra·tel /ráytl, raát'l/ *n.* ZOOL a carnivorous animal with short thick legs, a strong body with a thick furry coat, dark underneath and whitish on top, and a head similar to a badger's. Ratels are found in Asia and Africa, live on honey and small animals, and are noted for being very aggressive. Latin name: *Mellivora capensis.* [Late 18thC. From Afrikaans, of unknown origin.]

rate·mak·ing /ráyt máyking/ *n.* the process or business of establishing rates of payment for such things as public transportation or utilities

rate of change *n.* the ratio of the difference in values of a variable during a time period to the length of that time period

rate of ex·change *n.* = **exchange rate**

rate of re·turn *n.* the amount of income generated in a year by capital invested, expressed as a percentage of the total sum

rate·pay·er /ráyt pàyər/ *n.* somebody who pays for the use of a utility such as electricity or water on the basis of the amount consumed

rat·er /ráytər/ *n.* **1.** SOMEBODY WHO FIXES RATES somebody who establishes rates or ratings **2.** SOMEBODY OF A SPECIFIC ABILITY somebody who has a particular rank or level of ability (*often used in combination*) ○ *All of them are nothing but second-raters with delusions of grandeur.*

rat·fink /rát fingk/ *n.* an offensive term for somebody regarded as obnoxious or despicable (*insult*)

rat·fish /rát fish/ (*plural* **-fish** *or* **-fish·es**) *n.* a cartilaginous deep-sea fish with a long narrow tail, found worldwide. Family: Chimaeridae.

rat flea *n.* an insect of the flea family, found worldwide, that lives as a parasite on rodents, sometimes carrying the deadly bacterium that causes bubonic plague

rathe /rayth, raath/ *adj.* ripening or appearing early (*archaic*) [Old English *hræþ* "quick," from a prehistoric Germanic word that is perhaps also the ancestor of English *rash*]

Ra·then·au /raátə nòir/, **Walther** (1867–1922) German political economist and public servant. As foreign minister, he represented Germany at reparations conferences after World War I. He was assassinated by German nationalists.

rath·er /ráthər/ *adv.* **1.** MORE WILLINGLY more readily or willingly ○ *You go to the movies; I'd rather stay home tonight.* **2.** WITH MORE JUSTIFICATION with more logic, evidence, precision, or justification ○ *You should praise rather than blame them.* **3.** SOMEWHAT to some extent or degree ○ *rather disappointing* **4.** ON THE CONTRARY in contrast or opposition to what has been stated or expected ○ *You think she's snobbish? Rather, I'd say she's shy.* **5.** CONSIDERABLY to a great extent or degree ○ *I think the irises are rather attractive.* ■ *interj. U.K.* MOST CERTAINLY used to express complete or enthusiastic agreement with what has just been said (*dated*) [Old English *hræþor*, originally the comparative form of *hraep* (see RATHE and so meaning "more quickly," hence "earlier, sooner"]

Rath·lin Is·land /ráthlin-/ island in Northern Ireland, off the northern coast of Antrim County. It is home to three lighthouses. Length: 6 mi./10 km.

rat hole *n.* the entrance to a rat's nest

raths·kel·ler /raátskèlər, rátskèlər/ *n.* a beer hall or restaurant that serves German dishes, usually located below street level [Early 20thC. From obsolete German, literally "council cellar" (cellar of the town hall), from *Rat* "council" + *Keller* "cellar."]

rat·i·fy /ráttə fī/ (**-fied, -fy·ing, -fies**) *vt.* to give formal approval to something, usually an agreement negotiated by somebody else, in order that it can become valid or operative [14thC. Via French *ratifier* from medieval Latin *ratificare*, literally "to make fixed," from Latin *ratus* "fixed" (see RATE).] —**rat·i·fi·a·ble** /ráttə fīəb'l/ *adj.* —**rat·i·fi·ca·tion** /ràttəfə káysh'n/ *n.* —**rat·i·fi·er** /ráttə fīr/ *n.*

rat·i·né /ráttə náy, ráttə nay/, **rat·i·ne** *n.* a loosely woven cloth with a coarse nubby texture [Early 20thC. From French, past participle of *ratiner* "to raise a nap," from *ratine* (see RATINE.]

rat·ing /ráyting/ *n.* **1.** ASSESSMENT an assessment or classification of something on a scale according to how much or how little of a particular quality it possesses **2.** COMM CREDIT STANDING an assessment of the financial status and creditworthiness of a company or an individual **3.** MECH ENG PERFORMANCE LIMIT OF A MACHINE a stated performance limit of a machine or system, expressed as capacity, range, or working capability **4.** CLASSIFICATION OF SOMEBODY BY OCCUPATION a classification of somebody, e.g., a member of the military or a government worker, based on his or her specialization or occupation ■ **rat·ings** *npl.* TV, RADIO LIST SHOWING SIZE OF AN AUDIENCE a list or lists showing the estimated number of people who tuned in to a particular TV or radio program, used as an indication of its relative popularity

ra·tio /ráyshō, ráyshi ō/ (*plural* **-tios**) *n.* **1.** PROPORTIONAL RELATIONSHIP a proportional relationship between two different numbers or quantities ○ *The ratio of teachers to students at that school is 1 to 27* **2.** MATH ONE NUMBER DIVIDED BY ANOTHER a quotient of two numbers or expressions arrived at by dividing one by the other **3.** FIN RELATIVE VALUE OF GOLD AND SILVER the relative value of gold and silver in a monetary system based on these two metals [Mid-17thC. From Latin, "calculation," formed from *ratus* "reckoned" (see RATE).]

ra·ti·oc·i·nate /ràyti ṓs'nàyt, ráshi-/ (**-nat·ed, -nat·ing, -nates**) *vi.* to think or put forward an argument about something in a strictly logical way (*formal*) [Mid-17thC. From Latin *ratiocinat-*, past participle stem of *ratiocinari* "to compute," from *ratio* (see RATIO).] —**ra·ti·oc·i·na·tion** *n.* —**ra·ti·oc·i·na·tive** /ràyti ṓs'naytiv, ràshi-/ *adj.* —**ra·ti·oc·i·na·tor** /ràyti ṓs'naytər/ *n.*

ra·tion /rásh'n, ráysh'n/ *n.* **1.** FIXED AMOUNT ALLOCATED TO AN INDIVIDUAL a fixed and limited amount of something, especially food, given or allocated to somebody or a group from the stocks available, especially during a time of shortage or a war **2.** ADEQUATE AMOUNT the amount of anything that it seems normal or desirable for an individual to have ○ *more than your ration of bad luck* ■ **ra·tions** *npl.* AMOUNT OF FOOD OFFICIALLY ALLOCATED food, especially an amount of food allocated to somebody, e.g., a soldier or hiker, from a limited stock ■ *vt.* (**-tioned, -tion·ing, -tions**) **1.** RESTRICT AVAILABLE AMOUNT OF to restrict the amount of something, usually a commodity in short supply, that an individual is allowed to buy, consume, or use ○ *Gasoline was rationed, so long trips were out of the question.* **2.** LIMIT QUANTITY AVAILABLE TO to allow somebody only a limited quantity of something [Early 18thC. Via French from Spanish *ración*, from Latin *ratio* "calculation" (see RATIO). The modern meaning developed from "amount of provisions calculated for a soldier."]

ration out *vt.* to distribute something, especially something that is in short supply, in fixed or strictly limited quantities

ra·tion·al /rásh'n'l/ *adj.* **1.** REASONABLE AND SENSIBLE governed by, or showing evidence of, clear and sensible thinking and judgment, based on reason rather than emotion or prejudice **2.** ABLE TO THINK CLEARLY AND SENSIBLY able to think clearly and sensibly, because the mind is not impaired by physical or mental condition, violent emotion, or prejudice ○ *I can't be rational when so many people give me conflicting advice.* **3.** IN ACCORDANCE WITH REASON AND LOGIC presented or understandable in terms that accord with reason and logic or with scientific knowledge and are not based on appeals to emotion or, prejudice **4.** ABLE TO REASON endowed with the ability to reason, as opposed to being governed solely by instinct and appetite **5.** MATH EXPRESSIBLE AS RATIO OF POLYNOMIALS able to be expressed exactly as the quotient of two whole numbers or polynomials ○ *a rational function* ■ *n.* MATH RATIONAL NUMBER a rational number [14thC. From Latin *rationalis*, from *ratio* "calculation" (see RATIO).] —**ra·tion·al·ly** *adv.* —**ra·tion·al·ness** *n.*

ra·tion·al choice the·o·ry *n.* the hypothesis, derived from game theory, that there is a rational, definable, and calculable basis to human decision-making

ra·tion·ale /ràshə nál/ *n.* the reasoning or principle that underlies or explains a particular course of action, or a statement setting out these reasons or principles [Mid-17thC. From modern Latin, from Latin *rationalis*, (see RATIONAL).]

ra·tion·al-e·mo·tive be·hav·ior ther·a·py, ra·tion·al-e·mo·tive ther·a·py *n.* a form of cognitive-behavioral therapy in which the client is encouraged to examine and change irrational thought patterns and beliefs in order to reduce dysfunctional behavior

ra·tion·al ho·ri·zon *n.* ASTRON the celestial horizon (*technical*)

ra·tion·al·ism /rásh'n'lìzəm/ *n.* **1.** REASONING AS BASIS OF ACTION the belief that thought and action should be governed by reason **2.** REASON AS SOURCE OF TRUTH the belief that reason and logic are the primary sources of knowledge and truth and should be relied on in searching for and testing the truth of things —**ra·tion·al·ist** *n.* —**ra·tion·al·is·tic** /rásh'n'lístik/ *adj.* —**ra·tion·al·is·ti·cal·ly** /-istək'lee/ *adv.*

ra·tion·al·i·ty /ràshə nállətee/ (*plural* **-ties**) *n.* **1.** FACT OF BEING RATIONAL thinking or behaving in a rational way, or having the ability to think rationally **2.** SOMETHING RATIONAL a rational belief, opinion, or action (*often used in the plural*) **3.** CONDITION OF BEING LOGICAL the condition in which values, beliefs, and techniques are believed to be based on logical, explicable principles

ra·tion·al·i·za·tion /ràsh'n'lə záysh'n/ *n.* **1.** PROCESS OF RATIONALIZING the process of rationalizing something, or an effect of rationalizing something **2.** PSYCHOANAL DEFENSE MECHANISM in psychoanalytic theory, a defense mechanism whereby people attempt to hide their true motivations and emotions by providing reasonable or self-justifying explanations for irrational or unacceptable behavior

ra·tion·al·ize /rásh'n'lìz/ (**-ized, -iz·ing, -iz·es**) *v.* **1.** *vti.* OFFER A REASONABLE EXPLANATION to attempt to justify behavior normally considered irrational or unacceptable by offering an apparently reasonable explanation **2.** *vt.* **MAKE SOMETHING MORE LOGICAL OR RATIONAL** to make something rational, logical, or consistent **3.** *vt.* **INTERPRET SOMETHING LOGICALLY** to interpret something from a logical or rational perspective **4.** *vt.* MATH **ELIMINATE RADICALS** to eliminate irrational numbers from an expression or an equation —**ra·tion·al·iz·a·ble** *adj.* —**ra·tion·al·iz·er** *n.*

ra·tion·al num·ber *n.* a whole number or the quotient of any whole numbers, excluding zero as a denominator

ra·tio scale *n.* a scale for measuring data that makes it possible to compare different values and to state the difference between them in the form of a ratio

Rat Is·lands /rát-/ group of islands in Alaska, in the western Aleutian Islands, including Kiska, Amchitka, Semisopochnoi, and Rat Island

rat·ite /rá tīt/ *n.* a flightless bird such as the ostrich or emu that has a flat breastbone without the keel that flying birds have [Late 19thC. From Latin *ratitus* "having the figure of a raft," from *ratis* "raft."]

rat kan·ga·roo *n.* small kangaroo found in Australia and Tasmania that resembles a rat and has long hind legs for jumping. Genera: *Potorus* and *Bettongia.*

rat·line /ráttlən/, **rat·lin** *n.* any of the small ropes fastened horizontally between the shrouds in the rigging of a sailing ship to make a ladder for the crew going aloft [15thC. Origin unknown.]

RATO /ráytō/ *abbr.* rocket-assisted takeoff

ra·toon /rə to͞on/, **rat·toon** *n.* **1. SHOOT AT THE BASE OF A PLANT** a shoot growing up from the base of a crop plant such as sugar cane or bananas after the previous growth has been cut back **2. CROP PRODUCED ON RATOONS** a crop, e.g., sugar cane, bananas, or pineapple, that is produced on ratoons ■ *vti.* **(-tooned, -toon·ing, -toons) PRODUCE RATOONS** to propagate by inducing the formation of ratoons, or to send up ratoons [Mid-17thC. Via Spanish *retoño* "shoot" from, ultimately, Latin *autumnus* "autumn."]

rat race *n.* the struggle of individuals to survive and make progress in the competitive environment of modern life, seen as a dehumanizing and ultimately futile activity (*informal*) ○ *I'd like to get out of this rat race and retire to an isolated mountain cabin.*

rat·shit *adj. Aus* lacking in quality or excellence (*slang insult*)

rat snake *n.* a large nonvenomous snake of North America and Asia that eats rodents. Genera: *Elaphe* and *Ptyas.*

rat's nest *n.* **1. SOMETHING MESSY** something, such a room, house, or somebody's hair, that is very messy (*informal*) ○ *How can he live in such a rat's nest?* **2.** ZOOL **NEST OF RATS** a nest in which rats live and breed

rat·tail *n.* **HAIRLESS TAIL** a hairless tail on a horse ■ *adj.* **rat·tail, rat-tail, rat-tailed LIKE A RAT'S TAIL** looking like or having a part that resembles a rat's tail ○ *a rat-tail comb*

rat·tail cac·tus, rat's tail cac·tus (*plural* **rat·tail cac·ti** *or* **rat·tail cac·tus**) *n.* a commonly cultivated Mexican cactus that has thin creeping or hanging stems and bright crimson or pink flowers. Latin name: *Aporocactus flagelliformis.*

rat-tailed mag·got *n.* the larva of the drone fly that has an elongated rear end that it extends above the water surface like a snorkel while it feeds below. Latin name: *Eristalis tenax.*

rat·tan /ra tán, rə tán/ *n.* **1.** INDUST **STEMS USED FOR FURNITURE** long thin jointed and pliable stems used in wickerwork and for making furniture and canes **2.** HOUSEHOLD **ARTICLES MADE OF RATTAN** something made of rattan such as furniture **3.** PLANTS **TROPICAL ASIAN CLIMBING PALM** a tropical Asian climbing palm that is the source of rattan. Genera: *Calamus* and *Daemonorops* and *Plectomia.* [Mid-17thC. From Malay *rotan*, of uncertain origin: probably formed from *raut* "to trim, to strip."]

rat-tat *n., interj.* = **rat-a-tat-tat**

rat·ted /ráttəd/ *adj.* having had a comb used repeatedly to make tangles in the hair, making the hair stand up higher from the scalp [Late 20thC. Formed from RAT.]

rat·teen /ra te͞en/ *n.* ratiné (*archaic*) [Mid-17thC. From French *ratine*, of uncertain origin: perhaps ultimately from Latin *radere* "to scrape."]

rat·ter /ráttər/ *n.* an animal, especially a cat or dog, that is good at catching rats

rat·tle[1] /rátt'l/ *v.* **(-tled, -tling, -tles) 1.** *vti.* **MAKE SHORT SHARP KNOCKING SOUNDS** to make short sharp knocking or jangling sounds in quick succession, especially as a result of being moved or shaken, or to shake something so as to produce such sounds ○ *The windows and doors rattled in the wind.* **2.** *vi.* **MOVE WITH RATTLING SOUND** to move while making a rattling sound ○ *The old jalopy rattled noisily down the street.* **3.** *vt.* **DISCONCERT SOMEBODY** to make somebody lose his or her composure and feel frightened, worried, confused, or annoyed ○ *Reporters shouting questions rattled her.* ■ *n.* **1. SHORT SHARP KNOCKING OR JANGLING SOUNDS** a succession of short sharp knocking or jangling sounds, usually caused by something shaking or being shaken **2. BABY'S TOY** a baby's toy consisting of a hollow shape with small objects inside, usually attached to a handle, that makes a rattling noise when shaken **3.** MED **RATTLING NOISE IN THE THROAT** a raspy or rattling noise made in the throat caused by obstructed breathing and heard especially near death **4. NOISEMAKER** an object such as a musical instrument or a Shaman's implement that produces a loud rattling sound **5.** PLANTS **PLANT WITH RATTLING SEEDS** any of various European plants whose seeds make a rattling noise inside the seed capsule **6.** ZOOL **TIP OF RATTLESNAKE'S TAIL** a set of loosely attached horny segments at the end of a rattlesnake's tail that produce a buzzing or rattling sound when shaken [14thC. Origin uncertain: probably from Middle Low German *ratelen*, an imitation of the sound.]

rattle around *vi.* to be in a room, house, or building that is bigger than it needs to be (*informal*) ○ *There's just the two of us rattling around in this place.*

rattle off *vt.* to say, read aloud, or perform something very rapidly or with no apparent effort

rattle on *vi.* to talk rapidly and at length about something that is of little interest or importance to the listener

rat·tle[2] /rátt'l/ **(-tled, -tling, -tles)** *vt.* to attach ratlines to the shrouds in the rigging of a ship [Early 18thC. Back-formation from *ratling*, a variant of RATLINE.]

rat·tle·box /rátt'l bawks/ *n.* a tropical plant that has inflated seedpods containing seeds that make a rattling noise when the stem moves. Genus: *Crotalaria.*

rat·tle·brained *adj.* showing a lack of reason or sensibility by speaking rapidly and at length without much substance (*informal insult*)

rat·tler /rátlər/ *n.* **1.** = **rattlesnake 2. RATTLING THING** somebody or something that rattles **3.** a freight train (*informal*)

Rattlesnake

rat·tle·snake /rátt'l snayk/ *n.* a large venomous snake of the pit viper family, found in North and South America, whose tail has loosely attached horny segments that buzz or rattle when vibrated. Genus: *Crotalis* and *Sistrurus.*

rat·tle·snake plan·tain *n.* an orchid with striped or mottled leaves that resemble a rattlesnake's skin and spikes of white or yellow flowers. Genus:: *Goodyera.*

rat·tle·snake root *n.* a composite plant that has bitter-tasting tuberous roots and white or purple flowers resembling a strap, once believed to offer protection from rattlesnake bites. Genus: *Prenanthes.*

rat·tle·snake weed *n.* a North American plant that has purple-veined leaves and yellow flower heads. Latin name: *Hieracium venosum.*

rat·tle·trap /rátt'l trap/ *n.* an old noisy worn-out car or other vehicle (*informal*)

rat·tling /rátling/ *adj.* moving or talking at a very fast or lively pace ○ *a rattling TV debate* —**rat·tling·ly** *adv.*

rat·tly /rátlee/ **(-tlier, -tli·est)** *adj.* making a lot of noise, usually because of being in very bad condition or not firmly fixed ○ *a rattly air conditioner*

rat·toon *n.* = **ratoon**

rat·trap *n.* **1. SQUALID DWELLING** a dilapidated dirty unsafe dwelling (*informal*) ○ *They bought a rattrap and are fixing it up* **2. TRAP FOR RATS** a trap designed to catch rats

rat·ty /ráttee/ **(-ti·er, -ti·est)** *adj.* **1. MESSY** having an appearance that is messy and generally unkempt (*informal*) ○ *a ratty old sweater* **2. DILAPIDATED** in an unsafe, rundown condition and unfit for human habitation (*informal*) **3. INFESTED WITH RATS** full of or overrun with rats **4. OF RATS** relating to or believed to be characteristic of rats —**rat·ti·ly** *adv.* —**rat·ti·ness** *n.*

rau·cous /ráwkəss/ *adj.* loud and hoarse or unpleasant-sounding, or characterized by loud noise, shouting, and ribald laughter [Mid-18thC. Formed from Latin *raucus* "hoarse."] —**rau·ci·ty** /ráwsətee/ *n.* —**rau·cous·ly** /ráwkəslee/ *adv.* —**rau·cous·ness** *n.*

raunch /rawnch/ *n.* (*slang*) **1. SEXUAL EXPLICITNESS** sexual explicitness or suggestiveness of an earthy or vulgar kind, especially as part of a performer's material or act **2. SEXUALLY EXPLICIT MATERIAL** sexually explicit or lewd material or language **3. MESSINESS** lack of cleanliness or neatness [Mid-20thC. Back-formation from RAUNCHY.]

raun·chy /ráwnchee/ **(-chi·er, -chi·est)** *adj.* **1. SEXUALLY EXPLICIT OR OBSCENE** sexually explicit or obscene in a coarse vulgar way (*informal*) **2. DIRTY** lacking neatness or cleanliness (*slang*) [Mid-20thC. Origin unknown.] —**raun·chi·ly** *adv.* —**raun·chi·ness** *n.*

Robert Rauschenberg

Rausch·en·berg /rówsh'n búrg/, **Robert** (*b.* 1925) U.S. artist. His hybrid three-dimensional works such as *Monogram* (1955–59) had a strong influence on the pop art movement of the 1960s.

Raush·en·busch /rówsh'n bo͝osh/, **Walter** (1861–1918) U.S. clergyman. He was prominent in the Social Gospel movement, which advocated applying Christian principles to social problems.

rau·wol·fi·a /row wo͝olfee ə, raw-/ *n.* **1. TROPICAL SOUTHEAST ASIAN TREE** a tropical Southeast Asian tree or shrub belonging to the dogbane family. Latin name: *Rauwolfia serpentina.* **2. ROOT USED TO MAKE SEDATIVE DRUGS** root used to make various sedative drugs, including reserpine [Mid-18thC. From modern Latin, genus name, named for Leonhard *Rauwolf* (died 1596), a German botanist and physician.]

rav·age /rávvij/ *v.* **(-aged, -ag·ing, -ag·es) 1.** *vti.* **COMPLETELY WRECK OR DAMAGE SOMETHING** to wreck or utterly destroy something through a violent onslaught of some kind (*often passive*) ○ *a once-beautiful landscape ravaged by development* **2.** *vt.* **WRECK AND PLUNDER** to plunder or sack a place or area ■ *n.* **ACT OR HABIT OF DESTRUCTION** the act or habit of destroying or plundering something ■ **rav·ag·es** *npl.* **DAMAGING EFFECTS** the damaging or disfiguring effects of something, especially time [Early 17thC. From French *ravager*, alteration of *ravine* "rushing of water," from, ultimately, Latin *rapere* "to seize" (see RAPE[1]).] —**rav·age·ment** *n.* —**rav·ag·er** *n.*

rave /rayv/ *v.* **(raved, rav·ing, raves) 1.** *vi.* **GIVE HIGH PRAISE** to praise something in a very enthusiastic way ○ *All the critics raved about her performance.* **2.** *vti.* **SPEAK**

WILDLY AND INCOHERENTLY to speak in a loud or angry way that suggests lack of rationality or loss of self-control **3.** *vi.* **STORM** to be very stormy and make a loud roaring noise (*literary*) ■ *n.* **1. ENTHUSIASTIC PRAISE** something, especially a review, that expresses extremely enthusiastic praise for something (*informal*) (*often used before a noun*) ○ *gave the novel rave reviews* **2. LARGE-SCALE PARTY** a large-scale party or club event at which pop music is played, lasting sometimes all night (*slang*) **3. ACT OF RAVING** an act or instance of raving [14thC. From Old Northern French *raver*, of uncertain origin.]

rav·el /rávv'l/ (**-eled** *or* **-elled, -el·ing** *or* **-el·ling, -els**) *v.* **1.** *vti.* **FRAY** to come, or to cause threads to come, loose from a knitted or woven fabric **2.** *vti.* **TANGLE** to become tangled, or to cause threads or fibers of some kind to tangle ○ *My fishing line has raveled.* **3.** *vt.* **RESOLVE SOMETHING** to clarify or resolve something complicated [Late 16thC. Origin uncertain: probably from Dutch *ravelen*.] —**rav·el·er** *n.* —**rav·el·ment** *n.*

Maurice Ravel

Ra·vel /rə vél/, **Maurice** (1875–1937) French composer. A master of orchestration, he wrote impressionistic pieces that are classics of the 20th-century repertoire. His works include *Boléro* (1928) and *Daphnis et Chloé* (1912). Full name **Maurice Joseph Ravel**

rav·el·in /rávvlən/ *n.* a small outwork in fortifications consisting of two embankments shaped like an arrowhead that point outward in front of a larger defense work [Late 16thC. Via French from Italian *ravellina*, of unknown origin.]

Raven

ra·ven[1] /ráyv'n/ *n.* **LARGE BLACK BIRD OF CROW FAMILY** a large bird belonging to the crow family with glossy black plumage, a wedge-shaped tail, and a large beak. It is found throughout the northern hemisphere, chiefly in upland regions, and is a subject of legend and folklore, being often perceived as a bad omen. Latin name: *Corvus corax*. ■ *adj.* COLORS **SHINY BLACK** of a deep lustrous black (*literary*) [Old English *hræfn*. Ultimately from a prehistoric Germanic word, thought to be an imitation of its croaking.]

WORD KEY: CULTURAL NOTE

The Raven, a poem by Edgar Allen Poe (1845). This melancholy tale of lost love gained Poe national fame. As a young student mourns the death of his lover, a raven–a traditional symbol of doom–appears at his window. To every question that the student poses about his future and his lover, the bird responds "Nevermore."

rav·en[2] /rávv'n/ (**-ened, -en·ing, -ens**) *vti.* **1. EAT GREEDILY** to eat something voraciously or greedily **2. TAKE SOMETHING AWAY BY FORCE** to take something away by force, especially prey or plunder [15thC. Via Old French *raviner* "to seize" from, ultimately, Latin *rapere* (see RAPE[1]).] —**rav·en·er** *n.*

rav·en·ing /rávv'ning/ *adj.* living by hunting prey, especially in a greedy voracious way —**rav·en·ing·ly** *adv.*

Ra·ven·na /rə vénnə/ capital city of Ravenna Province, Emilia-Romagna Region, northeastern Italy. An ancient Roman city, it contains several early Christian churches. Population: 134,000 (1994).

rav·en·ous /rávv'nəss/ *adj.* **1. HUNGRY** extremely hungry **2. GREEDY FOR SOMETHING** hungry or greedy for something, especially for the gratification of wants or desires **3. PREDATORY** voracious and predatory —**rav·en·ous·ly** *adv.* —**rav·en·ous·ness** *n.*

rav·er /ráyvər/ *n.* somebody who goes to raves (*informal*)

rav·in /rávvin/ *n.* (*archaic or literary*) **1. PREYING** the act of preying on something **2. PREY** something taken as prey [14thC. From Old French *ravine* (see RAVINE).]

ra·vine /rə veén/ *n.* a deep narrow valley, especially one formed by running water [15thC. From Old French *ravine* "rapine, violent rush," from, ultimately, Latin *rapere* (see RAPE[1]).]

rav·ing /ráyving/ *adj.* **1. IRRATIONAL** wildly irrational, angry, or insulting **2. STUNNING** used to emphasize the sense of admiration and excitement felt for something (*informal*) ○ *a raving review of the play* ■ **rav·ings** *npl.* **WILDLY IRRATIONAL SPEECH** wildly irrational, angry, or insulting utterances ○ *the ravings of a person cheated* —**rav·ing·ly** *adv.*

ra·vi·o·li /ràvvee ṓlee/ (*plural* **-lis**) *n.* a food made from small squares of pasta sealed around a meat, cheese, or other filling [Mid-19thC. From Italian, the plural of dialectal *raviolo* "small turnip."]

rav·ish /rávvish/ (**-ished, -ish·ing, -ish·es**) *vt.* **1. RAPE** to force somebody to engage in sexual intercourse (*literary*) **2. OVERWHELM EMOTIONALLY** to overwhelm somebody with deep and pleasurable feelings or emotions (*usually passive*) **3. CARRY OFF** to carry off something by violent force (*archaic or literary*) [13thC. From the French stem *raviss-* "to seize," from, ultimately, Latin *rapere* (see RAPE[1]).] —**rav·ish·er** *n.* —**rav·ish·ment** *n.*

rav·ish·ing /rávvishing/ *adj.* extremely delightful or beautiful —**rav·ish·ing·ly** *adv.*

raw /ro/ *adj.* **1. UNCOOKED** not cooked **2. UNPROCESSED** not processed, refined, or treated in any way **3. HURT AND SORE** cut, scraped, or inflamed, often painfully so **4. COLD** extremely cold and harsh or damp **5. INEXPERIENCED** lacking training for or experience with something **6. BRUTALLY REALISTIC** factual and realistic, especially in connection with unpleasant matters ○ *a raw portrayal of a model's life* **7. CRUDE** coarse and vulgar **8. NOT CHANGED OR INTERPRETED** in an original state and not yet subjected to correction or analysis **9. NOT SUBTLE** not subtle, restrained, or refined ○ *the raw power of the music* [Old English *hrēaw*. Ultimately from an Indo-European word that also produced Latin *crudus* "raw" (source of English *crude* and *cruel*).] —**raw·ish** *adj.* —**raw·ly** *adv.* —**raw·ness** *n.* ◇ **in the raw 1.** not wearing clothes (*informal*) **2.** in a natural state, without embellishment or refinement

Ra·wal·pin·di /raàwəl píndee/, **Rā·wal·pin·di** city of Punjab Province, northern Pakistan. Population: 1,290,000 (1995).

raw bar *n.* a seafood restaurant or a counter in a restaurant where uncooked fish and shellfish are served or available

raw·boned /ráw bṑnd/ *adj.* having a lean body with prominent bones

raw deal *n.* an arrangement, situation, or treatment that is unfair

raw·hide /ráw hīd/ *n.* **1. UNTANNED HIDE** untanned animal hide **2. WHIP OR ROPE** a whip or rope made of rawhide ■ *vt.* (**-hid·ed, -hid·ing, -hides**) **BEAT SOMEBODY** to beat somebody with a rawhide

ra·win·sonde /ráywind sònd/ *n.* a balloon carrying meteorological instruments (**radiosonde**) that has a trackable radar target and is used to observe the velocity and direction of upper-air winds [Mid-20thC. A blend of RADAR, WIND, and *radiosonde*.]

Raw·lings /ráwlingz/, **Jerry** (*b.* 1947) Ghanaian soldier and statesman. He was elected president of Ghana (1992) and was chair of the Economic Community of West African States (1994–96). Full name **Jerry John Rawlings**

raw ma·te·ri·al *n.* **1. NATURAL UNPROCESSED MATERIAL** a natural unprocessed material that is used in a manufacturing process **2. SOMETHING POTENTIALLY USEFUL** something or somebody considered to have potential for use or development

raw si·en·na *n.* **1.** COLORS **YELLOWISH BROWN** a yellowish brown color **2.** INDUST **PIGMENT** a natural brownish yellow substance that is used as a pigment

raw silk *n.* **1. UNTREATED SILK FIBERS** silk fibers reeled from silkworm cocoons and left untreated **2. SILK FABRIC** fabric or yarn made from raw silk

ray[1] /ray/ *n.* **1. BEAM OF LIGHT** a narrow beam of light from the sun or an artificial light source **2.** PHYS **BEAM OF ENERGY** a thin beam of radiant energy or particles **3. TRACE OF SOMETHING POSITIVE** a slight indication of something positive in a difficult or worrying situation **4.** MATH **LINE EXTENDING FROM POINT** a straight line that extends from a point infinitely in one direction **5.** ZOOL **ARM OF STARFISH** any of the arms of a starfish or other animal with body parts radiating from the center **6.** ASTRON **BRIGHT STREAK FROM LUNAR CRATER** any of the bright streaks on the lunar surface that radiate from some craters **7.** BOT **RADIAL STRAND OF PLANT PITH** a distinct strand of tissue running radially through the conducting tissues in the stem of a plant ■ **rays** *npl.* **SUNSHINE** hot or warm sunshine, especially when thought of as a tanning agent (*slang*) ○ *catch some rays* ■ *v.* (**rayed, ray·ing, rays**) **1.** *vti.* **EMIT LIGHT** to shine or emit rays, e.g. of light or electromagnetic particles **2.** *vi.* **EXTEND IN LINES** to extend in radiating lines from a point [14thC. Via French *rai* from Latin *radius* (see RADIUS).] —**rayed** *adj.*

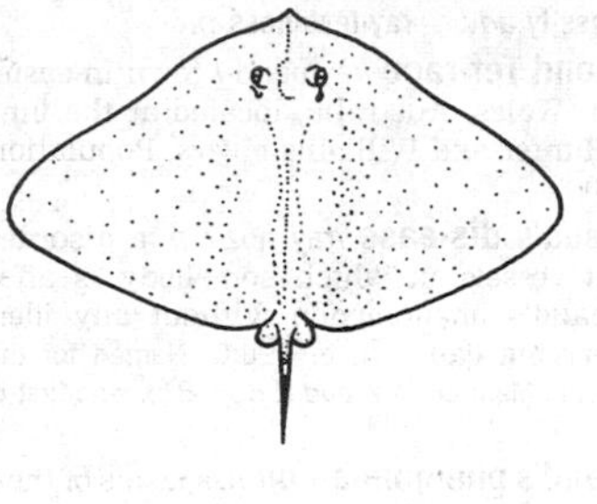
Ray

ray[2] /ray/ *n.* a fish with a cartilage skeleton, a flat head and body, broad pectoral fins, and a tapering tail. It lives near the sea floor, feeding on shellfish. The gill inlets are on top of the head behind the eyes, while the outlets are on the underside. Order: Rajiformes. ◊ **stingray** [14thC. Via French *raie* from Latin *raia*.]

ray[3] /ray/ *n. U.K.* MUSIC = **re**

Man Ray

Ray /ray/, **Man** (1890–1976) U.S. artist. Founder of the New York Dada movement, he is known for his avant-garde photographs and paintings. Real name **Emanuel Rudnitsky**

Ray, Satyajit (1921–92) Indian movie director. His Apu (1955–9) and Calcutta (1970–75) movie trilogies won him international acclaim.

ray flow·er, **ray flo·ret** *n.* any of the radiating parts of the flower of a composite plant such as the dandelion or daisy, comprising either the whole flower head or only its margin

ray gun *n.* in science fiction, a gun capable of firing rays of energy that stun or destroy

Ray·leigh /ráylee/, **John William Strutt, 3rd Baron** (1842–1919) British physicist. He performed research into

Satyajit Ray

resonance and vibration and, with Sir William Ramsay, discovered argon (1894).

Ray·leigh scat·ter·ing *n.* the scattering of electromagnetic radiation into different wavelengths by very small particles of matter, responsible for red sunrises and sunsets as well as the blue of the daytime sky. The particles must be very small relative to the wavelength of the radiation, and while there is no frequency change there is a phase change and a separation of colors. [Mid-20thC. Named for John William Strutt RAYLEIGH, who first described it.]

ray·less /ráyləss/ *adj.* **1.** WITHOUT LIGHT dark, gloomy, or lacking light (*literary*) **2.** BOT LACKING RAY FLOWERS lacking the ray flowers that typically form part of the flower heads of plants in the daisy family —**ray·less·ly** *adv.* —**ray·less·ness** *n.*

Ray·mond Ter·race /ràymənd-/ town in eastern New South Wales, Australia, located at the junction of the Hunter and Williams rivers. Population: 12,332 (1996).

Ray·naud's dis·ease /ray nṓz-/ *n.* a disorder of the blood vessels in which somebody is affected by Raynaud's phenomenon without any identifiable underlying cause [Late 19thC. Named for the French physician Maurice *Raynaud* (1834–81), who first described it.]

Ray·naud's phe·nom·e·non *n.* spasms of the arteries of the fingers and toes, typically brought on by cold, causing the hands and feet to become pale, cold, numb, and sometimes painful. Causes include diseases of the arteries, rheumatoid arthritis, and repeated trauma to the fingers. [Mid-20thC (see RAYNAUD'S DISEASE)]

ray·on /ráy òn/ *n.* **1.** SYNTHETIC TEXTILE FIBER a synthetic textile fiber made from cellulose **2.** SYNTHETIC FABRIC a synthetic fabric or yarn made from rayon fibers [Early 20thC. Coined from RAY[1], perhaps influenced by French *rayon* "ray"; from its sheen.]

raze /rayz/ (**razed, raz·ing, raz·es**), **rase** (**rased, rasing, rases**) *vt.* **1.** COMPLETELY DESTROY PLACE to destroy or level a building or settlement completely **2.** SCRAPE to scrape or shave something off something else [Mid-16thC. Via French *raser*, literally "to shave off," from, ultimately, Latin *radere* "to scrape, scratch" (source also of English *abrade, erase,* and *rash*).] —**raz·er** *n.*

ra·zor /ráyzər/ *n.* INSTRUMENT FOR SHAVING an instrument with a blade or powered cutting head that is used for shaving hair off the face or body ■ *vt.* (**-zored, -zor·ing, -zors**) SHAVE OR CUT HAIR to shave or cut hair, or remove something else, using a razor [13thC. From Old French *rasor*, from *raser* (see RAZE).]

ra·zor·back /ráyzər bàk/ *n.* **1.** FERAL HOG a feral hog of the southeastern United States that has a narrow body, ridged back, and long legs **2.** MARINE BIOL = **finback 3.** RIDGED HILL a hill that has a sharp ridge

ra·zor-billed auk, **ra·zor·bill** *n.* a seabird of the auk family, with black-and-white plumage and a sharp hooked beak. It inhabits coastal regions of the North Atlantic, feeding underwater on fish and shellfish. Latin name: *Alca torda.*

ra·zor blade *n.* a flat blade designed to be used in a safety razor

ra·zor clam *n.* a bivalve mollusk that has a long narrow tubular shell with squared ends. It burrows rapidly downward into the sand by extending a muscular foot. Family: Solenidae.

ra·zor cut *n.* HAIRCUT WITH RAZOR a haircut that is done using a razor rather than scissors ■ *vt.* CUT HAIR WITH RAZOR to cut or style hair with a razor rather than scissors

Razor-billed auk

ra·zor-shell *n. U.K.* = **razor clam**

ra·zor wire *n.* wire with sharp pieces of metal fixed along its length, used for fences and barriers

razz /raz/ *vt.* (**razzed, razz·ing, razz·es**) TEASE to tease or make fun of somebody (*informal*) ■ *n.* RASPBERRY a raspberry noise (*informal*) [Early 20thC. Shortening and alteration of RASPBERRY.]

raz·zle-daz·zle *n.* **1.** SHOWINESS THAT ASTONISHES an often gaudy showiness that is designed to impress and excite people **2.** CONFUSING ACTIONS actions intended to dazzle and confuse somebody, especially an opponent in a sport [Late 19thC. Rhyming compound formed from DAZZLE.]

razz·ma·tazz /ràzmə táz/ *n.* **1.** EXCITING SHOWINESS showiness that is designed to impress and excite people, especially in the context of a stage show or other spectacle **2.** DOUBLE-TALK language that is intended to confuse and conceal [Late 19thC. Origin uncertain: perhaps an alteration of RAZZLE-DAZZLE.]

Rb *symbol.* rubidium

RB *abbr.* FOOTBALL running back

RBC, **rbc** *abbr.* red blood (cell) count

RBE, **rbe** *abbr.* relative biological effectiveness

RBI, **rbi** *abbr.* BASEBALL run batted in

RC *abbr.* **1.** Red Cross **2.** Reserve Corps

rcd. *abbr.* received

RCMP, **R.C.M.P.** *abbr.* Royal Canadian Mounted Police

RCN, **R.C.N.** *abbr.* Royal Canadian Navy

r-col·or *n.* in phonetics, the effect of an "r" sound uttered simultaneously with a vowel by constricting the oral cavity with the tongue —**r-col·ored** *adj.*

R.C.P. *abbr.* Royal College of Physicians

rcpt. *abbr.* receipt

R.C.S. *abbr.* Royal College of Surgeons

rct. *abbr.* recruit

RD *abbr.* **1.** HEALTH registered dietician **2.** MAIL Rural Delivery

rd. *abbr.* **1.** rendered **2.** road **3.** round

Rd. *abbr.* Road (*in addresses*)

RDF *abbr.* **1.** RADIO radio direction finder **2.** MIL Rapid Deployment Force

re[1] /ray/ *n.* MUSIC a syllable that represents the second note in a scale, used for singing solfeggio. In fixed solfeggio it represents the note D, the second note in the scale of C, while in solfeggio with movable do, it is used to represent the second note of the key being sung. [15thC. Shortening of medieval Latin *resonare* (see GAMUT).]

re[2] /ray, ree/ *prep.* with reference to [Early 18thC. From Latin, literally "on the matter of," a form of *res* "thing, matter."]

WORD KEY: USAGE

Usage: The use of ***re*** meaning "with reference to" is largely restricted to the language of business, but it is also used informally as a convenient short form standing for "regarding, concerning": *Re your invitation, I'll be pleased to come.*

're *contr.* are ○ *They're planning to come.*

Re[1] *n.* MYTHOL = **Ra**

Re[2] *symbol.* **1.** CHEM ELEM rhenium **2.** MONEY rupee **3.** Reynolds number

R.E., **RE** *abbr.* real estate

re- *prefix.* **1.** again, anew ○ *rebuild* **2.** back, backward ○ *recall* [Via Old French from Latin]

reach /reech/ *v.* (**reached, reach·ing, reach·es**) **1.** *vti.* EXTEND to stretch out physically or extend as far as a particular place or point ○ *I can't reach the top shelf without a chair.* **2.** *vi.* MOVE TOWARD SOMETHING TO TOUCH IT to move toward something in order to touch or grasp it ○ *She reached for her coat.* **3.** *vt.* ARRIVE AT PARTICULAR PLACE to arrive or come to a particular place or point ○ *We reached home before midnight.* **4.** *vt.* ARRIVE AT PARTICULAR STATE to get into a particular state or condition ○ *I had reached the desperation point.* **5.** *vti.* INFLUENCE PEOPLE to have an influence or impact on people or on a group ○ *This campaign will reach millions of people.* **6.** *vt.* CONTACT to communicate with somebody ○ *I'll try to reach you at home.* **7.** *vi.* STRIVE FOR SOMETHING to strive too much to achieve or acquire something, especially without success ○ *reaching for fame* **8.** *vt.* PASS to pass or hand somebody something (*informal*) ○ *Just reach me down that file, would you.* **9.** *vi.* SAILING SAIL WITH WIND TO THE SIDE to sail on a tack with the wind blowing from the side ■ *n.* **1.** ACT OF STRETCHING OUT the act of stretching out or extending **2.** EXTENT OF REACHING the extent or range that somebody or something is able to reach ○ *The top shelf is just beyond his reach.* **3.** RANGE OF POWER the extent of somebody's, or something's, power or influence ○ *beyond the reach of the law* **4.** STRETCH OF WATER a stretch of open water, e.g., on a river **5.** SAILING TACK SAILED BY VESSEL a tack sailed by a vessel with the wind blowing from the side **6.** NUMBER OF VIEWERS the number of viewers who visit a Web site or watch a particular television program (*informal*) ○ *Reach is one factor determining whether companies invest in the Web.* ■ **reach·es** *npl.* AREA OR LEVEL an area or level of something ○ *the upper reaches of the Amazon* [Old English *rǣcan.* Ultimately from a prehistoric Germanic word that also produced German *reichen* "to reach."] —**reach·a·ble** *adj.* —**reach·er** *n.*

re·act /ree ákt/ (**-act·ed, -act·ing, -acts**) *vi.* **1.** RESPOND EMOTIONALLY to respond to something by showing the feelings or thoughts it arouses **2.** RESPOND BY TAKING ACTION to respond to something by taking action **3.** RESPOND PHYSICALLY to respond to the physical effects of something, e.g., a medication or air pollution **4.** CHEM CHANGE CHEMICALLY to undergo a chemical reaction

re·ac·tance /ree áktənss/ *n.* opposition to the flow of alternating current caused by the inductance and capacitance in a circuit, measured in ohms. The total opposition to the flow of current in the circuit is the impedance, which is the sum of the reactance and the resistance in the circuit. Symbol *X*

re·ac·tant /ree áktənt/ *n.* a substance that reacts with another in a chemical reaction

re·ac·tion /ree áksh'n/ *n.* **1.** EMOTIONAL RESPONSE an emotional or intellectual response that something arouses **2.** ACTIVE RESPONSE a response to something that involves taking action, or an action taken in response to something **3.** PHYSICAL RESPONSE a response to the physical effects of something such as heat, cold, or pollution **4.** MED BODILY RESPONSE TO SUBSTANCE a response by the body to a foreign substance, especially to an infection, medication, food, or something that causes an allergy **5.** PHYS FORCES ACTING ON A BODY an equal but opposite force exerted by a body when a force acts upon it **6.** POL STRONG CONSERVATISM strong opposition to social or political changes that the speaker considers liberal or progressive (*disapproving*) **7.** PHYS NUCLEAR PROCESS a nuclear process resulting in a change in structure of atomic nuclei —**re·ac·tion·al** *adj.*

re·ac·tion·ar·y /ree áksh'n èrree/ *adj.* OPPOSED TO LIBERAL OR PROGRESSIVE CHANGE opposed to social or political changes that the speaker considers liberal or progressive (*disapproving*) ■ *n.* (*plural* **-ies**) OPPONENT OF LIBERAL OR PROGRESSIVE CHANGE an opponent of social and political changes that the speaker considers liberal or progressive (*disapproving*)

re·ac·tion en·gine *n.* an engine that produces thrust by ejecting a stream of gas at high velocity, as do jet engines and rocket engines

re·ac·tion for·ma·tion *n.* in psychoanalysis, a defense mechanism in which somebody condemns something that has an unconscious appeal

re·ac·tion time *n.* PHYSIOL the interval of time between the application of a stimulus and the first indication of a response

re·ac·ti·vate /ree ákti vàyt/ (**-vat·ed, -vat·ing, -vates**) *vti.* to make something active again, or to become active again —**re·ac·ti·va·tion** /ree àkti váysh'n/ *n.*

re·ac·tive /ree áktiv/ *adj.* **1. REACTING TO EVENTS AND SITUATIONS** reacting to events, situations, and stimuli, especially when doing so spontaneously as they occur **2.** CHEM **REACTING CHEMICALLY** taking part in chemical reactions **3.** PSYCHOL **CAUSED BY STIMULI OR EVENTS** used to describe a psychiatric condition caused by particular situations or stimuli, e.g. the behavior of other people or the death of a loved one —**re·ac·tive·ly** *adv.* —**re·ac·tive·ness** *n.* —**re·ac·tiv·i·ty** /rèe ák tívvətee/ *n.*

re·ac·tor /ree áktər/ *n.* **1. SOMETHING THAT REACTS** somebody or something that reacts or takes part in a reaction **2.** MED **SOMEBODY SENSITIVE TO MEDICATION** a person or animal that displays a reaction to a medication, vaccine, or other substance, especially one that shows a positive reaction to a skin test for latent infection **3.** PHYS **DEVICE IN WHICH NUCLEAR REACTION OCCURS** a device in which self-sustained controlled nuclear fission or experimental nuclear fusion takes place, producing heat energy. Reactors are usually characterized by their fuel, moderator, and coolant, although sometimes their function, power, or size are employed. **4.** INDUST **CONTAINER IN WHICH CHEMICAL REACTION OCCURS** a vessel or other equipment in which an industrial chemical reaction takes place **5.** ELEC **COMPONENT IN ELECTRICAL CIRCUIT** a component in an electrical circuit used to create reactance, e.g., a capacitor or an inductor

read /reed/ *v.* (**read** /red/, **read·ing, reads**) **1.** *vti.* **INTERPRET WRITTEN MATERIAL** to interpret the characters in written or printed material, understanding the sense of what is written **2.** *vti.* **UTTER WRITTEN WORDS** to say the words of written or printed material either internally or out loud **3.** *vti.* **LEARN SOMETHING BY READING** to find something out by studying written or printed material ○ *I read it in a book.* **4.** *vt.* **INTERPRET NONWRITTEN MATERIAL** to interpret the information conveyed by movements, signs, or signals ○ *We could no longer read the trail.* **5.** *vti.* **INTERPRET PRINTED SIGNS** to interpret the meaning of signs and symbols in printed material, some of which may not be in verbal form ○ *to learn to read music* **6.** *vt.* **BE ABLE TO READ IN FOREIGN LANGUAGE** to know a foreign language well enough to be able to read in it ○ *Can you read French?* **7.** *vt.* **UNDERSTAND INTUITIVELY** to have an understanding of something by experience or intuitive means ○ *claiming to be able to read the future* **8.** *vti.* PUBL **PROOFREAD SOMETHING** to read through something in order to find poor grammar, misprints, and other errors **9.** *vti.* **INTERPRET SOMETHING IN PARTICULAR WAY** to interpret or understand something, or be interpreted or understood, in a particular way ○ *I read this passage as being extremely optimistic.* **10.** *vi.* **HAVE QUALITIES THAT AFFECT UNDERSTANDING** to have particular characteristics that affect the way something is understood ○ *In the original it reads as poetry rather than prose.* **11.** *vt.* EDUC **TAKE UNIVERSITY COURSE** to pursue a particular course of study at a university **12.** *vi.* **HAVE PARTICULAR WORDS** to have a particular wording ○ *a sign that reads DANGER* **13.** *vti.* RADIO **HEAR SOMETHING ON TWO-WAY RADIO** to receive and understand a message sent by somebody on a two-way radio **14.** *vt.* **INDICATE DATA** to indicate or display data, e.g., a temperature ○ *What does the thermometer read?* **15.** *vt.* PUBL **SUBSTITUTE WORD** to substitute a word or words for others that were printed incorrectly ○ *For "peasant" read "pheasant."* **16.** *vti.* COMPUT **TRANSFER DATA INTO COMPUTER MEMORY** to transfer program instructions or data from a storage device into a computer's main memory ■ *n.* **1. SOMETHING PRODUCING PARTICULAR REACTION** something that produces a particular reaction in the reader when read ○ *a thrilling read* **2. TIME SPENT READING** a period devoted to reading ○ *She settled down for a long read.* [Old English *rǣdan.* Ultimately from an Indo-European word that is also the ancestor of English *riddle.*] ◇ **take something as read** to assume something to be the case

read into *vt.* to detect meanings in speech or written text that were not necessarily intended by the speaker or writer

read out *vt.* **1. READ ALOUD** to read something aloud **2.** COMPUT **RETRIEVE INFORMATION FROM COMPUTER** to retrieve data from the memory or a disk or other storage device of a computer **3. EXPEL FROM ORGANIZATION** to expel somebody formally from a political party, organization, or other group

read up *vti.* to learn a lot about a subject by reading about it or researching it

Read /reed/, **George** (1733–98) American patriot. A delegate from Delaware, he signed the Declaration of Independence (1776).

read·a·bil·i·ty /rèedə bílləte e/ *n.* a measure of the ease with which a passage or whole text may be read

read·a·ble /rèedəb'l/ *adj.* **1. LEGIBLE** able to be read easily **2. ENJOYABLE TO READ** having a style that makes reading enjoyable and interesting —**read·a·ble·ness** *n.* —**read·a·bly** *adv.*

re·ad·dress /rèe ə dréss/ (**-dressed, -dress·ing, -dress·es**) *vt.* **1. PUT NEW ADDRESS ON LETTER** to put a new address on a letter, especially if the existing address is wrong or if the letter has to be forwarded **2. ATTEND TO AGAIN** to return to a problem or issue, especially with the intention of resolving it

read·er /rèedər/ *n.* **1. SOMEBODY WHO READS** somebody who reads or who reads in a particular manner **2.** COMPUT **READING DEVICE** a device that reads, especially one connected to a computer for reading media **3.** EDUC **EDUCATIONAL BOOK** an educational book intended as an aid in learning to read or learning a foreign language **4.** LITERAT **ANTHOLOGY** a collection of literary works by a single author or by several authors linked, e.g., by their period or style **5.** PUBL **SOMEBODY WHO READS FOR PUBLISHER** somebody who reads manuscripts for a publisher to assess whether they are publishable **6.** CHR = **lay reader 7.** *U.K.* UNIV **LECTURER AT BRITISH UNIVERSITY** a lecturer at a British university who ranks above a senior lecturer and below a professor

read·er·ship /rèedər shìp/ *n.* **1.** PRESS **PEOPLE WHO READ PARTICULAR NEWSPAPER** the group or number of people who read a particular newspaper, magazine, or journal **2.** *U.K.* UNIV **POSITION OF READER IN UNIVERSITY** the position of reader in a British university, ranking above a senior lectureship

read·i·ly /réddilee/ *adv.* **1. WITHOUT HESITATION** promptly and without any hesitation **2. EASILY** with little difficulty

read·ing /rèeding/ *n.* **1. IDENTIFYING OF WRITTEN OR PRINTED WORDS** the identifying of combinations of written or printed letters or characters as words in a language and understanding their meaning **2. MATERIAL THAT IS READ** printed or written material that can be read **3. OCCASION OF READING SOMETHING** an occasion when somebody reads something, especially a poem or a piece of literature, to an audience **4. TEXT READ TO AUDIENCE OR CONGREGATION** a piece of literature that is read to an audience, or a passage from a sacred text that is read to a congregation **5. INTERPRETATION OF SOMETHING** an interpretation or understanding of a situation or of something that has been written or said **6.** TECH **INFORMATION TAKEN FROM EQUIPMENT** information or a measurement taken from a piece of equipment or with the help of equipment

Read·ing /rédding/ **1.** city in northeastern Massachusetts, southeast of Andover and northwest of Boston. Population: 22,956 (1996). **2.** city in southeastern Pennsylvania. Population: 78,380 (1990).

read·ing desk *n.* = **lectern**

read·ing frame *n.* a group of three nucleotides that can be translated to produce a polypeptide, with the nucleotide composition of any one triplet dependent upon where translation is initiated. Shifts in the triplet reading frame on a sequence of DNA means a given sequence of DNA can code for a large number of different polypeptides needed for cellular operations.

re·ad·just /rèe ə júst/ (**-just·ed, -just·ing, -justs**) *v.* **1.** *vi.* **GET USED TO SOMETHING AGAIN** to get used to something after a period of absence from it **2.** *vt.* **REARRANGE** to rearrange or make small changes to something —**re·ad·just·a·ble** *adj.* —**re·ad·just·er** *n.* —**re·ad·just·ment** *n.*

READ·ME file /rèedmee-/ *n.* a computer text file supplied with the software for a program and containing information that a user may need in order to install or operate the program

read-on·ly *adj.* that can be retrieved and displayed but cannot be changed or deleted (*refers to computer storage or files*)

read-on·ly mem·o·ry *n.* a small computer memory for storing data permanently. Once data has been written onto it, the data cannot be altered or added to and can only be read. Because read-only memory retains its contents when the power is turned off, most personal computers use it to store essential programs such as the one that boots the computer.

read·out *n.* **1. DATA RETRIEVAL** the retrieving of data from a computer's memory, disk, or other storage device **2. DATA RETRIEVED BY COMPUTER** the data retrieved from a computer's memory, disk, or other storage system **3. DEVICE DISPLAYING INFORMATION** a part of a piece of equipment that displays information

read-through *n.* a reading of a play without acting, allowing actors to familiarize themselves with the dialog before full rehearsals begin

read-write head *n.* a magnetic device that can both read from and write data to a magnetic medium such as a computer floppy or hard disk. The head moves linearly between the hub and the rim of the disk to store and retrieve data from the disk's surface while the disk rotates beneath it.

read·y /réddee/ *adj.* (**-i·er, -i·est**) **1. PREPARED FOR SOMETHING** prepared for something that is going to happen ○ *Are you ready to leave?* **2. FINISHED AND AVAILABLE FOR USE** finished or completed and so able to be used immediately ○ *When will dinner be ready?* **3. ON THE POINT OF DOING SOMETHING** on the point of doing something or liable to do something ○ *This old roof is ready to cave in.* **4. WILLING TO DO SOMETHING** eager, willing, or prepared to do something ○ *Don't be so ready to give in!* **5. QUICKLY PRODUCED** quickly and easily given, provided, or available ○ *a ready response to questions about wrongdoing* **6. PREPARED IN ADVANCE** prepared or blended in advance, and able to be used with very little additional preparation (*often used in combination*) ○ *available ready-sliced in small packets* **7. INTELLIGENT** intelligent, alert, and quick-witted ○ *a ready wit* ■ *vt.* (**-ied, -y·ing, -ies**) **PREPARE** to prepare something, especially so that it is in a condition for something to happen to it [12thC. Formed from Old English *rǣde* "prompt." Ultimately from a prehistoric Germanic word meaning "arranged."] —**read·i·ness** *n.* ◇ **at the ready** prepared for immediate use or action

read·y cash *n.* cash or money that is available to be spent immediately, often as notes and coins

read·y-made *adj.* **1. ALREADY PREPARED** already prepared or made for convenience **2. PRECONCEIVED** thought out in advance ■ *n.* **READY-TO-WEAR GARMENT** an item of clothing that is offered for sale in a standard size and completely finished, as opposed to clothing that is made to the customer's specifications

read·y-mix *n.* a correct mixture of ingredients that is preblended and able to be used with very little additional preparation —**read·y-mixed** *adj.*

read·y mon·ey *n.* = **ready cash**

read·y-to-wear *adj.* **MADE IN STANDARD SIZES AND DESIGNS** already made in standard sizes, designs, and colors, rather than being specially made or designed for an individual ■ *n.* **READY-MADE CLOTHING** clothing that is already made in standard sizes and designs, rather than being specially designed or tailored for an individual

The White House

Ronald Reagan

Rea·gan /ráygən/, **Ronald** (*b.* 1911) U.S. statesman and 40th president of the United States. After a career as a movie actor, he served as Republican president twice (1981–89). Full name **Ronald Wilson Reagan**

Rea·gan·om·ics /ràygə nómmiks/ *n.* the free-market economic approach espoused by U.S. President Ronald Reagan, involving cuts in taxes and social spending together with deregulation of domestic markets [Late 20thC. A blend of REAGAN and ECONOMICS.]

re·a·gent /ree áyjənt/ *n.* a substance taking part in a chemical reaction, especially one used to detect, measure, or prepare another substance

re·a·gin /ree áyjin/ *n.* a type of antibody involved in allergic reactions such as hay fever. Reagins are produced following an initial exposure to an allergenic substance, and interact with allergenic substances to trigger the release of histamines, causing inflammation, swelling, and other symptoms. [Early 20thC. From German, formed from *reagieren* "to react."] —**re·a·gin·ic** /rée ə jínnik/ *adj.*

re·al[1] /rée əl/ *adj.* **1.** PHYSICALLY EXISTING having actual physical existence **2.** VERIFIABLE AS ACTUAL FACT verifiable as actual fact, e.g., legally or scientifically ○ *What is his real name?* **3.** NOT IMAGINARY existing as fact, rather than as a product of dreams or the imagination **4.** NOT ARTIFICIAL genuine and original, and so not artificial or synthetic **5.** TRADITIONAL AND AUTHENTIC prepared or made in a traditional or authentic way, rather than being mass-produced or artificial ○ *looking for some real food* **6.** ESSENTIAL of basic, essential, or critical importance **7.** UNDISPUTED based on fact, observation, or experience and so undisputed ○ *The real success of the evening was the comedy act.* **8.** SINCERE honest or sincere, not feigned or affected ○ *to express your real feelings* **9.** EMPHASIZING TRUTH used to emphasize the accuracy or appropriateness of a particular thing ○ *He's a real professional.* **10.** PROPERTY LAW RELATING TO FIXED PROPERTY relating to land and the fixed property associated with it ■ *adv.* VERY very or extremely (*informal*) ○ *I'm real tired.* ■ *adj.* **1.** ECON IN TERMS OF PURCHASING POWER regarded in terms of purchasing power rather than the actual amount **2.** MATH INVOLVING ONLY REAL NUMBERS involving, relating to, or having elements of the set of rational or irrational numbers only **3.** PHILOSOPHY ABOUT EXISTENCE concerned with independent objective existence ■ *n.* **1.** REALITY everything that exists in the actual world **2.** = **real number** [15thC. Directly or via Old French from late Latin *realis*, literally "related to things (in law)," from Latin *res* "thing, fact."] —**real·ness** *n.* ◇ **for real** seriously, not as a joke or as a practice (*informal*) ◇ **get real!** used to indicate strongly that what somebody said or thought is unrealistic, untrue, or out of date (*slang*) ◇ **(in) real life** in the course of normal life as opposed to imagined or fictional representations of life, e.g., in books and movies ◇ **the real thing, the real McCoy** something that is authentic and not an imitation

re·al[2] /ray áal, ree-/ (*plural* **-als** *or* **-al·es** /ray áales/) *n.* **1.** UNIT OF BRAZILIAN CURRENCY the unit of currency in Brazil. See table at **currency 2.** COIN OR BILL WORTH A REAL a coin or bill worth a real **3.** FORMER CURRENCY IN SPANISH-SPEAKING COUNTRIES in the past, a silver coin used as a unit of currency in several Spanish-speaking countries [Late 16thC. Via Spanish from Latin *regalis* (see ROYAL).]

re·al[3] /ray áal, ree áal/ (*plural* **re·als** *or* **reis** /rays/) *n.* a coin that was used as a unit of currency in Portugal [Mid-20thC. Via Portuguese from Latin *regalis* (see ROYAL).]

re·al es·tate *n. U.S., ANZ* land including all the property on it that cannot be moved and any attached rights

re·al-es·tate a·gent *n. ANZ, U.S.* a person who buys, sells, and leases property on behalf of somebody else

re·al fo·cus *n.* a point from which light diverges or at which it converges

re·al·gar /ree álgər, ree ál gaar/ *n.* a soft orange-red arsenic ore consisting of crystalline arsenic sulfide, used in tanning, as a pigment, and to make fireworks [14thC. Via medieval Latin *realger* from, ultimately, Arabic *rahj al-ġār*, literally "powder of the cave."]

re·a·lign /rée ə lín/ (**-ligned, -lign·ing, -ligns**) *v.* **1.** *vt.* STRAIGHTEN AGAIN to readjust or manipulate something so that it is in a straight line or is correctly oriented **2.** *vti.* CHANGE SOMETHING TO FIT SITUATION to alter or change something to fit particular circumstances **3.** *vti.* MAKE NEW ALLIANCES to form, or cause people or groups to form, new alliances or associations ○ *The party has realigned itself with several former ideological opponents.* —**re·a·lign·ment** *n.*

real im·age *n.* an optical image of something that is produced by reflection or refraction and can be transferred onto a surface such as inside a camera

re·al·ism /rée ə lìzzəm/ *n.* **1.** UNDERSTANDING OF NATURE OF REAL LIFE a practical understanding and acceptance of the actual nature of the world, rather than an idealized or romantic view of it **2.** ARTS, LITERAT LIFELIKE ARTISTIC REPRESENTATION in artistic and literary works, lifelike representation of people and the world, without any idealization **3.** PHILOSOPHY THEORY THAT THINGS EXIST OBJECTIVELY the theory that things such as universals, moral facts, and theoretical scientific entities exist independently of people's thoughts and perceptions **4.** PHILOSOPHY THEORY THAT PEOPLE PERCEIVE INDEPENDENT WORLD the theory that although there is an objectively existing world, not dependent on our minds, people are able to understand aspects of that world through perception **5.** PHILOSOPHY THEORY THAT STATEMENTS HAVE TRUTH VALUES the theory that every declarative statement is either true or false, regardless of whether this can be verified

re·al·ist /rée əlist/ *n.* **1.** PRAGMATIST somebody who is sensible, practical, and not concerned with abstract theories or idealistic views of life **2.** ADHERENT OF REALISM somebody who practices realism in the arts or believes in philosphical theories of realism

re·al·is·tic /rée ə lístik/ *adj.* **1.** PRACTICAL seeking what is achievable or possible, based on known facts ○ *set realistic goals when looking for a new job* **2.** SIMULATING REALITY simulating real things or imaginary things in a way that seems real ○ *computer games with realistic graphics* **3.** REASONABLE not priced or valued too low or high **4.** ARTS, LITERAT REPRESENTING REAL LIFE in the arts and literature, representing life as it really is, rather than an idealized picture of it **5.** PHILOSOPHY RELATING TO PHILOSOPHICAL REALISM relating to philosophical theories of realism —**re·al·is·ti·cal·ly** /-lístikəlee/ *adv.*

re·al·i·ty /ree állətee/ (*plural* **-ties**) *n.* **1.** REAL EXISTENCE actual being or existence, as opposed to an imaginary, idealized, or false nature **2.** ALL THAT ACTUALLY EXISTS OR HAPPENS everything that actually does or could exist or happen in real life **3.** SOMETHING THAT EXIST OR HAPPENS something that has real existence and must be dealt with in real life ○ *a vision that ignores the realities of the business world* **4.** TYPE OF EXISTENCE a kind of existence or universe, either connected with or independent from other kinds ○ *fantastic notions of alternative realities* **5.** PHILOSOPHY TOTALITY OF REAL THINGS the totality of real things in the world, independent of people's knowledge or perception of them ◇ **in reality** in actual fact

re·al·i·ty check *n.* an action taken to reconcile somebody's ideas or desires with reality (*informal*)

re·al·i·ty prin·ci·ple *n.* in Freudian theory, the ego's ability to postpone gratification to avoid unpleasant consequences or to gain greater reward

re·al·i·ty show *n.* a television show of a true story such as a police program or rescue show

re·al·i·za·tion /rée əli záysh'n/ *n.* **1.** REALIZING OF SOMETHING the realizing of something **2.** SOMETHING REALIZED something that has been realized

re·al·ize /rée ə lìz/ (**-ized, -iz·ing, -iz·es**) *v.* **1.** *vti.* KNOW AND UNDERSTAND SOMETHING to know, understand, and accept something ○ *doesn't realize how lucky he is* **2.** *vti.* BE OR BECOME AWARE OF SOMETHING to be aware or conscious of something, or to become aware of something ○ *Do you realize the problems you've caused?* **3.** *vt.* ACHIEVE SOMETHING HOPED FOR to achieve in actuality something that has been hoped or worked for **4.** *vt.* TURN WORK INTO PERFORMANCE to turn something such as a play or novel into a stage or film performance **5.** *vt.* CONVERT GAIN OR LOSS INTO CASH to convert a paper gain or loss into a cash gain or loss by closing out the original transaction **6.** *vt.* COMM TRANSLATE SOMETHING INTO MONEY to translate something into a particular amount of money, usually by selling it **7.** *vt.* MUSIC INTERPRET PIECE OF MUSIC to interpret a musical composition, especially the figured bass of a baroque composition [Early 17thC. Formed from REAL[1] on the model of French *réaliser*.] —**re·al·iz·a·ble** *adj.* —**re·al·iz·er** *n.*

WORD KEY: SYNONYMS

See Synonyms at ***accomplish***.

re·al-life *adj.* actual or true, as opposed to fictional or imaginary

re·al·ly /rée lee/ *adv.* **1.** IN FACT in fact or in reality, especially as distinct from what has been believed until now ○ *She's really going to Paris, not Bangkok.* **2.** GENUINELY used to emphasize the truthfulness or accuracy of what is being said ○ *She really is going to Paris next year.* **3.** UNDOUBTEDLY truly and without any doubt ○ *That's really interesting.* **4.** PROPERLY in order to act in the correct or proper manner ○ *You should really apply in writing.* ■ *interj.* EXCLAMATION OF SURPRISE used to express surprise, doubt, or exasperation ○ *You're getting married? Really!* ○ *Well really, how rude!*

realm /relm/ *n.* **1.** SCOPE OF SOMETHING a particular or stated area, range, or domain ○ *Here the scenario enters the realm of fantasy.* **2.** AREA OF INTEREST a defined area of interest or study ○ *the realm of pure mathematics* **3.** KINGDOM a country ruled by a monarch [13thC. Via Old French *realme* from Latin *regimen* "government," from *regere* "to rule" (source of English *rector, regent,* and *register*); the *l* was due to the influence of Old French *reiel* "royal."]

re·al num·ber *n.* a number that is either rational or irrational rather than imaginary. ◊ **imaginary number**

re·al·po·li·tik /ray áal polli teek/ *n.* politics based on pragmatism or practicality rather than on ethical or theoretical considerations [Early 20thC. From German, literally "real politics."] —**re·al·po·li·tik·er** *n.*

re·al pres·ence *n.* the doctrine that the body and blood of Jesus Christ are actually present in the elements of Communion

re·al-time *adj.* **1.** COMPUT RELATING TO IMMEDIATE DATA PROCESSING relating to the ability of certain computer systems to process and update data as soon as it is received from some external source, e.g. an air traffic control or antilock brake system. The time available to receive the data, process it, and respond to the external process is dictated by the time constraints imposed by the process. **2.** HAPPENING NOW happening at the very present time ○ *real-time coverage of the crisis*

Re·al·tor /rée əltər/ *tdmk.* a service mark for a real-estate agent who is a member of the National Association of Realtors

re·al·ty /rée əltee/ *n.* = **real estate**

re·al-world *adj.* relevant or practical in terms of everyday life

ream[1] /reem/ *n.* QUANTITY OF PAPER a quantity of paper, formerly 480 sheets but now usually 500 sheets ■ **reams** *npl.* LARGE QUANTITY a large quantity of material, especially written material [14thC. Via Old French *raime* from, ultimately, Arabic *rizma* "bundle."]

ream[2] /reem/ (**reamed, ream·ing, reams**) *vt.* **1.** FORM HOLE WITH REAMER to form, enlarge, or shape a hole with a reamer **2.** SQUEEZE CITRUS JUICE to squeeze the juice from a citrus fruit with a reamer **3.** CHEAT to cheat or swindle somebody (*slang*) **4.** REPRIMAND to reprimand somebody severely (*slang*) [Mid-18thC. Origin uncertain: perhaps from Old English *rȳman* "to widen."]

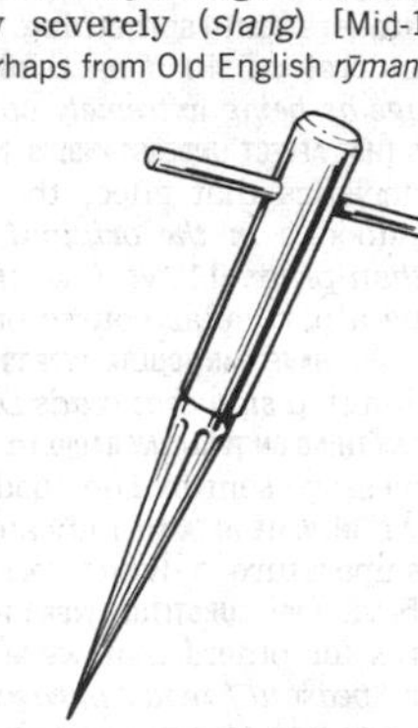

Reamer

ream·er /réemər/ *n.* **1.** TOOL FOR FORMING OR ENLARGING HOLES a tool that is used to form, enlarge, or shape holes **2.** COOK CITRUS FRUIT JUICE EXTRACTER a device for extracting juice from citrus fruit, consisting of a shallow dish with a pointed ridged center

reap /reep/ (**reaped, reap·ing, reaps**) *vt.* **1.** GATHER CROP to cut and gather a crop, especially a grain crop, from the land where it is growing **2.** OBTAIN AS RESULT to obtain something, especially as a consequence of previous effort or action [Old English *rīpan*. Origin uncertain: perhaps ultimately from an Indo-European word meaning "to tear."] —**reap·a·ble** *adj.*

reap·er /réepər/ *n.* somebody or something that reaps, especially, formerly, a machine for harvesting grain crops ◇ **the grim reaper, the reaper** death, or a personification of death

re·ap·por·tion·ment /ree ə páwrsh'nmənt/ *n.* periodic redistribution of congressional or legislative seats based on changing census figures, as constitutionally required (*formal*)

rear[1] /reer/ (**reared, rear·ing, rears**) *v.* **1.** *vt.* **RAISE YOUNG ANIMALS OR CHILDREN** to bring up and care for young animals or children until they are fully grown **2.** *vt.* **GROW** to raise a plant to full growth **3.** *vi.* **RISE ON HIND LEGS** to rise up on the hind legs (*refers to animals*) **4.** *vi.* **RISE HIGH** to rise high into the air ○ *tall office buildings rearing into the night sky* [Old English *rǣran*. Ultimately from an Indo-European word that is also the ancestor of English *raise* and *rise*.] —**rear·er** *n.*

rear[2] /reer/ *n.* **1. BACK OF SOMETHING** the back of something, or the area near the back of something **2.** MIL **PART OF ARMY FARTHEST FROM FRONT** the part of an army or a procession that is furthest from the front **3. BUTTOCKS** somebody's buttocks, or the similar part of an animal (*informal*) ■ *adj.* **BACK** situated at the back ○ *Do not join the rear four carriages.* [Late 16thC. Via Old French *rere* from Latin *retro* (see RETRO-).] ◇ **bring up the rear** to be at the back, particularly in a race or procession

rear ad·mi·ral *n.* a rank in the U.S. Navy or Coast Guard that is above captain or commodore and below vice admiral, or an officer holding this rank

rear end = **rear**[2] *n.* 1, **rear**[2] *n.* 3

rear-end (**rear-end·ed, rear-end·ing, rear-ends**) *vt.* to collide with the back of another vehicle

rear-end·er *n.* an accident in which one vehicle collides with the back of another (*informal*)

rear·guard /réer gaàrd/ *n.* **1.** MIL **TROOPS PROTECTING REAR** a portion of a military force on the move that is responsible for protecting against an attack from the rear **2. CONSERVATIVES** members of a political party or other organization who are strongly conservative and opposed to change and progress (*disapproving*)

rear lamp, rear light *n. U.K.* = **taillight**

re·arm /ree aárm/ (**-armed, -arm·ing, -arms**) *vti.* to equip people, an organization, or a nation with weapons and ammunition again, or to become so equipped —**re·ar·ma·ment** /ree aármәmənt/ *n.*

rear·most /réer mōst/ *adj.* farthest toward the back

re·ar·range /reè ə ráynj/ (**-ranged, -rang·ing, -rang·es**) *vt.* **1. CHANGE ORDER OF SOMETHING** to change the order or position of something **2. CHANGE TIME OF SOMETHING** to reschedule the time of something such as an event —**re·ar·range·ment** *n.*

rear·view mir·ror /réer wyoò-/ *n.* a mirror attached to the inside of the windshield or the outside of a front door of a vehicle, allowing the driver to see behind the vehicle

rear·ward /réerwərd/ *adv.* **rear·ward, rear·wards TOWARD REAR** toward or in the rear or back ■ *adj.* **LOCATED IN REAR** located in or near the rear or back ■ *n.* **REAR POSITION** a position at the back, especially of an army

rea·son /réez'n/ *n.* **1. JUSTIFICATION** an explanation or justification for something ○ *refused to give a reason for her behavior* **2. MOTIVE** a motive or cause for acting or thinking in a particular way ○ *His only reason for going was that she would be there.* **3. POWER OF ORDERLY THOUGHT** the power of being able to think in a logical and rational manner ○ *use reason rather than force* **4. CAUSE THAT EXPLAINS SOMETHING** a cause that explains a particular phenomenon ○ *What's the reason for grass being green?* **5. ABILITY TO THINK CLEARLY** the ability to think clearly and coherently **6.** PHILOSOPHY **INTELLECT AS BASIS FOR KNOWLEDGE** the ability to think logically regarded as a basis for knowledge, as distinct from experience or emotions ■ *v.* (**-soned, -son·ing, -sons**) **1.** *vi.* **THINK IN LOGICAL WAY** to think logically or use rational faculties **2.** *vi.* **USE RATIONAL ARGUMENT TO PERSUADE** to try to persuade or influence somebody by means of rational argument ○ *I tried to reason with him but he insisted on going ahead.* **3.** *vt.* **RESOLVE BY RATIONAL MEANS** to formulate or resolve something using rational means ○ *reason out a math problem* [13thC. Via Old French *reisun* from, ultimately, Latin *ratio* "calculation, thought" (source of English *rate* and *rational*), from *reri* "to think."] —**rea·son·er** *n.* ◇ **it stands to reason** used to emphasize that something seems obvious or logical ◇ **listen to reason** to take note of sensible advice ◇ **within reason** within reasonable limits

WORD KEY: USAGE

the reason is that or **the reason is because?** Particularly in writing, ***reason*** is more correctly followed by *that* than by *because* in sentences of the type *The reason I left is that* [not *because*] *I was bored.* Informally, however, and especially in conversation, *because* does occur.

WORD KEY: SYNONYMS

See Synonyms at ***deduce***.

rea·son·a·ble /reéz'nəb'l/ *adj.* **1. RATIONAL** sensible and capable of making rational judgments ○ *He did what any reasonable person would have done in that situation.* **2. IN ACCORD WITH COMMON SENSE** acceptable and according to common sense ○ *hoping to arrive at a reasonable time* **3. NOT EXPECTING MORE THAN IS POSSIBLE** not expecting or demanding more than is possible or achievable ○ *Come on, be reasonable!* **4. FAIRLY GOOD** fairly good but not excellent ○ *The food was reasonable.* **5. FAIRLY LARGE** large enough but not excessive ○ *He earns a reasonable amount of money.* **6. NOT EXORBITANT** fairly priced and not too expensive ○ *Three bottles for $12 is very reasonable.* —**rea·son·a·ble·ness** *n.* —**rea·son·a·bly** /reéz'nəblee/ *adv.*

WORD KEY: SYNONYMS

See Synonyms at ***valid***.

rea·son·ing /reéz'ning/ *n.* **1. LOGICAL THINKING** the use of logical thinking in order to find results or draw conclusions **2. ARGUMENT** an argument or other example of logical thinking ○ *Her reasoning was based on the available facts.*

re·as·sure /reè ə shoòr/ (**-sured, -sur·ing, -sures**) *vt.* **1. PUT SOMEBODY'S MIND AT EASE** to make a person feel less anxious or worried **2.** = **reinsure** —**re·as·sur·ance** *n.* —**re·as·sur·er** *n.*

re·as·sur·ing /reè ə shoòring/ *adj.* having the effect of making people feel less anxious or worried —**re·as·sur·ing·ly** /reè ə shoòringlee/ *adv.*

re·a·ta *n.* = **riata**

Ré·au·mur /ràу ō myoòr, -myoòr/ *adj.* using or measured on the Réaumur scale [Early 19thC. Named for the French physicist René Antoine Ferchault de *Réaumur* (1683–1757), who developed the scale.]

Ré·au·mur scale *n.* an obsolete temperature scale on which water freezes at 0 degrees and boils at 80 degrees under normal atmospheric conditions [Late 18thC. Named for the French physicist and inventor René Antoine Ferchault de *Réaumur* (1683–1757), who introduced it.]

reave[1] /reev/ (**reaved** *or* **reft** /reft/, **reav·ing, reaves**) *vt.* (*archaic*) **1. TAKE FORCIBLY** to plunder something or carry something off by force **2. DEPRIVE** to rob somebody or deprive somebody of something [Old English *rēafian*. Ultimately from a prehistoric Germanic word that is also the ancestor of English *rob*.] —**reav·er** *n.*

reave[2] /reev/ (**reaved** *or* **reft** /reft/, **reav·ing, reaves**) *vt.* to tear something apart (*archaic*) [13thC. Alteration of RIVE.] —**reav·er** *n.*

Reb /reb/, **reb** *n.* = **Johnny Reb** (*informal*) [Mid-19thC. Shortening of REBEL.]

re·bar·ba·tive /ri baárbətiv/ *adj.* unpleasant, annoying, or forbidding (*formal*) [Late 19thC. From French *rébarbatif*, from *rebarber*, literally "to face beard to beard," from *barbe* "beard."] —**re·bar·ba·tive·ly** *adv.*

re·bate[1] *n.* /reé bàyt/ **MONEY PAID BACK** money that is paid back, e.g., because somebody has overpaid a tax or is entitled to a refund ■ *vt.* /reè báyt/ (**-bat·ed, -bat·ing, -bates**) **GIVE REBATE TO** to give somebody a rebate [15thC. From French *rabattre*, literally "to beat down again," from *abattre* "to beat down" (source of English *abate* and *abattoir*), from Latin *battuere* "to beat."] —**re·bat·a·ble** *adj.* —**re·bat·er** *n.*

re·bate[2] *n.* = **rabbet** ■ *vt.* (**-bat·ed, -bat·ing, -bates**) = **rabbet** [Late 17thC. Alteration of RABBET.]

reb·be /rébbə/, **Reb·be** *n.* a rabbi or spiritual leader of a Hasidic Jewish community [Late 19thC. Via Yiddish from Hebrew *rabbī*, literally "my teacher."]

reb·bet·zin /rébbitsin/, **reb·bit·zin** *n.* the wife of a rabbi [Late 19thC. From Yiddish, formed from *rebbe* (see REBBE).]

re·bec /reé bèk/, **re·beck** *n.* a two- or three-stringed medieval instrument that looks like a lute and is played with a bow. It is one of the earliest bowed stringed instruments. [Early 16thC. Via French from, ultimately, Arabic *rabāb*.]

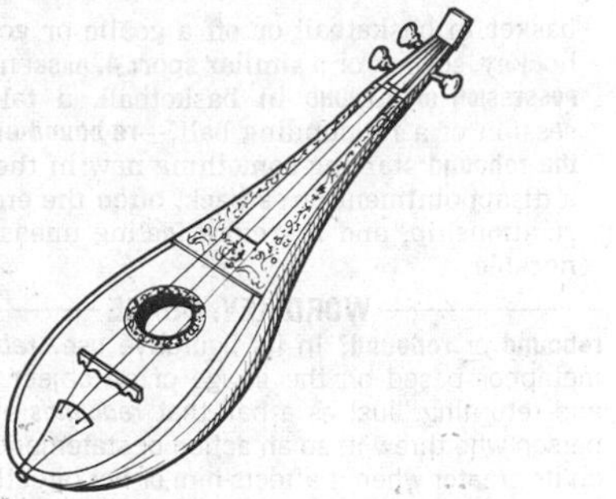

Rebec

Re·bec·ca, Re·be·kah *n.* in the Bible, the wife of Isaac, and mother of Jacob and Esau

reb·el *n.* /rébb'l/ **1. PROTESTER** somebody who protests against something by defying authority ○ *The rebels in the party voted against their leaders.* **2. SOLDIER WHO OPPOSES GOVERNMENT IN POWER** a soldier who belongs to a force seeking to overthrow a government or ruling power **3. UNCONVENTIONAL PERSON** somebody who refuses to conform to the codes and conventions of society ○ *always something of a rebel* ■ *vi.* /ri bél/ (**re·belled, re·bel·ling, re·bels**) **1. REVOLT AGAINST A GOVERNMENT** to fight to overthrow a government or ruling power **2. PROTEST BY DEFYING AUTHORITY** to protest something by defying a government or other form of authority ○ *students rebelling against education funding cuts* **3. REFUSE TO CONFORM** to refuse to conform to the usual codes and conventions of society **4. HAVE DISLIKE FOR SOMETHING** to experience or express an intense dislike or distaste for something [13thC. Via French *rebelle* from Latin *rebellis* from *bellum* "war" (source of English *belligerent*). The underlying idea is of the defeated "making war again" against their conquerors.]

re·bel·lion /ri béllyən/ *n.* **1. ATTEMPT TO OVERTHROW GOVERNMENT** an organized attempt to overthrow a government or other authority by the use of violence **2. DEFIANCE OF AUTHORITY** opposition or defiance of authority, accepted moral codes, or social conventions

re·bel·lious /ri béllyəss/ *adj.* **1. OPPOSING OR DEFYING AUTHORITY** opposing or defying authority, accepted moral codes, or social conventions **2. FIGHTING TO OVERTHROW GOVERNMENT OR AUTHORITY** fighting to overthrow a government or other authority —**re·bel·lious·ly** *adv.* —**re·bel·lious·ness** *n.*

reb·el yell *n.* an exuberant high-pitched yell such as was used during battle by soldiers of the Confederacy

re·bid *n.* /reé bid/ **FURTHER BID IN BRIDGE** a further bid in an auction at bridge, especially one of the same suit as a previous one ■ *vi.* /ree bíd/ (**-bid** *or* **-bid, -bid, -bid·ding, -bids**) **BID FURTHER** to make a bid in an auction at bridge after previously bidding no trump or a suit, especially one in the same suit

re·birth /ree búrth/ *n.* **1. REGENERATION OF SOMETHING DEAD OR DESTROYED** the regeneration of something that has died or has been destroyed **2. REVIVAL OF IDEAS OR FORCES** the revival of important ideas or forces, usually as part of broad and significant change **3.** RELIG **REINCARNATION** the act or process of reincarnation

re·blo·chon /rèbblə sháaN/ *n.* a soft delicately flavored washed-rind cheese with a pale pinkish skin, made in the Savoy region of France [Early 20thC. From French, from *reblocher* "to milk for a second time."]

re·boot /ree boòt/ *vti.* (**-boot·ed, -boot·ing, -boots**) **RESTART COMPUTER** to restart a computer or an operating system, or to be restarted ■ *n.* **RESTART OF COMPUTER** a restart of a computer or an operating system

re·born /ree báwrn/ *adj.* recreated or regenerated, especially in order to be more effective or modern, or renewed spiritually

re·bound *v.* /ree bównd/ (**-bound·ed, -bound·ing, -bounds**) **1.** *vi.* **SPRING BACK** to spring back or recoil **2.** *vi.* **MOVE BACK TO PREVIOUS LEVEL** to recover from a setback and move back to a previous or higher level or position **3.** *vti.* BASKETBALL **TAKE POSSESSION OF BALL OFF BACKBOARD** in basketball, to take possession of a ball that has bounced off the backboard or rim of the basket ■ *n.* /reé bòwnd/ **1. ACT OF REBOUNDING** the springing back or recoiling of something **2. UPWARD MOVEMENT** an upward movement or a recovery, especially after a setback **3.** SPORTS **BALL THAT BOUNCES** a ball that bounces back, particularly off a backboard or rim of the basket in basketball or off a goalie or goalpost in hockey, soccer, or a similar sport **4.** BASKETBALL **TAKING POSSESSION OF REBOUND** in basketball, a taking possession of a rebounding ball —**re·bound·er** *n.* ◇ **on the rebound** starting something new in the wake of a disappointment or setback, often the ending of a relationship, and therefore feeling uneasy or vulnerable

WORD KEY: USAGE

rebound or **redound**? In its figurative use, ***rebound*** is a metaphor based on the image of an object bouncing and returning. Just as a ball that ***rebounds*** affects the person who threw it, so an action or statement ***rebounds*** on its creator when it affects him or her directly, usually in an unpleasant or unwelcome way: *The city's decision to cut library services rebounded on city officials when they were unable to get the information they needed.* ***Redound*** does not have any physical meaning and is therefore not a metaphor. It is sometimes used in the same way as ***rebound***, but in its primary meaning it is followed by *to* and means "to contribute or lead to," with something good or creditable as the object (the opposite connotation of ***rebound***): *The individual performances redounded to the benefit of the team as a whole.* Note that only ***rebound*** can be used as a noun.

re·bo·zo /ray bṓssō, ri bṓssō/ (*plural* **-zos**) *n.* a long woolen or linen scarf worn over the head and shoulders, mainly by women in Mexico [Early 19thC. Via Spanish from, ultimately, Latin *bucca* "cheek, mouth."]

re·broad·cast /ree bráwd kàst/ *vti.* (**-cast** *or* **-cast·ed, -cast·ing, -casts**) **BROADCAST SOMETHING AGAIN** to broadcast something again, especially a radio or television show ■ *n.* **SOMETHING THAT IS BROADCAST AGAIN** something that is broadcast again, especially a radio or television show

re·buff *vt.* /ri búf/ (**-buffed, -buff·ing, -buffs**) **1. REJECT OR SNUB SOMETHING** to reject or snub an offer, advance, or approach made by somebody **2. REPEL ATTACK** to beat back or repel an attack or an attacking force ■ *n.* /rée bùf/ **1. REJECTION** a blunt rejection or snub of an offer, advance, or approach made by somebody else **2. SETBACK** a sudden severe setback to progress [Late 16thC. Via obsolete French *rebuffer* and Italian *ribuffare* "to scold" from, ultimately, *buffo* "puff," originally an imitation of the sound.]

re·build /ree bíld/ (**-built, -built** /ree bílt/, **-build·ing, -builds**) *vt.* **1. BUILD STRUCTURE AGAIN** to construct a building or other structure again because it has been damaged or destroyed **2. WORK TO RESTORE** to work to restore something that has been weakened, damaged, or ruined **3. MAKE MAJOR CHANGES TO** to make major alterations or improvements to something ○ *to rebuild society for the information age*

re·buke /ri byóōk/ *vt.* (**-buked, -buk·ing, -bukes**) **TELL OFF** to criticize or reprimand somebody, usually sharply ■ *n.* **A TELLING OFF** a reprimand or expression of criticism or disapproval [14thC. From Anglo-Norman and Old Northern French *rebuker*, literally "to chop wood," from, ultimately, Old French *busche* "log," of prehistoric Germanic origin.]

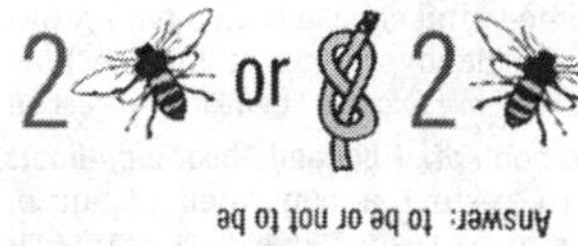

Answer: to be or not to be

Rebus

re·bus /réebəss/ (*plural* **-bus·es**) *n.* **1. WORD PUZZLE** a puzzle in which the syllables of words and names are represented either by pictures of things that sound the same, or by letters **2.** HERALDRY **HERALDIC EMBLEM** a heraldic emblem showing a picture that represents the name of the bearer, e.g., a picture of a lion for somebody named Lyon [Early 17thC. Via French from Latin, literally "by things," from *res* "thing." Perhaps from the phrase *non verbis sed rebus* "not by words but by things."]

re·but /ri bút/ (**-but·ted, -but·ting, -buts**) *vti.* to deny the truth of something, especially by presenting arguments that disprove it [13thC. Via Anglo-Norman *rebuter* from Old French *reboter*, from *boter* "to butt" (see BUTT[1]).] —**re·but·ta·ble** *adj.* —**re·but·tal** *n.*

re·but·ter /ri búttər/ *n.* **1.** LAW **DEFENDANT'S ANSWER** the defendant's answer in the third round of pleading in a legal action **2. SOMEBODY WHO REBUTS** somebody who rebuts something

rec /rek/ *n.* recreation (*informal*) (*often used before a noun*) ○ *rec room* [Early 20thC. Shortening.]

rec. *abbr.* **1.** receipt **2.** received **3.** recipe **4.** recommended **5.** MAIL recorded **6.** recorder **7.** recording **8.** recreation

re·cal·ci·trant /rə kálsitrənt/ *adj.* **1. RESISTING CONTROL** stubbornly resisting the authority or control of another **2. HARD TO DO OR HANDLE** difficult to deal with or operate ○ *struggling in front of the mirror with a recalcitrant necktie* ■ *n.* **STUBBORN OPPONENT** somebody who stubbornly resists authority or control by another ○ *A few recalcitrants refused to submit.* [Mid-19thC. Directly or via French from Latin *recalcitrant-* present participle stem of *recalcitrare*, literally "to kick back" (used of horses), from *calcitrare* "to kick (with the heels)," from the stem of *calc-* "heel."] —**re·cal·ci·trance** *n.*

WORD KEY: SYNONYMS

See Synonyms at ***unruly***.

re·cal·cu·late /ree kálkyə làyt/ (**-lat·ed, -lat·ing, -lates**) *vti.* to calculate something again in order to make sure it is correct, or to incorporate new information —**re·cal·cu·la·tion** /ree kàlkyə láysh'n/ *n.*

re·ca·lesce /rèekə léss/ (**-lesced, -lesc·ing, -lesc·es**) *vi.* to exhibit or undergo a sudden increase in temperature [Late 19thC. Back-formation from RECALESCENCE.]

re·ca·les·cence /rèekə léss'ns/ *n.* a sudden increase in the temperature and brightness of a cooling metal, caused by the release of latent heat as the metal undergoes a change in crystalline structure [Late 19thC. Formed from Latin *calescere* "to grow warm," from *calere* "to be warm" (source of English *nonchalant*).] —**re·ca·les·cent** *adj.*

re·call *v.* /ri káwl/ (**-called, -cal·ling, -calls**) **1.** *vti.* **REMEMBER SOMETHING** to remember something or bring something back to mind **2.** *vt.* **ORDER BACK** to order something or somebody to come back or be sent back **3.** *vt.* **REVOKE** to revoke or cancel a previous decision or instruction **4.** *vt.* **BRING ATTENTION BACK** to bring somebody's attention or thoughts back to an ongoing matter **5.** *vt.* **RESEMBLE** to remind another person of somebody or something familiar or previously seen ○ *Her face recalls that of her grandmother.* ■ *n.* /rée kàwl/ **1. MEMORY** somebody's memory or ability to remember ○ *a vague recall of the actual events* **2.** POL **DISMISSAL FROM OFFICE BY VOTE** the dismissal from office of an elected official by a popular vote, or the right of the electors to do this **3.** COMM **MANUFACTURER'S REQUEST TO RETURN PRODUCT** a request by a manufacturer to return a product because of a defect or contamination **4. RECALLING OF SOMETHING** the remembering of something or the calling back of somebody or something **5. REVOCATION** a revocation or cancellation of a previous decision or instruction **6.** MIL **SIGNAL TO RETURN** a signal, especially a bugle call, ordering troops to return to their positions or to a rallying point [Late 16thC. Formed from CALL on the model of French *rappeler* or Latin *revocare*.] —**re·call·a·ble** /riə káwləb'l/ *adj.* —**re·cal·ler** /-káwlər/ *n.* —**re·cal·la·bil·i·ty** /ri kàwlə bíllətee/ *n.*

re·ca·mi·er /ràykə myáy/ *n.* a couch with a high headrest and low footrest, often without a back [Early 20thC. Named for Jeanne *Récamier* (1777–1849), French hostess, portrayed reclining on a couch in a painting.]

re·ca·nal·i·za·tion /ree kànn'li záysh'n/ *n.* the surgical unblocking of an obstructed vessel within the body or the reconnection of a tube or duct

re·cant /ri kant/ (**-cant·ed, -cant·ing, -cants**) *vti.* to deny believing in something or withdraw something previously said [Mid-16thC. From Latin *recantare*, literally "to sing back" (modeled on Greek *palinōidein* "to recant"), from *cantare* "to sing."] —**re·can·ta·tion** /rèe kan táysh'n/ *n.* —**re·cant·er** /ri kántər/ *n.*

re·cap[1] /ree káp/ *vti.* (**-capped, -cap·ping, -caps**) **RESTATE MAIN POINTS** to go over the main points of something such as an argument or a proposal again ■ *n.* **SUMMARY** a summing-up of the main points of something previously put forward, e.g., a proposal [Mid-20thC. Shortening.]

re·cap[2] *n.* *ANZ, U.S.* TRANSP **RETREAD** a retread ■ *vt.* (**-capped, -cap·ping, -caps** /ri káp/) *ANZ, U.S.* **RETREAD** to retread a tire [Mid-20thC. Formed from CAP. Originally in the sense "to put a cap on something again."] —**re·cap·pa·ble** *adj.*

re·cap·i·tal·ize /ree káppit'l ìz/ (**-ized, -iz·ing, -iz·es**) *vt.* to supply a business with new capital or change the way in which its capital is held —**re·cap·i·tal·i·za·tion** /ree kàppit'li záysh'n/ *n.*

re·ca·pit·u·late /rèekə píchə làyt/ (**-lat·ed, -lat·ing, -lates**) *v.* **1.** *vti.* **RECAP** to recap (*formal*) **2.** *vt.* BIOL **REPEAT EVOLUTIONARY STAGES AS EMBRYO** to repeat stages from the evolution of the species during the embryonic period of an animal's life [Late 16thC. Partly from Latin *recapitulat-*, past participle stem of *recapitulare*, literally "to restate by chapters," from *capitulum* "chapter" (source of English *chapter*); partly a back-formation from RECAPITULATION.] —**re·ca·pit·u·la·tive** /rèekə píchə làytiv, -píchələtiv/ *adj.* —**re·ca·pit·u·la·to·ry** /-píchələ tàwree/ *adj.*

re·ca·pit·u·la·tion /rèekə pichə láysh'n/ *n.* **1. RECAP** a summation of the main points of something (*formal*) **2.** BIOL **REPEATING EVOLUTIONARY STAGES DURING EMBRYONIC PERIOD** the theoretical process of going through successive stages during the embryonic period of an animal's life that duplicate the evolutionary stages the species experienced **3.** MUSIC **REPETITION OF THEMES** the repetition of earlier themes in a piece of music, especially in sonata form at the end of a movement [14thC. Directly or via French from the late Latin stem *recapitulation* from Latin *recapitulat-* (see RECAPITULATE).]

re·cap·tion /ree kápshən/ *n.* LAW the taking back, by peaceful means, of property from somebody who has unlawfully taken it, or of a spouse or child from somebody who has unlawfully detained the person [Early 17thC. From the Anglo-Latin stem *recaption-* "capturing back," from Latin *captio* "capturing" Originally in English, "second legal seizure of another's goods."]

re·cap·ture /ree kápchər/ *vt.* (**-tured, -tur·ing, -tures**) **1. CAPTURE AGAIN** to capture again or take back somebody or something that has escaped or that has been taken away **2. EXPERIENCE AGAIN** to have, show, or experience again something that existed in the past or has been lost ○ *a failed attempt to recapture their youth* **3.** FIN **TAKE PART OF PROFITS** to take part of the profits, over a set amount, of a public-service corporation by law ■ *n.* **1. TAKING BACK OF SOMETHING** the capture of somebody or something that has escaped or that has been taken away ○ *the information that led to his recapture* **2. EXPERIENCING OF SOMETHING AGAIN** the having, showing, or experiencing again of something that is in the past or has been lost ○ *the recapture of youthful joys* **3.** FIN **TAKING OF PART OF PROFITS** the legal taking by government of part of the profits, over a set amount, of a public-service corporation

re·cast /ree kást/ (**-cast, -cast·ing, -casts**) *vt.* **1. CAST AGAIN** to repeat the casting process for an object formed in a mold **2. CHANGE** to change the form of something ○ *The experience led him to recast his philosophy of life.* **3. GIVE ROLES TO DIFFERENT ACTORS** to assign roles in something such as a play or film to different actors ○ *recast the play for a road tour*

rec·ce /rékee/ *n.* **RECONNAISSANCE** a reconnaissance (*slang*) ■ *vt.* (**-ced, -ce·ing, -ces**) **RECONNOITER** to reconnoiter something (*slang*) [Mid-20thC. Shortening and alteration.]

recd., **rec'd.** *abbr.* received

re·cede /ri séed/ (**-ced·ed, -ced·ing, -cedes**) *vi.* **1. GO BACK** to go back or down from a certain point or level ○ *waiting for the flood waters to recede* **2. GET FARTHER AWAY** to become more distant or unlikely ○ *As the ship gathered speed, the island receded in the distance.* **3. SLOPE** to slope backwards ○ *a receding forehead* **4. GO BALD** to gradually go bald from the front of the head backwards ○ *a hairline that was slowly receding* **5. BECOME LESS** to become less in value or quality **6. WITHDRAW** engage in a retreat [15thC. Directly or via Old French *receder* from Latin *recedere*, literally "to go back," from *cedere* (see CEDE).]

re·ceipt /ri séet/ *n.* **1. ACKNOWLEDGMENT OF RECEIPT** a written or printed acknowledgment that something such as money has been given to the person who issues the acknowledgment **2. ACT OF RECEIVING** the receiving of something ○ *The balance is payable on receipt of the goods.* **3.** COOK **RECIPE** a recipe (*dated*) ■ **re·ceipts** *npl.* **AMOUNT RECEIVED** the amount of money or goods received, especially in business ■ *v.* (-ceipt·ed, -ceipt·ing, -ceipts) 1. *vt.* ACKNOWLEDGE PAYMENT BY SIGNING to acknowledge, with a signature, that a bill has been paid 2. *vti.* GIVE RECEIPT to give a receipt for money or goods [14thC. From Anglo-Norman or Old Northern French *receite* "(medicinal) recipe, receipt," from, ultimately, Latin *recipere* (see RECEIVE).]

re·ceiv·a·ble /ri séevəb'l/ *adj.* 1. SUITABLE TO BE RECEIVED suitable to be received, especially as payment ○ *receivable notes* 2. AWAITING PAYMENT relating to a bill or account that is due to be paid ■ **re·ceiv·a·bles** *npl.* MONEY OWED business assets consisting of amounts of money that a company is owed

re·ceive /ri séev/ (-ceived, -ceiv·ing, -ceives) *v.* 1. *vti.* GET SOMETHING to take or accept something given 2. *vti.* CONVERT ELECTRONIC SIGNALS to pick up electronic signals and convert them into sound or pictures 3. *vt.* TAKE DELIVERY OF MESSAGE to take delivery of a message, e.g., a letter or telephone call 4. *vt.* LEARN OF to learn of something such as news or information 5. *vt.* MEET WITH to meet with or experience something ○ *We received a warm reception from the crowd.* 6. *vt.* ACQUIRE SOMETHING to come to have something, e.g., through effort 7. *vt.* REACT TO SOMETHING to react to something in a specified way ○ *The proposals were not well received by the members.* 8. *vti.* SPORTS PLAY BALL SENT BY OPPONENT to catch, hit, or kick a ball played by an opponent 9. *vt.* GREET GUESTS to greet and admit guests ○ *We were received by the duke himself.* 10. *vti.* ENTERTAIN VISITORS to be at home or available to entertain visitors ○ *Find out the hours during which patients can receive visitors.* 11. *vt.* HEAR AND ACKNOWLEDGE SOMETHING to hear and acknowledge something formally ○ *The priest received her confession.* 12. *vt.* BE HURT BY to be subjected to something such as an injury, blow, or pressure ○ *The parachutist received the full force of the earth's gravity upon landing.* 13. *vt.* CATCH to hold or take something ○ *The larger tank receives the overflow from the drainage system.* 14. *vt.* BEAR to bear or sustain something such as a burden ○ *The bridge is reinforced to receive the weight of heavy traffic.* 15. *vt.* ADMIT SOMEBODY to allow a person entry ○ *A knight had to prove himself worthy before being received into their fellowship.* 16. *vi.* CHR TAKE COMMUNION to partake of the Communion [14thC. Via Old French *receivre* from, ultimately, Latin *recipere*, literally "to take back," from *capere* "to take" (source of English *captive*, *capture*, and *conceive*).]

re·ceived /ri séevd/ *adj.* generally accepted as true ○ *The received wisdom in these matters is seldom wrong.*

Re·ceived Pro·nun·ci·a·tion *n.* the accent of British English that educated people from the southern part of England traditionally use, widely regarded as the least regionally modified of all British accents

re·ceiv·er /ri séevər/ *n.* 1. TELECOM PART OF A PHONE the part of a telephone that contains the earpiece and mouthpiece and receives and converts electronic signals into sound 2. ELECTRON ENG DEVICE FOR PICKING UP SIGNALS an electrical device that receives and converts electronic signals into sound or pictures 3. FOOTBALL PLAYER CATCHING FORWARD PASS a football player on the offensive team who is eligible to catch a forward pass 4. FIN SOMEBODY COURT APPOINTS TO RUN BUSINESS somebody appointed by a court to manage a business or property that is involved in a legal process such as bankruptcy 5. SOMEBODY WHO RECEIVES SOMETHING somebody who takes or accepts something given or takes delivery of something sent 6. BASEBALL CATCHER a catcher 7. LAW SOMEBODY DEALING IN STOLEN GOODS somebody who knowingly buys and sells stolen goods 8. CHEM COLLECTING VESSEL IN CHEMISTRY a vessel used during distillation to collect the distillate

re·ceiv·er·ship /ri séevər shìp/ *n.* LAW 1. BEING IN HANDS OF RECEIVER management by a receiver of a business or property that is involved in a legal process such as bankruptcy 2. OFFICE OF RECEIVER the office or duties of somebody appointed by a court to manage a business or property that is involved in a legal process such as bankruptcy

re·ceiv·ing blan·ket *n.* a light blanket in which an infant is wrapped, especially after a bath

re·ceiv·ing end *n.* the position of having to endure something ○ *We were on the receiving end of some harsh criticism.*

re·ceiv·ing line *n.* a group of people who stand in a line to greet individually the guests at a formal occasion such as a wedding reception

re·cen·sion /ri sénshən/ *n.* 1. CRITICAL REVISION a critical revision carried out on a literary text 2. REVISED TEXT a literary text that has been given a critical revision [Mid-17thC. From the Latin stem *recension-* "review," from *recensere*, literally "to reassess," from *censere* "to appraise, assess."]

re·cent /reés'nt/ *adj.* 1. HAVING HAPPENED NOT LONG AGO having happened or appeared not long ago ○ *the recent birth of her daughter* 2. MODERN from current times or the very near past ○ *recent political trends* [15thC. Directly or via French from Latin *recent-*, the stem of *recens*, of uncertain origin: perhaps related to Greek *kainos* "new."] —**re·cen·cy** *n.* —**re·cent·ly** *adv.* —**re·cent·ness** *n.*

Re·cent /reés'nt/ *adj., n.* = **Holocene**

re·cep·ta·cle /ri séptək'l/ *n.* 1. CONTAINER a container that holds, contains, or receives a liquid or solid 2. BOT FLOWER-BEARING PART OF PLANT the end of a flower stalk, bearing the parts of a flower or the florets of a composite flower 3. BOT PLANT PART BEARING REPRODUCTIVE ORGANS in a plant that reproduces through spores, e.g., an alga or liverwort, the part that bears the reproductive organs [14thC. Directly or via French from Latin *receptaculum*, literally "place in which to store something received," from, ultimately, *recipere* (see RECEIVE).]

re·cep·tion /ri sépshən/ *n.* 1. FORMAL PARTY a formal party to welcome somebody or celebrate an event, e.g., a wedding 2. WAY SOMEBODY OR SOMETHING IS RECEIVED the way in which somebody or something is received or greeted ○ *The audience gave her a warm reception.* 3. BROADCAST QUALITY OF SIGNAL the quality of the signal received by a radio or television set ○ *We don't get very good reception on this channel.* 4. ELECTRON ENG CONVERSION OF ELECTRONIC SIGNALS the receiving and conversion of electronic signals 5. FOOTBALL CATCHING OF FORWARD PASS in football, the catching of a pass made toward the opponent's goal 6. ACT OF RECEIVING the receiving of something given or sent 7. PLACE WHERE VISITORS ARE RECEIVED a place in a hotel, office, or public building where visitors are first received ○ *I'll be waiting for you in reception.* 8. = **reception room** [14thC. Directly or via French from the Latin stem *reception-*, from, ultimately, *recipere* (see RECEIVE).]

re·cep·tion·ist /ri sépshənist/ *n.* an employee who greets visitors, customers, or patients, answers the telephone, and makes appointments

re·cep·tion room *n.* a room in which clients, patients, or visitors are received and usually wait to see somebody

re·cep·tive /ri séptiv/ *adj.* 1. WILLING TO ACCEPT ready and willing to accept something, e.g., new ideas 2. QUICK TO LEARN quick to take in new information 3. ABLE TO RECEIVE able to receive something ○ *The United States was not immediately receptive to the refugees* 4. PHYSIOL ABLE TO RECEIVE STIMULI capable of transmitting and receiving stimuli (*refers to a sensory organ*) [15thC. Directly or via French from medieval Latin *receptivus*, from, ultimately, Latin *recipere* (see RECEIVE).] —**re·cep·tive·ly** *adv.* —**re·cep·tive·ness** *n.* —**re·cep·tiv·i·ty** /rèe sep tívvətee/ *n.*

re·cep·tor /ri séptər/ *n.* 1. PHYSIOL SENSITIVE NERVE ENDING a nerve ending that is sensitive to stimuli and can convert them into nerve impulses 2. ELECTRON ENG RECEIVING DEVICE a device designed to receive electronic signals 3. CHEM SPECIFIC CELL BINDING SITE OR MOLECULE a molecule, group, or site that is in a cell or on a cell surface and binds with a specific molecule, antigen, hormone, or antibody 4. ENVIRON RECEIVER OF POLLUTION somebody or something adversely affected by a pollutant [15thC. Directly or via Old French *receptour* "person who harbors criminals or stolen goods" (the original English sense) from Latin *receptor*, from, ultimately, *recipere* (see RECEIVE).]

re·cess /reé sèss, ri séss/ *n.* 1. EDUC BREAK FROM SCHOOL a break from classes during the school day or year ○ *played hopscotch during recess* 2. POL BREAK FROM BUSINESS a time during which no work or business is done, specifically a long period in which a legislative body is not sitting 3. LAW PERIOD WHEN COURT DOESN'T SIT a period of time of varying length when a court of law does not sit ○ *The court will stand in recess until noon on Friday.* 4. REMOTE PLACE a remote or secluded place (*often used in the plural*) ○ *A distant memory haunted the recesses of her mind.* 5. ARCHIT INDENTED OR HOLLOWED-OUT SPACE an area such as an alcove or niche, set into a wall or other flat surface ○ *a recess large enough to hold a vase* 6. ANAT BODY CAVITY a concave area or cavity in a part of the body ■ *v.* (-cessed, -cess·ing, -cess·es) 1. *vti.* SUSPEND PROCEEDINGS to take a break or suspend proceedings or work ○ *The meeting was recessed at midday.* ○ *The court recessed early for the weekend.* 2. *vt.* PUT IN RECESS to put something in a recess, especially in a wall ○ *recessed lighting* 3. *vt.* MAKE INDENTATION IN to make a recess in something, especially a wall ○ *The north wall of the chamber has been recessed to form an alcove.* [Mid-16thC. Directly or via Old French *reces* from Latin *recessus*, literally "going back," from *recedere* (see RECEDE).]

re·ces·sion /ri sésh'n/ *n.* 1. ECON DECLINE IN ECONOMIC ACTIVITY a period, shorter than a depression, during which there is a decline in economic trade and prosperity 2. WITHDRAWAL OF SOMEBODY IN CEREMONY the withdrawal of the participants in a ceremony, e.g., the clergy and choir after a church service 3. RECEDING a going back or becoming more distant

re·ces·sion·al /ri séshən'l, ri séshnəl/ *adj.* RELATING TO RECESSION involving or typical of a recession ■ *n.* 1. = **recession** *n.* 2 2. CHR TYPE OF HYMN a hymn sung as the clergy and choir withdraw from a church after a service

re·ces·sive /ri séssiv/ *adj.* 1. GENETICS PRODUCING EFFECT IN CERTAIN CONDITIONS ONLY producing an effect in an organism only when its matching allele is identical. The effect is masked when the matching allele is nonidentical. (*refers to a gene*) 2. GENETICS CONTROLLED BY RECESSIVE GENE determined by a recessive gene (*refers to a hereditary characteristic or trait*) 3. RECEDING tending to go backward or to recede ○ *recessive flood waters* 4. LING FALLING AT BEGINNING OF WORD used to describe stress that is placed at or near the beginning of a word ■ *n.* GENETICS 1. RECESSIVE GENE OR TRAIT a recessive gene or trait 2. ORGANISM WITH RECESSIVE GENE OR TRAIT an organism that has a recessive gene or trait —**re·ces·sive·ly** *adv.* —**re·ces·sive·ness** *n.*

re·charge /ree chaárj/ (-charged, -charg·ing, -charg·es) *vt.* 1. REPLENISH ELECTRICITY IN SOMETHING to replenish the amount of electric power in something, especially a battery 2. RENEW to renew something, e.g., somebody's energy ○ *We felt recharged after the weekend.* [15thC. Partly formed from CHARGE; partly modeled on French *recharger*. Originally in English, "to reload (a vessel)."] —**re·charge·a·ble** *adj.* —**re·charg·er** *n.*

ré·chauf·fé /rày shṓ fáy/ *n.* 1. REHEATED FOOD a dish of reheated leftovers 2. REUSED MATERIAL a piece of work, e.g., a piece of writing, that is merely a reuse of old material [Early 19thC. From French, the past participle of *réchauffer* "to reheat."]

re·cher·ché /rə shèr sháy/ *adj.* 1. RARE AND EXQUISITE marked by such rare and exquisite quality that it is known only to connoisseurs 2. APPRECIATING FINE THINGS having a deep appreciation of unusual or choice things ○ *a recherché taste in sculpture* 3. AFFECTED marked by excessive refinement or exaggerated importance ○ *Some of his ideas are a little recherché for my taste.* [Late 17thC. From French, the past participle of *rechercher*, literally "to seek thoroughly," from *chercher* "to seek."]

re·cid·i·vism /ri síddə vìzzəm/ *n.* the tendency to relapse into a previous undesirable type of behavior, especially crime [Late 19thC. Formed from *recidivist*, which came via French *récidiviste* from, ultimately, Latin *recidivus* "falling back," from *recidere* "to fall back," from *cadere* "to fall."] —**re·cid·i·vist** *n., adj.* —**re·cid·i·vis·tic** /ri sìddə vístik/ *adj.*

Re·ci·fe /rə seéfə/ capital city of Pernambuco State, northeastern Brazil, and the major city of the region. It is a port on the Atlantic Ocean. Population: 1,342,877 (1996).

recip. *abbr.* 1. MATH reciprocal 2. reciprocity

rec·i·pe /réssə pee/ *n.* 1. COOK INSTRUCTIONS FOR MAKING FOOD a list of ingredients and instructions for making something, especially a food dish 2. METHOD a method of doing something or a combination of circumstances likely to bring something about ○ *Hard work is the recipe for success.* 3. MED PRESCRIPTION a prescription for a therapeutic preparation [14thC. Directly or via French from Latin, "take!" (the original sense in English), a form of *recipere* (see RECEIVE).]

re·cip·i·ence /ri síppee əns/, **re·cip·i·en·cy** /-ənsee/ *n.* 1. ACT OF RECEIVING the receiving of something 2. RECEPTIVENESS the tendency or ability to receive

re·cip·i·ent /ri síppee ənt/ *n.* RECEIVER somebody or something that receives something ■ *adj.* RECEIVING tending or able to receive [Mid-16thC. Directly or via

French from Latin *recipient-*, the present participle stem of *recipere* (see RECEIVE).]

re·cip·ro·cal /ri sípprək'l/ *adj.* **1. GIVEN BY EACH SIDE** given or shown by each of two sides or individuals to the other ○ *reciprocal compliments* **2. IN RETURN** given or done in return for something else ○ *a reciprocal exchange of gifts* **3.** MATH **MULTIPLIED TO GIVE ONE** related to another by the fact that when multiplied together the product is one (*refers to a number or quantity*) **4.** MATH **COMPLEMENTING** serving to complement one another ○ *reciprocal angles* ■ *n.* **1. SOMETHING MUTUAL** something that is mutual or done in return **2.** MATH **NUMBER MULTIPLIED TO GIVE ONE** a number or quantity that is related to another by the fact that when multiplied together the product is one ○ *4 and $\frac{1}{4}$ are reciprocals* [Late 16thC. Formed from Latin *reciprocus*, literally "that goes backward and forward," from, ultimately, *re-* "backward" + *pro-* "forward."] —**re·cip·ro·cal·i·ty** /ri sìpprə kállətee/ *n.* —**re·cip·ro·cal·ly** /rə sípprəkəlee/ *adv.* —**re·cip·ro·cal·ness** /-k'lnəss/ *n.*

re·cip·ro·cal pro·noun *n.* a word or phrase such as "each other," representing two or more things that mutually correspond to one another

re·cip·ro·cate /ri sípprə kàyt/ (**-cat·ed, -cat·ing, -cates**) *v.* **1.** *vti.* **GIVE MUTUALLY** to give or feel something mutually or in return ○ *I couldn't accept such a generous gift without reciprocating.* **2.** *vti.* ENG **MOVE BACKWARDS AND FORWARDS** to move backwards and forwards in an alternating motion, or move something in this way **3.** *vi.* **BE COMPLEMENTARY** to be the same or complementary [Late 16thC. From Latin *reciprocat-*, the past participle stem of *reciprocare* "to move back and forth, reciprocate," from *reciprocus* (see RECIPROCAL).] —**re·cip·ro·ca·tion** /ri sìpprə káysh'n/ *n.* —**re·cip·ro·ca·tive** /ri sípprə kàytiv/ *adj.* —**re·cip·ro·ca·tor** /-kàytər/ *n.*

re·cip·ro·cat·ing en·gine *n.* an engine with one or more cylinders in which pistons move backwards and forwards

rec·i·proc·i·ty /rèssə próssətee/ (*plural* **-ties**) *n.* **1. RECIPROCAL RELATIONSHIP OR ACT** something done mutually or in return **2. RELATIONSHIP INVOLVING MUTUAL EXCHANGE** a relationship between people involving the exchange of goods, services, favors, or obligations, especially a mutual exchange of privileges between trading nations or recognition of licenses between states ○ *the long-standing tariff reciprocity between our two countries* [Mid-18thC. From French *réciprocité*, from, ultimately, Latin *reciprocus* (see RECIPROCAL).]

rec·i·proc·i·ty fail·ure *n.* in photography, the failure of light intensity and exposure time to act reciprocally when their values are extremely high or low, sometimes affecting the color characteristics of the resulting photograph

re·ci·sion /ri sízh'n/ *n.* the cancellation or rescinding of something, especially a contract [Early 17thC. Via the Latin stem *recision-*, literally "cutting back," from, ultimately, Latin *recidere*, literally "to cut back," from *caedere* "to cut" (source of English *circumcise*).]

recit. *abbr.* MUSIC recitative

re·cit·al /ri sít'l/ *n.* **1.** ARTS **SOLO PERFORMANCE** a performance given by a solo musician or dancer, or a series of solo performances by a group of musicians or dancers **2.** ARTS **PERFORMANCE BY MUSIC OR DANCE STUDENTS** a performance given by music or dance students to demonstrate the progress they have made **3. RECITING OF SOMETHING** the reading aloud or reciting from memory of something such as a poem **4. DETAILED ACCOUNT** a detailed account or report of something **5.** LAW **DETAILED PRESENTATION OF FACT** a statement in a judgment laying out jurisdictional facts. It also can mean a deed's preliminary part laying out the circumstances leading to its existence. —**re·ci·tal·ist** *n.*

rec·i·ta·tion /rèssə táysh'n/ *n.* **1. READING ALOUD** the public reading aloud of something or reciting of something from memory, especially poetry **2. MATTER READ ALOUD** material read aloud or recited from memory in public, especially poetry **3. REPORTING OF SOMETHING** the listing or reporting of something **4.** EDUC **STUDENT'S ORAL RESPONSE TO TEACHER'S QUESTIONS** the oral response by a student to questions on previously taught material **5.** EDUC **CLASS PERIOD FOR REVIEW** a class period during which previously taught material is reviewed [15thC]

rec·i·ta·tive[1] /rèssətə téev/, **re·ci·ta·ti·vo** /rèssətə téevō/ (*plural* **-vos**) *n.* **1. SINGING LIKE SPEECH** a style of singing that is close to the rhythm of natural speech, used in opera for dialogue and narration **2. PASSAGE SUNG LIKE SPEECH** a passage in a musical composition that is sung in the form of recitative [Mid-17thC. Formed from Italian *recitativo*, from Latin *recitat-*, the past participle stem of *recitare* (see RECITE).]

rec·i·ta·tive[2] /réssə tàytiv, ri sítətiv/ *adj.* relating to recital or recitation [Mid-17thC. Via Italian *recitativo* from, ultimately, Latin *recitare* (see RECITE).]

re·cite /ri sít/ (**-cit·ed, -cit·ing, -cites**) *v.* **1.** *vti.* **REPEAT OR READ ALOUD** to read something aloud or repeat something from memory, especially for an audience **2.** *vt.* EDUC **REPEAT SOMETHING LEARNED** to repeat aloud something learned, e.g., a lesson in school **3.** *vt.* **GIVE DETAILED ACCOUNT OF SOMETHING** to give a detailed account of an occurrence or event ○ *There's no need to recite every detail of your weekend.* **4.** *vt.* **LIST SOMETHING** to give a list of something ○ *He then recited all my faults.* [15thC. Directly or via French *réciter* from Latin *recitare*, literally "to summon again," from *citare* (see CITE).] —**re·cit·er** *n.*

reck /rek/ (**recked, reck·ing, recks**) *vti.* (*archaic*) **1. CARE** to care or mind about something **2. MATTER** to matter, or matter to somebody [Old English *rēcan* (recorded only in the past tense), *reccan* "to care, take care of, be interested in." From a prehistoric Germanic base that also produced English *reckless*.]

reck·less /rékləss/ *adj.* marked by a lack of thought about danger or other possible undesirable consequences ○ *with a reckless disregard for the established safety procedures* [Old English *rec(c)elēas*. From a prehistoric Germanic word (ancestor also of German *ruchlos* "dastardly" and Dutch *roekeloos* "reckless") formed from the base that produced English *reck*.] —**reck·less·ly** *adv.* —**reck·less·ness** *n.*

reck·on /rékən/ (**-oned, -on·ing, -ons**) *v.* **1.** *vti.* **COUNT** to count or calculate something ○ *I reckon the total at 200.* **2.** *vt.* **REGARD SOMEBODY OR SOMETHING AS SOMETHING** to consider somebody or something to be something (*often passive*) ○ *She's reckoned the best in her field.* **3.** *vt.* **INCLUDE** to include or class a person or thing as being part of a particular group ○ *I reckon him among my friends.* **4.** *vt.* **THINK OR BELIEVE** to suppose to be true (*regional*) ○ *I reckon we're finished now.* **5.** *vi.* **DEPEND** to expect with confident assurance (*informal*) ○ *You can reckon on my support.* [Old English *gerecenian* "to explain, recount, tell." From a prehistoric Germanic word (ancestor also of German *rechnen* "to work out, calculate, estimate").]

WORD KEY: USAGE

I reckon you're right: The informal use of ***reckon*** meaning "think, believe" and followed by a clause (with the word *that* present or suppressed), is chiefly dialectal in U.S. English, commonly occurring in Midland and Southern U.S. speech.

reckon with *vt.* **1. DEAL WITH** to deal or come to terms with somebody powerful ○ *If he lets you down he'll have me to reckon with.* **2. ALLOW FOR SOMEBODY OR SOMETHING** to take somebody or something into account ○ *We didn't reckon with the strength of the tide.*

reckon without *vt.* to fail to take something into account ○ *The legislators reckoned without the strength of public feeling against the new law.*

reck·on·er /rékənər/ *n.* a book of tables of calculations that are already worked out and are used as an aid in calculation [12thC. Originally in the sense "person who reckons."]

reck·on·ing /rékəning/ *n.* **1. CALCULATION** calculation of an aircraft's, a spacecraft's, or a vessel's position in the air, in space, or on the sea **2. SETTLEMENT OF AN ACCOUNT** the settlement of an account **3.** FIN **ACCOUNT OR BILL** a statement of debts owed or repaid **4. TIME TO ACCOUNT FOR WRONGS** a time to account for or be punished for wrongs ○ *day of reckoning*

re·claim /ree kláym/ *vt.* (**-claimed, -claim·ing, -claims**) **1. CLAIM SOMETHING BACK** to claim back something that has been taken away or temporarily given to another **2. CONVERT WASTELAND** to convert unusable land, e.g., desert or marsh, into land suitable for farming or other use **3. EXTRACT USEFUL SUBSTANCES** to extract useful substances from waste or refuse **4. MAKE SOMEBODY VIRTUOUS AGAIN** to make somebody stop doing things regarded as immoral and return to virtue **5. TAME BIRD** to tame a hawk or falcon ■ *n.* **RECOVERY OR CONVERSION** the reclaiming of something, or the state of being reclaimed ○ *polluted land beyond reclaim.* [14thC. Via the Old French stem *reclaim-* from Latin *reclamare* "to cry out against," from *clamare* (see CLAIM).] —**re·claim·a·ble** *adj.* —**re·claim·ant** *n.* —**re·claim·er** *n.*

rec·la·ma·tion /rèklə máysh'n/ *n.* **1.** ENVIRON **CONVERSION OF LAND** the conversion of unusable land, e.g., desert or marsh, into land suitable for farming or other uses **2.** ENVIRON **EXTRACTION FROM WASTE** the extraction of useful substances from waste or refuse **3. RECLAIMING OF SOMETHING** the claiming back of something taken or given away [Early 16thC. Directly or via French from the Latin stem *reclamation-*, from, ultimately, *reclamare* (see RECLAIM).]

ré·clame /ray klaám/ *n.* **1. FAME** public attention or fame **2. CAPACITY TO ATTRACT NOTORIETY** the capacity or gift for attracting public attention or fame [Late 19thC. From French, literally "advertisement," formed from *réclamer* "to claim" (see RECLAIM).]

rec·li·nate /réklə nàyt, -nət/ *adj.* BOT used to describe a leaf or stem that is bent or curved backward or down [Mid-18thC]

re·cline /ri klín/ (**-clined, -clin·ing, -clines**) *v.* **1.** *vi.* **LIE BACK** to lean back into a supported sloping or horizontal position, usually in order to rest or relax **2.** *vti.* **TILT BACK** to tilt back from an upright position, or make something tilt back ○ *These seats are more comfortable because they recline.* [15thC. Directly or via Old French *recliner* from Latin *reclinare*, literally "to bend back or against," from *clinare* "to bend" (source of English *incline*).] —**re·clin·a·ble** *adj.* —**rec·li·na·tion** /rèklə náysh'n/ *n.*

re·clin·er /ri klínər/ *n.* **1. RECLINING CHAIR** a chair that tilts back to a sloping or almost horizontal position, often with a footrest that can be raised, allowing the person sitting in it to rest more comfortably **2. SOMEBODY WHO RECLINES** somebody who lies back

re·clos·a·ble /ree klózəb'l/ *adj.* able to be closed and sealed again after being opened ○ *a reclosable package* [Mid-20thC]

re·cluse /ri klóoss, ri klóoz/ *n.* **1. SOMEBODY LIVING APART FROM OTHERS** somebody who lives alone and deliberately keeps away from other people **2. SOMEBODY LIVING A LIFE OF PRAYER** somebody who lives a solitary life devoted to prayer and meditation ■ *adj.* **RECLUSIVE** reclusive (*archaic*) [12thC. Via French *reclus*, the past participle of Old French *reclure* "to shut up," from Latin *recludere*, literally "to shut again," from *claudere* "to shut" (source of English *close*).] —**re·clu·sion** /ri klóozh'n/ *n.*

re·clu·sive /ri klóossiv, ri klóoziv/ *adj.* solitary and withdrawn from the rest of the world ○ *lead a reclusive existence* [Late 16thC. Formed from earlier English *recluse* "to shut up," from Latin *reclus-*, the past participle stem of *recludere* (see RECLUSE).] —**re·clu·sive·ly** *adv.* —**re·clu·sive·ness** *n.*

rec·og·ni·tion /rèkəg nísh'n/ *n.* **1. RECOGNIZING OF SOMETHING OR BEING RECOGNIZED** the perception that somebody or something has been seen before or an identification based on such perception **2. APPRECIATION** appreciation or fame earned by an achievement ○ *His pioneering work never got the recognition it deserved.* **3. ACKNOWLEDGMENT** acknowledgment of validity ○ *They'll need recognition from the committee in order to proceed.* **4. PERMISSION TO SPEAK** permission given by somebody chairing a meeting to somebody who has asked to speak **5.** POL **ACCEPTANCE OF A COUNTRY'S EXISTENCE** the formal acceptance by one country of the independent and legal status of another **6. TOKEN OF ACKNOWLEDGMENT** something given or awarded as a token of acknowledgment or gratitude **7.** COMPUT **SENSING OF DATA BY A COMPUTER** the sensing and conversion of data into machine-readable form by a computer **8.** BIOL **COMPATIBILITY OF MOLECULES** the ability of molecules with complementary shapes to attach to one another [15thC. Directly or via Old French from the Latin stem *recognition-*, from *recognit-*, the past participle stem of *recognoscere* (see RECOGNIZE).] —**re·cog·ni·tive** /ri kógnitiv/ *adj.* —**re·cog·ni·to·ry** /-tàwree/ *adj.*

re·cog·ni·zance /ri kógniz'ns/ *n.* **1.** LAW **FORMAL BOND** a formal agreement made by somebody before a judge or magistrate to do something, e.g., to appear in court at a set date ○ *He was released on his own recognizance.* **2.** FIN, LAW **MONEY PLEDGED** a sum of money pledged by somebody making a recognizance, to be forfeited if the agreed act is not carried out **3. RECOGNITION** recognition (*archaic*) [14thC. From Old French *recon(u)issance*, an alteration (influenced by medieval Latin *recognizare* "to recognize") of *reconoissance*, from the stem of *reconoistre* (see RECOGNIZE).] —**re·cog·ni·zant** *adj.*

rec·og·nize /rékəg nīz/ (**-nized, -niz·ing, -niz·es**) *vt.* **1. IDENTIFY SOMEBODY OR SOMETHING SEEN BEFORE** to identify a thing or person because of having perceived him, her, or it before ○ *If you saw him again, would you recognize him?* **2. ACKNOWLEDGE SOMEBODY'S ACHIEVEMENT** to show appreciation of or give credit to another's achievement ○ *I hope you recognize their contribution to the success of the campaign.* **3. ALLOW SOMEBODY TO SPEAK** to allow a person to speak to a meeting ○ *The chair recognizes the representative.* **4. ACCEPT STATE'S INDEPENDENCE** to accept formally the independent and legal status of a country or regime ○ *refused to recognize the military government* **5. REWARD SOMEBODY** to give or award something to a person as a token of acknowledgment of or gratitude ○ *recognized his bravery with a medal* **6. SHOW ACKNOWLEDGEMENT** to show in some way that somebody is personally known ○ *She recognized old friends in the crowd with a smile and a wave.* **7. ACCEPT SOMETHING** to accept the validity or truth of something ○ *I recognize that I am at fault.* **8.** BIOL **BIND ANOTHER MOLECULE** of a molecule, to bind another molecule that has a complementary structure [15thC. Via Old French *recon(n)iss-*, the stem of *reconnaistre*, from Latin *recognoscere* "to know again," from *cognoscere* "to know" (source of English *cognition* and *quaint*).] —**rec·og·niz·a·bil·i·ty** /rèkəg nīzə bíllətee/ *n.* —**rec·og·niz·a·ble** /rékəg nīzəb'l/ *adj.* —**rec·og·niz·a·bly** /-əblee/ *adv.* —**rec·og·niz·er** /-nīzər/ *n.*

re·coil *vi.* /ri kóyl/ (**-coiled, -coil·ing, -coils**) **1. MOVE BACK SUDDENLY** to move back suddenly and violently, e.g., after impact **2. MOVE BACK IN HORROR** to move back or away from something in horror or disgust **3.** PHYS **CHANGE MOMENTUM** to experience a change in momentum as a result of a nuclear collision or the emission of an elementary particle ■ *n.* /rée kòyl, ri kóyl/ **1. SUDDEN BACKWARD MOVEMENT** a sudden and violent backward movement, especially that of a firearm when it is fired **2. MOVEMENT AWAY IN HORROR** a movement back or away from something, especially in horror or disgust ○ *his rapid recoil from the cockroach* **3.** PHYS **CHANGE IN MOMENTUM** a change in the momentum of an atom, nucleus, or elementary particle as a result of a nuclear collision or the emission of an elementary particle [12thC. Via French *reculer* from assumed Vulgar Latin *reculare*, literally "to withdraw (your) backside," from Latin *culus* "backside." Originally in English, "to force back."] —**re·coil·er** /ri kóylər/ *n.*

WORD KEY: SYNONYMS

recoil, flinch, quail, shrink, wince

CORE MEANING: to draw back in fear or distaste

recoil is to draw back suddenly in fear, horror, disgust, or distaste. It can also mean to react mentally to something with fear or disgust, causing reluctance to do or deal with that thing; **flinch** is to draw back physically because of fear or pain. It can also mean to react mentally to something with fear or disgust, resulting in reluctance to do or deal with that thing; **quail** is to cower in fear. It also means to feel very reluctant to confront or face something repellant or frightening; **shrink** is to move away physically from something because of fear or disgust. It can also mean to indicate reluctance to do something because of fear or disgust; **wince** is to move the body slightly in an involuntary reaction to a stimulus such as pain or great embarrassment.

re·coil·less /ri kóylləss/ *adj.* relating to a heavy firearm, e.g., an antitank gun, whose recoil is reduced by venting the blast to the rear

re·coil-op·er·at·ed *adj.* using the movement caused by the recoil of a firearm to operate part of its mechanism

rec·ol·lect /rèkə lékt/ (**-lect·ed, -lect·ing, -lects**) *vti.* to bring something back to mind [Early 16thC. From Latin *recollect-*, the past participle stem of *recolligere* "to gather again" (later "to recall"), from *colligere* (see COLLECT).] —**rec·ol·lec·tive** *adj.* —**rec·ol·lec·tive·ly** *adv.*

re-col·lect (**re-col·lect·ed, re-col·lect·ing, re-col·lects**) *vt.* **1. REGAIN CONTROL OF SOMETHING** to regain control, especially of the self **2. COLLECT SOMETHING AGAIN** to collect again something that has been scattered or dispersed

rec·ol·lec·tion /rèkə lékshən/ *n.* **1. REMEMBERING OF SOMETHING** the remembering of something, or the ability to remember **2. MEMORY** something that a person remembers ○ *a recollection of having met him before*

re·com·bi·nant /ree kómbin'nt/ *adj.* **1. OF GENETIC RECOMBINATION** relating to or involved in genetic recombination ○ *a recombinant chromosome* **2. RELATING TO RECOMBINANT DNA** relating to recombinant DNA or produced by recombinant DNA technology ■ *n.* **1. RESULT OF GENETIC RECOMBINATION** a cell or organism exhibiting genetic recombination **2. GENETIC MATERIAL FROM GENE-SPLICING** genetic material resulting from the splicing of DNA fragments

re·com·bi·nant DNA *n.* DNA extracted from two or more different sources, e.g., genes from different organisms, and joined together to form a single molecule or fragment

re·com·bi·na·tion /rèe kombə náysh'n/ *n.* any process that gives rise to offspring that have combinations of genes different from those of either parent, such as crossing over and independent assortment of chromosomes during gamete formation —**re·com·bi·na·tion·al** *adj.*

re·com·bine /rèekəm bīn/ (**-bined, -bin·ing, -bines**) *vti.* **1. JOIN AGAIN** to become combined again or combine things again **2.** GENETICS **EXPERIENCE OR CAUSE GENETIC RECOMBINATION** to undergo or cause something to undergo genetic recombination

rec·om·mend /rèkə ménd/ (**-mend·ed, -mend·ing, -mends**) *vt.* **1. SUGGEST SOMETHING AS BEST IDEA** to suggest something as worthy of being accepted, used, or done **2. ENDORSE** to endorse a person or thing as being the most worthy or pleasing **3. MAKE SOMETHING APPEALING OR ATTRACTIVE** to make something worth doing or having because it is beneficial or pleasing ○ *Since the legislation has little to recommend it, it is unlikely to pass.* **4. ENTRUST ONE TO ANOTHER** to entrust a person or thing to the care of another (*formal*) ○ *She was recommended to our care until her family returned.* [14thC. From medieval Latin *recommendare*, literally "to commit thoroughly," from Latin *commendare* (see COMMEND).] —**rec·om·mend·a·ble** *adj.* —**rec·om·men·da·to·ry** *adj.* —**rec·om·mend·er** *n.*

WORD KEY: SYNONYMS

recommend, advise, advocate, counsel, suggest

CORE MEANING: to put foward ideas to somebody deciding on a course of action

recommend is to put forward a person or thing as being particularly suitable in the circumstances; **advise** is used in a similar way to "recommend," but usually suggests giving advice in a less forceful or definite way; **advocate** is a formal word meaning to recommend something in a forceful way; **counsel** is a fairly formal word meaning the same as "advise"; **suggest** is to recommend something in a tentative way without putting pressure on anybody to do what is recommended.

rec·om·men·da·tion /rèkəmən dáysh'n/ *n.* **1. RECOMMENDING OF SOMETHING** the suggestion or endorsement of something as the most worthy **2. SOMETHING THAT RECOMMENDS** a favorable reference about somebody or something, or other endorsement of desirability **3. SOMETHING RECOMMENDED** the best course of action recommended [15thC]

re·com·mit /rèekə mít/ (**-mit·ted, -mit·ting, -mits**) *vt.* **1. COMMIT SOMETHING AGAIN** to commit something or somebody again **2. SEND SOMETHING BACK** to return something, usually a bill, to a committee for more discussion —**re·com·mit·tal** *n.* —**re·com·mit·ment** *n.*

rec·om·pense /rékəm pèns/ *vt.* (**-pensed, -pens·ing, -pens·es**) **1. PAY OR REWARD SOMEBODY** to pay another for doing work or for performing a service **2. GIVE COMPENSATION** to give compensation to another for an injury or loss ○ *The state will recompense you for the accidental destruction of your property.* ■ *n.* **1. REMUNERATION** payment for services or work performed **2. COMPENSATION** compensation for a loss or injury [14thC. Directly or via French *récompenser* from late Latin *recompensare*, literally "to balance out again," from Latin *compensare* "to balance out" (source of English *compensate*).]

re·com·pose /rèekəm pṓz/ (**-posed, -pos·ing, -pos·es**) *vt.* **1. CAUSE SOMEBODY TO REGAIN COMPOSURE** to return to a calm or composed state of mind **2. CHANGE ARRANGEMENT** to change the arrangement or composition of a thing or group —**re·com·po·si·tion** /rèe kompə zísh'n/ *n.*

re·con[1] /rée kòn/ *n.* reconnaissance (*informal*) [Early 20thC. Shortening.]

re·con[2] /rée kòn/ (**-con·ned, -con·ning, -cons**) *vt.* COMPUT to transfer something from print to electronic form (*informal*) [Shortening of RECONFIGURE]

rec·on·cile /rékən sīl/ (**-ciled, -cil·ing, -ciles**) *v.* **1.** *vt.* **MAKE PEOPLE FRIENDLY** to bring about a friendly relationship between disputing people or groups (*often passive*) **2.** *vt.* **END CONFLICT** to solve a dispute or end a quarrel ○ *reconciled their differences* **3.** *vt.* **MAKE SOMEBODY ACCEPT SOMETHING** to make somebody accept that something undesirable cannot be changed ○ *He reconciled himself to the fact that his football career was over.* **4.** *vti.* **MAKE CONSISTENT OR COMPATIBLE** to make two or more apparently conflicting things consistent or compatible, or to become consistent or compatible ○ *trying to reconcile fitness with a penchant for fast food* **5.** *vi.* **BECOME FRIENDLY AGAIN** to return to a friendly relationship after a dispute or estrangement [14thC. Directly or via French *réconcilier* from Latin *reconciliare*, literally "to make friendly again," from *conciliare* "to make friendly" (source of English *conciliate*), from *concilium* "meeting" (source of English *council*).] —**rec·on·cil·a·bil·i·ty** /rèkən sīlə bíllətee/ *n.* —**rec·on·cil·a·ble** /rékən sīləb'l/*adj.* —**rec·on·cil·a·ble·ness** /-əb'lnəss/ *n.* —**rec·on·cil·a·bly** /-əblee/ *adv.* —**rec·on·cile·ment** /-mənt/ *n.* —**rec·on·cil·er** /-sīlər/ *n.*

rec·on·cil·i·a·tion /rèkən sillee áysh'n/ *n.* **1. RECONCILING OF PEOPLE** the ending of conflict or renewing of a friendly relationship between disputing people or groups ○ *a series of quarrels and reconciliations* **2. ACHIEVEMENT OF CONSISTENCY OR COMPATIBILITY** the making of two or more apparently conflicting things consistent or compatible ○ *the reconciliation of such action with his pacifist principles* **3.** CHR **SACRAMENT OF PENANCE** the sacrament in the Roman Catholic Church whereby an individual's sins are absolved through confession and penance [14thC. Directly or via French from the Latin stem *reconciliation-*, from, ultimately, *reconciliare* (see RECONCILE).] —**rec·on·cil·i·a·to·ry** /rèkən síllee ə tàwree/ *adj.*

rec·on·dite /rékən dīt, ri kón-/ *adj.* **1. UNDERSTOOD ONLY BY EXPERTS** requiring special detailed knowledge in order to be understood ○ *the recondite lore of the ancient Persians* **2. DEALING WITH DIFFICULT MATERIAL** dealing with material that is too difficult to be understood by those without special knowledge ○ *recondite learning* **3. HIDDEN** hidden from view or knowledge (*archaic*) [Mid-17thC. From Latin *reconditus*, the past participle of *recondere*, literally "to store away," from *condere* "to store, hide" (source of English *condiment*).] —**rec·on·dite·ly** *adv.* —**rec·on·dite·ness** *n.*

WORD KEY: SYNONYMS

See Synonyms at ***obscure***.

re·con·di·tion /rèe kən dísh'n/ (**-tioned, -tion·ing, -tions**) *vt.* to bring something back into good condition, especially by repairing it and replacing worn-out parts

WORD KEY: SYNONYMS

See Synonyms at ***renew***.

re·con·firm /rèekən fúrm/ (**-firmed, -firm·ing, -firms**) *vt.* **1. CONFIRM SOMETHING AGAIN** to confirm something such as an airline or hotel reservation again **2. STRENGTHEN COMMITMENT TO SOMETHING** to strengthen a commitment to or a belief in something ○ *reconfirmed their wedding vows* —**re·con·fir·ma·tion** /rèe konfər máysh'n/ *n.*

re·con·nais·sance /ri kónəss'ns/ *n.* **1.** MIL **EXPLORATION TO GATHER INFORMATION** the exploration or examination of an area, especially to gather information about the strength and positioning of enemy forces **2.** GEOG, GEOL **PRELIMINARY SURVEY** a preliminary inspection of a given area to obtain data concerning geographic, hydrographic, or similar information prior to a detailed or full survey [Early 19thC. From French, from *reconnaiss-*, the stem of *reconnaître* "to reconnoiter," from Latin *recognoscere* (see RECOGNIZE).]

re·con·nect /rèekə nékt/ (**-nect·ed, -nect·ing, -nects**) *vt.* to connect again something that has been disconnected or cut off, e.g., a telephone communication or an electricity supply —**re·con·nec·tion** *n.*

re·con·noi·ter /ri kə nóytər/ *vti.* (**-tered, -ter·ing, -ters**) MIL **EXPLORE TO GATHER INFORMATION** to explore an area in order to gather information, especially about the strength and positioning of enemy forces ○ *reconnoiter the drop zone* ■ *n.* MIL **RECONNOITERING OF AREA** an exploration of an area in order to gather information [Early 18thC. Via obsolete French *reconnoître* from Latin *recognoscere* (see RECOGNIZE).] —**re·con·noi·ter·er** *n.*

re·con·noi·tre *vti., n.* U.K. = **reconnoiter**

re·con·sid·er /rèekən síddər/ (**-ered, -er·ing, -ers**) *vti.* to think about something again, usually with the possibility or intention of changing a previous decision —**re·con·sid·er·a·tion** /rèekən siddə ráysh'n/ *n.*

re·con·sti·tute /ree kónstə to͞ot/ (**-tut·ed, -tut·ing, -tutes**) *vt.* **1. BRING SOMETHING BACK TO ORIGINAL STATE** to bring specified matter or a material back to its original state, usually by adding water to a concentrated, dried, or powdered form ○ *reconstituted the orange juice* **2. GIVE NEW FORM TO SOMETHING** to alter the form of something ○ *reconstitute the government* —**re·con·stit·u·ent** /reekən stíchoo ənt/ *adj., n.* —**re·con·sti·tu·tion** /rèe konstə to͞osh'n/ *n.*

re·con·struct /rèekən strúkt/ (**-struct·ed, -struct·ing, -structs**) *vt.* **1. PUT SOMETHING BACK TOGETHER** to put something back together from its component parts, pieces, or remains **2. ESTABLISH PLAUSIBLE SCENARIO** to create a plausible scenario of the details of something based on the known evidence ○ *reconstruct the culture of an ancient society* —**re·con·struc·ti·ble** *adj.* —**re·con·struc·tion** *n.* —**re·con·struc·tive** *adj.* —**re·con·struc·tor** *n.*

Re·con·struc·tion *n.* the period of U.S. history from 1865 through 1877, during which the states that had seceded during the Civil War were reorganized under federal control and later restored to the Union

Re·con·struc·tion·ism /rèekən strúkshə nìzzəm/ *n.* **1.** HIST **SUPPORT FOR RECONSTRUCTION** support of the policies of the Reconstruction in the southern United States after the Civil War **2.** JUDAISM **REFORMING MOVEMENT IN JUDAISM** a movement in the United States, begun in the 1920s by Mordechai Kaplan, emphasizing the idea that Judaism is a worldwide religious civilization and advocating continuous adaptation to contemporary conditions [Mid-20thC] —**Re·con·struc·tion·ist** *n., adj.*

re·con·struc·tive sur·ger·y *n.* the use of surgery to restore the appearance or use of a damaged body part

re·con·vene /rèekən véen/ (**-vened, -ven·ing, -venes**) *vti.* to convene something again or be convened again ○ *The hearing will reconvene tomorrow morning.*

re·con·vey /rèekən váy/ (**-veyed, -vey·ing, -veys**) *vt.* to transfer something, e.g., property, back to a former owner or location —**re·con·vey·ance** *n.*

rec·ord *n.* /rékərd/ **1. LASTING ACCOUNT** an account, preserved in a lasting form, e.g., in writing or on film ○ *She used a diary to keep a record of her life.* **2. BEST ACCOMPLISHMENT** something that represents the greatest attainment so far, especially in sports ○ *a world record* **3. MUSIC DISK** something on which sound is copied, especially a plastic disk with a groove that can be played using a phonograph **4. COPY OF MUSIC** a piece of music in a format that can be listened to repeatedly (*informal*) ○ *Their new record is only available on CD.* **5. BODY OF INFORMATION** a body of information or statistics, gathered over a period of time, about a particular subject (*often used in the plural*) ○ *the hottest summer since records began* **6. PAST PERFORMANCE** a person's accomplishments or performance to date **7.** CRIMINOL **PAST CRIMES** a background of criminal convictions, or a list of the crimes committed by a person **8.** LAW **WRITTEN ACCOUNT OF COURT PROCEEDINGS** an official written account of the proceedings of a court, available for use as evidence ○ *His remarks were struck from the record.* **9. DOCUMENT CONTAINING HISTORY** the document or book that bears the history of something ○ *The records are stored in the basement.* **10. ACCOUNT OF PROCEEDINGS** a written account of the proceedings of something ○ *the records of the Foundation* **11. EVIDENCE** something that acts as evidence or a memorial ○ *The Egyptian pyramids are a record of human engineering expertise.* **12.** COMPUT **COLLECTION OF DATA** a collection of related items of information treated as a unit by a computer, e.g., in a database ■ *v.* /ri káwrd/ (**re·cord·ed, re·cord·ing, re·cords**) **1.** *vti.* **COPY SOUNDS OR IMAGES** to make a copy of sounds or pictures, e.g., on magnetic tape ○ *I recorded my grandmother reminiscing about the war.* **2.** *vti.* **INDICATE MEASUREMENT** to register or show something, usually on a scale of a measurement **3.** *vt.* **NOTE SOMETHING** to make a note of something, often for official purposes or for subsequent consultation ○ *The clerk recorded their names in the register.* **4.** *vt.* **MAKE A LASTING ACCOUNT OF SOMETHING** to make a lasting account of something, e.g., in writing or on film ○ *Her journal records the last days of the Empire.* ■ *adj.* /rékərd/ **GREATEST YET** representing the greatest extreme yet accomplished ○ *A record crowd turned up for the game.* [12thC. Via French, from *recorder* "to bring to mind," from Latin *recordare, recordari,* literally "to bring back to the heart," from the stem of *cor* "heart, (metaphorically) mind."] —**re·cord·a·ble** /ri káwrdəb'l/ *adj.* ◇ **off the record** said informally or privately and not intended to be recorded or made public ◇ **on the record** said formally or publicly with the knowledge that it may be recorded or disseminated ◇ **set the record straight** to put right a mistake or misunderstanding

re·cord·ed /ri káwrdəd/ *adj.* copied to a record, tape, CD, or other form of permanent copy, rather than listened to or performed live ○ *recorded music* [Mid-16thC]

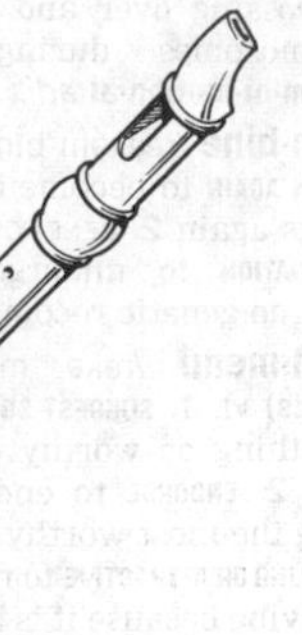

Recorder

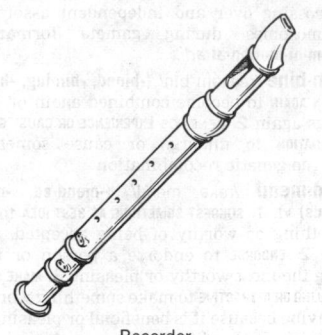

re·cord·er /ri káwrdər/ *n.* **1. MACHINE FOR RECORDING** a machine that makes a permanent copy of sounds or pictures, e.g., a tape recorder or a videotape recorder **2. PERSON NOTING SOMETHING** a person who makes a record of something, especially an official record **3.** MUSIC **TYPE OF FLUTE** a wind instrument of the flute family that has finger holes and is blown through a whistle-shaped mouthpiece at one end [15thC. Partly from Anglo-Norman *recordour,* Old French *recordeur* "person who records," from *recorder* (see RECORD); partly formed from RECORD.]

re·cord·ing /ri káwrding/ *n.* **1. COPY OF MUSIC** a permanent copy of sounds or images, e.g., a tape, CD, or videotape ○ *She was eager to buy the band's latest recording.* **2. MAKING OF RECORD** the making of a record, especially a permanent copy of sounds or images [14thC. The original sense was "remembrance, recollection."]

re·cord·ist /ri káwrdist/ *n.* somebody who records the sound during the making of a film or broadcast

rec·ord play·er *n.* a machine for reproducing the sounds recorded on records, consisting of a turntable on which the disk revolves and a needle that follows the groove to pick up sound

re·count (**-count·ed, -count·ing, -counts**) *vt.* /ree kównt/ to tell the story or details of something [15thC. From Anglo-Norman, Old Northern French *reconter,* literally "to relate again, count again," from *conter* (see COUNT).] —**re·count·al** *n.* —**re·count·er** *n.*

re·count *n.* /rée kòwnt/ **REPEAT COUNTING** a second counting of the votes cast in an election, usually done because the first counting indicated a very close result ■ *vti.* /ree kównt/ (**re·count·ed, re·count·ing, re·counts**) **COUNT AGAIN** to count something, especially the votes cast in an election, a second time

re·coup /ri ko͞op/ (**-couped, -coup·ing, -coups**) *v.* **1.** *vt.* **GET SOMETHING BACK** to regain something lost or an equivalent **2.** *vi.* **MAKE UP FOR A LOSS** to make up for something lost ○ *It will take us years to recoup.* **3.** *vt.* LAW **DEDUCT SOMETHING** to deduct legally part of what is due to a claim **4.** *vt.* **REIMBURSE ANOTHER** to give another party something to make up for that which has been lost ○ *We were adequately recouped for our losses.* [Early 17thC. From Old French *recouper* "to cut back," from *couper* "to cut," from *coup* "blow." Earlier also in the sense "to cut short, interrupt."] —**re·coup·a·ble** *adj.* —**re·coup·ment** *n.*

re·course /rée kàwrss, ri káwrss/ *n.* **1. CHANCE TO SEEK ASSISTANCE** a turning to another for assistance ○ *Can we resolve our financial problems without recourse to further borrowing?* **2. SOURCE OF HELP OR SOLUTION** somebody, something, or a course of action to which a person turns for help or to solve a problem ○ *She felt she had no recourse but to sue.* **3.** FIN, LAW **RIGHT TO DEMAND PAYMENT** the right to demand payment of a bill of exchange from the person who draws or endorses it, when the person who accepts it fails to pay [14thC. Directly or via French *recours* from Latin *recursus,* literally "a running back" (the original English sense), from *cursus* (see COURSE).]

re·cov·er /ri kúvvər/ (**-ered, -er·ing, -ers**) *v.* **1.** *vt.* **REGAIN SOMETHING** to get back something previously lost **2.** *vi.* **RETURN TO NORMAL** to return to a previous state of health, prosperity, or equanimity **3.** *vt.* **RECLAIM SOMETHING FROM WASTE** to extract useful substances from waste or refuse **4.** *vi.* **RETURN TO THE RIGHT POSITION** to return to a suitable or correct state or position ○ *The goalkeeper stumbled, but recovered enough to prevent the goal.* **5.** *vt.* **COMPENSATE FOR SOMETHING** to make up for that which is lost ○ *They'll have to work hard in order to recover their losses.* **6.** *vt.* LAW **OBTAIN SOMETHING THROUGH A COURT** to obtain something by the ruling of a court **7.** *vi.* LAW **SUCCEED IN LITIGATION** to be successful in a lawsuit **8.** *vr.* **BRING SELF BACK TO NORMAL** to bring the self back to a normal condition ○ *He soon recovered himself enough to feign a friendly welcome.* [13thC. Via Anglo-Norman *recoverer,* Old French *recovrer* from Latin *recuperare* (see RECUPERATE).] —**re·cov·er·a·bil·i·ty** /ri kùvvərə bíllətee/ *n.* —**re·cov·er·a·ble** /ri kúvvərəb'l/ *adj.* —**re·cov·er·er** /-kúvvərər/ *n.*

re·cov·er /ree kúvvər/ (**re·cov·ered, re·cov·er·ing, re·cov·ers**) *vt.* **1. GIVE SOMETHING A NEW COVER** to put a new cover on something **2. COVER SOMETHING AGAIN** to cover something again

re·cov·er·a·ble er·ror *n.* a program error that can be corrected without causing a computer program to fail. For example, if a user enters obviously wrong data, the program might request a different entry.

re·cov·er·y /ri kúvvəree/ (*plural* **-ies**) *n.* **1. RETURN TO HEALTH** the return to normal health of somebody who has been ill or injured ○ *a speedy recovery* **2. RETURN TO A NORMAL STATE** the return of something to a normal or improved state after a setback or loss ○ *an economic recovery* **3. GAINING BACK OF SOMETHING LOST** the regaining of something lost or taken away ○ *The arrests led to the recovery of large amounts of stolen property.* **4.** ENVIRON **RECLAMATION FROM WASTE** the extraction of useful substances from waste or refuse **5.** LAW **OBTAINING SOMETHING THROUGH A COURT** the obtaining of something by the ruling of a court **6.** GOLF **SHOT OUT OF AN OBSTACLE** a shot played out of the rough or an obstacle onto the green or fairway **7.** FENCING **RETURN TO GUARD** a return to the guard position after making an attack **8.** ROWING, SWIMMING **BRINGING THE ARM FORWARD** the bringing forward of the arm to make another stroke [14thC. The original English sense was "help, means of recovering."]

re·cov·er·y room *n.* a hospital room equipped for the care of patients who have just undergone surgery and are recovering from anesthesia

rec·re·ant /rékree ənt/, **rec·re·ance** /rékree ənssee/, **rec·re·an·cy** *adj.* (*archaic*) **1. DISLOYAL** disloyal to a cause or duty **2. COWARDLY** cowardly ■ *n.* (*archaic*) **1. DISLOYAL PERSON** somebody who is disloyal or deserts a cause **2. COWARD** a coward [13thC. Via Old French, the present participle of *recroire* "to surrender" from, ultimately, Latin *credere* "to entrust." Originally in English, "surrendering oneself (to an adversary)."] —**rec·re·ant·ly** *adv.*

rec·re·ate /rékree àyt/ (**-at·ed, -at·ing, -ates**) *v.* **1.** *vi.* **TAKE PART IN RECREATION** to take part in activities that are mentally or physically refreshing **2.** *vt.* **REFRESH SELF** to refresh somebody, especially the self, mentally or physically (*archaic*) [15thC. From Latin *recreat-,* the past participle stem of *recreare,* literally "to bring forth again," from *creare* (see CREATE); also, later, a back-formation from RECREATION.] —**rec·re·a·tive** *adj.* —**rec·re·a·tor** *n.*

re·cre·ate /ree kree áyt/ (**re·cre·at·ed, re·cre·at·ing, re·cre·ates**) *vt.* to create something again or reproduce it ○ *The decor aims to re-create a 19th-century interior.* —**re·cre·at·a·ble** *adj.* —**re·cre·a·tion** *n.* —**re·cre·a·tive** *adj.*

WORD KEY: SYNONYMS

See Synonyms at *copy.*

rec·re·a·tion /rèkree áysh'n/ *n.* **1. AMUSEMENT** an activity that a person takes part in for pleasure or relaxation rather than as work ○ *She took up sketching as a recreation.* **2. REFRESHMENT** the refreshment of the mind and body after work, especially by engaging in enjoyable activities ○ *after-work recreation* [14thC]

rec·re·a·tion·al /rèkree áyshən'l, -shnəl/ *adj.* **1. NOT FOR WORK** done or used for pleasure or relaxation rather than work **2.** DRUGS **NOT FOR MEDICAL PURPOSES** relating to controlled drugs taken illegally —**rec·re·a·tion·al·ly** *adv.*

rec·re·a·tion·al ve·hi·cle *n.* a large motor vehicle, usually with facilities for sleeping and eating, used for recreational activities such as camping

rec·re·a·tion room *n.* 1. ROOM IN HOUSE FOR RELAXATION a room used by the occupants of a house for relaxation and recreational activities ○ *a new TV for the recreation room* 2. ROOM FOR SOCIAL EVENTS a room set aside for games, social events, and other kinds of recreation in a public building

re·crim·i·nate /ri krímmə nàyt/ (-nat·ed, -nat·ing, -nates) *vi.* to accuse somebody who has already brought an accusation [Early 17thC. From medieval Latin *recriminat-*, the past participle stem of *recriminari*, literally "to accuse back or again," from Latin *criminari*, *criminare* "to accuse."] —**re·crim·i·na·tive** *adj.* —**re·crim·i·na·tor** *n.* —**re·crim·i·na·to·ry** /ri krímmənə tàwree/ *adj.*

re·crim·i·na·tion /ri krìmmə náysh'n/ *n.* 1. ACCUSING SOMEBODY IN RETURN an accusation made against somebody who has brought a previous accusation ○ *It started out as a calm discussion and ended in tears and recriminations.* 2. LAW COUNTERCHARGE an accusation that somebody accused of a crime makes against the accuser [Early 17thC]

rec room *n.* = **recreation room** *n.* 2

re·cru·desce /rèe kroo déss/ (-desced, -desc·ing, -desc·es) *vi.* to break out or become active again after a dormant period [Mid-17thC. Back-formation from *recrudescence*, from Latin *recrudescere*, literally "to become raw again," from, ultimately, *crudus* "raw, bloody" (source of English *crude*).] —**re·cru·des·cence** *n.* —**re·cru·des·cent** *adj.*

re·cruit /ri kro͞ot/ *v.* (-cruit·ed, -cruit·ing, -cruits) 1. *vti.* MIL ENLIST SOMEBODY to enlist somebody in a military force, or take part in enlisting people for a military force ○ *She was recruited by the Marines.* 2. *vti.* ENROLL OR TAKE ON SOMEBODY to enroll somebody as a worker or member, or to take on people as workers or members ○ *The company has stopped recruiting.* 3. *vt.* MIL RAISE AN ARMY to establish a military force 4. *vti.* RECOVER to recover in health or strength, or recover one's own health or strength (*archaic*) ■ *n.* 1. MIL NEW SOLDIER a member of a military force who has joined recently 2. NEW MEMBER a new member, worker, player, or supporter [Mid-17thC. Via French *recruter* from, ultimately, French *recrue*, literally "new growth," a noun use of the feminine past participle of *recroître* "to increase again," from, ultimately, Latin *crescere* "to grow."] —**re·cruit·er** *n.* —**re·cruit·ing** *n.* —**re·cruit·ment** *n.*

re·crys·tal·lize /ree kríst'l ìz/ (-lized, -liz·ing, -liz·es) *vti.* to crystallize something or become crystallized again —**re·crys·tal·li·za·tion** /ree krìst'li záysh'n/ *n.*

rec. sec. *abbr.* recording secretary

rect.[1], **rec't** *abbr.* receipt

rect.[2] *abbr.* rectangle

Rect. *abbr.* 1. Rector 2. Rectory

rec·ta *npl.* plural of **rectum**

rec·tal /rékt'l/ *adj.* relating to, involving, or in the rectum —**rec·tal·ly** *adv.*

rec·tan·gle /rék tàng g'l/ *n.* a four-sided plane figure in which each angle is a right angle, especially one with adjacent sides of different length [Late 16thC. Directly or via French from medieval Latin *rect(i)angulum*, a noun use of the neuter of late Latin *rectiangulus*, literally "straight angle," from Latin *rectus* "straight" + *angulus* "angle."]

rec·tan·gu·lar /rek táng gyələr/ *adj.* 1. SHAPED LIKE A RECTANGLE with four sides, usually with adjacent sides of different length, and four right angles 2. WITH OR AT RIGHT ANGLES involving, having, or meeting at right angles [Early 17thC. Formed from ANGULAR on the model of French *rectangulaire*.] —**rec·tan·gu·lar·i·ty** /rek tàng gyə lérrətee/ *n.* —**rec·tan·gu·lar·ly** /-táng gyələrlee/ *adv.*

rec·tan·gu·lar co·or·di·nate *n.* a Cartesian coordinate used in a system of axes that meet at right angles

rec·tan·gu·lar hy·per·bo·la *n.* a hyperbola with asymptotes that are at right angles

rec·ti /réktì/ plural of **rectus** [Formed from Latin *rectus* "straight, right, correct" (see RECTIFY)]

rec·ti·fi·er /réktə fìr/ *n.* 1. ELECTRON ENG ELECTRONIC DEVICE an electronic device that converts alternating current to direct current, e.g., semiconductor diodes connected in a bridge circuit 2. CHEM CONDENSING APPARATUS an apparatus that condenses vapor to liquid during distillation 3. ONE THAT RECTIFIES a person or thing that puts a matter or situation right

rec·ti·fy /réktə fì/ (-fied, -fy·ing, -fies) *vt.* 1. CORRECT SOMETHING to put something right 2. CHEM PURIFY to purify a substance, especially by distillation 3. ELECTRON ENG CONVERT A CURRENT to convert alternating current to direct current 4. MATH FIND THE LENGTH OF A CURVE to find the length of a curve [14thC. Directly or via French *rectifier* from medieval Latin *rectificare*, literally "to make right," from *rectus* "right" (source of English *rectangle* and *rectum*).] —**rec·ti·fi·a·bil·i·ty** /rèktə fì ə bíllətee/ *n.* —**rec·ti·fi·a·ble** /réktə fì əb'l/ *adj.* —**rec·ti·fi·ca·tion** /rèktəfi káysh'n/ *n.*

rec·ti·lin·e·ar /rèktə línnee ər/, **rec·ti·lin·e·al** /-əl/ *adj.* 1. WITH STRAIGHT LINES formed or consisting of straight lines 2. IN A STRAIGHT LINE moving in a straight line [Mid-17thC. Formed from late Latin *rectilineus*, from Latin *rectus* "straight" + *linea* "line" (source of English *line*).] —**rec·ti·lin·e·ar·ly** *adv.*

rec·ti·tude /réktə to͞od/ *n.* 1. RIGHTEOUSNESS strong moral integrity in character or actions 2. CORRECTNESS correctness in judgment ○ *the admirable rectitude of her assessments* 3. STRAIGHTNESS straightness in form or shape [15thC. Directly or via French from late Latin *rectitudo*, from Latin *rectus* "straight, correct."] —**rec·ti·tu·di·nous** /rèktə to͞od'nəss/ *adj.*

rec·to /réktō/ (*plural* -tos) *n.* ◊ **verso** 1. FRONT OF PRINTED SHEET the front side of a printed sheet 2. RIGHT-HAND PAGE the right-hand page of an open book [Early 19thC. From modern Latin *(folio) recto* "(the page) being on the right," a form of Latin *rectus* "straight, correct," the underlying idea being "right, proper."]

rec·tor /réktər/ *n.* 1. CHR CLERIC IN CHARGE OF AN EPISCOPAL PARISH a member of the Episcopal clergy who is in charge of a parish 2. CHR CLERIC IN CHARGE OF A CATHOLIC CONGREGATION a member of the Roman Catholic clergy who is in charge of a congregation, a college, or a religious community 3. CHR CLERIC IN CHARGE OF AN ANGLICAN PARISH a member of the clergy of the Church of England who is in charge of a parish 4. EDUC HEAD OF A SCHOOL the head of certain schools, colleges, or universities [14thC. Directly or via Old French, "captain (of a ship), head of a university," from Latin, "ruler, governor" (the original English sense), from, ultimately, *regere* "to rule."] —**rec·tor·ate** *n.* —**rec·to·ri·al** /rek táwree əl/ *adj.* —**rec·tor·ship** /réktər shìp/ *n.*

rec·to·ry /réktəree/ (*plural* -ries) *n.* 1. RECTOR'S HOUSE the house that a rector lives in, provided by church 2. RECTOR'S POST the post of rector and the income that goes with it [Late 16thC. Via Old French *rectorie* or medieval Latin *rectoria* from, ultimately, Latin *rector* (see RECTOR).]

rec·trix /rék triks/ (*plural* -tri·ces /-tri sèez, -trí sèez/) *n.* any of a bird's long stiff tail feathers that help to control direction during flight [Mid-18thC. From Latin, feminine of *rector* (see RECTOR).]

rec·tum /réktəm/ (*plural* -tums *or* -ta /-tə/) *n.* the lower part of the large intestine, between the colon and the anal canal [15thC. From Latin *(intestinum) rectum* "straight (intestine)," from *rectus* (see RECTUS).]

rec·tus /réktəss/ (*plural* -ti /-tì/) *n.* any straight muscle, e.g., the ones in the abdomen or the thigh [Early 18thC. From Latin, "straight" (source of English *rectify* and *correct*). Ultimately from an Indo-European base meaning "to go straight" (ancestor also of English *right, rich, rule,* and *regular*).]

re·cum·bent /ri kúmbənt/ *adj.* 1. LYING lying back or lying down (*literary*) ○ *a colossal recumbent statue* 2. BIOL RESTING OR LEANING used to describe a plant or animal part that rests or leans against something else 3. GEOL HORIZONTAL used to describe a fold whose axis is more or less horizontal [Early 18thC. From Latin *recumbere* "to lie back," from *-cumbere* "to lie down."] —**re·cum·bence** *n.* —**re·cum·bent·ly** *adv.*

re·cu·per·ate /ri ko͞opə ràyt/ (-at·ed, -at·ing, -ates) *v.* 1. *vi.* MED REGAIN HEALTH to recover from an illness or injury 2. *vt.* GET BACK to recover something lost, especially a sum of money [Mid-16thC. From Latin *recuperare*, literally "to take back," from *capere* (see CAPTURE).] —**re·cu·per·a·tion** /ri ko͞opə ráysh'n/ *n.* —**re·cu·per·a·tive** /ri ko͞opə ràytiv, -rətiv/ *adj.* —**re·cu·per·a·to·ry** /-rə tàwree/ *adj.*

WORD KEY: USAGE

Meaning trap: ***Recuperate*** is normally used intransitively, that is, without an object, as in *She needed several weeks to recuperate.* When used transitively, with a noun such as *health* as the object, *recover* is a better choice: *She needed several weeks to recover her health.*

re·cu·per·a·tor /ri ko͞opə ràytər/ *n.* 1. CHEM ENG HEAT EXCHANGER a device used to recover energy that would otherwise be lost, especially one that takes heat from exhaust gases and uses it to preheat incoming combustion air 2. ARMS RESETTING DEVICE IN GUN a device in a gun that returns it to its firing position following recoil

re·cur /ri kúr/ (-curred, -cur·ring, -curs) *vi.* 1. OCCUR AGAIN to happen or appear once again or repeatedly 2. MATH BE REPEATED INDEFINITELY to occur as an infinitely repeated digit or series of digits at the end of a decimal fraction 3. RETURN to return to a subject in speech, writing, or thought (*archaic or literary*) 4. RESORT to turn to something as an option after considering or trying other options (*archaic or literary*) [Early 16thC. From Latin *recurrere*, literally "to run back," from *currere* (see CURRENT).]

WORD KEY: USAGE

Redundancy trap: The sense of *again* being an integral part of the meaning of ***recur***, it is redundant to say things like "The disease recurred again." Simply say "recurred."

re·cur·rent /ri kúr ənt/ *adj.* 1. OCCURRING AGAIN happening or appearing again, especially repeatedly 2. ANAT TURNING AROUND used to describe a blood vessel or nerve that turns back on itself and runs in the opposite direction —**re·cur·rence** *n.* —**re·cur·rent·ly** *adv.*

re·cur·rent fe·ver *n.* = **relapsing fever**

re·cur·ring dec·i·mal *n.* = **repeating decimal**

re·cur·sion /ri kúrzh'n/ *n.* 1. RETURN OF SOMETHING the return of something, often repeatedly 2. LOGIC, MATH REPETITION OF STEPS TO GIVE RESULT the use of repeated steps, each based on the result of the one before, to define a function or calculate a number 3. COMPUT REPEATING OF COMPUTER PROCESS a routine's calling of itself in order to repeat a process in computing [Early 17thC. Via the late Latin stem *recursion-*, literally "a running back," from Latin *recurs-*, the past participle stem of *recurrere* (see RECUR).]

re·cur·sive /ri kúrssiv/ *adj.* 1. SELF-REPEATING repeating itself, either indefinitely or until a specified point is reached 2. MATH, LOGIC REPEATEDLY APPLYING FUNCTION TO ITSELF involving the repeated application of a function to its own values [Late 18thC. Formed from Latin *recurs-*, the past participle stem of *recurrere* (see RECUR).] —**re·cur·sive·ly** *adv.* —**re·cur·sive·ness** *n.*

re·cur·vate /ri kúr vàyt, -vət/ *adj.* curved backward, inward, or downward

re·curve /ri kúrv/ (-curved, -curv·ing, -curves) *vti.* to curve backward, inward, or downward, or cause something to curve in this way [Late 16thC. From Latin *recurvare*, literally "to curve back," from *curvus* (see CURVE).] —**re·cur·va·tion** /rèe kur váysh'n/ *n.* —**re·curved** /ri kúrvd/ *adj.*

rec·u·sant /rékyəz'nt, ri kyo͞o-/ *n.* 1. CHR DISSENTING ROMAN CATHOLIC a Roman Catholic who broke the law by refusing to attend Church of England services in England between the 16th and 18th centuries 2. SOMEBODY DISOBEYING AUTHORITY somebody who refuses to obey authority ■ *adj.* DISOBEYING AUTHORITY refusing to obey authority —**rec·u·sance** *n.*

re·cuse /ri kyo͞oz/ (-cused, -cus·ing, -cus·es) *vti.* to disqualify somebody from judging or participating in something because of bias or personal interest, or withdraw for that reason ○ *The judge recused herself because she knew the plaintiff socially.* [Early 19thC. From Latin *recusare* "to refuse," from *re-* "back" + *causa* "cause, case."] —**re·cus·al** *n.*

re·cy·cle /ree sík'l/ *v.* (-cled, -cling, -cles) 1. *vti.* PROCESS FOR REUSE to process used or waste material so that it can be used again 2. *vti.* SAVE FOR REUSE to save or collect used or waste material for reprocessing into something useful 3. *vti.* USE AGAIN DIFFERENTLY to adapt or convert something to a new use 4. *vt.* REUSE SOMETHING to use something again for the same purpose 5. *vt.* USE AGAIN UNIMAGINATIVELY to use something abstract again in the same form, often at the expense of freshness or originality 6. *vti.* REPEAT A PROCESS to repeat a process, or pass something through a process again ■ *n.* RECYCLING OF MATERIAL the recycling of material, especially used or waste materials —**re·cy·cla·ble** *adj.* —**re·cy·cler** *n.*

re·cy·cled /ree sī́k'ld/ *adj.* **1. MADE FROM WASTE** manufactured from used or waste materials that have been reprocessed **2. USED AGAIN** used again or repeatedly, often at the expense of freshness or originality

re·cy·cling /ree sī́kling/ *n.* **1. PROCESSING OF WASTE FOR REUSE** the processing of used or waste material so that it can be used again, instead of being wasted **2. SAVING FOR REPROCESSING** the saving or collecting of used or waste material for reprocessing. ◊ **recovery, reuse**

red /red/ *adj.* (**red·der, red·dest**) **1.** COLORS **OF THE COLOR OF BLOOD** of or near the color of blood, or a ripe tomato or strawberry **2. REDDISH BROWN** reddish brown, orange, or golden brown (*used of hair or fur*) **3. BLOODSHOT** bloodshot or with red rims, e.g., from tiredness **4. WITH A TEMPORARILY RED FACE** blushing, e.g., from shame or embarrassment **5.** WINE **MADE FROM BLACK GRAPES** made from black grapes. Pigments in the purple skins of these grapes give the wine a deep red color. **6.** ACCT **REPRESENTING DEBT** representing debt or financial loss **7. red, Red** POL **SOCIALIST** socialist or communist (*informal disapproving*) ◊ **white 8. red, Red** POL **SOVIET** relating or belonging to the former Soviet Union (*informal*) ■ *n.* **1.** COLORS **COLOR OF BLOOD** a color such as that of blood, or of a ripe tomato or strawberry. It lies at the far end of the visible spectrum and is one of the three primary colors of light and pigment. **2. RED COLORING** a pigment or dye that is of or near to the color of blood, or a ripe tomato or strawberry **3. RED FABRIC OR CLOTHES** fabric or clothing that is red in color **4. SOMETHING RED** a red object **5.** WINE **RED WINE** wine made from black grapes (*informal*) **6.** GAMBLING **SECTION OF GAMBLING TABLE** in roulette and other gambling games, one of the two colored areas on the table on which players may place bets. The other is black. **7.** ARCHERY **PART OF AN ARCHERY TARGET** a red ring immediately outside the gold disk at the center of a target **8.** CUE GAMES **RED BALL** in billiards, snooker, and other cue games, a red ball **9. red, Red** POL **SOCIALIST OR COMMUNIST** somebody with socialist or communist views (*informal disapproving*) [From Old English *rēad*. Ultimately from an Indo-European base that is also the ancestor of *ruddy, rouge,* and *erythro-*.] —**red·ly** *adv.* —**red·ness** *n.* ◇ **in the red** in debt, e.g., to a bank ◇ **see red** to suddenly become very angry (*informal*)

red. *abbr.* **1.** redeemable **2.** reduced **3.** reduction

re·dact /ri dákt/ (**-dact·ed, -dact·ing, -dacts**) *vt.* **1. EDIT SOMETHING** to edit or revise something in preparation for publication ○ *formerly classified documents that were redacted before release to protect still confidential material* **2. DRAFT SOMETHING** to compose or draft something for publication or for an announcement (*formal*) [Mid-19thC. From Latin *redact-*, the past participle stem of *redigere* "to reduce," literally "to bring down," from *agere* (see ACT).] —**re·dac·tion** /ri dákshən/ *n.* —**re·dac·tion·al** /ri dákshənəl/ *adj.* —**re·dac·tor** *n.*

red ad·mi·ral *n.* a brightly colored butterfly with broad orange-red bands on its forewings. It is native to Europe and North America. Latin name: *Vanessa atalanta.*

red a·lert *n.* a warning or alarm that indicates a situation of the highest priority or greatest urgency, especially an imminent attack, or the state of readiness to deal with such a situation

red al·gae *npl.* marine algae, e.g., dulse, laver, and carrageen, that contain a red pigment as well as chlorophyll. Family: Rhodophyceae.

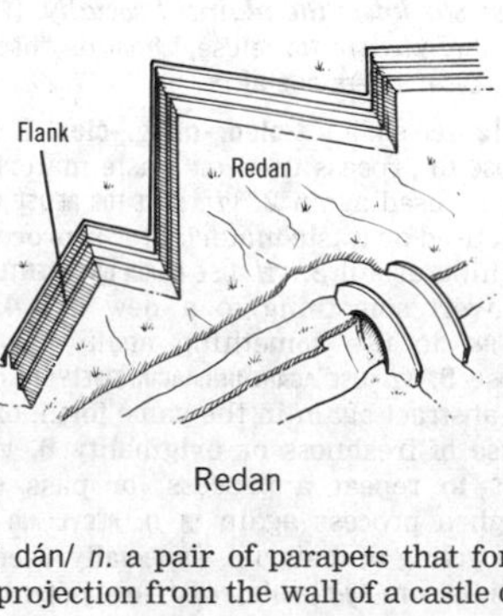

Redan

re·dan /ri dán/ *n.* a pair of parapets that form a V-shaped projection from the wall of a castle or other fortification [Late 17thC. From French, a variant of *redent*, from *dent* "tooth," from Latin *dens* (see DENTAL).]

Red Ar·my *n.* the military organization put into place by Leon Trotsky at the time of the Russian revolution. Its members were recruited from the worker and peasant classes.

red·back /réd bàk/, **red·back spi·der** *n.* a small venomous dark brown or black spider native to Australia and New Zealand. The female has a red stripe or patch on the back of the abdomen. Latin name: *Latrodectus hasselti.*

red-backed shrike *n.* a small bird, native to Europe, Asia, and Africa, the male of which has a chestnut-colored back and tail and a black-and-white face. Latin name: *Lanius collurio.*

red·bait /réd bàyt/ (**-bait·ed, -bait·ing, -baits**) *vti.* to attack or persecute somebody as a communist sympathizer (*dated*) —**red·bait·ing** *n.*

red bay *n.* a small tree that has red-stalked fruit and red heartwood and is widely grown as an ornamental plant. It is native to the southern United States. Latin name: *Persea borbonia.*

red-bel·lied black snake *n.* a large poisonous snake that is glossy black with an orangish-red underside. It is found in eastern Australian woodlands and can grow to almost 8 ft./2.5 m in length. Latin name: *Pseudechis porphyriacus.*

red·bel·ly dace /rèd bellee-/ *n.* either of two small brightly colored North American freshwater fish belonging to the minnow family. Genus: *Phoxinus.*

red·bird /réd bùrd/ *n.* any of various birds with red plumage, e.g., the card

red blood cell *n.* any of the red-colored cells in blood that contain hemoglobin and carry oxygen to the tissues

red-blood·ed *adj.* behaving in ways stereotypically associated with men, e.g., by showing strength or active sexual desire

red·bone /réd bōn/ *n.* a medium-sized hunting dog with a reddish coat, originally bred in the United States to hunt raccoons

red·breast /réd brèst/ (*plural* **-breasts** *or* **-breast**) *n.* **1. BIRD WITH RED CHEST** a bird with a reddish breast, especially the robin **2. FISH WITH RED BELLY** a freshwater sunfish with a reddish belly, found in the eastern United States. Latin name: *Lepomis auritus.*

red·brick /réd brìk/ *adj.* **1.** U.K. UNIV **OF 19THC BRITISH UNIVERSITY** relating to British universities that were founded in the late 19th and early 20th centuries, e.g., Manchester and Leeds. The term was originally intended to emphasize their modernity in contrast to the older British universities such as Oxford and St. Andrews, and now also distinguishes them from newer universities. **2. BUILT OF RED BRICKS** constructed of red bricks

Red Bri·gades *npl.* a left-wing urban organization that was active in Italy during the 1970s and was responsible for the kidnapping and murder of the Italian statesman Aldo Moro in 1978 [Translation of Italian *brigate rosse*]

red·bud /réd bùd/ (*plural* **-buds** *or* **-bud**) *n.* a North American tree that has heart-shaped leaves and small pale pink flowers. Genus: *Cercis.*

red·bug /réd bùg/ *n.* a stout red-and-black insect found throughout the tropics and subtropics. Some redbugs, such as the cotton stainer are pests. Family: Pyrrhocoridae.

WORD KEY: REGIONAL NOTE

The term outlines the entire South Midland and Southern speech areas, with *chigger* making substantial inroads into the south and **redbug** showing new strength in the Rocky Mountain states.

red·cap /réd kàp/ *n.* a porter at an airport or railroad station (*informal*) [From the red caps traditionally worn by such personnel]

red card *n.* in soccer, a red card displayed by the referee when ejecting a player from a game for a serious infringement of the rules. ◊ **yellow card**

red car·pet *n.* **1. VIP'S CARPET** a strip of red-colored carpet laid on the ground for an important visitor to walk on when arriving or departing **2. VIP TREATMENT** attentive or deferential treatment given to a dignitary, celebrity, or other important person (*hyphenated when used before a noun*)

red cell *n.* = **red blood cell**

red cent *n.* the smallest amount of money (*informal*) [From the fact that the one-cent coin is made of copper]

Red Cloud

Red Cloud /rèd klówd/ (1822–1909) U.S. Oglala Sioux leader. He resisted the U.S. government's occupation of Native North American territory in present-day Wyoming and Montana, but his defeat in the Sioux War (1875–76) resulted in the relocation of his people to South Dakota.

red clo·ver *n.* a variety of clover with fragrant red flowers, often grown as a forage crop for horses or cattle. It is native to Europe, Asia, and North America. Latin name: *Trifolium pratense.*

red·coat /réd kōt/ *n.* HISTORY a British soldier serving overseas in former times, especially during the American Revolution [From their bright red uniform coats]

red cor·al *n.* any coral whose hard pinkish-red skeletons are used to make ornaments and jewelry. Genus: *Corallium.*

red cor·pus·cle *n.* = **red blood cell**

Red Cres·cent *n.* the name under which any branch of the Red Cross functions in Islamic countries

Red Cross *n.* an international organization founded in 1864 and dedicated to the medical care of the sick or wounded in wars and natural disasters

red cur·rant *n.* **1.** FOOD **SHARP-TASTING RED BERRY** a small round red fruit with a tart flavor that grows in northern regions. It is often used to make jellies. **2.** PLANTS **FLOWERING SHRUB** a flowering shrub that grows in northern temperate regions and bears red currants. Latin name: *Ribes rubrum.*

redd[1] /red/ *vti.* (**redd** *or* **redd·ed, redd·ing, redds**) **TIDY SOMETHING** to straighten something up, or tidy things generally (*regional*) ■ *n.* **TIDYING SESSION** a spell of straightening something up (*regional*) [Early 16thC. From Old Norse *ryðja* (see RID), with the sense influenced by an obsolete verb meaning "to rescue," from Old English *hreddan*.] —**red·der** *n.*

redd[2] /red/ *n.* a hollow that is scooped out in the sand or gravel of a river bed for spawning by fish such as trout and salmon [Early 19thC. Origin unknown.]

red deer *n.* a large deer that has spreading antlers and a reddish-brown summer coat. It is native to Europe and Asia and has been introduced into Australia, New Zealand, and South America. Latin name: *Cervus elaphus.*

red·den /rédd'n/ (**-dened, -den·ing, -dens**) *v.* **1.** *vti.* **MAKE OR BECOME RED** to become red or redder, or make something red or redder **2.** *vi.* **BECOME FLUSHED** to go red in the face, e.g., with embarrassment, anger, or exertion

Red·ding /rédding/, **Otis** (1941–67) U.S. singer and

Otis Redding

songwriter. He won popular and critical acclaim for his Southern soul rhythm-and-blues style, an emotional blend of gospel, country, and traditional blues.

red·dish /réddish/ *adj.* of a color that is a shade of red or strongly tinged with red —**red·dish·ness** *n.*

red·dle *n., vt.* = **ruddle**

red-dog (**red-dogged, red-dog·ging, red-dogs**) *vt.* in football, to charge directly at the quarterback the moment the ball is put into play (*informal*)

rede /reed/ *n.* **1.** *dial* ADVICE advice **2.** EXPLANATION a story, account, or explanation (*archaic*) ■ *vt.* (**red·ed, red·ing, redes**) *dial* **1.** ADVISE SOMEBODY to advise or counsel somebody **2.** INTERPRET SOMETHING to explain, understand, or interpret something in a particular way [The noun is from Old English *rǣd*; the verb from Old English *rǣdan* (see READ)]

red·ear /réd èer/ (*plural* **-ears** *or* **-ear**), **red·ear sun·fish** *n.* a freshwater sunfish that has a scarlet margin around the gill cover. It is found in the southern and eastern United States. Latin name: *Lepomis microlophus.*

red earth *n.* a clayey soil found in tropical grasslands, colored red by the presence of iron compounds

re·dec·o·rate /ree dékə ràyt/ (**-rat·ed, -rat·ing, -rates**) *vti.* to change or renew the interior decoration of a building or room

re·deem /ri déem/ (**-deemed, -deem·ing, -deems**) *vt.* **1.** MAKE SOMETHING ACCEPTABLE to make something acceptable or pleasant in spite of its negative qualities or aspects **2.** RESTORE REPUTATION to restore yourself to favor or to somebody's good opinion **3.** BUY SOMETHING BACK to buy back an item given, e.g., to a pawnbroker, as security for a loan **4.** KEEP A PROMISE to fulfill a pledge or promise **5.** EXCHANGE SOMETHING FOR MONEY to exchange or convert something such as a voucher for money or its equivalent **6.** FIN PAY SOMETHING OFF to pay off the outstanding portion of a debt **7.** CHR ATONE FOR HUMAN SIN to pay for the sins of humanity with death on the Cross [15thC. Directly or via French *rédimer* from Latin *redimere*, literally "to buy back," from *emere* (see EXAMPLE).]

re·deem·a·ble /ri déeməb'l/ *adj.* able to be exchanged for money —**re·deem·a·bil·i·ty** /ri dèemə bíllətee/ *n.* —**re·deem·a·bly** /ri déeməblee/ *adv.*

re·deem·er /ri déemər/ *n.* somebody who redeems somebody or something, especially somebody who saves somebody else from unpleasantness or danger

Re·deem·er *n.* CHR Jesus Christ regarded as the savior of humanity through his death on the Cross

re·deem·ing /ri déeming/ *adj.* compensating for faults or flaws

re·de·fine /rèedi fín/ (**-fined, -fin·ing, -fines**) *vt.* to change the nature, appearance, or position of something consciously and sometimes arbitrarily

re·demp·tion /ri démpshən/ *n.* **1.** IMPROVING OF SOMETHING the saving or improving of something that has declined into a poor state **2.** REDEEMED STATE the improved state of somebody or something saved from apparently irreversible decline **3.** BUYING BACK OF SOMETHING the buying back of something given, e.g., to a pawnbroker, as security for a loan **4.** FIN ENDING OF FINANCIAL OBLIGATION the removal of a financial obligation, e.g., the repayment of a loan or promissory note **5.** CHR ATONEMENT FOR HUMAN SIN deliverance from the sins of humanity by the death of Jesus Christ on the Cross [14thC. Via French *rédemption* from, ultimately, Latin *redempt-*, the past participle stem of *redimere* (see REDEEM).] —**re·demp·tion·al** *adj.*

re·demp·tion·er /ri démpshənər/ *n.* an emigrant from Europe in the 18th and 19th centuries who worked as a servant on arriving in North America, to pay for the cost of the voyage

re·demp·tive /ri démptiv/ *adj.* bringing about the redemption of somebody or something [15thC. Formed from Latin *redempt-*, the past participle stem of *redimere* (see REDEEM).] —**re·demp·tive·ly** *adv.*

Re·demp·tor·ist /ri démptərist/ *n.* a member of the Congregation of the Most Holy Redeemer, a Roman Catholic order specializing in preaching and missionary work, founded in Italy in 1732 [Mid-19thC. Via French *rédemptoriste* from Latin *redemptor* "redeemer," from *redempt-*, the past participle stem of *redimere* (see REDEEM).]

red en·sign *n.* a red flag with the Union Jack in the upper corner of the vertical edge near the staff. It is flown by British merchant ships and pleasure craft.

re·de·ploy /rèedi plóy/ (**-ployed, -ploy·ing, -ploys**) *vti.* to move people or equipment from one area or activity to another —**re·de·ploy·ment** *n.*

re·de·sign /rèedi zín/ *vt.* (**-signed, -sign·ing, -signs**) CHANGE DESIGN OF to change or revise the design of something ■ *n.* NEW DESIGN a new or revised design

re·de·vel·op /rèedi véllәp/ (**-oped, -op·ing, -ops**) *vt.* to improve an area that has become run down by renovating buildings, making better use of wasteland, and encouraging inward investment —**re·de·vel·op·ment** *n.*

red-eye /réd ì/ *n.* **1.** AIR NIGHT FLIGHT a late night or overnight airline service, usually, because of early morning arrival due to the crossing of time zones, a long easterly flight (*informal*) **2.** PHOTOGRAPHY PHOTOGRAPHIC DEFECT red pupils in the eyes of a subject in flash photography, a common defect in photographs taken with simple cameras (*informal*) **3.** BEVERAGES CHEAP WHISKEY cheap inferior whiskey (*slang*)

red·eye gra·vy *n.* gravy made from the juices of baked or fried ham, often flavored with coffee [From the small bubbles of ham fat that form in it while cooking]

red fes·cue *n.* a grass plant that has creeping roots and green, reddish, or bluish-green flower clusters. It is native to Europe, Asia, and North America. Latin name: *Festuca rubra.*

red·fin /réd fin/ (*plural* **-fins** *or* **-fin**), **red·fin shin·er** *n.* a small freshwater fish with reddish fins that is native to central North America and is a popular aquarium fish. Genus: *Notropis.*

red fire *n.* a chemical mixture, especially one containing strontium salts, that burns with a vivid red flame and is used in fireworks and flares

red·fish /réd fish/ (*plural* **-fish·es** *or* **-fish**) *n.* **1.** REDDISH ROCKFISH any of various reddish North Atlantic rockfish, especially a species used as food **2.** = **channel bass 3.** SALMON a male salmon that has recently spawned

red flag *n.* **1.** FLAG SYMBOLIZING COMMUNISM OR SOCIALISM a plain red flag or banner used as an international symbol of communism or socialism **2.** INCITEMENT TO ANGER an incitement to anger or violence **3.** WARNING SIGNAL a flag waved as a danger signal or a command to stop

Red·ford /rédfərd/, **Robert** (*b.* 1937) U.S. actor, producer, and director. His many movies include *Butch Cassidy and the Sundance Kid* (1969). He also founded the Sundance Film Festival. Full name **Charles Robert Redford**

red fox *n.* the common fox of Europe, Asia, and North America, found in fields and open woods. It has sharply pointed ears, a reddish-orange to reddish-brown coat, and a white-tipped tail. Latin name: *Vulpes vulpes.*

red gi·ant *n.* a red-colored star with a relatively low surface temperature and a diameter much greater than that of the sun

Red·grave /réd gràyv/, **Sir Michael** (1908–85) British actor. One of the outstanding actors of his generation, he played both classical and contemporary roles in movies and on stage. Full name **Sir Michael Scudamore Redgrave**

Red·grave, Vanessa (*b.* 1937) British actor. The daughter of Michael Redgrave, she is acclaimed for her sensitive and intelligent portrayals of strong-willed independent women.

red-green col·or·blind·ness *n.* = **deuteranopia**

Red Guard *n.* **1.** CHINESE COMMUNIST YOUTH MOVEMENT the 1960s Chinese Communist youth movement that attempted to bring about the Cultural Revolution of Mao Zedong **2.** YOUNG CHINESE COMMUNIST a member of the Red Guard

red gum *n.* **1.** EUCALYPTUS TREE an Australian eucalyptus tree with aromatic leaves and distinctive red wood. Latin name: *Eucalyptus camaldulensis.* **2.** = **sweet gum**

red-hand·ed *adj.* in the act of committing a crime or doing something wrong ○ *caught red-handed* [From the notion of having blood on your hands]

red·head /réd hèd/ *n.* **1.** SOMEBODY WITH RED HAIR somebody, especially a woman, who has reddish-colored hair **2.** BIRDS AMERICAN DIVING DUCK a North American diving duck, the male of which has a bright chestnut head. Latin name: *Aythya americana.*

red·head·ed /rèd héddəd/ *adj.* **1.** WITH RED HAIR with reddish-colored hair **2.** ZOOL WITH RED HEAD used to describe an animal, especially a bird, with a red head

red heat *n.* the temperature at which something is red-hot, or the state of being at such a temperature

red her·ring *n.* **1.** MISLEADING CLUE something introduced, e.g., into a crime or mystery story, in order to divert attention or mislead **2.** FOOD SMOKED HERRING a herring salted and smoked to a reddish-brown color [From the practice of dragging smoked fish across a scent trail to teach hounds not to be distracted]

red·horse /réd hàwrss/ (*plural* **-hors·es** *or* **-horse**) *n.* ZOOL a large red-finned North American freshwater fish of the sucker family. Genus: *Moxostoma.*

red-hot, **red hot** *adj.* **1.** GLOWING RED WITH HEAT heated to such a high temperature as to glow red **2.** VERY HOT extremely hot **3.** EXTREMELY POPULAR in great demand (*informal*) **4.** VERY RECENT very recent and up to date (*informal*) **5.** PASSIONATE feeling or expressing intense enthusiasm, passion, or anger (*informal*) ■ *n.* FOOD **1.** HOT DOG a hot dog, especially one spiced with pepper **2. red hot** SPICY CANDY a small hot-tasting cinnamon-flavored candy

red-hot pok·er *n.* a tall perennial plant with spikes of drooping red or orange flowers. It is native to South Africa and cultivated elsewhere as a garden plant. Genus: *Kniphofia.*

re·di·a /réedee ə/ (*plural* **-ae** /-èe/) *n.* one of the forms that the larvae of trematode worms can take. Rediae are found as parasites in the gut of snails. [Late 19thC. From modern Latin, formed from the name of the Italian biologist Francesco *Redi* (1626–98).]

re·di·al /ree dí əl/ *vti.* (**-aled, -al·ing, -als**) DIAL TELEPHONE NUMBER AGAIN to dial a particular telephone number again, e.g., because the line was busy when the number was dialed earlier ■ *n.* DIALING OF NUMBER AGAIN the function that permits automatic redialing of a telephone number

re·did past tense of **redo**

Red In·di·an *n.* a highly offensive term formerly used to refer to a Native North American (*dated offensive*)

Redingote

red·in·gote /rédding gòt/ *n.* **1.** WOMAN'S DRESS OR COAT a belted woman's dress or coat of the 18th century that was open at the front to show a petticoat or dress **2.** MAN'S OVERCOAT a man's double-breasted coat of the 18th century that had wide flat cuffs and flared out below the waist [Late 18thC. From French, an alteration of English *riding-coat.*]

red ink *n.* financial loss or deficit [From accountants' traditional use of red ink to record deficits and losses]

re·di·rect /rèedi rékt, -dī-/ *vt.* (**-rect·ed, -rect·ing, -rects**) **1.** SEND SOMETHING ELSEWHERE to send something received to a different location, e.g., because the intended recipient has moved **2.** REROUTE TRAFFIC to send traffic along a different route **3.** CHANGE FOCUS to focus actions or activities on a different objective ■ *adj.* LAW CALLING WITNESS AGAIN questioning a witness again after cross-examination is completed —**re·di·rec·tion** /rèedi rékshən, -dī-/ *n.*

re·dis·cov·er /rèedi skúvvər/ (**-ered, -er·ing, -ers**) *vt.* to experience something again, especially finding a new source of pleasure in it —**re·dis·cov·er·y** *n.*

re·dis·trib·ute /rèedi strí byoot/ (**-ut·ed, -ut·ing, -utes**) *vt.* **1.** DISTRIBUTE SOMETHING AGAIN to distribute more of something previously distributed **2.** APPORTION SOMETHING DIFFERENTLY to divide something up or share something out in a different way, e.g., in more equal proportions or among a wider range of people —

re·dis·tri·bu·tion /reedistrə byo͞osh'n/ *n.* — **re·dis·trib·u·tive** /reedi stríbbyətiv/ *adj.*

red·i·vi·vus /rèddə vívəss, -veé-/ *adj.* revived, reborn, or brought back to life (*literary*) [Late 16thC. From Latin, literally "alive again," from *vivus* (see VIVID).]

red lead *n.* a bright red poisonous oxide of lead, used as a pigment in paints. Formula: Pb_3O_4.

red leaf *n.* a plant disease that causes abnormal reddening of the leaves

red·leg /réd lèg/ *n.* **1.** BIRDS **RED-LEGGED BIRD** a bird with red legs, e.g., the redshank **2.** MIL **ARTILLERYMAN** an artilleryman (*slang*) **3.** VET **FROG DISEASE** a bacterial disease of frogs that produces a red flush on the hind legs **4.** *Carib* **OFFENSIVE TERM** an offensive term for a poor Caucasian (*slang offensive*)

red-leg·ged grass·hop·per, **red-leg·ged lo·cust** *n.* a small migratory grasshopper that has reddish skin on the underside of the hind legs. It is native to the central United States, where it is an agricultural pest. Latin name: *Melanoplus femur-rubrum.*

red-let·ter day *n.* a very special day or occasion [From the marking of feast days in red on church calendars]

red light *n.* **1.** TRANSP **WARNING SIGNAL** a red warning signal, especially an instruction to drivers to stop **2. REJECTION** a sign of disapproval or rejection, e.g., an instruction not to proceed with something (*informal*)

red-light *adj.* relating to the part of a town or city where brothels and other commercial sex-based activities are concentrated [From the red lights traditionally displayed in the doors and windows of brothels]

red·line /réd lìn/ (**-lined, -lin·ing, -lines**) *v.* **1.** *vti.* POL, ECON **REFUSE FINANCIAL SERVICES IN AREA** to refuse loans, insurance, or other financial services to individuals or businesses in a supposedly high-risk area **2.** *vt.* INDUST **SELECT FOR REMOVAL** to select something such as an aircraft for removal from service **3.** *vt.* HR **EARMARK FOR DISMISSAL** to select somebody for dismissal as part of employee cutbacks [From the traditional use of red ink to cross out deleted items in a budget]

red man (*plural* **red men**) *n.* a highly offensive term formerly used to refer to a Native American (*dated offensive*)

red ma·ple *n.* a maple tree native to eastern North America, with red flowers, and leaves that turn bright red in fall. Latin name: *Acer rubrum.*

red mar·row *n.* the reddish bone marrow where red blood cells and some white blood cells are formed

red mass *n.* a special Roman Catholic mass celebrated in red vestments for the opening of a court or congress

red meat *n.* meat such as beef or lamb that is relatively dark red in color when raw

red mite *n.* any one of various reddish mites, e.g., the spider mite

red mul·ber·ry *n.* **1. N AMERICAN MULBERRY TREE** a North American mulberry tree that produces purple fruit **2. WOOD FROM RED MULBERRY** the soft but durable wood of the red mulberry tree

red mul·let *n.* *U.K.* = **goatfish**

red·neck /réd nèk/ *n.* (*informal insult*) **1. OFFENSIVE TERM** an offensive term for a Caucasian farm worker in the southern United States, especially one regarded as uneducated or aggressively prejudiced **2. OFFENSIVE TERM** an offensive term for somebody who is opposed to liberal social changes, especially somebody regarded as prejudiced [From the sunburned necks of those who work outdoors in sunny climates] —**red·necked** *adj.*

re·do /ree do͞o/ (**-did** /-díd/, **-done** /-dún/, **-do·ing, -does**) *vt.* **1. REPEAT SOMETHING** to do something again, e.g., in order to correct mistakes in an earlier effort **2. DO SOMETHING DIFFERENTLY** to change the appearance of something such as a hairstyle or the interior decoration of a room

red oak *n.* a North American oak tree that has bristly lobed leaves and acorns with small cups. Genus: *Quercus.*

red o·cher *n.* **1. REDDISH PAINT** a rich reddish-brown color used in painting **2. REDDISH EARTH** a reddish earth that is rich in iron oxide and used as a red pigment in paints

red·o·lent /rédd'lənt/ *adj.* **1. AROMATIC** with a strong pleasant aroma (*literary*) **2. SMELLING** with a particular scent or odor ○ *old oak furniture redolent of beeswax* **3. SUGGESTING** suggestive or reminiscent of something ○ *a report redolent of bias* [15thC. Via Old French from, ultimately, Latin *redolere* "to smell strongly," from *olere* (see OLFACTORY).] —**red·o·lence** *n.* —**red·o·lent·ly** *adv.*

re·done past participle of **redo**

red o·sier *n.* **1. REDDISH WILLOW** a willow tree whose reddish branches are used in basketry **2. red osier, red osier dogwood DOGWOOD PLANT** a North American dogwood plant with red branches and white fruits. Genus: *Cornus.*

re·dou·ble /ree dúbb'l/ *vti.* (**-bled, -bling, -bles**) **1. INCREASE** to increase something considerably, especially the amount of effort expended on something, or to become much greater **2.** CARDS **DOUBLE A DOUBLED BID** to double an opponent's double as a bid in bridge **3. ECHO** to echo or reecho, or cause something to echo or reecho ■ *n.* CARDS **DOUBLING OF A DOUBLE BID** a redoubling of a bid in bridge [15thC. From French *redoubler*, literally "to double again," from *double* (see DOUBLE).]

re·doubt /ri dówt/ *n.* **1. STRONGHOLD** a castle, fortress, or other stronghold (*literary*) **2.** MIL **TEMPORARY FORTIFICATION** a temporary fortification built to defend a position such as a hilltop [Early 17thC. Alteration (influenced by *redoubtable*) of French *redoute*, via Italian *ridotto* from medieval Latin *reductus* "refuge," from Latin, the past participle of *reducere* "to withdraw" (see REDUCE).]

re·doubt·a·ble /ri dówtəb'l/ *adj.* with personal qualities worthy of respect or fear [14thC. Via French *redoutable* from, ultimately, *douter* "to fear, doubt" (see DOUBT).] —**re·doubt·a·bly** *adv.*

re·dound /ri dównd/ (**-dound·ed, -dound·ing, -dounds**) *vi.* **1. HAVE A PARTICULAR RESULT** to have a particular consequence, usually something good or positive ○ *All the effort can only redound to her credit.* **2. HAVE A CONSEQUENCE FOR SOMEBODY** to return to affect somebody as a repercussion or consequence (*formal*) ○ *His attempts at revenge redounded upon his own head.* [14thC. Via French *redonder* from Latin *redundare* (see REDUNDANT).]

WORD KEY: USAGE

See Usage note at ***rebound.***

red·out /réd òwt/ *n.* sudden headache and reddening of the field of vision experienced by pilots or astronauts during rapid deceleration and other maneuvers. It is caused by blood being forced into the vessels of the head.

re·dox /reé dòks/ *n.* = **oxidation-reduction** [Early 20thC. Coined from REDUCTION + OXIDATION.]

red pan·da *n.* a reddish-brown mammal that resembles a raccoon in appearance and lives in forests in the Himalayas and nearby areas of eastern Asia. Latin name: *Ailurus fulgens.*

red-pen·cil (**red-pen·ciled, red-pen·cil·ing, red-pen·cils**) *vt.* to revise, correct, or censor written material. ◊ **blue-pencil**

red pep·per *n.* **1. EDIBLE RED POD** any red pod that belongs to the capsicum family of vegetables, especially a ripe sweet pepper. ◊ **bell pepper, green pepper** **2.** = **cayenne pepper**

red pine *n.* **1. REDDISH PINE TREE** a pine tree that has reddish bark and needles in clusters of two. It is native to northeastern North America. Latin name: *Pinus resinosa.* **2. NEW ZEALAND TREE** a coniferous tree of New Zealand with narrow pointed leaves. Latin name: *Dacrydium cupressinum.*

red plan·et *n.* the planet Mars (*informal*)

red·poll /réd pōl/ *n.* a small bird of the finch family with a red crown and a pink breast that breeds in the far northern regions of North America, Europe, and Asia. Genus: *Carduelis.*

Red Poll, **Red Polled** *n.* a hornless cow with short reddish hair belonging to a breed originating in England and bred for beef and milk

red puc·coon *n.* = **bloodroot** *n.*

re·draft /ree dráft/ *n.* **SECOND DRAFT** a second or further draft or rewriting ■ *vt.* (**-draft·ed, -draft·ing, -drafts**) **DRAFT SOMETHING AGAIN** to rewrite something

red rag *n.* *U.K.* = **red flag** *n.* 2 [From the notion that bulls are enraged at the sight of red objects]

re·draw /ree dráw/ *vt.* (**-drew** /-dro͞o/, **-drawn** /-dráwn/, **-draw·ing, -draws**) **1. REPOSITION BOUNDARY** to change the position of the boundaries of a region **2. DRAW SOMETHING AGAIN** to draw something again **3. REDESIGN SOMETHING** to redesign something, changing its shape or the positions of its constituent parts

re·dress /ri dréss/ *n.* **1. COMPENSATION** compensation or reparation for a loss or wrong a party has experienced **2. ACT OF COMPENSATING** the compensating of a party for a loss or wrong experienced ■ *vt.* (**-dressed, -dress·ing, -dress·es**) **1. MAKE UP FOR SOMETHING** to provide compensation or reparation for a loss or wrong experienced **2. IMPOSE FAIRNESS OR EQUALITY ON** to adjust a situation in order to make things fair or equal [14thC. From Old French *redrecier*, from *drecier* "to arrange" (see DRESS).] —**re·dress·er** *n.*

re·drew past tense of **redraw**

red rib·bon *n.* a red-colored ribbon, badge, or other decoration awarded to somebody who comes second in a competition

Red Riv·er /red/ **1.** river of the southern United States, flowing through Oklahoma, Arkansas, and Louisiana, and into the Mississippi. Length: 1,018 mi./1,638 km. **2.** river in North America, rising in Minnesota, United States, and emptying into Lake Winnepeg, Canada. Length: 545 mi./877 km. **3.** river in southeastern Asia. It rises in southern China and flows through northern Vietnam before emptying into the Gulf of Tonkin. Length: 500 mi./800 km.

red·root /réd ro͝ot/ *n.* **1. N AMERICAN BOG PLANT** a perennial bog plant with red roots and woolly yellow flowers, belonging to the bloodwort family. It grows in eastern North America. Latin name: *Lachnanthes caroliana.* **2. PLANT WITH RED ROOTS** a plant with red roots, e.g., the bloodroot or pigweed **3.** = **ceanothus**

red salm·on *n.* = **sockeye**

Red Sea inland sea between the Arabian peninsula and northeastern Africa. It is linked to the Mediterranean in the north by the Suez Canal. Area: 169,000 sq. mi./437,700 sq. km.

red set·ter *n.* = **Irish setter**

red·shank /réd shàngk/ *n.* a large wading bird of slender build with long red legs and red feet. Redshanks are native to Europe and Asia and belong to the sandpiper family. Genus: *Tringa.*

red shank *n.* *U.K.* = **lady's thumb**

red shift *n.* a shift in the spectrum of a celestial body toward longer wavelengths, or toward the red end of the spectrum, caused by its motion away from the Earth —**red·shift·ed** *adj.*

red·shirt /réd shùrt/ *n.* a college or university athlete who is kept out of competitions for one year in order to extend his or her period of eligibility [From the red jerseys that customarily distinguish these players at practices] —**red·shirt** *vt.*

red-should·ered hawk *n.* a large North American hawk with reddish shoulders and a banded tail. Latin name: *Buteo lineatus.*

Red Sin·dhi *n.* a small reddish-brown dairy cow of a breed developed in India. It is often used for crossbreeding with European stock in tropical countries.

red sis·kin *n.* a bright red finch whose head, wings, and tail are black. It is native to northern parts of South America. Latin name: *Carduelis cucullata.*

red·skin /réd skìn/ *n.* a highly offensive term formerly used to refer to a Native American (*dated offensive*)

red snap·per *n.* a large reddish-colored food fish found in the warm Atlantic coastal waters off North, South, and Central America. Genus: *Lutjanus.*

red snow *n.* fallen snow that is reddish in color, either from the presence of airborne dust or from red algae growing in it. It is commonly seen in Arctic and Alpine regions.

red spi·der, **red spi·der mite** *n.* = **spider mite**

Red Spot *n.* a large reddish oval and variable marking in the southern hemisphere of Jupiter. It does not rotate at the same rate as the planet and is thought to be an atmospheric phenomenon.

red spruce *n.* a spruce tree that has reddish-brown bark and cones and a light soft wood. It is native to eastern North America. Latin name: *Picea rubens.*

Red Square *n.* a large square in central Moscow, Russia, bordered by the Kremlin and Lenin's tomb. It was the site of military parades on public holidays in the former Soviet Union.

red squill *n.* a squill plant whose red bulbs are used as a source of rat poison. It belongs to the lily family. Latin name: *Urginea maritima.*

red squir·rel *n.* **1.** N AMERICAN SQUIRREL a squirrel with reddish fur found in coniferous forests of North America. It is smaller than the gray squirrel. Latin name: *Tamiasciurus hudsonicus.* **2.** EUROPEAN SQUIRREL a reddish-brown squirrel with tufted ears that is native to Europe and Asia. Latin name: *Sciurus vulgaris.*

red·start /réd staart/ *n.* **1.** THRUSH WITH REDDISH TAIL a bird of the thrush family that is native to Europe, Asia, and Africa. The male has a black throat and a reddish-brown tail. Genus: *Phoenicurus.* **2.** AMERICAN WARBLER a flycatching warbler native to North and South America. The male has reddish-orange patches on black and white plumage. Latin name: *Setophaga ruticilla.* [*Start* is an obsolete word for "tail" (from Old English *steort*)]

red steen·bras *n.* = **dentex**

red tape *n.* official procedure regarded as unnecessary, overcomplicated, or obstructive (*informal*) [From the red tape once widely used to seal official documents]

red tide *n.* a brownish-red discoloration in seawater, caused by the increased presence of plant-based plankton. It sometimes leads to the poisoning of fish and, consequently, of those who eat fish.

red·top /réd tòp/ *n.* a grass plant that has clusters of red flowers and is used for lawns and forage. Genus: *Agrostis.*

re·duce /ri dóoss/ (**-duced, -duc·ing, -duc·es**) *v.* **1.** *vti.* DECREASE to become or make something smaller in size, number, extent, degree, or intensity **2.** *vt.* PUT INTO A BAD STATE to bring somebody or something into a particular undesirable state ○ *The dreadful news reduced them all to tears.* ○ *Bombing had reduced the town to rubble.* **3.** *vt.* MAKE SOMETHING CHEAPER to lower the price or cost of an item for sale **4.** *vt.* SIMPLIFY SOMETHING to make something simpler, especially by extracting or summarizing essential elements **5.** *vt.* ANALYZE SOMETHING SYSTEMATICALLY to analyze something in terms of a system or rule, usually as an aid to explaining or understanding it **6.** *vt.* DEMOTE SOMEBODY to place somebody officially in a lower rank or grade, e.g., as a punishment for breaking rules **7.** *vti.* COOK THICKEN to make a sauce or stock thicker by boiling off some of the liquid, or to become thicker in this way **8.** *vt.* MATH SIMPLIFY AN EQUATION to simplify an expression or equation without changing its value **9.** *vti.* CHEM UNDERGO CHEMICAL REACTION to undergo, or cause a substance to undergo, a chemical reaction in which there is a gain in hydrogen or a loss of oxygen. ◊ **oxidize** *v.* 1 **10.** *vti.* CHEM GAIN ELECTRONS to undergo, or cause a substance to undergo, a chemical reaction in which there is an increase in the number of electrons. ◊ **oxidize** *v.* 2 **11.** *vt.* PHOTOGRAPHY DECREASE THE DENSITY OF to lessen the density of a photographic negative using a chemical substance **12.** *vt.* TAKE CONTROL OF to bring a place or people under a particular authority using force **13.** *vt.* METALL REFINE ORE to remove the impurities from an ore in order to obtain the pure metal **14.** *vti.* BIOL UNDERGO CELL DIVISION to undergo, or cause cells to undergo, a type of cell division (**meiosis**) [14thC. From Latin *reducere*, literally "to bring back," from *ducere* (see DUCT).] —**re·duc·i·bil·i·ty** /ri dóossə bíllətee/ *n.* —**re·duc·i·ble** /ri dóossəb'l/ *adj.*

re·duc·er /ri dóossər/ *n.* **1.** PHOTOGRAPHY PHOTOGRAPHIC CHEMICAL a chemical solution that lessens the density of a photographic negative by oxidizing it **2.** CONSTR PIPE FITTING a pipe fitting that connects two pipes of different diameters

re·duc·ing a·gent, **re·duc·tant** *n.* a chemical substance that reduces the amount of oxygen in another substance and becomes oxidized in the process

re·duc·tase /ri dúk tàyss, -tàyz/ *n.* an enzyme that catalyzes the reduction of an organic compound [Early 20thC. Formed from REDUCTION.]

re·duc·ti·o ad ab·sur·dum /ri dùkshee ō ad əb súrdəm, ri dùktee ō-/ (*plural* **re·duc·ti·o·nes ad ab·sur·dum**) *n.* **1.** TAKING SOMETHING TO ABSURD LENGTHS the application of a rule or principle so strictly or literally that the result is ridiculous **2.** PHILOSOPHY LOGICAL DISPROOF the disproving of a logical argument by showing that its ultimate conclusion is absurd **3.** PHILOSOPHY LOGICAL PROOF the proving of a logical argument indirectly, by showing that the contradictory argument is absurd [Mid-18thC. From Latin, "reduction to the absurd."]

re·duc·tion /ri dúkshən/ *n.* **1.** REDUCING OF SOMETHING the decreasing of something in size, number, extent, degree, or intensity **2.** AMOUNT BY WHICH SOMETHING IS REDUCED the amount by which something is made smaller or less **3.** SIMPLIFICATION a simplification or condensation of something **4.** SMALLER COPY a copy of something made on a smaller scale, e.g., a reduced photocopy **5.** MATH MAKING FRACTION SIMPLER the canceling of common factors in the numerator and denominator of a fraction **6.** COOK THICKENED SAUCE a sauce or stock that has been thickened by boiling off some of the liquid **7.** MATH DECIMALIZATION OF FRACTION the converting of a fraction into decimal form **8.** BIOL = **meiosis** *n.* 1 **9.** CHEM CHEMICAL REACTION a chemical reaction that brings about a gain in hydrogen, a loss of oxygen, or an increase in electrons [15thC. Via French from, ultimately, Latin *reducere* (see REDUCE).] —**re·duc·tion·al** *adj.*

re·duc·tion di·vi·sion *n.* BIOL = **meiosis** *n.* 1

re·duc·tion fir·ing *n.* the firing of pottery in an oxygen-starved atmosphere in order to change the nature of the glaze applied. It is achieved either by restricting the air intake or by introducing a substance that combines with oxygen.

re·duc·tion gear *n.* a set of gears in an engine used to reduce output speed relative to that of the engine while providing greater turning power when, e.g., climbing a hill

re·duc·tion·ism /ri dúkshə nizzəm/ *n.* **1.** SIMPLIFICATION the analysis of something into simpler elements or organized systems, especially with a view to explaining or understanding it **2.** OVERSIMPLIFICATION the oversimplifying of something complex, or the misguided belief that everything can be explained in simple terms —**re·duc·tion·ist** *n., adj.* —**re·duc·tion·is·tic** /ri dùkshə nístik/ *adj.*

re·duc·tive /ri dúktiv/ *adj.* **1.** ANALYZING IN SIMPLE TERMS seeking to explain complex things in terms of simple structures and systems **2.** OVERSIMPLIFYING oversimplifying complex things and ignoring their subtleties or important details [Mid-16thC. Via medieval Latin *reductivus* from, ultimately, Latin *reducere* (see REDUCE).] —**re·duc·tive·ly** *adv.* —**re·duc·tive·ness** *n.*

re·dun·dan·cy /ri dúndənsee/ (*plural* **-cies**) *n.* **1.** SUPERFLUOUSNESS the state or fact of not being or no longer being needed or wanted **2.** ELEC ENG DUPLICATION OF COMPONENTS the installation of duplicate electronic or mechanical components or backup systems that are designed to come into use to keep equipment working if their counterparts fail **3.** TELECOM DUPLICATION OF MESSAGE duplication of information in telecommunications in order to reduce the risk of error **4.** USE OF SUPERFLUOUS WORDS the use of a word whose meaning is already conveyed elsewhere in a passage, without a rhetorical purpose **5.** *U.K.* DISMISSAL FROM WORK dismissal from employment because the job or the worker has been deemed no longer necessary ○ *There may be more redundancies if sales do not improve.*

re·dun·dant /ri dúndənt/ *adj.* **1.** SUPERFLUOUS not needed or no longer needed **2.** ELEC ENG BACKUP fitted as a backup component or system **3.** LING REPEATING MEANING with the same meaning as a word used elsewhere in a passage and without a rhetorical purpose **4.** *U.K.* DISMISSED FROM WORK dismissed from employment because the job or the worker has been deemed no longer necessary [Late 16thC. From Latin *redundare* "to overflow," from *undare* "to rise in waves," from *unda* "wave" (see UNDULATE).] —**re·dun·dant·ly** *adv.*

redupl. *abbr.* reduplicate

re·du·pli·cate /ri dóopli kàyt/ *v.* (**-cat·ed, -cat·ing, -cates**) **1.** *vti.* REPEAT OR DOUBLE to repeat or double something, or be repeated or doubled **2.** *vt.* LING REPEAT SPEECH SOUND to repeat a vowel, syllable, or word in order to create a new word or linguistic element. For example, the first elements are reduplicated in the words "wishy-washy" and "goody-goody." ■ *adj.* **1.** LING REPEATED repeated in order to create a new word or other linguistic element **2.** BOT CURVING INWARD used to describe leaves or petals that have their edges curved inward [Late 16thC. From late Latin *reduplicare*, from Latin *duplicare* (see DUPLICATE).] —**re·du·pli·ca·tion** /ri dòopli káysh'n/ *n.* —**re·du·pli·ca·tive** /ri dóopli kàytiv/ *adj.* —**re·du·pli·ca·tive·ly** /-lee/ *adv.*

re·du·vi·id /ri dóovee id/ *n.* = **assassin bug** [Late 19thC. From modern Latin *Reduviidae*, family name, from Latin *reduvia* "hangnail."]

re·dux /ree dúks/ *adj.* brought back, especially in being restored to former importance or prominence (*literary*) [Late 19thC. From Latin, formed from *reducere* "to bring back" (see REDUCE).]

red va·le·ri·an *n.* a bushy plant with fragrant red or white flowers, native to Europe and Asia. Latin name: *Centranthus ruber.*

red·ware[1] /réd wàir/ *n.* MARINE BIOL = **kelp** *n.* 1 [*Red* because of its brown color; *ware* a northern English dialect word meaning "seaweed" (from Old English *wār*)]

red·ware[2] /réd wàir/ *n.* CRAFT reddish earthenware pottery made from clay with a high iron oxide content

red wa·ter *n.* a cattle disease characterized by the passage of reddish urine

red whor·tle·ber·ry *n.* = **cowberry**

red·wing /réd wìng/ *n.* **1.** THRUSH WITH REDDISH UNDERWINGS a bird of the thrush family that has reddish feathers under its wings and a spotted breast. It is native to Europe and Asia. Latin name: *Turdus iliacus.* **2.** = **red-winged blackbird**

red-winged black·bird, **red·wing black·bird** *n.* a North American blackbird, the male of which is black with scarlet and yellow patches on its wings. Latin name: *Agelaius phoeniceus.*

red wolf *n.* a small reddish-gray wolf found in southeastern North America, nearly eliminated by overhunting and hybridization with the coyote. Attempts at reintroduction are now in place. Latin name: *Canis rufus.*

red·wood /réd wòod/ *n.* **1.** TALL TREE WITH REDDISH BARK a very tall sequoia, with fibrous reddish bark. It grows in coastal California and can reach a height of over 330 ft./100 m. Latin name: *Sequoia sempervirens.* **2.** RED-COLORED WOOD durable red-colored wood, especially that from a redwood

Red·wood Na·tion·al Park /rèd wòod-/ national park in northern California, on the Pacific coast, established in 1968. It is noted for its ancient redwoods, including the world's tallest trees. Area: 172 sq. mi./446 sq. km.

REE *abbr.* rare-earth element

ree·bok *n.* = **rhebok**

re·ech·o /ree ékō/ (**-oed, -o·ing, -oes**) *v.* **1.** *vi.* ECHO BACK to resound or echo back **2.** *vt.* REPEAT SOMETHING AGAIN to repeat again something that has already been repeated

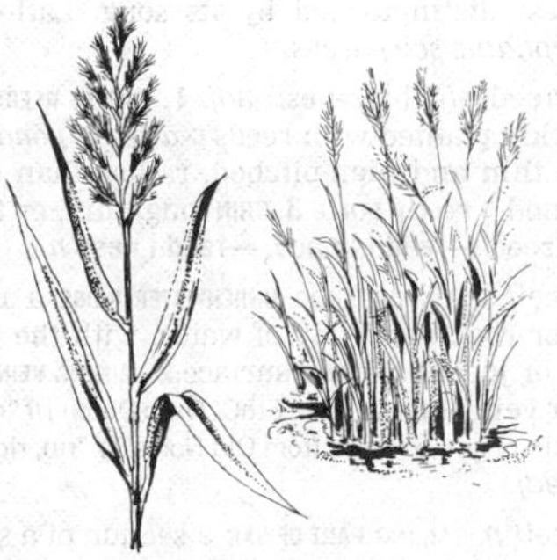

Reed

reed /reed/ *n.* **1.** BOT GRASS PLANT a tall slender grass plant with jointed stalks that grows in marshes and other wet areas. Genus: *Phragmites.* **2.** CRAFT STALK OF REED the stalk of a reed, or a number of such stalks, used for thatching, basketmaking, and other crafts **3.** MUSIC VIBRATING PART OF MUSICAL INSTRUMENT a thin piece of cane, metal, or plastic fitted inside some musical instruments that vibrates to produce sound, usually when the player blows into the instrument. Some woodwind instruments such as the clarinet have single reeds in the mouthpiece, while others such as the oboe and bassoon have double reeds. **4.** MUSIC MUSICAL INSTRUMENT a wind instrument such as an oboe or a clarinet, fitted with a reed (*informal*) **5.** TEXTILES WIRES ON A LOOM a series of parallel wires on a loom, used to separate the threads of the warp evenly **6.** MEASURE UNIT OF LENGTH an ancient Hebrew unit of length equal to six cubits [Old English *hrēod*, of prehistoric Germanic origin]

Reed /reed/, **Stanley Forman** (1884–1980) U.S. jurist. He was appointed to the Supreme Court by President Franklin D. Roosevelt, and served from 1938 to 1957.

Reed, Walter (1851–1902) U.S. army surgeon and bacteriologist. In the Army Medical Corps he researched epidemic diseases. His discovery in 1900 that yellow fever is transmitted by mosquitoes led to the near-eradication of the disease.

reed·buck /reéd bùk/ *n.* a tawny African antelope with long horns that curve slightly forward. Reedbucks live near rivers and lakes south of the Sahara. Genus: *Redunca.* [Mid-19thC. Translation of Afrikaans *rietbok.*]

reed bunt·ing *n.* a small bird with brown streaked plumage found near reed beds throughout Europe and Asia. The male has a black head with a white mustache. Latin name: *Emberiza schoeniclus.*

reed grass *n.* a tall grass plant that grows in rivers and ponds in Europe, Asia, and North America. Latin name: *Glyceria maxima.*

reed·ing /reéding/ *n.* **1.** ARCHIT **MOLDING** a set of small convex decorative moldings on a building **2.** COINS **COIN GROOVES** the narrow vertical grooves on the edge of a coin

reed·ling /reédling/ *n.* a small brownish-orange songbird with a long tail that lives in reed beds in Europe and Asia. The male has a black patch extending from the eye down the throat. Latin name: *Panurus biarmicus.*

reed mace *n.* a tall slender marsh plant whose flowers grow in brown tube-shaped spikes. Latin name: *Typha latifolia.*

reed·man /reédmən/ (*plural* **-men**) *n.* a musician who plays a reed instrument, especially a jazz clarinetist or saxophonist (*informal*)

reed or·gan *n.* a musical instrument such as the harmonium, harmonica, or accordion, in which sound is produced by air passing over a set of reeds

reed pipe *n.* an organ pipe containing a reed that vibrates to make the pipe sound

reed stop *n.* an organ stop that controls a set of reed pipes

re·ed·u·cate /ree éjjə kàyt/ (**-cat·ed, -cat·ing, -cates**), **re-ed·u·cate** *vt.* **1. TEACH SOMEBODY AGAIN** to teach somebody again, especially in order to change or update knowledge **2. RETRAIN SOMEBODY** to train or teach somebody again who has lost knowledge or a skill —**re·ed·u·ca·tive** *adj.*

reed war·bler *n.* a small brown European bird of the warbler family, commonly found in marsh reeds, and best distinguished by its song. Latin name: *Acrocephalus scirpaceus.*

reed·y /reédee/ (**-i·er, -i·est**) *adj.* **1. FULL OF REEDS** full of or thickly planted with reeds ○ *a reedy pond* **2. HIGH-PITCHED** thin and high-pitched, rather than deep or full-toned ○ *reedy voice* **3. THIN** long, thin, or flexible, like a reed —**reed·i·ly** *adv.* —**reed·i·ness** *n.*

reef[1] /reef/ *n.* **1.** OCEANOG **UNDERWATER RIDGE** a ridge of coral or rock in a body of water, with the top just below or just above the surface **2.** MINING **VEIN OF ORE** a lode or vein of ore [Late 16thC. From Dutch *rif* "ridge," of uncertain origin: perhaps from Old Norse *rif* "rib, ridge."] —**reef·y** *adj.*

reef[2] /reef/ *n.* SAILING **PART OF SAIL** a section of a sail that can be gathered in and tied down to reduce the sail's surface ■ *vt.* (**reefed, reef·ing, reefs**) SAILING **1. MAKE SAIL SMALLER BY GATHERING** to reduce the area of a sail by gathering part of it in **2. SHORTEN RIGGING PIECE** to shorten or bring in one of the pieces that support rigging on a ship [14thC. Via Dutch *reef* from Old Norse *rif* "reef (of a sail)," of uncertain origin: probably from *rif* "ridge" (see REEF[1]).] —**reef·a·ble** *adj.*

reef·er[1] /reéfər/ *n.* **1.** CLOTHES **DOUBLE-BREASTED WOOL COAT** a heavy, close-fitting double-breasted woolen jacket **2.** NAUT **SAILOR WHO REEFS SAILS** somebody who reefs the sails on a sailing ship [Early 19thC. Formed from REEF[2].]

reef·er[2] /reéfər/ *n.* (*slang*) **1.** DRUGS **MARIJUANA CIGARETTE** a marijuana cigarette **2. MARIJUANA** marijuana [Mid-20thC. Origin uncertain: perhaps from Mexican Spanish *grifo* "marijuana, drug addict," or from REEF[2], from the similarity of furling a sail and rolling such a cigarette.]

reef·er[3] /reéfər/ *n.* (*informal*) **1.** HOUSEHOLD **REFRIGERATOR** a refrigerator **2.** TRANSP **REFRIGERATED TRANSPORT VEHICLE** a refrigerated railroad car or truck trailer [Early 20thC. From REFRIGERATOR.]

reef·er jack·et *n. U.K.* = **reefer**[1] *n.* 1

reef knot *n.* = **square knot**

reek /reek/ *v.* (**reeked, reek·ing, reeks**) **1.** *vti.* **HAVE A VERY STRONG UNPLEASANT SMELL** to have a very strong and unpleasant smell, or give off such a smell ○ *The room reeked of smoke.* **2.** *vti.* **GIVE CLEAR EVIDENCE OF SOMETHING UNPLEASANT** to show very strong evidence of an unpleasant quality ○ *The whole document reeks of double standards.* **3.** *vi.* **GIVE OFF SMOKE** to give off smoke, steam, or fumes ○ *a reeking pile of old burning tires* **4.** *vt.* **TREAT SOMETHING WITH SMOKE** to process or treat something with smoke ■ *n.* **1. UNPLEASANT SMELL** a very strong and unpleasant smell ○ *a reek of disinfectant* **2. VISIBLE VAPOR** smoke, steam, or other visible vapor (*regional*) [Old English *rēocan.* Ultimately from an Indo-European word that is related to Latin *ructare* "to belch, vomit" (source of English *eructate*).] —**reek·er** *n.* —**reek·y** *adj.*

WORD KEY: SYNONYMS

See Synonyms at ***smell.***

reel[1] /reel/ *n.* **1. REVOLVING STORAGE DEVICE** a usually revolving wheel-shaped device around which something such as thread, film, or wire can be wound for storage **2. A REELFUL** the amount of a material that a reel can hold **3.** CINEMA **SECTION OF MOTION-PICTURE FILM** the amount of motion-picture film stored on one reel **4.** ANGLING **WINDER ON FISHING ROD** a winding device attached to a fishing rod that holds the fishing line and enables it to be cast and wound back ■ *vt.* (**reeled, reel·ing, reels**) **WIND SOMETHING ONTO A REEL** to wind something such as thread or fishing line onto or off of a reel [Old English *hrēol* "spool (for winding thread)," of unknown origin] —**reel·er** *n.*

reel in *vt.* **1. BRING SOMETHING CLOSER** to draw something, especially a fish, in by winding it in with a reel **2. BRING SOMEBODY OR SOMETHING IN** to bring in or acquire somebody or something by using the appropriate skills or offering suitable inducements

reel off *vt.* to list or utter in rapid succession and with no apparent effort

reel[2] /reel/ *vi.* (**reeled, reel·ing, reels**) **1. STAGGER BACKWARD** to move in a sudden and uncontrolled fashion, especially backward as if struck by a blow ○ *reeled back in horror* **2. MOVE UNSTEADILY** to move about unsteadily, staggering or swaying from side to side **3. FEEL GIDDY OR CONFUSED** to feel giddy or shocked and confused ○ *still reeling from the shock of his resignation* **4. WHIRL AROUND AND AROUND** to move or whirl around in circles ■ *n.* **STAGGERING MOTION** an unsteady or circling movement [14thC. Origin uncertain: probably from REEL[1].]

reel[3] /reel/ *n.* **1.** DANCE **SCOTTISH DANCE** a lively Scottish folk dance for sets of two, three, or four couples **2.** DANCE = **Virginia reel 3. DANCE MUSIC** a piece of music for a reel, written in quick duple meter ■ *vi.* (**reeled, reel·ing, reels**) DANCE **DANCE REEL** to dance a reel [Late 16thC. Origin uncertain: probably from REEL[2].]

re·e·lect /reè i lékt/ (**-lect·ed, -lect·ing, -lects**), **re-e·lect** *vt.* to elect somebody to the same office for another term —**re·e·lec·tion** *n.*

reel-to-reel *adj.* **HAVING TWO REELS** used to describe magnetic tape that must be wound off of a full source reel, threaded through the heads of the machine, and rewound on an empty takeup reel ■ *n.* **TAPE RECORDER WITH TWO REELS** a tape recorder or player that uses reel-to-reel tape

re·en·act /reè ə nákt/ (**-act·ed, -act·ing, -acts**), **re-en·act** *vt.* to act out an event that took place in the past, sometimes using the same people who originally took part in it —**re·en·act·ment** *n.*

re·en·force /reè ən fáwrs/ *vt.* = **reinforce**

re·en·gin·eer·ing, re-en·gin·eer·ing *n.* BUSINESS a business management theory that advocates the reorganization of a business on the basis of the market value each department adds to the products produced by the business —**re·en·gin·eer** *vt.*

re·en·ter /ree éntər/ (**-tered, -ter·ing, -ters**), **re-en·ter** *v.* **1.** *vti.* **RETURN** to come back into a place again ○ *The rocket reentered the atmosphere.* **2.** *vt.* **ENTER DATA AGAIN** to key or write something in again **3.** *vti.* **GO IN FOR AGAIN** to decide to take part in something again

re·en·trant /ree éntrənt/, **re-en·trant** *n.* MATH = **reentrant angle** ■ *adj.* MATH **POINTING INWARD INTO POLYGON** pointing inward into the interior of a polygon and thus greater than 180° when viewed or measured from inside the polygon

re·en·trant an·gle, re-en·trant an·gle, re-en·trant *n.* MATH an inward-pointing angle in a polygon that is greater than 180° when viewed or measured from inside the polygon

re·en·try /ree éntree/ (*plural* **-tries**), **re-en·try** (*plural* **re-en·tries**) *n.* **1. ENTERING AGAIN** the act of entering again **2.** SPACE TECH **RETURN TO EARTH'S ATMOSPHERE** the penetration of the earth's atmosphere by a spacecraft or missile returning from space (*often used before a noun*) ○ *reentry vehicle* **3.** LAW **REPOSSESSION OF LAND** the repossession of land or other real-estate property under the terms of a previous agreement, e.g., where the terms of a lease have not been complied with **4.** CARDS **TAKING LEAD IN A CARD GAME** in some card games such as bridge, the regaining of control by taking a trick, or the card played to take the trick

re·e·val·u·ate /reè ə vályoo àyt/ (**-at·ed, -at·ing, -ates**), **re-e·val·u·ate** *vt.* to think again, or from a different point of view, about the nature, purpose, or value of something, especially after changes have taken place. ◊ **revalue** —**re·e·val·u·a·tion** /reè ə vallyoo áysh'n/ *n.*

reeve[1] /reev/ *n.* **1. DISTRICT OFFICIAL** an administrative officer in a local district or parish who usually has the responsibility of enforcing the regulations connected with a particular area of activity **2. CANADIAN TOWN COUNCIL PRESIDENT** in Ontario and some western provinces of Canada, the elected president of a town or village council **3.** HIST **REPRESENTATIVE OF THE KING** in Anglo-Saxon times, the representative of the monarch in a shire **4.** HIST **STEWARD OF A FEUDAL MANOR** in medieval times, a steward responsible for running the everyday affairs of a feudal manor [Old English *gerēfa,* literally "official over an assembly of soldiers," from assumed *rōf* "array, number"]

reeve[2] /reev/ (**reeved** *or* **rove, reeved** *or* **rove** /rōv/, **reev·ing, reeves**) *vt.* NAUT **1. THREAD SOMETHING THROUGH AN OPENING** to thread a rope or rod through a ring or other opening **2. FASTEN SOMETHING BY REEVING** to fasten a line or rope by passing it around or through some solid object [Early 17thC. Origin uncertain: possibly from Dutch *reven* "reef" (sail).]

reeve[3] /reev/ *n.* BIRDS the female ruff sandpiper [Mid-17thC. Origin uncertain: perhaps a variant of RUFF[1].]

re·ex·am·ine /reè ig zámmin/ (**-ined, -in·ing, -ines**), **re-ex·am·ine** *vt.* **1. EXAMINE SOMEBODY OR SOMETHING AGAIN** to subject somebody or something to careful further consideration, scrutiny, or checks **2.** LAW **QUESTION SOMEBODY AGAIN AFTER CROSS-EXAMINATION** to question a witness in court again after he or she has been cross-examined by the other side —**re·ex·am·i·na·tion** /reè ig zammi náysh'n/ *n.*

re·ex·port /reè ik spáwrt, ree ék spàwrt/, **re-ex·port** *vt.* (**-port·ed, -port·ing, -ports**) **EXPORT SOMETHING AFTER IMPORTING** to export goods that were previously imported from another country, especially after reprocessing them ■ *n.* **1. PROCESS OF REEXPORTING** the business or process of reexporting imported goods **2. SOMETHING REEXPORTED** something that is reexported —**re·ex·por·ta·tion** /reè ek spawr táysh'n/ *n.*

ref /ref/ *n.* **REFEREE** a sports referee (*informal*) ■ *vti.* (**reffed, ref·ing, refs**) **REFEREE A GAME** to referee a sport or game (*informal*) [Late 19thC. Shortening of REFEREE.]

ref. *abbr.* **1.** reference **2.** referred **3.** refining **4.** reformed **5.** refunding

re·face /ree fáyss/ (**-faced, -fac·ing, -fac·es**) *vt.* **1.** CONSTR **RESTORE EXTERIOR OF BUILDING** to restore or replace the exterior surface of a building or monument **2.** SEW **SEW NEW FACING ON GARMENT** to replace the facing of a garment

Ref. Ch. *abbr.* Reformed Church

re·fec·tion /ri féksh'n/ *n.* (*literary*) **1. REFRESHMENT** refreshment, especially in the form of food and drink **2. LIGHT MEAL** a portion of food or a light meal [14thC. From the Latin stem *refection-* "restoration," from *reficere* (see REFECTORY).]

re·fec·to·ry /ri féktəree/ (*plural* **-ries**) *n.* a dining hall, especially in a monastery, convent, or college [15thC. From late Latin *refectorium,* literally "place where one is restored," ultimately from Latin *reficere* "to remake," from *facere* "to make."]

re·fec·to·ry ta·ble *n.* a long narrow dining table with straight heavy legs

re·fer /ri fúr/ (**-ferred, -fer·ring, -fers**) *v.* **1.** *vi.* **MENTION** to make a comment in speech or writing that either specifically mentions somebody or something, or is intended to bring somebody or something to mind ○ *referred to the subject only once in his speech* **2.** *vi.* **DESCRIBE** to describe somebody or something in a particular way ○ *tried to be respectful when referring to her colleague's thesis* **3.** *vi.* **BE RELATED** to relate to something or be connected with it ○ *This clause refers to your responsibilities as the homeowner.* **4.** *vi.* **CONSULT FOR INFORMATION** to consult a source in order to find information or assistance ○ *refer to the manual* **5.** *vt.* **DIRECT SOMEBODY TO SOURCE OF HELP** to direct somebody to something or somebody else for information, help, treatment, or judgment ○ *referred me to a specialist* **6.** *vt.* **ATTRIBUTE SOMETHING TO A CAUSE** to attribute the cause or source of something to something else ○ *They referred the high gains to the timing of their investment.* [14thC. From French *référer*, from Latin *referre* "to carry back," from *ferre* "to carry" (source of English *fertile*).] —**ref·er·a·ble** /réffərəb'l, ri fúrrəb'l/ *adj.* —**re·fer·rer** /ri fúrrər/ *n.*

WORD KEY: USAGE

Is **refer back** redundant? Some people think that *refer back* is redundant, because one of the implicit meanings of *re-* is "back." But a person may *refer* a problem or request, for example, to a new authority for a decision, or *refer* it *back* to the original decision-maker for reconsideration. If the meaning of *refer* is bringing an issue forward to a higher authority, use *refer forward* or *refer ahead* to avoid ambiguity. If the meaning of *refer* is "to make a mention or reference to something already mentioned," such as a text quoted, for example, in a class lecture, it is better to say *In referring* [not *back*] *to page 321 of my book, I might add the following information not mentioned in Tuesday's lecture.* There, context and meaning determine inclusion or exclusion of *back*.

ref·e·ree /rèffə rée/ *n.* **1.** SPORTS **OFFICIAL OVERSEEING SPORT** an official who oversees the play in a sport or game, judges whether the rules are being followed, and penalizes fouls or infringements **2. ARBITRATOR** somebody not directly involved in a matter who is called in to settle disputes, make decisions, or pass judgments concerning the matter **3.** *U.K.* COMM = **reference** *n.* 10 **4.** LAW **SOMEBODY WHO REVIEWS CASE** somebody appointed by a court to review and make a report or judgment on a case ■ *vti.* (**-reed, -ree·ing, -rees**) **ACT AS A REFEREE** to act as a referee in a sport, in a dispute, or for an applicant [Early 17thC]

ref·er·ence /réffərəns/ *n.* **1. MENTION** a spoken or written comment that either specifically mentions or calls attention to somebody or something, or is intended to bring somebody or something to mind **2. PROCESS OF MENTIONING** the process of mentioning or alluding to somebody or something ○ *The document makes reference to three methods for filing a complaint.* **3. APPLICABILITY** applicability or relevance to, or connection with, a particular subject or person ○ *Does what you're saying have any reference at all to the matter at hand?* **4. SOURCE OF INFORMATION** a source of information such as a dictionary or an encyclopedia (*often used before a noun*) ○ *the reference section of the library* **5.** PUBL **SOURCE REFERRED TO** a source of information referred to by a footnote or citation **6.** PUBL **FOOTNOTE OR BIBLIOGRAPHICAL CITATION** a note directing a reader's attention to a particular section of a work or to another source of information **7.** PUBL = **reference mark 8.** COMM **IDENTIFYING CODE** something, usually a set of letters or figures, that serves to identify somebody or something, e.g., a customer, client, business letter, or a spot on a map (*often used before a noun*) ○ *asked for a customer reference number* **9.** COMM **STATEMENT OF CHARACTER AND QUALIFICATIONS** a statement concerning somebody's character or qualifications, given, e.g., to a potential employer **10.** COMM **SOMEBODY WHO RECOMMENDS ANOTHER** somebody who comments on another's character and qualifications, e.g., for a job ○ *Please give the names and addresses of three references.* ■ *vt.* (**-enced, -enc·ing, -enc·es**) **1.** PUBL **COMPILE REFERENCES FOR BOOK** to compile a list of references for a book, essay, or thesis **2. USE SOMETHING AS A SOURCE** to use or refer to somebody or something as a source in the writing of something ○ *The author referenced some rather obscure works.* ■ *prep.* **WITH REFERENCE TO** in connection with ○ *Reference our discussion of June 5, I believe our prior decision stands.*

ref·er·ence book *n.* a book that is intended to be used for looking up facts, definitions, or other information

ref·er·ence mark *n.* a typographical symbol, such as an asterisk or number used to draw the attention of a reader to a note or bibliographic entry

ref·er·en·dum /rèffə réndəm/ (*plural* **-dums** *or* **-da** /-réndə/) *n.* a vote by the whole of an electorate on a specific question or questions put to it by a government or similar body [Mid-19thC. From Latin, literally "(something) to be referred (to the Senate)," a form of the gerundive of *referre* (see REFER).]

ref·er·ent /réffərənt/ *n.* the thing or idea that a symbol, word, or phrase denotes

ref·er·en·tial /rèffə rénshəl/ *adj.* **1. RELATING TO REFERENCE** relating to references or in the form of a reference **2. REFERRING TO OTHER WORKS** used to describe a work of art that imitates other works or contains oblique references or homages to them, often at the expense of original content or style —**ref·er·en·ti·al·i·ty** /rèffə renshee állətee/ *n.* —**ref·er·en·ti·al·ly** /rèffə rénshəlee/ *adv.*

re·fer·ral /ri fúr əl/ *n.* **1. PROCESS OF REFERRING** the act or process of referring somebody or something to somebody else, especially of sending a patient to consult a medical specialist **2. SOMEBODY OR SOMETHING REFERRED** somebody or something that has been referred, especially a patient who has been sent to a medical specialist

re·ferred pain *n.* pain that is felt not at its source but in another part of the body

re·fill *vti.* /ree fíl/ (**-filled, -fill·ing, -fills**) **FILL AGAIN** to fill a container again, or become filled again ■ *n.* /rée fìl/ **1. SOMETHING THAT FILLS AGAIN** a sufficient amount of something to fill a container again after it has been emptied **2.** BEVERAGES **ANOTHER DRINK** another drink to refill an empty glass or cup **3.** COMM **REPLACEMENT FOR CONTENTS OF CONTAINER** an amount of a product packaged as a replacement for the used up contents of a previously purchased product **4.** MED **FURTHER AMOUNT OF A PRESCRIBED MEDICINE** a further amount of a medication prescribed on a previous occasion —**re·fill·a·ble** /ree fílləb'l/ *adj.*

re·fi·nance /ree fī nàns, reefə nàns/ (**-nanced, -nanc·ing, -nanc·es**) *vti.* to obtain new financing for something on different terms, often involving the paying off of an existing high-interest loan by means of a new lower-interest one —**re·fi·nan·cer** *n.*

re·fine /ri fīn/ (**-fined, -fin·ing, -fines**) *vti.* **1.** INDUST **REMOVE IMPURITIES** to produce a purer form of something by removing the impurities from it, or to become pure through such a process **2. MAKE MORE ELEGANT AND CULTURED** to make somebody or something more cultured or elegant by eliminating less acceptable habits and tastes, or become more cultured in this way **3. MAKE SOMETHING MORE EFFECTIVE** to improve something through small changes that make it more effective or more subtle [Late 16thC. Literally "to make fine again," formed from *fine* "to make fine," from FINE.] —**re·fin·a·ble** *adj.* —**re·fin·er** *n.*

re·fined /ri fīnd/ *adj.* **1. CULTURED AND POLITE** cultured and polite in habits, tastes, or appearance **2. SOPHISTICATED AND EFFECTIVE** developed to or possessing a high degree of sophistication and effectiveness **3.** INDUST **PURIFIED** made purer by an industrial refining process

re·fine·ment /ri fīnmənt/ *n.* **1. ELEGANCE** elegance, politeness, and good taste **2. IMPROVEMENT** an addition or alteration that improves something by making it more sophisticated or effective **3.** INDUST **PROCESS OF REFINING** the process of refining something **4. SUBTLE, PRECISE POINT** a subtle or precise distinction in language or point in an argument

re·fin·er·y /ri fīnəree/ (*plural* **-ies**) *n.* an industrial site where substances such as oil or sugar are processed and purified

re·fin·ish /ree fínnish/ (**-ished, -ish·ing, -ish·es**) *vt.* to put a new finish such as varnish or paint on something such as furniture or wood —**re·fin·ish·er** *n.*

re·fit *vti.* /ree fít/ (**-fit·ted, -fit·ting, -fits**) **REPAIR AND REEQUIP** to make something, especially a ship, ready for further use by repairing and reequipping it, or to undergo a such a process ■ *n.* /rée fit, ree fít/ **THOROUGH OVERHAUL** a thorough overhaul of something, especially a ship, in which it is repaired and reequipped

refl. *abbr.* **1.** MATH reflection **2.** ANAT reflective **3.** MED reflex **4.** reflexive

re·flag /ree flág/ (**-flagged, -flag·ging, -flags**) *vt.* to register a ship or plane with a different national authority

re·fla·tion /ree fláysh'n/ *n.* the process of bringing an economy out of recession by increasing the amount of money in circulation within it [Mid-20thC. Coined from *-flation* (as in DEFLATION and INFLATION).] —**re·flate** *vti.*

re·flect /ri flékt/ (**-flect·ed, -flect·ing, -flects**) *v.* **1.** *vti.* **SEND SOMETHING BACK** to redirect something that strikes a surface, especially light, sound, or heat, usually back toward its point of origin ○ *The Moon reflects light from the Sun toward the Earth.* **2.** *vti.* **SHOW A MIRROR IMAGE OF** to show a reverse image of somebody or something on a mirror or other reflective surface **3.** *vt.* **SHOW SOMETHING** to express or be an indicator of something ○ *The election results reflect discontent among voters.* **4.** *vi.* **THINK SERIOUSLY** to think seriously, carefully, and relatively calmly ○ *The retreat will give us time to reflect.* **5.** *vi.* **SAY TO SELF THOUGHTFULLY** to have a particular thought which may or may not be voiced ○ *That, he reflected, was the only positive thing one could say about the matter.* **6.** *vti.* **BRING CREDIT OR DISCREDIT** to bring credit, discredit, or another judgment on somebody or something ○ *His current success reflects real credit on the school.* **7.** *vti.* **BEND BACK** to bend backward or bend something back (*archaic*) [14thC. Via Old French *reflecter* from Latin *reflectere* "to bend back," from *flectere* "to bend."]

re·flec·tance /rə flékt'ns/ *n.* PHYS = **reflectivity**

re·flect·ing tel·e·scope /ri flèkting-/ *n.* a telescope in which light from the object is initially focused by a concave mirror

re·flec·tion /ri flékshən/ *n.* **1.** PHYS **ACT OF REFLECTING SOMETHING** the process or act of reflecting something, especially light, sound, or heat **2. REFLECTED IMAGE** the image of somebody or something that appears in a mirror or other reflecting surface **3. CAREFUL THOUGHT** careful thought, especially the process of reconsidering previous actions, events, or decisions **4. CONSIDERED IDEA** an idea or thought, especially one produced by careful consideration of something **5. INDICATION** a clear indication or the result of something ○ *This award is a reflection of your hard work.* **6. CAUSE OF BLAME OR CREDIT** a cause of blame or credit to somebody or something ○ *Of course, it's no reflection on you that the project failed.* **7.** ANAT **BENDING BACK OF A STRUCTURE** the bending back upon itself of a membrane or other anatomical structure **8.** MATH **SYMMETRIC TRANSFORMATION** a symmetric transformation in which a figure is reversed along an axis so that the new figure produced is a mirror image of the original one —**re·flec·tion·al** *adj.*

re·flec·tive /ri fléktiv/ *adj.* **1. THOUGHTFUL** characterized by deep careful thought **2.** PHYS **ABLE TO REFLECT** able to reflect light, sound, or other forms of energy **3. BY REFLECTION** produced by reflection —**re·flec·tive·ly** *adv.* —**re·flec·tive·ness** *n.*

re·flec·tiv·i·ty /rèe flek tívvətee/ (*plural* **-ties**) *n.* the ratio of the energy of a wave reflected from a surface to the energy of the incident wave. Symbol **þ**

re·flec·tom·e·ter /rèe flek tómmətər/ *n.* an instrument used to measure the ratio of the energy of a wave after reflection to the energy of the wave before reflection

re·flec·tor /ri fléktər/ *n.* **1. SOMETHING THAT REFLECTS LIGHT** an object, usually glass, plastic, or metal, that reflects light **2.** ASTRON = **reflecting telescope**

re·flec·tor·ize /ri fléktə rīz/ (**-ized, -iz·ing, -iz·es**) *vt.* **1. MAKE SOMETHING REFLECTIVE** to treat something, especially with chemicals, so that it reflects light **2. EQUIP SOMETHING WITH REFLECTORS** to equip something with one or more reflectors

re·flet /ri fláy/ *n.* a shiny or iridescent effect, especially in ceramic finishes [Mid-19thC. Via French *reflet*, earlier *reflès*, from Italian *riflesso* "reflection."]

re·flex /rée flèks/ *adj.* **1.** PHYSIOL **AUTOMATIC AND INVOLUNTARY** occurring automatically and involuntarily as a result of the nervous system's reaction to a stimulus **2. EXTREMELY FAST** very fast in reacting **3. PRODUCED AUTOMATICALLY** produced automatically, unthinkingly, and totally predictably in response to events ○ *reflex opposition* **4.** MATH **BETWEEN 180° AND 360°** used to describe an angle of between 180° and 360° **5. re·flex, re·flexed** BOT **BENT BACK** bent or folded back ○ *reflex leaves* **6.** PHYS **REFLECTED** involving a reflection of energy, e.g., of light or a stream of electrons ○ *reflex light* ■ *n.* **1.** PHYSIOL **INVOLUNTARY BODILY REACTION** an involuntary physiological reaction such as a sneeze, triggered by a nerve impulse sent from a nerve center in response to a nerve receptor's reaction to a stimulus **2.** PHYS **SOMETHING REFLECTED** a reflected image, or a reflection of light, sound, or heat **3.** LING **WORD DEVELOPED FROM AN EARLIER FORM** a later form of a word or other linguistic element that has developed from an earlier one ■ *vti.* (**-flexed, -flex·ing, -flex·es**) BEND BACK to bend back, or cause something to bend back on itself [Early 16thC. From Latin *reflexus* "bent back," past participle of *reflectere* (see REFLECT).] —**re·flex·ly** *adv.*

re·flex arc *n.* a nerve pathway that is responsible for triggering a reflex action

re·flex cam·er·a *n.* a camera with an internal mirror that reflects the actual image from the lens into the viewfinder so that the photographer can check the composition and focus exactly. ◊ **single-lens reflex**

re·flexed *adj.* BOT = **reflex** *adj.* **5**

re·flex·ive /ri fléksiv/ *adj.* **1.** GRAM REFERRING TO PREVIOUS NOUN referring to the same person or thing as another noun or pronoun in the same sentence. The reflexive pronouns in English end in "-self" or "-selves," e.g., "myself," "yourself," "ourselves." **2.** GRAM DENOTING SELF-DIRECTED ACTION taking a reflexive pronoun as an object, thereby, indicating an action that the subject does to or for itself ○ *a reflexive verb* **3.** DONE BY REFLEX relating to a reflex **4.** WITHOUT THINKING automatic and involuntary or unthinking **5.** LOGIC, MATH BEING THE SAME used to describe an association between pairs of logical objects or numbers (**relation**) that are the same or the same size ■ *n.* GRAM REFLEXIVE VERB OR PRONOUN a reflexive verb or pronoun —**re·flex·ive·ly** *adv.* —**re·flex·ive·ness** *n.*

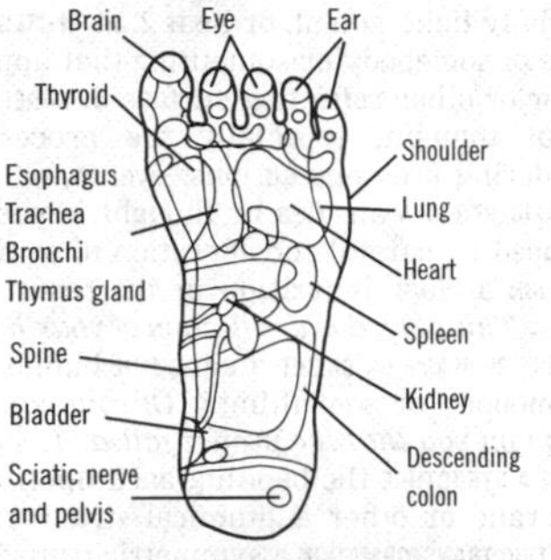

Reflexology

re·flex·ol·o·gy /rēe flek sóllәjee/ *n.* **1.** ALTERN MED MASSAGE THERAPY a form of massage in which pressure is applied to certain parts of the feet and hands in order to promote relaxation and healing elsewhere in the body **2.** PHYSIOL STUDY OF REFLEXES AND BEHAVIOR the scientific study of physiological reflexes and their relation to behavior **3.** PSYCHOL BEHAVIORAL THEORY a theory that explains human behavior as complex chains of conditioned and unconditioned reflexes

ref·lu·ent /ré floo әnt/ *adj.* flowing back [Late 17thC. From Latin *refluent-*, present participle stem of *refluere* "to flow back," from *fluere* "to flow."]

re·flux /rēe flùks/ *n.* **1.** BACKWARD FLOW a returning flow of something **2.** MED REGURGITATION OF STOMACH FLUID a backflow of liquid in the opposite direction to its normal movement such as the regurgitation of stomach and peptic juices associated with acid indigestion and hiatal hernia **3.** PHYS HEATING WHILE CONDENSING VAPOR a method of heating liquid so that escaping vapor is condensed and returned to the liquid ■ *vt.* (**-fluxed, -flux·ing, -flux·es**) PHYS HEAT SOMETHING WHILE CONDENSING VAPOR to heat a liquid in a container with a condenser that catches and returns escaping vapor [15thC. Coined from RE- + FLUX.]

re·fo·cus /ree fṓkәss/ (**-cused** *or* **-cussed, -cus·ing** *or* **-cus·sing, -cus·es** *or* **-cus·ses**) *vti.* **1.** CHANGE FOCUS OF CAMERA to change or adjust the focus of something such as a camera or telescope **2.** FOCUS ON SOMETHING DIFFERENT to concentrate attention or efforts on something different ○ *We need to refocus our marketing strategies.*

re·for·est /ree fáwrәst/ (**-est·ed, -est·ing, -ests**) *vti.* to replant an area with trees after its original trees have been cut down —**re·for·es·ta·tion** /rēe fawrәs táysh'n/ *n.*

re·form /ri fáwrm/ *v.* (**-formed, -form·ing, -forms**) **1.** *vt.* IMPROVE SOMETHING BY REMOVING FAULTS to change and improve something by correcting faults, removing inconsistencies and abuses, and imposing modern methods or values ○ *reform the law* **2.** *vti.* GET RID OF UNACCEPTABLE HABITS to adopt a more acceptable way of life and mode of behavior or persuade or force somebody else to do so **3.** *vt.* INDUST CHANGE THE MOLECULAR STRUCTURE OF PETROLEUM to subject petroleum to a chemical process such as catalytic cracking, in order to convert it into gasoline ■ *n.* **1.** REORGANIZATION AND IMPROVEMENT the reorganization and improvement of something, especially a political institution or system, that is considered to be faulty, ineffective, or unjust ○ *electoral reform* ○ *the reform candidate* **2.** IMPROVING CHANGE a particular change and improvement, especially in the social or political sphere ○ *reforms to prevent fraud* **3.** CHARACTER IMPROVEMENT the adoption by somebody of a more acceptable way of life [14thC. Directly or via French *réformer* from Latin *reformare*, literally "to form again," ultimately from *forma* "form."] —**re·form·a·bil·i·ty** /ri fàwrmә bíllәtee/ *n.* —**re·form·a·ble** /ri fáwrmәb'l/ *adj.* —**re·for·ma·tive** /-fáwrmәtiv/ *adj.*

Re·form *adj.* OF REFORM JUDAISM relating or belonging to Reform Judaism ■ *n.* = **Reform Judaism**

re·form /ree fáwrm/ (**re-formed, re-form·ing, re-forms**) *vti.* to return to or cause something to return to a previous form —**re-for·ma·tion** /rēe fàwr máysh'n/ *n.*

ref·or·ma·tion /rèffәr máysh'n/ *n.* **1.** ACT OF REFORMING the act or process of reforming somebody or something **2.** REFORMED STATE a reformed state, especially a general improvement in somebody's behavior —**ref·or·ma·tion·al** *adj.*

Ref·or·ma·tion *n.* the 16th-century religious movement in Europe that set out to reform some of the doctrines and practices of the Roman Catholic Church and resulted in the development of Protestantism

re·for·ma·to·ry /ri fáwrmә tàwree/ *n.* (*plural* **-ries**) INSTITUTION FOR YOUNG OFFENDERS a penal institution for young offenders ■ *adj.* INTENDED TO REFORM intended for the reform of somebody or something (*formal*)

re·formed /ri fáwrmd/ *adj.* **1.** IMPROVED improved by the removal of outdated, ineffective, or unjust qualities **2.** IMPROVED IN CHARACTER no longer behaving in an unacceptable way

Re·formed *adj.* relating or belonging to a Protestant Church, especially one based on the teachings of John Calvin rather than those of Martin Luther

re·form·er /ri fáwrmәr/ *n.* a person or movement that reforms or tries to reform others

Re·form·er *n.* somebody who was deeply involved in the Reformation that resulted in the development of Protestantism

re·form·ism /ri fáwr mìzzәm/ *n.* a philosophy or movement that advocates the reform of an existing institution

Re·form Ju·da·ism *n.* the branch of Judaism that seeks to adapt religious practice to modern times and rejects the belief that Moses was literally given the Torah by God. It was established in 19th-century Germany.

re·form school *n.* = **reformatory**

re·fract /ri fràkt/ (**-fract·ed, -fract·ing, -fracts**) *vt.* **1.** PHYS ALTER COURSE OF WAVE OF ENERGY to alter the course of a wave of energy that passes into something from another medium, as water does to light entering it from the air **2.** OPHTHALMOL MEASURE DEGREE OF REFRACTION IN SOMETHING to measure the degree of refraction in a lens or eye **3.** SHOW SOMETHING THROUGH A DIFFERENT MEDIUM to alter the appearance of something by viewing or showing it through a different medium [Early 17thC. From Latin *refractus*, perfect participle of *refringere* "to break off, break back," from *frangere* "to break."]

re·fract·ing tel·e·scope *n.* a telescope in which a lens receives and focuses light that is then viewed through a second, magnifying lens in the eyepiece

re·frac·tion /ri frákshәn/ *n.* **1.** PHYS CHANGE OF DIRECTION OF A WAVE the change in direction that occurs when a wave of energy such as light passes from one medium to another of a different density, e.g., from air to water **2.** PHYS DEGREE OF WAVE REDIRECTION the degree to which a wave of energy is refracted **3.** ASTRON DISTORTION OF A CELESTIAL BODY'S LOCATION the degree to which the apparent position of a celestial body is distorted by the redirection of its light as it passes through the Earth's atmosphere **4.** OPHTHALMOL EYE'S ABILITY TO BEND LIGHT the ability of the eye to change the direction of light in order to focus it on the retina **5.** OPHTHALMOL MEASURING OF EYE'S REFRACTIVE CAPACITY the process of measuring the eye's ability to refract light —**re·frac·tion·al** *adj.*

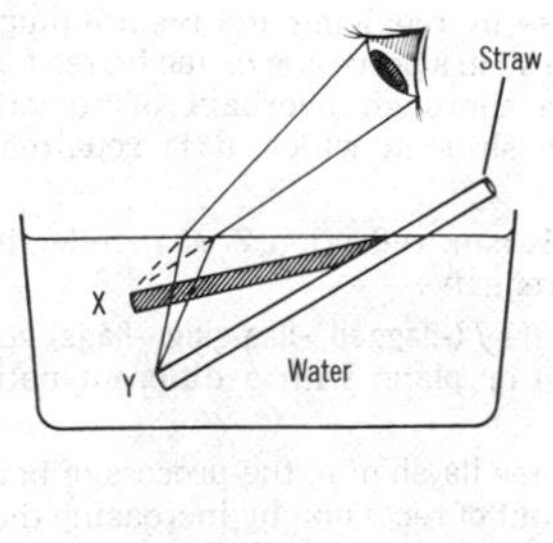

Refraction

re·frac·tive /ri fráktiv/ *adj.* PHYS relating to, involving, or capable of refraction —**re·frac·tive·ly** *adv.* —**re·frac·tive·ness** *n.* —**re·frac·tiv·i·ty** /rēe frak tívvәtee/ *n.*

re·frac·tive in·dex *n.* PHYS = **index of refraction**

re·frac·tom·e·ter /rēe frak tómmәtәr/ *n.* an instrument that measures the index of refraction of a medium —**re·frac·to·met·ric** /ri fràktә méttrik/ *adj.* —**re·frac·tom·e·try** /rēe frak tómmәtree/ *n.*

re·frac·tor /ri fráktәr/ *n.* **1.** = **refracting telescope 2.** PHYS LIGHT-REFRACTING DEVICE a device that alters the direction of a beam of light by passing it between two transparent materials of different density

re·frac·to·ry /ri fráktәree/ *adj.* **1.** UNCONTROLLABLE stubborn, rebellious, and uncontrollable **2.** PHYS HEAT-RESISTANT resistant to high temperatures, and therefore not easily melted or worked **3.** MED UNRESPONSIVE TO TREATMENT unresponsive to medical treatment ○ *a refractory infection* **4.** MED RESISTANT TO INFECTION resistant to infection or disease **5.** UNRESPONSIVE TO STIMULUS not able to respond to a stimulus ■ *n.* (*plural* **-ries**) INDUST, PHYS HIGHLY HEAT-RESISTANT MATERIAL a material that is able to withstand high temperatures without melting, such as the fire clay used to line furnaces [Early 17thC. Variant of earlier "refractary," from Latin *refractarius* "stubborn," from *refractus* "broken off" (see REFRACT).] —**re·frac·to·ri·ly** *adv.* —**re·frac·to·ri·ness** *n.*

re·frac·to·ry pe·ri·od *n.* the time after receiving a stimulus during which a nerve or muscle cell cannot respond to further stimuli

re·frain[1] /ri fráyn/ (**-frained, -frain·ing, -frains**) *vi.* to avoid or hold yourself back from doing something [14thC. Via Old French *refrener* from Latin *refrenare* "to hold back, curb," from *frenum* "bridle."] —**re·frain·ment** *n.*

re·frain[2] /ri fráyn/ *n.* **1.** POETRY RECURRING PIECE OF VERSE a line or group of lines that recurs at regular intervals in a poem, especially at the ends of verses **2.** MUSIC CHORUS the chorus in a song, or the music that accompanies it **3.** MUSIC MELODY a melody or tune **4.** SOMETHING REPEATED OFTEN something that is frequently repeated, such as a saying or an idea [14thC. From Old French, past participle of *refraindre* "to repeat," from assumed Vulgar Latin *refrangere*, alteration of Latin *refringere* "to break back" (see REFRACT).]

re·fran·gi·ble /ri fránjәb'l/ *adj.* able to be refracted [Late 17thC. From modern Latin *refrangibilis*, from *refrangere*, alteration of Latin *refringere* (see REFRACT).] —**re·fran·gi·bil·i·ty** /ri frànjә bíllәtee/ *n.*

re·fresh /ri frésh/ (**-freshed, -fresh·ing, -fresh·es**) *v.* **1.** *vt.* RENEW SOMEBODY'S ENERGY to make somebody feel more energetic, especially with rest, food, or drink ○ *feel refreshed after a nap* **2.** *vt.* REACTIVATE MEMORY to prompt or reactivate the memory with a piece of information ○ *Just refresh my memory.* **3.** *vt.* REPLENISH SOMETHING to replenish the supplies of something ○ *Can I refresh your drink?* **4.** *vi.* FOOD HAVE REFRESHMENTS to have or partake of refreshment, especially food or drink (*archaic*) **5.** *vti.* COMPUT UPDATE INFORMATION to update the information on a particular World Wide Web site, or to be updated ○ *This page refreshes every two minutes.* [14thC. From Old French *refreschir*, literally "to make fresh again," from *freis* "fresh."]

re·fresh·en /ri frésh'n/ (**-ened, -en·ing, -ens**) *vti.* to become or to make something fresh again

re·fresh·er /ri fréshәr/ *n.* something that refreshes

re·fresh·er course *n.* a course of instruction designed to bring somebody's knowledge and skills up to date

re·fresh·ing /ri fréshing/ *adj.* **1.** RESTORING ENERGY serving to restore energy and vitality **2.** PLEASING AND RATHER EXCITING pleasingly different and exciting

re·fresh·ment /ri fréshmənt/ *n.* **1.** SOMETHING REFRESHING something that refreshes, especially food and drink **2.** ACT OF REFRESHING the process of refreshing somebody or something, or a refreshing quality in something ■ **re·fresh·ments** *npl.* SOMETHING TO EAT AND DRINK something to eat and drink, usually snacks or a light meal and drinks

re·fresh rate *n.* the number of times per second that an image displayed on a screen needs to be regenerated to prevent flicker when viewed by the human eye. The refresh rate is dependent upon the persistence of the material used on the screen and the retina's retentivity.

re·fried beans *npl.* a Mexican dish of beans cooked with spices, mashed, then fried

re·frig·er·ant /ri fríjjərənt/ *n.* **1.** COOLING SUBSTANCE a substance used to cool or freeze, especially the liquid that circulates in a refrigerator **2.** MED FEVER-REDUCING MEDICATION a medication that alleviates fever or reduces body heat ■ *adj.* **1.** COOLING having a cooling or freezing effect **2.** MED REDUCING BODY HEAT reducing fever or body heat [Late 16thC. From Latin *refrigerant-*, present participle of *refrigerare* (see REFRIGERATE).]

re·frig·er·ate /ri fríjjə ràyt/ (**-at·ed, -at·ing, -ates**) *vt.* to cool food or other heat-sensitive products to prevent deterioration in quality [Mid-16thC. From Latin *refrigerare*, "to chill again, cool," from *friger-*, an obsolete stem of *frigus* "cold."] —**re·frig·er·a·tion** /ri frìjjə ráysh'n/ *n.* —**re·frig·er·a·tive** /ri fríjjə ràytiv/ *adj.*

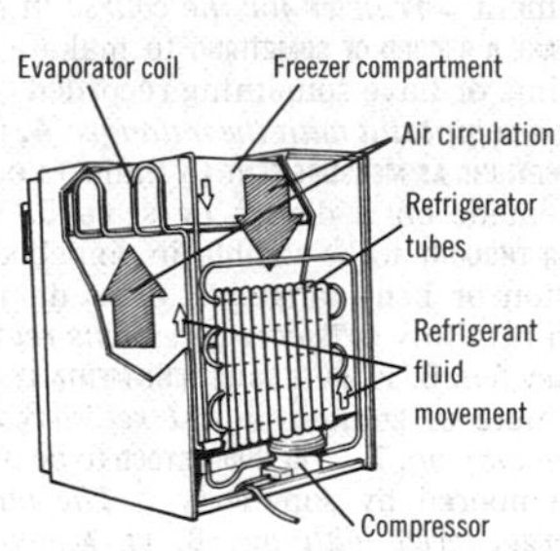

Refrigerator: Cross section of a refrigerator

re·frig·er·a·tor /ri fríjjə ràytər/ *n.* an electrical appliance in the form of an insulated cabinet that keeps items cool through artificial means, or an insulated walk-in chamber artificially cooled for this purpose

re·frin·gent /rə frínj'nt/ *adj.* refractive [Late 18thC. From Latin *refringent-*, present participle stem of *refringere* (see REFRACT).] —**re·frin·gence** *n.*

reft[1] past tense, past participle of **reave**[1]

reft[2] past tense, past participle of **reave**[2]

re·fu·el /ree fyóo əl/ (**-eled, -el·ing, -els**) *vti.* **1.** REFILL WITH FUEL to refill a vehicle's tank with fuel **2.** PROVIDE NEW MATERIAL FOR SOMETHING to provide additional material for or give a renewed impetus to something

ref·uge /réf fyooj/ *n.* **1.** SHELTER OR PROTECTION a sheltered or protected state safe from something threatening, harmful, or unpleasant **2.** SHELTERING PLACE a place, or sometimes a person, offering protection or safe shelter from something [14thC. Via Old French from Latin *refugium*, literally "place to flee back to," ultimately from *fugere* "to flee" (source of English *fugitive*).]

ref·u·gee /rèffyə jée/ *n.* somebody who is seeking or taking refuge, especially from war or persecution, by going to a foreign country (*often used before a noun*)

re·fu·gi·um /ri fyóojee əm/ (*plural* **-a** /-ə/) *n.* an area whose climate remains habitable for particular species, especially rare or endangered ones, when that of the surrounding areas has changed [Mid-20thC. From Latin (see REFUGE).]

re·ful·gent /ri fúljənt/ *adj.* shining brilliantly or splendidly (*literary*) [Early 16thC. From Latin *refulgent-*, present participle stem of *refulgere* "to shine back, reflect," from *fulgere* "to shine, flash."] —**re·ful·gence** *n.* —**re·ful·gent·ly** *adv.*

re·fund *vt.* /ri fúnd, rée fùnd/ (**-fund·ed, -fund·ing, -funds**) RETURN MONEY TO SOMEBODY to return money to somebody, usually because that person paid too much or did not receive what was paid for ■ *n.* /rée fùnd/ **1.** RETURNED MONEY an amount of money that is returned to somebody **2.** PROCESS OF REPAYMENT the act or process of returning money [14thC. Via Old French *refunder* from Latin *refundere* "to pour back," from *fundere* "to pour."] —**re·fund·er** *n.* —**re·fund·a·ble** *adj.*

re·fund (**re-fund·ed, re-fund·ing, re-funds**) *vt.* **1.** FUND SOMETHING ANEW to fund something again **2.** BORROW TO REPAY A DEBT to pay off a debt by new borrowing **3.** REPLACE BOND ISSUE WITH NEW ISSUE to replace an existing issue of bonds with a new issue

re·fur·bish /ree fúrbish/ (**-bished, -bish·ing, -bish·es**) *vt.* to restore something to a cleaner, brighter, or more functional state —**re·fur·bish·er** *n.* —**re·fur·bish·ment** *n.*

re·fus·al /ri fyóoz'l/ *n.* **1.** UNWILLINGNESS TO DO SOMETHING a declaration or an attitude of unwillingness to do or accept something **2.** FIRST OFFER OF SOMETHING the chance to accept or reject something before it is offered to others

re·fuse[1] /ri fyóoz/ (**-fused, -fus·ing, -fus·es**) *v.* **1.** *vti.* INDICATE UNWILLINGNESS to declare or make known a decision or intention not to do something **2.** *vt.* NOT ACCEPT SOMETHING to decline to accept something offered ○ *refused the promotion* **3.** *vt.* DENY to be unwilling to give, allow, or agree to something asked for by somebody ○ *I refused them the use of my tools.* **4.** *vti.* EQU BALK AT JUMP to stop and not jump over an obstacle (*refers to a horse*) [14thC. Via Old French *refuser* from assumed Vulgar Latin *refusare*, of uncertain origin: perhaps a blend of Latin *recusare* "to refuse" and *refutare* "to repel."] —**re·fus·a·ble** *adj.* —**re·fus·er** *n.*

ref·use[2] /réf fyooss/ *n.* things thrown away as being of no value or use, especially household garbage [14thC. From Old French *refus*, literally "refusal," from *refuser* (see REFUSE[1]).]

re·fuse·nik /ri fyóoznik/ *n.* **1.** JEW REFUSED EMIGRATION FROM FORMER USSR a citizen of the former Soviet Union, especially a Jew, who was not allowed by the government to emigrate **2.** SOMEBODY WHO REFUSES somebody who refuses to agree to, take part in, or cooperate with something, especially on grounds of principle (*informal*) [Late 20thC. Origin uncertain: perhaps a partial translation of Russian *otkaznik*, from *otkazat'* "to refuse."]

ref·u·ta·tion /rèffyə táysh'n/ *n.* **1.** PROOF AGAINST SOMETHING an argument, statement, or evidence that proves a claim to be wrong **2.** PROCESS OF REFUTING the act or process of refuting something

re·fute /ri fyóot/ (**-fut·ed, -fut·ing, -futes**) *vt.* **1.** PROVE SOMETHING WRONG to prove something to be false or somebody to be in error through logical argument or by providing evidence to the contrary **2.** DENY SOMETHING to deny an allegation or contradict a statement without disproving it ○ *military planners who tried to refute allegations of poor strategy by showing bomb-damage footage* [Early 16thC. From Latin *refutare* "to drive back, rebut," from the stem *-futare* "to beat."] —**re·fut·a·bil·i·ty** /ri fyòotə bíllətee, rèffyətə-/ *n.* —**re·fut·a·ble** /ri fyóotəb'l, réffyətəb'l/ *adj.* —**re·fut·a·bly** /-fyóotəblee/ *adv.*

reg /reg/ *n.* a regulation (*informal*) ○ *rules and regs* [Early 20thC. Shortening.]

reg. *abbr.* **1.** GEOG region **2.** registered **3.** EDUC registrar **4.** registry **5.** regular **6.** regularly **7.** GENETICS regulation **8.** regulator

Reg. *abbr.* **1.** Regent **2.** Regina

re·gain /rə gáyn, ree-/ (**-gained, -gain·ing, -gains**) *vt.* **1.** GET SOMETHING BACK to recover something after losing it **2.** REACH AGAIN to reach a place again ○ *She regained her seat and sat down.* —**re·gain·er** *n.*

re·gal /réeg'l/ *adj.* typical of or suitable for a king or queen, especially in splendor and magnificence [14thC. Via Old French from Latin *regalis*, from *reg-*, stem of *rex* "king" (source of English *reign* and *royal*).] —**re·gal·i·ty** /ree gállətee/ *n.* —**re·gal·ly** /réegəlee/ *adv.*

re·gale /ri gáyl/ *vt.* (**-galed, -gal·ing, -gales**) **1.** ENTERTAIN SOMEBODY to entertain or amuse somebody, especially by telling stories ○ *regaled us with stories from the early days* **2.** GIVE SOMEBODY PLENTY TO EAT AND DRINK to give somebody plenty of good things to eat and drink ■ *n.* FEAST a feast or a special delicacy (*archaic*) [Mid-17thC. From French *régaler* "to entertain," literally "to give pleasure again," from Old French *gale* "merriment, pleasure."]

re·ga·lia /ri gáylee ə/ *n.* ROYAL INSIGNIA the ceremonial and symbolic objects and clothing used and worn by royalty or other holders of high office on formal occasions (*takes a singular or plural verb*) ■ *npl.* (*takes a singular or plural verb*) **1.** DISTINCTIVE CLOTHING the distinctive clothing or trappings worn by a particular group of people, especially on formal occasions **2.** SPLENDID ATTIRE splendid attire for a formal occasion ○ *The general appeared in full regalia.* [Mid-16thC. From medieval Latin *regalia* "royal privileges, royal residence," originally a form of Latin *regalis* (see REGAL).]

re·gard /ri gaárd/ *vt.* (**-gard·ed, -gard·ing, -gards**) **1.** CONSIDER SOMEBODY OR SOMETHING to think of somebody or something as having a particular nature or quality, or a particular role or function ○ *I regard his gift as an apology.* **2.** HAVE FEELINGS IN RELATION TO SOMETHING to have a particular feeling toward somebody or something ○ *At first they regarded the idea of early retirement with horror.* **3.** JUDGE SOMEBODY OR SOMETHING to have an opinion as to the quality or worth of somebody or something ○ *I regard her highly.* **4.** LOOK AT SOMEBODY OR SOMETHING to look at something or somebody steadily or attentively ○ *regarded the photograph with interest* **5.** BE ABOUT SOMETHING to be about or concerned with something ○ *This memo regards your performance review.* ■ *n.* **1.** ATTENTION attention to or concern for somebody or something ○ *with no regard for my feelings* **2.** FAVORABLE OPINION respect, often coupled with affection ○ *I hold her in the highest regard.* **3.** GAZE a look, or somebody's gaze (*formal*) ■ **re·gards** *npl.* FRIENDLY GREETINGS friendly good wishes and greetings ○ *Give my regards to your father.* [14thC. From Old French *regarder*, literally "to look at fully," from *garder* "to look at, heed" (see GUARD).] ◇ **as regards** as far as somebody or something is concerned ◇ **in this** *or* **that regard** as far as this or that is concerned, or from this or that point of view (*formal*) ◇ **with** *or* **in regard to** concerning or in connection with somebody or something

WORD KEY: SYNONYMS

regard, admiration, esteem, favor, respect, reverence, veneration

CORE MEANING: referring to the recognition of the worth of somebody or something

regard a mixture of liking and appreciation of somebody or something; **admiration** a warm approval and appreciation of somebody or something, often suggesting a desire to copy or resemble somebody or to own something; **esteem** a high opinion and appreciation of somebody; **favor** a liking and preference for somebody or something; **respect** a strong acknowledgement and appreciation of somebody's abilities and achievements without necessarily suggesting a liking for the person; **reverence** a mix of strong feelings of admiration and respect that produces a slight sense of awe for the person or thing revered; **veneration** a formal word for profound feelings of the deepest admiration and highest awe.

re·gar·dant /ri gaárd'nt/ *adj.* used to describe a heraldic figure that is looking backward over its shoulder ○ *three lions regardant* [15thC. From Old French, present participle of *regarder* (see REGARD).]

re·gard·ful /ri gaárdfəl/ *adj.* **1.** MINDFUL paying due attention **2.** FULL OF ESTEEM full of esteem and often deferential respect for somebody —**re·gard·ful·ly** *adv.* —**re·gard·ful·ness** *n.*

re·gard·ing /ri gaárding/ *prep.* about or on the subject of ○ *I'd like a word with you regarding the schedule.*

re·gard·less /ri gaárdləss/ *adv.* IN SPITE OF EVERYTHING in spite of or ignoring setbacks, hindrances, or problems ■ *adj.* INDIFFERENT paying no attention, especially failing to pay proper attention —**re·gard·less·ly** *adv.* —**re·gard·less·ness** *n.*

WORD KEY: USAGE

See Usage note at ***irregardless***.

re·gard·less of *prep.* **1.** IN SPITE OF in spite of ○ *Regardless of what you were told, I cannot help you.* **2.** NO MATTER WHAT no matter what or taking no account of ○ *We're going on vacation regardless of the weather.*

re·gat·ta /ri gaátə, ri gáttə/ *n.* a sports event consisting of a series of boat or yacht races [Mid-17thC. From (Venetian) Italian, "gondola race (on the Grand Canal)," originally "contest for mastery," from *regattare* "to compete," of unknown origin.]

regd. *abbr.* registered

re·ge·la·tion /rèejə láysh'n/ *n.* **1.** GEOG **REFREEZING UNDER GLACIER** the process by which water, melted by pressure beneath a glacier, is refrozen **2.** CHEM **PRESSURE-INDUCED CHANGE IN FREEZING** reduction of the freezing point of water by force of pressure

re·gen·cy /rèejənsee/ (*plural* **-cies**) *n.* **1. GROUP SUBSTITUTING FOR MONARCH** a group of people ruling on behalf of a monarch who is unable to rule because of youth, illness, or absence **2. RESPONSIBILITIES OR RULE OF REGENT** the authority and responsibilities or period in office of a regent

Re·gen·cy *n.* **1. 1811–20 IN GREAT BRITAIN** the period from 1811–20 in Great Britain during which George, Prince of Wales, ruled as regent for his father King George III **2. 1715–23 IN FRANCE** the period from 1715–23 in France during which Philip, Duke of Orleans, ruled as regent on behalf of King Louis XV ■ *adj.* **IN STYLE OF REGENCY** in the style prevalent and fashionable during either of the Regency periods

re·gen·er·ate *v.* /ri jénnə ràyt/ (**-at·ed, -at·ing, -ates**) **1.** *vti.* **FORM AGAIN** to form or become formed again **2.** *vti.* **RECOVER FROM DECLINE** to return or bring something back from a state of decline to a revitalized state ○ *regenerating an inner city housing area* **3.** *vti.* BIOL **REPLACE BY NEW GROWTH** to replace lost tissue or a lost limb or organ with a new growth ○ *Some amphibians can regenerate limbs.* **4.** *vt.* RELIG **RESTORE SOMEBODY SPIRITUALLY** to restore and renew somebody morally or spiritually **5.** *vt.* ELECTRON ENG **RESTORE SOMETHING TO ORIGINAL WAVE SHAPE** to restore digital electrical signals to their original wave shape after transmission over long distances ■ *n.* /ri jénnərət/ **1.** RELIG **SOMEBODY SPIRITUALLY REFORMED** somebody who is spiritually reborn or renewed **2.** BIOL **REPLACEMENT TISSUE** tissue that has grown to replace lost tissue, or a regenerated part, organ, or organism ■ *adj.* /ri jénnərət/ **1.** RELIG **SPIRITUALLY REBORN OR RENEWED** spiritually reborn, renewed, or restored to health **2.** BIOL **NEWLY FORMED OR GROWN** newly formed or grown as a replacement for something lost —**re·gen·er·a·ble** *adj.* —**re·gen·er·a·cy** *n.* —**re·gen·er·ate·ly** *adv.* —**re·gen·er·ate·ness** *n.* —**re·gen·er·a·tive** *adj.* —**re·gen·er·a·tive·ly** *adv.* —**re·gen·er·a·tor** /-ràytər/ *n.*

re·gen·er·a·tion /ri jènnə ráysh'n/ *n.* **1. PROCESS OF REGENERATING** the act or process of regenerating, or a regenerated state **2.** BIOL **REGROWTH BY ANIMAL OR PLANT** regrowth of an organ, limb, or other tissue that has been injured or shed **3.** RELIG **SPIRITUAL RENEWAL** the spiritual renewal of somebody

Re·gens·burg /ràygənz búrg, ràygənss bo͝ork/ town in Bavaria, southeastern Germany, on the Danube River, about 65 mi./105 km northeast of Munich. Population: 126,000 (1995).

re·gent /rèejənt/ *n.* **1.** POL **SUBSTITUTE FOR MONARCH** somebody who rules on behalf of a monarch who is unable to rule because of youth, illness, or absence **2.** EDUC **UNIVERSITY OFFICIAL** any of various officers of a university, especially a member of the governing board ■ *adj.* **ACTING AS REGENT** ruling as a regent ○ *the prince regent* [14thC. Via Old French from Latin *regent-*, present participle stem of *regere* "to rule."] —**re·gent·al** *adj.*

WORD KEY: ORIGIN

The Latin word *regere*, from which ***regent*** is derived, is also the source of English *address, correct, direct, dirge, dress, erect, escort, realm, régime, regiment, region,* and *resurrect.*

reg·gae /ré gày/ *n.* popular music, originally from Jamaica, that combines elements of rock, calypso, and soul and is characterized by heavy accentuation of the second and fourth beats of a four-beat bar (*often used before a noun*) ○ *a reggae beat* [Mid-20thC. Origin uncertain: perhaps from Jamaican English *reggay*, alteration of *rege* "ragged fellow," from RAG^1.]

Reg·gio di Ca·la·bri·a /rèjji ō dee ka lábree a/ city and administrative center of Reggio di Calabria Province in Calabria Region, southern Italy. Population: 178,312 (1992).

Reg·gio nell'E·mi·lia /-nelle meelya/ capital city of Reggio nell'Emilia Province in Emilia Romagna Region, northern Italy. Population: 133,191 (1992).

reg·i·cide /réjji sīd/ *n.* **1. MURDER OF KING** the killing of a king **2. KING KILLER** somebody who kills a king [Mid-16thC. Formed from Latin *reg-*, the stem of *rex* "king" + -CIDE.] —**reg·i·ci·dal** *adj.*

re·gime /ray zhèem, ri-/, **ré·gime** *n.* **1.** POL **FORM OF GOVERNMENT** a system or style of government **2.** POL **OPPRESSIVE GOVERNMENT** a particular government, especially one that is considered to be oppressive **3. CONTROLLING GROUP** any controlling or managing group, or the system of control and management adopted by it **4. ESTABLISHED SYSTEM** an established system or way of doing things **5. CHARACTERISTIC CONDITIONS FOR A PROCESS** the characteristic conditions under which a natural, scientific, or industrial process occurs **6.** MED = **regimen** *n.* 1 [15thC. Via French from Latin *regimen* (see REGIMEN).]

reg·i·men /réjjəmən, réjjə mèn/ *n.* **1.** MED **PROGRAM TO IMPROVE HEALTH** a prescribed or recommended program of medication, diet, exercise, or other measures intended to improve health or fitness, or stabilize a medical condition **2.** POL **GOVERNMENT** a government or form of government (*archaic*) **3.** = **regime** *n.* 5 [14thC. From Latin *regimen* "rule, government," from *regere* "to rule."]

reg·i·ment *n.* /réjjəmənt/ **1.** MIL **ARMY UNIT** a permanent military unit usually consisting of two or three battalions of ground troops divided into smaller companies or troops and under the command of a colonel **2. LARGE NUMBER OF PEOPLE OR THINGS** a large number of people or things, especially an orderly group **3.** POL **GOVERNMENTAL RULE** governmental rule or administration (*archaic*) ■ *vt.* /réjjə mènt/ (**-ment·ed, -ment·ing, -ments**) **1. CONTROL SOMEBODY OR SOMETHING STRICTLY** to impose strict control or discipline on somebody or something, often to the extent of stifling flexibility, individuality, or imagination **2. GROUP SOMETHING SYSTEMATICALLY** to organize something systematically into groups **3.** MIL **GROUP SOLDIERS INTO REGIMENTS** to form regiments out of a group of soldiers [14thC. Via Old French from late Latin *regimentum*, from Latin *regere* "to rule" (see REGENT).] —**reg·i·ment·ed** *adj.*

reg·i·men·tal /rèjjə mént'l/ *adj.* **1.** MIL **OF REGIMENTS** belonging or relating to a military regiment **2. RIGID** marked by strict or excessive discipline ■ **reg·i·men·tals** *npl.* MIL **1. REGIMENT'S UNIFORM AND INSIGNIA** the uniform and insignia worn by the members of a particular regiment **2. MILITARY DRESS** military dress and insignia, especially as worn for ceremonial occasions —**reg·i·men·tal·ly** *adv.*

Re·gi·na /ri jīnə/ capital city of Saskatchewan Province, Canada. Population: 193,652 (1996).

re·gion /rèejən/ *n.* **1.** GEOG **GEOGRAPHIC AREA** a large land area that has particular geographic, political, or cultural characteristics that distinguish it from others, whether existing within one country or extending over several **2.** PUBLIC ADMIN **ADMINISTRATIVE UNIT** a large separate political or administrative unit within a country **3.** ECOL **ECOLOGICAL AREA** an area of the world with particular animal and plant life **4. LARGE INDEFINITE AREA** any large indefinite area of a surface **5. AREA OR ASPECT** an imprecisely defined area or part of something such as a sphere of activity **6. RANGE WITHIN WHICH FIGURE FALLS** the range within which something such as a figure, sum, or price might fall ○ *in the region of $1,000* **7.** ANAT **AREA OF THE BODY** an area of the body, usually an area surrounding a specific organ or part [14thC. Via Old French from the Latin stem *region-* "boundary, district," literally "area that is ruled," from *regere* (see REGENT).]

re·gion·al /rèejən'l/ *adj.* **1.** GEOG **RELATING TO REGION** belonging to or typical of a particular geographic region **2.** POL **CONNECTED WITH ADMINISTRATIVE REGION** serving or connected with one of the administrative regions of a country ○ *a regional authority* **3. TYPICAL OF PARTICULAR AREA** typical of or limited to a particular area of a country, especially typical of the speech and usage of a particular area and different from standard speech and usage —**re·gion·al·ly** *adv.*

re·gion·al·ism /rèejən'l ìzzəm/ *n.* **1.** POL **DIVISION INTO ADMINISTRATIVE AREAS** the policy of dividing a political territory into areas with separate administrations, or support for such a policy **2. LOYALTY TO HOME REGION** loyalty to or prejudice in favor of a particular region **3.** LING **LINGUISTIC FEATURE RESTRICTED TO ONE AREA** a linguistic feature such as a word, pronunciation, or expression that is only found in a particular region —**re·gion·al·ist** *n., adj.*

re·gion·al·ize /rèejən'l īz/ (**-ized, -iz·ing, -iz·es**) *vt.* **1. DIVIDE SOMETHING INTO REGIONS** to divide an area into administrative regions **2. ALLOCATE TO REGIONS** to allocate something to regional administrations —**re·gion·al·i·za·tion** /rèejən'li záysh'n/ *n.*

ré·gis·seur /ràyzhee súr, rézhee sṓr/ *n.* a director who is responsible for staging a theatrical work, especially a ballet [Early 19thC. From French, literally "agent, manager," from *régir* "to manage, rule."]

reg·is·ter /réjjistər/ *n.* **1. OFFICIAL LIST** an official record, often in the form of a list **2. BOOK FOR OFFICIAL RECORDS** a book in which a register of names, attendance, or events is kept **3. ITEM IN OFFICIAL LIST** an item recorded in an official register **4.** MEASURE **MEASURING DEVICE THAT RECORDS** a device that automatically records numbers, degrees, or quantities **5.** = **cash register 6. CORRECT ALIGNMENT** correct alignment or positioning with respect to something else **7. HEATING GRATE** a closable grill or grate through which warm or cool air is forced in a household heating system **8.** COMPUT **COMPUTER MEMORY LOCATION** a memory location in a processor or microprocessor that has a particular storage capacity, is usually intended for a particular purpose, and is accessible at very high speeds **9.** MUSIC **MUSICAL RANGE** the range of a voice or instrument, or a part of this range **10.** MUSIC **ORGAN STOP** one of a group of organ stops that are similar in tonal quality **11.** LING **SITUATION-SPECIFIC LANGUAGE VARIETY** language of a type that is used in particular social situations or when communicating with a particular set of people ■ *v.* (**-tered, -ter·ing, -ters**) **1.** *vti.* **ENTER IN REGISTER** to enter something in a register, or to have something entered there by an official ○ *They registered at the hotel.* **2.** *vti.* **ENROLL** to record a name with an organization in order, e.g., to enroll somebody for an academic course or fulfill a legal requirement ○ *register for the course in September* **3.** *vt.* **MAKE A RECORD OF SOMETHING** to make a record of something, or have something recorded ○ *I want to register a complaint with the manager.* **4.** *vt.* MEASURE **SHOW SOMETHING AS MEASUREMENT** to indicate or record a measurement on a device or scale **5.** *vti.* **DISPLAY FEELING OR THOUGHT** to be visible in somebody's facial expression or body language, or to display something in this way ○ *Their expressions registered the relief they felt.* **6.** *vt.* **NOTE SOMETHING MENTALLY** to make a mental note of something ○ *I registered the time before moving on.* **7.** *vi.* **BE UNDERSTOOD** to be understood or remembered by somebody ○ *The implications finally registered with me.* **8.** *vt.* **ACHIEVE SOMETHING** to achieve or accomplish something ○ *The team registered several notable successes last season.* **9.** *vt.* MAIL **SEND SOMETHING BY REGISTERED MAIL** to send a letter or package by registered mail **10.** *vi.* **BE ALIGNED** to be correctly aligned [14thC. Via Old French *regestre* from medieval Latin *registrum*, alteration of late Latin *regesta* "list," literally "things collected or brought back," ultimately from *gerere* "to bring."] —**reg·is·ter·er** *n.* —**reg·is·tra·ble** *adj.*

reg·is·tered /réjjistərd/ *adj.* **1. CERTIFIED** officially qualified as or for something and entered on an official list **2. HAVING OWNER'S NAME RECORDED** having the owner's name officially recorded **3. ENROLLED WITH BREEDERS' ASSOCIATION** enrolled with a breeders' association as a pedigree animal

reg·is·tered mail *n.* a service provided by post offices to ensure swift and secure delivery of letters and packages. Each item's route is recorded and it must be signed for on delivery.

reg·is·tered nurse *n. U.S., ANZ* a nurse who has passed a qualifying examination in order to be licensed by a state government to practice

reg·is·tered post *n. U.K.* = **registered mail**

reg·is·tered trade·mark *n.* = **trademark** *n.* 1

register ton *n.* = **ton**^{1} *n.* 5

reg·is·trant /réjjistrənt/ *n.* somebody who registers himself or herself, another person, or something such as a patent or trademark

reg·is·trar /réjji straar/ *n.* **1.** EDUC **OFFICIAL RESPONSIBLE FOR STUDENT RECORDS** a university, college, or school official responsible for keeping records of such things as student enrollments and examination results **2.** PUBLIC ADMIN **SOMEBODY WHO KEEPS OFFICIAL RECORDS** somebody who is responsible for keeping official records **3.** *U.K.* PUBLIC ADMIN **RECORDER OF BIRTHS, MARRIAGES, AND DEATHS** a public official who is in charge of the records of local births, marriages, and deaths **4.** BUSINESS **OFFICIAL RESPONSIBLE FOR STOCK RECORDS** a company official responsible for keeping records of stock issued **5.** MED **HOSPITAL ADMISSIONS OFFICER** an administrative officer in a hospital responsible for admitting patients —**reg·is·trar·ship** *n.*

Reg·is·trar Gen·er·al (*plural* **Reg·is·trars Gen·er·al**) *n.* in Canada, an official who keeps track of births, deaths, and marriages in a province

INTERNATIONAL VEHICLE REGISTRATION CODES

Australia **AUS**	Malaysia **MAL**
Bangladesh **BD**	New Zealand **NZ**
Canada **CDN**	Pakistan **PK**
Ghana **GH**	Singapore **SGP**
Hong Kong **HK**	South Africa **ZA**
India **IND**	United Kingdom **GB**
Ireland **IRL**	United States **USA**
Jamaica **JA**	Zimbabwe **ZW**

reg·is·tra·tion /rèjji stráysh'n/ *n.* **1.** ACT OF REGISTERING OR BEING REGISTERED the act or an instance of registering somebody or something, or the process of being registered **2.** CARS LEGAL PROOF FOR VEHICLE a certificate showing that a motor vehicle has been properly registered with a state's department of motor vehicles **3.** EDUC ENROLMENT PROCESS the process of enrolling at a college or university, choosing courses, and paying fees at the beginning of an academic term **4.** ENTRY IN REGISTER an entry in a register, or somebody or something whose name or designation is entered in a register **5.** PEOPLE REGISTERING TOGETHER the number of people who register for a particular thing or at a particular place at one time **6.** MUSIC COMBINATION OF ORGAN STOPS a particular combination of organ stops used to play a piece of music **7.** MUSIC CHOICE OF COMBINATIONS OF ORGAN STOPS the art of choosing combinations of organ stops appropriate for a particular piece or passage

reg·is·try /réjjistree/ (*plural* **-tries**) *n.* **1.** PUBLIC ADMIN RECORDS OFFICE a place where registers and other records are kept **2.** REGISTERING OF SOMETHING the act of registering somebody or something **3.** SHIPPING SHIP'S REGISTRATION IN PARTICULAR COUNTRY the nationality of a ship, as defined by where it is registered not by the nationality of its owner or its usual place of operation

reg·let /rég̀glət/ *n.* **1.** ARCHIT FLAT MOLDING a flat narrow architectural molding, or a narrow strip separating moldings or panels **2.** PRINTING PIECE OF WOOD FOR SPACING TYPE a piece of wood used to separate lines of type in traditional hot metal printing [Late 16thC. From Old French *régelet*, literally "small rule."]

reg·nal /régnəl/ *adj.* relating to a king or queen's reign, calculated from the date when he or she became the sovereign (*formal*) ○ *the third regnal year* [Early 17thC. Via Anglo-Latin *regnalis*, from Latin *regnum* "kingdom."]

reg·nant /régnənt/ *adj.* (*formal*) **1.** REIGNING actually reigning, usually as opposed to having a royal title by marriage ○ *queen regnant* **2.** WIDESPREAD widespread, predominant, or especially fashionable at a particular time ○ *according to the regnant custom* [Early 17thC. From Latin *regnant-*, present participle stem of *regnare* "to reign."]

Reg·o /ráygō/, **Paula** (*b.* 1935) Portuguese-born British painter. She was appointed first associate artist of the National Gallery, London, in 1990. An exhibition of her "Nursery Rhymes" etchings (1989) received international acclaim.

reg·o·lith /réggə lith/ *n.* the layer of loose rock particles that covers the bedrock of most land on Earth and the Moon [Late 19thC. From Greek *rhēgos* "blanket" + -LITH.]

re·gorge /ree gáwrj/ (**-gorged, -gorg·ing, -gorg·es**) *v.* **1.** *vt.* DISGORGE SOMETHING to bring up something that has been swallowed **2.** *vi.* FLOW BACK to flow or gush back along a channel or out of a pit [Early 17thC. Either from Old French *regorger*, ultimately from *gorge* "throat" (see GORGE), or coined from RE- + GORGE.]

re·gress *v.* /ri gréss/ (**-gressed, -gress·ing, -gress·es**) **1.** *vi.* RETURN TO EARLIER, WORSE CONDITION to return to an earlier and less advanced, less healthy, or generally worse state from a more advanced, healthier, or generally better one **2.** *vi.* GO BACK to move backward ○ *regress in time* **3.** *vti.* PSYCHOL GO BACK TO EARLIER PERIOD PSYCHOLOGICALLY to go back to or cause somebody to reenact an earlier emotional state and exhibit the type of behavior associated with it **4.** *vt.* PARAPSYCHOL SUPPOSEDLY MAKE RECALL APPARENTLY EARLIER LIVES to cause somebody to think of and describe supposed earlier lifetimes while under hypnosis **5.** *vi.* STATS TEND TOWARD MEAN to tend toward a statistical mean ■ *n.* /reé grèss/ **1.** MOVEMENT BACKWARD a going backward, especially from a more advanced or better state to a less advanced or worse one **2.** LOGIC REASONING FROM EFFECT TO CAUSE a process of reasoning backward from effects to their causes [Early 16thC. From Latin *regress-*, past participle stem of *regredi* "to move backward," from *gradi* "to walk."] —**re·gres·sor** *n.*

re·gres·sion /ri grésh'n/ *n.* **1.** REVERSION TO EARLIER STATE a return to an earlier or less developed condition or way of behaving **2.** MOVEMENT BACKWARD a going backward or a backward movement or progress, especially through the earlier stages or forms of something **3.** PSYCHOL REVERSION TO LESS MATURE STATE reversion to an earlier, less mature, and less adaptive emotional or mental level, often involving the appearance of forms of behavior associated with childhood **4.** STATS ASSOCIATION BETWEEN VARIABLES a process for determining the statistical relationship between a random variable and one or more independent variables that is used to predict the value of the random variable **5.** BIOL RETURN TO EARLIER PHYSICAL TYPE the recurrence of an earlier, less complicated physical type among the later generations of a particular population **6.** ASTRON RETROGRADE MOTION the apparent backward motion of a celestial body, caused by the differing orbital periods of the Earth and the body being observed **7.** ASTRON MOVEMENT OF MOON'S ORBIT the slow movement around the ecliptic of the two points where the orbit of the Moon crosses it. A complete revolution happens once in about every 19 years.

re·gres·sive /ri gréssiv/ *adj.* **1.** RETURNING TO PREVIOUS CONDITION reverting to an earlier, less developed condition or way of behaving **2.** FIN TAXING POORER PEOPLE MORE HARSHLY used to describe a tax system in which those with low incomes pay proportionally higher taxes than the wealthy —**re·gres·sive·ly** *adv.* —**re·gres·sive·ness** *n.*

re·gret /ri grét/ *vt.* (**-gret·ted, -gret·ting, -grets**) **1.** FEEL SORRY FOR SOMETHING to feel sorry and sad about something previously done or said that now appears wrong, mistaken, or hurtful to others **2.** USED POLITELY WHEN GIVING BAD NEWS used as a polite expression of sorrow when making an apology or delivering a piece of bad or unwelcome news ○ *We regret to inform you that this service is no longer available.* **3.** MOURN FOR SOMEBODY OR SOMETHING to feel sadness about something, or feel a sense of loss and longing for somebody or something that is no longer there (*formal*) ■ *n.* **1.** SAD OR DISAPPOINTED FEELING a feeling or expression of sorrow and guilt for a past action or event that you now wish had not happened or had happened differently **2.** FEELING OF SADNESS a feeling of sadness, disappointment, or of longing for somebody or something that is no longer there ■ **re·grets** *npl.* EXPRESSION OF SADNESS a polite expression of real or pretended sadness, used especially when refusing something such as an invitation ○ *My mother sends her regrets, but she can't come to dinner.* [15thC. From Old French *regreter*, of uncertain origin: perhaps literally "to weep much," from a prehistoric Germanic word meaning "to weep" that is also the ancestor of English *greet*.] —**re·gret·ter** *n.*

re·gret·ful /ri grétfəl/ *adj.* feeling or showing regret for something —**re·gret·ful·ly** *adv.* —**re·gret·ful·ness** *n.*

WORD KEY: USAGE

regretful or **regrettable**? *Regrettable* is used of something that is a cause for regret, whereas ***regretful*** describes somebody who has feelings of remorse or sadness about something: *These mistakes are regrettable. They felt regretful at missing the opportunity.* The adverbs *regrettably* and *regretfully* are even more vulnerable to confusion, but again *regrettably* relates to the cause of regret and *regretfully* to the feeling of regret: *The exam results are regrettably poor. She regretfully turned down the invitation.*

re·gret·ta·ble /ri gréttəb'l/ *adj.* unfortunate or blameworthy, and causing feelings of regret, embarrassment, or even shame ○ *It was a regrettable lapse by a person of otherwise exemplary character.* —**re·gret·ta·ble·ness** *n.* —**re·gret·ta·bly** *adv.*

WORD KEY: USAGE

See Usage note at ***regretful.***

re·group /ree gro͝op/ (**-grouped, -group·ing, -groups**) *v.* **1.** *vti.* MIL FORM INTO ORGANIZED BODY AGAIN to re-form, or re-form troops, into organized units or an effective fighting force, especially after their being dispersed or defeated **2.** *vi.* REORGANIZE to recover, reorganize, and prepare for a further effort after receiving a setback **3.** *vi.* RECOVER COMPOSURE to regain your composure e.g., after a shock or a period of stress ○ *Please pardon me a minute while I regroup here.* **4.** *vt.* ARRANGE THINGS IN NEW GROUPS to arrange people or things in new or different groups —**re·group·ment** *n.*

re·grow /ree gró/ (**-grew** /-gro͞o/, **-grown** /-grón/, **-grow·ing, -grows**) *vti.* to grow again, or cause something, especially a body part, to grow again —**re·growth** /ree gróth/ *n.*

Regt. *abbr.* **1.** Regent **2.** Regiment

reg·u·lar /réggyələr/ *adj.* **1.** HAVING EQUAL TIMES OR SPACES BETWEEN occurring in a fixed, unvarying, or predictable pattern, with equal amounts of time or space between each one ○ *the regular tick-tock of the clock* **2.** HAPPENING FREQUENTLY occurring or doing something frequently enough over a period of time to establish a pattern, though not necessarily a strict one ○ *Ice storms are becoming a regular occurrence around here.* **3.** USUAL normally expected, or most often used or done ○ *Following our regular practice, we'll start the meeting at noon.* **4.** FOLLOWING ROUTINE carried out according to an established routine or schedule ○ *keep very regular hours* **5.** PHYSIOL MENSTRUATING OR DEFECATING AT PREDICTABLE TIMES menstruating or having bowel movements at predictable times **6.** STANDARD OR MEDIUM of a standard or medium size or strength, as opposed, e.g., to something of a larger size or greater strength ○ *I'll have the regular fries.* **7.** SYMMETRICAL evenly and pleasingly shaped and symmetrical ○ *a regular facial profile* **8.** PROPER conforming to the normal or accepted rules or standards ○ *It may not be the regular way of doing long division but it works.* **9.** PROFESSIONAL officially or properly qualified to perform a specific job ○ *not a regular doctor* **10.** MIL FORMING PART OF PROFESSIONAL FORCE belonging to or constituting a full-time professional military or police force as opposed to, e.g., the reserves ○ *an officer in the regular army* **11.** COMPLETE AND UTTER thoroughly deserving a particular description (*informal*) ○ *a regular tyrant in the office* **12.** NICE pleasant, reliable, and thoughtful (*informal*) ○ *a regular guy* **13.** GRAM FOLLOWING NORMAL GRAMMATICAL PATTERNS following the normal or common grammatical patterns of a language. ◊ **irregular 14.** CHR OF RELIGIOUS ORDER belonging to a religious or monastic order ○ *the regular clergy* **15.** POL LOYAL TO PARTY OFFICIALS connected with or loyal to a particular political party **16.** GEOM HAVING EQUAL SIDES AND ANGLES having both equal sides and angles ○ *a regular polygon* **17.** GEOM COMPOSED OF IDENTICAL POLYGONS having faces that are congruent identical polygons and that make equal angles with each other ○ *a regular polyhedron* **18.** BOT HAVING RADIAL SYMMETRY having flower parts that are similar in size and shape and are arranged symmetrically ■ *n.* **1.** FREQUENT VISITOR somebody who visits a place frequently (*informal*) **2.** SOMETHING USUALLY ASKED FOR something such as a drink that somebody usually asks for or buys (*informal*) ○ *"I'll have my regular," he told the server.* **3.** MIL PROFESSIONAL SOLDIER a full-time professional soldier (*often used in the plural*) **4.** SOMETHING STANDARD OR MEDIUM something of a medium or standard size or strength, as opposed to something larger, smaller, stronger, or weaker **5.** CHR MEMBER OF RELIGIOUS ORDER somebody who belongs to a religious or monastic order **6.** POL SOMEBODY POLITICALLY LOYAL somebody who is loyal to a particular political party ○ *strong support from the party regulars* [14thC. Formed from Latin *rēgula* "rule" (source of English *rule*). Ultimately from an Indo-European word that is also the ancestor of English *royal* and *correct*.] —**reg·u·lar·i·ty** /règgyə lérrətee/ *n.* —**reg·u·lar·ly** *adv.*

reg·u·lar·ize /réggyələ rīz/ (**-ized, -iz·ing, -iz·es**) *vt.* to make something fit in with or conform to usual or accepted standards or practice —**reg·u·lar·i·za·tion** /règgyələri záysh'n/ *n.* —**reg·u·lar·iz·er** *n.*

reg·u·late /réggyə làyt/ (**-lat·ed, -lat·ing, -lates**) *vt.* **1.** ENG CONTROL SOMETHING to control something and bring it to the desired level, e.g., by adjusting the output of a machine or by imposing restrictions on the flow of something **2.** POL, LAW CONTROL SOMETHING BY RULES OR LAWS to organize and control an activity or process by making it subject to rules or laws (*formal*)

○ *Governments of socialist countries regulate their nations' economies.* 3. MECH ENG **ADJUST MACHINERY OR SELECT OUTPUT** to adjust a piece of machinery or a control device on it so that the machinery works correctly 4. **MAKE SOMETHING REGULAR** to cause something to occur at predictable intervals or in a regular way [15thC. From late Latin *regulat-*, past participle stem of *regulare*, from Latin *regula* (see REGULAR).] —**reg·u·la·tive** /-làytiv/ *adj.* —**reg·u·la·to·ry** /réggy lə tàwrree/ *adj.*

reg·u·la·tion /règgyə láysh'n/ *n.* 1. **RULE OR ORDER** an official rule, law, or order stating what may or may not be done or how something must be done (*often used in the plural*) 2. **REGULATING OF SOMETHING** the adjusting, organizing, or controlling of something, or the state of being adjusted, organized, or controlled 3. LAW **GOVERNMENT ORDER WITH FORCE OF LAW** an order issued by a government department or agency that has the force of law 4. BIOL **ABILITY OF EMBRYO TO GROW NORMALLY** the process or mechanism by which an embryo restores its ability to develop normally after being damaged or altered without creating new tissue ■ *adj.* 1. **OFFICIALLY APPROVED FOR USE** officially approved for use, or conforming to the official guidelines for something 2. **STANDARD AND UNADVENTUROUS** like everyone has or does, and completely standard and unadventurous

reg·u·la·tor /réggyə làytər/ *n.* 1. ENG **CONTROL MECHANISM** a mechanism that controls something such as pressure, temperature, speed, or voltage (*often used in combination*) 2. **CONTROLLING OFFICIAL** an official who controls an activity and makes certain that regulations are complied with (*often used in combination*) 3. TIME **VERY ACCURATE TIMEKEEPER** a very accurate watch or clock, used as a standard by which others are set 4. GENETICS = **regulator gene**

reg·u·la·tor gene, **reg·u·la·to·ry gene** *n.* a gene that regulates the expression of one or more structural genes, thereby controlling the synthesis of their corresponding proteins. In the simplest case, the regulator gene encodes a repressor molecule that binds to a site adjacent to the structural gene, so preventing transcription of the latter.

re·gu·lus /réggyələss/ (*plural* **-lus·es** *or* **-li** /-lī/) *n.* METALL 1. **IMPURE MASS OF METAL** the semipurified mass of metal that forms beneath the slag in the smelting of ore 2. **IMPURE METAL** an impure intermediate metal product created by the smelting process [Late 16thC. From Latin, diminutive of *rex* "king." Originally found in *regulus of antimony*, a metallic antimony so called because it combined readily with gold, a kingly metal.] —**reg·u·line** /réggyəlin, -līn/ *adj.*

Reg·u·lus /réggyələss/ *n.* ASTRON a bright double star of the first magnitude in the constellation Leo

re·gur·gi·tate /ree gúrji tàyt/ (**-tat·ed, -tat·ing, -tates**) *v.* 1. *vt.* ZOOL **BRING FOOD UP FROM STOMACH** to bring undigested or partially digested food up from the stomach to the mouth, as some birds and animals do to feed their young 2. *vt.* **REPEAT INFORMATION MECHANICALLY** to repeat or reproduce what has been heard, read, or taught, in a purely mechanical way, with no evidence of personal thought or understanding 3. *vi.* **FLOW OUT** to flow out or be ejected, especially from the mouth (*formal*) 4. *vi.* MED **FLOW IN OPPOSITE DIRECTION TO NORMAL** to flow in the opposite direction to the normal or usual direction, especially through a defective heart valve [Late 16thC. From medieval Latin *regurgitat-*, past participle stem of *regurgitare*, literally "to flood back," ultimately from *gurges* "whirlpool" (source of English *gorge*).] —**re·gur·gi·tant** *n., adj.* —**re·gur·gi·ta·tion** /ree gúrji tàysh'n/ *n.* —**re·gur·gi·ta·tive** *adj.*

re·hab /rée hàb/ *n.* (*informal*) 1. SOC WELFARE **REHABILITATION** the period or process of rehabilitation, e.g., for somebody addicted to a chemical substance (*often used before a noun*) ○ *a rehab clinic* 2. CONSTR **SOMETHING RECONSTRUCTED** something that has been rehabilitated, especially a rehabilitated building ■ *vt.* (**-habbed, -hab·bing, -habs**) **RESTORE BUILDING** to restore something, especially a building (*informal*) [Mid-20thC. Shortening.] —**re·hab·ber** *n.*

re·ha·bil·i·tate /rèe ə billə tàyt, rèe hə-/ (**-tat·ed, -tat·ing, -tates**) *vt.* 1. SOC WELFARE **HELP SOMEBODY RETURN TO NORMAL LIFE** to help somebody to return to good health or a normal life by providing training or therapy 2. **RESTORE SOMEBODY TO RANK OR RIGHTS** to restore somebody to a former position or rank and grant rights and privileges once more (*often passive*) 3. **RESTORE SOMEBODY'S REPUTATION** to restore somebody's good reputation and standing after he or she has been disgraced or neglected 4. CONSTR **RESTORE PLACE TO GOOD CONDITION** to restore a building, or part of a town, to its former good condition [Late 16thC. From medieval Latin *rehabilitat-*, past participle stem of *rehabilitare*, literally "to habilitate again" (see HABILITATE).] —**re·ha·bil·i·tat·a·ble** *adj.* —**re·ha·bil·i·ta·tive** *adj.* —**re·ha·bil·i·ta·tor** *n.*

re·ha·bil·i·ta·tion /rèe ə billə táysh'n, rèe hə-/ *n.* 1. SOC WELFARE **HELP FOR RECOVERY** training, therapy, or other help given to somebody, e.g., somebody who has survived a serious injury or illness or an addiction, that will enable him or her to live a healthy and productive life 2. CONSTR **RESTORING OF OLD BUILDINGS** the restoration of a building, or part of a town, to its former good condition 3. **RESTORATION OF LOST POSITION OR REPUTATION** the restoration of somebody's former position, rank, rights and privileges, influence, or good reputation

re·hash /ree hásh/ *vt.* (**-hashed, -hash·ing, -hash·es**) **REPEAT OR REUSE SOMETHING** to repeat something or reuse and rework old material, making some changes but without introducing anything new ■ *n.* **REUSE OF OLD IDEAS** a tiresome reuse of ideas or material to which nothing new or significant has been added

re·hear /ree héer/ (**-heard, -heard** /-húrd/, **-hear·ing, -hears**) *vt.* 1. LAW **CONSIDER SOMETHING AGAIN** to hear a case again in the same court 2. **HEAR SOMETHING AGAIN** to hear or, especially, listen to somebody or something again —**re·hear·ing** *n.*

re·hears·al /ri húrs'l/ *n.* 1. **PRACTICE PERFORMANCE** a session or series of sessions in which something that is to be done later, especially a public performance, is practiced 2. **TEDIOUS REPETITION** a detailed listing or repetition of something (*formal*)

re·hearse /ri húrs/ (**-hearsed, -hears·ing, -hears·es**) *v.* 1. *vti.* **PRACTICE SOMETHING BEFORE PERFORMING** to practice something before doing it, especially to practice something such as a play, speech, or piece of music before performing it for the public 2. *vt.* **TRAIN SOMEBODY FOR PERFORMANCE** to train or instruct somebody who is practicing before doing something, especially before giving a public performance 3. *vt.* **GO OVER LIST** to go over a list of items, often reasons, complaints, or troubles 4. *vti.* **REPEAT SOMETHING** to tell or repeat something such as a story (*literary*) [13thC. From Old French *rehercer*, literally "to rake over," from *herce* "harrow" (see HEARSE).] —**re·hears·er** *n.*

re·heat /ree héet/ (**-heat·ed, -heat·ing, -heats**) *vti.* to heat something, especially leftover food, again after cooling, or be heated up again —**re·heat·er** *n.*

Rehn·quist /rén kwìst/, **William** (*b.* 1924) U.S. jurist. He was appointed chief justice of the United States in 1986. Full name **William Hubbs Rehnquist**

re·ho·bo·am /rèe ə bṓ əm/ *n.* a large wine bottle, six times the size of a normal bottle [Mid-19thC. Named for *Rehoboam*, who "fortified the strongholds, and put captains in them ... and stores of oil and wine" (2 Chronicles 11:11).]

Re·ho·bo·am /rèe ə bṓ əm/ *n.* in the Bible, the son of Solomon and king of ancient Judah (922? B.C.-915? B.C.). His reign was marked by conflict with the rival kingdom of the northern tribes of Israel (1 Kings 11–14).

re·house /ree hówz/ (**-housed, -hous·ing, -hous·es**) *vt.* to provide a person or a group of people with a new or different place to live in, often one that is better than the previous dwelling

re·hy·drate /ree hī dràyt/ (**-drat·ed, -drat·ing, -drates**) *v.* 1. *vt.* **RETURN WATER TO SOMETHING** to add water to something that has been dried in order to return it to its natural state 2. *vt.* MED **REPLENISH SOMEBODY'S BODY FLUID** to restore the body fluids of somebody to a normal or healthy level 3. *vi.* **ABSORB WATER** to absorb water after dehydration —**re·hy·drat·a·ble** *adj.* —**re·hy·dra·tion** /rèe hī dráysh'n/ *n.*

Reich /rīk, rīkh/ *n.* the German state or empire, especially the Holy Roman Empire (926–1806) or First Reich, the German Empire (1871–1919) or Second Reich, or the Nazi state (1933–45) or Third Reich [Early 20thC. From German, "kingdom, state, empire."]

reichs·mark /rīks maark, rīkhs-/ (*plural* **-mark** *or* **-marks**) *n.* the basic unit of German currency from 1923 to 1948 [Mid-20thC. From German, from *Reich* "empire, kingdom" + *Mark* "mark."]

Reich·stag /rīk stàg, rīkh stàg/ *n.* 1. HIST **GERMAN LEGISLATIVE ASSEMBLY 1867–1919** the legislative assembly of both the North German Confederation, from 1867 to 1871, and the German Empire, from 1871 to 1919 2. HIST **LEGISLATIVE ASSEMBLY OF WEIMAR REPUBLIC** the sovereign legislative assembly of the Weimar Republic, from 1919 to 1933 3. **PARLIAMENT BUILDING IN BERLIN** the building in Berlin in which the Reichstag formerly met, destroyed by fire in 1933, and now rebuilt to house the parliament of the reunified German federal state [Mid-19thC. From German, from *Reich* "empire, kingdom" + *Tag* "diet, legislative assembly."]

Reid /reed/, **Whitelaw** (1837–1912) U.S. journalist and diplomat. He served as the U.S. minister to France (1889–92) and ambassador to Great Britain (1905–12).

re·i·fy /rée i fī/ (**-fied, -fy·ing, -fies**) *vt.* to think of or treat something abstract as if it existed as a real and tangible object [Mid-19thC. Coined from Latin *re-* (stem of *res* "thing") + -FY.] —**re·i·fi·ca·tion** /rèe ifi káysh'n/ *n.* —**re·i·fi·ca·to·ry** /ray íffikə tàwree, ree-/ *adj.* —**re·i·fi·er** /rée ə fī ər/ *n.*

reign /rayn/ *n.* 1. **PERIOD OF RULE** the period of time during which somebody, especially a king or queen, rules a nation 2. **CONTROL OR INFLUENCE** the fact of being the dominant or controlling power or factor in something, or the period of time during which this dominance persists ■ *vi.* (**reigned, reign·ing, reigns**) 1. **RULE A NATION** to exercise sovereign power or a controlling influence over something, especially to rule a country as its king or queen 2. **BE TITULAR SOVEREIGN** to hold a royal title and be head of state while possessing only limited powers, as in a constitutional monarchy 3. **BE MOST IMPORTANT FEATURE** to be the main or most noticeable feature of a situation, place, or period of time [13thC. Via Old French *reignier* from Latin *regnare* "to be king," from *regnum* "kingship."]

reign of ter·ror *n.* a time when systematic violence is used by a government, individual, or group to intimidate other people and obtain or maintain dominance over them

Reign of Ter·ror *n.* the period of the French Revolution between September 1793 and July 1794, during which thousands of people were executed as enemies of the revolution

rei·ki /ráykee/ *n.* a treatment in alternative medicine in which healing energy is supposedly channeled from the practitioner to the patient to enhance energy and reduce stress, pain, and fatigue [Late 20thC. From Japanese, "universal life force energy."]

re·i·mag·ine /rèe i májjin/ (**-ined, -in·ing, -ines**) *vt.* 1. **CREATE SOMETHING ANEW** to recreate something, or plan to recreate something, in a fundamentally different way ○ *to reimagine the Shakespearean corpus for television* 2. **REINVENT YOURSELF** to create a new and improved image or lifestyle for yourself

re·im·burse /rèe im búrs/ (**-bursed, -burs·ing, -burs·es**) *vt.* to pay somebody back money spent for an official or approved reason or taken as a loan, or give somebody money as compensation for loss or damage [Early 17thC. Formed from obsolete *imburse* "to pay, put in a purse," ultimately from Old French *borse* "purse," from medieval Latin *bursa* (source of English *purse*).] —**re·im·burs·a·ble** *adj.* —**re·im·burse·ment** *n.* —**re·im·burs·er** *n.*

re·im·port /ree ím pàwrt, rèe im páwrt/ *vt.* (**-port·ed, -port·ing, -ports**) **IMPORT GOODS MADE FROM EXPORTED MATERIALS** to bring back into a country finished goods made from raw materials that were originally exported from that country ■ *n.* 1. **IMPORTING OF GOODS USING EXPORTED MATERIALS** the business of bringing into a country goods made from raw materials originally exported from it 2. **REIMPORTED ITEM** something that has been reimported —**re·im·por·ta·tion** /rèe im pawr táysh'n/ *n.*

re·im·pres·sion /rèe im présh'n/ *n.* a reprint of a book without any changes in the text

Reims /reemz/ city in Marne Department, Champagne-Ardenne Region, northeastern France. Population: 185,164 (1990).

rein /rayn/ *n.* (*often used in the plural*) 1. EQU **STRAP FOR CONTROLLING HORSE** a strap, or either half of a strap, by which a horse is controlled by its rider or by the driver of a coach or cart it is pulling 2. **EXERCISE OF POWER** any means of guiding, controlling, or restraining somebody or something ■ **reins** *npl.* **STRAP FOR GUIDING CHILD** a harness that fits around the body of a very young child, with straps attached by means of which the child can be controlled and guided, especially when out walking ■ *vt.* **(reined, rein·ing, reins)** CONTROL SOMEBODY OR SOMETHING to guide, control, or restrain somebody or something [13thC. From Old French *rene*, earlier *resne*, of uncertain origin: perhaps ultimately from Latin *retinere* "to hold back."] —**rein·less** *adj.* ◇ **give (free) rein to somebody** *or* **something** to allow somebody or something complete freedom, imposing no restraints or limitations ◇ **have a (tight) rein on somebody** *or* **something, keep a (tight) rein on somebody** *or* **something** to maintain strict control of somebody or something

rein back *vt.* to subject something or somebody to stricter control, often to reduce the amount of something or restrict somebody's freedom of action

rein in *v.* **1.** *vti.* RIDING STOP OR SLOW HORSE to make a horse stop or slow down by pulling on the reins **2.** *vt.* CONTROL SOMEBODY OR SOMETHING to bring somebody or something under control

re·in·car·nate *vt.* /rèe in ka̅ar nàyt/ **(-nat·ed, -nat·ing, -nates) 1.** RELIG GIVE NEW BIRTH in some systems of belief, to return somebody to Earth to live another life in a different body (*often passive*) **2.** PUT INTO NEW FORM to present something again in a new form after it has been abandoned or discontinued ■ *adj.* /rèe in ka̅arnət/ **1.** RELIG REBORN in some systems of belief, returned to Earth in a new body after death **2.** REPACKAGED embodied or presented in a new form

re·in·car·na·tion /rèe in kaar náysh'n/ *n.* **1.** RELIG REBIRTH OF SOUL in some systems of belief, the cyclical return of a soul to live another life in a new body **2.** RELIG BODY IN WHICH SOMEBODY IS REBORN in some systems of belief, a person or animal in whose body somebody's soul is born again after he, she, or it has died **3.** APPEARANCE IN NEW GUISE a reappearance of something in a new form —**re·in·car·na·tion·ism** *n.* —**re·in·car·na·tion·ist** /rèe in kaar náysh'nist/ *n.*

rein·deer /ráyn dèer/ (*plural* **-deer** *or* **-deers**) *n.* a large deer with large branched antlers in both males and females, found in northern and Arctic regions of Europe and Asia, and in North America. Reindeer are domesticated by Sami and other Arctic peoples and used as beasts of burden and a source of food and materials. Latin name: *Rangifer tarandus.* [14thC. From Old Norse *hreinn* "reindeer" (perhaps of Finnish-Lappish origin) + *dýr* "animal."]

Rein·deer Lake lake in Canada, on the Saskatchewan-Manitoba border, discharging into the Reindeer River. Area: 2,568 sq. mi./6,651 sq. km.

rein·deer moss, rein·deer li·chen *n.* a gray lichen found in subarctic and Arctic regions that grows in large, erect, and branching tufts and provides food for reindeer and other animals. Latin name: *Cladonia rangiferia.*

re·in·dus·tri·al·ize /rèe in dústree ə lìz/ **(-ized, -iz·ing, -iz·es)** *vti.* to undergo a process of renewal, usually involving government help in the modernization of factories and equipment, or subject an industry or industrial society to such a process —**re·in·dus·tri·al·i·za·tion** /rèe in dustree əli záysh'n/ *n.*

Reines /rìnz/, **Frederick** (*b.* 1918) U.S. physicist. He shared a Nobel Prize in physics (1995) for providing evidence of the existence of the neutrino, a subatomic particle.

re·in·force /rèe in fáwrs/ **(-forced, -forc·ing, -forc·es)** *vt.* **1.** STRENGTHEN SOMETHING to make something stronger by providing additional external support or internal stiffening for it **2.** GIVE SOMETHING SUPPORT to give additional strength, force, or conviction to something such as an idea, opinion, or feeling, e.g., by providing further evidence to support it **3.** MIL MAKE MILITARY FORCE STRONGER to make a military force stronger by providing it with more troops or weapons **4.** PSYCHOL INFLUENCE BEHAVIOR BY REWARD OR PUNISHMENT to reward a particular action or type of behavior to increase the probability that it will be repeated, or punish an action in order to discourage it [15thC. Formed from ENFORCE, probably on the model of Italian *rinforzare.*] —**re·in·force·a·ble** *adj.*

re·in·forced con·crete *n.* concrete made with metal wire or rods embedded in it to increase its strength

re·in·forced plas·tic *n.* plastic with carbon or similar fibers embedded in it to make it stronger

re·in·force·ment /rèe in fáwrsmənt/ *n.* **1.** ADDED SUPPORT the addition of strengthening or supporting material to make something stronger or more durable **2.** SOMETHING ADDED TO INCREASE STRENGTH something that is added to strengthen or support something else **3.** PSYCHOL REWARD OR PUNISHMENT the rewarding (**positive reinforcement**) or punishing (**negative reinforcement**) of particular actions, especially in an experimental situation, for the purpose of changing a subject's behavior ■ **re·in·force·ments** *npl.* MIL ADDITIONAL TROOPS OR WEAPONS additional troops, police, or weapons provided to make an existing force stronger

re·in·forc·er /rèe in fáwrsər/ *n.* in behavioral psychology, a reward or stimulus used to encourage a particular action in order to increase the probability that it will be repeated

Reinga, Cape /ree áŋgə/ cape at the northwestern tip of the North Island, New Zealand. In Maori folklore, it is the departure point for the souls of the dead returning to the spiritual homeland of Hawaiki.

reins /raynz/ *npl.* the kidneys, lower abdomen, including the hips, or lower back [Pre-12thC. Via French from Latin *renes.*]

re·in·state /rèe in stáyt/ **(-stat·ed, -stat·ing, -states)** *vt.* **1.** GIVE SOMEBODY FORMER JOB BACK to give somebody back a job or position of influence that he or she once had and from which he or she was dismissed or deposed **2.** REINTRODUCE SOMETHING to bring something back into use or force again after it has been out of use —**re·in·state·ment** *n.* —**re·in·sta·tor** *n.*

re·in·sure /rèe in shóor/ **(-sured, -sur·ing, -sures)** *vt.* to insure something again, especially to obtain, as an insurer, additional coverage from another insurer for a risk that a customer has been insured against —**re·in·sur·ance** /rèe in shóorənss/ *n.* —**re·in·sur·er** /rèe in shóorər/ *n.*

re·in·te·grate /ree íntə gràyt/ **(-grat·ed, -grat·ing, -grates)** *vt.* **1.** BRING SOMEBODY BACK INTO GROUP to bring somebody or something back into a group or a larger entity of which he, she, or it once formed part after a period of exclusion from it **2.** MAKE SOMETHING WHOLE AGAIN to restore something to a state of wholeness or unity (*formal*) —**re·in·te·gra·tion** /ree ìntə gráysh'n/ *n.*

re·in·ter·pret /rèe in túrprət/ **(-pret·ed, -pret·ing, -prets)** *vt.* to interpret something again or in a different way, especially to find a new and different meaning in something —**re·in·ter·pre·ta·tion** /rèe in turprə táysh'n/ *n.*

re·in·tro·duce /rèe intrə dóoss/ **(-duced, -duc·ing, -duc·es)** *vt.* to bring or take somebody or something back to a place where he, she, or it used to be common, especially to reestablish a species in a habitat —**re·in·tro·duc·tion** /rèe intrə dúkshən/ *n.*

re·in·vent /rèe in vént/ **(-vented, -vent·ing, -vents)** *vt.* **1.** INVENT SOMETHING AGAIN to invent something again, or bring something back into existence, use, or popularity after a period of neglect or obscurity ○ *The party claims to have reinvented genuine popular democracy.* **2.** CREATE NEW VERSION OF SOMETHING to change radically the appearance, form, or presentation of something or somebody —**re·in·ven·tion** /rèe in vénshən/ *n.* ◇ **reinvent the wheel 1.** to waste time recreating something that already exists in a perfectly usable and acceptable form (*slang disapproving*) **2.** to produce a new version of something very basic and familiar (*slang disapproving*)

re·in·vest /rèe in vést/ **(-vest·ed, -vest·ing, -vests)** *vti.* **1.** STOCK EXCH BUY MORE SECURITIES WITH PROFIT to invest money again, especially to buy more shares with the income made on a previous investment **2.** BUSINESS, FIN INVEST IN IMPROVING BUSINESS to put income back into a business instead of distributing it as profit —**re·in·vest·ment** *n.*

re·in·vig·o·rate /rèe in víggə ràyt/ **(-rat·ed, -rat·ing, -rates)** *vt.* to imbue a person, organization or idea with new strength, energy, dynamism or appeal —**re·in·vig·o·ra·tion** /rèe in viggə ráysh'n/ *n.* —**re·in·vig·o·ra·tor** /rèe in víggə ràytər/ *n.*

reis plural of **real**^{2} *n.* 2

re·is·sue /ree íshoo/ *vt.* **(-sued, -su·ing, -sues)** PRODUCE SOMETHING AGAIN to produce, distribute, or make something available again, especially something such as a book or recording, sometimes in a different form ■ *n.* SOMETHING PRODUCED AGAIN something, especially a book or recording, that is reissued

REIT *abbr.* real estate investment trust

re·it·er·ate /ree íttə ràyt/ **(-at·ed, -at·ing, -ates)** *vt.* to say or do something again, once or several times, sometimes in a tiresome way —**re·it·er·ant** *adj.* —**re·it·er·a·tion** /ree ìttə ráysh'n/ *n.* —**re·it·er·a·tive** /ree íttə ràytiv/ *adj.* —**re·it·er·a·tive·ly** /-ràytivlee/ *adv.* —**re·it·er·a·tor** /-ràytər/ *n.*

WORD KEY: USAGE

Redundancy trap: The use of *again, once more, yet again,* and other such expressions with *reiterate,* whose innate meaning subsumes all of them, is a redudancy to be avoided.

Re·iter's syn·drome /rítərz-/, **Re·iter's dis·ease** *n.* a disease that begins as an infection in genetically predisposed people and is characterized by recurring bouts of arthritis, conjunctivitis, and urethritis [Early 20thC. Named for Hans *Reiter* (1881–1969), German bacteriologist.]

re·ject *vt.* /rə jékt/ **(-ject·ed, -ject·ing, -jects) 1.** NOT ACCEPT SOMETHING to refuse to accept, agree to, believe in, or make use of something **2.** TURN SOMEBODY DOWN to decide not to give somebody something asked or applied for, e.g., a job or membership of an organization **3.** BE UNKIND TO SOMEBODY to behave in an unkind and unfriendly way toward somebody who expects, or has a right to expect, love, kindness, and friendship **4.** NOT KEEP OR ACCEPT SOMETHING to put something aside, throw it away, or refuse to accept it because it is not good enough or not the right thing **5.** MED NOT ACCEPT TRANSPLANT to fail to accept foreign tissue or an organ transplant because of immunological incompatibility **6.** MED BRING UP FOOD to be unable to keep food down and vomit it up again ■ *n.* /rèe jèkt/ SOMETHING OR SOMEBODY NOT WANTED somebody who or something that is rejected as not meeting a required standard of quality, or as being generally unsuitable [15thC. From Latin *reject-*, past participle stem of *rejicere*, literally "to throw back," from *jacere* "to throw."] —**re·ject·a·ble** *adj.* —**re·ject·er** /ri jéktər/ *n.* —**re·jec·tive** /ri jéktiv/ *adj.* —**re·jec·tor** *n.*

WORD KEY: USAGE

See Usage note at ***refute.***

re·jec·tion /ri jékshən/ *n.* **1.** ACT OF REJECTING the rejecting of something or somebody, or the fact of being rejected **2.** MED FAILURE OF TRANSPLANT the destruction by immune mechanisms of transplanted tissue or a transplanted organ from another individual

re·jec·tion·ist /ri jékshənist/ *n.* somebody who refuses to accept a policy, proposal, or peace plan that other people have agreed to

re·jec·tion slip *n.* an official note stating that something has been rejected, e.g., a book submitted to a publisher or a painting submitted for exhibition

re·jig /ree jíg/ **(-jigged, -jig·ging, -jigs)** *vt.* = **rejigger** (*informal*)

re·jig·ger /ree jíggər/ **(-gered, -ger·ing, -gers)** *vt.* to alter, rearrange, or readjust something, or set it up differently, sometimes with the intention of deceiving a purchaser or user

re·joice /ri jóyss/ **(-joiced, -joic·ing, -joic·es)** *v.* **1.** *vi.* BE HAPPY to feel very happy or show great happiness about something (*literary*) **2.** *vt.* MAKE SOMEBODY HAPPY to fill somebody with happiness (*archaic*) [14thC. Via Old French *rejoir* "to be most joyful" from, ultimately, Latin *gaudere* "to rejoice" (source of English *joy*).] —**re·joic·er** *n.* —**re·joic·ing** *n.* —**re·joic·ing·ly** *adv.*

rejoice in *vt.* to be lucky enough to have or own something (*often used ironically*)

re·join^{1} /ree jóyn/ **(-joined, -join·ing, -joins)** *vti.* **1.** RETURN TO SOMEBODY AFTER BEING APART to meet up again with somebody, or go back to somebody or something, after a usually brief period of being away or apart **2.** BECOME MEMBER AGAIN to become a member again of an organization or group you formerly belonged to **3.** JOIN TOGETHER AGAIN to join two things together again, or become joined together or merged with something again [Formed from RE- + JOIN]

re·join^{2} /ri jóyn/ **(-joined, -join·ing, -joins)** *v.* **1.** *vti.* REPLY to say something in reply, especially to reply with a sharp, critical, angry, defensive, or clever remark (*formal*) **2.** *vi.* LAW RESPOND TO PLAINTIFF'S REPLY to respond to a plaintiff's reply or replication [15thC. From French *rejoign-*, stem of *rejoindre* "to join again," from *joindre* "to join" (see JOIN).]

re·join·der /ri jóyndər/ *n.* **1.** RETORT a reply to something said, especially one that is sharp, critical, angry, defensive, or clever (*formal*) **2.** LAW DEFENDANT'S RESPONSE the answer that a defendant makes during pleading to the plaintiff's reply or replication [15thC. Via Anglo-Norman from Old French, literally "to rejoin" (see REJOIN^{2}).]

WORD KEY: SYNONYMS

See Synonyms at *answer*.

re·ju·ve·nate /ri jóovə nàyt/ (**-nat·ed, -nat·ing, -nates**) *vt.* **1. MAKE SOMEBODY YOUNG AGAIN** to make somebody become, feel, or appear young again **2. RETURN SOMETHING TO ORIGINAL CONDITION** to restore something to its condition when new, or make it more vigorous, dynamic, and effective **3.** GEOL **CAUSE RIVER TO ERODE MORE** to cause a river to start eroding the land it runs over again, usually as a result of the land being uplifted **4.** GEOL **MAKE AREA DEVELOP TOPOGRAPHICALLY YOUNG FEATURES** to cause, through increased erosion of a landscape, the redevelopment of younger topographic features, that is, the more rugged ones typical of an early geologic stage [Early 19thC. Formed from RE- + Latin *juvenis* "young" (source of English *juvenile*) + -ATE.] —**re·ju·ve·na·tion** /ri jóovə náysh'n/ *n.* —**re·ju·ve·na·tive** /ri jóovə nàytiv/ *adj.* —**re·ju·ve·na·tor** /-nàytər/ *n.*

re·key /ree kée/ (**-keyed, -key·ing, -keys**) *vt.* to reenter lost text or data into a computer, or input text or data in a different form, using a keyboard

re·kin·dle /ree kínd'l/ (**-dled, -dling, -dles**) *vt.* **1. REVIVE SOMETHING** to revive or renew something, e.g., a feeling or interest **2. MAKE FIRE BURN AGAIN** to set a fire burning again

rel. *abbr.* **1.** relating **2.** relative **3.** relatively **4.** released **5.** religion **6.** religious

re·lapse *vi.* /ri láps/ (**-lapsed, -laps·ing, -laps·es**) **1. GO INTO FORMER STATE** to fall back into a former mood, state, or way of life, especially a bad or undesirable one, after coming out of it for a while **2.** MED **BECOME ILL AFTER RECOVERY** to become ill again after seeming to have made a recovery ■ *n.* /rée làps/ **1.** MED **WORSENING OF HEALTH** a sudden worsening in the condition of a patient who was ill but who seemed to have made a recovery from the illness **2. ACT OF RETURNING TO PREVIOUS CONDITION** a return to a former mood, state, or way of life, especially a bad or undesirable one, after coming out of it for a while [15thC. From Latin *relaps-*, past participle stem of *relabi* "to slip again," from *labi* "to slip."] —**re·laps·er** *n.*

re·laps·ing fe·ver *n.* an infectious disease, characterized by chills and recurring fever, caused by a bacterium transmitted to people by ticks and lice

re·late /ri láyt/ (**-lat·ed, -lat·ing, -lates**) *v.* **1.** *vi.* **HAVE A CONNECTION WITH SOMETHING** to have a significant connection with or bearing on something ○ *How does this story relate to our conversation?* **2.** *vt.* **FIND OR SHOW CONNECTION** to find or show a connection between two or more people or things **3.** *vi.* **INVOLVE SOMEBODY OR SOMETHING** to concern, involve, or apply to somebody or something specifically ○ *These regulations relate only to imported goods.* **4.** *vi.* **FORM FRIENDLY ASSOCIATION** to have a friendly relationship with or friendly feelings toward somebody, based on an understanding of the person or on shared views or concerns **5.** *vi.* **RESPOND TO SOMEBODY OR SOMETHING** to understand and respond favorably to something, or feel that it has a personal meaning or relevance (*informal*) ○ *I just can't seem to relate to the cynicism of that generation.* **6.** *vt.* **TELL OR DESCRIBE SOMETHING** to tell a story or describe an event [15thC. Via French *relater* "to report" from Latin *relatus* (source of English *translate*), use as past participle of *referre*, literally "to bring back" (see REFER).] —**re·lat·a·ble** *adj.* —**re·lat·er** *n.*

WORD KEY: USAGE

Jargon trap: The use of ***relate*** in the context of personal dealings between people is much used in the language of sociology but in general use has acquired the reputation of being an example of jargonistic, vague expression. The latter refers to the use of ***relate*** when it is not followed by *to* and a phrase, as in *Children who haven't learned to relate tend to be inadequately socialized.* A clearer way to express this would be *Children who haven't learned to relate to their peers tend to be inadequately socialized.*

re·lat·ed /ri láytəd/ *adj.* **1. ASSOCIATED** connected by similarities or a common source **2. BELONGING TO THE SAME FAMILY** belonging to the same family by birth or through adoption or marriage **3.** MUSIC **HAVING CLOSE HARMONIC CONNECTION** used to describe a musical key or chord that, harmonically speaking, is closely connected with another, e.g., by having particular notes in common with it —**re·lat·ed·ly** *adv.* —**re·lat·ed·ness** *n.*

re·la·tion /ri láysh'n/ *n.* **1. CONNECTION BETWEEN THINGS** a meaningful connection or association between two or more things, based, e.g., on the similarity or relevance of one thing to another **2. MEMBER OF FAMILY** somebody who belongs to the same family as somebody else, by birth or through adoption or marriage **3. CONNECTION BY FAMILY** connection by birth, adoption, or marriage **4. NARRATION OF SOMETHING** the narration of a story or description of something that has happened, or what is conveyed in the narration or description (*formal*) **5.** LAW **TAKING OF SOMETHING AS DONE EARLIER** a procedure whereby an act done at a particular time is, for legal purposes, deemed to have been done at an earlier time **6.** LOGIC, MATH **SHARED PROPERTY OF ASSOCIATION** a property of association, e.g., "greater than" or "less than," shared by ordered pairs of terms or objects ■ *npl.* **1. re·la·tions CONTACTS BETWEEN GROUPS OR PEOPLE** contacts or dealings between two or more people or groups **2. SEXUAL ACTS** sexual activities carried out by people (*used euphemistically*) ◇ **in** *or* **with relation to** with reference or regard to, or in comparison with something

re·la·tion·al /ri láyshən'l, ri láyshnəl/ *adj.* **1. INVOLVING A RELATIONSHIP** involving or expressing a relationship **2.** GRAM **CONVEYING SYNTACTIC RELATION** expressing or relating to a syntactic relation between elements in a phrase or sentence ○ *Prepositions are relational words.* **3.** COMPUT **OF ORGANIZATION OF DATABASE** used to describe a way of organizing and presenting information in a database so that the user perceives it as a set of tables —**re·la·tion·al·ly** *adv.*

re·la·tion·al gram·mar *n.* a theory of descriptive grammar in which syntactic relationships, e.g., subject and object, are used to define grammatical processes rather than syntactic structures

re·la·tion·ship /ri láysh'n shìp/ *n.* **1. CONNECTION** a significant connection or similarity between two or more things, or the state of being related to something else **2. BEHAVIOR OR FEELINGS TOWARD SOMEBODY ELSE** the connection between two or more people or groups and their involvement with each other, especially as regards how they behave and feel toward each other and communicate or cooperate **3. FRIENDSHIP** an emotionally close friendship, especially one involving sexual relations **4. CONNECTION BY FAMILY** the way in which two or more people are related by birth, adoption, or marriage, or the fact of being related by birth, adoption, or marriage **5.** LOGIC, MATH = **relation** *n.* **6**

rel·a·tive /rélləti v/ *adj.* **1. COMPARATIVE** measured or considered in comparison with each other or with something else ○ *discussing the relative merits of various methods of transportation* **2. CHANGING WITH CIRCUMSTANCES** not permanently fixed, but having a meaning or value that can only be established in relation to something else and will change according to circumstances or context ○ *"Big" and "small" are relative terms.* **3. DEPENDENT ON SOMETHING** depending on or in proportion to something else ○ *Payment will be relative to the value of the work done rather than the time taken to do it.* **4. CONNECTED WITH SOMETHING** connected with or referring to something ○ *The lawyers now have most of the data relative to the case.* **5.** GRAM **REFERRING TO PREVIOUSLY USED WORD** used to describe words, especially pronouns (**relative pronouns**) or clauses (**relative clauses**) that refer to another word previously used in the same sentence **6.** MUSIC **HAVING IDENTICAL KEY SIGNATURES** used to describe a key that has the same key signature as another, usually a minor key with the same sharps and flats as a major key, or vice versa ■ *n.* **1. MEMBER OF FAMILY** somebody who belongs to the same family by birth or through adoption or marriage **2. THING RELATED TO SOMETHING ELSE** one thing that is related to something else, especially a species that has developed from the same origin as another species **3.** GRAM **RELATIVE WORD** a relative word, especially a pronoun, or a relative clause —**rel·a·tive·ness** *n.*

rel·a·tive clause *n.* a clause that refers to and provides additional information about a preceding noun or pronoun, often beginning with a relative pronoun such as "who,""which," or "that"

rel·a·tive hu·mid·i·ty *n.* the ratio of the amount of water vapor in the air at a given temperature to the maximum amount air can hold at the same temperature, expressed as a percentage

rel·a·tive·ly /rélləti vlee/ *adv.* in comparison with other things ○ *a relatively cool day, given the summer weather*

rel·a·tive per·mit·tiv·i·ty (*plural* **rel·a·tive per·mit·tiv·i·ties**) *n.* PHYS symbol υ_r

rel·a·tive pitch *n.* **1. TONE'S PITCH COMPARED TO OTHER TONES** the pitch of a tone, determined by its position in a scale with respect to other tones **2. ABILITY TO PRODUCE TONE BY COMPARISON** the ability to identify or produce a tone by mentally comparing it to another tone recently heard

rel·a·tive pro·noun *n.* a pronoun such as "that,""which," or "who" that refers to a previously used noun and introduces a relative clause

rel·a·tiv·ism /rélləti vìzzəm/ *n.* the belief that concepts such as right and wrong, goodness and badness, or truth and falsehood are not absolute but change from culture to culture and situation to situation —**rel·a·tiv·ist** *n.*

rel·a·tiv·is·tic /rèlləti vístik/ *adj.* **1.** PHYS **MOVING CLOSE TO SPEED OF LIGHT** moving at a velocity approaching the speed of light, the point at which certain properties such as mass act in accordance with the theory of relativity **2.** PHYS **RELATING TO RELATIVITY** relating to or characterized by relativity **3.** PHILOS **RELATING TO RELATIVISM** involving or characterized by relativism —**rel·a·tiv·is·ti·cal·ly** *adv.*

rel·a·tiv·i·ty /rèllə tívvətee/ (*plural* **-ties**) *n.* **1.** PHYS **EQUIVALENCE OF MASS AND ENERGY** the first of Einstein's two theories describing the relationship of matter, time, and space, showing that mass and energy are equivalent, and that mass, length, and time change with velocity. The theory is based on two assumptions: that the speed of light in a vacuum is constant, and that physical laws have the same mathematical form throughout the universe. **2.** PHYS **THEORY OF GRAVITATION AND ACCELERATION** the principle put forward in the second of Einstein's two theories extending the principles of the first to gravitation and phenomena related to acceleration **3. DEPENDENCE ON CONTEXTUALLY VARIABLE FACTOR** dependence on a factor that varies according to context **4. FACT OF BEING RELATIVE** the fact or state of being relative to something else

re·la·tor /ri láytər/ *n.* **1. SOMEBODY WHO RELATES SOMETHING** somebody who tells a story or gives an account of something **2.** LAW **SOMEBODY WITH INTEREST IN PROCEEDING** somebody who stands to benefit from an action maintained on his or her behalf by a country or state

re·lax /ri láks/ (**-laxed, -lax·ing, -lax·es**) *v.* **1.** *vi.* **SPEND TIME AT EASE** to spend time resting or doing things for pleasure, especially in contrast to or as a relief from the effort and stress of everyday life **2.** *vti.* **MAKE OR BECOME LESS TENSE** to become, or make somebody or something, less anxious, hostile, defensive, or formal **3.** *vti.* **MAKE OR BECOME LESS STRICT** to make something such as a rule less strict or less severe, or become less strict **4.** *vti.* **BECOME OR MAKE SOMETHING LOOSER** to slacken something that is tensed or tight, e.g., a muscle or a grip on something, or become looser, less tense, or less tight **5.** *vti.* **MAKE OR BECOME LESS INTENSE** to become, or make something, less intense and concentrated **6.** *vt.* HAIR **STRAIGHTEN HAIR** to weaken or remove the curl from hair, usually by chemical means [14thC. From Latin *relaxare* "to loosen," ultimately from *laxus* "loose" (source of English *lax*).] —**re·lax·a·ble** *adj.* —**re·lax·er** *n.* —**re·lax·ing** *adj.*

re·lax·ant /ri láksənt/ *n.* **DRUG THAT RELAXES** a drug that reduces tension and strain, particularly in muscles ■ *adj.* **RELAXING** causing something such as a muscle to become less tense

re·lax·a·tion /rée lak sáysh'n/ *n.* **1. ENJOYABLE ACTIVITY** a form of activity that provides a change and relief from effort, work, or tension, and gives pleasure **2. LOOSENING OF SOMETHING** the process of becoming or of making something less firm, rigid, or tight **3. LESSENING OF SEVERITY** a lessening of the strictness or severity of regulations, restrictions, or controls **4. REDUCTION IN INTENSITY** a lessening or weakening of something that was previously concentrated or intense **5.** PHYS **RETURN OF SYSTEM TO EQUILIBRIUM** the return of a system to equilibrium after it has been displaced or changed **6.** MATH **WAY OF SOLVING EQUATIONS** a way of solving equations using a series of approximate solutions, each of which reduces the number of errors contained in the previous one, until the errors fall within acceptable limits [14thC.

Originally meaning "a rupture of a body part"; the sense of "enjoyable activity" was not recorded until mid-16thC.]

re·laxed /ri lákst/ *adj.* **1. WITHOUT STRAIN OR TENSION** under no strain or tension, and not exerting much strain or force on anything else **2. NOT FEELING ANXIOUS OR WORRIED** feeling no anxiety, tension, pressure, or sense of threat **3. ENCOURAGING INFORMALITY** encouraging informality and casual unhurried behavior **4.** CLOTHES **LOOSE-FITTING** loose-fitting and easy to wear —**re·lax·ed·ly** /ri láksədlee/ *adv.* —**re·lax·ed·ness** /ri láksədnəss/ *n.*

re·lax·in /ri láksin/ *n.* a polypeptide hormone that relaxes the pelvic ligaments of female mammals during pregnancy and is produced by the corpus luteum

re·lay *n.* /rée lày/ **1. PASSING OF SOMETHING TO SOMEBODY** the passing on of something, especially a message or information received, to somebody else, or the process of being passed on **2.** SPORTS **RELAY RACE** a relay race (*informal*) **3.** SPORTS **SECTION OF RELAY RACE** a section or lap of a relay race, run or swum by an individual athlete **4. REPLACEMENT TEAM** one of two or more teams of people or animals that relieve or replace each other in turn, e.g., as the previous team tires **5.** ELECTRON ENG **DEVICE THAT REGULATES ANOTHER** an electronic or electromechanical switching device, typically operated by a low voltage, that controls a higher-voltage circuit and turns it on or off **6.** TELECOM **APPARATUS THAT RECEIVES AND TRANSMITS SIGNALS** an apparatus consisting of a receiver and a transmitter, used to receive and retransmit signals **7.** TELECOM **SIGNAL** a message or broadcast passed on by an apparatus that receives and retransmits signals ■ *vt.* /ri láy, rée lày/ (**-layed, -lay·ing, -lays**) **1. PASS SOMETHING ON TO SOMEBODY** to pass information or a message on to somebody **2.** TELECOM **RETRANSMIT SIGNAL** to receive and retransmit a signal **3.** *U.K.* **BROADCAST** to transmit a broadcast through a transmitting station **4. REPLACE TEAM WITH FRESH PEOPLE** to replace or relieve a team, squad, or crew with a new one **5. ARRANGE PEOPLE INTO TEAMS** to organize somebody or something, especially workers, into relays [14thC. Via Old French *relayer* "to exchange tired horses," from, ultimately, Latin *relaxare* (see RELAX).]

re·lay /ree láy/ (**re-laid, re-lay·ing, re-lays** /ree láyd/) *vt.* to lay something such as a carpet again [Formed from RE- + LAY[1]]

re·lay race *n.* a race between teams of competitors in which each member of a team runs or swims only part of the total distance to be covered. There are usually four people in a relay-race team. In a running race, the current runner must pass a baton to the person running the next section.

re·lease /ri léess/ *vt.* (**-leased, -leas·ing, -leas·es**) **1. LET SOMEBODY OR SOMETHING GO** to set free a person or animal who is imprisoned, trapped, or confined in some way **2. STOP CLUTCHING SOMETHING** to stop gripping or holding something **3. LET SOMETHING OUT** to let out something that has been contained or confined within something or pent up or latent inside somebody **4. FREE SOMEBODY FROM OBLIGATION** to make somebody free of a debt, obligation, promise, or task **5. FIRE EMPLOYEE** to dismiss somebody from a job or position (*formal*) (*used euphemistically*) **6. MAKE SOMETHING AVAILABLE** to make something available, e.g., by putting it on sale, distributing it to the press or public, or allowing access to it **7. OPERATE CATCH TO LET MECHANISM WORK** to take the tension off a mechanism such as a spring, brake, or catch and so allow something to move, open, or operate **8.** LAW **RELINQUISH SOMETHING** to relinquish something, e.g., a right or claim, to another party ■ *n.* **1. LIBERATION** the act of setting somebody or something free, or the fact of being freed, from imprisonment, restraint, an obligation, or anything burdensome and oppressive **2. AUTHORIZATION FOR FREEDOM** a document or message stating that somebody is to be set free **3. REMOVAL OF BURDEN** the removal of something that makes somebody feel trapped, restricted, or burdened **4. ACT OF MAKING SOMETHING AVAILABLE** the act of making something available for the first time, or the fact of being made available in this way ○ *The release of his latest film is expected to be in the fall.* **5. SOMETHING MADE AVAILABLE TO PUBLIC** something such as a film, recording, or item of information that is made available to the public, put on show, or put on sale **6. EMISSION** the emission of something such as heat or radioactivity from the place where it is generated into the atmosphere or the environment **7.** ENG **CONTROL MECHANISM** a mechanism, catch, or handle that is moved or pressed so that something it controls can be used or allowed to operate **8. OPERATION OF A RELEASE** the moving or pressing of a mechanism so that what it controls can be used or allowed to operate **9.** LAW **RELINQUISHING OF CLAIM TO SOMETHING** the relinquishment of a right or claim to another party **10.** LAW **DOCUMENT CONFIRMING SURRENDER OF SOMETHING** a document stating that somebody has surrendered something, e.g., a claim or right [13thC. From Old French *relaisser* "to let go," from Latin *relaxare* (see RELAX).] —**re·leas·a·bil·i·ty** /ri léessə bíllətee/ *n.* —**re·leas·a·ble** /ri léesəb'l/ *adj.* —**re·leas·a·bly** /ri léessəblee/ *adv.* —**re·leas·ee** /ri lee sée/ *n.* —**re·leas·er** /ri léessər/ *n.* —**re·leas·or** *n.*

re-lease (**re-leased, re-leased, re-leas·ing, re-leas·es**) *vt.* to lease something such as an apartment again [Formed from RE- + LEASE]

re·leased time, re·lease time *n.* time given to somebody by an authority or manager allowing that individual to attend to personal matters or interests

re·lease print *n.* the version of a movie released for distribution to commercial theaters

re·leas·ing fac·tor *n.* a hormone produced by the hypothalamus that causes the pituitary gland to secrete other hormones

rel·e·gate /rélla gàyt/ (**-gat·ed, -gat·ing, -gates**) *vt.* **1. DEMOTE** to move somebody or something to a less important position, category, or status **2. HAND ON** to pass something on to somebody for the person to deal with it or provide information about it (*formal*) **3. EXILE** to banish somebody from a country or community [15thC. From Latin *relegat-*, past participle stem of *relegare* "to send away, refer," from *legare* "to send with a commission" (see LEGATE).] —**rel·e·ga·tion** /rèllə gáysh'n/ *n.*

re·lent /ri lént/ (**-lent·ed, -lent·ing, -lents**) *vi.* **1. BECOME LESS RIGID OR STRICT** to become more sympathetic or amenable and do something previously ruled out or allow something previously forbidden **2. BECOME LESS INTENSE** to slacken or become less intense ○ *At last my headache relented.* [14thC. Formed from RE- + Latin *lentare* "to bend, soften," from *lentus* "flexible" (source of English *lento*).]

re·lent·less /ri léntləss/ *adj.* **1. CEASELESS AND INTENSE** never slackening, but continuing always at the same intense, demanding, or punishing level **2. PERSISTENTLY HOSTILE** pursuing, attacking, or opposing somebody or something persistently and without mercy —**re·lent·less·ly** *adv.* —**re·lent·less·ness** *n.*

rel·e·vance /rélləvəns/, **rel·e·van·cy** /rélləvənsee/ *n.* **1. CONNECTION** the sensible or logical connection that one thing has with another, e.g., a matter being discussed or investigated **2. APPLICABILITY TO CURRENT ISSUES** applicability to or connection with real-world issues, present-day events, or the current state of society **3.** COMPUT **ABILITY TO FIND RELEVANT DATA** the ability of an information retrieval system to find and retrieve data that fit a user's requirements

rel·e·vant /rélləvənt/ *adj.* **1. CONNECTED** having some sensible or logical connection with something else, e.g., a matter being discussed or investigated **2. HAVING SOCIAL SIGNIFICANCE** having some bearing on or importance for real-world issues, present-day events, or the current state of society **3.** LING = **distinctive** *adj.* 2 [Early 16thC. From medieval Latin *relevant-*, present participle stem of Latin *relevare* "to relieve" (later, "to take possession of," hence the modern meaning of "connected with") (see RELIEVE).] —**rel·e·vant·ly** *adv.*

WORD KEY: USAGE

Spelling trap: The misspelling and mispronunciation "revelant" for *relevant* is increasingly common and should be avoided.

re·li·a·ble /ri lí əb'l/ *adj.* **1. DEPENDABLE** able to be trusted to do what is expected or has been promised ○ *She is extremely reliable and a hard worker.* **2. LIKELY TO BE ACCURATE** able to be trusted to be accurate or correct or to provide a correct result ○ *I don't think that clock's very reliable.* —**re·li·a·bil·i·ty** /ri lí ə bíllətee/ *n.* —**re·li·a·ble·ness** /rə lí əb'lnəss/ *n.* —**re·li·a·bly** /ri lí əblee/ *adv.*

re·li·ance /ri lí əns/ *n.* **1. DEPENDENCE** dependence on another person or on, e.g., a service or a device, and the need for something that he, she, or it provides **2. CONFIDENCE** trust or confidence in the eventual fulfillment of a promise or in the eventual success of a plan **3. PRIMARY SUPPORT** somebody or something needed or depended on

re·li·ant /ri lí ənt/ *adj.* depending on or needing somebody or something —**re·li·ant·ly** *adv.*

rel·ic /rélik/ *n.* **1. OLD THING SURVIVING FROM PAST** something that has survived from a long time ago, often a part of something old that has remained when the rest of it has decayed or been destroyed **2. OLD CUSTOM** a tradition, practice, or rule that dates from some time in the past, especially one that is considered out of date or inappropriate at the present time **3. KEEPSAKE** something that is kept for its interesting associations, e.g., with somebody famous or with a historic event **4.** RELIG **SOMETHING FROM DEAD HOLY PERSON** something that is kept and venerated because it once belonged to a saint, martyr, or religious leader, especially a part of his or her body ■ **rel·ics** *npl.* **CORPSE** the corpse of a deceased person (*archaic*) [13thC. Via Old French *relique*, from Latin *reliquiae* "remains" (particularly of a dead saint), a plural form of *reliquus* "remaining."]

rel·ict /réllikt/ *n.* **1.** GEOL **REMNANT OF PREEXISTING FORMATION** a remnant of a preexisting land or rock formation left behind after a destructive event has taken place **2.** GEOL **MINERAL UNALTERED BY METAMORPHISM** a mineral that did not change when the rock in which it occurs underwent metamorphosis **3.** BIOL **SURVIVING SPECIES** a species of organism surviving long after the extinction of related species, or a once widespread natural population surviving only in isolated localities because of environmental changes **4. WIDOW** the widow of somebody (*archaic*) ■ *adj.* BIOL **SURVIVING UNCHANGED** surviving in its original form when other related organisms have become extinct or its environment has changed completely [15thC. From Latin *relictus* "left behind," from *relinquere* "to relinquish." Originally meaning "widow."]

re·lic·tion /ri líkshən/ *n.* the gradual withdrawal of water from land, leaving it permanently dry

Relief: 9th-century Roman relief sculpture

re·lief /ri léef/ *n.* **1. FREEING OF SOMEBODY FROM ANXIETY** a release from anxiety or tension, or the feeling of release, lightness, and cheerfulness that accompanies this **2. FACTOR THAT ENDS ANXIETY** a factor that ends a painful or stressful experience such as pain, hunger, or boredom **3. DIVERTING CONTRAST** a factor forming a contrast to the general character of something else, especially something that breaks the monotony or tension of a longer experience **4.** HR **REPLACEMENT** a person who assumes a task or duty when a previous person completes his or her shift, or one person who replaces another who is unable to work **5. PROMINENCE CAUSED BY CONTRAST** uniqueness or prominence caused by contrast ○ *to bring out the differences in clear relief* **6.** ARTS **PROJECTION FROM SURFACE** the elevation of figures or shapes from a flat surface, as seen in sculpture, or their apparent elevation, as seen in painting. ◊ **bas-relief 7.** ARTS **WORK OF ART** a work of art with figures or shapes in relief. ◊ **bas-relief 8.** SOC WELFARE **AID TO THOSE IN NEED** public help in the form of money, food, clothing, shelter, or medicine, provided to people who are temporarily unable to care for themselves **9.** LAW **REDRESS AWARDED BY COURT** compensation or redress for a wrong or hardship, awarded to a party by a court **10.** MIL **FREEING FROM SIEGE** the freeing of a besieged town, castle, fort, or strategic position by soldiers belonging to the same side as those under siege **11.** PRINTING **PRINTING PROCESS** a printing process such as engraving that uses raised surfaces to apply ink to the paper **12.** GEOG, MAPS **ELEVATIONS OF LAND** the variations in height of a land surface and its being shaped into hills and valleys **13.** HIST **PAYMENT TO LORD** a payment made to a feudal lord by the descendant of a tenant in order to inherit a fief [14thC. From Old French *relief*, from *relever* (see RELIEVE). The sense "projection of a figure from a surface" was first recorded in the early 17thC.]

re·lief map *n.* a map that shows variations in land height, usually by means of contour lines or different colors

re·lief pitch·er *n.* in baseball or softball, a pitcher who replaces another pitcher during a game

re·lieve /ri léev/ (**-lieved, -liev·ing, -lieves**) *v.* **1.** *vti.* **STOP SOMETHING UNPLEASANT** to end, lessen, or provide a temporary break from something unpleasant such as pain, hunger, tension, or boredom **2.** *vt.* HR **REPLACE SOMEBODY** to replace somebody on a shift or at a job **3.** *vt.* **EASE SOMEBODY'S BURDEN** to remove something such as a burden or difficulty from the one on which it is imposed **4.** *vr.* PHYSIOL **URINATE** to empty the urinary bladder **5.** *vt.* HR **FIRE EMPLOYEE** to dismiss or suspend somebody from a job or position (*formal*) ○ *After the ship collision, the skipper was relieved of command.* **6.** *vt.* **REMOVE SOMEBODY'S LOAD OR BURDEN** to take something from somebody, usually something that the person is carrying or wearing **7.** *vt.* SOC WELFARE **HELP SOMEBODY** to provide help to people who are temporarily unable to care for themselves ○ *a scheme to relieve the poor* **8.** *vt.* MIL **SAVE SOMETHING FROM MILITARY SIEGE** to free a besieged town, castle, fort, or strategic field position **9.** *vt.* **MAKE SOMETHING PROMINENT** to make something stand out by contrast (*formal*) **10.** *vt.* **ROB VICTIM OF PROPERTY** to rob somebody of something, or steal something from somebody (*informal*) ○ *He relieved him of his wallet.* [14thC. Via Old French *relever* from Latin *relevare* "to raise again, help," literally "to make light again," ultimately from *levis* "light" (source of English *lever*).] —**re·liev·a·ble** *adj.*

re·liev·er *n.* **1. SOMEBODY WHO RELIEVES** somebody who or something that provides relief or relieves another person or thing **2.** BASEBALL = **relief pitcher**

re·lie·vo /rə lée vō/ (*plural* **-vos**), **ri·lie·vo** (*plural* **-vos**) *n.* the elevation of figures or shapes from a flat surface, as seen in sculpture, or their apparent elevation, as seen in painting [Early 17thC. From Italian *rilievo*, from *rilevare* "to raise," from Latin *relevare* (see RELIEVE).]

relig. *abbr.* religion

re·li·gion /ri líjjən/ *n.* **1.** RELIG **BELIEFS AND WORSHIP** people's beliefs and opinions concerning the existence, nature, and worship of a deity or deities, and divine involvement in the universe and human life **2.** RELIG **PARTICULAR SYSTEM** a particular institutionalized or personal system of beliefs and practices relating to the divine **3. PERSONAL BELIEFS OR VALUES** a set of strongly-held beliefs, values, and attitudes that somebody lives by **4. OBSESSION** an object, practice, cause, or activity that somebody is completely devoted to or obsessed by ○ *The danger is that you start to make fitness a religion.* **5.** CHR **MONK'S OR NUN'S LIFE** life as a monk or a nun, especially in the Roman Catholic Church [12thC. Via Anglo-Norman *religiun*, from Old French *religion*, from the Latin stem *religion-* "obligation, reverence," of uncertain origin: probably formed from *religare* "to bind together" (see RELY).] —**re·lig·ion·less** *adj.*
◇ **get religion 1.** to stop flouting the rules, regulations, customs, and expectations of society (*informal*) **2.** to become a believer or join a religious organization, and, usually, start to lead a life that follows its teachings (*informal*)

re·lig·ion·ism /ri líjjə nìzzəm/ *n.* excessive or affected religious enthusiasm (*disapproving*) —**re·lig·ion·ist** *n.*

re·li·gi·ose /ri líjjee òss/ *adj.* excessively, sentimentally, or affectedly pious (*disapproving*) [Mid-19thC. From Latin *religiosus*.] —**re·lig·i·os·i·ty** /ri lìjjee óssətee/ *n.*

re·lig·ious /ri líjjəss/ *adj.* **1. RELATING TO RELIGION** relating to belief in religion, the teaching of religion, or following the practices of a religion ○ *religious freedom* **2. BELIEVING IN A HIGHER BEING** believing in, and showing devotion or reverence for a deity or deities ○ *a religious family* **3. THOROUGH** very thorough or conscientious ○ *a religious attention to detail* **4.** CHR **BELONGING TO MONASTIC ORDER** used to describe Christians who have committed themselves to a monastic order. The vows taken when doing this include dedication to poverty, chastity, and obedience. ■ *n.* **re·lig·ious** (*plural* **-ious**) **MONK OR NUN** somebody who belongs to a monastic order —**re·lig·ious·ly** *adv.* —**re·lig·ious·ness** *n.*

re·lin·quish /ri língkwish/ (**-quished, -quish·ing, -quish·es**) *vt.* **1. CEDE** to renounce or surrender something **2. ABANDON SOMETHING** to give something up or put something aside **3. LET GO** to let go of something physically [15thC. Via the Old French stem *relinquiss-* from Latin *relinquere* "to leave behind," from *linquere* "to leave."] —**re·lin·quish·er** *n.* —**re·lin·quish·ment** *n.*

Reliquary: Reliquary bust of Charlemagne

rel·i·quar·y /rélli kwèrree/ (*plural* **-ies**) *n.* a container or shrine where relics, e.g., the remains of a saint, are kept

rel·ique /réllik/ *n.* something from an older time, kept for its religious, historical, or sentimental value (*archaic*) [13thC (see RELIC)]

re·liq·ui·ae /ri líkwee èe/ *npl.* the remains of something, especially fossil remains of plants or animals [Mid-17thC. From Latin (see RELIC).]

rel·ish /réllish/ *vt.* (**-ished, -ish·ing, -ish·es**) **1. ENJOY SOMETHING** to enjoy or take great pleasure in an experience ○ *relished every minute of their trip* **2. ENJOY EATING SOMETHING** to enjoy the taste of a particular food or drink **3. GIVE FLAVOR TO FOOD** to give a pleasing taste to food, e.g., by adding spice or relish ■ *n.* **1. ENJOYMENT** a liking or appreciation of food or of an experience ○ *a relish for Spanish food* **2.** FOOD **SPICY SIDE DISH** a spiced side dish, e.g., pickled or fresh vegetables with chili **3. STRONG TASTE** a pleasing sensation of strong taste or flavor **4. INTEREST OR EXCITEMENT** interest or excitement, especially when it makes something more enjoyable ○ *The incident added relish to an otherwise dull weekend.* [Early 16thC. From Old French *relais*, literally "remainder."] —**rel·ish·a·ble** *adj.*

re·live /ree lív/ (**-lived, -liv·ing, -lives**) *vt.* to experience something again, especially as a result of thinking about it

re·lo·cate /ree lṓ kàyt, rèe lō káyt/ (**-cat·ed, -cat·ing, -cates**) *vti.* to move or be moved to a new place on a long-term basis, especially to change the location of a business or a residence —**re·lo·ca·tion** /rèe lō káysh'n/ *n.*

re·lu·cent /ri lóos'nt/ *adj.* brightly shining or reflecting light (*archaic*) [Early 16thC. Via Old French *reluisant* from Latin *relucere* "to shine back."]

re·luct /ri lúkt/ (**-luct·ed, -luct·ing, -lucts**) *vi.* to offer opposition or resistance (*archaic*) [Early 16thC. From Latin *reluctari* "to struggle against," from *luctari* "to struggle."]

re·luc·tance /ri lúktənss/ *n.* **1. LACK OF ENTHUSIASM** unwillingness or lack of enthusiasm **2.** PHYS **MEASURE OF MAGNETIC RESISTANCE** a measure of the resistance of a closed magnetic circuit to a magnetic flux. It is equal to the ratio of the magnetic potential difference to the magnetic flux.

re·luc·tant /ri lúktənt/ *adj.* **1. NOT KEEN** feeling no willingness or enthusiasm to do something ○ *I am reluctant to drive in this weather.* **2. UNCOOPERATIVE** showing unwillingness to do something or cooperate ○ *a reluctant swimmer* **3. OPPOSED** opposing or resisting somebody or something (*archaic*) [Mid-17thC. From Latin *reluctant-*, the present participle stem of *reluctari* "to struggle against," from *luctari* "to struggle."] —**re·luc·tant·ly** *adv.*

WORD KEY: USAGE

See Usage note at ***reticent***.

WORD KEY: SYNONYMS

See Synonyms at ***unwilling***.

re·lume /ri lóom/ (**-lumed, -lum·ing, -lumes**), **re·lu·mine** (**-lum·ined, -lum·in·ing, -lum·ines**) *vt.* to light or light something up again [Early 17thC. Formed from ILLUME.]

re·ly /ri lī́/ (**-lied, -ly·ing, -lies**) *vi.* **1. DEPEND** to be dependent on somebody or something **2. TRUST** to have faith or confidence in somebody or something [14thC. Via Old French *relier* from Latin *religare* "to tie back," from *ligare* "to bind" (source of English *ally* and *religion*).]

rem /rem/ (*plural* **rem**) *n.* a unit for measuring amounts of radiation, equal to the effect that one roentgen of X-rays or gamma-rays would produce in a human being. It is used in radiation protection and monitoring. Full form **roentgen equivalent man**

REM /rem, àar ee ém/ *abbr.* rapid eye movement. ◊ **REM sleep**

re·made *v.* past tense, past participle of **remake**

re·main /ri máyn/ (**-mained, -main·ing, -mains**) *v.* **1.** *vi.* **STAY** to stay behind or wait somewhere **2.** *vti.* **CONTINUE IN A STATE** to continue in a particular state without changing **3.** *vi.* **BE LEFT** to be left after everything else has gone **4.** *vi.* **REQUIRE MORE WORK** to continue to need to be taken care of after everything else has been dealt with **5.** *vi.* **ENDURE** to endure and succeed at continuing on in spite of all ○ *In spite of everything, the city remains.* [14thC. Via Old French *remaindre*, *remanoir* from Latin *remanere*, from *manere* "to stay" (source of English *permanent*).]

re·main·der /ri máyndər/ *n.* **1. WHAT IS LEFT OF SOMETHING** the part of something that is left after other parts have gone or been used up **2.** MATH **AMOUNT LEFT OVER AFTER DIVISION** the amount left over when a number or quantity cannot be divided exactly by another **3.** PUBL **UNSOLD BOOK** a book sold by a publisher at a reduced price after demand has fallen off **4.** LAW **INTEREST IN SOMEBODY ELSE'S ESTATE** an interest in an estate that passes to somebody only after a prior interest terminates, e.g., when the current holder of the estate dies ■ *vt.* (**-dered, -der·ing, -ders**) PUBL **SELL BOOK AT REDUCED PRICE** to sell copies of a book at a reduced price after demand has fallen off [14thC. Via Anglo-Norman from Old French *remaindre* (see REMAIN).]

re·main·ing /ri máyning/ *adj.* still left or still existing

remains /ri máynz/ *npl.* **1. WHAT IS LEFT** all that is left of something ○ *the remains of the barn after the fire* **2. CORPSE** a decedent's body **3. ANCIENT RUINS** the parts of something old that are still left ○ *the remains of ancient Roman baths* **4. DEAD AUTHOR'S UNPUBLISHED WRITINGS** all of an author's work that was still unpublished at the time of the author's death

re·make *n.* /rée màyk/ **NEW VERSION OF SOMETHING** something that has been made again or differently, especially a new version of an old movie ■ *vt.* /ree máyk/ (**-made** /-máyd/, **-made, -mak·ing, -makes**) **PRODUCE AGAIN** to produce a remake of something

re·mand /ri mánd/ *vt.* (**-mand·ed, -mand·ing, -mands**) **1.** LAW **RETURN PRISONER TO CUSTODY** to return a prisoner or accused person to custody, or arrange for somebody to be released on bail when a court case is adjourned ○ *The judge ordered the prisoner to be remanded in custody.* **2.** LAW **SEND CASE BACK TO LOWER COURT** to return a case to a lower court with instructions for further action to be taken **3. SEND SOMEBODY BACK** to send or order somebody back ■ *n.* LAW **RETURNING OF SOMEBODY UNTRIED TO PRISON** the return of a prisoner or accused person to custody, or the arrangement of bail for somebody, while waiting for trial [15thC. Via Old French *remander* from late Latin *remandare* "to send word back," from Latin *mandare* "to command."] —**re·mand·ment** *n.*

re·mand home *n. U.K.* = **detention home**

rem·a·nence /rémmənəns/ *n.* the magnetic inductance that remains in a substance after the magnetizing field has been removed [Mid-16thC. From Latin *remanent-*, the present participle stem of *remanere* (see REMAIN).]

rem·a·nent mag·net·ism /rèmmənənt-/ *n.* magnetism shown by ferromagnetic minerals, which preserve the sense and direction of the earth's magnetic field from the time of their formation [*Remanent* from Latin, the present participle stem of *remanere* (see REMAIN)]

re·mark /ri máark/ *n.* **1. CASUAL COMMENT** a casual or brief observation **2. ACT OF COMMENTING** the act of making a remark about something, or an occasion on which this takes place ○ *They consumed their meal without remark.* **3.** COMPUT = **comment** *n.* 4 **4. ACT OF NOTICING** an act or instance of noticing something, especially something that deserves attention ○ *How could such a major change take place without remark?* ■ *v.* (**-marked, -mark·ing, -marks**) **1.** *vti.* **MAKE COMMENT ON**

SOMETHING to make a casual comment or observation about something **2.** *vt.* OBSERVE to notice or observe something (*formal*) [Late 16thC. From French *remarquer*, from *marquer* "to MARK."] —**re·mark·er** *n.*

re·mark·a·ble /ri maárkəb'l/ *adj.* **1.** WORTHY OF NOTICE worth noticing or commenting on **2.** UNUSUAL unusual or exceptional, and attracting attention because of this —**re·mark·a·ble·ness** *n.*

re·mark·a·bly /ri maárkəblee/ *adv.* **1.** TO A REMARKABLE DEGREE to an extent or degree that is remarkable **2.** IN A REMARKABLE WAY used to emphasize that something is worth noticing or commenting on ○ *Remarkably, no one was arrested.*

re·marque /ri maárk/ *n.* **1.** ENGRAVER'S MARK a mark in the margin of an engraved plate, made to indicate its stage of production and removed before the regular printing, or the plate with the mark itself **2.** PROOF OF ENGRAVING a proof of an engraving made from a plate with a remarque [Late 19thC. From French, formed from *remarquer* (see REMARK).]

Re·marque /rə maárk/, **Erich Maria** (1898–1970) German-born U.S. writer. After he was wounded fighting for Germany in World War I, he wrote *All Quiet on the Western Front* (1929), which became a classic war novel. He lived in the United States after 1939.

re·mas·ter /ree mástər/ (**-tered, -ter·ing, -ters**) *vt.* to make a new master copy of an earlier audio recording or movie to improve its quality of reproduction

re·match *n.* /reé màch/ SECOND MATCH a second or return contest between opponents ■ *vt.* /ree mách/ (**-matched, -match·ing, -match·es**) MATCH OPPONENTS AGAIN to arrange for opponents to meet in a second or return contest

Rembrandt van Rijn

Rem·brandt van Rijn /rém brànt vaan rín, rém braánt vaan rín/ (1606–69) Dutch artist. A major painter of the Dutch Golden Age, he imbued his portraits and religious and historical works with a moving spirituality. Full name **Rembrandt Harmenszoon van Rijn**

re·me·di·al /ri meédee əl/ *adj.* **1.** ACTING AS REMEDY acting as a remedy or solution to a particular problem **2.** EDUC HELPING TO IMPROVE SKILLS designed to help people with learning difficulties to improve their skills or knowledge, or relating to education designed to do this **3.** MED INTENDED TO IMPROVE HEALTH intended to cure or relieve the symptoms of somebody who is ill or is physically challenged ○ *remedial exercises* —**re·me·di·al·ly** *adv.*

re·me·di·a·tion /ri meédee áysh'n/ *n.* the use of remedial teaching or therapy to improve skills or health

rem·e·dy /rémmədee/ *n.* (*plural* **-dies**) **1.** MED TREATMENT FOR DISEASE a medication or treatment that cures a disease or disorder, or relieves its symptoms **2.** ALTERN MED HOMEOPATHIC TREATMENT a substance prescribed by a homeopath, and taken in minute quantities **3.** WAY OF PUTTING SOMETHING RIGHT a means of setting something right or getting rid of something undesirable ○ *no easy remedy for society's ills* **4.** LAW LEGAL REDRESS a legal means of enforcing a right or of providing redress **5.** COINS PERMITTED VARIATION IN COINS the legally permitted variation from an established standard in the weight or quality of a coin ■ *vt.* (**-died, -dy·ing, -dies**) **1.** MED CURE A DISEASE to cure or relieve a disease or disorder **2.** PUT SOMETHING RIGHT to set something right, or get rid of something undesirable [13thC. Via Anglo-Norman *remedie* from, ultimately, Latin *remedium* "medicine."] —**re·me·di·a·ble** /ri meédee əb'l/ *adj.* —**re·me·di·a·bly** /ri meédee əblee/ *adv.*

re·mem·ber /ri mémbər/ (**-bered, -ber·ing, -bers**) *v.* **1.** *vti.* RECALL SOMETHING FORGOTTEN to recall something to mind or become aware of something that had been forgotten **2.** *vti.* KEEP SOMETHING IN MEMORY to retain an idea in the memory without forgetting it **3.** *vt.* KEEP SOMEBODY IN MIND to keep somebody in mind for attention or consideration **4.** *vt.* GIVE SOMEBODY A GIFT to give somebody a gift, money, or a tip ○ *She always remembered him on his birthday.* **5.** *vt.* SEND GREETINGS TO to mention somebody to somebody else as a greeting to yet another person ○ *Remember me to your Dad.* **6.** *vt.* COMMEMORATE to commemorate somebody or something, e.g., in a ceremony or funeral service ○ *remembering our veterans on Memorial Day* [14thC. Via Old French *remembrer* from late Latin *rememorari*, from Latin *memor* "mindful" (source of English *memory*).] —**re·mem·ber·er** *n.*

re·mem·brance /ri mémbrəns/ *n.* **1.** REMEMBERING the act or process of remembering people, things, or events **2.** BEING REMEMBERED the state of being remembered, or of remaining in people's minds ○ *We hold her name in fond remembrance.* **3.** ACT OF HONORING the act of honoring the memory of a person or event ○ *a remembrance service* **4.** SOMETHING REMEMBERED something that is remembered **5.** EXTENT OF MEMORY the period of time over which memory extends **6.** MEMENTO something that reminds somebody of a thing, event, or another person **7.** GREETING a greeting, gift, or other expression of affection and friendship

WORD KEY: CULTURAL NOTE

Remembrance of Things Past, a series of novels by French writer Marcel Proust (1913–27). Regarded as one of the greatest works of 20th-century literature, this remarkable meditation on time and memory describes the narrator's childhood encounters with his aristocratic neighbors and his subsequent introduction to Parisian society. A series of unconscious recollections triggers the realization that the past is not lost but can be retrieved by memory and preserved as art.

Re·mem·brance Day *n.* November 11, observed in Canada as a legal holiday and with a two-minute silence in remembrance of those who died in World Wars I and II and subsequent conflicts

re·mex /reé mèks/ (*plural* **rem·i·ges** /rémmə jeèz/) *n.* any of the flight feathers of a bird's wing (*technical*) [Late 17thC. From Latin, literally "oarsman," formed from *remus* "oar."] —**re·mig·i·al** /ri míjjee əl/ *adj.*

re·mind /ri mínd/ (**-mind·ed, -mind·ing, -minds**) *vt.* to cause a person to remember or think of something or somebody else ○ *Remind me to collect the dry-cleaning.* ○ *He reminds me of his grandfather.*

re·mind·er /ri míndər/ *n.* **1.** SOMETHING USED TO REMIND SOMEBODY something that is used to remind somebody about something, e.g., a letter or message ○ *If they don't settle the bill next week, send them a reminder.* **2.** SOMETHING THAT REMINDS somebody who or something that makes somebody remember or think of another person or thing ○ *The monument is a reminder of their bravery.*

Rem·ing·ton /rémmingtən/, **Frederic** (1861–1909) U.S. artist. He produced paintings and sculptures of the old American West.

rem·i·nisce /rèmmə níss/ (**-nisced, -nisc·ing, -nisc·es**) *vi.* to talk or write about events remembered from the past [Early 19thC. Back-formation from REMINISCENCE.] —**rem·i·nis·cer** *n.*

rem·i·nis·cence /rèmmə níss'ns/ *n.* **1.** RECOLLECTION OF THE PAST the recollection of past experiences or events in speech or writing, or the act of recalling the past **2.** SOMETHING REMEMBERED an experience or event remembered from the past **3.** REMINDER something that recalls or suggests something similar **4.** PHILOS IDEA FROM PLATO the Platonic doctrine that anything we encounter is an imperfect recollection of an idea that our souls have encountered in a previous disembodied existence **5.** PSYCHOL ABILITY TO PERFORM TASK BETTER the ability to perform a task or remember information better some time after it has been learned than was possible immediately after it was learned

rem·i·nis·cent /rèmmə níss'nt/ *adj.* **1.** LIKE SOMETHING OR SOMEBODY ELSE suggesting similarities or comparisons with something or somebody else **2.** SUGGESTING MEMORIES OF THE PAST characterized by or containing recollections of the past ○ *scenes reminiscent of her childhood* **3.** RECALLING THE PAST given to reminiscing about the past [Mid-18thC. From Latin, the present participle stem of *reminisci* "to recollect."] —**rem·i·nis·cent·ly** *adv.*

re·mise /ri míz/ *n.* **1.** LAW DEEDING a transfer of property **2.** FENCING SECOND THRUST in fencing, a further thrust made on the same lunge to follow up a first thrust that has missed ■ *vi.* (**-mised, -mis·ing, -mis·es**) FENCING MAKE REMISE to make a remise when a first thrust has missed [15thC. Via French from, ultimately, Latin *remittere* (see REMIT).]

re·miss /ri míss/ *adj.* careless or negligent about doing something that is expected [15thC. From Latin *remissus*, the past participle of *remittere* (see REMIT).]

re·mis·si·ble /ri míssəb'l/ *adj.* worthy of forgiveness —**re·mis·si·bil·i·ty** /ri míssə bíllətee/ *n.*

re·mis·sion /ri mísh'n/ *n.* **1.** MED SLOWING OF DISEASE a lessening of the symptoms of a disease, or their temporary reduction or disappearance **2.** LESSENING OF SOMETHING a lessening or a reduction in the severity of something ○ *The afternoon sun beat down without remission.* **3.** RELEASE a release from a debt, penalty, or obligation **4.** FORGIVENESS pardon or forgiveness **5.** ACT OF REMITTING an instance or the action of remitting something

re·mit /ri mít/ *v.* (**-mit·ted, -mit·ting, -mits**) **1.** *vti.* SEND PAYMENT to send money to pay for merchandise or services, especially by mail **2.** *vt.* LAW SEND CASE BACK TO LOWER COURT to send a case back to a lower court for further action to be taken **3.** *vt.* CANCEL SOMETHING to cancel or hold back from enforcing something **4.** *vti.* REDUCE INTENSITY OF SOMETHING to reduce or allow the reduction in the intensity of something **5.** *vt.* RESTORE SOMETHING to restore something to a previous condition or position **6.** *vt.* DEFER SOMETHING to postpone or defer something **7.** *vt.* PARDON SOMETHING to pardon or forgive something (*archaic*) ■ *n.* **1.** LAW TRANSFER OF LEGAL CASE the transfer of a legal case from a higher to a lower court for further action to be taken **2.** SOMETHING REMITTED something sent to another person or authority for consideration [14thC. From Latin *remittere* "to send back," from *mittere* (see ADMIT).] —**re·mit·ment** *n.* —**re·mit·ta·ble** *adj.* —**re·mit·tal** *n.* —**re·mit·ter** *n.*

re·mit·tance /ri mítt'ns/ *n.* **1.** ACT OF PAYING the sending of money to pay for merchandise or services **2.** MONEY money sent as payment for merchandise or services **3.** REMITTING the act of remitting something

re·mit·tent /ri mítt'nt/ *adj.* lessening and then intensifying again at intervals ○ *slowed down by a remittent fever* —**re·mit·tence** *n.* —**re·mit·ten·cy** *n.* —**re·mit·tent·ly** *adv.*

re·mix *vt.* /ree míks/ (**-mixed, -mix·ing, -mix·es**) PRODUCE NEW VERSION OF MUSIC to produce a new version of a piece of music by altering the emphasis of the sound and, in pop music, often adding new tracks in place of existing ones ■ *n.* /reé mìks/ NEW RECORDING a recording that has been remixed

rem·nant /rémnənt/ *n.* **1.** SMALL PART STILL LEFT a small part of something that remains after the rest has gone **2.** SMALL AMOUNT OF CLOTH OR CARPET a small amount of unsold cloth or flooring material left at the end of a roll, often sold at a reduced price **3.** TRACE OF SOMETHING a small amount or trace of something such as a feeling or emotion **4.** SMALL SURVIVING GROUP OF PEOPLE a small isolated group of people surviving from a particular culture or group [14thC. From Old French *remanant*, the present participle of *remanoir* (see REMAIN).]

re·mod·el /ree módd'l/ (**-eled, -el·ing, -els**) *vt.* to renovate or alter the structure or style of something, e.g., a building, room, or design —**re·mod·el·er** *n.*

re·mon·e·tize /ree mónnə tìz, -múnnə-/ (**-tized, -tiz·ing, -tiz·es**) *vt.* to reinstate something as valid currency or legal tender —**re·mon·e·ti·za·tion** /ree mònnəti záysh'n, -mùnnəti-/ *n.*

re·mon·strance /ri mónstrəns/ *n.* **1.** ARGUMENT a forceful argument in favor or against something, or the act of making such an argument **2.** FORMAL PROTEST a formal protest, usually in the form of a document or petition

Re·mon·strance *n.* the statement expressing Arminian Protestant principles, drawn up in 1610 in Gouda, the Netherlands. The doctrines of Jacob Arminius rejected Calvinist predestination and supported the notion of free will, and had a profound effect on Wesleyan and Methodist theology.

re·mon·strant /ri mónstrənt/ *n.* PROTESTER somebody who remonstrates ■ *adj.* PROTESTING involved in or used for a protest (*formal*) [Early 17thC. From medieval Latin, the present participle stem of *remonstrare* (see REMONSTRATE).] —**re·mon·strant·ly** *adv.*

Re·mon·strant *n.* a Dutch dissenter and supporter of the Remonstrance of 1610

re·mon·strate /ri món stràyt/ (**-strat·ed, -strat·ing, -strates**) *vi.* to reason or argue forcefully with somebody about something [Late 16thC. From the past participle stem of medieval Latin *remonstrare* "to demonstrate," from *monstrare* "to show."] —**re·mon·stra·tion** /ri mòn stráysh'n, rèmmən-/ *n.* —**re·mon·stra·tive** /ri mónstrətiv/ *adj.* —**re·mon·stra·tive·ly** /-mónstrətivlee/ *adv.* —**re·mon·stra·tor** /ri món stràytər, rémmən-/ *n.*

WORD KEY: SYNONYMS

See Synonyms at ***object***.

rem·o·ra /rémmərə/ *n.* a bony salt-water fish with a suction disk on the top of its head that it uses to attach itself to a larger fish or a ship's hull. Family: Echeneidae. [Mid-16thC. From Latin, literally "hindrance"; from the belief that it slowed ships down when attaching itself to them.]

re·morse /ri máwrs/ *n.* **1.** GUILT a strong feeling of guilt and regret **2.** PITY compassion or pity (*archaic*) [14thC. Via Old French *remors* from, ultimately, Latin *remordere* "to torment," from *mordere* "to bite."] —**re·morse·ful** *adj.* —**re·morse·ful·ly** *adv.* —**re·morse·ful·ness** *n.*

re·morse·less /ri máwrsləss/ *adj.* **1.** WITHOUT COMPASSION showing no pity or compassion **2.** RELENTLESS continuing without lessening in strength or intensity —**re·morse·less·ly** *adv.* —**re·morse·less·ness** *n.*

re·mort·gage /ree máwrgij/ *vt.* (**-gaged, -gag·ing, -gag·es**) **1.** CHANGE MORTGAGE TERMS to revise the terms of a mortgage on a property **2.** MORTGAGE SOMETHING AGAIN to mortgage something again after the original mortgage has been paid off ■ *n.* NEW MORTGAGE a revised or second mortgage taken out on something

re·mote /ri mṓt/ *adj.* **1.** FAR AWAY situated a long way away **2.** OUT-OF-THE-WAY far away from civilization, society, or any other populated area **3.** DISTANTLY RELATED distantly related by blood, adoption, or marriage ○ *a remote relative on my father's side* **4.** LONG AGO distant in time **5.** SLIGHT faint or slight ○ *not the remotest possibility of her coming here* **6.** DISTANT distant in connection, relevance, or effect **7.** ALOOF distant in manner or behavior **8.** SEPARATED operated from a distance ■ *n.* **1.** HOUSEHOLD REMOTE CONTROL a remote control for an electronic device (*informal*) **2.** COMPUT COMPUTER FAR FROM CENTRAL COMPUTER a device or computer system that is situated at a distance from a central computer and that can be accessed via a network **3.** BROADCAST NOT FROM STUDIO a radio or television broadcast transmitted from outside the studio [15thC. From Latin *remotus*, the past participle of *removere* "to remove."] —**re·mote·ly** *adv.* —**re·mote·ness** *n.*

re·mote ac·cess *n.* access that is gained to a computer by means of a separate terminal

re·mote con·trol *n.* **1.** HOUSEHOLD HANDHELD CONTROL a handheld device used to operate a television set, videocassette recorder, or other electronic device from a distance **2.** OPERATION FROM DISTANCE the control of a device, system, or activity from a distance, usually by radio signals (*hyphenated when used before a noun*) ○ *a remote-control transmitter*

re·mote sen·sor *n.* an instrument, e.g., a radar or photographic device, that gathers information about the Earth or another astronomical body from an airborne platform or from space

ré·mou·lade /ràymoo la͡ad/ *n.* mayonnaise with herbs, mustard, capers, and pickles added, and sometimes chopped hard-boiled egg [Mid-19thC. From French, of uncertain origin: perhaps, ultimately, from Latin *armoracea* "wild radish."]

re·mount *v.* /ree mównt/ (**-mount·ed, -mount·ing, -mounts**) **1.** *vt.* PUT SOMETHING ON AGAIN to mount something again or anew **2.** *vti.* GET BACK INTO SADDLE to get back on a horse or bicycle ■ *n.* /rée mòwnt/ HORSE a replacement horse to ride

re·mov·a·ble /ri mo͞ovəb'l/ *adj.* designed in a way that allows it to be taken off and put back on again —**re·mov·a·bil·i·ty** /ri mo͞ovə bíllətee/ *n.* —**re·mov·a·ble·ness** /ri mo͞ovəb'lnəss/ *n.* —**re·mov·a·bly** /-mo͞ovəblee/ *adv.*

re·mov·al /ri mo͞ovəl/ *n.* **1.** REMOVING OF SOMETHING the taking away or getting rid of something **2.** CHANGE OF LOCATION a change in location, or in the place where somebody lives **3.** HR DISMISSAL dismissal from office or from a position

re·move /ri mo͞ov/ *v.* (**-moved, -mov·ing, -moves**) **1.** *vt.* TAKE SOMETHING AWAY to take something away from somebody or from a place **2.** *vti.* RELOCATE to transfer somebody or something to another place, or change a place of residence **3.** *vt.* TAKE SOMETHING OFF to take off an article of clothing **4.** *vt.* GET RID OF SOMETHING to make something go away or disappear ○ *a detergent that can remove stains even more quickly* **5.** *vt.* HR DISMISS SOMEBODY to dismiss somebody from office **6.** *vi.* DEPART to leave a place **7.** *vi.* BE REMOVED to go away or disappear ○ *The compound removed easily in solvent.* ■ *n.* **1.** DISTANCE the degree of distance or closeness between people or things ○ *He has only experienced war at one remove.* **2.** CHANGE OF LOCATION a change of residence or business (*formal*) **3.** FOOD INDIVIDUAL DISH IN MEAL a dish that is taken away during a formal meal to make way for another (*dated formal*)

re·moved /ri mo͞ovd/ *adj.* **1.** DISTANT separate or distant in space, time, or character from something or somebody else **2.** DISTANTLY RELATED separated from somebody to a specified degree by birth, adoption, or marriage ○ *a first cousin twice removed* —**re·mov·ed·ness** /ri mo͞ovdnəss/ *n.*

REM sleep *n.* a stage of sleep that recurs several times during the night and is marked by dreaming, rapid eye movements under closed lids, and elevated pulse rate and brain activity

re·mu·da /ri mo͞odə/ *n. Southwest U.S.* the herd of saddle horses from which ranch hands select their mounts for that day [Late 19thC. Via American Spanish, literally "change of horses," from, ultimately, Spanish *remudar* "to exchange."]

WORD KEY: REGIONAL NOTE

Remuda is an old-time common expression among working cattlemen in the Southwest and Rocky Mountain states. Alternative names are *caballado, cavvy,* and *caviard* (from Spanish *caballada*), and *string*.

re·mu·ner·ate /ri myo͞onə ràyt/ (**-at·ed, -at·ing, -ates**) *vt.* to pay somebody for goods or services, or compensate somebody for losses sustained or inconvenience caused in money [Early 16thC. Via Latin *remunerat-*, the past participle stem of *remunerari* "to reward," from, ultimately, *munus* "gift."] —**re·mu·ner·a·bil·i·ty** /ri myo͞onərə bíllətee/ *n.* —**re·mu·ner·a·ble** /ri myo͞onərəb'l/ *adj.* —**re·mu·ner·a·tor** /-ràytər/ *n.* —**re·mu·ner·a·to·ry** /-rə tàwree/ *adj.*

re·mu·ner·a·tion /ri myo͞onə ráysh'n/ *n.* **1.** PAY a payment or reward for goods or services or for losses sustained or inconvenience caused **2.** PAYING the paying or rewarding of somebody for goods or services or for losses sustained or inconvenience caused

WORD KEY: SYNONYMS

See Synonyms at ***wage***.

re·mu·ner·a·tive /ri myo͞onə ràytiv/ *adj.* paying somebody or rewarding somebody with money —**re·mu·ner·a·tive·ly** *adv.*

Re·mus /réeməss/ *n.* in Roman mythology, the son of Mars and twin brother of Romulus, the founder of the city of Rome. ◊ **Romulus**

ren·ais·sance /rénnə sa͡ans, rènnə sa͡ans, ri náyss'ns/, **re·nas·cence** /ri náss'ns, ri náyss'ns/ *n.* a rebirth or revival, e.g., of culture, skills, or learning forgotten or previously ignored [Late 19thC. From French, formed from *renaître* "to be reborn," from Latin *renasci* (see RENASCENT).]

Ren·ais·sance, Ren·as·cence *n.* **1.** END OF MIDDLE AGES the period in European history from about the 14th through 16th centuries regarded as marking the end of the Middle Ages and featuring major cultural and artistic change **2.** CLASSICAL REVIVAL the cultural and religious spirit that characterized the Renaissance, including the decline of Gothic architecture, the revival of classical culture, the beginnings of modern science, and geographical exploration. The new emphasis on individualism and secularism at this time led to the Reformation. ■ *adj.* **1.** RELATING TO THE RENAISSANCE relating to the history and culture of the Renaissance **2.** ARCHIT IN ARCHITECTURAL STYLE OF RENAISSANCE in the architectural style of classical revival that characterized the Renaissance

Renaissance: Detail of the bronze doors of the Baptistery, Florence, Italy, by Lorenzo Ghiberti

Ren·ais·sance man *n.* a man who has a wide range of accomplishments and intellectual interests

Ren·ais·sance wom·an *n.* a woman who has a wide range of accomplishments and intellectual interests

re·nal /rée n'l/ *adj.* relating to or affecting the kidneys [Mid-17thC. Via French from, ultimately, Latin *renes* "kidneys."]

re·nal clear·ance *n.* a measure of the removal of waste products from the blood by the kidneys, expressed as the volume of blood cleared of one particular substance in one minute

re·nal pel·vis *n.* the cavity in the kidney where urine collects before passing into the ureter

re·nas·cence *n.* = **renaissance**

Re·nas·cence *n.* HIST = **Renaissance**

re·nas·cent /ri náss'nt, -náys-/ *adj.* showing new life or activity [Early 18thC. From Latin, the present participle stem of *renasci* "to be reborn."]

re·na·ture /ree náychər/ (**-tured, -tur·ing, -tures**) *vt.* to restore the physical and chemical properties of an organic molecule, e.g., a denatured protein —**re·nat·u·ra·tion** /ree nàychə ráysh'n/ *n.*

ren·coun·ter /ren kówntər/ (**-tered, -ter·ing, -ters**) *n.* (*archaic*) **1.** HOSTILE MEETING a hostile meeting between adversaries **2.** CASUAL MEETING an unexpected casual meeting [Early 16thC. From French *rencontrer* "to have a (hostile) meeting," from *encontrer* (see ENCOUNTER).]

rend /rend/ (**rent** /rent/ *or* **rend·ed, rent** *or* **rend·ed, rend·ing, rends**) *v.* **1.** *vti.* TEAR SOMETHING APART to tear something apart violently, or be torn apart in this way ○ *The hurricane rent the flimsy houses in pieces.* **2.** *vt.* TEAR CLOTHES to tear or pull clothes or hair out of rage, frustration, or grief **3.** *vt.* WREST AWAY to tear or wrest something or somebody away **4.** *vt.* MAKE A PIERCING SOUND to disturb the silence or pierce the air with a loud sound ○ *a scream rent the air* **5.** *vt.* DISTRESS SOMEBODY to cause pain or distress to the heart or emotions [Old English. Ultimately, from a prehistoric Germanic word that is also the ancestor of English *rind*.]

WORD KEY: SYNONYMS

See Synonyms at ***tear***.

ren·der /réndər/ *v.* (**-dered, -der·ing, -ders**) **1.** *vt.* GIVE HELP to give help or provide a service (*formal*) **2.** *vt.* TRANSLATE SOMETHING to translate something into another language (*formal*) ○ *fragments of poetry, hastily rendered into English* **3.** *vt.* ARTS PORTRAY SOMETHING ARTISTICALLY to portray something or somebody in art, literature, music, or acting (*formal*) **4.** *vt.* GIVE DECISION to deliver a verdict or decision officially (*formal*) **5.** *vt.* SUBMIT SOMETHING FOR ACTION to submit something for consideration, approval, or payment (*formal*) ○ *render an invoice for payment* **6.** *vt.* PAY RESPECT to give what is due or appropriate to somebody who has authority or power (*formal*) ○ *"Render therefore unto Caesar the things which are Caesar's"* (Matthew 22:21, *The Bible*) **7.** *vt.* CAUSE TO BE to make somebody or something be or become something (*formal*) ○ *His actions rendered her powerless.* **8.** *vt.* PURIFY FAT to purify or extract something by melting, especially to heat solid fat slowly until as much liquid fat as possible has been extracted from it, leaving small crisp remains **9.** *vti.* GIVE UP SOMETHING to surrender something (*formal or literary*) **10.** *vt.* TRADE SOMETHING to give something in exchange for something else (*formal or literary*) **11.** *vt.* RETURN SOME-

THING to give something back (*formal or literary*) **12.** *vt.* BUILDING **COVER WALL WITH PLASTER** to cover masonry with a thin coat of plaster ■ *n.* **1.** BUILDING **COAT OF PLASTER** the first thin coat of plaster applied to masonry **2.** HIST **TENANT'S PAYMENT** a payment in goods, services, or money made by a tenant to a feudal lord [14thC. Via Old French *rendre* from, ultimately, Latin *reddere* "to give back," from *dare* "to give" (source of English *date*).] —**ren·der·a·ble** *adj.* —**ren·der·er** *n.*

ren·der·ing /réndəring/ *n.* **1.** ARTS **ARTISTIC PORTRAYAL** a portrayal of somebody or something in art, music, literature, or drama **2.** LITERAT **TRANSLATION** a translation of a literary work **3.** INDUST **HEATING ANIMAL REMAINS TO EXTRACT FAT** the process or business of separating fat from meat or animal remains by slow heating **4.** ARCHIT **ARCHITECT'S PERSPECTIVE DRAWING** an architect's representation of the inside and outside of a finished building, drawn in perspective **5.** BUILDING **COAT OF PLASTER** a coat of plaster applied to masonry

ren·dez·vous /ráan day voo, ráandə-/ *n.* (*plural* **-vous** /ráan day vooz, ráandə-/) **1. MEETING** a meeting arranged for a specified time and place **2. PLACE OF MEETING** the location of a prearranged meeting **3. PLACE WHERE PEOPLE MEET** a popular meeting place for people ■ *vti.* (**-voused, -voused** /ráan day vood, ráandə-/, **-vous·ing** /ráan day voo ing, ráandə-/, **-vous·es** /ráan day vooz, ráandə-/) **MEET SOMEBODY** to meet, or meet somebody, at a specified time and place, or cause this to happen [Late 16thC. From French, literally "present yourself."]

ren·di·tion /ren dísh'n/ *n.* **1.** ARTS **VERSION OF MUSICAL OR THEATRICAL PIECE** an interpretation or performance of a piece of music or drama **2.** LITERAT **TRANSLATION** a translation of a literary work **3. TRANSLATING** the act of translating something into another language (*formal*) **4. SURRENDER** a surrender (*archaic*) [Early 17thC. From French, formed from *rendre* (see RENDER).]

ren·dzi·na /ren jéenə/ *n.* a dark rich soil that develops beneath grassland above a layer of limestone or chalk [Early 20thC. From Polish *rędzina*.]

ren·e·gade /rénnə gàyd/ *n.* **1. TRAITOR** somebody who abandons previously held beliefs or loyalties **2. REBEL** somebody who chooses to live outside of the laws or coventions of a group [From Spanish *renegado*, from medieval Latin *renegatus*, from the past participle of Latin *renegare* (see RENEGE)]

re·nege /ri níg, -nég, -néeg/ (**-neged, -neg·ing, -neges**) *vi.* **1. BREAK A PROMISE** to go back on a promise or commitment **2.** CARDS **NOT FOLLOW SUIT** in cards, to fail to follow suit when able and required to do so [Mid-16thC. From medieval Latin *renegare* "to deny," from Latin *negare* (source of English *negate*).] —**re·nege** *n.* —**re·neg·er** *n.*

re·ne·go·ti·ate /reenə góshee àyt/ (**-at·ed, -at·ing, -ates**) *vti.* to negotiate an agreement again in order to change the terms

re·new /ri nóo/ (**-newed, -new·ing, -news**) *v.* **1.** *vti.* **RETURN TO DOING SOMETHING** to begin something again, or return to doing something **2.** *vti.* **EXTEND SOMETHING** to make something such as a contract, lease, or license effective for a longer period ○ *You'll need to renew your lease at the end of the year.* **3.** *vt.* **REPLACE SOMETHING WORN** to replace something that is worn out or no longer suitable for use **4.** *vt.* LIBRARIES **BORROW LIBRARY BOOK FOR LONGER** to extend the period of time a book or other item is borrowed from a library **5.** *vt.* **REPEAT PROMISE** to reaffirm or restate a promise or commitment ○ *renewed their marriage vows* **6.** *vt.* **GIVE SOMEBODY OR SOMETHING NEW ENERGY** to give somebody or something new energy, strength, or enthusiasm ○ *I felt quite renewed after the weekend.* **7.** *vt.* **GET NEW SUPPLY** to get a new supply of something **8.** *vt.* **MAKE SOMETHING NEW AGAIN** to make something new or as if new again —**re·new·ed·ly** /ri nóo ədlee/ *adv.* —**re·new·er** /ri nóo ər/ *n.*

WORD KEY: SYNONYMS

renew, recondition, renovate, restore, revamp

CORE MEANING: to improve the condition of something

renew to replace something worn or broken; **recondition** to bring something such as a machine or appliance back to a good condition or working state by means of repairs or replacement of parts; **renovate** to bring something such as a building back to a former better state by means of repairs, redecoration, or refurbishment; **restore** to bring something back to an original state after it has been damaged or fallen into a bad condition; **revamp** an informal word, to improve the appearance or condition of something.

re·new·a·ble /ri nóo əb'l/ *adj.* **1. ABLE TO BE RENEWED** capable of being renewed **2. NOT LIKELY TO RUN OUT** able to be sustained or renewed indefinitely, either because of inexhaustible supplies or because of new growth ○ *renewable resources* —**re·new·a·bil·i·ty** /ri nòo ə bíllətee/ *n.* —**re·new·a·bly** /ri nóo əblee/ *adv.*

re·new·a·ble re·source *n.* **1. RESOURCE THAT CAN BE SUSTAINED** a resource such as lumber that can be renewed as quickly as it is used up so that it can, in theory, last indefinitely, unlike mineral resources **2. NATURAL RESOURCE THAT REPLACES ITSELF** a natural resource that replaces itself unless overused, e.g., animal or plant life or fresh water **3. RENEWABLE FORM OF ENERGY** a source of energy, e.g., sunlight, wind, or tidal power, that can be used indefinitely to generate electricity because it does not involve burning fuel or damaging the environment

re·new·al /ri nóo əl/ *n.* **1. ACT OF RENEWING SOMETHING** the act or process of renewing something, or the state of being renewed **2. SOMETHING RENEWED** something that is being or has been renewed **3. URBAN REBUILDING** the rebuilding and revitalization of an urban area

ren·i·form /rénnə fàwrm, réenə-/ *adj.* shaped like or suggestive of a kidney

ren·in /rénnin/ *n.* an enzyme released by the kidneys that breaks down proteins and plays an important role in regulating blood pressure

ren·i·tent /rénnitənt, ri nít'nt/ *adj.* (*formal*) **1. RIGID IN STRUCTURE** resisting physical pressure, rather than being flexible or pliant **2. RIGID IN ATTITUDE** reluctant to have a change of mind or concede to others [Early 18thC. From Latin, the present participle stem of *reniti* "to struggle against."] —**ren·i·tence** *n.* —**ren·i·ten·cy** *n.*

Rennes /ren/ capital city of Ille-Vilaine Department, Brittany Region, western France. It is situated about 60 mi./97 km north of Nantes. Population: 203,533 (1990).

ren·net /rénnət/ *n.* **1.** ANAT **STOMACH LINING OF CALVES** the inner lining of the fourth stomach or abomasum of calves and other young ruminants **2.** FOOD, MANUF **SUBSTANCE FOR CURDLING MILK** a preparation made from rennet that contains the enzyme rennin and is used to curdle milk in making cheese **3. VEGETARIAN ALTERNATIVE TO RENNET** a substitute for rennet made from plants and used in the manufacture of cheese **4.** BIOCHEM = **rennin** [15thC. Origin uncertain: probably from an Old English word.]

ren·nin /rénnin/ *n.* an enzyme that is found in the gastric juice of the fourth stomach of calves and other young ruminants and is the constituent in rennet that curdles milk [Late 19thC. Formed from RENNET.]

Re·no /réenō/ city in western Nevada, located on the Truckee River, near Lake Tahoe in the Sierra Nevada Mountains. It is a resort and commercial center, and is home to the University of Nevada-Reno. Population: 145,029 (1994).

Re·no, Janet (*b.* 1938) U.S. attorney. She became the first female U.S. attorney general in 1993.

re·no·gram /réenə gràm/ *n.* **1. RECORD OF KIDNEY FUNCTION** a photographic record of kidney function, showing how quickly a radioactive substance injected into the bloodstream is removed when it passes through the kidneys **2. KIDNEY X-RAY** an X-ray image of a kidney [Early 20thC. *Reno-* formed from Latin *renes* "kidneys."]

Re·noir /rén wàar, rən wáar/, **Jean** (1894–1979) French movie director. The son of Pierre Auguste Renoir, he was a technical innovator known for the fluidity of his work. His greatest movie is *The Rules of the Game* (1939). He lived in the United States after 1941.

Re·noir, Pierre Auguste (1841–1919) French painter and sculptor. One of the leading Impressionists, he is noted for the harmony of his lines, the brilliance of his colors, and the intimate charm of his wide variety of subjects.

re·nounce /ri nówns/ *v.* (**-nounced, -nounc·ing, -nounc·es**) **1.** *vt.* **GIVE UP CLAIM TO SOMETHING** formally to give up a claim, title, position, or right **2.** *vt.* **REJECT BELIEF** to reject or disavow a belief or theory **3.** *vt.* **GIVE SOMETHING UP** to give up a habit, pursuit, or practice **4.** *vi.* CARDS **NOT FOLLOW SUIT** in cards, to be unable to follow suit and be forced to play a card from a different suit ■ *n.* CARDS **ACT OF NOT FOLLOWING SUIT** a failure to follow suit [14thC. Via French *renoncer* from

AKG London

Pierre Auguste Renoir

Latin *renuntiare* "to report," from *nuntiare* "to announce."] —**re·nounce·ment** *n.* —**re·nounc·er** *n.*

re·no·vas·cu·lar /reenō váskyələr/ *adj.* relating to the blood vessels of the kidneys [Mid-20thC. Coined from Latin *ren* "kidney" + VASCULAR.]

ren·o·vate /rénnə vàyt/ (**-vat·ed, -vat·ing, -vates**) *vt.* **1. MAKE SOMETHING LIKE NEW AGAIN** to restore something to good condition **2. RENEW** to give new vigor to somebody or something [15thC. From Latin *renovare*, from *novus* "new."] —**ren·o·va·tion** /rènnə váysh'n/ *n.* —**ren·o·va·tive** /rénnə vàytiv/ *adj.* —**ren·o·va·tor** /-vày tər/ *n.*

WORD KEY: SYNONYMS

See Synonyms at ***renew***.

re·nown /ri nówn/ *n.* widespread fame or honor [14thC. From Old French *renon*, from *renomer* "to make famous," from *nomer* "to name," from Latin *nominare* (source of English *nominate*).]

re·nowned /ri nównd/ *adj.* well known or famous, especially for a skill or expertise

rent[1] /rent/ *n.* **1. PAYMENT BY TENANT** a regular payment made by a tenant to an owner or landlord for the right to occupy or use property **2. PAYMENT TO USE EQUIPMENT** a regular payment to the owner for the right to use equipment or personal property **3. PROFIT FROM CULTIVATED LAND** the financial return from cultivated land after production costs have been deducted **4. INCOME OF LANDOWNERS** the portion of the national income that is earned by landowners **5.** ECON = **economic rent** ■ *vti.* (**rent·ed, rent·ing, rents**) **1. PAY TO USE SOMEBODY'S PROPERTY** to occupy somebody else's property or use somebody else's equipment in return for regular payments **2. ALLOW USE OF PROPERTY FOR PAYMENT** to allow somebody to occupy property or use equipment in return for regular payment [12thC. Via French *rente* from, ultimately, Latin *reddere* (see RENDER).]

WORD KEY: SYNONYMS

See Synonyms at ***hire***.

rent[2] /rent/ *n.* **1. HOLE MADE BY TEARING** an opening or hole made by tearing something **2. RELATIONSHIP RIFT** a rift in a relationship or breach in friendly relations [Mid-16thC. From the past participle of REND.]

rent[3] past tense, past participle of **rend**

rent·al /rént'l/ *n.* **1. RENT PAYMENT** the amount paid in rent **2. RENT INCOME** the amount received in rent **3. ACT OF RENTING SOMETHING** the renting of property or equipment **4. SOMETHING RENTABLE** something rented or available to rent ○ *The car is a rental.* **5. RENTING BUSINESS** a business that rents out property or equipment ■ *adj.* **1. FOR RENT** available to be rented **2. RELATING TO RENT** relating to property for rent or with rent payments

rent·al li·brar·y *n.* a library that lends books or other items for a fee

rent con·trol *n.* government regulation of the amount charged for housing rental and sometimes of eviction procedures —**rent-con·trolled** *adj.*

rent·er /réntər/ *n.* **1. SOMEBODY WHO RENTS FROM SOMEBODY** somebody who rents property or equipment from somebody else **2. SOMEBODY WHO RENTS TO SOMEBODY** somebody who rents property or equipment to somebody else

rent-free *adj.* **FREE OF CHARGE** not subject to rent payments ■ *adv.* **AT NO COST** without having to pay rent

ren·tier /rón tyày, roN tyáy/ *n.* somebody whose income is primarily from rent and securities [Mid-19thC. From French, formed from *rente* (see RENT[1]).]

rent strike *n.* an organized refusal by tenants to pay their rent

renumber /ree númbər/ *vt.* to number items according to a new sequence

re·nun·ci·a·tion /ri nùnsee áysh'n/ *n.* **1.** DENIAL OR REJECTION a denial or rejection of something, usually for moral or religious reasons **2.** DECLARATION GIVING SOMETHING UP an official declaration giving up a title, office, claim, or privilege —**re·nun·ci·a·to·ry** /-ə tàwree/ *adj.*

ren·voi /ren vóy/ *n.* the referral of a case or dispute from the country or state in which it arose to the laws of another [Late 19thC. From French, formed from *renvoyer* "to send back."]

Ren·wick /rén wik/, **James** (1818–95) U.S. architect. He designed the Smithsonian Institution in Washington, D.C. (1846), and St. Patrick's Cathedral in New York City (1858).

re·o·pen /ree ṓpən/ (**-pened, -pen·ing, -pens**) *vti.* **1.** OPEN AGAIN to open or open something once more **2.** START SOMETHING AGAIN to begin something again that was considered settled, or to be begun again **3.** OPEN SOMETHING CLOSED to open something that has been closed for a time, or to be opened after being closed for a long time

re·or·der /ree áwrdər/ *v.* (**-dered, -der·ing, -ders**) **1.** *vti.* REQUEST NEW SUPPLY to order the same goods again **2.** *vt.* REARRANGE SOMETHING to arrange something differently **3.** *vt.* ARRANGE SOMETHING AGAIN to put something in order again ■ *n.* ANOTHER ORDER another order for the same goods from the same supplier

re·or·gan·i·za·tion /ree àwrgəni záysh'n/ *n.* **1.** CHANGE IN SOMETHING a change in the way something is organized, arranged, or done **2.** BUSINESS RESTRUCTURING OF ORGANIZATION the thorough physical or financial restructuring of a business or organization —**re·or·gan·i·za·tion·al** *adj.*

re·or·gan·ize /ree áwrgə nìz/ (**-ized, -iz·ing, -iz·es**) *vti.* **1.** STRUCTURE AGAIN to organize something again **2.** STRUCTURE DIFFERENTLY to organize something differently —**re·or·gan·iz·er** *n.*

re·o·ri·ent /ree áwree ənt, ree áwree ènt/ (**-ent·ed, -ent·ing, -ents**), **re·o·ri·en·tate** /ree áwree ən tàyt, -áwree en-/ (**-tat·ed, -tat·ing, -tates**) *vti.* **1.** GET BEARINGS to find out where you are or where you are going after being lost **2.** ADAPT TO NEW SITUATION to change your behavior or ideas to deal with a new situation —**re·o·ri·en·ta·tion** /ree àwree ən táysh'n/ *n.*

re·o·vi·rus /reé ō vìrəss/ *n.* a virus that contains double-stranded RNA and is associated with various infections in plants and animals. Reoviruses are often found in people with breathing and stomach disorders. [Mid-20thC. *Reo-*, an acronym formed from *respiratory enteric orphan*.]

rep[1] /rep/, **repp** *n.* a ribbed or corded fabric made from silk, wool, rayon, or cotton [Mid-19thC. From French *reps*, of uncertain origin: probably from English *ribs*, plural of RIB.]

rep[2] /rep/ *n.* repertory theater (*informal*) [Early 20thC. Shortening.]

rep[3] /rep/ *n.* SALES REPRESENTATIVE a sales representative (*informal*) ■ *vi.* (**repped, rep·ping, reps**) BE A SALES REPRESENTATIVE to work as a sales representative (*informal*) [Late 19thC. Shortening.]

rep[4] /rep/ *n.* a reputation (*informal*) [Early 18thC. Shortening.]

rep[5] /rep/ *n.* a repetition of a fitness exercise (*informal*)

rep. *abbr.* **1.** repair **2.** report **3.** reported **4.** reporter **5.** reprint

Rep. *abbr.* **1.** Republic **2.** Republican **3.** Representative

re·pack·age /ree pákij/ (**-aged, -ag·ing, -ag·es**) *v.* **1.** PUT PRODUCT IN NEW PACKAGING to package a product in a new and differently designed container or wrapping **2.** *vt.* GIVE SOMEBODY NEW IMAGE to give somebody such as a politician or celebrity a new public image —**re·pack·ag·er** *n.*

re·paid *v.* past tense, past participle of **repay**

re·pair[1] /ri páir/ *vt.* (**-paired, -pair·ing, -pairs**) **1.** FIX OR MEND SOMETHING to restore something broken or damaged to good condition ○ *repair a flat tire* **2.** RESTORE RELATIONSHIP to restore a relationship or friendship by resolving a difficulty or disagreement **3.** ATONE FOR SOMETHING to make amends for something wrong ○ *How can I repair this wrong?* ■ *n.* **1.** JOB OF MENDING SOMETHING the process of mending something, or the job that is done in order to achieve this ○ *carry out repairs* **2.** REPAIRED ITEM something that has been repaired **3.** CONDITION OF SOMETHING the condition of something with respect to whether it needs mending or fixing ○ *an air conditioner no longer in good repair* [14thC. Via Old French *réparer* from Latin *reparare*, from *parare* "to make ready" (source of English *prepare*).] —**re·pair·a·ble** *adj.* —**re·pair·a·bil·i·ty** *n.* —**re·pair·er** *n.*

re·pair[2] /ri páir/ *vi.* (**-paired, -pair·ing, -pairs**) GO SOMEWHERE to go to a particular place (*formal*) ○ *repaired to the library after dinner* ■ *n.* (*archaic*) **1.** ACT OF GOING SOMEWHERE the act of going to a particular place **2.** MEETING PLACE a meeting place or a place where a person or animal is found [14thC. Via French *repairer* from late Latin *repatriare* (see REPATRIATE).]

re·pair·man /ri páir màn, ri páirmən/ (*plural* **-men** /-páir mèn, -páirmən/) *n.* a man whose job is making repairs to equipment or machinery

re·pair·per·son /ri páir pùrs'n/ (*plural* **-peo·ple** /-peép'l/ *or* **-per·sons**) *n.* a person whose job is making repairs to equipment or machinery

re·pair·wom·an /ri páir wŏŏmmən/ (*plural* **-en** /-wìmmin/) *n.* a woman whose job is making repairs to equipment or machinery

re·pand /ri pánd/ *adj.* BOT with a wavy edge ○ *a repand leaf* [Mid-18thC. Via Latin *repandus*, literally "curving back," from, ultimately, *pandere*, "to become curved."]

rep·a·ra·ble /réppərəb'l/ *adj.* able to be repaired, recovered, or put right —**rep·a·ra·bil·i·ty** /rèppərə bíllətee/ *n.* —**rep·a·ra·bly** /réppərəblee/ *adv.*

rep·a·ra·tion /rèppə ráysh'n/ *n.* **1.** AMENDS compensation for a wrong, or something that is done to achieve this **2.** REPAIR restoration of something to good condition, or the process of doing this (*formal*) ■ **rep·a·ra·tions** *npl.* COMPENSATION FOR WAR compensation demanded of a defeated nation by the victor in a war, especially that demanded of Germany by the Treaty of Versailles after World War I —**re·par·a·tive** /ri páirətiv/ *adj.* —**re·par·a·to·ry** /-tàwree/ *adj.*

rep·ar·tee /rèppər teé, -táy, -paar-/ *n.* **1.** WITTY TALK conversation consisting of witty remarks **2.** WIT skill in making witty remarks or conversation **3.** WITTY REMARK a witty remark or reply [Mid-17thC. From French *repartie*, from *repartir*, literally "to set out again," from *partir* (see PART).]

re·par·ti·tion /reè paar tísh'n/ *n.* **1.** DISTRIBUTION distribution or division of something **2.** DIVIDING OF SOMETHING AGAIN the act of dividing or distributing something again, either in the same way or differently ■ *vt.* (**-tioned, -tion·ing, -tions**) DIVIDE SOMETHING UP AGAIN to divide something up again, either in the same way or differently

re·past /ri pást/ *n.* FOOD a meal, or the food eaten at a meal (*archaic or literary*) ■ *vi.* (**-past·ed, -past·ing, -pasts**) EAT to eat or feast on food (*formal or literary*) [14thC. From Old French, formed from *repaistre* "to feed," from, ultimately, Latin *pascere* (source of English *pasture*).]

re·pa·tri·ate *vt.* /ree páytree àyt/ (**-at·ed, -at·ing, -ates**) **1.** SEND SOMEBODY BACK to send somebody back to his or her country of birth, the country of which he or she is a citizen, or the country from which he or she arrived **2.** FIN SEND BACK MONEY to send money that has been invested abroad back to its country of origin ■ *n.* /ree páytree ət, ree páytree àyt/ SOMEBODY REPATRIATED somebody who has been repatriated [Early 17thC. From Latin *repatriare* "to go back home," from *patria* "homeland."] —**re·pa·tri·a·tion** /ree pàytree áysh'n/ *n.*

re·pay /ri páy/ (**-paid** /ri páyd/, **-paid, -pay·ing, -pays**) *vt.* **1.** PAY BACK MONEY TO SOMEBODY to pay back money that is owed to somebody **2.** RETURN FAVOR to reward somebody for that person's effort, aid, or success **3.** RETURN IN KIND to return something in kind —**re·pay·a·ble** *adj.*

re·pay·ment /ri páymənt/ *n.* **1.** SUM PAID BACK TO LENDER a sum of money, especially one of a series of instalments, paid back by a borrower to a lender **2.** REPAYING OF SOMETHING the act or an instance of repaying something

re·peal /ri peél/ *vt.* (**-pealed, -peal·ing, -peals**) **1.** LAW UNDO LAW to officially revoke or abolish something such as a law **2.** RECALL FROM EXILE to recall somebody from exile (*archaic*) ■ *n.* LAW ABOLITION OF LAW the act of repealing something such as a law [14thC. From Anglo-Norman *repeler*, a variant of Old French *rapeler*, from *re-* "again, back," + *apeler* (see APPEAL).] —**re·peal·a·ble** *adj.* —**re·peal·er** *n.*

re·peat *v.* /ri peét/ (**-peat·ed, -peat·ing, -peats**) **1.** *vt.* SAY SOMETHING AGAIN to say or write something again **2.** *vti.* DO OR UNDERGO SOMETHING AGAIN to do, produce, or experience something again or several times ○ *She repeated the exercises every day.* **3.** *vti.* ECHO SOMEBODY'S WORDS to say again what somebody else has said **4.** *vt.* TELL WHAT HAS BEEN HEARD to tell another person something that was told to you, especially when it was done in confidence ○ *I'll tell you, but you mustn't repeat it to anyone else.* **5.** *vt.* SAY SOMETHING MEMORIZED to recite something that has been learned **6.** *vr.* SAY THE SAME THING OVER AGAIN to do or say something again, especially more than once ○ *You get tired of repeating yourself after a while.* **7.** *vr.* HAPPEN AGAIN AS BEFORE to happen again in the same way as previously **8.** *vti.* BROADCAST BROADCAST AGAIN to broadcast a television or radio program again, or be broadcast again **9.** *vi.* FOOD BE TASTED AGAIN to be tasted again after having been eaten, through wind or partial regurgitation (*informal*) ○ *Those spicy meatballs are repeating on me.* ■ *n.* /reé peét/ **1.** RECURRING EVENT OR SITUATION an event or situation that is the same as a previous one **2.** BROADCAST SOMETHING SHOWN AGAIN something that is broadcast, shown, or performed again **3.** MUSIC RECURRING MUSICAL PASSAGE OR ITS NOTATION a passage of music played again within a single piece, or the notation indicating that this is to be done. If a passage is to be repeated, the notation "||:" or ":||" is placed before or after it in a musical score. **4.** UNIFORMLY REPRODUCED PATTERN a pattern reproduced uniformly across a surface ○ *upholstery fabric with a large floral repeat* **5.** ACT OF REORDERING SOMETHING a reorder of the same goods or by the same customer [14thC. Via French *répéter* from Latin *repetere*, literally "to demand again," from *petere* "to demand" (source of English *petition*).] —**re·peat·a·bil·i·ty** /ri peètə bíllətee/ *n.* —**re·peat·a·ble** /ri peétəb'l/ *adj.*

re·peat·ed /ri peétəd/ *adj.* happening or done again and again

re·peat·ed·ly /ri peétədlee/ *adv.* again and again, or on several occasions

re·peat·er /ri peétər/ *n.* **1.** SOMEBODY OR SOMETHING REPEATING somebody who or something that repeats **2.** ARMS GUN FIRING SEVERAL SHOTS WITHOUT RELOADING a firearm such as a rifle with a magazine that can fire several shots before it has to be reloaded **3.** TIME TIMEPIECE THAT REPEATS CHIMES a clock or watch that can be made to repeat its latest chime when somebody presses a spring **4.** EDUC STUDENT MADE TO REPEAT STUDIES a student required to repeat a course or grade after failing it **5.** CRIMINOL RECIDIVIST a repeat offender **6.** ELEC ENG DEVICE FOR AMPLIFYING SIGNALS an electrical device that boosts and amplifies incoming communications signals and retransmits them. Such boosting is needed as the quality and strength of the analog signal decays over distance.

re·peat·ing dec·i·mal *n.* a decimal number in which one or more digits recur indefinitely after the decimal point, e.g., 3.77777... or 8.691691691...

re·peat·ing fire·arm *n.* = **repeater** *n.* **2**

re·peat pre·scrip·tion *n. U.K., Can* a prescription for a regularly needed medicine that has been prescribed before and can be renewed without the doctor having to see the patient

re·pe·chage /rèppə shaázh/ *n.* a heat within a competition such as a fencing, rowing, or cycling competition, during which runners-up in earlier heats have a final chance to qualify for the next round [Early 20thC. From French, from *repêcher*, literally "to fish out."]

re·pel /ri pél/ (**-pelled, -pel·ling, -pels**) *v.* **1.** *vt.* MIL RESIST ATTACK to ward off or force back an attack or invasion **2.** *vt.* KEEP SOMETHING AWAY to ward something off or keep something away ○ *a cream that is effective in repelling mosquitoes* **3.** *vti.* FAIL TO MIX to fail to mix or blend with something else ○ *Oil and water repel each other.* **4.** *vti.* PHYS EXERT OPPOSING FORCE to exert a force that tends to push something away ○ *Particles of like charge repel each other.* **5.** *vt.* SPURN SOMEBODY OR SOMETHING to reject or refuse to accept something or somebody **6.** *vti.* CAUSE GREAT DISTASTE to make somebody feel intense aversion, disgust, or revulsion [15thC. Via Old French *repeler* from Latin *repellere*, literally "to drive back," from *pellere* "to drive" (source of English *pulse*).] —**re·pel·ler** *n.*

WORD KEY: USAGE

See Usage note at ***repulse***.

re·pel·lent /ri péllənt/, **re·pel·lant** *adj.* **1.** RESISTANT TO SOMETHING resistant or impervious to something (*often used in combination*) ○ *water-repellent material* **2.** CAUSING DISGUST making somebody feel intense dislike, disgust, or revulsion **3.** PUSHING AWAY pushing something away or driving something back ■ *n.* **1.** SOMETHING THAT REPELS INSECTS a substance that drives away insects **2.** SUBSTANCE THAT RESISTS SOMETHING HARMFUL a substance that is applied to a surface of something to resist water, mold, or mildew —**re·pel·lence** *n.* —**re·pel·lent·ly** *adv.*

WORD KEY: USAGE

repellent or **repulsive**? Both words mean "causing disgust or revulsion," but ***repulsive*** is rather stronger in effect than ***repellent***, corresponding to the difference in strength between the root verbs *repulse* and *repel*. ***Repellent*** is common in combinations such as *insect-repellent* and *water-repellent*, denoting substances that repel or resist the things specified. ***Repulsive*** does not have a literal meaning corresponding to this, except in technical use in physics.

WORD KEY: USAGE

Spelling trap Note that the adjective is usually spelled *-ent* and not *-ant*. The *-ant* form is somewhat more common for the noun, but *-ent* is still preferable.

re·pent[1] /ri pént/ (**-pent·ed, -pent·ing, -pents**) *vti.* **1.** BE SORRY ABOUT to recognize the wrong in something you have done and be sorry about it **2.** RELIG CHANGE WAYS to feel regret about a sin or past actions and change your ways or habits [13thC. From French *repentir*, from *pentir*, from, ultimately, Latin *paenitere* (source also of English *penitent*).] —**re·pent·er** *n.*

re·pent[2] /reépənt/ *adj.* growing or lying along the ground [Mid-17thC. From Latin *repent-*, the present participle stem of *repere* "to creep" (source also of English *reptile*).]

re·pen·tance /ri pént'ns/ *n.* a feeling of regret or contrition for having done something wrong

re·pen·tant /ri péntənt/ *adj.* feeling or showing regret about having done something wrong —**re·pen·tant·ly** *adv.*

re·per·cus·sion /reèpər kúsh'n/ *n.* **1.** RESULT OF ACTION something, especially an unforeseen problem, that results from an action (*often used in the plural*) **2.** REBOUND the rebounding of a force after impact **3.** PHYS REFLECTION the reflection of light or sound **4.** MUSIC POINT OF REAPPEARANCE IN FUGUE in a fugue, the return of the theme after an episode [Mid-16thC. Directly or via French from Latin *repercuss-*, the past participle stem of *repercutere*, literally "to strike back through," from *percutere* "to strike through."] —**re·per·cus·sive** *adj.*

rep·er·toire /réppər twaàr/ *n.* **1.** MATERIAL AVAILABLE FOR PERFORMANCE a stock of musical or dramatic material that is known and can be performed **2.** BODY OF ARTISTIC WORKS the entire body of works in a specific area of the arts **3.** RANGE OF RESOURCES THAT SOMEBODY HAS the range of techniques, abilities, or skills that somebody or something has ○ *the surgeon's repertoire* [Mid-19thC. Via French from late Latin *repertorium* (see REPERTORY).] ◇ **in repertoire** used to refer to performances of different plays or ballets given on different days

rep·er·to·ry /réppər tàwree/ (*plural* **-ries**) *n.* **1.** THEATER = **stock 2.** THEATER GROUP OR THEATER USING STOCK SYSTEM a theater or company that uses the stock system **3.** ARTS = **repertoire** *n.* 1, **repertoire** *n.* 2 **4.** COLLECTION OF AVAILABLE THINGS a store or stock of available items ○ *a comedian with a large repertory of jokes* [Late 16thC. From late Latin *repertorium* "inventory," from, ultimately, Latin *reperire* "to get completely," from *parire* "to get" (source of English *parent*).] —**rep·er·to·ri·al** /réppər táwree əl/ *adj.*

rep·er·to·ry com·pa·ny *n.* = **stock company**

rep·e·tend /réppə tènd/ *n.* **1.** MATH REPEATED PART OF DECIMAL the part of a repeating decimal that is repeated infinitely, e.g., "37" in "0.373737" **2.** SOMETHING REPEATED something that is repeated [Early 18thC. From Latin *reperendum* "thing to be repeated," from *repetere* (see REPEAT).]

ré·pé·ti·teur /ri pèttee túr/ *n.* a musician in an opera company who coaches the singers and accompanies them on the piano in rehearsal [Mid-20thC. From French, literally "somebody who repeats."]

rep·e·ti·tion /rèppə tísh'n/ *n.* **1.** REPEATING OF SOMETHING an act of doing something again **2.** SOMETHING THE SAME AS BEFORE an event or situation that is the same as one that happened previously **3.** PROCEDURE OF STATING SOMETHING AGAIN the act or process of saying or writing something again **4.** REPEATED WORDS something that is repeated, especially unnecessary words **5.** REPLICA a replica or duplicate of something (*archaic*) [Early 16thC. Via French from, ultimately, Latin *repetere* (see REPEAT).]

rep·e·ti·tious /rèppə tíshəss/ *adj.* full of things that are said or written over and over again, especially in an unnecessary or tiresome way —**rep·e·ti·tious·ly** *adv.* —**rep·e·ti·tious·ness** *n.*

re·pet·i·tive /ri péttitiv/ *adj.* full of or involving things that are done over and over again ○ *a boring, repetitive task* —**re·pet·i·tive·ly** *adv.* —**re·pet·i·tive·ness** *n.*

re·pet·i·tive strain in·ju·ry, **re·pet·i·tive stress in·ju·ry** *n.* full form of **RSI**

re·phrase /ree fráyz/ (**-phrased, -phras·ing, -phras·es**) *vt.* to say or write something again using different words as a clarification or for variety

re·pine /ri pín/ (**-pined, -pin·ing, -pines**) *vi.* to feel dissatisfied or fretful about something and complain or grumble about it (*formal*) [Early 16thC. Formed from PINE[2] "to fret," on the model of *repent*.] —**re·pin·er** *n.*

re·place /ri pláyss/ (**-placed, -plac·ing, -plac·es**) *vt.* **1.** SUBSTITUTE FOR SOMETHING to take the place of or substitute for somebody or something ○ *The new ways rapidly replaced the old.* **2.** SUPPLANT SOMEBODY OR SOMETHING to fill the place of something or somebody with something or somebody else ○ *You can be replaced.* **3.** PUT SOMETHING IN ANOTHER'S PLACE to provide or find a substitute for something ○ *can't afford to replace his car* **4.** PUT SOMETHING BACK IN ITS PLACE to put an object back in its usual place ○ *She replaced the receiver slowly.* [Late 16thC. Formed from PLACE "to put," on the model of French *remplacer*.] —**re·place·a·ble** *adj.* —**re·plac·er** *n.*

WORD KEY: USAGE

See Usage note at ***substitute***.

re·place·ment /ri pláyssmənt/ *n.* **1.** SUBSTITUTION OF SOMEBODY OR SOMETHING the act or process of taking the place of or substituting for somebody or something **2.** SUBSTITUTE somebody who or something that replaces another **3.** CHEM CHANGE OF ONE MINERAL TO ANOTHER the partial or complete transformation of one mineral into another in response to changing conditions such as the presence of water **4.** MIL SOMEBODY FILLING MILITARY VACANCY somebody who fills a vacancy in a military force

re·plant /ree plánt/ (**-plant·ed, -plant·ing, -plants**) *vt.* **1.** GARDENING TRANSFER PLANT TO NEW PLACE to transfer a plant or part of a plant into new soil or a new area **2.** GARDENING PROVIDE WITH NEW PLANTS to put new plants in a place or container to replace previous plants ○ *replant the flower boxes every spring* **3.** MED, DENT REATTACH OR REINSERT BODY PART to reattach or reinsert a severed body part such as a limb or tooth —**re·plan·ta·tion** /reè plan táysh'n/ *n.*

re·play *vt.* /ree pláy/ (**-played, -play·ing, -plays**) **1.** SPORTS, GAME PLAY MATCH AGAIN to play a game, match, or contest again **2.** RECORDING PLAY RECORDING AGAIN to play again something that has been recorded on tape, video, or film ■ *n.* /reé plày/ **1.** SPORTS, GAME CONTEST PLAYED AGAIN a contest, match, or game that is played again **2.** RECORDING RECORDED MATERIAL REPLAYED something recorded on tape, video, or film that is played again **3.** REPEAT OF PREVIOUS EVENT an event that repeats or appears to repeat something in the past ○ *The latest business failure was a replay of the previous one.*

re·plen·ish /ri plénnish/ (**-ished, -ish·ing, -ish·es**) *vt.* **1.** REPLACE WITH NEW ITEMS to restock depleted items or material ○ *time for the campers to replenish their supplies* **2.** NOURISH SOMEBODY OR SOMETHING to fill somebody or something with needed energy or nourishment **3.** FURNISH NEW FUEL FOR FIRE to resupply a fire with fuel [Early 17thC. From Old French *repleniss-*, the stem of *replenir*, literally "to fill again," from *plenir* "to fill," from, ultimately, Latin *plenus* (source of English *full*).] —**re·plen·ish·er** *n.* —**re·plen·ish·ment** *n.*

re·plete /ri pleét/ *adj.* **1.** AMPLY OR FULLY EQUIPPED amply, completely, or fully supplied with something ○ *a kitchen replete with all the latest gadgets* **2.** FULL having eaten enough to be fully satisfied [14thC. Directly or via French from Latin *repletus*, the past participle of *replere*, literally "to fill up," from *plere* "to fill" (source of English *complete*).] —**re·plete·ness** *n.*

re·ple·tion /ri pleésh'n/ *n.* **1.** STATE OF BEING GORGED a condition of being overfull after eating too much **2.** STATE OF BEING SATISFIED the condition of being fully satisfied

re·plev·in /ri plévvin/ *n.* ACTION BY CLAIMANT TO RECOVER GOODS an act or writ to recover goods by somebody who claims to own them and who promises to have the claim later tested in court ■ *vt.* (**-ined, -in·ing, -ins**), *n.* = **replevy** *n.* [14thC. From Anglo-Norman, from *replevir* (see REPLEVY).]

re·plev·y /ri plévvee/ *vt.* (**-ied, -y·ing, -ies**) SEIZE CLAIMED GOODS BEFORE LEGAL TEST to seize goods on the grounds of ownership after promising to test the claim in court ■ *n.* (*plural* **-ies**) SEIZURE OF CLAIMED GOODS a seizure of claimed goods after a promise that the claim will be tested in court later [Late 16thC. Via Anglo-Norman *replevir*, literally "to recover thoroughly," from *plevir* "to recover." Ultimately from a prehistoric Germanic word (ancestor also of English *pledge*).] —**re·plev·i·a·ble** *adj.*

rep·li·ca /répplikə/ *n.* **1.** FAITHFUL COPY OF SOMETHING an accurate reproduction of an object **2.** ARTS FAITHFUL COPY OF ARTWORK a scrupulous copy of a work of art, especially one made, authorized, or supervised by the original artist [Early 19thC. Via Italian, "repeat," from, ultimately, Latin *replicare* (see REPLICATE).]

rep·li·cant /répplikənt/ *n.* an imaginary being, especially in science fiction, that has been constructed from organic and computerized components to look like a human being. ◊ **cyborg**

rep·li·case /réppli kàyss, -kàyz/ *n.* a polymerase enzyme, especially one that catalyzes the synthesis of a complementary RNA molecule from a template of an existing RNA strand, required for the replication of RNA viruses [Mid-20thC. Formed from REPLICATE.]

rep·li·cate *v.* /réppli kàyt/ (**-cat·ed, -cat·ing, -cates**) **1.** *vt.* DO SOMETHING AGAIN to do something again or copy something **2.** *vi.* BE DONE AGAIN to undergo a repetition or reproduction **3.** *vt.* BIOL COPY CELLULAR OR GENETIC MATERIAL to reproduce exactly an organism, genetic material, or a cell ■ *adj.* /répplikət/ BOT BENT BACK folded back on itself [Mid-16thC. From Latin *replicare*, literally "to fold back" (source also of English *reply*), from *plicare* "to fold." The underlying idea is of "going over again."] —**rep·li·ca·tive** /-kàytiv/ *adj.*

WORD KEY: SYNONYMS

See Synonyms at ***copy***.

rep·li·ca·tion /rèppli káysh'n/ *n.* **1.** PROCESS OF REPEATING the process of repeating, duplicating, or reproducing something **2.** BIOL MAKING OF CELLULAR OR GENETIC COPY the production of exact copies of molecules, genetic material, or cells **3.** LAW REPLY a reply (*dated*) **4.** BOT FOLD a fold or folding back **5.** REPLY TO ANSWER something said in reply to an answer (*archaic*)

rep·li·con /réppli kòn/ *n.* a segment of DNA or RNA that replicates itself as a unit, distinct from adjacent segments in a chromosome or other genetic element [Mid-20thC. Coined from REPLICATION + ON.]

re·ply /ri plí/ *v.* (**-plied, -ply·ing, -plies**) **1.** *vti.* RESPOND TO WHAT SOMEBODY SAYS to say or write something in response to what somebody else has said or written ○ *replied that she wouldn't be available to take the job* **2.** *vi.* RESPOND WITH ACTION OR GESTURE to respond to somebody's action with a countering action or gesture **3.** *vi.* LAW ANSWER DEFENDANT'S PLEA to speak in response to the plea of a defendant **4.** *vi.* ECHO to echo or return a sound ■ *n.* (*plural* **-plies**) **1.** SPOKEN OR WRITTEN RESPONSE something said or written as a response to something else **2.** ACTION PERFORMED AS RESPONSE something done as a response to somebody else's action ○ *Her only reply was to turn on her heel and leave.* **3.** LAW ANSWER TO DEFENDANT'S PLEA a statement made in response to the plea of a defendant [14thC. Via Old French *replier* from Latin *replicare* (see REPLICATE).] —**re·pli·er** *n.*

WORD KEY: SYNONYMS

See Synonyms at ***answer***.

re·po /reé pò/ (*plural* **-pos**) *n.* (*informal*) **1.** PROPERTY SUBJECT TO REPOSSESSION property that is repossessed because payments have not been made wholly or in part **2.** REPURCHASE AGREEMENT a repurchase agreement for something [Late 20thC. Shortening of REPOSSESS.]

re·point /ree póynt/ (**-point·ed, -point·ing, -points**) *vt.* to repair a brick wall by putting new mortar or cement between the bricks

re·port /ri páwrt/ *v.* (**-port·ed, -port·ing, -ports**) **1.** *vti.* TELL ABOUT WHAT HAPPENED to give information about something that has happened ○ *reported that negotiations were proceeding slowly* **2.** *vti.* BROADCAST, PRESS TELL PEOPLE NEWS USING MEDIA to find out facts and tell people about them in print or a broadcast **3.** *vt.* INFORM AUTHORITIES ABOUT SOMETHING OR SOMEBODY to inform somebody in authority about something that has happened, especially a crime or an accident, or about somebody who has done something wrong ○ *reported him missing two days ago* ○ *reported the break-in to the police* **4.** *vti.* TELL ABOUT RESEARCH OR INVESTIGATION to give detailed information about research or an investigation ○ *The committee will report their findings early next week.* **5.** *vti.* MAKE FULL OFFICIAL STATEMENT to make a formal statement or account of something **6.** *vt.* LAW RECORD COURT PROCEEDINGS to record the proceedings of a court **7.** *vi.* INFORM ABOUT ARRIVAL to let somebody know you have arrived ○ *Guests should report to reception on arrival.* **8.** *vi.* BE UNDER SOMEBODY'S AUTHORITY to be subordinate and responsible to somebody or something ○ *You'll be reporting to me from now on.* ■ *n.* **1.** ACCOUNT OF SOMETHING an account of an event, situation, or episode **2.** PRESS, BROADCAST NEWS ITEM OR BROADCAST an account of news presented by a journalist **3.** DOCUMENT GIVING INFORMATION ABOUT SOMETHING a document that gives information about an investigation or a piece of research, often put together by a group of people working together **4.** UNCONFIRMED ACCOUNT OF SOMETHING a widely-known account of something that may be true but has not been confirmed ○ *Report had it that the company was approaching bankruptcy.* **5.** BUSINESS PERIODIC STATEMENT OF COMPANY'S FINANCES a detailed periodic account of a company's activities, financial condition, and prospects that is made available to shareholders and investors ○ *a quarterly report* **6.** *U.K.* EDUC = **report card** **7.** LAW SHARP LOUD NOISE a very sharp loud noise, especially that of an explosion or gunshot **8.** REPUTATION reputation or character ■ **re·ports** *npl.* LAW ACCOUNTS OF COURT CASES written accounts of a court's adjudication, summarizing arguments and findings [14thC. Via Old French from Latin *reportare*, literally "to carry back," from *portare* "to carry." The underlying idea is of "bringing back news."] —**re·port·a·ble** *adj.*

re·port·age /ri páwrtij/ *n.* **1.** PROCESS OF TELLING NEWS the use of print and electronic media to inform people about news and current events **2.** THINGS REPORTED a body of reported news **3.** WAY OF GIVING NEWS a particular way of gathering and presenting news [Late 19thC. Formed from REPORT, in the model of French *reportage*.]

re·port card *n.* a record of a child's performance at school over a specified period, prepared by teachers and given to the child's parents

re·port·ed·ly /ri páwrtədlee/ *adv.* according to an unconfirmed report ○ *Reportedly he lost all his money.*

re·port·ed speech *n.* = **indirect speech**

re·port·er /ri páwrtər/ *n.* **1.** BROADCAST, PRESS SOMEBODY WHO REPORTS NEWS somebody whose job is to find out facts and use the print or broadcast media to tell people about them **2.** SOMEBODY WHO REPORTS somebody who makes a report of any kind **3.** LAW COMPILER OF COURT PROCEEDINGS somebody who compiles summarized records of court proceeding **4.** POL SOMEBODY WHO COMPILES LEGISLATIVE PROCEEDINGS an official who compiles the proceedings of a legislature —**rep·or·to·ri·al** /rèppər táwree əl, reépər-/ *adj.* —**rep·or·to·ri·al·ly** /rèppər táwree əlee, reéppər-/ *adv.*

re·pose[1] /ri pṓz/ *n.* **1.** REST a state of rest or inactivity **2.** TRANQUILITY a condition of peacefulness and tranquility, e.g., in a place **3.** PEACE OF MIND freedom from troubles or stress **4.** COMPOSURE calmness and composure of manner ■ *v.* (**-posed, -pos·ing, -pos·es**) (*formal*) **1.** *vti.* LIE RESTING to lie or lay something at rest **2.** *vi.* BE DEAD to lie dead (*used euphemistically*) **3.** *vi.* LIE RESTING ON TOP OF SOMETHING to lie while resting on or supported by something **4.** *vr.* SETTLE SELF AT REST to settle yourself in a relaxed or restful position **5.** *vi.* TAKE SUPPORT FROM SOMETHING to be supported or based on something ○ *Your argument reposes on false analogies.* [15thC. Via French *reposer* from Latin *repausare*, literally "to rest completely," from *pausare* "to rest" (source of English *pause*).] —**re·pos·al** *n.* —**re·pos·er** *n.*

re·pose[2] /ri pṓz/ (**-posed, -pos·ing, -pos·es**) *vt.* to place faith, confidence, or trust in somebody or something (*formal*) ○ *reposed a great deal of confidence in him* [Mid-16thC. Formed from Latin *repos-*, the stem of *reponere*, literally "to place again," from *ponere* "to place" (source of English *position*).]

re·pose·ful /ri pṓzfəl/ *adj.* showing or giving rise to restfulness or calm —**re·pose·ful·ly** *adv.* —**re·pose·ful·ness** *n.*

re·pos·it /ri pózzit/ (**-it·ed, -it·ing, -its**) *vt.* to put or store something somewhere (*formal*) [Mid-17thC. From Latin *reposit-*, the past participle stem of *reponere* (see REPOSE[2]).]

re·po·si·tion /reèpə zísh'n/ (**-tioned, -tion·ing, -tions**) *vt.* **1.** PUT SOMETHING SOMEWHERE DIFFERENT to put something in a new position **2.** MARKETING CHANGE MARKETING OF SOMETHING to change the marketing strategy of a company or product so as to have a wider or different appeal

re·pos·i·to·ry /ri pózzə tàwree/ (*plural* **-ries**) *n.* **1.** PLACE OR RECEPTACLE FOR STORAGE a place or container in which something is stored **2.** SOMEBODY WITH EXTENSIVE KNOWLEDGE somebody with, or something such as a book that contains, extensive detailed knowledge of something ○ *She was a repository of information about the history of the island.* **3.** SOMEBODY ENTRUSTED WITH SOMETHING somebody in whom something is confided **4.** *U.K.* COMM WAREHOUSE FOR COMMODITIES a place where goods are stored prior to sale **5.** TOMB a burial vault or sepulcher

re·pos·sess /reèpə zéss/ (**-sessed, -sess·ing, -sess·es**) *vt.* to take back goods or property from a buyer who has failed to keep up payments on them —**re·pos·ses·sion** *n.* —**re·pos·ses·sor** *n.*

re·pous·sé /rə poo sáy/ *adj.* **1.** FORMING PATTERN IN RELIEF formed as a raised pattern on a thin piece of metal by having been hammered through from the reverse side **2.** DECORATED WITH HAMMERED PATTERN decorated with a raised pattern that has been hammered through from the reverse side ■ *n.* **1.** HAMMERED DESIGN ON METAL a raised design on a piece of metal made by hammering the design through from the reverse side **2.** TECHNIQUE OF HAMMERING A DESIGN the technique of producing a raised design on a thin piece of metal by hammering it through from the reverse side [Mid-19thC. From French, the past participle of *repousser*, literally "to push back," from *pousser* "to push" (source of English *push*).]

repp *n.* = **rep**[1]

repr. *abbr.* **1.** representative **2.** represented **3.** representing **4.** reprint

rep·re·hend /rèppri hénd/ (**-hend·ed, -hend·ing, -hends**) *vt.* to criticize or reprove somebody or something [14thC. From Latin *reprehendere*, literally "to seize again," from *prehendere* "to seize" (source of English *prison*).] —**rep·re·hend·a·ble** *adj.* —**rep·re·hen·der** *n.*

rep·re·hen·si·ble /rèppri hénssəb'l/ *adj.* highly unacceptable and deserving censure [14thC. From late Latin *reprehensibilis*, from, ultimately, *reprehendere* (see REPREHEND).] —**rep·re·hen·si·bil·i·ty** /rèppri henssə bíllətee/ *n.* —**rep·re·hen·si·bly** /rèppri hénsəblee/ *adv.*

rep·re·hen·sion /rèppri hénshən/ *n.* reproof or criticism for wrongdoing [14thC. Formed from Latin *reprehension-*, the past participle stem of *reprehendere* (see REPREHEND).] —**rep·re·hen·sive** *adj.* —**rep·re·hen·sive·ly** *adv.*

rep·re·sent /rèppri zént/ (**-sent·ed, -sent·ing, -sents**) *v.* **1.** *vt.* ACT OR SPEAK FOR ANOTHER to act or speak on behalf of somebody or something **2.** *vt.* SYMBOLIZE SOMETHING to symbolize or stand for something ○ *The bear is often used to represent Russia.* **3.** *vt.* GO SOMEWHERE ON BEHALF OF ANOTHER to go or be present somewhere on behalf of somebody or something **4.** *vt.* ACT FOR ANOTHER OFFICIALLY to speak and act for somebody else in an official way ○ *Who will be representing France at the conference?* **5.** *vt.* EXPRESS OR EXPLAIN SOMETHING to express or explain what is happening or what people think ○ *Her views represent those of the majority of the community.* **6.** *vt.* BE PRESENT SOMEWHERE to be somewhere in large or small numbers **7.** *vt.* BE EQUIVALENT OF SOMETHING to be a sign or equivalent of something **8.** *vt.* DEPICT SOMETHING OR SOMEBODY to portray or present an image of somebody or something as being something in particular **9.** *vr.* UNTRUTHFULLY CLAIM TO BE SOMETHING to describe yourself as something you are not ○ *He was arrested at the airport despite trying to represent himself as a tourist.* **10.** *vt.* THEATER DEPICT SOMEBODY ON STAGE to portray or perform a character or role on stage [14thC. Directly or via French from Latin *repraesentare*, literally "to show back," from *praesentare* "to show" (source of English *present*[2]).] —**rep·re·sent·a·bil·i·ty** /rèppri zentə bíllətee/ *n.* —**rep·re·sent·a·ble** *adj.* —**rep·re·sent·er** *n.*

re·pre·sent /reèpri zént/ (**re·pre·sent·ed, re·pre·sent·ing, re·pre·sents**) *vt.* to send, offer, or present something again

rep·re·sen·ta·tion /rèpprəzən táysh'n/ *n.* **1.** FACT OF BEING SERVED BY REPRESENTATIVE the fact or right of being represented by somebody, especially of having a member in a legislature with power to vote or speak for an electorate **2.** VOTING SYSTEM OR BODY OF ELECTORS the system by which electors vote for people to represent them as legislators, administrators, or judges, or the group of people so elected **3.** PICTURE a visual depiction of somebody or something **4.** SOMETHING SPOKEN OR DONE FOR ANOTHER action or speech on behalf of another, especially as an agent or deputy **5.** SOMETHING DESCRIBED OR STATED a description, account, or statement of something real or alleged, especially one meant to induce a response from authority (*often used in the plural*) **6.** LAW STATEMENT INDUCING SOMEBODY TO MAKE CONTRACT a statement, real or implied, that encourages somebody to make an agreement **7.** THEATER PERFORMANCE a theatrical performance or production

rep·re·sen·ta·tion·al /rèpprəzən táyshən'l, -táyshnəl/ *adj.* **1.** CHARACTERIZED BY REPRESENTATION relating to or characterized by representation **2.** ARTS PORTRAYING RECOGNIZABLE OBJECTS depicting something in a physically recognizable form, especially in art ○ *representational painting* —**rep·re·sen·ta·tion·al·ly** *adv.*

rep·re·sen·ta·tion·al·ism /rèpprəzən táyshən'l ìzzəm, -táyshnə-/, **rep·re·sen·ta·tion·ism** /rèpprəzən táysh'n ìzzəm/ *n.* **1.** PHILOS THEORY OF DIRECT APPREHENSION OF OBJECTS the theory that the mind directly apprehends external objects only through ideas or data provided by the senses **2.** ARTS REALISTIC DEPICTION OF OBJECTS the practice or principle of depicting objects in recognizable form, especially in art —**rep·re·sen·tion·al·ist** /-táyshənəlist/ *n.* —**rep·re·sen·ta·tion·al·is·tic** /rèpprəzən táyshən'l ístik, -táyshnə-/ *adj.*

rep·re·sen·ta·tive /rèpprə zéntətiv/ *n.* **1.** SOMEBODY WHO SPEAKS FOR OTHERS somebody who votes or speaks on behalf of others **2.** POL MEMBER OF LEGISLATURE a member of a legislative assembly **3.** **rep·re·sen·ta·tive, Rep·re·sen·ta·tive** MEMBER OF HOUSE OF REPRESENTATIVES a member of the House of Representatives in the U.S. Congress, or of one of the state legislatures **4.** COMM COMMERCIAL AGENT OR SALESPERSON an agent or salesperson for a company. = **sales representative** **5.** EXAMPLE an example or type of something ■ *adj.* **1.** TYPICAL typical of something, especially of a class or kind **2.** MADE UP OF ELECTED PEOPLE composed of elected or authorized people ○ *a representative assembly* **3.** POL LETTING PEOPLE ELECT SOMEBODY allowing people to vote for somebody to represent them in a legislative body such as the Congress in the United States or the House of Commons in the United Kingdom ○ *a representative form of government* **4.** MADE UP OF ALL TYPES including a complete range of examples of something ○ *a representative sample* **5.** ACTING ON SOMEBODY'S BEHALF acting as somebody's agent, deputy, or delegate —**rep·re·sen·ta·tive·ly** *adv.* —**rep·re·sen·ta·tive·ness** *n.*

re·press /ri préss/ (**-pressed, -press·ing, -press·es**) *vt.* **1.** CURB ACTIONS THAT SHOW FEELINGS to check or restrain an action that would reveal feelings ○ *He had to repress a smile.* **2.** USE AUTHORITY TO CONTROL PEOPLE'S FREEDOM to control people's freedom by force or military means ○ *repress an uprising* **3.** PSYCHOL BLOCK SOMETHING FROM MIND to block unacceptable or painful impulses, desires, or memories from the conscious mind [14thC. From Latin *repress-*, the past participle stem of *reprimere*, literally "to press back," from *premere* "to press" (source of English *press*).] —**re·press·i·bil·i·ty** /ri prèssə bíllətee/ *n.* —**re·press·i·ble** /ri préssəb'l/ *adj.*

re·press·er /ri préssər/ *n.* = **repressor**

re·pres·sion /ri présh'n/ *n.* **1.** BEING KEPT DOWN BY FORCE the process of suppressing somebody or the condition of having political, social, or cultural freedom controlled by force **2.** PSYCHOL PSYCHOLOGICAL PROTECTIVE MECHANISM in Freudian psychology, a mechanism by which individuals protect themselves from threatening thoughts by blocking them out of their conscious minds. ◊ **denial**

re·pres·sive /ri préssiv/ *adj.* exerting strict control on the freedom of others —**re·pres·sive·ly** *adv.* —**re·pres·sive·ness** *n.*

re·pres·sor /ri préssər/ *n.* **1. re·pres·sor, re·press·er** REPRESSING PERSON OR THING somebody or something that represses **2.** BIOCHEM PROTEIN BLOCKING TRANSCRIPTION OF MESSENGER RNA a protein that binds to an operator gene and blocks transcription by messenger RNA. It is produced in the translation of a regulatory gene.

re·prieve /ri prèev/ *vt.* **(-prieved, -priev·ing, -prieves) 1.** STOP OR POSTPONE SOMEBODY'S PUNISHMENT to halt or delay somebody's punishment, especially when the punishment is death (*often passive*) **2.** OFFER RESPITE TO SOMEBODY to provide somebody with temporary relief from something harmful, especially danger or pain ■ *n.* **1.** STOPPING OR POSTPONEMENT OF PUNISHMENT the halting or delay of somebody's punishment, especially when the punishment is death **2.** WARRANT HALTING OR POSTPONING PUNISHMENT a warrant giving the authority to stop or postpone somebody's punishment, especially when the punishment is death **3.** RESPITE FROM SOMETHING HARMFUL a relief from something harmful, especially danger or pain [Mid-17thC. Alteration of earlier *repry* "to take back to prison" (hence "to escape the death sentence"), via Old French *repris* "taken back," from, ultimately, Latin *reprehendere* (see REPREHEND).] —**re·priev·a·ble** *adj.* —**re·priev·er** *n.*

rep·ri·mand /réppri mànd/ *vt.* **(-mand·ed, -mand·ing, -mands)** TELL SOMEBODY OFF to rebuke somebody for a wrongdoing ■ *n.* REBUKE a rebuke given for having done something wrong [Mid-17thC. Via French *réprimande* from, ultimately, Latin *reprimenda* "that is to be suppressed," from, ultimately, *reprimere* (see REPRESS).]

re·print *vt.* /ree prínt/ **(-print·ed, -print·ing, -prints)** PRINT SOMETHING AGAIN to print something again, especially with few or no changes ■ *n.* /rèe prìnt/ **1.** COPY OF SOMETHING ALREADY PUBLISHED a printed copy of something that has already been in print **2.** = **offprint 3.** REISSUE OF PRINTED WORK a book or other printed work that is the same as, or has only minor changes from, one that was previously issued **4.** IMPRESSION OF POSTAGE STAMP an impression of a postage stamp made from the original plates but after the stamp has been withdrawn from circulation —**re·print·er** *n.*

re·pri·sal /ri prīz'l/ *n.* **1.** MIL RETALIATION IN WAR a violent military action such as the killing of prisoners or civilians, carried out in retaliation for an enemy's action **2.** STRONG OR VIOLENT RETALIATION a strong or violent retaliation for an action that somebody has taken **3.** RETALIATORY SEIZURE FROM ANOTHER COUNTRY the forcible seizure of property or people from another country as retaliation for some injury [15thC. Via Anglo-Norman *reprisaille* from, ultimately, Latin *reprehendere* (see REPREHEND).]

re·prise /ri prīz/ *n.* **1.** MUSIC REPEAT OF MUSICAL PASSAGE a repeated passage of music, or a return to an earlier theme **2.** MUSIC = **chorus** *n.* 1 **3.** REPETITION a repetition or recurrence of something ■ *vt.* **(-prised, -pris·ing, -pris·es) 1.** MUSIC REPEAT MUSIC to repeat a passage of music or return to an earlier theme **2.** REPEAT ACTION to repeat an action or performance ○ *reprised her role as Gertrude in the New York production* [Mid-20thC. Via French, the past participle of *reprendre*, literally "to take again," used as a noun, from *prendre* "to take," from Latin *prehendere*.]

re·pri·va·tize /ree prīvə tīz/ **(-tized, -tiz·ing, -tiz·es)** *vt.* to return something from public to private ownership —**re·pri·va·ti·za·tion** /rèe prīvətə záysh'n/ *n.*

re·pro /rèe prō/ *n.* (*informal*) **1.** REPRODUCTION a reproduction, especially of a painting or piece of furniture **2.** PRINTING REPRODUCTION PROOF a reproduction proof [Mid-20thC. Shortening.]

re·proach /ri prṓch/ *v.* **(-proached, -proach·ing, -proach·es) 1.** *vt.* CRITICIZE SOMEBODY to criticize somebody for doing something wrong **2.** *vr.* FEEL BLAMEWORTHY to feel ashamed because you know you have done something wrong ○ *There's no reason to reproach yourself, because there was nothing you could do.* **3.** *vt.* DISGRACE SOMEBODY OR SOMETHING to bring disgrace upon somebody or something (*archaic*) ■ *n.* **1.** CRITICISM criticism or disapproval for having done something wrong or an expression of this **2.** SOMETHING DISGRACEFUL something that reflects badly on somebody who has failed to improve or deal with it **3.** DISCREDIT shame or disgrace that somebody or something incurs ○ *actions that brought reproach upon his family* [15thC. Via Old French *reprochier* from assumed Vulgar Latin *repropiare* "to bring back near" (hence "to force to face up to things"), from Latin *prope* "near."] —**re·proach·a·ble** *adj.* —**re·proach·a·ble·ness** *n.* —**re·proach·a·bly** *adv.* —**re·proach·er** *n.* —**re·proach·ing·ly** *adv.* ◇ **above** *or* **beyond reproach** so good that no criticism can be made

re·proach·ful /ri prṓchfəl/ *adj.* expressing disapproval or blame —**re·proach·ful·ly** *adv.* —**re·proach·ful·ness** *n.*

rep·ro·bate /réppra bàyt/ *n.* **1.** SOMEBODY IMMORAL a disreputable or immoral person **2.** RELIG SOMEBODY DAMNED somebody whose soul is believed to be damned ■ *adj.* **1.** DISREPUTABLE disreputable or immoral **2.** RELIG DAMNED with a soul that is damned ■ *vt.* **(-bat·ed, -bat·ing, -bates) 1.** CENSURE SOMEBODY to censure or condemn somebody (*formal*) **2.** RELIG DENY SALVATION TO SOMEBODY to condemn somebody to supposed eternal damnation [Mid-16thC. Via late Latin *reprobatus*, from Latin, the past participle of *reprobare* (see REPROVE).] —**rep·ro·bat·er** /-bàytər/ *n.* —**rep·ro·ba·tive** /-bàytiv/ *adj.*

rep·ro·ba·tion /rèpprə báysh'n/ *n.* **1.** DISAPPROVAL strong condemnation or disapproval of somebody or something **2.** RELIG DIVINE REJECTION the supposed condemnation of somebody's soul to eternal damnation [15thC. Directly or via French from, ultimately, Latin *reprobare* (see REPROVE).] —**rep·ro·ba·tion·ar·y** /rèpprə báysh'n èrree/ *adj.*

re·pro·duce /rèeprə dóoss/ **(-duced, -duc·ing, -duc·es)** *v.* **1.** *vti.* MAKE DUPLICATE OF SOMETHING to duplicate something, or be duplicated, by photographing, scanning, printing, or another process **2.** *vt.* REPEAT SOMETHING to do something in the same way as before **3.** *vi.* BIOL PRODUCE OFFSPRING to produce offspring or new individuals through a sexual or asexual process **4.** *vt.* REMEMBER to remember or imagine something again —**re·pro·duc·er** /rèeprə dóossər/ *n.* —**re·pro·duc·i·bil·i·ty** /-dòossə bíllətee/ *n.* —**re·pro·duc·i·ble** *adj.* —**re·pro·duc·i·bly** /-dóossəblee/ *adv.*

WORD KEY: SYNONYMS

See Synonyms at ***copy***.

re·pro·duc·tion /rèeprə dúkshən/ *n.* **1.** COPY OF OBJECT a copy of something in an earlier style, especially a painting or a piece of furniture **2.** REPRODUCING OF SOMETHING the act or process of reproducing something **3.** PRINT, ELECTRONIC, OR PHOTOGRAPHIC DUPLICATE a copy of something printed, scanned, photographed, or produced by other means **4.** RECORDING RECORDING OF SOUND the recording of sound or the quality of recorded sound **5.** BIOL PRODUCTION OF OFFSPRING the production of young plants and animals of the same kind through a sexual or asexual process [Mid-17thC. Formed from REPRODUCE, on the model of *production*.]

re·pro·duc·tion proof *n.* a printed proof, usually on glossy paper, of such high quality that it can be photographed for making a printing plate

re·pro·duc·tive /rèeprə dúktiv/ *adj.* relating to, taking part in, or enabling the production of new offspring or individuals ○ *reproductive organs* [Mid-18thC. Formed from REPRODUCE, on the model of *productive*.] —**re·pro·duc·tive·ly** *adv.* —**re·pro·duc·tive·ness** *n.*

re·pro·duc·tive sys·tem *n.* the combination of bodily organs and tissues used in the process of producing offspring

re·prog·ra·phy /ri próggrəfee/ *n.* the reproduction of something printed, e.g., by offset printing, microfilming, photography, or xerography [Mid-20thC. From German *Reprographie*, a blend of *Reproduktion* "reproduction" + *Photographie* "photography."] —**re·pro·graph·ic** /rèeprə gráffik, rèpprə-/ *adj.*

re·proof /ri próof/, **reproval** *n.* the act of criticizing somebody for having done something wrong, or something stated as a rebuke [14thC. From Old French *reprove*, from *reprover* (see REPROVE).]

re·prove /ri próov/ **(-proved, -prov·ing, -proves)** *vt.* to speak to somebody in a way that shows disapproval of something he or she has done [14thC. Via Old French *reprover* from Latin *reprobare*, literally "to prove to be unworthy," from *probare* "to prove" (source of English *prove*).] —**re·prov·a·ble** *adj.* —**re·prov·er** *n.* —**re·prov·ing·ly** *adv.*

rept. *abbr.* report

rep·tant /réptənt/ *adj.* creeping or lying along the ground [Mid-17thC. From Latin *reptare*, literally "to keep creeping," from *repere* "to creep" (see REPTILE).]

rep·tile /rép't'l, rép tīl/ *n.* **1.** COLD-BLOODED SCALY VERTEBRATE an air-breathing cold-blooded egg-laying vertebrate such as the crocodile, tortoise, snake, or lizard, with an outer covering of scales or plates and a bony skeleton. Class: Reptilia. **2.** OFFENSIVE TERM an offensive term that deliberately insults somebody's behavior or character (*informal insult*) ■ *adj.* BEING A REPTILE belonging to the class of reptiles [14thC. Via French from, ultimately, late Latin *reptilis* "creeping," from *rept-*, the past participle stem of *repere* "to creep."]

rep·til·i·an /rep tíllee ən/ *adj.* **1.** OF REPTILES relating to reptiles **2.** MEAN OR GROVELING displaying any of the characteristics traditionally attributed to or suggestive of reptiles, e.g., coldness and lack of emotion, or creeping, groveling behavior ■ *n.* = **reptile** *n.* 1

Repub. *abbr.* **1.** Republic **2.** Republican

re·pub·lic /ri púbblik/ *n.* **1.** POLITICAL SYSTEM WITH POWERFUL ELECTORATE a political system or form of government in which people elect representatives to exercise power for them **2.** STATE WITH POWERFUL ELECTORATE a state or other political unit with a form of government in which the supreme power is in the hands of representatives elected by the people **3. re·pub·lic, Re·pub·lic** COUNTRY WITH REPUBLICAN GOVERNMENT a country whose government or political system is that of a republic **4. re·pub·lic, Re·pub·lic** REPUBLICAN UNIT WITHIN LARGER COUNTRY a constituent political and territorial unit of a national federation or union **5.** GROUP OF EQUALS WITH COLLECTIVE INTERESTS a group of people who are considered to be equals and who have a collective interest, objective, or vocation (*formal*) ○ *the republic of letters* [Late 16thC. Via French *république* from Latin *res publica*, literally "public matter."]

WORD KEY: CULTURAL NOTE

The Republic, a political treatise by the Greek philosopher Plato (early 4th century B.C.). Presented in the form of a series of dialogues between Socrates and his pupils, it begins with a discussion of the nature of justice that leads in turn to an attempt to define the ideal society. For Plato, this would consist of an aristocracy run by a class of legislators groomed for leadership by a state education system.

re·pub·li·can /ri púbblikən/ *n.* SUPPORTER OF REPUBLIC AS GOVERNMENT somebody who believes that the best government is one in which supreme power is vested in an electorate ■ *adj.* OF A REPUBLIC relating to, belonging to, or characteristic of a republic

Re·pub·li·can[1] *adj.* **1.** OF REPUBLICAN PARTY belonging to or supporting the Republican Party in the United States **2.** *U.K.* DESIRING UNITED IRELAND supporting the idea that Northern Ireland should be united politically with the Republic of Ireland and should cease to form part of the United Kingdom ■ *n.* **1.** REPUBLICAN PARTY MEMBER a member or supporter of the Republican Party in the United States **2.** *U.K.* SUPPORTER OF UNITED IRELAND somebody who wants Northern Ireland to be united politically with the Republic of Ireland

Re·pub·li·can[2] /ri púbblikən/ river that flows from Colorado into Kansas, where it unites with the Smoky Hill River, to form the Kansas River. Length: 445 mi./715 km.

re·pub·li·can·ism /ri púbblikə nìzzəm/ *n.* **1.** BELIEF IN REPUBLIC AS POLITICAL SYSTEM the belief that the supreme power of a country should be vested in an electorate **2.** THEORY OF REPUBLICAN GOVERNMENT the theory and principles of republican government

Re·pub·li·can·ism *n.* **1.** REPUBLICAN PARTY SUPPORT support for the Republican Party in the United States **2.** *U.K.* SUPPORT FOR UNITED IRELAND support for the idea of uniting Northern Ireland politically with the Republic of Ireland

re·pub·li·can·ize /ri púbblikə nīz/ **(-ized, -iz·ing, -iz·es)** *vt.* to make a state or other political unit into a republic —**re·pub·li·can·i·za·tion** /ri pùbblikəni záysh'n/ *n.*

Re·pub·li·can Par·ty *n.* a political party at state and national level in the United States, founded in 1854–56

re·pub·li·ca·tion /rèe pubbli káysh'n/ *n.* **1.** REPUBLISHING OF SOMETHING the act or process of publishing something again **2.** SOMETHING PUBLISHED AGAIN something published again, especially in an unchanged form

re·pub·lish /ree púbblish/ **(-lished, -lish·ing, -lish·es)** *vt.* **1.** PUBLISH SOMETHING AGAIN to reissue a publication, especially in an unchanged form **2.** LAW EXECUTE WILL FOR SECOND TIME to execute a will again after it has been revoked —**re·pub·lish·er** /ree púbblishər/ *n.*

re·pu·di·ate /ri pyóodee àyt/ **(-at·ed, -at·ing, -ates)** *vt.* **1.** DISOWN SOMETHING to disapprove of something formally and strongly and renounce any connection with it

○ *She repudiated the committee's actions.* **2.** DENY SOMETHING to state that something is untrue **3.** REJECT SOMETHING to reject something that is offered **4.** DISOWN LOVED ONE to disown a family member or lover **5.** REJECT SOMETHING AS INVALID to refuse to accept the validity of something **6.** REFUSE TO PAY DEBT to refuse to acknowledge or pay a debt [Mid-16thC. Via Latin *repudiare* "to divorce" (the original meaning in English) from *repudium* "divorce."] —**re·pu·di·a·ble** *adj.* —**re·pu·di·a·tive** *adj.* —**re·pu·di·a·tor** *n.*

WORD KEY: USAGE

See Usage note at ***refute.***

re·pu·di·a·tion /ri pyo͝odee áysh'n/ *n.* **1.** FACT OF REPUDIATING SOMETHING the act or process of repudiating something **2.** REJECTION OF SOMETHING BY GOVERNMENT a refusal by a government to acknowledge and honor a claim or obligation because it is considered to be invalid —**re·pu·di·a·tion·ist** *n.*

re·pugn /ri pyo͞on/ (**-pugned, -pugn·ing, -pugns**) *vt.* to oppose or resist something (*archaic*) [14thC. Directly or via Old French from Latin *repugnare*, literally "to fight back," from *pugnare* "to fight" (source of English *pugnacious*).]

re·pug·nance /ri púgnənss/, **re·pug·nan·cy** *n.* a very strong dislike or distaste

WORD KEY: SYNONYMS

See Synonyms at ***dislike.***

re·pug·nant /ri púgnənt/ *adj.* **1.** OFFENSIVE offensive and completely unacceptable **2.** REVOLTING making somebody feel physically repelled ○ *a repugnant odor* [Late 18thC. Via Old French, "contrary," from, ultimately, Latin *repugnare* (see REPUGN).] —**re·pug·nant·ly** *adv.*

re·pulse /ri púls/ *vt.* (**-pulsed, -puls·ing, -puls·es**) **1.** MIL FORCE BACK MILITARY ATTACK to force back an attacking military force **2.** DISGUST SOMEBODY to cause disgust or revulsion in somebody **3.** SPURN SOMEBODY to reject or rebuff an approach from somebody ■ *n.* **1.** REJECTION a refusal or rejection of somebody **2.** MIL ACT OF FORCING BACK ATTACK the forcing back of an attacking military force [Mid-16thC. From Latin *repuls-*, the past participle stem of *repellere* (see REPEL).] —**re·puls·er** *n.*

WORD KEY: USAGE

repulse or **repel**? ***Repulse*** is a much stronger word than ***repel*** in all its meanings, physical and abstract. To ***repel*** people physically is to drive them back from the immediate vicinity; and its figurative equivalent is "to ward off" or "to be distasteful to." To ***repulse*** people physically is to drive them away with great force or strength, and it is normally used with reference to battles and warfare. The corresponding figurative meaning here is "to disgust."

re·pul·sion /ri púlshən/ *n.* **1.** FACT OF BEING REPULSED the act or condition of being repulsed **2.** REVULSION a feeling of disgust or very strong dislike **3.** PHYS REPELLING FORCE a force between two bodies of like electric charge or magnetic polarity that tends to repel or separate them. It is this repulsive force between atoms and molecules at very short distances that tends to keep them separated.

re·pul·sive /ri púlsiv/ *adj.* **1.** VERY UNPLEASANT making somebody feel disgust or very strong dislike **2.** REPELLENT tending to repel —**re·pul·sive·ly** *adv.* —**re·pul·sive·ness** *n.*

WORD KEY: USAGE

See Usage note at ***repellent.***

re·pur·chase a·gree·ment /ree púrchəss-/ *n.* **1.** AGREEMENT ABOUT REPURCHASE OF SECURITIES an agreement between a dealer and an investor in which the investor agrees to sell purchased securities back to the dealer on a fixed date for a specified profit **2.** AGREEMENT TO BUY BACK SOMETHING an agreement between a buyer and a seller in which the seller agrees to buy back the purchased item at the end of a specified period

rep·u·ta·ble /réppyətəb'l/ *adj.* known to be honest, reliable, or respectable [Late 17thC. Directly or via French from medieval Latin *reputabilis*, from Latin *reputare* (see REPUTE).] —**rep·u·ta·bil·i·ty** /rèppyətə bíllətee/ *n.* —**rep·u·ta·bly** *adv.*

rep·u·ta·tion /rèppyə táysh'n/ *n.* **1.** GENERAL OPINIONS ABOUT SOMEBODY OR SOMETHING the views that are generally held about somebody or something **2.** GOOD OPINION a high opinion that people hold about somebody or something **3.** SOMETHING THAT SOMEBODY IS KNOWN FOR the generally accepted estimation of somebody or something as having particular qualities or attributes ○ *The new manager has a reputation for being a stickler for details.* [14thC. From the Latin stem *reputation-* "consideration," from *reputare* (see REPUTE).]

re·pute /ri pyo͞ot/ *n.* (*formal*) **1.** REPUTATION estimation or character according to what people in general think **2.** GOOD REPUTATION good reputation or standing [Mid-16thC. Directly or via French *reputer* from Latin *reputare*, literally "to think repeatedly," formed from *putare* "to think." The underlying idea is "to think well or badly of."]

re·put·ed /ri pyo͞otəd/ *adj.* widely believed, although not necessarily established as fact [Late 16thC. Formed from REPUTE, used as a verb.]

req. *abbr.* **1.** request **2.** require **3.** required **4.** requirement **5.** requisition

re·quest /ri kwést/ *vt.* (**-quest·ed, -quest·ing, -quests**) **1.** ASK POLITELY FOR SOMETHING to ask formally or courteously for something to be given or done ○ *requested that he be excused* ○ *requested her favorite song* **2.** ASK SOMEBODY FOR SOMETHING to ask somebody to do something ○ *requested Father Peter to perform their marriage ceremony* ■ *n.* **1.** EXPRESSION OF A POLITE WISH OR DESIRE an act of politely or formally asking that something be done or given **2.** MUSIC THAT HAS BEEN ASKED FOR a piece of music played on a radio program, at a live performance, or at a disco because somebody asks for it ○ *We'll be taking several requests tonight.* **3.** ACT OF EXPRESSING A WISH the act of asking or petitioning for something to be done or given [14thC. Via Old French from, ultimately, Latin *requisitus*, the past participle of *requirere* (see REQUIRE).] —**re·quest·er** *n.*

re·quest stop *n. U.K.* = **flag stop**

req·ui·em /rékwee əm/, **Req·ui·em** *n.* **1.** CHR ROMAN CATHOLIC SERVICE FOR THE DEAD a Roman Catholic mass held to offer prayers for somebody who has died **2.** MUSIC, CHR MUSIC FOR A REQUIEM a piece of music written to accompany a requiem mass **3.** MUSIC SAD COMMEMORATIVE MUSIC a piece of music written to commemorate somebody who has died [14thC. From Latin, "rest," in a line of a prayer *Requiem aeternam dona eis Domine* "Grant them eternal rest, O Lord."]

req·ui·em shark *n.* a voracious shark of tropical waters. Hammerheads, tiger sharks, and soupfins are all requiem sharks. Family: Carcharhinidae. [By folk etymology from French *requin* "shark"]

req·ui·es·cat /rèkwee é skaat/ *n.* a prayer asking that the soul of a dead person might be at rest [Early 19thC. From Latin, "may he or she rest."]

re·quire /ri kwír/ (**-quired, -quir·ing, -quires**) *vt.* **1.** NEED SOMETHING OR SOMEBODY to be in need of something or somebody for a particular purpose ○ *The recipe requires a cup of milk.* **2.** MAKE SOMETHING NECESSARY to have something as a necessary precondition ○ *A password is required for entry to the system.* **3.** DEMAND SOMETHING BY LAW to demand something by a law or regulation (*often passive*) ○ *Notification was required by law.* **4.** INSIST ON SOMETHING to insist that somebody do something ○ *All applicants are required to pass a medical exam.* [14thC. From Old French *requ(i)er-*, the stem of *requere*, from, ultimately, Latin *requirere*, literally "to seek in return," from Latin *quaerere* "to seek" (source of English *query*).] —**re·quir·a·ble** *adj.* —**re·quir·er** *n.*

re·quired /ri kwírd/ *adj.* **1.** NEEDED necessary or appropriate ○ *He lacks the required degree of expertise.* **2.** COMPULSORY insisted upon or imposed as a condition ○ *required reading for a course*

re·quire·ment /ri kwírmənt/ *n.* **1.** SOMETHING NEEDED something that is needed for a particular purpose (*often used in the plural*) **2.** SOMETHING INSISTED UPON something that is obligatory or demanded (*often used in the plural*) ○ *a requirement for the job* **3.** FACT OF REQUIRING SOMETHING an act or process of requiring something

req·ui·site /rékwizit/ *adj.* ESSENTIAL necessary or indispensable for something (*formal*) ○ *the requisite skills for the job* ■ *n.* SOMETHING ESSENTIAL something that is necessary or indispensable [15thC. From Latin *requisitus*, the past participle of *requirere* (see REQUIRE).] —**req·ui·site·ly** *adv.* —**req·ui·site·ness** *n.*

WORD KEY: SYNONYMS

See Synonyms at ***necessary.***

req·ui·si·tion /rèkwi zísh'n/ *n.* **1.** DEMAND FOR SOMETHING a demand for something that is required **2.** OFFICIAL FORM a written or printed request for something that is needed **3.** FACT OF MAKING A FORMAL DEMAND the act or process of making a formal demand for something **4.** POL REQUEST FOR THE RETURN OF A FUGITIVE a request by a government that another government return a fugitive from the law ■ *vt.* (**-tioned, -tion·ing, -tions**) **1.** DEMAND AND TAKE SOMETHING OFFICIALLY to demand and take something that is needed, especially for official or military use **2.** REQUIRE AND OBTAIN SOMEBODY FOR A JOB to require and obtain the services of somebody to do something ○ *requisitioned a few friends for the weekend to help paint the house* [Mid-16thC. Directly or via French from, ultimately, Latin *requisit-*, the past participle stem of *requirere* (see REQUIRE).] —**req·ui·si·tion·ar·y** /rèkwi zísh'n èrree/ *adj.*

re·quit·al *n.* **1.** ACT DONE IN RESPONSE an act done in response, repayment, or retaliation (*formal*) **2.** REPAYMENT OR RETALIATION response, repayment, or retaliation

re·quite /ri kwít/ (**-quit·ed, -quit·ing, -quites**) *vt.* **1.** PAY BACK to return in kind a kindness or hurt that somebody has done **2.** RECOMPENSE to pay somebody back for a service performed [Early 16thC. Formed from an earlier form of QUIT, in the meaning "to pay up."] —**re·quit·a·ble** *adj.* —**re·quite·ment** *n.* —**re·quit·er** *n.*

re·ra·di·ate /ree ráydee àyt/ (**-at·ed, -at·ing, -ates**) *vt.* to emit radiation after absorbing incident radiation —**re·ra·di·a·tion** /ree ràydee áysh'n/ *n.*

re·read /ree réed/ (**-read, -read** /-réd/, **-read·ing, -reads**) *vt.* to read something again

Reredos

rere·dos /rérrə dòss, rírrə dòss/ *n.* **1.** CHR DECORATION FOR THE REAR OF AN ALTAR an artistic decoration behind the altar in a church, e.g., a wood or stone screen or a wall-hanging **2.** BACK OF A FIREPLACE the back of an open fireplace [14thC. Via Anglo-Norman from Old French *areredos*, from *arere* "behind" + *dos* "back" (from Latin *dorsum*).]

re·re·lease /rée ri léess/ *vt.* (**-leased, -leas·ing, -leas·es**) DISTRIBUTE AGAIN to release a music recording or a movie again for distribution to the public ■ *n.* RERELEASED RECORDING OR MOVIE a music recording or a movie that has been released again to the public

re·route /ree rówt, ree ro͞ot/ (**-rout·ed, -rout·ing, -routes**) *vt.* to direct people or vehicles along an alternate route, e.g., because of an accident, road construction, or for security reasons

re·run *vt.* /ree rún/ (**-ran** /-rán/, **-run, -run·ning, -runs**) **1.** CINEMA, TV SHOW RECORDED ENTERTAINMENT AGAIN to show or broadcast a TV series, video, or movie again **2.** SPORTS REPEAT A RACE to run a race again, or cause a race to be run again, after the result on the first occasion has been disallowed because of an infraction of the rules ■ *n.* /rée rùn/ (*plural* **-runs**) **1.** CINEMA, TV REPEAT SHOWING OF RECORDED ENTERTAINMENT a repeat showing of recorded entertainment, especially a TV series **2.** SPORTS REPEAT RUNNING OF A RACE the repeat running of a race after an infraction of the rules

res /rayss, reez/ (*plural* **res**) *n.* in law, a matter or thing [From Latin, "thing, legal matter"]

RES *abbr.* reticuloendothelial system

res. *abbr.* **1.** research **2.** reservation **3.** reserved **4.** reservoir **5.** residence **6.** resident **7.** resolution

res ad·ju·di·ca·ta *n.* LAW = **res judicata**

re·sale /rée sàyl/ *n.* **1.** SELLING AGAIN the selling of something again ○ *Not for resale.* **2.** SELLING SECOND-HAND the selling of something second-hand —**re·sal·a·ble** /ree sáyləb'l/ *adj.* —**re·sal·a·bil·i·ty** /ree sàylə bíllətee/ *n.*

re·scale /ree skáyl/ (**-scaled, -scal·ing, -scales**) *vt.* to modify the scale of something, especially to reduce it ○ *rescale a budget* ○ *rescale a drawing*

re·sched·ule /ree skéjool/ (**-uled, -ul·ing, -ules**) *vt.* **1.** CHANGE THE TIME FIXED FOR SOMETHING to arrange a new time slot for something **2.** FIN EXTEND A LOAN to extend the payment schedule of a loan

re·scind /ri sínd/ (**-scind·ed, -scind·ing, -scinds**) *vt.* **1.** CANCEL to remove the validity or authority of something **2.** REPEAL A DECISION OR ENACTMENT to declare a decision or enactment null and void [Mid-16thC. From Latin *rescindere*, literally "to cut back," from *scindere* "to cut."] —**re·scind·a·ble** *adj.* —**re·scind·er** *n.* —**re·scind·ment** *n.*

re·scis·sion /ri sízh'n/ *n.* the act of rescinding something [Early 17thC. Via the late Latin stem *rescission-* from, ultimately, Latin *rescindere* (see RESCIND).]

re·scis·so·ry /ri sízzəree, ri síssəree/ *adj.* relating to rescission or having the power to rescind (*formal*) [Early 17thC. Via late Latin *rescissorius* from, ultimately, Latin *rescindere* (see RESCIND).]

re·score /ree skáwr/ (**-scored, -scor·ing, -scores**) *vt.* to write new instrumentation for a piece of music

re·script /rée skrìpt/ *n.* **1.** REWRITE an act of rewriting something **2.** CHR ECCLESIASTICAL RULING a formal reply by the pope or some other high dignitary of the Roman Catholic Church on a matter of doctrine or discipline **3.** HIST, LAW ROMAN EMPEROR'S LEGAL RULING a formal reply by an ancient Roman or Holy Roman emperor on a point of law [14thC. From Latin *rescriptum*, the neuter past participle of *rescribere*, literally "to write back," from *scribere*.]

res·cue /réskyoo/ *v.* (**-cued, -cu·ing, -cues**) **1.** *vt.* REMOVE FROM DANGER to save somebody or something from a dangerous or harmful situation ○ *the boys had to be rescued from the rocks by helicopter* **2.** SAVE to prevent something from being discarded, rejected, or put out of operation ○ *At the last minute the factory was rescued from closure.* **3.** *vt.* LAW GET SOMEBODY OUT OF JAIL to release somebody from legal custody by force **4.** *vt.* LAW TAKE FORCIBLE POSSESSION OF to seize property or goods by force ■ *n.* REMOVAL FROM DANGER OR HARM an act or instance of saving somebody or something from a dangerous or harmful situation (*often used before a noun*) ○ *a daring rescue attempt* ■ an instance of helping somebody in an awkward or difficult situation ○ *I couldn't think what to say, but luckily he came to my rescue.* ■ *n.* LAW **1.** RELEASE FROM JAIL the release of somebody from legal custody by force **2.** SEIZURE OF GOODS the seizure of property or goods by force [14thC. From Old French *rescourre*, literally "to shake loose," from *escourre* "to shake," from Latin *escutere*, from *ex-* "out"+ *quatere* "to strike."] —**res·cu·a·ble** *adj.* —**res·cu·er** *n.*

res·cue grass *n.* a grass native to South America cultivated for hay. Latin name: *Bromus unioloides.*

re·search *n.* /rée sùrch, ri-/ ORGANIZED STUDY methodical investigation into a subject in order to discover facts, to establish or revise a theory, or to develop a plan of action based on the facts discovered ■ *vti.* /ri súrch, rée sùrch/ (**-searched, -search·ing, -search·es**) STUDY SOMETHING METHODICALLY to carry out research into a subject [Late 16thC. Via obsolete French *recerche* from Old French *recercher*, literally "to search closely," from *cerchier* (see SEARCH).] —**re·search·a·ble** *adj.* —**re·search·er** *n.* —**re·search·ist** *n.*

re·search and de·vel·op·ment *n.* the work in a company of investigating improved processes, products, and services and of developing new ones

re·seat /ree séet/ (**-seat·ed, -seat·ing, -seats**) *vt.* **1.** SEAT ELSEWHERE to seat somebody in another place **2.** SEAT SOMEBODY AS BEFORE to return somebody to the seat previously occupied **3.** REPLACE THE SEATS IN to fit new seats in an auditorium or hall **4.** PROVIDE A NEW SEAT FOR to replace the material on a seat **5.** REPLACE VALVE SEATING to return the seating of a valve to good condition

re·seau /ray zṓ, rə zṓ/ (*plural* **-seaux** /ray zṓz, rə zṓz, -zṓ/ *or* **-seaus** /ray zṓz, rə zṓz/) *n.* **1.** CRAFT NET FOR MAKING LACE a mesh foundation on which lace is made **2.** ASTRON PHOTOGRAPHIC REFERENCE PLATE a grid of lines photographed onto or cut into a glass plate and used as a reference for astronomical observations [Late 16thC. Via French *réseau* "network" from Old French *reseuil*, literally "little net," from *raiz* "net," from Latin *rete* "net."]

re·sect /ri sékt/ (**-sect·ed, -sect·ing, -sects**) *vt.* to cut through and surgically remove part of an organ, bone, or other body part [Mid-17thC. From Latin *resect-*, the past participle stem of *resecare*, literally "to cut back," from *secare* "to cut."]

re·sec·tion /ri sékshən/ *n.* **1.** SURG PARTIAL SURGICAL REMOVAL the surgical removal of part of an organ, bone, or other bodily part **2.** CIV ENG ESTABLISHMENT OF LOCATION OF POINT the establishment of the location of a point when surveying by sighting from that point to two other points whose locations are known

re·sec·to·scope /ri séktə skṑp/ *n.* a surgical instrument that allows a resection to be made without a bigger incision than that caused by the instrument itself

Reseda

re·se·da /ri séedə, ri séddə/ *n.* (*plural* **-das** *or* **-da**) **1.** PLANTS MEDITERRANEAN PLANT WITH GRAYISH-GREEN FLOWERS a Mediterranean plant that has small dense spikes of grayish-green flowers with divided petals. Genus: *Reseda.* **2.** COLORS GRAYISH GREEN a grayish-green color ■ *adj.* GRAYISH-GREEN of a grayish-green color [Mid-18thC. Via modern Latin, genus name, from Latin, of unknown origin.]

re·seed /ree séed/ (**-seed·ed, -seed·ing, -seeds**) *v.* **1.** *vt.* PLANT WITH SEEDS AGAIN to plant seeds on an area of land again **2.** *vti.* START A PLANT FROM ITS SEED to grow a plant or to grow from seed dropped by the previous generation

re·sem·blance /ri zémbləns/ *n.* **1.** SIMILARITY TO SOMEBODY OR SOMETHING similarity in appearance or quality to somebody or something else **2.** DEGREE OF SIMILARITY the extent to which somebody or something resembles somebody or something else ○ *the resemblance between them is striking* **3.** POINT OF SIMILARITY a respect in which somebody or something resembles somebody or something else **4.** SOMETHING SIMILAR something that resembles something else

re·sem·ble /ri zémb'l/ (**-bled, -bling, -bles**) *vt.* to be similar to somebody or something in appearance or behavior [14thC. From Old French *resembler*, literally "to be very like," from *sembler* "to seem" (source of English *semblance*), from Latin *simulare* "to simulate").] —**re·sem·bler** *n.*

re·send /ree sénd/ (**-sent,** /-sént/, **-send·ing, -sends**) *vt.* to send something again

re·sent /ri zént/ (**-sent·ed, -sent·ing, -sents**) *vt.* to feel aggrieved about something or toward somebody often because of a perceived wrong or injustice [Late 16thC. From obsolete French *ressentir*, literally "to feel strongly," from *sentir* "to feel," from Latin *sentire* "to feel."]

re·sent·ful /ri zéntf'l/ *adj.* **1.** ANNOYED feeling aggrieved and ill-used **2.** RESULTING FROM RESENTMENT characterized by feelings of annoyance or ill-use ○ *a resentful silence* —**re·sent·ful·ly** *adv.* —**re·sent·ful·ness** *n.*

re·sent·ment /ri zéntmənt/ *n.* aggrieved feelings about something or toward somebody, usually as a result of ill-usage or insult, or an instance of these [Early 17thC. From obsolete French *ressentiment* "strong feeling," from *ressentir* (see RESENT).]

res·er·va·tion /rèzzər váysh'n/ *n.* **1.** ARRANGEMENT MADE BEFOREHAND an advance booking, e.g., of a seat, table, hotel room, or a ticket on a plane, train, or bus **2.** PLACE ARRANGED BEFOREHAND something such as a seat, table, hotel room, or ticket booked in advance **3.** ARRANGING OF SOMETHING BEFOREHAND the act of booking something in advance **4.** LAND SET ASIDE an area of land set aside for a particular purpose, especially in North America for the use of a Native American people **5.** KEEPING SOMETHING BACK the act of withholding something, or an instance of so doing **6.** LIMITING CONDITION a limiting condition to an agreement **7.** LAW LEGAL INTEREST RETAINED IN SOMETHING GRANTED a clause in a deed by which somebody retains an interest in something being granted or leased, or such an interest itself **8.** CHR PRESERVATION OF CONSECRATED ELEMENTS FOR LATER the practice of retaining part of the consecrated bread and wine after celebrating Communion, in order to use it later, e.g., when visiting the sick ■ **res·er·va·tions** *npl.* MISGIVINGS THAT CAUSE HESITATION doubts that prevent wholehearted agreement to or approval of something —**res·er·va·tion·ist** *n.*

WORD KEY: SYNONYMS

See Synonyms at ***doubtful***.

re·serve /ri zúrv/ *vt.* (**-served, -serv·ing, -serves**) **1.** SET SOMETHING ASIDE to keep something back for future use or for some specific purpose **2.** BOOK A PLACE BEFOREHAND to make arrangements in advance to secure a place such as a seat, ticket, table, or hotel room **3.** RETAIN SOMETHING FOR YOUR OWN BENEFIT to retain the option of future action on somebody's or your own behalf ○ *I reserve the right to change my mind.* **4.** POSTPONE A DECISION to defer making a decision until all the issues have been considered ○ *reserve judgement* ■ *n.* **1.** FIN MONEY RETAINED FOR FUTURE USE an amount of capital or revenue retained by a company or financial institution to meet future contingencies (*often used in the plural*) **2.** EMERGENCY SUPPLY something kept back for later use, especially in an emergency **3.** COOLNESS OF MANNER emotional restraint, resulting in a reticent or composed manner **4.** SPORTS SUBSTITUTE PLAYER a team member called to play when a member of the original team withdraws, either before or during a game **5.** MIL INACTIVE PART OF THE ARMED SERVICES the part of a country's armed services that is not on active service at a given time **6.** MIL REINFORCEMENT FORCE the part of an armed force that is not initially committed during a military engagement but supplies reinforcements as necessary **7.** MIL MEMBER OF A RESERVE a member of a military reserve **8.** *U.K.* = **preserve 9.** ECON NATIONAL FUNDS a country's supply of gold and foreign currency that is held by the central bank against future liabilities or to support the currency when the exchange rates fluctuate **10.** GEOL UNEXPLOITED NATURAL RESOURCE a supply of a natural resource such as a mineral or petrochemical that is estimated to exist from geologic data but is not yet utilized **11.** *Can* LAND USED AS A RESERVATION an area of land set aside as a reservation for use by a Native American people **12.** NEXT RUNNER-UP a competitor or exhibit such as an animal at an agricultural show that places immediately after the prizewinners and will receive a prize if a prizewinner is disqualified ■ **re·serves** *npl.* EXTRA STAMINA, USABLE IN AN EMERGENCY additional personal resources of energy or strength that can be called upon in an emergency [14thC. Directly and via French *réserver* from Latin *reservare*, literally "to keep back," from *servare* "to keep."] —**re·serv·a·ble** *adj.* —**re·serv·er** *n.* ◇ **have** *or* **keep something in reserve** to use only part of something, keeping some of it back in case it is needed at a later time

re·serve bank *n.* one of the 12 banks in the U.S. Federal Reserve system

re·serve cur·ren·cy *n.* foreign currency that is acceptable for settling international transactions and that is held in reserve for that purpose by a central bank

re·served /ri zúrvd/ *adj.* **1.** BOOKED booked in advance **2.** EARMARKED FOR A SPECIFIC USE kept or set aside for a particular purpose **3.** HAVING A COOL MANNER having a tendency to emotional restraint and so appearing reticent or composed —**re·serv·ed·ly** /ri zúrvədlee/ *adv.* —**re·serv·ed·ness** /ri zúrvədnəss/ *n.*

reserve price *n.* the lowest price that a seller is willing to accept for something being sold at auction. ◊ **upset price**

re·serv·ist /ri zúrvist/ *n.* a member of a military force not on active service at a given time

res·er·voir /rézzər vwaar/ *n.* **1.** ENVIRON LAKE OR TANK FOR STORING WATER a large tank or natural or artificial lake used for collecting and storing water for human consumption or agricultural use **2.** LARGE BACKUP SUPPLY a substantial reserve supply of something intangible **3.** BIOL ORGANISM ACTING AS A PARASITE CARRIER an organism in which a parasite lives and develops without damaging it, but from which the parasite passes to another species that is damaged by it **4.** ANAT = **cisterna 5.** LIQUID STORE IN A DEVICE a part of a machine or device where liquid is stored for use by the machine or device **6.** GEOL, INDUST UNDERGROUND SUPPLY OF GAS OR OIL a natural chamber in porous rock where a supply of natural gas or crude oil collects [Mid-17thC. From French, formed from *réserver* (see RESERVE).]

re·set (**-set, -set·ting, -sets**) *vt.* /ree sét/ **1. SET AGAIN** to set something again **2. PUT BACK TO ZERO** to change the reading of dial or counter to zero or a different number —**re·set·ta·ble** *adj.* —**re·set·ter** *n.*

re·set·tle /ree sétt'l/ (**-tled, -tling, -tles**) *vt.* to provide a group or population with a new place to live and transfer it there —**re·set·tle·ment** *n.*

res ges·tae /ràyss gé stī, rèez jé stee/ *npl.* circumstances and facts that may be admitted as evidence in a lawsuit because they shed light on the matters in question [From Latin, literally "things done"]

resh /resh/ *n.* the 20th letter of the Hebrew alphabet, represented in the English alphabet as "r" [Early 19thC. From Aramaic *rēš* "head."]

re·shape /ree sháyp/ (**-shaped, -shap·ing, -shapes**) *vt.* **1. CHANGE OR RESTORE THE SHAPE OF SOMETHING** to alter or restore the shape of something **2. CHANGE THE ORGANIZATION OF SOMETHING** to change the form or organization of something

re·shuf·fle /ree shúff'l/ *n.* **1.** CARDS **SHUFFLING OF CARDS AGAIN** an act of shuffling something, especially cards, again **2.** POL **REDISTRIBUTION OF JOBS** a reorganization of the jobs of a group of people, especially a change by a president or prime minister of the positions or personnel of a cabinet ■ *vt.* (**-fled, -fling, -fles**) **1.** CARDS **SHUFFLE CARDS AGAIN** to shuffle something, especially cards, again **2.** POL **REDISTRIBUTE JOBS** to carry out a reshuffle of jobs

re·sid /ri zíd/ *n.* residual oil (*informal*) [Mid-20thC. Shortening.]

re·side /ri zíd/ (**-sid·ed, -sid·ing, -sides**) *vi.* **1. LIVE SOMEWHERE** to have a home in a particular place **2. BE PRESENT IN** to be present in or belong to somebody or something **3. BE VESTED IN** to be vested or placed in somebody or something [15thC. Origin uncertain: probably via French *résider* from Latin *residere*, literally "to remain behind," from *sedere* "to sit."]

res·i·dence /rézzid'ns/ *n.* **1. HOME** the house, apartment, or other dwelling in which somebody lives **2. LARGE HOUSE** a grand and imposing dwelling **3.** BUSINESS **CORPORATION'S OFFICIAL HEADQUARTERS** the official headquarters of a corporation **4. LIVING SOMEWHERE** the fact of living in a particular place **5. TIME LIVED IN PLACE** the period of time that somebody lives in a particular place **6.** MED = **residency** ◇ **in residence 1.** living in a place at a particular time **2.** employed as a creative artist by an educational or other institution to foster interest in a subject

res·i·den·cy /rézzid'nsee/ (*plural* **-cies**) *n.* **1.** MED **MEDICAL TRAINING FOLLOWING INTERNSHIP** a period of specialized training in clinical medicine or surgery in a hospital on completion of an internship **2.** ARTS **PERFORMING AND TEACHING ENGAGEMENT** an engagement at a university or conservatory for a performer or group of performers, usually for at least a semester, that involves performance, teaching, and master classes **3.** HIST **OFFICIAL RESIDENCE OF AN INDIAN GOVERNOR** formerly, the official residence of a governor in India **4.** *U.K.* POL, HIST **TERRITORY ADMINISTERED BY A RESIDENT AGENT** formerly, a territory such as the East Indies that was administered by the resident agent of a protecting state

res·i·dent /rézzid'nt/ *n.* **1. SOMEBODY LIVING IN A PARTICULAR PLACE** somebody who lives permanently or for a considerable period in a particular place **2.** MED **DOCTOR COMPLETING A RESIDENCY** a doctor or surgeon engaged in a residency **3.** SOC WELFARE **SOMEBODY WHO LIVES IN A RESIDENTIAL SITUATION** somebody who lives in a nursing home, children's home, retirement home, or other communal housing **4.** POL **DIPLOMAT** a diplomatic official based in a foreign country **5.** POL **LOCAL ORGANIZER OF GOVERNMENTAL INVESTIGATIVE AGENCY** a member of a government intelligence-gathering agency, domestic or foreign, who lives in a certain area and oversees operations for the agency there **6.** ZOOL **NONMIGRATORY BIRD OR OTHER ANIMAL** a bird or other animal that does not migrate seasonally **7.** *U.K.* HIST, INTERNAT REL **BRITISH COLONIAL REPRESENTATIVE** a representative of the British government in a British colony or protectorate ■ *adj.* **1. LIVING IN A PARTICULAR PLACE** living permanently or for a considerable period in a particular place **2. LIVE-IN** living somewhere as part of a particular job **3. INHERENT** present or inherent in something **4.** ZOOL **NONMIGRATORY** not migrating seasonally **5.** COMPUT **PERMANENTLY INSTALLED IN A COMPUTER'S MEMORY** used to describe a computer program or data intentionally retained in random-access memory after being loaded, even if another program is executing, so that it can be accessed quickly —**res·i·dent·ship** *n.*

res·i·dent com·mis·sion·er *n.* a representative from a dependency who is allowed to speak but not vote in the U.S. House of Representatives

res·i·den·tial /rèzzi dénshəl/ *adj.* **1. RELATING TO HOUSING** relating to or consisting of private housing rather than offices or factories **2. USED FOR LONG-TERM LIVING** used as a place to live for the long term **3. WITH LIVING ACCOMMODATIONS** providing living accommodations [Mid-17thC. Formed from RESIDENCE.] —**res·i·den·tial·ly** *adv.*

res·i·den·tial school *n.* a government-run school providing education and living accommodations for children who are physically or mentally challenged

res·i·den·ti·ar·y /rèzzi dénshee èrree, -dénshəree/ *adj.* **1. LIVE-IN** requiring the incumbent to live in an official residence **2. LIVING IN AN OFFICIAL RESIDENCE** residing in an official residence

re·sid·u·al /ri zíjjoo əl/ *adj.* **1. LEFT OVER** remaining after completion of a process that involves the removal of part of the original ○ *residual damp* **2.** GEOL **RELATING TO RESIDUE FROM ROCK WEATHERING** relating to the material left after weathering of a rock and removal of its soluble constituents ■ *n.* **1. SOMETHING LEFT OVER** something that remains after completion of a process that involves the removal of part of the original **2.** STATS **DIFFERENCE BETWEEN ACTUAL AND THEORETICAL RESULTS** the difference between results obtained through theoretical calculation and those obtained through observation **3.** CINEMA, TV **REPEAT FEE** a payment to performers, directors, or writers when their filmed work is shown again, especially on television —**re·sid·u·al·ly** *adv.*

re·sid·u·al oil *n.* the low-grade hydrocarbons that remain after the process of petroleum distillation, used, e.g., in asphalt or as a furnace fuel

re·sid·u·ar·y /ri zíjjoo èrree/ *adj.* **1.** LAW **ENTITLED TO THE REMAINDER OF AN ESTATE** entitled to the residue of a deceased person's estate after debts have been paid and bequests distributed **2. LEFT OVER** remaining after a process has been gone through [Early 18thC. Formed from RESIDUUM.]

res·i·due /rézzi dòo/ *n.* **1. SOMETHING LEFT OVER** something that remains after a process involving the removal of part of the original has been completed **2.** LAW **REMAINDER OF AN ESTATE** the remainder of a deceased person's estate after debts have been paid and bequests distributed **3. REMAINDER AFTER PROCESSING** something remaining after a chemical or physical process such as combustion, distillation, evaporation, or filtration removes part of the original [14thC. Via Old French from Latin *residuum* "something remaining," from *residere* (see RESIDE).]

re·sid·u·um /ri zíjjoo əm/ (*plural* **-a** /-ə/) *n.* LAW = **residue** *n.* 2 [Late 17thC. From Latin (see RESIDUE).]

re·sign /ri zín/ (**-signed, -sign·ing, -signs**) *v.* **1.** *vti.* **LEAVE A JOB** to give up a paid or unpaid position voluntarily **2.** *vr.* **ACCEPT SOMETHING RELUCTANTLY** to come to terms with something and acquiesce in it reluctantly ○ *She'd resigned herself to giving up work.* **3.** *vt.* **RELINQUISH A CLAIM** to give up a right or claim to something [14thC. Via Old French *resigner* from Latin *resignare* "to unseal, cancel, give back," from *signare* "to seal," from *signum* "mark."] —**re·sign·er** *n.*

re-sign (**re-signed, re-sign·ing, re-signs**) *v.* **1.** *vti.* SPORTS **SIGN ANOTHER CONTRACT** to sign or cause a player to sign another contract **2.** *vt.* **SIGN AGAIN** to sign a document again

res·ig·na·tion /rèzzig náysh'n/ *n.* **1. NOTIFICATION OF LEAVING A JOB** a formal notification of leaving a paid or unpaid position ○ *I've handed in my resignation.* **2. DEPARTURE FROM JOB** an instance of leaving a paid or unpaid position **3. UNPROTESTING ACCEPTANCE OF SOMETHING** agreement to something, usually given reluctantly but without protest

re·signed /ri zínd/ *adj.* acquiescing in something reluctantly, but without protest —**re·sign·ed·ly** /ri zínədlee/ *adv.* —**re·sign·ed·ness** /-zínədnəss/ *n.*

re·sile /ri zíl/ (**-siled, -sil·ing, -siles**) *vi.* (*formal*) **1. SPRING BACK INTO THE SAME SHAPE** to spring back into the same shape or position **2. JUMP BACK** to jump or leap back [Early 16thC. Directly or via obsolete French *resilir* from Latin *resilire* (see RESILIENT).]

re·sil·ience /ri zíllyəns/, **re·sil·ien·cy** /ri zíllyənsee/ *n.* **1. SPEEDY RECOVERY FROM PROBLEMS** the ability to recover quickly from setbacks **2. ELASTICITY** the ability of matter to spring back quickly into shape after being bent, stretched, or deformed

re·sil·ient *adj.* **1. RECOVERING QUICKLY** able to recover quickly from setbacks **2. ELASTIC** able to spring back quickly into shape after being bent, stretched, or deformed [Mid-17thC. From Latin *resilient-*, the present participle stem of *resilire*, literally "to jump back," from *salire* (see SALIENT).] —**re·sil·ient·ly** *adv.*

res·in /rézzin/ *n.* **1.** PLANTS **ORGANIC SUBSTANCE FROM PLANTS** a solid or semisolid natural organic substance secreted in the sap of some plants and trees that has a transparent or translucent quality and a yellow or brown color. It is used in varnishes, paints, adhesives, inks, and medicines. **2.** CHEM **SYNTHETIC COMPOUND RESEMBLING RESIN** a synthetic polymeric compound physically resembling natural resin, e.g., polyvinyl, polystyrene, or epoxy, used in the petrochemical and plastics industries ■ *vt.* (**-ined, -in·ing, -ins**) **TREAT WITH RESIN** to coat or rub something with resin [14thC. Via Old French *resine* and Latin *resina* from, ultimately, Greek *rhētinē*, of unknown origin (source also of English *rosin*).] —**res·in·ous** *adj.* —**res·in·ous·ly** *adv.* —**res·in·ous·ness** *n.*

res·in·ate /rézzi nàyt/ (**-at·ed, -at·ing, -ates**) *vt.* to impregnate, saturate, or flavor something with resin

res·in ca·nal *n.* a tubular space between cells of woody vascular seed plants that is lined with resin-secreting cells

res·in·if·er·ous /rèzzi níffərəss/ *adj.* producing, yielding, or secreting resin

res·in·oid /rézzi nòyd/ *adj.* **OF RESIN** relating to or containing resin ■ *n.* **SYNTHETIC RESIN** a resinous, usually synthetic, substance

res ip·sa lo·qui·tur /ràyss ípsə lókwə tòor, rèez-/ *n.* a rule of evidence that allows that mere proof that an accident occurred is enough to prove negligence on the part of the defendant [From Latin, literally "the thing speaks for itself"]

re·sist /ri zíst/ *v.* (**-sist·ed, -sist·ing, -sists**) **1.** *vti.* **FIGHT AGAINST SOMEBODY OR SOMETHING** to oppose and stand firm against somebody or something **2.** *vt.* **REFUSE TO GIVE IN TO SOMETHING** to refuse to accept or comply with something ○ *resisted all attempts to force them out of their homes* **3.** *vt.* **BE UNHARMED BY SOMETHING** to remain unaltered by the damaging effect of something ○ *ability to resist infection* **4.** *vti.* **SAY NO TO SOMETHING TEMPTING** to refrain from something in spite of being tempted ○ *I couldn't resist having a peek* ■ *n.* TECH **PROTECTIVE COATING** a protective coating, especially one used to prevent corrosion or oxidation, provide electrical insulation in a printed circuit, or prevent part of a fabric from accepting dye [14thC. Directly and via French *résister* from Latin *resistere*, literally "to stand against," from *sistere* "to make stand," from *stare* "to stand."] —**re·sist·i·ble** *adj.* —**re·sist·i·bil·i·ty** /ri zìstə bíllətee/ *n.* —**re·sist·i·bly** /ri zístəblee/ *adv.*

re·sis·tance /ri zístəns/ *n.* **1. OPPOSITION** opposition to somebody or something **2. REFUSAL TO GIVE IN** refusal to accept or comply with something **3.** MED, PHYSIOL **ABILITY TO WITHSTAND DAMAGING EFFECT** the ability to remain unaltered by the damaging effect of something, e.g., an organism's ability not to succumb to disease or infection **4. ABILITY TO SAY NO TO TEMPTATION** the ability to refrain from something in spite of being tempted **5.** PHYS **FORCE OPPOSING ANOTHER FORCE** a force that opposes or slows down another force. Symbol *R*, **r** **6.** ELEC **OPPOSITION TO AN ELECTRIC CURRENT** the opposition that a circuit, component, or substance presents to the flow of electricity. Symbol *R* **7.** ELEC **SOURCE OF RESISTANCE** something such as a resistor that is a source of opposition to the flow of electricity. Symbol *R* **8.** PSYCHOANAL **REPRESSION OF THOUGHTS** the process by which the ego keeps repressed thoughts and feelings from the conscious mind

Re·sis·tance *n.* an illegal secret organization that fights for national freedom against an occupying power, especially one that fought in France, the Netherlands, Denmark, or Italy during World War II

re·sis·tant /ri zístənt/ *adj.* **1. RESISTING** offering resistance to something ○ *resistant to change* **2. NOT DAMAGED BY SOMETHING** unaltered by or impervious to the damaging effect of something (*often used in combination*) ○ *moisture-resistant* ■ *n.* **SOMEBODY OR**

SOMETHING THAT RESISTS somebody or something that offers resistance

re·sis·tive /ri zístiv/ *adj.* **1.** = **resistant 2.** ELEC ELECTRICALLY RESISTANT having the property of electrical resistance —**re·sis·tive·ly** *adv.* —**re·sis·tive·ness** *n.*

re·sis·tiv·i·ty /ri zìs tívvətee/ *n.* **1.** ELEC ELECTRICAL RESISTANCE OF A STANDARD-LENGTH SUBSTANCE the electrical resistance of a substance of a standard length and cross section. Symbol ρ **2.** ABILITY TO RESIST capacity to resist

re·sist·less /ri zístləss/ *adj.* **1.** IRRESISTIBLE not able to be resisted **2.** UNABLE TO RESIST not able to resist something

re·sis·tor /ri zístər/ *n.* a component of an electrical circuit that has resistance and is used to control the flow of electric current

re·size /ree sīz/ (**-sized, -siz·ing, -sizes**) *vt.* to make something a different size, e.g., a dress pattern or graphics on a computer screen

res ju·di·ca·ta /ràyss joodee kaátə, reéz-/, **res ad·ju·di·ca·ta** /ràyss ə joodee kaátə, reéz-/ *n.* an issue already decided by a court [From Latin, literally "judged matter"]

re·sole /ree sṓl/ (**-soled, -sol·ing, -soles**) *vt.* to put a new sole on a shoe

re·sol·u·ble[1] /ri zóllyəb'l/ *adj.* able to be resolved or analyzed [Early 17thC. Directly or via French from Latin *resolubilis*, from *resolvere*, literally "to loosen up."] —**res·ol·u·bil·ity** /ri zòllyə bíllətee/ *n.* —**re·sol·u·ble·ness** /ri zóllyəb'lnəss/ *n.*

re·sol·u·ble[2] /ree sóllyəb'l/ *adj.* able to be dissolved again [15thC. Formed from SOLUBLE.] —**re·sol·u·bil·i·ty** /ree sòllyə bíllətee/ *n.* —**re·sol·u·ble·ness** /-sóllyəb'lnəss/ *n.* —**re·sol·u·bly** /-sóllyəblee/ *adv.*

res·o·lute /rézzə lòot/ *adj.* **1.** HAVING DETERMINATION possessing determination and purposefulness **2.** CHARACTERIZED BY DETERMINATION motivated by or displaying determination and purposefulness [15thC. From Latin *resolutus*, the past participle of *resolvere* (see RESOLVE).] —**res·o·lute·ly** *adv.* —**res·o·lute·ness** *n.*

res·o·lu·tion /rèzzə lóosh'n/ *n.* **1.** RESOLVING OF SOMETHING the process of resolving something ○ *the resolution of a difficulty* **2.** JOINT FORMAL EXPRESSION OF OPINION a formal expression of the consensus at a meeting, arrived at after discussion and usually as the result of a vote **3.** DECISION a firm decision to do something **4.** DETERMINATION firmness of mind or purpose **5.** ELECTRON ENG REPRODUCTION OF DETAIL IN AN IMAGE the level of reproduction of detail offered by a TV or computer screen or a film image **6.** SOLUTION an answer to a problem **7.** PHYS, CHEM SEPARATION INTO CONSTITUENT PARTS the process or act of separating something such as a chemical compound or a source of light into its constituent parts **8.** MED SUBSIDING the disappearance or coming to an end of symptom or condition such as fever or inflammation **9.** MUSIC SATISFACTORY CONCLUSION OF A HARMONIC PATTERN the movement from a dissonant to a consonant chord or note **10.** MUSIC FINAL NOTE IN A HARMONIC PROGRESSION the note or chord to which the harmony moves when progressing from dissonance to consonance **11.** THEATER PART OF A STORY WHEN CONFLICT IS RESOLVED the point in a dramatic work when the conflict is resolved **12.** PHYS = **resolving power 13.** POETRY SYLLABLE REPLACEMENT the substitution of a long syllable for two short ones in the rhythm of a line of poetry [14thC. Directly and via Old French from, ultimately, Latin *resolut-*, the past participle stem of *resolvere* (see RESOLVE).]

re·solve /ri zólv/ *v.* (**-solved, -solv·ing, -solves**) **1.** *vti.* MAKE A DECISION to come to or cause somebody to come to a firm decision about something ○ *he resolved to leave* **2.** *vti.* SPLIT INTO CONSTITUENT PARTS to cause something to separate into its constituent elements, or to become separated into constituent parts **3.** *vt.* EXPRESS A JOINT OPINION FORMALLY to express the opinion of a meeting formally as a consensus, after discussion and usually as the result of a vote **4.** *vt.* SOLVE A DIFFICULTY to find a solution to a problem **5.** *vt.* DISPEL DOUBTS to dispel doubts or anxieties **6.** *vt.* SETTLE AN ARGUMENT to bring a disagreement to an end **7.** *vr.* CHANGE to change into something else **8.** *vti.* MED REDUCE A SWELLING to subside or to cause an inflammation, swelling, or tumor to subside **9.** *vt.* CHEM SEPARATE A RACEMIC MIXTURE to separate a racemic compound or mixture into its two components **10.** *vti.* MUSIC MOVE FROM DISSONANT TO CONSONANT to move, or cause a chord or note to move, from dissonant to consonant **11.** *vt.* PHYS MAKE PARTS OF AN IMAGE DISTINCT to make parts of an image distinct, e.g., in a microscope or telescope **12.** *vt.* MATH SPLIT A VECTOR INTO DIRECTIONAL COMPONENTS to separate a vector into its directional components ■ *n.* **1.** DETERMINATION firmness of purpose **2.** DECISION a firm decision to do something [14thC. Directly and via Old French from Latin *resolvere*, literally "to loosen up," from *solvere* (see SOLVE).] —**re·solv·a·bil·i·ty** /ri zòlvə bíllətee/ *n.* —**re·solv·a·ble** /-zólvəb'l/ *adj.* —**re·solv·a·ble·ness** /-zólvəb'lnəss/ *n.* —**re·solv·er** /-zólvər/ *n.*

re·solved /ri zólvd/ *adj.* determined in purpose —**re·sol·ved·ly** /-zólvədlee/ *adv.* —**re·solv·ed·ness** /-zólvədnəss/ *n.*

re·sol·vent /ri zólvənt/ *adj.* **1.** SCI CAUSING SEPARATION INTO CONSTITUENT ELEMENTS causing or capable of causing something to separate into its constituent elements **2.** MED ANTI-INFLAMMATORY able to cause reduction in inflammation or swelling ■ *n.* **1.** SCI SOMETHING CAUSING SEPARATION INTO CONSTITUENT ELEMENTS a substance that causes or is capable of causing something to separate into its constituent elements **2.** MED ANTI-INFLAMMATORY MEDICINE a medicine that reduces inflammation or swelling

re·solv·ing pow·er *n.* the ability of an optical system such as a telescope or microscope to distinguish objects separated by small angular distances

res·o·nance /rézzənənss/ *n.* **1.** RESONANT QUALITY the quality or state of being resonant **2.** UNDERLYING MEANING the effect of an event or work of art beyond its surface meaning **3.** ACOUSTICS AMPLIFIED SOUND an intense and prolonged sound produced by sympathetic vibration **4.** ACOUSTICS, MUSIC RINGING QUALITY OF AN INSTRUMENT OR VOICE an amplification of a sound, e.g., that of an instrument or the human voice, caused by sympathetic vibration in a chamber such as an auditorium or a singer's chest **5.** PHYS LARGE OSCILLATION AT A NATURAL FREQUENCY increased amplitude of oscillation of a mechanical system when it is subjected to vibration from another source at or near its own natural frequency **6.** ELEC OSCILLATION IN AN ELECTRICAL CIRCUIT a state of oscillation that occurs at a very specific frequency in an electrical circuit consisting of inductive and capacitive components **7.** MED SOUND WHEN A BODY CAVITY IS TAPPED the sound heard during tapping (**percussion**) of a healthy chest or abdomen **8.** CHEM PROPERTY OF CERTAIN CHEMICAL COMPOUNDS the property of some chemical compounds of having characteristics of two or more electronic structures simultaneously

res·o·nant /rézzənənt/ *adj.* **1.** DEEP IN SOUND deep and rich in sound **2.** RESOUNDING continuing to sound for some time **3.** ACOUSTICS CAUSING ECHOES producing or increasing amplification of sound or echoes, usually by sympathetic vibration [Late 16thC. Directly or via French from, ultimately, Latin *resonare* (see RESONATE).] —**res·o·nant·ly** *adv.*

res·o·nate /rézzə nàyt/ (**-nat·ed, -nat·ing, -nates**) *v.* **1.** *vti.* RESOUND to resound or echo, or cause something to resound or echo **2.** *vti.* MECH ENG, ELEC, CHEM PRODUCE OR MAKE SOMETHING PRODUCE RESONANCE to produce or exhibit chemical, mechanical, or electrical resonance, or to cause a chemical compound or a electrical system to produce or exhibit resonance **3.** *vi.* BE FAMILIAR to produce a response in somebody, especially by reminding that person of something [Late 19thC. From Latin *resonare* "to resound," from *sonare* "to sound."]

res·o·na·tor /rézzə nàytər/ *n.* **1.** ELEC RESONATING DEVICE a device or part that resonates, especially one that produces sound or microwaves **2.** MUSIC RESONATING PART OF AN INSTRUMENT a part of a musical instrument designed to produce resonance, e.g., the hollow body of a violin or the tubes in a vibraphone

re·sorb /ri sáwrb, -záwrb/ (**-sorbed, -sorb·ing, -sorbs**) *vt.* to absorb something again [Mid-17thC. From Latin *resorbere*, literally "to drink in again," from *sorbere* (see ABSORB).] —**re·sor·bent** *adj.*

res·or·cin·ol /ri záwrsi nàwl/ *n.* a colorless crystalline phenol used in making dyes, resins, and drugs and in tanning. Formula: $C_6H_6O_2$. [Late 19thC. Coined from RESIN + *orcin* + -OL.]

re·sorp·tion /ri sáwrpshən, -záwrpshən/ *n.* **1.** RESORBING OR BEING RESORBED the process or state of resorbing or being resorbed **2.** GEOL PARTIAL FUSION OF A CRYSTAL IN A MAGMA the partial fusion of a crystal in a magma in response to changing conditions of temperature and pressure [Early 19thC. Formed from RESORB, on the model of *absorption*.] —**re·sorp·tive** /ri sáwrptəv, -záwrp-/ *adj.*

re·sort /ri záwrt/ *n.* **1.** VACATION PLACE a place that is popular for recreation and vacations and provides accommodations and entertainment **2.** SOURCE OF HELP a person, place, or course of action seen as a source of help in dealing with a problem ○ *As a last resort we could sell the car.* **3.** ACT OF HAVING RECOURSE TO the act of turning to somebody or something for help in dealing with a problem **4.** FREQUENT VISITING the act of going somewhere frequently or in large numbers **5.** MUCH-VISITED PLACE a place frequently visited [14thC. From Old French *resortir*, literally "to come back," from *sortir* "to go out" (source of English *sortie*).]

resort to *vt.* **1.** HAVE RECOURSE TO SOMETHING to turn to something, sometimes something extreme, for help in dealing with a problem **2.** GO SOMEWHERE FREQUENTLY VISITED to go somewhere that is frequently visited, or go somewhere in large numbers

re·sort (**re·sort·ed, re·sort·ing, re·sorts**) *vt.* to sort something again

re·sound /ri zównd/ (**-sound·ed, -sound·ing, -sounds**) *v.* **1.** *vi.* MAKE A REVERBERATING SOUND to produce a long reverberating sound **2.** *vi.* SOUND CLEARLY to sound loudly and clearly **3.** *vi.* BE FILLED WITH A REVERBERATING SOUND to be filled with a long reverberating sound ○ *the hall resounded to the cheers of the audience* **4.** *vi.* BE EXTREMELY WELL KNOWN to be extremely well known, especially over a long period or a wide area **5.** *vt.* SAY SOMETHING SO THAT IT ECHOES to say something loudly and in echoing tones [14thC. Alteration of Old French *resoner* (under the influence of SOUND), from Latin *resonare* (see RESONATE).]

re·sound·ing /ri zównding/ *adj.* **1.** CLEAR AND EMPHATIC clear and unequivocal ○ *a resounding defeat* **2.** ECHOING LOUDLY making a loud noise that echoes —**re·sound·ing·ly** *adv.*

re·source /reé sàwrs, ri sáwrs/ *n.* **1.** SOURCE OF HELP somebody who or something that can be used as a source of help or information **2.** BACKUP SUPPLY a reserve supply of something such as money, personnel, or equipment **3.** ABILITY TO FIND SOLUTIONS adeptness at finding solutions to problems **4.** = **natural resource** ■ *npl.* **1.** TALENT DRAWN ON WHEN NECESSARY an inner ability or capacity that is drawn on in time of need **2.** NATION'S NATURAL, ECONOMIC, OR MILITARY ASSET a natural, economic, political, or military asset enjoyed by a nation, e.g., mineral wealth, labor, capital, or military personnel **3.** COMM COMPANY'S ASSET a source drawn on by a company for making profit, e.g., personnel, capital, machinery, or stock [Early 17thC. Via French, from, ultimately, Latin *resurgere* "to rise again, be replenished," from *surgere*, literally "to rise up from below."] —**re·source·less** /reé sàwrsləss, ri sáwrsləss/ *adj.*

re·source·ful /ri sáwrsfəl/ *adj.* full of initiative and good at problem-solving, especially in difficult situations —**re·source·ful·ly** *adv.* —**re·source·ful·ness** *n.*

resp. *abbr.* **1.** respective **2.** respectively **3.** respiration **4.** respondent

re·spect /ri spékt/ *n.* **1.** CHARACTERISTIC an individual characteristic or point ○ *satisfactory in all respects* **2.** ESTEEM a feeling or attitude of admiration and deference toward somebody or something ○ *won the respect of her colleagues* **3.** STATE OF BEING ADMIRED the state of being admired deferentially **4.** THOUGHTFULNESS consideration or thoughtfulness ■ **re·spects** *npl.* REGARDS polite greetings offered to somebody ■ *vt.* (**-spect·ed, -spect·ing, -spects**) **1.** ESTEEM SOMEBODY OR SOMETHING to feel or show admiration and deference toward somebody or something **2.** NOT GO AGAINST OR VIOLATE to pay due attention to and refrain from violating something ○ *respect the law* ○ *respect another's privacy* **3.** BE CONSIDERATE IN DEALING WITH to show consideration or thoughtfulness in relation to somebody or something [14thC. Via Old French from Latin *respectus*, the past participle of *respicere* "to regard," literally "to look back at," from *specere* "to look at."] —**re·spect·er** *n.*

WORD KEY: SYNONYMS

See Synonyms at ***regard***.

re·spect·a·ble /ri spéktəb'l/ *adj.* **1.** MORALLY ABOVE REPROACH in accordance with accepted standards of correctness or decency ○ *a respectable district* **2.** SATISFACTORY meeting an adequate standard ○ *a respectable salary* **3.** WORTHY OF RESPECT deserving or receiving respect **4.** LARGE ENOUGH sufficiently large **5.** ACCEPTABLE IN APPEARANCE tidy and fit to be seen in public (*informal*) —**re·spect·a·bil·i·ty** /ri spèktə bíllətee/ *n.* —

re·spect·a·ble·ness /ri spéktəb'lnəss/ *n.* **—re·spect·a·bly** /-spéktəblee/ *adv.*

re·spect·ed /ri spéktəd/ *adj.* held in high regard by equals as well as subordinates

re·spect·ful /ri spéktfəl/ *adj.* showing appropriate deference and respect **—re·spect·ful·ly** *adv.* **—re·spect·ful·ness** *n.*

re·spect·ing /ri spékting/ *prep.* regarding or concerning somebody or something

re·spec·tive /ri spéktiv/ *adj.* varying according to each of the people or things concerned ○ *they returned to their respective homes* **—re·spec·tive·ness** *n.*

re·spec·tive·ly /ri spéktivlee/ *adv.* matching one list with another in the order given for both ○ *Joe and his wife are aged 52 and 51 respectively.*

re·spell /ree spél/ (**-spelled, -spell·ing, -spells**) *vt.* to spell something again or in a different way, especially using a different alphabet in order to give guidance on pronunciation **—re·spell·ing** *n.*

res·pi·ra·ble /résparəb'l, ri spírəb'l/ *adj.* fit or able to be breathed **—res·pi·ra·bil·i·ty** /rèsparə bíllətee, ri spīrə bíllətee/ *n.*

res·pi·ra·tion /rèspə ráysh'n/ *n.* **1. BREATHING** the act of breathing air in and out **2.** BIOL **DISTRIBUTION OF OXYGEN** the complete chemical and physical process in which oxygen is delivered to tissues or cells of the body and carbon dioxide and water are given off **3.** BIOL **OXIDATION PROCESS IN CELLS** an energy-producing oxidation process in cells **—res·pi·ra·tion·al** /rèspə ráyshən'l, -ráyshnəl/ *adj.*

res·pi·ra·tor /réspə ràytər/ *n.* **1. MACHINE PROVIDING ARTIFICIAL RESPIRATION** a machine used in hospitals to maintain breathing **2. PROTECTIVE MASK THROUGH WHICH TO BREATHE** a device placed over the nose and mouth to filter out noxious particles and fumes from inhaled air or to warm chilled air before it is inhaled

res·pi·ra·to·ry /résparə tàwree, ri spírə-/ *adj.* relating to or used in breathing or the system in the body that takes in and distributes oxygen

res·pi·ra·to·ry dis·tress syn·drome *n.* a respiratory disease of newborns, especially premature infants, caused by the inability of the lungs to take in oxygen and marked by cyanosis and difficult breathing

res·pi·ra·to·ry pig·ment *n.* a protein such as hemoglobin found in any of several colors in the cells of living organisms and serving to transfer oxygen atoms among some molecules active in cellular respiration

res·pi·ra·to·ry quo·tient *n.* the ratio of the volume of carbon dioxide released to the volume of oxygen absorbed by an organism, cell, or tissue over a given time period

res·pi·ra·to·ry sys·tem *n.* the system of organs in the body responsible for the intake of oxygen and the expiration of carbon dioxide. In mammals it consists of the lungs, bronchi, bronchioles, trachea, diaphragm, and nerve supply.

re·spire /ri spír/ (**-spired, -spir·ing, -spires**) *v.* **1.** *vti.* **BREATHE** to breathe air in and out **2.** *vi.* **BREATHE NORMALLY AFTER ANXIETY OR EXERTION** to breathe again in a normal way after anxiety or exertion (*literary*) [14thC. Directly or via French from Latin *respirare*, literally "to breathe again," from *spirare* "to breathe."]

res·pi·rom·e·ter /rèspə rómmətər/ *n.* an instrument for measuring and studying the process in which oxygen is taken into the body, delivered to tissues and cells, and used by them [Late 19thC. Coined from RESPIRATION + -METER.] **—res·pi·ro·met·ric** /rèsparō méttrik/ *adj.* **—res·pi·rom·e·try** /rèspə rómmətree/ *n.*

res·pite /réspit/ *n.* **1. BRIEF INTERVAL OF REST** a brief period of rest and recovery between periods of exertion or after something disagreeable **2. DELAY** a temporary delay **3.** LAW **REPRIEVE** a temporary stay of execution of a criminal [13thC. Via Old French, "refuge," from Latin *respectus*, the past participle of *respicere* "to look back."]

re·splen·dent /ri spléndənt/ *adj.* having a dazzlingly impressive appearance ○ *resplendent in his dress uniform* [15thC. From Latin *resplendere*, literally "to shine brightly," from *splendere* "to shine."] **—re·splen·dence** *n.* **—re·splen·dent·ly** *adv.*

re·spond /ri spónd/ *v.* (**-spond·ed, -spond·ing, -sponds**) **1.** *vti.* **PROVIDE AN ANSWER** to reply something or to something in spoken or written words **2.** *vi.* **REACT** to act or do something in reaction to something else ○ *was unsure of how to respond to his moods* **3.** *vi.* MED **HAVE A POSITIVE MEDICAL REACTION** to react positively to medical treatment ■ *n.* **1.** ARCHIT **PILASTER OR PILLAR SUPPORTING ARCH** a pilaster or pillar that supports an arch **2.** CHR, MUSIC **CHORAL PART OF AN ANTHEM** the choral part in an anthem for priest and choir following a lesson in a church service [Mid-16thC. Via Old French *respondre* from Latin *respondere*, literally "to promise in return," from *spondere* "to pledge."] **—re·spon·dence** *n.*

re·spon·dent /ri spóndənt/ *n.* **1. ANSWERER** somebody who replies to something **2.** LAW **DEFENDANT** the person against whom a divorce petition or an appeal is brought ■ *adj.* **1. RESPONDING** giving a response **2.** LAW **BEING A RESPONDENT** being a defendant in a divorce petition or appeal

re·spon·sa /ri spónsə/ plural of **responsum**

re·sponse /ri spóns/ *n.* **1. REPLY TO A QUESTION** something said or written in reply to a statement or question from somebody else **2. REACTION** something done in reaction to something else **3.** CARDS **BID IN BRIDGE** a bid in bridge that is in reply to a partner's bid or double **4.** CHR **REPLY MADE BY A CHURCH CHOIR** a phrase sung or spoken by the choir or congregation in reply to the officiant during a church service **5.** MED **BODY'S REACTION TO A STIMULUS** the reaction of an organism or any of its parts to a stimulus [14thC. Directly or via Old French from Latin *responsum*, from the past participle of *respondere* (see RESPOND).] **—re·sponse·less** /ri spónsləss/ *adj.*

WORD KEY: SYNONYMS

See Synonyms at ***answer***.

re·spon·si·bil·i·ty /ri spònsə bíllətee/ (*plural* **-ties**) *n.* **1. ACCOUNTABILITY** the state, fact, or position of being accountable to somebody or for something ○ *The responsibilities of parenthood* **2. BLAME** the blame for something that has happened ○ *took full responsibility for the mixup* **3. SOMETHING TO BE RESPONSIBLE FOR** somebody or something for which a person or organization is responsible **4. AUTHORITY TO ACT** authority to make decisions independently

re·spon·si·ble /ri spónsəb'l/ *adj.* **1. ANSWERABLE TO SOMEBODY** accountable to somebody for an action or for the successful carrying out of a duty **2. IMPORTANT** conferring the authority to take decisions independently and requiring conscientiousness and trustworthiness ○ *in a responsible position* **3. BEING TO BLAME FOR SOMETHING** being the cause of something, usually something wrong or disapproved of ○ *Who's responsible for this mess?* **4. IN CHARGE OF SOMEBODY OR SOMETHING** expected to deal with something or take care of somebody **5. RELIABLE** able to be counted on owing to qualities of conscientiousness and trustworthiness **6. RATIONAL AND ACCOUNTABLE FOR YOUR ACTIONS** capable of taking rational or moral decisions, and therefore accountable for your actions **7. HAVING AUTHORITY TO ACT** having the authority to take decisions independently **8.** FIN **FINANCIALLY SOUND** having adequate means to meet financial obligations [Late 16thC. Via obsolete French, "corresponding," from Latin *respons-*, the past participle stem of *respondere* (see RESPOND).] **—re·spon·si·ble·ness** /ri spónsəb'lnəss/ *n.* **—re·spon·si·bly** /ri spónsəblee/ *adv.*

re·spon·sive /ri spónsiv/ *adj.* **1. SHOWING A POSITIVE RESPONSE** reacting quickly, strongly, or favorably to something, especially a suggestion or proposal **2. DONE IN RESPONSE** serving to respond to something **3.** CHR **CONSISTING OF A CHOIR'S OR CONGREGATION'S RESPONSES** consisting of responses by a choir or congregation in a church service **—re·spon·sive·ly** *adv.* **—re·spon·sive·ness** *n.*

re·spon·so·ry /ri spónsəree/ (*plural* **-ries**) *n.* an anthem consisting of short verses sung or spoken by the officiant and responses sung or spoken by the choir, especially after the lesson in a church service **—re·spon·so·ri·al** /ri spòn sáwree əl/ *adj.*

re·spon·sum /ri spónsəm/ (*plural* **-sa** /ri spónsə/) *n.* a definitive written reply by a rabbinic authority to a question on religion [Late 19thC. From Latin, "reply," from the past participle of *respondere* (see RESPOND).]

res pub·li·ca /ràyss pōōbli kaà, reèz púbblikə/ *n.* **1.** POL **CONCEPT OF THE STATE** the state, a republic, or the commonwealth as a concept **2. PUBLIC GOOD** the public or common good [From Latin, literally "public matter"]

res·sen·ti·ment /rə saàNti maàN/ *n.* a feeling of resentment and hostility characterized by an inability to act to change the situation [Mid-20thC. Directly or via German from French, formed from *ressentir* (see RESENT).]

rest[1] /rest/ *n.* **1. CESSATION OF LABOR** a state or period of refreshing freedom from exertion ○ *a period of rest and recreation* **2. REFRESHING REPOSE OF SLEEP** the repose of sleep that is refreshing to body and mind and is marked by a reduction in metabolic activity **3. CESSATION OF MOVEMENT** the cessation of movement or action **4. REPOSE OF DEATH** death perceived as freedom from earthly toil **5. FREEDOM FROM ANXIETY** freedom from mental or emotional anxiety ○ *I put her mind at rest* **6.** MUSIC **PAUSE IN MUSIC** a rhythmic pause between musical notes, or the mark indicating a musical pause **7.** POETRY = **caesura 8. PLACE TO STOP AND REST** a stopping place for shelter and rest **9. SUPPORT** something used for support, especially on a piece of furniture ■ *v.* (**rest·ed, rest·ing, rests**) **1.** *vti.* **SLEEP OR RELAX** to restore energy to somebody or something by means of relaxation or sleep ○ *rest the sled dogs* ○ *Put your feet up and rest.* **2.** *vi.* **BE TRANQUIL** to be in a state of tranquility **3.** *vi.* **BE DEAD** to be dead, and so free from earthly concerns **4.** *vti.* **STOP MOVING** to cease activity, or cause something to cease activity **5.** *vi.* **BE LEFT ALONE** to be subject to no further discussion or attention ○ *Let the matter rest.* **6.** *vi.* **LIE FALLOW** to lie unfarmed **7.** *vti.* **SUPPORT OR BE SUPPORTED** to support something, or to be supported, on or against something ○ *the ornament was resting on a narrow ledge* **8.** *vi.* **LIGHT ON** to allow the eyes to come to a stop on somebody or something **9.** *vi.* **BE VESTED IN** to be vested or placed in somebody or something **10.** *vi.* **DEPEND ON SOMEBODY OR SOMETHING** to depend on somebody or something for action or as a burden or responsibility **11.** *vi.* **BE BASED ON SOMETHING** to rely on something for proof or explanation **12.** *vti.* LAW **CONCLUDE A LEGAL CASE** to conclude the presentation of evidence in a case ○ *I rest my case.* [The verb is from Old English *ræstan*; the noun from Old English *ræst*, both of prehistoric Germanic origin] **—rest·er** *n.*

rest[2] /rest/ *n.* **REMAINDER** something left as a remainder (*takes a singular or plural verb*) ■ *vi.* (**rest·ed, rest·ing, rests**) **CONTINUE TO BE** to remain or continue to be (*usually used as a command*) ○ *Rest assured that we're doing everything possible.* [15thC. From French *reste* "remnant," from *rester* "to remain," from Latin *restare* "to stay behind," literally "to stand back," from *stare* (see STATION).]

rest ar·e·a *n. U.S., ANZ* an area on the side of a major road where motorists can rest. These areas may be equipped with picnic tables, light refreshments, or toilet facilities.

re·start (**-start·ed, -start·ing, -starts**) *vti.* /ree staárt/ **1. RESUME SOMETHING** to begin doing something again after it was stopped or suspended **2. GET SOMETHING WORKING AGAIN** to start something or get it working again **—re·start** *n.* **—re·start·a·ble** *adj.*

re·state /ree stáyt/ (**-stat·ed, -stat·ing, -states**) *vt.* to say something again, especially in order to clarify or summarize what has already been said ○ *time to restate our goals*

res·tau·rant /réstərənt, -ròntl/ *n.* a place where meals and drinks are sold and served to customers [Early 19thC. From French, the present participle of *restaurer* "to restore" (see RESTORE).]

res·tau·rant car *n. U.K.* = **dining car**

res·tau·ra·teur /rèstərə túr/, **res·tau·ran·teur** /réstərəntər, -rontər/ *n.* somebody who owns or manages a restaurant [Late 18thC. From French, literally "restorer," from *restaurer* "to restore" (see RESTORE).]

rest cure *n.* a treatment involving complete rest, e.g., as a remedy for stress

rest·ed /réstəd/ *adj.* refreshed and relaxed following a period of rest

rest·ful /réstfəl/ *adj.* **1. PROVIDING REST** giving, promoting, or involving rest ○ *a restful vacation* **2. CALM** at rest or tranquil **—rest·ful·ly** *adv.* **—rest·ful·ness** *n.*

rest·har·row /rést hèrrō/ *n.* a pod-bearing plant of Europe and Asia that has three-lobed leaves, woody stems and roots, and clusters of white, purple, or pink flowers. Latin name: *Ononsis repens* and *Ononsis spinosa.* [So called because its tough roots can stop, or arrest, the progress of a harrow]

rest home *n.* a place where senior citizens and chronically ill people are housed and cared for (*dated*)

rest·ing /résting/ *adj.* **1.** BIOL **IMMOBILE** used to describe organisms that are not moving or active **2. DEAD** having recently died (*used euphemistically*) **3.** CELL BIOL **NOT DIVIDING** not undergoing cell division **4.** BOT

DORMANT used to describe spores, seeds, and eggs that are dormant before germination

res·ti·tu·tion /rèstə to͞osh'n/ *n.* **1. GIVING BACK** the return of something to its rightful owner **2. PAYING BACK** compensation for a loss, damage, or injury **3. RESTORATION** the return of something to the condition it was in before it was changed [13thC. Directly or via French from the Latin stem *restitution-*, ultimately from *restituere* "to restore," from *statuere* "to set up, establish" (see STATUE).] —**res·ti·tu·tive** /réstə to͞otiv/ *adj.* —**res·ti·tu·to·ry** /rèstə to͞otəree, ri stíchə tàwree/ *adj.*

res·tive /réstiv/ *adj.* **1. UNEASY** uneasy and on the verge of resisting control ○ *The people soon grew restive under the rule of the occupying force.* **2. IMPATIENT** having little patience and unwilling to tolerate annoyances **3. OBSTINATE OR AWKWARD** unwilling to be guided or controlled ○ *a restive horse* [Late 16thC. An alteration of earlier *restiff*, from Old French *restif*, from, ultimately, Latin *restare* "to rest."] —**res·tive·ly** *adv.* —**res·tive·ness** *n.*

rest·less /réstləss/ *adj.* **1. CONSTANTLY MOVING** constantly moving, or unable to be still ○ *Some waited patiently but others were restless.* **2. DISCONTENTED** seeking a change because of discontent ○ *He began to feel restless after only a few weeks in the job.* **3. SLEEPLESS** lacking rest or sleep ○ *She spent a restless night worrying.* —**rest·less·ly** *adv.* —**rest·less·ness** *n.*

rest mass *n.* the mass a body has when it is not moving, as opposed to the additional mass it gains as a result of its movement, according to the theory of relativity

re·stock /ree stók/ (**-stocked, -stock·ing, -stocks**) *vti.* to replace or refill something after it has been used or its contents emptied —**re·stock·able** *adj.*

res·to·ra·tion /rèstə ráysh'n/ *n.* **1. RESTORING OF SOMETHING** the return of something that was removed, or the restoring of something to a former condition ○ *calls for the restoration of curfews* **2. THING RESTORED** something, especially a building, that has been brought back to an earlier and usually better condition **3. MODEL** a model made to resemble or represent something in its original condition ○ *a restoration of a Neanderthal dwelling*

Res·to·ra·tion *n.* the reestablishment of monarchy in Great Britain under Charles II in 1660, or the period of his reign

re·stor·a·tive /ri stáwrətiv/ *adj.* **GIVING NEW STRENGTH** tending or meant to give somebody new strength or vigor ○ *restorative properties of a vacation* ■ *n.* **SOMETHING THAT RESTORES** something that gives somebody new strength or vigor, especially an activity or medication —**re·stor·a·tive·ly** *adv.* —**re·stor·a·tive·ness** *n.*

re·store /ri stáwr/ (**-stored, -stor·ing, -stores**) *vt.* **1. GIVE SOMETHING BACK** to return something to its proper owner or place **2. RETURN SOMETHING TO PREVIOUS CONDITION** to bring something back to an earlier and better condition ○ *techniques used to restore old oil paintings* **3. MAKE SOMEBODY FEEL BETTER** to give somebody new strength or vigor ○ *I felt restored after my weekend away.* **4. RETURN SOMEBODY TO PREVIOUS POSITION** to return somebody to a previously held rank, office, or position ○ *restore the ousted governor to his office* **5. PUT SOMETHING BACK** to reestablish or put back something that was once but is no longer there ○ *restore order in the capital* [13thC. Via Old French *restorer* from Latin *restaurare*, literally "to set upright again," from the stem *-staurare*.] —**re·stor·a·ble** *adj.* —**re·stor·er** *n.*

WORD KEY: SYNONYMS

See Synonyms at *renew*.

re·strain /ri stráyn/ (**-strained, -strain·ing, -strains**) *vt.* **1. HOLD SOMEBODY BACK** to prevent somebody or yourself from doing something ○ *I couldn't restrain myself from calling out.* **2. CONTROL SOMETHING** to keep something under control or within limits ○ *trying to restrain his desire to flee* **3. CONTROL SOMEBODY** to physically control the movements of a person or animal ○ *Restrain him before he hurts someone.* **4. IMPRISON SOMEBODY** to put somebody in prison or otherwise take away his or her freedom [14thC. Via Old French *restreindre* from Latin *restingere* "to bind fast, confine," from *stringere* "to draw tight" (see STRAIN).] —**re·strain·a·ble** *adj.*

re·strained /ri stráynd/ *adj.* characterized by control, especially in not being excessively emotional or aggressive ○ *the artist's restrained use of color* —**re·strain·ed·ly** /-stráynədlee/ *adv.*

re·strain·ing or·der *n.* a court order that commands somebody to stop doing something until the issuing court can determine its legality

re·straint /ri stráynt/ *n.* **1. HOLDING BACK** an act or the quality of holding back, limiting, or controlling something ○ *Although severely provoked, she showed admirable restraint in not retaliating.* **2. RESTRAINING THING** something that controls or limits somebody or something ○ *impose trade restraints* **3. HOLDING DEVICE** something that is fastened to limit somebody's freedom of movement [14thC. From Old French *restreinte*, the feminine past participle of *restreindre* (see RESTRAIN).]

re·straint of trade *n.* the limiting of commercial competition by means such as price-fixing or monopolistic practices

re·strict /ri stríkt/ (**-strict·ed, -strict·ing, -stricts**) *vt.* to keep something within fixed limits ○ *Entry is restricted to members only.* [15thC. From Latin *restrictus*, the past participle of *restringere* (see RESTRAIN).]

re·strict·ed /ri stríktəd/ *adj.* **1. LIMITED** limited or made smaller or less than might be desired ○ *It's difficult to turn the vehicle in such a restricted space.* **2. SUBJECT TO CONTROLS** subject to controls or limits, e.g., of time or availability ○ *restricted use of the facilities* **3. REQUIRING AUTHORIZATION** intended only for authorized people ○ *That information is restricted.* —**re·strict·ed·ly** *adv.*

re·stric·tion /ri stríkshən/ *n.* **1. SOMETHING THAT LIMITS** something that limits or controls something else ○ *There are restrictions on the use of the photocopier.* **2. ACT OR STATE OF RESTRICTING** a restricting of something, or the condition of being restricted ○ *the restriction of a person's freedom*

re·stric·tion en·zyme *n.* an enzyme that can be used to break down DNA into segments at precise locations for use in genetic engineering

re·stric·tion frag·ment *n.* a portion of a larger DNA molecule that has been separated at precise locations by a restriction enzyme

re·stric·tive /ri stríktiv/ *adj.* **1. TENDING TO LIMIT** acting as a limit or control on something **2.** GRAM **LIMITING A MEANING** limiting the range of reference or application of a word, phrase, or clause —**re·stric·tive·ly** *adv.* —**re·stric·tive·ness** *n.*

re·stric·tive cov·e·nant *n.* a stipulation on a party buying or leasing land to refrain from something, e.g., reselling or subletting it

re·strike *n.* /reé strìk/ a coin struck at a later date from a die that has already been used to produce the original issue —**re·strike** *vt.*

rest·room /rést ro͝om, -ro͞om/ *n.* a room that includes a toilet, especially in a building used by the public

re·struc·ture /ree strúkchər/ (**-tured, -tur·ing, -tures**) *v.* **1.** *vti.* **CHANGE SOMETHING'S BASIC STRUCTURE** to change the way in which something is organized or arranged ○ *restructure the company* **2.** *vt.* FIN **REORGANIZE A DEBT** to alter the terms of a loan, especially to relieve its burden on the debtor

re·struc·tur·ing /ree strúkchəring/ *n.* the process or an instance of changing the way in which something is organized or arranged

rest stop *n.* **1.** = **rest area 2. BREAK IN JOURNEY** a break in a journey for the use of a restroom or for refreshment

re·sult /ri zúlt/ *vi.* (**-sult·ed, -sult·ing, -sults**) **1. FOLLOW AS CONSEQUENCE** to follow as a consequence of a particular action, condition, or event ○ *This kind of error results from inattention.* **2. CAUSE AN OUTCOME** to produce a particular outcome ○ *Overgrazing results in soil erosion.* ■ *n.* **1. CONSEQUENCE** something that follows as a consequence of a particular action, condition, or event **2. NUMBER** a number arrived at by a calculation **3. SCORE** an outcome, especially the final score in a sporting competition or the grade awarded to somebody who has taken a test ○ *The results were in Saturday's paper.* ■ **re·sults** *npl.* **DESIRED OUTCOME** the desired outcome from an action ○ *The new policy is already showing results.* [15thC. From Latin *resultare* "to spring back, reverberate" ("to result" in medieval Latin), from *saltare* "to jump" (source of English *sauté*).]

re·sul·tant /ri zúltnət/ *adj.* **RESULTING FROM** happening as a consequence of something else ■ *n.* **1. OUTCOME OF SOMETHING ELSE** something that is an outcome of something else such as a calculation **2.** PHYS, MATH **SINGLE VECTOR EQUIVALENT TO OTHERS ADDED** a single vector that is equivalent to two or more other vectors

re·sul·tant tone *n.* a tone that is created by the sounding together of two other tones but is different from both of them

re·sume /ri zo͞om/ (**-sumed, -sum·ing, -sumes**) *v.* **1.** *vti.* **CONTINUE SOMETHING** to continue with something after a temporary halt **2.** *vt.* **TAKE SOMETHING AGAIN** to take, assume, or occupy a position again ○ *She came in and resumed her place at the head of the table.* [15thC. Directly or via French *résumer* from Latin *resumere* "to take up again," from *sumere* "to take" (source of English *assume*).] —**re·sum·a·ble** *adj.*

ré·su·mé /rézzə mày/, **re·su·mé, re·su·me** *n.* **1.** *U.S., Can, ANZ* **WORK HISTORY** a summary of somebody's educational and work experience, for the information of possible future employers. A résumé is typically used by people in all professions except academia and medicine. **2. SUMMARY** a summary of something such as events that have happened ○ *a résumé of the afternoon's activities* [Early 19thC. From French, the past participle of *résumer* "to sum up" (probably influenced by Old French *sommer* "to find the sum of") (see RESUME).]

re·sump·tion /ri zúmpshən/ *n.* the act or an instance of continuing with something that has been stopped for a while ○ *hoping for a resumption of negotiations* [15thC. Directly or via French *résumption* from Latin *resumpt-*, the past participle stem of *resumere* (see RESUME).]

re·su·pi·nate /ri so͞opə nàyt, -nət/ *adj.* used to describe a plant part, especially the flower of an orchid, that grows upside down or appears to do so [Late 18thC. From Latin *resupinatus*, the past participle of *resupinare* "to bend back," ultimately from *supinus* "turned upwards."] —**re·su·pi·na·tion** /ri so͞opə náysh'n/ *n.*

re·sur·face /ree súrfəss/ (**-faced, -fac·ing, -fac·es**) *v.* **1.** *vi.* **COME TO SURFACE AGAIN** to come back to the surface of a body of water after having submerged **2.** *vi.* **APPEAR AGAIN** to appear again after having disappeared or been absent ○ *He resurfaced in Bangkok after the war.* **3.** *vt.* **PUT NEW SURFACE ON SOMETHING** to put a new surface on something, especially a road

re·surge /ri súrj/ (**-surged, -surg·ing, -surg·es**) *vi.* **1. RISE AGAIN** to rise or grow strong again **2. SWEEP BACK** to sweep forward or back in a powerful way ○ *watched the waves dissipate and resurge along the rocky shore* [Late 16thC. From Latin *resurgere*, from *surgere* "to rise" (see SURGE).]

re·sur·gent /ri súrjənt/ *adj.* rising or becoming stronger again [Late 18thC. From Latin *resurgere* (see RESURGE).] —**re·sur·gence** *n.*

res·ur·rect /rèzzə rékt/ (**-rect·ed, -rect·ing, -rects**) *v.* **1.** *vti.* **RAISE SOMEBODY FROM DEAD** to come or bring somebody back to life after apparent death **2.** *vt.* **REINSTATE SOMETHING** to bring back into use something that had been stopped or discarded ○ *resurrect an old argument* [Late 18thC. Back-formation from RESURRECTION.]

res·ur·rec·tion /rèzzə rékshən/ *n.* **1. RISING FROM DEAD** in some systems of belief, a rising or raising from the dead, or the state of having risen from the dead **2. REVIVAL** the revival of something old or long disused ○ *the resurrection of a youthful dream* [13thC. Via Old French *résurrection* from, ultimately, Latin *resurrect-*, the past participle stem of *resurgere* (see RESURGE).] —**res·ur·rec·tion·al** *adj.*

Res·ur·rec·tion *n.* **1. JESUS CHRIST'S RISING FROM THE DEAD** in Christian belief, the rising of Jesus Christ from the dead after his crucifixion and entombment **2. RISING OF DEAD ON JUDGMENT DAY** the rising of the dead on Judgment Day, as anticipated by Christians, Jews, and Muslims

res·ur·rec·tion plant *n.* a plant that survives well in hot, dry conditions such as the Rose of Jericho

re·sus·ci·tate /ri sússə tàyt/ (**-tat·ed, -tat·ing, -tates**) *v.* **1.** *vti.* **REVIVE SOMEBODY OR BE REVIVED** to revive somebody or be revived from unconsciousness or apparent death **2.** *vt.* **RETURN SOMETHING TO POPULARITY** to revive waning interest in something such as a style or project [Early 16thC. From Latin *resuscitare*, from *suscitare* "to raise," literally "to move from under," from *citare* "to move" (see CITE).] —**re·sus·ci·ta·ble** /ri sússətəb'l/ *adj.* —**re·sus·ci·ta·tion** /ri sùssə táysh'n/ *n.* —**re·sus·ci·ta·tive** /ri sússə tàytiv/ *adj.*

re·sus·ci·ta·tor /ri sússə tàytər/ *n.* somebody who resuscitates somebody else, or more commonly, a machine used to reestablish normal breathing or heartbeat

ret /ret/ (**ret·ted, ret·ting, rets**) *vti.* to soak or moisten plant fibers such as flax or hemp so that they become easier to separate [15thC. From Middle Dutch *reeten.*]

ret. *abbr.* **1.** LAW retain **2.** retired **3.** LAW return **4.** COMM returned

re·ta·ble /rée tàyb'l, réttəb'l/ *n.* a shelf or setting behind an altar for holding candles, flowers, or religious images [Early 19thC. Via French *rétable* from, ultimately, Latin *retro-* "back" + *tabula* "table."]

re·tail /rée tàyl/ *n.* **SALE TO CONSUMERS** the selling of goods in small amounts directly to customers, e.g., in stores ○ *She works in retail.* ■ *adv.* **IN SMALL, NOT BULK, AMOUNTS** from an ordinary store or at the regular customer price and in small amounts rather than in bulk ○ *I bought it retail.* ■ *v.* (**-tailed, -tail·ing, -tails**) **1.** *vti.* **SELL GOODS** to sell goods, or be sold, to customers in small amounts and without a discount ○ *This item usually retails at a much higher price.* **2.** *vt.* **REPEAT GOSSIP** to regularly repeat what is heard, especially gossip [14thC. From Old French *retaille* "piece cut off," ultimately from *taillier* "to cut" (source of English *tailor*), the underlying idea being to sell in small quantities, not wholesale.] —**re·tail·er** *n.*

re·tail price in·dex *n. U.K.* a list of the prices of essential consumer goods that is published each month by the government to show how much prices have risen or fallen

re·tain /ri táyn/ (**-tained, -tain·ing, -tains**) *vt.* **1. KEEP SOMETHING** to keep possession of something ○ *Despite losing the court case he retains all rights to the magazine article.* **2. REMEMBER THINGS** to be able to keep ideas or information in mind or memory **3. KEEP SOMETHING IN POSITION** to keep or hold something in a place or position ○ *water retained by a dam* **4. HOLD SOMETHING WITHIN** to be able to hold or accumulate something, especially liquid **5. PAY SOMEBODY TO DO WORK** to pay somebody regularly to do work **6. HIRE PROFESSIONAL PERSON** to pay a preliminary fee to reserve the services of an attorney, accountant, or other professional whenever needed [14thC. Via the Anglo-Norman stem *retaign-* from, ultimately, Latin *retinere* "to hold back" (source of English *rein*), from *tenere* "to hold" (see TENANT).] —**re·tain·a·bil·i·ty** /-tàynə bíllətee/ *n.* —**re·tain·a·ble** /-táynəb'l/ *adj.* —**re·tain·ment** /-mənt/ *n.*

re·tained ob·ject *n.* the direct or indirect object of a passive verb, e.g., "letter" in "She was sent a letter by her brother"

re·tain·er[1] /ri táynər/ *n.* **1. HOLDER** a device for holding something in place **2.** DENT **DEVICE HOLDING TEETH IN POSITION** a device for holding a tooth or teeth in position after orthodontic treatment **3.** HR **SERVANT** a paid servant, especially one who has been employed for many years **4. FOLLOWER** in the past, a soldier or other person who supported or was dependent on somebody of high rank

re·tain·er[2] /ri táynər/ *n.* a fee paid to reserve the services of a professional whenever needed, especially an attorney or accountant ◇ **on (a) retainer** paid regularly in order to be consulted whenever necessary, rather than being paid for each job

re·tain·ing wall *n.* a wall built to keep earth or water from moving

re·take *vt.* /ree táyk/ (**-took** /-tŏŏk/, **-tak·en** /-táykən/, **-tak·ing, -takes**) **1.** MIL **RECAPTURE SOMETHING** to recapture a place that has been captured by an enemy **2.** RECORDING, CINEMA **FILM SOMETHING AGAIN** to record, photograph, or film something again in order to get it right **3.** SPORTS **TAKE SHOT AGAIN** to take a shot in a game again because of some infringement during the first attempt ○ *The referee ordered him to retake the penalty shot.* ■ *n.* /rée tàyk/ **ACT OF RECORDING SOMETHING AGAIN** an instance of recording, photographing, or filming something again, or the product that results from this

re·tal·i·ate /ri tállee àyt/ (**-at·ed, -at·ing, -ates**) *vi.* to deliberately harm somebody in response or revenge for a harm he or she has done [Early 17thC. From Latin *retaliare* "to pay back in kind," from *talio* "punishment in kind."] —**re·tal·i·a·tion** /ri tàllee áysh'n/ *n.* —**re·tal·i·a·tive** /ri tállee àytiv/ *adj.* —**re·tal·i·a·to·ry** /-ə tàwree/ *adj.*

re·tard /ri taárd/ *vt.* (**-tard·ed, -tard·ing, -tards**) **SLOW SOMETHING DOWN** to slow or delay the progress of something ■ *n.* **1.** MUSIC **SLOWING OF TEMPO** in music, a slowing down of a previously quick tempo **2. OFFENSIVE TERM** an offensive term that deliberately insults somebody's intelligence (*slang insult*) [15thC. Via French *retarder* from Latin *retardare*, from *tardus* "slow" (source of English *tardy*).]

re·tar·dant /ri taárd'nt/ *n.* **SLOWING AGENT** something designed to slow down a particular process or change, especially a chemical substance that inhibits change (*often used in combination*) ■ *adj.* **ABLE TO SLOW SOMETHING** capable of making something move or happen more slowly ○ *flame-retardant fabric*

re·tar·da·tion /rèe taar dáysh'n/ *n.* **1. SLOWING** the process or fact of slowing down **2.** PSYCHOL condition of being mentally challenged (*dated offensive*) **3. DELAY** something that acts as a delay or obstacle to progress **4. DECELERATION** deceleration, or the rate of deceleration

re·tard·ed /ri taárdəd/ *adj.* **1. UNDERDEVELOPED** not fully developed ○ *the retarded growth of the plant* **2.** PSYCHOL **MENTALLY CHALLENGED** mentally challenged (*dated offensive*)

retch /rech/ *v.* (**retched, retch·ing, retch·es**) **1.** *vi.* **EXPERIENCE A VOMITING SPASM** to experience a spasm of vomiting without actually bringing anything up **2.** *vti.* **VOMIT** to vomit, or vomit something ■ *n.* **VOMITING SPASM** a spasm of vomiting without bringing anything up [Mid-16thC. Variant of obsolete *reach* "to spit, vomit," from Old English *hrǣcan*, from prehistoric Germanic; originally an imitation of the sound.]

retd. *abbr.* **1.** retained **2.** retired **3.** COMM returned

re·te /réetee/ (*plural* **-ti·a** /réetee ə, réeshə/) *n.* a network of veins, arteries, or nerve fibers in the body [14thC. From Latin, "net." Originally in the meaning of "astrolabe."] —**re·tial** /réesh'l/ *adj.*

re·tell /ree tél/ (**-told, -told** /-tṓld/, **-tell·ing, -tells**) *vt.* to tell something such as a story or joke again, especially in a different form or to somebody who has not heard it

re·tell·ing /ree télling/ *n.* a repeating of an account or story that has been told before ○ *a modern retelling of an ancient fable*

re·tene /rée teen, ré-/ *n.* a yellow crystalline hydrocarbon that occurs in pine tar and in some fossil resins. Formula: $C_{18}H_{18}$. [Mid-19thC. Coined from Greek *rhētinē* "resin" + -ENE.]

re·ten·tion /ri ténshən/ *n.* **1. HOLDING IN OF SOMETHING** the act of retaining something or the condition of being retained **2. MEMORY** the ability to remember things **3.** PHYSIOL **ABNORMAL HOLDING OF WASTE** the abnormal holding in the body of waste that is normally excreted [14thC. Directly or via French from the Latin stem *retention-*, ultimately from *retinere* (see RETAIN).]

re·ten·tive /ri téntiv/ *adj.* **1. ABLE TO RETAIN SOMETHING** able to or tending to hold something ○ *a soil that is highly retentive of rainwater* **2. WITH GOOD MEMORY** able to remember a great deal of information [14thC. Via Old French *retentif* or medieval Latin *retentivus* from Latin *retent-*, the past participle stem of *retinere* (see RETAIN).] —**re·ten·tive·ly** *adv.* —**re·ten·tive·ness** *n.*

re·ten·tiv·i·ty /rèe ten tívvətee/ *n.* **1. POWER TO RETAIN** the power or condition of retaining something **2.** PHYS **MAGNETIZATION CAPACITY** the capacity of a material to remain magnetized after the force that magnetized it has been taken away

re·think *vti.* /ree thíngk/ (**-thought, -thought** /-tháwt/, **-think·ing, -thinks**) **RECONSIDER SOMETHING** to think about something again, especially using new information or in order to produce a better result ■ *n.* /rée thìngk/ **RECONSIDERATION** an attempt to rethink something, or an occasion on which something is rethought (*informal*) ○ *Let's have a rethink before we proceed.* —**re·think·er** *n.*

re·ti·a plural of **rete**

ret·i·cence /réttiss'ns/ *n.* **1. TENDENCY NOT TO COMMUNICATE** the tendency to not communicate very much or not reveal everything **2. RELUCTANCE** hesitation or uncertainty about acting in a matter [Early 17thC. From Latin *reticentia*, from *reticere* "to keep silent," from *tacere* "to be silent" (source of English *taciturn*).]

ret·i·cent /réttiss'nt/ *adj.* unwilling to communicate very much, talk a lot, or reveal all the facts ○ *rather reticent on the subject of her finances* —**ret·i·cent·ly** *adv.*

WORD KEY: USAGE

Extended senses In its traditional sense, ***reticent*** means a reluctance to speak. Thus it is more nearly a synonym for *silent* than it is for *reluctant*: *He was never reticent about wanting the job.* It is, however, increasingly seen in contexts in which it conveys other kinds of reluctance: *He was reticent to travel so much.* Many regard this as a misuse, and in fact such usages tend to convey nothing that *reluctant* would not convey better.

WORD KEY: SYNONYMS

See Synonyms at ***silent.***

ret·i·cle /réttik'l/ *n.* a grid of fine lines in the focus of an optical instrument, used for determining the scale or position of what is being looked at [Mid-17thC. From Latin *reticulum* (see RETICULUM).]

re·tic·u·la plural of **reticulum**

re·tic·u·lar /ri tíkyələr/ *adj.* **1. SIMILAR TO A NET** relating to, involving, or structurally resembling a net or network **2. COMPLEX** having a complicated, intricate structure [Late 16thC. From modern Latin *reticularis*, from Latin *reticulum* (see RETICULUM).]

re·tic·u·lar for·ma·tion *n.* a formation of neurons in the brainstem that regulates many body functions, including respiration, blood pressure, sleeping and waking, and transmission of stimuli

re·tic·u·late *adj.* /ri tíkyələt, ri tíkyə làyt/ = **reticular** *adj.* 1 ■ *v.* /ri tíkyə làyt/ (**-lat·ed, -lat·ing, -lates**) **1.** *vti.* **HAVE A NETWORK STRUCTURE** to form a network, or be formed into a network **2.** *vt.* **MARK SOMETHING WITH LINES** to mark something with lines so that it looks like a network [Mid-17thC. From Latin *reticulatus*, from *reticulum* (see RETICULUM).] —**re·tic·u·late·ly** *adv.* —**re·tic·u·la·tion** /ri tìkyə láysh'n/ *n.*

ret·i·cule /rétti kyool/ *n.* **1.** ACCESSORIES **WOMAN'S PURSE** a small purse made of netting or lightweight fabric, usually closed with a drawstring, carried by women in the late 18th and early 19th centuries (*archaic*) **2.** OPTICS = **reticle** [Early 18thC. Via French *réticule* from Latin *reticulum* (see RETICULUM).]

re·tic·u·lo·cyte /ri tíkyələ sīt/ *n.* an immature red blood cell containing a network of fibers of ribosomal remains that show up with laboratory staining [Early 20thC. Coined from RETICULUM + -CYTE.] —**re·tic·u·lo·cyt·ic** /ri tìkyələ síttik/ *adj.*

re·tic·u·lum /ri tíkyələm/ (*plural* **-la** /-tíkyələ/) *n.* **1. NETWORK** a network or something resembling a network in structure **2.** ANAT **SECOND STOMACH** the second stomach or stomach compartment in cows, sheep, and other ruminants [Mid-17thC. From Latin *reticulum*, literally "little net," from *rete* "net."]

Re·tic·u·lum /ri tíkyələm/ *n.* a small constellation of the southern hemisphere lying between Dorado and Horologium near to the Large Magellanic Cloud

retin- *prefix.* = **retino-** (*used before vowels*)

ret·i·na /rétt'nə/ (*plural* **-nas** *or* **-nae** /rétt'nee/) *n.* a light-sensitive membrane in the back of the eye containing rods and cones that receive an image from the lens and send it to the brain through the optic nerve [14thC. From medieval Latin, formed from Latin *rete* "net," from the network of blood-vessels.] —**ret·i·nal** *adj.*

ret·i·nac·u·lum /rètt'n ákyələm/ (*plural* **-la** /-ákyələ/) *n.* an anatomical structure of insects that holds small body parts together like a hook or clasp [Mid-18thC. From Latin, "band," literally "little thing that holds back," from *retinire* "to hold back" (see RETAIN).] —**ret·i·nac·u·lar** *adj.*

ret·i·nae plural of **retina**

ret·i·nene /rétt'n een/, **ret·i·nal** /rétt'nal/ *n.* an aldehyde derived from vitamin A that combines with proteins to form visual pigments in the eye. Formula: $C_{20}H_{28}O$.

ret·i·nite /rétt'n īt/ *n.* a fossil resin, especially one in which the plant matter has not formed a hard coal [Early 19thC. From French, formed from Greek *rhētinē* "resin."]

ret·i·ni·tis /rètt'n ītiss/ *n.* inflammation of the retina

ret·i·ni·tis pig·men·to·sa /-pigmən tṓzə/ *n.* an inherited disorder of the eye involving progressive disintegration of the retina and optic nerve and leading eventually to tunnel vision or inability to see [*Pigmentosa* from modern Latin, "pigmented"]

retino- *prefix.* retina ○ *retinoblastoma* [From RETINA]

ret·i·no·blas·to·ma /rètt'nō bla stṓmə/ (*plural* **-to·mas** *or* **-tom·a·ta** /-stṓmətə/) *n.* a malignant tumor of the eye, usually resulting from a genetic disorder and appearing in early childhood

ret·i·nol /rét'n awl/ *n.* = **vitamin A** [Mid-20thC. Formed from RETINA.]

ret·i·nop·a·thy /rètt'n óppəthee/ (*plural* **-thies**) *n.* a disease of the retina, especially one that is noninflammatory and usually associated with damage to the blood vessels of the retina ○ *diabetic retinopathy* —**ret·i·no·path·ic** /rètt'nō páthik/ *adj.*

ret·i·no·scope /rétt'nə skōp/ *n.* an instrument for identifying refractive errors in the eye by measuring the angle of a beam of light reflected from the retina and back out through the pupil

ret·i·nos·co·py /rètt'n óskəpee/ (*plural* **-pies**) *n.* a method of measuring refractive errors in the eye using a retinoscope —**ret·i·no·scop·ic** /rètt'nə skóppik/ *adj.* —**ret·i·no·scop·i·cal·ly** /-ə skóppikəlee/ *adv.* —**ret·i·no·scop·ist** /-óskəpist/ *n.*

ret·i·nue /rétt'n ōō/ *n.* a body of people who travel with and attend an important person [14thC. From Old French, literally "retained (in service)," from the past participle of *retenir* "to retain," from Latin *retinere* (see RETAIN).]

re·tire /ri tír/ (**-tired, -tir·ing, -tires**) *v.* **1.** *vi.* HR **STOP WORKING WILLINGLY** to leave a job or career voluntarily, at or near the usual age for doing so **2.** *vi.* **GO TO BED** to stop engaging in daily activities and go to bed **3.** *vi.* **WITHDRAW** to leave a place, position, or way of life and go to a place of less activity ○ *retire from public life* **4.** *vt.* **MAKE SOMEBODY STOP WORKING** to stop a person or an animal performing some activity because of an inability to continue or illness ○ *injuries so extensive that the horse was retired* **5.** *vt.* **WITHDRAW SOMETHING FROM SERVICE** to take a machine or piece of equipment out of service **6.** *vti.* MIL **GO BACK OR MOVE TROOPS BACK** to fall back, or move troops away from a position, action, or danger **7.** *vt.* **PUT SOMEBODY OUT** to end a batter's or team's turn at bat by getting batters out ○ *The pitcher retired eight batters in a row.* **8.** *vti.* SPORTS **WITHDRAW FROM SPORTS CONTEST** to withdraw or withdraw somebody from a sports contest, because of an inability to continue **9.** *vt.* FIN **WITHDRAW SOMETHING FROM CIRCULATION** to take a loan, stock, bond, or other financial instrument out of circulation by paying for it [Mid-16thC. From French *retirer* "retreat," from *tirer* "to draw" (source of English *tier* and *tirade*).] —**re·tir·er** *n.*

re·tired /ri tírd/ *adj.* **1. NO LONGER WORKING** having stopped working, typically after having worked many years ○ *a retired bus driver* **2. HAVING WITHDRAWN** having withdrawn from a busy way of life ○ *a retired lifestyle* ■ *n.* **RETIRED PEOPLE** used to refer to retired people as a group (*takes a plural verb*)

re·tir·ee /ri tì rée/ *n.* somebody who has retired from a job or career

re·tire·ment /ri tírmənt/ *n.* **1. LEAVING JOB OR CAREER** the act of leaving a job or career at or near the usual age for doing so **2. TIME AFTER HAVING STOPPED WORKING** the time that follows the end of somebody's working life **3. BEING AWAY FROM BUSY LIFE** a state of being withdrawn from the rest of the world or a former busy life ○ *He lives in retirement in the country.*

re·tir·ing /ri tíring/ *adj.* **1. SHY AND RESERVED** avoiding social contact with other people **2. UNDERGOING RETIREMENT** at, involving, or undergoing retirement from a job or career ○ *The retiring chairman made an emotional speech.* —**re·tir·ing·ly** *adv.* —**re·tir·ing·ness** *n.*

re·tool /ree tóōl/ (**-tooled, -tool·ing, -tools**) *v.* **1.** *vti.* **REFIT EQUIPMENT** to replace the tools or machinery in a factory, or to obtain new tools or machinery **2.** *vt.* **REORGANIZE SOMETHING** to reorganize something in order to make it more efficient or powerful ○ *The company will have to retool if it's to remain competitive.*

re·tor·sion /ri táwrsh'n/ *n.* an act of retaliation by a goverment against citizens of another country for a similar offense committed by the other country [Mid-17thC. Via French *rétorsion* from, ultimately, Latin *retort-*, the past participle stem of *retorquere* (see RETORT[1]).]

re·tort[1] /ri táwrt/ *vt.* (**-tort·ed, -tort·ing, -torts**) **1. RESPOND SHARPLY** to say something sharp, angry, witty, or insulting in quick response to something somebody else has said **2. ARGUE IN REPLY** to put forward something as an argument in reply to somebody else's argument ■ *n.* **SHARP ANSWER** something sharp, angry, witty, or insulting said quickly in response to something somebody else has said [15thC. From Latin *retort-*, the past participle stem of *retorquere*, literally "to twist again," from *torquere* "to twist" (see TORQUE).] —**re·tort·er** *n.*

WORD KEY: SYNONYMS

See Synonyms at *answer.*

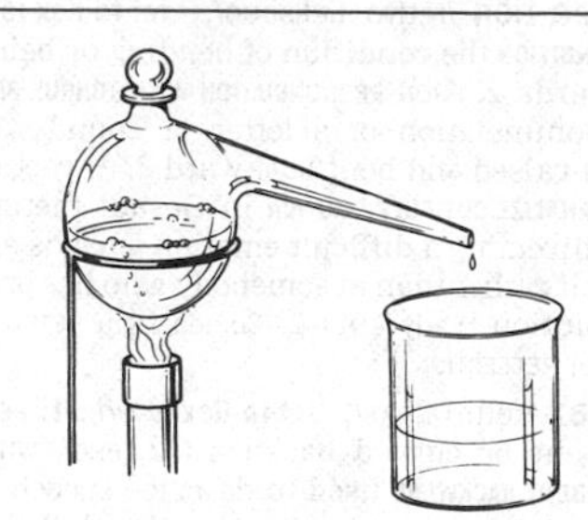

Retort

re·tort[2] /ri táwrt/ *n.* **1. GLASS VESSEL** a glass vessel with a long downward-pointing tapering spout, used for distilling by heat **2. CLOSED CONTAINER FOR HEATING SUBSTANCES** a closed container in which large quantities of a substance are heated to extract something, e.g., metal from ore ■ *vt.* (**-tort·ed, -tort·ing, -torts**) **HEAT SOMETHING IN RETORT** to heat or distill something in a retort [Early 17thC. Via French *retorte* from medieval Latin *retorta*, from Latin *retorquere* "to twist back" (see RETORT[1]), from the shape of the neck.]

re·tor·tion *n.* INTERNAT REL = **retorsion**

re·touch *vt.* /ree túch/ (**-touched, -touch·ing, -touch·es**) **1. IMPROVE SOMETHING** to make small finishing, correcting, or improving changes to something **2.** PHOTOGRAPHY **ALTER PHOTOGRAPH** to alter a photographic negative or print by removing imperfections or adding details **3. COLOR HAIR** to color new hair growth to match hair that is already bleached, tinted, or dyed ■ *n.* /rée tùch, ree túch/ **1. ACTIVITY OF RETOUCHING** the process of retouching something, or the occasion on which something is retouched **2.** PHOTOGRAPHY **SOMETHING ALTERED** something that has been retouched, especially a photograph **3. IMPROVING CHANGE** a small, finishing, correcting, or improving change to something —**re·touch·er** *n.*

re·trace /ri tráyss/ (**-traced, -trac·ing, -trac·es**) *vt.* **1. FOLLOW ROUTE AGAIN** to go back over a path or route again **2. REVIEW SOMETHING** to review something in the mind, e.g., an argument, account, or series of events ○ *retraced the events leading up to the war* —**re·trace·a·ble** *adj.* —**re·trac·er** *n.*

re·tract /ri trákt/ (**-tract·ed, -tract·ing, -tracts**) *v.* **1.** *vti.* **MOVE, OR MOVE SOMETHING, BACK INSIDE** to draw something in from an extended position, or be able to be drawn in ○ *Cats can retract their claws but dogs can't.* **2.** *vti.* **WITHDRAW STATEMENT** to withdraw or deny something previously said, published, or promised ○ *She has since retracted her earlier statement.* **3.** *vi.* **MOVE BACK** to move back from something **4.** *vt.* PHON **CHANGE VOWEL SOUND** to alter a vowel sound by drawing the tongue inward from the lips [15thC. From Latin *retract-*, the past participle stem of *retrahere* "to draw back," from *trahere* "to pull" (see TRACTOR).] —**re·tract·a·bil·i·ty** /ri tràktə bíllətee/ *n.* —**re·tract·a·ble** /ri tráktəb'l/ *adj.* —**re·trac·ta·tion** /rèe trak táysh'n/ *n.*

re·trac·tile /ri trákt'l/ *adj.* capable of being retracted —**re·trac·til·i·ty** /ri tràk tíllətee/ *n.*

re·trac·tion /ri trákshən/ *n.* **1. ACT OF RETRACTING** the act of retracting something or the condition of being retracted **2. RETRACTING STATEMENT** a statement, sometimes formal, that withdraws or denies a previous statement **3. SOMETHING RETRACTED** something that has been denied or taken back **4. POWER TO RETRACT** the ability or authority to draw back or be drawn back

re·trac·tor /ri tráktər/ *n.* **1.** SURG **SURGICAL INSTRUMENT** a surgical instrument used to hold back skin or tissue during surgery **2.** ANAT **MUSCLE THAT RETRACTS BODY PART** a muscle that retracts a body part, e.g., one that closes the jaw

re·train /ree tráyn/ (**-trained, -train·ing, -trains**) *vti.* to teach somebody or learn new skills ○ *decided to retrain as a systems analyst* —**re·train·a·ble** *adj.*

re·train·ing /ree tráyning/ *n.* the process or activity of learning new skills or of updating existing skills

re·trans·mit /ree tràns mít, -trànz-/ (**-mit·ted, -mit·ting, -mits**) *v.* **1.** *vt.* **TRANSMIT SOMETHING AGAIN** to transmit or broadcast something again, or transmit something onward to another place **2. TRANSMIT A BROADCAST BY CABLE** to transmit a television broadcast by cable —**re·trans·mis·sion** *n.*

re·tread *vt.* /ree tréd/ (**-tread·ed, -tread·ing, -treads**) **ADD LAYER TO TIRE** to add a new tread to a worn tire ■ *n.* /rée trèd/ **1. TIRE WITH NEW TREAD** a second-hand tire with a new tread bonded to it **2. RETRAINED WORKER** a worker who has been retrained for a new position **3. RETURNING WORKER** somebody who returns to a line of work previously given up (*informal*)

re·tread /ree tréd/ (**re·trod** /ree tród/, **re·trod·den** /ree tród'n/, **re·tread·ing, re·treads**) *vt.* to walk again on a route that has already been walked over

re·treat /ri trēet/ *n.* **1. MOVEMENT BACK** a movement away from danger or a confrontation, back along the original route ○ *The bear had the hunters in full retreat.* **2.** MIL **TROOP WITHDRAWAL** a withdrawal of military forces following a defeat or preceding a change of position **3.** MIL **SIGNAL TO MOVE BACK** a signal, usually a bugle call or drumbeat, telling soldiers to perform a retreat **4. WITHDRAWAL FROM POSITION** a withdrawal from a particular position or point of view to one intended to lessen conflict ○ *their retreat from a previously inflexible position* **5. QUIET TIME** a period of quiet rest and contemplation in a secluded place **6. QUIET PLACE** a quiet, secluded place where people go for rest and privacy **7. SAFE PLACE** a place where people or animals go to avoid danger or capture **8.** RELIG **PERIOD OF SECLUSION** a period away from normal activities, devoted to prayer and meditation, often spent in a religious community **9. SPECIAL HOSPITAL** a place for the long-term care and treatment of people who are incapable of caring for themselves (*dated*) **10.** MIL **FLAG-LOWERING CEREMONY** the ceremony of lowering the flag at a military institution, or the signal given to lower the flag ■ *v.* (**-treat·ed, -treat·ing, -treats**) **1.** *vi.* **MOVE BACK** to move back away from danger or a confrontation **2.** *vi.* MIL **MAKE MILITARY WITHDRAWAL** to withdraw following a defeat or prior to a change of position **3.** *vi.* **WITHDRAW FROM POSITION** to withdraw from a particular position or point of view to one intended to lessen conflict **4.** *vi.* **RECEDE** to recede or fall back from a previous position **5.** *vt.* CHESS **MOVE PIECE BACK** to move a chesspiece back to an earlier position [13thC. From Old French *retret*, from the past participle of *retraire*, from Latin *retrahere* (see RETRACT).] —**re·treat·er** *n.* ◇ **beat a (hasty) retreat 1.** to leave, especially in a hurry **2.** to back down or take something back that was said

re·treat·ant /ri trēet'nt/ *n.* somebody who takes part in a spiritual or religious retreat

re·trench /ri trénch/ (**-trenched, -trench·ing, -trench·es**) *v.* **1.** *vti.* **ECONOMIZE** to reduce something such as costs **2.** *vt.* **CUT SOMETHING OUT** to cut out, cut back, or omit something **3.** *vi.* **RETHINK SOMETHING** to stop doing something in order to reorganize or rethink something ○ *We retrenched and began reorganizing when we realized the plan wasn't working.* [Late 16thC. From French *retrancher* "to recut," from *trenchier* "to cut" (source of English *trench*).] —**re·trench·er** *n.*

re·trench·ment /ri trénchmənt/ *n.* the cutting back of expenses

re·tri·al /ree trí əl/ *n.* a second trial in a court of law that replaces a prior one that was flawed or ended in a hung jury

ret·ri·bu·tion /rèttrə byóosh'n/ *n.* something done or given to somebody as punishment or vengeance for something he or she has done ○ *a just retribution for their crime* [14thC. From the Latin stem *retribution-*, ultimately from *retribuere* "to hand back, repay," from *tribuere* "to allot" (source of English *tribute*).] —**re·trib·u·tive** /ri tríbbyətiv/ *adj.* —**re·trib·u·tive·ly** /-tríbbyətivlee/ *adv.* —**re·trib·u·to·ry** /-tríbbyə tàwree/ *adj.*

re·triev·al /ri trēev'l/ *n.* **1. RECOVERY OF SOMETHING** the act of getting something back, or a particular occasion on which this is done **2. POSSIBILITY OF BEING RESTORED** the possibility of something being brought back, saved, or restored to an original condition ○ *Their business seemed beyond retrieval.* **3.** COMPUT **DATA ACCESS** the process of reading data from a storage device and returning it to the program or device that requested it

re·trieve /ri trēev/ *v.* (**-trieved, -triev·ing, -trieves**) **1.** *vt.* **GET SOMETHING BACK** to get something back **2.** *vt.* **SAVE SOMETHING** to save something from being lost, damaged, or destroyed **3.** *vt.* **REMEDY SOMETHING** to set something right or make it better ○ *attempt to retrieve the situation before it worsens* **4.** *vt.* **RESTORE SOMETHING** to revive or restore something to its original condition ○ *She quickly retrieved her sense of humor.* **5.** *vt.* **REMEMBER SOMETHING** to recall something from memory 6. *vt.* COMPUT **GET DATA** to read data from a storage device and return it to the program or device that requested it 7. *vti.* RACKET GAMES **RETURN SHOT** to return a difficult shot in a game such as tennis or badminton 8. *vti.* HUNT **FETCH GAME** to fetch small game that has been shot by a hunter ■ *n.* **RETRIEVING OF SOMETHING** the act of retrieving something ○ *a successful retrieve* [15thC. From Old French *retroev-*, the stem of *retrover* "to find again," from *trover* "to find."] —**re·triev·a·bil·i·ty** /ri treevə bíllətee/ *n.* —**re·triev·a·ble** /ri treevəb'l/ *adj.* —**re·triev·a·bly** /-treevəblee/ *adv.*

Retriever

re·triev·er /ri treevər/ *n.* 1. ZOOL **LARGE DOG THAT RETRIEVES GAME** a large strong-bodied dog originally bred to retrieve game for a hunter 2. **SOMEBODY OR SOMETHING THAT RETRIEVES** any person who or thing that retrieves something

ret·ro *adj.* **MODELED ON SOMETHING FROM PAST** modeled on something from the past, e.g., a style of fashion or music ○ *retro clothing* ■ *n.* (*plural* **-ros**) 1. **USE OF PAST STYLES** the practice of modeling things such as clothes or music on styles from the past, or an example of such a practice ○ *The band is heavily into sixties retro.* 2. AEROSP = **retrorocket** [Late 20thC. From French *rétro*, a shortening of *rétrograde* "retrograde," from Latin *retrogradus* (see RETROGRADE); influenced by RETRO-.]

retro- *prefix.* 1. back, backward, after ○ *retrorocket* ○ *retrofit* 2. behind ○ *retrochoir* [From Latin *retro*]

ret·ro·ac·tion /rèttrō ákshən/ *n.* 1. **APPLICABILITY TO THE PAST** the applicability of something to past circumstances or events 2. **ACTION REACTING TO PAST SITUATION** an action that responds or reacts to something in the past 3. **COUNTEREFFECT** an action that goes against or balances a previous action

ret·ro·ac·tive /rèttrō áktiv/ *adj.* relating or applying to things that have happened in the past as well as the present ○ *a pay increase retroactive to the beginning of the year*

ret·ro·ac·tive in·hi·bi·tion *n.* the tendency of recently gained knowledge or skills to degenerate when new learning in a similar area is acquired

ret·ro·cede /réttrō seed/ (**-ced·ed, -ced·ing, -cedes**) *v.* 1. *vi.* **GO BACK** to go back or return 2. *vt.* **GIVE SOMETHING BACK** to give back something such as land or a territory [Mid-17thC. From French *rétrocéder*, from *céder* (see CEDE).] —**ret·ro·ce·dent** /rèttrō seed'nt/ *adj.* —**ret·ro·ces·sion** /-sésh'n/ *n.* —**ret·ro·ces·sive** /-séssiv/ *adj.*

ret·ro·choir /réttrō kwīr/ *n.* the area behind the high altar in a large church or cathedral [Mid-19thC. From medieval Latin *retrochorus*, literally "back choir," from *chorus* (see CHOIR).]

re·trod past tense of **re-tread**

re·trod·den past participle of **re-tread**

ret·ro·en·gine *n.* = **retrorocket**

ret·ro·fire /réttrō fīr/ (**-fired, -fir·ing, -fires**) *vti.* to fire a retrorocket to decelerate

ret·ro·fit /rèttrō fít/ *vt.* (**-fit·ted, -fit·ting, -fits**) 1. **MODIFY SOMETHING WITH NEW PARTS** to modify something such as a machine or a building by adding parts or devices of types not originally included ○ *older cars retrofitted with catalytic converters* 2. **INSTALL NEW PARTS** to install new parts or devices of types not originally included in existing equipment, machinery, or buildings ○ *retrofit a microchip in the alarm system* ■ *n.* 1. **NEW PART OR SOMETHING WITH ONE** something that has been equipped with a newly developed component, or such a component designed for something that is already in use 2. **PROCESS OF ADDING NEW PART** the process or an instance of modifying something such as a machine or a building by adding new parts or devices

ret·ro·flec·tion /rèttrō flékshən/, **ret·ro·flex·ion** *n.* 1. **BENT CONDITION** the condition of bending or being bent backwards 2. PHON **PRONUNCIATION WITH TONGUE BENT BACK** the pronunciation of a letter or sound with the tongue raised and bent backward 3. PSYCHOL **INABILITY TO EXTERNALIZE DIFFICULT EMOTION** in Gestalt therapy, the act of directing a difficult emotion such as anger at yourself rather than at somebody who has provoked the emotion [Early 19th C. Coined from RETRO- on the model of REFLECTION.]

ret·ro·flex /réttrō flèks/, **ret·ro·flexed** *adj.* 1. **BENT BACKWARD** bent or curved backward 2. PHON **WITH TIP OF TONGUE BENT BACKWARD** used to describe speech sounds that are pronounced with the tip of the tongue raised and bent backward [Late 18thC. From Latin *retroflex-*, the past participle stem of *retroflectere* "to bend back," from *flectere* "to bend."]

ret·ro·flex·ion /rèttrō fléksh'n/ *n.* = **retroflection**

ret·ro·grade /réttrō gràyd/ *adj.* 1. **MOVING BACKWARD** moving backward in space or time 2. **INVERSE** in writing, inverse or reversed, especially in syntactic order 3. **GETTING WORSE** worsening or returning to an earlier worse condition 4. ASTRON **HAVING A CONTRARY ORBIT** orbiting in a direction opposite to that of the Earth's orbit around the Sun or of the Moon's orbit around the Earth 5. ASTRON **MOVING EAST TO WEST** moving or appearing to move from east to west in the sky, counter to the direction of most astronomical bodies 6. MUSIC **REVERSING NOTES** reversing the sequence of notes of an earlier version of a musical composition ■ *vi.* (**-grad·ed, -grad·ing, -grades**) 1. **GO BACKWARD** to go back or appear to be moving backward in space or time 2. = **retrogress** *v.* 1 [14thC. From Latin *retrogradus* "going backwards," from *gradus* "step."] —**ret·ro·gra·da·tion** /rèttrō gray dáysh'n/ *n.* —**ret·ro·grade·ly** /réttrō gràydlee/ *adv.*

ret·ro·gress /rèttrō gréss/ (**-gressed, -gress·ing, -gress·es**) *vi.* 1. **REVERT OR DEGENERATE** to return to an earlier and usually worse condition 2. **GO BACKWARD** to move or travel backward 3. BIOL **HAVE LESS COMPLEX FEATURES** to show or develop the less complex features of simpler organisms [Early 19thC. Formed from RETRO- on the model of PROGRESS.] —**ret·ro·gres·sive** *adj.* —**ret·ro·gres·sive·ly** *adv.*

ret·ro·gres·sion /rèttrə grésh'n/ *n.* 1. **RETURN TO WORSE CONDITION** the process of returning to an earlier and usually worse condition 2. BIOL **DEVELOPMENT OF LESS COMPLEX FEATURES** the development of less complex features usually associated with simpler organisms

ret·ro·len·tal /rèttrō lént'l/ *adj.* located behind the lens of the eye, or the lens of an optical instrument [Mid-20thC. Coined from RETRO- + modern Latin *lent-*, the stem of *lens* (see LENS).]

ret·ro·nym *n.* a term that distinguishes a subclass from members of a superclass, e.g., "snail mail" is a retronym coined by those for whom "mail" is likely to mean "e-mail" [Combination of RETRO- + SYNONYM]

ret·ro·pack /réttrō pàk/ *n.* an array of retrorockets on a spacecraft, used for slowing down or for changing direction

ret·ro·pul·sion /rèttrō púlshən/ *n.* a tendency to walk backward involuntarily, associated with Parkinson's disease [Late 18thC. Blend of RETRO- and PROPULSION.]

ret·ro·rock·et /réttrō ròkət/ *n.* a small rocket engine on a spacecraft or missile that produces thrust to act against the main engines and is used for decelerating

re·trorse /ri tráwrs/ *adj.* used to describe plant parts that are turned back or down [Early 19thC. From Latin *retrorsus*, a contraction of *retroversus* "turning backward," from *versus* "turning."] —**re·trorse·ly** *adv.*

ret·ro·spect /réttrə spèkt/ *n.* the remembering of past events [Early 17thC. Formed from RETRO- on the model of PROSPECT.] —**ret·ro·spec·tion** *n.* ◇ **in retrospect** thinking about or reviewing the past, especially from a new perspective or with new information

ret·ro·spec·tive /rèttrə spéktiv/ *adj.* 1. **LOOKING TO THE PAST** looking back over things in the past 2. ARTS **CONTAINING PAST WORKS** containing examples of work from many periods of an artist's life ○ *a retrospective exhibition* 3. **APPLYING TO PAST EVENTS** applying to things that have happened in the past as well as the present ○ *a retrospective ruling* ■ *n.* ARTS **EXHIBITION OF ARTIST'S PAST WORK** an exhibition of the work of a particular artist or artistic movement, showing examples from all periods or styles ○ *a Degas retrospective* —**ret·ro·spec·tive·ly** *adv.*

re·trous·sé /rèttrə sáy/ *adj.* turned up at the end ○ *a retroussé nose* [Early 19thC. From French, literally "turned up."]

ret·ro·ver·sion /rèttrə vúrzh'n/ *n.* 1. **TURNING BACKWARD** the act or condition of being turned backward 2. MED **BACKWARD TILT OF BODY PART** the abnormal turning or tilting backward of a body part, e.g., the uterus, but without folding [Late 16thC. Formed from Latin *retroversus* (see RETRORSE).] —**ret·ro·verse** /rèttrə vúrs/ *adj.* —**ret·ro·vert·ed** /-vúrtəd/ *adj.*

ret·ro·vi·rus /rèttrō vīrəss, rèttrə vīrəss/ *n.* a type of virus whose genetic information is contained in RNA rather than DNA. Some retroviruses cause AIDS and cancer and they contain the enzyme reverse transcriptase for generating DNA from RNA. —**ret·ro·vi·ral** /rèttrō vīrəl/ *adj.*

re·try /ree trī/ *v.* (**-tried, -try·ing, -tries**) 1. *vt.* LAW **TRY SOMEBODY AGAIN** to try a person or case again in a court of law 2. *vti.* **ATTEMPT SOMETHING AGAIN** to try to do something again ■ *n.* (*plural* **-tries**) **SECOND ATTEMPT** another attempt to do something

ret·si·na /rétsinə, ret seenə/ *n.* a Greek wine flavored with pine resin [Early 20thC. Via modern Greek from, ultimately, Greek *rhētinē* "pine resin."]

re·turn /ri túrn/ *v.* (**-turned, -turn·ing, -turns**) 1. *vi.* **COME OR GO BACK** to come or go back to a place after leaving it or to a former condition 2. *vi.* **GO BACK** to go back to something that has already been mentioned or considered, especially in order to deal with it more thoroughly or conclusively ○ *Let's return to the matter at hand.* 3. *vi.* **APPEAR AGAIN** to appear or happen again 4. *vt.* **REPLY TO SOMEBODY** to answer or reply to something somebody has said ○ *"Do it yourself!" she returned.* 5. *vt.* **PUT SOMETHING BACK** to put, bring, send, or take something back to where it came from 6. *vt.* **REPAY SOMETHING** to give back something of equivalent value ○ *I hope that one day I'll be able to return the favor.* 7. *vt.* **YIELD PROFIT** to yield something as a profit on an investment ○ *returns 6% per annum* 8. *vt.* **REELECT SOMEBODY TO OFFICE** to reelect somebody to an office or position ○ *returned her to Congress for a second term* 9. *vt.* **REFLECT SOMETHING** to send back or reflect something such as as an echo ○ *The cliff wall returned the sound of their laughter.* 10. *vt.* LAW **PRODUCE VERDICT** to give a particular verdict in a court of law ○ *return a guilty verdict* 11. *vt.* **SUBMIT OFFICIAL REPORT** to give an official report, usually in response to a request or legal requirement 12. *vt.* COMPUT **GIVE RESPONSE** to give a particular response to a command, routine, or subroutine ○ *returns zero if the condition is false* 13. *vt.* ARCHIT **BUILD SOMETHING TO FACE OPPOSITE DIRECTION** to construct part of a building, e.g., a wall or decoration, so that it turns away from its original direction 14. *vti.* SPORTS **HIT BALL BACK** to hit a ball, especially a serve, back to an opponent in various games 15. *vt.* FOOTBALL **RUN FOOTBALL BACK UP FIELD** to run a football back up the field after it has been kicked, punted, fumbled, or intercepted 16. *vt.* CARDS **LEAD SAME SUIT** to lead the same suit as a partner in various card games, including bridge and pinochle ■ *n.* 1. **GOING OR COMING BACK** a going or coming back to a place after having left it or to a former condition 2. **REPLACEMENT** a putting, taking, sending, or bringing back of something to where it came from 3. **SOMETHING GIVEN BACK** something that has come or been brought back, especially unsold merchandise ○ *Returns go in that bin over there* 4. **REAPPEARANCE** a reappearance or recurrence of something 5. **RECIPROCATION** a response to something done or given ○ *If you are kind to your puppy it will give you love in return* 6. **ANSWER** something said in response to something else ○ *If you ask her an absurd question you can expect an angry return* 7. FIN **PROFIT** a profit made on an investment or business venture (*often used in the plural*) 8. FIN **TAX RETURN** a tax return 9. **FINANCIAL REPORT** a periodic financial report of an organization 10. **re·turn, re·turn key** COMPUT = **enter key** 11. ARCHIT **ANGLED PART** part of a building, e.g., a wall or decoration, built so that it turns away from its original direction 12. SPORTS **BALL PLAYED BACK** an instance of hitting or playing the ball back to an opponent in various games 13. LAW **LEGAL REPORT** a report on a legal document previously issued, e.g., a subpoena or writ, by an officer of that court of law 14. CARDS **LEAD OF SAME SUIT** an instance of leading the same suit as a partner in various card games ■ **re·turns** *npl.* ELECTION RESULTS the results from an election or election district ○ *We sat up late waiting for the election returns.* ■ *adj.* **1.** CONNECTED WITH GOING BACK AGAIN relating to an act of going or coming back to an earlier place or position ○ *I hope the return flight isn't delayed.* **2.** *U.K.* = **round-trip 3.** HAPPENING AGAIN given or done again or in order ○ *We enjoyed the resort so much that we decided to make a return visit the next year.* [14thC. Via Old French *reto(u)rner,* literally "to turn again," from *to(u)rner* "to turn," from Latin *tornare* (see TURN).] ◇ **in return (for something)** as an exchange for something ◇ **many happy returns (of the day)** a conventional way of expressing good wishes to somebody whose birthday it is, often as an exclamation

re·turn·a·ble /ri túrnəb'l/ *adj.* **1.** ABLE TO BE RETURNED capable of being returned ○ *a returnable deposit* **2.** REQUIRING RESPONSE requiring a response to a formal document, usually within a particular period of time, as do e.g., some court writs ■ *n.* CONTAINER RETURNED TO RECOVER DEPOSIT a bottle, jar, or other container on which a deposit is paid and that can be returned and reused

re·turn·ee /ri tùr nēe/ *n.* somebody who comes back, especially from military service or some other long absence

return key = **return** *n.* 10

re·turn tick·et *n.* **1.** = **round-trip ticket 2.** TICKET BACK the portion of a ticket for the journey back to your point of departure

re·tuse /ri to͞oss/ *adj.* used to describe leaves that have a blunt notched apex [Mid-18thC. From Latin *retusus,* past participle of *retundere* "to beat back," from *tundere* "to beat."]

Reu·ben[1] /ro͞obən/, **Reu·ben sand·wich** *n.* a grilled sandwich of rye bread filled with corned beef, sauerkraut, swiss cheese, and thousand island dressing [Mid-20thC. Origin uncertain: possibly named for the U.S. grocer *Reuben* Kulakofsky (died 1960).]

Reu·ben[2] /ro͞obən/ *n.* in the Bible, a Hebrew patriarch and the eldest son of Jacob and Leah. He was the ancestor of one of the tribes of Israel.

re·u·ni·fy /ree yo͞onə fī/ (**-fied, -fy·ing, -fies**) *vti.* to come together or bring people or factions together again, after they have been divided —**re·u·ni·fi·ca·tion** /ree yo͞onəfi káysh'n/ *n.*

re·un·ion /ree yo͞onyən/ *n.* **1.** A COMING TOGETHER AGAIN the coming together again of things or people that have been divided, or the condition of having come together in this way **2.** GATHERING a gathering of old friends, relatives, or people who were colleagues at one time ○ *a high-school class reunion*

re·un·ion·ist /ree yo͞onyənist/ *n.* a supporter of reunion between divided groups or parties, especially somebody who seeks reunion between the Anglican and Roman Catholic churches —**re·un·ion·ism** *n.* —**re·un·ion·is·tic** /ree yo͞onyə nístik/ *adj.*

re·u·nite /rēe yoo nīt/ (**-nit·ed, -nit·ing, -nites**) *vti.* to bring people together, or come together, after a separation

re-up (**re-upped, re-up·ping, re-ups**) *vi.* to sign up for another tour of duty in a military service (*informal*)

re·up·hol·ster /rēe up hṓlstər, -ə pṓlstər/ (**-stered, -ster·ing, -sters**) *vt.* to replace the worn or damaged upholstery on a chair or sofa

re·up·take /ree úp tàyk/ *n.* the reabsorption by nerve cells of a neurochemical after it has performed its function of transmitting a neural impulse

re·use *vt.* /ree yo͞oz/ (**-used, -us·ing, -us·es**) USE SOMETHING AGAIN to use something again, often for a different purpose and usually as an alternative to throwing it out ■ *n.* /ree yo͞oss/ USE OF SOMETHING AGAIN the using of something again, often for a different purpose and usually as an alternative to throwing it out —**re·us·a·bil·i·ty** /ree yo͞ozə bíllətee/ *n.* —**re·us·a·ble** /ree yo͞ozəb'l/ *adj.*

Reu·ter /róytər/, **Paul Julius, Baron von** (1816–99) German-born British journalist. In 1851 he established the pioneer Reuters Telegrams, now Reuters, the first news agency in the world. Real name **Isreal Beer Josaphat**

Reu·ters /róytərz/ *n.* a London news agency providing international news reports [Mid-19thC. Named for Paul Julius, Baron von REUTER.]

rev /rev/ *vti.* (**revved, rev·ving, revs**) MAKE VEHICLE ENGINE GO FASTER to increase a vehicle's engine speed by pressing down on the gas pedal or advancing the throttle, especially while the vehicle is stationary ■ *n.* ENGINE REVOLUTION a single revolution of a vehicle's engine (*informal*) (*usually plural*) [Early 20thC. Shortening of "revolutions per minute."]

rev up *vt.* (*informal*) **1.** INTENSIFY SOMETHING to increase the tempo, intensity, or amount of something ○ *We'd better rev up production if we're going to meet our deadline.* **2.** EMPASSION SOMEBODY to stir up intense feelings in somebody, usually feelings of excitement, desire, or anger

rev. *abbr.* **1.** revenue **2.** reverse **3.** MIL review **4.** PUBL revised **5.** EDUC revision **6.** revolution

Rev. *abbr.* Reverend

re·val·ue /ree vállyoo/ (**-ued, -u·ing, -ues**), **re·val·u·ate** /ree vállyoo àyt/ (**-at·ed, -at·ing, -ates**) *vt.* **1.** FIN RAISE VALUE OF CURRENCY to increase the value of a nation's currency. ◊ **reevaluate 2.** COMM REASSESS THE PRESENT VALUE to assign a new value to something such as assets

re·vamp /rēe vámp/ *vt.* (**-vamped, -vamp·ing, -vamps**) ALTER SOMETHING FOR THE BETTER to alter something in order to improve the way it looks or works ■ *n.* ALTERATION FOR THE BETTER a change made in something in order to improve its appearance or functioning [The word meant originally "to furnish a shoe with a new vamp"]

WORD KEY: SYNONYMS

See Synonyms at ***renew***.

re·vanche /ri vaánch/ *n.* a nation's or an ethnic group's policy of regaining lost territory [Mid-19thC. Via French from Old French *revancher* "to revenge," from *vengier* (see REVENGE).] —**re·vanch·ism** *n.* —**re·vanch·ist** *adj., n.*

Revd. *abbr.* Reverend

re·veal[1] /ri vēel/ (**-vealed, -veal·ing, -veals**) *vt.* **1.** MAKE SOMETHING KNOWN to disclose something that was unknown or secret **2.** EXPOSE SOMETHING to make something visible that had been hidden or covered **3.** RELIG MAKE KNOWN DIVINE TRUTH to make something known by divine or supernatural means [14thC. Via French *révéler* from Latin *revelare,* literally "to unveil," from *velum* (see VEIL).] —**re·veal·er** *n.*

re·veal[2] /ri vēel/ *n.* the vertical section of wall that lies between a doorframe or windowframe and the outer wall [Late 17thC. Alteration of earlier *revale* "to lower," from Old French *revaler,* from *val* "valley" (see VALE).]

re·vealed re·lig·ion *n.* a religion based on what its adherents believe to be the word of a supreme deity

re·veal·ing /ri vēeling/ *adj.* **1.** SHOWING BODY exposing part of the body that would normally be kept covered **2.** DISCLOSING INFORMATION giving away new, surprising, or valuable information **3.** FRANK exposing true emotions or intentions —**re·veal·ing·ly** *adv.*

rev·eil·le /révvəlee/ (*plural* **-les**) *n.* **1.** WAKE-UP CALL the sounding of a bugle to awaken and summon military personnel in a camp **2.** TIME OF REVEILLE the time of day at which reveille is sounded **3.** EARLY-MORNING MILITARY FORMATION the military formation that begins the day **4.** SIGNAL TO AWAKE any signal that it is time to get out of bed [Mid-17thC. Alteration of French *réveillez* "wake up!", from Old French *resveiller* "to awaken," from *esveiller,* via assumed Vulgar Latin *exvigilare* from, ultimately, Latin *vigil* (see VIGIL).]

rev·el /révv'l/ *vi.* (**-eled, -el·ing, -els**) **1.** ENJOY to take great pleasure in something **2.** BE AT A PARTY to have an enjoyable time in the company of others, especially at a party ■ *n.* NOISY CELEBRATION an uproarious party or celebration (*often used in the plural*) [14thC. Via Old French *reveler* "to rebel, carouse" from Latin *rebellare* (see REBEL).] —**rev·el·er** *n.*

rev·e·la·tion /rèvvə láysh'n/ *n.* **1.** INFORMATION REVEALED information that is newly disclosed, especially surprising or valuable information **2.** SURPRISING THING a surprisingly good or valuable experience **3.** DISCLOSURE the revealing of something previously hidden or secret **4.** CHR DEMONSTRATION OF DIVINE WILL a showing or revealing of divine will or truth [14thC. Via French from, ultimately, Latin *revelare* (see REVEAL).] —**rev·e·la·tion·al** *adj.*

Rev·e·la·tion, Rev·e·la·tions *n.* a book of the Bible that includes a description of the end of the world

rev·e·la·tor /révvə làytər/ *n.* somebody or something believed to reveal divine will or truth [15thC. From late Latin, formed from Latin *revelare* (see REVEAL).]

rev·e·la·to·ry /ri véllə tàwree, révvələ-/ *adj.* disclosing something not previously known

rev·el·er /révvələr/ *n.* somebody enjoying a noisy party or celebration

rev·el·ry /révv'lree/ (*plural* **-ries**) *n.* lively enjoyment or celebration, usually involving eating, drinking, dancing, and noise (*often used in the plural*)

rev·e·nant /révvənənt/ *n.* a dead person believed to have come back as a ghost (*literary*) [Early 19thC. From French, the present participle of *revenir* (see REVENUE).]

re·venge /ri vénj/ *vt.* (**-venged, -veng·ing, -veng·es**) **1.** SECURE REVENGE FOR SOMEBODY to avenge yourself or somebody else who has been harmed **2.** PUNISH SOMEBODY FOR HARM DONE to punish somebody in retaliation for harm or injury done ■ *n.* **1.** SOMETHING DONE IN RETALIATION something done to get even with somebody else who has caused harm **2.** DESIRE FOR RETALIATION the desire or urge to get even with somebody **3.** RETALIATORY PUNISHMENT the punishing of somebody in retaliation for harm done [14thC. From Old French *revengier,* from *vengier* "to avenge," from late Latin *vindicare* (see VINDICATE).] —**re·venge·ful** *adj.* —**re·venge·ful·ly** *adv.* —**re·veng·er** *n.*

rev·e·nue /révvə no͞o/ *n.* **1.** BUSINESS INCOME FROM BUSINESS money that comes into a business from the sale of goods or services **2.** POL GOVERNMENT INCOME the income of a government from all sources, used to pay for a nation's expenses **3.** FIN PERSONAL INCOME income or salary received from employment **4.** FIN YIELD ON INVESTMENT the total return produced by an investment **5.** TAX-COLLECTING DEPARTMENT the department of a nation's government that is responsible for collecting taxes [15thC. From French *revenu,* the past participle of *revenir* "to return," from Latin *revenire,* literally "to come back," from *venire* (see VENUE).]

rev·e·nue bond *n.* a bond issued by a government agency in order to build or improve a public property. The income from the property pays for the bond.

rev·e·nue cut·ter *n.* a small lightly armed boat used to patrol coastlines, enforce customs regulations, and prevent smuggling

rev·e·nu·er /révvə no͞o ər/ *n.* (*informal*) **1.** SHIPPING REVENUE CUTTER a revenue cutter **2.** POL GOVERNMENT AGENT a government agent who is in charge of stopping the illegal manufacture of alcoholic beverages

rev·e·nue shar·ing *n.* the practice of distributing a portion of federal income to state and city governments

rev·e·nue stamp *n.* a stamp put on something that proves a government tax has been paid

rev·e·nue tar·iff *n.* a tax or duty imposed to produce public revenue, as distinct from one imposed to protect a domestic economy

re·verb /ri vúrb/ *n.* **1.** ECHO IN MUSIC an echoing effect produced in live or recorded music by electronic means **2.** ECHO-PRODUCING DEVICE an electronic device used to produce an echoing effect in live or recorded music ■ *vi.* (**-verbed, -verb·ing, -verbs**) PRODUCE ELECTRONIC ECHO to produce an echoing effect in live or recorded music [Early 17thC. Shortening of REVERBERATE; earliest as verb meaning "to reverberate."]

re·ver·ber·ant /ri vúrbərənt/ *adj.* making an echoing sound —**re·ver·ber·ant·ly** *adv.*

re·ver·ber·ate /ri vúrbə ràyt/ (**-at·ed, -at·ing, -ates**) *v.* **1.** *vi.* ECHO to echo repeatedly **2.** *vi.* HAVE CONTINUING EFFECT to have a far-reaching or lasting impact, especially as a result of being circulated widely **3.** *vi.* PHYS BOUNCE BACK to be reflected repeatedly off different surfaces (*refers to heat, light, or sound waves*) **4.** *vt.* CAUSE SOUND TO ECHO to cause sound to bounce back from a surface **5.** *vt.* METALL HEAT OR REFINE METAL to treat metal in a furnace that reflects flame or heat (**reverberatory furnace**) [15thC. From Latin *reverberare,* literally "to beat again," from *verberare* "to beat," from *verber* "scourge."] —**re·ver·ber·a·tion** /ri vùrbə ráysh'n/ *n.* —**re·ver·ber·a·tive** /ri vúrbə ràytiv/ *adj.*

re·ver·ber·a·tion time *n.* the time it takes for a sound in a room to be reduced by 60 decibels

re·ver·ber·a·to·ry /ri vúrbərə tàwree/ *adj.* produced or functioning by the process of deflection of sound, light, or heat

re·ver·ber·a·to·ry fur·nace *n.* a furnace in which material is heated by heat reflected from above

re·vere /ri veér/ (**-vered, -ver·ing, -veres**) *vt.* to regard somebody with admiration and deep respect [Mid-17thC. Via French *révérer* from Latin *revereri*, from *vereri* "to be in awe of."]

Re·vere /ri véer/ city in eastern Massachusetts, east of Medford. It is a northeastern suburb of Boston. Population: 41,761 (1996).

Re·vere /ri veér/, **Paul** (1735–1818) American silversmith and patriot. A leading Boston silversmith, he made an historic midnight ride, on April 18, 1775, from Boston to Concord to warn of an impending British attack.

rev·er·ence /révvərəns/ *n.* **1.** RESPECT FELT feelings of deep respect or devotion **2.** RESPECT GAINED the respect or devotion that others show somebody or something **3. rev·er·ence, Rev·er·ence** CHR USED TO ADDRESS CHRISTIAN CLERGY used as a form of address for some members of the Christian clergy ■ *vt.* (**-enced, -enc·ing, -enc·es**) RESPECT SOMEBODY OR SOMETHING DEEPLY to regard somebody or something with deep respect (*formal*)

WORD KEY: SYNONYMS

See Synonyms at ***regard.***

rev·er·end /révvərənd/ *adj.* **1.** RESPECTED deserving to be shown respect (*formal*) **2.** CHR OF CLERGY relating or belonging to the Christian clergy ■ *n.* CHR CHRISTIAN PRIEST a member of the Christian clergy (*informal*) [15thC. Directly or via French from Latin *reverendus* "to be revered," from *revereri* (see REVERE).]

WORD KEY: USAGE

reverend or **reverent**? Care should be taken in distinguishing between ***reverend***, which refers to a member of the clergy, and ***reverent***, which is a descriptive adjective, meaning "showing reverence," applicable to anyone who merits it.

Rev·er·end *n.* used as a title and form of address for some members of the clergy in many Christian churches

Rev·er·end Moth·er *n.* CHR used as a title of respect to address the nun in charge of a convent

rev·er·ent /révvərənt/ *adj.* feeling or expressing profound respect or awe [14thC. From Latin *revereri* (see REVERE).] —**rev·er·ent·ly** *adv.*

WORD KEY: USAGE

See Usage note at ***reverend.***

rev·er·en·tial /rèvvə rénshəl/ *adj.* **1.** RESPECTFUL feeling or expressing deep respect or awe **2.** DESERVING RESPECT worthy of deep respect or awe —**rev·er·en·tial·ly** *adv.*

rev·er·ie /révvəree/ (*plural* **-ies**) *n.* a state of idle and pleasant contemplation [Early 17thC. From French, formed from *rêver* "to dream," of unknown origin.]

re·vers /ri veér, ri váir/ (*plural* **-vers** /-veérz, -váirz/) *n.* a part of a garment such as a lapel, turned back so that the reverse side shows [Mid-19thC. From French, (see REVERSE).]

re·ver·sal /ri vúrs'l/ *n.* **1.** CHANGE TO OPPOSITE DIRECTION a change to an opposite direction or state **2.** PROBLEM an unfortunate experience or setback, particularly in business or financial affairs **3.** REVERSING OF SOMETHING the changing of something to an opposite direction or state **4.** LAW CHANGE OF JUDICIAL DECISION a ruling made by a higher court that sets aside the decision of a lower court

re·verse /ri vúrs/ *adj.* **1.** OPPOSITE TO USUAL OR PREVIOUS ARRANGEMENT opposite to what is usual or what was previously said or arranged ○ *announce the results in reverse order* **2.** ON BACK SIDE on the other side or the back side of something **3.** FOR BACKWARD MOVEMENT used to make a machine or vehicle go backward ○ *reverse gear* ■ *n.* **1.** THE OPPOSITE the contrary of something ○ *She always does the reverse of what I tell her.* **2.** BACK SIDE the rear or back side of something ○ *The names are written on the reverse of the photo.* **3.** MONEY BACK SIDE OF COIN the side of a coin, medal, or seal on which the primary design does not appear ○ *The reverse of some coins carries the national motto.* ◊ **obverse 4.** CHANGE TO OPPOSITE DIRECTION a change or turn to the opposite direction, position, or condition **5.** SETBACK a change for the worse ○ *a military reverse* **6.** MECH ENG GEAR FOR BACKWARD MOVEMENT the gear in a vehicle or machine that makes it run backward ○ *It's easier to get out of here in reverse.* **7.** FOOTBALL OFFENSIVE PLAY IN FOOTBALL in football, a move in which a back receives the handoff from the quarterback and then hands the ball to another back running in the opposite direction ■ *v.* (**-versed, -vers·ing, -vers·es**) **1.** *vt.* CHANGE SOMETHING TO OPPOSITE to change something to the opposite direction, order, or position ○ *reversing the trend of population growth* **2.** *vti.* GO BACKWARD to go backward, or move something in a backward direction ○ *Reverse the car.* **3.** *vt.* TURN SOMETHING INSIDE OUT to change something so that the opposite side or part shows ○ *You can reverse the cloak and wear it with the lining on the outside.* **4.** *vt.* LAW REVOKE RULING to overturn a previous ruling made by a lower court **5.** *vt.* PRINTING PRINT SOMETHING WHITE AGAINST DARK BACKGROUND to print text or graphics in white against a dark or colored background **6.** *vt.* MIL TURN WEAPON UPSIDE DOWN to turn a weapon upside down, especially as a sign of mourning [14thC. Via Old French *revers* "reversed" from Latin *reversus*, the past participle of *revertere*, literally "to turn back," from *vertere* (see VERSE).] —**re·verse·ly** *adv.* —**re·vers·er** *n.*

re·verse-charge *adj. U.K.* TELECOM = **collect**

re·verse com·mut·ing *n.* the practice of traveling regularly between a home in a city and a job in the suburbs —**re·verse com·mut·er** *n.*

re·verse dis·crim·i·na·tion *n.* discrimination against a member of a social group generally regarded as dominant or privileged, e.g., in employment or admission to a university

re·verse en·gi·neer·ing *n.* the pirating of a competitor's technology by dismantling an existing product and reproducing its parts and construction to manufacture a replica —**re·verse-en·gi·neer** *vt.* —**re·verse-en·gi·neered** *adj.*

re·verse mort·gage *n.* a financial instrument in which a residential mortgage is transferred to a bank, which then pays an annuity to the homeowner

re·verse os·mo·sis *n.* a process of purifying water or other liquids such as fruit juices by passing them through a semipermeable membrane that filters out unwanted substances

re·verse take·o·ver *n.* the sale of a company to another company in order to avoid takeover by an unwanted predatory company

re·verse tran·scrip·tase *n.* an enzyme that assists in the formation of DNA using RNA as a template, used in genetic engineering because it reverses the natural flow of genetic information

re·verse vid·e·o *n.* the reversal of the usual character and background color combination on a computer display, used as a highlighting tool

re·ver·si /ri vúrsee/ *n.* a board game for two players, played on a checkerboard, in which captured pieces are transferred to the capturer [Early 19thC. From French, an alteration of *reversin*, via Italian *rovescina* "reversal" from, ultimately, Latin *reversus* (see REVERSE).]

re·vers·i·ble /ri vúrsəb'l/ *adj.* **1.** ABLE TO BE REVERSED able to be changed or undone **2.** CLOTHES USABLE INSIDE OUT made so that either side can be used as the outer or upper side **3.** CHEM UNDERGOING A REACTION AND REVERSING IT capable of going through a stage such as a chemical reaction and then reversing the process —**re·vers·i·bil·i·ty** /ri vùrsə bíllətee/ *n.* —**re·vers·i·ble·ness** /ri vúrsəb'lnəss/ *n.* —**re·vers·i·bly** /ri vúrsəblee/ *adv.*

re·ver·sion /ri vúrzh'n/ *n.* **1.** RETURN TO FORMER CONDITION a return to an earlier condition often perceived as less desirable or inferior **2.** REVERSAL a change to the opposite direction **3.** GENETICS RETURN TO ORIGINAL CHARACTERISTICS an organism's return to ancestral characteristics, usually by means of a second mutation that cancels out the effects of an earlier one **4.** GENETICS REVERTED ORGANISM an organism that has reverted to ancestral genetic characteristics **5.** LAW RETURN TO FORMER OWNER the return of property to its former owner or his or her heirs at the end of a specified period, usually when the present owner dies **6.** LAW PROPERTY RETURNED TO FORMER OWNER property that has been returned to its former owner or his or her heirs **7.** LAW RIGHT TO INHERIT PROPERTY the right to succeed to property, granted to somebody by the former owner —**re·ver·sion·al** *adj.* —**re·ver·sion·al·ly** *adv.* —**re·ver·sion·ar·y** *adj.*

re·ver·sion·er /ri vúrzh'nər/ *n.* somebody to whom ownership of property will be returned after a specified period of time

re·vert /ri vúrt/ (**-vert·ed, -vert·ing, -verts**) *vi.* **1.** GO BACK TO PREVIOUS STATE to return to a former state, often one perceived as less desirable or inferior **2.** RETURN IN DISCUSSION to return to an earlier topic in the course of a discussion **3.** GENETICS REACQUIRE ORIGINAL FEATURES to acquire or develop original genetic features again **4.** RETURN TO OLD HABITS to return to a former pattern of behavior, usually something less acceptable **5.** LAW BE RETURNED TO OWNER to become once again the property of the former owner or his or her heirs [14thC. Via Old French *revertir* from, ultimately, Latin *revertere*, literally "to turn back," from *vertere* (see VERSE).] —**re·vert·er** *n.* —**re·vert·i·ble** *adj.*

WORD KEY: USAGE

See Usage note at ***refer.***

re·ver·tant /ri vúrt'nt/ *adj.* HAVING REACQUIRED ORIGINAL FEATURES used to describe an organism or part of an organism that has acquired features that are original or simpler in the history of its kind ■ *n.* REVERTANT ORGANISM a revertant organism or part

re·vest /ree vést/ (**-vest·ed, -vest·ing, -vests**) *vt.* **1.** REINSTATE SOMEBODY to reinstate somebody in a position or office **2.** RESTORE SOMETHING TO SOMEBODY to restore power or property to somebody

re·vet /ri vét/ (**-vet·ted, -vet·ting, -vets**) *vti.* to give a structure additional support by adding a facing of bricks, stone, or concrete [Early 19thC. Via French *revêtir* from late Latin *revestire*, literally "to clothe again," from *vestire* "to clothe," from *vestis* (see VEST).]

re·vet·ment /ri vétmənt/ *n.* **1.** BUILDING SUPPORTING FACING ON STRUCTURE a facing added to a structure such as a wall or building that provides additional support **2.** MIL BARRICADE a barricade constructed to protect against damage or injury from explosives

re·view /ri vyoó/ *n.* **1.** SURVEY OF PAST a report or survey of past actions, performance, or events ○ *a review of the stock market for the past five years* **2.** ARTS JOURNALISTIC ARTICLE GIVING OPINION a journalistic article giving an assessment of a book, play, movie, concert, or other public performance ○ *The book got unexpectedly bad reviews.* **3.** PUBL PUBLICATION FEATURING REVIEWS a magazine or journal that publishes reviews ○ *the Literary Review* **4.** REEXAMINATION OF SOMETHING another look at or consideration of something **5.** COVERING OF LEARNED MATERIAL AGAIN a brief discussion of subject matter already learned, in preparation for a test ○ *This professor always has a review before a big test.* **6.** MIL MILITARY INSPECTION a formal military inspection **7.** MIL FORMAL MILITARY CEREMONY a formal military ceremony staged to honor a person or an occasion **8.** LAW JUDICIAL REEXAMINATION a critical examination by a higher court of a decision taken by a lower court **9.** THEATER = **revue** ■ *v.* (**-viewed, -view·ing, -views**) **1.** *vt.* LOOK AT SOMETHING CRITICALLY to examine something to make sure that it is adequate, accurate, or correct ○ *They need to review their sales strategy.* **2.** *vt.* ARTS GIVE OPINION ON QUALITY OF SOMETHING to write a journalistic report on the quality of a new play, book, movie, concert, or other public performance ○ *He reviews movies for a newspaper.* **3.** *vt.* CONSIDER SOMETHING AGAIN to consider, study, or check something again **4.** *vi.* EDUC STUDY NOTES FOR TEST to study for a test by looking over notes and course materials **5.** *vt.* LOOK BACK ON SOMETHING to discuss or examine something again ○ *She's writing an article reviewing the company's history.* **6.** *vt.* LAW RECONSIDER DECISION JUDICIALLY to reexamine a judicial decision made in a lower court in order to consider whether it should be overturned **7.** *vt.* MIL SUBJECT TROOPS TO MILITARY INSPECTION to make a formal inspection of a military force [15thC. From obsolete French *reveue* "inspection," from *revoir* "to inspect," from Latin *revidere*, literally "to see again," from *videre* (see VISION).] —**re·view·a·ble** *adj.*

re·view cop·y *n.* a copy of a new book that a publisher sends to potential critics and reviewers to encourage published reviews

re·view·er /ri vyoó ər/ *n.* somebody who writes journalistic articles giving opinions on plays, books, movies, concerts, and other events or works in the arts

re·vile /ri víl/ (**-viled, -vil·ing, -viles**) *v.* **1.** *vt.* ATTACK SOMEBODY OR SOMETHING VERBALLY to make a fierce or abusive verbal attack on somebody or something **2.** *vi.* USE ABUSIVE LANGUAGE to use insulting or abusive language [14thC. From Old French *reviler*, from *vil* (see VILE).] —**re·vile·ment** *n.* —**re·vil·er** *n.*

re·vise *v.* /ri vīz/ (**-vised, -vis·ing, -vis·es**) **1.** *vt.* RETHINK SOMETHING to come to different conclusions about somebody or something after thinking again **2.** *vt.* GIVE UPDATED VERSION OF SOMETHING to change a previous estimate in order to make it more accurate or realistic **3.** *vt.* ALTER SOMETHING FOR CORRECTION OR UPDATING to amend a text in order to correct, update, or improve it **4.** *vti. U.K.* EDUC = **review** *v.* 4 ■ *n.* /reē vīz, ri vīz/ **1.** SOMETHING REVISED something that has been revised **2.** PUBL LATE STAGE OF PRINTED PROOF a late stage of a printed proof that incorporates corrections to earlier proofs (*often used in the plural*) [Mid-16thC. Via French *réviser* from Latin *revisere*, literally "to look over again," from *visere* "to keep watching," from *videre* (see VISION).] —**re·vis·a·ble** *adj.* —**re·vis·er** *n.*

Re·vised Stan·dard Ver·sion *n.* a modern U.S. revision of the American Standard Version of the Bible, published in full in 1953

Re·vised Ver·sion *n.* a 19th-century British revision of the King James' Bible

re·vi·sion /ri vízh'n/ *n.* **1.** CHANGING OF SOMETHING the changing of a decision, estimate, statistic, or set of figures in order to correct it or make it more realistic **2.** CHANGING OF TEXT the amending of a text in order to correct, update, improve, or adapt it **3.** PUBL NEW EDITION a revised and republished version of a text **4.** *U.K.* EDUC = **review** *n.* 5 —**re·vi·sion·ar·y** *adj.*

re·vi·sion·ism /ri vízh'n ìzzəm/ *n.* **1.** RECONSIDERING OF ACCEPTED TRUTHS the reconsidering of long-established practices, views, or beliefs **2.** POL, HIST ANTI-MARXIST SOCIALIST MOVEMENT a socialist movement arguing against revolutionary Marxist theory and believing in the peaceful achievement of social progress through reforms —**re·vi·sion·ist** *adj., n.*

re·vis·it /ree vízzit/ *vt.* (**-it·ed, -it·ing, -its**) **1.** GO TO PLACE AGAIN to visit a place again **2.** RECONSIDER SOMETHING to reconsider something such as an issue of public policy or a course of action, especially when additional facts indicate that an earlier decision was inappropriate ■ *n.* SUBSEQUENT VISIT another visit to a place

re·vi·so·ry /ri vīzəree/ *adj.* carrying out a revision, or given the authority to revise something

re·vi·tal·ize /reē vīt'l īz/ (**-ized, -iz·ing, -iz·es**) *vt.* to give new life or energy to somebody or something —**re·vi·tal·i·za·tion** /ree vīt'li záysh'n/ *n.*

re·viv·al /ri vív'l/ *n.* **1.** RENEWAL OF INTEREST a renewal of interest in something that results in its becoming popular once more **2.** THEATER, MUSIC NEW PRODUCTION a new production of a play or opera that has not been performed recently **3.** REVIVING OF SOMEBODY the process of bringing somebody back to life, consciousness, or full strength **4.** RECOVERY the recovering of life, consciousness, or full strength **5.** RELIG RENEWED RELIGIOUS INTEREST a new interest in religion, or the reawakening of such interest **6.** CHR EVANGELICAL CHRISTIAN MEETING a meeting or a series of meetings of evangelical Christians intended to awaken religious fervor in those who attend **7.** LAW REESTABLISHING OF LEGAL VALIDITY the renewal of the validity of a contract or the effect of a judicial decision

re·viv·al·ism /ri vív'l ìzzəm/ *n.* **1.** DESIRE TO FOSTER NEW INTEREST a desire or tendency to renew interest in something old, e.g., old customs or beliefs **2.** RELIG EVANGELICAL RELIGIOUS MOVEMENT the efforts of a religious movement, especially an evangelical Christian movement, to reawaken religious commitment

re·viv·al·ist /ri vív'list/ *n.* **1.** SOMEBODY ADVOCATING RENEWED INTEREST somebody who wishes to revive old customs, ideas, or institutions **2.** RELIG EVANGELIST somebody who promotes, organizes, or preaches at a religious revival meeting, especially one for evangelical Christians ■ *adj.* RELIG REAWAKENING RELIGIOUS FAITH dedicated to reawakening or stimulating religious fervor in evangelical Christians —**re·viv·al·is·tic** /ri vīv'l ístik/ *adj.*

re·vive /ri vív/ (**-vived, -viv·ing, -vives**) *v.* **1.** *vti.* RECOVER CONSCIOUSNESS to come, or bring somebody, back to life, consciousness, or full strength **2.** *vti.* FLOURISH AGAIN to become, or make something, active, accepted, or popular once more **3.** *vt.* CAUSE EXPERIENCE TO RETURN to cause something to be experienced again as a memory or feeling **4.** *vt.* THEATER, MUSIC STAGE AGAIN to stage a new production of an old play or opera [15thC. Directly or via French *revivre* from late Latin *revivere*, literally "to make live again," from *vivere* (see VIVID).] —**re·viv·a·ble** *adj.* —**re·viv·er** *n.*

re·viv·i·fy /ree vívvə fī/ (**-fied, -fy·ing, -fies**) *vt.* to impart new life, energy, or spirit to something or somebody —**re·viv·i·fi·ca·tion** /reē vívvəfi káysh'n/ *n.*

rev·o·ca·ble /révvəkəb'l, ri vṓk-/ *adj.* able to be revoked or canceled —**rev·o·ca·bil·i·ty** /rèvvəkə bíllətee, ri vṓkə-/ *n.* —**rev·o·ca·bly** /révvəkəblee, ri vṓkəblee/ *adv.*

rev·o·ca·tion /rèvvə káysh'n, reē vō-/ *n.* the cancellation or withdrawal of something such as a law or license —**rev·o·ca·to·ry** /révvəkə tàwree, ri vṓkə-/ *adj.*

re·voke /ri vṓk/ *v.* (**-voked, -vok·ing, -vokes**) **1.** *vt.* LAW FORMALLY CANCEL SOMETHING to make something null and void by withdrawing, recalling, or reversing it **2.** *vt.* SUMMON SOMEBODY BACK to call somebody back, e.g., from exile or from an overseas position **3.** *vi.* CARDS NOT FOLLOW SUIT IN CARDS in a card game, to fail to follow suit though able to do so ■ *n.* CARDS FAILURE TO FOLLOW SUIT IN CARDS failure to follow suit in a card game when able to do so [14thC. Via French *révoquer* from Latin *revocare*, literally "to call back," from *vocare* (see VOCAL).] —**re·vok·er** *n.*

re·volt /ri vṓlt/ *v.* (**-volt·ed, -volt·ing, -volts**) **1.** *vi.* REBEL AGAINST THE STATE to try to overthrow an existing government **2.** *vi.* DEFY AUTHORITY to resist authority or rules **3.** *vti.* FEEL DISGUST to feel, or cause somebody to feel, disgust or repulsion ■ *n.* **1.** UPRISING AGAINST GOVERNMENT an uprising that attempts to overthrow a government **2.** DEFIANCE OF AUTHORITY a protest against authority or rules [Mid-16thC. Via French *révolter* from, ultimately, assumed Vulgar Latin *revolvitare* "to overturn," from Latin *revolvere* (see REVOLVE).] —**re·volt·er** *n.*

re·volt·ing /ri vṓlting/ *adj.* **1.** PROVOKING DISGUST arousing feelings of disgust, nausea, or repulsion **2.** NASTY unattractive or otherwise unpleasant (*informal*) —**re·volt·ing·ly** *adv.*

rev·o·lute /révvə lo͞ot/ *adj.* used to describe leaves and other plant parts that are rolled backward and downward from the tip or edge [Mid-18thC. From Latin *revolutus*, the past participle of *revolvere* (see REVOLVE).]

rev·o·lu·tion /rèvvə lo͞osh'n/ *n.* **1.** POL OVERTHROW OF GOVERNMENT the overthrow of a ruler or political system **2.** MAJOR CHANGE a dramatic change in ideas or practice **3.** COMPLETE CIRCULAR TURN one complete circular movement made by something round or cylindrical, e.g., a wheel, around a fixed point **4.** CIRCLE AROUND SOMETHING a complete circle made around something, e.g., the orbit made by a planet or satellite around another body **5.** GEOL PERIOD OF MAJOR GEOLOGIC CHANGE a period during which the Earth's crust changes considerably and major features such as mountain ranges may emerge [14thC. Via French from, ultimately, Latin *revolut-*, the past participle stem of *revolvere* (see REVOLVE).]

rev·o·lu·tion·ar·y /rèvvə lo͞osh'n èrree/ *adj.* **1.** POL OF A POLITICAL REVOLUTION relating to or involving a political or social revolution **2.** POL STIRRING REBELLION causing, supporting, or advocating revolution **3.** NEW AND DIFFERENT so new and different as to cause a major change in something ■ *n.* (*plural* **-ies**) POL REBEL somebody committed to a political or social revolution —**rev·o·lu·tion·ar·i·ly** *adv.* —**rev·o·lu·tion·ar·i·ness** *n.*

Rev·o·lu·tion·ar·y *adj.* **1.** OF THE AMERICAN REVOLUTION relating to the war with Great Britain fought by the American colonists **2.** OF PARTICULAR NATIONAL REVOLUTION relating to a particular revolution that has taken place such as the Russian Revolution or the French Revolution

Rev·o·lu·tion·ar·y Cal·en·dar *n.* = **French Republican Calendar**

rev·o·lu·tion·ist /rèvvə lo͞osh'nist/ *n.* = **revolutionary**

rev·o·lu·tion·ize /rèvvə lo͞osh'n īz/ (**-ized, -iz·ing, -iz·es**) *vt.* **1.** CHANGE SOMETHING RADICALLY to cause a radical change in something such as a method or approach **2.** POL INCITE PEOPLE TO REBELLION to inspire people with revolutionary ideas **3.** POL CAUSE REBELLION IN COUNTRY to bring about a revolution in a country —**rev·o·lu·tion·iz·er** *n.*

re·volve /ri vólv/ *v.* (**-volved, -volv·ing, -volves**) **1.** *vti.* MOVE IN CIRCULAR FASHION to move, or send something, in a circular movement, either around an object or on a central axis **2.** *vi.* BE FOCUSED to have something as a primary focus or theme **3.** *vi.* RECUR to happen in cycles or regular periodic intervals ■ *n.* THEATER TURNING STAGE a circular part of a stage that can be turned mechanically in order to change a scene [14thC. From Latin *revolvere*, literally "to roll back," from *volvere* (see VOLUTE).] —**re·volv·a·ble** *adj.*

re·volv·er /ri vólvər/ *n.* a handgun with a revolving cylinder of chambers, allowing several shots to be fired without reloading

re·volv·ing cred·it *n.* a credit scheme that imposes regular repayments and a predetermined spending limit

re·volv·ing door *n.* **1.** DOOR THAT GOES AROUND a door, usually in a large building, consisting of four panels that intersect at right angles and turn on a central pivot **2.** HR CIRCULAR SYSTEM any system in which people frequently enter and leave, e.g., a corporation that repeatedly hires and fires staff or a criminal justice system that returns offenders to society (*hyphenated when used before a noun*)

re·volv·ing fund *n.* a fund that can be drawn upon and repaid as desired, established for a particular purpose

re·vue /ri vyo͞o/ (*plural* **-vues**) *n.* a musical variety show consisting of skits, dance routines, and songs that often satirize current events and personalities [Late 19thC. From French, formed from *revoir* (see REVIEW).]

re·vulsed /ri vúlst/ *adj.* disgusted or appalled by something

re·vul·sion /ri vúlshən/ *n.* **1.** FEELING OF DISGUST a sudden and violent feeling of extreme loathing **2.** WITHDRAWAL a pulling or turning back (*formal*) **3.** MED DIVERSION OF BLOOD the diversion of blood or disease from one part of the body to another [Mid-16thC. Via French from, ultimately, Latin *revuls-*, the past participle stem of *revellere*, literally "to pull back," from *vellere* "to tear, pull."] —**re·vul·sive** *adj.*

Rev. Ver. *abbr.* Revised Version

re·wake /ree wáyk/ (**-woke** /-wṓk/ *or* **-waked, -wok·en** /-wṓkən/ *or* **-waked, -wak·ing, -wakes**) *vti.* to wake again, or wake somebody again

re·wak·en /reē wáykən/ (**-ened, -en·ing, -ens**) *vi.* to waken up again

re·ward /ri wáwrd/ *n.* **1.** THING GIVEN IN RETURN something desirable given in return for what somebody has done **2.** MONEY OFFERED IN RETURN money offered for information about the whereabouts of a criminal or the return of something lost or stolen **3.** BENEFIT RECEIVED a benefit obtained as a result of an action taken or a job done **4.** PSYCHOL SOMETHING REINFORCING DESIRED BEHAVIOR something positive that follows a desired response and acts to encourage desired behavior ■ *vt.* (**-ward·ed, -ward·ing, -wards**) **1.** GIVE SOMEBODY SOMETHING AS REWARD to give somebody something in return, especially in thanks for kindness or help **2.** REPAY EFFORT to be worth the effort or attention that is given [14thC. From Anglo-Norman, a variant of Old French *reguard* (see REGARD).] —**re·ward·a·ble** *adj.* —**re·ward·er** *n.*

re·ward·ing /ri wáwrding/ *adj.* **1.** SATISFYING providing somebody with personal satisfaction or great pleasure **2.** GIVEN AS REWARD intended as a reward for something —**re·ward·ing·ly** *adv.*

re·wind *vt.* /ree wīnd/ (**-wound** /-wównd/, **-wound, -wind·ing, -winds**) WIND SOMETHING BACK to wind something such as video or audio tape back onto its original spool or back to an earlier point ■ *n.* /reē wīnd/ **1.** REWINDING PROCESS the process of rewinding something **2.** REWINDING FUNCTION a function, e.g., on a camera or video recorder, that rewinds film or tape

re·wire /ree wīr/ (**-wired, -wir·ing, -wires**) *vt.* to install new electrical wiring in a building, vehicle, or electrical device

re·word /ree wúrd/ (**-word·ed, -word·ing, -words**) *vt.* to change the wording of something written or spoken

re·work /ree wúrk/ *vt.* (**-worked, -work·ing, -works**) **1.** MAKE IMPROVEMENTS TO SOMETHING to alter or revise something in order to improve or update it **2.** AMEND SOMETHING FOR REUSE to alter something in order to reuse it in a different context ■ *n.* REVISED VERSION a new version of something, especially a spoken or written text

re·work·ing /reē wúrking/ *n. U.K.* = **rework**

re·write *vt.* /ree rīt/ (**-wrote** /-rṓt/, **-writ·ten** /-rítt'n/, **-writ·ing, -writes**) **1.** AMEND WORDING OF TEXT to redraft a text by changing the wording or structure **2.** PRESS EDIT FOR PUBLICATION to edit a reporter's copy for publication in a newspaper or magazine **3.** ALTER FACTS ABOUT SOMETHING to change the way the past is perceived or known about ■ *n.* /rée rìt/ **AMENDED TEXT** an amended version of a written document —**re·writ·er** *n.*

Rex /reks/ *n.* a word used in the formal title of a reigning king, especially on coins and official documents (*formal*) [Early 17thC. From Latin, "king" (source of English *regal, royal, viceroy,* and *reign*). Ultimately from an Indo-European word that is also the ancestor of *rich, Reich,* and *rajah.*]

Reye's syn·drome /rī́z-/ *n.* a rare and serious childhood disease, usually following a respiratory infection, causing vomiting, fatty deposits in the liver, disorientation, and swelling of the kidneys and brain [Named for the Australian pediatrician Ralph Douglas *Reye* (1912–78), who first described the condition]

Rey·kja·vik /ràykyə vík/ capital city of Iceland, situated on Faxaflói Bay, in the southwest of the country. Population: 103,000 (1994).

Rey·nolds /rénn'ldz/, **Burt** (*b.* 1936) U.S. actor. In his early movies such as *Deliverance* (1972), he played action roles, but later moved on to comedies. Full name **Burton Leon Reynolds Jr.**

Rey·nolds, Sir Joshua (1723–92) British painter. He painted portraits of many notable people of his day, and was the founding president of the Royal Academy of Arts (1768).

Reyn·old's num·ber *n.* a number used to indicate the flow of fluid through a pipe or around an obstruction. Symbol *Re* [Named for the Irish physicist Osborne *Reynolds* (1842–1912)]

re·zone /ree zṓn/ (**-zoned, -zon·ing, -zones**) *vt.* to change the zoning of a neighborhood or a piece of property

Rf[1] *symbol.* CHEM ELEM rutherfordium

Rf[2] *abbr.* MONEY rufiyaa

RF[1] *abbr.* **1.** RADIO radio frequency **2.** MIL reconnaissance fighter **3.** MIL regular forces **4.** GENETICS releasing factor **5.** MAPS representative fraction **6.** République française **7.** MIL Reserve Force **8.** CHEM retention factor **9.** BASEBALL right fielder

RF[2] MONEY symbol **Rwanda franc**

rf. *abbr.* **1.** reef **2.** COMM refund

r.f. *abbr.* **1.** RADIO radio frequency **2.** MIL rapid fire **3.** PAPER rough finish

R fac·tor *n.* a combination of genes that makes some bacteria resistant to antibiotics. It can be transferred to other bacteria through conjugation. [*R* abbreviation of *resistance*]

RFC *abbr.* **1.** Reconstruction Finance Corporation **2.** SPORTS Rugby Football Club

RFD *abbr.* **1.** RADIO radio-frequency device **2.** MIL reporting for duty **3.** MAIL rural free delivery

Rfn. *abbr.* Rifleman

r.g., RG *abbr.* right guard

RGB *abbr.* red, green, blue (*used to describe a color monitor or color value*)

RGS *abbr.* Royal Geographical Society

Rgt. *abbr.* regiment

Rh[1] *symbol.* rhodium

Rh[2] *abbr.* rhesus (factor)

RH *abbr.* **1.** METEOROL relative humidity **2.** right hand **3.** Royal Highness

r.h. *abbr.* **1.** METEOROL relative humidity **2.** right hand

rhab·dom /rábdəm, ráb dòm/ *n.* a transparent rod-shaped part of the compound eye of insects, spiders, and other arthropods [Late 19thC. From late Greek *rhabdōma,* from *rhabdos* "rod."]

rhab·do·man·cy /rábdə mànsee/ *n.* the use of a divining rod to locate underground water or mineral ores [Mid-17thC. From Greek *rhabdomanteia,* from *rhabdos* "rod" + *-manteia* (see -MANCY).] —**rhab·do·man·cer** *n.* —**rhab·do·man·tist** *n.*

rhab·do·vi·rus /rábdə vìrəss/ *n.* a rod-shaped virus that contains RNA such as the virus that causes rabies [Mid-20thC. Coined from Greek *rhabdos* "rod" + VIRUS.]

Rhad·a·man·thus /ràddə mánthəss/ *n.* in Greek mythology, the son of Zeus and Europa, and brother of Minos. According to Homer, he lived in Elysium, the home of the blessed dead. Later legend states that he was one of the three judges of the dead in the underworld.

Rhae·tian /réeshee ən, réesh'n/ *n.* = **Rhaeto-Romance** ■ *adj.* **1.** LANG **OF RHAETO-ROMANCE** relating or belonging to Rhaeto-Romance **2. OF RHAETIA** relating to Rhaetia, an alpine province of ancient Rome, or the section of the Alps in this area [Late 16thC. Formed from *Rhaetia,* an alpine province of ancient Rome.]

Rhae·to-Ro·mance /réetō rō mánss/ *n.* a group of Romance dialects, sometimes considered to be separate languages, spoken in some Alpine regions of Switzerland and Italy. The group comprises Romansch, Ladin, and Friulian. —**Rhae·to-Ro·mance** *adj.*

rham·nose /rám nòss/ *n.* a crystalline sugar found in the cells of most plants. Formula: $C_6H_{12}O_5$. [Late 19thC. Formed from modern Latin *rhamnus,* genus name of the buckthorn (in whose berries the substance is found), from Greek *rhamnos.*]

rhap·sode /ráp sṑd/ *n.* = **rhapsodist** *n.* 2 [Mid-19thC. From Greek *rhapsōidēs,* from *rhapsōidein* "to recite" (see RHAPSODY).]

rhap·sod·ic /rap sóddik/, **rhap·sod·i·cal** /-ik'l/ *adj.* **1.** MUSIC **OF A RHAPSODY** relating to a rhapsody, or with the emotional and improvisational qualities of a rhapsody **2. ENTHUSIASTIC** joyfully enthusiastic or ecstatic about something —**rhap·sod·i·cal·ly** *adv.*

rhap·so·dist /rápsədist/ *n.* **1. ENTHUSIASTIC PERSON** somebody who is joyfully enthusiastic or ecstatic about something (*literary*) **2.** HIST **ANCIENT GREEK RECITER** an ancient Greek poet who recited epic poetry professionally

rhap·so·dize /rápsə dìz/ (**-dized, -diz·ing, -diz·es**) *v.* **1.** *vi.* **EXPRESS ENTHUSIASM** to speak or write in an enthusiastic or ecstatic manner **2.** *vti.* POETRY **RECITE RHAPSODY** to write or recite a rhapsody

rhap·so·dy /rápsədee/ (*plural* **-dies**) *n.* **1.** MUSIC **FREE-FORM MUSICAL COMPOSITION** a composition that is often irregular in form, emotional in effect, and improvisational in nature **2. ENTHUSIASTIC TALK** an expression of intense enthusiasm (*often used in the plural*) **3.** POETRY **ANCIENT GREEK RECITED POEM** in ancient Greece, an epic poem recited by a professional reciter **4.** LITERAT **EXALTED LITERARY COMPOSITION** any literary work written in an intense or exalted style [Mid-16thC. Via Latin from Greek *rhapsōidia,* from *rhapsōidein* "to recite poems," from *rhaptein* "to stitch together" + *ōidē* "song" (see ODE).]

WORD KEY: CULTURAL NOTE

Rhapsody in Blue, a musical composition by U.S. composer George Gershwin (1924). Originally written for piano and jazz band, it was later rearranged for orchestra by Ferde Grofé. One of the first classical works to incorporate jazz influences such as syncopated rhythms, it was inspired by the vibrancy of contemporary urban life, particularly that of New York City.

rhat·a·ny /rátt'nee/ (*plural* **-ny** *or* **-nies**) *n.* **1. S AMERICAN SHRUB** a South American shrub with two-sided symmetrical flowers, spiny globular fruits, and thick roots. Genus: *Krameria.* **2. DRIED RHATANY ROOT** the dried root of the rhatany, formerly used as an astringent but now commonly used in dental products, including toothpaste and mouthwash [Early 19thC. Via modern Latin *rhatania* from, ultimately, Quechua *ratánya.*]

rhe·a /ree ə/ (*plural* **-as** *or* **-a**) *n.* a large flightless bird that looks like an ostrich but is slightly smaller. It is native to South America and lives in open country. Rheas have long legs and can run at high speeds. Family: Rheidae. [Early 19thC. From modern Latin, genus name, of uncertain origin: probably from RHEA[1].]

Rhe·a[1] *n.* in Greek mythology, a Titan who was the wife of Cronus and mother of the gods. Roman equivalent **Cybele**

Rhe·a[2] /rée ə/ *n.* the second-largest natural satellite of Saturn, discovered in 1672. It is 1528 km (949 mi.) in diameter and occupies an intermediate orbit.

re·bok /rée bòk/ (*plural* **-boks** *or* **-bok**), **ree·bok** (*plural* **-boks** *or* **-bok**) *n.* a straight-horned antelope that lives in upland meadows and rocky outcrops in southern Africa. It has brownish-gray woolly hair. Rheboks are related to reedbucks. Latin name: *Pelea capreolus.* [Late 18thC. From Dutch *reebok* "roebuck."]

Rhee /ree/, **Syngman** (1875–1965) Korean statesman. He led the fight for Korean independence from Japan and served as South Korea's first president (1948–60).

rheme /reem/ *n.* the part of a sentence, often the predicate, that adds the greatest amount of new information to what is already available in the discourse. ◊ **theme** [Late 19thC. From Greek *rhēma* "what is said." Ultimately from an Indo-European base meaning "to speak," which is also the ancestor of English *word, verb,* and *irony.*]

Rhen·ish /rénish/ *adj.* coming from or relating to the Rhineland area of Germany [14thC. Via Anglo-Norman *reneis,* from, ultimately, Latin *Rhenus* "Rhine."]

rhe·ni·um /réenee əm/ *n.* a rare heavy silvery-white metallic chemical element that has a high melting point and is used as a catalyst and with tungsten in thermocouples. Symbol **Re** [Early 20thC. Via German, which was coined by its discoverers, from Latin *Rhenus* "the Rhine."]

rheo- *prefix.* flow, current ○ *rheometer* [From Greek *rheos* "stream, current," which was formed from *rhein* "to flow." Ultimately from an Indo-European word that is also the ancestor of English *stream.*]

rhe·o·base /rée ō bàyss/ *n.* the minimum electrical nerve impulse necessary to cause a twitch in a muscle

rhe·ol·o·gy /ree óllajee/ *n.* a branch of physics dealing with the way matter flows and changes shape —**rhe·o·log·i·cal** /rée ə lójjik'l/ *adj.* —**rhe·o·log·i·cal·ly** /-lójjikəlee/ *adv.* —**rhe·ol·o·gist** /ree óllajist/ *n.*

rhe·om·e·ter /ree ómmətər/ *n.* an instrument that measures the flow of thick liquids such as blood —**rhe·o·met·ric** /rée ə méttrik/ *adj.*

rhe·o·mor·phism /rée ə máwr fìzzəm/ *n.* the liquefying of rock

rhe·o·stat /rée ə stàt/ *n.* a resistor designed to allow variation in resistance without breaking the electrical circuit of which it is a part. An example is the volume control of a radio. —**rhe·o·stat·ic** /rée ə státtik/ *adj.*

rhe·o·tax·is /rée ə táksiss/ *n.* the motion of an organism toward or away from a current of water or air —**rhe·o·tac·tic** /-táktik/ *adj.*

rhe·ot·ro·pism /ree óttrə pìzzəm/ *n.* growth of a plant, or of an immobile animal such as a coral, in the direction of a flow of water

Rhe·sus /réessəss/ *n.* in Greek mythology, one of the kings of Thrace

Rhe·sus fac·tor *n.* = **Rh factor** [From the fact that the antigens were first discovered in the blood of rhesus monkeys]

rhe·sus mon·key *n.* a brownish monkey of the macaque family, found in southern Asia and used in medical research. It is the most common monkey in India. Latin name: *Macaca mulatta.* ["Rhesus" from modern Latin genus name, arbitrarily for RHESUS]

Rhe·sus neg·a·tive *adj.* = **Rh negative**

Rhe·sus pos·i·tive *adj.* = **Rh positive**

rhet·o·ric /réttərik/ *n.* **1. PERSUASIVE SPEECH OR WRITING** speech or writing that communicates its point persuasively **2. PRETENTIOUS WORDS** complex or elaborate language that only succeeds in sounding pretentious **3. EMPTY TALK** fine-sounding but insincere or empty language **4. SKILL WITH LANGUAGE** the ability to use language effectively, especially to persuade or influence people **5. STUDY OF WRITING OR SPEAKING EFFECTIVELY** the study of methods employed to write or speak effectively and persuasively [14thC. Via Old French *rethorique,* from, ultimately, Greek *rhētorikē (tekhnē)* "(art) of public speaking," from *rhētor* "speaker."]

rhe·tor·i·cal /ri táwrik'l/ *adj.* **1. OF EFFECTIVE USE OF LANGUAGE** relating to the skill of using language effectively and persuasively **2. BOMBASTIC** relating to or using language that is elaborate or fine-sounding but insincere —**rhe·tor·i·cal·ly** *adv.*

rhe·tor·i·cal ques·tion *n.* a question asked for effect that neither expects nor requires an answer

rhet·o·ri·cian /réttə rísh'n/ *n.* **1.** EDUC **RHETORIC TEACHER** somebody who teaches the art of using language effectively and persuasively **2. SKILLED SPEAKER OR WRITER** a skilled and effective speaker or writer **3. PRETENTIOUS SPEAKER OR WRITER** somebody who speaks or writes using elaborate or fine-sounding but insincere language

rheum /room/ *n.* watery discharge coming from the eyes, nose, or mouth [14thC. Via Old French *reume* from, ultimately, Greek *rheuma* "flow, bodily humor."]

rheu·mat·ic /roo máttik/ *adj.* **OF RHEUMATISM** relating to or affected with rheumatism ■ *n.* **SOMEBODY WITH RHEUMATISM** somebody who is affected with rheumatism —**rheu·mat·i·cal·ly** *adv.*

rheu·mat·ic fe·ver *n.* an acute infectious disease that causes a sore throat, fever, pain, swelling in the joints, and often damage to the heart valves. It affects children particularly.

rheu·mat·ic heart dis·ease *n.* damage to the valves or muscular tissue of the heart caused by rheumatic fever

rheu·ma·tism /ro͝omə tìzzəm/ *n.* **1. STIFFNESS IN JOINTS OR MUSCLES** any painful condition of the joints or muscles that is not caused by infection or injury **2. RHEUMATOID ARTHRITIS** a popular name for rheumatoid arthritis

rheu·ma·toid /ro͝omə tòyd/ *adj.* relating to or affected with rheumatism or rheumatoid arthritis —**rheu·ma·toi·dal·ly** /ro͝omə tóyd'lee/ *adv.*

rheu·ma·toid ar·thri·tis *n.* a chronic disease of the joints that causes stiffness, swelling, weakness, loss of mobility, and eventual destruction and deformity of the joints

rheu·ma·toid fac·tor *n.* an antibody found in the blood serum of many people who have rheumatoid arthritis. It is used to diagnose the disease.

rheu·ma·tol·o·gy /ro͝omə tólləjee/ *n.* a branch of medicine dealing with the study and treatment of rheumatic diseases —**rheu·ma·tol·o·gist** *n.*

Rh fac·tor *n.* a group of antibody-producing substances (**antigens**) present in most people's red blood cells. Rh compatability is important in matching blood for transfusions and between pregnant women and their fetuses. ◊ **Rh negative, Rh positive** ["Rh" from *rhesus*]

rhin- *prefix.* = **rhino-** (*used before vowels*)

rhi·nal /rín'l/ *adj.* relating to the nose

Rhine /rīn/ river and major economic waterway in western Europe, flowing through Switzerland, Austria, Liechtenstein, France, Germany, and the Netherlands. Length: 820 mi./1,320 km.

Rhine, Joseph Banks (1895–1980) U.S. psychologist. He was a pioneer in the field of parapsychology, including the study of extrasensory perception, ESP.

rhi·nen·ceph·a·lon /rī nen séffə lòn, -séffələn/ (*plural* **-lons** *or* **-la** /-lə/) *n.* the area of the forebrain that controls the sense of smell —**rhi·nen·ce·phal·ic** /rī nensə fállik/ *adj.*

rhine·stone /rín stòn/ *n.* a small piece of paste or glass used as an imitation diamond [Late 19thC. Translation of French *caillou du Rhin*, so called because the stones were first made in the city of Strasbourg, on the Rhine.]

rhi·ni·tis /rī nítiss/ *n.* inflammation of the mucous membranes of the nose, usually accompanied by a discharge of mucus

rhi·no /rí nō/ (*plural* **-no** *or* **-nos**) *n.* a rhinoceros (*informal*) [Late 19thC. Shortening.]

rhino- *prefix.* nose, nasal ○ *rhinoplasty* [From Greek *rhin-*, the stem of *rhis* 'nose,' of unknown origin]

Rhinoceros

rhi·noc·er·os /rī nóssərəss/ (*plural* **-os·es** *or* **-os** *or* **-i** /-nóssə rī/) *n.* a very large herbivorous mammal with very thick skin and one or two horns on its snout. It is native to Africa and Asia. Family: Rhinocerotidae. [13thC. Via Latin from Greek *rhinokerōs*, from *rhin-*, the stem of *rhis* "nose" + *keras* "horn" (see KERATO-).] —**rhi·noc·e·rot·ic** /rī nòssə róttik/ *adj.*

rhi·noc·er·os bee·tle *n.* any large tropical scarab beetle that has horns on its head and thorax

rhi·noc·er·os bird *n.* = **oxpecker**

rhi·nol·o·gy /rī nólləjee/ *n.* the branch of medicine dealing with conditions and structures of the nose

rhi·no·phar·yn·gi·tis /rī nō ferrən jítiss/ *n.* inflammation of the mucous membranes in the nose and pharynx

rhi·no·plas·ty /rí nō plàstee, rínə-/ (*plural* **-ties**) *n.* plastic surgery performed on the nose, whether for medical or cosmetic reasons —**rhi·no·plas·tic** /rī nō plástik, rīnə-/ *adj.*

rhi·no·scope /rínə skōp/ *n.* a device used by physicians to examine the nasal passages —**rhi·no·scop·ic** /rīnə skóppik/ *adj.* —**rhi·nos·co·py** /rī nóskəpee/ *n.*

rhi·no·vi·rus /rī nō vírəss/ *n.* a virus containing RNA that causes infections of the upper respiratory system, including the common cold

rhiz- *prefix.* = **rhizo-** (*used before vowels*)

rhizo- *prefix.* root ○ *rhizosphere* [From Greek *rhiza* "root" (source also of English *licorice*). Probably ultimately from an Indo-European word that is also the ancestor of *root*, *wort*, and *radical*.]

rhi·zo·bi·um /rī zṓbee əm/ (*plural* **-a** /-zṓbee ə/) *n.* a soil bacterium that forms nodules on the roots of legumes such as beans and clover and takes up nitrogen from the atmosphere. Genus: *Rhizobium*. [Early 20thC. From modern Latin, genus name, from Greek *rhiza* "root" + *bios* "life."]

rhi·zo·car·pous /rī zō kaárpəss/ *adj.* used to describe plants that produce their fruit underground

rhi·zo·ceph·a·lan /rīzō séffələn/ *n.* a small crustacean that lives in water as a parasite on crabs. Order: Rhizocephala. [Late 19thC. Formed from modern Latin *Rhizocephala*, order name, from Greek *rhiza* "root" + *kephalē* "head."] —**rhi·zo·ceph·a·lous** *adj.*

rhi·zo·gen·ic /rī zō jénnik/, **rhi·zo·ge·net·ic** /rī zō jə néttik/, **rhi·zog·e·nous** /rī zójjənəss/ *adj.* used to describe plant cells and tissues from which roots develop

rhi·zoid /rí zòyd/ *n.* a slender outgrowth on mosses, liverworts, and the reproductive cells of ferns that absorbs nourishment in much the same way as a root —**rhi·zoi·dal** /rī zóyd'l/ *adj.*

rhi·zome /rí zōm/ *n.* a thick underground horizontal stem that produces roots and has shoots that develop into new plants. In some plants such as the iris it is fleshy and survives the winter. [Mid-19thC. Via Greek *rhizōma* "mass of roots" from, ultimately, *rhiza* "root" (see RHIZO-).] —**rhi·zom·a·tous** /rī zómmətəss, -zṓmətəss/ *adj.*

rhi·zo·morph /rízə màwrf/ *n.* a structure in some pathogenic fungi that allows them to move from host to host —**rhi·zo·mor·phous** /rīzə máwrfəss/ *adj.*

rhi·zoph·a·gous /rī zóffəgəss/ *adj.* feeding on roots

rhi·zo·plane /rízə plàyn/ *n.* the part of a plant's root that lies at the surface of the soil, where many microorganisms adhere to it

rhi·zo·pod /rízə pòd/ *n.* a single-celled organism (**protozoan**) that moves and eats by means of filaments that it can extend temporarily. Subphylum: Rhizopoda. —**rhi·zop·o·dous** /rī zóppədəss/ *adj.*

rhi·zo·pus /rízōpəss, rízəpəss/ *n.* a mold that causes decay such as the common bread mold. Genus: *Rhizopus*. [Late 19thC. From modern Latin, genus name, from Greek *rhiza* "root" + *pous* "foot"; so called because of its shape.]

rhi·zo·sphere /rízə sfeer/ *n.* the area of soil that immediately surrounds and is affected by a plant's roots

rhi·zot·o·my /rī zóttəmee/ (*plural* **-mies**) *n.* surgery in which spinal nerves are cut in order to relieve pain or high blood pressure

Rh neg·a·tive *adj.* lacking the Rh factor in the blood. ◊ **Rh factor, Rh positive**

rho /rō/ (*plural* **rhos**) *n.* the 17th letter of the Greek alphabet, represented in the English alphabet as "r." See table at **alphabet** [14thC. From Greek *rhō*, of Phoenician origin.]

rhod- *prefix.* = **rhodo-** (*used before vowels*)

rho·da·mine /rṓdə meen/ *n.* a red or pink fluorescent dye used to color wool and silk, and also used as a biological stain [Late 19thC. Coined from Greek *rhodon* "rose" + -AMINE.]

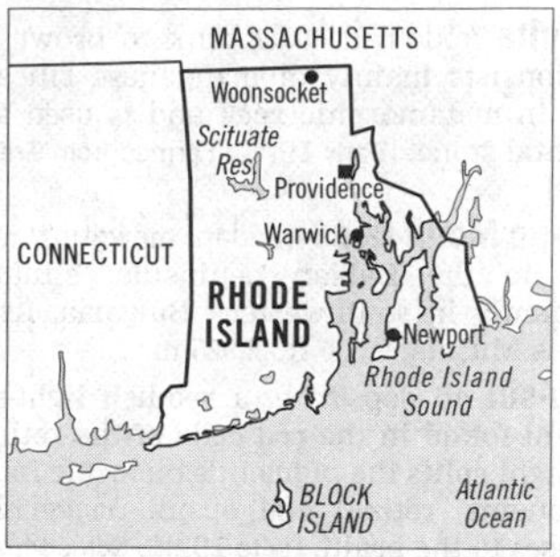

Rhode Island

Rhode Is·land /rōd-/ state in the northeastern United States, bordered by Massachusetts, Connecticut, and the Atlantic Ocean. The country's smallest state, its territory was bought from Native North American peoples by religious dissidents from Massachusetts in the 1630s. Capital: Providence. Population: 987,429 (1997). Area: 1,231 sq. mi./3,188 sq. km. Official name **State of Rhode Island and Providence Plantations** —**Rhode Is·land·er** *n.*

Rhodes /rōdz/ **1.** island in Greece, the largest of the Dodecanese Islands. Population: 87,831 (1981). Area: 540 sq. mi./1,400 sq. km. **2.** city in Greece, the capital of the island of Rhodes. Population: 40,656 (1981).

Rhodes, Cecil (1853–1902) British colonial statesman. He made a fortune mining diamonds in South Africa, where he formed De Beers Consolidated Mining Company (1888). He was prime minister of Cape Colony (1890–96) and helped to develop Rhodesia after 1889. Full name **Cecil John Rhodes**

Rho·de·sia /rō deéz͟hə/ former name for Zimbabwe —**Rho·de·sian** *adj.*, *n.*

Rho·de·sian man *n.* an early human being sharing features with the Neanderthals and with modern human beings and living in Africa in the late Pleistocene period. Latin name: *Homo sapiens rhodesiensis*. [Early 20thC. Named for RHODESIA, where the fossils were found.]

Rho·de·sian ridge·back *n.* a large dog with a ridge of hair growing down its back, belonging to a breed originally developed in Africa

rho·di·nal /rṓd'n àl/ *n.* = **citronellal**

rho·di·um /rṓdee əm/ *n.* a hard silvery-white metallic chemical element that is resistant to corrosion. It is found in platinum and nickel ores and is used with platinum in alloys and in plating other metals. Symbol **Rh** [Early 19thC. Formed from Greek *rhodos* "rose," from the pink color of its compounds.]

rhodo- *prefix.* red, rosy ○ *rhodolite* [From Greek *rhodon* "rose." Ultimately related to Latin *rosa* (source of English *rose*).]

rho·do·chro·site /rṑdə krṓ sīt/ *n.* a pink, red, brown, or gray mineral that is an ore of manganese. It consists of manganese carbonate. [Mid-19thC. Formed from Greek *rhodokhrōs* "rose-colored."]

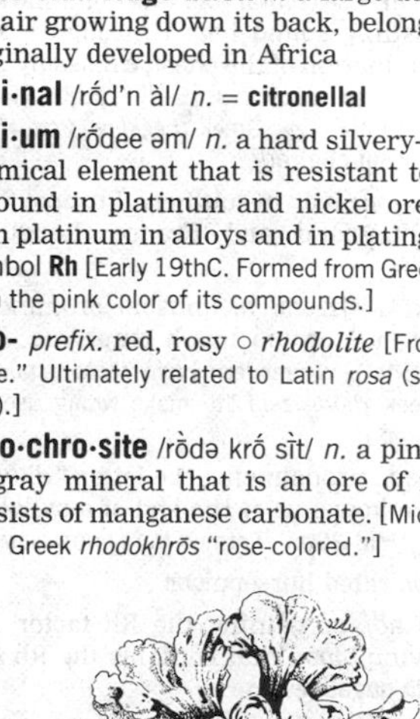

Rhododendron

rho·do·den·dron /rṑdə déndrən/ *n.* an evergreen shrub of the heath family that is native to southern Asia but is widely grown in temperate regions for its clusters of brightly colored flowers. Genus: *Rhododendron*. [Early 17thC. Via Latin, "oleander," from Greek, from *rhodon* "rose" + *dendron* "tree."]

rho·do·lite /rṓd'l īt/ *n.* a variety of garnet, used as a gem, with a color ranging from pink to rose red [Late 19thC. Coined from RHODO- + -LITE.]

rho·do·nite /ródd'n ìt/ *n.* a pink to brown mineral that consists mainly of manganese silicate. It is found in metamorphic rock and is used as an ornamental stone. [Early 19thC. Formed from Greek *rhodon* "rose."]

Rhod·o·pe Moun·tains /raadəpi mównt'nz/ mountain range in the Balkan peninsula, situated predominantly in southwestern Bulgaria. Its highest point is Musala, 9,596 ft./2,925 m.

rho·dop·sin /rō dópsin/ *n.* a reddish light-sensitive pigment found in the rod cells of the retina of the eye. Light splits the pigment's molecule into its two components, retinal and opsin, triggering nerve impulses to the brain. [Late 19thC. Coined from RHODO- + Greek *opsis* "sight" + -IN.]

rho·do·ra /rō dáwrə/ *n.* a shrub of the rhododendron family, native to marshy regions of northeastern North America, with deep pink flowers that bloom in spring before the leaves emerge. Latin name: *Rhododendron canadense.* [Late 18thC. From modern Latin, former genus name, of uncertain origin: possibly an alteration of Latin *rodarum*, a kind of plant, or formed from Greek *rhodon* "rose."]

rhomb *n.* = **rhombus**

rhom·ben·ceph·a·lon /ròmb en séffə lòn, rómb en séffələn/ *n.* = **hindbrain** [Late 19thC. Coined from RHOMBUS + ENCEPHALON.]

rhombi plural of **rhombus**

rhom·bo·he·dron /ròmbō hée dròn/ *n.* a prism with six faces, each one a rhombus [Mid-19thC. Coined from RHOMBUS, on the model of *polyhedron.*]

rhom·boid /róm bòyd/ *n.* **PARALLELOGRAM WITH UNEQUAL ADJACENT SIDES** a parallelogram with adjacent sides that are not equal ■ *adj.* **1. RHOMBOID-SHAPED** shaped like a rhomboid **2. RELATING TO RHOMBUS** relating to or characteristic of a rhombus [Late 16thC. From Greek *rhomboeidēs* "lozenge-shaped," from *rhombos* (see RHOMBUS).]

rhom·bus /rómbəss/ (*plural* **-bus·es** *or* **rhom·bi** /róm bì/) *n.* a parallelogram that has four equal sides and oblique angles [Mid-16thC. Via Latin from Greek *rhombos.* Ultimately, from an Indo-European word meaning "to bend," which is also the ancestor of English *warp.*] —**rhombic** *adj.*

rhon·chus /róngkəss/ (*plural* **-chi** /-kì/) *n.* a harsh rattling or whistling sound heard through a stethoscope on examination of the chest, caused by partial obstruction of the airways [Early 19thC. Via Latin, "snoring," from, ultimately, Greek *rhegkhos*, from *rhegkein* "to snore."] —**rhon·chal** *adj.*

Rhône /rōn/ major river in southern Europe, flowing through Switzerland and France. Length: 505 mi./813 km.

rho·ta·cism /rṓtə sìzzəm/ *n.* unusual pronunciation of the letter "r," or too much emphasis on this sound [Mid-19thC. Via modern Latin *rhotacismus*, from, ultimately, Greek *rhōtakizein* "to make wrong use of the letter *r*," from *rhō.*]

rho·tic /rṓtik/ *adj.* pronouncing the letter "r" when it occurs after a vowel or at the end of a syllable ○ *a rhotic accent* [Mid-20thC. Formed from RHOTACISM.]

rhp, **r.h.p.** *abbr.* rated horsepower

Rh pos·i·tive *adj.* containing the Rh factor in the blood or having blood that contains the Rh factor. ◊ **Rh factor, Rh negative**

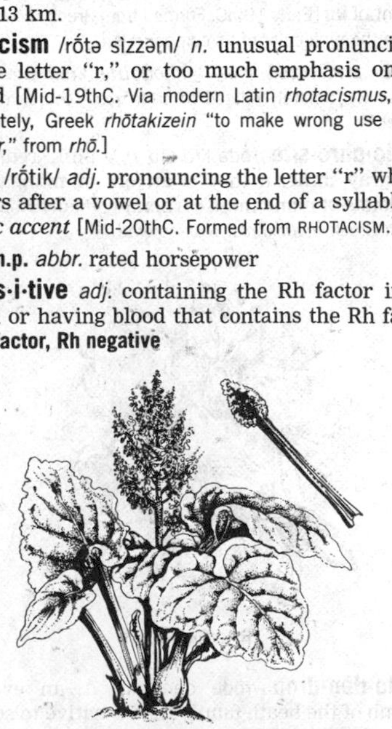

Rhubarb

rhu·barb /róo baarb/ *n.* **1.** PLANTS **PLANT WITH EDIBLE STALKS** a perennial plant, found in the wild and cultivated, with green or pink leaf stalks that are edible when cooked. The leaves are toxic. Genus: *Rheum.* **2.** FOOD **RHUBARB STALKS AS FOOD** the pink stalks of the common rhubarb plant, cooked and eaten as fruit **3.** PHARM **MEDICINAL ASIAN PLANT** a rhubarb plant found in central and eastern Asia whose underground stems may be dried and used as a laxative **4. QUARREL** a serious disagreement, quarrel, or fight (*informal*) [14thC. Via Old French *reubarbe*, from, ultimately, Latin *rha barbarum* "barbarian rhubarb," from Greek *Rha*, the ancient name of the river Volga, because rhubarb was once grown on its banks.]

WORD KEY: ORIGIN

The Greeks had two words for ***rhubarb***: "rhēon" (which evolved into Latin "rheum," now the plant's scientific name) and *rha*, which is said to have come from *Rha*, an ancient name of the river Volga, in allusion to the fact that ***rhubarb*** was once grown on its banks (***rhubarb*** is native to China, and was once imported to Europe via Russia). In medieval Latin ***rhubarb*** became known as *rha barbarum* "barbarian rhubarb, foreign rhubarb," again with reference to the plant's exotic origins; and in due course association with Latin *rheum* altered this to *rheubarbarum.*

rhumb /rum, rumb/ *n.* **1.** NAVIG = **rhumb line** *n.* 2 **2. COMPASS POINT** any of the 32 points of a compass

rhumb line *n.* **1.** GEOG **IMAGINARY GEOMETRIC LINE** an imaginary line on the surface of the Earth intersecting all meridians at the same angle **2.** NAVIG **STEADY COURSE** a steady course along one compass setting taken by a ship or aircraft

rhyme /rīm/, **rime** *n.* **1. SIMILARITY IN SOUND** similarity in the sound of word endings, especially in poetry **2. WORD SOUNDING SAME AS ANOTHER** a word with an ending that sounds similar to the ending of another word **3. POEM** a poem, or poetry generally, of a lighthearted kind with a pattern of similar sounds at the ends of the lines ■ *v.* (**rhymed, rhym·ing, rhymes; rimed, rim·ing, rimes**) **1.** *vti.* **SOUND SIMILAR** to have an ending that sounds similar to the ending of another word or line of poetry ○ *"Rough" rhymes with "cuff."* **2.** *vt.* **CHOOSE RHYMING WORD** to find or choose a word with an ending that sounds similar to another **3.** *vti.* **WRITE POETRY** to write rhyming poetry or express something in rhyme [12thC. Alteration (influenced by RHYTHM) of earlier *rime*, from Old French, of Germanic origin. Ultimately from an Indo-European base meaning "to put in order" that is also the ancestor of English *arithmetic* and *rite.*] ◇ **without rhyme or reason** without any rational explanation or apparent sense

rhym·er, **rim·er** *n.* = **rhymester**

rhyme roy·al *n.* a form of poetry using verses with seven lines of iambic pentameter with a rhyme scheme ababbcc, or one of these verses [Mid-19thC. From the use of the form by James I of Scotland.]

rhyme scheme *n.* the pattern of rhyming lines in a poem or verse of a poem often indicated with matching letters to show which lines rhyme. For example, ababcc means the first and third, second and fourth, and fifth and sixth lines rhyme with each other.

rhyme·ster, **rime·ster** *n.* somebody who writes poems with rhyming lines, especially lighthearted or poor quality verse

rhym·ing /rīming/ *adj.* with lines that end in similar sounding words, forming a pattern

rhym·ing slang *n.* a form of slang that replaces a word with an expression that rhymes with the word but has no meaningful connection with it, used especially in Cockney. Sometimes the rhyming part of the original expression is eventually dropped, e.g., "whistle," originally "whistle and flute," means "suit."

rhyn·cho·ce·pha·lian /rìngkō sə fáyliən/ *adj.* **OF NEARLY EXTINCT REPTILE ORDER** relating to an order of primitive reptiles resembling lizards with only one living representative, the tuatara of New Zealand. Order: Rhynchocephalia. ■ *n.* **NEARLY EXTINCT REPTILE** a member of the rhynchocephalian order [Mid-19thC. Formed from modern Latin *Rhyncocephalia*, order name, from Greek *rhugkhos* "snout" + *kephalē* "head."]

rhy·o·lite /rī ə lìt/ *n.* a fine-grained acid volcanic rock that is the molten form of granite [Mid-19thC. Coined from Greek *rhuax* "stream (of lava)" (formed from *rhein* "to flow" + -LITE.] —**rhy·o·lit·ic** /rī ə líttik/ *adj.*

rhythm /ríthəm/ *n.* **1.** MUSIC **PATTERN OF BEATS IN MUSIC** the regular pattern of beats and emphasis in a piece of music ○ *The audience clapped in rhythm as we sang.* **2.** MUSIC **PARTICULAR MUSIC PATTERN** a particular pattern of beats in a piece or kind of music **3.** POETRY **PATTERN OF STRESS IN POETRY** in poetry, the pattern formed by stressed and unstressed syllables **4.** POETRY **PARTICULAR POETRY PATTERN** a particular pattern of stress in a poem or kind of poetry **5. REGULAR PATTERN** any regularly recurring pattern of activity such as the cycle of the seasons, night and day, or repeated functions of the body **6. CHARACTERISTIC PATTERN** the characteristic pattern of a particular activity **7.** ARTS **PATTERN IN ART** a pattern of elements suggesting movement or pace in something such as a work of art **8.** LANG **SOUND PATTERN** the pattern of sound that characterizes a language, dialect, or accent **9.** CINEMA, LITERAT **PATTERN FROM REPEATED ELEMENTS** a mood or effect in a book, play, or film created from repeated elements [Mid-16thC. Via Latin from Greek *rhuthmos.* Ultimately from an Indo-European word meaning "to flow" that is also the ancestor of English *stream* and *hemorrhoid.*]

rhythm and blues *n.* a style of music combining elements of blues and jazz, originally developed by African American musicians

rhythm gui·tar *n.* chordal accompaniment from a guitar that does not play the melody

rhyth·mic /ríthmik/, **rhyth·mi·cal** /ríthmik'l/ *adj.* **1. WITH RECURRING PATTERN** with a regularly recurring pattern or beat **2. OF RHYTHM** relating to rhythm —**rhyth·mi·cal·ly** *adv.* —**rhyth·mic·i·ty** /rith míssətee/ *n.*

rhyth·mics /ríthmiks/ *n.* the study of rhythms and rhythmic forms (*takes a singular verb*)

rhyth·mist /ríthmist/ *n.* somebody who studies or creates rhythm

rhythm meth·od *n.* a method of contraception in which sexual intercourse is avoided at the times when a woman is most likely to conceive

rhythm sec·tion *n.* the instruments in a band such as the drums, bass, piano, or guitar that provide the basic rhythm

rhythm stick *n.* either of a pair of wooden sticks, often with notches, used as a simple percussion instrument

rhy·ti·dec·to·my /rìti déktəmee/ (*plural* **-mies**) *n.* a face-lift (*technical*) [Mid-20thC. Coined from Greek *rhutid-*, the stem of *rhutis* "wrinkle" + -ECTOMY.]

rhy·ton /rī tòn/ *n.* a drinking vessel in ancient Greece with a hole in the bottom through which to drink [Mid-19thC. From Greek *rhuton*, from *rhutos* "flowing."]

RI, **R.I.** *abbr.* **1.** Rhode Island **2.** religious instruction

ri·a /ree ə/ *n. U.K.* a narrow inlet running inland from the coastline, formed when a valley is permanently flooded as a result of a rise in sea-level. Rias are a feature of the coastlines of southwestern England and southwestern Ireland. [Late 19thC. From Spanish *ría* "estuary," feminine of *río* "river," from Latin *rivus* "stream" (see RIVAL).]

RIA *abbr.* radioimmunoassay

ri·al /ree aál/, **ry·al** (*unmarked inflection* **-als**) *n.* **1. UNIT OF MIDDLE EASTERN CURRENCY** the main unit of currency in Iran, Oman, Qatar, Saudi Arabia, and Yemen. See table at **currency 2. COIN WORTH ONE RIAL** a coin worth one rial [Mid-20thC. Via Persian and Arabic *riyāl* from Spanish *real* (REAL[2]).]

ri·al·to /ree áltō/ (*plural* **ri·al·tos**) *n.* **1. ri·al·to, Ri·al·to** THEATER **THEATER DISTRICT** the part of a town or city where its theaters are located **2.** COMM **MARKETPLACE** a market or marketplace [Mid-16thC. Named for *Rialto*, the district of Venice in which the market was located.]

ri·a·ta /ree áttə, -aátə/, **re·a·ta** *n.* a lasso or lariat [Mid-19thC. From Spanish *reata* (source of English *lariat*), from *reatar*, literally "to retie," from *atar* "to tie," via Latin *aptare* "to join" from, ultimately, *apere* "to tie."]

rib /rib/ *n.* **1.** ANAT **CURVED BONE OF CHEST** any of the curved

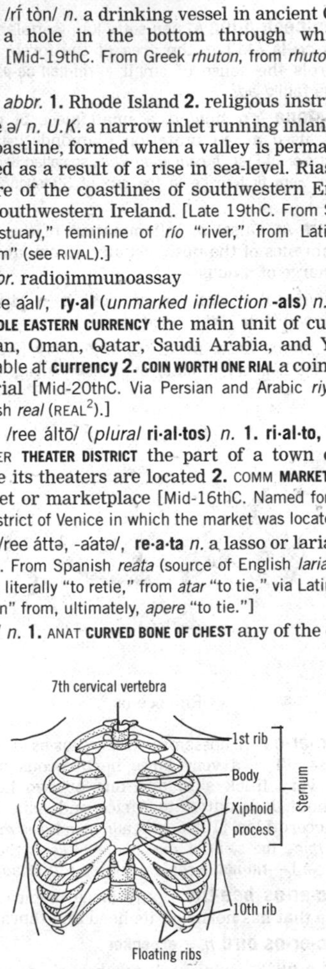

Rib

bones extending from the vertebrae and in some cases meeting the sternum, forming a cavity housing vital organs in many vertebrates **2.** FOOD **MEAT** a cut of meat that contains ribs **3.** KNITTING **RIDGED KNITTING** a portion of knitted material with raised vertical lines of stitches, made by alternating purl stitches with plain stitches **4.** BOT **LEAF VEIN** a raised vein on a leaf **5.** ARCHIT **MOLDING ON VAULT** a ridge or molding on the underside of a vault or arched ceiling **6.** NAUT **PART OF A SHIP'S HULL** any of the beams extending from the keel to the top of the hull of a ship, giving it its shape **7.** AIR **PART OF AIRCRAFT WING** a part of an aircraft wing crossing from the leading to the trailing edge of the wing **8. PIECE RESEMBLING RIB** a bar, rod, or other supporting part that has the shape or function of a rib ○ *a broken rib on the umbrella* **9. TEASING COMMENT** a comment or action meant as a joke or to tease somebody (*informal*) ■ **ribs** *npl.* **RIBS WITH LITTLE MEAT** ribs of an animal from which most of the meat has been removed, eaten as food ■ *v.* **(ribbed, rib·bing, ribs) 1.** *vti.* **TEASE** to make playful teasing remarks to somebody about something (*informal*) ○ *They ribbed me about my haircut.* **2.** *vti.* KNITTING **KNIT PLAIN AND PURL STITCHES** to knit plain stitches alternately with purl stitches to make raised lines in knitting **3.** *vt.* **PROVIDE WITH RIBS** to provide or strengthen something with ribs [Old English *ribb*, from a prehistoric Germanic word meaning "covering (of the chest cavity)"]

rib·ald /ríbbəld, rī́ bàwld/ *adj.* **COARSE AND FUNNY** humorous but rude and vulgar, often involving jokes about sex ■ *n.* **RIBALD PERSON** somebody who often uses ribald language [14thC. From Old French *ribau(l)t*, from *riber* "to sleep around," of Germanic origin.] —**rib·ald·ly** *adv.*

rib·ald·ry /ríbbəldree, rī́bəl-/ *n.* language or behavior that is humorous but rude and vulgar, often involving jokes about sex

rib·and, **rib·band** *n.* a ribbon, especially one that is used for decorative purposes (*old*) [14thC. Variant of *riban* (see RIBBON).]

Ri·bault /rī́ bṓ/, **Jean** (1520?–65) French-born American explorer and colonizer. He explored the Florida coast and settled Port Royal, South Carolina (1562).

ri·ba·vi·rin /rī́bə vī́rin/ *n.* a synthetic antiviral agent that is used to treat certain viral diseases, notably Lassa fever. It inhibits the synthesis of DNA and RNA. [Late 20thC. Coined from *riba-*, of uncertain origin: probably from *rib(onucleic) a(cid)* + VIRUS + -IN.]

rib·band *n.* = **riband**

ribbed /ribd/ *adj.* **1. HAVING RIBS** with structural support or decoration in the form of ribs **2.** KNITTING **KNITTED INTO PATTERN OF VERTICAL LINES** knitted to form a pattern of raised vertical lines, giving a stretchy fabric **3. STRIPED** with a surface marked by raised, roughly parallel bands

rib·bing /ríbbing/ *n.* **1.** KNITTING **SECTION OF RIB IN KNITTING** a section of knitting in a pattern of raised vertical lines, making a stretchy fabric **2. RIB FRAMEWORK** a supporting structure or framework of ribs, e.g., in the hull of a boat **3. TEASING** playful or friendly teasing (*informal*)

rib·bon /ríbbən/ *n.* **1.** TEXTILES **DECORATIVE STRIP OF FABRIC** a strip of fabric, often in a bright color, used for tying hair, trimming gifts, and other decorative purposes **2.** COMM **STRIP OF INKED MATERIAL** a strip of material with ink on it, used in some printers and typewriters **3.** COMPUT **FLAT CABLE** a flat cable in which all the wires are parallel to one another in a single plane **4. RIBBON AS AWARD OR BADGE** a decorative strip of fabric given to somebody as an award or worn as a sign of rank or membership **5. LONG NARROW STRIP** something that is long, narrow, and thin, in the shape of a ribbon **6.** CONSTR = **ledger board** ■ **rib·bons** *npl.* **1. BADLY DAMAGED STATE** a damaged state in which something is cut or torn very badly ○ *My shirt was in ribbons.* **2.** EQU **REINS** reins for controlling a horse (*informal*) ■ *vt.* **(-boned, -bon·ing, -bons) 1. DECORATE WITH RIBBONS** to decorate something by attaching ribbons to it **2. TEAR INTO STRIPS** to tear something into strips [Early 16thC. Variant of earlier *riban*, from Old French, a variant of *ruban*, of uncertain origin: probably from a Germanic source.] —**rib·bon·y** *adj.*

rib·bon de·vel·op·ment *n. U.K.* a planning scheme or development with houses built in a single row on each side of main roads leading out of a town or city center

Rib·bon Falls /ríbbən-/ falls in eastern California, and the highest in Yosemite National Park. It often dries up in summer. Height: 1,612 ft./491 m.

rib·bon·fish /ríbbən fish/ (*plural* **-fish** *or* **-fish·es**) *n.* a marine fish that has a long tapering ribbon-shaped body and, typically, a dorsal fin extending from head to tail. Some species can exceed 32 ft./10 m in length. Family: Trachypteridae.

rib·bon grass *n.* a grass that is grown as an ornamental in northern temperate regions for its drooping cream-striped leaves. Latin name: *Phalaris arundinacea picta.*

rib·bon snake *n.* a nonvenomous North American snake with longitudinal reddish or yellow stripes extending the full length of its body. It bears live young and feeds on frogs and worms. Latin name: *Thamnophis sauritus.*

rib·bon worm *n.* = **nemertean**

rib cage /ríb kàyj/ *n.* the ribs as a whole, forming a protective bony enclosure surrounding the heart and lungs

rib·grass /ríb gràss/ (*plural* **-grass·es** *or* **-grass**) *n.* a Eurasian plant with long slender ribbed leaves and a dense rounded spike of small white flowers that grows as a weed. Latin name: *Plantago lanceolata.* [Early 16thC. From the plant's ribbed leaves.]

rib·let /ríblət/ *n.* veal or lamb cut from the end of a rib

ribo- *prefix.* ribose ○ *riboflavin* [From RIBOSE]

ri·bo·fla·vin /rī̀bə fláyvin/, **ri·bo·fla·vine** /-fláy veen/ *n.* an orange-yellow crystalline pigment in the vitamin B complex, essential for normal growth in humans and an important component of many of the body's enzymes. It is found in foods such as spinach, eggs, milk, and liver. Formula: $C_{17}H_{20}N_4O_6$.

ri·bo·nu·cle·ase /rī̀bō nóoklee àyss, -nóoklee àyz/ *n.* any enzyme that catalyzes the breakdown of RNA

ri·bo·nu·cle·ic ac·id /rī̀bō noo klee ik-/ *n.* full form of **RNA**

ri·bo·nu·cle·o·pro·tein /rī̀bō nooklee ō prṓ teen/ *n.* a conjugated protein found in chromosomes, made up of RNA molecules together with protein molecules

ri·bo·nu·cle·o·side /rī̀bō nóoklee ə sīd/ *n.* a nucleoside in which the sugar group is ribose. Ribonucleosides are important in living organisms as precursors of ribonucleotides.

ri·bo·nu·cle·o·tide /rī̀bō nóoklee ə tīd/ *n.* a nucleotide that contains the sugar ribose and makes up many important cellular molecules including RNA and energy coenzymes such as ATP

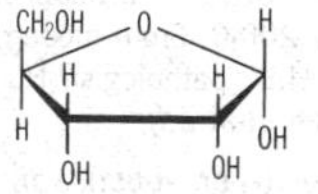

Ribose

ri·bose /rī́ bōss/ *n.* a five-carbon sugar found in all living cells as a constituent of RNA and many other metabolically important compounds, including ribonucleotides, nucleic acids, and riboflavin. Formula: $C_5H_{10}O_5$. [Late 19thC. Via German, from ARABINOSE.]

ri·bo·so·mal RNA /rī̀bə sṓm'l-/ *n.* an RNA that is a structural and functional component of ribosomes

ri·bo·some /rī́bə sōm/ *n.* a submicroscopic cluster of proteins and RNA, occurring in great numbers in the cytoplasm of living cells, that takes part in the manufacture of proteins. Ribosomes bind to messenger RNA molecules, which carry encoded transcripts of the cell's genes, and direct the assembly of amino acids into proteins according to the code. [Mid-20thC. Coined from RIBONUCLEIC ACID + -SOME.] —**ri·bo·so·mal** /rī̀bə sṓm'l/ *adj.*

ri·bo·zyme /rī́bə zīm/ *n.* a strand of RNA that attaches to and catalyzes site-specific cleavages of other strands of RNA. Ribozymes are the only nonenzyme biological catalysts known. [Late 20thC. Coined from RIBONUCLEIC ACID + ENZYME.]

rib roast *n.* a large cut of red meat that includes the part along the outer edge of the rib

rib-tick·ler *n.* a very funny joke or story (*informal*)

Ric·ci /reechee/, **Matteo** (1552–1610) Italian priest. A Jesuit missionary, he lived in China from 1583, and provided the West with early descriptions of the country.

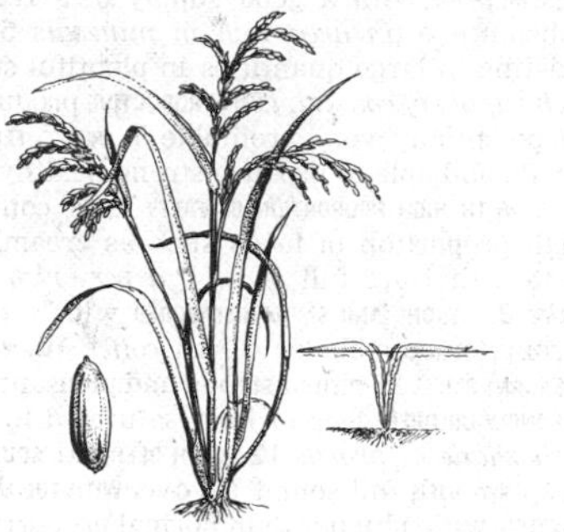
Rice

rice /rīss/ *n.* (*plural* **ric·es** *or* **rice**) **1.** BOT **TALL GRASS** an annual grass probably native to India but long cultivated for its grain in tropical and warm regions of the world. Latin name: *Oryza sativa.* **2.** FOOD **EDIBLE GRAINS** the edible grains obtained from the rice plant, served hot or cold after cooking in water or other liquid ■ *vt.* **(riced, ric·ing, ric·es)** COOK **SIEVE FOOD** to push food through a sieve or ricer to make it into a coarse purée [13thC. Via Old French *ris* and Italian *riso* from, ultimately, Greek *oruza*, of Iranian origin.]

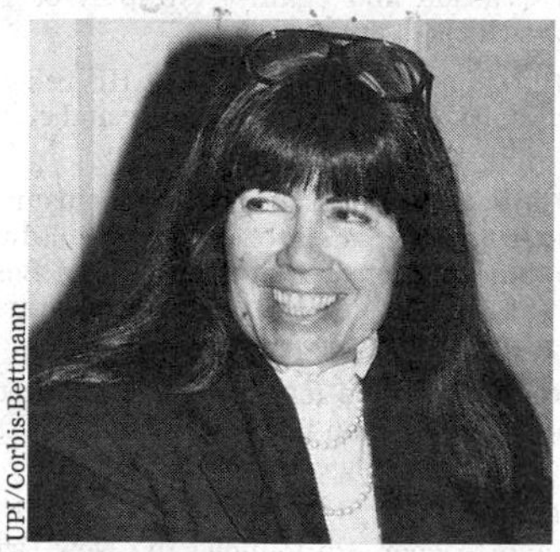
UPI/Corbis-Bettmann
Anne Rice

Rice /rīss/, **Anne** (*b.* 1941) U.S. writer. She is best known for the Vampire Chronicles, beginning with *Interview with the Vampire* (1976). Born **Howard Allen O'Brien**

Rice, Elmer (1892–1967) U.S. playwright. He won a Pulitzer Prize for the play *Street Scene* (1929), and is also known for *The Adding Machine* (1923). Real name **Elmer Reizenstein**

rice·bird /rīss bùrd/ *n.* a bird, especially the bobolink, that is commonly seen in rice fields

rice pa·per *n.* **1.** FOOD **EDIBLE PAPER** thin brittle edible paper made from plant sources, used to undercoat baked foods such as almond macaroons that would otherwise stick to the pan during baking. The paper bakes into the mixture providing an edible, slightly crisp base. **2.** INDUST **PAPER FROM RICE-PAPER PLANT** thin paper made from the rice-paper plant

rice-pa·per plant *n.* a Chinese shrub grown for its fiber that is used to make rice paper. Latin name: *Tetrapanax papyriferus.*

rice pud·ding *n.* a hot dessert made by baking rice slowly in milk and sugar

ric·er /rī́ssər/ *n.* a kitchen utensil consisting of a perforated plate in one end of an open cylinder through which foods can be pressed to form long strings

rice rat *n.* a rat that inhabits the marshes of the southern United States and Central and South America where rice fields are located. Genus: *Oryzomys.*

ric·er·care /rèechər kaá rày/ (*plural* **ric·er·ca·ri** /-rèe/) *n.* a fugal composition for musical instruments, analogous to a motet for voices, involving lines of melody interwoven in an often complicated pattern [Late 18thC. From Italian, literally "to seek out."]

rice wee·vil *n.* an insect of the weevil family that infests stored rice, wheat, and other grains. Latin name: *Sitophilus oryzae.*

rich /rich/ *adj.* **1.** WEALTHY owning a lot of money or expensive property **2.** WORTH MUCH worth a great deal **3.** COSTLY AND FINE made from or consisting of things of the highest quality ○ *rich fabrics* **4.** WITH GOOD SUPPLY OF SOMETHING with a good supply of a resource or substance ○ *an area rich in minerals* **5.** PLENTIFUL existing in large quantities in plentiful supply ○ *a rich supply of conscripts* **6.** PRODUCTIVE productive and so potentially very profitable **7.** AGRIC FERTILE very fertile and able to produce strong healthy plants **8.** FOOD WITH HIGH PROPORTION OF FATTY FOODS containing a high proportion of foods such as cream, eggs, or butter, that are full of fat ○ *a very rich chocolate cake* **9.** STRONG AND SMOOTH-FLAVORED with a pleasantly strong, smooth flavor ○ *rich coffee* **10.** WITH STRONG PLEASANT SMELL having a strong and pleasant smell **11.** STRONGLY COLORED deep or fully saturated in color ○ *a rich shade of brown* **12.** WITH DEEP FULL SOUND with a deep smooth full sound **13.** CARS WITH TOO MUCH FUEL IN MIXTURE with a higher than normal proportion of fuel to air in the mixture supplied to an engine **14.** UNLIKELY hard to believe because ridiculous (*informal*) ○ *That's rich, coming from her!* ■ *npl.* WELL-OFF wealthy people in general ○ *a playground for the rich and famous.* ◊ **riches** [Old English *rīce* "strong, powerful" and Old French *riche*, of Germanic origin. Ultimately, from an Indo-European word meaning "king" that is also the ancestor of English *royal, rajah,* and *bishopric.*] —**rich·ness** *n.*

Rich·ard I /rícherd/, **King of England** (1157–99). He spent most of his reign (1189–99) overseas, fighting in the Third Crusade and against Philip II of France. Known as **Richard the Lionheart**

Rich·ard II, King of England (1367–99). His reign (1377–99) was marked by national disunity and civil strife that culminated in his being deposed.

Rich·ard III, King of England (1452–85). He usurped the throne while protector of the young Edward V (1483), but was defeated at the Battle of Bosworth Field (1485) in a rebellion led by the future King Henry VII.

Rich·ard Roe /rìchərd rṓ/ *n.* LAW a name used for a second unknown man in legal proceedings, the first unknown man being called John Doe

Rich·ards /ríchərdz/, **I. A.** (1893–1979) British critic, poet, and teacher. He founded the New Criticism movement, which was influential on the teaching of English literature in universities. Full name **Ivor Armstrong Richards**

Rich·ard·son /ríchərdss'n/, **H.H.** (1838–86) U.S. architect. He was a leader of the romanesque revival movement in the United States, which led to a distinctively American style of architecture. Full name **Henry Hobson Richardson**

Rich·ard·son, John (1796–1852) Canadian writer. He is known for his historical and autobiographical novels.

Rich·ard·son, Robert C. (*b.* 1937) U.S. physicist. He shared a Nobel Prize in physics (1996) for his research into the superfluidity of helium-3.

Rich·ard·son's ground squir·rel /rìchərdss'nz-/ *n.* a ground squirrel found in the northwestern United States and Canadian prairies that can be a pest of grain crops. Latin name: *Citellus richardsoni.* [Mid-20thC. Named for the Scottish naturalist Sir John *Richardson* 1787–1865, who first collected it.]

Rich·e·lieu /ríshə lòo, réeshə lyö/, **Armand Jean du Plessis, Duc de** (1585–1642) French cardinal and statesman. He was named a cardinal in 1622. As chief minister to Louis XIII after 1624, he wielded supreme power in France. He strengthened the monarchy and made France the preeminent military power in Europe. Known as **Cardinal Richelieu**

rich·es /ríchəz/ *npl.* **1.** GREAT WEALTH great wealth or many valuable possessions **2.** PLENTIFUL NATURAL THINGS things occurring naturally in abundance ○ *enjoy the riches of the forest* [12thC. Originally singular, misunderstood as plural; variant of *richesse*, from Old French *richeise*, from *riche* "rich," from the prehistoric Germanic ancestor of English *rich* (see RICH).]

Rich·ler /ríchlər/, **Mordecai** (*b.* 1931) Canadian writer. He drew on his working-class Jewish background in *The Apprenticeship of Duddy Kravitz* (1959) and other works.

rich·ly /ríchlee/ *adv.* **1.** ELABORATELY beautifully and elaborately ○ *richly decorated* **2.** WITH DEEP COLOR with a deep, fully saturated color **3.** COMPLETELY completely and suitably ○ *a richly deserved award* **4.** PLENTIFULLY plentifully or very fully [Old English *ricilce*]

Rich·mond /ríchmənd/ **1.** capital city of the state of Virginia, situated in the eastern part of the state. Population: 201,108 (1994). **2.** city in central Kentucky, southwest of Winchester and southeast of Lexington. Population: 26,227 (1996). **3.** city in eastern Indiana, west of the Indiana-Ohio border, on the East Fork River, east of Indianapolis. Population: 37,312 (1996). **4.** market town in North Yorkshire, northern England, on the banks of the Swale River. Population: 7,862 (1991). **5.** town in eastern New South Wales, Australia, on the Hawkesbury River. Population: (including Windsor) 21,317 (1996).

Rich·ter scale /ríktər-/ *n.* a scale from 1 to 10 used to measure the severity of earthquakes according to the amount of energy released, with a higher number indicating stronger tremors. Each increment of the scale is a 32-fold increase over the previous one. ◊ **Mercalli scale** [Mid-20thC. Named for the U.S. seismologist Charles Francis *Richter* (1900–85), who devised it.]

ri·cin /rīss'n, ríss'n/ *n.* a white poisonous protein extracted from the beans of the castor plant for use as a biochemical reagent that acts in the body to clump red blood cells [Late 19thC. Formed from Latin *ricinus* "castor oil plant," of unknown origin.]

ric·in·o·le·ic ac·id /rīss'n ō lée ik-/ *n.* an unsaturated fatty acid that is the main constituent of castor oil and is used in making soap, plastics, and in textile finishing. Formula: $C_{18}H_{34}O_3$. [Coined from Latin *ricinus* "castor oil plant" + OLEIC]

rick /rik/ *n.* STACK OF HAY OR STRAW a large quantity of hay or straw stacked into a rectangular shape for storage and covered at the top to protect it from the weather ■ *vt.* (**ricked, rick·ing, ricks**) FORM A RICK to stack hay or straw to form a rick [Old English *hrēac*, of unknown origin]

rick·ets /ríkits/ *n.* a disease, especially of children, caused by a deficiency in vitamin D that makes the bones become soft and prone to bending and structural change. Technical name **rachitis** [Mid-17thC. Origin unknown.]

rick·ett·si·a /ri kétsee ə/ (*plural* **-as** *or* **-ae** /-ee/ *or* **-a**) *n.* a parasitic bacterium that typically lives inside ticks and can be transmitted to humans, causing Rocky Mountain spotted fever, certain forms of typhus, and other diseases. Order: Rickettsiales. [Early 20thC. From modern Latin, genus name, named for the U.S. pathologist H. T. *Ricketts* (1871–1910).] —**rick·ett·si·al** *adj.*

rick·et·y /ríkətee/ (**-i·er, -i·est**) *adj.* **1.** UNSTABLE in bad condition, unstable, and likely to collapse ○ *a rickety chair* **2.** INFIRM weakened by the aging process or illness **3.** MED WITH RICKETS affected by rickets **4.** MED RELATING TO RICKETS relating to or resembling rickets [Late 17thC. Formed from RICKETS, from the unsteadiness that the disease causes.] —**rick·et·i·ness** *n.*

rick·ey /ríkee/ (*plural* **-eys**) *n.* a cocktail made from soda water, lime or lemon juice, sugar, and gin or vodka [Late 19thC. Origin uncertain: probably from the name *Rickey.*]

rick·rack /rík ràk/, **ric·rac** *n.* a narrow decorative braid in a zigzag shape [Late 19thC. Doubling of RACK[1].]

rick·shaw /rík shàw/, **rick·sha** *n.* **1.** TWO-WHEELED PASSENGER VEHICLE a small vehicle with two wheels and a seat for passengers, pulled along by somebody walking in front of it, used especially in Asia **2.** THREE-WHEELED PASSENGER VEHICLE a small three-wheeled vehicle, like a tricycle with a seat at the back for passengers, that is driven by somebody sitting at the front and pedalling [Late 19thC. Shortening of Japanese *jinrikisha*, from *jin* "man" + *riki* "strength" + *sha* "vehicle."]

RICO /rée kō/ *abbr.* Racketeer Influenced and Corrupt Organizations (Act)

ric·o·chet /ríkə shày, rìkə sháy/ *vi.* (**-cheted,** /ríkə shàyd, rìkə sháyd/, **-chet·ing** /ríkə shày ing, rìkə sháy ing/, **-chets** /ríkə shàyz, rìkə sháyz/) REBOUND to hit a surface and bounce, traveling away in a different direction ■ *n.* REBOUNDING ACTION the rebounding action of something that hits a surface and bounces off in a different direction [Mid-18thC. From Old French, "give-and-take, repetition," of unknown origin.]

ri·cot·ta /ri kóttə/ *n.* a soft white mild-tasting Italian cheese made from whey and used mostly in cooking, or a cheese made to resemble this [Late 19thC. Via Italian, literally "recooked," from Latin *recocta*, the feminine past participle of *recoquere* "to recook," from *coquere* (see COOK).]

ric·tus /ríktəss/ (*plural* **-tus** *or* **-tus·es**) *n.* **1.** STRANGE GRIN OR GRIMACE a fixed open-mouthed grin or grimace, especially an expression of horror **2.** ZOOL GAPE OF BIRD'S BEAK the gape of a bird's beak [Mid-18thC. From Latin, from the past participle of *ringi* "to gape," of unknown origin.] —**ric·tal** *adj.*

rid /rid/ (**rid** *or* **rid·ded** *archaic*, **rid·ding, rids**) *vt.* **1.** EMPTY OF SOMETHING to free, relieve, or empty a place or thing of something, usually something undesirable ○ *an attempt to rid the town of crime* **2.** FREE YOURSELF FROM SOMETHING to free somebody or yourself from something undesirable ○ *trying to rid myself of the habit* [12thC. From Old Norse *ryðja* "to clear land," from *hrjóða* "to strip."] —**rid·der** *n.* ◇ **be** *or* **get rid of 1.** to make somebody or something burdensome, unpleasant, or unnecessary go away **2.** to throw something out

rid·dance /rídd'ns/ *n.* the removal or destruction of something unwanted ◇ **good riddance (to somebody** *or* **something)** used to show that you are glad to be free of somebody or something

rid·den past participle of **ride**

rid·dle[1] /rídd'l/ *n.* **1.** WORD PUZZLE a puzzle in the form of a question or rhyme that contains clues to its answer **2.** PUZZLING THING something that is difficult to understand or presents a problem that needs to be solved ■ *v.* (**-dled, -dling, -dles**) **1.** *vti.* ANSWER RIDDLE to find or explain the answer to a riddle **2.** *vi.* TALK IN RIDDLES to speak in a deliberately obscure way [Old English *rǣdels.* Ultimately from an Indo-European word that is also the ancestor of English *read, reason,* and *rathskeller.*] —**rid·dler** *n.*

WORD KEY: SYNONYMS

See Synonyms at ***problem***.

rid·dle[2] /rídd'l/ *vt.* (**-dled, -dling, -dles**) **1.** MAKE HOLES IN SOMETHING to damage something by making a large number of small holes in it **2.** AFFECT EVERY PART to affect every part of something, e.g., by spreading throughout **3.** SIFT SOIL OR STONES to put soil or stones through a sieve to separate the large pieces from the small ones **4.** SHAKE ASHES FROM FIRE to shake ashes from the bottom of a fire by poking it with a metal rod or moving a mechanism under the grate ■ *n.* SIEVE a large flat shallow sieve for sifting soil or stones [Old English *hriddel* "sieve," an alteration of *hridder.* Ultimately from an Indo-European word meaning "to sort" that is also the ancestor of English *discriminate, criterion,* and *crime.*] —**rid·dler** *n.*

ride /rīd/ *v.* (**rid·den** /rídd'n/ *or* **rode** /rōd/, **rid·ing, rides**) **1.** *vti.* EQU SIT ON AND CONTROL HORSE to sit on a horse or other animal and control it as it moves along **2.** *vti.* TRANSP TRAVEL ON BIKE to travel mounted on a bicycle or motorcycle **3.** *vti.* TRAVEL AS PASSENGER to travel as a passenger in a vehicle **4.** *vt.* SPORTS USE SPORTS EQUIPMENT to use any of various kinds of gliding or rolling sports equipment such as a skateboard or surfboard **5.** *vti.* TRAVEL IN AN ELEVATOR to travel in an elevator **6.** *vt.* TRAVEL OVER AREA to travel across an area of land ○ *ride the range* **7.** *vt.* SPORTS BE IN RACE to take part in a race or other event on a horse or bike **8.** *vi.* CARS HANDLE WELL OR BADLY to function in a particular way while moving ○ *a car that rides well over rough ground* **9.** *vt.* TO CARRY SOMEBODY ALONG to carry or take somebody along ○ *His mother rode him around on her bicycle.* **10.** *vi.* APPEAR TO BE FLOATING to appear to be floating in the sky or moving like a floating object ○ *Birds soared above our heads, riding the currents.* **11.** *vi.* DO SOMETHING EFFORTLESSLY to do something successfully and apparently effortlessly, as if carried along by a wave ○ *riding on a tide of sympathy* **12.** *vi.* DEPEND ON SOMETHING to depend on something for success ○ *Her future is riding on the outcome of the interview.* **13.** *vi.* BE ALLOWED TO CONTINUE to continue without intervention or alteration ○ *let it ride for a* *few days* **14.** *vt.* DEAL WITH PROBLEM AND SURVIVE to manage to deal with a difficult situation successfully and survive without too much harm ○ *to ride the storm* **15.** *vt.* TEASE OR TORMENT to tease or torment somebody with criticism or mockery (*informal*) ○ *My sister always rides me about my hair.* **16.** *vt.* SAILING RISE ON TOP OF WAVE to rise up on a wave and move forward with it **17.** *vti.* NAUT ANCHOR to be moored with the anchor down, or to moor a ship by dropping its anchor ○ *a ship riding at anchor* **18.** *vi.* ENG BE SUPPORTED BY SOMETHING to be supported by something such as a pivot or an axle ○ *Most of the weight rides on the central shaft.* **19.** *vt.* CARS PARTIALLY DEPRESS CLUTCH OR BRAKE to put your foot on the clutch or brake, partially depressing it, while driving **20.** *vt.* OVERLAP to overlap or encroach on something such as another part **21.** *vt.* YIELD TO BLOW to move in the direction of something forceful such as a blow, in order to lessen the impact ■ *n.* **1.** TRANSP JOURNEY BY VEHICLE OR ANIMAL a journey or outing in a motor vehicle or on an animal ○ *to go for a ride* **2.** TRANSP MEANS OF TRANSPORTATION transportation as a passenger in a vehicle, especially when this is offered to somebody who would otherwise have to walk or use public transportation ○ *Do you want a ride?* **3.** CARS QUALITY OF TRAVEL the quality of travel in a motor vehicle ○ *The new model offers a very smooth ride.* **4.** LEISURE FAIRGROUND ENTERTAINMENT an entertainment such as a rollercoaster at an amusement park or carnival, offering a thrilling experience **5.** EQU PATH FOR HORSES a broad grassy path where horses can be ridden **6.** MUSIC JAZZ CYMBAL one of the three cymbals in a drum set, used to keep time and mark rhythmic accents in jazz [Old English *rīdan*. Ultimately from an Indo-European base that is also the ancestor of English *road, raid, ready,* and *array*.] —**rid·a·ble** *adj.* ◇ **be riding high** to be enjoying a period or feeling of success ◇ **ride herd on somebody** to keep a close eye on or control over somebody ◇ **ride roughshod over somebody** to treat somebody very arrogantly without regard to that person's feelings ◇ **ride roughshod over something** to disregard a rule, law, or agreement ◇ **ride shotgun** to sit in the front passenger seat of a car (*informal*) ◇ **take somebody for a ride** to cheat or deceive somebody

ride down *vt.* **1.** TRAMPLE to hit and knock down somebody while riding, especially on horseback **2.** CATCH UP WITH OR OVERTAKE to catch up with or overtake somebody

ride out *vti.* to manage to deal with a difficult situation successfully and survive without too much harm ○ *ride out the storm*

ride up *vi.* to gradually move up out of the correct position ○ *Her skirt was riding up.*

Ri·deau Hall /ri dṓ-/ *n.* the official residence of the Governor General of Canada

rid·er /rídər/ *n.* **1.** TRANSP SOMEBODY ON HORSE OR BIKE somebody who rides or is riding on an animal or vehicle **2.** ADDITIONAL COMMENT an extra comment or clause added to a document or statement **3.** LAW ADDITIONAL CLAUSE TO BILL an extra clause added to a legislative bill, often not directly related to the main issue **4.** SOMETHING RESTING ON OR STRENGTHENING SOMETHING something that rests on or strengthens something else, e.g., the horizontal rail of a fence or additional timbers in the frame of a ship **5.** SLIDING ADJUSTMENT a small sliding weight on the arm of a chemical balance, used for adjusting the scales **6.** GEOL THIN SEAM a thin seam of a mineral lying above a thicker one

rid·er·ship /rídər shìp/ *n.* the number of passengers using a particular form of public transportation

ride·shar·ing /ríd shàiring/ *n.* an arrangement in which commuters take turns using their cars for going to work, taking along one another as passengers to cut down the number of cars on the roads

ridge /rij/ *n.* **1.** RAISED STRIP a long narrow raised area of something **2.** GEOG RAISED LAND FORMATION a long narrow hilltop or range of hills **3.** GEOG RIDGE ON OCEAN FLOOR an elevation on the ocean floor resembling a ridge on land and resulting from volcanic eruption along the fissures between tectonic plates **4.** METEOROL AREA OF HIGH PRESSURE a long area of high pressure in a weather system **5.** ANAT RAISED PART ON BONE a long narrow protuberance or crest, e.g., on a bone **6.** ZOOL BACKBONE OF ANIMAL the backbone of an animal, especially a whale **7.** CONSTR TOP OF ROOF the line along the top of a roof or a tent where the two sloping sides meet ■ *vti.* (**ridged, ridg·ing, ridg·es**) FORM RIDGES to mark, form, or provide something with ridges, or make something into the shape of a ridge [Old English *hrycg*. From a prehistoric Germanic word meaning "back, spine" that is also the ancestor of English *rucksack*.] —**ridg·y** *adj.*

ridge·back /ríj bàk/ *n.* = **Rhodesian ridgeback**

ridg·el /ríjjəl/ *n.* = **ridgeling**

ridge·line /ríj lìn/ *n.* = **ridge** *n.* 2

ridge·ling /ríjling/, **ridg·ling** *n.* a male animal in which one or both testes fail to descend into the scrotum at the usual time. The condition is most common in horses and pigs. [Mid-16thC. Formed from earlier *ridgel*, of uncertain origin.]

ridge·pole /ríj pṓl/, **ridge·tree** /ríj trèe/ *n.* **1.** BUILDING BEAM ALONG RIDGE OF ROOF a long beam of wood that runs along the ridge of a roof, supporting the upper ends of the rafters **2.** CAMPING HORIZONTAL TENT POLE the horizontal pole supporting the top of a tent

Ridg·way /ríj wày/, **Matthew Bunker** (1895–1993) U.S. army officer. He commanded an airborne assault on Normandy (1944) and was supreme commander of United Nations ground forces in Korea (1950–52).

rid·i·cule /ríddi kyoòl/ *vt.* (**-culed, -cul·ing, -cules**) MOCK to make fun of or mock somebody or something in a contemptuous way ■ *n.* MOCKING LAUGHTER, BEHAVIOR, OR COMMENTS mocking laughter, mimicry, or comments intended to make fun of somebody in a contemptuous way [Late 17thC. Directly or via French from Latin *ridiculum* "joke," from *ridiculus* (see RIDICULOUS).] —**rid·i·cul·er** *n.*

WORD KEY: SYNONYMS

ridicule, deride, laugh at, mock, send up

CORE MEANING: to belittle or make fun of somebody or something

ridicule to belittle somebody or something in a cruel contemptuous way in order to make that person or thing an object of fun; **deride** a formal word used to talk about ridiculing somebody or something in strong harsh terms; **laugh at** to ridicule somebody in an amused or contemptuous way; **mock** to treat somebody or something with scorn or contempt, often involving cruel mimicking. It is often used to suggest something more subtle than *ridicule* or *deride*; **send up** an informal phrase meaning to make fun of or mock somebody or something, usually by means of parody or mimicking.

ri·dic·u·lous /ri díkyələss/ *adj.* **1.** UNREASONABLE completely unreasonable and not at all sensible or acceptable **2.** COMPLETELY SILLY silly and amusing [Mid-16thC. Formed from Latin *ridiculus* "laughable," from *ridere* "to laugh" (source of English *risible*), of unknown origin.] —**ri·dic·u·lous·ly** *adv.* —**ri·dic·u·lous·ness** *n.*

rid·ing[1] /ríding/ *n.* **1.** EQU BEING ON A HORSE the sport or hobby of sitting on a horse and controlling it as it moves along **2.** TRANSP TRAVELING ON ANIMAL OR VEHICLE the act of traveling on an animal or vehicle ■ *adj.* EQU USED ON HORSEBACK used while riding a horse ○ *riding breeches*

rid·ing[2] /ríding/ *n.* **1.** **ri·ding, Rid·ing** AREA OF YORKSHIRE one of the three administrative districts into which the British county of Yorkshire was formerly split **2.** *Canadian* CANADIAN CONSTITUENCY a constituency represented by either a federal member of parliament or a member of the provincial legislature [Pre-12thC. From Old Norse *þriðungr* "third part," from *þriði* "third."]

rid·ing crop *n.* a straight short riding whip with a loop at the end

rid·ing hab·it *n.* outfit worn for horseback riding

Rid·ing Moun·tain Na·tion·al Park /ríding-/ national park in Canada, in southwestern Manitoba. Area: 1,148 sq. mi./2,973 sq. km.

rid·ley /ríddlee/ (*plural* **-leys**) *n.* **1.** a small marine turtle, especially the gray-shelled Kemp's ridley found in the Atlantic, or the larger greenish olive ridley found in the Pacific **2.** = **olive ridley**

ri·dot·to /ri dóttō/ (*plural* **ri·dot·tos**) *n.* a musical entertainment with dancing, popular in the 18th century [Early 18thC. Via Italian, "retreat, entertainment," from medieval Latin *reductus*, from the past participle of Latin *reducere* (see REDUCE).]

rieb·eck·ite /réebə kìt, rée be-/ *n.* a blue-black silicate mineral of the amphibole group, found in acidic igneous rocks and metamorphic schists. Tiger's eye is a mixture of riebeckite and silica. [Late 19thC. Named for the German explorer Emil *Riebeck* (died 1885).]

Rief·en·stahl /réef'n shtaàl/, **Leni** (*b.* 1902) German movie director and photographer. Her documentary films of a Nazi rally and of the 1936 Berlin Olympic Games glorified the Nazis, but are nevertheless masterpieces of cinematic technique. Born **Helena Bertha Amalia Riefenstahl**

Riel /ree él/, **Louis David** (1844–85) Canadian political leader. He headed provisional governments of Manitoba (1869, 1885), and led the North West Rebellion.

Rie·mann·ian ge·om·e·try /ree maànee ən-, -mànnee ən-/ *n.* a type of non-Euclidean geometry in which it is assumed that in a plane all pairs of straight lines intersect [Early 20thC. Named for G. F. B. *Riemann* (1826–66), the German mathematician who founded it.]

ries·ling /réezling, réessling/, **Riesling** *n.* **1.** WHITE WINE a fruity dry to sweet white wine produced from a white grape grown mainly in Germany, Austria, Alsace, and Australia **2.** RIESLING GRAPE the grape used to make riesling [Mid-19thC. From German, alteration of obsolete *Rüssling*.]

Ries·man /réess mən/, **David** (*b.* 1909) U.S. sociologist. His controversial work *The Lonely Crowd* (1950) describes a U.S. society evolving from individualism to conformism.

ri·fam·pi·cin /ri fámpissin/ *n.* = **rifampin** [Mid-20thC. Blend of RIFAMYCIN and PIPERAZINE.]

ri·fam·pin /ri fámpin/ *n.* an antibiotic derived from soil bacteria and used to treat various bacterial infections, including tuberculosis. It works by interfering with RNA synthesis in the infecting bacteria. [Mid-20thC. Blend of RIFAMYCIN and PIPERAZINE.]

rif·a·my·cin /rìffə míss'n/ *n.* an antibiotic produced by a soil bacterium and used to treat various bacterial infections, including leprosy and tuberculosis. Latin name: *Streptomyces mediterranei.* [Mid-20thC. Origin uncertain: probably coined from Italian *riformare* "to reform," from *formare* "to form" from Latin (see REFORM) + -MYCIN.]

rife /rīf/ *adj.* **1.** WIDESPREAD AND PLENTIFUL occurring everywhere in plentiful supply ○ *areas where poverty is rife* **2.** FULL OF SOMETHING full of or severely affected by something undesirable ○ *an organization rife with corruption* [Old English *rȳfe*] —**rife·ly** *adv.* —**rife·ness** *n.*

WORD KEY: SYNONYMS

See Synonyms at ***widespread***.

riff /rif/ *n.* **1.** MUSIC SERIES OF NOTES a short, often repeated series of notes in pop music or jazz that forms a distinctive part of the accompaniment **2.** QUIP a quick, witty remark, especially when exchanged rapidly ■ *vi.* (**riffed, riff·ing, riffs**) USE RIFFS to play or make use of riffs [Early 20thC. Origin uncertain: possibly a shortening of RIFFLE, or perhaps an alteration of REFRAIN.]

Rif·fi·an /ríffee ən/ *n.* a dialect of Berber spoken in Morocco, especially in the Riff Mountains of northern Morocco —**Rif·fi·an** *adj.*

rif·fle /ríff'l/ *v.* (**-fled, -fling, -fles**) **1.** *vti.* FLICK THROUGH PAGES to flick through the pages of a book, magazine, or newspaper, glancing casually at the contents **2.** *vt.* CARDS SHUFFLE CARDS to shuffle playing cards by halving the deck, lifting the corners, and flicking the cards so that they overlap as they fall **3.** *vi.* BECOME CHOPPY to become rough and choppy when passing over submerged rocks ○ *Water riffles over the rocks.* ■ *n.* **1.** OCEANOG SUBMERGED ROCKS OR SANDBAR an area of rocks or a sandbar lying just below the surface of the water **2.** OCEANOG ROUGH WATER an area of rough water caused by submerged rocks or a sandbar **3.** QUICK LOOK AT BOOK a quick flick through the pages of a book, magazine, or newspaper **4.** CARDS SHUFFLING the shuffling of playing cards **5.** MINING GROOVED PART OF SLUICE the bottom part of a sluice that has grooves for collecting gold or other mineral particles [Mid-18thC. Origin uncertain: perhaps a blend of RIPPLE and RUFFLE[1].]

rif·fler /rífflər/ *n.* a curved file for smoothing concave surfaces [Late 18thC. From French *rifloir*, from *rifler* "to scratch" (see RIFLE[2]).]

riff·raff /ríf ràf/ *n.* **1.** OFFENSIVE TERM an offensive term that deliberately insults somebody's social status, importance, and manners (*insult*) **2.** WORTHLESS THINGS rubbish or worthless objects (*informal*) [15thC. From French *rif et raf* "pieces of plunder of small value," from *rifler* "to plunder" and *raffler* "to snatch."]

ri·fle[1] /rī́f'l/ *n.* **1.** GUN a gun with a long barrel that is fired from the shoulder. Spiral grooves inside the barrel make the bullet spin, improving its accuracy over a long distance. **2.** CANNON a large cannon with spirals cut into the bore ■ **ri·fles, Ri·fles** *npl.* ARMY UNIT OF ARMED SOLDIERS a unit of soldiers carrying rifles ■ *vt.* (**-fled, -fling, -fles**) **1.** ARMS CUT GUN BARREL to cut the inside of a gun barrel with spiral grooves **2.** SPORTS THROW FAST BALL to hit or throw a ball hard, making it travel very fast [Late 17thC. From French *rifler* "to scratch" (see RIFLE[2]).]

ri·fle[2] /rī́f'l/ (**-fled, -fling, -fles**) *v.* **1.** *vti.* SEARCH THROUGH VIGOROUSLY to search vigorously through something such as a drawer or room, often leaving things in disorder and sometimes with the intent to steal **2.** *vt.* ROB to rob or plunder somebody or something [14thC. From French *rifler* "to plunder, scratch," of uncertain origin: probably from prehistoric Germanic.] —**ri·fler** *n.*

ri·fle·bird /rī́f'l bùrd/ *n.* a bird of paradise found in parts of Australia and New Guinea, the male of which performs an elaborate courtship dance. Genus: *Ptiloris.* [Mid-19thC. *Rifle* of uncertain origin: probably from RIFLE[1], either an imitation of the sound of the bird's cry, or because its plumage resembles a military uniform.]

ri·fle gre·nade *n.* a grenade propelled to its target by a rifle-fired bullet, requiring special adapting hardware

ri·fle·man /rī́f'lmən/ (*plural* **ri·fle·men** /-mən/) *n.* **1.** ARMY SOLDIER WITH RIFLE a soldier who has been trained to use a rifle **2.** ARMS RIFLE USER somebody skilled in the use of a rifle

ri·fle range *n.* an area with targets where people can practice shooting rifles

ri·fle·ry /rī́f'lree/ *n.* **1.** FIRING RIFLES the skill or practice of firing rifles **2.** RIFLE FIRE fire from rifles

ri·fle·scope /rī́f'l skōp/ *n.* a telescopic sight designed to be used on a rifle [Mid-20thC. Coined from RIFLE + TELESCOPE.]

ri·fling /rī́fling/ *n.* **1.** CUTTING GROOVES the cutting of spiral grooves in the barrel of a gun **2.** SPIRAL GROOVES a series of spiral grooves cut in the barrel of a gun

rift[1] /rift/ *n.* **1.** GAP OR BREAK a gap or break in something where it has split apart **2.** DISAGREEMENT a serious disagreement that disrupts good relations **3.** GEOL = **fault** *n.* 6 ■ *vti.* (**rift·ed, rift·ing, rifts**) SPLIT to split or make something split apart [14thC. Of Scandinavian origin.]

rift[2] /rift/ *n.* **1.** SHALLOW WATER a shallow, often rapidly flowing area of water **2.** BACKWASH the backward flow of water caused by a wave when it breaks [Early 18thC. Origin uncertain: probably from Dutch *rif* (see REEF).]

rift val·ley *n.* a valley formed by geological faulting, where the land between two parallel faults drops down to give a broad central plain with steep sides

rift zone *n.* an area of the earth's surface, often associated with the margins of continental plates, that is especially heavily faulted and may be subject to earth tremors

rig[1] /rig/ *vt.* (**rigged, rig·ging, rigs**) **1.** SAILING EQUIP VESSEL WITH RIGGING to fit a boat or its mast with sails and rigging **2.** EQUIP to equip or fit out something so it is ready to use **3.** MAKE to make something temporary and serviceable, usually done in haste and lacking the proper materials **4.** AIR PREPARE AIRCRAFT FOR USE to make an aircraft ready for use by making sure that all the parts are correctly adjusted **5.** CLOTHES DRESS to dress or adorn something or somebody (*usually passive*) ○ *rigged in striped pajamas* ■ *n.* **1.** INDUST DRILLING STRUCTURE FOR OIL a structure and apparatus used for drilling for oil and gas **2.** SAILING ARRANGEMENT OF SAILS AND MASTS the arrangement of sails and masts on a boat **3.** CLOTHES OUTFIT OF CLOTHING an outfit that somebody is wearing (*informal*) **4.** SPECIALIST EQUIPMENT the special equipment used for an activity, especially fishing tackle or the radio equipment used by an amateur radio operator **5.** TRANSP TRUCK a tractor-trailer, or a tractor without a trailer (*informal*) **6.** TRANSP HORSE CARRIAGE in former times, a carriage or cart pulled by one or more horses [15thC. Origin uncertain: probably from a Scandinavian source.]

rig out *vt.* (*informal*) **1.** DRESS SOMEBODY UP to put a special kind of clothing on somebody ○ *rigged himself out for a heavyweight bout* **2.** PROVIDE EQUIPMENT FOR SOMEBODY OR SOMETHING to fit a person, place, or object with proper or necessary equipment ○ *rigged out for a trekking expedition*

rig[2] /rig/ *vt.* (**rigged, rig·ging, rigs**) ARRANGE OUTCOME DISHONESTLY to affect the outcome of something by intervening dishonestly or unfairly to gain an advantage ■ *n.* TRICK a trick or swindle [Early 18thC. Origin unknown.]

rig[3] /rig/ *n.* a male animal in which one or both testes fail to descend into the scrotum at the usual time. The condition is most common in horses and pigs. (*informal*) [15thC. Variant of RIDGE.]

Ri·ga /réegə/ capital city of Latvia, on its eastern coast. Population: 839,675 (1995).

rig·a·doon /rìggə dóon/, **rig·au·don** /rèe gaw dáwN/ *n.* in former times, a lively couple dance, or the music for it, with two or four beats to the bar. Traditionally from the Provence region of France, in the 17th and 18th centuries it was popular in the French court where it was danced in a more dignified manner. [Late 17thC. From French *rigaudon*, of uncertain origin: perhaps named for *Rigaud*, a dancing-master in Marseilles who is said to have invented it.]

rig·a·ma·role *n.* = **rigmarole**

rig·a·to·ni /rìggə tṓnee/ *n.* short rounded tubes of pasta with narrow ridges running along them [Mid-20thC. From Italian, from *rigato* "ridged," the past participle of *rigare* "to draw a line," from *riga* "line."]

rig·au·don *n.* = **rigadoon**

Ri·gel /rī́jəl/ *n.* a blue-white double star of the first magnitude in the constellation Orion [From Arabic *rijl*, literally "foot," because it appears at the base of the constellation]

rig·ger /ríggər/ *n.* **1.** ROWING BRACKET ON ROWING BOAT a bracket supporting a rowlock on a rowing boat **2.** SAILING SOMEBODY WHO RIGS BOATS somebody whose job is to rig a boat **3.** SAILING SHIP a ship, especially one with a specific kind of rigging **4.** CONSTR SCAFFOLDING WORKER somebody whose job is to erect and maintain scaffolding and lifting equipment **5.** INDUST OIL-RIG WORKER somebody who works on an oil or gas rig

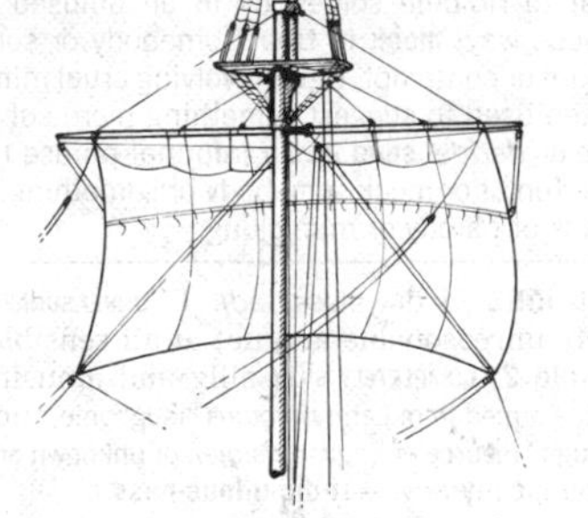

Rigging

rig·ging /rígging/ *n.* **1.** SAILING ROPES, WIRES, AND PULLEYS the ropes, wires, and pulleys that support the masts and control the sails of a boat **2.** THEATER THEATER EQUIPMENT the system of ropes, pulleys, and other equipment used to shift scenery on a stage **3.** SUPPORTING EQUIPMENT any system of ropes, pulleys, or other equipment used as a support for something, e.g., construction scaffolding **4.** CLOTHES SPECIAL-PURPOSE CLOTHING clothing, especially when designed for a special purpose

right /rīt/ *adj.* **1.** TRUE consistent with facts or belief ○ *gave the right answer* **2.** SOCIALLY APPROVED adhering to or consistent with conventional ideas of morality, propriety, or decorum ○ *right conduct between nations* **3.** USUAL conforming to what is usual or expected ○ *Something didn't seem right when I walked in.* **4.** PROPER proper with regard to use, function, or operation ○ *You're not holding the thing by the right end.* **5.** BEST most suitable or desirable ○ *waiting for the right offer to come along* **6.** SUPERIOR holding a view or position that is superior, more proper, or more moral ○ *hard to tell who's right in this situation* **7.** HEALTHY in good physical and mental health ○ *hasn't felt right in weeks* **8.** IN A SATISFACTORY CONDITION being in a satisfactory condition or proper state, or going into one ○ *make things right for them* **9.** PROMINENT prominent in business, society, or some other sphere ○ *knows all the right people* **10.** EAST WHEN FACING NORTH on the side of the body that is east when you face north **11.** MAIN main or most prominent ○ *has to be stored right side up* **12.** GEOM PERPENDICULAR being perpendicular or forming an angle of 90 degrees ■ *adv.* **1.** PROPERLY in the proper or conventional way, or a way that will be successful ○ *You didn't do it right.* **2.** IMMEDIATELY OR EXACTLY used to emphasize immediacy or exactness ○ *right at that moment* **3.** STRAIGHT without deviating from a course ○ *went right to work from the hospital* **4.** CORRECTLY in conformity with fact or expectation ○ *If you'd answered right you would have won $100.* **5.** MORALLY AND APPROPRIATELY in conformity with conventional morality, propriety, or justice ○ *I want to do right by my children.* **6.** DESIRABLY desirably or advantageously ○ *afraid that it won't turn out right* **7.** TOWARD EAST WHEN FACING NORTH in or toward the east when you are facing or moving north, and correspondingly for other directions ○ *turn right at the church* **8.** VERY very (*regional*) ○ *a right good deal* **9.** INTENSELY used to intensify the meaning of another term ○ *He just kept right on going and didn't even think about anyone else.* **10.** USED AS PART OF TITLE used as part of a title of respect ○ *Right Reverend* ■ *n.* **1.** MORALLY APPROPRIATE THING that which is conventionally moral or appropriate ○ *She's too young to know right from wrong.* **2.** ACCURATE OR TRUE something that is correct, completely true, and accurate **3.** ENTITLEMENT an entitlement, freedom, or privilege to do something (*often used in the plural*) ○ *human rights* **4.** ENTITLEMENT UNDER LAW an entitlement granted under law ○ *the right to an appeal* **5.** LAW CLAIM somebody's interest in a property (*often used in the plural*) **6.** FIN SECURITIES OPTION the entitlement or option to purchase or receive securities not offered for sale openly, or the certificate indicating this (*often used in the plural*) **7. Right, right** CONSERVATIVES political conservatives generally, or the opinions they hold **8.** EAST WHEN FACING NORTH the side of something that lies east when you are facing north **9.** RIGHT-HAND TURN a turn to the right **10.** CLOTHES ONE OF PAIR the member of a pair designed for the right hand or foot **11.** BLOW WITH RIGHT HAND a blow delivered with the right hand ■ *v.* (**right·ed, right·ing, rights**) **1.** *vti.* MAKE OR BECOME UPRIGHT to put something upright, or to return to an upright position ○ *I righted the vase and mopped up the water.* **2.** *vt.* BRING JUSTICE to bring justice or proper results to a situation **3.** *vt.* CORRECT MISTAKE to change something that is wrong so that it is correct **4.** *vt.* MAKE AMENDS FOR WRONG to redress an error or misdeed ■ *interj.* **1.** USED TO AGREE used to indicate assent or understanding (*informal*) **2.** SEEKING CONFIRMATION used to solicit confirmation of a statement ○ *You just got here, right?* [Old English *riht.* Ultimately, from an Indo-European word meaning "to go straight," which is also the ancestor of English *direct* and *rectify.*] —**right·er** *n.* —**right·ness** *n.* ◇ **be in the right** to be correct in what you say or do ◇ **have** *or* **catch somebody dead to rights** to catch a criminal in the act of committing a crime (*informal*) ◇ **in somebody's own right** because of somebody's birth, ability, or other entitlement, without reference to anyone else ◇ **set** *or* **put something to rights** to put something into a correct or ordered state

right·a·ble /rī́təb'l/ *adj.* designed to be able to be restored to an upright position

right·a·bout /rī́tə bòwt/ *n.* TURN THROUGH 180° a turn through 180° to face in the opposite direction ■ *adj., adv.* FACING OPPOSITE facing in the opposite direction

right an·gle *n.* an angle of 90° —**right-an·gled** *adj.*

right as·cen·sion *n.* one of the two reference points in the equatorial coordinate system for specifying the position of an astronomical object on the celestial sphere. Corresponding to longitude on the earth, it is measured in hours, minutes, and seconds eastward from the vernal equinox, the point where the ecliptic intersects the celestial equator.

right a·tri·o·ven·tric·u·lar valve *n.* = **tricuspid valve**

right a·way *adv.* immediately, without waiting or any delay

right-brain *adj.* relating to or involving emotions or creative ability that are believed to be associated with the right half of the cerebrum

right cir·cu·lar cone *n.* = **cone** *n.* 2

right·eous /rī́chəss/ *adj.* **1.** STRICTLY OBSERVANT OF MORALITY always behaving according to a religious or moral code **2.** JUSTIFIABLE considered to be correct or justifiable **3.** RESPONDING TO INJUSTICE arising from the perception of great injustice or wrongdoing ○ *righteous indignation* **4.** GREAT good or outstanding (*dated slang*) ■ *n.* MORALLY UPRIGHT GROUP righteous people viewed as a group ○ *believing that the righteous will prevail* [Alteration of Old English *rihtwīs*, from earlier forms of RIGHT + -WISE] —**right·eous·ly** *adv.* —**right·eous·ness** *n.*

right face *n.* MILITARY COMMAND a military command to turn 90° to the right ■ *interj.* TURN 90° TO RIGHT used as a military command to turn 90° to the right

right field *n.* **1.** RIGHT SIDE OF OUTFIELD the right side of the outfield on a baseball field, when looking from home plate **2.** BASEBALL POSITION the position covered by the right fielder in baseball —**right field·er** *n.*

right·ful /rítfəl/ *adj.* **1.** HAVING CLAIM with a legal or moral claim to something ○ *the rightful owner* **2.** OWNED BY SOMEBODY WITH RIGHT owned by somebody who has a right to it ○ *rightful property* **3.** FAIR considered to be right and fair ○ *a rightful objection* —**right·ful·ly** *adv.* —**right·ful·ness** *n.*

right hand *n.* **1.** RIGHT SIDE the side of something that lies east when you are facing north **2.** SOMEBODY INVALUABLE somebody who is of invaluable assistance to another

WORD KEY: SYNONYMS

See Synonyms at ***assistant***.

right-hand *adj.* **1.** ON OR TO THE RIGHT on the right or bending to the right **2.** FOR THE RIGHT HAND designed for or done with the right hand **3.** MOST IMPORTANT AND TRUSTED most important and trusted, and relied upon to the greatest extent

right-hand·ed *adj.* **1.** PREFERRING TO USE RIGHT HAND using the right hand in preference to the left for writing, throwing, and other activities that require skill and careful control **2.** DONE WITH RIGHT HAND carried out with the right hand **3.** DESIGNED FOR RIGHT HAND designed to be done with or used by the right hand **4.** TOWARD THE RIGHT turning toward the right in a clockwise direction **5.** SWINGING TOWARD LEFT swinging a bat or other implement to the left ■ *adv.* **1.** WITH RIGHT HAND using the right hand **2.** TOWARD THE LEFT with a swing or direction toward the left ○ *hit a ball right-handed* —**right-hand·ed·ly** *adv.* —**right-hand·ed·ness** *n.*

right-hand·er *n.* **1.** SOMEBODY RIGHT-HANDED a right-handed person, especially an athlete **2.** BLOW WITH RIGHT HAND a blow delivered with the right hand

Right Hon·our·a·ble *n. Can* a title of respect used to refer to the governor general, prime minister, or chief justice of Canada, and some other eminent Canadians

right·ist /rítist/ *adj.* RELATING TO CONSERVATISM favoring or relating to political conservatism ■ *n.* POLITICAL CONSERVATIVE somebody with politically conservative views —**right·ism** *n.*

right·ly /rítlee/ *adv.* **1.** CORRECTLY correctly, properly, and appropriately **2.** UNDERSTANDABLY with very good reason **3.** CERTAINLY certainly or positively (*informal*)

right-mind·ed *adj.* with opinions and attitudes considered to be sensible and fair —**right-mind·ed·ly** *adv.* —**right-mind·ed·ness** *n.*

right·most /rít mōst/ *adj.* in the position that is farthest to the right

right off *adv.* immediately, without waiting or any delay

right of search *n.* the right of a country at war to stop and search the merchant ships of neutral nations to determine if they are carrying forbidden goods that may be seized

right of way, right-of-way (*plural* **rights-of-way** *or* **right-of-ways**) *n.* **1.** TRANSP PERMISSION TO GO FIRST the legal or accepted right of a vehicle or craft to proceed ahead of another **2.** LAW RIGHT TO CROSS PROPERTY the right to cross somebody else's property by a specific route, e.g., as a means of accessing your own property **3.** LAWFUL ROUTE ACROSS SOMEBODY'S PROPERTY a lawful route that may be taken across somebody else's property **4.** TRANSP LAND USED FOR ROAD OR LINE a narrow length of land used for the route of a railroad, electric power line, or public road

right on *interj.* used to show enthusiastic agreement with something said or done (*dated informal*)

right-on *adj.* **1.** UP-TO-DATE socially and politically fashionable and forward-looking, particularly in a way that corresponds to the attitudes of the political left (*dated informal*) **2.** TRUE perfectly true (*informal*)

Right Rev·er·end *n.* a form of address for a Roman Catholic, Anglican, or Episcopal bishop, or for a Roman Catholic abbot or monsignor

right shoul·der arms *n.* the command or act of bringing a weapon to rest on the right shoulder during a military drill

rights is·sue *n.* an instance of an organization offering stock to existing holders on favorable terms so that they can maintain their percentage share of ownership

right-size (**right-sized, right-siz·ing, right-siz·es**) *vi.* to achieve an optimal size appropriate to a particular company, usually an effort considered to require dismissal of employees

right stuff *n.* exactly the psychological and physical characteristics called for by a task (*informal*)

right-think·ing *adj.* = **right-minded**

right-to-life *adj.* = **pro-life**

right-to-work *adj.* relating to the right of workers to gain or keep a job regardless of whether they belong to a union

right tri·an·gle *n.* a triangle having one angle that is a right angle

right·ward /rítwərd/ *adj.* DIRECTED TO THE RIGHT moving toward or positioned on the right ■ *adv.* **right·ward, right·wards** TOWARD THE RIGHT in a direction toward the right

right whale *n.* a large-headed whale of the northern Atlantic and Pacific oceans with a deeply curved jawline and notched tail. Family: Balaenidae.

right wing *n.* **1.** POL CONSERVATIVE PART the conservative membership of a group or political party **2.** SPORTS PLAYER OR POSITION AT RIGHT in certain team games, the player or position occupying the right-hand part of a playing area when facing an opponent **3.** MIL RIGHT-HAND MILITARY FORCE OR POSITION the right-hand part or position of a military force while facing the enemy

right-wing *adj.* **1.** POL CONSERVATIVE conservative in conviction or temperament **2.** SPORTS ON RIGHT WHILE FACING OPPONENT occupying the right-hand part of a playing area when facing an opponent **3.** MIL OCCUPYING RIGHT DURING MILITARY ENGAGEMENT occupying the right-hand part or position of a military force when it is facing the enemy —**right-wing·er** *n.*

right·y /rítee/ *n.* (*plural* **-ies**) (*informal*) **1.** RIGHT-HANDED PERSON somebody who is right-handed **2.** RIGHT-WING PERSON somebody who holds right-wing views ■ *adv.* WITH RIGHT HAND using the right hand (*informal*)

rig·id /ríjjid/ *adj.* **1.** FIRM AND STIFF not bending or easily moved into a different shape or position ○ *lengths of rigid plastic pipe* **2.** INFLEXIBLE applied or carried out strictly, with no allowances or exceptions ○ *a rigid set of rules* **3.** HELD INFLEXIBLY inflexibly adhered to ○ *rigid opinions* **4.** REFUSING TO CHANGE unchanging in behavior, opinions, or attitudes ○ *Despite arguments to the contrary, she remained rigid in her stand.* [15thC. From Latin *rigidus*, from *rigere* "to be stiff" (source of English rigor).] —**ri·gid·i·ty** /ri jíddətee/ *n.* —**rig·id·ness** /ríjjidnəss/ *n.*

rig·id des·ig·na·tor *n.* in philosophy, a name that stands for the same thing in every possible world as opposed to a description that could stand for somebody or something else in some possible world

ri·gid·i·fy /ri jíddə fì/ (**-fied, -fy·ing, -fies**) *vti.* to become or cause something to become stiff and inflexible

rig·ma·role /rígmə rōl/, **rig·a·ma·role** /ríggəmə-/ *n.* **1.** RIDICULOUSLY COMPLICATED PROCESS an irritating, tedious, or confusing sequence of tasks, especially tasks that seem unnecessary or absurd **2.** OVERELABORATE ACCOUNT OF SOMETHING a tediously long, complicated, or unhelpful explanation [Mid-18thC. Origin uncertain: probably an alteration of earlier *ragman roll*, a parchment scroll used in the gambling game of *ragman*.]

WORD KEY: ORIGIN

A *ragman roll* was a parchment scroll used in a medieval gambling game. The roll had things such as names written on it, with pieces of string attached to them, and participants had to select a string at random. The word *ragman* may have been a contraction of *ragged man*, perhaps in allusion to the appearance of the scroll, with all its bits of string hanging from it. *Ragman roll* eventually came to be used for any list or catalog, and *ragman* itself denoted a "long rambling discourse" in 16th-century Scottish English – a meaning that seems to have transferred itself eventually to ***rigmarole***.

rig·or /ríggər/ *n.* **1.** USE OF DEMANDING STANDARDS the application of precise and exacting standards in the doing of something **2.** LACK OF TOLERANCE severity, strictness, or harshness in dealing with somebody **3.** HARDSHIP great hardship or difficulty **4.** METEOROL SEVERE WEATHER harshness of weather or climate **5.** MED RIGIDITY OF BODY stiffness and lack of response to stimuli in body organs or tissues **6.** MED SUDDEN FEELING OF CHILLINESS an abrupt attack of shivering and coldness, typically marking a rise in body temperature, e.g., at the onset of fever **7.** BOT INERTIA IN PLANTS insensitivity of a plant due to unfavorable conditions [14thC. Directly and via Old French from Latin *rigor* "stiffness," from *rigere* "to be stiff" (source also of English *rigid*).]

rig·or·ism /ríggə rìzzəm/ *n.* **1.** SEVERITY great strictness or severity **2.** CHR ADOPTION OF STRICT MORALITY in Roman Catholic philosophy, the theory that in matters of moral choice the stricter course should be taken —**rig·or·is·tic** /riggə rístik/ *adj.*

rig·or mor·tis /-máwrtiss/ *n.* the progressive stiffening of the body that occurs several hours after death, due to the coagulation of protein in the muscles. It usually starts to wane after about 24 hours. [From Latin, literally "stiffness of death"]

rig·or·ous /ríggərəss/ *adj.* **1.** STRICT harsh, strict, or difficult in nature ○ *a rigorous training program* **2.** EXACTING extremely precise and exacting ○ *rigorous standards of cleanliness* **3.** SEVERE severe and extreme to experience ○ *climbing in rigorous conditions* **4.** LOGIC PRECISE precise and formalized ○ *a rigorous proof* —**rig·or·ous·ness** *n.*

rig·our *n.* U.K. = **rigor**

Rig-Ve·da /rig váydə, rig véedə/ *n.* a large collection of Hindu hymns dating from 2000 B.C. or earlier [Late 18thC. From Sanskrit *ṛgvedaḥ*, from *ṛc* "verse" + *vedaḥ* "knowledge" (see VEDA).]

Riis /rees/, **Jacob August** (1849–1914) Danish-born U.S. journalist and social reformer. He reported on life in overcrowded areas of U.S. cities.

Ri·je·ka /ree yékə/ city and port in northwestern Croatia, situated on the Gulf of Kvarner, on the Adriatic Sea. Population: 167,964 (1991).

rijst·ta·fel /rí staaf'l/, **rijs·ta·fel** *n.* a Dutch meal of Indonesian origin based on rice with many small side dishes, e.g., Indonesian-style curry, seafood, satay, soups, sauces, and condiments [Late 19thC. From Dutch, from *rijs* "rice" + *tafel* "table."]

rile /rīl/ (**riled, ril·ing, riles**) *vt.* **1.** GET SOMEBODY ANGRY to irritate somebody enough that it provokes anger (*informal*) (*often passive*) **2.** MAKE WAVES IN WATER to stir up water or other liquid violently [Early 19thC. Variant of ROIL.]

rile·y /rílee/ *adj.* **1.** FULL OF SEDIMENT cloudy with stirred-up sediment **2.** ANNOYED annoyed or angered by something

Ri·ley [Early 20thC. Origin uncertain: probably from a popular late 19th-century song.] ◇ **the life of Riley** a comfortable well-off life with no worries

Ri·ley /rílee/, **Bridget** (*b.* 1931) British painter. She was a leading figure in the 1960s art movement known as op art. Full name **Bridget Louise Riley**

Ri·ley, James Whitcomb (1849–1916) U.S. poet. Best known for his Hoosier dialect and whimsical sense of humor, he published several collections of poems.

rilievo *n.* = **relievo**

rill /ril/ *n.* **1.** STREAM a little stream or brook **2.** GEOG GROOVE IN SOIL a small channel cut in soil **3. rill, rille** ASTRON TRENCH ON MOON a long narrow valley on the moon's surface ■ *vt.* GEOG FORM CHANNELS IN FIELD to form small channels in a plowed field as a result of the runoff of rainwater [Mid-16thC. From Low German *rille*. Ultimately from an Indo-European word meaning "to run," which is also the ancestor of English *run* and *rivulet*.]

rill·et /rìllət/ *n.* **1.** TINY STREAM a little rill **2.** ASTRON SHORT VALLEY ON MOON a short narrow valley on the moon's surface

ril·lettes /ri léts/ *n.* seasoned pork or goose cooked in its own fat until very tender and potted as a type of soft spreadable pâté (*takes a singular or plural verb*) [Late 19thC. From French, literally "small pieces of pork," from *rille* "piece of pork," a variant of *reille* "board," from Latin *regula* (see RULE).]

rim /rim/ *n.* **1.** OUTER EDGE OF SOMETHING CIRCULAR an outer edge, often slightly raised, that runs along the outside of something curved or circular **2.** LIMIT the farthest limit of something (*literary*) **3.** TRANSP PART AROUND A WHEEL'S EDGE the curved outer edge of a wheel of a motor vehicle or bicycle **4.** PART OF GLASSES FRAME a usually curved part that holds and forms an edge to lenses in a pair of glasses **5.** BASKETBALL **METAL HOOP FOR BASKETBALL NET** the metal hoop to which a basketball net is attached ■ *vt.* **(rimmed, rim·ming, rims) FORM SOMETHING'S OUTER EDGE** to form an edge, usually a slightly raised edge, along the edge of something curved or circular [Old English *rima* "border, coast," of unknown origin]

ri·maye /ri máy/ *n.* GEOG = **bergschrund** [Early 20thC. From French, literally "group of fissures," from Latin *rima* (see RIMOSE).]

rime[1] /rīm/ *n.* **FROST COATING** a thin coating of frost formed on cold objects exposed to fog or cloud ■ *vt.* **(rimed, rim·ing, rimes) COAT SOMETHING WITH THIN FROST** to cover something with a thin frost or with something resembling it (*often passive*) [Old English *hrīm*, from a prehistoric Germanic word of unknown origin]

rime[2] /rīm/ *n.* POETRY a rhyme (*archaic*)

rime riche /reem reésh/ (*plural* **rimes riches** /reem reésh/) *n.* the use of rhyme in which stressed syllables or words are identical in pronunciation, as in "weigh" and "away," and sometimes in spelling, as in "back" and "track" [From French, literally "rich rhyme"]

rim·fire /rím fīr/ *adj.* designed for or using a cartridge with its primer located in the rim of the base, rather than in the center

Ri·mi·ni /rímmənee/ city and port in Forli Province, Emilia-Romagna Region, northern Italy, on the Adriatic Sea. Population: 129,876 (1992).

rim job *n.* an offensive term for the use of the lips and tongue on or in the anus of a sexual partner (*slang taboo*)

rimmed /rimd/ *adj.* made with an outer rim or border, sometimes of a different material, substance, or color

ri·mose /rī mṓss, rī mṓss/ *adj.* covered with cracks, fissures, or crevices [Early 18thC. From Latin *rimosus*, from *rima* "fissure." Ultimately from an Indo-European word meaning "to scratch," which is also the ancestor of English *row*[1].] —**ri·mose·ly** *adv.* —**ri·mos·i·ty** /rī móssətee/ *n.*

Ri·mous·ki /ri mόoskee/ city in Canada, in Quebec State, on the St. Lawrence River, northeast of Quebec City. Population: 48,104 (1996).

rim·ple /rímpəl/ (**-pled, -pling, -ples**) *n.* (*regional archaic*) **1. WRINKLE** a wrinkle **2.** *vti.* **TO WRINKLE** to wrinkle, rumple, or crease something [Old English *hrympel*. From a prehistoric Germanic word that is also the ancestor of English *rumple*.]

rim·rock /rím ròk/ *n.* a layer of rock that forms a vertical boundary to a plateau, valley, or deposit of gravel

Rim·sky-Kor·sa·kov /rìmskee káwssə kàwf/, **Nikolay** (1844–1908) Russian composer. He was renowned as a consummate orchestrator. His works, often inspired by Russian folk music, include *Scheherazade* (1888). Full name **Nikolay Andreyevich Rimsky-Korsakov**

rim·y /rímee/ (**-i·er, -i·est**) *adj.* with a thin coating of frost (*literary*)

rind /rīnd/ *n.* **1. TOUGH OUTSIDE LAYER OF FRUIT** the thick tough outer skin of a fruit **2.** FOOD **HARD OUTER LAYER OF FOOD** a tough outer protective layer of a food product, e.g., a cheese [Old English *rind(e)*, literally "something torn off." Ultimately from an Indo-European word meaning "to tear," which is also the ancestor of English *rend*.]

rin·der·pest /ríndər pèst/ *n.* a sometimes fatal viral disease mainly affecting cattle, sheep, and goats that occurs chiefly in central Africa and Asia and is marked by fever, hemorrhage, and diarrhea. Animals can be vaccinated against rinderpest, and importation of animals from affected regions is strictly controlled. [Mid-19thC. From German, from *Rinder* "cattle" + *Pest* "plague."]

Rine·hart /rīn haart/, **Mary Roberts** (1876–1958) U.S. writer. She wrote mystery stories and coauthored the play *The Bat* (1920).

rin·for·zan·do /reén fawr tsáan dō/ *adj., adv.* loud and with emphasis (*used as a musical direction*) [Early 19thC. From Italian "getting stronger."]

ring[1] /ring/ *n.* **1. SMALL BAND OF SOMETHING** a durable circular band of something, especially a small band made of a specified material or for some special use **2.** ACCESSORIES **SMALL CIRCULAR PIECE OF JEWELRY** a band, usually made of metal, worn as an ornament on a part of the body, especially around a finger. Rings are made in a variety of decorative designs, sometimes with mounted gemstones on the outer part of the band. **3. ENCIRCLING MARK** an outline, mark, or figure in the shape of a circle (*often used in the plural*) **4. CIRCLE OF SOMETHING** a circular arrangement of people or objects ○ *a ring of chairs* **5. CIRCULAR MOTION** a movement of steps, especially by people skipping or dancing, that goes around in a continuous circle ○ *dancing in a ring* **6.** CRIMINOL **GROUP OF PEOPLE OPERATING DISHONESTLY** an organized group of people who work together in a dishonest or unethical way ○ *a gambling ring* **7.** ARTS **CIRCULAR AREA FOR PERFORMANCE** a round stage or piece of ground, usually surrounded by seating, on which a spectator event such as a circus or a theatrical performance takes place ○ *a three-ring circus* **8.** BOXING, WRESTLING **PLATFORM FOR BOXING OR WRESTLING** a raised square roped platform on which a boxing or wrestling match takes place **9.** BOXING **BOXING** the sport of boxing ○ *choose the ring as a career* **10.** ASTRON **BAND OF MATTER CIRCLING PLANET** a band of dust, particles, and small bodies revolving around a planet. Such bands are known to circle Saturn, Jupiter, Uranus, and Neptune. **11.** TREES = **growth ring 12.** SPORTS = **bullring 13. CONTEST** a competition or contest, especially a political one **14.** AGRIC **ENCLOSURE FOR LIVESTOCK AT FAIR** an enclosure at a fair in which livestock are shown, paraded, or auctioned **15. TURN OF SPIRAL** a single turn of a spiral **16.** MATH **SET OF MATHEMATICAL ELEMENTS** a set of elements that is associative under multiplication and distributive under addition **17.** CHEM **CLOSED LOOP OF ATOMS** a collection of bound atoms represented graphically in cyclic form **18.** GEOM **SPACE BETWEEN CIRCLES** a space between two concentric circles ■ **rings** *npl.* SPORTS **GYMNASTIC APPARATUS** a pair of wooden rings that are suspended from a ceiling and used to perform gymnastic routines ■ *v.* **(ringed, ring·ing, rings) 1.** *vti.* **ENCIRCLE** to encircle something, or be encircled by something ○ *We were ringed by the herd of cattle.* **2.** *vt.* LEISURE **ENCIRCLE SOMETHING WITH RING** to throw a ring or horseshoe so that it encircles a peg or stake [Old English *hring*. Ultimately from an Indo-European base meaning "to curl," which is also the ancestor of English *shrink* and *curve*.]

WORD KEY: CULTURAL NOTE

The Ring of the Nibelung, a series of musical dramas by German composer Richard Wagner (1813–83). Based on Teutonic legends, this massive tetralogy — *The Rhinegold* (1869), *The Valkyrie* (1870), *Siegfried* (1876) and *The Twilight of the Gods* (1876) — a full performance of which lasts up to 15 hours, recounts the complex chain of events triggered by the theft of a magical gold ring. It represents Wagner's most successful attempt to create a new form of theater in which poetic drama is set to a musical score unified by recurring themes or leitmotifs.

ring back *vti.* to make a return telephone call to somebody (*informal*) ○ *I left several messages but she never rang back.*

ring in *vt.* **1. CELEBRATE THE BEGINNING OF SOMETHING** to make bells ring in celebration of the beginning of something **2.** *Aus* **FRAUDULENTLY SUBSTITUTE SOMETHING** to substitute something fraudulently, especially a horse in a race

ring out *v.* **1.** *vi.* **SOUND LOUDLY** to be heard loudly and clearly **2.** *vt.* **CELEBRATE THE END OF SOMETHING** to make bells ring in celebration of the end of something

ring up *v.* **1.** *vt.* **ACCOMPLISH** to accomplish or achieve something **2.** *vt.* COMM **ENTER SUM PAID FOR SOMETHING** to press keys on a cash register to record the amount of money being paid for something (*dated*) **3.** *vti. U.K.* **PHONE** to telephone somebody

ring[2] /ring/ *v.* **(rang** /rang/, **rung** /rung/, **ring·ing, rings) 1.** *vti.* **MAKE THE SOUND OF A BELL** to make, or cause something such as a bell to make, a metallic sound when struck or played **2.** *vti.* **MAKE A SOUND TO ALERT SOMEBODY** to produce or make something produce a continuous or regular high-pitched sound to alert somebody **3.** *vi.* **ECHO LOUDLY** to be full of a loud, high-pitched, or reverberating sound, especially laughter or applause ○ *The hall rang with applause.* **4.** *vi.* **MAKE CALL FOR SOMETHING** to call for somebody or something by sounding a bell or buzzer **5.** *vi.* **IMPRESS SOMEBODY AS SOMETHING** to make a particular impression on somebody ○ *His excuse didn't ring true.* **6.** *vti. U.K.* UTIL **TELEPHONE** to telephone somebody ○ *He rang me to cancel the appointment.* **7.** *vi.* **HAVE SENSATION OF HIGH-PITCHED SOUNDS** to have a sensation of a repeated or continuous high-pitched sound ○ *It made my ears ring.* ■ *n.* **1. ACT OF SOUNDING BELL** the act of making a bell sound **2. BELL SOUND** the sound of a bell or something like a bell **3. GENERAL IMPRESSION** a general impression made by somebody or something ○ *It had a familiar ring to it.* **4. REPEATED SOUND** a loud continuous repeated or reverberating sound **5. SET OF BELLS IN TOWER** a set of bells in a tower or belfry [Old English *hringan*, of uncertain origin: probably from a prehistoric Germanic word meaning "to make a noise," which is also the ancestor of English *raven* and *cricket*[1]] ◇ **ring down the curtain on something** to bring an end to something (*informal*)

ring-a-levio /rìng ə leévee ō/ *n.* a children's game in which members of one team hide and the other team tries to find and capture them. A captured player must stand inside a circle drawn on the ground until tagged by a free teammate. [Early 20thC. Alteration of earlier *ring relievo*, from RING[1] + RELIEVE.]

ring-a-ring-a-roses *n.* = **ring-around-the-rosey**

ring-a·round-the-rosey, ring-a·round-the-ros·y, ring-a·round-a-ros·y *n.* a young children's game in which players sing while moving around in a circle and abruptly squat when the words "all fall down" are sung [Late 19thC. Origin uncertain: popularly thought to refer to the "rosy" (rash) of the bubonic plague, but probably originally simply a singing game with a curtsy at the end.]

ring-bill *n.* = **ring-necked duck**

ring-billed gull *n.* a white gull that nests by inland lakes of North America, lives on the coast in winter, and has a black ring around its bill. Latin name: *Larus delawarensis*.

ring bind·er *n.* a stiff cover with metal rings inside the spine that snap open for insertion or removal of punched looseleaf paper

ring·bolt *n.* a bolt with a ring fitted through the eye at its head

ring·bone /ríng bōn/ *n.* **1. HORSE'S BONE DISORDER** a condition of a horse's pastern bone in which bony outgrowths develop, sometimes leading to pain and lameness. It is treated with rest, medication, or surgery. **2. BONY OUTGROWTH** a bony outgrowth characteristic of ringbone [So called because the outgrowths encircle the bone]

ring dance *n.* = **round dance**

ring·dove /ríng dùv/ *n.* **1.** = **wood pigeon 2. BLACK-COLLARED PIGEON** a domesticated variety of the collared dove that has a semicircular black collar. Latin name: *Streptopelia risoria*.

ringed /ringd/ *adj.* **1. WEARING RING** wearing one or more rings **2. ENCIRCLED** encircled by a ring **3.** ZOOL **WITH MARKS THAT FORM RING** with markings that form a ring around the neck, bill, or other body part

ringed plov·er *n.* a plover of sandy or pebbly shores of Europe, Asia, and Africa with a gray back and wings, white undersides, a black breast band, and a black-tipped orange bill. Latin name: *Charadrius hiaticula*.

ringed seal *n.* a seal of Arctic and subarctic regions that has a dark grayish coat with lighter markings that encircle the body. Latin name: *Pusa hispida*.

rin·gent /rínjənt/ *adj.* with an opening bordered by parts resembling the lips of a gaping mouth, as has, e.g., the flower of a snapdragon [Mid-18thC. From Latin *ringent-*, the present participle stem of *ringi* "to gape" (source of English *rictus*).]

ring·er[1] /ríngər/ *n.* **1.** = **bander 2.** CRIMINOL **FRAUDULENT ENTRY** somebody or something fraudulently substituted in a competition (*informal*) **3.** LEISURE **GAME OF MARBLES** a game in which marbles are formed like a cross inside a circle and each player uses a marble to shoot the laid out marbles outside the circle

ring·er[2] /ríngər/ *n.* a horseshoe or quoit thrown skillfully so that it encircles a peg or stake

ring·ers /ríngərz/ *n.* = **ringer**[1] *n.* 3 (*takes a singular verb*)

Ring·er's so·lu·tion, Ring·er so·lu·tion *n.* a solution of inorganic salts used to sustain cells, tissues, or organs outside the body [Late 19thC. Named for Sydney *Ringer* (1834–1910), the British physician who introduced this type of solution.]

ring fin·ger *n.* the third finger of the hand, especially the left hand, on which an engagement or wedding ring is traditionally worn

ring·hals /ríng hàls/ (*plural* **-hals** *or* **-hals·es**) *n.* a southern African snake related to the cobra that has a small rough-skinned black or brown body and can spit jets of venom from its fangs at an aggressor. Latin name: *Hemachatus hemachatus*. [Late 18thC.

From Afrikaans, literally "ring-neck," from the one or two white rings across the snake's neck.]

ring-in *n. Aus* an outsider brought into a team or group, usually to replace somebody or make up the numbers (*informal*)

ring·ing /ríngíng/ *n.* **CONTINUING SOUND** a clear continuing usually high-pitched sound ■ *adj.* **STATED LOUDLY AND UNMISTAKABLY** expressed in a definite and unrestrained way —**ring·ing·ly** *adv.*

ring·lead·er /ríng lèedər/ *n.* the member of a circle or gang who organizes and encourages others to do something unlawful or rebellious [From the phrase *lead the ring* "to go first"]

ring·let /rínglət/ *n.* **1. CURLY LOCK OF HAIR** a spiral curl of hair **2. SMALL RING** a small ring or circle

ring·let·ed /rínglətəd/ *adj.* wearing the hair in ringlets

ring·mas·ter /ríng màstər/ *n.* somebody who presides over a circus show from a ring, announcing and commenting on the events

Ring Neb·u·la *n.* a nebula in the constellation Lyra that has a ring-shaped appearance

ring-necked /ríng nèkt/, **ring·neck** *adj.* with markings resembling a ring around the neck in a color that contrasts with adjacent feathers, scales, or hair

ring-necked duck *n.* a North American diving duck found on woodland ponds that has coppery ring neck markings and two white rings on the bill. The males are mainly black, the females mostly brown. Latin name: *Aythya collaris.*

ring-necked pheas·ant *n.* an Asian pheasant widely introduced elsewhere as a game bird. Males have a white neck collar, a red head, and lustrous coppery-red and green plumage; females are mottled brown. Latin name: *Phasianus colchicus.*

ring·neck snake, ring-necked snake *n.* a small non-venomous North American snake that has a yellowish or orange neck band. Genus: *Diadophis.*

ring ou·zel *n.* = **ousel**

ring-po·rous *adj.* with annual rings marked by prominent bands of large pores. These rings are readily apparent when a cross section of a trunk or branch is examined.

ring-pull *n. U.K.* = **pull-tab**

ring road *n. U.K.* = **beltway**

ring·side /ríng sìd/ *n.* **1. AREA NEXT TO RING** the row of seats or area directly in front of a boxing, wrestling, or circus ring **2. PLACE OFFERING GOOD VIEW OF SOMETHING** a place or location offering a clear and close view of something (*informal*) —**ring·sid·er** *n.*

ring spot *n.* **1. ROUND PLANT DISCOLORATION** a pale or yellowish ring-shaped discoloration occurring in plants infected with a virus disease **2. FUNGAL DISEASE OF CABBAGE** a fungus disease affecting members of the cabbage family, with brown spots appearing on the leaves

ring·ster /ríngstər/ *n.* somebody who belongs to an illegal or unethical business or political group that manipulates something to its own advantage (*dated*)

ring·tail /ríng tàyl/ *n.* **1. RING-TAILED ANIMAL** a ring-tailed mammal, especially a member of the family that includes the cacomistle and raccoon. Family: Procyonidae. **2.** = **ringtail possum**

ring-tailed *adj.* with a tail encircled by colored bands or markings in a color that contrasts with adjacent feathers, scales, or hair

ring-tailed lemur *n.* a lemur with a gray coat and a long tail with black and white bands. Latin name: *Lemur catta.*

ring·tail pos·sum *n.* an opossum found in Australasia and New Guinea that has a curly-tipped prehensile tail that it uses for grasping branches and carrying objects. Family: Pseudocheiridae.

ring·toss /ríng tòss/ *n.* a game in which rope or metal rings are thrown to encircle a peg, popular at carnivals

ring·worm /ríng wùrm/ *n.* a fungal disease of the skin, scalp, or nails in which intensely itchy ring-shaped patches develop. Infection is transmitted to humans from pets or livestock, or from infected bedding.

rink /ringk/ *n.* **1.** ICE SKATING **AREA OF ICE USED FOR SPORTS** a smooth, enclosed, and often artificially prepared ice surface used for ice-skating, hockey, or curling **2.** SPORTS **SURFACE USED FOR ROLLER-SKATING** a smooth, enclosed, usually wooden surface used for roller-skating **3.** SPORTS **BUILDING FOR ICE SPORTS** a building or arena in which ice-skating, hockey, or curling takes place **4.** SPORTS **PLAYING SIDE** a team of players in curling, bowls, or quoits [14thC. Origin uncertain: perhaps ultimately from Old French *renc* "line, row" (see RANK[1]). The English word originally meant "racecourse."]

rin·ky-dink *adj.* (*informal*) **1. OUT-OF-DATE** broken down or no longer useful **2. OLD-FASHIONED** old-fashioned or outmoded **3. INSIGNIFICANT** small and insignificant ■ *n.* **INFERIOR PERSON OR THING** something or somebody considered shoddy and inferior (*informal*) [Late 19thC. Origin uncertain: perhaps an alteration of RICKETY.]

rinse /rinss/ *vt.* (**rinsed, rins·ing, rins·es**) **1. LIGHTLY CLEAN SOMETHING IN LIQUID** to wash something lightly by dipping it in a liquid, especially clean water, or by running liquid over it **2. FLUSH MOUTH WITH WATER** to flush the mouth or teeth with clean water **3.** TEXTILES **DIP SOMETHING INTO DYE** to dip fabrics or garments into a dye solution ■ *n.* **1. GENTLE WASH** the act of washing something lightly by running a liquid, usually clean water, over or around it **2.** HAIR **COSMETIC TREATMENT FOR HAIR** a solution that is applied to somebody's wet hair to alter or enhance its color or condition temporarily **3. CLEANSING LIQUID** a liquid, usually water or a water-based solution, used to wash away something lightly [13thC. Via Old French *reincier*, of uncertain origin: possibly via assumed Vulgar Latin *recentiare* "to freshen," from Latin *recens* (see RECENT).] —**rins·a·ble** *adj.* —**rins·er** *n.* —**rins·i·ble** *adj.*

Ri·o de Ja·nei·ro /rèe ō day zhə náir ō, -nír ō/ city and port in Brazil, in the southeast of the country. It is the capital of Rio de Janeiro State, and the former capital of the country. Population: 5,533,011 (1996).

Ri·o Grande /rèe ō gránd, -grándee/ river of North America, rising in Colorado, flowing through New Mexico and along the Texas-Mexico boundary, and emptying into the Gulf of Mexico. Length: 1,885 mi./3,034 km.

Ri·o·ja /ree ó ha'a/ *n.* a dry red or white wine with a distinctive flavor, produced in northern Spain [Early 20thC. Named after *Rioja*, the district in northern Spain where the wine is produced.]

Rí·o Mu·ni /rèe ō móonee/ mainland region of Equatorial Guinea, in western central Africa. Population: 240,804 (1983). Area: 10,045 sq. mi./26,017 sq. km.

ri·ot /rí ət/ *n.* **1. VIOLENT DISTURBANCE** a public disturbance during which a group of angry people becomes noisy and out of control, often damaging property and acting violently. In law, a riot is typically defined as a group of three or more persons disturbing the peace for private purposes. **2. SOMETHING EXTREMELY ENJOYABLE** a social occasion, event, or experience that people enjoy in a wild, noisy, and energetic way (*informal*) **3. FUNNY PERSON** somebody who is very amusing (*informal*) **4. GREAT DISPLAY** a spectacular visual display **5. WILD ENJOYABLE AMUSEMENT** uninhibited fun, especially involving dancing, drinking, and eating (*dated*) **6. UNCONTROLLED WAY OF LIFE** behavior that shows complete lack of control, especially financially or sexually (*archaic*) ■ *vi.* (**-ot·ed, -ot·ing, -ots**) **1. TAKE PART IN PUBLIC DISTURBANCE** to act as part of a crowd in an unruly, violent, and unrestrained way **2. BE WILD AND SELF-INDULGENT** to behave without any personal control, especially financially or sexually (*archaic*) [12thC. From Old French, "quarrel," from *rioter* "to quarrel," of uncertain origin.] ◇ **run riot 1.** to behave in a wild and uncontrolled way **2.** to grow in profusion

Ri·ot Act *n.* an English law, passed in 1713, providing that persons making a public disturbance had to disperse within one hour of having had the act read to them by a magistrate ◇ **read (somebody) the riot act** to reprimand somebody severely for doing something, often including a threat of punishment if the offending behavior does not stop

ri·ot gun *n.* a short-barrelled gun used to disperse crowds. It fires plastic or rubber bullets.

ri·ot·ous /rí ətəss/ *adj.* **1. UNRESTRAINED** loud, conspicuous, and unrestrained **2. RIOTING OR LIKELY TO RIOT** involved in or taking part in serious public unrest (*formal*) —**ri·ot·ous·ly** *adv.* —**ri·ot·ous·ness** *n.*

ri·ot po·lice *n.* a police reserve specially equipped for controlling a rioting crowd

rip[1] /rip/ *v.* (**rips, ripped, rip·ping, rips**) **1.** *vti.* **TEAR OR BE TORN** to tear something or become torn with a sudden or rough splitting action, especially occurring accidentally and usually accompanied by a distinct tearing noise **2.** *vt.* **USE FORCE TO REMOVE SOMETHING** to remove something from a place where it had been firmly set, especially by tearing it out forcibly without taking time or care ○ *Most of the original features of the house were ripped out.* **3.** *vi.* **MOVE WITH EXTREME SPEED** to move with dangerous or violent speed ○ *The tornado ripped through northern Nebraska.* **4.** *vt.* WOODWORK **DIVIDE TIMBER LENGTHWAYS** to make a split along the grain of a piece of wood using a saw or chopping tool ■ *n.* **1. ROUGHLY TORN PLACE** a rough tear or split, especially one that is caused suddenly and forcefully **2. RIPSAW** a ripsaw (*informal*) [14thC. Origin uncertain. Ultimately from an Indo-European base meaning "to snatch away," which is also the ancestor of English *rob* and *bereave*.] ◇ **let her rip** to proceed without hesitation or restraint (*informal*) ◇ **let rip** to speak rapidly and without restraint, especially with a series of curses (*informal*)

WORD KEY: SYNONYMS

See Synonyms at ***tear***.

rip into *vt.* to attack somebody or something, especially with a sudden and damaging criticism (*informal*)

rip off *vt.* (*informal*) **1. TREAT SOMEBODY UNFAIRLY OVER MONEY** to charge somebody an unfair price or cheat somebody financially **2. STEAL SOMETHING** to rob somebody or steal something

rip up *vt.* to tear something up with the hands into pieces or strips

rip[2] /rip/ *n.* **1. ROUGH WATER** an area of rough water caused by winds or opposing currents **2.** = **rip current, riptide** [Late 18thC. Origin uncertain: probably from RIP[1].]

rip[3] /rip/ *n.* (*archaic informal*) **1. DISSOLUTE PERSON** somebody considered to be corrupt and dissolute **2. SOMETHING OLD AND WORTHLESS** something, especially a horse, that is old and of no value [Late 18thC. Origin uncertain: perhaps an altered shortening of REPROBATE.]

R.I.P. *abbr.* rest in peace [Latin *requiescat in pace* or *requiescant in pace*]

ri·par·i·an /ri pérree ən, rī-/ *adj.* **ALONG RIVERBANK** situated or taking place along or near the bank of a river ■ *n.* **LAND OWNER BY RIVER** somebody who owns land along a river [Mid-19thC. Formed from Latin *riparius* (source of English *river*), from *ripa* "riverbank." Ultimately from an Indo-European word meaning "to cut," which is also the ancestor of *rift*[1].]

rip·cord /ríp kàwrd/ *n.* **1. CORD TO OPEN PARACHUTE** a cord that, when pulled, opens a parachute **2. CORD RELEASING GAS IN BALLOON** a cord used to release gas from a hot air balloon during an emergency

rip cur·rent *n.* a narrow current strongly flowing from the shore to the sea, visible as a band of agitated water [From RIP[2]]

ripe /rīp/ (**rip·er, rip·est**) *adj.* **1. READY AND PLEASANT TO EAT** ready to be picked and eaten because it is mature and has reached optimum flavor **2.** BOT, AGRIC **READY TO HARVEST** having developed to the stage for harvesting and subsequent storage or sale **3.** FOOD **MATURE AND MELLOW** matured enough to have developed the best flavor and body ○ *ripe cheese* **4. IMPOLITE OR LEWD** full of rude words, swearwords, sexual references, or outrageous opinions (*informal*) **5. EXACTLY READY** at the most suitable stage of preparation or development ○ *The occasion was ripe for asking for a raise* **6. ADVANCED IN YEARS** representing or constituting a long life **7. EXPERIENCED AND KNOWLEDGEABLE** showing plenty of experience and knowledge accumulated gradually over time **8. SMELLY** giving off a strong and unpleasant smell, especially caused by sweat from part of the body (*informal*) **9. FULL AND RED** full and ruddy, suggesting ripe fruit [Old English *rīpe*. Ultimately from a prehistoric Germanic word that is also the ancestor of English *reap* and *ripple*[2].] —**ripe·ly** *adv.* —**ripe·ness** *n.*

rip·en /rípən/ (**-ened, -en·ing, -ens**) *vti.* **1. MAKE OR BECOME READY TO EAT** to reach, or cause fruit or other food to reach, a ripe or mature condition **2. REACH RIGHT CONDITION** to become or make something fully developed, mature, or ready (*often passive*) —**rip·en·er** *n.* —**rip·en·ing** *adj.*, *n.*

ri·pie·no /rip yáynō/ *n.* in a baroque concerto, the full ensemble, as contrasted with the soloist or group of soloists (**concertino**) [Mid-18thC. From Italian, literally "filled up," from *pieno* "full."]

Rip·ken /rípkən/, **Cal, Jr.** (*b.* 1960) U.S. baseball player.

He broke Lou Gehrig's major league record of 2,130 consecutive games played (1995).

rip-off *n.* (*informal*) **1. UNFAIRLY PRICED ITEM** something that is not worth the price asked or paid **2. ACT OF BEING DISHONESTLY TREATED** an act or example of being cheated, tricked, or exploited **3. IMITATION OF SOMETHING** an imitation of something more inventive, successful, or famous perpetrated in order to make a financial gain based on the other's reputation

Rip·on /ríppən/ city in North Yorkshire, England, on the River Ure. Population: 13,806 (1991).

ri·poste /ri pṓst/ (**-post·ed, -post·ing, -postes**) *n.* **1. SMART ANSWER** something said or done quickly and effectively in response **2.** FENCING **QUICK FENCING THRUST** a quick deft thrust made after parrying the lunge of a fencing opponent [Early 18thC. Via French from Italian *risposta*, the past participle of *rispondere* "to respond," from Latin *respondere* (see RESPOND).]

WORD KEY: SYNONYMS

See Synonyms at ***answer***.

rip·per /ríppər/ *n.* a murderer who uses a knife to kill and mutilate people (*informal*)

rip·ping /rípping/ *adj.* *U.K.* wonderful or excellent (*dated informal*) —**rip·ping·ly** *adv.*

rip·ple[1] /rípp'l/ *v.* (**-pled, -pling, -ples**) **1.** *vti.* **FLOW IN TINY GENTLE WAVES** to flow with, or be lightly disturbed by, a succession of tiny waves moving quickly and gently ○ *a breeze rippled the water* **2.** *vti.* **SHAPE SOMETHING INTO GENTLE WAVY PATTERN** to take on or give something an appearance of very small wavy shapes across its surface or length **3.** *vi.* **MAKE LAPPING SOUND** to make a gentle lapping sound **4.** *vi.* **BE HEARD BRIEFLY AMONG CROWD** to begin as a sound made by a few people, spreading and briefly becoming slightly louder before dying away ○ *Laughter rippled around the room.* ■ *n.* **1. TINY WAVE OR SERIES OF WAVES** a small wave or series of gentle waves across a surface **2. GENTLE WAVY SHAPE OR MARK** something that resembles a ripple in its smooth undulating shape **3. GENTLE PATTERN OF SOUND** a sound that starts quietly and then spreads, becoming slightly louder for a few seconds before dying away ○ *a ripple of scorn* **4.** GEOL **SHALLOW BROKEN RIVER WATER** an area of shallow water in a river broken by rocks or sand bars **5.** ELEC **OSCILLATION OF CURRENT** a small oscillation of electrical current ■ **rip·ples** *npl.* **CONSEQUENCES** a series of repercussions or consequences ○ *The ripples of the sector's downturn continue to be felt.* ■ *adj.* FOOD **WITH SECOND FLAVOR MIXED IN** with a second flavor partly combined or marbled through ○ *raspberry ripple ice cream* [Late 17thC. Origin unknown.] —**rip·pler** *n.* —**rip·ply** *adj.*

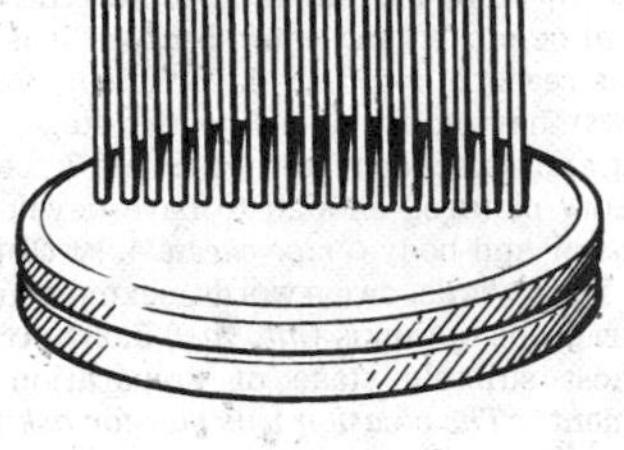

Ripple

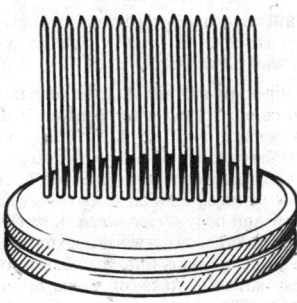

rip·ple[2] /rípp'l/ *vt.* (**-pled, -pling, -ples**) **REMOVE PLANT'S SEEDS** to use a comb-shaped tool to remove seeds from a plant ■ *n.* **TOOL TO REMOVE PLANT'S SEEDS** a comb-shaped tool used to remove seeds from a plant [Mid-17thC. Origin uncertain.]

rip·ple ef·fect *n.* a spreading series of effects or consequences caused by a single event [From the ripples that spread across the surface of a pool when something is dropped into the water]

rip·ple mark *n.* a series of small wavy ridges created in sand or silt by wind or water. Ripple marks can be preserved in sedimentary rocks. —**rip·ple-marked** *adj.*

rip·plet /rípplət/ *n.* a small ripple (*literary*)

rip·rap /ríp ràp/ *n.* **1. BROKEN STONE USED IN CONSTRUCTION** broken stone used in making protective foundations and embankments for riverbeds and riverbanks **2. SOMETHING BUILT OF BROKEN STONE** a protective foundation or embankment made from broken stone loosely or irregularly combined ■ *vt.* (**-rapped, -rap·ping, -raps**) **CONSTRUCT SOMETHING WITH BROKEN STONE** to build or strengthen a riverbed or riverbank with broken stone [Late 16thC. Doubling of RAP[1].]

rip-roar·ing *adj.* full of boisterous excitement or energy (*informal*) [Mid-19thC. Formed from RIP[1] + UPROAROUS.] —**rip-roar·ing·ly** *adv.*

rip·saw /ríp sàw/ *n.* a saw with coarse teeth used to cut along the grain of wood

rip·snort·er /ríp snàwrtər/ *n.* something or somebody exceptionally impressive (*informal*) [Mid-19thC. Formed from RIP[1] + SNORT "something big and impressive."]

rip·stop /ríp stòp/ *adj.* woven with extra threads to make tearing less likely ○ *ripstop nylon*

rip·tide /ríp tīd/ *n.* a strong narrow tide that opposes other currents and produces turbulence, especially sea water that rushes seaward after incoming waves mount up on the shore [From RIP[2]]

Rip·u·ar·i·an /rìppyoo áiree ən/ *adj.* belonging or relating to the Frankish people who lived beside the Rhine in the 4th century B.C. [Late 18thC. Formed from medieval Latin *Ripuarius*, of unknown origin.]

RISC /risk/ *abbr.* reduced-instruction-set computer

rise /rīz/ *v.* (**rose** /rōz/, **ris·en** /rízz'n/, **ris·ing, ris·es**) **1.** *vi.* **STAND UP** to assume a standing or nearly vertical position after sitting, kneeling, or lying **2.** *vi.* **ASCEND** to go up to a higher position or location ○ *Disturbed by our footsteps, the birds rose above the trees.* **3.** *vi.* **GET HIGHER** to gain a greater height or level ○ *After heavy rains the river rose dangerously.* **4.** *vi.* **GROW LARGER** to increase in amount, degree, or quantity ○ *Prices are rising.* **5.** *vi.* **ACHIEVE GREATER SOCIAL PROMINENCE** to achieve higher wealth, status, or importance ○ *He rose steadily through the ranks.* **6.** *vi.* **EXTEND UPWARD** to become elevated or extend upward ○ *The church tower rose above the village.* **7.** *vi.* **GROW LOUDER OR MORE INTENSE** to increase in volume or intensity of sound ○ *Their voices rose.* **8.** *vi.* **BECOME MENTALLY MORE INTENSE** to become more intense or powerful in the mind ○ *Her spirits rose.* **9.** *vi.* **GROW OR INTENSIFY** to grow or intensify, especially until a particular state is reached ○ *By morning a blizzard had risen.* **10.** *vi.* **BECOME LARGER AND PUFFIER** to swell and puff out, e.g., in the manner of dough containing yeast ○ *The bread is rising.* **11.** *vi.* **REBEL OR REVOLT** to make an organized rebellion against something or somebody ○ *They rose against the government.* **12.** *vi.* **END A MEETING** to adjourn after a meeting or assembly **13.** *vi.* **BECOME ERECT** to become stiff and erect ○ *He felt the hair rise on the back of his neck.* **14.** *vi.* **ORIGINATE** to have an origin or beginning ○ *The stream rises a few miles back.* **15.** *vi.* **GROW** to spring up or grow **16.** *vi.* **BECOME APPARENT** to become visible or apparent ○ *After many days at sea, Africa rose before their astonished eyes.* **17.** *vi.* BUILDING **BE BUILT** to become larger during the process of building **18.** *vi.* ASTRON **APPEAR OVER HORIZON** to appear above the horizon ○ *The sun was rising when we went to bed.* **19.** *vt.* NAUT = **raise** *v.* **19** **20.** *vi.* **BE RESURRECTED** to become resurrected ○ *rise from the dead* ■ *n.* **1. INCREASE** an increase in amount ○ *a rise in prices* **2. PROCESS OF BEING NOTICED** the process of becoming noticed and successful ○ *the rise of a new talent* **3. INCREASE IN SOCIAL IMPORTANCE** an increase in wealth, status, or importance ○ *the rise and fall of the empire* **4. UPWARD SLOPE** an upward slope or gradient ○ *a rise in the road* **5. HIGHER GROUND** a hill or piece of raised or rising ground **6. UPWARD MOVEMENT** an ascent or upward movement **7. INCREASE IN A QUALITY** an increase in degree, intensity, or force ○ *a rise in her fever* **8. INCREASE OF SOUND** an increase in loudness or pitch **9. HEIGHT** the vertical extent of something **10.** ASTRON **APPEARANCE ABOVE HORIZON** the appearance of something above the horizon **11. ORIGIN** a beginning or origin of something **12. REBELLION** a rebellion against authority **13.** *U.K.* **SALARY INCREASE** an increase in salary or wages **14.** CLOTHES **DISTANCE BETWEEN CROTCH AND WAIST** the length between the crotch and the waist of a pair of pants [Old English *rīsan*. Ultimately from a prehistoric Germanic word that is also the ancestor of English *raise* and *rear*[1].] ◇ **give rise to something** to cause something ◇ **take** *or* **get a rise out of somebody** to produce a desired response, usually anger or annoyance, by teasing or taunting somebody (*informal*)

rise above *vt.* to overcome something unpleasant by not letting it become too important

rise to *vt.* to behave well in response to a challenge or difficulty (*informal*) ○ *rose to the occasion*

ris·er /rízər/ *n.* **1. SOMEBODY WHO RISES FROM BED** somebody who gets up in a particular way after sleeping for the night ○ *We are late risers on weekends.* **2. VERTICAL PART OF STEP** the vertical part of a step or stair **3.** CONSTR **VERTICAL PIPE** a vertical pipe, duct, or conduit **4. SOMEBODY RISING** somebody who or something that rises

ris·i·bil·i·ty /rìzzə bíllətee/ (*plural* **-ties**) *n.* **1. ABILITY TO LAUGH** an ability or tendency to laugh (*formal*) ○ *"I believe that the humorous peculiarities of my countenance excited the infant's risibilities; at any rate, the young mother assured me that he smiled when he looked at me."* (George van Schaick, *A Top-Floor Idyl*; 1917) **2. LUDICROUSNESS** laughable or ludicrous quality

ris·i·ble /rízzəb'l/ *adj.* **1. LUDICROUS** causing or capable of causing laughter **2. INCLINED TO LAUGH** able or inclined to laugh (*formal*) [Mid-16thC. From late Latin *risibilis*, from Latin *ris-*, the past participle stem of *ridere* "to laugh" (source of English *ridiculous*).]

ris·ing /rízing/ *adj.* **1. GETTING MORE IMPORTANT** becoming increasingly respected or significant in an occupation or activity **2. BECOMING POWERFUL** becoming more influential and powerful **3. GETTING HIGHER** going up or becoming higher ■ *n.* **1. REVOLT** a rebellion or revolt **2. SOMETHING GETTING HIGHER** something that rises in height **3. UPWARD MOVEMENT** the action of something that moves upward or to a higher level **4. ACTION OF STANDING UP** the action of assuming a standing or nearly vertical position after sitting, kneeling, or lying **5.** FOOD **LEAVENING PROCESS** the process of leavening bread

ris·ing damp *n.* moisture that is absorbed from the ground into walls, resulting in structural damage

ris·ing diph·thong *n.* a diphthong in which the second of two sounds has more stress or sonority than the first

ris·ing rhythm *n.* a rhythmic pattern produced by a succession of metrical feet, each foot having an accented syllable preceded by one or more syllables that are unaccented

ris·ing trot *n.* a horse-riding technique used while trotting, in which the rider rises from the saddle every second beat. ◊ **sitting trot**

risk /risk/ *n.* **1. CHANCE OF SOMETHING GOING WRONG** the danger that injury, damage, or loss will occur **2. SOMEBODY OR SOMETHING HAZARDOUS** somebody or something likely to cause injury, damage, or loss **3.** INSUR **CHANCE OF LOSS TO INSURER** the probability, amount, or type of possible loss incurred and covered by an insurer **4.** FIN **POSSIBILITY OF INVESTMENT LOSS** the possibility of loss in an investment or speculation **5. STATISTICAL ODDS OF DANGER** the statistical chance of danger from something, especially from the failure of an engineered system ■ *vt.* (**risked, risk·ing, risks**) **1. PUT SOMETHING IN DANGER** to place something valued in a position or situation where it could be damaged or lost, or exposed to damage or loss **2. DO SOMETHING DESPITE DANGER** to incur the chance of harm or loss by taking an action [Mid-17thC. Via French *risque* from Italian *rischo*, from *rischiare* "to run into danger," of uncertain origin.] —**risk·er** *n.* ◇ **at risk 1.** in danger of damage or loss **2.** SOC SCI in danger of being harmed or of harming others ◇ **run** *or* **take a risk** to do something that involves the possibility of injury, damage, or harm

risk ar·bi·trage *n.* the technique of using price discrepancies in a market in order to profit, e.g., by buying shares in a company being acquired while selling shares in the acquiring company —**risk ar·bi·tra·geur** *n.*

risk-ben·e·fit *adj.* studying or testing whether the benefits of a procedure, process, or treatment outweigh the risks involved

risk cap·i·tal *n.* = **venture capital**

risk fac·tor *n.* a feature of somebody's habits, genetic makeup, or personal history that increases the probability that disease or harm to health will occur

risk man·age·ment *n.* the profession or technique of determining, minimizing, and preventing accidental loss in a business, e.g., by taking safety measures and buying insurance

risk·y /rískee/ (**-i·er, -i·est**) *adj.* likely to cause damage, injury, or loss —**risk·i·ly** *adv.* —**risk·i·ness** *n.*

Ri·sor·gi·men·to /ree sàwrjə mén tō/ *n.* the movement for, and period of, political unification in Italy beginning about 1750 and culminating in the occupation of Rome by Italian troops in 1870 [Late 19thC. From Italian, literally "resurgence."]

ri·sot·to /ri zóttō/ (*plural* **-tos**) *n.* a moist Italian dish of short-grained rice and other ingredients cooked gently in stock [Mid-19thC. From Italian, formed from *riso* (see RICE).]

ris·qué /ri skáy/ *adj.* alluding to sexual conduct in a way that is close to being indecent or in bad taste [Mid-19thC. From French, the past participle of *risquer* "to risk," from *risque* (see RISK).]

Riss /riss/ *n.* one of the four major glacial periods in Europe, at its peak 150,000 years ago [Early 20thC. Named for the river *Riss*, a tributary of the Danube in Germany where signs of the glaciation were observed.]

ris·sole /ri sṓl, rí sṑl/ *n.* a small fried cake of minced seasoned meat or poultry, often coated or mixed with breadcrumbs [Early 18thC. Via French from assumed Vulgar Latin *russeola (pasta)* "reddish (pastry)," from Latin *russus* "red."]

ri·sus sar·don·i·cus /reéssəss saár dónnikəss/ *n.* a distorted grinning expression caused by involuntary prolonged contraction of the facial muscles, especially as a result of tetanus [From modern Latin, literally "sardonic grin"]

rit. *abbr.* **1.** ritardando **2.** ritenuto

Rit·a·lin /ríttʹlin/ *tdmk.* a trademark for methylphenidate

ri·tar·dan·do /reè taar daán dō/ *adj., adv.* becoming gradually slower (*used as a musical direction*) [Early 19thC. From Italian, the present participle of *ritardare* "to slow down," from Latin *retardare* (see RETARD).]

rite /rīt/ *n.* **1. CEREMONIAL ACT** a solemn and ceremonial act or procedure that follows the rule customary to a community, especially a religious group (*often used in the plural*) ○ *the rite of baptism* **2. FORMAL PROCEDURE** a formal, customary observance or procedure (*often used in the plural*) ○ *rites of courtship* **3. CEREMONIAL WAY OF PROCEEDING** a system of ceremonial procedure ○ *Roman rite* **4. rite, Rite** CHR **LITURGICAL PROCEDURE** a liturgy or version of a liturgy, especially of a Eucharistic service **5. rite, Rite** CHR **DIVISION OF CHURCHES** a historical division of Christian churches based on their liturgies [14thC. Directly or via French from Latin *ritus*. Ultimately from an Indo-European base meaning "to fit together," which is also the ancestor of English *arithmetic* and *rhyme*.]

ri·te·nu·to /reètə nóotō/ *adj., adv.* played slightly slower than the rest of a piece of music (*used as a musical direction*) [Early 19thC. From Italian, "held back."]

rite of pas·sage *n.* **1. SIGNIFICANT TRANSITIONAL EVENT** an event or act that marks a significant transition in a human life **2.** ANTHROP **CEREMONY MARKING CHANGED STATUS** a ceremony that marks somebody's passage from one stage of life to another, e.g., from childhood to puberty or from unmarried to married life [Translation of French *rite de passage*]

ri·tor·nel·lo /reè tawr néllō/ (*plural* **-los** *or* **-li** /-néllee/) *n.* **1. MUSICAL REFRAIN** a short musical passage used as an orchestral refrain between verses of a song or aria **2. RETURN OF ORCHESTRAL MUSIC AFTER SOLO** in a concerto grosso, the return of full orchestral music after a solo [Late 17thC. From Italian, literally "little return."]

rit·u·al /ríchoo əl/ *n.* **1. ESTABLISHED FORMAL BEHAVIOR** an established and prescribed pattern of observance, e.g., in a religion **2. ACTIONS DONE FORMALLY AND REPEATEDLY** the performance of actions or procedures in a set, ordered, and ceremonial way (*often used before a noun*) ○ *a ritual dance* **3. UNCHANGING PATTERN** a formalized pattern of actions or words followed regularly and precisely (*informal*) ○ *the weekend car-washing ritual* **4.** BIOL **SET FORM OF COMMUNICATION** a set sequence of actions that an animal uses to communicate information or to reinforce social cohesion ○ *mating rituals* **5.** PSYCHOL **REPETITIVE BEHAVIOR** an inflexible, stylized, and often repetitive sequence of actions, e.g., repeated hand-washing, that may indicate an obsession **6. BOOK OF CEREMONIES** a book containing rites or ceremonial procedures, especially religious rites ■ *adj.* **CONCERNED WITH RITE** concerned with or practicing a rite ○ *ritual observance* [Late 16thC. From Latin *ritualis*, from *ritus* (see RITE).] —**rit·u·al·ly** *adv.*

rit·u·al a·buse *n.* the alleged physical or alleged abuse of children by adults taking part in supposed satanic rituals

rit·u·al·ism /ríchoo ə lìzzəm/ *n.* a devotion or adherence to rituals

rit·u·al·is·tic /rìchoo ə lístik/ *adj.* forming part of or adhering to a ritual —**rit·u·al·is·ti·cal·ly** *adv.*

rit·u·al·i·za·tion /rìchoo əli záysh'n/ *n.* **1. TURNING SOMETHING INTO RITUAL** the act of making something into a ritual **2.** ETHNOL **PROCESS OF MODIFYING BEHAVIOR INTO RITUALS** the process in which different forms of behavior are modified and combined to form a ritual

rit·u·al·ize /ríchoo ə lìz/ (**-ized, -iz·ing, -iz·es**) *v.* **1.** *vt.* **MAKE SOMETHING A RITUAL** to make a ritual of something **2.** *vi.* **PROMOTE RITUALS** to promote the use of rituals

rit·u·al mur·der *n.* **1.** RELIG **OFFERING OF HUMAN LIFE** a human sacrifice, especially to appease a deity **2.** CRIMINOL **MURDER WITH RITUALISTIC APPEARANCE** a murder performed in a methodical, formalized, or ritualistic way

ritz /rits/ *n.* an extravagant or ostentatious show or display of something (*informal*) [Early 20thC. Back-formation from RITZY.] ◇ **put on the ritz** to make a show of wealth and extravagance (*dated informal*)

ritz·y /rítsee/ (**-i·er, -i·est**) *adj.* expensively stylish and elegant (*informal*) [Early 20thC. Formed from *Ritz*, name of the luxurious hotels established by the Swiss-born entrepreneur César *Ritz* (1850–1918).] —**ritz·i·ly** *adv.* —**ritz·i·ness** *n.*

riv. *abbr.* river

riv·age /rívvij/ *n.* a shore, coastline, or bank (*archaic literary*) [13thC. From French, formed from *rive* "bank," from Latin *ripa* (see RIPARIAN).]

ri·val /rívʹl/ *n.* **1. COMPETING PERSON OR GROUP** a person or group competing with another for something or somebody **2. SOMEBODY EQUAL OR BETTER** somebody who or something that can equal or surpass another in a particular respect ■ *v.* (**-valed, -val·ing, -vals**) **1.** *vt.* **EQUAL OR SURPASS** to equal or better somebody or something in a particular respect **2.** *vti.* **COMPETE** to compete with somebody **3.** *vt.* **TRY TO EQUAL** to try to equal or surpass somebody or something in a particular respect ■ *adj.* **COMPETING** competing with somebody or something [Late 16thC. From Latin *rivalis*, literally "using the same stream," from *rivus* "stream" (source of English *derive*). Ultimately from an Indo-European word that is also the ancestor of English *run*.] —**ri·val·rous** *adj.*

WORD KEY: CULTURAL NOTE

The Rivals, a play by Irish dramatist Richard Brinsley Sheridan (1775). This lively comedy of manners portrays the attempts of Captain Jack Absolute to woo Lydia Languish, the idealistic niece and ward of Mrs. Malaprop. The latter's habit of misusing similar-sounding words created one of the most memorable characters in English drama and gave rise to a new term: *malapropism*.

ri·val·ry /rívəlree/ (*plural* **-ries**) *n.* **1. CONDITION OF COMPETITIVENESS** the condition or fact of competing with somebody or something **2. COMPETITIVE ACTION** an act of competitiveness

rive /rīv/ (**rived, riv·en** /rívv'n/ *or* **rived, riv·ing, rives**) *v.* **1.** *vt.* **TEAR SOMETHING APART** to tear something apart (*archaic*) **2.** *vti.* **SPLIT** to split or become split (*literary*) [12thC. From Old Norse *rífa*. Ultimately from an Indo-European base meaning "to cut," which is also the ancestor of English *rift* and *river*.]

riv·en *adj.* torn apart (*literary*) ○ *a political party riven by dissent* [Past participle of RIVE]

riv·er /rívvər/ *n.* **1.** GEOG **LARGE NATURAL CHANNEL OF WATER** a natural formation in which fresh water forms a wide stream that runs across the land until it reaches the sea or another area of water **2. FLOW** a large flow or stream of something (*often used in the plural*) ○ *a river of mud* [13thC. Via Anglo-Norman *rivere* from, ultimately, Latin *riparius* (see RIPARIAN).] ◇ **sell somebody down the river** to betray or desert somebody, usually for a selfish or mercenary motive (*informal*)

Ri·ve·ra /ri vérrə/, **Diego** (1886–1957) Mexican artist. He is known for his murals portraying Mexican social issues, influenced by Native American art.

riv·er·bank /rívvər bàngk/ *n.* a piece of sloping ground at the edge of a river

riv·er ba·sin *n.* a large area of land that drains exclusively to a particular river

riv·er·bed /rívvər bèd/ *n.* the ground or part of the ground covered by a river along its course and between its banks

WORLD'S LONGEST RIVERS

	River	Length	Location
1	Nile	[4,160 mi. / 6,695 km]	Africa
2	Amazon	[4,000 mi. / 6,400 km]	South America
3	Yangtze (Chang Jiang)	[3,900 mi. / 6,300 km]	Asia
4	Mississippi-Missouri	[3,710 mi. / 5,970 km]	North America
5	Huang He (Yellow River)	[3,395 mi. / 5,464 km]	Asia
6	Ob'-Irtysh	[3,362 mi. / 5,410 km]	Asia
7	Congo	[2,710 mi. /4,374 km]	Africa
8	Amur	[2,700 mi. /4,345 km]	Asia
8	Lena	[2,700 mi. /4,400 km]	Asia
10	Mekong	[2,600 mi. /4,200 km]	Asia
10	Niger	[2,600 mi. /4,200 km]	Africa

CORBIS/Bettmann
Diego Rivera

riv·er birch *n.* a tree of the eastern United States, found on the banks of rivers and streams, that has a fissured reddish brown lower trunk and smooth pinkish upper trunk and branches. The river birch is grown as an ornamental, and the wood is used to make furniture and other items. Latin name: *Betula nigra*.

riv·er blind·ness *n.* = **onchocerciasis**

riv·er·boat /rívvər bṑt/ *n.* a boat built with a flat bottom or shallow draft, used for traveling on rivers

riv·er catch·ment *n.* = **river basin**

riv·er·front /rívvər frùnt/ *n.* the area of a town, property, or built-up area directly facing a river

riv·er·head /rívvər hèd/ *n.* the upstream source of a river or the area of land around it

Rive·rina /rìvvə reénə/ region in southern New South Wales, Australia. It is heavily irrigated and predominantly agricultural.

riv·er·ine /rívvə rīn, -reèn/ *adj.* **1. OF A RIVER** relating to or produced by a river **2. BESIDE A RIVER** located beside a river

Riv·ers /rívvərz/, **Larry** (*b.* 1923) U.S. artist. A versatile painter and sculptor, he was both an early exponent of pop art, a realist, and an abstract expressionist. Real name **Yitzroch Loisa Grossberg**

riv·er·side /rívvər sìd/ *n.* LAND BY RIVER the area of land beside a river ■ *adj.* BY A RIVER located beside a river

Riv·er·side /rívvər sìd/ city in southwestern California, on the Santa Ana River. It is a citrus-growing center, and is home to the University of California-Riverside. Population: 241,644 (1994).

riv·er·ward /rívvərwərd/, **riv·er·wards** /-wərdz/ *adv., adj.* moving or facing toward a river (*literary*)

riv·er·weed /rívvər weed/ *n.* a small many-branched freshwater plant that clings to rock with roots that function as suckers. Genus: *Podostema.*

riv·et /rívvit/ *n.* SHORT METAL FASTENING a fastening in the form of a short metal rod with a head. The shaft is passed through holes in materials and flattened into a second head on the other side. Rivets are commonly used in aircraft, building, and bridge construction. ■ *vt.* (**-et·ed, -et·ing, -ets**) **1.** FIRMLY FIX ATTENTION to fix or hold the attention completely (*informal; often passive*) **2.** FASTEN WITH RIVET to fasten something using a rivet or rivets **3.** PULL AND HOLD ONTO SOMETHING FIRMLY to draw and hold people's eyes or attention in a powerful, absorbing way (*informal*) ○ *"Old Grannis dared not move, but sat rigid, his eyes riveted on his empty soup plate."* (Frank Norris, *McTeague – A Story of San Francisco*; 1899) **4.** FIX SOMETHING FIRMLY to fix or secure something firmly [14thC. From Old French, formed from *river* "to fasten," of unknown origin.]

riv·et·ing /rívviting/ *adj.* completely fixing and holding the attention (*informal*) —**riv·et·ing·ly** *adv.*

riv·i·er·a /rìvvee érrə/ *n.* a stretch of coastland where the climate and beaches are good and there are fashionable resort towns

ri·vière /rìvvee áir, ri vyáir/ *n.* a necklace made of a string of diamonds or other gemstones that gradually increase in size up to a large centered gem [Mid-19thC. Via French, literally "river," from, ultimately, Latin *riparius* (see RIPARIAN).]

Riv·ière-du-Loup /ree vvyàir dyoo lóo/ city in Quebec, Canada, on the southern shore of the St. Lawrence River. Population: 22,378 (1996).

riv·u·let /rívvyələt/ *n.* **1.** LITTLE STREAM a small stream of flowing water (*literary*) **2.** SMALL FLOW a small quick-flowing stream of something [Late 16thC. Origin uncertain: perhaps via Italian *rivoletto*, literally "little stream," from, ultimately, Latin *rivus* (see RIVAL).]

rix-dol·lar /ríks-/ *n.* any of several silver coins formerly used in Denmark, the Netherlands, and Germany [Late 16thC. From obsolete Dutch *rijksdaler* "dollar of the realm."]

Ri·yadh /ree yaad/ capital city of Saudi Arabia, located in the eastern central part of the country. Population: 2,500,000 (1994).

ri·yal *n.* MONEY = **rial**

RJ *abbr.* road junction

RL *abbr.* real life (*used in e-mail and Internet chat*)

Rm *abbr.* BIBLE Romans

RM *abbr.* **1.** Madagascar (*international vehicle registration*) **2.** Registered Midwife

rm. *abbr.* **1.** ream **2.** room

rms *abbr.* root mean square

RMS *abbr.* **1.** Royal Mail Ship **2. RMS, R.M.S.** Railway Mail Service **3. RMS, R.M.S.** Royal Mail Service

Rn *symbol.* radon

RN, R.N. *abbr.* **1.** MED registered nurse **2.** NAVY Royal Navy

RNA *n.* a nucleic acid that contains the sugar ribose, is found in all living cells, and is essential for the manufacture of proteins according to the instructions carried by genes. RNA also acts instead of DNA as the genetic material in certain viruses. Full form **ribonucleic acid**

RNA pol·y·mer·ase *n.* a polymerase, found in living cells, that catalyzes the synthesis of RNA from its constituent nucleotides, using DNA or RNA as a template

RN·ase *abbr.* ribonuclease

RNA vi·rus *n.* a virus in which the core of nucleic acid consists of RNA

R'n'B, R & B *abbr.* rhythm and blues

rnd, rnd. *abbr.* round

RNP *abbr.* ribonucleoprotein

ro. *abbr.* MEASURE rood

roach[1] /rōch/ (*plural* **roach** *or* **roach·es**) *n.* **1.** FOOD FISH a northern European freshwater fish of the carp family that has an olive-green or gray-green back and reddish fins. It is a popular game fish. Latin name: *Rutilus rutilus.* **2.** SMALL N AMERICAN FISH a small sunfish of eastern North America that resembles a European roach. Latin name: *Hesperoleucus symmetricus.* [12thC. From Old French *roche*, of unknown origin.]

roach[2] /rōch/ *n.* **1.** INSECTS COCKROACH a cockroach (*informal*) **2.** DRUGS MARIJUANA CIGARETTE BUTT the end of a marijuana cigarette after the rest of it has been smoked (*slang*) [Mid-19thC. Shortening of COCKROACH.]

roach[3] /rōch/ *n.* SAILING CURVE OF SAIL the upward curve at the foot of a square sail ■ *vt.* (**roached, roach·ing, roach·es**) EQU CUT HORSE'S MANE to cut a horse's mane short so that the hairs stand up [Late 18thC. Origin uncertain: perhaps from ROACH[1], perhaps from the shape of its back.]

road /rōd/ *n.* **1.** HARD TRACK FOR USE OF VEHICLES a long surfaced route broad enough for vehicles to be driven on it (*often used in placenames*) **2.** COURSE OF ACTION a route or way that heads toward some predictable outcome ○ *the road to financial success* **3.** RAIL = **railroad 4.** MINING MINE TUNNEL a tunnel used for hauling coal or ore in a mine **5.** SHIPPING = **roadstead** (*often used in the plural*) [Old English *rād* "a riding" (source also of English *raid*). Ultimately from an Indo-European word meaning "to ride," which is also the ancestor of English *ride* and *ready*.] ◇ **down the road** in the future ◇ **one for the road** an alcoholic drink taken just before leaving (*informal*) ◇ **on the road** traveling from place to place ○ *The band has been on the road all summer.*

WORD KEY: CULTURAL NOTE

On the Road, a novel by Jack Kerouac (1957). A thinly disguised and rapidly composed memoir, it describes a series of cross-country trips undertaken by a group of people united by their quest for new experiences and disregard for traditional values. It is both an engaging chronicle of the Beat generation and a lyrical evocation of the energy and passion of youth.

road·a·bil·i·ty /rōdə bílləteе/ *n.* the ability of a motor vehicle to maintain a steady, balanced, and comfortable ride over a variety of routes

road ap·ple *n.* a round piece of horse manure on a road (*informal*)

road·bed /rōd bèd/ *n.* a foundation of soil, cinders, or crushed rock that supports a road or railroad

road·block /rōd blòk/ *n.* **1.** BARRIER ACROSS ROAD TO STOP TRAFFIC a temporary barrier used to prevent vehicles from continuing along a road so that they can be checked or their drivers questioned, usually by police or military personnel **2.** OBSTACLE a hindrance or obstacle to something

road com·pa·ny *n.* a group of actors who tour with a show, usually performing a play that has been successful in a large city

road·e·o /rōdee ō/ (*plural* **-os**) *n.* a competition in driving skill for professional truck drivers [Mid-20thC. Alteration of RODEO.]

road hock·ey *n. Can* a game that uses the rules of ice hockey and is played on a road or street by children wearing shoes or in-line skates

road hog *n.* somebody who drives in an inconsiderate and dangerous way, usually by refusing to let other motorists pass or go first, or by forcing them to move out of the way (*informal*)

road·house /rōd hòwss/ (*plural* **-hous·es** /-hòwzəz/) *n.* a hotel or tavern located beside a main road (*dated*)

road·ie /rōdee/ *n.* somebody who loads, unloads, and sets up the equipment used by a musical or theatrical group on tour, especially a rock band

road·kill /rōd kìl/ *n.* a bird or animal that has been hit and killed by a motor vehicle on the road

road map /rōd map/, **road·map** *n.* **1.** MAP SHOWING ROADS a motorists' map or atlas that shows routes, mileage, and often other features of interest to travelers **2.** GUIDE a plan or guide for something (*informal*) ○ *"the national bank at a profit sells roadmaps for the soul to the old folks home"* (Bob Dylan, *Lyrics 1962–85*; 1987)

road met·al *n.* the cinders, crushed rock, and other materials used in the construction of roads

road mov·ie *n.* a movie that depicts the adventures of a person or people who leave home and travel from place to place by road, often to find or escape from something

road rac·ing *n.* a race for motor vehicles or bicycles that takes place on a public road temporarily reserved for the purpose, or on a racing course resembling a public road

Roadrunner

road·run·ner /rōd rùnnər/ *n.* a swift-running bird of the cuckoo family, found in deserts of the western United States and Mexico. It has streaked brown-and-white plumage, a head crest, small, round wings, and a long tail. Latin name: *Geococcyx californianus.*

road show /rōd shō/, **road·show** *n.* **1.** THEATER PERFORMANCE BY TRAVELING ACTORS a show staged by a touring company of entertainers, or the company performing such a show **2.** BROADCAST TRAVELING RADIO BROADCAST a live open-air radio show that travels to a series of locations. The following location is announced in advance to ensure an audience. **3.** TRAVELING PROMOTIONAL GROUP a group of people who travel from place to place in order to broadcast, publicize, or promote something, or to conduct a political campaign

road·stead /rōd stèd/ *n.* a partly sheltered area for anchored vessels

road·ster /rōdstər/ *n.* **1.** CARS SPORTS CAR a small open-topped car with a single seat in front and often with an additional folding seat (**rumble seat**) at the back (*dated*) **2.** EQU HORSE FOR RIDING ON ROAD a sturdy horse for riding on a road (*archaic*)

road test *n.* **1.** CARS TEST OF VEHICLE OR TIRE PERFORMANCE a test of a motor vehicle or tire under actual operating conditions **2.** CARS PRACTICAL DRIVING TEST an offical test on the road to determine whether a driver of a motor vehicle is competent to be issued a license to drive **3.** MANUF TEST OF HOW WELL SOMETHING WORKS a series of tests carried out on a new product or design to determine how well it performs during actual use

road-test *vt.* to carry out a test of a vehicle or other product under actual operating conditions

road·way /rōd wày/ *n.* the main part of a road area meant to be driven on

road·work /rōd wùrk/ *n.* **1.** TRANSP REPAIRS TO A ROAD construction or repair work being carried out on a section of public road, or on the utilities located near it, creating a temporary obstruction for road users **2.** SPORTS TRAINING EXERCISE a form of exercise consisting of long runs on roads, chiefly used as part of training for boxers

road·wor·thi·ness /rōd wùrtheenəss/ *n.* the condition of a motor vehicle in terms of whether it can be driven safely on public roads

road·wor·thy /rōd wùrthee/ *adj.* in a safe condition to be driven on public roads [Early 19thC. Modeled on "seaworthy."]

roam /rōm/ *vti.* (**roamed, roam·ing, roams**) WANDER AIMLESSLY to move over a large area, especially without any particular purpose or definite destination ■ *n.* AIMLESS WANDER an act of roaming [14thC. Origin unknown.] —**roam·er** *n.*

roan /rōn/ *adj.* WITH LIGHT SPECKLES IN DARK COAT having a reddish brown, brown, or black coat speckled with white or gray hairs ○ *a* ■ *n.* **1.** ROAN HORSE an animal, especially a horse, that has a roan coat **2.** COLORS ROAN COLOR the color of a roan animal **3.** INDUST FINE-GRAINED LEATHER a soft pliable kind of sheepskin leather used in bookbinding. It has a close grain resembling that of morocco. [Early 16thC. Via French from Old

Spanish *roano*, of uncertain origin: possibly from Germanic.]

Ro·a·noke /rṓ ə nṑk/ **1.** river in the United States, rising in western Virginia and flowing through eastern North Carolina to Albemarle Sound. Length: 410 mi./660 km. **2.** city in southwestern Virginia, on the Roanoke River. Population: 96,397 (1990).

roar /rawr/ *v.* (**roared, roar·ing, roars**) **1.** *vi.* **GROWL LOUDLY** to make a loud natural growling noise, e.g., as a lion makes **2.** *vti.* **SHOUT LOUDLY** to make a loud shouting noise, or utter something with a loud shouting noise, especially in anger **3.** *vi.* **LAUGH LOUDLY** to give a loud, prolonged, and unrestrained laugh **4.** *vi.* **BURN NOISILY** to burn noisily while giving off a lot of heat ○ *a roaring fire* **5.** *vi.* **CRASH LOUDLY** to make a loud crashing or blowing noise, e.g., as wind, waves, and other natural phenomena do **6.** *vi.* VET **BREATHE NOISILY** to breathe with difficulty, making a rasping or wheezing noise, as some diseased horses do **7.** *vi.* **MOVE NOISILY** to move quickly and with a loud mechanical noise, especially a harsh or droning noise **8.** *vr.* **BECOME BY ROARING** to cause the voice to be in a specified condition through shouting, cheering, or making some other loud vocal noise ○ *roared themselves hoarse* ■ *n.* **1.** **LOUD SHOUT** a loud, often prolonged, shout or cry, especially one made by a person or crowd that is cheering, angry, or upset **2.** **LOUD LAUGH** a loud, prolonged, and unrestrained laugh **3.** **LOUD GROWL** a loud growling noise made by a large animal, especially a lion **4.** **NOISE OF SOMETHING BURNING** a loud continuous noise made by something burning intensely **5.** **LOUD CRASHING NOISE** a loud crashing or blowing noise made by waves, the wind, or some other natural phenomenon [Old English *rārian*, of uncertain origin: possibly an imitation of the sound] —**roar·er** *n.*

roar·ing /ráwring/ *n.* **1.** **ACT OF MAKING ROAR** an act of making a roar **2.** VET **BREATHING DIFFICULTIES IN HORSES** noisy breathing in horses, especially when caused by paralysis of the recurrent laryngeal nerve ■ *adj.* **1.** **WITH A ROAR** making or characterized by a roar **2.** **WITH FAST SALES** selling vigorously and making a good profit ○ *It's a hot day and the ice-cream sellers are doing a roaring trade.* **3.** **HUGE** conspicuously great ○ *Her new novel proved a roaring success.* ◊ **rip-roaring** ■ *adv.* **EXCEEDINGLY** to an extreme degree —**roar·ing·ly** *adv.*

Roar·ing Twen·ties *npl.* the 1920s, especially when thought of as being a time of exuberance, hedonism, and prosperity in contrast to the hardship of World War I

roast /rōst/ *v.* (**roast·ed, roast·ing, roasts**) **1.** *vti.* COOK **COOK IN OVEN** to cook something, especially meat or vegetables, by dry heat, usually in an oven or over an open fire, basting it with fat, or be cooked in this way **2.** *vti.* COOK, INDUST **PREPARE BY DRYING OR BROWNING** to heat something until it is dry or brown, especially coffee beans or nuts, as part of a manufacturing process, or be heated in this way **3.** *vt.* METALL **HEAT ORE IN FURNACE** to heat ore in a furnace without fusing in order to concentrate, dehydrate, or purify it or to cause a chemical change that will facilitate smelting. When sulfide ores are roasted to covert them to oxides, the escaping sulfur laden gases are often used to make sulfuric acid. **4.** *vti.* **OVERHEAT** to become too warm or make something or somebody too warm at a source of heat such as the sun or a fire ○ *roast in front of the log fire* **5.** *vt.* **DISPARAGE** to criticize somebody or something harshly (*informal*) **6.** *vt.* **MOCK** to make fun of somebody (*informal*) ■ *n.* **1.** COOK, FOOD **OVEN-COOKED MEAT** something such as a piece of meat that is suitable for roasting, or that has been roasted **2.** **OPEN-AIR MEAL** an outside gathering or party with food cooked on open fires **3.** **PARTY FOR SOMEBODY** a gathering, party, or other celebration where the guest of honor is the subject of speeches that alternate between praise and humorous criticism ■ *adj.* **OVEN-COOKED** cooked by dry heat, usually in an oven or over an open fire, and basted with fat [13thC. From Old French *rostir*, of prehistoric Germanic origin.]

roast·er /rṓstər/ *n.* **1.** **SOMEBODY OR SOMETHING THAT ROASTS** somebody who or something that roasts a food or ore **2.** **SOMETHING FOR ROASTING FOOD** a pan, dish, or oven for roasting food in **3.** **ROASTED CHICKEN** an item of food, especially a chicken, that is suitable for roasting

roast·ing /rṓsting/ *adj.* **VERY HOT** feeling or causing somebody to feel very hot (*informal*) ■ *n.* **HARSH CRITICISM** a harsh criticism of somebody (*informal*) ■ *adv.* **EXTREMELY** to a high degree of temperature (*informal*) ○ *roasting hot*

rob /rob/ (**robbed, rob·bing, robs**) *v.* **1.** *vt.* **DEPRIVE SOMEBODY ILLEGALLY** to take something illegally from a person or place, especially by using force, threats, or violence **2.** *vt.* **STEAL SOMETHING** to steal something (*nonstandard*) ○ *They broke in and robbed the TV and video.* **3.** *vi.* **COMMIT ROBBERY** to commit robbery, especially habitually **4.** *vt.* **DEPRIVE SOMEBODY UNFAIRLY** to deprive somebody of something unfairly or harmfully ○ *The wet weather robbed her of her holiday.* [12thC. From Old French *rober*, from a prehistoric Germanic word that is also the ancestor of English *bereave* and *rover*.]

ro·ba·lo /rō báa lō/ (*plural* **-los** *or* **-lo**) *n.* any fish in a large diverse family that ranges from large ocean fish such as the snook to the tiny glass fish popular with aquarists. Family: Centropomidae. [Late 19thC. From Spanish *robalo*, of uncertain origin: probably from assumed *lobaro* "wolflike fish," from *lobo* "wolf," from Latin *lupus*.]

ro·band /rṓbən, rób-, rṓbənd, rób-/ *n.* a piece of rope used to attach a sail to a spar [15thC. Origin uncertain: probably from Dutch *raband*, from *ra* "sailyard" + *band* "band."]

Ro·bards /róbbərds/, **Jason** (*b.* 1922) U.S. actor. Primarily a stage actor known especially for his roles in plays by Eugene O'Neill, he also won an Academy Award for his role in the movie *All the President's Men* (1976).

rob·ber /róbbər/ *n.* somebody who commits robbery

rob·ber bar·on *n.* **1.** **UNSCRUPULOUS 19THC U.S. INDUSTRIALIST** a wealthy industrialist or businessman of the late 19th century who used unscrupulous business practices **2.** **MEDIEVAL NOBLEMAN STEALING FROM TRAVELERS** a landholding nobleman who, in feudal Europe, habitually stole from people traveling through his lands

rob·ber fly *n.* a predatory fly that catches other insects in its long bristly legs and pierces them with its sharp mouthparts. Family: Leptidae.

rob·ber·y /róbbəree/ (*plural* **-ies**) *n.* the act or an instance of illegally taking something that belongs to somebody else, especially by using force, threats, or violence

WORD KEY: SYNONYMS

See Synonyms at ***theft***.

Rob·bins /rób binz/, **Jerome** (1918–98) U.S. choreographer and theatrical director. Among the Broadway musicals he choreographed are *The King and I* (1951), *West Side Story* (1957), and *Fiddler on the Roof* (1964). Real name **Jerome Rabinowitz**

robe /rōb/ *n.* **1.** CLOTHES **CEREMONIAL DRESS** a long loose outer garment worn on ceremonial occasions or as a symbol of authority, especially by the judiciary, academics, and members of the clergy (*often used in the plural*) **2.** CLOTHES **DRESSING GOWN OR BATHROBE** a loose garment for wear at home, especially a dressing gown or bathrobe **3.** CLOTHES, CHR = **christening robe** **4.** CLOTHES, HIST **WOMAN'S OUTER DRESS** in the 17th and 18th centuries, a woman's outer dress, especially a heavy brocade and ornately decorated one worn over a plainer one **5.** ACCESSORIES **MATERIAL FOR KEEPING LEGS WARM** a fur or fabric covering for keeping the lower part of the body warm, especially while driving or riding in an open vehicle ■ *v.* (**robed, rob·ing, robes**) **1.** *vti.* **DRESS IN ROBE** to dress somebody in a robe, or be dressed in a robe **2.** *vt.* **COVER SOMETHING** to cover or adorn something ○ *robed in glory* [13thC. From Old French, literally "(clothes taken as) booty, spoil," ultimately from a prehistoric Germanic word that is also the ancestor of English *rob*.]

Rob·ert I /róbbərt thə fúrst/, **King of Scotland** (1274–1329). He fought successfully for Scottish independence from the English, whom he defeated at the Battle of Bannockburn (1314). Known as **Robert the Bruce**

Rob·ert II /róbbərt thə sékənd/, **King of Scotland** (1316–90). The grandson of Robert I , he founded the Stuart dynasty.

Rob·ert III /róbbərt thə thúrd/, **King of Scotland** (1337–1406). The son of Robert II and father of James I of Scotland, he ruled Scotland (1390–1406) during a time of civil strife and war with England.

Rob·erts /róbbərts/, **Sir Charles George Douglas** (1860–1943) Canadian poet. He wrote poems about New Brunswick and Nova Scotia.

Rob·erts, Julia (*b.* 1967) U.S. movie actor. She is best known for her role in *Pretty Woman* (1990).

Rob·erts, Owen Josephus (1875–1955) U.S. jurist. Associate justice of the United States Supreme Court (1930–45), he was a leading exponent of conservation in jurispudence.

AKG London

Paul Robeson

Robe·son /rṓbsən/, **Paul** (1898–1976) U.S. singer and actor. He acted in both musicals and Shakespeare, and gave recitals of spirituals. His openly communist sympathies and opposition to racial discrimination forced him from public life. Full name **Paul Bustill Robeson**

Robes·pierre /rṓbz peer/, **Maximilien** (1758–94) French lawyer and revolutionary. He was elected as first deputy for Paris to the National Convention after the fall of the monarchy in 1792. As commissioner of public safety (1793) he instituted the Reign of Terror and was later guillotined. Full name **Maximilien François Marie Isidore de Robespierre**

Robin

rob·in /róbbin/ *n.* **1.** **LARGE N AMERICAN THRUSH** a large North American thrush with a rust-colored breast and dark gray or brown upper parts. Latin name: *Turdus migratorius.* **2.** **EUROPEAN SONGBIRD** a small thrush, native mainly to Europe, the adult male of which has an reddish orange breast and head. Latin name: *Erithacus rubercula.* **3.** **BIRD WITH REDDISH BREAST LIKE ROBIN** a bird with a reddish breast that is similar to the European or North American robin, especially numerous Australian species [Mid-16thC. Shortening of ROBIN REDBREAST, from the name *Robin*, a diminutive of *Robert*.]

Rob·in Good·fel·low /róbbin go͝od féllō/ *n.* = **Puck**

rob·in red·breast *n.* = **robin** *n.* 1, **robin** *n.* 2

rob·in's-egg blue *n.* a pale greenish-blue color —**rob·ins-egg blue** *adj.*

Rob·in·son /róbbinss'n/, **Edward G.** (1893–1973) Romanian-born U.S. actor. He is best known as the tough-talking gangster in the movie *Little Caesar* (1930). Real name **Emmanuel Goldenberg**

Rob·in·son, Edwin Arlington (1869–1935) U.S. poet. His collection *Captain Craig and Other Poems* (1902) attracted the attention of Theodore Roosevelt. He won Pulitzer Prizes (1922, 1925, and 1928) for subsequent works.

Rob·in·son, Jackie (1919–72) U.S. baseball player and civil rights activist. He broke baseball's color barrier, stole home 19 times, and was elected to the Baseball Hall of Fame (1962). Full name **Jack Roosevelt Robinson**

Rob·in·son, Mary (*b.* 1944) Irish lawyer and politician. After her tenure as president of the Republic of Ireland (1990–97), the first woman to serve in that role, she became the United Nations High Com-

Mary Robinson

missioner for Human Rights in 1997. Born **Mary Bourke**

Rob·in·son, Sugar Ray (1921–89) U.S. boxer. He was the welterweight champion (1946–51) and middleweight champion (1951–60) of the world. Real name **Walker Smith**

Rob·in·son Cru·soe /ròbbinsən kroó sō/ *n.* the eponymous hero of Daniel Defoe's novel of 1719, in which the ingenuity, loneliness, survival, and eventual rescue of the shipwrecked sailor on a desert island are chronicled. The novel, which is often regarded as the first English novel, is based on the true story of Alexander Selkirk's five-year stay on the uninhabited island of Juan Fernandez.

Rob·in's plan·tain *n.* a plant of eastern North America with rayed purple flower heads. Latin name: *Erigeron pulchellus.* [Late 18thC. Origin unknown.]

ro·ble /rṓ blày, rṓb'l/ *n.* **1. CALIFORNIAN OAK** an oak, native to California, that has a short trunk, leathery leaves, and thin tapering acorns. Latin name: *Quercus lobata.* **2. TREE LIKE TRUE ROBLE** any of various oaks of California and Mexico similar or related to the roble [Mid-19thC. Via Spanish and Portuguese from Latin *robur* "oak tree, hardness, strength."]

rob·o·rant /róbbərənt, rṓbərənt/ *adj.* **FORTIFYING OR STRENGTHENING** used to describe medications or other remedies that have the effect of restoring somebody's strength or vigor ■ *n.* **STRENGTHENING SUBSTANCE** a medication or other remedy that restores strength or vigor [Mid-17thC. From Latin *roborant-*, present participle stem of *roborare* "to strengthen," from *robur* "oak tree, hardness, strength."]

Robot: Part of an automated car assembly line

ro·bot /rṓ bòt, -bət/ *n.* **1. MECHANICAL DEVICE PROGRAMMED TO PERFORM TASKS** any machine that can be programmed to carry out instructions and perform specified duties, especially one that can take over tasks normally done by people. These mechanical devices are best suited to sensing, gripping, and moving objects or to performing repetitive tasks such as welding. ◊ **automaton 2. IMAGINARY MACHINE LIKE HUMAN** a machine that resembles a human in appearance and can function like a human, especially in science fiction. ◊ **android 3. PERSON LIKE A MACHINE** somebody who works or behaves mechanically, showing little or no emotion and often responding to orders without question [Early 20thC. Via German from Czech, from *robota* "forced labor"; coined by Karel Čapek in his play *R.U.R.* (Rossum's Universal Robots) (1920).] —**ro·bot·ic** /rō bóttik/ *adj.* —**ro·bot·i·cal·ly** *adv.* —**ro·bo·tism** /rṓbə tìzzəm/ *n.* —**ro·bot·is·tic** /rṓbə tístik/ *adj.* —**ro·bot·like** /rṓ bòt lìk, rṓbət-/ *adj.* —**ro·bot·ry** /rṓbətree/ *n.*

ro·bot bomb *n.* a jet-propelled bomb whose flight to a target is governed by a gyroscopic guidance system, e.g., the V-1 used by Germany against London in World War II

ro·bot·ics /rō bóttiks/ *n.* the science and technology relating to computer-controlled mechanical devices, e.g., the automated tools commonly found on automobile assembly lines (*takes a singular verb*)

ro·bot·ize /rṓbə tìz/ (**-ized, -iz·ing, -iz·es**) *vt.* **1. AUTOMATE SOMETHING** to introduce automation into something, especially a factory or factory process **2. MAKE BEHAVE LIKE ROBOT** to make somebody act in an automated and unemotional or insensitive fashion —**ro·bot·i·za·tion** /rṓbəti záysh'n/ *n.*

Rob Roy /rob róy/ *n.* a cocktail made with Scotch whisky, sweet vermouth, and a dash of bitters. ◊ **Manhattan** [Mid-19thC. Named for the Scottish brigand ROB ROY.]

Rob Roy /rob róy/ (1671–1734) Scottish brigand. Forced into life as an outlaw by debts, he led raids against both the English and the Scots. His life was romanticized in a novel by Sir Walter Scot. Real name **Robert MacGregor**

ro·bust /rō búst, rṓ bùst/ *adj.* **1. STRONG AND HEALTHY** strong, healthy, and hardy in constitution **2. STRONGLY CONSTRUCTED** built, constructed, or designed to be sturdy, durable, or hard-wearing **3. NEEDING PHYSICAL STRENGTH** involving or requiring great physical strength and stamina ○ *Football is a robust sport.* **4.** FOOD **FULL-FLAVORED** rich, strong-tasting, and full-bodied **5. DETERMINED** characterized by firmness and determination and a refusal to make concessions **6. STRAIGHTFORWARD** showing clear thought and common sense **7. BLUNT OR CRUDE** rough and direct or crude **8.** COMPUT **CAPABLE OF RECOVERY** able to recover from unexpected conditions during operation ○ *a robust operating system* [Mid-16thC. From Latin *robustus* "oaken, hard, strong," from *robur* "oak tree, hardness, strength."] —**ro·bust·ly** *adv.* —**ro·bust·ness** *n.*

ro·bus·ta /rō bústə/ *n.* **1. AFRICAN COFFEE PLANT** a coffee plant, native to western central Africa, that has white flowers and red berries. Latin name: *Coffea canephora.* **2. COFFEE** beans from the robusta coffee plant, or coffee made from them [Early 20thC. From Latin, feminine of *robustus* "robust."]

ro·bus·tious /rō búschəss/ *adj.* **1. ENERGETIC** rowdy, unruly, or out of control (*old or humorous*) **2. HEALTHY** strong, healthy, and hardy in constitution (*archaic or humorous*) **3. VULGAR** vulgar or crude (*archaic or humorous*) —**ro·bus·tious·ly** *adv.* —**ro·bus·tious·ness** *n.*

roc /rok/ *n.* in Arabian legend, a large bird of prey strong enough to lift and fly with an elephant in its talons [Late 16thC. Via Arabic *rukk* from Persian *ruk*, source of English *rook*[2].]

ro·caille /rō kī́/ *n.* **1. DECORATIVE STONEWORK** decorative rococo stonework or shellwork, especially scrollwork **2.** = **rococo** [Mid-19thC. From French, literally "pebble work, rock work," from *roc* "rock" (see ROCK).]

roc·am·bole /rókəm bōl/ *n.* a leek or Europe and Asia grown for its bulb that resembles garlic and is used to flavor food. Latin name: *Allium scorodoprasum.* [Late 17thC. Via French from German *Rockenbolle* "distaff bulb" (from its shape), formed from *Rocken* "distaff" + *Bolle* "bulb."]

Roche lim·it /ráwsh-, rṓsh-/ *n.* the closest a satellite can come to the celestial body it is orbiting before being torn apart by tidal forces generated by the gravitational attraction of the celestial body. The distance varies with relative density but is approximately 2.45 times the radius of the primary for bodies of similar density. [Late 19thC. Named for Édouard *Roche* (1820–83), French astronomer who first made the calculation.]

Ro·chelle salt /rə shél-, rō-/ *n.* a white powder used in medicine as a mild laxative, as a food preservative, and in electronics. Formula: $KNaC_4H_4O_6$. [Mid-18thC. Named for *La Rochelle*, a French seaport, at which the salt is mined.]

roche mou·ton·née /rōsh moot'n áy/ *n.* an elongated mound of bare rock, modified by glacial erosion, that is smooth and striated on one side and shattered rubble on the other [Mid-19thC. From French, literally "fleecy rock" (that is, rounded like a sheep's back).]

Roch·es·ter /ráach estər/ **1.** city on the Zumbro River in southeastern Minnesota. It is the site of the Mayo Clinic, founded in 1914. Population: 70,745 (1990). **2.** city and port in western New York, south of Lake Ontario and northeast of Buffalo. Population: 221,594 (1996).

roch·et /róchət/ *n.* a white linen garment, similar to a surplice but with tight-fitting sleeves, worn on ceremonial occasions by bishops and other high-ranking members of the clergy [14thC. From Old French, "little mantle," from *roc* "mantle," of prehistoric Germanic origin.]

rock[1] /rok/ *n.* **1. HARD MINERAL AGGREGATE** any consolidated material such as granite or limestone, or unconsolidated material such as sand or mud, consisting of more than one mineral and sometimes organic material **2. PROJECTING MASS OF ROCK** a large mass of mineral material, especially an isolated or projecting one (*often used in placenames*) **3. BOULDER** a large stone or boulder **4. SOMEBODY DEPENDABLE** somebody who or something that is considered to be stable, dependable, or supportive, especially in times of trouble **5.** *U.K.* **HARD CANDY** a hard, often brightly colored, candy made from boiled sugar, usually in the form of a long cylindrical stick, sometimes with the name of a seaside resort through it **6. DIAMOND** a large gemstone, especially a diamond (*informal*) **7. CRACK COCAINE** crack cocaine, or a small piece of crack cocaine (*slang*) ■ **rocks** *npl.* **1. MONEY** money (*informal*) **2. OFFENSIVE TERM** an offensive term for the testicles (*slang offensive*) [14thC. Via Old French *ro(c)que* from assumed Vulgar Latin *rocca*, of unknown origin.] ◇ **between a rock and a hard place** faced with a choice between two equally unpleasant or undesirable alternatives ◇ **get your rocks off 1.** an offensive term meaning to have an orgasm (*slang offensive; refers to a male*) **2.** to get a great deal of pleasure or excitement from some activity (*slang offensive*) ◇ **on the rocks 1.** in great difficulties and heading for ruin or disaster, especially financially or emotionally (*informal*) **2.** served with ice cubes

rock[2] /rok/ *v.* (**rocked, rock·ing, rocks**) **1.** *vti.* **SWAY TO AND FRO** to swing or sway, or cause something or somebody to swing or sway, backward and forward or from side to side, especially with a slow gentle rhythm **2.** *vt.* **BRING TO A STATE BY ROCKING** to cause somebody to be in a specified condition by rocking ○ *rocked the child to sleep* **3.** *vti.* **SHAKE OR TREMBLE** to move or shake, or cause somebody or something to move or shake, violently ○ *An earth tremor rocked the city.* **4.** *vt.* **SHOCK** to disturb, upset, or shock somebody (*informal*) ○ *The ruling rocked the legal profession.* **5.** *vi.* **PLAY OR DANCE TO ROCK MUSIC** to sing, play, or dance to music, especially to rock music (*informal*) **6.** *vi.* **BE FILLED WITH ROCK MUSIC** to contain people performing or enjoying music, especially rock music (*informal*) ○ *The joint was really rocking.* **7.** *vi.* MUSIC **HAVE STRONG BEAT** to have or play music with a strong solid beat (*informal*) **8.** *vi.* **TRAVEL** to advance steadily or quickly (*informal*) ○ *rocking along at 60 miles an hour* **9.** *vti.* MINING **WASH ORE IN CRADLE** to wash gold-bearing or gem-bearing sands or gravel in a pivoting cradle (**rocker**) **10.** *vt.* ARTS **ROUGHEN COPPER PLATE** in engraving a mezzotint, to prepare a copper plate with a tool with a short, curved, jagged blade (**rocker**) ■ *n.* **1. ACT OF ROCKING** an act or the process of rocking somebody or something **2.** MUSIC **TYPE OF POP MUSIC** a style of pop music, derived from rock and roll, usually played on electric or electronic instruments and equipment [Old English *roccian*, of uncertain origin: probably from a prehistoric Germanic word meaning "to move"]

Rock /raak/ river rising in Wisconsin, flowing through Illinois and into the Mississippi River. Length: 300 mi./483 km.

rock·a·bil·ly /róka bìllee/ *n.* a style of pop music, originating in the late 1950s, that combines elements of rock and roll with elements of country music [Mid-20thC. Blend of ROCK AND ROLL + HILLBILLY.]

rock·a·bye /róka bī/, **rock·a·by** *interj.* used to encourage a baby or child to go to sleep [Early 19thC. Blend of ROCK[2] + LULLABY.]

Rock·all /ráak àwl/ rocky islet in the Atlantic Ocean, 220 mi./354 km west of the Outer Hebrides. Area: 8,000 sq. ft./743 sq. m.

rock and roll /ròkən rṓl, rókən rṑl/, **rock'n'roll** *n.* **1.** MUSIC **POP MUSIC WITH HEAVY BEAT** a style of pop music that has its roots mainly in blues music and is characterized by heavily stressed beats. It is played on electric instruments, and has simple, often repetitive, lyrics. **2.** DANCE **DANCE DONE TO ROCK AND ROLL** a style of dancing done to rock and roll music ■ *vi.* (**rocked and rolled, rock·ing and roll·ing, rocks and rolls;**

rock'n'rolled, rock'n'roll·ing, rock'n'rolls) DANCE TO ROCK AND ROLL to do a rock and roll dance —**rock and roll·er** *n.*

rock and rye *n.* a type of rye whiskey that contains pieces of rock candy and, occasionally, fruits

rock·a·way /rókə wày/ *n.* a light, four-wheeled, horse-drawn carriage for two or four passengers that usually has a fixed top and open sides [Mid-19thC. Named for *Rockaway,* a town in northern New Jersey where the carriage was first made.]

rock bass /-bàss/ *n.* a sunfish with a dark olive back, white undersides, and red eyes. It is a freshwater food and game fish native to eastern and central North America. Latin name: *Ambloplites rupestris.*

rock bot·tom *n.* the lowest level or price possible —**rock-bot·tom** *adj.*

rock·bound /rók bòwnd/ *adj.* **1.** SURROUNDED BY ROCKS entirely, or almost entirely, surrounded by rocks **2.** TOO ROCKY TO GET AT being so rocky as to be inaccessible

rock brake *n.* a fern that has compound fronds and grows on rocky ground. Genus: *Crytogramma.*

rock can·dy *n.* a hard candy consisting of dissolved sugar that is cooled to form large crystals. It is sometimes made on a piece of string or a stick.

rock climb·ing *n.* the activity of scaling rock faces, usually using ropes and other specialized equipment and often in a team —**rock climb·er** *n.*

Rock Cor·nish *n.* a small chicken developed by crossbreeding Cornish and white Plymouth Rock fowls, used especially as a roasting chicken

rock crab *n.* a crab found in rocky coastal areas of North America. Genus: *Cancer.*

rock crys·tal *n.* a colorless transparent variety of quartz, used in electronic and optical instruments

rock dove *n.* a bluish gray dove of Europe and Asia from which domestic and wild pigeons are descended. Latin name: *Columba livia.*

Rock·e·fel·ler /rókə fèllər/, **John D.** (1839–1937) U.S. industrialist and philanthropist. He founded Standard Oil and established the Rockefeller Foundation (1913). Full name **John Davison Rockefeller**

rock elm *n.* **1.** TREES EASTERN N AMERICAN ELM TREE a deciduous tree of eastern North America with corky branches. Latin name: *Ulmus thomasii.* **2.** INDUST TIMBER the wood of the rock elm tree

rock·er /rókər/ *n.* **1.** ROCKING DEVICE a device that functions by way of a rocking movement **2.** FURNITURE STAND an upwardly curved piece of wood or metal that allows something such as a rocking chair or baby's cradle to move backward and forward or from side to side **3.** FURNITURE = **rocking chair 4.** MINING = **cradle** *n.* 8 **5.** ARTS ENGRAVER'S TOOL a tool with a short, curved, jagged blade used in the engraving of mezzotints for roughening the copper plates **6.** ICE SKATING TYPE OF ICE SKATE an ice skate with a curved blade, or the curved blade itself (*often used in the plural*) **7.** MUSIC ROCK MUSICIAN a rock singer or musician (*informal*) **8.** MUSIC ROCK FAN a fan of rock music or rock and roll (*informal*) **9.** ROCK SONG a rock music song ◇ **be off your rocker** an offensive phrase that deliberately insults somebody's mental balance (*informal or offensive*)

rock·er arm *n.* a pivoted lever, e.g., in an internal-combustion engine, that transmits motion from a cam or pushrod at one end to open and close a valve at the other

rock·er cam *n.* a cam that oscillates or rocks but does not revolve

rock·er pan·el *n.* on a passenger vehicle, the exterior panel located below the doorsill of the passenger compartment

rock·er·y /rókəree/ (*plural* **-ies**) *n.* = **rock garden** *n.* 1

rock·et[1] /rókət/ *n.* **1.** SPACE TECH SPACE VEHICLE a device or vehicle designed for space travel, propelled by a device that carries both fuel and oxidizer and produces thrust by expelling expanding hot gases (**rocket engine**) **2.** = **rocket engine 3.** MIL ROCKET-PROPELLED WEAPON a weapon consisting of an explosive, nuclear, or other warhead that is propelled by a rocket engine **4.** SELF-PROPELLED FIREWORK OR FLARE a firework, flare, or similar device containing combustible propellants. Rockets are usually cylindrical in shape with a lightable fuse at the bottom. ■ *v.* (**-et·ed, -et·ing, -ets**) **1.** *vi.* MOVE FAST to move or begin to move at great speed **2.** *vti.* ATTAIN OR MAKE ATTAIN SOMETHING QUICKLY to get to, or cause

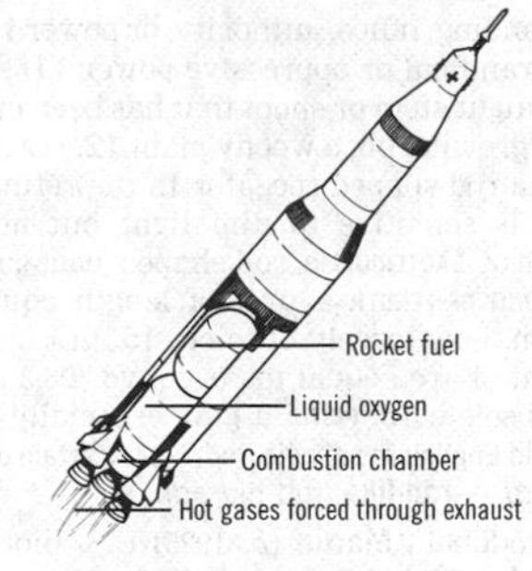

Rocket

somebody or something to get to, a specified condition or position very quickly (*informal*) **3.** *vi.* INCREASE QUICKLY to increase very quickly and dramatically (*informal*) **4.** *vt.* MIL, AEROSP POWER SOMETHING USING ROCKET ENGINE to send something, especially a spacecraft, warhead, or missile, into the air or atmosphere by means of a rocket engine or rocket engines **5.** *vt.* BOMBARD WITH ROCKET to fire a rocket at a target **6.** *vi.* FLY UP QUICKLY to fly up vertically at speed (*refers to game birds*) [Early 17thC. From Italian *rocchetta* "small distaff" (from its shape), from *rocca* "distaff," of prehistoric Germanic origin.]

rock·et[2] /rókət/ *n.* **1.** YELLOW-FLOWERED FAST-GROWING PLANT a fast-growing plant with pale yellow flowers, typically growing on waste ground. Genus: *Sisymbrium.* **2.** = **dame's violet 3.** = **sea rocket 4.** *U.K.* = **arugula** [Early 16thC. Via French *roquette* from Italian *ruchetta,* literally "small ruca" (a cabbage), ultimately from Latin *eruca* "caterpillar, cole."]

rock·et·eer /ròkə téer/ *n.* **1.** SOMEBODY WHO DESIGNS SPACE ROCKETS a scientist or engineer who designs space rockets **2.** SOMEBODY TRAVELING IN SPACE ROCKET somebody who launches, operates, or travels in a space rocket

rock·et en·gine *n.* a device that carries both fuel and oxidizer that it burns in a combustion chamber, producing thrust by expelling the expanding hot gases through a nozzle. The fuel and oxidizer may be liquefied gases, such as oxygen and hydrogen, or solids, such as powdered aluminum and ammonium perchloride.

rock·et plane *n.* **1.** AIRCRAFT POWERED BY ROCKET ENGINES an aircraft that is powered by a rocket engine or engines **2.** ROCKET-CARRYING AIRCRAFT an aircraft that is designed to carry and launch rockets, missiles, or warheads

rock·et·ry /rókətree/ *n.* the science and technology of the design, construction, operation, flying, and maintenance of rockets

rock·et sci·ence *n.* a complex and intellectually demanding activity (*informal*) ○ *Using the Internet isn't exactly rocket science.* [Late 20thC. From the idea that rocket science is the province of a few highly qualified specialists.]

rock·et sci·en·tist *n.* somebody who is highly intelligent (*informal*) ○ *It doesn't take a rocket scientist to figure that one out!*

rock·et ship *n.* a spaceship powered by rocket engines

rock·et sled *n.* a rocket-propelled vehicle that runs on a rail or rails and can be accelerated rapidly to high speeds, used in aeronautical applications such as crash and G-force tolerance testing

rock·et·sonde /rókət sond/ *n.* an instrument transported by rocket to the upper atmosphere to carry out weather observations

rock·fall /rók fàwl/ *n.* **1.** FALLEN ROCKS a collection or mass of fallen rocks **2.** FALLING ROCKS an avalanche of falling rocks

rock·fish /rók fish/ (*plural* **-fish** *or* **-fish·es**) *n.* **1.** FOOD FISH LIVING AMONG ROCKS a fish that lives among rocks. Many are important food fishes. **2.** = **striped bass**

rock flour *n.* fine powdery rock produced by grinding or abrasion, e.g., by the movement of a glacier

Rock·ford /ráakfərd/ city in northern Illinois, south of the Wisconsin border, east of Freeport and northwest of Chicago. Population: 143,531 (1996).

rock gar·den *n.* **1.** DECORATIVE STONY GARDEN a garden or area of a garden in which plants, especially low-growing colorful hardy ones grow between carefully arranged large stones **2.** GARDEN WITH ROCKS a garden in which large stones are a prominent feature

Rock Hill /ráak híl/ city in northern South Carolina, north of Columbia and southwest of Charlotte, North Carolina. Population: 44,061 (1996).

rock·hop·per /rók hòppər/ *n.* a small penguin, native to Antarctica, New Zealand, and the Falkland Islands, that has a stout bill and a yellow crest. Latin name: *Eudyptes crestatus.*

rock hound *n.* (*informal*) **1.** ROCK COLLECTOR somebody who has an interest in, or whose hobby is, collecting rocks and minerals **2.** GEOL a geologist —**rock·hound·ing** /rók hòwnding/ *n.*

rock hy·rax *n.* a small plant-eating African hyrax that lives in large colonies in rocky outcrops. Genus: *Procavia.*

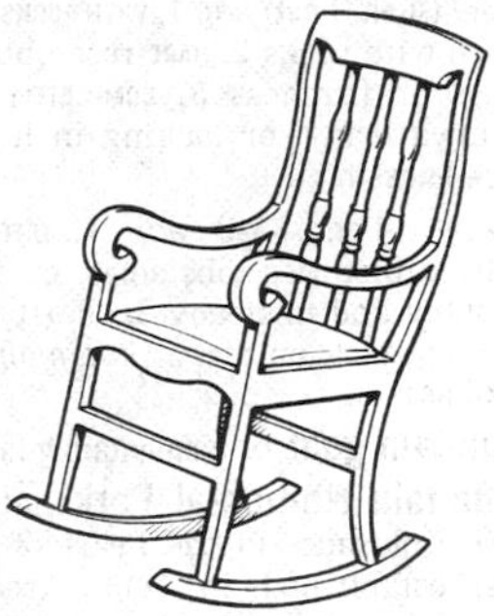
Rocking chair

rock·ing chair *n.* a chair that is set on a pair of curved pieces of wood so that somebody sitting in it can be rocked backward and forward

rock·ing horse *n.* a small model horse fitted with reins and a saddle and set on a pair of rockers on which a child can sit and rock backward and forward

Rock Is·land city in northwestern Illinois, on the eastern bank of the Mississippi River. It forms the Illinois-Iowa border, southwest of Moline. Population: 39,679 (1996).

rock·ling /rókling/ (*plural* **-lings** *or* **-ling**) *n.* any of various small North Atlantic fishes of the cod family. Family: Gadidae.

rock lob·ster *n.* = **spiny lobster**

rock ma·ple *n.* = **sugar maple**

rock'n'roll *n., vi.* = **rock and roll**

rock·oon /ro kóon/ *n.* an upper-atmosphere research system consisting of a large plastic balloon, launched at a high altitude, that carries a small rocket fitted with scientific equipment [Mid-20thC. Blend of ROCKET[1] + BALLOON.]

rock pi·geon *n.* = **rock dove**

rock rab·bit *n.* = **rock hyrax**

rock-ribbed *adj.* **1.** FIRM IN BELIEFS rigid and inflexible in beliefs or principles **2.** ROCKY characterized by rocks or rocky outcrops

rock·rose /rók rōz/ *n.* a woody shrub or plant grown for its small light-yellow or reddish flowers that are shaped like roses. Genera: *Cistus* and *Helianthemum.*

rock salt *n.* = **halite**

rock·slide /rók slīd/ *n.* **1.** ROCKS THAT HAVE SLID DOWNWARD a collection or mass of rocks that have slid downward **2.** SLIDING AVALANCHE OF ROCKS an avalanche of rocks as a result of surface movement

rock-sol·id *adj.* **1.** COMPLETELY SOLID firm and unshakable **2.** UNLIKELY TO BREAK extremely hard and unlikely to break

Rock·ville /ráak víl/ city in western central Maryland, south of Gaithersburg. It is a northwestern suburb of Washington, D.C. Population: 46,019 (1996).

Rock·ville Cen·tre village on Long Island, southeastern New York, directly east of the borough of Queens, New York City. Population: 24,787 (1996).

rock wal·la·by *n.* a medium-sized Australian marsupial that is found in open rocky country and has large well-padded hind feet with stiff hairs to prevent it from slipping on the rocks. Genus: *Petrogale.*

rock·weed /rók wèed/ *n.* any of various coarse brown seaweeds that grow on coastal rocks. Genera: *Fucus* and *Ascophyllum.*

Rock·well /rók wèl, rókwəl/, **Norman** (1894–1978) U.S. illustrator. He is best known for his magazine covers and illustrations of everyday small-town life, published in U.S. periodicals such as *The Saturday Evening Post* and the *Ladies' Home Journal.*

rock wool *n.* = **mineral wool**

rock·work /rók wùrk/ *n.* **1. DECORATIVE STONEWORK** artificial or decorative stonework designed to resemble the irregularity of natural rocks **2. MASS OF STONES** a collection or mass of large stones or rocks

rock wren *n.* a gray wren of western North America, commonly found in rocky barrens and canyons. Latin name: *Salpinctes obsoletus.*

rock·y[1] /rókee/ (**-i·er, -i·est**) *adj.* **1. WITH ROCKS** consisting of or covered with rocks **2. HARD** resembling rock in its hardness or firmness **3. COMPLETELY STEADY** unyielding, unwavering, or lacking in human emotions —**rock·i·ness** *n.*

rock·y[2] /rókee/ (**-i·er, -i·est**) *adj.* **1. DIFFICULT** characterized by difficulties, obstacles, or troubles **2. UNSTEADY** wobbly and unsteady **3. UNWELL** unwell, especially feeling sick or dizzy (*informal*) —**rock·i·ly** *adv.* —**rock·i·ness** *n.*

Rock·y Moun·tain goat *n.* = **mountain goat**

Rock·y Moun·tain Na·tion·al Park national park in northern Colorado, in the heart of the Rocky Mountains, established in 1915. Area: 414 sq. mi./1,073 sq. km.

Rock·y Moun·tains major mountain system of North America. Its highest point is Mount Elbert, at 14,433 ft./4,399 m. Length: 3,000 mi./4,800 km.

Rock·y Moun·tain spot·ted fe·ver *n.* an acute infectious disease transmitted by the bite of ticks infected with the microorganism *Rickettsia rickettsi.* Symptoms include chills, fever, muscle and joint pain, skin rash, and prostration. [Because first reported in the area of the ROCKY MOUNTAINS]

AKG London

Rococo: Detail of stuccowork at Wies church, Bavaria, Germany (1745–54)

ro·co·co /rə kṓkō, rō kṓkō, rṓkə kṓ/ *n.* **1. ro·co·co, Ro·co·co** ARTS **ORNATE 18C ART STYLE** a style of architecture and the decorative arts characterized by intricate ornamentation that was popular throughout Europe in the early 18th century **2. ro·co·co, Ro·co·co** MUSIC **ORNATE 18C MUSIC STYLE** a style of music characterized by the use of ornamentation and embellishment that was popular in the 18th century **3. ORNATE STYLE** any overly ornate or fancy style ■ *adj.* **1. ro·co·co, Ro·co·co** ARTS, MUSIC **IN STYLE OF ROCOCO** belonging to, relating to, or in the style of 18th-century rococo **2. ORNATE** overly ornate or fancy [Mid-19thC. From French, a fanciful alteration of ROCAILLE.]

rod /rod/ *n.* **1. THIN STICK** a narrow, usually cylindrical, length of wood, metal, plastic, or other material **2.** ANGLING = **fishing rod 3. WHIPPING STICK** a stick, or bundle of sticks tied together, used for whipping somebody as a punishment **4.** BUILDING **SURVEYING POLE** a graduated pole used by surveyors for sighting with a leveling instrument to determine elevation differences **5.** MEASURE = **measuring rod 6.** JOINERY **BOARD MARKED WITH FULL-SCALE JOINERY PATTERN** a board on which the dimensions of a joinery assembly, e.g., a window or door frame, are marked in full scale **7.** = **lightning rod 8.** FREIGHT, RAIL **METAL BAR SUPPORTING RAILROAD CAR** one of the metal bars that form the framework of the underside of a railroad car, especially one on a freight car (*often used in the plural*) **9.** POL **STAFF OF OFFICE** a staff, especially one that indicates somebody's standing, office, authority, or power **10. POWER WIELDED** tyrannical or oppressive power **11.** BOT **PLANT STEM** a straight stem or shoot that has been cut from, or that is growing on, a woody plant **12.** ANAT **RECEPTOR CELL IN EYE** a rod-shaped receptor in the retina of the eye that is sensitive to dim light but not color **13.** MICROBIOL **BACTERIUM** a rod-shaped bacterium **14.** MEASURE **UNIT OF LENGTH** a unit of length equal to $5\frac{1}{2}$ yd./5.03 m, now largely obsolete **15.** MEASURE **UNIT OF AREA** a unit of area equal to $30\frac{1}{4}$ sq. yd./25.3 m^2, now largely obsolete **16. PISTOL** a gun, especially a pistol (*slang*) [Old English *rodd* "pole, rod," of uncertain origin] —**rod·less** *adj.* —**rod·like** /ród lìk/ *adj.*

Rod·bell /róddbel/, **Martin** (*b.* 1925) U.S. biochemist. He shared a Nobel Prize (1994) in physiology or medicine for discovering a chemical transducer.

rode[1] past tense of **ride**

rode[2] /rōd/ *n.* a rope or chain, especially one attached to an anchor [Early17thC. Of uncertain origin.]

ro·dent /rṓd'nt/ *n.* a small mammal such as a mouse, rat, squirrel, or marmot with large gnawing incisor teeth that continue growing throughout the animal's life. Rodents make up more than a third of all living mammal species and are adapted to all terrestrial habitats. Order: Rodentia. [Mid-19thC. From modern Latin *Rodentia,* order name, from Latin *rodent-,* the present participle stem of *rodere* "to gnaw."]

ro·den·ti·cide /rō déntə sìd/ *n.* a substance designed to kill rodents, especially rats and mice

ro·dent ul·cer *n.* a persistent, usually cancerous ulcer of the skin, especially of the face [*Rodent* literally "gnawing" (see RODENT)]

ro·de·o /rṓdee ō, rō dáy ō/ *n.* (*plural* **-os**) **1. COMPETITION IN COWBOY SKILLS** a competition or display of lassoing, bronco-riding, calf-roping, and steer-wrangling **2. MOTORCYCLING COMPETITION** a competition or display of motorcycle riding that often includes stunts **3.** AGRIC **CATTLE ROUND-UP** an occasion when cattle are rounded up, especially so that they can be branded, counted, or have their health checked **4.** AGRIC **CATTLE PEN** a pen for rounded-up cattle ■ *vi.* (**-od, -o·ing, -os**) AGRIC, SPORTS to take part in a rodeo [Mid-19thC. From Spanish, literally "cattle ring," from *rodear* "to go round, surround," from Latin *rotare* (see ROTATE).]

Rodg·ers /rójjərz/, **Richard** (1902–79) U.S. composer. His collaborations with Lorenz Hart (1920–40) and Oscar Hammerstein II (1943–59) produced popular musicals such as *Pal Joey* (1940) and *Oklahoma!* (1943).

AKG London

Auguste Rodin: Bronze portrait bust (1888–89) by Camille Claudel

Ro·din /rō dáN/, **Auguste** (1840–1917) French sculptor. Among his bronze sculptures are *The Thinker* (1880), *The Kiss* (1880), and *The Burghers of Calais* (1886). Full name **François Auguste René Rodin**

rod·man /ródmən, ród màn/ (*plural* **-men** /-mən/) *n.* a surveyor's assistant whose job is to hold the graduated pole, or rod

Rod·ney /ródnee/, **Caesar** (1728–84) American patriot. He signed the Declaration of the Continental Congress of Independence (1776) and presided over Delaware (1778–82).

rod·o·mon·tade /ròddəmən táyd, ròddə mon-, -taád/, **rho·do·mon·tade** *n.* **BOASTFULNESS** pretentious, self-important, or self-indulgent boasting, speech, or behavior (*literary*) ■ *vi.* (**-tad·ed, -tad·ing, -tades**) **BOAST** to boast or speak in a pretentious, self-important, or self-indulgent way (*literary*) ■ *adj.* **BOASTFUL** boastful in a pretentious, self-important, or self-indulgent way (*literary*) [Early 17thC. Via French from obsolete Italian *rodomontada,* from *rodomonte* "braggart," from *Rodomonte,* a boastful Saracen king in Boiardo's *Orlando Innamorato* and Ariosto's *Orlando Furioso.*]

roe[1] /rō/ *n.* **1.** ZOOL, FOOD **FISH EGGS** a mass of mature fish eggs, especially when still inside the ovarian sac, sometimes eaten cooked **2.** ZOOL **FISH SPERM** a mass of mature fish sperm, especially when it is still inside the testicular sac **3.** ZOOL **CRUSTACEAN EGGS** a mass of mature eggs of certain crustaceans, e.g., the lobster, especially when still inside the ovarian sac [15thC. From Middle Dutch or Middle Low German *roge,* of unknown origin.]

roe[2] /rō/ (*plural* **roe** *or* **roes**) *n.* = **roe deer** [Old English *rā,* from prehistoric Germanic]

Roeb·ling /rṓbling/, **John Augustus** (1806–69) German-born U.S. civil engineer. He pioneered the construction of suspension bridges, and designed the Brooklyn Bridge (1869).

roe·buck /rṓ bùk/ (*plural* **-buck** *or* **-bucks**) *n.* a male roe deer, especially an adult one

Roe·de·an /rō dáyən/ *n.* private school in southern England: a private school for girls in southern England. It was founded in 1885.

roe deer *n.* a medium-sized reddish brown European and Asian deer found in deciduous woodlands. Latin name: *Capreolus capreolus.*

roent·gen /réntgən, réntjən/, **rönt·gen** *n.* a unit of radiation, used to measure the exposure of somebody or something to X-rays and gamma rays, defined in terms of the ionization effect on air. It is equal to the quantity of radiation that produces ionization equal to one electrostatic unit of charge at 0° and standard atmospheric pressure. Symbol **R** [Late 19thC. Named for W.C. ROENTGEN.]

Roent·gen /réntgən, réntjən/, **Wilhelm Conrad** (1845–1923) German physicist. He was awarded a Nobel Prize in 1901 for his discovery of X-rays, originally known also as Roentgen rays.

roentgen- *prefix.* = **roentgeno-** (*used before vowels*)

roentgeno- *prefix.* X-ray ○ *roentgenotherapy* [From ROENTGEN]

Roes·lare /rŏŏssə laárə/ city in West Flanders Province, western Belgium, 18 mi./29 km south of Bruges. Population: 53,706 (1996).

Roeth·ke /rétkə/, **Theodore** (1908–63) U.S. poet. His volume of poetry, *The Waking: Poems* (1953), won a Pulitzer Prize.

ro·ga·tion /rō gáysh'n/ *n.* **1.** CHR **SOLEMN PRAYER** in the Christian church, a solemn prayer or supplication, especially one made as part of the observation of the three days preceding Ascension Day (**Rogation Days**) (*often used in the plural*) **2.** HIST **SUBMISSION OF LAW FOR APPROVAL** in ancient Rome, the submission of a law by a consul or tribune to the people for their approval, or a law so submitted [14thC. From the Latin stem *rogation-,* from *rogare* "to ask, beg."]

Ro·ga·tion Day *n.* any of the three days preceding Ascension Day on which Christians are expected to pray (*often used in the plural*)

Ro·ga·tion Sun·day *n.* the Sunday before the Christian festival of Ascension Day, falling five weeks after Easter

ro·ga·to·ry /róggə tàwree/ *adj.* requesting information, especially information that might be pertinent to a court case [Mid-19thC. Via French *rogatoire* from medieval Latin *rogatorius,* from Latin *rogare* "to ask, beg."]

rog·er /rójjər/ *interj.* **1.** TELECOM **AS CODE WORD IN TELECOMMUNICATIONS** used in telecommunications to indicate that the speaker has received and understood a transmitted message **2. OK** used to indicate the speaker's agreement to something (*informal*) ■ *vti.* (**-ered, -er·ing, -ers**) **OFFENSIVE TERM** an offensive term meaning to have sexual intercourse with a woman (*dated slang offensive*) [Mid-20thC. From the name *Roger,* used in radio communications for the letter *r* and meaning *received.*]

Rog·ers /ráajərz/ city in northwestern Arkansas, west of Beaver Lake and north of Springdale. Population: 35,355 (1996).

Rog·ers, Ginger (1911–95) U.S. dancer and actor. She was Fred Astaire's dance partner in many Hollywood musicals (1933–49), including *Top Hat* (1935). Born **Virginia Katherine McMath**

Rog·ers, Will (1879–1935) U.S. humorist. He was known for his vaudeville performances and rope tricks. Full name **William Penn Adair Rogers**

Rog·ers Moun·tain mountain in southwestern Virginia, near the North Carolina border. It is the highest point in the state. Height: 5,927 ft./1,807 m.

Ro·get /rō zháy/, **Peter Mark** (1779–1869) British scholar and doctor. He compiled the *Thesaurus of English Words and Phrases* (1852), now known as Roget's Thesaurus.

rogue /rōg/ *n.* **1.** **SOMEBODY DISHONEST** somebody who is unscrupulous or dishonest, especially somebody who is nevertheless likable **2.** **SOMEBODY MISCHIEVOUS** somebody who is mischievously playful, especially a naughty child **3.** PLANTS, ZOOL **BIOLOGICALLY INFERIOR VARIANT** a plant or animal that is a biologically inferior variant as compared to the rest of its species **4.** ZOOL **DANGEROUS SOLITARY ANIMAL** a vicious or uncontrolled animal that lives apart from the rest of its herd or group, especially an elephant **5.** **TRAMP** a tramp or vagrant (*archaic*) ■ *adj.* **1.** ZOOL **DANGEROUS AND SOLITARY** vicious and uncontrolled and living apart from the rest of the herd or group **2.** **MAVERICK** acting independently and using unorthodox methods that often cause trouble **3.** **STRAY** different and unwanted, and often dangerous or destructive ■ *vt.* **(rogued, rogu·ing, rogues) 1.** AGRIC, PLANTS **CLEAR AWAY PLANTS FROM LAND** to remove inferior plants from a piece of land or a group of plants **2.** **DEFRAUD** to swindle or defraud somebody [Mid-16thC. Originally "vagrant," of uncertain origin: possibly from *roger* ("g" pronounced hard) "beggar posing as an impoverished student," from Latin *rogare* "to beg."]

Rogue /rōg/ river in southwestern Oregon, rising in the Cascade Mountains and emptying into the Pacific Ocean. Length: 200 mi./320 km.

rogu·er·y /rṓgəree/ (*plural* **-ies**) *n.* **1.** **DISHONEST ACTION** an act or behavior that is unscrupulous or dishonest **2.** **MISCHIEVOUS ACTION** an act or behavior that is mischievously playful

rogues' gal·ler·y *n.* a set of photographs of known criminals that the police show to witnesses to crimes for possible identification (*archaic*)

rogue site *n.* a World Wide Web site that redirects users to its site by having a similar domain name as a popular site

rogu·ish /rṓgish/ *adj.* **1.** **DISHONEST** unscrupulous or dishonest in the manner of a rogue **2.** **MISCHIEVOUS** mischievously playful —**rogu·ish·ly** *adv.* —**rogu·ish·ness** *n.*

ROI *abbr.* return on investment

roil /royl/ **(roiled, roil·ing, roils)** *v.* **1.** *vti.* PHYS **MAKE OR BECOME OPAQUE** to stir up a liquid so that the sediment becomes dispersed through the liquid and makes it cloudy, or become cloudy with sediment by being stirred **2.** *vt.* **MAKE SOMEBODY ANGRY** to anger or annoy somebody. ◊ **rile** [Late 16thC. Origin uncertain: perhaps from French *rouiller* "to make muddy, rust," from assumed Vulgar Latin *robicula*, alteration of Latin *robigo* "rust."] —**roil·y** *adj.*

rois·ter /róystər/ **(-tered, -ter·ing, -ters)** *vi.* **1.** **CELEBRATE ROWDILY** to take part in loud rowdy partying or celebrations **2.** **BRAG LOUDLY** to behave in a loud bragging manner [Mid-16thC. Origin uncertain: probably from Old French *ru(i)stre* "boor, churl," ultimately from Latin *rusticus* "rustic."] —**rois·ter·er** *n.* —**rois·ter·ous** *adj.* —**rois·ter·ous·ly** *adv.*

role /rōl/, **rôle** *n.* **1.** ARTS **ACTING PART** an individual part in a play, movie, opera, or other performance played by an actor, singer, or other performer **2.** **SPECIFIC FUNCTION** the usual or expected function of somebody or something, or the part somebody or something plays in a particular action or event **3.** PSYCHOL, SOCIOL **PART PLAYED IN SOCIAL CONTEXT** the part played by somebody in a given social context, with any characteristic or expected pattern of behavior that it entails [Early 17thC. From French *rôle* "(paper) roll on which an actor's part is written," from Old French *rol(l)e* (see ROLL).]

role mod·el *n.* somebody who is regarded as somebody to look up to and often as an example to emulate

role-play *n.* **ACTING OUT OF PART** role-playing, or an instance of it ■ *vti.* **ACT OUT PART** to engage or act out a part in role-playing

role-play·ing *n.* the acting out of a part, especially that of somebody with a particular social role, in order to understand the role or person better. This process is used in psychotherapy and in training people in interpersonal skills.

Rolfe /rolf/, **John** (1585–1622) English-born American colonist. He devised a method for curing tobacco, and was married to the Native North American princess, Pocahontas (1614).

Rolf·ing /rólfing/ *tdmk.* a service mark for a type of therapy using vigorous massage to alleviate physical or psychological tension

roll /rōl/ *v.* **(rolled, roll·ing, rolls) 1.** *vti.* **TURN OVER AND OVER** to move or cause something to move with repeated turning or rotating motions **2.** *vti.* **MOVE ON WHEELS** to move, or cause something to move, on wheels or rollers **3.** *vi.* **DRIVE IN VEHICLE** to move in a wheeled vehicle **4.** *vi.* ZOOL **WRITHE** to lie on the back and move about or from side to side, but without moving very far, often with a writhing motion (*refers to animals*) **5.** *vti.* NAUT **ROCK FROM SIDE TO SIDE** to move with a sideways swaying or rocking motion on waves or a swell, or cause something, especially a ship, to move in this way **6.** *vi.* **WALK UNSTEADILY** to walk with an unsteady or staggering motion **7.** *vi.* **WALK WITH A SWAY** to sway rhythmically in walking **8.** *vi.* **STRETCH OUT OR AWAY IN UNDULATIONS** to have or take the form of a succession of gentle slopes ○ *green hills rolling away into the distance* **9.** *vti.* **MOVE WITH UNDULATIONS** to move, or cause something to move, in a steady flowing motion **10.** *vi.* **ELAPSE** to go by or elapse, especially uneventfully or imperceptibly (*refers especially to time*) **11.** *vi.* **TRAVEL AROUND** to travel from place to place **12.** *vi.* **CARRY ON** to proceed or continue successfully (*informal*) ○ *Now this project is finally rolling.* **13.** *vi.* **MOVE AS CROWD** to move or arrive in large numbers or in a crowd **14.** *vt.* PHON **TRILL SOUND** to pronounce a sound, especially an "r," with a trill **15.** *vi.* **REVERBERATE LOUDLY** to make a low prolonged rumbling noise **16.** *vi.* MUSIC, MIL **BEAT DRUM** to make a series of quick beats on a drum **17.** *vt.* MUSIC **PLAY CHORD WITH SPREAD NOTES** to play a chord with its notes in rapid succession **(arpeggio)** rather than simultaneously **18.** *vti.* GAME **THROW DICE** to throw a die or dice **19.** *vt.* GAME **SCORE NUMBER BY THROWING DICE** to achieve a specified number, position, or score by throwing a die or dice **20.** *vi.* **BE CARRIED BY RIVER** to be transported by river **21.** *vti.* **ROTATE** to turn or cause something to turn in a complete or partial rotation **22.** *vi.* ASTRON **ORBIT** to revolve in an orbit (*refers to celestial bodies*) **23.** *vti.* AIR **ROTATE AIRCRAFT** to cause an aircraft to perform a single complete rotation about its lengthwise axis while maintaining the same altitude and direction, or perform such a rotation **24.** *vt.* **FLATTEN SOMETHING WITH ROLLER** to flatten or spread something, especially by using a roller or rolling pin **25.** *vt.* PRINTING **INK SOMETHING WITH ROLLER** to apply ink to type or a plate with a roller **26.** *vti.* **FORM INTO ROUND SHAPE** to form something, or be formed, into a ball, tube, cylinder, or other rounded shape, or form something with such a shape **27.** *vt.* **WRAP SOMETHING INTO CYLINDER** to make something into a cylinder shape, especially by wrapping something over and over on itself **28.** *vt.* **TURN BETWEEN OR ON SOMETHING** to revolve something between two surfaces or on a coating material **29.** *vti.* **OPERATE SOMETHING** to function or cause something, especially a motion picture camera or printing press, to function **30.** *vti.* CINEMA, TV **SEND OR GO UP ON SCREEN** to cause credits, titles, or other captions to move in a continuous upward direction on a cinema or television screen, or move in this way **31.** *vt.* CRIMINOL **ROB SOMEBODY** to take money or belongings from somebody who cannot offer any resistance (*informal*) **32.** *vti.* **HAVE SEX** to have sexual intercourse or engage in sexual foreplay with somebody (*informal; offensive in some contexts*) ■ *n.* **1.** **OFFICIAL LIST** an official register or list of names, especially of school pupils, members of a club, or of people entitled to vote **2.** **TOTAL ON OFFICIAL LIST** the total number of people registered on a school, club, or electoral roll **3.** **SOMETHING TUBE-SHAPED** a tube, cylinder, or coil of something, especially something that is wrapped around itself **4.** **ROUNDED LAYER** a thick rounded layer of something, especially of flesh **5.** **WAD OF MONEY** a cylindrical wad of bills formed by coiling the wad around itself (*informal*) **6.** FOOD **FILLED FOOD** a food made by wrapping pastry around a filling or by spreading a filling on something, e.g., sponge cake, and wrapping it around itself (*usually used in combination*) **7.** FOOD **INDIVIDUAL LOAF** a small individual-sized loaf of bread, usually round or long in shape, or a sandwich made from one **8.** **EQUIPMENT HOLDER WITH POCKETS** a length or belt of fabric or leather that has pockets to hold tools, medical instruments, or other equipment and can usually be wrapped around itself and tied up **9.** ARCHIT **SPIRAL SCROLL** in Greek architecture, a spiral scroll on an Ionic column **10.** **ACT OF FLATTENING** an act of flattening or spreading something, especially by using a roller or rolling pin **11.** **REPEATED TURN** a repeated turning or rotating motion **12.** GAME **TOSS OF DICE** a throw of a die or dice **13.** AIR **ROTATION OF AIRCRAFT** a midair flight maneuver in which an aircraft maintains the same height and direction while doing a single complete rotation about its lengthwise axis. ◊ **pitch, yaw 14.** GYMNASTICS **SOMERSAULT** a gentle somersault **15.** **MOVEMENT ON WHEELS** a movement on wheels or rollers **16.** **SINGLE TURN** a complete or partial rotation **17.** **WRITHING MOTION** an action that involves writhing while turning backward and forward or from side to side, but without moving very far **18.** **MOVEMENT FROM SIDE TO SIDE** a swaying or rocking motion, especially by a ship. ◊ **pitch, yaw 19.** **SWAYING WALK** a rhythmical sway in walking **20.** **SOMETHING UNDULATING** a gentle rounded hump on a surface, often one of a series **21.** **UNDULATING MOVEMENT** a steady, flowing, undulating movement **22.** **RHYTHMICAL STREAM OF WORDS** a continuous stream of words with a rhythmical quality **23.** INDUST **ROLLER FOR METAL** a cylinder or roller used for pressing, shaping, or flattening something, especially one used for shaping metal in a rolling mill **24.** CRAFT **BOOKBINDER'S TOOL** a bookbinder's tool for embossing book covers **25.** **TRILLING SOUND** a trilling noise, especially the sound of a trilled "r" or the song of a canary **26.** **RUMBLING NOISE** a low prolonged rumbling noise **27.** MUSIC, MIL **DRUM BEATS** a series of quick beats on a drum **28.** MUSIC **CHORD WITH SPREAD NOTES** a chord played with its notes in rapid succession **(arpeggio)** rather than simultaneously **29.** CRIMINOL **ACT OF ROBBERY** an act or the process of taking money or belongings from somebody who cannot offer any resistance (*informal*) **30.** **SEX ACT** an act of sexual intercourse or foreplay (*informal; offensive in some contexts*) [12thC. Via Old French *rolle* "scroll," from the Latin stem *rotul-* "little wheel," ultimately from Latin *rota* "wheel."] ◇ **on a roll** enjoying a period of good luck or of doing something well (*informal*) ◇ **rolled into one** forming a single unit consisting of a number of different aspects or qualities

roll back *vt.* **1.** **DECREASE SOMETHING** to cause something, especially prices or wages, to decrease **2.** **FORCE TO WITHDRAW** to cause somebody or something to retreat **3.** **PUT STOP TO SOMETHING** to reduce or nullify the influence or effectiveness of something

roll in *vi.* **1.** **ARRIVE LATE** to come home or arrive at a destination, especially in a leisurely way, often later than expected **2.** **ARRIVE IN LARGE NUMBERS** to arrive or attend in large numbers or quantities

roll off *vi.* **1.** **MOVE EASILY OR IN QUANTITY** to flow, especially with ease or in large numbers **2.** **REDUCE AMPLITUDE-FREQUENCY RESPONSE** to display a gradually decreasing response in the upper and lower portions of the amplitude-frequency range of an electronic system or transducer

roll out *v.* **1.** *vt.* **FLATTEN PASTRY** to flatten pastry, dough, or other uncooked food by shaping it with a rolling pin **2.** *vt.* **UNCOIL** to unfold or uncoil something **3.** *vi.* FOOTBALL **RUN TOWARD SIDELINE** to perform a play in which a quarterback runs toward either sideline **4.** *vt.* MARKETING **LAUNCH PRODUCT GRADUALLY** to launch a new product or service by gradually increasing the number of outlets where it is available to the public **5.** *vt.* AEROSP **SHOW NEW AIRCRAFT TO PUBLIC** to put a new aircraft or spacecraft on public display for the first time

roll over *v.* **1.** *vi.* **CAPSIZE** to capsize, tip over, or overturn **2.** *vt.* FIN **EXTEND LOAN** to allow a loan to be paid at a later date **3.** *vt.* **DEFEAT SOMEBODY** to defeat a person or team overwhelmingly **4.** *vt.* FIN **NEGOTIATE NEW FINANCIAL TERMS FOR SOMETHING** to achieve new terms for a financial contract through discussion **5.** *vt.* FIN **REINVEST FUNDS** to transfer funds from one investment to a similar investment

roll up *v.* **1.** *vi.* **ARRIVE** to come to a place or destination, often in a vehicle and especially when later than expected or when not expected at all **2.** *vt.* **PRODUCE CYLINDER SHAPE** to turn something into a cylindrical form **3.** *vt.* **ACCUMULATE MONEY** to accumulate something, especially money

roll·a·way /rṓlə wày/ *adj.* fitted with wheels or casters so as to be easily moved or stored

roll·back /rṓl bàk/ *n.* **1.** **MONEY CUT** a decrease in something, especially in something such as prices and wages involving money **2. REDUCTION OF INFLUENCE OR EFFECTIVENESS** a reduction or nullification of the influence or effectiveness of something

roll bar *n.* a reinforcing bar across the top of a vehicle, especially an open-top sports car or off-road vehicle, to protect the occupants if the vehicle overturns

roll cage *n.* a protective network of metal bars enclosing the driver of a racing car

roll call *n.* **1. ATTENDANCE CHECK** a check on attendance, especially in a school or military establishment, by calling out the names of those expected to be present, with each of those present responding **2. TIME FOR ROLL CALL** a time when a roll call is read out, especially one that is fixed at a regular time of day

rolled oats *npl.* oats that have had the husks removed and been flattened. They are especially used in making oatmeal.

rolled steel *n.* steel produced to a desired thickness by being passed through a set of rollers

roll·er /rṓlər/ *n.* **1. SOMEBODY OR SOMETHING THAT ROLLS** somebody who or something that rolls **2. DEVICE FOR APPLYING PAINT** a painting tool in the form of a revolving tube with a soft absorbent covering and a handle, used for applying paint to large surface areas **3.** PRINTING **INKED TUBE** a hard tube, usually of compressed rubber, on which ink is spread. It is used for inking type or a plate. **4. SPOKELESS WHEEL** a small wheel without spokes, especially on a skate or piece of heavy furniture **5.** GARDENING **DEVICE FOR FLATTENING LAWNS** a large heavy revolving cylinder or pair of cylinders with a handle, used for flattening a lawn or green **6.** ENG **CYLINDER THAT TRANSMITS FORCE AND MOTION** a cylindrically shaped rotating device that transmits force and motion via its rotation and is often used in sets or pairs and machine-operated **7.** HAIR **HAIR CURLER** a short tube around which hair is wrapped in order to make it curly or wavy **8.** MED **COILED BANDAGE** a long bandage that is rolled up tightly upon itself to form a dense cylinder. The required amount is then cut off for use. **9.** EQU **BELT FOR HORSE BLANKET** a strap around the belly of a horse to hold a blanket in place **10. HEAVY WAVE** a long heavy wave that does not break until it reaches the shoreline **11.** BASEBALL **BALL HIT WITH LITTLE FORCE** in baseball, a batted ball that rolls along the ground slowly **12.** BIRDS **BRIGHTLY COLORED BIRD KNOWN FOR TUMBLING FLIGHT** a brightly colored European bird with a hooked bill that performs rolling dives and erratic flight during the breeding season as a courtship display. Family: Coraciidae.

roll·er bear·ing *n.* a set of rotating cylindrically shaped parallel steel rollers contained within a closed track, used to prevent friction between machine parts

Roll·er·blade /rṓlər blàyd/ *tdmk.* a trademark for a type of roller skate on which the wheels are arranged in one straight line

roll·er coast·er *n.* **1.** LEISURE **FAIRGROUND RIDE** an amusement park ride consisting of a narrow rail track on a metal framework shaped into extreme peaks and troughs and sharp bends **2. SITUATION WITH EXTREME HIGHS AND LOWS** a situation that is characterized by sudden, extreme, and often repeated, changes (*hyphenated when used before a noun*)

roller der·by *n.* competition between two teams of roller skaters

roll·er hock·ey *n.* hockey played on a roller rink or other hard surface by players wearing roller skates

roll·er rink *n.* a place where people can go to roller-skate

roll·er skate *n.* **1. SET OF WHEELS ATTACHED TO SHOE** a metal or plastic frame with wheels attached, usually one pair at the front and another at the back, fastened onto a shoe and used for skating **2. SHOE FOR ROLLER-SKATING** a specially designed shoe or boot to which a roller skate is attached —**roll·er skat·er** *n.* —**roll·er skat·ing** *n.*

roll·er-skate *vi.* to go around on roller skates

roll·er tow·el *n.* a continuous roll of material, usually linen or toweling, housed inside a metal box and used, especially in public bathrooms, for drying the hands. Each user pulls down a fresh section of towel.

roll film *n.* a length of film rolled around a spool and put inside a protective case ready to be loaded into a camera

rol·lick /róllik/ (**-licked, -lick·ing, -licks**) *vi.* to have fun, especially in a loud, rowdy way [Early 19thC. Origin uncertain: probably a blend of ROLL or ROMP and FROLIC.] —**rol·lick** *n.* —**rol·lick·some** *adj.* —**rol·lick·y** *adj.*

rol·lick·ing *adj.* loud and rowdy —**rol·lick·ing·ly** *adv.*

roll·ing /rṓling/ *adj.* **1. UNDULATING** characterized by undulating slopes **2. RICH** rich or very well-off (*informal*) **3. GRADUALLY DEVELOPING** proceeding in successive phases and usually gaining in momentum, intensity, or effectiveness **4. REVERBERATING** characterized by a low, prolonged, rumbling noise ■ *adv.* **EXTREMELY** to the extent of staggering (*informal*) ○ *rolling drunk* ◇ **be rolling in it** *or* **something** to have plenty of something, especially money, assets, or wealth (*informal*)

roll·ing hitch *n.* a knot used for joining two pieces of rope together or for attaching a rope to a spar

Roll·ing Mead·ows city in northeastern Illinois, northeast of Hoffman Estates. It is a northwestern suburb of Chicago. Population: 22,560 (1996).

roll·ing mill *n.* **1. METAL-PRESSING FACTORY** a factory, or part of a factory, where metal, usually in ingot form, is processed by being rolled into sheets or bars of the desired shape and size **2. METAL PRESS EMPLOYING ROLLERS** a machine with rollers that press metal into sheets or bars of the desired shape and size

roll·ing pa·per *n.* a small piece of fine paper used for rolling a handmade cigarette (*often used in the plural*)

roll·ing pin *n.* a cylinder, sometimes with small handles at either end, used for rolling out and flattening dough, pastry, or other uncooked food

roll·ing stock *n.* **1. RAILROAD VEHICLES** railroad vehicles such as locomotives, passenger cars, and freight cars thought of collectively, especially those belonging to a particular company **2. ROAD VEHICLES** road vehicles thought of collectively, especially those belonging to a particular company

roll·ing stone *n.* somebody who is unable to stay in the same job, or live in the same place, for any length of time [Originally in the proverb, *a rolling stone gathers no moss*]

Rol·ling Stones /rṑling stṓnz/ British rock group, formed in 1962, that rivaled the popularity of the group's early contemporaries, the Beatles. The group was formed by Mick Jagger, Keith Richards, Brian Jones, Charlie Watts, and Bill Wyman, who left the band in late 1992. After Jones' death (1968), Mick Taylor replaced him until 1975, when Ron Wood took his place.

roll·mops /rṓl mòps/ *n.* a fillet of raw herring wrapped around a slice of onion or a pickle and left to marinate in spiced vinegar. It is usually served as an hors d'oeuvre. [Early 20thC. From German, from *rollen* "to roll" + *Mops* "pug dog."]

roll-neck *n.* **1. FOLD-DOWN COLLAR** a garment neck that is high, tight-fitting, and worn rolled down. ◊ **crew neck, turtleneck 2. ROLL-NECK GARMENT** a garment, especially a sweater, with a roll-neck ■ *adj.* **WITH ROLL-NECK** having a roll-neck. ◊ **crew-neck, turtleneck** —**roll-necked** *adj.*

roll-on *adj.* **WITH ROTATING-BALL APPLICATOR** that is applied to the skin by means of a rotating ball in the top of the container ■ *n.* **DEODORANT WITH ROTATING-BALL APPLICATOR** a deodorant, cosmetic, or other product that comes in a container with a rotating ball in its top

rollout *n.* **1.** AEROSP **SHOWING OF NEW AIRCRAFT** the first public display of a new aircraft or spacecraft **2.** MARKETING **GRADUAL LAUNCH OF NEW PRODUCT** a launch of a new product that involves gradually increasing the number of outlets where it is available to the public **3.** FOOTBALL **PASSING PLAY IN FOOTBALL** in football, a play in which a quarterback runs with the ball toward the side of the field in order to pass it

roll·o·ver /rṓl ṑvər/ *n.* **1.** FIN **TRANSFER OF FUNDS** a transfer of funds from one investment to another similar investment, often without taking possession of the funds **2. ACCIDENT WHERE A VEHICLE OVERTURNS** a road accident involving a vehicle that has overturned **3. CAPSIZING INCIDENT** an act or the process of capsizing, tipping over, or overturning

roll-top desk, roll-top *n.* a desk with a rounded cover consisting of connected parallel wooden slats that can be pulled down over the writing area and, usually, locked

roll·way /rṓl wày/ *n.* **1. SLOPE FOR LOGS** a natural or artificial sloping area along which cylindrical objects are rolled, especially a slope used by lumberjacks to move felled timber to water for transportation **2. SET OF ROLLERS** a series of parallel rollers used to facilitate the transportation of heavy loads

Ro·lo·dex /rṓlə dèks/ *tdmk.* a trademark for a type of desktop card-index system in which cards containing names, addresses, and telephone numbers are attached to but removable from a central cylinder

Röl·vaag /rṓl vaag/, **O. E.** (1876–1931) Norwegian-born U.S. writer and educator. He wrote epic novels about Norwegian settlers in the United States. Full name **Ole Edvart Rölvaag**

ro·ly-po·ly *adj.* of greater body weight than is desirable (*insult*) [Early 17thC. Origin uncertain: probably a rhyming compound of ROLL and POLL, originally meaning "rascal," and the name of several games of rolling balls.] —**ro·ly-po·ly** *n.*

Rom /rōm/ (*plural* **Rom** *or* **Ro·ma** /rṓmə/) *n.* a member of the Romany people, especially a Romany man [Mid-19thC. From Romany, literally "married man."]

ROM /rom/ *abbr.* COMPUT read-only memory

rom., **rom** *abbr.* PRINTING roman

Rom. *abbr.* **1.** GEOG Roman **2.** LANG Romance **3.** Romania **4.** LANG Romanian **5.** BIBLE Romans

Ro·ma plural of **Rom**

Ro·ma·ic /rō máy ik/ *n., adj.* modern Greek (*archaic*) [Early 19thC. From Greek *Rhōmaïkos* "Roman" (in reference to the Eastern Roman Empire).]

ro·maine /rō máyn/, **ro·maine let·tuce** *n.* a variety of lettuce that has a long slender head and loose leaves. Latin name: *Latuca sativa longifolia.* [Early 20thC. From French, feminine of *romain* "Roman"; perhaps because this lettuce was introduced into France during the Avignon papacy (1309–77).]

ro·ma·ji /rṓməjee/ *n.* the Roman alphabet as used for transliterating Japanese [Late 19thC. From Japanese, from *roma* "Roman" + *ji* "character."]

ro·man[1] /rṓmən/ *adj.* **IN OR OF UPRIGHT TYPE** relating to a type with upright as opposed to slanting characters that is the standard type used in printing books, newspapers, and magazines ■ *n.* **ROMAN TYPE** roman type or characters [Early 16thC. So called because it imitates the style of Roman inscriptions.]

ro·man[2] /rō maán/ *n.* **1. NOVEL** a novel, especially a French one or one in a French genre (*literary*) **2. MEDIEVAL FRENCH POEM** a medieval French narrative poem, especially one that has heroic exploits as its main theme [Mid-18thC. From French, literally "romance, novel."]

Ro·man /rṓmən/ *adj.* **1. OF MODERN ROME** relating or belonging to the modern city of Rome and its inhabitants **2.** HIST **OF ANCIENT ROME** belonging to or characteristic of the ancient city of Rome and its territories and inhabitants **3.** ARCHIT **IN ANCIENT ROMAN ARCHITECTURAL STYLE** relating to, belonging to, or built in a style characteristic of the buildings of ancient Rome, especially in having rounded arches, vaults, and domes **4.** CHR **OF THE ROMAN CATHOLIC CHURCH** belonging to or characteristic of the Roman Catholic church ■ *n.* **1. SOMEBODY FROM MODERN ROME** somebody who was born in or is a citizen of the modern city of Rome **2.** HIST **SOMEBODY FROM ANCIENT ROME** somebody who was born in or was a citizen of ancient Rome **3.** CHR **OFFENSIVE TERM** an offensive term for a member of the Roman Catholic church (*offensive*) [Pre-12thC. From Latin *Romanus* "Roman, a Roman," from *Roma* "Rome"; later reinforced by French *Romain.*]

ro·man à clef /rō maan ə kláy/ *n.* a novel in which some or all of the characters are based on real people and that usually includes clues to the characters' true identities [From French, literally "novel with a key"]

Ro·man al·pha·bet *n.* the writing system that represents sounds by the letters A-Z and is used for the languages of most Western European countries and many elsewhere. It is based on the alphabet developed in ancient Rome and now has 26 letters.

Ro·man cal·en·dar *n.* the lunar calendar, comprising 10 months and an intercalated month, that was used by the ancient Romans until the introduction of the Julian calendar in 46 B.C. ◊ **Julian calendar, Gregorian calendar**

Ro·man can·dle *n.* a short cylindrical firework that when placed on the ground and lit produces showers of sparks and occasional colored balls or stars of fire

Ro·man Cath·o·lic *adj.* **OF THE CATHOLIC CHURCH** relating to the Roman Catholic Church, its members, or its beliefs ■ *n.* **MEMBER OF THE CATHOLIC CHURCH** a member of the Roman Catholic Church

Ro·man Cath·o·lic Church *n.* a Christian church that has a pope as the head of a hierarchy of bishops and priests and is administered from the Vatican City in Rome

Ro·man Ca·thol·i·cism *n.* the system of beliefs, practices, and organization of the Roman Catholic Church

ro·mance *n.* /rō mánss, rṓ mànss/ **1. LOVE AFFAIR** a love affair, especially a brief and intense one ○ *This is more than just a holiday romance.* **2. LOVE** sexual love, especially when the other person or the relationship is idealized or when it is exciting and intense ○ *The secret of a happy marriage is to keep the romance alive.* **3. SPIRIT OF ADVENTURE** a spirit or feeling of adventure, excitement, the potential for heroic achievement, and the exotic ○ *the romance of cruising down the Nile* **4. FASCINATION WITH SOMETHING** a particular fascination or enthusiasm for something, especially of an uncritical or inexplicable kind ○ *his lifelong romance with football* **5. STORY OF LOVE** a novel, movie, or play with a love story as its main theme ○ *a writer of cheap romances* **6. LOVE STORIES COLLECTIVELY** love stories considered as a genre **7.** LITERAT **MEDIEVAL ADVENTURE STORY** a story of the adventures of chivalrous heroes written in verse or prose in a vernacular language in the Middle Ages **8.** LITERAT **MEDIEVAL ADVENTURE STORIES COLLECTIVELY** the genre of medieval adventure stories ○ *Arthurian romance* **9. NARRATIVE OF ADVENTURES** a fictional narrative dealing with exciting and extravagant adventures ○ *a romance of piracy on the high seas* **10. FICTITIOUS ACCOUNT** an extravagant or absurd fictitious account of something **11.** MUSIC **SHORT LYRICAL PIECE** a short lyrical song or instrumental composition, usually expressing or evoking tender emotions ■ *v.* /rō máns/ (**-manced, -manc·ing, -manc·es**) **1.** *vi.* **TELL ROMANTIC OR ADVENTUROUS STORIES** to tell or write extravagant or idealized fictitious accounts **2.** *vi.* **TELL LOVE STORIES** to tell or write stories about love **3.** *vi.* **THINK ROMANTICALLY** to think or behave in a romantic way **4.** *vt.* **TREAT SOMEBODY ROMANTICALLY** to treat somebody in a special way during a love relationship or with a view to entering on one **5.** *vt.* **HAVE AN AFFAIR WITH SOMEBODY** to have a love affair with somebody [13thC. From Old French *romanz* "(work composed) in French," from assumed Vulgar Latin *romanice* "in the vernacular," a form of Latin *romanicus* "Roman," ultimately from ROME.] —**ro·manc·er** /rō mánsər/ *n.*

Ro·mance *n.* the Italic branch of the Indo-European group of languages that includes French, Italian, Portuguese, Romanian, and Spanish, all of which are descended from Latin. About 500 million people speak one of the Romance languages. —**Ro·mance** *adj.*

Ro·man col·lar *n.* = **clerical collar**

Ro·man Em·pire *n.* **1. TERRITORY RULED BY ROMAN EMPERORS** the territories ruled by ancient Rome under its emperors, from 27 B.C. to A.D. 395. In 395, these territories were split into the Byzantine or Eastern Roman Empire and the Western Roman Empire. ◊ **Holy Roman Empire** **2. RULE OF ROMAN EMPERORS** the rule or form of government of ancient Rome under its emperors

Ro·man·esque /rṑmə nésk/ *adj.* **1. TYPICAL OF AN EARLY EUROPEAN ARCHITECTURAL STYLE** relating to or built in the style of European architecture that combines Roman and Byzantine elements, prevalent from the 9th century to the 12th and featuring rounded arches and barrel vaults **2. RELATING TO THE PERIOD OF ROMANESQUE ARCHITECTURE** characteristic of or relating to the style of European painting, sculpture, or decorative arts contemporary with Romanesque architecture. Romanesque works of art show a Byzantine influence and often feature elaborate ornamentation. ■ *n.* **ROMANESQUE STYLE** the Romanesque style in architecture or art

ro·man-fleuve /rō maan flṓv/ (*plural* **ro·mans-fleuves**) *n.* a long novel or series of novels telling the stories of a linked group of people over many years [From French, literally "river-novel"]

CORBIS/Andrea Jemolo

Romanesque: Carved stone capital (1127–45) from Pamplona Cathedral, Spain

Ro·man hol·i·day *n.* **1. ENTERTAINMENT INVOLVING CRUELTY** a type of entertainment in which people are killed, e.g., a gladiatorial contest **2. PLEASURE IN WATCHING BLOODSHED** a feeling of pleasure derived from watching others be maimed or killed

Rom·a·ni *n.* = **Romany** [See ROMANY]

Romania

Ro·ma·ni·a /rō máynee ə/ republic in southeastern Europe, bordered by Ukraine, Moldova, the Black Sea, Bulgaria, Yugoslavia, and Hungary. Language: Romanian. Currency: Romanian leu. Capital: Bucharest. Population: 22,600,000 (1997). Area: 91,700 sq. mi./237,500 sq. km.

Ro·ma·ni·an /rō máynee ən, -máynyən/ *n.* **1.** PEOPLES **SOMEBODY FROM ROMANIA** somebody who was born or raised in Romania, or who has Romanian citizenship **2.** LANG **LANGUAGE OF ROMANIA** the official language of Romania, belonging to the Romance group of Indo-European languages that developed from Latin —**Ro·ma·ni·an** *adj.*

Ro·man·ic /rō mánnik/ *adj.* **1.** HIST **OF ANCIENT ROME** belonging or relating to ancient Rome or the ancient Romans **2.** LANG **OF ROMANCE LANGUAGES** belonging or relating to the Romance family of languages ■ *n.* LANG **ROMANCE LANGUAGES COLLECTIVELY** the Romance family of languages as a group

Ro·man·ism /rṓmə nìzzəm/ *n.* an offensive term for Roman Catholicism, especially its ritual (*offensive*)

Ro·man·ist /rṓmənist/ *n.* **1. OFFENSIVE TERM** an offensive term for a member of the Roman Catholic Church (*offensive*) **2. STUDENT OF ANCIENT ROME** somebody who studies or is an expert in ancient Roman history or law ■ *adj.* **1. OFFENSIVE TERM** an offensive term meaning belonging or relating to the Roman Catholic Church (*offensive*) **2. OF ANCIENT ROMAN HISTORY** relating to or involving ancient Roman history or law —**Ro·man·is·tic** /rṑmə nístik/ *adj.*

Ro·man·ize /rṓmə nīz/ (**-ized, -iz·ing, -iz·es**) *v.* **1.** *vt.* CHR **MAKE SOMETHING ROMAN CATHOLIC** to make something such as a service take on a Roman Catholic character or influence **2.** *vti.* CHR **CONVERT TO ROMAN CATHOLICISM** to become a Roman Catholic, or convert somebody to Roman Catholicism **3. ro·man·ize, Ro·man·ize** *vt.* LANG **TRANSCRIBE SOMETHING INTO THE ROMAN ALPHABET** to transcribe something such as a language or text in the characters of the Roman alphabet **4.** *vti.* HIST **MAKE OR BECOME ROMAN** to take on Roman characteristics, or make somebody or something take on Roman characteristics ○ *the Romanized Celts* —**Ro·man·i·za·tion** /rṑməni záysh'n/ *n.*

Ro·man law *n.* **1. LAW OF ANCIENT ROME** the system of law established in ancient Rome, forming the basis of many modern legal systems **2.** = **civil law** *n.* 3

Ro·man mile *n.* a measure of distance used in ancient Rome, approximately equal to 1,620 yards/1,481 meters

Ro·man nose *n.* a nose with a high and prominent bridge

Ro·man nu·mer·al *n.* any of the letters or sequences of letters used by the ancient Romans to represent cardinal numbers, including I for 1, V for 5, and X for 10

Ro·ma·no /rō maá nō/ *n.* a type of hard and sharp-tasting Italian cheese, similar to Parmesan and often used grated [Early 20thC. Via Italian, literally "Roman," from Latin *Romanus* (source of English *Roman*).]

Ro·mans *n.* in the Bible, a letter from St. Paul to the Church at Rome. Written in about A.D. 58, it is an exposition of his theory of religious thinking. See table at **Bible**

Ro·mansch /rō mánsh, -maansh/, **Ro·mansh** *n.* one of the official languages of Switzerland, belonging to the Romance group of Indo-European languages and existing in several dialectal forms. Romansch is spoken by about 50,000 people. [Mid-17thC. From Romansch, via medieval Latin *romanice* from assumed Vulgar Latin (see ROMANCE).] —**Ro·mansch** *adj.*

ro·mans-fleuves plural of **roman-fleuve**

ro·man·tic /rō mántik/ *adj.* **1. INVOLVING SEXUAL LOVE** involving or characteristic of a love affair or sexual love, especially when the relationship is idealized or exciting and intense ○ *I don't think there's any romantic attachment between them.* **2. SUITABLE FOR LOVE** characterized by or suitable for lovemaking or the expression of tender emotions ○ *a romantic candlelit dinner for two* **3. INVOLVING ENTHUSIASM** relating to or characterized by a fascination or enthusiasm for something, especially of an uncritical or indefinable kind ○ *a romantic attachment to the mountains* **4. INVOLVING ADVENTURE** relating to or characterized by adventure, excitement, the potential for heroic achievement, and the exotic ○ *a romantic tale about life in the Outback* **5. IDEALISTIC** characterized by or arising from idealistic or impractical attitudes and expectations ○ *a romantic dreamer* **6. IMAGINARY** imaginary or fictitious in an extravagant or glamorizing way ○ *a romantic version of the events of her life* **7.** ARTS = **Romantic** *adj.* ■ *n.* **1. ROMANTIC PERSON** somebody who has a romantic personality or outlook **2.** ARTS = **Romantic** *n.* [Mid-17thC. Formed from *romaunt* Mid-16thC. From Old French, variant of *romanz* (see ROMANCE).] —**ro·man·ti·cal·ly** *adv.*

Ro·man·tic /rō mántik/, **ro·man·tic** *adj.* **OF AN 18C ARTISTIC MOVEMENT** relating to the movement in late 18th- and early 19th-century music, literature, and art that departed from classicism and emphasized sensibility, the free expression of feelings, nature, and the exotic ■ *n.* ARTS **ARTIST INVOLVED IN THE ROMANTIC MOVEMENT** a writer, composer, or artist who was involved in the Romantic movement during the late 18th and early 19th centuries

ro·man·tic com·e·dy *n.* a humorous movie, play, or novel about a love story that ends happily, or the genre itself

ro·man·ti·cism /rō mánti sìzzəm/ *n.* the quality of being romantic or having romantic inclinations

Ro·man·ti·cism *n.* in the arts, the style and theories of the Romantic movement, or the movement itself —**Ro·man·ti·cist** *n.*

ro·man·ti·cize /rō mánti sīz/ (**-cized, -ciz·ing, -ciz·es**) *v.* **1.** *vt.* **MAKE SOMETHING APPEAR GLAMOROUS** to make something seem or believe something to be more glamorous or ideal than it really is ○ *The movie tends to romanticize a rather sordid period in history.* **2.** *vi.* **THINK ROMANTICALLY** to think or express something in an amorous, idealistic, or sentimental way —**ro·man·ti·ci·za·tion** /rō màntissi záysh'n/ *n.*

Rom·a·ny /rómmənee, rṓmənee/ (*plural* **-nies**) *n.* **1.** PEOPLES **MEMBER OF A NOMADIC PEOPLE** a member of a nomadic people who probably originated in northwestern India. They appeared in Western Europe in the fifteenth century and there are now Romany communities throughout the world. **2. Rom·any, Rom·a·ni** LANG **LANGUAGE OF THE ROMANIES** the Indic language spoken by the Romany people. It belongs to the Indo-European family of languages and is spoken by around 250,000 people. [Early 19thC. From Romany *Romani*, a form of *Romano* "Romany" (adjective), from *Rom* "man."]

Rom·berg /róm bùrg/, **Sigmund** (1887–1951) Hungarian-born U.S. composer. His operettas include *The Student Prince* (1924), *The Desert Song* (1926), and *Up in Central Park* (1945).

Rome /rōm/ **1.** capital city of Italy, located in the center of the country. The former capital of the Roman Empire, it includes within its boundaries the independent state of the Vatican City. Population: 2,687,881 (1993). **2.** city in New York, on the Mohawk River, northwest of Utica and northeast of Syracuse. Population: 40,979 (1996). ◇ **fiddle while Rome burns** to occupy yourself with unimportant things when there are extremely important things requiring to be done ◇ **when in Rome (do as the Romans do)** used to indicate the advisability of adopting the behavior and customs of the place or circumstances in which you find yourself

Rom·el·dale /rómm'l dàyl/ *n.* an American breed of sheep that produces fine wool and high-grade lamb [Mid-20thC. Blend of ROMNEY MARSH, RAMBOUILLET, and CORRIEDALE.]

Ro·me·o /rṓmee ō/ (*plural* **-os**) *n.* **1. AMOROUS MAN** a man with a reputation for having or seeking romantic or sexual involvement with a large number of women ○ *the office Romeo* **2.** COMMUNICATION **CODE WORD FOR THE LETTER "R"** a code word for the letter "R," used in international radio communications [Mid-18thC. Named for *Romeo*, lover of Juliet in William Shakespeare's play *Romeo and Juliet* 1594.]

Rom·ish /rṓmish/ *adj.* an offensive term meaning belonging to, characteristic of, or influenced by the Roman Catholic Church, (*offensive*) —**Rom·ish·ly** *adv.* —**Rom·ish·ness** *n.*

Rom·mel /rómməl/, **Erwin** (1891–1944) German military leader. He is renowned for his victories in the African deserts during World War II. Known as **the Desert Fox**

Rom·ney Marsh /rómnee-/ *n.* a sheep of a breed that has long wool and is bred for mutton, originally from the Romney Marsh area in southern England

romp /romp/ *vi.* **(romped, romp·ing, romps) 1. PLAY BOISTEROUSLY** to run around or play in a boisterous way ○ *kids romping in the playground* **2. RUN EASILY** to run or move forward easily and smoothly ○ *The horse romped toward the finishing line.* **3. WIN** to win a contest easily (*informal*) ○ *Their team just romped all over us.* **4. MAKE EASY PROGRESS** to progress swiftly and effortlessly ○ *romped through her final exam* ■ *n.* **1. BOISTEROUS ACTIVITY** boisterous or playful activity ○ *The dogs had a romp in the park* **2. LIGHTHEARTED WORK** a book, play or movie that is lighthearted and lively as opposed to serious or weighty (*informal*) ○ *The novel is an exhilarating romp through the pages of recent history.* **3. CASUAL SEX** a casual or lighthearted sexual encounter (*informal*) **4. EASY VICTORY** a victory that is remarkably or unexpectedly easy (*informal*) **5. EASY PACE** an easy smooth pace **6. SOMEBODY PLAYFUL** a playful or boisterous person, especially a woman (*archaic*) [Early 18thC. Origin uncertain: perhaps an alteration of RAMP[2] in the sense "to stand menacingly."]

romp·ers /rómpərz/ *npl.* a one-piece suit usually with short pants and a bib held up by shoulder straps, worn by babies and small children

Ro·mu·lo /róm yoo lō/, **Carlos Pena** (1899–1985) Filipino politician. He served as president of the United Nations General Assembly (1949–50), and was ambassador to the United States in 1952.

Rom·u·lus /rómmyələss/ *n.* in Roman mythology, the founder of the city of Rome. He was the son of Mars and twin brother of Remus, whom he is said to have killed. ◊ **Remus**

ron·deau /rón dō, ron dṓ/ (*plural* **-deaux** /rón dōz, ron dṓz/) *n.* **1.** LITERAT **POEM WITH A REFRAIN** a poem of 13 or 10 lines in three stanzas, with two rhymes and with the opening phrase repeated twice as an unrhyming refrain **2.** MUSIC **MEDIEVAL FRENCH SONG** a medieval French song, especially a trouvère song with a two-part refrain [Early 16thC. From French, later form of *rondel* (see RONDEL).]

ron·del /rónd'l, ron dél/, **ron·delle** /ron dél/ *n.* a poem, similar to a rondeau, that has 13 or 14 lines in 3 stanzas, with 2 rhymes and with the opening 2 lines repeated as a refrain [14thC. From Old French, literally "small round" (from the repetition of the opening two lines), from *rond* "round," from, ultimately, Latin *rotundus* (see ROUND).]

ron·de·let /róndə lèt, ròndə lét/ *n.* a short form of rondeau, with five or seven lines and the first line repeated as a refrain. The first line is of four syllables and is repeated as line three and, in the longer form, line seven, while the other lines have eight syllables.

ron·do /rón dō/ (*plural* **-dos**) *n.* an instrumental piece or movement in which the principal theme is repeated between at least two sections that contrast with it, often forming the last movement of a sonata [Late 18thC. Via Italian from French *rondeau* "rondeau," a later form of Old French *rondel* (see RONDEL).]

ron·dure /rónjər/ *n.* something that has a circular, curved, or round shape (*literary*) [Late 16thC. From French *rondeur* "roundness," from *rond* (see RONDEL).]

rönt·gen *n.* = **roentgen**

roo /roo/ (*plural* **roos**) *n. Aus* a kangaroo (*informal*) [Early 20thC. Shortening.]

rood /rood/ *n.* **1.** ARCHIT **CRUCIFIX** a crucifix, especially one mounted at the entrance to the choir or chancel of a church **2. JESUS CHRIST'S CROSS** the cross on which Jesus Christ was crucified (*archaic*) **3.** MEASURE **QUARTER OF AN ACRE** a unit of area equal to 0.25 acre/0.10117 hectares [Old English *rōd* "cross, pole"]

rood screen *n.* a partition with a cross mounted on it and often decorated, separating the choir or chancel of a church from the nave or main part

WORD KEY: CULTURAL NOTE

Cat on a Hot Tin Roof, a play by Tennessee Williams (1955). Set in the U.S. South, it depicts the Pollitt family gathering to celebrate the 65th birthday of patriarch Big Daddy. The simmering conflicts between Daddy and sons Gooper and Buck and their wives reflect the lies and deceit that underpin many family relationships. It was made into a movie by Richard Brooks in 1958. One of its most famous lines is the last one from Act III: "Nothing's more determined than a cat on a tin roof–is there? Is there, baby?".

roof·er /roofər, rŏof-/ *n.* somebody whose job is to build or repair the roofs of buildings

roof gar·den *n.* **1. GARDEN ON TOP OF A BUILDING** a garden on the flat roof of a building **2. RESTAURANT AT THE TOP OF A BUILDING** a restaurant, bar, or public area at the top of a building, usually with access to an outdoor area

roof·ing /roofing, rŏof-/ *n.* **1.** CONSTR **MATERIAL FOR A ROOF** material used to make a roof **2. TOP OF SOMETHING** something forming a top or roof **3. OCCUPATION OF MAKING OR REPAIRING ROOFS** the business or occupation of making or repairing roofs

roof·line /roof līn, rŏof-/ *n.* the outline of the roof of a building or a series of roofs

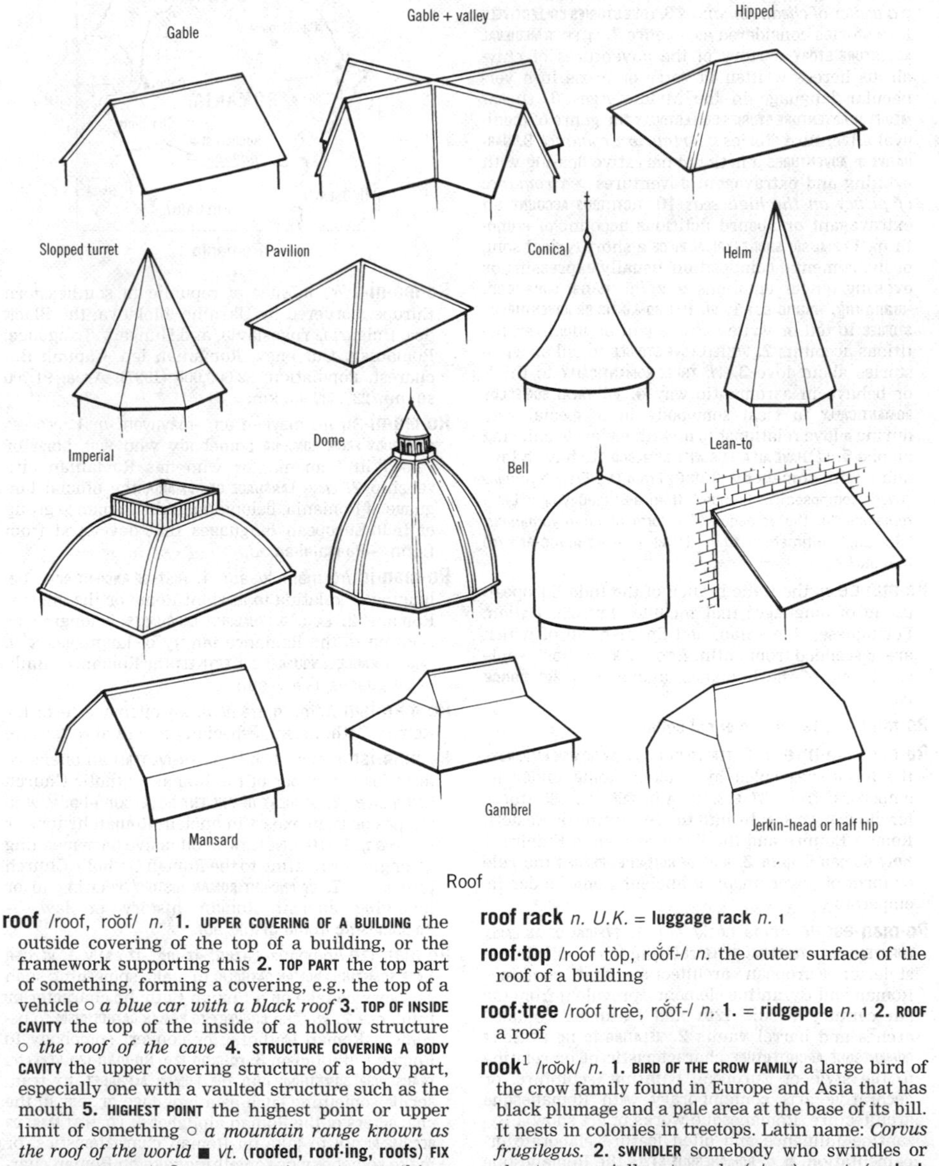

Roof

roof /roof, rŏof/ *n.* **1. UPPER COVERING OF A BUILDING** the outside covering of the top of a building, or the framework supporting this **2. TOP PART** the top part of something, forming a covering, e.g., the top of a vehicle ○ *a blue car with a black roof* **3. TOP OF INSIDE CAVITY** the top of the inside of a hollow structure ○ *the roof of the cave* **4. STRUCTURE COVERING A BODY CAVITY** the upper covering structure of a body part, especially one with a vaulted structure such as the mouth **5. HIGHEST POINT** the highest point or upper limit of something ○ *a mountain range known as the roof of the world* ■ *vt.* **(roofed, roof·ing, roofs) FIX ROOF ON SOMETHING** to fix a top covering onto something, especially a building ○ *The house is roofed with slate tiles.* [Old English *hrōf* "roof, ceiling, top," from prehistoric Germanic] —**roof·less** *adj.* —**roof·like** /roof līk, rŏof-/ *adj.* ◇ **hit the roof** to be extremely angry ◇ **go through the roof** to rise to an extremely high level

roof rack *n. U.K.* = **luggage rack** *n.* 1

roof·top /roof tòp, rŏof-/ *n.* the outer surface of the roof of a building

roof·tree /roof trēe, rŏof-/ *n.* **1.** = **ridgepole** *n.* 1 **2. ROOF** a roof

rook[1] /rŏok/ *n.* **1. BIRD OF THE CROW FAMILY** a large bird of the crow family found in Europe and Asia that has black plumage and a pale area at the base of its bill. It nests in colonies in treetops. Latin name: *Corvus frugilegus.* **2. SWINDLER** somebody who swindles or cheats, especially at cards (*slang*) ■ *vt.* **(rooked, rook·ing, rooks) CHEAT SOMEBODY** to overcharge, swindle, or cheat somebody (*slang*) ○ *If you paid that amount you've been rooked.* [Old English *hrōc*, from a prehistoric Germanic word of uncertain origin: probably an imitation of the sound] —**rook·y** *adj.*

Rook

rook[2] /ro͝ok/ *n.* any one of four chess pieces that begin a game in the corner squares and that can move in a straight line in any direction over any number of unoccupied squares [13thC. From Old French *rok,* ultimately from Arabic *rukk* (of unknown original meaning).]

rook·er·y /ro͝okəree/ (*plural* **-ies**) *n.* **1.** COLONY OF ROOKS a colony of nesting rooks **2.** ROOKS' BREEDING PLACE a place, especially in the tops of trees, where rooks breed **3.** ANIMALS' COLLECTIVE BREEDING PLACE a breeding or living area for large numbers of animals, especially birds or mammals that come together in colonies to nest or breed **4.** SLUM a slum or overcrowded group of rundown houses, especially tenements (*dated informal*)

rook·ie /ro͝okee/ *n.* (*informal*) **1.** SOMEBODY INEXPERIENCED somebody who is new to an activity or job, e.g., a new recruit to the army **2.** INEXPERIENCED PLAYER a player, especially a professional, who is in the first year of participation in a sport [Late 19thC. Origin uncertain: perhaps an alteration of RECRUIT, influenced by ROOK[1] in the obsolete sense "dupe, person easily cheated."]

room /room, ro͝om/ *n.* **1.** USABLE SPACE space that may or may not be filled with something ○ *There's room for another passenger in my car.* **2.** PART OF A BUILDING an area within a building that is enclosed by a floor, walls, and a ceiling ○ *a hotel room* **3.** PEOPLE IN A ROOM the people in a room considered as a group ○ *Her entrance silenced the room.* **4.** SCOPE the scope, opportunity, or possibility for something to exist, happen, or be done ○ *there's room for improvement* ■ **rooms** *npl.* ACCOMMODATIONS part of a house or hotel that may be rented as separate accommodations ○ *I managed to find myself rooms in town.* ■ *vi.* (**roomed, room·ing, rooms**) SHARE LIVING QUARTERS WITH SOMEBODY to occupy or share living quarters with one person or several people ○ *She rooms with her aunt.* [Old English *rūm,* from a prehistoric Germanic word meaning "spacious," of uncertain origin: perhaps ultimately from an Indo-European word that is also the ancestor of English *rural*] ◇ **not enough room to swing a cat** very little space

room and board *n.* accommodations with all meals provided, sometimes paid for and sometimes given in return for work ○ *Do you prefer bed and breakfast or room and board?*

room·er /róomər, ró͝omər/ *n.* a person who rents a room in another person's house, sharing the accommodations with the owner

room·ette /roo mét, ro͝o-/ *n.* a private single compartment in a railroad sleeping car

room·ful /róom fo͝ol, ró͝om-/ *n.* **1.** CONTENTS OF A FULL ROOM as many people or things as a room can hold ○ *a roomful of desks* **2.** THOSE IN A ROOM all the people or things in a room

room·ie /róomee, ró͝o-/ *n.* a roommate (*informal*)

room·mate /róom mayt, ró͝om-/ *n.* somebody with whom a person shares a room, apartment, or house

room ser·vice *n.* **1.** PROVIDING OF REFRESHMENTS a service providing food and drinks served to hotel guests in their rooms ○ *Room service is available throughout the day.* **2.** STAFF PROVIDING FOOD AND DRINK TO ROOMS the staff or department of a hotel responsible for serving food and drinks to guests in their rooms ○ *Call room service and order lunch.*

room tem·per·a·ture *n.* the average normal temperature of a living room, usually thought of as around 68°F/20°C or slightly above ○ *This wine should be served at room temperature.*

room·y /róomee, ró͝om-/ (**-i·er, -i·est**) *adj.* having plenty of space in which to move around —**room·i·ly** *adv.* —**room·i·ness** *n.*

roor·back /ró͝or bàk/ *n.* a false and defamatory story made public to gain a political advantage [Mid-19thC. From an attack on U.S. presidential candidate James K. Polk in 1844, which pretended to quote from a nonexistent work by a Baron von *Roorback.*]

Library of Congress

Eleanor Roosevelt

Roo·se·velt /rṓzə vèlt/, **Eleanor** (1884–1962) U.S. first lady, social activist, and writer. As the first lady of President Franklin D. Roosevelt, her national broadcasts and syndicated newspaper column established her reputation as a campaigner for progressive social causes. She was a U.S. delegate to the United Nations (1945–53) and chaired the commission that drafted the Universal Declaration of Human Rights. Born **Anna Eleanor Roosevelt**

Library of Congress

Franklin D. Roosevelt

Roo·se·velt, Franklin D. (1882–1945) U.S. statesman and 32nd president of the United States. He served longer than any other president (1933–45), with an unprecedented election to four terms. He held office during the Great Depression of the 1930s and World War II. Full name **Franklin Delano Roosevelt**

Library of Congress

Theodore Roosevelt

Roo·se·velt, Theodore (1858–1919) U.S. statesman and 26th president of the United States During his presidency (1901–09) he expanded U.S. involvement in world affairs, established domestic reforms, and promoted conservation. Known as **Teddy Roosevelt**

roost /roost/ *n.* **1.** PLACE WHERE BIRDS SLEEP a place where a bird rests or sleeps such as a perch or a building with perches for domestic fowl **2.** BIRDS SHARING A ROOST a group of birds sharing a roost **3.** TEMPORARY ACCOMMODATIONS a place where somebody may rest or sleep temporarily ■ *vi.* (**roost·ed, roost·ing, roosts**) GO TO SLEEP to rest or sleep on or in a roost ○ *Starlings were roosting in the trees* [Old English *hrōst*] ◇ **come home to roost** to result in undesirable or negative effects, usually after a fairly long period of time ◇ **rule the roost** to be the person who is in charge and who must be obeyed

roost·er /róostər/ *n.* **1.** MALE BIRD an adult male bird, especially a domestic fowl **2.** ARROGANT MAN a cocky or vain man

root[1] /root/ *n.* **1.** BOT UNDERGROUND BASE OF A PLANT the part of a plant that has no leaves or buds and usually spreads underground, anchoring the plant and absorbing water and nutrients from the soil **2.** BOT UNDERGROUND STEM OF A PLANT an underground plant part that behaves like a root, e.g., a rhizome or tuber, especially a fleshy edible one such as that of a carrot or turnip **3.** ANAT EMBEDDED BODY PART the portion of a body part such as a tooth or hair that is embedded in tissue **4.** BASE OF SOMETHING the bottom or base of something, or the part by which something is attached to the body ○ *the root of the tongue* **5.** CAUSE the fundamental cause, basis, or essence of something, or the source from which something derives ○ *the roots of discontent* **6.** ANCESTOR an ancestor or progenitor, especially one from whom many people are descended **7.** MATH NUMBER MULTIPLIED BY ITSELF a number that when multiplied by itself a given number of times equals another number ○ *2 is the square root of 4.* **8.** MATH NUMBER SUBSTITUTABLE FOR A VARIABLE a number that can take the place of the variable in an equation and solve the equation **9.** LING BASIC PART OF A WORD in linguistics, the basic meaningful part of a word that is left when any affixes are removed and that cannot be analyzed further into other meaningful elements **10.** LING ORIGINAL FORM OF A WORD in historical linguistics, the original reconstructed form from which a recorded word is derived, e.g., by phonetic change or the addition of affixes **11.** MUSIC FOUNDATION OF A CHORD the note that forms the foundation of a chord **12.** ANAT END OF A NERVE the end of a nerve that is nearer to the center of the body ■ **roots** *npl.* **1.** FEELING OF BELONGING a feeling of belonging in a particular place or culture ○ *I live in the city but my roots are in the country.* **2.** SOMEBODY'S GENETIC ORIGIN somebody's origins or ancestry ■ *v.* (**root·ed, root·ing, roots**) **1.** *vti.* GROW ROOTS to develop a root or roots or cause a plant to grow roots **2.** *vti.* BE FIXED to become fixed, embedded, or immobile or to cause somebody or something to become fixed, embedded, or immobile ○ *news that rooted me to the spot* **3.** *vi.* BE BASED to have a basis or origin in something ○ *herbal remedies that are rooted in folk medicine* [Pre-12thC. From Old Norse *rót.* Ultimately from an Indo-European word meaning "branch, root," which is also the ancestor of English *eradicate, radical,* and *wort.*] —**root·er** *n.* ◇ **root and branch** in every respect or to the fullest extent ○ *reformed the system root and branch* ◇ **take root** to become established and accepted

WORD KEY: SYNONYMS

See Synonyms at ***origin.***

root out *vt.* **1.** ERADICATE SOMETHING to eradicate or remove somebody or something completely ○ *He ruthlessly rooted out all opposition.* **2.** FIND SOMETHING EVENTUALLY to find or remove something after rummaging for it ○ *I'll root out some old photos of him.*

root up *vt.* to pull or dig up a whole plant, including its roots

root[2] /root/ (**root·ed, root·ing, roots**) *v.* **1.** *vti.* DIG IN THE GROUND WITH THE SNOUT to dig in the surface of the ground with the snout or nose out of curiosity or in search of food ○ *The pigs were rooting for beech nuts.* **2.** *vi.* RUMMAGE to move things about unsystematically while looking for something ○ *rooting in the drawer for a pencil* [Mid-16thC. Alteration (influenced by ROOT[1]) of *wroten,* from Old English *wrōtan.*] —**root·er** *n.*

root[3] /root/ (**root·ed, root·ing, roots**) *vi.* **1.** SUPPORT SOMEBODY OR SOMETHING NOISILY to cheer, shout, or applaud in support of a contestant or team **2.** LEND SUPPORT TO SOMEBODY to provide support to or be actively in favor of somebody or something [Late 19thC. Origin uncertain: perhaps an alteration of rout "to low loudly."] —**root·er** *n.*

Root /root/, **Elihu** (1845–1937) U.S. lawyer and politician. He won the Nobel Peace Prize (1912) for his work with the League of Nations.

root·age /róotij/ *n.* **1.** PLANTS PLANT ROOTS a system of plant roots **2.** PLANTS GROWTH OF ROOTS the developing of roots **3.** ACT OR PROCESS OF BECOMING FIXED the act or process of becoming rooted or established

root ball *n.* the tightly packed mass of roots and soil produced by a plant, especially when grown in a container

root beer *n.* a sweet carbonated soft drink made from the extracts of various roots and herbs

root ca·nal *n.* **1.** PULP CAVITY OF A TOOTH the cavity in the root of a tooth, containing pulp, nerves, and blood vessels **2.** DENTAL TREATMENT a dental treatment in which the diseased tissue in a root canal is removed and replaced with an inert material

root cap *n.* a thick protective mass of cells that covers the growing tip of the root of a plant

root cel·lar *n.* a pit or underground cellar used for storing root crops and vegetables

root climb·er *n.* a vine such as an ivy that climbs up a structure by developing small roots on its stems that grip the structure

root crop *n.* a crop grown for its edible roots, e.g., turnips, potatoes, or sugar beets

root·ed /ro͝otəd/ *adj.* **1.** HAVING ROOTS on which strong roots have developed ○ *a rooted plant* **2.** WELL ESTABLISHED arising from firmly held beliefs or long-standing traditions or practices ○ *a rooted conviction* **3.** UNABLE TO MOVE unable to move because of shock or fear **4.** HAVING STRONG TIES having strong emotional or cultural roots —**root·ed·ness** *n.*

root hair *n.* a fine growth from the outer cells of a plant root that resembles a hair and absorbs nutrients. Root hairs are elongated epidermal cells that increase the surface area of roots to improve absorption of water and minerals.

root·hold /ro͝ot hōld/ *n.* the anchoring of a plant in the soil by the spreading of its roots

root knot *n.* a disease of plants caused by nematodes in which the roots become enlarged and plant growth is stunted

root·less /ro͝otləss/ *adj.* **1.** PLANTS WITHOUT ROOTS with roots cut off or underdeveloped **2.** LACKING A BOND WITH PEOPLE lacking close ties to people or places —**root·less·ly** *adv.* —**root·less·ness** *n.*

root·let /ro͝otlət/ *n.* a small root or part of a root

root mean square *n.* the square root of the mean of the squares of a set of numbers. Sometimes the root mean square is a more useful measure of central tendency than the mean or the median.

root nod·ule *n.* a swelling on the roots of leguminous plants such as alfalfa, soybeans, and peas, caused by symbiotic bacteria that can fix nitrogen in the soil

root pres·sure *n.* the pressure that forces water upward through the conducting tissues of a plant, caused by the water potential in the stem being lower than in the root. Root pressure causes exudation of sap from cut stems and secretion of water droplets from leaves.

root rot *n.* a disease of plants that causes the roots to break or decay, often caused by fungi

roots mu·sic *n.* world music (*dated*)

root·stock /ro͝ot stŏk/ *n.* **1.** PLANTS = **rhizome 2.** PLANTS ROOT USED IN GRAFTING a root or piece of root used as a stock in propagation by grafting. ◊ **stock** *n.* 13 **3.** SOURCE OF SOMETHING a source or origin of something

root sys·tem /root sĭstəm/ *n.* the network of roots that a plant develops

root veg·e·ta·ble *n.* a vegetable such as a carrot, turnip, or beet that is grown for its fleshy edible root or tuber. Some are also used for their young leaves.

root·worm /ro͝ot wùrm/ *n.* a beetle whose larvae feed on the roots of crops, including corn. Genus: *Diabrotica.*

root·y /rootee/ (-i·er, -i·est) *adj.* **1.** HAVING MANY ROOTS full of or having many roots **2.** SIMILAR TO A ROOT resembling a root or roots —**root·i·ness** *n.*

ro·pa·ble /rṓpəb'l/, **rope·a·ble** *adj.* able to be caught or restrained using a rope

rope /rōp/ *n.* **1.** STRONG CORD a strong cord made by twisting together strands of hemp or other fibers or wire **2.** STRING OF SOMETHING a row of things strung or twisted together ○ *a rope of pearls* **3.** STRAND OF STICKY MATERIAL a stringy strand of a sticky substance ○ *a rope of saliva* **4.** CORD FOR HANGING SOMEBODY a cord with a noose at one end, used to execute people by hanging **5.** DEATH BY HANGING execution by hanging **6.** FREEDOM TO DO SOMETHING freedom or latitude to do something ■ **ropes** *npl.* **1.** LASSO a lasso or lariat **2.** BOXING CORDS OF A RING USED FOR FIGHTING the cords used to enclose a boxing or wrestling ring **3.** HOW TO DO SOMETHING the appropriate means and procedures for doing something or for functioning in an environment (*informal*) ○ *Her task was to show the new employee the ropes.* ■ *v.* (**roped, rop·ing, ropes**) **1.** *vt.* SECURE SOMETHING WITH A ROPE to tie, link, or bind somebody or something with rope ○ *the two climbers were roped together for the ascent* **2.** *vt.* ENCLOSE AN AREA to enclose or partition an area using ropes as barriers ○ *Museum staff had roped off the area.* **3.** *vt.* CATCH AN ANIMAL WITH A LASSO to catch an animal with a lasso ○ *rope a steer* **4.** *vi.* FORM STRANDS SIMILAR TO ROPE to form strands that resemble rope in shape or texture [Old English *rāp* (source of English *stirrup*)] —**rop·er** *n.* ◇ **give somebody enough rope** to allow somebody enough freedom or latitude to accomplish something or do something well ◇ **give somebody enough rope to hang himself** *or* **herself** to give somebody enough freedom to make mistakes or reveal his or her shortcomings ◇ **on the ropes** in a desperate or hopeless position and likely to fail (*informal*)

rope in *vt.* **1.** INVOLVE SOMEBODY to involve somebody in an activity, especially if he or she was initially reluctant or unwilling ○ *We got roped in to help with the cleaning up.* **2.** FOOL SOMEBODY to trick or deceive somebody into doing something

rope·danc·er /rṓp dànsər/ *n.* an acrobat who dances or performs feats on a rope, especially a tightrope, stretched above the ground —**rope·danc·ing** *n.*

rope tow *n.* = **ski tow**

rope·walk /rṓp wàwk/ *n.* a long shed or covered walk where ropes are made

rope·walk·er /rṓp wàwkər/ *n.* an acrobat who performs on a rope stretched above the ground, especially a tightrope walker [Early 17thC]

rope·way /rṓp wày/ *n.* a system of cables strung from high supports and used to carry heavy objects such as logs from one place to another through the air

rop·y /rṓpee/ (-i·er, -i·est), **rop·ey** (-i·er, -i·est) *adj.* **1.** SIMILAR TO ROPE resembling a rope or ropes **2.** FORMING STICKY THREADS forming into sticky, stringy strands —**rop·i·ly** *adv.* —**rop·i·ness** *n.*

roque /rōk/ *n.* a game developed from croquet and played on a hard court with a surrounding wall from which the ball can rebound and still be in play [Late 19thC. Alteration of CROQUET.]

Roque·fort /rṓkfərt/ *n.* a moist, strongly flavored, blue-veined cheese made from ewes' milk and matured in caves [Mid-19thC. Named for ROQUEFORT-SUR-SOULZON, where it was first made.]

Roque·fort-sur-Soul·zon /rṓkfərt syoor so͞o zoN/ town in Aveyron Region, in southwestern France, famous for its blue cheese. Population: 880 (1998).

ro·que·laure /rókə làwr, rṓkə-/ *n.* a knee-length hooded cloak worn by men in Europe in the 18th and 19th centuries [Early 18thC. Named for Antoine-Gaston (1656–1738), Duc de *Roquelaure* and Marshal of France.]

ro·quet /rō kāy/ *vti.* (**-queted, -quet·ing, -quets**) STRIKE AN OPPONENT'S CROQUET BALL in croquet, to strike another player's ball with your own ball ■ *n.* CROQUET STROKE HITTING ANOTHER BALL in croquet, a stroke that makes the player's ball strike that of another player [Mid-19thC. Origin uncertain: probably an alteration of CROQUET.]

ror·qual /ráwrkwəl/ *n.* any large streamlined baleen whale that has a small pointed dorsal fin and longitudinal grooves on the throat, e.g., the blue whale or the humpback whale. Genus: *Balaenoptera.* [Early 19thC. Via French from Norwegian *røyrkval*, from Old Norse *reyðarhvalr*, from *reyðr* "rorqual" (which was formed from *rauðr* "red") + *hvalr* "whale"; from its reddish color.]

Ror·schach test /ráwr shaak-, -shaakh-/ *n.* a projective test of personality or mental state based on somebody's interpretation of a series of standard inkblots. ◊ **projective test** [Early 20thC. Named for its inventor, Hermann *Rorschach* (1884–1922), a Swiss psychiatrist.]

ro·sa·ce·a /rō záyshə/ *n.* a recurring inflammatory disorder of the skin of the nose, cheeks, and forehead that is characterized by swelling, dilation of capillaries, pimples, and a reddened appearance [Late 19thC. Via modern Latin *(acne) rosacea* "rose-colored (acne)" from Latin *rosacea*, feminine of *rosaceus.*]

ro·sa·ceous /rō záyshəss/ *adj.* **1.** OF ROSES belonging or relating to the rose family (**Rosaceae**) of flowering plants **2.** SIMILAR TO A ROSE resembling a rose flower [Mid-18thC. From Latin *rosaceus.*]

Ro·sa·lind /rózzə lind, rṓzə-/ *n.* a small inner natural satellite of Uranus, discovered in 1986 by the Voyager 2 planetary probe. It is approximately 58 km (36 mi.) in diameter.

ros·an·i·line /rōz ánn'lin/, **ros·an·i·lin** /rō zánnələn/ *n.* a brownish-red crystalline compound derived from aniline and used as a dye, in the preparation of other dyes, as an antifungal drug, and in Schiff's reagent. Formula: $C_{20}H_{21}N_3O$. [Mid-19thC. From ROSE + ANILINE.]

ro·sar·i·an /rō zérree ən/ *n.* somebody who cultivates roses or who is an expert on their cultivation [Mid-19thC. Formed from Latin *rosarium* "rose garden," a form of *rosarius* "of roses," from *rosa* (see ROSE).]

Ro·sa·ri·o /rō záaree ō, -sáaree-/ city in east central Argentina, situated on the Parana River. Population: 894,645 (1991).

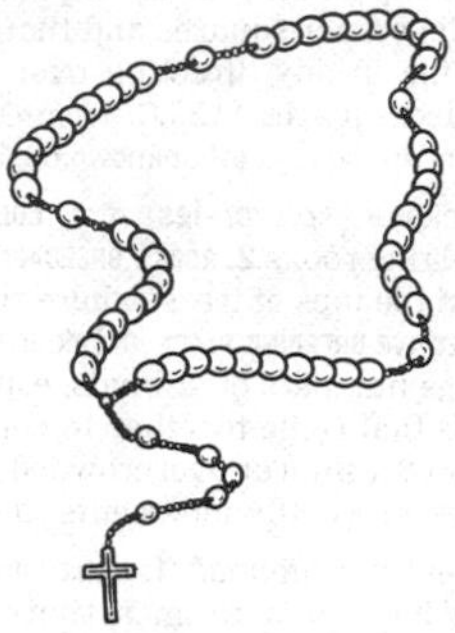
Rosary

ro·sa·ry /rṓzəree/ (*plural* **-ries**) *n.* **1.** SERIES OF PRAYERS a series of Roman Catholic prayers, usually made up of 5 or 15 decades of Hail Marys, each decade beginning with an Our Father and ending with a Gloria **2.** CATHOLIC PRAYER BEADS a string of beads used in counting the prayers said in a rosary **3. ro·sa·ry, ro·sa·ry bead** NON-CATHOLIC PRAYER BEADS a string of beads used in praying by members of religions or denominations other than Roman Catholicism [15thC. From Latin *rosarium* and Anglo-Latin *rosarius* "rose garden" (see ROSARIAN).]

WORD KEY: ORIGIN

It was a common stylistic device in the Middle Ages to name collections of verse or similar short pieces after bunches of flowers (*anthology* comes from the Greek word for "flower," and a similar inspiration underlies *florilegium*). This was the background against which a collection of Roman Catholic prayers came to be known as a ***rosary.*** The metaphor was probably encouraged by the symbolic association of roses and rose gardens with, respectively, the Virgin Mary and paradise.

ro·sa·ry pea *n.* **1.** TROPICAL PLANT a tropical vine naturalized in Florida that produces scarlet and black poisonous seeds used as beads and a root that is used as a substitute for licorice. Latin name: *Abrus precatorius.* **2.** ROSARY PEA SEED a seed of the rosary pea

Ros·com·mon /raass káamən/ town and administrative center of County Roscommon, in the Republic of Ireland. Population: 1,363 (1986).

Rose

rose[1] /rōz/ *n.* **1.** PLANTS PRICKLY SHRUB WITH ORNAMENTAL FLOWERS a prickly shrub or bush with compound leaves that is cultivated in many varieties and hybrids for its flowers. Genus: *Rosa.* **2.** PLANTS FLOWER OF A ROSE SHRUB the flower of the rose shrub. Roses are usually red, pink, yellow, or white and are often fragrant. The wild rose has five petals, but cultivated varieties are usually double or partly double. **3.** PLANTS **PLANT SIMILAR TO A ROSE** a member of the family of flowering plants that includes the rose, or a plant that resembles it, especially in having similar flowers. Family: Rosaceae. **4.** COLORS **REDDISH COLOR** a reddish-pink color **5. ORNAMENT RESEMBLING A ROSE** a representation of a rose flower as an emblem or decoration, or an ornament or design resembling a rose flower **6.** MINERALS **FORM OF VARIOUS MINERALS** a mineral form that is round and resembles a rose **7. SPRINKLER NOZZLE** a perforated nozzle on a watering can or hose for producing a spray **8.** CRAFT, INDUST = **rose cut 9.** ARCHIT **ROSE WINDOW** a rose window **10.** = **compass card ■ roses** *npl.* **1. EASY CIRCUMSTANCES** favorable, comfortable, or easy circumstances **2. PINK COLORING** pink coloration, especially in the cheeks ■ *adj.* **1. REDDISH-PINK** having a reddish-pink color **2. HAVING OR RESEMBLING ROSES** containing roses or resembling roses, especially in smell **3. RELATING TO ROSES** relating to or used for roses [Old English *rōse*, via prehistoric Germanic from Latin *rosa* (source of English *rosary*, and *rosé*), of uncertain origin: probably ultimately from Greek *rhodon*, of Iranian origin] ◇ **everything's coming up roses** everything is going very well

rose² past tense of **rise**

ro·sé /rō záy/ *n.* a pink-colored wine, especially one made by fermenting red grapes and removing the skins from the juice before all the color has been extracted [Late 19thC. From French, from *(vin) rosé* "pink (wine)."]

Rose /rōz/, **Pete** (*b.* 1941) U.S. baseball player and manager. He had a record-breaking 4,256 career hits, but was banned from baseball for betting (1989). Full name **Peter Edward Rose**

rose a·ca·cia *n.* a prickly shrub of the southeastern United States that has clusters of pale purple or rose-pink flowers. Latin name: *Robinia hispida*.

Rose·anne /rō zán/ (*b.* 1952) U.S. comedian and actor. She is best known for her television comedy series *Roseanne* (1988–97). Full name **Roseanne Barr**

rose ap·ple *n.* **1. SE ASIAN TREE** an evergreen tree of Southeast Asia that is widely grown for its decorative flowers and edible fruit. Latin name: *Eugenia jambos* and *Syzygium jambos*. **2. FRUIT OF THE ROSE APPLE TREE** the edible oval fruit of the rose apple tree, used in jellies and confections

ro·se·ate /rṓzee àyt, -ee ət/ *adj.* **1. ROSE-COLORED** of the reddish-pink color of roses **2. OPTIMISTIC** optimistic or idealistic, especially to an absurd degree [15thC. Formed from Latin *roseus* "rosy," from *rosa* "rose" (see ROSE).] —**ro·se·ate·ly** *adv.*

ro·se·ate spoon·bill *n.* an American wading bird that has rosy plumage and a spoon-shaped bill. Latin name: *Ajaia ajaja*.

rose·bay /rṓz bày/ *n.* **1.** = **rosebay rhododendron 2.** = **fireweed 3.** = **oleander**

rose·bay rho·do·den·dron *n.* a rhododendron of the eastern United States that has rose-pink bell-shaped flowers. Latin name: *Rhododendron maximum*.

rose·bay wil·low·herb *n.* = **fireweed**

rose bee·tle *n.* = **rose chafer**

Rose·ber·y /rṓz bèrree/ lake in the center of the North Island, New Zealand, originally formed by a volcanic eruption. It is a major tourist center. Area: 31 sq. mi./80 sq. km.

Rose·ber·y, Archibald Philip Primrose, 5th Earl of (1847–1929) British statesman. He succeeded W. E. Gladstone as Liberal Party leader and prime minister (1894–95) before retiring from a long political career.

rose-breast·ed gros·beak *n.* a North American woodland finch with a heavy bill, the male of which is black and white with a rose-red patch on its breast. The female is grayish brown with a streaked breast. Latin name: *Pheucticus ludovicianus*.

rose·bud /rṓz bùd/ *n.* the unopened flower of a rose

rose bug *n.* = **rose chafer**

rose·bush /rṓz bo͝osh/ *n.* any variety of rose that grows as a bush

rose cam·pi·on *n.* a plant that has white woolly down on its stems and leaves and is grown for its pink flowers. It is native to Europe and Asia but naturalized in northeastern North America. Latin name: *Lychnis coronaria*.

rose cha·fer *n.* a North American beetle that feeds on the roots, leaves, and flowers of roses and other garden plants. Latin name: *Macrodactylus subspinosus*.

rose cold *n.* = **rose fever**

rose-col·ored *adj.* **1.** COLORS **REDDISH PINK** a reddish-pink color **2. OPTIMISTIC** optimistic or idealistic, especially to an unjustifiable degree

Rose·crans /rṓz krànz/, **William Starke** (1819–98) U.S. Civil War Union general. He captured Chattanooga, Tennessee (1863) from the Confederates, but his troops were later beseiged there.

rose cut *n.* a way of cutting gemstones that gives them a flat base and a hemispherical crown with facets rising to a low point —**rose-cut** *adj.*

rose fe·ver *n.* hay fever experienced in the spring or early summer, caused by pollen, usually of grasses, that is airborne when roses are in bloom

rose·fish /rṓz fìsh/ (*plural* **-fish** *or* **-fish·es**) *n.* **1. N ATLANTIC FISH** a spiny-finned red food fish of the North Atlantic. Latin name: *Sebastes marinus*. **2.** = **redfish** *n.* 1

rose ge·ra·ni·um *n.* a shrub grown for its pink flowers and fragrant leaves that are used for scenting cosmetics and for flavoring. Latin name: *Pelargonium graveolens*.

rose·hip /rṓz hìp/ *n.* the fleshy fruit of a rose, resembling a berry and used to make jelly, herbal tea, or a medicinal syrup

ro·selle /rō zél/ *n.* a hibiscus of tropical Africa and Southeast Asia that has flowers with yellow petals and a red calyx from which jelly and beverages are made. Latin name: *Hibiscus sabdariffa*. [Mid-19thC. Origin uncertain: perhaps by folk etymology from French *l'oseille (de Guinée)* "sorrel (of Guinea)," alteration of popular Latin *acidula*, literally "sourish (plant)," from, ultimately, Latin *acidus* "sour."]

Ro·selle /rō zél/ village in northeastern Illinois, south of Schaumburg. It is a western suburb of Chicago. Population: 23,044 (1996).

rose mal·low *n.* **1. MARSH PLANT** a tall plant that grows in marshy areas of eastern North America and has downy leaves and pink or white flowers. Genus: *Hibiscus*. **2.** = **hollyhock**

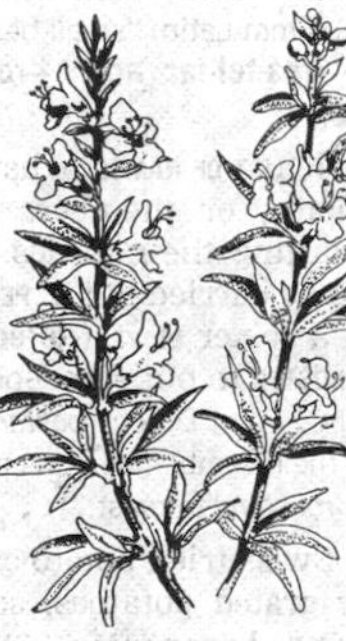

Rosemary

rose·mar·y /rṓz mèrree/ (*plural* **-ies**) *n.* a southern European aromatic shrub of the mint family grown for its fragrant gray-green needle-shaped leaves and used as a flavoring in cooking and in making perfume. Latin name: *Rosmarinus officinalis*. [14thC. By folk etymology from *rosmarine*, ultimately from Latin *rosmarinus*, from *ros* "dew" + *marinus* "of the sea," from its growth near sea coasts and its blossom's resemblance to dew.]

rose moss *n.* PLANTS = **portulaca**

Ro·sen·berg /rṓz'n bùrg/, **Julius** (1917–53) U.S. convicted spy. He and his wife Ethel Rosenberg (1916–53), both members of the Communist Party, were convicted in 1951 of passing nuclear weapons information to the Soviets during World War II. They were the first U.S. civilians to be executed for espionage (1953).

Ro·sen·wald /rṓz'n wàwld/, **Julius** (1862–1932) U.S. merchant and philanthropist. He financed various educational projects, including the Museum of Science and Industry (1929) in Chicago.

rose of Jer·i·cho *n.* a plant of desert regions that curls up into a ball in dry conditions and unfolds and grows in wet conditions. One variety is found in North Africa and southwest Asia, and the other in southwest North America and northern South America. Latin name: *Anastatica hierochuntica* and *Selaginella lepidophylla*. [Named for *Jericho*, an ancient city in Palestine]

rose of Shar·on /-shérrən/ *n.* **1. EUROPEAN SHRUB WITH YELLOW FLOWERS** a creeping southern European shrub, widely grown as ground cover and for its large yellow flowers. Latin name: *Hypericum calycinum*. **2. HIBISCUS** a Syrian shrub that is widely grown for its large red, purple, or white flowers. Latin name: *Hibiscus syriacus*. [Early 17thC. Translation of the Hebrew name in the *Song of Solomon*; *Sharon* refers to the fertile plain south of Mount Carmel in Israel.]

rose oil *n.* an essential oil made from rose flowers, used in perfumes, flavorings, and medicines

ro·se·o·la /rṑzee ṓlə, rō zée ələ/ *n.* a red rash on the skin, seen in diseases such as measles, scarlet fever, and syphilis [Early 19thC. Formed on the model of RUBEOLA from Latin *roseus* "rosy," from *rosa* (see ROSE).] —**ro·se·o·lar** *adj.*

ro·se·o·la in·fan·tum /-in fántoom/ *n.* a mild disease of young children, typically involving a three-day fever and the eruption of pink spots

rose per·i·win·kle *n.* = **Madagascar periwinkle**

rose quartz *n.* a pink translucent variety of quartz used as a gemstone and for ornaments

rose·root /rṓz ro͞ot/ *n.* a perennial mountain plant of Europe and Asia with yellow flowers, fleshy leaves, and a pinkish underground stem. Latin name: *Sedum rosea*. [Late 16thC. *Rose* from its root, which smells of roses when bruised.]

rose slug *n.* the larva of the sawfly, which feeds on the leaves of roses. Latin name: *Claudius isomerus* and *Endelomyia aethiops*.

rose to·paz *n.* a pink form of topaz made by applying heat to yellowish-brown topaz

Ro·set·ta /rō zéttə/ town in Egypt, on the Mediterranean coast. Population: 52,014 (1986).

Ro·set·ta stone *n.* a stone tablet found in 1799 near Rosetta in Egypt that contained the same text repeated in Egyptian hieroglyphics, Egyptian demotic script, and Greek, thereby supplying the key to deciphering hieroglyphics

ro·sette /rō zét/ *n.* **1. ROSE-SHAPED BADGE** a circular badge made from gathered loops of ribbon or pleated material, worn to demonstrate support for a team or political party or to indicate having won a prize **2. ORNAMENT RESEMBLING A ROSE** a carved or painted ornament resembling the open flower of a rose **3.** ZOOL **MARKING RESEMBLING A ROSE** a patch of color or a marking resembling the open flower of a rose, especially a cluster of spots on the fur of a leopard **4.** BOT **CLUSTER OF LEAVES** a circular or spiral cluster of leaves at the base of the stem of a plant [Mid-18thC. From French, literally "small rose," from *rose* "rose," from Latin *rosa* (see ROSE).]

Rose·wall /rṓz wàwl/, **Ken** (*b.* 1934) Australian tennis player. He won the Australian, French, and U.S. championships, and was also a successful doubles player. Full name **Kenneth Robert Rosewall**

rose wa·ter *n.* a fragrant liquid made by distilling or steeping rose petals in water, used as toilet water and in cooking

Rose window

rose win·dow, rose *n.* a round window with tracery radiating from the center in a pattern that resembles a rose. Often made of stained glass, rose windows are a feature of the Gothic style of church architecture.

rose·wood /rṓz wŏŏd/ *n.* **1. DARK WOOD OF TROPICAL TREES** a dark, heavy, rose-scented wood used in cabinetmaking that is obtained from various tropical trees, especially blackwood. Genus: *Dalbergia.* **2. ROSEWOOD TREE** a tree that yields rosewood

Rosh Cho·desh /ràwsh k͟hàw dèsh/ *n.* the first day of a new month in the Jewish religious calendar [From Hebrew *rō'š ḥōdeš*, literally "head of the month"]

Rosh Ha·sha·nah /ràwsh hə sháwnə, -hə shaánə/, **Rosh Ha·sha·na, Rosh Ha·sho·na, Rosh Ha·sho·nah** *n.* the festival that celebrates the Jewish New Year, observed on the first and second days of Tishri in the autumn. It marks the beginning of the Days of Awe, a period concerned with confessions of sin and redemption. [Mid-18thC. From Hebrew *rō'š haššānāh*, literally "head of the year."]

Ro·si·cru·cian /rṓzi krŏŏsh'n, ròzzi-/ *n.* a member of an international organization concerned with esoteric wisdom derived from ancient mystical and philosophical doctrines [Early 17thC. Formed from modern Latin *rosa crucis* "rose of the cross," translation of German *Rosenkreuz*, named for the organization's reputed founder, Christian *Rosenkreuz.*] —**Ro·si·cru·cian·ism** *n.*

ros·in /rózzin/ *n.* **HARD RESIN** a hard translucent resin ranging in color from amber to dark brown that is derived from the sap, stumps, or other parts of pine trees. It is used in making varnishes and other products and to increase friction, e.g., between the bow and strings of some stringed instruments. ■ *vt.* **(-ined, -in·ing, -ins) TREAT SOMETHING WITH ROSIN** to treat something with rosin, in particular to rub rosin on the bow of a stringed instrument to increase friction [13thC. Alteration of Old French *raisine*, variant of *resine*, from Latin *resina* (source of English *resin*); also via Anglo-Latin *rosina* from, ultimately, Latin *resina.*] —**ros·in·y** *adj.*

Ros·i·nan·te /ròzz'n ántee, rṓz'n-/ *n.* **1. DON QUIXOTE'S HORSE** the bony old horse that belongs to Don Quixote, the hero of the novel by Cervantes published in 1605 **2. OLD HORSE** any worn-out old horse (*literary*)

ros·in oil *n.* a thick yellowish sticky liquid distilled from rosin and used in making varnishes, inks, and other products

ros·in·weed /rózzin weèd/ *n.* a North American plant that smells of resin or has resinous juice, e.g., the compass plant. Genera: *Silphium* and *Grindelia.*

Ros·kil·de /rŏŏss keèlə/ city in Denmark, in eastern Sjaelland, situated about 15 mi./24 km west of Copenhagen. Population: 49,080 (1990).

Ross /ross/, **Betsy** (1752–1836) U.S. seamstress. She is credited with sewing the first flag of the United States of America (1776). Born **Elizabeth Griscom**

Diana Ross

Ross, Diana (*b.* 1944) U.S. pop singer. Known for her seductive vocal style and glamorous appearance, she helped her 1960s female group the Supremes become one of the most successful acts in the history of popular music before pursuing a solo career. Real name **Diane Ernestine Ross**

Ross, George (1730–79) American patriot. A member of the Continental Congress (1774–77) from Delaware, he signed the Declaration of Independence (1776).

Ross, Sir James Clark (1800–62) British explorer. He determined the position of the magnetic North Pole (1831) and discovered Victoria Land, Ross Island, and the Ross Sea (1839–43).

Ross, John (1790–1866) U.S. Native American leader. He led the Cherokee on the Georgia–Oklahoma "Trail of Tears" to a new home (1838–39) and became Chief of the United Cherokee nation.

Christina Rossetti

Ros·set·ti /rō zéttee/, **Christina** (1830–94) British lyric poet. She wrote in a variety of styles and forms, often exploring the themes of religion and death. She was the sister of Dante Gabriel Rossetti. Full name **Christina Georgina Rossetti**

Ros·set·ti, Dante Gabriel (1828–82) British painter and poet. A founder of the Pre-Raphaelite Brotherhood (1848), he brought medieval and Italianate influences to bear on idealized, emotionally charged paintings such as *The Annunciation* (1850) and *Proserpina* (1874). His last volume of verse was *Ballads and Sonnets* (1881). He was the brother of Christina Rossetti. Full name **Gabriel Charles Dante Rossetti**

Ros·si·ni /rō seénee/, **Gioacchino Antonio** (1792–1868) Italian composer. The most successful operatic composer of his time, he was a master of the bel canto style and excelled in comedy. His 37 operas, all written before 1831, include *The Barber of Seville* (1816) and *William Tell* (1829).

Ross Sea southern extension of the Pacific Ocean, bordering Antarctica. A large part of its surface is frozen, forming the Ross Ice Shelf. Ross Island, in the Ross Sea, is the location of the volcano Mt. Erebus.

ros·tel·lum /rò stélləm/ (*plural* **-la** /-stéllə/) *n.* a part of an animal or plant that resembles a beak, e.g., the hooked projection from the head of a tapeworm [Mid-18thC. From Latin, "small beak," from *rostrum* (see ROSTRUM).] —**ros·tel·lar** *adj.* —**ros·tel·late** /róstə làyt, ro stéllət/ *adj.*

ros·ter /róstər/ *n.* **1. LIST OF NAMES** a list, especially of employees, athletes, or members of the armed forces, often detailing their duties and the times when they are to be carried out **2. PEOPLE ON A LIST** the people listed on a roster ■ *vt.* **(-tered, -ter·ing, -ters) PUT SOMEBODY ON A ROSTER** to put somebody's name on a roster [Early 18thC. From Dutch *rooster*, originally "gridiron," hence (from the resemblance of its pattern to lines on paper) "list," from *roosten* "to roast."]

rös·ti /rṓstee/ *n.* a Swiss fried potato cake made from thinly sliced or grated potatoes, sometimes with added onions and bacon [Mid-20thC. From Swiss German.]

Ros·tock /róst òk, ráwst àwk/ city and port in northeastern Germany, in the state of Mecklenburg-Western Pomerania, on the Baltic Sea. Population: 236,100 (1994).

Ros·tov /rə stáwf/ city in southwestern European Russia, on the Don River. Population: 1,027,100 (1992).

ros·tra plural of **rostrum**

ros·trate /rós tràyt, róstrət/ *adj.* having a part that is shaped like a beak

ros·trum /róstrəm/ (*plural* **-trums** *or* **-tra** /róstrə/) *n.* **1. PLATFORM FOR PUBLIC SPEAKING** a platform or raised area where somebody stands to address an audience **2.** MUSIC **CONDUCTOR'S PLATFORM** a platform on a stage or in front of an orchestra where the conductor stands **3.** HIST **PROW OF ROMAN SHIP** the beak-shaped prow of an ancient Roman ship, especially a war galley **4. BEAK-SHAPED PART** a beak or beak-shaped part of something [Mid-16thC. From Latin, "beak, ship's prow," in plural, "platform" (because ships' prows decorated the orator's platform in the Forum), from *rodere* "to gnaw."] —**ros·tral** *adj.* —**ros·tral·ly** *adv.*

Ros·well /rṓz wèll, rózwəl/ city in southeastern New Mexico, directly west of the Pecos River and southeast of Albuquerque. Population: 47,559 (1996).

ros·y /rṓzee/ (**-i·er, -i·est**) *adj.* **1. ROSE-COLORED** of the reddish-pink color of roses ○ *the sunset turning the sky a rosy hue* **2. HAVING A PINKISH COMPLEXION** having a pinkish complexion that is regarded as indicating good health in Caucasian people **3. PROMISING** likely to be characterized by success or happiness ○ *predicts a rosy future for the business* **4. OPTIMISTIC** optimistic, especially to an unreasonable degree ○ *takes a rosy view of things* **5. LIKE A ROSE** resembling roses, characteristic of roses, or full of roses — **ros·i·ly** *adv.* —**ros·i·ness** *n.*

rosy pastor *n.* BIRDS = **pastor**

rot /rot/ *v.* (**rot·ted, rot·ting, rots**) **1.** *vti.* **DECOMPOSE** to be broken down or to break something organic down by the action of bacteria or fungi ○ *rotting vegetation* **2.** *vti.* **CHANGE BY DECOMPOSITION** to be reduced, damaged, or broken by the action of bacteria or fungi, or to affect something organic in this way ○ *allow the compost to rot down* **3.** *vi.* **LANGUISH** to endure the effects of complete neglect ○ *thrown into prison and left to rot* ■ *n.* **1. PROCESS OF DECAYING** the process or condition of decaying or a decayed area **2. NONSENSE** irrelevant or ridiculous talk (*informal*) **3. FUNGAL DISEASE** disease caused by fungi, e.g., foot rot of sheep, dry rot of timber and plants, and wet rot of timber **4.** ZOOL **ANIMAL DISEASE** infestation with liver flukes **5.** BOT **BACTERIAL PLANT DISEASE** a plant disease in which the tissue is broken down by the action of bacteria ■ *interj.* **EXPRESSION OF DISAGREEMENT** used to disagree with what somebody has said or to express annoyance or exasperation (*informal*) [Old English *rotian* (verb), ultimately of uncertain origin: perhaps from an Indo-European word that is also the ancestor of English *rude.* The noun perhaps came from Scandinavian.]

rot. *abbr.* MATH rotation

rota /rṓtə/ *n.* *U.K.* a list of people's names and the order in which they are to carry out specified duties [Mid-17thC. From Latin, "wheel."]

WORD KEY: ORIGIN

The Latin word *rota* from which ***rota*** is derived is also the source of English *control, rodeo, roll, rondo, rotate, rotund, roué,* and *round.*

Ro·ta *n.* the supreme ecclesiastical tribunal of the Roman Catholic Church

Ro·tar·i·an /rō térree ən/ *n.* somebody who belongs to a Rotary Club —**Ro·tar·i·an·ism** *n.*

ro·ta·ry /rṓtəree/ (*plural* **-ries**) *n.* **1. ROTATING PART** a machine or part of a machine that rotates around an axis or a fixed point **2.** TRANSP = **traffic circle** [Mid-18thC. From medieval Latin *rotarius*, from Latin *rota* "wheel."]

Ro·ta·ry Club *n.* a local club that is a member of Rotary International, an international organization of business and professional people originally formed in the United States to encourage service to the community [*Rotary* from the organization's early practice of holding meetings in rotation at members' business premises]

ro·ta·ry cul·ti·va·tor *n.* AGRIC = **rototiller**

ro·ta·ry cut·ter *n.* a disk blade encased in a handle and used for speed-cutting of strips of fabric, especially in patchwork

ro·ta·ry en·gine *n.* **1. INTERNAL-COMBUSTION ENGINE WITH ROTATING CYLINDERS** an internal-combustion engine with cylinders that rotate about a fixed crankshaft **2. ENGINE POWERING A ROTATING PART** an engine that produces torque or power entirely by a rotating mechanism rather than by a crankshaft and reciprocating piston arrangement. ◊ **radial engine**

Ro·ta·ry In·ter·na·tion·al *n.* an international organization of business and professional people formed in the United States in 1905 to encourage service to the community [See ROTARY CLUB]

ro·ta·ry mow·er *n.* a lawn mower with a single blade attached in the middle and sharpened at both ends that rotates as the mower is moved

ro·ta·ry plow *n.* AGRIC = **rototiller**

ro·ta·ry press *n.* a printing press that prints from curved plates mounted on a revolving cylinder, often onto a continuous roll of paper

ro·ta·ry pump *n.* a pump that imparts motion by internal sets of rotating vanes or screws, used to move water or other fluids

ro·ta·ry til·ler *n.* AGRIC = **rototiller**

ro·ta·ry-wing air·craft *n.* an aircraft, especially a helicopter, that is lifted or propelled by rotating airfoils

ro·tate /rṓ tàyt/ *v.* (**-tat·ed, -tat·ing, -tates**) **1.** *vti.* **TURN AROUND AN AXIS** to turn like a wheel around an axis or a fixed point, or make something turn around an axis or a fixed point ○ *The earth rotates around the axis through its poles.* ○ *The windmill's sails are rotated by the wind.* **2.** *vti.* AGRIC **VARY THE CROP GROWN** to vary the crops grown on the same piece of ground so as not to exhaust the soil or make it susceptible to disease **3.** *vti.* **FOLLOW IN ORDER** to follow in a sequence, taking turns, or make things follow in such a sequence ○ *Rotate the plates in the pile so that they all get used.* **4.** **REPLACE PERSONNEL** to be replaced by somebody else, or replace one person or group by another, e.g., in a sports team or military unit ○ *The manager rotates first-team players with promising newcomers in less important games.* ■ *adj.* **WHEEL-SHAPED** having parts that radiate from a central point [Late 17thC. Origin uncertain: either from Latin *rotat-*, past participle stem of *rotare*, from *rota* "wheel"; or a back-formation from ROTATION.] —**ro·tat·a·ble** *adj.*

ro·ta·tion /rō táysh'n/ *n.* **1.** **TURNING MOTION** a turning motion like that of a wheel around an axis or a fixed point, or the act or process of turning in such a way ○ *the rotation of the earth* **2.** **SINGLE REVOLUTION** a single turn of something around an axis or a fixed point ○ *one full rotation of the wheel* **3.** **REGULAR VARIATION** a regular or planned recurrent sequence of events or changes of position ○ *The families use the vacation home in strict rotation.* **4.** AGRIC **CROP ROTATION** crop rotation **5.** MATH **MATHEMATICAL TRANSFORMATION** a mathematical transformation in which axes are rotated by a fixed angle while the origin remains unchanged **6.** CUE GAMES **WAY OF PLAYING POOL** a way of playing pool in which the balls are shot in ascending numerical order —**ro·ta·tion·al** *adj.*

ro·ta·tive *adj.* = **rotatory** —**ro·ta·tive·ly** *adv.*

ro·ta·tor /rṓ tàytər/ *n.* **1.** **SOMEBODY OR SOMETHING ROTATING** somebody or something that rotates or causes rotation **2.** (*plural* **-tor·es**) ANAT **MUSCLE FOR ROTATION** a muscle that rotates part of the body on an axis

ro·ta·tor cuff *n.* the deep muscles of the shoulder and their tendons, which connect the arm to the shoulder joint, encircle it, and provide strength and stability while permitting rotation of the arm

ro·ta·to·ry /rṓtə tàwree/, **ro·ta·tive** /rṓ tàytiv/ *adj.* **1.** **ROTATING LIKE A WHEEL** involving, characterized by, or causing rotation around an axis or a fixed point **2.** **VARYING REGULARLY** involving, characterized by, or causing rotation of people or things in sequence

ro·ta·vi·rus /rṓtə vìrəss/ *n.* a wheel-shaped RNA virus that causes gastroenteritis, especially in infants. It is the most common cause of viral gastroenteritis. [Late 20thC. From modern Latin, literally "wheel-virus," from Latin *rota* "wheel" + *virus* "poison, virus."]

ROTC *abbr.* Reserve Officers' Training Corps

rote[1] /rōt/ *n.* mechanical repetition of something so that it is remembered, often without real understanding of its meaning or significance ○ *learned it by rote* [13thC. Origin uncertain: perhaps from Old French *ro(u)te* (see ROUTE) or Latin *rota* "wheel."]

rote[2] /rōt/ *n.* the noise of waves breaking on the shore [Early 17thC. Variant of *rut*, of uncertain origin: perhaps from Scandinavian.]

rote[3] /rōt/ *n.* a medieval stringed instrument played by plucking [14thC. From Old French, of uncertain origin: probably ultimately from late Latin *chrotta* "British musical instrument," from Welsh *crwth* "(type of) Celtic stringed instrument" or Old Irish *crot* "harp, cithara."]

ro·te·none /rṓt'n ōn/ *n.* a white crystalline insecticide extracted from the roots of derris. Formula: $C_{23}H_{22}O_6$. [Early 20thC. Formed from Japanese *roten* "derris."]

ROTFL, **ROFL** *abbr.* rolling on the floor laughing

rot·gut /rót gùt/ *n.* cheap and rough alcoholic drink (*informal*)

Roth /rawth/, **Philip** (*b.* 1933) U.S. writer. His novels, which often concern American Jewish life, include *Goodbye Columbus* (1959) and *Portnoy's Complaint* (1969). Full name **Philip Milton Roth**

Roth·ko /róth kō/, **Mark** (1903–70) Russian-born U.S. artist. He is known for large color-field abstract expressionist paintings, often in somber tones.

ro·ti /rṓtee/ (*plural* **-tis**) *n.* a type of unleavened bread originally from the northern parts of the Indian subcontinent, also eaten in the Caribbean [Early 20thC. From Hindi *roṭī*.]

ro·ti·fer /rṓtəfər/ *n.* a microscopic invertebrate animal that has a wheel-shaped crown of projecting threads (**cilia**) at the anterior end and lives mostly in freshwater habitats. The cilia aid in locomotion and food ingestion. Phylum: Rotifera. [Late 18thC. From modern Latin, literally "wheel-bearing, wheel-bearer," from, ultimately, Latin *rota* "wheel."] —**ro·tif·er·al** /rō tíffərəl/ *adj.* —**ro·tif·er·ous** /-fərəss/ *adj.*

ro·tis·se·rie /rō tíssəree/ *n.* **1.** **ROASTING SPIT** a cooking appliance for roasting meat using a rotating spit **2.** **PLACE ROASTING MEAT** a shop or restaurant where meat is roasted and sold [Mid-19thC. From French *rôtisserie*, from *rôtir* "to roast," from Old French *rostir*, from a prehistoric Germanic word that is also the ancestor of English *roster*.]

rot·l /rótt'l/ *n.* a unit of weight used in many Islamic countries, varying from approximately 1 to 5 lbs/0.45 to 2.25 kg [Early 17thC. From Arabic *raṭl*, of uncertain origin: perhaps an alteration of Greek *litra* "pound (unit of weight)" (source of English *liter*).]

ro·to·gra·vure /rṑtəgrə vyŏŏr/ *n.* **1.** **PRINTING PROCESS WITH A ROTARY PRESS** a printing process in which images are etched photomechanically onto copper cylinders mounted in a rotary press, from which they are printed onto a moving web of paper **2.** **SOMETHING PRINTED BY ROTOGRAVURE PROCESS** something printed using rotogravure, e.g., a magazine or a photographic section of a newspaper [Early 20thC. From German *Rotogravur*, company name, of uncertain origin: perhaps a blend of the company names *Rotophot* and *(Deutsche) Photogravur*.]

ro·tor /rṓtər/ *n.* **1.** AIR **ROTATING AIRFOILS** an assembly of airfoils that rotate about a hub to give lift to an aircraft, especially a helicopter **2.** AIR **ROTOR BLADE** a blade or airfoil of a rotor (*informal*) **3.** **ROTATING PART OF MACHINE** a rotating part of an electrical apparatus, e.g., the armature of a generator, or of a mechanical device **4.** METEOROL **WAVE OF AIR** a wave of air in which air rotates around a horizontal axis [Late 19thC. Contraction (perhaps modeled on VECTOR) or ROTATOR.]

Ro·to·ru·a /rṑtə rŏŏ ə/ city in the center of the North Island, New Zealand, noted for its volcanic activity and thermal springs. Population: 56,928 (1996).

Ro·to·ru·a, Lake lake in the center of the North Island, New Zealand, originally formed by a volcanic eruption. It is a major tourist center. Area: 31 sq. mi./80 sq. km.

ro·to·till /rṓtə tìl/ (**-tilled, -till·ing, -tills**) *vt.* to break up or till soil using a rototiller [Mid-20thC. Back-formation from ROTOTILLER.]

ro·to·till·er /rṓtə tìllər/ *n.* a machine for breaking up and tilling soil, consisting of a series of blades mounted on a revolving power-driven shaft [Early 20thC. From, ultimately, Latin *rota* "wheel" (see ROTA) + TILLER.]

rot·ten /rótt'n/ *adj.* **1.** **DECAYED** affected by rot or decay ○ *a rotten apple* **2.** **FOUL** extremely unpleasant, unfortunate, or nasty (*informal*) ○ *rotten weather* **3.** **INFERIOR** below the acceptable standard (*informal*) ○ *He's a rotten driver.* **4.** **NOT FEELING WELL** feeling unwell, usually without a specific complaint (*informal*) **5.** **UNHAPPY** feeling unhappy or uncomfortable, especially through guilt or embarrassment (*informal*) ○ *I feel rotten about letting you down.* **6.** **UNETHICAL** lacking ethical principles in the treatment of other people or animals ■ *adv.* **TO A GREAT DEGREE** to a great degree, especially so much as to be disapproved of (*informal*) ○ *The grandmother spoils those kids rotten.* [13thC. From Old Norse *rotinn*, of uncertain origin: probably the past participle of an assumed verb.] —**rot·ten·ly** *adv.* —**rot·ten·ness** *n.*

rot·ten bor·ough *n.* HIST a political constituency with few electors but the same right to elect a representative as a more populous constituency

rot·ten·stone /rótt'n stōn/ *n.* a form of silica-rich limestone that has been decomposed by weathering and is used in powdered form for polishing metal

rot·ter /róttər/ *n.* *U.K.* somebody who behaves in a nasty or unpleasant way (*informal dated*) [Early 17thC. Originally in the sense "causer of rotting."]

Rot·ter·dam /ráwtər daàm/ city and port in Zuid-Holland Province, southwestern Netherlands. Population: 1,074,387 (1994).

rott·wei·ler /rótt wìlər, -vìlər/ *n.* a large powerful dog of a breed that has a black smooth coat with tan markings. Rottweilers are often used as guard dogs.

ro·tund /rō túnd/ *adj.* **1.** **OVERWEIGHT** with a greater body weight than is advisable **2.** **RICH IN SOUND** having a full, rich sound [15thC. Directly or via Italian *rotondo* from Latin *rotundus* "round," from *rotare* "to rotate," from *rota* "wheel."] —**ro·tun·di·ty** *n.* —**ro·tund·ly** *adv.* —**ro·tund·ness** *n.*

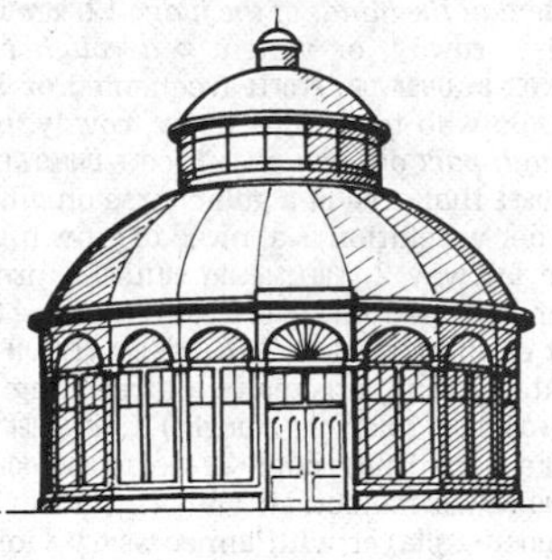

Rotunda

ro·tun·da /rō túndə/ *n.* **1.** **ROUND BUILDING** a round building, usually covered with a dome **2.** **ROUND ROOM** a large round hall or room **3.** **OPEN AREA IN A PUBLIC BUILDING** a large open area at an airport, railroad station, or other public building [Early 17thC. Alteration (modeled on Latin *rotundus* "round") of Italian *rotonda*, from Latin *rotunda*, the feminine of *rotundus* "round."]

ro·tu·rier /rō tŏŏree ày, -tyŏŏrə-/ *n.* a commoner or peasant [Late 16thC. From French, from *roture* "land tenure by somebody of low social class," hence "newly cultivated land," from Latin *ruptura* "breaking" (source of English *rupture*).]

Rou·baix /roo bé/ city in Nord Department, Nord-Pas-de-Calais Region, northern France, situated northeast of Lille. Population: 98,179 (1990).

rou·ble /rŏŏb'l/ *n.* = **ruble** [Mid-16thC. Via French from Russian *rubl*.]

rou·é /roo áy/ *n.* a man who regularly engages in drinking, gambling, and womanizing (*literary*) [Early 19thC. From French, noun use of the past participle of *rouer* "to break on the wheel" (a medieval instrument of torture), from, ultimately, Latin *rotare* (see ROTATE).]

WORD KEY: ORIGIN

The term ***roué*** is thought to stem from Philip II, Regent of France (1715–23), who humorously designated his debauched companions as *roués*, either to suggest that they deserved to be broken upon the wheel or because their behavior was so exhausting that they felt they had undergone this torture.

Rou·en /roo aàN/ capital of Seine-Maritime Department, Haute-Normandie Region, northwestern France. Population: 105,470 (1990).

rouge /roozh/ *n.* **1.** **REDDISH MAKEUP FOR THE CHEEKS** red or pink makeup in powder or cream form used to add color to the cheeks or lips or to accentuate the shape of the cheekbones (*dated*) **2.** **POLISH IN POWDER FORM** any of various kinds of polish in powder form containing metallic oxides, especially a polish for metal called jeweler's rouge that contains ferric oxide ■ *v.* (**rouged, roug·ing, roug·es**) **1.** *vt.* **COLOR SOMETHING WITH ROUGE** to put rouge on the cheeks or lips (*dated*) **2.** *vti.* **BLUSH** to blush or cause somebody to blush (*archaic*) [Mid-18thC. Via French from Latin *rubeus* "red."]

rouge et noir /rŏŏzh ay nwaàr/ *n.* a card game in which gamblers place their stakes on a table marked with two red and two black diamonds and all betting is against the house at even money [From French, literally "red and black"]

rough /ruf/ *adj.* **1.** **NOT SMOOTH OR FLAT** having a bumpy, knobby, or uneven surface rather than being smooth, flat, and regular **2.** **NOT SOFT** not soft and smooth, but rather coarse in texture ○ *a dog with a rough, bristly coat* **3.** **WINDY OR TURBULENT** stormy, or unpleasantly turbulent as a result of stormy conditions ○ *The weather had been rough for days.* **4.** **DIFFICULT TO TRAVEL OVER** in a wild and natural state and difficult to travel across ○ *marching over rough terrain* **5.** **NOT GENTLE** done with or using a lot of force or violence ○ *toys that will stand up to rough handling* **6.** **NOT POLITE** not refined or polite in manner and behavior ○ *rough talk* **7. SOUNDING OR TASTING HARSH** harsh on the ears or to the taste **8. NOT DETAILED** not exact, precise, or detailed, but broadly correct ○ *a rough estimate* **9. JUST BARELY SERVICEABLE** made quickly or without using proper or good-quality materials, or providing for only the most basic needs ○ *used branches to build a rough shelter* **10. LACKING FINISH OR REFINEMENT** hastily or incompletely made ○ *a rough wooden carving* **11. SEVERE OR UNPLEASANT** severe, unfair, or generally unpleasant ○ *received rough treatment at the hands of the judge* **12. ROWDY** tending to noisy, rowdy, or violent ○ *a rough crowd* **13. FREQUENTED BY UNSAVORY PEOPLE** frequented or inhabited by people who tend to be noisy, rowdy, or violent ○ *a rough part of town* ■ *n.* **1.** GOLF **UNMOWED PART OF A GOLF COURSE** that area of a golf course on which grass and other vegetation is allowed to grow higher than on the fairway **2. PRELIMINARY OUTLINE** a preliminary version of something, e.g., a sketch giving the broad layout of an artwork **3.** *U.K.* **VIOLENT PERSON** a violent or brutal person, especially a hired thug (*regional*) ■ *vt.* **(roughed, rough·ing, roughs) 1. ROUGHEN SOMETHING** to make something rough **2.** SPORTS **USE VIOLENCE ON AN OPPOSING PLAYER** in football and ice hockey, to treat an opposing player with unnecessary violence [Old English *rūh*. Ultimately from a prehistoric Germanic word that is also the ancestor of Dutch *ruw* and German *rauh*.] —**rough·ish** *adj.* —**rough·ness** *n.* ◇ **in the rough** in a crude, unfinished, or uncultivated state ◇ **rough it** to live in a less comfortable or less sophisticated way than usual (*informal*) ◇ **rough or smooth** RACKET GAMES used as a call when spinning a racquet in a game of tennis or squash to decide which player should serve first or choose the end to serve from

rough out *vt.* to prepare a rough model, plan, or sketch of something ○ *The scriptwriters meet to rough out a scene-by-scene narrative long before a word of dialogue is written.*

rough up *vt.* **1. BEAT SOMEBODY VIOLENTLY** to subject somebody to a violent beating (*informal*) **2. GIVE SOMETHING AN UNTIDY LOOK** to make something such as somebody's hair look untidy

rough·age /rúffij/ *n.* MED = **fiber** *n.* 7 [Late 19thC. Originally in the sense "rough grass, weeds."]

rough-and-read·y *adj.* **1. CRUDE BUT SERVICEABLE** not elegant or stylish but practical or usable ○ *rough-and-ready accommodations in a hostel* **2. LACKING POLITENESS BUT NOT FRIENDLINESS** not polite or well-mannered but friendly or kindhearted

rough-and-tum·ble *n.* a situation characterized by a lack of restraint and a ruthless disregard for rules and conventions —**rough-and-tumble** *adj.*

rough blue·grass *n.* a grass native to Eurasia and northern Africa and naturalized in the United States, where it is used in lawns and as forage. Latin name: *Poa trivialis.*

rough breath·ing *n.* in ancient Greek, a sound like that of the English "h," occurring with an initial vowel or the letter ρ and indicated by the symbol ʽ. ◊ **smooth breathing**

rough·cast /rúf kàst/ *n.* **1. PEBBLED SURFACE ON WALLS** a surface of coarse plaster covered with pebbles on the outside walls of a building (*often used before a noun*) ○ *roughcast walls* **2. ROUGH MODEL** a preliminary form or model of something ○ *made a roughcast in clay before starting to work the marble* ■ *vt.* **(-cast, -cast·ing, -casts) 1. COVER A WALL WITH ROUGHCAST** to cover the surface of a wall or the walls of a building with roughcast **2. FORM SOMETHING ROUGHLY** to shape or form something in a crude fashion or as a preliminary to more polished work —**rough·cast·er** *n.*

rough col·lie *n.* a long-haired collie dog that is black and white or black, white, and tan and has a band of thick hair around its neck and shoulders

rough cut *n.* the preliminary version of a movie, with only basic editing done to put the scenes together in sequence

rough di·a·mond *n. U.K.* = **diamond in the rough**

rough-dry *vt.* to dry washed laundry but not iron it —**rough-dry** *adj.*

rough·en /rúff'n/ **(-ened, -en·ing, -ens)** *vti.* to make something rough, or become rough

rough fish *n.* a species of fish that is neither caught for food nor fished for by anglers

rough-hew **(rough-hewed, rough-hewn, rough-hew·ing, rough-hews)** *vt.* **1. CUT SOMETHING ROUGHLY, WITHOUT SMOOTHING** to cut or carve something roughly without smoothing the surface or edges ○ *He rough-hewed the wood to make a crude table.* **2. MAKE SOMETHING CRUDELY** to shape or form something crudely

rough-hewn *adj.* **1. CUT NOT SMOOTHED** cut or shaped only roughly, with the surface and the edges not smoothed ○ *blocks of rough-hewn sandstone* **2. CRUDELY MADE** crudely shape or formed **3. RUGGED** rugged or rough and unrefined in character

rough·house /rúf hòwss/ *n.* **ROWDINESS** rough behavior or excessively boisterous play (*informal*) ○ *The party turned into a roughhouse.* ■ *vti.* **(-housed, -hous·ing, -hous·es** /-hòwzez/**) BEHAVE OR TREAT SOMEBODY ROUGHLY** to behave or treat somebody in a rough boisterous way (*informal*) [Late 19thC. From the idea of an establishment such as a bar or brothel where disorderly behavior occurs.]

rough-leg·ged buz·zard *n. U.K.* = **rough-legged hawk**

rough-leg·ged hawk *n.* a large Arctic hawk that has a dark body, feathers covering its legs, and a white tail with a broad dark band at the end. Latin name: *Buteo lagopus.*

rough·ly /rúfflee/ *adv.* **1. CRUDELY** in a crude or incomplete way ○ *shape the ground beef roughly into balls* **2. VIOLENTLY OR RUDELY** in a violent way or a manner lacking in gentleness and politeness **3. APPROXIMATELY** as a guess without any claim to exactness ○ *Roughly one third of the funding comes from government.*

rough·neck /rúf nèk/ *n.* **1. HIRED THUG** somebody who is violent, especially a hired thug (*informal*) **2. COARSE PERSON** somebody who behaves in a rough, bad-mannered way (*informal*) **3.** INDUST **OIL-FIELD WORKER** an unskilled worker on an oil-drilling rig or at an oil well (*slang*) [Mid-19thC. *Neck* used here for "person."]

rough·rid·er /rúf rìdər/ *n.* somebody who breaks wild horses, or who is skilled at riding horses that have not been trained

Rough Rid·er *n.* a soldier in the 1st U.S. Volunteer Cavalry recruited by Theodore Roosevelt to fight in the Spanish-American War

rough·shod /rúf shòd/ *adj.* **1. WEARING SPIKED HORSESHOES** fitted with horseshoes that have short spikes to prevent slipping in wet weather **2. BRUTAL** displaying great forcefulness and a lack of consideration ◇ **ride roughshod over somebody** *or* **something** to dispose of somebody or something forcefully and inconsiderately

rough sled·ding *n.* a hard or difficult time or experience (*informal*)

rough stuff *n.* violent behavior or acts (*informal*)

rough trade *n.* an offensive term for a tough or sometimes violent sexual partner for a gay man (*slang offensive*)

rough-winged swal·low *n.* a small brown bird in the swallow family commonly found near water in North America. Genus: *Stelgidopteryx.* [From the barb-shaped hooks on the outer feathers]

rouille /ro͝o ee/ *n.* a sauce made from chilies, garlic, and olive oil served as an accompaniment to many Provençal foods, especially bouillabaisse and other fish soups [Mid-20thC. Via French, literally "rust" (from its color), from, ultimately, Latin *robigo*.]

rou·lade /roo laád/ (*plural* **-lades**) *n.* **1.** FOOD **FOOD IN THE FORM OF A ROLL** a dish in which a piece of food is coated with a sauce or filling and rolled up before being cooked, so that each slice has a spiral appearance **2.** MUSIC **VOCAL MUSICAL ORNAMENT** a run of several musical notes sung rapidly to one syllable [Early 18thC. Via French, from *rouler* "to roll," from, ultimately, Latin *rota* "wheel" (source of English *rota* and *rotate*).]

rou·leau /roo lṓ/ (*plural* **-leaux** /-lṓ/ *or* **-leaus** /-lṓz/) *n.* **1. ROLL OF COINS** a stack of coins wrapped in a paper cylinder **2.** SEW **PIPING** rolled or folded ribbon used as decorative piping or trimming [Late 17thC. Via French, literally "small roll," from, ultimately, Latin *rotula* "small wheel," from *rota* (see ROULADE).]

rou·lette /roo lét/ *n.* **1.** GAMBLING **GAMBLING GAME WITH A SPINNING WHEEL** a game in which a ball is rolled onto a spinning horizontal wheel divided into compartments, with players betting on which compartment the ball will come to rest in (*often used before a noun*) **2. TOOL WITH A TOOTHED WHEEL** a tool with a toothed wheel used for making dots, e.g., in engraving, or for making perforations in paper, e.g., on a sheet of postage stamps **3. SLITS CUT IN PAPER** a line of slits or perforations made by a cutting tool on a sheet of paper ■ *vt.* **(-let·ted, -lett·ing, -lettes) MARK SOMETHING WITH DOTS OR PERFORATIONS** to use a roulette to mark a surface with a line of dots or make perforations in a sheet of paper [Mid-18thC. Via French, literally "small wheel" (the original sense in English), from, ultimately, late Latin *rotella*, from Latin *rota* "wheel" (source of English *rota*).]

Rou·ma·ni·an /rō máynee ən, roo-/ *n., adj.* Romanian (*dated*)

round[1] /rownd/ CORE MEANING: a grammatical word used to indicate that a circle of people, a place, or an object surrounds or encloses something ○ (prep) *She sat clasping her hands round her knees.* ○ (prep) *an area of green belt round the town* ○ (adv) *a crowd soon gathered round*

1. *prep.* **IN A PARTIAL CIRCUIT** to move to the other side of a corner or obstacle in a partial circuit, or be reached by such a movement ○ *The truck came round the bend at breakneck speed.* **2.** *prep., adv.* **TURNING ON AN AXIS** revolving around a center or axis ○ (prep) *the movement of the planets round the sun* ○ (adv) *cylinders going round at 1,000 revolutions per minute.* [13thC. Via Old French *ro(u)nd-*, the stem of *ro(o)nt*, from, ultimately, Latin *rotundus* (source of English *rotund*, *rondo*, and *roundelay*).]

round off *vt.* **1. MAKE SOMETHING MORE ROUNDED** to make the edges, sides, or corners of something less straight or angular and more rounded **2. FINISH SOMETHING IN PLEASING WAY** to bring something to a pleasant or satisfactory end by doing or adding one last thing

round on *vt.* to attack somebody suddenly, either physically or verbally, in a fit of anger

round out *vti.* to achieve or cause something to achieve a more complete or satisfactory form

round up *vt.* to gather people or animals together in one place

round[2] /rownd/ *adj.* **1. CIRCULAR OR SPHERICAL** shaped like a circle or a ball ○ *a big, perfectly round bowl* **2. CURVED** curved rather than square or angular ○ *round hips and a small waist* **3. IN A CIRCULAR MOTION** done with or involving a circular motion **4. COMPLETE** not less or more than ○ *I'll have a round 100 of them.* **5.** MATH **EXPRESSED BY AN INTEGER** expressed as an approximate value, especially to the nearest integer or power of ten ○ *use 1500 as a round number* **6. CONSIDERABLE** large in amount or size ○ *a round sum* **7. FULLY DEVELOPED** fully developed in terms of personality, or fully depicted, as in a character in a book ○ *His heroes are always very round and colorful.* **8. RATHER PLUMP** full and plump, especially in facial features ○ *kindly eyes surrounded by a round face* **9. SONOROUS** mellow and rich in tone **10. BRISK** lively and rather fast ○ *We set off at a round pace.* **11. STRAIGHTFORWARD** plain and outspoken ○ *"I said in good round English 'I'm going to knock the stuffing out of you'."* (John Buchan, *Greenmantle*) **12.** PHON **PRONOUNCED WITH ROUNDED LIPS** articulated with the lips forming an oval opening ○ *a round vowel sound*

round[3] /rownd/ *n.* **1. A ROUND SHAPE** a round shape or object ○ *little rounds of cheese* **2. A SESSION** a session or instance of a particular event, usually in a series of similar or related events ○ *the Uruguay round of global talks* ○ *the dreary round of fruitless calls* **3.** SPORTS **STAGE OF A COMPETITION** a game or series of games in a competition ○ *He beat last year's champion in the first round of the competition.* **4.** WRESTLING, BOXING **PERIOD OF BOXING OR WRESTLING** a time period, usually three minutes, during which boxers or wrestlers fight **5.** GOLF **GAME OF GOLF** a playing of all the holes on a golf course constituting one game **6.** LEISURE **TURN OF PLAY** a single turn of play, as in a game of cards **7.** ARCHERY **ARROWS SHOT** a specified number of arrow shot from a specified distance **8.** ARMS **CHARGE OF AMMUNITION** a bullet, blank cartridge, or other charge of ammunition ○ *a city that has received more than its share of mortar rounds* **9.** ARMS **GUN DISCHARGE** a single discharge by a gun or guns ○ *loose off a few rounds* **10. SERIES OF VISITS** a series of visits made on a regular basis to different places or people (*often used in the plural*) **11. DRINKS BOUGHT** a number of drinks bought for each member of a group of people **12.** FOOD **SLICE OF BREAD** a slice of bread or toast, or a sandwich made from two slices of bread **13. APPLAUSE** an outburst of applause or cheering ○ *She entered the hall to a huge round of applause.* **14.** MUSIC **A PART SONG** a song sung by several people whereby each person sings a different part of the song at the same time **15. MOVEMENT IN A CIRCLE** movement in a circle or around an axis **16.** MUSIC **BELLS RUNG** a sequence of bells rung in order of treble to tenor **17.** DANCE **CIRCULAR DANCE** a dance involving a sequence of movements in a circle **18.** FOOD **CUT OF BEEF** a cut of beef from between the rump and the shank ◇ **make** *or* **do** *or* **go the rounds 1.** to circulate and become widespread ○ *a new rumor making the rounds* **2.** to go from place to place in a regular pattern ◇ **in the round 1.** THEATER with the stage in the center and the audience seated around it **2.** with full detail and perspective from all sides

round[4] /rownd/ (**rounded, round·ing, rounds**) *v.* **1.** *vt.* **MOVE PAST AN OBSTACLE** to move in a curve past the edge or corner of something ○ *as they rounded the corner* **2.** *vti.* MATH **EXPRESS AS A LARGER OR SMALLER NUMBER** to express a number containing several units as the nearest significant number above or below it, e.g., treating 5,753 as 6,000, or 6.375 as 6 ○ *The estimate was rounded to the nearest dollar.* **3.** *vt.* **PRONOUNCE SOUNDS** to pronounce a sound with rounded lips ○ *Try to round your vowels.* **4.** *vt.* **PURSE LIPS** to purse the lips

round down *vt.* to express a number as a smaller and less exact number for ease of calculation

round up *vt.* to express a number containing several units as the nearest significant number above it, regarding, e.g., 5,924 as 6,000, or 7.57 as 8

round·a·bout /równdə bòwt/ *adj.* **CIRCUITOUS** indirect and not straightforward ○ *went by a roundabout route* ○ *answered in a roundabout way* ■ *n. U.K.* **1.** LEISURE = **merry-go-round 2.** TRANSP = **traffic circle** —**round·a·bout·ness** *n.*

round clam *n.* = **quahog** [From its rounded shell]

round dance *n.* **1.** DANCING **FOLK DANCE IN A CIRCLE** any folk dance in which several dancers or couples come together to form a circle **2.** DANCING **BALLROOM DANCE WITH A REVOLVING MOTION** any ballroom dance in which couples revolve as they move around the room, as they do in a waltz **3.** ZOOL **BEE'S SEQUENCE OF MOVEMENTS** a more or less circular sequence of movements that a honey bee performs in or near the hive to show others that food is nearby

round·ed /równdəd/ *adj.* **1. CURVED, OR WITH CURVED PARTS** having curved, not straight or angular, surfaces or edges ○ *a rounded lawn* **2. COMPLEX OR DIVERSE** having many different features or aspects that together form a whole that is complete and interestingly complex or diverse ○ *received a rounded education* **3.** PHON **PRONOUNCED WITH PURSED LIPS** pronounced with the lips pursed to form a round shape —**round·ed·ness** *n.*

roun·del /równd'l/ *n.* **1. ROUND PART** a round part or piece such as a round section in a stained-glass window or a round panel in a section of wood paneling **2.** POETRY **MODIFIED FORM OF RONDEAU** an English form of the rondeau that has eleven lines arranged in three stanzas of three lines and a one-line refrain after the first and third stanzas **3.** POETRY **TYPE OF RONDEL** a modified form of the rondel that has ten lines arranged in two stanzas of three lines and one of four lines, with the opening line repeated as a refrain **4.** DANCE = **roundelay** [13thC. From Old French *rondel*, literally "small circle," from *ro(u)nd-*, the stem of *ro(o)nt* (see ROUND[1]).]

roun·de·lay /równdə lày, róndə lày/ *n.* **1.** MUSIC **SONG WITH A VERSE REPEATED AS A CHORUS** a simple song in which the chorus consists of one of the verses repeated, or the music for this song **2.** DANCE **MEDIEVAL DANCE WITH DANCERS IN A CIRCLE** a slow medieval dance performed by a group arranged in a circle [15thC. Anglicization of French *rondelet* "small roundel," from *rondel*, literally "small circle," from *ro(u)nd-*, the stem of *ro(o)nt* (see ROUND[1]).]

round·er /równdər/ *n.* **1.** SPORTS **COMPLETE CIRCUIT IN ROUNDERS** a score in the game of rounders made when the batter runs around all four bases after a single hit of the ball **2. TOOL MAKING THINGS ROUND** a tool that makes edges or surfaces round **3. SOMEBODY LIVING A DEBAUCHED LIFE** somebody who lives a life of crime or debauchery (*informal*) [Early 17thC. Originally in the sense "somebody who makes the rounds of sentries."]

round·ers /równdərz/ *n.* a British ball game in which batters score a point, or rounder, if they run around all four marked fielding positions or bases after a single hit of the ball

round hand *n.* handwriting with broad rounded letters as opposed to, e.g., copperplate

Round·head /równd hèd/ *n.* somebody who supported Oliver Cromwell and the parliamentary party against King Charles I during the English Civil War of 1642 to 1649. ◊ **Cavalier** [Mid-17thC. From their close-cropped hair (contrasted with that of the Cavaliers).]

round her·ring *n.* a small silvery fish that is similar and related to the herring but does not have its sharp keeled abdomen. Family: Dussumieriidae.

round·house /równd hòwss/ (*plural* **-hous·es** /-hòwzəz/) *n.* **1.** RAIL **BUILDING FOR LOCOMOTIVES** a circular building in which railroad locomotives are stored or repaired, consisting of a central turntable with several sections of track radiating from it **2.** SHIPPING **CABIN ON A SAILING SHIP** a large cabin or set of cabins at the rear of an old-fashioned sailing ship **3.** BOXING **PUNCH DELIVERED WITH A CIRCULAR SWING** a punch made with a wide circular swing of the arm (*slang*) **4.** CARDS **PINOCHLE MELD** a meld of four kings and four queens in all suits in the card game pinochle [Late 16thC. Originally in the sense "prison."]

round·ish /równdish/ *adj.* somewhat round ○ *large roundish eyes* —**round·ish·ness** *n.*

round·let /równdlət/ *n.* a small circular or disk-shaped object (*literary*)

round lot *n.* STOCK EXCH a regular number of stocks or bonds as a trading unit, usually 100 shares of stock or 5 bonds

round·ly /równdlee/ *adv.* **1. SEVERELY** forcefully and thoroughly ○ *They were roundly criticized for their failure.* **2. AS A CIRCLE OR SPHERE** so as to form a circle or sphere (*dated*)

round rob·in *n.* **1.** SPORTS **TOURNAMENT WITH EVERYONE PLAYING ONE ANOTHER** a tournament in which each player or team plays against every other player or team in turn **2. PETITION WITH SIGNATURES IN A CIRCLE** a letter, especially a petition or letter of protest, on which the signatures are arranged in a circle in order to hide the identity of the first person to sign **3. DOCUMENT EACH PERSON PASSES ON** a letter or other document circulated in turn to all members of a group, with each of them adding comments if they wish [From the male first name *Robin*]

round-shoul·dered *adj.* with the shoulders hunched or drooping and the upper back bent forward slightly

rounds·man /równdzmən/ (*plural* **-men** /-mən/) *n.* **1. SOMEBODY DOING THE ROUNDS OF PLACES** somebody who makes regular visits to places on a set route, e.g., to make deliveries or carry out inspections **2. POLICE OFFICER SUPERVISING A PATROL** a police officer, especially a sergeant, in charge of all the officers patrolling a particular area

round·ta·ble /równd tàyb'l/ *n.* a discussion or negotiation between several parties or groups who all take part on equal terms [From ROUND TABLE]

Round Ta·ble *n.* **1. KING ARTHUR'S TABLE** the legendary table at which King Arthur and his knights sat, made round so that no one would appear to have precedence **2. KING ARTHUR'S KNIGHTS** the knights of King Arthur as a group

round-the-clock *adj.* lasting or operating throughout the day and night ○ *mounted round-the-clock surveillance on the house*

round trip *n.* **1.** TRANSP **TRIP THERE AND BACK** a trip to a place and back again, usually returning by the same route **2.** CARDS = **roundhouse** *n.* 4

round-trip tick·et *n.* a ticket that entitles a passenger to travel both to and back from a particular destination

round·up /równd ùp/ *n.* **1. A GATHERING OF PEOPLE OR ANIMALS** a gathering together of people or animals, e.g., suspects in a criminal investigation or livestock on a farm or ranch **2. SUMMARY** a gathering together of things of any kind, especially information or news ○ *a news roundup on the hour*

round·worm /równd wùrm/ *n.* a parasitic round-bodied worm (**nematode**) that infests the intestines of people and some animals. Latin name: *Ascaris lumbricoides.*

roup /roop/ *n.* an infectious respiratory disease that affects poultry [14thC. Origin uncertain: probably from a Scandinavian source. Originally in the sense "to shout, croak."]

rouse /rowz/ (**roused, rous·ing, rous·es**) *v.* **1.** *vti.* **WAKE, OR WAKE SOMEBODY** to wake up, or wake somebody from sleep or unconsciousness **2.** *vt.* **SHAKE SOMEBODY OUT OF APATHY** to stir somebody into action or a more active state, or to become more active ○ *Anger roused her to write a letter of complaint.* **3.** *vt.* **PROVOKE FEELING IN SOMEBODY** to cause somebody to feel a particular emotion ○ *the feelings of guilt that the whole affair roused in us* [15thC. Origin uncertain: perhaps via Old French *r(e)user* "to repel," from, ultimately, Latin *recusare*, literally "to cause to go back," formed from *causa* "cause" (source of English *cause*).] —**rous·er** *n.*

rous·ing /rówzing/ *adj.* **1. INCITING EMOTION** filling people with passion, emotion, and enthusiasm ○ *a rousing speech* **2. LIVELY** suggesting energy and vigor, especially by its fast pace —**rous·ing·ly** *adv.*

Rous sar·co·ma /rówss-/ *n.* a cancerous tumor found in chickens, caused by a specific tumor-producing RNA virus [Early 20thC. Named for Francis Peyton *Rous* (1879–1970), the U.S. physician who first described it.]

Rous·seau /roos ṓ/, **Jean Jacques** (1712–78) French philosopher and writer. He was one of the great authors of the Age of Enlightenment. His works include *The Social Contract* (1762), *The New Heloise* (1761), and *Émile* (1762).

roust /rowst/ *vt.* (**roust·ed, roust·ing, rousts**) **1. FORCE SOMEBODY TO GET UP** to make somebody get up, make a move, or take action, especially abruptly or roughly **2. HARASS SOMEBODY** to bother, annoy, or jostle somebody (*slang*) ■ *n.* **HARASSING** a harassing of somebody (*slang*) [Mid-17thC. Origin uncertain: probably an alteration of ROUSE.]

roust·a·bout /rówstə bòwt/ *n.* an unskilled laborer, especially on an oil-drilling rig, on a ship or wharf, or in a circus

roust·er /rówstər/ *n.* a deckhand or longshoreman

rout[1] /rowt/ *n.* **1. DEFEATED ARMY'S RETREAT** a swift and disorderly retreat by a defeated army **2. CRUSHING DEFEAT** any severe and humiliating defeat ○ *The game quickly turned into a rout.* **3. RABBLE** a noisy and disorganized group of people ■ *vt.* (**rout·ed, rout·ing, routs**) **1. FORCE AN ARMY TO RETREAT** to defeat an army completely and force it to make a swift and disorderly retreat **2. DEFEAT SOMEBODY THOROUGHLY** to subject an opponent to a thorough and humiliating defeat [13thC. Via Anglo-Norman *rute* and Old French *route* "dispersed group," from, ultimately, Latin *rumpere* "to break" (source of English *rupture*).]

rout out *vt.* **1. FORCE SOMEBODY OUT** to drive a person or animal from a place, especially by the use of force **2. REVEAL SOMETHING AFTER SEARCHING** to reveal or uncover something, especially after a search ○ *routed out his true motives*

rout[2] /rowt/ (**rout·ed, rout·ing, routs**) *v.* **1.** *vt.* CONSTR **MAKE A GROOVE IN SOMETHING** to cut a groove in wood or metal, especially with a router **2.** *vti.* **SEARCH BY POKING** to search for something by poking around or digging through something, as pigs do with their snouts [Mid-16thC. Variant of ROOT[2].]

route /root, rowt/ *n.* **1. WAY TO TRAVEL** a way, path, or road for traveling from one place to another **2. GENERAL COURSE SOMETHING FOLLOWS** the course that something follows, or the way it progresses or develops ○ *My career might have taken an entirely different route.* **3. REGULAR JOURNEY OR SEQUENCE OF CALLS** a journey somebody regularly makes, especially a set sequence of stops made, e.g., by somebody delivering something ○ *Their store wasn't on my usual route.* ■ *vt.* (**rout·ed, route·ing, routes**) **SEND SOMEBODY OR SOMETHING ALONG A ROUTE** to direct or arrange for somebody or something to follow a particular course ○ *All phone calls were routed through my office.* [12thC. Via Old French *route* from assumed Vulgar Latin *rupta*, literally "broken" (from frequent use), the feminine past participle of Latin *rumpere* "to break" (source of English *rupture*).]

route·man /ro͞otmən/ (*plural* **-men** /-mən/) *n.* somebody who makes a regular set of calls or stops in the course of a job, especially somebody selling or delivering something

route march *n.* a long march over rough ground, often used as training in physical endurance for soldiers, in which discipline is often relaxed and route step is allowed —**route-march** *vti.*

rout·er[1] /ro͞otər, rówtər/ *n.* **1. SOMEBODY ARRANGING DELIVERY** somebody who routes, especially somebody who arranges deliveries **2.** COMPUT **COMPUTER SWITCHING PROGRAM** a computer switching program that transfers incoming messages to outgoing links via the most efficient route possible, e.g., over the Internet

rout·er[2] /rówtər/ *n.* CONSTR a tool that cuts shaped grooves and hollows in wood or metal, originally a hand tool but now usually a power tool

route step *n.* a mode of marching in formation where there is no requirement to keep in step and talking and singing are allowed

rou·tine /roo te͞en/ *n.* **1. USUAL SEQUENCE OF ACTIVITIES** the usual way tasks or activities are arranged **2. SOMETHING REPETITIVE** something that is unvarying or boringly repetitive ○ *a life of mindless routine* **3. REGULAR PATTERN OF BEHAVIOR** a typical pattern of behavior that somebody adopts in particular circumstances, especially insincere or affected behavior (*informal*) ○ *The salesman went into his routine about the car's unique reliability and performance.* **4. REHEARSED PERFORMANCE** a rehearsed set of movements, actions, or speeches that make up a performance ○ *her gymnastic routine on the parallel bars* **5.** COMPUT **PART OF A COMPUTER PROGRAM** a part of a computer program that performs a particular task ○ *a dump routine* ■ *adj.* **1. USUAL OR STANDARD** regular or standard and nothing out of the ordinary ○ *carrying out routine questioning* **2. REPETITIVE** boringly predictable, monotonous, and unchanging ○ *found the work pretty routine* [Late 17thC. From French, from *route* (see ROUTE).] —**rou·tine·ly** *adv.*

WORD KEY: SYNONYMS

See Synonyms at ***habit*** and ***usual***.

rou·tin·ize /ro͞ot'n ɪ̄z, roo te͞e nɪ̄z/ (**-ized, -iz·ing, -iz·es**) *vt.* to arrange or plan something so that it follows a regular or unchanging pattern —**rou·tin·i·za·tion** /ro͞ot'ni záysh'n, roo te͞eni-/ *n.*

roux /roo/ (*plural* **roux** /roo, rooz/) *n.* a mixture of flour and fat that is cooked briefly and used as the thickening base of a sauce or soup [Early 19thC. Via French, "browned," which evolved from Old French *rous* "reddish brown," from Latin *russus* "red" (source of English *russet* and *rissole*).]

Rou·yn /ro͞o in, rwaN/ city in eastern Quebec, Canada, in a gold- and copper-mining district near the Ontario border. Population: 39,096 (1996).

rove[1] /rōv/ (**roved, rov·ing, roves**) *v.* **1.** *vti.* **WANDER OR TRAVEL AIMLESSLY** to wander or travel about with no definite purpose, often over a wide area **2.** *vi.* **MOVE IN CHANGING DIRECTIONS** to move, especially to look, in changing directions ○ *The officer's trained gaze roved around the room, taking it all in.* [Early 16thC. Origin uncertain: perhaps originally a dialect word meaning "to wander," probably of Scandinavian origin. Originally, "to shoot at random targets."]

rove[2] /rōv/ *vt.* (**roved, rov·ing, roves**) TEXTILES **TWIST FIBERS PRIOR TO SPINNING** to twist fibers slightly before they are spun into yarn or thread ■ *n.* TEXTILES **FIBERS TWISTED FOR SPINNING** wool, cotton, or other fibers twisted slightly in preparation for spinning [Late 18thC. Origin unknown.]

rove[3] /rōv/ NAUT past tense, past participle of **reeve**

rove bee·tle *n.* a carnivorous or scavenging beetle with a long body and short wing covers. Family: Staphylinidae. [Origin uncertain: perhaps from ROVE[1]]

rov·er[1] /rṓvər/ *n.* **1. WANDERER** somebody who wanders from place to place, never settling anywhere for long **2.** ARCHERY **ARCHERY TARGET** a mark or object selected randomly as a target in archery **3.** SPORTS **CROQUET BALL** a ball in croquet that has been through all the hoops but has not yet hit the final peg **4.** SPACE TECH **VEHICLE FOR EXPLORING A PLANET** a small vehicle launched from a lander and used to explore the surface of the moon or a planet

rov·er[2] /rṓvər/ *n.* a pirate or pirate ship (*archaic*) [14thC. From Middle Low German or Middle Dutch *röver*, from *röven* "to rob."]

rov·er[3] /rṓvər/ *n.* TEXTILES a machine or attachment for twisting fibers slightly in preparation for spinning [Mid-18thC. Originally in the sense "somebody who twists fibers for spinning."]

rov·ing /rṓving/ *adj.* **1. MOVING ABOUT** moving or traveling from one place or thing to another ○ *a bulletin from our roving reporter* **2. ERRATIC OR FICKLE** tending to wander or waver rather than settle or concentrate on one thing

rov·ing eye *n.* a wide and often promiscuous sexual interest

row[1] /rō/ *n.* **1. LINE OF THINGS** things or people that are arranged in a line that is usually straight, or the line itself ○ *cabbages planted in a row* **2. LINE OF SEATS** a line of seats in a theater, lecture hall, or similar public place ○ *the second row in the balcony* **3. NARROW STREET BETWEEN LINES OF HOUSES** a narrow street that is lined with houses or other buildings on both sides **4. STREET WITH A PARTICULAR CHARACTER** a street where a particular occupation or type of person predominates ○ *lawyer's row* **5.** MUSIC = **tone row** [Old English *rāw*] ◇ **in a row** one after the other in succession ◇ **a tough** *or* **hard row to hoe** something that is difficult to do

row[2] /rō/ (**rowed, row·ing, rows**) *v.* **1.** *vti.* **PROPEL A BOAT WITH OARS** to propel a boat across water by using oars **2.** *vi.* **ROW AS SPORT** to take part in the sport of rowing [Old English *rōwan*. Ultimately from a prehistoric Germanic base meaning "to steer."] —**row·er** *n.*

row[3] /row/ *n.* **1. LOUD FIGHT** a noisy quarrel or dispute **2. RACKET** an unpleasant or excessively loud noise ■ *vi.* (**rowed, row·ing, rows**) **ARGUE NOISILY** to have a noisy argument [Mid-18thC. Origin unknown.]

row·an /rów ən, rṓ ən/ *n.* **1.** = **mountain ash** *n.* **2. row·an, row·an·ber·ry** (*plural* **-ries**) **BERRY OF ROWAN** a red to orange berry from a rowan tree [Early 19thC. From a Scandinavian source. Ultimately from an Indo-European base meaning "red." Originally a Scots and northern English dialect word.]

row·boat /rṓ bṑt/ *n.* a small lightweight boat designed to be propelled through the water by one or more people rowing with oars

row·dy /rówdee/ *adj.* (**-di·er, -di·est**) **UNRULY** noisy and disorderly ○ *The debate was a pretty rowdy affair.* ■ *n.* (*plural* **-dies**) **NOISY PERSON** somebody who is rough and noisy and often causes disturbances ○ *a bar full of local rowdies* [Early 19thC. Origin uncertain: probably formed from ROW[3].] —**row·di·ly** *adv.* —**row·di·ness** *n.* —**row·dy·ism** *n.*

row·el /rów əl, rowl/ *n.* **SPIKED WHEEL ON A SPUR** a small spiked revolving wheel on the end of a horse rider's spur ■ *vt.* (**-eled, -el·ing, -els**) **SPUR A HORSE ON** to urge a horse on by digging rowels into its sides [14thC. Via Old French *roel(e)* "small wheel" (the original English sense), from late Latin *rotella* (source of English *roulette*), formed from Latin *rota* "wheel" (source of English *rota*).]

row·en /rów ən/ *n.* *New England* a second mowing of hay or grass in the same season [14thC. From Old Norman French, a variant of French *regain*, literally "to till again," formed from Old French *gaignier* "to till" (source of English *gain*[1]).]

WORD KEY: REGIONAL NOTE

The word ***rowen*** is the dominant form in New England, extending across upstate New York and the northernmost counties of Pennsylvania. See also ***aftermath***.

row house /rō-/, **row home** *n.* one of a line of houses joined to each other by their side walls

row·ing /rṓ ing/ *n.* the propelling of a small boat through the water using oars, especially the sport of racing in specially designed lightweight boats (*often used before a noun*) ○ *a member of the rowing team* [Old English *rōwing*]

row·ing boat *n.* *U.K.* = **rowboat**

row·ing ma·chine *n.* a fitness machine that imitates the action of rowing a boat

Row·land /rṓlənd/, **F. Sherwood** (*b.* 1927) U.S. chemist. He shared a Nobel Prize in chemistry (1995) for his research into chlorofluorocarbons and the depletion of the ozone layer. Full name **Frank Sherwood Rowland**

row·lock /rṓ lòk/ *n.* *U.K.* = **oarlock** [Mid-18thC. Alteration of OARLOCK by substituting ROW for OAR.]

Popperfoto

Arundhati Roy

Roy /roy/, **Arundhati** (*b.* 1961) Indian writer. She achieved success with her first novel, *The God of Small Things* (1997), which won the Booker Prize.

Roy, Gabrielle (1909–83) Canadian writer. She wrote novels about poverty among the working classes.

roy·al /róy əl/ *adj.* **1. OF KINGS AND QUEENS** relating to, belonging to, or consisting of a king, queen, or other member of a monarch's family ○ *members of the royal household* **2. ENJOYING ROYAL PATRONAGE** a word used in the titles of organizations and societies established by a monarch or a member of a monarch's family, or given his or her formal approval and support **3. LARGEST OR BEST** of the largest size or of the highest standard **4. EXCELLENT** of the most excellent kind ○ *given a royal welcome* **5. EXTREMELY BAD** used to emphasize how extremely bad something is (*informal*) ○ *a royal pain in the neck* **6.** SAILING **ABOVE THE TOPGALLANT** located in the area of rigging that is above the topgallant ■ *n.* **1. MONARCH OR MEMBER OF MONARCH'S FAMILY** a monarch or a member of a monarch's family, especially his or her immediate family (*informal*) **2.** HUNT **STAG WITH LARGE ANTLERS** a stag with large antlers that have 12 or more points on them **3.** SAILING **SAIL ABOVE TOPGALLANT SAIL** the sail above the topgallant sail on a full-rigged ship **4.** PRINTING **SIZE OF PAPER** a size of printing paper 20 x 25 in./508 x 635 mm [13thC. Via Old French *roial* from Latin *regalis* (source of English *regal* and *regalia*), from *reg-*, the stem of *rex* "king" (source of English *regicide*).]

roy·al blue *adj.* of a bright, deep blue color —**roy·al blue** *n.*

Roy·al Ca·na·di·an Mount·ed Po·lice *n.* a police force that operates throughout Canada except in cities and provinces with their own police forces

roy·al fern *n.* a deep-rooted fern with branched stems, found throughout the world. Latin name: *Osmunda regalis.*

roy·al flush *n.* in poker, a hand that consists of a ten, jack, queen, king, and ace of the same suit

Roy·al High·ness *n.* a title used when speaking or referring to a member of a royal family other than a king or queen

roy·al·ist /róy əlist/ *n.* somebody who supports the monarchy or who thinks a country should keep its king or queen rather than become a republic (*often used before a noun*) —**roy·al·ism** /róy ə lìzzəm/ *n.*

Roy·al·ist /róy əlist/ *n.* **1. CAVALIER** a Cavalier, or supporter of Charles I during the English Civil War **2.** = **Tory** *n.* 1 **3. FRENCH LOYALIST** in France, a supporter of the Bourbon dynasty after the Revolution

roy·al jel·ly *n.* a protein-rich substance that worker bees secrete and feed to larvae in the early stages of their development and to the larvae of queen bees in all stages of their development

roy·al·ly /róy əlee/ *adv.* with impressive generosity and hospitality ○ *royally entertained*

roy·al mast *n.* the highest section of a mast that is immediately above the topgallant

roy·al palm *n.* a palm tree with a tall naked trunk, found in the tropical regions of the Americas. Genus: *Roystonea.*

roy·al poin·ci·an·a *n.* a tropical tree native to Madagascar but widely grown in other tropical regions for its bright red flower clusters. Latin name: *Delonix regia.*

roy·al pur·ple *adj.* of a deep vivid reddish-purple color —**roy·al pur·ple** *n.*

roy·al road *n.* the route or method by which progress or a particular result is guaranteed, often by virtue of special privileges ○ *a young singer on the royal road to stardom*

roy·al·ty /róy əltee/ (*plural* **-ties**) *n.* **1. ROYAL PERSON OR PEOPLE** a king, queen, or other member of a monarch's family, or members of a royal family generally ○ *mixing with royalty at garden parties* **2. ROYAL PERSON'S STATUS** the status or authority of a king, queen, or other member of a monarch's family **3. KINGLY OR QUEENLY QUALITIES** the personal qualities conventionally ascribed to a king or queen, especially great dignity **4. MONARCH'S PERMISSION TO HAVE SOMETHING** the right to have or take something, especially minerals, granted by a king or queen to a person or company **5. PERCENTAGE OF INCOME PAID TO CREATOR** a percentage of the income from a book, piece of music, or invention that is paid to the author, composer, or inventor (*often used in the plural*) ○ *still living on the royalties from her first novel* **6. MINING COMPANY'S PAYMENT TO LANDOWNER** money paid to a landowner by a company taking minerals, oil, or gas from his or her land (*often used in the plural*)

royal war·rant *n.* a king's or queen's official authorization to a company to supply goods to a royal household

Royce /royss/, **Josiah** (1855–1916) U.S. philosopher and teacher. A proponent of idealism, he wrote many philosophical works, including *The Religious Aspect of Philosophy* (1885).

R.P. *abbr.* Received Pronunciation

RPG *n.* a high level computer language used primarily to produce business reports. Full form **report program generator**

rpm, **r.p.m.** *abbr.* revolutions per minute

rps, **r.p.s.** *abbr.* revolutions per second

rpt. *abbr.* **1.** repeat **2.** report

RPV *abbr.* MIL remotely piloted vehicle

R.Q. *abbr.* MED respiratory quotient

RR, **R.R.** *abbr.* **1.** railroad **2.** rural route

R.R. *abbr.* Right Reverend

RRB *abbr.* Railroad Retirement Board

-rrhagia *suffix.* abnormal or excessive flow or discharge ○ *metrorrhagia* [From Greek, formed from *rhag-*, the stem of *rhēgnunai* "to burst forth"]

-rrhoea, **-rrhea** *suffix.* flow, discharge ○ *pyorrhoea* [Via modern Latin from, ultimately, Greek *rhein* "to flow" (see RHEO-)]

rRNA *abbr.* ribosomal RNA

RRSP *abbr.* Registered Retirement Savings Plan

Rs *symbol.* rupees

RS *abbr.* **1.** recording secretary **2.** right side **3. RS, R.S.** Royal Society

RSA[1] *abbr.* Republic of South Africa

RSA[2] *n.* COMPUT a system of encryption based on the difficulty of factoring very large numbers

RSC *n., abbr.* **1.** Royal Shakespeare Company **2.** Royal Society of Canada ■ *abbr.* Royal Society of Chemistry

RSFSR, **R.S.F.S.R.** *abbr.* Russian Soviet Federated Socialist Republic

RSI *n.* a painful condition affecting some people who overuse muscles as a result of, e.g., regularly operating a computer keyboard and mouse or playing the piano. Full form **repetitive strain injury.** ◊ **tenosynovitis**

RSM *abbr.* **1.** regimental sergeant major **2.** MED Royal Society of Medicine

RSV, **R.S.V.** *abbr.* BIBLE Revised Standard Version

R.S.V.P., **r.s.v.p.** used on an invitation to request a response to it. Abbr of **please reply** [French, *répondez s'il vous plaît*]

RT *abbr.* **1.** radiotelephone **2.** radio telephony **3.** room temperature

rt. *abbr.* right

RTA *abbr.* ready to assemble

RTDS *abbr.* COMPUT real-time data system

rte. *abbr.* route

rtf *suffix.* COMPUT used after the period in a computer file name to show that the file contains codes identifying different fonts, layouts and other presentational features. Full form **rich text format**

RTFM COMPUT an offensive term used as a response in e-mail communications to an obvious technical question (*slang offensive*) Abbr of **read the fucking manual**

Rt. Hon. *abbr.* Right Honorable

Rt. Rev. *abbr.* Right Reverend

RTW *abbr.* ready-to-wear

Ru *symbol.* ruthenium

RU-486 *tdmk.* a trademark for a drug that blocks the body's use of progesterone and is used to induce an early-term abortion

Ru·a·hine Range /ro͞o ə hee̅ nay-/ mountain range in the south of the North Island, New Zealand. Its highest point is Mount Mangaweka, 5,686 ft./1,733 m.

ru·a·na /roo a̅ana/ *n.* a cape or poncho worn in Peru and Colombia [Mid-20thC. Via American Spanish from Spanish, "woolen fabric," from, ultimately, Latin *ruga* "wrinkle."]

rub /rub/ *v.* (**rubbed, rub·bing, rubs**) **1.** *vt.* PRESS AND MOVE HAND ON SOMETHING to move the hand or an object over the surface of something, pressing down with a repeated circular or backward and forward motion ○ *rubbing ointment into his skin* **2.** *vi.* TOUCH SOMETHING WITH DRAGGING PRESSURE to make dragging contact with a surface ○ *metal parts rubbing against one another* **3.** *vti.* CLEAN SOMETHING WITH REPEATED STROKES to clean, dry, or polish something, or be able to be cleaned, dried, or polished, by moving a cloth, sponge, or other implement over the surface repeatedly ○ *Rub the flaking paint off with sandpaper.* **4.** *vti.* CAUSE DISCOMFORT ON SKIN BY SCRAPING to cause discomfort or pain by repeatedly scraping the skin ○ *These shoes are rubbing my heels.* **5.** *vt.* ANNOY SOMEBODY to cause annoyance to somebody (*informal*) ○ *Her brusqueness was beginning to rub me.* ■ *n.* **1.** RUBBING ACTION a rubbing motion, or a rubbing of something with or against something else **2.** MASSAGE a massaging of part of the body ○ *a soothing back rub* **3.** DIFFICULTY a problem or difficulty ○ *That's the rub: too little time.* **4.** IRRITATING THING something that somebody does or says that irritates or offends somebody else [14thC. Origin uncertain: perhaps from Low German *rubben*, of unknown origin.] ◇ **rub somebody the wrong way** to irritate or annoy somebody

rub down *vt.* **1.** MASSAGE SOMEBODY to massage somebody or part of the body vigorously **2.** DRY BODY WITH VIGOROUS RUBBING to dry a person's or animal's body by vigorous rubbing with a towel

rub in *v.* to keep reminding somebody of something that person does not want to be reminded of, usually because it is embarrassing (*informal*)

rub off *vi.* to be passed to somebody or be an influence on somebody who is exposed to it

rub out *v.* **1.** *vti.* OBLITERATE to remove or obliterate something, e.g., by rubbing or wearing away, or to be removed or obliterated **2.** *vt.* KILL to murder somebody (*slang*)

rub up *vti.* to refresh old knowledge of something, or to bring a skill back up to its former standard ○ *rubbing up on his high-school French*

Rub al-Khali /ro͝ob al ka̅alee/ desert in the Arabian Peninsula. Also called the Empty Quarter, it extends from central Saudi Arabia into Yemen, the United Arab Emirates, and Oman. Area: 900,000 sq. mi./2,300,000 sq. km.

ru·basse /roo báss, ro͝o bàss/ *n.* MINERALS a variety of quartz with a high iron-oxide content that gives it a ruby red color [Late 19thC. Via French *rubace*, from *rubis* "ruby," from, ultimately, the base of Latin *rubeus*, *ruber* "red" (source of English *rubric* and *ruby*).]

ru·ba·to /roo ba̅atō/ *n.* DIVERGENCE FROM STRICT BEAT rhythmic freedom in musical performance, often against a steady accompaniment ■ *adj., adv.* WITH RUBATO performed with rubato [Late 18thC. From Italian *(tempo) rubato*, literally "robbed (time)," the past participle of *rubare* "to rob."]

rub·ber[1] /rúbbər/ *n.* **1.** INDUST NATURALLY OCCURRING ELASTIC SUBSTANCE a strong elastic material made by drying the sap from various tropical trees, especially the rubber tree **2.** INDUST ELASTIC SYNTHETIC SUBSTANCE a strong elastic synthetic substance made either by improving the qualities of natural rubber or by an industrial process using petroleum and coal products **3.** CLOTHES WATERPROOF OVERSHOE a waterproof overshoe worn over normal shoes to protect them in wet weather (*usually used in the plural*) **4.** BASEBALL SPOT PITCHER STANDS ON the rectangle of hard rubber on the mound that the pitcher stands on to throw the ball in baseball **5.** FURNITURE RUBBING OR POLISHING CLOTH a cloth or pad used for rubbing or polishing something, especially the pad that a cabinetmaker uses to apply varnish or polish **6.** DEVICE THAT RUBS SOMETHING any machine or device that rubs a surface **7.** = **eraser 8.** CONDOM a contraceptive sheath that fits over a man's penis (*slang; offensive in some contexts*) [Mid-16thC. Formed from RUB.]

rub·ber[2] /rúbbər/ *n.* **1.** CARDS BRIDGE MATCH OF THREE GAMES a match of three or five games in cards, especially bridge and whist **2.** CARDS DECIDING GAME IN CARDS MATCH in some card games, an extra game played to decide a tied match **3.** CARDS SESSION OF PLAY IN CARD GAME a match or session of playing in a card game (*informal*) **4.** SPORTS SET OF GAMES a set or series of games in some sports (*informal*) [Late 16thC. Origin uncertain: perhaps from RUBBER[1].]

rub·ber band *n.* a loop of thin rubber that is wrapped around objects to hold them together

rub·ber bridge *n.* a form of contract bridge in which a new hand is dealt for each round

rub·ber bul·let *n.* a cylindrical block of hard rubber fired by police officers or troops during crowd-control operations, designed as a deterrent but capable of inflicting serious injury

rub·ber ce·ment *n.* an adhesive made by dissolving rubber in an organic solvent

rub·ber check *n.* a check that is returned by a bank because the person who wrote it has insufficient funds in his or her account to cover it (*informal humorous*) [Because it bounces]

rub·ber-chick·en cir·cuit *n.* a series of events that people feel obliged to attend, especially lunches or dinners for politicians or other public figures (*informal*) [Because the food served is usually unappetizing]

rub·ber·ize /rúbbə rīz/ (**-ized, -iz·ing, -iz·es**) *vt.* to coat or impregnate something, especially fabric, with rubber

rub·ber·neck /rúbbər nèk/ *n.* = **rubbernecker** (*informal*) ■ *vi.* (**-necked, -neck·ing, -necks**) GAWK AT SOMETHING to stare at somebody or something in an over-inquisitive or insensitive way (*informal*) [Late 19thC. From craning or turning the neck as if it were made of rubber.] —**rub·ber·neck·ing** *n.*

WORD KEY: SYNONYMS

See Synonyms at ***gaze***.

rub·ber-necked /rúbbər nèkt/ *adj.* staring insensitively or in an over-inquisitive way (*informal*) ○ *a crowd of rubbernecked onlookers*

rub·ber·neck·er /rúbbər nèkər/ *n.* somebody who stares at somebody or something in an over-inquistive, stupid, or insenstive way (*informal*)

rub·ber plant *n.* **1.** TROPICAL PLANT GROWN AS HOUSEPLANT a tropical plant with thick glossy leaves and a rubbery sap, widely grown as a houseplant but growing as a full-size tree in Southeast Asia. Latin name: *Ficus elastica.* **2.** PLANT WITH RUBBERY SAP any plant that produces a rubbery sap

rub·ber stamp *n.* **1.** STAMPING DEVICE a device for stamping words or numbers on paper, consisting of an embossed flat rubber pad that is inked **2.** AUTOMATIC AUTHORIZATION authorization or approval that is given automatically **3.** SOMEBODY GIVING APPROVAL AUTOMATICALLY a person or group who gives authorization or approval automatically, without thinking, questioning, or dissenting

rub·ber-stamp (**rub·ber-stamped, rub·ber-stamp·ing, rub·ber-stamps**) *vt.* **1.** GIVE SOMETHING AUTOMATIC APPROVAL to authorize or approve something automatically, without thinking, questioning, or dissenting **2.** TO STAMP SOMETHING WITH IMPRINT to mark a document with an imprint from a rubber stamp

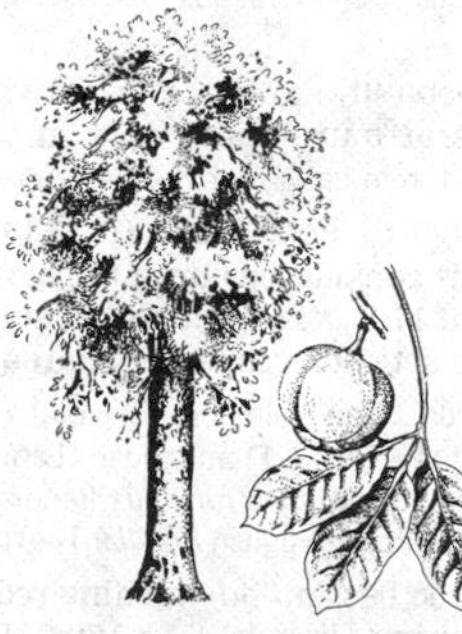

Rubber tree

rub·ber tree *n.* **1.** TROPICAL AMERICAN TREE SUPPLYING RUBBER a tropical American tree whose sap is the world's largest commercial source of natural rubber. Latin name: *Hevea brasiliensis.* **2.** ANY TREE PRODUCING RUBBER any tree that produces a sap from which rubber is made

rub·ber·y /rúbbəree/ *adj.* **1.** TOUGH OR ELASTIC with the elastic or tough texture of rubber **2.** WOBBLY lacking firmness or stiffness ○ *Suddenly, my legs felt rubbery.*

rub·bing /rúbbing/ *n.* an impression of a textured surface, e.g., a raised design on a tombstone, made by placing paper over the surface and rubbing with a drawing implement [14thC. Originally in the sense "action of rubbing."]

rub·bing al·co·hol *n.* a liquid, usually consisting of 70% denatured ethyl alcohol or isopropanol, used for massaging and as an antiseptic

rub·bish /rúbbish/ *n.* **1.** TRASH trash, garbage, or other unwanted things (*often used before a noun*) **2.** WORTHLESS THINGS things that are worthless or of very poor quality ○ *Most of what he's written is utter rubbish.* **3.** NONSENSE foolish things said or written, or things dismissed as wrong or not to be believed ○ *Don't talk rubbish!* [14thC. From Anglo-Norman *rubbous,* of uncertain origin: perhaps from, ultimately, Old French *robe* "stolen objects" (source of English *robe*), from Vulgar Latin *rauba*).] —**rub·bish·y** *adj.*

rub·ble /rúbb'l/ *n.* **1.** FRAGMENTS OF BROKEN BUILDINGS broken stones, bricks, and other materials from buildings that have fallen down or been demolished **2.** CONSTR ROUGH STONES AS FILLER OR BULK rough unfinished stones used to fill space between walls or to build the bulk of a wall that will have a finishing surface of dressed stone **3.** **rub·ble, rub·ble·work** CONSTR MASONRY OF ROUGH STONES masonry that is constructed using rough unfinished stones [14thC. Origin uncertain: perhaps from Anglo-Norman, an alteration of Old French *robe* (see RUBBISH).] —**rub·bly** *adj.*

rub·down /rúb dòwn/ *n.* a brisk rubbing down, usually of a person's or animal's body after exercising

rube /roob/ *n.* an offensive term for somebody who is naive or unsophisticated, especially somebody from a rural area and not used to city ways (*slang*) [Late 19thC. From "Rube," a pet form of the male forename *Reuben*; perhaps because it was considered a common name among country people.]

ru·be·fa·cient /rùbbə fáysh'nt/ *adj.* REDDENING THE SKIN causing the skin to become red (*formal*) ■ *n.* SOMETHING THAT MAKES SKIN RED a substance that causes the skin to become red, particularly a cream or ointment used as a counterirritant [Early 19thC. From Latin *rubefacient-*, the present participle stem of *rubefacere* "to make red," from *rubeus* "red" + *facere* "to make."] —**ru·be·fac·tion** /rùbbə fákshən/ *n.*

ru·be·fy /ro͞obə fī/ (**-fied, -fy·ing, -fies**) *vti.* MED to use a rubefacient on skin [14thC. Formed from Old French *rube-*, the stem of *rubifier* from, ultimately, Latin *rubeus* "red."]

Rube Gold·berg /roob gṓld bùrg/ *adj.* unnecessarily intricate and complicated [Mid-20thC. Named for *Reuben Goldberg* (1883–1970), a U.S. cartoonist known for his depictions of complex devices performing elementary tasks.]

ru·bel·la /roo béllə/ *n.* a highly contagious viral disease especially of children that causes swelling of the lymph glands and a reddish-pink rash on the skin. It can be harmful to the unborn baby of a pregnant woman who contracts it. [Late 19thC. From modern Latin, "rash," noun use of the neuter plural of Latin *rubellus* "reddish," from *rubeus* "red" (source of English *rubeola*).]

ru·bel·lite /ro͞obə līt, roo bé-/ *n.* a red variety of the glassy mineral tourmaline, used in jewelry [Late 18thC. Formed from Latin *rubellus* (see RUBELLA).]

Ru·bens /ro͞obənz/, **Peter Paul** (1577–1640) Flemish painter. He is considered one of the most important artists of the 17th century, and his style has come to define the sensuous aspects of baroque painting.

ru·be·o·la /roo bée ələ, ro͞obi ṓlə/ *n.* measles (*technical*) [Late 17thC. From modern Latin, noun use of the neuter plural of assumed *rubeolus* "reddish," from Latin *rubeus* "red" (source of English *rubella*).] —**ru·be·o·lar** *adj.*

ru·bes·cent /roo béss'nt/ *adj.* turning red or reddish, e.g., by blushing (*literary*) [Mid-18thC. From Latin *rubescent-*, the present participle stem of *rubescere* "to redden," from, ultimately, *ruber* "red."] —**ru·bes·cence** /roo béss'ns/ *n.*

Ru·bi·con[1] /ro͞obi kòn/, **ru·bi·con** *n.* a point at which any action taken commits the person taking it to a further particular course of action that cannot be avoided [Early 17thC. Named for the RUBICON[2].] ◇ **cross the Rubicon** to do something that commits you to a particular course of action

WORD KEY: ORIGIN

The ***Rubicon*** was a stream in northern Italy that formerly constituted part of the boundary between Cisalpine Gaul and Italy. By crossing it with his army en route to Rome in 49 B.C., Julius Caesar broke a law forbidding a general to lead an army out of his own province and so committed himself to civil war against the Senate and Pompey. The expression *crossing the Rubicon* has come to mean making an irrevocable step that commits you to a course of action.

Ru·bi·con[2] /ro͞obi kaán/ stream in northeastern Italy that in ancient times marked the frontier between Italy and Cisalpine Gaul. Now called the Rubicone, it empties into the Adriatic Sea just north of Rimini. See Origin note above.

ru·bi·cund /ro͞obikənd/ *adj.* with the reddish skin color that is widely regarded as a sign of good health in Caucasian people (*literary*) [15thC. From Latin *rubicundus,* from, ultimately, *ruber* "red" (source of English *rubescent*).] —**ru·bi·cun·di·ty** /ro͞obi kúndətee/ *n.*

ru·bid·i·um /roo bíddee əm/ *n.* a soft silvery-white radioactive chemical element of the alkali metal group that reacts strongly with water, bursts into flame when exposed to air, and is used in photocells. Symbol **Rb** [Mid-19thC. From modern Latin, from Latin *rubidus* "red," from *rubere* "to be red"; from the two red lines in its spectrum.]

ru·big·i·nous /roo bíjjənəss/ *adj.* reddish-brown, like the color of rust (*formal*) [Mid-17thC. Formed from Latin *rubigin-*, the stem of *rubigo* "rust," a variant of *robigo* (source of English *rouille*). Originally in the sense "(of a plant) affected by blight."]

Ru·bik's cu·be /ro͞obiks-/ *tdmk.* a trademark for a puzzle that is a cube composed of smaller rotating colored cubes, the aim being to rotate them to make each of the large cube's faces a uniform color

Ru·bin·stein /ro͞obin stīn/, **Arthur** (1887–1982) Polish-born U.S. pianist. He is known for his interpretations of works by the romantic composers, notably Frédéric Chopin.

ru·bi·ous /ro͞obee əss/ *adj.* dark red, like the color of rubies (*literary*) [Early 17thC. Formed from RUBY.]

ru·ble /ro͞ob'l/, **rou·ble** *n.* **1.** UNIT OF RUSSIAN CURRENCY the main unit of currency in Russia, Belarus, and some other former republics of the U.S.S.R. See table at **currency 2.** COIN WORTH ONE RUBLE a coin worth one ruble

ru·bric /ro͞obrik/ *n.* **1.** TITLE OR HEADING a printed title or heading, usually distinguished from the body of the text in some way, especially the heading of a section of a legal statute, originally underlined in red **2.** SET OF PRINTED INSTRUCTIONS a set of printed rules or instructions, e.g., the rules governing how Christian services are to be conducted, often printed in red in a prayer book **3.** ESTABLISHED CUSTOM a well-established custom or tradition that provides rules for conduct **4.** CATEGORY a class or category of things ■ *adj.* IN RED printed or marked in red [13thC. Directly or via Old French from Latin *rubrica* "red ochre," from the base of *rubeus, ruber* "red" (source of English *ruby*).] —**ru·bri·cal** *adj.* —**ru·bri·cal·ly** *adv.*

ru·bri·cate /ro͞obri kàyt/ (**-cat·ed, -cat·ing, -cates**) *vt.* (*formal*) **1.** ADD HEADINGS TO TEXT to add titles or heading to a text, or to print them in red **2.** MARK SOMETHING IN RED to print or mark something in red **3.** REGULATE SOMETHING to apply a set of rules to something —**ru·bri·ca·tion** /ro͞obri káysh'n/ *n.* —**ru·bri·ca·tor** /ro͞obri kàytər/ *n.*

ru·bri·cian /roo brísh'n/ *n.* somebody who is an authority on the way religious services should be conducted

ru·by /ro͞obee/ *n.* (*plural* **-bies**) **1.** MINERALS RED GEMSTONE a glassy red stone that is a variety of corundum, highly valued for its use in jewelry as well as in the making of watches and other precision instruments (*often used before a noun*) ○ *a ruby ring* **2.** COLORS DEEP RED a deep glowing red color tinged with dark purple, like that of a ruby ■ *adj.* COLORS DEEP RED IN COLOR of a deep glowing red color tinged with purple, like that of a ruby [14thC. Via Old French from, ultimately, Latin *ruber, rubeus* "red" (source also of English *rubella* and *rubric*).]

ru·by port *n.* a port that is matured for a minimal period in the barrel and then bottled for immediate drinking

ru·by spi·nel *n.* a red transparent variety of the mineral spinel, used in jewelry

ru·by-throat·ed hum·ming·bird *n.* the most common hummingbird in North America, with a red throat and a shiny green back. Latin name: *Archilochus colubris.*

ruche /roosh/ *n.* GARMENT'S FRILLY TRIMMING a strip of gathered, pleated, or frilled fabric used as a decorative trimming on a garment ■ *vt.* (**ruched, ruch·ing, ruch·es**) TRIM GARMENT WITH RUCHES to decorate the edges of a garment with ruches [Early 19thC. Via French from medieval Latin *rusca* "tree bark," of Celtic origin.]

ruch·ing /ro͞oshing/ *n.* decorative edges of gathered, pleated, or frilled fabric

ruck[1] /ruk/ (**rucked, ruck·ing, rucks**) *n.* **1.** LARGE NUMBER a large number of people or things **2.** ORDINARY PEOPLE OR THINGS the great mass of unexceptional people or things **3.** FOLLOWERS the group of competitors behind the leader in a race [13thC. Origin uncertain: probably from a Scandinavian language. Originally in the meaning "pile of combustible material."]

ruck[2] /ruk/ *vti.* (**rucked, ruck·ing, rucks**) WRINKLE to become wrinkled or creased, or cause something, especially fabric, to become wrinkled or creased ○ *The carpet is rucked up under your chair.* ■ *n.* UNWANTED FOLD a crease or wrinkle, especially in a fabric [Late 18thC. From Old Norse *hrukka* "wrinkle."]

ruck·sack /rúk sàk, ro͝ok-/ *n.* a large bag, usually with two straps and often with a supporting frame, carried on the back and used especially by walkers and climbers [Mid-19thC. From German, literally "back-sack."]

ruck·us /rúkəss/ *n.* a noisy and unpleasant disturbance [Late 19thC. Origin uncertain: perhaps a blend of RUCTION and RUMPUS.]

ruc·tion /rúkshən/ *n.* a noisy, often violent, quarrel or fight [Early 18thC. Origin uncertain: perhaps an alteration of INSURRECTION.]

rud·beck·i·a /rud békee ə, rood-/ (*plural* **-as** *or* **-a**) *n.* a North American plant with showy yellow flowers that have green or black centers. It has alternate leaves and belongs to the composite family of flowering plants. Genus: *Rudbeckia.* [Mid-19thC. From modern Latin, named for the Swedish botanists Olof *Rudbeck* the elder (1630–1702) and the younger (1660–1740).]

rudd /rud/ (*plural* **rudds** *or* **rudd**) *n.* a European freshwater fish of the carp family with a thin greenish-brown body and red fins. Latin name: *Scardinius erythrophthalmus.* [Early 16thC. Variant of obsolete *rud* "redness." Ultimately from a prehistoric Germanic word that is also the ancestor of English *red.*]

rud·der /rúddər/ *n.* **1.** MEANS OF STEERING BOAT OR SHIP a means of steering a boat or ship, usually in the form of a pivoting blade under the water, mounted at the stern and controlled by a wheel or handle (**tiller**) **2.** AIRFOIL FOR STEERING AIRPLANE an airfoil, usually on the tail of an airplane, that pivots vertically and controls left-to-right movement **3.** CONTROLLING FORCE a guiding or controlling force or influence [Old English *rōþer.* Ultimately from a prehistoric Germanic word that is also the ancestor of English *row.*] —**rud·der·less** *adj.*

rud·der·fish /rúddər fish/ (*plural* **-fish** *or* **-fish·es**) *n.* a small-to-medium oval fish known for its habit of following oceangoing ships in schools. Family: Kyphosidae.

rud·dle /rúdd'l/, **red·dle** /rédd'l/, **rad·dle** /rádd'l/ *n.* COLORING SUBSTANCE a type of red ocher used as a dye. It was formerly used to mark sheep. ■ *vt.* (**-dled, -dling, -dles; -dled, -dling, -dles; -dled, -dling, -dles**) COLOR SOMETHING WITH RUDDLE to dye or mark something such as a sheep with ruddle [Mid-16thC. Formed from obsolete *rud* (see RUDD).]

rud·dy /rúddee/ *adj.* (**-di·er, -di·est**) **1.** ROSY WITH HEALTH with a healthy reddish glow ○ *ruddy cheeks* **2.** REDDISH red or reddish in color ○ *ruddy sky* ■ *adj.* (**-di·er, -di·est**), *adv.* *U.K.* SWEARWORD used as a mild swearword to emphasize how good, bad, or severe something is (*slang*) (*offensive in some contexts*) [Old English *rudig.* Ultimately from a prehistoric Germanic word that is also the ancestor of English *red.*] —**rud·di·ly** *adv.* —**rud·di·ness** *n.*

rud·dy duck *n.* a North American duck with a broad bill, upright tail, and white cheeks. During the mating season the male is brownish-red with a black crown and blue bill. Latin name: *Oxyura jamaicensis.*

rude /rood/ (**rud·er, rud·est**) *adj.* **1.** ILL-MANNERED disagreeable or discourteous in manner or action ○ *Don't be rude!* **2.** INDECENT offensive to accepted standards of decency ○ *rude words* **3.** UNREFINED lacking refinement or social skills **4.** SUDDEN AND UNPLEASANT happening with unexpected suddenness and unpleasantness ○ *a rude awakening* **5.** ROUGHLY MADE in a rough or incomplete state ○ *a rude wooden bench* **6.** UNSKILLED showing a lack of skill or training

○ *rude paintings* **7.** INEXPERIENCED without schooling or experience ○ *a rude youth raised in the wilderness* **8.** RAW in a raw or unprocessed state ○ *rude fibers* **9.** VAGUE lacking precision ○ *a rude guess* **10.** UNDEVELOPED technologically or economically undeveloped **11.** ROBUST strong and energetic ○ *in rude health* [13thC. Via French from Latin *rudis* "raw, rough" (source of English *rudiment* and *erudite*).] —**rude·ly** *adv.* —**rude·ness** *n.*

ru·der·al /ródərəl/ *adj.* GROWING IN TRASH growing in wasteland, trash, or disturbed ground ■ *n.* RUDERAL PLANT a plant that grows in wasteland, trash, or disturbed ground [Mid-19thC. Formed from the Latin stem *ruder-* "rubble."]

ru·di·ment /ródəmənt/ *n.* **1.** SOMETHING BASIC TO SUBJECT a basic principle or skill, especially in a particular field or subject (*often used in the plural*) ○ *the rudiments of computer programming* **2.** BEGINNING an early stage in the development of something such as a plan (*often used in the plural*) **3.** BIOL UNDEVELOPED BODY PART a body part that does not develop fully and performs no useful function. The mammary gland in males is a rudiment. **4.** BIOL EMBRYO OF ORGAN an embryonic stage of an organ or body part [Mid-16thC. Directly or via French from, ultimately, Latin *rudis* (see RUDE).]

ru·di·men·ta·ry /ródə méntəree/, **ru·di·men·tal** /-mént'l/ *adj.* **1.** BASIC existing at an elementary or basic level **2.** DEVELOPING in an early or partially developed stage **3.** BIOL UNDEVELOPED not fully developed ○ *a rudimentary tail* **4.** BIOL IN FORM OF EMBRYO in an embryonic state —**ru·di·men·tar·i·ly** *adv.* —**ru·di·men·ta·ri·ness** *n.*

Ru·dolf I /róo dolf/, **King of Germany and Holy Roman Emperor** (1218–91). His acquisition of Bohemian territories in 1278 greatly strengthened the house of Hapsburg. He is considered the founder of the Hapsburg dynasty.

Ru·dolf, Lake former name for **Turkana, Lake**

rue[1] /roo/ *vti.* (**rued, ru·ing, rues**) FEEL REGRET FOR to feel regret or sorrow for something in the past ○ *I rue the day I offered to help.* ■ *n.* FEELING OF REGRET a feeling of regret or sorrow (*archaic*) [Old English *hrēowan*. Ultimately from a prehistoric Germanic word that also produced German *reuen* "to repent." Originally in the meaning "to induce pity."]

rue[2] /roo/ (*plural* **rues** *or* **rue**) *n.* a woody plant with small yellow flowers, native to Europe and Asia. Its bitter, strongly scented leaves yield an oil formerly used as a narcotic and stimulant. Latin name: *Ruta graveolens.* [14thC. Via French and Latin *ruta* from Greek *rhutē.*]

rue·ful /róof'l/ *adj.* **1.** REGRETFUL feeling, showing, or causing regret **2.** INDUCING PITY causing people to feel pity —**rue·ful·ly** *adv.* —**rue·ful·ness** *n.*

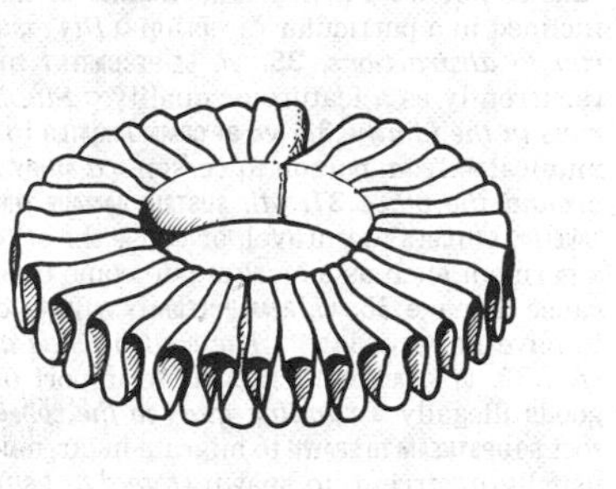

Ruff

ruff[1] /ruf/ *n.* **1.** FANCY PLEATED COLLAR a separate collar of starched pleated linen or lace worn by men and women from the middle of the 16th century to the early 17th century **2.** ZOOL NECK HAIR OR FEATHERS a growth of long, colorful, or bushy hair or feathers on the neck of a bird or other animal **3.** (*plural* **ruffs** *or* **ruff**) BIRDS BIRD WITH ELABORATE RUFF a bird of the sandpiper family, the male of which has a ruff of feathers that are erected during courtship displays. It is native to Europe and Asia. Latin name: *Philomachus pugnax.* [Early 16thC. Origin uncertain: probably a variant of ROUGH, or perhaps a shortening of RUFFLE.] —**ruffed** *adj.*

ruff[2] /ruf/ *n.* **1.** PLAYING OF TRUMP CARD in bridge or whist, the act of playing a trump card **2.** CARDS CARD GAME an old card game similar to whist ■ *vti.* (**ruffed, ruff·ing, ruffs**) PLAY TRUMP ON DIFFERENT SUIT in bridge or whist, to play a trump card on a card from a different suit [Late 16thC. From Old French *roffle*, a card game, of uncertain origin: perhaps from *renfler* "to rise" (from, ultimately, Latin *inflare* "to inflate"), or from Italian *trionfo* "trump."]

ruf·fi·an /rúffee ən/ *n.* somebody who behaves in a rough, bullying, or violent way, often a member of a gang of criminal thugs (*dated*) [15thC. Via French from, ultimately, Italian *ruffiano*, of Germanic origin.] —**ruf·fi·an·ism** *n.* —**ruf·fi·an·ly** *adj.*

ruf·fle[1] /rúff'l/ *v.* (**-fled, -fling, -fles**) **1.** *vti.* MAKE WAVES IN A SURFACE to disturb or ripple something, especially a surface, or to become disturbed or rippled **2.** *vt.* MAKE FEATHERS ERECT to erect feathers, e.g., in defense, as a display, or for warmth or grooming **3.** *vti.* ANNOY SOMEBODY to bother or fluster somebody, or to become bothered or flustered ○ *gets ruffled so easily* **4.** *vt.* GLANCE QUICKLY THROUGH SOMETHING to flip rapidly through the pages of a book or magazine (*dated*) **5.** *vt.* SEW GATHER OR PLEAT to draw a strip of material into pleats or gathers to use as trim **6.** *vt.* CARDS SHUFFLE CARDS to shuffle playing cards (*dated*) ■ *n.* **1.** WAVE IN SURFACE a disturbance or ripple in something, especially a surface **2.** IRRITATING THING a source of irritation or annoyance **3.** SEW TRIM OF PLEATED FABRIC a strip of closely pleated or gathered material used as trim **4.** ZOOL = **ruff**[1] *n.* 2 [14thC. Origin uncertain: perhaps thought to suggest the action.] —**ruf·fled** *adj.* —**ruf·fly** *adj.*

ruf·fle[2] /rúff'l/ *n.* LOW DRUMBEAT a low continuous drumbeat ■ *vt.* (**-fled, -fling, -fles**) BEAT RUFFLE ON A DRUM to play a ruffle on a drum [Early 18thC. Origin uncertain: probably an imitation of the sound.]

ruf·fle[3] /rúff'l/ (**-fled, -fling, -fles**) *vi.* to behave in an ostentatiously arrogant or boastful way (*archaic*) [15thC. Origin unknown. It disappeared by 1700 but was revived in the 19thC by Sir Walter Scott.]

ru·fi·yaa /roo fee yaa, ró fee yaa/ (*plural* **-yaa**) *n.* **1.** UNIT OF CURRENCY OF MALDIVES the main unit of currency in the Maldive Islands, worth 100 laari. See table at **currency 2.** BILL WORTH ONE RUFIYAA a bill worth one rufiyaa [Late 20thC. Via Maldivian from Hindi *rupiya* (see RUPEE).]

rug /rug/ *n.* **1.** FABRIC FLOOR COVERING a thick heavy fabric covering for a floor, especially one that is smaller than a carpet **2.** ANIMAL SKIN MAT an animal skin used as a mat or small carpet **3.** BLANKET a thick blanket, especially one formerly used by car or carriage passengers to cover their legs and feet **4.** HAIRPIECE a toupee or wig (*informal*) [Mid-16thC. Origin uncertain: probably from a Scandinavian word.]

ru·ga /róogə/ (*plural* **-gae** /-gee, -gī/) *n.* a natural crease or ridge in a body part, especially in the internal organs (*often used in the plural*) [Late 18thC. From Latin, "wrinkle."] —**ru·gate** /ró gayt/ *adj.*

Rugby: A player attempts a kick

Rug·by[1] /rúgbee/, **Rug·by foot·ball** *n.* a team sport in which players run with an oval ball, pass it laterally from hand to hand, and kick it (*often used before a noun*) [Mid-19thC. Named for RUGBY School, where it was reputedly invented.]

Rug·by[2] /rúgbee/ town in Warwickshire, central England. Rugby School, a leading independent school, is located there. Population: 84,300 (1991).

rug·ged /rúggəd/ *adj.* **1.** WITH IRREGULAR SURFACE with a sharply rising and falling, rough, or jagged surface ○ *over rugged terrain* **2.** STRONG-FEATURED with furrowed facial features thought to suggest physical strength or strength of character, especially in men ○ *their rugged faces* **3.** PHYSICALLY RESILIENT physically strong enough to endure harsh conditions, or used to enduring them **4.** SEVERE IN MANNER harsh and forbidding in manner **5.** METEOROL STORMY affected by violent and dangerous storms **6.** LACKING REFINEMENT coarse or unrefined in behavior **7.** TESTING requiring strength, skill, or endurance **8.** ENG STRONGLY BUILT designed and manufactured to withstand hard use or harsh environments [13thC. Origin uncertain: probably from a Scandinavian word. The underlying idea is of a bristled surface.] —**rug·ged·ly** *adv.* —**rug·ged·ness** *n.*

rug·ged·ize /rúggə dīz/ (**-ized, -iz·ing, -iz·es**) *vt.* to make something such as a piece of equipment capable of withstanding rough treatment —**rug·ged·i·za·tion** /rùggədi záysh'n/ *n.*

ru·go·sa rose /roo gṓssə-/ *n.* a common hedge rose that has not been cultivated. It is thorny with fragrant pink or white blossoms and is found across eastern North America. Latin name: *Rosa rugosa.* [*Rugosa* from Latin, the feminine form of *rugosus* (see RUGOSE)]

ru·gose /ró gòss/, **ru·gous** /róogəss/ *adj.* **1.** CREASED with creases, wrinkles, or ridges **2.** BOT WITH RIDGED SURFACE used to describe a leaf or other plant part that has a surface of alternating depressions and ridges [15thC. From Latin *rugosus*, from *ruga* "wrinkle."] —**ru·gose·ly** *adv.* —**ru·gos·i·ty** /roo góssətee/ *n.*

rug rat *n.* an offensive term for a young child, especially an infant or toddler (*slang offensive*)

Ruhr /róor/ river in western Germany. The Ruhr valley contains the largest coalfield and industrial region in western Europe. Length: 146 mi./235 km.

ru·in /ró in/ *n.* **1.** BROKEN REMAINS the physical remains of something such as a building or city that has decayed or been destroyed (*often used in the plural*) **2.** COMPLETE DEVASTATION a state of complete destruction, decay, collapse, or loss ○ *The buildings had gone to ruin* **3.** COMPLETE FAILURE complete moral, social, or economic failure ○ *facing financial ruin* **4.** SOMEBODY OR SOMETHING DESTROYED somebody or something completely lost or destroyed **5.** CAUSE OF DESTRUCTION a cause of complete loss or destruction ○ *Alcohol was their ruin.* **6.** LOSS OF VIRGINITY a woman's loss of virginity to a man other than her husband (*archaic*) ■ **ru·ins** *npl.* COMPLETE DEVASTATION a state of complete destruction, decay, collapse, or loss ○ *Her dreams lay in ruins.* ■ *v.* (**-ined, -in·ing, -ins**) **1.** *vt.* DESTROY SOMETHING to cause something to be destroyed or lost **2.** *vt.* DESTROY SOMEBODY FINANCIALLY to bring about somebody's financial demise **3.** *vt.* DAMAGE SOMETHING BEYOND REPAIR to spoil something so severely that it cannot be restored **4.** *vi.* DECLINE to fall into a state of complete destruction or loss (*literary*) **5.** *vt.* SEDUCE THEN ABANDON A WOMAN to induce a woman to engage in sex before marriage, then abandon her (*archaic*) [14thC. Via French *ruine* from Latin *ruina*, from *ruere* "to fall."] —**ru·ined** *adj.* —**ru·in·er** *n.*

ru·in·a·tion /rò ə náysh'n/ *n.* **1.** LOSS the destruction or loss of something **2.** CAUSE OF LOSS something that brings about destruction or loss

ru·in·ous /ró inəss/ *adj.* **1.** DAMAGING causing severe damage or complete destruction or loss **2.** DECAYED decayed or deteriorated beyond repair —**ru·in·ous·ly** *adv.* —**ru·in·ous·ness** *n.*

rule /rool/ *n.* **1.** PRINCIPLE GOVERNING CONDUCT an authoritative principle set forth to guide behavior or action ○ *the rules of the game* **2.** USUAL CONDITION a prevailing condition or quality **3.** GOVERNING POWER a governing or reigning power ○ *under Communist rule* **4.** REIGN OR GOVERNMENT a period during which a person or group reigns or governs **5.** RELIG RELIGIOUS PRINCIPLES a body of principles governing a religious order or group ○ *the Benedictine rule* **6.** MATH METHOD OF CALCULATING a mathematical procedure for performing an operation or solving a problem **7.** = **ruler** *n.* 2 **8.** PRINTING LINE BETWEEN PRINTED COLUMNS a thin strip or design used for borders or for separating columns of type **9.** LAW LAW GOVERNING COURT PROCEDURE a law made to govern procedure in court **10.** LAW COURT ORDER an order issued by a court of law or by a judge ■ *v.* (**ruled, rul·ing, rules**) **1.** *vti.* GOVERN to exercise controlling authority over somebody or something ○ *She ruled for almost 50 years.* **2.** *vt.* CONTROL SOMETHING to subject something to control or to restrain something **3.** *vt.* MARK WITH LINES to make a straight line or mark something with straight lines **4.** *vti.* DOMINATE to prevail or be the prevailing influence over something ○ *He let his heart rule his head.* **5.** *vti.* LAW MAKE LEGAL DECISION to issue a legal decision or order ○ *The judge ruled against the plaintiff.* [13thC. Via French *riule* from, ultimately, Latin *regula* "straight stick, standard" (source of English *regular* and *regulate*).] —**rul·a·ble** *adj.*

rule out *vt.* **1. EXCLUDE SOMETHING** to exclude something or take a decision not to consider something **2. PREVENT SOMETHING** to make something impossible

rule of thumb *n.* **1. COMMON PRACTICE** a way of proceeding based on experience or sound judgment **2. GENERALLY RELIABLE METHOD** any practical, though not entirely accurate, method that can be relied on for an acceptable result [Said to derive from the workman's practice of using the thumb as a rough measure] —**rule-of-thumb** *adj.*

rul·er /ro͞olər/ *n.* **1. SOMEBODY WHO RULES** somebody such as a sovereign who governs a state or nation **2. STRAIGHT TOOL FOR MEASURING AND DRAWING** a strip of plastic, wood, or metal with at least one straight edge and units of length marked on it. It is used for measuring and for drawing straight lines.

rul·ing /ro͞oling/ *adj.* **1. IN POWER** exercising controlling or governing authority ○ *the ruling party* **2. MOST POWERFUL** exerting the strongest influence ○ *a ruling passion* ■ *n.* LAW **DECISION BY AUTHORITY** an official or binding decision made, e.g., by a court or judge

rum[1] /rum/ *n.* **1. LIQUOR MADE FROM SUGAR CANE** an alcoholic liquor made from sugar cane or molasses. It can be clear but is usually colored brownish-red by storage in oak casks or by the addition of caramel. **2. LIQUOR** any intoxicating liquor [Mid-17thC. Shortening of obsolete *rumbullion*, of unknown origin.]

rum[2] /rum/ (**rum·mer, rum·mest**) *adj. U.K.* out of the ordinary (*dated informal*) [Late 18thC. Origin unknown.]

rum·ba /rúmbə, ro͝om-, ro͞om-/, **rhum·ba** *n.* **1. CUBAN DANCE** a rhythmically complex Cuban dance **2. RHYTHMIC BALLROOM DANCE** a ballroom dance based on the Cuban rumba. It is danced more or less on the spot, with exaggerated swinging of the hips. **3. MUSIC FOR RUMBA** a piece of music for or in the rhythm of a rumba ■ *vi.* (**-baed, -ba·ing, -bas**) **DANCE RUMBA** to dance a rumba [Early 20thC. Via American Spanish and Spanish *rumbo* "course, direction" from, ultimately, Latin *rhombus* "rhombus."]

rum·ble /rúmb'l/ *v.* (**-bled, -bling, -bles**) **1.** *vi.* **MAKE DEEP SOUND** to make a deep rolling sound ○ *thunder rumbling in the distance* **2.** *vi.* **MOVE NOISILY** to travel, e.g., along a road, with a deep rolling sound ○ *Trucks rumbled past.* **3.** *vt.* **UTTER WITH A RUMBLE** to say something with a deep rolling voice **4.** *vt. U.K.* **FIND OUT ABOUT SOMEBODY OR SOMETHING** to discover the truth about somebody or something (*informal*) ○ *We've been rumbled!* **5.** *vi. U.S., NZ* **BE IN A FIGHT** to be involved in a street fight, especially one between members of rival gangs (*slang*) **6.** *vt.* MINERALS, MECH ENG **TO CLEAN STONES OR METAL** to polish stones or metal in a rotating drum (**tumbling barrel**) ■ *n.* **1. DEEP SOUND** a deep rolling sound **2. MURMUR OF DISSATISFACTION** a feeling of dissatisfaction quietly expressed by several people (*informal*) **3.** *U.S., NZ* **STREET FIGHT** a street fight, especially one fought by members of rival gangs (*slang*) **4.** MINERALS, MECH ENG = **tumbling barrel** [14thC. Origin uncertain: probably from obsolete Dutch *rommelen*, an imitation of the sound.] —**rum·bler** *n.* —**rum·bly** *adj.*

rum·ble seat *n.* a folding passenger seat on the back of some early automobiles

rum·bling /rúmbling/ *n.* **1. DEEP SOUND** a deep rolling sound **2. FIRST INDICATION** an early sign of growing discontent, or an indication of an unpleasant event that is about to happen (*often used in the plural*) ■ *adj.* **MAKING DEEP SOUND** making a deep rolling sound ○ *rumbling stomach*

rum·bus·tious /rum búschəss/ *adj.* full of noisy uncontrollable exuberance [Late 18thC. Origin uncertain: probably an alteration of ROBUSTIOUS.] —**rum·bus·tious·ly** *adv.* —**rum·bus·tious·ness** *n.*

ru·men /ro͞omen, ro͞omən/ (*plural* **-mi·na** /-mənə/ *or* **-mens**) *n.* the large first chamber of a ruminant animal's stomach in which microorganisms break down plant cellulose before the food is returned to the mouth as cud for additional chewing [Early 18thC. From Latin.] —**ru·mi·nal** *adj.*

ru·mi·nant /ro͞omənənt/ *n.* ZOOL **HOOFED ANIMAL THAT CHEWS CUD** any cud-chewing hoofed mammal with an even number of toes and a stomach with multiple chambers. Cattle, camels, and giraffes are ruminants. Suborder: Ruminantia. ■ *adj.* **1.** ZOOL **OF RUMINANTS** relating or belonging to the suborder of animals that chew the cud **2. THOUGHTFUL** inclined to be thoughtful and reflective [Mid-17thC. From the present participle stem of Latin *ruminare* (see RUMINATE).] —**ru·mi·nant·ly** *adv.*

ru·mi·nate /ro͞omə nàyt/ (**-nat·ed, -nat·ing, -nates**) *v.* **1.** *vi.* ZOOL **CHEW PARTIALLY DIGESTED FOOD** to regurgitate partially digested food and chew it again (*refers to ruminants*) **2.** *vti.* **MULL SOMETHING OVER** to think carefully and at length about something [Mid-16thC. From Latin *ruminat-*, the past participle stem of *ruminare*, from *rumen* "rumen."] —**ru·mi·na·tion** /ro͞omə náysh'n/ *n.* —**ru·mi·na·tive** /ro͞omə nàytiv/ *adj.* —**ru·mi·na·tive·ly** /-nàytivlee/ *adv.*

rum·mage /rúmmij/ *v.* (**-maged, -mag·ing, -mag·es**) **1.** *vti.* **GO THROUGH THINGS LOOKING FOR SOMETHING** to make a rapid search for or through something by carelessly moving and disarranging things **2.** *vt.* **FIND SOMETHING** to find something by searching ■ *n.* **1. THOROUGH SEARCH** a thorough search for or through something **2. SECOND-HAND ARTICLES** articles sold at a rummage sale **3. GROUP OF THINGS** a miscellaneous collection of items [15thC. Via Old French *arrumage* "arrangement of cargo in a ship" from, ultimately, *run* "ship's hold," from Dutch *ruim* "space."] —**rum·mag·er** *n.*

rum·mage sale *n.* a sale of miscellaneous donated items to raise money for charity

rum·mer /rúmmər/ *n.* a large drinking glass, especially one with a short stem [Mid-17thC. Directly or via German *Römer* from Dutch *roemer*, from *roemen* "to praise."]

rum·my[1] /rúmmee/ *n.* a card game in which the players try to get three or more cards of the same rank or a sequence of three or more cards of the same suit [Early 20thC. Origin unknown.]

rum·my[2] /rúmmee/ *n.* (*plural* **-mies**) **DRUNKARD** a drunkard (*slang*) ■ *adj.* **OF OR LIKE RUM** tasting or smelling of rum, or similar to rum in smell or taste

ru·mor /ro͞omər/ *n.* **1. UNVERIFIED REPORT** a generally circulated story, report, or statement without facts to confirm its truth **2. IDLE SPECULATION** general talk or opinion of uncertain reliability **3. UPROAR** a loud noise or disturbance (*archaic*) ■ *vt.* (**-mored, -mor·ing, -mors**) **TO PASS ON RUMORS** to pass along information by rumor (*usually passive*) ○ *It is rumored that they are leaving the company.* [14thC. Via Old French *rumur* from Latin *rumor* "noise, rumor."]

ru·mor·mon·ger /ro͞omər mùng gər, -mòng-/ *n.* **SOMEBODY SPREADING RUMORS** somebody who habitually spreads rumors ■ *vi.* (**-gered, -ger·ing, -gers**) **SPREAD RUMORS** to participate actively in spreading rumors

ru·mour *n., vt.* U.K. = **rumor**

rump /rump/ *n.* **1.** ZOOL **ANIMAL'S HINDQUARTERS** the fleshy hindquarters of a four-legged mammal, not including its legs **2.** FOOD **BEEF FROM THE HINDQUARTERS** a cut of beef that is tender and contains some fat, taken from the rump ○ *rump steak* **3. BUTTOCKS** somebody's buttocks (*informal*) **4.** LAW **REMAINS OF LEGISLATURE** the remnant of a legislative body after the majority of its members have resigned or been expelled **5.** BIRDS **BIRD'S TAIL END** the lower part of a bird's back, nearest the tail. It is sometimes colored distinctively. [15thC. Origin uncertain: probably from a Scandinavian language.]

rum·ple /rúmp'l/ *vti.* (**-pled, -pling, -ples**) **MAKE OR BECOME UNKEMPT** to take on a disheveled appearance, or to make clothes or hair untidy, e.g., by creasing clothes or pulling hair out of style ■ *n.* **A CREASE** a wrinkle or crease [Early 16thC. Origin uncertain: perhaps from Dutch *rumpelen*.]

rum·pus /rúmpəss/ *n.* an outcry or noisy disturbance [Mid-18thC. Origin unknown.]

rum·pus room *n. Can, ANZ, U.S.* a room in a house for recreational activities such as parties and children's play

rum·run·ner /rúm rùnnər/ *n.* **1. SMUGGLER OF LIQUOR** somebody who smuggles liquor across a border **2.** SHIPPING **BOAT USED IN CARRYING ILLEGAL LIQUOR** a boat used to smuggle liquor across a border

run /run/ *v.* (**ran** /ran/, **run, run·ning, runs**) **1.** *vi.* **GO AT FAST PACE** to move rapidly on foot so that both feet are momentarily off the ground in each step **2.** *vi.* **GALLOP** to go at a fast pace in which all four feet are momentarily off the ground in each stride (*refers to four-footed animals*) **3.** *vt.* **TRAVEL DISTANCE BY RUNNING** to cover a particular distance while running **4.** *vti.* **PARTICIPATE IN RACE** to compete in a race on foot, or on a horse or other animal **5.** *vt.* **ENTER ANIMAL IN RACE** to enter a horse or other animal in a race **6.** *vi.* **BE IN RELATIVE POSITION** to be or end in a particular position, e.g., in a race, election, or contest ○ *running behind until the last lap* **7.** *vt.* **PERFORM SOMETHING** to carry out or accomplish something ○ *run a test* **8.** *vi.* **LEAVE QUICKLY** to leave a place quickly or in a hurry, usually in order to escape notice or capture ○ *take the money and run* **9.** *vi.* **MOVE FREELY** to move around without restraint ○ *allow the cats to run* **10.** *vt.* **SPEED ACROSS SOMETHING** to travel quickly across, over, or through something ○ *running the rapids* **11.** *vt.* **TRANSPORT SOMEBODY OR SOMETHING** to take or transport somebody or something, usually by motor vehicle ○ *ran me into town* **12.** *vi.* **GO TO FOR HELP** to turn to somebody for assistance, especially in desperation or as a dependant to a protector ○ *He always runs to his brother for money.* **13.** *vi.* **VISIT** to make a brief trip or visit somewhere ○ *ran out to the mountains for the weekend* **14.** *vti.* **MOVE SMOOTHLY** to pass, or cause something to pass, quickly or smoothly through or over something ○ *ropes running easily through the pulleys* **15.** *vti.* **BE A CANDIDATE** to be a candidate, or enter somebody as a candidate, in an election ○ *running for president* **16.** *vi.* **COME INTO PARTICULAR STATE** to enter into a particular state or condition ○ *Supplies were running low.* **17.** *vti.* **OPERATE** to be functioning, or to put or leave something in a functioning mode ○ *Let the engine run.* **18.** *vt.* **CONTROL SOMETHING** to direct the activities, affairs, or operation of something ○ *responsible for running the whole department* **19.** *vti.* **POUR OR FLOW** to flow, or cause water or another liquid to flow from or to something ○ *run a faucet* **20.** *vi.* MED **RELEASE MUCUS** to discharge a fluid such as pus or mucus ○ *a nose that was constantly running* **21.** *vti.* **GO BACK AND FORTH** to travel, or cause somebody or something to travel, regularly over a set route ○ *running a shuttle between stations* **22.** *vi.* **ROLL FREELY** to roll unhindered or unchecked ○ *could only stand and watch it run down the hill* **23.** *vti.* **GO OR TAKE OFF COURSE** to deviate, or allow something such as a ship or automobile to deviate, from the usual or proper course ○ *run a car off the road* **24.** *vi.* **SPREAD OR LEAK UNDESIRABLY** to spread as a result of unwanted dissolving or mixing ○ *The red stripes ran into the white.* **25.** *vi.* **RANGE** to range between specified limits ○ *The work ran from difficult to impossible.* **26.** *vi.* **KEEP COMPANY** to associate with a particular person or group **27.** *vti.* **EXTEND SOMETHING** to route something or be routed in a particular direction or for a particular distance ○ *They plan to run the cable under the road.* **28.** *vi.* **CONTINUE FOR A TIME** to continue for a particular length or period ○ *a report running ten pages* **29.** *vti.* PUBL, BROADCAST **SHOW PUBLICLY** to print, broadcast, or exhibit something, or to be printed, broadcast, or exhibited ○ *run a news story* **30.** *vt.* **EXPERIENCE SOMETHING** to experience, undergo, or be subject to something ○ *a child running a high temperature* **31.** *vti.* **TOTAL** to total a specified amount ○ *The bill runs to four figures.* **32.** *vt.* **BREACH SOMETHING** to break through a barrier of some kind ○ *run a checkpoint* **33.** *vi.* **BE WORDED** to be worded in a particular way ○ *in a statement that runs as follows* **34.** *vi.* **EXHIBIT TENDENCY** to tend or be inclined in a particular direction ○ *His tastes in art run to abstractions.* **35.** *vi.* **BE RECURRENT** to appear recurrently as a feature or quality ○ *Stubbornness runs in the family.* **36.** *vi.* **BE COMMUNICATED** to be communicated from person to person ○ *a story running around the office* **37.** *vti.* **SUSTAIN DAMAGE THROUGH UNRAVELING STITCHES** to unravel, or cause the stitching in a garment such as a stocking, to come undone and cause damage **38.** *vi.* **REMAIN LEGALLY VALID** to continue to have force in law ○ *The contract has a year to run.* **39.** *vt.* **TRADE GOODS ILLEGALLY** to import or export goods illegally ○ *running guns to the rebels* **40.** *vi.* ZOOL **GO UPSTREAM TO SPAWN** to migrate in large numbers, usually upstream, to spawn (*refers to fish*) **41.** *vti.* FOOTBALL **CARRY FOOTBALL DOWNFIELD** to advance the football while running as opposed to passing **42.** *vt.* METALL **PRODUCE METAL BY CASTING** to cast or mold molten metal ■ *n.* **1. FAST PACE** a rapid pace faster than a walk or jog **2. GALLOPING PACE** an animal's fastest pace **3. SPELL OF RUNNING** a spell of running, especially for pleasure or exercise **4. RACE** a race in which the competitors run **5. REGULAR TRIP** a regular or scheduled trip or route ○ *the run to work each day* **6. TRIP FOR PLEASURE** a trip in a vehicle, especially for pleasure ○ *went for a run along the coast road* **7. DISTANCE OR TIME COVERED** a distance or period covered while traveling or running **8. ERRAND** a brief trip made in order to get something ○ *a quick run to the store* **9. FREE USE OF A PLACE** unrestricted access to, use of, and movement around a place ○ *given the run of the whole house* **10. UNINTERRUPTED PERIOD** an extended period during which a specified condition or circumstance prevails ○ *a run of bad luck* **11.** MANUF, PRINTING **QUANTITY MANUFACTURED** an amount of something produced in a period of continuous operation of a machine or factory ○ *an initial print run of five thousand copies* **12.** MANUF **OPERATING PERIOD** a period of continuous operation of a machine or factory **13.** CARDS **SEQUENCE OF CARDS** in card games, a sequence of playing cards in one suit **14.** CUE GAMES **SUCCESSIVE SHOTS** a series of successful shots in some games such as billiards **15.** ARTS **SERIES OF PERFORMANCES** a series of continuous showings or performances **16.** **URGENT REQUIREMENT** a sudden large demand for something such as goods or payment ○ *Rumors of a shortage led to a run on coffee.* **17.** **FLOW** a flow of liquid **18.** **PIPE FOR LIQUID** a channel or pipe in which a liquid flows **19.** **PERIOD OF FLOW** a period during which a liquid flows **20.** **AMOUNT OF LIQUID** an amount of liquid in a flow **21.** SPORTS **STEEP ROUTE** a sloping course or track for a specific activity ○ *a ski run* **22.** SPORTS **PASSAGE DOWN TRACK** a single trip along a course or down a slope **23.** **DIRECTION SOMETHING LIES IN** the natural direction of a pattern in something, e.g., wood grain **24.** **TENDENCY** the general direction in which things or events are moving ○ *the usual run of things* **25.** **SOMETHING ORDINARY** an average or typical kind of person or thing ○ *the general run of merchandise* **26.** **UNRAVELING OF STITCHES** a damaged section of a stocking or other knitted garment caused by unraveling stitches **27.** AGRIC **ANIMAL ENCLOSURE** an outdoor enclosure for domestic animals, often one attached to or used as a temporary break from a standard enclosure that allows less freedom of movement **28.** ZOOL **ANIMAL TRAIL** a trail followed regularly by a group or herd of animals **29.** POL **ELECTION CAMPAIGN** a campaign for election to public office ○ *a run for Congress* **30.** MUSIC **RAPID MUSICAL PASSAGE** a rapid musical scale or melodic passage, especially one for the piano **31.** FOOTBALL **GAIN WHILE RUNNING** an offensive player's advance of the ball while running **32.** BASEBALL **SCORE IN BASEBALL** a score in baseball made by traveling around all the bases to home plate ■ **runs** *npl.* MED **DIARRHEA** an attack of diarrhea (*informal*) (*takes a singular or plural verb*) ○ *have the runs* ■ *adj.* **1.** **MELTED** in a melted state **2.** **WORN OUT** exhausted or out of breath, especially from running [Old English *rinnan.* Ultimately from a prehistoric Germanic word that is also the ancestor of English *runnel.*] ◇ **be on the run** to be fleeing from something, especially the law ◇ **give somebody a run for his** *or* **her money** to provide somebody with some serious, sometimes unexpected, competition ◇ **run yourself** *or* **somebody ragged** to work yourself or somebody else to the point of exhaustion

WORD KEY: REGIONAL NOTE

Run, a small fast-flowing stream, is a South Midland and Southern term, common from Pennsylvania south to Virginia, as in *Bull Run*. Terms such as Northern *creek* and Southern *branch* identify larger streams.

run across *vt.* to meet somebody or find something unexpectedly

run after *vt.* **1.** **PURSUE SOMEBODY OR SOMETHING** to chase after somebody or something **2.** **PURSUE SOMEBODY ROMANTICALLY** to pursue somebody romantically or sexually (*informal*)

run along *vi.* to go away (*usually used as a command*)

run around *vi.* (*informal*) **1.** **BE PROMISCUOUS** to behave promiscuously **2.** **ASSOCIATE** to spend a lot of time with somebody ○ *running around with a bad crowd*

run away *vi.* to escape or flee from somebody or something

run away with *vt.* **1.** **TAKE SOMETHING AND LEAVE** to steal something and escape with it **2.** **ELOPE WITH SOMEBODY** to leave secretly with a lover, especially in order to marry **3.** **TAKE CONTROL OF SOMEBODY** to cause somebody to lose self-control ○ *His excitement ran away with him.* **4.** **WIN EASILY** to win a competition, contest, or election easily

run down *v.* **1.** *vti.* **STOP FUNCTIONING** to lose power and cease to function, or allow a device to lose its power **2.** *vt.* **HIT SOMEBODY WITH A VEHICLE** to knock somebody or something to the ground with a vehicle **3.** *vti.* **REDUCE** to shrink in size or amount, or reduce the size or amount of something **4.** *vt.* **BELITTLE SOMEBODY** to speak of somebody in a disparaging or critical manner **5.** *vt.* **CATCH SOMEBODY EVENTUALLY** to find or capture somebody after a long search or chase **6.** *vt.* **TRACE SOMETHING** to find the source of something ○ *run down a lead* **7.** *vt.* **READ SOMETHING QUICKLY** to read or review something quickly **8.** *vt.* SHIPPING **CAUSE SHIP TO SINK** to collide with a ship and cause it to sink **9.** *vt.* BASEBALL **REMOVE BASEBALL PLAYER** to chase and tag out a base runner trapped between two bases

run in *v.* **1.** *vt.* **ARREST SOMEBODY** to take somebody into police custody (*informal*) **2.** *vi.* **VISIT** to pay somebody a casual visit (*informal*) **3.** *vt.* PRINTING **ADD SOMETHING AS TEXT** to insert additional text in printed matter

run into *v.* **1.** *vt.* **MEET SOMEBODY BY CHANCE** to meet somebody unexpectedly **2.** *vti.* **COLLIDE WITH SOMETHING** to have, cause, or allow a collision between people or things **3.** *vt.* **ENCOUNTER SOMETHING** to encounter something unanticipated, usually problems or trouble **4.** *vt.* **AMOUNT TO SOMETHING** to add up to something or be approximately equal to something ○ *left debts running into millions*

run off *v.* **1.** *vi.* **LEAVE IN HASTE** to leave quickly without notifying anyone **2.** *vt.* **MAKE COPIES** to produce or print copies, e.g., on a photocopier **3.** *vt.* **FORCE SOMEBODY TO LEAVE** to force trespassers off property **4.** *vt.* **SETTLE TIED CONTEST** to settle a tied competition or election by running a final deciding contest

run off with *vt.* **1.** **STEAL SOMETHING** to steal and escape with something **2.** **ELOPE WITH SOMEBODY** to leave secretly with a lover, especially in order to marry

run on *v.* **1.** *vi.* **TALK AT LENGTH** to talk at length, especially about trivial things **2.** *vi.* **CONTINUE** to continue without interruption, often boringly or frustratingly **3.** *vt.* PRINTING **PRINT TEXT WITHOUT PARAGRAPH BREAK** to print or typeset following text without a paragraph break

run out *v.* **1.** *vi.* **COME TO AN END** to be consumed completely ○ *Time is running out.* **2.** *vi.* **EXHAUST SUPPLIES** to consume all of a supply of something ○ *We've run out of milk.* **3.** *vi.* **BECOME INVALID** to become invalid because of time restrictions **4.** *vt.* **CHASE SOMEBODY AWAY** to expel somebody using force

run out on *vt.* to leave somebody or something in a helpless state or at a time when support is needed (*informal*)

run over *v.* **1.** *vt.* **KNOCK SOMEBODY DOWN WITH VEHICLE** to hit somebody or something with a vehicle while driving it **2.** *vi.* **OVERFLOW** to overflow the limits or capacity of a container **3.** *vti.* **TAKE LONGER THAN PLANNED** to go beyond a limit or time previously set **4.** *vt.* **REVIEW SOMETHING** to examine or consider something again, especially reviewing its main points

run through *vt.* **1.** **USE SOMETHING UP** to exhaust a supply of something, especially money, quickly and without much consideration **2.** **REVIEW SOMETHING** to examine or consider something again, especially reviewing its main points **3.** ARTS **REHEARSE SOMETHING QUICKLY** to read or perform at speed the whole or part of a play, script, piece of music, lecture or other prepared text in order to rehearse it **4.** ARMS **STAB SOMEBODY WITH SWORD** to push a sword all the way through somebody's body (*literary*)

run to *vt.* to have the specified length

run up *vt.* **1.** FIN **INCUR AS EXPENSE** to amass or accumulate a large expense **2.** SEW **SEW** to make something, usually a garment, by means of fast sewing **3.** **RAISE ON FLAGPOLE** to hoist a flag on a flagpole

run up against *vt. U.K.* to suddenly encounter an unexpected problem

run·a·bout /rúnnə bòwt/ *n.* **1.** **SMALL VEHICLE** a small car, motorboat, or aircraft, especially one used for short trips **2.** **WANDERER** somebody who moves from place to place

run·a·round /rúnnə ròwnd/ *n.* **1.** **DELAYING OR MISLEADING TACTICS** inconvenience deliberately engineered in order to mislead or delay somebody (*informal*) ○ *They've been giving me the runaround.* **2.** PRINTING **ARRANGEMENT OF TYPE AROUND A PICTURE** an arrangement of printed type in which lines are shortened to leave room for an illustration or symbol

run·a·way /rúnnə wày/ *n.* **SOMEBODY WHO ESCAPES** somebody who leaves a place, e.g., to escape confinement or harm (*often used before a noun*) ■ *adj.* **1.** **OUT OF CONTROL** moving too fast to be stopped or controlled **2.** **EASILY WON** won by an overwhelming margin (*informal*)

Run·a·way, Cape /rúnnə wày/ cape on the north-eastern coast of the North Island, New Zealand, situated at the eastern end of the Bay of Plenty

run·back /rún bàk/ *n.* a run made in football after catching an opponent's kick or intercepting a pass

run·ci·ble spoon /rùnssib'l-/ *n.* a fork with three curved prongs, one of which is sharp ["Runcible" is a nonsense word coined by Edward Lear in *The Owl and the Pussy Cat* (1871)]

run·down /rún dòwn/ *n.* **1.** **REVIEW** a summary of the main points of a subject **2.** BASEBALL **OUT IN BASEBALL** a baseball play in which a runner is tagged out after being chased back and forth between two bases

run-down *adj.* **1.** **EXHAUSTED** tired out, e.g., from overwork or poor health **2.** **SHABBY** in poor repair from neglect or hard use **3.** **OUT OF POWER** depleted of energy or power and unable to operate

Rune

rune /roon/ *n.* **1.** LANGUAGE **OLD GERMANIC ALPHABET CHARACTER** a character in any of several ancient Germanic alphabets used from about the 3rd to the 13th centuries. The earliest Anglo-Saxon texts and inscriptions were written in runes. **2.** **MAGICAL SYMBOL OR SPELL** a mysterious symbol, inscription, or incantation, especially one believed to have magical power **3.** POETRY **POEM IN FINNISH** a Finnish poem or stanza [Old English *rūn.* From a prehistoric Germanic word that also produced German *raunen* "to whisper." Its "runic character" sense, once obsolete, was reintroduced from Old Norse *rún* in the 17thC.] —**run·ic** *adj.*

rung[1] /rung/ *n.* **1.** **LADDER STEP** any of the steps of a ladder **2.** **CROSSPIECE OF CHAIR** a horizontal bar used to strengthen the legs of a chair or stool **3.** **LEVEL IN HIERARCHY** a position in a hierarchy, e.g., of a profession **4.** NAUT **PART OF SHIP'S WHEEL** a spoke or handle on the wheel of a ship by which the wheel is turned [Old English *hrung.* Ultimately from a prehistoric Germanic word that also produced German *Runge* "rung."]

rung[2] past participle of **ring**

run-in *n.* **1.** **ARGUMENT** a heated argument or quarrel (*informal*) **2.** PRINTING **ADDITION TO PRINTED TEXT** a section of text added to a page that has already been typeset or printed

run·let /rúnnlət/ *n.* a small river or stream (*regional*)

run·nel /rúnn'l/ *n.* **1.** **STREAM** a small brook or stream **2.** **WATER CHANNEL** any narrow channel for water such as a gutter [Late 16thC. Alteration of obsolete *rindle.* Ultimately from a prehistoric Germanic word that is also the ancestor of English *run.*]

run·ner /rúnnər/ *n.* **1.** **RACER** somebody or something that runs, especially an athlete or a horse in a race **2.** POL **CANDIDATE** somebody entered as a candidate in an election **3.** **MESSENGER** somebody who carries messages or does errands for a bank, brokerage firm, or other business **4.** BASEBALL = **base runner** **5.** FOOTBALL = **ball carrier** **6.** **SMUGGLER** somebody involved in smuggling (*often used in combination*) ○ *gun runner* **7.** SHIPPING **SMUGGLER'S VESSEL** a boat or ship used for smuggling (*often used in combination*) **8.** OPERATOR somebody who manages or operates something such as a business or a machine **9.** DOOR OR DRAWER SLIDE a guide on which a drawer or door slides **10.** STRIP UNDER A SLED either of the long blades beneath a sled or sleigh, on which it rides **11.** SKATE BLADE the blade of an ice skate **12.** CARPET STRIP a long narrow piece of carpet **13.** FABRIC STRIP a strip of fabric, often linen or lace, used to protect or decorate the top of a piece of furniture such as a dresser **14.** BOT CREEPING STEM THAT GROWS ROOTS a thin horizontal stem that grows roots from nodes at regular intervals **15.** BOT PLANT GROWING FROM STEM NODES a plant such as a strawberry that has runners or grows by runners **16.** BOT CLIMBING PLANT any plant that climbs and twists, e.g., a bean plant **17.** ZOOL DEEP-WATER MARINE FISH a swift streamlined deep-water marine fish of the jack family, especially either of two edible bluish species. Latin name: *Caranx crysos* and *Elagatis bipinnulata*. **18.** MOUNTAINEERING ANCHORING LOOP a continuous loop of webbing used to provide an anchor to a rock, tree, or other point

WORD KEY: SYNONYMS

See Synonyms at ***candidate***.

run·ner-up (*plural* **run·ners-up**) *n.* a contestant or competitor who comes second, e.g., in a sports event or an election

run·ning /rúnning/ *n.* **1.** FAST MOVEMENT rapid movement on foot, with long strides and both feet momentarily off the ground **2.** SPORT RUNNING AS EXERCISE the sport or exercise of running **3.** MANAGEMENT the managing of a business or organization ■ *adj.* **1.** FLOWING flowing continuously in a stream **2.** FUNCTIONING in operation or in working order **3.** FOR USE OR WEAR BY RUNNERS relating to or intended for the sport or exercise of running ○ *running shoes* **4.** SPORTS WHILE RUNNING begun with a run or performed during a run ○ *a running jump* **5.** LONG-STANDING begun long ago and still continuing ○ *a running joke* **6.** MADE DURING AN EVENT made while something is operating or happening ○ *a running commentary* **7.** MED OPEN open and discharging fluid or pus ○ *a running sore* **8.** BOT CREEPING growing by means of horizontal stems that creep along the ground **9.** FOOTBALL GAINING YARDS WHILE RUNNING advancing the ball while running rather than passing ■ *adv.* CONSECUTIVELY in succession ○ *for five days running* [Old English] ◇ **be in** *or* **out of the running** to have or not have a chance of success

run·ning back *n.* in football, an offensive back who advances the ball in running plays

run·ning board *n.* a narrow step beneath the doors of some motor vehicles, typically vintage cars

run·ning hand *n.* handwriting done without lifting the pen or pencil from the writing surface

run·ning head, **run·ning ti·tle** *n.* a heading printed on every page or every other page of a book

run·ning light *n.* a light displayed on a ship or aircraft at night to show its location and size

run·ning mate *n.* **1.** POL NOMINEE FOR LESSER OFFICE a candidate for the lesser of two associated political offices, e.g., a vice-presidential candidate **2.** HORSERACING PACESETTING HORSE in horseracing, a horse that is entered in a race for the purpose of setting the pace for a stronger horse from the same stable

run·ning start *n.* = **flying start**

run·ning stitch *n.* a simple sewing stitch that goes down and up evenly through cloth without being looped

run·ning ti·tle *n.* PUBL = **running head**

run·ny /rúnnee/ (**-ni·er, -ni·est**) *adj.* **1.** OF A LIQUID CONSISTENCY of a liquid or semiliquid consistency that pours or flows **2.** WATERY of a consistency that is too thin **3.** RELEASING MUCUS producing excessive flowing mucus ○ *a runny nose*

run-off /rún àwf, -òf/ *n.* **1.** GEOG WATER NOT ABSORBED BY SOIL rainfall that does not soak into the soil but flows into surface waters **2.** ENVIRON, MANUF, AGRIC WATER POLLUTION agricultural or industrial waste products that are carried by rainfall and melting snow into surface waters **3.** SPORTS, POL SECOND CONTEST TO DETERMINE THE WINNER an election, race, or other contest held after an earlier one that produced no clear winner

run-of-the-mill *adj.* with no exceptional or distinguishing qualities

run-on *adj.* PRINTING ON THE SAME LINE added to a line of text without a line break ■ *n.* **1.** PRINTING TEXT ADDED WITHOUT A LINE BREAK an added section of text that continues a line, without a line break **2.** LING WORD UNDERSTOOD BUT UNDEFINED an undefined word appearing at the end of a dictionary entry, whose meaning can be understood from the previous defined senses (*often used before a noun*)

runt /runt/ *n.* **1.** SMALLEST ANIMAL an animal that is considerably smaller than others of the same kind, especially the smallest or weakest animal in a litter **2.** OFFENSIVE TERM an offensive term for a short person or somebody regarded as lacking physical strength (*informal insult*) [Mid-16thC. Origin uncertain: perhaps from Dutch *rund* "bull, cow, small ox."] —**runt·i·ness** *n.* —**run·tish** *adj.* —**runt·y** *adj.*

run-through *n.* **1.** REHEARSAL a practice or rehearsal of something, especially a dramatic performance **2.** BRIEF SURVEY a brief review of something such as an agenda or report

run-time *n.* **1.** = **execution time** **2.** RUNNING TIME OF PROGRAM the time during which a program runs **3.** PROGRAM VERSION WITH LIMITED FUNCTIONS a version of a computer program that allows a user to perform some, but not all, of the program's functions ○ *a run-time module*

run-up *n.* **1.** SUDDEN RISE a sudden increase in something such as price, sales, or value **2.** RUN PRECEDING SOMETHING a run taken to gather momentum, e.g., for a jump or kick in an athletic event **3.** *U.K.* TIME IMMEDIATELY BEFORE SOMETHING the period of time that leads up to an important event

run·way /rún wày/ *n.* **1.** STRIP FOR AIRCRAFT LANDINGS AND TAKEOFFS a long wide level roadway or other strip of land on which aircraft land and take off **2.** EXTENSION OF STAGE INTO AUDIENCE a narrow ramp or platform that is part of a stage and extends into the auditorium of a theater or nightclub **3.** PLATFORM USED IN FASHION SHOWS a long platform along which fashion models walk during a show **4.** CHUTE FOR LOGS a chute down which logs are slid **5.** TRACK a track, passageway, or channel along which something runs

Popperfoto

Damon Runyon

Run·yon /rúny'n/, **Damon** (1884–1946) U.S. journalist and short story writer. His writings, mainly about low life, are distinguished by their use of slang and colorful characterizations. Full name **Alfred Damon Runyon**

ru·pee /roo peé, róopee/ *n.* **1.** CURRENCY OF INDIA AND PAKISTAN the standard unit of currency in India, Pakistan, the Maldive Islands, Mauritius, Nepal, Bhutan, the Seychelles, and Sri Lanka. See table at **currency** **2.** BILL WORTH A RUPEE a bill worth a rupee [Early 17thC. From Hindi *rūpiyā*, from Sanskrit *rūpya*, "wrought silver," from *rūpa*, "shape."]

Ru·pes Rec·ta /róopez réktə/ *n.* a fault on the surface of the Moon running north – south for 75 mi./120 km along the eastern edge of Mare Nubium

ru·pi·ah /roo peé ə/ (*plural* **-ahs** *or* **-ah**) *n.* **1.** UNIT OF INDONESIAN CURRENCY the standard unit of currency in Indonesia. See table at **currency** **2.** BILL WORTH A RUPIAH a bill worth a rupiah [Mid-20thC. Via Malay from Hindi *rūpiyā* (see RUPEE).]

ru·pic·o·lous /roo píkələss/ *adj.* used to describe organisms that live or grow on or among rocks [Mid-19thC. Formed from Latin *rupi-* "rock, cliff" + -COLOUS.]

rup·ture /rúpchər/ *n.* **1.** BROKEN STATE OF SOMETHING a break in or breaking apart of something ○ *a rupture in a water main* **2.** TORN TISSUE a tear in or tearing of bodily tissue ○ *the rupture of a blood vessel* **3.** = **hernia** **4.** BREACH IN RELATIONS a breakdown in a friendly or peaceful relationship ■ *vti.* (**-tured, -tur·ing, -tures**) **1.** BREAK, BURST, OR TEAR SOMETHING to break, burst, or tear something or to become broken, burst, or torn **2.** CAUSE RIFT IN RELATIONSHIP to cause or undergo a breakdown in a friendly or peaceful relationship **3.** TEAR TISSUE to cause or suffer a tearing of bodily tissue **4.** PRODUCE OR HAVE HERNIA to cause or suffer a hernia [15thC. Via Old French from Latin *ruptura*, from *rumpere* "to break."] —**rup·tur·a·ble** *adj.*

WORD KEY: ORIGIN

Latin *rumpere*, from which ***rupture*** is derived, is also the source of English *corrupt*, *disrupt*, *erupt*, *rout*, *route*, and *routine*.

ru·ral /róorəl/ *adj.* **1.** OUTSIDE THE CITY found in or living in the country **2.** TYPICAL OF COUNTRY relating to or characteristic of the country or of country living **3.** AGRICULTURAL relating to, characteristic of, or involving farming [15thC. Via Old French from Latin *rural-*, from *rur-*, stem of *rus* "country, countryside" (source of English *rustic*).] —**ru·ral·i·ty** /roo rállətee/ *n.* —**ru·ral·ly** /róorəlee/ *adv.*

ru·ral free de·liv·er·y *n.* free mail delivery in rural areas

ru·ral·ist /róorəlist/ *n.* **1.** SOMEBODY LIVING IN COUNTRY somebody who lives in the country **2.** SOMEBODY FAVORING RURAL LIFE somebody who supports or promotes a rural lifestyle and rural interests

ru·ral·ize /róorə līz/ (**-ized, -iz·ing, -iz·es**) *v.* **1.** *vt.* MAKE SOMETHING RURAL to make something rural in character or habit **2.** *vi.* LIVE IN COUNTRYSIDE to live or pass time in the country after having lived in a city or town —**ru·ral·i·za·tion** /róorələ záysh'n/ *n.*

ru·ral route *n.* a route for mail delivery in rural areas

Ru·rik /róorik/ *n.* a Scandinavian leader who died in A.D. 879 after establishing the first kingdom and royal dynasty of Russia, which continued until 1598

Ru·ri·tan /róorətən/ *n.* a member of the Ruritan National club, a service organization with emphasis on education for underprivileged people [Mid-20thC. From *Ruritan National*, a service club.]

Ru·ri·ta·ni·a /róorə táynee ə/ *n.* a place of romance, adventure, and intrigue [Late 19thC. Named for *Ruritania*, fictional central European kingdom in the novels *The Prisoner of Zenda* 1894 and *Rupert of Hentzau* 1898 by Anthony Hope.] —**Ru·ri·ta·ni·an** *adj., n.*

ruse /rooz, rooss/ *n.* a clever trick or plot used to deceive others [15thC. Originally "doubling of hunted game in its tracks," from Old French *ruser* "to repulse, retreat, dodge" (source of English *rush*[1]).]

Ru·se /róoss ay/ city in Ruse Province, northern Bulgaria. Population: 168,000 (1996).

rush[1] /rush/ *v.* (**rushed, rush·ing, rush·es**) **1.** *vi.* MOVE FAST to move, act, or proceed quickly **2.** *vt.* HURRY SOMEBODY OR SOMETHING ALONG to make somebody or something move, act, or proceed quickly ○ *Don't rush me.* **3.** *vt.* TAKE SOMEBODY OR SOMETHING URGENTLY to take or send somebody or something to a place quickly and urgently ○ *We rushed him to the airport to catch his flight.* **4.** *vt.* DO SOMETHING HASTILY to do something in a hurry and without careful thought ○ *rush a job* **5.** *vi.* GO RECKLESSLY to proceed in a quick and reckless way ○ *We mustn't rush into things.* ○ *"For fools rush in where angels fear to tread."* (Alexander Pope, *An Essay on Criticism*; 1711) **6.** *vi.* FLOW FAST to flow somewhere quickly **7.** *vt.* CAPTURE AN ENEMY QUICKLY to seize a position or overcome an enemy by a sudden quick attack **8.** *vt.* ENCOURAGE SOMEBODY TO JOIN SOMETHING to encourage somebody to become a member of something, especially a fraternity or sorority, with parties and entertainment **9.** *vt.* SEEK TO JOIN AN ASSOCIATION to seek to become a member of something, especially a fraternity or sorority, by, e.g., attending its parties ○ *I'm rushing Sigma Chi, what about you?* **10.** *vti.* FOOTBALL CARRY A BALL FORWARD to carry the football forward in a running play **11.** *vt.* FOOTBALL CHARGE THE PASSER OR KICKER to move aggressively toward the opposing passer or kicker in football to try to block the ball or tackle the player before the ball is passed or kicked ■ *n.* **1.** HURRY a hurry or need for hurry **2.** SUDDEN FAST MOVEMENT BY A CROWD a sudden and quick movement of a person or group of people toward a place or objective ○ *there was a rush to the door* **3.** BUSY TIME a very busy period, e.g., a time when large numbers of people try to do something at the same time ○ *a rush during the store's sale* **4.** SUDDEN ATTACK a sudden quick forward movement in an attack **5.** SUDDEN FLOW a sudden quick flow or movement of something **6.** SUDDEN FEELING a sudden powerful onset of an emotion **7.** SUDDEN PLEASURABLE SENSATION a sudden feeling of elation and pleasure (*informal*) **8.** FOOTBALL FOOTBALL PLAY WITHOUT A PASS a football play in which the ball is carried rather than passed **9.** FOOTBALL DEFENSIVE PLAY a football defense in which linemen move aggressively toward the opposing passer or kicker to try to block the ball or tackle the player before the ball is passed or kicked **10.** RECRUITMENT DRIVE a concentrated effort by a fraternity or sorority to recruit new members ○ *a rush party* **11. rushes** CINEMA UNEDITED PRINTS OF MOVIE SCENES the first unedited prints of a scene or scenes shot for a movie ■ *adj.* **1.** DONE QUICKLY done or needing to be done quickly ○ *a rush job* **2.** VERY BUSY very busy, especially with many people traveling at the same time [14thC. From Old French *re(h)usser* "to repel," of uncertain origin: perhaps from Latin *recusare* "to object to"; or from assumed Vulgar Latin *rursare*, from Latin *rursus* "backward."] —**rush·er** *n.*

rush into *vt.* to do or agree to something or to cause somebody to do or agree to something quickly, with little consideration of the consequences

rush through *vt.* **1.** GET SOMETHING APPROVED QUICKLY to get something approved or put in place hurriedly, often without allowing time for full consideration ○ *The plans for the new building were rushed through.* **2.** DO SOMETHING QUICKLY to do something quickly and with little thought or preparation

rush[2] /rush/ *n.* **1.** PLANT GROWING IN WET AREAS a marsh plant with a cylindrical stem that is sometimes hollow and leaves that resemble blades of grass. Genus: *Juncus.* **2.** STEM OF THE RUSH PLANT the stem of a rush plant, used in weaving baskets and mats and in caning chairs (*often used before a noun*) ○ *a rush mat* [Old English *rysc*, from prehistoric Germanic]

Rush /rush/, **Geoffrey** (*b.* 1951) Australian actor. In 1997 he won an Academy Award for his role in *Shine* (1996).

rush can·dle *n.* = **rushlight**

Rush·die /rúshdee/, **Salman** (*b.* 1947) Indian-born British novelist. A master of the magic realist style, his novels include *Midnight's Children* (1981), which won the Booker Prize, *The Satanic Verses* (1988), *The Moor's Last Sigh* (1996), and *The Ground Beneath Her Feet* (1999).

rushed /rusht/ *adj.* **1.** DONE IN A HURRY done very quickly, usually too quickly **2.** VERY BUSY feeling a need or obligation to do something quickly

rush·ee /ru sheé/ *n.* a college or university student who is being rushed by a fraternity or sorority

rush hour *n.* a period of heavy traffic in the morning and evening during which people are traveling to and from work

rush·light /rúsh līt/ *n.* a candle made from pith of the stem of a rush that has been dipped in tallow

Mount Rushmore

Rush·more, Mount /rúsh màwr/ mountain in the Black Hills, western South Dakota, carved with the faces of presidents George Washington, Thomas Jefferson, Theodore Roosevelt, and Abraham Lincoln. Height: 5,600 ft./1,700 m.

rush·y /rúshee/ (**-i·er, -i·est**) *adj.* overgrown with, made of, or resembling rushes

rusk /rusk/ *n.* a sweet crisp golden-brown bread, often given to children and babies and made from bread that is baked, sliced, left to dry out, and then baked again [Late 16thC. Alteration of Portuguese or Spanish *rosca* "screw, coil, bread twist," of uncertain origin.]

Rus·kin /rússkin/, **John** (1819–1900) British art and social critic. He argued for the moral and religious significance of art in works such as *Modern Painters* (1843–60) and *The Stones of Venice* (1851–53).

Russ. *abbr.* **1.** Russia **2.** Russian

Rus·sell /rúss'l/, **Bertrand, 3rd Earl Russell** (1872–1970) British philosopher and mathematician. A pacifist and winner of a Nobel Prize in literature (1950), he wrote many highly influential philosophical works. Full name **Bertrand Arthur William Russell**

Rus·sell, Bill (*b.* 1934) U.S. basketball player. He played for the Boston Celtics (1957–69), during which time the team won 11 NBA championships. Full name **William Felton Russell**

Rus·sell, Charles Taze (1852–1916) U.S. religious leader. He founded the International Bible Students Association, now known as Jehovah's Witnesses (1872). Known as **Pastor Russell**

Rus·sell, Henry Norris (1877–1957) U.S. astronomer. He studied the evolution of stars by plotting them on a special graph, which became known as the Hertzsprung-Russell diagram.

Rus·sell, Ken (*b.* 1927) British movie director. His vivid adaptations of the novels of D. H. Lawrence and biographies of composers often attracted controversy. Full name **Henry Kenneth Alfred Russell**

Rus·sell, Lillian (1861–1922) U.S. singer. Her most famous roles included leading parts in the operettas of Gilbert and Sullivan. Real name **Helen Louise Leonard**

Rus·sell's vi·per *n.* a venomous snake common in India. Latin name: *Vipera russelli.* [Early 20thC. Named for Patrick *Russell* (1727–1805), Scottish naturalist and physician.]

Rus·sel·lville /rúss'l vìl/ city in northern Arkansas, directly north of the Arkansas River and north of Hot Springs. Population: 24,794 (1996).

rus·set /rússət/ *n.* **1.** COLORS REDDISH BROWN a reddish-brown color **2.** BOT POTATO a usually small reddish-brown potato **3. rus·set, rus·set ap·ple** BOT APPLE WITH ROUGH SKIN an apple with a rough brownish skin, a deep sweet-sharp flavor, and a firm texture **4.** TEXTILES HOMESPUN FABRIC a coarse homespun fabric with a reddish-brown color ■ *adj.* REDDISH-BROWN of a reddish-brown color [13thC. From Old French *rousset*, literally "small red," from *rous* "red," from Latin *russus* (source of English *roux*).]

Rus·sia /rúshə/ republic in eastern Europe and northern and western Asia. In the past the term referred to the Russian Empire, a state that included several republics that are now independent. Language: Russian. Currency: ruble. Capital: Moscow. Population: 147,501,000 (1997). Area: 6,592,850 sq. mi./17,075,400 sq. km. Official name **Russian Federation**

Rus·sia leath·er *n.* a smooth brownish-red leather impregnated with oil from birch bark, used for binding books

Rus·sian /rúsh'n/ *n.* **1.** PEOPLES SOMEBODY FROM RUSSIA somebody who was born or raised in Russia or who has Russian citizenship **2.** LANG OFFICIAL LANGUAGE OF RUSSIA the official language of Russia, also spoken by people of Russian descent in other parts of the world. It belongs to the Balto-Slavic branch of Indo-European languages. There are about 160 million native speakers of Russian and appoximately another 110 million people use it as a second language. ■ *adj.* **1.** PEOPLES OF RUSSIA relating to Russia, or its people or culture **2.** LANG OF RUSSIAN relating to the Russian language **3.** PEOPLES OF THE FORMER SOVIET UNION relating to the former Soviet Union, or its peoples or cultures (*dated*)

Rus·sian blue *n.* a cat belonging to a breed of short-haired domestic cats with a slender body and bluish-gray fur

Rus·sian dress·ing *n.* a salad dressing with a mayonnaise or vinaigrette base and sometimes with added chili sauce or pickles

Rus·sian·ize /rúsh'n īz/ (**-ized, -iz·ing, -iz·es**) *vti.* to become or make somebody or something become Russian in style, character, or appearance —**Rus·sian·i·za·tion** /rùsh'nə záysh'n/ *n.*

Rus·sian ol·ive *n.* BOT = **oleaster** *n.* **3**

Rus·sian Or·tho·dox Church *n.* the national church of Russia, an independent section of the Eastern Orthodox Church with the Patriarch of Moscow at its head

Rus·sian rou·lette *n.* **1.** DEADLY GAME USING A REVOLVER a deadly game in which people take turns firing a revolver loaded with only one bullet at their own heads, after spinning the cylinder **2.** SOMETHING DANGEROUS a dangerous or reckless action or activity [*Russian* because it was reportedly played by Russian officers in Romania in 1917, except that only one bullet was removed from the revolver]

Rus·sian this·tle, Rus·sian tum·ble·weed *n.* a European saltwort of the goosefoot family that has narrow spiny leaves and has become a troublesome weed in western North America. Latin name: *Salsola kali.*

Rus·sian wolf·hound *n.* = **borzoi**

Rus·ski /rúskee, rŏŏskee/, **Rus·sky** (*plural* **-skies**) *n.* an offensive term referring to a Russian person (*slang offensive*) [Mid-19thC. From Russian *russkiĭ.*]

Russo- *prefix.* Russia, Russian ○ *Russophile* [From RUSSIA]

Rus·so-Jap·a·nese War *n.* a war fought in 1904–05 between Russia and Japan, mainly over control of Korea, in which Russia was unexpectedly defeated

Rus·so·phile /rússə fīl/, **Rus·so·phil** /rússəfil/ *n.* somebody who likes or admires Russia, its people, or its culture —**Rus·so·phile** *adj.*

Rus·so·phobe /rússə fōb/ *n.* somebody who dislikes or is afraid of Russia, its people, or its culture —**Rus·so·pho·bi·a** /rùssə fṓbee ə/ *n.* —**Rus·so·pho·bic** /-fṓbik/ *adj.*

rust /rust/ *n.* **1.** REDDISH-BROWN COATING ON METAL a reddish-brown coating of iron oxide on the surface of iron or steel that forms when the metal is exposed to air and moisture **2.** SOMETHING RESEMBLING RUST something that resembles rust, especially in color, e.g., another type of corrosion or a stain **3.** COLORS REDDISH BROWN a reddish-brown color **4.** BOT PLANT DISEASE a disease of plants caused by rust fungus, in which reddish-brown spots form on the leaves and stems **5.** BOT = **rust fungus** ■ *v.* (**rust·ed, rust·ing, rusts**) **1.** *vti.* CORRODE WITH RUST to cause something to corrode with rust or to become corroded with rust **2.** *vi.* BOT DEVELOP A PLANT DISEASE to become infected with a disease caused by rust fungus **3.** *vi.* DETERIORATE to deteriorate from neglect or lack of use ○ *His knowledge of German rusted over the years.* ■ *adj.* REDDISH-BROWN of a reddish-brown color [Old English *rūst*, from a prehistoric Germanic word that is also the ancestor of English *red*]

rust belt, Rust Belt *n.* an area of heavy industry where unprofitable factories have closed down or are closing down

rust buck·et *n.* a car that is badly affected by rust (*informal humorous*)

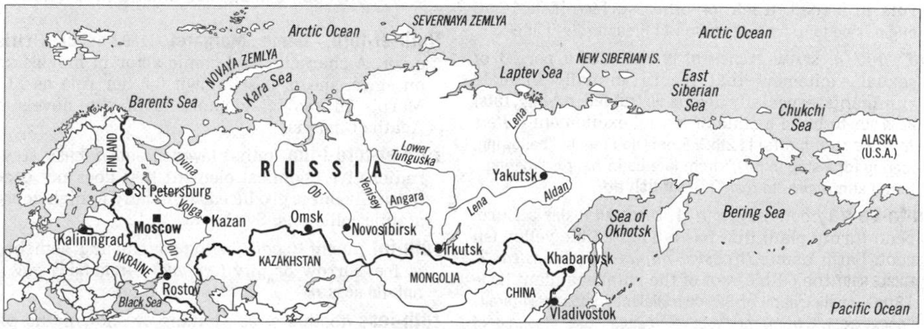

Russia

rust fun·gus *n.* a fungus that lives as a parasite on many plants, causing reddish-brown spots on the plant parts. Order: Uredinales.

rus·tic /rústik/ *adj.* **1.** RELATING TO A COUNTRY LIFESTYLE relating to, characteristic of, or appropriate to the country or country living **2.** PLAIN AND SIMPLE lacking excessive refinement or elegance **3.** MADE OF ROUGH BRANCHES made of rough wood, especially branches with the bark left on them **4.** CONSTR HAVING A ROUGH SURFACE with a rough finish ○ *rustic bricks* ■ *n.* SOMEBODY LIVING IN COUNTRY somebody who lives in the country, especially somebody who is considered to be unsophisticated (*offensive in some contexts*) [15thC. From Latin *rusticus*, from *rus* "country" (see RURAL).] —**rus·ti·cal·ly** *adv.* —**rus·tic·i·ty** /ru stíssətee/ *n.*

rus·ti·cate /rústi kàyt/ (**-cat·ed, -cat·ing, -cates**) *v.* **1.** *vi.* MOVE TO THE COUNTRY to go to the country to live **2.** *vt.* SEND SOMEBODY TO THE COUNTRY to send somebody to the country to live **3.** *vt.* MAKE SOMEBODY OR SOMETHING APPEAR RUSTIC to become or to cause somebody or something to become rustic in appearance or quality **4.** *vt. U.K.* SUSPEND STUDENT FROM UNIVERSITY to suspend a student from university for a set time as a punishment **5.** *vt.* CONSTR FINISH A WALL WITH ROUGH MASONRY to finish the outside of a wall with large blocks of masonry that are left with a rough surface, beveled, and have deep joints between them —**rus·ti·ca·tion** /rùsti káysh'n/ *n.* —**rus·ti·ca·tor** /rústi kàytər/ *n.*

rus·tle[1] /rúss'l/ *v.* (**-tled, -tling, -tles**) **1.** *vti.* MAKE SWISHING SOUND to make or cause something to make a swishing or soft crackling sound, e.g., that made by dry leaves rubbing together **2.** *vi.* MOVE WITH RUSTLING SOUND to move with a swishing or soft crackling sound ■ *n.* RUSTLING SOUND a swishing or soft crackling sound ○ *the rustle of paper money* [14thC. An imitation of the sound.] —**rus·tling·ly** *adv.*

rustle up *vt.* (*informal*) **1.** PREPARE FOOD QUICKLY to prepare a meal or snack quickly using any food that is immediately available **2.** GET THINGS OR PEOPLE TOGETHER to quickly find and bring together things or people

rus·tle[2] /rúss'l/ (**-tled, -tling, -tles**) *v.* **1.** *vti.* STEAL LIVESTOCK to steal livestock, especially cattle or horses **2.** *vi.* MOVE QUICKLY AND ENERGETICALLY to move or work quickly and energetically [Early 20thC. From RUSTLE[1].]

rus·tler /rússlər/ *n.* somebody who steals livestock, especially cattle or horses

rust mite *n.* a gall mite that produces brown spots on leaves and fruit by burrowing into them

Rus·ton /rústən/ city in northern Louisiana, east of Shreveport and west of Monroe. Population: 19,853 (1996).

rust·proof /rúst pro͞of/ *adj.* TREATED TO INHIBIT RUST not susceptible to rust or treated so as not to be susceptible to rust ■ *vt.* (**-proofed, -proof·ing, -proofs**) MAKE METAL RUSTPROOF to treat metal to prevent it rusting —**rust·proof·ing** *n.*

rust·y /rústee/ (**-i·er, -i·est**) *adj.* **1.** CORRODED covered with or corroded by rust **2.** OUT OF PRACTICE out of practice or impaired because of old age, neglect, or lack of use ○ *My German is very rusty.* **3.** RUST-COLORED of the color of rust **4.** BOT INFECTED WITH RUST FUNGUS affected by rust fungus **5.** DISCOLORED faded and threadbare from wear and age [Old English] —**rust·i·ly** *adv.* —**rust·i·ness** *n.*

rut[1] /rut/ *n.* **1.** NARROW GROOVE a narrow channel or groove in something, especially one made by the wheels of vehicles **2.** BORING SITUATION a routine procedure, situation, or way of life that has become uninteresting and tiresome ○ *I felt in a rut* ■ *vt.* (**rut·ted, rut·ting, ruts**) MAKE RUTS IN SOMETHING to make ruts in a road, track, or other surface [Late 16thC origin uncertain: probably from Old French *rote* "route"]

rut[2] /rut/ *n.* SEXUAL EXCITEMENT IN MALE DEER a period of sexual excitement that recurs annually in male ruminants, especially deer ■ *vi.* (**rut·ted, rut·ting, ruts**) BE IN RUT to be in a state of sexual excitement (*refers to male ruminants*) [12thC. From Old French, "bellowing, roaring (of a stag in rut)," from late Latin *rugitus* "roaring," from Latin *rugire* "to roar."] —**rut·tish** *adj.*

ru·ta·ba·ga /roótə bàygə/ *n.* **1.** EUROPEAN TURNIP a European turnip plant that has a large edible yellowish root. Latin name: *Brassica napus napobrassica.* **2.** EDIBLE ROOT the edible root of the rutabaga plant [Late 18thC. Anglicization of Swedish dialect *rotabagge*, literally "baggy root," from *rot* "root" + *bagge* "bag" (source of English *bag*).]

ruth /rooth/ *n.* (*archaic*) **1.** SADNESS FOR ANOTHER pity for another person's troubles **2.** SORROW sorrow or remorse for having done something wrong [12thC. Formed by adding *-th* (on the model of words like TRUTH) from RUE.]

Ruth /rooth/ *n.* **1.** WOMAN IN THE BIBLE in the Bible, a Moabite widow who left her own people to live with her mother-in-law Naomi, married Boaz, and was an ancestor of King David **2.** BOOK OF BIBLE the book of the Bible that tells the story of Ruth

Babe Ruth

Ruth /rooth/, **Babe** (1895–1948) U.S. baseball player. While playing for the New York Yankees in the 1920s and 1930s, his legendary home run hitting dominated the sport and made him one of the most popular players in the history of baseball. Real name **George Herman Ruth**

Ru·the·ni·an /roo theénee ən/ *n.* **1.** SOMEBODY FROM RUTHENIA somebody who was born or raised in the former region of Ruthenia, or who was a citizen of Ruthenia **2.** UKRAINIAN DIALECT a dialect of Ukranian spoken in the former region of Ruthenia —**Ru·the·ni·an** *adj.*

ru·then·ic /roo thénnik, -theénik/ *adj.* relating to or containing ruthenium, especially with a high valence [Mid-19thC. Formed from RUTHENIUM + -IC.]

ru·the·ni·ous /roo theénee əss/ *adj.* relating to or containing ruthenium, especially with a low valence [Mid-19thC. Formed from RUTHENIUM + -OUS.]

ru·the·ni·um /roo theénee əm/ *n.* a brittle white metallic chemical element found in platinum ores and used to harden platinum and palladium alloys. Symbol **Ru** [Mid-19thC. Named for RUTHENIA, where the ore was first found.]

Ruth·er·ford /rú*th*ər fùrd/, **Ernest, 1st Baron Rutherford of Nelson and Cambridge** (1871–1937) New Zealand-born British physicist. He discovered the nuclear structure of the atom (1909), and was awarded a Nobel Prize in chemistry (1908).

Dame Margaret Rutherford

Ruth·er·ford, Dame Margaret (1892–1972) British actor. A character and comic actor in movies and on stage, she is best known for her role as Miss Marple in movie adaptations of the novels by Agatha Christie.

ruth·er·ford·i·um /rù*th*ər fáwrdee əm/ *n.* CHEM ELEM a radioactive chemical element that does not occur naturally but is produced artificially in high-energy atomic collisions. Symbol **Rf**

ruth·ful /roóthf'l/ *adj.* feeling or causing somebody to feel sorrow or pity (*archaic*) —**ruth·ful·ly** *adv.* —**ruth·ful·ness** *n.*

ruth·less /roóthləss/ *adj.* having or showing no pity or mercy —**ruth·less·ly** *adv.* —**ruth·less·ness** *n.*

ru·ti·lant /ro͞ot'lənt/ *adj.* shining or glowing with a red light [15thC. From Latin *rutilant-*, present participle stem of *rutilare* "to redden," from *rutilus* "reddish."]

ru·tile /ro͞o teel, -tīl/ *n.* a dark reddish-brown or lustrous black form of titanium dioxide that occurs widely in igneous and metamorphic rocks as needle-shaped crystals and is used as a source of titanium [Early 19thC. Via French and German from Latin *rutilus* "reddish."]

Rut·ledge /rút lìdj/, **Edward** (1749–1800) U.S. politician. He signed the Declaration of Independence (1776) and was governor of South Carolina (1798–1800).

Rut·ledge, John (1739–1800) U.S. jurist. He was associate justice (1789–91) and chief justice (1795) of the U.S. Supreme Court.

rut·ting /rútting/ *adj.* used to describe male ruminants, especially deer, that are in a state of sexual excitement

rut·ty /rúttee/ (**-ti·er, -ti·est**) *adj.* with a surface marked by ruts —**rut·ti·ness** *n.*

Ru·wen·zo·ri Range /ro͞o ən záwree/ mountain range in central Africa, on the northeastern border of the Democratic Republic of the Congo and the southwestern border of Uganda, between Edward and Albert lakes

RV *abbr.* **1.** recreational vehicle **2.** reentry vehicle **3.** **RV, R.V.** BIBLE Revised Version

Rv. *abbr.* Revelation

R-val·ue *n.* a measure of the ability of a material such as insulation to retard heat flow. A higher number indicates better insulating properties. [Mid-20thC. R is the symbol for RESISTANCE.]

R.W. *abbr.* **1.** Right Worshipful **2.** Right Worthy

Rwan·da[1] /roo aándə/ *n.* LANG one of the official languages of Rwanda, also spoken in other parts of east central Africa. It is a Bantu language belonging to the Benue-Congo branch of Niger-Congo languages and is spoken by about 15 million people. [Early 20thC. From Bantu.]

Rwanda

Rwan·da[2] /ro͞o aándə/ republic in east central Africa bordered by Uganda, Tanzania, Burundi, Lake Kivu, and the Democratic Republic of Congo. Language: Rwanda, French. Currency: Rwanda franc. Capital: Kigali. Population: 6,727,000 (1996). Area: 10,169 sq. mi./26,338 sq. km. Official name **Rwandese Republic** —**Rwand·an** *n., adj.* —**Rwand·ese** *n., adj.*

r.w.d. *abbr.* TRANSP rear-wheel drive

rwy., Rwy. *abbr.* railway

Rx *n.* a prescription [Early 20thC. Alteration of a symbol used at the beginning of prescriptions, abbreviation of Latin *recipe*, literally "take" (source of English *recipe*).]

ry., Ry. *abbr.* railway

-ry *suffix.* = **-ery**

ry·a /reé ə/ *n.* **1.** HANDWOVEN SCANDINAVIAN RUG a type of handwoven Scandinavian rug with a deep pile and a colorful pattern **2.** WEAVING PATTERN USED FOR A RYA the weaving pattern or style used in making a rya [Mid-20thC. Named for *Rya*, a city in Sweden where the craft originated.]

Ry·an /rī ən/, **Nolan** (*b.* 1947) U.S. baseball player. Considered one of the greatest pitchers in major league history, he retired in 1993 with the record for most career strikeouts (2,714) and most career no-hitters (7). Real name **Lynn Nolan Ryan, Jr.**

Ry·der /rīdər/, **Albert Pinkham** (1847–1917) U.S. painter. His idiosyncratic style of painting, often seen in depictions of the sea, involved the application of several layers of paint.

rye[1] /rī/ *n.* **1.** BOT **HARDY ANNUAL GRASS** a tall hardy annual cereal grass that has bluish-green leaves and is widely cultivated for its light brown grain. Latin name: *Secale cereale.* **2. RYE GRAIN** the grain of the rye plant, used to make flour and whiskey and also as fodder **3.** = **rye whiskey 4.** FOOD = **rye bread** [Old English *ryge*]

WORD KEY: CULTURAL NOTE

Catcher in the Rye, a novel by J. D. Salinger (1951). A moving and realistic account of a young boy's attempt to come to terms with encroaching adulthood, it describes two days in the life of disaffected teenager Holden Caulfield. Holden absconds to New York, then resolves to leave home for good; his failure to accomplish this results in his mental collapse.

rye[2] /rī/ *n.* a word used by Romany people to mean gentleman [Mid-19thC. From Romany *rai*, from Sanskrit *rājan* "rajah."]

rye bread *n.* a dark or light bread made using rye flour, often flavored with caraway seed

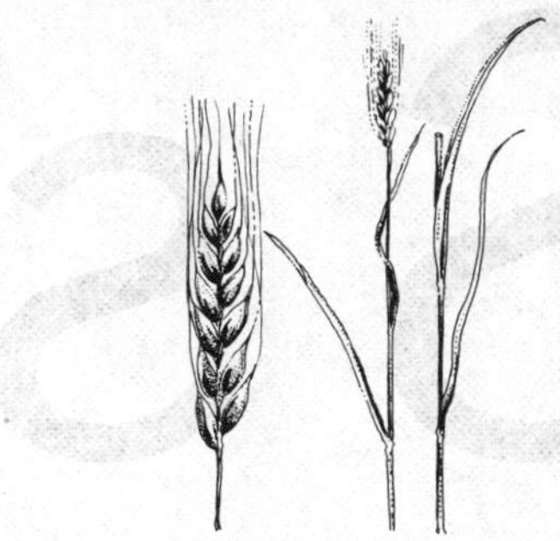

Rye

rye grass *n.* a European grass that is widely cultivated as forage, as a cover crop, and for lawns. Latin name: *Lolium perenne.*

Ry·er·son /rī́rssən/, **Adolphus Egerton** (1803–82) Canadian clergyman and educator. As superintendent of education for Canada West (1844–76), he promoted universal and compulsory education.

rye whis·key *n.* whiskey distilled from fermented rye

Ryle /rīl/, **Sir Martin** (1918–84) British astronomer. As Astronomer Royal (1972–82) he received the Nobel Prize in physics (1974) for his development of aperture synthesis in radio astronomy.

Ryu·kyu Islands /ree ŏŏ koo-/ chain of islands in southwestern Japan, between Kyushu and Taiwan. Population: 1,222,458 (1990). Area: 870 sq. mi./2,260 sq. km.

Ss

s[1] /ess/ (*plural* **s's**), **S** (*plural* **S's** *or* **Ss**) *n.* **1. 19TH LETTER OF ENGLISH ALPHABET** the 19th letter of the modern English alphabet **2. SPEECH SOUND CORRESPONDING TO LETTER "S"** the speech sound that corresponds to the letter "S" **3. LETTER "S" WRITTEN** a written representation of the letter "S"

s[2] *symbol.* TIME, GEOM second

s[3] *abbr.* **1.** MEASURE stere **2.** QUANTUM PHYS strange quark

S[1], **s** *symbol.* PHYS siemens

S[2] *symbol.* **1.** QUANTUM PHYS entropy **2.** MONEY schilling **3.** sulfur **4.** MONEY sucre

S[3] *abbr.* **1.** BIBLE Samuel **2.** EDUC satisfactory **3.** QUANTUM PHYS strangeness **4.** small

S[4], **S.** *abbr.* South

s. *abbr.* **1.** semi- **2.** MUSIC solo **3.** shilling **4.** GRAM singular **5.** MUSIC soprano **6.** sire **7.** sister **8.** small **9.** son **10.** stock **11.** GRAM substantive

S. *abbr.* **1.** Sabbath **2.** Saturday **3.** Saxon **4.** September **5.** Saint **6.** Sea **7.** Sunday

SA *abbr.* **1.** Salvation Army **2.** Sturmabteilung

s.a. *abbr.* **1.** semiannual **2.** without date **3.** COMM subject to approval

SAA *abbr.* COMPUT systems application architecture

Saa·di·a ben Jo·seph /saádee ə ben jṓzif/ (882–942) Arabian philosopher and scholar, whose *Book of Opinions and Beliefs* (933) is a classic exegesis of Jewish traditions and laws.

Saa·mi /saámee/ (*plural* **-mi** *or* **-mis**) *n.* **1. SOMEBODY FROM LAPLAND** a member of the indigenous people of Lapland who are traditionally nomadic herders of reindeer **2. SAAMI LANGUAGE** the Finno-Ugric language of the Saami. Saami is spoken by about 80,000 people. [Late 18thC. From Saami.]

Saar·brück·en /saá broǒkən, za brykən/ capital city of Saarland State, in southwestern Germany. Population: 189,900 (1994).

Saa·ri·nen /saárənən/, **Eero** (1910–61) Finnish-born U.S. architect. He is known for his innovative and elegant buildings such as the TWA terminal at New York's Kennedy International Airport (1962). He was the son of Eliel Saarinen.

Saa·ri·nen, Eliel (1873–1950) Finnish-born U.S. architect, whose most admired work was the Helsinki Railway Station (1915). He emigrated to the U.S. (1923), where he headed the Cranmore Academy of Art (1932–48). He often worked in collaboration with his son, Eero Saarinen. Full name **Gottlieb Eliel Saarinen**

Sab. *abbr.* Sabbath

sab·a·dil·la /sàbbə díllə, -deé yə/ (*plural* **-las** *or* **-la**) *n.* **1. MEXICAN PLANT** a Mexican plant of the lily family with long flower spikelets and bitter brown seeds. Latin name: *Schoenocaulon officinale.* **2. SEEDS OF SABADILLA PLANT** the seeds of the sabadilla plant, used in insecticides and the source of the toxic compound veratrine [Early 19thC. From Spanish *cebadilla*, a diminutive of *cebada* "barley," ultimately from Latin *cibatus* "food, fodder," from *cibus* "food."]

Sa·bah /saá baá/ the second largest state in Malaysia, on the northeast of the island of Borneo. Capital: Kota Kinabalu. Population: 1,736,902 (1991). Area: 28,800 sq. mi./73,711 sq. km. Former name **North Borneo** (until 1963)

Sa·ba·tier /saa baa tyáy/, **Paul** (1854–1941) French chemist. His research on the catalytic hydrogenation of oils made possible the manufacture of margarine. He shared the Nobel Prize in chemistry (1912).

sab·bat /sábbət/ *n.* = **witches' Sabbath** [Via French from Latin *sabbatum* (see SABBATH)]

Sab·ba·tar·i·an /sàbbə táiree ən/ *n.* **1. STRICT OBSERVER OF THE SABBATH** somebody who believes in the strict observance of Sunday, in most Christian denominations, or Saturday, in Judaism and some Christian denominations, as a day of worship and rest **2. OBSERVER OF SATURDAY AS SABBATH** somebody who observes Saturday as the Sabbath, e.g., in Judaism ■ *adj.* **OF SABBATH OR SABBATARIANS** relating to the Sabbath, its observance, or to Sabbatarians [Early 17thC. Formed from late Latin *Sabbatarius*, from Latin *sabbatum* (see SABBATH).] —**Sab·ba·tar·i·an·ism** *n.*

Sab·bath /sábbəth/ *n.* **1. SUNDAY AS DAY OF RELIGIOUS WORSHIP** Sunday, observed by most Christians as the day of worship and rest from work **2. SATURDAY AS DAY OF RELIGIOUS WORSHIP** Saturday, observed as a day of religious worship and rest from work in Judaism and some Christian denominations **3.** = **witches' Sabbath** [Pre-12thC. Via Latin *sabbatum* from Greek *sabbaton*, from Hebrew *šabbāṯ* "rest," from *šāḇaṯ* "to rest."]

sab·bath school, Sab·bath School *n.* in the tradition of the Seventh-Day Adventists, a school for religious teaching held on Saturday

sab·bat·i·cal, sab·bat·ic *n.* **LEAVE FROM WORK** a period of leave from work for research, study, or travel, often with pay and usually granted to college professors every seven years ■ *adj.* **OF SABBATICAL** relating to a sabbatical [Late 16thC. Ultimately from Greek *sabbatikos* "of the Sabbath," from *sabbaton* (see SABBATH).]

Sab·bat·i·cal, Sab·bat·ic *adj.* relating to or suitable for the Sabbath

sab·bat·i·cal year, sab·bat·i·cal leave *n.* = **sabbatical** *n.*

Sab·bat·i·cal Year *n.* every seventh year, during which the ancient Israelites allowed their land to lie fallow

sa·ber /sáybər/ *n.* **1. HEAVY SWORD WITH CURVED BLADE** a heavy cavalry sword with a slightly curved blade that is sharp on one edge **2. FENCING SWORD WITH TAPERING BLADE** a light sword with a guard to cover the hand and a tapering flexible blade, used in fencing **3. FENCING WITH SABER** the sport or technique of fencing with a saber ■ *vt.* **(-bered, -ber·ing, -bers) INJURE SOMEBODY WITH SABER** to jab, injure, or kill somebody with a saber [Late 17thC. Via French *sabre* from obsolete German *Sabel*, of uncertain origin: perhaps from Slavic (Polish *szabla* or Russian *sablya*) or from Hungarian *szablya*.]

sa·ber rat·tling *n.* an aggressive display or threat of force, especially military force

sa·ber-toothed ti·ger, sa·ber-toothed cat *n.* an extinct animal of the cat family that lived in the Oligocene and Pleistocene epochs and had long curving upper canine teeth. Genus: *Smilodon.*

sa·bin /sáybin/ *n.* a unit of sound absorption equal to the absorption of one square foot of a perfectly absorbing surface [Mid-20thC. Named for Wallace Clement Ware *Sabine* 1868–1919, U.S. physicist who established the discipline of architectural acoustics.]

Sa·bin /sáybin/, **Albert** (1906–93) Russian-born U.S. microbiologist and immunologist. Best known for developing an oral, live-virus polio vaccine (1957), he also developed vaccines against dengue and sandfly fever. Full name **Albert Bruce Sabin**

Sa·bine[1] /sáy bīn, -beén/ *n.* **1.** PEOPLES **MEMBER OF ANCIENT ITALIAN PEOPLE** a member of an ancient people that occupied lands in central Italy, to the northeast of Rome. By the 3rd century B.C., after centuries of rivalry and fighting, the Romans had defeated them. **2.** LANG **SABINE LANGUAGE** the Italic language of the Sabines [14thC. From Latin *Sabinus.*] —**Sa·bine** *adj.*

Sa·bine[2] /sə beén/ river rising in Texas, forming the Texas-Louisiana border, flowing into the Gulf of Mexico. Length: 380 mi./612 km.

Sabin vac·cine /sáybin-/ *n.* an oral vaccine used to immunize against poliomyelitis and containing live poliovirus [Mid-20thC. Named for Albert SABIN who developed the vaccine.]

sab·ji /súbjee/ *n. S Asia* a raw or cooked vegetable [Early 19thC. From Urdu *sabzī*; "greenness," from *sabz* "green," from Persian *sebz.*]

sa·ble /sáyb'l/ *n.* (*plural* **-bles** *or* **-ble**) **1.** ZOOL **NORTHERN ASIAN MARTEN** a marten of northern Asia that has soft dark fur. Latin name: *Martes zibellina.* **2. FUR OF SABLE** the fur of the sable, which is highly valued **3. SABLE GARMENT** a garment made of sable fur **4.** ARTS **ARTIST'S BRUSH** an artist's brush made with the hairs of a sable **5.** COLORS **BLACK COLOR** a black color, the color of sable fur (*literary*) **6.** HERALDRY **COLOR BLACK IN HERALDRY** in heraldry, the color black ■ **sa·bles** *npl.* **MOURNING CLOTHES** black clothes worn in mourning (*archaic*) ■ *adj.* **1.** COLORS **OF A BLACK COLOR** of a black color, like that of sable fur (*literary*) **2. DARK** very dark or gloomy (*literary*) **3.** HERALDRY **OF HERALDIC BLACK COLOR** in heraldry, of a black color [15thC. Via Old French from medieval Latin *sabelum*, from a Baltic (Lithuanian *sàbalas*) or a Slavic (Russian *sobol*) source.]

sa·ble an·te·lope *n.* a large African antelope with long backward-curving horns. The male has a black coat. Latin name: *Hippotragus niger.*

sa·ble·fish /sáyb'l fish/ (*plural* **-fish** *or* **-fish·es**) *n.* a large dark-colored fish of the North American Pacific coast that is important for commercial fisheries. Latin name: *Anaplopoma fimbria.*

sa·bot /sa bṓ, sá bṓ/ *n.* **1. WOODEN SHOE** a wooden shoe, or a shoe with a wooden sole, formerly worn in Belgium, France, the Netherlands, and Germany **2. SUPPORT FOR PROJECTILE IN WEAPON** a sleeve placed around a projectile so that it can be fired from a weapon with a larger bore. The sabot drops away shortly after the projectile is fired. **3. SANDAL OR STRAP** a strap across the instep of a sandal, or a sandal with a strap across the instep [Early 17thC. Via French from Old French *çabot*, the source of English *sabotage*, a blend of *savate* "old shoe," of unknown origin, and *bot* (source of English *boot*).]

sab·o·tage /sábbə taa͟zh/ *n.* **1. DELIBERATE DESTRUCTION** the deliberate damaging or destroying of property or equipment, e.g., by resistance fighters, enemy agents, or disgruntled workers **2. ACTION TO HINDER** an action taken to undermine or destroy somebody's efforts or achievements ■ *vt.* **(-taged, -tag·ing, -tag·es) 1. DAMAGE SOMETHING** to damage, destroy, or disrupt something deliberately, especially in a war **2. HINDER SOMETHING** to undermine or destroy somebody's efforts or achievements [Mid-19thC. From French from *saboter* "to clatter in clogs," hence "to act clumsily, work badly, ruin," from *sabot* (see SABOT).]

sab·o·teur /sàbbə túr/ *n.* somebody who carries out an act of sabotage [Early 20thC. From French, from *sabot* (see SABOTAGE).]

sa·bra /saábrə/ *n.* a Jewish person who was born in Israel [Mid-20thC. Directly or via colloquial modern Hebrew *ṣābrāh* from Arabic *ṣabr* "prickly pear" (widespread in the Negev).]

sa·bre *n., vt.* U.K. = **saber**

sab·u·lous /-ləss/, **sab·u·lose** /sábbyə lṑss/ *adj.* having a gritty texture like sand [Mid-19thC. Formed from

Latin *sabulum* "sand."] —**sab·u·los·i·ty** /sàbbyə lóssətee/ *n.*

sac /sak/ *n.* a small bag or pouch, especially one that contains a fluid, formed by a membrane in an animal or plant ○ *amniotic sac* [Mid-18thC. Via French from Latin *saccus*. See SACK[1].]

Sac /sak, sawk/ (*plural* **Sacs** *or* **Sac**) *n.* PEOPLES, LANG = **Sauk**

SAC /sak/ *abbr.* Strategic Air Command

Sac·a·ga·we·a /sàkəjə wée ə/ (1784–1812?) Shoshone interpreter and guide. She was the guide and interpreter for the Lewis and Clark expedition (1804–05). Born **Boinaiv**

sac·a·ton /sákə tṓn/ *n.* a coarse perennial grass grown in the southwestern United States and Mexico and used for hay and pasture in dry alkaline areas. Latin name: *Sporobolus wrightii.* [Mid-19thC. From American Spanish *zacatón*, literally "large coarse grass" from *zacate* "coarse grass," from Nahuatl *zacatl* "straw."]

sac·cade /sa káad, sə-/ *n.* a rapid irregular movement of the eye as it focuses from one point to another, e.g., while reading [Early 18thC. From French, literally "twitch" (literally "pulling as if drawing a sack closed violently"), ultimately from *sac*, "sack" from Latin *saccus* (see SACK[1]).] —**sac·cad·ic** *adj.* —**sac·cad·i·cal·ly** *adv.*

sac·cate /sá kàyt/ *adj.* enclosed in or resembling a sac [Early 19thC. From modern Latin *saccatus*, a derivative of *saccus* (see SACK[1]).]

sacchar- *prefix.* = **saccharo-** (*used before vowels*)

sac·cha·rase /sákə ràyss, -ràyz/ *n.* = **invertase**

sac·cha·rate /sákə ràyt, -rət/ *n.* a chemical compound that is a salt or ester of saccharic acid [Early 19thC. Formed from SACCHARIC ACID + -ATE.]

sac·char·ic ac·id /sə kèrrik-, sa kèrrik-/ *n.* a white soluble solid formed by the oxidation of sugar or starch. Formula: $COOH(CHOH)_4COOH$.

sac·cha·ride /sákə rīd/ *n.* a water-soluble carbohydrate with a sweet taste and a chemical structure comprising a ring of four or five carbon atoms and one oxygen atom

sac·char·i·fy /sə kérrə fī, sa-/ (**-fied, -fy·ing, -fies**) *vt.* to convert a complex substance such as starch into simple sugars —**sac·char·i·fi·ca·tion** /sə kèrrəfə káysh'n, sa-/ *n.*

sac·cha·rim·e·ter /sàkə rímmitər/ *n.* an instrument, e.g., a polarimeter, used to measure the concentration of sugar in a solution —**sac·cha·rim·e·try** *n.*

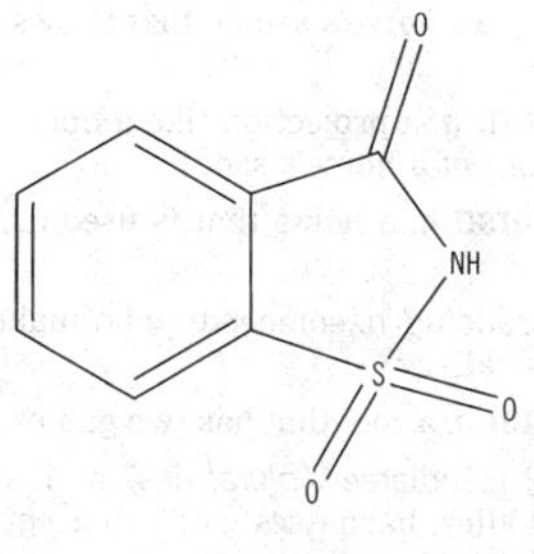

Saccharin

sac·cha·rin /sákərin/ *n.* a white crystalline compound that is several hundred times sweeter than sugar, used as a sugar substitute. Formula: $C_7H_5NO_3S$.

sac·cha·rine /sákərin, -reen/ *adj.* **1. OF OR LIKE SUGAR** relating to, resembling, or containing sugar **2. TOO SWEET** excessively sweet and ingratiating ○ *a saccharine smile* **3. TOO SENTIMENTAL** excessively sentimental and cloying —**sac·cha·rine·ly** *adv.* —**sac·cha·rin·i·ty** /sàkə rínnətee/ *n.*

saccharo- *prefix.* sugar ○ *saccharometer* [Via Latin and Greek from, ultimately, Sanskrit *śarkarā* "sugar"]

sac·cha·roid /sákə ròyd/, **sac·cha·roi·dal** /sàkə róyd'l/ *adj.* used to describe rocks and minerals that have a texture resembling loaf sugar

sac·cha·rom·e·ter /sàkə rómmitər/ *n.* a hydrometer used to determine the strength of a sugar solution by measuring its density

sac·cha·ro·my·cete /sákərō mī séet/ (*plural* **-cetes**) *n.* a single-celled yeast that has no mycelium, reproduces asexually, and ferments sugar. Genus: *Saccharomyces.* [Late 19thC. Coined from SACCHARO- + Greek *mukēs* "mushroom, fungus."]

sac·cha·rose /sákə rōss, -rōz/ *n.* = **sucrose** [Late 19thC. Formed from SACCHARO- + -OSE.]

Sac·co /sákō/, **Nicola** (1891–1927) Italian-born U.S. anarchist. He was executed (1927) for murder in what was considered an unjust and political trial. Full name **Ferdinando Nicola Sacco**

sac·cu·lar /sákyələr/ *adj.* resembling a sac or saccule [Mid-19thC. Formed from Latin *sacculus* (see SACCULE).]

sac·cu·late /sákyələt, -làyt/, **sac·cu·lat·ed** /-làytəd/ *adj.* containing or resembling a saccule or saccules [Late 19thC Formed from Latin *sacculus* (see SACCULE)] —**sac·cu·la·tion** /sàkyə láysh'n/ *n.*

sac·cule /sá kyool/, **sac·cu·lus** /sákyələss/ (*plural* **-li** /-lī, -lee/) *n.* **1. SMALL SAC** a small membranous bag or pouch in an animal or plant **2. SAC IN INNER EAR** the smaller of two sacs in the vestibule of the inner ear [Mid-19thC. From Latin *sacculus*, literally "little sack" from *saccus* (see SACK[1].]

sac·er·do·tal /sàssər dṓt'l, sàkər-/ *adj.* relating to or characteristic of a priest or the priesthood [14thC. Via Old French from Latin *sacerdotalis* "priestly," from the stem *sacerdot-* the stem of *sacerdos* "priest."] —**sac·er·do·tal·ly** *adv.*

sac·er·do·tal·ism /sàssər dṓt'l ìzzəm, sákər dṓt'l ìzzəm/ *n.* **1. PRINCIPLES OF PRIESTHOOD** the beliefs or methods of priests **2. BELIEF IN PRIEST'S POWER AS MEDIATOR** the belief that a priest is able to mediate between God and human beings —**sac·er·do·tal·ist** *n.*

SAC·EUR *abbr.* Supreme Allied Commander, Europe

sac fun·gus *n.* = **ascomycete**

sa·chem /sáychəm/ *n.* **1. NATIVE N AMERICAN CHIEF** a chief of a Native North American tribe or confederation, especially of Algonquian people **2.** POL **LEADER OF TAMMANY SOCIETY** a leader or official of the Tammany Society [Early 17thC. From an Algonquian word.] —**sa·chem·ic** /say chémmik/ *adj.*

sa·cher torte /saákər tàwrt, zaákhər tàwrtə/ *n.* a dark rich chocolate cake, sometimes with a filling of apricot jam, covered with glossy chocolate frosting [Early 20thC. From German, named for Franz *Sacher*, the pastry chef who invented the cake.]

sa·chet /sa sháy/ *n.* a small bag containing perfumed powder or potpourri, used to scent clothes in wardrobes or drawers [15thC. From Old French, literally "little sack," a diminutive of *sac* "bag" from Latin *saccus* (see SACK[1]).]

sack[1] /sak/ *n.* **1. LARGE BAG** a large bag, especially one that is made from coarse cloth or thick heavy-duty paper **2. AMOUNT IN SACK** the amount that a sack will hold **3. JOB DISMISSAL** dismissal from a job (*informal*) ○ *to get the sack* **4. BED** bed (*informal*) **5.** FOOTBALL **TACKLE OF PASSER** in football, a tackle of the quarterback behind the line of scrimmage during the quarterback's attempt to pass the ball **6.** BASEBALL **BASE IN BASEBALL** a base on a baseball diamond (*informal*) **7. WOMAN'S DRESS** a woman's loose-fitting dress that narrows below the knee **8. 18TH-CENTURY WOMAN'S GOWN** a gown worn by women in the 18th century that had a bodice with loose pleats at the back ■ *vt.* (**sacked, sack·ing, sacks**) **1. FIRE SOMEBODY** to dismiss somebody from a job (*informal*) **2. PUT SOMETHING IN A SACK** to put something into a sack, e.g., for storage or transport **3.** FOOTBALL **TACKLE PASSER BEHIND LINE OF SCRIMMAGE** in football, to tackle the quarterback behind the line of scrimmage during the quarterback's attempt to pass the ball [Pre-12thC. Via Latin *saccus* "sack, bag, wallet" influenced by Old French *sac*, also from Latin *saccus* from Greek *sakkos* "packing material," from a Semitic word.] —**sack·er** *n.* ◇ **hit the sack** to go to bed (*informal*)

sack out *vi.* to go to sleep or to bed (*informal*)

sack[2] /sak/ *vt.* (**sacked, sack·ing, sacks**) **DESTROY AND PLUNDER PLACE** to destroy a captured town or city and plunder its goods and valuables ■ *n.* **DESTRUCTION AND PLUNDERING** the destruction of a captured town or city and the plundering of its goods and valuables [Mid-16thC. Via Old French *(a) sac*, call to plunder, literally "(to the) bag," from, ultimately, Italian *saccomano* "plunderer," literally "bag-man," via German from, ultimately, Latin *saccus* "sack."]

sack[3] /sak/ *n.* dry white wine from Spain, Portugal, or the Canary Islands (*archaic*) [Mid-16thC. An alteration of earlier *wine seck*, a partial translation of French *(vin) sec* "dry (wine)," from Latin *siccus* "dry" (source of English *desiccate*).]

sack·but /sák bùt/ *n.* a wind instrument with a long slide like a trombone, played in medieval times [Early 16thC. From Old French *saqueb(o)ute* "hooked lance for pulling riders from their horses," of uncertain origin: perhaps from *saquer* "to pull" + assumed Vulgar Latin *bottare* "to push against."]

sack·cloth /sák klòth/ *n.* **1. CLOTH FOR SACKS** coarse cloth used to make sacks **2. MOURNING CLOTHES** clothes made from the type of coarse cloth usually used for sacks, which were worn in the past as a sign of mourning or penitence ◇ **sackcloth and ashes** a show of mourning or repentance

sack·ing /sáking/ *n.* coarse cloth used for making sacks, usually woven from hemp or jute

sack race *n.* a race in which each competitor stands in a sack and jumps toward the finish line while holding up the sack

E. O. Hoppe/Corbis

Vita Sackville-West

Sack·ville-West /sàk vil wést/, **Vita** (1892–1962) British writer. She is remembered for poems such as "The Land" (1926) and novels including *The Edwardians* (1930). Virginia Woolf celebrated their friendship in her novel *Orlando* (1928). Full name **Victoria Mary Sackville-West**

Sa·co /sáykō/ city in southwestern Maine, on the northern shore of the Saco River, opposite Biddeford. Population: 15,681 (1996).

sa·cra plural of **sacrum**

sa·cral[1] /sákrəl, sáyk-/ *adj.* relating to or near the sacrum

sa·cral[2] /sákrəl, sáyk-/ *adj.* relating to or used in sacred rites [Late 19thC. From Latin *sacr-*, the stem of *sacer* "sacred" (source of English *sacred*).]

sac·ra·ment /sákrəmənt/ *n.* **1. RELIGIOUS RITE OR CEREMONY** in Christianity, a rite that is considered to have been established by Jesus Christ to bring grace to those participating in or receiving it. In the Protestant Church, the sacraments are baptism and Communion. The Roman Catholic and Eastern Churches also include penance, confirmation, holy orders, matrimony, and the anointing of the sick. **2. sac·ra·ment, Sac·ra·ment CONSECRATED ELEMENTS OF COMMUNION** the bread and wine consecrated at Communion **3. SOMETHING SACRED** something considered to be sacred or have a special significance [12thC. Via Old French from Late Latin *sacramentum* "rite, mystery, (gospel) revelation, sacrament" from Latin, "soldier's oath of loyalty, solemn obligation" (see SACRED).]

sac·ra·men·tal /sàkrə mént'l/ *adj.* **1. USED IN SACRAMENT** relating to or used in a sacrament **2. SACRED** bound by a sacrament or in a way considered inviolable ■ *n.* **RITUAL ACTION OR SIGN** in the Roman Catholic Church, an object, act, or ritual such as the sign of the cross that is used to show religious devotion —**sac·ra·men·tal·i·ty** /sàkrəmən tállətee, -men-/ *n.* —**sac·ra·men·tal·ly** /sàkrə mént'lee/ *adv.*

sac·ra·men·tal·ism /sàkrə mént'l ìzzəm/ *n.* in Christianity, the belief in the necessity of the sacraments to attain salvation and God's grace —**sac·ra·men·tal·ist** *n.*

Sac·ra·men·tar·i·an /sàkrəmən táiree ən, sàkrə men-/ *n.* **1. BELIEVER IN THE SYMBOLIC NATURE OF COMMUNION** somebody who believes that the consecrated bread and wine of the Communion are only symbolic of the body and blood of Jesus Christ **2. SACRAMENTALIST** somebody who believes in sacramentalism ■ *adj.* **OF SACRAMENTARIANS** relating to or characteristic of Sacramentarians —**Sac·ra·men·tar·i·an·ism** *n.*

Sac·ra·men·to /sàkrè méntō/ **1.** river in California, rising near Mount Shasta and flowing south into San Francisco Bay. Length: 382 mi./615 km. **2.** capital city of California, at the confluence of the Sacramento and American rivers. Population: 369,365 (1990).

Sac·ra·men·to Moun·tains mountain range in southern New Mexico, between the Pecos River and the Rio Grande

sa·crar·i·um /sə kráiree əm/ (*plural* **-a** /-ə/) *n.* **1. SANCTUARY OR SACRISTY** a Christian church's sanctuary or sacristy **2.** = **piscina** *n.* 1 [Early 18thC. From Latin, literally "place for keeping sacred things, shrine," from *sacer* "holy, sacred."]

sa·cred /sáykrid/ *adj.* **1. DEVOTED TO DEITY** dedicated to a deity or religious purpose **2. OF RELIGION** relating to or used in religious worship **3. WORTHY OF WORSHIP** worthy of or regarded with religious veneration, worship, and respect **4. DEDICATED TO SOMEBODY** dedicated to or in honor of somebody **5. INVIOLABLE** not to be challenged or disrespected [14thC. Originally the past participle of archaic *sacre* "to consecrate," via Old French *sacrer* from Latin *sacrare*, from *sacr-*, the stem of *sacer* "holy, sacred."] —**sa·cred·ly** *adv.* —**sa·cred·ness** *n.*

WORD KEY: ORIGIN

The Latin word *sacer*, from which ***sacred*** is derived, is also the source of English *consecrate*, *execrate*, *sacrament*, *sacrifice*, *sacrilege*, *sacristan*, and *sexton*.

sa·cred ba·boon *n.* = **hamadryas baboon** [Late 19thC. From its being held sacred by the ancient Egyptians.]

sa·cred cow *n.* somebody or something exempt from any criticism by, or interference from, others [Early 20thC. From the sacrosanctity of cattle for Hindus.]

Sa·cred Heart *n.* **1. HEART OF JESUS CHRIST** in the Roman Catholic Church, the heart of Jesus Christ, seen as a symbol of his love **2. IMAGE OF SACRED HEART** an image representing the Sacred Heart, often shown as bleeding

sa·cred i·bis *n.* a large wading bird of sub-Saharan Africa and Arabia with bold black-and-white plumage, a large downward-curving beak, and decorative plumes on its back. Latin name: *Threskiornis aethiopica*. [*Sacred* from its being held sacred by the ancient Egyptians]

sa·cred mush·room *n.* a hallucinogenic American mushroom eaten in the past in Native American rituals. Genus: *Psilocybe*.

sac·ri·fice /sákrə fìss/ *n.* **1. GIVING UP OF SOMETHING VALUED** a giving up of something valuable or important for somebody or something else considered to be of more value or importance **2. SOMETHING VALUED AND GIVEN UP** something valuable or important given up as a sacrifice **3. OFFERING TO GOD** an offering to honor or appease a god, especially of a ritually slaughtered animal or person **4. SOMETHING OR SOMEBODY OFFERED TO A GOD** something or somebody offered to honor or appease a god **5. SYMBOLIC OFFERING** a symbolic offering made to a god **6. LOSS IN GIVING UP SOMETHING VALUED** a loss incurred by giving away or selling something below its value **7.** CHESS **STRATEGIC GIVING UP OF CHESS PIECE** in chess, an act or instance of allowing or forcing an opponent to take one of your pieces or pawns so that you can gain an advantage position ■ *v.* (**-ficed, -fic·ing, -fic·es**) **1.** *vt.* **GIVE UP SOMEBODY OR SOMETHING VALUED** to give up somebody or something important or valued in exchange for somebody or something else that is considered more important or valuable **2.** *vt.* **ABANDON SOMEBODY OR SOMETHING FOR ADVANTAGE** to allow somebody or something to be hurt, killed, or destroyed for your own advantage **3.** *vti.* **MAKE OFFERING TO GOD** to make an offering of a ritually slaughtered animal or person to a god **4.** *vt.* **STRATEGICALLY GIVE UP CHESS PIECE** in chess, to allow or force one of your pieces or pawns to be taken by an opponent so that you can gain an advantage in position **5.** *vi.* BASEBALL **HIT A SACRIFICE BUNT** in baseball, to bunt the ball, expecting to be put out, in order to advance a base runner [13thC. Via Old French from Latin *sacrificium*, literally "making sacred," from *sacr-*, stem of *sacer* "sacred."] —**sac·ri·fice·a·ble** *adj.* —**sac·ri·fic·er** *n.*

sac·ri·fice bunt, **sac·ri·fice hit** *n.* in baseball, an act of bunting the ball, expecting to be put out, in order to advance a base runner

sac·ri·fice fly *n.* in baseball, a fly ball that is caught in the outfield and on which a runner scores

sac·ri·fice hit *n.* = **sacrifice bunt**

sac·ri·fi·cial /sàkrə físh'l/ *adj.* relating to, used in, or offered as a sacrifice —**sac·ri·fi·cial·ly** *adv.*

sac·ri·lege /sákrəlij/ *n.* **1. TREATING HOLY THING WITHOUT RESPECT** the violation, desecration, or theft of something considered holy or sacred **2. DISRESPECT** the disrespectful or irreverent treatment of something others consider worthy of respect or reverence [14thC. Via Old French from Latin *sacrilegium* "temple robbery," from *sacrilegus*, literally "collector of sacred things," from *sacr-* the stem of *sacer* "sacred."] —**sac·ri·le·gist** /sàkrə léejist/ *n.*

sac·ri·le·gious /sàkrə líjjəss/ *adj.* relating to, involving, or committing sacrilege —**sac·ri·le·gious·ly** *adv.* —**sac·ri·le·gious·ness** *n.*

sac·ris·tan /sákristən/, **sac·rist** /sáykrist, sá-/ *n.* **1. SOMEBODY RESPONSIBLE FOR CHRISTIAN CHURCH CONTENTS** somebody who looks after the contents of a Christian church, especially those kept in the sacristy **2. SEXTON** a sexton (*dated*) [14thC. From medieval Latin *sacristanus*, from *sacrista* "keeper of sacred things," from *sacer* "sacred."]

sac·ris·ty /sákristee/ (*plural* **-ties**) *n.* a room in a Christian church in which sacred objects such as vessels and vestments are kept [15thC. Via French from medieval Latin *sacristia*, from *sacrista*. See SACRISTAN.]

sac·ro·il·i·ac /sàkrō íllee àk/ *adj.* **RELATING TO SACRUM AND ILIUM** relating to the sacrum and the upper portion of the hip bone (**ilium**), or to the joint between the sacrum and ilium ■ *n.* **JOINT WHERE SACRUM AND ILIUM MEET** the joint in the back where the sacrum and the ilium meet [Mid-19thC. Coined from *sacrum* + ILIUM.]

sac·ro·sanct /sákrō sàngkt/ *adj.* **1. SACRED** very holy and sacred **2. INVIOLABLE** not to be criticized or tampered with [Early 17thC. From Latin *sacrosanctus*, from *sacro sanctus* "made holy through religious rites," from *sacer* "sacred."] —**sac·ro·sanc·ti·ty** /sàkrō sángktətee/ *n.* —**sac·ro·sanct·ness** /sákrō sangktnəss/ *n.*

sa·crum /sáykrəm, sák-/ (*plural* **-crums** *or* **-cra** /-krə/) *n.* a triangular bone at the base of the spine that joins to a hip bone on either side and forms part of the pelvis. In human beings it consists of five fused vertebrae. [Mid-18thC. From Latin *(os) sacrum*, a translation of Greek *hieron (osteon)* "sacred (bone)" (from the belief that the soul resided there).]

sad /sad/ (**sad·der, sad·dest**) *adj.* **1. UNHAPPY** feeling or showing unhappiness, grief, or sorrow ○ *a sad expression* **2. CAUSING UNHAPPINESS** causing or containing unhappiness ○ *sad news* **3. REGRETTABLE** unfortunate, or to be deplored ○ *The sad fact is that there are not enough funds available to support this project.* **4. DULL IN COLOR** dull or dark in color [Old English *sæd* "weary, heavy, sated." Ultimately from an Indo-European word that is also the ancestor of English *satisfy*. The meaning "unhappy" developed in the 14thC.] —**sad·ly** *adv.* —**sad·ness** *n.*

SAD *abbr.* seasonal affective disorder

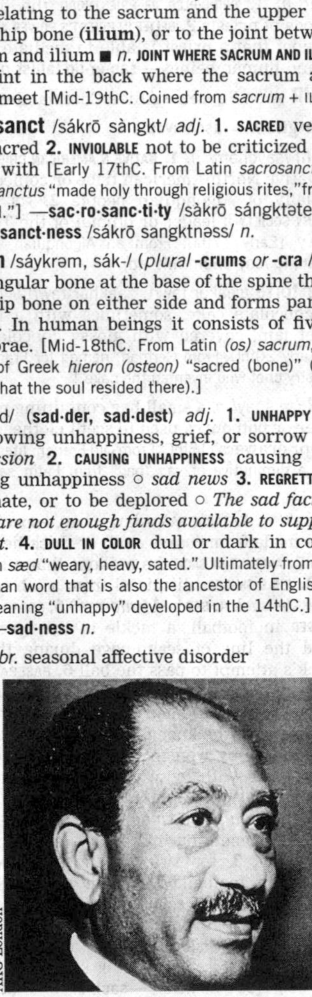

Anwar al-Sadat

Sa·dat /sə dát, sə daát/, **Anwar al-** (1918–81) Egyptian statesman. As president of Egypt (1970–81), he was the first Arab leader to recognize Israel, and he shared the Nobel Peace Prize with Israeli prime minister Menachem Begin in 1978 for the negotiations that culminated in the signing of their historic peace treaty in 1979. He was assassinated by members of his own army.

sad·den /sádd'n/ (**-dened, -den·ing, -dens**) *vti.* to become sad or to cause somebody to become sad (*often passive*)

sad·dhu *n.* = **sadhu**

sad·dle /sádd'l/ *n.* **1. SEAT FOR RIDING AN ANIMAL** a seat, usually made of leather, used by a rider on the back of an animal such as a horse or donkey **2. SEAT ON A BICYCLE OR MOTORCYCLE** a padded seat for a rider on a vehicle such as a bicycle, motorcycle, or tractor **3. PART OF AN ANIMAL'S BACK** the part of an animal where a saddle is placed **4. PART OF A HARNESS** a pad that forms part of a harness and fits across the back of an animal carrying or pulling something **5. SOMETHING RESEMBLING A SADDLE** something that looks like or is used like a saddle **6.** GEOG **LOW POINT OF A RIDGE** a low point of a ridge connecting two peaks **7. CUT OF MEAT** a cut of meat that includes part of the backbone and both loins **8. BACK PART OF A CHICKEN** the back part of a chicken or other fowl nearest its tail ■ *v.* (**-dled, -dling, -dles**) **1.** *vt.* **STRAP A SADDLE ONTO AN ANIMAL** to put a saddle onto a horse or other animal **2.** *vi.* **MOUNT AN ANIMAL** to mount a horse, or other animal, that has a saddle on it [Old English *sadol*. Ultimately from an Indo-European word meaning "to sit," which is also the ancestor of English *sit*.] —**sad·dle·less** *adj.* ◇ **in the saddle** in control of something

saddle up *vti.* to put a saddle on a horse to prepare for riding it

saddle with *vt.* to give somebody an unwelcome or unpleasant task or responsibility

sad·dle·back /sádd'l bàk/ *n.* **1. ANIMAL WITH A SADDLE-SHAPED MARKING** an animal such as a bird, fish, or other vertebrate that has a saddle-shaped marking on its back **2.** ARCHIT = **saddle roof 3.** GEOG = **saddle** *n.* 6

sad·dle-backed /sádd'l bàkt/ *adj.* **1. HAVING BACK LIKE A SADDLE** with its back curved into a shape like a saddle **2. HAVING SADDLEBACK** with a saddle-shaped marking on its back

sad·dle·bag /sádd'l bàg/ *n.* a bag, sometimes one of a pair, carried near or attached to an animal's saddle or attached to a frame over a wheel of a bicycle or motorcycle

sad·dle-billed stork /sádd'l bild-/, **sad·dle·bill** /sádd'l bil/ (*plural* **-bills** *or* **-bill**) *n.* a stork of sub-Saharan Africa that has black-and-white plumage, long black legs with red joints, and a red bill with a black band. Latin name: *Ephippiorhynchus senegalensis*.

sad·dle blan·ket *n.* a blanket or other pad placed under a saddle to prevent it from chafing the animal's back

sad·dle·bow /sádd'l bō/ *n.* the high arch or raised part (**pommel**) at the front of a horse's saddle [Old English]

sad·dle·cloth /sádd'l klòth/ *n.* a cloth placed under or over a racehorse's saddle that shows the horse's number

sad·dle horn *n.* a projection like a horn on the arch at the front of a horse's saddle

sad·dle horse *n.* a horse that is used or trained for riding

sad·dler /sáddlər/ *n.* somebody who makes, sells, or repairs saddlery

sad·dle roof *n.* a roof that has two gables and a ridge

sad·dler·y /sáddləree/ (*plural* **-ies**) *n.* **1. EQUIPMENT FOR HORSES** saddles, harnesses, and other equipment for horses **2. JOB OF SADDLER** the work done by a saddler **3. SADDLER'S SHOP** a shop that sells equipment for horses **4. PLACE FOR STORING SADDLES** a room in or near a stable used for making, repairing, or storing equipment for horses

sad·dle shoe *n.* a white or light-colored laced shoe with a band of contrasting leather across the instep

sad·dle soap *n.* a mild soap containing neat's-foot oil, used for cleaning, softening, and preserving leather

sad·dle sore *n.* **1. SORE ON A RIDER** a sore on the buttocks, groin, or inner thighs of a rider, caused by the rubbing of the saddle **2. SORE ON A HORSE** a sore on a horse's body, caused by the rubbing of an ill-fitting saddle

sad·dle-sore *adj.* **1. SORE FROM RIDING** sore from having ridden something with a saddle such as a horse or bicycle **2. SORE FROM HAVING WORN A SADDLE** sore, or affected by sores, from the wearing of a saddle

sad·dle stitch *n.* **1. RUNNING STITCH** a long running stitch, usually made with a contrasting color for ornamentation **2. BINDING BY STITCHING ON A FOLD** in bookbinding, a method of binding the pages of a small book or magazine together by folding it in half and stitching along the line of the fold

sad·dle-stitch (**sad·dle-stitched, sad·dle-stitch·ing, sad·dle-stitch·es**) *vti.* to sew something using a saddle stitch

sad·dle·tree /sádd'l trée/ *n.* the frame of a saddle

Sad·du·cee /sájjəssee, sáddyəssee/ *n.* a member of an ancient Jewish group of priests and aristocrats who accepted the literal interpretation of the Torah but rejected Oral Law and belief in the afterlife. Sadducees favored accommodation with the Roman occupiers of Palestine. [Pre-12thC. Via late Latin from late Greek *Saddoukaios*, from post-Biblical Hebrew *Ṣĕdūqī* "follower of Zadok," from *Ṣādōq* "Zadok" (the high priest who supposedly founded the group), literally "righteous."] —**Sad·du·ce·an** /sàjjə sée ən, sàddyə-/ *adj.* —**Sad·du·cee·ism** /sájjəssee ìzzəm, sáddyə-/ *n.*

Sade /saad, sad/, **Marquis de** (1740–1814) French philosopher and novelist. His own cruel sexual practices, for which he was imprisoned, were reflected in such novels as *Juliette* (1797). Full name **Donatien Alphonse François, Comte de Sade**

sa·dhe /saádee, saádə/, **sade, tsa·de** /tsaádee, tsaádə/ *n.* the 18th letter of the Hebrew alphabet, represented in the English alphabet as "s" or "ts." See table at **alphabet** [Late 19thC. From Hebrew *ṣādhē*.]

sa·dhu /saá dōō/, **sad·hu** *n.* a Hindu holy man who lives by begging [Mid-19thC. From Sanskrit *sādhu* "good, holy," literally "straight."]

Sa·di /saa dée/, **Saa·di, Mosharref al-Din ebn Mosleh al-Din** (1213?–92) Persian poet. His contributions to classical Persian literature include the *The Rose Garden* (1258). Pseudonym of **Mosharref al-Din ebn Mosleh**

sad·i·ron /sád ìrn/ *n.* a heavy iron that curves to a point at both ends, has a removable handle, is heated on an external source, and is used for pressing clothes and linens [Mid-18thC. From SAD in the obsolete sense "solid, heavy" + IRON.]

sa·dism /sáy dìzzəm/; *formerly also* /sá dìzzəm/ *n.* **1.** PSYCHOL **HURTING OTHERS FOR SEXUAL PLEASURE** the gaining of sexual gratification by causing physical or mental pain to other people, or the acts that produce such gratification **2. BEING CRUEL FOR FUN** the gaining of pleasure from causing physical or mental pain to people or animals **3. CRUELTY** great physical or mental cruelty [Late 19thC. From French *sadisme*, named for the Marquis de SADE.] —**sa·dist** *n.* —**sa·dis·tic** /sə dístik/ *adj.* —**sa·dis·ti·cal·ly** /sə dístikəlee/ *adv.*

sa·do·mas·o·chism /sàydō mássə kìzzəm, sáddō-/ *n.* PSYCHOL **1. SEXUAL PRACTICES INVOLVING SADISM AND MASOCHISM** the gaining of sexual gratification by alternately or simultaneously enduring pain and causing pain to somebody else, or the acts that produce such gratification **2. COMBINATION OF SADISTIC AND MASOCHISTIC TENDENCIES** a combination of sadistic and masochistic sexual tendencies within an individual, who may derive sexual pleasure both from inflicting and from enduring pain and cruelty [Mid-20thC. From SADISM + MASOCHISM.] —**sa·do·mas·o·chist** *n.* —**sa·do·mas·o·chis·tic** /sàydō mássə kístik, sàydō mázzə kístik/; *formerly also* /sàddō mássə kístik, sàddō mázzə kístik/ *adj.*

sad sack *n.* somebody, especially a soldier, who means well but is hopelessly inept (*informal*) [Mid-20thC. From the name of a melancholy cartoon GI created by the U.S. cartoonist George Baker during World War II.]

SAE *abbr.* Society of Automotive Engineers

s.a.e., SAE *abbr.* stamped addressed envelope

Sa·far /sə faár/, **Sa·phar** *n.* CALENDAR in the Islamic calendar, the second month of the year, made up of 29 days [Late 18thC. From Arabic *safar*.]

sa·fa·ri /sə faáree/ *n.* **1. CROSS-COUNTRY EXPEDITION** a journey across a stretch of land, especially in East Africa, for the purpose of hunting or observing wild animals ○ *go on safari* **2. PEOPLE ON EXPEDITION** a group of people on a safari, together with the animals or vehicles that transport them [Late 19thC. Via Swahili from Arabic *safar* "journey."]

sa·fa·ri jack·et *n.* a casual jacket, usually made of tough light-colored fabric, with four large pockets and a belt

sa·fa·ri park *n.* a large enclosed area of land where wild animals wander relatively freely and people pay to drive around and observe them

sa·fa·ri suit *n.* a short-sleeved safari jacket in a light-colored fabric, with matching pants, shorts, or skirt

Sa·fa·vid dy·nas·ty /sə faá wìd-/ *n.* a Persian dynasty, originally part of a Turkic nomadic group, that ruled from 1500 to 1722 and established the Shiite branch of Islam as the state religion [Early 20thC. Formed from Arabic *ṣafaw i*, from *Ṣ i* al-Din Isḥ aq, the name of the dynasty's founder.]

safe /sayf/ *adj.* **1. NOT DANGEROUS** unlikely to cause or result in harm, injury, or damage ○ *Is it safe to open the window?* **2. NOT IN DANGER** in a position or situation that offers protection, so that harm, damage, loss, or unwanted tampering is unlikely ○ *You'll be safe with me.* ○ *It's hidden in a safe place.* **3. UNHARMED OR UNDAMAGED** in an unharmed, uninjured, or undamaged condition ○ *They're safe, but the car's beyond repair* **4. SURE TO BE SUCCESSFUL** certain to be successful or profitable, and not at risk of failure or loss ○ *a safe investment* **5. UNLIKELY TO CAUSE TROUBLE** unlikely to cause trouble or controversy ○ *Is it safe to talk about politics with them?* **6. PROBABLY CORRECT** unlikely to be wrong ○ *It's safe to assume that the weather will be good.* **7. CAUTIOUS AND CONSERVATIVE** cautious with regard to risks or unforeseen problems, conservative with regard to estimates, or unadventurous with regard to choices and decisions ○ *The safe option is just to put the money in the bank.* **8. DEPENDABLE** able to be trusted or depended on ○ *Don't worry, your child's in safe hands.* **9.** BASEBALL **HAVING REACHED BASE SUCCESSFULLY** having reached a base or home plate without being put out ■ *n.* **1. CONTAINER FOR VALUABLES** a strong metal container, often with a complex locking system, for the storage of money and other valuables **2. STORAGE CONTAINER** a container for storage or protection, especially a ventilated box or small cupboard for keeping food cool or fresh (*dated*) **3. CONDOM** a condom (*slang*) [13thC. Via Old French *sauf* from Latin *salvus*.] —**safe·ly** *adv.* —**safe·ness** *n.* ◇ **be on the safe side** to take as few risks, or eliminate as many risks, as possible

safe-con·duct *n.* **1. GUARANTEE OF TRAVELER'S SAFETY** official protection from harm or immunity from arrest for somebody passing through a dangerous area, such as enemy territory in wartime **2. SOMETHING GUARANTEEING TRAVELER'S SAFETY** a document or escort providing safe-conduct

safe·crack·er /sáyf kràkər/ *n.* somebody who breaks into a safe, with or without the use of force, so that the contents can be stolen —**safe·crack·ing** *n.*

safe-de·pos·it *n.* the placement of money and other valuables in storage without risk of loss or damage by fire or theft e.g., in a bank vault

safe-de·pos·it box *n.* a strong metal container for valuables, e.g., jewelry or documents, usually kept in a bank vault

safe·guard /sáyf gaàrd/ *n.* **1. PROTECTIVE MEASURE** something intended to prevent undesirable consequences from happening, e.g., a safety device or measure, or a proviso in a legal document **2. SAFE-CONDUCT DOCUMENT** a document providing safe-conduct ■ *vt.* (**-guard·ed, -guard·ing, -guards**) **KEEP SOMETHING SAFE** to prevent something or somebody from being harmed, damaged, or lost [14thC. From Anglo-Norman *salve garde* and French *sauve garde*, from *sauf* "safe" (see SAFE) + *garde* (see GUARD).]

WORD KEY: SYNONYMS

safeguard, protect, defend, guard, shield

CORE MEANING: to keep safe from actual or potential injury, danger, or attack

safeguard a fairly formal word, often used to talk about preventative or precautionary planning, usually against potential harm or damage; **protect** a general word, used to talk about working to prevent harm, or something that is intended to prevent harm; **defend** to take measures to ward off defeat or an actual or threatened attack; **guard** to work to prevent harm, damage, or attack by being vigilant and taking defensive measures; **shield** to prevent harm, damage, or attack by doing something that forms a barrier between the person or thing being defended and the source of the threat.

safe house *n.* a house or other place of refuge where people in danger can hide or meet in secret

safe·keep·ing /sàyf kéeping, sáyf kéeping/ *n.* **1. KEEPING SOMETHING SAFE** protection from harm, damage, loss, or theft ○ *I put the documents in my desk for safe-keeping.* **2.** BANKING **NOT RETURNING CHECKS** a system whereby banks keep checks that people write, rather than returning them to the account holder with the monthly statement

safe·light /sáyf lìt/ *n.* a type of light used in darkrooms that filters out the rays that are harmful to sensitive film and photographic paper

safe sex *n.* sexual activity in which precautions are taken to avoid spreading sexually transmitted diseases, e.g., by using a condom

safe·ty /sáyftee/ (*plural* **-ties**) *n.* **1. FREEDOM FROM DANGER** protection from or nonexposure to the risk of harm or injury ○ *a safety device* ○ *The captain is responsible for the safety of the crew.* **2. LACK OF DANGER** inability to cause or result in harm, injury, or damage ○ *People are beginning to question the safety of the medication.* **3. SAFE PLACE** a place or situation where harm, damage, or loss is unlikely ○ *She led the passengers to safety.* **4. BEING UNHARMED OR UNDAMAGED** the fact of being or remaining unharmed, uninjured, or undamaged ○ *There are fears for their safety.* **5. DEVICE PREVENTING UNINTENTIONAL OPERATION** a device designed to prevent a mechanism from being operated unintentionally, e.g., one that keeps a gun from being fired by accident or an elevator from falling **6.** FOOTBALL **DEFENSIVE BACK** in football, a player defending the back of the field **7.** FOOTBALL **PLAY AWARDING POINTS FOR DEFENSIVE TEAM** in football, a play in which a member of the offensive team downs the ball intentionally or unintentionally in his own end zone, resulting in the defensive team being awarded two points **8. CONDOM** a condom (*slang*) [14thC. Via French *sauveté* from medieval Latin *salvitas*, from Latin *salvus* (see SAFE).]

safe·ty belt *n.* **1.** = **seat belt 2. STRAP TO PREVENT SOMEBODY FROM FALLING** a strong strap attached to a fixed point, worn by a person in danger of falling, such as somebody working in a high place

safe·ty cur·tain *n.* a fireproof curtain that can be lowered at the front of the stage in a theater to isolate the auditorium from the stage in the event of fire

safe·ty-de·pos·it *n.* = **safe-deposit**

safe·ty-de·pos·it box *n.* = **safe-deposit box**

safe·ty film *n.* nonflammable movie film made with a cellulose acetate or polyester base. Formerly, film was made with cellulose nitrate and was prone to catch fire upon aging.

safe·ty glass *n.* **1. SHATTERPROOF GLASS** a type of strong laminated glass designed not to shatter, made with a layer of clear plastic sandwiched between two glass sheets **2. SPLINTERPROOF GLASS** a type of glass that, if it breaks, forms rounded fragments rather than sharp splinters

safe·ty is·land *n.* an area within a road that is marked off and from which vehicular traffic is prohibited, used especially for the safety of pedestrians

safe·ty lamp *n.* a miner's lamp in which the flame is enclosed in fine wire gauze to prevent the combustion of flammable gases

safe·ty·man /sáyfti màn/ (*plural* **-men** /-mèn/) *n.* = **safety**

safe·ty match *n.* a match that will only produce a flame if it is struck against a specially prepared surface

safe·ty net *n.* **1. NET TO CATCH FALLING PERSON** a net installed below a high place, such as a circus tightrope or trapeze from which somebody might fall or jump **2. PROTECTION FOR PEOPLE IN DIFFICULTY** something intended to help people in the event of hardship or misfortune, especially something providing financial security, such as insurance or welfare payments

safe·ty pin *n.* **1. PIN WITH COVERED POINT** a loop-shaped pin that fastens into itself with its point under a protective cover to prevent accidental opening or injury **2.** ARMS **PIN PREVENTING DETONATION** a pin, e.g., in a grenade, that when properly seated prevents accidental or premature detonation

safe·ty ra·zor *n.* a razor in which the blade is partially covered to minimize the risk of accidental injury

safe·ty valve *n.* **1.** ENG **FLUID RELEASE VALVE** a valve that will automatically open and release a fluid when the pressure in a chamber, e.g., a steam engine or a boiler, approaches a dangerous level **2.** PSYCHOL **MEANS OF RELEASING EMOTION OR ENERGY** something that enables people to get rid of strong feelings such as anger, grief, anxiety, or excitement without harming themselves or others

saf·fi·an /sáffee ən/ *n.* hides of sheep or goats tanned with sumac and often dyed in bright colors [Late 16thC. Via Russian *saf'yan* from, ultimately, Persian *saktiyān*.]

saf·flow·er /sá flòwr/ *n.* **1.** PLANTS **PLANT YIELDING OIL AND DYE** an annual composite plant with orange or red flowers, native to the Indian subcontinent, from which dye and an oil used in cooking, paints, and medicine are obtained. Latin name: *Carthamus tinctorius*. **2. DRIED FLOWERS** the dried flowers of the safflower plant, used to make a red dye **3. RED DYE** a red dye made from the dried flowers of the safflower plant, used to color fabric, food, and cosmetics [15thC. Via Dutch or German from Old French *saffleur*, via obsolete Italian *asfiore* from, ultimately, Arabic *asfar* "yellow plant"; influenced by SAFFRON and FLOWER.]

saf·fron /sáffrən/ *n.* (*plural* **-frons** *or* **-fron**) **1. SPICE-PRODUCING CROCUS** a crocus introduced into Europe from Asia Minor, with showy purple or white flowers bearing stigmas that are used as spice. Latin name: *Crocus sativus*. **2. COOKING SPICE** the deep orange-colored stigmas of the saffron plant, or an orange or yellow powder obtained from these, used to color and flavor food **3.** COLORS **BRIGHT ORANGE-YELLOW COLOR** a bright orange-yellow color ■ *adj.* COLORS **ORANGE-YELLOW** of a bright orange-yellow color [Pre-12thC. Via Old French *safran* and medieval Latin *safranum* from, ultimately, Arabic *za'farān*.]

Sa·fi /saa fée/ capital city of Safi Province and a port on the Atlantic Ocean, in western Morocco. Population: 278,000 (1993).

S. Afr. *abbr.* South Africa

saf·ra·nine /sáffrə neen, -nin/, **saf·ra·nin** /sáffrənin/ *n.* red organic dye derived from phenazine, used to color textiles and as a biological stain [Mid-19thC. From French, formed from *safran* (see SAFFRON).]

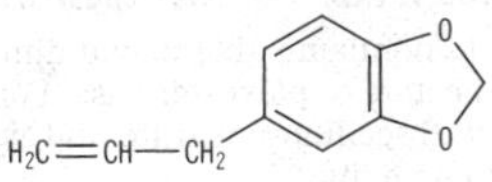

Safrole

saf·role /sá frōl/ *n.* a colorless or yellow poisonous oily liquid found in sassafras oil and used in making perfumes and soap. Formula: $C_{10}H_{10}O_2$. [Mid-19thC. Coined from SASSAFRAS + -OLE.]

sag /sag/ *v.* (**sagged, sag·ging, sags**) **1.** *vti.* **BEND UNDER WEIGHT** to bend downward in the middle, or to hang or droop instead of remaining firm or level, or to make something bend in this way, usually through having to support excessive weight ○ *The skirt's hem sags in the back.* **2.** *vi.* **BECOME WEAKER OR LOSE INTENSITY** to become weaker or lose intensity or enthusiasm **3.** *vi.* **FALL IN VALUE** to decrease in value **4.** *vi.* NAUT **DRIFT LEEWARD** to drift to leeward ■ *n.* **1. PLACE WHERE SOMETHING SAGS** a bend, depression, or slackness in something where it has sagged **2. DECLINE IN STRENGTH** a decline in strength, intensity, or value ○ *a sag in the stock market* **3.** NAUT **LEEWARD DRIFT** a tendency to drift to leeward [14thC. Origin uncertain: possibly from a Scandinavian source or from Middle Low German *sacken* "to sink."] —**sag·gy** *adj.*

sa·ga /saágə/ *n.* **1. NORSE LITERARY GENRE** an epic tale in Old Norse literature, usually in prose, recounting events in the lives of historical and mythological figures from medieval Iceland and Norway **2. LONG NOVEL OR SERIES OF NOVELS** a long story or novel, or a series of stories or novels, often following the lives of a family or community over several generations **3. SERIES OF EVENTS** a complicated series of events or personal experiences stretching over a considerable period of time, or a detailed account of such a series of events or experiences (*informal*) ○ *Have you heard the saga of our coast-to-coast relocation?* [Early 18thC. From Old Icelandic *saga* "saga, story" (see SAW).]

WORD KEY: CULTURAL NOTE

The Forsyte Saga, a series of novels by English writer John Galsworthy (1906–22). Set in early 20th-century England, it charts the decline of Victorian values in upper-middle-class society through the story of three generations of the Forsyte family. It was made into a popular television series in 1967.

sa·ga·cious /sə gáyshəss/ *adj.* having or based on a profound knowledge and understanding of the world combined with intelligence and good judgment (*formal*) [Early 17thC. Formed from Latin *sagac-*, the stem of *sagax* "of quick perception." Ultimately from an Indo-European word meaning "to seek," which is also the ancestor of English *seek*.] —**sa·ga·cious·ly** *adv.* —**sa·ga·cious·ness** *n.*

sa·gac·i·ty /sə gássətee/ *n.* profound knowledge and understanding, coupled with foresight and good judgment [15thC. Via Old French *sagacité* from Latin *sagacitas*, from the stem *sagac-* (see SAGACIOUS).]

sag·a·more /sággə màwr/ *n.* among the Native North American Algonquian people, a subordinate chief [Early 17thC. From Algonquian (Abnaki) *sangman* literally "he overcomes" or "chief."]

Françoise Sagan

Sa·gan /saa gaán/, **Françoise** (*b.* 1935) French writer. Among her best known novels are *Bonjour Tristesse* (1954) and *A Certain Smile* (1956). Pseudonym of **Françoise Quoirez**

sa·ga nov·el *n.* = **roman-fleuve**

sage[1] /sayj/ *n.* **WISE PERSON** somebody who is regarded as knowledgeable, wise, and experienced, especially a man of advanced years revered for his wisdom and good judgment (*literary*) ■ *adj.* **WISE** having or showing great wisdom, especially that gained from long experience of life (*literary*) [14thC. Via Old French from, ultimately, Latin *sapere* "to be wise, have taste" (source of English *savor* and *savvy*).] —**sage·ly** *adv.* —**sage·ness** *n.*

sage[2] /sayj/ (*plural* **sa·ges** *or* **sage**) *n.* **1. PLANT WITH AROMATIC LEAVES** a plant or shrub with blue, purple, or white flowers and aromatic grayish-green leaves that are used as a flavoring. Latin name: *Salvia officinalis*. **2. LEAVES USED AS COOKING HERB** the fresh or dried leaves of the sage plant used in cooking as a flavoring **3.** = **sagebrush 4.** = **sage green** [14thC. Via Old French *sauge* from Latin *salvia* "healing plant," from *salvus*.]

sage·brush /sáyj brùsh/ (*plural* **-brush·es** *or* **-brush**) *n.* a bushy composite plant native to dry regions of North America that has silvery wedge-shaped leaves and large clusters of small white flowers. Genus: *Artemisia*.

Sage·brush Re·bel·lion *n.* a populist campaign in the late 1970s waged in the western states by ranchers and farmers with mining and timber interests who protested the imposition of more federal regulations on land management

sage green, **sage** *adj.* of a grayish-green color, like sage leaves —**sage green** *n.*

sage grouse *n.* a large grouse of western North America that has mottled plumage, a black belly, and a long pointed tail that it spreads during courtship. Latin name: *Centrocercus urophasianus*.

sage thrash·er *n.* a grayish-brown thrasher of western North America that nests in sagebrush and other low-growing desert plants. Latin name: *Oreoscoptese montanus*.

sag·gar /sággər/, **sag·ger** *n.* a clay box into which delicate ceramic objects are placed to protect them in the kiln during firing. It is seldom used now that fuels are cleaner. [Mid-18thC. Origin uncertain: probably a contraction of SAFEGUARD.]

Sa·git·ta /sə jíttə/ *n.* a small but conspicuous constellation in the sky of the northern hemisphere lying in the Milky Way between Aquila and Vulpecula

sag·it·tal /sájjət'l/ *adj.* **1.** ZOOL **RELATING TO MEDIAN PLANE** relating to or situated on the imaginary plane that divides a human or animal body into right and left halves **2. RESEMBLING ARROW** resembling an arrow or an arrowhead in shape [Mid-16thC. From medieval Latin *sagittalis*, from Latin *sagitta* "arrow."] —**sag·it·tal·ly** *adv.*

Sag·it·tar·i·an /sàjjə táiree ən/ *n.* = **Sagittarius**

Sag·it·tar·i·us /sàjjə táiree əss/ *n.* **1.** ASTRON **CONSTELLATION IN THE SOUTHERN HEMISPHERE** a large zodiacal constellation in the sky of the southern hemisphere between Scorpius and Capricornus, crossed by the Milky Way and lying in the direction of the center of the galaxy **2. NINTH SIGN OF ZODIAC** the ninth sign of the zodiac, represented by an archer and lasting from approximately November 22 to December 21. Sagittarius is classified as a fire sign and its ruling planet is Jupiter. **3. SOMEBODY BORN UNDER SAGITTARIUS** somebody whose birthday falls between November 22 and December 21 [Pre-12thC. From Latin, "archer," from *sagitta* "arrow."] —**Sag·it·tar·i·an** *adj.*

sag·it·tate /sájjə tàyt/, **sag·it·ti·form** /sə jíttə fàwrm/ *adj.* used to describe a leaf that is shaped like an arrowhead [Mid-18thC. Formed from Latin *sagitta* "arrow."]

sa·go /sáygō/ *n.* a powdery substance obtained from the pith of the sago palm, used in cooking as a thickener, e.g., in soups, and also used for stiffening textiles [Mid-16thC. From Malay *sagu*.]

sa·go palm *n.* a tall Asian palm tree that yields sago. Genus: *Metroxylan*.

sa·gua·ro /sə gwaárō, -waárō/ (*plural* **-ros** *or* **-ro**), **sa·hua·ro** /sə waárō/ (*plural* **-ros** *or* **-ro**) *n.* a large cactus of the southwestern United States and northern Mexico growing up to 60 ft./18 m tall with upward-curving branches, white nocturnal flowers, and edible red fruit. Latin name: *Carnegiea gigantea*. [Mid-19thC. From Mexican Spanish, of uncertain origin: probably from Uto-Aztecan.]

Sa·har·a /sə haárə/ the largest desert in the world, covering much of northern Africa between the Atlantic Ocean and the Red Sea. Area: 3,500,000 sq. mi./9,100,000 sq. km.

Sa·har·an /sə hérrən, -haárən/ *n.* **GROUP OF LANGUAGES SPOKEN IN CHAD** a group of languages spoken in parts of Chad and neighboring countries. It is thought to be a branch of the Nilo-Saharan family. ■ *adj.* **1. RELATING TO SAHARA** relating to or found in the Sahara **2. BELONGING TO SAHARAN GROUP OF LANGUAGES** relating to or belonging to the Saharan group of languages

Sa·hel /sá hil, sè híl/ semiarid zone, extending from Sudan in the east to Senegal in the west, and separating the Sahara from the tropical regions of western and central Africa

sa·hib /saá hìb, saá ìb/ *n.* *S Asia* a respectful form of address for men in the Indian subcontinent, formerly widely used to Caucasian men during the colonial period. The term is also used as a title, placed after the man's name. [Late 17thC. Via Hindi from Arabic "friend."]

Sahl /saal/, **Mort** (*b.* 1927) Canadian-born U.S. comedian. He was known for his satirical monologues based on current events.

said[1] *v.* past tense, past participle of **say** ■ *adj.* LAW **PREVIOUSLY MENTIONED** previously named or mentioned ○ *The said car was later found abandoned.*

said[2] *n.* = **sayyid**

sai·ga /sígə/ (*plural* **-gas** *or* **-ga**) *n.* an antelope of central Asia, with a thick tawny coat and enlarged snout, considered a genetic link between the antelope and the sheep. Genus: *Saiga*. [Early 19thC. From Russian, of uncertain origin: probably from a Finnic language.]

sail /sayl/ *n.* **1. FABRIC CATCHING WIND ON BOAT** a large piece of strong fabric, usually triangular or rectangular in shape, fixed by rigging, masts, and booms to catch the wind and propel a vessel forward **2. JOURNEY IN VESSEL** a trip or voyage in a boat or ship, especially a sailing vessel ○ *a pleasant sail across the bay* **3.** (*plural* **sail**) **VESSEL WITH SAILS** a boat or ship with sails, or such vessels considered collectively ○ *go by sail*

4. **SAILS OF VESSEL** the sails of a boat or ship considered collectively ○ *a ship under full sail* **5.** **THING OR PART RESEMBLING SAIL** something that resembles a sail of a boat or ship in form, function, or position **6.** **BLADE OF WINDMILL** any of the long flat structures on the outside of a windmill that are turned by the wind **7.** NAUT **PART OF SUBMARINE** the conning tower of a submarine ■ *v.* **(sailed, sail·ing, sails) 1.** *vti.* **GO BY VESSEL ON WATER** to travel in a boat or ship across a stretch of water **2.** *vti.* **MOVE ON WATER** to move across the surface of water, or across a particular stretch of water, driven by wind or engine power ○ *pirate ships that sailed the high seas* **3.** *vt.* **DRIVE BOAT OR SHIP** to control the movement of a boat or ship, especially one with sails ○ *She sailed the boat into the harbor.* **4.** *vi.* **BEGIN SEA JOURNEY** to depart in a boat or ship, or to leave a harbor, mooring, or anchorage ○ *The ferry sails at noon.* **5.** *vi.* **MOVE SMOOTHLY** to move smoothly or swiftly and usually in a graceful way ○ *The ball sailed over the fence.* [Old English *segl*, from a prehistoric Germanic word perhaps meaning "cut cloth"] —**sail·a·ble** *adj.* ◇ **set sail** to depart in a boat or ship, or to leave a harbor, mooring, or anchorage ◇ **under sail** with sails hoisted, and not propelled by an engine

sail into *vt.* (*informal*) **1.** **ATTACK SOMEBODY VIOLENTLY** to make a violent physical or verbal attack on somebody ○ *She sailed into me for forgetting to mail the letter.* **2.** **GET ON WITH SOMETHING** to start to do something with vigor and enthusiasm ○ *He sailed into the task of redesigning the building.*

sail through *vti.* to do something, especially to pass a test, with ease ○ *He sailed through the exam.*

sail·board /sáyl bàwrd/ *n.* **SURFBOARD WITH A SAIL** a large surfboard with a keel and a mast and a sail mounted on it that is operated by one person standing up in the sport of windsurfing ■ *vi.* **RIDE ON SAILBOARD** to ride on a sailboard or take part in the sport of windsurfing —**sail·board·er** *n.*

sail·board·ing /sáyl bàwrding/ *n.* = **windsurfing**

sail·boat /sáyl bŏt/ *n.* a boat with one or more masts and sails that is propelled by the wind, chiefly used for sport and leisure. Larger sailboats often have an engine as well.

sail·cloth /sáyl klòth, -klàwth/ *n.* **1.** **FABRIC FOR SAILS** any strong fabric used to make sails, originally a heavy cotton canvas **2.** **FABRIC FOR CLOTHES** a lightweight cotton fabric with a texture like that of canvas, used to make clothes

sail·er /sáylər/ *n.* a boat or ship, especially a sailing vessel, that has particular sailing characteristics

sail·fish /sáyl fìsh/ (*plural* **-fish** *or* **-fish·es**) *n.* a warm-water marine fish with a large high dorsal fin resembling a sail and an elongated upper jaw that projects forward like a spear. Genus: *Istiophorus.*

sail·ing /sáyling/ *n.* **1.** **TRAVELING IN A VESSEL WITH SAILS** the sport, leisure activity, or occupation of traveling in or operating a boat or ship propelled by sails **2.** **SKILL OF OPERATING VESSEL** the art or a method of controlling a boat or ship, especially one with sails ○ *Expert sailing is required in such conditions.* **3.** **SHIP'S DEPARTURE OR DEPARTURE TIME** the departure of a ship, or the time at which a ship is scheduled to leave port ○ *The next sailing is at noon.* [Old English *segling*]

sail·ing boat *n.* = **sailboat**

sail·ing ship *n.* a ship with masts and sails that is propelled by the wind, formerly used for transporting passengers and goods

sail·or /sáylər/ *n.* **1.** **SOMEBODY WHO WORKS ON SHIP** somebody who works aboard a boat or ship, especially a low-ranking member of the crew of a merchant or naval ship **2.** **SOMEBODY TRAVELING ON WATER** somebody who frequently sails or travels on a boat or ship, especially with reference to his or her susceptibility to seasickness ○ *I'm not a good sailor.*

sail·or col·lar *n.* a collar that is V-shaped in front and has a broad square shape at the back, traditionally worn by sailors

sail·or hat *n.* a hat with a flat top, a low crown, and wide brim that is either straight or rolled upward all around

sail·or's-choice *n.* a small fish of Atlantic coastal regions of North America such as the pinfish or pigfish

sail·or suit *n.* an outfit for children resembling the traditional sailor uniform, made up of a top with a sailor collar and pants or a skirt, usually in dark blue and white

sail·plane /sáyl plàyn/ *n.* **LIGHT GLIDER** a light glider particularly well adapted to making use of rising air currents, used for soaring ■ *vi.* **(-planed, -plan·ing, -planes)** **TRAVEL BY SAILPLANE** to travel in a sailplane —**sail·plan·er** *n.*

Sai·maa, Lake /sīmaa-/ lake in southeastern Finland. Area: 500 sq. mi./1,300 sq. km.

sain·foin /sáyn fòyn/ (*plural* **-foins** *or* **-foin**) *n.* a plant of the pea family that is grown as forage. It has clusters of pink flowers and is native to Europe and Asia. Latin name: *Onobrychis viciifolia.* [Early 17thC. From obsolete French, from modern Latin *sanctum foenum*, literally "holy hay," alteration of *sanum foenum* "wholesome hay."]

saint /saynt/; *in French names often* /saN/ *n.* **1.** **SOMEBODY HONORED BY CHURCH AFTER DEATH** somebody who has been particularly holy in life and after death is declared by a Christian church to have a privileged place in heaven and be worthy of veneration **2.** **SOMEBODY IN HEAVEN** somebody who is thought to have gone to heaven after death **3.** **VIRTUOUS PERSON** a particularly good or holy person, or one who is kind and patient in dealing with difficult people or situations ■ *vt.* **(saint·ed, saint·ing, saints)** **RECOGNIZE SOMEBODY AS SAINT** to declare somebody officially to be a saint of a Christian church [Pre-12thC. From Latin *sanctus* "holy," literally "consecrated," past participle of *sancire* "to confirm, consecrate."] —**saint·dom** *n.*

Saint Ag·nes's Eve /-ágnəssəz-/ *n.* CALENDAR January 20, the eve of St. Agnes's Day, on which, according to British folklore, people dream of their future partners if they have performed particular rituals before going to sleep.

Saint An·drew's cross /-àn drooz-/ *n.* a diagonal cross with arms of equal length, especially a white one on a blue background as on the flag of Saint Andrew and Scotland

Saint An·tho·ny's cross /-ànthəniz-/ *n.* = **tau cross**

Saint An·tho·ny's fire /-ánthəniz-/ *n.* any acutely painful inflammatory skin disorder such as cellulitis, shingles, or erysipelas (*archaic*)

St. Au·gus·tine /saynt áwgə stèen/ city and resort in northeastern Florida, on the Matanzas and San Sebastian rivers, near the Atlantic coast. Population: 11,692 (1990).

Saint Bar·thol·o·mew's Day Mas·sa·cre /-baar thòllə myooz-/ *n.* a massacre of Huguenots that began in Paris on Saint Bartholomew's Day, August 24, 1572

Saint Ber·nard /-bər naárd/ *n.* a very large working dog belonging to a breed developed in Switzerland to rescue lost mountain travelers [Mid-19thC. Named for the Hospice of the Great St. Bernard Pass.]

St. Ber·nard Pass /sènt burnèrd-/ either of two mountain passes running between Italy and Switzerland

St. Cath·a·rines /-káthèrènz/ city in Ontario, Canada, on the Welland Ship Canal, across Lake Ontario from Toronto. Population: 129,300 (1996).

St. Charles /-chaárlz/ city in eastern Missouri, on the Missouri River, near its confluence with the Mississippi River. It is a suburb of St. Louis. Population: 54,555 (1990).

St. Clair, Lake /-kláir/ lake in central North America, astride the border between Michigan and Ontario. Area: 430 sq. mi./1,114 sq. km.

St. Clair Shores city in southeastern Michigan, on Lake Saint Clair, near Detroit. Population: 68,107 (1990).

St. Cloud /-klówd/ city in central Minnesota, on the Mississippi and Sauk rivers. Since 1870, it has been an important center for quarrying and polishing granite. Population: 48,812 (1990).

St. Croix /-króy/ the largest island of the U.S. Virgin Islands, situated in the West Indies. Population: 50,139 (1990). Area: 84 sq. mi./218 sq. km.

St. Denis /sàN də neé/, **Ruth** (1878–1968) U.S. dancer and choreographer. A pioneer of 20th-century dance, she cofounded the Denishawn Dance School (1915) with her husband, Ted Shawn. Born **Ruth Dennis**

Saint-De·nis /sa dè neé/ city in north central France, in Seine-Saint-Denis Department, on the Seine River. It is a northern suburb of Paris. Population: 90,806 (1990).

saint·ed /sáyntəd/ *adj.* **1.** **RECOGNIZED AS SAINT** officially declared to be a saint of a Christian church **2.** **IN HEAVEN** dead and thought to be in heaven **3.** **VIRTUOUS** good, virtuous, or holy (*literary*)

Sain·te-Foy /sàNt fwaá/ city in the southern part of the province of Quebec, Canada, located on the St. Lawrence and Cap-Rouge rivers. Population: 72,330 (1996).

St. E·li·as, Mount /-è líèss/ the second highest mountain in Canada, in the Saint Elias Range, on the Alaska-Yukon Territory border. Height: 18,008 ft./5,489 m.

Saint El·mo's fire /-élmōz-/ *n.* a luminous region of electrical discharge that appears during stormy weather around a narrow pointed object, such as a church spire or the mast of a ship [Early 19thC. Named for *St. Elmo* (died A.D. 303), patron saint of sailors.]

Saint-E·mil·ion /-e meélyən/ *n.* a red wine produced in the area around Saint-Emilion in the Bordeaux region of France

Saint-É·tienne /saN etee én/ city and administrative center of Loire Department, Rhône-Alpes Region, east central France. Population: 201,695 (1990).

Saint-Ex·u·pé·ry /saN teg zoópə reé/, **Antoine Marie Roger de** (1900–44) French aviator and writer. He wrote novels, essays and autobiographical works, but is chiefly remembered for his much-loved children's story, *The Little Prince* (1943).

St. Fran·cis /-fránsiss/ river rising in southeastern Missouri and flowing south through Arkansas to join the Mississippi River. Length: 425 mi./684 km.

St. Gal·len, St. Gall /-gaálèn, -gáwl/ capital of St. Gallen Canton, northeastern Switzerland, situated about 40 mi./64 km east of Zürich. Population: 75,541 (1990).

Saint-Gau·dens /-gáwd'nz/, **Augustus** (1848–1907) Irish-born U.S. sculptor. His works, mostly in bronze, include various U.S. public monuments such as the Shaw Memorial in Boston, Massachusettts (1897) and "Grief" in Washington, D.C. (1891).

St. Georg·e's Chan·nel /-jáwrjèz-/ sea passage between southeastern Ireland and southwestern Wales

Saint Geor·ge's cross /-jàwrjəz-/ *n.* a red cross on a white background, as on the flags of Saint George and England

St. Gott·hard Pass /sènt góttèrd-/ pass through the central Alps between southern Switzerland and Italy. Length: 16 mi./26 km.

St. Hel·ens, Mount /sènt héllènz-/ active volcano in southwestern Washington State, in the Cascade Range. Its last major eruption was in 1980. Height: 8,365 ft./2,550 m.

saint·hood /sáynt hŏŏd/ *n.* **1.** **STATUS OF BEING SAINT** the condition or status of being a saint or saintly **2.** **SAINTS COLLECTIVELY** saints regarded as a group

St. John /saynt jón/ **1.** river in east central North America, that rises in northwestern Maine, flows northeastward into New Brunswick, and empties into the Atlantic Ocean. It forms part of the border between the United States and Canada. Length: 418 mi./673 km. **2.** largest city and principal port of New Brunswick, Canada, situated on the Bay of Fundy. Population: 74,969 (1991).

St. John, Lake lake in south central Quebec Province, Canada. It drains to the St. Lawrence River on the east by the Saguenay River. Area: 414 sq. mi./1,070 sq. km.

St. Johns /saynt jónz/ river flowing in eastern Florida to Jacksonville, emptying into the Atlantic Ocean. Length: 276 mi./444 km.

St. John's /saynt jónz/ **1.** capital city and principal port of Newfoundland, Canada, situated on the Atlantic Ocean. Population: 174,051 (1996). **2.** capital city of Antigua and Barbuda. It is situated in the northwestern part of Antigua, on an inlet of the Caribbean Sea. Population: 21,514 (1991).

Saint John's-wort /-jónz wùrt, -wàwrt/ *n.* an herb or shrub with showy five-petaled yellow flowers. Genus: *Hypericum.* [*Saint John's* from its being said to flower on the feast of St. John the Baptist.]

St. Jo·seph /sènt jóssèf/ city in Buchanan County, northwestern Missouri, on the Missouri River. Population: 71,852 (1990).

St. Kil·da /sènt kíldè/ group of small, now uninhabited islands in the Outer Hebrides, Scotland. They are home to a seabird sanctuary and a National Nature Reserve.

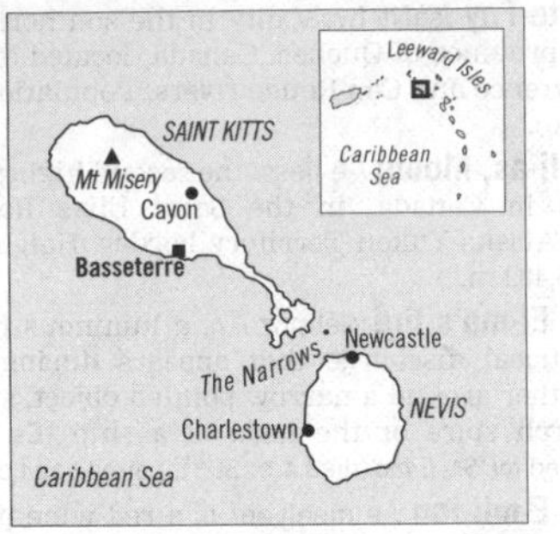

St. Kitts and Nevis

St. Kitts and Ne·vis /saynt kìts and néeviss/ independent state in the West Indies, comprising two islands that are part of the Leeward Islands group. Language: English. Currency: East Caribbean dollar. Capital: Basseterre. Population: 39,400 (1996). Area: 104 sq. mi./269 sq. km. Official name **Federation of St. Kitts and Nevis**

St. Laurent /sàN law ráaN/, **Louis Stephen** (1882–1973) Canadian lawyer and statesman. He served as the prime minister of Canada (1948–57).

Saint-Lau·rent /sànt law rént, sàN law ráaN/ city in Île-de-Montreal County, southern Quebec Province, on Montreal Island. Population: 74,240 (1996).

St. Law·rence /saynt láwrènss/ major river of North America, linking the outflow from the Great Lakes with the Atlantic Ocean. Length: 800 mi./1,300 km.

St. Law·rence, Gulf of /saynt láwrənss/ deep inlet of the Atlantic Ocean between Newfoundland and the Canadian mainland

St. Law·rence Is·lands Na·tion·al Park national park incorporating part of the shore of the St. Lawrence River and 13 of the Thousand Islands, Ontario, Canada. Area: 3 sq. mi./8 sq. km.

St. Law·rence Sea·way system of canals bypassing unnavigable sections of the St. Lawrence River and allowing oceangoing vessels to reach the Great Lakes, sometimes also including the canals between the Great Lakes

Saint-Le·o·nard /saynt lénnərd, sàN layō naár/ city in Île-de-Montreal County, southern Quebec Province, on Montreal Island. Population: 71,327 (1996).

Saint-Lô /saN lṓ/ city and administrative center of Manche Department, Basse-Normandie Region, northwestern France. Population: 22,819 (1990).

St. Lou·is /saynt lóo iss/ city in eastern Missouri, extending along the western bank of the Mississippi River. It is one of the principal industrial and cultural centers of the Midwest. Population: 368,215 (1994).

Saint-Lou·is /saN loo ée/ town and port in northwestern Senegal, situated 110 mi./177 km northeast of Dakar. Population: 132,444 (1994).

St. Lou·is en·ceph·a·li·tis *n.* a viral inflammation of the brain found in parts of North America and transmitted by mosquitoes [Mid-20thC. Named for St. Louis, Missouri.]

St. Lou·is Park city in southeastern Minnesota, on Minnehaha Creek. It is a residential and industrial suburb of Minneapolis. Population: 43,787 (1990).

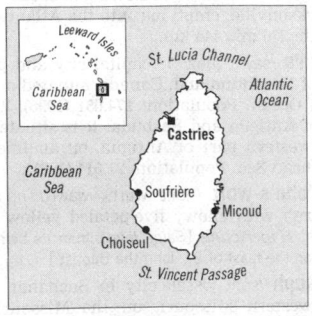

St. Lu·cia /saynt lóoshə/ independent island state in the West Indies. It is one of the Windward Islands. Language: English. Currency: East Caribbean dollar. Capital: Castries. Population: 143,000 (1995). Area: 238 sq. mi./617 sq. km.

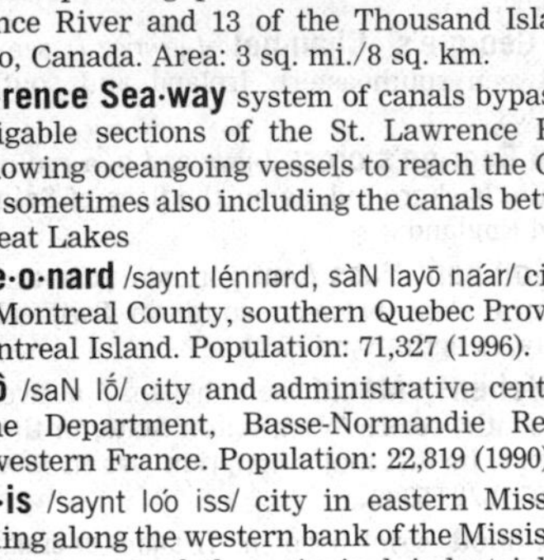

St. Lucia

saint·ly /sáyntlee/ (**-li·er, -li·est**) *adj.* **1.** OF CHRISTIAN SAINT characteristic of or associated with a saint of a Christian church **2.** VERY VIRTUOUS very good, virtuous, or holy —**saint·li·ly** *adv.* —**saint·li·ness** *n.*

St. Mar·tin /saynt maárt'n/ island in the West Indies, one of the Leeward Islands, between the islands of Anguilla and Saint-Barthélemy. It is a dependency of Guadeloupe. Area: 20 sq. mi./52 sq. km.

St. Mar·ys /sènt máiriz/ **1.** river rising in the Okefenokee Swamp in Georgia, United States, winding eastward into the Atlantic Ocean. Length: 175 mi./282 km. **2.** river in North America connecting Lake Superior with Lake Huron, forming part of the border between the United States and Canada. Length: 63 mi./101 km.

St. Mat·thews /sènt máth yooz/ city in northern Kentucky, south of the Illinois border. It is an eastern suburb of Louisville. Population: 16,562 (1996).

St. Mo·ritz /saN mè ríts/ spa town in southeastern Switzerland, situated 9 mi./14 km from the Italian border. Population: 5,600 (1996).

Saint-Na·zaire /saN na záir/ city and port in Loire-Atlantique Department, Pays de la Loire Region, western France. Population: 66,087 (1990).

St. Pat·rick's Day *n.* CALENDAR March 17, the Christian feast day of St. Patrick, the patron saint of Ireland

St. Paul /saynt páwl/ capital city of Minnesota, in the southeastern part of the state on the banks of the Mississippi River. Population: 262,071 (1994).

St. Paul's Cathedral /sàynt páwlz/ *n.* a large, domed, baroque cathedral in the City of London, England, designed by Christopher Wren and completed in 1710

St. Peter's, Vatican, Rome, Italy

St. Pe·ter's /-péetərz/ *n.* a large Baroque basilica in the Vatican City, Rome, Italy that was completed in 1612. It is one of the largest churches in the world.

St. Pe·ters·burg /saynt péetərz bùrg/ **1.** the second largest city in Russia, located in the northwestern part of the country. Situated at the head of the Gulf of Finland, an arm of the Baltic Sea, it is also the country's largest port. It was the capital of Russia for two centuries, from 1712 until 1918. Population: 4,672,000 (1997). Former name **Leningrad** (1924–90) **2.** city in western Florida, located on Pinellas Peninsula between Tampa Bay and the Gulf of Mexico. Population: 238,585 (1994).

St.-Pi·erre town and tourist center in the French West Indies, on Martinique Island, in the Caribbean Sea, near the base of the volcano, Montagne Pelée. Population: 5,007 (1990).

St.-Pi·erre and Mi·que·lon /san peér ənd méekə lon, saN pyàir and mée klòN/ overseas territory of France, in the North Atlantic Ocean, off the coast of Newfoundland, Canada. It consists of two small groups of islands. Population: 6,392 (1990). Area: 93 sq. mi./242 sq. km.

Saint-Saëns /saN saáNss, -saáN/, **Camille** (1835–1921) French composer. His works, including symphonies, church music, concertos, songs, and operas, are in the classical French tradition. Full name **Charles Camille Saint-Saëns**

saint's day *n.* a day of the year on which a particular saint is remembered or honored. Some saints' days are marked by traditional festivities or associated with popular superstitions.

St. Si·mons Is·land /sènt símənz-/ island off southeastern Georgia, United States, in the Atlantic Ocean. It is home to Fort Frederica, a national monument. Area: 36 sq. mi./93 sq. km.

St. Thomas /saynt tómməss-/ island of the U.S. Virgin Islands, situated in the West Indies. Population: 48,166 (1990). Area: 28 sq. mi./73 sq. km.

Saint-Tro·pez /saN trō páy/ resort town on the Mediterranean coast, southern France. It is situated 60 mi./155 km east of Marseille. Population: 5,790 (1990).

St. Val·en·tine's Day /-vállən tīnz-/ *n.* CALENDAR = **Valentine's Day**

St. Vin·cent, Cape /sènt vínsènt-/ cape at the southwesternmost point of Portugal

St. Vin·cent, Gulf of /sènt vínsènt-/ gulf in southern Australia, located between the Yorke and Fleurieu peninsulas

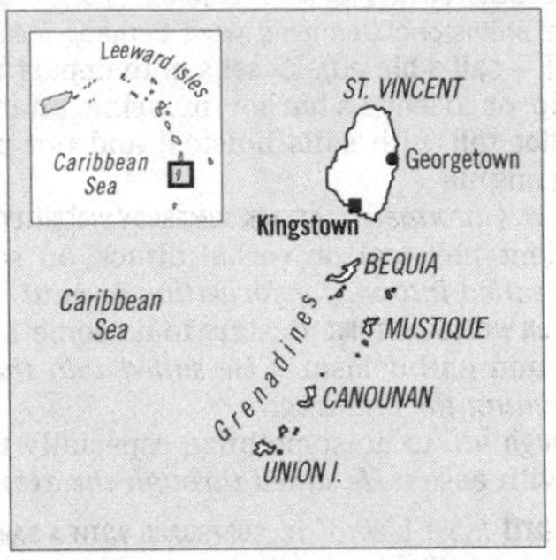

St. Vincent and the Grenadines

St. Vin·cent and the Gren·a·dines /saynt vínss'nt ənd thə grènnə déenz/ independent state in the West Indies comprising the island of St. Vincent and 32 of the islands of the Grenadine group. Language: English. Currency: East Caribbean dollar. Capital: Kingstown. Population: 112,000 (1995). Area: 150 sq. mi./389 sq. km.

St. Vi·tus's dance /-vítəssəz-/ *n.* Sydenham's chorea (*no longer in technical use*) [Early 17thC. Named for *St. Vitus* (3rdC), patron saint of those affected by this condition.]

saith /seth, sáy ith/ 3rd person present singular of **say** (*archaic*)

Sai·va /sívə/ *n.* a member of a Hindu religious group that worships Shiva [Late 18thC. From Sanskrit *saiva-* "sacred to Shiva."] —**Sai·va** *adj.* —**Sai·vism** *n.* —**Sai·vite** *n.*

sa·kai /saá kī/ *n.* a member of an aboriginal people who live in the forests of Malaysia [Mid-19thC. From Malay, "dependent, subject."]

Sa·kai /saa kí/ southern suburb of Osaka, situated on Osaka bay in Osaka Prefecture, on western Honshu, Japan. Population: 807,765 (1990).

sake[1] /sayk/ *n.* **1.** SOMEBODY'S OR SOMETHING'S INTEREST the good, benefit, or welfare of somebody or something ○ *I hope you're right, for all our sakes!* **2.** MOTIVE OR OBJECTIVE the purpose of doing, obtaining, achieving, or maintaining something ○ *It's not worth risking your life for the sake of getting there a few minutes earlier.* [Old English *sacu*, from a prehistoric Germanic word meaning "seeking," hence "accusation, cause," which is also the ancestor of English *seek*]

sa·ke[2] /saákee/, **sa·ki** *n.* a Japanese alcoholic beverage made from fermented rice and usually served warm [Late 17thC. From Japanese.]

sa·ker /sáykər/ *n.* a large falcon from central Asia and eastern Europe with brown body plumage and a pale-colored head, used in falconry. Latin name: *Falco cherrug*. [15thC. Via (Old) French *sacre* from Arabic *sakr* "hawk, falcon."]

sa·ki *n.* = **sake**

Sak·ka·ra /sə kaárə/ village near Cairo, Egypt. It is the site of a stepped pyramid built by King Zoser between 2737 and 2717 B.C., the first monumental royal tomb, and one of the oldest stone structures in Egypt.

Sak·ta /shaáktə/, **Shak·ta** *n.* INDIAN RELIG a member of a Hindu religious group who particularly worship the female principle or the female gods

Sak·ti /saáktee/, **Shak·ti** /shúktə, shaáktee/ *n.* in Hinduism, the vital generative and creative principle at work in the universe, typically associated with the femine component of the divine, often embodied as a goddess [Early 19thC. From Sanskrit *śaktiḥ*, literally "power," from *śak-* "to be strong" (source of English *Sikh*).]

Sak·ya·mu·ni /saákya moónee/ *n.* one of the names of the Buddha, deriving from Sakya, the name of his clan

sal /sal/ *n.* PHARM used in pharmacology to denote salt (*usually used in combination*) ○ *sal ammoniac* [14thC. From Latin, "salt."]

sa·laam /sə laám/ *n.* **1.** **DEEP BOW WITH HAND ON FOREHEAD** a deeply respectful or deferential gesture of greeting or acknowledgment, used especially in Islamic countries, made by bowing low with the palm of the right hand against the forehead **2.** **RESPECTFUL GREETING** the word "salaam," meaning "peace," used as a respectful greeting ■ *vti.* **(-laamed, -laam·ing, -laams)** **MAKE SALUTATION OF GREETING OR RESPECT** to perform a salaam, or to greet somebody with a salaam [Early 17thC. From Arabic *salām* "peace."]

sal·a·ble, sale·a·ble *adj.* suitable for selling or capable of being sold —**sal·a·bil·i·ty** /sàylə bíllətee/ *n.* —**sal·a·bly** /sáyləblee/ *adv.*

sa·la·cious /sə láyshəss/ *adj.* **1.** **WITH SEXUAL CONTENT** intended to titillate or arouse people sexually, usually by having an explicit erotic content **2.** **EXPLICITLY SEXUAL** having or showing explicit or crude sexual desire or interest [Mid-17thC. Formed from the Latin stem *salac-*, from *salire* "to leap" (source of English *salient*).] —**sa·la·cious·ly** *adv.* —**sa·la·cious·ness** *n.*

sal·ad /sálləd/ *n.* **1.** **MIXTURE OF RAW VEGETABLES** a cold savory dish consisting mainly of a mixture of raw vegetables whole, sliced, chopped, or in pieces, usually served with a dressing for moisture and flavor. Many other ingredients may be incorporated into a salad, which can be served as a separate course or as an accompaniment to other food. **2.** **DISH OF COLD INGREDIENTS** a cold dish consisting of a particular type of food, e.g., a single vegetable or a selection of fruit, cut into pieces or slices, and served usually with a dressing ○ *potato salad* **3.** **LEAFY VEGETABLES** any of the leafy vegetables commonly used to make a green salad, typically the many types of lettuce, watercress, chicory, and endive **4.** **CONFUSED MIXTURE** a confused or varied mixture ○ *a salad of ideas* [14thC. Via French *salade* from assumed Vulgar Latin *salata* "salted," ultimately from Latin *sal* "salt" (source of English *salami*).]

sal·ad bar *n.* a counter in a restaurant or grocery store where salads of various types are available, set up as a buffet where customers can choose their own ingredients ○ *The menu offered typical meals but we could also choose the salad bar.*

sal·ad days *npl.* the period of a person's life when he or she is young, innocent, naive, and inexperienced (*dated*) [From the words of Cleopatra in Shakespeare's *Antony and Cleopatra*: "My salad days, When I was green in judgement, cold in blood"]

sal·ad dress·ing *n.* a well-seasoned sauce poured over or mixed with the ingredients of a salad, e.g., one made from oil and vinegar or mayonnaise

sal·ade ni·çoise /sə laád nee swaáz/ *n.* a cold dish originally from the region around Nice in France, containing anchovies, tuna fillets, olives, green beans, and sometimes other ingredients, served with a dressing of olive oil and garlic [Early 20thC. From French, named for *Nice*, city in France.]

Sal·a·din /sálləd̲in/, **Sultan of Egypt and Syria** (1137–93). During his sultanate (1174–93), he led the Muslims successfully against the Christian crusaders in Palestine until he was defeated and captured at Acre (1191). Full name **Salah ed-din Yussuf ibn Ayub**

sal·ad oil *n.* a light or pleasantly flavored vegetable oil used to make a salad dressing, e.g., olive, sunflower, or canola oil

sa·lal /sə lál/ (*plural* **sal·als** *or* **sal·al**) *n.* an evergreen shrub of the heath family native to the west coast of North America, with leathery leaves, clusters of pink or white flowers, and edible purple berries. Latin name: *Gaultheria shallon.* [Early 19thC. From Chinook jargon *sallal.*]

Sal·a·man·ca /salè mángkè/ city in the autonomous region of Castile-León, west central Spain. It is the site of the University of Salamanca, founded in 1218. Population: 167,316 (1995).

Salamander

sal·a·man·der /sállə màndər/ *n.* **1.** **SMALL ANIMAL RESEMBLING LIZARD** an amphibian that resembles a lizard but has porous moist skin instead of scales, and that lives in water as a larva and on land as an adult. Order: Caudata. **2.** MYTHOL **MYTHICAL REPTILE LIVING IN FIRE** a mythical lizard that can live in fire **3.** **BUILDING PORTABLE STOVE** a stove that is used on construction projects to heat or dry out buildings or to thaw frozen water pipes [14thC. Directly and via Old French from Latin and Greek *salamandra.*] —**sal·a·man·drine** /sàllə mándrin, sállə màndrin/ *adj.*

sa·la·mi /sə laámee/ *n.* a large thick highly seasoned sausage, Italian in origin and very often cured, usually served cold in thin slices [Mid-19thC. From Italian, plural of *salame*, from, ultimately, Latin *sal* "salt" (source of English *sauce*).]

Sal·a·mis /sállèmèss/ island in eastern Greece 8 mi./13 km west of the port of Piraeus. It was the location of a major sea battle in 480 B.C. in which the Greeks defeated the Persians. Population: 28,574 (1981). Area: 39 sq. mi./10 sq. km.

sal am·mo·ni·ac /sàl ə mṓnee àk/ *n.* = **ammonium chloride** [From Latin *sal ammoniacus*, literally "salt of Ammon" (see AMMONIA)]

sal·a·ried /sálləreed, sállreed/ *adj.* receiving a regular salary for employment, e.g., as opposed to being paid by the hour

sal·bu·ta·mol /sal byoótə mòl/ *n.* a bronchodilating drug used as a component in inhalers to relieve asthma, emphysema, and chronic bronchitis. Formula: $C_{13}H_{21}NO_3$. [Mid-20thC. Coined from *salicylic acid* + BUTYL + AMINE +-OL.]

sal·chow /sál kòw/ *n.* a jump in figure skating in which the skater takes off from one skate, does a complete rotation in the air, and lands on the opposite skate [Early 20thC. Named for the Swedish figure skater Ulrich *Salchow* (1877–1949).]

sale /sayl/ *n.* **1.** **SELLING OF SOMETHING** the exchanging of goods or services for an agreed amount of money, or a single transaction of this nature **2.** **OPPORTUNITY TO BUY GOODS AT DISCOUNT** a period of time when a store sells goods at reduced prices, often in order to clear its stock ○ *We always look for bargains at the after-Christmas sales.* **3.** **OPPORTUNITY TO BUY SECONDHAND GOODS** an event at which personal possessions or other secondhand items are sold, usually at low prices, sometimes to raise money for a charitable or other cause **4.** **AUCTION** an event at which goods are sold to the highest bidder **5.** **MARKET OR DEMAND** demand that creates an opportunity to sell something **6.** **AMOUNT SOLD OR RATE OF SELLING** a quantity of things sold, or the rate at which they are sold ■ **sales** *npl.* **1.** **DEPARTMENT SELLING THINGS** the department of a company involved with selling its products or services **2.** **THINGS SOLD** the total number or value of items sold ○ *Sales fell by 10 percent last month.* [Pre-12thC. From Old Norse *sala*, from a prehistoric Germanic word that is also the ancestor of English *sell.*] ◇ **for sale** available for purchase ◇ **on sale** available for purchase, especially at a reduced price

Sa·lé /saa láy/ city on the Atlantic coast of Morocco. Population: 521,000 (1993).

sale·a·ble *adj.* = **salable**

sale and lease·back *n.* the sale of an asset that the vendor rents back from the buyer immediately after the sale, thereby raising cash and allowing a tax deduction

Sa·lem /sáyləm/ **1.** city in northeastern Massachusetts, on Massachusetts Bay, northeast of Boston. It was the site of witchcraft trials and executions in 1692. Population: 38,008 (1996). **2.** capital city of Oregon, on the Willamette River, in the northwest of the state. Population: 107,786 (1990).

sal·ep /sálləp/ *n.* the dried ground tubers of various orchids used as food and formerly in medicine [Mid-18thC. Via French from Turkish *sālep*, from Arabic *ta'lab* "fox," a shortening of *kuṣa* "t-ta'lab""orchid," literally "fox's testicles."]

sal·er·a·tus /sàllə ráytəss/ *n.* baking soda (*archaic*) [Mid-19thC. From modern Latin *sal aeratus*, literally "aerated salt."]

Sa·ler·no /sè lÚrnō/ capital city and port in Salerno Province, Campania Region, southern Italy. Population: 147,564 (1994).

sale·room /sáyl ro͝om, -ro͞om/ *n. U.K.* = **salesroom**

sales as·sis·tant *n. U.K.* = **salesclerk**

sales check *n.* = **sales slip**

sales·clerk /sáylz klùrk/ *n.* somebody who is employed to assist and sell goods to customers in a retail store

sales force *n.* the body of salespeople employed by a company to sell its goods and services

sales·girl /sáylz gùrl/ *n.* a young woman employed to sell goods to customers in a store (*dated or offensive*)

Sa·le·sian /sə leézh'n/ *n.* a member of the Roman Catholic order of Saint Francis de Sales founded in Turin, Italy, in 1845 and dedicated to educational and missionary work —**Sa·le·sian** *adj.*

sales·man /sáylzmən/ (*plural* **-men** /-mən/) *n.* a man who sells goods or services, either in a store or by contacting potential customers within a particular area —**sales·man·ship** *n.*

WORD KEY: CULTURAL NOTE

Death of a Salesman, a play by Arthur Miller (1949). The tragic story of Willy Loman, an aging salesman tormented by an overwhelming sense of failure, highlights the false values of contemporary consumer society and questions traditional ideas of success and failure. It was made into a movie by Volker Schlöndorff in 1985. As a result of the power of the play, the term *Willy Loman* came to mean a man who has tragically sacrificed or sold his own life, and that of his family, in pursuit of the so-called American Dream.

sales·per·son /sáylz pùrss'n/ (*plural* **-peo·ple** /-peep'l/ *or* **-per·sons**) *n.* somebody who sells goods or services, usually in a store or by contacting customers within a particular area

sales pitch *n.* the statements made, arguments used, and assurances given by somebody trying to sell something

sales rep·re·sen·ta·tive *n.* somebody employed by a company to visit prospective customers with a view to selling them the company's products

sales re·sis·tance *n.* reluctance or refusal to buy, especially when aggressive selling techniques are used

sales·room /sáylz ro͝om, -ro͞om/ *n.* **1.** **PLACE DISPLAYING GOODS FOR SALE** a large room where goods for sale are put on display **2.** **PLACE OF AUCTION** a large room where goods are sold by auction

sales slip *n.* a record of a purchase or sale made in a store, usually given to the customer as a receipt

sales tax *n.* a tax on retail merchandise that is levied by the federal, state, or local government and collected at the point of sale by the retailer

sales·wom·an /sáylz wo͝omən/ (*plural* **-en** /-wìmmin/) *n.* a woman who sells goods or services, usually in a store or by contacting potential customers within a particular area

sal·et *n.* = **sallet**

Sa·li·an /sáylee ən, sáylyən/ *n.* a member of the branch of Frankish people, the Salii, who invaded and then settled in an area of the Rhine valley in the Netherlands during the 4th century A.D. They subsequently spread into and conquered large parts of Northern Gaul. [Early 17thC. Formed from late Latin *Salii* "Salian Franks."]

Sal·ic /sáylik, sállik/, **Sal·ique** /sáylik, sállik, sə leék, sa-/ *adj.* **1.** PEOPLES **RELATING TO SALIANS** relating to or typical of the Salians, or their culture **2.** HIST **RELATING TO SALIC LAW** relating to Salic Law [Mid-16thC. Via French *salique* or medieval Latin *Salicus* from late Latin *Salii* (plural) "Salian Franks."]

sal·i·ca·ceous /sàlli káyshəss/ *adj.* used to describe trees or woody shrubs that have catkins, e.g., the willow and poplar. Family: Salicaceae. [Mid-19thC. Formed from modern Latin *salicaceus*, from Latin *salic-*, stem of *salix* "willow."]

sal·i·cin /sállissin/ *n.* a colorless crystalline substance obtained from the bark of certain poplar and willow trees and formerly used as an analgesic. Formula: $C_{13}H_{18}O_7$. [Mid-19thC. Via French *salicine* from Latin *salic-* the stem of *salic* "willow."]

sa·li·cion·al /sə lishən'l, -líshnəl/ *n.* a stop and pipes on an organ that produce a soft, gentle tone [Mid-19thC. Via German from Latin *salic-*, the stem of *salix* "willow."]

Sal·ic law *n.* a law excluding women from the right to succeed to the throne that formerly applied in France and some other European monarchies. The prohibition was supposedly founded on a law of the Salians that prevented women from inheriting land in some areas.

sa·lic·y·late /sə líssə làyt, -lət/ *n.* a salt or ester of salicylic acid [Mid-19thC. Via French *salicyle* from Latin *salictum*, from *salic-*, the stem of *salix* "willow."]

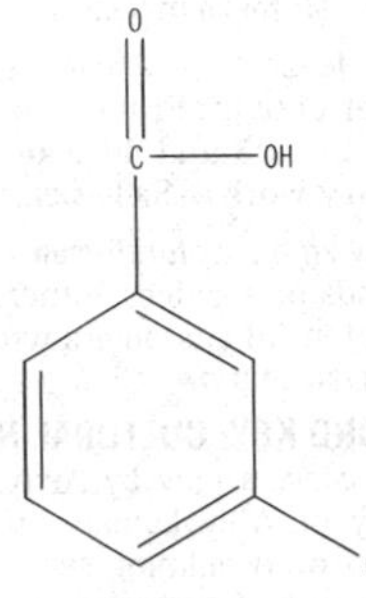

Salicylic acid

sal·i·cyl·ic ac·id /sàlli sillik-/ *n.* a white crystalline acid used in making aspirin and dyes and to preserve foods. Formula: $C_7H_6O_3$. [Formed from French *salicyle* (see SALICYLATE)]

sa·li·ence /sáylyənss/, **sa·li·en·cy** /-ssee/ (*plural* **-cies**) *n.* **1. BEING IMPORTANT** the quality of being particularly important or striking **2. IMPORTANT OR STRIKING FEATURE** a particularly important or striking feature

sa·li·ent /sáylyənt/ *adj.* **1. NOTICEABLE OR STRIKING** particularly noticeable, striking, or relevant **2. PROJECTING** sticking out from a surface **3.** GEOM **PROJECTING OUTWARD** used to describe an angle that projects outward from a polygon **4.** HERALDRY **JUMPING** represented as a jumping or leaping animal ■ *n.* **1.** MIL **PROJECTING PART OF DEFENSIVE ALIGNMENT** a part of a front, line, or fortification that projects outward into enemy-held territory or toward the enemy **2.** GEOM **SALIENT ANGLE** a salient angle [Mid-17thC. From Latin *salient-*, present participle stem of *salire* "to jump" (source of English *salacious*).] —**sa·li·ent·ly** *adv.*

WORD KEY: ORIGIN

The Latin word *salire*, from which ***salient*** is derived, is also the source of English *assail*, *assault*, *desultory*, *insult*, *salacious*, *sally*, and *sauté*.

sa·li·en·tian /sàylee énsh'n/ *adj.* = **anuran** [Mid-20thC. Formed from modern Latin *Salentia* from the Latin stem *salient-* (see SALIENT).]

Sal·i·er·i /sàllee áiree/, **Antonio** (1750–1825) Italian composer. As a successful writer of operas and church music in Vienna, he was a rival of Mozart.

sa·lif·er·ous /sə liffərəss/ *adj.* used to describe a geological formation that contains or produces salt [Early 19thC. Coined from Latin *sal* "salt" + -FEROUS.]

sa·lim·e·ter /sə límmətər/ *n.* = **salinometer** [Mid-19thC. Coined from Latin *sal* "salt" + -METER.] —**sal·i·met·ric** /sàllə méttrik/ *adj.* —**sa·lim·e·try** /sə límmətree/ *n.*

sa·li·na /sə léenə, -línə/ *n.* a salt marsh, lake, pond, or spring [Late 16thC. Via Spanish from medieval Latin, "salt pit."]

Sa·li·na /sə línə/ city in central Kansas, on the Smoky Hill River, southwest of Abilene and north of McPherson. Population: 44,176 (1996).

Sa·li·nas /sə léenəss/ river in western California, rising in the Santa Lucia Mountains and flowing into Monterey Bay. Length: 150 mi./241 km.

Sa·li·nas de Gor·ta·ri /sə léenəss də gawr táaree/, **Carlos** (*b.* 1948) Mexican statesman. He was president of Mexico (1988–94), and signed the North American Free Trade Agreement (NAFTA) with the United States and Canada in 1992.

sa·line /sáy leen, -līn/ *adj.* **1. CONTAINING SALT** containing or impregnated with salt **2.** CHEM **CONTAINING SALTS** relating to or containing alkali metal salts or magnesium salt ■ *n.* MED **SOLUTION OF SALT AND DISTILLED WATER** a solution of common salt (**sodium chloride**) and distilled water, especially one having the same concentration as body fluids. It is used as a diluent for drugs and as a plasma substitute. [15thC. From Latin *salinum* "salt cellar," from *sal* "salt" (source of English *salad*).] —**sa·lin·i·ty** /sə línnətee/ *n.*

Sal·in·ger /sállinjər/, **J. D.** (*b.* 1919) U.S. writer. After great success with such works as *The Catcher in the Rye* (1951), in the mid-1960s he became a complete recluse. Full name **Jerome David Salinger**

sal·i·nize /sállə nīz/ (**-nized, -niz·ing, -niz·es**) *vt.* to treat or contaminate something with salt —**sal·i·ni·za·tion** /sàllənə záysh'n/ *n.*

sal·i·nom·e·ter /sàllə nómmətər/ *n.* an instrument used to measure the concentration of salt in salt solutions —**sal·i·no·met·ric** /sàllənə méttrik/ *adj.* —**sal·i·nom·e·try** /-nómmətree/ *n.*

Sa·lique *adj.* = **Salic**

Salis·bur·y /sáwlzbèree, -bree/ city and port in southeastern Maryland, on the Delmarva Peninsula, on the Wicomico River. Population: 21,160 (1996). Former name **Sarum**

Salis·bur·y steak /sáwlz bèrree-/ *n.* a mixture of ground beef, egg, bread crumbs, onion, and seasoning that is formed into a flat round cake, cooked by broiling or frying, and usually served with gravy [Late 19thC. Named for the U.S. physician, J. H. Salisbury, known for his work on food chemistry.]

Sa·lish /sáylish/ *n.* **1. Salish, Salishan** LANG **FAMILY OF NATIVE N AMERICAN LANGUAGES** a family of Native North American languages spoken in the northwestern United States and British Columbia. Around 2,000 people speak one of the remaining 20 Salish languages. **2.** PEOPLES **NATIVE N AMERICANS SPEAKING SALISH LANGUAGES** the group of Native North American peoples who speak the Salish languages (*takes a plural verb*) [Mid-19thC. From Salish *sé'liš* "Flatheads."]

Sa·lish·an *n.* = **Salish** *n.* 1 ■ *adj.* **TYPICAL OF SALISH** relating to or typical of the Salish languages or the Salish peoples and their culture

sa·li·va /sə līvə/ *n.* the clear liquid secreted into the mouth by the salivary glands, consisting of water, mucin, protein, and enzymes. It moistens food and starts the breakdown of starches. [15thC. Via French *salive* and directly from Latin *saliva* "spittle."]

sal·i·var·y /sállə vèrree/ *adj.* relating to saliva or the salivary glands

sal·i·var·y gland *n.* any of the glands in mammals that produce and secrete saliva into the mouth

sal·i·vate /sállə vàyt/ (**-vat·ed, -vat·ing, -vates**) *v.* **1.** *vi.* **PRODUCE SALIVA** to produce saliva in the mouth, especially at an increased rate, e.g., when food is seen, smelled, or expected **2.** *vt.* **CAUSE ANIMAL TO SALIVATE** to cause something, e.g., an animal in an experiment, to produce large amounts of saliva **3.** *vi.* **LONG FOR** to feel or show an immense desire for or appreciation of something (*informal*) ○ *I'm practically salivating over that set of golf clubs in the shop window.* [Mid-17thC. Back-formation from *salivation*, directly and via French from, ultimately, Latin *saliva* "saliva."] —**sal·i·va·tion** /sàllə váysh'n/ *n.*

Salk /sawk, sok/, **Jonas** (1914–95) U.S. physician and epidemiologist. He developed the first vaccine against poliomyelitis. Full name **Jonas Edward Salk**

Jonas Salk

Salk vac·cine *n.* a vaccine against poliomyelitis containing a form of the virus that causes it, which has been made inactive by treatment with a solution of formaldehyde. ◊ **Sabin vaccine** [Mid-20thC. Named for Jonas *Salk*.]

sal·let /sállət/, **sal·et** *n.* a light helmet protecting the head and the back of the neck, worn in the late Middle Ages [15thC. Via French *salade* from, ultimately, Latin *caelata* "engraved (helmet)," from *caelum* "chisel."]

Sal·lie Mae /sàlli máy/ *n.* the Student Loan Marketing Association, the U.S. government agency providing liquidity to the student loan market (*informal*) [From a pronunciation of the acronym *SLMA*]

sal·low[1] /sállō/ *adj.* **UNNATURALLY YELLOW** unnaturally pale and yellowish ○ *a sallow complexion* ■ *vt.* (**-lowed, -low·ing, -lows**) **MAKE SOMETHING SALLOW** to make something unnaturally pale and yellowish ○ *The illness had sallowed her skin.* [Old English *salo* "dark, dusky," from prehistoric Germanic] —**sal·low·ly** *adv.* —**sal·low·ness** *n.*

sal·low[2] /sállō/ (*plural* **-lows** *or* **-low**) *n.* a small European willow tree with broad leaves and large catkins that yields a hard wood used to produce charcoal. Latin name: *Salix caprea.* [Old English *salh.* Ultimately from an Indo-European word meaning "willow," which is also the ancestor of English *salicaceous*.] —**sal·low·y** *adj.*

Sal·lust /sállәst/ (86–35? B.C.) Roman historian. His histories of Catiline's conspiracy and a Roman war in Africa, written after he retired from holding colonial governorships, influenced the work of later historians. Full name **Gaius Sallustius Crispus**

sal·ly /sállee/ *n.* (*plural* **-lies**) **1.** MIL **ATTACK FROM DEFENSIVE POSITION** an offensive thrust from a defensive position, especially, formerly, a sudden attack by the defenders of a besieged position on the people besieging them **2. SUDDEN RUSH FORWARD** a sudden rush or spring forward **3. SUDDEN ACTION** a sudden burst of activity or springing into action **4. SUDDEN EXPRESSION** a sudden outburst of speech or expression of emotion **5. WITTY REMARK** a witty remark, reply, or retort **6. EXPEDITION** an expedition or excursion ■ *vi.* (**-lied, -ly·ing, -lies**) **1.** MIL **MAKE SALLY** to make an offensive thrust from a defensive position **2. SET OUT** to go out after being indoors or set out on a journey or excursion **3. RUSH OUT SUDDENLY** to rush or spring out suddenly [Mid-16thC. From French *saillie*, from the past participle of *saillir* "to leap," ultimately from Latin *salire* (source of English *salient*).] —**sal·li·er** *n.*

Sal·ly Lunn /sàlli lún/ *n.* a sweet bread leavened with yeast that is typically baked in a round pan with a hole in the center and served warm in slices with butter [Late 18thC. Origin uncertain: perhaps named for the woman in Bath, England, who first sold these cakes.]

sal·ly port /sálli pàwrt/ *n.* an opening in a fortification from which the defenders can make sallies

sal·ma·gun·di /sàlmə gúndee/ *n.* **1. MIXED SALAD** a mixed salad of many ingredients, such as meat, poultry, fish, and vegetables, arranged in rows on a platter **2. MIXTURE** a mixture or miscellany (*literary*) [Late 17thC. From French *salmagondis*, originally "seasoned salt meats," of uncertain origin.]

Sal·man·a·zar /sàlmə názzər/, **sal·man·a·zar** *n.* a large wine bottle that holds the equivalent of 12 standard bottles, used especially for champagne [Mid-20thC. From late Latin *Salmanasar*, a variant of *Shalmaneser*, a king of Assyria in the Bible.]

sal·mi /sálmee/, **sal·mis** (*plural* **-mis**) *n.* a dish made from pieces of partly roasted game stewed with mushrooms and served with a rich wine sauce [Mid-18thC. Shortening of French *salmagondis* (see SALMAGUNDI).]

salm·on /sámmən/ (*plural* **-on** *or* **-ons**) *n.* **1.** ZOOL **LARGE ATLANTIC FOOD AND GAME FISH** a large North Atlantic fish, popular for fishing and eating, that has soft fins and pink flesh and migrates up freshwater rivers to spawn. Family: Salmonidae. **2.** ZOOL **LARGE PACIFIC FOOD AND GAME FISH** a food fish of the salmon family found in the North Pacific, e.g., the Chinook, sockeye, coho, or chum. Genus: *Oncorhynchus.* **3.** FOOD **SALMON AS FOOD** the red or pink flesh of the salmon eaten as food **4.** COLORS = **salmon pink** [13thC. Via French *saumon* from Latin *salmon-*, stem of *salmo*, of uncertain origin: perhaps from *salire* "to leap."]

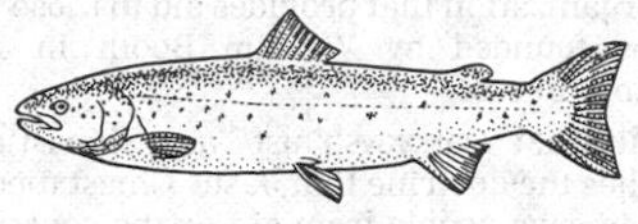

Salmon

Salm·on /sámmən/ river in Idaho flowing into the Snake River on the Washington border. Length: 420 mi./676 km.

salm·on·ber·ry /sámmən bèrree/ (*plural* **-ries**) *n.* **1.** PLANTS **N AMERICAN RASPBERRY** a raspberry plant from the Pacific coast of North America that has showy red flowers and salmon-pink fruit. Latin name: *Rubus spectabilis.* **2.** FOOD **FRUIT OF SALMONBERRY** the edible salmon-pink fruit of the salmonberry

sal·mo·nel·la /sàlmə néllə/ (*plural* **-lae** /-néllee/) *n.* **1.** BIOL **BACTERIUM CAUSING FOOD POISONING** a rod-shaped bacterium found in the intestine that can cause food poisoning, gastroenteritis, and typhoid fever. Genus: *Salmonella.* **2.** MED = **salmonellosis** [Early 20thC. From modern Latin, named for Daniel Elmer *Salmon* (1850–1914), the U.S. veterinary surgeon who isolated a strain of these bacteria.]

sal·mo·nel·lo·sis /sàlmə ne lṓssiss/ *n.* food poisoning caused by infection with salmonella organisms, usually characterized by gastrointestinal upset, diarrhea, fever, and occasionally death. It is usually contracted by eating undercooked contaminated food.

salm·o·nid /sámmənid, sálmə-/ *n.* a bony soft-finned fish belonging to the family that includes salmon, trout, whitefish, and char. Family: Salmonidae.

salm·on pink *n.* a pale orange-pink color, like the flesh of a salmon —**salm·on-pink** *adj.*

Sa·lo·me /sə lṓmee, sállə mày/ *n.* in the New Testament, the daughter of Herodias who demanded and received John the Baptist's head as reward for her dancing before her stepfather, Herod Antipas (Matthew 14:6–11 and Mark 6:21–28)

sa·lom·e·ter /sə lómmətər/ *n.* = **salinometer** [Mid-19thC. Coined from Latin *sal* "salt" + -METER.]

sa·lon /sə lón, sa láwN/ *n.* **1. GRAND SITTING ROOM** an elegantly furnished room in a large house where guests are received and entertained **2. SOCIAL GATHERING OF INTELLECTUALS** a regular gathering of prominent people from the worlds of literature, art, music, or politics, especially one held at the home of a wealthy woman. Salons were especially popular in the 17th, 18th, and 19th centuries. **3. PLACE FOR HAIRDRESSING OR BEAUTY TREATMENTS** a commercial establishment where hairdressers or beauticians work, sometimes part of a larger store or a hotel **4.** FASHION **EXPENSIVE CLOTHES SHOP** a shop selling elegant or fashionable women's clothes, especially expensive designer clothes **5.** ARTS **ART EXHIBITION OR GALLERY** an art exhibition, especially one devoted to the work of living artists, or the hall in which the exhibits are displayed [Late 17thC. Via French from Italian *salone* "large hall," from *sala,* ultimately from prehistoric Germanic.]

Sa·lo·ni·ka /sə lónnikə, sàllə néékə/ = **Thessaloniki**

sa·lon mu·sic *n.* light classical music for easy listening

sa·loon /sə lóon/ *n.* **1. DRINKING PLACE** a commercial establishment serving alcoholic drinks to the general public **2. PART OF SHIP OR TRAIN** a large room on a ship where passengers can sit and relax [Early 18thC. Anglicization of SALON.]

sa·loop /sə lóop/ *n.* a hot drink prepared from aromatic herbs or plant parts such as salep or sassafras, formerly used for medicinal purposes (*archaic*) [Early 18thC. Alteration of French *salep* (see SALEP).]

sa·lo·pettes /sàllə péts/ *npl. U.K.* a garment worn by skiers, comprising a pair of usually padded, water-resistant pants that reach up to the chest with straps passing over the shoulders [Late 20thC. From French.]

salp /salp/, **sal·pa** /sálpə/ (*plural* **-pae** /-pee/ *or* **-pas**) *n.* a tiny free-swimming organism (**tunicate**) that inhabits warm seas and has a transparent barrel-shaped body. Genus: *Salpa.* [Mid-19thC. Via French from modern Latin *salpa* from, ultimately, Greek *salpē* "fish."] —**sal·pi·form** /sálpə fàwrm/ *adj.*

sal·pin·gec·to·my /sàlpin jéktəmee/ (*plural* **-mies**) *n.* the severing or surgical removal of a fallopian tube [Late 19thC. Coined from Greek *salpigg-*, the stem of *salpinx* "trumpet" + -ECTOMY.]

sal·pin·gi·tis /sàlpin jī́tiss/ *n.* inflammation of a fallopian tube [Mid-19thC. Coined from the Greek stem *salpigg-* "trumpet" + -ITIS.] —**sal·pin·git·ic** /sàlpin jíttik/ *adj.*

sal·sa /saálssə/ *n.* **1.** FOOD **SPICY SAUCE** a spicy sauce of finely chopped vegetables including tomatoes, onions, and chilis, eaten with tortilla chips and other Mexican foods **2.** MUSIC **LATIN AMERICAN DANCE MUSIC** a type of Latin American dance music combining elements of jazz and rock with rhythmic African-Cuban melodies **3.** DANCING **DANCE TO SALSA MUSIC** a dance performed to salsa music [Late 20thC. Via Spanish, "sauce," from Latin, "salted," from the past participle of *sallere* "to salt," from *sal* "salt" (source of English *sauce*).]

sal·si·fy /sálssəfee, -fī/ (*plural* **-fies** *or* **-fy**) *n.* **1.** PLANTS **EUROPEAN HERB WITH EDIBLE ROOT** a European composite plant that has leaves resembling grass, purple flowers, and a long edible root. Latin name: *Tragopogon porrifolius.* **2.** FOOD **ROOT EATEN AS VEGETABLE** the long pale edible root of the salsify plant, which can be eaten boiled or fried as a vegetable [Early 18thC. Via French *salsifis* from Italian *salsefica,* of unknown origin.]

sal so·da *n.* = **washing soda**

salt /sawlt/ *n.* **1.** FOOD **WHITE CRYSTALS USED IN FOOD PREPARATION** a substance, usually in the form of small white crystals, with a sharp tangy taste that is used to season or preserve food. Salt consists mainly of sodium chloride and is abundant in sea water. ◊ **sodium chloride 2.** CHEM **CRYSTALLINE CHEMICAL COMPOUND** a crystalline chemical compound formed as a result of the neutralization of an acid by a base containing a metal or group acting like a metal **3. SOMETHING THAT ADDS ZEST** something that adds zest, piquancy, liveliness, or vigor **4. DRY WIT** sharp or dry wit **5.** = **old salt 6.** HOUSEHOLD = **saltcellar** ■ **salts** *npl.* **SUBSTANCE RESEMBLING SALT** a chemical or crystalline solution used for a particular purpose ○ *smelling salts* ■ *adj.* **1. PRESERVED WITH SALT** preserved with salt or a salt solution ○ *salt cod* **2. CONTAINING SALT** containing or consisting of salt ○ *salt tears* **3. CONTAINING OR ASSOCIATED WITH SALT WATER** containing, covered with, or growing near salt water **4. TASTING OF SALT** tasting or smelling of salt ■ *vt.* (**salt·ed, salt·ing, salts**) **1. SEASON FOOD WITH SALT** to add salt to food, during or after preparation, to emphasize its flavor **2. PRESERVE FOOD WITH SALT** to preserve food by treating it with salt or a salt solution **3. PUT SALT ON COLD GROUND** to scatter salt over a road or sidewalk to melt ice or prevent it from forming **4. ADD ZEST TO SOMETHING** to add a more lively or entertaining quality to something ○ *She salted her speech with jokes.* **5.** MINING **ENRICH ORE SAMPLE** to enrich a mining area or sample with a valuable ore artificially introduced in order to increase its apparent value [Old English *sealt.* Ultimately from an Indo-European word meaning "salt."] —**salt·ness** *n.* ◇ **rub salt in the wound** to add to somebody's distress, embarrassment, or sense of shame, often deliberately ◇ **take something with a grain** *or* **pinch of salt** to listen to something without fully believing it ◇ **the salt of the earth** a very good, worthy person or group of people ◇ **worth your salt** efficient and doing the job well

WORD KEY: ORIGIN

The Indo-European ancestor of *salt* is also the ultimate source of English *halogen, salad, salami, salary, saline, sauce, saucer, sausage, silt,* and *souse,* and also of the *cellar* of *saltcellar.*

salt away *vt.* to hoard or save money for future use, often secretly or illegally [Origin uncertain: probably from the practice of preserving food in salt]

salt out *vt.* to cause a dissolved substance to come out of solution by adding a salt

SALT /sawlt/ *abbr.* Strategic Arms Limitation Talks (or Treaty)

salt-and-pep·per *adj.* = **pepper-and-salt**

sal·ta·rel·lo /saàltə réllō, sàwltə-/ (*plural* **-los** *or* **-li** /-réllee/) *n.* **1.** DANCE **QUICK DANCE WITH MEDIEVAL ORIGINS** a quick dance in triple meter dating from the medieval period and especially popular in Spain and Italy **2.** MUSIC **MUSIC FOR SALTARELLO DANCE** a piece of music for a saltarello [Late 16thC. Via Italian from, ultimately, Latin *saltare* "to dance," (see SALTATION).]

sal·ta·tion /sal táysh'n, sawl-/ *n.* **1. JUMPING OR JUMP** leaping or jumping, or a sudden jump or leap (*formal*) **2. SUDDEN CHANGE** development or transition that takes place in jumps or leaps (*formal*) **3.** BIOL **ABRUPT EVOLUTIONARY DEVELOPMENT** the abrupt evolutionary development of a new species or property, especially as a result of genetic mutation **4.** GEOL **JUMPING MOTION OF PARTICLES** the transportation of particles of soil or sand in the wind or in running water, characterized by bouncing movements [Early 17thC. From the Latin stem *saltation-*, from *saltare* literally "to keep leaping," from *salire* "to leap" (source of English *salient*).]

sal·ta·to·ri·al /sàltə táwree əl, sàwltə-/, **sal·ta·to·ry** /sáltə tàwree, sáwltə-, sóltə-/ *adj.* **1.** ZOOL **RELATING TO JUMPING** relating to or adapted for jumping ○ *an insect with saltatorial legs* **2. ASSOCIATED WITH JUMPING OR DANCING** associated with or involving jumping, leaping, or dancing **3. DEVELOPING IN JUMPS OR LEAPS** involving or characterized by sudden change rather than gradual transition

salt·box /sáwlt bòks/ *n.* **1. BOX FOR SALT** a box in which salt is stored, especially one with a sloping lid **2.** ARCHIT **FRAME HOUSE DESIGN** a wood-frame house that has two floors at the front but only one in the back, and with a long, typically broken rear slope to the roof

salt·bush /sáwlt bòosh/ (*plural* **-bush·es** *or* **-bush**) *n.* = **orach**

salt cake *n.* an impure form of sodium sulfate used in the manufacture of glass, paper pulp, soap, and ceramic glazes

salt·cel·lar /sáwlt sèllər/ *n.* a small container for salt, especially one used at the table to season food after it is served

salt·chuck /sáwlt chùk/ *n. Can* a stretch of salt water flowing into a freshwater lake or river

salt·chuck·er /sáwlt chùkər/ *n. Can* an angler who fishes in salt water

salt de·ple·tion *n.* the dangerous loss of salt from the body by excessive sweating, diarrhea, and vomiting, causing muscular weakness and cramps

salt dome *n.* a dome-shaped structure formed in sedimentary rock when buried salt deposits move up through overlying rocks, owing to their low density and high buoyancy

salt·ed /sáwltəd/ *adj.* **1. TREATED WITH SALT** with salt added for seasoning, preservation, or some other purpose **2. HARDENED OR EXPERIENCED** hardened or experienced, e.g., in a trade or profession

salt·er /sáwltər/ *n.* **1. DEALER IN SALT** somebody who produces or sells salt **2. SOMEBODY TREATING FOOD WITH SALT** somebody who treats food with salt to preserve it

salt·ern /sáwltərn/ *n.* **1.** INDUST **SALTWORKS** a place wherre salt is produced commercially **2.** GEOG **SOURCE OF SALT PRODUCED BY EVAPORATION** a place where salt is produced naturally when pools of sea water evaporate [Old English, from *sealt* (see SALT) + *ærn* "building" (source of English *barn*)]

salt·fish /sáwlt fish/ *n. Carib* cod or other fish preserved with salt

salt flat *n.* a broad flat area in hot deserts encrusted with salt left after the evaporation of water from shallow saline lakes (*often used in the plural*)

salt gland *n.* a gland in certain marine animals, e.g., birds or reptiles, used to excrete excess ingested salt

salt glaze *n.* a glaze formed by throwing salt into a kiln during the firing process

salt grass *n.* any grass native to salt marshes or alkaline regions

salt hay *n.* hay produced from salt grass, used as fodder

Sal·ti·llo /sal téel yō/ capital of Coahuila State in northern Mexico, founded in 1575. Population: 420,845 (1990).

sal·tim·boc·ca /saàltim bṓkə, sàwl-, -bókə/ *n.* a dish consisting of thin slices of veal rolled up with prosciutto ham and fresh sage leaves, lightly fried and braised in white wine [Mid-20thC. From Italian, from *saltare* "to leap" + *in* "into" + *bocca* "mouth."]

sal·tine /sawl teen/ *n.* a thin crisp cracker sprinkled with salt

sal·tire /sál tìr, sáwl-/ *n.* one of the basic designs used on coats of arms consisting of a diagonal cross [15thC. Via Old French *sau(l)toir* "stirrup, style" from, ultimately, Latin *saltare* (see SALTATION).]

salt lake *n.* a lake with no outlet and having a high salt content as a result of evaporation, e.g., the Dead Sea

Salt Lake Ci·ty capital city of Utah, located in the northern central part of the state, 15 mi./24 km east of the Great Salt Lake. Population: 171,849 (1994).

salt lick *n.* **1. PLACE WHERE ANIMALS LICK SALT DEPOSITS** a place where animals go to lick salt deposits that occur naturally **2. SALT FED TO FARM ANIMALS** a block of salt or other preparation that livestock lick in order to supplement their salt intake. It may also contain other essential minerals such as magnesium or iodine.

salt marsh *n.* a marshy grassland area regularly flooded with salt water

Sal·ton Sea /sáwlt'n-/ saltwater lake in southern California, formed when the Colorado River flooded in 1905. Area: 360 sq. mi./932 sq. km.

salt·pan /sáwlt pàn/ *n.* a basin in a semiarid region where salts are precipitated after saline floodwaters evaporate

salt·pe·ter /sàwlt peetər/ *n.* **1.** = **Chile saltpeter 2.** = **potassium nitrate** [14thC. Alteration, influenced by SALT, of *salpetre*, from, ultimately, Latin *sal* "salt" + *petra* "rock," from its appearance as a crust on rock.]

salt pork *n.* a fat cut of pork from the belly, back, or sides, cured by salting

salt·shak·er /sáwlt shàykər/ *n.* a small container with holes in the top for sprinking salt over food at the table

salt·wa·ter /sáwlt wàwtər, -wòttər/ *adj.* **1. OF SALT WATER** containing or involving salt water **2.** BIOL **LIVING IN SALT WATER** living or growing in salt water

salt wa·ter *n.* **1. WATER CONTAINING SALT** water containing a lot of salt **2. SEAWATER** the water of the sea and coastal inlets

salt·wa·ter croc·o·dile *n.* a large crocodile that inhabits the coastal waterways of northern Australia and Southeast Asia and feeds on fish, birds, reptiles, and small mammals. Latin name: *Crocodylus porosus.*

salt·works /sáwlt wùrks/ *n.* a place or factory where salt is produced commercially (*takes a singular or plural verb*)

salt·wort /sáwlt wùrt, -wàwrt/ (*plural* **-worts** *or* **-wort**) *n.* a plant of the goosefoot family with prickly leaves and small flowers that is native to seashores. Genus: *Salsosa.*

salt·y /sáwltee/ (**-i·er, -i·est**) *adj.* **1. TASTING OF SALT** containing or tasting of salt **2. OF SEA OR SAILORS** associated with the sea or with nautical life **3. LIVELY AND AMUSING** lively, amusing, and sometimes mildly indecent ○ *salty jokes* —**salt·i·ly** *adv.* —**salt·i·ness** *n.*

sa·lu·bri·ous /sə lóobree əss/ *adj.* beneficial to or promoting health or well-being (*formal*) [Mid-16thC. Formed from Latin *salubris*, from *salus* "health" (source of English *salutary* and *salute*).] —**sa·lu·bri·ous·ly** *adv.* —**sa·lu·bri·ous·ness** *n.* —**sa·lu·bri·ty** *n.*

Sa·lu·da /sè lóodè/ river in South Carolina, rising in the Blue Ridge Mountains and flowing into the Congaree River. Length: 200 mi./322 km.

sa·lu·ki /sə lóokee/ *n.* a tall slender dog belonging to a breed originally developed in Arabia and Egypt. It has a smooth coat and long fur on the ears and tail. [Early 19thC. From Arabic *salūkī*, from *Salūk*, a town in Yemen.]

sal·u·tar·y /sállyə tèrree/ *adj.* **1. USEFUL** of value or benefit to somebody or something ○ *We asked if military service had been a salutary experience for him.* **2. HEALTHFUL** promoting good health (*formal*) [15thC. Directly or via French *salutaire* from Latin *salutaris*, from *salus* "health" (source of English *salubrious*).] —**sal·u·tar·i·ly** *adv.* —**sal·u·tar·i·ness** *n.*

sal·u·ta·tion /sàllyə táysh'n/ *n.* **1. SIGN OF GREETING** a gesture or phrase that is used to greet, welcome, or recognize somebody **2. ACT OF GREETING SOMEBODY** the expression of greetings, welcome, or recognition **3. OPENING GREETING** the opening phrase of a letter or speech, used to address the recipient or audience, e.g., "Dear Sir or Madam" or "Ladies and Gentlemen" ■ *interj.* **sal·u·ta·tions** *npl.* **GREETINGS** greetings or regards (*formal*) ○ *Salutations from us all!* —**sal·u·ta·tion·al** *adj.*

sa·lu·ta·to·ri·an /sə lòotə táwree ən/ *n.* a student in a graduating class who is second highest in academic ranking, usually required to give a salutatory at the graduation ceremony

sa·lu·ta·to·ry /sə lóotə tàwree/ *adj.* **EXPRESSING GREETINGS** expressing or conveying greetings ■ *n.* (*plural* **-ries**) **WELCOMING SPEECH AT GRADUATION** a welcoming speech, especially one given at a graduation ceremony

sa·lute /sə lóot/ *v.* (**-lut·ed, -lut·ing, -lutes**) **1.** *vti.* MIL **GIVE FORMAL SIGN OF RESPECT** to formally signal respect to another member of the armed forces or to a flag, usually by raising the right hand to the forehead or by presenting arms **2.** *vt.* **GREET SOMEBODY** to greet, welcome, or acknowledge somebody, either with a gesture or in words **3.** *vt.* **FORMALLY PRAISE OR HONOR SOMEBODY** to praise or honor somebody for something, especially in a formal ceremony ○ *We salute you for your contribution.* ■ *n.* **1. GESTURE OF RESPECT** a gesture used by members of the armed forces and some other organized groups as a formal sign of respect **2. FIRING GUNS AS MILITARY HONOR** a military display of honor for a dignitary or on a special occasion, e.g., the firing of guns into the air at the funeral of an officer ○ *a 21-gun salute* **3. ACT OF SALUTING** an act or an occasion of saluting [14thC. From Latin *salutare*, from *salut-*, stem of *salus* "health" (source of English *salubrious*).] —**sa·lut·er** *n.*

sal·va·ble /sálvəb'l/ *adj.* capable of being saved or salvaged (*formal*) [Mid-17thC. Formed from late Latin *salvare* "to save" (see SALVAGE).]

Sal·va·dor /sálvèdawr/ port and capital city of Bahia State in eastern Brazil, on the Atlantic Ocean. Population: 2,209,465 (1996).

Sal·va·dor, El ♦ **El Salvador**

Sal·va·do·ran /sàlvə dáwrən/, **Sal·va·do·ri·an** /sàlvə dáwree ən/, **Sal·va·do·re·an** *n.* **SOMEBODY FROM EL SALVADOR** somebody who was born or raised in El Salvador, or who is a citizen of El Salvador ■ *adj.* **OF EL SALVADOR** relating to or typical of El Salvador or its people or culture

sal·vage /sálvij/ *vt.* (**-vaged, -vag·ing, -vag·es**) **1. SAVE SOMETHING FOR FURTHER USE** to save used, damaged, or rejected goods for recycling or further use ○ *Maybe we can salvage some spare parts from your old car.* **2. RESCUE SOMETHING FROM BAD SITUATION** to save something of worth or merit from a situation or event that is otherwise a failure **3. SAVE SOMETHING FROM DESTRUCTION** to save a ship, cargo, crew, or other property or goods from destruction or loss (*often passive*) ○ *They salvaged what they could from the wreckage.* ■ *n.* **1. RESCUE OF PROPERTY FROM DESTRUCTION** the rescue of property or goods from destruction or loss, e.g., because of a flood or fire **2.** SHIPPING **RESCUE OF SHIP FROM SEA** the rescue of a ship, its cargo, or crew from loss at sea **3. RESCUED GOODS** something such as a ship or goods that have been saved from destruction or loss ○ *a salvage yard* **4. SOMETHING REUSED** something that would otherwise be destroyed or discarded but is recycled or put to further use **5. PAYMENT TO RESCUERS** payment made to volunteers who help in the rescue of ships, property, or goods from destruction or loss **6. MONEY FROM SALE OF RESCUED GOODS** money from the sale of goods or property that have been saved from destruction or loss [Mid-17thC. Via French from, ultimately, late Latin *salvare* "to save," from Latin *salvus* "safe."] —**sal·vage·a·bil·i·ty** /sàlvijə billətee/ *n.* —**sal·vage·a·ble** /sálvijəb'l/ *adj.* —**sal·vag·er** *n.*

sal·va·tion /sal váysh'n/ *n.* **1. ACT OF SAVING FROM HARM** the saving of somebody or something from harm, destruction, difficulty, or failure ○ *The business was clearly beyond salvation.* **2. MEANS OF SAVING SOMEBODY OR SOMETHING** somebody or something that protects or delivers somebody or something else from harm, destruction, difficulty, or failure ○ *Those long walks were my salvation.* **3.** CHR **DELIVERANCE FROM SIN THROUGH JESUS CHRIST** in the Christian religion, deliverance from sin or the consequences of sin through Jesus Christ's death on the cross **4. CHRISTIAN SCIENCE PHILOSOPHY OF LIFE** in the Christian Science religion, belief in the supremacy of life, truth, and love, and in their destruction of such illusions as sin, illness, and death [13thC. Via Old French *salvacion* from, ultimately, Latin *salvare* "to save" (see SALVAGE).] —**sal·va·tion·al** *adj.*

Sal·va·tion Ar·my *n.* a worldwide evangelical Christian organization that provides aid to those in need. It was founded by William Booth in London, England, in 1865.

sal·va·tion·ist /sal váysh'nist/ *n.* a Christian who preaches the doctrine that Jesus Christ died on the cross to save people from sin or the consequences of sin —**sal·va·tion·ism** *n.*

Sal·va·tion·ist *n.* a member of the Salvation Army

salve[1] /sav, salv/ *n.* **1. SOOTHING OINTMENT** an ointment for soothing or healing wounds or sores **2. SOMETHING THAT SOOTHES OR CALMS** anything that eases pain or anxiety ○ *Her forgiveness was a salve to my conscience.* ■ *vt.* (**salved, salv·ing, salves**) **EASE PAIN OR WORRY** to soothe or ease pain or anxiety ○ *salve your wounded pride* [Old English *salf*, of prehistoric Germanic origin]

salve[2] /salv/ (**salved, salv·ing, salves**) *vt.* to save something from destruction or loss [Early 18thC. Back-formation from SALVAGE.] —**sal·vor** /sálvər, sál vàwr/ *n.*

sal·ver /sálvər/ *n.* a tray, especially a silver one, used to serve food or drinks, or to present things such as letters or visiting cards [Mid-17thC. Via French *save* "tray for presenting things to the king" from, ultimately, late Latin *salvare* "to save" (see SALVAGE).]

sal·ver·form /sálvər fàwrm/ *adj.* used to describe the corolla of a flower with joined petals that is long and tube-shaped with a spreading upper part

sal·vi·a /sálvee ə/ (*plural* **-as** *or* **-a**) *n.* an ornamental plant of the mint family with opposite leaves and whorled red flowers, each of which has a two-lipped corolla and two anthers. Latin name: *Salvia splendens.* [Mid-19thC. Via modern Latin *Salvia*, genus name, from Latin *salvia* "sage," from *salvus* "safe."]

sal·vif·ic /sal víffik/ *adj.* having the power or desire to bring salvation (*formal*) [Late 16thC. From late Latin *salvificus*, from Latin *salvus* "safe."]

sal·vo[1] /sálvō/ (*plural* **-vos** *or* **-voes**) *n.* **1. SIMULTANEOUS DISCHARGE OF WEAPONS** the firing of several weapons simultaneously, especially at a formal military ceremony **2. HEAVY BURST OF FIRING OR BOMBING** a concentrated burst of firing or bombing from several different sources during a battle **3. NUMBER OF BOMBS RELEASED AT ONCE** a number of bombs or projectiles released simultaneously **4. OUTBURST** a sudden burst of applause or cheering ○ *a salvo of applause* **5. VERBAL ATTACK** a vigorous written or spoken attack ○ *a blistering salvo* [Late 16thC. Via French *salve* or Italian *salva* "greeting, salutation" from, ultimately, Latin *salvus* "safe."]

sal·vo[2] /sálvō/ (*plural* **-vos**) *n.* something that is used to save a reputation or soothe somebody's conscience or wounded pride [Early 17thC. From Latin, a form of *salvus* "safe."]

sal vo·la·tile /sàl və látt'lee/ *n.* **1.** = **ammonium carbonate 2. SMELLING SALTS** a solution of ammonium carbonate in alcohol and ammonia in water, often mixed with aromatic oils, that is used as smelling salts [Mid-17thC. From modern Latin, literally "volatile salt."]

Sal·ween /sálween/ river in Southeast Asia, flowing through China, including Tibet, and Myanmar (Burma). Length: 1,800 mi./2,900 km.

Salz·burg /sáltsburg, záaltsberg/ capital city of Salzburg Province in western Austria. The Salzburg Festival, which concentrates on the music of Mozart, who was born in the city, is held there annually. Population: 143,978 (1991).

Salz·git·ter /záalts gitər/ city in Lower Saxony State, northern central Germany, situated 105 mi./169 km south of Hamburg. Population: 117,700 (1994).

SAM /sam, èss ay ém/ *abbr.* surface-to-air missile

Sam. *abbr.* BIBLE Samuel

Sa·mar·i·a /sə márree ə/ ancient city and state in Palestine, located north of present-day Jerusalem, east of the Mediterranean Sea —**Sam·ar·i·an** *n., adj.*

Sa·mar·i·tan /sə mérrətən/ *n.* **1.** PEOPLES **SOMEBODY FROM SAMARIA** somebody who was born in or was a citizen of Samaria **2. SOMEBODY WHO HELPS THOSE IN NEED** somebody who helps others who are in difficulty, without expecting any reward or recognition. = **Good Samaritan** [Pre-12thC. Via late Latin *Samaritanus* from, ultimately, Greek *Samareia* "Samaria."] —**Sa·mar·i·tan·ism** *n.*

sa·mar·i·um /sə máiree əm/ *n.* a silvery-gray metallic chemical element that is found in monazite and bastnaesite and is used particularly in making strong magnets. It is also used in carbon-arc lighting, as a dopant for laser materials, and as a neutron absorber. Symbol **Sm** [Late 19thC. Coined from SAMARSKITE + -IUM.]

Sa·mar·kand /sámmər kànd/, **Sa·mar·qand** capital city of Samarkand Oblast, central Uzbekistan. Located in the valley of the Zeravshan River, it is the oldest city in central Asia. Population: 371,000 (1991).

sa·mar·skite /sə maar skīt, sámmər-/ *n.* a black mineral that contains uranium and a mix of rare-earth elements and is found in pegmatites [Mid-19thC. Named for the Russian mining engineer V. E. Samarskii-Vykhovets (1803–70).]

Sa·ma-Ve·da /saàmə váydə/ *n.* one of the four collections of chants (**Veda**) used during Hindu sacrifices. It contains songs based on the Rig-Veda with instructions on their recitation. [Late 18thC. From Sanskrit, formed from *sāman* "chant" + *vedaḥ* "knowledge" (see RIG-VEDA).]

sam·ba /sámbə, saàmbə/ *n.* **1.** DANCE **BRAZILIAN DANCE** a lively Brazilian ballroom dance with strong African influences **2.** MUSIC **MUSIC FOR SAMBA** a piece of music in 4/4 time written for the samba ■ *vi.* (**-baed, -ba·ing, -bas**) DANCE **DANCE THE SAMBA** to dance the samba [Late 19thC. From Portuguese, of uncertain origin: perhaps from an African language.]

sam·bal /saàm baàl, saam baàl/, **sam·bol** *n.* a spicy condiment or relish of Southeast Asia made of chili, spices, vinegar, tomato, onion, and other vegetables [Early 19thC. From Malay.]

sam·bar /sámbər, saàmbər/ (*plural* **-bars** *or* **-bar**), **sam·bur** (*plural* **-burs** *or* **-bur**) *n.* a large deer that has a reddish-brown coat and three-pronged antlers. It is native to Southeast Asia. Latin name: *Cervus unicolor.* [Late 17thC. Via Hindi *sāmbar* from Sanskrit *śambaraḥ.*]

sam·bo /sámbō/, **sam·bo wres·tling** *n.* a form of wrestling based on judo that originated in the former Soviet Union and is now practiced internationally [Mid-20thC. An acronym from Russian *samozashchita bez oruzhiya,* literally "unarmed self-defence."] —**sam·bo wres·tler** *n.*

sam·bol *n.* = **sambal**

Sam Browne belt /sàm brówn-/, **Sam Browne** *n.* a wide belt supported by a diagonal strap that passes from the left-hand side over the right shoulder, worn as part of military or police uniforms [Named for the British military commander Sir *Samuel Browne* (1824–1901), who invented it]

sam·bu·ca /sam bóokə, -byóokə/ *n.* an Italian liqueur made from elderberries and flavored with licorice or aniseed [Late 20thC. Via Italian from Latin *sambucus* "elder tree."]

sam·bur *n.* = **sambar**

same /saym/ CORE MEANING: a word indicating that one thing or person is involved rather than two or more different things or people ○ *I can't drive and talk at the same time.* ○ *two men in love with the same woman* ○ *He lives on the same street as I do.*

1. *adj., pron.* **PREVIOUSLY MENTIONED** previously mentioned, or as previously described (*used as pronoun without "the" in business contexts*) ○ *She left because she was bored, and I left two months later for the same reason.* ○ *Wool should always be washed carefully. The same applies to silk.* **2.** *adj., pron., adv.* **IDENTICAL** resembling something exactly ○ *They turned up at the party wearing the same dress.* ○ *All the houses looked exactly the same.* ○ *Look – their curtains are the same as ours!* ○ *All the experts say the same.* **3.** *adj.* **UNCHANGED** unchanged or unchanging ○ *After the accident, he just wasn't the same person.* ○ *The house looked the same as always.* ○ *I want things to stay the same.* [12thC. From Old Norse *samr.* Ultimately from an Indo-European base meaning "one," which is also the ancestor of English *simple* and *homo-*.] ◇ **the same as** in the identical way that (*informal*) ○ *He wants to win, the same as I do.*

WORD KEY: USAGE

We have received your order and have pleasure in completing same. This use of ***same*** as a pronoun is characteristic of commercial language and is not normally suitable for general use, except for special or humorous effect: *She poured out a large glass of water and drank same.*

sa·mekh /saà mèk, -mèkh/ *n.* the 15th letter of the Hebrew alphabet, represented in the English alphabet as "s." See table at **alphabet** [Early 19thC. From Hebrew *sāmekh,* literally "a support."]

same·ness /sáymnəss/ *n.* **1. QUALITY OF BEING THE SAME** the quality or condition of being very similar or the same ○ *There was a sameness about the two accounts.* **2. LACK OF VARIETY** a lack of variety or change ○ *There's a certain sameness about all his paintings.*

same-sex *adj.* homosexual or lesbian ○ *involved in a same-sex relationship*

Sam Hill /sàm híl/, **sam hill** *n.* used for emphasis, especially in questions, as a euphemism for "hell" (*slang*) ○ *What the Sam Hill is wrong with my computer?* [Mid-19thC. Origin unknown.]

Sa·mi·an /sáymee ən/ *n.* PEOPLES somebody who was born or raised on the Greek island of Samos —**Sa·mi·an** *adj.*

sam·iel /saàm yèl, səm yél/ *n.* METEOROL = **simoom** [Late 17thC. From Turkish *samyeli,* literally "poisonous wind."]

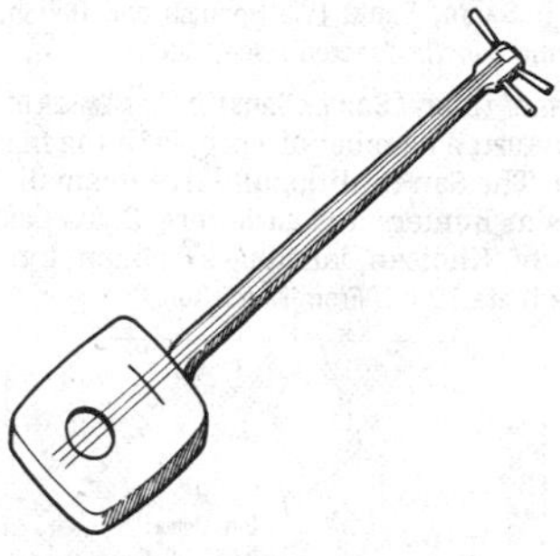

Samisen

sam·i·sen /sámmi sèn/ *n.* a Japanese three-stringed musical instrument that has a long fretless neck and is played with a plectrum [Early 17thC. Via Japanese from Chinese *sānxián* literally "three strings."]

sam·ite /sá mīt, sáy-/ *n.* a heavy silk fabric, often interwoven with gold or silver threads, that was used for clothing in the Middle Ages [12thC. Via Old French *samit* and medieval Latin *examitum* from, ultimately, Greek *hexamiton* literally "six threads."]

sa·miz·dat /saàmiz dàt, -daàt/ *n.* **1. UNDERGROUND PUBLISHING IN FORMER USSR** in the former Soviet Union, the printing and distribution of secret or banned literature **2. BANNED LITERATURE** literature produced by the samizdat system **3. SECRET PRINTING PRESS** a secret printing press, especially in the former Soviet Union [Mid-20thC. From Russian, formed from *sam-* "self" + *izdatel'stvo* "publishing house."]

sam·let /sámmlət/ *n.* a young salmon, feeding in fresh water [Mid-17thC. Contraction of *salmonlet.*]

Sam·nite /sám nīt/ *n.* **MEMBER OF PEOPLE IN ANCIENT ITALY** a member of an ancient people who occupied an area of central and southern Italy known as Samnium. They repeatedly tried to spread into territory held by Rome during the 4th and 3rd centuries B.C. and were eventually defeated by the Romans around 290 B.C. ■ *adj.* **OF THE SAMNITES** relating to the Samnites, or their culture or empire ○ *the Samnite Wars* [14th C. From Latin *Samnites* "the Samnites."]

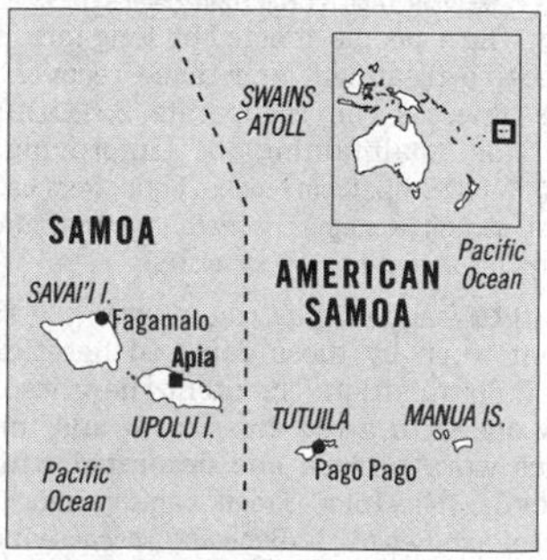

Samoa

Sa·mo·a /sə mṓ ə/ independent island state in the southern Pacific Ocean, situated west of American Samoa. Language: Samoan, English. Currency: tala. Capital: Apia. Population: 167,400 (1996). Area: 1,093 sq. mi./2,831 sq. km. Official name **Independent State of Samoa.** Former name **Western Samoa**

Sa·mo·an /sə mṓ ən/ *n.* **1.** PEOPLES **SOMEBODY FROM SAMOA** somebody who was born or raised in Samoa or is a citizen of American Samoa or the Independent State of Samoa **2.** LANG **LANGUAGE OF SAMOA** the language of Samoa, belonging to the Polynesian family of languages. About 300,000 people speak Samoan. —**Sa·mo·an** *adj.*

Sa·mos /sáymoss/ Greek island in the Aegean Sea, separated from the southwestern coast of Turkey by the narrow Samos Strait. Population: 41,965 (1991). Area: 195 sq. mi./505 sq. km.

sa·mo·sa /sə mṓssə, sə móssə/ (*plural* **-sas** *or* **-sa**) *n.* an Indian snack consisting of a thin pastry case filled with spiced vegetables or meat and then deep-fried [Mid-20thC. From Urdu.]

Sam·o·thrace /sámmè thrayss/ Greek island in the northeastern Aegean Sea, situated 25 mi./40 km from mainland Greece. Population: 2,871 (1981). Area: 69 sq. mi./178 sq. km.

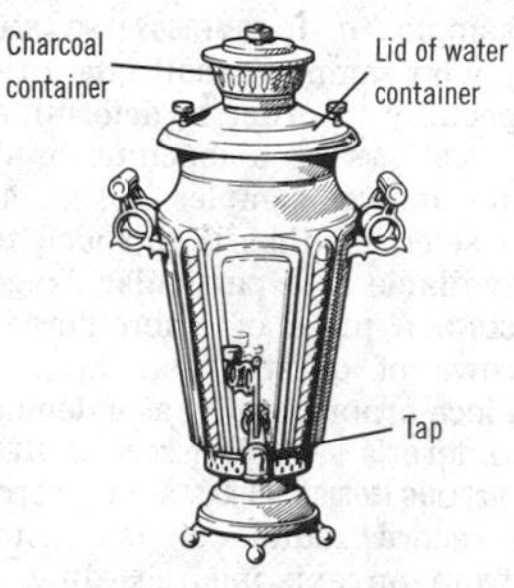

Samovar

sam·o·var /sámmə vaàr/ *n.* a large and often ornate Russian tea urn. In older models the water was heated by a built-in charcoal burner, but many modern models are electrically operated. [Mid-19thC. From Russian, formed from *samo-* "self" + *varit* "to boil."]

Sam·o·yed /sámmə yèd, sám oy-/ *n.* **1.** (*plural* **-yeds** *or* **-yed**) PEOPLES **MEMBER OF A SIBERIAN PEOPLE** a member of a people living traditionally as reindeer herders in far northeastern European Russia and western Siberia **2.** LANG **SAMOYED LANGUAGE** the group of languages spoken by the Samoyed peoples. They belong to the Uralic family of languages, are related to Finno-Ugric, and are sometimes classified as belonging to the Ural-Altaic group. **3.** ZOOL **SIBERIAN DOG** a dog belonging to a Siberian breed that has a thick creamy-white coat, distinctive ruff, and tightly-curled tail [Late 16thC. From Russian.] —**Sam·o·yed** *adj.*

samp /samp/ *n. New England* cornmeal mush [Mid-17thC. From Algonquian *nasàump.*]

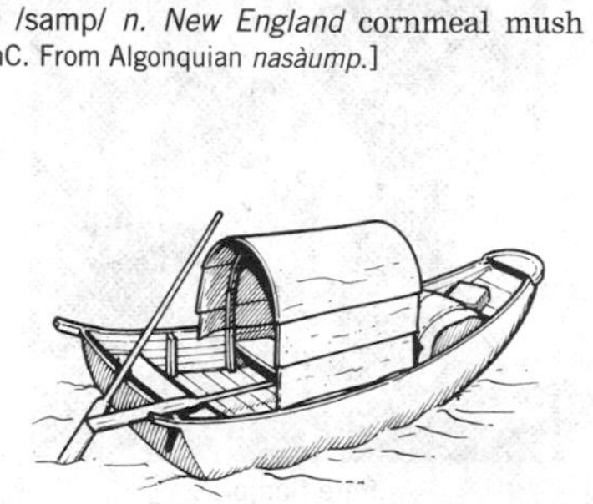

Sampan

sam·pan /sám pàn/ *n.* a small flat-bottomed boat (**skiff**) propelled by two oars or a single rear-mounted oar (**scull**) [Early 17thC. From Chinese *sānbǎn,* literally "three-board (boat)."]

sam·phire /sám fīr/ (*plural* **-phires** *or* **-phire**) *n.* **1. EUROPEAN PLANT WITH WHITE FLOWERS** a European coastal plant that has small white flowers, and fleshy leaves that are used in pickles. Latin name: *Crithmum maritimum.* **2.** = **glasswort** [Mid-16thC. Contraction of French *herbe de Saint Pierre.*]

sam·ple /sámp'l/ *n.* **1. EXAMPLE OF SOMETHING** a small amount of something, used as an example of more general character, features, or quality ○ *a free sample of the new shampoo* **2.** **SPECIMEN FOR ANALYSIS** a small part or quantity of something, e.g., blood or soil, for scientific or medical examination or analysis ○ *took a blood sample* **3.** RECORDING **PIECE OF RECORDED SOUND** a piece of recorded sound or a musical phrase taken from an existing recording, especially in digital form, used as part of a new recording ○ *a CD of drum samples* **4.** STATS **GROUP SELECTED FOR TESTING** a representative selection of a population that is examined to gain statistical information about the whole ■ *vti.* (**-pled, -pling, -ples**) **1.** **GET A SAMPLE OF SOMETHING** to take a sample of something, especially to determine its character, features, or quality ○ *sample the river water* **2.** RECORDING **TAKE SAMPLE OF SOMETHING FOR RECORDING** to take a sample of recorded music, especially in order to use it in another recording ○ *sampled whatever albums happened to be lying around* **3.** RECORDING **CONVERT SOUND INTO DIGITAL INFORMATION** to convert sound into digital information in order to store or manipulate it electronically [13thC. Shortening of Norman French *assample* "example."]

sam·pler /sámplər/ *n.* **1.** **SOMEBODY WHO ANALYZES SAMPLES** somebody who samples small quantities of something, especially in order to determine quality **2.** **DEVICE FOR TAKING SAMPLES** a machine or device used to take and analyze samples **3.** STATS **REPRESENTATIVE SELECTION** a selection that is intended to represent what is available in a particular range **4.** SEW **EMBROIDERED CLOTH** a piece of embroidered cloth containing rows of different stitches, either as a practice piece or, originally, as a demonstration of the embroiderer's skill **5.** RECORDING **ELECTRONIC EQUIPMENT FOR SAMPLING MUSICAL PHRASES** an electronic device that can record sounds or take short musical phrases from an existing recording, and allows them to be manipulated digitally before being used to make a new recording **6.** RECORDING **MACHINE CONVERTING SOUND TO DIGITAL INFORMATION** an electronic device that converts sound to digital information for electronic storage or manipulation

sam·ple space *n.* the set of all possible outcomes of a statistical experiment, represented by points

sam·pling /sámpling/ *n.* **1.** **PROCESS OF SELECTING SAMPLE GROUP** the process of selecting a group of people or products to be used as a representative or random sample **2.** **SOMETHING USED AS A SAMPLE** a small part, number, or quantity of something that has been taken or selected as a sample **3.** RECORDING **REUSE OF RECORDED MUSICAL PHRASES** the process of taking a short musical phrase from one recording and using it in another recording, often in repeated sequences and sometimes in an adapted or edited form ○ *recent advances in sampling technology*

Pete Sampras

Sam·pras /sámprəss/, **Pete** (*b.* 1971) U.S. tennis player. At 19, he became the youngest player to win the U.S. Open championship. He was ranked the world's number one player in 1993 and 1994. Full name **Peter Sampras**. Known as **Pistol Pete**

sam·sa·ra /səm saárə/ *n.* **1.** **HINDU CYCLE OF DEATH AND REBIRTH** in Hinduism, the endless cycle of birth, life, death, and rebirth **2.** **REBIRTH** in Buddhism, somebody's rebirth [Late 19thC. From Sanskrit *saṃs araḥ*, from *sam* "together" + *sarati* "it flows."]

Sam·son /sámss'n/ *n.* **1.** **BIBLICAL WARRIOR** in the Bible, an Israelite judge and warrior. He used his enormous strength to fight the Philistines, to whom he was ultimately betrayed by his mistress, Delilah (Judges 13–16). **2.** **STRONG MAN** any very strong man — **Sam·so·ni·an** /sam sṓnee ən/ *adj.*

Sam·u·el *n.* in the Bible, the leader of the Israelites in the 11th century B.C. He was the first prophet after Moses.

Sam·uel·son /sámmyəls'n, -yoo əls'n/, **Paul** (*b.* 1915) U.S. economist, who is best known for his widely used and constantly updated textbook, *Economics*, first published in 1948. He won the Nobel Prize in economics (1970). Full name **Paul Anthony Samuelson**

sam·u·rai /sámmə rī/ (*plural* **-rai** *or* **-rais**) *n.* **1.** **ARISTOCRATIC JAPANESE WARRIOR** an aristocratic Japanese warrior of a class that dominated the military aristocracy from the 11th to the 19th centuries **2.** **FORMER JAPANESE WARRIOR CLASS** the powerful class of Japanese warriors that dominated the military aristocracy from the 11th to the 19th centuries [Early 18thC. From Japanese.]

san /saan/, **-san** *n.* used in Japanese after somebody's first name, last name, or title, as a polite form of address [Late 19thC. From Japanese, contraction of *sama*.]

San[1] /san/ *n.* used as a title, usually in place names, before the name of a man who has been made a saint. ◊ **Santo, Santa** [Via Spanish and Italian, "Saint," from Latin *sanctus* "sacred" (see SAINT)]

San[2] /saan/ (*plural* **San** *or* **Sans**) *n.* **1.** **MEMBER OF SOUTHERN AFRICAN PEOPLE** a member of a people living in southern Africa. The San traditionally live in small nomadic groups as hunters and gatherers. **2.** **SAN LANGUAGE** the group of Khoisan languages spoken by the San people [Late 19thC. From Nama *san*.]

San Andreas Fault

San An·dre·as Fault /sàn an dráy əss-/ *n.* a geologic fault zone between two tectonic plates that runs from San Francisco south to San Diego in California. It is an area of frequent earthquakes caused by the plates sliding past each other. Length: 600 mi./970 km. [So called because it runs along the San Andreas valley]

San An·ge·lo /san ánjəlō/ city in western Texas, on the Concho River. Population: 84,474 (1990).

San An·to·ni·o /sàn an tṓnee ō/ city in southern central Texas. It is the cultural and commercial center for the Rio Grande Valley, and is where the battle of the Alamo was fought. Population: 935,933 (1990).

san·a·tive /sánnətiv/ *adj.* able to restore health (*archaic formal*) [15thC. Directly, or via Old French *sanatif*, from late Latin *sanativus*, from Latin *sanare* "to heal."]

san·a·to·ri·um /sànnə táwree əm/ (*plural* **-ums** *or* **-a** /-ə/), **san·i·tar·i·um** /sànnə táiree əm/ (*plural* **-ums** *or* **-a** /-ə/) *n.* **1.** **MEDICAL FACILITY FOR LONG-TERM ILLNESS** a medical facility where people affected by long-term illnesses can receive treatment and those recovering from severe illnesses can recuperate **2.** **HEALTH RESORT** a resort for maintaining or improving health (*dated*) [Mid-19thC. From modern Latin, from Latin *sanat-*, the past participle stem of *sanare* "to cure," from *sanus* "healthy" (source of English *sane*).]

san·be·ni·to /sànbə neétō/ (*plural* **-tos**) *n.* a sackcloth garment worn by those declared heretics by the Spanish Inquisition. Penitent heretics wore a yellow one with a red cross on it and impenitent heretics wore a black one decorated with flames and devils. [Mid-16thC. From Spanish *sambenito*, an alteration of *San Benito* "St. Benedict," because it resembles the scapular of a Benedictine monk.]

San Ber·nar·di·no /sàn bərnər deénō/ city in southern California, located at the foot of the San Bernardino Mountains in the eastern extreme of a large metropolitan region centered on Los Angeles. Population: 181,718 (1994).

San Ber·nar·di·no Moun·tains mountain range in southern California. The highest peak is San Gorgonio Mountain, 11,485 ft./3,506 m. Length: 100 mi./160 km.

San Bru·no /san broōnō/ city in San Mateo County, western California, on San Francisco Bay. Population: 38,961 (1990).

San Car·los /san kaárləss/ city in San Mateo County, western California, on the San Francisco Peninsula. Population: 26,167 (1990).

San Cle·men·te /sàn klə méntee/ city and resort in Orange County, southwestern California, on the Pacific Ocean. Population: 41,100 (1990).

san·coche /sang kóch, -kósh, -kóchee/ *n. Carib* a Caribbean soup made with a variety of vegetables, split peas, and salted meat, or sometimes with chicken or beef [Mid-20thC. Via American Spanish *sancocho* from, ultimately, Spanish *sancochar* "to parboil."]

San Cri·sto·bal /san krístə baál/ one of the Galapagos Islands, off the coast of Ecuador. Area: 195 sq. mi./505 sq. km.

San Cri·stó·bal /san kri stṓb'l/ capital city of Táchira State, western Venezuela. Population: 238,670 (1992).

sanc·ta plural of **sanctum**

sanc·ta sanc·to·rum plural of **sanctum sanctorum**

sanc·ti·fy /sángktə fī/ (**-fied, -fy·ing, -fies**) *vt.* **1.** RELIG **BLESS SOMETHING** to make something holy **2.** RELIG **FREE SOMEBODY FROM SIN** to free somebody from sin, e.g., by a ritual act of purification **3.** RELIG **BLESS SOMETHING THROUGH RELIGIOUS VOW** to give a religious blessing to something, e.g., a marriage, usually through an oath or vow **4.** **OFFICIALLY APPROVE SOMETHING** to give social, moral, or official approval to something **5.** RELIG **MAKE SOMETHING ROUTE TO HOLINESS** to make something a means of achieving holiness or a source of grace **6.** **CAUSE SOMETHING TO BE REVERED** to designate something an object of reverence (*archaic*) [14thC. Via Old French *saintifier* from, ultimately, Latin *sanctus* "sacred" (see SAINT).] —**sanc·ti·fi·a·ble** *adj.* —**sanc·ti·fi·ca·tion** /sàngktəfə káysh'n/ *n.* —**sanc·ti·fi·er** /sángktə fī ər/ *n.*

sanc·ti·mo·ni·ous /sàngktə mṓnee əss/ *adj.* making an exaggerated show of holiness or moral superiority (*disapproving*) [Early 17thC. Formed from Latin *sanctimonia* "sanctity," from *sanctus* "sacred" (see SAINT).] —**sanc·ti·mo·ni·ous·ly** *adv.* —**sanc·ti·mo·ni·ous·ness** *n.* —**sanc·ti·mo·ny** /sángktə mōnee/ *n.*

sanc·tion /sángksh'n/ *n.* **1.** **AUTHORIZATION** official permission or approval for a course of action ○ *unable to proceed without the sanction of the board* **2.** **SUPPORT** something that serves as approval or encouragement, e.g., social acceptance or custom **3.** **LAW** a law or rule that leads to a penalty being imposed when it is disobeyed **4.** **PENALTY IMPOSED FOR BREAKING RULE** a punishment imposed as a result of breaking a law or rule **5.** INTERNAT REL **PUNITIVE MEASURE TO PRESSURE A COUNTRY** a measure taken by one or more nations to apply pressure on another nation to conform to international law or opinion. Such measures usually include restrictions on or withdrawal of trade rights, diplomatic ties, and membership of international organizations or forums. (*often used in the plural*) ○ *to impose trade sanctions* **6.** ETHICS **PRINCIPLE DETERMINING BEHAVIOR** an ethical principle or consideration that determines or influences somebody's conduct ■ *vt.* (**-tioned, -tion·ing, -tions**) **1.** **AUTHORIZE SOMETHING** to grant official approval or permission for something ○ *The county government refused to sanction the proposed design of the new building.* **2.** **APPROVE OF SOMETHING** to allow something to be tolerated or accepted ○ *The school's inaction further sanctions this behavior.* [15thC. Via Old French from, ultimately, Latin *sanctus* "sacred" (see SAINT).] —**sanc·tion·a·ble** *adj.* —**sanc·tion·er** *n.* —**sanc·tion·less** *adj.*

sanc·ti·ty /sángktətee/ (*plural* **-ties**) *n.* **1.** **SACREDNESS** the condition of being considered sacred or holy, and therefore entitled to respect and reverence **2.** **HOLY THING** something considered holy or sacred (*formal*) [14thC. Directly and via Old French *sainctité* from Latin *sanctitas*, from *sanctus* "sacred" (see SAINT).]

sanc·tu·ar·y /sángkchoo èrree/ (*plural* **-ies**) *n.* **1.** **REFUGE** a safe place, especially for people being persecuted **2.** **PLACE WHERE WILDLIFE IS PROTECTED** a place or area of land where wildlife is protected from predators and from being destroyed or hunted by human beings

○ *a bird sanctuary* **3.** RELIG **HOLY PLACE** a holy place such as a church, mosque, or temple **4.** RELIG **MOST SACRED PART OF HOLY BUILDING** the most sacred part of a consecrated building, e.g., the area around the altar in a Christian church **5.** CHR **CHURCH PROTECTING FUGITIVES** in medieval times, a holy place, usually a church, that provided immunity from the law **6.** JUDAISM, HIST **ISRAELITE HOLY OF HOLIES** the holy of holies in the Israelite temple at Jerusalem [14thC. Via Anglo-Norman *sanctuarie* from, ultimately, Latin *sanctus* "sacred" (see SAINT).]

sanc·tum /sángktəm/ (*plural* **-tums** *or* **-ta** /-tə/) *n.* **1.** RELIG **SACRED INNER PLACE** a sacred place inside a church, temple, or mosque **2. QUIET PRIVATE PLACE** a quiet private place where somebody is free from interference or interruption [Late 16thC. Via late Latin from Latin *sanctus* "sacred" (see SAINT).]

sanc·tum sanc·to·rum /sàngktəm sangk táwrəm/ (*plural* **sanc·ta sanc·to·rum** /sàngktə-/ *or* **sanc·tum sanc·to·rums**) *n.* **1.** = **holy of holies** *n.* 1 **2. PRIVATE, QUIET PLACE** a very private, quiet place in which to be alone or relax [14thC. From late Latin, literally "holy of holies."]

Sanc·tus /sángktəss/ *n.* in some Christian churches, a musical setting that forms part of the Mass and praises the power and holiness of God [14thC. Via late Latin from Latin *sanctus* "sacred" (see SAINT), the first word of the hymn.]

Sanc·tus bell *n.* in the Roman Catholic Church, a bell rung at the beginning of the Sanctus and at other times during Mass, e.g., at the elevation of the consecrated elements

sand /sand/ *n.* **1. MATERIAL MADE OF TINY GRAINS** a substance consisting of fine loose grains of rock or minerals, found on beaches, in the desert, and in soil, and also used as a building material. Sand is a sedimentary material, usually quartz fragments, that is finer than gravel but coarser than silt, with particle sizes between 0.06 mm and 2 mm. **2.** COLORS **BROWNISH YELLOW** a brownish-yellow color like that of sand **3. DETERMINATION** courage and determination (*dated informal*) **4. PARTICLES IN HOURGLASS** the tiny grains in an hourglass **5.** GEOG **AREA OF SAND** an area covered with or made up of sand, e.g., a beach or a desert ○ *playing on the sand and swimming in the sea* ■ **sands** *npl.* **TIME REMAINING** remaining or allotted portion of time (*literary*) ○ *the sands of time* ■ *v.* (**sand·ed, sand·ing, sands**) **1.** *vt.* **SMOOTH SOMETHING USING SANDPAPER** to rub a surface with sandpaper or sand to make it smoother **2.** *vt.* **SPRINKLE SOMETHING WITH SAND** to cover or sprinkle something such as an icy road with sand **3.** *vt.* **ADD SAND TO SOMETHING** to add sand to something, e.g., to a mixture of building materials when making mortar **4.** *vti.* **FILL WITH SAND** to become filled with sand, or fill something with sand ■ *adj.* COLORS **OF THE COLOR OF SAND** of a brownish-yellow color, like sand [Old English, of prehistoric Germanic origin] ◇ **kick sand in somebody's face** to show contempt for or dominance over somebody less strong or powerful, especially somebody already in a weak position

George Sand: Portrait (1839) by Auguste Charpentier

Sand /sand/, **George** (1804–76) French writer. She wrote many volumes of essays, novels, and plays, which reflect her feminist and libertarian ideals. Pseudonym of **Amandine Aurore Lucile, Baroness Dudevant**

san·dal /sánd'l/ *n.* **1. LIGHT SHOE WITH STRAPS** a light open shoe that is held on by straps across the instep or around the heel or ankle, usually worn during warm weather **2. STRAP FOR FASTENING SHOE** a strap for going around the ankle or across the instep to keep a shoe on a foot [14thC. Via Latin *sandalium* from, ultimately, Greek *sandalon*, of uncertain origin: probably from an Asian language.] —**san·daled** *adj.*

san·dal·wood /sánd'l wòod/ *n.* **1.** TREES **TROPICAL EVERGREEN TREE** a tropical evergreen tree native to southern Asia and Australia that has a fragrant wood. Genus: *Santalum.* **2.** INDUST **WOOD OF SANDALWOOD TREE** the wood of the sandalwood tree, used extensively in the manufacture of furniture, and burned as incense **3. AROMATIC OIL OF SANDALWOOD TREE** the aromatic oil that is extracted from the wood of sandalwood trees and used in perfumes and incense and as an essential oil in aromatherapy **4.** TREES **TREE RESEMBLING SANDALWOOD TREE** any tree native to southern Asia and Australia that resembles the sandalwood and that is harvested for wood. Genera: *Adenanthera* and *Myroporum* and *Pterocarpus.*

san·da·rac /sándə ràk/ *n.* **1. EVERGREEN TREE OF AFRICA AND SPAIN** a coniferous tree that is native to northwestern Africa and Spain and has flat branches, leaves with overlapping scales, and dark hard aromatic wood. Latin name: *Tetraclinis articulata.* **2. RESIN FROM SANDARAC TREE** a brittle yellowish translucent resin that oozes from the bark of the sandarac and is used in varnishes and incense **3. WOOD FROM SANDARAC TREE** the wood from the sandarac, used as a building material [Mid-17thC. Via Latin *sandaraca* from Greek *sandarakē.*]

sand·bag /sánd bàg/ *n.* **1. SACK OF SAND** a sealed bag full of sand, used in building defenses against gunfire or flooding, or as ballast in hot air balloons **2. BAG OF SAND USED AS WEAPON** a small bag filled with sand and used as a weapon in the same way as a cosh ■ *v.* (**-bagged, -bag·ging, -bags**) **1.** *vt.* **PROTECT SOMETHING WITH SANDBAGS** to put sandbags in or around something as protection **2.** *vt.* **KNOCK SOMEBODY OR SOMETHING DOWN** to attack or hit somebody or something with a sandbag (*informal*) **3.** *vti.* **DELAY NEGOTIATIONS** to delay negotiations or a business deal in the hope of receiving a more favorable offer from somebody else (*slang*) **4.** *vt.* **COERCE SOMEBODY** to force somebody to do something using coercive or crude tactics (*dated slang*) —**sand·bag·ger** *n.*

sand·bank /sánd bàngk/ *n.* a mound or bank of sand, especially one that is submerged at most states of the tide

sand·bar /sánd baar/ *n.* a long ridge of sand formed in a body of water by currents or tides

sand·blast /sánd blàst/ *vti.* (**-blast·ed, -blast·ing, -blasts**) **POLISH WITH SAND** to clean, polish, or mark glass, metal, or a stone surface by applying a jet of pressurized air or steam mixed with sand or grit ■ *n.* **1. JET OF SAND FIRED UNDER PRESSURE** a jet of pressurized air or steam mixed with sand or grit that is used to sandblast something **2. MACHINE FOR SANDBLASTING** a machine that is used for sandblasting —**sand·blast·er** *n.*

sand-blind *adj.* having reduced ability to see (*archaic or literary*) [15thC. Alteration of Old English *samblind*, from *sam-* "half" + *blind* "blind." Ultimately from an Indo-European word meaning "half," which is also the ancestor of English *semi-* and *hemi-*.] —**sand-blind·ness** *n.*

sand·box /sánd bòks/ *n.* an area of sand for children to play in, usually contained in a box or frame

sand·box tree *n.* a tropical American tree with spiny bark, milky sap that can irritate the skin, and woody seed capsules that explode when ripe. Latin name: *Hura crepitans.* [So called because the seed capsules formerly served as boxes for sand]

sand·bur /sánd bùr/ *n.* **1. GRASS WITH SEED-CONTAINING BUR** a grass that is native to the eastern United States and tropical America. Its single-grained spikelet is enclosed by a spiny bur. Genus: *Cenchrus.* **2. BUR OF SANDBUR** a bur of the sandbur plant

Sand·burg /sánd burg/, **Carl** (1878–1967) U.S. poet, folklorist, and historian. He wrote poems, collected and sang American folksongs, and won a Pulitzer Prize for his six-volume biography *Abraham Lincoln* (1926–39).

sand-cast *vt.* to make a casting by pouring molten metal into a sand mold

sand cast·ing *n.* a casting made by pouring molten metal into a sand mold

sand crack *n.* a crack in a horse's hoof that starts at the top (**coronet**) and extends vertically toward the sole

sand dab *n.* a small flatfish that is native to North American Pacific coastal waters and is caught for food. Genus: *Citharichthys.*

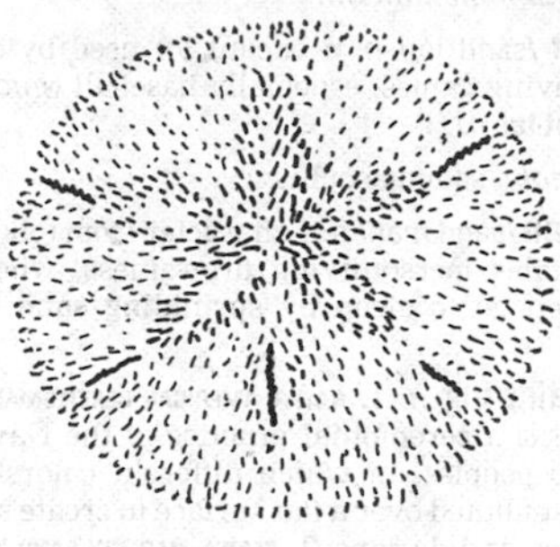
Sand dollar

sand dol·lar *n.* a flat circular animal (**echinoderm**) related to the starfish and sea urchin, found in shallow sandy North American coastal waters. Its shell looks like a white disk with an imprint that resembles a flower. Genus: *Citharichthys.*

sand eel *n.* = **sand lance**

sand·er /sándər/ *n.* **1. POWER TOOL FOR SMOOTHING SURFACES** an electric power tool that is used to smooth wooden or metal surfaces **2. TRUCK THAT SPREADS SAND ON ROADS** a truck or a truck attachment that spreads sand on roads **3. SOMEBODY WHO SANDS SOMETHING** somebody who sands something or operates a sander

sand·er·ling /sándərling/ (*plural* **-lings** *or* **-ling**) *n.* a small bird, found in coastal regions worldwide, that is similar to but smaller than a sandpiper and has gray and white plumage. Latin name: *Calidris alba.* [Early 17thC. Origin uncertain: perhaps formed from SAND + -LING.]

sand flea *n.* **1.** = **chigoe 2. TINY JUMPING CRUSTACEAN** a tiny jumping crustacean that lives on sandy tidal beaches. Genus: *Orchestia.*

sand fly *n.* a hairy fly that resembles a moth and lives in tropical regions. Bloodsucking females transmit several tropical diseases. Genus: *Phlebotomus.*

sand·fly fe·ver /sánd flī-/ *n.* a mild viral illness transmitted by the bite of a female sand fly. It causes fever, headaches, eye pain, and general discomfort.

sand·glass /sánd glàss/ *n.* = **hourglass**

sand·grouse /sănd gròwss/ (*plural* **-grouses** *or* **-grouse**) *n.* a bird related to the pigeon that is native to the arid and semiarid regions of Europe and Asia. Sandgrouses have long pointed wings and tails, and short feet and bills. Genus: *Pterocles.*

san·dhi /sándee, saan-, sún-/ *n.* the modification of the sound or form of a word under the influence of a preceding or following sound. The variation between "a" and "an" for the indefinite article in English is a form of sandhi. [Early 19thC. From Sanskrit *saṃdhiḥ* "combination."]

sand·hill crane /sánd hìl-/ *n.* a crane of North America and northeastern Siberia that has gray drooping plumage and a bald red crown. Latin name: *Grus canadensis.* [So called because the bird is commonly found among sand dunes]

sand·hog /sánd hòg/ *n.* somebody who works inside a caisson in underwater building projects such as tunnels (*slang*)

sand hop·per *n.* = **sand flea**

San Di·e·go /san dee áygō/ city in southwestern California, on San Diego Bay. It is the second largest city in California, and the sixth largest in the United States. Population: 1,151,977 (1994).

San Di·mas /san deéməss/ city in Los Angeles County, southwestern California, 25 mi./40 km east of Los Angeles. Population: 32,397 (1990).

San·din·is·ta /sàndə neéstə, saandə-/ *n.* a member of a socialist movement in Nicaragua that successfully overthrew the government of President Anastasio Somoza in 1979 and fought a United-States-backed insurgent force in the 1980s [Early 20thC. Named for the Nicaraguan revolutionary leader Augusto César *Sandino* (1893–1934).]

S & L *abbr.* savings and loan association

sand lance *n.* a small slender marine fish that resembles an eel. Sand lances travel in large schools and burrow in sand or shingle. Genus: *Ammodytes.*

sand lil·y *n.* a low-growing stemless plant of western North America that has long thin leaves and fragrant white star-shaped flowers. Latin name: *Leucocrinum montanum.*

sand·lot /sánd lòt/ *n.* a vacant lot used by children for playing games, especially baseball (*informal*) —**sand·lot·ter** *n.*

S & M *abbr.* sadomasochism

sand·man /sánd màn/ *n.* a character from folklore and fairy tales, personifying drowsiness, who makes children go to sleep by sprinkling sand in their eyes

sand paint·ing *n.* **1.** **NATIVE AMERICAN CEREMONIAL PRACTICE USING SAND** a ceremonial practice of the Navajo and Pueblo peoples, in which different colors of sand are distributed over a flat surface to create symbolic pictures and designs **2.** **DESIGN MADE BY SAND PAINTING** a picture or design made by sand painting

sand·pa·per /sánd pàypər/ *n.* **STRONG PAPER COATED WITH ABRASIVE MATERIAL** strong paper coated on one side with sand or another abrasive, used for smoothing surfaces ■ *vt.* (**-pered, -per·ing, -pers**) **SMOOTH SOMETHING USING SANDPAPER** to rub a surface, e.g., a piece of wood or a wall, with sandpaper —**sand·pa·per·y** *adj.*

sand pear *n.* **1.** TREES **CHINESE TREE WITH EDIBLE FRUIT** a Chinese tree, related to the rose, that bears edible fruit. Latin name: *Pyrus pyrifolia.* **2.** FOOD **FRUIT OF THE SAND PEAR TREE** the fruit of the sand pear with the shape of an apple and the coloring of a pear, thin skin, crisp juicy flesh, and a delicate flavor

sand·pi·per /sánd pìpər/ (*plural* **-pers** *or* **-per**) *n.* a wading shore bird with a long slender sensitive bill that it uses to catch insects, worms, and soft mollusks in sand and mud. Family: Scolopacidae. [*Piper* from its piping voice]

sand·pit /sánd pìt/ *n.* **1.** = **sandbox** **2.** **PIT FOR EXCAVATING SAND** a large deep pit from which sand is excavated

sand shark *n.* a shark that lives mainly in the shallow coastal waters of the central and southern Atlantic and western Pacific. Although it has very sharp teeth, it is not generally considered dangerous. Genus: *Carcharias.*

sand·shoe /sánd shoo/ *n. U.K., ANZ* a light low-cut canvas shoe with a rubber sole

sand·stone /sánd stōn/ *n.* a type of sedimentary rock made up of particles of sand, mostly quartz, bound together with a mineral cement, along with some feldspar, mica, and rock debris. It is widely used as a building material.

sand·storm /sánd stàwrm/ *n.* a strong windstorm, especially in the desert, that carries clouds of sand or dust, reducing visibility

sand ta·ble *n.* **1.** MIL **TABLE WITH SAND IMITATING BATTLEGROUND TERRAIN** a table covered with a layer of sand molded to imitate the relief of a battleground terrain, used to plan military tactics **2.** **RAISED BOX OF SAND** a table whose top is a shallow box filled with sand for children to play with

sand trap *n.* a depression on a golf course that is partly filled with sand, usually located near a green as a hazard

sand ver·be·na *n.* a low trailing plant of the four-o'clock family that is native to western North America and has fragrant usually red, yellow, or white flowers resembling those of verbena. Genus: *Abronia.*

sand vi·per *n.* = **horned viper**

sand wedge *n.* a golf club with a face angle of more than 50° that is used for chipping the ball out of a sand trap

sand·wich /sándwich, sám-/ *n.* **1.** FOOD **BREAD SLICES WITH FILLING IN BETWEEN** a snack or light meal usually made of two slices of bread or a split roll with a filling, or a single slice of bread with a topping. ◊ **club sandwich** **2.** **SOMETHING LIKE A SANDWICH** something resembling a sandwich, especially something in which various things are squashed together or arranged in layers ■ *vt.* (**-wiched, -wich·ing, -wich·es**) **PLACE SOMEBODY OR SOMETHING BETWEEN THINGS** to fit something or somebody tightly between two other things or people in space or time ○ *I'll see if I can sandwich you in on Tuesday.* [Mid-18thC. Named for John Montague, fourth Earl of *Sandwich* (1718–92).]

WORD KEY: ORIGIN

The Earl of ***Sandwich*** is said to have been so addicted to the gambling table that in order to sustain him through an entire 24-hour session uninterrupted, he had a portable meal of cold beef between slices of toast brought to him. The idea was not new, but the earl's patronage ensured that it became a vogue, and by the early 1760s we have the first evidence of his name being attached to it: the historian Edward Gibbon recorded in his diary in 1762 how he dined at the Cocoa Tree and saw "twenty or thirty of the best men in the kingdom ... supping at little tables ... upon a bit of cold meat, or a ***Sandwich.***"

Sand·wich /sán wich/ market town in southern Kent, England. It was one of the original Cinque Ports. Population: 4,164 (1991).

sand·wich board *n.* **1.** **NOTICES HANGING FROM SHOULDERS** a pair of boards, usually displaying advertisements or notices, joined by straps and hung from the shoulders with one displayed in front and one behind **2.** **ONE BOARD OF A SANDWICH BOARD** either of the two boards that make up a sandwich board [So called because the boards sandwich the person wearing them]

sand·wich coin *n.* a three-layered coin such as a U.S. twenty-five cent piece that has a middle layer made of a different metal from the outside layers

sand·wich man *n.* a man who carries a sandwich board

sand·worm /sánd wùrm/ *n.* a segmented worm living in coastal sand or mud, often used as fishing bait. Genera: *Nereis* and *Anicola.*

sand·wort /sánd wùrt, sánd-/ (*plural* **-worts** *or* **-wort**) *n.* a plant that grows in thick tufts close to the ground on sandy soil and has single white or pink flowers. Genus: *Arenaria.*

sand·y /sándee/ (**-i·er, -i·est**) *adj.* **1.** **FULL OF SAND** made up of, covered in, or full of sand **2.** **LIKE SAND** having a grainy texture or consistency similar to that of sand **3.** **OF THE COLOR OF SAND** of a yellow color tinged with red or brown —**sand·i·ness** *n.*

sane /sayn/ (**san·er, san·est**) *adj.* **1.** **MENTALLY BALANCED** mentally healthy and able to make rational decisions **2.** **REASONABLE** based on sensible, reasonable, or rational thinking ○ *a sane and practical solution to the problem* **3.** **HEALTHY** in good health (*archaic*) [Early 17thC. From Latin *sanus* "healthy" (source of English *sanatorium*).] —**sane·ly** *adv.* —**sane·ness** *n.*

San Fer·nan·do Val·ley residential and industrial region in southern California, north of Los Angeles. It is bounded by the Transverse Range on the north, the Santa Susana Mountains on the west, and the Santa Monica Mountains on the south. Population: 1,300,000 (1998).

San·ford /sánfèrd/ city in southwestern Maine, southwest of Biddeford and Saco. Population: 20,801 (1996).

San·for·ized /sánfə rìzd/ *tdmk.* a trademark used to describe fabric preshrunk by a patented process

San Fran·cis·co /san frèn sískō/ city in western California, in a spectacular location on San Francisco Bay. Population: 723,959 (1990). —**San Fran·cis·can** *n., adj.*

San Fran·cis·co Bay inlet linked to the Pacific Ocean by the Golden Gate Strait, in California. Length: 50 mi./80 km.

sang past tense of **sing**

San Gab·ri·el /san gáybree əl/ city in Los Angeles County, southwestern California, a residential community near Los Angeles. Population: 37,120 (1990).

san·ga·ree /sàng gə rée/ *n.* **1.** **DRINK OF WINE WITH FRUIT JUICE** a chilled drink of wine mixed with fruit juice, nutmeg, and sometimes a hard liquor **2.** = **sangria** [Mid-18thC. Alteration of Spanish *sangría* (see SANGRIA).]

San·ger /sángər/, **Margaret** (1883–1966) U.S. social reformer. She founded and led the U.S. birth control movement in the 1910s and 1920s. Born **Margaret Louise Higgins**

sang-froid /sàng frwáa, sàang-/ *n.* self-possession or calmness, especially in a dangerous or stressful situation (*formal*) [Mid-18thC. From French, literally "cold blood."]

san·go·ma /sang gṓmə/ *n. S Africa* in South Africa, a traditional healer (**shaman**) or herbalist [Late 19thC. From Nguni.]

Library of Congress

Margaret Sanger

San·greal /san gráyl/, **San·graal** /san gráal/ *n.* CHR = **Grail** *n.* [15thC. From Old French *saint graal* "Holy Grail."]

San·gre de Cris·to Moun·tains /sàng gri dè krístō-/ range of the Rocky Mountains. Its highest point is Blanca Peak, 14,345 ft./4,372 m. Length: 220 mi./354 km.

san·gri·a /sang grée ə/ *n.* a chilled Spanish drink of red wine, fruit juice, carbonated water, sugar, and brandy or another liquor, usually served in a jug with pieces of fruit [Mid-20thC. Via Spanish, literally "a bleeding," from, ultimately Latin *sanguis* "blood" (source of English *sanguine*).]

san·gui·nar·i·a /sàng gwə náiree ə/ *n.* **1.** PLANTS = **bloodroot** **2.** MED **ROOT OF BLOODROOT USED MEDICINALLY** the dried rhizome and roots of the bloodroot plant, formerly used internally as a medicine, now used as an antiplaque agent in toothpaste [Early 19thC. Via modern Latin *Sanguinaria,* order name, from, ultimately, Latin *sanguis* "blood."]

san·gui·nar·y /sáng gwə nèrree/ *adj.* (*formal*) **1.** **INVOLVING BLOODSHED** involving death or bloodshed **2.** **BLOODTHIRSTY** bloodthirsty or eager to kill **3.** **BLOODIED** consisting of or stained with blood —**san·gui·nar·i·ly** *adv.* —**san·gui·nar·i·ness** *n.*

san·guine /sáng gwin/ *adj.* **1.** **CONFIDENT** cheerfully optimistic **2.** **RUDDY** flushed with a healthy rosy color **3.** COLORS **BLOOD-RED** of a blood-red color **4.** **BLOODTHIRSTY** eager to shed blood (*archaic*) **5.** PHYSIOL, HIST **HAVING BLOOD AS DOMINANT HUMOR** in medieval physiology, having blood as the dominant humor and therefore characterized by a ruddy complexion and a courageous, optimistic, and romantic temperament. ◊ **phlegmatic, melancholic, choleric** [14thC. Via French from, ultimately, Latin *sanguin-,* the stem of *sanguis* "blood."] —**san·guine·ly** *adv.* —**san·guine·ness** *n.* —**san·guin·i·ty** /sang gwínnətee/ *n.*

san·guin·e·ous /sang gwínnee əss/ *adj.* **1.** MED **CONTAINING BLOOD** relating to or containing blood, especially mixed with other fluids (*often used in combination*) ○ *a sero-sanguineous discharge* **2.** COLORS **BLOOD-COLORED** of the color of blood **3.** **BLOODTHIRSTY** involving or enjoying bloodshed (*literary*) [Early 16thC. Formed from Latin *sanguineus,* from *sanguin,* the stem of *sanguis* "blood."]

San·hed·rin /san héedrin, -héddrin/ *n.* the supreme Jewish judicial, ecclesiastical, and administrative council in ancient Jerusalem before A.D. 70, having 71 members from the nobility and presided over by the high priest [Late 16thC. Via Hebrew from Greek *sunedrion* "council," from *sun* "together" + *hedra* "seat."]

san·i·cle /sánnik'l/ *n.* a widely distributed plant with clusters of small, variously colored flowers, oval fruits, and hooked bristles. It was formerly used as an astringent. Genus: *Sanicula.* [15thC. Via Old French from medieval Latin *sanicula,* of uncertain origin: probably formed from Latin *sanus* "healthy."]

san·i·dine /sánni deen, -din/ *n.* a glassy high-temperature form of the potassium feldspar variety of orthoclase, found in lava deposits. When translucent it is known as moonstone. Formula: $KAlSi_3O_8$. [Early 19thC. From Greek *sanid-,* stem of *sanis* "board," from the shape of the mineral's crystals.]

sanit. *abbr.* **1.** sanitary **2.** sanitation

san·i·tar·i·a plural of **sanitarium**

san·i·tar·i·an /sànnə táiree ən/ *adj.* **OF PUBLIC HEALTH** relating to public health and hygiene, especially sanitation (*formal*) ■ *n.* **PUBLIC HEALTH OFFICIAL** a public health official or inspector, especially one involved in sanitation (*formal*)

san·i·tar·i·um *n.* = sanatorium

san·i·tar·y /sánnə tèrree/ *adj.* **1. CONNECTED WITH PUBLIC HEALTH** relating to public health, especially general hygiene and the removal of human waste through the sewage system **2. CLEAN AND HYGIENIC** clean and free from agents that cause disease or infection [Mid-19thC. Via French *sanitaire* from, ultimately, Latin *sanus* "healthy" (source of English *sane*).] —**san·i·tar·i·ly** *adv.* —**san·i·tar·i·ness** *n.*

san·i·tar·y en·gi·neer·ing *n.* the branch of civil engineering concerned with the building, maintenance, and development of water and sewage systems and other public health services —**san·i·tar·y en·gi·neer** *n.*

san·i·tar·y land·fill *n.* = **landfill** (*dated*)

san·i·tar·y pad, **san·i·tar·y nap·kin** *n.* a disposable or cotton pad worn by women to absorb the blood flow during menstruation

san·i·ta·tion /sànnə táysh'n/ *n.* **1. STUDY OF WATER AND SEWAGE SYSTEMS** the study and maintenance of public health and hygiene, especially the water supply and sewage systems ○ *sanitation laws* **2. SEWAGE AND GARBAGE COLLECTION AND DISPOSAL** conditions or procedures related to the collection and disposal of sewage and garbage [Mid-19thC. Formed from SANITARY.]

san·i·ta·tion work·er *n.* = **garbage man**

san·i·tize /sánnə tìz/ (**-tized, -tiz·ing, -tiz·es**) *vt.* **1. CLEAN SOMETHING BY DISINFECTING OR STERILIZING** to clean something thoroughly by disinfecting or sterilizing it **2. MAKE SOMETHING LESS LIKELY TO OFFEND** to make something more likely to be acceptable by removing anything that might be considered offensive or controversial (*usually passive*) ○ *a sanitized version of the article* [Mid-19thC. Formed from SANITARY.] —**san·i·ti·za·tion** /sànnətə záysh'n/ *n.*

san·i·ty /sánnətee/ *n.* **1. STATE OF GOOD MENTAL BALANCE** the condition of being mentally healthy and able to make rational decisions **2. GOOD SENSE** common sense, reasonableness, and predictability ○ *to restore a little sanity to the situation* [Early 17thC. via Old French *sanite* from, ultimately, Latin *sanus* "whole, sound."]

San Ja·cin·to /san yè síntō/ river flowing from southeastern Texas into the Gulf of Mexico at Galveston Bay. Length: 85 mi./137 km.

San Joa·quin /sàn waw kéen/ river in central California flowing from the Sierra Nevada Mountains into the Sacramento River. Length: 350 mi./563 km.

San Jo·sé /sàn hō sáy/ capital city of Costa Rica, and of San José Province, situated in the center of the country. It is the country's largest city and its economic and political hub. Population: 324,011 (1996).

San Jo·se scale *n.* a scale insect that originated in Asia and is destructive to fruit trees and other fruit-bearing plants. Latin name: *Quadraspidiotus perniciosus.* [Late 19thC. Named for the city of *San Jose* in California, where it was first identified in the United States.]

San Juan /san hwáan/ **1.** river flowing from Colorado into New Mexico and back into Colorado, joining the Colorado River in Utah. Length: 360 mi./580 km. **2.** capital city and port of Puerto Rico, located in the northeast of the island. Population: 433,705 (1996).

San Ju·an Ca·pist·ra·no /-kàppi stráanō/ city in Orange County, southwestern California. It is the site of a Spanish mission, and is known for its swallows that regularly fly off in October and return in March. Population: 26,183 (1990).

San Juan Is·lands group of 172 islands in Washington State, between Haro and Rosario straits, east of Vancouver Island. Population: 10,035 (1990).

San Ju·an Moun·tains mountain range in the southwestern United States, in southwestern Colorado and northwestern New Mexico. Volcanic in origin, it is part of the Rocky Mountains. The highest point is Uncompahgre Peak, 14,309 ft./4,361 m.

sank past tense of **sink**

WORD KEY: USAGE

See Usage note at *sink.*

San·khya /sáangkyə/ *n.* one of six systems of orthodox Hindu philosophy, based on the perpetual interaction of spirit and matter [Late 18thC. From Sanskrit *sāṁkhya*, literally "relating to number."]

San Le·an·dro /sàn lee ándrō/ city in Alameda County, western California, on San Francisco Bay, near Oakland. Population: 68,223 (1990).

San Lu·is Ob·is·po /san lòo iss ə bíspō/ city in western California, on San Luis Obispo Creek, near the Pacific coast. Population: 41,958 (1990).

San Lu·is Po·to·sí /san loo èess póttō see/ industrial center and capital city of San Luis Potosí State, central Mexico. Population: 489,238 (1990).

San Marino

San Ma·ri·no /san mè réenō/ small independent republic entirely surrounded by Italy. It has been independent since A.D. 885 and a republic since the 14th century. Language: Italian. Currency: Italian lira. Capital: San Marino. Population: 24,521 (1996). Area: 24 sq. mi./61 sq. km. Official name **Republic of San Marino** —**Sam·ma·ri·nese** /sa mèrrə néez/ *n., adj.* —**San Ma·ri·nese** /san mèrrə néez/ *n., adj.*

San Mar·tín /san maar téen/, **José Francísco de** (1778–1850) Argentine statesman and soldier. He helped to liberate Argentina (1812), Chile (1818), and Peru (1821) from Spanish rule. Frustrated by political quarrels, he retired to France in 1824.

San Ma·te·o /san mə táyō/ city in San Mateo County, western California, on San Francisco Bay. Population: 85,486 (1990).

San Mig·uel de Tu·cu·mán /san mi gèl də too koo máan/ capital city of Tucumán Province, northwestern Argentina, on the Río Salí. Population: 626,143 (1990).

san·nup /sánnəp/ *n.* a married Native North American man [Early 17thC. From Massachusetts Algonquian *sanomp.*]

sann·ya·si /sun yáassee/, **sann·ya·sin** /-yáassin/ *n.* in Hinduism, a brahmin who has reached the fourth and final stage of life as a mendicant and will be absorbed into the Universal Soul instead of being reborn [Early 17thC. From Sanskrit *saṃnyāsī*, literally "somebody who renounces."]

S-A node *abbr.* sinoatrial node

San Pe·dro Su·la /san pèddrō sòo laa/ capital city of Cortés Department, northwestern Honduras, in the Sula Valley. Population: 353,800 (1993).

San Ra·fa·el /san rə fél/ city in western California, on San Francisco Bay, near San Francisco. Population: 48,404 (1990).

San Re·mo /san réemō/ town and port in Imperia Province, Liguria Region, northwestern Italy. Population: 59,600 (1990).

sans /sanz, saaN / *prep.* without (*archaic or literary or humorous*) ○ *looking forward to a well-earned break sans children* [13thC. Via Old French *sanz* from, ultimately, Latin *sine* "without," influenced by *absentia* "absence."]

San Sal·va·dor /san sálvèdawr/ **1.** capital city of El Salvador and of San Salvador Department, located in central El Salvador. Population: 422,520 (1992). **2.** island of the Bahamas, in the Atlantic Ocean, near Cat Island. Population: 465 (1990). Area: 60 sq. mi./155 sq. km.

sans-cu·lotte /sànzkyə lót, sànkyə-/ *n.* **1. REVOLUTIONARY IN FRENCH REVOLUTION** during the French Revolution, a revolutionary either from the poorer classes or with extreme republican sympathies **2. REVOLUTIONARY EXTREMIST** a revolutionary in any country who has extremist views (*formal*) [Late 18thC. From French, literally "without breeches."] —**sans-cu·lot·tic** *adj.* —**sans-cu·lot·tism** *n.* —**sans-cu·lot·tist** *n.*

San Se·bas·tián /san sè báschèn/ city and administrative center of Guipúzcoa Province in the Basque Country, northern Spain. It is the site of an annual international film festival. Population: 178,470 (1995).

San·sei /san sáy/ (*plural* **-seis** *or* **-sei**) *n.* somebody born in North America whose grandparents immigrated from Japan. The word is mainly used by Japanese American people. ◊ **Nisei, Issei** [Mid-20thC. From Japanese, literally "third generation."]

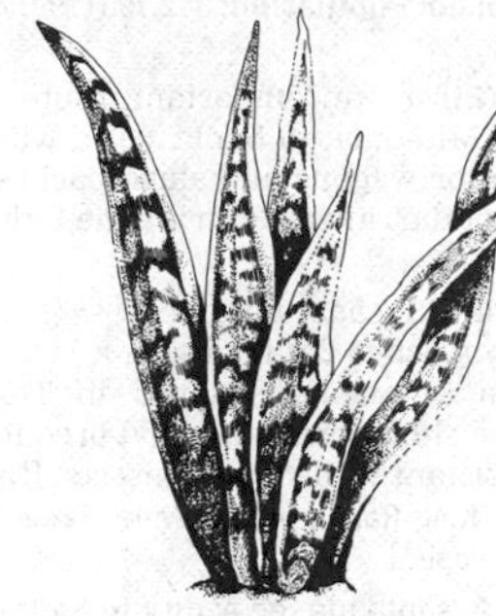
Sansevieria

san·se·vie·ri·a /sànsə véeree ə/ (*plural* **-as** *or* **-a**) *n.* a plant, native to tropical Africa and Asia, with thick variegated blade-shaped leaves. It is commonly grown as a houseplant or as a source of bowstring hemp. Genus: *Sansevieria.* [Early 19thC. Named for the Italian patron of horticulture, Raimondo de Sangro, Prince of *Sanseviero* (1710–70).]

San·skrit /sánskrit/ *n.* the extinct Indo-European language of ancient India. Sanskrit was spoken between the fourteenth and fifth centuries B.C., and survives as the language of classical Indian literature and Hindu religious texts. [Early 17thC. From Sanskrit *saṃskṛta* "perfected."] —**San·skrit·ic** /san skríttik/ *n., adj.* —**San·skrit·ist** /sánskritist/ *n.*

sans ser·if /san sérrif/, **san·ser·if** *n.* any style of typeface in which there are no fine lines (**serifs**) at the ends of the main strokes of the characters

San·ta[1] /sántə/ *n.* used as a title, usually in place names, before the name of a woman who has been made a saint. ◊ **San, Santo** [From Spanish and Italian, a form of *San* "Saint"]

San·ta[2] /sántə/ *n.* Santa Claus (*informal*) [Early 20thC. Shortening.]

San·ta An·a[1] /-ánnə/ *n.* a strong hot dry wind that blows from the deserts of California to the coast during the winter months. It is often responsible for spreading dangerous wildfires. [Named for the *Sant Ana* mountains in southern California]

San·ta A·na[2] /sàntə ánnə/ city in Orange County, southwestern California, located in the southern portion of a large metropolitan region centered around Los Angeles. Population: 290,827 (1994).

San·ta An·na /sàntə ánnə/, **Antonio Lopez de** (1794–1876) Mexican general and politician. Alternately viewed as a national hero and national scapegoat, he served as president of Mexico (1833–36, 1844, 1847, and 1853–55).

San·ta Bar·ba·ra Is·lands /sàntè baárbèrè-/ group of eight U.S. islands in the Pacific Ocean, off the southern coast of California

San·ta Cat·a·li·na Is·land /sàntè katè leénè-/ island off the coast of California in the Pacific, south of Long Beach. It is one of the Santa Barbara Islands. Population: 2,918 (1990).

San·ta Cla·ra /sàntə klárrə/ city in Silicon Valley, western California, on the Guadalupe River, near San Jose. Population: 93,613 (1990).

San·ta Cla·ri·ta /sàntə klə réetə/ city in southern California, in Los Angeles County, situated on a valley floor and along canyons reaching into the San Gabriel and Santa Susanna mountains. Population: 123,676 (1994).

San·ta Cruz /sàntə kròoz/ **1.** river in southern Argentina that flows eastward out of Lake Argentino in western Santa Cruz Province, and empties into the Atlantic Ocean at the port of Santa Cruz. Length: 250 mi./400 km. **2.** city in Santa Cruz Department, central Bolivia, on the Piray River, in the tropical plains region east of the Andes Mountains. Population: 694,616 (1992). **3.** city and tourist center in Santa Cruz County, western California, on Monterey Bay. Population: 49,040 (1990).

San·ta Cruz de Te·ne·ri·fe /-dè tenè rēef/ capital city and port of Tenerife Island and of Santa Cruz de Tenerife Province, in the Canary Islands, Spain. Population: 204,948 (1995).

San·ta Fe /sàntè fáy/ **1.** capital city of New Mexico, on the Santa Fe River, in the north of the state. Population: 66,522 (1996). **2.** capital city of Santa Fe Province in northeastern Argentina. It is a port on the River Salado. Population: 342,796 (1991). —**San·ta Fe·an** *n., adj.*

San·ta Fe Trail *n.* an important route from Independence, Missouri, to Santa Fe in what is now New Mexico for wagons and stagecoaches prior to the opening of the railroad during the 19th century. ◊ **Route 66**

San·ta Ger·tru·dis /sàntə gər trōōdəss/ (*plural* **San·ta Ger·tru·dis·es** *or* **San·ta Ger·tru·dis**) *n.* a large red cow belonging to a breed developed in Texas from Brahman and shorthorn cattle and bred for beef. It is highly resistant to heat and insects. [Named for a section of the King Ranch in Kingsville, Texas, where the breed was developed]

San·ta Ma·ri·a /sàntə mə rēe ə/ city in Santa Barbara County, southwestern California. Population: 61,284 (1990).

San·ta Mar·ta /sàntè maártè/ port and capital city of Magdalena Department in northern Colombia, on the Caribbean Sea. Population: 309,372 (1995).

San·ta Mo·ni·ca /santə mónnikə/ city near Los Angeles in southwestern California, on Santa Monica Bay. It is chiefly a resort and residential city. Population: 86,905 (1990).

San·tan·der /sàntèn dáir/ port and capital city of Santander Province in the autonomous region of Cantabria, northern Spain. Population: 194,837 (1995).

San·ta Pau·la /sàntə páwlə/ city in Ventura County, southern California, situated on the Santa Clara River, northwest of Los Angeles. Population: 25,062 (1990).

San·ta Ro·sa /sàntə rṓzə/ city in Sonoma County, northwestern California. Population: 116,962 (1994).

San·tee /sántee/ river flowing from southern South Carolina into the Atlantic Ocean, south of Georgetown. Length: 143 mi./230 km.

San·te·rí·a /sàntə rēe ə, saàntə-/, **san·te·rí·a** *n.* a religion that combines the West African Yoruba religion with Roman Catholicism. The religion recognizes a supreme God as well as other spirits. Originally developed in Cuba by West African enslaved laborers, it is now practiced in the Caribbean and the United States. [Mid-20thC. Via Spanish *santería* "holiness" from, ultimately, Latin *sanctus* "sacred" (see SAINT).]

San·ti·a·go /sàntee aágō/ capital and largest city of Chile, on the Mapocho River, in the central part of the country. Population: 4,295,593 (1992).

San·ti·a·go de Com·postela /santee aágō day kompo stáylè/ capital city of the autonomous region of Galicia, northwestern Spain. Its cathedral has been a major place of pilgrimage since medieval times. Population: 94,057 (1995).

San·ti·a·go de Cu·ba /santee aágō day kōōbè/ the second largest city in Cuba, situated in the southeast of the country. It is a major port. Population: 440,084 (1993).

san·tim /sán teem/ *n.* **1.** SUBUNIT OF LATVIAN CURRENCY a subunit of currency in Latvia, 100 of which are worth one lat. See table at **currency** **2.** COIN WORTH A SANTIM a coin worth a santim

San·to /sántō/ (*plural* **-tos**) *n.* used as a title, usually in place names, before the name of a man who has been made a saint. ◊ **San, Santa** [Via Spanish and Italian from Latin *sanctus* (see SAINT)]

San·to Do·min·go /sàntō də míng gō/ capital and largest city of the Dominican Republic, situated in the south of the country. Population: 2,100,000 (1993).

san·ton·i·ca /san tónnikə/ (*plural* **-cas** *or* **-ca**) *n.* **1.** WORMWOOD PLANT WITH ABUNDANT FLOWERS a shrubby wormwood plant native to Europe and Asia that has twin needle-shaped leaves and abundant flower heads. Genus: *Artemisia.* **2.** SOURCE OF SANTONIN the dried unopened flower heads of the santonica plant which contain santonin [Mid-17thC. Via modern Latin from, ultimately, Latin *santonicus* "of the Santoni," a tribe of the Gauls.]

san·to·nin /sántənin/ *n.* a white crystalline compound that is extracted from the dried flower heads of the santonica plant, formerly used to eradicate parasitic worms. Formula: $C_{15}H_{18}O_3$. [Mid-19thC. Coined from SANTONICA + -IN.]

San·tor·in·i /sàntə rēe nee/ = **Thera**

San·tos /sántooss/ city and port in São Paulo State, in southeastern Brazil, situated on the Atlantic island of São Vicente. Population: 412,288 (1996).

São Mi·guel /sow mi gél/ the largest island of the Azores, located in the North Atlantic Ocean 740 mi./1,200 km from the western coast of Portugal. Population: 126,388 (1991). Area: 288 sq. mi./746 sq. km.

São Pau·lo /sow pówlō/ capital of São Paulo State in southeastern Brazil. It is the largest city in South America, and an industrial and commercial metropolis. Population: 9,811,776 (1996).

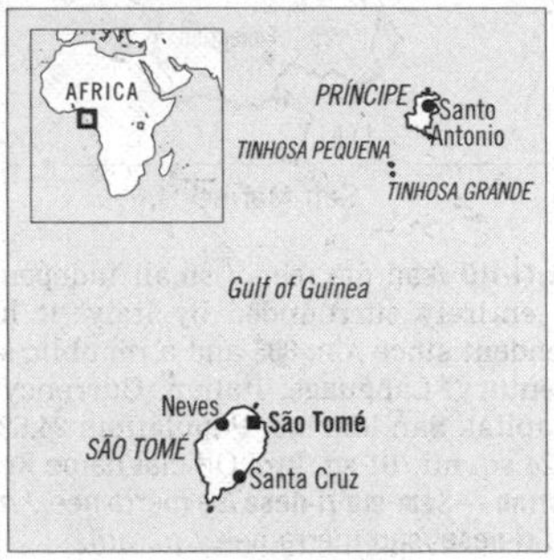

São Tomé and Príncipe

São Tomé and Príncipe /sow tō mày ènd prínchè pay/ island republic in the Gulf of Guinea, approximately 180 mi./290 km west of Gabon, western Africa. Formerly Portuguese, the territory became an independent republic in 1975. Language: Portuguese. Currency: dobra. Capital: São Tomé. Population: 134,000 (1996). Area: 372 sq. mi./964 sq. km. Official name **Democratic Republic of São Tomé and Príncipe**

sap[1] /sap/ *n.* **1.** PLANT FLUID a watery liquid containing mineral salts, sugars, and other nutrients that circulates through the conducting tissues of a plant **2.** BODY FLUID any essential body fluid **3.** ENERGY bodily strength or vitality ○ *feel the sap rising* **4.** OFFENSIVE TERM an offensive term that deliverately insults somebody's intelligence and ability to recognize the truth (*informal insult*) **5.** COSH a weapon such as a cosh or blackjack ■ *vt.* (**sapped, sap·ping, saps**) **1.** DRAIN PLANT OF SAP to drain a plant of sap **2.** HIT SOMEBODY WITH A SAP to hit or knock somebody out with a sap [Old English *sæp.* From a prehistoric Germanic word that is also the ancestor of German *Saft* "juice."] —**sap·less** *adj.*

sap[2] /sap/ *n.* COVERED TRENCH LEADING TO ENEMY TERRITORY a deep narrow covered trench, dug to approach or get inside enemy territory, especially during a siege ■ *v.* (**sapped, sap·ping, saps**) **1.** *vti.* DIG A SAP to dig a sap, or undermine the foundations of an enemy fortification by digging a tunnel **2.** *vt.* TAKE AWAY SOMEBODY'S ENERGY to gradually weaken or reduce something, especially somebody's strength or energy ○ *The long hours were sapping his strength.* [Late 16thC. Via obsolete French *sappe* and Italian *zappa* from late Latin *sappa*, of uncertain origin: perhaps from Arabic *sarab* "burrow."]

sap·a·jou /sáppə jōō, sàppə zhōō/ (*plural* **-jous** *or* **-jou**) *n.* = **capuchin** [Late 17thC. From French, of uncertain origin: perhaps from Tupi.]

sa·pe·le /sə pēelee/ (*plural* **-les** *or* **-le**) *n.* **1.** TREES WEST AFRICAN TREE WITH HARD WOOD a tree native to western Africa that produces a hard wood. Genus: *Entandrophragma.* **2.** INDUST WOOD FROM SAPELE TREE the wood from the sapele tree, which is similar to mahogany and is used for making furniture [Early 20thC. Named for *Sapele*, a port on the Benin River in Nigeria.]

sap·head /sap hèd/ *n.* an offensive term that deliverately insults somebody's intelligence or cunning (*slang insult*) —**sap·head·ed** *adj.*

sa·phe·na /sə fēenə/ (*plural* **-nae** /-nee/) *n.* = **saphenous vein** —**sa·phe·nous** *adj.*

sa·phe·nous vein /sə fēenəss-/ *n.* either of two major veins in the leg that run from the foot to the thigh near the surface of the skin [From medieval Latin, "vein"]

sap·id /sáppəd/ *adj.* (*formal*) **1.** FLAVORFUL having a strong and pleasant taste **2.** PLEASANT TO THINK ABOUT engaging or pleasant to think about [Early 17thC. From Latin *sapidus*, from *sapere* "to taste" (source of English *insipid*).] —**sa·pid·i·ty** /sə píddətee/ *n.* —**sap·id·ness** /sáppədnəss/ *n.*

sa·pi·ent /sáypee ənt/ *adj.* wise or learned [15thC. Via Old French from Latin *sapiens-*, the present participle stem of *sapere* "to be wise, taste."] —**sa·pi·ence** *n.* —**sa·pi·ent·ly** *adv.*

sa·pi·en·tial /sàypee énsh'l/ *adj.* having or giving wisdom (*formal*) —**sa·pi·en·tial·ly** *adv.*

sa·pin·da·ceous /sàppin dáyshess/ *adj.* belonging to an order of trees and shrubs that includes the soapberry. Order: Sapindaceae. [19thC. Formed from modern Latin *Sapindaceae*, order name, from *Sapindus*, literally "Indian soap," from *sapo* "soap" + *Indus* "India."]

Sa·pir-Whorf hy·poth·e·sis /sə pēer wáwrf-/ *n.* the theory that the structure of a language helps determine how its native speakers perceive and categorize experience. It was proposed by Edward Sapir in 1929 and further developed by Benjamin Lee Whorf.

sap·ling /sápling/ *n.* **1.** TREES SMALL TREE a young tree with a slender trunk **2.** YOUNG PERSON a young person (*literary*)

sap·o·dil·la /sàppə díllə, -dēe yə/ *n.* **1.** TREES TROPICAL EVERGREEN TREE an evergreen tree of Mexico, Central America, and the Caribbean that yields chicle and has a brown rough-skinned fruit with sweet yellowish pulp **2.** FOOD SAPODILLA FRUIT a small round edible fruit with a brown skin that grows on the sapodilla tree [Late 17thC. From Spanish *zapotillo*, from *zapote*, from Nahuatl *tzapotl*.]

sap·o·na·ceous /sàppə náyshəss/ *adj.* with the consistency of soap (*formal*) [Early 18thC. Formed from modern Latin from Latin *sapon- saponaceus*, from "hair dye" (see SAPONATED).] —**sap·o·na·ceous·ness** *n.*

sap·o·na·ted /sáppə nàytəd/ *adj.* treated or mixed with soap [Mid-18thC. Formed from Latin *sapon-*, the stem of *sapo* "hair dye," from a prehistoric Germanic word.]

sa·pon·i·fy /sə pónni fì/ (**-fied, -fy·ing, -fies**) *vti.* to be converted into soap or to convert a fat into soap, especially by reaction with an alkali [Early 19thC. Via French *saponifier* from, ultimately, Latin *sapo-* "hair dye" (see SAPONATED).] —**sa·pon·i·fi·a·ble** *adj.* —**sa·pon·i·fi·er** *n.*

sap·o·nin /sáppənin, sə pṓnin/ *n.* any of a group of chemical substances (**glucosides**) extracted from plants that form a soapy lather when mixed with water and are used to make detergents [Mid-19thC. Via French *saponine* from, ultimately, the Latin stem *sapon-* "hair dye" (see SAPONATED).]

sap·o·nite /sáppə nìt/ *n.* a soft soapy clay mineral found in the veins and cavities of certain rocks that have undergone hydrothermal alteration [Mid-19thC. Formed from the Latin stem *sapon-* "hair dye" (see SAPONATED).]

sa·por /sáy pər/ *n.* taste or flavor as a characteristic of something (*formal*) [15thC. From Latin (also the source of English *savor*), formed from *sapere* "to taste."] —**sa·po·rif·ic** /sàypə ríffik, sàppə-/ *adj.* —**sa·po·rous** /sáypərəss, sáppə-/ *adj.*

sa·po·ta /sə pṓtə/ (*plural* **-tas** *or* **-ta**) *n.* **1.** = **sapodilla** *n.* 1 **2.** = **sapote** *n.* 1

sap·o·ta·ceous /sàppə táyshəss/ *adj.* belonging to an order of trees that includes the balata tree. Order: Sapotaceae. [Mid-19thC. From modern Latin, formed from *sapota* (see SAPOTA).]

sa·po·te /sə pṓtee, sə pṓtay/ *n.* **1.** TREES TROPICAL AMERICAN TREE a Mexican and Central American tree that has a sweet brown fruit. Latin name: *Poulteria sapota.* **2.** FOOD FRUIT OF SAPOTE TREE an oval brown edible fruit that grows on the sapote tree [Mid-16thC. Via modern Latin from Spanish *zapote*, from Nahuatl *tzapotl*.]

sap·pan·wood /sə pán wŏŏd/ *n.* **1.** TREES TROPICAL ASIAN TREE a tropical Asian tree. Latin name: *Caesalpina sappan.* **2.** INDUST TROPICAL WOOD the wood of the sappanwood tree, which yields a red dye [Late 16thC. Via Dutch from Malay *sapang*.]

sap·per /sápper/ *n.* **1.** SPECIALIST IN TRENCHES AND TUNNELS a military engineer who specializes in fortifications, especially tunnels dug under enemy territory **2.** SPECIALIST IN MINES a military engineer who lays, detects, and disarms mines [Early 17thC. Formed from SAP[2].]

Sap·phic /sáffik/ *adj.* **1.** RELATING TO SAPPHO'S POETRY relating to the Greek poet Sappho or her poetry, largely written in 11-syllable lines, with stanzas of three such lines and a shorter fourth line **2.** LESBIAN lesbian (*literary*) ■ *n.* GREEK POEM a Sapphic line, stanza, or poem

sap·phire /sá fīr/ *n.* **1.** MINERALS DEEP BLUE JEWEL a clear hard precious stone that is a variety of the mineral corundum and is usually deep blue in color **2.** COLORS BRILLIANT BLUE COLOR a brilliant blue color like that of a sapphire ■ *adj.* **1.** WITH A SAPPHIRE made of or set with a sapphire **2.** COLORS OF BRILLIANT BLUE of a brilliant blue color like that of a sapphire [13thC. Via Old French *safir* and Latin *sapphirus* from Greek *sappheiros.*]

sap·phi·rine /sáffə rīn, -reen, -rin/ *adj.* LIKE A SAPPHIRE resembling a sapphire, especially in being a brilliant blue color ■ *n.* KIND OF MINERAL a rare blue or green mineral that is a silicate of aluminum and magnesium

sap·phism /sá fizzəm/ *n.* lesbianism (*literary*) [Late 19thC. Named for the Greek poet SAPPHO.]

Sap·pho /sáffō/ (*fl.* 7th century B.C.) Greek poet. She wrote odes, wedding songs, and hymns notable for their depth of feeling. Few fragments of her work remain.

Sap·po·ro /sáppōrō, sa pṓrō/ commercial center and capital of Hokkaido Prefecture, on western Hokkaido Island, Japan. Population: 1,748,000 (1995).

sap·py /sáppee/ (**-pi·er, -pi·est**) *adj.* **1.** PLANTS FULL OF SAP full of sap **2.** OFFENSIVE TERM an offensive term describing somebody as thoughtless or unintelligent (*informal insult*) —**sap·pi·ly** *adv.*

sapr- *prefix.* = **sapro-** (*used before vowels*)

sa·pre·mi·a /sə preemee ə/ *n.* blood poisoning thought to be caused by the toxic products of microorganisms in decaying tissue (*archaic*) [Late 19thC. Coined from SAPRO- + -EMIA.] —**sa·pre·mic** *adj.*

sapro- *prefix.* **1.** death, decay, putrefaction ○ *saprozoic* **2.** dead or decaying organic matter ○ *saprophagous* [From Greek *sapros* "rotten"]

sap·robe /sáp rōb/ *n.* an organism that gets its nourishment from inorganic or decaying organic matter [Mid-20thC. Formed from SAPRO-, on the model of *microbe.*] —**sap·ro·bic** *adj.*

sap·ro·bi·ol·o·gy /sàpprō bī óllәjee/ *n.* the study of environments that support organisms (**saprobes**) that feed on decaying organic matter —**sap·ro·bi·o·log·i·cal** /sàpprō bī ə lójjik'l/ *adj.* —**sap·ro·bi·ol·o·gist** /sàpprō bī óllәjist/ *n.*

sap·ro·gen·ic /sàpprə jénnik/ *adj.* causing or resulting from decay —**sap·ro·ge·nic·i·ty** /sàpprəjə níssətee/ *n.*

sap·ro·lite /sáppra līt/ *n.* soft disintegrating igneous rock that remains where it was located when solid, formed by heavy weathering in a humid environment —**sap·ro·lit·ic** *adj.*

sap·ro·pel /sápprə pèl/ *n.* a soft black layer of decaying organic matter at the bottom of a body of water [Early 20thC. From German, from Greek *sapros* "rotten" (see SAPRO-) + *pēlos* "mud."] —**sap·ro·pel·ic** /sàpprə péllik, -peelik/ *adj.*

sa·proph·a·gous /sa prófəgəs/ *adj.* feeding on or obtaining food from decaying organic matter

sap·ro·phyte /sápprə fīt/ *n.* a plant, especially a fungus, or bacterium that obtains food from dead or decaying organic matter —**sap·ro·phyt·ic** /sàpprə fíttik/ *adj.* —**sap·ro·phyt·i·cal·ly** /-fíttikəlee/ *adv.*

sap·ro·zo·ic /sàpprə zṓ ik/ *adj.* getting nourishment by absorbing dissolved organic matter and salts

sap·sa·go /sap sáygō, sápsə gō/ (*plural* **-gos** *or* **-go**) *n.* a hard green Swiss cheese made with sour skim milk and flavored with sweet clover [Mid-19thC. Alteration of German *Schabzieger*, from *schaben* "to scrape" and *zieger* "curd cheese."]

sap·suck·er /sáp sùkər/ *n.* a small North American woodpecker that drills holes in trees in order to drink the sap and eat insects attracted by the sap. Genus: *Sphyrapicus.*

sap·wood /sáp wŏŏd/ *n.* the soft wood of a tree between the inner bark and the heartwood. It is lighter in color than the heartwood and more active in conducting water.

SAR *abbr.* Sons of the American Revolution

sar·a·band /sárrə bànd/, **sar·a·bande** *n.* **1.** DANCE SPANISH COURT DANCE a slow and dignified dance in triple time, favored by the Spanish nobility in the 17th and 18th centuries **2.** MUSIC MUSIC FOR SARABAND music for the saraband, written in triple time with an accent on the second beat of the measure [Early 17thC. Via French from Spanish *zarabanda.*]

Sar·a·cen /sárrəss'n/ *n.* **1.** MUSLIM OPPOSING CHRISTIAN CRUSADES a Muslim who fought against the Christian Crusaders in the Middle Ages **2.** MEMBER OF ANCIENT DESERT PEOPLE a member of an ancient nomadic desert people of Syria and Arabia living on the fringes of the Roman Empire. They resisted periodic Roman attempts to incorporate their territories. **3.** ARAB an Arab (*archaic*) ■ *adj.* **1.** RELATING TO SARACENS relating to or typical of the ancient or medieval Saracens or their culture **2.** ISLAMIC OR ARAB relating to Muslims or Arabs or their cultures (*archaic*) [Pre-12thC. Via Old French *sarazin* from, ultimately, late Greek *sarakēnos*, of uncertain origin: perhaps from Arabic *sarki* "eastern."] —**Sar·a·cen·ic** /sàrrə s-nnik/ *adj.* —**Sar·a·cen·i·cal** /-sénnik'l/ *adj.*

Sar·a·gos·sa /sàrrè gósse/ = **Zaragoza**

Sa·rah /sáirə/ *n.* in the Bible, the wife and half-sister of Abraham, and mother of Isaac (Genesis 17:15–22)

Sa·ra·je·vo /sàrrè yáyvō/ capital city of Bosnia-Herzegovina, in the eastern central part of the country. Population: 415,631 (1991).

sa·ran /sə rán/ *n.* a thermoplastic resin created from a vinyl compound and used to make fabrics, plastic wrap, and other articles [Mid-20thC. Originally a trademark.]

Sa·ran·don /sə rándən/, **Susan** (*b.* 1946) U.S. movie actor. She won an Academy Award for *Dead Man Walking* (1995). Born **Susan Tomaling**

sar·an·gi /sə ráng gee/ (*plural* **-gis**) *n.* a musical instrument of the Indian subcontinent that is similar to a violin with a rectangular soundbox and three strings with additional sympathetic strings [Mid-19thC. From Sanskrit *sāraṅgī.*]

Sar·a·to·ga Springs /sàrrè tṓgə-/ city in eastern New York, in the Adirondack Mountain foothills, north of Albany. Two battles were fought in its vicinity during the Revolution. Population: 25,118 (1996).

Sar·a·to·ga trunk /sàrrə tṓgə-/ *n.* a large traveling trunk with a rounded top, once widely used by women [Named for SARATOGA SPRINGS, New York, a popular resort destination in the 19thC]

Sa·ra·wak /sə raawaak/ state in Malaysia, in the northwestern portion of the island of Borneo. Capital: Kuching. Population: 1,648,217 (1990). Area: 48,050 sq. mi./124,449 sq. km.

Sa·ra·zen /sárrəz'n/, **Gene** (*b.* 1902) U.S. golfer. He was the first golfer to win the four championships that comprise the Grand Slam of golf. Born **Eugene Saraceni**

sarc- *prefix.* = **sarco-** (*used before vowels*)

sar·casm /saar kàzzəm/ *n.* remarks that mean the opposite of what they seem to say and are intended to mock or deride [Mid-16thC. Via French from, ultimately, Greek *sarkazein* "to tear flesh," from *sarx* "flesh" (source of English *sarcoma* and *sarcophagus*).]

sar·cas·tic /saar kástik/ *adj.* **1.** MOCKING characterized by words that mean the opposite of what they seem to say and make fun of something or somebody or express irritation **2.** FOND OF SARCASM fond of or habitually using sarcasm —**sar·cast·ic·al·ly** *adv.*

WORD KEY: SYNONYMS

sarcastic, ironic, sardonic, satirical, satiric, caustic

CORE MEANING: used to describe remarks that are designed to hurt or mock

sarcastic used to describe remarks that are contemptuous, scornful, or mocking and that are intended to hurt or belittle the person or thing they are directed at; **ironic** used to describe remarks that deliberately state the opposite of the truth, usually with the intention of being amusing rather than contemptuous or mocking; **sardonic** used to describe remarks or behavior that are mocking and cynical or disdainful. It does not suggest such deliberate hurtfulness as ***sarcastic***; **satirical** used to describe writing, drama, drawing, or any other form of expression that uses ridicule and irony to criticize somebody's or something's faults; **satiric** a more formal word used in the same way as *satirical*; **caustic** used to describe remarks that are harsh and bitter and intended to mock, offend, or belittle the person or thing they are directed at.

sar·ce·net /saarssnət/, **sar·se·net** *n.* a soft delicate silk cloth once widely used for veils, linings, and ribbons [15thC. From Old French *sarzinet*, of uncertain origin: perhaps formed from *Sarazin* (see SARACEN).]

sarco- *prefix.* **1.** striated muscle ○ *sarcolemma* **2.** flesh ○ *sarcoid* [From Greek *sark-*, the stem of *sarx* "flesh." Ultimately from an Indo-European word meaning "to cut, tear," which is also the ancestor of English *sarcasm* and *sarcophagus.*]

sar·co·din·i·an /saarkə dínnee ən/ *adj.* OF AMOEBA CLASS OF PROTOZOANS belonging to the class of protozoans that includes amoebas ■ *n.* SARCODINIAN PROTOZOAN a protozoan that belongs to the same class as amoebas [Formed from modern Latin *Sarcodina*, superclass name, from Greek *sarkōdēs*, "fleshy," from *sarx* "flesh"]

sar·coid /saar kòyd/ *n.* INFECTED AREA a small area of chronic infection in the body of a person affected by sarcoidosis ■ *adj.* LIKE FLESH relating to or resembling flesh

sar·coid·o·sis /saar koy d-ssəss/ *n.* a disease in which lumps of fibrous tissue and collections of cells (**granulomas**) appear on the skin and internal organs

sar·co·lac·tic ac·id /saarkə làktik-/ *n.* a form of lactic acid produced by muscle tissue during anaerobic activity

sar·co·lem·ma /saarkə lémmə/ *n.* a thin clear membrane that covers a striated muscle fiber

sar·co·ma /saar kṓmə/ (*plural* **-mas** *or* **-ma·ta** /-mətə/) *n.* a malignant tumor that begins growing in connective tissue such as muscle, bone, fat, or cartilage. Sarcomas may occur in any part of the body, and are typically fast-growing and quick to spread. —**sar·co·ma·toid** *adj.* —**sar·co·ma·tous** *adj.*

sar·co·ma·to·sis /saar kṓmə tṓssəss/ *n.* a disease marked by the growth of sarcomas in various parts of the body

sar·co·mere /saarkə meer/ *n.* any of the tiny segments that make up a fibril of striated muscle

sar·coph·a·gus /saar kóffəgəss/ (*plural* **-gi** /-gī/ *or* **-gus·es**) *n.* an ancient stone or marble coffin, often decorated with sculpture and inscriptions [Early 17thC. Via Latin from Greek *sarkophagos*, literally "flesh-eater." The word originally referred to a kind of limestone used for making coffins in which bodies were thought to decompose quickly.]

sar·co·plasm /saarkə plàzzəm/ *n.* the cytoplasm of a striated muscle fiber —**sar·co·plas·mic** /saarkə plázmik/ *adj.* —**sar·co·plas·mous** /-plázməss/ *adj.*

sar·co·plas·mic re·tic·u·lum *n.* the endoplasmic reticulum of a striated muscle fiber

sar·cop·tic mange /saar kòptik-/ *n.* a form of mange caused by a parasitic mite that burrows into the skin [Formed from modern Latin *Sarcoptes*, genus name of the mite that causes the disease, from Greek *sarx* "flesh" + *koptein* "to cut"]

sar·co·style /saarkə stīl/ *n.* = **myofibril**

sar·cous /saarkəss/ *adj.* consisting of or relating to flesh or muscle tissue

sard /saard/ *n.* a deep orange-red variety of chalcedony used in making jewelry [15thC. Via Latin *sarda* from Greek *sardios*, of uncertain origin: perhaps from SARDIS.]

sar·dar *n.* = **sirdar** [Late 16thC. From Persian, literally "holding the position of chief."]

sar·dine /saar deen/ *n.* a small marine fish related to the herring, especially the European pilchard. Sardines are netted in large numbers for food and preserved in cans, packed tightly in oil. Latin name: *Sardinia pilchardus.* [15thC. Via French from, ultimately, Greek *Sardō* "Sardinia."] ◇ **be packed like sardines** to be crowded closely together

Sar·din·i·a /saar dínnee è/ Italian island in the Mediterranean Sea. It is the second largest island in the Mediterranean after Sicily. Capital: Cagliari. Population: 1,659,466 (1995). Area: 9,194 sq. mi./23,813 sq. km.

Sar·din·i·an /saar dínnee ən/ *n.* **1.** PEOPLES SOMEBODY FROM SARDINIA somebody who was born in or who lives in Sardinia **2.** LANG SPOKEN LANGUAGE OF SARDINIA the language spoken in Sardinia. It belongs to the Romance family of languages and is regarded by some linguists as a dialect of Italian. ■ *adj.* RELATING TO

SARDINIA relating to Sardinia, or its people or culture

Sar·dis /sa̋ardiss/ ancient city of Asia Minor, in present-day Turkey. It was the capital city of Lydia and an early seat of Christianity.

sar·di·us /sa̋ardee əss/ *n.* = **sard** [15thC. From Latin, formed from *sarda* (see SARD).]

sar·don·ic /saar dónnik/ *adj.* disdainfully or ironically mocking [Mid-17thC. Via French *sardonique* from, ultimately, Greek *sardanios* "scornful." Originally meaning "Sardinian," its later meaning derives from the "Sardinian plant," which caused facial contortions resembling a scornful grin.] —**sar·don·i·cal·ly** *adv.* —**sar·don·i·cism** *n.*

WORD KEY: SYNONYMS

See Synonyms at *sarcastic.*

sar·don·yx /saar dónniks/ *n.* a variety of onyx with alternating bands of light orange-brown sard and white chalcedony, once widely used in making cameos [14thC. Via Latin from Greek *sardonux*, from *sardios* (see SARD) + *onux* (see ONYX).]

sa·ree *n.* = **sari**

sar·gas·so /saar gássō/, **sar·gas·so weed** *n.* = **gulfweed** [Late 16thC. From Portuguese *sargaço*, of unknown origin.]

Sar·gas·so Sea /sar gàssō-/ section of the North Atlantic Ocean, between the West Indies and the Azores. It is noted for its predominantly still waters.

sar·gas·sum /saar gássəm/ *n.* = **gulfweed** [Early 20thC. From modern Latin, from SARGASSO.]

sar·gas·sum fish *n.* a brown and black fish that lives in floating gulfweed in the Atlantic and western Pacific oceans. Latin name: *Histrio histrio.*

sarge /saardg/ *n.* a sergeant in the armed forces or police (*informal*) [Mid-19thC. Shortening of SERGEANT.]

Library of Congress

John Singer Sargent

Sar·gent /sa̋arjənt/, **John Singer** (1856–1925) Italian-born U.S. artist. Possessing a brilliant technique, he was known for oil portraits of well-known people such as *Madame Gautreau* (1882–83). He later turned to watercolors.

Sar·go·dha /saar gṓdè/ city in Punjab Province, Pakistan, about 110 mi./177 km northwest of Lahore. Population: 291,361 (1981).

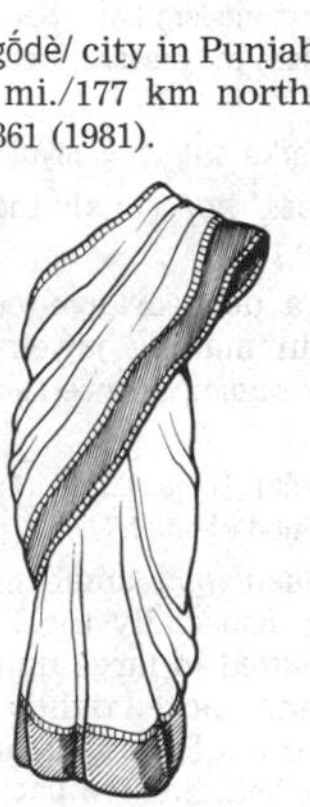

Sari

sa·ri /sa̋aree/, **sa·ree** *n.* a traditional garment worn by women in or from the Indian subcontinent, consisting of a long rectangle of fabric reaching the feet, wrapped and pleated around the waist over an underskirt and choli, and draped over the shoulder [Late 18thC. Via Hindi *sāṛī* from, ultimately, Sanskrit *śāṭī* "garment."]

sar·in /sa̋arin/ *n.* an extremely toxic gas that attacks the central nervous system, causing convulsions and death. It has been used for chemical warfare. Formula: $C_4H_{10}FO_2P$. [Mid-20thC. From German, of unknown origin.]

sar·men·tose /saar méntōss/, **sar·men·tous** /saar méntəss/ *adj.* producing long slender stems that reach out and take root along the ground [Mid-18thC. Formed from Latin *sarmentosus* "full of twigs," from *sarmentum* "twig."]

Sar·ni·a /sa̋arniè/ city at the southern tip of Lake Huron, on the St. Clair River, Ontario, Canada. Population: 86,480 (1996).

Sar·noff /sa̋arn of/, **David** (1891–1971) Russian-born U.S.entrepreneur. A pioneer in radio and television, he headed the Radio Corporation of America (1930–70) and established the National Broadcasting Company (1926).

sa·rod /sə rṓd/ *n.* a stringed instrument of northern India that resembles a lute with two resonating gourds but is played with a bow [Mid-19thC. Via Urdu from Persian *sar ud.*]

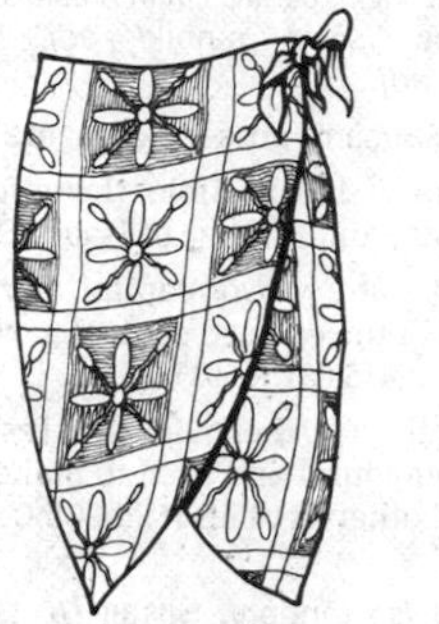

Sarong

sa·rong /sə ráwng/ *n.* **1. TRADITIONAL MALAYSIAN GARMENT** a traditional garment of Java and the Malay archipelago, consisting of a length of fabric wrapped and tied around the body at the waist or under the arms. It is worn by men and women. **2.** CLOTHES **FASHION VERSION OF SARONG** a fashion version of the sarong worn by a woman as a wrapped skirt, often for the beach **3. CLOTH FOR MALAYSIAN GARMENTS** cloth for a sarong, often brightly colored [Mid-19thC. From Malay "covering."]

Sa·ron·ic Gulf /sè rónik-/ gulf of the Aegean Sea, on the coast of southeastern Greece

sa·ros /sáir oss, sa̋arōss/ *n.* the cycle of 6,585.32 days, or approximately 18 years 11 days, after which a sequence of eclipses of the sun and moon repeats itself. It was known to the Babylonians and some other ancient civilizations. [Early 19thC. Via Greek from Babylonian *sāru* "the number 3600." The modern sense, "eclipse cycle," derives from a 19thC misunderstanding of the Babylonian word.] —**sa·ron·ic** /sə rónnik/ *adj.*

Sa·roy·an /sə róy ən/, **William** (1908–81) U.S. playwright and novelist, whose often flamboyant works include the play *The Time of Your Life* (1938). He refused its Pulitzer Prize because he disapproved of such awards.

sar·panch /sa̋ar pùnch/ *n.* the head of a village council (**panchayat**) in India [Mid-20thC. From Urdu, formed from *sar* "head" + *panch* "five."]

sar·ra·ce·ni·a /sàrrə seénee ə/ (*plural* **-as** *or* **-a**) *n.* any of the pitcher plants that are native to eastern North America and have hollow tubular leaves that trap insects. Genus: *Sarracenia.* [Mid-18thC. From modern Latin, named for the 17thC Canadian botanist D. *Sarrazin.*]

sar·ru·so·phone /sə ro͞ozə fōn/ *n.* a woodwind musical instrument similar to a bassoon but made of brass [Late 19thC. Named for M. *Sarrus*, the 19thC French bandmaster who invented the instrument.]

sar·sa·pa·ril·la /sa̋aspə rílə/ (*plural* **-las** *or* **-la**) *n.* **1. TROPICAL VINE** tropical American vine with aromatic roots and heart-shaped leaves. Genus: *Smilax.* **2. PLANT SIMILAR TO SARSAPARILLA** a plant similar to sarsaparilla, especially American sarsaparilla and Australian sarsaparilla **3. MEDICINAL ROOT** the dried root of any sarsaparilla plant, used in traditional or herbal medicine and to make a soft drink **4.** BEVERAGES **KIND OF SODA POP** a carbonated drink flavored with sarsaparilla root, similar to root beer [Late 16thC. From Spanish *zarzaparilla*, from *zarza* literally "little bramble vine."]

sar·sen /sa̋arss'n/ *n.* any of the many large sedimentary rocks that have been broken into blocks by frost action and are found scattered across the chalk downs of southern England [Late 17thC. Alteration of SARACEN. The association is unclear.]

sar·sen·et *n.* = **sarcenet**

sar·tor /sa̋artər/ *n.* a tailor (*literary*) [Mid-17thC. From Latin, formed from *sart-*, the past participle stem of *sarcire* "to patch."]

sar·to·ri·al /saar táwree əl/ *adj.* **1.** CLOTHES **OF TAILORING** relating to tailoring or clothing in general **2.** ANAT **OF SARTORIUS MUSCLE** relating to the sartorius muscle in the thigh

sar·to·ri·us /saar táwree əss/ (*plural* **-i** /-ī/) *n.* a flat narrow muscle that extends from the hip to the inner thigh and helps rotate the leg to a cross-legged position. It is the longest muscle in the human body. [Early 18thC. From modern Latin *musculus sartorius* "tailor's muscle," from *sartor* (see SARTOR). The term derives from the cross-legged seating posture tailors traditionally assumed when sewing.]

AKG London

Jean-Paul Sartre

Sar·tre /sa̋artrə, saart/, **Jean-Paul** (1905–80) French philosopher, playwright, and novelist. The principal exponent of existentialism, he wrote *Being and Nothingness* (1943) and the novel *Nausea* (1938).

Sar·vo·day·a *n.* the name that Mohandas K. Gandhi and his followers gave to the new social order that they sought to establish in India. [Early 20thC. From Sanskrit, literally "prosperity for all."]

SAS *n.* a British military force that is specially trained to undertake dangerous clandestine operations. Full form **Special Air Service**

SASE *abbr.* self-addressed stamped envelope

sash /sash/ *n.* **1. FABRIC BELT** a strip of cloth tied around the waist, e.g., as part of ceremonial dress **2. WIDE RIBBON WORN ACROSS THE CHEST** a band of cloth draped over one shoulder and across the chest as a symbol of rank or office **3. FRAME FOR GLASS** a frame holding the glass panes of a window or door [Late 17thC. From Arabic "muslin."]

sa·shay /sa sháy/ *vi.* (**-shayed, -shay·ing, -shays**) **1. FLOUNCE GRACEFULLY** to walk in a way that is intended to attract attention, especially by swaying the hips or swinging the elbows (*informal*) **2. PERFORM STEPS IN SQUARE DANCING** to dance a sequence of steps in square dancing ■ *n.* **1.** = **chassé 2. PATTERN IN SQUARE DANCING** a figure in square dancing in which partners circle each other using sideways steps [Mid-19thC. From French *chassé*, literally "chasing, chase."]

sash cord *n.* a weighted cord that runs through a groove on either side of a window frame, to provide balance as the window is raised and lowered

sa·shi·mi /saa sheémee/ *n.* a Japanese dish consisting of slices of raw fish, usually served with a dipping sauce such as a seasoned soy sauce. Small quantities of other ingredients, e.g., finely shredded white radish or selected pickles, may also be added as garnishes and palate-refreshing accompaniments. [Late 19thC. From Japanese.]

sash saw *n.* a small saw with a thin blade, used in making window sashes

sash weight *n.* a small metal weight attached to the sash cord on either side of a window frame to provide balance so that the window can be raised and lowered smoothly

sash win·dow *n.* a window that consists of two frames, one above the other in vertical grooves, allowing either to be opened or shut by sliding it up or down

sa·sin /sáyssin/ *n.* = **blackbuck**

Sask. *abbr.* Saskatchewan

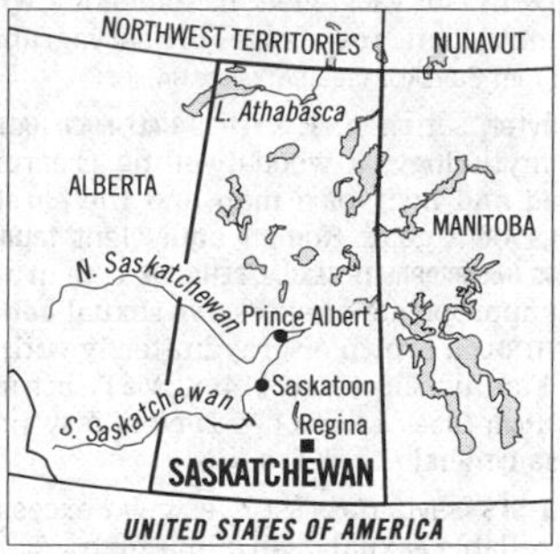

Saskatchewan

Sas·katch·e·wan[1] /sas káchèwàn/ the central Prairie province of Canada, along with Alberta and Manitoba. Capital: Regina. Population: 990,237 (1996). Area: 251,865 sq. mi./652,330 sq. km. —**Sas·katch·e·wa·ni·an** /sa skàche wáanee ən/ *n., adj.*

Sas·katch·e·wan[2] /sès káchèwàn/ river in Canada, rising in central Saskatchewan and flowing into Lake Winnipeg, in Manitoba. Length: 340 mi./547 km.

sas·ka·toon /sàskə to͞on/ *n.* **1.** TREES **N AMERICAN SHRUB** a small bush that grows in northwest North America, with white flowers and sweet purple-black fruit. Latin name: *Amelanchier alnifolia.* **2. WILD N AMERICAN FRUIT** the sweet purple-black fruit of the saskatoon [Early 19thC. From Cree *misaaskwatoomin,* "amelanchier berry."]

Sas·ka·toon /sàskè to͞on/ the second largest city in Saskatchewan, Canada, 150 mi./242 km northwest of Regina. Population: 219,056 (1996).

sas·quatch /sás kwòch, sás kwàwch/ *n.* a large hairy humanoid creature said to live in the mountains of western Canada [Early 20thC. From Salish.]

sass /sass/ *n.* **BACK TALK** disrespectful or impudent remarks, especially in reply to an older person or somebody in authority (*informal*) ■ *vt.* **(sassed, sass·ing, sass·es) TALK BACK TO SOMEBODY** to talk disrespectfully or impudently, especially to somebody who is older or in authority (*informal*) [Mid-19thC. Alteration of SAUCE.]

sas·sa·by /sássəbee/ (*plural* **-bies**) *n.* = **topi**[1] *n.* [Early 19thC. Alteration of Tswana *tsessébi.*]

sas·sa·fras /sássə fràss/ (*plural* **-fras**) *n.* **1. N AMERICAN TREE** an eastern North American tree with aromatic bark, unevenly lobed leaves, and small bluish fruits. Latin name: *Sassafras albidum.* **2. FLAVORED BARK** the dried root bark of the sassafras tree, used for flavoring and in perfumes and medicines [Late 16thC. From Spanish *sasafrás,* of uncertain origin: perhaps from Latin *saxifraga* (see SAXIFRAGE).]

sas·sa·fras oil *n.* a clear oil made from the root of the sassafras tree

Sas·sa·nid /sássənid/ *n.* a member of a Persian dynasty that ruled from A.D. 224–651. The dynasty superseded the Parthian Empire, and challenged Roman power in the East. It was the last line of Persian kings before the Arab conquests. [Late 18thC. Named for the Persian monarch *Sasan,* grandfather of the first Sassanian king.] —**Sas·sa·ni·an** /sə sáynee ən/ *adj.*

Sas·sa·ri /sássèree/ capital of Sassari Province, Sardinia, Italy, situated near the northwestern coast of the island. Population: 121,961 (1992).

Sas·soon /sə so͞on/, **Siegfried** (1886–1967) British poet and novelist. He is known for his searing poems about the horrors of World War I and for his semi-autobiographical fictional trilogy, collected as *The Memoirs of George Sherston* (1928–36). Full name **Siegfried Lorraine Sassoon**

sass·wood /sáss wo͝od/ *n.* = **sassy**[2]

sas·sy[1] /sássee/ (*plural* **-sies**, *comparative* **-si·er**, *superlative* **-si·est**) *adj.* **1. IMPUDENT** impudent or disrespectful **2. HIGH-SPIRITED** lively and high-spirited ○ *The show has refreshingly sassy hoedown-style choreography.* **3. STYLISH** stylish or fashionable ○ *a sassy look for spring* [Mid-19thC. Alteration of SAUCY.]

sas·sy[2] /sássee/ (*plural* **-sies**) *n.* a western African tree with poisonous bark and hard insect-resistant wood used for building. Latin name: *Erythrophleum suaveolens.* [Mid-19thC. Origin uncertain: perhaps from Twi *sese* "plane tree."]

sas·sy wood *n.* **1.** = **sassy**[2] **2. W AFRICAN POISON** a drink made with the poisonous extract of the sassy tree. In West African tradition it was used as a poison in trial by ordeal, and the ability to drink it and survive was thought to be a proof of innocence.

sas·tra *n.* = **shastra**

sas·tru·ga /sas tro͞ogə, sástrəgə/ *n.* a long wave-shaped ridge of hard snow formed by the wind and common in polar regions [Mid-19thC. Via German from Russian *zastruga.*]

sat past tense, past participle of **sit**

SAT *n.* a test of performance given to high school students, used to determine eligibility for admission to a college or university. Full form **Scholastic Aptitude Test**

sat. *abbr.* **1.** saturated **2.** saturation **3.** satellite

Sat. *abbr.* CALENDAR Saturday

Sa·tan /sáyt'n/ *n.* in Christianity, the enemy of God, the lord of evil, and the tempter of human beings. He is sometimes identified with Lucifer, the leader of the fallen angels. [Pre-12thC. Via Latin from, ultimately, Hebrew *śāṭān* "to accuse."]

sa·tang /sə táang/ (*plural* **-tang**) *n.* **1. SUBUNIT OF THAI CURRENCY** a subunit of currency in Thailand, 100 of which are worth one baht. See table at **currency 2. COIN WORTH A SATANG** a coin worth a satang

sa·tan·ic /sə tánnik/ *adj.* **1. RELATING TO SATAN WORSHIP** relating to Satan or the worship of Satan **2. EXTREMELY EVIL** extremely evil or cruel —**sa·tan·i·cal·ly** *adv.* —**sa·tan·i·cal·ness** *n.*

Sa·tan·ism /sáyt'n ìzzəm/ *n.* the worship of Satan, especially as a parody of Christian rites

sa·tay /saá tay/ *n.* a dish popular in Indonesia and Malaysia, consisting of marinated well-seasoned pieces of meat, chicken, or fish grilled on wooden skewers and served with peanut sauce [Mid-20thC. From Malay.]

SATB *abbr.* soprano, alto, tenor, bass

satch·el /sáchəl/ *n.* a small bag, often with a shoulder strap, used for carrying books and personal belongings [14thC. Via Old French *sachel* from Latin *sacellus,* from *saccus* "bag" (source of English *sack*).]

sate /sayt/ **(sat·ed, sat·ing, sates)** *vt.* **1. FULLY GRATIFY DESIRE** to satisfy completely somebody's hunger or some other desire **2. GLUT SOMEBODY** to provide somebody with more than enough, to the point of exhaustion or disgust [Old English *sadian.* Ultimately from an Indo-European word that is also the ancestor of English *sad, satisfy,* and *asset.*]

sa·teen /sə te͞en/ (*plural* **-teens** *or* **-teen**) *n.* a cotton or polyester fabric with a shiny side intended to look like satin [Late 19thC. Formed from SATIN, on the model of "velveteen."]

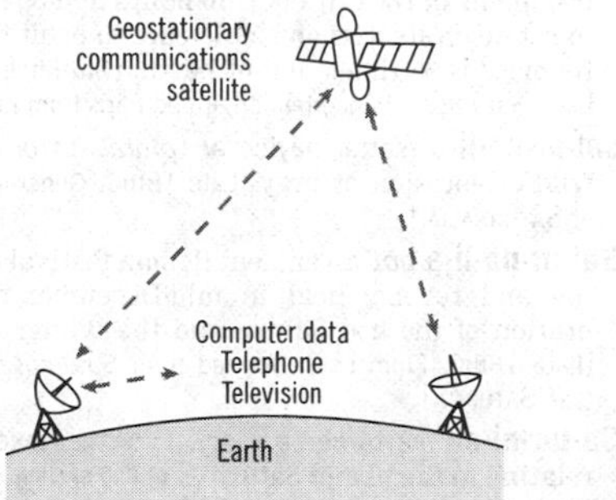

Satellite

sat·el·lite /sátt'l ìt/ *n.* **1.** TELECOM **DEVICE THAT ORBITS A PLANET** an object put into orbit around Earth or any other planet in order to relay communications signals or transmit scientific data **2.** ASTRON **MOON ORBITING OTHER BODY** a celestial body that orbits a larger one **3. COUNTRY DEPENDENT ON ANOTHER COUNTRY** a nation or political unit that is dependent economically and politically on another more powerful nation **4.** GEOG **SUBURB** a town or small city located near and dependent on a larger city **5. ATTENDANT** somebody who attends a person of importance, often obsequiously [Mid-16thC. Via French from Latin *satelles* "attendant."]

sat·el·lite broad·cast·ing *n.* the global transmission of television programs via satellite

sat·el·lite cell *n.* one of the cells forming the capsule that encloses the nerve cells in many spinal ganglia

sat·el·lite dish *n.* a dish-shaped device for receiving television signals broadcast via satellite

sat·el·lite DNA *n.* a component of an animal's DNA that differs in density from surrounding DNA, consists of short repeating sequences of nucleotide pairs, and does not undergo transcription

sat·el·lite sta·tion *n.* a radio or television station that receives programs from another station and rebroadcasts them immediately on a different wavelength

sat·el·li·ti·um /sàttə líttee əm/ *n.* in astrology, a group of planets in one sign of the zodiac (*archaic*)

sa·tem /saátəm/ *adj.* relating to Indo-European languages in which the consonant sounding like "k" developed into the sound "s" or "sh" [Early 20thC. From Avestan *satem* "hundred."]

sa·ti *n.* = **suttee**

sa·tia·ble /sáyshəb'l/ *adj.* able to be satisfied [Late 16thC. Formed from Latin *satiare* "to satisfy" (see SATIATE).] —**sa·tia·bil·i·ty** /sàyshə bíllətee/ *n.* —**sa·tia·bly** /sáyshəblee/ *adv.*

sa·ti·ate /sáyshee àyt/ *vt.* **(-at·ed, -at·ing, -ates) 1. GRATIFY DESIRE** to satisfy hunger or another appetite completely **2. GLUT SOMEBODY** to provide somebody with too much of something desirable, to the point of overindulgence (*often passive*) ■ *adj.* **HAVING TOO MUCH** having had enough or too much [15thC. From Latin *satiat-*, the past participle stem of *satiare,* from *satis* "enough" (source of English *satisfy*).]

sa·ti·e·ty /sə tī́ ətee/ *n.* a state in which somebody has had enough or too much [Mid-16thC. Via French *satiété* from, ultimately, Latin *satis* "enough."]

sat·in /sátt'n/ *n.* **GLOSSY SILK OR RAYON FABRIC** a fabric woven of silk or rayon, with a smooth glossy finish and a dull back ■ *adj.* **1. OF SATIN** made of satin fabric **2. GLOSSY LIKE SATIN** smooth and glossy like satin [14thC. Via Old French from Arabic *zaytūnī* "of the town of Zaytun," of uncertain location: probably the Chinese city of Tsinkiang.] —**sat·in·y** *adj.*

sat·in·et /sàtt'n ét/, **sat·in·ette** *n.* **1. IMITATION SATIN** an imitation satin made from cotton and wool **2. INFERIOR SATIN** thin or inferior satin

sat·in flow·er *n.* **1. N AMERICAN PLANT** a North American plant that grows on the Pacific coast and has red flowers. Latin name: *Clarkia amoena.* **2.** = **honesty** *n.* **3**

sat·in spar *n.* a variety of sulfate or carbonate of calcium. ◊ **gypsum**

sat·in stitch *n.* an embroidery stitch that is worked in close parallel lines to fill in an area or form a solid line

sat·in wal·nut *n.* the wood of the sweet gum tree, often used to make furniture. ◊ **sweet gum**

sat·in weave *n.* a weave in which the face of the fabric is covered entirely with warp threads, producing a smooth finish

sat·in·wood /sátt'n wo͝od/ *n.* **1. E INDIAN TREE** a tree that grows in India and Sri Lanka and has hard yellow-brown wood. Latin name: *Chloroxylon swietenia.* **2. WOOD FROM SATINWOOD TREE** the smooth hard wood of the East Indian satinwood tree, used in fine carpentry **3. W INDIAN TREE** a tree that grows in the West Indies and has smooth lustrous wood. Latin name: *Zanthoxylum flavum.*

sat·in·y /sátt'nee/ *adj.* smooth and lustrous like satin

sat·ire /sá tīr/ *n.* **1. USE OF WIT** the use of wit, especially irony, sarcasm, and ridicule, to attack the vices and follies of humankind **2. LITERARY WORK USING SATIRE** a literary work that uses satire, or the branch of literature made up of such works [Early 16thC. Directly or via French from Latin *satira* "poetic medley, satire," of uncertain origin: perhaps a variant of *satura* "a mixed dish."]

sa·tir·i·cal /sə tírik'l/ *adj.* relating to satire or the use of wit to attack the vices and follies of humankind

WORD KEY: SYNONYMS

See Synonyms at ***sarcastic***

sat·i·rist /sáttərist/ *n.* somebody who writes satirical works

sat·i·rize /sáttə rīz/ (**-rized, -riz·ing, -riz·es**) *vt.* to attack or criticize somebody or something by means of satire —**sat·i·ri·za·tion** /sàrtərə záysh'n/ *n.* —**sat·i·riz·er** /sáttə rīzər/ *n.*

sat·is·fac·tion /sàttəs fáksh'n/ *n.* **1.** GRATIFICATION the feeling of pleasure that comes when a need or desire is fulfilled ○ *job satisfaction* **2.** FULFILLMENT the fulfillment of a need, claim, or desire **3.** HAPPINESS WITH SOMETHING happiness with the way that something has been arranged or done ○ *organized to her satisfaction* **4.** FREEDOM FROM DOUBT the assurance that something has been fully explained or settled ○ *a solution that was never explained to my satisfaction* **5.** COMPENSATION compensation for an injury or loss ○ *demanded satisfaction for their mistreatment* [14thC. Via French from, ultimately, Latin *satisfacere*, from *satis* "enough" + *facere* "to make."]

sat·is·fac·to·ry /sàttəs fáktəree/ *adj.* good enough to meet a requirement or to be considered acceptable [15thC. Via French *satisfactoire* from, ultimately, Latin *satisfacere* "to satisfy" (see SATISFACTION).]

sat·is·fied /sáttəs fīd/ *adj.* **1.** CONTENT WITH SOMETHING contented or pleased with what has happened **2.** FULLY CONVINCED fully convinced that something is right, proper, or true **3.** FULLY PAID paid in full

sat·is·fy /sáttəs fī/ (**-fied, -fy·ing, -fies**) *v.* **1.** *vt.* MAKE SOMEBODY FEEL CONTENT to do or offer enough to make somebody feel pleased or content **2.** *vti.* FULFILL NEED to fulfill a need or gratify a desire **3.** *vt.* RESOLVE DOUBTS to convince somebody by resolving questions or doubts **4.** *vt.* BE GOOD ENOUGH TO MEET CONDITION to achieve or be of sufficient standard to meet a requirement or condition **5.** *vt.* MATH SOLVE MATHEMATICAL PROBLEM to make both sides of an equation equal by finding the quantities of the unknown variables **6.** *vt.* LAW PAY DEBT to pay a debt in full **7.** *vt.* COMPENSATE SOMEBODY to compensate somebody for an injury or loss [15thC. Via Old French *satisfier* from Latin *satisfacere* "to satisfy" (see SATISFACTION).] —**sat·is·fi·er** *n.*

Sa·to Ei·sa·ku /saàtō áyss aakōō/ (1901–75) Japanese prime minister, who was awarded the Nobel Peace Prize (1974) for his role in negotiating a nuclear nonproliferation pact.

sa·to·ri /saa táwree/ *n.* in Zen Buddhism, a state of spiritual enlightenment that is a spiritual objective [Early 18thC. From Japanese "awakening."]

sa·trap /sá tràp, sáy-/ *n.* **1.** PERSIAN GOVERNOR the governor of a province in ancient Persia **2.** POLITICAL HENCHMAN a subordinate official, especially a self-important one [15thC. Via French and Latin from, ultimately, Old Persian *kšatrapāvan*, literally "protector of the country."]

sa·tra·py /sáttrəpee, sáy-/ (*plural* **-pies**) *n.* the province or territory ruled by a satrap

sat·su·ma /sat sōōmə/ *n.* **1.** FOOD KIND OF TANGERINE a citrus fruit with a thin orange skin **2.** TREES JAPANESE CITRUS TREE a small Japanese tree that bears satsumas. Latin name: *Citrus reticulata.* [Late 19thC. Named for a province in the island of Kiusiu, in Japan.]

Sat·su·ma ware, Sat·su·ma *n.* a kind of cream-colored Japanese pottery

sat·u·ra·ble /sáchərəb'l/ *adj.* capable of being saturated, or of reaching the point where nothing more can be absorbed [Late 16thC. Formed from Latin *saturat-*, the past participle stem of *saturare* "to saturate" (see SATURATE).] —**sat·u·ra·bil·i·ty** /sàchərə bíllətee/ *n.*

sat·u·rant /sáchərənt/ *n.* SOMETHING THAT SATURATES a substance that is used to saturate another substance ■ *adj.* SATURATING causing saturation [Mid-18thC. From Latin *saturant-*, the present participle stem of *saturare* "to saturate" (see SATURATE).]

sat·u·rate *vt.* /sáchə ràyt/ (**-rat·ed, -rat·ing, -rates**) **1.** MAKE SOMETHING WET to make something soaked with liquid **2.** FILL SOMETHING COMPLETELY to fill something with so many people or things that no more can be added **3.** COMM SUPPLY MARKET FULLY to supply a market fully, so that all existing demand for a product is met **4.** CHEM FILL SOLUTION WITH ANOTHER SUBSTANCE to add a liquid, solid, or gas to a solution until it reaches the point where nothing more can be absorbed **5.** MIL BOMB ENEMY HEAVILY to overwhelm an enemy with intensive bombing ■ *adj.* SATURATED saturated with liquid (*archaic*) [Mid-16thC. From Latin *saturat-*, the past participle stem of *saturare*, from *satur* "satiated" (probable source of English *satire*).]

sat·u·rat·ed /sáchə ràytəd/ *adj.* **1.** WET soaked with liquid **2.** CHEM CONTAINING MAXIMUM SOLUTE containing the maximum amount of absorbed solute **3.** PACKED FULL completely packed or full so that no more can be added **4.** FOOD CONTAINING FATTY ACIDS containing a relatively large number of fatty acids

sat·u·rat·ed fat *n.* a kind of fat, often found in meat and other animal products, that cannot incorporate any additional hydrogen atoms. A diet heavy in saturated fat is thought to raise cholesterol in the bloodstream.

sat·u·ra·tion /sàchə ráysh'n/ *n.* **1.** STATE OF TOTAL WETNESS a state in which something is completely soaked with liquid **2.** STATE OF BEING PACKED FULL a state in which something is so full or packed that no more can be added **3.** MIL HEAVY BOMBING intensive bombing of a military target in order to overwhelm an enemy **4.** COMM FULL SUPPLYING OF MARKET the full supplying of a market, to the point where all existing demand for a product is met **5.** CHEM MAXIMUM ABSORPTION the absorption of the greatest possible amount of a liquid, solid, or gas by a solution **6.** PHYS STATE OF MAGNETIZATION a state of complete magnetization **7.** METEOROL 100 PERCENT HUMIDITY the condition of the atmosphere when it contains as much water vapor as it can hold at a specific temperature **8.** PHYS COLOR INTENSITY the intensity of a color **9.** ELECTRON ENG CONDITION OF STABLE OUTPUT CURRENT a condition where the output current of an electronic device is substantially constant and no longer increases as a function of increasing input ■ *adj.* COMPREHENSIVE comprehensive in the use of outlets or other resources ○ *The event had saturation coverage in the press.*

sat·u·ra·tion div·ing *n.* a method of diving in which the diver's bloodstream is saturated with an inert gas so that the time required for decompression is unaffected by the duration of the dive

sat·u·ra·tion point *n.* **1.** LIMIT TO SCOPE FOR EXPANSION the point at which no more can be added **2.** CHEM LIMIT TO ABSORPTION the point at which the greatest possible amount of a substance has been absorbed in a solution

sat·u·ra·tion zone *n.* the zone below the water table that is saturated with groundwater

Sat·ur·day /sáttər dày, -dee/ *n.* CALENDAR the day of the week after Friday and before Sunday [Pre-12thC. Translation of Latin *Saturni dies*, literally "day of Saturn" (see SATURN).]

Sat·ur·day night spe·cial *n.* a small cheap handgun that is easy to obtain and conceal [Because the guns are most often used in urban attacks, fights and robberies, the types of crime that typically occur on a Saturday night]

Sat·ur·days /sáttər dàyz, -deez/ *adv.* CALENDAR every Saturday

Sat·urn /sáttərn/ *n.* **1.** ROMAN GOD OF AGRICULTURE in Roman mythology, the god of agriculture and ruler of the universe during the Golden Age. Greek equivalent **Cronus 2.** PLANET 6TH FROM SUN the second largest planet in the solar system and the sixth planet from the sun. Saturn has bright rings made up of orbiting fragments of rock. It takes 10 hours and 39 minutes to rotate on its axis and 29.5 years to orbit the Sun. Its mass is 95 times that of Earth. [Old English. From Latin *Saturnus*, of uncertain origin: perhaps from Etruscan.]

sat·ur·na·li·a /sàttər náylee ə/ (*plural* **-as** *or* **-a**) *n.* a wild celebration or orgy [Late 18thC. Generalized use of SATURNALIA.]

Sat·ur·na·li·a *npl.* an ancient Roman festival of feasting and revelry held in mid-December in celebration of the god Saturn and the winter solstice [Late 16thC. From Latin, formed from *Saturnus* "Saturn" (see SATURN).]

Sa·tur·ni·an /sa túrnee ən/ *adj.* **1.** OF THE PLANET SATURN relating to the planet Saturn **2.** OF GOD SATURN relating to the Roman god Saturn or the Golden Age of his reign

sa·tur·ni·id /sa túrnee id/ *n.* a large brightly colored moth that has a stout hairy body. Family: Saturniidae. [Late 19thC. From modern Latin *Saturniidae*, from Latin *Saturnus* "Saturn" (see SATURN).]

sat·ur·nine /sáttər nīn/ *adj.* **1.** MELANCHOLY gloomy and morose **2.** CAUSED BY LEAD POISONING caused by the absorption of lead or suffering from lead poisoning (*archaic*) [15thC. Directly or via French from medieval Latin *saturninus*, from Latin *Saturnus* "Saturn" (see SATURN).] —**sat·ur·nine·ly** *adv.*

sa·tya·gra·ha /sut jaágrəhə/ *n.* the doctrine of nonviolent resistance originated by Mohandas K. Gandhi and used in the opposition to British rule in India. [Early 20thC. From Sanskrit *satyāgrahaḥ*, literally "force born out of truth."]

sa·tya·gra·hi /sut yaágrəhee/ *n.* somebody who practices nonviolent resistance or satyagraha [Early 20thC. From Sanskrit (see SATYAGRAHA).]

sa·tyr /sáytər, sáttər/ *n.* **1.** MYTHOL HALF-MAN, HALF-GOAT in Greek mythology, a wood-dwelling creature with the head and body of a man and the ears, horns, and legs of a goat. Roman equivalent **faun 2.** MAN DISPLAYING INAPPROPRIATE SEXUAL BEHAVIOR a man who displays inappropriate or excessive sexual behavior **3.** ZOOL BUTTERFLY a brown or gray butterfly with spotted wings. Family: Satyridae. [14thC. Via French from Latin *satyrus*, from Greek *saturos*.] —**sa·tyr·ic** /say tírrik, sə-/ *adj.* —**sa·tyr·i·cal** /-tírrik'l/ *adj.*

sa·ty·ri·a·sis /sàytə rī́əssiss/ *n.* PSYCHIAT excessive and uncontrollable sexual desire in a man

sa·tyr·id /sáytərid, sáttə-/ *n.* a small brown butterfly. Family: Satyridae.

sa·tyr play *n.* in ancient Greece, a comic play that mocked a mythological subject and included a chorus of satyrs

sauce /sawss/ *n.* **1.** FLAVORING LIQUID FOR FOOD a thick liquid that is served with food to add extra flavor **2.** STEWED FRUIT stewed fruit served with a meal ○ *cranberry sauce* **3.** IMPUDENT REMARKS impudent or disrespectful remarks (*informal*) **4.** ZEST something that adds zest or excitement **5.** LIQUOR alcoholic liquor (*slang*) ■ *vt.* (**sauced, sauc·ing, sauc·es**) **1.** SPEAK TO SOMEBODY DISRESPECTFULLY to make impudent or disrespectful remarks to somebody (*informal*) **2.** ADD SAUCE TO FOOD to add flavor to food using a sauce **3.** ENLIVEN SOMETHING to add zest or interest to something [14thC. Via Old French from, ultimately, Latin *salsus*, past participle of *sallere* "to salt," from *sal* "salt."]

Sauceboat

sauce·boat *n.* a low boat-shaped pitcher used for serving sauce or gravy

sauce·pan /sáwss pàn/ *n.* a cooking pot with a handle, used on top of a stove

sauce·pot /sáwss pòt/ *n.* a cooking pot with two handles and a close-fitting lid

sau·cer /sáwssər/ *n.* **1.** SMALL CIRCULAR DISH a small shallow dish designed to hold a matching cup **2.** ROUND FLAT OBJECT anything circular and shallow like a saucer

sauce su·prême *n.* = **suprême sauce**

sauc·y /sáwssee/ (**-i·er, -i·est**) *adj.* **1.** IMPUDENT showing a lack of respect **2.** PERT cheerfully pert ○ *a hat at a saucy angle* **3.** SEXUALLY EXPLICIT intended to be amusingly vulgar, especially in sexual innuendo [Early 16thC] —**saucily** *adv.* —**sauciness** *n.*

Saud /saa ōōd/, **King of Saudia Arabia** (1902–69). The son of King Ibn Saud, he ruled (1953–63) until he was peacefully deposed and replaced by his brother Faisal.

Sa·u·di /sówdee/ *n.* SOMEBODY FROM SAUDI ARABIA somebody who was born or raised in Saudi Arabia, or who is a citizen of Saudi Arabia ■ *adj.* RELATING TO SAUDI ARABIA relating to or typical of Saudi Arabia, or its people or culture [Mid-20thC. Named for *Sa'ūd*, founder of the dynasty that has ruled Saudi Arabia since 1932.]

Sa·u·di A·ra·bi·a /sòwdee ə ráybee ə/ monarchy in the Middle East, on the Arabian Peninsula. Language: Arabic. Currency: riyal. Capital: Riyadh. Population: 18,426,000 (1996). Area: 864,869 sq. mi./2,240,000 sq. km. Official name **Kingdom of Saudi Arabia** —**Sa·u·di A·ra·bi·an** *n.*, *adj.*

sau·er·bra·ten /sówər braàt'n/ *n.* a German dish of beef roast marinated and cooked in a vinegar

Saudi Arabia

mixture [Late 19thC. From German, literally "sour roast meat."]

sau·er·kraut /sówər kròwt/ *n.* a German dish of shredded cabbage fermented in its own juice with salt [Mid-17thC. From German, literally "sour cabbage."]

sau·ger /sáwgər/ *n.* a North American freshwater fish similar to but smaller than a walleyed pike and valued in sport fishing. Latin name: *Stizostedion canadense.* [Late 19thC. Origin unknown.]

Sau·gus /sáwgèss/ town in northeastern Massachusetts, on the Saugus River. It is a northeastern suburb of Boston. Population: 26,223 (1996).

Sauk /sawk/ (*plural* **Sauk** *or* **Sauks**), **Sac** (*plural* **Sac** *or* **Sacs**) *n.* **1. MEMBER OF NATIVE N AMERICAN PEOPLE** a member of a Native North American people that originally occupied lands in Wisconsin, Illinois, and Iowa, and whose members now live mainly in Oklahoma. The Sauk joined with the Fox to fight in the Black Hawk War of 1832, following U.S. attempts to move the Fox from their lands in Illinois. **2. SAUK LANGUAGE** the Algonquian language of the Sauk, related to Fox [Early 18thC. Via Canadian French *Saki* from Ojibwa *osāki.*]

Saul /sawl/ (*fl.* 11th century B.C.) Israeli monarch, mentioned in 1 Samuel 8–15. He defeated the Philistines but later died in battle against them. He was succeeded by his son-in-law, David.

sault /soo/ *n.* a waterfall or rapids [14thC. Via Old French from Latin *saltus* "leap," from *salire* "to leap" (source of English *somersault* and *insult*).]

Sault Sainte Ma·rie /soo sàynt me rée/ **1.** city in Ontario, Canada, between Lakes Superior and Huron, on the St. Mary's River. Population: 83,619 (1996). **2.** city in northern Michigan, opposite Sault Sainte Marie, Ontario. Population: 14,689 (1990).

Sault Sainte Ma·rie Ca·nals series of ship canals in North America, two in the United States and one in Canada, on St. Mary's River, between Lakes Superior and Huron.

sau·na /sáwnə, sówna/ *n.* **1. STEAM BATH** a kind of bath involving a spell in a hot steamy room followed by a plunge into cold water or a light brushing with birch or cedar boughs **2. ROOM FOR SAUNA** a room designed or prepared for having a sauna [Late 19thC. From Finnish.]

saun·ter /sáwntər/ *vi.* (**-tered, -ter·ing, -ters**) **STROLL** to walk at an easy unhurried pace ■ *n.* **1. EASY PACE** an easy unhurried pace ○ *walk at a saunter* **2. SLOW WALK** a slow leisurely walk ○ *go for a saunter around the grounds* [Mid-17thC. Origin unknown.] —**saun·ter·er** *n.*

sau·rel /sáwrəl, saw rél/ *n.* **1.** = **jack mackerel 2.** = **horse mackerel** [Late 19thC. Via Latin *saurus* from Greek *sauros* "lizard, horse mackerel" (source of English *dinosaur*).]

sau·ri·an /sáwree ən/ *n.* **LIZARD** any of a former suborder of reptiles that included all lizards. Suborder: Sauria. ■ *adj.* **OF LIZARDS** relating to or resembling a lizard [Early 19thC. Formed from modern Latin *Sauria*, name of the suborder, from Latin *saurus* "lizard," from Greek *sauros.*]

saur·is·chi·an /saw rískee ən/ *n.* **KIND OF DINOSAUR** a dinosaur that had a pelvis like that of a modern lizard. Order: Saurischia. ■ *adj.* **OF SAURISCHIANS** relating to the saurischians [Late 19thC. Formed from modern Latin *Saurischia*, name of the order, literally "lizard hip-joint."]

sau·ro·pod /sáwrə paad/ *n.* **KIND OF DINOSAUR** a gigantic plant-eating dinosaur that had a long neck and tail and a small head. Suborder: Sauropoda. ■ *adj.* **OF SAUROPODS** relating to the sauropods [Late 19thC. Formed from modern Latin *Sauropoda*, name of the suborder, literally "lizard foot."] —**sau·rop·o·dous** /saw róppədəss/ *adj.*

sau·ry /sáwree/ (*plural* **-ries**) *n.* a small offshore tropical or temperate marine fish that resembles a needlefish but has shorter jaws and a series of finlets behind the dorsal and anal fins. Family: Scomberosocidae. [Late 18thC. Formed from modern Latin *saurus* "lizard," from Greek *sauros.*]

sau·sage /sóssij/ *n.* **1. SPICY MEAT IN A CASING** seasoned pork or other meat chopped fine and stuffed into a tube of animal intestine or another tube-shaped skin **2.** = **sausagemeat** [15thC. Via Old French *saussiche* from medieval Latin *salsicius* "made by salting," from Latin *salsus* "salted."]

sau·sage dog *n.* = **dachshund** (*informal*)

sau·sage tree *n.* a tropical African tree with clusters of scarlet flowers and long fruits with hard shells. Latin name: *Kigelia pinnata.*

sau·té /sō táy/ *vt.* (**-téed, -té·ing, -tés**) **FRY SOMETHING LIGHTLY** to cook food quickly and lightly in a little butter, oil, or fat ■ *n.* **SAUTÉED DISH** a dish consisting of food, usually meat, that has been sautéed and prepared with a sauce ■ *adj.* **BEING COOKED LIGHTLY** cooked by being sautéed [Early 19thC. From French, the past participle of *sauter* "to leap," from, ultimately, Latin *salire.*]

sau·terne /sō túrn/ *n.* **1. KIND OF WHITE WINE** a sweet white wine made from grapes grown in the Sauternes region of France **2. WINE SIMILAR TO SAUTERNE** a category of wines similar to sauterne [Early 18thC. Named for the French region of *Sauternes* where the wine is produced.]

Sauve /sōv/, **Jeanne-Mathilde Benoit** (*b.* 1922) Canadian journalist and politician. She was the first woman governor-general of Canada (1984–90). Born **Jeanne-Mathilde Benoit**

sauve qui peut /sōv kee pő/ *n.* a disordered or panicked escape [Early 19thC. From French, literally "save who can."]

Sau·vi·gnon blanc /sōvi nyōn blaángk/ *n.* a variety of grape from which white wine is made [Mid-20thC. From French, literally "white Sauvignon."]

sav·age /sávvij/ *adj.* **1. VIOLENT** unrestrained, violent or vicious **2. BRUTAL** brutal and severe ○ *savage cuts in funding* **3. UNDOMESTICATED** living wild, beyond the control of people ○ *savage beasts* **4. OFFENSIVE TERM** an offensive term referring to a culture perceived as inferior to one's own (*offensive*) ■ *n.* **1. VICIOUS OR VIOLENT PERSON** somebody who enjoys treating other people and animals in a cruel violent way **2. OFFENSIVE TERM** an offensive term referring to a member of a people considered inferior or not as advanced as your own group (*offensive*) ■ *vt.* (**-aged, -ag·ing, -ag·es**) **1. ATTACK SOMEBODY OR SOMETHING VIOLENTLY** to attack somebody or something violently, viciously, and without restraint **2. CRITICIZE SOMEBODY OR SOMETHING CRUELLY** to criticize somebody or something cruelly and unrestrainedly ○ *The same critics who praised her first book savaged her second.* [13thC. Via French *sauvage* from, ultimately, Latin *silvaticus* "wild," from *silva* "forest" (source of English *sylvan*).] —**sav·age·ly** *adv.* —**sav·age·ness** *n.*

WORD KEY: USAGE

Sensitivity trap: The use of ***savage*** to refer to primitive peoples was a feature of 19th-century and earlier English (*Vouchsafe to show the sunshine of your face, that we, like savages, may worship it*, Shakespeare, *Love's Labour's Lost* Act 5, scene 2), but is regarded as inappropriate and offensive in current use.

sav·age·ry /sávvijəree/ *n.* **1. VIOLENT CRUELTY** barbarity or violent cruelty **2. OFFENSIVE TERM** an offensive term referring to a culture perceived to be inferior to or less advanced than your own (*offensive*)

sa·van·na /sə vánnə/, **sa·van·nah** *n.* a flat grassland, sometimes with scattered trees, in a tropical or subtropical region [Mid-16thC. Via Spanish *zavana* from Taino.]

Sa·van·nah /sə vánnə/ **1.** river rising in northeastern South Carolina, emptying into the Atlantic Ocean below Savannah, Georgia. Length: 314 mi./505 km. **2.** city and seaport in southeastern Georgia, United States, on the Savannah River near its mouth on the Atlantic Ocean. Population: 140,597 (1994).

sa·vant /sa vaánt/ *n.* a wise or scholarly person [Early 18thC. From French, the present participle of *savoir* "to know," from, ultimately, Latin *sapere* "to be wise."]

sa·vate /sə vát, sə vaát/ *n.* a form of boxing in which kicking as well as hitting is allowed [Mid-19thC. From French, originally a kind of shoe.]

save[1] /sayv/ *v.* (**saved, sav·ing, saves**) **1.** *vt.* **RESCUE SOMEBODY OR SOMETHING** to rescue somebody or something from harm or danger ○ *The entire crew was saved.* **2.** *vti.* **ACCUMULATE MONEY** to set aside money for later use, often adding to the sum periodically ○ *She's saving for a new computer.* **3.** *vt.* **CONSERVE SOMETHING** to avoid wasting something or using it unnecessarily ○ *take a shortcut to save time* **4.** *vt.* **KEEP SOMETHING BACK FOR LATER** to set something aside, keep something back, or protect something so that it can be used later ○ *Save some of the pie for tomorrow.* **5.** *vti.* **REDUCE EXPENSE** to reduce or limit the expense of something ○ *Extra insulation helps us to save on fuel.* **6.** *vt.* **COLLECT ITEMS FOR LATER** to collect as many items of a particular kind as possible, usually in order to do something with them later ○ *She saves old jam jars for when she makes marmalade.* **7.** *vti.* COMPUT **COPY DATA FOR STORAGE** to store a copy of a data file on a storage medium such as a hard drive or disk **8.** *vt.* **SPARE SOMEBODY FROM SOMETHING** to make it possible for somebody to be spared from a situation or activity ○ *It will save me from having to decide.* **9.** *vt.* **PRESERVE SOMETHING** to treat something carefully or stop using it in order to keep it from being used up or worn out ○ *Turn the radio off to save the batteries.* **10.** *vt.* SPORTS **PREVENT GOAL** to prevent an opponent from scoring a goal **11.** *vt.* RELIG **REDEEM SOMEBODY** to free somebody from the consequences of sin **12.** *vt.* **MAINTAIN LEAD SUCCESSFULLY** in baseball, to maintain the lead in completing a game started by another pitcher ■ *n.* **1.** SPORTS **BLOCK** an action that keeps an opponent from scoring **2. MAINTENANCE OF LEAD** in baseball, the successful maintenance of a team's lead by a relief pitcher [13thC. Via Old French *salver* from late Latin *salvare*, which was formed from Latin *salvus* "safe."]

save[2] /sayv/ *prep., conj.* except ○ *Everyone agreed save one.*

save-all *n.* **1. CONTAINER FOR SALVAGING WASTE** a receptacle for catching waste products so that they can be reused **2. SOMETHING PREVENTING WASTE** something that prevents waste or loss

sav·e·loy /sávvə lòy/ *n.* a spicy smoked pork sausage [Mid-19thC. Via French *cervelas* from Italian *cervellata* "sausage."]

Save the Chil·dren Fund *n.* an organization in the United Kingdom that provides international aid directed toward children's well-being

sav·in /sávvin/, **sav·ine** *n.* an evergreen shrub found in Europe, northern Asia, and North America that yields an oil formerly used as a medicine and in perfumes. Latin name: *Juniperus sabina.* [Pre-12thC. Via Old French *savine* from Latin *herba Sabina* "Sabine plant."]

sav·ing /sáyving/ *n.* **1. SOMETHING KEPT FROM BEING WASTED** an amount of time or money that is reduced or not spent or used **2. RESCUE FROM DANGER** rescue of somebody or something from harm or danger **3.** LAW **LEGAL EXCEPTION** an exception or reservation in law ■ **sav·ings** *npl.* **MONEY SET ASIDE** money set aside for future use ■ *prep., conj.* **EXCEPT** except (*literary*)

sav·ing grace *n.* a quality or feature that redeems a person or situation

sav·ings ac·count *n.* a bank account that earns interest on money saved

sav·ings and loan as·so·ci·a·tion *n.* a financial institution that issues shares to members who deposit savings and invests the money mainly in home mortgage loans. Members receive interest on their savings in the form of dividends.

sav·ings bank *n.* a bank that invests the savings of individual depositors and pays interest on the deposits

sav·ings bond *n.* **1. U.S. GOVERNMENT BOND** a registered bond issued by the U.S. government in denominations of $50 to $10,000. It allows people to earn interest on the savings they entrust to the government in exchange for the bond. **2.** *Can* **CANADIAN GOVERNMENT-ISSUED BOND** a bond issued by the Canadian government in denominations of $100 to $100,000. The bond is offered to most working Canadians through a payroll deduction plan.

sav·ings meth·od *n.* a method of testing memory by assessing how much faster somebody can learn information already previously learned, seen, or read

sav·ings ra·tio *n.* the ratio of national disposable income to consumer spending, used as a measure of national saving

sav·ior /sáyvyər/ *n.* somebody who rescues somebody or something from harm or danger [13thC. Via Old french *sauveour* from, ultimately, late Latin *salvare* "to save" (see SAVE).]

Sav·ior /sáyvyər/ *n.* a name used by Christians for the teacher and prophet Jesus Christ

sav·iour *n.* U.K. = **savior**

sa·voir-faire /sàv waar fáir/ *n.* the ability to act appropriately and adroitly in any situation [Early 19thC. From French, literally "to know how to do."]

sa·vor /sáyvər/ *v.* **(-vored, -vor·ing, -vors) 1.** *vt.* ENJOY SOMETHING UNHURRIEDLY to enjoy something with unhurried appreciation ○ *savor the moment* **2.** *vi.* SHOW TRACES to show traces of something ○ *something in his manner that savored of deceit* **3.** *vt.* RELISH SOMETHING to enjoy the taste or smell of something **4.** *vi.* HAVE TASTE OR SMELL to have a specific taste or smell (*literary*) **5.** *vt.* SEASON SOMETHING to add flavor or scent to, especially by seasoning (*archaic*) ■ *n.* **1.** ENJOYMENT enjoyment and relish **2.** TASTE OR SMELL SOMETHING HAS the way that something tastes or smells **3.** DISTINCTIVE QUALITY a quality that identifies or distinguishes something [12thC. Via Old French *savour* from Latin *sapor* "taste," from *sapere* "to have a taste."] —**sa·vor·less** *adj.* —**sa·vor·ous** *adj.*

sa·vor·y[1] /sáyvəree/ *adj.* **1.** NOT SWEET salty or sharp-tasting rather than sweet **2.** APPETIZING having an appetizing taste or smell **3.** RESPECTABLE respectable or morally acceptable ○ *not a very savory character* ■ *n.* (*plural* **-ies**) *U.K.* FOOD DISH THAT ADDS RELISH a light dish served before or at the end of a meal [13thC. Via Old French *savoure*, the past participle of *savourer* "to taste" from, ultimately, Latin *sapor* (see SAVOR).] —**sa·vor·i·ly** *adv.* —**sa·vor·i·ness** *n.*

sa·vor·y[2] /sáyvəree/ *n.* **1.** KIND OF MINT a Mediterranean herb with pale lavender and white flowers and aromatic leaves used for seasoning. Latin name: *Satureja hortensis.* **2.** SAVORY LEAVES the leaves of savory used as an herb [14thC. From Latin *satureia.*]

sa·vour *n., vti.* U.K. = **savor**

sa·vour·y *adj., n.* U.K. = **savory**

sa·voy /sə vóy/, **sa·voy cab·bage** *n.* a winter cabbage with crinkled leaves [16thC. Named for the *Savoy* region of southeast France.]

Sa·voy·ard /sàv oy aárd/ *n.* **1.** SOMEBODY FROM SAVOY somebody who was born or lives in the French region of Savoy **2.** MUSIC DEVOTEE OF GILBERT AND SULLIVAN a performer, producer, or admirer of the operettas of W. S. Gilbert and Arthur Sullivan. [Early 17thC. From French, formed from *Savoie* "the region of Savoy."]

sa·voy cab·bage *n.* = **savoy**

Sa·voy o·pe·ra *n.* an operetta by Gilbert and Sullivan or a work composed in the same style

sav·vy /sávvee/ *n.* SHREWDNESS shrewdness and practical knowledge (*informal*) ■ *adj.* SHREWD shrewd and well informed (*informal*) ■ *vti.* **(-vied, -vy·ing, -vies)** COMPREHEND SOMETHING to understand something, especially what somebody has said (*informal*) [Late 18thC. Originally an African American dialect form of Spanish *sabe usted*, literally "you know."]

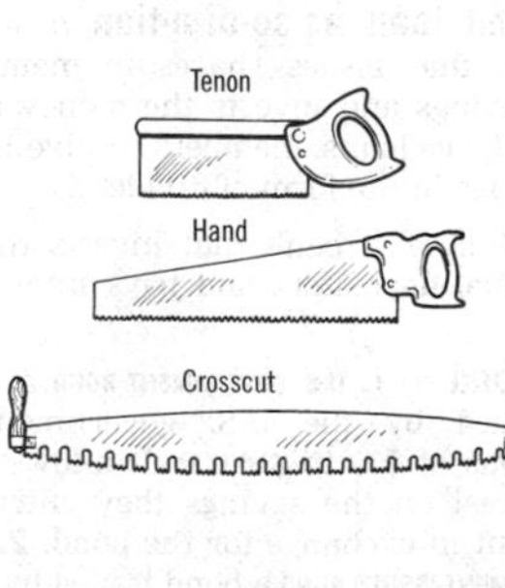

Saw

saw[1] /saw/ *n.* TOOL FOR CUTTING WOOD a hand-operated or power-driven tool with a toothed metal blade, used to cut wood or other hard materials ■ *v.* **(sawed, sawed** *or* **sawn** /sawn/, **saw·ing, saws) 1.** *vti.* CUT SOMETHING USING SAW to cut something using a saw **2.** *vt.* MOVE FORWARD AND BACK to make back-and-forth motions, as if using a handsaw [Old English *saga.* Ultimately from an Indo-European word that is also the ancestor of English *section* and *sickle.*]

saw[2] *n.* an old saying, especially a cliché [Old English *sagu.* Ultimately from a prehistoric Germanic word that is also the ancestor of English *say.*]

saw[3] /saw/ past tense of **see**

SAW *abbr.* surface acoustic wave

saw·bones /sáw bònz/ (*plural* **-bones** *or* **-bones·es**) *n.* a surgeon or physician (*slang*) [Mid-19thC. From early surgeons' role as amputators.]

saw·buck /sáw bùk/ *n.* **1.** = **sawhorse 2.** 10 DOLLARS a ten-dollar bill (*slang*) [Mid-19thC. From Dutch *zaagbok*; in sense 2, from the resemblance between the X-shaped end of a sawhorse and the roman numeral for "ten."]

saw·dust /sáw dùst/ *n.* tiny particles of wood produced when wood is sawed

sawed-off *adj.* **1.** CUT SHORT relating to a shotgun with the barrel cut short. This increases the gun's field of fire as well as making it less cumbersome or obtrusive. **2.** SHORT of small stature (*slang offensive*)

Sawfish

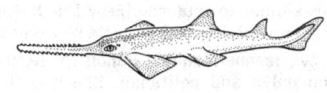

saw·fish /sáw fìsh/ (*plural* **-fish** *or* **-fish·es**) *n.* a ray that inhabits tropical seas and is characterized by a long snout with projections resembling teeth that it uses as a weapon. Family: Pristidae.

saw·fly /sáw flī/ (*plural* **-flies**) *n.* an insect in which the female has a prominent, often serrated appendage at the tip of its abdomen, for boring holes and laying eggs in wood and plants. Family: Tenthredinidae.

saw grass *n.* any one of various sedges that have serrated leaves. Genus: *Cladium.*

saw·horse /sáw hàwrss/ *n.* a support for wood during sawing

saw·ine /sáy wīn, saá-/ *n. Carib* a Trinidadian dessert consisting mostly of milk with fried vermicelli, spiced with cinnamon, raisins, and other additions, usually made and shared with others during the Muslim festival of Eid-ul-Fitr

saw log *n.* a log of sufficient size to be suitable for sawing

saw·mill /sáw mìl/ *n.* **1.** FACTORY WHERE WOOD IS SAWED a factory in which wood is sawed into planks or boards by machine **2.** SAWING MACHINE a powerful sawing machine

sawn past participle of **saw**

saw pal·met·to *n.* a small palm tree of the southeastern United States that has spiny-toothed leafstalks. Latin name: *Serenoa repens.*

saw-scaled vi·per *n.* a small venomous snake of arid North Africa and Central Asia that is believed to have the most powerful venom of all the vipers. Latin name: *Echis carinaus.*

saw set *n.* an instrument that bends alternating teeth of a saw in opposite directions

Saw·tell /saw tél/ coastal town in northeastern New South Wales, Australia. Population: 13,240 (1996).

saw·tooth /sáw tòoth/ *n.* (*plural* **-teeth** /-teeth/) TOOTH OF A SAW any one of the teeth of a saw ■ *adj.* **saw·tooth, saw·toothed** ZIGZAG in a zigzag shape, like the teeth of a saw

saw-toothed *adj.* **1.** WITH TEETH LIKE A SAW'S having notched teeth like a saw **2.** = **sawtooth** *adj.*

saw-toothed grain bee·tle *n.* a tiny red beetle with prominent teeth on either side of the front of the middle part of its body. It is a common pest in grain warehouses and processing plants. Latin name: *Oryzaephilus surinamensis.*

saw-whet owl *n.* a small North American owl with a call that is a long series of short whistles. Latin name: *Aegolius acadicus.* [*Saw-whet* because its call was considered to resemble the sound of a saw being sharpened]

saw·wort *n.* a European plant of the daisy family with serrated leaves that yield a yellow dye. Latin name: *Serratula tinctoria.*

saw·yer /sáwyər/ *n.* **1.** SOMEBODY WHO SAWS WOOD somebody who saws wood for a living **2.** HORNED BEETLE a horned beetle whose larvae bore into coniferous trees. Genus: *Monochamus.* [13thC. Formed from SAW + *-yer*, a variant of -IER.]

sax /saks/ *n.* a saxophone (*informal*) [Early 20thC. Shortening.]

Sax. *abbr.* **1.** Saxon **2.** Saxony

sax·a·tile /sáksə tĭl, sáksət'l/ *adj.* growing on or living in rocks [Mid-17thC. Directly or via French from Latin *saxatilis*, from *saxum* "rock, stone."]

saxe blue /sàks-/ *adj.* of a light blue color with a tinge of gray [*Saxe* via French from German *Sachsen* "Saxony," because the color is produced from SAXON BLUE] —**saxe blue** *n.*

sax·horn /sáks hàwrn/ *n.* any of a family of valved brass wind instruments, often used in military brass bands [Mid-19thC. Named for the Belgian instrument makers Charles Joseph *Sax* 1791–1865, who invented these instruments, and his son Antoine Joseph *Sax* 1814–94 (known as "Adolphe"), who improved them.]

sax·ic·o·lous /sak síkələss/, **sax·ic·o·line** /-síkə līn/ *adj.* = **saxatile** [Mid-19thC. From modern Latin *saxicola*, from Latin *saxum* "rock, stone" + *colere* "to inhabit."]

sax·i·frage /sáksi fràyj, -frìj/ (*plural* **-frages** *or* **-frage**) *n.* a plant growing on rocky ground that has small white, yellow, purple, or red flowers. Genus: *Saxifraga.* [14thC. Directly or via French from Latin *saxifraga* "rock-breaking," from *saxum* "rock, stone" (because the plants often grow in rock crevices).]

sax·i·tox·in /sàksi tóksin/ *n.* a strong neurotoxin that is produced by certain organisms found in plankton **(dinoflagellates)** and accumulates in shellfish feeding on them, causing food poisoning in humans. It is found in red tides. [Mid-20thC. From modern Latin *Saxodomus*, genus of clams (from Latin *saxum* "rock" + *domus* "home") + TOXIN.]

Sax·on /sáks'n/ *n.* **1.** MEMBER OF ANCIENT GERMANIC PEOPLE a member of a West Germanic people that originally came from the southern part of the Jutland Peninsula, and who started to spread west during Roman times. During the 5th century A.D., they made incursions into Gaul and Britain and by the 7th century they had settlements in southern Britain, where, with the Angles, they established powerful kingdoms. ◊ **Angle, Jute 2.** LANGUAGE OF ANCIENT SAXONS the group of West Germanic dialects spoken by the ancient Saxons. ◊ **Anglo-Saxon 3.** SOMEBODY FROM SAXONY somebody who was born or who lives in the region of Saxony in Germany [12thC. Via French from Latin *Saxones* (plural), from a prehistoric Germanic word perhaps meaning "to cut" (perhaps because they were armed with swords).] —**Sax·on** *adj.*

Sax·on blue *n.* a dye made from a solution of indigo in sulfuric acid

Sax·on·ism /sáksə nìzzəm/ *n.* a word, phrase, or idiom in English supposedly from an Anglo-Saxon rather than Latin source

sax·o·ny /sáksənee/ *n.* **1.** FINE YARN a fine three-ply knitting yarn **2.** FINE WOOLEN FABRIC a fine woolen fabric used for coats [Mid-19thC. Originally "fine kind of wool," named for the state of SAXONY in Germany, where it was first made.]

Sa·xo·ny /sáks'nee/ state in eastern Germany. It was a kingdom until 1918, although part of the North German Confederation from 1866. Between 1945 and 1989 the area was part of East Germany. Population: 5,000,000 (1990).

sax·o·phone /sáksə fòn/ *n.* a metal wind instrument with keys and a reed that comes in several sizes and registers, the alto and tenor saxophones being the most popular. It is particularly associated with jazz. [Mid-19thC. Named for Adolphe *Sax* (see SAXHORN), who invented it.] —**sax·o·phon·ic** /sàksə fónnik/ *adj.* —**sax·o·phon·ist** /sáksə fònist/ *n.*

sax·tu·ba /sáks tòobə/ *n.* a large bass saxhorn [Mid-19thC. Blend of SAXHORN and TUBA.]

say /say/ *v.* (**said** /sed/, **said, say·ing, says** /sez/) **1.** *vt.* UTTER SOMETHING to utter something in a normal voice, not singing, shouting, or whispering **2.** *vti.* EXPRESS VERBALLY to convey information or express feelings in spoken words **3.** *vt.* STATE SOMETHING to utter something as a matter of fact, belief, or prediction ○ *said to be the largest in captivity* **4.** *vt.* INDICATE SOMETHING to convey information in written or printed words, numbers, or symbols ○ *The clock said midnight.* ○ *The rules say that you should not kick your opponent.* **5.** *vt.* MAKE CASE FOR OR AGAINST SOMETHING to utter something by way of argument, explanation, or excuse ○ *There's much to be said for being rich.* **6.** *vt.* COMMAND SOMETHING to utter something as an instruction ○ *She said to buy some wine for tonight.* **7.** *vt.* SUPPOSE SOMETHING to assume something for the sake of argument, or take something as a suitable example ○ *Let's say that it will cost you $500.* **8.** *vt.* RECITE SOMETHING to utter something that has a formula or set form of words ○ *says his prayers* **9.** *vt.* CONVEY SOMETHING INDIRECTLY to convey something over and above the immediate words or superficial sound or appearance ○ *The finale says that we can all triumph in the end.* **10.** *vt.* CONVEY SOMETHING IMPORTANT to convey something substantial or significant in what is said or written ○ *We talked for hours but didn't really say anything.* ■ *n.* **1.** CHANCE TO SPEAK a chance or turn to say something, especially to give an opinion ○ *You've already had your say.* **2.** RIGHT TO GIVE OPINION the right to express an opinion and have it considered by others ○ *The junior staff appeared to have no say in the way things were done.* ■ *interj.* (*informal*) **1.** EXPRESSING SURPRISE used to express surprise, admiration, or protest **2.** ATTRACTING ATTENTION used to attract somebody's attention [Old English *secgan*, from a prehistoric Germanic word that is also the ancestor of English *saga* and *scold*] —**say·er** *n.* ◇ **enough said, 'nuff said** used to indicate that nothing more need be said for a situation to be understood ◇ **I say 1.** *U.K.* used to express surprise, admiration, or protest (*dated*) **2.** *U.K.* used to attract somebody's attention (*dated*) ◇ **it goes without saying** used to emphasize that there should be no doubt concerning something ◇ **say when** used to ask somebody to indicate when enough drink has been poured or food served (*informal*) ◇ **that is to say** used to indicate that you are repeating something more clearly or in other words ◇ **there's no saying** used to emphasize the uncertainty of a situation ◇ **you can say that again!** used to indicate complete agreement with what has just been said (*informal*)

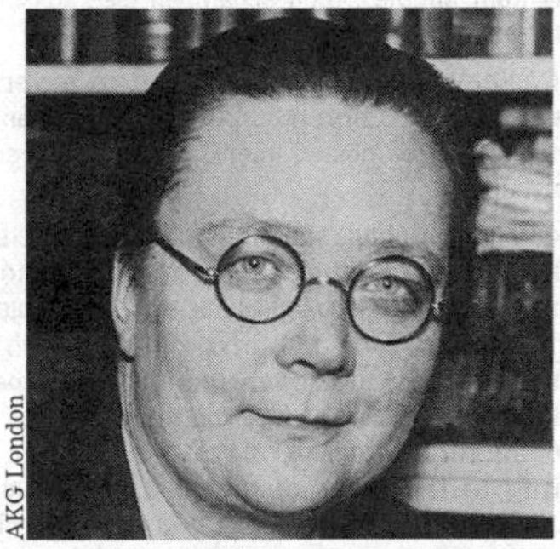

Dorothy L. Sayers

Say·ers /sáy ərz/, **Dorothy L.** (1893–1957) British writer. She wrote detective stories, including *Whose Body?* (1923) and *Gaudy Night* (1935). Full name **Dorothy Leigh Sayers**

say·est /sáy əst/, **sayst** 2nd person present singular of **say** (*archaic*)

say·id *n.* = **sayyid**

say·ing /sáy ing/ *n.* a frequently offered piece of advice or information, or a frequently heard reflection on the way things are

sa·yo·na·ra /sì ə naárə/ *n.* good-bye [Late 19thC. From Japanese, literally "if it be so."]

say-so *n.* (*informal*) **1.** AUTHORIZATION permission or authorization from somebody **2.** ASSERTION a mere assertion by somebody that something is so

say·yid /saáyid, sáyid/, **sayid, said** /saá id/ *n.* **1.** DESCENDANT OF MUHAMMAD'S GRANDSON a Muslim who claims to be descended from Muhammad's grandson Husain **2.** ISLAMIC TITLE an Islamic title of respect for a man [Mid-17thC. From Arabic, literally "prince."]

Saz·er·ac /sázzə ràk/ *tdmk.* a trademark for a cocktail of bourbon, bitters, Pernod, and sugar, with a twist of lemon

Sb *symbol.* antimony [Shortening of Latin *stibium* "antimony"]

SB *abbr.* simultaneous broadcast

s.b. *abbr.* BASEBALL stolen base

S.B. *abbr.* Bachelor of Science [Latin, Scientiae Baccalaureus]

SBA *abbr.* Small Business Administration ■ *n.* RADIO NAVIGATION SYSTEM a system of radio navigation that provides an aircraft with lateral guidance and marker beam indicators at set points during its landing approach. Abbr of **standard beam approach**

SbE *abbr.* south by east

SBS *abbr. Aus* Special Broadcasting Service

SbW *abbr.* south by west

sc, s.c. *abbr.* small capital

Sc *symbol.* scandium

SC *abbr.* **1. SC S.C.**, South Carolina **2.** Security Council **3.** Signal Corps

sc. *abbr.* **1.** scene **2.** MEASURE scruple **3.** that is to say

Sc. *abbr.* **1.** Scots **2.** Scottish

S.C. *abbr.* **1. S.C., SC** South Carolina **2.** Supreme Court

scab /skab/ *n.* **1.** CRUST OVER HEALING WOUND a hard crust of dried blood, serum, or pus, that forms over a wound during healing **2.** OFFENSIVE TERM an offensive term for somebody who continues to work during a strike, or who does a striker's job during a strike (*insult offensive*) **3.** BOT PLANT DISEASE CAUSING CRUSTY SPOTS a fungal plant disease causing crusty spots on the affected parts **4.** VET SKIN DISEASE OF SHEEP a skin disease of sheep and other animals that resembles mange **5.** DISLIKABLE PERSON a despicable or dislikable person (*slang insult*) **6.** BOT CRUSTY SPOT ON A PLANT a crusty spot on a plant caused by a fungal disease ■ *vi.* (**scabbed, scab·bing, scabs**) **1.** BECOME COVERED WITH SCAB to become covered with a scab during healing **2.** WORK DURING STRIKE to continue to work during a strike, or do a striker's job during a strike (*disapproving*) [13thC. From Old Norse *skabb*; ultimately "something that is scratched," from an Indo-European word meaning "to scrape," which is also the ancestor of English *scabies* and *shabby*.]

Scabbard

scab·bard /skábbərd/ *n.* SHEATH FOR SWORD a sheath, hanging from a belt, for a sword, dagger, or bayonet ■ *vt.* (**-bard·ed, -bard·ing, -bards**) PUT SWORD INTO SHEATH to put a sword, dagger, or bayonet into a sheath [13thC. From Anglo-Norman *escauberge*, of uncertain origin: probably originally "blade protector," from prehistoric Germanic.]

scab·bard fish *n.* any of various marine fishes that have an elongated body and long sharp teeth. Family: Trichiuridae.

scab·ble /skább'l/ (**-bled, -bling, -bles**) *vt.* to give a rough shape to stone [Early 17thC. Alteration of Middle English *scapple*, from Old French *escapeler* "to shape timber," from *capler* "to cut."]

scab·by /skábbee/ (**-bi·er, -bi·est**) *adj.* **1.** WITH SCABS having or covered in scabs **2.** DISLIKABLE despicable or dislikable (*slang*) —**scab·bi·ly** *adv.* —**scab·bi·ness** *n.*

sca·bies /skáybiz/ *n.* a contagious skin disease marked by intense itching, inflammation, and red papules. It is caused by the itch mite, which burrows into the skin. [14thC. From Latin, from *scabere* "to scratch" (see SCAB).] —**sca·bi·et·ic** /skàybee éttik/ *adj.*

sca·bi·ous /skáybee əss, skábbee əss/ *adj.* COVERED IN SCABS having scabs or scabies ■ *n.* (*plural* **-ous·es** *or* **-ous**) PLANT WITH DOME-SHAPED FLOWERS a plant with blue, pink, or white dome-shaped flowers. Genera: *Scabiosa* and *Knautia*. [14thC. Directly and via French *scabieux* from Latin *scabiosus*, from *scabies* (see SCABIES); the plant was formerly used in cures for skin diseases.]

scab·lands /skáb làndz/ *npl.* tracts of elevated land with bare rock, thin soil, and sparse vegetation, crossed by dry channels formed by glacial floodwaters

scab·rous /skábbrəss, skáybrəss/ *adj.* **1.** WITH A ROUGH SURFACE having a rough surface because of scales or short stiff hairs **2.** OBSCENE dealing with sex or referring to sex in an obscene way (*literary*) **3.** REQUIRING TACT requiring something to be handled with tact and care [Late 16thC. Directly or via French *scabreux* from late Latin *scabrosus*, from Latin *scaber* "scurfy, scaly, rough."] —**scab·rous·ly** *adv.* —**scab·rous·ness** *n.*

scad /skad/ (*plural* **scad** *or* **scads**) *n.* **1.** FISH WITH LONG BODY a fish that has a long body and sharp bony plates on either side of the narrow point of the tail, found in tropical and subtropical seas. Family: Caringidae. **2.** = **horse mackerel** [Early 17thC. Origin unknown.]

scads /skadz/ *npl.* large numbers or quantities (*informal*) ○ *scads of money* [Mid-19thC. Origin uncertain: earlier also "money"; perhaps from Scandinavian.]

scaf·fold /skáff'ld, -fōld/ *n.* **1.** FRAMEWORK TO SUPPORT WORKERS a temporary framework of poles and planks that is used to support workers and materials during the erection, repair, or decoration of a building **2.** PLATFORM FOR EXECUTIONS a raised platform on which somebody is executed by hanging or beheading **3.** DEATH BY HANGING death by hanging or beheading as a form of punishment **4.** SUPPORT any supporting framework ■ *vt.* (**-fold·ed, -fold·ing, -folds**) ERECT SCAFFOLD AROUND BUILDING to put up a scaffold around or against a building [13thC. Via Old French *(e)schaffaut* from, ultimately, assumed Vulgar Latin *catafalcum* (source of English *catafalque*).] —**scaf·fold·er** *n.*

scaf·fold·ing /skáff'lding, ská fōlding/ *n.* **1.** SYSTEM OF SCAFFOLDS a scaffold or a system of scaffolds **2.** MATERIALS FOR BUILDING SCAFFOLD the poles and planks used to build a scaffold

scag /skag/, **skag** *n.* = **heroin** (*slang*) [Early 20thC. Origin unknown.]

scagl·io·la /skàl yṓlə/ *n.* imitation marble made of gypsum mixed with glue with a polished surface of marble or granite dust [Late 16thC. From Italian, literally "tiny scale, small chip of marble," ultimately from a prehistoric Germanic word that is also the ancestor of English *scale*[3].]

scal·a·ble /skáyləb'l/ *adj.* **1.** CLIMBABLE able to be climbed up or over **2.** VARIABLE used to describe computer graphics fonts generated by an algorithm that permits the size to vary proportionately over a wide range **3.** EXPANDABLE used to describe a computer, component, or network that can be expanded to meet future needs —**scal·a·bil·i·ty** /skàyl ə bíl ətee/ *n.* —**scal·a·ble·ness** *n.* —**scal·ab·ly** *adv.*

scal·age /skáylij/ *n.* **1.** COMM PERCENTAGE OFF COST FOR SHRINKAGE an allowance in the form of a percentage deducted from the cost of goods to reflect loss in amount or size during storage or shipping **2.** FORESTRY ESTIMATED LUMBAR YIELD the estimated yield of lumber from a log

sca·lar /skáylər/ *n.* QUANTITY WITH MAGNITUDE BUT NOT DIRECTION a quantity, e.g., mass or time, that has magnitude but no direction ■ *adj.* WITH MAGNITUDE BUT NOT DIRECTION used to describe a quantity that has magnitude but no direction [Mid-17thC. From Latin *scalaris*, from *scala* (see SCALE[2]).]

sca·la·re /skə lérree, -laáree/ (*plural* **-re** *or* **-res**) *n.* = **angelfish** [Early 20thC. From Latin, a form of *scalaris* "of a ladder" (from its parallel markings), from *scala* (see SCALE[2]).]

sca·lar·i·form /skə lérrə fàwrm/ *adj.* used to describe the walls of a cell that have parallel structural formations resembling the rungs of a ladder [Mid-19thC. Formed from Latin *scalaris* "of a ladder," from *scala* (see SCALE[2]).]

sca·lar prod·uct *n.* a number (**scalar**) equal to the product of the magnitudes of any two vectors and the cosine of the angle formed between them

scal·a·wag /skállə wàg/, **scal·ly·wag** /skálli wàg/ *n.* **1.** MISCHIEVOUS PERSON somebody who behaves in inappropriate or disruptive ways (*dated informal*) **2.** SOUTHERNER WHO COLLABORATED WITH GOVERNMENT a Caucasian person in the South who worked with the federal government during the Reconstruction period after the Civil War [Mid-19thC. Origin uncertain: perhaps an alteration of Scottish *scallag* "farm servant," from Old Scottish *scolloc* "tenant of church land," originally "monastery student," from Latin *schola* (see SCHOOL).]

scald /skawld/ *v.* (**scald·ed, scald·ing, scalds**) **1.** *vt.* **BURN SOMEBODY WITH HOT LIQUID** to burn somebody or a part of the body with hot liquid or steam **2.** *vt.* **STERILIZE SOMETHING WITH BOILING LIQUID** to subject something to the action of boiling liquid or steam in order to clean or sterilize it **3.** *vt.* **HEAT LIQUID TO NEAR BOILING POINT** to heat a liquid to just below the boiling point **4.** *vt.* **TREAT FRUIT WITH BOILING WATER** to plunge a fruit or vegetable into boiling water or pour boiling water over it and leave it briefly before draining to prevent cooking. Scalding is used to loosen skin on fruit and to stop naturally present enzymes working on fruit and vegetables during freezing. **5. BREW TEA** to pour boiling water on to tea and leave it to brew (*informal*) ■ *n.* **1. BURN CAUSED BY LIQUID** a burn caused by hot liquid or steam **2. PLANT DISEASE** any of various plant diseases or conditions that produce brownish discoloration of leaves and fruit [12thC. Via Anglo-Norman *escalder* from, ultimately, late Latin *excaldere* "to bathe in hot water," literally "to be very hot," from *calidus* "hot" (see CAULDRON).]

scald·ing /skáwlding/ *adj.* **1. EXTREMELY HOT** extremely hot, especially hot enough to scald somebody **2. SCATHING** severely critical

scale[1] /skayl/ *n.* **1. WEIGHING MACHINE** a device on which something or somebody can be weighed (*sometimes used in the plural*) **2. PAN OF BALANCE** either of the dishes or pans of a balance ■ *vt.* (**scaled, scal·ing, scales**) **1. WEIGH SO MUCH** to have a particular weight when put on a scale **2. WEIGH SOMETHING OR SOMEBODY** to weigh something or somebody with a scale [12thC. From Old Norse *skál* "bowl" (plural "pair of scales"), from a prehistoric Germanic word that is also the ancestor of English *scale*[3].] ◇ **tip the scales at something** to weigh a particular amount

scale[2] /skayl/ *n.* **1. MEASURING INSTRUMENT** an instrument or apparatus with graduated markings for measuring something **2. SIZE RATIO** a ratio representing the size of an illustration or reproduction, especially a map or a model, in relation to the object it represents ○ *The scale of the map is 1:50,000.* **3. MEASURING SYSTEM** a system of measurement based on a series of marks laid down at regular intervals and representing numerical values **4. MINIMUM PAYMENT** the minimum payment for work, as agreed on during labor negotiations **5. LEVEL** the extent or relative size of something **6. SERIES OF MUSICAL NOTES** a series of musical notes, usually sequential, arranged in ascending or descending order of pitch ■ *v.* (**scaled, scal·ing, scales**) **1.** *vt.* **CLIMB SOMETHING** to climb up something, especially a steep incline, often using a ladder **2.** *vt.* **MAKE SOMETHING TO SCALE** to make a model or draw a map in a regular proportion to the size of the original **3.** *vi.* **RISE IN STAGES** to go upward in stages or steps [14thC. From Latin *scala* "staircase, ladder."] ◇ **to scale** with the same proportion of reduction or enlargement throughout, e.g., in a map or model

scale down, scale back *vt.* to reduce something in size, amount, or extent

scale[3] /skayl/ *n.* **1. BONY PLATE ON FISH** any one of the small flat bony or horny overlapping plates that cover the bodies of fish and some reptiles and mammals **2. FLAKE** a thin flat piece or flake of something such as dead skin **3.** ZOOL **COVERING OF BUTTERFLY WING** any of the small overlapping structures that cover the wings of butterflies and moths **4.** METALL **BLACK OXIDE ON HEATED IRON** a flaky oxide that forms on the surface of some metals undergoing heat treatment, especially the black oxide that forms on iron or steel at high temperatures **5. DEPOSIT INSIDE A KETTLE OR BOILER** a white deposit sometimes formed on the inside of a kettle or boiler by the action of heat on the water **6.** DENT = **tartar** *n.* 1 **7.** BOT = **scale leaf 8.** INSECTS = **scale insect 9.** BOT **PLANT DISEASE** the diseased condition of plants caused by scale insects ■ *v.* (**scaled, scal·ing, scales**) **1.** *vt.* **CLEAN SCALES OR SCALE FROM SOMETHING** to remove the scales or scale from something **2.** *vi.* **FLAKE OFF** to come off in scales **3.** *vi.* ZOOL **SHED SCALES** to shed scales **4.** *vi. Aus* **DODGE FARE** to travel by public transport without paying (*informal*) [13thC. Via Old French *escale* from, ultimately, a prehistoric Germanic word that is also the ancestor of English *shield, shell,* and *skill.*] —**scale·less** *adj.*

scale·board /skáyl bàwrd/ *n.* **1. THIN BOARD FOR BACKING PICTURES** very thin board used to back a picture or mirror **2. STRIP FOR JUSTIFYING TYPE** a thin strip of wood used to justify hand-set type

scale in·sect, scale *n.* any of various plant-sucking insects found worldwide that cover themselves with a waxy secretion resembling scales. They are extremely destructive, especially to fruit trees. Superfamily: Coccoidea.

scale leaf, scale *n.* a kind of leaf that protects a plant bud before the bud expands

scale moss *n.* any of various liverworts with leaves resembling scales. Order: Jungermanniales.

sca·lene /skáy lèen, skày léen/ *adj.* used to describe a triangle in which each side is a different length [Mid-17thC. Via Latin *scalenus* from Greek *skalenos* "uneven, unequal."]

scal·er /skáylər/ *n.* an electronic circuit that produces an output pulse for every specified number of input pulses received. It is typically used in counting applications and the implementation of electronic counters.

Scales /skaylz/ *npl.* = **Libra**

Sca·li·a /skə lée ə/, **Antonin** (*b.* 1936) U.S. jurist. Known as an articulate legal conservative, he was appointed associate justice of the U.S. Supreme Court in 1986.

scal·ing /skáyling/ *n.* the creation of a measurement device for such things as attitudes and strength of feeling, where there is no existing scale. These devices are used in social research.

scal·ing lad·der *n.* a ladder used to climb high walls, especially those of a besieged fortress

scal·lion /skállyən/ *n.* any onion with a small bulb and long green leaves, e.g. , spring onions and shallots [13thC. From Anglo-Norman *scal(o)un*, variant of Old French *escalo(i)gne* (source of English *shallot*) from, ultimately, Latin *Ascalonia (caepa)*, literally "(onion) of Ascalon" from *Ascalon*, port in ancient Palestine.]

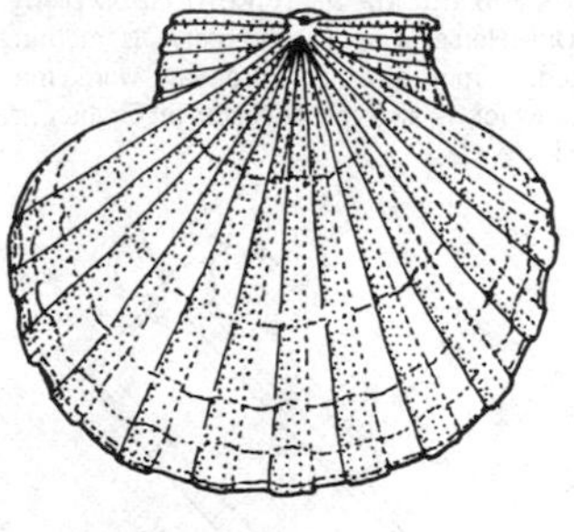

Scallop

scal·lop /skólləp/, **scol·lop** *n.* **1. MARINE MOLLUSK** a marine bivalve mollusk that has a fan-shaped shell with radial ribs and wavy edges. Scallops move by opening and closing the valves. Family: Pectinidae. **2. SCALLOP AS FOOD** the round white edible muscle of a scallop, often with bright red roe around one side **3.** = **scallop shell** *n.* **4. DISH SHAPED LIKE SCALLOP SHELL** a dish shaped like a scallop shell, used for cooking and serving food in **5. FABRIC EDGING** an ornamental undulating edging in fabric **6. THIN SLICE OF MEAT** a thin boneless slice of meat or poultry **7. PILGRIM'S BADGE** a representation of a scallop shell worn as a badge by pilgrims in the Middle Ages ■ *v.* (**-loped, -lop·ing, -lops**) **1.** *vt.* **MAKE EDGE WAVY** to decorate the edge of a fabric or object with an undulating pattern **2.** *vt.* **COOK FOOD IN SCALLOP SHELL** to cook food in a scallop shell or in a dish shaped like a scallop shell **3.** *vi.* **COLLECT SCALLOPS** to gather or dredge for scallops [14thC. From Old French *escalope*, of uncertain origin.] —**scal·loped** *adj.* —**scal·lop·er** *n.* —**scal·lop·ing** *n.*

scal·lop shell *n.* either of the fan-shaped shell valves of the scallop, with radial ribs and a wavy edge. Scallop shells are used for cooking and serving seafood dishes in.

scal·ly·wag *n.* = **scalawag**

scal·o·gram /skáylə gràm/ *n.* a test of attitudes or opinions in which the questions are ranked so that the answer to one implies the same answer to all questions lower on the scale [Mid-20thC. Formed from SCALE[2], probably modeled on CARDIOGRAM.]

scalp /skalp/ *n.* **1. SKIN ON TOP OF HEAD** the skin and underlying tissues covering the dome of the skull **2. SCALP CUT OFF AS TROPHY** the scalp of an enemy cut off as a trophy **3. TROPHY** a trophy or achievement belonging to somebody that somebody else wants to win or taken away ■ *vt.* (**scalped, scalp·ing, scalps**) **1. CUT OFF SOMEBODY'S SCALP** to cut off the scalp of an enemy as a trophy **2. RESELL SOMETHING FOR QUICK PROFIT** to resell something quickly or at an inflated price in order to make a quick profit [14thC. Origin uncertain: probably from a Scandinavian language.] —**scalp·er** *n.*

scal·pel /skálpəl/ *n.* a surgical knife with a short, very sharp blade [Mid-18thC. Directly or via French from Latin *scalpellum* "small cutting tool."]

scalp lock *n.* a tuft or braid of hair left on the otherwise shaven scalp by the men among some Native North American peoples

scal·y /skáylee/ (**-i·er, -i·est**) *adj.* covered in scales or flakes —**scal·i·ness** *n.*

scal·y ant·eat·er *n.* = **pangolin**

scam /skam/ *n.* **DISHONEST SCHEME** a scheme for making money by dishonest means (*slang*) ■ *vt.* (**scammed, scam·ming, scams**) **TRICK SOMEBODY** to obtain money from somebody by dishonest means (*slang*) [Mid-20thC. Origin unknown.] —**scam·mer** *n.*

scam·mo·ny /skámmənee/ (*plural* **-nies** *or* **-ny**) *n.* **1. TWINING PLANT** a twining Asian plant that has arrow-shaped leaves and white, pink, or purple funnel-shaped flowers. Latin name: *Convulvulus scammonia.* **2. PURGATIVE FROM SCAMMONY ROOT** a resin obtained from the roots of the scammony or similar plants and used as a purgative [Pre-12thC. Via Old French *escamonie* or Latin *scammonia* from Greek *skammōnia*.]

scamp[1] /skamp/ *n.* **1. MISCHIEVOUS CHILD** a mischievous person, especially a child who misbehaves in harmless or humorous ways (*informal*) **2. ROGUE** a rascally or dishonest person (*dated informal*) [Mid-18thC. Origin uncertain: probably via Middle Dutch *schampen* "to slip away, decamp" from Old French *esc(h)amper*, ultimately from Latin *campus* "field" (source of English *camp, campus,* and *champion*).] —**scamp·ish** *adj.*

scamp[2] /skamp/ (**scamped, scamp·ing, scamps**) *vt.* to do something hastily, carelessly, or in a perfunctory manner [Mid-19thC. Origin uncertain: perhaps from SCAMP[1]; or related to SKIMP.]

scam·per /skámpər/ *vi.* (**-pered, -per·ing, -pers**) **RUN PLAYFULLY** to run quickly or playfully ■ *n.* **PLAYFUL RUN** a quick or playful run [Late 17thC. Origin uncertain: probably from Middle Dutch *schampen* (see SCAMP[1]).] —**scam·per·er** *n.*

scam·pi /skámpee/ *n.* shrimp cooked in a very garlicky sauce with lemon [Mid-20thC. From Italian, plural of *scampo*, a kind of lobster, from Greek *kampē* "bending"; from its shape.]

scan /skan/ *v.* (**scanned, scan·ning, scans**) **1.** *vt.* **EXAMINE SOMETHING IN DETAIL** to subject something to a thorough examination **2.** *vt.* **LOOK THROUGH SOMETHING QUICKLY** to look through or read something quickly **3.** *vt.* **LOOK AT SOMETHING INTENTLY** to look over and around something intently **4.** *vi.* **CONFORM TO VERSE RULES** to conform to the rules of meter **5.** *vt.* **ANALYZE VERSE** to analyze verse according to the rules of meter **6.** *vti.* **SEARCH AREA USING RADAR** to search a region for specific objects, such as aircraft, by systematically sweeping a radar or sonar beam across it **7.** *vt.* **OBTAIN IMAGE OF BODY** to obtain an image of internal organs with any of various devices, especially in order to make a diagnosis without the need for exploratory surgery. ◊ **CT scan, MRI 8.** *vt.* **EXAMINE SOMETHING WITH BEAM OF LIGHT** to direct a light-sensitive device over a surface in order to convert an image into digital or electronic form for further storage, retrieval, and transmission **9.** *vt.* **EXAMINE STORED DATA** to make an automatic search of a computer storage medium such as a magnetic disk or tape for data in anticipation of retrieving that data ■ *n.* **1. IMAGE OF BODY** an image of an internal body part taken using a scanner, or the process involved in obtaining one **2. BRIEF PERUSAL** a quick look at or through something [14thC. From late Latin *scandere* "to scan a verse" from Latin "to climb." Originally, in English, "to mark off a verse into metrical feet," hence "to analyze."] —**scan·na·ble** *adj.*

Scan., Scand. *abbr.* **1.** Scandinavia **2.** Scandinavian

scan·dal /skánd'l/ *n.* **1. SOMETHING CAUSING PUBLIC OUTRAGE** a situation or event that causes public outrage or censure **2. PUBLIC OUTRAGE** an outburst of public outrage or censure as a consequence of some event

3. **MALICIOUS TALK** malicious talk, especially about other people's private lives [12thC. Via French *scandale* (later form of *escandle*, source of English *slander*) from, ultimately, Greek *skandalon* "trap, temptation."]

WORD KEY: CULTURAL NOTE

School for Scandal, a play by Irish dramatist Richard Brinsley Sheridan (1777). In this satire on contemporary middle-class mores, Sir Oliver Surface attempts to spy on his nephews Charles and Joseph in order to discover their true characters. Among the play's many targets are the hypocrisy and vindictiveness of gossipmongers, personified by the characters of Lady Sneerwell, Sir Benjamin Backbite, and Mrs. Candour. When a media outlet or a society is characterized as a *school for scandal*, the reference is to this play.

scan·dal·ize /skánd'l ìz/ (**-ized, -iz·ing, -iz·es**) *vt.* to shock people by outrageous or improper behavior —**scan·dal·i·za·tion** /skànd'lə záysh'n/ *n.* —**scan·dal·iz·er** /skánd'l ìzər/ *n.*

scan·dal·mon·ger /skánd'l mùng gər, -móng-/ *n.* somebody who indulges in malicious talk about other people's private lives

scan·dal·ous /skánd'ləss/ *adj.* 1. **SHOCKING** causing or deserving to cause public outrage or censure 2. **DEFAMATORY** causing or having the potential to cause damage to somebody's reputation —**scan·dal·ous·ly** *adv.* —**scan·dal·ous·ness** *n.*

scan·dal sheet *n.* a periodical publication that features scandalous stories about people's private lives (*disapproving*)

scan·dent /skándənt/ *adj.* used to describe a plant that climbs as it grows [Late 17thC. From Latin *scandent-*, present participle stem of *scandere* "to climb."]

scan·dic /skándik/ *adj.* containing the element scandium

Scan·di·na·vi·a /skàn də náyvee ə/ region in northern Europe comprising Norway, Sweden, Denmark, Finland, Iceland, and the Faroe Islands —**Scan·di·na·vi·an** *n., adj.*

scan·di·um /skándee əm/ *n.* a rare silvery-white metallic chemical element found in various minerals in association with rare-earth elements. Symbol **Sc** [Late 19thC. Formed from Latin *Scandia*, shortening of SCANDINAVIA, because it is found in various minerals in Scandinavia.]

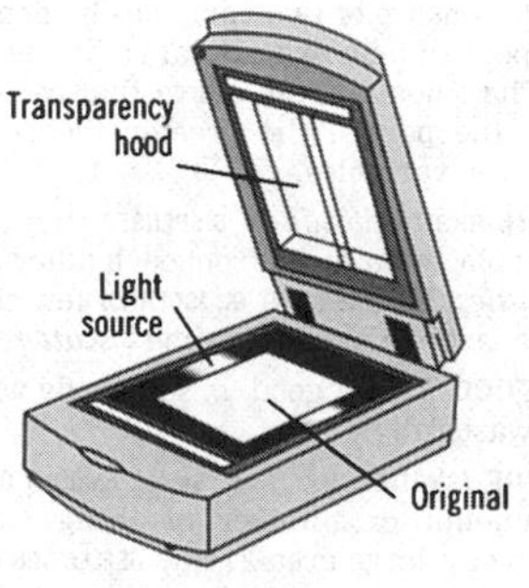

Scanner

scan·ner /skánnər/ *n.* 1. **DATA-SCANNING DEVICE** a device for examining written or recorded data, e.g., for reading a product bar code for inventory and pricing purposes 2. **DEVICE PUTTING SOMETHING INTO DIGITAL FORM** a device used to convert an image into digital form for storage, retrieval, and transmission 3. **BODY-SCANNING DEVICE** a device used to obtain information about the internal parts of the body without the need for surgery, or the contents of something without the need for opening it. ◊ **CAT scanner** 4. **RADAR SEARCHING DEVICE** a rotating directional radar antenna that emits a beam to search for or locate objects 5. **SOMEBODY WHO SCANS TEXTS** somebody who scans texts, e.g., for errors or in poetic analysis

scan·ning e·lec·tron mi·cro·scope *n.* a microscope that uses a beam of electrons to scan an object and produce an enlarged image of it on a cathode-ray tube. It can work at much greater magnifications than a light microscope while avoiding depth of field problems. —**scan·ning e·lec·tron mi·cros·co·py** *n.*

scan·sion /skánshən/ *n.* 1. **ANALYSIS OF VERSE** analysis of verse according to the rules of meter 2. **METRICAL STRUCTURE** the way that a line, verse, or poem scans [Late 17thC. From late Latin *scansion-*, the stem of *scansio*, from Latin, "act of climbing," from *scandere* "to climb," the underlying idea being "moving along in steps."]

scant /skant/ *adj.* 1. **INADEQUATE** not sufficient 2. **ONLY OR NOT QUITE** just about or just below the amount stated ○ *a scant twenty votes* ■ *vt.* (**scant·ed, scant·ing, scants**) **NOT PROVIDE ENOUGH OF SOMETHING** to provide an insufficient supply of something (*archaic*) [14thC. From Old Norse *skamt*, a form of *skammr* "short, brief."] —**scant·ly** *adv.*

scant·ies /skánteez/ *npl.* very brief panties for women (*dated informal*) [Early 20thC. Formed from SCANTY on the model of PANTIES.]

scant·ling /skántling/ *n.* 1. **THIN PIECE OF TIMBER** a piece of timber with a small cross-section, e.g., a rafter 2. **SIZE** the dimension of a building material or a structural part of a ship 3. **SMALL AMOUNT** a small amount or quantity [Early 16thC. Alteration of obsolete *scantillon* "gauge," via Old French *escantillon* "sample" from, ultimately, late Latin *scandaculum* "ladder, gauge," from Latin *scandere* "to climb."]

scant·y /skántee/ (**-i·er, -i·est**) *adj.* 1. **REVEALING** not covering much of the part of the body that it is worn on 2. **INADEQUATE** not much and less than is needed 3. **MEAGER** only just enough —**scant·i·ly** *adv.* —**scant·i·ness** *n.*

scape[1] /skayp/ *n.* 1. BOT **LEAFLESS FLOWER STALK** a leafless flower stalk rising directly from the root 2. ZOOL **PART OF FEATHER OR ANTENNA** a shaft of a feather or other animal part, or a segment of an antenna 3. ARCHIT **ARCHITECTURAL COLUMN** the shaft of an architectural column [Early 17thC. Via Latin *scapus* from Greek *skapos* "rod."] —**sca·pose** /ská pōss/ *adj.*

scape[2] /skayp/ (**scaped, scap·ing, scapes**) *vti.* to escape (*archaic*) [13thC. Shortening of ESCAPE.]

-scape *suffix.* a scene or view ○ *seascape* ○ *lunarscape* [From LANDSCAPE]

scape·goat /skáyp gòt/ *n.* 1. **SOMEBODY MADE TO TAKE THE BLAME** somebody who is made to take the blame for others 2. PSYCHOL **SOMEBODY WRONGLY BLAMED** somebody who is unjustly blamed for causing upset or distress by another person who is unwilling or unable to take personal responsibility for his or her own actions 3. BIBLE **GOAT GIVEN SINS IN JEWISH RITUAL** on the Jewish Day of Atonement, a goat on which the high priest symbolically loaded all the sins of the community before sending the animal out into the wilderness ■ *v.* (**-goat·ed, -goat·ing, -goats**) 1. *vt.* **MAKE SOMEBODY TAKE THE BLAME** to force somebody to take the blame for others 2. PSYCHOL **BLAME SOMEBODY TO AVOID TAKING RESPONSIBILITY** to blame another person unjustly for causing upset or distress as a way of avoiding taking personal responsibility [Mid-16thC. "Scape" from SCAPE[2], because in Jewish ritual the goat, having had the sins of the people symbolically laid on it, was allowed to "escape" into the desert.]

scape·grace /skáyp gràyss/ *n.* a lazy, mischievous, or irresponsible person, especially a child (*archaic*) [Early 19thC. From SCAPE[2] + GRACE; literally "someone who has escaped God's grace."]

scaph·oid /ská fòyd/ *adj.* ANAT navicular (*archaic*) [Mid-18thC. Via modern Latin *scaphoides* from Greek *skaphoeidēs*, from *skaphē* "boat."]

scap·o·lite /skáppə lìt/ *n.* any of a group of variously colored aluminosilicate minerals found in metamorphic rocks and as weathering products of basic igneous rocks. They include semiprecious gemstones. [Early 19thC. From Greek *skapos* "rod" + *lithos* "stone."]

scap·u·la /skáppyələ/ (*plural* **-lae** /-lee/ *or* **-las**) *n.* 1. **BONE FORMING BACK OF SHOULDER** either of two large flat triangular bones that form the back of the shoulder in humans. Each forms a joint with the respective upper arm and provides attachment for muscles. 2. **SHOULDER BLADE IN VERTEBRATES** a bone in vertebrates that corresponds to the human shoulder blade [Late 16thC. From late Latin, singular of Latin *scapulae* "shoulder blades."]

scap·u·lar[1] /skáppyələr/ *n.* **BIRD'S SHOULDER FEATHER** any one of the feathers on a bird's shoulder ■ *adj.* **OF SHOULDER BLADE** relating to or associated with the shoulder blade

scap·u·lar[2] /skáppyələr/, **scap·u·lar·y** /-ləree/ (*plural* **-ies**) *n.* 1. **MONK'S GARMENT** a loose sleeveless garment worn by monks 2. **CLOTHS SHOWING AFFILIATION TO RELIGIOUS ORDER** two pieces of cloth joined together and worn over the shoulder and back underneath other garments to signify membership in a particular religious order or some other devotional purpose [15thC. From late Latin *scapulare*, from *scapula* "shoulder" (see SCAPULA), because it covers the shoulders.]

scar[1] /skaar/ *n.* 1. **MARK ON SKIN AFTER WOUND HEALS** a mark left on the skin after a wound, burn, or sore has healed over 2. **MENTAL EFFECT OF DISTRESSING EXPERIENCE** a lasting effect left on somebody's mind by a personal misfortune or unpleasant experience 3. **MARK ON SURFACE** a mark on a surface caused by damage 4. BOT **MARK OF FORMER ATTACHMENT ON PLANT** the mark on a plant indicating the place where a part such as a leaf was formerly attached ■ *v.* (**scarred, scar·ring, scars**) 1. *vt.* **MARK SOMEBODY OR SOMETHING WITH SCARS** to leave somebody or something with a physical or emotional scar 2. *vi.* **FORM A SCAR** to form or become marked by a scar [14thC. Via Old French *escharre* "scar, scab," from, ultimately, Greek *eskhara* "hearth, brazier, scab formed after a burn."]

scar[2] /skaar/ *n.* 1. **STEEP CRAGGY ROCK FORMATION** a steep bare rocky cliff, typically in the limestones of the Yorkshire Dales, England 2. **ROCK SUBMERGED IN SEA** a rock submerged or partly submerged in the ocean [14thC. From Old Norse *sker* "low reef," from a prehistoric Germanic word that is also the ancestor of English *shear*.]

scar·ab /skérrəb/ *n.* 1. **SACRED BEETLE** any of several beetles regarded as sacred by the ancient Egyptians. Many scarabs roll dung into balls to provision their larvae. Family: Scarabaeidae. 2. **REPRESENTATION OF A BEETLE** a representation of a beetle used on amulets and signets by the ancient Egyptians [Late 16thC. Via Latin *scarabaeus* from Greek *karabos* "crab, beetle."]

scar·a·bae·id /skèrrə bée id/, **scar·a·bae·an** /-bée ən/ *n.* = **scarab** *n.* 1 [Mid-19thC. Via modern Latin *Scarabaeidae*, family name, from Latin *scarabaeus* (see SCARAB).]

scar·a·bae·us /skèrrə bée əss/ (*plural* **-us·es** *or* **-i** /-bée ì/) *n.* = **scarab** *n.* 2 [Late 16thC. Via Latin (see SCARAB).]

Scar·a·mouch /skérrə mòoch, -mòosh/, **Scar·a·mouche** *n.* a boastful and cowardly man (*archaic*) [Mid-17thC. Directly or via French *Scaramouche* from Italian *Scaramuccia*, character in the commedia dell'arte, literally "skirmish" (see SKIRMISH).]

scarce /skairss/ *adj.* 1. **INSUFFICIENT** being in insufficient supply 2. **RARE** rarely found or rarely occurring ■ *adv.* **SCARCELY** scarcely (*archaic or literary*) [13thC. Via Anglo-Norman *(e)scars* from, ultimately, Latin *excerpere* "to pick out" (source of English *excerpt*), from *carpere* "to pluck" (source of English *carpet*).] —**scarce·ness** *n.* ◇ **make yourself scarce** to go or stay away, often in order to avoid some kind of trouble or difficulty (*informal*)

scarce·ly /skáirsslee/ *adv.* 1. **SURELY NOT** surely or almost certainly not ○ *That is scarcely a good reason for taking the day off.* 2. **HARDLY AT ALL** only to the slightest degree ○ *I scarcely slept all night.*

WORD KEY: USAGE

See Usage note at ***hardly***.

scarce·ment /skáirssmənt/ *n.* a ledge in a wall [Early 16thC. Formed from obsolete *scarce* "to make scarce."]

scar·ci·ty /skáirssətee/ (*plural* **-ties**) *n.* 1. **INSUFFICIENT SUPPLY** an insufficient supply of something 2. **RARITY** an infrequency of occurrence of something

scare /skair/ *v.* (**scared, scar·ing, scares**) 1. *vt.* **FRIGHTEN SOMEBODY** to make somebody afraid or alarmed 2. *vi.* **BE FRIGHTENED** to be or become frightened ■ *n.* 1. **FRIGHT** a sudden fright or feeling of fear 2. **SOMETHING THAT FRIGHTENS** a situation causing general fear or alarm [12thC. From Old Norse *skirra* "to frighten, to avoid," from *skjarr* "timid, shy."] —**scar·er** *n.*

scare off, scare away *vt.* to frighten a person or an animal into going away

scare up *vt.* to manage to find something or put something together from whatever is available (*informal*)

scare·crow /skáir krò/ *n.* 1. **OBJECT FOR SCARING BIRDS AWAY** an object in the shape of a person dressed in old clothes, set up in a field to scare birds away from the crops 2. **POORLY DRESSED PERSON** somebody who wears ragged clothes (*informal*) 3. **SOMETHING FRIGHTENING BUT NOT DANGEROUS** somebody or something that may have a frightening effect but is not dangerous

scared /skaird/ *adj.* feeling full of worry or fear —**scared·ly** *adv.* —**scared·ness** *n.*

scare·dy-cat /skáirdi kàt/ *n.* = **fraidy-cat** (*informal*)

scare·mon·ger /skáir mùng gər, -mòng-/ *n.* somebody who deliberately spreads alarming rumors —**scare·mon·ger·ing** *n.*

scarf[1] /skaarf/ *n.* (*plural* **scarfs** *or* **scarves** /skaarvz/) **1. CLOTH WORN AROUND THE NECK** a piece of cloth of various shapes, worn around the neck or on the head for warmth or decoration **2. CLOTH COVERING FOR SURFACE** a cloth covering a surface such as a table or a piano **3. MILITARY SASH** an official sash, usually indicating military rank ■ *vt.* (**scarfed, scarf·ing, scarfs**) **WRAP SOMETHING IN SCARF** to wrap a scarf around something (*literary*) [Mid-16thC. Via Old Northern French *escarpe* from Old French *escherpe* "pilgrim's bag hung around the neck," from assumed Frankish *skirpja* "bag woven from rushes," from Latin *scirpus* "rush."]

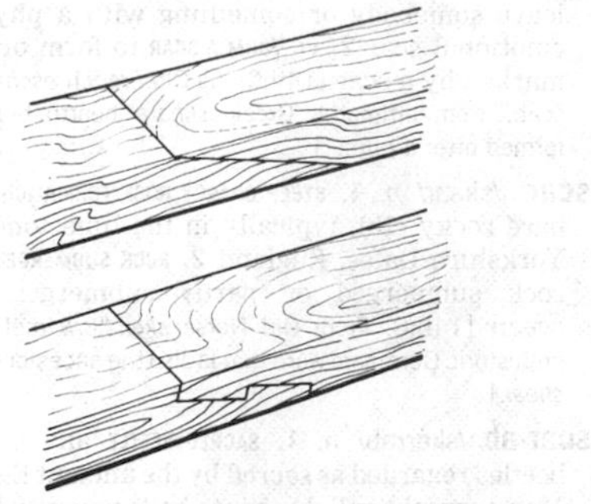

Scarf

scarf[2] /skaarf/ *n.* **1. scarf, scarf joint JOINT MADE BETWEEN NOTCHED ENDS** a joint made by joining two notched boards together **2. NOTCHED END** either of the notched ends of a scarf joint ■ *vt.* (**scarfed, scarf·ing, scarfs**) **JOIN BOARDS USING NOTCHES** to join boards together by means of a scarf joint [13thC. Origin uncertain: probably via Old French from a Scandinavian language.]

scarf[3], **scarf down** *vt.* to eat or drink something greedily or noisily (*slang*) ["Scarf": variant of SCOFF]

scarf joint *n.* = **scarf**[2] *n.* **2**

scarf·skin /skaárf skìn/ *n.* the outermost layer of skin, especially the cuticle of a nail [Early 16thC. "Scarf" from SCARF[1], with the underlying sense of a light outer covering.]

scar·i·fi·ca·tor /skérrəfi kàytər/ *n.* a surgical instrument formerly used to make superficial incisions in the skin

scar·i·fy[1] /skérrə fì/ (**-fied, -fy·ing, -fies**) *vt.* **1. MAKE SCRATCHES ON SKIN** to make scratches on or superficial incisions in the skin, done in the past, e.g., to promote an improved blood supply in the underlying tissues **2. LOOSEN SOIL** to break up and loosen the surface of soil **3. SCRATCH SEEDS** to break the outer cover of hard seeds to aid germination [14thC. Via French *scarifier* from, ultimately, Greek *skarisphasthai* "to scratch an outline, sketch lightly," from *skariphos* "stylus."] —**scar·i·fi·ca·tion** /skèrrəfi káysh'n/ *n.* —**scar·i·fi·er** /skérri fìr/ *n.*

scar·i·fy[2] /skérri fì/ (**-fied, -fy·ing, -fies**) *vt.* to make somebody afraid or alarmed (*informal*) [Late 18thC. Formed from SCARE, perhaps modeled on TERRIFY.] —**scar·i·fy·ing·ly** *adv.*

scar·i·ous /skérree əss/, **scar·i·ose** /-ōss/ *adj.* used to describe parts of plants that have a thin dry membranous appearance [Late 18thC. Via French *scarieux* from modern Latin *scariosus*.]

scar·la·ti·na /skaàrlə teénə/ *n.* = **scarlet fever** (*technical*) [Early 19thC. Via modern Latin from Italian *scarlattina* "little scarlet things," from *scarlatto* "scarlet," from, ultimately, Arabic *siqillāt* (see SCARLET).] —**scar·la·ti·nal** *adj.*

Scar·lat·ti /skaar laátee/, **Alessandro** (1659–1725) Italian composer. The father of Domenico Scarlatti, he was a major contributor to the establishment of the Neapolitan style of opera. He also wrote over 700 works of church music. Full name **Pietro Alessandro Gaspare Scarlatti**

Scar·lat·ti /skaar làttee/, **Domenico** (1685–1757) Italian composer. The son of Alessandro Scarlatti, he composed operas and church music, but is best known for over 550 sonatas for harpsichord.

scar·let /skaárlət/ *n.* **1. BRIGHT RED COLOR** a bright red color tinged with orange **2. SCARLET CLOTH** scarlet clothing or cloth, especially the traditional red uniforms of the British army ■ *adj.* **BRIGHT RED IN COLOR** of a bright red color tinged with orange ○ *scarlet lipstick* [13thC. Via Old French *escarlate* from Arabic *siqillāt*, a rich cloth (scarlet being its usual color), from Latin *sigillatus* "decorated with raised figures," ultimately from *signum* "sign."]

scar·let fe·ver *n.* a contagious bacterial infection marked by fever, a sore throat, and a red rash, mainly affecting children

scar·let hat *n.* CHR = **red hat**

scar·let i·bis *n.* BIRDS an ibis that is bright red when mature. It nests in swamps and is the national bird of Trinidad and Tobago, displayed on the national coat-of-arms. Latin name: *Eudocimus ruber*.

scar·let let·ter *n.* a scarlet letter A that a woman convicted of adultery was formerly made to wear, especially among the Puritans of 17th-century New England

WORD KEY: CULTURAL NOTE

The Scarlet Letter, a novel by Nathaniel Hawthorne (1850). The title of this eloquent plea for tolerance refers to the red letter A that Hester Prynne, a woman living in mid-17th-century New England, is forced to wear as punishment for an adulterous affair. While her husband and lover are consumed by anger and guilt respectively, Hester's honesty and strength of character help her to survive the scandal. The term *scarlet letter*, used generically to denote adultery or evidence of it, derives from this novel.

scar·let pim·per·nel *n.* a common pimpernel that has small scarlet, purple, or white flowers that close in cloudy weather. Latin name: *Anagallis arvensis*.

scar·let run·ner *n.* = **string bean**

scar·let tan·a·ger *n.* a medium-sized songbird of the eastern United States. The male is bright red with black wings and tail during the breeding season. Latin name: *Piranga olivacea*.

scar·let wom·an *n.* an offensive term referring to a woman believed to be an adulterer or prostitute or to engage excessively in sexual activity, especially a prostitute (*disapproving*) [From the Bible, *Revelations* 17:1–6, in which a whorish woman, representing the Roman Church, appears "in purple and scarlet color"]

scarp /skaarp/ *n.* **1.** GEOG **STEEP CLIFF** a steep slope or cliff, formed by erosion or faulting. ◊ **escarpment 2.** MIL **STEEP SLOPE IN A FORTIFICATION** a steep slope, e.g., the inner wall of a ditch, in front of a fortification [Late 16thC. From Italian *scarpa* (source of English *escarp*), of uncertain origin.]

scarp·er /skaárpər/ (**-ered, -er·ing, -ers**) *vi. U.K.* to leave a place quickly (*slang*) [Mid-19thC. Origin uncertain: probably from Italian *scappare* "to escape," influenced by rhyming slang "Scapa Flow," "go."]

scart /skaart/ (**scarted, scart·ing, scarts**) *vti. Scotland* to scratch something or the self (*nonstandard*) [14thC. Alteration of dialect *scrat*, of unknown origin.]

scar tis·sue *n.* dense fibrous tissue that forms the scar over a healed wound

scarves plural of **scarf**

scar·y /skáiree/ (**-i·er, -i·est**) *adj.* (*informal*) **1. FRIGHTENING** causing fear or alarm **2. TIMID** easily frightened —**scar·i·ly** *adv.* —**scar·i·ness** *n.*

scat[1] /skat/ (**scat·ted, scat·ting, scats**) *vi.* to leave immediately and quickly (*informal*) (*usually used as a command*) [Mid-19thC. Origin unknown.]

scat[2] /skat/ *n.* **JAZZ VOCAL STYLE** a style of jazz singing that uses nonsense syllables to approximate the sound of a solo instrument. Ella Fitzgerald and Mel Tormé are considered consummate scat singers. ■ *vi.* (**scat·ted, scat·ting, scats**) **SING SCAT** to sing in scat style [Early 20thC. Origin uncertain: probably an imitation of the sound.]

scat[3] /skat/ (*plural* **scats** *or* **scat**) *n.* a small tropical Indo-Pacific marine fish, popular for aquariums because of its bright color. Family: Scatophagidae. [Mid-20thC. Shortening of modern Latin *Scatophagidae*, family name, from Greek *scatophagos*, "dung-eating," because it frequents sewage outlets.]

scat[4] /skat/ *n.* a fecal dropping of an animal [Mid-20thC. From the Greek stem *skat-* (see SCATOLOGY).]

scathe /skayth/ *vt.* (**scathed, scath·ing, scathes**) **1. CRITICIZE SOMEBODY** to subject somebody to severe criticism (*literary*) **2. DAMAGE SOMETHING BY BLASTING** to damage something by blasting or scorching it (*archaic*) ■ *n.* **HARM** injury or harm (*archaic*) [12thC. From Old Norse *skaða* "to harm or damage."] —**scathe·less** *adj.*

scath·ing /skáything/ *adj.* severely critical and scornful —**scath·ing·ly** *adv.*

scato- *prefix.* excrement ○ *scatology* [Formed from Greek *skat-*, the stem of *skōr* "excrement." Ultimately from an Indo-European word meaning literally "something cut off," which is also the ancestor of English *dreck*.]

sca·tol·o·gy /ska tóllәjee, skə-/ *n.* **1. VULGAR LANGUAGE** vulgar language related to excretory functions **2. OBSESSION WITH EXCREMENT** preoccupation with excrement or obscenity **3. STUDY OF EXCREMENT** the scientific study of excrement, especially for diagnostic purposes —**scat·o·log·i·cal** /skàtt'l ójjik'l/ *adj.* —**sca·tol·o·gist** /ska tóllәjist/ *n.*

scat·ter /skáttər/ *v.* (**-tered, -ter·ing, -ters**) **1.** *vt.* **THROW THINGS AROUND** to throw things around so that they land with an irregular distribution over a relatively wide area **2.** *vt.* **SCATTER SOMETHING OVER AN AREA** to cover an area by throwing things around over it ○ *scatter seed* **3.** *vti.* **DISPERSE** to separate and move suddenly in different directions, or cause people or animals to move in this way **4.** *vti.* PHYS **DEVIATE** to cause waves or a beam of particles to be irregularly deflected, dispersed, or reflected, or to be turned aside in such a fashion ■ *n.* **THINGS SCATTERED AROUND** a number of things spread untidily around an area (*literary*) [12thC. Origin uncertain: probably a variant of SHATTER.] —**scat·ter·a·ble** *adj.* —**scat·ter·er** *n.*

WORD KEY: SYNONYMS

scatter, broadcast, distribute, disseminate

CORE MEANING: to spread around

scatter to spread things around physically, especially in a random widespread manner; **broadcast** used in old-fashioned or formal English with the meaning to scatter seeds. It is now commonly used with the meaning to spread or transmit information, especially by means of radio or television; **distribute** to allocate something or give it out in a structured or organized way. It can also be used in formal English in a similar way to **scatter**, to talk about physically spreading something over a surface or area; **disseminate** a formal word with the meaning to spread abstract things such as ideas, information, or good will.

scat·ter·brain /skáttər bràyn/ *n.* somebody who is incapable of serious or organized thought, or of remembering important things —**scat·ter·brained** *adj.*

scat·ter cush·ion *n.* = **throw pillow**

scat·ter di·a·gram *n.* a graph that represents the joint relationship of two variables by depicting the data as points along two axes at right angles to each other. The smoother the curve that can be drawn through the points, the greater the relationship between the variables.

scat·tered /skáttərd/ *adj.* **1. DISPERSED** in a number of different places far away from each other ○ *scattered communities* **2. INFREQUENT OR ISOLATED** few in number and far apart in distance or time ○ *scattered showers*

scat·ter·good /skáttər good/ *n.* somebody who spends money wastefully

scat·ter·ing /skáttəring/ *n.* **1. SMALL AMOUNT OR NUMBER** a small amount or number of things irregularly spread over a large area **2.** PHYS **DEFLECTION OF PARTICLES** the deflection of a wave or beam of particles caused by collisions with other particles

scat·ter·ing lay·er *n.* an undersea zone where there is a high concentration of plankton that causes sound waves to become scattered. This makes strong acoustic echoes possible.

scat·ter pin *n.* a small decorative pin typically worn as part of a cluster on clothing

scat·ter rug *n.* a small decorative rug

scat·ter·shot /skáttər shòt/ *adj.* indiscriminate and lacking in focus ○ *a scattershot approach to the operation*

scat·ter·site /skáttər sīt/ *adj.* relating to low-income housing distributed across a large urban area so as to avoid concentration of poverty

scat·ty /skáttee/ (**-ti·er, -ti·est**) *adj. U.K., Can* lacking in serious or organized thought, forgetful, and often eccentric in behavior (*informal*) [Early 20thC. Origin uncertain: probably formed from a shortening of *scatterbrained*.] —**scat·ti·ly** *adv.* —**scat·ti·ness** *n.*

scaup /skawp, skaap/ (*plural* **scaups** *or* **scaup**), **scaup duck** *n.* a diving duck native to Europe and North America. The male has a black-and-white body. Genus: *Aythya*. [Late 17thC. Variant of *scalp* "shellfish-bed," of uncertain origin: perhaps because it feeds on shellfish.]

scau·per /skáwpər, skaápər/ *n.* an engraving tool used to clear away lines or other unwanted areas on wood [Mid-19thC. Variant of scalper from SCALP.]

scaur *n. Scotland* a steep eroded hill or precipice (*often used in placenames*) [Early 18thC. Variant of SCAR².]

scav·enge /skávvənj/ (-enged, -eng·ing, -eng·es) *vti.* **1.** LOOK FOR SOMETHING USABLE to search for or through discarded material in order to find something usable **2.** FEED ON CARRION OR SCRAPS to feed on dead and rotting flesh or discarded food scraps **3.** CLEAN UP to remove waste material and dirt from an area **4.** CHEM GET RID OF IMPURITIES to neutralize or remove impurities in a chemical reaction or mixture [Mid-17thC. Back-formation from SCAVENGER.]

scav·en·ger /skávvənjər/ *n.* **1.** ANIMAL FEEDING ON CARRION OR SCRAPS an animal, bird, or other organism that feeds on dead and rotting flesh or discarded food scraps **2.** SOMEBODY LOOKING FOR SOMETHING USABLE somebody who searches for or through discarded material in order to find something usable **3.** CHEM SUBSTANCE REMOVING IMPURITIES something that is added to a chemical reaction or mixture to neutralize or remove impurities **4.** *U.K.* STREET CLEANER somebody who works as a street cleaner or refuse collector (*archaic*) [Mid-16thC. Alteration of *scavager* "tax collector," from Anglo-Norman *scawager*, from, ultimately, Flemish *scauwen* "to look at."] —**scav·en·ge·ry** *n.*

WORD KEY: ORIGIN

The term *scavenger* was originally, in the Middle Ages, an official who collected taxes levied on overseas merchants. Later the term came to denote a street-cleaner, and by the time it had metamorphosed into ***scavenger*** (by the same process as produced *messenger* from *messager* and *passenger* from *passager*) it had completed its descent to its modern meaning.

scav·en·ger bee·tle *n.* a dark oval-shaped beetle that lives in water and feeds on decaying vegetation. Family: Hydrophilidae.

scav·en·ger hunt *n.* a game in which people must obtain items on a list within a time limit and without buying them

scav·en·ger moth *n.* a small moth that is commonly found scavenging stored food, e.g., grains and oils. The clothes moth is a kind of scavenger moth. Family: Tineidae.

Sc.B. *abbr.* Bachelor of Science [Latin, *Scientiae Baccalaureus*]

SCC *abbr.* storage connecting circuit

Sc.D. *abbr.* Doctor of Science [Latin, *Scientiae Doctor*]

sce·na /sháynə/ (*plural* -ne /sháynay/) *n.* **1.** SCENE IN OPERA a division of an opera that is equivalent in length or structure to a scene in a play **2.** DRAMATIC CONCERT PIECE a dramatic concert piece written and performed in the style of an operatic scena [Early 19thC. Via Italian from Latin *scaena* (see SCENE¹).]

sce·nar·i·o /sə nárree ō, -nérree-, -naáree-/ (*plural* -os) *n.* **1.** POSSIBLE SITUATION an imagined sequence of possible events ○ *the worst-case scenario* **2.** PLOT OUTLINE an outline of the plot of a play or opera **3.** CINEMA SCREENPLAY a screenplay [Late 19thC. From Italian, formed from *scena* "scene," from Latin *scaena* (see SCENE¹).]

sce·nar·ist /sə nárrəst, -nérrəst/ *n.* somebody who writes movie scripts

scend /send/, **send** *n.* SHIP'S UPWARD PITCH the upward movement of a ship that is pitching in heavy seas ■ *vi.* (**scend·ed, scend·ing, scends**) RISE HIGH ON WAVE to rise up high under the force of a strong wave (*refers to ships*) [15thC. Origin uncertain: probably an alteration of DESCEND or ASCEND.]

scene¹ /seen/ *n.* **1.** ARTS DIVISION OF AN ACT OF A PLAY any of the divisions of an act of a play or opera, presenting continuous action in one place **2.** ARTS SHORT SECTION OF A PLAY OR MOVIE a short section of a play, movie, opera, or work of literature that presents a single event ○ *the love scene* **3.** ARTS SETTING IN A DRAMATIC WORK a setting for the whole or a part of a play, movie, opera, or work of literature **4.** PLACE WHERE SOMETHING HAPPENS a location at which an event or action happens ○ *the scene of many battles* **5.** ARTS SCENERY FOR DRAMATIC WORK the backgrounds, sets, or props for a play, movie, or opera (*often used before a noun*) ○ *a couple of quick scene changes* **6.** VIEW OR PICTURE a view of a place or an activity, especially one presented in a painting or photograph **7.** EMBARRASSING PUBLIC DISPLAY an embarrassing or disconcerting public display of emotion ○ *Don't make a scene, but I think they lost your coat.* **8.** MILIEU the characteristic environment in which an activity or pursuit is carried out ○ *new to the fashion scene* **9.** SITUATION a set of circumstances of any kind (*informal*) ○ *We seem to have stumbled into a bad scene.* [Mid-16thC. Via Latin *scaena* from Greek *skēnē* "tent, stage." The underlying idea is of something that gives shade.] ◇ **behind the scenes 1.** out of sight of the audience at a performance or spectacle **2.** in private and away from public view ◇ **set the scene 1.** to describe a situation or the background to an event **2.** to create the circumstances in which something can or does happen

scene² plural of **scena**

scen·er·y /seénəree/ *n.* **1.** ARTS THEATRICAL BACKDROP the set or decorated background for a play, movie, or opera **2.** SURROUNDINGS landscape or natural surroundings, especially when regarded as picturesque ○ *admired the scenery from the hotel balcony* [Mid-18thC. Alteration of *scenary*, from Italian *scenario* (see SCENARIO).]

scene-steal·er *n.* a performer who, by his or her performance or personal qualities, takes the audience's attention away from another performer who is supposedly the focus of the scene

sce·nic /seénik, sénnik/ *adj.* **1.** PICTURESQUE with attractive or impressive natural scenery **2.** OF NATURAL SCENERY relating to the natural scenery of an area ○ *famous for its scenic beauty* **3.** ARTS OF DRAMATIC SCENES relating to scenes in a play, movie, or opera **4.** THEATER OF STAGE SCENERY relating to stage scenery — **sce·ni·cal·ly** *adv.*

sce·nic rail·road, sce·nic rail·way *n.* **1.** TRAIN TRAVELING A SCENIC ROUTE a railroad that has been restored for passenger use, especially for tourists, because of its passage through attractive scenery **2.** MINIATURE RAILROAD IN A PARK a miniature railroad that carries customers past artificial scenery in an amusement park or other place of entertainment

sce·nog·ra·phy /see nóggrəfee/ *n.* **1.** PAINTING PAINTING OR DRAWING IN PERSPECTIVE the artistic representation of objects according to the rules of perspective **2.** THEATER SCENERY-PAINTING the painting of theatrical scenery —**sce·nog·raph·er** *n.* —**sce·no·graph·ic** /seènə gráffik/ *adj.* —**sce·no·graph·i·cal** /-gráffik'l/ *adj.* —**sce·no·graph·i·cal·ly** *adv.*

scent /sent/ *n.* **1.** CHARACTERISTIC PLEASANT SMELL a distinctive odor, especially a pleasant one ○ *the scent of jasmine* **2.** SMELL USED AS TRAIL a smell left behind by a person or animal and used especially for tracking ○ *They followed the scent deep into the forest.* **3.** PERFUME cosmetic fragrances, especially women's perfume **4.** SMELLING SENSE the sense of smell **5.** ABILITY TO SENSE SOMETHING an ability to sense or detect something as likely to happen **6.** HINT a faint indication that something is likely to happen ○ *There was the scent of danger in the air.* ■ *v.* (**scent·ed, scent·ing, scents**) **1.** *vti.* SMELL SOMEBODY OR SOMETHING to perceive somebody or something by smelling **2.** *vt.* DETECT SOMETHING AS IMMINENT to sense that something is likely to happen ○ *they could scent victory* **3.** *vt.* IMBUE SOMETHING WITH A PLEASANT SMELL to fill something with a distinctive odor, especially a pleasant one ○ *Roses scented the room.* [14thC. Via French *sentir* from Latin *sentire* "to feel" (source of English *sense* and *sentiment*).] ◇ **put** *or* **throw somebody off the scent** to divert somebody from finding or discovering something

WORD KEY: SYNONYMS

See Synonyms at ***smell***.

scent gland *n.* a specialized skin gland that enables an animal to secrete a scent designed to send social or sexual signals or serve as a deterrent

scent strip *n.* a strip of perfumed paper used to advertise a commercially available perfume to potential customers

scep·ter /séptər/ *n.* **1.** STAFF USED AS A ROYAL EMBLEM a ceremonial staff, rod, or wand used as an emblem of a monarch's authority **2.** ROYAL AUTHORITY royal or imperial power or authority ■ *vt.* (**-tered, -ter·ing, -ters**) GIVE SOMEBODY ROYAL AUTHORITY to endow somebody with royal power or authority [13thC. Via Old French *sceptre* from, ultimately, Greek *skēptron* "staff, scepter," from *skēptein* "to lean on."] —**scep·tered** *adj.*

scep·tic *n., adj.* = **skeptic**

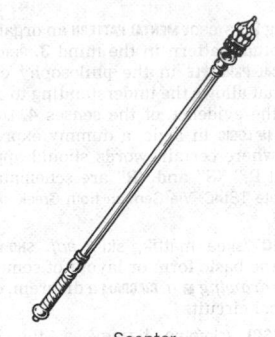

Scepter

Scep·tic *n., adj.* = **Skeptic**

scep·ti·cal *adj.* = **skeptical**

WORD KEY: SYNONYMS

See Synonyms at ***doubtful***.

scep·tre *n., vt.* U.K. = **scepter**

SCF *abbr.* Save the Children Fund

sch. *abbr.* school

scha·den·freu·de /shaád'n frŏydə/, **Scha·den·freu·de** *n.* malicious or smug pleasure taken in somebody else's misfortune [Late 19thC. From German, formed from *Schaden* "harm" + *Freude* "joy."]

Schaff·hau·sen /shaáf hòwzən/ capital of Schaffhausen Canton, in northern Switzerland. Population: 34,396 (1983).

schappe /shap, shaápə/, **schappe silk** *n.* yarn or fabric made from the waste products of silk [Late 19thC. From German.]

Schaum·burg /shówm bùrg/ village in northeastern Illinois, south of Hoffman Estates. It is a western suburb of Chicago. Population: 74,294 (1996).

schav /shav, shchaav/ *n.* a chilled soup made from sorrel or spinach, to which chopped egg, sour cream, lemon juice, and chopped green onions are sometimes added [Via Yiddish *shtshav* "sorrel, soup made with sorrel" from Polish *szczaw*]

schechita *n.* = **shechita**

sched·ule /skéjool, skéjjəl/ *n.* **1.** WORK PLAN a plan of work to be done in a specified order and by specified times **2.** LIST OF MEETINGS, COMMITMENTS, OR APPOINTMENTS an outline description of the things somebody is to do and the times at which they are to be done ○ *Her busy work schedule didn't permit us to meet for lunch.* **3.** LIST OF ARRIVALS AND DEPARTURES a list of the times of arrivals and departures, e.g., of buses or trains **4.** EDUC STUDENT'S TIMETABLE a list of the classes that are the responsibility of a student or a teacher in a given period **5.** LIST OF ITEMS a table of items of information ○ *a schedule of tariffs* **6.** DRUGS LIST OF RESTRICTED DRUGS a list of drugs that are subject to legal restrictions **7.** LAW SUPPLEMENTARY LIST a list of details, often in the form of an appendix to a legal or legislative document ■ *vt.* (**-uled, -ul·ing, -ules**) **1.** PLAN SOMETHING FOR A PARTICULAR TIME to plan something to happen at a particular time ○ *They are scheduled to arrive at midday.* **2.** MAKE A LIST OF THINGS to put together a table of items of information, or place an item in the table [14thC. Via Old French *cēdule* from late Latin *schedula* "small piece of paper," from, ultimately, Greek *skhedē* "page."] —**sched·u·lar** *adj.* —**sched·u·ler** *n.*

sched·uled castes *npl.* castes in India that are officially considered disadvantaged and granted special treatment

schee·lite /sháy līt, sheé-/ *n.* a variously colored mineral that occurs in veins and is the chief ore of tungsten [Mid-19thC. Named for Karl Wilhelm *Scheele* (1742–86), the German-born Swedish chemist who first isolated tungstic acid from this mineral.]

schef·fle·ra /shef leérə, shéfflərə/ (*plural* -ras *or* -ra) *n.* a tropical tree or shrub with glossy leaves, often cultivated as a house plant. Genus: *Schefflera*. [Mid-20thC. From modern Latin, named for German botanist J. C. *Scheffler* (1742–86).]

Schel·te /skéltə/ river in Europe that flows through France, Belgium, and the Netherlands. Length: 270 mi./435 km.

sche·ma /skeémə/ (*plural* -ma·ta /-mətə/) *n.* **1.** DIAGRAM a diagram or plan showing the basic outline of

ST

something **2.** PSYCHOL **MENTAL PATTERN** an organizational or conceptual pattern in the mind **3.** PHILOS **KANTIAN PHILOSOPHICAL PRINCIPLE** in the philosophy of Kant, a method that allows the understanding to apply concepts to the evidence of the senses **4.** LOGIC **DUMMY EXPRESSION IN LOGIC** in logic, a dummy expression indicating where certain words should appear, e.g., in "S and R," "S" and "R" are schemata for sentences [Late 18thC. Via German from Greek *skhēma* (see SCHEME).]

sche·mat·ic /skee máttik, ski-/ *adj.* **SHOWING LAYOUT** showing the basic form or layout of something ○ *a schematic drawing* ■ *n.* **DIAGRAM** a diagram, especially of electrical circuits

sche·ma·tism /skéemə tìzzəm/ *n.* the basic arrangement or layout of parts in a complex object or system [Mid-17thC]

sche·ma·tize /skéemə tìz/ (**-tized, -tiz·ing, -tiz·es**) *vt.* to arrange or organize something according to a system —**sche·ma·ti·za·tion** /skèemətə z áysh'n/ *n.*

scheme /skeem/ *n.* **1. SECRET PLOT** a secret and cunning plan, especially one designed to cause damage or harm **2. PLAN** a systematic plan of action **3. SYSTEM** a systematic and coherent arrangement of parts **4. DIAGRAM** a diagram, chart, or map **5.** *U.K.* **GOVERNMENT OR BUSINESS PROGRAM** a plan, policy, or program carried out by a government or business ○ *training scheme* **6.** ASTRON **ASTROLOGER'S CHART** an astrological chart of the sky ■ *v.* (**schemed, schem·ing, schemes**) **1.** *vi.* **MAKE A SECRET PLAN** to devise a secret and cunning plan, especially one intended to cause damage or harm **2.** *vt.* **PLAN SOMETHING SYSTEMATICALLY** to devise a systematic plan for something [Mid-16thC. Via Latin *schema* (stem *schemat-*) "form," from Greek *skhēma*. Ultimately from an Indo-European word meaning "to hold," which is also the ancestor of English *school*.]

schem·ing /skéeming/ *adj.* making secret and cunning plans, especially to do damage or cause harm —**schem·ing·ly** *adv.*

Sche·nec·ta·dy /skə néktədee/ city in eastern New York, on the Mohawk River, northwest of Albany. Population: 62,893 (1996).

Scher·er·ville /shúrrə vìl/ town in northwestern Indiana, near the Indiana-Illinois border, southeast of Chicago. Population: 23,322 (1996).

scher·zan·do /skair tsaándō/ *adj., adv.* **IN PLAYFUL STYLE** performed in a playful musical style and tempo (*used as a musical direction*) ■ *n.* (*plural* **-di** /-tsaándee/ *or* **-dos**) **SCHERZANDO PIECE** a scherzando piece or passage of music [Early 19thC. From Italian, formed from *scherzare* (see SCHERZO).]

scher·zo /skáirtsō/ (*plural* **-zos** *or* **-zi** /-tsee/) *n.* **1. LIGHTHEARTED MUSICAL MOVEMENT** a rapid, playful, or humorous movement, usually the third of four, in a musical work **2. LIGHTHEARTED MUSICAL PIECE** an independent musical work in a rapid, playful, or humorous style [Mid-19thC. From Italian, formed from *scherzare* "to joke," of uncertain origin: probably of Germanic origin.]

Sche·ven·in·gen /skáyvən ingən/ resort town in the western Netherlands, on the North Sea. It is now a district of The Hague.

Popperfoto

Elsa Schiaparelli

Schia·pa·rel·li /skee aàpə réllee, skàppə-/, **Elsa** (1896–1973) Italian fashion designer. Her designs were often extravagant with deliberately overstated effects.

Schick test /shík-/ *n.* an injection of nontoxic diphtheria under the skin, used to determine whether a patient is immune to diphtheria. A patch of reddened skin at the point of injection indicates no immunity. [Early 20thC. Named for Bela *Schick* (1877–1967), the Hungarian-born U.S. pediatrician who devised the test.]

Schie·le /sheélə/, **Egon** (1890–1918) Austrian painter. His depictions of the human figure, in the expressionist style, have a strongly erotic quality.

Schiff's re·a·gent /shìffs-/, **Schiff re·a·gent** *n.* an acid solution of fuchsine used to test for the presence of aldehydes [Late 19thC. Named for the German chemist Hugo *Schiff* (1834–1915).]

schil·ler /shíllər/ *n.* a metallic iridescent luster in some minerals [Early 19thC. From German, "iridescence."]

Schil·ler /shíllər/, **Friedrich von** (1759–1805) German poet, dramatist, historian, and philosopher. Regarded as Germany's greatest playwright, he wrote works in praise of the freedom of the human spirit, including the dramas *Wallenstein, Maria Stuart* (both 1800), and *William Tell* (1804). Full name **Johann Christoph Friedrich von Schiller**

schil·ling /shílling/ *n.* **1. AUSTRIAN UNIT OF CURRENCY** a unit of currency in Austria worth 100 groschen. See table at **currency 2. COIN WORTH SCHILLING** a coin worth one schilling [Mid-18thC. From German.]

Schipperke

schip·per·ke /shíppər kee/ (*plural* **-kes** *or* **-ke**) *n.* a small black tailless dog of a breed with pointed ears and a thick coat [Late 19thC. From Dutch dialect, a diminutive of Dutch *schipper* "skipper" (see SKIPPER[1]). From the use of the dog as a watchdog on boats.]

schism /skízzəm, sízzəm/ *n.* **1. SPLITTING INTO FACTIONS** the division of a group into mutually antagonistic factions **2. FACTION** a faction formed as a result of a schism **3.** RELIG **DIVISION IN OR FROM A RELIGIOUS DENOMINATION** a division within a religious denomination or a breaking away from it, usually on the grounds of differing beliefs or practices [14thC. Via Old French *scisme* from late Latin *schisma* from, ultimately, Greek *skhizein* (see SCHIZO-).]

schis·mat·ic /skiz máttik, siz-/, **schis·mat·i·cal** /-máttik'l, -/ *adj.* **OF A SCHISM** relating to, involved in, or causing schism ■ *n.* **MEMBER OR PROMOTER OF A SCHISM** somebody who is involved in a schism or who causes a schism —**schis·mat·i·cal·ly** *adv.* —**schis·mat·i·cal·ness** *n.*

schist /shist/ *n.* any rock whose minerals have aligned themselves in one direction in response to deformation stresses, with the result that the rock can be split in parallel layers [Late 18thC. Via French *schiste* from Latin *(lapis) schistos* "fissile (stone)," from Greek *skhistos*, from *skhizein* (see SCHIZO-).] —**schis·tose** /shíss tōss, -tōz/ *adj.* —**schis·tos·i·ty** /shiss tóssətee/ *n.*

schis·to·cyte /shístə sìt/ *n.* a red blood cell undergoing fragmentation, or any of the fragments that are formed as a result

schis·to·some /shístə sòm/ *n.* a tiny flatworm that often lives as a parasite in the blood of birds and mammals. In humans, it causes the disease schistosomiasis.

schis·to·so·mi·a·sis /shìstəsō mí əssiss/ *n.* an often chronic illness that results from infection of the blood with a parasitic flatworm (**schistosome**). It causes debilitation and can cause liver and intestinal damage. It is most common in Asia, Africa, and South America, especially in areas where the water is contaminated by freshwater snails that carry the parasite.

schiz- *prefix.* = **schizo-** (*used before vowels*)

schi·zan·thus /skit sánthəss, ski zánth-/ (*plural* **-thus**) *n.* a Chilean plant with small flowers that resemble orchids. Genus: *Schizanthus.* [Early 19thC. From modern Latin, name of the genus; coined from SCHIZO- + Greek *anthos* "flower."]

schiz·o /skítsō/ *n.* (*plural* **-os**) **AN OFFENSIVE TERM** an offensive term for somebody who has schizophrenia (*slang offensive*) ■ *adj.* **OFFENSIVE TERM** an offensive term referring to characteristics often erroneously thought of as symptomatic of schizophrenia (*slang offensive*) [Mid-20thC. Shortening of SCHIZOPHRENIC.]

schizo- *prefix.* **1.** split, cleft ○ *schizocarp* **2.** cleavage, fission ○ *schizogenesis* **3.** schizophrenia ○ *schizo-affective* [Via modern Latin from Greek *skhizein* "to split." Ultimately from an Indo-European base that is also the ancestor of English *schism* and *rescind*.]

schiz·o·carp /skítsə kaárp/ *n.* a dry fruit that splits into individually seeded parts (**carpels**) when ripe —**schiz·o·car·pic** /skìtsə kaárpik/ *adj.* —**schiz·o·car·pous** /-kaárpəss/ *adj.*

schi·zog·o·ny /ski zóggənee, skit sóggənee/ *n.* a form of asexual reproduction that occurs in certain single-celled organisms (**protozoans**), in which the nucleus of an individual divides many times before the cytoplasm divides to form the daughter cells. This process enables certain parasites, including the malaria parasite, to undergo rapid proliferation in the body tissues of an infected host.

schiz·oid /skíts òyd/ *adj.* **1.** PSYCHIAT **TENDING TOWARD SCHIZOPHRENIA** with some of the symptoms of schizophrenia, e.g., withdrawal into the self and a tendency to fantasize ○ *exhibits a schizoid personality* **2. OFFENSIVE TERM** an offensive term describing a personality that suggests inner conflicts and exhibits outer contradictions (*offensive*)

schiz·ont /skíz ònt, skít zònt/ *n.* a cell formed during the asexual phase of the life cycle of certain single-celled organisms (**protozoans**)

schiz·o·phre·ni·a /skìtsə fréenee ə/ *n.* **1. PSYCHIATRIC DISORDER AFFECTING THE COHERENCE OF THE PERSONALITY** a severe psychiatric disorder with symptoms of emotional instability, detachment from reality, often with delusions and hallucinations, and withdrawal into the self **2. OFFENSIVE TERM** an offensive term for contradictory or conflicting attitudes, behavior, or qualities (*offensive*) [Early 20thC. Coined from SCHIZO- + Greek *phrēn* "mind" (see PHRENO-).]

schiz·o·phren·ic /skìtsə frénnik/ *adj.* **1.** PSYCHIAT **OF SCHIZOPHRENIA** relating to schizophrenia or resulting from schizophrenia **2. OFFENSIVE TERM** an offensive term meaning characterized by conflicts and contradictions (*offensive*)

schiz·o·phyte /skítsə fìt/ *n.* a microorganism that reproduces by fission. Bacteria and bluish-green algae are schizophytes. —**schiz·o·phyt·ic** /skìtsə fíttik, skìzzə-/ *adj.*

schiz·o·pod /skítsə pòd, skízzə-/ (*plural* **-pods** *or* **-pod**) *n.* any of numerous kinds of crustacean that resemble shrimp, including krill. Order: Mysidacea and Euphausiacea.

schiz·o·thy·mi·a /skìtsə thímee ə/ *n.* an introverted psychiatric condition that resembles a mild form of schizophrenia [Mid-20thC. Ultimately from Greek *skhizein* "to split" + *thumos* "soul, mind."] —**schiz·o·thy·mic** *adj.*

schiz·y /skítssee/ (**-i·er, -i·est**) *adj.* offensive term meaning emotionally sensitive or moody to a degree that makes others feel uneasy (*slang offensive*) [Mid-20thC. Shortening of SCHIZOPHRENIC or SCHIZOID with alteration.]

schle·miel /shlə méel/, **schle·mihl** *n.* an offensive term referring to somebody regarded as bungling, inept, or unlucky (*insult slang*) [Late 19thC. From Yiddish *shlemiel*, of uncertain origin: probably from *Shelumiel*, biblical figure identified in the Talmud with a prince who was killed while committing adultery.]

schlep /shlep/ *v.* (**schlepped** *or* **shlepped, schlep·ping** *or* **shlep·ping, schleps** *or* **shleps**) (*informal*) **1.** *vt.* **MOVE SOMETHING WITH DIFFICULTY** to lug or haul something from one place to another **2.** *vi.* **GO WITH DIFFICULTY** to move slowly, clumsily, or tediously ■ *n.* (*plural* **schleps** *or* **shleps**) **1. TEDIOUS JOURNEY** a long, tedious, or difficult journey (*informal*) ○ *It's such a schlep all the way across town.* **2. OFFENSIVE TERM** an offensive term referring to somebody who is regarded as unintelligent or clumsy (*insult*) [Early 20thC. Via Yiddish *shlepn* from German *schleppen* "to drag."] —**schlep·per** *n.*

Schles·wig-Hol·stein /shlèzvig hólstìn/ state in northern Germany occupying the southern part of the Jutland peninsula. Capital: Kiel. Population: 2,708,000 (1994). Area: 6,066 sq. mi./15,710 sq. km.

schlie·ren /shleérən/ *npl.* **1.** PHYS **STREAKS IN FLUID** zones of different density and refraction in a transparent fluid, visible as streaks and caused by pressure or temperature variations **2.** GEOL **LINEAR FEATURES IN ROCKS** a texture observed in some igneous rocks where the darker, more basic minerals form linear aggregates in the paler host rock [Late 19thC. Via German, "streaks," from, ultimately, Middle High German *slier* "mud," of uncertain origin.]

schlie·ren pho·tog·ra·phy *n.* a form of flash photography that records schlieren present in a fluid

schli·ma·zel /shlə maázəl/ *n.* an offensive term for somebody regarded as prone to mistakes, errors and bad luck (*slang insult*) [Mid-20thC. From Yiddish, formed from Middle High German *slim* "crooked" + Hebrew *mazzāl* "luck."]

schlock /shlok/ *n.* **JUNK** something that has no value and is shoddily made (*slang*) ■ *adj.* **LACKING IN SUBSTANCE** cheap and lacking any redeeming quality (*slang*) ○ *a schlock horror film* [Early 20thC. Origin uncertain: possibly from Yiddish *shlak* "stroke, evil," from Middle High German *slag*.] —**schlock·y** *adj.*

schlock·meis·ter /shlók mìstər/ *n.* somebody who sells shoddy goods of little value (*slang*) [Mid-20thC. *Meister* from German, "master."]

schmaltz /shmaalts, shmawlts/, **schmalz, shmaltz** *n.* **1.** **SENTIMENTALITY** cloying or exaggerated sentimentality (*informal*) **2.** COOK **COOKING FAT** melted chicken fat used for cooking [Mid-20thC. Via Yiddish *shmalts*, literally "melted fat," from German *Schmalz*.] —**schmaltz·y** *adj.*

schmat·te /shmaátə/, **shmat·te** *n.* a rag or worthless thing (*informal*) [Late 20thC. Via Yiddish from Polish *szmata* "rag."]

schmeer /shmeer/, **schmear, shmeer** *n.* **1.** **WHOLE SET** an entire set or group of related things (*slang*) ○ *the whole schmeer* **2.** **BRIBE** a bribe (*slang*) **3.** FOOD **SPREAD OR PASTE** something such as cream cheese spread on a roll or bagel [Mid-20thC. Via Yiddish *schmirn* "to smear" from Middle High German *smiren*.]

Schmidt /shmit/, **Helmut** (*b.* 1918) German statesman. He was chancellor of West Germany (1974–82), a prominent leader of the European Union, and, from 1983, publisher of *Die Zeit*. Full name **Helmut Heinrich Waldemar Schmidt**

Schmidt cam·er·a /shmít-/ *n.* = **Schmidt telescope**

Schmidt sys·tem *n.* an optical system that uses a special concave spherical mirror to correct optical aberrations [Mid-20thC. Named for Bernhard Voldemar *Schmidt* (1879–1935), an Estonian-born German specialist in optics.]

Schmidt tel·e·scope *n.* a wide-angle photographic telescope used in astronomy. It has a special internal mirror to correct optical aberrations. [Mid-20thC (see SCHMIDT SYSTEM)]

Schmitt trig·ger /shmít-/ *n.* an electronic circuit that produces an output when the input exceeds a predetermined turn-on or threshold level. The output is maintained until the input falls below the threshold level. [Mid-20thC. Named for Otto H. *Schmitt* (b. 1913), U.S. biophysicist and electronics engineer.]

schmo /shmō/ (*plural* **schmoes**), **shmo** (*plural* **shmoes**) *n.* an offensive term referring to somebody regarded as boring, easily deceived, or having otherwise objectionable qualities (*slang insult*) [Mid-20thC. Alteration of SCHMUCK.]

schmooze /shmooz/ *v.* (**schmoozed, schmooz·ing, schmooz·es**) **1.** *vi.* **CHAT INFORMALLY** to chat socially and agreeably (*slang*) **2.** *vt.* **BE INGRATIATING TOWARD SOMEBODY** to talk persuasively to somebody, often to gain personal advantage ■ *n.* **A CHAT** an informal chat about trivial matters (*slang*) [Late 19thC. Via Yiddish *schmuesn* "to talk" from, ultimately, Hebrew *šəmū'āh* "rumor."] —**schmooz·er** *n.*

schmuck /shmuk/, **shmuck** *n.* an offensive term referring to somebody who is regarded as being unworthy of respect (*slang insult*) [Late 19thC. From Yiddish *shmok* "penis," of unknown origin.]

Schna·bel /shnaáb'l/, **Artur** (1882–1951) Austrian pianist and composer. He was known for his interpretations of Beethoven, Schubert, and Mozart. His own compositions include chamber music and piano works. After 1939 he settled in the United States.

schnapps /shnaps/ (*plural* **schnapps**) *n.* **1.** **FLAVORED LIQUOR** a strong liquor in which flavoring, e.g., peppermint, is distilled in rather than added later **2.** **GLASS OF SCHNAPPS** a glass or measure of schnapps [Early 19thC. Via German from Low German or Dutch *snaps*, "mouthful" (of uncertain origin).]

schnau·zer /shnówtsər, shnówzər/ *n.* a wiry-coated dog with bushy eyebrows and whiskers that grow like a beard, belonging to any of three breeds that originated in Germany. They are bred in giant, standard, and miniature sizes. [Early 20thC. From German, formed from *Schnauze* "snout."]

schneck·en /shnékən/ *npl.* sweet bread rolls flavored with layers of butter, chopped nuts, and cinnamon between the spiraled strands [From German, plural of *Schnecke* "snail"]

schnit·zel /shníts'l/ *n.* a piece of meat, typically veal, beaten flat and served fried, usually coated in egg and breadcrumbs [Mid-19thC. From German, formed from, ultimately, Old High German *snidan* "to cut."]

schnook /shnŏŏk/ *n.* an offensive term referring to somebody who is regarded as easily duped, or unimportant (*slang insult*) [Mid-20thC. Origin uncertain: perhaps from Yiddish *shnuk* "snout."]

schnor·rer /shnáwrər/ *n.* an offensive term referring to somebody who seems unable or unwilling to support him – or herself (*slang insult*) [Late 19thC. Via Yiddish, "beggar," from, ultimately, Middle High German *snurren* "to hum," from the beggar's practice of playing a musical instrument while begging.]

schnoz·zle /shnózz'l/, **schnoz** /shnoz/ (*plural* **schnoz·es**) *n.* a nose, especially a large one (*slang*) [Mid-20thC. From Yiddish *shnoytsl*, a diminutive of *shnoyts* "snout," from German *Schnauze*.]

Schoen·berg /shúrn bùrg, shŏn bairk/, **Arnold** (1874–1951) Austrian composer. He is known for his revolutionary 12-tone, or serial, system and the discordant works it produced. Full name **Arnold Franz Walter Schoenberg**

scho·la can·to·rum /skōlə kan táwrəm/ (*plural* **scho·lae can·to·rum** /skōlee-/) *n.* a choir, or choir school, housed in a church or cathedral [Late 18thC. From medieval Latin, literally "school of singers."]

schol·ar /skólər/ *n.* **1.** **LEARNED PERSON** somebody who has a great deal of knowledge, especially an academic who specializes in a particular arts subject **2.** **SCHOLARSHIP STUDENT** a student who receives a scholarship **3.** **STUDENT** a student (*formal*) [Pre-12thC. From late Latin *scholaris*, from Latin *schola* (see SCHOOL).]

schol·ar·ly /skólərlee/ *adj.* **1.** **LEARNED** with a great deal of knowledge, especially knowledge of an academic subject **2.** **OF SCHOLARS** relating to scholars or to formal study ○ *scholarly journals* **3.** **ACCORDING TO PRINCIPLES OF FORMAL STUDY** in keeping with a rigorous and systematic approach to acquiring knowledge or to setting out the results of formal study — **schol·ar·li·ness** *n.*

schol·ar·ship /skólər shìp/ *n.* **1.** **FINANCIAL HELP FOR A STUDENT** a sum of money awarded to a student to help with living expenses, study, or travel **2.** **FORMAL STUDY** academic learning or achievement **3.** **ACADEMIC WORKS** a body of learning on an academic subject ○ *a review of German scholarship on the topic*

scho·las·tic /skə lástik, sko-/ *adj.* **1.** **OF SCHOOLS OR STUDYING** relating to students, schools, or studying **2.** **PEDANTIC** too concerned with details or fine distinctions and too ready to criticize minor errors **3.** HIST **OF SCHOLASTICISM** relating to the medieval movement of religious and philosophical learning known as scholasticism ■ *n.* **1.** HIST **STUDENT OR TEACHER UNDER SCHOLASTICISM** a student or teacher in the medieval intellectual movement known as scholasticism **2.** **PEDANT** somebody who is quibbling or pedantic **3.** CHR **SOMEBODY UNDERGOING ROMAN CATHOLIC SCHOLASTICATE** somebody who is undergoing a scholasticate at a Roman Catholic seminary [Late 16thC. Via Latin *scholasticus* from Greek *skholastikos* "learned," from, ultimately, *skholē* (see SCHOOL).] —**scho·las·ti·cal·ly** *adv.*

Scho·las·tic Ap·ti·tude Test *n.* full form of **SAT**

scho·las·ti·cate /skə lásti kàyt, -kət/ *n.* **1.** **PERIOD OF STUDY AT A SEMINARY** a probationary period of study for a Jesuit student at a Roman Catholic seminary **2.** **JESUIT SEMINARY** a seminary where a scholasticate is undertaken

scho·las·ti·cism /skə lásti sizzəm, sko-/ *n.* **1.** HIST **MEDIEVAL THEOLOGY AND PHILOSOPHY** a medieval theological and philosophical system of learning based on the authority of St. Augustine and other leaders of the early Christian Church, and on the works of Aristotle. It sought to bridge the gap between religion and reason. **2.** **TRADITIONAL LEARNING** narrowly traditional learning, or adherence to traditional educational methods

scho·li·a plural of **scholium**

scho·li·ast /skōlee àst, -əst/ *n.* a medieval scholar who wrote commentaries on ancient Greek and Latin texts [Late 16thC. From medieval Greek *skholiastēs*, from, ultimately, *skholion* (see SCHOLIUM).] —**scho·li·as·tic** /skōlee ástik/ *adj.*

scho·li·um /skōlee əm/ (*plural* **-a** /-lee ə/) *n.* a medieval annotation or commentary written on an ancient Greek or Latin text [Mid-16thC. From Greek *skholion* "interpretation," from *skholē* (see SCHOOL).]

school[1] /skool/ *n.* **1.** EDUC **BUILDING FOR TEACHING CHILDREN** a building or institution in which children and teenagers are taught, usually up to the age of 17 (*often used before a noun*) **2.** UNIV **COLLEGE OR UNIVERSITY** any college or university **3.** UNIV **DEPARTMENT SPECIALIZING IN AN ACADEMIC SUBJECT** a faculty, department, or institution that offers specialized instruction in an academic subject ○ *medical school* **4.** **INSTITUTION TEACHING A NONACADEMIC SKILL** an institution that specializes in teaching a specific skill, especially a practical or sports skill ○ *tennis school* **5.** **STAFF AND STUDENTS** all the staff and students of an educational institution (*often used before a noun*) **6.** **DAY IN SCHOOL** the part of a day spent teaching or being taught in a school ○ *School was over for another day.* **7.** **YEARS SPENT AT SCHOOL** the part of somebody's life spent being taught in a school ○ *After school, he went abroad for two years.* **8.** **INSTRUCTIVE PLACE OR PERIOD** any place or period of activity regarded as providing knowledge or experience ○ *the school of life* **9.** **ARTISTS OR WRITERS SHARING SAME APPROACH** a group of people, especially artists, writers, or philosophers, who share the same principles, methods, ideals, or style ○ *the Impressionist school* ○ *the Aristotelian school* ■ *vt.* (**schooled, school·ing, schools**) **1.** **INSTRUCT SOMEBODY** to train or instruct somebody in a specific skill ○ *schooled in the art of debate* **2.** **EDUCATE SOMEBODY IN SCHOOL** to educate a child or teenager formally in a school **3.** **DISCIPLINE SOMEBODY** to exert control or discipline over somebody or yourself **4.** EQU **TRAIN A HORSE** to train a horse, especially for riding and dressage [Pre-12thC. Via Latin *schola* from Greek *skholē* "leisure, learned discussion, school." Ultimately from an Indo-European base meaning "to hold," which is also the ancestor of English *epoch*.]

WORD KEY: SYNONYMS

See Synonyms at ***teach***.

school[2] /skool/ *n.* **SHOAL OF AQUATIC ANIMALS** a group of fish, whales, porpoises, or other aquatic animals of a single type ■ *vi.* (**schooled, school·ing, schools**) **FORM OR SWIM IN A SCHOOL** to congregate in a school or swim in a school [14thC. From Middle Dutch *schole*, from prehistoric West Germanic, perhaps from a base meaning "to divide" (ancestor also of English *scale*[2]), in which case the underlying meaning is "division."]

school age *n.* the age at which a child is required legally to attend school —**school-age** *adj.*

school board *n.* = **board of education**

school·boy /skŏŏl bòy/ *n.* **YOUNG MALE STUDENT** a boy who attends school ■ *adj.* **IMMATURE** at a level of maturity typical of, or designed to appeal to, male children of school age ○ *schoolboy humor*

school·child /skŏŏl chìld/ (*plural* **-chil·dren** /-chìldrən/) *n.* a child who attends school

School·craft /skŏŏl kràft/, **Henry Rowe** (1793–1864) U.S. ethnologist. His studies of Native North American life included *Historical and Statistical Information Respecting the Indian Tribes of the United States* (1851–57). In 1832 he discovered the source of the Mississippi River in Minnesota.

school dis·trict *n.* an area that includes a number of public schools that are administered together

school·fel·low /skŏŏl fèllō/ *n.* a schoolmate

school fig·ure *n.* any one of a number of basic movements in figure-skating that are performed in competition (*often used in the plural*)

school·girl /skŏŏl gùrl/ *n.* a girl who attends school

school·house /skŏŏl hòwss/ (*plural* **-houses** /-hòwzəz/) *n.* **1.** **BUILDING USED AS A SCHOOL** a building that houses a school, especially a rural elementary school **2.** **TEACHER'S HOUSE ATTACHED TO A SCHOOL** a house attached to a school where a teacher lives, often the principal

school·ies week /skóoleez week/ *n. Aus* the week after the final-year school examinations, when school pupils traditionally congregate in holiday resorts to celebrate quitting school (*informal*)

school·ing /skóoling/ *n.* **1.** EDUC **EDUCATION AT SCHOOL** the education or instruction that is acquired in school **2. INSTRUCTION** instruction or training in anything, carried out systematically and in a disciplined way **3.** EQU **TRAINING OF A HORSE** the training of a horse, especially for riding and dressage

school·kid /skóol kid/ *n.* a child or teenager who attends school (*informal*)

school-leav·er *n. U.K.* a student who has quit school or is about to do so, especially one who quits at the minimum age and does not go on to further or higher education

School·man /skóol màn/ (*plural* **-men** /-mèn/) *n.* somebody who taught or studied as part of the medieval intellectual movement known as a scholasticism

school·marm /skool maarm/ *n.* **1. OFFENSIVE TERM** an offensive term for a woman schoolteacher, especially one considered too proper and old-fashioned (*dated insult*) **2. OFFENSIVE TERM** an offensive term for a woman thought to live in a way regarded as old-fashioned (*informal insult*)

school·mas·ter /skóol màstər/ *n.* **1. MAN SCHOOLTEACHER** a man who teaches school, especially in a private school (*dated*) **2.** (*plural* **-ters** *or* **-ter**) ZOOL **TROPICAL FOOD FISH** a Caribbean and tropical Atlantic food fish with yellow fins. It belongs to the snapper family. Latin name: *Lutjanus apodus*.

school·mate /skóol màyt/ *n.* a friend or companion at school

school·mis·tress /skóol mìstrəss, -mìss triss/ *n.* a woman who teaches school, especially in a private school (*dated*)

school of arts *n. Aus* a building used for adult education classes in a rural town

school of hard knocks *n.* difficult or challenging experiences that are considered to be instructive

School of the Air *n. Aus* an education service provided for children living in remote parts of Australia. Lessons are carried out by radio as well as through video, tape, fax, and computer networks.

school of thought *n.* a way of thinking about something, or a group of people who share the same attitude or opinion

school psy·chol·o·gist *n.* a psychologist who specializes in the assessment and problems of schoolchildren

school·room /skóol ròom, -ròom/ *n.* a classroom in a school

school·teach·er /skóol teechər/ *n.* somebody who teaches in a school —**school·teach·ing** *n.*

school·work /skóol wùrk/ *n.* the work that a student does in or after school

school·yard /skóol yaard/ *n.* a playground adjacent to a school

school year *n.* **1. PERIOD WHEN SCHOOLS ARE OPEN** the months during which instruction is given at a school, college, or university **2. TWELVE-MONTH EDUCATIONAL PERIOD** a period of twelve months, beginning usually in late August or early September, throughout which students are assigned to the same class

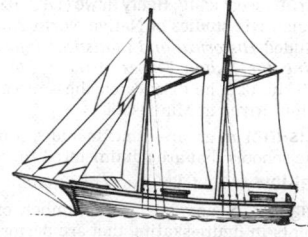

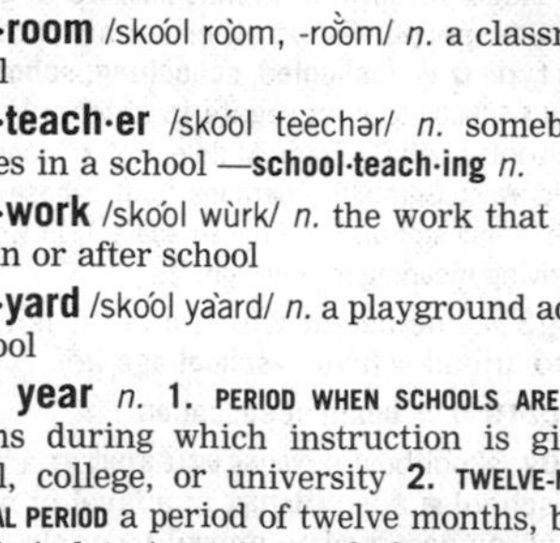

Schooner

schoo·ner /skóonər/ *n.* **1.** SAILING **SAILING VESSEL** a fast sailing ship with at least two masts and with sails set lengthways (**fore and aft**) **2.** *U.S., Aus* **BEER GLASS** a tall slim glass for beer **3.** HIST = **prairie schooner** [Early 18thC. Origin unknown.]

schoo·ner rig *n.* an arrangement of masts and sails (**rig**) in which the mainmast is taller than the foremast —**schoo·ner-rigged** *adj.*

Scho·pen·hau·er /shópən hòwər/, **Arthur** (1788–1860) German philosopher. His atheistic, deeply pessimistic philosophy was most fully expounded in *The World as Will and Idea* (1819).

schorl /shawrl/ *n.* a black opaque form of the mineral tourmaline, often occurring in needle-shaped radiating crystals [Late 18thC. From German *Schörl*, of unknown origin.] —**schor·la·ceous** /shawr láyshəss/ *adj.*

schot·tische /shótish, sho teésh/ *n.* **1. GERMAN FOLK DANCE** a round dance of German origin, resembling a slow polka **2. MUSIC FOR A SCHOTTISCHE** a piece of music for a schottische [Mid-19thC. From German *(der) Schottische(tanz)*, literally "the Scottish dance."]

Schot·tky ef·fect /shótkee-/ *n.* a reduction in the energy needed to remove an electron from a solid surface caused by the application of an electric field [Mid-20thC. Named for Walter *Schottky* (1886–1976), the German physicist who described the phenomenon.]

schrod *n.* = **scrod**

schtick *n.* = **shtick**

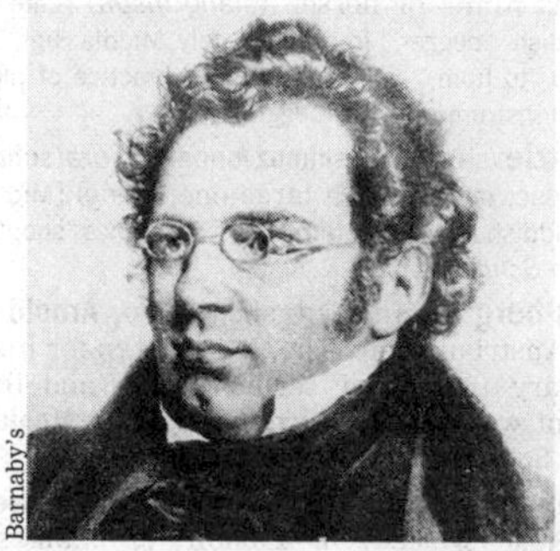

Franz Schubert

Schu·bert /shóobərt/, **Franz** (1797–1828) Austrian composer. He is particularly noted for his songs and chamber works, although he also wrote choral and orchestral music. Full name **Franz Peter Schubert**

schul *n.* = **shul**

Schultz /shóolts/, **Charles** (*b.* 1922) U.S. cartoonist. He created the successful *Peanuts* comic strip (1950), featuring Snoopy and Charlie Brown. Full name **Charles Monroe Schultz**

Schu·man /shóomən/, **William** (1910–92) U.S. composer. He is known for his Pulitzer Prize-winning *Secular Cantata, No. 2 (A Free Song)* (1943). He headed the Juilliard School of Music in New York City (1945–62). Full name **William Howard Schuman**

Schu·mann /shoom aan, shóomən/, **Robert** (1810–56) German composer. He was a major exponent of the romantic style, noted for his songs, piano music, and orchestral and chamber works. Full name **Robert Alexander Schumann**

Schum·pe·ter /shóomp aytər/, **Joseph Alois** (1883–1950) Austrian-born U.S. economist. A professor at Harvard University (1932–50), he promoted entrepreneurship for the "creative destruction" by which it drives economies forward.

Schurz /shurts, shóorts/, **Carl** (1829–1906) German-born U.S. statesman and journalist. He was a U.S. senator from Missouri (1869–75) and secretary of the interior (1877–81). He continued to advocate for progressive policies as an editor and journalist.

schuss /shòoss, shooss/ *vi.* (**schussed, schuss·ing, schuss·es**) **SKI DOWNHILL** to ski straight downhill at high speed ■ *n.* **DOWNHILL RUN IN SKIING** a straight fast downhill run on skis [Mid-20thC. From German *Schuß* "shot."]

schuss·boom·er /shóoss boomər, shooss-/ *n.* a skier adept at making fast straight downhill runs (*informal*)

schwa /shwaa, shvaa/, **shwa** *n.* an unstressed vowel, e.g., "a" in "above" or "e" in "sicken." It is represented in the International Phonetic Alphabet by the symbol ə. [Late 19thC. Via German from Hebrew *šəwā'*, of uncertain origin: probably an alteration of *šāw'* "emptiness."]

Schwann cell /shwaan-, shvaan-/ *n.* a cell of the peripheral nervous system that wraps around a nerve fiber and forms the myelin sheath [Early 20thC. Named for Theodor *Schwann* (1810–82), the German physiologist and histologist who described the structure.]

Schwarz·en·eg·ger /shwáwrtsə nèggər/, **Arnold** (*b.* 1947) Austrian-born U.S. body builder and movie actor. He has appeared in action movies such as *The Terminator* (1984).

Schwarzs·child ra·di·us /shwáwrts chīld-, shvaarts shīld-/ *n.* the critical radius within which the gravitational force of a gravitationally collapsing celestial body becomes so great that neither matter nor energy can escape, creating a black hole [Mid-20thC. Named for the German astronomer Karl *Schwarzschild* (1873–1916).]

Albert Schweitzer

Schweit·zer /shwítsər/, **Albert** (1875–1965) German-born theologian, musicologist, and missionary. He wrote important works on J.S. Bach and New Testament theology before setting up a hospital in 1913 at Lambaréné, in present-day Gabon, where he spent most of the rest of his life. He was awarded a Nobel Peace Prize (1952).

sci. *abbr.* **1.** science **2.** scientific

s.c.i. *abbr.* PRINTING single column inch

sci·ae·nid /sī eenid/ *n.* a carnivorous tropical or subtropical fish that produces loud sounds by snapping muscles attached to its air bladder. Croakers, drums, and grunts are all members of the family. Family: Sciaenidae. [Early 20thC. Via modern Latin *Sciaenidae* from *Sciaena*, name of the genus, from Greek *skiaina*, a kind of fish.] —**sci·ae·nid** *adj.*

sci·am·a·chy /sī ámmakee, skī-/ (*plural* **-chies**), **ski·am·a·chy** (*plural* **-chies**) *n.* (*literary*) **1. SHADOW-BOXING** practice fighting with a shadow or with an imaginary opponent **2. FUTILE FIGHTING** fighting with an imagined foe or against a foe who cannot be defeated, or an instance of this [Early 17thC. From Greek *skiamakhia*, literally "shadow fight," from *makhia* "fight."]

sci·at·ic /sī áttik/ *adj.* **1. OF THE HIP OR SCIATIC NERVE** relating to or affecting the back of the hip or the sciatic nerve **2. OF SCIATICA** causing sciatica or caused by sciatica [Early 16thC. Via French *sciatique* from, ultimately, Greek *iskhion* "hip joint."]

sci·at·i·ca /sī áttikə/ *n.* pain and tenderness extending from the back of the hip down to the calf, usually caused by a protrusion of vertebral disk substance pressing on the roots of the sciatic nerve [15thC. From medieval Latin, the feminine of *sciaticus* (see SCIATIC).]

sci·at·ic nerve *n.* either of two nerves that run from the back of the hip down the thigh to the calf

SCID *abbr.* severe combined immunodeficiency

sci·ence /sī ənss/ *n.* **1. STUDY OF THE PHYSICAL WORLD** the study of the physical world and its manifestations, especially by using systematic observation and experiment (*often used before a noun*) **2. BRANCH OF SCIENCE** a branch of science of a particular area of study ○ *the life sciences* **3. KNOWLEDGE GAINED FROM SCIENCE** the knowledge gained by the study of the physical world **4. SYSTEMATIC BODY OF KNOWLEDGE** any systematically organized body of knowledge about a specific subject ○ *the social sciences* **5. SOMETHING STUDIED OR PERFORMED METHODICALLY** any activity that is the object of careful study or that is carried out according to a developed method ○ *treated me to a lecture on the science of dressing for success* [14thC. Via Old French from Latin *scientia*, from *scient-*, present participle stem of *scire* "to know," ultimately "to discern," from an Indo-European word meaning "to cut."] ◇ **blind somebody with science** to confuse or overwhelm somebody by giving an impenetrable explanation using technical terms and concepts

sci·ence fic·tion *n.* a form of fiction, usually set in the future, that deals with imaginary scientific and technological developments and contact with other worlds (*often used before a noun*)

sci·ence park *n.* an area, usually associated with a university, where scientific research is carried out by commercial companies

sci·en·ter /sī éntər/ *adv.* LAW with full knowledge or awareness [Early 19thC. From Latin, "knowingly," formed from the stem *scient-* (see SCIENCE).]

sci·en·tial /sī énsh'l/ *adj.* **1. OF SCIENCE** relating to science or knowledge **2. KNOWLEDGEABLE** possessing considerable knowledge or skill (*formal*)

sci·en·tif·ic /sī ən tíffik/ *adj.* **1. OF SCIENCE** relating to, using, or conforming to science or its principles **2. METHODICAL** proceeding in a systematic and methodical way —**sci·en·tif·i·cal·ly** *adv.*

sci·en·tif·ic meth·od *n.* the system of advancing knowledge by formulating a question, collecting data about it through observation and experiment, and testing a hypothetical answer

sci·en·tif·ic no·ta·tion *n.* a way of expressing a given number as a number between 1 and 10 multiplied by 10 to the appropriate power. 5,743.6 expressed in scientific notation is 5.7436×10^3.

sci·en·tif·ic rev·o·lu·tion *n.* the period of advances in science that was at its height in the 17th century and produced widespread change in traditional beliefs held since the Middle Ages

sci·en·tism /sī ən tìzzəm/ *n.* **1. USE OF THE SCIENTIFIC METHOD** the use of the scientific method of acquiring knowledge, whether in the traditional sciences or in other fields of inquiry **2. RELIANCE ON SCIENCE FOR ANSWERS** the belief that science alone can explain phenomena, or the application of scientific methods to fields unsuitable for it (*disapproving*) ○ *"We feel that the attitude that predominates in science at present is arrogance, which has fostered dogmatism and scientism."* (Brian D. Josephson, Beverly A. Rubik, *The Challenge of Consciousness Research*; 1992) —**sci·en·tis·tic** /sī ən tístik/ *adj.*

sci·en·tist /sī əntist/ *n.* somebody who has had a scientific training or who works in one of the sciences ○ *a social scientist*

sci-fi /sī fī/ *n.* science fiction (*informal*) [Shortening of SCIENCE FICTION]

scil·i·cet /sílli sèt, skéeli kèt/ *adv.* used to introduce a word or phrase of clarification, or a missing word or phrase [14thC. From Latin, a contraction of *scire licet*, literally "it is permitted to know."]

scil·la /síllə/ (*plural* **-las** *or* **-la**) *n.* a plant of the lily family with flowers shaped like small bells. It is native to Europe and Asia. Genus: *Scilla.* [Early 19thC. Via Latin from Greek *skilla* "squill."]

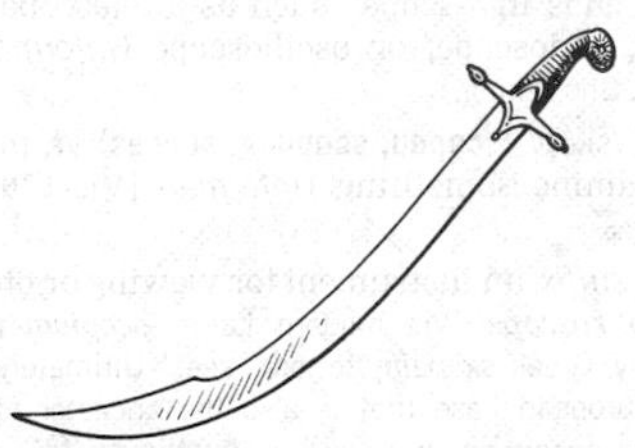

Scimitar

scim·i·tar /símmətər, símmə tàar/, **sim·i·tar** *n.* an Arab or Turkish sword with a curved blade that broadens out as it nears the point [Mid-16thC. From French *cimeterre* or Italian *scimitarra*, of uncertain origin: perhaps from Persian *šimšir*.]

scin·dap·sus /skin dápsəss/ (*plural* **-sus·es** *or* **-sus**) *n.* a climbing plant that has heart-shaped, often variegated leaves and is popular as a house plant. It is native to Asia. Genus: *Scindapsus.* [Mid-20thC. Via modern Latin *Scindapsus*, name of the genus, from Greek *skindapsos*, an ivylike plant.]

scin·ti·gram /sínti gràm/ *n.* a two-dimensional image of the distribution of a radioactive tracer in a body organ such as the brain or a kidney, obtained using a special scanner (**scintiscanner**) [Mid-20thC. Coined from SCINTILLATION + -GRAM.]

scin·til·la /sin tíllə/ *n.* a tiny amount of something ○ *There's not a scintilla of truth in what he said.* [Late 17thC. From Latin, "spark."]

scin·til·late /sínt'l àyt/ (**-lat·ed, -lat·ing, -lates**) *v.* **1.** *vi.* **SPARKLE** to give off or reflect light in sparks or flashes **2.** *vt.* PHYS **EMIT LIGHT FLASHES** to produce sparks of light when hit by particles or photons **3.** *vi.* **BE VERY DAZZLINGLY CLEVER** to be dazzlingly lively, clever, or witty [Early 17thC. Formed from Latin *scintillat-*, past participle stem of *scintillare*, from *scintilla* "spark."] —**scin·til·lant** *adj.* —**scin·til·lant·ly** *adv.*

scin·til·lat·ing /sínt'l àyting/ *adj.* possessing or displaying dazzling liveliness, cleverness, or wit —**scin·til·lat·ing·ly** *adv.*

scin·til·la·tion /sìnt'l áysh'n/ *n.* **1.** ASTRON **TWINKLING OF STARS** the twinkling of stars, caused by refraction of light rays from the stars because of different densities in the Earth's atmosphere **2.** PHYS **FLASH OF LIGHT** a flash of light caused by the impact of particles or photons **3. LIVELINESS** dazzling liveliness, cleverness, or wit (*literary*)

scin·til·la·tion count·er *n.* a device that detects and measures high-energy radiation through flashes of light produced when ionizing radiation impacts on a phosphorescent substance

scin·til·la·tor /sínt'l àytər/ *n.* a phosphorescent substance that produces flashes of light when struck by particles or photons

scin·ti·scan /sínt' skàn/ *n.* MED = **scintigram** [Mid-20thC. Coined from SCINTILLATION + SCAN.]

scin·ti·scan·ner /sínti skànnər/ *n.* an apparatus used in diagnosing certain diseases that produces an image (**scintigram**) of the distribution in the body of a radioactive tracer that has been administered to the patient

sci·o·lism /sī ə lìzzəm/ *n.* displays of sham learning designed to deceive or impress [Early 19thC. From late Latin *sciolus*, a diminutive of *scius* "having knowledge," from *scire* (see SCIENCE).] —**sci·o·list** *n.* —**sci·o·lis·tic** /sī ə lístik, sī ō-/ *adj.*

sci·on /sī ən/ *n.* **1.** BOT **PART OF A PLANT FOR GRAFTING** a living shoot or twig of a plant used for grafting to a stock **2. YOUNGER MEMBER OF A FAMILY** a child or descendant of a family, especially a rich, famous, or important family [13thC. From Old French *ciun*, of unknown origin.]

sci·o·phyte /sī ə fīt/ *n.* a plant that prefers shady conditions [Early 20thC. Coined from Greek *skia* "shadow" + -PHYTE.] —**sci·o·phy·tic** /sī ə fíttik/ *adj.*

Scip·i·o /síppee ō, skíppee ō/, **Publius Cornelius** (*d.* 211 B.C.) Roman general. He was the father of Scipio Africanus the Elder. Although he failed to defeat the Carthaginians in northern Italy and Spain, he helped to check their advances on Rome.

Scip·i·o Af·ri·ca·nus (the El·der) /-afri kaánəss/ (234?–183 B.C.) Roman general. He was the grandfather by adoption of Scipio Africanus the Younger. His defeat of Hannibal in 202 B.C. ended the Second Punic War. Full name **Publius Cornelius Scipio**

Scip·i·o Af·ri·ca·nus (the Youn·ger) (185?–129 B.C.) Roman general. He was the grandson by adoption of Scipio Africanus the Elder. A successful military commander, he destroyed Carthage to end the Third Punic War (146 B.C.). As a government official in Rome, he opposed the populist Gracchi brothers. Full name **Publius Cornelius Scipio Aemilianus**

sci·re fa·ci·as /sīree fàyshee àss/ *n.* LAW the judicial proceeding that produces a writ of scire facias [15thC. From Latin, literally "you should cause (him) to know."]

sci·roc·co *n.* = **sirocco**

scir·rhous /skírrəss, sírrəss/ *adj.* used to describe a cancerous tumor (**carcinoma**) that is hard and fibrous [Mid-16thC. Via French from modern Latin *scirrhosus*, ultimately via Latin from Greek *skirros* "hard coat or covering."] —**scir·rhos·i·ty** /ski róssətee, si-/ *n.*

scis·sel /síss'l, sízz'l/ *n.* metal clippings left over after disks, especially coins, have been punched out of sheets of metal [Early 17thC. From French *cisaille*, from *cisailler* "to clip with shears."]

scis·sile /síss'l, sí sīl/ *adj.* capable of being easily and smoothly cut, separated, or divided [Early 17thC. From Latin *scissilis*, from the stem *sciss-* (see SCISSION).]

scis·sion /sízh'n, sísh'n/ *n.* the act or process of cutting, separating, or dividing [15thC. Via French or directly from the Latin stem *scission-*, from *sciss-*, past participle stem of *scindere* "to cut."]

scis·sor /sízzər/ (**-sored, -sor·ing, -sors**) *vti.* **1. CUT WITH SCISSORS** to use scissors to cut something **2. MAKE A MOVEMENT LIKE SCISSORS** to move the legs, arms, or body in the way that the blades of a pair of scissors open and shut ○ *The swimmer scissored through the water.* [Early 17thC. From the singular of SCISSORS.]

scis·sors /sízzərz/ (*plural* **-sors**) *n.* **1. INSTRUMENT FOR CUTTING SOMETHING** a hand-held cutting instrument made up of two crossed connected blades, each with a ring-shaped handle, that cut as they slide and pivot (*takes a singular or plural verb*) **2.** GYMNASTICS **GYMNASTICS MOVEMENT** in gymnastics, a movement of the legs that resembles the opening and closing of scissors **3.** SPORTS **TECHNIQUE IN HIGH-JUMPING** in the high jump, a simple technique of clearing the bar sideways with each leg separately in a fast scissors movement. This technique is now rarely used. **4.** WRESTLING = **scissors hold** [14thC. Via French *cisoires* from the plural of late Latin *cisorium* "cutting tool," from Latin *caedere* "to cut" (source of English *concise* and *decide*).]

scis·sors-and-paste *adj.* crudely or hastily put together

scis·sors hold *n.* a wrestling hold in which the legs are wrapped and the feet locked around an opponent's head or body

scis·sors kick *n.* SWIMMING in swimming, a kicking motion that resembles the opening and closing of scissors, used especially when doing the sidestroke

scis·sor·tail /sízzər tàyl/ (*plural* **-tails** *or* **-tail**) *n.* any bird with a long forked tail, especially a scissor-tailed flycatcher

scis·sure /sízhər, síshər/ *n.* a long slit, especially one running lengthwise (*archaic*) [14thC. Via French or directly from Latin *scissura*, from the stem *sciss-* (see SCISSION).]

sci·u·rine /sī yŏŏ rīn/, **sci·u·rid** /sī yŏŏ rìd/ *n.* **RODENT OF THE SQUIRREL FAMILY** any rodent belonging to the family that includes squirrels, marmots, and chipmunks. Family: Sciuridae. ■ *adj.* **OF THE SQUIRREL FAMILY** relating to or belonging to the squirrel family of rodents [Mid-19thC. Formed from Latin *sciurus* (see SQUIRREL).]

sclaff /sklaf/ *vti.* (**sclaffed, sclaff·ing, sclaffs**) **HIT THE GROUND WITH A GOLF CLUB** in golf, to play a faulty stroke in which the clubhead scrapes the ground before coming into contact with the ball ■ *n.* **FAULTY GOLF STROKE** a golf stroke that is sclaffed [Early 19thC. Origin uncertain: probably an imitation of the sound produced when a club strikes the ground.] —**sclaff·er** *n.*

SCLC *abbr.* Southern Christian Leadership Conference

scler- *prefix.* = **sclero-** (*used before vowels*)

scle·ra /skleérə/ *n.* the dense outer coating of the eyeball that forms the white of the eye [Late 19thC. Via modern Latin from Greek *sklēros* "hard."]

scler·e·id /sklérree ìd/ *n.* any of a group of mainly short thick-walled plant cells that help to make up a plant's supporting tissue (**sclerenchyma**) [Late 19thC. Coined from Greek *sklēros* "hard" + -ID.]

scle·ren·chy·ma /sklə réngkəmə/ *n.* strengthening or supporting walls of plant tissue made up of long cells or fibers and short cells (**sclereids**) [Mid-19thC. Formed from SCLERO- on the model of *parenchyma*.] —**scle·ren·chym·a·tous** /skleérən klímmətəss/ *adj.*

scle·ri·a·sis /sklə rī əssəss/ *n.* = **scleroderma**

scle·rite /skleér ìt/ *n.* a hard plate or layer of chitin or calcium on the outer skeleton of an arthropod —**scle·rit·ic** /sklə ríttik/ *adj.*

scle·ri·tis /sklə rítiss/ *n.* inflammation of the tough outer coat of the eyeball that forms the white of the eye (**sclera**) [Mid-19thC. Formed from SCLERA.]

sclero- *prefix.* **1.** hard ○ *scleroderma* **2.** hardness ○ *sclerometer* **3.** sclera ○ *scleritis* [From Greek *sklēros* "hard." Ultimately from an Indo-European base meaning "dried up, withered," which is also the ancestor of English *skeleton*.]

scle·ro·der·ma /skleérə dúrmə/ *n.* a disease in which the skin becomes progressively hard and thickened

scle·ro·der·ma·tous /skleérə dúrmətəss/ *adj.* **1.** BIOL **SCALY** with a hard external covering of scales or plates **2.** MED **OF SCLERODERMA** relating to or characteristic of the skin disease scleroderma

scle·ro·der·mi·a /sklèerə dúrmee ə/ *n.* = **scleroderma**

scle·roid /skléer oyd/ *adj.* used to describe tissues or body parts that have become harder than is normal

scle·rom·e·ter /sklə rómmətər/ *n.* an instrument that determines the hardness of a metal or mineral by measuring the force required to scratch or pierce it —**scle·ro·met·ric** /sklèerə méttrik/ *adj.*

scle·ro·phyll /skléerə fìl/ *n.* any woody plant of arid areas with thick leathery evergreen foliage that retains water —**scle·ro·phyl·lous** /sklèerə fílləss/ *adj.*

scle·ro·pro·tein /sklèerrō-, sklèerō prṓtèen/ *n.* any one of a group of fibrous insoluble proteins, such as keratin, elastin, and collagen that are found in body tissue

scle·rosed /sklə rṓst, -rṓzd/ *adj.* used to describe tissues and body parts that have become harder and thicker than normal [Late 19thC. Formed from SCLEROSIS.]

scle·ro·sis /sklə rṓssəss/ (*plural* **-ses**) *n.* **1.** MED **HARDENING OF BODY TISSUE** the hardening and thickening of body tissue as a result of unwarranted growth, degeneration of nerve fibers, or deposition of minerals, especially calcium **2.** BOT **HARDENING OF PLANT CELL WALL** the hardening and thickening of a plant cell wall that occurs as lignin is deposited, turning young green growth woody —**scle·ro·sal** *adj.*

scle·ro·ti·a plural of **sclerotium**

scle·rot·ic /sklə róttik/ *adj.* **1.** BOT **OF PLANT CELL WALL HARDENING** relating to the hardening and thickening of plant cell walls that turns young green growth woody **2.** BIOL **OF THE WHITE OF THE EYE** relating to the dense outer coating of the eyeball that forms the white of the eye (**sclera**) **3.** MED **OF SCLEROSIS OF BODY TISSUE** relating to or suffering from sclerosis of body tissue **4.** **INFLEXIBLE** having become unresponsively rigid, especially from longevity ○ *a political party grown sclerotic from too many years in power* ■ *n.* BIOL = **sclera** [Mid-16thC. From modern Latin *sclerotica*, ultimately from Greek *sklēros* "hard"; or formed from SCLERA.]

scler·o·tin /sklèerətin, sklérrətin/ *n.* an insoluble protein that hardens and darkens the chitin on the outer skeleton of arthropods [Mid-20thC. Formed from SCLERO- on the model of words such as *keratin*.]

scle·ro·ti·um /sklə rṓshee əm, -shəm/ (*plural* **-a** /-shee ə, -shə/) *n.* in fungi, a compact hard mass that contains stored food [Mid-19thC. From modern Latin, originally the name of a genus of fungi, formed from Greek *sklērotēs* "hardness," from *sklēros* (see SCLERA).] —**scle·ro·ti·al** *adj.* —**scle·ro·ti·oid** *adj.*

scle·ro·tize /sklérrə tīz/ (**-tized, -tiz·ing, -tiz·es**) *vt.* to harden and darken an arthropod's outer skeleton [Mid-20thC. Ultimately from SCLEROTIC.] —**scler·o·ti·za·tion** /sklèrrətə záysh'n/ *n.*

scle·rot·o·my /sklə róttəmee/ (*plural* **-mies**) *n.* a surgical operation in which the outer coat (**sclera**) of the eyeball is cut, e.g., in order to remove an underlying tumor

scle·rous /skléerəss, sklérrəss/ *adj.* **1.** ZOOL **HARD** used to describe animal parts that are bony or scaly **2.** MED **HARDENED** used to describe body tissue or body parts that have become especially hardened, as a result of the deposition of minerals

scoff[1] /skof, skawf/ *vi.* (**scoffed, scoff·ing, scoffs**) **BE DERISIVE OR SCORNFUL** to express derision or scorn about somebody or something ○ *She scoffed at all our suggestions.* ■ *n.* **1.** **EXPRESSION OF SCORN** an expression of derision or scorn **2.** **OBJECT OF SCORN** somebody or something that is derided or scorned [14thC. Origin uncertain: probably from Scandinavian.] —**scoff·er** *n.* —**scoff·ing·ly** *adv.*

scoff[2] /skof, skawf/ (**scoffed, scoff·ing, scoffs**) *vti.* to eat food quickly and hungrily or greedily (*informal*) [Late 18thC. Variant of dialect *scaff*, of unknown origin.]

scoff·law /skóf làw, skáwf-/ *n.* somebody who ignores or disregards the law (*informal*) [Early 20thC. From SCOFF[1].]

Sco·field /skṓ feeld/, **Sir Paul** (*b.* 1922) British actor. He won an Academy Award for *A Man for All Seasons* (1966) and is known for his versatility in numerous stage and screen roles, from Shakespeare to contemporary drama. Full name **Sir David Paul Scofield**

scold /skōld/ *v.* (**scold·ed, scold·ing, scolds**) **1.** *vt.* **TELL SOMEBODY OFF** to rebuke somebody angrily **2.** *vi.* **SPEAK HARSHLY** to use harsh language, especially when complaining or finding fault ■ *n.* **1.** **REBUKING PERSON** somebody who is constantly rebuking others **2.** **OFFENSIVE TERM** an offensive term for a woman who is said to make a habit of using abusive language, especially when she is constantly reminding a man to do something (*archaic*) [13thC. Origin uncertain: probably from Old Norse *skáld* "poet," from the poet's role of satirizing or poking fun at people.] —**scold·er** *n.* —**scold·ing·ly** *adv.*

scol·e·cite /skáwlə sīt, skṓlə-/ *n.* a white zeolite mineral consisting of hydrated calcium aluminum silicate and found in both crystalline and massive forms [Early 19thC. Formed from Greek *skōlēk-*, stem of *skōlēx* "worm."]

sco·lex /skṓ lèks/ (*plural* **-li·ces** /skṓ-/ *or* **-le·ces** /skō lée seez/) *n.* the head of a tapeworm, with suckers or hooks that enable the parasitic worm to attach itself to its host [Mid-19thC. Via modern Latin from Greek *skōlēx* "worm."]

sco·li·o·sis /skōlee óssəss/ *n.* an excessive, sideways curvature of the spine. ◊ **kyphosis, lordosis** [Early 18thC. Via modern Latin from Greek *skoliōsis*, from *skolios* "bent, curved."] —**sco·li·ot·ic** /skōlee óttik/ *adj.*

scol·lop *n.* = **scallop**

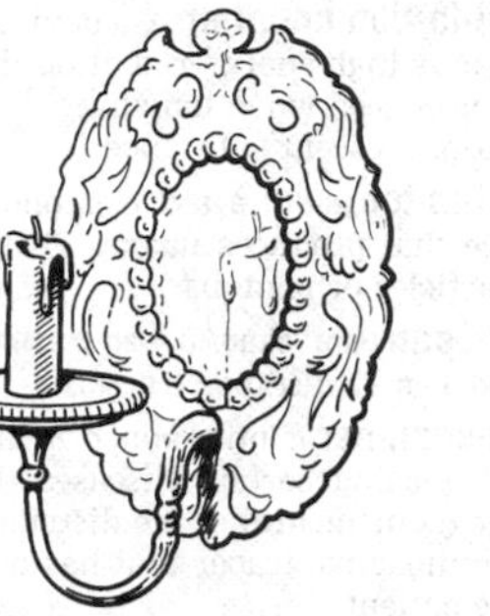

Sconce

sconce[1] /skonss/ *n.* a wall bracket for holding candles or, sometimes, electric light bulbs [14thC. From Old French *esconse* "hiding place, lantern," or from medieval Latin *absconsa laterna* "dark lantern," from *abscondere* (see ABSCOND).]

sconce[2] /skonss/ *n.* MIL a small defensive fort or earthwork [Late 16thC. From Dutch *schans* "brushwood, earthwork," of unknown origin.]

sconce[3] /skónss/ *n.* (*archaic*) **1.** **HEAD OR SKULL** the head or skull of a human being **2.** **INTELLIGENCE** wit or brains [Mid-16thC. Origin uncertain: perhaps a humorous use of SCONCE[1].]

scone /skōn/ *n.* a small baked quick bread, similar to a rich biscuit and traditionally served split and buttered. Plain scones are served with jam and clotted cream as part of the traditional British cream tea. [Early 16thC. Origin uncertain: perhaps from Middle Dutch *schoonbroot* "fine bread."]

Scone /skoon/ village in central Scotland, near the Tay River. It is famous for the Stone of Destiny on which Scottish kings were crowned, which was originally located there.

scoop /skoop/ *n.* **1.** **UTENSIL RESEMBLING A TROWEL** a utensil with a short handle and deep rounded sides, used for shoveling or ladling grain, flour, or other dry or semisolid substances **2.** COOK **LADLE** a utensil with a long handle and round bowl, used for transferring liquids **3.** COOK **UTENSIL WITH A BOWL-SHAPED HEAD** a utensil with a long handle and a small hemispherical bowl, used for serving such things as ice cream and mashed potatoes or making melon balls **4.** AUTOMOT **DIGGING PART** the part of a dredge or digging machine that is used for excavating **5.** **QUANTITY LIFTED IN A SCOOP** the quantity that is taken by a scoop ○ *three scoops of ice cream* **6.** **DIGGING MOTION** a curving digging movement of a scoop or the hand **7.** **CAVITY** a shallow cavity, hole, or other hollow area in something **8.** CARS **OPENING TO TAKE IN A SUBSTANCE** an opening that allows a substance to flow or be sucked inside, such as an air intake on the hood of a hot rod **9.** BROADCAST, PRESS **EXCLUSIVE** a news story that is published by a newspaper, magazine, or news program before its rivals (*informal*) ○ *scoop of the year* **10.** MUSIC **SLIDING UP TO PITCH** in vocal and instrumental music, a sliding up to a pitch **11.** **NEWS** the latest news or gossip (*informal*) ○ *What's the scoop?* **12.** **QUICK PROFIT** a large amount of money made quickly (*informal*) ■ *v.* (**scooped, scoop·ing, scoops**) **1.** *vt.* **HOLLOW SOMETHING OUT** to create a shallow hole in something with a scoop or similar object, or a cupped hand ○ *He scooped out a hole in the earth.* **2.** *vt.* **REMOVE SOMETHING** to remove an amount of a liquid or solid substance with a scoop or similar object, or a cupped hand ○ *scooping up water with a ladle* **3.** *vt.* **LIFT SOMEBODY OR SOMETHING SWIFTLY** to pick somebody or something up swiftly and without ceremony ○ *She scooped him up in her arms.* **4.** *vt.* BROADCAST **PUBLISH OR BROADCAST SOMETHING FIRST** to publish or broadcast an item of news before any other newspaper, magazine, or news program ○ *The newspaper scooped its rivals for the second time in a week.* ○ *scooping the hottest story of the year* **5.** *vt.* **GET A GREAT DEAL OF MONEY** to win or otherwise obtain a large amount of money **6.** *vti.* SPORTS **HIT A BALL UP IN THE AIR** to hit a ball upward from underneath so that it rises into the air [14thC. From Middle Low German and Middle Dutch *schōpe* "bucket for bailing, bucket of a waterwheel."] —**scoop·er** *n.*

scoop neck *n.* a low curved neckline on an article of women's clothing

scoosh /skoosh/ (**scooshed, scoosh·ing, scoosh·es**) *n.* *Scotland* an act of squirting (*informal*) [19thC. An imitation of the sound.]

scoot /skoot/ *v.* (**scoot·ed, scoot·ing, scoots**) (*informal*) **1.** *vi.* **LEAVE** to go away quickly (*often used as a command*) **2.** *vi.* **MOVE QUICKLY** to move, run, or go somewhere quickly **3.** *vt.* **SEND QUICKLY** to move or send something quickly ○ *Scoot that file to me as soon as you can.* ■ *n.* **SWIFT MOVEMENT** a swift movement or trip (*informal*) ○ *a quick scoot to the supermarket* [Mid-18thC. Origin uncertain: perhaps of Scandinavian origin.]

scoot·er /skóotər/ *n.* **1.** **WHEELED TOY** a child's toy consisting of handlebars attached by a long rod to a footboard on two wheels. One foot is placed on the board and the other propels it along. **2.** AUTOMOT = **motor scooter** **3.** SAILING **SAILBOAT FOR WATER OR ICE** a sailboat that can be used on water or ice [Early 19thC. Formed from SCOOT.]

scop /skop/ *n.* a bard or poet in Anglo-Saxon England [Old English *sc(e)op*, from a prehistoric Germanic word that may also be the ancestor of English *scoff*. Obsolete by the 14thC but revived in the 18thC.]

scope[1] /skōp/ *n.* **1.** **ROOM TO ACT** freedom, space, or capacity to act ○ *not much scope for originality* **2.** **RANGE COVERED** the range covered by an activity, subject, or topic ○ *a question that is beyond the scope of this lecture* **3.** **MENTAL CAPACITY** the extent of somebody's mental capacity **4.** SHIPPING **MOORING CABLE** the length of a ship's mooring cable **5.** LOGIC **RANGE OF A LOGICAL OPERATOR** the range of application or boundaries of a logical operator, usually indicated by parentheses. The scope of "and" in "(p and q) or r" is limited to "p" and "q." [Mid-16thC. Via Italian *scopo* "aim, purpose" from Greek *skopos* "target." The underlying sense is "something aimed at or kept in view," hence "range of view."]

scope[2] /skōp/ *n.* any optical device or tool whose name ends in "-scope" such as a telescope, microscope, endoscope, or oscilloscope (*informal*) [Early 17thC. Shortening.]

scope[3] /skōp/ (**scoped, scop·ing, scopes**) *vt.* to look at or examine something (*informal*) [Mid-17thC. From SCOPE[1].]

-scope *suffix.* an instrument for viewing or observing ○ *nephroscope* [Via modern Latin *-scopium* from, ultimately, Greek *skopein* "to look, see." Ultimately from an Indo-European base that is also the ancestor of English *inspect*, *specimen*, and *spy*.] —**-scopic** *suffix.* —**-scopy** *suffix.*

sco·pol·a·mine /skə pólə mèen, skə páwləmən/ *n.* a colorless thick liquid poisonous alkaloid found in some plants of the nightshade family and used as a truth serum, to prevent motion sickness, and as a sedative. Formula: $C_{17}H_{21}NO_4$. [Late 19thC. From modern Latin *Scopolia japonica*, scientific name of the Japanese belladonna, from which scopolamine was first extracted, and which was named for G. A. Scopoli (1723–88), Italian naturalist.]

scop·u·la /skópyələ/ (*plural* **-las** *or* **-lae** /-lèe/) *n.* a tuft of dense hairs on the back of the legs of some insects or spiders [Early 19thC. From late Latin, literally "little broom."]

scor·bu·tic /skawr byóotik/, **scor·bu·ti·cal** /skawr byóotik'l/ *adj.* relating to, affected with, or causing scurvy [Mid-17thC. Via modern Latin *scorbuticus* from medieval Latin *scorbutus* "scurvy," of uncertain origin: perhaps ultimately from a prehistoric Germanic word that is also the ancestor of English *scurf*.] —**scor·bu·ti·cal·ly** *adv.*

scorch /skawrch/ *v.* (**scorched, scorch·ing, scorch·es**) **1.** *vti.* **BURN SOMETHING ON ITS SURFACE** to burn the surface of something, or to be burnt so as to cause pain, injury, or discoloring ○ *scorched the handkerchief with the iron* **2.** *vti.* **DRY OUT** to dry or parch something with intense heat, or to become dried out or parched because of intense heat ○ *The plains had been scorched by the sun.* **3.** *vt.* **CRITICIZE SOMEBODY** to subject somebody to severe criticism (*informal*) ■ *n.* **1. SURFACE BURN** a burn, or burn mark on the surface of something ○ *The iron left a slight scorch on the blouse.* **2.** BOT **DISCOLORATION ON PLANTS** a brown marking on plants or vegetables caused by disease, insecticide, or heat [12thC. Origin uncertain: probably of Scandinavian origin.]

scorched-earth pol·i·cy *n.* **1.** MIL **LEAVING NOTHING FOR AN ENEMY** a policy of destroying crops or buildings, especially by burning, or of removing anything that might be useful to an advancing enemy in wartime **2.** BUSINESS **TAKEOVER-AVOIDANCE STRATEGY** a strategy adopted by a company facing a hostile takeover whereby it makes itself appear a financially less attractive acquisition until the threat has gone

scorch·er /skáwrchər/ *n.* **1. SOMETHING THAT BURNS** somebody or something that scorches **2. HOT DAY** an extremely hot day (*informal*) ○ *Yesterday was fairly warm but today is a scorcher!* **3. CRITICAL REMARK** a severely critical remark

scorch·ing /skáwrching/ *adj.* extremely hot (*informal*)

score /skawr/ *n.* **1.** SPORTS, GAME **POINTS MADE** the total number of points made by a player or team at the end of or during a match or game **2.** SPORTS, GAME **TALLY OF POINTS MADE** a record of the number of points made by a player or team in a match or game ○ *Who's keeping score?* **3.** SPORTS, GAME **GAINING OF POINT** the gaining of a point or points in a match or game **4.** EDUC **EXAM RESULT** the result of a test or examination, usually presented in numerical form **5.** (*plural* **score** *or* **scores**) **GROUP OF 20** a group of twenty things or people (*often used in combination*) ○ *A score or more people showed up.* **6.** MUSIC **PRINTED MUSIC** a written or printed copy of a musical composition ○ *distributed copies of the score to the chorus* **7.** MUSIC **MUSIC COMPOSED** the music that has been composed for a movie, play, or musical ○ *a film with a breathtaking score* **8.** DANCE **COPY OF CHOREOGRAPHIC NOTATION** a written record of the choreography for a dance or ballet **9. NOTCH** a notch or incision cut into the surface of something **10. PARTIAL CUT** a crease or superficial cut made in something, such as a piece of paper to enable it to be folded or separated easily **11. GRUDGE** a grievance that is not resolved and incurs resentment **12. RECORD OF MONEY OWED** a record of an amount of money due for payment **13. MONEY OWED** an amount of money due for payment **14. PRESENT SITUATION** the present state or actual facts of a situation (*informal*) ○ *What's the score, are you coming or not?* **15. SUCCESS** a successful result or achievement, especially one that is significant (*informal*) **16.** DRUGS **DRUG DEAL** a purchase of illegal drugs (*slang*) **17.** CRIMINOL **ROBBERY** the successful theft of something (*informal*) **18. SEXUAL CONQUEST** a successful seduction of somebody or the sexual encounter itself (*informal*) **19.** SAILING **GROOVE FOR ROPE** a groove cut in wood to hold a rope ■ **scores** *npl.* **MANY** a great many ○ *Scores of members protested at the decision.* ■ *v.* (**scored, scor·ing, scores**) **1.** *vti.* SPORTS, GAME **MAKE POINTS** to make a point or points in a match or game ○ *scored twice in the second half* **2.** *vt.* SPORTS, GAME **MAKE A TOTAL OF POINTS IN GAME** to make a total number of points in a match, game, or other competition **3.** *vti.* SPORTS, GAME **RECORD POINTS** to keep a record of the number of points made in a match, game, or other competition ○ *Who's scoring?* **4.** *vt.* SPORTS, GAME **ASSIGN SOMEBODY POINTS** to award a particular number of points to somebody in a match, game, or other competition ○ *Three of the judges scored her a perfect 10.* **5.** *vt.* SPORTS, GAME **BE WORTH CERTAIN POINTS IN A GAME** to count for a particular number of points in a match, game, or other competition ○ *Hitting the red area scores ten.* **6.** *vt.* EDUC **EXAM GRADE** to grade or evaluate a test or examination **7.** *vti.* **GET POINTS IN EXAM** to achieve a particular number of points in a test or examination **8.** *vt.* **CUT LINES IN SOMETHING** to make notches, cuts, or lines in a surface **9.** *vt.* **CUT SOMETHING SUPERFICIALLY TO SEPARATE IT** to make a superficial cut or crease in something, such as a piece of paper in order to fold, tear, or break it easily **10.** *vt.* **WRITE SOMETHING BY MAKING INCISIONS** to write something by means of notches, incisions, or lines cut into a surface ○ *names scored on the back of the bench with a penknife* **11.** *vti.* **CROSS SOMETHING OUT** to draw a line through something in order to mark it as canceled or deleted **12.** *vt.* **RECORD MONEY OWED** to keep a record of an amount of money owed by somebody by making a series of marks next to his or her name **13.** *vi.* **DO WELL** to secure an advantage in a particular field or area of activity (*informal*) ○ *She scores because she can communicate.* **14.** *vt.* MUSIC **ORCHESTRATE SOMETHING** to orchestrate or arrange a piece of music **15.** *vt.* MUSIC **COMPOSE THE MUSIC FOR SOMETHING** to write the music for a movie, play, or musical **16.** *vt.* DANCE **WRITE THE CHOREOGRAPHY FOR SOMETHING** to write out the choreography for a dance or ballet **17.** *vt.* **GET SOMETHING** to succeed in getting something (*informal*) ○ *scored front-row tickets for the concert* **18.** *vti.* DRUGS **BUY DRUGS** to buy illegal drugs (*slang*) **19.** *vi.* **HAVE SEX** to succeed in having sex with somebody, especially a new sexual partner (*slang*) **20.** *vt.* **CRITICIZE SOMEBODY** to subject somebody to severe criticism (*informal*) [Pre-12thC. From Old Norse *skor* "notch, tally, 20."] ◇ **on this** *or* **that score** as far as this or that is concerned ○ *Her health is fine, so there's no need to worry on that score.*

score·board /skáwr bàwrd/ *n.* a board at a sporting venue on which the score of a game, match, or other competition in progress is displayed. Scores of other games in progress elsewhere may also be shown.

score·card /skáwr kaàrd/ *n.* **1. CARD TO KEEP SCORE WITH** a small card used by a player to keep a record of his or her own score, e.g., in golf **2. CARD LISTING PLAYERS IN A GAME** a card listing the players in a game or match that enables a spectator to identify who is who and to keep a record of the progress of play

score·keep·er /skáwr keèpər/ *n.* somebody who is responsible for keeping a note of the score in a game, match, or other competition —**score·keep·ing** *n.*

score·less /skáwrləss/ *adj.* having no points scored ○ *The game remained scoreless at the half.*

scor·er /skáwrər/ *n.* **1.** SPORTS, GAME **SOMEBODY SCORING POINT** somebody who scores a point or points in a game or match **2.** SPORTS, GAME = **scorekeeper 3.** EDUC **SOMEBODY SCORING POINTS IN AN EXAM** somebody who gets a particular score in a test or examination ○ *a consistently high scorer in math* **4.** TECH **CUTTING DEVICE** a device for cutting a notch or incision into something

Scores·by Sound /skàwrzbee-/ arm of the Norwegian Sea touching eastern Greenland. It is the largest fjord in the world. Length: 280 mi./451 km.

sco·ri·a /skáwree ə/ (*plural* **-ae** /skáwree eè/) *n.* **1.** GEOL **POROUS ROCK** loose rubbly porous solidified lava that is ejected from a volcano and builds up around the crater **2.** METALL = **slag** *n.* 1 [14thC. Via Latin from Greek *skōria* "refuse, dross," from *skōr* "dung."] —**sco·ri·a·ceous** /skàwree áyshəss/ *adj.*

sco·ri·fy /skáwrə fì/ (**-fied, -fy·ing, -fies**) *vt.* to purify ore by separating it out into metal and slag —**sco·ri·fi·ca·tion** /skàwrəfə káysh'n/ *n.* —**sco·ri·fi·er** /skáwrə fì ər/ *n.*

scorn /skawrn/ *n.* **1. DISDAIN** a strong feeling of contempt ○ *poured scorn on my attempts at writing* **2. OBJECT OF CONTEMPT** somebody or something that is held in contempt ○ *Their behavior made them the scorn of the entire community.* ■ *v.* (**scorned, scorn·ing, scorns**) **1.** *vt.* **DISDAIN SOMEBODY OR SOMETHING** to hold somebody or something in contempt **2.** *vti.* **REJECT SOMETHING CONTEMPTUOUSLY** to reject something with contempt ○ *They had scorned our attempts at peace.* [12thC. From Old French *escharnir* "to mock or despise."] —**scorn·er** *n.*

scorn·ful /skáwrnf'l/ *adj.* feeling or expressing great contempt for somebody or something —**scorn·ful·ly** *adv.* —**scorn·ful·ness** *n.*

scor·pae·nid /skawr peénid/ *n.* a marine fish with spiny fins such as the scorpion fish, redfish, or rockfish. Family: Scorpaenidae. [Late 19thC. From modern Latin *Scorpaenidae*, from Latin *scorpaena*, a kind of fish, from Greek *skorpios* (see SCORPION).] —**scor·pae·nid** *adj.*

Scor·pi·o /skáwrpee ò/ *n.* **1.** ASTRON = **Scorpius 2.** ZODIAC **EIGHTH SIGN OF THE ZODIAC** the eighth sign of the zodiac, represented by a scorpion and lasting from approximately October 23 to November 21. Scorpio is classified as a water sign and its ruling planets are Mars and Pluto. **3. Scor·pi·o** (*plural* **-os**), **Scor·pi·an** ZODIAC **SOMEBODY BORN UNDER SCORPIO** somebody whose birthday falls between October 23 and November 21 [14thC. From Latin, from *scorpio* (see SCORPION).] —**Scor·pi·o** *adj.*

scor·pi·oid /skáwrpee òyd/ *adj.* **1.** BOT **WITH A COILED MAIN STEM** having the main stem curled at the end ○ *a scorpioid cyme* **2.** ZOOL **OF OR LIKE A SCORPION** relating to or resembling a scorpion [Mid-19thC. From Greek *skorpioeidēs*, from *skorpios* (see SCORPION).]

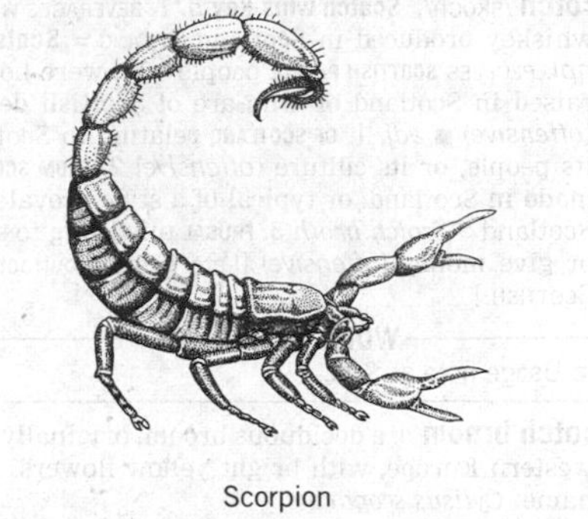

Scorpion

scor·pi·on /skáwrpee ən/ *n.* a nocturnal arachnid of warm dry regions that has a long body with pincers in front and a thin segmented upturned tail tipped with a venomous sting. Order: Scorpionida. [12thC. Via French from, ultimately, Greek *skorpios* "sea fish, scorpion."]

Scor·pi·on /skáwrpee ən/ *n.* **1.** ASTRON = **Scorpius 2.** ZODIAC = **Scorpio** *n.* 2

scor·pi·on fish *n.* a small brightly colored fish with venomous spines in its fins. Family: Scorpaenidae.

scor·pi·on fly *n.* a nonvenomous fly that has downward-pointing mouthparts and a reproductive organ in the male resembling the sting of a scorpion. Order: Mecoptera.

scor·pi·on grass *n.* = **forget-me-not**

Scor·pi·us /skáwrpee əss/ *n.* a distinctive bright zodiacal constellation between Libra and Sagittarius lying partly in the Milky Way. Scorpius contains the bright red star Antares. [15thC. From Latin *scorpius* (see SCORPION).]

Scor·se·se /skawr sáysee, -sézzee/, **Martin** (*b.* 1942) U.S. movie director. His movies, including *Taxi Driver* (1976) and *Goodfellas* (1990), often depict urban violence.

scot /skot/ *n.* money assessed or paid for something, e.g., as a tax or fine (*archaic*) [Pre-12thC. Partly from Old Norse *skot* "shot," partly from Old French *escot*.]

Scot /skot/ *n.* **1. SOMEBODY FROM SCOTLAND** somebody who was born or raised in Scotland, or is of Scottish descent **2. MEMBER OF ANCIENT BRITISH PEOPLE** a member of a people who lived in Ireland and who periodically invaded western Britain from the 3rd century A.D., before settling in northern Britain during the 6th century [Pre-12thC. Via medieval Latin from late Latin *Scottus*, of unknown origin.]

WORD KEY: USAGE

Scot, Scotch, or **Scottish**? All these words mean "of Scotland," but they are used in different ways. ***Scottish*** is the most generally used word to describe the country and people of Scotland (*Scottish history*; *a Scottish poet*; *Scottish Gaelic*), whereas ***Scots*** is normally applied to people or to the form of English spoken in Scotland (*Scots Guard*; *a Scots accent*). A ***Scot*** is a person from Scotland; more specific words are *Scotsman* and *Scotswoman*. ***Scotch*** is a literary word more closely associated with the writing of Robert Burns and Sir Walter Scott, and has fallen out of general use, usually being considered offensive unless used in fixed expressions such as *Scotch pine* and *Scotch mist*.

Scot. *abbr.* **1.** Scotch **2.** Scotland **3.** Scottish

scotch[1] /skoch/ *vt.* (**scotched, scotch·ing, scotch·es**) **1. STOP SOMETHING** to put a stop to something such as a rumor **2. DISABLE SOMEBODY** to disable somebody by wounding (*archaic*) **3. GASH SOMETHING** to make a gash or score in something (*archaic*) ■ *n.* (*archaic*) **1. SCORE IN SOMETHING** a cut or score in something **2. LINE** a line drawn on the ground, especially one used to mark out a grid for hopscotch [15thC. Origin uncertain: perhaps from Anglo-Norman *escocher* "to notch," ultimately from Latin *coccum* "scarlet oak berry" (that has notches), from Greek *kokkos.*]

WORD KEY: USAGE

See Usage note at ***Scot.***

scotch² /skoch/ *n.* TECH **WEDGE** a wedge used to prevent something from moving ■ *vt.* (**scotched, scotch·ing, scotch·es**) TECH **WEDGE SOMETHING** to wedge something in order to prevent it from moving [Early 17thC. Origin uncertain.]

Scotch /skoch/, **Scotch whis·key** *n.* **1.** BEVERAGES **WHISKEY** whiskey produced in Scotland **2.** LANG = **Scots** *n.* ■ *npl.* PEOPLES **SCOTTISH PEOPLE** people who were born or raised in Scotland or who are of Scottish descent (*offensive*) ■ *adj.* **1. OF SCOTLAND** relating to Scotland, its people, or its culture (*offensive*) **2. FROM SCOTLAND** made in Scotland, or typical of a style prevalent in Scotland ○ *Scotch broth* **3. FRUGAL** unwilling to spend or give money (*offensive*) [Late 16thC. Contraction of SCOTTISH.]

WORD KEY: USAGE

See Usage note at ***Scot.***

Scotch broom *n.* a deciduous broom, originally from western Europe, with bright yellow flowers. Latin name: *Cytisus scoparius.*

Scotch egg *n.* a hard-boiled egg wrapped in sausagemeat, coated with breadcrumbs, and deep fried. It is served cut in half, either hot or cold.

Scotch-I·rish /skòts-/, **Scots-I·rish** *npl.* Irish people of Scottish descent, or U.S. citizens descended from these people —**Scotch-Irish** *adj.*

Scotch·man /skóchmən/ (*plural* **-men** /-mən/) *n.* a Scotsman (*archaic or offensive*)

Scotch mist *n.* **1. DRIZZLY MIST** a fine, damp mist **2. SOMETHING IMAGINED** a figment of somebody's imagination (*humorous*)

Scotch pine *n.* **1.** TREES **PINE WITH HARD YELLOW WOOD** a pine native to Europe and Asia that has a reddish trunk, twisted bluish-green needles, and yellow wood valued as timber. Latin name: *Pinus sylvestris.* **2.** INDUST **TYPE OF WOOD** the wood of the Scotch pine

Scotch tape *tdmk.* a trademark for a type of transparent adhesive tape

Scotch ter·ri·er *n.* = **Scottish terrier**

Scotch ver·dict *n.* **1.** LAW **VERDICT OF "NOT PROVEN"** a verdict of "not proven" in a case in which there is insufficient evidence to prove the defendant's guilt **2. INCONCLUSIVE JUDGMENT** a judgment or statement that is inconclusive

Scotch whis·key *n.* = **Scotch**

Scotch·wom·an /skóch wòommən/ (*plural* **-en** /-wìmmin/) *n.* a Scotswoman (*archaic or offensive*)

Scotch wood·cock *n.* a snack or light meal of toast spread with an anchovy paste and topped with scrambled eggs [Fanciful name for a meal, thought to originate in Scotland, that is completely different to what its name suggests]

sco·ter /skṓtər/ (*plural* **-ters** *or* **-ter**) *n.* a large sea duck of the northern coasts of North America, Asia, and Europe the male of which has black plumage with white spots on its head. Genus: *Melanitta.* [Late 17thC. Origin unknown.]

scot-free *adv.* without punishment being exacted or payment being made [The original meaning was "without having to pay SCOT"]

sco·tia /skṓshə/ *n.* a deep concave molding, especially on the base of a column [Mid-16thC. Via Latin from Greek *skotia,* from *skotos* "darkness" (from the shadow inside the molding).]

Sco·tia /skṓshə/ *n.* a former name for Scotland, still sometimes used in literary contexts (*archaic or literary*) [Early 17thC. From medieval Latin *Scotia.*] —**Sco·tian** *adj.*

Sco·tism /skṓtizzəm/ *n.* the philosophical tenets of, or school of scholastic philosophy founded by, Duns Scotus, the 13th-century Scottish philosopher and theologian —**Sco·tist** *adj.* —**Sco·tis·tic** /skə tístik/ *adj.*

Scot·land /skótlənd/ one of the four countries that comprise the United Kingdom of Great Britain and Northern Ireland. It consists of the northern third of Great Britain, as well as hundreds of islands. It became united with England in 1707. Capital: Edinburgh. Population: 5,132,400 (1994). Area: 29,750 sq. mi./77,080 sq. km.

Scot·land Yard *n.* the headquarters of the Metropolitan Police in London, from which national criminal investigations are coordinated. The headquarters moved to new premises in 1890 and 1967 and is officially known as New Scotland Yard. [Because it was originally located in *Great Scotland Yard,* a street in which the palace used by visiting kings of Scotland in medieval times formerly stood]

sco·to·ma /skə tṓmə/ (*plural* **-mas** *or* **-ma·ta** /-mətə/) *n.* a permanent or temporary area of diminished sight in the field of vision [Mid-16thC. Via late Latin from Greek *skotōma* "dizziness," ultimately from *skotos* "darkness."] —**sco·to·ma·tous** *adj.*

sco·to·pi·a /skə tṓpee ə, skō-/ *n.* the ability to see in poor light or in the dark [Early 20thC. Coined from Greek *skotos* "darkness" + -OPIA.] —**sco·to·pic** /-tóppik/ *adj.*

Scots /skots/ *adj.* **OF SCOTLAND** relating to Scotland, its people, or its culture ■ *n.* LANG **SCOTTISH DIALECT OF ENGLISH** the dialect of English spoken in Scotland [14thC. Contraction of SCOTTISH.]

WORD KEY: WORLD ENGLISH

Scots is the Germanic speech of the Scottish Lowlands, in contrast to Gaelic, the traditional Celtic speech of the Highlands. It is regarded by some as a dialect of English, by others as a distinct language. Many scholars regard Scots of the period before the Union of the Crowns (1603) as a language in its own right and after that date as a more limited vernacular. It is, however, listed alongside languages such as Basque, Catalan, and Gaelic by the Bureau of Lesser Used European Languages (an institution of the European Union). Scots has its own dialects, from the Borders (linked with the dialects of Northern England) to Orkney and Shetland (mixed with elements of Old Norse). Its literature includes two medieval epic poems, copious 16th-century verse, the works of Robert Burns, and more recent poetry and fiction.

Scots Gael·ic *n.* = **Scottish Gaelic**

Scots-I·rish *npl., adj.* = **Scotch-Irish**

Scots·man /skótsmən/ (*plural* **-men** /-mən/) *n.* a man who was born or raised in Scotland, or who has Scottish ancestry

WORD KEY: USAGE

See Usage note at ***Scot.***

Scots pine *n. U.K.* = **Scotch pine**

Scots·wom·an /skóts wòommən/ (*plural* **-en** /-wìmmin/) *n.* a woman who was born or raised in Scotland, or who has Scottish ancestry

WORD KEY: USAGE

See Usage note at ***Scot.***

Scott /skot/, **George C.** (*b.* 1926) U.S. actor. He specialized in tough-guy roles such as the title role in *Patton* (1970), for which he won an Academy Award, but refused to accept it. Full name **George Campbell Scott**

Scott, Robert Falcon (1868–1912) British naval officer and explorer. On his second expedition to Antarctica (1910–12) he was beaten to the South Pole by Roald Amundsen. He died on the return journey.

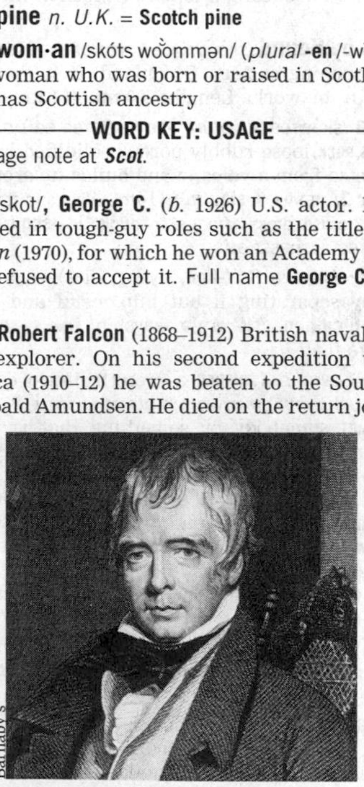

Sir Walter Scott

Scott, Sir Walter (1771–1832) Scottish novelist and poet. His ballads and historical novels, which mainly dealt with Scottish subjects, made him one of the most popular writers of his day and did much to establish widespread European interest in Scottish history and culture.

Scott, Winfield (1786–1866) U.S. general. A veteran of the War of 1812, he conducted a masterful campaign in the Mexican War (1846–48). He unsuccessfully ran for U.S. president (1852). Known as **Old Fuss and Feathers**

Scot·ti·cism /skótti sìzzəm/ *n.* a word, phrase, or idiom that is characteristic of English as spoken in Scotland

Scot·tie /skótee/, **Scot·ty** (*plural* **-ties**) *n.* **1.** ZOOL **SCOTTISH TERRIER** a Scottish terrier (*informal*) **2.** PEOPLES **SCOTSMAN** somebody, especially a man, who is Scottish (*informal offensive*)

Scot·tish /skóttish/ *adj.* **OF SCOTLAND** relating to Scotland, or its people or culture ■ *npl.* PEOPLES **PEOPLE OF SCOTLAND** people who were born, raised, or live in Scotland ■ *n.* (*plural* **-tish**) LANG = **Scots** *n.* [12thC. Formed from SCOT.] —**Scot·tish·ness** *n.*

WORD KEY: USAGE

See Usage note at ***Scot.***

Scot·tish deer·hound *n.* = **deerhound**

Scot·tish Eng·lish *n.* a variety of English spoken in Scotland

WORD KEY: WORLD ENGLISH

Scottish English is the English language as used in Scotland, considered by some to include traditional (Lowland) Scots, by others to be distinct from it, despite overlap. A compromise with the English of England began to emerge after the Union of the Crowns in 1707, when many among the upper and middle classes began to take on the pronunciation, grammar, and vocabulary of so-called refined London. The Scottish aristocracy became socially and linguistically indistinguishable from their peers in England, while the middle class developed a shaky compromise.

Scot·tish Gael·ic *n.* the Celtic language still spoken in parts of the Highlands and Western Isles of Scotland

Scot·tish rite *n.* a type of Masonic rite

Scottish terrier

Scot·tish ter·ri·er, **Scotch ter·ri·er** *n.* a terrier of a breed with short sturdy legs, pointed ears and thick, wiry, usually black hair

Scotts·bor·o /skótsbərə/ city in northeastern Alabama, on the western bank of the Tennessee River, southeast of Huntsville. Population: 14,133 (1996).

Scotts·dale /skóts dàyl/ city in southern Arizona, on the Salt River, east of Phoenix. Population: 179,012 (1996).

Scot·ty (*plural* **-ties**) *n.* ZOOL = **Scottie** (*informal*)

scoun·drel /skówndrəl/ *n.* somebody who behaves dishonorably toward other people [Late 16thC. Origin unknown.] —**scoun·drel·ly** *adj.*

scour¹ /skowr/ *v.* (**scoured, scour·ing, scours**) **1.** *vti.* **CLEAN BY RUBBING** to clean or brighten something by rubbing it with an abrasive substance or material **2.** *vti.* **REMOVE SOMETHING BY RUBBING** to remove something by rubbing with an abrasive substance or material **3.** *vt.* **FREE SOMETHING FROM DIRT OR IMPURITIES** to remove dirt or impurities from something by washing **4.** *vt.* **FLUSH SOMETHING OUT** to clear something out by using water **5.** *vi.* VET **HAVE DIARRHEA** to be affected by diarrhea (*refers to cattle*) ■ *n.* **1. SCOURING** a scouring of something **2. CLEANING SUBSTANCE** a substance or tool that can be used for cleaning **3. PLACE SCOURED** a place that has been scoured, especially by water ■ **scours** *npl.* VET **DIARRHEA** diarrhea affecting cattle and pigs (*takes* *a singular or plural verb*) [12thC. Via Middle Low German or Middle Dutch from, ultimately, late Latin *excurare*, literally "to clean out, take care of," ultimately from Latin *cura* "care" (source of English *cure*).] —**scour·er** *n.*

scour[2] /skowr/ (**scoured, scour·ing, scours**) *vti.* **1. SEARCH SOMETHING CAREFULLY** to search something thoroughly and quickly for somebody or something ○ *They scoured the countryside for him, but to no avail.* **2. MOVE ABOUT AT SPEED** to move quickly over or through an area [15thC. Origin uncertain: probably from a Scandinavian language.] —**scour·er** *n.*

scourge /skurj/ *n.* **1. TORMENTOR** somebody or something that is perceived as an agent of punishment, destruction, or severe criticism ○ *the scourge of my childhood* **2. WHIP** a whip that is used for inflicting punishment ■ *vt.* (**scourged, scourg·ing, scourg·es**) **1. PUNISH SOMEBODY** to punish or criticize somebody severely **2. WHIP SOMEBODY** to whip somebody severely [12thC. From Old French *escorgier* "to whip," ultimately from Latin *corrigia* "thong, whip."] —**scourg·er** *n.*

scour·ing rush *n.* a horsetail that has a rough stem and was, in the past, used for scouring. Genus: *Equisetum.*

scour·ings /skówringz/ *npl.* the material removed or left after scouring something, especially that left after scouring grain

scouse /skowss/ *n. U.K.* a stew made from leftover meat with potatoes and vegetables (*regional*) [Mid-19thC. Shortening of LOBSCOUSE (the original meaning).]

Scouse /skowss/ *n.* (*informal*) **1. Scouse, Scous·er SOMEBODY FROM LIVERPOOL** somebody who was born, raised, or lives in the English city of Liverpool **2.** *U.K.* **LIVERPOOL DIALECT** the dialect spoken in the English city of Liverpool ■ *adj. U.K.* **LIVERPUDLIAN** relating to the English city of Liverpool, or its inhabitants or their English dialect (*informal*) [Mid-19thC. Shortening of LOBSCOUSE (the original meaning).]

scout[1] /skowt/ *n.* **1.** MIL **SOLDIER SENT TO GATHER INFORMATION** somebody, especially a soldier, who is sent to gather information about an enemy's position or movements **2.** SPORTS, ARTS = **talent scout 3.** SPORTS **SOMEBODY SENT TO EVALUATE OPPOSING TEAM** somebody sent to discover and evaluate the performance, tactics, and players of an opposing team **4.** MIL **RECONNAISSANCE CRAFT OR VEHICLE** a ship, aircraft, or vehicle designed and used for reconnaissance purposes **5.** MIL **RECONNOITERING** a gathering of information concerning an enemy's position or movements **6. PERSON** a person, usually a boy or man (*dated informal*) ○ *Be a good scout and give me a hand here.* ■ *v.* (**scout·ed, scout·ing, scouts**) **1.** *vti.* **SEARCH AREA** to make a search of an area for somebody or something ○ *scouting around for a place to camp* **2.** *vi.* **GATHER INFORMATION** to seek out information about somebody or something, especially about an enemy's position or movements **3.** *vti.* SPORTS, ARTS **SEEK OUT NEW TALENT** to look for talented players for a sports team, or for talented performers for a show or group **4.** *vt.* SPORTS **EVALUATE OPPOSING TEAM** to discover and evaluate the performance, tactics, and players of an opposing team [14thC. Via Old French *escouter* from, ultimately, Latin *auscultare* "to listen."] —**scout·er** *n.*

scout[2] /skowt/ (**scout·ed, scout·ing, scouts**) *vt.* to reject somebody or something with scorn or derision (*archaic*) [Early 17thC. Origin uncertain: probably from a Scandinavian language.]

Scout /skowt/, **scout** *n.* a member of the Boy Scouts or Girl Scouts. ◊ **Boy Scout, Girl Scout** [Early 20thC. From SCOUT[1].]

Scout·ing /skówting/ *n.* the activities of the Boy Scouts or Girl Scouts

scout·mas·ter /skówt màstər/ *n.* a man who is in charge of a troop of Boy Scouts

scow /skow/ *n.* **1.** SHIPPING **FREIGHT BARGE** a barge for transporting freight **2.** SAILING **SAILBOAT** a flat-bottomed sailboat [Mid-17thC. From Dutch *schouw.*]

scowl /skowl/ *n.* **FROWN** an expression of anger, displeasure, or menace made by drawing the eyebrows together toward the middle of the forehead ■ *v.* (**scowled, scowl·ing, scowls**) **1.** *vi.* **MAKE A FROWN** to draw the eyebrows together toward the middle of the forehead in an expression of anger, displeasure, or menace **2.** *vt.* **REVEAL FEELING WITH SCOWL** to give expression to an emotion by means of a scowl [14thC. Origin uncertain: probably from a Scandinavian language.] —**scowl·er** *n.*

SCPO *abbr.* Senior Chief Petty Officer

scrab·ble /skrább'l/ *v.* (**-bled, -bling, -bles**) **1.** *vi.* **SCRATCH AT SOMETHING** to scrape or scratch at something with small, hurried movements of the fingers, toes, or claws ○ *The cat was scrabbling at the door.* **2.** *vi.* **FEEL WITH FINGERS** to grope around frantically in an effort to find something ○ *She scrabbled around trying to find the flashlight.* **3.** *vi.* **CLIMB OVER SOMETHING** to climb hastily or clumsily up or over something **4.** *vi.* **STRUGGLE TO GET SOMETHING** to struggle desperately to get something **5.** *vt.* **PRODUCE SOMETHING WITH DIFFICULTY** to produce something hastily and with difficulty from scarce resources **6.** *vti.* **SCRIBBLE** to scribble something ■ *n.* **1. A SCRATCHING AT SOMETHING** a scraping or scratching at something with short hurried movements of the fingers, toes, or claws **2. A SEARCH WITH FINGERS** a frantic groping around in an effort to find something **3. A CLIMB OVER SOMETHING** a climbing hastily or clumsily up or over something **4. A STRUGGLE TO GET SOMETHING** a desperate struggle to acquire or gain something **5. A SCRIBBLING** a scribbling of something **6. SOMETHING SCRIBBLED** something that somebody has scribbled [Mid-16thC. From Middle Dutch *schrabbelen*, literally "to scratch repeatedly," from *schrabben* "to scratch or scrape."] —**scrab·bler** *n.*

Scrab·ble /skrább'l/ *tdmk.* a trademark for a board game in which the players try to form words by placing tiles, each with a single letter on it, on the squares of a board

scrab·bly /skrábblee/ (**-bli·er, -bli·est**) *adj.* **1. SCRATCHY** characterized by a scratching sound **2. SCRUBBY** thinly covered with vegetation

scrag /skrag/ *n.* **1. scrag, scrag end BONY CUT OF MUTTON** the bony neck joint, especially of mutton, usually cut up and used in soups and stews **2. THIN PERSON OR ANIMAL** an unattractively thin person or animal **3. NECK** somebody's neck (*informal*) ■ *vt.* (**scragged, scrag·ging, scrags**) **STRANGLE SOMEBODY** to throttle or strangle somebody (*informal*) [Mid-16thC. Origin uncertain: probably from dialect *crag* "neck," from Middle Dutch *crăghe* "throat."]

scrag·gly /skrágglee/ (**-gli·er, -gli·est**) *adj.* messy and uneven in appearance or shape [Mid-19thC. Formed from SCRAG.] —**scrag·gli·ness** *n.*

scrag·gy /skrággee/ (**-gi·er, -gi·est**) *adj.* **1. SCRAWNY** bony and thin ○ *a scraggy little cat* **2. JAGGED** having sharp points or edges [Early 17thC. Formed from SCRAG.] —**scrag·gi·ly** *adv.* —**scrag·gi·ness** *n.*

WORD KEY: SYNONYMS

See Synonyms at ***thin.***

scram /skram/ *v.* (**scrammed, scram·ming, scrams**) **1.** *vi.* **LEAVE QUICKLY** to get out or leave quickly (*informal*) (*often used as a command*) **2.** *vti.* PHYS **SHUT DOWN NUCLEAR REACTOR** to shut down a nuclear reactor rapidly in an emergency, or be shut down rapidly ■ *n.* PHYS **REACTOR SHUTDOWN** a rapid shutdown of a nuclear reactor in an emergency [Early 20thC. Origin uncertain: perhaps a shortening of SCRAMBLE.]

scram·ble /skrámb'l/ *v.* (**-bled, -bling, -bles**) **1.** *vi.* **CLAMBER** to climb or advance over something using both hands and feet ○ *We managed to scramble over the fence.* **2.** *vi.* **HURRY** to move in haste and with a sense of urgency **3.** *vi.* **COMPETE FRANTICALLY** to struggle or compete frantically in order to get something ○ *Everyone was scrambling for the best seats.* **4.** *vt.* **JUMBLE THINGS TOGETHER** to mix or gather two or more things together haphazardly **5.** *vi.* FOOTBALL **RUN WHEN UNABLE TO PASS** to run with the ball after the pass protection breaks down, trying to avoid being tackled and pass the ball, or to gain yardage (*refers to a quarterback*) **6.** *vt.* COOK **BEAT AND COOK EGGS** to beat eggs, usually with some milk, and cook in a pan until set **7.** *vt.* TELECOM **ENCODE TRANSMITTED SIGNALS** to render a telecommunications or broadcast signal unintelligible by means of an electronic device **8.** *vti.* AIR FORCE **LAUNCH AIRCRAFT AGAINST ATTACK** to launch a large number of aircraft in a short space of time in response to an impending attack, or to be launched in these circumstances ■ *n.* **1. HARD CLIMB** a difficult climb or walk that involves using the hands as well as the feet but no ropes **2. DASH OR STRUGGLE** a hasty, undignified, or disorganized struggle for something or in order to do something **3.** MOTORCYCLES **MOTORCYCLE RACE** a motorcycle race over rough terrain **4.** AIR FORCE **LAUNCH OF AIRCRAFT** the scrambling of military aircraft **5. CONFUSED MASS** a jumbled mass of people or things [Late 16thC. Thought to suggest the action.]

scram·bled eggs *npl.* gold braid attached to the peak of the cap of a senior military officer (*slang*)

scram·bler /skrámblər/ *n.* TELECOM an electronic device that renders telecommunications or broadcast signals unintelligible without a special receiver

scram·jet /skrám jèt/ *n.* a ramjet aircraft in which fuel is burned in air that is moving at supersonic speeds [Mid-20thC. From the initial letters of SUPERSONIC and COMBUSTION + RAMJET.]

Scran·ton /skránt'n/ city in northeastern Pennsylvania. A mining city until the 1940s, it is now a manufacturing center. Population: 81,805 (1990).

scrap[1] /skrap/ *n.* **1. FRAGMENT** a small piece or remnant that has been detached or torn off from a larger piece **2. WASTE MATERIAL** waste material, especially metal awaiting reprocessing **3. SMALL PIECE** a very small piece of something ○ *There's not a scrap of evidence to prove it.* **4. BIT OF WRITTEN OR PRINTED MATERIAL** a short piece of writing, or a cutting from something printed ■ **scraps** *npl.* COOK **1. LEFTOVERS** pieces of leftover food ○ *table scraps* **2. CRACKLINGS** the crisp remains of animal fat after the oil has been rendered ■ *vt.* (**scrapped, scrap·ping, scraps**) **1. GET RID OF SOMETHING** to discard or discontinue something because it is considered useless or ineffective **2. CONVERT SOMETHING TO SCRAP** to convert something into scrap material ○ *scrapping old warships* [14thC. From Old Norse *skrap* "scraps, trifles."]

scrap[2] /skrap/ *n.* **MINOR FIGHT** a minor fight or disagreement (*informal*) ■ *vi.* (**scrapped, scrap·ping, scraps**) **FIGHT OR DISAGREE** to have a minor fight or disagreement with somebody [Late 17thC. Origin uncertain: perhaps a variant of SCRAPE.]

scrap·book /skráp bòŏk/ *n.* a blank book or album for pasting in photos, pictures, cuttings, or other material

scrape /skrayp/ *v.* (**scraped, scrap·ing, scrapes**) **1.** *vti.* **RUB SOMETHING ON SURFACE** to move something hard, sharp, or rough across a surface, especially in order to clean it ○ *scraping the wall to remove the paint* **2.** *vt.* **TAKE SOMETHING OFF** to remove something by applying a hard or sharp edge to it and rubbing with it ○ *My efforts to scrape the paint off failed.* **3.** *vt.* **SCRATCH SOMETHING** to scratch, cut, or damage something by bringing it into contact with a rough or abrasive surface ○ *fell and scraped my knees* **4.** *vti.* **MAKE GRATING NOISE** to make a harsh grating sound or cause something to make such a sound ○ *scraping his chair along the floor* **5.** *vi.* **SCRIMP** to live economically in an effort to save money ○ *scraping by on a single income* **6.** *vti.* **BARELY DO SOMETHING** to manage only just to do or achieve something ○ *He just scraped through law school.* ■ *n.* **1. SCRAPING** a scraping of something ○ *I'll give the paint a quick scrape.* **2. LIGHT SCRATCH** a light cut, graze, or area of damage caused by contact with a rough or abrasive surface **3. GRATING SOUND** a sharp, grating sound ○ *the scrape of chairs on the bare floor* **4. DANGEROUS SITUATION** a dangerous, difficult, or awkward situation (*informal*) **5. MINOR FIGHT** a minor fight or disagreement (*informal*) [Old English *scrapian* "to scratch," from a prehistoric Germanic word that is also the ancestor of English *shear.* Reinforced by related Old Norse *skrapa* or Dutch *schrapen.*] —**scrap·er** *n.*

scrape together, scrape up *vt.* to manage with difficulty to collect together an amount of something, especially money, or a number of people or things

scrap·er·board /skráypər bàwrd/ *n.* **1.** *U.K.* = **scratchboard 2. SCRAPERBOARD DRAWING** a drawing produced on a scraperboard

scrap·heap /skráp hèep/ *n.* **1. PILE OF TRASH** a large pile of unwanted or discarded items, especially those being used as scrap material **2. PLACE FOR DISCARDED THINGS** an imagined place to which people and things discarded as worn out and useless are consigned (*informal*) ○ *workers who are relegated to the scrapheap at 50*

scra·pie /skráypee/ *n.* a usually fatal disease affecting the nervous system of sheep and goats that is marked by intense itching and loss of muscular control. It is now thought to be one of the diseases caused by a prion, and is similar to bovine spongiform encephalopathy in cattle and Creutzfeldt-Jakob disease in humans. [Early 20thC. Formed from SCRAPE, from the animals' rubbing against objects to alleviate itching.]

scrap·per /skráppər/ *n.* an enthusiastic, determined fighter, especially a boxer (*slang*) [Late 19thC. Formed from SCRAP[2].]

scrap·ple /skrápp'l/ *n.* pork trimmings cooked with cornmeal and seasonings, formed into a loaf, and cooled. It is sliced and fried before serving. [Mid-19thC. Formed from SCRAP[1].]

WORD KEY: REGIONAL NOTE

Also called *Philadelphia scrapple*, the term emerges from Pennsylvania and the Middle Atlantic states, extending southward as far as East Tennessee where it preserves remarkable currency.

scrap·py[1] /skráppee/ (**-pi·er, -pi·est**) *adj.* **1. IN SCRAPS** consisting of scraps or fragments **2. DISCONNECTED** poorly held together or structured —**scrap·pi·ly** *adv.* —**scrap·pi·ness** *n.*

scrap·py[2] /skráppee/ (**-pi·er, -pi·est**) *adj.* (*informal*) **1. PLUCKY** fighting with enthusiasm and determination **2. BELLIGERENT** too ready to fight or quarrel —**scrap·pi·ly** *adv.* —**scrap·pi·ness** *n.*

scratch /skrach/ *v.* (**scratched, scratch·ing, scratch·es**) **1.** *vt.* **MAKE MARK IN SOMETHING** to scrape or make a slight mark in the surface of something ○ *He scratched the tabletop with the knife.* **2.** *vti.* **TEAR SKIN** to make a thin tear in the surface of the skin of a person or animal ○ *The cat scratched me.* **3.** *vti.* **MAKE SCRAPING MOVEMENT** to rub or scrape a surface, e.g., with claws or a scraping instrument ○ *The cat was scratching at the door.* **4.** *vi.* **MAKE HARSH NOISE** to make a scraping sound **5.** *vti.* **RELIEVE ITCHING** to rub the skin with nails or claws, especially to relieve itching or discomfort **6.** *vti.* MUSIC **PRODUCE SCRAPING SOUND FROM RECORD** to run a record backward and forward on a turntable in order to repeat and distort the original sound of the record **7.** *vti.* **CAUSE ITCHING** to irritate the surface of the skin by being rough or prickly **8.** *vt.* **DRAG SOMETHING ALONG SURFACE** to drag something along a rough surface so that the object is scraped **9.** *vt.* **WRITE SOMETHING WITH SHARP INSTRUMENT** to write or draw something by marking a surface with a pointed or sharp instrument ○ *names scratched on the tree* **10.** *vti.* **PEN SOMETHING QUICKLY** to write or draw something hastily **11.** *vt.* **DELETE SOMETHING** to delete or erase something by scraping it off, crossing it out, or rendering it illegible **12.** *vt.* **CANCEL SOMETHING** to cancel or abandon a project, plan, or proposal completely **13.** *vi.* **SEARCH AIMLESSLY** to search for something in an unsystematic way by picking through things or looking on the ground ○ *scratching around for evidence* **14.** *vti.* SPORTS **WITHDRAW FROM COMPETITION** to withdraw an individual or team from a race or competition **15.** *vi.* CUE GAMES **INCUR PENALTY** to make a billiard shot that incurs a penalty, e.g., by hitting the cue ball into a pocket **16.** *vi.* CUE GAMES **MAKE FLUKE SHOT** in billiards, to make a mishit that produces a score **17.** *vti.* **JUST GET BY** to make a barely adequate living ○ *scratching out a living* ■ *n.* **1. MARK ON SURFACE** a slight cut or mark on a surface **2. TEAR IN SKIN** a thin cut or tear in the surface of the skin of a person or animal **3. SCRAPING SOUND** a scraping sound, especially one made with the claws or nails **4. ACTION TO RELIEVE ITCHING** a rubbing of the skin with the nails or claws, especially to relieve itching or discomfort **5. SCRIBBLY WRITING** something written hastily or illegibly **6.** SPORTS = **scratch line 7.** SPORTS **WITHDRAWN COMPETITOR** an individual or team withdrawn from a race or competition **8.** GOLF **HANDICAP OF ZERO** in golf, a zero handicap **9.** CUE GAMES **SHOT INCURRING PENALTY** a billiard shot that incurs a penalty **10.** MUSIC **TYPE OF POP MUSIC** music produced by running a record backward and forward on a turntable, repeating and distorting the original sound. Scratch is performed especially by disk jockeys in clubs. **11. MONEY** money or cash (*slang*) ■ *adj.* **1. DONE RANDOMLY** done randomly or by chance **2. FOR JOTTED NOTES** used for making quick or preliminary notes ○ *scratch paper* **3.** SPORTS **ASSEMBLED HASTILY** assembled hastily from available resources ○ *a scratch team* **4.** GOLF **WITH NO HANDICAP** playing golf with a handicap of zero [14thC. Origin uncertain: probably a blend of "scrat" (of unknown origin) and "cratch" (probably from Middle Dutch *kratsen*), both meaning "to scratch."] ◇ **from scratch 1.** right from the beginning, or with nothing having previously been done (*informal*) **2.** using basic ingredients instead of a prepared mix (*informal*) ◇ **up to scratch** of or up to a satisfactory standard (*informal*) ○ *exam results that aren't really up to scratch*

scratch together, scratch up *vt.* = **scrape together**

scratch-and-sniff *adj.* designed to release a smell when scratched, especially as a complement to a visual experience

scratch·board /skrách bàwrd/ *n.* a drawing board that is covered with a layer of white clay on top of which is a layer of black that can be scraped away to make line drawings

scratch card *n.* a card containing one or more sections covered in an overlay that can be scratched off to reveal a possible prize printed beneath

scratch line *n.* **1. scratch line, scratch STARTING LINE** a starting line in a race **2. LINE NOT TO BE OVERSTEPPED** a line that a competitor may not step over without committing a foul

scratch·proof /skrách proof/ *adj.* resistant to being scratched

scratch sheet *n.* in horseracing, a program listing horses withdrawn from races and giving odds on those horses still entered

scratch test *n.* a test to discover if somebody is allergic to a substance (**allergen**), in which a small amount of the substance is rubbed into a lightly scratched area of skin. A reaction, e.g., the formation of a welt, indicates an allergy to the substance.

scratch·y /skráchee/ (**-i·er, -i·est**) *adj.* **1. ITCHY** causing or feeling itchiness on the skin ○ *a scratchy sweater* **2. SOUNDING LIKE SCRATCHES** making a scratching or scraping sound ○ *a scratchy recording* **3. PENNED QUICKLY** written or drawn hastily or illegibly **4. IRREGULAR** done haphazardly or not smoothly —**scratch·i·ly** *adv.* —**scratch·i·ness** *n.*

scrawl /skrawl/ *vti.* (**scrawled, scrawl·ing, scrawls**) **WRITE OR DRAW SOMETHING MESSILY** to write or draw something untidily or hastily, especially in large letters that are difficult to read ■ *n.* **MESSY WRITING** messy or hurried-looking handwriting or drawing [Early 17thC. Origin uncertain: perhaps from obsolete "scrawl" "to gesticulate, sprawl," blend of SPRAWL and CRAWL.] —**scrawl·er** *n.* —**scrawl·y** *adj.*

scraw·ny /skráwnee/ (**-ni·er, -ni·est**) *adj.* unpleasantly or unhealthily thin and bony [Mid-19thC. Variant of dialect "scranny," of uncertain origin: probably from a Scandinavian language.] —**scraw·ni·ly** *adv.* —**scraw·ni·ness** *n.*

WORD KEY: SYNONYMS

See Synonyms at ***thin***.

screak /skreek/ *vi.* (**screaked, screak·ing, screaks**) **1. TO SCREECH** to produce a screech **2. TO CREAK** to produce a creak ■ *n.* **1. SCREECH** a screeching sound **2. CREAK** a creaking sound [15thC. From Old Norse *skrækja*, an imitation of the sound.] —**screak·y** *adj.*

scream /skreem/ *n.* **1. PIERCING CRY** a loud, piercing, high-pitched cry, uttered especially in fear, pain, excitement, or amusement **2. HIGH-PITCHED NOISE** a very loud, high-pitched sound such as that of a siren or jet engine **3. SOMEBODY OR SOMETHING HIGHLY AMUSING** an extremely funny or entertaining person, event, or activity (*informal*) ■ *v.* (**screamed, scream·ing, screams**) **1.** *vi.* **CRY** to utter a loud, piercing, high-pitched cry, especially in fear, pain, or excitement ○ *He screamed for help.* **2.** *vt.* **SHOUT SOMETHING IN PIERCING VOICE** to utter something in a loud, piercing, high-pitched voice, especially in fear, panic, desperation, or excitement ○ *"Get out!" he screamed.* **3.** *vi.* **LAUGH LOUDLY** to laugh shrilly and loudly **4.** *vi.* **MAKE HIGH-PITCHED SOUND** to make a loud high-pitched sound ○ *The ambulance went by, sirens screaming.* **5.** *vi.* **MOVE AT SPEED** to move extremely quickly while producing a loud high-pitched sound ○ *The police car screamed by.* **6.** *vi.* **BE OBVIOUS** to be extremely obvious or noticeable ○ *The mistakes just scream out at you.* [13thC. Origin uncertain: perhaps from Middle Dutch *schreem* or Old Norse *scræma*, both imitations of the sound.] —**scream·ing·ly** *adv.*

WORD KEY: CULTURAL NOTE

The Scream, a painting by the Norwegian painter Edvard Munch (1893). Painted in a bold, expressionist style, it depicts a panic-stricken human figure standing on a bridge or pier. The skull-like face appears to emit a cry that reverberates through the surrounding landscape. A powerful symbol of despair, it is one of the best-known icons of modern art.

scream·er /skreémər/ *n.* **1. SOMETHING THAT SCREAMS** somebody or something that screams **2.** BIRDS **BIRD RESEMBLING GOOSE** a South American aquatic bird that resembles a goose, but with a smaller bill, and has a harsh call. Family: Anhimidae. **3.** PRESS **SENSATIONAL HEADLINE** a sensational headline set in large letters (*slang*) **4.** PRINTING **EXCLAMATION POINT** an exclamation point (*slang*)

scream·ing mee·mies /-meémeez/ *npl.* an attack of nervous anxiety (*informal*) (*takes a singular or plural verb*) ["Meemies" of unknown origin]

scree /skree/ *n.* **1. ROCK DEBRIS AT BASE OF HILL** an accumulation of rock debris at the base of a cliff, hill, or mountain slope, often forming a heap **2. SCREE-COVERED SLOPE** a slope covered with a layer of scree [Early 18thC. From Old Norse *skriða* "landslip."]

screech /skreech/ *n.* **1. SHRILL SCREAM** a high-pitched grating cry or scream, uttered especially in fear, pain, excitement, or amusement ○ *the screech of an owl* **2. HIGH-PITCHED SOUND** a loud high-pitched grating sound ○ *a screech of brakes* **3.** *Can* BEVERAGES **DARK RUM** a dark rum bottled in Newfoundland, Canada ■ *v.* (**screeched, screech·ing, screech·es**) **1.** *vi.* **UTTER SHRILL SCREAM** to utter a high-pitched grating cry or scream, especially in fear, pain, excitement, or amusement **2.** *vt.* **SHRIEK SOMETHING** to utter something in a high-pitched and grating tone of voice **3.** *vi.* **MAKE SCREECHING SOUND** to make a loud high-pitched grating sound **4.** *vi.* **PRODUCE SCREECHING SOUND BY MOVING FAST** to move, usually extremely fast, while producing a screeching sound ○ *The car screeched to a stop.* [Mid-16thC. Alteration of archaic *scritch*, ultimately an imitation of the sound.] —**screech·er** *n.* —**screech·i·ness** *n.* —**screech·y** *adj.*

screech owl *n.* a small North American owl with a high-pitched whistling call and feather tufts on the head that resemble ears. Genus: *Otus*.

screed /skreed/ *n.* **1. LENGTHY PIECE OF WRITING** a long and often tedious piece of writing or speech **2.** CONSTR **GUIDE FOR PLASTERING** a strip of plaster, wood, or other material placed on a surface as a guide to the correct thickness of plaster or concrete to be applied there **3.** CONSTR **BOARD FOR LEVELING** a board or tool used to level a layer of concrete, sand, or other loose material **4.** CONSTR **TOP LAYER** a smooth top layer on a concrete floor or other surface [14thC. Variant of SHRED; originally in the sense "torn strip."]

screen /skreen/ *n.* **1. PARTITION OR SHELTER** a fixed or movable partition or frame that is used to conceal, divide, separate, or provide shelter ○ *You may change your clothes behind the screen.* **2. SOMETHING THAT CONCEALS** anything that serves to conceal, divide, separate, or provide shelter ○ *A screen of leaves protected her from the sun.* **3. MESH FRAME OR MESH** a frame with a fine wire or plastic mesh designed to prevent the entry of mosquitoes or other insects, or the mesh itself **4.** ELECTRON ENG **ELECTRONIC DISPLAY SURFACE** the broad flat end of a cathode-ray tube or liquid crystal display on which images are displayed, e.g., in a television set or computer monitor **5.** COMPUT **DATA DISPLAYED ON MONITOR** the data displayed on the screen of a computer monitor ○ *to print the screen* **6.** CINEMA, PHOTOGRAPHY **SURFACE FOR PROJECTING MOVIE ONTO** a large flat white or silver surface onto which a movie or slide is projected **7.** CINEMA **MOVIES** the movie industry **8.** ARCHIT **DECORATIVE FRAME** a decorative frame or partition, e.g., in a church choir ○ *a rood screen* **9. CONCEALMENT** a measure taken to conceal something ○ *This report is just a screen for the government's inaction.* **10. SELECTION SYSTEM** a system for selecting suitable people, e.g., for a post, membership in an organization, or rental of an apartment **11. SIEVE** a sieve used to filter out fine particles, e.g., of sand or gravel **12.** SPORTS **BLOCKING TACTIC** a tactic in a team game in which players of one team block a player from the opposing team **13.** FOOTBALL = **screen pass 14.** PHOTOGRAPHY **CAMERA PLATE FOR FOCUSING** a ground-glass plate in a camera that is used for getting an image properly focused before it is photographed **15.** PRINTING **GLASS PLATE FOR HALF-TONE REPRODUCTIONS** a glass plate marked with very fine lines and used in producing half-tone reproductions **16.** MIL **ADVANCE DETACHMENT** a military detachment sent in advance of a main force to protect it from the enemy or give warning of an enemy approach **17.** PSYCHOANAL **EMOTIONAL BLOCK** something that prevents somebody from understanding his or her real feelings ■ *v.* (**screened, screen·ing, screens**) **1.** *vt.* **CONCEAL OR SHELTER SOMEBODY OR SOMETHING** to provide shelter, protection, or concealment from somebody or something **2.** *vt.* **PARTITION SOMETHING OFF** to partition, separate, or divide something off from something else ○ *They had screened* *the area into cubicles.* **3.** *vt.* **FIT SOMETHING WITH SCREEN** to provide something with a screen **4.** *vt.* **PROTECT SOMEBODY** to protect somebody from something unpleasant or dangerous **5.** *vti.* CINEMA **SHOW IN MOVIE THEATER** to project a movie onto a screen in a theater **6.** *vti.* TV **SHOW ON TELEVISION** to broadcast a movie, program, or other item on television **7.** *vti.* **TEST FOR DISEASE** to test somebody or something for a particular illness or disease **8.** *vti.* **SELECT BY WEEDING OUT** to select somebody as being suitable for something, e.g., a post, membership in an organization, or renting an apartment **9.** *vt.* **SIFT SOMETHING** to filter something through a sieve **10.** *vti.* SPORTS **BLOCK OPPONENT** to block a member of an opposing team so that he or she cannot see or respond to a particular move **11.** *vt.* PRINTING **PHOTOGRAPH SOMETHING FOR HALF-TONE REPRODUCTION** to photograph something through a glass plate to make a half-tone reproduction [14thC. From Old Northern French *escren.*] —**screen·a·ble** *adj.* —**screen·er** *n.*

screen dump *n.* the process of printing or saving the contents of a computer display screen

screen·ing /skréening/ *n.* **1.** CINEMA **A SHOWING IN A CINEMA** a projection of a movie on a screen in a cinema **2.** TV **A SHOWING ON TELEVISION** a showing of a movie, program, or other item on television **3.** MED **TEST FOR DISEASE** a test or testing carried out routinely on supposedly healthy people in order to establish, as early as possible, whether or not an illness or disease is present **4.** **PROTECTING SCREENS** screens for providing shelter, protection, or concealment, or for separating or dividing **5.** **WIRE MESH** fine wire or plastic mesh used on a door or window to prevent the entry of mosquitoes or other insects ■ **screen·ings** *npl.* **SIFTED MATERIAL** waste material that has been screened from something

screen mem·o·ry *n.* an early childhood memory that is used subconsciously to mask another related, often distressful, memory

screen pass *n.* FOOTBALL a forward pass to a player who is protected from being tackled by a screen of members of his or her own team

screen·play /skréen plày/ *n.* a script or scenario for a film

screen-print *n.* a print produced by silk-screen printing —**screen-print·ing** *n.* —**screen-print** *vti.*

screen sav·er *n.* a computer utility that automatically makes the screen go blank or display a particular image after a particular period of time. Originally developed to prevent the permanent etching of a pattern on the screen of older monochrome monitors, screen savers now are an adornment with which to personalize a computer.

screen test *n.* an audition for a movie role in which an actor is filmed, or the film made of the audition —**screen-test** *vti.*

screen·writ·er /skréen rìtər/ *n.* the writer of a script that is intended to be filmed —**screen·writ·ing** *n.*

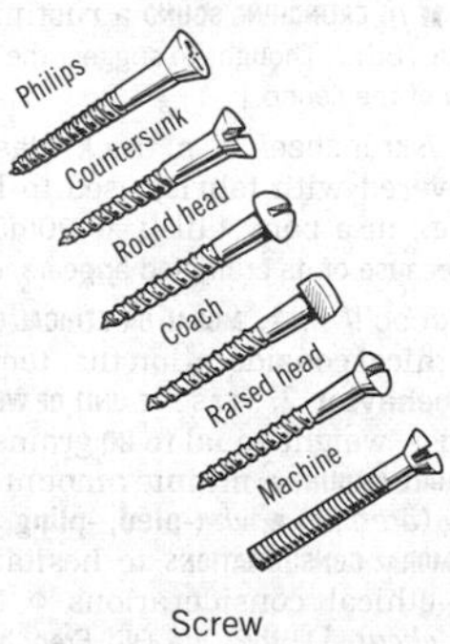

Screw

screw /skroo/ *n.* **1.** CONSTR **THREADED FASTENER INSERTED INTO MATERIAL** a piece of metal with a tapering threaded body and grooved head by which it is turned into something in order to fasten things together **2.** CONSTR **SCREW FOR NUT** a screw with a blunt end onto which a nut is fitted to hold two objects together **3.** **DEVICE SIMILAR TO SCREW** anything that has a form similar to a tapering metal screw, e.g., a corkscrew **4.** **TWISTING ACTION** a turn of a screw or of a device like a screw **5.** ENG = **propeller 6.** **OFFENSIVE TERM** an offensive term for an act or instance of sexual intercourse (*slang offensive*) **7.** **OFFENSIVE TERM** an offensive term for a sexual partner with regard to his or her sexual performance (*slang offensive*) **8.** CRIMINOL **GUARD** a prison guard (*slang*) ■ *v.* (**screwed, screw·ing, screws**) **1.** *vti.* **FASTEN WITH SCREWS** to fasten or tighten something with a screw or screws ○ *He screwed the shelf to the wall.* **2.** *vti.* **FASTEN BY ROTATING** to rotate something along a thread in order to fasten or tighten it ○ *screwed the bulb in carefully* **3.** *vt.* **CRUSH SOMETHING** to crumple or crush something into a tight ball **4.** *vti.* **CONTORT** to contort or crumple a part of or all of the face, or to be contorted or crumpled ○ *She screwed her eyes up against the glare.* **5.** *vti.* **OFFENSIVE TERM** an offensive term meaning to have sexual intercourse with somebody (*slang offensive*) **6.** *vt.* **CHEAT SOMEBODY** to cheat or swindle somebody (*slang*) **7.** *vt.* **EXTORT SOMETHING** to get something out of somebody with great difficulty (*slang*) ○ *We managed to screw some money out of him in the end.* **8.** *vt.* **OFFENSIVE TERM** an offensive term used to express anger or frustration (*slang offensive*) [15thC. From Old French *escroue*, directly or via prehistoric Germanic from Latin *scrofa* "sow" (because of its curly tail shaped like a corkscrew).] —**screw·a·ble** *adj.* —**screw·er** *n.* ◇ **have a screw** *or* **few screws loose** to be irrational or lack common sense or good judgment (*informal*) ◇ **put the screws on somebody** to use force or pressure on somebody (*slang*)

screw around *vi.* (*slang offensive*) **1.** **OFFENSIVE TERM** an offensive term meaning to have sex with a number of different people, especially when married or in an established relationship **2.** **OFFENSIVE TERM** an offensive term meaning to waste time in trivial or pointless activities

screw up *v.* **1.** *vti.* **OFFENSIVE TERM** an offensive term meaning to mismanage, disrupt, or make a mess of something (*slang offensive*) **2.** *vt.* **OFFENSIVE TERM** an offensive term meaning to disturb somebody psychologically or emotionally (*slang offensive*) **3.** **MUSTER SOMETHING** to gather courage or nerve before doing something

screw·ball /skróo bàwl/ *n.* **1.** **OFFENSIVE TERM** an offensive term for somebody who is regarded as behaving in an unconventional, irrational, or strange way (*informal insult*) **2.** BASEBALL **PITCH IN OPPOSITE DIRECTION TO CURVEBALL** in baseball, a pitch that curves in a direction opposite to that of a regular curveball, traveling instead to the same side as the hand with which it is thrown ■ *adj.* **STRANGE** regarded as unconventional, irrational, or strange (*informal*)

screw·ball com·e·dy *n.* a movie, especially a Hollywood comedy of the 1930s, featuring the amusing antics of appealing characters in a glamorous world. These films often feature an emancipated and strong-willed heroine.

screw bean *n.* **1.** **SHRUB PRODUCING PODS USED AS FODDER** a shrub of the legume family that is native to the southwestern United States and Mexico and produces twisted pods that are used as fodder. Latin name: *Prosopis pubescens.* **2.** **SEED POD** a pod of the screw bean plant

screw·driv·er /skróo drìvər/ *n.* **1.** TECH **TOOL FOR FASTENING SCREWS** a tool for driving screws that consists of a handle or power tool with a metal rod shaped at the tip to fit into the head of a screw **2.** BEVERAGES **VODKA AND ORANGE COCKTAIL** a cocktail made from vodka and orange juice

screwed up *adj.* (*hyphenated when used before a noun*) **1.** **OFFENSIVE TERM** an offensive term meaning affected by or displaying symptoms of psychological or emotional disorder (*slang offensive*) **2.** **OFFENSIVE TERM** an offensive term meaning mismanaged, disrupted, or made a mess of (*informal*)

screw eye *n.* a screw with a looped instead of a flat head

screw jack *n.* a jack used for lifting heavy items such as vehicles, operated by a screw mechanism

screw pine *n.* = **pandanus**

screw pro·pel·ler *n.* = **propeller**

screw thread *n.* **1.** **OUTER RIDGE OF SCREW** the continuous helical outer surface of a screw or the inner surface of a nut **2.** **TURN OF SCREW THREAD** a full turn of a screw thread

screw·up /skróo ùp/ *n.* (*slang offensive*) **1.** **OFFENSIVE TERM** an offensive term for a mess, blunder, or bungled event **2.** **BUNGLER** an offensive term for somebody who habitually messes up, blunders, or bungle things

screw·worm /skróo wùrm/ *n.* the larva of the screwworm fly, that grows under the skin of livestock and other mammals, causing injury and death [Late 19thC. *Screw* from the spiny hairs of the larva, which encircle each segment.]

screw·worm fly *n.* a bluish blowfly whose eggs, laid on the skin of livestock and other large mammals, hatch as larvae (**screwworms**) that grow under the skin. Latin name: *Cochliomyia hominivorax.*

screw·y /skróo ee/ (**-i·er, -i·est**) *adj.* (*informal*) **1.** **OFFENSIVE TERM** an offensive term meaning irrational, unconventional, or strange **2.** **IMPROPER OR ILLEGAL** not quite right or correct, especially in being improper or illegal —**screw·i·ly** *adv.* —**screw·i·ness** *n.*

scrib·ble /skríbb'l/ *v.* (**-bled, -bling, -bles**) **1.** *vti.* **WRITE MESSILY** to write something hastily or untidily, often in smallish letters **2.** *vti.* **MAKE MEANINGLESS MARKINGS** to write or draw meaningless or undecipherable marks on something ○ *Don't scribble on the wall!* **3.** *vi.* **BE WRITER** to be a writer, especially one of little merit (*humorous*) ■ *n.* **1.** **MESSY HANDWRITING** messy or careless handwriting **2.** **HASTY NOTE** something written messily or hastily **3.** **DOODLES** meaningless marks written or drawn on something [15thC. Ultimately from Latin *scribere* "to write" (source of English *scribe*).] —**scrib·bler** *n.*

scribe /skrīb/ *n.* **1.** HIST **BOOK COPIER** somebody who copies or writes out documents, especially somebody who copied manuscripts in medieval times **2.** JUDAISM **COPIER OF JEWISH RELIGIOUS DOCUMENTS** somebody who copies the Sefer Torah and other religious documents using a quill pen on parchment **3.** **CLERK** an official public clerk **4.** **JOURNALIST** a writer, especially a journalist (*humorous*) **5.** TECH = **scriber** ■ *vti.* (**scribed, scrib·ing, scribes**) TECH **MARK LINES ON SOMETHING** to mark something such as wood or metal with a line using a pointed instrument, especially as a guide for cutting [12thC. From Latin *scriba* "official or public writer," from *scribere* "to write."]

scrib·er /skrībər/ *n.* a sharp instrument for marking lines on wood or other material

scrim /skrim/ *n.* **1.** THEATER **THEATRICAL CURTAIN** a drop curtain in a theater that appears opaque to the audience when lit from the front but transparent when lit from behind **2.** TEXTILES **COTTON OR LINEN FABRIC** a durable open-weave cotton or linen fabric used for curtains, clothing, upholstery lining, and in industry [Late 18thC. Origin unknown.]

scrim·mage /skrímmij/ *n.* **1.** SPORTS **PRACTICE GAME** a practice game between two squads, often from the same team **2.** FOOTBALL **PLAY IN FOOTBALL** the action in a football game from the moment the ball is snapped to the moment the ball is dead **3.** **STRUGGLE** a rough or confused struggle **4.** **FIGHT** a skirmish or minor battle **5.** RUGBY **SCRUM** a scrum (*archaic*) ■ *vti.* (**-maged, -mag·ing, -mag·es**) **TAKE PART IN SCRIMMAGE** to engage in a scrimmage or play a scrimmage against somebody [15thC. Alteration of SKIRMISH.]

scrim·mage line *n.* = **line of scrimmage**

scrimp /skrimp/ (**scrimped, scrimp·ing, scrimps**) *v.* **1.** *vi.* **ECONOMIZE** to economize drastically or be extremely frugal ○ *scrimp on food* **2.** *vt.* **BE STINGY TO SOMEBODY** to treat somebody meanly or limit provision to somebody severely **3.** *vt.* **MAKE SOMETHING TOO SMALL** to make something too small or scanty [Mid-18thC. From obsolete *scrimp* "scant, meager," of uncertain origin: perhaps ultimately from a Scandinavian source.] —**scrimp·i·ly** *adv.* —**scrimp·i·ness** *n.* —**scrimp·y** *adj.*

scrim·shand·er /skrím shàndər/ *n.* somebody who makes carved or engraved articles from the teeth or bones of whales [Mid-19thC. Formed from a variant of SCRIMSHAW.]

scrim·shaw /skrím shàw/ *n.* **1.** **CARVED WHALE IVORY** a carved or engraved article made originally by North American whalers from the teeth and bones of whales, or such articles collectively **2.** **MAKING OF SCRIMSHAW** the skill or pastime of making scrimshaw ■ *v.* (**-shawed, -shaw·ing, -shaws**) **1.** *vi.* **MAKE SCRIMSHAW** to make scrimshaw **2.** *vt.* **CARVE OR ENGRAVE SOMETHING** to carve or engrave something into scrimshaw [Mid-19thC. From earlier *scrimshonting* "carving whale ivory," ultimately of unknown origin: perhaps influenced by the surname *Scrimshaw.*]

scrip[1] /skrip/ *n.* **1.** **TEMPORARY PAPER CURRENCY** paper currency issued for temporary emergency use, e.g., by an occupying force **2.** **BRIEF PIECE OF WRITING** a list, receipt, or other short piece of writing **3.** **PRESCRIPTION**

a doctor's prescription (*slang*) [Late 16thC. Alteration of SCRIPT, influenced by SCRAP.]

scrip[2] /skrip/ *n.* a document or certificate representing a fraction of a share or stock [Mid-18thC. Shortening of *subscription receipt*.]

scrip[3] /skrip/ *n.* a wallet or small satchel or bag (*archaic*) [14thC. From Old French *escrep(p)e* "alms purse," from *escherpe* "scarf."]

scrip·oph·i·ly /skri póffəlee/ *n.* the hobby of collecting share and bond certificates, especially those of historical interest [Late 20thC. Coined from SCRIP[2] + -PHILY.] —**scrip·o·phile** /skríppə fīl/ *n.*

Scripps /skrips/, **E.W.** (1854–1926) U.S. newspaper publisher. He gradually acquired newspapers and in 1894 established what became the Scripps-Howard newspaper chain. In 1897 he founded a news service that became the United Press Association. Full name **Edward Wyllis Scripps**

script /skript/ *n.* **1.** TEXT OF PLAY OR BROADCAST the printed version of a stage play, movie screenplay, or radio or television broadcast, including the words to be spoken and often also technical directions **2.** MANUSCRIPT an original document or manuscript **3.** HANDWRITING characters written by hand, especially in cursive form **4.** SYSTEM OF WRITING any system of characters used in writing **5.** PRINTED TYPE RESEMBLING WRITING printed type designed to imitate handwriting ■ *vt.* (**script·ed, script·ing, scripts**) WRITE SCRIPT FOR SOMETHING to write or prepare a script for something [14thC. Via Old French *escri(p)t* from Latin *scriptus*, from *scribere* "to write" (source of English *description* and *scripture*).]

Script. *abbr.* Scripture

script doc·tor *n.* a writer who revises an unsatisfactory script for a play or movie

scrip·to·ri·um /skrip táwree əm/ (*plural* **-ums** *or* **-a** /-ə/) *n.* a room in a monastery for storing, copying, illustrating, or reading manuscripts [Late 18thC. From medieval Latin, where it was formed from Latin *scribere* (see SCRIPTURE).]

scrip·tur·al /skrípchərəl/ *adj.* **1.** RELIG OF SACRED WRITINGS relating to, contained in, or according to sacred writings, especially the biblical scriptures **2.** OF WRITING written or relating to writing [Mid-17thC. From late Latin *scripturalis*, from *scriptura* (see SCRIPTURE).] —**scrip·tur·al·ly** *adv.*

scrip·ture /skrípchər/, **Scrip·ture** *n.* **1.** BIBLICAL WRITINGS the sacred writings of the Bible **2.** BIBLICAL TEXT a passage from the Bible **3.** SACRED WRITING any sacred writing or book ○ *Buddhist scripture* **4.** AUTHORITATIVE STATEMENT a statement regarded as authoritative [14thC. From Latin *scriptura* "that which is written," from the past participle of *scribere* "to write."]

script·writ·er /skrípt rītər/ *n.* somebody who writes scripts for material to be broadcast

scriv·en·er /skrívvənər/ *n.* **1.** PROFESSIONAL COPYIST OR SCRIBE in former times, somebody whose job involved writing or making handwritten copies of documents, books, or other texts **2.** NOTARY PUBLIC a notary public (*archaic*) [14thC. Via Old French *escrivein*, ultimately from Latin *scriba* (see SCRIBE).]

scro·bic·u·late /skrō bíkyə làyt, -lət/ *adj.* BIOL with a grooved or pitted surface [Late 19thC. Via *scrobicule* "small pit or groove," from late Latin *scrobiculus* "little trench," from *scrobis* "trench."]

scrod /skrod/, **schrod** *n.* a young cod or haddock, especially when split, cooked, and served as food [Mid-19thC. Origin uncertain: perhaps via Dutch *schrood*, "piece cut off," from Middle Dutch *scrōde*, "shred," because the fish was usually sliced up before preparation.]

scrof·u·la /skróffyələ/ *n.* tuberculosis of the lymph glands, especially of the neck. If untreated, the glands burst through the skin to form running sores. [14thC. From medieval Latin *scrofula* "swelling of glands," from *scrofa* "breeding sow," because the glands resemble a pig's back, or because "scrofula" meant "swine disease."]

scrof·u·lous /skróffyələss/ *adj.* **1.** HAVING OR RESEMBLING SCROFULA affected with or characteristic of scrofula **2.** SHABBY IN APPEARANCE run-down, diseased, or shabby in appearance **3.** MORALLY CORRUPT morally corrupt and degenerate —**scrof·u·lous·ly** *adv.* —**scrof·u·lous·ness** *n.*

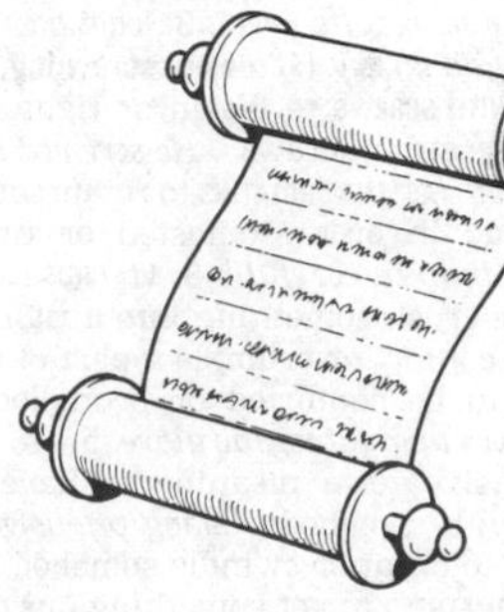

Scroll

scroll /skrōl/ *n.* **1.** ROLL OF PARCHMENT a roll of paper, parchment, leather, or other material for writing a document **2.** LIST a list, roll, or roster **3.** ORNAMENTAL DESIGN RESEMBLING ROLL OF PAPER an ornamental design shaped like a rolled or partially rolled piece of paper **4.** MUSIC CURVED HEAD OF STRINGED INSTRUMENT the curved head of a stringed musical instrument such as a violin where the tuning pegs are set **5.** HERALDRY HERALDIC RIBBON WITH MOTTO in heraldry, a ribbon with rolled ends inscribed with a motto ■ *vti.* (**scrolled, scroll·ing, scrolls**) MOVE TEXT OR GRAPHICS to cause text or graphics to move up, down, or across a computer display screen, or to be moved in this way [15thC. Alteration of *scrowe*, influenced by ROLL, via Old French *escroe* "strip of parchment" from medieval Latin *scroda* "strip," ultimately from a prehistoric Germanic word meaning "something cut."]

scroll bar *n.* a horizontal or vertical bar on a computer display screen containing a box used to make text or graphics move up, down, or across the screen

scroll saw *n.* a saw with a narrow blade used for cutting curved ornamental designs

scroll·work /skrṓl wùrk/ *n.* ornamental designs characterized by scrolls, especially in wood

scrooch /skrooch/ (**scrooched, scrooch·ing, scrooch·es**) *vi.* to crouch or bend down [Mid-19thC. Alteration of SCROUGE.]

scrooge /skrooj/, **Scrooge** *n.* somebody who is regarded as very miserly (*informal*) [Mid-19thC. From *Ebenezer Scrooge*, a character in *A Christmas Carol* (1843), by Charles DICKENS.]

scroop /skroop/ *n.* RUSTLING SOUND OF SILK a rasping sound like that of rustling silk ■ *vi.* (**scrooped, scroop·ing, scroops**) RUSTLE to make a rustling or rasping noise [Late 18thC. An imitation of the sound.]

scro·tum /skrṓtəm/ (*plural* **-tums** *or* **-ta** /-tə/) *n.* the external pouch of skin and muscle containing the testes in mammals. It allows sperm to develop at a temperature lower than that of the body. [Late 16thC. From Latin. Ultimately from an Indo-European word that is also the ancestor of English *shroud*.] —**scro·tal** *adj.*

scrounge /skrownj/ (**scrounged, scroung·ing, scroung·es**) *vti.* (*informal*) **1.** BEG OR BORROW to acquire something from somebody by begging or borrowing without intending to make repayment or return **2.** GET FROM ANY AVAILABLE SOURCE to seek and acquire something from any available source, e.g., by foraging [Early 20thC. Alteration of *scringe*, "to prowl around," from CRINGE.] —**scroung·er** *n.*

scroung·y /skrównjee/ (**-i·er, -i·est**) *adj.* shabby, dirty, and neglected (*informal*) ○ *a scroungy hovel*

scrub[1] /skrub/ *v.* (**scrubbed, scrub·bing, scrubs**) **1.** *vti.* CLEAN BY RUBBING to clean something by rubbing hard **2.** *vt.* REMOVE DIRT BY RUBBING to remove dirt by rubbing hard, usually with a brush **3.** *vt.* REMOVE IMPURITIES FROM GAS to remove impurities from a gas by passing it over or through a liquid **4.** *vi.* CLEANSE FOR SURGERY to cleanse the arms and hands in preparation for surgery **5.** *vt.* CANCEL SOMETHING to cancel or postpone something (*informal*) ■ *n.* ACT OF SCRUBBING the act of cleaning something by rubbing hard ■ **scrubs** *npl.* CLOTHING WORN WHILE PERFORMING SURGERY the clothing, usually a matching green shirt and pants, worn by surgeons and nurses in an operating room (*informal*) [13thC. Origin uncertain: probably from Middle Low German or Middle Dutch *schrubben*.]

scrub[2] /skrub/ *n.* **1.** STUNTED TREE a stunted tree or shrub **2.** AREA OF LOW VEGETATION low, stunted, or straggly vegetation or an area of such vegetation **3.** MONGREL a domestic animal of mixed breeding **4.** OFFENSIVE TERM an offensive term for somebody small or insignificant **5.** SPORTS PLAYER NOT ON FIRST STRING a player not on the first string or a team made up of such players **6.** *Aus* REMOTE PLACE a remote part of the countryside (*informal*) [14thC. Alteration of SHRUB.]

scrub·ber /skrúbbər/ *n.* **1.** SOMEBODY OR SOMETHING THAT SCRUBS somebody or something that cleans by rubbing hard, often with a brush **2.** APPARATUS FOR PURIFYING GAS a device for removing impurities from a gas [Mid-19thC]

scrub·by /skrúbbee/ (**-bi·er, -bi·est**) *adj.* **1.** STUNTED OR STRAGGLY inferior in size or quality **2.** COVERED WITH LOW TREES covered with or consisting of low or undersized shrubs or trees **3.** SHABBY shabby, messy, or wretched in appearance —**scrub·bi·ness** *n.*

scrub·land /skrúb lànd/ *n.* land covered with low trees and shrubs

scrub nurse *n.* a nurse who helps a surgeon in the operating room

scrub oak *n.* a small North American oak found in scrubland. Latin name: *Quercus ilicifolia.*

scrub pine *n.* a stunted, straggly, or undersized pine tree that is unsuitable for use as lumber

scrub ty·phus *n.* a common infectious disease in Asia that is caused by the microorganism *Rickettsia tsutsugamushi* and spread by a biting mite. Symptoms include fever, painful swollen lymph nodes, and a skin rash.

scrub·wom·an /skrúb wŏŏmmən/ (*plural* **-en** /-wìmmin/) *n.* a woman hired to do cleaning (*archaic*)

scruff /skruf/ *n.* the back of the neck, especially when used to seize, drag, or lift a person or animal [Late 18thC. Alteration of earlier *scuff*, from Old Norse *skoft*, "hair of the head."]

scruff·y /skrúffee/ (**-i·er, -i·est**) *adj.* messy, shabby, or run-down in appearance [Mid-17thC. Formed from SCRUFF. The modern meaning, "shabby," evolved from "scaly, covered with scurf."] —**scruf·fi·ly** *adv.* —**scruf·fi·ness** *n.*

scrum /skrum/ *n.* PLAY IN RUGBY TO GET BALL a part of a rugby game in which the two sets of forwards gather around the ball with heads down and arms linked and try to obtain possession of it ■ *vi.* (**scrummed, scrum·ming, scrums**) FORM RUGBY SCRUM to form a scrum in rugby [Late 19thC. Shortening of SCRUMMAGE.]

scrum·mage /skrúmmij/ *n.*, *vi.* (**-maged, -mag·ing, -mag·es**) = **scrum** *n.* [Early 19thC. Alteration of SCRIMMAGE.] —**scrum·mag·er** *n.*

scrump·tious /skrúmpshəss/ *adj.* very pleasing, especially to the taste (*informal*) [Mid-19thC. Origin uncertain: probably an alteration of SUMPTUOUS.] —**scrump·tious·ly** *adv.* —**scrump·tious·ness** *n.*

scrunch /skrunch/ *v.* (**scrunched, scrunch·ing, scrunch·es**) **1.** *vt.* SQUEEZE SOMETHING to crumple, crush, or squeeze something together tightly **2.** *vi.* MOVE WITH CRUNCHING SOUND to move with or make a crunching sound **3.** *vi.* HUNKER DOWN to hunker down, hunch, or crouch ■ *n.* CRUNCHING SOUND a rustling, crunching sound [Late 18thC. Thought to suggest the action, or to be an imitation of the sound.]

scrunch·ie /skrúnchee/ *n.* a thick elasticated band loosely covered with fabric, used to hold a bunch of hair, e.g., in a pony tail [Late 20thC. Formed from SCRUNCH, because of its crumpled appearance.]

scru·ple /skrŏŏp'l/ *n.* **1.** MORAL OR ETHICAL CONSIDERATION a moral or ethical consideration that tends to restrain action or behavior **2.** MEASURE UNIT OF WEIGHT a unit of apothecaries' weight equal to 20 grains/or about 1.3 g **3.** VERY SMALL AMOUNT a minute amount or portion of something (*archaic*) ■ *vi.* (**-pled, -pling, -ples**) HESITATE BECAUSE OF MORAL CONSIDERATIONS to hesitate because of moral or ethical considerations ○ *She wouldn't scruple to cheat.* [15thC. Via Old French *scrupule* from Latin *scrupulus* "small sharp stone, uneasiness," from *scrupus* "sharp stone." The underlying idea is of a sharp stone causing discomfort.]

scru·pu·lous /skrŏŏpyələss/ *adj.* **1.** HAVING MORAL INTEGRITY having or showing careful regard for what is morally right **2.** VERY PRECISE rigorously precise and exact —**scru·pu·lous·ly** *adv.* —**scru·pu·los·i·ty** /skrŏŏpyə lóssətee/ *n.* —**scru·pu·lous·ness** /skrŏŏpyələssnəss/ *n.*

WORD KEY: SYNONYMS

See Synonyms at ***careful***.

scru·ta·ble /skrŏŏtəb'l/ *adj.* capable of being understood by careful observation, examination, or study [Late 16thC. Back-formation from INSCRUTABLE.] —**scru·ta·bil·i·ty** /skròotə bíllətee/ *n.*

scru·ti·neer /skròot'n éer/ *n.* somebody who inspects or examines something very carefully [Mid-16thC. Coined from SCRUTINY + -EER.]

scru·ti·nize /skròot'n ìz/ (**-nized, -niz·ing, -niz·es**) *vt.* to examine somebody or something closely and carefully [Late 17thC. Formed from SCRUTINY.] —**scru·ti·niz·er** *n.*

scru·ti·ny /skròot'nee/ (*plural* **-nies**) *n.* **1. CAREFUL INSPECTION** close, careful, searching examination or inspection **2. OBSERVATION** careful study or surveillance **3. GAZE** a searching look [15thC. From Latin *scrutinium* "search, inquiry," from *scrutinari* "to search, examine," literally "to pick through rags," which was in turn formed from *scruta* "trash."]

SCSI /skúzzee/ *n.* a specification for a high-speed computer interface used to connect peripheral devices to a computer. Full form of **small computer systems interface**

scu·ba /skóobə/ *n.* an apparatus for breathing underwater consisting of a portable canister of compressed air and a mouthpiece [Mid-20thC. Acronym formed from *Self-Contained Underwater Breathing Apparatus.*]

scu·ba div·er *n.* somebody who swims underwater using scuba equipment —**scu·ba div·ing** *n.*

scud /skud/ *vi.* (**scud·ded, scud·ding, scuds**) **1. MOVE SWIFTLY** to move swiftly and smoothly **2.** SAILING **SAIL BEFORE GALE** to sail with a gale or strong wind blowing from behind ■ *n.* **1. SWIFT MOVEMENT** a swift smooth movement **2.** METEOROL **CLOUDS DRIVEN BY WIND** low clouds that are driven swiftly by the wind **3.** METEOROL **SUDDEN SHOWER OR GUST** a sudden shower of rain or gust of wind [Mid-16thC. Origin uncertain: perhaps literally "to race like a hare," alteration of SCUT in the obsolete sense "hare."]

Scud mis·sile /skúd-/ *n.* a surface-to-surface missile that can take a nuclear, conventional, or chemical warhead [*Scud*: a NATO codename, from SCUD]

scu·do /skóodō/ (*plural* **-di**) *n.* a gold or silver coin introduced in the early 16th century and formerly current in various Italian states, now only appearing occasionally as a commemorative coin issued by the republic of San Marino [Mid-17thC. Via Italian from Latin *scutum*, "shield" (source of *écu* and *escudo*).]

scuff /skuf/ *vti.* (**scuffed, scuff·ing, scuffs**) **1. SCRAPE OR RUB** to scrape, rub, or wear away the surface of something, or to become scraped, rubbed, or worn with use **2. SCRAPE FEET WHILE WALKING** to scrape the feet on the ground while standing or walking or to walk in a manner that makes the feet scrape **3. POKE THE FOOT** to move or shift the foot tentatively in embarrassment or exploration ■ *n.* **1. ACT OF SCUFFING** a scraping or shuffling movement or sound **2. MARK FROM SCRAPING OR RUBBING** a mark or scratch made by scuffing **3. FLAT SHOE** a flat-soled shoe with no strap or back [Late 16thC. Origin uncertain: possibly from Scandinavian, from a prehistoric Germanic base thought to suggest the action. Originally "to evade," the modern meaning may have evolved via "sidestep."]

scuf·fle[1] /skúff'l/ *n.* **DISORDERLY FIGHT** a disorderly confused fight or struggle at close quarters ■ *v.* (**-fled, -fling, -fles**) **1.** *vti.* **FIGHT IN CONFUSION** to struggle or fight at close quarters and in confusion **2.** *vi.* **SHUFFLE QUICKLY** to shuffle along hurriedly [Late 16thC. Origin uncertain: probably from SCUFF + *-le*, with the original meaning "to evade or dodge repeatedly."] —**scuf·fler** *n.*

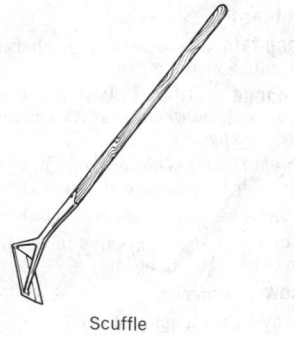

scuf·fle[2] /skúff'l/, **scuf·fle hoe** *n.* a hoe that is used by pushing it back and forth [Late 18thC. From Dutch *schoffel.*]

Scuffle

scull /skul/ *n.* **1. SINGLE OAR AT BACK OF BOAT** a single oar that is moved from side to side at the stern of a boat to propel the boat forward **2. EITHER OF A PAIR OF OARS** either one of a pair of relatively short oars used by a single rower **3. LIGHT RACING BOAT** a light narrow racing boat propelled by one, two, or four rowers using sculls ■ *vti.* (**sculled, scull·ing, sculls**) **PROPEL BOAT WITH SCULLS** to propel a boat using a scull or sculls [14thC. Origin unknown.] —**scull·er** *n.*

scul·ler·y /skúlləree/ (*plural* **-ies**) *n.* a small room for washing and storing dishes and utensils and doing other kitchen chores such as preparing vegetables [15thC. From French *escuelerie* "duty of servant in charge of plates," from *escuelle* "dish," from Latin *scutella* "serving platter" (source of English *skillet*).]

scul·lion /skúllyən/ *n.* a servant employed to perform menial kitchen chores [15thC. Via Middle French *escouillon, escouvillon* "swab, washcloth," from *escouve* "broom," from Latin *scopae* (plural).]

sculp. *abbr.* **1.** sculptor **2.** sculptress **3.** sculpture

scul·pin /skúlpin/ (*plural* **-pin** *or* **-pins**) *n.* **1. FLAT-HEADED FISH** a marine and freshwater fish, mostly bottom-dwelling, with a large flat head, large pectoral fins, and spines. Family: Cottidae. **2. SCORPION FISH** a scorpion fish with venomous spines that lives off the southern California coast and is caught for food and for sport. Latin name: *Scorpaena guttata.* [Late 17thC. Origin uncertain: perhaps from *scorpene* "scorpion-fish," via Spanish *scorpena* or Latin *scorpæna* from Greek *skorpios* "scorpion."]

sculpt /skulpt/ (**sculpt·ed, sculpt·ing, sculpts**) *v.* **1.** *vti.* **MAKE SCULPTURE** to carve, model, cast, or otherwise create a three-dimensional representation of something as a work of art **2.** *vti.* **CARVE OR MODEL MATERIAL** to use a material to create a three-dimensional work of art **3.** *vi.* **BE SCULPTOR** to create three-dimensional works of art as a profession or pastime **4.** *vt.* **CHANGE SHAPE OF SOMETHING NATURALLY** to change the shape or contours of something by natural processes such as erosion [Mid-19thC. Via French *sculpter*, from Latin *sculpere* "to carve" (see SCULPTURE).]

sculp·tor /skúlptər/ *n.* an artist who creates three-dimensional works of art, especially by carving, modeling, or casting [Mid-17thC. From Latin, where it was formed from *sculpere*. See SCULPTURE.]

Sculp·tor *n.* a faint constellation in the sky of the southern hemisphere between Grus and Cetus

sculp·tress /skúlptrəss/ *n.* a woman artist who creates three-dimensional works of art, especially by carving, modeling, or casting

sculp·ture /skúlpchər/ *n.* **1. CREATION OF THREE-DIMENSIONAL ART** the creation of a three-dimensional work of art, especially by carving, modeling, or casting **2. THREE-DIMENSIONAL WORK OF ART** a work of art created by sculpture, or such works collectively **3.** BOT, ZOOL **NATURAL MARKING ON A PLANT OR ANIMAL** a natural indentation or other marking on a plant or animal, e.g., a ridge on a seashell ■ *v.* (**-tured, -tur·ing, -tures**) **1.** *vt.* **REPRESENT SOMETHING IN THREE-DIMENSIONAL ART** to carve, model, cast, or otherwise create a representation of something as a three-dimensional work of art **2.** *vi.* = **sculpt** *v.* 1 **3.** *vti.* = **sculpt** *v.* 2 **4.** *vt.* = **sculpt** *v.* 4 [14thC. From Latin *sculptura* "sculpture," from *sculpere* "to carve, scratch," variant of *scalpere* "to carve" (source of English *scalpel*).] —**sculp·tur·al** *adj.* —**sculp·tur·al·ly** *adv.*

sculp·tur·esque /skùlpchə résk/ *adj.* resembling sculpture —**sculp·tur·esque·ly** *adv.* —**sculp·tur·esque·ness** *n.*

scum /skum/ *n.* **1. FILMY LAYER ON SURFACE OF LIQUID** a filmy layer of extraneous matter or impurities that rises to or is formed on the surface of a liquid **2. OFFENSIVE TERM** an offensive term for a person or group of people regarded as contemptible, vile, or worthless (*insult offensive*) **3. REFUSE** refuse or worthless items **4.** METALL **REFUSE FROM MOLTEN METAL** dross or refuse from molten metals ■ *v.* (**scummed, scum·ming, scums**) **1.** *vi.* **HAVE SCUM** to become covered with scum **2.** *vt.* **CLEAR SOMETHING OF SCUM** to remove scum from something [14thC. Via Middle Dutch *scūme*, "foam, froth," ultimately from Germanic. The meaning evolved from "froth on liquid" through "film on top of liquid" and "film of dirt."] —**scum·mer** *n.*

scum·bag /skúm bàg/ *n.* an offensive term referring to somebody who is seen as unpleasant or malicious (*slang insult offensive*) [Mid-20thC. From its original slang meaning "(used) condom."]

scum·ble /skúmb'l/ *vt.* (**-bled, -bling, -bles**) **1. SOFTEN SOMETHING WITH OPAQUE COLOR** to soften the colors or outlines of a painting or drawing by covering it with a film of opaque or semiopaque color **2. SOFTEN COLORS BY RUBBING** to soften the colors or outlines of a painting or drawing by rubbing ■ *n.* **1. TECHNIQUE OF SCUMBLING** the technique or effect of scumbling **2. SCUMBLING MATERIAL** a material used for scumbling [Late 17thC. Origin uncertain: perhaps literally "to skim the surface repeatedly," formed from SCUM.]

scun·gil·li /skun jíllee/ *n.* conch eaten as food [Mid-20thC. Plural of *scungille*, from Italian dialect *scunciglio*, of uncertain origin: perhaps an alteration of Italian *conchiglia* "seashell, shellfish."]

scup /skup/ (*plural* **scups** *or* **scup**) *n.* a fish of the porgy family that is caught for food along the Atlantic coast from Maine to North Carolina. Latin name: *Stenotomus chrysops.* [19thC. From Narraganset *mishcup*, "big and close together," because of the shape of the fish's scales.]

scup·per[1] /skúppər/ *n.* **1. OPENING FOR DRAINING WATER FROM DECK** an opening in the bulwarks of a ship that allows water on the deck to drain overboard **2. OPENING ALLOWING DRAINAGE FROM BUILDING** an opening allowing water to drain from the roof or floor of a building [15thC. Origin uncertain: perhaps formed from SCOOP, or from Anglo-Norman and Old French *escopir* "to spit out."]

scup·per[2] /skúppər/ (**-pered, -per·ing, -pers**) *vt.* **1.** NAUT **SINK SHIP** to sink a ship, especially to sink your own vessel intentionally **2. WRECK OR RUIN SOMETHING** to wreck, defeat, or ruin something [Late 19thC. Origin uncertain: perhaps from SCUPPER[1].]

scup·per·nong /skúppər nàwng, -nòng/ *n.* **1. MUSCADINE GRAPE** a cultivated variety of the muscadine grape that has sweet yellowish-green fruit **2. WINE MADE FROM SCUPPERNONG GRAPES** a sweet amber-colored wine made from scuppernong grapes [Early 19thC. Named for the *Scuppernong*, a river in North Carolina, where the the vine is found.]

scurf /skurf/ *n.* **1. DANDRUFF** thin dry flaking scales of skin, usually as a result of a specific skin condition such as dandruff **2. FLAKY INCRUSTATION** a flaky or scaly incrustation on a surface **3.** BOT **SCALY DEPOSIT ON PLANT** a scaly deposit or covering on a plant **4.** BOT **PLANT DISEASE** a plant disease characterized by a scaly deposit or covering [Old English]

scur·ril·i·ty /skə ríllətee/ (*plural* **-ties**) *n.* **1. COARSENESS** coarseness, vulgarity, or a lack of refinement **2. VULGAR REMARK OR LANGUAGE** language that is coarse and vulgar, or a remark made in coarse vulgar language

scur·ri·lous /skúr ələss, skúrrələss/ *adj.* **1. ABUSIVE OR DEFAMATORY** containing abusive language or defamatory allegations **2. FOUL-MOUTHED OR VULGAR** using or containing coarse, vulgar, or obscene language **3. WICKED** behaving in ways thought to be evil or immoral [Late 16thC. Formed from *scurrile*, directly or via French from Latin *scurrilis*, from *scurra* "buffoon."] —**scur·ri·lous·ly** *adv.* —**scur·ri·lous·ness** *n.*

scur·ry /skúr ee, skúrree/ *vi.* (**-ried, -ry·ing, -ries**) **1. MOVE BRISKLY** to move at a hurried pace, usually with small fast steps **2. MOVE AROUND AGITATEDLY** to move around in an agitated manner or with a swirling motion ■ *n.* (*plural* **-ries**) **SCURRYING MOVEMENT** a hurried, agitated, or swirling movement [Early 19thC. Origin uncertain: perhaps a shortening of *hurry-scurry* "to rush about frantically," variant of HURRY.]

scur·vy /skúrvee/ *n.* **DISEASE CAUSED BY VITAMIN DEFICIENCY** a disease caused by insufficient vitamin C, the symptoms of which include spongy gums, loosening of the teeth, and bleeding into the skin and mucous membranes ■ *adj.* (**-vi·er, -vi·est**) **DESPICABLE** behaving in ways thought to be mean or contemptible [15thC. Coined from SCURF + -Y. "Disease" evolved from "covered with scurf, wretched," and was influenced by French *scorbut* and Dutch *scheurbuik* "scurvy."] —**scur·vi·ly** *adv.* —**scur·vi·ness** *n.*

scur·vy grass *n.* a northern European plant that was formerly used to treat scurvy. Latin name: *Cochlearia officinalis.*

scut /skut/ *n.* a short erect tail such as that of a rabbit [15thC. Origin uncertain: perhaps from obsolete *scut* "short," or from Scandinavian.]

scu·ta plural of **scutum**

scu·tage /skyóotij/ *n.* in feudal times, a tax paid by a knight or vassal to his lord that freed him from military service [15thC. From medieval Latin *scutagium*, literally "shield-tax," from Latin *scutum* "shield."]

scu·tate /skyóo tàyt/ *adj.* **1.** BOT **SHIELD-SHAPED** shaped like a shield ○ *a scutate leaf* **2.** ZOOL **COVERED BY BONY PLATES** covered or protected by external bony or horny plates or scales [Early 19thC. Coined from SCUTUM + -ATE.] —**scu·ta·tion** /skyoo táysh'n/ *n.*

scutch /skuch/ *vt.* (**scutched, scutch·ing, scutch·es**) **PROCESS FLAX BY BEATING** to beat flax in order to separate the valuable fibers from the woody parts ■ *n.* **TOOL FOR BEATING FLAX** a tool or machine for scutching flax or cotton [Late 17thC. Via Old French *escoucher*, ultimately from Latin *excutere* "to shake." The meaning "to process flax" evolved from "to remove moss from bark."]

scutch·eon /skúchən/ *n.* an escutcheon (*archaic*) [14thC. From Anglo-Norman *escuchoune* (see ESCUTCHEON).]

scutch grass *n.* = **Bermuda grass**

scute /skyoot, skoot/ *n.* an external bony or horny plate or scale in some animals, especially snakes and other reptiles [14thC. From Latin *scutum*, "shield."]

scu·tel·lum /skyoo téllәm/ (*plural* **-la** /-téllә/) *n.* **1.** ZOOL **HARD PLATE OR SCALE** a hard plate or scale, e.g., on the thorax of an insect or a toe of a bird **2.** BOT **LEAF OF DEVELOPING GRASS SEED** the shield-shaped embryonic leaf (**cotyledon**) of a grass seed [Mid-18thC. From modern Latin, where it was formed from Latin *scutella* "platter"; mistaken as literally "small shield," formation from Latin *scutum* "shield."] —**scu·tel·lar** *adj.* —**scu·tel·late** /skyoo téllət, skyóot'l àyt/ *adj.* —**scu·tel·la·tion** /skyóotə láysh'n/ *n.*

scu·ti·form /skyóotə fàwrm/ *adj.* shaped like a shield [Mid-17thC. Coined from Latin *scutum* "shield" + -FORM.]

scut·ter /skúttər/ (**-tered, -ter·ing, -ters**) *vi.* to move hastily in a scurrying manner [Late 18thC. Variant of medieval sense of SCUTTLE "to scamper about."]

scut·tle[1] /skútt'l/ *n.* **1.** **SMALL HATCH** a small hatchway with a cover in the deck or hull of a ship or in some part of a building such as the roof or a wall **2.** NAUT **SCUTTLE COVER ON SHIP** the cover for a scuttle on a ship ■ *vt.* (**-tled, -tling, -tles**) **1.** NAUT **SINK SHIP BY LETTING WATER IN** to sink a ship by making or opening holes in the bottom **2.** **DESTROY SOMETHING** to destroy or bring something to an end ○ *had effectively scuttled his plans* [15thC. Via French *escoutille*, or directly from Spanish *escotilla* "hatchway," from *escotar* "to cut out," from a prehistoric Germanic word that is the ancestor of English *sheet*.]

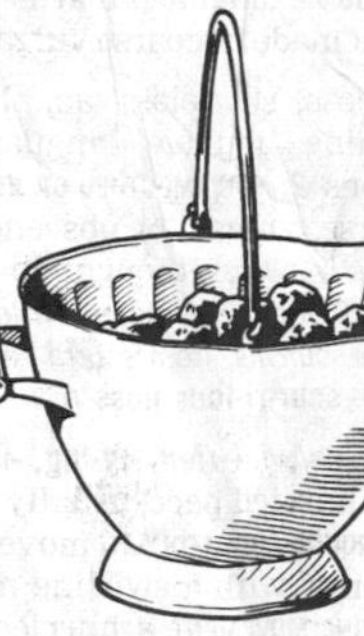
Scuttle

scut·tle[2] /skútt'l/ *n.* **1.** **COAL CONTAINER** a metal container shaped like a wide-rimmed pail with a lip and a handle, used to carry or store coal indoors **2.** **SHALLOW BASKET** an open shallow basket used to carry foods or small items [15thC. Via Old English *scutel* and Old Norse *skutill* from Latin *scutella* "dish, tray."]

scut·tle[3] /skútt'l/ *vi.* (**-tled, -tling, -tles**) **MOVE WITH SHORT FAST STEPS** to run or move quickly with short steps ■ *n.* **A RUSH OR RUN** a hurried pace or scuttling movement

scut·tle·butt /skútt'l bùt/ *n.* **1.** **GOSSIP** rumors about somebody's activities, often of an intimate and scandalous nature (*slang*) **2.** **DRINKING FOUNTAIN ON SHIP** a drinking fountain on a ship **3.** **CASK OF WATER ON SHIP** a cask on a ship containing a day's supply of fresh water (*archaic*) [Early 19thC. From SCUTTLE[2] + BUTT.]

scu·tum /skyóotəm/ (*plural* **-ta** /-tə/) *n.* **1.** ZOOL = **scute** **2.** ARMS **ANCIENT ROMAN SHIELD** a large shield used by legionaries in ancient Rome [Late 18thC. From Latin, "shield."]

Scu·tum *n.* a small faint constellation in the sky of the southern hemisphere lying partly in the Milky Way, located between Sagittarius and Aquila

scut·work /skút wùrk/ *n.* routine monotonous menial chores or work (*informal*) [Mid-20thC. *Scut* of uncertain origin: perhaps from *scut*, "silly or objectionable person."]

scuzz /skuz/ *n.* **1.** **SOMETHING DISGUSTING** something dirty, disgusting, or disreputable (*slang*) **2.** **scuzz, scuzz·ball, scuzz·buck·et, scuzz·bag** **OFFENSIVE TERM** an offensive term referring to somebody regarded as disgusting and contemptible (*slang insult offensive*) [Mid-20thC. Origin uncertain: perhaps a shortening of DISGUSTING, or a blend of SCUM and FUZZ.] —**scuzz·i·ly** *adv.* —**scuz·zi·ness** *n.* —**scuz·zy** *adj.*

Scyl·la /síllə/ *n.* in Greek mythology, a sea monster who attacked sailors. In later times, Scylla was thought to be a rock on the Italian side of the Straits of Messina. ◇ **be between Scylla and Charybdis** to be faced with the necessity of choosing between two equally undesirable or unpleasant things (*formal*)

scy·phis·to·ma /sī fístəmə/ (*plural* **-mae** /-mee/ *or* **-mas**) *n.* the form in the life cycle of a marine invertebrate such as a jellyfish that remains fixed in one place and reproduces asexually to produce free-swimming offspring [Late 19thC. Coined from SCYPHUS + STOMA.]

scy·pho·zo·an /sīfə zō ən/ *n.* a marine invertebrate animal such as a jellyfish that is free-swimming and does not have a significant sedentary stage [Early 20thC. From modern Latin, from SCYPHUS and Greek *zōa* "animals."]

scy·phus /sīfəss/ (*plural* **-phi** /-fī/) *n.* **1.** **ANCIENT GREEK DRINKING VESSEL** a drinking vessel with a deep body, flat bottom, and two small handles near the rim, used by the ancient Greeks **2.** BOT **CUP-SHAPED STRUCTURE** a cup-shaped enlargement in lichens [Late 18thC. Via Latin, from Greek *skuphos* "large drinking vessel."]

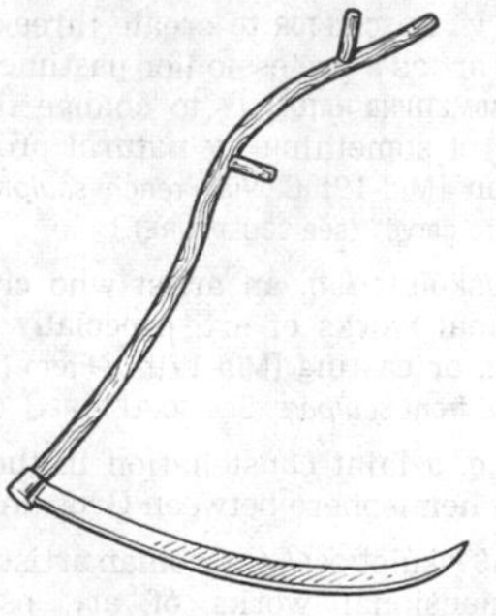
Scythe

scythe /sīth/ *n.* **TOOL FOR MOWING OR REAPING** an implement with a long handle and a long curved single-edged blade, used to cut grass, crops, or similar plants by swinging the blade horizontally close to the ground ■ *vti.* (**scythed, scyth·ing, scythes**) **CUT WITH SCYTHE** to cut or reap something with a scythe [Old English *sipe*. Ultimately from an Indo-European word meaning "to cut" that is also the ancestor of English *section*, *sickle*, and *insect*. Influenced by SCISSORS.]

Scyth·i·an /síthee ən, sīthee ən/ *n.* **INHABITANT OF SCYTHIA** a member of an ancient people that lived in Scythia, an area of present-day Ukraine ■ *adj.* **RELATING TO SCYTHIA** relating to the ancient region of Scythia, or its people or culture

SD *abbr.* **1.** **SD, S.D.** South Dakota **2.** **SD, S.D.** special delivery **3.** STATS standard deviation

S.Dak. *abbr.* South Dakota

SDI, **S.D.I.** *abbr.* Strategic Defense Initiative

SDR, **SDRs** *abbr.* ECON special drawing rights

SDS *abbr.* Students for a Democratic Society

Se *symbol.* selenium

SE *abbr.* **1.** southeast **2.** southeastern

sea /see/ *n.* **1.** **SALT WATERS OF EARTH** the great body of salt water that covers a large portion of the Earth **2.** **PARTICULAR BODY OF SALT WATER** a body of salt water that is surrounded by land on all or most sides, or that is part of one of the oceans **3.** **LARGE LAKE** a large inland body of fresh water **4.** ASTRON = **mare**[2] *n.* **5.** **TURBULENCE OF OCEAN** the motion and disturbance of a large body of water such as the ocean, or the waves themselves **6.** **SEAFARER'S JOB OR LIFE** the occupation or way of life of a sailor **7.** **VAST BODY** a large area or great number of something [Old English *sǣ*, from prehistoric Germanic] ◇ **be at sea 1.** be traveling on the ocean **2.** be bewildered and confused

sea an·chor *n.* a device such as a conical canvas bag that is thrown overboard and dragged behind a ship to control its speed or heading

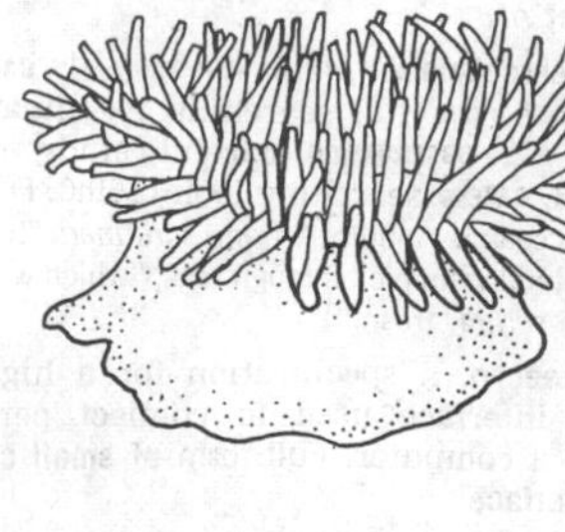
Sea anemone

sea a·nem·o·ne *n.* a solitary and often colorful sea animal with a squat cylindrical body that bears a ring of tentacles and is attached to rock or other nonliving material. Order: Actiniaria.

sea as·ter *n.* a biennial or perennial plant of the daisy family with narrow fleshy leaves and purple-and-yellow flowers that is found in salt marshes throughout Europe. Latin name: *Aster tripolium.*

sea bass /-bàss/ *n.* a bony marine fish with a long body, large mouth, and spiny dorsal fin, caught for food or sport in Atlantic coastal waters of North America. Latin name: *Centropristis striata.*

sea·bed /sée bèd/ *n.* the surface of the earth at the bottom of the sea

Sea·bee /sée bèe/ *n.* a member of one of the construction battalions of the United States Navy that builds naval shore facilities in combat zones [Mid-20thC. From the abbreviation CB, "Construction Battalion," influenced by "(worker) bee."]

sea·bird /sée bùrd/ *n.* a bird such as a gull, albatross, or petrel that frequents the open ocean

sea bis·cuit *n.* = **hardtack**

sea·blite /sée blīt/ *n.* an annual plant of the goosefoot family that grows in salt marshes. Latin name: *Suaeda maritima.* [Mid-18thC. From SEA + *blite*.]

sea·board /sée bàwrd/ *n.* land that borders the sea

sea·borne /sée bàwrn/ *adj.* **1.** **CARRIED BY SEA** carried over, on, or in the sea **2.** **TRANSPORTED BY SHIP** transported by ship across the sea

sea bream *n.* **1.** **ATLANTIC PORGY** a porgy of Atlantic coastal waters, harvested as a food fish. Latin name: *Archosargus rhomboidalis.* **2.** **MARINE FOOD FISH** a marine food fish of European waters. Family: Sparidae.

sea breeze *n.* a cooling breeze that blows inland from the sea during the daytime when the land is warmer than the surface of the water

sea buck·thorn *n.* a shrub found on seashores of Europe and Asia that has silvery leaves, greenish flowers, and orange-red edible berries, and yields a yellow dye. Latin name: *Hippophaë rhamnoides.*

Sea·bur·y /sée bèree, -bəree/, **Samuel** (1729–96) U.S. clergyman. He served as a Loyalist under the British during the Revolution (1776–83). Afterwards he became the first Episcopal bishop of Connecticut and Rhode Island (1783).

sea but·ter·fly *n.* = **pteropod**

sea cap·tain *n.* the person in charge of a ship, especially a merchant ship

sea change *n.* **1.** **GREAT CHANGE** a substantial transformation **2.** **CHANGE CAUSED BY SEA** a change caused by the sea (*archaic*)

sea chest *n.* a large box or trunk in which a sailor's personal belongings are stored

sea·coast /sée kōst/ *n.* the land that borders the sea

sea·cock /sée kòk/ *n.* a valve in the hull of a ship used to let water in or out

sea cow *n.* = **sirenian**

sea cray·fish *n.* = **spiny lobster**

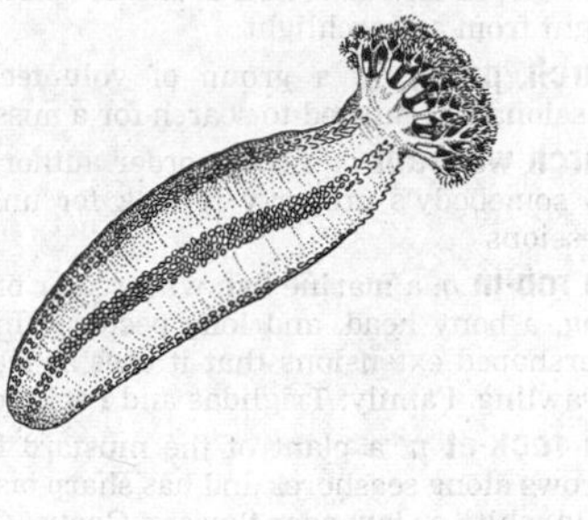
Sea cucumber

sea cu·cum·ber *n.* a marine invertebrate (**echinoderm**) that has a long tough muscular body and a mouth encircled by tentacles, and lives on the seabed. Class: Holothuroidea.

sea de·vil *n.* = **devilfish**

sea dog *n.* somebody who has been a sailor for a long time

sea·dog /sée dòg/ *n.* METEOROL = **fogbow** [Mid-16thC. The original meaning was "animal like a seal." The modern meaning evolved through "experienced sailor" to "phenomenon recognized by experienced sailors."]

sea ea·gle *n.* a fish-eating eagle that lives near the sea

sea el·e·phant *n.* = **elephant seal**

sea fan *n.* a coral with a fan-shaped skeleton that inhabits the waters of Florida and the West Indies. Genus: *Gorgonia.*

sea·far·er /sée fàirər/ *n.* **1.** SEA TRAVELER somebody who travels by sea **2.** SAILOR a sailor (*archaic or literary*)

sea·far·ing /sée fàiring/ *adj.* **1.** REGULARLY GOING TO SEA regularly traveling by sea or working at sea **2.** OF SEA TRAVEL OR TRANSPORTATION relating to travel or transportation by sea ■ *n.* SAILOR'S WAY OF LIFE the work and way of life of a sailor

sea fire *n.* light that is produced by marine organisms

sea·floor /sée flàwr/ *n.* the surface of the Earth at the bottom of the sea

sea·floor spread·ing *n.* a process in which molten material from the Earth's mantle rises up at ocean ridges, causing volcanic and seismic activity, spreads out, and creates a new seafloor

sea·food /sée fòod/ *n.* fish and shellfish from the sea eaten as food

sea·fowl /sée fòwl/ (*plural* **-fowl** *or* **-fowls**) *n.* = **seabird**

sea·front /sée frùnt/ *n.* the part of a town that faces the edge of the sea

sea·girt /sée gùrt/ *adj.* encircled by the sea (*literary*)

sea·go·ing /sée gō ing/ *adj.* **1.** FOR OCEAN TRAVEL made or fit for sailing on the open sea **2.** = **seafaring** *adj.* 1

sea grape *n.* a tree that grows on sandy shores from Florida to South America and has large rounded leaves and clusters of purple-to-whitish edible berries. Latin name: *Coccoloba uvifera*

sea green *n.* a blue-green color in which the green is predominant —**sea-green** *adj.*

sea·gull /sée gùl/ *n.* = **gull**

WORD KEY: CULTURAL NOTE

The Seagull, a play by the Russian writer Anton Chekhov (1896). The plot centers on the young writer Triplev's love for the aspiring actress Nina, who, to Triplev's dismay, allows herself to be seduced by an older, more famous writer, Trigorin. One of Chekhov's most successful plays, it typically eschews melodrama for social and psychological analysis.

sea hare *n.* a large marine mollusk that has an arched back, a reduced or absent external shell, and two tentacles resembling rabbit ears. Genus: *Aplysia.*

sea hog *n.* = **porpoise** *n.* 1

sea hol·ly *n.* a perennial plant of the carrot family with spiny leaves and blue flowers, found on European seashores. The roots were formerly thought to have aphrodisiac properties. Latin name: *Eryngium maritimum.*

Sea horse

sea horse *n.* **1.** FISH RESEMBLING HORSE a small bony fish with a head shaped like that of a horse, a vertical swimming position, and a prehensile tail that it uses to cling to seaweed. Genus: *Hippocampus.* **2.** MYTHOL MYTHOLOGICAL CREATURE a mythological creature with the head and forelegs of a horse and the body of a fish **3.** WALRUS a walrus (*archaic*)

sea-is·land cot·ton *n.* a type of cotton with long silky fibers grown chiefly in the West Indies. Latin name: *Gossypium barbadense.* [Named for the SEA ISLANDS]

Sea Is·lands chain of more than 100 islands in the southern United States, in the Atlantic Ocean

sea kale *n.* a plant related to the cabbage that grows along the seashores of Europe and Asia and has edible leaves and shoots. Latin name: *Crambe maritima.*

sea king *n.* a Norse pirate chief of the early Middle Ages

seal[1] /seel/ *n.* **1.** TIGHT OR PERFECT CLOSURE a closure that prevents the entrance or escape of something such as air or water, or a substance or device that forms such a closure **2.** SPECIAL CLOSURE THAT REVEALS TAMPERING a closure for something such as a package or container that must be broken to open it and can thereby reveal tampering **3.** AUTHENTICATING STAMP a ring or stamp with a raised or engraved symbol or emblem that is pressed into wax in order to certify a signature or authenticate a document **4.** WAX MARKED WITH SEAL a piece of wax bearing the mark of a seal **5.** SYMBOL OF OFFICE a device, emblem, or symbol that is a mark of office **6.** ORNAMENTAL ADHESIVE STAMP an ornamental adhesive stamp used to close a letter or package, sometimes created as part of fund-raising campaigns or by charities **7.** SOMETHING GIVING CONFIRMATION something that gives confirmation or assurance ○ *Mother gave our plans for the party her seal of approval.* ■ *vt.* (**sealed, seal·ing, seals**) **1.** CLOSE SOMETHING FIRMLY to close something tightly or securely with a seal, e.g., to prevent tampering **2.** MAKE SOMETHING WATERTIGHT OR AIRTIGHT to make something watertight, airtight, or nonporous, e.g., by filling gaps or applying a special substance to the surface **3.** ATTACH AUTHENTICATING SEAL TO SOMETHING to affix a marked piece of wax to something in order to authenticate or certify it **4.** CONFIRM SOMETHING to confirm a decision or come to an agreement on something **5.** SETTLE SOMETHING to determine something irrevocably ○ *His fate was sealed when his lies were discovered.* **6.** RELIG SOLEMNIZE MARRIAGE OR ADOPTION to solemnize a marriage or adoption in the Church of Jesus Christ of Latter-Day Saints [12thC. Via Anglo-Norman from Latin *sigillum* "little mark or picture," from *signum* "sign, token, mark."] —**seal·a·ble** *adj.*

seal off *vt.* to prevent people or things from entering or leaving a place, e.g., by surrounding it or closing it securely ○ *Police sealed off the area.*

seal[2] /seel/ *n.* **1.** FISH-EATING MARINE MAMMAL a carnivorous marine mammal with a sleek body adapted for swimming and living in cold regions and webbed feet modified as flippers. Families: Otariidae and Phocidae. ◊ **common seal 2.** SEAL'S PELT the pelt or fur of a seal **3.** LEATHER FROM SEAL'S SKIN leather made from the skin of a seal ■ *vi.* (**sealed, seal·ing, seals**) HUNT SEALS to hunt seals, usually for their skins or blubber [Old English *seolh*]

SEAL /seel/ *abbr.* NAVY sea, air, land (team)

sea lam·prey *n.* a large eel-shaped jawless marine fish that swims up rivers along Atlantic coasts to spawn and is sometimes used as food. It lives as a parasite on other fish as an adult, and has been

Seal

introduced to some landlocked ecosystems such as the Great Lakes. Latin name: *Petromyzon marinus.*

sea lane *n.* an established and commonly used sea route for large ships

seal·ant /séelənt/ *n.* a substance used to seal something, e.g., by filling gaps or making a surface nonporous

sea lav·en·der *n.* a perennial plant of the thrift family with a rosette of slender leaves at the base and branching spikes of bluish-purple flowers, found in temperate salt marshes. Genus: *Limonium.*

sea law·yer *n.* an argumentative sailor (*informal*)

sealed-beam head·light *n.* a vehicle headlight with a prefocused reflector and lens sealed in one unit

sealed or·ders *npl.* written instructions not to be opened or read before a particular time, e.g., instructions to the captain of a ship whose destination is not revealed before it leaves harbor

sealed road *n. ANZ* a road with a surface of bitumen or tar

sea legs *npl.* the ability to move with ease on a ship and not feel seasick despite its pitching and rolling motion (*informal*)

seal·er[1] /séelər/ *n.* **1.** SOMEBODY OR SOMETHING THAT SEALS a person, substance, or device that seals something, e.g., a substance used to make a surface nonporous **2.** OFFICIAL WHO CERTIFIES SOMETHING an official who inspects and certifies weights and measures

seal·er[2] /séelər/ *n.* somebody who hunts seals, or a boat used for this purpose

seal·er·y /séeləree/ (*plural* **-ies**) *n.* **1.** REARING OR BREEDING PLACE FOR SEALS a place where seals are reared or where seals congregate and breed **2.** PLACE WHERE SEALS ARE HUNTED a place where seals are hunted **3.** HUNTING OF SEALS the occupation or practice of hunting seals

sea let·tuce *n.* a seaweed sometimes used as food in salads. Genus: *Ulva.*

sea lev·el *n.* the level of the surface of the sea relative to the land, halfway between high and low tide, used as a standard in calculating elevation

sea lil·y *n.* a marine invertebrate that has a stalk anchored to the seabed and a flower-shaped body. Class: Crinoidea.

seal·ing wax *n.* a resinous substance that is soft when heated and used for sealing letters, documents, batteries, or jars

Sea lion

sea lion *n.* a large gregarious seal that has external ears and coarse hair with no underfur. Family: Otariidae.

seal point *n.* a Siamese cat with a cream or fawn body and a dark brown face, paws, and tail. ◊ **blue point**

seal ring *n.* = **signet ring**

seal·skin /seél skìn/ *n.* the pelt or fur of a seal, or a garment made from this

Sea·ly·ham ter·ri·er /seéli hàm-, seélee əm-/ *n.* a dog with short legs, a long head, powerful jaws, and a wiry mostly white coat, belonging to a breed developed in Wales for catching rabbits and similar animals [Late 19thC. Named for the village in Wales where the dog was first bred.]

seam /seem/ *n.* **1. PLACE WHERE PIECES JOIN** the line along which pieces of cloth or leather are joined by sewing **2. STITCHES FORMING SEAM** the stitches used to form a seam **3. LINE FORMED BY ADJACENT SECTIONS** any line, groove, or ridge formed by joining or fitting together two sections along their edges **4. LINEAR INDENTATION** a scar, wrinkle, or other linear indentation **5.** GEOL **THIN LAYER OF ROCK** a thin layer of a rock or mineral such as a coal deposit occurring between different strata of bedrock ■ *v.* **(seamed, seam·ing, seams) 1.** *vt.* **JOIN THINGS ALONG EDGES** to join two parts or pieces along their edges, e.g., by sewing them together **2.** *vti.* **MARK WITH LINES** to mark something with wrinkles, scars, furrows, or other lines, or to become marked in this way [Old English *sēam*, from a prehistoric Germanic word that is also the ancestor of English *sew*] ◇ **come** *or* **fall apart at the seams** enter into a state of collapse

sea·man /seémən/ (*plural* **-men** /-mən/) *n.* **1.** = **sailor 2. SOMEBODY RANKING BELOW PETTY OFFICER** somebody enlisted in the U.S. Navy or Coast Guard who ranks below petty officer and above seaman apprentice [Old English]

sea·man ap·pren·tice *n.* somebody enlisted in the U.S. Navy or Coast Guard who ranks above a seaman recruit and below a seaman

sea·man re·cruit *n.* somebody enlisted in the U.S. Navy or Coast Guard who holds the lowest rank

sea·man·ship /seémən shìp/ *n.* the skill of handling, working on, or navigating a boat or ship

sea·mark /seé maark/ *n.* an object on land easily visible from the sea that serves as an aid to navigation

seam·er /seémər/ *n.* a person or machine that makes seams or the operator of such a machine [Old English]

sea mew *n.* a seagull, especially the common gull

sea mile *n.* = **nautical mile**

sea milk·wort *n.* a plant of the primula family with small pink flowers that grows on northern temperate coasts. Latin name: *Glaux maritima.*

seam·less /seémləss/ *adj.* **1. WITHOUT SEAMS** having no seams **2. PERFECTLY SMOOTH** free from awkward transitions and creating perfectly smooth continuity — **seam·less·ly** *adv.* —**seam·less·ness** *n.*

sea·moss /seé mòss/ *n. Carib* a drink popular in the Caribbean, made of seaweed that is boiled until it dissolves and then mixed with milk and spices

sea moth *n.* a small tropical marine fish with large wing-shaped pectoral fins, a long snout, and an armor of bony plates. Family: Pegasidae.

sea·mount /seé mòwnt/ *n.* an isolated undersea mountain of volcanic origin that rises from the seabed to a height of up to 3,300 ft./1,000 m, usually 3,300 ft./1,000 m to 6,500 ft./2,000 m below the surface of the sea

sea mouse *n.* a large marine worm with a broad flat body that is covered in bristles resembling hair. Genus: *Aphrodite.*

seam·stress /seémstrəss/ *n.* a woman who sews or whose occupation is sewing [Late 16thC. Formed from *seamster* "tailor, person who sews," from SEAM.]

seam·y /seémee/ (**-i·er, -i·est**) *adj.* having unpleasant qualities associated with a degraded or degenerate way of living [Late 16thC. Coined from SEAM + -Y. The meaning "degraded" evolved from "rough side of a garment, where the seams show."] —**seam·i·ness** *n.*

se·ance /sáy aanss, -aaNss/ *n.* **1. MEETING TO SPEAK WITH DEAD** a meeting at which a spiritualist attempts to receive communications from the spirits of the dead **2. SESSION** a sitting, session, or meeting, e.g., of a society or a legislative body [Late 18thC. Via French, "sitting," and Old French *seoir* "to sit," from Latin *sedere* "to sit" (source of English *session, sedentary,* and *sediment*).]

sea net·tle *n.* a stinging jellyfish that inhabits Atlantic estuaries from Cape Cod to the West Indies

Sea of Japan *n.* the sea between Korea and Japan that has been the subject of a dispute between the two countries for much of the 20th century

sea on·ion *n.* a Mediterranean plant of the lily family that bears dense spikes of small white flowers. It has an onion-shaped bulb with medicinal properties. Latin name: *Urginea maritima.*

sea ot·ter *n.* a marine animal of the weasel family with a thick brown coat that inhabits northern Pacific coasts and feeds mainly on shellfish. Latin name: *Enhydra lutris.*

sea pea *n. U.K.* = **beach pea**

sea pen *n.* a marine organism related to coral that forms feathery colonies in warm seas. Genus: *Pennatula.*

sea pink *n.* = **thrift** *n.* 3

sea·plane /seé plàyn/ *n.* a plane designed in such a way that it can take off from and land on water

sea poach·er *n.* a small slender marine fish that has an armor of bony plates and is found near the bottom of the North Pacific and other cold waters. Family: Agonidae.

sea·port /seé pàwrt/ *n.* a port, town, or harbor that can accommodate seagoing ships

sea pow·er *n.* **1. NATION WITH NAVAL STRENGTH** a nation that has formidable naval strength **2. NAVAL STRENGTH** the military power that a nation can deploy to fight on water

sea purse *n.* the egg pouch of a shark or ray that often has curly tendrils so that it can attach itself to seaweed

sea·quake /seé kwàyk/ *n.* an earthquake occurring under the sea

sear[1] /seer/ *v.* **(seared, sear·ing, sears) 1.** *vt.* **BURN SOMETHING** to burn or scorch something with an application of intense heat **2.** *vt.* **HAVE AN UNPLEASANT EFFECT ON** to have a sudden painful or unpleasant effect on somebody or something **3.** *vti.* **WITHER** to wither, shrivel, or dry up, or to cause something to wither, shrivel, or dry up ■ *n.* **BURN OR SCORCH MARK** a mark or scar made by searing [Old English *sēarian* "to wither away," from a prehistoric Germanic word that is also the ancestor of English *sere* "dried up"]

sear[2] /seer/ *n.* the catch that holds a gunlock cocked or at half-cock [Mid-16thC. From French *serre* "grasp, lock," from *serrer* "to grasp," ultimately from Latin *sera* "bar for a door."]

sea rav·en *n.* a large fish found along the Atlantic coast of North America that swallows air and blows up like a balloon when removed from the water. Latin name: *Hemitripterus americanus.*

search /surch/ *v.* **(searched, search·ing, search·es) 1.** *vti.* **EXAMINE THOROUGHLY** to look into, over, or through something carefully in order to find somebody or something **2.** *vt.* **EXAMINE SOMETHING FOR CONCEALED ITEMS** to examine the clothing, personal effects, or body of somebody in order to discover something such as weapons or illegal drugs that have been deliberately concealed **3.** *vt.* **EXAMINE PUBLIC RECORD** to examine a public record to find information about something **4.** *vt.* **DISCOVER SOMETHING BY EXAMINATION** to discover, come to know, or find something by examination **5.** *vt.* COMPUT **EXAMINE COMPUTER FILE** to examine a computer file, disk, database, or network for particular information ■ *n.* **1. THOROUGH EXAMINATION** a careful and thorough examination in order to find somebody or something **2.** COMPUT **EXAMINATION OF COMPUTER FILE** the examination of a computer file, disk, database, or network in order to find particular information **3.** LAW **BOARDING OF SHIP TO SEARCH IT** the boarding of a ship in accordance with international law in order to search it, especially during wartime [14thC. Via Anglo-Norman *sercher*, and Old French *cerchier* "to explore," from Latin *circare* "to go around in circles," from *circus* "circle" (source of English *circular*).] —**search·a·ble** *adj.* —**search·er** *n.* ◇ **search me** used to emphasize your lack of knowledge about something (*informal*)

search en·gine *n.* a computer program that searches for specified keywords and returns a list of documents in which they were found, especially a commercial service that scans documents on the Internet

search·ing /súrching/ *adj.* observing acutely or examining thoroughly —**search·ing·ly** *adv.*

search·light /súrch lìt/ *n.* **1. APPARATUS FOR PROJECTING LIGHT** an apparatus for projecting a high-intensity beam of light in any direction **2. INTENSE PROJECTED LIGHT** the light from a searchlight

search par·ty *n.* a group of volunteers or professionals organized to search for a missing person

search war·rant *n.* a court order authorizing entry to somebody's property to look for unlawful possessions

sea rob·in *n.* a marine fish with red or brown coloring, a bony head, and long pectoral fins with fingershaped extensions that it uses as feelers or for crawling. Family: Triglidae and Peristediidae.

sea rock·et *n.* a plant of the mustard family that grows along seashores and has sharp-tasting leaves and white or lavender flowers. Genus: *Cakile.*

sea·room /seé ro͝om, -ro͞om/ *n.* open space at sea in which to turn or maneuver a ship

sea rov·er *n.* a pirate or a pirate ship (*literary*)

sea salt *n.* coarse salt obtained from the evaporation of seawater

sea·scape /seé skàyp/ *n.* a painting or picture of the sea, or a view of the sea [Late 18thC. Formed from SEA, on the model of LANDSCAPE.]

Sea Scout *n.* a member of a scouting organization who learns sailing, boating, canoeing, and other water activities

sea ser·pent *n.* **1.** MYTHOL **MYTHICAL CREATURE** a giant creature resembling a snake often reported to have been seen at sea, but never proven to exist **2.** ZOOL = **sea snake** *n.* 1

sea·shell /seé shèl/ *n.* the empty shell of a sea creature, especially a mollusk

sea·shore /seé shàwr/ *n.* **1. LAND LYING NEXT TO SEA** the land lying next to the sea, especially a beach **2.** LAW **LAND BETWEEN TIDEMARKS** the land lying between the usual high and low water marks

sea·sick /seé sìk/ *adj.* nauseated or dizzy as a result of the rocking movement of a vessel on water — **sea·sick·ness** *n.*

sea·side /seé sìd/ *n.* **LAND ALONG SEA** the area of land bordering the sea ■ *adj.* **AT THE SEASIDE** situated or taking place at the seaside ○ *a seaside cottage*

sea·side spar·row *n.* a sparrow that lives along the Atlantic coast of North America. Latin name: *Ammodramus maritimus.*

sea slug *n.* a marine mollusc without gills that resembles a sea snail with no shell and is often brightly colored. Order: Nudibranchia.

sea snail *n.* a small sea creature such as a whelk or perwinkle with a spiral shell resembling that of a snail. Class: Gastropoda.

sea snake *n.* **1. POISONOUS TROPICAL SNAKE** a venomous snake found in tropical seas that swims by means of an oar-shaped tail and bears live young. Family: Hydrophidae. **2.** MYTHOL = **sea serpent** *n.* 1

sea·son /seéz'n/ *n.* **1. TRADITIONAL DIVISION OF YEAR** any one of the periods marked by particular weather conditions into which the year is traditionally divided. In temperate regions, there are four seasons, spring, summer, fall, and winter, while in tropical countries there are often only two, a dry season and a rainy season. **2. PERIOD FOR PARTICULAR ACTIVITY** a time or period of the year during which a particular activity usually takes place in the human world or among plants and animals ○ *planting season* ○ *mating season* **3. PERIOD SET ASIDE FOR ACTIVITY** a fixed period of every year during which particular activities, especially sports, take place or are permitted ○ *baseball season* **4. PLAYER'S OR TEAM'S PERFORMANCE** the performance of a player or team during a sporting season in relation to others ○ *had his best season ever* **5. TIME FOR FOOD** the time of year when something, especially a kind of food, is abundant and at its best ○ *asparagus season* **6.** *U.K.* ARTS **CONNECTED SERIES OF PERFORMANCES** a period of time during which works that are all by or featuring the same person, or are connected by theme or period, are shown or performed **7. HIGH SEASON AT RESORTS** the time of year at which resorts receive most visitors and charge their highest rates **8. SOCIAL SEASON** the time during which the important social events of the year involving members of high society take place (*dated*) **9. TIME AROUND HOLIDAY** the period of time just before, after, and including a holiday ○ *the Christmas season* **10. PERIOD OF TIME** a period of time of unspecified length ○ *a brief season* **11. SUITABLE TIME** a fit or appropriate time for something or to do something (*literary*) ■ *v.* (**-soned, -son·ing, -sons**) **1.** *vti.* ADD FLAVORINGS to add flavorings such as salt, spices, or herbs to food **2.** *vt.* ENLIVEN SOMETHING to liven up something such as a speech or piece of writing by inserting exciting or amusing material ○ *a speech seasoned with wit* **3.** *vti.* DRY OUT BEFORE USE to allow wood to dry out fully before use, or to become fully dried out before being used **4.** *vt.* PREPARE NEW PAN FOR USE to prepare a new frying pan or wok for use by rubbing vegetable oil into the heated cooking surface **5.** *vt.* CAUSE SOMEBODY TO GAIN EXPERIENCE to cause or enable somebody to gain experience and become more skilled, or to gain toughness and strength ○ *seasoned troops* **6.** *vt.* MODERATE SOMETHING to temper something such as a strong emotion (*literary*) [14thC. Via Old French from the Latin stem *sation-* "sowing," from *sat-*, past participle stem of *serere* "to sow."] —**sea·son·er** *n.* ◇ **in season 1.** plentifully available and at a peak of quality ○ *Strawberries are in season now.* **2.** allowed to be hunted, caught, or killed **3.** VET sexually receptive to males **4.** at an appropriate time (*literary*) ◇ **out of season 1.** not widely available or not of good quality because of the time of year ○ *Tulips are out of season at this time of year.* **2.** not allowed to be hunted, caught, or killed because of the time of year **3.** at an inappropriate time (*literary*)

WORD KEY: CULTURAL NOTE

The Four Seasons, a violin concerto by the Italian composer Antonio Vivaldi (1725). Vivaldi's best-known work (Opus 8) consists of four movements, each of which describes a season with appropriate music. The section called "Spring," for example, features birdsong while "Autumn" incorporates sounds that suggest rustling leaves. Vivaldi provided a commentary on each movement in a series of sonnets he wrote to accompany the concerto.

sea·son·a·ble /séez'nəb'l/ *adj.* **1.** TYPICAL OF PARTICULAR SEASON typical of or appropriate for a particular season of the year **2.** OPPORTUNE done, given, or occurring at a time when needed or appropriate —**sea·son·a·ble·ness** *n.* —**sea·son·a·bly** *adv.*

sea·son·al /séezən'l, séeznəl/ *adj.* **1.** DEPENDENT ON SEASON dependent on or determined by the time of year **2.** LIMITED TO PARTICULAR TIMES available or employed only during a particular time or at particular times of the year —**sea·son·al·ly** *adv.* —**sea·son·al·ness** *n.*

sea·son·al af·fec·tive dis·or·der, sea·son·al af·fec·tive dis·or·der syn·drome *n.* a type of depression associated with the onset of winter and thought to be caused by decreasing amounts of daylight

sea·son·ing /séez'ning/ *n.* **1.** FLAVORING salt, pepper, or any herb or spice used to give additional flavor to food **2.** REMOVING MOISTURE FROM LUMBER the process of treating lumber to reduce its moisture sufficiently so that it is suitable for the function for which it will be used

sea·son tick·et, sea·son pass *n.* a ticket or pass valid for a season or specified period of time for use of sport or leisure facilities or attendance at sporting or cultural events

sea spi·der *n.* a sea creature resembling a spider, with a fairly small body and four to six pairs of long jointed legs. Class: Pycnogonida.

sea squill *n.* = **sea onion**

sea squirt *n.* a tiny sea creature that has a transparent sac-shaped body with openings through which water passes in and out. It squirts out a stream of water when disturbed. Class: Ascidiacea.

sea star *n.* = **starfish**

sea swal·low *n.* a tern, especially the common tern. Latin name: *Sterna hirundo.*

seat /seet/ *n.* **1.** PLACE TO SIT something for sitting on, especially something designed for this such as a chair or bench **2.** PART OF CHAIR SAT ON the usually horizontal part of a chair or other seat that takes most of the weight of the person sitting on it **3.** VIEWER'S OR TRAVELER'S SITTING PLACE a place to sit and watch an event or travel in a vehicle, for which a ticket is usually required ○ *We don't really want seats in the front row.* **4.** PART OF GARMENT COVERING BUTTOCKS the part of a garment that covers the buttocks **5.** MEMBERSHIP IN OFFICIAL GROUP a position as a member of an official body or group, especially in an elected legislature ○ *won a seat in the legislature* **6.** BASE a place where something is located or based (*formal*) ○ *the seat of consciousness* **7.** CENTER OF POWER a place from which administrative power is exercised ○ *a county seat* **8.** RESIDENCE a residence, especially a large house associated with a particular family **9.** OBJECT ON WHICH SOMETHING RESTS an object, part, or space on which something such as a part of a machine or device rests or into which it fits **10.** RIDER'S POSITION the position in which a rider sits on a horse ■ *v.* (**seat·ed, seat·ing, seats**) **1.** *vt.* PLACE SOMEBODY IN SEAT to place somebody or yourself in a chair or other seat **2.** *vt.* PROVIDE SEATS FOR PEOPLE to have or provide seats for a specified number of people ○ *The hall seats five hundred.* **3.** *vti.* REST OR FIT SECURELY to rest something securely on or fit something firmly into something else, or to be firmly resting on or fitted into something ○ *The valve isn't seating properly.* **4.** *vt.* INSTALL SOMEBODY IN POWERFUL POSITION to establish somebody in a position of power or authority (*literary*) **5.** *vt.* FIT SEAT ON SOMETHING to put or refurbish a seat in or on something such as a chair or garment [12thC. From Old Icelandic *sæti*; from a prehistoric Germanic word that is also the ancestor of English *sit*.] ◇ **by the seat of your pants 1.** using intuition and guesswork rather than theory or specialized knowledge **2.** without the help of any instruments or technical aids

seat·back /séet bàk/ *n.* the part of a seat against which the back rests

seat belt *n.* a strong strap or harness designed to keep the wearer securely in a seat, especially in a vehicle or aircraft

seat·ing /séeting/ *n.* **1.** SEATS the places provided for people to sit, especially in a public building or a vehicle **2.** ARRANGEMENT OF SEATS OR SITTERS the way in which seats or people sitting are arranged ○ *a seating plan* **3.** ACT OR TIME OF SITTING a time or instance when everyone sits down and an activity such as meal service begins ○ *a restaurant with two seatings for dinner* **4.** SOMETHING OBJECT RESTS ON something on which an object rests or into which it fits **5.** UPHOLSTERING MATERIAL material for upholstering the seat of a chair

seat·mate /séet màyt/ *n.* somebody in an adjacent seat, e.g., on an airplane

SEATO /séetō/ *abbr.* Southeast Asia Treaty Organization

seat-of-the-pants *adj.* relying on intuition and guesswork rather than mechanical aids, rules and procedures, or planning [The expression comes from pilots' cant, presumably because the intuitive understanding of the plane's motions is rumored to be located in that spot]

sea·train /sée tràyn/ *n.* a ship carrying loaded railroad freight cars

sea trout *n.* **1.** N AMERICAN MARINE FISH a North American marine fish of the Atlantic coast that resembles a trout but belongs to the croaker family. Latin name: *Cynoscion regalis.* **2.** EUROPEAN AND N AFRICAN TROUT a large silvery-colored European and North African trout that lives mainly in the sea but returns to fresh water to spawn. Latin name: *Salmo trutta.*

Se·at·tle /see átt'l/ city in west central Washington, between Puget Sound and Lake Washington. The most important city in the Pacific Northwest, it is a major seaport and commerical center. Population: 516,259 (1990).

sea tur·tle *n.* a large turtle with limbs shaped like paddles that is usually found in tropical and subtropical seas. Family: Cheloniidae and Dermochelyidae.

seat·work /séet wùrk/ *n.* tasks to be done by students while sitting at their desks in the classroom

sea ur·chin *n.* a small sea animal with a soft body enclosed in a spiny spherical shell. Class: Echinoidea.

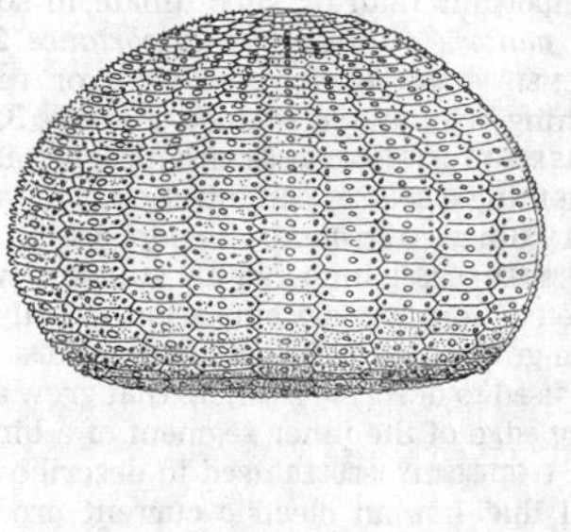

Sea urchin

sea wall *n.* a wall built to prevent flooding or coastal erosion by the sea

sea·ward /séewərd/ *adv.* TOWARD THE SEA in a direction toward the sea ■ *adj.* **1.** SITUATED TOWARD THE SEA situated toward the sea **2.** BLOWING FROM SEA used to describe wind that blows in toward the shore from the sea

sea·ware /sée wàir/ *n.* seaweed collected from the shore and used as fertilizer

sea wasp *n.* a jellyfish that has a cube-shaped body with tentacles hanging from the lower corners. Its sting is very venomous and sometimes fatal. Order: Cubomedusae.

sea·wa·ter /sée wàwtər, -wòttər/ *n.* salt water in or from the sea [Old English]

sea·way /sée wày/ *n.* **1.** INLAND CHANNEL FOR SHIPS an inland canal, passage, or channel large enough for seagoing ships to navigate ○ *the St. Lawrence Seaway* **2.** ROUTE ACROSS SEA a shipping route across a sea **3.** SHIP'S PROGRESS the progress of a ship through the sea **4.** ROUGH SEAS seas that are moderate to rough [Old English]

Seaweed

sea·weed /sée wèed/ *n.* plants such as kelp that grow in the sea

sea whip *n.* a coral that forms long flexible structures with few or no branches and is common on Atlantic reefs

sea·wor·thy /sée wùrthee/ *adj.* suitable or in a fit state to sail safely on the sea —**sea·wor·thi·ness** *n.*

sea wrack *n.* seaweed, especially clumps of the larger varieties, found cast up on shore

se·ba·ceous /sə báyshəss/ *adj.* relating to or producing a waxy yellowish body secretion **(sebum)** [Early 18thC. Formed from Latin *sebaceus*, from *sebum* (see SEBUM).]

se·ba·ceous gland *n.* a gland that secretes sebum into hair follicles to lubricate the hair and skin. Sebaceous glands are found all over the human body except for the palms of the hands and the soles of the feet.

se·bac·ic ac·id /sə bàssik-, -bàysik-/ *n.* a white crystalline acid that is used in the making of some polyester resins, rubbers, and plasticizers. Formula: $COOH(CH_2)_8COOH$. [*Sebacic* formed from SEBACEOUS]

Se·bas·to·pol /sə bástə pol/, **Se·vas·to·pol** city and port on the Black Sea, in the southern Ukraine, on the southern coast of the Crimean Peninsula. Population: 366,200 (1991).

SEbE *abbr.* southeast by east

seb·or·rhe·a /sèbbə rée ə/ *n.* excessively oily skin caused by heavy discharge from the sebaceous glands [Late 19thC. Coined from SEBUM + -RRHEA.] —**seb·or·rhe·al** *adj.* —**seb·or·rhe·ic** *adj.*

seb·or·rhoe·a /sèbbə rée ə/ *n. U.K.* = **seborrhea**

SEbS *abbr.* southeast by south

se·bum /séebəm/ *n.* an oily substance secreted by the sebaceous glands that lubricates the hair and skin and gives some protection against bacteria [Late 19thC. From Latin, "grease, tallow."]

sec[1] /sek/ *n.* a second (*informal*) [Late 19thC. Shortening.]

sec[2] /sek/ *adj.* used to describe a wine, especially champagne, that is dry in taste [Mid-19thC. Via French from Latin *siccus* "dry."]

sec[3] *abbr.* secant

SEC *abbr.* Securities and Exchange Commission

sec. *abbr.* **1.** second **2.** secondary **3.** secretary **4.** section **5.** sector **6.** secundum **7.** security

SECAM /sé̱e kàm/ *n.* a broadcasting system for color television used in France, Russia, and a number of other countries. Full form **séquentiel couleur à mémoire**

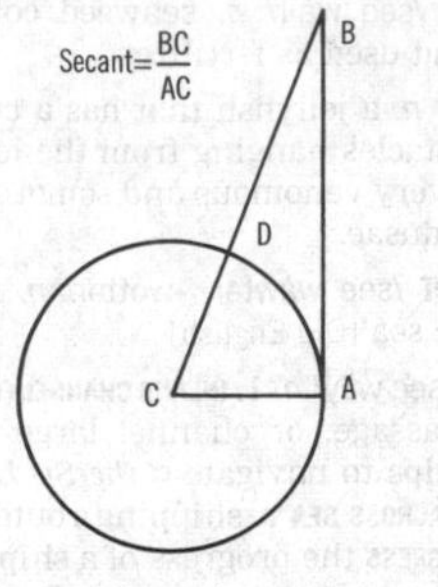

Secant

se·cant /sé̱ekənt/ *n.* GEOM **1.** STRAIGHT LINE CUTTING CURVE a straight line that intersects with a curve in two or more places **2.** TRIGONOMETRIC FUNCTION the ratio of the hypotenuse to the side adjacent to a given angle in a right triangle [Late 16thC. Via French from, ultimately, Latin *secare* (see SECTION).]

sec·co /sékō/ *n.* (*plural* **-cos**) **1.** PAINTING WALL PAINTING TECHNIQUE the technique of wall painting on dry plaster using tempera or pigments ground in limewater **2.** PAINTING PICTURE PAINTED ON WALL a painting on a wall made by the secco method **3.** MUSIC RECITATIVE STYLE a style of vocal recitative in which the natural stress of the words is paramount and, if accompanied at all, is supported only by occasional chords of continuo instruments ■ *adj.* MUSIC **1.** ACCOMPANIED ONLY BY CONTINUO INSTRUMENTS used to refer to vocal recitatives that are unaccompanied or accompanied only by occasional chords of continuo instruments **2.** STACCATO played and released quickly and lacking resonance (*used as a musical direction*) ■ *adv.* MUSIC IN STACCATO MANNER with the notes played and released quickly and without resonance (*used as a musical direction*) [Mid-19thC. Via Italian from Latin *siccus* "dry."]

se·cede /si sé̱ed/ (**-ced·ed, -ced·ing, -cedes**) *vi.* to make a formal withdrawal of membership from an organization, state, or alliance [Early 18thC. From Latin *secedere*, literally "to go apart," from *cedere* (see CEDE).] —**se·ced·er** *n.*

se·cern /si súrn/ (**-cerned, -cern·ing, -cerns**) *vt.* to identify or perceive something as separate (*archaic*) [Early 17thC. From Latin *secernere*, literally "to separate apart," from *cernere* "to separate" (source of English *discern*).] —**se·cern·ment** *n.*

se·ces·sion /si sésh'n/ *n.* a formal withdrawal from an organization, state, or alliance [Mid-16thC. Directly or via French from, ultimately, Latin *secedere* (see SECEDE).] —**se·ces·sion·al** *adj.*

Se·ces·sion *n.* the withdrawal from the Union of 11 Southern States in 1860–61 that led to the formation of the Confederacy and the beginning of the Civil War

Seck·el pear /sék'l-/ *n.* a small sweet North American variety of pear with a reddish skin [Early 19thC. Named for an early grower from Philadelphia.]

se·clude /sə kló͞od/ (**-clud·ed, -clud·ing, -cludes**) *vt.* **1.** ISOLATE SOMEBODY to remove somebody from contact with others **2.** MAKE SOMETHING PRIVATE to make a place private and quiet by screening or isolating it [15thC. From Latin *secludere*, literally "to shut apart," from *claudere* "to shut" (source of English *conclusive* and *recluse*).]

se·clud·ed /sə kló͞odəd/ *adj.* **1.** PRIVATE AND QUIET cut off from other places and therefore private and quiet **2.** HAVING LITTLE CONTACT having or involving little or no contact with others —**se·clud·ed·ly** *adv.* —**se·clud·ed·ness** *n.*

se·clu·sion /sə kló͞ozh'n/ *n.* **1.** CONDITION OF BEING SECLUDED the condition of being cut off from others, or from other places **2.** ACT OF SECLUDING an act of setting somebody or something apart from others **3.** SECLUDED PLACE a quiet place removed from activity and people [Early 17thC. From Latin *seclusion-*, from *secludere* (see SECLUDE).]

se·clu·sive /sə kló͞ossiv/ *adj.* disposed to be solitary (*literary*) [Mid-19thC. Formed from SECLUDE, on the model of INCLUSIVE.] —**se·clu·sive·ly** *adv.* —**se·clu·sive·ness** *n.*

sec·o·bar·bi·tal /sèkō baárbə tòl/ *n.* a barbiturate that in its form as a sodium salt is used as a sedative. Formula: $C_{12}H_{18}N_2O_3$. [Mid-20thC. Contraction of SECONDARY + BARBITAL.]

Sec·o·nal /sékə nàl, sékən'l/ *tdmk.* a trademark for a barbiturate sedative made from secobarbital

sec·ond[1] /sékənd/ *adj.* **1.** COMING AFTER FIRST coming after the first in a series **2.** ANOTHER additional to, repeating, or following one that came before or was previously mentioned ○ *I need a second look at those figures.* **3.** ADDITIONAL AND LESS IMPORTANT additional to and less important than the first or main one ○ *a second home* **4.** SIMILAR TO PREDECESSOR similar or comparable in many respects to a particular renowned personality or event ○ *a second Watergate* **5.** INFERIOR TO inferior to or less important than somebody or something else ○ *second only to the president* **6.** MUSIC PERFORMING LOWER OR LESS IMPORTANT PART singing or playing a lower or less important part ■ *n.* **1.** SECOND MEMBER OF SERIES the second member or item in a series **2.** ANOTHER PERSON OR THING another person or thing of the same kind as one previously mentioned **3.** COMPETITOR'S OR DUELIST'S ASSISTANT an official assistant to a contestant in a boxing match or a duel **4.** SECONDER a seconder for a proposal, a motion, or nomination in a debate **5.** ARTICLE WITH FAULT an imperfectly manufactured article that is sold at a discount **6.** TRANSP FORWARD GEAR a forward gear of a transmission that is higher than first gear and lower than third gear **7.** BASEBALL = **second base** *n.* 1 **8.** MUSIC INTERVAL OF TWO NOTES in a standard musical scale, the interval between one note and another that lies one note above or below it. In the scale of C major, C and D form a second. **9.** MUSIC NOTE A SECOND AWAY FROM ANOTHER in a standard musical scale, a note that is a second away from another note **10.** BALLET = **second position** ■ **sec·onds** *npl.* FOOD ANOTHER HELPING OR SERVING another helping or serving of a dish or type of food (*informal*) ■ *vt.* (**-ond·ed, -ond·ing, -onds**) **1.** ACT AS SECONDER OF SOMETHING to state support officially for a proposal, motion, or nomination introduced by somebody else, so that discussion or voting can take place **2.** EXPRESS AGREEMENT AND SUPPORT FOR SOMETHING to express agreement and support for something that somebody has just said (*informal*) ○ *I second that.* **3.** ACT AS COMPETITOR'S OR DUELIST'S SECOND to act as second to a contestant in a boxing match or duel **4.** ASSIST OR SUPPORT to assist or support somebody or something (*formal*) ○ *seconded her efforts* ■ *adv.* **1.** EXCEPT FOR ONE the one that exceeds all the rest, except for one, in a particular way (*used to qualify a superlative*) ○ *the second highest mountain in the world* **2.** = **secondly** [14thC. Directly or via Old French from Latin *secundus* "the following, second," from *sequi* "to follow" (source of English *consequence* and *sequential*).] ◇ **second to none** better than anyone or anything else

sec·ond[2] /sékənd/ *n.* **1.** 60TH OF MINUTE a unit of time that is equal to one sixtieth of a minute. Symbol **s** **2.** MEASURE UNIT OF MEASUREMENT OF ANGLES a unit of measurement of angles equal to one sixtieth of a minute or one 360th of a degree. Symbol **s** **3.** VERY SHORT TIME a very short period of time [14thC. Via French from medieval Latin *secunda* (see SECOND[1]), from *secunda pars minuta*, literally, "second diminished part." The word denotes the second division of an hour by sixty.]

se·cond[3] /sə kónd/ (**-cond·ed, -cond·ing, -conds**) *vt.* *U.K.* to transfer an employee, official, or soldier temporarily to other duties [Early 19thC. From French *en second* "in the second rank."] —**se·cond·ment** *n.*

Sec·ond Ad·vent *n.* = **Second Coming**

sec·ond·ar·y /sékən dèrree/ *adj.* **1.** NOT PRIMARY OR MAJOR less important than or subordinate to something else ○ *matters of secondary importance* **2.** DERIVED FROM SOMETHING ORIGINAL derived from or reliant on something original ○ *a secondary source* **3.** MED HAPPENING AS RESULT OF PRIMARY DISORDER happening as a result of something else, e.g. , an infection starting after a primary illness ○ *secondary tumors* **4.** EDUC OCCURRING AFTER PRIMARY SCHOOL intended for students who have completed their primary education, usually for children in grades 7 to 12 **5.** BIRDS GROWING ALONG INNER EDGE OF WING used to describe feathers that grow along the trailing edge of the inner segment of a bird's wing **6.** ELEC ELECTRICALLY INDUCED used to describe a circuit or coil that has an electric current produced by induction **7.** INDUST INVOLVED IN MANUFACTURING involved in the manufacture of goods from raw materials **8.** CHEM ORGANIC CARBON COMPOUND used to describe an organic compound having a carbon atom to which three organic groups of atoms are attached, at least one of which is chemically active **9.** CHEM RELATING TO ORGANIC NITROGEN COMPOUND used to describe an amine having two organic groups of atoms and one hydrogen atom attached to a nitrogen atom **10.** BOT OF RAPIDLY DIVIDING TISSUE relating to or derived from rapidly dividing tissue (**cambium**) that gives rise to increased girth, not increased length ■ *n.* (*plural* **-ies**) **1.** SOMEBODY OR SOMETHING SECONDARY somebody or something that is secondary or subordinate **2.** MED SECONDARY TUMOR a cancerous growth at a site remote from that of the original malignant tumor **3.** BIRDS SECONDARY FEATHER a secondary feather **4.** ELEC INDUCED COIL OR CIRCUIT a coil or circuit in which an induced current flows [14thC. Formed from SECOND[1].] —**sec·ond·ar·i·ly** /sèkən dáirrəlee/ *adv.* —**sec·ond·ar·i·ness** *n.*

sec·ond·ar·y ac·cent *n.* **1.** WEAKER STRESS ON SYLLABLE an accentuation on a syllable that is weaker than that on the syllable receiving the main accent. For example, in the word "secondary," the main accent falls on the first syllable and the secondary accent on the third. **2.** STRESS MARK a mark used to indicate where the secondary accent is placed

sec·ond·ar·y bat·ter·y *n.* = **storage battery**

sec·ond·ar·y boy·cott *n.* a strike or boycott against a company that is a supplier or customer of a company involved in a labor dispute

sec·ond·ar·y cell *n.* an electric cell in which electricity is produced by a reversible chemical reaction. It is therefore rechargeable and able to store electrical energy.

sec·ond·ar·y col·or *n.* a color such as orange, green, or purple produced by mixing two primary colors in roughly equal quantities

sec·ond·ar·y e·lec·tron *n.* an electron released by secondary emission

sec·ond·ar·y e·mis·sion *n.* the emission of electrons from the surface of a substance bombarded with electrons or ions

sec·ond·ar·y in·fec·tion *n.* an infection that is acquired during the course of a separate initial infection

sec·ond·ar·y of·fer·ing *n.* the sale of securities to dealers outside the stock exchange

sec·ond·ar·y school *n.* a school for students who have completed their primary education, usually attended by children in grades 7 to 12

sec·ond·ar·y sex·u·al char·ac·ter·is·tic *n.* a characteristic that develops at puberty but is not directly concerned with reproduction, e.g., a woman's breasts or a man's facial hair

sec·ond·ar·y stress *n.* = **secondary accent**

sec·ond·ar·y syph·i·lis *n.* the second, highly infectious stage of syphilis that appears several weeks or months after primary infection and is marked by a faint skin rash, fever, and muscular pain

sec·ond bal·lot *n.* a second round of voting in an election in which no candidate obtained a winning majority in the first round. In a second ballot, the candidates who received the fewest votes in the first round are usually left out.

sec·ond ba·nan·a *n.* (*slang*) **1.** ASSISTANT OR SUBORDINATE somebody who plays a less prominent role or acts as an assistant or subordinate to somebody else **2.** COMEDIAN'S STOOGE somebody who plays the straight man or stooge to a comedian in burlesque or vaudeville

sec·ond base *n.* **1.** BASE DIRECTLY OPPOSITE HOME PLATE the base opposite home plate in the baseball diamond, or the position of the infielder playing nearest to second base on the first base side **2.** = **second baseman**

sec·ond base·man *n.* in baseball, the player positioned closest to second base, on the first-base side of it

sec·ond best *adj.* (*hyphenated when used before a noun*) **1.** NEXT IN QUALITY TO BEST next in quality to, or surpassed only by, the best **2.** INFERIOR TO BEST inferior to the best or the favorite ○ *had to make do with a second-best alternative* ■ *n.* **1.** SOMEBODY OR SOMETHING NEXT TO BEST somebody or something that is next in quality to, or surpassed only by, the best **2.** SOMEBODY

OR SOMETHING INFERIOR TO BEST somebody or something inferior to the best or the favorite

sec·ond child·hood *n.* a condition associated with aging that manifests itself in behavior regarded as resembling that of a child (*offensive*)

sec·ond class *n.* **1. CATEGORY AFTER BEST** the category or standard of something, especially of accommodation or travel, that comes immediately below the best **2. MAIL SERVICE** a mail delivery service for newspapers and periodicals ■ *adj.* (*hyphenated when used before a noun*) **1. BELONGING TO SECOND CLASS** belonging to or meeting the standards of second class, especially regarding mail service or travel accommodations ○ *second-class accommodations* **2. INFERIOR** inferior to, or less important than somebody or something else ■ *adv.* **sec·ond-class BY SECOND-CLASS MEANS OF TRAVEL** by second-class mail delivery service or travel accommodations ○ *traveled second-class*

sec·ond-class cit·i·zen *n.* somebody who does not have or is perceived not to have the same rights, privileges, or opportunities as a full citizen

Sec·ond Com·ing *n.* in Christian belief, the anticipated and prophesied return of Jesus Christ to judge humanity at the end of the world

sec·ond cous·in *n.* a child of a first cousin of either of your parents

sec·ond-de·gree burn *n.* a burn that causes blistering on the skin, but does not damage the deeper layers of the skin or require grafting

se·conde /sə kónd/ *n.* the second of the eight classic parrying positions in fencing [Early 18thC. From French, a form of *second* (see SECOND[1]).]

Sec·ond Em·pire *n.* **1.** HIST **REIGN OF NAPOLEON III** the reign or the government of the Emperor Napoleon III of France, lasting from 1852 until 1870 **2.** ARTS **STYLE OF SECOND EMPIRE** the weighty, grandiose, and highly ornamented style of architecture, furnishing, and decoration typical of the Second Empire

se·con·der /sékəndər/ *n.* somebody who officially states support for a proposal, motion, or nomination introduced by somebody else, so that discussion or voting can take place

sec·ond es·tate *n.* the nobility, as one of the three broad traditional classes of people within a monarchical state

sec·ond fid·dle *n.* a less important or less prominent role or somebody or something in such a role

sec·ond floor *n.* (*hyphenated when used before a noun*) **1. NEXT FLOOR ABOVE GROUND LEVEL** the floor of a building immediately above the floor at ground level **2.** *U.K.* = **third floor**

sec·ond gen·er·a·tion *n.* **1. CHILDREN OF IMMIGRANTS** the children of immigrants to a particular country **2. LATER STAGE OF DEVELOPMENT** a later stage in the development of something that benefits from what was learned from the first stage of development —**sec·ond-gen·er·a·tion** *adj.*

sec·ond growth *n.* the trees and plants that grow back naturally in an area of forest after the original trees have been removed by cutting or fire

sec·ond-guess (**sec·ond-guessed, sec·ond-guess·ing, sec·ond-guess·es**) *vti.* **1. CRITICIZE AFTER THE EVENT** to criticize, assess, or correct somebody or something after an event is over and the outcome is known **2. MAKE A PREDICTION** to predict a course of events, outcome, or what someone will do, from a position of relative ignorance ○ *no point in trying to second-guess what they'll do* —**sec·ond-guess·er** *n.*

sec·ond hand *n.* the hand of a clock or watch that shows time passing second by second and rotates once around the dial in the space of a minute

sec·ond·hand /sèkənd hánd/ *adj.* **1. PREVIOUSLY OWNED** previously owned or used **2. SELLING USED GOODS** selling or dealing in used goods **3. NOT ORIGINAL** received from or reliant on somebody or something other than the original source ○ *secondhand accounts of the incident* ■ *adv.* **1. IN USED CONDITION** after being owned or used by somebody else ○ *bought it secondhand* **2. THROUGH INTERMEDIARY** from or through somebody or something else and not by direct experience or personal effort ○ *acquires the information secondhand* ◇ **at secondhand, at second hand** from or through somebody or something else

sec·ond·hand smoke *n.* tobacco smoke unintentionally inhaled by people who do not smoke

se·con·di plural of **secondo**

sec·ond-in-com·mand *n.* somebody who is in charge in the absence of the person usually in charge

Sec·ond In·ter·na·tion·al *n.* an international socialist association established in 1889 in Paris and lasting until World War I

sec·ond lan·guage *n.* (*hyphenated when used before a noun*) **1. LANGUAGE LEARNED AFTER FIRST LANGUAGE** a language learned by somebody after the first language he or she learns at home **2. LANGUAGE OF SECONDARY IMPORTANCE** a language in widespread use in a country that sometimes has official status after the main language of the country

sec·ond lieu·ten·ant *n.* **1. OFFICER OF LOWEST COMMISSIONED RANK** an officer of the lowest commissioned rank in various military forces such as the U.S. and British armies, the U.S. Marine Corps and Air Force, or the British Royal Marines **2. LOWEST COMMISSIONED RANK** the lowest commissioned rank in various military forces, e.g. , the U.S. and British armies, the U.S. Marine Corps and Air Force, or the British Royal Marines

sec·ond·ly /sékəndlee/ *adv.* used to introduce the second point in an argument or discussion

sec·ond mate *n.* the officer on a merchant ship next in the line of command after the first mate, usually the third-highest-ranking officer on board

sec·ond mort·gage *n.* an additional mortgage on a property that has been mortgaged once already and secondary to the main lien for settlement

sec·ond na·ture *n.* a habit or tendency so well-developed and long-practiced that it seems to be done unconsciously

se·con·do /si kóndō/ (*plural* **-di** /-dee/) *n.* the second or lower part in a piece of music for two players, especially a piano duet [Late 18thC. From Italian, "second."]

sec·ond o·pin·ion *n.* an opinion, especially one of a professional nature, from somebody other than the usual or first person consulted

sec·ond per·son *n.* **1. GRAMMATICAL CLASS OF VERB OR PRONOUN** the grammatical class of a verb or pronoun used when addressing somebody **2. ADDRESSING FORM OF VERB OR PRONOUN** a form of a pronoun or verb in the second person, e.g., "you" or "are"

sec·ond po·si·tion *n.* a position in ballet in which the feet are turned outward with the feet slightly apart

sec·ond-rate *adj.* inadequate in quality or performance ○ *a second-rate pianist* —**sec·ond-rat·er** *n.*

sec·ond read·ing *n.* the second presentation of a bill to a legislature as part of the process of turning the bill into law. In the U.S. Congress, it follows the committee stage and precedes a full debate and opportunity for amendment.

Sec·ond Re·pub·lic *n.* the period of the Republican government in France from 1848 to 1852

sec·ond sight *n.* the supposed ability to see things that the physical eye cannot see, especially events taking place in the future or elsewhere —**sec·ond-sight·ed·ness** *n.*

sec·ond-strike *adj.* relating to, involving, or intended for use in, a retaliatory nuclear attack with weapons designed to survive a first nuclear strike by an enemy ○ *second-strike capabilities*

sec·ond string *n.* a substitute or reserve group of team members —**sec·ond-string** *adj.* —**sec·ond-string·er** *n.*

sec·ond thought *n.* a reconsideration of something tentatively decided, e.g., in light of new developments or something not previously taken into account (*often used in the plural*) ○ *having second thoughts about getting married* ◇ **on second thought** after reconsideration

sec·ond u·nit *n.* CINEMA a smaller secondary crew that films locations or crowd scenes in which the main actors do not appear or for which the major production personnel are not required

sec·ond wind *n.* a renewal of energy following a period of effort and exertion

Sec·ond World War *n.* = **World War II**

Se·cord /sék awrd, seék-/, **Laura** (1775–1868) Massachusetts-born Canadian patriot. She became a hero in British Canada during the War of 1812 when she walked a substantial distance to warn the British after overhearing plans for a U.S. attack. Born **Laura Ingersoll**

se·cre·cy /seékrəssee/ *n.* **1. STATE OF CONCEALMENT** the state of being concealed or secret ○ *talks held in secrecy* **2. KEEPING OF SECRETS** the keeping of a secret or secrets ○ *sworn to secrecy* **3. SECRETIVENESS** a tendency to keep things secret [Late 16thC. Formed from SECRET.]

se·cret /seékrət/ *adj.* **1. NOT WIDELY KNOWN** known by only a few people and intentionally withheld from general knowledge **2. UNDERCOVER** working or operating without the knowledge of the general public **3. UNADMITTED** acting or feeling in a particular way without admitting to it ○ *a secret admirer* **4. PRIVATE AND SECLUDED** known to very few people and consequently quiet and secluded **5. SECRETIVE** tending by nature to keep things secret (*informal*) **6. MYSTERIOUS** mysterious and often beyond common understanding ■ *n.* **1. INFORMATION NOT WIDELY KNOWN** a piece of information that is known only to a few people and is intentionally withheld from general knowledge **2. MYSTERY** something that is unknown, hidden, or not understood **3. SOMETHING ENSURING SUCCESS** a little-known technique, approach, or piece of information that is the key to success in a particular endeavor [14thC. Via French from Latin *secretus* "separate, hidden," from *secernere* (see SECERN).] —**se·cret·ly** *adv.* ◇ **in secret** without anyone else's knowledge ○ *meet in secret*

WORD KEY: SYNONYMS

secret, clandestine, covert, furtive, stealthy, surreptitious

CORE MEANING: conveying a desire or need for concealment

secret a general word describing actions or events that are or should be concealed. It can also describe things, places, and information; **clandestine** describes something such as a meeting between two people that is illicit, unauthorized, or unacceptable, and therefore must be concealed; **covert** a formal word used to describe something that is done secretly, especially in order to emphasize a lack of honesty or openness; **furtive** the cautious nervous behavior of a guilty person trying to avoid attention; **stealthy** describes behavior that is quiet and slow in order to avoid notice, especially when this behavior is associated with wrongdoing; **surreptitious** describes something forbidden or unacceptable done at an opportune moment.

Se·cret /seékrət/, **se·cret** *n.* a variable prayer said at the conclusion of the Offertory and before the Preface in the Roman Catholic Mass [From ecclesiastical Latin *secreta oratio*, literally, "concealed speech," from the low voice used]

se·cret a·gent *n.* somebody engaged in espionage for a government or organization

se·cre·ta·gogue /sə kreétə gàwg, -gòg/ *n.* a substance such as a hormone that causes or stimulates secretion [Early 20thC. Coined from SECRETE + Greek *agōgos* "leading, eliciting," from *agein* "to lead."] —**se·cre·ta·gog·ic** /sə kreétə gójjik/ *adj.*

se·cré·taire /sèkrə táir/ *n.* FURNITURE = **secretary** [Late 18thC. Via French from late Latin *secretarius* (see SECRETARY).]

sec·re·tar·i·at /sèkrə térree ət/ *n.* **1. ADMINISTRATIVE DEPARTMENT** a department that carries out the administrative and clerical work of an organization or legislature **2. SECRETARIAL STAFF** the secretarial staff under the direction of a secretary-general **3. BUILDING HOUSING SECRETARIAT** the headquarters or offices of a secretariat [Early 19thC. Via French from medieval Latin *secretariatus*, from late Latin *secretarius* (see SECRETARY).]

sec·re·tar·y /sékri tèrree/ (*plural* **-ies**) *n.* **1. CLERICAL WORKER** somebody who does general clerical and administrative work such as word-processing, filing, and arranging appointments for an individual or an organization **2. OFFICER OF CLUB, SOCIETY, OR COMMITTEE** somebody elected or appointed to keep the records of the meetings of an organization such as a club, society, or committee, and to write or answer letters on its behalf **3.** = **company secretary** **4. Sec·re·tar·y, sec·re·tar·y** POL **CABINET MEMBER** a cabinet-level official of a national government **5.** *U.K.* = **secretary of state** **6.** *U.K.* **CIVIL SERVANT ASSISTING GOVERNMENT MINISTER** a senior civil servant who advises a government minister **7.** FURNITURE **CABINET INCORPORATING WRITING DESK** a large cabinet with a fold-down desktop, usually with drawers below and an enclosed bookcase above [14thC. From late Latin *secretarius* "confidential officer," from, ultimately, *secretus* (see SECRET).] —**sec·re·tar·i·al** /sèkrə térree əl/ *adj.* —**sec·re·tary·ship** *n.*

Secretary bird

sec·re·tar·y bird *n.* a large long-legged African bird of prey that feeds mainly on snakes. It has gray-and-black plumage and a crest projecting from the back of its head. Latin name: *Sagittarius serpentarius.* [*Secretary* from the supposed resemblance of the bird's crest to quill pens stuck behind a secretary's ear]

sec·re·tar·y-gen·er·al (*plural* **sec·re·tar·ies-gen·er·al**) *n.* the chief executive officer of an organizations such as the United Nations, who oversees a secretariat

sec·re·tar·y of state *n.* **1.** STATE OFFICIAL a state government official with administrative responsibilities that vary from state to state **2.** BRITISH GOVERNMENT OFFICIAL a member of the British government and cabinet who is in charge of a major department such as Education or Defense

Sec·re·tary of State *n.* the U.S. government official and cabinet member who is in charge of foreign affairs

se·crete[1] /sə kréet/ (**-cret·ed, -cret·ing, -cretes**) *vti.* to produce and discharge a secretion [Early 18thC. From Latin *secret-*, the past participle stem of *secernere* (see SECERN).] —**se·cret·or** *n.*

se·crete[2] /sə kréet/ (**-cret·ed, -cret·ing, -cretes**) *vt.* **1.** HIDE SOMETHING to conceal somebody or something **2.** REMOVE SOMETHING SECRETLY to remove or steal something secretly or without being observed (*archaic*) [Mid-18thC. Alteration (on the model of Latin *secretus* "hidden") of obsolete *secret* "to hide," from SECRET.] —**se·cre·tion** *n.*

se·cre·tin /sə kréet'n/ *n.* a hormone secreted in the duodenum that stimulates the pancreas and the bowel to produce digestive enzymes and the liver to produce bile [Early 20thC. Formed from SECRETION.]

se·cre·tion /sə kréesh'n/ *n.* **1.** PROCESS OF SECRETING the process of producing a substance from the cells and fluids within a gland or organ and discharging it **2.** SECRETED SUBSTANCE a substance formed and discharged by a cell, tissue, gland, or organ [Mid-17thC. Via French from, ultimately, Latin *secernere* (see SECERN).] —**se·cre·tion·ar·y** *adj.*

se·cre·tive /séekrətiv/ *adj.* tending to keep information secret —**se·cre·tive·ly** *adv.* —**se·cre·tive·ness** *n.*

se·cre·to·ry /sə kréetəree/ *adj.* involved in, producing, or produced by secretion [Late 17thC. Formed from SECRETE[1].]

se·cret part·ner *n.* a partner whose involvement in a business is kept secret

se·cret po·lice *npl.* a police force that operates in secret and whose function is to prevent subversion or suppress political opposition to a regime

se·cret serv·ice *n.* a government department that carries out secret investigations and covert operations

Se·cret Ser·vice *n.* a branch of the U.S. Treasury Department whose main function is the protection of the president and vice president and their families

se·cret so·ci·e·ty *n.* an organization that requires its members to keep all or some of its activities secret from nonmembers

sect /sekt/ *n.* **1.** RELIG NONMAINSTREAM RELIGIOUS GROUP a religious group with beliefs and practices at variance with those of a more established main group **2.** RELIG RELIGIOUS DENOMINATION a denomination of a larger religious group **3.** SOC SCI CLOSE-KNIT GROUP a small close-knit group with strongly held views that are sometimes regarded as extreme by the majority [14thC. Directly or via French from Latin *secta* "school of thought," originally "way, road," from *sequi* "to follow" (source of English *sequence* and *second*).]

sect. *abbr.* **1.** section **2.** sectional

-sect *suffix.* **1.** to cut or divide ○ *quadrisect* **2.** cut, divided ○ *pinnatisect* [From Latin *sectus*, the past participle of *secare* "to cut" (see SECTION)]

sec·tar·i·an /sek térree ən/ *adj.* **1.** RELIG OF RELIGIOUS GROUP relating to or involving relations between religious groups or denominations **2.** RELIG OF SINGLE RELIGIOUS GROUP relating to, involved with, or devoted to a particular religious group or denomination **3.** DOGMATIC AND INTOLERANT rigidly adhering to a particular set of doctrines and intolerant of other views ■ *n.* **1.** MEMBER OF RELIGIOUS GROUP a member of a religious group or denomination **2.** SOMEBODY DOGMATIC AND INTOLERANT somebody who rigidly adheres to a particular set of doctrines and is intolerant of other views —**sec·tar·i·an·ism** *n.*

sec·tar·i·an·ize /sek térree ə nīz/ (**-ized, -iz·ing, -iz·es**) *vt.* to cause somebody or something to become sectarian

sec·ta·ry /séktəree/ (*plural* **-ries**) *n.* a member of a religious group or denomination (*archaic*)

sec·tile /sékt'l/ *adj.* used to describe minerals that can be cut so as to leave a smooth surface [Early 18thC. From Latin *sectilis*, from the stem *sect-* (see SECTION).] —**sec·til·i·ty** /sek tíllətee/ *n.*

sec·tion /séksh'n/ *n.* **1.** DISTINCT PART a distinct part that can be separated or considered separately from the whole of something **2.** UNIT OF PEOPLE a group of people forming a unit within a larger group, e.g., a subdivision of a military unit, or the musicians playing a particular kind of instrument in an orchestra **3.** SUBDIVISION OF DOCUMENT a major subdivision of a written work such as a book or newspaper, or of an official or legal document, often numbered **4.** GEOG FUNCTIONAL AREA an area of a country, county, city, or town, usually characterized by the type of activity mainly carried on there ○ *a residential section of the city* **5.** AREA OF ONE SQUARE MILE an area of land, for purposes of land surveying, equal to one square mile, 2.59 square kilometers, or one thirty-sixth of a township **6.** VIEW OF SOMETHING CUT THROUGH a view or representation of something cut through to show its internal structure or workings **7.** SCI VERY THIN SLICE a very thin slice of something removed for examination under a microscope ○ *a tissue section* **8.** SURG SURGICAL CUT a surgical incision **9.** RAIL LENGTH OF RAIL TRACK a length of railroad track maintained by a single crew **10.** BOT SEGMENT OF CITRUS FRUIT a segment of an orange, grapefruit, or other citrus fruit **11.** PRINTING = **section mark** ■ *vt.* (**-tioned, -tion·ing, -tions**) **1.** DIVIDE SOMETHING to divide something up into separate parts **2.** CUT SOMETHING SURGICALLY to make a surgical incision in something [14thC. Directly or via French from the Latin stem *section-*, from *sect-*, past participle stem of *secare* "to cut."]

WORD KEY: ORIGIN

The Latin word *secare*, from which ***section*** is derived, is also the source of English *bisect, dissect, insect, intersect, secateurs, sector,* and *segment.*

sec·tion·al /sékshən'l/ *adj.* **1.** SECTION OF relating to a particular group or section **2.** INVOLVING DIFFERENT SECTIONS involving different groups or sections **3.** CONSISTING OF SECTIONS divided into or made up of sections ■ *n.* FURNITURE IN PARTS a piece of furniture made up of coordinated sections that can be used together or apart —**sec·tion·al·ly** *adv.*

sec·tion·al·ism /sékshn'lìzzəm/ *n.* excessive concern for the interests of a particular group or area to the detriment of the whole —**sec·tion·al·ist** *n., adj.*

sec·tion·al·ize /sékshən'l īz/ (**-ized, -iz·ing, -iz·es**) *vt.* to divide something, especially a geographic area, into sections —**sec·tion·al·i·za·tion** /sèkshən'lə záysh'n/ *n.*

Sec·tion Eight *n.* **1.** MILITARY DISCHARGE a discharge from military service on physical or psychological grounds **2.** DISCHARGED SOLDIER a soldier discharged under Section Eight regulations

sec·tion gang *n.* a gang of railroad workers responsible for maintaining a particular section of track

sec·tion hand *n.* a worker on a section gang

sec·tion mark *n.* a symbol (§) sometimes used in printing to mark the beginning of a section of a book or one of a series of footnotes, and for various other purposes

sec·tor /séktər/ *n.* **1.** COMPONENT PART a component of an integrated system such as an economy or a society **2.** MIL PART OF AREA OF MILITARY OPERATIONS a part of an area where military forces are operating or in control **3.** GEOM PART OF CIRCLE a part of a circle bounded by two radii and the part of the circumference that lies between them **4.** MEASURING INSTRUMENT a measuring instrument consisting of two arms marked with graduations, hinged together at one end **5.** COMPUT UNIT OF MAGNETIC STORAGE DEVICE the smallest addressable unit of a magnetic storage device ■ *vt.* (**-tored, -tor·ing, -tors**) DIVIDE SOMETHING to divide something into sectors [Late 16thC. From late Latin, "section of a circle," originally "cutter," from the stem *sect-* (see SECTION).] —**sec·tor·al** *adj.*

sec·to·ri·al /sek táwree əl/ *adj.* **1.** OF SECTOR relating to a sector or consisting of sectors **2.** ZOOL USED FOR CUTTING adapted or specialized for cutting ○ *sectorial teeth*

sec·u·lar /sékyələr/ *adj.* **1.** NOT CONCERNED WITH RELIGION not controlled by a religious body or concerned with religious or spiritual matters **2.** NOT RELIGIOUS not religious or spiritual in nature ○ *secular music* **3.** NOT MONASTIC not belonging to a monastic order **4.** OCCURRING ONCE A CENTURY occurring only once in the course of an age or century **5.** OCCURRING OVER LONG PERIOD taking place over an extremely or indefinitely long period of time ■ *n.* **1.** MEMBER OF SECULAR CLERGY a member of the secular clergy **2.** LAYPERSON a member of the laity [14thC. Formed from Old French *seculer*, from Latin *saecularis*, from *saeculum* "world, generation, age."] —**sec·u·lar·i·ty** /sèkyə lérrətee/ *n.* —**sec·u·lar·ly** *adv.*

sec·u·lar hu·man·ism *n.* a philosophy or world view that stresses human values without reference to religion or spirituality

sec·u·lar·ism /sékyələ rìzzəm/ *n.* **1.** EXCLUSION OF RELIGION FROM PUBLIC AFFAIRS the belief that religion and religious bodies should have no part in political or civic affairs or in running public institutions, especially schools **2.** REJECTION OF RELIGION the rejection of religion or its exclusion from a philosophical or moral system —**sec·u·lar·ist** *n.* —**sec·u·lar·is·tic** /sèkyələ rístik/ *adj.*

sec·u·lar·ize /sékyələ rīz/ (**-ized, -iz·ing, -iz·es**) *vt.* **1.** TRANSFER SOMETHING TO CIVIL USE to transfer something from a religious to a nonreligious use, or from control by a religious body to control by the state or a lay body or person **2.** MAKE SOMETHING SECULAR to remove the religious dimension or element from something, or otherwise make it secular —**sec·u·lar·i·za·tion** /sèkyələrə záysh'n/ *n.* —**sec·u·lar·iz·er** *n.*

se·cund /sée kùnd, sé-, sə kúnd/ *adj.* arranged on or curving toward only one side of an axis [Late 18thC. From Latin *secundus* (see SECOND).] —**se·cund·ly** *adv.*

se·cure /sə kyóor/ *adj.* **1.** NOT WORRIED untroubled by feelings of fear, doubt, or vulnerability **2.** FIRMLY FIXED firmly fixed or placed in position and unlikely to come loose or give way ○ *made the rope secure* **3.** RELIABLE reliable and unlikely to fail or be lost ○ *a secure investment* **4.** WELL GUARDED AND FORTIFIED well guarded and strongly fortified or protected **5.** SAFE safe, especially against attack or theft **6.** SAFE FOR SECRET COMMUNICATIONS safe to use for secret or confidential communication ○ *a secure line* **7.** ASSURED certain to be achieved or gained ○ *Just when victory seemed secure, we let it slip from our grasp.* ■ *v.* (**-cured, -cur·ing, -cures**) **1.** *vt.* FIX SOMETHING FIRMLY to fix something firmly in position **2.** *vti.* MAKE SOMETHING SAFE to make a building or area safe to occupy, usually by ensuring that all internal sources of danger are removed or that it is defended against attack **3.** *vt.* ACQUIRE SOMETHING to obtain something, especially after using considerable effort to persuade somebody to grant or allow it ○ *secure an agreement* **4.** *vt.* FIN ENSURE PAYMENT FOR SOMETHING to provide security for something or otherwise guarantee payment ○ *a loan secured against your house* **5.** *vti.* GUARANTEE to guarantee or ensure something **6.** *vt.* PREVENT SOMEBODY FROM ESCAPING to ensure that somebody cannot escape ○ *secure a prisoner* **7.** *vt.* MAKE SOMETHING SAFE FOR SECRET COMMUNICATIONS to ensure that a means of communication can be safely used for secret or confidential messages ○ *secure a telephone line* **8.** *vt.* MAKE THINGS SAFE ON BOARD to make sure that everything on board a ship is safely stowed and that openings are covered ○ *secure a ship* ○ *secure the cargo* [Mid-16thC. From Latin *securus*, literally "without care," from *cura* "care" (source of English *cure*).] —**se·cur·a·ble** *adj.* —**se·cure·ly** *adv.* —**se·cure·ment** *n.* —**se·cure·ness** *n.* —**se·cur·er** *n.*

WORD KEY: SYNONYMS

See Synonyms at ***get***.

Se·cu·ri·ties and Ex·change Com·mis·sion *n.* an agency of the U.S. government set up to regulate transactions in securities and protect investors against malpractice

se·cu·ri·ti·za·tion /sə kyŏorətə záysh'n/ *n.* the preparation of readily marketable securities representing an ownership interest in some asset such as credit card loans or timberland that is not otherwise conveniently traded

se·cu·ri·ty /sə kyŏorətee/ (*plural* **-ties**) *n.* **1.** STATE OR FEELING OF SAFETY the state or feeling of being safe and protected **2.** FREEDOM FROM WORRY ABOUT POSSIBLE LOSS the assurance that something of value will not be taken away **3.** SOMETHING GIVING ASSURANCE something that provides a sense of protection against loss, attack, or harm **4.** SAFETY protection against attack from without or subversion from within ○ *a matter of national security* **5.** PRECAUTIONS TO MAINTAIN SAFETY precautions taken to keep somebody or something safe from crime, attack, or danger ○ *security measures* **6.** GUARDS people or an organization entrusted with the job of protecting somebody or something, especially a building or institution, against crime **7.** ASSET DEPOSITED TO GUARANTEE REPAYMENT something pledged to guarantee fulfillment of an obligation, especially an asset guaranteeing repayment of a loan that becomes the property of the creditor if the loan is not repaid **8.** GUARANTOR somebody who guarantees to fulfill an obligation entered into by somebody else if that person fails to do so **9.** FINANCIAL INSTRUMENT a tradable document such as a stock certificate or bond that shows evidence of debt or ownership

se·cu·ri·ty blan·ket *n.* a familiar blanket, toy, or other object that a child carries around for the feeling of security it gives, or any object that fulfills the same function for an adult

se·cu·ri·ty clear·ance *n.* official permission allowing somebody to have access to a secue facility or to information that has been classified for reasons of national security

Se·cu·ri·ty Coun·cil *n.* the permanent committee of the United Nations that oversees its peacekeeping operations throughout the world. The Security Council has five permanent members: Great Britain, China, France, Russia, and the United States, and ten other members chosen in rotation from among the other member states.

se·cu·ri·ty guard *n.* somebody employed by a private organization to guard and protect a building or other property

se·cu·ri·ty risk *n.* somebody or something considered a threat to security, especially somebody whose behavior is thought likely to compromise the security of a country

secy., **sec'y.** *abbr.* secretary

sed. *abbr.* **1.** sediment **2.** sedimentation

se·dan[1] /sə dán/ *n.* *U.S., Can, ANZ* a car with a fully enclosed passenger compartment, a permanent roof, two or four doors, front and rear seats, and a separate trunk [Mid-17thC. Origin uncertain: perhaps via an Italian dialect word from, ultimately, Latin *sedes* "seat."]

se·dan[2], **se·dan chair** *n.* in the 17th and 18th centuries, an enclosed chair carried by porters at the front and rear on two long poles passed through handles on the sides of the box

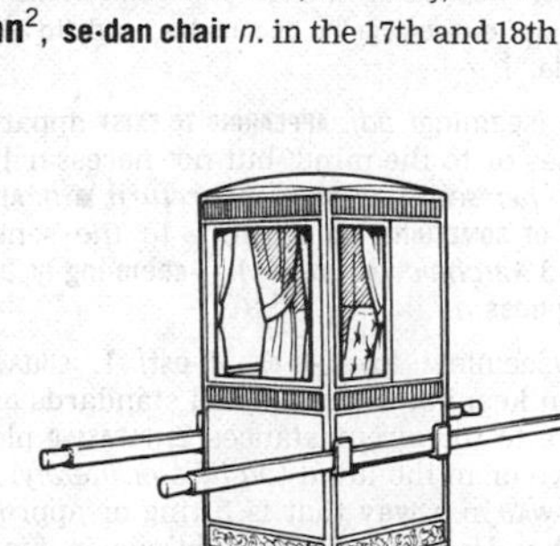

Sedan

Se·dan /sè dán, sè doN/ town in Ardennes Department, Champagne-Ardenne Region, northeastern France. It was the location of a decisive French defeat in 1870 during the Franco-Prussian war. Population: 22,407 (1990).

se·date[1] /sə dáyt/ *adj.* dignified, subdued, and lacking any sense of hurry or urgency [Mid-17thC. From Latin *sedatus*, past participle of *sedare* "to calm," literally "to force to sit," from *sedere* "to sit" (source of English *session*).] —**se·date·ly** *adv.* —**se·date·ness** *n.*

se·date[2] /sə dáyt/ (**-dat·ed, -dat·ing, -dates**) *vt.* to administer a sedative to somebody [Mid-20thC. Back-formation from SEDATIVE and SEDATION.]

se·da·tion /sə dáysh'n/ *n.* **1.** STATE OF CALM a state of calm, restfulness, or drowsiness, especially as induced by a sedative or tranquilizing drug **2.** USE OF SEDATIVES the use of a sedative or tranquilizing drug to induce a state of calm, restfulness, or drowsiness

sed·a·tive /séddətiv/ *n.* DRUG INDUCING SEDATION a drug or other agent that induces sedation ■ *adj.* INDUCING SEDATION inducing sedation, especially by means of a tranquilizing drug ○ *a sedative effect*

sed·en·tar·y /sédd'n tèrree/ *adj.* **1.** INVOLVING SITTING involving a lot of sitting and correspondingly little exercise ○ *sedentary work* **2.** USUALLY SITTING tending to sit most of the time and getting little exercise ○ *a sedentary person* **3.** ZOOL NOT MOVING used to describe shellfish that remain in one place, usually attached to a rock, for most of their lives **4.** BIRDS NONMIGRATORY remaining in the same area throughout the year and not migrating [Late 16thC. Directly or via French *sédentaire* from Latin *sedentarius*, from, ultimately, *sedere* (see SEDATE[2]).] —**sed·en·tar·i·ly** *adv.* —**sed·en·tar·i·ness** *n.*

Se·der /sáydər/ (*plural* **-ders** *or* **-der·im** /sə daárim/) *n.* CALENDAR in Judaism, a ceremonial meal eaten on either of the first two nights of Passover, commemorating the exodus of the Jews from Egypt [Mid-19thC. From Hebrew, literally "order, procedure."]

sedge /sej/ *n.* a wetland plant that resembles grass and has a triangular stem, leaves growing in three vertical rows, and inconspicuous spikes of flowers. Genus: *Carex*. [Old English *secg*. Ultimately from an Indo-European word meaning "to cut" that is also the ancestor of English *section*. Probably from the plant's sharpness.] —**sedg·y** *adj.*

sedge wren *n.* a wren of eastern North America that is similar to a sparrow in coloration and lives in grassy meadows and sedge marshes. Latin name: *Cistothorus platensis.*

se·di·lia /sə díllyə, -ee əl/ *npl.* a set of three seats placed near the altar of a church and often recessed into the wall used by priests celebrating Mass or Holy Communion [Late 18thC. From Latin, plural of *sedile* "seat," from *sedere* "to sit."]

sed·i·ment /séddimənt/ *n.* **1.** SETTLED MATTER AT BOTTOM OF LIQUID material, originally suspended in a liquid, that settles at the bottom of the liquid when it is left standing for a long time **2.** ERODED MATERIAL material eroded from preexisting rocks that is transported by water, wind, or ice and deposited elsewhere [Mid-16thC. Directly or via French from Latin *sedimentum* "settling," from *sedere* "to sit."] —**sed·i·men·tous** /sèddi méntəss/ *adj.*

sed·i·men·ta·ry /sèddə méntəree/ *adj.* **1.** FORMING IN LIQUID forming at the bottom of a liquid **2.** FORMED FROM ERODED MATERIAL used to describe rocks formed from material, including debris of organic origin, deposited as sediment by water, wind, or ice and then consolidated by pressure —**sed·i·men·ta·ri·ly** /sèddə men térrilee/ *adv.*

sed·i·men·ta·tion /sèddəmən táysh'n/ *n.* **1.** FORMATION OF ROCKS the process by which rocks are formed by the accumulation of sediment **2.** PROCESS OF FORMING SEDIMENT IN LIQUID the process by which particles in suspension in a liquid form sediment

sed·i·men·ta·tion tank *n.* a tank in which sewage is left in order to allow its solid constituents to separate out

sed·i·men·tol·o·gy /sèddəmən tólləjee/ *n.* the branch of geology concerned with the nature and formation of sedimentary rocks —**sed·i·men·to·log·ic** /sèddəmənt'l ójjik/ *adj.* —**sed·i·men·tol·o·gist** /sèddəmən tólləjist/ *n.*

se·di·tion /sə dísh'n/ *n.* actions or words intended to provoke or incite rebellion against government authority, or such a rebellion [14thC. Directly or via Old French from the Latin stem *sedition-* "civil disorder," literally, "a going apart, separation," from, ultimately, *ire* "to go."]

se·di·tious /sə díshəss/ *adj.* **1.** INVOLVING SEDITION involving or encouraging rebellion against a government or other authority **2.** INVOLVED IN SEDITION taking part in activities that are directed against a government or other authority [15thC Via French *seditieux* from, ultimately, Latin *seditio* "discord" (see SEDITION)] —**se·di·tious·ly** *adv.* —**se·di·tious·ness** *n.*

se·duce /sə dŏoss/ (**-duced, -duc·ing, -duc·es**) *vt.* **1.** INDUCE SOMEBODY TO HAVE SEX to persuade somebody to have sex, especially by using a romantic or deceptive approach **2.** LEAD SOMEBODY ASTRAY to persuade somebody into doing something wrong **3.** WIN SOMEBODY OVER to persuade somebody into giving support or agreement [15thC From Latin *seducere* "to lead astray," from *ducere* "to lead" (source of English *educate*)] —**se·duc·er** *n.* —**se·duc·i·ble** *adj.*

se·duce·ment /sə dŏossmənt/ *n.* **1.** SOMETHING THAT SEDUCES something that tempts or persuades ○ *"ere any flattering seducement, or vain principle seize them"* (John Milton, *Civil War Polemic, part I*) **2.** SEDUCTION a seduction

se·duc·tion /sə dúksh'n/ *n.* **1.** LEADING ASTRAY OF SOMEBODY the act of persuading somebody to do something wrong ○ *their easy seduction into a life of crime* **2.** LURING OF SOMEBODY INTO SEX the act of persuading somebody to have sex, especially by using a romantic or deceptive approach **3.** TEMPTING THING something that tempts, persuades, or attracts

se·duc·tive /sə dúktiv/ *adj.* **1.** SEXUALLY ENTICING aiming to be or regarded as being sexually inviting ○ *his seductive smile* **2.** TEMPTING serving to tempt, persuade, or attract ○ *made me a very seductive offer* —**se·duc·tive·ly** *adv.* —**se·duc·tive·ness** *n.*

se·duc·tress /sə dúktrəss/ *n.* a woman who seduces others [Early 19thC. Formed from obsolete "sedutor" + -ESS.]

sed·u·lous /séjjələss/ *adj.* (*literary*) **1.** WORKING PERSISTENTLY working with great zeal and persistence **2.** PAINSTAKING carried out with great care, concentration, and commitment ○ *sedulous attention to detail* [Mid-16thC. From Latin *sedulus*, from, ultimately, *se* "without" + *dolus* "deception."] —**se·du·li·ty** /sə dŏolətee/ *n.* —**sed·u·lous·ly** /séjjələsslee/ *adv.* —**sed·u·lous·ness** /séjjələssnəss/ *n.*

se·dum /seédəm/ *n.* any one of a genus of low-growing herbaceous plants that grow naturally in rocky places and have fleshy leaves and clusters of white, yellow, or pink flowers. Genus: *Sedum*. [Mid-16thC. From Latin, "houseleek."]

see[1] /see/ (**saw** /saw/, **seen** /seen/, **see·ing, sees**) *v.* **1.** *vti.* PERCEIVE WITH EYES to perceive, or perceive something, with the eyes **2.** *vi.* HAVE VISION to be able to perceive things with the eyes ○ *sees fine without his glasses* **3.** *vti.* VIEW OR WATCH to examine, look at, or watch somebody or something using the eyes ○ *He asked to see my passport.* **4.** *vti.* COMPREHEND to have a clear understanding of something ○ *I'm not sure I see what you mean.* **5.** *vti.* REALIZE BY SEEING to realize that something is true or exists by using the eyes, e.g., by reading about it ○ *I see from his letter that he's worked here before.* **6.** *vt.* PERCEIVE SOMETHING AS PLEASING OR GOOD to perceive or find a trait in somebody, especially one that is interesting or pleasing ○ *I don't understand what she sees in him.* **7.** *vt.* MEET OR CONSULT WITH SOMEBODY to meet somebody or spend time with somebody, either socially or professionally ○ *I'm seeing an old friend for lunch.* **8.** *vt.* HAVE A RELATIONSHIP WITH SOMEBODY to meet with somebody in a romantic context or have a romantic or sexual relationship with somebody ○ *Is he seeing anyone at the moment?* **9.** *vt.* HAVE INTERVIEW WITH SOMEBODY to meet with somebody in order to raise or discuss an issue such as a complaint ○ *She asked to see the manager.* **10.** *vt.* RECEIVE SOMEBODY FOR INTERVIEW to admit or receive somebody who has come for a visit or an interview ○ *The doctor can't see you until next week.* **11.** *vt.* IMAGINE SOMETHING to picture something in the mind ○ *I couldn't see someone like him in a jacket and tie.* **12.** *vt.* BELIEVE SOMETHING to regard it as likely that somebody will do something ○ *We couldn't see them agreeing to that.* **13.** *vt.* CONSIDER SOMEBODY OR SOMETHING to regard somebody or something in a particular way ○ *We don't really see them as good friends.* **14.** *vt.* **UNDERGO SOMETHING** to experience something firsthand ○ *They've seen a lot of unhappiness in their short lives.* **15.** *vt.* **ESCORT SOMEBODY** to go somewhere with somebody, usually as a guide, for company, or for protection ○ *Would you see me to my car?* **16.** *vt.* **MAKE SURE OF SOMETHING** to remember to do something or be sure to do it ○ *See that they wipe their feet before they come in.* **17.** *vt.* **REFER TO SOMETHING** to consult something or refer to something ○ *See our main advertisement on page 25.* **18.** *vti.* **ASCERTAIN** to find something out ○ *See if you can get this book locally.* **19.** *vi.* **WAIT UNTIL LATER TO DECIDE** to allow time to elapse, either in order to be better able to judge what the outcome will be or in order to delay making a decision ○ *I don't know; we'll have to see.* **20.** *vt.* GAMBLING **MATCH BET** to match an opponent's bet by staking the same amount [Old English *sēon.* From a prehistoric Germanic base that is also the ancestor of German *sehen.*] —**see·a·ble** *adj.* ◇ **what you see is what you get** used to emphasize that nothing is disguised, hidden, or insincere. ◊ **WYSIWYG**

see about *vt.* **1. ATTEND TO SOMETHING** to take care of a particular matter **2. INVESTIGATE SOMETHING** to make inquiries about a particular matter

see after *vt.* to take care of somebody or something, especially children or animals

see into *vt.* **1. PERCEIVE TRUTH ABOUT SOMETHING** to discern the true nature or content of something hidden, e.g., somebody's thoughts **2. FORETELL EVENTS** to be able to predict future events

see off *vt.* to accompany somebody to a place of departure and say goodbye

see out *vt.* **1. ESCORT SOMEBODY OUT** to accompany somebody who is leaving a room, building, or other place **2. STAY UNTIL THE END OF SOMETHING** to stay in a place or stay committed to something until the end

see through *vt.* **1. FINISH SOMETHING** to continue with something until it is completed ○ *a professional who sees every job through personally* **2. PERCEIVE TRUTH BENEATH EXTERIOR** to discern the true nature of somebody or something beneath a façade or disguise ○ *I saw through all his bravado.* **3. HELP SOMEBODY THROUGH DIFFICULTY** to provide somebody with help, advice, and support, especially in times of trouble ○ *He's seen me through some bad times.*

see to *vt.* to do what is required in order to deal with something or take care of somebody successfully ○ *We need an usher to see to guests as they arrive.*

see[2] /seel/ *n.* **1. BISHOP'S DIOCESE** the area that is under the jurisdiction of a bishop or archbishop **2. BISHOP'S POWER** the position or authority of a bishop or archbishop [13thC Via Old French *se* from, ultimately, Latin *sedere* "to sit"]

See·beck ef·fect /sée bèk-/ *n.* the production of an electric current in a circuit containing junctions between different metals or semiconductors kept at different temperatures. The effect is used in thermocouples. [Early 20thC. Named for Thomas J. *Seebeck* (1770–1831), the Russian-born German physicist who first discovered the phenomenon.]

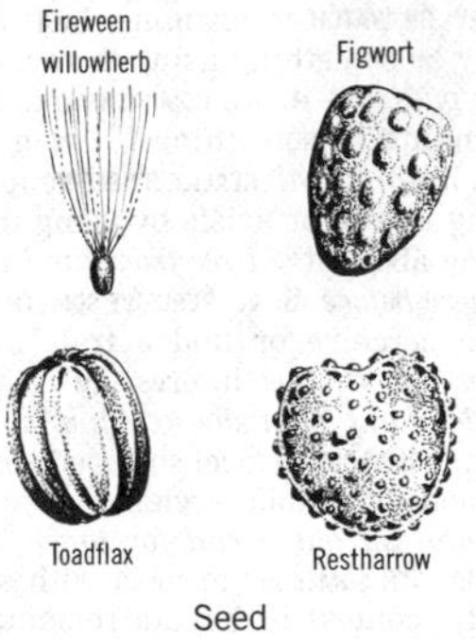

Seed

seed /seed/ *n.* **1.** BOT **PLANT PART CONTAINING EMBRYO** the body produced by reproduction in most plants that contains the embryo and gives rise to a new individual. In flowering plants, it is enclosed within the fruit. The seed develops from the fertilized ovule, contains a food supply, and is itself enclosed in a protective coat **(testa)**. **2.** BOT **FRUIT OF GRASS PLANT** the small dry hard fruit produced by cereal plants or grasses **3.** BOT **PROPAGATIVE PART OF PLANT** any compact part of a plant such as a bulb, tuber, or spore that is used for propagation **4.** BOT **PROPAGATIVE PLANT PARTS COLLECTIVELY** propagative plant parts as a whole, including seeds, tubers, rhizomes, spores, and bulbs ○ *a dry place to store seed* **5. SOURCE** something that is the source of a significant change in outlook or action ○ *sowing the seeds of doubt in her mind* **6. SOMETHING RESEMBLING SEED** something that resembles a seed in shape, size, or function **7.** CHEM **CRYSTAL** a small crystal added to a supersaturated or supercooled solution to induce further crystallization **8. DESCENDANTS** descendants (*literary*) ○ *the seed of Abraham* **9.** SPORTS **GRADED COMPETITOR** a competitor who is graded according to the perceived likelihood of his or her winning a particular tournament **10. SPERM** sperm or semen as a vehicle of reproduction (*literary*) **11.** ZOOL = **seed oyster** ■ *v.* **(seed·ed, seed·ing, seeds) 1.** *vt.* **PLANT SEEDS** to plant seeds in soil or plant something by sowing seeds ○ *The lower field was seeded with barley.* **2.** *vi.* **DROP SEEDS** to shed seeds that develop into new plants (*refers to plants*) ○ *Those poppies have seeded themselves everywhere.* **3.** *vt.* **REMOVE SEEDS FROM SOMETHING** to take the seeds out of a fruit or vegetable before eating or cooking **4.** *vt.* CHEM **ADD CRYSTAL TO SOLUTION** to add a small crystal to a supersaturated or supercooled solution to induce further crystallization **5.** *vt.* METEOROL **SPRINKLE CLOUD WITH CRYSTALS** to release silver iodide into clouds to encourage precipitation **6.** *vt.* SPORTS **STRUCTURE TOURNAMENT** to arrange the draw of a tournament so that the best players meet in the later rounds **7.** *vt.* SPORTS **RANK PLAYER** to rank a player according to the perceived likelihood of his or her winning a tournament **8.** *vt.* BUSINESS **ENCOURAGE ENTERPRISE** to give financial or other assistance to something such as a business during the early stages of its development ■ *adj.* AGRIC **RESERVED FOR USE AS SEED** reserved for planting to grow the next crop ○ *seed potatoes* [Old English *sǣd.* From a prehistoric Germanic base that is also the ancestor of English *sow.*] —**seedless** *adj.* ◇ **go to seed 1.** to reach the stage of producing seeds. At this stage, flowering plants have lost their flowers and the vegetables on vegetable plants have become inedible. **2.** to become shabby or unhealthy from lack of proper care or attention

seed·bed /séed bèd/ *n.* **1.** GARDENING **GROUND FOR PLANTING** a plot of ground in which seeds and seedlings are cultivated before being transplanted **2. PLACE WHERE SOMETHING DEVELOPS** a place where conditions encourage the development of a significant change in outlook or action

seed·cake /séed kàyk/ *n.* a cake or cookie flavored with seeds, usually caraway seeds

seed cap·i·tal *n. U.K.* = **seed money**

seed coat *n.* = **testa**

seed·eat·er /séed èetər/ *n.* a bird such as the finch that relies on seeds for its food and usually has a stout conical bill adapted to cracking the seeds open

seed·er /séedər/ *n.* **1.** AGRIC **MACHINE FOR SOWING SEEDS** a mechanical device designed to scatter seed on the surface of the ground, usually either one pulled by a tractor or one with wheels and a handle that is pushed **2.** HOUSEHOLD **DEVICE FOR REMOVING SEEDS** a kitchen device used to remove the seeds from fruit and vegetables **3. SOMEBODY OR SOMETHING THAT SEEDS** somebody or something that seeds, especially somebody who seeds clouds [Old English *sǣdere*]

seed fern *n.* = **pteridosperm**

seed leaf *n.* = **cotyledon**

seed·ling /séedling/ *n.* a young developing plant that is grown from a seed

seed mon·ey *n.* money provided to enable a business venture to be developed

seed oys·ter *n.* a small young oyster, especially one that is transplanted to a commercial oyster bed

seed pearl *n.* a very small round pearl, natural or cultured, weighing less than one quarter of a grain

seed plant *n.* = **spermatophyte**

seed·pod /séed pòd/ *n.* = **pod**[1] *n.* 1

seed stock *n.* **1. SEED SUPPLY** a supply of seed for planting **2. SUPPLY OF BREEDING ANIMALS** a supply of animals kept or provided for breeding purposes, capable of founding a new population or sustaining an existing population

seed tick *n.* the tiny larva of a tick

seed·time /séed tìm/ *n.* **1. SOWING SEASON** the time of the year when seeds are planted **2. DEVELOPMENT PERIOD** a period of new development or growth

seed ves·sel *n.* the part of a plant that contains its seeds, especially a part that is not an edible fruit or vegetable

seed wasp *n.* any one of several species of wasp such as the gall wasp that bore into the seeds of plants to lay their eggs. Superfamily: Chalcidoidea.

seed wee·vil *n.* any one of several species of insect of the weevil family that lays its eggs in seeds, where the larvae then develop

seed·y /séedee/ **(-i·er, -i·est)** *adj.* **1. SHABBY** shabby, dirty-looking, and often disreputable ○ *He discovered her singing in some seedy bar.* **2. HAVING SEEDS** containing many seeds ○ *seedy raspberry jam* **3. UNWELL** somewhat ill, especially with a stomach complaint (*informal*) —**seed·i·ly** *adv.* —**seed·i·ness** *n.*

See·ger /séegər/, **Pete** (*b.* 1919) U.S. singer and songwriter. He led the 1960s folk music revival with songs including "Where Have All the Flowers Gone?" (1956).

see·ing /sée ing/ *n.* **1. VISION** vision or perception with the eyes ○ *My seeing isn't too good.* **2.** ASTRON **ATMOSPHERIC CONDITIONS** the clarity of the Earth's atmosphere for astronomical observations using an optical telescope, or the quality of the images obtained ■ *conj.* **IN VIEW OF** used to introduce a statement that takes into account something mentioned before or after ○ *Seeing that you're an old friend, I can give you a special price.*

WORD KEY: USAGE

Perhaps a bonus on my wages might be an idea, seeing that I shall be doing this out of hours (Paula Marshall, *An American Princess*). The use of ***seeing that*** as a conjunction not grammatically attached to a particular subject is established in current English and conforms to a pattern used also by *given that, granted that,* and others. On the other hand, ***seeing as***, used in the same way, is informal only: *I'll leave now seeing as you look tired.*

seek /seek/ **(sought** /sawt/, **sought, seek·ing, seeks)** *v.* **1.** *vti.* **SEARCH FOR SOMETHING** to try to find a particular thing or place **2.** *vt.* **STRIVE FOR SOMETHING** to try to achieve or obtain something ○ *candidates seeking election* **3.** *vt.* **ASK FOR SOMETHING** to consult somebody in order to obtain something such as help or advice ○ *His advice was regularly sought on such matters.* **4.** *vt.* **HEAD FOR SOMETHING** to go to or toward a place or thing ○ *As the water rose, they sought higher ground.* **5.** *vt.* **ATTEMPT SOMETHING** to try to do something ○ *seeking to exploit the rift between them* [Old English *sēcan.* Ultimately from an Indo-European base meaning "to seek out" that is also the ancestor of English *sagacity.*] —**seek·er** *n.*

seek out *vt.* to find somebody or something as a result of active searching

seel /seel/ **(seeled, seel·ing, seels)** *vt.* to sew shut the eyelids of a hawk or falcon in order to make it tame [15thC. Via Old French *siller, ciller* from medieval Latin *ciliare*, from Latin *cilium* "eyelid."]

seem /seem/ **(seemed, seem·ing, seems)** *v.* **1.** *vti.* **APPEAR TO BE SOMETHING** to give a particular impression, either of a quality or of something happening ○ *It's not as difficult as it seems.* **2.** *vt.* **APPEAR TO BE TRUE** to appear to exist or be true, used expecially to lessen the force of a following statement, usually by suggesting uncertainty or mitigating criticism, often for the sake of politeness ○ *We seem to have a misunderstanding.* [12thC. From Old Norse *sœma* "to conform to," from *sœmr* "fitting." The modern meaning "to appear to be" evolved via "to be suitable" and "to appear to be suitable."]

seem·ing /séeming/ *adj.* **APPEARING TO EXIST** apparent to the senses or to the mind, but not necessarily true or real ○ *her seeming joy at his return* ■ *n.* **APPARENT EXISTENCE OF SOMETHING** appearance to the senses or the mind (*archaic or literary*) —**seem·ing·ly** *adv.* —**seem·ing·ness** *n.*

seem·ly /séemlee/ *adj.* **(-li·er, -li·est) 1. SUITABLE AND CORRECT** in keeping with accepted standards and appropriate to the circumstances **2. PLEASING** pleasing to the eye or to the mind (*archaic or literary*) ■ *adv.* **IN SEEMLY WAY** in a way that is fitting or appropriate (*archaic*) ○ *He was seemly courteous in his greeting.* [12thC. From Old Norse *sœmiligr*, from *sœmr* "fitting."] —**seem·li·ness** *n.*

seen past participle of **see**

seep /seep/ *vi.* **(seeped, seep·ing, seeps) 1. PASS THROUGH** to pass or escape through an opening very slowly and in small quantities (*refers to liquids or gases*) ○ *water seeping out of the cracks* **2. DISAPPEAR** to diminish slowly but steadily ○ *with her resistance gradually seeping away* **3. GO SLOWLY** to enter or escape slowly but inexorably ○ *new sensations seeping into his consciousness* ■ *n.* **1.** GEOL **PLACE WHERE LIQUID ESCAPES** a small pool or spring where liquid escapes from the ground **2.** = **seepage** [Late 18thC. Variant of dialect *sipe*, of uncertain origin: perhaps from Old English *sipian* "to seep."]

seep·age /seépij/ *n.* the escape of liquid or the amount of liquid that escapes

seer /seer, seé ər/ *n.* **1. PREDICTER OF FUTURE** somebody who claims or is assumed to be able to see into the future **2. OCCULTIST** somebody who claims to have supernatural powers

seer·suck·er /seér sùkər/ *n.* a lightweight cotton, linen, or synthetic fabric with a pattern of alternate puckered and smooth stripes [Early 18thC. Via Hindi *śīrśakar* from, ultimately, Persian *shīr o shakar*, literally "milk and sugar."]

see·saw /seé sàw/ *n.* **1. PLAYGROUND TOY** a playground toy in which two people sit at either end of a bar balanced in the middle and take turns riding up into the air **2. SEESAW RIDING** the game of riding a seesaw **3. UP-AND-DOWN MOVEMENT** an up-and-down, back-and-forth, or otherwise alternating movement, e.g., in the popularity of one political party over another ■ *vi.* **(-sawed, -saw·ing, -saws) 1. RIDE A SEESAW** to ride up and down on a seesaw **2. MOVE LIKE SEESAW** to move in an alternating fashion, especially back and forth or up and down **3. TO ALTERNATE** to change regularly and repeatedly from one thing to another, e.g., one state of mind to another ○ *seesawing between one plan and another* [Mid-17thC. Thought to suggest the repetitive action and sound of using a two-handled saw.]

seethe /seeth/ *v.* **(seethed, seeth·ing, seethes) 1.** *vi.* **BE ANGRY** to be in a state of extreme emotion, especially unexpressed anger ○ *I sat in my office quietly seething.* **2.** *vi.* **BE BUSY** to be full of bustling activity, especially with crowds of people moving in many different directions **3.** *vi.* **MAKE BOILING MOVEMENTS** to boil or to churn or foam as if boiling **4.** *vi.* **BEGIN BOILING** to come to a boil (*archaic*) **5.** *vt.* COOK **BOIL SOMETHING** to cook food by boiling it or boil something to extract its essence (*archaic*) **6.** *vt.* **SOAK SOMETHING** to soak something in liquid ■ *n.* **SEETHING MOVEMENT OR ACTION** an act of seething [Old English *sēothan*]

seeth·ing /seéthing/ *adj.* **1. ANGRY** full of anger, especially pent-up anger **2. BOILING** boiling and bubbling or foaming **3. BUSTLING** moving in all directions, busily or frantically ○ *"the seething crowd of Paris"* (Baroness Orczy, *The Scarlet Pimpernel*; 1905) —**seeth·ing·ly** *adv.*

see-through *adj.* made of transparent material, especially so as to reveal clothes or skin underneath

Se·fer Tor·ah /sàyfər táwrə/ (*plural* **Se·fer Tor·ahs** *or* **Si·frei Tor·ah** /sì fray-/) *n.* a parchment scroll on which the Pentateuch is handwritten [Mid-17thC. From Hebrew *sēper tōrāh*, literally "book of (the) Law."]

seg·ment *n.* /ségmənt/ **1. COMPONENT PART** any one of the parts or sections into which an object or group is divided **2.** ZOOL **ORGANISM'S BODY PART** any one of the individual units that make up an animal's body or part of its body. These units can follow a repeated pattern, as with a centipede, or can be variously shaped, as with the mouth parts of a spider. **3.** GEOM **PART OF GEOMETRIC FIGURE** the portion of a line or curve between any two of its points or the portion of a solid cut by a plane **4.** LING **SPEECH SOUND** any one of the individual speech sounds that make up a longer string of sounds ■ *vt.* /seg mént/ **(-ment·ed, -ment·ing, -ments) SPLIT SOMETHING INTO SEGMENTS** to divide an object or group into segments [Late 16thC. From Latin *segmentum*, from *secare* "to cut."] —**seg·men·tar·y** /ségmən tèrree/ *adj.*

seg·men·tal /seg mént'l/ *adj.* **1. OF SEGMENTS** relating to segments or in the form of segments **2.** LING **RELATING TO SPEECH SOUNDS** relating to individual speech sounds or to the dividing of strings of speech into isolable sounds —**seg·men·tal·ly** *adv.*

seg·men·ta·tion /sèg men táysh'n, -mən-/ *n.* **1. SPLITTING INTO SEGMENTS** the dividing of something into segments **2. SEGMENTED STRUCTURE** the structure of something that is made up of a series of similar segments **3.** EMBRYOL = **wraparound 4.** ZOOL **BODY STRUCTURE** the structure of the body of an organism such as a worm or centipede that consists of a linear series of similar subunits

seg·men·ta·tion cav·i·ty *n.* = **blastocoel**

se·gno /sáynyō/ (*plural* **-gnos** *or* **-gni** /sáynyee/) *n.* a symbol used on sheet music to mark the beginning or end of a repeated section [Early 20thC. Via Italian fromLatin *signum* "sign."]

se·go lil·y /seégō-/ *n.* a lily native to the western United States that has mottled, variously colored flowers and an edible bulb. Latin name: *Calochortus nuttallii*. [Early20thC. *Sego* from Southern Paiute *sigho'o*.]

Sé·gou /sáy goo/ capital city of Ségou Region, in southwestern Mali. Population: 88,877 (1987).

Se·go·vi·a /sə gốviè/ capital of Segovia Province, in the autonomous region of Castile-León, central Spain. Population: 54,750 (1989).

Se·go·vi·a /si gốvee ə, se gáwvyaa/, **Andrés** (1893–1987) Spanish guitarist. His successful international career revived interest in the classical guitar. He made many transcriptions for guitar, and a number of contemparary composers wrote works specially for him.

seg·re·gant /séggrəgənt/ *adj.* **HAVING DIFFERENT GENETIC MAKEUP** having a genetic makeup that differs from that of either parent because of genetic segregation ■ *n.* **DISTINCT ORGANISM** an organism having a genetic makeup that differs from that of either parent because of genetic segregation

seg·re·gate /séggrə gàyt/ **(-gat·ed, -gat·ing, -gates)** *v.* **1.** *vt.* **SEPARATE PEOPLE OR THINGS** to separate one person or group from the rest or to keep different people or groups separate **2.** *vti.* SOCIOL **KEEP GROUPS SEPARATE** to enforce a policy of keeping different groups within a population separate, especially different ethnic, racial, religious or gender groups **3.** *vti.* GENETICS **UNDERGO GENETIC SEGREGATION** to undergo or cause cells to undergo genetic segregation [Mid-16thC. From Latin *segregat-*, the past participle stem of *segregare* "to separate from the flock.", from *grex* "flock."] —**seg·re·ga·ble** *adj.* —**seg·re·ga·tive** *adj.* —**seg·re·ga·tor** /-gàytər/ *n.*

seg·re·ga·tion /sèggrə gáysh'n/ *n.* **1.** SOCIOL **ENFORCED SEPARATION OF RACIAL GROUPS** the practice of keeping ethnic, racial, religious, or gender groups separate especially by enforcing the use of separate schools, transportation, housing, and other facilities, and usually discriminating against a minority group **2. SEGREGATED STATE** the state or position of somebody or something kept separate from others **3. ACT OF SEGREGATING** the separating of one person, group, or thing from others or the dividing of people or things into separate groups kept apart from each other **4.** GENETICS **GENE SEPARATION** the separation of the two versions (**alleles**) of each gene and their distribution to separate sex cells during formation (**meiosis**) of these cells in organisms with paired chromosomes —**seg·re·ga·tion·al** *adj.*

seg·re·ga·tion·ist /sèggrə gáysh'nist/ *n.* somebody who advocates or enforces segregation, especially racial segregation —**seg·re·ga·tion·ist** *adj.*

se·gue /sé gwày, sáy-/ *vi.* **(-gued, -gue·ing, -gues) 1.** MUSIC **CONTINUE PLAYING** to continue by playing the following piece or passage of music without a pause **2. MOVE SMOOTHLY** to make a smooth, almost imperceptible transition from one state, situation, or subject to another ○ *segued into a discussion of the playoffs without skipping a beat* ■ *n.* **1.** MUSIC **CONTINUATION OF MUSIC** the act of moving from one musical piece or passage into another, without a pause **2.** MUSIC **INSTRUCTION TO CONTINUE** an instruction to a musician to begin playing a following piece or passage without a pause **3. SMOOTH TRANSITION** the act of making a smooth transition from one state or situation to another [Mid-18thC. From Italian, the third person singular of *seguire* "to follow," from Latin *sequi*.]

se·gui·dil·la /sèggə deéyə, sàygə-, -deélyə/ *n.* **1.** DANCE **SPANISH DANCE** a Spanish dance in moderate 3/4 time, usually accompanied by castanets and guitars **2.** MUSIC **DANCE MUSIC FOR SEGUIDILLA** a piece of music written for a seguidilla **3.** POETRY **SPANISH VERSE FORM** a poem with either four or seven very short verses that makes use of assonance rather than rhyme. It is a popular form in Spanish poetry. [Mid-18thC. Via Spanish, literally "little sequence," from, ultimately, Latin *sequi* "to follow."]

sei·cen·to /say chéntō/ *n.* the 17th century, with reference to Italian art and literature [Early 20thC. Shortening of Italian *milseicento*, literally "one thousand six hundred."]

seiche /saysh, seech/ *n.* a movement on the surface of an enclosed body of water such as a lake, usually caused by intense storm activity [Mid-19thC. From Swiss French, of uncertain origin: perhaps from German *Seiche* "sinking."]

sei·del /sīd'l, zīd'l/ *n.* a large beer glass [Early 20thC. Via German *Seidel* from Latin *situla* "bucket."]

Seid·ler /zīdlər/, **Harry** (*b.* 1923) Austrian-born Australian architect. He was a modernist who studied under Walter Gropius at Harvard. He designed Australia Square in Sydney.

Seid·litz pow·der /séddlits-/ *n.* a laxative preparation in powder form that contains sodium bicarbonate, tartaric acid, and potassium sodium tartrate (**Rochelle salt**). It is taken dissolved in water. [Late 18thC. Named for the village of *Seidlitz* in Bohemia, which has a mineral spring noted for its laxative properties.]

seif dune /sáyf-, sīf-/ *n.* a sand dune with curved edges, found in hot deserts in a series of parallel ridges and often several miles long and up to 300 ft./100 m in height [Early 20thC. From Arabic *sayf* "sword" + DUNE. From its shape.]

seign·eur /sayn yúr/, **Seign·eur** *n.* **1.** HIST = **seignior 2. FORMER FRENCH CANADIAN ESTATE OWNER** in French Canada until 1854, the owner of an estate originally granted by the king of France and farmed by tenants holding a form of feudal tenure over the land [Late 16thC. Via French from Latin *senior* "older" (the ancestor of English *sire, sir*, and *surly*).]

seign·eur·y /sáynyəree, sén-/ (*plural* **-ies**) *n.* **1. SEIGNEUR'S LAND** the estate of a seigneur **2. SEIGNEUR'S RANK** the rank or authority of a seigneur

seign·ior /sàyn yáwr/ *n.* a feudal lord, especially in England [13thC. Via Old French from Latin *senior* "older" (source of English *seigneur*).] —**sei·gnio·ri·al** *adj.*

seign·ior·age /sáynyərij/ *n.* **1. MONARCH'S PERCENTAGE OF BULLION** a monarch's right to a percentage of the bullion brought to a mint for the minting of coins **2. COINING PROFIT** the profit represented by the difference between the value of bullion and the face value of the coins minted from it **3.** HIST **ARISTOCRAT'S PRIVILEGE** a right or privilege claimed by a sovereign or other person of high rank

seign·ior·y /sáynyəree/ (*plural* **-ies**), **sign·ior·y** /seényəree/ (*plural* **-ies**), **sign·or·y** (*plural* **-ies**) *n.* **1. SEIGNIOR'S LAND** the estate of a seignior **2. SEIGNIOR'S RANK** the rank or authority of a seignior **3. LORDS COLLECTIVELY** lords considered as a group, especially English lords under the feudal system

seine /sayn/ *n.* **FISHING NET** a large commercial fishing net that is weighted so that it hangs vertically in the water. Its ends are then hauled together to form a trap like a large bag. ■ *vti.* **(seined, sein·ing, seines) FISH WITH SEINE** to catch fish with a seine [Pre-12thC. Via Latin *sagena* from Greek *sagēnē*.] —**sein·er** *n.*

Seine /sayn, sen/ river in northern France, flowing from near Dijon into the English Channel. Length: 482 mi./776 km.

Sein·feld /sīn feld/, **Jerry** (*b.* 1955) U.S. comedian. His comedy series *Seinfeld* (1990–98) was one of the most popular television shows of its time.

seise *vt.* LAW = **seize** *v.* **9** [Early 17thC. Variant of SEIZE.]

sei·sin /seézin/, **sei·zin** *n.* LAW **1. POSSESSION OF LAND** the legal possession of land, or the act of taking possession of it **2. OWNED LAND** land that is wholly and legally owned, especially land taken possession of legally [13thC. Via Anglo-Norman *sesine* or Old French *seisine* from *saisir* (see SEIZE).]

seism /sīzəm/ *n.* an earthquake (*technical*) [Late 19thC. From Greek *seismos* "earthquake," from *seiein* "to shake."]

seism- *prefix.* = **seismo-** (*used before vowels*)

seis·mic /sīzmik/, **seis·mi·cal** /-mik'l/ *adj.* **1. RELATING TO EARTHQUAKES** relating to or caused by an earthquake or earth tremor **2. LARGE** extremely large or great (*informal*) ○ *This had a seismic impact on the music world.* —**seis·mi·cal·ly** *adv.*

seis·mic ar·ray *n.* a network of seismometers positioned to maximize the sensitivity of each of them and best monitor seismic activity in a particular region of the world

seis·mic·i·ty /sīz míssətee/ *n.* the distribution and frequency of seismic events

seis·mic wave *n.* a shock wave traveling through the Earth from the epicenter of an earthquake

seis·mo·gram /sízmə gràm/ *n.* a record of an earthquake made by a seismograph

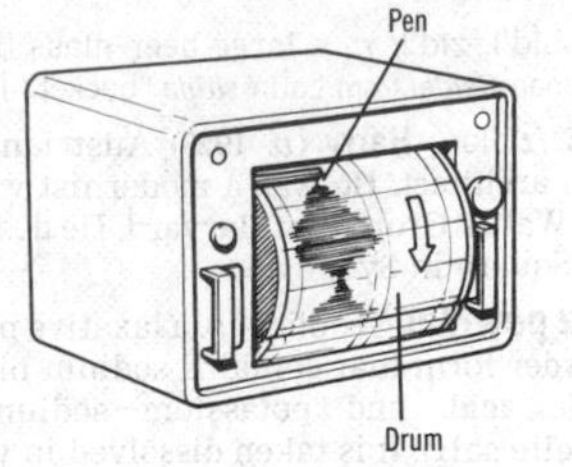

Seismograph

seis·mo·graph /sízmə gràf/ *n.* an instrument that detects the presence of an earthquake and measures and records its magnitude —**seis·mog·ra·pher** /sīz móggrəfər/ *n.* —**seis·mo·graph·ic** /sìzmə gráffik/ *adj.* —**seis·mog·ra·phy** /sīz móggrəfee/ *n.*

seis·mol·o·gy /sīz mólləjee/ *n.* the scientific study of earthquakes —**seis·mo·log·i·cal** /sìzmə lójjik'l/ *adj.* —**seis·mo·log·i·cal·ly** /sìzmə lójjikəlee/ *adv.* —**seis·mol·o·gist** /sīz mólləjist/ *n.*

seis·mom·e·ter /sīz mómmətər/ *n.* an instrument used to measure vibrations caused by an earthquake —**seis·mo·met·ric** /sìzmə méttrik/ *adj.*

sei whale /sáy-/ *n.* a dark bluish-gray whale similar to the blue whale but smaller and more streamlined. It feeds on tiny marine organisms by filtering them through bony plates on the jaw. It lives in all but the polar oceans and belongs to the rorqual family of whales. Latin name: *Balaenoptera borealis.* [Early 20thC. From Norwegian *sejhval,* from *sei* "coalfish" + *hval* "whale."]

seize /seez/ (**seized, seiz·ing, seiz·es**) *v.* **1.** *vt.* **TAKE A HOLD OF SOMETHING** to take a hold of an object quickly and firmly ○ *seized the letter from his hand* **2.** *vt.* **EXPLOIT SOMETHING IMMEDIATELY** to take advantage of something such as a chance eagerly and immediately ○ *seize an opportunity* **3.** *vt.* **AFFECT SOMEBODY SUDDENLY** to overwhelm the mind or emotions suddenly ○ *seized by panic* **4.** *vt.* **AFFECT SOMEBODY PHYSICALLY** to overwhelm somebody physically ○ *Yet another spasm seized him.* **5.** *vt.* **APPROPRIATE SOMETHING** to take official or legal possession of something, often something held illegally such as arms, drugs, or stolen goods ○ *The shipment was seized by customs officials.* **6.** *vt.* **ARREST SOMEBODY** to take somebody into custody ○ *Attempts to seize the attackers have so far failed.* **7.** *vti.* **COMPREHEND SOMETHING** to understand an idea or concept, especially quickly **8.** *vi.* MECH ENG **STOP WORKING** to become jammed, especially as a result of great heat, pressure, or friction, often arising from lack of lubrication **9.** *vi.* **STIFFEN UP** to become painfully stiff and immobile **10.** *vi.* **STOP** to come to a sudden and sometimes permanent halt ○ *The negotiations seized up after the most recent incident.* **11.** *vt.* LAW **GIVE SOMEBODY LEGAL POSSESSION** to make somebody the legal owner of property or goods ○ *The families were seized of all the relevant documentation.* **12.** *vt.* SAILING **LASH SOMETHING WITH THIN ROPE** to tie or secure something by lashing it using several turns of thin rope or wire [13thC. Via Old French *saisir* from medieval Latin *sacire* "to claim," of Germanic origin.] —**seiz·a·ble** *adj.* —**seiz·er** *n.*

WORD KEY: SYNONYMS

See Synonyms at ***catch***.

sei·zin *n.* LAW = **seisin**

seiz·ing /seézing/ *n.* a knot or lashing made using thin rope or wire, e.g., to join two ropes or to secure an item of ship's gear

sei·zure /seézhər/ *n.* **1.** **ACT OF SEIZING SOMETHING** the seizing of something, especially the taking of something by force or the official or legal appropriation of something **2.** **FACT OF BEING SEIZED** capture or appropriation ○ *so far managed to avoid seizure* **3.** MED **DISEASE ATTACK** a sudden attack of an illness or of particular symptoms, especially of the kind experienced by people with epilepsy **4.** **EMOTIONAL FIT** a sudden and intense rush of emotion ○ *a seizure of panic*

se·jant /seéjənt/, **se·jeant** *adj.* HERALDRY used to describe a figure on a coat of arms that is in a sitting position [15thC. Variant of French *séant* from, ultimately, Latin *sedere* "to sit."]

Sejm /saym/ *n.* the national parliament of Poland. It has a single legislative chamber. [Late 19thC. From Polish, "Assembly."]

Sek·on·di-Ta·ko·ra·di /sekèn deé takè raádee/ port and capital of Western Region, southwestern Ghana, situated 120 mi./193 km southwest of Accra. Population: 116,500 (1990).

se·la·chi·an /sə láykee ən/ *n.* a fish that belongs to the order that includes all sharks, rays, and skates. Order: Selachii. [Mid-19thC. Modeled on French *selacien.* Via modern Latin *selachii,* from the genus name *selache,* from Greek *selakhē* "shark."]

se·lag·i·nel·la /sə làjjə néllə/ *n.* a mossy plant with branching stems and small leaves bearing spores. It is related to the club mosses. Genus: *Selaginella.* [Mid-19thC. Via modern Latin *Selaginella,* genus name, from, ultimately, Latin *selago,* a herb similar to savin.]

se·lah /seélə, -laá/ *interj.* an ancient Hebrew word of unknown meaning and uncertain grammatical status that appears in some books of the Bible and is therefore, when included in English translations, left untranslated. It is used to perform a punctuating function between verses. [Mid-16thC. From Hebrew *selāh.*]

sel·dom /séldəm/ *adv.* not often [Old English *seldum.* Variant of *seldan,* of Germanic origin.] —**sel·dom·ness** *n.*

se·lect /sə lékt/ *vti.* (**-lect·ed, -lect·ing, -lects**) **CHOOSE FROM OTHERS** to choose somebody or something from among several ○ *select a chocolate from the box* ■ *adj.* **1.** **OF GOOD QUALITY** chosen on grounds of particularly high quality **2.** **HAVING LIMITED MEMBERSHIP** admitting only a few carefully chosen members ○ *one of the more select country clubs* **3.** **SPECIALLY CHOSEN** chosen from several others and given special treatment or a special privilege ○ *advance copies sent to a select few* **4.** **DISCRIMINATING** showing care and discernment when choosing ○ *"foreign films which generally attract a select audience"* (James Berardinelli, *Review: Deception*; 1993) **5.** FOOD **LEAN** used to describe meat with a relatively low amount of fat (**marbling**) [Mid-16thC. From Latin *select-,* the past participle stem of *seligere,* from *legere* "to choose."] —**se·lect·ness** *n.* —**se·lec·tor** *n.*

se·lect com·mit·tee *n.* a small group of members of Congress instructed by either the Senate or the House of Representatives to investigate and report on a particular matter

se·lect·ee /sə lèk teé/ *n.* somebody who is selected, especially for compulsory military service

se·lec·tion /sə léksh'n/ *n.* **1.** **ACT OF CHOOSING** an act of choosing somebody or something from a wide variety of others **2.** **CHOSEN STATE** the status of somebody or something chosen from among others **3.** **SOMEBODY OR SOMETHING CHOSEN** somebody or something chosen from among others **4.** **AVAILABLE CHOICE** the range from which somebody or something can be selected ○ *a fantastic selection of carpets* **5.** BIOL **SURVIVAL OF THE FITTEST** the production of more offspring by organisms with particular desirable characteristics, resulting in a better gene pool for the species. This can be a natural process or can be accomplished through human intervention, e.g., when breeding plants or animals for a particular trait.

se·lec·tion·ist /sə léksh'nist/ *n.* somebody who accepts or promotes the theory that natural selection is the major or only force governing biological development or change

se·lec·tive /sə léktiv/ *adj.* **1.** **NOT UNIVERSAL** applying to some but not others **2.** **DISCERNING** tending to make careful choices **3.** ELECTRON ENG **RECEIVING ON SOME FREQUENCIES ONLY** capable of selecting certain frequencies or frequency bands and blocking out all others, and therefore eliminating interference in reception —**se·lec·tive·ly** *adv.* —**se·lec·tive·ness** *n.*

se·lec·tive at·ten·tion *n.* the ability to pay attention to those things that are considered important and to ignore those that are not

se·lec·tive ser·vice *n.* a system for calling up men for U.S. military service

se·lec·tiv·i·ty /sə lèk tívvətee/ *n.* **1.** **CHOOSING ONLY SOME** the choosing of only some, not all, and the exercising of judgment in making the choice **2.** ELEC ENG **ABILITY TO DISTINGUISH FREQUENCIES** the degree to which an electronic device or circuit can distinguish a desired frequency from others

se·lect·man /si léktmàn, -mən/ (*plural* **-men** /-mèn, -mən/) *n.* in most New England states, any one of a number of officers elected by the public to manage local affairs

se·lec·tor /sə léktər/ *n.* a person or device that selects

se·lect·wom·an /si lékt wòommən/ (*plural* **-women** /-wìmmin/) *n.* in most New England states, a woman who is one of a number of officers elected by the public to manage local affairs

selen- *prefix.* = **seleno-** (*used before vowels*)

sel·e·nate /séllə nàyt/ *n.* a chemical compound that is a salt or ester of selenic acid [Early 19thC. Coined from SELENIUM + -ATE.]

Se·len·e /sə leénee/ *n.* in Greek mythology, the goddess of the Moon. Roman equivalent **Luna**

se·le·nic /sə lénnik, -leénik/ *adj.* relating to or containing the nonmetallic chemical element selenium, especially in the form in which it has a valence of six [Early 19thC. Coined from SELENIUM + -IC.]

se·le·nic ac·id *n.* a highly corrosive acid usually found in the form of a whitish solid. Formula: H_2SeO_4.

sel·e·nif·er·ous /sèllə níffərəss/ *adj.* containing or producing selenium [Early 19thC. Coined from SELENIUM + -FEROUS.]

se·le·ni·ous /sə leénee əss/ *adj.* relating to or containing the nonmetallic chemical element selenium, especially in the form in which it has a low valence [Early 19thC. Coined from SELENIUM + -OUS.]

sel·e·nite /séllə nīt/ *n.* a transparent colorless variety of gypsum that cleaves in a particular way to reveal lustrous crystal faces [Mid-16thC. Via Latin from Greek *selēnitēs lithos* "moon stone," from *selēnē* "moon." So named because its luster resembles that of the Moon (see SELENIUM).]

se·le·ni·um /sə leénee əm/ *n.* a nonmetallic chemical element that occurs in several forms ranging from a red powder to gray-black crystals. It is an essential trace element, although toxic in excess, and is used in photocells and photocopiers owing to its light-sensitive properties. Symbol **Se** [Early 19thC. From modern Latin, formed from Greek *selēnē* "moon," from *selas* "light."]

se·le·ni·um cell *n.* a photoelectric cell based on the light-sensitive properties of selenium and containing a strip of selenium mounted between two metal electrodes

seleno- *prefix.* **1.** the moon ○ *selenography* **2.** selenium ○ *selenite* [From Greek *selēnē* "moon" (see SELENIUM)]

sel·e·nog·ra·phy /sèllə nóggrəfee/ *n.* the branch of astronomy that is concerned with mapping the surface features of the Moon —**sel·e·no·graph·ic** /sèllənə gráffik, sə leénə-/ *adj.* —**sel·e·no·graph·i·cal·ly** /-gráffikəlee/ *adv.* —**sel·e·nog·ra·phist** *n.*

sel·e·nol·o·gy /sèllə nólləjee/ *n.* the branch of astronomy concerned with the origin and physical characteristics of the Moon —**sel·e·no·log·i·cal** /sèllənə lójjik'l, sə leénə-/ *adj.* —**sel·e·nol·o·gist** *n.*

Se·les /sél ess/, **Monica** (*b.* 1973) Yugoslavian-born U.S. tennis player. She was the winner of the French Open (1990, 1991, 1992), Australian Open (1991, 1992, 1993, 1996), U.S. Open (1991 and 1992), and Canadian Open (1995).

Se·leu·cid /sə lóossid, -lyóossid/ *n.* any one of a dynasty of rulers who ruled Asia Minor from 312 to 64 B.C., after the death of Alexander the Great [Mid-19thC. Via Latin *Seleucides* from Greek *Seleukidēs,* from *Seleukos,* the name of the founder of the dynasty.] —**Se·leu·cid** *adj.*

Se·leu·cus I /sə lóokəss/ (358?–280 B.C.) Macedonian general. One of Alexander the Great's successors, he founded the Seleucid dynasty. He became king of Babylonia in 312 B.C. and gained control of territory from India to Asia Minor, but died trying to seize the throne of Macedonia. Known as **Seleucus Nicator**

Se·leu·cus II (265?–226? B.C.) Syrian monarch. During his reign over the Seleucid kingdom (247–

226 B.C.), the Bactrians and Parthians won independence.

self /self/ *n.* (*plural* **selves** /selvz/) **1. PERCEIVED PERSONALITY** somebody's personality or an aspect of it, especially as perceived by others ○ *He's not his usual cheery self this morning.* **2. SELF-INTEREST** somebody's own individual interests and welfare, especially when placed before those of other people **3. COMPLETE PERSONALITY** a complete and individual personality, especially one that somebody recognizes as his or her own and with which there is a sense of ease ○ *A person needs to develop a sense of self.* **4. IMMUNOL OWN BODY PARTS** the set of organs and tissues that the body recognizes as its own and does not attack with antibodies ■ *pron.* **ONESELF** myself, yourself, himself, or herself (*informal*) ○ *not enough to sustain self and family* ■ *adj.* **1. SELF-COLORED** having the same color all over **2. OF SAME FABRIC** made of the same material as the garment it is worn with **3. SAME** same or identical (*archaic*) [Old English. Ultimately from an Indo-European pronoun that is also the ancestor of English *suicide* and *sober.*]

WORD KEY: USAGE

Grammar The two main uses of **-self** compounds such as *himself, herself,* and *myself* are, first, to serve as a reflexive pronoun when the object of the verb is the same as the subject (*He saw himself in the mirror*) and, second, to reinforce or emphasize a noun (*Jane herself had wanted to go with them*). Compounds with ***-self*** should not be used simply as alternatives for other pronouns, such as *him, her, me,* and *I*: *It was up to her [not herself] whether she came or not. This is between him and me [not myself].*

self- *prefix.* **1.** of, by, for, or in itself ○ *self-assured* **2.** automatic ○ *self-winding* [From SELF]

self-a·ban·doned *adj.* showing little self-control and tending to give in to impulse —**self-a·ban·don·ment** *n.*

self-a·base·ment *n.* the humbling of yourself in response to feelings of guilt or shame

self-ab·sorbed *adj.* excessively concerned with your own life and interests

self-ab·sorp·tion *n.* **1. PREOCCUPATION WITH SELF** excessive concern with your own life and interests **2. PHYS ABSORPTION OF OWN RADIATION** a radioactive material's absorption of part of the radiation that it emits

self-a·buse /-ə byo͞oss/ *n.* **1. MASTURBATION** masturbation when viewed as being detrimental to character (*dated*) (*sometimes used humorously*) **2. CRITICISM OF SELF** somebody's deprecation or deliberate misuse of his or her talents and abilities —**self-a·bus·er** *n.*

self-act·ing *adj.* operating itself —**self-ac·tion** *n.*

self-ac·tu·al·i·za·tion *n.* the successful development and use of personal talents and abilities

self-ad·dressed *adj.* addressed to the sender for return by mail

self-ad·he·sive *adj.* having adhesive on one side and able to stick in a position without needing to be moistened or to have adhesive applied

self-ad·min·is·ter (**self-ad·min·is·tered, self-ad·min·is·ter·ing, self-ad·min·is·ters**) *vt.* to administer something, especially medical treatment, to yourself —**self-ad·min·is·tered** *adj.*

self-ag·gran·dize·ment *n.* the ambitious or ruthless pursuit of increased personal importance, wealth, reputation, or power —**self-ag·gran·diz·ing** *adj.*

self-an·ni·hi·la·tion *n.* **1. DETACHMENT FROM SELF** loss of awareness of being an individual, achieved through meditation or other mystical means **2. SUICIDE** an act or instance of suicide

self-ap·point·ed *adj.* assuming a role personally, rather than being given it or being regarded as worthy of it by others ○ *a self-appointed arbiter of good taste*

self-as·ser·tive *adj.* tending to be aggressively confident in making your views heard and your presence felt —**self-as·ser·tive·ly** *adv.* —**self-as·ser·tive·ness** *n.*

self-as·sur·ance *n.* relaxed confidence that your views and abilities are of value

self-as·sured *adj.* behaving in a relaxed manner that displays confidence that your views and abilities are of value —**self-as·sur·ed·ly** *adv.* —**self-as·sur·ed·ness** *n.*

self-a·ware *adj.* having a balanced and honest view of your own personality, and often an ability to interact with others frankly and confidently —**self-a·ware·ness** *n.*

self-bast·ing *adj.* commercially prepared with added fat to prevent drying out when cooked in an oven ○ *a self-basting turkey*

self-ca·ter·ing *adj.* *U.K.* used to describe accommodations, especially for vacationers or students, in which meals are not provided but cooking facilities are

self-cen·tered *adj.* tending to concentrate selfishly on your own needs and affairs and to show little or no interest in those of others —**self-cen·tered·ly** *adv.* —**self-cen·tered·ness** *n.*

self-clean·ing *adj.* designed to stay clean when being used, usually by virtue of being coated with materials that shed dirt ○ *a self-cleaning oven*

self-clos·ing *adj.* used to describe a door, gate, or window fitted with a mechanism that returns it to a closed position after it has been opened

self-col·ored *adj.* **1. UNIFORM IN COLOR** of the same color all over or throughout **2. BOT RETAINING NATURAL COLOR** used to describe a flower whose color has not been artificially changed by hybridization **3. TEXTILES UNDYED** used to describe cloth that has not been dyed and so retains its natural color

self-com·mand *n.* the ability to present your ideas and intentions clearly and effectively

self-com·pat·i·ble *adj.* used to describe a plant that is capable of pollinating itself

self-con·cept *n.* the whole inner picture that somebody has of himself or herself, including a complete evaluation of such traits as competence, worth, and attractiveness

self-con·fessed *adj.* admitting freely to possessing a particular quality or to behaving in a certain way

self-con·fi·dence *n.* confidence in yourself and your own abilities

self-con·fi·dent *adj.* having or showing confidence in yourself and your abilities, usually with a readiness to be assertive —**self-con·fi·dent·ly** *adv.*

self-con·grat·u·la·tion *n.* the frequent mentioning of personal achievements and the displaying of the smug satisfaction taken in them —**self-con·grat·u·la·to·ry** *adj.*

self-con·scious *adj.* **1. ILL AT EASE** feeling acutely and uncomfortably aware of failings and shortcomings when in the company of others and believing that others are noticing them too ○ *too self-conscious to speak in public* **2. EXCESSIVELY CONCERNED WITH APPEARANCES** highly conscious of the impression made on others and tending to act in a way that reinforces this impression ○ *swinging his car keys in a self-conscious manner* —**self-con·scious·ly** *adv.* —**self-con·scious·ness** *n.*

self-con·tained *adj.* **1. HAVING EVERYTHING REQUIRED** possessing all the features and facilities required to function independently **2. KEEPING FEELINGS PRIVATE** able or tending to keep feelings and opinions private or to control feelings and reactions in front of others **3. HAVING OWN FACILITIES AND ENTRANCE** used to describe accommodations that have their own kitchen, bathroom, and entrance ○ *All of our units are self-contained* —**self-con·tain·ment** *n.*

self-con·tra·dic·tion *n.* **1. LACK OF CONSISTENCY** speech, thoughts, or actions that contradict what their author previously said, thought, or did **2. SOMETHING CONTRADICTORY** a statement, idea, or theory that contradicts itself —**self-con·tra·dic·to·ry** *adj.*

self-con·trol *n.* the ability to control your own behavior, especially in terms of reactions and impulses —**self-con·trolled** *adj.*

self-cor·rect·ing *adj.* **1. CORRECTING ERRORS AUTOMATICALLY** used to describe a word processor that automatically corrects typing errors as they occur **2. CORRECTING OWN MISTAKES** able or tending to notice personal mistakes and correct them

self-crit·i·cal *adj.* tending to notice and dwell on your own shortcomings —**self-crit·i·cism** *n.*

self-de·ceiv·ing *adj.* **1. IGNORING TRUTH** refusing to recognize the truth, usually because to do so would be painful or difficult **2. TENDING TO GLORIFY SELF** cherishing self-indulgent beliefs about yourself —**self-de·cep·tion** *n.*

self-de·feat·ing *adj.* defeating the very aim or purpose it is designed to serve

self-de·fense *n.* **1. LAW LEGAL RIGHT TO DEFEND SELF** the use of reasonable force to defend yourself, your family, and your property against physical attack, or the right to do this **2. FIGHTING TECHNIQUES** fighting techniques used to defend yourself against physical attack, especially unarmed combat techniques such as any of the martial arts **3. JUSTIFYING OF SELF** the defending of your own ideas, principles, or actions —**self-de·fen·sive** *adj.*

self-de·ni·al *n.* the setting aside of your own wishes, needs, or interests, whether voluntary, altruistic, or enforced by circumstances —**self-de·ny·ing** *adj.* —**self-de·ny·ing·ly** *adv.*

self-dep·re·cat·ing, **self-dep·re·ca·to·ry** *adj.* tending to belittle yourself or your achievements

self-de·struct *vi.* (**self-de·struc·ted, self-de·struc·t·ing, self-de·structs**) **1. DESTROY ITSELF AUTOMATICALLY** to destroy itself by means of a built-in mechanism **2. RUIN OWN LIFE** to behave in a way that destroys any chance of your success, credibility, or effectiveness ■ *adj.* **CAUSING DESTRUCTION OF ITSELF** causing a device or machine to destroy itself if certain conditions are met

self-de·struc·tion *n.* **1. RUINING OF OWN LIFE** the ruining of your own life or an aspect of it such as your health, happiness, or career **2. AUTOMATIC DESTRUCTION OF DEVICE** the automatic destruction of a device fitted with a self-destruct mechanism **3. SUICIDE** an act or instance of suicide

self-de·struc·tive *adj.* causing or tending to cause harm to yourself

self-de·ter·mi·na·tion *n.* **1. RIGHT TO DECIDE FOR SELF** the ability or right to make your own decisions without interference from others **2. POL RIGHT TO CHOOSE OWN GOVERNMENT** the right of a people to determine its own form of government without interference from outside

self-dis·ci·pline *n.* the ability to do what is necessary or sensible without needing to be urged by somebody else —**self-dis·ci·plined** *adj.*

self-dis·cov·er·y *n.* the process of learning about your true personality and motives

self-doubt *n.* feelings of doubt about your own worth and abilities

self-ef·fac·ing *adj.* tending to be modest about your achievements and to avoid drawing attention to yourself in company —**self-ef·face·ment** *n.* —**self-ef·fac·ing·ly** *adv.*

self-ef·fi·ca·cy *n.* the belief that you can influence your own thoughts and behavior

self-em·ployed *adj.* earning a living by working independently of an employer, either freelance or by running a business —**self-em·ploy·ment** *n.*

self-es·teem *n.* confidence in your own merit as an individual

self-e·val·u·a·tion *n.* the process of evaluating your own character, work, achievements, or goals

self-ev·i·dent *adj.* obvious without explanation or proof —**self-ev·i·dence** *n.* —**self-ev·i·dent·ly** *adv.*

self-ex·am·i·na·tion *n.* **1. REFLECTION ON OWN CONDITION** careful reflection on your own thoughts, beliefs, behavior, and circumstances **2. MEDICAL EXAMINATION OF OWN BODY** the regular examination of parts of your own body for signs of disease —**self-ex·am·in·ing** *adj.*

self-ex·cit·ed *adj.* used to describe an electrical device with a field system that is excited by a current the device generates for itself

self-ex·e·cut·ing *adj.* legally effective without intervention ○ *self-executing clauses in the contract*

self-ex·ile *n.* **1. SOMEBODY WHO LEAVES OWN COUNTRY VOLUNTARILY** somebody who leaves his or her own country voluntarily to live elsewhere, especially for political reasons **2. VOLUNTARY EXILE** a voluntary state of exile —**self-ex·iled** *adj.*

self-ex·plan·a·to·ry *adj.* clear and easy to understand with no need for explanation

self-ex·pres·sion *n.* the expressing of your own ideas, emotions, or individuality through behavior or an activity such as painting, music, or writing

self-feed·er *n.* a machine or device that automatically supplies or replaces materials as they are needed, e.g., a device for feeding animals

self-fer·til·i·za·tion *n.* fertilization of a plant or animal ovum using pollen or sperm from the same individual —**self-fer·til·ized** *adj.* —**self-fer·til·iz·ing** *adj.*

self-fi·nanc·ing *adj.* paid for or run without outside financial support

self-flag·el·la·tion *n.* 1. SELF-CRITICISM very strong or harsh self-criticism 2. PUNISHING OF OWN BODY severe self-administered physical punishment. The practice of self-flagellation was formerly used as an act of penance, often in the form of beatings or floggings.

self-flat·ter·y *n.* the exaggerating of positive personal traits while overlooking negative traits

self-fo·cus·ing *adj.* focusing automatically rather than manually

self-for·get·ful *adj.* putting the interests of others first (*archaic*) —**self-for·get·ful·ly** *adv.* —**self-for·get·ful·ness** *n.*

self-ful·fill·ing *adj.* 1. HAPPENING BECAUSE EXPECTED brought about or proved true because of having been expected or predicted 2. SATISFYING providing satisfaction or pleasure through personal labor, initiative, or talent

self-ful·fill·ment *n.* contentment or happiness as a result of personal work, initiative, or talent

self-giv·ing *adj.* willing to act unselfishly for the benefit of others

self-glo·ri·fi·ca·tion *n.* promotion of your own qualities and abilities, especially beyond what is true or appropriate

self-gov·erned *adj.* 1. NOT INFLUENCED BY OTHERS not needing or wanting the advice or influence of others 2. INDEPENDENT run by the people who live or work in a particular area or place rather than by external government 3. USING SELF-CONTROL capable of exercising self-control

self-gov·ern·ing *adj.* 1. USING SELF-CONTROL able to control your own actions and behavior 2. GOVERNED BY OWN INHABITANTS OR EMPLOYEES run by its own members, employees, or citizens, rather than being run from outside

self-gov·ern·ment *n.* 1. AUTONOMY the ability or right of the citizens of a region to choose their own government rather than having it imposed from outside 2. SELF-CONTROL the ability to exercise self-control (*archaic*)

self-grat·i·fi·ca·tion *n.* the satisfying of your own desires for the sake of pleasure, especially sexual pleasure (*used euphemistically*)

self-hard·en·ing *adj.* becoming harder without special treatment after being heated above a certain temperature

self-harm·ing *n.* the practice of causing physical harm to yourself, usually as a symptom of a psychiatric disorder

self-ha·tred, self-hate *n.* hatred or contempt for your own weaknesses or innate characteristics such as ethnicity or race

self·heal /sélf hèel/ *n.* a low-growing creeping mint with small spikes of purple-blue flowers that is native to Europe and Asia but grows as a weed in North America. Latin name: *Prunella vulgaris.* [14thC. Applied to various plants believed to have medicinal properties.]

self-help *n.* 1. GROUP HELP AND SUPPORT the practice of meeting or working with others who share a common problem rather than relying on the government or professionals for help 2. ACTION OUTSIDE LEGAL SYSTEM an action that is usually left to the legal authorities and may not be permitted by law, but that is undertaken by an individual to protect a legal or moral right 3. SOLVING PROBLEMS WITHOUT OTHERS' HELP the practice of dealing with your own problems and challenges without seeking outside help

self·hood /sélf hòod/ *n.* 1. INDIVIDUALITY the possession of a unique identity, distinct from others 2. COMPLETE SENSE OF SELF the possession of a fully developed personality and sense of identity 3. SOMEBODY'S CHARACTER OR PERSONALITY all the qualities and characteristics that make up somebody's character or personality

self-hyp·no·sis *n.* = **autohypnosis**

self-i·den·ti·fied *adj.* 1. IDENTIFYING WITH SOMEBODY OR SOMETHING having somebody or something particular as the focus of a sense of self 2. ADMITTING IDENTITY having voluntarily acknowledged an identity without coercion ○ *a self-identified thief*

self-i·den·ti·ty *n.* 1. INDIVIDUALITY the awareness that an individual or group has of being unique 2. SENSE OF BEING ONE the quality that something has of being one with itself

self-im·age *n.* the opinion that you have of your own worth, attractiveness, or intelligence

self-im·mo·la·tion *n.* suicide, usually by burning, as an act of sacrifice or protest (*formal*)

self-im·por·tance *n.* an unrealistically high evaluation of your own importance or worth —**self-im·por·tant** *adj.* —**self-im·por·tant·ly** *adv.*

self-im·posed *adj.* chosen willingly as a burden or limit ○ *a self-imposed deadline*

self-im·prove·ment *n.* improvement of yourself or advancement in career or status as a result of your own effort

self-in·crim·i·na·tion *n.* speech or action that suggests your own guilt, especially during court testimony —**self-in·crim·i·nat·ing** *adj.* —**self-in·crim·i·na·to·ry** *adj.*

self-in·duced *adj.* 1. RESULTING FROM OWN ACTIONS brought on by your own actions 2. ELECTRON ENG CAUSED BY SELF-INDUCTION produced by the process of self-induction

self-in·duc·tion *n.* ELECTRON ENG induction of an electromotive force in a circuit by means of a changing current in that circuit —**self-in·duc·tive** *adj.*

self-in·dul·gence *n.* 1. PURSUIT OF OWN PLEASURE lack of self-control in pursuing your own pleasure or satisfaction 2. SOMETHING SHOWING NO SELF-CONTROL something that reveals lack of self-restraint —**self-in·dul·gent** *adj.* —**self-in·dul·gent·ly** *adv.*

self-in·flict·ed *adj.* caused or done by your own actions

self-in·sur·ance *n.* the saving of money to protect against a loss instead of buying an insurance policy

self-in·ter·est *n.* 1. SELFISHNESS the placing of your own needs or desires before those of others 2. OWN NEEDS OR DESIRES your own needs and desires —**self-in·ter·est·ed** *adj.* —**self-in·ter·est·ed·ness** *n.*

self-in·volved *adj.* = **self-absorbed**

self·ish /sélfish/ *adj.* 1. LOOKING AFTER OWN DESIRES concerned with your own interests, needs, and wishes while ignoring those of others 2. DEMONSTRATING SELFISHNESS showing that personal needs and wishes are thought to be more important than those of other people —**self·ish·ly** *adv.* —**self·ish·ness** *n.*

self·ish DNA *n.* a segment of DNA that increases itself, e.g., as repeated sequences, within the total genetic material of a population over successive generations without apparent benefit to the organisms concerned

self·ish gene *n.* a gene that exploits the organism in which it occurs as a vehicle for its self-perpetuation. Posited by the biologist Richard Dawkins in 1976, it overturns the traditional concept of the gene serving as a vehicle of inheritance for the organism.

self-jus·ti·fi·ca·tion *n.* 1. MAKING OF EXCUSES FOR ACTIONS an attempt to explain your own behavior or actions by making excuses 2. SOMETHING DONE AS JUSTIFICATION something that somebody does or says in an attempt to explain personal behavior or actions

self-jus·ti·fy·ing *adj.* 1. ATTEMPTING TO EXPLAIN making excuses in an attempt to explain your own behavior or actions 2. AUTOMATICALLY MAKING TEXT UNIFORM ON MARGIN automatically providing an even right or left margin for text printed on a page 3. LOGICALLY COMPLETE used to describe an argument or rule that justifies or explains itself without referring to something else because of being regarded as completely logical or obvious

self-knowl·edge *n.* knowledge or understanding of your own motives and behavior

self·less /sélfləss/ *adj.* putting other people's needs first —**self·less·ly** *adv.* —**self·less·ness** *n.*

self-lim·it·ed, self-lim·it·ing *adj.* 1. LIMITED BY OWN NATURE limited by internal or personal characteristics rather than by outside influences 2. HAVING PARTICULAR LIFESPAN used to describe a disease that lasts for a particular length of time time whether or not it is treated

self-lim·it·ing *adj.* 1. SELF-IMPOSED imposing personal limitations or restrictions 2. = **self-limited** —**self-lim·i·ta·tion** *n.*

self-liq·ui·dat·ing *adj.* 1. ABLE TO MAKE MONEY BEFORE DUE used to describe a loan to fund a transaction that is expected to make money before the loan is due to be repaid 2. PAYING FOR ITSELF used to describe a business transaction that makes enough money to cover its costs

self-load·ing *adj.* used to describe a firearm that automatically ejects a spent cartridge and puts a new round into the chamber each time it is fired —**self-load·er** *n.*

self-loath·ing *n.* = **self-hatred**

self-lock·ing *adj.* used to describe a window or door that locks automatically when closed

self-love *n.* concern with only your own wishes and desires

self-lu·bri·cat·ing *adj.* not requiring external application of lubrication to parts that experience friction

self-made *adj.* 1. SUCCESSFUL AS A RESULT OF WORK successful or wealthy through your own efforts, rather than through birth or from the work of others 2. MADE UNAIDED made without the help of others

self-mas·ter·y *adj.* control over your own emotions, needs, or desires and their expression

self-med·i·ca·tion *n.* the practice of treating illnesses and medical complaints without consulting a doctor, e.g., by buying treatments from a drugstore —**self-med·i·ca·tor** *n.*

self-mor·ti·fi·ca·tion *n.* self-administered punishment, often as prescribed by religious precepts, because of some perceived fault or flaw

self-mo·ti·vat·ed *adj.* energetic and ambitious, and so able to make plans and get things done without being directed by others —**self-mo·ti·va·tion** *n.*

self-mur·der *n.* suicide (*archaic or disapproving*)

self-mu·ti·la·tion *n.* self-inflicted injury, especially with a sharp object

self-oc·cu·pied *adj.* busy with your own thoughts or problems

self-o·pin·ion *n.* a very high opinion of your own abilities or worth

self-o·pin·ion·at·ed, self-opin·ioned *adj.* 1. CERTAIN OF BEING RIGHT confident of holding the correct opinions 2. VAIN very conceited

self-or·dained *adj.* claiming the authority to speak as an expert without qualifications or the support of others

self-par·o·dy *n.* unintentional exaggeration or overemphasis by somebody of his or her worst characteristics

self-per·pet·u·at·ing *adj.* continuing because of having the power to preserve or renew itself indefinitely

self-pit·y *n.* the self-indulgent belief that your life is harder and sadder than everyone else's —**self-pit·y·ing** *adj.* —**self-pit·y·ing·ly** *adv.*

self-pol·li·na·tion *n.* pollination that takes place within a flower through the transfer of pollen from its anthers to its stigmas —**self-pol·li·nate** *vi.* —**self-pol·li·nat·ing** *adj.*

self-por·trait *n.* a visual image, sculpture, or written description of somebody, produced by that person

self-pos·sessed *adj.* confident and in control of your own emotions —**self-pos·sess·edly** *adv.*

self-pos·ses·sion *n.* the ability to remain calm and confident, especially in difficult or emotional circumstances

self-pow·ered *adj.* = **self-propelled** *adj.* 1

self-pres·er·va·tion *n.* the instinctive need to do what is necessary to survive danger

self-pro·claimed *adj.* claiming to be something, often without justification

self-pro·mo·tion *n.* behavior shown or action taken by somebody in order to attract attention, especially in relation to work or business

self-pro·nounc·ing *adj.* using only letters of the ordinary alphabet to represent a pronunciation, rather than using symbols from the phonetic alphabet

self-pro·pelled *adj.* 1. MOVING UNDER OWN POWER able to move or travel using its own power source such as a motor or batteries, rather than needing power from an external source 2. MOUNTED ON VEHICLE relating to a piece of heavy military equipment that is mounted on a vehicle rather than needing to be towed —**self-pro·pel·ling** *adj.* —**self-pro·pul·sion** *n.*

self-pro·tec·tion *n.* action taken to protect against attack on or injury to yourself —**self-pro·tect·ing** *adj.* —**self-pro·tec·tive** *adj.*

self-pub·lished *adj.* published without a publisher, and therefore at the author's own expense

self-rais·ing *adj. U.K.* = **self-rising**

self-re·al·i·za·tion *n.* fulfillment of personal potential

self-ref·er·en·tial *adj.* used to describe an art form that employs references to the art itself or to personal experience or character —**self-ref·er·ence** *n.* —**self-ref·er·en·tial·ly** *adv.*

self-re·flec·tion *n.* = **self-examination** *n.* 1

self-re·gard *n.* 1. LACKING REGARD FOR OTHERS self-interest rather than concern for the well-being of others 2. SELF-RESPECT belief in your own worth and dignity —**self-re·gard·ing** *adj.*

self-reg·u·lat·ing, self-reg·u·la·to·ry *adj.* 1. REGULATING ITSELF WITHOUT LAWS regulating its own affairs rather than being regulated by an outside organization or by law 2. REGULATING SELF AUTOMATICALLY capable of regulating its functions automatically —**self-reg·u·la·tion** *n.*

self-re·li·ance *n.* the ability to make your own decisions confidently and independently —**self-re·li·ant** *adj.* —**self-re·li·ant·ly** *adv.*

self-re·nun·ci·a·tion *n.* the giving up of your own rights, claims, or property to benefit others

self-rep·li·cat·ing *adj.* used to describe a molecule or bacterium that reproduces on its own by making copies of itself —**self-rep·li·ca·tion** *n.*

self-re·proach *n.* self-criticism or blame —**self-re·proach·ful** *adj.* —**self-re·proach·ful·ly** *adv.*

self-re·spect *n.* belief in your own worth and dignity —**self-re·spect·ing** *adj.*

self-re·straint *n.* self-control over speech, behavior, or action

self-right·eous *adj.* sure of the moral superiority of your own beliefs and actions (*disapproving*) —**self-right·eous·ly** *adv.* —**self-right·eous·ness** *n.*

self-right·ing *adj.* able to right itself after being capsized

self-ris·ing *adj.* used to describe flour that has a leavening agent added to it so that baking powder is not needed when making cakes. *U.K. term* **self-raising**

self-rule *n.* = **self-government** *n.* 1

self-sac·ri·fice *n.* the giving up of personal wants and needs, either from a sense of duty or in order to benefit others —**self-sac·ri·fic·ing** *adj.* —**self-sac·ri·fic·ing·ly** *adv.*

self·same /sélf sàym/ *adj.* being the very same

self-sat·is·fac·tion *n.* a feeling of satisfaction in personal achievements and good fortune —**self-sat·is·fied** *adj.*

self-seal·ing *adj.* 1. SEALING WITHOUT BEING MOISTENED used to describe an envelope that has a flap coated with adhesive that can be closed without being moistened 2. ABLE TO SEAL SELF used to describe a tire that can seal itself after being punctured. The tire contains a compound that hardens in contact with air.

self-seed·ed *adj.* = **self-sown**

self-seek·ing *adj.* SELFISH interested only in gaining an advantage over others, rather than in sharing or cooperating ■ *n.* SELF-SEEKING BEHAVIOUR behavior intended to secure an advantage over others —**self-seek·er** *n.*

self-se·lec·tion *n.* 1. = **self-service** 2. SELECTING OF SELF choice of, by, or for yourself —**self-se·lect·ed** *adj.* —**self-se·lec·tive** *adj.*

self-serv·ice *adj.* used to describe a retail outlet or device used by customers or users helping themselves ○ *a self-service gas station* ○ *a self-service drink dispenser* —**self-serv·ice** *n.*

self-serv·ing *adj.* putting personal concerns and interests before those of others

self-sown *adj.* used to describe plants that grow from seeds that reach the soil by themselves, without being carried there by people or animals

self-start·er *n.* 1. SOMEBODY ENTERPRISING somebody with the initiative and motivation to work without needing help or supervision 2. AUTOMOT ELECTRIC STARTER an electrically operated device for starting an internal-combustion engine —**self-start·ing** *adj.*

self-stick, self-stick·ing *adj.* coated with adhesive so as to adhere to something without being moistened

self-styled *adj.* using a particular name or title or professing knowledge of a subject without having training or independent proof

self-suf·fi·cient, self-suf·fic·ing *adj.* 1. NOT NEEDING THINGS FROM OTHERS able to provide what is needed, e.g., by making enough money or growing enough food, without having to borrow or buy from others 2. ABLE TO MANAGE ALONE able to live independently of others —**self-suf·fi·cien·cy** *n.* —**self-suf·fi·cient·ly** *adv.*

self-sug·ges·tion *n.* = autosuggestion

self-sup·port·ing *adj.* 1. GETTING ALONG FINANCIALLY earning enough money to live or operate without external financial support 2. STANDING WITHOUT BEING HELD able to stand or stay upright without being supported —**self-sup·port** *n.* —**self-sup·port·ed** *adj.*

self-sus·tain·ing *adj.* able to live or continue existing without outside support

self-talk *n.* the things that an individual says to himself or herself mentally

self-taught *adj.* having learned a skill, job, or subject without formal instruction

self-ten·der *n.* an offer made by a company to buy back shares from its shareholders, e.g., to avoid a hostile takeover bid

self-test *n.* 1. MED SELF-ADMINISTERED TEST a diagnostic test, e.g., for blood pressure, that you give yourself to determine your health 2. TEST OF KNOWLEDGE a test you give yourself to find out how well you know a particular subject ■ *v.* (**self-test·ed, self-test·ing, self-tests**) 1. *vti.* MED TEST ON YOURSELF to perform a diagnostic test on yourself in order to determine your health 2. *vr.* TEST YOURSELF ON KNOWLEDGE to test yourself on a particular subject to find out how well you know it

self-treat·ment *n.* an individual's treating of his or her own illnesses or injuries rather than seeking the advice of a doctor

self-will *n.* stubborn determination to hold to personal views and behavior —**self-willed** *adj.*

self-wind·ing *adj.* not needing to be wound ○ *a self-winding watch*

self-worth *n.* confidence in personal value and worth as an individual

Sel·juk /sél jòok, -jóok/ *n.* a member of one of the Turkish dynasties that ruled large areas of Asia during the 11th, 12th, and 13th centuries before the Ottoman Empire [Mid-19thC. From Turkish *Selčük*, the name of the reputed founder of the dynasty.] —**Sel·juk** *adj.*

Sel·kirk Moun·tains /sèl kurk-/ mountain range in southeastern British Columbia, Canada, west of the Rocky Mountains. The highest point is Mount Sandford, 11,555 ft./3,522m.

sell /sel/ *v.* (**sold** /sōld/, **sold, sell·ing, sells**) 1. *vti.* EXCHANGE SOMETHING FOR MONEY to exchange a product or service for money 2. *vt.* OFFER SOMETHING FOR SALE to offer a particular product or range of products for sale 3. *vi.* BE BOUGHT IN QUANTITY to be bought in large numbers ○ *The book is selling well.* 4. *vt.* MAKE PEOPLE WANT TO BUY SOMETHING to increase the sale of or the demand for a particular product ○ *Advertising sells products.* 5. *vt.* PERSUADE SOMEBODY TO ACCEPT SOMETHING to persuade somebody to accept an idea or proposal ○ *You've convinced me but now you have to sell it to the shareholders.* 6. *vt.* GIVE SOMETHING UP FOR MONEY to sacrifice an important personal quality in order to obtain wealth or success ○ *He's sold his integrity for a long-term contract.* ■ *n.* PROCESS OF SELLING the activity or process of persuading people to buy a product or service (*informal*) ○ *use an aggressive sell* [Old English *sellan* "to grant, give up, hand over," from a prehistoric Germanic word that is also the ancestor of English *sale*. Current senses developed via "to betray for money."] —**sell·a·ble** *adj.* ◇ **sell somebody** *or* **something short** 1. to make an estimate of the quality and worth of somebody or something that is too low 2. to sell goods or securities without owning them, expecting to buy them at a price lower than the selling price ◇ **sell yourself** to work hard to persuade others that you are talented, pleasant, well-qualified, or suitable for a particular job ◇ **sell your soul** to abandon your principles in order to obtain wealth or success

sell off *vt.* to sell something, especially at a low price, in order to get rid of it

sell on *vt.* to convince somebody that a plan or product is the best (*usually passive*)

sell·back /séll bàk/ *n.* the act of selling something back to the person it was bought from

sell-by date *n. U.K.* a date displayed on food and pharmaceutical products, after which they should not be sold

sell·er /séllər/ *n.* 1. SOMEBODY WHO IS SELLING a person, store, or company that offers something for sale 2. ITEM THAT IS SELLING a product that sells in a specified way, especially well or badly

sell·er's mar·ket *n.* a situation or market in which the demand for something is greater than the supply, so that its price can be forced up. ◊ **buyer's market**

sell·ing cli·max *n.* a large volume of trading at the end of a downturn in the stock markets (*informal*)

sell·ing point *n.* a feature of something such as a product or an idea that makes people more likely to want to buy or support it

sell·ing race, sell·ing plate *n.* a horse race in which the winner is auctioned and sold

sell·out /sél òwt/ *n.* 1. EVENT WITH NO TICKETS LEFT a show, concert, or sports event for which all the tickets are sold 2. BETRAYAL betrayal of personal principles or another person (*informal*) 3. TRAITOR TO PRINCIPLE somebody who has betrayed a principle or cause for money or something else of value (*informal*)

Sel·ma /sélmə/ city in central Alabama, northwest of Montgomery, on the northern bank of the Alabama River. Population: 22,745 (1996).

sel·syn /sél sìn/ *n.* a system used to transmit angular rotation or position in a generator to a motor [Early 20thC. Blend of SELF and SYNCHRONOUS.]

selt·zer /séltsər/ *n.* 1. NATURALLY FIZZY MINERAL WATER mineral water that contains naturally occurring dissolved gases that make it slightly fizzy, often used for medicinal purposes 2. SODA WATER soda water (*dated*) [Mid-18thC. Alteration of German *Selterser*, literally "from Selters," alluding to mineral springs in the village of Nieder- *Selters* near Wiesbaden in Germany.]

sel·va /sélvə/ *n.* a dense tropical rain forest, especially in the Amazon Basin [Mid-19thC. Via Spanish or Portuguese from Latin *silva* "wood" (source of English *sylvan* and *savage*).]

sel·vage /sélvij/, **sel·vedge** *n.* 1. NONFRAYING EDGE OF FABRIC an edge of a piece of fabric that is woven so that it will not fray 2. STRIP OF MATERIAL an edge or strip of material included when manufacturing something such as a metal or plastic article or a sheet of postage stamps that allows it to be handled 3. LOCK PLATE a slotted plate or surface through which the bolt of a lock passes 4. RUG FRINGE a decorative fringe on the ends of an oriental rug [15thC. Alteration of "self-edge" (because it "edges" itself and does not need hemming).] —**sel·vaged** *adj.*

selves plural of **self**

David O. Selznick

Selz·nick /sélznik/, **David O.** (1902–65) U.S. movie producer. His many classic productions included *Gone With the Wind* (1939). Full name **David Oliver Selznick**

SEM *abbr.* scanning electron microscope

sem. *abbr.* 1. semester 2. semicolon 3. seminary

Sem. *abbr.* 1. Semitic 2. Seminary

se·man·teme /sə mán teem/ *n.* the smallest possible unit of meaning in language [Early 20thC. From French *sémantème*, formed from Greek *semantikos* (see SEMANTIC), on the model of *morphème* (see MORPHEME).]

se·man·tic /sə mántik/ *adj.* **1.** LING **RELATING TO WORDS' MEANINGS** relating to meaning or the differences between meanings of words or symbols **2.** LING **OF SEMANTICS** relating to semantics **3.** LOGIC **RELATING TO TRUTH** relating to the conditions in which a system or theory can be said to be true [Mid-17thC. Via French *semantique* from Greek *semantikos* "significant," from *sēmainein* "to show or signify," from *sēma* "sign, mark."] — **se·man·ti·cal·ly** *adv.*

se·man·tics /sə mántiks/ *n.* **1.** LING **STUDY OF MEANING IN LANGUAGE** the study of how meaning in language is created by the use and interrelationships of words, phrases, and sentences **2.** LOGIC **STUDY OF SYMBOLS** the study of the relationship between symbols and what they represent **3.** LOGIC **STUDY OF LOGIC** the study of ways of interpreting and analyzing theories of logic — **se·man·ti·cist** *n.*

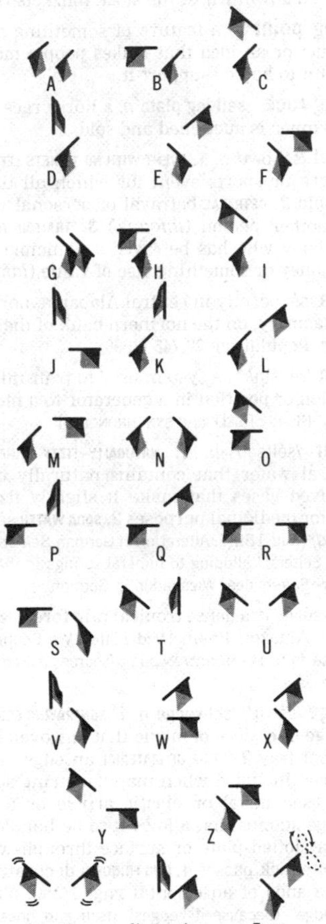

Semaphore

sem·a·phore /sémmə fawr/ *n.* **1. SYSTEM OF SIGNALING** a system for sending messages using hand-held flags that are moved to represent letters of the alphabet **2. MECHANICAL SIGNALING DEVICE** a signaling device for sending information over distances using mechanically operated arms or flags mounted on a post, especially on a railroad ■ *vti.* (**-phored, -phor·ing, -phores**) **USE SEMAPHORE TO SIGNAL** to send messages using semaphore [Early 19thC. From French *sémaphore*, literally "sign-bearer," from Greek *sēma* "mark, sign, signal."] — **sem·a·phor·ic** /sèmmə fáwrik/ *adj.* —**sem·a·phor·i·cal·ly** *adv.*

Se·ma·rang /sèmmə ráng/ city and port on the island of Java, Indonesia, located east of Jakarta. Population: 1,250,971 (1990).

se·ma·si·ol·o·gy /sə màyssee óllәjee, -màyzee-/ *n.* = **semantics** *n.* 1, **semantics** *n.* 2 [Mid-19thC. From German *Semasiologie*, literally "science of meaning," from Greek *sēmasia* "meaning," from *sēmainein* (see SEMANTIC).] — **se·ma·si·o·log·i·cal** /sə màyssee ə lójjik'l, -màyzee-/ *adj.* —**se·ma·si·o·log·i·cal·ly** *adv.* —**se·ma·si·ol·o·gist** /sə màyssee óllәjist, sə màyzee-/ *n.*

se·mat·ic /sə máttik/ *adj.* used to describe bright colorings on particular animals that act as a warning to predators, e.g., because the animals are poisonous [Late 19thC. Formed from Greek *sēmat-*, stem of *sēma* "mark, sign."]

sem·bla·ble /sémbləb'l/ *n.* **SOMEBODY OR SOMETHING LOOKING LIKE ANOTHER** somebody who or something that closely resembles somebody or something else (*archaic*) ■ *adj.* **1. LIKE ANOTHER** resembling or similar to something or somebody else (*formal*) **2. NOT REAL** apparent rather than real (*archaic*) [13thC. From Old French, formed from *sembler* (see SEMBLANCE).] —**sem·bla·bly** *adv.*

sem·blance /sémbl ənss/ *n.* **1. TRACE OF SOMETHING** a small amount of something ○ *a semblance of dignity* **2. LOOK OF BEING SOMETHING** an outward appearance or imitation of something ○ *a semblance of competence* **3. COPY** a representation, likeness, or copy (*literary*) [14thC. From Old French, formed from *sembler* "to seem" (source of English *resemble*), from Latin *simulare* (see SIMULATE).]

se·mé /sə máy, sé mày/ *adj.* covered with many small dots or delicate designs [15thC. From French, past participle of *semer* "to sow," from Latin *semere*.]

se·meme /sée meem/ *n.* the meaning that a morpheme has in a linguistic system [Early 20thC. Formed from Greek *sēma* "mark, sign."]

se·men /séemən/ *n.* the thick white fluid containing sperm that a male ejaculates [14thC. From Latin, literally "seed."]

se·mes·ter /sə méstər/ *n.* either one of two periods of 15 to 18 weeks into which the academic year is often divided. ◊ **term** [Early 19thC. Via German from Latin *semestris*, literally "of six months," from *mensis* "month" (source of English *menstrual*).] —**se·mes·tral** *adj.*

sem·i /sémmee, sémmī/ *n.* **1.** = **tractor-trailer 2. SEMIFINAL** a semifinal (*informal*) **3.** = **semitrailer** *n.* 1 [Early 20thC. Shortening.]

semi- *prefix.* **1.** partial, partially, somewhat ○ *semisweet* ○ *semiterrestrial* **2.** half ○ *semiround* **3.** resembling, having some characteristics of something ○ *semitropical* ○ *semivowel* **4.** occurring twice during a particular period ○ *semiweekly* [From Latin, "half." Ultimately from an Indo-European word that is also the ancestor of English *hemi-* and *sand-blind*.]

sem·i·ab·stract /sèmmee ab strákt, sèmmī-/ *adj.* used to describe art that has heavily stylized but still recognizable subject matter —**sem·i·ab·strac·tion** *n.*

sem·i·an·nu·al /sèmmee ánnyoo əl, sèmmī-/ *adj.* **1. HAPPENING TWICE A YEAR** happening or issued every six months or twice a year **2. LASTING SIX MONTHS** lasting for half a year —**sem·i·an·nu·al·ly** *adv.*

sem·i·a·quat·ic /sèmmee ə kwóttik, sèmmī-/ *adj.* growing or living near water as well as in it

sem·i·ar·id /sèmmee érrid, sèmmī-/ *adj.* with little rainfall and scrubby vegetation —**sem·i·a·rid·i·ty** /sèmmee ə ríddәtee, sèmmī-/ *n.*

sem·i·at·tached /sèmmee ə tácht, sèmmī-/ *adj.* partly joined to something else

sem·i·au·to·bi·o·graph·i·cal /sèmmee àwtō bī ə gráffik'l, sèmmī-/ *adj.* used to describe something such as a novel or film that is based in part on the life or experiences of its author

sem·i·au·to·mat·ic /sèmmee àwtə máttik, sèmmī-/ *adj.* **1. RELOADING AUTOMATICALLY** automatically ejecting a spent shell from a weapon's chamber and replacing it with another round each time the weapon is fired **2. PARTIALLY AUTOMATED** operated partly automatically and partly manually ■ *n.* **SEMIAUTOMATIC WEAPON** a weapon that is semiautomatic — **sem·i·au·to·mat·i·cal·ly** *adv.*

sem·i·au·ton·o·mous /sèmmee aw tónnəməss, sèmmī-/ *adj.* **1. PARTLY SELF-GOVERNING** ruled partly by its own citizens or rulers and partly by another country or region **2. ACTING AS SELF-GOVERNING PART** self-governing but remaining within a larger organization of which it is part — **sem·i·au·ton·o·mous·ly** *adv.* —**sem·i·au·ton·o·my** *n.*

sem·i·bold /sèmmee bōld, sèmmī-/ *adj.* darker than ordinary type but not as dark as a bold type

sem·i·breve /sémmee breev, sémmī-/ *n. U.K.* = **whole note**

sem·i·cen·ten·ni·al /sèmmee sen ténnee əl, sèmmī-/ *adj.* **MARKING 50TH ANNIVERSARY** marking the date or year that is 50 years after a particular event ■ *n.* **50TH ANNIVERSARY OF EVENT** the 50th anniversary of an important event

sem·i·cir·cle /sémmi sùrk'l/ *n.* **1. HALF CIRCLE** half of the area or circumference of a circle **2. CURVED LINE** a curved or crescent-shaped line of things or people in the shape of a semicircle [Early 16thC. From Latin *semicirculus*, from *circulus*, literally "small circle."] — **sem·i·cir·cu·lar** /sèmmi súrk jələr/ *adj.* —**sem·i·cir·cu·lar·ly** *adv.*

sem·i·cir·cu·lar ca·nal *n.* any one of three tubes in the inner ear, semicircular in shape and set at right angles to one another, that help to maintain balance

sem·i·clas·si·cal /sèmmee klássik'l, sèmmī-/ *adj.* classical in musical style, pleasant, easy to listen to, and usually written relatively recently — **sem·i·clas·si·cal·ly** *adv.*

sem·i·co·lon /sémmi kōlən/ *n.* a punctuation mark (;) used to separate parts of a sentence or list and indicating a pause longer than a comma but shorter than a period

sem·i·co·ma /sèmmee kṓmə, sèmmī-/ *n.* a partial or light comatose state from which it is sometimes possible to rouse people by stimulating them

sem·i·co·ma·tose /sèmmee kṓmə tòss, sèmmī-/ *adj.* **1. BEING IN SEMICOMA** bordering on being unconscious but capable of being awakened **2. NEARLY UNCONSCIOUS** almost unconscious or half asleep

sem·i·con·duc·tor /sèmmee kən dúktər, sèmmī-/ *n.* a solid such as silicon or germanium that has electrical conductivity between that of a conductor and an insulator —**sem·i·con·duct·ing** *adj.* — **sem·i·con·duc·tion** *n.* —**sem·i·con·duc·tive** *adj.* — **sem·i·con·duc·tiv·i·ty** /sèmmee kùndək tívvətee, sèmmī-/ *n.*

sem·i·con·scious /sèmmee kónshəss, sèmmī-/ *adj.* only partly conscious —**sem·i·con·scious·ly** *adv.* — **sem·i·con·scious·ness** *n.*

sem·i·con·ser·va·tive /sèmmi kən súrvətiv, sèmmī-/ *adj.* relating to the replication of a nucleic acid molecule such as DNA in which a double stranded molecule separates into two templates for the formation of complementary strands — **sem·i·con·ser·va·tive·ly** *adv.*

sem·i·dark·ness /sèmmee daárknəss, sèmmī-/ *n.* a state in which it is neither fully dark nor fully light

sem·i·des·ert /sèmmee dézzərt, sèmmī-/ *n.* a region that is not completely arid, usually one lying between desert and a more heavily vegetated area

sem·i·de·tached /sèmmee di tácht, sèmmī-/ *adj.* **SHARING A WALL** joined to a neighboring building by a shared wall ■ *n.* **SEMIDETACHED HOUSE** a house with a wall in common with the next house

sem·i·di·am·e·ter /sèmmee dī ámmətər, sèmmī-/ *n.* half of the angular diameter of the visible disk of a celestial body as measured by an observer

sem·i·di·ur·nal /sèmmee dī úrn'l, sèmmī-/ *adj.* **1. LASTING ONE-HALF DAY** continuing or happening over half a day **2. OCCURRING AT 12-HOUR INTERVALS** happening approximately once every twelve hours

sem·i·doc·u·men·ta·ry /sèmmee dòkyə méntəree, sèmmī-/ (*plural* **-ries**) *n.* a film or TV program that is fictional but makes use of or is based on factual details or events

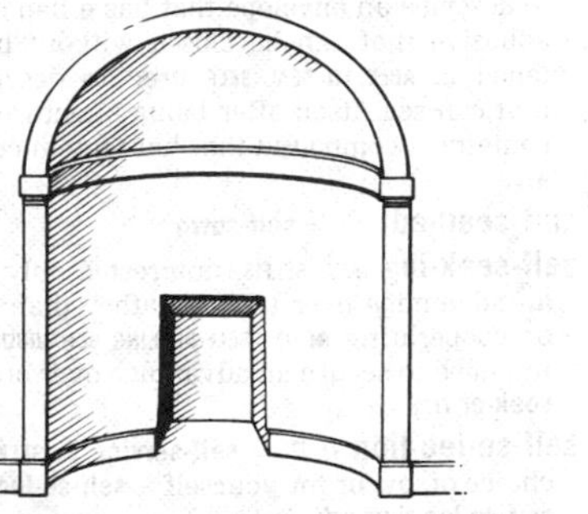
Semidome

sem·i·dome /sémmee dōm, sémmī-/ *n.* a half dome, especially one used as the roof for a semicircular space or recess

sem·i·do·mes·ti·cat·ed /sèmmee də mésti kàytəd, sèmmī-/ *adj.* still wild but living with and bred by humans for animal products — **sem·i·do·mes·ti·ca·tion** /sèmmee də mèsti káysh'n, sèmmī-/ *n.*

sem·i·dry /sèmmee drī́, sèmmī-/ *adj.* used to describe wine that is partially or moderately dry

sem·i·el·lip·ti·cal /sèmmee i líptik'l, sèmmī-/ *adj.* resembling half an ellipse in shape, especially one that is divided along its major axis

sem·i·fi·nal /sèmmee fī́n'l, sèmmī-/ *n.* either one of two matches or games, the winners of which will play each other in the final round of a competition —**sem·i·fi·nal** *adj.* —**sem·i·fi·nal·ist** *n.*

sem·i·fin·ished /sèmmee fínnisht, sèmmī-/ *adj.* partially finished, treated, or processed

sem·i·flu·id /sèmmee flo͞o id, sèmmī-/ *adj.* having properties between those of a fluid and a solid —**sem·i·flu·id** *n.* —**sem·i·flu·id·i·ty** /sèmmee floo íddətee, sèmmī-/ *n.*

sem·i·for·mal /sèmmee fáwrm'l, sèmmī-/ *adj.* SUITABLE FOR FAIRLY FORMAL OCCASIONS designed to be worn on moderately formal occasions ■ *n.* DANCE a dance to which people, often students, wear semiformal attire

sem·i·gloss /sèmmee glóss, sèmmī-/ *n.* a paint or varnish with a finish that is midway between gloss and matte when it dries

sem·i·hard /sèmmee haárd, sèmmī-/ *adj.* used to describe cheese that has a consistency firm enough to slice but that is moist and pliable. Hard cheese is not pliable even when moist.

sem·i·in·fi·nite *adj.* unbounded in one dimension or direction

sem·i·le·thal /sèmmee leéth'l, sèmmī-/ *adj.* lethal in more than 50 percent but fewer than 100 percent of cases

sem·i·liq·uid /sèmmee líkwid, sèmmī-/ *adj.* = **semifluid** —**sem·i·liq·uid** *n.* —**sem·i·liq·uid·i·ty** /sèmmee li kwíddətee, sèmmī-/ *n.*

sem·i·lit·er·ate /sèmmee líttərət, sèmmī-/ *adj.* **1.** NOT FULLY LITERATE unable to read or write properly **2.** HAVING ONLY LIMITED UNDERSTANDING having only limited understanding of a particular subject, especially a technical one —**sem·i·lit·er·a·cy** *n.* —**sem·i·lit·er·ate** *n.*

Sé·mil·lon /sáy meel yòN/, **Se·mil·lon** *n.* a late-maturing French grape variety used to produce white wine [Mid-19thC. Via French *Sémillon* from, ultimately, Latin *semen* "seed"; probably from the grape's high productivity.]

sem·i·lu·nar /sèmmee lo͞onər, sèmmī-/ *adj.* shaped like a crescent or a half moon

sem·i·lu·nar car·ti·lage *n.* either one of two crescent-shaped pieces of cartilage in the knee joint

sem·i·lu·nar valve *n.* either one of two crescent-shaped valves in the heart that prevent blood from flowing back into the ventricles. The two valves are called the aortic valve and the pulmonary valve.

sem·i·month·ly /sèmmee múnthlee, sèmmī-/ *adj.* HAPPENING TWICE IN MONTH happening or published twice each month, usually at equal intervals ■ *adv.* TWICE DURING MONTH twice each month, usually at equal intervals ■ *n.* (*plural* **-lies**) PUBL SEMIMONTHLY PUBLICATION a publication that appears twice each month, usually at equal intervals

sem·i·nal /sémminəl/ *adj.* **1.** INFLUENTIAL highly original and influential **2.** CAPABLE OF DEVELOPMENT containing an idea or set of ideas that forms a basis for later developments **3.** BIOL OF SEMEN OR SEEDS relating to, containing, or carrying semen or seeds [14thC. Via French from Latin *seminalis*, from *semin-*, stem of *semen* "seed" (source of English *seminary* and *disseminate*).] —**sem·i·nal·i·ty** /sèmmee nállətee/ *n.* —**sem·i·nal·ly** /sémmən'lee/ *adv.*

sem·i·nal ves·i·cle *n.* either one of a pair of glands that secrete the fluid component of semen into the ejaculatory duct in males

sem·i·nar /sémmi naàr/ *n.* **1.** MEETING ON SPECIALIZED SUBJECT a single session or short, often one-day meeting devoted to presentations on and discussion of a particular topic, usually at an advanced or professional level ○ *a seminar on the industrial applications of biotechnology* **2.** SPECIALIZED EDUCATIONAL CLASS a course of specialized graduate or undergraduate study under faculty supervision, in which ideas, approaches, and advances are regularly shared among participants **3.** MEETING OF STUDENTS AND ACADEMIC SUPERVISOR a meeting of university or college students for study or discussion with an academic supervisor, or the group that participates in it [Late 19thC. Via German, "advanced class," from Latin *seminarium* "seed plot, breeding ground," ultimately from the stem *semin-* (see SEMINAL).]

sem·i·nar·i·an /sèmmi náiree ən/, **sem·i·nar·ist** /sémmənərist/ *n.* a student who is training in a seminary to be a priest, minister, or rabbi

sem·i·nar·y /sémmə nèrree/ (*plural* **-ies**) *n.* **1.** SCHOOL FOR CLERGY a school for the training of priests, ministers, or rabbis **2.** GIRLS' SCHOOL a private residential school for girls (*archaic*) [15thC. From Latin *seminarium* "seed plot, breeding ground," ultimately from the stem *semin-* (see SEMINAL).]

sem·i·nif·er·ous /sèmmee níffərəss/ *adj.* **1.** BIOL PRODUCING SEMEN carrying, containing, or producing semen **2.** BOT PRODUCING SEEDS bearing or producing seeds [Late 17thC. Coined from the Latin stem *semin-* (see SEMINAL) + -FEROUS.]

Sem·i·nole /sémmi nòl/ *n.* (*plural* **-nole** *or* **-noles**) **1.** NATIVE N AMERICAN PEOPLE a member of a Native North American people who originally occupied lands to the east of the Mississippi River, and whose members now live mainly in Oklahoma. The Seminole were one of the Five Civilized Nations who, under the Removal Act of 1830, settled in Indian Territory. **2.** SEMINOLE LANGUAGE either one of the two Muskogean languages spoken by the Seminole ■ *adj.* **1.** OF SEMINOLE relating to the Seminole or their languages or culture **2.** SEW PATCHWORK STYLE used to describe a type of patchwork in which long strips of fabric are joined together, then cut up and reformed to create new patterns. It was originally developed by the Seminole. [Mid-18thC. From Creek *simanóli*, alteration of *simalóni*, alteration of Spanish-American *cimarrón* "wild, untamed."]

sem·i·no·ma /sèmmi nṓmə/ (*plural* **-mas** *or* **-ma·ta** /-mətə/) *n.* a malignant tumor of the sperm-producing tissue in the testicle [Early 20thC. Via French *séminome* from modern Latin *seminoma*, from the Latin stem *semin-* "seed" + -OMA.]

sem·i·no·mad·ic /sèmmee nō máddik, sèmmī-/ *adj.* belonging or relating to an ethnic group or people who migrate seasonally as well as cultivating crops during periods of settlement

sem·i·nude /sémmi no͞od, sémmī-/ *adj.* HALF-DRESSED only partly clothed, usually in underclothes or skimpy outer clothing ■ *n.* STATE OF PARTIAL UNDRESS the state of being only partly clothed, usually in underclothes or skimpy outer clothing —**sem·i·nu·di·ty** /sèmmee no͞odətee, sèmmī-/ *n.*

sem·i·o·chem·i·cal /sèmmee o kémmik'l/ *n.* an organic chemical such as pheromone that plays a role in animal communication [Late 20thC. Coined from Greek *sēmeion* "sign" + CHEMICAL.]

sem·i·of·fi·cial /sèmmee ə físh'l, sèmmī-/ *adj.* with only some degree of authority or official status and therefore not completely reliable —**sem·i·of·fi·cial·ly** *adv.*

se·mi·ol·o·gy /seèmee óllәjee, sèmmee-/ *n.* = **semiotics** [Late 17thC. Coined from Greek *sēmeion* "sign" + -LOGY.] —**se·mi·o·log·ic** /seèmee ə lójjik, sèmmee-/ *adj.* —**se·mi·o·log·i·cal** /-lójjik'l/ *adj.* —**se·mi·o·log·i·cal·ly** /-lójjikəlee/ *adv.* —**se·mi·ol·o·gist** /seèmee óllәjist, sèmmee-/ *n.*

se·mi·ot·ic /sèmmee óttik, seèmee-/ *adj.* **1.** RELATING TO SIGNS OR SYMBOLS relating to signs or symbols, especially in speech or writing **2.** OF SEMIOTICS relating to semiotics **3.** MED RELATING TO SYMPTOMATOLOGY relating to the field of symptomatology [Early 17thC. From Greek *sēmeiōtikos*, from *sēmeiousthai* "to interpret signs," from *sēmeion* "sign."]

se·mi·ot·ics /sèmmee óttiks, seèmee-/ *n.* (*takes a singular verb*) **1.** STUDY OF SIGNS the study of signs and symbols of all kinds, what they mean, and how they relate to the things or ideas they refer to **2.** MED STUDY OF SYMPTOMS OF DISEASES the study of identifying the ways that various symptoms indicate the diseases that underlie them —**se·mi·o·ti·cian** /sèmmee ə tísh'n, seèmee-/ *n.*

sem·i·pal·mate /sèmmee pál màyt, -paá-, sèmmī-/, **sem·i·pal·mat·ed** /sèmmee pál màytəd, -paá-, sèmmī-/ *adj.* with feet or toes that are partially webbed. Some shorebirds have semipalmate feet.

sem·i·per·ma·nent /sèmmee púrmənənt, sèmmī-/ *adj.* set up or arranged to last quite a long time but not indefinitely ○ *Dozens of refugees have taken up semipermanent residence in the grounds of the embassy.*

sem·i·per·me·a·ble /sèmmee púrmee əb'l, sèmmī-/ *adj.* used to describe a membrane or tissue that allows some types of particle to pass through, but not others —**sem·i·per·me·a·bil·i·ty** /sèmmee pùrmee ə bíllətee, sèmmī-/ *n.*

sem·i·po·lar bond *n.* = **coordinate bond**

sem·i·por·ce·lain /sèmmee páwrsslən, sèmmī-/ *n.* a durable glazed ceramic material widely used for tableware. It resembles porcelain but is opaque.

sem·i·post·al /sèmmee pṓst'l, sèmmī-/ *n.* a postage stamp sold for more than its face value, with the consequent proceeds going to a charity

sem·i·pre·cious /sèmmee préshəss, sèmmī-/ *adj.* used to describe stones, gems, and minerals that have commercial value but are not valued as highly as those called precious

sem·i·pri·vate /sèmmee prī́vət, sèmmī-/ *adj.* shared with at least one other person, e.g., another patient ○ *She had a semiprivate room in the hospital.*

sem·i·pro /sèmmee prṓ, sèmmī-/ *n.* (*plural* **-pros**) SOMEBODY SEMIPROFESSIONAL a semiprofessional (*informal*) ■ *adj.* SEMIPROFESSIONAL relating to or being semiprofessional (*informal*)

sem·i·pro·fes·sion·al /sèmmee prə féshən'l, sèmmī-/ *adj.* **1.** PAID BUT NOT FULL-TIME participating in a sport or artistic activity for pay but not as a full-time professional **2.** FOR SEMIPROFESSIONAL ATHLETES played in or contested by semiprofessional athletes **3.** LIKE A PROFESSIONAL displaying some aspects of a professional ■ *n.* PART PROFESSIONAL somebody, especially an athlete or performing artist, who is intermediate between an amateur and a professional —**sem·i·pro·fes·sion·al·ly** *adv.*

sem·i·qua·ver /sémmee kwàyvər, sémmī-/ *n.* = **sixteenth note**

sem·i·re·tired /sèmmee ri tī́rd, sèmmī-/ *adj.* working only part-time following the end of a full-time career —**sem·i·re·tire·ment** *n.*

sem·i·rig·id /sèmmee ríjjid, sèmmī-/ *adj.* **1.** PARTLY RIGID partly rigid or rigid only in some parts **2.** AEROSP WITH RIGID KEEL used to describe an airship with a rigid keel that maintains its shape

sem·i·round /sèmmee równd, sèmmī-/ *adj.* SEMICIRCULAR semicircular, with one flat side ■ *n.* SOMETHING SEMIROUND something with one round side and one flat side

sem·i·ru·ral /sèmmee ro͝orəl, sèmmī-/ *adj.* intermediate between rural and urban

sem·i·se·cret /sèmmee seékrət, sèmmī-/ *adj.* intended or supposedly intended to be secret but actually known about

sem·i·skilled /sèmmee skíld, sèmmī-/ *adj.* with or requiring relatively few skills or little training ○ *semiskilled workers* ○ *a semiskilled job*

sem·i·soft /sèmmee sáwft, sèmmī-/ *adj.* softer than most things, especially foods, of its type

sem·i·sol·id /sèmmee sóllid, sèmmī-/ *adj.* HALF SOLID, HALF LIQUID not quite solid or liquid, but somewhere in between, like a gel ■ *n.* THICK STICKY SUBSTANCE a substance that has most of the qualities of a solid but can also flow, e.g., a gel

sem·i·staged /sèmmee stáyjd, sèmmī-/ *adj.* performed without all of the elements of a full stage production such as costumes, props, or minor characters ○ *They performed a semistaged version of Faust.*

sem·i·sub·mers·i·ble /sèmmee sub múrssəb'l, sèmmī-/, **sem·i·sub·mers·i·ble rig** *n.* a self-propelled oil-drilling platform resting on vertical pontoons that can be flooded for stability in deep water

sem·i·syn·thet·ic /sèmmee sin théttik, sèmmī-/ *adj.* **1.** SYNTHESIZED USING NATURAL INGREDIENTS chemically synthesized from natural ingredients **2.** PART NATURAL made up of some natural and some synthetic ingredients

Sem·ite /sé mīt/ *n.* **1.** MEMBER OF SEMITIC-SPEAKING PEOPLE a member of any of several Semitic-speaking peoples of the Middle East, including the Arab and Jewish peoples, and the ancient Assyrians, Babylonians, Carthaginians, Ethiopians, and Phoenicians **2.** OFFENSIVE TERM an offensive term for a Jewish person (*slang offensive*) [Mid-19thC. Ultimately via modern Latin *Semita* from Greek *Sēm* "Shem," son of Noah traditionally believed to be the ancestor of this group.]

sem·i·ter·res·tri·al /sèmmee tə réstree əl, sèmmī-/

adj. living partly on land but requiring a watery environment

Se·mit·ic /sə míttik/ *n.* LANG **LANGUAGES SPOKEN BY SEMITES** a group of languages belonging to the Afro-Asiatic family and spoken in North Africa and southwestern Asia, including Hebrew, Arabic, Aramaic, Maltese, and Amharic ■ *adj.* **1.** LANG **OF SEMITIC** in or relating to Semitic **2.** PEOPLES **OF PEOPLES WHO SPEAK SEMITIC LANGUAGES** relating to the peoples who speak Semitic languages

Se·mit·ics /sə míttiks/ *n.* the study of the Semitic peoples, languages, and culture (*takes a singular verb*) —**Se·mit·i·cist** /sə míttissist/ *n.* —**Sem·i·tist** /sémmitist/ *n.*

Sem·i·tism /sémmi tìzzəm/ *n.* **1.** **SEMITIC CULTURE** the customs, traditions, and characteristics of Semitic people **2.** **LANGUAGE FEATURE OF SEMITIC ORIGIN** a word or other language feature of Semitic origin, especially one occurring in a non-Semitic language

sem·i·tone /sémmee tòn, sémmī-/ *n.* the smallest interval of the diatonic scale, half of a whole tone. It is the difference in pitch between adjacent frets on fretted string instruments such as guitars, or between adjacent black or white notes on the piano. [15thC. Directly or via Old French, "half tone," from medieval Latin *semitonus*, from *tonus* (see TONE).] —**sem·i·ton·al** /sèmmee tṓn'l, sèmmī-/ *adj.* —**sem·i·ton·al·ly** /-tṓn'lee/ *adv.* —**sem·i·ton·ic** /-tónnik/ *adj.*

sem·i·trail·er /sémmee tràylər, sémmī-/ *n.* **1.** **TRAILER WITHOUT FRONT WHEELS** a large rectangular vehicle with wheels only at the rear and a hitch at the front that attaches to a tractor or other towing vehicle **2.** **TRACTOR WITH SEMITRAILER** a tractor with an attached semitrailer

sem·i·trans·par·ent /sèmmee trans pérrənt, sèmmī-/ *adj.* partly, but not completely, transparent

sem·i·trop·i·cal /sèmmee tróppik'l, sèmmī-/ *adj.* = **subtropical** —**sem·i·trop·ics** *npl.*

sem·i·vow·el /sémmee vòw əl, sémmī-/ *n.* a sound that is like a vowel in involving no major obstruction of the airflow but that functions as a consonant in preceding vowels that form the nucleus of syllables. Examples in English are initial "w" and "y."

sem·i·week·ly /sèmmee wéeklee, sèmmī-/ *adj.* **HAPPENING TWICE PER WEEK** happening or published twice each week ■ *adv.* **TWICE PER WEEK** twice each week

sem·o·li·na /sèmmə léenə/ *n.* gritty ground grains of wheat that are a byproduct of flour milling, used in making pasta, couscous, and other foods [Late 18thC. Alteration of Italian *semolino*, literally "small bran," formed from *semola* "bran," from Latin *simila* "fine wheat flour," of uncertain origin: probably from Semitic.]

sem·per fi·del·is /sèmpər fi dáyliss/ *adj.* "always faithful," the motto of the United States Marine Corps [From Latin]

sem·per par·a·tus /sèmpər pə ráatəss, -ráytəss/ *adj.* "always prepared," the motto of the United States Coast Guard [From Latin]

Sempervivum

sem·per·viv·um /sèmpər vívəm/ *n.* a widely-grown ornamental garden plant that has rosettes of fleshy leaves and clusters of pink flowers growing on stems. Genus: *Sempervivum.* [Late 16thC. From Latin, a form of *sempervivus* "ever-living," from *semper* "ever" + *vivus* "living" (see VIVACIOUS).]

sem·pi·ter·nal /sèmpi túrn'l/ *adj.* lasting forever (*literary*) [15thC. Directly or via Old French from late Latin *sempiternalis*, from Latin *sempiternus*, from *semper* "always" + *-ternus*, suffix of time.] —**sem·pi·ter·nal·ly** *adv.* —**sem·pi·ter·ni·ty** *n.*

sem·pli·ce /sémplə chày/ *adv.* in a simple manner, without rubato (*used in musical directions*) [Mid-18thC. From Italian, "simple."]

sem·pre /sém pràỳ/ *adv.* to be played or sung throughout in the manner indicated (*used in musical directions*) ○ *sempre largo* [Early 19thC. From Italian, "always, throughout."]

semp·stress /sémpstrəss, sémstrəss/ *n.* a seamstress (*archaic*) [Mid-17thC. Formed from *sempster*, variant of *seamster.*]

Sem·tex /sém tèks/ *tdmk.* a trademark for a type of plastic explosive of Czech origin

sen /sen/ (*plural* **sen**) *n.* **1.** **SUBUNIT OF SE ASIAN CURRENCIES** a subunit of currency in Cambodia, 100 of which are worth one riel, in Indonesia, 100 of which are worth one rupiah, in Japan, 100 of which are worth one yen, and in Malaysia, 100 of which are worth one ringgit. See table at **currency 2.** **COIN WORTH A SEN** a coin worth a sen [Early 18thC. From Japanese, ultimately from Mandarin Chinese *qián* "money, coin."]

Sen. *abbr.* **1.** POL senator **2.** senior **3.** POL senate

sen·a·ry /séenəree, sénnəree/ *adj.* based on six (*formal*) [Mid-17thC. From Latin *senarius* "based on six," from *seni* "six each," from *sex* "six."]

sen·ate /sénnət/ *n.* **1.** **LEGISLATIVE BODY** the sole or upper law-making chamber of government in many countries or states, past or present **2.** **U.S. STATE LEGISLATURE** the higher of two elected legislative bodies in many states of the United States **3.** HIST **ANCIENT ROMAN ASSEMBLY** the highest council of the ancient Roman Republic and of the Roman Empire **4.** **SENATE BUILDING** the building where a senate meets **5.** EDUC **UNIVERSITY BODY** the main faculty governing body in some universities and colleges [12thC. Via Old French from Latin *senatus*, literally "assembly of elders," from *senex* "male elder" (source of English *senile* and *senior*).]

Sen·ate *n.* **1.** **U.S. LEGISLATURE** the higher of the two elected legislative bodies of the United States government. It is made up of two senators from each state. **2.** **UPPER HOUSE OF CANADIAN PARLIAMENT** the upper chamber of the federal parliament of Canada. It is made up of 104 senators appointed by the ruling government.

sen·a·tor /sénnətər/ *n.* an elected or appointed member of a senate, e.g., in the United States, Australia, or ancient Rome

sen·a·to·ri·al /sènnə táwree əl/ *adj.* **1.** **OF SENATORS OR A SENATE** relating to or characteristic of a senate or with the post of senator ○ *senatorial privileges* **2.** **CONSISTING OF SENATORS** made up of senators —**sen·a·to·ri·al·ly** *adv.*

sen·a·to·ri·al cour·te·sy *n.* a custom in the U.S. Senate allowing it to refuse to approve a presidential appointment if objections are raised by a particular party or parties. These are either the senior senator in the president's party from the appointee's state, or both senators from that state.

sen·a·to·ri·al dis·trict *n.* a state electoral district in the United States, represented in a state senate by a senator

send[1] /send/ *v.* (**sent** /sent/, **sent, send·ing, sends**) **1.** *vt.* **CAUSE SOMEBODY OR SOMETHING TO GO** to cause somebody or something to be moved or taken to another place **2.** *vt.* **COMMUNICATE SOMETHING** to transmit information to somebody who is somewhere else **3.** *vt.* **COMMAND SOMEBODY TO GO** to ask or command somebody to come or go **4.** *vt.* **ENABLE SOMEBODY TO GO** to enable somebody to go somewhere special ○ *Let's send the children to camp this summer.* **5.** *vt.* **REFER SOMEBODY SOMEWHERE** to suggest that somebody go somewhere or see somebody, usually for a specific kind of information **6.** *vt.* **BRING SOMETHING ABOUT** to make something happen ○ *Our blessings were sent by a higher power.* **7.** *vt.* **PROPEL SOMETHING** to make something move or travel by pushing it or hitting it ○ *A gust of wind sent the papers swirling around the office.* **8.** *vt.* **DRIVE SOMEBODY INTO PARTICULAR STATE** to make somebody enter a particular condition ○ *The delay is sending her into fits of frustration.* **9.** *vt.* **EXCITE SOMEBODY GREATLY** to excite or thrill somebody intensely (*dated slang*) **10.** *vi.* COMPUT **BE TRANSMITTED** to be transmitted or transmittable ○ *This e-mail won't send.* **11.** *vi.* TELECOM **BROADCAST INFORMATION** to transmit information by telecommunication ○ *The operator was still sending when the power was cut off.* ■ *n.* COMPUT **COMMAND TO TRANSMIT COMPUTER DATA** a command, key, or icon on a computer monitor or keyboard that is used to start the transmission of data [Old English *sendan*, from a prehistoric Germanic word meaning "to cause to go"] ◇ **send flying** to make somebody or something fly through the air by force of impact ◇ **send somebody packing 1.** to tell somebody to go in a firm, not very polite way (*informal*) **2.** to force or frighten somebody into going away (*informal*)

send away for *vt.* to order something by mail or through a mail order catalog

send for *vt.* to request the delivery, dispatch, or appearance of somebody or something ○ *send for reinforcements*

send forth *vt.* to give out or produce somebody or something (*archaic or literary*) ○ *sent forth a cry of joy*

send in *vt.* to mail something, e.g., an application form, for processing along with those sent by other people

send off *vt.* **1.** MAIL **DISPATCH SOMETHING** to dispatch something in the mail **2.** **SEND SOMEBODY AWAY** to send somebody away, either on an errand, or by way of dismissal ○ *We sent him off to buy some things.* **3.** **BID SOMEBODY FAREWELL** to say goodbye or good luck to somebody who is leaving ○ *Who was there to send her off?*

send out for *vt.* to order food by telephone, to be delivered to a particular address and paid for when it arrives (*informal*) ○ *Let's send out for a pizza.*

send up *vt.* **1.** **MAKE SOMETHING GO UP** to make something rise or climb, especially a scale or index such as on a thermometer or a listing of stock market values ○ *News of lower interest rates sent the stock market index up 60 points.* **2.** **SEND SOMEBODY TO PRISON** to imprison somebody following conviction (*informal*) ○ *He was sent up for armed robbery.* **3.** **MOCK SOMEBODY OR SOMETHING BY IMITATION** to make fun of somebody or something by humorous imitation (*informal*)

WORD KEY: SYNONYMS

See Synonyms at ***ridicule.***

send[2] *vi., n.* = **scend**

Sen·dai /sen dí/ capital city of Miyagi Prefecture, on northeastern Honshu Island, Japan. Population: 918,398 (1990).

send·off /sénd ŏf/ *n.* an act of showing goodwill toward somebody who is leaving or something that is starting, especially in a group at a place such as an airport or at a farewell party

send·up /sénd ùp/ *n.* a parody done as a joke (*informal*)

se·ne /sáy nay/ (*plural* **-ne**) *n.* **1.** **SUBUNIT OF SAMOAN CURRENCY** a subunit of currency in Samoa, 100 of which are worth one tala. See table at **currency 2.** **COIN WORTH A SENE** a coin worth one sene [Mid-20thC. From Samoan, "cent."]

Sen·e·ca /sénnəkə/ (*plural* **-ca** *or* **-cas**) *n.* **1.** PEOPLES **MEMBER OF NATIVE N AMERICAN PEOPLE** a member of a Native North American people who originally occupied lands in western New York State, and whose members mainly continue to live there and in southern Ontario. The Seneca were one of the five peoples who formed the Iroquois Confederacy, which later became known as the Six Nations. **2.** LANG **SENECA LANGUAGE** the Iroquoian language of the Seneca. it now has few speakers. [Mid-17thC. From Dutch *Sennecaas* (plural) "the Upper Iroquois peoples," of uncertain origin: possibly from Mahican.] —**Sen·e·can** *adj.*

Sen·e·ca /sénnəkə/ (4? B.C.–A.D. 65) Spanish-born Roman statesman, philosopher, and dramatist. He was Nero's tutor, and influenced the early years of his reign, but committed suicide after being condemned for conspiracy against the state. His writings as a dramatist, rhetorician, and Stoic moralist were influential in shaping the thought and literature of the European Renaissance. Full name **Lucius Annaeus Seneca**. Known as **Seneca the Younger**

Sen·e·ca Lake lake in New York. It is one of the Finger Lakes. Area: 67 sq. mi./174 sq. km.

Sen·e·ca snake·root *n.* a flowering plant of eastern North America with small white flowers, and roots with various medicinal uses. Latin name: *Polygala senega.* [From the plant's use by the Seneca people as an antidote to snakebite]

se·ne·ci·o /si néeshi ō, -shō/ (*plural* **sen·ec·i·os**) *n.* = **ragwort** [Mid-16thC. From Latin, "groundsel," literally "male elder" (from the plant's white hairs), from *senex* (see SENATE).]

sen·e·ga /sénnəgə/ *n.* = **Seneca snakeroot** [Mid-18thC. Origin uncertain: probably an alteration of SENECA.]

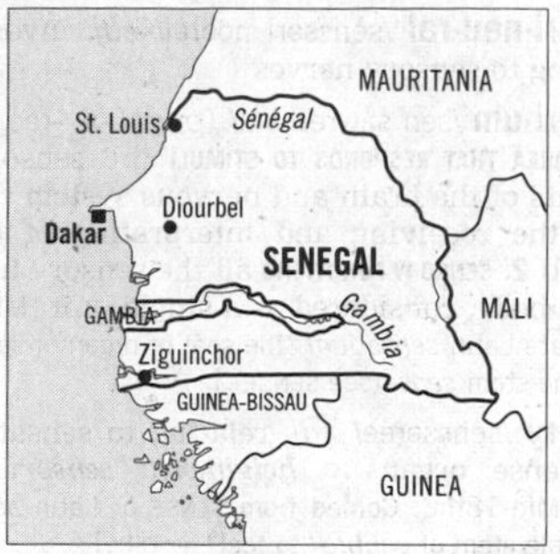

Senegal

Sen·e·gal /sénni gaal, seni gáwl/ republic in western Africa. Formerly a French territory, it became an independent republic in 1960. Language: French. Currency: C.F.A. franc. Capital: Dakar. Population: 8,532,000 (1996). Area: 75,750 sq. mi./196,192 sq. km. Official name **Republic of Senegal** —**Sen·e·gal·ese** /sènni gaal éez/ *n., adj.*

se·nes·cent /sə néss'nt/ *adj.* approaching an advanced age [Mid-17thC. From Latin *senescent-*, present participle stem of *senescere*, ultimately from *senex* "advanced in age."] —**se·nes·cence** *n.*

sen·e·schal /sénnəshəl/ *n.* a steward in medieval times who managed the retainers of a noble house [14thC. Via Old French from medieval Latin *seniscalcus*, from prehistoric Germanic words meaning "old" and "servant."]

sen·hor /sayn yáwr, sin-/ (*plural* **-hors** *or* **-hor·es** /-yáw rayss/) *n.* a Portuguese title equivalent to English "Mr." [Late 18thC. Portuguese, via medieval Latin *senior* "lord, superior" from Latin, "elder, older" (source of English *sir*).]

sen·ho·ra /sayn yáwrə, sin-/ *n.* a Portuguese title equivalent to English "Mrs." [Early 19thC. From Portuguese, formed from SENHOR.]

sen·ho·ri·ta /sàynyə réetə, sènnyə-/ *n.* a Portuguese title equivalent to English "Miss" [Late 19thC. From Portuguese, literally "little senhora," formed from SENHORA.]

se·nile /sée nīl, sé-/ *adj.* **1. MENTALLY LESS ACUTE IN LATER LIFE** forgetful, confused, or otherwise mentally less acute in later life **2. RELATING TO LATER LIFE** occurring in or believed to be characteristic of later life, especially the period after the age of 65 years [Mid-17thC. Directly or via French *sénile* from Latin *senilis* "advanced in age," from *senex* (see SENATE).] —**se·nile·ly** *adv.* —**se·nil·i·ty** /sə níllətee/ *n.*

se·nile de·men·tia *n.* a form of brain disorder marked by progressive and irreversible mental deterioration, memory loss, and disorientation, known to affect some people after the age of about 65 years

sen·ior /séenyər/ *adj.* **1. MORE ADVANCED IN AGE** of a more advanced age **2. HIGHER IN RANK** of higher rank or having longer service or employment than another ○ *Everyone on the committee is senior to me* **3. sen·ior, Sen·ior RELATING TO EARLIER GENERATION** used to distinguish the elder of two members of the same family with the same name from the younger person of that name ■ *n.* **1. SOMEBODY OF GREATER AGE** somebody who is more advanced in age than somebody else **2. HIGHER-RANKING PERSON** somebody who is of a higher rank than somebody else or who has worked in the same place longer than another person ○ *She is my only senior in the department.* **3.** EDUC **FINAL-YEAR STUDENT** a student in the last year of high school or college **4.** = **senior citizen 5.** *Aus* LAW **AUSTRALIAN BARRISTER** in Australia, a barrister who has qualified as a Queen's Counsel [14thC. From Latin, "elder, older," the comparative from of *senex* (see SENATE).]

sen·ior chief pet·ty of·fi·cer *n.* an enlisted person in the United States Navy intermediate between a chief petty officer and a master chief petty officer, or the rank of such a person

sen·ior cit·i·zen *n.* somebody of retirement age or beyond

sen·ior debt *n.* an indebtedness with no claims ahead of it and the first in line to be paid off

sen·ior high school *n.* a school for the last three or four years of secondary education, grades 9 or 10 through 12

sen·ior·i·ty /seen yáwrətee/ (*plural* **-ties**) *n.* **1. HIGHER STATUS** status accorded to greater age, higher rank, or longer service or employment ○ *Days off will be awarded on the basis of seniority.* **2. STATE OF BEING SENIOR** the state of being of greater age or higher rank than somebody else

sen·ior lec·tur·er *n. U.K.* in the United Kingdom, a university teacher ranking above a lecturer and below a reader or professor

sen·ior man·age·ment *n.* the tier of management in an organization that makes important decisions about direction, focus, and general policy

sen·ior mas·ter ser·geant *n.* somebody holding a rank in the United States Air Force intermediate between a master sergeant and a chief master sergeant, or the rank itself

sen·i·ti /sénnee tee/ (*plural* **seniti**) *n.* **1. TONGAN SUBUNIT OF CURRENCY** a subunit of currency in Tonga, 100 of which are worth a pa'anga. See table at **currency 2. COIN WORTH A SENITI** a coin worth one seniti

sen·na /sénnə/ *n.* **1. FLOWERING PLANT USED AS LAXATIVE** a leguminous plant, usually with clusters of yellow flowers, found widely in temperate regions and sometimes used as a laxative. Genus: *Cassia.* **2. DRIED LEAVES OR PODS** the dried leaves or pods of a senna plant used as a purgative or laxative [Mid-16thC. Via modern Latin *sena* from Arabic *sanā.*]

Ayrton Senna

Sen·na /sénnə/, **Ayrton** (1960–94) Brazilian racing driver. One of the most celebrated Brazilian athletes of the 20th century, he won the World Grand Prix Formula One championship three times (1988, 1990, 1991). Full name **Ayrton Senna da Silva**

Sen·na·che·rib /sə nákə rib/, **King of Assyria** (*d.* 681 B.C.). During his reign (705–681 B.C.) he conquered Babylon (689 B.C.) and rebuilt Nineveh.

sen·net[1] /sénnət/ *n.* a trumpet call that announced the exits and entrances of actors in Elizabethan drama [Late 16thC. Origin uncertain: possibly from assumed Anglo-Norman *senet*, variant of *signet* in the obsolete sense "signal."]

sen·net[2] /sénnət/ *n.* a barracuda that is found in the waters of the western Atlantic Ocean. Latin name: *Sphyraena borealis.* [Late 17thC. Origin unknown: probably from a Caribbean language.]

Sen·nett /sénnit/, **Mack** (1880–1960) Canadian-born U.S. movie director. A leading director of silent movies, he was known for slapstick movies featuring Charlie Chaplin and the Keystone Cops. Born **Mikall (or Michael) Sinnott**

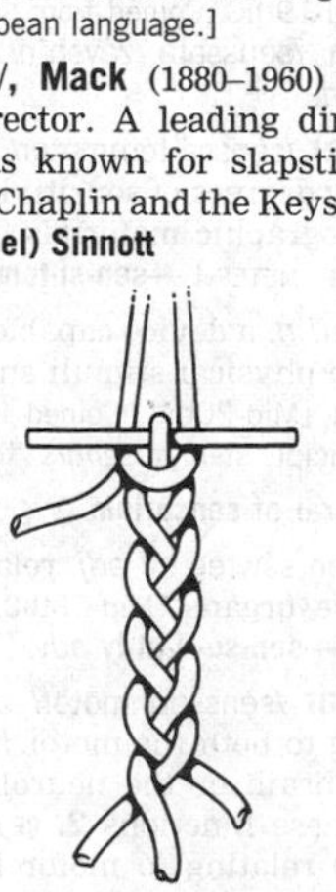

Sennit

sen·nit /sénnət/ *n.* **1. BRAIDED CORD USED ON SHIPS** braided cord in flat strands, used on ships **2. BRAIDED STRAW** braided straw, reeds, or leaves, used to make hats [Mid-18thC. Variant of *sinnet*, of unknown origin.]

se·ñor /sayn yáwr, sin-/ (*plural* **-ñors** *or* **-ñor·es** /sayn yáw rayss, sin-/) *n.* a Spanish title equivalent to English "Mr." [Early 17thC. From Spanish, via medieval Latin *senior* (see SENHOR).]

se·ño·ra /sayn yáwrə, sin-/ *n.* a Spanish title equivalent to English "Mrs." [Late 16thC. From Spanish, formed from SEÑOR.]

se·ño·ri·ta /sàynyə réetə, sènnyə-/ *n.* a Spanish title equivalent to English "Miss" [Early 19thC. From Spanish, literally "little señora," formed from SEÑORA.]

sen·ryu /sén ryoo/ (*plural* **-ryu**) *n.* a three-line ironic or satirical Japanese poem, similar in structure to a haiku [Mid-20thC. Named for the Japanese poet Karai *Senryu* (1718–90).]

sen·sate /sén sàyt/ *adj.* perceived through any of the senses [15thC. From late Latin *sensatus* "equipped with senses," from Latin *sensus* (see SENSE).] —**sen·sate·ly** *adv.*

sen·sa·tion /sen sáysh'n/ *n.* **1. PHYSICAL FEELING** a physical feeling caused by having one or more of the sense organs stimulated ○ *a burning sensation in my mouth and throat* **2. POWER TO PERCEIVE** the capacity to receive impressions through the sense organs ○ *He has lost all sensation in his legs.* **3. MENTAL IMPRESSION** a vague or general feeling, especially one not attributable to an obvious cause ○ *a sensation of falling* **4. PUBLIC INTEREST** a state of avid public interest in a phenomenon ○ *Her speech caused a sensation.* **5. INTERESTING PHENOMENON** a phenomenon that creates avid public interest [Early 17thC. Directly, or via French, from the medieval Latin stem *sensation-* "perception," from Latin *sensus* (see SENSE).]

sen·sa·tion·al /sen sáyshən'l/ *adj.* **1. OUTSTANDING** exceptionally good ○ *sensational results* **2. EXTRAORDINARY** attracting a great deal of attention and interest ○ *a sensational defeat* **3. EMPHASIZING LURID DETAILS** giving too much emphasis to the most shocking and lurid aspects of something ○ *sensational coverage of the murder trial* **4. SENSORY** connected with the senses or sense impressions —**sen·sa·tion·al·ly** *adv.*

sen·sa·tion·al·ism /sen sáyshən'l ìzzəm/ *n.* **1. USE OF SHOCKING MATERIAL** the practice of emphasizing the most lurid, shocking, and emotive aspects of anything under discussion or investigation, especially by the media **2.** PHILOS **THEORY OF KNOWLEDGE** the belief that all knowledge is obtained only through the senses —**sen·sa·tion·al·ist** *n., adj.* —**sen·sa·tion·al·is·tic** /sen sàyshən'l ístik/ *adj.*

sen·sa·tion·al·ize /sen sáyshən'l īz/ (**-ized, -iz·ing, -iz·es**) *vt.* to place excessive emphasis on the most shocking and emotive aspects of a subject —**sen·sa·tion·al·i·za·tion** /sen sàyshən'lə záysh'n/ *n.*

sense /senss/ *n.* **1. PHYSICAL FACULTY** one of the faculties by which a person or animal obtains information about the physical world **2. FEELING DERIVED FROM THE SENSES** a feeling derived from multiple or subtle sense impressions ○ *Flying filled him with a sense of insecurity.* **3. ABILITY TO APPRECIATE SOMETHING** the faculty whereby somebody appreciates a particular quality ○ *She has no sense of humor.* **4. MORAL DISCERNMENT** an ability to perceive and be motivated by moral or ethical principles ○ *instill a sense of right and wrong in the children* **5. INTELLIGENCE** the ability to make intelligent decisions or sound judgments ○ *He's got no sense at all.* **6. POINT** useful purpose or good reason ○ *There's no sense in waiting any longer.* **7. REASONED OPINION** an opinion arrived at through reflection or perception, often as a consensus ○ *The sense of the meeting was clearly against the proposal.* **8. MAIN IDEA** the essence or gist of something ○ *What was the sense of her argument?* **9. MEANING** a single meaning of a word or phrase that may have many **10.** LOGIC **TERM'S MEANING** the meaning as opposed to the reference of a term or sentence ■ **sens·es** *npl.* **RATIONAL MIND** a sensible, rational state of mind ○ *I must be out of my senses.* ■ *vt.* (**sensed, sens·ing, sens·es**) **1. PERCEIVE SOMEBODY OR SOMETHING** to perceive somebody or something with a sense or the senses ○ *I sensed a movement behind me.* **2. INFER SOMETHING** to understand something intuitively ○ *He must have sensed that I was disappointed.* **3. DETECT AND IDENTIFY CHANGE** to detect and identify a change in something ○ *The device senses when the door is opened and sounds the alarm.* [14thC. Directly, and via Old French, from Latin *sensus* "feeling, perception," from *sens-*, past participle stem of *sentire* "to feel."] ◇ **in a sense 1.** considered from a point of view that may not be the most obvious or the most popular **2.** used when saying that something could be described in a particular way, but that the description is not complete or accurate ◇ **make sense** to be understandable and consistent with reason ◇ **make sense of something** to understand something well enough to be able to act on it or evaluate it

WORD KEY: ORIGIN

The Latin word *sentire*, from which ***sense*** is derived, is also the source of English *assent, consensus, consent, dissent, resent, sensible, sentence, sentiment,* and *sensual*.

WORD KEY: CULTURAL NOTE

Sense and Sensibility, a novel by English writer Jane Austen (1811). Set in Devonshire, in southwestern England, Austen's first novel describes the emotional development of two sisters, Elinor and Marianne Dashwood, who live with their widowed mother in a modest cottage. Outwardly, Elinor appears dull and practical, Marianne sensitive and passionate, but the story of their involvement with two seemingly appropriate suitors warns against simplistic character judgments.

sense da·tum *n.* in the doctrine of phenomenalism, a sensation

sen·sei /sen sáy/ (*plural* **-sei**) *n.* **1. MARTIAL ARTS TEACHER** somebody who teaches one of the martial arts such as karate or tai-chi **2. FORM OF ADDRESS** used as a title to address somebody who is a teacher, especially in the martial arts [Late 19thC. From Japanese, "teacher, instructor," from *sen* "previous" + *sei* "birth."]

sense·less /sénssləss/ *adj.* **1. WITHOUT INTELLIGENCE** demonstrating a lack of reason and intelligence ○ *a senseless decision* **2. UNCONSCIOUS** unconscious, or unable to perceive anything ○ *was knocked senseless by the blow* **3. WITH NO APPARENT PURPOSE** apparently or really without purpose or meaning ○ *a senseless activity*

sense or·gan *n.* an organ such as an eye or ear that is specialized to receive stimuli from the physical world and transmit them via nerve impulses to the brain. Sense organs include the eye, ear, nose, skin, and taste buds of the tongue, which respond to light, sound, airborne chemicals, touch, and chemicals in food and drink, respectively.

sen·si·bil·i·a /sènssə bíllee ə/ *npl.* things that can be sensed, considered collectively [Mid-19thC. From Latin, a plural form of *sensibilis* "perceptible by the senses," from *sensus* (see SENSE).]

sen·si·bil·i·ty /sènssə bíllətee/ *n.* (*plural* **-ties**) **1. CAPACITY TO FEEL** the capacity to perceive or feel **2. EMOTIONAL RESPONSIVENESS** the capacity to respond emotionally or aesthetically ○ *the sensibility of a child* **3.** BOT **PLANTS' CAPACITY FOR RESPONSE** the sensitivity of plants to external stimuli ■ **sen·si·bil·i·ties** *npl.* **MORAL SENSE** sensitivity about moral or ethical issues ○ *careful not to offend their sensibilities*

WORD KEY: USAGE

sensibility or **sensitivity**? ***Sensitivity*** is used in ways corresponding to the meanings of the adjective *sensitive*, and is mainly concerned with physical or emotional reactions of various kinds: *a sensitivity to bright light.* ***Sensibility*** is less closely related in meaning to *sensible* than ***sensitivity*** is to *sensitive*, and chiefly denotes somebody's acute perceptions or finer feelings, corresponding to a particular meaning of *sensible*, as in *poetry that appealed to his sensibility.*

sen·si·ble /sénssəb'l/ *adj.* **1. SHOWING GOOD SENSE** having or demonstrating sound reason and judgment ○ *a sensible decision* ○ *She's not very sensible.* **2. PRACTICAL** practical, usually comfortable and hard-wearing, and not worn as an adornment ○ *a pair of sensible shoes* **3. SUBJECT TO PERCEPTION** able to be perceived through the senses ○ *sensible objects in the world around us* **4. AWARE OF SOMETHING** aware or conscious of something (*formal*) ○ *not sensible of the tragic mistake he'd made* **5. CONSCIOUS** awake or conscious, and having the capacity to understand [14thC. Directly, and via French *sensible*, from late Latin *sensibilis* "perceptible by the senses, able to perceive," from the stem *sens-* (see SENSE).] —**sen·si·ble·ness** *n.* —**sen·si·bly** *adv.*

WORD KEY: USAGE

sensible or **sensitive**? The two words overlap in meaning to some extent in the sense illustrated by the sentence *I am sensible of your difficult situation* ("I can appreciate your difficult situation"). In this meaning, ***sensible*** is normally used to express emotional or intellectual awareness. In a comparable use, ***sensitive*** is followed by *to* and denotes a more involved and finely attuned feeling about or for something: *He was always sensitive to their needs.*

WORD KEY: SYNONYMS

See Synonyms at ***aware***.

sen·si·ble ho·ri·zon *n.* ASTRON = **horizon** *n.* 2

sen·sil·lum /sen síllәm/ (*plural* **-la** /-síllə/) *n.* a simple sense organ made up of one or a few cells connected by a nerve cell, often found in insects [Early 20thC. From modern Latin, literally "little sense," from Latin *sensus* (see SENSE).]

sen·si·tive /sénssətiv/ *adj.* **1. ABLE TO SENSE** with the capacity to perceive via the sense organs **2. DELICATE** easily damaged or irritated physically ○ *a toothpaste for people with sensitive teeth* **3. ACUTELY PERCEPTIVE** unusually responsive to stimuli from the physical world ○ *a sensitive nose* **4. SUBTLE IN ARTISTIC EXPRESSION** subtly expressive in one of the arts **5. ARTISTICALLY IMPRESSIONABLE** susceptible to artistic effects, e.g., in music, writing, or painting **6. AFFECTED BY AN EXTERNAL STIMULUS** affected in some way by a particular external stimulus such as an allergen (*often used in combination*) ○ *eyes sensitive to light* ○ *a touch-sensitive screen* ○ *a price-sensitive product* **7. THOUGHTFUL AND SYMPATHETIC** tactful and sympathetic in relation to the feelings of others **8. TOUCHY** easily offended or annoyed if something is spoken about ○ *He's very sensitive about his driving.* **9. SECRET OR CONFIDENTIAL** not to be mentioned or divulged ○ *sensitive matters of national security* **10. REQUIRING TACTFULNESS** needing to be dealt with tactfully to avoid embarrassment ○ *a sensitive issue* **11. ABLE TO MEASURE SMALL DIFFERENCES** capable of detecting minute changes in levels, conditions, or amounts ○ *a sensitive scientific instrument* **12.** FIN **FLUCTUATING** volatile and subject to fluctuation ○ *a sensitive market* **13.** PHOTOGRAPHY **RESPONSIVE TO LIGHT** extremely responsive to radiation, especially to light of a specific wavelength **14.** ELECTRON ENG **RESPONSIVE TO SIGNALS** able to respond to transmitted signals ■ *n.* **PSYCHIC PERSON** somebody who has clairvoyant or psychic powers [14thC. Directly, and via French, from medieval Latin *sensitivus*, from the Latin stem *sens-* (see SENSE).] —**sen·si·tive·ly** *adv.* —**sen·si·tive·ness** *n.* —**sen·si·tiv·i·ty** /sènsə tívvətee/ *n.*

WORD KEY: USAGE

See Usage note at ***sensible***.

sen·si·tive plant *n.* **1. FLOWERING PLANT SENSITIVE TO THE TOUCH** a tropical American shrub with purplish flowers that recoils when touched. Latin name: *Mimosa pudica*. **2. UNDULY SENSITIVE PERSON** somebody who is easily upset (*informal*)

sen·si·tize /sénssə tìz/ (**-tized, -tiz·ing, -tiz·es**) *vt.* **1. MAKE SOMEBODY SENSITIVE** to make somebody sensitive, especially to a situation **2. MAKE SOMEBODY ALLERGIC** to induce undue sensitivity in somebody to a particular substance such as a food ingredient or drug so that subsequent exposure to the substance triggers an allergic reaction **3.** PHOTOGRAPHY **MAKE FILM SENSITIVE TO LIGHT** to make a film, plate, or other medium sensitive to light by coating it with an emulsion [Mid-19thC. Coined from SENSITIVE + -IZE.] —**sen·si·ti·za·tion** /sènssətə záysh'n/ *n.* —**sen·si·tiz·er** /sénssə tìzər/ *n.*

sen·si·tom·e·ter /sènssə tómmətər/ *n.* an instrument for measuring degrees of sensitivity, especially one used on photographic materials [Late 19thC. Coined from SENSITIVE + -METER.] —**sen·si·tom·e·try** *n.*

sen·sor /sénssər/ *n.* a device capable of detecting and responding to physical stimuli such as movement, light, or heat [Mid-20thC. Coined from SENSE or Latin *sens-*, past participle stem of *sentire* "to sense," + -OR.]

sen·so·ri·a plural of **sensorium**

sen·so·ri·al /sen sáwree əl/ *adj.* relating to sensation and the sense organs [Mid-18thC. Coined from SENSORIUM + -AL.] —**sen·so·ri·al·ly** *adv.*

sen·so·ri·mo·tor /sènssəri mṓtər/ *adj.* **1. SENSORY AND MOTOR** relating to both the motor and sensory functions in the brain or the neurological structures underlying these functions **2. OF MOVEMENT CAUSED BY SENSORY STIMULI** relating to motor functions arising from sensory stimuli

sen·so·ri·mo·tor stage *n.* the first major stage in Piaget's theory of cognitive development, from birth to approximately two years, in which children begin to understand their world through sensory and motor experience

sen·so·ri·neu·ral /sènssəri nŏŏrəl/ *adj.* involving or relating to sensory nerves

sen·so·ri·um /sen sáwree əm/ (*plural* **-a** /-ree ə/) *n.* **1. BRAIN AREA THAT RESPONDS TO STIMULI** the sensory components of the brain and nervous system that deal with the receiving and interpreting of external stimuli **2. SENSORY FUNCTIONS** all the sensory functions in the body, considered as a single unit [Mid-17thC. From late Latin *sensorium* "the seat or organ of sensation," from the stem *sens-* (see SENSE).]

sen·so·ry /sénssəree/ *adj.* relating to sensation and the sense organs ○ *heightened sensory awareness* [Mid-18thC. Coined from SENSE or Latin *sens-*, past participle stem of *sentire* "to feel" + -ORY.]

sen·so·ry ad·ap·ta·tion *n.* the tendency of a sensory system to adjust as a result of repeated exposure to a particular type of stimulus such as low levels of light

sen·so·ry dep·ri·va·tion *n.* the elimination of or a sharp reduction in sensory stimulation, usually as part of an experiment in psychology or as part of repressive interrogation procedures or brainwashing

sen·so·ry reg·is·ter, **sen·so·ry store** *n.* a memory store for each sense such as touch, vision, or hearing. It is presumed to hold large quantities of information, but only for milliseconds.

sen·so·ry thresh·old *n.* the minimum intensity of a stimulus at which it can be detected

sen·su·al /sénshoo əl/ *adj.* **1. SENSORY** relating to the body and the senses as opposed to the mind or the intellect **2. CARNAL** relating to physical or, especially, sexual pleasure [15thC. From late Latin *sensualis* "equipped with feeling or sensation," from Latin *sensus* (see SENSE).] —**sen·su·al·ness** *n.*

WORD KEY: USAGE

sensual or **sensuous**? Both words are connected with gratification of the human senses. ***Sensual*** is the older word, and in the seventeenth century it developed special meanings associated with the bodily appetites, especially eating and above all sexual satisfaction: *Her mouth looked sensual and inviting. They enjoyed the sensual pleasures of the table.* About this time the poet John Milton seems to have invented the word ***sensuous*** to refer more specifically to the aesthetic and spiritual senses (seeing, hearing, thinking), and it was taken up by Samuel Taylor Coleridge in the nineteenth century. In current use, it is almost impossible to keep the two sets of meanings apart, since the senses cannot readily be compartmentalized in this way, but it is prudent to have regard for the main distinction when using these words. ***Sensuous***, for example, is the word to use in connection with music or poetry: *The conductor relished the sensuous parts of Ravel's score.*

sen·su·al·ism /sénshoo ə lìzzəm/ *n.* **1. PLEASURE-SEEKING** devotion to sensual gratification **2.** PHILOS, ETHICS = **sensationalism** *n.* 2 —**sen·su·al·ist** *n.* —**sen·su·al·is·tic** /sènshoo ə lístik/ *adj.*

sen·su·al·i·ty /sènshoo állətee/ *n.* **1. BEING SENSUAL** the capacity for enjoying the pleasures of the senses **2. BEING PLEASING TO THE SENSES** the quality of being pleasing to the senses

sen·su·ous /sénshoo əss/ *adj.* **1. OF SENSE STIMULATION** relating to stimulation of the senses **2. APPRECIATING STIMULATION** enjoying or appreciating pleasurable stimulation of the senses ○ *a sensuous lover* **3. CAUSING STIMULATION** causing pleasurable stimulation of the senses ○ *a sensuous experience* [Mid-17thC. Coined from Latin *sensus* (see SENSE) + -OUS, apparently by John Milton, in order to avoid the lustful overtones that SENSUAL had at the time.] —**sen·su·ous·ly** *adv.* —**sen·su·ous·ness** *n.*

WORD KEY: USAGE

See Usage note at ***sensual***.

Sen·sur·round /sénssə ròwnd/ *tdmk.* a trademark for a movie sound effect system emitting low-frequency sound signals that are felt by the audience as vibrations

sent past tense, past participle of **send**[1]

sen·te /séntee/ (*plural* **li·sen·te** /li séntee/) *n.* **1. LESOTHO SUBUNIT OF CURRENCY** a subunit of currency in Lesotho, 100 of which are worth one loti. See table at **currency** **2. COIN WORTH A SENTE** a coin worth one sente [Late 20thC. From Sesotho, "cent."]

sen·tence /sént'nss/ *n.* **1.** GRAM **MEANINGFUL LINGUISTIC UNIT** a group of words or a single word that expresses a complete thought, feeling, or idea. It usually contains an explicit or implied subject and a predicate containing a finite verb. **2.** LAW **JUDGMENT** a judgment by a court specifying the punishment of somebody convicted of a crime, or the punishment itself ○ *a sentence of 15 years in prison* **3.** LOGIC **WELL-FORMED EXPRESSION** a well-formed expression in a symbolic language ■ *vt.* **(-tenced, -tenc·ing, -tenc·es)** LAW **ALLOCATE SOMEBODY PUNISHMENT** to allocate a particular punishment to somebody convicted of a crime, usually stating its nature and its duration ○ *was sentenced to two years in prison* [13thC. Via French from Latin *sententia* "feeling, opinion," from *sentient-*, present participle stem of *sentire* "to feel."] —**sen·tenc·er** *n.*

sen·tence ad·verb *n.* an adverb that modifies an entire sentence. "Frankly" is a sentence adverb in "Frankly, I don't care."

WORD KEY: USAGE

See Usage note at ***clearly, hopefully,*** and ***thankfully.***

sen·tence sub·sti·tute *n.* a single word that, when used in the proper context, meets all the semantic requirements of a sentence. Words such as "yes" and "no" are sentence substitutes.

sen·tenc·ing /sént'nssing/ *n.* the phase of a court trial in which a sentence is arrived at and pronounced, or the act of making such a pronouncement

sen·ten·tia /sen ténshee ə/ (*plural* **-ti·ae** /-ee/) *n.* a short memorable saying (*formal*) [Early 20thC. From Latin (see SENTENCE.]

sen·ten·tial /sen ténsh'l/ *adj.* relating to sentences in natural language or logic —**sen·ten·tial·ly** *adv.*

sen·ten·tial cal·cu·lus *n.* LOGIC = **propositional calculus**

sen·ten·tious /sen ténshəss/ *adj.* **1. FULL OF APHORISMS** tending to use, or full of, maxims and aphorisms **2. OVERLY MORALIZING** inclined to moralize more than is merited or appreciated **3. PITHY** expressing much in few words [15thC. Directly, and via Old French *sententieux*, from Latin *sententiosus* "meaningful, pithy," from *sententia* (see SENTENCE).] —**sen·ten·tious·ly** *adv.*

sen·tience /sénshənss, sénshee ənss/ *n.* **1. AWARENESS** the condition of being conscious or aware **2. FEELING** the quality of emotional response, distinguished from intellectual processes

sen·tient /sénshənt, sénshee ənt/ *adj.* **1. CONSCIOUS** capable of feeling and perception ○ *a sentient being* **2. RESPONDING WITH FEELING** capable of responding emotionally rather than intellectually [Mid-17thC. From Latin *sentient-*, present participle stem of *sentire* "to feel."] —**sen·tient·ly** *adv.*

sen·ti·ment /séntəmənt/ *n.* **1. MENTAL FEELING** a thought or idea based on a feeling or emotion **2. GENERAL FEELING** a feeling or opinion prevailing among a group of people ○ *The sentiment emerged that we were acting too soon.* **3. UNDERLYING FEELING** an underlying feeling, as distinct from the action that it brings about ○ *His speech was awkward but the sentiment was right.* **4. APPEAL TO FEELING** a calculated appeal to feeling or emotion, especially one that is excessive and unreasoning ○ *The book ends on a note of cheap sentiment.* **5. DEEP FEELING, ESPECIALLY IN ART** refined or tender feeling, especially when expressed in a work of art (*formal*) ■ **sen·ti·ments** *npl.* **OPINION** a point of view or judgment on something ○ *What are her sentiments on the matter?* [14thC. Via French from medieval Latin *sentimentum* "opinion, feeling," from Latin *sentire* (see SENSE).]

sen·ti·men·tal /sèntə mént'l/ *adj.* **1. MAWKISH IN FEELING** affected acutely by emotional matters, often to the point of mawkishness **2. MAWKISH IN EXPRESSION** displaying too much uncontrolled or self-indulgent emotion **3. APPEALING TO TENDER FEELINGS** appealing to or expressing tender, often romantic, feelings ○ *a sentimental portrait of our town* **4. NOSTALGIC** expressing or experiencing tender sadness or nostalgia **5. EXPRESSING DEEP FEELING** expressing deep, refined feeling (*formal*) —**sen·ti·men·tal·ly** *adv.*

WORD KEY: CULTURAL NOTE

A Sentimental Journey, a novel by English writer Laurence Sterne (1768). Sterne's second and last novel was intended as a riposte to Tobias Smollett's ill-tempered *Travels Through France and Italy* (1766) and even features a Smollett-like curmudgeon called Smellfungus. A rambling account of a trip through France from Calais to Lyons, it is transformed into an engaging work of art by the author's wit, sensitivity, and sharp social observation. Not surprisingly, the word *smellfungus* came to mean a carping faultfinder in the general parlance.

sen·ti·men·tal·ism /sèntə mént'l ìzzəm/ *n.* **1. EXCESSIVE DISPLAY OF SENTIMENT** a tendency to express or use obvious or powerful feelings or emotions without appealing to reason **2. SOMETHING WITH TOO MUCH EMOTION** something that expresses excessive emotion, especially something that is self-indulgent or nostalgic —**sen·ti·men·tal·ist** *n.*

sen·ti·men·tal·i·ty /sèntəmən tállətee/ *n.* the tendency or practice of indulging in emotion or nostalgia

sen·ti·men·tal·ize /sèntə mént'l ìz/ **(-ized, -iz·ing, -iz·es)** *v.* **1.** *vi.* **BE SENTIMENTAL** to indulge excessively in emotion or nostalgia **2.** *vt.* **TREAT SOMEBODY OR SOMETHING TOO EMOTIONALLY** to treat somebody or something, or express something, with undue emphasis on feeling —**sen·ti·men·tal·i·za·tion** /sèntə mènt'lə záysh'n/ *n.*

sen·ti·men·tal val·ue *n.* a value placed on something because of its emotional associations rather than its monetary worth

sen·ti·nel /séntən'l, sént'nəl/ *n.* **SENTRY** somebody who is assigned the duty of keeping guard ■ *vt.* **(-neled, -nel·ing, -nels) 1. GUARD SOMETHING** to stand guard over something or a group of people **2. PROVIDE A GUARD FOR SOMETHING** to provide a guard for something or for a group of people [16thC. Via French *sentinelle* from Italian *sentinella*, of uncertain origin: possibly ultimately from Italian *sentire* "to watch," from Latin, "to perceive."]

sen·try /séntree/ (*plural* **-tries**) *n.* a member of the armed services who is assigned to keep watch to warn of danger and to guard entrances and exits [Early 17thC. Origin uncertain: perhaps a back-formation from *centrinel*, variant of SENTINEL.]

sen·try box *n.* a covered shelter for a sentry, typically at an entrance or crossing

Sen·us·si /sə nóossee/, **Sen·u·si** *n.* a member of an Islamic religious group in Arabia and North Africa, founded in the 19th century [Late 19thC. From the name of the founder Sīdī Muḥammad ibn ʻAlī as- *Sanūsī* (*d.* 1859).] —**Sen·us·si·an** *adj.*

sen·za /séntsə, sénzə/ *prep.* MUSIC without something indicated by a following Italian noun (*used in musical directions*) ○ *senza ritenuto* [Early 18thC. From Italian, "without," of uncertain origin: possibly ultimately from Latin *absentia* "absence," influenced by *sine* "without."]

Seoul /sōl/ capital city of South Korea, on the Han River, in the northwest of the country. Capital of Korea from 1392, it became capital city of the newly formed republic, South Korea, when Korea was partitioned in 1947. Population: 10,229,260 (1995).

SEP *abbr.* simplified employee pension

sep. *abbr.* **1.** sepal **2.** separate **3.** separation

Sep. *abbr.* **1.** CALENDAR September **2.** Septuagint

se·pal /seep'l, sépp'l/ *n.* a modified leaf in the outermost whorl (**calyx**) of a flower. The sepals enclose the petals and other parts. [Early 19thC. Via French from modern Latin *sepalum*, blend of Greek *skepē* "covering" (perhaps influenced by Latin *separare* "to separate") and French *pétale* "petal."] —**se·paled** *adj.* —**sep·a·lous** *adj.*

se·pal·oid /séppə lòyd/ *adj.* resembling or functioning as a sepal

-sepalous *suffix.* having a particular number or kind of sepals ○ *trisepalous*

sep·a·ra·ble /sépparəb'l/ *adj.* capable of being divided, taken apart, or removed, either from each other or from something else —**sep·a·ra·bil·i·ty** /sèppərə bíllətee/ *n.* —**sep·a·ra·ble·ness** /sépparəb'lnəss/ *n.* —**sep·a·ra·bly** /sépparəblee/ *adv.*

sep·a·rate *adj.* /séppərət/ **1. APART** not touching or connected, not together, or not in the same place ○ *They slept in separate rooms.* **2. NOT RELATED TO SOMETHING ELSE** distinct from or unrelated to something else ○ *I think we should treat that as a separate issue.* **3. DIFFERENT** not shared with somebody or something else ○ *The book will be sent to you under separate cover.* ■ *v.* /séppə ràyt/ **(-rat·ed, -rat·ing, -rates) 1.** *vt.* **MOVE OR KEEP SOMETHING APART** to move two or more people or things away from each other or prevent them from coming into contact with each other ○ *Somehow we got separated in the crowd.* **2.** *vt.* **BE BETWEEN THINGS** to stand or lie between one person or thing and another **3.** *vt.* **MAKE SOMEBODY OR SOMETHING DIFFERENT** to be the factor that makes two people or things different from one another ○ *There was something about her that separated her from the other interviewees.* **4.** *vi.* **COME APART** to come apart or stop being attached or connected **5.** *vi.* **PART COMPANY** to leave one another and go off in different directions ○ *A crowd had gathered but it separated as soon as the police arrived.* **6.** *vi.* LAW **CEASE LIVING AS A COUPLE** to stop living together as a couple **7.** *vt.* **CATEGORIZE SOMEBODY OR SOMETHING** to put somebody or something into different categories or groups **8.** *vt.* **SHOW HOW THINGS DIFFER** to see or show that two or more things are different or not ○ *We must separate these two issues in the mind of the public.* **9.** *vti.* **DIVIDE** to split something, or to be split, into component parts **10.** *vti.* **MAKE OR BECOME INDEPENDENT** to leave a larger group and become independent, or to cause part of a larger group to leave and form an independent unit **11.** *vt.* **RELEASE OR FIRE SOMEBODY** to dismiss somebody from a job or release somebody from military service ■ **sep·a·rates** *npl.* CLOTHES **INDIVIDUAL ITEMS OF CLOTHING** articles of women's clothing such as blouses, skirts, jackets, and pants that can be bought as individual items and worn in various combinations [15thC. From Latin *separare*, literally "to arrange apart," from *parare* "to make ready" (source of English *prepare*).] —**sep·a·rate·ly** /séppərətlee/ *adv.* —**sep·a·rate·ness** /séppərətnəss/ *n.*

separate out *vti.* to come out of a mixture and form a distinct mass, or to make something do so

sep·a·rat·ed /séppə ràytəd/ *adj.* no longer living together as a couple but still legally married

sep·a·rate school *n. Can* a school run according to the beliefs of a denomination or religion, especially Roman Catholicism, that receives public funding

sep·a·rat·ing fun·nel *n.* a large funnel that has a valve in its output tube, used to separate liquids that do not mix

sep·a·ra·tion /sèppə ráysh'n/ *n.* **1. ACTION THAT SEPARATES OR SEPARATE CONDITION** the act of separating things or people **2. STATE OF BEING APART** the state of not being with somebody else, or the period of time spent apart **3. PLACE OF MEETING OR SPACE BETWEEN** a place, line, or mark that shows where two things meet, or the gap between them **4.** LAW **AGREEMENT NOT TO LIVE TOGETHER** the act of stopping living together as husband and wife while remaining married, or a formal agreement to do so, especially one made in a court of law **5. DIVISION** splitting into component parts **6. DEPARTURE FROM GROUP** dismissal from a job or release from military service **7. DUMPING PART OF ROCKET** the act of detaching the rear section of a multistage rocket when it is burned out, or the time when this happens

sep·a·ra·tion anx·i·e·ty *n.* a state of anxiety caused in somebody, especially a young child, by the thought or fact of being separated from his or her mother or primary caregiver

sep·a·ra·tion·ist /sèppə ráysh'nist/ *n., adj.* = **separatist**

sep·a·ra·tion of pow·ers *n.* the constitutional requirement that each of the three branches of government, executive, judicial, and legislative, be autonomous and distinct from the others

sep·a·ra·tist /sépparətist/ *n.* **1. ADVOCATE OF BREAKING AWAY** somebody who breaks away from or who is in favor of breaking away from a religious group, a country, or a group or organization of any sort **2. SUPPORTER OF SEPARATION OF DIFFERENT GROUPS** somebody who is in favor of keeping members of different racial, religious, sexual, or cultural groups separate —**sep·a·ra·tism** *n.* —**sep·a·ra·tis·tic** *adj.*

Sep·a·ra·tist *n. Can* somebody who is in favor of the secession of a province, especially Quebec, from Canada

sep·a·ra·tive /sépparətiv/ *adj.* tending to become separate or make something become separate —**sep·a·ra·tive·ly** *adv.* —**sep·a·ra·tive·ness** *n.*

sep·a·ra·tor /séppə ràytər/ *n.* somebody or something that separates one thing from another, e.g., a machine for separating cream from milk

sepd. *abbr.* separated

Se·phar·di /si faar dee/ (*plural* **-dim** /-dim/) *n.* a Jewish person of Spanish or Portuguese origin, now used loosely to refer to any Jewish person who is not of

German or Eastern European descent. ◊ **Ashkenazi** [Mid-19thC. From modern Hebrew, formed from *sĕpārad*, a land of exile mentioned in the Bible, assumed to be Spain.] —**Se·phar·dic** *adj.*

se·pi·a /seépee ə/ *n.* **1.** REDDISH-BROWN PIGMENT a deep reddish-brown pigment made from the dark liquid in the ink sacs of various species of cuttlefish, or an artificial form of it, used in painting. The ink is used by the cuttlefish as a means of protection. When disturbed, it ejects a stream of ink, which confuses its attacker. **2.** ARTS SEPIA DRAWING OR PHOTOGRAPH a drawing done in sepia or a photograph with a brownish tone **3.** COLORS DARK BROWN a dark brown color with a tinge of yellow or red **4.** PHOTOGRAPHY BROWNISH COLOR IN PHOTOGRAPHS a brownish tone produced, especially in early photographs, by some photographic processes ■ *adj.* DEEP REDDISH-BROWN of a deep reddish-brown color [14thC. Via Latin from Greek *sēpia* "cuttlefish" (the original sense in English).]

se·pi·o·lite /seépee ə līt/ *n.* = **meerschaum** *n.* 1 [Mid-19thC. Via German *Sepiolith* from Greek *sēpion* "cuttlefish bone" (because of its similar texture).]

se·poy /seé pòy/ *n.* an Indian soldier under British command, especially one who served in the British East India Company [Early 18thC. From Persian and Urdu *sipāhī* "horseman, soldier."]

sep·pu·ku /se pŏŏkoo, séppə koo/ *n.* = **hara-kiri** [Late 19thC. From Japanese, literally "to cut the abdomen."]

sep·sis /sépsiss/ *n.* the condition or syndrome caused by the presence of microorganisms or their toxins in the tissue or the bloodstream [Late 19thC. From Greek *sēpsis*, from *sēpein* "to make rotten."]

sept /sept/ *n.* **1.** DIVISION OF A PEOPLE a section of a people that believes itself to be descended from one particular ancestor **2.** CELTIC CLAN a branch of a Scottish or Irish clan [Early 16thC. Origin uncertain: probably an alteration of SECT.]

Sept., **Sept** *abbr.* **1.** CALENDAR September **2.** BIBLE Septuagint

sep·ta plural of **septum**

sep·tal /sépt'l/ *adj.* relating to a septum

sep·tar·i·um /septáiree əm/ (*plural* **-a** /-ree ə/) *n.* a roughly spherical mass of mineral substance containing cracks that have been filled with a crystalline mineral, usually calcite [Late 18thC. From modern Latin, formed from Latin *septum* (see SEPTUM).] —**sep·tar·i·an** *adj.*

sep·tate /sép tàyt/ *adj.* ANAT, BOT, ZOOL divided into sections or compartments by septa

Sep·tem·ber /sep témbər/ *n.* CALENDAR in the Gregorian calendar, the ninth month of the year, made up of 30 days [Pre-12thC. Directly or via French *septembre* from Latin *September*, from *septem* "seven"; September was originally the seventh month of the Roman year.]

Sep·tem·ber Mas·sa·cre *n.* the massacre of hundreds of prisoners by Paris mobs in September 1792, during the French Revolution. The killings were caused by fears of a counterrevolution by royalist prisoners, but most of those who were killed were ordinary criminals.

Sep·tem·brist /sep témbrist/ *n.* a member of the Paris mob that carried out the September Massacre in 1792

sep·te·na·ry /sép teenəree/ *adj.* **1.** RELATING TO 7 relating to the number seven **2.** CONTAINING SEVEN made up of seven people or things ■ *n.* (*plural* **-ries**) **1.** NUMBER 7 the number seven **2.** GROUP OF 7 a group of seven people or things **3.** 7 YEARS a period of seven years **4.** POETRY LINE OF VERSE CONTAINING SEVEN FEET a line of verse that contains seven metrical feet [15thC. From Latin *septenarius*, from *septeni* "seven each," from *septem* "seven."]

sep·ten·ni·al /sep ténnee əl/ *adj.* **1.** FOR 7 YEARS lasting seven years **2.** HAPPENING EVERY 7 YEARS occurring once every seven years ■ *n.* SOMETHING HAPPENING EVERY 7 YEARS something that happens every seven years [Mid-17thC. Formed from Latin *septennium*.] —**sep·ten·ni·al·ly** *adv.*

sep·tet /sep tét/, **sep·tette** *n.* **1.** MUSIC 7 MUSICAL PERFORMERS a group of seven instrumentalists or singers **2.** MUSIC MUSIC FOR 7 PERFORMERS a musical piece composed for seven instrumentalists or singers **3.** GROUP OF 7 a group of seven people or things [Early 19thC. Via German *Septett* from Latin *septem* "seven."]

septi- *prefix.* seven ○ *septivalent* [From Latin *septem* (see SEPTET]

sep·tic /sép tik/ *adj.* **1.** POISONED full of or generating pus **2.** INVOLVING SEPSIS relating to, involving, or causing sepsis [Early 17thC. Via Latin *septicus* from Greek *sēptikos*, from *sēpein* "to make rotten."] —**sep·ti·cal·ly** *adv.* —**sep·tic·i·ty** /sep tíssitee/ *n.*

sep·ti·ce·mi·a /sèptə seémee ə/ *n.* a disease caused by toxic microorganisms in the bloodstream [Mid-19thC. Formed from Latin *septicus* (see SEPTIC).] —**sep·ti·ce·mic** *adj.*

sep·ti·ci·dal /sèptə sīd'l/ *adj.* used to describe a fruit that splits open along the septa, dividing the component carpels [Early 19thC. Formed from SEPTUM + Latin *-cidere*, from *caedere* "to cut."] —**sep·ti·ci·dal·ly** *adv.*

sep·tic tank *n.* a tank, usually underground, in which human waste matter is decomposed by bacteria

Sept-Îles /se teél/ city on the northern shore of the St. Lawrence River in southeastern Quebec, Canada. Population: 28,005 (1996).

sep·til·lion /sep tíllyən/ (*plural* **-lions** *or* **-lion**) *n.* **1.** 10^{24} the number equal to 10^{24}, written as 1 followed by 24 zeros **2.** *U.K.* 10^{42} the number equal to 10^{42}, written as 1 followed by 42 zeros (*dated*) [Late 17thC. From French, formed from *sept* "seven" + *-illion* as in *million*.] —**sep·til·lion** *adj., pron.* —**sep·til·lionth** *adj.*

sep·time /sep teém/ *n.* in fencing, the seventh of eight positions from which a parry or attack can be made [Mid-18thC. From Latin *septimus* "seventh," from *septem* "seven."]

sep·tu·a·ge·nar·i·an /sèp too əjə nérree ən, sèp choo-/ *n.* SOMEBODY IN THE EIGHTH DECADE OF LIFE somebody who is between 70 and 79 years old ■ *adj.* BETWEEN 70 AND 79 between 70 and 79 years old [Early 18thC. Formed from Latin *septuaginarius*, ultimately from *septuaginta* "seventy."]

Sep·tu·a·ges·i·ma /sèp too ə jéssimə, sèp choo-/ *n.* CALENDAR the third Sunday before Lent in the Christian calendar [14thC. From Latin *septuagesima (dies)* "seventieth (day)," from *septuaginta* "seventy." Perhaps because it precedes Sexagesima, or perhaps referring to the seventy days between Septuagesima and the Saturday after Easter.]

Sep·tu·a·gint /sép too ə jìnt, sép choo-/ *n.* a Greek translation of the Hebrew Bible made in the 3rd and 2nd centuries B.C. to meet the needs of Greek-speaking Jewish people outside Palestine. The Septuagint contains some books not in the Hebrew canon. [Mid-16thC. From Latin *septuaginta* "seventy" (because it is said that about seventy translators worked on it).]

sep·tum /séptəm/ (*plural* **-ta** /-tə/) *n.* **1.** ANAT, BOT THIN PARTITION IN AN ORGANISM a thin partition or membrane dividing something into two or more cavities such as the tissue separating the nostrils or the internal dividing walls in the seed heads of poppies **2.** ENG PARTITION IN A MACHINE a thin partition that separates components in a machine [Mid-17thC. From Latin, literally "partition," formed from *sepire* "to enclose," from *sepes* "hedge."]

sep·tu·ple /sèp tŏŏp'l, -túp'l/ *adj.* **1.** 7 TIMES AS MUCH seven times as many or as much as something else **2.** HAVING 7 PARTS consisting of seven parts ■ *vti.* (**-pled, -pling, -ples**) INCREASE BY 7 TIMES to multiply something by seven, or become seven times as much or as many (*formal*) [Early 17thC. From late Latin *septuplus*, from Latin *septem* "seven."]

sep·tu·plet /sep túpplət, -tŏŏplət/ *n.* **1.** ONE OF 7 BORN TOGETHER any one of seven people or animals born to the same mother at one time **2.** GROUP OF 7 a group of seven people or things **3.** MUSIC GROUP OF SEVEN NOTES a group of seven notes to be played or sung in the time of four, six, or eight of the same notated value [Late 19thC. Formed from SEPTUPLE, modeled on *triplet*.]

sep·ul·cher /sépp'l kər/ *n.* **1.** BURIAL PLACE a vault in which somebody is buried **2.** CONTAINER FOR RELICS a container for sacred relics, especially one in an altar ■ *vt.* (**-chered, -cher·ing, -chers**) PUT A CORPSE IN A BURIAL VAULT to put a dead body into a sepulcher (*literary*) [12thC. Via Old French *sépulchre* from Latin *sepulc(h)rum*, from *sepult-*, past participle stem of *sepelire* "to bury."]

se·pul·chral /sə púlkrəl, sə pŏŏl-/ *adj.* **1.** DISMAL suggesting or possessing the characteristics associated with the grave, e.g., gloominess **2.** OF SEPULCHERS relating to burial vaults or funerals and burials (*formal*) —**se·pul·chral·ly** *adv.*

sep·ul·chre *n., vt.* U.K. = **sepulcher**

sep·ul·ture /sépp'lchər, sépp'l-/ *n.* the act of putting a dead body in a grave or tomb (*formal or archaic*) [14thC. Via French from Latin *sepultura*, from *sepult-* (see SEPULCHER).]

seq. *abbr.* sequel

se·qua·cious /si kwáyshəss/ *adj.* **1.** LOGICAL argued, or developing an argument, in a logically consistent and coherent way (*formal*) **2.** UNTHINKINGLY OBEDIENT too willing to follow a leader uncritically (*archaic*) [Early 17thC. Formed from Latin *sequax*, "inclined to follow," from *sequi* "to follow."] —**se·qua·cious·ly** *adv.* —**se·qua·cious·ness** *n.* —**se·quac·i·ty** /si kwássətee/ *n.*

se·quel /seékwəl/ *n.* **1.** CONTINUATION OF A STORY a movie, novel, or play that continues a story begun in a previous movie, novel, or play **2.** SOMETHING FOLLOWING SOMETHING ELSE something that happens after something else, especially as a consequence of it [15thC. Directly or via Old French from Latin *sequel(l)a*, from *sequi* "to follow."]

se·quel·a /si kwéllə/ (*plural* **-ae** /-lee/) *n.* a disease or disorder that is caused by a preceding disease or injury in the same individual [Late 18thC. From Latin (see SEQUEL).]

se·quence /seékwənss/ *n.* **1.** SERIES OF THINGS a number of things arranged in a particular order or connected in some way, or a number of actions or events that happen one after another ○ *Can you recall the sequence of events?* **2.** ORDER OF THINGS the order in which things are arranged, actions are carried out, or events happen **3.** CINEMA SECTION OF MOVIE a section of a movie showing a single incident or set of related actions or events ○ *a chase sequence* **4.** CARDS CARDS OF CONSECUTIVE VALUES three or more consecutive playing cards, usually of the same suit **5.** MUSIC REPEATED MUSICAL PHRASE a musical passage or chant consisting of three or more related short phrases repeated several times at successively higher or lower pitch levels **6.** CHR HYMN in the Roman Catholic Church, a hymn sung or said between the gradual and the gospel **7.** MATH ORDERED SET OF ELEMENTS an ordered set of elements that can be put into a one-to-one correspondence with the set of positive integers **8.** BIOCHEM ORDER OF MOLECULAR ELEMENTS the order of the constituent subunits of a large biological molecule, e.g., the order of amino acids in a protein or the order of nucleotides in a nucleic acid. The sequence determines the molecule's biological properties, e.g., its catalytic properties, or the nature of its genetic information. ■ *vt.* (**-quenced, -quenc·ing, -quenc·es**) **1.** PUT OR DO THINGS IN ORDER to arrange things or perform actions in a definite order **2.** BIOCHEM DETERMINE MOLECULE'S SEQUENCE to determine the sequence of a biological molecule such as a protein or nucleic acid [14thC. Via late Latin *sequentia* "what follows" from Latin *sequent-*, present participle stem of *sequi* "to follow." The word originally denoted a hymn or chant that followed the gradual.]

WORD KEY: ORIGIN

The Latin word *sequi*, from which ***sequence*** is derived, is also the source of English *consecutive, consequence, ensue, obsequious, persecute, prosecute, pursue, second, sect, sequal, set, subsequent, sue,* and *suit.*

se·quence of tens·es *n.* the grammatical relationship that causes the tense of a verb in a subordinate clause to be influenced or dictated by the tense of the verb in the related main clause

se·quenc·er /seékwənssər/ *n.* **1.** ELECTRON ENG DEVICE FOR SORTING DATA an instrument for sorting information into the correct order for data processing **2.** MUSIC ELECTRONIC DEVICE FOR STORING MUSIC an electronic device or software that digitally stores sequences of musical notes, chords, or rhythms that can be transmitted as required to an electronic musical instrument such as a synthesizer **3.** BIOCHEM DEVICE FOR DETERMINING SEQUENCES an apparatus for automatically determining the sequence of the constituent subunits of a protein, nucleic acid, or other biological molecule

se·quent /seékwənt/ *adj.* **1.** CONSEQUENT following as a consequence or result (*formal*) **2.** FOLLOWING following one after another (*formal or archaic*) ■ *n.* **1.** CONSEQUENCE a consequence or result (*formal*) **2.** LOGIC FORMAL LOGICAL REPRESENTATION a formal representation of an argument showing that an element is a theorem [Mid-16thC. Directly or via French from Latin *sequent-* (see SEQUENCE).] —**se·quent·ly** *adv.*

se·quen·tial /si kwénnsh'l/ *adj.* **1.** IN SEQUENCE happening in a particular order or forming a particular sequence **2.** RESULTING being a consequence or result of something else [Early 19thC. Formed from SEQUENCE, modeled on *consequence, consequential.*] —**se·quen·ti·al·i·ty** /si kwènshee állətee/ *n.* —**se·quen·tial·ly** /si kwénnsh'lee/ *adv.*

se·quen·tial ac·cess *n.* a way of accessing and reading a computer file by starting at the beginning. ◊ **direct access**

se·quen·tial scan·ning *n.* a system that scans a television picture using lines in a numerical sequence. ◊ **interlaced scanning**

se·ques·ter /si kwéstər/ (**-tered, -ter·ing, -ters**) *vt.* **1.** PUT SOMEBODY INTO ISOLATION to put somebody in an isolated or lonely place away from other people, the pressures of everyday life, or possible disturbances (*formal*) **2.** LAW TAKE SOMEBODY'S PROPERTY TO COVER AN OBLIGATION to take legal possession of somebody's property temporarily until a debt that person owes is paid, a dispute is settled, or a court order obeyed **3.** INTERNAT LAW TAKE AN ENEMY'S PROPERTY to demand or seize the property of an enemy [14thC. Directly or via French *séquestrer* from late Latin *sequestrare* "to place in safe keeping," from *sequester* "trustee," literally "follower."] —**se·ques·tra·ble** *adj.*

se·ques·trant /si kwésstrənt/ *n.* an agent that removes ions from a chemical solution, often used in horticulture to treat soil that has lime in it

se·ques·trate /seékwə strȧyt, sékwə-/ (**-trat·ed, -trat·ing, -trates**) *vt.* **1.** *U.K.* TAKE SOMEBODY'S PROPERTY TEMPORARILY to take legal possession of somebody's property temporarily until a debt that person owes is paid, a dispute is settled, or a court order obeyed **2.** ISOLATE SOMEBODY OR SOMETHING to isolate or separate somebody or something (*archaic*) [15thC. From late Latin *sequestrat-*, past participle stem of *sequestrare* (see SEQUESTER).] —**se·ques·tra·tor** *n.*

se·ques·tra·tion /seékwə stráysh'n, sèkwə-/ *n.* **1.** CONFISCATING OR BEING CONFISCATED the act or process of legally confiscating somebody's property temporarily until a debt that person owes is paid, a dispute is settled, or a court order obeyed **2.** INTERNAT LAW SEIZING OR BEING SEIZED the seizing of an enemy's property, or the fact or process of being seized **3.** GOING INTO OR BEING IN ISOLATION the act of going into or putting somebody in an isolated place, away from people or everyday pressures, or the fact of being in such a place (*formal*) **4.** CHEM ION-BINDING PROCESS the chemical process of binding an ion, especially a metallic ion, in a coordination complex

se·ques·trum /si kwésstrəm/ (*plural* **-tra**) *n.* a fragment of dead tissue, usually bone, that separates from surrounding living tissue. It may be seen in X-rays of inflammatory bone disease as a dense region surrounded by a fibrous envelope. [Mid-19thC. From medieval Latin *sequestrum* "sequestration," from late Latin *sequester* (see SEQUESTER).] —**se·ques·tral** *adj.*

se·quin /seékwin/ *n.* **1.** FASHION SMALL SHINY CLOTHING DECORATION a small round flat piece of shiny metal or plastic that is sewn onto clothing as a decoration, usually in large numbers **2. sequin, zech·in, zec·chi·no** (*plural* **-ni** *or* **-nos**) MONEY FORMER GOLD COIN a gold coin that was used in Venice and Turkey between the 16th and 18th centuries [Late 16thC. Via French from Italian *zecchino*, from *zecca* "mint," from Arabic *sikka* "coin, die for making coins."] —**se·quined** *adj.*

se·quoi·a /si kwóy ə/ (*plural* **-a** *or* **-as**) *n.* a large coniferous tree of the bald cypress family, native to California. Genus: *Sequoia.* [Mid-19thC. From modern Latin, named for SEQUOYA.]

Se·quoi·a Na·tion·al Park park in south central California, established in 1890. It includes Mt. Whitney, and is noted for its giant sequoia trees. Area: 629 sq. mi./1629 sq. km.

Se·quoy·a /si kwóy ə/, **Se·quoi·a** (1766?–1843) U.S. Cherokee leader. He tried to integrate Native North American and European culture, and invented the Cherokee alphabet. The giant tree and the national park in California are named for him. Known as **George Gist, George Guess**

ser. *abbr.* **1.** serial **2.** series **3.** sermon

se·ra plural of **serum**

se·rac /sə raák, say-/, **sérac** *n.* a ridge, pinnacle, or block of ice in the crevasses or slope of a glacier [Mid-19thC. From Swiss French *sérac*, originally "kind of firm white cheese," of uncertain origin: probably from Latin *serum* "whey" (source of English *serum*).]

se·ra·glio /sə r ályō, sə raályō/ (*plural* **-glios**) *n.* **1.** HAREM the women's quarters in a Muslim house, or the women themselves **2.** PALACE a Turkish palace, especially the Ottoman sultan's palace at Istanbul [Late 16thC. From Italian *serraglio*, alteration of Turkish *saray* "palace," from Persian *sarāī* "inn"; influenced by Italian *serraglio* "cage," ultimately from Latin *sera* "bolt."]

se·ra·pe /sə raápee, sə-/, **sa·ra·pe** *n.* a usually brightly colored woolen blanket worn as a cloak by men in Mexico and Central and South America [Early 19thC. From Mexican Spanish *sarape.*]

ser·aph /sérrəf/ (*plural* **-aphs** *or* **-a·phim** /sérrəffim/) *n.* an angel of the highest rank in the traditional medieval hierarchy of nine categories of angels. In the Book of Isaiah they are described as having six wings. [Pre-12thC. Via late Latin *seraphim* (plural) from Hebrew *sĕrāpīm.*] —**se·raph·ic** /sə ráffik/ *adj.* —**se·raph·i·cal·ly** /-ráffiklee/ *adv.*

Serb /surb/ *n.* a member of a Slavic people living mainly in Serbia, where they constitute the largest ethnic group, and other areas of the Balkan region [Early 19thC. From Serbo-Croat *Srb.*]

Serb. *abbr.* **1.** Serbia **2.** Serbian

Ser·bi·a /súrbiə/ republic in southeastern Europe that, together with Montenegro, makes up the Federal Republic of Yugoslavia. Capital: Belgrade. Population: 9,979,116 (1996). Area: 34,116 sq. mi./88,361 sq. km.

Ser·bi·an /súrbee ən/ *n.* LANG DIALECT OF SERBO-CROATIAN the dialect of Serbo-Croatian as it is spoken in Serbia and adjacent areas, written in a Cyrillic alphabet ■ *adj.* OF SERBIA relating to Serbia or its people, language, or culture

Ser·bo-Cro·a·tian /sùrbō krō áysh'n/, **Ser·bo-Cro·at** /sùrbō krṓ at/ *n.* **1.** LANG SLAVIC LANGUAGE the language spoken by the Serbians and Croatians, which belongs to the Slavic branch of Indo-European **2.** PEOPLES SPEAKER OF SERBO-CROATIAN somebody whose native language is Serbo-Croatian ■ *adj.* OF SERBO-CROATIAN relating to the Serbo-Croatian language or its speakers

sere[1] /seer/, **sear** *adj.* dry and withered (*archaic or literary*) [Old English *sēar* "withered." Ultimately from an Indo-European word that is also the ancestor of English *austere.*]

WORD KEY: SYNONYMS

See Synonyms at ***dry.***

sere[2] /seer/ *n.* the series of different communities of plants and animals that occupy a given site and create a stable system during the process of ecological succession [Early 20thC. From Latin *serere* "to join or connect" (source of English *series*).] —**ser·al** *adj.*

se·rein /sə rán/ *n.* in the tropics, a very fine rain that falls from a clear sky at dusk [Late 19thC. Via French from, ultimately, Latin *serum* "evening," a form of *serus* "late" (source of English *soirée*).]

ser·e·nade /sèrrə náyd, sérrə nàyd/ *n.* **1.** LOVE SONG a song or the performance of a song used to court somebody, traditionally sung by a man in the evening outside a woman's window **2.** INSTRUMENTAL COMPOSITION FOR A SMALL ENSEMBLE an instrumental work similar to a sonata, designed for evening outdoor performance by a small ensemble of musicians **3.** = **shivaree** (*regional*) ■ *vti.* (**-nad·ed, -nad·ing, -nades**) PERFORM A LOVE SONG to sing or play a serenade ○ *A mockingbird serenades us every evening.* [Mid-17thC. Via French *sérénade* from Italian *serenata* (see SERENATA).] —**ser·e·nad·er** *n.*

ser·e·na·ta /sèrrə naátə/ *n.* **1.** 18C CHORAL WORK a choral work popular during the 18th century, often based on a religious text and having solos and duets **2.** = **serenade** *n.* 1, **serenade** *n.* 2 [Mid-18thC. From Italian, formed from *sereno* "serene," from Latin *serenus* (source of English *serene*). The meaning of the Italian word was influenced by Italian *sera* "evening."]

ser·en·dip·i·ty /sèrrən díppətee/ *n.* a natural gift for making useful discoveries by accident [Mid-18thC (but rare before the 20thC). From *The Three Princes of Serendip*, an originally Persian story about three princes who had this ability; "Serendip" is supposedly a former name of Sri Lanka.] —**ser·en·dip·i·tous** *adj.* —**ser·en·dip·i·tous·ly** *adv.*

WORD KEY: USAGE

Extended senses: The phrase *serendipitous discovery*, which is often seen, manages to suggest that ***serendipity*** is nothing other than good luck. However, the idea of a discovery is necessary to the word, and ***serendipity*** and ***serendipitous*** are nonstandard in senses unrelated to making happy discoveries by chance.

se·rene /sə reén/ *adj.* **1.** CALM AND UNTROUBLED without worry, stress, or disturbance **2.** CLOUDLESS bright and without clouds [15thC. From Latin *serenus* "clear, calm."] —**se·rene·ly** *adv.* —**se·rene·ness** *n.* —**se·ren·i·ty** /sə rénnə tee/ *n.*

WORD KEY: SYNONYMS

See Synonyms at ***calm.***

Se·rene /sə reén/ *adj.* a word used in the titles of members of certain European royal families, e.g., that of Monaco

Se·ren·ge·ti Na·tion·al Park /sèrrəng gèttee-/ national park on the plains of western Tanzania. Established in 1941, it is home to many species of large mammals and other wildlife. Area: 5,700 sq. mi./14,750 sq. km.

serf /surf/ *n.* **1.** MEDIEVAL FARMWORKER an agricultural worker, especially in feudal Europe, who cultivated land belonging to a landowner, and who was bought and sold with the land. A serf was little better off than an enslaved laborer. Without the landowner's permission, a serf could not leave his or her plot of land or village, marry, or change occupation. **2.** ENSLAVED LABORER somebody who is, or is like, an enslaved laborer [15thC. Via French from Latin *servus* "slave."] —**serf·dom** *n.* —**serf·hood** *n.*

serge /surj/ *n.* a strong cloth, usually made of wool but sometimes of other fibers, used especially to make coats, jackets, and pants [14thC. Via Old French *sarge* from, ultimately, Latin *serica lana* "silken wool," from *sericus* (see SILK).]

ser·geant /saárjənt/ *n.* **1.** MILITARY RANK in the U.S. Army or Marine Corps, the rank immediately above corporal, or any of various ranks above that, or any of various equivalent ranks in the U.S. Air Force **2.** POLICE RANK the rank below lieutenant, captain, or inspector in a police force **3.** = **sergeant at arms** [12thC. Via Old French *sergent* "servant" (the original sense in English) from Latin *servient-*, present participle stem of *servire* (see SERVE).] —**ser·gean·cy** /saár jən see/ *n.* —**ser·geant·ship** *n.*

ser·geant at arms (*plural* **ser·geants at arms**) *n.* somebody appointed to keep order within an organization, e.g., a legislative body or court of law, and to perform certain other duties, e.g., making arrests

ser·geant first class (*plural* **ser·geants first class**) *n.* a rank in the U.S. Army between staff sergeant and master sergeant or first sergeant, or a soldier who has this rank

ser·geant fish *n.* **1.** = **cobia 2.** = **snook** [Said to be so named because of the stripes on its body, like those on a sergeant's arm]

ser·geant ma·jor (*plural* **ser·geants ma·jor** *or* **ser·geant ma·jors**) *n.* **1.** MILITARY ADMINISTRATIVE OFFICER the chief noncommissioned administrative officer at a U.S. Army, Air Force, or Marine Corps headquarters unit **2.** ARMY RANK in the British armed forces, the second highest rank of noncommissioned officer, immediately below regimental sergeant major, or somebody who holds this rank **3.** ZOOL LARGE TROPICAL FISH a large damselfish of tropical Atlantic waters that ranges from blue-green to yellow in color with black vertical stripes. Latin name: *Abudefduf saxatilis.*

se·ri·al /seéree əl/ *n.* PUBL **1.** STORY IN PARTS a story that is published or broadcast in parts, normally at regular intervals **2.** REGULAR NEWSPAPER OR MAGAZINE a magazine or newspaper published at regular intervals, especially weekly or monthly ■ *adj.* **1.** IN A SERIES in or forming a series, or done or doing something repeatedly in a series **2.** PRODUCED IN PARTS published or broadcast in parts, usually at regular intervals **3.** COMPUT SENDING COMPUTER INFORMATION SEQUENTIALLY used to describe a form of data communication in which the individual bits that comprise each byte or character travel one after another through a single wire. ◊ **parallel 4.** MUSIC RELATING TO MUSICAL COMPOSITION used to describe a method of musical composition in which all 12 chromatic tones of the octave appear in strict order with no note repeated before the sequence is completed [Mid-19thC. Formed from SERIES.] —**se·ri·al·ly** *adv.*

se·ri·al·ism /seéree əlìzzəm/ *n.* a method of musical composition in which all 12 chromatic tones of the octave appear in strict order with no note repeated before the sequence is completed —**se·ri·al·ist** *n.*

se·ri·al·ize /seéree ə lìz/ (**-ized, -iz·ing, -iz·es**) *vti.* to publish or broadcast a story in parts at intervals, or to be divided into parts suitable for publishing or broadcasting —**se·ri·al·i·za·tion** /seèree ələ záysh'n/ *n.*

se·ri·al kill·er *n.* somebody who murders a number of people over a period of time, especially somebody who uses the same method each time —**se·ri·al kill·ing** *n.*

se·ri·al mo·nog·a·my *n.* the idea or practice of having only one sexual partner at a time and entering another relationship when one comes to an end

se·ri·al num·ber *n.* a set of numbers assigned to, and usually marked on, each of a series of identical products, e.g., television sets, cars, paper money, or computers

se·ri·ate /sírree àyt, -it/ *adj.* arranged in rows or a series (*formal*) —**se·ri·ate·ly** *adv.*

se·ri·a·tim /seèrree áytəm, -áttim/ *adv.* one after another, or in a series [15thC. From medieval Latin, formed from Latin *series* (see SERIES).]

se·ri·ceous /sə ríshəss/ *adj.* **1.** COVERED WITH SOFT HAIRS covered with small soft silky hairs **2.** SILKY having the soft smooth feel of silk (*formal*) [Late 18thC. Formed from Latin *sericus* "silken," ultimately from Greek *Sēres*, Greek name of the Asian people who originally made silk, thought to be the Chinese.]

ser·i·cin /sérrəssin/ *n.* a gelatinous protein that binds together the filaments of a silk fiber [Mid-19thC. Formed from Latin *sericum* "silk," a form of *sericus* (see SERICEOUS).]

ser·i·cul·ture /sérrə kùlchər/ *n.* the commercial breeding of silkworms for their silk [Mid-20thC. Shortening of French *sériciculture*, from Latin *sericum* "silk," a form of *sericus* (see SERICEOUS).] —**ser·i·cul·tur·al** /sèrrə kúlchərəl/ *adj.* —**ser·i·cul·tur·ist** *n.*

ser·i·e·ma /sèrree eémə/ (*plural* **-ma** *or* **-mas**) *n.* either one of two large, crested, mainly ground-dwelling birds native to South America that have long tails and legs. Family: Cariamidae. [Mid-19thC. Via modern Latin from Tupi *siriema*, probably meaning "crested."]

se·ries /seér eez/ (*plural* **-ries**) *n.* **1.** THINGS ONE AFTER ANOTHER a number of similar or related things coming one after another ○ *a series of lectures on modern philosophy* **2.** BROADCAST SET OF BROADCAST PROGRAMS a set of regularly broadcast programs, each of which is complete in itself **3.** PUBL SIMILAR PUBLICATIONS FROM ONE ORGANIZATION a number of books, pamphlets, or periodicals brought out by one company or organization on the same or related topics or in the same format **4.** SPORTS SET OF GAMES BETWEEN SAME TEAMS in some sports, e.g., cricket and baseball, a set of games between the same teams **5.** COLLECTING RELATED ITEMS PRODUCED AT ONE TIME a number of related items, e.g., stamps or coins of different values, brought out at one time **6.** CHEM RELATED CHEMICALS a group of related chemical compounds that are similar in structure or properties **7.** MATH SUM OF SEQUENCE OF TERMS the indicated sum of a finite or infinite sequence of terms, each term being added to those that precede it. ◊ **geometric series 8.** GEOL ROCK LAYER a succession of rock strata deposited during a particular period of geologic time **9.** ELECTRON ENG ARRANGEMENT OF ELECTRIC ELEMENTS a set of two or more electronic components through which current flows in sequence **10.** MUSIC SET OF 12 NOTES a set of 12 notes, the 12 chromatic pitches of an octave, in which no pitch is repeated. This forms the basis for serial composition. **11.** GRAM TWO OR MORE COORDINATE ELEMENTS a sequence of two or more elements in a sentence that have the same grammatical structure. ◊ **parallelism** [Early 17thC. From Latin, formed from *serere* "to join or connect."] ◇ **in series** connected in a circuit so that the same current flows through each component in sequence

WORD KEY: ORIGIN

The Latin word *serere*, from which ***series*** is derived, is also the source of English *assert*, *insert*, and *serial*.

Serif

ser·if /sérrif/ *n.* a short decorative line at the start or finish of a stroke in a letter [Mid-19thC. Origin uncertain: perhaps from Dutch *schreef* "dash, line."]

ser·i·graph /sérrə graàf/ *n.* = **silkscreen** [Late 19thC. Formed from Latin *sericum* "silk," a form of *sericus* (see SERICEOUS).] —**se·rig·ra·pher** /sə ríggrəfər/ *n.* —**se·rig·ra·phy** /-ríggrəfee/ *n.*

ser·in /sérrin/ (*plural* **-ins** *or* **-in**) *n.* a yellowish or grayish finch found in North Africa and the Mediterranean region. The best-known serin is the canary. Genus: *Serinus.* [Mid-16thC. From French, literally "canary" (the original sense in English), of uncertain origin: perhaps ultimately from Greek.]

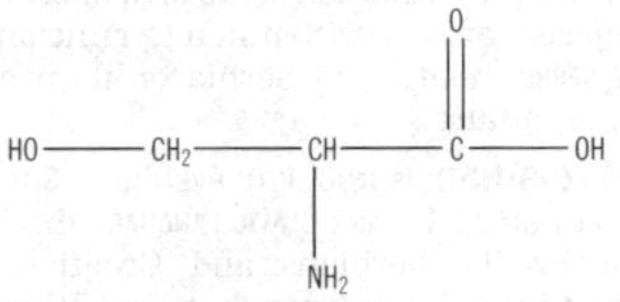

Serine

ser·ine /sə reén/ *n.* an amino acid that is obtained in the hydrolysis of proteins and is a precursor in the biosynthesis of glycine, choline, and other metabolites. Formula: $C_3H_7O_3N$. [Late 19thC. From German *Serin*, from Latin *sericum* "silk," a form of *sericus* (see SERICEOUS).]

se·rin·ga /sə ríng gə/ *n.* a Brazilian tree that yields rubber. Genus: *Hevea.* [Mid-18thC. Via French and Portuguese from Latin *syringa* (see SYRINGA).]

se·ri·o·com·ic /seèree ō kómik/, **se·ri·o·com·i·cal** /-ō kómik'l/ *adj.* with both serious and comic elements —**se·ri·o·com·i·cal·ly** /-kómiklee/ *adv.*

se·ri·ous /seéree əss/ *adj.* **1.** VERY BAD OR GREAT very great, bad, dangerous, harmful, or difficult to handle **2.** IMPORTANT important or grave enough to require thought and attention ○ *There are serious arguments against this proposal.* **3.** LIKELY TO SUCCEED having a possibility of success or showing an intention to succeed ○ *Only two of the five applicants can be considered serious candidates for the job.* **4.** THOUGHTFUL OR THOUGHT-PROVOKING discussing or dealing with matters in a thoughtful or thought-provoking way as opposed to a superficial or merely entertaining manner ○ *a serious discussion of the issues* **5.** NOT LIGHTHEARTED quiet, thoughtful, not laughing or making jokes very often, and always being sensible **6.** MEANING SOMETHING LITERALLY not joking, pretending, or exaggerating about something ○ *Do you think she's serious about helping us out?* **7.** SUBSTANTIAL substantial or sustained rather than trivial or insignificant (*informal*) ○ *I've invested serious money in this endeavor.* **8.** DEDICATED TO SOMETHING showing great interest in or commitment to an endeavor, skill, or pastime ○ *a serious stamp collector* [15thC. Via French *sérieux* or late Latin *seriosus* from Latin *serius.*] —**se·ri·ous·ness** *n.*

se·ri·ous·ly /seéree əsslee/ *adv.* **1.** BADLY in a great, bad, dangerous, harmful, or problematic way ○ *seriously ill* **2.** GRAVELY in a grave and thoughtful way, without being lighthearted or dismissive ○ *We have to take this threat seriously.* **3.** TRULY in a true or literal way, without exaggeration or deceit ○ *Do you seriously expect me to go along with this?* **4.** EXTREMELY to a great or remarkable extent (*informal*) ○ *I'm getting seriously fed up with her arrogance.*

se·ri·ous-mind·ed *adj.* earnest and taking an interest in matters that are weighty and important

Ser·kin /súrkin/, **Rudolf** (1903–91) Czechoslovakian-born U.S. pianist. He was known especially for his interpretations of the classical Austro-German repertoire.

ser·mon /súrmən/ *n.* **1.** RELIGIOUS TALK a talk on a religious or moral subject given by a member of the clergy as part of a religious service **2.** LONG LECTURE ON BEHAVIOR a long and tedious talk, especially one telling somebody how or how not to behave [12thC. Via Anglo-Norman *sermun* from Latin *sermo* "talk, conversation."] —**ser·mon·ic** /sur mónnik/ *adj.*

ser·mon·ette /sùrmə nét/ *n.* a short and usually unwelcome sermon or scolding

ser·mon·ize /súrmə nìz/ (**-ized, -iz·ing, -iz·es**) *vti.* to give somebody a long tedious talk about how or how not to behave —**ser·mon·iz·er** *n.*

Ser·mon on the Mount *n.* a collection of Jesus Christ's religious and moral teachings recorded in Matthew's Gospel in the Bible, much of which Jesus Christ set out in a speech to his disciples from a hillside

sero- *prefix.* serum ○ *serology* [From SERUM]

se·ro·con·vert /seèrōkən vúrt/ (**-vert·ed, -vert·ing, -verts**) *vi.* to produce specific antibodies in response to the presence of an antigen such as a bacterium or virus —**se·ro·con·ver·sion** /seèrō kən vúr shən/ *n.*

se·rol·o·gy /sə rólləjee/ *n.* the branch of medicine concerned with the study of blood serum and its constituents, especially its role in protecting the human body against disease —**se·ro·log·ic** /seèrə lójjik/ *adj.* —**se·rol·o·gist** /sə rólləjist/ *n.*

se·ro·neg·a·tive /seèrō néggətiv/ *adj.* after a blood test, showing no immunological evidence of infection, either current or previous, with a particular bacterium, virus, or other infective agent

se·ro·pos·i·tive /seèrō paázətiv/ *adj.* after a blood test, showing immunological evidence of infection, either current or previous, with a particular bacterium, virus, or other agent

se·ro·pu·ru·lent /seèrō pyoórələnt/ *adj.* consisting of a mixture of blood serum and pus

se·ro·sa /sə róssə, sə rózə/ (*plural* **-sae** /-róssee, -rózee/ *or* **-sas**) *n.* = **serous membrane** [Late 19thC. From modern Latin *(membrana) serosa* "serous (membrane)."]

se·rot·i·nal *adj.* = **serotinous** [Late 19thC. Formed from Latin *serotinus* (see SEROTINE).]

ser·o·tine /sérrətin, -tìn/ *n.* a small brown bat found in Europe and Asia. Genus: *Eptesicus.* [Late 18thC. Via French *sérotine* from a late Latin sense "in or of the evening" of Latin *serotinus* "belated, late flowering," from, ultimately, *serus* "late."]

se·rot·i·nous /sə rótt'nəss/, **se·rot·i·nal** /sə rótt'nəl/, **ser·o·tine** /sérrətin, -tìn/ *adj.* developing or blooming during the late part of a growing season [Mid-17thC. From Latin *serotinus* (see SEROTINE).]

se·ro·to·ner·gic /sèrrətə núrjik/, **se·ro·to·ni·ner·gic** /sèrrə tōə núrjik/ *adj.* used to describe neurons or nerves that are capable of releasing serotonin as a neurotransmitter at their endings

se·ro·to·nin /sèrrə tṓnin/ *n.* a chemical derived from the amino acid tryptophan, and widely distributed in tissues. It acts as a neurotransmitter, constricts blood vessels at injury sites, and may affect emotional states. LSD and certain antidepressants work by interfering with serotonin in the brain. Formula: $C_{10}H_{12}N_2O$. [Mid-20thC. Coined from SERO- + TONIC + -IN.]

se·rous /seérəss/ *adj.* relating to, resembling, or producing serum [15thC. From French *séreux* or medieval Latin *serosus*, both formed from Latin *serum* "whey, watery fluid" (source of English *serum*).]

se·rous flu·id *n.* any bodily fluid that resembles serum

se·rous mem·brane *n.* a thin moist transparent membrane that lines the body cavities and surrounds the internal organs, e.g., the peritoneum that lines the abdomen and the pericardium that surrounds the heart. Serous membranes secrete a lubricating fluid that provides for virtually frictionless movement of the internal organs against both the body wall and each other.

se·row /sérrō, sə rṓ/ (*plural* **se·rows** *or* **se·row**) *n.* a goat antelope that lives in the mountains of tropical and subtropical east Asia. Genus: *Capricornus.* [Mid-19thC. Origin uncertain: probably from Lepcha *sā-ro.*]

Ser·pens /súr penz/ *n.* a constellation of the equatorial region that is unique in being split into two separate parts **(Serpens Caput)** (the head) and **(Serpens Cauda)** (the tail), located either side of Ophiuchus

Serpent

ser·pent /súrpənt/ *n.* **1.** SNAKE a snake **2.** TREACHEROUS PERSON somebody who is sly or treacherous **3.** OLD WIND INSTRUMENT a woodwind instrument shaped like a curving snake, dating back to the medieval period. The sound is produced as in a brass instrument, but there are key holes instead of valves, as in a wind instrument. [13thC. Via French from Latin *serpent-*, present participle stem of *serpere* "to creep."]

Ser·pent *n.* **1.** BIBLICAL GUISE OF EVIL in the Bible, the reptile said to have tempted Eve **2.** SATAN Satan (*literary*) **3.** ASTRON = **Serpens**

ser·pen·tine /súrpən teèn, -tīn/ *adj.* **1.** WINDING winding and twisting, with many bends and curves **2.** RESEMBLING SNAKE like a snake in motion or shape (*literary*) **3.** CUNNING untrustworthy and cunning, as a snake is conventionally thought to be (*literary*) **4.** MATH CURVING relating to or being a complex curve that is symmetric about the x-axis and the central part of which is convex ■ *n.* MINERALS GREEN OR BROWN MINERAL a dull green or brownish mineral consisting of hydrous magnesium silicate. It is often used as an ornamental stone. [15thC. In the noun sense, from French *serpentin*; from its being mottled like a snake's skin.]

Ser·pen·tine Ridge /sùrpən tīn-/ *n.* on the moon, a low ridge running north to south across the eastern side of the Mare Serenitatis, or Sea of Tranquility

ser·pul·id /súrpyəlid/ *n.* a round segmented marine worm that produces a flat, spirally coiled, limy shell, from which it projects a crown of tentacles, typically found on rocks and seaweed. Family: Serpulidae. [Late 19thC. From late Latin *serpula* "small serpent."]

Ser·ra /sérrə/, **Junípero** (1713–84) Spanish-born North American missionary. He was a Franciscan who established Roman Catholic missions throughout California, beginning in San Diego in 1769. Born **Miguel José Serra**

ser·ran·id /sə ránnid, sérrə-/ *n.* a robust large-mouthed marine fish such as a sea bass or a grouper, living in temperate and tropical seas. Family: Serranidae. [Mid-20thC. From modern Latin *Serranidae*, ultimately from Latin *serra* "saw" (source of English *serrate*).] —**ser·ran·id** *adj.*

ser·rate /sé ràyt/ *adj.* LIKE TEETH OF SAW with notches or projections like the teeth of a saw ■ *vt.* (**-rat·ed, -rat·ing, -rates**) GIVE SOMETHING TOOTHED EDGE to give something an edge that is notched like the teeth of a saw [14thC. From late Latin *serrat-*, past participle stem of *serrare*, from Latin *serra* "saw."]

ser·rat·ed /sé raytəd/ *adj.* with notches like the teeth of a saw

ser·ra·tion /sə ráysh'n/ *n.* **1.** NOTCHES LIKE SAW TEETH a row of notches like the teeth of a saw **2.** TOOTH OR NOTCH a tooth or notch in a series or row that is like the teeth of a saw **3.** STATE OF BEING NOTCHED the state of having a sharp notched edge like the teeth of a saw

ser·ried /sérreed/ *adj.* crowded together with little space between each (*literary*) [Mid-17thC. Past participle of obsolete *serry* "to close ranks," from French *serrer* "to press close together," from, ultimately, Latin *sera* "bolt."]

ser·ri·form /sérrə fàwrm/ *adj.* with notches like the teeth of a saw [Early 19thC. Coined from Latin *serra* "saw" + -FORM.]

ser·ru·late /sérryələt, -làyt/, **ser·ru·lat·ed** /sérryə làytəd/ *adj.* having an edge with tiny notches like the teeth of a saw [Late 18thC. From modern Latin *serrulatus*, from Latin *serrulus* "small saw," from *serra* "saw."]

ser·ru·la·tion /sèrryə láysh'n/ *n.* **1.** NOTCH ON EDGE OF SOMETHING any of a row of tiny notches around the edge of something **2.** CONDITION OF HAVING TINY NOTCHES the condition of having tiny notches like the teeth of a saw

se·rum /seèrəm/ (*plural* **-rums** *or* **-ra** /seèrə/) *n.* **1.** PHYSIOL LIQUID PART OF BLOOD the fluid that separates from clotted blood, similar to plasma but without clotting agents **2.** MED = **antiserum 3.** BIOL BODY FLUID any clear watery body fluid, especially that exuded by serous membranes **4.** WHEY whey (*archaic*) [Late 17thC. From Latin, literally "whey, watery fluid."] —**se·rum·al** *adj.*

se·rum al·bu·min *n.* the most abundant protein in blood serum. It helps determine the osmotic pressure of blood, and is used in transfusions to treat shock.

se·rum glob·u·lin *n.* a globular soluble protein or mixture of proteins that can be separated from blood serum and contains most of the blood's antibodies

se·rum hep·a·ti·tis *n.* = **hepatitis B**

serv. *abbr.* **1.** servant **2.** service

ser·val /súrv'l/ (*plural* **-vals** *or* **-val**) *n.* an African wild cat that has a reddish-brown coat with black spots, long legs, a long neck, and a relatively small head with large ears. The serval lives in the African bush south of the Sahara Desert. It hunts at night, preying on birds and small animals. Latin name: *Felis serval.* [Late 18thC. Via modern Latin or French from Portuguese *lobo cerval* "lynx" (literally "deerlike wolf"), ultimately from Latin *cervus* "deer."]

ser·vant /súrvənt/ *n.* **1.** SOMEBODY WHO SERVES ANOTHER somebody who serves another, especially somebody employed to do household jobs such as cooking, cleaning, and serving meals **2.** SOMEBODY WORKING FOR PUBLIC somebody in the public employ. ◊ **civil servant, public servant** [12thC. From Old French, present participle of *servir* "to serve" (see SERVE).]

serve /surv/ *v.* (**served, serv·ing, serves**) **1.** *vti.* WORK FOR SOMEBODY to work, or work for somebody **2.** *vti.* BE OF USE to be useful or helpful for a particular purpose **3.** *vti.* PREPARE AND SUPPLY FOOD to prepare and supply food or drinks **4.** *vti.* GIVE SOMEBODY FOOD OR DRINK to bring food or drink to somebody **5.** *vt.* PROVIDE CUSTOMERS WITH GOODS to wait on customers in a store, and provide them with goods, supplies, or services **6.** *vi.* CHR ASSIST DURING MASS to assist a Roman Catholic priest during the celebration of Mass **7.** *vti.* SPEND TIME IN PRISON to spend a certain length of time in a place, especially in prison **8.** *vti.* WORK AS SERVANT to work as a servant **9.** *vi.* BE IN ARMED FORCE to be a member of an armed force, especially in wartime **10.** *vt.* WORSHIP SOMEBODY OR SOMETHING to worship or follow somebody or something (*formal*) **11.** *vt.* COPULATE WITH FEMALE to copulate with a female animal **12.** *vti.* HAVE PARTICULAR EFFECT to have a particular effect or result ○ *This letter will serve to remind you of our appointment.* **13.** *vt.* LAW DELIVER LEGAL DOCUMENT TO SOMEBODY to deliver to somebody a legal document such as a summons, writ, or warrant (*formal*) **14.** *vti.* RACKET GAMES PUT BALL OR SHUTTLECOCK IN PLAY to hit a ball or shuttlecock towards an opponent in a racket game as a way of beginning play **15.** *vt.* NAUT BIND ROPE WITH WIRE OR CORD to bind a rope with something such as fine wire to keep it from wearing or fraying ■ *n.* RACKET GAMES HIT THAT STARTS POINT in racket games, the shot used to begin every point [12thC. Directly or via Old French *servir* from Latin *servire*, from *servus* "slave."] —**serv·a·ble** *adj.* ◇ **serve somebody right** to be a deserved punishment for doing something wrong

WORD KEY: ORIGIN

The Latin word *servire*, from which ***serve*** is derived, is also the source of English *deserve, dessert, sergeant*, and *serviette* (but not of *conserve, observe, preserve*, and *reserve*, which come from the unrelated Latin *servare*).

serv·er /súrvər/ *n.* **1.** SOMEBODY WHO SERVES somebody who serves something, e.g., food at a meal **2.** RACKET GAMES SOMEBODY WHO STARTS GAME the player who starts a game in a sport such as tennis or badminton by hitting the ball or shuttlecock across the net to an opponent **3.** DOMESTIC TRAY FOR SERVING SOMETHING a tray for serving food or drinks on **4.** DOMESTIC FOOD UTENSIL a utensil for serving food **5.** CHR ASSISTANT AT MASS somebody who assists a Roman Catholic priest at Mass. ◊ **acolyte, altar boy 6.** COMPUT = **file server 7.** COMPUT = **print server**

ser·vice[1] /súrvəss/ *n.* **1.** WORK DONE FOR SOMEBODY ELSE work done by somebody for somebody else as a job, a duty, a punishment, or a favor **2.** MEETING OF PUBLIC NEED the system or operation by which people are provided with something they need, e.g., public transportation, or the organization that runs such a system **3.** GOVERNMENT AGENCY an official organization, especially a government department, or the work performed for such an organization ○ *the diplomatic service* **4.** MIL ONE OF THE ARMED FORCES one of a country's armed forces ○ *Which branch of the service is your daughter in?* **5.** DOMESTIC DOMESTIC SERVANT'S WORK the work done as a servant in a private house **6.** MAINTENANCE OF MACHINERY the act of cleaning, checking, adjusting, or making minor repairs to a piece of machinery, especially a motor vehicle, to make sure that it works properly **7.** USE OR OPERATION current use or operation ○ *The number you have dialed is not in service at this time.* **8.** RELIG PUBLIC WORSHIP CEREMONY a religious ceremony usually involving specific forms for worship and prayer **9.** RELIG RELIGIOUS RITUAL a specific religious ritual that is performed according to a prescribed form **10.** DOMESTIC SET OF DISHES a set of dishes and cups for use in serving a particular meal ○ *dinner service* **11.** FOOD SERVING SOMEBODY FOOD the act of bringing food to somebody or the way in which this is done **12.** RACKET GAMES ACT OF SERVING BALL OR SHUTTLECOCK the act or manner of serving in a racket game, or the right to do so **13.** RACKET GAMES GAME a game in which a player serves **14.** LAW SERVING OF LEGAL DOCUMENT TO SOMEBODY the delivery of a legal document such as a writ or summons **15.** NAUT MATERIAL USED TO BIND ROPE something such as fine wire or cord used to bind a rope to prevent it from fraying ■ **serv·ic·es** *npl.* **1.** TRANSP FACILITIES FOR TRAVELERS facilities such as stores, restaurants, and toilets available at certain places along a highway ○ *There are no services at the next exit.* **2.** COMM WORK THAT DOES NOT MAKE ANYTHING jobs and businesses such as banking and insurance that provide something for other people but do not produce tangible goods **3.** THINGS PROVIDED BY GOVERNMENT things such as education, health care, and roads that are provided by national or local government and paid for by taxation **4.** ARMED FORCES the armed forces of a country ■ *vt.* (**serv·iced, serv·ic·ing, serv·ic·es**) **1.** PROVIDE SOMETHING FOR COMMUNITY to provide a community or organization with something that it needs ○ *The electric company services all nine counties.* **2.** CLEAN AND ADJUST MACHINERY to clean, check, adjust, and make minor repairs to a piece of machinery in order to make sure that it works properly ○ *It's time to have my car serviced.* **3.** FIN PAY INTEREST ON DEBT to pay interest on a debt **4.** AGRIC COPULATE WITH FEMALE to copulate with a female animal ■ *adj.* **1.** PROVIDING A SERVICE NOT GOODS relating to jobs or businesses such as banking and insurance that do something useful for people but that do not manufacture any goods **2.** FOR MAINTENANCE AND REPAIR providing maintenance and repair for manufactured products **3.** USED BY EMPLOYEES OR FOR DELIVERIES intended for employees or deliveries rather than for members of the public ○ *a service elevator* [Pre-12thC. Directly or via French from Latin *servitium* "slavery," from *servus* "slave."] ◇ **press somebody *or* something into service** to use something or somebody for an unusual purpose, especially in an emergency situation ○ *At the last minute, she was pressed into service as the organist at her brother's wedding.*

ser·vice[2] /súrvəss/ *n.* = **service tree** [Mid-16thC. Plural of obsolete "serve," ultimately from Latin *sorbus*, "service tree."]

Ser·vice /súrviss/, **Robert William** (1874–1958) British-born Canadian writer. He is remembered for the popular poems such as "The Shooting of Dan McGrew" (1907) that gained him the epithet "the Canadian Kipling."

serv·ice·a·ble /súrvəssəb'l/ *adj.* **1.** MADE TO WEAR WELL suitable for everyday use and hard wear **2.** WORKING in working condition **3.** EFFECTIVE useful or effective —**serv·ice·a·ble·ness** *n.* —**serv·ice·a·bly** *adv.*

ser·vice ar·e·a *n.* **1.** TRANSP FACILITIES FOR HIGHWAY TRAVELERS a place beside a highway where there are facilities for travelers such as a restaurant, toilets, and a service station **2.** BROADCAST **AREA OF SATISFACTORY SIGNAL** the area over which a radio or television broadcasting station can transmit a satisfactory signal for reception

serv·ice·ber·ry /súrvəss bèrree/ (*plural* **-ries**) *n.* **1. PLANT WITH SMALL EDIBLE BERRIES** a small tree or shrub of the rose family, mostly native to North America, that bears clusters of white flowers and produces small, edible, dark blue fruits. Genus: *Amelanchier.* **2. ROUND FRUIT** the round fruit of the serviceberry **3. FRUIT OF SERVICE TREE** the fruit of the service tree [*Service* from SERVICE[2]]

ser·vice break *n.* a game won by a player in a racket game when an opponent was serving

ser·vice cap *n.* a round, flat-topped military cap with a visor

ser·vice charge *n.* **1. MONEY ADDED TO BILL FOR SERVICE** a sum of money, usually calculated as a percentage of a customer's bill, added to the bill in a restaurant or hotel to pay the staff for their service **2.** COMM **MONEY CHARGED FOR PERFORMING SERVICE** a sum of money charged by a business or bank for handling a transaction

ser·vice con·tract *n.* a contract with a company or manufacturer to maintain equipment in working order at an agreed price over a fixed period

ser·vice court *n.* in racket games, the area within which a served ball or shuttlecock must land

ser·vice in·dus·try *n.* an industry that provides a service rather than goods, or such industries as a whole

ser·vice line *n.* in racket games and volleyball, a line on a court that the server must not cross before serving

serv·ice·man /súrvəssmən/ (*plural* **-men** /-mən/) *n.* **1.** MIL **SOLDIER** a man serving in the armed forces **2. serv·ice·man, ser·vice man** BUSINESS **REPAIRMAN** a man whose job is repairing and servicing equipment

ser·vice mark *n.* a sign or symbol used by people or companies who provide a particular service to identify themselves and set them apart from other companies

ser·vice mod·ule *n.* the section of an Apollo spacecraft in which elements of the propulsion and navigation systems are kept until the unit has reentered the earth's atmosphere and is jettisoned. ◊ **lunar module, command module**

ser·vice·per·son /súrvəss pùrss'n/ (*plural* **-peo·ple** /-peep'l/ *or* **-per·sons**) *n.* **1.** MIL **SOLDIER** somebody serving in the armed forces **2. ser·vice·per·son, ser·vice per·son** BUSINESS **REPAIR PERSON** somebody whose job is maintaining and servicing equipment

ser·vice road *n.* a minor road that runs alongside a main road, especially a major highway, giving access to houses, stores, offices, and other businesses

ser·vice sta·tion *n.* a place where gasoline, oil, and other requirements for motor vehicles can be bought, and often where maintenance and repair work are also done

ser·vice stripe *n.* a stripe worn on the sleeve of somebody's uniform to show that he or she has been a member of the armed forces for a certain number of years

ser·vice tree, service *n.* a tree, native to central and southern Europe, that has compound leaves of up to 20 toothed leaflets and produces edible fruit. The fruits are fermented with grain to produce an alcoholic beverage. Latin name: *Sorbus domestica.*

ser·vice·wom·an /súrvəss wòommən/ (*plural* **-en** /-wìmmin/) *n.* **1.** MIL **WOMAN SOLDIER** a woman serving in the armed forces **2. ser·vice·woman, ser·vice wom·an** BUSINESS **REPAIR WOMAN** a woman whose job is repairing and servicing equipment

ser·vi·ette /sùrvee étt/ *n. U.K.* = **napkin** *n.* 1 [15thC. From French, formed from *servir* "to serve" (see SERVE).]

ser·vile /súrv'l, -vīl/ *adj.* **1. TOO OBEDIENT** too willing to agree with somebody or to do whatever demeaning thing somebody wants **2. FOR SERVANTS** relating to dirty degrading work that is considered fit only for servants or enslaved laborers ○ *servile tasks* **3. RELATING TO SLAVERY** relating to enslaved labor or the condition of enslaved labor [14thC. From Latin *servilis,* from *servus* "slave."] —**ser·vile·ly** *adv.* —**ser·vile·ness** *n.*

serv·ing /súrving/ *n.* an amount of food served to one person

ser·vi·tor /súrvitər, -tawr/ *n.* a servant or attendant (*dated*) [14thC. Via Old French from late Latin, formed from Latin *servire* "to serve" (see SERVE).]

ser·vi·tude /súrvi tòod/ *n.* **1. STATE OF SLAVERY** the state of being a slave **2. SUBJECTION** the state of being ruled or dominated by somebody or something **3. WORK IMPOSED AS PUNISHMENT** work imposed as a punishment for a crime **4.** LAW **RESTRICTION OR OBLIGATION ON PROPERTY** a restriction or obligation attached to a property that entitles somebody other than the owner to a specified use of it, e.g., the right to cross it [15thC. Via Old French from Latin *servitudo,* from *servus* "slave."]

ser·vo[1] /súrvō/ *adj.* **RELATING TO SERVOMECHANISM** relating to, forming part of, or activated by a servomechanism ■ *n.* (*plural* **-vos**) **1.** = **servomechanism 2.** = **servometer** [Late 19thC. Shortening of French *servomoteur* "servomotor" (an auxiliary motor); *servo-* from Latin *servus* "slave."]

ser·vo[2] /súr vō/ (*plural* **-vos**) *n. Aus* a service station (*informal*) [Late 20thC. Shortening.]

ser·vo·mech·a·nism /súrvō mèkə nìzzəm/ *n.* a closed-circuit device in which a small input power controls a much larger power, as in a radio telescope — **ser·vo·me·chan·i·cal** /sùrvōmə kánnik'l/ *adj.*

ser·vo·mo·tor /súrvō mōtər/ *n.* a motor that supplies the initial power in a servomechanism

SES *abbr.* socioeconomic status ■ *n., abbr.* Senior Executive Service

Sesame

ses·a·me /séssəmee/ (*plural* **-mes** *or* **-me**) *n.* **1.** PLANTS **TROPICAL PLANT CULTIVATED FOR SEEDS** an herbaceous plant of tropical Asia, cultivated for its seeds. Latin name: *Sesamum indicum.* **2.** FOOD **SEED OF SESAME PLANT** the seed of the sesame plant. Both the seed and its oil are used in cooking. [15thC. Via Latin *sesamum* from Greek *sēsamon,* of Near Eastern origin.]

ses·a·me oil *n.* a strongly flavored oil from sesame seeds, widely used in Asian and Southeast Asian cooking

ses·a·moid /séssə mòyd/ *n.* **SMALL ROUGHLY SPHERICAL BONE** a small, roughly spherical bone lying within a tendon to assist in its mechanical action or to bear pressure ■ *adj.* **RELATING TO VARIOUS SMALL BONES** relating to or being various small bones or cartilages in a tendon or joint such as the kneebone [Late 17thC. Formed from SESAME.]

Se·so·tho /sə sṓtō, sə sóo tòo/ *n.* the dialect of Sotho spoken by the Basotho in Lesotho [Mid-19thC. From Sesotho.] —**Se·so·tho** *adj.*

sesqui- *prefix.* one and a half ○ *sesquicentennial* [From Latin, from *semis* "half" + *-que* "and"]

ses·qui·cen·ten·ni·al /sèskwi sen ténnee əl/, **ses·qui·cen·ten·ar·y** /-ténnəree/ *n.* (*plural* **-ies**) **1. 150TH ANNIVERSARY** a 150th anniversary or the celebration of one **2. 150 YEARS** a period of 150 years ■ *adj.* **OCCURRING EVERY 150 YEARS** relating to or happening after a period of 150 years —**ses·qui·cen·ten·ni·al·ly** *adv.*

ses·qui·pe·da·lian /sèskwipə dáylee ən/, **ses·quip·e·dal** /-pédd'l/ *adj.* (*literary*) **1. USING LONG WORDS** characterized by the use of very long words **2. LONG** relating to or being a long word ■ *n.* **LONG WORD** a word with many letters or syllables (*literary*) [Early 17thC. From Latin *sesquipedalis* "measuring one and one-half feet," from the stem *ped-* "foot."] —**ses·qui·pe·da·lian·ism** *n.*

sess. *abbr.* session

ses·sile /séssīl, séss'l/ *adj.* **1.** BOT **LACKING STALK** used to describe a leaf or flower that has no stalk but is attached directly to the stem **2.** ZOOL **PERMANENTLY ATTACHED** used to describe an animal that is permanently attached to something rather than free-moving, e.g., a barnacle [Early 18thC. From Latin *sessilis* "lying close to the ground," from *sess-,* past participle stem of *sedere* "to sit" (source of English *séance, hostage,* and *obsession*).] —**ses·sil·i·ty** /sə síllətee/ *n.*

ses·sion /sésh'n/ *n.* **1. MEETING** a meeting of an official body, especially a court or legislature **2. PERIOD OF MEETING** a period during which an official body meets or does business **3. SERIES OF MEETINGS** a series of meetings of an official body **4.** EDUC **TEACHING PERIOD** the time of year or the time of day during which a school or university holds classes **5. PERIOD OF DOING SOMETHING** a period of time during which people are involved in doing something together **6. PERIOD OF PLAYING MUSIC** a period during which musicians play together, especially in a recording studio **7.** CHR **GOVERNING BODY OF PRESBYTERIAN CONGREGATION** the governing body of a Presbyterian congregation, consisting of the minister and elders ■ **ses·sions** *npl.* LAW **SITTINGS OF ENGLISH JUSTICE OF PEACE** in England, the sittings of a justice of the peace in court. ◊ **petty sessions, quarter sessions** ■ *adj.* MUSIC **1. RELATING TO FREELANCE MUSICIAN** relating to or being a musician paid to play or sing on recordings in a studio but not a permanent member of a band **2. RELATING TO FREELANCE MUSIC** relating to playing or singing done by a session musician [14thC. Via Old French from Latin *session-* "a sitting," from the stem *sess-* (see SESSILE).] —**ses·sion·al** *adj.*

WORD KEY: ORIGIN

The Latin word *sedere,* from which *session* is derived, is also the source of English *assess, assiduous, assize, insidious, séance, sedentary, size, subsidy,* and *supersede.*

Ses·sions /sésh'nz/, **Roger** (1896–1985) U.S. composer. He is known for his 12-tone compositions. He won two Pulitzer Prizes. Full name **Roger Huntington Sessions**

ses·terce /sés tùrss/, **ses·ter·ti·us** /sestúrshəss, -shee əss/ (*plural* **-i** /-shə, -shee ə/) *n.* an ancient Roman coin, originally silver but later bronze, worth a quarter of a denarius [Late 16thC. From Latin *sestertius* "two and one-half times as great," literally "one-half third," from *semis* "half" + *tertius* "third"; originally equivalent to two and a half asses.]

ses·ter·tium /se stúrshəm, -shee əm/ (*plural* **-tia** /-shə, -shee ə/) *n.* an ancient Roman unit of currency equal to 1,000 sesterces [Mid-16thC. From the Latin phrase *(mille) sestertium,* literally "(a thousand) of sesterces" (see SESTERCE).]

ses·tet /se stét/ *n.* a stanza or poem of six lines, especially the last six lines of a Petrarchan sonnet [Early 19thC. From Italian *sestetto,* literally "little sixth," from *sesto* "sixth," from Latin *sextus* "sixth."]

ses·ti·na /se steenə/ *n.* a poem of six six-line stanzas and a three-line envoy, with the last words of the first six lines repeated, in different order, at the ends of the other lines [Mid-19thC. From Italian, formed from *sesto* "sixth" (see SESTET).]

set[1] /set/ *v.* (**set, set·ting, sets**) **1.** *vt.* **PLACE SOMETHING** to put somebody or something somewhere ○ *Set the books on the table.* **2.** *vt.* **PUT SOMEBODY INTO CONDITION** to get or put somebody or something into a particular condition ○ *set the hostages free* **3.** *vt.* **MAKE SOMETHING HAPPEN** to cause something to happen ○ *set an unfortunate train of events in motion* **4.** *vt.* **FOCUS ON SOMETHING** to focus on a goal or task ○ *had set his mind on it* **5.** *vt.* **ARRANGE FOR USE** to arrange, place, or prepare something to be used ○ *set a trap for them* **6.** *vti.* **BECOME OR MAKE SOLID** to form or cause something to be formed in a solid state ○ *Let the concrete set.* **7.** *vt.* **ADJUST MEASURING DEVICE** to adjust a device such as a clock to a desired time, level, or position ○ *Remember to set the alarm.* **8.** *vt.* **DECIDE ON OR IMPOSE SOMETHING** to decide on a particular time or impose a rule as a condition for something ○ *We've set a date for the wedding.* **9.** *vt.* **BE EXAMPLE** to be an example of a type of behavior ○ *tried to set an example for her younger siblings* **10.** *vt.* **DETERMINE PRICE OF SOMETHING** to determine or state the price of something ○ *set the price at $20* **11.** *vt.* **CONSIDER AS HAVING VALUE** to consider something as having a particular value ○ *set a high value on his own work* **12.** *vt.* **DETERMINE COURSE** to determine a direction or course to travel ○ *set a course for home* **13.** *vt.* **ESTABLISH RECORD** to establish a record ○ *set a new 100-meter record* **14.** *vt.* EDUC **ASSIGN SOMETHING FOR STUDY** to assign something such as a book or subject to be studied **15.** *vt.* HAIR **ARRANGE HAIR** to arrange hair in a particular style by using styling products or clips **16.** *vt.* **PUT GEM IN SETTING** to put a gem or stone in a metal setting **17.** *vt.* MED **PUT BROKEN BONE IN POSITION** to put a broken bone back in its normal position so it can heal properly **18.** *vi.* MED **HEAL** to heal up and become solid after being broken (*refers to a bone*) **19.** *vt.* MUSIC **PROVIDE MUSIC FOR SOMETHING** to provide the music for something such as lyrics or a poem ○ *set his words to music* **20.** *vt.* **ADORN** to adorn something with decorations ○ *set a gown with sequins* **21.** *vt.* ARTS **PORTRAY IN PARTICULAR SETTING** to portray something as happening in a particular place or time period (*usually passive*) ○ *The play is set in the 19th century.* **22.** *vt.* THEATER **PLACE SCENERY ON** to place scenery on stage **23.** *vt.* PRINTING **ARRANGE TYPE** to arrange type for printing **24.** *vti.* SAILING **POSITION SAIL** to rig a sail to catch the wind, or to be rigged in this way **25.** *vi.* **GO BELOW HORIZON** to go below the horizon ○ *watched the sun set* **26.** *vi.* CLOTHES **FIT WELL OR POORLY** to fit in a particular way (*refers to clothes*) ○ *The skirt sets well.* **27.** *vi.* **START** to begin something, especially work ○ *set to work with a will* **28.** *vi.* SPORTS **GET READY TO START RACE** to get into a position ready to start a race ○ *Ready, get set, go!* **29.** *vi.* **BECOME PERMANENT** to become permanent (*refers to a dye or color*) **30.** *vt.* COOK **LET DOUGH RISE** to place dough aside to allow it to rise **31.** *vt.* **SHARPEN SOMETHING** to sharpen a blade **32.** *vt.* **DISPLACE TEETH ON SAW** to bend the teeth of a saw alternately to either side of the blade **33.** *vt.* **DRIVE NAIL HEAD BELOW SURFACE** to drive the head of a nail below the surface **34.** *vti.* AGRIC, PLANTS **PRODUCE FRUIT OR SEEDS** to produce fruit or seeds after being pollinated, or be produced in this way **35.** *vi.* **END** to come to an end (*literary*) **36.** *vt.* **SIT SOMEBODY** to cause somebody to sit somewhere (*regional*) ○ *Set yourself here.* **37.** *vt.* AGRIC, GARDENING **PLANT** to plant something **38.** *vti.* AGRIC **SIT OR MAKE SIT ON EGGS** to put a hen on eggs to keep them warm, or to sit on eggs **39.** *vti.* GAME **INDICATE GAME** to indicate the presence of game by turning toward it and holding that position **40.** *vt.* BRIDGE **BEAT IN BRIDGE** to prevent an opponent from meeting the contract in bridge **41.** *vi.* METALL **BECOME BENT** to become bent from strain ■ *n.* **1. CONDITION OF SOLIDITY** the condition of being solid **2. POSTURE** the posture or bearing of somebody or an animal **3.** CLOTHES **FIT OF CLOTHES** the way something hangs when worn **4.** THEATER, CINEMA **THEATRICAL SCENERY** scenery for a play or film or the place where this has been put up **5.** PRINTING **WIDTH OF PIECE OF TYPE** the width of a piece of type **6.** PRINTING **WIDTH OF LINE OF TYPE** the width of a column or a page of type **7.** SAILING **ARRANGEMENT OF SAILS** the way the sails and other rigging are arranged on a sailboat **8. DIRECTION** the direction of a wind, tide, or current **9. PREFERENCE** a preference for or increased ability in a particular activity **10.** PSYCHOL **BIAS INFLUENCING REACTION TO STIMULUS** the psychological state that causes an organism to react to a stimulus in a particular way **11.** AGRIC, GARDENING **SEEDLING READY FOR PLANTING** a plant such as a seedling that is ready to be planted **12.** METALL **DISTORTION DUE TO STRESS** a distortion or bending that occurs in metal as a result of stress **13.** HAIR **HAIRSTYLE** a way of styling the hair **14.** AGRIC **CLUTCH** the number of eggs that a hen lays at one time **15.** = **sett** ■ *adj.* **1. ESTABLISHED** previously established such as by tradition, agreement, or authority **2. INFLEXIBLE** being rigid and unwilling to change, especially in the way of doing things ○ *They're so set in their ways, they'll never change.* **3. READY** prepared for somebody or something, or to do something ○ *We're all set to go.* **4. STEREOTYPED** conforming to an established often conventional formula ○ *a set speech* **5. DETERMINED** determined to do something ○ *We're set on the idea and won't consider changing.* **6.** EDUC **ASSIGNED TO STUDY** assigned for students to study ○ *a set text* [Old English *settan*, literally "to cause to sit." From a prehistoric Germanic word (ancestor also of German *setzen*) "to sit."]

set about *vt.* to begin doing something

set against *vt.* **1. COMPARE** to consider one thing in relation to another, especially when the other thing is very important **2. MAKE PEOPLE FIGHT ONE ANOTHER** to make people or groups start to fight with or be hostile to people they used to be on friendly terms with

set apart *vt.* **1. RESERVE FOR SPECIFIC USE** to keep something for a specific use or purpose **2. MAKE SOMEBODY CONSPICUOUS** to make somebody conspicuous or different ○ *Her knowledge sets her apart.*

set aside *vt.* **1. RESERVE** to keep something, especially time or money, for a particular purpose **2. PUT TO ONE SIDE** to put something to one side **3. REJECT PREVIOUS DECISION** to discard, reject, or annul a previous decision or judgment

set back *vt.* **1. DELAY** to block or delay the progress of something or somebody **2. COST SOMEBODY** to cost somebody a lot of money (*informal*)

set down *vt.* **1. PUT DOWN** to put something down on a surface **2. WRITE DOWN** to write something down **3. SUSPEND** to take somebody, e.g., a jockey, out of competition as a punishment **4. JUDGE** to judge somebody or something as being something specified ○ *set the whole thing down as a failure* **5. ATTRIBUTE** to attribute an event or quality to something specified ○ *set his mistake down to inexperience* **6. SIT** to cause or allow somebody to sit down **7.** *U.K.* **SCOLD SOMEBODY** to snub or rebuke somebody **8. LAND AIRCRAFT** to land an aircraft

set forth *v.* **1.** *vt.* **STATE** to state or present an argument or a set of figures in speech or writing **2.** *vi.* **LEAVE** to leave on a journey (*literary*)

set in *v.* **1.** *vi.* **BEGIN** to begin and become established ○ *once the winter snows set in* **2.** *vt.* CLOTHES **ADD ON** to add a separately made part to a garment **3.** *vi.* **MOVE SHOREWARD** to move in a shoreward direction (*refers to a wind, tide, or current*)

set off *v.* **1.** *vi.* **START OUT ON TRIP** to start out on a journey **2.** *vt.* **MAKE SOMETHING WORK** to make something such as an alarm or fireworks operate or explode **3.** *vt.* **MAKE SOMEBODY START DOING SOMETHING** to make somebody start doing something such as laughing, crying, or talking about something ○ *When she started crying it set us all off too.* **4.** *vt.* **START SOMETHING** to make something start happening ○ *set off a chain of events that eventually led to war* **5.** *vt.* **MAKE SOMETHING LOOK ATTRACTIVE** to provide a contrast to something in a way that makes it look more attractive ○ *The new frame really sets off the painting.* **6.** *vt.* ACCT **COUNTERBALANCE CREDIT** to counterbalance a credit in the accounts of one person or organization against a debit in those of another

set on *vt.* **1. ATTACK** to attack somebody or encourage a person or animal to attack somebody or something **2. INCITE SOMEBODY** to encourage somebody to do something

set out *v.* **1.** *vi.* **BEGIN JOURNEY** to begin something, especially a journey **2.** *vi.* **INTENTIONALLY START DOING SOMETHING** to intentionally start doing something or planning to do something ○ *deliberately set out to ruin the performance* **3.** *vt.* **DISPLAY** to arrange, display, or decorate something ○ *merchants setting out their wares* **4.** *vt.* **LAY OUT** to lay out something in a planned way ○ *The gardens are beautifully set out.* **5.** *vt.* **PRESENT** to present or explain something, especially in a full way ○ *a book that clearly sets out the author's philosophy* **6.** *vt.* GARDENING **PLANT** to plant out small plants

set to *vi.* **1. BEGIN TASK** to start doing something, especially work **2. START FIGHTING** to start fighting

set up *v.* **1.** *vt.* **ERECT** to erect something or put something in an upright or usable position ○ *set up road blocks* **2.** *vti.* **PREPARE EQUIPMENT FOR EVENT** to prepare the equipment needed for an event ○ *The band is setting up on stage.* **3.** *vt.* **ORGANIZE** to arrange, establish, or bring about something ○ *I've set up a meeting for next week.* **4.** *vt.* **CAUSE TO BE BLAMED** to cause somebody to be caught and blamed for something (*informal*) ○ *claims he was set up* **5.** *vt.* **GIVE DRINKS** to buy or provide an alcoholic beverage for somebody (*informal*) **6.** *vt.* **PLAN** to make necessary arrangements for something, e.g., a meeting or conference **7.** *vti.* **CLAIM TO BE SOMETHING** to claim to be something, especially an expert or authority on something ○ *set herself up as an expert* **8.** *vti.* **START BUSINESS** to start a business or give somebody everything needed to start a business ○ *His family set him up in business.* **9.** *vt.* **PRESENT AS MODEL** to present something or somebody as an example to a group **10.** *vt.* **PROPOSE** to put an idea, theory, or proposal to a group for consideration **11.** *vt.* **PRODUCE SOMETHING** to produce or create something ○ *The spectators set up a howl of protest.* **12.** *vt.* **PUT IN POSITION OF POWER** to put a person or group in a position of power **13.** *vt.* **MAKE HEALTHY** to make somebody feel healthy or invigorated, especially after having been ill

set upon *vt.* to attack somebody violently

set[2] /set/ *n.* **1. COLLECTION CONSIDERED AS UNIT** a collection of people or things considered together and usually having something in common **2. SOCIAL GROUP** a group of people who form a social group ○ *They were the first in our set to have kids.* **3.** ELECTRON ENG **DEVICE RECEIVING SIGNALS** a device that receives radio or television signals **4.** RACKET GAMES **PART OF TENNIS MATCH** a part of a tennis match that is won when one player or couple wins a minimum of six games **5. PREFERENCE** a preference for or increased ability in a particular activity **6.** MUSIC **SONGS PLAYED IN ONE SESSION** a number of songs or acts that an entertainer or band performs on a single occasion **7.** SPORTS **NUMBER OF REPETITIONS OF EXERCISE** a number of repetitions of an exercise done at one time **8.** MATH, LOGIC **COLLECTION OF ELEMENTS** a collection of elements in mathematics or logic, e.g., numbers or terms **9.** DANCE **COUPLES REQUIRED FOR DANCE** a number of couples required for certain dances ○ *We need another couple to complete our set.* ■ *vi.* (**set, set·ting, sets**) DANCE **DANCE FACING PARTNER** to perform a series of moves while facing another dancer [14thC. Via Old French *sette* from Latin *secta* "sect" (see SECT).]

se·ta /séetə/ (*plural* **-tae** /-tee/) *n.* a slender, usually rigid bristle or hair [Late 18thC. From Latin, "bristle."] —**se·tal** *adj.*

se·ta·ceous /si táyshəss/ *adj.* **1.** BIOL **HAVING BRISTLES** having bristles or made up of bristles **2. RESEMBLING BRISTLES** having the appearance or feel of bristles (*formal*) [Mid-17thC. Formed from modern Latin *setaceus*, from Latin *seta* "bristle."]

set·back /sét bàk/ *n.* **1. SOMETHING THAT DELAYS PROGRESS** something that reverses or delays the progress of somebody or something **2.** ARCHIT **SHELF OR RECESS IN WALL** a place in the wall of a building where there is a shelf or recess **3. THERMOSTAT REDUCTION** an automatic adjustment made by a thermostat to reduce a temperature, e.g., in a domestic heating system at night **4.** ARCHIT **DISTANCE FROM BUILDING TO PROPERTY LINE** the distance required by law between the edge of a building and the property line

se ten·ant /sə ténnənt, sətə naáN/ *adj.* **JOINED BUT DIFFERENT** used to describe two stamps that are joined together but have different values or designs ■ *n.* **JOINED PAIR OF DIFFERENT STAMPS** a pair of stamps that are joined together but have different values or designs [Early 20thC. From French, literally "holding together."]

SETI /séttee/ *n.* a scientific attempt to detect or communicate with intelligent beings from beyond Earth, especially using radio signals. Full form **Search for Extraterrestrial Intelligence**

se·tif·er·ous /sə tíffərəss/, **se·tig·er·ous** /sə tíjjərəss/ *adj.* used to describe a living organism that has bristles or projections that resemble bristles [Early 19thC. *setiferous* coined from SETA + -FEROUS; *setigerous* from Latin *setiger* "bristly," from *seta* "bristle."]

se·ti·form /séeti fàwrm/ *adj.* having the shape of a bristle [Early 19thC. Coined from SETA + -FORM.]

se·tig·er·ous *adj.* = **setiferous**

set-in *adj.* **1.** BUILDING **BUILT-IN** built or inserted into a space in something else **2.** CLOTHES **STITCHED IN** used to describe a part of a garment that is made separately and stitched in

set·off /sét òf/ *n.* **1. COUNTERBALANCE** something that compensates for something else **2. SOMETHING IMPROVING APPEARANCE** something that contrasts with something else in a way that improves its appearance **3.** PRINTING = **offset** *n.* 4 **4.** ACCT **COUNTERBALANCING CLAIM** a claim brought by a debtor against a creditor that counterbalances the debt owed

Se·ton /séet'n/, **Ernest Thompson** (1860–1946) British-born U.S. writer and illustrator. He was one of the founders of the Boy Scouts of America (1910). He is known for his stories about animals for young people such as *Wild Animals I Have Known* (1898). Real name **Ernest Seton-Thompson**

se·tose /sée tōss/ *adj.* covered with bristles [Mid-17thC. From Latin *setosus*, formed from *seta* "bristle."]

set piece *n.* **1. PLANNED ACTION** a carefully planned and rehearsed performance or action, especially a military or diplomatic operation **2.** ARTS **FORMAL WORK OF ART** a work of art with a formal theme, undertaken to show the artist's skill **3.** THEATER **PIECE OF SCENERY** a piece of stage scenery that can stand unsupported

set point *n.* **1.** TENNIS **POINT TO WIN SET** a time in a tennis or paddle tennis match when a player can win a set by winning the next point, or the point itself **2.** PHYSIOL **LEVEL OF VARIABLE** the level of some variable such as weight that the body attempts to maintain **3.** PHYSIOL **NATURAL BODYWEIGHT** the natural weight that somebody's body will assume if provided with a balanced diet

set·screw /sét skrōō/ *n.* **1. SCREW PREVENTING RELATIVE MOTION** a screw that fixes one part of a mechanism to another and prevents it moving relative to the part to which it is fixed **2. SCREW REGULATING TENSION** a screw that regulates the tension in a spring or the opening of a valve

set square *n. U.K.* = **triangle**

sett /set/, **set** *n.* **1. PAVING STONE** a rectangular stone paving block **2.** ZOOL **BADGER'S BURROW** the burrow of a badger [Variant of SET[1]]

set·tee /se tée/ *n.* **1. COMFORTABLE SEAT FOR TWO PEOPLE** a comfortable seat for two or more people, with a cushioned back and arms **2. BENCH WITH BACK** a long wooden bench with a back [Early 18thC. Origin uncertain: perhaps an alteration of SETTLE.]

set·ter /séttər/ *n.* **1. SOMEBODY OR SOMETHING THAT SETS** somebody or something that sets something **2.** ZOOL **BIRD DOG** a long-haired bird dog belonging to various breeds that is trained to crouch in a set position when it finds game

set the·o·ry *n.* **1.** MATH **MATHEMATICS OF SETS** the branch of mathematics that deals with the properties and relationships of sets **2.** LOGIC **SYSTEM OF SET AXIOMS** the system of axioms for sets

set·ting /sétting/ *n.* **1. SURROUNDINGS** the surroundings or environment in which something exists **2. LEVEL ON SCALE** a chosen point or level in the operation of a machine **3. SURROUNDINGS OF JEWEL** the metal fixture into which a jewel is fixed **4. UTENSILS** the utensils, napkin, table mat, and any other items placed on a table to be used by one person during a meal **5.** ARTS **PERIOD OR PLACE OF STORY** the period in time or the place in which the events of a story take place **6.** ARTS **SET FOR PERFORMANCE** the set, including props and scenery, where actors perform for a film or play **7.** MUSIC **MUSIC FOR POEM** the music composed for a particular text, e.g., a poem or hymn **8.** BIRDS, AGRIC **CLUTCH OF EGGS** a batch of eggs in a bird's nest, especially a hen's

set·ting cir·cle *n.* a scale on the mounting of an equatorial telescope, used to show right ascension or declination

set·tle /sett'l/ *v.* (**-tled, -tling, -tles**) **1.** *vt.* **DECIDE ON SOMETHING** to decide on something so that other arrangements can be made **2.** *vti.* **SOLVE** to solve a problem or end a dispute **3.** *vti.* **MAKE OR BECOME RESIDENT** to become or cause somebody to become a resident of a place **4.** *vt.* **COLONIZE** to populate an area with permanent residents **5.** *vti.* **STOP FLOATING** to stop floating and sink to the bottom or the ground, or to cause something to do this ○ *waited for the dust to settle before opening their eyes* **6.** *vti.* **PAY** to pay a bill, debt, or claim **7.** *vi.* **MOVE DOWNWARD** to move downward and spread over something ○ *A blanket of mist settled over the field.* **8.** *vi.* **SINK INTO GROUND** to sink slowly to a lower level **9.** *vi.* **STOP MOVING** to stop moving and come to rest somewhere **10.** *vti.* **MAKE OR BECOME CLEAR** to cause a cloudy liquid to become clear after a sediment has sunk to the bottom, or to become clear in this way **11.** *vti.* LAW **END LEGAL DISPUTE** to end a legal dispute by mutual agreement out of court **12.** *vti.* **GET REVENGE** to get revenge on somebody for an injury or offense **13.** *vti.* **MAKE OR BECOME CALM** to become or cause somebody or something to become calm, quiet, or stable **14.** *vt.* **PUT IN ORDER** to put all the details of a piece of business in order or into a desired arrangement **15.** *vti.* **MAKE SOMEBODY COMFORTABLE** to make somebody feel comfortable in a particular position **16.** *vt.* **PUT IN PLACE** to put something in a place firmly or permanently **17.** *vti.* **ESTABLISH OR BECOME ESTABLISHED** to establish somebody or become established in a place, occupation, or way of life **18.** *vt.* **COMPACT** to press something such as loose soil down and make it firm **19.** *vt.* LAW **ASSIGN PROPERTY** to give something, especially property or money, to somebody legally and formally ○ *settled her with a substantial inheritance* **20.** *vt.* **IMPREGNATE OR BE IMPREGNATED** to make an animal pregnant, or become pregnant **21.** *vi.* **CONCEIVE** of an animal, to become pregnant ■ *n.* FURNITURE **LONG WOODEN SEAT WITH HIGH BACK** a long wooden seat with a high back, and often with storage space inside the box-shaped seat [Old English *setlan*, formed from *setl* "chair, bench." Ultimately from an Indo-European base meaning "to sit" that is also the ancestor of English *saddle* and *Upanishad*.] —**set·tle·a·ble** *adj.*

settle down *v.* **1.** *vti.* **MAKE OR BECOME CALM** to become or to cause somebody or something to become calm, quiet, or orderly **2.** *vi.* **LIVE ORDERLY LIFE** to begin a stable, orderly, and often conventional way of life **3.** *vi.* **DO SOMETHING DILIGENTLY** to begin doing something in a diligent and orderly way ○ *settled down to her morning's work*

settle for *vt.* to accept or agree to something that is not ideal or exactly what was wanted

settle in *v.* **1.** *vti.* **ADAPT** to adapt or cause somebody to adapt to a new environment ○ *settling in at a new school* **2.** *vi.* **REMAIN SOMEWHERE FOR LONG TIME** to get comfortable in a place because the intention is to stay there for a long time ○ *decided to settle in for the night*

set·tle·ment /sétt'lmənt/ *n.* **1. SETTLING** an act of settling or the state of being settled **2. COLONY** a place that has recently been populated with permanent residents **3.** LAW **AGREEMENT OUT-OF-COURT** an agreement reached without completing legal proceedings **4. AGREEMENT** an agreement reached after discussion or negotiation **5. PAYMENT** the payment of a bill, debt, or claim **6. POPULATING** the act of populating a place with permanent residents **7. SMALL COMMUNITY** a small community **8. set·tle·ment, set·tle·ment house** SOC WELFARE **WELFARE SERVICES BUILDING** a public building in which social workers provide welfare services in a deprived area **9.** *U.K.* BUILDING **SUBSIDENCE** subsidence in a building **10.** LAW **SETTLING OF PROPERTY ON SOMEBODY** a conveyance of property to a person or trustees for somebody **11.** LAW **CONVEYANCE DOCUMENT** a document recording a conveyance of property

set·tler /séttlər/ *n.* somebody who comes to live in a new place, especially a place that is unpopulated or populated by people of a different race or civilization

set·tlings /séttlingz/ *npl.* solid material that has sunk to the bottom of a liquid

set·tlor /séttlər/ *n.* somebody who creates a trust or settlement

set-to (*plural* **set-tos**) *n.* a brief and hot-tempered argument or fight (*informal*)

Se·tú·bal /se tōōb'l/ city and port in western Portugal, situated 20 mi./32 km southeast of Lisbon. Population: 83,550 (1991).

set·up /sét ùp/ *n.* **1. ORGANIZATION OF SOMETHING** the way that something is organized or arranged **2. SET OF PREPARED OBJECTS FOR TASK** an assembly of prepared tools or apparatus required for performing a task **3. ERECT CARRIAGE OF BODY** the way that somebody walks and stands, especially when it is particularly soldierly **4. TABLE SETTING** a table setting for a single person **5.** BEVERAGES **SET OF REQUIREMENTS FOR COCKTAIL** a glass, mixer, ice, or soda water provided to customers who provide their own liquor **6. SOMETHING DELIBERATELY MADE EASY** something such as a task or contest that is deliberately made easy to accomplish or win **7. STRATEGY** a planned course of action **8. DISHONEST PLAN OR TRICK** something that is planned to bring about a desired result dishonestly (*informal*) **9.** CINEMA **POSITION OF CAMERA FOR SCENE** the position of a camera at the beginning of a scene

set width *n.* = **set**[1] *n.* **5, set**[1] *n.* **6**

Georges Seurat: Portrait drawing (1890?) by Maximilien Luce

Seu·rat /sə ráa/, **Georges** (1859–91) French painter. He developed the theory and practice of pointillism, or divisionism, seen in a work such as *Sunday Afternoon at the Grande Jatte (1886)*.

Seuss /sooss/, **Dr.** (1904–91) U.S. writer and illustrator. His children's books, replete with fanciful word play and illustrated with his own drawings, include *Horton Hatches the Egg* (1940) and *The Cat in the Hat* (1957). Pseudonym of **Theodor Seuss Geisel**

Se·van, Lake /se vaán-/ the largest lake in Armenia, in the north of the country, in the Caucasus Mountains. It is drained by the Razdau River. Area: 540 sq. mi./1,397 sq. km.

Se·vas·to·pol = **Sebastopol**

sev·en /sévv'n/ *n.* **1. NUMBER 7** the number 7 **2. SOMETHING WITH VALUE OF 7** something in a numbered series, e.g., a playing card, with a value of 7 ○ *the seven of clubs* ○ *to play the seven* **3. GROUP OF 7** a group of seven objects or people [Old English *seofon*. Ultimately from an Indo-European word meaning "seven," which is also the ancestor of English *septi-* and *hepta-*.] —**sev·en** *adj., pron.*

sev·en dead·ly sins *npl.* = **deadly sins**

sev·en·fold /sévv'n fōld/ *adj.* **1. BEING SEVEN TIMES AS MUCH** relating to something that is seven times as much as something else **2. CONSISTING OF SEVEN PARTS** relating to something that is made up of seven parts ■ *adv.* **BY SEVEN TIMES** by seven times as much or as many [Old English]

sev·en seas *npl.* all the oceans of the world. They are the North and South Atlantic, North and South Pacific, Arctic, Antarctic, and Indian Oceans.

Seven Sisters *n.* ASTRON = **Pleiades**

sev·en·teen /sèvv'n téen/ *n.* **1. NUMBER 17** the number 17 **2. GROUP OF 17** a group of seventeen objects or people [Old English *seofontīene*, literally "ten more than seven," from *-tīene* "ten more than"]

sev·en·teenth /sèvv'n téenth/ *n.* one of 17 equal parts of something [Old English] —**sev·en·teenth** *adj., adv.*

sev·en·teen-year lo·cust *n.* a cicada of eastern North America that spends most of its 17 years of life as an underground nymph, living as a winged adult for only a few weeks. In the southern United States the nymph lasts 13 years. Latin name: *Magicicada septendecim.*

sev·enth /sévv'nth/ *n.* **1. ONE OF 7 PARTS OF SOMETHING** one of seven equal parts of something **2.** = **seventh chord** **3.** MUSIC **INTERVAL OF SEVENTH NOTES** in a standard musical scale, the interval between one note and another that lies six notes above or below it. In the scale of C major, C and B form a seventh. **4.** MUSIC **NOTE A SEVENTH AWAY FROM ANOTHER** in a standard musical scale, a note that is a seventh away from another note [Old English] —**sev·enth** *adj., adv.*

sev·enth chord *n.* a chord with a seventh note above the base note

Sev·enth-Day Ad·vent·ist *n.* a member of a Protestant denomination that believes in the imminent Second Coming of Jesus Christ and observes Saturday as the Sabbath

sev·enth heav·en *n.* **1. PERFECT HAPPINESS** a state of extreme happiness **2.** RELIG **HIGHEST HEAVEN** the highest of the seven heavens in Muslim and Talmudic belief

sev·en·ti·eth /sévv'ntee əth/ *n.* one of seventy equal parts of something —**sev·en·ti·eth** *adj., adv.*

sev·en·ty /sévv'ntee/ *n.* (*plural* **-ties**) **1. NUMBER 70** the number 70 **2. GROUP OF 70** a group of seventy objects or people ■ **sev·en·ties** *npl.* **1. NUMBERS 70 TO 79** the numbers 70 to 79, particularly as a range of temperature ○ *in the low seventies* **2. YEARS 1970 TO 1979** the years 1970 to 1979 **3. PERIOD FROM AGE 70 TO 79** the period of somebody's life from the age of 70 to 79 [Old English *hundseofontig*, from *hund* (of uncertain origin and lost in Middle English) + *seofon* "seven" (see SEVEN) + *-tig* "ten"] —**sev·en·ty** *adj., pron.*

sev·en·ty-eight, 78 *n.* a phonograph record designed to be played at 78 revolutions per minute, a former standard speed

sev·en-up *n.* a card game in which the first person to reach seven points wins the game

Sev·en Years' War *n.* a war fought from 1756 to 1763 by Prussia, assisted by British subsidies and Hanoverian troops, against France and Austria

sev·er /sévvər/ (**-ered, -er·ing, -ers**) *vti.* **1. CUT THROUGH OR OFF** to cut through something or cut off, or be cut through or off **2. BREAK OFF TIE** to break off a tie, or to become broken off ○ *severed her relationship with him* **3. SEPARATE** to separate or put things or people apart, or to become separated or put apart [14thC. Via Anglo-Norman *severer* from Old French *sevrer* from, ultimately, Latin *separare* "to separate" (see SEPARATE).]

sev·er·a·ble /sévvərəb'l/ *adj.* **1. CAPABLE OF BEING SEVERED** able to be severed **2. LEGALLY SEPARABLE** capable of being legally separated without invalidating what remains, e.g., clauses in an agreement [Mid-16thC] —**sev·er·a·bil·i·ty** /sèvvərə bíllətee/ *n.*

sev·er·al /sévvərəl/ CORE MEANING: a grammatical word indicating a small number ○ (pron) *Several of the apples were bruised.*
adj. **1.** VARIOUS various or separate ○ *They all went their several ways.* **2.** LAW SEPARATE relating to separate individuals ○ *joint and several liability* [15thC. Via Anglo-Norman from, ultimately, Latin *separ* "separate," from *separare* "to separate" (see SEPARATE).]

sev·er·al·fold /sévvərəl fòld/ *adj.* **1.** BEING SEVERAL TIMES AS MUCH relating to something that is several times as much as something else **2.** CONSISTING OF SEVERAL PARTS relating to something that is made up of several parts ■ *adv.* BY SEVERAL TIMES by several times as much or as many

sev·er·al·ly /sévvərəlee/ *adv.* (*formal or literary*) **1.** SEPARATELY in a separate or individual way **2.** RESPECTIVELY in turn or respectively

sev·er·al·ty /sévvərəltee/ *n.* the state of being several or separate

sev·er·ance /sévvərənss/ *n.* **1.** ACT OF SEVERING an act of severing or the state of being severed **2.** = **severance pay** **3.** LAW SPLITTING INTO PARTS the splitting into separate parts of something held jointly, e.g., an estate

sev·er·ance pay, **sev·er·ance** *n.* money paid as compensation, usually on the basis of length of service, to an employee who is fired

sev·er·ance tax *n.* a tax imposed by a state on natural resources, e.g., oil or gas, extracted for use in another state

se·vere /sə veér/ *adj.* **1.** HARSH very harsh or strict **2.** DANGEROUS extremely bad or dangerous ○ *severe injuries* **3.** EXTREMELY UNPLEASANT causing great discomfort by being extreme ○ *a severe frost* **4.** DIFFICULT TO ENDURE difficult to do or endure ○ *severe hardship* **5.** EXACTING having standards or other criteria that are difficult to meet ○ *a severe test* **6.** STERN looking stern or serious **7.** PLAIN plain or austere in style, with little or no decoration ○ *severe clothing* [Mid-16thC. Via French *sévère* or directly from Latin *severus* "serious," of uncertain origin.] —**se·vere·ly** *adv.* —**se·vere·ness** *n.*

se·ver·i·ty /sə vérritee/ *n.* **1.** STATE OR EXTENT OF BADNESS the state of being very bad, or the extent to which something is bad **2.** STRICTNESS OR STERNNESS the state of being very strict or stern **3.** PLAINNESS the plainness or austerity of something such as a building or style of dress **4.** (*plural* **-ties**) HARSH ACT OR CRITICISM an instance of harsh treatment or censure

Sev·ern /sévvurn/ river that originates in lakes in western Ontario, in Canada, and flows northeast into Hudson Bay. Length: 610 mi./982 km.

Se·ve·so /se váyzō/ town situated near Milan, in northern Italy. It was the scene of an industrial accident in 1976, when the poisonous gas dioxin escaped into the atmosphere.

se·vi·che *n.* = **ceviche**

Se·ville /sè víl/ city and river port in the autonomous region of Andalusia, southwestern Spain. Population: 719,590 (1995).

Se·ville or·ange *n.* TREES = **bitter orange** [Late 16thC. Named for SEVILLE, known for the quality of its oranges.]

Sè·vres /sévvrə/ *n.* a highly decorated French porcelain

sew /sō/ (**sewed, sewn** /sōn/ *or* **sewed, sew·ing, sews**) *vti.* to join things or repair or make something by using a needle to pass thread repeatedly through material [Old English *siowan.* Ultimately from an Indo-European word meaning "to sew" that is also the ancestor of English *hymen* and *suture.*] —**sew·a·ble** *adj.*

sew up *vt.* to finish a business or plan successfully

sew·age /soó ij/ *n.* human and domestic waste matter from buildings, especially houses, that is carried away through sewers [Mid-19thC. Formed from SEWER.]

Sew·all /soó əl/, **Samuel** (1652–1730) English-born U.S. jurist. He was a primary judge in the witchcraft trial in Salem, Massachusetts (1692). In 1697 he confessed his error, and in 1700 he wrote one of the earliest antislavery tracts. His diary remains a revealing picture of his times.

Se·ward /soó ərd/, **William H.** (1801–72) U.S. statesman. As secretary of state (1861–69) under presidents Lincoln and Johnson, he negotiated foreign policy during the Civil War, and in 1867 purchased Alaska from Russia for $7.2 million, an act widely derided at the time as "Seward's folly." Full name **William Henry Seward**

Sew·ard Pen·in·su·la peninsula in western Alaska that projects into the Bering Sea. Length: 200 mi./320 km.

Sew·ell /soó əl/, **Anna** (1820–78) British writer. Her only book, *Black Beauty* (1877), was written to advocate humane treatment of animals and became a children's classic.

se·wel·lel /sə wélləl/ *n.* = **mountain beaver** [Early 19thC. From Chinook *šwalál* "robe made of sewellel skin."]

sew·er[1] /soó ər/ (**-ered, -er·ing, -ers**) *n.* a pipe or drain, usually underground, that carries away waste or rainwater [15thC. Via Anglo-Norman *sever* from, ultimately, assumed Vulgar Latin *exaquare* "to remove water, drain," from Latin *ex-* "out" + *aqua* "water" (source of English *aquarium*).]

sew·er[2] /soó ər/ *n.* a medieval servant who served meals [14thC. From Anglo-Norman *asseour,* from French *asseoir* "to place a seat for," literally "to sit to," ultimately from Latin *sedere* "to sit."]

sew·er[3] /sō ər/ *n.* somebody or something that sews

sew·er·age /soó ərij/ *n.* **1.** SEWER SYSTEM a system of sewers **2.** REMOVAL OF WASTE the removal of waste by means of sewers **3.** = **sewage**

sew·ing /sō ing/ *n.* **1.** USE OF NEEDLE AND THREAD the act or work of using a needle and thread to join or repair material **2.** MATERIAL BEING SEWN a piece of material that somebody is sewing

sew·ing cir·cle *n.* a group of people who meet regularly to sew items, often for charity

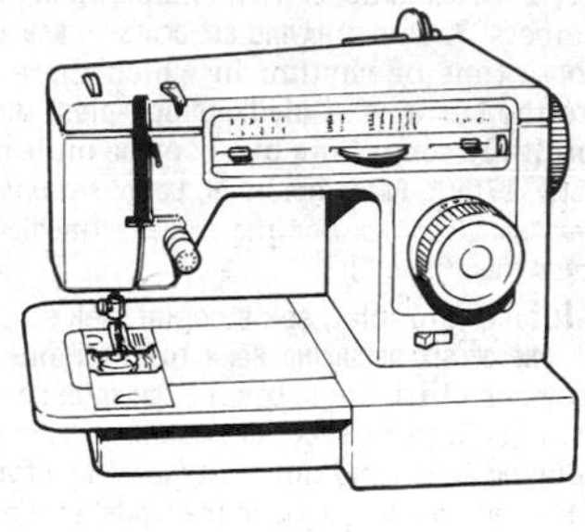

Sewing machine

sew·ing ma·chine *n.* a machine, now usually electric, for sewing material

sewn past participle of **sew**

sex /seks/ *n.* **1.** MALE OR FEMALE GENDER either of the two reproductive categories, male or female, of animals and plants **2.** INTERCOURSE sexual intercourse **3.** SEXUAL BEHAVIOR sexual activity or behavior leading to it **4.** GENITALS the genitals (*literary*) **5.** BIOL REPRODUCTIVE CHARACTERISTICS the set of characteristics that determine whether the reproductive role of an animal or plant is male or female ■ *adj.* OF SEX relating to sexual matters or the sexes ■ *vt.* (**sexed, sex·ing, sex·es**) DETERMINE SEX OF to determine the sex of an animal or plant [14thC. Via French *sexe* or directly from Latin *sexus.* The meaning of "sexual intercourse" (first recorded in the works of D. H. Lawrence) is a 20th-century development.]

WORD KEY: USAGE

See Usage note at ***gender.***

sex up *v.* **1.** *vti.* SEXUALLY AROUSE to arouse somebody sexually or become aroused **2.** *vt.* MAKE SOMEBODY OR SOMETHING APPEALING to made somebody or something more appealing or stimulating, especially sexually

sex- *prefix.* six ○ *sexangular* [From Latin *sex* "six." Ultimately from the Indo-European word for "six," which is also the ancestor of English *six* and *hexa-*.]

sex·a·ge·nar·i·an /sèksəjə náiree ən/, **sex·ag·e·nar·y** /sek sájjə nèrree/ *n.* somebody aged between 60 and 69 —**sex·a·ge·nar·i·an** *adj.*

Sex·a·ges·i·ma /sèksə jéssimə/ *n.* CALENDAR in the Christian calendar, the second Sunday before Lent, eight weeks before Easter [14thC. From ecclesiastical Latin, a form of Latin *sexagesimus* "sixtieth" (see SEXAGESIMAL); probably because the day occurs two Sundays before *Quadragesima,* literally "fortieth (day)."]

sex·a·ges·i·mal /sèksə jéssim'l/ *adj.* BASED ON 60 relating to or based on the number 60 ■ *n.* FRACTION WITH DENOMINATOR POWER OF 60 a fraction in which the denominator is a power of 60 [Late 17thC. Formed from Latin *sexagesimus* "sixtieth," from *sexaginta* "sixty" (see SEXAGENARY).]

sex ap·peal *n.* **1.** SEXUAL ATTRACTIVENESS the quality of being sexually attractive **2.** APPEAL attractiveness in general ○ *Their new product has real sex appeal.*

sex·a·va·lent /sèksə váylənt/ *adj.* = **hexavalent**

sex cell *n.* = **gamete**

sex·cen·te·nar·y /sèk sen ténnəree, sek sént'n èrree/ *adj.* **1.** OF 600 relating to the number 600 or a period of 600 years **2.** OF 600TH ANNIVERSARY relating to a 600th anniversary ■ *n.* (*plural* **-ies**) 600TH ANNIVERSARY a 600th anniversary or the celebration of one

sex change *n.* an operation with accompanying hormonal treatment that changes somebody's physical characteristics from those of one sex to the other

sex chro·ma·tin *n.* = **Barr body**

sex chro·mo·some *n.* a chromosome that determines the sex of an organism such as the X and Y chromosomes in humans and other mammals. In each cell nucleus, a male mammal has one X and one Y chromosome, and a female has two X chromosomes.

sex·duc·tion /seks dúksh'n/ *n.* the transfer of a fragment of chromosome from one bacterial cell to another by its incorporation into a special DNA particle (**plasmid**) that initiates sexual conjugation between the cells [Mid-20thC. Blend of SEX and TRANSDUCTION.]

sexed /sekst/ *adj.* **1.** INTERESTED IN SEX having a specified degree of interest in sex ○ *highly sexed* **2.** BIOL HAVING SEXUAL CHARACTERISTICS possessing sexual characteristics [Late 16thC]

sex·en·ni·al /sek sénnee əl/ *adj.* OCCURRING EVERY SIX YEARS happening every six years or over a period of six years ■ *n.* SOMETHING OCCURRING EVERY SIX YEARS something that happens every six years or over a period of six years [Mid-17thC. Formed from Latin *sexennium* "a period of six years," from *annus* "year" (see ANNUAL).] —**sex·en·ni·al·ly** *adv.*

sex fac·tor *n.* a genetic element found in certain bacteria that enables the cell to put out a fine tube to another bacterial cell and transfer some of its genetic material

sex gland *n.* = **gonad**

sex hor·mone *n.* a hormone that affects the development of the reproductive organs and sexual characteristics

sex·ism /sék sìzzəm/ *n.* **1.** SEX DISCRIMINATION discrimination against women or men because of their sex **2.** SEXUAL STEREOTYPING the tendency to treat people as cultural stereotypes of their sex

sex·ist /séksist/ *adj.* **1.** BELIEVING ONE SEX IS INFERIOR believing that one sex is inferior to the other in a variety of attributes **2.** RESULTING FROM SEXIST BELIEF resulting from or relating to the belief that one sex is inferior to the other in a variety of attributes ■ *n.* SOMEBODY WHO IS SEXIST somebody who believes that one sex is weaker to the other in a variety of attributes

sex·i·va·lent /sèksi váylənt/ *adj.* = **hexavalent**

sex kit·ten *n.* an offensive term referring to a young woman perceived as sexually appealing (*offensive*)

sex·less /séksləss/ *adj.* **1.** WITHOUT SEXUAL ACTIVITY living without sexual intercourse or interest in sex **2.** NOT SEXY sexually unattractive **3.** WITHOUT SEXUAL CHARACTERISTICS used to describe an animal or plant that has no, or no obvious, sexual characteristics —**sex·less·ly** *adv.* —**sex·less·ness** *n.*

sex-lim·i·ted *adj.* used to describe genetically inherited traits or conditions that appear in one sex only, although the genes themselves may be found in either sex

sex-linked *adj.* relating to a gene located on a sex chromosome, typically the X chromosome, or inheritance determined by such a gene —**sex-link·age** *n.*

sex ob·ject *n.* somebody treated or seen as worthy of notice because of characteristics perceived as sexually appealing

sex of·fend·er *n.* somebody who commits a crime involving a sexual act

sex·ol·o·gy /sek sólləjee/ *n.* the study of human sexual behavior —**sex·o·log·i·cal** /sèksə lójjik'l/ *adj.* —**sex·ol·o·gist** /-sólləjist/ *n.*

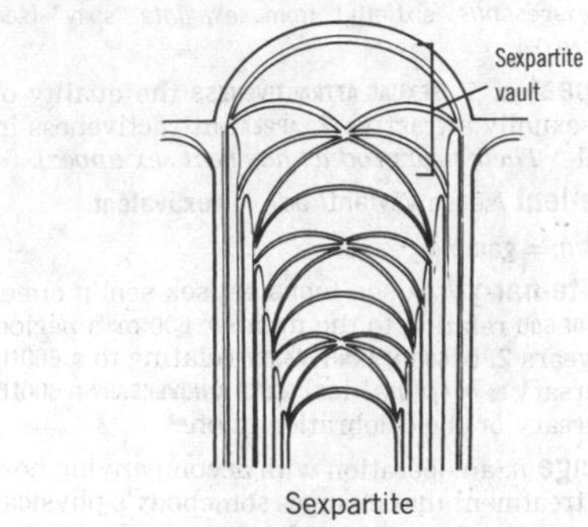

Sexpartite

sex·par·tite /seks paar tīt/ *adj.* **1.** ARCHIT **CONSISTING OF SIX PARTS** divided into or made up of six parts ○ *a sexpartite vault* **2. HAVING SIX PARTICIPANTS** involving six participants [Mid-18thC. Formed from SEX- + PARTITE.]

sex·ploi·ta·tion /sèks ploy táysh'n/ *n.* the deliberate use of sexual material to make a product, especially a movie, commercially successful [Mid-20thC. Blend of SEX and EXPLOITATION.]

sex·pot /séks pòt/ *n.* an offensive term referring to a woman who appears to radiate sexuality (*offensive*)

sex role *n.* a set of behaviors characteristic of or expected of members of one sex or the other

sex shop *n.* a shop that sells items intended to aid sexual arousal or add to the pleasure of sexual intercourse

sex-starved *adj.* lacking sexual activity even though it is desired

sex sym·bol *n.* somebody such as a movie star whose fame is linked to a widely perceived sex appeal

sext /sekst/ *n.* in Christianity, especially Roman Catholicism, the fourth of the seven canonical hours of the divine office, or the prayers said then. This was originally the sixth hour of the day, midday. [14thC. Formed from Latin *sexta (hora)* "sixth (hour)," the feminine of *sextus*.]

sex·tain /sék stàyn/ *n.* = **sestina** [Mid-17thC. Origin uncertain: probably formed from SEX- on the model of *quatrain* and similar forms.]

Sex·tans /sék stànz/ *n.* a faint constellation of the equatorial region lying between Leo and Hydra

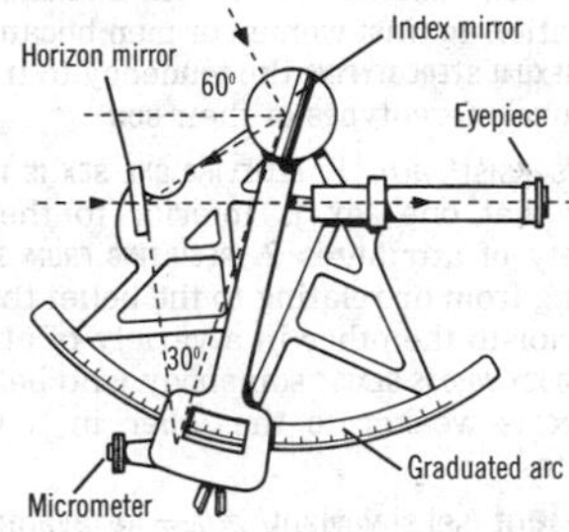

Sextant

sex·tant /sékstənt/ *n.* a navigational instrument incorporating a telescope and an angular scale that is used to work out latitude and longitude. A celestial body is viewed through the telescope and its angular distance above the horizon is read off the scale. The data is then used to calculate position. [Late 16thC. From the Latin stem *sextant-* "sixth part (of a circle)" (referring to the arc on which the scale is marked), from *sextus*.]

sex·tet /sek stét/, **sex·tette** *n.* **1. SIX PLAYERS OR SINGERS** a group of six musicians or singers, or a piece of music composed for them **2. SIX PEOPLE OR THINGS** any group of six people or things [Mid-19thC. Alteration of SESTET under the influence of Latin *sex* "six" (see SEX-).]

sex ther·a·py *n.* the treatment of sexual problems through counseling and psychotherapy —**sex ther·a·pist** *n.*

sex·tile /sékst'l, -stīl/ *n.* **1.** STATS **STATISTICAL DIVISION** any of the six equal groups into which a statistical sample can be divided **2.** STATS **STATISTICAL VALUE** any of the five statistical values that divide a frequency distribution into six parts, with each containing a sixth of the sample population **3.** ASTRON **ANGLE BETWEEN PLANETS** a position of two celestial bodies in which they are 60 degrees apart as viewed from the Earth [Mid-16thC. From Latin *sextilis*, from *sextus* "sixth."] —**sex·tile** *adj.*

sex·til·lion /sek stíllyən/ (*plural* **-lions** *or* **-lion**) *n.* **1. 1 FOLLOWED BY 21 ZEROS** the number equal to 10^{21}, written as 1 followed by 21 zeros **2.** *U.K.* **1 FOLLOWED BY 36 ZEROS** the number equal to 10^{36}, written as 1 followed by 36 zeros (*dated*) [Late 17thC. From French, formed from Latin *sex* "six" (see SEX-) on the model of *million* and similar numerals.] —**sex·til·lion** *adj., pron.* —**sex·til·lionth** *n., adj.*

sex·to·dec·i·mo /sèkstō déssi mō/ (*plural* **-mos**) *n.* a size of book page obtained by folding a sheet of paper into 16 leaves, producing 32 pages [Mid-17thC. From Latin *sexto decimo*, a form of *sextus decimus* "sixteenth," literally "sixth tenth" (*decimus*: source of English *decimal*).]

sex·ton /sékstən/ *n.* the caretaker of a church and its graveyard whose duties often include ringing the bell and digging graves [14thC. Via Anglo-Norman *segerstein* from, ultimately, medieval Latin *sacristanus* "sacristan" (see SACRISTAN).]

Sex·ton /sékstən/, **Anne** (1928–74) U.S. poet. Much of her intense poetry dealt with the psychiatric disorder that led to her suicide. Born **Anne Harvey**

sex·tu·ple /sek stóop'l, sek stúpp'l, sék stùpp'l/ *n.* MATH **NUMBER SIX TIMES ANOTHER** a number or quantity that is six times another number or quantity ■ *adj.* **1.** MATH **BEING SIX TIMES ANOTHER** relating to or being a number or quantity that is six times another number or quantity **2. CONSISTING OF SIX PARTS** made up of six parts or members **3.** MUSIC **HAVING SIX BEATS TO BAR** used to describe a time or rhythm in which there are six beats to the bar ■ *vti.* **(-pled, -pling, -ples) MULTIPLY BY SIX** to multiply something by six or be multiplied by six [Early 17thC. From medieval Latin *sextuplus*, from Latin *sex* "six" (see SEX-) on the model of medieval Latin *quintuplus* "quintuple."]

sex·tup·let /sek stúpplət, sek stóoplət, sék stùpplət/ *n.* **1.** BIOL **ONE OF SIX OFFSPRING BORN TOGETHER** one of six offspring born in a single birth **2. GROUP OF SIX** a group of six things **3.** MUSIC **GROUP OF SIX NOTES** a group of six notes played in a time normally given to four [Mid-19thC. Formed from SEXTUPLE on the model of *triplet*.]

sex·tu·pli·cate /sek stóoplikət, -stúpplikət/ *n.* **SET OF SIX COPIES** a set of six things, especially identical copies ■ *adj.* MATH **BEING SIX TIMES ANOTHER** relating to or being a number or quantity that is six times another number or quantity ■ *v.* **(-cat·ed, -cat·ing, -cates) 1.** *vti.* MATH **MULTIPLY BY SIX** to multiply something by six or be multiplied by six **2.** *vt.* **MAKE SIX COPIES** to make six copies of something [Mid-17thC. Formed from medieval Latin *sextuplicat-*, the past participle stem of *sextuplicare* "to increase sixfold," from, ultimately, Latin *sex* "six" (see SEX-).]

sex-typed *adj.* intended for or conventionally perceived as appropriate for one sex and not the other —**sex-typ·ing** *n.*

sex·u·al /sékshoo əl, séksh'l/ *adj.* **1. OF SEX** relating to sex, sexuality, or the sexual organs **2. RELATING TO EITHER SEX** relating to the two sexes or to either of them **3.** BIOL **INVOLVING REPRODUCTIVE UNION** relating to the union of male and female gametes in reproduction [Mid-17thC. From late Latin *sexualis*, from Latin *sexus* "sex."] —**sex·u·al·ly** *adv.*

sex·u·al as·sault *n.* an incident that involves sexual contact that is forced on somebody or to which somebody cannot consent

sex·u·al di·mor·phism *n.* the existence of differences in the appearance of the male and female of a species

sex·u·al ha·rass·ment *n.* unwanted sex-related behavior toward somebody, e.g., touching somebody or making suggestive remarks, especially by somebody with authority to a subordinate

sex·u·al in·ter·course *n.* an act carried out for reproduction or pleasure involving penetration, especially one in which a man inserts his erect penis into a woman's vagina

sex·u·al·i·ty /sèkshoo állətee/ *n.* **1. STATE OF BEING SEXUAL** the state of being sexual **2. INVOLVEMENT IN SEXUAL ACTIVITY** involvement or interest in sexual activity **3. SEXUAL APPEAL** sexual appeal or potency

sex·u·al·ize /sékshoo ə līz/ **(-ized, -iz·ing, -iz·es)** *vt.* to impose a sexual interpretation or perception on something or somebody

sex·u·al·ly trans·mit·ted dis·ease *n.* a disease such as syphilis or genital herpes that is normally passed from one person to another through sexual activity

sex·u·al o·ri·en·ta·tion *n.* the direction of somebody's sexual desire, toward people of the opposite sex, or of the same sex, or of both sexes

sex·u·al re·la·tions *npl.* = **sexual intercourse**

sex·u·al re·pro·duc·tion *n.* reproduction that involves the union of male and female gametes, each contributing half of the genetic makeup of the resulting zygote

sex·u·al se·lec·tion *n.* the choice by a female animal of a mate on the basis of a characteristic, e.g., a bird song or bright plumage

sex·va·lent *adj.* = **hexavalent**

sex work *n.* the work of somebody in one of the sex industries such as pornography or prostitution —**sex work·er** *n.*

sex·y /séksee/ **(-i·er, -i·est)** *adj.* **1. AROUSING DESIRE** arousing or intended to arouse sexual desire **2. AROUSED** sexually aroused **3. APPEALING** appealing especially because of being new, interesting, or trendy (*informal*) —**sex·i·ly** *adv.* —**sex·i·ness** *n.*

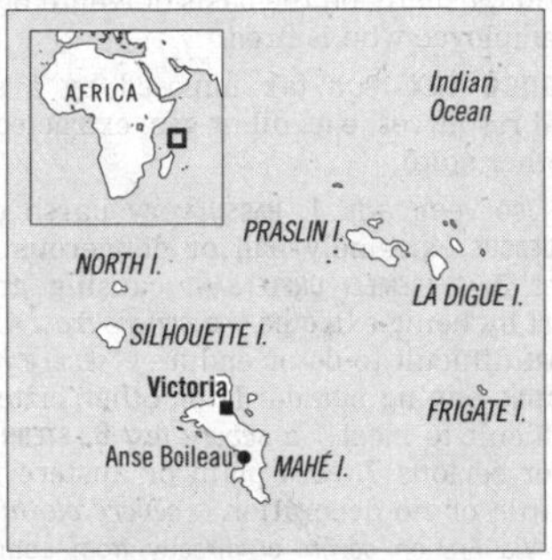

Seychelles

Sey·chelles /say shélz/ island republic in the Indian Ocean. It contains four main islands and many islets. Language: Creole, English, French. Currency: Seychelles rupee. Capital: Victoria. Population: 76,100 (1996). Area: 175 sq. mi./455 sq. km. Official name **Republic of Seychelles** —**Sey·chell·ois** *adj., n.*

Sey·fert gal·ax·y /sééfərt-, sīfərt-/ *n.* a small spiral galaxy that varies in brightness and emits radio waves and X-rays [Mid-20thC. Named for Carl K. *Seyfert* (1911–60), the U.S. astronomer who first described this type of galaxy.]

Sey·mour /séem awr/, **Jane, Queen of England and Ireland** (1509?–37). She was the third wife of Henry VIII of England, and died shortly after giving birth to Edward VI, Henry's only male heir.

sf *abbr.* **1.** sforzando **2.** science fiction

SF *abbr.* **1.** science fiction **2.** sinking fund **3.** BASEBALL sacrifice fly

Sfax /sfaks/ port and capital city of Safaqis Governorate, east-central Tunisia. Population: 230,900 (1994).

SFC *n., abbr.* sergeant first class

sfer·ics *npl.* = **spherics**

sfor·zan·do /sfawrt saándō/ *adv.* **WITH STRONG ACCENT** with a sudden strong accent (*used as a musical direction*) ■ *n.* (*plural* **-dos** *or* **-di** /-dee/) **SUDDEN STRONG NOTE** a note or chord that is to be played with a sudden strong accent, or a symbol indicating this [Early 19thC. From Italian, formed from *sforzare* "to use force," from, ultimately, Latin *fortis* "strong" (see FORTIS).] —**sfor·zan·do** *adj.*

sfu·ma·to /sfoo maátō/ *n.* the gradual blending of one area of color into another without a sharp outline [Mid-19thC. From Italian, past participle of *sfumare* "to tone down," literally "to smoke out," from, ultimately, Latin *fumus* "smoke" (see FUME).]

sfz. *abbr.* sforzando

sg *abbr.* specific gravity

Sg *abbr.* Song of Songs

SG *abbr.* **1.** EDUC senior grade **2.** solicitor general ■ *n., abbr.* SURG Surgeon General ■ *abbr.* singular

S.G. *n., abbr.* LAW **1.** solicitor general **2.** Secretary General

sgd. *abbr.* signed

SGHWR *abbr.* steam-generating heavy-water reactor

SGML *n.* an international standard for the definition of system-independent methods of representing texts in electronic form by describing the relationship between a document's form and its structure. SGML is used widely to manage large documents that are subject to frequent revisions and need to be printed in different formats. Full form **Standard Generalized Markup Language**

SGP *abbr.* Singapore (*international vehicle registration*)

sgraf·fi·to /zgraa féetō, skraa féetō/ (*plural* **-ti** /-féetee/) *n.* **1.** DECORATION TECHNIQUE a technique used to decorate ceramics or plaster walls, in which the top layer has patterns scratched into it, revealing the different-colored layer beneath **2.** DECORATION a decoration made using the sgraffito technique **3.** DECORATED OBJECT an object decorated using the sgraffito technique [Mid-18thC. From Italian, the past participle of *sgraffire* "to scratch," from *sgraffio* "scratch," from *sgraffiare* "to scratch" from Old Italian, literally "to scratch completely," from *graffiare* (see GRAFFITO).]

Sgt. *abbr.* Sergeant

Sgt. Maj. *abbr.* Sergeant Major

sh, shh *interj.* used to tell somebody to be silent or quieter [Mid-19thC. A naturally produced interjection.]

sh. *abbr.* **1.** sheep **2.** sheet **3.** shilling **4.** share

SHA *abbr.* sidereal hour angle

Shaan·xi /shaa áanshee/ province in China bordering Ningsia Hui, Inner Mongolia, Shanxi, Henan, Hubei, Sichuan, and Gansu. Capital: Xi'an. Population: 34,810,000 (1994). Area: 75,598 sq. mi./195,799 sq. km.

Sha'·ban /shə báan, shaa-/, **Sha·ban, Shaa·ban** *n.* CALENDAR in the Islamic calendar, the eighth month of the year [Mid-18thC. From Arabic *ša'bān*.]

Shab·bat /shə báat/ (*plural* **-ba·tot** /shàbba tṓt/ *or* **-bes** /shaábəss/) *n.* CALENDAR the Jewish Sabbath, celebrated on Saturday [Mid-19thC. From Hebrew *šabbāt*, literally "day of rest" (source of English *Sabbath*).]

shab·by /shábbee/ (**-bi·er, -bi·est**) *adj.* **1.** WORN AND THREADBARE worn out, frayed, or threadbare after long use **2.** WEARING WORN CLOTHES wearing worn-out clothing and perceived as being unappealing to the eye **3.** INCONSIDERATE inconsiderate and unfair ○ *won't put up with shabby treatment* **4.** INFERIOR IN QUALITY inferior in quality ○ *shabby goods* **5.** RUN DOWN poorly maintained and thus falling apart or dirty ○ *a shabby section of town* [Mid-17thC. Formed from obsolete *shab* "disreputable person," from Old English *sceabb* "scab." Ultimately from a prehistoric Germanic word that is also the ancestor of English *scab*.]

Sha·cha·ris /shaákhriss/ *n.* the Jewish morning liturgy [From Hebrew *šaḥărīṯ*, literally "morning time"]

shack /shak/ *n.* a small crude building typically made of boards or sheets of material, usually without a foundation [Late 19thC. Origin uncertain: perhaps via Mexican Spanish *jacal* "wooden hut" from Nahuatl *xacalli*.]

shack up *vi.* to live with a lover without being married (*informal disapproving*) [From the practice of military personnel living with local women off base]

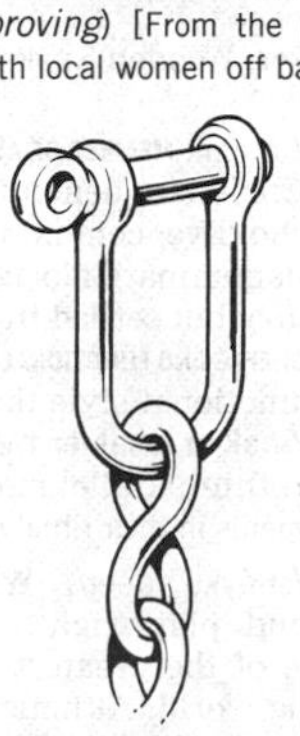

Shackle

shack·le /shák'l/ *n.* **1.** METAL BRACELET FOR HOLDING PRISONERS a round metal band that can be opened or locked in order to hold the wrist or ankle of a captive, usually attached by chains in pairs or fours (*often used in the plural*) **2.** RIDING BINDER FOR ANIMAL LEGS a device used to hold together the legs of horses and other animals **3.** U-SHAPED FASTENER a U-shaped bar that is fastened with a straight pin or bolt to hold something securely **4.** RESTRAINT ON FREEDOM an oppressive restraint on something or somebody (*often plural*) ○ *mental shackles* ■ *vt.* (**-led, -ling, -les**) **1.** RESTRICT FREEDOM to restrict the freedom of somebody or something ○ *felt shackled by the inflexible rules* **2.** RESTRAIN WITH SHACKLES to restrain somebody or an animal using shackles **3.** SECURE WITH SHACKLE to connect or secure something with a shackle [Old English *sceacul*. Ultimately from a prehistoric Germanic word denoting "a fastening."] —**shack·ler** *n.*

Shack·le·ton /shák'ltən/, **Sir Ernest Henry** (1874–1922) Irish explorer. He was the leader of an expedition that almost reached the South Pole (1907–09). He was the first to cross South Georgia (1916), but died there on his fourth expedition.

shad /shad/ (*plural* **shads** *or* **shad**) *n.* any of various North Atlantic fishes similar to herring, commonly used as food. They leave salt water to spawn upstream in rivers. Genus: *Alosa*. [Old English *sceadd*]

shad·ber·ry /shád bèrree/ (*plural* **-ries**) *n.* = **serviceberry** *n.* 2 [Mid-19thC. From its flowering when shad appear in the rivers to spawn.]

shad·blow /shád blō/ *n.* = **serviceberry** *n.* 1 [Mid-19thC. "blow," from BLOW.]

shad·bush /shád bŏŏsh/ *n.* = **serviceberry** *n.* 1

shad·chan /shaádkhən/ (*plural* **-cha·nim** /-khənim/ *or* **-chans**), **shad·khan** (*plural* **-ka·nim** *or* **-khans**) *n.* a marriage broker for Jewish couples [Mid-19thC. Via Yiddish *shadkhn* from medieval Hebrew *šaddəkān*, from *šiddēk* "to make marriage proposals."]

shad·dock /sháddək/ *n.* = **pomelo** *n.* 1, **pomelo** *n.* 2 [Late 17thC. Named for a 17th-century English ship captain named *Shaddock*, who brought the seed to Barbados.]

shade /shayd/ *n.* **1.** AREA OUT OF DIRECT SUNLIGHT an area of relative darkness where direct sunlight is blocked or obscured **2.** SLIGHTLY DIFFERENT COLOR a color that is a variation on a basic color, e.g., by being more or less bright or dark ○ *a pretty shade of blue* **3.** SOMETHING THAT BLOCKS LIGHT something, e.g., a lampshade, used to block a direct light source **4.** WINDOW DEVICE a flexible piece of material mounted on a window that can be rolled down to block light or up to admit light **5.** ARTS DARK PARTS OF PAINTING the darker areas of a painting, drawing, or photograph **6.** SMALL AMOUNT a slight degree or amount ○ *a shade too close* **7.** VARIATION a slight variation on something similar ○ *different shades of opinion* **8.** OBSCURITY relative obscurity **9.** PARANORMAL GHOST a ghost or phantom (*literary*) **10.** SHADOW a shadow (*archaic*) ■ **shades** *npl.* SUNGLASSES sunglasses (*informal*) ■ *v.* (**shad·ed, shad·ing, shades**) **1.** *vt.* PROTECT FROM SUNLIGHT to protect something or block it off from direct light, particularly from direct sunlight ○ *The awning shades the porch well.* **2.** *vt.* DARKEN PART OF PICTURE to darken part of a drawing or picture using pencil, ink, or some other dark medium ○ *He shaded in the trees in the background.* **3.** *vi.* CHANGE SLIGHTLY OR GRADUALLY to change imperceptibly into something slightly different ○ *The cream gradually shades into gold.* **4.** *vt.* DARKEN to make a place or area darker **5.** *vt.* BUSINESS REDUCE PRICE to reduce a price slightly [Old English *sceadu* (source also of English *shadow*). Ultimately from an Indo-European word meaning "darkness, shadow."] ◇ **put somebody *or* something in the shade** to make somebody or something seem unimportant by appearing much more special or attractive ◇ **shades of somebody *or* something** used to say that something is reminiscent of something, especially a time in the past or the work of a writer or other artist ○ *You can take tea on the terrace – shades of E. M. Forster – or ride on an elephant.*

Shades /shaydz/ *npl.* the underworld (*literary*) [Late 16thC. Originally in the meaning "darkness" (as of the underworld).]

shade tree *n.* a tree with a broad crown that is planted to shade an area from sunlight

shad·fly /shád flī/ (*plural* **-flies**) *n.* = **mayfly** [Early 19thC. From its appearance when shad appear in the rivers to spawn.]

shad·ing /sháyding/ *n.* **1.** DARKENED AREA IN PICTURE an area of relatively dark tone or close lines, dots, or hatching that produces darkness or shadow in a drawing or picture **2.** SLIGHT DIFFERENCE a subtle difference or variation

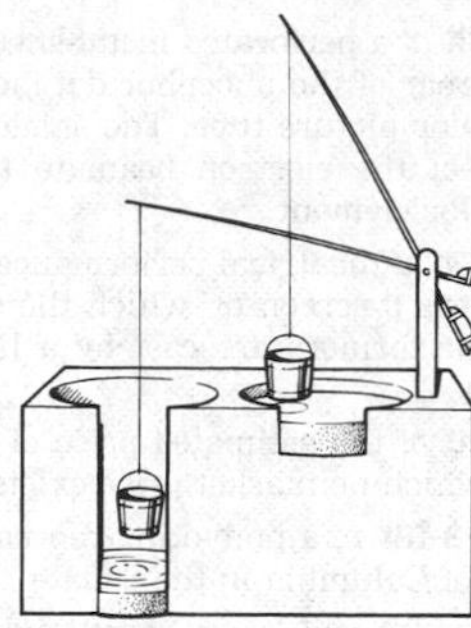

Shadoof

sha·doof /shə dóof, shaa-/, **sha·duf** *n.* a water-raising device used in ancient Egypt consisting of a suspended pivoting pole with a bucket on one end and a counterweight on the other [Mid-19thC. From Egyptian Arabic *šādūf*.]

shad·ow /sháddō/ *n.* **1.** DARKENED SHAPE OF SOMETHING IN LIGHT a darkened shape on a surface that falls behind somebody or something blocking the light **2.** DARKNESS relative darkness in a place that is being screened or blocked off from direct sunlight ○ *Part of the room was in shadow.* **3.** HINT OF SOMETHING a slight suggestion or hint of something ○ *beyond the shadow of a doubt* **4.** OMINOUS GLOOM a depressing or ominous gloom ○ *The news cast a shadow over the party.* **5.** THREAT an ever-present threat or blight ○ *living under the shadow of environmental disaster* **6.** DARK AREA UNDER EYES a darkened area of skin under the eyes usually caused by fatigue **7.** OVERSHADOWED STATE a state in which somebody is always overshadowed by another person ○ *grew up in his brother's shadow* **8.** SOMEBODY ALWAYS FOLLOWING AFTER ANOTHER somebody who constantly follows another person around wanting to be with the other person **9.** PERSON SECRETLY TRAILING ANOTHER somebody, e.g., a detective or spy, who secretly follows somebody **10.** ARTS = **shade** *n.* 5 **11.** PARANORMAL = **shade** *n.* 9 **12.** REFLECTION a reflection of something in water ○ *the shadow of the stars in the dark lake* **13.** COPY an imitation or copy of something **14.** INFERIOR REMNANT a remnant of somebody or something formerly greater or more important ○ *now a shadow of her former self* **15.** BUSINESS SOMEBODY LEARNING JOB BY FOLLOWING WORKER somebody who learns a job by following and observing somebody else who knows or regularly does the job **16.** MED ABNORMAL AREA IN X-RAY an abnormal area showing up on an X-ray **17.** PSYCHOL JUNGIAN ARCHETYPE in Jungian psychology, the archetype that represents sexual and aggressive instincts inherited from a more primitive stage of humanity **18.** SHELTER something that provides protection ■ *vt.* (**-owed, -ow·ing, -ows**) **1.** PROTECT FROM LIGHT to shade something from the light ○ *Her face was shadowed by a wide-brimmed straw hat.* **2.** FOLLOW to follow somebody secretly ○ *The police had been shadowing him for days.* **3.** BUSINESS LEARN JOB BY FOLLOWING WORKER to learn a job by following somebody who is actually doing the job **4.** REPRESENT VAGUELY to represent something vaguely or in outline **5.** SHELTER SOMETHING to provide protection from something (*archaic*) ■ *adj. U.K.* POL IN CAPACITY OF OPPOSITION COUNTERPART used to describe a member of an opposition party who speaks on a particular area of policy and would hold a ministerial job if the party were in government ○ *the shadow cabinet* [Old English *sceaduwe*, a form of *sceadu* (see SHADE)] —**shad·ow·er** *n.*

WORD KEY: SYNONYMS

See Synonyms at ***follow***.

shad·ow·box /sháddō bòks/ (**-boxed, -box·ing, -box·es**) *vi.* to practice boxing moves by sparring with an imaginary partner

shad·ow box *n.* a shallow box consisting of a frame and a glass front in which small objects can be displayed and protected

shad·ow dance *n.* a dance performance in which the dancers' shadows are seen on a screen

shad·ow·graph /sháddō gràf/ *n.* **1.** IMAGE CAST IN SHADOW an image of a shape made by casting a shadow onto a surface, e.g., by shaping the hands so that their shadow resembles the silhouette of an animal **2.** = **radiograph**

shad·ow mask *n.* a perforated metal sheet mounted close to the rear of the phosphor dot faceplate of a three gun color picture tube. The shadow mask is used to direct the electron beam to the desired phosphor color element.

shad·ow play *n.* a theatrical performance where the audience views a screen on which the shadows of puppets or performers are cast by a light source behind them

shad·ow price *n.* the estimated price of goods or a service for which no market price exists

shad·ow sen·a·tor *n.* a nonvoting representative of the District of Columbia in the Senate

shad·ow·y /sháddō ee/ (-i·er, -i·est) *adj.* **1.** FULL OF SHADOWS full of shadows or shade **2.** NOT CLEARLY SEEN not clearly or only vaguely seen **3.** MYSTERIOUS mysteriously little-known or obscure —**shad·ow·i·ness** *n.*

sha·duf *n.* = **shadoof**

shad·y /sháydee/ (-i·er, -i·est) *adj.* **1.** HAVING SHADE having little natural light, often giving shelter from harsh sunlight **2.** DISHONEST probably dishonest or illegal ○ *shady dealings with foreign investors* **3.** PROVIDING SHADE providing shade —**shad·i·ly** *adv.* —**shad·i·ness** *n.*

SHAEF /shayf/ *abbr.* Supreme Headquarters Allied Expeditionary Forces

shaft /shaft/ *n.* **1.** LONG HANDLE the long slender handle on various instruments and tools, e.g., golf clubs and hammers **2.** VERTICAL PASSAGE a vertical passage, especially one in which an elevator travels or one that gives access to a mine **3.** PASSAGE FOR VENTILATION IN BUILDING a small passageway in a building, particularly in a wall, ceiling, or floor, to allow for air circulation **4.** MECH ENG ROTATING ROD IN MACHINE a rotating rod that provides motion or power for a machine **5.** LIGHT BEAM a beam of light ○ *a shaft of sunlight* **6.** SHARP COMMENT a sharp or barbed comment directed at somebody ○ *a shaft of wit* **7.** POLE FOR HARNESSING HORSE either of the two parallel bars by which an animal is harnessed to a cart or wagon **8.** HARSH TREATMENT unkind or harsh treatment or dismissal (*informal*) ○ *His girlfriend gave him the shaft.* **9.** ARROW an arrow (*literary*) **10.** BODY OF PROJECTILE a long narrow rod that forms the body of a spear, arrow, harpoon, or other projectile **11.** ANAT MIDDLE OF LONG BONE the middle part of a long bone **12.** ANAT BODY OF PENIS the cylindrical body of the penis **13.** ANAT MAIN PART OF HAIR the part of a hair that is visible above the skin **14.** ARCHIT BODY OF COLUMN the main body of a column, between the capital and base **15.** ARCHIT COLUMN a column, especially one of a pair supporting an arch **16.** BIRDS FEATHER RIB the central rib of a feather **17.** TREES TREE TRUNK the trunk of a tree **18.** UPRIGHT PART OF CROSS the upright bar in a cross ■ *vt.* (shaft·ed, shaft·ing, shafts) TREAT UNFAIRLY to cheat somebody or treat somebody unfairly (*slang*) ○ *She got shafted on her book contract.* [Old English *sceaft*]

shag[1] /shag/ *n.* **1.** LONG-PILED CARPET a carpet or rug with a long thick pile **2.** TEXTILES LONG PILE ON TEXTILE a long rough nap or pile on a textile **3.** HAIR LAYERED HAIRCUT a hairstyle with layers that are cut progressively shorter from base to crown **4.** DRUGS SHREDDED TOBACCO a strong, coarse tobacco that is finely shredded **5.** MATTED TANGLE OF HAIR a rough matted tangle of hair or wool ■ *vt.* (shagged, shag·ging, shags) **1.** MAKE ROUGH to cause something to be rough looking and shaggy **2.** PROVIDE WITH SHAFT to provide something such as a tool with a shaft [Old English *sceacga*]

shag[2] /shag/ (shagged, shag·ging, shags) *vt.* **1.** RETRIEVE to run and retrieve something **2.** BASEBALL CATCH FLY BALLS to chase, catch, and return fly balls in baseball practice **3.** CHASE AWAY to chase somebody or something away (*regional*) [Early 20thC. Origin unknown.]

shag[3] /shag/ *n.* a small crested cormorant mainly found in Europe and North Africa. Latin name: *Phalacrocorax aristotelis.* [Mid-16thC. Origin uncertain: perhaps from SHAG[1], because of the bird's shaggy crest.]

shag[4] /shag/ (shagged, shag·ging, shags) *vti. U.K.* an offensive term referring to sexual intercourse (*slang taboo*) [Late 18thC. Origin unknown.]

shag[5] /shag/ *n.* 1930S DANCE a 1930s dance step involving hopping alternately on each foot ■ *vi.* (shagged, shag·ging, shags) DANCE THE SHAG to dance the shag [Early 20thC. Origin uncertain.] —**shag·ger** *n.*

shag·bark /shág baark/, **shag·bark hick·o·ry** *n.* **1.** TREES HICKORY WITH SHAGGY BARK a hickory of eastern North America that has gray shaggy bark. Latin name: *Carya ovata.* **2.** INDUST SHAGBARK WOOD the valuable hard light-colored wood of the shagbark **3.** FOOD HICKORY NUT the round hard-shelled edible nut of the shagbark

shag·gy /shággee/ (-gi·er, -gi·est) *adj.* **1.** LONG AND TANGLED growing long and unevenly **2.** HAVING COARSE LONG FIBERS covered with or resembling coarse, long, and usually uneven hair, wool, or similar fibers **3.** TEXTILES ROUGH NAPPED having a rough, relatively long nap or pile **4.** DONE WITHOUT PLANNING done in a haphazard way, with little thought or planning

shag·gy cap *n.* = **shaggymane**

shag·gy-dog sto·ry *n.* a long drawn-out absurd story or joke, often with an ending or punchline that is anticlimactic [From one such anecdote involving a shaggy dog]

shag·gy·mane /shággi màyn/ *n.* a common edible mushroom with shaggy scales on its cap that contain black spores. Latin name: *Coprinus comatus.*

sha·green /shə greén/ *n.* **1.** ROUGH SHARK SKIN the rough skin of certain sharks and rays, used as an abrasive or as leather **2.** ROUGH, UNTANNED LEATHER rough, untanned leather with a grainy surface, made from the hide of various animals and often dyed green [Late 17thC. Via French *chagrin* "untanned leather" from Turkish *sağri* "back of a horse."]

shah /shaa/ *n.* formerly, the hereditary monarch of certain Middle Eastern nations, especially Iran [Mid-16thC. Via Persian *šāh* from Old Persian *xšāyathiya-* "king" (source of English *check*).] —**shah·dom** *n.*

Shahn /shaan/, **Ben** (1898–1969) Lithuanian-born U.S. artist. He is known for employing bold colors and a poster-like style in paintings that often had political themes.

shai·tan /shī taán, shày-/ *n.* in Islamic countries, an evil spirit or person [Mid-17thC. Via Arabic *šaytān* from Hebrew *śāṭān.*]

Shai·tan *n.* in Islamic belief, the Devil

shake /shayk/ *v.* (shook /shòok/, shak·en /sháykən/, shak·ing, shakes) **1.** *vti.* MOVE BACK AND FORTH to move or make something or somebody move back and forth or up and down in short quick movements ○ *I shook my coat to see if my keys were in the pockets.* **2.** *vi.* TREMBLE to tremble uncontrollably ○ *shaking with fright* **3.** *vti.* BECOME BY SHAKING to achieve a particular state by shaking, or shake something in order to achieve a particular state ○ *The door finally shook free of its hinges* **4.** *vt.* SHAKE TO DISLODGE to shake something in order to make parts attached to it come off ○ *We shook the apples from the tree.* **5.** *vi.* QUAVER WITH EMOTION to sound uncertain, nervous, angry, or distressed ○ *Her voice was shaking.* **6.** *vt.* SHOCK AND UPSET SOMEBODY to shock and upset or disturb somebody ○ *He was badly shaken by the accident.* **7.** *vt.* MAKE SOMEBODY LESS CONFIDENT to cause somebody to lose confidence or certainty ○ *Nothing could shake his faith.* **8.** *vti.* CLASP HANDS AS GREETING to grasp another person's hand and move it up and down as a greeting or sign of trust **9.** *vt.* GET RID OF SOMETHING to get rid of something undesired ○ *I can't shake this cold.* **10.** *vt.* MIX BY SHAKING to mix ingredients together in a container by shaking the container **11.** *vt.* MOVE HEAD TO EXPRESS "NO" to move the head from side to side in order to express disagreement, disbelief, commiseration, or sorrow **12.** *vt.* WAVE SOMETHING THREATENINGLY to wave something in the air in a threatening way ○ *She shook her fist at them.* **13.** *vti.* RATTLE DICE BEFORE THROWING to rattle a die or dice in the hand or in a dice cup before throwing **14.** *vti.* MUSIC TRILL to trill a note ■ *n.* **1.** ACT OF SHAKING a shaking of something ○ *She gave the bag a good shake.* **2.** VIBRATION a trembling motion or vibration ○ *The device moves smoothly along the track without shake.* **3.** MOMENT a brief moment (*informal*) ○ *I'll do it in two shakes.* **4.** BEVERAGES = **milk shake** *n.* 1 **5.** BEVERAGES SHAKEN BEVERAGE a beverage made without milk or ice cream but blended or shaken like a milk shake ○ *a fruit and yogurt shake* **6.** HANDSHAKE an act of grasping somebody's hand as a greeting **7.** REASONABLE CHANCE reasonable treatment or a reasonable opportunity to succeed ○ *give everybody a fair shake* **8.** GEOL, FORESTRY FISSURE OR CRACK a fissure or crack in a rock or timber **9.** MUSIC TRILL a trilled note **10.** SEISMOL EARTHQUAKE an earthquake (*informal*) **11.** BUILDING WOODEN SHINGLE a rough wooden shingle cut with a hatchet ■ **shakes** *npl.* UNCONTROLLABLE TREMBLING uncontrollable trembling caused, e.g., by fear or illness [Old English *sceacan*] —**shak·a·ble** *adj.* ◇ **be no great shakes** to be not very good or not very important (*informal*)

shake down *v.* **1.** *vt.* EXTORT MONEY FROM SOMEBODY to extort money from somebody (*slang*) **2.** *vt.* SEARCH FOR SOMETHING to search somebody or a place, especially for contraband (*informal*) **3.** *vt.* TAKE SOMETHING FOR TRIAL RUN to subject a ship or aircraft to a trial run in order to look for defects or train the crew **4.** *vi.* BECOME ACCUSTOMED to become comfortable in a new setting (*informal*) **5.** *vi.* SLEEP IN MAKESHIFT BED to go to bed in a makeshift bed

shake out *vt.* to open something, spread something, or dislodge things from something by holding it and shaking it

shake up *vt.* **1.** MAKE MAJOR CHANGES to make major changes in an organization or institution, especially with the intention of improving or modernizing it **2.** UPSET SOMEBODY to make somebody feel upset and disturbed **3.** MIX BY SHAKING to mix something by shaking it in a container

shake·down /sháyk dòwn/ *n.* **1.** ACT OF EXTORTION an act of extorting money from somebody using threats (*slang*) **2.** THOROUGH SEARCH a thorough search of somebody or a place (*informal*) **3.** TRIAL RUN OF VESSEL a trial run of a ship or aircraft in order to locate and fix problems or to familiarize the crew with their duties **4.** MAKESHIFT BED a makeshift bed such as a pile of blankets on a floor

shak·en past participle of **shake**

shak·en ba·by syn·drome *n.* in young babies, a series of often life-threatening internal head injuries sustained through being shaken violently

shake·out /sháyk òwt/ *n.* a major change in an organization or system resulting in the falling away of some elements ○ *a shakeout in the voluntary sector*

shak·er /sháykər/ *n.* **1.** CONTAINER FOR DISPERSING FINE PARTICLES a container with small holes in its lid that can be shaken to disperse the contents **2.** CONTAINER FOR MIXING DRINKS a container with a lid in which drinks are mixed by shaking the container **3.** SOMEBODY CAUSING CHANGE somebody who is active in some field, especially somebody who brings about change (*informal*) ○ *a real shaker in the industry* **4.** SOMETHING THAT SHAKES somebody or something that shakes or shakes something

Philadelphia Museum of Art/Corbis

Shaker: Wooden Shaker box

Shak·er /sháykər/ *n.* CHR MEMBER OF ASCETIC DENOMINATION a member of a Christian denomination related to the Quakers who live communally, simply, and celibately. The denomination originated in England in the 18th century but settled in the United States. ■ *adj.* **1.** DESIGN SIMPLE AND FUNCTIONAL designed or made in the simple, functional style that originated with the Shakers **2. Shak·er, shak·er** PARALLEL RIBBED knit at a large gauge in thin parallel ribs [Late 18thC. From the shaking movements in their ritual dances.]

Shake·speare /sháyks peer/, **William** (1564–1616) English poet and playwright. He is widely recognized as one of the greatest dramatists in the English-speaking world. Although much of his life is obscure, he was born in Stratford-upon-Avon, England. He was established as an actor-playwright in London by about 1590, and over the next 23 years wrote 36 tragedies, histories, and comedies, including *Hamlet* (1601?), *Richard III* (1595–96?), and *Twelfth Night* (1600?). His poetry includes over 150 sonnets.

Shake·spear·e·an /shayk speéree ən/, **Shake·spear·i·an** *adj.* RELATING TO SHAKESPEARE relating to or written by William Shakespeare, or typical of his works ■ *n.*

William Shakespeare

STUDIER OF SHAKESPEARE a scholar who studies Shakespeare and his works

Shake·spear·e·an·a /shayk speeree ánnə, -áanə/, **Shake·spear·i·an·a** *n.* collectively, things relating to William Shakespeare

Shake·spear·e·an son·net *n.* a sonnet in iambic pentameter composed of three quatrains followed by a couplet. The rhyme pattern is abab cdcd efef gg. This is the form perfected by William Shakespeare.

Shake·spear·i·an *adj.* = **Shakespearean**

Shake·spear·i·an·a *n.* = **Shakespeareana**

shake-up, shake·up *n.* a major reorganization or change

shak·ing pal·sy *n.* Parkinson's disease (*informal dated*) [From its characteristic tremor]

shak·o /shákō, sháykō/ (*plural* **-os** *or* **-oes**) *n.* a tall cylindrical military hat made of stiff material with a short visor and a plume in front [Early 19thC. Via French *schako* from Hungarian *csákós (süveg)* "peaked (cap)," of uncertain origin: probably from German *Zacken* "peak, point."]

Shak·ta /shúktə, shaáktə/, **Sak·ta**, /súktə, saáktə/ *n.* a Hindu who worships Shakti, the female consort of Shiva [Early 19thC. From Sanskrit *śāktaḥ*, from *śaktiḥ* (see SHAKTI).] —**Shak·tism** *n.* —**Shak·tist** *n.*

Shak·ti *n.* = **sakti**

sha·ku·ha·chi /shaákoo haáchee/ (*plural* **-chis**) *n.* a Japanese bamboo flute [Late 19thC. From Japanese, from *shaku*, a unit of measure + *hachi* "eight"; so called because it is one and eight-tenths of a "shaku" in length.]

shak·y /sháykee/ (**-i·er, -i·est**) *adj.* **1. TREMBLING** trembling or unsteady **2. NOT STURDY** not sturdy or firm and likely to collapse **3. WEAK AND NOT LIKELY TO LAST** weak or wavering and unlikely to last long or to be successful ○ *a shaky financial venture* **4. UNRELIABLE** unreliable or uncertain ○ *made us a pretty shaky promise* —**shak·i·ly** *adv.* —**shak·i·ness** *n.*

shale /shayl/ *n.* a dark fine-grained sedimentary rock composed of layers of compressed clay, silt, or mud [Mid-18thC. Origin uncertain: ultimately from a prehistoric Germanic word meaning "to split," which is also the ancestor of English *scale* and *shell*.] —**shal·y** /sháylee/ *adj.*

shale oil *n.* crude oil distilled from heated shale

shall *stressed* /shal/; *unstressed* /shəl/ **CORE MEANING:** will happen in the future, or intended to happen ○ *I shall as president promote measures that keep families whole.*

vi. **1. MUST** used especially in formal speech and writing to indicate determination on the part of the speaker that something will happen or somebody will do something ○ *If you want to behave like that you shall certainly not do it here.* **2. RULES AND LAWS** indicating that something must happen or somebody is obliged to do something because of a rule or law ○ *The department shall issue an account number to the vehicle owner.* **3. OFFERS AND SUGGESTIONS** used to make offers and suggestions or to ask for advice (*used in questions*) ○ *Shall I arrange it for you?* ○ *What shall I do next?* **4. CERTAINTY** indicating the certainty or inevitability of something happening in the future ○ *If you want a new outfit that badly then you shall have one.* [Old English *sceal*. From a prehistoric Germanic word meaning "to owe."]

WORD KEY: USAGE

shall or will? The traditional rule, often stated in grammars and usage books, is that to express a simple future tense ***shall*** is used after *I* and *we* and ***will*** in other cases, and to express intention or wish their roles are reversed; but it is unlikely that this rule has ever been regularly observed, and many examples of written English can be found that contradict it. (The distinction is often difficult to establish, especially in the first person when the speaker is also the performer of the future action and intention must always be involved to some extent.) Although ***will*** and (occasionally) ***shall*** are used as auxiliary verbs with reference to future action or state, there are other ways of expressing this that are often preferred as more natural, such as *am going to*. When ***shall*** and ***will*** are used in conversation, they are normally contracted to *'ll*, so that the difference between the two words becomes irrelevant. In all parts of the English-speaking world other than England, ***shall*** has been more or less driven out by ***will***. It survives mostly in the contracted negative form *shan't*, but this is not used in American English. In the English of England (note: England, not Britain), ***shall*** is fighting a rearguard action in such uses as *They shall apologize immediately* (a command) and *Shall you bring the children?* (an inquiry rather than a request), but even these sound very old-fashioned and affected, and ***will*** is now more common, especially in speech.

shal·loon /shə lóon/ *n.* a light wool twill, usually used as a garment lining [Mid-17thC. From French *chalon*, of uncertain origin: perhaps named for the French city of *Châlons*-sur-Marne, where it is said to have first been made.]

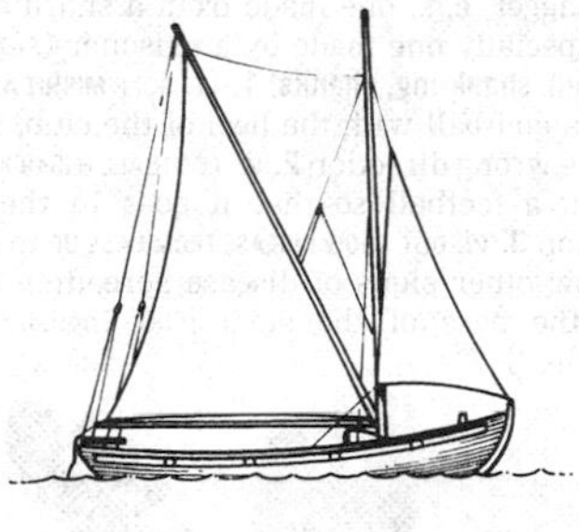
Shallop

shal·lop /shállәp/ *n.* a light boat with oars, sails, or both, used in shallow waters [Late 16thC. From French *chaloupe*, of uncertain origin: perhaps an alteration of Dutch *sloep* (see SLOOP).]

shal·lot /shə lót/ *n.* **1. PLANTS PLANT IN ONION FAMILY** a plant of the onion family widely cultivated for use in cooking. Latin name: *Allium ascalonicum.* **2. FOOD SHALLOT BULB USED AS FOOD** the bulb of the shallot that divides into small sections and is used in cooking for its delicate onion flavor [Mid-17thC. From French *échalotte*, an alteration of Old French *esc(h)aloigne*, from assumed Vulgar Latin *escalonia* (see SCALLION).]

shal·low /shállō/ *adj.* **1. NOT DEEP** with little space between the bottom and the surface or top **2. NOT THINKING OR FEELING DEEPLY** having or displaying little intellectual or emotional complexity or value **3. TAKING IN LITTLE AIR** characterized by the inhaling and exhaling of an abnormally small amount of air ■ **shal·lows** *npl.* **AREA OF SHALLOW WATER** an area of shallow water ■ *vti.* (**-lowed, -low·ing, -lows**) **MAKE OR BECOME SHALLOW** to become less deep or to make water less deep [15thC. Origin uncertain: ultimately.] —**shal·low·ly** *adv.* —**shal·low·ness** *n.*

sha·lom /shaa lṓm/ *interj.* used as a Jewish greeting or leave-taking [Late 19thC. From Hebrew *šālōm* "peace."]

shalt /shalt/ 2nd person present singular, 2nd person present plural of **shall** (*archaic*)

sham /sham/ *n.* **1. A FAKE** something that is presented as genuine but that is not **2. IMPOSTOR** somebody who pretends to be a completely different person or different type of person **3.** = **pillow sham** ■ *adj.* **NOT GENUINE** not genuine and used for deception ○ *sham credentials* ■ *vti.* (**shammed, sham·ming, shams**) **FEIGN** to pretend to be experiencing a condition, e.g., illness or an emotion, in order to deceive [Late 17thC. Origin uncertain: probably a northern English variant of SHAME.] —**sham·mer** *n.*

sha·man /shaáman, sháymən/ *n.* somebody who acts as a go-between for the physical and spiritual realms, and who is said to have particular powers such as prophecy and healing [Late 17thC. Via Russian from Tungus *šaman*, ultimately from Sanskrit *śramaṇáḥ* "Buddhist ascetic," from *śrámas* "religious exercise."] —**sha·man·ic** /shə mánnik, shay-/ *adj.*

sha·man·ism /shaámə nizzəm, sháymə-/ *n.* **1. SPIRITUALIST RELIGION OF ASIA** a religion of northern Asia, in which shamans can intercede between humanity and powerful good and evil spirits **2. ANIMISTIC BELIEF SYSTEM** any animistic belief system involving shamans

sha·mash *n.* = **shammash**

sham·ble /shámb'l/ *vi.* (**-bled, -bling, -bles**) **SHUFFLE ALONG CLUMSILY** to walk clumsily keeping the feet close to the ground ■ *n.* **SHUFFLING WALK** a shuffling, awkward walking style [Late 16thC. Origin uncertain: probably from the obsolete expression *shamble legs* "ungainly legs," alluding to the rickety legs of a meat vendor's stall (see SHAMBLES).]

sham·bles /shámb'lz/ *n.* **1. DISORGANIZED FAILURE** a failure caused by inadequate planning or organization **2. MESSY DISORDER** a state of messy disorder or chaos **3. PLACE OF CARNAGE** a place of great destruction and carnage **4. SLAUGHTERHOUSE** a slaughterhouse (*dated*) **5. MEAT MARKET** a meat or fish market (*archaic*) [15thC. Formed from obsolete *shamble* "meat vendor's stall," from, ultimately, Latin *scamellum* "small bench").]

WORD KEY: ORIGIN

The Old English ancestor of ***shamble*** still meant simply "stool, table." It gradually acquired the specialized meaning "meat table," being applied to meat sellers' stalls at markets (a street in the old butchers' quarter of York is still known as the Shambles). By a natural extension the plural form ***shambles*** came to denote a "slaughterhouse," and hence metaphorically any "scene of bloodshed and slaughter," but the milder modern sense "scene of disorder or ruin" did not emerge until as recently as the early 20th century.

sham·bol·ic /sham bóllik/ *adj. U.K.* poorly organized and in a messy or chaotic state (*informal*) [Late 20thC. Formed from SHAMBLES, perhaps on the model of "symbolic."]

shame /shaym/ *n.* **1. NEGATIVE EMOTION** a negative emotion that combines feelings of dishonor, unworthiness, and embarrassment **2. CAPACITY TO FEEL UNWORTHY** the capacity or tendency to feel shame ○ *He has no shame.* **3. STATE OF DISGRACE** a state of disgrace or dishonor ○ *bring shame on the family* **4. CAUSE FOR REGRET** a cause for regret or disappointment ○ *It's a shame you couldn't stay for lunch.* **5. CAUSE OF SHAME** somebody or something that causes somebody to feel shame ■ *vt.* (**shamed, sham·ing, shames**) **1. MAKE SOMEBODY FEEL ASHAMED** to make somebody feel ashamed ○ *It shamed her that she had cheated.* **2. FORCE SOMEBODY THROUGH SHAME** to make somebody do something by exploiting the fact that he or she would be ashamed not to do it ○ *He shamed us into making higher donations to the ministry.* **3. MAKE SOMEBODY FEEL INFERIOR** to be so much better or more successful than others as to expose their comparative inadequacy ■ *interj.* **1. USED IN SYMPATHETIC REACTION** used to react sympathetically to something disappointing ○ *Shame, man, we would have invited you if we'd known you were free.* **2.** *S Africa* **USED TO SHOW SENTIMENTAL APPROVAL** used to show that you think that something or somebody is attractive in an endearing way ○ *"Have you seen our new puppy?" "Oh, shame! Isn't it cute!"* [Old English *sceamu*] ◇ **put somebody** *or* **something to shame** to make somebody or something seem inferior or of inferior quality by comparison

shame·faced /sháym fàyst/ *adj.* **1. SHOWING SHAME** showing a feeling of shame or embarrassment **2. TIMID** timid or easily embarrassed [Mid-16thC. Alteration (influenced by SHAME) of obsolete *shamefast* "bashful," literally "held fast by shame," from Old English *sceamfæst*.] —**shame·fac·ed·ly** /sháym fàysədlee, -fàystlee/ *adv.* —**shame·fac·ed·ness** /-fàysədnəss/ *n.*

shame·ful /sháymf'l/ *adj.* **1. DISGRACEFUL OR SCANDALOUS** bad enough to inspire shame in those responsible **2. ASHAMED** feeling shame (*archaic*) [Old English *sceamful*] —**shame·ful·ly** *adv.* —**shame·ful·ness** *n.*

shame·less /sháymləss/ *adj.* **1. NOT FEELING SHAME** untroubled or unaffected by shame, especially in situations where others would be shamed **2. DONE WITHOUT SHAME** done without shame, especially where others would feel shame [Old English *sceamlēas*] —**shame·less·ly** *adv.* —**shame·less·ness** *n.*

sha·mi·a·na /shàmmee aánə/ *n. S Asia* a decorative circus-style tent used for outdoor entertaining or weddings [Early 17thC. From Persian and Urdu *shāmiyāna*.]

Sha·mir /shə meér/, **Yitzhak** (*b.* 1914) Polish-born Israeli political leader. He held many government positions, including foreign minister (1980–92), leader of the Likud Party (1983–93), and prime minister (1983–84, 1986–92). Real name **Yitzhak Jazernicki**

sham·mash /shaáməss/ (*plural* **-ma·shim** /shaa maássim/), **sha·mash** (*plural* **-ma·shim**), **sham·mes** (*plural* **-mo·sim** /shaa mṓssim/) *n.* **1. SYNAGOGUE CARETAKER** the sexton of a synagogue **2. CANDLE USED TO LIGHT OTHERS** the candle used to light the candles in the Hanukkah candlestick [Mid-17thC. Via Yiddish *shames* from Hebrew *šāmmāš* "attendant," from *šimmēš* "to serve."]

sham·my /shámmee/ (*plural* **-mies**) *n.* = **chamois**

sham·poo /sham poó/ *n.* **1. HAIR-CLEANING SOAP** soap for cleaning the hair and scalp, usually in liquid or gel form **2. SUDSY DETERGENT** sudsy detergent for cleaning upholstery and carpets **3. USE OF SHAMPOO** a cleaning of the hair with shampoo ■ *vt.* (**-pooed, -poo·ing, -poos**) **CLEAN WITH SHAMPOO** to clean something with shampoo [Mid-18thC. Via Anglo-Indian from Hindi *cāpō*, from *cāpnā* "to knead, press, massage."]

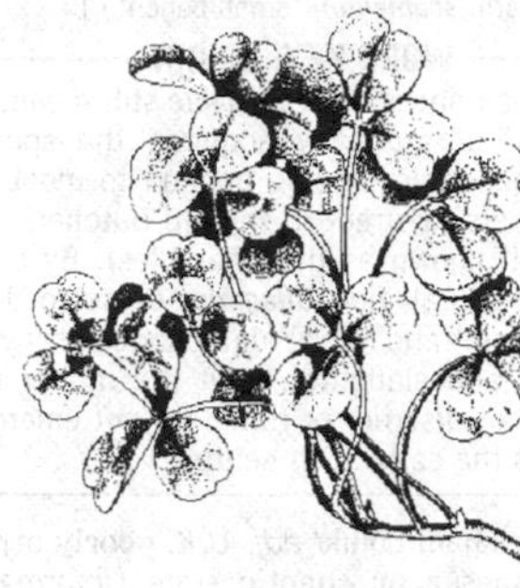

Shamrock

sham·rock /shám ròk/ *n.* a three-leafed clover or a plant similar to clover that serves as the national emblem of Ireland [Late 16thC. From Irish *seamróg* "small clover," from *seamar* "clover."]

sha·mus /sháyməss/ *n.* (*slang*) **1. POLICE OFFICER** a police officer **2. PRIVATE DETECTIVE** private detective [Early 20thC. Origin uncertain: possibly an alteration of SHAMMASH, or perhaps from the Irish name *Séamus*, in allusion to the many Irish immigrants who became police officers.]

Shan /shaan, shan/ (*plural* **Shan** *or* **Shans**) *n.* **1. MEMBER OF SOUTHEAST ASIAN PEOPLES** a member of a group of peoples living mainly in the hilly regions of northeastern Myanmar, and also in neighboring parts of China, Laos, and Thailand **2.** LANG **SHAN LANGUAGE** the tai language of the Shan people. Shan is spoken by 2.5 million people. [Early 19thC. From Burmese.] —**Shan** *adj.*

Shan·dong /shan dóong/ province on the eastern coast of China, bordered by Hebei, Henan, and Jiangsu. Capital: Jinan. Population: 86,710,000 (1994). Area: 59,200 sq. mi./153,300 sq. km.

shan·dy /shándee/ (*plural* **-dies**) *n.* **1. BEER CONCOCTION** a drink made of beer and lemon-lime soda **2.** = **shandygaff** [Late 19thC. Shortening of SHANDYGAFF.]

shan·dy·gaff /shándi gàf/ *n.* a drink made of beer and ginger beer [Mid-19thC. Origin unknown.]

Shang /shaang/ *n.* a Chinese dynasty that ruled from 1766? to 1027? B.C., a period that coincided with the development of China's system of handwriting and bronzework (*often used before a noun*) [Mid-17thC. From Chinese *Shāng*.]

Shan·gaan /shàng gaán/ (*plural* **-gaan** *or* **-gaans**) *n.* = **Tsonga** [Late 19thC. Of Bantu origin.]

shang·hai /shang hī́, sháng hī́/ (**-haied, -hai·ing, -hais**) *vt.* **1.** NAVY **FORCE INTO NAVAL SERVICE** to recruit somebody forcibly into a navy **2. TRICK OR FORCE TO DO SOMETHING** to trick or force somebody to do something or go somewhere [Late 19thC. Named for SHANGHAI, a typical destination of ships crewed in this way.]

Shang·hai /shang hī́/ city and port on Huang-p'u River in eastern China. Population: 8,760,000 (1993).

Shan·go /shaáang gṓ/ *n.* a religious group in the Caribbean characterized by a blend of West African religious practice and Christianity. Rituals involve drumming, dancing, and chanting, as well as the sacrifice of small animals. Some participants enter a state of trance. [Mid-20thC. From Yoruba, name of the god of thunder.]

Shan·gri-la /shàng gri laá/ *n.* an imaginary and remote paradise on earth [Mid-20thC. From the name given to an imaginary land in the novel *Lost Horizon* (1933) by the English novelist James Hilton.]

shank /shangk/ *n.* **1. LONG, NARROW PART** the long narrowest part of something such as a key or pipe, especially when it connects two functional parts **2.** FOOD **CUT OF MEAT** a cut of meat from the leg of cattle or sheep **3.** ZOOL **BOTTOM OF ANIMAL LEG** the lower part of an animal's leg, between the bottom and middle joints **4. LOWER LEG** the lower part of the human leg, from ankle to knee **5. LEG** a human leg (*informal*) **6.** MECH ENG **BODY OF PIN OR NAIL** the long, narrow part of a pin, nail, screw, or bolt, between the head and the pointed or threaded part **7.** MECH ENG **PART CONNECTING TOOL HEAD TO HANDLE** a part sticking out from the head of a tool, by which it can be fitted into a handle **8.** ACCESSORIES **RING BAND** the plain band part of a ring, not including the jewels and their settings **9.** ACCESSORIES **NARROW PART OF SOLE** the narrow part of the sole of a shoe, beneath the arch of the foot, or any fitting at this part of a shoe **10.** = **shankpiece 11.** NAUT **ANCHOR'S STEM** the stem of an anchor **12.** PRINTING **PART OF PRINTING TYPE** the body of a piece of type, between the foot and shoulder **13.** CLOTHES **BUTTON STEM** a loop or stem at the back of a button, by which it is sewn to the cloth **14. EARLY PART OF SOMETHING** the early part of a period (*regional*) **15. LATER PART** the later or remaining part of a period (*regional*) **16. HOMEMADE DAGGER** a makeshift dagger, e.g., one made from a shard of glass, and especially one made by a prisoner (*slang*) ■ *v.* (**shanked, shank·ing, shanks**) **1.** *vt.* GOLF **MISHIT A GOLF BALL** to hit a golf ball with the heel of the club, sending it in the wrong direction **2.** *vt.* FOOTBALL **MISKICK FOOTBALL** to kick a football so that it goes in the wrong direction **3.** *vi.* BOT **SHOW DISEASE FROM BASE UP** to shrivel, or show other signs of disease spreading upward from the base of the stem [Old English *sceanca*. "shinbone."]

Ravi Shankar

Shan·kar /shángk aar/, **Ravi** (*b.* 1920) Indian sitarist, composer, and teacher. His international tours popularized Indian music in the West. His compositions include movie scores and sitar concertos.

shank·piece /shángk peess/ *n.* a shoe insert that supports the arch of the foot

shank's mare *n.* the feet, as a means of transportation (*dated or informal*)

shan·na·chie /shánna k͟hee/ *n. Ireland* a traditional Irish story-teller [From Irish *seanchaidhe*]

shan·ny /shánnee/ (*plural* **-nies** *or* **-ny**) *n.* a European fish with a small tapering body and a long dorsal fin that lives in rocky coastal areas. Latin name: *Blennius pholis*. [Mid-19thC. Origin unknown.]

shan't /shant/ *contr.* contraction of "shall not"

shan·tey *n.* = **chantey**

shan·tung /shan túng/ *n.* **1. NUBBY SILK** heavy silk cloth with a nubby uneven weave **2. FABRIC RESEMBLING SHANTUNG** cotton or synthetic fabric made to resemble silk shantung [Late 19thC. Named for the Chinese province of *Shantung* (Shandong), where it was originally manufactured.]

shan·ty /shántee/ (*plural* **-ties**) *n.* a crudely built shack or hut [Early 19thC. Origin uncertain: possibly from Canadian French *chantier* "lumberjack's hut," via French, "timberyard," from, ultimately, Latin *cant(h)erius* "rafter."]

shan·ty·town /shánti tòwn/ *n.* a settlement consisting of crudely built shacks

Shan·xi /shánshee/ agricultural province of northeastern China, bordered by Inner Mongolia, Hebei, Henan, and Shaanxi. Capital: Taiyuan. Population: 28,759,014 (1990). Area: 60,656 sq. mi./157,099 sq. km.

shape /shayp/ *n.* **1. OUTLINE OF SOMETHING'S FORM** the outline of something's form ○ *His face has a square shape.* **2. SOMETHING NOT CLEARLY SEEN** something that has bulk but is not clearly seen in outline ○ *She could see a shape through the fog.* **3.** GEOM **GEOMETRIC FORM** a geometric form such as a square, triangle, cone, or cube **4. GENERAL CHARACTER OF SOMETHING** the broad character that something has ○ *the overall shape of the proposals* **5. ORIGINAL FORM** the original or optimal form of something ○ *The pleats lost their shape in the wash.* **6. HEALTH** the condition of somebody's health or fitness ○ *She exercises regularly and is in good shape.* **7. CONDITION OF SOMETHING** the condition of something ○ *The lawn is in great shape.* **8. PHYSIQUE** the figure of a person **9. MOLD** a mold or pattern for making or giving something its form **10. GHOST** a ghostly form or phantom ■ *vt.* (**shaped, shap·ing, shapes**) **1. INFLUENCE SOMETHING GREATLY** to have a profound or crucial influence over something ○ *His beliefs were shaped by his upbringing.* **2. PLAN FOR NATURE OF SOMETHING** to plan or decide on what the character of something should be ○ *They are meeting to shape the nation's future.* **3. GIVE SOMETHING PARTICULAR SHAPE** to mold something into a different shape ○ *She shapes the clay into little animals.* **4.** PSYCHOL **TRAIN WITH REWARD AND PUNISHMENT** to change somebody's behavior gradually using reward as the person comes closer to the desired behavior, and punishment for moving away from it [Old English *gesceap* "creation," literally "something cut out." From a prehistoric Germanic word meaning "to cut out," which is also the ancestor of English *-ship* and *-scape*.] ◇ **knock** *or* **lick** *or* **whip somebody** *or* **something into shape** to bring somebody or something to a desired state quickly, roughly, or haphazardly (*informal*) ◇ **take shape** to take a definite form

shape up *vi.* **1. IMPROVE** to improve or develop in the way that is wanted (*informal*) **2. REACH ACCEPTABLE STANDARD** to reach an acceptably high standard of behavior, skill, or attitude **3. DEVELOP IN PARTICULAR WAY** to seem to be developing in the way specified ○ *It's shaping up to be an environmental disaster.*

shape·less /sháypləss/ *adj.* **1. LACKING PRECISE SHAPE** with an indefinite or imprecise shape **2. LACKING STRUCTURE** put together in a very haphazard way —**shape·less·ly** *adv.* —**shape·less·ness** *n.*

shape·ly /sháyplee/ (**-li·er, -li·est**) *adj.* having a shape that is visually appealing —**shape·li·ness** *n.*

shape-up, **shape·up** *n.* a method of hiring dock workers in which those seeking work arrive at the docks in the morning and employers select from among them

shard /shaard/, **sherd** /shurd/ *n.* **1. BROKEN PIECE OF GLASS** a sharp broken piece of glass or metal **2.** ARCHEOL = **potsherd 3.** ZOOL **SCALE OR SHELL** an animal's scales, shell, or other tough outer covering **4.** INSECTS **BEETLE'S OUTER WING** the outer wing covering of a beetle [Old English *sceard* "cut, notch." Ultimately from an Indo-European word meaning "to cut," which is also the ancestor of English *shear, scar, score,* and *short*.]

share[1] /shair/ *v.* (**shared, shar·ing, shares**) **1.** *vti.* **USE SOMETHING ALONG WITH OTHERS** to have or use something in common with other people ○ *We shared an apartment.* **2.** *vti.* **TAKE RESPONSIBILITY TOGETHER** to take equal responsibility for something along with other people ○ *We shared the blame.* **3.** *vti.* **LET SOMEBODY USE SOMETHING** to allow somebody to use something or have part of something ○ *I shared my ice cream with him.* **4.** *vt.* **DIVIDE SOMETHING EQUALLY BETWEEN PEOPLE** to allocate equal parts of something to different people or groups ○ *She shared the money between her six grandchildren.* **5.** *vt.* **HAVE SIMILAR FEELING OR EXPERIENCE** to have something the same as or in common with somebody else ○ *He shared my view that the plan would not work.* **6.** *vt.* **TELL SOMEBODY SOMETHING** to express something to another person rather than keeping silent ○ *Do you want to share your feelings?* ■ *n.* **1. PART OF SOMETHING ALLOTTED** a part of something that is owned by, paid for by, done by, or set aside for each of several people ○ *He hasn't had his share of the cake.* **2.** FIN **PART OF COMPANY'S STOCK** any of the equal, usually small, parts into which a company's capital stock is divided ○ *100 shares of General Motors* **3. REASONABLE OR APPROPRIATE PORTION** the portion that somebody deserves or should be responsible for ○ *She does more than her share of the work.* [Old English *scearu* "division, portion." Ultimately from an Indo-European word meaning "to cut," which is also the ancestor of English *shear, scar, score,* and *shirt*.] —**shar·er** *n.*

share[2] /shair/ *n.* = **plowshare** [Old English *scear.* Ultimately from an Indo-European word meaning "to cut," which is also the ancestor of *shear* and *share*[1].]

share·crop /sháir kròp/ (**-cropped, -crop·ping, -crops**) *vti.* to farm land as a sharecropper [Early 20thC. From SHARE[1], because the crop was shared with the landowner.]

share·crop·per /sháir kròppər/ *n.* a tenant farmer who farms land for the owner and is paid a share of the value of the yielded crop

share·hold·er /sháir hòldər/ *n.* somebody who owns one or more shares of a company's stock

share·ware /sháir wàir/ *n.* software made available for free trial with the understanding that users will voluntarily pay a fee to the author or publisher if they continue to use it

sha·ri·a /shəaa reé ə/, **sha·ri'·a, sha·ri'·ah** *n.* Islamic religious law, based on the Koran (*often used before a noun*) [Mid-19thC. Via Arabic *šarʻīya* "lawfulness" from, ultimately, *aš-šarʻ* "Islamic law."]

sha·rif *n.* = **sherif**

Shar·jah /shaárjə/ one of the seven member states of the United Arab Emirates. Population: 125,000 (1995).

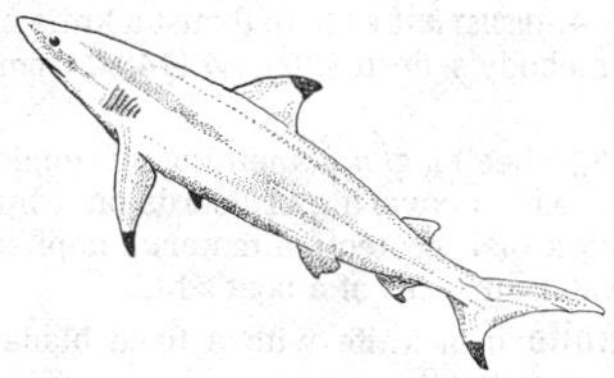

Shark

shark /shaark/ *n.* **1.** ZOOL **CARNIVOROUS FISH** a carnivorous fish that has a long body, two dorsal fins, sharp teeth, a cartilaginous skeleton, and thick, rough skin. Class: Chondrichthyes. **2. RUTHLESS PERSON** a ruthless greedy person (*informal*) **3. LOANSHARK** a loanshark (*informal*) **4. ESPECIALLY TALENTED PERSON** somebody with a particular talent ■ *v.* (**sharked, shark·ing, sharks**) **1.** *vt.* **GET SOMETHING ILLICITLY** to get something illegally or unethically (*archaic*) **2.** *vi.* **CHEAT OTHERS PROFESSIONALLY** to make a living as a cheater or fraud [Mid-16thC. Origin unknown. Introduced to English in a ballad about the things seen by a group of explorers. In the sense "ruthless person," perhaps from German *schurke* "scoundrel."]

shark net *n.* a net strung across a bay to keep sharks out

shark si·ren *n. Aus* a siren or similar mechanism sounded to warn swimmers and surfers that sharks have been spotted offshore

shark·skin /shaárk skin/ *n.* **1.** TEXTILES **GLOSSY FABRIC** a smooth glossy fabric made from a mixture of acetate and rayon **2.** INDUST **SHARK LEATHER** leather made from shark's skin

shark·suck·er /shaárk sùkər/ *n.* = **remora** [Mid-19thC. From its habit of attaching itself to sharks by means of a sucking disk.]

Helen Sharman

Shar·man /shaármən/, **Helen** (*b.* 1963) British astronaut. With her participation in the Russian scientific space mission Project Juno (1991), she became Britain's first astronaut. Full name **Helen Patricia Sharman**

sharp /shaarp/ *adj.* **1. ABLE TO CUT** with an edge or point that is very acute and able to cut or puncture things ○ *a sharp blade* **2. POINTED** ending in a point or sharp angle ○ *a sharp nose* **3. ABRUPT IN CHANGING DIRECTION** making a change in direction that forms an acute angle ○ *a sharp turn* **4. QUICK-WITTED** quick-witted and intelligent or quick to notice and understand **5. CRITICAL** critical and unsympathetic ○ *a sharp rebuke* **6. IRRITABLE** irritable or angry ○ *a sharp temper* **7. SUDDEN** sudden and significant ○ *a sharp rise in prices* **8. SURPRISED** abrupt or unexpected ○ *a sharp intake of breath* **9. DISTINCT** clearly and definitely distinct ○ *Her soft voice was in sharp contrast to her forbidding expression.* **10. CLEARLY DETAILED** with the detail clear and distinct ○ *a sharp image* **11. PIERCING** loud, piercing, and abrupt or unexpected ○ *a sharp cry* **12. STRONG IN TASTE** strong and slightly bitter in taste ○ *a sharp cheese* **13. INTENSE** penetrating and intense ○ *a sharp frost* **14.** MUSIC **HIGHER BY SEMITONE** higher in pitch by a half step ○ *F sharp* **15.** MUSIC **TOO HIGH PITCHED** a little too high in pitch and therefore slightly out of tune **16. STYLISH** neat, stylish, and fashionable ○ *a sharp dresser* **17. FRAUDULENT** deceitful or fraudulent ○ *sharp business practice* ■ *adv.* **1. PRECISELY** exactly, and not before or after ○ *at 9 o'clock sharp* **2.** MUSIC **AT SLIGHTLY TOO HIGH A PITCH** at higher than the usual pitch and therefore slightly out of tune ○ *She's singing sharp.* ■ *n.* **1.** MUSIC **NOTE HIGHER BY HALF STEP** a note or tone that is a half step higher in pitch than the natural or unmodified pitch. Symbol ♯ **2.** MUSIC **SHARP SYMBOL** the symbol for a sharp note. Symbol ♯ **3.** SEW **LONG SEWING NEEDLE** a long thin needle for hand sewing **4.** MED **SHARP MEDICAL INSTRUMENT** a sharp medical instrument such as a hypodermic or surgical blade that requires careful disposal (*usually used in the plural*) ○ *a container labeled "sharps only"* **5. SHARPER** a sharper (*informal*) **6. EXPERT** somebody expert at something (*informal*) [Old English *scearp.* Ultimately from an Indo-European word meaning "to cut," which is also the ancestor of English *sharp, scarf,* and *shard.*] —**sharp·ly** *adv.* —**sharp·ness** *n.*

Sharp /shaarp/, **Phillip** (*b.* 1944) U.S. molecular biologist. He shared in the Nobel Prize in physiology or medicine (1933) for his research on the genetic structure of DNA. Full name **Phillip Allen Sharp**

sharp·bill /shaárp bìl/ *n.* a small fruit-eating bird of the Central and South American rainforest with a straight sharp bill, green and yellow plumage, and a red crest. Latin name: *Oxyruncus cristatus.*

shar-pei /shaar páy/, **Shar-Pei** *n.* a medium-sized dog with a squarish snout, blue tongue, short hair, and loose skin that falls in folds over its body, especially when young. It belongs to a breed originating in China. [Late 20thC. From Chinese *shā pí*, literally "sand skin."]

sharp·en /shaárpən/ (**-ened, -en·ing, -ens**) *v.* **1.** *vti.* **BECOME OR MAKE SHARPER** to become or make something sharp or sharper **2.** *vt.* **IMPROVE SOMETHING** to improve something so that it is more efficient or stylish than before

sharp·er /shaárpər/ *n.* a skillful cheat, especially in gambling

Sharpe·ville /shaárp vil/ African township near Vereeniging, South Africa. It was the scene of a massacre of antiapartheid demonstrators in 1960. Population: 42,000 (1972).

sharp-eyed *adj.* **1. ALERT TO DETAIL** alert and able to notice detail **2. HAVING GOOD EYESIGHT** with very keen eyesight

sharp·ie /shaárpee/, **sharp·y** (*plural* **-ies**) *n.* **1.** NAUT **FLAT FISHING SAILBOAT** a long narrow fishing boat with a flat bottom and one or two masts with triangular sails **2. QUICK-WITTED PERSON** somebody who is quick-witted and alert **3. SHARPER** a sharper (*informal*)

sharp-nosed puff·er *n.* any tropical marine fish that can inflate its body like other puffers but also has a characteristic long snout with prominent nostrils. Family: Canthigasteridae.

sharp-set *adj.* eagerly wanting something, especially food

sharp-shinned hawk *n.* a small bird-hunting hawk of North America with short wings, a long square tail, and gray feathers with a brown underside. Latin name: *Accipiter striatus.* [From its slender legs]

sharp·shoot·er /shaárp shòotər/ *n.* **1. SOMEBODY WHO SHOOTS PRECISELY** somebody who is very good at hitting precise targets using firearms **2.** SPORTS **GOOD TARGET-HITTER** somebody who is accurate in hitting any type of target, e.g., a basketball player who can make baskets from long distances

sharp-sight·ed *adj.* **1. HAVING GOOD VISION** with very good eyesight **2. ALERT TO DETAIL** quick to notice detail —**sharp-sight·ed·ly** *adv.* —**sharp-sight·ed·ness** *n.*

sharp-tailed grouse *n.* a light-colored grouse with a narrow tapered tail and dark breast markings, found on prairies and scrubland of the northwestern United States and Canada

sharp-tailed spar·row *n.* a North American marsh-dwelling sparrow with tail feathers that have pointed ends. Latin name: *Ammodramus caudacutus.*

sharp-tongued *adj.* critical or sarcastic and unsympathetic in speech

sharp-wit·ted *adj.* quick to think, understand, or react —**sharp-wit·ted·ly** *adv.*

sharp·y *n.* = **sharpie**

shash·lik /shaásh lìk, shaash lík/, **shash·lick** *n.* = **shish kebab** [Early 20thC. Via Russian *shashlyk* from Crimean Turkish *şişlik* "small skewer," from *şiş* "skewer."]

Shas·ta, Mount /shástə-/ mountain and extinct volcano in the Cascade Range, northern California. It has five glaciers. Height: 14,162 ft./4,317 m.

Shas·ta dai·sy *n.* a chrysanthemum with large white flower heads. Latin name: *Chrysanthemum maximum.* [Early 20thC. Named for Mount SHASTA, or the *Shasta* peoples of northern California, where the flower is commonly found.]

shas·tra /shaástrə/, **sas·tra** *n.* in Hinduism, a sacred text [Mid-17thC. From Sanskrit *śāstra* "lesson," from *śās-* "to instruct."]

shat past tense, past participle of **shit** (*taboo*)

Shatt al-Ar·ab /shàt al árrəb, shaát-/ river in southwestern Asia. It rises at the confluence of the Euphrates and Tigris rivers, flows along the border between Iran and Iraq, and empties into the Persian Gulf, near Kuwait. Length: 106 mi./170 km.

shat·ter /sháttər/ *v.* (**-tered, -ter·ing, -ters**) **1.** *vti.* **SMASH INTO PIECES** to break or cause something to break suddenly into many small, brittle pieces **2.** *vt.* **DESTROY HOPE OR BELIEF** to destroy something that somebody believed in or hoped for **3.** *vt.* **SHOCK SOMEBODY** to shock and distress somebody badly **4.** *vi.* AGRIC **SHED PLANT PARTS** to drop petals, ripe fruit, or leaves ■ **shat·ters** *npl.* **FRAGMENTS** fragments made by shattering something [Assumed Old English *sceaterian.* Ultimately from an Indo-European word meaning "to split apart," which is also the ancestor of English *shingle*[1].] —**shat·ter·er** *n.*

shat·ter cone *n.* a cone-shaped rock piece that has stripes running from its point, created by volcanic pressure or meteoric impact

shat·ter·proof /sháttər pròof/ *adj.* made to resist shattering

shave /shayv/ *v.* (**shaved, shaved** *or* **shav·en** /sháyv'n/, **shav·ing, shaves**) **1.** *vti.* **REMOVE HAIR WITH RAZOR** to remove hair from the body using a razor **2.** *vt.* **REDUCE AMOUNT SLIGHTLY** to reduce an amount, price, or time taken by a very slight amount ○ *shaved two seconds off her best time* **3.** *vt.* **BARELY TOUCH IN PASSING** to barely touch something when passing **4.** *vt.* **REMOVE A THIN LAYER OF** to remove a thin layer from something using a razor, rasp, or similar tool **5.** *vt.* **TRIM SOMETHING CLOSELY** to trim something closely ■ *n.* **1. ACT OF SHAVING** the act, process, or result of shaving **2.** = **shaving** *n.* 1 **3. SHAVING TOOL** any tool for shaving or scraping [Old English *sceafan.* Ultimately from an Indo-European word meaning "to scrape, scratch," which is also the ancestor of English *scabies.*]

shav·en /sháyv'n/ *v.* past participle of **shave** ■ *adj.* (*often used in combination*) **1. WITH NO BEARD OR HAIR** with the beard or the hair shaved off **2. TRIMMED** trimmed or cropped

shav·er /sháyvər/ *n.* **1. DEVICE FOR SHAVING** a device that is used to shave the beard or hair, especially an electric razor (*often used before a noun*) **2. YOUNG BOY** a boy who is not old enough to shave (*dated informal*) [The meaning of "young boy" developed from "fellow"]

Sha·vi·an /sháyvee ən/ *adj.* **1. BY OR LIKE G. B. SHAW** written by or in the style of the work of the playwright George Bernard Shaw **2. OF SHAW** relating to or studying Shaw or his works ■ *n.* ADMIRER OR STUDENT OF SHAW an admirer of Shaw, or a scholar who studies his works [Early 20thC. Formed from *Shavius*, Latinized form of SHAW.]

shav·ing /sháyving/ *n.* **1.** SHAVED-OFF PIECE a thin slice shaved off **2.** HAIR REMOVAL WITH RAZOR the removing of hair or a beard with a razor (*often used before a noun*)

Sha·vu·oth /shə vo͝o ōt, -ōth/, **Sha·vu·ot** /-ōt/ *n.* CALENDAR a Jewish festival held on the 6th day of Sivan, in May or June, and commemorating the Law being given by God to Moses on Mount Sinai [Late 19thC. From Hebrew *šāḇūʿōt*, plural of *šāḇūaʿ* "week," alluding to the weeks between Passover and Pentecost.]

shaw /shaw/ *n. U.K., Midwest* a thicket of shrubs or small trees [Old English *sceaga*. Ultimately from a prehistoric Germanic word meaning "something sticking out," which is also the ancestor of English *shag* "long coarse pile."]

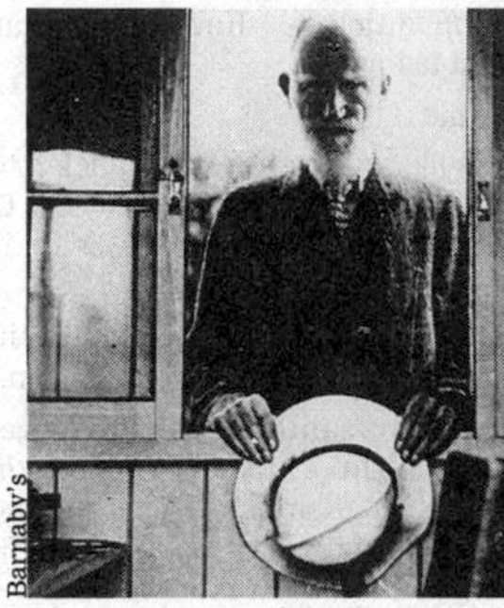

George Bernard Shaw

Shaw /shaw/, **George Bernard** (1856–1950) Irish playwright. His plays, including *Pygmalion* (1913) and *Heartbreak House* (1919), established him as the leading English-language playwright of his time. He promoted socialism in works such as *The Intelligent Woman's Guide to Socialism and Capitalism* (1928).

Sha·wa·no *n., adj.* = **Shawnee**

Sha·win·i·gan /shə wínnigən/ city in southern Quebec, Canada, northwest of Trois Rivières on the St. Maurice River. Population: 19,931 (1991).

shawl /shawl/ *n.* GARMENT FOR THE HEAD AND SHOULDERS a fabric square worn by women over the shoulders or head and shoulders or used to wrap a baby in ■ *vt.* **(shawled, shawl·ing, shawls)** WRAP IN A SHAWL to cover somebody or something with a shawl or with something performing a similar function [Early 17thC. From Persian and Urdu *šāl*.]

shawm /shawm/ *n.* a woodwind instrument of the Middle Ages and Renaissance that has a double reed and was the predecessor of the modern oboe [14thC. Origin uncertain: probably a back-formation from *schalmys*, plural of *shalemie*, from Old French *chalemie*, ultimately from Latin *calamus* "reed" (see CALAMUS).]

Shawn /shawn/, **Ted** (1891–1972) U.S. dancer and choreographer. He founded the Denishawn Dance School (1915) with his wife, Ruth St. Denis, and they were leading exponents of modern dance. Real name **Edwin Myers Shawn**

Shaw·nee[1] /shaw née/ (*plural* **-nee** *or* **-nees**), **Sha·wa·no** /shə wáanō/ (*plural* **-no** *or* **-nos**) *n.* **1.** PEOPLES MEMBER OF NATIVE N AMERICAN PEOPLE a member of a Native North American people who originally occupied lands along the Ohio, Cumberland, and Tennessee Rivers, and whose descendants now live mainly in Oklahoma **2.** LANG LANGUAGE OF SHAWNEE the language of the Shawnee people, belonging to the Algonquian family. Few people now speak Shawnee. [Late 17thC. From Delaware *šawanow*.] —**Shaw·nee** *adj.*

Shaw·nee[2] /shaw née/ city in northeastern Kansas. It is a western suburb of Kansas City. Population: 43,006 (1996).

Shaw·wal /shə wól/ *n.* in the Islamic calendar, the tenth lunar month of the year [Late 18thC. From Arabic *shawwāl*.]

she *stressed* /shee/; *unstressed* /shee/ *pron.* (*used as the subject of a verb*) **1.** PREVIOUSLY MENTIONED FEMALE PERSON OR ANIMAL used to refer to a female person or animal who has been previously mentioned or whose identity is known ○ *Ms Jones continues to enjoy high approval ratings as she starts her third year in office.* **2.** OBJECT PERCEIVED AS FEMALE used to refer to something previously mentioned or known that has been traditionally thought of as female, e.g., a nation, a car, a machine, a boat, or a ship ○ *Iran stated that she is ready to start talks on the issue.* ○ *She'll have to go to the scrap yard; she can't be repaired any longer.* ■ *n.* SOMETHING FEMALE a female animal or person, sometimes used of a new baby ○ *Is it a he or a she?* [12thC. Origin uncertain: probably a variant of Old English *hēo*.]

s/he /shée awr hée/ *pron.* used in writing as a pronoun to mean "she or he" (*intended to avoid sexism in writing*) ○ *If a student wishes to change courses s/he should consult me before the end of term.*

shea *n.* = **shea tree** [Late 18thC. From Mande *si*.]

shea but·ter *n.* a white fat obtained from the seeds of the shea tree. It is used as a food and in the manufacture of soap and candles.

sheaf /sheef/ *n.* (*plural* **sheaves** /sheevz/) **1.** BUNDLE OF HARVESTED GRAIN STALKS a bundle of the harvested stalks of a plant, especially wheat, barley, or another cereal, with the heads still containing their seeds **2.** ANY BUNDLE a bundle of objects gathered or tied together ■ *vt.* = **sheave**[1] *v.* [Old English *sceaf*. Ultimately from a prehistoric Germanic word that is also the ancestor of English *shove*. The underlying idea is of things shoved together.]

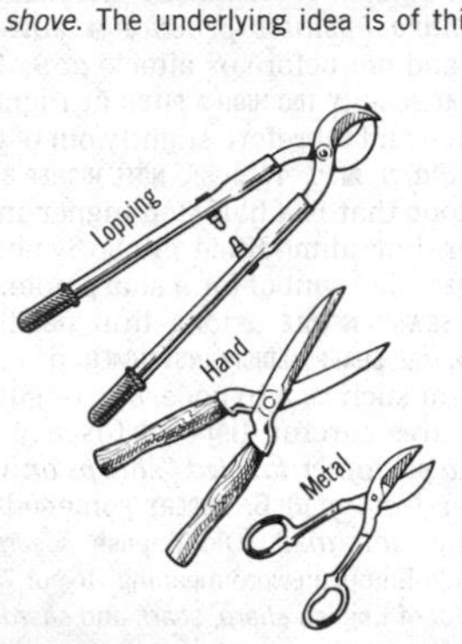

Shears

shear /sheer/ *v.* **(sheared, sheared** *or* **shorn** /shawrn/, **shear·ing, shears) 1.** *vti.* CUT OFF to remove something with a sharp tool **2.** *vti.* CUT HAIR, WOOL, OR FOLIAGE FROM to cut hair, fleece, or foliage from the surface of something using a sharp tool **3.** *vt.* DEPRIVE to take something valuable or prized away from somebody ○ *sheared of all self-respect* **4.** *vti.* MOVE CLEANLY THROUGH SOMETHING to move quickly and cleanly through something **5.** *vti.* DEFORM BY APPLYING TWISTING FORCE to cause something to deform or break by applying a twisting force ■ *n.* **1.** REMOVAL OF FLEECE a cutting off of a sheep's wool, often used as a measure of the age of a sheep **2.** WOOL CUT OFF a quantity of wool cut off **3.** = **shear strain 4.** = **shear stress 5.** SHEARS a pair of shears ■ **shears** *npl.* **1.** CUTTING TOOL a tool like a large pair of scissors, used for cutting or trimming **2.** SHEERLEGS a sheerlegs [Old English *sceran*. Ultimately, from an Indo-European word meaning "to cut" that is also the ancestor of English *score, short*, and *curtail*.]

shear force *n.* a force, or a component of a force, that acts parallel to a plane

shear·legs *n.* = **sheerlegs**

shear·ling /sheerling/ *n.* **1.** YOUNG SHEEP SHORN FOR FIRST TIME a young sheep, usually between six and twelve months old, after its first shearing **2.** TANNED SKIN WITH WOOL ATTACHED the tanned skin of a recently sheared lamb or sheep, with the short wool that remains after shearing still attached

shear mod·u·lus *n.* the ratio of the shear stress to the shear strain, taken as an indication of the strength of a material under shear forces

shear pin *n.* a pin inserted in a machine as a safety device. If safe loads are exceeded, the pin breaks and the machine shuts down.

shear strain *n.* the angular deformation of a body, quantitatively taken to be the sideways displacement of two adjacent planes divided by the distance between them

shear stress *n.* the forces acting on a body that produce shear strain

shear·wa·ter /sheer wáwtər, -wòttər/ (*plural* **-ters** *or* **-ter**) *n.* a long-winged dark-colored sea bird with a short hooked bill. It flies low over the water in search of food. Genus: *Puffinus*. [From the impression given when the bird flies that its wings are shearing the water]

sheath /sheeth/ *n.* (*plural* **sheaths** /sheethz, sheeths/) **1.** CASE FOR A BLADE a case for the blade of a knife, sword, or other cutting implement **2.** CLOSE-FITTING COVERING a covering or case that fits closely around something in the way that a sheath covers a blade **3.** CLOSELY FITTING DRESS a woman's closely fitting dress, originally floor-length, but now also knee-length **4.** *U.K.* = **condom 5.** BIOL PROTECTIVE TUBE a tubular covering that protects some body parts and plant parts, e.g., certain nerves and blood vessels in animals or leaf stems in some grasses ■ *vt.* = **sheathe** [Old English *scǣð*. Ultimately from a prehistoric Germanic word that probably meant "to divide, split" (ancestor also of *shed*[1]), the underlying idea being of something split open.]

sheath·bill /shéeth bil/ *n.* a squat shore bird with a horny sheath on its face, around the bill. It is a gregarious scavenger native to rocky antarctic and subantarctic coasts. Latin name: *Chionis alba* and *Chionis minor*.

sheathe /sheeth/ **(sheathed, sheath·ing, sheathes), sheath** /sheeth/ **(sheathed, sheath·ing, sheaths)** *vt.* **1.** PUT INTO A SHEATH to put a knife, sword, or other cutting implement into a sheath **2.** ENCLOSE WITH A COVERING OR CASE to enclose something in a protective covering or case **3.** RETRACT to retract the claws, in the way a cat does **4.** THRUST INTO FLESH to thrust a knife or sword into somebody's flesh (*literary*) [14thC. Formed from SHEATH.]

sheath·ing /shéething/ *n.* something that encloses and protects, e.g., a covering of boards on a building's framework or a protective material applied to the underwater surfaces of a boat's hull

sheath knife *n.* a knife with a fixed blade that is carried in a sheath

shea tree /shée-, sháy-/, **shea** *n.* a tropical West African tree with seeds from which shea butter is obtained. Latin name: *Vitellaria paradoxa* and *Butytrospermum parkii*.

sheave[1] /sheev/ **(sheaved, sheav·ing, sheaves), sheaf** /sheef/ **(sheafed, sheafing, sheafs)** *vt.* to gather something, especially the cut stalks of a cereal crop, into a sheaf [Late 16thC. Back-formation from SHEAVES.]

sheave[2] /sheev/ *n.* a wheel with a grooved rim for a rope, cable, or belt, especially one used as a pulley [13thC. Ultimately from a prehistoric Germanic word meaning "disk, slice of bread."]

sheaves plural of **sheaf**

She·ba /shéebə/ ancient kingdom of southwestern Arabia, in present-day Yemen. It reached the height of its wealth and power in the 8th century B.C. In the Bible, it is the meeting place of Solomon and the Queen of Sheba (1 Kings 10:1–13).

she·bang /shə báng/ [Mid-19thC. Origin uncertain: perhaps a variant of SHEBEEN. Originally used for "hut, shed."] ◇ **the whole shebang** the whole of something (*informal*)

She·bat *n.* CALENDAR, JUDAISM = **Shevat**

she·been /shə béen/ *n.* a small establishment that sells alcoholic beverages illegally or without a license, traditionally operating in the poorer regions of Ireland, Scotland, and South Africa [Late 18thC. From Irish *síbín*, literally "little mug," from *séibe* "mug."]

She·chi·na /shə kheénə, -kéenə, -kínə/, **She·chi·nah, She·khi·nah** *n.* in Jewish theology, God's presence in and throughout the world [Mid-17thC. From late Hebrew *šěḵīnāh*, from *šākan* "to rest, dwell."]

she·chi·ta /shə kheétə/, **sche·chi·ta** *n.* the prescribed method of slaughter of animals and birds under Jewish dietary laws. The act is performed by a trained and licensed slaughterer (**shochet**) who draws a very sharp knife across the animal's throat and allows the blood to drain out. [Late 19thC. From Hebrew *šěḥīṭāh*, literally "slaughter," from *šāḥaṭ* "to slaughter."]

shed[1] /shed/ *v.* **(shed, shed·ding, sheds) 1.** *vt.* CAUSE TO FLOW to cause tears or blood to pour out **2.** *vt.* RADIATE to radiate or disperse something, especially light **3.** *vt.* GET RID OF to get rid of somebody or something that is unwanted or unnecessary **4.** *vti.* REPEL OR BE REPELLED to flow off or drop off, or cause something, especially water, to flow off or drop off **5.** *vt. U.K.* LOSE ACCIDENTALLY to have a transported load accidentally fall off onto the road **6.** *vt. Scotland* PART HAIR to part the hair ■ *n. Scotland* DIVISION IN HAIR a part in the hair [Old English *scēadan* "to divide, separate." Ultimately from a prehistoric Germanic word that is also the ancestor of English *ski* and, probably, *sheath.*]

shed[2] /shed/ *n.* **1. SMALL BUILDING** a small structure, either free-standing or attached to a larger building, used especially for storage or shelter **2. LARGE OPEN BUILDING** a large building with an open interior, used for storage or shelter or as a work area. Some sides often have no walls. [15thC. Origin uncertain: probably a variant of SHADE.]

she'd /sheed/ *contr.* a short form of "she had" or "she would"

Shed dormer

shed dor·mer *n.* a dormer with a flat roof that slopes in the same direction as the main roof that surrounds it

she-dev·il *n.* a woman who is perceived as treating people with cruelty or contempt

Sheel·er /sheélər/, **Charles** (1883–1965) U.S. painter and photographer. He is known for his precisionist images of urban and rural structures.

sheen /sheen/ *n.* **1. GLOSSY APPEARANCE** a bright, softly shining surface or appearance **2. FINE CLOTHING** fine or brightly colored clothing (*literary*) ■ *vi.* **(sheened, sheen·ing, sheens)** *U.K.* **SHINE** to have a sheen (*regional*) [14thC. From earlier *sheen* "beautiful," via Old English *scēne* from a prehistoric Germanic word meaning "to see" (ancestor of English *show*).] —**shee·ny** *adj.*

shee·ny /sheénee/ (*plural* **-nies**) *n.* a highly offensive term for a Jewish person (*dated or offensive*)

Sheep

sheep /sheep/ (*plural* **sheep**) *n.* **1. MAMMAL RAISED FOR WOOL AND MEAT** a stocky hooved mammal with ribbed horns that is raised for its wool and meat. Genus: *Ovis.* **2. LEATHER FROM SHEEP** leather made from the skin of a sheep **3. SUBMISSIVE PERSON** somebody who is timid, submits readily to others, or is easily led [Old English *scēap.* Ultimately from a prehistoric Germanic word perhaps meaning "to make," in which case the underlying idea is "something made or created."]

sheep·ber·ry /sheep bèrree/ (*plural* **-ries**) *n.* a North American shrub or tree of the honeysuckle family that has white flower clusters and edible black berries. Latin name: *Viburnum lentago.* [*Sheep* from the berry's supposed resemblance to a sheep-dropping]

sheep-dip *n.* **1. DISINFECTANT FOR SHEEP** a disinfectant in which sheep are immersed to rid them of external parasites such as mites, ticks, and flies **2. BATH CONTAINING SHEEP-DIP** a bath containing a disinfectant in which sheep are immersed to rid them of external parasites

sheep·dog /sheép dáwg/ *n.* a dog that is used to herd sheep, or one of a type traditionally bred to herd sheep

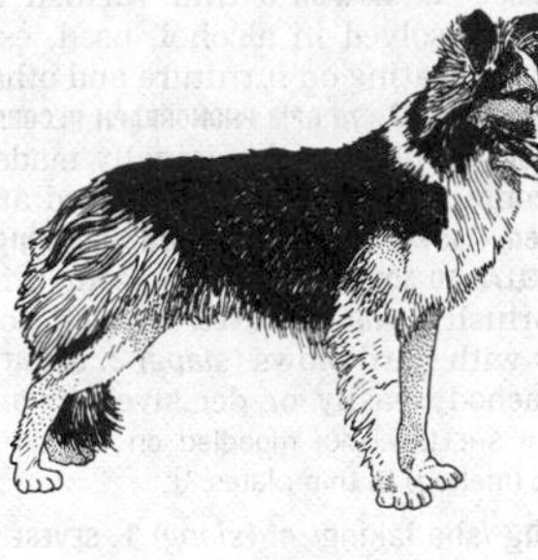

Sheepdog

sheep·fold /sheép fōld/ *n.* an enclosure or shelter for sheep

sheep·herd·er /sheép hùrdər/ *n.* somebody who herds and guards sheep, especially a large flock of sheep on the open range

sheep·ish /sheépish/ *adj.* **1. EMBARRASSED** showing embarrassment as a result of having done something awkward or wrong **2. TIMID** showing the meekness popularly associated with sheep —**sheep·ish·ly** *adv.* —**sheep·ish·ness** *n.*

sheep ked /sheép kèd/ *n.* = **sheep tick** [*Ked* "sheep tick" of unknown origin]

sheep lau·rel *n.* a low-growing evergreen shrub of the heath family that is native to the eastern United States and Canada and is poisonous to young grazing animals. Latin name: *Kalmia angustifolia.*

sheep's eyes *npl.* shy glances full of love and longing [From the large size and the docile appearance of the eyes of sheep]

sheep·shank /sheép shàngk/ *n.* a knot used to shorten a rope in which the rope is doubled up upon itself

sheep·skin /sheép skìn/ *n.* **1. SHEEP LEATHER WITH OR WITHOUT WOOL** the skin of a sheep used as leather, with or without the wool still attached (*often used before a noun*) **2. SHEEPSKIN GARMENT OR RUG** a rug or a garment, especially a coat or jacket, made from sheepskin with the wool attached **3. PARCHMENT** a parchment made from the skin of a sheep (*often used before a noun*) **4. DIPLOMA** a diploma, traditionally made of sheepskin parchment (*informal*)

sheep tick *n.* a wingless fly that lives as a blood-sucking parasite on sheep and can cause serious skin irritations. Latin name: *Melophagus ovinus.*

sheer[1] /sheer/ *adj.* **1. COMPLETE AND UTTER** used to emphasize the unlimited extent or unmitigated quality of something ○ *That explanation is sheer nonsense.* **2. EXCLUSIVE OF ANYTHING ELSE** considered by itself without reference to anything else, or acting by itself without help from anything else ○ *She won the race by sheer endurance.* **3. PURE OR UNADULTERATED** free from any impurities, or not mixed with anything else **4. VERTICAL** rising nearly straight up or falling nearly straight down over a long distance ○ *They looked over the edge and there was a sheer drop.* **5. THIN AND ALMOST TRANSPARENT** so thin and fine as to be almost transparent ○ *a sheer summer blouse* ■ *adv.* **1. VERTICALLY** with an almost vertical rise or fall **2. COMPLETELY** completely and utterly ■ *n.* **NEARLY TRANSPARENT FABRIC** a fabric or piece of clothing that is very thin and fine and almost transparent [Mid-16thC. Origin uncertain: perhaps from Old English *scīr* "bright, shining" from, ultimately, a prehistoric Germanic base that is also the ancestor of English *shimmer.*] —**sheer·ly** *adv.* —**sheer·ness** *n.*

sheer[2] /sheer/ *vti.* **(sheered, sheer·ing, sheers) SWERVE FROM A COURSE** to swerve from a course, or cause a vehicle or vessel to swerve from its course ■ *n.* **1. CHANGE OF COURSE** an abrupt or sudden change of course **2.** NAUT **POSITION OF SHIP AT ANCHOR** the position of a ship in relation to its anchor [Early 17thC. Origin uncertain: perhaps from Low German *scheren.*]

sheer[3] /sheer/ *n.* the upward curve of a boat's hull as seen from the side, or the degree to which the hull curves upward [Late 17thC. Origin uncertain: perhaps from SHEAR.]

sheer·legs /sheér lègz/, **shear·legs** *n.* a lifting device consisting of two poles tied together at the top and spread apart at the bottom with a pulley suspended from the apex (*takes a singular or plural verb*)

sheet[1] /sheet/ *n.* **1.** HOUSEHOLD **CLOTH USED ON BED** a large rectangular piece of cloth that is used to cover the mattress of a bed or somebody sleeping on the mattress **2. FLAT THIN RECTANGULAR PIECE** a broad flat thin piece of a material, especially a rectangular piece of paper, metal, or glass **3. BROAD THIN EXPANSE** a broad flat thin expanse of a substance, especially ice or water **4. EXPANSE OF SOMETHING MOVING** a broad expanse of something that is in motion, e.g., falling water **5.** COOK **FLAT BAKING PAN** a large flat metal rectangle with very shallow sides or none at all, used for baking **6.** STAMPS **PAGE OF STAMPS** an entire rectangular page of postage stamps that were printed as a unit **7.** PUBL **NEWSPAPER** a newspaper or periodical, especially one dismissed as trivial ■ *v.* **(sheet·ed, sheet·ing, sheets) 1.** *vt.* **PUT A SHEET OVER** to cover or wrap something in a sheet **2.** *vt.* **COVER WITH THIN LAYER** to cover something with a thin layer of a material **3.** *vt.* **MAKE INTO FLAT THIN PIECES** to form something, especially metal, into broad flat thin pieces **4.** *vi.* **FALL OVER BROAD EXPANSE** to fall, flow, or spread out over a broad area ■ *adj.* **1. BROAD, FLAT, AND THIN** made in broad, flat, thin, usually rectangular pieces **2. COVERING THINLY** covering a broad area thinly [Old English *scēte* "cloth." Ultimately from a prehistoric Germanic word meaning "to project" (ancestor also of English *shoot, shout,* and *scuttle*).]

sheet[2] /sheet/ *n.* **ROPE FOR CHANGING SAIL'S POSITION** a rope or line attached to a bottom corner of a sail and used to change the sail's position ■ **sheets** *npl.* **SPACES AT BOW AND STERN** the spaces in the bow and stern of an open boat that are not occupied by the seats [Old English *scēata* "corner; lower part of a sail"]

sheet an·chor *n.* **1. LARGE EMERGENCY ANCHOR** a large anchor that is dropped only in emergencies **2. HELP IN EMERGENCY** somebody who or something that is relied on for help in a time of crisis or danger [*Sheet* of unknown origin: perhaps influenced by SHEET[2]]

sheet·ing /sheéting/ *n.* **1. CLOTH FOR SHEETS** wide cotton or linen cloth used primarily for making bedsheets **2. THIN MATERIAL FOR COVERING** thin material used for covering or lining the surface of something

sheet light·ning *n.* lightning that appears in a broad sheet as a result of being diffused by cloud cover

sheet met·al *n.* metal that has been formed into a sheet by being pressed between rollers until it is thinner than plate but thicker than foil

sheet mu·sic *n.* music printed on folded or unfolded sheets of paper that have not been bound into a book

Sheet·rock /sheét ròk/ *tdmk.* a trademark for a type of plasterboard

she·getz /sháygəts/ (*plural* **shkotz·im** /shkáwtsim/), **shey·getz** (*plural* **shkotz·im**) *n.* an offensive Jewish term for a boy or man who is not Jewish (*taboo insult*) [Early 20thC. Via Yiddish *sheygets* from Hebrew *šeqeṣ* "abomination, detested thing."]

sheik /sheek, shayk/, **sheikh, shaikh** *n.* **1. ARAB CHIEF** the leader of an Arab tribe or village **2.** ISLAM **ISLAMIC RELIGIOUS LEADER** a senior official in an Islamic religious organization **3. PHYSICALLY APPEALING MAN** a handsome and physically appealing man (*dated informal*) [Late 16thC. From, ultimately, Arabic *šayḵ,* literally "old man," from *šāḵa* "to be old."]

shei·ka /sháy kaa/, **shei·kha, shai·kha** *n.* the wife of a sheik [Mid-19thC. From Arabic *šayḵa.*]

sheik·dom /sheékdəm, sháyk-/, **sheikh·dom, shaikh·dom** /sháydəm, shīk-/ *n.* a territory ruled by an Islamic religious leader. The emirates of the United Arab Emirates are sheikdoms.

sheikh *n.* = **sheik**

shei·kha *n.* = **sheika**

sheikh·dom *n.* = **sheikdom**

shei·la /sheélə/ *n.* *ANZ* a woman, especially a girl or young woman (*informal*) [Mid-19thC. Origin uncertain: perhaps from *Sheila,* female name.]

shek·el /shék'l/ *n.* **1. ISRAELI CURRENCY UNIT** the main unit of currency of the modern state of Israel, worth 100 agorot. See table at **currency 2. COIN WORTH A SHEKEL** a coin worth one shekel **3. ANCIENT JEWISH UNIT OF WEIGHT** an ancient Jewish unit of weight equivalent to approximately .5 oz/16g **4. ANCIENT JEWISH COIN** an ancient Jewish coin that was a unit of currency between 66 A.D. and 130 A.D. ■ **shek·els** *npl.* **MONEY** money or cash (*slang*) [Mid-16thC. From Hebrew *šeqel,* from *šaqal* "to weigh."]

shel·drake /shél dràyk/ (*plural* **-drakes** *or* **-drake**) *n.* **1.** LARGE EUROPEAN DUCK a large thick-set often brightly colored or variegated European duck with a thick bill. Genus: *Tadorna.* **2.** = **merganser** [14thC. Origin uncertain: perhaps from earlier *sheld* "variegated" + DRAKE.]

shelf /shelf/ (*plural* **shelves** /shelvz/) *n.* **1.** FLAT SURFACE FOR HOLDING OBJECTS a flat usually rectangular board on which things are stored or displayed. It can be attached to a wall or can form part of a cabinet. **2.** CONTENTS OF SHELF the contents of a shelf, or the quantity of something that a shelf holds **3.** GEOG LEDGE ON THE LANDSCAPE a ledge of rock, ice, or sand **4.** MINING LAYER OF UNDERGROUND ROCK a layer of underground rock encountered when sinking a shaft **5.** ARCHERY HEEL OF HAND the part of the heel of the hand on which the back end of an arrow is supported before being fired from a bow [14thC. From Low German *Schelf* "shelf, shelves," of uncertain origin: perhaps, ultimately, from a prehistoric Germanic word meaning "to split," the underlying idea being "split piece of wood."] —**shelf·ful** *n.* ◇ **be (left) on the shelf 1.** to be thought too old to have any chance of marrying (*insult*) **2.** to be no longer wanted, used, or taken account of

shelf ice *n.* a large plate of floating ice that has broken off from an ice shelf

shelf life *n.* **1.** STORAGE TIME OF PRODUCT the length of time a product may be stored before it begins to lose its freshness or effectiveness **2.** PERIOD OF POPULARITY the length of time that somebody or something is popular or lasts (*informal*)

shell /shel/ *n.* **1.** ZOOL COVERING OF TURTLE OR CRAB the hard protective outer covering of turtles, crabs, and other mollusks and crustaceans, or the calcium-based material this covering is made of **2.** INSECTS COVERING OF INSECT'S BODY the hard outer covering (**exoskeleton**) of an insect's body **3.** ZOOL COVERING OF EGG the hard or tough protective outer covering of the eggs of birds, reptiles, and a few mammals **4.** BIOL NUT'S OUTER COVERING the hard or fibrous protective outer covering of some seeds and fruits such as nuts **5.** PROTECTIVE CASING any hard casing or covering that protects or holds its contents, or the material composing it **6.** CONSTR FRAMEWORK OF BUILDING the basic framework of a building, especially while under construction or after damage by fire **7.** SHIPPING SHIP'S HULL the outer hull of a ship **8.** COOK PASTRY CASE a casing of pastry that has a filling put into it **9.** HOLLOW OR EMPTY THING an external form that contains nothing ○ *a mere shell of her former self* **10.** RESERVED MANNER a reserved manner behind which a shy person hides feelings or thoughts ○ *eventually came out of her shell and joined in* **11.** ARMS LARGE EXPLOSIVE PROJECTILE an explosive projectile fired from a large-bore gun such as a field gun or tank gun **12.** ARMS GUN CARTRIDGE a piece of ammunition fired by a gun, especially a shotgun cartridge, which holds the shot and explosive powder **13.** INDUST FIREWORK CARTRIDGE the cartridge that forms the outside of a firework and contains the explosive powder **14.** HOUSEHOLD SMALL GLASS a small beer glass **15.** CLOTHES UNLINED JACKET an unlined usually lightweight jacket **16.** CLOTHES SLEEVELESS BLOUSE a sleeveless blouse or sweater for a woman **17.** BUSINESS = **shell company 18.** ROWING NARROW RACING BOAT a narrow light boat used for racing, rowed by one or more persons **19.** PHYS GROUP OF ELECTRONS IN SIMILAR ORBITS a group of electrons orbiting the nucleus of an atom and having the same principal quantum number **20.** COMPUT COMMAND PROGRAM a computer program that simplifies the interface between a user and the operating system by allowing the user to pick from a set of menus instead of entering commands ■ *v.* (**shelled, shell·ing, shells**) **1.** *vti.* TAKE SOMETHING OUT OF A SHELL to take something out of a shell, or be taken out of a shell ○ *shell peas* **2.** *vti.* SEPARATE KERNELS FROM A COB to separate kernels from a cob, or be separated from a cob ○ *shell sweet corn* **3.** *vti.* MIL BOMBARD TARGET to fire artillery shells at something **4.** *vi.* FLAKE OFF to fall off in thin scales **5.** *vi.* COLLECT SEASHELLS to look for and gather shells at the seashore **6.** *vt.* BASEBALL MAKE MANY HITS AGAINST to make many hits against an opposing pitcher in baseball and score many runs [Old English *scell*, originally "something that splits off"]

shell out *vti.* to pay out money, especially a great deal of money (*informal*)

she'll /sheel/ *contr.* a short form of "she will" or "she shall"

shel·lac /shə lák/, **shel·lack** *n.* **1.** PURIFIED RESIN yellowish-orange flakes of a resin (**lac**) secreted by a tropical insect **2.** VARNISH a thin varnish made of purified lac dissolved in alcohol, used, especially formerly, as a coating on furniture and other items made from wood **3.** 78 RPM PHONOGRAPH RECORD an old type of phonograph record originally made from a material containing purified lac, played at 78 rpm ■ *vt.* (**-lacked, -lack·ing, -lacs; -lacked, -lack·ing, -lacks**) **1.** APPLY SHELLAC TO SOMETHING to coat something with shellac varnish **2.** HIT REPEATEDLY to beat somebody repeatedly with hard blows (*slang*) **3.** DEFEAT EASILY to defeat somebody easily or decisively (*slang*) [Mid-17thC. From SHELL + LAC, modeled on French *laque en écailles* "lac (melted) in thin plates."]

shel·lack·ing /shə láking/ *n.* (*slang*) **1.** SEVERE BEATING a severe physical beating **2.** DECISIVE DEFEAT an easy or decisive defeat

shell·back /shél bàk/ *n.* **1.** SAILOR WHO HAS CROSSED EQUATOR a sailor who has crossed the equator, especially one whose crossing was marked by a traditional initiation ceremony **2.** EXPERIENCED SAILOR an old or experienced sailor [From the idea that limpets and barnacles have grown on the sailor's back during the long time at sea]

shell·bark /shél baárk/ *n.* = **shagbark** *n.* 1

shell bean *n.* **1.** BEAN GROWN FOR SEEDS a bean plant that is grown for its seeds not its pods **2.** SEED OF A SHELL BEAN PLANT a seed of a shell bean plant, used as food

shell com·pa·ny *n.* a company that has no independent assets or operations of its own but is used by its owners to conduct certain business dealings or maintain control of other companies

Mary Shelley

Shel·ley /shéllee/, **Mary** (1797–1851) British writer. Her most famous work is *Frankenstein* (1818). She was the daughter of Mary Wollstonecraft and the wife of Percy Bysshe Shelley. Born **Mary Wollstonecraft Godwin**

Shel·ley, Percy Bysshe (1792–1822) British poet. His lyric poetry was at the forefront of the English romantic movement, and included odes such as "To a Skylark" (1820) and an elegy on Keats, "Adonais" (1821). He was the husband of Mary Shelley.

shell·fire /shél fìr/ *n.* **1.** FIRED ARTILLERY SHELLS artillery shells or projectiles fired at a target **2.** FIRING OF ARTILLERY SHELLS the firing or exploding of artillery shells or projectiles

shell·fish /shél fish/ (*plural* **-fish** *or* **-fish·es**) *n.* an aquatic invertebrate animal with a shell, especially an edible mollusk or crustacean such as an oyster, shrimp, or lobster

shell game *n.* **1.** GAMBLING GAME a form of the game thimblerig in which spectators bet on the final location of an object hidden under one of three walnut shells or cups that have been shuffled **2.** FRAUDULENT SCHEME a scheme for defrauding or deceiving people

shell jack·et *n.* a tight-fitting military jacket that extends only to the waist and is worn on semiformal occasions

shell pink *adj.* of a delicate pale pink color (*hyphenated when used before a noun*) —**shell pink** *n.*

shell shock *n.* a psychiatric disorder caused by exposure to warfare, especially shellfire (*dated*)

shell-shocked *adj.* **1.** STUNNED OR EXHAUSTED stunned, upset, or exhausted as a result of a stressful experience (*informal*) **2.** AFFECTED BY BATTLE FATIGUE experiencing severe psychological effects from exposure to warfare, especially shellfire

shell steak *n.* a cut of steak from the short loin area

shell·work /shèl wúrk/ *n.* seashells stuck on furniture and other items to give a decorative finish

Shel·ta /shéltə/ *n.* an ancient secret language used by Romany and other traveling people in Ireland and the United Kingdom. It is based on Gaelic with consonants systematically inverted or changed. [Late 19thC. Origin uncertain: perhaps an alteration of Old Irish *bélre* "language."]

shel·ter /shéltər/ *n.* **1.** STRUCTURE THAT PROTECTS OR COVERS a structure or building that provides cover from weather or protection against danger **2.** REFUGE an establishment providing accommodations and food for people who need to leave a violent or otherwise dangerous situation **3.** REFUGE FOR ANIMALS an establishment that takes in and looks after lost or unwanted animals **4.** PROTECTION OR COVER the protection, cover, refuge, or safety that a shelter provides **5.** DWELLING OR HOUSING a place to live, considered as one of life's necessities ■ *v.* (**-tered, -ter·ing, -ters**) **1.** *vt.* PROVIDE WITH PROTECTION to provide somebody or something with protection, cover, refuge, or safety **2.** *vi.* FIND PROTECTION to find protection, cover, refuge, or safety **3.** *vt.* FIN INVEST TO AVOID TAXES to put money into an investment that is subject to a lower tax rate or is free from taxes [Late 16thC. Origin uncertain: perhaps an alteration of earlier *sheltron* "troops protected by shields," from Old English *scieldtruma*, from *scield* "shield" + *truma* "troop."]

shel·tered /shéltərd/ *adj.* **1.** PROTECTED FROM ELEMENTS protected from the adverse effects of the weather, especially wind **2.** NOT EXPOSED TO RIGORS OF LIFE protected from the unpleasant, upsetting, or testing experiences of life

shel·tered work·shop *n.* a workplace specially designed to provide a noncompetitive environment where people who have various limitations can acquire job skills and experience

shel·ter tent *n.* a small tent for two people usually made from two similar pieces of waterproof fabric

shel·tie /shéltee/, **shel·ty** (*plural* **-ties**) *n.* a Shetland pony or a Shetland sheepdog (*informal*) [Early 16thC. Origin uncertain: probably via Orkney dialect from Old Norse *Hjalti* "Shetlander."]

shelve[1] /shelv/ (**shelved, shelv·ing, shelves**) *vt.* **1.** PUT ON SHELF to put or store something on a shelf **2.** SET ASIDE to put something off until later, or set something aside **3.** DISMISS to dismiss or withdraw somebody or something from active service [Late 16thC. Back-formation from SHELVES.]

shelve[2] /shelv/ (**shelved, shelv·ing, shelves**) *vi.* to descend with a flat, usually gradual slope [Late 16thC. Origin uncertain: perhaps from earlier SHELF "grassy bank."]

shelves plural of **shelf**

shelv·ing /shélving/ *n.* **1.** SHELVES the shelves in a place, or shelves in general **2.** MATERIAL FOR SHELVES material used for making shelves

She·ma /shə maá/ *n.* the confession of faith made in Jewish religious practice [Early 18thC. From Hebrew *šěma*, from the Bible (Deuteronomy 6:4), literally "Hear!".]

Shen·an·do·ah Na·tion·al Park /shénnən dō ə-/ national park in the Blue Ridge Mountains of northern Virginia, established in 1935. Area: 304 sq. mi./788 sq. km.

Shen·an·do·ah Val·ley valley of the Shenandoah River in Virginia, between the Allegheny and Blue Ridge mountains, southwest of Harpers Ferry. Length: 140 mi./225 km.

she·nan·i·gan /shə nánnigən/ *n.* (*informal*) **1.** QUESTIONABLE ACT something that is deceitful, underhanded, or otherwise questionable (*usually used in the plural*) **2.** TRICK OR PRANK a playful trick, mischievous prank, or other display of high spirits [Mid-19thC. Origin uncertain: perhaps from Spanish *chanada* "trick, deceit," contraction of *charranada*.]

Shen·yang /shèn yúng/ city in Liaoning Province, northeastern China. Population: 3,860,000 (1993).

She·ol /sheé ōl, shee ól/ *n.* in ancient Hebrew theology, the dwelling place of the dead [Late 16thC. From Hebrew *šĕ'ōl*.]

Shep·ard /shéppərd/, **Alan, Jr.** (1923–98) U.S. astronaut. He was the first U.S. astronaut in space (May 5, 1961) and the fifth person to walk on the Moon (1971). Full name **Alan Bartlett Shepard, Jr.**

Shep·ard, Sam (*b.* 1943) U.S. playwright and actor. His offbeat plays include the Pulitzer Prize-winning

Buried Child (1978). Full name **Samuel Shepard Rogers, Jr.**

shep·herd /shéppərd/ *n.* **1.** **SOMEBODY TENDING SHEEP** somebody who looks after sheep **2.** **SOMEBODY PROVIDING GUIDANCE** somebody who is responsible for caring for and guiding a group of people, especially a Christian minister ■ *v.* (**-herd·ed, -herd·ing, -herds**) **1.** *vti.* **TEND SHEEP** to look after sheep **2.** *vt.* **GUIDE** to guide a group of people somewhere **3.** *vt.* **TAKE CARE OF OTHERS** to look after the well-being of a group of people [Old English *scēaphirde*, from *scēap* (see SHEEP) + *hierde* "herder"]

shep·herd·ess /shéppərdəss/ *n.* a girl or woman who looks after sheep (*dated*)

shep·herd's check *n.* (*often used before a noun*) **1.** **PATTERN OF SQUARES** a pattern of small black and white squares **2.** **SHEPHERD'S CHECK FABRIC** a fabric in a shepherd's check pattern

shep·herd's pie *n.* a baked dish made of cooked ground meat, traditionally lamb or mutton, in gravy with a topping of mashed potato

shep·herd's plaid *n.* = **shepherd's check** (*often used before a noun*)

shep·herd's purse *n.* an annual plant of the mustard family that has white flowers and heart-shaped seed pods and is commonly found as a weed in gardens. Latin name: *Capsella bursa-pastoris.* [From the pod's resemblance to a bag used by shepherds to carry food]

Shep·par·ton /shéppərtən/ city in northern Victoria, Australia. It is an industrial, agricultural, and food processing center. Population: 30,510 (1991).

Popperfoto

Sheraton

Sher·a·ton /shérrət'n/ *adj.* relating to furniture designed by or in the graceful simple style of Thomas Sheraton, who favored straight lines, understated classical ornamentation, and light thin legs

Sher·a·ton /shérrət'n/, **Thomas** (1751–1806) British cabinetmaker. He wrote *The Cabinet-Maker and Upholsterer's Drawing Book* (1793–94), which was influential in formulating the neoclassical style in English furniture.

sher·bet /shúrbət/ *n.* **1.** **sher·bet, sher·bert** **FROZEN DESSERT** a frozen dessert made with fruit syrup, milk and the white of an egg, whisked until smooth and opaque **2.** *U.K.* **FIZZY POWDER** a fruit-flavored sweet powder that fizzes when moistened on the tongue and is eaten as a confection or is stirred into water to make a fizzy drink (*often used before a noun*) **3.** *U.K.* **FRUIT DRINK** a drink made from fruit juice, water, and sugar and served chilled **4.** **sher·bet, sher·bert** *U.K., Aus* **BEER** beer (*dated humorous slang*) [Early 17thC. Via Turkish *şerbet* and Persian *šerbet* from Arabic *šarbat* "drink," from *šariba* "to drink" (source of English *syrup*).]

Sher·brooke /shúr brŏŏk/ city situated south of the St. Lawrence River in Quebec, Canada, 100 mi./160 km east of Montreal. Population: 76,429 (1991).

sherd *n.* = **potsherd**

Sher·i·dan /shérrid'n/, **Richard Brinsley** (1751–1816) Irish-born British playwright. His comedies of manners include *The Rivals* (1775) and *The School for Scandal* (1777). He was a Whig member of Parliament (1780–1812).

she·rif /shə réef/, **sha·rif, she·reef** *n.* **1.** ISLAM **DESCENDANT OF MUHAMMAD** a descendant of the prophet Muhammad through his daughter Fatima **2.** **GOVERNOR OF MECCA** the governor or chief magistrate of Mecca during the years of Ottoman Turkish rule **3.** **ARAB RULER** an Arab prince or ruler [Late 16thC. From Arabic *šarīf*, literally "illustrious."]

sher·iff /shérrif/ *n.* **1.** **U.S. COUNTY LAW ENFORCEMENT OFFICER** in the United States, the chief law enforcement officer for a county, whose duties are sometimes restricted to the enforcement of the orders of the courts **2.** **SENIOR OFFICIAL OF ENGLISH COUNTY** in England and Wales, the senior representative of the monarch in a county, who performs ceremonial and some judicial duties **3.** **SCOTTISH JUDGE** in Scotland, a judge who presides over one of the lower courts for civil and criminal cases **4.** **CANADIAN COURT OFFICER** in Canada, an officer of the courts who assists with the administration of the justice system, e.g., by serving writs **5.** **AUSTRALIAN COURT OFFICIAL** in Australia, a court official charged with managing juries and implementing orders from the Supreme Court [Old English *scīrgerēfa*, literally "reeve of the shire," from *scīr* "shire" + *gerēfa* "reeve"] —**sher·iff·dom** *n.*

AKG London

Cindy Sherman

Sher·man /shúrmən/, **Cindy** (*b.* 1954) U.S. photographer. Her carefully staged and composed photographs, featuring herself in various roles, gained widespread notice in the 1980s.

Sher·man, James S. (1855–1912) U.S. statesman and vice president. He was William Howard Taft's vice president (1909–12). Full name **James Schoolcraft Sherman**

Sher·man, John (1823–1900) U.S. statesman. The brother of General William T. Sherman, he served as secretary of the treasury (1877–81) and secretary of state (1897–98). As a Republican U.S. senator (1861–77, 1881–97), he wrote the Sherman Antitrust Act (1890) and the Sherman Silver Purchase Act (1890).

Sher·man, Roger (1721–93) American patriot. He signed the Declaration of Independence (1776) and represented Connecticut at the Constitutional Convention (1787).

Sher·man, William T. (1820–91) U.S. soldier. A Mexican War veteran, he rejoined the army in 1861 as the Civil War broke out and became one of the Union army's most aggressive and successful generals, marching on Atlanta and then to the sea (1864). Full name **William Tecumseh Sherman**

Sher·pa (*plural* **-pas** *or* **-pa**) *n.* **1.** PEOPLES **MEMBER OF HIMALAYAN MOUNTAIN PEOPLE** a member of a people originally from Tibet who live on the southern Himalayan slopes in Nepal and Sikkim. Sherpas are noted for their mountaineering skills. **2.** **Sher·pa, sher·pa** MOUNTAINEERING **HIMALAYAN MOUNTAIN GUIDE** a Sherpa who works as a guide for mountaineers in the Himalayas **3.** **Sher·pa, sher·pa** POL **EXPERT POLITICAL AIDE** an expert who helps a government leader prepare for a summit meeting [Mid-19thC. From Tibetan *sharpa* "inhabitant of an eastern country."]

sher·ry /shérree/ (*plural* **-ries**) *n.* a wine, especially one made near Jerez, Spain, that has a higher alcohol content as a result of adding brandy, and ranges from very sweet to very dry [Late 16thC. Alteration of earlier *sherris*, interpreted as plural, named for *Xeres* (now Jerez), Spain, where the wine was produced.]

Sher·wood /shúrwŏŏd/, **Robert E.** (1896–1955) U.S. playwright. His Pulitzer Prize-winning plays include *Idiot's Delight* (1936). Full name **Robert Emmet Sherwood**

she's /sheez/ *contr.* a short form of "she is" or "she has"

Shet·land /shétlənd/ *n.* **1.** ZOOL = **Shetland sheepdog** **2.** TEXTILES = **Shetland wool** **3.** CLOTHES **GARMENT OF SHETLAND WOOL** an item of clothing made of Shetland wool, especially a sweater ■ *adj.* **MADE OF SHETLAND WOOL** made of Shetland wool

Shet·land Is·lands /shét lənd-/ group of about 150 islands lying 130 mi./209 km north of mainland Scotland. The islands serve as a base for the North Sea oil industry. Mainland is the chief island. Capital: Lerwick. Population: 23,232 (1996). Area: 555 sq. mi./1,438 sq. km. —**Shet·land·er** *n.*

Shetland pony

Shet·land po·ny *n.* a small sturdy pony with a long shaggy mane and tail, belonging to a breed that originated in Shetland

Shet·land sheep·dog *n.* a small herding dog with a heavy coat that resembles a collie, belonging to a breed that originated in Shetland

Shet·land wool *n.* fine wool from sheep raised in Shetland, or a yarn spun from this wool

Shev·ard·na·dze /shèvvərd naádzə/, **Eduard** (*b.* 1928) Georgian statesman. As foreign minister (1985–90, 1991) during the last years of the Soviet Union, he helped to implement democratic reforms in East European countries and cultivate warmer relations with the West. After his native Georgia became an independent republic, he became its head of state (1992). Full name **Eduard Amvrosiyevich Shevardnadze**

She·vat /shə vót/, **She·bat** /-bót, -vót/ *n.* JUDAISM, CALENDAR the eleventh month of the Jewish religious calendar, covering part of January and February [Mid-16thC. From Hebrew *šĕbāṭ*.]

shew /shō/ (**shewed, shewed** *or* **shewn** /shōn/, **shew·ing, shews**) *vti.* to show (*archaic*) [Variant spelling]

shew·bread /shṓ brèd/ *n.* in the Bible, the twelve loaves of bread placed in the tabernacle every Sabbath by the Hebrew priests of ancient Israel (*archaic*)

shey·gets *n.* = **shegetz** (*taboo insult*)

SHF, **shf** *abbr.* superhigh frequency

Shi·a /shée ə/, **Shi·'a, Shi·'ah** *n.* (*plural* **-a** *or* **-as**; *plural* **-'a** *or* **-'as**; *plural* **-'ah** *or* **-'ahs**) **1.** **MAJOR BRANCH OF ISLAM** the branch of Islam that considers Ali, the cousin of Muhammad, and his descendants as Muhammad's true successors. ◊ **Sunni** **2.** = **Shiite** *n.* ■ *adj.* = **Shiite** *adj.* [Early 17thC. From Arabic *šī'a* "faction, party" (of Ali, Muhammad's son-in-law and the fourth caliph).]

shi·at·su /shee aát sōō/, **shi·at·zu** *n.* a form of healing massage in which the hands are used to apply pressure at acupuncture points on the body in order to stimulate and redistribute energy. Originating in Japan, it is used to treat various conditions, e.g., back pain, migraine, insomnia, depression, and digestive problems. [Mid-20thC. From Japanese, literally "finger pressure."]

shib·bo·leth /shíbbə lèth/ *n.* **1.** **CATCHWORD OR SLOGAN** a word or phrase frequently used, or a belief strongly held, by members of a group that is usually regarded by outsiders as meaningless, unimportant, or misguided **2.** **COMMON SAYING OR BELIEF** a saying that is widely used or a belief that is widely held, especially one that interferes with somebody's ability to speak or think about things without preconception **3.** **IDENTIFYING WORD OR CUSTOM** a unique pronunciation, word, behavior, or practice used to distinguish one group of people from another and to identify individuals as either members of the group or outsiders [Mid-17thC. From Hebrew *šibbōleṯ* "stream."]

WORD KEY: ORIGIN

According to the Bible, the Gileadites used the word *šibbōleṯ* as a password, for they knew their enemies the Ephraimites could not pronounce the "sh" properly ("And it was so, that when those Ephraimites which were escaped said, Let me go over; that the men of

Gilead said unto him, Art thou an Ephraimite? If he said, Nay, then they said unto him, Say now Shibboleth; and he said Sibboleth: for he could not frame to pronounce it right" (*Judges* 12:5–6).

shid·duch /shíddək/ (*plural* **-duch·im** /shíddəkim/) *n.* a prospective Jewish marriage that was formerly usually arranged by a professional matchmaker (**shadchan**) [Late 19thC. Via Yiddish from Hebrew *šiddūk* "negotiation (of an arranged marriage)."]

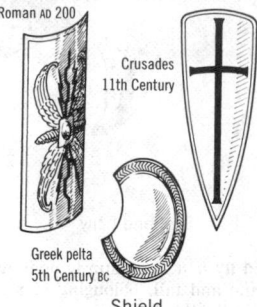

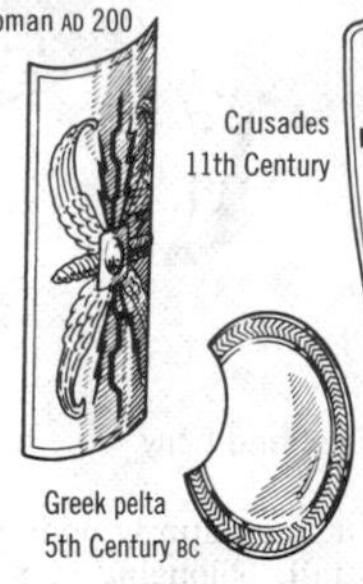

Shield

shield /sheeld/ *n.* **1.** ARMS **PIECE OF ARMOR CARRIED ON ARM** a flat or convex piece of armor carried on the arm and used as a protection against weapon blows, arrows, bullets, or projectiles **2. PROTECTION OR DEFENSE** somebody or something that serves as protection or acts as a defense **3.** HERALDRY **COAT OF ARMS** a shield or a shield-shaped insignia that contains somebody's coat of arms **4. PRIZE OR TROPHY** a prize or trophy, especially in a sports competition, that is made in the shape of a shield **5. DECORATIVE OFFICIAL EMBLEM** a decorative device used as an official emblem by a government or organization, usually containing symbolic images associated with the government's territory or the organization's purpose **6.** PUBLIC ADMIN **U.S. POLICE OFFICER'S BADGE** the official badge that a U.S. law enforcement officer wears or carries **7.** CLOTHES = **dress shield 8.** ARMS **PROTECTIVE PLATE ATTACHED TO ARTILLERY** a steel plate attached to a piece of artillery to protect those operating the artillery from bullets and shrapnel **9.** MECH ENG **MACHINE'S SAFETY BARRIER** a protective barrier such as a screen or housing around the moving parts of a piece of machinery **10.** ELEC ENG **ANTISTATIC OR ANTIMAGNETIC SCREEN** a screen used to protect equipment or persons from unwanted electric or magnetic fields **11.** NUCLEAR PHYS **WALL PROTECTING FROM RADIATION** an encasing structure or wall, usually made of lead or concrete that is put around a nuclear reactor or other source of radiation to prevent the release of radiation **12.** GEOL **FLAT AREA OF ROCK** a broad flat area of exposed Precambrian basement rock that lies at the center of each continent **13.** ZOOL **ANIMAL'S PROTECTIVE COVERING** the protective covering of an animal, e.g., a shell, scale, or plate **14.** BOT = **apothecium** ■ *v.* (**shield·ed, shield·ing, shields**) **1.** *vt.* **PROTECT WITH SHIELD** to defend or protect somebody or something with a shield or by using the body or another object as a shield **2.** *vi.* **ACT AS SHIELD** to serve or act as a protection or defense **3.** *vt.* **HIDE** to conceal or shelter somebody or something from view [Old English *scield.* Ultimately from a prehistoric Germanic word, probably originally used for "board," from a word meaning "to split."] —**shield·er** /sheéldər/ *n.*

WORD KEY: SYNONYMS

See Synonyms at ***safeguard***.

shield·ing /sheélding/ *n.* the use of material such as lead or concrete around a source of radiation to prevent the harmful release of radiation

shield law *n.* in North America, a law that protects a journalist from being forced to reveal the name of a source who provided information confidentially

Shield of Da·vid *n.* = **Star of David**

shiel·ing /sheéling/ *n. Scotland* **1. COWHERD'S MOUNTAIN HUT** a mountain hut used by a cowherd **2. MOUNTAIN PASTURE** a mountain pasture that is used by cattle in the summer [Mid-16thC. Formed from earlier *shiel*, of unknown origin.]

shift /shift/ *v.* (**shift·ed, shift·ing, shifts**) **1.** *vti.* **MOVE** to move somebody or something to a different position, or be moved to a different position **2.** *vti.* **CHANGE OR EXCHANGE** to change or exchange something for something else of the same group, set, or class ○ *I've shifted jobs three times in the last year.* **3.** *vti.* AUTOMOT **CHANGE GEARS** to change gears in a motor vehicle **4.** *vi.* **PROVIDE FOR OWN NEEDS** to provide personal needs or manage personal affairs ○ *You need to learn to shift for yourself.* **5.** *vi.* **GET BY WITH DECEIT** to get by through the use of deceit, tricks, or underhanded methods **6.** *vi.* **PRESS SHIFT KEY** to press the shift key on a computer or typewriter keyboard to produce capital letters and certain other characters **7.** *vti.* LING **ALTER PHONETICALLY** to alter a sound phonetically in the course of the development of a language, or be altered phonetically **8.** *vi.* BASEBALL **CHANGE FIELDING POSITIONS** to change positions on a baseball diamond to respond to a new batter or forestall an expected change of tactics by the opposing team (*refers to fielders*) **9.** *vi. Malaysia, Singapore* **MOVE HOUSE** to move house ○ *We are going to shift to Penang.* ■ *n.* **1. CHANGE MADE** a change in position, direction, makeup, or circumstances **2.** INDUST **PERIOD OF TIME WORKED** a period of working time, especially any of the fixed periods that the day is divided into in workplaces that operate 24 hours a day. There are usually two twelve-hour or three eight-hour shifts. **3. PEOPLE WORKING DURING PERIOD** the group of people who are working during a particular period of time **4. KEY ON COMPUTER KEYBOARD** a key on a computer or typewriter keyboard that is depressed to produce capital letters and certain other characters **5.** CLOTHES **DRESS** a loose-fitting dress that hangs down from the shoulders **6.** CLOTHES **WOMAN'S UNDERGARMENT** a woman's shirt-shaped undergarment of the17th and 18th centuries **7. TRICK** a deceitful or underhanded scheme or plan **8.** BASEBALL **CHANGE IN FIELDERS' POSITION** a change in the positions of the fielders on a baseball diamond to respond to a new batter or forestall an expected change of tactics by the opposing team **9.** FOOTBALL **CHANGE IN PLAYERS' POSITION** a change in the position of a player or players on a football field after the teams have lined up but before the ball is snapped **10.** GEOL **ROCK DISPLACEMENT AT FAULT** a displacement of rocks on a fault line **11.** MUSIC **CHANGE IN HAND POSITION** a change in hand position in order to play a different set of notes in a different register on a keyboard or string instrument **12.** LING **CHANGE IN PRONUNCIATION** a change in the pronunciation of a sound in the course of the development of a language **13.** PHYS **CHANGE IN FREQUENCY** a change in the position of a spectral line representing a change of frequency, e.g., that caused by the Doppler effect [Old English *sciftan* "to divide, arrange." Ultimately from prehistoric Germanic. The main modern meanings evolved from "arrange" via "change."]

WORD KEY: SYNONYMS

See Synonyms at ***change***.

shift key *n.* a key on a computer or typewriter keyboard that is pressed to produce capital letters or certain other characters

shift·less /shíftləss/ *adj.* **1. LACKING AMBITION** unwilling to make the effort to be successful or do something properly **2. INEFFICIENT** lacking the abilities or knowledge required to do something successfully or properly —**shift·less·ly** *adv.* —**shift·less·ness** *n.*

shift·y /shíftee/ (**-i·er, -i·est**) *adj.* **1. UNTRUSTWORTHY** likely to try to deceive or avoid responsibility **2. CHANGING DIRECTION OR POSITION** changing direction or position often or quickly, or able to do so **3. RESOURCEFUL** with the abilities and knowledge needed to do something successfully —**shift·i·ly** *adv.* —**shift·i·ness** *n.*

shi·gel·la /shi géllə/ (*plural* **-lae** /-lee/ *or* **-las**) *n.* a rod-shaped bacterium that lives in the intestinal tracts of human beings and animals and causes dysentery. There are four species, all causing dysentery but with varying degrees of severity. Genus: *Shigella.* [Mid-20thC. From modern Latin *Shigella*, genus name, which was named for Kiyoshi *Shiga* (1870–1957), Japanese bacteriologist who discovered the bacterium.]

shig·el·lo·sis /shìggə lóssəss/ (*plural* **-ses** /-ló seez/) *n.* a highly infectious form of dysentery caused by the shigella bacterium. It occurs mainly in tropical countries, especially under unsanitary conditions and among children and people with weakened immune systems.

shih tzu /sheè tsoó/ (*plural* **shih tzus** *or* **shih tzu**) *n.* a small short-legged dog with a short muzzle, long dense coat, and a tail that curls over its back, belonging to a breed developed in Tibet [Early 20thC. From Chinese *shīzigǒu*, literally "lion dog."]

Shi·ism /sheè ìzzəm/, **Shi·'ism** *n.* = **Shia** *n.* 1 [Late 19thC. Formed from SHIA OR SHIITE.]

shi·i·ta·ke /shi taákee/, **shi·i·ta·ke mush·room** *n.* a dark-colored mushroom with an edible fleshy cap, native to eastern Asia. Latin name: *Lentinus edodes.* [Late 19thC. From Japanese, literally "oak-tree mushroom."]

Shi·ite /sheè ìt/, **Shi·'ite** *n.* **FOLLOWER OF MAJOR BRANCH OF ISLAM** a follower of the Shia branch of Islam, which considers Ali, the cousin of Muhammad, and his descendants as Muhammad's true successors. ◊ **Sunni** ■ *adj.* **OF SHIITES** relating or belonging to Shiites or to the Shia branch of Islam —**Shi·it·ic** /shee íttik/ *adj.*

Shi·jia·zhuang /shèjiè joó ung/ industrial center and capital of Hebei Province, southwest of Beijing, in northeastern China. Population: 1,320,000 (1990).

shi·ka·ri /shi kaáree/, **shi·ka·ree** *n. S Asia* a big-game hunter, especially a professional hunter who works as a guide [Early 19thC. Via Urdu from Persian *šikārī* "of hunting," from *šikār* "hunting."]

shik·sa /shíksə/, **shik·se** *n.* a highly offensive Jewish term for a girl or woman who is not Jewish (*taboo insult*) [Late 19thC. From Yiddish *shikse*, feminine of *sheygets* (see SHEGETZ).]

shill /shil/ *n.* **1. PRETENDED CUSTOMER OR GAMBLER** somebody who pretends to be an interested customer or gambler in order to lure others into buying or gambling **2. SELF-INTERESTED PROMOTER** somebody who promotes somebody or makes a sales pitch for something for reasons of self-interest ■ *v.* (**shilled, shill·ing, shills**) **1.** *vi.* **BE SHILL** to be or work as a shill **2.** *vt.* **PROMOTE AS SHILL** to promote or sell something using the tactics of a shill [Early 20thC. Origin uncertain: perhaps a shortening of the name of Benjamin Penhallow *Shillaber* (1814–90), U.S. humorist who was accused of plagiarism.]

shil·le·lagh /shə láylee, -láylə/, **shil·la·lah** *n. Ireland* a stick or club, traditionally made of oak or blackthorn wood [Late 18thC. Named for *Shillelagh*, town in east-central Ireland famous for oaks.]

shil·ling /shílling/ *n.* **1. FORMER BRITISH COIN** a former British coin and subunit of currency, in use until 1971, that was equivalent to one-twentieth of a pound **2. FORMER U.S. COIN** an old U.S. coin **3. UNIT OF CURRENCY IN EAST AFRICA** a unit of currency in Kenya, Somalia, Tanzania, and Uganda. See table at **currency 4. COIN WORTH A SHILLING** a coin worth a shilling in Kenya, Somalia, Tanzania, or Uganda **5.** *Malaysia, Singapore* **COIN** a coin (*informal*) [Old English *scilling.* Ultimately from a prehistoric Germanic word perhaps meaning "to divide," in which case the underlying idea is "division of a standard unit of weight or currency."]

Shil·long /shi lóng/ capital of Meghalaya State, northeastern India. Population: 132,000 (1991).

Shil·luk /shi loók/ (*plural* **-luk** *or* **-luks**) *n.* **1.** PEOPLES **MEMBER OF NE AFRICAN PEOPLE** a member of a people who live in northeastern Africa, mainly along the western bank of the Nile River in Sudan **2.** LANG **SHILLUK LANGUAGE** the language spoken by the Shilluk, belonging to the Nilo-Saharan family of languages. Shilluk is spoken by about 110,000 people. [Late 18thC. From Shilluk.] —**Shil·luk** *adj.*

shil·ly-shal·ly /shílli shàllee/ *vi.* (**shil·ly-shal·lied, shil·ly-shal·ly·ing, shil·ly-shal·lies**) **1. HESITATE OR VACILLATE** to be unable to make a choice or decision when one is needed **2. WASTE TIME** to waste time on unimportant things ■ *adv.* **IRRESOLUTELY** with hesitation or a lack of decision ■ *adj.* **LACKING DECISIVENESS** feeling or showing a lack of decisiveness ■ *n.* (*plural* **shil·ly-shal·lies**) **HESITATION** a failure or inability to make a choice or decision [Early 18thC. Alteration (perhaps influenced by DILLY-DALLY) of "shall I? shall I?".] —**shil·ly-shal·li·er** *n.*

shim /shim/ *n.* **THIN WEDGE-SHAPED PIECE** a thin usually wedge-shaped piece of wood, metal, plastic, or other material that is used to help position something properly, usually by adjusting a level or filling a gap ■ *vt.* (**shimmed, shim·ming, shims**) **POSITION SOMETHING USING SHIM** to position or adjust something using a shim [Early 18thC. Origin unknown. Originally used for "piece of iron attached to a tool for scraping soil."]

shim·mer /shímmər/ *vti.* (**-mered, -mer·ing, -mers**) **1. SHINE WITH A WAVERING LIGHT** to shine softly with a wavering or flickering light, or cause something to shine in this way **2. BE VISIBLE AS WAVERING IMAGE** to be visible as a wavering or flickering and sometimes distorted image, or make something visible in this way ■ *n.*

1. WAVERING LIGHT OR GLOW a wavering or flickering soft light or glow **2. WAVERING IMAGE OR APPEARANCE** a wavering or flickering and sometimes distorted image, e.g., that caused by hot air rising from the ground [Old English *scymrian*, originally "to shine repeatedly." Ultimately from a prehistoric Germanic word meaning "to shine," which is also the ancestor of English *shine* and *sheer*.] —**shim·mer·y** *adj.*

shim·my /shímmee/ *n.* **1.** AUTOMOT **WOBBLING OF A VEHICLE** a wobbling motion or vibration, especially in the front wheels of a motor vehicle **2.** DANCE **POPULAR 1920S DANCE** a jazz dance, popular in the 1920s in which the body was held straight and shaken rhythmically and rapidly from the shoulders down **3.** CLOTHES **CHEMISE** a chemise (*informal*) ■ *vi.* **(-mied, -my·ing, -mies) 1.** AUTOMOT **WOBBLE** to wobble or be shaken with a wobbling motion, especially in the front wheels (*refers to vehicles*) **2.** DANCE **DANCE THE SHIMMY** to dance the shimmy **3. MOVE SHAKINGLY** to move the body in shaking or swaying way [Early 20thC. Origin unknown.]

shin[1] /shin/ *n.* **1.** ANAT **FRONT OF LOWER LEG** the front portion of the leg from below the knee to above the ankle, or the leg bone (**tibia**) located there **2.** FOOD **CUT OF BEEF** the lower portion of the foreleg in cattle, used as a cut of beef in stews ■ *v.* **(shinned, shin·ning, shins) 1.** *vti.* **CLIMB USING ARMS AND LEGS** to climb a rope, tree, or pole with speed and agility by gripping with the arms and legs and then pulling up with the arms and sliding upward **2.** *vt.* **HIT IN SHIN** to kick or hit somebody in the shin **3.** *vi.* **WALK BRISKLY OR RUN** to walk at a fast pace or run [Old English *scinu*. Ultimately from a prehistoric Germanic word probably meaning "thin piece."]

shin[2] /shin/ *n.* the 22nd letter of the Hebrew alphabet, represented in the English alphabet as "sh" [Early 19thC. From Hebrew *shīn*.]

shin·bone /shín bōn/ *n.* the flat surface of the bone immediately under the skin on the front of the lower leg. Technical name **tibia** [Old English *scinbān*]

shin·dig /shín dìg/ *n.* **1. NOISY PARTY** a noisy and festive party or celebration (*informal*) **2.** = **shindy** *n.* 1 [Late 19thC. Origin uncertain: probably an alteration of SHINDY.]

shin·dy /shíndee/ (*plural* **-dies**) *n.* **1. DISTURBANCE** a disturbance or commotion (*informal*) **2.** = **shindig** *n.* 1 [Early 19thC. Origin uncertain: probably a variant of SHINNY.]

shine /shīn/ *v.* **(shone, shone** /shōn/, **shin·ing, shines) 1.** *vi.* **EMIT LIGHT** to give out light **2.** *vi.* **BE BRIGHT** to be bright or reflect light **3.** *vt.* **DIRECT LIGHT** to direct the light emitted by something ○ *Shine the flashlight over here.* **4.** *vi.* **EXCEL** to be very good at or do very well in some form of activity **5.** *vi.* **APPEAR CLEARLY** to appear clearly **6.** *vi.* **HAVE RADIANT QUALITY** to appear to have a specially bright or radiant quality as a result of good health or a strong positive emotion ○ *Her face shone with happiness.* **7.** (*past and past participle* **shined**) *vt.* **POLISH SOMETHING** to make something bright and gleaming by polishing it ■ *n.* **1. BRIGHTNESS FROM LIGHT SOURCE** brightness or radiance emitted by a source of light **2. BRIGHT SURFACE** the bright or gleaming surface of something **3. ACT OF POLISHING SOMETHING** an act of polishing something to make it shiny **4.** BEVERAGES **MOONSHINE** moonshine (*informal*) ■ **shines** *npl.* **TRICKS** mischievous or amusing tricks played on somebody [Old English *scīnan*. Ultimately from an Indo-European base meaning "to glimmer, shine faintly" that is also the ancestor of English *shimmer* and *skiagram*.] ◇ **come rain or shine** whatever the weather or other attending circumstances ◇ **take a shine to somebody** to take a liking to somebody (*informal*)

shin·er /shínər/ *n.* **1. BLACK EYE** a black eye (*informal*) **2. SHINY FRESHWATER FISH** a small silvery freshwater fish. Genus: *Notropis*. **3. SOMETHING SHINY** something that shines or makes something shine

shin·gle[1] /shíng g'l/ *n.* **1. ROOF OR WALL TILE** a small flat tile, especially one made of wood or asphalt, used in overlapping rows to cover a roof or wall **2. SIGN OR NAMEPLATE** a nameplate or a small sign giving the name of a doctor, lawyer, or other professional person, fixed outside that person's office **3. HAIRSTYLE** a short hairstyle for women, popular in the 1920s, in which the back hair was cut to taper at the nape of the neck ■ *vt.* **(-gled, -gling, -gles) 1. COVER SOMETHING WITH TILES** to cover something with small overlapping tiles **2. TAPER HAIR AT BACK** to cut hair so that it is tapered at the nape of the neck [12thC. Alteration of late Latin *scindula*, a variant of Latin *scandula*. Ultimately from an Indo-European word meaning "to split" that is also the ancestor of English *shatter*.] —**shin·gler** *n.* ◇ **hang out your shingle** to begin working as a professional from your own office (*informal*)

shin·gle[2] /shíng g'l/ *n.* **1. PEBBLES** small round pebbles on a beach **2. PEBBLY AREA** an area of beach covered in shingle [Mid-16thC. Origin unknown.] —**shin·gly** *adj.*

shin·gle[3] /shíng g'l/ **(-gled, -gling, -gles)** *vt.* to remove the slag from iron by hammering or squeezing it in the process of making wrought iron [Late 17thC. Via French *cingler* from German *zängeln*, from *Zange* "tongs."]

shin·gles /shíng g'lz/ *n.* a disease of adults caused by the reactivation of chickenpox viruses in a nerve ganglion and resulting in inflammation, pain, and a rash of small skin blisters. Technical name **herpes zoster, zoster** [14thC. Alteration of Latin *cingulum* "girdle" (a translation of Greek *zōstēr*), from *cingere* "to gird." So called because the skin eruptions often encircle the body.]

shin·leaf /shín lèef/ (*plural* **-leafs** *or* **-leaves** /-lèevz/) *n.* a plant of the wintergreen family found in Europe, Asia, and North America that has a base of evergreen leaves and white or pink flowers. Family: Pyrolaceae. [Early 19thC. From its formerly being used to treat shin soreness.]

shin·ny[1] /shíntee/, **shin·ney** *n.* (*plural* **-nies**) **1. GAME RESEMBLING FIELD HOCKEY** a game similar to field hockey, played with a small hard ball and curved wooden sticks **2. STICK USED IN SHINNY** the stick that is used to play shinny ■ *vi.* **(-nied, -ny·ing, -nies** /shínnee/; **-neyed, -ney·ing, -neys) PLAY SHINNY** to play the game of shinny [Late 17thC. Origin uncertain: probably from the phrase *shin (t')ye!*, uttered by players of the game, of unknown origin.]

shin·ny[2] /shínnee/ **(-nied, -ny·ing, -nies)** *vi.* to climb up or down something using the hands and legs [Late 19thC. Formed from SHIN[1].]

shin·plas·ter /shín plàstər/ *n.* a piece of low-value paper money, especially one issued in the United States during the Civil War [Early 19thC. From its resemblance to the plaster used for leg plasters.]

shin splints *n.* a painful inflammation of the muscles surrounding the shinbone, often caused by running or jogging on hard roads (*takes a singular or plural verb*)

shin·tai·do /shin tī dō/ *n.* a form of exercise based on the movements used in Japanese martial arts, performed by a group [From Japanese]

Shin·to /shín tō/ *n.* a Japanese religion in which devotees worship and make offerings to numerous gods and spirits associated with the natural world [Early 18thC. From Japanese *shintō*, literally "way of the gods."] —**Shin·to·ism** *n.* —**Shin·to·ist** *n., adj.*

shinty /shíntee/, **shinny** *n. Scotland* SPORTS a game resembling hockey traditionally played in the Highlands

shin·y /shínee/ **(-i·er, -i·est)** *adj.* **1. BRIGHT AND POLISHED** bright and polished or with a glossy or glistening surface **2. WORN SMOOTH AND GLOSSY** smooth and glossy on the surface through too much wear ○ *a shiny patch on the seat of his pants* **3. SUNNY** bright with sunlight **4. LIGHT** filled with light —**shin·i·ness** *n.*

ship /ship/ *n.* **1. LARGE BOAT** a large wind-driven or engine-powered vessel designed to carry passengers or cargo over water, especially across the ocean **2. LARGE SQUARE-RIGGED SAILBOAT** a large sailing vessel with three, four, or five square-rigged masts **3. SHIP'S CREW** the crew of a ship **4. AIRCRAFT OR SPACECRAFT** a large aircraft or spacecraft ■ *v.* **(shipped, ship·ping, ships) 1.** *vti.* **TRANSPORT OVER WATER** to transport something by ship **2.** *vt.* **TRANSPORT OVERLAND OR BY AIR** to send or transport something overland or by air, using a common carrier **3.** *vt.* **SEND SOMEBODY** to send somebody to a place ○ *shipped the children off to summer camp* **4.** *vt.* **TAKE IN WATER** to take in water over the sides of a ship or boat ○ *We're shipping water.* **5.** *vt.* **BRING OARS INSIDE BOAT** to bring oars inside a boat and lay them down **6.** *vi.* **GO ON SHIP** to travel on a ship **7.** *vi.* **WORK ON SHIP** to take a job aboard a ship [Old English *scip*. From a prehistoric Germanic word that is also the ancestor of English *skipper* and *skiff*.] —**ship·pa·ble** *adj.* ◇ **desert** *or* **leave a sinking ship** to leave an organization that is having difficulties ◇ **when your ship comes in** when you become rich

WORD KEY: SYNONYMS

See Synonyms at *boat*.

-ship *suffix.* **1.** condition, state, or quality ○ *companionship* **2.** skill, art, craft ○ *musicianship* **3.** office, title, position, profession ○ *governorship* **4.** a group of people collectively ○ *membership* **5.** person holding a particular title ○ *ladyship* **6.** something showing a particular quality or condition ○ *township* [Old English *-scipe*]

ship bis·cuit *n.* = **hardtack**

ship·board /shíp bàwrd/ *adj.* used, intended for, or occurring on board a ship ◇ **on shipboard** on board a ship

ship·borne /shíp bàwrn/ *adj.* transported by ship

ship·build·er /shíp bìldər/ *n.* a person or business that constructs ships —**ship·build·ing** *n.*

ship ca·nal *n.* a canal that is wide and deep enough for ships to pass through

ship chan·dler *n.* a person, store, or company that sells supplies for ships —**ship chan·dler·y** *n.*

ship fit·ter *n.* **1. SHIP PART ASSEMBLER** somebody who assembles the structural parts of a ship **2. U.S. SAILOR WHO MAINTAINS METAL FITTINGS** a sailor in the U.S. Navy who maintains ship metal fittings

Ship·ley /shíplee/, **Jenny** (*b.* 1952) New Zealand political leader. A Liberal Party politician, she became prime minister of New Zealand in 1997. Full name **Jennifer Mary Shipley**

ship·load /shíp lōd/ *n.* the quantity of cargo carried by a ship

ship·mas·ter /shíp màstər/ *n.* the captain or master of a ship

ship·mate /shíp màyt/ *n.* a fellow sailor in a ship's crew

ship·ment /shípmənt/ *n.* **1. GOODS SHIPPED TOGETHER** a quantity of goods that are shipped together as part of the same cargo **2. ACT OF SHIPPING** the act of shipping something

ship of the line *n.* formerly, a sailing warship large enough to be in the front line of battle

ship·per /shíppər/ *n.* a person or company that sends or receives goods by ship, land, or air [Old English *scipere* "seaman"]

ship·ping /shípping/ *n.* **1. ACT OF TRANSPORTING GOODS** the act or business of transporting goods **2. GROUP OF SHIPS** ships considered collectively, especially those belonging to a single port, country, or industry, and often referred to in terms of their tonnage

ship·ping ar·ti·cles *npl.* = **ship's articles**

ship·ping clerk *n.* somebody who is employed to prepare, send, receive, and record shipments of goods

ship-rigged *adj.* used to describe a sailing ship with three, four, or five masts and square sails set at right angles to the hull

ship's ar·ti·cles, **ship·ping ar·ti·cles** *npl.* the terms of shipboard service agreed to by a sailor

ship·shape /shíp shàyp/ *adj.* **BEING IN GOOD ORDER** neat and in good order ■ *adv.* **IN ORDERLY WAY** in a neat and orderly way [Mid-17thC. Shortening of obsolete *shipshapen* "made appropriate for use aboard ship."]

ship·side /shíp sīd/ *n.* the area, especially at a dock, beside a ship

ship's pa·pers *npl.* documents stating the ownership, nationality, cargo, and destination of a ship, required by international law to be carried by all ships

ship·way /shíp wày/ *n.* **1. STRUCTURE ON WHICH SHIPS ARE BUILT** a structure on which a ship is built and down which it slides when it is launched **2.** = **ship canal**

ship·worm /shíp wùrm/ *n.* a burrowing marine mollusk that drills into wood, damaging wharves and ships. Family: Teredinidae.

ship·wreck /shíp rèk/ *n.* **1. SINKING OR DESTRUCTION OF SHIP** the sinking, destruction, or damaging of a ship while at sea **2. SUNKEN SHIP** a ship that has been destroyed or sunk **3. DESTRUCTION** the destruction or failure of something ■ *v.* **(-wrecked, -wreck·ing, -wrecks) 1.** *vti.* **INVOLVE SOMEBODY IN SHIPWRECK** to experience the sinking or destruction of a ship or cause somebody to experience this (*usually passive*) ○ *shipwrecked on a desert island* **2.** *vti.* **DESTROY SHIP** to sink or destroy a ship, or to be sunk or destroyed, at sea (*usually passive*) **3.** *vt.* **RUIN SOMETHING** to ruin or destroy something utterly (*literary*) [Old English *scipwræc*]

ship·wright /shíp rīt/ *n.* somebody who builds or repairs ships [Old English *scipwyrhta*]

ship·yard /shíp yaàrd/ *n.* a place where ships are built or repaired

shire /shīr/ *n.* **1.** BRITISH COUNTY a county in Great Britain, especially one with a name ending in "-shire" such as Hertfordshire or Berkshire **2. shire, Shire = shire horse** [Old English *scīr* "administrative office, district," of unknown origin]

Shire /shéeray/ river flowing from Malawi to Mozambique in south central Africa. Length: 250 mi./402 km.

Shire High·lands plateau in southern Malawi, east of the Shire River. Height: 3,000 ft./900 m.

shire horse, Shire horse *n.* a large heavy cart horse with long hair growing from its fetlocks, belonging to a breed originating in the Midlands of England

shirk /shurk/ **(shirked, shirk·ing, shirks)** *v.* **1.** *vt.* AVOID SOMETHING to avoid having to carry out something such as an obligation, task, or responsibility through lack or initiative, cowardice, or distaste for it **2.** *vi.* AVOID RESPONSIBILITY to lack initiative or deliberately avoid work or duty [Mid-17thC. Origin uncertain: possibly from German *Schurke* "scoundrel."] —**shirk·er** *n.*

Shir·ley pop·py /shúrli-/ *n.* an annual poppy with red, pink, or white single or double flowers [Late 19thC. Named for the district of *Shirley* in Croydon, Surrey, England,where it was developed.]

shirr /shur/ **(shirred, shirr·ing, shirrs)** *v.* **1.** *vti.* SEW GATHER FABRIC to gather fabric into two or more parallel rows for decoration on a garment such as a skirt, usually using elasticated thread **2.** *vt.* COOK BAKE EGG IN DISH to bake an egg without its shell, e.g., in a ramekin dish [Mid-19thC. Origin unknown.]

shirt /shurt/ *n.* **1.** CLOTHING FOR UPPER BODY an article of clothing for the upper part of the body usually made of a fairly light material and having a collar, sleeves, and buttons down the front **2.** MAN'S UNDERGARMENT a usually loose linen garment for the upper body with sleeves that was worn by men as underwear until the early 20th century **3.** NIGHTSHIRT a nightshirt [Old English *scyrte.* Ultimately from an Indo-European base meaning "to cut" that is also the ancestor of English *short* and *cortex.*] ◇ **lose your shirt** to lose everything you have, especially as a result of losing a bet ◇ **keep your shirt on** to keep your temper (*informal*) (*usually used as a command*)

shirt·dress /shúrt drèss/ *n.* a woman's dress that is tailored to resemble a shirt, with buttons fastening down the front

shirt·front /shúrt frùnt/ *n.* the front part of a shirt, especially the stiffened fabric on the front of a dress shirt

shirt·ing /shúrting/ *n.* fabric used in making men's shirts

shirt·sleeve /shúrt slèev/ *n.* SLEEVE OF SHIRT the part of a shirt that covers all or part of the arm ■ *adj.* NEEDING NO JACKET sufficiently warm or sufficiently informal for a shirt without a jacket to be the appropriate wear ○ *shirtsleeve wearer* ◇ **in shirtsleeves** not wearing a jacket

shirt·tail /shúrt tàyl/ *n.* **1.** CLOTHES BOTTOM PART OF SHIRT the lower part of a shirt, usually cut in a curved shape, that extends below the waist at the back and is usually tucked into pants **2.** PIECE AT END OF NEWSPAPER ARTICLE a short additional and related piece of writing at the end of a newspaper article ■ *adj.* **1.** TOO SMALL small and inadequate ○ *living on a shirttail allowance* **2.** YOUNG very young

shirt·waist /shúrt wàyst/ *n.* **1.** BLOUSE RESEMBLING MAN'S SHIRT a woman's blouse styled like a man's shirt **2.** = **shirtdress**

shirt·waist·er /shúrt wàystər/ *n. U.K.* = **shirtdress**

shirt·y /shúrtee/ **(-i·er, -i·est)** *adj. U.K.* aggressive or bad-tempered because of being annoyed about something (*informal*) [Mid-19thC. Origin uncertain: probably from the expression "get your shirt out""to lose your temper."] —**shirt·i·ly** *adv.* —**shirt·i·ness** *n.*

shish ke·bab /shísh-/ *n.* a dish of cubes of marinated meat and vegetables grilled and served on a skewer [Early 20thC. Via Armenian from Turkish *şiş kebabiu,* from *şiş* "skewer" + *kebab* "roast meat."]

shit /shit/ *n.* **1.** OFFENSIVE TERM a highly offensive term referring to human or animal excrement (*taboo offensive*) **2.** OFFENSIVE TERM a highly offensive term referring to an act of defecating (*taboo offensive*) **3.** OFFENSIVE TERM a mean or unpleasant person (*taboo insult*) **4.** OFFENSIVE TERM an offensive term for something that is unpleasant, of no value, or of inferior quality (*taboo offensive*) **5.** OFFENSIVE TERM a highly offensive term referring to useless or unnecessary things (*taboo*) **6.** OFFENSIVE TERM a highly offensive term referring to nonsense or lies (*taboo offensive*) **7.** OFFENSIVE TERM a highly offensive term referring to difficulty or trouble (*taboo offensive*) **8.** OFFENSIVE TERM a highly offensive term referring to criticism perceived as unhelpful or mean-spirited (*taboo offensive*) **9.** OFFENSIVE TERM a highly offensive term referring to illegal drugs, especially cannabis (*taboo offensive*) ■ **shits** *npl.* OFFENSIVE TERM a highly offensive term referring to diarrhea (*taboo offensive*) ■ *interj.* OFFENSIVE TERM used as a swearword (*slang offensive*) ■ *v.* **(shit** *or* **shat, shit** *or* **shat** /shat/, **shit·ting, shits)** (*taboo offensive*) **1.** *vti.* OFFENSIVE TERM a highly offensive term meaning to eliminate waste from the body via the rectum **2.** *vr.* OFFENSIVE TERM a highly offensive term meaning to be extremely scared **3.** *vt.* OFFENSIVE TERM a highly offensive term meaning to tease somebody or deceive somebody for amusement **4.** *vi.* OFFENSIVE TERM a highly offensive term meaning to behave toward or criticize somebody with arrogant contempt and a total disregard for his or her feelings, especially from a position of power ■ *adj.* OFFENSIVE TERM a highly offensive term meaning very bad or inferior (*taboo offensive*) [Old English *scitte.* Ultimately from an Indo-European base meaning "to cut, split," which is also the ancestor of English *schism* and *science.*] ◇ **get your shit together** a highly offensive phrase meaning to get organized (*taboo offensive*) ◇ **no shit** an offensive exclamation of surprise, disbelief, or sarcasm (*taboo offensive*) ◇ **tough shit** a highly offensive phrase indicating in an unfriendly way that there is no alternative to a difficult or undesirable situation (*taboo offensive*) ◇ **when the shit hits the fan** a highly offensive phrase indicating that trouble is just beginning (*taboo offensive*)

shit·faced /shít fàyst/ *adj.* a highly offensive term describing somebody who is completely drunk (*taboo offensive*) [Mid-20thC. From the facial numbness that accompanies extreme drunkenness.]

shit·head /shít hèd/ *n.* a highly offensive term that deliberately insults somebody's intelligence or character (*taboo insult*)

shit·house /shít hòwss/ *n.* a highly offensive term referring to an outhouse (*taboo offensive*)

shit·less /shítləss/ *adv.* a highly offensive term expressing extreme fear (*taboo offensive*) [Mid-20thC. From the tendency to lose control of the bowels when terror-stricken.]

shit·list /shít lìst/ *n.* a highly offensive term referring to a list of people who are out of favor, especially in the view of somebody in authority (*taboo*)

shit·load /shít lòd/ *n.* a highly offensive term referring to an undesirably large amount or quantity of something (*taboo offensive*)

shit·tah /shíttə/ (*plural* **-tahs** *or* **-tim** /shíttim/) *n.* the tree that yielded the shittim wood of the Bible, probably a species of acacia [Early 17thC. From Hebrew *šiṭṭāh.*]

shit·tim·wood /shíttim wòod/ *n.* **1.** WOOD IN BIBLE the wood of the shittah tree that according to the Bible was used to make the Ark of the Covenant **2.** (*plural* **shittimwoods** *or* **shittimwood)** N AMERICAN TREE WITH HARD WOOD a North American tree that has hard dense wood and black fruit. Genus: *Bumelia.*

shit·ty /shíttee/ *adj.* **1.** OFFENSIVE TERM a highly offensive term describing something inferior, unpleasant, or unenjoyable (*taboo offensive*) **2.** OFFENSIVE TERM a highly offensive term describing a feeling of misery (*taboo*) **3.** OFFENSIVE TERM of very poor quality (*taboo*) **4.** OFFENSIVE TERM a highly offensive term describing something covered with excrement (*taboo*) —**shit·ti·ly** *adv.* —**shit·ti·ness** *n.*

shiv /shiv/ *n.* a switchblade knife or sharp object used as a weapon (*slang*) [Late 17thC. Alteration of CHIV.]

shiv·a /shívə/, **shiv·ah** *n.* seven days of formal mourning observed by close relatives of a deceased Jewish person during which they sit on low stools and do not go out, work, bathe, or shave [Late 19thC. Via Yiddish *shive* from Hebrew *šiḇ'āh* "seven."]

Shi·va /shéevə/, **Si·va** /séevə/ *n.* an important Hindu deity, worshipped as the god of destruction. Shiva is one of the Trimurti trinity. [Late 18thC. From Sanskrit, literally "the auspicious one."]

shiv·a·ree /shìvvə rée, shívvə rèe/ *n.* a noisy mock-serenade to wish newlyweds well, involving the banging of saucepans, kettles, and other objects [Mid-19thC. Alteration of French *charivari,* of uncertain origin.]

shive *n.* = **shiva**

shiv·er[1] /shívvər/ *v.* **(-ered, -er·ing, -ers) 1.** *vi.* TO TREMBLE to tremble or shake slightly because of cold, fear, or illness **2.** *vti.* FLAP OR MAKE SAIL FLAP to flap, or make a sail flap, when a sailing vessel is too close to the wind ■ *n.* BODY TREMOR a tremor or shudder in the body caused by fear, cold, or illness ■ **shiv·ers** *npl.* ATTACK OF SHIVERING an attack of shivering caused by fear, cold, or illness (*informal*) [13thC. Origin uncertain.] —**shiv·er·er** *n.* —**shiv·er·ing·ly** *adv.*

shiv·er[2] /shívvər/ *n.* FRAGMENT a very small piece of something such as glass that has splintered off a larger piece ■ *vti.* **(-ered, -er·ing, -ers)** SHATTER to splinter into fragments or cause something to splinter into fragments [12thC. From assumed Old English *scifer;* ultimately from an Indo-European base meaning "to split" that is also the ancestor of English *schism* and *science.*]

shiv·er·y /shívvəree/ *adj.* trembling from cold, fear, or illness

Shi·zu·o·ka /shee zoo ṓkə/ capital city of Shizuoka Prefecture, west of Suruga Bay, on southeastern Honshu Island, Japan. Population: 472,196 (1990).

Shkod·ër /shkṓdair/ capital city of Shkodër District, northwestern Albania, situated near the southern end of Lake Shkodër. Population: 83,700 (1991).

shkotz·im plural of **shegetz**

shle·miel *n.* = **schlemiel** (*informal*)

shlep *vti.* = **schlep** (*slang*)

Shluh /shloo/ (*plural* **Shluh** *or* **Shluhs**) *n.* **1.** MEMBER OF NORTH AFRICAN PEOPLE a member of a people that is a subgroup of the Berbers and lives mainly in the Atlas Mountains of Morocco and Algeria **2.** SHLUH LANGUAGE the Berber dialect of the Shluh people [Early 18thC. From Berber.]

SHM *n., abbr.* simple harmonic motion

shmaltz *n.* = **schmaltz**

shmat·te *n.* = **schmatte**

shmo (*plural* **shmoes**) *n.* = **schmo** (*informal*)

shmuck *n.* = **schmuck**

Sho·ah /shṓ ə, -aàl/ *n.* a Hebrew word for the Holocaust [Mid-20thC. From Hebrew *šōāh,* literally "catastrophe."]

shoal[1] /shōl/ *n.* **1.** GROUP OF FISH a large group of fish or other marine animals swimming together **2.** GROUP OF PEOPLE a large group of similar people or things ○ *a shoal of reporters* ■ *vi.* **(shoaled, shoal·ing, shoals)** FORM SHOAL to group together to form a shoal [Late 16thC. From Middle Dutch *scōle* or Middle Low German *schōle* (see SCHOOL[2]).]

shoal[2] /shōl/ *n.* **1.** SHALLOW WATER an area of shallow water in a larger body of water **2.** UNDERWATER SANDBANK an underwater sandbank or sandbar that is visible at low water ■ *v.* **(shoaled, shoal·ing, shoals) 1.** *vti.* MAKE OR BECOME SHALLOW to become shallow or shallower, or to make something shallow **2.** *vi.* ENTER SHALLOWER WATER to enter a shallower area of water ■ *adj.* **shoal, shoal·y** SHALLOW shallow [Old English *sceald*]

shoat /shōt/, **shote** *n.* a young pig that has just been weaned [15thC. Origin unknown.]

shoch·et /shṓkət, shṓkhət/ (*plural* **-et·im** /shṓkətim, shṓkh-/) *n.* somebody licensed to perform the ritual kosher slaughter of animals for food **(shechita)** [Late 19thC. From Hebrew *šōḥēṭ,* the present participle of *šāḥaṭ* "to slaughter."]

shock[1] /shok/ *n.* **1.** SOMETHING SURPRISING AND UPSETTING an unexpected, intense, and distressing experience that has a sudden and powerful effect on somebody's emotions or physical reactions ○ *The news of her death came as a great shock to us all.* **2.** DISTRESSING FEELINGS AFTER SHOCK the feeling of distress or numbness experienced by somebody who has had a shock **3.** MED PHYSIOLOGICAL COLLAPSE a state of physiological collapse, marked by a weak pulse, coldness, sweating, and irregular breathing, and resulting from, e.g., blood loss, heart failure, allergic reaction, or emotional trauma ○ *in shock* **4.** PHYSICAL IMPACT a sudden and violent impact, collision, or blow **5.** MOVEMENT AFTER IMPACT the movement or violent shaking felt after a collision, explosion, or earthquake **6.** SOMETHING THREATENING OR DAMAGING an unexpected event that threatens or damages a system, organization, or conventional situation ○ *The economy cannot take any more shocks.* **7.** ELECTRIC SHOCK an electric shock **8.** = **shock absorber** ■ *v.* **(shocked, shock·ing, shocks) 1.** *vt.* UPSET SOMEBODY to make somebody feel suddenly and acutely distressed or upset **2.** *vti.* OFFEND OR BE OFFENDED to make somebody feel deeply offended or disgusted, or to be likely to feel offended or disgusted ○ *He shocks easily.* **3.** *vt.* GIVE SOMEBODY ELECTRIC SHOCK to give an electric shock to a person or animal **4.** *vt.* MED PUT SOMEBODY INTO SHOCK to cause a state of shock in somebody **5.** *vti.* COLLIDE to collide, or to cause people or things to collide (*archaic*) [Mid-16thC. The noun is via French *choc*, the verb directly from French *choquer* "to strike," of uncertain origin.] —**shock·a·bil·i·ty** /shòkə bíllətee/ *n.* —**shock·a·ble** /shókəb'l/ *adj.*

shock[2] /shok/ *n.* SHEAVES OF DRYING GRAIN OR CORN a group of sheaves of grain or corn set upright in a field for drying ■ *vt.* **(shocked, shock·ing, shocks)** ARRANGE GRAIN SHEAVES IN SHOCK to arrange sheaves of grain or corn in a shock [14thC. Origin uncertain: perhaps from Middle Dutch or Middle Low German *schok.*]

shock[3] /shok/ *n.* a large amount of thick shaggy hair [Early 19thC. Origin uncertain.]

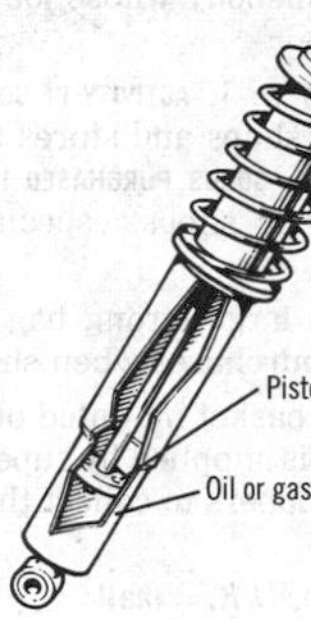

Shock absorber

shock ab·sorb·er *n.* a device on a vehicle designed to absorb jarring or jolting e.g., that caused by wheels moving over a rough surface

shock·er /shókər/ *n.* (*informal*) **1.** SOMETHING UNPLEASANT a highly unpleasant experience, thing, or person **2.** SHOCKING STORY, PLAY, OR MOVIE a story, play, or movie that is particularly lurid and intended to shock people **3.** *Aus* BAD SPORTS PERFORMANCE a very poor performance, especially at sport

shock hor·ror *interj.* used humorously to feign shock about something that others might really find shocking (*informal*)

shock-hor·ror *adj.* lurid, sensational, and apparently intended to cause a shocked or horrified reaction (*informal; used ironically*)

shock·ing /shóking/ *adj.* **1.** OUTRAGEOUS provoking a deeply offended or outraged response **2.** DISTRESSING emotionally distressing or horrifying **3.** VERY BAD very bad or unpleasant (*informal*) ■ *adj., adv.* VERY BRIGHT very bright or glaring in shade of color —**shock·ing·ly** *adv.* —**shock·ing·ness** *n.*

shock·ing pink *adj.* of a bright garish pink color —**shock·ing pink** *n.*

shock jock *n.* a disk jockey or radio host who uses provocative language and broadcasts his or her extreme views (*slang*)

Shock·ley /shóklee/, **William B.** (1910–89) U.S. physicist. He codeveloped the transistor (1948) and shared the Nobel Prize in physics (1956). He went on to promote controversial theories about intelligence and race. Full name **William Bradford Shockley**

shock·proof /shók proof/ *adj.* designed or able to withstand the effects of jarring or impact

shock tac·tics *npl.* the use of methods that are likely to shock people in order to achieve something

shock ther·a·py, **shock treat·ment** *n.* a method of treating patients affected with psychiatric disorders that involves passing an electric current through the brain

shock troops *npl.* soldiers who are specially trained and equipped to be in the forefront of an attack [Translation of German *Stosstruppen*]

shock wave *n.* **1.** WAVE OF HEAT AND AIR PRESSURE a wave of increased temperature or pressure as a result of an explosion or earthquake or the movement of a supersonic body **2.** SURPRISED REACTION a widespread reaction of shock or distress caused by an event or piece of news (*often used in the plural*)

shod past participle, past tense of **shoe**

shod·dy /shóddee/ *adj.* **(-di·er, -di·est) 1.** POORLY MADE poorly or carelessly made or done **2.** MADE FROM INFERIOR MATERIAL made of inferior material **3.** DISHONEST dishonest or disgraceful ○ *shoddy treatment* ■ *n.* (*plural* **-dies**) **1.** CLOTH MADE WITH OLD WOOL cloth made using a yarn composed of a mixture of old unraveled woolen cloth and new wool **2.** SOMETHING INFERIOR something that is of inferior quality, especially if it is imitating something better [Mid-19thC. Origin unknown.] —**shod·di·ly** *adv.* —**shod·di·ness** *n.*

Shoe

shoe /shoo/ *n.* **1.** STIFF OUTER COVERING FOR THE FOOT an outer covering for the foot, usually made of leather, fabric, or plastic, with a stiff sole and usually not reaching above the ankle **2.** = **horseshoe** *n.* 1 **3.** PROTECTIVE PART IN AN ENGINE a lining or part in an engine or machine that protects another part from being worn down **4.** PLAYING CARD DISPENSER a special box that dispenses playing cards one at a time **5.** POWER COLLECTOR ON AN ELECTRIC TRAIN the part of an electric train or streetcar that connects with the electrified rail from which it draws power **6.** METAL STRIP ON SLED a strip of metal along the runner of a sled **7.** PART OF A BRIDGE a base that supports the upper part of a bridge ■ *vt.* **(shod** *or* **shoed, shod** /shod/ *or* **shoed, shoe·ing, shoes) 1.** PROVIDE A HORSE WITH HORSESHOES to fix a horseshoe on a horse **2.** SUPPLY SOMEBODY WITH SHOES to provide somebody with shoes (*usually passive*) **3.** MECH ENG PUT A PROTECTIVE COVERING ON SOMETHING to cover something with a hard, especially metal, plate to protect against wear [Old English *scōh*] ◇ **be in somebody's shoes** to be in somebody else's position (*informal*)

shoe·bill /shoó bìl/ *n.* a large East African tropical wading bird with shaggy gray plumage, a large head, long black legs, and a broad hooked bill. Latin name: *Balaeniceps rex.*

shoe·black /shoó blàk/ *n.* = **bootblack** (*dated*)

shoe·box /shoó bòks/ *n.* **1.** BOX FOR SHOES a box, usually made of cardboard, in which shoes are packed for sale **2.** CRAMPED SPACE a small and cramped living or working space (*informal*)

shoe·horn /shoó hàwrn/ *n.* DEVICE TO HELP HEEL INTO SHOE a curved piece of plastic, metal, or horn used to help ease the heel into a tight-fitting shoe or boot ■ *vt.* **(-horned, -horn·ing, -horns)** SQUEEZE SOMEBODY OR SOMETHING INTO SPACE to squeeze somebody or something into a space that is barely large enough

shoe·lace /shoó làyss/ *n.* a thin cord of leather or fabric used to fasten together the two top flaps of a shoe

shoe·mak·er /shoó màykər/ *n.* somebody who makes or repairs boots or shoes

Shoe·ma·ker /shoó maykər/, **Willie** (*b.* 1931) U.S. jockey. He won a record 8,833 horse races during his 42-year career. Real name **William Lee Shoemaker**

shoe·pac /shoó pàk/, **shoe·pack** *n.* a heavy laced waterproof boot [Mid-18thC. Alteration of pidgin Delaware *seppock* "shoes," from Unami Delaware *čipahko* "moccasins."]

shoe·shine /shoó shìn/ *n.* **1.** ACT OF POLISHING SHOES the act of giving a clean or shiny finish to shoes by polishing them **2.** POLISH ON SHOES a polished finish on shoes

shoe·string /shoó string/ *adj.* **1.** CONSISTING OF LITTLE MONEY consisting of or running on a very limited amount of money ○ *a shoestring allocation for new classrooms* **2.** FOOD LONG AND NARROW cut or made long and narrow in shape ○ *shoestring licorice* ■ *n.* = **shoelace** ◇ **on a shoestring** using very little money

shoe·string catch *n.* BASEBALL a catch of a fly or pass made near the ground by a running player

shoe·tree /shoó trèe/ *n.* a wooden or metal block that is inserted into a boot or shoe to stretch it or help it to keep its shape when not being worn

sho·far /shṓ faàr/ (*plural* **-fars** *or* **-froth** /shō frót/) *n.* a horn, usually a ram's horn, blown in a synagogue on Rosh Hashanah and Yom Kippur [Mid-19thC. From Hebrew *šōpār*, literally "ram's horn."]

sho·gi /shṓgee/ *n.* a Japanese board game for two players that resembles chess [Mid-19thC. From Japanese *shōgi.*]

sho·gun /shṓgən, shṓ ùn/ *n.* any one of the hereditary military commanders in feudal Japan who ruled the country under the nominal rule of an Emperor between the years 1192 and 1867 [Mid-17thC. Via Japanese *shōgun* from Chinese *jiāng jūn* "general."] —**sho·gun·al** *adj.*

sho·gun·ate /shṓgənət, -nàyt/ *n.* the office, period in office, or rule of a shogun

sho·ji /shṓ jee/ (*plural* **-ji** *or* **-jis**) *n.* a ricepaper screen in a wooden frame used as a sliding partition or door in traditional Japanese houses [Late 19thC. From Japanese *shōji.*]

Sho·la·pur /shōlē poór/ city and administrative headquarters of Sholapur District, Maharashtra State, western India. Population: 603,870 (1991).

Sho·na /shṓnə/ (*plural* **-na** *or* **-nas**) *n.* **1.** MEMBER OF CENTRAL AFRICAN PEOPLE a member of a people that live in parts of southern central Africa, mainly in Zimbabwe, where they are the dominant ethnic group, and in Mozambique **2.** SHONA LANGUAGE the Bantu language of the Shona people. Shona is spoken by about eight million people. [Mid-20thC. Of Bantu origin.] —**Sho·na** *adj.*

shone *v.* past tense, past participle of **shine**

shon·een /shō neén/ *n. Ireland* an Irish person who, in order to seem of a higher social class, imitates an English person, especially in accent [Mid-19thC. From Irish *seóinín*, literally "little John," from *Seón* "John, John Bull."]

shoo /shoo/ *interj.* USED TO GET ANIMAL TO LEAVE used to tell a child or animal to go away ■ *vti.* (**shooed, shoo·ing, shoos**) WAVE AWAY to say shoo and gesture to a child or animal to go away [15thC. An instinctive exclamation.]

shoo·fly /shoó flī/ (*plural* **-flies**) *n.* a child's rocker with the seat between two flat sides cut in the shape of an animal [Late 19thC. From the exclamation "shoo-fly."]

shoo·fly pie *n.* a pie made with a filling of crumbs, butter, and brown sugar or molasses [From its sweet filling, which is apt to attract flies]

shoo-fly plant *n.* = **apple of Peru** [So called because it is supposed to repel flies]

shoo-in *n.* somebody who is certain to win something such as an election or be chosen for something such as a job [Origin uncertain]

shook[1] past tense of **shake**

shook[2] /shŏŏk/ *n.* **1.** AGRIC = **shock 2.** SET OF TIMBER PARTS FOR BARREL a set of timber parts for assembling a barrel or box [Late 18thC. Origin uncertain; perhaps from the phrase *shook cask*, a cask broken down for shipment, from *shake* in the archaic sense "to split apart."]

shook-up *adj.* disturbed and upset (*informal*)

shoot /shoot/ *v.* (**shot, shoot·ing, shoots**) **1.** *vti.* FIRE A WEAPON OR PROJECTILE to fire a projectile such as a bullet, missile, or arrow from a weapon, or make a weapon fire a projectile ○ *Don't shoot!* **2.** *vt.* HIT SOMEBODY OR SOMETHING WITH A BULLET to fire a weapon at and hit, injure, or kill a person or animal ○ *She shot herself.* **3.** *vti.* HUNT ANIMALS WITH A GUN to hunt animals or birds with a gun for sport **4.** *vti.* MOVE FAST to move or cause something to move quickly and suddenly ○ *She shot out her hand to catch the ball.* **5.** *vi.* DASH to go somewhere quickly and suddenly (*informal*) ○ *He shot off to his interview.* **6.** *vt.* TRAVEL OVER SOMETHING FAST to travel quickly over a stretch of water where the current is fast ○ *shoot the rapids* **7.** *vi.* PROGRESS VERY RAPIDLY to make extremely rapid progress or undergo a startlingly rapid change of state ○ *She shot to fame.* **8.** *vi.* MOVE SWIFTLY THROUGH THE BODY to seem to move very swiftly, and usually painfully, through the body ○ *Pain shot up her leg.* **9.** *vti.* SEND SOMETHING OUT RAPIDLY to send out something rapidly or forcefully or in a beam or ray **10.** *vt.* DIRECT SOMETHING QUICKLY to direct a look or glance at something briefly and rapidly ○ *He shot a glance at her.* **11.** *vt.* ASK OR SAY SOMETHING RAPIDLY to say something rapidly or ask a question rapidly **12.** *vti.* RECORD SOMETHING ON FILM to record a shot, scene, movie, or program on film with a camera **13.** *vti.* SPORTS KICK BALL TO GET POINT to kick, hit, or throw a ball in a sport such as soccer or basketball in an attempt to score a goal or point **14.** *vt.* SCORE A POINT IN A SPORT to score a goal or point in a sport **15.** *vi.* STRIVE TO ACHIEVE SOMETHING to try to achieve something difficult (*informal*) ○ *shooting for a five percent increase in productivity* **16.** *vt.* MOVE A BOLT INTO PLACE to move something such as a bolt into or out of a fastening **17.** *vi.* GERMINATE to germinate or begin to grow **18.** *vt.* DRUGS = **shoot up** *v.* 4 (*slang*) **19.** *vt.* TRAVEL OVER SOMETHING FAST to travel quickly over water where the current is fast ○ *shoot the rapids* **20.** *vt.* CUE GAMES PLAY CUE GAME to play a game of pool or billiards **21.** *vti.* THROW DICE to throw a die or dice **22.** *vt.* MEASURE THE DISTANCE TO HEAVENLY BODY to measure the altitude of a star or other heavenly body ■ *n.* **1.** NEW PLANT GROWTH a newly grown aerial part of a plant, e.g., a leaf bud or branch **2.** ACT OF FIRING an act of firing a weapon **3.** *U.K.* HUNTING PARTY a party of people gathered together to hunt animals with guns for sport **4.** *U.K.* HUNTING AREA an area where people shoot animals with guns for sport **5.** GEOL VEIN OF ORE a narrow vein of ore ■ *interj.* (*informal*) **1.** USED TO TELL SOMEBODY TO START used to tell somebody to go ahead and start talking **2.** USED TO EXPRESS ANNOYANCE used as an exclamation of annoyance or disappointment [Old English *scēotan*. Ultimately from a prehistoric Germanic base that is also the ancestor of English *shot*, *shut*, and *shuttle*.]

shoot down *vt.* **1.** BRING DOWN AN AIRCRAFT to bring down an aircraft while it is in the air by firing a weapon or missile **2.** KILL SOMEBODY OR SOMETHING BY SHOOTING to fire a weapon at and hit, injure, or kill a person or animal **3.** DESTROY ARGUMENT to destroy somebody's argument, theory, or idea by disproving, criticizing, or discrediting it

shoot through *vi. Aus* to leave a place, usually abruptly (*informal*)

shoot up *v.* **1.** *vi.* INCREASE SUDDENLY to increase suddenly by a large amount **2.** *vi.* GET TALLER to grow considerably taller in a short space of time **3.** *vt.* HARM SOMEBODY OR SOMETHING BY GUNFIRE to cause serious injuries to somebody or damage to something with gunfire **4.** *vti.* DRUGS INJECT A DRUG to inject an illegal drug (*slang*)

shoot-'em-up /shoótəm ùp/ *n.* **1.** MOVIE WITH SHOOTING a movie or television show featuring a large amount of shooting and bloodshed (*dated*) **2.** COMPUTER GAME WITH SHOOTING a video or computer game in which a player scores points by shooting at figures on the screen

shoot·er /shoótər/ *n.* **1.** GUN a pistol or other gun (*informal*) **2.** SOMEBODY SHOOTING somebody or something that shoots

shoot·ing gal·ler·y *n.* **1.** PLACE TO PRACTICE SHOOTING a place used for target practice using guns or rifles **2.** PLACE WHERE DRUG ADDICTS SHOOT UP a place such as an abandoned building where addicts inject drugs (*slang*)

shoot·ing i·ron *n.* a handgun (*informal*)

shoot·ing script *n.* the final screenplay for a cinema or television film that includes directions for shooting and is broken down into scenes with the shots numbered consecutively

shoot·ing star *n.* **1.** = **meteor 2.** N AMERICAN PRIMROSE a North American plant in the primrose family that has oblong leaves and flowers with petals that curve backward. Genus: *Dodeatheon.*

Shooting stick

shoot·ing stick *n.* a walking stick with handles at one end that fold out to form a small seat, often used by a spectator at an outdoor sporting event

shoot-out *n.* **1.** DECISIVE FIGHT WITH GUNS a fight to the finish with guns **2.** SOCCER TIE-BREAKER WITH PENALTY SHOTS a means of resolving a tie in a soccer game in which five players from each side take alternate penalty shots at the goal **3.** FIGHT TO SETTLE DISPUTE an argument or fight that finally settles a long-drawn-out dispute (*informal*)

shoot-the-chute, chute-the-chute *n.* an amusement ride in which visitors slide down a steep slope in a boat into a pool at the bottom of the slide

shoot-to-kill *adj.* relating to or involving the aiming of a gun to kill, not wound, somebody

shop /shop/ *n.* **1.** COMM RETAIL BUSINESS a retail business that sells consumer merchandise and sometimes services **2.** MANUF WORKSHOP a place where goods are manufactured or repaired **3.** EDUC INDUSTRIAL ARTS SCHOOL SUBJECT a school subject in which students are taught to work with tools and machinery, especially on wood **4.** EDUC SCHOOLROOM FOR LEARNING INDUSTRIAL ARTS a schoolroom or building with tools and equipment for students to learn industrial arts ■ *v.* (**shopped, shop·ping, shops**) **1.** *vi.* VISIT STORES to visit stores and shops in order to look at and usually buy things **2.** *vt.* VISIT PARTICULAR STORE to buy goods from a particular store **3.** *vt. U.K.* INFORM ON SOMEBODY to inform on somebody to the police or authorities (*slang*) **4.** *vt.* TRY TO SELL SOMETHING to try to sell something such as a company or creative work by bringing it to the attention of potential buyers [Old English *sceoppa* "booth, peddler's stall" (related to German *Schuppen* "shed")] ◇ **close** *or* **shut up shop 1.** to stop working or doing something **2.** to close down a business ◇ **talk shop** to talk about your work or some other specialized activity

shop around *vi.* **1.** LOOK AROUND FOR THE BEST DEAL to look around for the best deal or bargain **2.** CONSIDER SEVERAL POSSIBILITIES BEFORE CHOOSING to review a number of possibilities before making a choice

shop·a·hol·ic /shòppə hóllik/ *n.* somebody who enjoys or compulsively engages in shopping (*informal*)

shop as·sis·tant *n. U.K.* = **salesclerk**

shop-bought *adj. U.K.* = **store-bought**

shop floor *n.* **1.** MANUFACTURING AREA IN A FACTORY the area in a factory where goods are manufactured **2.** MANUAL WORKERS the manual workers in a factory

shop·keep·er /shóp keépər/ *n.* = **storekeeper**

shop·lift /shóp lìft/ (**-lift·ed, -lift·ing, -lifts**) *vti.* to steal something from a shop or store while pretending to shop for goods —**shop·lift·er** *n.* —**shop·lift·ing** *n.*

shoppe /shop/ *n.* a shop (*archaic*) [Early 20thC. Alteration of SHOP.]

shop·per /shóppər/ *n.* **1.** SOMEBODY DOING SHOPPING somebody who is looking for things to buy in a shop or store **2.** COMM SOMEBODY WHO SHOPS FOR OTHERS somebody who shops on behalf of a customer or employer as a job **3.** LOCAL NEWSPAPER a usually free newspaper that carries advertising and some local news **4.** SOMEBODY FILLING MAIL ORDERS somebody whose job is to fill mail or telephone orders

shop·ping /shópping/ *n.* **1.** ACTIVITY OF GOING TO SHOP the activity of visiting shops and stores to look at and buy things **2.** *U.K.* GOODS PURCHASED IN SHOPS goods bought in a shop or shops, especially food and household items

shop·ping bag *n.* a large strong bag with handles used for carrying purchases when shopping

shop·ping cart *n.* a basket mounted on wheels with a push handle that is supplied by supermarkets and other stores for shoppers to collect their purchases in

shop·ping cen·ter *n. U.K.* = **mall**

shop·ping list *n.* **1.** LIST OF ITEMS TO SHOP FOR a list of all the things somebody wants to buy when shopping **2.** LIST OF THINGS WANTED a list of demands, requirements, or things wanted

shop·ping trol·ley *n. U.K.* = **shopping cart**

shop-soiled /shóp sòyld/ *adj. U.K.* = **shopworn**

shop stew·ard /shóp stoó ərd/ *n.* a worker elected by fellow union members as their representative in dealings with the management

shop·talk /shóp tàwk/ *n.* **1.** TALK ABOUT WORK conversation about work or another specialized activity at a time when more lighthearted chat is the norm, especially outside working hours **2.** JOB'S JARGON jargon used in a particular field, job, or profession

shop·walk·er /shóp wàwkər/ *n. U.K.* = **floorwalker**

shop·worn /shóp wàwrn/ *adj.* faded, tarnished, or otherwise slightly spoiled from being on display in a shop

sho·ran /sháw ràn/ *n.* a short-range navigational system in which a ship's or aircraft's precise location is determined by the time taken for a signal to travel to two fixed stations and back [Mid-20thC. Contraction of *short-range navigation*.]

shore[1] /shawr/ *n.* **1.** LAND AT EDGE OF WATER the land that runs along the edge of the ocean, a sea, or lake **2.** DRY LAND dry land as opposed to water ○ *on shore* **3.** COUNTRY a land or country (*literary; often used in the plural*) ○ *having reached our native shores* **4.** *U.K.* LAW COAST BETWEEN LOW AND HIGH TIDES the area of land that lies between normal low and high tide marks [Old English *scora*. Ultimately from an Indo-European base meaning "to cut" that is also the ancestor of English *shear* and *scarp*.]

shore[2] /shawr/ *vt.* (**shored, shor·ing, shores**) **1.** PROP UP A STRUCTURE to stop something such as a wall from falling down or over by propping a support against it **2.** HELP TO STOP SOMETHING FAILING to give support or help in order to stop something failing ■ *n.* PROP TO SUPPORT SOMETHING a beam or other prop set at an angle to support something such as a wall or tree [14thC. From Middle Low German or Middle Dutch *schōre* "prop," of unknown origin.]

shore bird *n.* a bird that lives and feeds near the shores of coastal or inland waters, e.g., the plover, sandpiper, avocet, or snipe. Suborder: Charadrii.

shore din·ner *n.* a meal consisting mainly of fish and seafood

shore·front /sháwr frùnt/ *n.* land situated immediately next to a body of water

shore ice *n.* a large sheet of sea ice attached to a shore

shore leave *n.* **1.** PERMISSION TO GO ASHORE permission for a member of a ship's crew to go ashore **2.** TIME SPENT ASHORE a period of time spent ashore by a member of a ship's crew

shore·less /sháwrləss/ *adj.* having no flat shore on which a boat can land

shore·line /sháwr lìn/ *n.* the edge of a body of water, especially the ocean, where it meets the shore

shore pa·trol *n.* the military police of the the U.S. Navy, Coast Guard, or Marine Corps, or the British Royal Navy while on shore

shore·ward /sháwrwərd/ *adj.* FACING SHORE facing or near the shore ■ *adv.* **shore·ward, shore·wards** TOWARD SHORE toward the shore

shor·ing /sháwring/ *n.* a structure or arrangement designed to shore something up

shorn /shawrn/ past participle of **shear** ■ *adj.* **1.** HAVING SHORT HAIR with hair cut short **2.** DEPRIVED OF SOMETHING having had something removed or taken away

short /shawrt/ *adj.* **1.** NOT LONG having little or relatively little length, or extending only a small distance ○ *short hair* **2.** NOT TALL having little or relatively little height ○ *shorter than her sister* **3.** NOT LASTING LONG lasting for only a small amount of time ○ *a short stay* **4.** NOT SEEMING LONG IN DURATION seeming or imagined not to last very long ○ *in a few short weeks* **5.** CONCISE expressed economically and briefly ○ *a short summary* **6.** ABBREVIATED expressed in fewer words or using fewer letters or characters than the full form ○ *Typo is short for typographical error.* **7.** HAVING LESS THAN NEEDED having less than the amount needed, expected, or thought to be sufficient ○ *I'm rather short of cash at the moment.* **8.** INSUFFICIENTLY LONG OR TALL not long or tall enough by a particular amount ○ *All the beams are six inches short.* **9.** NOT REMEMBERING MORE DISTANT EVENTS unable or unwilling to recall events that happened before the comparatively recent past ○ *a short memory* **10.** DISCOURTEOUS rude and abrupt when speaking to somebody ○ *She was very short with the cashier.* **11.** FULL OF FAT made with lots of fat so as to be flaky or crumbly when baked ○ *short pastry* **12.** FIN SOLD WITHOUT POSSESSING THE SHARES SOLD involving a seller who, at the time of sale, does not possess the shares he or she is selling and has to borrow them before being able to deliver. Once the share price has fallen, the short seller buys the shares and returns them to the person from whom they were borrowed, resulting in a gain on the deal. ○ *short sale* **13.** FIN MATURING SOON being due for payment or repayment within a comparatively short space of time ○ *short bill* **14.** LING PRONOUNCED WITH A RELATIVELY BRIEF SOUND used to describe phonemes or syllables that, when spoken, are comparatively brief in duration or are categorized as being of this type. The vowel "a" in the word "hat" is short compared with the same vowel in the word "hate." ■ *adv.* **1.** ABRUPTLY abruptly and unexpectedly ○ *stop short* **2.** NOT REACHING THE TARGET before reaching a goal, target, or destination ○ *The pass fell 3 yards short.* **3.** FIN WITHOUT ACTUAL POSSESSION without actually possessing the things being sold when the sale is agreed on ○ *sell short* ■ *n.* **1.** FILM OF SHORT DURATION a film whose running time is approximately 30 minutes or less. = **short subject 2.** = **short circuit** *n.* **3.** BASEBALL = **shortstop 4.** *U.K.* SMALL DRINK a drink consisting of a small measure of spirits in a small glass (*informal*) **5.** GARMENT SIZE a size of garment for a short person ■ *npl.* **1. shorts** SHORT PANTS pants that end somewhere between the upper thigh and the knee **2. shorts** UNDERPANTS men's underpants **3.** AGRIC MIXTURE OF BRAN AND COARSE FLOUR a mixture of bran and coarse flour left over from the milling of wheat **4.** STOCK EXCH SHORT-DATED ITEMS bills or securities that are due to mature within a comparatively short space of time ■ *v.* (**short·ed, short·ing, shorts**) **1.** *vt.* PROVIDE WITH LESS to give somebody less than expected or due **2.** *vti.* = **short-circuit** [Old English *sceort.* Ultimately from an Indo-European base meaning "to cut" that is also the ancestor of English *shirt, skirt,* and *curt.*] —**short·ness** *n.* ◇ **cut something short** to end something earlier than expected or desired ◇ **for short** as an abbreviation or shortened form ◇ **go short** to have insufficient money or food ◇ **in short** used to introduce a rephrasing of something in a more concise form ◇ **short and sweet** pleasant or bearable because brief ◇ **short of 1.** not having something, or not having enough of something **2.** less than **3.** without actually doing something, usually something unpleasant or wrong

short-act·ing *adj.* effective for a short period

short·age /sháwrtij/ *n.* a lack of something that is needed or required

WORD KEY: SYNONYMS

See Synonyms at ***lack***.

short-billed marsh wren *n.* = **sedge wren**

short·bread /sháwrt brèd/ *n.* a rich crumbly cookie made with a high proportion of butter to flour and a comparatively small proportion of sugar

short·cake /sháwrt kàyk/ *n.* **1.** DESSERT WITH FRUIT AND CREAM a dessert consisting of a spongecake base topped with fruit and cream **2.** SPONGY CAKE a round, spongy cake that serves as a base for a shortcake dessert

short·change /shàwrt cháynj/ (**-changed, -chang·ing, -chang·es**) *vt.* **1.** GIVE SOMEBODY TOO LITTLE CHANGE to give somebody less change than is due to him or her **2.** TREAT SOMEBODY UNFAIRLY to behave unfairly toward somebody by giving him or her less of something than he or she deserves or expects —**short·chang·er** *n.*

short cir·cuit *n.* a failure in an electrical circuit caused by an accidental connection of low resistance such as when there is a break in the insulation across which an excessive current can flow

short-cir·cuit (**short-cir·cuit·ed, short-cir·cuit·ing, short-cir·cuits**) *v.* **1.** *vti.* HAVE OR CAUSE FAILURE IN A CIRCUIT to have or cause a failure in an electrical circuit by creating a connection of low resistance across which an excessive current flows **2.** *vt.* USE SHORTCUT TO DO SOMETHING to use a much quicker or more direct method to achieve something **3.** *vt.* FRUSTRATE OR HINDER PLANS to hinder a plan or project by erecting obstacles

short·com·ing /sháwrt kùmming/ *n.* a defect or failure in somebody's character or in a system or organization (*often used in the plural*)

short·cut /shàwrt kùt/ *n.* **1.** SHORTER ROUTE a route that is shorter or more direct than the usual one **2.** TIMESAVER a way of saving time and effort in doing something —**short·cut** *vti.*

short-day *adj.* able to flower only upon exposure to relatively short periods of sunlight, e.g., during spring or autumn

short·en /sháwrt'n/ (**-ened, -en·ing, -ens**) *v.* **1.** *vti.* BECOME OR MAKE SHORTER to make something shorter or become shorter **2.** *vti.* MAKE ODDS SHORTER to reduce the odds on a bet, or to be reduced in this way **3.** *vt.* REDUCE SAIL AREA to reduce the area of a sail **4.** *vt.* MAKE PASTRY SHORTER to make pastry more crumbly by adding more shortening —**short·en·er** *n.*

short·en·ing /sháwrt'ning/ *n.* fat such as lard that is solid at room temperature such as lard used for making pastry

short·fall /sháwrt fàwl/ *n.* **1.** AMOUNT LACKING an amount by which something falls short of what is required **2.** FAILURE TO MEET A GOAL a failure to meet a goal or requirement

short fuse *n.* a tendency to get angry quickly and with little provocation (*informal*)

short·hair /sháwrt hàr, -hèr/ *n.* a medium-sized muscular domestic cat with a short thick coat

short·haired /shàwrt hàrd, sháwrt hèrd/ *adj.* having a coat of short hair ○ *a shorthaired cat*

short·hand /sháwrt hànd/ *n.* **1.** QUICK WAY OF TAKING NOTES a fast method of writing, using symbols to represent letters, words, or phrases **2.** SHORTER WAY OF SAYING SOMETHING a shorter or quicker way of referring to something

short-hand·ed *adj.* having fewer than the usual or required number of staff, helpers, or players —**short-hand·ed·ness** *n.*

short·hand typ·ist *n.* *U.K.* = **stenographer**

short-haul *adj.* traveling or used for traveling a short distance

short·horn /sháwrt hàwrn/ (*plural* **-horns** *or* **-horn**) *n.* a reddish-brown or white breed of cattle with short curved horns developed in northern England and used for beef or milk production

short-horned grass·hop·per *n.* a winged grasshopper with short antennae belonging to the family that includes the locust and many other common crop pests. Family: Acrididae.

short hun·dred·weight *n.* = **hundredweight** *n.* 1

short·ie *n.* = **shorty**

short in·ter·est *n.* the number of shares in a particular security that have been borrowed and sold and must eventually be returned to the lender

short·leaf pine /shàwrt leef-/ *n.* **1.** SOUTHEASTERN U.S. PINE TREE a pine tree native to the southeastern United States, that has reddish bark and short bluish-green flexible needles in groups of two. Latin name: *Pinus echinata.* **2.** WOOD USED IN BUILDING the yellow wood of the shortleaf pine, used in construction

short list *n.* a list of the best candidates for a position or award after all others have been eliminated

short-list (**short-list·ed, short-list·ing, short-lists**) *vt.* to put somebody or something on a final list of candidates for a position or award

short-lived /sháwrt lívd, shàwrt lívd/ *adj.* lasting or living for only a short period of time

short·ly /sháwrtlee/ *adv.* **1.** IN SHORT TIME soon or in a short time ○ *The guests will arrive shortly.* **2.** CURTLY in a curt or discourteous manner ○ *"I wish you'd stop interrupting me," he said shortly.* **3.** BRIEFLY using only a few words [Old English]

short-nosed cat·tle louse *n.* a sucking louse that infests large grazing mammals, sometimes to the detriment of their health. Latin name: *Haematopinus eurysternus.*

short or·der *n.* food in a restaurant that is prepared and served quickly (*hyphenated when used before a noun*)

short po·si·tion *n.* an open position in a security in which the investor borrowed the security from somebody, sold it, and promised to replace the borrowed security at a later time

short ra·di·us *n.* the perpendicular distance or line from the center of a regular polygon to one of its sides

short-range *adj.* **1.** FOR SHORT DISTANCE OPERATION designed for or capable of traveling or operating only over a short distance **2.** ABOUT THE NEAR FUTURE concerned with the near future ○ *short-range plans*

short ribs *npl.* a cut of beef consisting of tough fatty meat on rib ends from between the rib roast and plate

short sale *n.* the sale of a borrowed security in anticipation that the security price will fall and can be paid back from the profits earned after repurchasing it at the lower price

short score *n.* a condensed orchestra score omitting some of the less important instruments and often combining several parts on one staff

short shrift *n.* **1.** UNSYMPATHETIC TREATMENT brief and inconsiderate or unsympathetic treatment **2.** BRIEF PERIOD FOR CONFESSION a short period of time before execution during which a condemned prisoner could confess (*archaic*) ◇ **make short shrift of something** deal with a matter quickly, giving it little attention

short sight *n.* an inability to see distant objects clearly

short-sight·ed *adj.* **1.** *U.K.* OPHTHALMOL = **nearsighted 2.** FOR SHORT TERM ONLY without taking the future into account —**short-sight·ed·ly** *adv.* —**short-sight·ed·ness** *n.*

short-spo·ken *adj.* inclined to speak abruptly

short-staffed *adj.* lacking the normal or required number of staff

short·stop /sháwrt stòp/ *n.* **1.** INFIELDER POSITION the position of the infielder in baseball playing closest to second base on the side toward third base **2.** PLAYER AT SHORTSTOP the baseball player playing at shortstop

short sto·ry *n.* a work of prose fiction that is shorter than a novel

short sub·ject *n.* a short movie of approximately 30 minutes or less, sometimes a documentary, shown before a full-length feature movie

short-tem·pered *adj.* easily made angry or impatient

short-term *adj.* **1.** NOT LASTING LONG lasting for or affecting a relatively short period of time **2.** FIN MATURING OR DUE SOON maturing or payable within a relatively short period of time **3.** FIN FROM ASSETS HELD BRIEFLY realized from assets held for a short time and then sold

short-term mem·o·ry *n.* the part of the mind used for retaining temporary information over a short period

short ton *n.* = **ton**[1] *n.* 1

short-waist·ed *adj.* unusually short between the shoulders and the waist

short·wave /shάwrt wàyv/ *adj.* SHORTER THAN 200 M transmitting or receiving wavelengths shorter than 200 m ■ *n.* RADIO a radio capable of transmitting or receiving short waves

short-wind·ed *adj.* **1.** SHORT OF BREATH experiencing shortness of breath, especially after mild exertion **2.** BRIEF expressed in few words

short·y /shάwrtee/ (*plural* **-ies**), **short·ie** *n.* somebody or something very short or shorter than average (*informal*)

Sho·sho·ne /shō shṓnee/ (*plural* **-nes** *or* **-ne**), **Sho·sho·ni** (*plural* **-nis** *or* **-ni**) *n.* **1.** MEMBER OF NATIVE N AMERICAN PEOPLE a member of a Native North American people living mainly in Nevada, Idaho, Wyoming and Utah **2.** SHOSHONE LANGUAGE the Uto-Aztecan group of languages spoken by the Shoshone. Shoshone languages are spoken by about 3,000 people. [Early 19thC. Origin unknown.] —**Sho·sho·ni·an** *n., adj.*

Sho·sho·ne, Lake /shō shṓni-/ lake in the Rocky Mountains, west of Yellowstone Lake, in Yellowstone National Park, northwestern Wyoming. Length: 12 mi./19 km.

Sho·sho·ne Falls /shō shṓni-/ falls on the Snake River in southern Idaho, named for the Shoshone people. Height: 212 ft./65 m.

Shost·ako·vich /shòstə kṓvich/, **Dmitry** (1906–75) Russian composer. A major figure in 20th-century music, he wrote prolifically in many different forms despite repeated criticism of his work by the Soviet government. His works include 15 symphonies and an equal number of string quartets. Full name **Dmitry Dmitrievich Shostakovich**

shot[1] /shot/ *n.* **1.** SHOOTING OF GUN a firing of a gun or other weapon **2.** SOMEBODY WHO SHOOTS somebody who shoots in a particular way ○ *a good shot* **3.** SHOOTING OF A PROJECTILE AT A TARGET an aimed discharge of a projectile, e.g., a bullet from a gun **4.** BULLET OR CANNONBALL a single solid metal missile for a gun or cannon, e.g., a bullet or cannonball **5.** SMALL METAL PELLETS small steel or lead pellets used in shotgun shells **6.** SPORTS ATTEMPT TO SCORE an attempt to score points in a sport by throwing, hitting, kicking, or shooting something ○ *Jordan's foul shot went right into the hoop.* **7.** SPORTS ACT OF HITTING BALL an act of hitting the ball in certain sports such as golf, tennis, or snooker ○ *His shot from the fairway was perfectly placed.* **8.** SPORT = **shot put 9.** PHOTOGRAPHY PARTICULAR VIEW ON FILM a particular view recorded on film with a camera ○ *The cameraman bent down to get a low shot of the damaged wheels.* **10.** CINEMA CONTINUOUS UNINTERRUPTED FILM SEQUENCE a continuous action or image on the screen that appears to be the result of a single uninterrupted operation of the camera **11.** PHOTOGRAPHY CAMERA VIEW the range of, or view from, a camera **12.** ATTEMPT an opportunity to attempt something ○ *He had a shot at repairing the vacuum cleaner.* **13.** GUESS a wild guess or speculation, usually based on little or no information (*informal*) **14.** MED INJECTION an injection of a medication or vaccine (*informal*) **15.** BEVERAGES SMALL AMOUNT OF ALCOHOL a small glass or drink of a strong alcoholic beverage (*informal*) **16.** SHARP COMMENT an angry or critical remark **17.** SPACE TECH ROCKET LAUNCH the launching of a rocket or probe to a specified destination **18.** MINING BLASTING EXPLOSION a charge of explosives used in blasting **19.** PROJECTILE FLIGHT PATH a flight or path of a projectile **20.** GAMBLING CHANCE AT WINNING something such as a racehorse to bet on at particular odds (*informal*) ○ *The horse was a 3 to 1 shot.* **21.** SMALL QUANTITY OF SOMETHING a small amount given or taken on one occasion (*informal*) ○ *You need a shot of energy.* **22.** MEASURE MEASUREMENT IN FATHOMS a unit of chain length equal to 15 fathoms in the United States and 12.5 fathoms in the United Kingdom ■ **shots** *npl.* SMALL CANDIES small candies sprinkled on something such as ice cream or cake [Old English *sceot, gesceot* "act of shooting," also "payment." Ultimately, from a prehistoric Germanic word meaning "to project," which is also the ancestor of English *shoot* and *shuttle.*] ◇ **a shot in the arm** something that has a sudden good effect on somebody or something ◇ **a shot in the dark 1.** a guess made without any information **2.** an attempt made in desperation but with little hope of success ◇ **deliver** *or* **fire a shot across somebody's bows** give somebody a warning of what might happen ◇ **like a shot** very eagerly and quickly

shot[2] /shot/ past tense, past participle of **shoot** ■ *adj.* **1.** TWO-TONE IN COLOR woven of two colors in such a way that when the fabric is viewed from different angles the visible colors change **2.** MARKED WITH VARYING COLOR streaked or flecked with a different color **3.** FILLED WITH PARTICULAR QUALITY filled with or permeated by an emotion or quality **4.** MADE USELESS brought to a state of ruin or exhaustion (*informal*) ○ *I've been so busy my nerves are shot.* **5.** USED UP no longer full or operating properly (*informal*) ○ *This tube of toothpaste is shot.*

shot clock *n.* a clock used in basketball to limit the time a team may take before it must either shoot or lose possession of the ball

shote *n.* = **shoat**

shot·gun /shót gùn/ *n.* **1.** GUN THAT SHOOTS PELLET LOAD a short-range smoothbore gun that discharges a load of small pellets **2.** FOOTBALL FORMATION IN FOOTBALL an offensive formation in football, usually used when passing, in which the quarterback receives the snap a few yards behind the line of scrimmage ■ *adj.* **1.** INVOLVING INTIMIDATION brought about by pressure, threats, or force **2.** HIT-OR-MISS having no clear design, purpose, or objective

shot·gun house *n.* a house with all the rooms in a line, usually from front to back, found especially in the southern United States

shot·gun wed·ding, shot·gun mar·riage *n.* a marriage that takes place at short notice, usually because the bride is pregnant [Because the parties are or feel compelled, as if at gunpoint, to marry]

shot hole *n.* **1.** MINING HOLE FOR EXPLOSIVE CHARGE a hole bored into rock in which an explosive charge is placed **2.** PARASITE OR INSECT DAMAGE a small hole made in wood or leaves by insects or parasites (*informal*)

Shot put

shot put *n.* **1.** COMPETITION FOR THROWING BALL an athletic field event in which contestants compete to throw a heavy metal ball as far as possible **2.** BALL FOR THROWING COMPETITION a heavy metal ball used in the shot put —**shot-put·ter** *n.*

shot·ten /shótt'n/ *adj.* having recently spawned and therefore less valuable as food ○ *a shotten fish* [15thC. From the obsolete past participle of SHOOT.]

shot tow·er *n.* a tower formerly used for making lead shot, in which molten lead was dropped from the top into water at the bottom in which the drops solidified

should /shŏŏd, shəd/ CORE MEANING: modal verb indicating that something is the right thing for somebody to do ○ *You should get more exercise.* ○ *I should have told her I was leaving.* ○ *The report recommended that children should be tested regularly.*

v. **1.** EXPRESSING LIKELIHOOD OR PROBABILITY to be scheduled or expected to be or do something ○ *I should be back by 12.* ○ *The scissors should be in the second drawer down.* ○ *They should have arrived at Grandma's by now.* **2.** EXPRESSING CONDITIONS OR CONSEQUENCES used to express the conditionality of an occurrence and suggest it is not a given, or to indicate the consequence of something that might happen (*used in conditional clauses*) ○ *If anything should happen to my car, I'd be heartbroken.* ○ *Should you have any questions, our staff will be available to help.* ○ *"If I should die, think only this of me..."* (Rupert Brooke, "The Soldier"; 1887–1915) **3.** WOULD used to mean the same thing as the verb would (*used with "I" or "we"*) ○ *If we spent that much every month, we should soon run out of money.* ○ *I should love to meet her.* **4.** REPORTING PAST VIEWPOINT ABOUT FUTURE used when reporting something from a past perspective, e.g., somebody's words or thoughts, about a future event ○ *It was intended that the library should be for the use of everyone.* ○ *He was keen that I should meet his publisher friend.* **5.** USED TO SOFTEN HARSH WORDS used to soften a blunt statement or make one more polite ○ *I should hope you're sorry now.* ◇ **I should** used to advise somebody to do something ○ *I should take him up on his offer, if I were you.*

WORD KEY: USAGE

should or **would**? The same general pattern is true here as for *shall* and *will*. As an auxiliary verb, ***would*** is more usual than ***should*** when stating a condition or proposition and is the only choice when asking a question (*They would like to come. I would think so. Would you like to go to the movies?*). ***Should*** has the special role of denoting obligation or likelihood (*I should stay until they arrive. Should you be lifting that? That should be our visitors now*) and must be used in inverted constructions expressing a condition: *Should it rain, the party will be held indoors.* ***Would*** has to be used when referring to habitual action in the past: *On Wednesdays I would go to the library.* In conversational English, the contracted form *I'd, you'd*, etc., are regularly used instead of the full forms in making simple statements (*They'd like to come*), but these are not available in place of ***should*** in its sense of obligation or likelihood.

shoul·der /shṓldər/ *n.* **1.** ANAT PLACE WHERE AN ARM ATTACHES TO THE TRUNK either one of the two parts of the human body immediately below and at each side of the neck, where the arm joins the trunk **2.** ZOOL JOINT ATTACHING A FORELIMB TO THE TRUNK the part of the body of a vertebrate animal equivalent to the shoulder, where the forelimb joins the pectoral girdle **3.** PART OF GARMENT FITTING SHOULDER a part of a piece of clothing that covers the shoulder **4.** MEAT FROM SHOULDER a fairly fatty cut of meat consisting of the upper part of a foreleg of an animal **5.** SOMETHING SLOPED LIKE SHOULDER something resembling a shoulder in position or slope, e.g., the part of a stringed instrument between the neck and body or the slope near the top of a hill **6.** TRANSP LAND BESIDE ROAD a strip of land along the side of a road **7.** PRINTING TYPE SURFACE THAT IS NOT LETTER a flat surface of printers' type below the base of the raised letter or character **8.** WIDER PORTION OF SHAFT any portion of a shaft or other instrument for transmitting force that has an increase in diameter to withstand thrust ■ **shoul·ders** *npl.* **1.** ANAT UPPER AREA OF BACK the upper back, including both shoulders and the area between them **2.** CAPACITY TO HANDLE RESPONSIBILITY the capacity to carry responsibility for something, especially something unpleasant or worrying ○ *The blame rests on her shoulders.* ■ *v.* (**-dered, -der·ing, -ders**) **1.** *vt.* CARRY OR PLACE SOMETHING ON SHOULDERS to carry, lift, or place something on the shoulders **2.** *vt.* ACCEPT RESPONSIBILITY to accept and bear a burden or responsibility **3.** *vti.* MOVE SOMETHING WITH SHOULDER to push something or make way using a shoulder ○ *She successfully shouldered her way to the front of the crowd.* [Old English *sculdor.* Ultimately, from a prehistoric West Germanic word meaning "shoulder blade."] ◇ **put your shoulder to the wheel** work hard ◇ **rub shoulders with somebody** associate with somebody of a particular type or social class ◇ **shoulder to shoulder 1.** side by side **2.** in a cooperative effort ◇ **straight from the shoulder** in a frank or blunt way

shoul·der bag *n.* a bag carried by a long strap hung over the shoulder

shoul·der belt *n.* = **shoulder harness**

shoul·der blade *n.* either one of two large flat triangular bones over the upper outer parts of the ribs at the top of the back that joins with the upper arm bone. Technical name **scapula**

shoul·der board *n.* one of a pair of stiff cloth patches worn on the shoulders of a military uniform to indicate rank

shoul·der gir·dle *n.* an incomplete ring of bones formed by the two shoulder blades (**scapulas**), the two collar bones (**clavicles**), and the upper edge of the breastbone (**sternum**)

shoul·der har·ness, **shoul·der belt** *n.* a safety belt in a motor vehicle that is worn diagonally across the shoulder and chest and is attached at the waist to the seat belt

shoul·der hol·ster *n.* a holster hung from a shoulder strap and worn under the arm, used to hide a gun under a coat or jacket

shoul·der knot *n.* a decoration of braided cord worn on the shoulder of a uniform

shoul·der pad *n.* a pad inserted into the shoulder of a piece of clothing to improve its shape, often making it appear larger

shoul·der patch *n.* a cloth patch with an identifying emblem on it, worn on the upper part of the sleeve of a uniform

shoul·der strap *n.* **1.** STRAP TO SUPPORT CLOTHING a strap that goes over a shoulder for carrying a bag or holding up a garment **2.** = **shoulder board**

should·n't /shŏŏd'nt/ *contr.* should not

shouldst 2nd person present singular of **should** (*archaic*)

shout /showt/ *v.* (**shout·ed, shout·ing, shouts**) **1.** *vt.* SAY SOMETHING LOUDLY to say or utter something very loudly **2.** *vi.* SPEAK LOUDLY to speak in a loud or angry voice **3.** *vti. ANZ* PAY FOR FOOD OR DRINK to buy something for somebody else, especially a drink in a bar or a meal in a restaurant (*informal*) ■ *n.* **1.** LOUD CRY a loud call or cry **2.** *ANZ, U.K.* TURN TO PAY somebody's turn to buy something, especially a drink or meal (*informal*) ○ *"It's my shout. What would you like to drink?"* [14thC. Origin unknown: perhaps from, ultimately, a prehistoric Germanic word meaning "to project," which is also the ancestor of English *shoot*, or from Old Norse *skúta* "to taunt."] —**shout·er** *n.* ◇ **be all over bar the shouting** *U.K.* used to say that something is nearly over, and the outcome is clear ◇ **nothing to shout about** not good enough to speak of with pride (*informal*)

shout down *vt.* to prevent somebody from being heard by shouting loudly

shove /shuv/ *vti.* (**shoved, shov·ing, shoves**) **1.** MOVE SOMETHING WITH FORCE to push somebody or something along or forward with force **2.** PUSH SOMEBODY OR SOMETHING ROUGHLY to push somebody or something in a rude or careless way ■ *n.* PUSH a strong push [Old English *scūfan* "to push away." Ultimately, from a prehistoric Germanic word that is also the ancestor of English *scuffle*.] —**shov·er** *n.*

shove off *vi.* **1.** LEAVE to leave (*informal; sometimes used as a command*) **2.** LEAVE SHORE to move from shore or a mooring in a boat

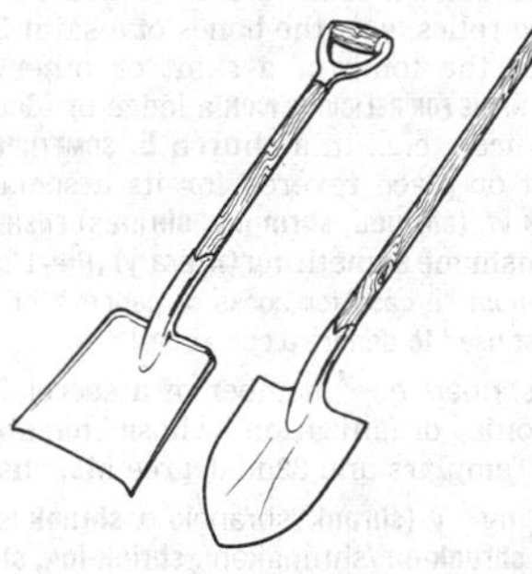

Shovel

shov·el /shúvv'l/ *n.* (*plural* **-els** *or* **-els**) **1.** LONG-HANDLED SCOOP a hand tool consisting of a broad, usually curved blade attached to a long handle, used for lifting and moving loose material **2.** MACHINE FOR EARTH DIGGING a power-driven machine that operates with a scooping motion, especially one used for digging or moving earth **3.** AMOUNT HELD BY SHOVEL the amount that a shovel is capable of holding ■ *v.* (**-eled** *or* **-elled, -el·ing** *or* **-el·ling, -els**) **1.** *vti.* DIG WITH SHOVEL FOR SOMETHING to lift, move, or clear something with a shovel **2.** *vt.* THROW SOMETHING CARELESSLY to move large amounts of something from one place to another in a careless or clumsy way [Old English *scofl*. The underlying sense is "an implement for shoving."]

shov·el·er /shúvvələr/ *n.* **1.** SOMEBODY OR SOMETHING THAT SHOVELS somebody or something that uses a shovel to move or throw something **2.** BIRDS BROAD-BILLED DUCK a small freshwater duck with a broad spoon-shaped bill that inhabits marshes in the northern hemisphere. Latin name: *Anas clypeata.*

shov·el·ful /shúvv'l fŏŏl/ (*plural* **-el·fuls** *or* **-els·ful**) *n.* an amount that a shovel can hold

shov·el hat *n.* a black felt hat with a low crown and a wide brim turned up at the sides, formerly worn by some English clergymen

shov·el·head /shúvv'l hèd/ (*plural* **-heads** *or* **-head**) *n.* a common hammerhead shark of Atlantic and Pacific waters with a broad shovel-shaped head. It grows to about 6 ft./1.6 m long, is not dangerous to human life, and inhabits shallow waters. Latin name: *Sphyrna tiburo.*

shov·el·nose /shúvv'l nōz/ *n.* (*plural* **-nose** *or* **-noses**) = **shovel-nosed sturgeon** [Early 18thC. From its broad, flat snout.]

shov·el-nosed *adj.* having a broad shovel-shaped head, snout, or bill

shov·el-nosed stur·geon *n.* a freshwater sturgeon of North America with a broad shovel-shaped snout. Latin name: *Scaphirhynchus platorhynchus.*

show /shō/ *v.* (**showed, shown** /shōn/ *or* **showed, show·ing, shows**) **1.** *vti.* MAKE VISIBLE to cause or allow something to come into view ○ *Show me your hand.* **2.** *vti.* BE VISIBLE to be visible or allow something to be seen easily ○ *Does the spot on my shirt show?* **3.** *vti.* EXHIBIT to put on an exhibition or performance or to present something for the public to see ○ *She's showing her paintings all over the world now.* ○ *A new movie is showing.* **4.** *vti.* DISPLAY FOR SALE to present something for sale to the public ○ *His work was showing at the Museum of Modern Art.* **5.** *vt.* GUIDE SOMEBODY to guide or accompany somebody ○ *Show them to the office.* **6.** *vt.* POINT SOMETHING OUT TO SOMEBODY to call somebody's attention to something ○ *She showed him the mistake.* **7.** *vt.* DEMONSTRATE QUALITIES to make somebody's or something's fundamental qualities or characteristics evident ○ *He has shown that he is honest.* **8.** *vt.* ESTABLISH SOMETHING USING REASON to explain, demonstrate, or prove something in a logical way ○ *The teacher showed them the solution.* **9.** *vt.* DEMONSTRATE SOMETHING FOR INSTRUCTION to give a demonstration of something in order to teach others ○ *She showed us how to apply the glaze to the pot.* **10.** *vt.* GIVE INFORMATION to register information ○ *This chart shows the sudden increase in temperature.* **11.** *vt.* DISPLAY ATTITUDE to display a personal feeling or attitude ○ *She's never shown much interest in art.* **12.** *vi.* APPEAR IN CERTAIN WAY to have a particular appearance when being viewed ○ *The horse shows well.* **13.** *vi.* ARRIVE to put in an appearance at a place (*informal*) ○ *They never showed.* **14.** *vi.* COME IN THIRD to finish at least third in a race, especially a horse race or a dog race **15.** *vt.* LAW PLEAD SOMETHING IN LAWSUIT to allege or plead something in a legal document ■ *n.* **1.** DEMONSTRATION an expression or demonstration of something ○ *a show of force* **2.** PUBLIC PRESENTATION a public entertainment such as a theater performance, movie, or radio or television program ○ *Shall we go to a show tonight?* **3.** EXHIBITION an exhibition, e.g., of art, flowers, animals, or an industry's products ○ *a flower show* **4.** *U.K.* = **fair 5.** APPEARANCE an appearance given, either as an outward display of an emotion or trait, or as a demonstration of falseness and pretense ○ *a show of diligence* **6.** SIZABLE VENTURE an undertaking or task, especially one of some size and complexity (*informal*) ○ *You decide – it's your show!* **7.** IMPRESSIVE DISPLAY an extravagant or impressive display **8.** SPECTACLE a display or exhibition designed to evoke laughter or ridicule **9.** THIRD PLACE a third place finish in a race, especially a horse race or a dog race **10.** *ANZ, U.S.* OPPORTUNITY a chance or opportunity (*informal*) ○ *no show of winning* **11.** INDICATION a trace of something indicating its presence, e.g., oil in the ground **12.** MED BLOOD INDICATING START OF LABOR a bloody mucous discharge indicating the onset of labor in childbirth [Old English *scēawian* "to look at." Ultimately, from a prehistoric West Germanic word meaning "to look," which is also the ancestor of English *sheen*.] —**show·a·ble** *adj.* ◇ **get the** *or* **this show on the road** begin an activity or start an event (*informal*) ◇ **steal the show** attract the most attention or admiration

show off *v.* **1.** *vi.* ATTRACT THE ATTENTION OF OTHERS to try to impress others by behaving in a way that attracts attention **2.** *vt.* PRESENT SOMETHING FOR APPROVAL to display somebody or something proudly for others to admire **3.** *vt.* PRESENT SOMETHING IN AN APPEALING WAY to display something in a way that enhances it

show up *v.* **1.** *vi.* ARRIVE to arrive or put in an appearance (*informal*) **2.** *vt.* BRING SOMETHING TO LIGHT to expose or reveal something, especially an error or personal shortcoming **3.** *vi.* BE SEEN to be easily seen **4.** *vt.* EMBARRASS SOMEBODY BEFORE OTHERS to embarrass or humiliate somebody publicly **5.** *vt.* MAKE SOMEBODY LOOK BAD to perform in a superior way and make somebody look inferior by comparison

show-and-tell, **show and tell** *n.* **1.** INFORMATIVE CLASSROOM ACTIVITY a classroom activity for children in which each child brings an object to school and tells the other children about it **2.** PUBLIC PRESENTATION an informative meeting or presentation to which the public is invited (*informal*)

show bill *n.* a poster advertising or publicizing something

show biz *n.* show business (*informal*)

show·boat /shṓ bŏt/ *n.* **1.** RIVERBOAT THEATER a river steamboat equipped with a theater and carrying an acting company that performs for communities along the river **2.** SHOW-OFF somebody who behaves flamboyantly in order to attract attention (*informal*) ■ *vi.* (**-boat·ed, -boat·ing, -boats**) SHOW OFF FOR ATTENTION to behave flamboyantly in order to attract attention (*informal*)

show busi·ness *n.* the entertainment industry, including movies, radio, television, theater, and music recording

show·case /shṓ kàyss/ *n.* **1.** GLASS CASE FOR DISPLAYING OBJECTS a box or case, usually one made of glass, used to display objects, especially in a museum or shop **2.** MOST FAVORABLE SETTING an event, setting, or medium in which something or somebody is presented to advantage ■ *vt.* (**-cased, -cas·ing, -cas·es**) PRESENT SOMETHING TO ADVANTAGE to present something or somebody in a way that is designed to attract attention and admiration

show·down /shṓ dòwn/ *n.* **1.** CONFRONTATION a confrontation to settle a conflict or dispute **2.** PLACING OF CARDS FACE UP in poker, the moment at the end of a round when the players show their cards to see who has the best hand

show·er[1] /shówər/ *n.* **1.** BATH UNDER SPRAY a method of washing in which somebody stands upright under a spray of water from a nozzle **2.** PLACE AND EQUIPMENT FOR SHOWER an enclosure or the plumbing apparatus for a shower **3.** METEOROL PERIOD OF PRECIPITATION a short period of rain, snow, hail, or sleet **4.** SOMETHING LIKE RAIN a sudden spray or fall of something, e.g., meteors, sparks, or bullets **5.** LARGE AMOUNT OF SOMETHING something that somebody receives all at once in quantity **6.** *ANZ, Can, U.S.* PARTY WITH GIFTS a party given by friends, especially in honor of a woman who is about to be married or is expecting a baby, at which gifts are given **7.** *U.K.* DISAGREEABLE GROUP a group of people considered unpleasant, worthless, or inferior (*informal*) **8.** PHYS IONIZING PARTICLES CAUSED BY COSMIC RAY a large number of ionizing particles and photons caused by the collision of a cosmic-ray particle with the upper atmosphere ■ *v.* (**-ered, -er·ing, -ers**) **1.** *vi.* WASH UNDER SHOWER to wash using a shower **2.** *vti.* RAIN DOWN ON SOMEBODY to fall or make things fall in a spray **3.** *vt.* GIVE SOMEBODY SOMETHING PLENTIFULLY to give somebody something in abundance ○ *They were showered with gifts.* [Old English *scūr*. Ultimately from a prehistoric West Germanic word that is also the ancestor of German *schauer* and Dutch *schoer*.] —**show·er·y** *adj.*

show·er[2] /shṓ ər/ *n.* somebody or something that shows, especially an exhibitor at a public exhibition [Old English *scēawere* "scout, watchman," from *scēawian* "to look at" (see SHOW)]

show·er bath *n.* = **shower**[1] *n.* 1

show·er gel *n.* a liquid soap with the consistency of a gel, used especially when in the shower and often scented

show·er·head /shówər hèd/ *n.* a spray nozzle that is part of an overhead plumbing fixture used in a shower

show·er tea *n. ANZ* a party given by friends for a woman soon to be married at which they give her gifts, usually small items for the kitchen

show·girl /shṓ gùrl/ *n.* a young woman who performs in the chorus of a stage show, usually a musical, as a dancer or singer

show·ing /shṓ ing/ *n.* **1.** DISPLAY a presentation or exhibition, e.g., of a movie or artwork **2.** TYPE OF PERFORMANCE the way a person, group, or team performs **3.** PRESENTATION OF FACTS a presentation of facts [Old English *scēawung*]

show jump·ing /shṓ jùmping/ *n.* a competitive sport in which riders on horseback take turns jumping over a series of obstacles on a set course and are judged on speed and ability —**show·jump·er** *n.*

show·man /shṓmən/ (*plural* **-men** /-mən/) *n.* **1.** GIFTED ENTERTAINER somebody who has a natural talent for dramatic presentation or entertainment **2.** PRODUCER OF SHOW a producer or promoter of commercial entertainment ventures, especially in musical theater —**show·man·ship** *n.*

shown past participle of **show**

show-off *n.* somebody who behaves in a way that attracts attention and invites admiration (*informal*)

show of hands *n.* a form of voting that involves counting the hands raised by people to vote for or against a proposal

show·piece /shṓ pèess/ *n.* something considered or offered as a fine example of something

show·place /shṓ plàyss/ *n.* **1.** SPECIAL PLACE a place visited for its beauty or historical significance **2.** SOMETHING EXCEPTIONALLY BEAUTIFUL a place that is considered or offered as an example of beauty

show po·ny *n. Aus* somebody who looks and sounds good but lacks substance or depth

show·room /shṓ ròom, -rŏŏm/ *n.* a room in which goods for sale, especially cars or electrical appliances, are displayed

show·stop·per /shṓ stòppər/ *n.* **1.** ACT GETTING PROLONGED APPLAUSE a performance receiving so much applause from an audience that the show is interrupted **2.** SOMETHING SO STRIKING IT STOPS ACTION somebody or something so spectacular as to attract and hold everyone's attention

show·time /shṓw tīm/ *n.* **1.** STARTING TIME FOR ENTERTAINMENT the scheduled time for an entertainment such as a movie or play to begin **2.** TIME TO START SOMETHING the scheduled time for any event or activity to begin (*informal*)

show tri·al *n.* a trial with a predetermined verdict held for propaganda purposes

show win·dow *n.* a window in a store used to display merchandise

show·y /shṓ ee/ (**-i·er, -i·est**) *adj.* **1.** IMPRESSIVE making an attractive or impressive display **2.** OSTENTATIOUS appearing tasteless and ostentatious —**show·i·ly** *adv.* —**show·i·ness** *n.*

sho·yu /shṓ yŏŏ/ *n.* a Japanese variety of soy sauce [Early 18thC. From Japanese.]

shp, **s.hp.** *abbr.* shaft horsepower

shpil·kes /shpíl'kəss/ *npl.* a state of great nervousness or anxiety

shpt. *abbr.* shipment

shr. *abbr.* share

shrank past participle of **shrink**

shrap·nel /shrápnəl/ *n.* **1.** FRAGMENTS FROM AN EXPLOSIVE DEVICE metal balls or fragments that are scattered when a shell, bomb, or bullet explodes **2.** SHELL THAT SCATTERS METAL FRAGMENTS an artillery shell designed to explode before impact producing a shower of metal balls and fragments [Early 19thC. Named for General Henry Shrapnel, 1761–1842, the British artillery officer who invented the shell.]

shred /shred/ *n.* **1.** LONG TORN STRIP a ragged scrap or strip cut or torn from something **2.** SMALL PART a very small amount or fragment of something ■ *v.* (**shred·ded, shred·ding, shreds**) **1.** *vt.* TEAR SOMETHING INTO SHREDS to cut or tear something into shreds **2.** *vt.* PUT SOMETHING THROUGH SHREDDER to reduce a document to unreadable strips in a shredder **3.** *vti. Aus, U.S.* SPORTS SURF OR SNOWBOARD EXPERTLY to ride a wave on a surfboard or descend a slope on a snowboard with expert skill (*informal*) [Old English *scrēade*. Ultimately, from a prehistoric West Germanic word meaning "cut," which is also the ancestor of English *scroll*.]

shred·ded wheat *n.* a breakfast cereal made from cooked dried whole wheat that has been shredded, shaped into biscuits, and baked

shred·der /shréddər/ *n.* **1.** MACHINE FOR DESTROYING DOCUMENTS an office machine used to destroy documents by cutting them into very small pieces so that they cannot be read **2.** *Aus, U.S.* SPORTS GOOD SURFER an expert surfer or snowboarder (*informal*) [Late 16thC. Originally, "instrument for shredding."]

Shreve·port /shréev pawrt/ city in northwestern Louisiana, on the western bank of the Red River, east of the Texas border. The city is an important producer of oil, natural gas, and cotton. Population: 191,558 (1996).

Shrew

shrew /shroo/ *n.* **1.** SMALL MAMMAL WITH POINTED NOSE a small nocturnal mammal resembling a mouse but really an insectivore, with velvety fur, a long pointed snout, and small eyes and ears. Family: Soricidae. **2.** OFFENSIVE TERM an offensive term referring to a woman who is regarded as quarrelsome, nagging, or ill-tempered (*offensive*) [Old English *scrēawa*, of unknown origin. The sense "quarrelsome woman" derives from the belief that the shrew had a poisonous bite.]

WORD KEY: CULTURAL NOTE

The Taming of the Shrew (1593–94?), a play by English dramatist William Shakespeare. The central story of this play within a play is set in Verona and describes Petruchio's attempts to woo the wealthy but haughty and temperamental Katharina (the "shrew" of the title). The rounded and convincing protagonists make this an intriguing character study as well as a boisterous farce. The expression "Kiss me, Kate" comes from line 318, scene i, Act II: "Kiss me, Kate, we will be married o' Sunday."

shrewd /shrood/ *adj.* **1.** GOOD AT JUDGING PEOPLE OR SITUATIONS showing or possessing intelligence, insight, and sound judgment, especially in business or politics **2.** CLEVER AND PROBABLY ACCURATE based on good judgment and probably correct ○ *a shrewd assessment of the situation* **3.** CRAFTY inclined to deal with others in a clever underhanded way **4.** SHARP piercing or sharp (*archaic*) [13thC. From SHREW in the obsolete sense of "wicked man." The meaning evolved from "wicked, dangerous" via "cunning."] —**shrewd·ly** *adv.* —**shrewd·ness** *n.*

shrew·ish /shrŏŏ ish/ *adj.* with a quarrelsome ill-tempered disposition —**shrew·ish·ly** *adv.* —**shrew·ish·ness** *n.*

Shrews·bur·y /shrŏŏzbèree, shrṓz-/ town in central Massachusetts, southeast of Leominster and northeast of Worcester. Population: 26,771 (1996).

shriek /shreek/ *v.* (**shrieked, shriek·ing, shrieks**) **1.** *vi.* MAKE SHRILL SOUND to make a loud high-pitched piercing sound **2.** *vt.* SAY SOMETHING IN LOUD SHRILL VOICE to utter something in a loud high-pitched piercing voice ■ *n.* LOUD SHRILL CRY a loud high-pitched piercing cry or sound [15thC. From a Scandinavian source, probably of imitative origin.] —**shriek·er** *n.*

shrieve /shreev/ *vti.* to shrive or shrive somebody (*archaic*) [Alteration of SHRIVE]

shrift /shrift/ *n.* (*archaic*) **1.** SHRIVING SOMEBODY the act of shriving or of being shriven **2.** CONFESSION confession to a priest **3.** ABSOLUTION absolution granted by a priest [Old English *scrift* from *scrīfan* (to SHRIVE)]

shrike /shrīk/ (*plural* **shrikes** *or* **shrike**) *n.* a brown or gray songbird with a screeching call and a hooked bill. It eats insects and small animals that it impales on sharp objects such as thorns. Family: Laniidae. [Mid-16thC. Origin uncertain.]

shrill /shril/ *adj.* **1.** PENETRATINGLY HIGH-PITCHED with a high-pitched penetrating quality **2.** MAKING A SHRILL SOUND making a high-pitched penetrating sound **3.** INSISTENT with an obtrusive insistent quality **4.** STRIDENT having a harsh intense quality perceived as unpleasant ■ *v.* (**shrilled, shrill·ing, shrills**) **1.** *vi.* MAKE A SHRILL SOUND to make a high-pitched penetrating sound (*literary*) **2.** *vt.* SAY SOMETHING IN A PIERCING VOICE to utter something in a high-pitched penetrating voice [13thC. Origin uncertain.] —**shrill·ness** *n.* —**shril·ly** *adv.*

Shrike

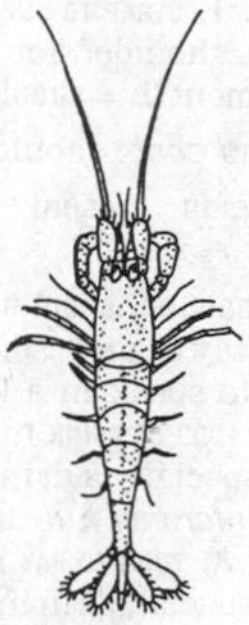

Shrimp

shrimp /shrimp/ *n.* (*plural* **shrimp** *or* **shrimps**) **1.** ZOOL SMALL MARINE CRUSTACEAN WITH TEN LEGS a small mainly marine crustacean with ten legs belonging to a suborder that includes several edible species. A shrimp has a long thin semitransparent body, five pairs of jointed legs, a tail resembling a fan, and a pair of pincers. Suborder: Natantia. **2.** SOMETHING UNDERSIZE somebody or something very small or considered insignificant (*informal*) ■ *vi.* (**shrimped, shrimp·ing, shrimps**) FISH FOR SHRIMP to fish for shrimp [14thC. Origin uncertain.] —**shrimp·er** *n.*

shrimp plant *n.* a tropical American plant, grown in gardens and as a houseplant, with long curving spikes of white flowers that grow out from overlapping pink bracts. Latin name: *Beloperone guttata.*

shrine /shrīn/ *n.* **1.** HOLY PLACE OF WORSHIP a sacred place of worship associated with a holy person or event **2.** CONTAINER FOR HOLY RELICS a case or other container for sacred relics, e.g., the bones of a saint **3.** TOMB OF HOLY PERSON the tomb of a saint or other revered figure **4.** NICHE FOR RELIGIOUS ICON a ledge or alcove for a religious icon, e.g., in a church **5.** SOMETHING REVERED an object or place revered for its associations or history ■ *vt.* (**shrined, shrin·ing, shrines**) ENSHRINE SOMETHING to enshrine something (*literary*) [Pre-12thC. From Latin *scrinium* "a case for books or papers," of uncertain origin. First used to denote a container.]

Shrin·er /shrī́nər/ *n.* a member of a secret fraternal non-Masonic organization whose members are Knights Templars and 32nd-degree Masons

shrink /shringk/ *v.* (**shrank** /shrangk/ *or* **shrunk** /shrungk/, **shrunk** *or* **shrunk·en** /shrúngkən/, **shrink·ing, shrinks**) **1.** *vti.* MAKE OR BECOME SMALLER to become smaller or cause something to become smaller, e.g., when exposed to cold, heat, or damp **2.** *vti.* REDUCE SIZE to decrease or cause something to decrease in amount, extent, value, or weight **3.** *vi.* DRAW AWAY FROM SOMETHING to move back and away, especially out of disgust, fear, or horror **4.** *vi.* BE DISINCLINED TO DO SOMETHING to be unwilling or reluctant to do something, especially something difficult or unpleasant ■ *n.* **1.** PSYCHIATRIST a psychiatrist (*slang*) (*considered offensive by some people*) **2.** ACT OF SHRINKING AWAY an act of shrinking away from something **3.** AMOUNT SOMETHING SHRINKS the amount by which something shrinks [Old English *scrincan* "to wither." Ultimately, from an Indo-European word meaning "to turn, bend," which is also the ancestor of English *curve*.] —**shrink·a·ble** *adj.* —**shrink·er** *n.*

WORD KEY: SYNONYMS

See Synonyms at ***recoil***.

shrink·age /shríngkij/ *n.* **1.** DECREASE AFTER SHRINKING the amount lost when something is decreased or reduced, or when it shrinks **2.** ACT OF SHRINKING the shrinking of something **3.** **MERCHANDISE STOLEN OR BROKEN** the loss of goods due to theft or breakage **4.** **LOSS OF VALUE** the decrease in value of something **5.** AGRIC **WEIGHT REDUCTION IN CARCASSES** the loss in body weight of livestock carcasses during shipping, storage, and preparation for sale **6.** **REDUCED SIZE OF CLAY ITEM** the reduction in size of a clay object when it is fired in a kiln, caused by the moisture burning off

shrink fit *n.* the fit of two interlocking parts in which the outer is heated and therefore expands before being put in position, the contraction during cooling ensuring that it is tight

shrink·ing vi·o·let *n.* somebody who is very shy or retiring (*informal*)

shrink-wrap *n.* **TRANSPARENT PLASTIC PACKAGING MATERIAL** a clear thermoplastic film that is wrapped around a product and shrunk to its original smaller size using heat, thereby forming a tightly sealed package ■ *vt.* **WRAP SOMETHING IN SHRINK-WRAP** to wrap goods in shrink-wrap

shrive /shrīv/ (**shrove** /shrōv/ *or* **shrived, shriv·en** /shrívv'n/ *or* **shrived, shriv·ing, shrives**) *v.* **1.** *vt.* **ABSOLVE SOMEBODY OF SINS** in Christianity, to hear somebody's confession of sins and give the person absolution **2.** *vt.* **IMPOSE PENANCE** in Christianity, to impose a penance on a sinner **3.** *vi.* **CONFESS** to confess sins to a priest (*archaic*) [Pre-12thC. Ultimately, from Latin *scribere* "to write" (source of English *scribe*). The meaning evolved via the sense "to prescribe penances."] —**shriv·er** *n.*

shriv·el /shrívv'l/ (**-eled, -el·ing, -els**) *vti.* **1.** **SHRINK** to become or cause somebody or something to become shrunken or wrinkled, especially from drying out or aging **2.** **WEAKEN** to become or cause somebody to become useless or ineffectual **3.** **BECOME OR MAKE SMALLER** to become or cause something to become gradually smaller or less [Mid-16thC. Origin unknown.]

WORD KEY: SYNONYMS

See Synonyms at ***dry***.

shriv·en past participle of **shrive**

Shriv·i·jay·a /shreévi jáyə/ *n.* a trading empire centered on the Malacca Straits between Malaya and Sumatra with a Buddhist government that opened up Southeast Asia to Muslim conversion when it fell [Late 19thC. From Hindi.]

shroff /shrof, shrawf/ *n.* **1.** **INDIAN BANKER** a banker or moneychanger in India **2.** **EXPERT IN COUNTERFEIT COINS** somebody employed in eastern Asia to separate counterfeit from real coins ■ *vt.* (**shroffed, shroff·ing, shroffs**) **SEPARATE COUNTERFEIT COINS** to separate counterfeit from real coins [Early 17thC. Alteration of Hindi *śarāf*, from Arabic *ṣarrāf*.]

Shrop·shire /shróp sheer, -shər/ *n.* a dark-faced sheep belonging to a breed kept for wool and meat [Mid-18thC. From the name of the place in England where the breed originated.]

shroud /shrowd/ *n.* **1.** **BURIAL CLOTH** a cloth in which a dead body is wrapped before burial **2.** **COVERING** something that covers or conceals something or somebody **3.** **PROTECTIVE COVERING** a protective covering such as a guard for a piece of machinery **4.** SPACE TECH **PROTECTIVE COVERING FOR SPACECRAFT** a shield that protects a spacecraft from heat during launch **5.** SAILING **MAST STAY** any one of the supporting ropes or wires that extend down from the top of a mast **6.** **CABLE TO STOP SWAY** a supporting cable that extends from the top of a tall structure such as a smokestack to the ground **7.** **PART OF AIRFOIL SURFACE** a rearward extension of a fixed airfoil surface covering the leading edge of a movable surface hinged to it **8.** AIR **PARACHUTE LINE** any one of the lines by which the harness of a parachute is attached to the canopy ■ *v.* (**shroud·ed, shroud·ing, shrouds**) **1.** *vt.* **WRAP CORPSE** to wrap a dead body in a cloth **2.** *vt.* **COVER OR CONCEAL SOMETHING** to cover or conceal somebody or something **3.** *vti.* **SHELTER** to shelter somebody or to seek shelter (*archaic*) [Old English *scrūd* "garment." Ultimately, from a prehistoric West Germanic word meaning "to cut," which is also the ancestor of English *shred*.]

shrove past tense of **shrive**

Shrove·tide /shrṓv tīd/ *n.* CALENDAR in the Christian calendar, the three-day period preceding Ash Wednesday and the season of Lent

Shrove Tues·day /shrṑv-, -tóozdee/ *n.* in the Christian calendar, the last day before the beginning of Lent [From the practice of going to confession at the beginning of Lent]

shrub[1] /shrub/ *n.* any woody plant without a trunk but with several stems growing from the base [Old English *scrybb* "shrubbery." Ultimately, from an Indo-European word meaning "to cut," which is also the ancestor of English *short*.]

shrub[2] /shrub/ *n.* a drink made with fruit juice, sugar, spices, and rum or other alcohol [Early 18thC. From Arabic *surb* "a drink," which is also the ancestor of English *syrup*.]

shrub·ber·y /shrúbbəree/ (*plural* **-ies**) *n.* **1.** **PART OF GARDEN WITH SHRUBS** a part of a garden where shrubs grow **2.** **SHRUBS COLLECTIVELY** shrubs considered collectively

shrub·by /shrúbbee/ (**-bi·er, -bi·est**) *adj.* **1.** **WITH SHRUBS** having shrubs or covered with shrubs **2.** **LIKE A SHRUB** resembling a shrub in size or in having little or no trunk —**shrub·bi·ness** *n.*

shrug /shrug/ *vti.* (**shrugged, shrug·ging, shrugs**) **RAISE AND DROP SHOULDERS BRIEFLY** to raise and drop the shoulders briefly, especially to indicate indifference or lack of knowledge ■ *n.* **GESTURE OF RAISING AND DROPPING SHOULDERS** a gesture of raising and dropping the shoulders briefly [14thC. Origin unknown.]

shrug off *vt.* **1.** **DISMISS SOMETHING** to reject or disregard something as unimportant **2.** **GET FREE OF SOMETHING** to become free of something such as a disease **3.** **REMOVE CLOTHING** to get out of clothing by wriggling

shrunk past tense, past participle of **shrink**

shrunk·en past participle of **shrink**

sht. *abbr.* sheet

shtetl /shtétt'l, shtáyt'l/ (*plural* **shtetls** *or* **shtet·lach** /shtét laak, shtáyt-/), **schtetl** (*plural* **schtetls** *or* **schtet·lech** /shtétlak/) *n.* formerly, a small Jewish town or village in Eastern Europe [Mid-20thC. Via Yiddish, "little town" from German *Stadt* "town."]

shtg. *abbr.* shortage

shtick /shtik/, **schtick, shtik** *n.* **1.** **ENTERTAINER'S ROUTINE** a comedian's or entertainer's act, routine, or gimmick (*informal*) **2.** **SPECIAL ATTRIBUTE OF SOMEBODY** something, e.g., an interest, talent, trait, job, or hobby, that especially characterizes somebody (*slang*) **3.** **EXAGGERATION** an exaggerated complaint or extreme position (*humorous*) [Mid-20thC. Via Yiddish "a routine, a piece," from, ultimately, Old High German *stucki* "piece."]

shtink·er /stíngkər/ *n.* a reprehensible person (*insult*)

shuck /shuk/ *n.* **1.** **OUTER COVERING OF GRAIN OR FRUIT** the husk, pod, or shell of something such as a nut, pea, or ear of corn **2.** **OYSTER OR CLAM SHELL** the shell of a clam or oyster ■ **shucks** *npl.* **SOMETHING WITH LITTLE VALUE** something of little or no value (*informal*) ■ *vt.* (**shucked, shuck·ing, shucks**) **1.** **TAKE SOMETHING FROM HUSK** to remove the husk, pod, or shell from something **2.** **GET RID OF SOMETHING** to get rid of or remove something or throw something off (*informal*) [Late 17thC. Origin unknown.] —**shuck·er** *n.*

WORD KEY: REGIONAL NOTE

Shuck, as both noun and verb, is a strong Southern marker that extends from Southern Delaware above Virginia into West Virginia. In the North, it identifies the northern reaches of South Midland territory, from Ohio to Iowa; in the South, the term is virtually unchallenged.

shucks /shuks/ *interj.* used to express disappointment, bashfulness, or irritation (*informal*) [Mid-19thC. From *shuck* "something worthless."]

shud·der /shúddər/ *vi.* (**-dered, -der·ing, -ders**) **1.** **SHIVER VIOLENTLY** to shake or tremble uncontrollably from a reaction such as cold, fear, or disgust **2.** **VIBRATE** to vibrate rapidly ■ *n.* **1.** **VIOLENT SHAKING MOVEMENT** an uncontrolled shaking or trembling movement **2.** **VIBRATION** a rapid vibrating movement [12thC. Origin uncertain: probably from Middle Low German *schōderen* "to keep on shuddering" or Middle Dutch *shūderen*.] —**shud·der·y** *adj.*

shuf·fle /shúff'l/ *v.* (**-fled, -fling, -fles**) **1.** *vi.* **WALK WITHOUT LIFTING FEET** to walk slowly without picking up the feet **2.** *vti.* **DRAG FEET** to move the feet without picking them up **3.** *vi.* **MOVE AWKWARDLY** to move in an awkward clumsy way **4.** *vi.* DANCE **DANCE BY SHUFFLING THE FEET** to slide the feet in a dance step **5.** *vt.* **CHANGE WHERE SOMETHING IS LOCATED** to move things around from one place to another **6.** *vt.* **MIX THINGS UP** to mix things together carelessly **7.** *vti.* CARDS **REARRANGE ORDER OF PLAYING CARDS** to rearrange playing cards randomly so the order is not known **8.** *vt.* **AVOID OR HIDE SOMETHING** to put something aside in order to avoid or hide it **9.** *vi.* **BEHAVE EVASIVELY** to be deliberately evasive or shifty in addressing an issue ■ *n.* **1.** **FOOT-DRAGGING WALK** a slow walk while dragging the feet **2.** DANCE **SLIDING DANCE STEP** a dance or dance step in which the feet drag or slide on the floor **3.** **JUMBLE OF THINGS** a careless mixture of things **4.** CARDS **REORDERING OF CARDS** a random reordering of playing cards **5.** CARDS **SOMEBODY'S CHANCE TO SHUFFLE SOMETHING** a player's turn to shuffle playing cards **6.** **EVASION** a deliberate evasion of an issue [Mid-16thC. Origin uncertain: perhaps from Low German *schuffeln* "to walk with dragging feet." Ultimately, from a prehistoric Germanic word that is also the ancestor of English *shove*.] —**shuf·fler** *n.*

shuf·fle·board /shúff'l bàwrd/ *n.* **1.** **GAME PLAYED WITH DISKS** a game in which players use a long pronged cue to push disks along a smooth hard surface into numbered scoring areas **2.** **SURFACE FOR SHUFFLEBOARD** the surface on which shuffleboard is played [Mid-19thC. Alteration of *shovelboard*, an alteration of obsolete *shove-board*, an earlier name for the game.]

shul /shool/, **schul** *n.* a synagogue [Late 19thC. Via Yiddish from German *Schule* "school." From its use as a place of learning.]

Shull /shul/, **Clifford G.** (*b.* 1915) U.S. physicist. He shared a Nobel Prize (1994) for his research on shattering neutrons and atomic structure.

shun /shun/ (**shunned, shun·ning, shuns**) *vt.* to avoid somebody or something intentionally [Old English *scunian*, of unknown origin] —**shun·ner** *n.*

shun·pike /shún pīk/ *n.* a secondary road taken to avoid traffic or to avoid paying a toll on a main highway or turnpike

shunt /shunt/ *v.* (**shunt·ed, shunt·ing, shunts**) **1.** *vt.* **MOVE SOMEBODY OR SOMETHING ELSEWHERE** to move somebody or something to a different place, especially for convenience rather than fairness or kindness **2.** *vti.* RAIL **CHANGE TRACKS** to move rolling railroad cars from one track to another, either by using a locomotive or by means of an automatic switch, especially when assembling trains **3.** *vt.* **GET RID OF RESPONSIBILITY** to avoid something by ignoring it or shifting responsibility for it to somebody else **4.** *vt.* ELECTRON ENG **DIVERT CURRENT** to use an electrical device to divert electrical current from an instrument **5.** *vt.* **SURGICALLY DIVERT FLOW** to use an artifically created passage to redirect the circulation of blood or cerebrospinal fluid ■ *n.* **1.** **DIVERSION OF SOMETHING** a turning aside or means of turning something aside **2.** RAIL **SORTING OF RAILWAY VEHICLES** the act of a locomotive pushing railway vehicles in the process of sorting them **3.** ELECTRON ENG **DEVICE FOR DIVERTING ELECTRIC CURRENT** a component in an electric circuit that is connected in parallel with an instrument and diverts the majority of current from the instrument **4.** **BYPASS FOR BODILY FLUID** a passage in the body that diverts the flow of blood or other bodily fluid form one channel to another, created either as a result of disease or injury or artificially by surgery. Artificial shunts are used to facilitate regular connection to a kidney dialysis machine or to relieve the pressure of cerebrospinal fluid on the brain in the condition of hydrocephalus. [13thC. Origin uncertain: perhaps from SHUN.]

shush /shŏŏsh, shush/ *interj.* **BE QUIET** used to tell somebody to be quiet ■ *vti.* (**shushed, shush·ing, shush·es**) **SILENCE SOMEBODY** to silence somebody or to become silent (*informal*) [Early 20thC. Of imitative origin.]

shut /shut/ *v.* (**shut, shut·ting, shuts**) **1.** *vti.* **CLOSE OPENING** to move something or move into a position that blocks or covers an opening ○ *leaned over to shut the window* **2.** *vt.* **STOP ACCESS OR EXIT** to prevent entrance to or exit from something, e.g., by locking doors ○ *Rising water levels meant that they had to shut the tunnel.* **3.** *vt.* **FOLD PARTS CLOSED** to close something by bringing its covering or parts together ○ *had to shut her eyes against the light* **4.** *vt.* **LOCK SOMETHING** to secure something with a lock or latch ○ *The gate had not been shut properly.* **5.** *vti.* **STOP OPERATION** to discontinue or cause something to discontinue operation temporarily or permanently ○ *another factory shut because it was losing money* ■ *adj.* **SECURED** closed or fastened against entrance or exit ■ *n.* METALL **CONNECTION REGION BETWEEN WELDED METAL PIECES** the region of connection between pieces of metal that are welded together [Old English *scyttan*. Ultimately, from a prehistoric Germanic word that is also the ancestor of English *shoot*. From the sense of shooting a bolt across a door to fasten it.]

shut down *v.* **1.** *vti.* **STOP OPERATION** to cease or cause something to cease operation or activity **2.** *vi.* **SETTLE OVER PLACE** to settle over and blanket a place **3.** *vt.* PHYS **CUT REACTOR OUTPUT** to reduce the power output of a nuclear reactor by maintaining it at its lowest possible level

shut in *vt.* to confine or enclose somebody or something

shut off *v.* **1.** *vti.* **STOP SOMETHING WORKING** to stop operating or to cause something to stop operating **2.** *vt.* **CUT OFF FLOW** to stop the passage, flow, or supply of something **3.** *vt.* **BLOCK SOMETHING OFF** to impede the flow or progress of something **4.** *vt.* **ISOLATE SOMEBODY** to put somebody or something into a state of isolation

shut out *vt.* **1.** **EXCLUDE SOMEBODY** to exclude somebody or something **2.** **STOP SOMEBODY ENTERING** to prevent somebody or something from entering a place **3.** **HIDE SOMETHING** to hide something from sight **4.** SPORTS **KEEP SOMEBODY FROM SCORING** to prevent an opponent from scoring in a game

shut up *v.* **1.** *vi.* **STOP TALKING** to be quiet or stop talking (*informal*) ○ *I shut up before saying something I would regret.* **2.** *vt.* **SILENCE SOMEBODY** to cause somebody to be quiet or stop talking (*informal*) ○ *She shot me a look that shut me up instantly.* **3.** *vt.* **CONFINE SOMEBODY** to confine or imprison somebody or something ○ *She shut the dog up in the pen.* **4.** *vt.* **CLOSE SOMETHING** to close or prevent entrance to something ○ *The building is all shut up.*

shut·down /shút dòwn/ *n.* **1.** **BUSINESS CLOSING** the cessation or suspension of activities at a business, factory, or plant **2.** **MAINTENANCE LEVEL OF REACTOR POWER** the reduction of power in a nuclear reactor by maintaining the core at the lowest level possible

shut·eye *n.* a short sleep (*informal*)

shut-in *n.* somebody who cannot leave a dwelling because of illness or physical limitations on mobility

shut·off *n.* **1.** **DEVICE THAT STOPS SOMETHING WORKING** a device, usually a valve, that shuts something off **2.** **TEMPORARY STOP** an interruption or stoppage, e.g., in flow or supply

shut·out *n.* **1.** = **lockout** *n.* **2.** SPORTS **GAME SCORELESS ON ONE SIDE** a game in which one team does not score

shut·ter /shúttər/ *n.* **1.** **DOOR OR WINDOW COVER** a hinged cover for a door or window, often with louvers and usually fitted in pairs **2.** PHOTOGRAPHY **CAMERA DEVICE** a mechanical part of a camera that opens and closes the lens aperture to expose the film or plate to light ■ *vt.* **(-tered, -ter·ing, -ters)** **1.** **CLOSE SOMETHING USING SHUTTERS** to close or protect something by means of shutters **2.** **FIT SOMETHING WITH SHUTTERS** to equip something with shutters

shut·ter·bug /shúttər bùg/ *n.* an active and enthusiastic amateur photographer (*informal*)

shut·tle /shútt'l/ *n.* **1.** **WEAVING DEVICE** a device in weaving that holds the weft thread and is used to pass it between the warp threads **2.** **SPINDLE OR BOBBIN HOLDING THREAD** a thread holder, e.g., in tatting or netting or for the lower thread in a sewing machine **3.** **ROUTE TAKEN OR VEHICLE USED** the route taken or the aircraft, bus, or train used to travel frequently between two places, often relatively near each other **4.** = **space shuttle** **5.** **GOING BACK AND FORTH** frequent travel by vehicle between two places **6.** RACKET GAMES = **shuttlecock** ■ *vti.* **(-tled, -tling, -tles)** **1.** **GO BACK AND FORTH** to move or cause somebody or something to move between two places frequently **2.** TRANSP **GO BY SHUTTLE** to transport somebody or something or to be transported by a shuttle [Old English *scytel* "arrow, dart." Ultimately, from a prehistoric Germanic word meaning "to project," which is also the ancestor of English *shoot.*]

shut·tle·cock /shútt'l kòk/ *n.* **OBJECT HIT IN BADMINTON** a small rounded piece of cork or rubber attached to a cone of feathers that is hit back and forth in badminton and in the old game of battledore ■ *vt.* **(-cocked, -cock·ing, -cocks)** **SEND SOMETHING BACK AND FORTH** to toss or send something back and forth [Early 16thC. *Shuttle* probably from its going back and forth, like the shuttle in a loom; *cock* from the feathers, like a bird's crest.]

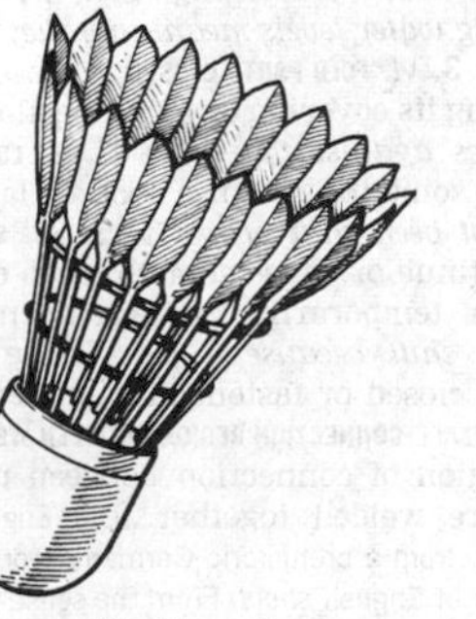

Shuttlecock

shut·tle·craft /shútt'l kràft/ (*plural* **-craft**) *n.* a reusable spacecraft for carrying astronauts or material between Earth and space or between objects in space

shut·tle di·plo·ma·cy *n.* diplomatic negotiations carried on between countries by a mediator who travels back and forth between the countries

shvart·se /shvaártsə/ *n.* an offensive term referring to somebody of African ancestry (*slang offensive*) [Mid-20thC. From the Yiddish pronunciation of the feminine form of German *schwarz* "black."]

shwa *n.* = **schwa**

shy[1] /shī/ *adj.* **(shi·er, shi·est)** **1.** **UNCOMFORTABLE WITH OTHERS** reserved, diffident, and uncomfortable in the company of others **2.** **TIMID** easily frightened ○ *The deer were shy and ran when we tried to approach them.* **3.** **CAUTIOUS** unwilling to trust or put confidence in somebody or something ○ *The children were shy of their new classmates.* **4.** **RELUCTANT** fearful of making a commitment ○ *Don't be shy of speaking your mind.* **5.** **SHORT OF SOMETHING** short of the full or a particular amount ○ *We are $100 shy of the down payment.* **6.** BIOL **NOT REPRODUCING EASILY** used to describe plants and animals that do not breed readily or freely ■ *vi.* **(shied, shy·ing, shies)** **1.** **MOVE SUDDENLY** to move suddenly in fright or alarm ○ *The horse shied when the firecracker went off in the next field.* **2.** **STAY AWAY** to avoid or evade something ○ *He always shies away from public speaking.* ■ *n.* (*plural* **shies**) **SUDDEN MOVE** a sudden movement in fright or alarm [Old English *scēoh.* From a prehistoric Germanic base that is also the ancestor of English *eschew* and *skew.*] —**shy·er** *n.* —**shy·ly** *adv.* —**shy·ness** *n.*

shy[2] /shī/ *vt.* **(shied, shy·ing, shies)** **THROW SOMETHING** to toss something quickly and suddenly ■ *n.* (*plural* **shies**) **QUICK THROW** a quick sudden throw of something [Late 18thC. Origin uncertain: perhaps from SHY[1], applied to timid cockerels, from the custom of throwing sticks at them to make them fight.] —**shy·er** *n.*

shy·lock /shī lòk/ *n.* **HEARTLESS CREDITOR** a ruthless and demanding moneylender or creditor ■ *vi.* **(-locked, -lock·ing, -locks)** **PRACTICE USURY** to charge exorbitant interest on borrowed money [Late 18thC. Named for *Shylock*, a moneylender in Shakespeare's play *The Merchant of Venice.*]

shy·ster /shīstər/ *n.* an unscrupulous person, especially a lawyer or political representative (*slang insult*) [Mid-19thC. Origin uncertain: perhaps from the name *Scheuster*, a New York lawyer in the 1840s known for his unethical methods. Alternatively from German *Scheisser* "bastard," formed from *Scheisse* "excrement."]

si /see/ *n.* MUSIC = **ti** [Early 18thC. From the initial letters of Latin *Sancte Iohannes* "St. John," which are the words sung to this note in the hymn for St. John's day.]

Si *symbol.* silicon

SI *abbr.* International System of Units [French *Système International (d'Unités)*]

si·al /sī àl/ *n.* a term used in the past for rocks rich in silicon and aluminum that form the crust of the continental masses [Early 20thC. A blend of *silicon* and *aluminum.*] —**si·al·ic** /sī állik/ *adj.*

si·al·a·gogue /sī állə gòg/, **si·al·o·gogue** *n.* a drug or agent that stimulates the flow of saliva —**si·al·a·gog·ic** /sī àllə gójjik, -góggik/ *adj.*

si·al·ic ac·id *n.* an amino acid found in animal blood and tissues

Si·al·kot /see álkot/ town in Punjab Province, northeastern Pakistan, situated about 60 mi./97 km north of Lahore. Population: 302,009 (1981).

si·al·o·gogue *n.* = **sialagogue**

si·a·loid /sī ə lòyd/ *adj.* resembling saliva

Si·am /sī ám/ former name for **Thailand**

Si·am, Gulf of former name for **Thailand, Gulf of**

si·a·mang /seé ə màng, -maàng/ *n.* the largest species of gibbon, found in Sumatra and Malaysia. It has a large throat sac that inflates during calls and webbing between its second and third toes. Latin name: *Hylobates syndactylus.* [Early 19thC. From Malay.]

siamese /sī ə meéz/ *adj.* connecting two or more hoses or pipes into a Y-shaped adapter that permits a discharge in a single stream

Si·a·mese /sī ə meéz/ *adj.* PEOPLES = **Thai** (*dated*) ■ *n.* (*plural* **-mese**) **1.** PEOPLES = **Thai** (*dated*) **2.** = **Siamese cat** [Late 17thC. The original meaning is "of Siam."]

Siamese cat

Si·a·mese cat *n.* a short-haired domestic cat with blue eyes and a long cream-colored body with dark ears, paws, face, and tail, belonging to a breed that originated in Thailand (formerly Siam) [Named for its place of origin]

Si·a·mese fight·ing fish *n.* a brightly colored long-finned freshwater fish, native to Thailand and Malaysia. The male of this popular aquarium fish is very aggressive. Latin name: *Betta splendens.*

Si·a·mese twins *npl.* a term used mainly in the past for twins physically joined together at birth [Named for two twins, Chang and Eng (1811–74), born in Siam (Thailand), who were physically joined together near the waist at birth]

sib /sib/ *n.* **1.** **BROTHER OR SISTER** a brother or sister **2.** GENETICS **INDIVIDUAL WITH SAME PARENTS AS ANOTHER** an individual that has the same parents as another individual **3.** ANTHROP **GROUP WITH SINGLE COMMON ANCESTER** a group of persons who trace their descent lineally from a single real or presumed ancestor ■ **sibs** *npl.* **WIDER FAMILY** members of an extended family considered as a group (*takes a plural verb*) ■ *adj.* **CLOSELY RELATED** with the same parents or closely related [Old English *sib(b)*, of unknown origin] —**sib·ship** *n.*

Sib. *abbr.* **1.** Siberia **2.** Siberian

Jean Sibelius

Si·be·li·us /sə báylee əss/, **Jean** (1865–1957) Finnish composer. One of the leading symphonic composers of the 20th century, his works are much influenced by the culture and landscape of his native Finland. Full name **Jean Julius Christian Sibelius**

Si·be·ri·a /sī beéree ə/ vast region of eastern Russia, extending from the Ural Mountains in the west to the Pacific Ocean in the east, and from the Arctic Ocean in the north, to China, Mongolia, and Kazakhstan in the south. Much of it is frozen for over half the year. Sparsely populated, it was used during Soviet rule (1917–91) as a place of exile, and now has no administrative significance. —**Si·be·ri·an** *n., adj.*

Si·be·ri·an hus·ky *n.* any of a breed of medium-sized dogs with a thick soft coat, erect ears, and a bushy tail that were first bred in Siberia to pull sleds

sib·i·lant /síbbilənt/ *adj.* **1.** **PRONOUNCED WITH HISSING SOUND** used to describe consonants that are pronounced with a hissing sound **2.** PRODUCING HISSING SOUND producing a hissing sound ○ *the sibilant sound of air escaping from a tire* ■ *n.* SIBILANT CONSONANT a sibilant consonant [Mid-17thC. From the present participle stem of Latin *sibilare* "to hiss," thought to be imitative of the sound.] —**sib·i·lance** *n.* —**sib·i·lant·ly** *adv.*

sib·i·late /síbbi làyt/ (**-lat·ed, -lat·ing, -lates**) *vti.* to pronounce sounds with a hiss [Mid-17thC. From the past participle stem of Latin *sibilare* (see SIBILANT).]

sib·ling /síbbling/ *n.* **1.** BROTHER OR SISTER a brother or sister (*often used before a noun*) **2.** ANTHROP MEMBER OF SIB a member of a group of persons who trace their descent from a single real or presumed ancestor [Old English. Formed from *sib(b)* (see SIB). The word disappeared by the end of the 15thC and was re-introduced by anthropologists in the early 20thC.]

sib·ling spe·cies *n.* a species that closely resembles another in appearance and other characteristics but cannot interbreed with it

sib·yl /síbbil/ *n.* **1.** GREEK OR ROMAN PROPHET a woman of ancient Greece and Rome believed to be an oracle or a prophet **2.** FORTUNETELLER a woman prophet or fortuneteller [13thC. Directly or via Old French *Sibile* from Latin *Sibylla*, which came from Greek *Sibulla*.] —**si·byl·lic** /si bíllik/ *adj.* —**syb·il·line** /síbbi lìn, -leen/ *adj.*

sic[1] /sik/ *adv.* thus or so, used within brackets to indicate that what precedes it is written intentionally or is copied verbatim from the original, even if it appears to be a mistake [Late 19thC. From Latin.] ◇ **sic passim** used to show that a particular word or term is used in the same form throughout a printed work (*formal*) ◇ **sic transit gloria mundi** thus passes the glory of the world, used, e.g., when a distinguished person dies or an important era comes to an end

sic[2] /sik/ (**sicced** *or* **sicked, sic·cing** *or* **sick·ing, sics**), **sick** *vt.* **1.** ATTACK SOMEBODY to attack somebody physically, usually used as a command to a dog **2.** INCITE SOMEBODY TO ATTACK to urge a person or animal, especially a dog, to attack somebody physically [Mid-19thC. Originally a dialect form of SEEK.]

Sic. *abbr.* **1.** Sicilian **2.** Sicily

sic·ca·tive /síkətiv/ *n.* DRYING AGENT a substance added to paints and other liquids to speed drying ■ *adj.* ABSORBENT absorbing moisture to promote drying [15thC. From late Latin *siccativus*, from Latin *siccare* "to dry."]

sice *n.* = **syce**

Si·chuan /sè chwáan/ province of southern China bordered by Qinghai, Gansu, Shaanxi, Hubei, Hunan, Guizhou, Yunnan, and Tibet. Capital: Chengdu. Population: 112,140,000 (1994). Area: 219,691 sq. mi./569,000 sq. km.

si·cil·i·a·no /si sìllee áa nō/ (*plural* **-nos**), **si·cil·i·a·na** /si sìllee áanə/ *n.* **1.** SICILIAN DANCE an old Sicilian folk dance **2.** MUSIC FOR DANCING a piece of music for a siciliano, in a minor key with six or twelve beats to the measure [Early 18thC. From Italian, literally "Sicilian."]

Si·ci·ly /síssəlee/ the largest island in the Mediterranean Sea, in southern Italy. Capital: Palermo. Population: 5,082,697 (1995). Area: 9,830 sq. mi./25,460 sq. km. —**Si·cil·ian** /si síllee ən/ *n., adj.*

sick[1] /sik/ *adj.* **1.** ILL affected by an illness **2.** RELATING TO ILLNESS relating to illness or to people who are ill ○ *The company gives employees five sick days a year.* **3.** LIKELY TO VOMIT feeling on the point of vomiting **4.** OFFENSIVE TERM an offensive term referring to somebody thought to have a psychiatric disorder that makes him or her dangerous to others **5.** IN BAD TASTE dealing with subjects regarded by most people as bizarre, gruesome, or otherwise unsuitable for lighthearted treatment (*informal*) **6.** DISTRESSED spiritually or emotionally distraught ○ *sick with worry* **7.** VERY BORED WITH SOMETHING utterly tired of something because of having had too much of it ○ *I am sick of watching television.* **8.** YEARNING feeling a deep or passionate longing for something or somebody ○ *sick for my family* **9.** DISGUSTED filled with disgust or repulsion ○ *His rudeness makes me sick.* **10.** IMPAIRED in need of repair ○ *a sick economy* **11.** SUGGESTING ILLNESS pale and unhealthy looking **12.** AGRIC UNPRODUCTIVE unable to produce a profitable crop ○ *a sick field* **13.** MED FORMING UNHEALTHFUL ENVIRONMENT used to describe a building or other location that is seen as an unhealthful environment for people ○ *a sick office building* ■ *n.* ILL PEOPLE people who are ill [Old English *sēoc*, ultimately of unknown origin]

sick[2] *vt.* = **sic**[2]

sick·bay /sík bày/ *n.* **1.** SHIP'S HOSPITAL a hospital and dispensary on a ship **2.** TREATMENT FACILITY a place for treating the sick or injured

sick·bed /sík bèd/ *n.* a bed on which a sick person lies

sick build·ing syn·drome *n.* a group of symptoms typically including headaches and respiratory problems that affect workers in usually new or remodeled office buildings and are attributed to toxic building materials or poor ventilation

sick call *n.* a daily lineup or formation for military personnel in need of medical attention, or the scheduled time at which they may receive medical attention

sick·en /síkən/ (**-ened, -en·ing, -ens**) *vti.* **1.** MAKE OR BECOME NAUSEATED to become ill or nauseated, or make somebody feel ill or nauseated ○ *I sicken at the sight of blood.* **2.** MAKE OR FEEL DISGUSTED to feel disgust for something or somebody, or inspire disgust in somebody **3.** MAKE OR BECOME BORED to grow weary of somebody or something, or make somebody weary ○ *We soon sickened of their chatter.*

sick·en·er /síkənər/ *n.* a widely distributed poisonous mushroom with a fragile red cap. Latin name: *Russula emetica* and *Russula fragilis.* [Early 19thC. Originally in the meaning "nauseating thing."]

sick·en·ing /síkəning/ *adj.* **1.** DISGUSTING inspiring feelings of disgust or repulsion ○ *sickening cruelty* **2.** CAUSING ILLNESS bringing on illness —**sick·en·ing·ly** *adv.*

sick head·ache *n.* a headache accompanied by feelings of nausea

sick·ie *n.* = **sicko** (*offensive*)

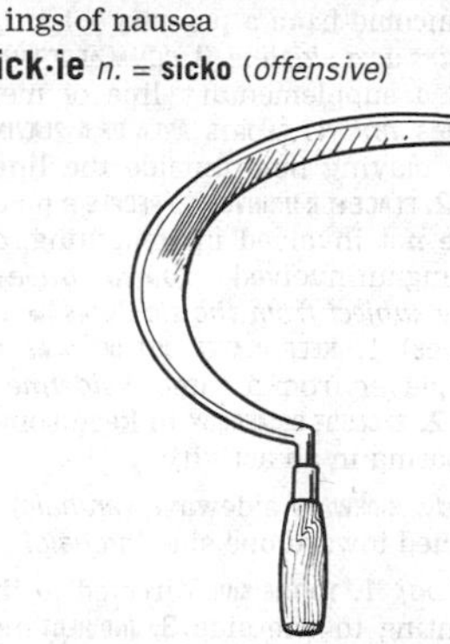

Sickle

sick·le /sík'l/ *n.* **1.** TOOL FOR CUTTING GRASS a short-handled implement with a curved blade used for cutting tall grass or grain **2.** BLADES OF FARM IMPLEMENT the cutting mechanism of a combine, reaper, or mower ■ *v.* (**-led, -ling, -les**) **1.** *vt.* CUT SOMETHING WITH SICKLE to cut something using a sickle **2.** *vti.* DEFORM RED BLOOD CELL to change a red blood cell into a sickle cell, or become a sickle cell ■ *adj.* CURVED curved in shape like a sickle (*literary*) [Old English *sicol*. Via prehistoric Germanic from Latin *secula*, from *secare* "to cut" (source of English *section* and *insect*).]

sick leave *n.* absence from work for reasons of illness

sick·le·bill /sík'l bìl/ *n.* a name given to various birds that have long curved bills, e.g., the curlew and the honeycreeper

sick·le cell *n.* an abnormal red blood cell that is crescent-shaped as a result of an inherited defect in the cell's hemoglobin

sick·le-cell a·ne·mi·a *n.* a chronic hereditary form of anemia that occurs mainly in people of African descent. It is caused by a gene inherited from both parents.

sick·le cell trait *n.* a hereditary condition of the blood in which some red cells become sickle-shaped, but not enough cells to cause anemia. This trait, which usually gives some resistance to malaria, occurs when the responsible gene is inherited from only one parent.

sick·le feath·er *n.* a long curving feather in the tail of a rooster

sick·le med·ic, sick·le med·ick *n.* a small plant with three-lobed leaves, yellow flowers, and curved pods. It is native to Europe and Asia. Latin name: *Medicago falcata.*

sick·le·mi·a /sìkə leémee ə/ *n.* = **sickle cell trait**

sick list *n.* a list of people who are sick, especially in the military

sick·ly /síklee/ *adj.* (**-li·er, -li·est**) **1.** OFTEN ILL unhealthy or tending to be frequently ill ○ *a sickly child* **2.** FROM ILLNESS produced by or related to illness ○ *a sickly complexion* **3.** BRINGING ILLNESS causing or conducive to illness ○ *a sickly climate* **4.** CAUSING DISGUST provoking feelings of disgust or nausea ○ *a sickly smell* **5.** FEEBLE lacking in strength or intensity **6.** OVERLY SENTIMENTAL sentimental to a degree that inspires disgust or scorn ○ *a sickly display of affection* ■ *adv.* FEEBLY in a weak or feeble way —**sick·li·ness** *n.*

sick·ly-sweet *adj.* excessively sweet or sentimental ○ *a sickly-sweet smile*

sick·ness /síknəss/ *n.* **1.** ILLNESS an illness or a disease **2.** NAUSEA feelings of nausea **3.** IMPAIRED CONDITION an unsound or corrupt condition [Old English]

sick note *n. U.K.* = **excuse** *n.* 4

sick·o /síkō/ (*plural* **-os**), **sickie** *n.* an offensive term referring to somebody though to have a psychiatric disorder that makes him or her dangerous to others (*offensive*)

sick-out *n. U.S., Carib* an organized absence from work by employees on the pretext of illness in an effort to force an employer to grant demands

sick pa·rade *n. U.K.* = **sick call**

sick pay *n.* wages paid to an employee who is absent from work due to illness

sick·room /sík ròom, -ròom/ *n.* a room to which an ill person is confined

Sarah Siddons

Sid·dons /sídd'nz/, **Sarah** (1755–1831) British actor. An acclaimed tragic stage actor, she was noted particularly for her role as Lady Macbeth. Born **Sarah Kemble**

sid·dur /sí dòor, síddər/ (*plural* **-du·rim** /si dóorim/ *or* **-durs**) *n.* a Jewish daily and Sabbath prayer book [Mid-19thC. From Hebrew *siddūr*, literally "arrangement, order."]

side /sīd/ *n.* **1.** PERIMETER OF FIGURE a line segment that forms the perimeter of a plane geometric figure ○ *A square has four sides.* **2.** SURFACE OF FIGURE a surface of a solid geometric figure ○ *A cube has six sides.* **3.** SURFACE OF SOMETHING FLAT either of the two surfaces of a flat object **4.** LEFT OR RIGHT OF SOMETHING the left or right of an object as opposed to the top, bottom, front, or back **5.** EITHER DIVISION either of two parts or areas into which something can be divided relative to the observer ○ *The playing field is on the far side of the park.* **6.** PLACE RELATIVE TO CENTER a location, place, or direction relative to a central point ○ *We live on the east side of the city.* **7.** PLACE SEPARATED BY BARRIER a place or area on either side of a barrier or boundary ○ *We live on the east side of the river.* **8.** VERTICAL SURFACE a vertical surface of something ○ *the side of a building* **9.** EDGE the area at the edge of something ○ *the side of the road* **10.** HALF OF BODY either half of the body of an animal or person, especially the area of a person's body between the shoulder and the hip ○ *My side aches.* **11.** HALF OF CARCASS half of a meat carcass ○ *a side of pork* **12.** NEARBY POSITION the place next to somebody or something ○ *Come stand at my side.* **13.** PARTY IN CONTEST any one of two or more opposing individuals, teams, groups, or factions **14.** OPINION IN A DISPUTE any one of the positions or opinions held in a dispute **15.** SUPPORTERS the group of people who support a particular party in a dispute ○ *I'm on your side.* **16.** ASPECT an aspect or view of an issue or event ○ *the funny side of a situation* **17.** PART OF FAMILY a line of descent ○ *He gets his red hair from his father's side.* **18.** = **side dish 19.** *U.K.* CUE GAMES = **English** ■ *adj.* **1.** AT THE SIDE situated at or on a side ○ *The side door is open.* **2.** FROM THE SIDE directed to or from the side ○ *a side blow* **3.** INCIDENTAL having only minor or subsidiary importance ○ *a side issue* ■ *v.* **(sid·ed, sid·ing, sides) 1.** *vi.* ALIGN WITH OR AGAINST SOMEBODY to align with or against one or other of the individuals, teams, groups, or factions in a contest or dispute ○ *We all sided with the home team.* **2.** *vt.* FIT BUILDING WITH OUTER WALLS to fit the boards **(siding)** that form the outer skin of a building ○ *side the barn* [Old English *sīde*. From a prehistoric Germanic word, of uncertain origin: probably formed from an adjective meaning "long, deep, low."] ◇ **get on the right side of somebody, keep on the right side of somebody** to get into or keep in somebody's favor ◇ **get on the wrong side of somebody** to make yourself disliked by somebody ◇ **on the side 1.** illegally or secretly **2.** in addition to a main job or activity **3.** as an additional separate dish ◇ **to one side** out of the focus of attention for the moment, to be dealt with later ◇ **side by side** close beside each other ◇ **take sides** to support one person or group against another ◇ **this side of** almost or just short of

side arm *n.* a weapon such as a pistol that is worn at the waist, usually on a belt

side·arm /sīd àarm/ *adj.* THROWN WITH SIDEWAYS MOTION in baseball, thrown with a sweep of the arm at the side while keeping it between the shoulder and the hip ○ *a sidearm pitch* ■ *adv.* WITH SWEEPING MOTION used to describe a way of throwing a baseball with a sweeping motion at the side and the arm kept below shoulder height ○ *He pitches sidearm.*

side·band /sīd bànd/ *n.* the band of frequencies on either side of the carrier frequency, produced by modulation of a carrier wave

side·bar /sīd bàar/ *n.* **1.** SUPPLEMENTARY NEWS STORY a short news story containing supplementary information that is printed alongside a featured story **2.** JUDGE-LAWYER DISCUSSION a conversation among a judge and lawyers at a trial that those on the jury cannot hear [Mid-20thC. From the practice of printing such articles boxed off to the side.]

side·board /sīd bàwrd/ *n.* a piece of dining room furniture with a flat top and drawers and cupboards to store tableware and linens [14thC. The meaning evolved from "side table" via "dining-room table."]

side·boards /sīd bàwrdz/ *npl. U.K.* = **sideburns**

side·burns /sīd bùrnz/ *npl.* hair grown down the side of a man's face in front of his ears [Late 19thC. Alteration of *burnsides*, named for General Ambrose E. *Burnside* (1824–81), who wore them.]

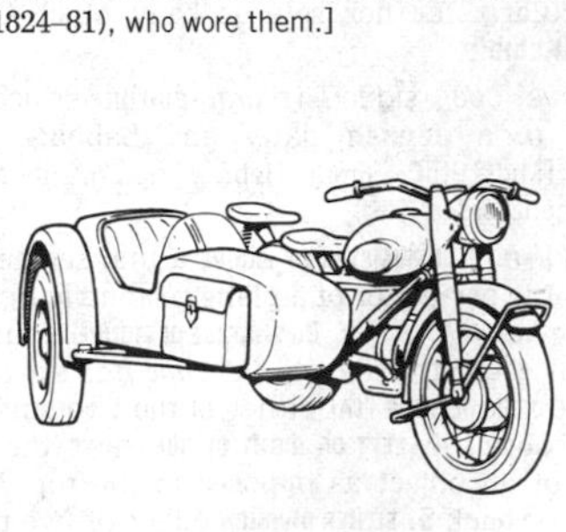

Sidecar

side·car /sīd kàar/ *n.* **1.** VEHICLE ATTACHED TO MOTORCYCLE a one-wheeled passenger vehicle attached to the side of a motorcycle **2.** COCKTAIL a cocktail of brandy, orange liqueur, and lemon juice [Late 19thC. Originally in the meaning "carriage with lengthwise seats."]

side chain *n.* a group of atoms attached to an atom in a principal chain or to a ring in a molecule

side chair *n.* a straight-backed chair with no arms, especially at a dining table

side deal *n.* a mutually beneficial agreement made between two people aside from an agreement negotiated by them on behalf of the parties or organizations they represent

side dish *n.* accompanying food, e.g., vegetables or salad, served with the main dish of a meal

side-dress *vt.* to fertilize plants by applying nutrients to the soil near the roots

side-dress·ing *n.* **1.** FERTILIZER ADDED AT ROOTS fertilizer that is put into the soil near the roots of a growing crop **2.** USE OF SIDE-DRESSING the adding of fertilizer near the roots of growing crops

side drum *n.* = **snare drum** [From its place at the drummer's side]

side ef·fect *n.* **1.** SECONDARY MEDICAL EFFECT an undesirable secondary effect of a drug or other form of medical treatment **2.** SECONDARY EFFECT a usually undesirable secondary effect produced by something

side-glance *n.* **1.** SIDEWAYS GLANCE a glance directed sideways **2.** INDIRECT REFERENCE a casual or indirect reference or allusion

side-impact *adj.* relating to or designed to protect somebody from an impact from the side

side is·sue *n.* a matter that tends to distract from the important issue

side·kick /sīd kìk/ *n.* an associate or companion who is sometimes considered subordinate (*informal*) [Early 20thC. Back-formation from "side-kicker," which was coined by the American writer O. Henry (1862–1910).]

side·light /sīd līt/ *n.* **1.** INCIDENTAL INFORMATION incidental information, usually additional to what is known already **2.** LIGHT FROM SIDE light coming from the side **3.** SIDE WINDOW a window at the side of a door **4.** NAUT SHIP'S LIGHT either of a ship's two navigational running lights, red on the port bow and green on the starboard bow **5.** *U.K.* = **parking light**

side·line /sīd līn/ *n.* **1.** SPORTS FIELD'S SIDE BOUNDARY either of two lines marking the side limits of a playing field **2.** SUPPLEMENTARY SOURCE OF INCOME a job or activity that supplements income from a primary job ○ *He does television repairs as a sideline.* **3.** COMM ADDITIONAL RANGE OF MERCHANDISE a supplementary line of merchandise ■ **side·lines** *npl.* **1.** SPORTS AREA OF A PLAYING FIELD the area of a playing field outside the lines marking its limits **2.** PLACE FOR UNINVOLVED PEOPLE a place for people who are not involved in something, or the condition of being uninvolved ○ *You can always get opinions on any subject from the sidelines.* ■ *vt.* **(-lined, -lin·ing, -lines) 1.** KEEP PLAYER OUT OF GAME to remove or keep a player from a game ○ *sideline a player for injuries* **2.** EXCLUDE SOMEBODY to keep somebody from participating in an activity

side·ling /sīdling/ *adv.* SIDEWAYS sideways (*archaic*) ■ *adj.* TO ONE SIDE directed toward one side (*archaic*)

side·long /sīd lòng/ *adj.* **1.** TO THE SIDE directed to the side **2.** SLOPING slanting to one side **3.** INDIRECT not direct or straightforward ○ *a sidelong remark* ■ *adv.* OBLIQUELY toward an area that lies at the side

side·man /sīd màn/ (*plural* **-men** /-mèn/) *n.* a member of a jazz or dance band who is neither the leader nor a soloist

side meat *n.* salt pork or bacon (*regional*) [From the part of the animal from which the meat is cut]

side or·der *n.* a portion of food ordered as an accompaniment to the main dish in a restaurant or other food outlet

sider- *prefix.* = **sidero-** (*used before vowels*)

si·de·re·al /sī dēeree əl/ *adj.* relating to the stars, especially measured with reference to the apparent motion of the stars [Mid-17thC. Directly or via French from Latin *sidereus*, from *sidus* "star."]

si·de·re·al day *n.* the time it takes for the Earth to make one complete revolution in relation to a given star, equal to 23 hours, 56 minutes, 4.1 seconds

si·de·re·al hour *n.* a 24th part of a sidereal day

si·de·re·al month *n.* the time it takes for the Moon to make one revolution around the Earth in relation to a given star, equal to 27 days, 7 hours, 43 minutes, 4.5 seconds

si·de·re·al time *n.* time measured by the daily rotation of the Earth in relation to a given star

si·de·re·al year *n.* the time it takes the Earth to make one revolution around the Sun with reference to fixed stars, equal to 365 days, 6 hours, 9 minutes, 9.5 seconds

sid·er·ite /sídə rīt/ *n.* **1.** ORE OF IRON a yellow-brown mineral that is an important source of iron. It consists mainly of ferrous carbonate and is widespread in sedimentary rock. Formula: $FeCO_3$. **2.** METEORITE a meteorite consisting of dense metallic masses composed chiefly of iron alloyed with nickel [Late 18thC. Coined from Greek *sidēros* "iron" + -ITE.] —**sid·er·it·ic** /sīdə ríttik/ *adj.*

sidero- *prefix.* iron ○ *siderolite* [From Greeek *sidēros* "iron"]

side·road /sīd rōd/ *n.* **1.** SMALLER ROAD a secondary road off the main road **2.** *Can* ROAD ALONGSIDE BOUNDARY a road along the side boundary of a concession road

sid·er·o·lite /síddərə līt/ *n.* a meteorite that is made up of approximately equal amounts of iron and stone

sid·e·roph·i·lin /sīddə róffəlin/ *n.* = **transferrin**

sid·er·o·sis /síddə rōssəss/ *n.* **1.** LUNG DISEASE a chronic lung disease caused by inhaling dust particles of iron or other metals. It is a form of pneumoconiosis. **2.** IRON ACCUMULATION IN SOMEBODY'S BODY an abnormal accumulation of iron in the blood and tissues —**sid·er·ot·ic** /síddə róttik/ *adj.*

sid·er·o·stat /síddərə stàt/ *n.* an astronomical instrument consisting of a plane mirror driven by a clock mechanism that keeps a celestial object within the same field of view of a telescope [Mid-19thC. Coined from *sidero-*, from the Latin stem *sider-* "star" + -STAT.] —**sid·er·o·stat·ic** /síddərə státtik/ *adj.*

side·sad·dle /sīd sàdd'l/ *n.* WOMEN'S RIDING SADDLE a saddle designed for women wearing long skirts so that the rider sits with both legs on the same side of the horse ■ *adv.* WITH LEGS ON ONE SIDE seated with both legs on the same side of a horse

side·show /sīd shō/ *n.* **1.** SMALLER SHOW a minor attraction offered in addition to the main entertainment at a circus or fair **2.** SOMETHING OUTRAGEOUS an action or behavior that is outrageous or bizarre (*informal*) ○ *that sideshow he calls a home life* **3.** MINOR EVENT a subordinate event or spectacle

side·slip /sīd slìp/ *vi.* **(-slipped, -slip·ping, -slips) 1.** SLIDE SIDEWAYS to skid or slide sideways **2.** AIR SLIP SIDEWAYS IN AIRPLANE to move sideways and downward while banking steeply in an airplane **3.** SKIING SLIDE SIDEWAYS DOWN SLOPE to slide at an angle down a slope ■ *n.* **1.** SIDEWAYS SKID a skid sideways ○ *The car went into a sideslip.* **2.** AIR SIDEWAYS MOVEMENT OF AIRPLANE a sideways and downward movement made by a steeply banking aircraft **3.** SKIING ANGLED SLIDE DOWN SLOPE a sideways slide at an angle down a slope

side·split·ting /sīd splìtting/ *adj.* extremely funny [The idea is of bursting with laughter] —**side·split·ting·ly** *adv.*

WORD KEY: SYNONYMS

See Synonyms at ***funny***.

side·step /sīd stèp/ *vti.* **(-stepped, -step·ping, -steps) 1.** STEP ASIDE to step aside or out of the way of somebody or something ○ *I sidestepped to avoid the running children.* **2.** EVADE SOMETHING to avoid saying or discussing something ○ *sidestep the question* ■ *n.* SIDEWAYS MOVEMENT a movement to one side —**side·step·per** *n.*

side·strad·dle hop *n.* = **jumping jack**

side·stream smoke /sīd strēem-/ *n.* smoke from a cigarette or cigar that the smoker does not inhale

side street *n.* a secondary street, often off a main street

side·stroke /sīd strōk/ *n.* a swimming stroke performed on the side by thrusting the arms alternately forward and downward while doing a scissors kick

side·swipe /sīd swīp/ *n.* **1.** GLANCING BLOW a glancing blow from or on the side **2.** GIBE a critical or insulting remark made in passing (*informal*) ○ *They were all taking sideswipes at my golfing skills.* ■ *vt.* **(-swiped, -swip·ing, -swipes)** STRIKE SIDE OF SOMETHING to strike a glancing blow to or from the side of something ○ *sideswiped a car in the parking lot* —**side·swip·er** *n.*

side·track /sīd tràk/ *v.* **(-tracked, -track·ing, -tracks) 1.** *vt.* DISTRACT SOMEBODY to divert somebody from the original subject or activity ○ *The interruption sidetracked the discussion.* **2.** *vti.* SHUNT A TRAIN to shunt a train to a railroad siding or to run into a siding ■ *n.* **1.** CAUSE OF DIVERSION something that causes a diversion from the original subject or activity **2.** SIDING a railroad siding

side·walk /sīd wàwk/ *n.* a paved path for pedestrians alongside a street

side·walk su·per·in·ten·dent *n.* somebody, often a passing pedestrian, who watches or gives unsolicited advice to workers on a construction site [From the onlooker's demeanor]

side·wall /sīd wàwl/ *n.* the side surface of a vehicle's tire, between the edge of the tread and the rim [15thC. Originally any wall forming the side of a structure.]

side·ward /sīdwərd/ *adj.* AT SIDE toward one side or at one side ■ *adv.* **side·ward, side·wards** TOWARD SIDE toward one side

side·ways /sīd wàyz/ *adj., adv.* **1.** TO ONE SIDE to or toward one side ○ *a sideways jump* **2.** FROM SIDE from one side ○ *a sideways approach* **3.** WITH SIDE FACING FRONT with or into a position with the side toward the front ○ *See if it will fit in sideways.* **4.** INTO NEW BUT EQUAL POSITION into a job or position with the same rank or status as previously held ○ *not a promotion but more of a sideways move into another department*

side·wheel /sīd hweel/ *n.* PADDLE WHEEL either of the paddle wheels on the sides of a sidewheeler ■ *adj.* WITH PADDLE WHEELS propelled by a paddle wheel on each side ○ *a sidewheel steamboat*

side·wheel·er /sīd hweelər/ *n.* a steamboat driven by a paddle wheel on each side

side whis·kers *npl.* sideburns, especially long ones

side·wind·er /sīd wīndər/ *n.* **1.** ZOOL RATTLESNAKE a small rattlesnake of the southwestern United States and northern Mexico that moves forward with a diagonal looping motion. Latin name: *Crotalus cerastes.* **2.** MIL AIR-TO-AIR MISSILE an air-to-air missile that uses a heat-seeking device to home in on a target **3.** BOXING PUNCH IN BOXING a hard swinging punch from the side **4.** SOMEBODY SNEAKY somebody who does things regarded as sneaky, especially a treacherous person or a sidearm pitcher in baseball (*slang*)

side·wise /sīd wīz/ *adj., adv.* = **sideways**

Si·di-bel-Ab·bès /seedi bele béss/ capital of Sidi-bel-Abbès Province, northwestern Algeria, situated 50 mi./80 km south of Oran. Population: 152,778 (1995).

sid·ing /sīding/ *n.* **1.** MATERIAL FORMING BUILDING'S OUTER SKIN sheets of wood, vinyl, aluminum, or other material used to surface the outside of a building **2.** SHORT RAILROAD TRACK a short stretch of railroad track that connects with the main track

si·dle /sīd'l/ *v.* (**-dled, -dling, -dles**) **1.** *vi.* MOVE FURTIVELY to edge along in a furtive way ○ *I sidled to the door in the hope that no one would notice me.* **2.** *vti.* MOVE SIDEWAYS to move, or move something, sidewards ■ *n.* SIDLING MOVEMENT a sideways or furtive movement [Late 17thC. Origin uncertain: probably a back-formation from *sideling,* modeled on verbs such as *paddle* and *mumble.*]

Sid·ney /sídnee/, **Sir Philip** (1554–86) English soldier, courtier, and poet. He was a favorite of Elizabeth I and an accomplished diplomat and soldier. His *Arcadia,* posthumously published in 1590, became the model for later English pastoral poetry.

Si·don /sīd'n/ city and seaport in southwestern Lebanon, on the Mediterranean Sea south of Beirut. It was a Phoenician city-state in the 3rd millenium B.C. Population: 38,000 (1988).

Sid·ra, Gulf of /sídrə–/ arm of the Mediterranean Sea that forms a bay on the coast of Libya, northern Africa

SIDS /sidz/ *n., abbr.* sudden infant death syndrome

siege /seej/ *n.* **1.** MILITARY OPERATION a military or police operation in which an army or the police surround a place and cut off all outside access to force surrender (*often used before a noun*) ○ *siege warfare* **2.** PROLONGED EFFORT a prolonged effort to gain or overcome something **3.** TIRESOME PERIOD a prolonged and tedious period **4.** SEAT a seat, especially a formal or ceremonial seat, e.g., a throne (*archaic*) ■ *vt.* (**sieged, sieg·ing, sieg·es**) SUBJECT PLACE TO SIEGE to assail or assault an enemy's fortifications militarily ○ *a town sieged with troops* [12thC. Via Old French *sege* "seat" from, ultimately, Latin *sedere* "to sit" (source of English *session size subsidy*).] ◇ **lay siege to 1.** to besiege a place **2.** to make a persistent attempt to gain something

Sieg·fried /seeg freed, síg-/ *n.* in German legend, a prince who kills the dragon guarding the treasure of the Nibelungs, and wins Brunhild for Gunther

Sieg·fried line *n.* the line of fortifications constructed by Germany before and during World War II on its western frontier, facing the Maginot line in France [Mid-20thC. Named for *Siegfried,* the (nearly) invincible hero of Germanic legend.]

Sieg Heil /seeg hīl/ *interj.* hail to victory, a Nazi salute usually accompanied by the right arm raised with the palm facing downward [Mid-20thC. From German.]

sie·mens /seemənz/ (*plural* **-mens**) *n.* the SI unit of electrical conductance equal to one ampere per volt. Symbol **S** [Mid-20thC. Named for the German inventor Werner von *Siemens* (1816–92).]

Si·en·a /see énnə/ capital of Siena Province, Tuscany Region, in north central Italy. Population: 58,300 (1990). —**Si·e·nese** /see ə néez/ *n., adj.*

si·en·na /see énnə/ *n.* **1.** EARTH USED AS PIGMENT a kind of iron-rich soil that is used as a pigment in paints. It is brownish-yellow in its natural state (**raw sienna**) and reddish-brown when roasted (**burnt sienna**). **2.** PAINT artists' paint made with either color of sienna, or either color itself [Late 18thC. Named for *Siena,* a city in western Italy where the pigment was first produced.] —**si·en·na** *adj.*

si·er·ra /see érrə/ *n.* **1.** MOUNTAINS a range of mountains with jagged peaks, or the country surrounding such a range **2.** SPANISH MACKEREL a large Spanish mackerel valued as game fish and for food. Genus: *Scomberomorus.* [Mid-16thC. Via Spanish from Latin *serra* "saw" (source of English *serrate*).] —**si·er·ran** /see érrən/ *adj.*

Si·er·ra *n.* a code word for the letter "S," used in international radio communications

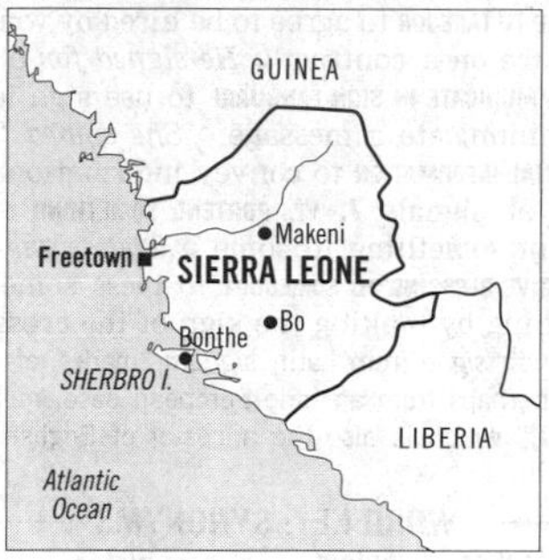

Sierra Leone

Si·er·ra Le·one /siàirə li ṓn/ republic in western Africa, situated south of Guinea, northwest of Liberia, and with the Atlantic Ocean on its western coast. Language: English. Currency: leone. Capital: Freetown. Population: 4,630,000 (1996). Area: 27,699 sq. mi./71,740 sq. km. Official name **Republic of Sierra Leone** —**Si·er·ra Le·on·e·an** *n., adj.*

Si·er·ra Ma·dre /see èrrə maa dray/ mountain system in Mexico that stretches southeastward from the U.S. border in the north to the border with Guatemala in the south. Length: 1,500 mi./2,500 km.

Si·er·ra Ne·va·da /-nè vaadə/ **1.** mountain range in southeastern Spain. Its highest peak is Cerro de Mulhacén, 11,411 ft./3,480 m. **2.** mountain range in eastern California, extending from the Mojave Desert to the Coast Range. Its highest peak is Mount Whitney, 14,491 ft./4,417 m. Length: 400 mi./640 km.

Si·er·ra Vis·ta /siàirè veestè/ city in southeastern Arizona, north of the Mexican border and southeast of Tucson. Population: 37,434 (1996).

si·es·ta /see éstə/ *n.* an early afternoon rest or nap [Mid-17thC. Via Spanish from Latin *sexta (hora),* literally "sixth (hour of the day), noon." From its customary time.]

sieve /siv/ *n.* MESHED UTENSIL a utensil consisting of a round frame surrounding a mesh or used to separate solids from liquids, large particles from small particles, or to purée foods ■ *vt.* (**sieved, siev·ing, sieves**) PUT SOMETHING THROUGH A SIEVE to pass something through a sieve [Old English *sife.* From a prehistoric Germanic base that is also the ancestor of English *sift.*]

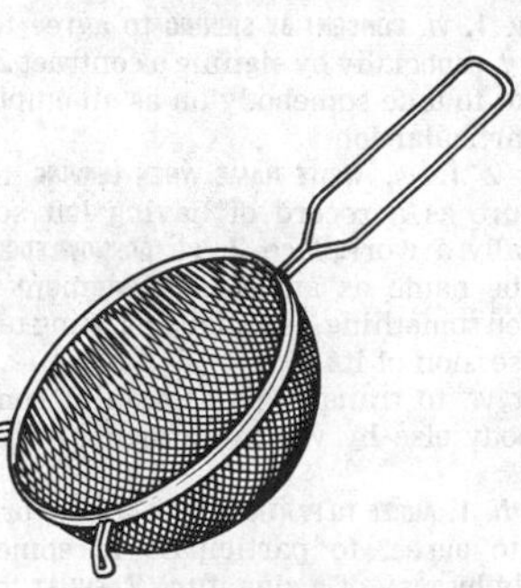

Sieve

sieve plate *n.* an area of perforations in the end walls of the cells that make up a sieve tube in plants

siev·ert /seevərt/ *n.* the SI unit measuring the probability that a stated dose of a particular radiation type will cause a biological effect. 1 sievert is equal to 1 joule per kilogram. Symbol **Sv** [Mid-20thC. Named for the Swedish radiologist R. M. *Sievert* (1896–1966).]

sieve tube *n.* a sap-conducting tube within the phloem tissue of a plant. It is composed of numerous cells (**sieve tube elements**) connected end to end and separated by porous sieve plates.

si·fa·ka /si fákə/ *n.* a large rare tree-dwelling lemur of Madagascar. It has a black face and long soft fur variously patterned in white, black, or brown. Latin name: *Propithecus verreauxi* and *Propithecus diadema.* [Mid-19thC. From Malagasy.]

sift /sift/ (**sift·ed, sift·ing, sifts**) *v.* **1.** *vti.* SEPARATE PARTICLES to pass a substance through a sieve to separate out or break up coarse particles **2.** *vt.* TAKE SOMETHING OUT to separate something out with a sieve, or by a process of selection or elimination ○ *sift the good from the bad* **3.** *vt.* SCATTER SOMETHING to scatter something with or as if with a sieve ○ *We sifted sugar on the candies.* **4.** *vti.* EXAMINE to sort or examine something carefully ○ *sift evidence* **5.** *vi.* PASS THROUGH to pass or fall through or as if through a sieve [Old English *siftan.* From a prehistoric Germanic base that is also the ancestor of English *sieve.*] —**sift·er** *n.*

sift·ings /síftingz/ *npl.* parts or elements separated out using a sieve or by a process of elimination

SIG *n., abbr.* special interest group

sig. *abbr.* **1.** signature **2.** signal **3. sig., Sig.** signor **4. sig., Sig.** signore

Sig. used on prescriptions before instructions that should be written on the label of the medicine given to a patient. Abbr of **Signa** [Shortening of Latin *signa* "mark or label it"]

sigh /sī/ *v.* (**sighed, sigh·ing, sighs**) **1.** *vi.* BREATHE LONG AND LOUD to take in and let out a deep audible breath in relief or weariness **2.** *vi.* MAKE EXHALING SOUND to make a sound like the exhalation of a deep breath ○ *The wind sighed in the trees.* **3.** *vi.* YEARN to long for somebody or something ○ *sigh for simpler times* **4.** *vt.* EXPRESS FEELING IN SIGHS to express an emotion by sighs ○ *She sighed her relief when she found us.* ■ *n.* **1.** EXHALATION an audible exhalation of a deep breath **2.** SOUND OF EXHALING a sound like that of somebody exhaling a deep breath [13thC. Origin uncertain: probably a back-formation from the past tense form of Old English *sīcan* "to sigh," which is of unknown origin.]

sight /sīt/ *n.* **1.** FACULTY OF SEEING the ability to see using the eyes **2.** SEEING the perception of something using the visual sense **3.** RANGE OF SEEING the range or field of vision ○ *Home is within sight.* **4.** SOMETHING SEEN something that somebody sees **5.** SOMETHING WORTH SEEING something that is worth seeing, especially the landmarks of a particular place (*often used in the plural*) ○ *the sights of the city* **6.** SOMETHING UNPLEASANT TO LOOK AT something or somebody that has an unpleasant, distressing, or disarranged appearance (*informal*) ○ *He was a sight after the fight.* **7.** ALIGNMENT DEVICE an alignment device on a gun or surveying instrument used to guide the eye in aiming or determining direction **8.** AIM a determination of direction made with a gun or surveying instrument **9.** OPPORTUNITY FOR OBSERVATION an opportunity to observe or inspect **10.** OPINION a point of view ○ *In the sight of his followers he was infallible.* **11.** INSIGHT expert knowledge or sharp perception (*archaic*) ■ *v.* (**sight·ed, sight·ing, sights**) **1.** *vt.* SEE SOMETHING to see or notice somebody or something ○ *They sighted the plane in the distance.* **2.** *vti.* OBSERVE USING OPTICAL DEVICE to observe something or take measurements of something using an optical device **3.** *vti.* AIM AT SOMETHING WITH GUN to take aim at something with a firearm **4.** *vt.* ADJUST GUN'S SIGHTS to adjust the sights of a gun **5.** *vi.* DIRECT THE EYES to look carefully in a particular direction ○ *sight down a line* [Old English *(ge)sih*] ◇ **a sight** a great deal or quantity (*informal*) ○ *He's feeling a far sight better today.* ◇ **a sight for sore eyes** a very welcome sight ◇ **at sight, on sight** as soon as something is able to be seen ◇ **in sight 1.** able to be seen **2.** likely to happen in the near future ◇ **know somebody by sight** be able to recognize somebody whom you have never actually met or spoken to ◇ **out of sight 1.** no longer able to be seen **2.** used to express approval and surprise (*informal*) ◇ **set your sights on something, have your sights on something** to decide to try to get something ◇ **sight unseen** without seeing or inspecting first ○ *buy something sight unseen*

sight draft *n.* a written order for the payment of money that is payable upon presentation

sight·ed /sítəd/ *adj.* **1.** ABLE TO SEE having the faculty of sight **2.** WITH SPECIFIED VISION having sight of a particular kind (*used in combination*) ○ *clear-sighted* —**sight·ed·ness** *n.*

sight gag *n.* a joke or comic episode that depends on it being seen to be funny (*informal*)

sight·ing /síting/ *n.* an occasion on which something is seen, usually something unusual or searched for ○ *sightings of UFOs*

sight·less /sítləss/ *adj.* **1.** UNABLE TO SEE without the faculty of sight **2.** UNSEEN invisible (*literary*) ○ *"heaven's cherubim, hors'd upon the sightless couriers of the air"* (William Shakespeare, *Macbeth*; 1623) —**sight·less·ly** *adv.* —**sight·less·ness** *n.*

sight·line /sít lìn/ *n.* a line of vision between a person and an object, especially between a member of an audience and the stage in a theater

sight·ly /sítlee/ (**-li·er, -li·est**) *adj.* **1.** ATTRACTIVE pleasing to look at **2.** WITH GOOD VIEW affording a fine view

sight-read /sít rèed/ *vti.* to read or perform something, e.g., music or a foreign language, without having practiced or seen it beforehand —**sight read·er** *n.*

sight rhyme *n.* = **eye rhyme**

sight·see /sít sèe/ (**-saw** /-sàw/, **-seen** /-sèen/, **-see·ing, -sees**) *vi.* to visit a place's interesting sights —**sight·se·er** *n.*

sight·see·ing /sít sèe ing/ *n.* visiting places of interest (*often used before a noun*) ○ *a sightseeing tour*

sig·il /síjjəl/ *n.* **1.** SEAL a seal or signet **2.** MAGICAL SIGN a sign or image that is supposed to have magical power [16thC. Via late Latin from Latin *sigillum*, literally "small sign," from *signum* (see SIGN).] —**sig·il·la·ry** /sí jìlleree/ *adj.*

Sig·is·mund /síggissmənd/ (1368–1437). As king of Hungary (1387–1437), he conquered much Balkan territory, but was defeated by the Ottoman Turks at Nicopolis (1396). He was Holy Roman Emperor from 1411 to 1437. His rule over Bohemia (1419–37) was constantly challenged by Bohemians opposed to his role in the execution of the religious reformer John Huss (1415).

sig·los /síglloss/ (*plural* **-loi** /sígllòy/) *n.* a silver coin used in ancient Persia between the sixth and fourth centuries B.C. [Early 20thC. From Greek.]

sig·ma /sígmə/ *n.* **1.** 18TH GREEK LETTER the 18th letter of the Greek alphabet, represented in the English alphabet as "s." See table at **alphabet 2.** MATH SYMBOL SHOWING SUMMATION the symbol σ indicating the addition of the numbers or quantities indicated **3.** = **sigma hyperon** [Early 17thC. Via Latin from Greek.]

sig·ma hy·per·on, sig·ma, sig·ma par·ti·cle *n.* any of three unstable elementary particles of the baryon group, with a mass of 2328 to 2343 times that of an electron, and a positive, negative, or neutral electric charge

sig·mate /síg màyt/ *adj.* shaped like the Greek letter sigma or the Roman S —**sig·ma·tion** /sig máysh'n/ *n.*

sig·moid /síg mòyd/ *adj.* **1.** S-SHAPED shaped like the letter S **2.** RELATING TO SIGMOID COLON relating to the sigmoid colon of the large intestine

sig·moid co·lon *n.* the final S-shaped portion of the large intestine leading to the rectum

sig·moid flex·ure *n.* **1.** = **sigmoid colon 2.** S-SHAPED CURVE an S-shaped curve or bend, e.g., in the neck of a bird or turtle

sig·moid·o·scope /sig móydə skòp/ *n.* a fiber-optic tubular instrument inserted through the anus for examining the interior of the rectum and sigmoid colon —**sig·moid·o·scop·ic** /sig mòydə skóppik/ *adj.* —**sig·moid·os·co·py** /sìg moy dóskəpee/ *n.*

sign /sīn/ *n.* **1.** SOMETHING REPRESENTING SOMETHING ELSE something that indicates or expresses the existence of something else not immediately apparent ○ *a sign of wealth* **2.** SOMETHING CONVEYING IDEA an action or gesture used to convey an idea, information, a wish, or a command ○ *His kick under the table was a sign we should leave.* **3.** ADVERTISING NOTICE a publicly displayed structure, e.g., a painted board or neon lights, carrying lettering or designs intended to advertise a business or product **4.** INFORMATION NOTICE a publicly displayed notice or board bearing directions, instructions, or warnings ○ *a highway sign* **5.** INDICATION something that indicates the presence of something or somebody ○ *no sign of life* **6.** TRACE LEFT BY ANIMAL a trace of a wild animal, e.g., the droppings, scent, or footprints **7.** OMEN something interpreted as being an omen **8.** DIVISION OF ZODIAC any of the 12 equal parts into which the zodiac is divided, each represented by a symbol **9.** EVIDENCE OF DISEASE an indication of the presence of a disease or disorder, especially one observed by a doctor but not apparent to the patient ○ *Fever is a sign of an infection.* **10.** SYMBOL USED IN MATH OR LOGIC a symbol indicating an operation or relation in mathematics or logic ○ *the plus sign* **11.** MUSICAL NOTATION SYMBOL a symbol used in musical notation **12.** = **sign language** ■ *v.* (**signed, sign·ing, signs**) **1.** *vti.* WRITE NAME to write a signature on something **2.** *vti.* APPROVE DOCUMENT to affirm or approve a document formally by affixing a signature or seal ○ *sign a bill into law* **3.** *vt.* HIRE SOMEBODY to engage somebody or somebody's services by written agreement ○ *The college signed him to coach the team.* **4.** *vi.* AGREE TO TAKE JOB to agree to be hired by writing the signature on a contract ○ *He signed for a year.* **5.** *vti.* COMMUNICATE IN SIGN LANGUAGE to use sign language to communicate a message ○ *She signed "yes."* **6.** *vti.* SIGNAL INFORMATION to convey information using a signal or signals **7.** *vt.* PORTEND SOMETHING to be an omen of something to come ○ *That signs danger.* **8.** *vt.* GIVE BLESSING TO SOMEBODY to bless somebody or something by making the sign of the cross [13thC. Via French *signe* from Latin *signum* "mark," of uncertain origin: perhaps from an Indo-European base, meaning "to say, tell," which is also the ancestor of English *say*.] —**sign·er** *n.*

WORD KEY: SYNONYMS

sign, indication, symptom

CORE MEANING: something that suggests the presence or occurrence of something

sign a general word for something that suggests the presence or occurrence of another thing. It can refer to concrete or abstract things; **indication** used in a similar way to *sign*, but most commonly used to talk about abstract things; **symptom** used to refer to a physical sign that suggests the presence of a particular medical condition. It can also refer to something that suggests the presence of a particular problem.

WORD KEY: ORIGIN

The Latin word *signum*, from which ***sign*** is derived, is also the source of English *assign, consign, design, designate, ensign, insignia, resign, seal, signal, signature, signet*, and *significant*.

sign away *vt.* to convey rights or property to somebody by signing a document ○ *He signed away his property to pay his debts.*

sign in *vi.* to write a signature in a register, usually as way of recording presence or attendance

sign off *vi.* **1.** END SOME FORM OF COMMUNICATION to bring a communication or transmission, e.g., a radio or TV program, a letter, or an e-mail message, to an end by announcing its conclusion **2.** AGREE TO SOMETHING to give approval to something (*informal*) ○ *Several members have not yet signed off on the proposed changes.*

sign on *v.* **1.** *vi.* CONSENT BY SIGNING to agree to do some activity, especially by signing a contract **2.** *vt.* EMPLOY SOMEBODY to take somebody on as an employee or to do a particular job

sign out *v.* **1.** *vi.* WRITE NAME WHEN LEAVING to write a signature as a record of having left somewhere, especially a workplace **2.** *vt.* ACKNOWLEDGE RECEIPT to sign the name as an acknowledgment of having received something, especially as being temporarily in possession of it

sign over *vt.* to transfer possession of something to somebody else by writing a signature on a document

sign up *vti.* **1.** AGREE TO PARTICIPATE to agree, or get somebody to agree, to participate in something, especially by way of a signature **2.** ENLIST to enlist, or enlist somebody, for military service

sign·age /sínij/ *n.* **1.** SIGNS signs collectively ○ *the signage along a highway* **2.** SIGN-DESIGNING the design and display of signs

sig·nal /sígn'l/ *n.* **1.** MEANS OF COMMUNICATION an action, gesture, or sign used as a means of communication ○ *Yellow is a signal for caution.* **2.** COMMUNICATED INFORMATION a piece of information communicated by an action, gesture, or sign **3.** INCITEMENT something that incites somebody to action ○ *The threat of a shortage was a signal to hoard.* **4.** TRANSMITTED INFORMATION information transmitted by means of a modulated current or an electromagnetic wave and received by telephone, telegraph, radio, television, or radar ■ *adj.* NOTABLE of considerable importance ○ *a signal accomplishment* ■ *v.* (**-naled, -nal·ing, -nals**) **1.** *vti.* COMMUNICATE to communicate a message to somebody **2.** *vt.* SEND MESSAGE USING SIGNAL to communicate something by sending a signal of some kind **3.** *vt.* INDICATE SOMETHING to be a sign that something has happened or is about to happen ○ *This event signaled the end of the conflict.* [14thC. Via Old French *seignal* from, ultimately, Latin *signum* (see SIGN). The adjective came via French *signalé* and Italian *segnalato* "made famous."] —**sig·nal·er** *n.*

sig·nal box *n. U.K.* = **signal tower**

sig·nal gen·er·a·tor *n.* a device used to test electronic equipment by generating a signal whose frequency, wave shape, and amplitude are independently adjustable over a wide range of settings

sig·nal·ize /sígnə lìz/ (**-ized, -iz·ing, -iz·es**) *vt.* **1.** MAKE SOMETHING STAND OUT to make something conspicuous or remarkable **2.** POINT SOMETHING OUT to indicate something distinctly **3.** PROVIDE TRAFFIC SIGNALS to provide a place with traffic signals —**sig·nal·i·za·tion** /sìgnələ záysh'n/ *n.*

sig·nal·ly /sígnəlee/ *adv.* completely and unmistakably

sig·nal·man /sígnəlmən/ (*plural* **-men** /-mən/) *n.* **1.** SOMEBODY WHO SENDS AND RECEIVES SIGNALS a member of the armed forces who sends and receives signals **2.** RAILROAD EMPLOYEE a railroad employee who is in charge of operating signals

sig·nal·ment /sígnəlmənt/ *n.* a detailed physical description of somebody for purposes of identification [Late 18thC. From French *signalement*, from *signaler* "to mark out."]

sig·nal-to-noise ra·tio *n.* the ratio of the strength of a signal carrying information to unwanted interference in an electronic circuit

sig·nal tow·er *n.* an electrically and semiautomatically operated control point for a large system of railroad track

sig·na·to·ry /sígnə tàwree/ *n.* (*plural* **-ries**) PARTY TO TREATY OR CONTRACT a person, government, or organization that has signed a treaty or contract and is bound by it ■ *adj.* BOUND BY TREATY bound by the terms of a treaty or contract ○ *a signatory nation*

sig·na·ture /sígnəchər, sígnə chòor/ *n.* **1.** SIGNED NAME somebody's name signed by him or her or by somebody authorized by him or her to sign **2.** SIGNING OF NAME a signing of somebody's name **3.** DISTINCTIVE CHARACTERISTIC a distinctive mark, characteristic, or thing that identifies somebody (*often used before a noun*) ○ *a signature song* **4.** MED DIRECTIONS ON PRESCRIPTION the part of a doctor's prescription that contains the directions for use **5.** MUSIC = **key signature 6.** MUSIC = **time signature 7.** PRINTING MARK INDICATING PAGE ORDER a letter or mark printed on what will become the first page of a section of a book, indicating its order in binding **8.** PRINTING SHEET PRINTED WITH MULTIPLE PAGES a sheet of paper printed with several pages that, when folded, will become a section of a book **9.** PRINTING SECTION OF BOOK a section of a book consisting of a folded sheet with several pages printed on it [Mid-16thC. Directly or via French from medieval Latin *signatura*, from Latin *signare* (see SIGN).]

sig·na·ture tune *n. U.K.* = **theme song**

sign·board /sín bàwrd/ *n.* a board carrying a notice or advertisement

signed /sīnd/ *adj.* **1.** HAVING PLUS OR MINUS SIGN with a positive or negative value, as indicated by a plus or minus sign **2.** WITH SIGNATURE ON IT bearing a signature, e.g., written to authenticate a document or as an autograph

sign·ed-ranks test *n.* = **Wilcoxon test**

sig·net /sígnət/ *n.* **1.** SMALL SEAL a small seal, e.g., one that is engraved on a ring **2.** STAMP FOR DOCUMENTS a seal used to stamp official documents **3.** IMPRESSION MADE BY SEAL the impression made on a document with a seal ■ *vt.* (**-net·ed, -net·ing, -nets**) STAMP DOCUMENT WITH SEAL to stamp a document with a seal [14thC. Directly or via French from medieval Latin *signetum*, literally "small seal," from Latin *signum* (see SIGN).]

sig·net ring *n.* a finger ring containing a small seal

sig·nif·i·cance /sig nífikənss/, **sig·nif·i·can·cy** /-nífikənssee/ *n.* **1.** IMPORTANCE the quality of having importance or being regarded as having great meaning **2.** MEANING implied or intended meaning **3.** STATS VALUE AS STATISTICAL POINTER status as a statistical value that is not accidental or random (*often used before a noun*)

sig·nif·i·cance lev·el *n.* = **level of significance**

sig·nif·i·can·cy *n.* = **significance**

sig·nif·i·cant /sig nífikənt/ *adj.* **1.** MEANINGFUL having or expressing a meaning **2.** COMMUNICATING SECRET MEANING having a hidden or implied meaning ○ *a significant nod of the head* **3.** MOMENTOUS AND INFLUENTIAL having a major or important effect ○ *a significant idea* **4.** SUBSTANTIAL relatively large in amount ○ *Her work was a significant contribution to the project.* **5.** STATS OCCURRING NOT MERELY BY CHANCE relating to the occurrence of events or outcomes that are too closely linked statistically to be mere chance [Late 16thC. From the present participle stem of Latin *significare* (see SIGNIFY).]

sig·nif·i·cant dig·its *npl.* the digits necessary in a decimal number to express accuracy, beginning with the first nonzero digit to the right of the decimal and ending with the digit farthest to the right

sig·nif·i·cant fig·ures *npl. U.K.* = **significant digits**

sig·nif·i·cant·ly /sig nífikəntlee/ *adv.* **1.** GREATLY to a large extent or degree ○ *significantly higher* **2.** IMPORTANTLY in an important or fundamental way ○ *Your ideas will contribute significantly.*

sig·nif·i·cant oth·er *n.* **1.** HUSBAND, WIFE, PARTNER, OR LOVER a spouse or someone with whom somebody has a long-term sexual relationship **2.** SOMEBODY IMPORTANT an influential or supportive person in somebody's life

sig·ni·fi·ca·tion /sìgnifi káysh'n/ *n.* **1.** MEANING the meaning of something, e.g., a word, event, or other phenomenon **2.** SIGNIFYING the signifying or indicating of something [13thC. Either directly or via Old French from the Latin stem *signification-* "indication, sign," from *significare* (see SIGNIFY).]

sig·nif·i·ca·tive /sig níffi kàytiv/ *adj.* **1.** MEANINGFUL OR IMPORTANT carrying meaning or importance **2.** SIGNIFYING OR INDICATING SOMETHING used to describe signs, symbols, or other marks that signify or indicate something —**sig·nif·i·ca·tive·ly** *adv.* —**sig·nif·i·ca·tive·ness** *n.*

sig·ni·fy /sígni fī/ (**-fied, -fy·ing, -fies**) *v.* **1.** *vt.* MEAN SOMETHING to have something as a particular meaning **2.** *vt.* BE SIGN OF SOMETHING to be a sign or symbol of something **3.** *vi.* BE IMPORTANT to be important or significant **4.** *vi.* EXCHANGE INSULTS to exchange insults with somebody playfully (*slang*) [13thC. Either directly or via Old French *signifier* from Latin *significare*, from *signum* (see SIGN).] —**sig·ni·fi·a·ble** *adj.* —**sig·ni·fi·er** *n.*

sign·ing /sīning/ *n.* = **sign language**

sign·ing bo·nus *n.* FIN an extra amount paid to somebody when he or she signs a contract, especially in entertainment and sports

si·gnior *n.* = **signor**

si·gnio·ry *n.* = **seigniory**

sign lan·guage, sign *n.* communication, or a system of communication, by gestures as opposed to written or spoken language, especially the highly developed system of hand signs used by or to people who are hearing-impaired

sign man·u·al *n.* somebody's signature, especially that of a king or queen on an official document [Translation of Anglo-Latin *signum manuale*, literally "sign made with the hand"]

sign-off (*plural* **sign-offs**) *n.* **1.** END OF TRANSMISSION PERIOD OR COMMUNICATION the end of a transmission period or communication **2.** APPROVAL approval or agreement (*informal*)

sign of the cross *n.* in Christianity, a movement of the hand as if tracing a cross in the air or on the body, usually by touching the forehead, chest, and shoulders in turn. The gesture is made, mainly by Roman Catholics, in order to invoke the blessing of God or as a declaration of Christian faith.

si·gnor /seen yáwr/ (*plural* **-gnors** *or* **-gno·ri** /-ree/), **si·gnior** (*plural* **-gniors** *or* **-gnio·ri**), **Si·gnor** (*plural* **-gnors** *or* **-gno·ri**), **Si·gnior** (*plural* **-gniors** *or* **-gnio·ri**) *n.* the usual Italian form of title or address for a man. It is the equivalent of English "Mr." ◊ **signore, signora, signorina** [Late 16thC. From Italian, a reduced form of *signore*.]

si·gno·ra /seen yáwrə/ (*plural* **-ras** *or* **-re** /-ray/), **Si·gno·ra, Si·gno·re** *n.* the usual Italian form of title or address for a married or older woman. It is equivalent to English "Mrs." or "madam." ◊ **signor, signore, signorina** [Mid-17thC. From the Italian feminine form of *signore*.]

si·gno·re /seen yáw ray/ (*plural* **-ri** /-ree/) *n.* the Italian form of title or address for a highly respected man or a man of advanced age. It is equivalent to English "sir." ◊ **signor, signora, signorina** [Late 16thC. Via Italian from Latin *senior* (source of English *senior*), the comparative form of *senex* "old."]

si·gno·ri·na /seènyə reènə/ (*plural* **si·gno·ri·nas** *or* **sig·no·ri·ne** /seènyə reè nay/) *n.* the usual Italian form of title or address for a young or unmarried woman. It is equivalent to English "Miss." ◊ **signor, signore, signora** [Early 19thC. From Italian, literally "little signora," formed from *signora*.]

si·gno·ry *n.* = **seigniory**

sign-out *n.* the act or an instance of signing out, or of signing somebody or something out

sign paint·ing *n.* the activity or profession of designing and painting signs, especially for advertising —**sign paint·er** *n.*

sign·post /sīn pōst/ *n.* **1.** INFORMATION SIGN a pole with a sign on it, especially one that gives directions or other information **2.** SOMETHING THAT INDICATES SOMETHING something that gives a clue, indication, hint, or guide ■ *vt.* (**-post·ed, -post·ing, -posts**) DIRECT SOMEBODY TO PLACE to direct somebody or mark the way to a place with signposts or similar indications ○ *a series of notices signposting patients to the X-ray department*

signwriting /sīn rīting/ *n. U.K.* = **sign painting**

Si·ha·nouk /seè ənòok/, **Norodom, King of Cambodia** (*b.* 1922). As king of Cambodia (1941–55) and intermittently prime minister and head of state, he helped win independence from French rule (1954) and protested the Vietnamese occupation (1975–82). He was restored to the throne after negotiating a political settlement in 1993.

si·ka /seékə/ *n.* a small deer native to Japan and China that has a brown, often spotted coat with a white patch on the rump. Latin name: *Cervus nippon*. [Late 19thC. From Japanese, "deer."]

sike /sīk/ *n. N England, Scotland* **1.** SMALL STREAM a small, usually slow-moving stream, especially one that tends to dry up in summer. ◊ **burn 2.** DITCH a ditch [Old English *sīc*]

Sikh /seek/ *n.* MEMBER OF INDIAN RELIGION a member of a religious group that broke away from Hinduism during the 16th century and advocated a monotheistic doctrine, incorporating some aspects of Islam ■ *adj.* OF SIKHS belonging or relating to the Sikhs or their religion, beliefs, customs, or history [Late 18thC. Via Panjabi or Hindi from Sanskrit *śiṣya* "disciple."] —**Sikh·ism** *n.*

Sik·kim /síkim/ mountainous state in northeastern India, in the eastern Himalayas, bordered by Tibet, Bhutan, and Nepal. Capital: Gangtok. Population: 406,457 (1991). Area: 2,740 sq. mi./7,096 sq. km. —**Sik·kim·ese** *n., adj.*

Si·kor·sky /si káwrskee/, **Igor** (1889–1972) Russian-born U.S. aeronautical engineer. He built the first multi-engined airplane (1913) and produced the first helicopter that could be controlled during sustained flight (1939). Full name **Igor Ivanovich Sikorsky**

si·la *n.* in Buddhism, morality, one of the three major divisions of the noble eightfold path, which consists of right speech, right action, and right livelihood. ◊ **samadhi, panna** [Mid-20thC. From Pali.]

si·lage /sílij/ *n.* animal fodder that is made by storing green plant material in a silo where it is preserved by partial fermentation [Late 19thC. Via French *ensilage* from, ultimately, Spanish *ensilar* "to store in a silo." The alteration from *ensilage* to "silage" was probably influenced by SILO.]

si·lane /sí làyn/ *n.* a compound containing silicon and hydrogen, analogous to a paraffin hydrocarbon. Formula: Si_nH_{2n+2}. [Early 20thC. Coined from SILICON + -ANE.]

Sil·bur·y Hill /sílbəri-/ artificial mound near Avebury, in Wiltshire, England. It was made about 2100 B.C. Height: 130 ft./40 m.

sild /sild/ (*plural* **silds** *or* **sild**) *n.* an immature herring, especially one that has been processed and canned. ◊ **sprat, sardine** [Early 20thC. Via Danish and Norwegian from Old Norse *sīld* "herring."]

sil·den·a·fil cit·rate /sil dènnə fil-/ *n.* a drug used to treat impotence [Late 20thC. *Sildenafil* an invented name.]

si·lence /sīlənss/ *n.* **1.** QUIETNESS the absence or lack of noise **2.** NOT SPEAKING a refusal, failure, or inability to speak **3.** ABSENCE OF ACKNOWLEDGMENT OF SOMETHING an absence of notice or acknowledgment of something ○ *Most remarkable was the statement's silence about the recent policy change.* ■ *vt.* (**-lenced, -lenc·ing, -lenc·es**) **1.** STOP SOMETHING OR SOMEBODY MAKING NOISE to stop something or somebody from making a noise **2.** SUPPRESS SOMETHING to suppress the expression of something or stop a person or group from speaking out ○ *silence criticism* **3.** END SOMEBODY'S HOSTILE BEHAVIOR to cause somebody to stop hostile or aggressive behavior [13thC. Via Old French from Latin *silentium*, from the stem of *silens*, the present participle of *silere* "to be silent."]

si·lenc·er /sīlənssər/ *n.* **1.** ARMS FIREARM MUFFLER a device that muffles the noise of a gun **2.** *U.K.* CARS PART OF EXHAUST SYSTEM the drum-shaped part of a vehicle's exhaust system that is designed to lessen noise. ◊ **muffler 3.** SOMEBODY OR SOMETHING IMPOSING SILENCE somebody or something that causes silence or lessens noise

si·lent /sīlənt/ *adj.* **1.** UTTERLY QUIET lacking any noise or sound ○ *a silent country lane* **2.** NOT SPEAKING not speaking or communicating, especially through choice ○ *The children all remained silent.* **3.** SAYING LITTLE not inclined to say much ○ *the strong silent type* **4.** UNSPOKEN not expressed or voiced, though felt or believed ○ *rolled her eyes in silent disbelief* **5.** CINEMA WITHOUT SOUNDTRACK relating to movies made without sound, typically those made before 1927 **6.** RELIG UNABLE TO SPEAK unable or not allowed to speak ○ *a silent order of monks* **7.** INACTIVE currently inactive or not operating ○ *a silent volcano* **8.** QUIETLY EXPRESSED drawing attention inconspicuously, without making noise ○ *a silent warning* **9.** NOT PRONOUNCED used to describe a letter that appears in a word but is not pronounced, e.g., the "k" in "knight" or the "b" in "debt" ■ *n.* CINEMA SILENT MOVIE a motion picture made without sound [15thC. From Latin *silent-*, the stem of *silens* (see SILENCE).] —**si·lent·ly** *adv.* —**si·lent·ness** *n.*

WORD KEY: SYNONYMS

silent, quiet, reticent, taciturn, uncommunicative

CORE MEANING: not speaking or not saying much

silent describes somebody who is refraining from speech at a particular time or in a particular situation, or somebody who is not disposed to speak much; **quiet** describes somebody who is not disposed to speak much, often because of shyness. It can also be used to describe somebody who is not speaking much in a particular situation, especially when this seems out of character; **reticent** describes somebody who is reluctant to speak on a particular occasion or about a particular subject. It can also describe somebody whose disposition is not to reveal much about himself or herself; **taciturn** describes a person who is not inclined to say very much, usually as a matter of disposition, especially when this creates an impression of gruffness or bad-temper; **uncommunicative** describes somebody who is deliberately withholding information or refusing to talk about something. It can also be used in a similar way to *taciturn* to describe somebody who tends not to say much.

si·lent auc·tion *n.* an auction that is conducted by submitting bids in sealed envelopes before the sale

si·lent but·ler *n.* a small container, usually with a hinged lid, for crumbs from the table and the contents of ashtrays (*dated*)

si·lent ma·jor·i·ty *n.* a significant number of a given population who choose not to express their views, often because of apathy or because they do not believe their views matter

si·lent part·ner *n.* somebody who invests capital in a business but who takes no part in managing it

si·lent ser·vice *n.* the submarine service of the U.S. Navy (*informal*)

si·lent treat·ment *n.* a prolonged spell of refusing to communicate as a way of expressing contempt, anger, disapproval, or some other negative emotion (*informal*)

si·le·nus /sī leénəss/ (*plural* **-ni** /-nī/) *n.* in Greek mythology, a woodland god resembling an elderly satyr [Early 18thC. Via Latin from Greek *silenos*, from *Silēnos*, name of a woodland satyr, the tutor of Dionysius.]

Silenus /sī leénəss/ *n.* in Greek mythology, an old woodland god in charge of Dionysus' education. In art, Silenus is often depicted as a drunken old man.

si·le·sia /sī leézhə/ *n.* a hard-wearing cotton twill fabric, used especially for pockets and linings of garments [Late 17thC. Named for *Silesia*, where it was manufactured.]

Si·le·sia /sī leéshə/ historic region in east central Europe, lying mostly within present-day southwestern Poland —**Si·les·i·an** *n., adj.*

si·lex /sí lèks/ *n.* **1. POWDERED SILICA** powdered silica or tripoli, used as a filter material **2. HEAT-RESISTANT GLASS** a heat-resistant glass with high quartz content [Late 16thC. From Latin, "flint."]

Silhouette

sil·hou·ette /sìlloo ét/ *n.* **1. SHADOWED CONTOUR** an outline of somebody or something filled in with black or a dark color on a light background, especially when done as a likeness or work of art **2. SOMETHING DARK ON LIGHT BACKGROUND** something lit in such a way as to appear dark but surrounded by light, or the effect produced by such lighting ○ *silhouettes dancing in front of the bonfire* ■ *vt.* (**-et·ted, -et·ting, -ettes**) **MAKE SOMETHING APPEAR AS A SILHOUETTE** to cause somebody or something to appear surrounded by light (*often passive*) ○ *The buildings were silhouetted against the rising sun.* [Late 18thC. Via French, named for Etienne de *Silhouette* (1709–67), French finance minister.]

WORD KEY: ORIGIN

As French finance minister in the late 1750s, Étienne de ***Silhouette*** gained a reputation for stinginess, and ***silhouette*** came to be used for anything skimped. One account of the application of the word to a "simple cut-out picture" is that it carries on this notion of "simplicity" or "lack of finish," but an alternative theory is that ***Silhouette*** himself was in the habit of making such pictures.

silic- *prefix.* = **silici-**

sil·i·ca /síllikə/ *n.* silicon dioxide found naturally in various crystalline and amorphous forms, e.g., quartz, opal, sand, flint, and agate [Early 19thC. From modern Latin, from the stem of Latin *silex* "flint."]

sil·i·ca gel *n.* gelatinous silica in a form that readily absorbs water from the air, used as a drying agent, a carrier for catalysts, and an anticaking agent

sil·i·cate /sílli kàyt, síllikət/ *n.* any of the most important and common of the rock-forming minerals, formed from silicon and oxygen combined with various elements, classified by their crystalline structures

si·li·ceous /sə líshəss/, **si·li·cious** *adj.* **1. OF SILICA OR SILICATES** connected with or consisting of silica or a silicate **2. REQUIRING SILICA** used to describe plants that require silica-rich soil in order to grow [Mid-17thC. From Latin *siliceus* "of flint," from the stem of *silex* "flint."]

silici- *prefix.* **1.** silica ○ *silicosis* **2.** silicon ○ *silicate* [From SILICON and SILICA]

si·lic·ic /sə líssik/ *adj.* relating to or containing silica or silicon

si·lic·ic ac·id *n.* a weak gelatinous acid obtained by adding an acid to sodium silicate

sil·i·cide /síllə sīd/ *n.* a binary compound of silicon with another element

sil·i·cif·er·ous /sìllə síffərəss/ *adj.* containing or yielding silica

si·lic·i·fy /sə líssə fī/ (**-fied, -fy·ing, -fies**) *vti.* to convert something or become converted into silica —**si·lic·i·fi·ca·tion** /sə lìssəfə káysh'n/ *n.*

sil·i·cle *n.* = **silicula**

sil·i·con /síllikən, sílli kòn/ *n.* an abundant brittle nonmetallic chemical element found naturally in sand, granite, clay, and many minerals, and used in alloys, semiconductors, and building materials. Symbol **Si** [Early 19thC. Coined from SILICA + -ON.]

sil·i·con car·bide *n.* an extremely hard bluish-black crystalline compound used as an abrasive, refractory, and semiconductor. Formula: SiC.

sil·i·con chip *n.* a small wafer of silicon forming the base on which an integrated circuit is laid out, or such a wafer together with its integrated circuit

sil·i·con di·ox·ide *n.* a colorless transparent solid that melts at a very high temperature. It is an important material in microchip manufacture. Formula: SiO_2.

sil·i·cone /sílli kōn/ *n.* a silicon-based synthetic substance in the form of a heat- and water-resistant grease, oil, or plastic. Silicones are used as lubricants, insulators, water-repellents, resins, adhesives, coatings, and paints. ◊ **siloxane** [Mid-20thC. Coined from SILICON + -ONE.]

Sil·i·con Val·ley /sìlli kōn-/ region in Santa Clara County, western California, that is an important center for electronics and computer manufacturing industries

sil·i·co·sis /sìlli kṓsiss/ *n.* a lung disease caused by prolonged inhalation of dust containing silica, and marked by the development of fibrous tissue in the lungs resulting in chronic shortness of breath —**sil·i·cot·ic** /sìlli kóttik/ *adj.*

si·lic·u·la /si líkyələ/ (*plural* **-lae** /si líkyə leè/ *or* **-las**), **sil·i·cule** /sílli kyoòl/, **sil·i·cle** /síllik'l/ *n.* a type of dry fruit, e.g., that of honesty, consisting of a broad flat pod divided by a membrane into two seed chambers [Mid-18thC. From Latin, literally "little pod," from *siliqua* (see SILIQUE).]

si·lique /sə leék, síllik/, **si·li·qua** /síllikwə/ (*plural* **-quae** /sílli kweè/ *or* **-quas**) *n.* a long dry seed capsule of plants of the mustard family that has two valves that open, leaving a central partition to which seeds are attached [Late 18thC. Via French from, ultimately, Latin *siliqua* "seed pod."] —**si·li·qua·ceous** /sìlli kwáyshəss/ *adj.* —**si·li·quose** /síllikwṑss/ *adj.* —**si·li·quous** /sílli kwəss/ *adj.*

silk /silk/ *n.* **1. THREAD FROM SILKWORMS** the fine fiber that silkworms secrete to make their cocoons. Because of its strength and elasticity and soft, shiny appearance, it is used in the manufacture of threads and fabrics. **2.** TEXTILES **SILK THREAD OR FABRIC** thread or fabric made from the fiber that silkworms secrete **3.** ZOOL **THREAD FROM SPIDERS** a fine fiber that spiders secrete and use to make their webs, nests, and cocoons **4.** PLANTS **TUFT ON CORN** the tuft of long soft hairs that forms at the end of ears of corn. = **corn silk 5.** *U.K.* LAW **KING'S OR QUEEN'S COUNSEL** somebody who has the right to practice as a King's or Queen's Counsel in British courts (*informal*) **6.** *U.K.* LAW **HIGH BARRISTER'S GARMENT** the gown worn by a King's or Queen's Counsel in British courts ■ **silks** *npl.* HORSE-RACING **JOCKEY'S SILK GARMENTS** distinctively colored clothes made from silk or a similar fabric, worn by a jockey as a mark of identification [Old English *seoloc*. Origin uncertain: probably via a Slavic language, from, ultimately, Chinese.] ◇ **hit the silk** to jump from an aircraft with a parachute

silk·a·line /sílkə leén/, **silk·a·lene** *n.* a fine cotton fabric with a glossy finish [Late 19thC. Coined from SILK + -OLINE.]

silk cot·ton *n.* = **kapok**

silk-cot·ton tree *n.* a tropical tree with large fruit capsules containing seeds coated with silky hairs, the source of kapok. Genera: *Bombax* and *Ceiba.*

silk·en /sílkən/ *adj.* **1. MADE OF SILK** made or consisting of silk **2. LIKE SILK IN TEXTURE OR APPEARANCE** resembling silk, especially in smoothness, softness, or shininess ○ *Spaniels have lovely silken ears.* **3. IN SILK CLOTHES** dressed in garments made of silk **4. SOFT OR GENTLE** pleasingly soft, gentle, or delicate ○ *silken phrases* **5. LUXURIOUS** luxurious or opulent (*dated*)

silk gland *n.* a salivary gland of a cocoon-spinning insect or an abdominal gland of a web-spinning spider that produces a viscous liquid that is expelled in a thread and polymerizes into a filament

silk hat *n.* a man's top hat with an outer covering made of silk or a fabric resembling silk

silk-screen *vti.* **PRINT DESIGN BY SILK-SCREEN PRINTING** to print a design on paper or fabric using the silk-screen printing technique ■ *n.* **1.** = **silk-screen printing 2. SILK-SCREEN PRINT** a print made using the silk-screen printing technique

silk-screen print·ing, **silk-screen** *n.* a method of printing on paper or fabric in which ink is forced through areas of a silk screen that are not blocked out with an impermeable substance

silk-stock·ing *adj.* affluent, wealthy, or aristocratic

silk tree *n.* an Asian tree of the mimosa family that is widely cultivated for its showy pink flowers with silky filaments. Latin name: *Albizia julibrissin.*

silk·weed /sílk weéd/ *n.* = **milkweed**

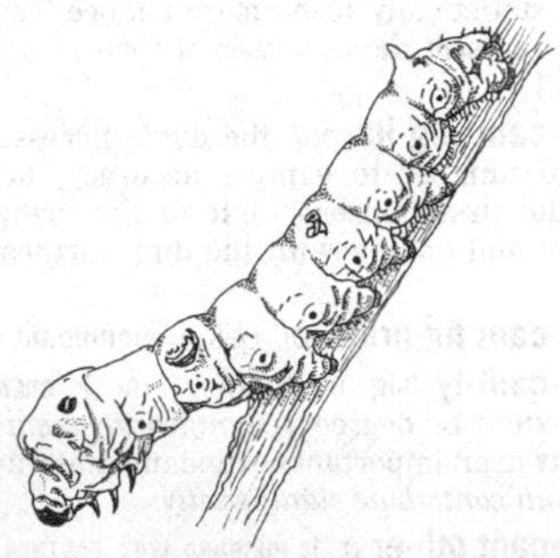

Silkworm

silk·worm /sílk wùrm/ *n.* **1. MOTH LARVA THAT SPINS SILK** a yellowish caterpillar, the larva of an Asian moth, that feeds on mulberry leaves and is a commercial source of silk. Latin name: *Bombyx mori.* **2. SILK-SPINNING LARVA** a moth larva that excretes a substance resembling silk. Family: Bombycidae.

silk·worm moth *n.* a moth with larvae that spin silk for cocoons. Family: Bombycidae.

silk·y /sílkee/ (**-i·er, -i·est**) *adj.* **1. LOOKING OR FEELING LIKE SILK** resembling silk, especially in smoothness, softness, or shininess ○ *silky hair* **2.** TEXTILES **MADE OF SILK** made of silk or a similar fiber or fabric ○ *a silky blouse* **3. SMOOTH IN MANNER** smooth, refined, elegant, or sophisticated, often to the extent of being unctuous ○ *a silky manner* **4. COVERED WITH FINE HAIRS** covered with delicate downy hairs or feathers —**silk·i·ly** *adv.* —**silk·i·ness** *n.*

silk·y oak *n.* an Australian evergreen tree grown for its feathery leaves, orange flowers, and smooth silky timber. Latin name: *Grevillea robusta.*

silk·y ter·rier *n.* a small slender Australian terrier with a long silky gray or gray-and-tan coat

sill /sil/ *n.* **1.** BUILDING **WINDOW LEDGE** a ledge below a window, especially one on the inside of a building **2.** BUILDING **BOTTOM OF FRAME** the horizontal part at the bottom of a window or door frame **3.** GEOL **LAYER OF IGNEOUS ROCK** a more or less horizontal layer of igneous rock forced between layers of sedimentary rock or older volcanic beds [Old English *syll* "foundation of a wall"]

sil·la·bub *n.* = **syllabub**

sil·li·man·ite /síllәmə nīt/ *n.* a white or greenish-brown fibrous mineral consisting of aluminum silicate and found in metamorphic rock [Mid-19thC. Coined from the name of U.S. geologist Benjamin *Silliman* (1779–1864) + -ITE.]

Sil·li·toe /síllitō/, **Alan** (*b.* 1928) British novelist, short story writer, and poet. The theme of social exclusion and of the individual's rebellion against society runs through much of his work, including *Saturday Night and Sunday Morning* (1958).

Sills /silz/, **Beverly** (*b.* 1929) U.S. soprano. She was known for her coloratura voice during a 27-year operatic career, and was manager of the New York City Opera (1979–88). Real name **Belle Miriam Silverman**

sil·ly /síllee/ *adj.* (**-li·er, -li·est**) **1. RIDICULOUS** lacking common sense **2. TRIVIAL** unworthy of serious concern **3. DAZED OR HELPLESS** in or into a stunned, dazed, or helpless condition ○ *be scared silly* ■ *n.* (*plural* **-lies**) **SILLY PERSON** somebody who lacks sense or acts foolishly (*informal*) [Old English *sælig* "happy." Ultimately from a prehistoric West Germanic word meaning "luck, happiness."] —**sil·li·ly** *adv.* —**sil·li·ness** *n.*

WORD KEY: ORIGIN

Silly has undergone one of the most astonishing semantic about-faces in the history of the English lexicon. In a thousand years it has gone from "blessed, happy" to "foolish." The transformation began with "blessed" becoming "pious." This led on via "innocent, harmless," "pitiable," and "feeble" to "feeble in mind, foolish." The related German *selig* retains its original meaning "happy, blessed."

Silly Putty *tdmk.* a trademark for a soft colored modeling material that can be stretched and bounced

sil·ly sea·son *n.* a period in summer when newspapers print frivolous articles because there is a lack of political news

si·lo /sílō/ *n.* (*plural* **-los**) **1. CONTAINER FOR GRAIN OR ANIMAL FEED** a tall cylindrical tower used for storing grain, animal feed, or other material or for making silage **2. MISSILE SAFETY CHAMBER** a reinforced, protective underground chamber where a missile or missiles can be stored and from which they can be launched ■ *vt.* (**-loed, -lo·ing, -los**) **STORE IN SILO** to store something in a silo [Mid-19thC. Via Spanish from, ultimately, Latin *sirus*, from Greek *siros* "pit to keep corn in."]

si·lox·ane /si lók sàyn, sī-/ *n.* a compound containing silicon atoms alternating with oxygen atoms and attached to organic groups or hydrogen. ◊ **silicone** [Early 20thC. Coined from SILICON + OXYGEN + METHANE.]

silt /silt/ *n.* **RIVER DEPOSITS** fine-grained sediment, especially of mud or clay particles at the bottom of a river or lake ■ *vti.* (**silt·ed, silt·ing, silts**) **CLOG UP** to become full or obstructed, or to fill or obstruct something, with silt [15thC. Origin uncertain: probably from a Scandinavian source.] —**sil·ta·tion** /sil táysh'n/ *n.* —**silt·y** /síltee/ *adj.*

silt·stone /sílt stōn/ *n.* a form of fine-grained sandstone consisting of compressed silt

Sil·u·res /síllyə reez/ *npl.* an ancient people that occupied lands in western Britain, especially South Wales, and who put up a strong defense against the invading Romans during the 1st century A.D. [Late 19thC. From Latin.]

Si·lu·ri·an /si lóoree ən, sī-/ *n.* **1.** GEOL **GEOLOGIC PERIOD** the period of geologic time when fishes first appeared, 439 to 408.5 million years ago **2.** PEOPLES **MEMBER OF SILURES** a member of the Silures [Early 18thC. Formed from Latin *Silures*; from the discovery of rocks of this period in southeast Wales, where the Silures lived.] —**Si·lu·ri·an** *adj.*

si·lu·rid /si lóorid, sī-/ *n.* **EURASIAN FRESHWATER CATFISH** a freshwater catfish of Europe and Asia with an elongated scaleless body, a short dorsal fin, and a long anal fin. Family: Siluridae. ■ *adj.* **OF SILURIDS** relating or belonging to the silurids [From Latin *silurus* "type of catfish," which came from Greek *silouros*]

sil·va, syl·va (*plural* **-vas** *or* **-vae**) *n.* **1. REGIONAL FOREST** the forests or trees of a particular region **2. BOOK DESCRIBING TREES** a book or treatise on the trees or forests of a particular region

sil·van *adj.* = **sylvan**

Sil·va·nus, Syl·va·nus *n.* in Roman mythology, the god of fields and forests, protector of flocks and cattle. He later came to be identified with the gods Pan and Faunus.

sil·ver /sílvər/ *n.* **1. SHINY ELEMENT** a shiny grayish-white metallic element that has the highest thermal and electric conductivity of any substance and is used in coins, ornaments, jewelry, dental materials, solders, photographic chemicals, and conductors. Symbol **Ag** **2.** HOUSEHOLD **SILVER ARTICLES** items of tableware or other household goods that are made of silver, coated with silver plate, or made of a silver-colored metal **3.** COINS **COINS** money, especially coins made of silver or a silver-colored metal **4.** COLORS **LUSTROUS GRAYISH-WHITE** a pale or lustrous grayish-white color **5. SILVER MEDAL** a silver medal (*informal*) **6.** PHOTOGRAPHY **SILVER COMPOUND** a compound of silver used in photography, e.g., to make paper sensitive to light ■ *adj.* **1. MADE OF SILVER** made of, plated with, or containing some silver ○ *a silver bracelet* **2.** COLORS **WITH COLOR OF SILVER** of a pale or lustrous grayish-white color **3. SHINY** shining like silver ○ *silver moonlight* **4. OF 25TH ANNIVERSARY** connected with or describing the 25th anniversary of something ○ *silver wedding anniversary* **5. RESONANT** pleasingly resonant and clear in tone **6. FLUENT** fluently or persuasively eloquent ○ *a silver tongue* ■ *v.* (**-vered, -ver·ing, -vers**) **1.** *vt.* **COAT SOMETHING WITH SILVER** to coat something with a layer of silver or a similar shiny material **2.** *vti.* **MAKE OR BECOME LIKE SILVER** to become, or cause something to become, like silver in color or sheen ○ *Frost silvered the trees.* [Old English *siolfor*. Probably ultimately from an Asian source.] —**sil·ver·er** *n.* —**sil·ver·ing** *n.*

Sil·ver Age *n.* in classical mythology, the epoch following the Golden Age that was characterized by a refusal to serve the gods and a love of luxury

sil·ver·back /sílvər bàk/ *n.* an older adult male gorilla with grayish-white hair on its back

sil·ver·bell /sílvər bèl/, **sil·ver·bell tree** *n.* a deciduous tree or shrub of the storax family of the southeastern United States and Asia with toothed leaves and drooping white bell-shaped flowers. Genus: *Halesia*.

sil·ver·ber·ry /sílvər bèrree/ (*plural* **-ries**) *n.* **1. SILVERY N AMERICAN SHRUB** a North American shrub of the oleaster family that has silvery leaves and berries. Latin name: *Elaeagnus commutata*. **2.** = **oleaster** *n.* 3

sil·ver birch *n.* a deciduous tree of Europe and Asia that has peeling silvery-white bark. Latin name: *Betula pendula*.

sil·ver bro·mide *n.* a yellowish light-sensitive powder that is used in photographic emulsions because it darkens when exposed to light. Formula: $AgBr$.

sil·ver bul·let *n.* a magical solution to a problem, e.g., a cure for cancer (*informal*) [From the idea that silver possesses magical qualities, rendering the bullet effective against such enemies as vampires in modern fiction]

sil·ver cer·tif·i·cate *n.* a bill redeemable for a fixed quantity of silver. They were issued as legal tender by the U.S. government under the former silver standard.

sil·ver chlo·ride *n.* a white light-sensitive powder that is used in photographic emulsions because it darkens when exposed to light. Formula: $AgCl$.

sil·ver cord *n.* the mutual bond that unites a mother and child (*dated or literary*) [From the title of a play (1926) by Sidney Howard, probably based on the earlier sense "cord whose loosening allows life to depart," inspired by a Bible passage, *Ecclesiastes* 12:6]

sil·ver dol·lar *n.* **1.** COINS **AMERICAN COIN** a one-dollar coin with high silver content, minted from time to time in various designs and sizes in the United States **2.** *Can* COINS **COMMEMORATIVE CANADIAN COIN** in Canada, a dollar coin issued annually, as a collector's item, to commemorate different subjects **3.** PLANTS = **honesty** [In sense 3, from the shape and color of its seedcases]

sil·ver dol·lar fish *n.* a tropical freshwater fish from Central or South America with a flattened round silver body. It is similar to the piranha but has a more docile nature and plant-eating habits. Genera: *Metynnis* and *Myleus*.

sil·ver fir *n.* a fir tree with leaves that have a white or silvery underside. Genus: *Abies*.

sil·ver·fish /sílvər fìsh/ (*plural* **-fish** *or* **-fish·es**) *n.* **1.** INSECTS **WINGLESS INSECT** a small silvery wingless insect with three long tail bristles and two long antennae that feeds on the starch of books, wallpaper, food, and other materials. Latin name: *Lepisma saccharina*. **2.** ZOOL **SILVER-SCALED FISH** a silvery fish, e.g., the moonfish, tarpon, or silversides

sil·ver fox *n.* **1.** ZOOL **FOX WITH WHITE-TIPPED FUR** an American red fox in the color phase in which the black fur is silver-tipped **2. PELT OF SILVER FOX** the pelt of the silver fox, once valued for making fur coats and other articles

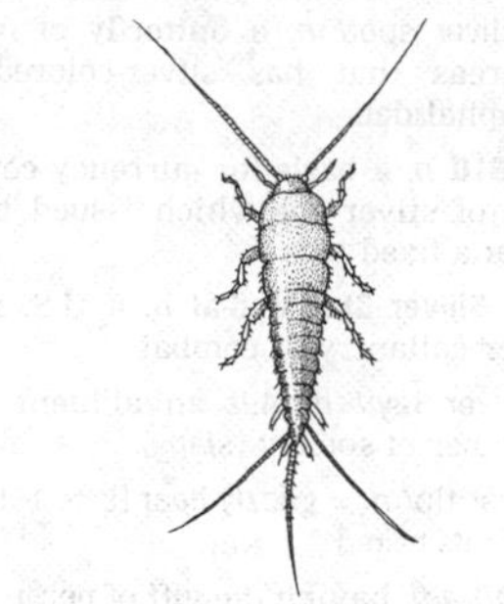

Silverfish

sil·ver-gilt *n.* **1. SILVER COATED WITH GOLD** silver that has been coated with a very thin layer of gold **2. SILVER COATING** a decorative coating of silver leaf

silver-gray *adj.* **PALE LUSTROUS GRAY** of a pale lustrous gray color ■ *n.* **PALE LUSTROUS GRAY COLOR** a pale lustrous gray color

sil·ver gull *n.* a common Australian seagull that has a white head and breast, a gray back, black-tipped wing feathers, and red beak, legs, and eye-ring. Latin name: *Larus novaehollandiae*.

sil·ver hake *n.* a common fish resembling a cod with silvery scales. It is found in North American Atlantic coastal waters and is an important food fish. Latin name: *Merluccius bilinearis*.

sil·ver i·o·dide *n.* a yellow light-sensitive powder that is used in photographic emulsions and as an antiseptic. It can also be scattered in clouds to cause rainfall. Formula: AgI.

sil·ver lin·ing *n.* something that offers hope or benefit in a situation that is generally adverse [From the proverb "Every cloud has a silver lining"]

sil·ver ma·ple *n.* **1. N AMERICAN MAPLE WITH SILVERY LEAVES** a common North American maple tree with deeply cut five-lobed leaves that are light green above and silvery-white underneath. Latin name: *Acer saccharinum*. **2. HARD WOOD** the hard wood of the silver maple tree

sil·ver med·al *n.* an award for taking second place in a race or other competition, usually in the form of a silver disk on a ribbon —**sil·ver med·al·ist** *n.*

sil·vern /sílvərn/ *adj.* made of or resembling silver (*archaic or literary*) [Old English *silfren*, formed from *siolfor* (see SILVER)]

sil·ver ni·trate *n.* a white poisonous light-sensitive compound used in photographic emulsions, as a chemical reagent, and in medicine as an antiseptic and astringent. Formula: $AgNO_3$.

sil·ver perch *n.* **1. SILVERY FISH RESEMBLING PERCH** a silvery fish resembling a perch, e.g., the white crappie and white perch **2. U.S. COASTAL FISH** a drum fish found along the southern Atlantic coast of the United States. Latin name: *Bairdiella chrysoura*.

sil·ver plate *n.* **1. THIN LAYER OF SILVER** a thin layer of silver, especially one that is used to coat a base metal **2. ITEMS COATED IN SILVER** items, especially of tableware, that are made from a base metal coated with a thin layer of silver

sil·ver-plate (**sil·ver-plat·ed, sil·ver-plat·ing, sil·ver-plates**) *vt.* to coat something, especially a base metal, with a thin layer of silver, usually by electroplating

sil·ver·point /sílvər pòynt/ *n.* **1. DRAWING TECHNIQUE USING SILVER-TIPPED PENCIL** a drawing technique that involves using a silver-tipped pencil on specially prepared paper or parchment **2. DRAWING IN SILVERPOINT** a drawing made using the silverpoint technique

sil·ver sal·mon *n.* = **coho salmon**

sil·ver screen *n.* **1. MOVIES** movies or the movie industry in general **2. FILM PROJECTION SCREEN** the screen that movies are projected onto

sil·ver·side /sílvər sīd/ *n.* a small bony fish with a broad silvery stripe along each side of its body. Family: Atherinidae.

sil·ver·smith /sílvər smìth/ *n.* somebody who is skilled in making or repairing silver or silver-plated objects [Old English *seolforsmi*] —**sil·ver·smith·ing** *n.*

sil·ver spoon *n.* inherited wealth and high social status [From the expression *be born with a silver spoon in your mouth* "to be born advantageously into a wealthy family"]

sil·ver·spot /sílvər spòt/ *n.* a butterfly of northern temperate areas that has silver-colored spots. Family: Nymphalidae.

sil·ver stan·dard *n.* a basis for currency consisting of a reserve of silver for which issued bills are redeemable at a fixed rate

Sil·ver Star, Sil·ver Star Med·al *n.* a U.S. military decoration for gallantry in combat

sil·ver·tail /sílvər tàyl/ *n.* *Aus* an affluent and influential member of society (*slang*)

sil·ver·tip /sílvər tìp/ *n.* = **grizzly bear** [Late 19thC. From the white tips of its hairs.]

sil·ver-tongued *adj.* having the gift of persuading or complimenting people eloquently and with charm

sil·ver·ware /sílvər wàir/ *n.* **1. METAL TABLEWARE** metal knives, forks, and other items of tableware **2. SILVER ITEMS** items made of silver or silver plate, especially tableware

sil·ver·weed /sílvər weèd/ *n.* a creeping plant of the rose family that has yellow flowers and leaves with silvery undersides. Latin name: *Potentila anserina.*

sil·ver·y /sílvəree/ *adj.* **1. LIKE SILVER** resembling silver, especially in color or sheen **2. WITH SILVER** containing some silver or coated with a thin layer of silver **3. CLEAR AND RESONANT** clear and ringing in tone ○ *silvery peals of laughter* —**sil·ver·i·ness** *n.*

sil·vex /síl vèks/ *n.* an herbicide used to control woody plants that is toxic to animals. Its use is now widely banned or severely restricted. Formula: $C_9H_7Cl_3O_3$. [Mid-20thC. Coined from Latin *silva* "a wood" + *-ex*, as in *exterminate*.]

sil·vic·o·lous /sil víkələss/ *adj.* used to describe plants and animals that grow or live in woods or forests [Formed from Latin *silvicola* "living in woods"]

sil·vi·cul·ture /sílvi kùlchər/, **syl·vi·cul·ture** *n.* the study, cultivation, and management of forest trees [Late 19thC. From French, from Latin *silva* "a wood" + French *culture* "cultivation."] —**sil·vi·cul·tur·al** /sìlvi kúlchərəl/ *adj.* —**sil·vi·cul·tur·ist** /-kúlchərist/ *n.*

sim. *abbr.* similar

si·ma /símə/ *n.* an area consecrated for the ordination of Buddhist monks, and for other formal monastic activities

si·ma·rou·ba /sìmmə roòbə/, **si·ma·ru·ba** *n.* a tropical American tree of the quassia family with bark that has various medicinal properties. Genus: *Simaruba.*

Sim·chat To·rah /sìm khaat-/, **Sim·chas To·rah** /sìm khaas-/, **Sim·chath To·rah** /sìm khaat-/ *n.* a Jewish festival at the end of Succoth celebrating the end of the annual cycle of reading from the Torah and the beginning of a new one [Late 19thC. From Hebrew *śimḥath tōrā*, literally "rejoicing of the Torah."]

Sim·coe /símkō/, **John Graves** (1752–1806) British military officer. He was lieutenant governor of Upper Canada (1791–96).

Georges Simenon

Si·me·non /seemə náwN/, **Georges** (1903–89) Belgian-born French writer. He published more than 500 novels under a variety of pseudonyms, but is best known for the 80 crime novels featuring his tough and intuitive sleuth, Inspector Maigret. Full name **Georges Joseph Christian Simenon**

Sim·e·on Sty·li·tes /sìmmee ən stī lít eez/, **St.** (390?–459) Syrian ascetic. He was the first "pillar saint," so called for the stone pillar near Antioch on which he resided for long periods of time and from which he preached.

Sim·fer·o·pol /sìmfə ráwpəl/ city on the Crimean Peninsula, in southern Ukraine, situated about 30 mi./48 km northeast of Sevastopol. Population: 353,000 (1991).

sim·i·an /símmee ən/ *adj.* **OF OR LIKE MONKEYS AND APES** belonging to or characteristic of monkeys or apes, or resembling such animals in appearance or behavior ■ *n.* **MONKEY** a monkey or an ape [Early 17thC. Formed from Latin *simia* "ape," from, ultimately, Greek *simos* "snub-nosed."]

sim·i·lar /símmələr/ *adj.* **1. ALIKE** sharing some qualities, but not exactly identical **2.** GEOM **THE SAME PROPORTIONALLY** used to describe geometric figures that differ in size or proportion but not in shape or angular measurements **3.** *Malaysia, Singapore* **IDENTICAL** exactly the same [Late 16thC. Directly or via French *similaire* from medieval Latin *similaris*, from Latin *similis* "like."]

WORD KEY: USAGE

similar to In its meaning "of the same kind, having resemblances," ***similar*** is followed by *to*: *My own experience has been similar to yours.* Use with *as*, though occasionally found, is incorrect: *I had a similar experience as yours.*

sim·i·lar·i·ty /sìmmə lérrətee/ (*plural* **-ties**) *n.* **1. LIKENESS** the possession of one or more qualities in common **2. SHARED CHARACTERISTIC** a quality or feature that two or more things or people have in common

sim·i·lar·ly /símmələrlee/ *adv.* **1. IN A SIMILAR WAY** so as to share some qualities but not exactly identical **2. CORRESPONDINGLY** used to indicate that something corresponds to or is similar to something else

sim·i·le /símməlee/ *n.* a figure of speech that draws a comparison between two different things, especially a phrase containing the word "like" or "as," e.g., "as white as a sheet." ◊ **metaphor** [14thC. From Latin *simile* "a like thing," from *similis* "like."]

si·mil·i·tude /si míllə toòd/ *n.* **1. BEING SIMILAR** likeness or resemblance (*formal*) **2. SOMETHING OR SOMEBODY THAT RESEMBLES ANOTHER** something or somebody that is like something or somebody else **3. A SIMILARITY** a shared characteristic (*formal*) **4. FORM OR SEMBLANCE** a form or semblance of somebody or something (*formal or literary*) **5. SIMILE OR ALLEGORY** a simile, allegory, or parable (*archaic*) [14thC. Directly or via Old French from Latin *similitudo* "likeness," from *similis* "like."]

sim·i·ous /símmee əss/ *adj.* simian (*archaic*)

sim·i·tar *n.* = **scimitar**

Sim·la /símlə/ capital city of Himachal Pradesh State, northwestern India. Population: 81,463 (1991).

Sim·men·tal /zímmən taàl/ (*plural* **-tals** *or* **-tal**), **Sim·men·thal** (*plural* **-thals** *or* **-thal**) *n.* a large cow with a yellowish-brown or reddish coat, a white head, and white legs. It belongs to a breed originating in Switzerland and is bred for beef and milk. [Early 20thC. Named for the *Simmental* valley in central Switzerland.]

sim·mer /símmər/ *v.* (**-mered, -mer·ing, -mers**) **1.** *vti.* COOK **COOK JUST BELOW BOIL** to cook gently or cook something gently just below boiling point, usually with the occasional bubble breaking on the surface **2.** *vti.* COOK **STAY OR KEEP SOMETHING BELOW BOIL** to stay just below boiling point, or to cause a liquid to stay just below boiling point **3.** *vi.* **BE GROWING ANGRY** to have anger, or some other strong emotion, building up inside ○ *simmering with rage* **4.** *vi.* **BUILD UP** to build up or ferment, often without being expressed ○ *"with grief and rage and laughter all simmering within me like a boiling pot"* (Arthur Conan Doyle, *The Lost World*; 1912) ■ *n.* COOK **GENTLE COOKING TEMPERATURE** a cooking temperature that cooks food or keeps liquid at just below boiling point [Mid-17thC. Alteration of obsolete English *simper* "to simmer," which may have been an imitation of the sound.]

simmer down *v.* **1.** *vi.* **BECOME CALM** to become calm, e.g., after an outburst of anger or a state of excitement **2.** *vti.* COOK **CONDENSE BY SIMMERING** to condense something by simmering or boiling it gently, or to reduce the volume of something in this way

sim·nel cake /símnəl-/ *n.* *U.K.* a fruitcake covered with marzipan or with a layer of marzipan baked in the middle, usually served during the Christian festivals of Lent or Easter. It is traditionally decorated with 11 balls of marzipan representing the loyal apostles of Jesus Christ, excluding Judas Iscariot. [13thC. "Simnel" via Old French *simenel* from, ultimately, Latin *simila* "fine flour" (source of English *semolina*).]

si·mo·le·on /sə mólee ən/ *n.* a dollar (*dated slang*) [Late 19thC. Origin unknown.]

Si·mon /símən/ *n.* in the New Testament, one of the 12 apostles, traditionally believed to have been martyred in Persia with St. Jude. Known as **Simon the Zealot**

Si·mon /símən/, **Neil** (*b.* 1927) U.S. playwright. Plays such as *The Odd Couple* (1965) and *Sweet Charity* (1966) made him the country's most successful writer of comedies. He later wrote more serious works including the Pulitzer Prize-winning *Lost in Yonkers* (1991). Full name **Marvin Neil Simon**

Nina Simone

Si·mone /si mṓn/, **Nina** (*b.* 1933) U.S. jazz singer and composer. She wrote and sang protest songs against racism in the 1960s, using her smoky contralto voice to great dramatic effect. Real name **Eunice Kathleen Waymon**

si·mo·ni·ac /sī mónee àk, si-/ *n.* **SOMEBODY TRADING IN SACRED THINGS** somebody who buys and sells sacred things or who has been found guilty of buying and selling sacred things ■ *adj.* **si·mo·ni·ac, si·mo·ni·a·cal CONNECTED WITH SIMONY** relating or belonging to the buying or selling of sacred or spiritual things [14thC. From French *simoniaque*, from late Latin *simonia* (see SIMONY).]

Si·mon Le·gree /-lə greé/ *n.* somebody who is considered to be a hard taskmaster and a stickler for discipline [Named for the brutal owner of enslaved people in Harriet Beecher Stowe's *Uncle Tom's Cabin* (1852) who had the eponymous African American hero beaten to death]

si·mon-pure *adj.* completely genuine or authentic, often used to describe somebody who is an amateur as opposed to a professional [Late 18thC. From *Simon Pure*, the name of a character in Susannah Centlivre's play *A Bold Stroke for a Wife* (1717).]

Si·mon's Town town and naval base in Western Cape Province, South Africa, situated about 20 mi./32 km south of Cape Town. Population: 6,500 (1997).

si·mo·ny /símənee/ *n.* in Christianity, the buying or selling of sacred or spiritual things [13thC. Via French *simonie* from late Latin *simonia*, from *Simon* Magus, the name of a Samaritan who tried to buy the power of conferring the Holy Spirit.] —**si·mo·nist** *n.*

si·moom /si moòm/, **si·moon** /si moòn/ *n.* a hot dry wind that blows across North Africa and the Arabian peninsula, carrying dust and sand particles [Late 18thC. From Arabic *samūm*, from *samma* "to poison."]

simp /simp/ *n.* a simpleton (*informal offensive*) [Early 20thC. Shortening.]

sim·pa·ti·co /sim paàtikō, -pátti-/ *adj.* sharing similar temperaments or interests and, therefore, able to get on well together [Mid-19thC. Via Spanish *simpático* or Italian *simpatico* "sympathetic" from, ultimately, Latin *sympathia*.]

sim·per /símpər/ *v.* (**-pered, -per·ing, -pers**) **1.** *vt.* **SAY SOMETHING COYLY** to say something while simpering **2.** *vi.* **SMILE COYLY** to smile in an affected, coy, and usually irritating way ■ *n.* **AFFECTED SMILE** a coy and affected smile [Mid-16thC. Origin uncertain: perhaps from Scandinavian source.] —**sim·per·er** *n.* —**sim·per·ing** *adj., n.* —**sim·per·ing·ly** *adv.*

sim·ple /símp'l/ *adj.* (**-pler, -plest**) **1. EASY** easy to do, understand, or work out because not complicated ○ *a simple task* **2. NOT ELABORATE** lacking decoration or embellishment and therefore plain in appearance ○ *a simple black dress* **3. NOT COMPLEX** made up of or having only one part or element ○ *a simple organism* **4.** **WITHOUT COMPLICATIONS** with no complications, luxuries, or embellishments ○ *the simple life* **5.** **STRAIGHTFORWARD** ordinary or straightforward ○ *It's a simple case of the flu and I should be back to work in a couple of days.* **6.** **OFFENSIVE TERM** an offensive term referring to somebody with an intellectual capacity that does not allow somebody to perform higher level cognitive processes (*offensive*) **7.** **NAIVE** naive and lacking in depth and detail **8.** **HUMBLE** humble and unsophisticated ○ *simple folk* **9.** **GUILELESS** direct, sincere, or lacking any form of deceitfulness **10.** CHEM **CONTAINING ONE COMPOUND ONLY** consisting of a single chemical compound **11.** BIOL **NOT DIVIDED** not divided, either totally or partially, into separate segments ○ *a simple leaf.* ◊ **compound** ■ *n.* (*archaic*) **1.** **NAIVE OR UNINTELLIGENT PERSON** a naive, unsophisticated, or unintelligent person **2.** **SIMPLE THING** something that has no additions, complications, or separate parts **3.** **HERBAL MEDICINE** an herbal medicine or an herb that yields medicine [Pre-12thC. Via French from Latin *simplus.* Ultimately from an Indo-European base that is also the ancestor of English *assemble, same, single,* and *some.*] —**sim·ple·ness** *n.*

WORD KEY: USAGE

See Usage note at *simplistic.*

sim·ple closed curve *n.* a plane curve, e.g., a circle or ellipse, that is closed and does not intersect itself

sim·ple e·qua·tion *n.* = **linear equation**

sim·ple frac·tion *n.* a fraction that consists of two whole numbers separated by a horizontal or slanting line, as opposed to a decimal fraction

sim·ple frac·ture *n.* a fracture of a bone in which the fragments remain in their correct alignment, with little damage to the surrounding tissue

sim·ple fruit *n.* a fruit, e.g., a pea pod or a tomato, that forms from a single pistil

sim·ple har·mon·ic mo·tion *n.* = **harmonic motion**

sim·ple-heart·ed *adj.* honest, open, and lacking deceit or deviousness

sim·ple in·ter·est *n.* interest on an investment that is calculated once per period, usually annually, on the amount of the capital alone and not on any interest already earned

sim·ple ma·chine *n.* any one of the six devices formerly considered to be the elements from which all machines were composed. They were the inclined plane, lever, pulley, screw, wedge, and wheel and axle.

sim·ple-mind·ed *adj.* **1.** **LACKING DUE THOUGHT** showing a lack of intelligent thinking or proper consideration **2.** **OFFENSIVE TERM** an offensive term referring to somebody whose intellectual ability is limited (*offensive*) **3.** **UNSOPHISTICATED** without guile or complexity —**sim·ple-mind·ed·ly** *adv.* —**sim·ple-mind·ed·ness** *n.*

sim·ple pro·tein *n.* a protein such as globulin that yields only amino acids on complete hydrolysis

sim·ple sen·tence *n.* a sentence that takes the form of a single main clause with no relative or subordinate clause, e.g., "I read the book." ◊ **complex sentence, compound sentence**

Sim·ple Si·mon *n.* an offensive term referring to somebody, especially a man or boy, who is perceived as lacking intelligence or sophistication (*insult*) [From the name of a character in a nursery rhyme]

sim·ple sug·ar *n.* = **monosaccharide**

sim·ple tense *n.* a grammatical form of a verb that expresses a relationship of time without using any auxiliary or modal verbs. In English, there are only two simple tenses, the simple present, as in "I walk," and the simple past, as in "I walked."

sim·ple time *n.* a musical tempo in which the main beats are divisible by two, e.g., 2/2 or 4/4 time

sim·ple·ton /símp'ltən/ *n.* an offensive term referring to somebody who seems to lack intelligence or common sense (*insult*)

sim·plex /sím plèks/ *adj.* **1.** **SIMPLE** containing, using, or designed for a single element or component **2.** TELECOM **ALLOWING TRANSMISSION IN ONE DIRECTION** allowing transmission of signals or communication in only one direction at a time ■ *n.* **1.** LING **ROOT FORM OF WORD** a word in its base form, without any inflections, prefixes, or suffixes, and not formed by putting two distinct words together. The words "book" and "mark" are simplexes, whereas "bookmark," "books," "marked," and "remark" are not. **2.** GEOM **GEOMETRIC FIGURE OR ELEMENT** a geometric element in a Euclidean space that exhibits the minimum number of dimensions of the space, e.g., a line in one-dimensional space or a triangle in two-dimensional space **3.** **APARTMENT ON ONE FLOOR** an apartment with all rooms on one floor [Late 16thC. From Latin, formed from *simplus* (see SIMPLE).]

sim·plic·i·ty /sim plíssətee/ (*plural* **-ties**) *n.* **1.** **BEING SIMPLE** lack of complexity, complication, embellishment, or difficulty **2.** **SIMPLE THING** a simple quality or thing [14thC. Directly or via French *simplicité* from Latin *simplicitas* "simpleness," from *simplex* (see SIMPLEX).]

sim·pli·fy /símpli fì/ (**-fied, -fy·ing, -fies**) *vt.* **1.** **MAKE SOMETHING EASIER** to make something less complicated or easier to understand **2.** MATH **REDUCE MATHEMATICAL EXPRESSION TO SIMPLER TERMS** to convert a mathematical expression, e.g., a fraction or equation, to a simpler form by removing common factors or regrouping elements [Mid-17thC. Via French *simplifier* from medieval Latin *simplificare,* from Latin *simplus* (see SIMPLE).] —**sim·pli·fi·ca·tion** /sìmplifi káysh'n/ *n.* —**sim·pli·fic·a·tive** /símplifi kàytiv/ *adj.* —**sim·pli·fi·er** /-fìr/ *n.*

sim·plism /sím plìzzəm/ *n.* a tendency to avoid or ignore the complexities of something —**sim·plist** *n.*

sim·plis·tic /sim plístik/ *adj.* **1.** **NAIVELY SIMPLE** characterized by naive simplicity **2.** **SIMPLIFYING TOO MUCH** tending to oversimplify something, especially by avoiding or ignoring its complexities —**sim·plis·ti·cal·ly** *adv.*

WORD KEY: USAGE

simple or **simplistic**? ***Simplistic*** is normally a derogatory word, implying that something is artificially oversimplified rather than naturally simple: *He argued that it was simplistic to reject these methods as unscientific.* It should not be used as an alternative or supposedly stronger word for ***simple***: *A simplistic* [use *simple*] *approach would be helpful here.*

Sim·plon Pass /sìm plon-/ mountain pass in the Swiss Alps, between Brig in Switzerland, and Iselle in northern Italy. Height: 6,590 ft./2,009 m.

sim·ply /símplee/ *adv.* **1.** **NOTHING OTHER THAN** with nothing else involved ○ *It was simply a misunderstanding.* **2.** **PLAINLY** in an uncomplicated, straightforward, or plain way ○ *To put it simply, I can't afford it.* **3.** **AT ALL OR TOTALLY** to any or the fullest degree or extent ○ *simply astonishing* **4.** **FRANKLY** frankly and without embellishment ○ *It was, quite simply, the best they had in stock.* **5.** **NAIVELY** without full understanding

Simp·son /símps'n/, **Sir George** (1787?–1860) British-born Canadian administrator and explorer. He was the governor of the Hudson's Bay Company from 1821 to 1856. In 1841–42 he traveled overland around the world. Known as **Little Emperor**

Simp·son, O.J. (*b.* 1947) U.S. football player, sportscaster, and actor. He was one of the NFL's greatest running backs in a ten-year career, mostly with the Buffalo Bills. He was acquitted of murdering his wife after a controversial criminal trial (1995), but convicted in a civil trial (1997). Full name **Orenthal James Simpson**

Simp·son Des·ert desert in central Australia, centered on the junction of the South Australia, Northern Territory, and Queensland borders. Area: 29,723 sq. mi./77,000 sq. km.

sim·u·la·crum /sìmmyə láykrəm, -lákrəm/ (*plural* **-cra** /-krə/) *n.* **1.** **REPRESENTATION OR IMAGE** a representation or image of something **2.** **SOMETHING VAGUELY SIMILAR** something that has a vague, tentative, or shadowy resemblance to something else [Late 16thC. From Latin, formed from *simulare* (see SIMULATE).]

sim·u·lant /símmyələnt/ *adj.* **SIMULATING** serving to imitate or reproduce the essential features of something (*formal*) ■ *n.* = **simulator** *n.* 1 [Mid-18thC. From the present participle stem of Latin *simulare* (see SIMULATE).]

sim·u·lar /símmyələr/ *n.* **SOMEBODY OR SOMETHING FAKE** somebody or something that mimics, simulates, or pretends to be another person or thing, especially for deceptive purposes (*archaic*) ■ *adj.* **FAKE** mimicking, simulating, or pretending to be somebody or something else, especially for deceptive purposes (*archaic*) [Early 16thC. Formed from Latin *simulare* (see SIMULATE), perhaps on the model of SIMILAR.]

sim·u·late /símmyə làyt/ *vt.* (**-lat·ed, -lat·ing, -lates**) **1.** **REPRODUCE FEATURES OF SOMETHING** to reproduce an essential feature or features of something, e.g., as an aid to study or training ○ *a computer model simulating the process of continental drift* **2.** **FAKE SOMETHING** to feign something, or pretend to experience something ○ *simulating enjoyment* **3.** **MIMIC SOMEBODY OR SOMETHING** to mimic or imitate somebody or something ■ *adj.* **FAKE OR DECEPTIVE** mimicking, simulating, or pretending to be something or somebody else (*archaic*) [15thC. From Latin *simulat-,* the past participle stem of *simulare* "to simulate," from *similis* "like" (source of English *similar*).] —**sim·u·la·tive** *adj.* —**sim·u·la·tive·ly** *adv.*

sim·u·lat·ed /símmyə làytəd/ *adj.* **1.** **REPRODUCED BY SIMULATION** reproduced or realized by simulation, especially computer simulation **2.** **NOT GENUINE** artificial, especially made in imitation of a genuine article, fabric, or other substance **3.** **FALSE** feigned or faked

sim·u·la·tion /sìmmyə láysh'n/ *n.* **1.** **REPRODUCTION OF FEATURES OF SOMETHING** the reproduction of the essential features of something, e.g., as an aid to study or training **2.** **FALSE APPEARANCE** the imitation or feigning of something **3.** **FAKE** an artificial or imitation object **4.** COMPUT, STATS **CONSTRUCTION OF MATHEMATICAL MODEL** the construction of a mathematical model to reproduce the characteristics of a phenomenon, system, or process, often using a computer, in order to infer information or solve problems [14thC]

sim·u·la·tor /símmyə làytər/ *n.* **1.** **DEVICE THAT SIMULATES SOMETHING** a device, instrument, or piece of equipment designed to reproduce the essential features of something, e.g., as an aid to study or training. ◊ **emulator** *n.* 2 **2.** **SOMEBODY WHO SIMULATES SOMETHING** somebody who feigns or imitates something —**sim·u·la·to·ry** /símmyələ tàwree/ *adj.*

si·mul·cast /sím'l kàst/ *n.* **1.** **SIMULTANEOUS TV AND RADIO BROADCAST** a program that is broadcast simultaneously on both television and radio, on multiple channels, or in multiple languages **2.** **LIVE BROADCAST** a live broadcast of an event on closed-circuit television ■ *vt.* (**-cast, -cast·ing, -casts**) **MAKE SIMULTANEOUS BROADCAST** to broadcast a simulcast program [Mid-20thC. Blend of SIMULTANEOUS and BROADCAST.]

si·mul·ta·ne·ous /sìm'l táynee əss/ *adj.* **1.** **AT THE SAME TIME** done, happening, or existing at the same time **2.** MATH **TAKING SAME VARIABLES** used to describe equations that are satisfied by the same values of the variables [Mid-17thC. From medieval Latin *simultaneus,* from Latin *simul* "at the same time," probably on the model of *momentaneus* "momentary."] —**si·mul·ta·ne·i·ty** /sìm'ltə née ətee/ *n.* —**si·mul·ta·ne·ous·ly** /sìm'l táynee əsslee/ *adv.* —**si·mul·ta·ne·ous·ness** /-táynee əssnəss/ *n.*

sin[1] /sin/ *n.* **1.** **TRANSGRESSION OF THEOLOGICAL PRINCIPLES** an act, a thought, or behavior that goes against the law or teachings of a particular religion, especially when the person who commits it is aware of this **2.** **SHAMEFUL OFFENSE** something that offends a moral or ethical principle **3.** **ESTRANGEMENT FROM GOD** in Christian theology, the condition of being denied God's grace because of a sin or sins committed ■ *vi.* (**sinned, sin·ning, sins**) **1.** **KNOWINGLY DO WRONG** to commit a sin, especially by knowingly violating a law or the teachings of a particular religion **2.** **COMMIT SHAMEFUL OFFENSE** to commit any serious moral or ethical offense [Old English *synn.* Ultimately from an Indo-European base that also produced German *Sünde* "sin" and perhaps Latin *sons* "guilty."] ◇ **live in sin** to live together as husband and wife without being married (*dated or humorous*)

sin[2] *abbr.* sine. ◊ **cos, tan**

Si·nai /sí nì/ peninsula in the Middle East bounded on the east by the Gulf of Aqaba, on the north by the Mediterranean Sea, and on the west by the Gulf of Suez. A sparsely populated wilderness, it has long been the land bridge between Africa and Asia. Area: 23,500 sq. mi./60,863 sq. km.

Si·nai, Mount mountain in northeastern Egypt on the south central Sinai Peninsula, about 7,500 ft./2,888 m high. According to the Bible, it is the place where Moses received the Ten Commandments (Exodus 19).

si·na·may /seénə mí, sínnə mì/ *n.* a stiff open-weave fabric spun from the fibers of the banana plant, used in making hats [Mid-20thC. From Tagalog.]

Sin·an·thro·pus /sin ánthrəpəss/ *n.* the original scientific name for Peking man [Early 20thC. From modern

Latin, coined from late Latin *Sinae* "the Chinese" + Greek *anthrōpos* "person."]

Frank Sinatra

Si·na·tra /si naátrə/, **Frank** (1915–98) U.S. singer and actor. He won an Academy Award for *From Here to Eternity* (1953), and is generally recognized as the supreme master of the popular song. Full name **Francis Albert Sinatra**

sin bin *n.* an area with a bench beside an ice-hockey rink where penalized players must stay during the period they have to serve as a time penalty for an offense (*slang*)

since /sinss/ CORE MEANING: a grammatical word used to indicate that a situation has continued from a particular time or event in the past ○ (prep) *Karen has lived in London since 1988.* ○ (adv) *She left the firm in 1980 and has since been self-employed.* ○ (conj) *He has been on a high since he got married in January.*

1. *prep., conj.* HAPPENING AFTER happening at some point or points after the stated period of time or event ○ *The rate of job growth is higher than under any administration since 1920.* ○ *Since Ryland became commissioner in 1994, all complaints are investigated fully.* **2.** *adv.* SUBSEQUENTLY at some point between then and now ○ *even when the department had an engineer, who has since retired* **3.** *conj.* BECAUSE because, seeing that ○ *He recalls that since it was fall, it was already dark by 6:00 p.m.* [15thC. Contraction of earlier *sithence*, from Old English *siððan*, from *sīð* "after" + *þam* "that."] ◇ **long since** a long time ago

WORD KEY: USAGE

See Usage note at ***because***.

sin·cere /sin séer/ (**-cer·er, -cer·est**) *adj.* **1.** HONEST AND OPEN honest and unaffected in a way that shows what is said is really meant **2.** NOT FEIGNED based on what is truly and deeply felt [Mid-16thC. From Latin *sincerus* "pure, whole."] —**sin·cere·ly** *adv.* —**sin·cere·ness** *n.*

sin·cer·i·ty /sin sérrətee/ *n.* honesty in the expression of true or deep feelings

sin·ci·put /sínssəpət/ (*plural* **-ci·puts** *or* **-cip·i·ta** /-síppətə/) *n.* the part of the skull that includes the forehead and the area above it [Late 16thC. From Latin, literally "half head."] —**sin·cip·i·tal** /sin síppət'l/ *adj.*

Sin·clair /sin kláir, sing-/, **Upton** (1878–1968) U.S. writer and reformer. His social and political novels include *The Jungle* (1906). He ran unsuccessfully for several public offices including governor of California (1934). Full name **Upton Beall Sinclair**

Sind /sind/ historical region of southeastern Pakistan in the lower Indus valley. A province of British India from 1843, it became part of Pakistan after partition in 1947. Capital: Karachi. Population: 21,682,000 (1985). Area: 54,407 sq. mi./140,914 sq. km.

Sin·dhi /síndee/ (*plural* **-dhi** *or* **-dhis**) *n.* **1.** SOMEBODY FROM SIND somebody who was born or raised in Sind **2.** SINDHI LANGUAGE the Indic language spoken in Sind and parts of western India. Sindhi is spoken by about 14 million people. [Early 19thC. Via Persian and Urdu *sindī* from *Sind* (see SIND), from Sanskrit *sindhu* "river," specifically "the Indus."]

sine /sīn/ *n.* **1.** TRIGONOMETRIC FUNCTION FOR ANGLES for a given angle in a right triangle, a trigonometric function equal to the length of the side opposite the angle divided by the hypotenuse **2.** MATHEMATICAL FUNCTION ON CIRCLE a mathematical function equal to the vertical coordinate of a circumference point divided by the radius of a circle with its center at the origin of a Cartesian coordinate system [Late 16thC. From Latin *sinus* "a curve, fold" (source of English *sinus*) later "fold in a garment." From the confusion of Arabic *jiba* "sine" with *jayb* "fold in a garment."]

si·ne·cure /sínə kyoor/ *n.* **1.** PAID JOB REQUIRING LITTLE WORK a job or position that provides a regular income but requires little or no work **2.** PAID CHURCH OFFICE WITHOUT DUTIES a church office whose holder is paid but is not required to do pastoral work [Mid-17thC. From the medieval Latin phrase *beneficium sine cura*, literally "benefice without cure (of souls)."]

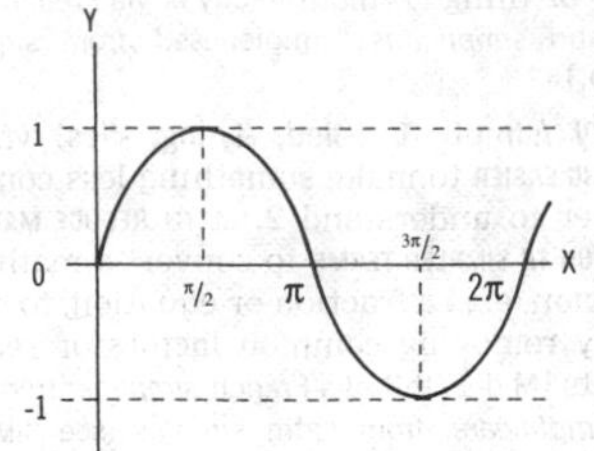

Sine curve

sine curve *n.* a graph of the sine equation "y = a sin bx," with "a" and "b" being constants

si·ne di·e /sínee dí ee, sìn ay dée ày/ *adv.* without a day being fixed for a further meeting (*formal*) ○ *The committee was adjourned sine die.* [From Latin, literally "without day"]

si·ne pro·le /sínee prō lee, sín prō lay/ *adv.* LAW without offspring ○ *She died in 1985, aged 59, sine prole.* [From Latin, literally "without offspring"]

si·ne qua non /sìnnee kwaa nṓn, sìnni kwaa nón, sínə kwaa nṓn, síni kwaa nón/ *n.* an essential condition or prerequisite ○ *The suspension of industrial activity is considered a sine qua non for talks to proceed.* [From Latin, literally "without which (cause) not"]

sin·ew /sínnyoo/ *n.* **1.** = **tendon 2.** STRENGTH strength, power, or resilience (*literary*) **3.** SOURCE OF POWER a source of strength or power (*literary*) (*often used in the plural*) ■ *vt.* (**-ewed, -ew·ing, -ews**) STRENGTHEN SOMEBODY OR SOMETHING to give added strength to somebody or something [Old English *sin(e)we, sionwe*. Ultimately from a prehistoric Germanic word that is also the ancestor of Dutch *zenuw* and German *Sehne*.] —**sin·ew·less** *adj.*

sine wave *n.* a waveform with the shape of a sine curve, representing a single frequency indefinitely repeated in time

sin·ew·y /sínnyoo ee/ *adj.* **1.** THIN AND STRONG lean, tough, and muscular ○ *a sinewy 20-year-old.* **2.** CONTAINING OR RESEMBLING TENDONS consisting of or containing tendons or stringy parts resembling tendons ○ *a rather sinewy steak* **3.** FORCEFUL vigorous and forceful (*literary*) ○ *rich, sinewy prose* —**sin·ew·i·ness** *n.*

sin·fo·ni·a /sin fónee ə/ (*plural* **-as** *or* **-e** /-àyl/) *n.* **1.** OVERTURE OR INTERLUDE a piece of orchestral music used as an overture or interlude in an opera **2.** SYMPHONY OR SYMPHONIC WORK a complex instrumental composition, usually for a group of stringed instruments or an orchestra [Late 18thC. Via Italian from Latin *symphonia* "sound of instruments, harmony" (source of English *symphony*).]

sin·fo·ni·et·ta /sìnfən yéttə, sìnfōn-/ *n.* **1.** SHORT SYMPHONY an orchestral piece that resembles a symphony but is shorter or written for fewer instruments, often for strings only **2.** SMALL ORCHESTRA a small symphony orchestra, often composed of stringed instruments only [Early 20thC. From Italian, literally "little sinfonia," from *sinfonia* (see SINFONIA).]

sin·ful /sínf'l/ *adj.* **1.** COMMITTING OR CHARACTERIZED BY SIN engaging in or characterized by behavior that goes against the law or teachings of a particular religion **2.** WRONG morally or ethically wrong ○ *a sinful waste of an expensive education* [Old English] —**sin·ful·ly** *adv.* —**sin·ful·ness** *n.*

sing /sing/ *v.* (**sang** /sang/, **sung** /sung/, **sing·ing, sings**) **1.** *vti.* MAKE MUSIC WITH VOICE to use the voice to produce words or sounds in a musical way **2.** *vti.* PERFORM SONGS PROFESSIONALLY to perform songs as a trained or professional singer **3.** *vti.* MAKE TUNEFUL ANIMAL SOUND to make a melodious sound that is typical of a species (*refers to animals*) **4.** *vi.* MAKE CONTINUOUS MUSICAL SOUND to make a continuous whistling, humming, or ringing sound ○ *a strong wind making the wires sing* **5.** *vi.* MAKE BRIEF SPEEDING SOUND to make a brief whistling or whizzing sound **6.** *vi.* EXPERIENCE RINGING OR HUMMING IN HEAD to experience a continuous ringing or humming sound in the head **7.** *vt.* INTONE SOMETHING to chant something, especially a religious text, on a single note or a small range of notes **8.** *vt.* SING FOR PARTICULAR PURPOSE to bring something to a particular condition by singing ○ *sing the baby to sleep* **9.** *vi.* CONFESS OR IMPLICATE SOMEBODY to confess to or implicate others in a crime (*slang*) **10.** *vti.* TELL ABOUT SOMETHING to praise somebody or proclaim something, especially in verse **11.** *vi.* BE HAPPY to rejoice in something ■ *n.* PERFORMANCE OF SONGS a session of singing, especially by a group gathered for this purpose (*informal*) [Old English *singan*. Ultimately from an Indo-European word that is also the ancestor of English *song*.] —**sing·a·ble** *adj.* —**sing·a·bil·i·ty** /sìngə bíllətee/ *n.* —**sing·ing·ly** /síngingIee/ *adv.*

sing along /síng ə làwng/ *vi.* to join in a song that somebody else is singing

sing out *vi.* to call out in a loud voice, especially to warn somebody

sing. *abbr.* singular

sing·a·long *n.* a meeting of a group of people to sing songs together for fun, or an impromptu session of singing

Singapore

Sin·ga·pore /síng gə pàwr/ city-state in Southeast Asia, comprising one major island and several islets, situated south of Malaysia. Language: Chinese, Malay, Tamil. Currency: Singapore dollar. Population: 2,986,500 (1995). Area: 247 sq. mi./640 sq. km. Official name **Republic of Singapore** —**Sin·ga·por·e·an** *n., adj.*

Sing·a·pore Eng·lish *n.* a variety of English spoken in Singapore

WORD KEY: WORLD ENGLISH

The English language as used in the city-state of Singapore, where it has been co-official since 1965 with Mandarin Chinese, Malay, and Tamil, having already been a regional lingua franca since the early 19th century. As the key language of government, business, and education, it has uniquely acquired a large fully native-speaking community of non-Western origin. There are two varieties: educated, more formal usage and a patois influenced by Chinese and Malay. Singapore English is "non-rhotic" (i.e., "r" is not pronounced in words such as *art, door,* and *worker*). It tends to have full vowels in all syllables (e.g., *7* is pronounced "seh-ven" not "sevn"). Words ending in *k, p,* and *t* are generally pronounced with "glottal stops," as in "ki?" (kick), "sto?" (stop), and "pu?" (put). Those words ending in clusters such as *-st* and *-ld* are reduced to the vowel and the first of the last two consonants e.g., "fas" for *fast*, "sol" for *sold*. Colloquial usage diverges considerably from the standard, as in: "You come or not?" for "Are you coming?"; "My dad, he come from Penang" for "My dad comes from Penang"; "This hotel cheap" for "This hotel is cheap." Compare MALAYSIAN ENGLISH.

singe /sinj/ *v.* (**singed, singe·ing, sing·es**) **1.** *vti.* SCORCH SOMETHING SLIGHTLY to burn or cause something to burn slightly so that only the surface, edge, or tip is affected **2.** *vt.* REMOVE FEATHERS OR HAIR WITH FLAME to expose the carcass of a bird or animal to a flame in order to remove unwanted feathers, bristles, or hair **3.** *vt.* BURN ENDS OF CLOTH FIBERS to burn the short fuzzy ends of fibers from cloth in the process of manufacturing it ■ *n.* SCORCH a superficial burn [Old English *sencgan*]

sing·er /síngər/ *n.* **1.** PERFORMER OF SONGS somebody who sings, especially professionally **2.** SINGING BIRD a bird that sings **3.** POET OR VERSIFIER somebody who writes poetry or other verse (*literary*)

Sing·er /síngər/, **Isaac Bashevis** (1904–91) Polish-born U.S. writer. His novels often concern Polish-Jewish subjects, and, like most of his works, were written first in Yiddish. He won the Nobel Prize in literature (1978).

Sing·er, Isaac M. (1811–75) U.S. inventor and entrepreneur. He patented a home sewing machine (1851) and founded the Singer Manufacturing Company. Full name **Isaac Merritt Singer**

Singh *n.* a title adopted as a surname by a Sikh boy when he is initiated at puberty into the fraternity of warriors [Early 17thC. Via Panjabi *siṅgh* "lion" from Sanskrit *siṃha*.]

Singh. *abbr.* Singhalese

Sin·gha·lese *n., adj.* PEOPLES, LANG = **Sinhalese**

sing·ing /sínging/ *n.* **1.** USE OF VOICE TO PRODUCE SONGS the technique of producing musical sounds with the voice, or the performance of songs **2.** MELODIC SOUNDS the melodic or other sounds made by somebody or something that sings ■ *adj.* MAKING MUSICAL SOUND performing songs or making a melodic, whistling, humming, or ringing sound

sing·ing tel·e·gram *n.* a message sung by a messenger paid to do so, or the service of providing sung messages

sin·gle /síng g'l/ *adj.* **1.** UNMARRIED unmarried or characteristic of being unmarried **2.** FOR ONE PERSON suitable or designed for one person ○ *We have a single room on the third floor.* **3.** CONSIDERED INDIVIDUALLY considered separately as something distinct or unique ○ *every single time* **4.** ONE only one ○ *in the space of a single day* **5.** CONSISTING OF ONE THING consisting of one part, element, or quality **6.** BETWEEN ONLY TWO PEOPLE taking place as a contest or competition between two persons only, one to each side ○ *a single competition* **7.** FORMING ONE UNDIVIDED UNIT forming a whole and left undivided or unbroken ○ *The swan had been carved from a single block of ice.* **8.** UNIFORM sole and the same for all ○ *a single rate for the job* **9.** BOT WITH ONE PETAL ROW used to describe a flower that has only one whorl or row of petals ■ *n.* **1.** ACCOMMODATION FOR ONE a room, cabin, or bed for one person ○ *Do you have any singles left?* **2.** MUSIC RECORDING WITH ONE SONG ON A SIDE a record, cassette, or CD with only one song on it, or the song recorded **3.** ONE DOLLAR a one-dollar bill **4.** BASEBALL HIT a hit in baseball that allows the batter to reach first base **5.** GOLF TWO-PLAYER MATCH a match between two golfers **6.** *U.K.* OUTWARD-BOUND TICKET a ticket that covers the outward-bound part of a journey to a destination but not the return **7. sin·gles** RACQUET GAME BETWEEN TWO PLAYERS a match between two players in a racquet game ■ **sin·gles** *npl.* UNMARRIED PEOPLE unmarried people considered as a group ■ *vti.* (**-gled, -gling, -gles**) HIT BASEBALL SINGLE to hit a single in baseball or advance a runner by hitting a single [13thC. Via Old French *sengle, single* from Latin *singulus*, from the stem of *simplus* (see SIMPLE).] —**sin·gle·ness** *n.*

single out *vt.* to select an individual from a group for a particular reason

sin·gle-ac·tion *adj.* REQUIRING COCKED HAMMER OF FIREARM requiring the hammer of a firearm to be cocked by hand before each shot can be fired ■ *n.* FIREARM REQUIRING COCKED HAMMER a firearm that cannot be fired until the hammer is cocked by hand

sin·gle-blind *adj.* used to describe an experiment or clinical trial in which the subjects are not told whether the tested substance or procedure they receive is active, in order to avoid subjective bias in the results. Single-blind experiments are often used to test people's reaction to drugs so as to eliminate the placebo effect. ◊ **double-blind**

sin·gle bond *n.* a covalent bond between two atoms formed through the sharing of a pair of electrons

sin·gle-breast·ed *adj.* with a small overlap at the front and fastened with a single row of buttons

sin·gle-cell pro·tein *n.* a protein derived from one-celled organisms grown in various cultures. It is used as food supplement.

sin·gle cross *n.* the first generation of offspring resulting from hybridization between two inbred lines

sin·gle-cut file *n.* a file that has all its teeth pointing in one direction. It is used on soft materials.

sin·gle en·try *n.* a system of bookkeeping in which the amounts owed or due are kept in a single account (*hyphenated when used before a noun*)

sin·gle-fam·i·ly *adj.* designed or suitable for a single family ○ *a number of single-family units*

sin·gle file *n.* SINGLE LINE a line of people, animals, or vehicles standing or moving one behind another ■ *adv.* MOVING IN SINGLE LINE moving in a line, one behind another

sin·gle-foot *n.* = **rack**[4] *n.* ■ *vti.* (**sin·gle-foot·ed, -foot·ing, -foots**) = **rack**[4] *v.*

sin·gle-hand·ed *adj.* **1.** UNAIDED accomplished alone and unaided ○ *the first single-handed circumnavigation of the world* **2.** WITH ONE-HAND ONLY with only one hand or the use of one hand **3.** FOR ONE HAND ONLY using or requiring only one hand ■ *adv.* WITHOUT HELP without any help from anyone ○ *sailed round the world single-handed* —**sin·gle-hand·ed·ly** *adv.* —**sin·gle-hand·ed·ness** *n.*

sin·gle-heart·ed *adj.* sincere, faithful, and straightforward [*Single* in the obsolete sense of "honest"] —**sin·gle-heart·ed·ly** *adv.* —**sin·gle-heart·ed·ness** *n.*

sin·gle-is·sue *adj.* concerned with only a single public issue ○ *the multiplication of single-issue groups*

sin·gle knot *n.* = **overhand knot**

sin·gle-lens re·flex *n.* a camera in which the light passes through one lens to the film and, by means of a mirror and prism system, to the focusing screen. ◊ **reflex camera**

sin·gle-mind·ed *adj.* **1.** WITH SINGLE AIM with only one goal in mind **2.** DEDICATED with the mind fixed on one task or preoccupation —**sin·gle-mind·ed·ly** *adv.* —**sin·gle-mind·ed·ness** *n.*

sin·gle par·ent *n.* a parent who brings up a child or children alone, usually because he or she is unmarried, widowed, or divorced (*hyphenated when used before a noun*)

sin·gle-phase *adj.* with, generating, or powered by a single alternating voltage

sin·gle pho·ton e·mis·sion com·put·ed to·mog·ra·phy *n.* a technique used in diagnosing certain diseases that generates a three-dimensional computer-generated image of the distribution of a radioactive tracer in a particular organ

sin·gles bar *n.* a bar frequented by men and women, usually unmarried, who are seeking romance, companionship, or sex

sin·gle-sex *adj.* restricted to either men or to women

sin·gle-shot *adj.* reloaded after each shot is fired

sin·gle-space (**sin·gle-spaced, sin·gle-spac·ing, sin·gle-spac·es**) *vt.* to type or print text without a blank space between the lines

sin·gle·stick /síng g'l stìk/ *n.* **1.** FENCING STICK a stick fitted with a handguard, formerly used in fencing **2.** PRACTICE OF FENCING WITH SINGLESTICK the former sport or skill of fencing with a singlestick

sin·glet /síng glət/ *n.* **1.** LIGHT SLEEVELESS SHIRT a sleeveless shirt worn with shorts in sports such as basketball or amateur boxing **2.** *U.K.* SLEEVELESS UNDERGARMENT a sleeveless undershirt [Mid-18thC. Formed from SINGLE on the model of DOUBLET, because it originally referred to an unlined, one-layered garment.]

sin·gle tax *n.* **1.** TAXATION WITH SOLE SOURCE OF REVENUE a taxation system in which all revenue is raised from a tax on one thing, usually the value of land **2.** TAX ON ONE TYPE OF THING a tax applied to one thing only, especially the value of land

sin·gle·ton /síng g'ltən/ *n.* **1.** SINGLE OCCURRENCE OF SOMEBODY OR SOMETHING somebody or something that occurs singly and not as part of a group, e.g., the only child in a family **2.** CARDS ONE CARD OF A SUIT a playing card that is the only one of its suit in a hand

Sin·gle·ton /síng gèltən/ town in eastern New South Wales, in Australia. It is a center for coal mining, agriculture, and light industry. Population: 12,519 (1996).

sin·gle-tongue (**sin·gle-tongued, sin·gle-tongu·ing, sin·gle-tongues**) *vti.* to articulate notes on a wind instrument by raising the tip of the tongue against the palate, temporarily obstructing the flow of air

sin·gle-track *adj.* **1.** FIXED ON SINGLE IDEA fixed on one thought or idea only **2.** RAIL WITH ONE TRACK ONLY with only one track and passing places for trains coming from opposite directions

sin·gle·tree /síng g'l trèe/ *n.* = **whiffletree** [Mid-19thC. Alteration of SWINGLETREE "a whiffletree," by association with DOUBLETREE "crosspiece to which the whiffletree is attached."]

sin·gly /síng glee/ *adv.* **1.** INDIVIDUALLY IN SEQUENCE one at a time or one by one **2.** WITHOUT HELP alone and by unaided efforts **3.** SEPARATELY solely and separately

sing·song /síng sàwng/ *adj.* WITH REPEATEDLY RISING AND FALLING INTONATION with an intonation that regularly rises and falls in pitch ■ *n.* **1.** SINGSONG WAY OF SPEAKING a voice with an intonation that rises and falls regularly in pitch **2.** SINGSONG VERSE RHYTHMS OR RHYMES a singsong rhythm or rhyme in verse, or a verse marked by such monotony **3.** *U.K.* = **sing-along**

sing·spiel /síng speel, zíng-/, **Sing·spiel** *n.* an 18th-century German comic opera consisting of folksongs or classical music performed in a popular or folk style interspersed with spoken dialogue [Late 19thC. From German, literally "singing play."]

sin·gu·lar /síng gyələr/ *adj.* **1.** LING REFERRING TO ONE PERSON OR THING used to describe a word or form that refers to one person or thing **2.** EXCEPTIONAL remarkably good or admirable **3.** UNUSUAL unusual, odd, or striking **4.** LOGIC STANDING FOR INDIVIDUAL THING used to describe a term intended to stand for an individual thing, or a proposition containing such a term ■ *n.* **1.** SINGULAR WORD OR FORM the form of a word that is used when referring to one person or thing **2.** LOGIC THING IN ISOLATION something considered solely by itself [14thC. Via Old French from Latin *singularis* "alone of its kind," from *singulus* (see SINGLE).] —**sin·gu·lar·ly** *adv.* —**sin·gu·lar·ness** *n.*

sin·gu·lar·i·ty /sìng gyə lárrətee/ (*plural* **-ties**) *n.* **1.** SINGULAR QUALITY singular, exceptional, or unusual quality **2.** SOMETHING UNIQUE OR UNUSUAL something that is unique, distinctive, or remarkable **3.** CHARACTERISTIC a distinguishing trait **4.** ASTROPHYS HYPOTHETICAL POINT IN SPACE a hypothetical region in space in which gravitational forces cause matter to be infinitely compressed and space and time to become infinitely distorted **5.** MATH FUNCTION THAT IS NOT DIFFERENTIABLE a point at which a complex function is undefined because it is neither differentiable nor single-valued while the function is defined in every neighborhood of the point [13thC. Via Old French from, ultimately, Latin *singularis* (see SINGULAR).]

sin·gu·lar·ize /síng gyələ rīz/ (**-ized, -iz·ing, -iz·es**) *v.* **1.** *vti.* MAKE OR BECOME SINGULAR to make a word singular or to become singular **2.** *vt.* MAKE CONSPICUOUS to distinguish somebody or something or make somebody or something stand out from the rest (*formal*) —**sin·gu·lar·i·za·tion** /sìng gyələrə záysh'n/ *n.*

sin·gu·lar point *n.* MATH = **singularity** *n.* 5

Sin·ha·lese /sìnhə léez, sìnghə-/ (*plural* **-lese**), **Sin·gha·lese** /sìng gə léez, sìnghə-/ (*plural* **-lese**) *n.* **1.** MEMBER OF SRI LANKAN PEOPLE a member of a people who live mainly in Sri Lanka, where they are the dominant ethnic group **2.** SINHALESE LANGUAGE the language of the Sinhalese people and the official language of Sri Lanka. It belongs to the Indic branch of the Indo-European family of languages. [Late 18thC. Via Portuguese *Singhalez* from Sanskrit *Siṁhala*, a variant of *Siṁhala* "Sri Lanka."] —**Sin·ha·lese** *adj.*

Si·ni·cism /sínə sìzzəm, sínnə-/ *n.* a custom, usage, or idiom peculiar to or characteristic of the Chinese [Late 19thC. Formed from obsolete English *Sinic* "Chinese," from late Latin *Sinae* "the Chinese" (see SINO-).]

Si·ni·cize /sínə sìz, sínnə-/ (**-cized, -ciz·ing, -ciz·es**) *vti.* to acquire, or give somebody or something, a Chinese idiom, form, or cultural trait (*often passive*) [Late 16thC. Formed from obsolete English *Sinic* (see SINICISM).]

Si·ni·fi·ca·tion /sínəfə kàysh'n, sìnnə-/ *n.* the adoption, imposition, or acquisition of Chinese idioms, forms, or cultural traits [Early 20thC. Formed from English *sinify*, from late Latin *Sinae* (see SINO-).]

sin·is·ter /sínnəstər/ *adj.* **1.** SUGGESTING EVIL threatening or suggesting malevolence, menace, or harm **2.** HERALDRY ON LEFT PART OF SHIELD on the left side of a heraldic shield as seen by the holder ○ *a bend sinister* [15thC. Directly and via Old French from Latin, "left," from the superstition that the left side of the body is unlucky.] —**sin·is·ter·ly** *adv.* —**sin·is·ter·ness** *n.*

sin·is·tral /sínnistrəl, si nístrəl/ *adj.* **1.** OF OR ON LEFT SIDE relating to or located on the left side, especially the left side of the body (*archaic*) **2.** LEFT-HANDED left-handed (*archaic*) **3.** MARINE BIOL COILING CLOCKWISE coiling in a clockwise direction from the apex to the aperture —**sin·is·tral·ly** *adv.*

sin·is·trorse /sínnə strawrss/ *adj.* growing upward in a clockwise spiral [Mid-19thC. From Latin *sinistrorsus*, from *sinister* (see SINISTER).] —**sin·is·trorse·ly** *adv.*

sin·is·trous /sínnəstrəss, si nís-/ *adj.* sinister or ill-omened (*archaic*) —**sin·is·trous·ly** *adv.*

Si·nit·ic /si níttik, sī-/ *n.* the branch of the Sino-Tibetan language group that includes the Chinese languages [Late 19thC. Formed from late Latin *sinæ* (see SINO-).]

sink /singk/ *v.* (**sank** /sangk/ *or* **sunk** /sungk/, **sink·ing, sinks**) **1.** *vti.* FALL BENEATH SURFACE OF LIQUID to go beneath the surface of a liquid or a soft substance and become partly or wholly submerged **2.** *vi.* APPEAR TO FALL to appear to descend toward or below the horizon ○ *We watched the sun sink in the sky.* **3.** *vi.* FALL TO LOWER LEVEL to become lower in height or depth ○ *The water level in the lake must have sunk six inches.* **4.** *vi.* GO DOWN GRADUALLY to slowly subside or settle at a lower level **5.** *vi.* FALL GENTLY to fall or collapse slowly ○ *He sank to his knees in exhaustion.* **6.** *vt.* DRILL INTO GROUND to drill a well, tunnel, or shaft in the ground **7.** *vt.* DRIVE INTO GROUND to force something into the ground ○ *We need to sink more piles.* **8.** *vti.* PENETRATE OR MAKE PENETRATE to penetrate something or cause something to penetrate something **9.** *vi.* BE ABSORBED to become absorbed in something **10.** *vi.* BECOME QUIETER to sound quieter or weaker ○ *voice sank to a whisper* **11.** *vi.* SUBSIDE to diminish in degree, volume, or strength **12.** *vi.* DECLINE PHYSICALLY to deteriorate physically, usually because of fatigue, injury, or ill health ○ *There's a danger he'll sink into a coma.* **13.** *vi.* FEEL DISCOURAGEMENT to pass gradually into a condition of hopelessness, dejection or despair **14.** *vi.* LOSE SOCIAL STATUS to gradually pass from a higher to a lower social status or position **15.** *vt.* INVEST IN SOMETHING to invest or lose money in a business or project ○ *He must have sunk millions into these theaters.* **16.** *vi.* DECLINE IN VALUE to decline in value or amount ○ *The pound sank again yesterday.* **17.** *vt.* BRING TO RUIN to defeat, undo, or ruin somebody or something ○ *If they won't accept our offer, we're sunk.* **18.** *vt.* DEFEAT IN CONTEST to defeat an opponent easily in a game or contest (*informal*) **19.** *vt.* SHOOT OR HIT SUCCESSFULLY to take aim at something and make a successful shot or stroke (*informal*) ○ *sink a critical putt* ■ *n.* **1.** BASIN FOR WASHING SOMETHING a basin that is fixed or mounted against a wall, and has a piped water supply and drainage **2.** CESSPOOL a cesspool, drain, or sewer **3.** BAD OR CORRUPT PLACE a place considered to be wicked and corrupt (*dated*) **4.** GEOG POORLY DRAINED LAND WHERE WATER COLLECTS an area of low-lying, poorly drained land in which water collects, sometimes in the form of a salt lake, and evaporates or sinks into the ground **5.** GEOG = **sinkhole** *n.* 1 **6.** PHYS DEVICE ABSORBING ENERGY OR OTHER ENTITY a device or component of a system at which a physical entity such as energy or neutrons is absorbed **7.** MINING MINE SHAFT a shaft in a mine [Old English *sincan*] —**sink·a·ble** *adj.* ◇ **sink or swim** to have no alternative but to succeed or fail without help from anyone else

WORD KEY: USAGE

sank, sunk, or **sunken**? The inflections of the verb ***sink*** have been variable over many centuries of use. In current usage, the preferred past tense is ***sank***, although ***sunk*** is also used and is not incorrect. For the past participle, ***sunk*** is used (*Six enemy ships were sunk on a single day*); the alternative form ***sunken*** is used only as an adjective: *a sunken garden.*

sink in *vi.* to become fully understood ○ *I don't think the news of her death has sunk in yet.*

sink·age /síngkij/ *n.* the process of sinking or the extent to which something sinks

sink·er /síngkər/ *n.* **1.** WEIGHT USED IN FISHING a weight used to take a fishing line or net to the bottom **2.** DOWNWARD CURVING BASEBALL PITCH in baseball, a pitched ball that curves sharply downward as it reaches the plate **3.** DOUGHNUT a doughnut (*informal*) [Early 16thC. Originally in the meaning "someone who engraves designs on dies."]

sink·hole /síngk hōl/ *n.* **1.** GEOG DEPRESSION IN GROUND WITH UNDERGROUND STREAM a natural depression in the land surface, especially in limestone, where a stream flows underground into a passage or cave **2.** SUNKEN AREA a sunken area where waste collects

sink·ing fund *n.* a fund created by setting aside regular sums for investment, usually in bonds, in order to repay a debt that will fall due at a future date

sin·ner /sínnər/ *n.* somebody who commits a sin or who habitually does wrong

Sinn Féin /shìn fáyn/ *n.* a nationalist Irish republican party founded in 1905 [Early 20thC. From Irish *sinn féin*, literally "we ourselves."] —**Sinn Féin·er** *n.* —**Sinn Féin·ism** *n.*

si·no·a·tri·al /sìnō áytree əl/ *adj.* relating to the sinus venosus and the right atrium of the heart [Early 20thC. Coined from SINO-, from SINUS, + *atrial*, from ATRIUM.]

si·no·a·tri·al node *n.* a small mass of specialized cardiac muscle fibers located in the wall of the right atrium of the heart. It originates the regular electrical impulses that stimulate the heartbeat.

Si·nol·o·gy /sī nóllәjee/ *n.* the study of Chinese civilization, literature, and language —**Si·no·log·i·cal** /sìnə lójjik'l, sīnə-/ *adj.* —**Si·nol·o·gist** /sī nólləjist/ *n.*

Si·no·pe /si nṓpee/ *n.* the outermost known natural satellite of Jupiter, discovered in 1914. It is 28 km (17 mi.) in diameter.

Si·no·phile /sínə fīl/ *n.* somebody who admires China or the Chinese

Si·no·phobe /sínə fōb/ *n.* somebody who hates or fears China and the Chinese

Si·no-Ti·bet·an /sínō tə bétt'n/ *n.* a family of languages of East and Southeast Asia. There are two main branches, Chinese (**Sinitic**) and Tibeto-Burman. Over twelve hundred million people speak a Sino-Tibetan language.

sin·se·mil·la /sìnssə mee yə, -míllə/ *n.* a very strong form of marijuana obtained from unpollinated female hemp plants [Late 20thC. From American Spanish, literally "without seed."]

sin tax *n.* a tax on something such as tobacco, alcoholic beverages, or gambling that is considered to have harmful personal and social effects

sin·ter /síntər/ *vti.* (**-tered, -ter·ing, -ters**) BOND METAL PARTICLES to use pressure and heat below the melting point to bond and partly fuse masses of metal particles, or to be bonded in this way ■ *n.* **1.** BONDED METAL PARTICLES a mass of metal particles bonded and partly fused by the use of pressure and heat below the melting point **2.** POROUS MINERAL SEDIMENT a whitish chemical sediment consisting of porous silica or calcium carbonate deposited by a mineral spring [Late 18thC. From German, "cinder," from the same prehistoric Germanic word that produced English *cinder*.]

Sin·tra /síntrə/ city in Portugal, situated 15 mi./24 km west of Lisbon. Population: 20,000 (1981).

sin·u·ate *adj.* /sínnyoo ət, -àyt/ **sin·u·ate, sin·u·at·ed** BOT WITH WAVY INDENTED EDGE used to describe a leaf with a wavy indented margin ■ *vi.* /sínnyoo àyt/ (**-at·ed** /-àytəd/, **-at·ing, -ates**) WIND SINUOUSLY to wind in and out [Late 16thC. From Latin *sinuat-* the past participle stem of Latin *sinuare*, "to bend, curve," from *sinus* (see SINUS).] —**sin·u·ate·ly** *adv.* —**sin·u·a·tion** /sìnnyoo áysh'n/ *n.*

sin·u·os·i·ty /sìnnyoo óssətee/ (*plural* **-ties**) *n.* **1.** SINUOUSNESS the condition of being winding or curving in shape or movement **2.** SOMETHING SINUOUS a winding bend or curving movement

sin·u·ous /sínnyoo əss/ *adj.* **1.** MOVING IN GRACEFUL CURVES with graceful winding or curving movements ○ *the sinuous movements of the dancer's arm* **2.** WINDING OR SERPENTINE full of bends and curves ○ *the sinuous course of a stream* **3.** DEVIOUS indirect and devious **4.** BOT = **sinuate** [Late 16thC. From Latin *sinuosus*, from *sinus* (see SINUS).] —**sin·u·ous·ly** *adv.* —**sin·u·ous·ness** *n.*

si·nus /sínəss/ *n.* **1.** ANAT CAVITY IN BONE OF SKULL a cavity filled with air in the bones of the face and skull, especially one opening into the nasal passages **2.** ANAT CHANNEL FOR BLOOD a widened channel containing blood, especially venous blood **3.** MED CHANNEL LEADING FROM BODY CAVITY an elongated tract leading from a pus-filled region of the body to the exterior or to the cavity of a hollow organ **4.** BOT NOTCH BETWEEN LEAVES a cleft or indentation between the lobes of a leaf or the fused petals of a corolla [15thC. From Latin, "curve, fold, hollow."]

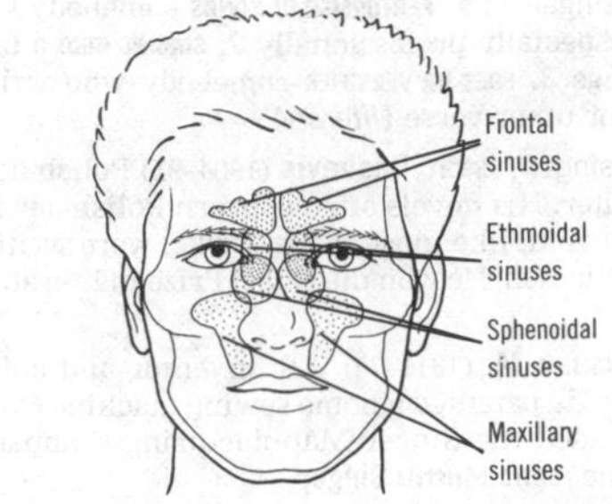

Sinus

Si·nus I·rid·um /sínəss írridəm/ *n.* ASTRON a large half-crater on the Moon adjoining the northwest side of Mare Imbrium. Its walled perimeter forms the Montes Jura and it is approximately 160 mi./260 km in diameter.

si·nus·i·tis /sìnə sítiss/ *n.* inflammation of the membrane lining a sinus of the skull

si·nus node *n.* = **sinoatrial node**

si·nu·soid /sínə sòyd/ *n.* **1.** SMALL VESSEL IN ORGAN TISSUE a small blood vessel or cavity in the tissue of an organ such as the liver, heart, or pancreas **2.** = **sine curve** ■ *adj.* LIKE SINUS resembling a sinus in shape or function —**si·nu·soi·dal** *adj.* —**si·nus·oi·dal·ly** *adv.*

si·nu·soi·dal pro·jec·tion *n.* a map projection on which equal areas appear equal, the parallels of latitude are regularly spaced straight lines, and all the lines of longitude except the prime meridian are curved

si·nus ve·no·sus /-və nṓssəss/ (*plural* **si·nus ve·no·si** /-ee/) *n.* an enlarged pouch attached to the heart of fish, amphibians, and reptiles through which blood from the veins is forced into the atrium [From Latin, literally "veined sinus"]

Siou·an /sóo ən/ *n.* **1.** FAMILY OF NATIVE N AMERICAN LANGUAGES a family of Native North American languages that includes Dakota, Omaha, and Choctaw. About 30,000 people speak a Siouan language. **2.** SOMEBODY SPEAKING SIOUAN LANGUAGE somebody who speaks a Siouan language ■ *adj.* RELATING TO SIOUX relating to any of the Sioux peoples or their cultures

Sioux /soo/ (*plural* **Sioux**) *n.* a member of a group of Native North American peoples that originally occupied vast tracts of the Great Plains, and whose members now live mainly in North and South Dakota [Early 18thC. From North American French, shortening of *Nadouessioux*, from Ojibwa (Ottawa dialect) *natowèssiwak*.]

Sioux Cit·y city in western Iowa, across the Missouri River from South Dakota and Nebraska, and northwest of Council Bluffs. Population: 83,791 (1996).

Sioux Falls city in southeastern South Dakota, on the Big Sioux River, southeast of Mitchell. Population: 113,223 (1996).

sip /sip/ *vti.* (**sipped, sip·ping, sips**) DRINK SLOWLY IN VERY SMALL AMOUNTS to drink something slowly, taking only a small amount at a time ■ *n.* SMALL AMOUNT OF DRINK a very small amount of liquid taken into the mouth [14thC. Origin uncertain: probably a variant of SUP, thought to suggest a less vigorous action.] —**sip·per** *n.*

SIPC *abbr.* Securities Investor Protection Corporation

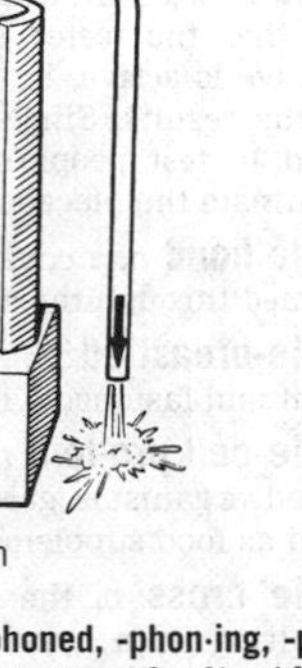
Siphon

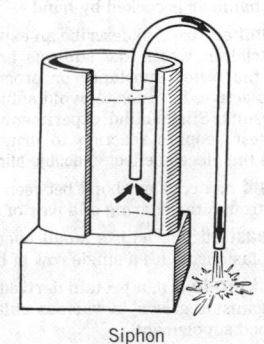

si·phon /sífən/, **sy·phon** *v.* (**-phoned, -phon·ing, -phons**) **1.** *vt.* DRAW LIQUID THROUGH TUBE to transfer liquid from one container to another through a tube using atmospheric pressure to make it flow **2.** *vti.* ILLEGALLY TAP FUNDS OR RESOURCES to convey or draw money or resources from something, especially illegally ■ *n.* **1.** BENT TUBE FOR DRAWING OFF LIQUID a bent tube or pipe used to transfer liquid from one container to another using atmospheric pressure to make it flow **2.** = **siphon bottle 3.** MARINE BIOL TUBULAR ORGAN a tubular organ, especially of arthropods and mollusks, by which water is taken in or expelled [14thC. Directly or via French from Latin *sipho,* from Greek *siphōn* "pipe, tube."] —**si·phon·age** *n.* —**si·phon·al** *adj.* —**si·phon·ic** /sī fónnik/ *adj.*

si·phon bot·tle *n.* a heavy sealed bottle fitted with a valve and nozzle at the top and containing pressurized carbonated water. When the valve is opened the water begins to flow.

si·phon·o·phore /sī fónnə fàwr, sīffənə-/ *n.* a marine hydrozoan such as the Portuguese man-of-war that forms floating or swimming transparent or lightly-colored colonies. Order: Siphonophora. [Mid-19thC] —**si·pho·noph·o·rous** /sīfə nóffərəss/ *adj.*

sip·pet /síppət/ *n. U.K.* a small piece of toast or fried bread cut in a triangle or small neat shape and usually eaten with stews or dishes served with sauce (*dated*) [Mid-16thC. Formed from an alteration of SOP, literally "small sop."]

Si·quei·ros /si káyrōss/, **David Alfaro** (1896?–1974) Mexican painter and political activist. He was a major figure among Mexican mural painters. His works include *The March of Humanity* (1968).

sir (*stressed*) /sur/; (*unstressed*) /sər/ *n.* **1.** POLITE FORM OF ADDRESS TO MAN a form of address to a man often used in speech as a sign of respect or as a salutation in a letter ○ *Excuse me, sir, do you know what time it is?* **2.** *U.K.* WAY TO ADDRESS MAN TEACHER a form of address to a man teacher, mainly used by his students [13thC. Variant of SIRE.] ◇ **yes sir, no sir** used to emphasize emphatic confirmation or denial of something

Sir *n.* a title of honor used before the name a knight or baronet

sir·dar /súr daar, sər daar/ *n.* **1.** HIGH-RANKING LEADER in India or Pakistan, somebody of high rank such as a political or military leader **2.** FORMER BRITISH COMMANDER OF EGYPTIAN ARMY the title formerly given to the British commander of the Egyptian army **3.** TITLE FOR SIKH MAN a title of respect for a Sikh man [Early 17thC. Via Hindi *sardār* from Persian, literally "head holder."]

sire /sīr/ *vt.* (**sired, sir·ing, sires**) FATHER OFFSPRING to father young, especially animals ■ *n.* **1.** MALE PARENT OF FOUR-LEGGED ANIMAL the male parent of a four-legged animal, especially a domesticated animal such as a stallion or bull **2. sire, Sire** ADDRESS TO KING OR LORD a respectful form of address for a king or lord (*archaic*) [12thC. Via Old French from, ultimately, Latin *senior* "older" (source of English *senior*).]

si·ren /sīrən/ *n.* **1.** STATIONARY WARNING DEVICE a mounted warning device that produces a loud wailing sound when a current of compressed air or steam is forced through a rotating perforated disk **2.** PORTABLE WARNING DEVICE an electronic warning device, often mounted or placed on a moving vehicle, that produces a loud wailing sound **3.** SEA NYMPH LURING SAILORS ONTO ROCKS a sea nymph, half-woman half-bird, who was believed to sing beguilingly to passing sailors in order to lure them to their doom on the rocks she sat on **4.** OFFENSIVE TERM an offensive term used to refer to a woman who is considered to be attractive in a dangerous way (*offensive*) **5.** BIOL SALAMANDER RESEMBLING EEL a salamander with a long thin body and tail, permanent external gills, lungs, small forelegs, and no hind limbs. Family: Sirenidae. [14thC. Via Old French *sereine* "sea nymph" and Latin *Siren* from Greek *Seirēn*. The modern meaning evolved from the idea of the sea nymph's cries.]

si·ren call *n.* = **siren song**

si·re·ni·an /sī reenee ən/ *n.* an aquatic herbivorous placental mammal that has forelimbs like paddles, no hind limbs, and a broad flat tail. The dugong and manatee are sirenians. Order: Sirenia. [Late 19thC. Formed from modern Latin *Sirenia*, order name, from Latin *Siren* (see SIREN).] —**si·re·ni·an** *adj.*

si·ren song *n.* an alluring appeal that something possesses, even though it may have unfortunate effects ○ *She yielded to the siren song of a higher salary.*

Sir·i·us /sírree əss/ *n.* a binary star in the constellation Canis Major that appears as the brightest star in the sky

sir·loin /súr lòyn/ *n.* an expensive prime cut of beef used for roasting or steaks, taken from the lower part of the ribs or the upper loin [15thC. From an assumed Old French word, literally "loin above."]

WORD KEY: ORIGIN

One of the most persistent of etymological fictions is that the ***sirloin*** got its name because a particular English king found the joint of beef so excellent that he knighted it. The monarch in question has been variously identified as Henry VIII, James I, and Charles II, but none of these is chronologically possible, and in fact the story has no truth in it at all. The spelling *sir-*, which began to replace the original *sur-* (from Old French *sur* "above") in the 18th century, no doubt owes something to the "knighting" story.

si·roc·co /sə rókō/ (*plural* **-cos** /shə rókō, sə-/), **sci·roc·co** (*plural* **-cos**) *n.* a hot dusty humid southeast wind in southern Europe that begins in the Sahara and picks up moisture as it crosses the Mediterranean [Early 17thC. Via French *sirocco* and Italian *scirocco* from Arabic *šarūq* "the east," hence "east wind."]

sir·rah /sírrə/ *n.* a form of address for a man or boy that was used to express contempt (*archaic*) [Early 16thC. Alteration of SIRE, its original second syllable associated with AH, as an expression of contempt.]

sir·ree /sə rée/ *n.* sir, used to express emphasis [Early 19thC. Extension of SIR, thought to suggest emphasis.] ◇ **yes sirree!, no sirree!** used to emphasize agreement or disagreement (*informal*)

Sir Rog·er de Cov·er·ley /sər ròjjər də kúvvərlee/ *n.* an English country dance, similar to a Virginia reel, that is danced to a traditional tune and performed by two rows of dancers facing each other [Alteration of earlier English *roger of coverley*, probably from *Roger*, the personal name + OF + *Coverley*, a fictitious place name (or perhaps that of *Calverley* in YORKSHIRE)]

sir·up *n.* syrup (*archaic*)

sir·vente /sər vént, -vaaNt/, **sir·vent·es** /sər véntəss/ *n.* a poem in stanza form written by troubadors in Provence that chiefly satirized moral or political matters [Early 17thC. Via French from Provençal *sirventes*, literally "servant's song" (from the position of a lover in relation to his mistress).]

sis /siss/ *n.* a form of address for a sister (*informal*) [Mid-17thC. Shortening.]

si·sal /sīss'l, sīz'l/, **si·sal hemp** *n.* **1.** PLANT YIELDING FIBERS a Mexican agave plant widely grown for its large sword-shaped leaves that yield a stiff fiber. Latin name: *Agave sisalana.* **2.** FIBER FROM SISAL a strong white fiber obtained from the leaves of the sisal plant, used to make rope and rugs [Mid-19thC. Named for Sisal, a town in Yucatán.]

sis·kin /sískin/ *n.* **1.** FINCH a yellow-and-black finch of Europe, Asia, and northern Africa that is related to the goldfinch. Latin name: *Carduelis spinus.* **2.** = **pine siskin** [Mid-16thC. From Middle Dutch *siseken* and early Flemish *sijsken*, literally "little siskin." Ultimately of Slavic origin.]

sis·si·fied /síssə fīd/ *adj.* = **sissy**

sis·sy /síssee/, **cis·sy** *n.* (*plural* **-sies**) OFFENSIVE TERM an offensive term used to refer to a boy or man who is considered not to exhibit stereotypical masculine behavior, especially by other boys or men (*informal offensive*) ■ *adj.* OFFENSIVE TERM an offensive term used to refer to a boy, man, behavior, or object that is considered not to exhibit or be characteristic of stereotypical masculinity (*informal offensive*) [Mid-19thC. Formed from SIS, originally in the sense "sister."] —**sis·sy·ish** *adj.* —**sis·si·ness** *n.*

sis·sy bar *n.* a U-shaped bar that chiefly acts as a backrest for the rider or passenger of a motorcycle or bicycle [Because the passenger is supported by the bar]

sis·ter /sístər/ *n.* **1.** FEMALE SIBLING a girl or woman who has the same parents as another person **2.** STEPSISTER OR HALF-SISTER a girl or woman who has one parent in common with another person **3.** NUN a female member of a religious community, or a form of address to such a person ○ *Sister Brigit joined us a few weeks ago.* **4.** *U.K.* MED WOMAN SENIOR NURSE a woman who holds the most senior grade of hospital nurse, above staff nurse, often in charge of a ward **5.** WOMAN MEMBER OF SAME ORGANIZATION a woman who belongs to the same organization as another **6.** WOMAN SUPPORTER OF FEMINISM a woman who advocates or supports feminist principles **7.** AFRICAN AMERICAN WOMAN a form of address or way of referring to an African American woman, used especially by other African Americans **8.** CLOSE WOMAN FRIEND a close woman friend, especially of another woman ■ *adj.* **1.** CLOSELY LINKED belonging to or closely associated with something ○ *her sister ship, The Princess* **2.** GENETICS WITH PAIRED CELL used to describe either of an identical pair of cells or cell components formed by division of a parent cell or component [Old English *sweostor, sweoster.* Ultimately from an Indo-European word that is also the ancestor of English *sorority*.]

WORD KEY: CULTURAL NOTE

The Three Sisters, a play by the Russian dramatist Anton Chekhov (1900). Set in rural Russia, this powerful and compassionate study of the quiet desperation of bourgeois life centers on the three Pozarov sisters. Stifled by the dreariness of local society, they look to the officers of the local garrison for romance and entertainment. But when the army departs, the sisters are left with only their dreams and each other.

sis·ter·hood /sístər hòòd/ *n.* **1.** SOLIDARITY AMONG WOMEN the empathy and loyalty that women feel for other women who have shared goals, experiences, or viewpoints **2.** WOMEN'S GROUP a group of women who have shared goals, experiences, or viewpoints **3.** STATUS AS SISTER the status of a sister or the relationship of sisters **4.** COMMUNITY OF NUNS a religious community of women

sis·ter-in-law (*plural* **sis·ters-in-law**) *n.* **1.** SPOUSE'S SISTER the sister of somebody's husband or wife **2.** BROTHER'S WIFE the wife of somebody's brother

sis·ter·ly /sístərlee/ *adj., adv.* relating to, coming from, or characteristic of a sister, especially in an affectionate, kind, or caring way —**sis·ter·li·ness** *n.*

Sis·tine /sís teen/ *adj.* **1.** OF POPE SIXTUS relating to any of the popes named Sixtus, especially Sixtus IV who was pope 1471–84 **2.** OF SISTINE CHAPEL relating to the Sistine Chapel [Late 18thC. From Italian *Sistino* "of Sixtus," from Latin *Sextus*, a Roman personal name, from *sextus* "sixth."]

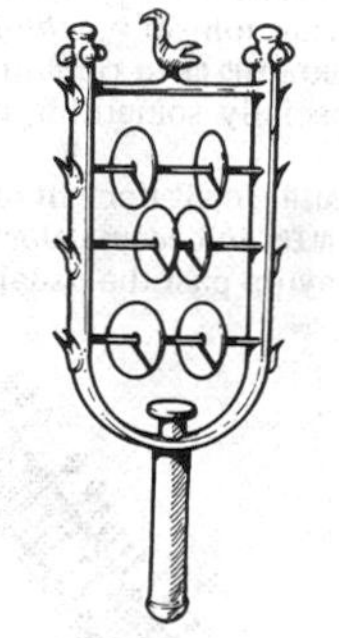

Sistrum

sis·trum /sístrəm/ (*plural* **-tra** /-trə/) *n.* an ancient Egyptian percussion instrument consisting of a thin metal frame with rods or loops attached that jingle when shaken [14thC. Via Latin from Greek *seistron*, from *seiein* "to shake."]

Sis·y·phe·an /sìssə fée ən/ *adj.* involving endless but futile labor [Late 16thC. Formed from Latin *Sisypheius*, from, ultimately, Greek *Sisuphos* (see SISYPHUS).]

Sis·y·phus /síssəfəss/ *n.* in Greek mythology, a cruel king of Corinth who was condemned for eternity to roll a boulder up a hill only to have it roll down again just before it reached the top

sit /sit/ *v.* (**sat, sat** /sat/, **sit·ting, sits**) **1.** *vi.* REST WITH WEIGHT ON BUTTOCKS to assume a position of rest in which the weight is largely supported by the buttocks, usually with the body vertical and the thighs horizontal **2.** *vt.* PLACE IN SEAT to place somebody or yourself in a seat or a sitting position **3.** *vi.* REST BODY ON HINDQUARTERS to rest the body with the weight supported by the lowered hindquarters (*refers to four-legged animals*) **4.** *vi.* PERCH, ROOST, OR COVER EGGS to perch, roost, or cover and warm eggs for hatching **5.** *vi.* POL, LAW EXERCISE AUTHORITY to occupy a position of authority while deciding or legislating something **6.** *vi.* ARTS, PHOTOGRAPHY POSE FOR SOMETHING to pose for a portrait or picture **7.** *vi.* BE IDLE to be or remain idle **8.** *vi.* BE

PLACED OR SITUATED to be located or positioned somewhere ○ *The dinner dishes were still sitting on the table.* **9.** *vi.* BABY-SIT to baby-sit (*informal*) **10.** *vt.* HAVE SEATING SPACE FOR to have seats or seating space for a specified number of people ○ *We can sit 10 around the dining table.* **11.** *vi.* BE TAKEN AS SPECIFIED to be accepted or considered in the way specified ○ *The news didn't sit well with me.* **12.** *vi.* BE DIGESTIBLE to be digestible (*informal*) ○ *The heavy meal didn't sit well with me.* **13.** *vi.* BE IN SPECIFIED WAY to rest, weigh, or lie as specified ○ *Authority sits lightly on his shoulders.* **14.** *vi.* CLOTHES FIT OR HANG to fit or hang on somebody in a specified way ○ *The gown sat beautifully on the model.* **15.** *vt.* BE ASTRIDE SOMETHING to keep astride of a horse or similar animal ○ *She sat her gelding with great poise.* **16.** *vi.* SET IN SPECIFIED DIRECTION to be in a specified direction (*archaic*) ○ *The wind sat in the east.* ■ *n.* **1.** TIME SPENT BEING SEATED a period of being seated, especially while waiting ○ *We had a long sit waiting for the dentist.* **2.** CLOTHES WAY GARMENT FITS the way a garment hangs on somebody **3.** MOUNTED POSITION a position astride a horse or similar animal [Old English *sittan.* Ultimately from an Indo-European word that is also the ancestor of English *saddle.* Related to German *sitzen* "to sit."] ◇ **be sitting pretty** to be in a fortunate or favorable situation (*informal*) ◇ **sit tight** refrain from moving or acting until the right time (*informal*)

sit back *vi.* to take no action ○ *sat back and watched the crisis develop*

sit down *vti.* to become seated, or make somebody become seated ○ *time to sit him down and tell him the truth*

sit in *vi.* **1.** ATTEND WITHOUT TAKING PART to attend something but not take an active part in it ○ *Do you mind if I sit in on your meeting?* **2.** TEMPORARILY REPLACE SOMEBODY to do a job for the person who normally does it ○ *sitting in for the regular announcer on the show* **3.** OCCUPY BUILDING AS PROTEST to take part in a sit-in

sit on *vt.* **1.** BE PART OF DECISION-MAKING GROUP to be a member of a group that decides something **2.** SUPPRESS to suppress something or delay dealing with it ○ *The government sat on the information for weeks.* **3.** NAG SOMEBODY to nag somebody continually (*informal*) ○ *If you want to be sure I'll do it, you'll have to sit on me.*

sit out *v.* **1.** *vt.* NOT PARTICIPATE IN to remain seated during something and not join in ○ *I think I'll sit this one out.* **2.** *vt.* STAY UNTIL END OF to remain until the end of something, especially something unpleasant **3.** *vi.* *U.K.* = **hike out**

sit up *vi.* **1.** SIT STRAIGHT to sit upright or rise from lying down **2.** BECOME ALERT to become alert or interested **3.** STAY UP LATE to stay up past the usual time of going to bed

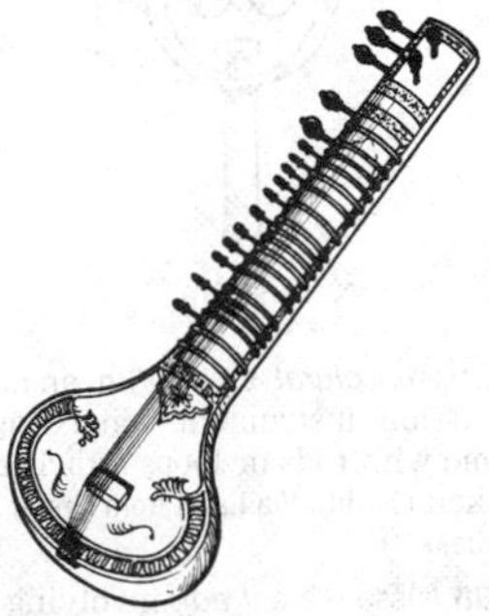

Sitar

si·tar /si taar/ *n.* an Indian stringed instrument with a rounded resonating body and a long fretted neck. There are several playing strings and a larger number that vibrate sympathetically. [Mid-19thC. Via Hindi from Persian, literally "three-stringed," from the original design.] —**si·tar·ist** *n.*

sit·com /sít kòm/ *n.* a situation comedy (*informal*) [Mid-20thC. Shortening.]

sit-down *adj.* SERVED WHILE SITTING DOWN served to people sitting at a table ○ *There's a sit-down dinner before the dancing.* ■ *n.* **1.** = **sit-down strike** **2.** = **sit-in** **3.** PERIOD OF RELAXATION BY SITTING a short spell of sitting in order to relax (*informal*) ○ *After all that shopping I could do with a sit-down.*

sit-down strike *n.* a form of protest in which people refuse to leave a place, often sitting or lying down, until their demands are granted or negotiated

site /sīt/ *n.* **1.** PLACE WHERE SOMETHING STANDS an area or piece of land where something was, is, or will be located ○ *The whole area has become one vast building site.* **2.** PLACE OF SIGNIFICANT EVENT a place where something important happened **3.** COMPUT = **Web site** ■ *vt.* (**sit·ed, sit·ing, sites**) POSITION SOMETHING to locate something in a particular place or position ○ *The plan is to site all further malls in the suburbs.* [14thC. Directly or via Anglo-Norman from Latin *situs* "place, position," from the past participle of *sinere* "to put."]

si·tel·la /si téllə/ *n.* a small gregarious songbird found in Australasia, similar to the nuthatch in its stout body, short tail, and habit of hopping up and down trees. Family: Neosittidae. [Mid-19thC. From modern Latin *Sittella,* former genus name, literally "little nuthatch," from, ultimately, Greek *sittē* "nuthatch."]

sit·fast /sít fàst/ *n.* *U.K.* a sore on a horse's back caused by the rubbing of a saddle

sith /sith/ *adv., conj., prep.* since (*archaic*) [Old English Shortening of Old English *siððan* "since" (source also of English *since*)]

sit-in *n.* a form of protest in which people occupy a building or public place and refuse to leave until their demands have been met or negotiated

Sit·ka /sítkə/ city in southeastern Alaska, on the western coast of Baranof Island, in the Alexander Archipelago. Population: 8,588 (1996).

sit·ka spruce /sítkə-/ *n.* a tall spruce tree of the northwest Pacific coast of North America. It has reddish-brown bark and silvery-white needles and yields soft, pale-brown timber. Latin name: *Picea sitchensis.* [Late 19thC. Named for SITKA.]

si·tol·o·gy /sī tólləjee/ *n.* the scientific study of food, diet, and nutrition as they relate to health [Mid-19thC. Coined from Greek *sitos* "food, grain" + -LOGY.]

si·to·ma·ni·a /sìtə máynee ə/ *n.* an eating disorder marked by excessive craving for food (*dated*) [Late 19thC. Coined from Greek *sitos* "food, grain" + -MANIA.]

sit spin *n.* a spin on one ice skate made in a squatting position with one leg stretched out in front of the body

sit·ter /sittər/ *n.* **1.** HIRED MINDER somebody hired to look after something (*often used in combination*) **2.** = **baby-sitter** **3.** MED SOMEBODY HIRED TO WATCH PATIENTS somebody hired to watch over patients in order to respond to urgent needs or to prevent them from harming themselves accidentally **4.** ARTS, PHOTOGRAPHY ARTIST'S OR PHOTOGRAPHER'S MODEL somebody who poses for a portrait **5.** AGRIC BROODING HEN a hen or other bird sitting on eggs to hatch them

sit·ting /sítting/ *n.* **1.** TURN TO EAT any of the periods when a meal is served in a place where there is insufficient room for everyone to eat at the same time ○ *The first sitting is at 12 o'clock.* **2.** ARTS, PHOTOGRAPHY TIME FOR POSING a period of time during which somebody is seated in posing for a portrait ○ *I'd like to get another sitting in this afternoon.* **3.** POL, LAW SESSION OF PUBLIC BODY a meeting or session of an official body such as a legislature or court **4.** PERIOD OF BEING SEATED a period of being seated while engaged in an activity ○ *It took him three sittings to read the book.* **5.** AGRIC SET OF EGGS a clutch of eggs under a brooding bird **6.** AGRIC INCUBATION OF EGGS the period of time during which a hen sits on eggs to hatch them ■ *adj.* **1.** SEATED seated or for being seated ○ *a sitting area* **2.** IN OFFICE holding office at the present

Library of Congress

Sitting Bull

Sit·ting Bull /sìtting bóol/ (1831?–90) Sioux leader. He defeated General George Custer at the Battle of Little Big Horn in 1876. He was killed during a later outbreak of hostilities.

sit·ting duck *n.* somebody or something that is defenseless, exposed to danger, and easy to attack or exploit (*informal*)

sit·ting room *n.* a small room in a house, apartment, or office that is used for sitting, especially one that forms part of a connecting suite. ◊ **living room**

sit·ting trot *n.* EQU a slow trot during which the rider does not rise from the horse's saddle. ◊ **rising trot**

sit·u·ate /síchoo àyt/ (**-at·ed, -at·ing, -ates**) *vt.* to place something in a context or set of circumstances and show its connections (*formal*) [15thC. From late Latin *situat-,* the past participle stem of *situare* "to place," from Latin *situs* "position" (see SITE).]

sit·u·at·ed /síchoo àytəd/ *adj.* (*often used in combination*) **1.** LOCATED located in a place or position ○ *a conveniently situated building* **2.** IN SPECIFIED FINANCIAL STATE in a specified financial condition ○ *comfortably situated, living off their investments*

sit·u·a·tion /síchoo áysh'n/ *n.* **1.** EXISTING CONDITIONS the general conditions that prevail in a place or society **2.** CIRCUMSTANCES OF SOMEBODY'S LIFE the circumstances that somebody is in at a particular moment **3.** LOCATION the location of a property **4.** COMBINATION OF DIFFICULT CIRCUMSTANCES a difficult or problematic set of circumstances ○ *I'm afraid we have a situation here.* **5.** *U.K.* JOB a job or position of employment (*formal*) **6.** ARTS SET OF CIRCUMSTANCES IN PLOT a significant combination of circumstances in a drama, movie, or work of literature —**sit·u·a·tion·al** *adj.*

sit·u·a·tion com·e·dy *n.* a television or radio comedy series in which a regular cast of characters, usually working or living together, respond to everyday situations in a humorous way

sit·u·a·tion eth·ics, sit·u·a·tion·al eth·ics *n.* a system of ethics in which moral judgments are thought to depend on the context in which they are to be made, rather than on general moral principles (*takes a singular verb*)

sit·u·la /síchələ, sítt'lə/ (*plural* **-lae** /-lee/) *n.* an ancient decorated metal or pottery vessel shaped like a deep bucket, urn, or vase [Late 19thC. From Latin, "bucket."]

sit-up *n.* an exercise in which you lie flat on your back with your legs bent and then raise the upper part of your body to a sitting position without using your hands

si·tus /sítəss/ (*plural* **-tus·es** *or* **-tus**) *n.* **1.** POSITION OF ORGAN the position of an organ or part of the body, especially the normal position **2.** LAW RIGHTFUL PLACE the place where a thing or a right properly belongs [Early 18thC. From Latin (see SITE).]

si·tus in·ver·sus /-in vúrsəss/ *n.* an uncommon reversal of organs in the body in which the apex of the heart points to the right and the liver and appendix are on the left side [From Latin, shortening of *situs inversus viscerum* "inverted position of the internal organs"]

Popperfoto

Dame Edith Sitwell

Sit·well /sít wel, síttwəl/, **Dame Edith** (1887–1964) British writer. Unconventional in her writing, behavior, and dress, she is best known for her poetic work *Façade* (1922), which was set to music by Sir William Walton. She was the sister of Osbert and Sacheverell Sitwell. Full name **Dame Edith Louisa Sitwell**

Sit·well, Sir Osbert (1892–1969) British writer. He wrote satirical and serious poetry and five volumes of memoirs (1944–50). He was the brother of Edith and Sacheverell Sitwell.

Sit·well, Sir Sacheverell (1897–1988) British writer. He was known for his biographies and studies in baroque art, which included *Sacred and Profane Love* (1940). He was the brother of Osbert and Edith Sitwell.

sitz bath /síts-, zíts-/ *n.* **1.** BATHTUB SHAPED LIKE A CHAIR a bathtub shaped like a chair in which the bather sits immersed up to the waist in water, to which salts may be added for therapeutic purposes **2.** THERAPEUTIC BATH an act of immersion in a sitz bath, especially for therapeutic purposes [Partial translation of German *Sitzbad*, literally "sitting bath"]

sitz·krieg /síts krèeg, zíts-/ *n.* a period in a war during which there is little offensive activity or change in the positions of the combatants [Mid-20thC. Coined from German *sitzen* "to sit" on the model of BLITZKRIEG.]

sitz·mark /síts maàrk, zíts-/ *n.* a depression in the snow made by a skier who has fallen backward [Mid-20thC. Partial translation of German *Sitzmarke*, literally "sitting mark."]

SI u·nit *n.* a unit adopted for international use under the Système International d'Unités in science and technology. There are seven fundamental units: the meter, kilogram, second, ampere, kelvin, candela, and mole, and two supplementary units, the radian and steradian.

Si·va *n.* = **Shiva**

Si·van /sívv'n/ *n.* in the Jewish calendar, the third month in biblical reckoning and the ninth month in the civil year, made up of 30 days and usually falling around May [14thC. From Hebrew *sīwān*.]

si·wash /sí wàwsh, -wòsh/ *n.* **1.** *Northwest U.S., Can* OFFENSIVE TERM an offensive term for an Aboriginal person (*offensive*) **2.** *Can* SIWASH SWEATER a siwash sweater (*informal*) ■ *vi.* (**-washed, -wash·ing, -wash·es**) *Northwest U.S., Can* CAMP WITHOUT A TENT to travel and camp out without a tent (*informal*) [Mid-19thC. Via Chinook Jargon from Canadian French *sauvage*, "savage."]

si·wash sweat·er *n.* a heavy sweater made from unbleached wool, originally by the North Americans of British Columbia, decorated with symbolic designs

six /siks/ *n.* **1.** NUMBER 6 the number 6 **2.** SOMETHING WITH VALUE OF 6 something in a numbered series, e.g., a playing card, with a value of 6 **3.** GROUP OF SIX a group of six objects or people, e.g., an ice hockey team **4.** GROUP OF CUBS OR BROWNIES a division of a Cub Scout pack or Brownie Guide troop **5.** CRICKET BALL CROSSING BOUNDARY a stroke in cricket that clears the boundary without bouncing or the six runs scored by this stroke [Old English *si(e)x*. Ultimately from an Indo-European word that is also the ancestor of English *semester*.] —**six** *adj., pron.* ◇ **at sixes and sevens 1.** disorganized or in disarray (*informal*) **2.** in disagreement (*informal*) ◇ **be six of one and half-a-dozen of the other** used when there is not much difference between two choices

six·ain /sík sàyn/ *n.* a six-line stanza in poetry [Late 16thC. From French, from *six* "six."]

Six Day War *n.* a war between Israel and the states of Egypt, Jordan, and Syria that lasted six days in June 1967. The Six Day War resulted in Israel's occupation of the Gaza Strip, the Sinai Peninsula, the West Bank of the Jordan River, and the Golan Heights.

six·fold /síks fòld/ *adj.* **1.** SIX TIMES GREATER with six times as much or as many **2.** WITH SIX PARTS with six parts or elements ■ *adv.* MULTIPLIED BY SIX by six times as much or as many

six-foot·er *n.* somebody who is six feet tall or taller (*informal*)

six-gun *n.* = **six-shooter**

Six Na·tions *n.* a confederacy of six Native North American peoples, the Cayuga, Mohawk, Oneida, Onondaga, Seneca, and Tuscarora, that lived together in New York State. It was formed in 1722 when the Tuscarora joined the Five Nations of the Iroquois Confederacy.

six-pack *n.* **1.** UNIT OF SIX CANS OR BOTTLES six cans or bottles, usually of beer, sold together in a pack **2.** ABDOMINAL MUSCLES a well-developed block of abdominal muscles (*informal*)

six·pen·ny nail /síkspənee-, -pènnee-/ *n.* a nail that is 2 in./5 cm long [From the original price of a hundred such nails]

six-shoot·er *n.* a handgun whose bullets are loaded into a revolving cylinder containing six chambers (*informal*)

sixte /sikst/ *n.* the sixth of the eight basic defensive positions in fencing [Late 19thC. From French, "sixth."]

six·teen /siks tèen, síks tèen/ *n.* **1.** NUMBER 16 the number 16 **2.** SOMETHING WITH VALUE OF 16 something in a numbered series with a value of 16 **3.** GROUP OF 16 a group of sixteen objects or people [Old English *si(e)xtiene, syxtiene*] —**six·teen** *adj., pron.*

six·teen·mo /siks tèenmō/ (*plural* **-mos**) *n.* = **sextodecimo** [Mid-19thC. English reading of the symbol *16mo*.]

six·teenth /siks tèenth, síks tèenth/ *n.* one of 16 equal parts of something —**six·teenth** *adj., adv.*

six·teenth note *n.* a note that has the time value of one-sixteenth of a whole note

sixth /siksth/ *n.* **1.** MUSIC INTERVAL OF SIX NOTES in a standard musical scale, the interval between one note and another that lies five notes above or below it. In the scale of C major, C and A form a sixth. **2.** ONE OF 6 PARTS OF SOMETHING one of six equal parts of something **3.** MUSIC NOTE A SIXTH AWAY FROM ANOTHER in a standard musical scale, a note that is a sixth away from another note **4.** HARMONY OF A SIXTH the harmony created by playing two notes a sixth apart **5.** ONE NOTE IN A SIXTH one of the two notes in a sixth —**sixth** *adj., adv.*

sixth chord *n.* a musical chord made up of a note plus a note a third above and a note a sixth above

sixth sense *n.* a supposed special ability to perceive something not using any of the five senses of sight, hearing, touch, smell, and taste

six·ti·eth /síkstee əth/ *n.* one of 60 equal parts of something —**six·ti·eth** *adj., adv.*

Six·tus V /síkstəss/, **Pope** (1521–90). He reformed the church administration, ordered the construction of public buildings in Rome, and supported missions abroad.

six·ty /síkstee/ *n.* (*plural* **-ties**) **1.** NUMBER 60 the number 60 **2.** GROUP OF 60 a group of sixty objects or people ■ **six·ties** *npl.* **1.** NUMBERS 60 TO 69 the numbers 60 to 69, particularly as a range of temperature ○ *in the low sixties* **2.** YEARS 1960 TO 1969 the years 1960 to 1969 **3.** PERIOD FROM AGE 60 TO 69 the period of somebody's life from the age of 60 to 69 [Old English *sixtig*] —**sixty** *adj., pron.*

six·ty-four·mo /-fàwrmō/ (*plural* **six·ty-four·mos**) *n.* **1.** PAPER SIZE a book or paper size that results from a sheet of paper being folded 64 times **2.** BOOK OF SIXTY-FOURMO SIZE paper or a book that is sixty-fourmo in size [English reading of the symbol 64mo]

six·ty-fourth note *n.* MUSIC a note written as a filled note-head with a stem and four tails, whose time value is one 64th that of a whole note

six·ty-nine *n.* an offensive term used to refer to a sexual activity in which two people simultaneously stimulate each other's genitals orally (*slang offensive*) [From the position of the couple, with their heads at opposite ends from each other]

siz·a·ble /sízəb'l/, **size·a·ble** *adj.* fairly large —**siz·a·ble·ness** *n.* —**siz·a·bly** *adv.*

siz·ar /sízər/, **siz·er** *n.* an undergraduate student at some universities who receives a grant for expenses from a college [Late 16thC. Coined from SIZE in the obsolete sense "quantity of bread or ale" (probably because the student's "sizes" were free) + -AR.] —**siz·ar·ship** *n.*

size[1] /sīz/ *n.* **1.** HOW MUCH SOMETHING MEASURES the amount, scope, or degree of something, in terms of how large or small it is **2.** HOW BIG SOMETHING IS the large quality or extent of a particular thing **3.** STANDARD MEASUREMENT OF MANUFACTURED ITEM a set of measurements used when making or classifying articles that are produced and sold, such as clothing or shoes. Manufacturers make goods in a fixed set of graduated sizes, with particular dimensions. ■ *vt.* (**sized, siz·ing, siz·es**) **1.** SORT ACCORDING TO SIZE to put things into different groups according to their size **2.** MAKE TO A PARTICULAR SIZE to cut, shape, or manufacture goods so that they have the necessary or chosen measurements [13thC. From Old French *sise*, an alteration of *assise*, from Latin *assidere* "to sit beside" (see ASSIZE). Originally "sitting down to make a judgment (later, on the standardization of amounts)," hence "dimension."] ◇ **cut somebody down to size** to make somebody be less self-important and arrogant ◇ **that's about the size of it** used to indicate that something describes a situation very well (*informal*) ◇ **try something (on) for size 1.** to put something on to see whether it fits you or not **2.** to find out how much you like something, or how well it suits you

size up *vt.* to assess a person or situation and form a judgment

size[2] /sīz/ *n.* GELATINOUS MIXTURE FOR FILLING POROUS SURFACES a gelatinous mixture made from glue, starch, or varnish that is used to fill the pores in the surface of paper, textiles, or plaster ■ *vt.* (**sized, siz·ing, siz·es**) COAT WITH SIZE to coat a porous surface such as paper, textile, or plaster with size [15thC. Origin uncertain: perhaps the same as SIZE[1].]

size·a·ble /sízəb'l/ *adj.* = **sizable**

sized /sīzd/, **size** *adj.* having a specified size (*often used in combination*)

size·ism /sí zìzzəm/ *n.* discrimination against somebody on the basis of the person's size, especially the person's unusual tallness, shortness, fatness or thinness —**size·ist** *adj.*

siz·er *n.* = **sizar**

siz·ing /sízing/ *n.* **1.** = **size**[2] *n.* **2.** USE OF SIZE the process of coating something with size

siz·zle /sízz'l/ *v.* (**-zled, -zling, -zles**) **1.** *vti.* MAKE THE NOISE OF FOOD FRYING to make the hissing and spattering sound typical of frying fat, or to cook food so that it makes a hissing sound **2.** *vi.* BE FURIOUS to show or feel great anger (*informal*) **3.** *vi.* BE HOT to be extremely hot (*informal*) **4.** *vi.* BE PHYSICALLY APPEALING to be physically appealing or very popular (*informal*) ■ *n.* **1.** PHYSICAL APPEAL appeal based on physical attributes (*informal*) **2.** HISSING, FRYING NOISE the sound of something frying, or a sound resembling this [Early 17thC. An imitation of the sound.]

siz·zler /sízzlər/ *n.* **1.** SOMETHING THAT SIZZLES something that sizzles **2.** HOT DAY an extremely hot day (*informal*)

siz·zling /sízzling/ *adj.* (*informal*) **1.** HOT extremely hot **2.** PHYSICALLY APPEALING physically appealing or very popular —**siz·zling·ly** *adv.*

S.J. *abbr.* Society of Jesus

Sjael·land /syéllènd/ the main island of Denmark, on which Copenhagen is situated. Population: 2,159,260 (1994). Area: 2,700 sq. mi./7,000 sq. km.

sjam·bok /sham bók, -búk/ (**-bokked, -bok·king, -boks**) *n. S Africa* a sturdy whip or riding crop made from the hide of a rhinoceros or hippopotamus [Late 18thC. Via Afrikaans from Malay *chambuk*, from, ultimately, Persian *chābuk* "whip."]

SK *abbr.* Saskatchewan

ska /skaa/ *n.* dance music in 4/4 time originating in Jamaica in the late 1950s, marked by emphasis on the second and fourth beats. It combines traditional Caribbean music and jazz, and was a predecessor of reggae. [Mid-20thC. Origin unknown.]

Skag·er·rak /skággè rak/ arm of the North Sea between Norway and the Jutland Peninsula, Denmark. Length: 150 mi./240 km.

skald /skawld/, **scald** *n.* a medieval Scandinavian poet or traveling minstrel (*archaic or literary*) [Mid-18thC. From Old Norse *skáld*. Perhaps ultimately from a prehistoric Germanic word meaning "to say" that is the ancestor of English *say* and *saga*.] —**skald·ic** *adj.*

Skåne /skónə/ province forming the southern tip of Sweden. It consists of the counties of Kristianstad and Malmöhus. Population: 1,084,755 (1993). Area: 4,241 sq. mi./10,984 sq. km.

skank /skangk/ (**skanked, skank·ing, skanks**) *vi.* to dance to reggae music, especially in a jerky way [Late 20thC. Origin unknown.]

skat /skat/ *n.* a card game for three players played with 32 cards and involving bids, contracts, and the taking of tricks [Mid-19thC. Via German from Italian *scarto* "discarded card," from, ultimately, Latin *charta* "paper" (see CARD).]

skate[1] /skayt/ *n.* **1.** ICE SKATE an ice skate **2.** ROLLER SKATE a roller skate **3.** METAL BLADE FOR AN ICE SKATE a steel runner that is fastened to the sole of a boot or shoe to make an ice skate **4.** TIME SPENT SKATING a period of time spent skating ■ *v.* (**skat·ed, skat·ing, skates**) **1.** *vi.* MOVE AROUND ON SKATES to glide along a surface wearing ice skates or roller skates **2.** *vi.* SLIDE SMOOTHLY to slide along a slippery surface **3.** BEHAVE IDLY OR IRRESPONSIBLY to behave in an idle, irresponsible manner (*informal*) ○ *Instead of studying, he's skating.* [Mid-17thC. Back-formation from Dutch *schaats* (taken as plural), from Old French *eschasse* "stilt," probably from prehistoric Germanic.]

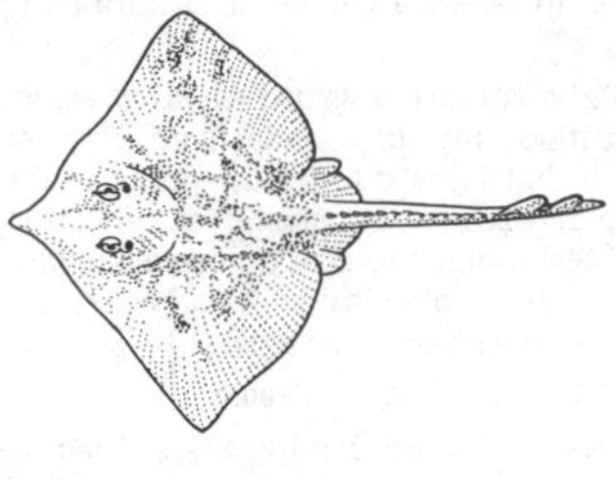

Skate

skate[2] /skayt/ (*plural* **skates** *or* **skate**) *n.* a bottom-dwelling marine cartilaginous fish that has a flattened body, very large flat pectoral fins, two small dorsal fins, a long snout, and short slender tail. Family: Rajidae. [14thC. From Old Norse *skata.*]

skate·board /skáyt bàwrd/ *n.* **WHEELED BOARD FOR RIDING** a short narrow board to which a set of small wheels is fitted on the underside, used to move rapidly or to perform jumps and stunts ■ *vi.* (**-board·ed, -board·ing, -boards**) **RIDE ON SKATEBOARD** to ride on a skateboard —**skate·board·er** *n.*

skate·board·ing /skáyt bàwrding/ *n.* the sport or pastime of riding a skateboard

skat·er /skáytər/ *n.* **1. SOMEBODY MOVING ALONG ON SKATES** somebody who ice-skates or roller-skates as a sport, hobby, or profession **2.** INSECTS = **water strider**

skat·ing /skáyting/ *n.* the pastime or sport of sliding on ice skates or rolling on roller skates

skat·ole /ská tòl, -tàwl/ *n.* an organic crystalline solid that has a strong fecal odor, is found in feces, beetroot, and coal tar, and is used as a fixative in making perfumes. Formula: C_9H_9N. [Late 19thC. Coined from the Greek stem *skat-* "dung" (see SCATO-) + -OLE.]

skean /skeen/ *n. Scotland* a dagger with a double-edged blade used in the past in Scotland and Ireland [Early 16thC. Via Gaelic *scian* from Old Irish. Ultimately from an Indo-European base meaning "to cut" that is also the ancestor of English *shin* and *schism.*]

ske·dad·dle /skə dádd'l/ *vi.* (**-dled, -dling, -dles**) **RUN AWAY** to run away quickly (*slang*) ■ *n.* **QUICK DEPARTURE** a very quick or agitated departure (*slang*) [Mid-19thC. Origin unknown.] —**ske·dad·dler** *n.*

skeet /skeet/, **skeet shoot·ing** *n.* a form of sport shooting in which clay targets are tossed into the air at speeds and angles intended to simulate the flight of birds [Early 20thC. Said to be from *skeet* (invented as a supposedly archaic form of SHOOT), the winning entry in a contest held to choose a name for this sport.]

skeet·er /skéetər/ *n.* a mosquito (*slang*) [Mid-19thC. Dialect variant of MOSQUITO.]

skeet shooting *n.* = **skeet**

skeg /skeg/ *n.* **1.** NAUT **PART CONNECTING KEEL AND RUDDERPOST** a part of the keel of a ship, near the stern, that connects the keel with the rudderpost **2. FIN ON SURFBOARD** the short stabilizing fin on the rear underside of a surfboard or sailboard [Early 17thC. Via Dutch *scheg* from Old Norse *skegg* "beard, point of a ship's stern."]

skein /skayn/ *n.* **1. TWISTED BUNDLE OF YARN** a length of yarn or thread wound loosely and coiled together **2.** BIRDS **GROUP OF GEESE IN FLIGHT** a flock of wild birds flying across the sky in a line **3. A TANGLE** tangled or complex mass of material [15thC. From Old French *escaigne*, of unknown origin.]

skel·e·tal /skéllət'l/ *adj.* **1. OF A SKELETON** relating to a skeleton **2. VERY THIN** extremely thin or emaciated —**skel·e·tal·ly** *adv.*

skel·e·ton /skéllət'n/ *n.* **1.** ZOOL **BONES OF PERSON OR ANIMAL** the rigid framework of interconnected bones and cartilage that protects and supports the internal organs and provides attachment for muscles in humans and other vertebrate animals **2.** ZOOL **SUPPORTIVE PROTECTIVE STRUCTURE OF INVERTEBRATES** something that provides support, gives protection, or maintains shape in an invertebrate animal, such as the shell of a snail or cuticle of a crab **3. BASIC FRAME SOMETHING IS BUILT AROUND** a structure that is needed to support and hold something together as an internal framework, onto which the connecting or covering parts are attached **4. SOMETHING WITH ONLY ESSENTIAL PARTS LEFT** a plan, organization, or structure that has been reduced so that only its most basic and necessary elements are still functioning or in place **5. OUTLINE OR LAYOUT OF SOMETHING** a description that gives the main points but no details of something such as a book or plan **6. SOMEBODY VERY THIN** an emaciated person or animal (*informal*) [Late 16thC. Via modern Latin from Greek *skeleton (sōma)* "dried up (body)," from *skellein* "to dry up."] ◇ **a skeleton in the closet** a closely kept secret that is a source of shame or embarrassment

skel·e·ton·ize /skéllət'n ìz/ (**-ized, -iz·ing, -iz·es**) *vt.* **1. CUT BACK TO ABSOLUTE BASICS** to reduce something until only its most basic structure or outline remains **2. CREATE OUTLINE OF** to create something in basic outline **3. REDUCE TO A SKELETAL FORM** to reduce something to a skeleton

skel·e·ton key *n.* a key with the usually serrated part that connects with the lever of a lock (**bit**) filed down so that it can open many different unsophisticated locks [From its basic cut-back shape]

skell /skel/ *n.* somebody who has no home or job so must live on the street (*slang*) [Late 20thC. Origin uncertain.]

skep·tic /sképtik/ *n.* **1. SOMEBODY WHO DOUBTS SOMETHING IS TRUE** somebody who questions the validity or truth of things that most people accept **2. SOMEBODY WHO DOUBTS RELIGIOUS TEACHINGS** somebody who is not willing to accept the doctrines and principles that form the basis of a religion [Late 16thC. Via French *sceptique* or directly from Latin *scepticus* "follower of the Greek philosopher Pyrrho," from Greek *skeptikos*, from *skeptesthai* "to look about."]

Skep·tic /sképtik/ *n.* **SOMEBODY DENYING KNOWLEDGE IS POSSIBLE** a member of an ancient Greek school of philosophy holding the doctrine that real knowledge is impossible, or a later follower of this doctrine ■ *adj.* **RELATING TO SKEPTICS** relating to an ancient Greek school of philosophy or its members, who believed that knowledge is impossible [Late 16thC] —**Skeptic** *adj.*

skep·ti·cal /sképtik'l/ *adj.* **1. DOUBTFUL** tending not to believe things but to question them **2. SHOWING DOUBT** marked by a doubting attitude —**skep·ti·cal·ness** *n.* —**skep·ti·cal·ly** *adv.*

WORD KEY: SYNONYMS

See Synonyms at ***doubtful***.

skep·ti·cism /sképti sìzzəm/ *n.* **1. DOUBTING ATTITUDE** an attitude marked by a tendency to doubt what others accept to be true **2.** RELIG **DOUBT OF RELIGION** a doubting attitude toward religious beliefs **3. skep·ti·cism, Skep·ti·cism** PHILOS **DOCTRINE THAT KNOWLEDGE IS IMPOSSIBLE** the doctrine that holds that true knowledge is not possible [Mid-17thC]

sker·ry /skérree/ (*plural* **-ries**) *n. Scotland* a rocky islet or reef [Early 17thC. Via Scots dialect from Old Norse *sker* "reef." Ultimately from an Indo-European base meaning "to cut" that is also the ancestor of English *sharp* and *scrape.*]

sketch /skech/ *n.* **1.** DRAWING **PICTURE DONE QUICKLY AND ROUGHLY** a drawing or painting that is done quickly without concern for detail. A sketch might be made to capture the general mood of a scene, or to help the artist work out an idea for a finished composition. **2.** ARTS **SHORT PERFORMANCE** a quick comic routine or piece of acting that is part of a variety show or comedy revue **3. ROUGH DESCRIPTION OR EXPLANATION OF SOMETHING** a short written or spoken account that conveys just a general outline or idea, with little detail **4.** LITERAT **SHORT PIECE OF WRITING** a short, often descriptive, piece of writing **5.** MUSIC **SHORT MUSICAL COMPOSITION** a short piece of instrumental music, often for piano ■ *vti.* (**sketched, sketch·ing, sketch·es**) ARTS **MAKE A SKETCH** to create a sketch of something [Mid-17thC. Via Dutch *schets* or German *Skizze* from Italian *schizzo*, from, ultimately, Vulgar Latin *schediare* "to do hastily," from Latin *schedius*, from Greek *skhedios* "on the spur of the moment."] —**sketch·a·ble** *adj.* —**sketch·er** *n.*

sketch·book /skéch bòòk/, **sketch·pad** /skéch pàd/ *n.* a book of plain paper for making sketches on

sketch·y /skéchee/ (**-i·er, -i·est**) *adj.* **1. SUPERFICIAL** lacking in substance, clarity, or detail **2. RESEMBLING A SKETCH** giving only the main points with little detail —**sketch·i·ly** *adv.* —**sketch·i·ness** *n.*

skew /skyoo/ *v.* (**skewed, skew·ing, skews**) **1.** *vti.* **SLANT OR CAUSE TO SLANT** to make something uneven, sloping, or unsymmetrical, or to be in this state **2.** *vt.* **MAKE INCORRECT OR DISTORTED** to misrepresent the true meaning or nature of something **3.** *vi.* **SQUINT** to look sideways at something ■ *adj.* **1. IN A SLANTED POSITION OR LINE** being in a slanted or unsymmetrical position **2.** MATH **NOT PARALLEL OR INTERSECTING** used to describe a line that is neither parallel nor intersecting ■ *n.* **1. TILTED OR INACCURATE POSITION** a position that is not straight but that slants or twists out of correct alignment **2.** MECH ENG **SLANTING DIRECTION** a slanting movement, line, or direction [14thC. Shortening of Old Northern French *eskiuer*, a variant of Old French *eschiver* "to eschew" (see ESCHEW).]

skew arch *n.* an arch, e.g., on a bridge or tunnel, with sides that are not at right angles to the span

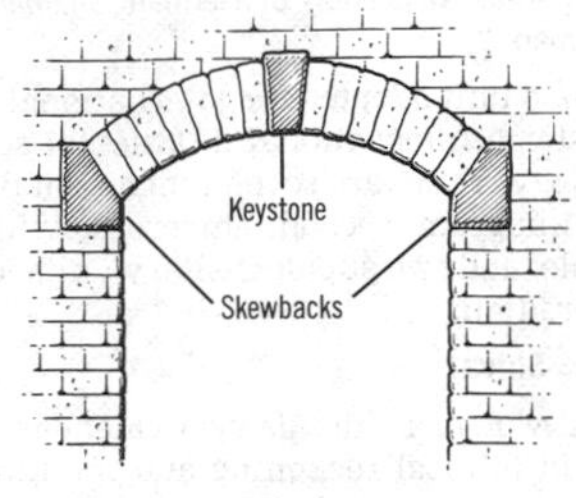

Skewback

skew·back /skyóo bàk/ *n.* either of the sloping surfaces on which the sides of a segmental arch abut

skew·bald /skyóo bàwld/ *adj.* **WITH WHITE AND BROWN PATCHES** used to describe a horse that has a spotted coat consisting of white and another color other than black, generally brown ■ *n.* **SKEWBALD HORSE** a skewbald horse [Mid-17thC. Formed from obsolete *skewed* "having mixed colors," of unknown origin, on the model of PIEBALD.]

skew·er /skyóo ər/ *n.* **1. THIN PIN TO COOK FOOD ON** a thin metal or wooden rod with a sharp end used to hold meat or meat and vegetables during cooking **2. SOMETHING SIMILAR TO SKEWER** a thin pointed object used to pierce something or hold it in place ■ *vt.* (**-ered, -er·ing, -ers**) **1. PIERCE WITH SKEWER** to pierce somebody or something with a skewer or with something else that is thin and sharp **2. CRITICIZE POINTEDLY** to make a pointed and effective criticism [15thC. Origin unknown.]

skew lines *npl.* two straight lines that do not lie in the same plane, are not parallel, and do not intersect, the distance between them being the unique segment perpendicular to both lines

skew·ness /skyóonəss/ *n.* **1. CROOKEDNESS** the way or amount that something is tilted or distorted from the true or straight position **2.** STATS **LACK OF SYMMETRY** a lack of symmetry, especially about the mean in a frequency distribution

ski /skee/ *n.* (*plural* **skis**) **1. BOARD USED TO SLIDE ACROSS SNOW** either of a pair of long thin boards made of wood, metal, or other material that curve up at the front and are used to slide across snow **2.** = **water-ski 3. RUNNER FOR VEHICLES TRAVELING ON SNOW** a runner fitted to vehicles such as snowmobiles and airplanes for landing or traveling on snow and ice ■ *vti.* (**skied, ski·ing, skis**) **MOVE ALONG ON SKIS** to glide over the surface of snow or water wearing skis, as a means of travel or as a leisure pursuit or sport [Mid-18thC. Via Norwegian from Old Norse *skíð* "piece of split wood, snowshoe." Ultimately from an Indo-European base meaning "to cut" that is also the ancestor of English *sheath* and *shiver.*] —**ski·a·ble** *adj.* —**ski·er** *n.*

ski·bob /skée bòb/ *n.* a vehicle similar to a bicycle that has skis instead of wheels and is used to travel over snow [Mid-20thC. *Bob* is a shortening of BOBSLED.] —**ski·bob·ber** *n.* —**ski·bob·bing** *n.*

skid /skid/ *n.* **1.** TRANSP **UNCONTROLLED SLIDE** an uncontrolled slide across a surface in a wheeled vehicle **2.** AIR **AIRCRAFT RUNNER** a runner on the underside of an aircraft, used as part of its landing gear **3.** TECH **PALLET** a low pallet on which goods are loaded for handling or transport **4. POLE USED TO FORM TRACK** one of two or more logs or poles used to form a track for sliding or rolling something along, e.g., from a truckbed to the ground **5.** MECH ENG **BLOCK USED TO PREVENT WHEEL TURNING** a shoe or block used to prevent a wheel from turning, e.g., when a vehicle is descending a hill **6.** SHIPPING **SHIP'S FENDER** a wooden structure hung over the side of a ship to protect the ship in loading and unloading cargo ■ *v.* **(skid·ded, skid·ding, skids) 1.** *vti.* AUTOMOT **SLIDE DANGEROUSLY ACROSS SURFACE** to slide or make a vehicle slide across a surface, usually unintentionally, so that the wheels lose their grip and control is lost **2.** *vi.* TRANSP **SLIDE OVER SURFACE WITHOUT ROLLING** to slide across a surface without turning around and gripping it in the proper way **3.** *vti.* AIR **SLIDE SIDEWAYS** to slide or make an aircraft slide sideways away from the center of curvature when it is insufficiently banked in making a turn **4.** *vt.* **MOVE SOMETHING ON SKIDS** to lift or move something along using a track made of poles or logs **5.** *vt.* **DRAG LOGS** to move logs by dragging them [Early 17thC. Origin uncertain: perhaps from Old Norse.] —**skid·dy** *adj.* ◇ **be on the skids** to be in difficulties and heading for failure (*slang*)

skid marks *npl.* dark heavy lines marked on a road surface by the wheels of a vehicle that has skidded

Ski-Doo *tdmk. Can* a trademark for a kind of snowmobile [Mid-20thC]

skid·proof /skíd proòf/ *adj.* designed to prevent skidding

skid road *n.* **1.** = **skid row** (*informal*) **2. TRACK FOR HAULING LOGS ALONG** a road with logs embedded in it, along which timber is hauled to a mill or loading area

skid row *n.* an area of a city that has cheap bars and rundown hotels and is frequented by members of the city's underclass (*informal*) [Alteration of SKID ROAD. The word originally referred to an area of a town that loggers typically frequented.]

skied[1] /skeed/ past tense, past participle of **ski**

skied[2] /skīd/ past participle, past tense of **sky**

skies[1] present tense of **ski**

skies[2] plural of **sky**

skiff /skif/ *n.* a small flatbottom boat of shallow draft that is usually propelled with oars, a sail, or a motor [Late 15thC. Via French *esquif* from Italian *schifo*, probably from Old High German *schif*. Related to English *ship*.]

skif·fle /skíff'l/ *n.* a type of music that was popular in the 1950s, usually played by a small group on guitars as well as improvised instruments such as a washboard used as percussion [Early 20thC. Origin unknown.]

Barnaby's

Skiing

ski·ing /skee ing/ *n.* the activity, sport, or pastime of traveling on skis

ski·jor·ing /skee jàwring/ *n.* a sport in which a skier is towed across a frozen surface by a horse or vehicle [Early 20thC. From Norwegian *skikjøring*, literally "ski driving."] —**ski·jor·er** *n.*

ski jump *n.* **1. TRACK FOR SKIERS TO JUMP FROM** a steep artificial slope with a sharp upturn at the bottom. People ski down this and then leap into the air, competing with one another to travel the longest distance. **2. JUMP MADE FROM SKI JUMP** a jump made by a skier from a ski jump ■ *vi.* **(ski jumped, ski jump·ing, ski jumps) PERFORM SKI JUMP** to perform a ski jump —**ski jump·er** *n.*

Skik·da /skik daa/ city and port in northeastern Algeria, situated about 220 mi./354 km east of Algiers. Population: 128,747 (1987).

skil·ful *adj.* U.K. = **skillful**

ski lift *n.* a motor-driven apparatus consisting of a continuously moving cable with seats, gondolas, or tow bars suspended from it, built to transport skiers to the top of a ski run

skill /skil/ *n.* **1. ABILITY TO DO SOMETHING WELL** the ability to do something well, usually gained through experience and training **2. SOMETHING REQUIRING TRAINING TO DO WELL** something such as an art or trade that requires training and experience to do well [12thC. From Old Norse *skil* "discernment." Ultimately from an Indo-European base meaning "to cut" that is also the ancestor of English *shell* and *scalpel*.] —**skill-less** *adj.* —**skill-less·ness** *n.*

WORD KEY: SYNONYMS

See Synonyms at ***ability***.

skilled /skild/ *adj.* **1. VERY GOOD AT DOING SOMETHING** having or showing a special ability and competence in a particular type of work or activity **2. REQUIRING TRAINING AND EXPERIENCE** characterized by the need for special abilities developed and practiced over time

skil·let /skíllit/ *n.* **1.** = **frying pan 2.** *U.K.* **SMALL FRYING PAN** a small shallow pan with a long handle, used for frying or braising food [15thC. Origin uncertain: probably from Old French *escuelete*, literally "small platter," from *escuele* "platter," from Latin *scutella* "flat dish" (see SCUTTLE).]

skill·ful /skíff'l/ *adj.* **1. PARTICULARLY ADEPT AT SOMETHING** with a special ability and dexterity in a particular type of work or activity **2. INVOLVING SPECIAL SKILL** requiring or done with specialized techniques and abilities developed over a period of time —**skill·ful·ly** *adv.* —**skill·ful·ness** *n.*

skim /skim/ *v.* **(skimmed, skim·ming, skims) 1.** *vt.* COOK **SCOOP FROM TOP OF LIQUID** to remove a substance such as a fatty accumulation forming a layer on the surface of a liquid, usually with a large shallow spoon **2.** *vt.* **RID LIQUID OF FLOATING MATERIAL** to rid a liquid of material accumulating on its surface **3.** *vti.* **PASS CLOSELY OVER SURFACE OF SOMETHING** to pass or make something pass quickly across and just above the surface of something, sometimes touching it lightly and briefly **4.** *vt.* **GLANCE THROUGH A BOOK OR PAPER** to read something very quickly looking only at occasional lines or words, to get a general idea of its contents **5.** *vt.* **SEND SOMETHING BOUNCING ALONG** to throw something so that it bounces lightly along the surface of water **6.** *vt.* **GIVE LITTLE OR NO ATTENTION TO** to deal with something in a superficial way **7.** *vti.* **COAT OR BECOME COATED WITH LAYER** to develop a thin surface layer of something, or coat an object so that its surface is covered in a thin layer of something **8.** *vti.* **EMBEZZLE** to embezzle some of the proceeds from a business (*informal*) **9.** *vt.* **HIDE PROFITS TO AVOID TAXES** to hide earnings or profits in order to avoid paying taxes on them (*informal*) ■ *n.* **1. THIN FILM** a layer coating a surface **2. CURSORY LOOK** a cursory look at or treatment of something ○ *a quick skim over the main topics on the agenda* **3. SUBSTANCE REMOVED FROM SURFACE OF SOMETHING** the matter that forms a layer on a surface and is skimmed off **4. SKIMMING PROCESS** the process of removing a substance from a surface [15thC. From Old French *escumer*, from *escume* "scum," from a prehistoric Germanic word that is also the ancestor of English *scum*.]

skim off *vt.* to cull the best people or items from a group

ski mask *n.* a protective covering for the face and sometimes the head, worn by skiers and made of knitted or other material and often having openings for the eyes, nose, and mouth

skim·mer /skímmər/ *n.* **1. SOMEBODY OR SOMETHING THAT SKIMS** a person, object, or device that skims **2.** CLOTHES **FLAT STRAW HAT** a flat hat usually made of straw **3.** BIRDS **LONG-WINGED MARINE BIRD** a long-winged marine bird that has a bill with the lower half longer than the upper, used for skimming food from the surface of water while in flight. Genus: *Rynchops*. **4.** COOK **UTENSIL USED FOR SKIMMING** a broad flat spoon with small perforations in it used to skim something such as fat from the surface of a liquid

skim milk, **skimmed milk** *n.* milk with most or all of its fat content removed

skim·mings /skímmingz/ *npl.* the floating fat or debris skimmed off the surface of a liquid

skimp /skimp/ **(skimped, skimp·ing, skimps)** *v.* **1.** *vti.* **USE TOO LITTLE OF SOMETHING** to use or provide hardly enough of something **2.** *vt.* **DO SOMETHING IMPROPERLY** to carry out a piece of work poorly, without spending enough time, trouble, or materials on it **3.** *vt.* **NOT PROVIDE WITH ENOUGH** to give or allow somebody only an inadequate amount of money, food, or other necessary items [Late 18thC. Origin unknown.]

skimp·y /skímpee/ **(-i·er, -i·est)** *adj.* **1. HARDLY ADEQUATE** made or done using barely enough of the necessary materials **2. STINGY** not giving somebody enough of something through meanness —**skimp·i·ly** *adv.* —**skimp·i·ness** *n.*

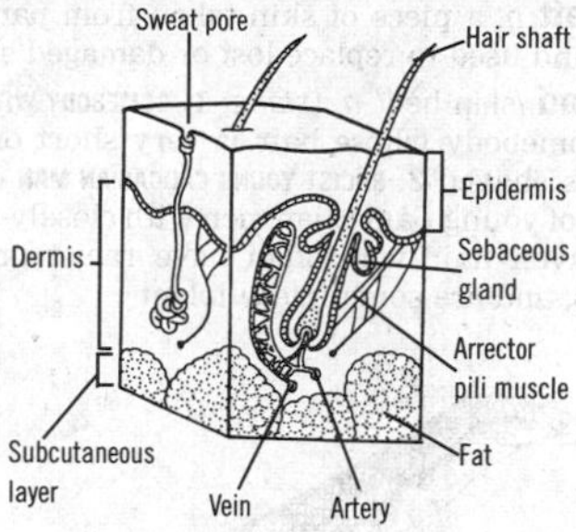

Skin: Cross section of human skin

skin /skin/ *n.* **1. NATURAL LAYER COVERING AN ANIMAL'S BODY** the external protective membrane or covering of an animal's body, consisting of the dermis and epidermis and often covered in hair, fur, scales, or feathers **2. SKIN ON FACE** somebody's skin, especially on the face, in terms of its color and appearance **3.** BOT **THIN NATURAL COVERING** a relatively thin but protective layer closely surrounding the flesh of a fruit or vegetable **4.** INDUST **FUR OR LEATHER FROM DEAD ANIMAL** skin or a piece of skin removed from an animal's body, especially once it has been cleaned and treated to use as fur or leather **5. SOLID SURFACE LAYER ON A LIQUID** a thin pliant surface that forms on the top of some liquids, e.g., on hot milk left to cool **6. TIGHT-FITTING COVERING** a thin tough casing or cover that fits closely around something such as a sausage to hold in, protect, or preserve the enclosed material **7. SMALL LEATHER SACK** a bag made from animal hide used to hold liquid such as wine or water **8. OUTER COVERING OF STRUCTURE** the outer protective covering of a structure such as an aircraft ■ **skins** *npl.* MUSIC **JAZZ DRUMS** drums, especially in a jazz band (*informal*) ■ *v.* **(skinned, skin·ning, skins) 1.** *vt.* **TAKE THE SKIN OFF** to remove the skin from a fruit or vegetable, or from an animal or person, especially by cutting or ripping it **2.** *vt.* MED **SCRAPE THE SKIN** to make the skin on a part of the body red, sore, and broken, especially by falling on it or scraping it **3.** *vt.* CRIMINOL **SWINDLE** to trick somebody out of money or property (*slang*) **4.** *vt.* **REMOVE OUTSIDE PART OF** to strip off an outer, covering layer that resembles a skin **5.** *vti.* **PUT SKIN ON** to grow or become covered with a skin, or cover somebody or something with a skin ■ *adj.* **PORNOGRAPHIC** relating to or containing pornographic material (*informal*) [12thC. From Old Norse *skinn*. Ultimately from an Indo-European word meaning "to cut" (see SKI). The underlying idea is of something peeled off (presumably a pelt from a hunted animal).] —**skin·less** *adj.* ◇ **be no skin off your nose** to be a matter that does not harm you at all and therefore may be of little interest (*informal*) ◇ **by the skin of your teeth** by a very narrow margin, or only just (*informal*) ◇ **get under your skin 1.** to annoy or irritate you (*informal*) **2.** to make you feel great interest or attraction (*informal*) ◇ **jump out of your skin** to get a bad fright or a shock (*informal*) ◇ **save somebody's skin** to prevent somebody suffering hurt, loss, or punishment by giving vital help (*informal*) ◇ **skin up** *vi.* to roll a marijuana joint or cigarette (*informal*)

skin-deep *adj.* **WITHOUT DEEP MEANING OR IMPORTANCE** appearing to be important, meaningful, or valuable but having little deep or lasting importance ■ *adv.* **NOT DEEPLY** in a superficial way

skin div·ing *n.* the sport of underwater diving using flippers and a mask and snorkel —**skin-dive** *vi.* —**skin div·er** *n.*

skin ef·fect *n.* the tendency of a high-frequency alternating current to flow near the surface of the conductor rather than in its interior

skin flick *n.* a pornographic movie (*slang*)

skin·flint /skín flìnt/ *n.* somebody who hates parting with money, whether by spending it or by giving it to other people [Late 17thC. From the phrase "skin a flint," used of somebody so miserly as to try to remove the skin from a piece of flint.]

skin fric·tion *n.* a frictional force, or drag, acting on the surface of an airfoil or other object immersed in a large volume of fluid that is in motion relative to the object

skin game *n.* a confidence trick or scheme used to cheat people of their money (*slang*) [From SKIN "to swindle"]

skin graft *n.* a piece of skin taken from part of the body and used to replace lost or damaged skin

skin·head /skín hèd/ *n.* (*slang*) **1. SOMEBODY WITH SHAVED HEAD** somebody whose hair is very short or whose head is shaved **2. RACIST YOUNG CAUCASIAN MAN** one of a group of young Caucasian men with closely-cropped or shaven hair who often have racist or fascist beliefs, and are sometimes violent

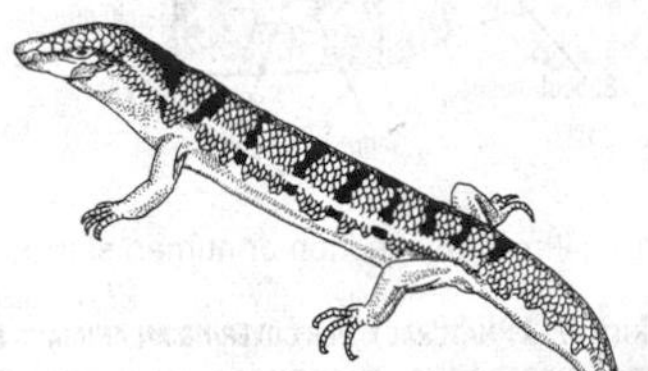

Skink

skink /skingk/ *n.* a small smooth insect-eating lizard with a long thin body and small limbs. It lives in temperate and tropical regions, especially in Asia and Africa. Family: Scincidae. [Late 16thC. Directly or via obsolete French *scinc* from Latin *scincus*, from Greek *skigkos*.]

skin·ner /skínnər/ *n.* **1. SOMEBODY WHO SKINS** somebody who skins animals or deals in animal skins **2.** *Western U.S.* **MULE DRIVER** somebody who drives a team of mules

Skin·ner /skínnər/, **B. F.** (1904–90) U.S. psychologist. His stimulus-response experiments and behaviorist theories profoundly influenced methods of education and behavior therapy. His works include *Beyond Freedom and Dignity* (1971). Full name **Burrhus Frederic Skinner** —**Skin·ner·i·an** /ski néeree ən/ *adj.*, *n.*

Skin·ner, Cornelia Otis (1901–79) U.S. writer and actor. Known for her one-woman shows, she was coauthor of *Our Hearts Were Young and Gay* (1942).

Skin·ner box *n.* an enclosure for isolating an animal during studies of learning behavior, or operant conditioning, that contains a device the animal may operate to receive a reward or avoid punishment [Mid-20thC. Named for B. F. SKINNER.]

skin·ny /skínnee/ *adj.* (**-ni·er, -ni·est**) **VERY THIN** thin, especially in an unappealing or unhealthy way ■ *n.* **RELIABLE INFORMATION** the truth about something (*slang*) [Mid-16thC. Formed from SKIN.] —**skin·ni·ness** *n.*

WORD KEY: SYNONYMS

See Synonyms at ***thin***.

skin·ny-dip *vi.* (**skin·ny-dipped, skin·ny-dip·ping, skin·ny-dips**) **SWIM NUDE** to go swimming in the nude (*informal*) ■ *n.* **NUDE SWIM** a swim in the nude (*informal*) [From SKINNY in its original sense "pertaining to the skin"] —**skin·ny-dip·per** *n.* —**skin·ny-dip·ping** *n.*

skin-pop (**skin-popped, skin-pop·ping, skin-pops**) *vti.* to take narcotic drugs by inserting the needle under the skin, not straight into a vein (*slang*)

skin test *n.* a test in which a substance is applied to the skin to determine somebody's allergic sensitivity or immunity to it

skin-tight /skīn tít/ *adj.* fitting tightly to the body

skip[1] /skip/ *v.* (**skipped, skip·ping, skips**) **1.** *vi.* **MOVE WITH SMALL HOPPING STEPS** to move along by hopping from one foot to the other **2.** *vti.* **JUMP REPEATEDLY OVER CIRCLING ROPE** to jump repeatedly over a rope as it is swung around over the head and under the feet **3.** *vti.* **OMIT** to pass over or leave something out that should properly follow as part of a sequence or a complete work **4.** *vt.* **NOT ATTEND OR BE AT** to choose or decide to miss an event or activity (*informal*) **5.** *vt.* **OMIT SCHOOL GRADE** to promote a student to a grade that is one beyond the next in succession, or to omit a grade in this way **6.** *vti.* **LEAVE SOMEWHERE SECRETLY** to make a secret getaway, especially for some dishonest reason, e.g., to avoid being punished for something (*informal*) **7.** *vi.* RECORDING **NOT PLAY CORRECTLY** to fail to play a CD or record properly by jumping from one place to another, or to undergo this kind of faulty playing **8.** *vti.* **MOVE IN SERIES OF SMALL HOPS** to move lightly across a surface in a series of small hops, or make something move in this way **9.** *vt.* **NIMBLY JUMP OVER** to jump nimbly over something **10.** *vt.* **DEAL WITH CURSORILY** to deal with or look at something in a cursory way ■ *n.* **1. SMALL HOPPING STEP** a small forward hopping step **2. ACT OF OMITTING SOMETHING** an act of omitting part of something [13thC. Origin uncertain: probably from Old Norse.] —**skip·pa·ble** *adj.*

skip[2] /skip/ *n.* (*plural* **skips** *informal*) NAUT **SKIPPER** a skipper (*slang*) ■ *vi.* (**skipped, skip·ping, skips**) NAUT **BE SKIPPER OF** to be the skipper of a vessel (*slang*) [Early 19thC. Shortening.]

ski pants *npl.* **1.** = **stirrup pants 2. PANTS FOR SKIING** pants that are worn for skiing and other cold weather activities and that are often lined, windproof, and water-resistant

skip dis·tance *n.* the shortest distance between a radio transmitter and receiver that permits waves of a particular frequency to be sent and received by reflection from the ionosphere

skip·jack /skíp jàk/ (*plural* **-jacks** *or* **-jack**) *n.* **1.** ZOOL **LEAPING MARINE FISH** any of various marine fishes that leap out of the water such as the bonito, ladyfish, or bluefish **2. skip·jack, skip·jack tu·na** FOOD, ZOOL **MARINE FOOD FISH** a tropical marine sport and food fish of the tuna family that is blue and silver with dark stripes on its abdomen. Latin name: *Euthynnus pelamus*. **3.** SAILING **SAILBOAT** a sailboat with straight sides and a V-shaped bottom

ski·plane /skée plàyn/ *n.* an aircraft equipped with skis for taking off from and landing on snow

ski pole *n.* one of a pair of lightweight poles held by skiers for balance and control. The bottom end has a point surrounded by a disk for gaining purchase on the snow.

skip·per[1] /skíppər/ *n.* **1.** NAUT **SOMEBODY IN CHARGE OF SHIP** somebody in charge of a ship or boat **2. LEADER OF A TEAM** somebody in charge of a squad or group of others, especially the captain or coach of a sports team (*informal*) ■ *vt.* (**-pered, -per·ing, -pers**) **BE SKIPPER OF** to be in charge of a ship, team or aircraft (*informal*) [14thC. From Middle Dutch *schipper*, from *schip* "ship."]

skip·per[2] /skíppər/ *n.* **1. SOMEBODY OR SOMETHING THAT SKIPS** somebody or something that skips **2.** INSECTS **INSECT RESEMBLING MOTH** a quick-flying insect that has a stout hairy body and clubbed antennae with hooked tips, and is closely related to true butterflies. Families: Hesperiidae and Megathymidae. **3.** ZOOL = **saury** [Mid-18thC. Formed from SKIP[1]. The word was used to designate these animals because of their jumping and darting movements.]

skip·ping-rope *n. U.K.* = **jump rope**

skirl /skurl/ *n. Scotland* **SHRILL WAILING NOISE** the high-pitched wailing sound that bagpipes typically make ■ *vti.* (**skirled, skirl·ing, skirls**) *Scotland* **PRODUCE SHRILL WAILING NOISE** to produce a high-pitched wailing sound on the bagpipes [14thC. Origin uncertain: probably from a Scandinavian language.]

skir·mish /skúrmish/ *n.* **1.** MIL **SMALL, RELATIVELY UNIMPORTANT BATTLE** an incident where fighting breaks out briefly between two small contingents away from the main battlefield in a war **2. SHORT ARGUMENT** a brief fight or disagreement between people ■ *vi.* (**-mished, -mish·ing, -mish·es**) **ENGAGE IN MINOR BATTLE** to become involved in a skirmish [14thC. From the Old French stem *eskermiss-* "to fence," from, ultimately, a prehistoric Germanic word meaning "to defend"; the noun was later reinforced by Old French *escar(a)muche*, from Italian *scaramuccia*.] —**skir·mish·er** *n.*

WORD KEY: SYNONYMS

See Synonyms at ***fight***.

skirr /skur/ (**skirred, skir·ring, skirrs**) *n.* a whirring sound [Mid-16thC. Origin unknown.]

skir·ret /skúr ət/ *n.* a plant cultivated in Europe for its sweetish edible root. Latin name: *Sium sisarum*. [14thC. Earlier *skirwhit*, of uncertain origin: probably by folk etymology (from obsolete *scir* "pure" + WHITE) from Old French *eschervi*, from Arabic *karawiyā* "caraway" (see CARAWAY).]

skirt /skurt/ *n.* **1.** CLOTHES **GARMENT THAT HANGS FROM THE WAIST** a piece of clothing that hangs from the waist and does not divide into two separate legs, usually worn by women and girls **2.** CLOTHES **AREA OF FABRIC FALLING FROM WAISTLINE** the section from the waist to the hem on a dress, coat, or robe **3.** TECH **SOMETHING SIMILAR TO SKIRT** an attachment shaped like a skirt, or covering the lower part of something like a skirt **4. OFFENSIVE TERM** an offensive term used to refer to a girl or woman, or women in general, by suggesting that they are objects (*slang offensive*) **5.** *U.K.* FOOD **CUT OF BEEF** a stewing cut of beef taken from the flank, below the sirloin and rump, and cut from the inside of flank steak **6.** ENG **FLAP AROUND BOTTOM OF HOVERCRAFT** the lower outer section of a rocket or the flap around the bottom of a hovercraft **7.** EQU **FLAP ON SADDLE** one of a pair of leather flaps that hang from a saddle ■ *v.* (**skirt·ed, skirt·ing, skirts**) **1.** *vti.* **BE AROUND THE OUTSIDE OF SOMETHING** to form a border along the edge of an area or object **2.** *vti.* **MOVE AROUND THE OUTSIDE OF SOMETHING** to travel along the edge of something such as an area, structure, or geographic feature **3.** *vt.* **AVOID GIVING PROPER ATTENTION TO** to avoid dealing with a particular subject in any depth, usually because it is tricky or unpleasant **4.** *vt.* TECH **GIVE AN EDGE TO** to provide something with an attachment shaped like a skirt or border [13thC. From Old Norse *skyrta* "shirt," from a prehistoric Germanic word that is also the ancestor of English *shirt*.] —**skirt·er** *n.*

skirt-chas·er *n.* an offensive term used to refer a man who is regarded as being excessively interested in pursuing women sexually (*slang offensive*) —**skirt-chas·ing** *n.*

skirt·ing /skúrting/ *n.* **1.** *U.K.* CONSTR = **skirting board 2.** INDUST **MATERIAL FOR SKIRTS** material used to make skirts ■ **skirt·ings** *npl. ANZ* **PIECES OF FLEECE** pieces trimmed from a shorn fleece

skirt·ing board *n. U.K.* = **skirting**

skit /skit/ *n.* **1.** THEATER **SHORT COMIC SKETCH** a short, usually comic, dramatic sketch **2.** LITERAT **COMIC SATIRICAL WRITING** a short piece of comic writing that satirizes somebody or something [Early 18thC. Origin uncertain: perhaps from a Scandinavian language.]

ski tour·ing *n.* traveling over long distances on skis, especially in wilderness areas

ski tow *n.* an apparatus consisting of a motor-driven rope that skiers hang onto to be towed up a mountain

skit·ter /skíttər/ (**-tered, -ter·ing, -ters**) *v.* **1.** *vi.* **RUN WITH TINY STEPS** to move about or run off quickly with small scampering steps **2.** *vti.* **SKID LIGHTLY ACROSS SOMETHING** to pass quickly across something, touching its surface very lightly and briefly, or to send something skidding rapidly over the surface of something [Mid-19thC. Origin uncertain.]

skit·tish /skíttish/, **skit·ter·y** /skíttəree/ *adj.* **1. NERVOUS** easily agitated or alarmed **2. SILLY AND IRRESPONSIBLE** with moods or ideas that constantly change, in a frivolous and unreliable way **3. LIVELY** tending to dash about in an energetic or restless way [14thC. Origin uncertain: perhaps formed from an alteration of Old Norse *skjóta* "to shoot."] —**skit·tish·ly** *adv.* —**skit·tish·ness** *n.*

skit·tle /skítt'l/ *n. U.K.* = **ninepin** [Mid-17thC. Origin uncertain: perhaps from a Scandinavian language.]

skive /skīv/ (**skived, skiv·ing, skives**) *vt.* to scrape thin slices off leather in preparing it [Early 19thC. Of Scandinavian origin.]

skiv·er /skívər/ *n.* **1. THIN SOFT LEATHER** a thin soft tanned leather taken from the outer side of a skin **2. SOMEBODY OR SOMETHING THAT SKIVES** somebody or something that skives leather

Skiv·vies /skívviz/ *tdmk.* a trademark for underwear, especially men's underwear

skiv·vy /skívvee/ (**-vied, -vy·ing, -vies**, *plural* **-vies**) *n. ANZ* a long-sleeved, usually cotton piece of clothing with a rolled neck worn on the upper part of the body [Mid-20thC. Origin unknown.]

skoal /skōl/ *interj.* used as a drinking toast [Early 17thC. Via Danish *skaal* and Swedish and Norwegian *skål* from Old Norse *skál* "bowl" (source of English *scale*).]

Sko·kie /skṓkee/ village in northeastern Illinois, south of Wilmette, on the northern border of Chicago. Population: 58,635 (1996).

Sko·mer /skṓmər/ islet in St. Bride's Bay, off the Pembrokeshire coast, Wales.

Skop·je /skóp yee/ capital of the Republic of Macedonia, situated in the north-central part of the country. Population: 563,102 (1994).

skosh /skōsh/ *n.* a little bit (*slang*) ○ *I'd like just a skosh more, please.* [Mid-20thC. From Japanese *sukoshi.*]

Skr., **Skt.** *abbr.* Sanskrit

skul·dug·ger·y /skul dúggəree/, **skull·dug·ger·y** *n.* unfair and dishonest practices carried out in a secretive way so as to trick other people (*humorous*) [Mid-19thC. Alteration of *sculduddery* "sexual impropriety, indecency," of unknown origin.]

skulk /skulk/ *vi.* (**skulked, skulk·ing, skulks**) **1. MOVE FURTIVELY** to move about in a furtive way **2. HIDE FOR SINISTER PURPOSE** to hide, especially in order to do something sinister **3.** *U.K.* **SHIRK** to avoid work or responsibilities ■ *n.* **1. SOMEBODY WHO SKULKS** somebody who moves about furtively or conceals a sinister purpose **2.** ZOOL **GROUP OF FOXES** a pack of foxes [12thC. Of Scandinavian origin.]

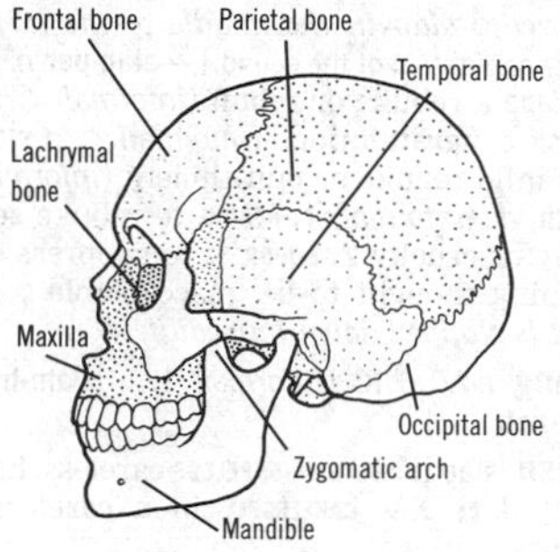

Skull

skull /skul/ *n.* **1.** ANAT **BONY PART OF THE HEAD** the skeletal part of the head in humans and other vertebrates, consisting of the cranium, which encases the brain, and the bones of the face and jaws **2. HEAD** a person's head or mind (*informal*) ○ *tried to din the principles of thermodynamics into his skull* [13thC. Origin uncertain: probably from a Scandinavian language.]

skull and cross·bones *n.* **1. SYMBOLIC SIGN REPRESENTING DANGER** a representation of a human skull above two human thighbones crossed over each other, used as a symbol of danger or death **2.** = **Jolly Roger**

skull·cap /skúl kàp/ *n.* **1.** CLOTHES **SMALL ROUND BRIMLESS HAT** a simple hat consisting of a small circle of fabric shaped to fit over the crown of the head **2.** JUDAISM **YARMULKE** a yarmulke **3.** PLANTS **PERENNIAL MINT** a perennial plant of the mint family. Its blue or pinkish flowers have a calyx shaped like a helmet. Genus: *Scutellaria.* **4.** ANAT **TOP OF SKULL** the top part of the skull

skull ses·sion *n.* (*informal*) **1. BUSINESS PLANNING MEETING** a meeting to talk over and think about policies and procedures **2.** SPORTS **STRATEGY MEETING FOR SPORTS TEAM** a meeting for a coach to instruct team members on strategy

Skunk

skunk /skungk/ *n.* (*plural* **skunks** *or* **skunk**) **1.** ZOOL **BLACK-AND-WHITE MAMMAL WITH FOUL-SMELLING SPRAY** a North and South American black-and-white mammal of the weasel family that ejects a foul-smelling liquid from an anal gland as a defensive action **2. DESPICABLE PERSON** somebody who is despised (*slang*) ■ *vt.* (**skunked, skunk·ing, skunks**) (*slang*) **1. DEFEAT SOUNDLY** to defeat an opponent soundly, especially by not allowing him or her to score any points in a sports competition **2. CHEAT** to cheat somebody out of something [Mid-17thC. From Massachusett.]

skunk cab·bage, **skunk·weed** /skúngk wèed/ (*plural* **-weeds** *or* **-weed**) *n.* **1. FOUL-SMELLING PERENNIAL HERB** a foul-smelling perennial herb of swampy areas of eastern North America that has broad leaves and small flowers enclosed in a greenish spathe. Latin name: *Symplocarpus foetidus.* **2. A PLANT SIMILAR TO SKUNK CABBAGE** a plant of western North America, similar to skunk cabbage and with a large yellow spathe. Latin name: *Lysichitum americanum.*

skunk·works /skúngk wùrks/ *npl.* a department or laboratory involved in usually secret cutting-edge research and development (*informal*) (*usually takes singular verb*) [Mid-20thC. From Al Capp's comic strip *L'il Abner*, where "Skonk Works" was the name of the site at which Big Barnsmell brewed his Kickapoo Joy Juice.]

sky /skī/ *n.* (*plural* **skies**) **1. REGION ABOVE THE EARTH** the area high above the trees, buildings, landscape, or horizon. The sky is made up of the various layers of the Earth's atmosphere and the part of space beyond it, as seen from one place on the Earth's surface. **2. WAY SKY APPEARS** the way the sky looks in a particular part of the world (*often used in the plural*) **3. sky, Sky HEAVEN** the plane, thought of as being high above the Earth, in which immortal powers or beings exist, such as God or immortal souls (*literary*) (*often used in the plural*) **4. HIGHEST LIMIT** the topmost limit or the best and most it is possible to achieve ○ *to the sky* ■ *vti.* (**skied, sky·ing, skies**) **MAKE SOMETHING GO VERY HIGH** to hit or throw a ball high up into the air [13thC. From Old Norse *ský* "cloud." Ultimately from an Indo-European base meaning "to conceal" that is also the ancestor of English *scum* and *hide.*] ◇ **praise somebody to the skies** to praise somebody very highly ◇ **the sky's the limit** there is no upper limit on something (*informal*)

sky blue *adj.* **PALE BLUE** of a pale blue color like that of the sky on a clear day ■ *n.* **PALE BLUE COLOR** a pale blue color like that of the sky on a clear day

sky·box /skī̀ bòks/ *n.* a raised room or balcony area in a stadium, which is private and separate from the main seating areas [Late 20thC]

sky·cap /skī́ kàp/ *n.* somebody who works at an airport helping travelers with their baggage [Mid-20thC. Formed from SKY on the model of *redcap.*]

sky·dive /skī́ dīv/ (**-dived** *or* **-dove, -dived** *or* **-dove** /-dōv/, **-div·ing, -dives**) *vi.* to jump from an airplane and descend in free fall, sometimes performing acrobatic maneuvers, before pulling the ripcord of a parachute —**sky·div·er** *n.* —**sky·div·ing** *n.*

Skye /skī/ the largest island in the Inner Hebrides, in Scotland. Portree is the chief town and port. Population: 8,843 (1991). Area: 647 sq. mi./1,676 sq. km.

Skye ter·ri·er *n.* a small terrier with short legs, a long body, and a long straight coat belonging to a breed originating in Scotland [Mid-19thC. Named for the Isle of SKYE, where the dog was bred.]

sky-high *adv., adj.* **EXTREMELY HIGH** up to or at the highest level ○ *They charge sky-high prices.* ■ *adv.* **INTO PIECES** high into the air or in all directions, forcefully and often in pieces

sky-hook *n.* a helicopter that is specially configured with a hook-and-cable apparatus in its fuselage, used to lift, drop, and transport heavy objects

sky·jack /skī́ jàk/ (**-jacked, -jack·ing, -jacks**) *vt.* to use force to take over control of an aircraft, especially a commercial aircraft, when it is in the air [Mid-20thC. Formed from SKY on the model of HIJACK.] —**sky·jack·er** *n.* —**sky·jack·ing** *n.*

Sky Ken·nel *tdmk.* a trademark for animal transport cages

sky·lark /skī́ laàrk/ *n.* BIRDS **COMMON LARK** a lark that is common in Europe and Asia. It has streaked brown-and-white plumage and is noted for singing melodiously while hanging high in the air. Latin name: *Alauda arvensis.* ■ *vi.* (**-larked, -lark·ing, -larks**) **HAVE BOISTEROUS FUN** to take part in lively physical playful behavior (*dated informal*) —**sky·lark·er** *n.*

sky·light /skī́ līt/ *n.* an opening in a roof or ceiling, fitted with glass to let in daylight

sky·light fil·ter *n.* a photographic filter that is slightly pink and is used to filter out ultraviolet light and reduce blueness

sky·line /skī́ līn/ *n.* **1. SHAPE OF OBJECTS AGAINST THE SKY** the pattern of shapes made by the various features of a landscape such as hills or buildings against the sky **2. EDGE WHERE SKY AND LANDSCAPE MEET** the apparent line where the Earth joins the sky

sky mar·shal *n.* an armed federal officer whose job is to prevent or deal with skyjackings

sky pi·lot *n.* an offensive term used to refer to a priest or chaplain, especially in the armed forces (*slang offensive*) [In supposedly humorous reference to concern with spiritual matters]

sky·rock·et /skī́ ròkət/ *vti.* (**-et·ed, -et·ing, -ets**) **GO UP DRAMATICALLY AND QUICKLY** to rise or make something rise suddenly to a very high level or value (*informal*) ■ *n.* = **rocket**[1] *n.* 4

Sky·ros /skī́rəss, skeé ross/ the largest and most easterly of the Greek Sporades Islands, in the west central Aegean Sea. Population: 2,757 (1981). Area: 79 sq. mi./205 sq. km.

sky·sail /skī́ sàyl, skī́ss'l/ *n.* a small light square sail that goes above the royal on a square-rigged sailing vessel

sky·scape /skī́ skàyp/ *n.* a scene or picture showing chiefly sky, especially an artistic study of a section of sky

sky·scrap·er /skī́ skràypər/ *n.* a modern building, especially a block of city offices or apartments, that is extremely tall [Late 18thC. Like *moonraker, skyscraper* originally referred to a sail positioned high above the deck (the *skysail*). The meaning "tall building" first appeared in the early 19thC.]

sky·walk /skī́ wàwk/ *n.* a raised walkway, usually joining two buildings

sky·ward /skī́wərd/ *adv., adj.* in the direction of the sky

sky wave *n.* a radio wave that is transmitted around the curved surface of the Earth by being reflected back to Earth by the ionosphere

sky·way /skī́ wày/ *n.* **1.** AIR **AIRCRAFT ROUTE** a route used by aircraft **2.** TRANSP **ELEVATED HIGHWAY** an elevated highway, supported by tall spans ○ *the Chicago Skyway* **3.** ARCHIT = **skywalk**

sky·writ·ing /skī́ rīting/ *n.* **1. WRITING WITH AIRCRAFT SMOKE** the use of an aircraft releasing colored smoke to form letters in the sky **2. WRITING MADE WITH AIRCRAFT SMOKE** letters or a message formed in the sky by colored smoke released from an aircraft —**sky·write** *vti.* —**sky·writ·er** *n.*

SL *abbr.* **1.** GEOG sea level **2.** LING source language **3.** GEOG south latitude

sl. *abbr.* **1.** slightly **2.** slow

slab /slab/ *n.* **1. THICK PIECE** a thick flat broad piece of something, especially when cut or trimmed **2.** ARCHIT **STONE BASE FOR SOMETHING** a flat rectangular base or foundation of concrete or stone **3.** GEOL **SHEET OF ROCK** a smooth flat sheet of rock sharply angled to the horizontal **4. WASTE FROM LOG** any of the large outer sections of a log that are sawed off in manufacturing lumber **5.** *Aus* **PACK OF BEER** a pack or box of 24 cans or bottles of beer (*informal*) ■ *vt.* (**slabbed, slab·bing, slabs**) **1. MAKE INTO SLABS** to cut or make something into slabs **2. COVER WITH SLABS** to cover something by laying stone or concrete slabs on it **3. TRIM BY SAWING** to saw off the rough outer parts of a log [13thC. Origin unknown.]

slab·ber /slábbər/ *vi.* **TO SLOBBER** to slobber (*regional*) ■ *n.* **SLOBBER** slobber (*regional*) [Mid-16thC. Origin uncertain: probably related to dialect *slab* "muddy place, puddle," of Scandinavian origin.]

slab·bing /slábbing/ *n.* **1. LAYING OF SLABS** the laying of stone or concrete slabs to form a surface such as a pathway **2. SLABS** stone or concrete slabs, collectively

slab pot·ter·y *n.* pottery made by hand using rolled-out sheets of clay

slab-sid·ed *adj.* **1. WITH LONG FLAT SIDES** having long, flat sides **2. TALL AND THIN** tall and thin (*informal*)

slack /slak/ *adj.* **1. NOT TIGHT** not tight or stretched taut, but hanging loosely or having a good deal of give ○ *The reins are too slack.* **2. NOT SHOWING ENOUGH CARE** not showing enough care, attention, or rigor ○ *They've been rather slack about keeping to performance targets.* **3. NOT BUSY** not busy or active, or less busy than usual ○ *the slack period following the main tourist season* **4. MOVING SLOWLY** moving slowly or sluggishly **5.** PHON = **lax** *adj.* 4 ■ *adv.* **LOOSELY** in a loose or limp way ○ *His clothes hung slack on him.*

■ *n.* **1.** LOOSENESS looseness or give in something such as a rope, or the extra length or fullness in it that needs to be taken in to make it taut **2.** UNUSED POTENTIAL productive potential in an organization or system that is not being fully made use of ○ *take in some of the slack in the administrative division* **3.** QUIET TIME a period of time that is not busy **4.** STILL WATER a stretch of water that is still or moving only slowly ■ *vti.* (**slacked, slack·ing, slacks**) **1.** AVOID WORK to be lazy, to avoid work, or to work with insufficient vigor or concentration **2.** = **slacken** *v.* 1 **3.** CHEM = **slake** *v.* 2 [Old English *slæc*. Ultimately from an Indo-European word meaning "to be loose" that is also the ancestor of English *lax* and *languid*.]

slack·en /slákən/ (**-ened, -en·ing, -ens**) *vti.* **1.** MAKE OR BECOME SLOWER OR QUIETER to become or to make something become less intense, vigorous, or fast **2.** LOOSEN OR RELAX to become or to make something become looser or more relaxed

slack·er /slákər/ *n.* **1.** SHIRKER somebody who shirks or avoids doing something, especially work or military service **2.** OFFENSIVE TERM an offensive term used to describe a young educated person who is regarded as being disaffected or apathetic, and underachieving (*slang offensive*)

slacks /slaks/ *npl.* casual pants, especially loose-fitting ones [Early 19thC. From the idea of being loose and slack.]

slack wa·ter *n.* the period of time during which the tide is turning and the water is still or slow-moving because of this

slag /slag/ *n.* **1.** INDUST WASTE MATERIAL FROM SMELTING fused glassy material that is produced when a metal is separated from its ore during smelting **2.** MINING COAL WASTE the mixture of coal dust and mineral waste produced after coal has been mined **3.** GEOL = **scoria** *n.* 2 ■ *vti.* (**slagged, slag·ging, slags**) INDUST TURN SOMETHING INTO SLAG to convert something into slag or become slag [Mid-16thC. From Middle Low German *slagge*, from a prehistoric Germanic word meaning "to strike" that is also the ancestor of English *sledgehammer* and *slay*.]

slag heap *n.* a large mound of waste material from a coal mine or factory

slain past participle of **slay**

slake /slayk/ (**slaked, slak·ing, slakes**) *v.* **1.** *vt.* SATISFY NEED to satisfy a desire for something, especially a drink **2.** *vti.* CHEM MAKE CALCIUM HYDROXIDE to treat lime with water to produce calcium hydroxide, or to undergo this process [Old English *slacian* "to relax, slacken," formed from *slæc*, (see SLACK)] —**slak·a·ble** *adj.*

slaked lime *n.* = **calcium hydroxide**

Slalom

sla·lom /sláaləm/ *n.* **1.** ZIGZAG SKI RACE a downhill ski race in which competitors follow a winding course and zigzag through flags on poles or through other obstacles **2.** ZIGZAG RACE any race that involves following a zigzag course through obstacles, e.g., in canoes ■ *vi.* (**-lomed, -lom·ing, -loms**) FOLLOW ZIGZAG COURSE to follow a zigzag or winding course, especially in a race [Early 20thC. From Norwegian *slalåm*, literally "sloping track."]

slam[1] /slam/ *v.* (**slammed, slam·ming, slams**) **1.** *vti.* CLOSE FORCEFULLY to close something forcefully and noisily **2.** *vti.* PUT SOMETHING DOWN VIOLENTLY to put something down violently and noisily **3.** *vti.* HIT to hit with sudden or violent force ○ *The waves slammed into the dock.* **4.** *vt.* CRITICIZE to criticize somebody or something forcefully (*informal*) ○ *The press slammed the President's performance.* ■ *n.* **1.** IMPACT a heavy, noisy, or violent blow or impact **2.** CRITICISM a forceful criticism [Late 17thC. Origin uncertain.]

slam[2] /slam/ *n.* CARDS the winning of all, or all but one, of the tricks in a hand of bridge or whist [Mid-17thC. Origin unknown.]

slam-bang *adv.* (*informal*) **1.** VIOLENTLY in a sudden, noisy, or violent way **2.** CARELESSLY in a careless and reckless way **3.** EXCITINGLY in an exciting and vigorous way ○ *The novel ended slam-bang with a fight to the finish.* ■ *adj.* (*informal*) **1.** SUDDEN AND NOISY sudden, noisy, or violent ○ *a slam-bang fight* **2.** CARELESS AND RECKLESS careless and reckless ○ *a slam-bang approach to his work* **3.** EXCITING exciting and vigorous ○ *slam-bang action scenes*

slam danc·ing *n.* boisterous dancing to rock music in which young people hurl their bodies against one another, more out of enthusiasm than aggression —**slam dance** *vi.*

slam-dunk, **slam dunk** *n.* **1.** BASKETBALL FORCEFUL DUNK SHOT in basketball, a dunk shot carried out with great force **2.** SOMETHING EASILY DONE something done without any effective opposition (*informal*) ■ *vt.* (**slam-dunked, slam-dunking, slam-dunks**) **1.** MAKE FORCEFUL DUNK SHOT in basketball, to make a forceful dunk shot **2.** TREAT SOMEBODY HARSHLY to speak of or treat somebody in a dramatic, hostile, or disrespectful way (*slang*) ○ *The two legislators have done nothing but slam-dunk each other during the session.* **3.** DEFEAT SOMEBODY COMPLETELY to defeat a person or a group of people completely (*slang*) ○ *The prosecutor slam-dunked the defense in the trial.* ■ *adj.* CERTAIN OF SUCCESS without risk and sure to be successful ○ *a slam-dunk scenario*

slam·mer /slámmər/ *n.* a jail or prison (*slang*) [Mid-20thC. From the idea of the doors slamming shut.]

s.l.a.n. *abbr.* without place, year, or name [Shortening of Latin *sine loco, anno, vel nomine*]

slan·der /slándər/ *n.* **1.** LAW SAYING OF SOMETHING FALSE AND DAMAGING the act of saying something false or malicious that damages somebody's reputation **2.** FALSE AND DAMAGING STATEMENT a false and malicious statement that damages somebody's reputation ■ *vt.* (**-dered, -der·ing, -ders**) UTTER A SLANDER AGAINST to make a false and malicious oral statement about somebody [13thC. Via Old French *esclandre* from, ultimately, ecclesiastical Latin *scandalum* "cause of offense" (see SCANDAL).] —**slan·der·er** *n.* —**slan·der·ous** *adj.* —**slan·der·ous·ly** *adv.* —**slan·der·ous·ness** *n.*

WORD KEY: SYNONYMS

See Synonyms at **malign.**

slang /slang/ *n.* **1.** VERY CASUAL SPEECH OR WRITING words, expressions, and usages that are casual, vivid, racy, or playful replacements for standard ones, are often short-lived, and are usually considered unsuitable for formal contexts **2.** LANGUAGE OF AN EXCLUSIVE GROUP a form of language used by a particular group of people, often deliberately created and used to exclude people outside the group ○ *a word that came from surfers' slang* ■ *adj.* IN SLANG belonging to, expressed in, or containing slang ○ *a slang dictionary* ■ *vti.* (**slanged, slang·ing, slangs**) USE ABUSIVE LANGUAGE to use abusive language, usually slang, or to use this to attack somebody verbally [Mid-18thC. Origin unknown.] —**slang·i·ly** *adv.* —**slang·i·ness** *n.* —**slang·y** *adj.*

slant /slant/ *v.* (**slant·ed, slant·ing, slants**) **1.** *vti.* BE OR SET SOMETHING AT AN ANGLE to be at an angle, or set something at an angle **2.** *vt.* CAUSE SOMETHING TO HAVE A PARTICULAR APPEAL to make something appeal to a particular group of people ○ *a magazine slanted toward the youth market* **3.** *vt.* PRESENT WITH BIAS to present something in a way that is biased toward a particular person, group, or viewpoint ○ *The news report was slanted in favor of the nationalists.* ■ *n.* **1.** ANGLED POSITION an angled position or a direction that is at an angle to something else ○ *the roof was built on a slant* **2.** BIASED PERSPECTIVE a particular bias, or a perspective on something that is likely to appeal to a particular group ○ *The news was given a progovernment slant.* **3.** POINT OF VIEW a point of view or way of looking at something ○ *Her diaries give us a new slant on the events of the time.* **4.** FOOTBALL RUNNING PLAY a play in football in which an offensive player runs forward with the ball at an angle to the line of scrimmage ■ *adj.* **slant, slant·ing, slant·y** SLOPING sloping, or at an angle (*informal*) [15thC. Variant of earlier *slent*, of uncertain origin: probably from a Scandinavian language.] —**slan·ted** *adj.* —**slant·ing·ly** *adv.*

slant rhyme *n.* POETRY = **half rhyme**

slant·wise /slánt wīz/, **slant·ways** /slánt wàyz/ *adv.* at an angle to something else

slap /slap/ *n.* **1.** BLOW MADE WITH THE OPEN HAND a blow made with the open hand or a flat object **2.** NOISE OF A SLAP the noise made by a slap, or something that sounds like it ○ *the slap of a wave on the side of the boat* **3.** REBUKE something that rebukes, insults, or hurts ■ *v.* (**slapped, slap·ping, slaps**) **1.** *vt.* HIT WITH THE OPEN HAND to hit somebody or something with the open hand or a flat object **2.** *vi.* STRIKE SHARPLY to strike sharply and noisily, as if with a slap **3.** *vt.* PUT DOWN SHARPLY to put something down sharply or noisily on something else ○ *He slapped the money on the table and walked away.* **4.** *vt.* APPLY CARELESSLY to put something on or make something, quickly and carelessly ○ *I slapped on some makeup and ran for the car.* **5.** *vt.* APPLY AS A PENALTY to apply something as a punishment, penalty, or restriction to somebody or something (*informal*) ○ *The company was slapped with a fine.* ■ *adv.* (*informal*) **1.** FORCEFULLY forcefully, and often with the sound or effect of a slap ○ *landed slap on the floor* **2.** EXACTLY exactly, and usually with suddenness and force ○ *slap in the middle of the target* [Mid-17thC. An imitation of the sound.] —**slap·per** *n.* ◇ **a slap in the face** a rebuke or rebuff (*informal*) ◇ **a slap on the back** congratulations (*informal*) ◇ **a slap on the wrist** a mild rebuke or punishment (*informal*)

slap down *vt.* (*informal*) **1.** REBUKE to rebuke somebody sharply or cruelly **2.** SUPPRESS to suppress or check something thought to be unacceptable ○ *Any disrespect is slapped down immediately.*

slap-bang *adv.* *U.K.* (*informal*) **1.** = **slam-bang 2.** = **smack-dab**

slap·dash /sláp dàsh/ *adj.* CARELESS careless, hasty, and unskillful ■ *adv.* CARELESSLY in a careless, hasty, and unskillful way

slap·hap·py /sláp hàppee/ *adj.* (*informal*) **1.** CHEERFULLY IRRESPONSIBLE irresponsible or careless in a cheerful way **2.** DAZED dazed or disoriented, like a boxer who has been hit in the head too many times

slap·jack /sláp jàk/ *n.* **1.** COOK = **flapjack 2.** CARDS CARD GAME USING JACKS a card game in which players compete to be first in slapping a hand on a face-up jack ["Flapjack": early 19thC. Alteration of FLAPJACK. "Card game": late 19thC. Coined from SLAP + JACK.]

slap shot *n.* a shot in ice hockey in which the player swings the stick with a fast powerful stroke [*Slap* from the loud sound made when the stick hits the ice]

slap·stick /sláp stìk/ *n.* comedy with the emphasis on fast physical action, farcical situations, and obvious jokes that do not depend on language (*often used before a noun*) ○ *slapstick comedy* [Early 20thC. From earlier *slapstick* "device made of two flat linked pieces of wood, formerly used in comic performances to simulate the sound of a blow."]

slash /slash/ *vt.* (**slashed, slash·ing, slash·es**) **1.** MAKE CUTS IN to make long deep cuts in something **2.** ATTACK WITH A SHARP OBJECT to cut or attack somebody with the sharp sweeping strokes of a sword, knife, stick, or whip **3.** CRITICIZE to criticize somebody or something severely **4.** REDUCE OR SHORTEN to greatly reduce or shorten something ○ *All prices slashed!* **5.** CLOTHES MAKE A SLIT IN CLOTH to make a slit in fabric or a garment to reveal the lining **6.** FORESTRY CLEAR A FOREST BY CUTTING to cut bushes and undergrowth from a wooded area ■ *n.* **1.** SHARP SWEEPING STROKE a sharp sweeping stroke of a sword, knife, stick, or whip **2.** LONG AND DEEP CUT a long deep cut or wound **3.** CLOTHES SLIT IN FABRIC a slit in fabric or a garment, made to reveal the lining **4.** FORESTRY DEBRIS FROM CUT TREES the debris left after trees have been cut down **5.** PRINTING PRINT CHARACTER a character, (/), that is used to separate optional items in a list or to express fractions or division, and that has various uses in computer programming. Technical name **virgule 6.** SWAMPY GROUND swampy ground covered with bushes and small trees (*often used in the plural*) [Late 16thC. Origin uncertain: possibly from French *esclachier* "to break," variant of Old French *esclater*, from *esclat* "splinter" (source of English *slat*).] —**slash·er** *n.*

slash-and-burn *adj.* **1.** AGRIC CUTTING, BURNING, AND TILLING used to describe a form of agriculture characterized by the cutting down and burning of trees and vegetation in order to plant crops **2.** TENDING TO DESTROY SOMETHING COMPLETELY having or showing the intention to deal with somebody or something drastically and ruthlessly or to destroy somebody or something completely (*informal*) ○ *her slash-and-burn approach to budget cuts*

slash·er mov·ie *n.* a horror film featuring gory effects such as people being slashed with blades (*slang*)

slash·ing /sláshing/ *n.* **1.** SPORTS **ILLEGAL ACT IN HOCKEY AND LACROSSE** the illegal striking or swinging of a stick at an opposing player in hockey or lacrosse **2. CUTTING ATTACK** an act of attacking and cutting somebody with a blade ■ *adj.* **1. CRITICAL** aggressively critical **2. REDUCING** severely reducing or shortening something ○ *make slashing cuts to the budget* —**slash·ing·ly** *adv.*

slash pine *n.* **1.** TREES **PINE FOUND IN SWAMPS** a pine that grows mainly in swamps in the southeastern United States and is a source of turpentine and timber. Latin name: *Pinus elliottii.* **2.** INDUST **WOOD FROM SLASH PINE** the hard and durable wood of the slash pine [*Slash* from *slash* "swamp," of unknown origin]

slash pock·et *n.* a pocket in a garment fitted with a diagonal slit for easy access

slat /slat/ *n.* **1. THIN STRIP** a light thin narrow strip of wood or metal **2.** TECH **AIRFOIL ON AN AIRCRAFT WING** an auxiliary airfoil fixed to the leading edge of a wing to give extra lift ■ *vt.* (**slat·ted, slat·ting, slats**) **ADD SLATS TO** to put slats in something [Mid-18thC. From Old French *esclat* "splinter, piece broken off," of uncertain origin: possibly from prehistoric Germanic.]

slate /slayt/ *n.* **1.** GEOL **LAYERED ROCK** a fine-grained metamorphic rock that splits easily into layers and is widely used as a roofing material **2.** BUILDING **ROOFING TILE** a roofing tile made of slate **3. WRITING TABLET** a small square piece of slate used in the past for writing on, especially by school students. It could be wiped clean and reused indefinitely. **4.** COLORS **DARK GRAY** a dark gray or bluish-gray color **5.** POL **LIST OF CANDIDATES** a list of the candidates in an election **6.** CINEMA **IDENTIFYING BOARD ON A MOVIE SET** an identifying board used on a movie set showing information such as the shot number that is held in front of a camera at the beginning or end of a shot ■ *vt.* (**slat·ed, slat·ing, slates**) **1. COVER A ROOF WITH SLATE** to cover a roof with tiles made of slate **2.** POL **INCLUDE SOMEBODY IN LIST OF A CANDIDATES** to put somebody's name on a list of candidates for election **3. DESIGNATE SOMEBODY** to choose or schedule somebody for a particular task or position ○ *You've been slated for the next vacant management position.* ■ *adj.* COLORS **DARK GRAY** of a dark gray or bluish-gray color [14thC. From Old French *esclate*, feminine form of *esclat* "splinter, piece broken off" (source of *slat*).] ◇ **a clean slate** an imaginary record of somebody's past, with no bad marks recorded on it or with all previous bad marks forgotten (*informal*) ◇ **wipe the slate clean** to forget about what has happened and make a fresh start (*informal*)

slate black *adj.* of a purplish-black color —**slate black** *n.*

slate blue *adj.* of a dark bluish-gray color —**slate blue** *n.*

slate-col·ored jun·co *n.* an eastern North American subspecies of junco with dark gray plumage. Latin name: *Junco hyemalis.*

slat·er /sláytər/ *n.* somebody whose job is to lay roofing tiles made of slate

Slat·er /sláytər/, **Samuel** (1768–1835) British-born U.S. engineer and entrepreneur. He founded the first North American cotton mill in Pawtucket, Rhode Island (1789), after emigrating there and reconstructing British textile machinery from memory.

slath·er /sláthər/ *vt.* (**-ered, -er·ing, -ers**) **1. SPREAD SOMETHING THICKLY** to spread something thickly or excessively on something else **2. SQUANDER SOMETHING** to use something wastefully (*informal*) ■ **slath·ers** *npl.* **LARGE AMOUNT** a large or generous quantity (*informal*) [Mid-19thC. Origin unknown.]

slat·ing /sláyting/ *n.* the process of covering something with slates, or the slates themselves

slat·tern /sláttərn/ *n.* (*dated insult*) **1. OFFENSIVE TERM** an offensive term referring to a woman regarded as ignoring conventional standards of hygiene and grooming **2. OFFENSIVE TERM** an offensive term referring to a woman regarded as being sexually promiscuous [Mid-17thC. Origin uncertain: possibly from a dialect word meaning "to slop, be slovenly."] —**slat·tern·li·ness** *n.* —**slat·tern·ly** *adj.*

slat·y /sláytee/ (**-i·er, -i·est**) *adj.* made of slate or like slate, especially in color —**slat·i·ness** *n.*

slaugh·ter /sláwtər/ *n.* **1. KILLING OF ANIMALS** the killing of animals for their meat **2. KILLING OF PEOPLE** the brutal killing of a person or large numbers of people **3. MAJOR DEFEAT** an overwhelming defeat (*slang*) ■ *vt.* (**-tered, -ter·ing, -ters**) **1. KILL AN ANIMAL FOR MEAT** to kill an animal or animals, usually for their meat **2. KILL PEOPLE BRUTALLY** to kill a person or large numbers of people brutally **3. DEFEAT SOMEBODY CONVINCINGLY** to defeat a person or a group of people overwhelmingly (*slang*) [13thC. From Old Norse *slátr* "meat, butchery."] —**slaugh·ter·er** *n.* —**slaugh·ter·ous** *adj.*

WORD KEY: SYNONYMS

See Synonyms at ***kill***.

slaugh·ter·house /sláwtər hòwss/ (*plural* **-hous·es** /-hòwzəz/) *n.* = **abattoir**

WORD KEY: CULTURAL NOTE

Slaughterhouse 5, a novel by Kurt Vonnegut (1970). In this highly original blend of realism and science fiction, World War II veteran Billy Pilgrim is kidnapped by aliens who enable him to revisit his past. He subsequently relives the Allied firebombing of Dresden in 1945, an event witnessed by Vonnegut himself and here presented as a symbol of the endless cruelty and suffering of humanity.

Slav /slaav/ *n.* a member of any of the peoples of Eastern Europe and North Western Asia that speak one of the Slavonic languages [14thC. Via medieval Latin *Sclavus* (source of English *slave*) from medieval Greek *Sklabos*, ultimately of Slavic origin.]

Slav. *abbr.* **1.** Slavic **2.** Slavonic

slave /slayv/ *n.* **1. PERSON FORCED TO WORK FOR ANOTHER** in former times, one person who was forced to work for another person for no payment and was regarded as the property of the person he or she worked for **2. DOMINATED PERSON** somebody who is completely dominated by somebody or something **3. SOMEBODY ACCEPTING ANOTHER'S RULE** somebody who meekly accepts being ruled by somebody else **4. VERY HARD WORKER** somebody who works or has to work very hard, often in bad conditions and for low pay **5. DEVICE CONTROLLED BY ANOTHER** a device that is totally controlled by another (*often used before a noun*) ■ *vi.* (**slaved, slav·ing, slaves**) **WORK VERY HARD** to work very hard ○ *I've been slaving away over this manuscript all day.* ■ *adj.* **1. USING ENSLAVED LABORERS** using or relating to enslaved laborers **2. HARSH** very harsh and unfair ○ *slave conditions* [13thC. Via Old French *esclave* from medieval Latin *sclavus* "Slav, captive" (see SLAV), because Slavic peoples were widely captured and enslaved during the Middle Ages.]

slave ant *n.* an ant captured and forced to work for an ant colony of another species

slave driv·er *n.* **1. SOMEBODY WHO MAKES PEOPLE WORK HARD** somebody who makes employees work excessively hard **2.** HIST **OVERSEER OF LABORERS** in the past, somebody who was employed to make sure that enslaved people worked hard

slave·hold·er /sláyv hòldər/ *n.* somebody owning slaves

slave la·bor *n.* **1. WORKFORCE OF ENSLAVED LABORERS** a workforce consisting of people who are forced to work against their will ○ *The pyramids were built by slave labor.* **2. HARD WORK** hard or demanding work, in poor conditions, that is not well paid (*informal*) ○ *It's nothing but slave labor in that department.*

slave-mak·ing ant, **slave-mak·er ant** *n.* a species of ant that raids the colonies of other ant species, capturing larvae and pupae to be used in its own colony

slav·er[1] /sláyvər/ *n.* HIST **1. SLAVE OWNER** somebody who owned or bought and sold slaves in former times **2.** = **slave ship**

slav·er[2] /slávvor, sláyvər/ *vi.* (**-ered, -er·ing, -ers**) **1. DRIBBLE SALIVA** to dribble saliva from the mouth **2. BEHAVE OBSEQUIOUSLY** to fawn or behave obsequiously to somebody ■ *n.* **DRIPPING SALIVA** saliva that drips from somebody's mouth [14thC. Origin uncertain; probably from Scandinavian.]

slav·er·y /sláyvəree/ *n.* **1. SYSTEM BASED ON ENSLAVED LABOR** a system based on using the enforced labor of other people **2. CONDITION OF BEING AN ENSLAVED LABORER** the condition of being forced to work for somebody else in past times **3. HARD WORK** very hard work, especially for low pay and under bad conditions **4. STATE OF BEING DOMINATED** a state of being completely dominated by another

slave ship *n.* HIST a ship used to carry captured and enslaved people, especially from Africa

slave state *n.* any of the 15 states where slavery was legal until the Civil War

slave trade *n.* the business of capturing people and buying and selling them as enslaved laborers

Slav·ic /slaávik/, **Sla·von·ic** /slə vónnik/ *n.* LANG **E EUROPEAN LANGUAGE GROUP** a branch of the Indo-European family of languages that includes Bulgarian, Russian, and Polish ■ *adj.* **TYPICAL OF SLAVIC LANGUAGES OR PEOPLE** relating to the Slavic languages or the people who speak them

slav·ish /sláyvish/ *adj.* an offensive term comparing something to the stereotypical traits attributed to an enslaved person —**slav·ish·ly** *adv.* —**slav·ish·ness** *n.*

Slav·ism /slaá vìzzəm/ *n.* a feature or characteristic of the Slavs or Slavic languages

slav·oc·ra·cy /slay vókrəssee/ *n.* slave owners considered collectively as a ruling group, or rule by slave owners

Sla·von·ic *n., adj.* LANG, PEOPLES = **Slavic** [Early 17thC. From medieval Latin *S(c)lavonicus*, from *S(c)lavonia* "country of the Slavs."]

Slav·o·phile /slaávə fīl/, **Slav·o·phil** /slaávə fil/ *n.* (*often used before a noun*) **1. ADMIRER OF SLAVIC CULTURE OR PEOPLE** somebody who admires Slavic culture or people **2.** HIST **ADVOCATE OF SLAVIC SUPREMACY** somebody who, in 19th-century Russia, asserted the superiority of Slavic people and worked for their supremacy —**Sla·voph·i·lism** /slə vóffə lìzzəm/ *n.*

slaw /slaw/ *n.* FOOD = **coleslaw** [Late 18thC. From Dutch *sla*, a contraction of French *salade* "salad" (see SALAD).]

slay /slay/ (**slew** /sloo/, **slain** /slayn/, **slay·ing, slays**) *vt.* **1. KILL SOMEBODY** to kill somebody or something (*formal or literary*) **2.** (*past* **slayed**, *past participle* **slayed** *or* **slain**) **AMUSE SOMEBODY** to amuse somebody very much (*informal*) [Old English *slēan*, from a prehistoric Germanic word meaning "to strike," which is also the ancestor of English *onslaught* and *sledge*[2]] —**slay·er** *n.*

WORD KEY: SYNONYMS

See Synonyms at ***kill***.

slay·ing /sláying/ *n.* a killing or murder

SLBM *abbr.* submarine-launched ballistic missile

SLCM *abbr.* sea-launched cruise missile

sld. *abbr.* **1.** sailed **2.** sealed **3.** sold

SLE *abbr.* MED systemic lupus erythematosus

sleaze /sleez/ *n.* **1. DISHONESTY OR CORRUPTION** corruption, dishonesty, or scandal, especially among public figures such as politicians **2.** = **sleazebag** (*slang insult*) [Mid-20thC. Back-formation from SLEAZY.]

sleaze·bag /sleéz bàg/, **sleaze·ball** /sleéz bàwl/ *n.* an offensive term referring to somebody whose behavior is perceived as immoral, unethical, or disreputable (*slang insult*)

slea·zy /sleézee/ (**-zi·er, -zi·est**) *adj.* **1. SORDID** dirty, disreputable, or sordid in character or appearance **2. DISHONEST OR IMMORAL** dishonest or immoral ○ *You get some pretty sleazy types in here.* [Mid-17thC. Originally "flimsy in texture," of uncertain origin: perhaps ultimately from *Silesia*, region in present-day Poland, where a good linen fabric was made that was later imitated cheaply.] —**slea·zi·ly** *adv.* —**slea·zi·ness** *n.*

sled *n.* **1. SMALL VEHICLE SLIDING OVER SNOW** a small low vehicle on ski-style or other runners, designed to be pulled over snow or ice by people or dogs **2. CHILD'S TOY VEHICLE FOR SNOW** a child's toy vehicle on runners, used for sliding down snowy hills ■ *vti.* (**sled·ded, sledding, sleds**) **MOVE BY SLED** to ride, travel, or transport something by sled [14thC. From Middle Low German *sledde*, from a prehistoric Germanic base meaning "to slip, slide," which is also the ancestor of English *slide, sleigh*, and *sledge*[1].] —**sled·der** *n.*

sled·ding /slédding/ *n.* **1. USE OF A SLED** the use of a sled for work or recreation **2. CONDITIONS FOR USING A SLED** conditions in which a sled may be used ○ *The sledding is good right now.* **3. PROGRESS** a particular kind of progress ○ *It was hard sledding for a while, but now things are easier.*

sled dog *n.* a dog trained to pull a sled, especially when part of a dog team

sledge[1] /slej/ **(sledged, sledg·ing, sledg·es)** *n.* **1. LARGE TRANSPORT SLED** a large sled pulled by animals, used for transporting loads across snow or ice **2. = sled** *n.* 1 [Late 16thC. From Dutch dialect *sleedse*.]

sledge[2] /slej/ *n.* **= sledgehammer** [Old English *slecg*, from a prehistoric Germanic word meaning "to strike," which is also the ancestor of English *slay, slaughter*, and *onslaught*]

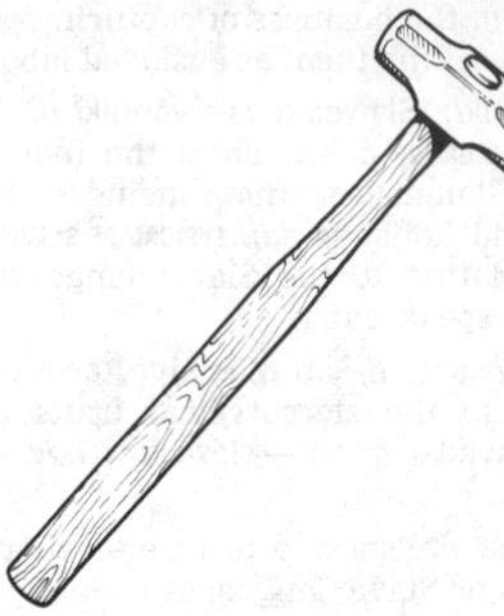

Sledgehammer

sledge·ham·mer /sléj hàmmər/ *n.* **LARGE HAMMER** a large heavy hammer swung with both hands ■ *vt.* **(-mered, -mer·ing, -mers) STRIKE WITH A SLEDGEHAMMER** to hit something with a sledgehammer or with the force of one ■ *adj.* **VERY FORCEFUL** extremely forceful ○ *sledgehammer blows* [15thC. Coined from SLEDGE[2] + HAMMER.]

sleek /sleek/ *adj.* **1. SMOOTH AND SHINY** attractively smooth and shiny **2. WELL-GROOMED** well-groomed and healthy looking **3. SUAVE** smooth and polished in behavior or speech, often insincerely or suspiciously so ○ *a sleek sales pitch* ■ *vt.* **(sleeked, sleek·ing, sleeks) MAKE SOMETHING SLEEK** to make something appear smooth or shiny [Late 16thC. Variant of SLICK.] —**sleek·ly** *adv.* —**sleek·ness** *n.*

sleep /sleep/ *n.* **1.** PHYSIOL **STATE OF NOT BEING AWAKE** a state of partial or full unconsciousness in people and animals during which voluntary functions are suspended and the body rests and restores itself, or a period in this state **2. STATE RESEMBLING SLEEP** any state that is inactive or dormant, like sleep **3. DEATH** death (*literary*) (*also used euphemistically*) **4. MUCUS IN EYES** small amounts of dried mucus that often collect in the eyes during sleep (*informal*) **5.** BOT **= nyctitropism** ■ *v.* **(slept, slept** /slept/**, sleep·ing, sleeps) 1.** *vi.* PHYSIOL **BE IN A STATE OF SLEEP** to go into or be in a state of sleep **2.** *vi.* **BE INACTIVE** to be in an inactive or dormant state ○ *a city that never sleeps* **3.** *vi.* BOT **CHANGE POSITION AT NIGHT** to assume a position at night that is different from the daytime position **4.** *vt.* **PROVIDE BEDS FOR PEOPLE** to provide sleeping accommodations for a particular number of people ○ *The yacht sleeps eight.* **5.** *vi.* **BE DEAD** to be dead (*literary*) (*also used euphemistically*) ○ *He sleeps in the bosom of Abraham.* **6.** *vt.* **SPEND TIME IN SLEEP** to spend a period of time sleeping ○ *We slept the night in a hotel.* [The noun is from Old English *slǣp*, the verb from Old English *slǣpan*, both from prehistoric Germanic] ◇ **get to sleep, go to sleep** begin sleeping ◇ **in your sleep 1.** while you are sleeping **2.** with ease, as if not having to be fully awake (*informal*) ○ *I could find my way there in my sleep, I've been so often.* ◇ **not lose (any) sleep over something** to not worry about something because it is thought to be trivial or irrelevant ◇ **put something to sleep** kill an animal in a humane way, especially because it is ill, injured, or in pain ◇ **sleep on it** postpone a decision until at least the next day in order to give it more thought

sleep around *vi.* to have a lot of casual sexual relationships with different people (*informal*)

sleep in *vi.* **1. SLEEP LONGER THAN USUAL** to sleep longer than you usually do **2. SLEEP WHERE YOU WORK** to sleep at the place where you are employed

sleep off *vt.* to get rid of illness by sleeping until it is gone

sleep out *vi.* **1. SLEEP OUTSIDE** sleep out of doors **2. SLEEP AWAY FROM YOUR PLACE OF WORK** to sleep somewhere other than the place where you are employed

sleep over *vi.* to sleep at somebody else's house as part of a visit

sleep together *vi.* to have sex (*informal*) (*used euphemistically*)

sleep with *vt.* to have sex with somebody (*informal*) (*used euphemistically*)

sleep ap·ne·a *n.* a temporary cessation of breathing that happens to some people while they are sleeping

sleep·er /sleépər/ *n.* **1. SOMEBODY SLEEPING** somebody who is sleeping, or somebody who sleeps in a particular way ○ *a light sleeper* **2.** RAIL **TRAIN CAR WITH BEDS** a train car or compartment with beds for passengers **3.** *U.K.* RAIL **= tie** *n.* 5 **4.** BUILDING **HEAVY BEAM** a heavy beam used as a sill, footing, or support **5. SURPRISING SUCCESS** somebody or something that is not immediately successful but, often surprisingly, becomes so after a while (*informal*) **6. SPY INACTIVE UNTIL CALLED INTO ACTION** a spy or secret agent who lives an ordinary life until called into action (*informal*) **7.** ZOOL **TROPICAL FISH** a marine or freshwater tropical fish related to the goby that often lies immobile. Family: Eleotridae. **8.** FURNITURE **CONVERTIBLE BED** a piece of furniture that converts into a bed **9.** WRESTLING **WRESTLING HOLD INDUCING UNCONSCIOUSNESS** a wrestling hold in which pressure is applied to the sides of an opponent's neck so as to induce real or simulated unconsciousness ■ **sleep·ers** *npl.* **CHILDREN'S COVERALL PAJAMAS** children's one-piece pajamas with feet

sleep-in *adj.* living in the house of an employer ○ *a sleep-in maid*

sleep·ing bag *n.* a long padded or lined fabric bag, often zippered, for sleeping in, especially when camping

sleep·ing car *n.* a railroad car that has bunks or compartments in which passengers can sleep

sleep·ing part·ner *n. U.K.* BUSINESS **= silent partner**

sleep·ing pill *n.* a pill containing a drug that is meant to induce sleep

sleep·ing sick·ness *n.* **1. TROPICAL DISEASE** a disease in tropical Africa caused by parasitic protozoans that are carried by tsetse flies. Affected people and animals experience fever, weight loss, and lethargy. **2. ENCEPHALITIS CAUSING LETHARGY** an epidemic form of encephalitis causing lethargy, muscular weakness, and impaired vision

sleep-learn·ing *n.* a method of learning something that involves the continuous playing of recordings of it to a sleeping learner

sleep·less /sleépləss/ *adj.* **1. LACKING SLEEP** without sleep, or unable to sleep ○ *a sleepless night* **2. AWAKE** always awake, active, or busy —**sleep·less·ly** *adv.* —**sleep·less·ness** *n.*

sleep-out *n. ANZ* a part of a veranda or yard that has been turned into an outdoor sleeping area, usually partially or fully enclosed with glass or insect screens

sleep·o·ver /sleép òvər/ *n.* an overnight stay at somebody else's house after a children's party (*informal*)

sleep·suit /sleép soot/ *n. U.K.* **= sleeper** *npl.*

sleep ter·ror dis·or·der *n.* a condition of persistent nightmares from which the sleeper awakens in a state of terror and disorientation but remembers nothing of the episode in the morning

sleep·walk /sleép wàwk/ **(-walked, -walk·ing, -walks)** *vi.* **1. WALK WHILE ASLEEP** to walk while you are asleep **2. BE INATTENTIVE** to do something in an inattentive or lethargic way (*informal*) —**sleep·walk·er** *n.* —**sleep·walk·ing** *n.*

sleep·wear /sleép wàir/ *n.* clothes for people to wear while sleeping

sleep·y /sleépee/ **(-i·er, -i·est)** *adj.* **1. DROWSY** feeling drowsy and wanting to sleep **2. QUIET AND WITHOUT MUCH ACTIVITY** quiet and not very lively or exciting ○ *a sleepy mining town* **3. CAUSING SLEEP** tending to make somebody fall asleep —**sleep·i·ly** *adv.* —**sleep·i·ness** *n.*

sleep·y·head /sleépi hèd/ *n.* somebody who has just woken up and is drowsy, or somebody who is nearly falling asleep (*informal*) —**sleep·y·head·ed** *adj.*

sleet /sleet/ *n.* **1. PARTLY FROZEN RAIN** partly frozen rain **2. THIN COATING OF ICE** the thin coating of ice formed when rain freezes on something ■ *vi.* **(sleet·ed, sleet·ing, sleets) FALL AS SLEET** to fall as sleet [13thC. Origin uncertain: probably from an Old English word.]

sleeve /sleev/ *n.* **1.** CLOTHES **COVERING FOR THE ARM** either of the two parts of a garment that wholly or partially cover the arms **2.** ENG **TUBULAR PIECE** a tubular piece designed to fit inside or over a cylinder **3.** RECORDING **= jacket** *n.* 3 ■ *vt.* **(sleeved, sleev·ing, sleeves) FIT WITH A SLEEVE** to provide something with a sleeve [Old English *slēfe*. Ultimately from an Indo-European word meaning "to slide, slip," which is also the ancestor of English *slop, sloop*, and *lubricate*.] —**sleeve·less** *adj.* ◇ **roll up your sleeves** get ready to do something energetically (*informal*) ◇ **up your sleeve** kept hidden or secret but available for use

sleeve notes *npl. U.K.* RECORDING **= liner notes**

sleeve valve *n.* a valve for an internal-combustion engine, fitted and reciprocating inside a cylinder

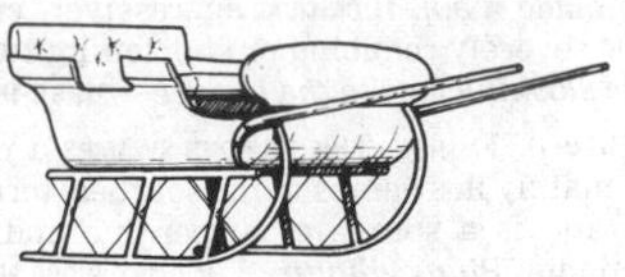

Sleigh

sleigh /slay/ *n.* **SNOW VEHICLE PULLED BY HORSES** an open, usually horse-drawn vehicle on runners, used for travel on snow and ice ■ *vi.* **(sleighed, sleigh·ing, sleighs) TRAVEL IN SLEIGH** to move over snow or ice in a sleigh [Early 18thC. Via Dutch *slee* from, ultimately, Middle Dutch *slēde*. From a prehistoric Germanic base meaning "to slip, slide," which is also the ancestor of English *slide* and *sled*.]

sleigh·bell /sláy bèl/ *n.* one of several small bells attached to a sleigh or to the harness of horses pulling it. Sometimes a number of them are used together as a musical instrument.

sleight /slīt, slayt/ *n.* (*archaic*) **1. TRICK** a trick or cunning act **2. SKILL** dexterity or skill in doing something **3. TRICKERY** cunning or trickery [13thC. From Old Norse *slǿgð* "cunning," from *slǿgr* "crafty" (see SLY).]

sleight of hand *n.* **1. SKILL WITH THE HANDS** skill or dexterity with the hands in performing magic tricks, card tricks, or juggling **2. DECEPTIVE SKILL** any kind of skill by which something happens without it being obvious how it is done

slen·der /sléndər/ *adj.* **1. SMALL IN WIDTH** small or slight in width in proportion to height or length ○ *a flower with a slender stem* **2. SLIM** thin in a graceful way **3. LIMITED** small or limited in degree, extent, or size ○ *The home team won by a slender margin.* [13thC. Origin unknown.] —**slen·der·ly** *adv.* —**slen·der·ness** *n.*

WORD KEY: SYNONYMS

See Synonyms at ***thin***.

slen·der·ize /sléndə rīz/ **(-ized, -iz·ing, -iz·es)** *vti.* to become slender, or make somebody or something slender (*dated*)

slen·der lo·ris *n.* a small tailless slow-moving primate found in the rain forests of India and Sri Lanka. Latin name: *Loris tardigradus.*

slept past tense, past participle of **sleep**

sleuth /slooth/ *n.* **1. DETECTIVE** a detective (*informal*) **2. = sleuthhound** *n.* 1 ■ *v.* **(sleuthed, sleuth·ing, sleuths) 1.** *vi.* **INVESTIGATE** to investigate as or in a similar way to a detective **2.** *vt.* **TRACK SOMEBODY** to track or find somebody or something [Early 19thC. Shortening of SLEUTHHOUND.]

sleuth·hound /slooth hòwnd/ *n.* **1. DOG FOR TRACKING PEOPLE** a dog used for tracking people, especially a bloodhound **2. = sleuth** *n.* 1 (*informal*) [14thC. *Sleuth* from *sleuth* "track, trail," from Old Norse *slóð*, of unknown origin.]

slew[1] past tense of **slay**

slew[2] /sloo/, **slue** *n.* a large quantity or number of something (*informal*) ○ *They hit us with a whole slew of complaints.* [Mid-19thC. Via Irish *sluagh* "multitude" from Old Irish *slúag* "host, army" (source of English *slogan*).]

slew[3] /sloo/ *vti.* **= slue**[1] ■ *n.* **= slue**[1] [Mid-18thC. Origin unknown.]

slew[4] **= slough**[1] [Early 18thC. Alteration of SLOUGH.]

slice /slīss/ *n.* **1. PIECE CUT FROM SOMETHING** a thin broad piece cut from something larger ○ *a slice of ham* **2. SHARE** a part, portion, or share of something ○ *a slice of the profits* **3.** COOK **SERVING UTENSIL** a utensil with a thin, flat, triangular blade, used for cutting and serving food, especially cake **4.** SPORTS **OBLIQUE WAY OF HITTING A BALL** a stroke in which the ball is hit off-center so that it follows a curving path **5.** SPORTS **FLIGHT OF A BALL** the flight of a ball that has been sliced

6. TENNIS **TENNIS SHOT** a tennis shot that makes the ball spin and stay low when it bounces in the opponent's court ■ *v.* **(sliced, slic·ing, slic·es) 1.** *vti.* **CUT INTO PORTIONS** to cut something, or to be cut, into slices or portions **2.** *vti.* **CUT CLEANLY** to cut something cleanly and effortlessly ○ *The sword sliced the rope in half.* **3.** *vi.* **MOVE SWIFTLY AND CLEANLY** to move swiftly and cleanly, especially through a medium such as air or water **4.** *vti.* **CUT OFF** to cut something off something else ○ *The spinning blade sliced off log after log.* **5.** *vt.* SPORTS **SET ON A CURVING PATH** to hit a ball off-center so that it follows a curving path, whether intentionally or as a result of a bad swing or stroke **6.** *vti.* TENNIS **HIT WITH A CHOPPING ACTION** to hit a tennis shot with a chopping stroke so that the ball spins and stays low when it bounces in the opponent's court **7.** *vt.* ROWING **PUT IN THE WATER AT AN ANGLE** to put the blade of an oar into the water at an angle [15thC. From Old French *esclice* "splinter," from *esclicier* "to splinter," ultimately from a prehistoric Germanic word that is also the ancestor of English *slit*.] —**slice·a·ble** *adj.* —**slicer** *n.*

slice of life *n.* a realistic portrayal of life, especially a harsh or unpleasant life, e.g., in a movie [From the idea of cutting into something to see inside]

slick /slik/ *adj.* **1. SLIPPERY** having a smooth, glossy, or slippery surface ○ *a slick runway* **2. CRAFTY** clever and resourceful but not entirely trustworthy (*informal*) **3. GLIB** superficially impressive or persuasive but lacking substance or sincerity ○ *a slick sales pitch* **4. POLISHED** done or able to do things with great skill and apparently effortlessly ○ *a slick presentation* **5. SUAVE** smooth or refined in manners or behavior ■ *n.* **1. SLIPPERY PATCH** a thinly spread or slippery patch of something, especially a quantity of oil floating on top of water **2.** PUBL **EXPENSIVE MAGAZINE** a magazine containing high-quality color photographs, especially a fashion magazine, printed on smooth-coated paper **3.** MOTOR SPORTS **TREADLESS TIRE** a wide treadless tire used in auto racing **4.** AIR, MIL **UNARMED AIRCRAFT** an unarmed aircraft ■ *vt.* **(slicked, slick·ing, slicks) MAKE SOMETHING SMOOTH** to make something smooth, glossy, or presentable ○ *He wears his hair slicked back.* [14thC. Ultimately from an Indo-European word denoting "slippery," which is also the ancestor of English *slime, slip,* and *oblivion*.] —**slick·ly** *adv.* —**slick·ness** *n.*

slick·en·side /slíkən sìd/ *n.* a rock surface that is smooth and marked with fine scratches caused by friction with another rock surface [Early 19thC. Coined from a dialect variant of SLICK + SLIDE.]

slick·er /slíkər/ *n.* **1. RAINCOAT** a shiny raincoat, often made of a plastic or rubber material **2. SOPHISTICATED BUT UNTRUSTWORTHY PERSON** somebody who appears to be very sophisticated, stylish, or clever, but is not very honest or trustworthy (*informal*) ◊ **city slicker 3. SMOOTHING TOOL** a tool used for smoothing something

slick·head fish /slík hèd-/ *n.* a small slender deep-sea fish with dark coloration and no scales on its head, which gives it a slick appearance. Family: Alepocephalidae.

slide /slīd/ *v.* **(slid /slid/, slid, slid·ing, slides) 1.** *vti.* **MOVE SMOOTHLY** to move or make something move smoothly across a surface ○ *The car slid for 50 yards when the brakes locked.* **2.** *vti.* **MOVE UNOBTRUSIVELY** to move or move something unobtrusively ○ *He slid the letter into his pocket.* **3.** *vi.* **TO CHANGE TO A DIFFERENT CONDITION** to change to a different, usually worse, state or condition ○ *unable to stop the economy from sliding into recession* **4.** *vi.* **SLIP** to lose your grip or secure footing on a surface ○ *It seemed to slide right off the window ledge.* **5.** *vi.* **DECREASE** to decrease in value or quantity ○ *Stock prices are sliding for the third straight day.* **6.** *vi.* MUSIC **PLAY A GLIDE BETWEEN NOTES** to make a gliding change from one note to another **7.** *vti.* BASEBALL **APPROACH A BASE HORIZONTALLY** to approach a base in baseball or softball while skidding feet first, low to the ground ○ *The runner avoided the tag with a beautiful hook slide.* ■ *n.* **1. SLIDING** a sliding movement **2.** LEISURE **STRUCTURE THAT CHILDREN PLAY ON** a structure with a metal slope that children slide down for fun **3.** PHOTOGRAPHY **SMALL POSITIVE PHOTOGRAPH** a positive photograph reproduced on a small piece of film, mounted in a frame or on a plate and viewed by projection on a screen or through a magnifying device **4.** GEOL **FALL OF ROCK, MUD, OR EARTH** a downhill displacement of rock, mud, or earth, often caused by rainfall or erosion **5.** SCI **SPECIMEN HOLDER** a small glass plate on which a specimen is mounted for viewing under a microscope **6. SLIDING MACHINE PART** a machine part that slides, or the part on which it moves **7.** ROWING = **sliding seat 8.** MUSIC **TROMBONE MECHANISM** the U-shaped tube of a trombone that is pushed in and out to allow for changes in pitch **9.** MUSIC **MUSICAL FEATURE** a sliding change from one note to another [Old English *slīdan*, from a prehistoric Germanic word that is also the ancestor of English *sled* and *sleigh*] ◇ **let things** *or* **something slide** to let a situation gradually go back to its previous worse state ◇ **on the slide** in the process of becoming worse (*informal*)

slide-ac·tion *adj.* used to describe a shotgun or rifle with a lever that ejects the case of a spent round and loads a new one

Sli·dell /slī dél/ city in southeastern Louisiana, on the northeastern shore of Lake Pontchartrain, opposite New Orleans. Population: 25,846 (1996).

Sli·dell, John (1793–1871) U.S. politician and diplomat. He was the Confederacy's commissioner to France during the Civil War.

slid·er /slídər/ *n.* **1. SOMETHING THAT SLIDES** somebody or something that slides **2.** BASEBALL **FAST REVERSE CURVE** a fast pitch in baseball that curves outward from the side of the pitcher's throwing arm as it reaches the batter

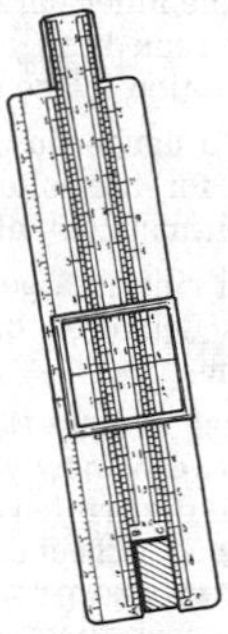

Slide rule

slide rule *n.* a manual calculating device, now largely obsolete, consisting of two rulers marked with graduated logarithmic scales, one sliding inside the other

slide show *n.* a sequence of photographic slides projected on a screen or wall as education or entertainment

slide trom·bone *n.* a trombone with a slide that is moved to select different pitches as distinct from a trombone fitted with valves

slid·ing /slíding/ *adj.* **1. VARYING ACCORDING TO SOMETHING ELSE** varying according to changing conditions **2. MOVED BY SLIDING** moved by sliding ○ *a sliding door* [Old English]

slid·ing scale *n.* any scale, e.g., of wages, costs, or fees, that varies according to changes in some other factor

slid·ing seat *n.* a seat in a rowboat that slides back and forth, allowing a rower to lengthen the stroke of the oars

sli·er comparative of **sly**

sli·est superlative of **sly**

slight /slīt/ *adj.* **1. VERY SMALL** very small in size, degree, amount, or importance ○ *a slight resemblance* **2. THIN** having a slim body that does not look very strong **3. INSUBSTANTIAL** not very substantial or convincing ○ *an assertion made without the slightest evidence* ■ *vt.* **(slight·ed, slight·ing, slights) 1. SNUB SOMEBODY** to treat somebody rudely, e.g., by deliberately ignoring him or her **2. TREAT SOMETHING AS UNIMPORTANT** to think of or treat something as unimportant **3. DO SOMETHING CARELESSLY** to handle duties or responsibilities carelessly ■ *n.* **IMPOLITE ACT** an action that shows contempt for somebody or something [14thC. Origin uncertain; possibly from Scandinavian.] —**slight·ly** *adv.* —**slight·ness** *n.*

slight·ing /slíting/ *adj.* showing contempt or disrespect ○ *make slighting remarks about it* —**slight·ing·ly** *adv.*

slim /slim/ *adj.* **(slim·mer, slim·mest) 1. SMALLER IN WIDTH THAN HEIGHT** small in width, thickness, or girth and generally long and narrow in shape **2. PLEASINGLY THIN** slender and well-proportioned **3. SMALL** small in degree, quality, or extent ○ *Chances for their survival were slim.* ■ *v.* **(slimmed, slim·ming, slims) 1.** *vi.* **LOSE WEIGHT** to lose weight, especially by dieting **2.** *vt.* **REDUCE** to reduce the size or scope of something ○ *slim down the bloated bureaucracy* [Mid-17thC. Via Dutch, "inferior, small," from Middle Dutch, "crooked." Ultimately from an Indo-European base meaning "to hang loose," which is also the ancestor of English *lump* and *limp*.] —**slim·ly** *adv.* —**slim·ness** *n.*

WORD KEY: SYNONYMS

See Synonyms at ***thin***.

slime /slīm/ *n.* **1. SLIPPERY LIQUID** a fluid that is thick and slippery, especially one that is unpleasant to touch **2.** BIOL **MUCOUS SECRETION OF SOME LIVING THINGS** a mucous substance secreted by some living things such as fish, snails, and fungi ■ *vt.* **(slimed, slim·ing, slimes) 1. COVER SOMETHING WITH SLIME** to cover or smear something with slime **2. REMOVE SLIME FROM SOMETHING** to remove slime from something such as a fish before preparing it for cooking [Old English *slīm*. Ultimately from an Indo-European base meaning "slippery" (see SLICK).]

slime·ball /slīm bàwl/ *n.* an offensive term that deliberately insults somebody regarded as despicable or repellent (*slang insult*) [Late 20thC. Coined from SLIME, on the model of *sleazeball*, variant of SLEAZEBAG.]

slime mold *n.* a simple organism that forms a small slimy amoeboid mass, e.g., on fallen logs, and produces spore-bearing reproductive organs similar to those of a fungus

slim·mer /slímmər/ *n. U.K.* = **dieter**

slim·sy /slímzee/ **(-si·er, -si·est), slimp·sy** /slímpzee/ **(-si·er, -si·est)** *adj.* both slight and flimsy (*informal*) [Mid-19thC. Blend of SLIM and FLIMSY.]

slim·y /slímee/ **(-i·er, -i·est)** *adj.* **1. LIKE SLIME** covered with or resembling slime ○ *a slimy secretion* **2. DISGUSTING** having the semiliquid, sticky consistency of slime ○ *a slimy mess* **3. OFFENSIVE TERM** an offensive term referring to somebody thought to behave in an excessively ingratiating way (*insult*) —**slim·i·ly** *adv.* —**slim·i·ness** *n.*

sling[1] /sling/ *n.* **1.** MED **SUPPORTING BANDAGE** a wide bandage suspended from somebody's neck to support an injured arm or hand **2. CARRYING STRAP** a carrying strap attached to something such as a rifle **3. LOOP FOR CARRYING SOMETHING HEAVY** a loop of rope, leather, chain, or net used to lift, lower, or carry something heavy **4. LOOP USED AS WEAPON** a weapon used for throwing a stone or other object, consisting of a loop of leather or other material in which the missile is twirled before being released **5.** = **slingshot 6.** NAUT **SUPPORT FOR A YARD** a rope or chain that supports a ship's beam ■ **slings** *npl.* MOUNTAINEERING **ANCHORING LOOP** a fixed loop of webbing used to provide an anchor to a rock, tree, or other point ■ *vt.* **(slung /slung/, slung, sling·ing, slings) 1. THROW WITH FORCE** to throw something with a lot of force **2. USE A CARRYING LOOP ON SOMETHING** to attach something to, carry something with, or hang something from a carrying loop **3.** *U.K.* **PASS OR PUT SOMETHING CASUALLY** to throw or pass something or to put or place something somewhere in a casual or careless way (*informal*) [13thC. Origin uncertain: the noun is possibly from Low Dutch or Middle Low German *slinge*; the verb partly from Old Norse *slyngva* and partly from the noun.] —**sling·er** *n.*

sling[2] /sling/ *n.* a mixed alcoholic drink made with liquor, sugar, lemon or lime juice, and water [Mid-18thC. Origin unknown.]

sling·back /slíng bàk/ *n.* a woman's shoe that is open at the heel and is held on the foot by a strap (*often used before a noun*)

sling·shot /slíng shòt/ *n.* a Y-shaped weapon with a loop of elastic attached to the two prongs, used to propel stones or other objects

slink /slink/ *v.* **(slunk /slunk/** *or* **slinked, slunk** *or* **slinked, slink·ing, slinks) 1.** *vi.* **MOVE FURTIVELY** to move or behave quietly and secretively ○ *I could see her trying to slink away through the back door.* **2.** *vi.* **MOVE SEXILY** to walk in a sexually alluring way **3.** *vt.* VET **BEAR PREMATURELY** to give birth to young prematurely, especially to a calf ■ *n.* VET **PREMATURE ANIMAL** a prematurely born animal, especially a calf ■ *adj.* VET **BORN EARLY** used to describe an animal, especially a calf, that is born prematurely [Old English *slincan*, from a prehistoric Germanic word meaning "to slide, throw," which is also the ancestor of English *sling*]

slink·y /slínkee/ **(-i·er, -i·est)** *adj.* **1. SEDUCTIVE** having a seductive appearance or way of moving **2. CLOSE-FITTING** close-fitting and emphasizing the curves of the body ○ *a slinky outfit* —**slink·i·ly** *adv.* —**slink·i·ness** *n.*

Slink·y *tdmk.* a trademark for a spring toy

slip[1] /slip/ *v.* **(slipped, slip·ping, slips) 1.** *vti.* MOVE SMOOTHLY to move or make something move smoothly and easily and usually with a sliding motion ○ *It slips easily in and out of its case.* **2.** *vti.* PUT ON OR TAKE OFF to put on or take off something quickly and easily **3.** *vi.* LOSE YOUR FOOTING to lose your footing or grip on a slippery surface ○ *I slipped and fell.* **4.** *vi.* MOVE FROM ITS PROPER POSITION to slide or move accidentally out of the proper or desired position ○ *This strap keeps slipping off my shoulder.* **5.** *vti.* BE FORGOTTEN to be forgotten or overlooked by somebody ○ *It slipped my mind.* **6.** *vi.* GO QUIETLY to go somewhere in a quiet, furtive, or unnoticed way ○ *He slipped out while nobody was looking.* **7.** *vt.* PASS SOMETHING SECRETLY to give somebody something furtively or secretly ○ *I saw the man slip her an envelope* **8.** *vi.* ERR to make a mistake or to do something wrong ○ *You must have slipped up when you were making a note of the number.* **9.** *vi.* GET WORSE to decline from a previous standard, e.g., of performance or awareness ○ *He's slipping – two years ago he would have spotted that mistake at once* **10.** *vt.* DISLOCATE A BONE to dislocate or displace a bone, especially in the spine **11.** *vti.* AUTOMOT DISENGAGE THE CLUTCH to disengage the clutch of a motor vehicle or be disengaged **12.** *vi.* MECH ENG FAIL TO ENGAGE to fail to engage properly, usually because of wear (*refers to mechanical parts*) **13.** *vt.* NAUT, SAILING LET A RESTRAINING CABLE GO to let a line or cable that is securing a vessel to a mooring or anchor fall over the side **14.** *vti.* RELEASE to release an animal from a restraint, or be released in this way ■ *n.* **1.** ACT OF SLIPPING an act of slipping, especially a sudden slide on a slippery surface **2.** ERROR an error or oversight **3.** LAPSE a moral lapse or instance of misconduct **4.** CLOTHES UNDERGARMENT a light sleeveless woman's undergarment worn under a dress **5.** NAUT = **slipway 6.** CRYSTALS DEFORMATION OF A CRYSTAL the deformation of a metallic crystal by shearing along a plane **7.** CLOTH COVERING a cloth covering for something **8.** AIR = **sideslip** *n.* 2 [13thC. Origin uncertain: probably from Middle Dutch or Middle Low German *slippen.*] ◇ **give somebody the slip** to get away from somebody who is chasing or pursuing you ◇ **let slip 1.** to say something without meaning to, or reveal something that should be kept secret **2.** to allow somebody or something to escape ◇ **slip one over on somebody** to trick or deceive somebody (*informal*)

WORD KEY: SYNONYMS

See Synonyms at ***mistake***.

slip up *vi.* to make a mistake (*informal*) ○ *Somebody slipped up and forgot to put your name on the guest list.*

slip[2] /slip/ *n.* **1.** BOT CUTTING a stem or branch of a plant broken off and used to start a new plant **2.** NARROW PIECE a narrow strip of something ○ *a slip of paper* **3.** DELICATE YOUNG PERSON somebody who is both young and slightly built ○ *a slip of a lad* **4.** SMALL PIECE OF PAPER a small piece of paper, especially a small form, document, or record of a transaction **5.** NARROW CHURCH PEW a church pew that is narrow ■ *vt.* **(slipped, slipping, slips)** BOT REMOVE A SLIP to remove a slip from a plant in order to grow a new plant

slip[3] /slip/ *n.* a mixture of clay and water, used as a decorative layer on pottery or for casting in molds to form an actual piece

SLIP /slip/ *n.* the older of two protocols for dial-up access to the Internet using a modem. It has now been largely replaced by a higher-level protocol (**PPP**). Full form **serial line Internet protocol**

slip·case /slíp kàyss/ *n.* a box for protecting a book or set of books, usually made of sturdy cardboard, with one or more open ends

slip·cov·er /slíp kùvvər/ *n.* COVER FOR FURNITURE a fitted protective cover for a piece of upholstered furniture, usually made of cloth ■ *vt.* **(-ered, -er·ing, -ers)** COVER FURNITURE to provide a piece of furniture with a slipcover

slip·knot /slíp nòt/, **slip knot** *n.* a knot that slips easily along the rope or cord around which it is tied

slip-on *n.* GARMENT EASY TO PUT ON a shoe or piece of clothing that is easy to put on or remove ■ *adj.* EASILY DONNED easy to put on and take off

slip·o·ver /slíp ōvər/ *n.* = **pullover**

slip·page /slíppij/ *n.* **1.** SLIDE the process or an instance of slipping, especially from a stable or desired position ○ *Recent thunderstorms have caused slippage in the banks along rivers.* **2.** AMOUNT OF SLIPPING an amount or extent that something slips **3.** DECLINE a decrease in the quality, performance, or production of something **4.** MECH ENG LOSS OF POWER a loss of power or forward motion caused by the slipping of a mechanical part

slip·per /slíppər/ *n.* a flat shoe of soft or lightweight material, usually worn indoors —**slip·pered** *adj.*

slip·per flow·er *n.* = **calceolaria**

slip·per·wort /slíppər wùrt, -wàwrt/ *n.* = **calceolaria**

slip·per·y /slíppəree/ **(-i·er, -i·est)** *adj.* **1.** CAUSING SLIDING likely to cause somebody or something to slip **2.** HARD TO HOLD FIRMLY sliding easily from the grasp or from a position **3.** PRECARIOUS unstable and liable to change ○ *We're in a slippery situation; things could go either way.* **4.** UNTRUSTWORTHY behaving in a devious or deceitful way ○ *a slippery character* —**slip·per·i·ly** *adv.* —**slip·per·i·ness** *n.*

slip·per·y dip *n. Aus* a long children's slide in a playground or funfair

slip·per·y elm *n.* **1.** TREES N AMERICAN TREE a deciduous North American hardwood tree with a moist sticky inner bark. Latin name: *Ulmus rubra.* **2.** ALTERN MED BARK OF SLIPPERY ELM the inner bark of the slippery elm used as a natural remedy in alternative medicine to relieve inflammation in the digestive tract

slip·pery slope *n.* a dangerous situation, e.g., in a military, political, foreign-policy, or legal situation, that can lead to ultimate downfall

slip ring *n.* a metal ring in a generator or motor to which current is delivered or from which it is removed by brushes

slip·sheet /slíp shèet/ *n.* BLANK PAPER a sheet of blank paper placed between newly printed sheets to prevent wet ink on the printed sheets from rubbing off or smearing ■ *vt.* **(-sheet·ed, -sheet·ing, -sheets)** INSERT BLANK PAPER BETWEEN PRINTED SHEETS to place a blank sheet of paper between newly printed papers on which the ink is still wet

slip·shod /slíp shòd/ *adj.* **1.** CARELESS done in a sloppy way without attention to details **2.** UNTIDY not neat in appearance [Late 16thC. From SLIP "to slide" + SHOD "wearing shoes."] —**slip·shod·di·ness** *n.* —**slip·shod·ness** *n.* —**slip·shod·ly** *adv.*

slip·slop /slíp slòp/ *n.* (*archaic*) **1.** WATERY FOOD weak or watery food or drink **2.** TRIVAL TALK OR WRITING inconsequential speech or writing [Late 17thC. Doubling of SLOP. "Trivial talk" from the character Mrs. Slipslop in *Joseph Andrews* (1742) by Henry Fielding (1707–54).]

slip stitch *n.* a stitch used to connect two layers of fabric in such a way that the stitches are hidden from the right side

slip·stream /slíp strèem/ *n.* **1.** AIR AIR FROM PROPELLER a stream of air driven backward by an aircraft's propeller **2.** AREA BEHIND FAST-MOVING VEHICLE an area of reduced air pressure and forward suction that is directly behind and caused by a rapidly moving vehicle ■ *vi.* **(-streamed, -stream·ing, -streams)** FOLLOW IN SLIPSTREAM to follow in another vehicle's slipstream so as to take advantage of the decreased air resistance

slip-up *n.* an accidental mistake or blunder (*informal*)

slip·ware /slíp wàir/ *n.* pottery that has been coated or decorated with slip

slip·way /slíp wày/ *n.* a sloping surface used to build or repair boats before returning them to the water

slit /slit/ *vt.* **(slit, slit·ting, slits) 1.** SLICE SOMETHING to make a long straight cut in something ○ *She slit the bag open with a knife.* **2.** CUT SOMETHING INTO STRIPS to cut something into thin strips ■ *n.* NARROW CUT OR OPENING a long narrow cut or opening [12thC, ultimately of prehistoric Germanic origin] —**slit·ter** *n.*

WORD KEY: SYNONYMS

See Synonyms at ***tear***.

slith·er /slíthər/ *v.* **(-ered, -er·ing, -ers) 1.** *vti.* SLIDE OR CAUSE SOMETHING TO SLIDE to move along a slippery or uneven surface, or make something slide along ○ *We slithered down the muddy river bank.* **2.** *vi.* GLIDE to slide along easily, using friction to move forward, as a snake does ■ *n.* GLIDING MOVEMENT a gliding, effortless movement [12thC. From Old English *slidrian*, literally "to slide repeatedly," from *slidan*, an earlier form of SLIDE.]

slit trench *n.* a narrow trench dug as protection against shelling during a battle

sliv·er /slívvər/ *n.* **1.** SPLINTER a thin piece of something that has been split, cut, or broken off **2.** SMALL PIECE a small narrow portion or piece of something **3.** LOOSE FIBER a loose strand of wool, cotton, or some other material prepared for drawing and twisting by carding ■ *vti.* **(-ered, -er·ing, -ers)** BREAK INTO SPLINTERS to break something into splinters, or become splintered [14thC. From Old English *-slīfan* "to cleave, split," from prehistoric Germanic.]

sliv·o·vitz /slívvə vits/ *n.* a dry colorless plum brandy made in eastern Europe [Late 19thC. From Serbo-Croat *sljivovica* "plum brandy," from *sljiva* "plum."]

Sloan /slōn/, **John** (1871–1951) U.S. artist. A member of the group of artists called The Eight, he is known for his paintings of urban life, which gave rise to the epithet "the Ashcan School". Full name **John French Sloan**

slob /slob/ *n.* an offensive term that deliberately insults somebody's personal habits, hygiene, and manners (*informal insult*) [Late 18thC. Via Irish *slab* "mud" from English *slab* "bog," from Scandinavian, and related to Swedish *slabb* "slime."] —**slob·bish** *adj.*

slob·ber /slóbbər/ *v.* **(-ber·ed, -ber·ing, -bers) 1.** *vti.* DRIBBLE SALIVA to drool or allow saliva or a liquid to run from the mouth **2.** *vi.* EXPRESS EXTREME EMOTION to be overly sentimental or emotional **3.** *vt.* SMEAR SOMETHING WITH SALIVA to soak or cover something with saliva or liquid from the mouth ■ *n.* **1.** SALIVA saliva or liquid that has been drooled from the mouth **2.** SENTIMENTAL WRITING OR TALK overemotional or sentimental talk or writing ○ *I can't stand to read such slobber.* [14thC. Origin uncertain: probably from Middle Dutch *slobberen* "to feed noisily, walk through mud."] —**slob·ber·er** *n.* —**slob·ber·y** *adj.*

slob ice *n. Can* floating ice in slushy masses

sloe /slō/ (*plural* **sloes** *or* **sloe**) *n.* **1.** = **blackthorn 2.** N AMERICAN PLUM TREE either of two eastern North American plum trees or shrubs that bear dark purple, red, or yellow fruit. Latin name: *Prunus alleghaniensis* and *Prunus americana.* **3.** SMALL TART PLUM the small sour fruit of the blackthorn or either species of sloe [Old English *slāh*. Ultimately from an Indo-European word meaning "bluish," which is also the ancestor of English *livid* and *slivovitz.*]

sloe-eyed *adj.* with dark almond-shaped eyes [Refers to the blue-black color of the fruit]

sloe gin *n.* a liqueur made of gin flavored with sloes

slog /slog/ *v.* **(slogged, slog·ging, slogs) 1.** *vi.* PLOD to walk slowly with great effort ○ *How long did it take us to slog up that mountain?* **2.** *vi.* WORK LONG AND HARD to work at something for a long time with little progress ○ *They've all been down at the office, slogging through endless reams of paperwork.* **3.** *vt.* MAKE YOUR WAY to make headway or progress through something with great difficulty ○ *We had to slog our way through several muddy fields.* **4.** *vt.* HIT SOMEBODY OR SOMETHING HARD to hit somebody or something with great force ○ *It was like being slogged by a heavyweight boxer.* ■ *n.* **1.** LONG HARD WALK a long difficult trip or walk ○ *It was quite a slog from the station to the hostel.* **2.** HARD WORK a long period of hard work ○ *It was a hard long slog during law school* **3.** HARD HIT a hard blow or swipe [Early 19thC. Origin uncertain: perhaps a variant of SLUG[3].] —**slog·ger** *n.*

slo·gan /slṓgən/ *n.* **1.** MOTTO a short distinctive phrase used to identify a company or organization or its goals **2.** ADVERTISING PHRASE a short catchy phrase used in advertising to promote something **3.** *Scotland* SCOTTISH BATTLE CRY the battle cry of a Highland clan (*archaic*) [Early 16thC. From Gaelic *sluagh-ghairm*, from *sluagh* "army" + *gairm* "cry." Originally "a battle cry."]

slo·gan·eer /slṓgə néer/ *n.* MAKER OF SLOGANS somebody who creates or frequently uses slogans ○ *the kind of politician who is little more than a clever sloganeer* ■ *vi.* **(-eered, -eer·ing, -eers)** MAKE UP SLOGANS to create or use slogans

slo·gan·ize /slṓgə nīz/ **(-ized, -iz·ing, -iz·es)** *vt.* to express something in a slogan or make a slogan of something ○ *the sloganizing of political ideals* —**slo·gan·iz·er** *n.*

sloop /sloop/ *n.* a single-masted sailing boat, rigged fore-and-aft, with one headsail extending from the foremast to the bowsprit [Early 17thC. Via Dutch *sloep* from French *chaloupe*, from Old French *chalupe* "sloop-rigged boat" (source of English *shallop*).]

sloop of war *n.* a small armed sailing ship that is

larger than a gunboat and carries guns on only one deck

slop[1] /slop/ *n.* **1. SOMETHING SPILLED** a liquid that has spilled or overflowed ○ *Look at all the slop on the floor!* **2. MUD OR SLUSH** soft mud or slushy snow ○ *How far do we have to wade through this slop?* **3. UNAPPEALING FOOD** poor-quality unappetizing or watery food (*often used in the plural*) **4.** BEVERAGES **MASH** what remains of the mash after an alcoholic beverage has been distilled (*often used in the plural*) **5. HUMAN WASTE** human waste such as urine **6. OVERLY SENTIMENTAL WRITING OR SPEECH** overly emotional or sentimental speech or writing without any literary value (*informal*) ○ *He has gotten rich by writing pure slop and is proud of it.* ■ **slops** *npl.* **HOG FEED** leftover food, especially kitchen waste, that is fed to hogs ■ *v.* **(slopped, slop·ping, slops) 1.** *vti.* **SPILL LIQUID** to spill a liquid, or be spilled on or over somebody or something **2.** *vi.* **WALK THROUGH MUD OR WATER** to trudge or splash through water, mud, or slush **3.** *vi.* **WRITE GUSHILY** to write or speak about something in an overly emotional or sentimental way (*informal*) **4.** *vt.* **SERVE FOOD MESSILY** to serve food in a careless and unappetizing way **5.** *vt.* AGRIC **FEED ANIMALS SLOPS** to feed kitchen waste to hogs and other livestock [14thC. From Old English *-sloppe* "dung," from a prehistoric Germanic word that is also the ancestor of English *slip* "clay and water."]

slop[2] /slop/ *n.* **SMOCK** a loose smock or overalls (*archaic*) ■ **slops** *npl.* **ITEMS SOLD TO SAILORS** clothes and personal articles that are sold from the ship's store to sailors on a merchant ship (*archaic*) [14thC. Origin uncertain: probably from Middle Dutch.]

slop ba·sin *n. U.K.* = **slop bowl**

slop bowl *n.* a bowl or other container into which tea or coffee dregs are emplied at the table

slope /slōp/ *n.* **1. SLANTED GROUND** ground that inclines slightly **2. SIDE OF A HILL OR MOUNTAIN** the part of a hill or mountain that is at an angle ○ *Let's hit the slopes and do some skiing!* **3. SLANT** a slant upward or downward, or the degree of such a slant **4. SOMETHING SLANTED** a line, surface, direction, or plane that is inclined **5.** MATH **TANGENT** the tangent of the angle between a straight line and the x-axis **6.** MATH **FIRST DERIVATIVE OF CURVE** the first derivative of a curve at a point **7. OFFENSIVE TERM** a highly offensive term that deliberately insults somebody of Asian, particularly Vietnamese, descent (*slang insult*) ■ *v.* **(sloped, slop·ing, slopes) 1.** *vti.* **GO UP OR DOWN** to ascend or descend, or make something ascend or descend ○ *From here, the road slopes gently down to the valley.* **2.** *vt.* **TAKE SOMETHING UP OR DOWN** to make something rise or descend gradually ○ *We had a landscaper slope the path through our garden.* **3.** *vi.* **BE AT A SLANT** to be at or have an angle that deviates from horizontal ○ *Does the floor in this room slope?* [Late 16thC. From assumed Old English *aslopen*, past participle of *aslupan* "to slip away," from *slupan* "to slip."] —**slop·er** *n.* —**slop·ing** *adj.*

slo-pitch *n.* = **slow-pitch**

slop·py /slóppee/ **(-pi·er, -pi·est)** *adj.* **1. MESSY** lacking order or tidiness **2. WET** slushy, muddy, or very wet **3. NOT DONE WELL** carelessly or badly done (*informal*) **4. GUSHY** overly sentimental or emotional (*informal*) **5.** COOK **WATERY** cooked or prepared in a way that results in excessive wateriness **6.** CLOTHES **BAGGY** loose-fitting so as to be casual and comfortable ○ *a big sloppy sweater* **7. DIRTY** splashed or covered with liquid

slop·py joe *n.* ground beef cooked in a spicy tomato sauce and served on a bun [Origin uncertain: *joe* probably from the name *Joe*]

slop·work /slóp wùrk/ *n.* **1. CHEAP CLOTHES OR THEIR MANUFACTURE** clothing or the manufacture of clothing that is cheap and of inferior quality (*dated*) **2. QUICK LOW-QUALITY WORK** any kind of work that has been done quickly and carelessly —**slop·work·er** *n.*

slosh /slosh/ *v.* **(sloshed, slosh·ing, slosh·es) 1.** *vt.* **SPILL LIQUID CLUMSILY** to spill or splash a liquid on or over something **2.** *vti.* **STIR SOMETHING IN LIQUID** to move or splash something, or move or splash in a liquid (*informal*) ○ *Slosh the shirt in some warm water before the stain sets.* **3.** *vi.* **WADE IN LIQUID** to wade or splash around in water, mud, or slush (*informal*) ■ *n.* **1. SLUSH** wet snow or mud **2. LIQUID SPLASHING** liquid splashing, or its sound ○ *We could hear the slosh of water against the docks all night because of the storm.* [Early 19thC. Probably a blend of SLOP "bog" and SLUSH.] —**slosh·y** *adj.*

sloshed /slosht/ *adj.* thoroughly intoxicated (*slang*)

slot[1] /slot/ *n.* **1. OPENING** a narrow vertical or horizontal opening into which something can be inserted ○ *Put the coin in the slot.* **2.** AEROSP **AIR PASSAGE** an air passage in an airfoil that directs air from the lower to the upper surface **3. SCHEDULED TIME** an assigned place and time in a sequence or schedule ○ *The station is moving the new comedy to a prime-time slot next month.* **4.** BUSINESS **JOB** a job or a position in a company or other organization **5.** ELEC ENG = **expansion slot** ■ *v.* **(slot·ted, slot·ting, slots) 1.** *vti.* **ASSIGN A PLACE TO SOMETHING** to put something in a specific place, position, or time ○ *We've slotted your appointment for three o'clock tomorrow afternoon.* **2.** *vt.* **MAKE SLOT IN SOMETHING** to cut a slot or slots in something [14thC. From Old French *esclot* "hollow of the breastbone," of unknown origin.]

slot in *vti.* to find a suitable time or place for somebody or something in a plan, organization, or series of events ○ *The doctor is busy this morning but she could slot you in at 2 o'clock.*

slot[2] /slot/ *n.* the track of an animal, especially a deer [Late 16thC. From Old French *esclot* "horse's hoofprint," of uncertain origin: probably from Old Norse *slóð* "track" (source of English *sleuth*).]

slot car *n.* an electronic toy racing car that is operated by a rheostat and has a pin underneath that fits into a groove on a slotted track

Sloth

sloth /slawth, slōth, sloth/ *n.* **1. SLOW-MOVING MAMMAL** a slow-moving mammal found in Central and South America that uses its long claws to hang upside down from tree branches. Genera: *Bradypus* and *Choloepus.* **2. LAZINESS** a dislike of work or any kind of physical exertion [12thC. Coined from SLOW + -TH.]

sloth bear *n.* a bear, native to India and Sri Lanka, with long shaggy fur and a long snout that enables it to feed on plants and insects. Latin name: *Melursus ursinus.*

sloth·ful /slóthf'l/ *adj.* disliking work or any form of physical exertion (*formal*) —**sloth·ful·ly** *adv.* —**sloth·ful·ness** *n.*

slot ma·chine *n.* **1. GAMBLING MACHINE** a gambling machine in which a player inserts coins or bills in a slot and pulls a lever that spins symbols in matching combinations that determine winnings **2. VENDING MACHINE** a coin-operated vending machine

slot rac·ing *n.* the racing of slot cars

slot·ter /slóttər/ *n.* somebody who places bets on a slot machine (*informal*)

slouch /slowch/ *v.* **(slouched, slouch·ing, slouch·es) 1.** *vti.* **WALK OR SIT IN A LAZY WAY** to stand, sit, or walk in a careless drooping way or make a part of the body droop carelessly ○ *He slouched his back and shoulders and leaned against the wall.* **2.** *vi.* **DROOP** to hang casually, often at an angle ○ *That child slouched all over the chair, watching TV all day.* ■ *n.* **1. EXTREMELY CASUAL POSTURE** an extremely relaxed or ungainly way of sitting, standing, or walking **2. LAZY OR INEPT PERSON** somebody who is unwilling or unable to do something well (*informal*) (*usually used in negative statements*) ○ *very good with children and no slouch around the house, either* [Early 16thC. Origin uncertain: probably from Scandanavian.] —**slouch·er** *n.* —**slouch·i·ly** *adv.* —**slouch·i·ness** *n.* —**slouch·y** *adj.*

slouch hat *n.* a hat made of a soft material, e.g., felt, that has a broad drooping brim

slough[1] /sloo, slow/, **slew** /sloo/ *n.* **1. DEEP MUDDY HOLE** a hole or low area in the ground filled with mud or water **2. slough, slew, slue SWAMPY AREA** a stagnant area of water connected to a larger body of water such as a marsh, inlet, bayou, or backwater **3. ESTUARY** a saltwater estuary **4. HOLE FILLED WITH WATER** on the prairies, a low area filled with water, especially from melting snow **5. SPIRITUAL LOW POINT** deep despair or disgrace [Old English *slōh*, ultimately of unknown origin] —**slough·y** *adj.*

slough[2] /sluf/, **sluff** *n.* **1.** ZOOL **DEAD OUTER COVERING** the dead outer skin shed by a reptile or an amphibian **2.** MED **DEAD TISSUE LAYER** a layer of dead skin that separates from healthy skin after an infection or inflammation **3.** CARDS **DISCARDED CARD** in card games, a card that has been discarded **4. SOMETHING CAST OFF** something discarded or shed ■ *v.* **(sloughed, slough·ing, sloughs; sluffed, sluff·ing, sluffs) 1.** *vti.* **CAST SOMETHING OFF** to shed something, or be shed ○ *Snakes slough off their dead skins.* **2.** *vi.* MED **SEPARATE FROM HEALED TISSUE** to separate from surrounding healthy skin (*refers to dead skin*) **3.** *vt.* **DISCARD SOMETHING OR SOMEBODY** to get rid of somebody or something that is no longer wanted or needed ○ *She sloughs off friends when she no longer has a use for them.* **4.** *vt.* **IGNORE SOMETHING** to pay no attention to something **5.** *vti.* CARDS **DISCARD CARD** to get rid of an unwanted card **6.** *vt.* **SKIP SOMETHING UNWANTED** to skip something unwanted, especially school (*regional*) [14thC. Origin uncertain.]

WORD KEY: REGIONAL NOTE

To *slough* school is a Nevada usage.

slough of de·spond /slòò-, slòw-/ *n.* a state of extreme despair and depression [Named for the deep bog in *Pilgrim's Progress, Part 1* (1678) by John Bunyan (1628–88) that Christian has to cross to reach the Wicket Gate]

Slo·vak /slṓ vàk/, **Slo·va·ki·an** /slō vákee ən/ *n.* **1.** PEOPLES **SOMEBODY FROM SLOVAKIA** somebody who was born or raised in Slovakia or who is a citizen of Slovakia **2.** LANG **LANGUAGE OF SLOVAKIA** the national language of Slovakia, a member of the Slavic group of Indo-European languages. Slovak is spoken by over five million people. ■ *adj.* **1. OF SLOVAKIA** relating to or typical of Slovakia or its people or culture **2.** LANG **OF SLOVAK** relating to the Slovak language

Slovakia

Slo·vak·i·a /slō vaákee ə/ republic in eastern central Europe. It was part of Czechoslovakia until 1993. Language: Slovak. Currency: Slovak koruna. Capital: Bratislava. Population: 5,343,000 (1996). Area: 18,932 sq. mi./49,035 sq. km. Official name **Slovak Republic**

Slo·va·ki·an *n., adj.* PEOPLES, LANG = **Slovak**

slov·en /slúvv'n/ *n.* an offensive term that deliberately insults somebody who is not concerned about conventional standards of personal hygiene and tidiness (*insult*) [15thC. Origin uncertain: probably from Middle Flemish *sloovin* "a scold."]

Slo·vene /slṓ veen/, **Slo·ve·ni·an** /slō veénee ən/ *n.* **1.** PEOPLES **SOMEBODY FROM SLOVENIA** somebody who was born, raised in, or is a citizen of Slovenia **2.** LANG **LANGUAGE OF SLOVENIA** the national language of Slovenia, belonging to the Slavic group of Indo-European languages. Slovene is spoken by about two million people. ■ *adj.* **1. OF SLOVENIA** relating to Slovenia or its people or culture **2.** LANG **OF SLOVENE** relating to the Slovene language

Slo·ve·ni·a /slō veénee ə/ republic in eastern Europe, on the Balkan Peninsula. It was part of Yugoslavia until 1991. Language: Slovene. Currency: tolar. Capital: Ljubljana. Population: 1,991,000 (1996). Area: 7,820 sq. mi./20,254 sq. km. Official name **Republic of Slovenia**

Slovenia

Slo·ve·ni·an *n., adj.* PEOPLES, LANG = **Slovene**

slov·en·ly /slúvv'nlee/ (**-li·er, -li·est**) *adj.* an offensive term used to describe somebody who is not concerned about conventional standards of personal hygiene and tidiness

slow /slō/ *adj.* **1. NOT FAST** not moving quickly or at a fast pace **2. LENGTHY** taking a long time to do or create something ○ *Writing software is a slow process.* **3. TAKING TOO MUCH TIME** requiring more time than is usual or expected **4. NOT KEEPING ACCURATE TIME** showing a time that is earlier than the correct time ○ *I was late for my appointment because my watch was slow.* **5. HESITANT** doing something hesitantly or unwillingly ○ *Why were you so slow to answer my question?* **6. SLUGGISH** lacking the usual volume of sales or customers ○ *Business is usually slow during the summer months.* **7. OFFENSIVE TERM** an offensive term that deliberately insults somebody's imagination or intelligence **8. DULL** lacking in interest or activity ○ *The acting was good but the plot was terribly slow.* **9.** COOK **WARM** operating at a low temperature that ensures thorough cooking throughout ○ *Turkey should be cooked in a slow oven.* **10.** SPORTS **REDUCING SPEED OF BALL OR RUNNER** tending to reduce the speed or ability to travel of a ball, runner, or other competitor ○ *That horse usually wins on a slow track.* ■ *adv.* **1. BEHIND** behind the correct time or pace ○ *My watch seems to be running slow.* **2. AT A LOW SPEED** at a reduced speed or pace ○ *The law requires motorists to drive slow through school zones.* ■ *vti.* (**slowed, slow·ing, slows**) **1. MAKE SOMETHING SLOW** to make somebody or something slow or slower, or become slow or slower ○ *Could you slow your speed a little on those sharp turns?* **2. DELAY OR BE DELAYED** to reduce the speed or progress of something, or become reduced in speed or progress [Old English *slaw* "sluggish"] —**slow·ly** *adv.* —**slow·ness** *n.*

WORD KEY: USAGE

slowly or **slow**? The normal adverb is ***slowly***: *The car moved slowly up the hill.* ***Slow*** is used as an adverb (*Don't walk so slow*) in expressions such as *go slow,* and *slow-moving.*

slow burn, slow boil *n.* a steadily growing anger (*informal*) ○ *doing a slow burn*

slow·coach /slṓ kòch/ *n. U.K.* = **slowpoke** (*informal*)

slow·down /slṓ dòwn/ *n.* an intentional reduction in pace or production by workers in order to win demands from their employer

slow-foot·ed *adj.* happening or proceeding at an extremely slow pace ○ *Congress has been slow-footed in passing the bill.* —**slow-foot·ed·ness** *n.*

slow lo·ris *n.* a small slow-moving primate found in Indonesia that has a rounded, almost tailless body. Latin name: *Nycticebus coucang.*

slow match *n.* a flameless match or fuse that burns very slowly or at a known rate, used to set off explosives

slow mo·tion *n.* a method of filming action at a rate faster than the normal projection rate, so that it appears on the screen at a slower-than-normal rate

slow-mo·tion *adj.* **1. SLOWED-DOWN** photographed or shown in slow motion **2. HAPPENING SLOWLY** taking place at a slower pace than normal ○ *her slow-motion reaction*

slow neu·tron *n.* a relatively slow-moving neutron that possesses less than 100 electronvolts of kinetic energy and is capable of bringing about nuclear fission

slow-pitch, slo-pitch *n.* a kind of softball in which there are ten players on a team and the pitched ball must travel in an arc from three to ten feet high

slow·poke /slṓ pòk/ *n.* somebody who moves, acts, responds, or works very slowly (*informal*) ○ *C'mon you slowpokes! We'll be late for the movie.* [Mid-19thC. *Poke* from POKE in the sense "dawdling person."]

slow vi·rus *n.* any virus or agent resembling a virus that causes diseases with very long incubation periods. Technical name **lentivirus**

slow·worm /slṓ wùrm/ *n.* a legless lizard with a smooth body resembling that of a snake. It feeds chiefly on slugs and is found in Europe, northern Africa, and western Asia. Latin name: *Anguis fragilis.* [Old English *slāwyrm* (altered by folk etymology), from *slā* "slowworm" (of unknown origin) + *wyrm* "worm"]

SLR *abbr.* single-lens reflex

slub /slub/ *n.* **1. KNOT IN YARN** a lump in yarn or fabric that is sometimes an imperfection, but is often made to provide a knobby effect **2. TWISTED THREAD** a loosely twisted roll of fiber, e.g., of silk or cotton, prepared for spinning ■ *vt.* (**slubbed, slub·bing, slubs**) **PREPARE FIBER FOR SPINNING** to draw out and twist a strand of fiber to prepare it for spinning [Early 19thC. Origin unknown.]

sludge /sluj/ *n.* **1. SLUSH** wet material, especially watery mud or snow **2. SOLID WASTE** the solids in sewage that separate out during treatment **3. SEDIMENT** a solid deposit found at the bottom of a liquid **4. BROKEN ICE** a layer of broken or half-formed ice on a body of water, especially the sea **5.** MED **MASS OF BLOOD CELLS** a sticky grouping of blood cells that form a mass and hinder the circulation of blood [Mid-17thC. Origin uncertain: possibly from obsolete *slutch* "mud, mire," or a variant of SLUSH.] —**sludg·y** *adj.*

slue[1] /sloo/, **slew** *vti.* (**slued, slu·ing, slues; slewed, slew·ing, slews**) **1. PIVOT AROUND AN AXIS** to pivot or turn, or cause something to pivot or turn, around an axis **2. VEER OR SKID** to swerve or skid sideways, or cause something to swerve or skid sideways off course ■ *n.* **1. VEERING OR SKIDDING** an act of swerving or skidding sideways **2. POSITION AFTER SOMETHING SLUES** a position in which something stops after it slues [Variant of SLEW "alternative for slough" and SLEW "to turn"]

slue[2] *n.* = **slough**[1] *n.* 2

slue[3] *n.* = **slew**[2]

sluff *n., vti.* = **slough**[2]

slug[1] /slug/ *n.* **1.** ARMS **BULLET** a metal projectile that is fired from a gun or rifle **2.** BEVERAGES **DRINK OF SOMETHING** a single shot of a strong alcoholic drink (*informal*) **3. DISK USED AS ILLEGAL COIN** a small metal disk, made in the shape and size of a coin, used to purchase something illegally, especially from a vending machine **4.** PRINTING **TYPE METAL** a strip of type metal, less than type-high, used for spacing in traditional hot-metal printing **5.** PRINTING **LINE OF TYPE** a strip of cast type in a single strip of metal in traditional hot-metal printing **6.** PRINTING **TEMPORARY TYPE LINE** a temporary type line inserted in copy that carries identifying marks or a compositor's instructions **7.** MANUF **METAL OR GLASS BLANK FOR PROCESSING** a metal or glass blank that will receive further processing **8.** MEASURE **UNIT OF MASS** a foot-pound-second unit of mass equal to 32.17 pounds that will acquire an acceleration of one foot per second per second when acted on by a 1 pound force ■ *vt.* **1. DRINK SOMETHING QUICKLY** to gulp down a drink (*informal*) **2.** PRINTING **ADD SLUGS** to add printers' slugs to copy in traditional hot-metal printing [Early 17thC. Originally "bullet," of uncertain origin: perhaps from SLUG[2], from the similarity in shape. "Drink" may have come from Gaelic *slog* "swallow."]

slug[2] /slug/ *n.* **1.** ZOOL **MOLLUSK WITHOUT A SHELL** a small slow-moving terrestrial mollusk that resembles a snail but has no shell, or only a rudimentary one. Order: Stylommatophora. **2.** INSECTS **LARVA** a soft smooth larva of some insects, e.g., that of the sawfly **3.** CELL BIOL **CELLS THAT DEVELOP INTO SPORE-BEARING STRUCTURE** a sticky mass of cells from which the sporophore of a slime mold develops **4. OFFENSIVE TERM** an offensive term that deliberately insults somebody's level of energy or activity (*insult*) [15thC. Origin uncertain: probably from Scandinavian, and related to Norwegian dialect *slugg* "large heavy body."]

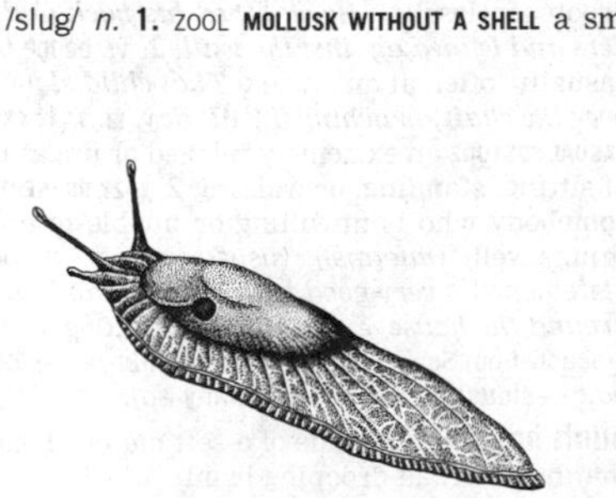
Slug

slug[3] /slug/ *vt.* (**slugged, slug·ging, slugs**) **HIT SOMEBODY OR SOMETHING HARD** to strike somebody or something very hard with the fist or a bat ■ *n.* **HARD HIT** a hard strike or blow [Mid-19thC. Origin uncertain: probably ultimately from a prehistoric Germanic word meaning "to hit," which is also the ancestor of English *slog* and *slay.*] ◇ **slug it out** to fight to a conclusion (*informal*)

slug[4] /slug/ *n.* a commuter who is not a member of an organized car pool and who hitches rides at established pickup points, hoping for an empty seat (*slang*) [Origin unknown]

slug·a·bed /slúggə bèd/ *n.* somebody who likes to stay in bed later than other people (*archaic*) [Late 16thC. From SLUG[2] + ABED.]

slug·fest /slúg fèst/ *n.* **1. BRAWL** a long fight in which many heavy blows are exchanged (*slang*) **2.** BASEBALL **BASEBALL GAME WITH MANY HITS** a baseball game in which both teams make many hits and score many runs **3. HEATED ARGUMENT** an intense debate or dispute

slug·gard /slúggərd/ *n.* **LAZY PERSON** somebody who avoids work or physical exertion (*archaic*) ■ *adj.* **LAZY** sluggishly lazy [14thC. Formed from SLUG[2].] —**slug·gard·li·ness** *n.* —**slug·gard·ly** *adj.* —**slug·gard·ness** *n.*

slug·ger /slúggər/ *n.* **1. FIGHTER** somebody who delivers very hard blows during a fight **2.** BASEBALL **GOOD HITTER** a baseball player who hits many extra-base hits [Formed from SLUG[3]]

slug·ging av·er·age, slug·ging per·cent·age *n.* the total number of bases reached on hits by a baseball player divided by the number of official times at bat, expressed as a three-digit decimal

slug·gish /slúggish/ *adj.* **1. NOT MOVING MUCH** inactive and moving slowly or very little **2. NOT VERY RESPONSIVE** slow to react or to respond to stimulation **3. LACKING ALERTNESS AND ENERGY** not alert and showing little energy or vitality —**slug·gish·ly** *adv.* —**slug·gish·ness** *n.*

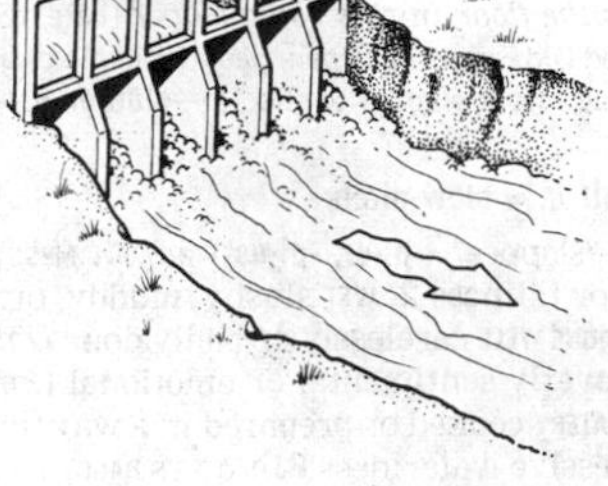
Sluice

sluice /slooss/ *n.* **1. WATER CHANNEL** an artificial channel for a flow of water that is controlled by a valve or gate **2. FLOODGATE** a valve or floodgate that controls the water in a sluice **3. WATER BEHIND FLOODGATE** a body of water contained by a floodgate **4. DRAINAGE CHANNEL** a channel for carrying away excess water **5. TROUGH** a long inclined trough used to separate gold ore from sand or gravel **6. CHANNEL TO MOVE LOGS** an artificial stream or channel for floating logs ■ *v.* (**sluiced, sluic·ing, sluic·es**) **1.** *vt.* **FLUSH SOMETHING WITH WATER** to flood or clean something with a sudden heavy flow of water **2.** *vt.* **WASH GOLD** to wash gold or other minerals in water flowing in a sluice **3.** *vti.* **RELEASE SOMETHING FROM A SLUICE** to flow from or let something out of a sluice **4.** *vt.* **MOVE SOMETHING IN SLUICE** to float something, especially logs, down a sluice [14thC. Via Old French *escluse* from Latin *exclus-*, past participle stem of *excludere* "to shut out" (see EXCLUDE). Altered by folk etymology by association with JUICE.]

sluice·gate /slooss gàyt/ *n.* = **sluice** *n.* 2

sluice·way /slo͞os wày/ *n.* an artificial channel into which water flows from a sluice

slum /slum/ *n.* POOR AREA an overcrowded area of a city in which the housing is typically in very bad condition (*often used in the plural*) ■ *v.* (**slummed, slum·ming** *or* **slummed, slums**) **1.** ACCEPT LOWER STANDARDS THAN USUAL to stay in or go to a place that you would usually consider unacceptable (*often used humorously*) ○ *We'll have to slum it and stay here until we can find a better place.* **2.** *vi.* VISIT SLUMS to go into a slum out of curiosity [Mid-19thC. From the earlier expression *back slum* "street housing poor people" in which *slum* meant "room" (of unknown origin).] —**slum·mer** *n.*

slum·ber /slúmbər/ *vi.* (**-bered, -ber·ing, -bers**) **1.** SLEEP to be asleep **2.** BE IN QUIET STATE to be in a state of inactivity or rest ■ *n.* **1.** SLEEPING the state of being asleep, or a period of sleep ○ *A loud noise disturbed my slumber.* **2.** INACTIVITY a state of being dormant or quiet [14thC. Alteration of obsolete *sloom*, from Old English *slūma* "light sleep," from prehistoric Germanic.] —**slum·ber·less** *adj.*

slum·ber·ous /slúmbərəss/ *adj.* **1.** DROWSY feeling sleepy **2.** INACTIVE characterized by inactivity or sluggishness ○ *A slumberous atmosphere seemed to stifle sound and motion in the town.* **3.** CAUSING SLEEP inducing lethargy or sleep ○ *She dozed in the slumberous heat of the afternoon.* —**slum·ber·ous·ly** *adv.* —**slum·ber·ous·ness** *n.*

slum·ber par·ty *n.* a party at which a group of teenage girls, wearing nightgowns or pajamas, talk, eat, and stay overnight at one of the girls' homes

slum·gul·lion /slum gúllyən, slúm gùllyən/ *n.* a watery meat stew (*informal*) [Mid-19thC. Origin uncertain: perhaps from *slum* "sludge" (from German *Schlamm*) + obsolete *gullion* "mud, cesspool," from Irish Gaelic *goilín* "pit."]

slum·lord /slúm làwrd/ *n.* somebody who owns housing in slum areas, especially somebody who overcharges for rent and does not maintain or repair the buildings [Mid-20thC. Blend of SLUM and LANDLORD.]

slump /slump/ *vi.* (**slumped, slump·ing, slumps**) **1.** COLLAPSE to sink or fall suddenly and heavily **2.** SLOUCH to have a hunched drooping posture ○ *She was slumped over her desk.* **3.** DECREASE to decline suddenly and sharply in value ○ *stock prices slumped* ■ *n.* **1.** SLOUCHED POSTURE a drooping or hunched posture **2.** ECONOMIC RECESSION a sudden decline in business, stock prices, or productivity ○ *an economy fluctuating between boom and slump* **3.** PERIOD OF POOR PERFORMANCE a relatively long period of time during which somebody or something, e.g., an employee, athlete, or team fails to perform well ○ *If he doesn't pull out of his slump, his job may be in jeopardy.* [Mid-17thC. Origin uncertain: perhaps from Scandinavian.]

slump·fla·tion /slùmp fláysh'n/ *n.* an economic situation in which an economic depression is accompanied by increasing inflation [Late 20thC. Blend of SLUMP and INFLATION.]

slung past tense, past participle of **sling**

slung·shot /slúng shòt/ *n.* a weight or weights attached to the end of a cord and used as a weapon

slunk past tense, past participle of **slink**

slur /slur/ *v.* (**slurred, slur·ring, slurs**) **1.** *vti.* SPEAK INDISTINCTLY to pronounce sounds or words so that they cannot be distinguished **2.** *vt.* DEMEAN SOMEBODY to speak of somebody in an insulting or demeaning way **3.** *vt.* GLOSS OVER SOMETHING to ignore something or treat it superficially ○ *The committee slurred over my protests.* **4.** *vt.* MUSIC PERFORM MUSIC SMOOTHLY to play musical notes in a smooth, uninterrupted way **5.** *vti.* SMEAR OR BE SMEARED to blur or smear wet ink on a page, or be blurred or smeared ■ *n.* **1.** INSULT an insulting or demeaning statement about somebody **2.** SLURRED PRONUNCIATION an indistinct pronunciation or sound **3.** MUSIC MUSIC SYMBOL a curved line that connects two or more notes on a score, indicating that they are to be performed smoothly **4.** BLURRED IMAGE an image that has been smeared or blurred [Early 17thC. Origin uncertain.]

slurb /slurb/ *n.* an ugly suburban area in which the housing is crowded or badly built (*informal*) [Mid-20thC. Blend of SLUM and SUBURB.]

slurp /slurp/ *vti.* (**slurped, slurp·ing, slurps**) DRINK SOMETHING NOISILY to make a loud sucking sound while drinking or eating something ○ *Would you stop slurping your milkshake?* ■ *n.* **1.** SUCKING SOUND a loud sucking sound made while drinking or eating **2.** LIQUID MOUTHFUL a mouthful of a liquid (*informal*) ○ *Can I have a slurp of your soda?* [Mid-17thC. From Dutch *slurpen*, of uncertain origin: perhaps an imitation of the sound.] —**slurp·ing·ly** *adv.*

slur·ry /slúr ree/ (*plural* **-ries**) *n.* a liquid mixture of water and an insoluble solid material, e.g., cement or clay [15thC. Formed from SLUR.]

slush /slush/ *n.* **1.** MELTING SNOW OR ICE snow or ice that has begun to melt **2.** SEMILIQUID SUBSTANCE a solid substance such as mud that has become wet and sloppy **3.** NAUT GREASE FROM SHIP'S GALLEY the waste grease or fat produced by a ship's galley **4.** GREASE a greasy substance used to lubricate machine parts **5.** OVERLY SENTIMENTAL EXPRESSION extremely sentimental speech or writing **6.** BEVERAGES ICE DRINK a drink made of finely crushed ice with a flavored syrup poured over it ■ *v.* (**slushed, slush·ing, slush·es**) **1.** *vt.* ENG GREASE MACHINERY to lubricate the parts of a machine **2.** *vt.* BUILDING PUT MORTAR IN JOINTS to fill masonry joints with mortar, or cover a surface with cement **3.** *vt.* SOAK SOMETHING WITH SLUSH to splash or cover something with mud or slush **4.** *vi.* WALK THROUGH SLUSH to walk through wet snow or mud ○ *It had been raining so hard we had to slush through mud to get there.* **5.** *vi.* MAKE A SPLASHING SOUND to make a splashing or squelching sound [Mid-17thC. Origin uncertain: perhaps an imitation of the sound of splashing, or from Scandinavian.]

slush fund *n.* **1.** CRIMINOL MONEY FOR ILLEGAL ACTIVITIES money set aside by a business or other organization for corrupt activities such as the bribery of public officials **2.** FIN MONEY FOR ENTERTAINMENT money set aside to use for fun or entertainment expenses **3.** NAUT LUXURY FUND FOR SHIP'S CREW money raised by selling refuse and garbage from a ship to pay for small luxuries for the crew [From the money gained from selling a ship's *slush*, the grease collected in a ship's galley. "Money used for bribes" comes from "greasing" somebody's palm with money.]

slush pile *n.* a pile of unsolicited manuscripts accumulated in a publisher's office (*informal*)

slush·y /slúshee/ (**-i·er, -i·est**) *adj.* **1.** FULL OF SLUSH covered with or full of melting snow and ice **2.** RESEMBLING SLUSH with the consistency of slush **3.** OVERLY SENTIMENTAL filled with or expressing excessive sentiment ○ *a slushy love story* —**slush·i·ness** *n.*

slut /slut/ *n.* **1.** OFFENSIVE TERM a highly offensive term for a woman thought by others to be sexually promiscuous (*insult*) **2.** OFFENSIVE TERM an offensive term for a woman who charges for engaging in sexual activities (*insult*) **3.** OFFENSIVE TERM a highly offensive term for a woman who is not concerned about conventional standards of domestic cleanliness (*insult dated*) [15thC. Origin uncertain.] —**slut·tish** *adj.* —**slut·tish·ly** *adv.* —**slut·tish·ness** *n.* —**slut·ty** *adj.*

SLV *abbr.* standard launch vehicle *or* space launch vehicle

sly /slī/ (**sli·er, sli·est**) *adj.* **1.** CRAFTY cleverly skillful and cunning **2.** EVASIVE lacking honesty or straightforwardness **3.** MISCHIEVOUS full of playful mischief [13thC. From Old Norse *slœgr* "clever, crafty," literally "able to strike" (source of English *sleight*).] —**sly·ly** *adv.* —**sly·ness** *n.* ◇ **on the sly** without the knowledge or permission of others

sly·boots /slī bo͝ots/ *n.* an offensive term for somebody considered to be cunning or devious (*informal insult*) (*takes a singular verb*)

slype /slīp/ *n.* a covered passage in a cathedral or church that joins the transept to a chapter house [Mid-19thC. Origin uncertain: perhaps a variant of obsolete *slipe*, from SLIP; or from Dutch dialect or West Flemish *slijpe* "secret path."]

Sm *symbol.* samarium

SM[1] *abbr.* **1.** station master **2.** stage manager **3.** service mark

SM[2], **S.M.** *abbr.* **1.** sergeant major **2.** Soldier's Medal **3.** Master of Science

sm. *abbr.* small

S/M, S-M *abbr.* sadomasochism

SMA *abbr.* sergeant major of the army

smack[1] /smak/ *v.* (**smacked, smack·ing, smacks**) **1.** *vti.* SLAP SOMEBODY to hit somebody with a quick stinging and usually noisy blow with the palm of the hand **2.** *vi.* HIT AGAINST SOMETHING NOISILY to strike against, collide with, or land in something with a sharp loud noise **3.** *vt.* PRESS LIPS TOGETHER to press together and then open the lips with a short loud noise ■ *n.* **1.** SLAP a sharp quick blow with the palm of the hand **2.** NOISY SOUND a sharp loud noise made when one thing strikes another **3.** LOUD KISS a brief noisy kiss ■ *adv.* **1.** WITH A LOUD NOISE with a sharp loud noise or collision **2.** DIRECTLY directly or precisely ○ *I was smack in the middle of getting ready to leave when you called.* [Mid-16thC. From Middle Low German *smacken* "to open the lips noisily," an imitation of the sound.]

smack[2] /smak/ *n.* **1.** DISTINCTIVE TASTE a unique flavor or taste of something **2.** HINT a small amount or trace ■ *vi.* (**smacked, smack·ing, smacks**) **1.** BE DISTINCTIVELY FLAVORED to have a unique flavor or taste **2.** EXPRESS SOMETHING INDIRECTLY to suggest or hint at something ○ *an editorial that smacked of snobbery* [Old English *smæc* "taste," from prehistoric Germanic]

smack[3] /smak/ *n.* a sailing vessel used for fishing, usually for carrying the catch to market [Early 17thC. From Dutch *smak*, of unknown origin.]

smack[4] /smak/ *n.* heroin (*slang*) [Mid-20thC. Origin uncertain: probably an alteration of *schmeck* "drug," from Yiddish, "sniff," ultimately from Middle High German *smecken* "to smell."]

smack-dab *adj.* straight or directly (*informal*) ○ *I landed smack-dab in a huge mud puddle.*

smack·er /smákər/ *n.* (*informal*) **1.** LOUD KISS a noisy smacking kiss **2.** DOLLAR a dollar

smack·ing /smáking/ *adj.* very brisk or lively ○ *a smacking breeze*

small /smawl/ *adj.* **1.** LITTLE of a relatively little size ○ *a small animal* **2.** NOT MUCH little in quantity or value ○ *a small sum of money* **3.** INSIGNIFICANT unimportant or trivial ○ *a small matter* **4.** LIMITED operating on a limited scale ○ *small businesses* **5.** MINOR lacking in power, influence, or status **6.** NOT YET MATURE young or not fully grown ○ *small children* **7.** ORDINARY humble or modest ○ *He came from small beginnings.* **8.** MEAN petty and mean-spirited **9.** LOWER-CASE in lower case rather than capitals ○ *small letters* **10.** WITHOUT SELF-RESPECT humiliated or feeling little self-worth ○ *Her criticisms and ridicule made me feel very small.* **11.** NOT STRONG lacking in strength (*archaic*) ○ *a small sound* ■ *adv.* **1.** IN SMALL PIECES in or into little pieces ○ *Cut it up small.* **2.** IN A SMALL WAY in a moderate or limited way ○ *start out small* **3.** QUIETLY quietly or softly (*archaic*) ■ *n.* **1.** NARROW PART a part of something that is narrower or smaller than the rest of it ○ *the small of the back* **2.** CLOTHES SIZE FOR SOMEBODY SMALL a size or a garment in a size that fits somebody who is of less than average proportions ■ **smalls** *npl.* **1.** LITTLE THINGS small things or products (*informal*) **2.** *U.K.* UNDERGARMENTS items of underwear (*informal or humorous*) [Old English *smæl* "slender, small," from a prehistoric Germanic word meaning "small animal"] —**small·ish** *adj.* —**small·ness** *n.*

small arms *n.* firearms such as pistols and rifles that can be held in one or both hands while firing

small beer *n.* **1.** TRIVIA something of little or no importance (*informal*) ○ *A thousand dollars is small beer to folks like him.* **2.** WEAK BEER weak or inferior beer (*dated*)

small-bore *adj.* used to describe .22-caliber firearms or ammunition.

small cal·o·rie *n.* = **calorie** *n.* 1

small cap·i·tal *n.* a capital letter that is the same height as a lower-case letter

small-claims court *n.* a local court that has jurisdiction to try civil actions involving claims worth only a small sum of money

small·clothes /smáwl klṓthz/ *npl.* close-fitting knee breeches worn by men in the 18th century (*archaic*)

Smal·ley /smáwlee/, **Richard E.** (*b.* 1943) U.S. chemical physicist. He discovered the molecular family of carbon called fullerenes, and shared a Nobel Prize in chemistry (1996).

small fry *npl.* **1.** CHILDREN young children (*informal*) **2.** YOUNG FISH young, immature, or small fish **3.** TRIVIAL THINGS people, events, or issues that are thought to be of little importance

small game *n.* small animals and birds that are hunted for sport

small hours *n.* the early morning hours after midnight

small in·tes·tine *n.* the part of the intestine between the stomach and large intestine, consisting of the duodenum, jejunum, and ileum, where digestion of food and most absorption of nutrients takes place

small-mind·ed *adj.* an offensive term for somebody who is considered to be petty and intolerant of the ideas and beliefs of others —**small-mind·ed·ly** *adv.* —**small-mind·ed·ness** *n.*

small·mouth bass /smáwl mowth bàss/ *n.* a greenish-brown freshwater bass of North America that is found in clear streams and lakes and is a popular gamefish. Latin name: *Micropterus dolomieu.*

small po·ta·toes *npl.* somebody or something considered to be unimportant or trivial (*informal*) ○ *A thousand dollars is small potatoes to him.* [Refers to potatoes too small to be worth cleaning or peeling]

small·pox /smáwl pòks/ *n.* a highly contagious disease caused by a poxvirus and marked by high fever and the formation of scar-producing pustules. A worldwide inoculation program has virtually eradicated the smallpox virus from the human population. Technical name **variola**

small print *n.* = **fine print**

small-scale *adj.* **1.** LIMITED limited in scope or size **2.** SMALL IN SIZE made or constructed on a small scale ○ *She built a small-scale replica of the ship.*

small screen *n.* the medium of television, especially as distinct from the movies (*informal*)

small slam *n.* = **little slam**

small stores *npl.* small items such as clothing sold on a ship or at a naval base

small·sword /smáwl sàwrd/ *n.* a light sword used in the 17th and 18th centuries for dueling and fencing (*archaic*)

small talk *n.* polite conversation about matters of little importance, especially between people who do not know each other well

small-time *adj.* of minor importance or influence (*informal*) ○ *He's just a small-time crook.*

smalt /smawlt/ *n.* **1.** BLUE GLASS a kind of silica glass that has been colored a deep blue by cobalt oxide **2.** PIGMENT a deep blue pigment made by crushing smalt [Mid-16thC. Via French from Italian *smalto* SMALTO.]

smalt·ite /smáwl tìt/ *n.* a naturally occurring blue-gray arsenide of cobalt and nickel that is an important ore of cobalt

smal·to /smáwltō/ *n.* small bits of pottery, glass, and tiles used in mosaics [Early 18thC. From Italian, ultimately from prehistoric Germanic.]

sma·ragd /smá ràgd/ (*plural* **-ragds** *or* **-rag·des** /-ràgdəz/) *n.* any green gemstone, e.g., an emerald (*archaic*) [13thC. From Latin *smaragdus*, from Greek *smaragdos*, ultimately from Hebrew *bāreqet* "emerald," from *bāraq* "flash, sparkle."] —**sma·rag·dine** /smə rág din/ *adj.*

sma·rag·dite /smə rág dìt/ *n.* a fibrous green amphibole mineral

smarm /smaarm/ (**smarmed, smarm·ing, smarms**) *n.* (*informal*) **1.** SELF-SERVING FLATTERY ingratiating or servile flattery **2.** INSINCERE CHARM charm that is distastefully self-conscious or insincere [Early 20thC. Origin unknown.]

smarm·y /smáarmee/ (**-i·er, -i·est**) *adj.* **1.** EXCESSIVELY INGRATIATING self-servingly earnest and ingratiating in manner **2.** INSINCERELY CHARMING charming in a distastefully self-conscious or insincere way (*informal*) [Early 20thC. Formed from SMARM.] —**smarm·i·ly** *adv.* —**smarm·i·ness** *n.*

smart /smaart/ *adj.* **1.** CLEVER showing intelligence and mental alertness ○ *smart students* **2.** KEEN shrewd and calculating in business and other dealings ○ *a smart dealer* **3.** WITTY AND AMUSING amusingly clever and possessing a quick wit **4.** INSOLENT disrespectful or impertinent ○ *Whatever you say to him he has some smart answer.* **5.** TIDY with a neat and well-cared-for appearance **6.** FASHIONABLE fashionable and stylish ○ *smart restaurants* **7.** LIVELY vigorous and brisk ○ *a smart pace* **8.** STINGING causing a sharp stinging sensation ○ *a smart slap* **9.** MIL LASER- OR RADIO-GUIDED used to describe a missile or weapon that is guided to its target by laser or radio beams **10.** ELECTRON ENG ELECTRONIC with a built-in microprocessor ○ *smart traffic signals* ■ *vi.* (**smart·ed, smart·ing, smarts**) **1.** CAUSE OR HAVE SHARP PAIN to feel, cause, or be the site of a sharp stinging pain ○ *My hand smarts.* **2.** BE EMBARRASSED to feel acute embarrassment or distress ○ *She still smarted when she remembered his criticism.* **3.** BE PUNISHED to be punished severely ■ *adv.* SMARTLY in a smart manner ■ *n.* **1.** PAIN a sharp stinging localized pain **2.** EMBARRASSMENT OR MENTAL DISCOMFORT a feeling such as embarrassment, remorse, or shame ■ **smarts** *npl.* INTELLIGENCE practical intelligence or expertise (*informal*) ○ *She has the smarts to succeed.* [Old English *smeortan* "to be painful," ultimately of uncertain origin: perhaps from an Indo-European word meaning "to harm," which is also the ancestor of English *nightmare* and perhaps *remorse*] —**smart·ly** *adv.* —**smart·ness** *n.*

WORD KEY: SYNONYMS

See Synonyms at ***intelligent***.

smart al·eck /smáart àllik/, **smart al·ec** *n.* somebody who shows off his or her knowledge or always has the right answer in a way that annoys other people (*informal*) [Mid-19thC. Origin uncertain: perhaps named for an infamous New York pimp and confidence man of the 1840s *Aleck* Hoag.]

smart-al·eck /smaárt àllikee/, **smart-al·eck·y** *adj.* pretentiously clever and annoyingly self-assertive (*informal*) —**smart-al·eck·y** *adj.*

smart·ass /smaárt àss/, **smart-ass** *n.* somebody who makes an annoying show of knowledge (*slang*)

smart bomb *n.* a missile that is guided to its target by laser or radio beams

smart card *n.* a small plastic card containing a microchip that can store personal data and bank-account details, enabling it to be used for identification and to pay for purchases

smart·en /smaárt'n/ (**-ened, -en·ing, -ens**) *vt.* **1.** IMPROVE APPEARANCE to improve the appearance of somebody or something **2.** SPEED SOMETHING UP to increase the speed of something

smarten up *vti.* **1.** IMPROVE APPEARANCE to improve your appearance, or the appearance of somebody or something else **2.** MAKE OR BECOME LIVELIER to make somebody or something brighter or livelier, or become brighter or livelier **3.** MAKE OR BECOME WISER to make somebody wiser or more knowing, or become wiser or more knowing

smart growth *n.* economic growth that consciously seeks to avoid wastefulness and damage to the environment and communities

smart mon·ey *n.* **1.** WISE INVESTMENT OR BET money bet on or invested in something likely to yield a good profit **2.** WISE INVESTORS those with privileged information to make wise bets or investments **3.** LAW DAMAGES AWARDED TO PUNISH A DEFENDANT damages awarded to a plaintiff in excess of the normal level of compensation to punish a defendant in cases of serious negligence or willful misconduct

smart·weed /smaárt weèd/ *n.* any of various plants of the buckwheat family that grow in marshy temperate regions and have acidic juice that can irritate the skin. Genus: *Polygonum.* [From SMART "stinging pain," because of its acidic juice]

smart·y pants /smaártee-/ (*plural* **smart·y pants**), **smarty** (*plural* **smarties**) *n.* somebody who is annoying because he or she is always trying to be clever (*informal*) (*takes a singular verb*)

smash /smash/ *v.* (**smashed, smash·ing, smash·es**) **1.** *vti.* BREAK INTO PIECES to break, or break something, into many small pieces **2.** *vti.* BREAK WITH FORCE to break something, or break through something, with great force or violence **3.** *vti.* HIT AGAINST SOMETHING to hit something, or make something hit something else, with great force **4.** *vt.* DEFEAT OR DESTROY to ruin, defeat, or put an end to somebody or something completely **5.** *vt.* RACKET GAMES HIT WITH OVERHAND STROKE in games such as tennis and badminton, to hit a ball or shuttlecock with great force, especially with an overhand stroke ■ *n.* **1.** LOUD NOISE the loud sound of something hitting or being hit by something else and breaking into pieces ○ *The mirror hit the floor with a smash.* **2.** BUSINESS, THEATER GREAT SUCCESS an unqualified success ○ *The new show was a smash hit.* **3.** BLOW a heavy blow **4.** COLLISION a crash or collision ○ *There's been a bad smash on the freeway.* **5.** RACKET GAMES OVERHAND STROKE in games such as tennis and badminton, a strong overhand stroke hit downward into the opponent's court **6.** BUSINESS BIG FAILURE a major failure, especially one involving finances **7.** BEVERAGES COCKTAIL a cocktail made with sugar, seltzer, mint leaves, and usually brandy ■ *adv.* WITH A SMASH with the sound of a smash [Late 17thC. Origin uncertain: perhaps a blend of such words as SMACK, SMITE, and others such as BASH, MASH.] —**smash·a·ble** *adj.* —**smash·er** *n.*

smash up *v.* **1.** *vti.* DAMAGE BY COLLISION to damage something severely, or become badly damaged, because of a collision with something solid **2.** *vt.* DAMAGE BY BREAKING to damage or destroy something by breaking

smashed /smasht/ *adj.* very drunk or under the influence of drugs (*informal*)

smash·ing /smáshing/ *adj.* **1.** CRUSHING crushing or serving to smash something ○ *a smashing blow to the jaw* **2.** *U.K.* VERY GOOD extremely good or pleasing

smash·up /smásh ùp/ *n.* **1.** WRECK a collision between vehicles in which all those involved are badly damaged **2.** DESTRUCTION complete ruin, collapse, or destruction

smat·ter /smáttər/ *vt.* (**-tered, -ter·ing, -ters**) **1.** STUDY LIGHTLY to study a subject or language in a not very serious way **2.** SPEAK LANGUAGE POORLY to speak a language badly ■ *n.* = **smattering** *n.* **1**, **smattering** *n.* **2** [15thC. Origin uncertain.] —**smat·ter·er** *n.*

smat·ter·ing /smáttəring/ *n.* **1.** SLIGHT KNOWLEDGE a slight knowledge of something such as a subject or language **2.** SMALL AMOUNT a small amount or number ○ *a smattering of rain* ■ *adj.* SUPERFICIAL concerned only with surface issues and not going into depth or substance

SMATV *abbr.* satellite master antenna television

smear /smeer/ *v.* (**smeared, smear·ing, smears**) **1.** *vti.* SPREAD OVER to spread over, or spread something liquid or greasy over something ○ *This lipstick is made not to smear.* **2.** *vt.* SPREAD DAMAGING RUMORS to deliberately spread damaging rumors about somebody **3.** *vt.* DEFEAT to severely defeat a competitor or enemy (*informal*) (*usually passive*) ○ *We got smeared.* ■ *n.* **1.** PATCH OF SMEARED SUBSTANCE an act of smearing, or a smeared patch of something **2.** MED SAMPLE OF CELLS a sample of cells taken from body tissue or a bodily secretion or discharge and smeared on a microscope slide for examination **3.** HARMFUL RUMOR a harmful rumor or story about somebody [The verb is from Old English *smeirwan*, the noun from *smeoru*, both from a prehistoric Germanic word that is also the ancestor of English *smorgasbord*] —**smear·er** *n.*

smear cam·paign *n.* a concerted effort to diminish somebody's reputation by spreading harmful information about him or her

smear·case /sméer kàyss/ *n.* cottage cheese (*regional*) [Early 19thC. By folk-etymology from German *schmierkäse*, from *schmieren* "to smear" (because it is easily spread) + *käse* "cheese."]

WORD KEY: REGIONAL NOTE

Concentrated in Eastern Pennsylvania, ***smearcase*** has spread with migrations throughout Appalachia into the Western Carolinas and East Tennessee. It is German-American usage, for example, in Cincinnati, Chicago, Milwaukee, and East Texas, and the Pennsylvania Dutch form occurs across much of the Eastern United States.

smear·y /sméeree/ (**-i·er, -i·est**) *adj.* **1.** SMEARED OR LIABLE TO SMEAR smeared on, easily smeared, or likely to smear **2.** COVERED WITH SMEARS having or covered with smears

smec·tic /sméktik/ *adj.* used to describe materials whose liquid phase consists of elongated molecules arranged in layers and with their axes parallel to each other. Liquid crystals are smectic. [Late 17thC. Via Latin *smecticus*, from Greek *smēktikos*, from *smēkhein* "to rub, cleanse."]

smec·tite /smék tìt/ *n.* any of a group of clay minerals that includes montmorillonite and saponite. These clays swell, or take up liquids between their layers, and are used in ion exchange processes. [Early 19thC. Formed from Greek *smēktis* "fuller's earth."]

smeg·ma /smégmə/ *n.* a cheesy secretion of the sebaceous glands that collects under the foreskin or around the clitoris [Early 19thC. Via Latin from Greek *smēgma* "soap," from *smēkhein* "to rub, cleanse."]

smell /smel/ *v.* (**smelled** *or* **smelt, smell·ing, smells**) **1.** *vti.* DETECT BY NOSE to detect or recognize something by means of sensitive nerves in the nose **2.** *vt.* USE NOSE to use the sensitive nerves in the nose to assess something ○ *Smell that and see if it's still good.* **3.** *vi.* BE DETECTED WHEN BREATHED IN to seem to be in a particular condition, or give a particular impression, when judged by somebody breathing in through the nose ○ *Something smells good.* **4.** *vi.* **GIVE UNPLEASANT IMPRESSION** to be considered unpleasant when breathed in through the nose **5.** *vi.* **GIVE IMPRESSION** to give off a suggestion or impression of something ○ *It smells dangerous.* **6.** *vt.* **FEEL OR DETECT** to detect the presence or existence of something, usually something bad **7.** *vi.* **SEEM DISHONEST** to seem dishonest or illegal ○ *Her excuse really smells.* ■ *n.* **1. SENSE BASED ON NERVES IN NOSE** the sense based on the sensitive nerves in the nose that distinguish odors **2. QUALITY DETECTED BY NOSE** the quality of something that can be detected by the sensitive nerves in the nose **3. ACT OF SMELLING** an act or instance of breathing something in through the nose in order to make a judgment about it **4. SUGGESTION OF SOMETHING** a suggestion or impression of something [12thC. Origin uncertain.] —**smel·ler** *n.*

WORD KEY: SYNONYMS

smell, odor, aroma, bouquet, scent, perfume, fragrance, stink, stench, reek

CORE MEANING: the way something smells

smell is a general word that describes the way something smells, whether this is neutral, pleasant, or unpleasant; **odor** is a fairly formal word, usually describing either neutral or unpleasant smells; **aroma** is a distinctive pleasant smell, especially one related to cooking or food; **bouquet** is a characteristic pleasant smell, usually associated with fine wines; **scent** is the characteristic smell given off by a particular animal. It is also used to describe a pleasant, sweet smell, for example, the smell of flowers; **perfume** is a sweet, pleasant, and heady smell, especially the smell of flowers or plants; **fragrance** is a sweet pleasant smell, especially a delicate or subtle one; **stink** is a strong unpleasant smell; **stench** is a strong unpleasant smell, especially one associated with burning or decay; **reek** is a strong unpleasant smell, especially one associated with people's bodies or homes.

smell up *vt.* to fill something with an unpleasant smell

smell·ing salts *npl.* a mixture of ammonium carbonate and perfume used, especially in the past, to revive somebody who felt faint or had become unconscious

smell·y /sméllee/ (**-i·er, -i·est**) *adj.* giving off a strong or unpleasant smell —**smell·i·ness** *n.*

smelt[1] /smelt/ (**smelt·ed, smelt·ing, smelts**) *v.* **1.** *vt.* **PRODUCE METAL** to melt ore in order to get metal from it, or produce metal in this way. The separation of the metal usually requires a chemical change. **2.** *vi.* **MELT** to undergo fusing or melting in the process of smelting [Mid-16thC. From Middle Low German *smelten.*]

smelt[2] /smelt/ (*plural* **smelts** *or* **smelt**) *n.* a small silvery marine or freshwater fish found in northern waters that has oily flesh and is used extensively for food. Family: Osmeridae. [Old English, of uncertain origin]

smelt[3] past tense, past participle of **smell**

smelt·er /sméltər/ *n.* **1. SOMEBODY WHO SMELTS ORE** somebody who smelts ore or who owns a factory where ore is smelted **2. SMELTING APPARATUS OR FACTORY** a place where smelting is carried out, or an apparatus used for smelting

smew /smyoo/ (*plural* **smews** *or* **smew**) *n.* a European and Asian duck related to the mergansers that has a hooked serrated bill and, in the male, predominantly white plumage with black markings. Latin name: *Mergus albellus.* [Late 17thC; probably ultimately of prehistoric West Germanic origin]

smid·gen /smíjjən/, **smid·gin, smid·geon, smidge** /smij/ *n.* a small amount (*informal*) [Mid-19thC. Origin uncertain, perhaps formed from *smitch* "particle."]

smi·lax /smī́ làks/ *n.* **1. CLIMBING PLANT** a climbing plant of temperate and tropical regions with small white or yellowish flowers, red or bluish-black berries, and in many cases prickly stems. Genus: *Smilax.* **2. FLORIST'S VINE** a South African vine prized by florists for its glossy bright green leaves. Latin name: *Asparagus asparagoides.* [Late 16thC. From Latin, from Greek, "bindweed."]

smile /smīl/ *v.* (**smiled, smil·ing, smiles**) **1.** *vti.* **HAVE OR MAKE PLEASANT EXPRESSION** to have or make an expression with the corners of the mouth raised, usually expressing amusement, pleasure, or approval **2.** *vi.* **HAVE PLEASANT APPEARANCE** to appear to be in a state of happiness or enjoying good fortune or pleasure **3.** *vi.* **FAVOR SOMEBODY** to be favorably disposed to somebody ○ *Fortune smiled on their trip* **4.** *vt.* **EXPRESS SOMETHING BY SMILING** to express something by or while smiling ■ *n.* **1. PLEASANT EXPRESSION** a facial expression in which the corners of the mouth are raised, usually expressing amusement, pleasure, or approval **2. PLEASANT APPEARANCE** an appearance of pleasure or approval (*often used in the plural*) **3. SIGN OF FAVOR** an expression or sign of favor [13thC. Origin uncertain: probably from Scandinavian, from a prehistoric Germanic word that is also the ancestor of English *smirk.*] —**smil·er** *n.* —**smil·ing·ly** *adv.*

smil·ey /smīlee/ *adj.* (**-i·er, -i·est**) **SMILING** smiling or often smiling ■ *n.* (*plural* **-eys**) COMPUT **COMPUTER FACE SYMBOL** a symbol (**emoticon**), often in the form :-) keyed by a computer user to communicate feelings such as pleasure, approval, or humor

Smil·ey /smīlee/, **Jane** (*b.* 1949) U.S. writer. Her novels include *A Thousand Acres* (1991) and *Moo* (1995).

smil·ey face *n.* **1.** COMPUT = **smiley 2. CIRCULAR REPRESENTATION OF FACE** a round yellow image representing a smiling face, generally consisting of two dots and an upward-curving arc, representing eyes and a mouth

smi·lo·don /smīlə dòn/ *n.* a large saber-toothed tiger existing during the Pleistocene epoch, between about two million and ten thousand years ago. Genus: *Smilodon.* [Mid-19thC. From modern Latin, literally "knife-toothed," from Greek *smilē* "knife."]

smirch /smurch/ *vt.* (**smirched, smirch·ing, smirch·es**) (*archaic or literary*) **1. DAMAGE REPUTATION** to damage somebody's or something's reputation or good name **2. DIRTY SOMETHING** to make something dirty by smearing or staining it **3. SPOIL** to spoil or harm something ■ *n.* (*archaic or literary*) **1. DIRTY STAIN** a dirty stain or smear **2. SOMETHING DAMAGING** something that damages a reputation [15thC. Origin uncertain: perhaps from Old French *esmorcher* "to torture."]

smirk /smurk/ *n.* **INSOLENT SMILE** an insolent smile expressing feelings such as superiority, self-satisfaction, or conceit ■ *v.* (**smirked, smirk·ing, smirks**) **1.** *vi.* **SMILE INSOLENTLY** to smile in an insolent, smug, or contemptuous way **2.** *vt.* **EXPRESS WITH SMIRK** to express something with a smirk [Old English *smearcian* "to smile," from a prehistoric Germanic word that is also the ancestor of English *smile*]

smite /smīt/ (**smote** /smōt/, **smit·ten** /smítt'n/ *or* **smote** /smōt/, **smit·ing, smites**) *v.* **1.** *vti.* **HIT HARD** to hit somebody or something hard (*regional archaic or literary*) **2.** *vt.* **AFFECT OR AFFLICT** to affect somebody strongly or disastrously, or afflict somebody with something (*archaic or literary*) (*often passive*) **3.** *vt.* **FILL SOMEBODY WITH LOVE** to fill somebody with love or longing (*humorous or archaic or literary*) (*usually passive*) [Old English *smītan* "to smear, pollute," from prehistoric Germanic] —**smit·er** *n.*

smith /smith/ *n.* **1. METAL WORKER** somebody who repairs and fashions metal objects **2.** = **blacksmith** [Old English *smiþ*, from a prehistoric Germanic word meaning "coppersmith"]

Smith /smith/, **Adam** (1723–90) British philosopher and economist. He articulated his theory of free trade in *The Wealth of Nations* (1776).

Smith, Bessie (1894–1937) U.S. singer. The leading blues singer of her day, she recorded widely with major jazz bands. Known as **Empress of the Blues**

Smith, David (1906–65) U.S. sculptor. Originally inspired by Picasso, his abstract scuptures of the 1930s, made of iron and steel, greatly influenced later 20th-century sculptors. Full name **David Roland Smith**

Smith, Donald Alexander, 1st Baron Strathcona and Mount Royal (1820–1914) Scottish-born Canadian business executive and diplomat who was a financial backer of the Canadian Pacific Railway (1885), governor of Hudson's Bay Company (1889), and Canadian high commissioner in Britain (1896).

Smith, Jedediah Strong (1799–1831) U.S. explorer and fur trader. He was an early explorer of the Far West, including California and Oregon (1826–30).

Smith, John (1580–1631) English-born North American colonist. He was president of the Virginia colony at Jamestown (1608–09). The tale of his rescue from Native North Americans by Pocahontas is his own. His explorations and accounts influenced many English people to settle in North America.

Smith, Joseph (1805–44) U.S. religious leader. He was the visionary founder of the Church of the Latter-Day Saints (1830). Amid local controversy, he established communities in Missouri and Illinois. He was killed by a mob opposed to his philosophy.

Dame Maggie Smith

Smith, Dame Maggie (*b.* 1934) British actor. Her work in classical theater was complemented by her comedy performances and extensive movie appearances. Real name **Dame Margaret Nathalie Smith**

Smith, Stevie (1902–71) British poet and novelist. Her works include the autobiographical *Novel on Yellow Paper* (1936) and collections of sharp, wry verse such as *Not Waving but Drowning* (1957). Her *Collected Poems* (1975) were published posthumously. Real name **Florence Margaret Smith**

smith·er·eens /smìthə reénz/ *npl.* very small broken pieces (*informal*) [Early 19thC. Origin uncertain: probably formed from Irish *smidirín*, literally "small fragment," from *smiodar* "fragment."]

smith·er·y /smítharee/ (*plural* **-ies**) *n.* **1. SMITH'S WORK** the work or craft of a smith **2.** = **smithy** *n.* 1

Smithson /smíths'n/, **Robert** (1938–73) U.S. sculptor. He reshaped large areas of land into earthworks such as *Spiral Jetty* (1970). Full name **Robert Irving Smithson**

Smith·so·ni·an In·sti·tu·tion /smith sōnee ən-/, **Smith·so·ni·an** *n.* a government trust founded in Washington, D.C., by an act of congress in 1846 to promote research and education. It sponsors scientific research and publications and maintains the national collections. The fourteen museums it administers include the National Museum of American History and the National Air and Space Museum in Washington, D.C., and the National Museum of the Native American in New York City. [Early 19thC. Named for James L. M. *Smithson* (1765–1829), British chemist and mineralogist who endowed the institution.]

smith·son·ite /smíthsə nīt/ *n.* a white or yellow to brown zinc carbonate mineral, an important ore of zinc. The honeycombed variety of smithsonite is also known as dry-bone ore. Formula: $ZnCO_3$. [Mid-19thC. Named for James L. M. *Smithson* (see SMITHSONIAN INSTITUTION).]

smith·y /smíthee, smíthee/ (*plural* **-ies**) *n.* **1. BLACKSMITH'S WORKPLACE** the place where a blacksmith works **2.** = **blacksmith**

smit·ten past participle of **smite**

SMN *abbr.* seaman

smock /smok/ *n.* **1. OVERSHIRT** a loose garment worn to protect the clothes **2. UNDERGARMENT** a woman's loose-fitting undergarment or chemise of a type used until the 18th century ■ *vt.* (**smocked, smock·ing, smocks**) **SEW WITH GATHERING STITCHES** to sew or decorate something with decorative gathering stitches [Old English *smoc*, from a prehistoric Germanic word meaning "to creep." The underlying idea is of a garment that you put on by creeping into it.]

smock·ing /smóking/ *n.* decorative stitching in a

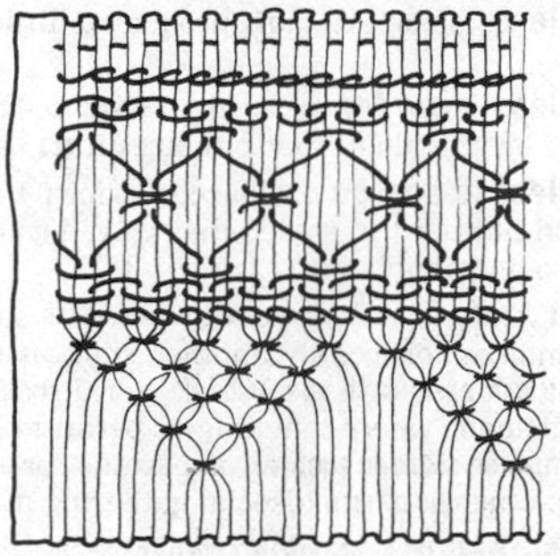
Smocking

honeycomb or zigzag pattern, used to gather fabric evenly

smog /smog/ *n.* a mixture of fog and smoke or other airborne pollutants such as exhaust fumes [Early 20thC. Blend of SMOKE and FOG.] —**smog·gy** *adj.*

smoke /smōk/ *n.* **1. CLOUD OF TINY PARTICLES** a mass of tiny particles in the air that rises up from something burning **2. VAPOR RESEMBLING SMOKE** something that resembles smoke, usually consisting of minute particles suspended in a gas ○ *a white, stinging smoke of chemical fumes* **3. INHALING OF BURNING TOBACCO FUMES** an act of smoking a cigarette, cigar, or pipe **4. CIGARETTE** a cigarette or other tobacco product (*informal*) **5. SMOKABLE SUBSTANCE** something that can be smoked (*informal*) **6. SOMETHING THAT OBSCURES** something that obscures or obstructs information, understanding, or awareness **7. SOMETHING TRANSIENT** something transient or illusory **8.** COLORS **GRAY COLOR** a gray color with a tinge of blue or brown ■ *v.* (**smoked, smok·ing, smokes**) **1.** *vti.* **USE TOBACCO** to have the habit of inhaling the smoke of a burning tobacco in cigarettes, cigars, or pipes **2.** *vti.* **INHALE VAPORS** to inhale the smoke of any substance that can burn and be inhaled **3.** *vi.* **GIVE OFF SMOKE** to give off smoke, often in a way that indicates some malfunction **4.** *vt.* FOOD **CURE FOOD WITH SMOKE** to cure or treat food such as meat, fish, or cheese with wood smoke **5.** *vt.* **FUMIGATE WITH SMOKE** to fumigate, clean, or clear something with smoke **6.** *vt.* CRAFT **DARKEN** to darken something to give it the color of smoke **7.** *vt.* **STUPEFY SOMETHING** to stupefy something with smoke ■ *adj.* **GRAYISH** of a gray color tinged with blue or brown [Old English *smoca*, from prehistoric Germanic. Its use as a verb in connection with tobacco is first recorded in the early 17thC.] —**smok·a·ble** *adj.* ◇ **go up in smoke 1.** to fail completely to happen as planned or hoped **2.** to be destroyed by burning **3.** to get into a very bad temper

smoke out *vt.* **1. DRIVE FROM HIDING** to drive somebody or something from a hiding place by using smoke **2. BRING TO LIGHT** to bring something to light by clever or assertive inquiry

smoke a·larm *n.* = **smoke detector**

smoke and mir·rors *n.* something that is intended to draw people's attention away from something else that somebody would prefer remained unnoticed [The allusion is to the use of smoke and mirrors in magic acts]

smoke bomb *n.* a device that gives off dense clouds of irritating chemical smoke, used to drive people or animals out of a place

smoke de·tec·tor *n.* a device that sets off an alarm when it detects smoke

smoke-dried *adj.* cured with or dried in smoke

smoked rub·ber *n.* crude rubber prepared by drying coagulated latex sheets in smokehouses before they are packed into bales. The smoking process hinders the formation of bacteria and molds and aids in the preservation of the rubber against oxidation.

smoke-filled room *n.* a room where deals are negotiated in private, traditionally considered to be filled with the smoke of the negotiators' cigarettes, cigars, and pipes

smoke·house /smōk hòwss/ (*plural* **-hous·es** /-hòwzəz/) *n.* a small building where meat, fish, or other materials are cured in smoke

smoke·jack /smōk jàk/ *n.* a device that turns a roasting spit and is powered by rising gases in a chimney

smoke·jump·er /smōk jùmpər/ *n.* a firefighter who parachutes into inaccessible areas to extinguish forest fires —**smoke·jump·ing** *n.*

smoke·less /smókləss/ *adj.* producing little or no smoke

smoke·less pow·der *n.* a nitrocellulose-based explosive or propellant that produces little smoke

smoke·less to·bac·co *n.* tobacco in a form that is not smoked but used in some other way, e.g., chewing tobacco and snuff

smok·er /smókər/ *n.* **1. SOMEBODY WHO SMOKES** somebody who smokes tobacco or another substance **2.** RAIL **RAILROAD CAR DESIGNATED FOR SMOKING** a railroad car or compartment where smoking is permitted **3.** COOK **APPARATUS FOR SMOKING FOOD** an apparatus for smoking food **4. GATHERING OF MEN** a social gathering of men

smoke screen *n.* **1. ACTION INTENDED TO OBSCURE** an action taken to mislead somebody or obscure something **2.** MIL **SMOKE HIDING SOMETHING** a mass of smoke produced to conceal the movements of ships, troops, or equipment

smoke·stack /smōk stàk/ *n.* **1. OUTLET OF STEAM ENGINE** a funnel mounted to the boiler of a locomotive or steamboat that provides draft to the firebox and exhausts the combustion gases from the cylinders of an engine **2. TALL INDUSTRIAL CHIMNEY** a tall, often cylindrical industrial chimney, often attached to a factory

smoke tree *n.* a shrub or small tree whose clusters of small flowers resemble puffs of smoke. Genus: *Cotinus.*

Smok·ey /smókee/ *n.* the police (*slang*) [Late 20thC. Shortening of *Smokey the Bear*, a fictional character used in a campaign about fire prevention, with a hat resembling that worn by fictional state police.]

smok·ing car *n.* = **smoker** *n.* 2

smok·ing com·part·ment *n.* = **smoker** *n.* 2

smok·ing gun *n.* conclusive evidence or proof, especially of some wrongdoing [From the idea of finding a recently fired gun in a suspect's hand]

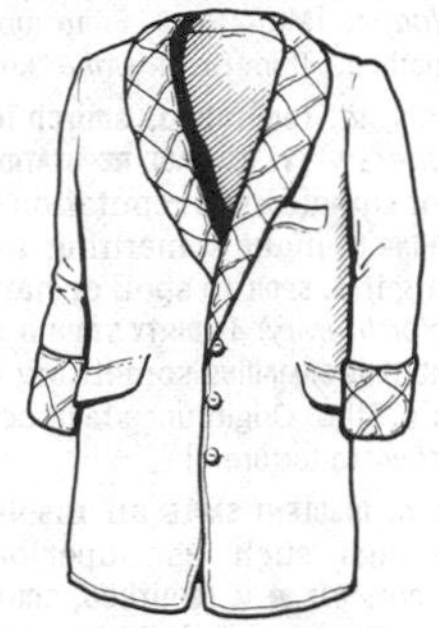

Smoking jacket

smok·ing jack·et *n.* a loose-fitting jacket made of a rich fabric such as velvet or silk, worn in the past by men while smoking

smok·ing room *n.* a room designated for people to smoke in

smok·y /smókee/ (**-i·er, -i·est**) *adj.* **1. FILLED WITH SMOKE** filled with smoke, or smelling as if it had been filled with smoke **2.** COLORS **COLORED LIKE SMOKE** of a gray color, like smoke **3.** FOOD **TASTING OF SMOKE** having or suggesting a taste imparted by smoke or an open flame **4. GIVING OFF EXCESSIVE SMOKE** giving off smoke, especially excessively **5. AFFECTED BY SMOKE** discolored or marked with smoke —**smok·i·ly** *adv.* —**smok·i·ness** *n.*

Smok·y Hill /smókee-/ river rising in eastern Colorado and flowing eastward into the Kansas River, in eastern Kansas. Length: 540 mi./870 km.

smol·der /smóldər/, **smoul·der** *vi.* (**-dered, -dering, -ders**) **1. BURN SLOWLY** to burn slowly and gently, usually with some smoke but without a flame **2. HAVE SUPPRESSED EMOTION** to have or show a strong emotion that is suppressed but liable to flare up at any time **3. EXIST IN BACKGROUND** to exist in the background, liable to appear or reappear at any moment ■ *n.* **1. THICK SMOKE** thick smoke from a slow-burning fire **2. SMOKY FIRE** a slow-burning fire [From Old English *smorian* "to smoke, suffocate"]

Smo·lensk /smō lénsk/ city in western Russia, on the Dnieper River. It is the capital of Smolensk Oblast. Population: 350,000 (1991).

smolt /smōlt/ *n.* a young salmon before it has swum to the sea. It is characterized by physiological changes in preparation for living in salt water, such as silver coloration. [15thC. Origin uncertain.]

smooch /smooch/ *vti.* (**smooched, smooch·ing, smooch·es**) **TO KISS** to kiss and caress somebody (*informal*) ■ *n.* **KISS** an instance of kissing (*informal*) [Mid-20thC. An imitation of the sound of kissing.] —**smooch·y** *adj.*

smooth /smooth/ *adj.* **1. NOT ROUGH OR BUMPY** not having a rough or uneven surface **2. WITHOUT LUMPS** without lumps or pieces of solid matter ○ *Beat the mixture to a smooth paste.* **3. WITHOUT UPHEAVAL OR DIFFICULTIES** proceeding without interruption, upheaval, or problems **4. WITHOUT JERKS OR JOLTS** in a steady flowing motion, without jolts or interruptions **5. NOT HARSH** without harshness **6. NOT SHARP OR SOUR** not tasting sharp or sour **7. NOT EASILY UPSET** not easily ruffled or upset ○ *a smooth and serene personality* **8. INSINCERELY CONVINCING** using insincere flattery and pleasantness, especially in order to persuade somebody to do something **9. HAIRLESS** without a beard or mustache ○ *a smooth-faced young man* **10. FRICTIONLESS** offering no apparent resistance to sliding **11.** PHON **UNASPIRATED** spoken without audible breath ■ *vt.* (**smoothed, smooth·ing, smoothes**) **1. EVEN OUT ROUGHNESS** to remove bumps, unevenness, or roughness **2. PRESS OUT CREASES** to remove lines and creases **3. MAKE CREAMY** to remove lumps from something **4. REMOVE DIFFICULTIES** to remove obstacles and difficulties ○ *Influential allies smoothed his path to power.* **5. LESSEN BAD FEELINGS** to remove or lessen bad feeling or disagreement between people ○ *I tried to smooth things over with her.* **6.** STATS **REMOVE IRREGULARITIES FROM DATA** to modify a sequential set of numerical data by reducing the differences in magnitude between adjacent numbers **7.** PHYS, ELEC ENG **REMOVE IRREGULARITIES IN CURRENT** to remove the slight irregularities (**ripples**) in a rectified current ■ *adv.* **WITHOUT PROBLEMS** without problems or difficulties ○ *The path of true love never runs smooth.* ■ *n.* **1. ACT OF SMOOTHING** the action of smoothing something **2. SOMETHING SMOOTH** a smooth part of something [Old English *smōþ*, of unknown origin] —**smooth·a·ble** *adj.* —**smooth·er** *n.* —**smooth·ly** *adv.* —**smooth·ness** *n.*

smooth down *v.* **1.** *vti.* **FLATTEN BY SMOOTHING** to make something flat by a smoothing action, or become flat by being smoothed **2.** *vt.* **CALM SOMEBODY** to calm or placate somebody

smooth out *vti.* **1. MAKE OR BECOME SMOOTH** to make something smooth, or become smooth, by the removal of lines and creases **2. MAKE OR BECOME EASIER** to make something easier or calmer, or become easier or calmer, after a period of difficulty

smooth over *vt.* to remove or lessen difficulties or tensions

smooth·bore /smooth bàwr/ *adj.* **SMOOTH IN INTERIOR OF BARREL** having a barrel with no ridges or grooves in the bore. Early firearms and modern shotguns and mortars are characterized by smooth bores. ■ *n.* **SMOOTHBORE GUN** a gun with a smooth surface inside its barrel

smooth breath·ing *n.* a mark ʼ written over some initial Greek vowels to show that they are not aspirated. ◊ **rough breathing**

smooth col·lie *n.* a dog belonging to a breed of collie with a thick short-haired coat

smooth·en /smooth'n/ (**-ened, -en·ing, -ens**) *vti.* to make something smooth, or become smooth

smooth fox ter·ri·er *n.* a dog belonging to a breed of English fox terrier with a mostly white short coat

smooth hound *n.* any of several small sharks, including some types of dogfish without a spine in front of the dorsal fin. Genus: *Mustelus.*

smooth·ie /smoothee/ *n.* **1. smooth·ie, smooth·y** (*plural* **-ies**) **CHARMING MAN** an attractive and charming man perceived as being insincere (*informal*) **2.** BEVERAGES **MILK SHAKE** a drink similar to a milk shake made with fruit, cream, or milk, and ice cream

smooth·ing cir·cuit *n.* a circuit used to remove the alternating current component from a direct current power source

smooth mus·cle *n.* a type of muscle functioning involuntarily and made up of layers of spindle-shaped cells lacking cross striations. It is found in the viscera, e.g., the stomach and bladder. Smooth muscle functions by slow contraction, and is not under voluntary control. It is activated by the autonomic nervous system, hormones, and drugs.

smooth-tongued *adj.* speaking or spoken skillfully and persuasively

smooth·y *n.* = **smoothie** *n.* 1 (*informal*)

smor·gas·bord /smáwrgəss bàwrd/ *n.* **1. BUFFET MEAL** a meal served buffet style, consisting of a large variety of hot and cold dishes **2. RESTAURANT SERVING BUFFET** a restaurant featuring a smorgasbord **3. VARIETY** a wide variety [Late 19thC. From Swedish *smörgåsbord* (see SMEAR).]

smote past tense of **smite**

smoth·er /smúthər/ *v.* (**-ered, -er·ing, -ers**) **1.** *vti.* **ALLOW OR GET TOO LITTLE AIR** to deprive somebody or something of air, or be deprived of air **2.** *vti.* **SUFFOCATE** to kill somebody or something, or die, by suffocation **3.** *vti.* **OVERWHELM WITH AFFECTION** to give somebody too much love or affection with the effect that he or she feels restricted **4.** *vti.* **PUT OUT OR BE PUT OUT** to extinguish something such as a fire, or go out from lack of oxygen **5.** *vt.* **SUPPRESS OR HIDE** to suppress or hide the expression of something **6.** *vt.* **COVER THICKLY** to cover something with a thick layer of something else ■ *n.* **1. DENSE SMOKE** dense smoke or gas **2. THICK COATING** a thick coating of something [12thC. Formed from Old English *smorian* "to suffocate, choke (with smoke)."] —**smoth·er·er** *n.* —**smoth·er·ing·ly** *adv.* — **smoth·er·y** *adj.*

smoul·der *vi., n.* = **smolder**

sm·ri·ti /smríttee/ *n.* a group of Hindu scriptures giving instruction on social and domestic matters

SMSA *abbr.* standard metropolitan statistical area

S.M.Sgt., **SMSGT** *abbr.* Senior Master Sergeant

SMTP *n.* the main protocol used to send electronic mail on the Internet, consisting of rules for how programs sending mail should interact with programs receiving mail. Full form **Simple Mail Transfer Protocol**

smudge /smuj/ *n.* **1. SMEARED INK OR PAINT** a patch of smeared ink or paint blurring what has been written or painted **2. DIRTY MARK** a dirty or greasy mark **3. INDISTINCT AREA** something visible but blurred or indistinct and not easily identifiable **4.** AGRIC **SMOKE OR FIRE** smoke produced to protect trees from frost or insect damage, or a fire that produces such smoke ■ *v.* (**smudged, smudg·ing, smudg·es**) **1.** *vti.* **SMEAR OR BE SMEARED** to smear or blur something by rubbing it, or become smeared or blurred by being rubbed **2.** *vti.* **MAKE OR BECOME DIRTY** to smear something, or become smeared, with dirt or grease **3.** *vt.* AGRIC **PROTECT WITH SMOKE** to fill an orchard with smoke to protect the trees from frost or insects [15thC. Origin unknown.] —**smudg·i·ly** *adv.* —**smudg·i·ness** *n.* — **smudg·y** *adj.*

smudge pot *n.* a container in which material is burned to produce smoke for protecting trees from frost or insects

smug /smug/ (**smug·ger, smug·gest**) *adj.* conceited and self-satisfied [Mid-16thC. Origin uncertain: perhaps ultimately from Low German *smuk* "pretty," from Middle Low German *smucken* "to adorn."] —**smug·ly** *adv.* — **smug·ness** *n.*

smug·gle /smúgg'l/ (**-gled, -gling, -gles**) *v.* **1.** *vti.* **BRING INTO A COUNTRY ILLEGALLY** to carry goods into a country secretly because they are illegal or in order to avoid paying duty on them **2.** *vt.* **TAKE OR BRING SECRETLY** to take, bring, or carry somebody or something secretly into or out of a place [Late 17thC. From Low German *smukkelen* or Dutch *smokkelen*, of uncertain origin: perhaps literally "to sneak repeatedly," formed from a word.] —**smug·gler** *n.*

smurf /smurf/ (**smurfed, smurfing, smurfs**) *vi.* (*slang*) **1. LAUNDER MONEY** to launder money in nations requiring reports for large transactions, by using a number of people to open small accounts and then drawing checks on them for small amounts **2. ENGAGE IN HACKING ATTACK** to route data to a computer or a network of computers in such a way as to flood the target's machine or system with messages, causing a crash [Late 20thC. From *Smurf* the name of a children's tiny blue toy; money laundering sense dates to 1985; computer hacking sense, to 1999.]

smut /smut/ *n.* **1. OBSCENE MATERIAL** obscene jokes, stories, or pictures **2.** BOT **PLANT DISEASE** a plant disease, especially of cereals and other grasses, caused by fungi and characterized by sooty black masses of spores forming on leaves and other parts **3. FUNGUS BEARING DISEASE** a parasitic fungus that causes smut. Order: Ustilaginales. **4. SMALL PIECE OF SOOT** a speck of dirt or soot ■ *v.* (**smut·ted, smut·ting, smuts**) **1.** *vt.* **MAKE DIRTY** to mark or dirty something with smuts **2.** *vi.* BOT **BECOME AFFECTED WITH SMUT** to become affected with smut [15thC. Ultimately from prehistoric Germanic. Its original meaning was "to debase, defile."]

smutch /smuch/ *n.* **SMUDGE** a smudge of something dirty or greasy ■ *vt.* (**smutched, smutch·ing, smutch·es**) **MARK WITH A SMUDGE** to mark something with a smudge of something dirty or greasy [Mid-16thC. Origin uncertain: perhaps thought to suggest a dirty mark.] — **smutch·y** *adj.*

Smuts /smutss, smōtss/, **Jan** (1870–1950) South African statesman and general. He was instrumental in forming the Union of South Africa (1910), and as prime minister (1919–24, 1939–48) was sometimes unpopular for his pro-British policies. Full name **Jan Christiaan Smuts**

smut·ty /smúttee/ (**-ti·er, -ti·est**) *adj.* **1. OBSCENE** obscene or pornographic (*informal*) **2. MARKED WITH SMUTS** covered with sooty marks of dirt **3.** BOT **AFFECTED BY SMUT** affected by the disease smut —**smut·ti·ly** *adv.* — **smut·ti·ness** *n.*

SMV *n., abbr.* slow-moving vehicle

Smyr·na /smúrnə/ former name for **Izmir**

Sn *symbol.* tin

SNA *abbr.* COMPUT systems network architecture

snack /snak/ *n.* **1. SMALL MEAL** a small meal of prepared or easy-to-prepare food eaten in place of a regular meal or between regular meals **2. FOOD FOR SNACK** any sort of food suitable for eating between meals or instead of a main meal ■ *vi.* (**snacked, snack·ing, snacks**) **EAT BETWEEN MEALS** to eat between the times that meals are usually served, or eat a snack instead of a main meal ○ *I've been snacking all afternoon.* [15thC. From Middle Dutch *snac* "bite."]

snack bar *n.* a small restaurant or food outlet that sells snacks

snaf·fle /snáff'l/ *n.* **snaf·fle, snaf·fle bit** EQU **BIT FOR HORSES** a bit for a horse that is jointed in the middle and has rings on either end where the reins are attached ■ *vt.* (**-fled, -fling, -fles**) **1.** EQU **FIT WITH BIT** to fit a horse or pony with a snaffle bit **2.** *U.K.* **STEAL** to steal or take something, usually something relatively unimportant (*informal*) [Mid-16thC. Formed from a Low Dutch word. The early 18thC meaning "to steal" may be a different word.]

sna·fu /sna fóo/ *n.* **BAD SITUATION CAUSED BY INCOMPETENCE** a mishap or mistake generally caused by incompetence and resulting in delay or confusion (*informal*) ■ *vti.* (**-fued, -fu·ing, -fus**) **SPOIL OR BE SPOILED** to cause a situation or process to become confused or delayed, generally by incompetence, or become confused or delayed (*informal*) [Mid-20thC. Originally a U.S. military acronym formed from the initial letters of "situation normal all fouled up."]

snag /snag/ *n.* **1. SMALL PROBLEM** a minor problem or obstacle to progress **2. UNWANTED SHARP POINT** a sharp projection on which something may catch and tear **3. HOLE IN FABRIC** a hole in a fabric resulting from catching it on something sharp **4.** SHIPPING **NAVIGATIONAL OBSTRUCTION** an object underwater, e.g., a tree stump, that may obstruct boats **5.** *ANZ* **SAUSAGE** a sausage (*slang*) ■ *v.* (**snagged, snag·ging, snags**) **1.** *vti.* **CATCH ON A SNAG** to catch on or collide with a sharp projection ○ *snagged my sleeve on a nail* **2.** *vt.* **OBSTRUCT** to obstruct the progress of something **3.** *vt.* **OBTAIN** to obtain by luck, skillful maneuvering, or both **4.** *vt.* **CLEAR OF OBSTRUCTIONS** to clear a river or lake of underwater obstructions **5.** *vi.* **MEET A PROBLEM** to come up against a problem or obstacle that deters progress **6.** *vi.* **GET TANGLED** to become tangled or entangled [Late 16thC. Origin uncertain: probably from Scandinavian.] —**snag·gy** *adj.*

snag·gle·tooth /snágg'l tòoth/ (*plural* **-teeth** /-teéth/) *n.* a broken, projecting, or crooked tooth [Early 19thC. Snaggle: literally "to snag repeatedly," formed from SNAG.] —**snag·gle·toothed** *adj.*

snag·gle-toothed fish *n.* an elongated deep-sea fish with a long chin barbel, a large mouth with sharp projecting teeth, and a large stomach for digesting prey. Family: Astronesthidae.

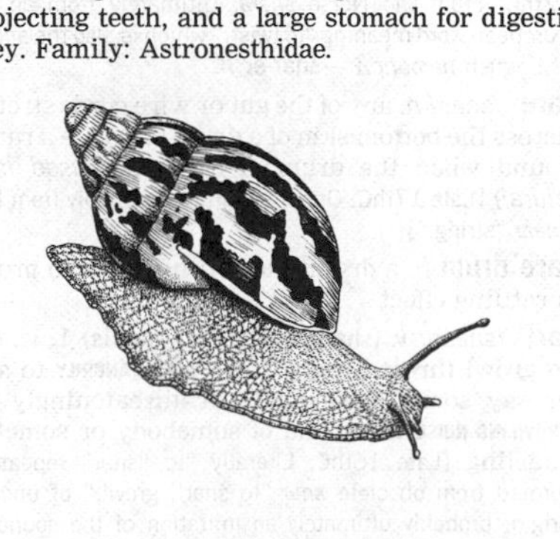

Snail

snail /snayl/ *n.* **1. CRAWLING CREATURE WITH SHELL** any of a large class of land and water creatures (**gastropods**) that have a coiled shell and a retractable muscular foot on which they crawl. Class: Gastropoda. **2. SLOW-MOVING PERSON OR THING** somebody or something that moves very slowly (*informal*) [Old English *snægel*, from a prehistoric Germanic base meaning "to crawl," which is also the ancestor of English *snake*]

snail dart·er *n.* a small snail-eating fish found in eastern Tennessee. Latin name: *Percina tanasi.*

snail fe·ver *n.* = **schistosomiasis**

snail·fish /snáyl fish/ (*plural* **-fish** *or* **-fish·es**) *n.* a small elongated flabby bottom-dwelling marine fish, often with ventral fins modified to form a sucking disk, found in cold oceans, mostly the northern Pacific. Family: Liparidae. [Snail perhaps because of its soft and oily texture]

snail-hunt·er *n.* a small spherical ground beetle with specialized elongated mandibles for extracting snails from their shells. Genus: *Saphinotus.*

snail kite *n.* a tropical American bird of prey that has a sharp hooked bill, travels in flocks, and feeds on snails. Latin name: *Rostrhamus sociabilis.*

snail mail *n.* mail sent through the postal service, as distinct from the faster electronic mail (*informal*)

snail's pace *n.* a speed that is thought unbearably or unaccountably slow —**snail-paced** *adj.*

snake /snayk/ *n.* **1. LEGLESS REPTILE** a legless reptile with a scaly tubular body tapering toward the tail, lidless eyes, and often venomous fangs. Suborder: Serpentes. **2. OFFENSIVE TERM** an offensive term that deliberately insults somebody's reliability and honesty, especially in personal dealings **3. PLUMBER'S TOOL** a plumber's tool consisting of a long flexible wire that can be inserted into and rotated inside drains to unblock them ■ *v.* (**snaked, snak·ing, snakes**) **1.** *vi.* **MOVE LIKE SNAKE** to move or lie like a snake, with many bends or twists **2.** *vt.* **DRAG** to drag something by a rope or chain **3.** *vt.* **TUG** to pull or jerk something suddenly [Old English *snaca*, from a prehistoric Germanic word meaning "to crawl," which is also the ancestor of English *snail*] ◇ **a snake in the grass** somebody who betrays or deceives others

Snake /snayk/ river in the northwestern United States, rising in Wyoming and flowing into the Columbia River in Washington State. Length: 1,038 mi./1,670 km.

snake·bird /snáyk bùrd/ *n.* = **anhinga**

snake·bite /snáyk bīt/ *n.* the bite of a poisonous snake, or illness resulting from this

snake charm·er *n.* an entertainer who elicits a swaying movement from snakes, especially cobras, by means of music and rhythmic body movements

snake dance *n.* **1. NATIVE N AMERICAN RITUAL** a ritual dance of some Native North American peoples in which live snakes are handled **2. DANCE IN LINE** a group dance in which participants follow a leader in a single file, often hanging onto the person in front and sometimes moving in a zigzag

snake doc·tor *n.* *Southern U.S.* a dragonfly

WORD KEY: REGIONAL NOTE

This Piedmont designation for "dragonfly" has spread across the Upper and Middle South, from Virginia to Arkansas and Texas. The Pennsylvania term *snake feeder* endures in eastern sections of Kentucky and Tennessee and the western parts of the Carolinas. Elsewhere, along the Atlantic and Gulf coasts, *mosquito hawk* prevails, with the clipped form *skeeter hawk*. The New England terms *darning needle* and *devil's darning needle* extend across the Inland North into the Upper Midwest.

snake eyes *n.* a throw of two dice that turns up one spot on each (*slang*)

snake feed·er *n.* a dragonfly (*regional*)

snake fence *n.* = **worm fence**

snake·fish /snáyk fish/ (*plural* **-fish** *or* **-fish·es**) *n.* an elongated predatory fish in the lizardfish family, found in the eastern Pacific and western Atlantic inshore regions. Latin name: *Trachinocephalus myops.*

snake fly *n.* an insect with a small head and long prothorax. Family: Raphidiidae.

snake·head /snáyk hèd/ *n.* **1.** = **turtlehead 2. TROPICAL FISH WITH PROTRUDING LOWER JAW** any of a group of tropical freshwater African or Asian fish that have a protruding lower jaw and are able to breathe air for long periods of time. Family: Channidae.

snake liz·ard *n.* a legless lizard found in Australia and New Guinea, not easily distinguished from a snake except that its tongue is flat and fleshy like a lizard's. Family: Pygopodidae.

snake oil *n.* **1.** WORTHLESS MEDICINE any worthless liquid preparation sold as a medicine, especially in the past by traveling peddlers **2.** DECEIVING WORDS something said or written with the intention of deceiving, pacifying, or persuading others

snake pit *n.* **1.** HORRIBLE CONFUSION a place or situation of horrible confusion (*informal*) **2.** OFFENSIVE TERM an offensive term for a place used to house and care for people judged to have a psychiatric disorder (*informal disapproving*)

snake·root /snáyk ro͝ot/ *n.* a plant with roots used in folk medicine to treat snakebite, or the root of any of these plants used as medicine

snake's head *n.* a European plant that grows in damp areas with drooping, purplish, checkered flowers. Latin name: *Fritillaria meleagris.*

snake·skin /snáyk skìn/ *n.* **1.** SNAKE'S SKIN the skin of a snake **2.** LEATHER MADE OF SNAKES' SKINS the skin of a snake or snakes made into leather, e.g., for shoes

snake·weed /snáyk wèed/ *n.* a plant used in folk medicine to cure snakebite, especially bistort

snak·y /snáykee/ (**-i·er, -i·est**) *adj.* **1.** RESEMBLING A SNAKE resembling a snake in being long and narrow with bends or coils, or like a snake's twisting and turning movements **2.** TREACHEROUS treacherous and deceitful —**snak·i·ly** *adv.* —**snak·i·ness** *n.*

snap /snap/ *v.* (**snapped, snap·ping, snaps**) **1.** *vti.* BREAK WITH SHARP NOISE to break or break something suddenly with a sharp cracking sound **2.** *vti.* DO SOMETHING WITH A SHARP NOISE to move, strike, or operate something in a way that makes a sharp noise **3.** *vti.* BREAK to break under force or pressure, or break something by excessive force or pressure **4.** *vi.* LOSE CONTROL to lose control or erupt in anger suddenly **5.** *vti.* SPEAK ANGRILY to say something or reply in anger or irritation **6.** *vt.* PHOTOGRAPHY TAKE A PHOTOGRAPH to take a photograph of somebody or something, especially in a casual way (*informal*) **7.** *vi.* BITE to bite or try to bite somebody or something with a quick movement or movements **8.** *vti.* TAKE SOMETHING to take or grasp something eagerly, or take something away from somebody suddenly **9.** *vti.* MOVE SHARPLY to move or be moved quickly and sharply **10.** *vi.* APPEAR ANGRY to flash, especially in anger (*refers to eyes*) **11.** *vt.* FLICK SOMETHING AWAY to flick something away with a finger coming forward sharply from the thumb **12.** *vt.* FOOTBALL PLAY THE BALL in football, to put the ball into play by passing it back to the quarterback behind the line of scrimmage ■ *n.* **1.** SHARP SOUND a short sharp sound, e.g., of something brittle suddenly breaking or of something clicking shut **2.** FASTENER THAT CLICKS TOGETHER a circular fastener consisting of two halves that close when pressed together and open when pulled apart **3.** SOMETHING EASY something easily done ○ *The test was a snap.* **4.** SHORT TIME a short period of time, especially one with cold weather ○ *a sudden cold snap* **5.** PHOTOGRAPHY = **snapshot** *n.* 1 **6.** LIVELINESS liveliness and vigor ○ *His campaign needs more snap.* **7.** CARDS CARD GAME a game where players lay cards face up in a pile. When two identical cards are played one after the other, the first player to shout "snap" takes the pile. The object of the game is to win the whole deck of cards. **8.** FOOD SWEET COOKIE a crisp, thin sweet cookie **9.** FOOTBALL FOOTBALL PLAY in football, the action required to start play in football, when the ball is passed to the quarterback behind the line of scrimmage ■ *adj.* **1.** DECIDED WITHOUT REFLECTION arrived at quickly and without reflection ○ *a snap decision* **2.** COMING WITHOUT WARNING coming suddenly and without warning **3.** OPERATING WITH A SHARP SOUND operating with interlocking parts that snap when being shut **4.** EASILY DONE easily done with success ■ *adv.* WITH A SNAP so as to make a sharp sound [15thC. Partly an imitation of the sound, and partly from Middle Dutch *snappen* "to seize" (source of English *snack*).]

snap up *v.* **1.** *vt.* TAKE SOMETHING HASTILY to quickly buy or take up something offered or available **2.** *vti.* GO FASTER to make something be or go faster (*informal*) ○ *Snap it up or we'll be late.*

snap bean *n.* an edible bean with long tubular pods that are harvested and eaten when immature [*Snap* either from its crispness, or because the pods are broken in pieces before being cooked]

snap-brim, snap-brim hat *n.* a man's hat with a flexible brim all around that is usually turned up in back and down in front

Snapdragon

snap·drag·on /snáp dràggən/ *n.* a common perennial plant with spikes of flowers of various colors. Genus: *Antirrhinum.* [Late 16thC. So called because the flowers are said to be similar to a dragon's mouth.]

snap·per /snáppər/ *n.* **1.** (*plural* **-pers** *or* **-per**) TROPICAL FOOD FISH a carnivorous fish common in tropical waters and caught for food. Family: Lutjanidae. **2.** = **snapping turtle 3.** SOMETHING THAT SNAPS somebody who or something that snaps

snap·ping be·etle *n.* = **click beetle**

snap·ping tur·tle *n.* a North American freshwater turtle with a large head and powerful hooked jaws. Family: Chelydridae.

snap·pish /snáppish/ *adj.* **1.** SHOWING IRRITATION showing a sharpness or curtness caused by irritation or impatience **2.** TENDING TO SNAP inclined to snap at things —**snap·pish·ly** *adv.* —**snap·pish·ness** *n.*

snap·py /snáppee/ (**-pi·er, -pi·est**) *adj.* **1.** STYLISH fashionable and stylish (*informal*) ○ *a snappy dresser* **2.** INTERESTING interesting and to the point, or able to write something interesting and to the point (*informal*) **3.** SHOWING IMPATIENCE expressing or showing impatience or irritation **4.** HASTY done or produced without delay —**snap·pi·ly** *adv.* —**snap·pi·ness** *n.* ◇ **make it snappy** to do something quickly (*informal*)

snap ring *n.* = **carabiner**

snap roll *n.* an aerial maneuver in which an airplane turns a complete circle longitudinally while maintaining altitude and direction of flight

snap·shot /snáp shòt/ *n.* **1.** PHOTOGRAPHY PHOTOGRAPH a photograph, especially one taken by an amateur with simple equipment **2.** RECORD OF POINT IN PROCESS a record or view of a particular point in a sequence of events or continuing process [Early 19thC. Originally meaning "quick shot from a gun," the sense was extended to "casual photograph" at the end of the 19thC.]

snare[1] /snair/ *n.* **1.** ANIMAL TRAP a trap for small animals that operates like a noose **2.** TRAP FOR UNWARY a situation that is both alluring and dangerous **3.** SURG SURGICAL DEVICE a surgical instrument for removing small polyps and tumors by means of a noose that is tightened by being pulled into a narrow tube ■ *vt.* (**snared, snar·ing, snares**) **1.** CATCH IN TRAP to catch somebody or something in a snare **2.** ENTRAP SOMEBODY to entrap somebody by alluring deception [Pre-12thC. From Old Norse *snara.* Ultimately from an Indo-European word meaning "to twist," which is also the ancestor of English *narcotic.*] —**snar·er** *n.*

snare[2] /snair/ *n.* any of the gut or wire cords stretched across the bottom skin of a drum to create a rattling sound when the drum is hit (*often used in the plural*) [Late 17thC. Origin uncertain: probably from Dutch *snaar* "string."]

snare drum *n.* a drum fitted with snares to produce a rattling effect

snarl[1] /snaarl/ *v.* (**snarled, snarl·ing, snarls**) **1.** *vi.* GROWL to growl threateningly **2.** *vti.* SPEAK ANGRILY to speak or say something angrily or threateningly ■ *n.* GROWLING NOISE the sound of somebody or something snarling [Late 16thC. Literally "to 'snar' repeatedly," formed from obsolete *snar* "to snarl, growl," of uncertain origin: probably ultimately an imitation of the sound.] —**snarl·er** *n.* —**snarl·ing·ly** *adv.*

snarl up *vti. U.K.* = **snarl**

snarl[2] /snaarl/ *n.* **1.** TANGLE a tangled mass of something such as hair or wool **2.** CONFUSION a state of confusion and obstruction from which there is no easy exit **3.** KNOT IN WOOD a knot in wood ■ *vti.* (**snarled, snarl·ing, snarls**) **1.** TANGLE SOMETHING to tangle something or become tangled **2.** GET CONFUSED OR CONGESTED to become or make something complicated, confused, or too congested to move [14thC. Origin uncertain: probably literally "small snare," formed from SNARE[1]. Its orginal meaning was "moral snare, temptation."]

snarl-up *n. U.K.* = **snarl**

snatch /snach/ *vt.* (**snatched, snatch·ing, snatch·es**) **1.** TAKE QUICKLY to grab or grasp somebody or something hastily **2.** MOVE SOMETHING QUICKLY to move or remove something quickly **3.** TAKE WHEN OPPORTUNITY ARISES to take or get something while there is an opportunity ○ *snatched a few hours of sleep* **4.** KIDNAP to kidnap somebody (*informal*) ■ *n.* **1.** GRABBING an instance of grabbing or grasping somebody or something **2.** SMALL AMOUNT a small, incomplete bit or short period of something **3.** KIDNAPPING an act of kidnapping (*informal*) **4.** LIFTING FEAT a weightlifting feat in which the barbell is raised from the floor to over the lifter's head in one motion **5.** OFFENSIVE TERM a highly offensive term referring to the outer sexual organs a woman (*taboo offensive*) [12thC. Origin uncertain: perhaps from Middle Dutch *snacken* "to snatch, chatter."] —**snatch·er** *n.*

snatch block *n.* a block that can be opened on one side to insert a rope, thereby avoiding the necessity of threading the rope through from one end

snatch·y /snáchee/ (**-i·er, -i·est**) *adj.* occurring or done in short spells

snath /snath/, **snathe** /snay*th*/ *n.* the handle of a scythe [Late 16thC. Variant of *snead,* from Old English *snǣd,* of unknown origin.]

snaz·zy /snázzee/ (**-zi·er, -zi·est**) *adj.* attractively new, bright, or fashionable (*informal*) [Mid-20thC. Origin unknown.]

SNCC /snik/ *abbr.* Student Nonviolent Coordinating Committee

SNCF *n.* Société Nationale des Chemins de Fer, the rail system in France

Snead /sneed/, **Sam** (*b.* 1912) U.S. golfer. He won 84 Professional Golf Association (PGA) tournaments. Real name **Samuel Jackson Snead.** Known as **Slammin' Sammy**

sneak /sneek/ *v.* (**sneaked** *or* **snuck, sneak·ing, sneaks**) **1.** *vi.* GO STEALTHILY to go or act in a stealthy, secretive way **2.** *vt.* DO SOMETHING FURTIVELY to do something stealthily, furtively, and without being noticed ○ *He sneaked a look over the wall.* **3.** *vt.* BRING STEALTHILY to get or carry somebody or something secretly, furtively, and without being noticed ○ *sneak friends into the house for a surprise party* ■ *n.* **1.** UNTRUSTWORTHY PERSON a cunning and deceitful person **2.** STEALTHY DEPARTURE a departure intended to be unobserved **3.** CLOTHES SNEAKER a sneaker (*informal*) ■ *adj.* STEALTHILY DONE done stealthily or furtively [Late 16thC. Origin uncertain.]

sneak up on *vt.* **1.** APPROACH SECRETLY to approach stealthily with the intention of surprising or frightening somebody or something **2.** ARRIVE UNEXPECTEDLY to arrive more quickly than expected ○ *The weekend sneaked up on me.*

sneak·er /snéekər/ *n. U.S., Can, ANZ* a shoe with a rubber sole and, usually, a cloth upper (*often used in the plural*)

sneak·ing /snéeking/ *adj.* **1.** HIDDEN FROM OTHERS unknown to or hidden from others **2.** SLIGHT BUT PERSISTENT slight but persistent ○ *a sneaking suspicion* **3.** DECEPTIVE deceptive or given to cunning and deception —**sneak·ing·ly** *adv.*

sneak pre·view *n.* a public screening of a movie prior to its general release, in order to test public reaction to it

sneak thief *n.* a thief who surreptitiously steals unguarded or unsecured articles when the opportunity arises

sneak·y /snéekee/ (**-i·er, -i·est**) *adj.* done, doing something, or in the habit of behaving, in an underhanded and unfair way —**sneak·i·ly** *adv.* —**sneak·i·ness** *n.*

sneer /sneer/ *n.* EXPRESSION OF SCORN a facial expression of scorn or hostility in which the upper lip may be raised ■ *v.* (**sneered, sneer·ing, sneers**) **1.** *vi.* FEEL OR SHOW SCORN to feel or show scorn, contempt, or hostility, either in speech or facial expression **2.** *vt.* SAY WITH SCORN to speak or say something with scorn or contempt [14thC. Origin uncertain: perhaps suggestive of the expression; or an alteration of Old English *fnǣran* "to snort."] —**sneer·er** *n.* —**sneer·ing** *adj.* —**sneer·ing·ly** *adv.*

sneeze /sneez/ *n.* **EXPLOSIVE EXPULSION OF AIR** a sudden involuntary expulsion of air through the nose and mouth, caused by irritation of the nasal passages ■ *vi.* (**sneezed, sneez·ing, sneez·es**) **MAKE A SNEEZE** to suddenly, forcefully, and involuntarily expel air through the nose and mouth because of irritation of the nasal passages [15thC. Alteration of *fnesan*, from Old English *fneosan*, an imitation of the sound of breathing or sneezing.] —**sneez·er** *n.* —**sneez·y** *adj.*

sneeze·guard /sneéz gaàrd/ *n.* a plastic or glass cover hanging over a food display such as a salad bar or a buffet to protect it from contamination

sneeze·weed /sneéz weèd/ *n.* a perennial plant growing wild in North America that makes some people sneeze. Genus: *Helenium.*

sneeze·wort /sneéz wùrt, -wàwrt/ *n.* a European and Asian composite plant with small white flowers similar to those of a daisy and silvery leaves that when powdered induce sneezing. Latin name: *Achillea ptarmica.*

snell /snel/ *n.* a short piece of gut or nylon used to connect a fishhook or lure to a longer line [Mid-19thC. Origin unknown.]

Snel·len chart /snéllən-/ *n.* a chart for vision testing on which are printed rows of letters and numbers in decreasing size from top to bottom [Mid-19thC. Named for Herman *Snellen* 1834–1908, Dutch opthalmologist.]

Snell's law /snélz-/ *n.* the law stating that for a light ray passing between two media the ratio of the sines of the angle of incidence and the angle of refraction is a constant [Late 19thC. Named for Willebrord Van Roijen *Snell* 1591–1626, Dutch astronomer and mathematician.]

SNG *n., abbr.* synthetic (or substitute) natural gas

snick /snik/ *n.* **1. SMALL CUT** a small cut or notch **2. CLICKING NOISE** a small clicking noise ■ *v.* (**snicked, snick·ing, snicks**) **1.** *vt.* **CUT SOMETHING** to cut something slightly **2.** *vi.* **MAKE CLICKING NOISE** to make a small clicking noise [Late 17thC. Origin uncertain: probably from obsolete *snick or snee* (see SNICKERSNEE).]

snick·er /sníkər/, **snig·ger** /sníggər/ *v.* (**-ered, -er·ing, -ers; -gered, -ger·ing, -gers**) **1.** *vi.* **LAUGH DISRESPECTFULLY** to laugh disrespectfully in a covert way **2.** *vt.* **SAY SOMETHING WITH DERISION** to speak derisively or with disrespectful laughter of somebody or something ■ *n.* **DISRESPECTFUL LAUGH** an instance of laughing disrespectfully or the sound of disrespectful laughter [Late 17thC. Origin uncertain: possibly an imitation of the sound.]

snick·er·snee /sníkər sneè, sníkər sneé/ *n.* a long knife used as a cutting or thrusting weapon (*archaic*) [Early 18thC. Alteration of *snick or snee* "cut or thrust in knife-fighting," an alteration of *stick or snee*, from Dutch *steken* "to thrust" + *snee*, variant of *snijden* "to cut."]

snide /snīd/ (**snid·er, snid·est**) *adj.* derisively sarcastic [Mid-19thC. Origin unknown. Originally in the meaning of "counterfeit."] —**snide·ly** *adv.*

sniff /snif/ *v.* (**sniffed, sniff·ing, sniffs**) **1.** *vti.* **BREATHE IN THROUGH NOSE** to breathe in through the nose, e.g., to see how something smells **2.** *vt.* **SUSPECT SOMETHING** to have a suspicion of something, especially something bad ○ *sniff trouble* ■ *n.* **1. ACT OR SOUND OF SNIFFING** an instance or the sound of inhaling through the nose **2. SUSPICION** a hint or suspicion, especially of something bad [14thC. An imitation of the sound.]

sniff at *vt.* to show contempt or disdain for somebody or something

sniff out *vt.* to discover something, especially something bad, by investigation (*informal*)

sniff·er /sníffər/ *n.* somebody who sniffs, especially somebody who takes drugs by inhaling them through the nose

snif·fle /snífʼl/ *vi.* (**-fled, -fling, -fles**) **1. INHALE MUCUS** to inhale through the nose to prevent mucus from dripping out of it **2. WEEP QUIETLY** to sniff repeatedly while gently weeping ■ *n.* **ACT OR SOUND OF SNIFFLING** an instance or the sound of sniffling ■ **snif·fles** *npl.* **SLIGHT COLD** a slight cold that causes sniffling (*informal*) [Mid-17thC. An imitation of the sound.] —**snif·fler** *n.*

sniff·y /sníffee/ (**-i·er, -i·est**) *adj.* (*informal*) **1. HAUGHTY** behaving in a haughty, disdainful way **2. SNIFFING** tending to sniff a lot, e.g., because of a cold —**sniff·i·ly** *adv.* —**sniff·i·ness** *n.*

snif·ter /snífter/ *n.* **1. GLASS FOR SERVING BRANDY** a stemmed glass with a bowl that tapers upward, typically used for brandy **2. SMALL DRINK** a small amount of drink, especially of alcohol (*informal*) [Mid-18thC. Originally in the meaning of "strong breeze," from archaic *snifter* "to sniff, snuffle," an imitation of the sound.]

snig·ger *vi.* = **snicker** [Early 18thC. A later variant of SNICKER.]

snig·gle /sníggʼl/ *vti.* (**-gled, -gling, -gles**) **FISH FOR EELS** to fish for eels by putting a baited hook into crevices where they hide, or to catch eels using this method ■ *n.* **HOOK** a baited hook used for catching eels [Mid-17thC. Formed from *snig* "young eel," of unknown origin.] —**snig·gler** *n.*

snip /snip/ *vti.* (**snipped, snip·ping, snips**) **CUT USING SMALL STROKES** to cut with scissors or shears, especially using small strokes, or cut something using small strokes ■ *n.* **1. A CUT** a short quick cut, made with scissors **2. SMALL PIECE** a small piece of something that has been snipped off **3. ACT OR SOUND OF SNIPPING** the act or sound of using scissors to snip something **4. DEMEANING TERM** young girl regarded as behaving in ways inappropriate to her age or class (*insult*) ■ *interj.* **SOUND OF SNIPPING** used to represent the sound that scissors make [Mid-16thC. From Dutch or Low German *snippen*, an imitation of the sound.]

snipe /snīp/ *n.* (*plural* **snipes** *or* **snipe**) **1. WADING BIRD** a wading bird with a long straight bill. It lives in marshy areas and on river banks throughout the northern hemisphere. Latin name: *Gallinago gallinago.* **2. BIRD RELATED TO SNIPE** a bird related to the snipe such as a sandpiper or curlew **3. SHOT FIRED FROM CONCEALMENT** a shot fired from a concealed place ■ *vi.* (**sniped, snip·ing, snipes**) **SHOOT FROM CONCEALED PLACE** to shoot at people from a concealed position [14thC. Origin uncertain: probably from Old Norse *snípa*. The verb came from the idea of hunting snipe.]

snipe·fish /snīp fish/ (*plural* **-fish** *or* **-fish·es**) *n.* a fish with a long snout and a spine extending from its dorsal fin to its tail. It lives in tropical and temperate seas and is related to the seahorse. Family: Macrorhamphosidae.

snipe fly *n.* a fly with a long body and long legs that eats other insects. Some also suck the blood of mammals. Family: Leptidae.

snip·er *n.* somebody who shoots at people from a concealed position

snip·pet·y *adj.* = **snippy** *adj.* —**snip·pet·i·ness** *n.*

snip·ping *n.* = **snip** *n.* **2**

snip·py /snípee/ (**-pi·er, -pi·est**) *adj.* behaving in a curt and irritable way (*informal*) —**snip·pi·ly** *adv.* —**snip·pi·ness** *n.*

snips *npl.* shears used for cutting sheet metal (*takes a singular or plural verb*)

snit /snit/ *n.* a state of mild irritation or bad temper [Mid-20thC. Origin unknown.]

snitch /snich/ *v.* (**snitched, snitch·ing, snitch·es**) (*slang*) **1.** *vt.* **PILFER SOMETHING** to steal something in a sneaky way especially something of little value **2.** *vi.* **INFORM** to inform on somebody ○ *Friends don't snitch on each other.* ■ *n.* **INFORMER** somebody who informs on others (*slang*) [Late 17thC. Origin unknown.] —**snitch·er** *n.*

sniv·el /snívʼl/ *vi.* (**-eled** *or* **-elled, -el·ing** *or* **-el·ling, -els**) **1. SNIFF** to sniff audibly **2. WHINE** to behave in a whining, tearful, or self-pitying way **3. SNIFFLE** to have a runny nose ■ *n.* **WHINE OR SNIFF** an act of sniveling [Assumed Old English *snyflan*] —**sniv·el·er** *n.* —**sniv·el·ing** *n., adj.* —**sniv·el·y** *adj.*

snob /snob/ *n.* **1. SOMEBODY WHO LOOKS DOWN ON OTHERS** somebody who admires and cultivates relationships with those considered socially superior, and disdains those considered inferior **2. SOMEBODY WHO FEELS SUPERIOR** somebody who looks down on people considered to have inferior knowledge or tastes [Mid-19thC. Origin unknown. Its meaning developed from "cobbler's apprentice," through "lower-class person," to "somebody who tries to imitate those of higher status."]

WORD KEY: ORIGIN

Snob originally meant "shoemaker" (a sense that survives in places). Cambridge University students of the late 18th century adopted it as a slang term for a "townsman, someone not a member of the university," and it seems to have been this usage that formed the basis in the 1830s for the emergence of the new general sense "member of the lower classes." The modern sense "someone who apes social superiors" received a considerable boost when William Thackeray used it in his *Book of Snobs* (1848). As for the origins of the word itself, the suggestion that it comes from *s.nob.*, short for Latin *sine nobilitate* "without nobility," is ingenious but ignores the word's early history.

snob ap·peal *n.* qualities intended to appeal to a sense of snobbery in people and make them want to be part of or have something

snob·ber·y (*plural* **-ies**) *n.* the attitude or behavior of somebody who looks down on those considered inferior, or a particular example of this

snob·bish *adj.* displaying an offensively superior condescending manner —**snob·bish·ly** *adv.* —**snob·bish·ness** *n.*

snob·bism *n.* = **snobbery**

snob·by (**-bi·er, -bi·est**) *adj.* snobbish (*informal*)

SNOBOL /snṓ bawl/ *n.* a computer programming language designed for dealing with strings of symbols. Full form **String Oriented Symbolic Language** [Mid-20thC. Modeled on "COBOL."]

Sno-Cat /snṓ kat/ *tdmk.* a trademark for a motorized vehicle that has tractor treads for moving easily on snow

snoek /snook/ (*plural* **snoeks** *or* **snoek**) *n.* a long predatory edible fish of Australia, New Zealand, and South Africa that belongs to the snake mackerel family. Latin name: *Thyrsites atun.* [Late 18thC. Via Afrikaans from Middle Dutch *snoec* "pike" (source of English *snook*).]

snol·ly·gos·ter /snóli gòstər/ (*plural* **-ters** *informal*) *n.* somebody, especially a politician, whose actions are motivated by self-interest rather than by high principles (*slang*) [Mid-19thC. Origin uncertain: possibly an alteration of earlier *snallygaster*, perhaps from Pennsylvania Dutch.]

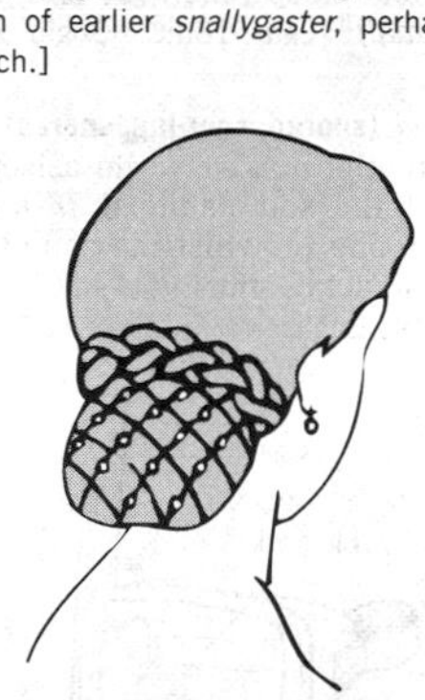

Snood

snood /snood/ *n.* **1. DECORATIVE HAIR NET** a net that holds a woman's hair at the back of her head **2. RIBBON WORN BY UNMARRIED SCOTTISH WOMEN** a hairband or ribbon that unmarried women in Scotland wore in the 17th and 18th centuries ■ *vt.* (**snood·ed, snood·ing, snoods**) **WEAR A SNOOD OVER THE HAIR** to fasten the hair with a snood [Old English *snōd*. Ultimately from an Indo-European base meaning "to spin, sew," which is also the ancestor of English *needle*.]

snook[1] /snook, snoŏk/ (*plural* **snook** *or* **snooks**) *n.* a large bony fish that lives in warm seas and rivers. Latin name: *Centropomus undecimalis.* [Late 17thC. Via Dutch *snoek* "pike" from Middle Dutch *snoec*.]

snook[2] /snook, snoŏk/ *n.* a gesture made as a sign of contempt, by putting the thumb to the nose with the fingers outstretched [Late 18thC. Origin unknown.]

snook·er /snoŏkər/ *n.* **1. GAME LIKE POOL** a pool game in which a white cue ball is used to hit 15 red balls and 6 balls of different colors into any of 6 pockets **2. POSITION IN SNOOKER** a position in snooker in which a player is forced to play an indirect shot because another ball is between the cue ball and the target ball ■ *vt.* (**-ered, -er·ing, -ers**) **1. TRICK SOMEBODY** to deceive somebody through trickery (*informal*) ○ *snookered by a fast-talking salesman into buying something he didn't really need* **2. PUT SOMEBODY AT DISADVANTAGE IN SNOOKER** to put a snooker player in the position of being forced to play an indirect shot because another ball is between the cue ball and the target ball [Late 19thC. Origin unknown.]

WORD KEY: ORIGIN

The most widely canvassed theory of the origins of the word ***snooker*** is that it is an adaptation of late 19th-century British army slang *snooker* "new recruit." The game was invented, as a diversion perhaps from the monotony of billiards, by British army officers serving in India in the 1870s, and the story goes that the term ***snooker*** was applied to it by Colonel Sir Neville Chamberlain (1856–1944), at that time a subaltern in the Devonshire Regiment stationed in Jubbulpore, in allusion to the inept play of one of his brother officers.

snoop /snoop/ *vi.* (**snooped, snoop·ing, snoops**) **PRY** to pry into other people's business or affairs, especially in a furtive way (*informal*) ■ *n.* (*informal*) **1. SOMEBODY WHO SNOOPS** somebody who pries into other people's business or affairs, especially in a sneaky way **2. SNEAKY PRYING INTO SOMEBODY'S AFFAIRS** a furtive search or investigation of somebody's private property or affairs [Mid-19thC. From Dutch *snoepen* "to eat on the sly."] —**snoop·er** *n.*

snoop·er·scope /snóopər skōp/ *n.* a device that converts infrared radiation into a visual image and is used for seeing in the dark

snoop·y (**-i·er, -i·est**) *adj.* tending to pry into the affairs of others

snoot /snoot/ *n.* **NOSE** a nose or snout (*informal*) ■ *vt.* (**snoot·ed, snoot·ing, snoots**) **CONDESCEND TO SOMEBODY** to treat somebody haughtily (*informal*) [Mid-19thC. Variant of SNOUT. In the meaning of "condescend," a back-formation from SNOOTY.]

snoot·y /snóotee/ (**-i·er, -i·est**) *adj.* (*informal*) **1. SUPERCILIOUS** showing a haughty, condescending manner **2. EXCLUSIVE** excluding some people out of snobbery [Early 20thC. Formed from SNOOT, from the notion of looking down one's nose at others.] —**snoot·i·ly** *adv.* —**snoot·i·ness** *n.*

snooze /snooz/ *vi.* (**snoozed, snooz·ing, snooz·es**) **TO NAP** to have a short sleep (*informal*) ■ *n.* **A NAP** a short sleep (*informal*) [Late 18thC. Origin unknown.] —**snooz·er** *n.*

snore /snawr/ *vi.* (**snored, snor·ing, snores**) **BREATHE NOISILY IN SLEEP** to breathe noisily while asleep because of vibrations of the soft palate ■ *n.* **A SOUND MADE BY SNORING** a snorting or whistling sound made while sleeping, or an act of snoring [14thC. Origin uncertain: possibly from Old English *fnora* "sneezing."] —**snor·er** *n.*

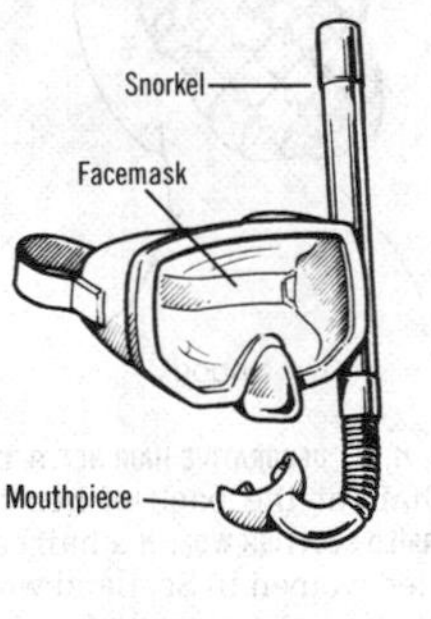

Snorkel

snor·kel /snáwrk'l/ *n.* **1. BREATHING APPARATUS** a device allowing somebody to swim just below water, consisting of a face mask and a breathing tube held in the mouth while the other end projects above the water **2. VENTILATOR ON SUBMARINE** a ventilation device on a submarine. It projects above the surface while the vessel is submerged, allowing air in and gases out. **3. DEVICE ON TANK** a device on a tank or other vehicle that functions like the snorkel on a submarine and enables the vehicle to go through shallow water ■ *vi.* (**-keled, -kel·ing, -kels**) **SWIM WITH SNORKEL** to swim underwater breathing air through a snorkel [Mid-20thC. From German *Schnorchel*, from a dialect word meaning "nose"; originally "intake and exhaust shaft of a submarine"; from its resemblance to a nose.] —**snor·kel·er** *n.*

snor·kel·ing *n.* the activity or pastime of swimming with a snorkel

snort /snawrt/ *v.* (**snort·ed, snort·ing, snorts**) **1.** *vi.* **FORCE AIR THROUGH NOSE** to make a harsh sound by forcing air out through the nostrils **2.** *vi.* **SHOW CONTEMPT** to express a feeling, especially of contempt or impatience, by snorting **3.** *vti.* DRUGS **INHALE DRUG** to inhale a powdered drug through the nostrils (*slang*) ■ *n.* **1. HARSH SOUND** a harsh sound made by snorting, or an instance of this **2. GULP OF ALCOHOL** a short drink, especially of alcohol, taken all at once (*informal*) **3.** DRUGS **INHALATION OF DRUG** an act of inhaling a powdered drug through the nostrils (*slang*) **4. SUBMARINE SNORKEL** the snorkel of a submarine (*slang*) [14thC. Origin uncertain: probably a variant of SNORE.] —**snort·er** *n.* —**snort·ing** *n., adj.*

snot /snot/ *n.* **1. OFFENSIVE TERM** an offensive term referring to mucus produced in the nose (*slang offensive*) **2. OFFENSIVE TERM** an offensive term referring to somebody whose behavior is regarded as arrogant or condescending (*slang insult*) [Old English *gesnot*. Ultimately from a prehistoric Germanic word that is also the ancestor of English *snout* and *snoot*.]

snot-nosed *adj.* an offensive term describing somebody who is regarded as being young and precocious but not to be taken seriously (*slang offensive*)

snot·ty /snóttee/ (**-ti·er, -ti·est**) *adj.* (*slang offensive*) **1. OFFENSIVE TERM** an offensive term describing something that is wet or dirty with nasal mucus **2. OFFENSIVE TERM** an offensive term describing somebody who is regarded as behaving in an arrogant and condescending manner **3. OFFENSIVE TERM** an offensive term describing actions that are regarded as mean or rude —**snot·ti·ly** *adv.* —**snot·ti·ness** *n.*

snout /snowt/ *n.* **1.** ZOOL **ANIMAL'S NOSE** the projecting part of a vertebrate's head, consisting of the nose and mouth **2.** INSECTS **PROJECTING PART OF INSECT'S HEAD** the projecting part of the head of an insect or other invertebrate such as a weevil **3. LARGE NOSE** somebody's nose (*slang*) **4. PROJECTION SIMILAR TO A SNOUT** something that sticks out like a snout such as the muzzle of a gun **5.** GEOL **STEEP END OF GLACIER** the leading face of a glacier, usually heavily loaded with rock debris [13thC] —**snout·ed** *adj.*

snout bee·tle *n.* = **weevil** *n.* 1 ["Snout" from the shape of its head]

snow /snō/ *n.* **1.** METEOROL **ICE CRYSTAL FLAKES** water vapor in the atmosphere that has frozen into ice crystals and then falls to the ground in the form of flakes **2.** METEOROL **FALL OF SNOW** an amount of snow that falls at one time ○ *had a heavy snow last night* **3.** METEOROL **SNOW ON GROUND** a layer of snow on the ground **4. SOMETHING RESEMBLING SNOW** something that resembles snow in color or texture **5.** ELEC **WHITE SPECKS ON TELEVISION SCREEN** random patterns of small white specks on a television or radar screen caused by electrical interference **6. DESSERT RESEMBLING SNOW** a dessert made of whipped egg whites, sugar, and fruit **7.** DRUGS **NARCOTIC DRUG** cocaine or heroin in the form of a white powder (*slang*) ■ *v.* (**snowed, snow·ing, snows**) **1.** *vi.* METEOROL **TO FALL IN THE FORM OF SNOW** to be marked by the falling of snow ○ *It's snowing!* **2.** *vt.* **COVER SOMETHING WITH SNOW** to cover, close in, or block with a fall of snow ○ *We were snowed in for two days.* **3.** *vti.* **FALL LIKE SNOW** to fall as snow or like snow, or make something fall in this way **4.** *vt.* **PERSUADE SOMEBODY WITH GLIB TALK** to overwhelm or deceive somebody especially with flattery or charm (*slang*) ○ *She actually snowed us into buying worthless stock.* [Old English *snāw*. Ultimately from an Indo-European word meaning "snow."] ◇ **be snowed under (with something)** to be overwhelmed with something, especially work

snow under *vt.* (**snowed un·der, snow·ing un·der, snows un·der**) **DEFEAT OPPONENT** to defeat an opposing team soundly ■ **OVERWHELM SOMEBODY WITH SOMETHING** to inundate somebody with something such as work beyond the point at which the person can deal with it

snow·ball /snṓ bàwl/ *n.* **1. BALL OF SNOW** a soft lump of snow for throwing at somebody or something, made from handfuls of snow pressed together **2. FROZEN SNACK** a frozen snack made from crushed ice and colored, flavored syrup ■ *v.* (**-balled, -ball·ing, -balls**) **1.** *vi.* **INCREASE RAPIDLY** to grow or multiply rapidly or at an accelerating rate ○ *The event snowballed until hundreds of people were involved.* **2.** *vt.* **CAUSE TO INCREASE** to cause something to increase rapidly or at an accelerating rate **3.** *vti.* **THROW SNOWBALLS** to throw snowballs at each other or at somebody else ◇ **not have a snowball's chance (in hell)** to have no chance at all (*informal*)

Snowbelt, **Snow Belt** *n.* the northern regions of the United States, especially the Midwest and Northeast, which have a large amount of snow in winter

snow·ber·ry /snṓ beree/ (*plural* **-ries**) *n.* **1. SHRUB WITH WHITE BERRIES** a North American shrub with small pink flowers and white berries. Genus: *Symphoricarpos*. **2. WHITE BERRY** the white berry that grows on the snowberry shrub

snow·bird /snṓ bùrd/ *n.* **1. WINTER TRAVELER TO A WARMER CLIMATE** somebody who travels to a place that has a warmer climate in the winter (*informal*) **2. BIRD SEEN IN WINTER** any bird that is seen chiefly in winter such as the snow bunting, fieldfare, and junco

snow-blind, **snow-blind·ed** *adj.* effected with temporary blindness and pain in the eyes caused by bright light reflected from snow and ice

snow blind·ness *n.* a condition of temporary blindness caused by the bright sunlight and intense radiation reflected from snow or ice, which causes swelling of parts of the eyeball and severe pain

snow·blink /snṓ blìngk/ *n.* a white glow in the sky, especially in polar regions, caused by reflection of light from distant snowfields

snow·blow·er /snṓ blō ər/ *n.* a machine that clears snow from roads by scooping it into a fast-rotating spiral blade and ejecting it to one side

snow·board /snṓ bàwrd/ (**-board·ed, -board·ing, -boards**) *n.* **1. BOARD FOR SLIDING ON SNOW** a board that somebody stands on to slide down snow slopes. It has bindings for the feet and is used without ski poles. **2.** *vi.* **USE A SNOWBOARD** to slide down snow slopes using a snowboard —**snow·board·er** *n.* —**snow·board·ing** *n.*

snow·bound /snṓ bòwnd/ *adj.* prevented from moving or leaving a place by heavy snow

snow bunt·ing *n.* a white finch with dark markings that nests on tundra and winters in coastal regions. Latin name: *Plectrophenax nivalis*.

snow·bush /snṓ bòosh/ *n.* a spiny shrub that has small white flowers and is native to California and Oregon. Latin name: *Ceanothus cordulatus*.

snow·cap /snṓ kàp/ *n.* a covering of snow on a mountain peak —**snow·capped** *adj.*

snow cone *n.* a snack consisting of crushed flavored ice served in a paper cone

snow·drift /snṓ drìft/ *n.* a bank of snow piled up by the wind

snow·drop /snṓ dròp/ *n.* a bulbous plant of Europe and Asia with small white drooping flowers that appear early in spring. Latin name: *Galanthus nivalis*.

snow·drop tree *n.* = **silverbell**

snow·fall /snṓ fàwl/ *n.* **1. FALL OF SNOW** a period during which show falls or an instance of snow falling **2. AMOUNT OF FALLEN SNOW** the amount of snow that falls in a particular place or in a given period ○ *What is the average snowfall for the area?*

snow fence *n.* a portable flexible fence made of upright slats, designed to stop snow from drifting onto roads or ski runs

snow·field /snṓ feeld/ *n.* a large area permanently covered in snow

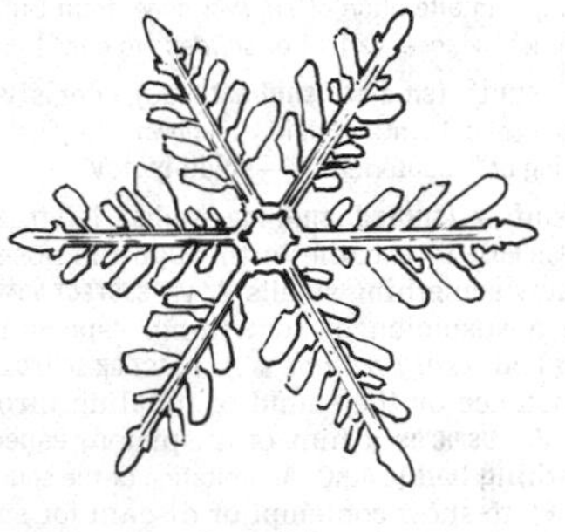

Snowflake

snow·flake /snṓ flàyk/ *n.* **1. CRYSTAL OF SNOW** any of the individual masses of ice crystals that together fall as snow **2. PLANT WITH BELL-SHAPED FLOWERS** a bulbous garden plant with white flowers like those of a snowdrop but larger. Genus: *Leucojum*. **3.** = **snow bunting**

snow goose *n.* a North American goose that breeds in Arctic regions and migrates to coastal areas in winter. The adults have white plumage and black wingtips. Latin name: *Anser caerulescens*.

snow-in-sum·mer *n.* a perennial European plant with wooly stems, notched silvery-green leaves, and white flowers. Latin name: *Cerastium tomentosum*.

snow job *n.* an attempt to mislead or persuade somebody by insincere talk or flattery (*slang*)

snow leop·ard *n.* a large cat that lives in mountainous regions of central Asia and has a thick pale-gray or brown coat marked with dark splotches. Latin name: *Panthera uncia.*

snow line *n.* the line of altitude above which there is permanent snow, or the line of latitude that marks the extent of permanent snow in the polar regions

snow·mak·ing /snów màukiln/ *n.* the science or process or making artificial snow, e.g., at a ski area

snow·man /snṓ màn/ (*plural* **-men** /-mèn/) *n.* a roughly human figure made by piling up and shaping snow

snow·melt /snṓ mèlt/ *n.* **1.** RUNOFF runoff produced when snow melts **2.** SEASON the season when snow melts

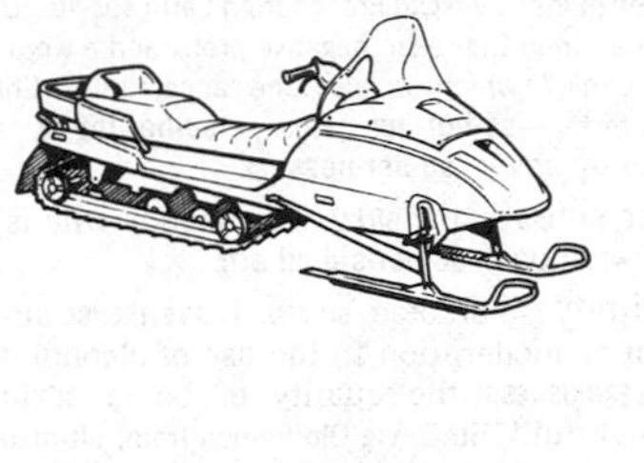

Snowmobile

snow·mo·bile /snṓmə bèel, -mō-/ *n.* a small vehicle used for traveling over snow. It has runners at the front and a caterpillar track underneath. —**snow·mo·bil·er** *n.* —**snow·mo·bil·ing** *n.*

snow-on-the-moun·tain *n.* a North American shrub that has white-edged leaves and white bracts. Latin name: *Euphorbia marginata.*

snow·pack /snów pàk/ *n.* accumulated snow, usually in a mountainous area

snow pea *n. U.S., Can, ANZ* a variety of garden pea that has an edible thin flat pod. Latin name: *Pisum sativum.*

snow pel·let *n.* a soft white round mass of ice that falls as precipitation (*often used in the plural*)

snow plant *n.* a plant with scarlet flowers and a fleshy reddish stalk. It grows in the mountains of western North America and often flowers before the snow has melted. Latin name: *Sarcodes sanguinea.*

snow·plow /snó plòw/ *n.* **1.** VEHICLE FOR CLEARING SNOW a vehicle or an implement that can be fixed to a vehicle, used for clearing snow from roads or paths **2.** CONTROL TECHNIQUE IN SKIING a technique used in skiing in which the points of the skis are brought together to make a V, enabling the skier to turn or stop ■ *vi.* (**-plowed, -plowing, -plows**) SKI IN SNOWPLOW POSITION to use the snowplow position to turn or stop in skiing

snow·shed /snṓ shèd/ *n.* a shelter over an open section of a railroad track, especially on a mountainside, to prevent it from getting covered in snow

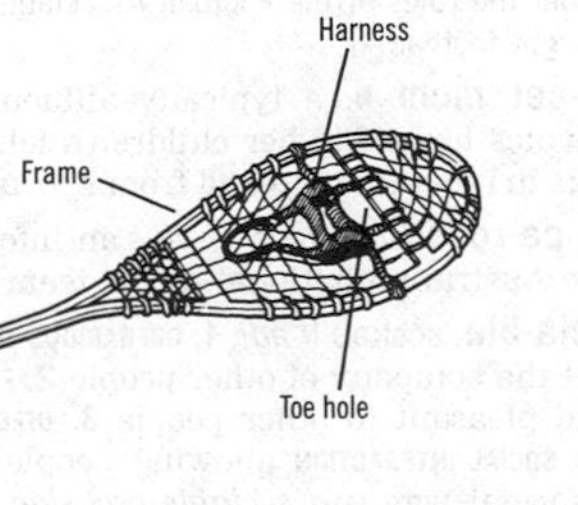

Snowshoe

snow·shoe /snṓ shoo/ *n.* SHOE FOR WALKING IN SNOW a metal or wood framework with interwoven straps that is attached to a boot and allows the wearer to walk on snow without sinking ■ *vi.* (**-shoed, -shoe·ing, -shoes**) WALK IN SNOWSHOES to walk on snow wearing snowshoes —**snow·sho·er** *n.*

snow·shoe hare, snow·shoe rabbit *n.* a North American hare with a white winter coat that turns brown in summer and large heavily furred hind feet that allow it to move quickly in snow. Latin name: *Lepus americanus.*

snow·storm /snṓ stàwrm/ *n.* a storm with heavy snow and sometimes strong winds

snow·suit /snṓ sòot/ *n.* an insulated, often water-resistant, garment of one or two pieces worn by children in cold snowy weather

snow throw·er *n.* = **snow blower**

snow tire *n.* a tire with a deep tread pattern or studs to provide extra traction for a vehicle driving in snowy conditions

snow-white *adj.* as white as fresh snow —**snow white** *n.*

snow·y *adj.* **1.** MARKED BY SNOW characterized by the presence of snow ○ *a snowy day* **2.** LIKE SNOW resembling snow, especially in color or purity ○ *a snowy beard* —**snow·i·ly** *adv.* —**snow·i·ness** *n.*

snow·y e·gret *n.* a small egret of North and South America that has white feathers, black legs, and yellow feet. Latin name: *Egretta thula.*

Snow·y Moun·tains range of peaks within the Australian Alps, in southeastern New South Wales, Australia. Mount Kosciusko is both its highest peak and the highest peak in Australia, 7,310 ft./2,228 m.

snow·y owl *n.* a large white owl that lives in the Arctic. It builds nests on the ground and feeds mainly on lemmings. Latin name: *Nyctea scandiaca.*

snow·y plov·er *n.* a small shorebird with white underparts found on sandy coasts, sand flats, and alkali ponds in the United States and Mexico. Latin name: *Charadrius alexandrinus.*

snub /snub/ *vt.* (**snubbed, snub·bing, snubs**) **1.** TREAT SOMEBODY RUDELY to treat somebody with deliberate coldness or contempt **2.** BRING SOMETHING TO A STOP to stop a line from paying out by wrapping it around something, or to stop something attached to a line such as a boat or horse from getting away by wrapping the line around something **3.** STUB SOMETHING OUT to extinguish something by stubbing it out ■ *n.* HUMILIATING ACTION a remark or act intended to humiliate or insult, e.g., ignoring somebody ■ *adj.* SMALL short and flat or turned up at the end [14thC. From Old Norse *snubba*, of uncertain origin: probably from a prehistoric Germanic base of words concerning the nose, which is also the ancestor of English *sniff*.] —**snub·ber** *n.*

snub·by (**-bi·er, -bi·est**) *adj.* **1.** TENDING TO SNUB PEOPLE tending to treat people with a lack of regard, e.g., by ignoring or insulting them **2.** = **snub-nosed**

snub-nosed *adj.* **1.** WITH SHORT BARREL OR BLUNT END having a very short barrel or a blunt end ○ *snub-nosed pliers* **2.** WITH TURNED UP NOSE with a nose that is short and flat or turned up

snuck /snuk/ past tense, past participle of **sneak**

snuff[1] /snuf/ *vt.* (**snuffed, snuff·ing, snuffs**) **1.** EXTINGUISH FLAME to extinguish a flame, e.g., that of a burning candle **2.** TRIM CANDLEWICK to remove the burned end from the wick of a candle **3.** DESTROY SOMETHING to put an end to somebody or something (*informal*) ○ *snuff out enthusiasm* ■ *n.* SOOTY WICK the sooty, charred end of a candlewick [14thC. Origin unknown.]

snuff[2] /snuf/ *n.* **1.** POWDERED TOBACCO tobacco in the form of powder, taken by sniffing it up the nostrils **2.** AMOUNT OF SNUFF a portion of snuff ■ *vi.* (**snuffed, snuff·ing, snuffs**) TAKE SNUFF to inhale snuff [Late 17thC. From Dutch *snuf*, shortening of *snuftabak*, literally "sniffing tobacco." The verb came from Dutch *snuffen* "to snuffle."]

snuff[3] *v.* (**snuffed, snuff·ing, snuffs**) **1.** *vt.* INHALE SOMETHING to inhale something through the nose **2.** *vti.* SNIFF to sniff, especially noisily, or to examine something by sniffing it ○ *The hounds snuffed the ground searching for the trail.* ■ *n.* SNIFFING SOUND a sound made by sniffing noisily [Early 16thC. From Dutch *snuffen* "to snuffle," ultimately from a prehistoric Germanic base concerning the nose (see SNUB).]

snuff·box /snúf boks/ *n.* a small ornamental box for powdered tobacco

snuff-col·ored *adj.* of a dark yellowish-brown color

snuff·er /snúfər/ *n.* LONG-HANDLED CANDLE EXTINGUISHER a device used to extinguish a candle, consisting of a long handle with a cone shape at one end ■ **snuff·ers** *npl.* CANDLE EXTINGUISHER LIKE SCISSORS an instrument resembling a pair of scissors, used for trimming wicks or extinguishing candles or oil lamps (*takes a singular or plural verb*)

snuf·fle /snúf'l/ *v.* (**-fled, -fling, -fles**) **1.** *vi.* BREATHE NOISILY to breathe noisily through a partially blocked nose **2.** *vti.* SPEAK NASALLY to speak or say something in a nasal or whining way **3.** *vi.* SNIFF to make repeated sniffing sounds ■ *n.* SOUND OF SNUFFLING the act of snuffling, or the sound made by breathing noisily through the nose [Late 16thC. Origin uncertain: possibly from Dutch *snuffelen*, literally "to keep sniffing about," from *snuffen* "to sniff."] —**snuf·fler** *n.* —**snuf·fly** *adj.*

snuff movie, snuff film *n.* a pornographic movie or video that allegedly ends with the murder of one of the participants in a sex act (*slang*)

snuff·y /snúfee/ (**-i·er, -i·est**) *adj.* **1.** DISAGREEABLE in a bad temper and acting irritably **2.** LIKE SNUFF like snuff in color or smell **3.** COVERED WITH SNUFF soiled or marked with snuff —**snuff·i·ness** *n.*

snug /snug/ *adj.* (**snug·ger, snug·gest**) **1.** COZY warm and comfortable **2.** SMALL BUT COMFORTABLE small in size but offering a comfortable well-arranged space ○ *a snug cottage* **3.** SHELTERED protected from the weather ○ *The fishing boats were snug in the harbor.* **4.** CLOSE-FITTING fitting comfortably close or too close ○ *The sweater was perhaps a little too snug.* **5.** SEAWORTHY seaworthy because of being well-built **6.** CONCEALED offering a safe and private hiding place **7.** FINANCIALLY SECURE allowing one to live comfortably and securely, without having to worry about money ■ *n.* **1.** *U.K.* SMALL ROOM a small room or enclosed area in a pub allowing a small number of people to sit in private **2.** PEG FOR HOLDING A BOLT a small peg used to hold the head of a bolt in place while a nut is tightened onto the end ■ *v.* (**snugged, snug·ging, snugs**) **1.** *vi.* SNUGGLE to lie closely together or curl up in a cozy way ○ *snug in the overstuffed chair* **2.** *vt.* MAKE SNUG to make somebody or something comfortable and warm **3.** *vti.* SECURE A BOAT to make a boat secure to weather a storm [Late 16thC. Origin uncertain: probably from Scandinavian or Low Dutch.]

snug·ger·y /snúgəree/ (*plural* **-ies**) *n. U.K.* **1.** COZY PLACE a place that is warm and comfortable **2.** = **snug** [Early 19thC. Formed from SNUG.]

snug·gle /snúg'l/ (**-gled, -gling, -gles**) *v.* **1.** *vi.* CUDDLE UP to get into a comfortable, cozy position, especially close to another person **2.** *vt.* GET CLOSE TO SOMEBODY to draw close to somebody or something to offer or receive comfort and affection ○ *snuggled in front of the fireplace* [Late 17thC. Formed from SNUG.]

Sny·der /snídər/, **Gary** (*b.* 1930) U.S. writer. His poetry, translations, and essays showed the influence of his interests in ecology, Zen Buddhism, and Native American culture, and included the Pulitzer Prize-winning verse collection *Turtle Island* (1975).

so[1] /sō/ CORE MEANING: a conjunction indicating the reason for an action or situation, or its result ○ *Let's go upstairs and talk, so we can have a little privacy.* ○ *Keep your password secret so that others cannot use your user name.* ○ *I had the flu, so I couldn't attend the meeting.*

1. *conj.* IN ORDER THAT introduces the reason for doing what has just been mentioned ○ *The poles are joined together so as to enclose an area of about twenty feet in diameter.* ○ *He held her tight so that she wouldn't fall.* **2.** *conj.* INTRODUCES RESULT introduces the result of the situation that has just been mentioned ○ *Everything is done on a shoestring, so their prices are very low.* **3.** *adv.* REFERS BACK refers back to something that has just been mentioned ○ *Lunch may be purchased on the island, for those who desire to do so.* **4.** *adv.* INDICATES IDENTITY indicates that what is true of one person or thing is also true of another person or thing (*followed by auxiliary or modal, or by the main verb "do, have," or "be"*) ○ *If you can keep a secret, so can I.* **5.** *adv.* AS IT IS indicates that something is the way it has been described ○ *Nebraska has the potential to be very important, and will soon be so, both politically and commercially.* **6.** *adv.* TO SUCH AN EXTENT emphasizes the degree of something by mentioning its result ○ *He is so busy working at Nathan's, he doesn't have time to take classes.* ○ *He's not so unobservant as to miss seeing the change.* **7.** *adv.* EMPHASIZES A QUALITY adds emphasis to the meaning of an adverb or adjective ○ *I was so scared.* ○ *He acts so stubbornly sometimes.* **8.** *adv.* THEREFORE OR IN CONSEQUENCE introduces an event in a sequence ○ *It's not working out. So we'll have to go back to the beginning and start again.* ○ *She said she would like to see me again. So I gave her my phone number.* **9.** *adv.* INTRODUCES COMMENT introduces a new topic, or a question or comment about something ○ *So what* *are we going to do about it?* ○ *So I see you've changed your mind.* **10.** *adv.* **INDICATES POSITION OR DIMENSIONS** indicates the position or dimensions of something, using actions or gestures ○ *Hold onto the boat like so, and hoist yourself up.* **11.** *conj.* **INDICATES SIMILARITY** indicates that two events or situations are alike in some way ○ *Just as my circumstances have changed, so too have my aims in life.* **12.** *adv.* **INDEED** used to contradict a negative statement (*nonstandard*) ○ *"You never explained what to do." "I did so!"* [Old English *swā*. Ultimately from an Indo-European word that is also the ancestor of English *such* and *quasi*.] ◇ **and so on, and so forth** used at the end of a list to indicate that there are other things that could be mentioned ○ *These systems are traditionally used in industries such as insurance, banking, universities and so on.* ○ *Remove any additional hardware from the system (mouse, network card, fax board, modem, and so forth.)* ◇ **or so** approximately ○ *That pair of neutron stars at 1,600 light-years isn't expected to crash for another billion years or so.* ◇ **so be it** expresses agreement or resignation ○ *I wish you'd think again, but never mind – so be it!* ◇ **so much, so many** a certain degree or amount ○ *The government can only do so much.* ○ *I can only take so many insults.* ◇ **so much for 1.** indicates that there is nothing more that can be said or done about something (*informal*) ○ *So much for the morning. I still had the afternoon to get through.* **2.** indicates that something has not been successful or helpful (*informal*) ○ *Well, so much for simple fairness!* ◇ **so what?** used to ask rather rudely why something is important, implying that it is not ○ *You amass all these facts, but the question is, 'so what?'*

so[2] *n.* = **sol**[1] *n.*

So., **so.** *abbr.* **1.** south **2.** southern

s.o. *abbr.* **1.** seller's option **2.** BASEBALL strike-out

S.O. *abbr.* standing order

soak /sōk/ *v.* (**soaked, soak·ing, soaks**) **1.** *vti.* **TO STEEP** to immerse something in liquid or be immersed in liquid for a period of time **2.** *vt.* **MAKE SOMETHING WET** to make something or somebody completely wet (*often passive*) ○ *We got soaked in the rain on the way home.* **3.** *vti.* **ABSORB** to draw something such as moisture in through the pores or other small holes ○ *This sponge soaks up moisture.* **4.** *vti.* **PERMEATE SOMETHING** to penetrate something by saturating it and passing into pores or small holes ○ *The water quickly soaked through her shoes.* **5.** *vti.* **REMOVE STAIN BY SOAKING** to remove something, especially a mark or a stain from an item of clothing, by leaving it in liquid for a time **6.** *vt.* **OVERCHARGE** to overcharge or tax somebody heavily (*slang*) **7.** *vti.* **GET DRUNK** to drink too much alcohol, or to make somebody drunk (*informal*) ■ *n.* **1. ACT OF SOAKING** an act or the process of immersing something in liquid ○ *had a long, leisurely soak in the bathtub* **2. SOAKING LIQUID** a solution or liquid for soaking something in **3. HARD DRINKER** somebody who habitually drinks too much alcohol (*slang*) [Old English *socian*, from *sūcan*, an earlier form of SUCK] —**soak·er** *n.*

soak·age /sṓkij/ *n.* **1. PROCESS OF SOAKING** the process of soaking or the condition of being soaked **2. AMOUNT OF LIQUID** the amount of liquid soaking into or out of something

soak·ing /sṓking/ *n.* **1. INSTANCE OF OVERPAYING** an instance of being overcharged for something (*informal*) **2. DRENCHING** an instance of being made very wet (*informal*) **3. STEEPING** an act or the process of steeping something in liquid ■ *adj.* **VERY WET** very wet, especially because of being rained on (*informal*)

WORD KEY: SYNONYMS

See Synonyms at ***wet***.

so-and-so (*plural* **so-and-sos**) *n.* **1. UNNAMED PERSON OR THING** somebody or something not named or specified (*informal*) **2. SOMEBODY UNPLEASANT** somebody regarded as annoying or disagreeable (*informal insult*)

soap /sōp/ *n.* **1. CLEANSING AGENT** a solid, liquid, or powdered cleaning preparation that is made by potassium or sodium hydroxide reacting with animal or vegetable oils. Soaps are usually used with water and may contain perfumes or other additional ingredients. **2. SOAP OPERA** a soap opera (*informal*) **3. METALLIC SALT COMBINED WITH FATTY ACID** a metallic salt of a fatty acid, often made with calcium, aluminum and lithium, used as a waterproofing agent and as a base for greases **4. MONEY USED TO BRIBE** money, especially when it is used as a bribe or for paying somebody secretly (*slang*) ■ *v.* (**soaped, soap·ing, soaps**) **1.** *vt.* **PUT SOAP ON** to put soap on something or somebody **2.** *vti.* **CAJOLE** to flatter somebody especially with the intention of persuading or soothing (*slang*) [Old English *sāpe*, from a prehistoric Germanic word meaning "soap," which is also the ancestor of Latin *sapo* (source of English *saponaceous*)]

soap·bark /sṓp baàrk/ *n.* **1. EVERGREEN TREE** a South American evergreen tree of the rose family that has small white flowers and bark high in saponin. Latin name: *Quillaja saponaria.* **2. BARK OF SOAPBARK** the bark of the soapbark, which contains saponin and was used in the past as soap

soap·ber·ry /sṓp bèree/ (*plural* **-ries**) *n.* **1. TROPICAL AMERICAN TREE** a tropical American tree or shrub that has pulpy fruit containing saponin. Latin name: *Sapindus saponaria.* **2. BERRY** the fruit of the soapberry

soap boil·er *n.* a soap manufacturer

soap·box /sṓp bòks/ *n.* **1. PLATFORM FOR SPEAKING** something, such as a wooden box, used as a platform for making an impromptu speech **2. BOX FOR SOAP** a box in which soap is packed ■ *vi.* (**-boxed, -box·ing, -box·es**) **SPEAK UNOFFICIALLY** to make an unofficial speech in public (*informal*)

soap bub·ble *n.* **1. BUBBLE** a bubble formed with soapy water **2. SOMETHING ILLUSORY** something that is beautiful but that does not last

soap op·e·ra *n.* **1. SERIAL DRAMA** a serial on television or radio that deals with the lives of a group of characters, especially in a melodramatic or sentimental way **2. SOMETHING LIKE SOAP OPERA** an event or series of events that resembles the events of a soap opera in melodrama or sentimentality ["Soap" from the fact that they were originally often sponsored by soap manufacturing companies]

soap plant *n.* any of several plants that have bulbs or other parts used as soap. Genus: *Chlorogalum.*

Soapstone: Nigerian carving (12th to 15th centuries)

soap·stone /sṓp stòn/ *n.* a dark gray or green soft compact variety of talc that has a soapy texture and is used to make objects including ornaments and hearths

soap·suds /sṓp sùdz/ *npl.* = **suds** *npl.* —**soap·suds·y** *adj.*

soap·wort /sṓp wùrt, -wàwrt/ *n.* = **bouncing Bet**

soap·y /sṓpee/ (**-i·er, -i·est**) *adj.* **1. WITH SOAP** full of or covered with soap **2. LIKE SOAP** with the look or feel of soap ○ *a soapy texture* **3. INSINCERE** given to excessive insincere flattery (*slang*)

soar /sawr/ *vi.* (**soared, soar·ing, soars**) **1. FLY** to fly or rise high in the air **2. GLIDE HIGH** to glide, on rising currents of air **3. INCREASE RAPIDLY** to increase rapidly in number, volume, size, or amount ○ *soaring prices* **4. BECOME MORE INTENSE** to rise to a higher, more intense, or exalted level ■ *n.* **ACT OF SOARING** the act of soaring, or the height or range reached by soaring [14thC. Via Old French *essorer* from assumed Vulgar Latin *exaurare*, from Latin *ex-* "out, up" + *aura* "air" (see AURA).] —**soar·er** *n.*

So·a·ve /sō aá vay, swaá vay/ *n.* a dry white wine made in Italy [Mid-20thC. Named for the village of *Soave*, near Verona in Italy, where it is produced.]

So·ay /sṓ ay, sóy/ *n.* a small dark brown sheep of a breed found in the Outer Hebrides, especially on the island of Soay

sob /sob/ *v.* (**sobbed, sob·bing, sobs**) **1.** *vi.* **GASP WHILE CRYING** to draw in breath while crying, making gasping sounds **2.** *vt.* **UTTER SOMETHING WHILE SOBBING** to say something while sobbing **3.** *vr.* **BECOME BY SOBBING** to get into a particular state by sobbing ○ *to sob yourself to sleep* ■ *n.* **SOUND OF SOBBING** a convulsive breath made while sobbing, or the sound of this breath ○ *stifled a sob* [12thC. Origin uncertain: possibly from Low German or Low Dutch.] —**sob·bing·ly** *adv.*

SOB, **s.o.b.** *n.*, *abbr.* son of a bitch (*slang insult*)

so·ber /sṓbər/ *adj.* **1. NOT INTOXICATED** not under the influence of drugs or alcohol **2. TENDING NOT TO DRINK** not in the habit of drinking much alcohol or using drugs **3. SERIOUS** serious and thoughtful in demeanor or quality ○ *a sober face* **4. DULL** lacking vitality or brightness in appearance ○ *He always dresses in sober colors.* **5. NOT FANCIFUL OR SPECULATIVE** based on facts and rational thinking rather than on speculation ○ *a sober assessment of the situation* ■ *vti.* (**-bered, -ber·ing, -bers**) **LESSEN INTOXICATION** to become or make somebody become less intoxicated or completely sober [14thC. Via Old French from Latin *sobrius*. Ultimately from an Indo-European negative prefix and a word meaning "to drink," which is also the ancestor of English *inebriate*.] —**so·ber·ing** *adj.* —**so·ber·ing·ly** *adv.* —**so·ber·ly** *adv.* —**so·ber·ness** *n.*

so·ber·sides /sṓbər sīdz/ *n.* somebody who is solemn and serious —**so·ber·sid·ed** *adj.*

so·bri·e·ty /sə brī́ ətee, sō-/ *n.* **1. ABSTINENCE** abstinence from or moderation in the use of alcohol or drugs **2. SERIOUSNESS** the quality of being serious and thoughtful [15thC. Via Old French from, ultimately, Latin *sobrius* "sober" (see SOBER).]

so·bri·quet /sṓbri kay, -ket, sòbri káy, -két/, **sou·bri·quet** *n.* an unofficial name or nickname, especially a humorous one [Mid-17thC. From French, literally "a tap under the chin."]

sob sis·ter *n.* (*informal*) **1. JOURNALIST WHO WRITES SENTIMENTAL STORIES** a journalist who writes or edits sentimental stories or answers problems sent in by readers **2. OVERLY SENTIMENTAL DO-GOODER** somebody who tries to help others but is often ineffective

sob sto·ry *n.* a story told to gain somebody's sympathy or pity, especially when offered as an excuse (*informal*)

soc., **Soc.** *abbr.* **1.** society **2.** socialist

so·ca /sṓkə/ *n.* a style of Caribbean music that combines calypso and soul and has a fast beat [Late 20thC. Blend of SOUL and CALYPSO.]

soc·age /sókij, sṓkij/, **soc·cage** *n.* a feudal system of holding land in which the tenant either paid rent or performed a fixed service, usually agricultural and nonmilitary in nature [14thC. From Anglo-Norman, where it was formed from *soc*, variant of SOKE.] —**soc·ag·er** *n.*

so-called *adj.* **1. POPULARLY** popularly known as, but not necessarily by the speaker or writer ○ *the so-called Information Superhighway* **2. INCORRECTLY** incorrectly known as ○ *a so-called art expert*

soc·cer /sókər/ *n.* a game in which two teams of 11 players try to score by kicking or butting a round ball into the net goals on either end of a rectangular field. Only the goalkeeper may play the ball with a hand or arm. [Late 19thC. Formed from *Assoc.*, an abbreviation of *Association football*, because it was played under the rules of the Football Association, as opposed to "Rugby football."]

soc·cer mom *n.* a typically affluent mother who devotes herself to her children's leisure activities, e.g., driving them to and from sports activities

Soc·ce·roos /sòkə ro͞oz/ *n. Aus* an informal name for the Australian national soccer team (*informal*)

so·cia·ble /sṓshəb'l/ *adj.* **1. GREGARIOUS** inclined to seek out the company of other people **2. FRIENDLY** friendly and pleasant to other people **3. OFFERING OPPORTUNITY FOR SOCIAL INTERACTION** allowing people to mix in an informal way ○ *a sociable occasion* [Mid-16thC. Directly or via French from Latin *sociabilis*, from *socius* "companion" (see SOCIAL).] —**so·cia·bil·i·ty** /sṑshə bíllətee/ *n.* —**so·cia·ble·ness** /sṓshəb'lnəss/ *n.* —**so·cia·bly** /sṓshəblee/ *adv.*

WORD KEY: USAGE

sociable or **social**? ***Social*** is a neutral word that classifies a person or thing as being concerned in some way with society or its organization. A *social club* is a place provided for people to enjoy themselves, and a *social worker* is involved in work done for people's welfare. ***Sociable***, by contrast, is a judgmental word referring to a person's capacity to deal in social ways with other people, so a *sociable worker* is a worker who enjoys the company of colleagues.

so·cial /sṓshəl/ *adj.* **1.** RELATING TO SOCIETY relating to human society and how it is organized **2.** RELATING TO INTERACTION OF PEOPLE relating to the way people in groups behave and interact ○ *the social sciences* **3.** LIVING IN A COMMUNITY living or preferring to live as part of a community or colony, rather than alone ○ *social insects such as ants* **4.** OFFERING OPPORTUNITY FOR INTERACTION allowing people to meet and interact with others in a friendly way ○ *a social club* **5.** RELATING TO HUMAN WELFARE relating to human welfare and the organized welfare services that a community provides ○ *social services* **6.** TO DO WITH RANK relating to or thought appropriate to a particular rank in society, especially the upper classes **7.** SOCIABLE tending to seek out the company of others (*informal*) ○ *a very social person* **8.** GROWING IN CLUMPS used to describe plants that grow in clumps or masses ■ *n.* INFORMAL GET-TOGETHER an informal gathering or party, usually of a particular group of people who meet regularly [Mid-17thC. Via French from Latin *socialis*, from *socius* "companion." Ultimately from an Indo-European word meaning "to follow," which is also the ancestor of English *sequel*.] —**so·cial·ly** *adv.* —**so·cial·ness** *n.*

WORD KEY: USAGE

See Usage note at ***sociable***.

so·cial an·thro·pol·o·gy *n. U.K.* the scientific study of human society or a particular society, including study of kinship systems, traditional political and economic practices, rituals, and beliefs

so·cial as·sis·tance *n. Can* social security

social capital *n.* the educational, social, and cultural advantages tha somebody from the upper classes is believed to possess

so·cial climb·er *n.* somebody who tries to join a higher social class by setting out to mix with people that belong to it (*disapproving*) —**so·cial climb·ing** *n.*

so·cial cog·ni·tion *n.* thought processes involved in understanding and dealing with other people

so·cial cog·ni·tive the·o·ry *n.* a theory of how individuals make sense of their social experiences and how the resulting understanding influences their behavior and development. It is an extension of the earlier social learning theory.

so·cial con·tract, so·cial com·pact *n.* an agreement among individuals in a society or between the people and their government that describes the rights and duties of each party. It derives from the ideas of Hobbes, Locke, and Rousseau and involves individuals giving up certain freedoms in return for benefits such as state protection.

so·cial Dar·win·ism *n.* a discredited social theory stating that the political and economic advantages in a developed society are derived from the biological advantages of its collective membership —**so·cial Dar·win·ist** *n.*

so·cial de·moc·ra·cy, So·cial De·moc·ra·cy *n.* the political belief that a change from capitalism to socialism can be achieved gradually and democratically —**so·cial dem·o·crat** *n.* —**so·cial dem·o·crat·ic** *adj.*

So·cial Dem·o·crat·ic Party *n.* a German political party advocating gradual reform to socialism

so·cial dis·ease *n.* **1.** VENEREAL DISEASE a venereal disease (*informal; used euphemistically*) **2.** DISEASE AFFECTED BY SOCIOECONOMIC CONDITIONS a disease, such as tuberculosis, brought about or affected by the socioeconomic conditions in which people live

so·cial drink·er *n.* somebody who only drinks in company and in moderation

so·cial en·gi·neer·ing *n.* the use of policies that are based on the findings of social science to deal with social problems

so·cial in·sur·ance *n.* state insurance that uses compulsory contributions to pay for benefits for unemployed and retired people

so·cial·ism /sṓshə lìzəm/ *n.* **1.** POLITICAL SYSTEM OF COMMUNAL OWNERSHIP a political theory or system in which the means of production and distribution are controlled by the people and operated according to equity and fairness rather than market principles **2.** MOVEMENT BASED ON SOCIALISM any of several political movements or theories of the 19th and 20th centuries based on principles of socialism, typically advocating an end to private property and the exploitation of workers **3.** STAGE BETWEEN CAPITALISM AND COMMUNISM in Marxist theory, the stage after the proletarian revolution when a society is changing from capitalism to communism, marked by pay distributed according to work done rather than need

so·cial·ist /sṓshəlist/, **So·cial·ist** *n.* BELIEVER IN SOCIALISM somebody who believes in and supports socialism or a socialist party ■ *adj.* **1.** ADVOCATING SOCIALISM relating to, based on, or advocating socialism **2. so·cial·ist, So·cial·ist** RELATING TO SOCIALISTS relating to socialists or a socialist party —**so·cial·is·tic** /sṑshə lístik/ *adj.* —**so·cial·is·ti·cal·ly** /-lístiklee/ *adv.*

So·cial·ist La·bor Par·ty *n.* a Marxist political party in the United States

so·cial·ist re·al·ism *n.* an artistic doctrine officially sanctioned in many Communist countries, especially during the 1930s-50s, that proposed the idea that art and literature should serve to promote and glorify the ideals of a socialist state

so·cial·ite /sṓshə lìt/ *n.* somebody who is well-known in fashionable society

so·ci·al·i·ty /sṑshee álətee/ (*plural* **-ties**) *n.* **1.** QUALITY OF BEING SOCIAL the quality of being social, or an instance of it **2.** TENDENCY TO FORM SOCIAL GROUPS the tendency to form social groups or live in a community

so·cial·i·za·tion /sṑshələ záysh'n/ *n.* the process involved when young children are becoming aware of society and learning how they are expected to behave

so·cial·ize /sṓshə lìz/ (**-ized, -iz·ing, -iz·es**) *v.* **1.** *vi.* TAKE PART IN SOCIAL ACTIVITIES to take part in social activities or behave in a friendly way to others ○ *a group of friends who like to socialize after work* **2.** *vt.* TRAIN TO BE SOCIAL to teach somebody to be a fit member of society ○ *socialize a child* —**so·cial·iz·er** *n.*

so·cial·ized med·i·cine *n.* a system of national health care that provides medical care to all and is regulated and subsidized by the government

so·cial-mind·ed *adj.* concerned with the conditions of human society and the welfare of others

so·cial psy·chol·o·gy *n.* the area of psychology that deals with how groups behave and how individuals are affected by the group —**so·cial psy·chol·o·gist** *n.*

so·cial re·al·ism *n.* the use of realistic portrayals of life in art or literature to make a social or political point

so·cial sci·ence *n.* **1.** STUDY OF SOCIETY the study of people in society and how individuals relate to one another and to the group **2.** DISCIPLINE STUDYING SPECIFIC AREA OF SOCIETY any of the disciplines within social science that study a specific area of human society such as sociology, psychology, economics, political science, history, or anthropology —**so·cial sci·en·tist** *n.*

so·cial sec·re·tar·y *n.* somebody whose job is to arrange social activities and handle correspondence for a person or organization

so·cial se·cu·ri·ty *n.* **1. so·cial se·cu·ri·ty, So·cial Se·cu·ri·ty** GOVERNMENT PROGRAM PROVIDING ECONOMIC SECURITY a government program providing for the economic welfare of the individual, e.g., through payments to people who are retired, unemployed, or unable to work. The U.S. Social Security program was established in 1935 and its funds come from employers and employees. **2.** MONEY PAID BY GOVERNMENT TO INDIVIDUAL money paid by a government to an individual through a Social Security program

so·cial ser·vice *n.* SERVICE FOR WELFARE OF COMMUNITY a service provided by a government agency for the welfare of an individual or community. Such services include housing, child protection, free school lunches, or health care. (*often used in the plural*) ■ **so·cial ser·vic·es** *npl.* AGENCY PROVIDING SOCIAL SERVICES a government agency that provides social services to individuals or a community (*takes a singular or plural verb*)

so·cial stud·ies *npl.* an academic subject devoted to the study of society and including geography, economics, and history (*takes a singular or plural verb*)

so·cial wel·fare *n.* the social services provided by a state or by a private organization

so·cial work *n.* the profession or work of providing people in need with social services —**so·cial work·er** *n.*

so·ci·e·tal /sə sí ət'l/ *adj.* relating to society, especially its organization, structure, or function —**so·ci·e·tal·ly** *adv.*

so·ci·e·ty /sə sí ətee/ (*plural* **-ties**) *n.* **1.** RELATIONSHIPS AMONG GROUPS the sum of social relationships among groups of humans or animals **2.** STRUCTURED COMMUNITY OF PEOPLE a structured community of people bound together by similar traditions, institutions, or nationality **3.** CUSTOMS OF A COMMUNITY the customs of a community and the way it is organized, e.g., its class structure ○ *the role of women in society* **4.** SUBSET OF SOCIETY a particular section of a community that is distinguished by specific qualities ○ *In those days, the subject was never mentioned in polite society.* **5.** PROMINENT PEOPLE the prominent or fashionable people in a community and their social life **6.** COMPANIONSHIP the state of being with other people ○ *seek the society of coworkers* **7.** GROUP SHARING INTERESTS an organized group of people who share an interest, aim, or profession [Mid-16thC. Via French from Latin *societas*, literally "companionship," from *socius* "companion" (see SOCIAL).]

So·ci·e·ty of Friends *n.* the Christian group also known as the Quakers (*formal*)

So·ci·e·ty of Je·sus *n.* the Roman Catholic religious order also known as the Jesuits (*formal*)

So·cin·i·an /sō sínee ən/ *n.* FOLLOWER OF SOCINUS a follower of Laelius and Faustus Socinus, Italian theologians who preached belief in God but rejected other traditional Christian doctrines such as the Trinity and the divinity of Christ ■ *adj.* RELATING TO THE SOCINIANS relating to the Socinians and their beliefs —**So·cin·i·an·ism** *n.*

socio- *prefix.* society, social ○ *sociopath* ○ *sociopsychological* [Via French from, ultimately, Latin *socius* "companion" (see SOCIAL)]

so·ci·o·bi·ol·o·gy /sṑsi ō bī óləjee, -shi-/ *n.* the study of the social behavior of animals and humans and how this is related to genetics and the survival of species —**so·ci·o·bi·o·log·i·cal** *adj.*

so·ci·o·cul·tur·al *adj.* involving cultural and social factors —**so·ci·o·cul·tur·al·ly** *adv.*

so·ci·o·ec·o·nom·ic /sṑsi ō ékə nómiks, -shi-, -ḗkə nómiks/ *adj.* involving economic and social factors —**so·ci·o·ec·o·nom·i·cal·ly** *adv.*

sociol. *abbr.* sociology

so·ci·o·lin·guis·tics /sṑsi ō ling gwístiks, -shi-/ *n.* the study of the relationships between language and the social and cultural factors that affect it —**so·ci·o·lin·guist** /sṓsi ō líng gwist, -shi-/ *n.* —**so·ci·o·lin·guis·tic** /sṑsi ō ling gwístik, -shi-/ *adj.*

so·ci·ol·o·gy /sṑsee óləjee, -shee-/ *n.* **1.** STUDY OF SOCIETY the study of the origin, development, and structure of human societies and the behavior of individuals and groups in society **2.** STUDY OF INDIVIDUAL SOCIAL INSTITUTION the study of a particular social institution and the part it plays in society [Mid-19thC. From French *sociologie*, literally "science of companions," from Latin *socius* "companion" (see SOCIO-).] —**so·ci·o·log·ic** /sṑssee ə lójjik/ *adj.* —**so·ci·o·log·i·cal·ly** /-lójjikəlee/ *adv.* —**so·ci·ol·o·gist** /sṑssee óllәjist/ *n.*

so·ci·om·e·try /sṑsee ómətree, -shee-/ *n.* the statistical study of behavior and relationships within social groups, especially expressed in terms of preferences —**so·ci·o·met·ric** /sṑsi ō métrik, -shi-/ *adj.* —**so·ci·om·e·trist** /sṑsee áwmətrəst, sṑsheeáwmətrəst/ *n.*

so·ci·o·path /sṓsi ō pàth, -shi-/ *n.* = **psychopath** [Mid-20thC. Modeled on PSYCHOPATH.] —**so·ci·o·path·ic** /sṑsi ō páthik/ *adj.* —**so·ci·op·a·thy** /sṑsee óppəthee, -shee-/ *n.*

so·ci·o·po·lit·i·cal /sṑsi ō pə líttik'l, -shi-/ *adj.* relating to or involving both social and political factors

so·ci·o·psy·cho·log·i·cal /sṑsi ō sīkə lójik'l, -shi-/ *adj.* **1.** RELATING TO SOCIAL PSYCHOLOGY relating to or involving social psychology **2.** SOCIAL AND PSYCHOLOGICAL relating to or involving both social and psychological factors

sock[1] /sawk/ *n.* **1.** (*plural* **socks** *or* **sox**) SOFT FOOT COVERING a soft, usually knitted covering for the foot and ankle that may reach as high as the knee. It is usually worn inside a shoe. **2.** METEOROL = **windsock** [Old English *socc* "light shoe, slipper," via prehistoric

Germanic from Latin *soccus* (source of English *socle*), from Greek *sukkhos* "(kind of) shoe"]

sock away *vt. U.S., Can, NZ* to save money for the future (*informal*) [From the practice of storing savings in a sock]

sock in *vt.* to close an airport to air traffic temporarily because of poor visibility (*usually passive*)

sock[2] /sáwk/ *vti.* (**socked, sock·ing, socks**) STRIKE SOMEBODY to hit somebody or something hard, usually with the fist (*informal*) ■ *n.* HARD HIT OR BLOW a hard hit or blow, usually with the fist (*informal*) [Late 17thC. Origin unknown.] ◇ **sock it to somebody** to subject somebody to a physical or verbal attack (*informal*)

sock·dol·a·ger /sawk dóləjər/, **sock·dol·o·ger** *n.* (*dated informal*) **1.** DECISIVE ARGUMENT a decisive blow or argument **2.** SOMETHING OUTSTANDING something outstanding or remarkable [Mid-19thC. Origin uncertain: probably a fanciful formation from SOCK.]

sock·et /sókət/ *n.* **1.** SHAPED HOLE FOR CONNECTION a hole or recess in something specially shaped to receive a particular object or part, e.g., the hole that receives a light bulb or one that receives a plug on an electrical device **2.** ELEC = **outlet 3.** HOLLOW IN BODY a bony hollow in the body into which another part fits ■ *vt.* (**-et·ed, -et·ing, -ets**) PUT IN SOCKET to insert something into a socket, or to provide something with a socket [13thC. From Anglo-Norman *soket*, literally "small plowshare," from Old French *sok* "plowshare," of uncertain origin: probably ultimately from Gaulish. Originally "spearhead," later "socket supporting a spear."]

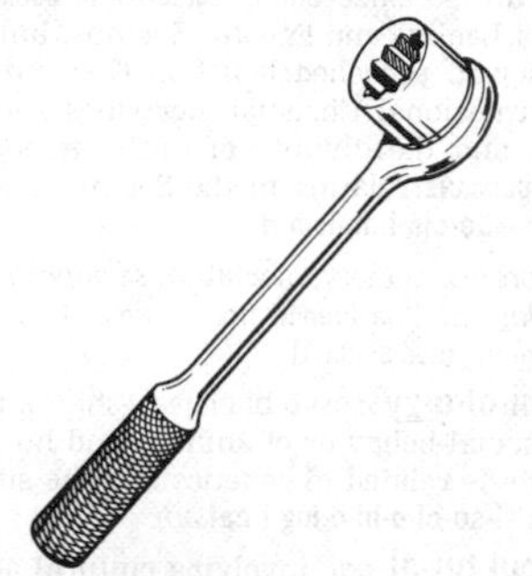

Socket wrench

sock·et wrench *n.* a long-handled wrench with interchangeable heads that fit over various sized nuts and bolts and a ratchet that makes tightening nuts and bolts easier

sock·eye /sáwk ī/ (*plural* **-eyes** *or* **-eye**), **sock·eye salm·on** *n.* a Pacific food fish in the salmon family that has red flesh. Latin name: *Oncorhynchus nerka*. [Late 19thC. By folk etymology from Salish *sukai*, literally "fish of fishes."]

sock·o /sáwkō/ *adj.* producing a strong impression (*informal*) [Early 20thC. Formed from SOCK[2].]

so·cle /sáwk'l/ *n.* a base that sticks out from under the bottom of a wall, or the lowest part of the base of a column or pedestal [Early 18thC. Via French from, ultimately, Latin *socculus* "small light shoe," from *soccus* (see SOCK[1]).]

Soc·ra·tes /sókrə teez/ (469–399 B.C.) Greek philosopher. His philosophy has survived through the writings of his pupils, especially Plato. He employed what became known as the "Socratic method" to question conventional assumptions about morality, justice, and other social concepts. Charged with atheism and corrupting youth, he was condemned to death.

So·crat·ic /sə kráttik/ *adj.* RELATING TO SOCRATES relating to Socrates, to his philosophy, or to his method of arriving at truth ■ *n.* SOMEBODY STUDYING SOCRATES a student or follower of Socrates —**So·crat·i·cal·ly** *adv.* —**So·crat·i·cism** *n.* —**So·crat·ist** /sókrətəst/ *n.*

So·crat·ic i·ro·ny *n.* ignorance feigned in order to elicit explanations from somebody whose own ignorance can then be exposed through subsequent clever questioning

So·crat·ic meth·od *n.* a means of arriving at truth by continually questioning, obtaining answers, and criticizing the answers

So·cred /sṓkred/ *n. Can* MEMBER OF SOCIAL CREDIT MOVEMENT a member or supporter of a Social Credit movement or political party ■ *adj. Can* OF SOCIAL CREDIT PARTY relating to the Social Credit political party [Mid-20thC. Contraction of SOCIAL CREDIT.]

sod[1] /sáwd/ *n.* **1.** TURF a surface section or strip of earth with growing grass and roots **2.** GROUND ground or soil (*literary*) ■ *vt.* (**sod·ded, sod·ding, sods**) COVER WITH TURF to cover ground with sods [15thC. From Middle Dutch or Low German *sode* "turf," of unknown origin.]

sod[2] /sáwd/ *n. U.K.* **1.** OFFENSIVE TERM an offensive term referring to somebody regarded as stupid, annoying, or obnoxious (*slang insult*) **2.** ANY PERSON used, often humorously or affectionately, to refer to a person (*slang; considered offensive in some contexts*) ■ *vt. U.K.* DAMN used as a swearword to express anger or defiance (*slang offensive*) [Early 19thC. Shortening of SODOMITE.]

so·da /sṓdə/ *n.* **1.** SOFT DRINK a flavored and carbonated drink, served cold. ◊ **tonic 2.** = **soda water** *n.* 1 **3.** ICE CREAM IN FLAVORED CARBONATED WATER a refreshment made with flavored carbonated water and ice cream, usually served in a tall glass **4.** SODIUM sodium that is chemically combined with other elements **5.** = **sodium bicarbonate 6.** = **sodium carbonate 7.** = **sodium hydroxide 8.** CARDS CARD THAT STARTS FARO the card from the top of the pack that is turned face up in the dealing box at the start of the card game faro [15thC. Via Italian "saltwort" (from which sodium carbonate is obtained) from Arabic *suwwād*.]

so·da ash *n.* sodium carbonate when sold commercially, e.g., for use as a manufacturing ingredient in the soap and paper industries

so·da bis·cuit *n.* **1.** BISCUIT MADE USING BAKING SODA a biscuit leavened with baking soda **2.** = **soda cracker**

so·da bread *n.* bread leavened with soda rather than yeast, associated especially with Irish cooking

so·da crack·er *n.* a cracker leavened slightly with baking soda and cream of tartar

so·da foun·tain *n.* **1.** SODA WATER DISPENSER a device for dispensing soda water **2.** FOOD AND DRINK COUNTER a counter or stand where beverages, ice cream, and snacks are sold (*dated*)

so·da jerk *n.* somebody who serves food and beverages at a soda fountain (*dated slang*)

so·da lime *n.* a mixture of sodium hydroxide and calcium hydroxide used commercially and industrially to absorb moisture and carbon dioxide

so·da·list /sṓdələst/ *n.* somebody who belongs to a sodality

so·da·lite /sṓdəlīt/ *n.* a blue, grayish, or yellow translucent mineral consisting of sodium and aluminum silicates with chlorine. It is found in alkaline igneous rocks. [Early 19thC. Coined from SODA + -LITE.]

so·dal·i·ty /sō dállətee/ (*plural* **-ties**) *n.* **1.** RELIGIOUS SOCIETY a Roman Catholic lay society that is run as a charity or a religious fellowship **2.** ORGANIZED GROUP an association or fellowship of any kind [Early 17thC. Directly or via French *sodalité* from Latin *sodalitas* "fellowship," from *sodalis* "fellow, companion."]

so·da ni·ter *n.* = **Chile saltpeter**

so·da pop *n.* a flavored and carbonated drink, served cold (*informal*)

so·da si·phon *n.* = **siphon bottle**

so·da wa·ter *n.* **1.** WATER CHARGED WITH CARBON DIOXIDE carbonated water drunk as a beverage or used as a mixer in alcoholic drinks **2.** DIGESTIVE AID a weak solution of water, baking soda, and acid, taken to aid digestion

sod·bus·ter *n.* **1.** FARMER somebody who farms the land **2.** PLOW a plow that is used to break the sod **3.** *Can* HOMESTEADER a prairie homesteader, especially one who raised crops (*informal*)

sod·den /sáwd'n/ *adj.* **1.** THOROUGHLY WET saturated with moisture **2.** DRUNK with dulled senses from excessive drinking ■ *vti.* (**-dened, -den·ing, -dens**) MAKE OR BECOME SODDEN to make something or somebody sodden or to become sodden [13thC. The obsolete past participle of SEETHE. Originally "boiled"; the sense "thoroughly wet" dates from the 19thC.] —**sod·den·ly** *adv.* —**sod·den·ness** *n.*

WORD KEY: SYNONYMS

See Synonyms at ***wet***.

so·di·um /sṓdee əm/ *n.* a soft silver-white metallic chemical element that reacts readily with other substances. It is essential to the body's fluid balance and occurs in abundance, especially in common salt. Symbol **Na** [Early 19thC. Coined from SODA (from its being isolated from caustic soda) + -IUM.]

so·di·um ben·zo·ate *n.* a white crystalline powder used as a food preservative, as an antiseptic, and in pharmaceutical preparations. Formula: $C_7H_5O_2Na$.

so·di·um bi·car·bon·ate *n.* a white crystalline slightly alkaline salt used as a leavening agent, in effervescent drinks and fire extinguishers, and medicinally as an antacid. Formula: $NaHCO_3$.

so·di·um car·bon·ate *n.* **1.** SALT OF CARBONIC ACID a white crystalline salt of carbonic acid used in making glass, ceramics, soap, and paper. It is also used as a water softener, and in cleaning, bleaching, and photography. Formula: Na_2CO_3. **2.** = **washing soda**

so·di·um chlo·rate *n.* a colorless crystalline salt used as a weed killer, a bleaching agent, and in explosives. Formula: $NaClO_3$.

so·di·um chlo·ride *n.* a colorless crystalline compound, found naturally in sea water and halite and used as a preservative and food seasoning. Formula: NaCl. ◊ **salt**

so·di·um cit·rate *n.* a crystalline salt used in photography, and in medicine as an anticoagulant in stored blood. Formula: $Na_3C_6H_5O_7$.

so·di·um cy·a·nide *n.* a poisonous white salt used in fumigating, in manufacturing steel and dyes, and in extracting gold and silver from ore. Formula: NaCN.

so·di·um cy·cla·mate *n.* = **cyclamate**

so·di·um di·chro·mate *n.* a red or orange crystalline salt used in tanning leather, in making dyes and inks, and as an oxidizing agent and corrosion inhibitor. Formula: $Na_2Cr_2O_7$.

so·di·um fluor·ide *n.* a poisonous colorless crystalline salt used in small quantities in the fluoridation of water, in preventing tooth decay, in metallurgy, and as a pesticide. Formula: NaF.

so·di·um fluor·o·ac·e·tate *n.* a white poisonous powder used to kill rodents. Formula: $C_2H_2FNaO_2$. [Mid-20thC. "Fluoroacetate" coined from FLUORO- + ACETATE.]

so·di·um glu·ta·mate *n.* = **monosodium glutamate**

so·di·um hy·drox·ide *n.* a brittle white alkaline solid used in making paper, rayon, soap, chemicals, pharmaceuticals, and in petroleum refining. Formula: NaOH.

so·di·um hy·po·chlo·rite *n.* a green crystalline salt used in bleaching, disinfecting, and water purification. Formula: NaOCl.

so·di·um hy·po·sul·fite *n.* = **sodium thiosulfate**

so·di·um ni·trate *n.* a white crystalline salt used in curing meat, in rocket propellants, as a fertilizer, and in making explosives, pottery, and glass. Formula: $NaNO_3$.

So·di·um Pen·to·thal *tdmk.* a trademark for thiopental sodium

so·di·um per·ox·ide *n.* a yellowish odorless powder used in bleaching and as an antiseptic and disinfectant. Formula: Na_2O_2.

so·di·um phos·phate *n.* any of several sodium salts of phosphoric acid that are used in medicine and manufacturing

so·di·um pro·pi·o·nate *n.* a colorless crystalline powder used to kill bacteria and fungi in the preservation of food. Formula: $C_3H_5NaO_2$.

so·di·um pump *n.* a molecular process by which sodium ions are transported across cell membranes and exchanged with potassium ions

so·di·um sil·i·cate *n.* any of several compounds of silicate glass used as preservatives, in processing textiles, and in cement

so·di·um sul·fate *n.* a bitter white salt used in making glass, wood pulp, rayon, dyes, detergents, ceramic glazes, and in pharmaceuticals as a cathartic. Formula: Na_2SO_4.

so·di·um thi·o·sul·fate *n.* a white crystalline salt used as a fixer in photography and as a bleach. Formula: $Na_2S_2O_3$.

so·di·um-va·por lamp *n.* an electric lamp containing neon gas and sodium vapor through which a current runs to produce an orange-yellow light used for street lighting

Sod·om /sódəm/ *n.* **1.** CITY OF DEPRAVITY in the Bible, a city full of moral corruption and evil that was destroyed along with Gomorrah by God **2. CORRUPT PLACE** a place that is regarded as corrupt

sod·om·ite /sóddəmìt/ *n.* somebody who engages in sodomy [14thC. Via French from, ultimately, Greek *Sodomitēs* "inhabitant of Sodom," from *Sodoma* "Sodom."] —**sod·o·mit·ic** /sòddə míttik/ *adj.*

sod·om·ize /sóddəmìz/ (**-ized, -iz·ing, -iz·es**) *vt.* to engage in sodomy with somebody

sod·om·y /sóddəmee/ *n.* **1. ANAL INTERCOURSE** anal intercourse engaged in by heterosexual or homosexual partners **2. INTERCOURSE WITH ANIMALS** sexual intercourse with an animal [13thC. Directly or via French *sodomie* from medieval Latin *sodomia*, which was formed from ecclesiastical Latin *peccatum Sodomiticum* "sin of Sodom."]

Sod's Law *n. U.K.* = **Murphy's Law** (*informal*)

so·ev·er /sō évvər/ *adv.* in any way or to any degree possible [13thC. Originally two words (from SO + EVER).]

so·fa /sṓfə/ *n.* a long upholstered seat that has a back and arms and is made to seat more than one person [Early 17thC. Via French from, ultimately, Arabic *ṣuffa*, literally "long bench." First attested in English denoting a "cushioned dais for reclining (as found especially in Arab countries)."]

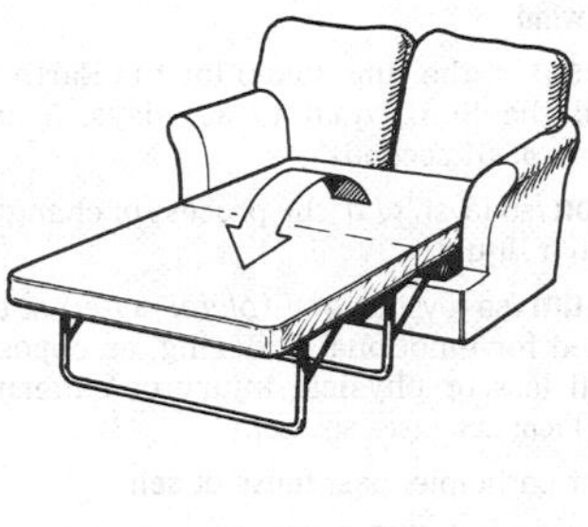

Sofa bed

so·fa bed *n.* a sofa that can be temporarily converted into a bed as required, e.g., by unfolding its seat

so·far /sṓfaar/ *n.* a way of locating survivors at sea by measuring the time it takes sound waves to reach three shore locations from an explosion set off underwater by the survivors [Mid-20thC. Acronym formed from *Sound fixing and ranging.*]

sof·fit /sáwfət/ *n.* the underside of a structural component of a building, e.g., the underside of a roof overhang or the inner curve of an arch [Early 17thC. Via French *soffite* or Italian *soffitto* from, ultimately, Latin *suffixus* "fixed under" (see SUFFIX).]

So·fi·a /sṓfee è/ capital city of Bulgaria, situated in the Sofia basin, about 40 mi./64 km from the Yugoslavian border. Population: 1,116,000 (1995).

S. of Sol. *abbr.* BIBLE Song of Solomon

soft /sáwft/ *adj.* **1. MALLEABLE** easily shaped, bent, or cut **2. YIELDING** giving way to externally applied pressure or weight ○ *a soft cushion* **3. SMOOTH-TEXTURED** having a texture that is smooth to the touch ○ *soft fur* **4. WITH SMOOTH OUTLINE** with no sharp or jagged edges ○ *furniture designed with soft lines* **5. QUIET-SOUNDING** quiet and soothing in sound **6. EASY ON THE EYES** without glare or intensity of light or color **7. MILD** not blowing strongly nor falling heavily ○ *a soft rain* **8. AFFECTIONATE** conveying love and tenderness **9. EMOTIONAL** easily moved to tender emotions **10. COWARDLY** lacking determination or strength of character **11. LENIENT** lenient in treatment or punishment, often too lenient **12. UNDEMANDING** requiring little effort or attention (*informal*) ○ *a soft job* **13. NOT WELL TONED** out of good physical condition **14. INCAPABLE OF ENDURING HARDSHIP** unable or unwilling to put up with hardship or privation, especially from having lived a life of ease **15. LACKING GOOD SENSE** lacking intelligence or sound judgment (*informal*) **16. LACKING SIGNIFICANCE** dealing with other than serious issues or facts ○ *soft news* **17. NOT EASILY VERIFIABLE** dealing with data that is not easily proved or disproved using scientific method **18. CONCILIATORY** based on negotiation, flexibility, and good will rather than on coercion ○ *a soft sell* **19.** = **soft-core 20. VULNERABLE** unprotected against violent attack **21.** MIL **UNARMORED** used to describe military vehicles and sites with little or no protection against military attack **22.** FIN **RELATING TO PAPER MONEY** relating to currency or a monetary system that is not backed by gold, and is therefore not easily convertible to a foreign currency **23.** COMM **DECLINING ECONOMICALLY** exhibiting a downward trend, e.g., in price, demand, or economic activity **24.** PHON **SIBILANT OR FRICATIVE** used to describe the consonant sounds "c" and "g" when pronounced as a fricative, as in "dance" and "age," rather than as a stop, as in "cat" and "get" **25.** PHON **PALATALIZED** used to describe a consonant that is palatalized in a Slavic language **26.** PHYS **LOW-ENERGY** used to describe radiation that has low energy and lacks penetrating ability ■ *adv.* **SOFTLY** in a quiet, tender, or lenient way ■ *n.* **SOMETHING SOFT** a soft thing or part of something [Old English *sōfte* (earlier *sēfte*), from prehistoric Germanic. The underlying idea is perhaps "fitting, arranged (so as to be pleasing)."] —**soft·ly** *adv.* —**soft·ness** *n.* ◇ **be soft on somebody** to be romantically attracted to somebody

soft·back /sáwft bàk/ *adj., n.* = **paperback**

soft·ball /sàwft báwl/ *n.* **1. BALLGAME** a kind of baseball played on a smaller field with a larger and softer ball that is pitched underhand **2. BALL USED FOR SOFTBALL** the ball used to play softball

soft-boiled *adj.* **1. WITH SOFT YOLK** boiled so that the yolk is soft but the white is firm **2. TENDING TO SYMPATHIZE** with a sympathetic or sentimental nature

soft·bound *adj.* = **paperback** *adj.*

soft chan·cre *n.* = **chancroid** ["Soft" from the softness of the ulcer]

soft coal *n.* = **bituminous coal**

soft cop·y *n.* data stored on a computer disk, as distinct from data that is printed on paper

soft-core *adj.* sexually suggestive or provocative without being explicit

soft·cov·er /sáwft kùvvər/ *adj., n.* = **paperback**

soft drink *n.* any nonalcoholic and usually carbonated beverage, usually served chilled

soft drug *n.* any illicit drug that is thought by some to be less addictive and harmful than the narcotic drugs heroin and cocaine

soft·en /sáwf'n/ (**-ened, -en·ing, -ens**) *vti.* **1. MAKE OR BECOME LESS HARD** to become soft or softer, or to make something soft or softer **2. BE KINDER** to become gentler or less harsh, or to make something gentler or less harsh **3. WEAR SOMEBODY DOWN** to make somebody's resolve less firm, or to become less firmly resolved **4. HARASS ENEMY** to weaken an enemy's resistance or morale by continuous bombardment, or to have resistance or morale weakened **5. REDUCE SOMETHING** to decline, e.g., in price, demand, or economic activity, or to cause something such as a market to decline

soft·en·er /sáwf'nər/ *n.* a substance added to something such as water or laundry to make it softer

soft fo·cus *n.* a deliberate slight blurring of a photograph or a filmed image giving it a hazy appearance, in order to achieve a special effect such as romance or nostalgia (*hyphenated when used before a noun*)

soft goods *npl.* textiles and the items such as clothing and bedding that are made from them

soft hail *n.* = **graupel**

soft-heart·ed *adj.* showing sympathy, kindness, or generosity —**soft-heart·ed·ly** *adv.* —**soft-heart·ed·ness** *n.*

soft·ie *n.* = **softy**

soft-kill *adj.* intended to disable rather than kill an enemy

soft land·ing *n.* a landing of a spacecraft, especially on the moon, without enough impact to cause damage

soft line *n.* a flexible and reasonable approach, especially to a political issue —**soft-lin·er** *n.*

soft pal·ate *n.* the fleshy rear portion of the roof of the mouth, extending from the hard palate at the front and tapering to the hanging uvula at the rear. It elevates to close off the nasal passages when swallowing, sucking, and pronouncing certain sounds.

soft ped·al *n.* a pedal on a piano that reduces the usual volume. It either shifts the hammers so that they do not strike all the strings of each note or so that they strike the strings with less force.

soft-ped·al (**soft-ped·aled, soft-ped·al·ing, soft-ped·als**) *vti.* **1. PLAY PIANO'S SOFT PEDAL** to reduce the volume of music played on a piano by operating the soft pedal **2. PLAY SOMETHING DOWN** to try to make something seem less important, noticeable, or objectionable (*informal*)

soft rock *n.* rock music that tends to be slower and more melodic than hard rock, often influenced by folk or country and western music

soft rot *n.* any bacterial or fungal plant disease that causes plant parts, especially fruits and vegetables, to decay into a pulpy mass

soft sell *n.* a method of selling or advertising goods and services that uses subtlety and persuasion, rather than aggressive insistence (*informal; hyphenated when used before a noun*)

soft-shell *adj.* used to describe an aquatic animal with a soft or thin and brittle shell, sometimes as a result of having recently molted

soft-shelled tur·tle *n.* a freshwater turtle with sharp claws, a pointed snout, and a soft flat shell covered with leathery skin. Family: Trionychidae.

soft-shoe *n.* a type of tap dancing for which soft-soled shoes without metal taps are worn (*often used before a noun*)

soft shoul·der *n.* a soft strip of ground alongside a road

soft soap *n.* **1. TYPE OF SOAP** a liquid or semiliquid soap, usually made with potassium hydroxide **2. MANIPULATIVE FLATTERY** flattery used for the purpose of persuading or distracting somebody (*informal*)

soft-soap (**soft-soaped, soft-soap·ing, soft-soaps**) *vt.* to use flattery to persuade or distract somebody (*informal*)

soft-spo·ken *adj.* speaking or said with a quiet gentle voice

soft spot *n.* a place, position, or area in which something is weak or vulnerable ◇ **have a soft spot for somebody** *or* **something** to have especially tender feelings or affection for somebody or something

soft touch *n.* somebody who can be easily swayed or imposed upon to do something

soft·ware /sáwft wàir/ *n.* computer programs and applications, such as word processing or database packages, that can be run on a particular computer system (*often used before a noun*) [Mid-19thC. Originally, in plural, "soft goods." The modern sense dates from the mid-20thC.]

soft·ware en·gi·neer·ing *n.* the application of mathematics and technology to the design, implementation, and testing of computer programs to optimize their production and support

soft·ware pi·ra·cy *n.* the illegal duplication of copyrighted software or the installation of copyrighted software on more computers than authorized under terms of the software license agreement

soft wa·ter *n.* water that contains very low levels of calcium and magnesium salts, either naturally or because they have been removed. Soap lathers easily in soft water.

soft wheat *n.* a type of wheat with soft kernels and weak gluten that is relatively low in protein. It is used mainly for cakes, biscuits, pastries, and as a livestock feed.

soft·wood /sáwft wòōd/ *n.* **1. WOOD OF CONIFEROUS TREE** the open-grained wood of a pine, cedar, or other coniferous tree. Many softwoods are, in fact, hard and durable. **2. CONIFEROUS TREE** any tree that yields softwood, such as a pine or cedar

soft·y /sáwftee/ (*plural* **-ies**), **soft·ie** *n.* somebody who is weak, timid, or sentimental (*informal*)

Sog·di·an /sógdee ən/ *n.* **1.** PEOPLES **MEMBER OF ANCIENT ASIAN PEOPLE** a member of a people that lived in Sogdiana, an ancient region of central Asia **2.** LANG **SOGDIAN LANGUAGE** the Iranian language of the Sogdian people, now extinct [Mid-16thC. Via Latin from Greek *Sogdianos*, from Old Persian *Suguda.*] —**Sog·di·an** *adj.*

sog·gy /sóggee/ (**-gi·er, -gi·est**) *adj.* **1. THOROUGHLY WET** soaked through with moisture **2. WITH TOO MUCH LIQUID** unpleasantly wet and heavy in texture **3. UNINTERESTING** lacking animation or vitality [Early 18thC. Formed from obsolete *sog* "area of marshy ground."] —**sog·gi·ly** *adv.* —**sog·gi·ness** *n.*

Sog·ne Fjord /sóngnè-/ inlet of the North Sea in southwestern Norway. Length: 125 mi./200 km.

soh *n. U.K.* = **sol**

So·ho /sṓhō/ *n.* **1. AREA IN LONDON** an area of central London well known for its theaters, restaurants and clubs **2. So·ho, So·Ho AREA IN NEW YORK** an area of the lower west side of Manhattan well known for its art studios and galleries [In sense 2, from the first letters of SOUTH and of *Houston Street*, from its location]

soi·di·sant /swàadee zàaN, -zàan/ *adj.* self-styled or so-called (*literary*) [From French, literally "saying oneself"]

soi·gné /swaa nyáy, swàanyay/, **soi·gnée** *adj.* **1. WELL GROOMED** neat and smart in dress and appearance **2. WELL FURNISHED** designed or furnished in an elegant style [Early 19thC. From French, past participle of *soigner* "to care for," from, ultimately, Germanic.]

soil[1] /soyl/ *n.* **1. TOP LAYER OF LAND** the top layer of most of the earth's land surface, consisting of the unconsolidated products of rock erosion and organic decay, along with bacteria and fungi (*often used before a noun*) **2. KIND OF EARTH** earth or ground of a particular kind **3. COUNTRY** somebody's country or land (*literary*) **4. FARMING** agricultural life and work (*literary*) **5. NURTURING MEDIUM** any medium in which growth and development takes place (*literary*) [13thC Via Anglo-Norman, "piece of land," from Latin *solium* "seat," by association with *solum* "ground, soil"]

soil[2] /soyl/ *vt.* (**soiled, soil·ing, soils**) **1. MAKE DIRTY** to make something dirty or stained **2. BRING DISHONOR ON** to damage somebody's reputation, character, or good name ■ *n.* **1. DIRT** dirt or dirty condition ○ *remove soil from linens* **2. MORAL CORRUPTION** immoral behavior or lack of moral standards (*literary*) [13thC. From Old French *soill(i)er* "to soil, wallow" (probable source of English *sully*), of uncertain origin: probably from assumed Vulgar Latin *suculare* "to make dirty," from Latin *sus* "pig, boar."]

soil[3] /soyl/ *n.* excrement or sewage [15thC. From Old French *souille* "muddy place," from *soill(i)er* (see SOIL[2]).]

soil bank *n.* land retired from crop production and planted with soil-building plants under a program that provides subsidies for the retired land

soil·ure /sóylyər/ *n.* **1. DIRTYING OF SOMETHING** the soiling or staining of something (*literary*) **2. DIRTY MARK** a stain or smudge (*archaic*) [14thC. From Old French *soilleure*, from *soillier* (see SOIL[2]).]

soi·ree, **soi·rée** *n.* a party or gathering held in the evening, especially in somebody's home (*formal*) [Late 18thC. From *French*, from *soir* "evening," from Latin *sero* "at a late hour," from *serus* "late" (partial source of English *serenade*).]

soix·ante-neuf /swàas aaN nőf/ *n.* = **sixty-nine** (*slang offensive*) [From French, literally "sixty-nine"]

so·journ /sṓ jùrn/ *n.* **BRIEF VISIT** a short stay at a place (*literary*) ■ *vi.* (**-journed, -journ·ing, -journs**) **STAY FOR TIME** to stay at a place for a time (*literary*) [13thC. Via Anglo-Norman *sujurn* or Old French *sojorn* (noun) from *sojourner* (verb), from assumed Vulgar Latin *subdiurnare* "to spend the day," from late Latin *diurnum* "day."] — **so·journ·er** *n.*

So·ko·to /sṓkètō/ capital city of Sokoto State, northwestern Nigeria, situated about 300 mi./483 km northwest of Abuja. Population: 207,000 (1995).

sol[1] /sōl/ *n.* the fifth note in the diatonic musical scale. In fixed solfeggio it corresponds to the note "g." [14thC. From medieval Latin, being the first syllable of Latin *solve* "purge!, release!", the word sung to this note in a medieval hymn to St. John the Baptist.]

sol[2] /sawl, sōl/ *n.* a liquid colloidal solution [Late 19thC. Shortening of SOLUTION.]

sol[3] /sol/ *n.* a copper or silver coin formerly used in France, worth 12 deniers [Late 16thC. Via obsolete French from Latin *solidus* (see SOLDIER).]

sol[4] /sōl/ (*plural* **soles** /sṓlays/) *n.* MONEY **1. PERUVIAN UNIT OF CURRENCY** the main unit of currency in Peru, worth 100 centimos. See table at **currency 2. COIN WORTH A SOL** a coin worth one sol

Sol /sol/ *n.* **1. SUN PERSONIFIED** the personification of the sun (*literary*) **2. ROMAN SUN GOD** in Roman mythology, the god of the sun. Greek equivalent **Helios** [14thC. From Latin, literally "sun."]

sol. *abbr.* **1.** soluble **2.** solution

Sol. *abbr.* **1.** solicitor **2.** BIBLE Solomon

so·la[1] /sṓlə/ *adj.* used as a stage direction to indicate that a female character appears alone on stage

so·la[2] plural of **solum**

sol·ace /sólləss/ *n.* **1. RELIEF FROM EMOTIONAL DISTRESS** comfort at a time of sadness, grief, or disappointment **2. SOURCE OF COMFORT** somebody or something that provides comfort in times of sadness, grief, or disappointment ■ *vt.* (**-aced, -ac·ing, -ac·es**) **PROVIDE WITH COMFORT** to comfort somebody at a time of sadness, grief, or disappointment [13thC. Via Old French *solas* from Latin *solatium*, from *solari* "to comfort" (source of English *console*).] —**sol·ac·er** *n.*

so·lan /sṓlən/, **so·lan goose** *n.* a gannet found in the North Atlantic. Latin name: *Morus bassanus.* [15thC. Origin uncertain: probably from Old Norse *súla* "gannet" + *and-*, the stem of *ǫnd* "duck."]

sol·a·na·ceous /sòllə náyshəss/ *adj.* relating to or belonging to the nightshade family of plants, a family that includes the potato, tomato, and tobacco [Early 19thC. Formed from modern Latin *Solanaceae* (family name), from Latin *solanum* (see SOLANUM).]

so·lan goose *n.* = **solan**

so·la·nine /sṓlənèen/ *n.* a bitter poisonous alkaloid found in several plants of the nightshade family. It was formerly used to treat epilepsy, bronchitis, and asthma. Formula: $C_{45}H_{73}NO_{15}$.

solanum /sə láynəm, sə làanəm/ (*plural* **solanums** *or* **solanum**) *n.* a plant of the nightshade family. Some species such as the potato and eggplant are cultivated for food. Genus: *Solanum.* [Late 16thC. Via modern Latin, genus name, from Latin, from *sol* "sun" (see SOLAR).]

so·lar /sṓlər/ *adj.* **1. FROM THE SUN** relating to or originating from the Sun **2. OPERATING USING ENERGY FROM THE SUN** using the Sun's radiation as a source of energy **3. MEASURED BY THE SUN'S POSITION** measured with reference to the Earth's movement in relation to the Sun [15thC. From Latin *solaris*, from *sol* "sun" (source of English *parasol*, *solarium*, and *solstice*).]

so·lar a·pex *n.* the point in space toward which the Sun appears to be moving. It is in the constellation Hercules.

so·lar bat·ter·y *n.* an arrangement of several solar cells for converting solar radiation into electricity

so·lar cell *n.* an electric cell that converts solar radiation directly into electricity. Solar cells are mounted on solar panels used, e.g., on satellites and spacecraft.

so·lar cy·cle *n.* a calendar system based on the solar year, typical of most civilizations. Variations of solar calendars in western civilization are the Julian and Gregorian calendars.

so·lar day *n.* the time taken for the Earth to make a complete revolution on its axis, measured with respect to the Sun

so·lar e·clipse *n.* an eclipse in which the Moon blocks all or part of the Sun's light from reaching the Earth's surface, because it passes directly between the Earth and the Sun

so·lar flare *n.* a brief sudden eruption of high-energy hydrogen gas from the surface of the Sun, associated with sunspots. It causes interruptions of communication systems on Earth.

so·lar fur·nace *n.* a furnace equipped with a series of concave mirrors that are motorized to follow the Sun and focus its radiation to obtain and maintain extremely high temperatures

so·lar·i·a plural of **solarium**

so·lar·im·e·ter /sòlə rímmətər/ *n.* an instrument used to measure solar radiation [Early 20thC. Coined from SOLAR + -METER.]

so·lar·i·um /sə lérree əm, sō lérree əm/ (*plural* **-a** /-ə/ *or* **-ums**) *n.* a room built for the purpose of enjoying sunlight, usually with large windows or glass walls, especially a room in a hospital or other healthcare establishment [Mid-19thC. From Latin, "sundial (the original English sense), sunny roof, terrace," from *sol* "sun" (see SOLAR).]

so·lar·ize /sṓlə rīz/ (**-ized, -iz·ing, -iz·es**) *vt.* **1. OVEREXPOSE TO SUNLIGHT** to affect or damage something with solar radiation **2.** PHOTOGRAPHY **OVEREXPOSE** to overexpose photographic materials to light for deliberate effect, usually in order to exaggerate highlights — **so·lar·i·za·tion** /sōlərə záysh'n/ *n.*

so·lar month *n.* one-twelfth of a solar year, equal to 30 days, 10 hours, 29 minutes, 3.8 seconds

so·lar pan·el *n.* a large panel containing solar cells or heat-absorbing plates that convert the sun's radiation into electricity, for use, e.g., in heating buildings and powering satellites and spacecraft

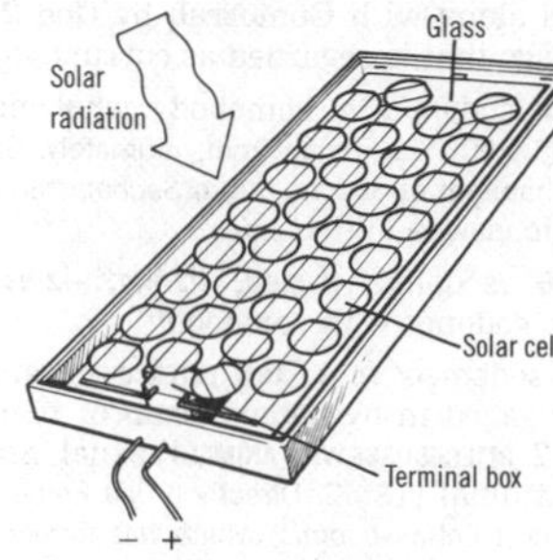

Solar panel

so·lar plex·us *n.* **1. NERVES IN UPPER ABDOMEN** a mass of nerve cells in the upper abdomen behind the stomach, kidneys, and other internal organs **2. ABDOMINAL AREA** a point on the upper abdomen just below where the ribs separate. A sharp blow to this region can cause loss of consciousness. ["Solar" from its radial network of nerves, likened to the sun's rays]

so·lar sys·tem *n.* the Sun and all the planets, satellites, asteroids, meteors, and comets that are subject to its gravitational pull

so·lar wind *n.* the flow of high-speed ionized particles from the sun's surface into interplanetary space. ◊ **stellar wind**

so·lar year *n.* the time taken for the Earth to move around the Sun, equal to 365 days, 5 hours, 48 minutes, 45.51 seconds

so·la·tion /sō láysh'n/ *n.* the process of changing from a gel to a liquid

so·la·ti·um /sə láyshee əm/ (*plural* **-a** /-e/) *n.* damages awarded for emotional suffering, as opposed to financial loss or physical injury or suffering [Early 19thC. From Latin (see SOLACE).]

sold past participle, past tense of **sell**

sol·der /sáwdər/ *n.* **1. ALLOY FOR JOINING METAL** an alloy with a low melting point, typically a mixture of tin and lead, used to join electrical components to a circuit board or to join metal objects together **2. SOMETHING THAT UNITES** something that forms a bond or union ■ *vti.* (**-dered, -der·ing, -ders**) **1. JOIN THINGS WITH SOLDER** to work with solder or to join things using solder **2. UNITE TO FORM WHOLE** to come together in unity, or to establish a bond of unity between people or things [Via Old French from Latin *solidare* "to fasten together, make solid," from *solidus* "solid" (see SOLID)] — **sol·der·er** *n.*

sol·der·ing iron *n.* a tool with a point that is heated for melting and applying solder

sol·dier /sṓljər/ *n.* **1.** MIL **SOMEBODY SERVING IN ARMY** somebody who serves in an army or other military service **2.** ARMY **ARMY MEMBER BELOW OFFICER RANK** a member of an army who ranks below a commissioned officer **3. DEDICATED WORKER** somebody who works with dedication for a cause **4. SKILLED WARRIOR** a skilled and experienced fighter or military strategist **5.** INSECTS **ANT THAT PROTECTS COLONY** a sterile member of an ant or termite colony with a large head and powerful jaws. Its role is to defend the colony. ■ *vi.* (**-diered, -dier·ing, -diers**) **1.** MIL **BE MEMBER OF AN ARMY** to serve as a soldier in an army **2. PRETEND TO WORK** to give the appearance of working while really idling [13thC. From Old French, literally "somebody having pay," from *soulde* "(soldier's) pay," from Latin *solidus (nummus)* "Roman gold coin," literally "solid (coin)" (see SOLID).] —**sol·dier·ly** *adj.*

WORD KEY: CULTURAL NOTE

The Good Soldier, a novel by Ford Madox Ford (1915). Considered Ford's masterpiece, it describes an American couple's tragic involvement with an English army captain (the good soldier of the title) and his domineering wife. A powerful study of the conflict between sexuality and contemporary moral values, it is admired in particular for its innovative and intricate narrative structure.

soldier on *vi.* to persevere despite difficulties or setbacks

sol·dier·fish /sṓljər fish/ (*plural* **-fish·es** *or* **-fish**) *n.* = **squirrelfish** [*Soldier* from its sharp spines and rough scales]

sol·dier of for·tune *n.* somebody who will serve in any army in which there is profit or adventure

sol·diers' home *n.* an institution funded by the government for the care of war veterans

sol·dier·y /sṓljəree/ *n.* **1.** SOLDIERS COLLECTIVELY soldiers as a group **2.** SOLDIER'S WORK the profession or skill of a soldier

sol·do /sṓldō/ (*plural* **-di** /-dee/) *n.* a copper coin used in the former Italian states until the 19th century, worth one-twentieth of a lira [Late 16thC. Via Italian from Latin *solidus* (see SOLDIER).]

Sol·dot·na /sol dótnə/ city in southern Alaska on the Kenai Peninsula, southeast of Anchorage. Population: 4,295 (1996).

sold-out *adj.* for which all available tickets have been sold

sole[1] /sōl/ *n.* **1.** ANAT BOTTOM OF THE FOOT the underside of the foot, stretching from the toes to the heel **2.** BOTTOM OF A SHOE the underside of a shoe, boot, or other piece of footwear, sometimes excluding the heel **3.** GOLF BOTTOM SURFACE OF A GOLF CLUB the underside of the head of a golf club ■ *vt.* (**soled, sol·ing, soles**) **1.** PUT SOLE ON SHOE to put a sole on a shoe, boot, or other piece of footwear **2.** GOLF PLACE ON THE GROUND to put the sole of a golf club on the ground in preparation for a stroke [14thC. Via Old French from Latin *solea* "sandal, sole of an animal's foot," from *solum* "ground, foot, shoe sole."]

sole[2] /sōl/ *adj.* **1.** ONLY of which there is only one ○ *the sole reason* **2.** EXCLUSIVE belonging to one person or group ○ *has sole responsibility for the department* **3.** UNFETTERED free from the interference of others **4.** LAW UNMARRIED without husband or wife **5.** UNACCOMPANIED without a companion (*archaic*) [13thC. Via Old French *soule* from Latin *sola*, the feminine of *solus* (source of English *desolate, solitary*, and *sullen*).] —**sole·ness** *n.*

sole[3] /sōl/ (*plural* **soles** *or* **sole**) *n.* **1.** FISH WITH FLAT BODY a brownish marine fish with a small mouth and both eyes on the upper side of its flat body. It is valued as a food fish. Family: Soleidae. **2.** FOOD FISH LIKE THE SOLE a name used for fishes similar to the sole when they are sold as food [14thC. Via French from, ultimately, Latin *solea* "sandal" (see SOLE), from its being likened to the sole of a sandal.]

sol·e·cism /sóllə sìzzəm, sṓlə-/ *n.* **1.** GRAMMATICAL MISTAKE a mistake in grammar or syntax **2.** ERROR something incorrect, inappropriate, or inconsistent **3.** BREACH OF GOOD MANNERS an action that breaks the rules of etiquette or good manners [Mid-16thC. Ultimately via Latin *soloecismus* from Greek *soloikismos*, from *soloikos* "speaking incorrectly," literally "inhabitant of Soloi" (in ancient Cilicia, southern Turkey), whose Attic dialect was considered barbarous.] —**sol·e·cist** *n.* —**sol·e·cis·ti·cal** /sòllə sístik'l, sṑlə-/ *adj.* —**sol·e·cis·ti·cal·ly** /-sístiklee, -/ *adv.*

sole·ly /sṓl lee/ *adv.* **1.** ONLY for nothing other than ○ *sold the company solely for commercial reasons* **2.** EXCLUSIVELY to the exclusion of all else or others ○ *He is solely to blame.*

sol·emn /sólləm/ *adj.* **1.** EARNEST demonstrating sincerity and gravity **2.** HUMORLESS without joy or humor **3.** FORMAL characterized by ceremony or formality **4.** RELIGIOUS observed with sacred or religious ceremony **5.** AWE-INSPIRING inspiring wonder or reverence [14thC. Via Old French *solemne* from Latin *sol(l)emnis* "customary, religious," from *sollus* "whole, entire" (source of English *solicit*) + an element of unknown origin.] —**sol·emn·ly** *adv.* —**sol·emn·ness** *n.*

so·lem·ni·fy /sə lémnə fī/ (**-fied, -fy·ing, -fies**) *vt.* to make something serious or solemn

so·lem·ni·ty /sə lémnətee/ (*plural* **-ties**) *n.* **1.** SOLEMN QUALITY the solemn nature or quality of something **2.** SOLEMN CEREMONY a formal or solemn ceremony held to observe an occasion or event (*often used in the plural*) **3.** LAW LEGAL FORMALITY a formality that must be complied with before a contract or agreement can become effective

sol·em·nize /sólləm nīz/ (**-nized, -niz·ing, -niz·es**) *v.* **1.** *vt.* CELEBRATE WITH CEREMONY to observe an event or occasion with ceremony or formality **2.** *vt.* PERFORM A MARRIAGE CEREMONY to celebrate a marriage with a religious ceremony **3.** *vt.* MAKE DIGNIFIED to bring dignity or formality to something **4.** *vi.* SPEAK SOLEMNLY to speak or reflect with great seriousness —**sol·em·ni·za·tion** /sòlləmnə záysh'n/ *n.*

so·le·no·don /sō lénə dòn, -lénnə-/ *n.* a rare nocturnal insect-eating mammal native to the West Indies, with a long snout and a long scaly tail. It looks like a large shrew. Family: Solenodontidae. [Mid-19thC. From modern Latin, genus name, literally "pipe-tooth," from, ultimately, Greek *sōlēn* "pipe, channel."]

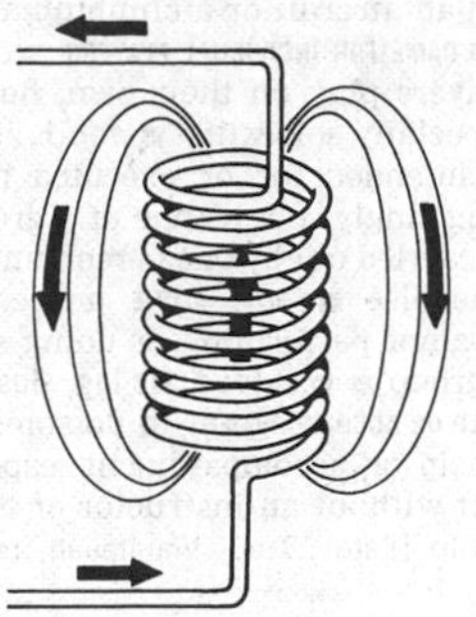

Solenoid

so·le·noid /sṓlə nòyd/ *n.* a device consisting of a cylindrical coil of wire surrounding a moveable iron core that moves along the length of the coil when an electric current is passed through it. Solenoids are used as switches and relays, e.g., in a motor vehicle to complete the circuit between the battery and starter motor. [Early 19thC. From French *solénoïde*, literally "pipe-shaped," from Greek *sōlēn* "pipe, channel."] —**so·le·noi·dal** /sṑlə nóyd'l/ *adj.* —**so·le·noi·dal·ly** /sṑlə nóyd'lee/ *adv.*

sole·plate /sṓl plàyt/ *n.* **1.** HOUSEHOLD BOTTOM OF AN IRON the underside of an iron for pressing clothes **2.** BUILDING PLATE ON WHICH STUDS REST the plate that supports the bases of the studs used in framing a wall

so·le·us /sṓlee əss/ (*plural* **-i** /-lee ī/) *n.* a broad flat muscle in the calf of the leg that helps to flex the ankle and depress the sole of the foot [Late 17thC. Via modern Latin from Latin *solea* (see SOLE[1]).]

sol-fa /sōl fáa/ *n.* = **tonic sol-fa** ■ *vti.* (**sol-faed, sol-fa·ing, sol-fas**) SING USING SOL-FA to sing a tune using the sol-fa syllables

sol·fa·ta·ra /sṑlfə táarə, sṓlfə-/ *n.* a vent in a volcano through which sulfur-rich gases and steam escape, leaving bright yellow sulfur deposits [Late 18thC. From Italian, "sulfurous volcano," from *solfo* "sulfur," from Latin *sulfur* (source of English *sulfur*).] —**sol·fa·ta·ric** *adj.*

sol·feg·gio /sōl féjjee ō, -féjjō/ (*plural* **-gi** /sōl féjjee/ *or* **-gios**) *n.* an exercise in singing using the sol-fa syllables [Late 18thC. From Italian, from *sol-fa* "sol-fa."]

sol·fe·ri·no /sṑlfə rée nō/ *adj.* of a red color tinged with purple [Mid-19thC. Named for *Solferino*, an Italian town at which a dye of this color was invented.] —**sol·fe·ri·no** *n.*

so·li plural of **solo**

so·lic·it /sə líssit/ (**-it·ed, -it·ing, -its**) *v.* **1.** *vti.* PLEAD FOR SOMETHING to try to get something by making insistent requests or pleas **2.** *vt.* ASK SOMEBODY FOR SOMETHING to plead with or petition a person or group for something **3.** *vti.* OFFER SEX FOR MONEY to offer to participate in sexual activities in return for money **4.** *vt.* GET SOMEBODY TO DO SOMETHING WRONG to attempt to draw somebody into participating in illegal or immoral acts [15thC. Via French *solliciter* from Latin *sollicitare* "to disturb," from *sollicitus*, literally "completely moved," from *sollus* "whole" + *citus*, past participle of *ciere* "to move" (source of English *excite*).] —**so·lic·i·ta·tion** /sə lìssə táysh'n/ *n.*

so·lic·i·tor /sə líssətər/ *n.* **1.** TOP LEGAL OFFICER the chief officer for legal matters in a city, town, or county, or in a government department **2.** SOMEBODY WHO SOLICITS CONTRIBUTIONS somebody who solicits, especially somebody who asks for financial contributions **3.** *U.K.* LAWYER a lawyer who gives legal advice, draws up legal documents, and does preparatory work for barristers. A solicitor who holds an advocacy qualification may also represent clients in court. —**so·lic·i·tor·ship** *n.*

so·lic·i·tor gen·er·al (*plural* **so·lic·i·tors gen·er·al**) *n.* **1.** U.S. LAW OFFICER a law officer appointed to the U.S. Department of Justice who is in charge of appeals, including those before the U.S. Supreme Court **2.** STATE LAW OFFICER a high-ranking law officer equivalent to a state attorney general

so·lic·i·tous /sə líssətəss/ *adj.* **1.** CONCERNED expressing an attitude of concern and consideration **2.** READY AND WILLING full of eagerness and anticipation to do something **3.** METICULOUS paying very careful attention to details **4.** NOT AT EASE troubled by uneasiness or apprehension (*archaic*) [Mid-16thC. Formed from Latin *sollicitus* (see SOLICIT).] —**so·lic·i·tous·ly** *adv.* —**so·lic·i·tous·ness** *n.*

so·lic·i·tude /sə líssə tood/ *n.* **1.** EXPRESSED CONCERN concern and consideration, especially when expressed **2.** ANXIETY a state of uneasiness or anxiety (*archaic*) **3.** SOMETHING CAUSING CONCERN a cause of concern or uneasiness (*often used in the plural*)

sol·id /sóllәd/ *adj.* **1.** NOT SOFT OR YIELDING consisting of compact unyielding material **2.** NOT HOLLOW having no open interior spaces **3.** UNADULTERATED OR UNMIXED made of the same material throughout **4.** OF STRONG AND SECURE CONSTRUCTION built out of strong substantial material and not likely to break or collapse **5.** UNINTERRUPTED continuing without breaks or openings ○ *It took a solid two hours to crack the code.* **6.** NOURISHING providing ample nourishment **7.** UNANIMOUS in complete agreement ○ *Support for the amendment was solid.* **8.** RELIABLE able to be relied or depended upon **9.** FINANCIALLY SECURE in sound financial condition **10.** GEOM THREE-DIMENSIONAL with the three dimensions of length, breadth, and depth, or relating to geometric figures that have three dimensions **11.** CHEM RETAINING ITS SHAPE with a shape that resists moderate stress or deformation, and therefore distinct from a liquid or a gas **12.** LANG AS SINGLE WORD written as one word without a space or hyphen **13.** PRINTING WITHOUT SPACES without spaces between lines of type in printing ■ *n.* **1.** SOLID THING something that is solid **2.** GEOM SOLID FIGURE a three-dimensional geometric figure or object **3.** CHEM SUBSTANCE THAT RETAINS SHAPE a substance that resists moderate stress and deformation, unlike a liquid or a gas [14thC. Directly or via French *solide* from Latin *solidus* "firm, whole" (source of English *soldier*).] —**so·lid·i·ty** /sə líddətee/ *n.* —**sol·id·ly** /sólləd lee/ *adv.* —**sol·id·ness** /sólləd nəss/ *n.*

sol·id an·gle *n.* a three-dimensional angle formed at the vertex of a cone or the intersection of three planes

sol·i·dar·i·ty /sòllə dérrətee/ *n.* harmony of interests and responsibilities among individuals in a group, especially as manifested in unanimous support and collective action for something

Sol·i·dar·i·ty *n.* a federation of trade unions in Poland, founded in 1980. Under the leadership of Lech Walesa it challenged the Soviet-backed government of the day. [Late 20thC. Translation of Polish *Solidarność*.]

sol·id ge·om·e·try *n.* the branch of geometry dealing with three-dimensional figures

sol·i·di plural of **solidus**

so·lid·i·fy /sə líddə fī/ (**-fied, -fy·ing, -fies**) *vti.* **1.** MAKE OR BECOME SOLID to become compact or firm, or make something compact or firm **2.** STRENGTHEN to become strong and united, or make something strong and united —**so·lid·i·fi·a·ble** *adj.* —**so·lid·i·fi·ca·tion** /sə lìddəfə káysh'n/ *n.* —**so·lid·i·fi·er** /sə líddə fī ər/ *n.*

sol·id of rev·o·lu·tion *n.* a three-dimensional mathematical figure formed by rotating a plane figure around an axis in its plane

sol·id so·lu·tion *n.* a crystalline substance such as glass or an alloy in which certain atoms or molecules have been replaced by others but the structure has not changed

sol·id-state *adj.* **1.** USING TRANSISTORS OR SEMICONDUCTORS working by means of the flow of electric current through solid material, as happens with semiconductors and transistors. The term is usually used to distinguish modern electronic equipment from earlier devices that made use of vacuum tubes or heated filaments. **2.** OF ELECTRONICS AND SOLIDS relating to the electronic characteristics of solids, especially at the atomic or molecular level

sol·i·dus /sólləd əss/ (*plural* **-di** /-dī/) *n.* **1.** PRINTING = **virgule 2.** MONEY ROMAN GOLD COIN a gold coin used in the Roman Empire from the fourth century B.C. It remained in use in Europe until the 12th century A.D. [14thC. From Latin (see SOLDIER).]

so·li·fluc·tion /sṑlə flúksh'n/ *n.* the slow movement of soil downhill as a result of water saturation after rainfall or the melting of ice [Early 20thC. Formed from Latin *solum* "ground" + *fluct-*, the past participle stem of *fluere* "to flow" (source of English *fluctuate*).]

so·lil·o·quize /sə lílə kwīz/ (**-quized, -quiz·ing, -quiz·es**) *vi.* to speak a soliloquy in the course of a play —**so·lil·o·quist** *n.* —**so·lil·o·quiz·er** *n.*

so·lil·o·quy /sə lílləkwee/ (*plural* **-quies**) *n.* **1.** **TALKING WHEN ALONE** the act of speaking while alone, especially when used as a theatrical device that allows a character's thoughts and ideas to be conveyed to the audience **2.** **SECTION IN PLAY** a section of a play or other drama in which a soliloquy is spoken [14thC. From late Latin *soliloquium,* literally "a speaking alone," from Latin *solus* "alone" (see SOLE²) + *loqui* "to speak" (source of English *eloquent*).]

So·ling·en /zṓlingən/ city in North Rhine-Westphalia State, western central Germany. Population: 166,000 (1994).

sol·ip·sism /sóllәp sìzzəm, sáwl-/ *n.* the belief that the only thing somebody can be sure of is that he or she exists, and that true knowledge of anything else is impossible [Late 19thC. Formed from Latin *solus* "alone" + *ipse* "self."] —**sol·ip·sist** *n.* —**sol·ip·sis·tic** /sòllәp sístik, sòləp-/ *adj.* —**sol·ip·sis·ti·cal·ly** /-sístiklee, -/ *adv.*

sol·i·taire /sáwlə tàir/ *n.* **1.** CARDS **CARD GAME FOR ONE** a card game played by one person. The object is to form sequences of cards, using up all the cards from several piles dealt face down. **2.** ACCESSORIES **SINGLE GEMSTONE** a gem, especially a diamond, that is set alone in a ring **3.** BIRDS **SONGBIRD** a thrush that is native to North and Central America, well known for its attractive song. Genus: *Myadestes.* [14thC. Via French, "recluse," from Latin *solitarius* (see SOLITARY). The original English sense was "widow."]

sol·i·tar·y /sóllə tèrree/ *adj.* **1.** **DONE ALONE** done without the company of other people **2.** **SHUNNING COMPANY** preferring to be or live alone **3.** **SECLUDED** in a remote location, apart from others **4.** **SINGLE** existing as the only one of its kind ○ *a solitary boat on the sea* **5.** ZOOL **NOT LIVING IN SOCIAL GROUPS** used to describe animals that live alone or in pairs rather than in colonies or social groups **6.** BOT **GROWING SINGLY** used to describe flowers that grow singly rather than as a cluster ■ *n.* (*plural* **-ies**) **1.** **RECLUSE** somebody who lives or prefers to live away from others **2.** = **solitary confinement** [14thC. Directly or via French *solitaire* from Latin *solitarius* (source of English *solitaire*), from *solus* "alone" (see SOLE²).]

sol·i·tar·y bee *n.* a flower-visiting bee that does not live in a colony, but raises its young independently

sol·i·tar·y con·fine·ment *n.* confinement of a prisoner in an area or cell isolated from other prisoners, used as a punishment or for protection

sol·i·tar·y wasp *n.* = **hunting wasp**

sol·i·tude /sóllə tòod/ *n.* **1.** **STATE OF BEING ALONE** the state of being alone, separated from other people, whether considered as a welcome freedom from disturbance or as an unhappy loneliness **2.** **REMOTENESS** a quality of quiet remoteness or seclusion in places from which human activity is generally absent **3.** **LONELY PLACE** a remote or uninhabited place (*literary*) [14thC. Directly or via Old French from Latin *solitudo,* from *solus* "alone."] —**sol·i·tu·di·nous** /sòllə tòod'nəss/ *adj.*

WORD KEY: CULTURAL NOTE

One Hundred Years of Solitude, a novel by Colombian writer Gabriel Garcia Marquez (1967). It recounts 100 years in the lives of the Buendía family, founders of the town of Macondo in Colombia, a story that mirrors the history of the nation. Marquez's skillful use of fantasy and myth to convey the depth of his characters' experiences make this a key work in the magical realism school of literature.

sol·i·tud·i·nar·i·an /sòllə toodə nérree ən/ *n.* somebody who likes to be alone (*literary*)

sol·ler·et /sòllə rét/ *n.* a shoe made of steel plates riveted together, forming part of a suit of armor [14thC. Via the diminutive of Old French *soller,* "shoe" from, ultimately, late Latin *subtel* "hollow of the foot," from *sub* "under" + *talus* "ankle."]

sol·mi·za·tion /sòlmə záysh'n/ *n.* the assignment of separate syllables to different musical pitches for singing or training the ear, as, e.g., in solfeggio [Mid-18thC. French *solmisation* from *solmiser* "to sing sol-fa."]

soln. *abbr.* solution

so·lo /sṓlō/ *n.* (*plural* **-los** *or* **-li** /sṓlee/) **1.** MUSIC **MUSICAL PIECE PERFORMED BY ONE PERSON** a piece of music performed by one musician or singer, or a passage for a single player or singer within a longer piece for two or more, a choir, or an orchestra **2.** ARTS **PERFORMANCE BY ONE ARTIST** a performance by a single artist such as a musician, singer, or dancer with or without accompaniment **3.** **ACT DONE BY SINGLE PERSON** an action or feat carried out by one person alone, e.g., a flight in an aircraft or a climb up a mountain **4.** CARDS **CARD GAME FOR INDIVIDUAL PLAYERS** a card game in which players play on their own, not in pairs or teams, especially solo whist ■ *adj.* **1.** ARTS **FOR A SINGLE PERFORMER** intended for or executed by somebody performing singly, not as one of a group **2.** **DONE BY ONE PERSON** carried out by one person unaccompanied by anyone else ■ *adv.* **ALONE** unaccompanied by anyone, or not performing or doing something as one of a group ■ *vi.* (**-loed, -lo·ing, -los**) **DO SOMETHING WITHOUT HELP OR ACCOMPANIMENT** to do something alone, without help or accompaniment, especially to fly an aircraft without an instructor or to perform an artistic solo [Late 17thC. Via Italian from Latin *solus* "alone."]

so·lo·ist /sṓlō ist/ *n.* somebody who performs a solo —**so·lo·is·tic** /sṓlō ístik/ *adj.*

So·lo man /sṓlō màn/ *n.* an extinct variety of the human species Homo sapiens that lived 50,000 years ago during the late Pleistocene epoch and whose fossils were discovered near the Solo River in Java

Sol·o·mon /sólləmən/ *n.* somebody who is very wise (*informal*)

So·lo·mon /sólləmən/, **King of Israel** (*fl.* 10th century B.C.) The second son of David and Bathsheba, he ruled Israel from 961 B.C. to 922 B.C. Famed for his wisdom, he is generally acknowledged as the builder of the Temple in Jerusalem. He is credited with writing the biblical *Song of Solomon* and *Proverbs.*

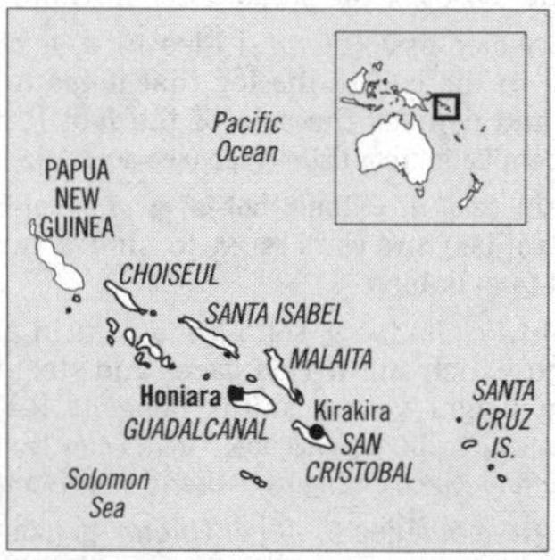

Solomon Islands

Sol·o·mon Is·lands /sólləmən-/ monarchy comprising over 35 islands and atolls in the southern Pacific Ocean. Language: English. Currency: Solomon Islands dollar. Capital: Honiara. Population: 412,902 (1996). Area: 10,980 sq.mi./28,446 sq. km. —**Sol·o·mon Is·land·er** *n.*

Sol·o·mon's seal *n.* **1.** **SIX-POINTED STAR** a six-pointed symbol resembling a star, made up of one triangle laid on top of another facing the other way. Examples are the Star of David that is the symbol of Judaism, and the hexagram that healers of former times believed had the power to cure diseases. **2.** PLANTS **WOODLAND PLANT WITH DROOPING FLOWERS** a perennial plant found in woodlands in northern countries that has drooping whitish flowers that grow in pairs. Latin name: *Polygonatum multiflorum.*

so·lon /sṓlən/ *n.* (*literary*) **1.** **MEMBER OF A LEGISLATURE** a member of a law-making body **2.** **SOMEBODY WISE** somebody wise, especially an experienced and wise legislator or politician [Early 17thC. Named for *Solon* (638?–558?B.C.), Athenian statesman, legal reformer, and poet.]

so·lon·chak /sòlən chák, -chàk/ *n.* an intrazonal soil with a grayish crust that develops in semiarid and desert areas and contains large amounts of soluble salts [Early 20thC. From Russian literally "salt marsh, salt lake," from *sol* "salt."]

so·lo·netz /sàwlə néts, sáwlə nèts/, **so·lo·nets** *n.* an intrazonal soil with a blackish crust developed from solonchak soil by leaching of the salts [Early 20thC. From Russian, literally "salt marsh, salt lake," from *sol* "salt."]

so long *interj.* **GOODBYE** used to say goodbye (*informal*) ■ *adv.* *S Africa* **IN THE MEANTIME** in the meantime, for the time being (*informal*)

so·lo stop *n.* a stop on an organ with a penetrating tone, used in isolated passages of organ pieces to give the effect of a single instrument playing the melody

sol·stice /sólstiss, sṓlstiss/ *n.* **1.** **LONGEST OR SHORTEST DAY** either of the times when the sun is furthest from the equator, on or about June 21 or December 21. The summer solstice falls in June in the northern hemisphere but in December in the southern hemisphere, and vice versa for the winter solstice. **2.** **POINT ON THE ECLIPTIC** either of the two points on the ecliptic when the sun reaches its northernmost or southernmost point relative to the celestial equator [13thC. Via Old French from Latin *solstitium,* from *sol* "sun" + the past participle stem of *sistere* "to stand still."] —**sol·sti·tial** /sòl stísh'l, sōl-/ *adj.*

Georg Solti

Sol·ti /shṓltee/, **Sir Georg** (1912–97) Hungarian conductor. Associated particularly with the music of late romantic composers, he held important posts in Germany, the United Kingdom, and the United States, where he long conducted the Chicago Symphony Orchestra (1969–91).

sol·u·bil·i·ty /sòlyə bíllətee/ (*plural* **-ties**) *n.* **1.** **CAPACITY TO DISSOLVE** the extent to which one substance is able to dissolve in another **2.** **MEASURE OF CAPACITY TO DISSOLVE** a measure of one substance's ability to dissolve in a specific amount of another substance at standard temperature and pressure

sol·u·bi·lize /sólyəbə lìz/ (**-lized, -liz·ing, -liz·es**) *vti.* to make a substance soluble or more soluble, or become soluble or more soluble

sol·u·ble /sólyəb'l/ *adj.* **1.** **DISSOLVING IN LIQUID** able to be dissolved in another substance. The level of solubility often varies with temperature. (*often used in combination*) ○ *water-soluble* **2.** **DESIGNED TO DISSOLVE** designed to be dissolved in water **3.** **SOLVABLE** able to be solved or answered [14thC. Via Old French from Late Latin *solubilis,* from *solvere* "to loosen, dissolve."] —**sol·u·bly** *adv.*

sol·u·ble glass *n.* = **sodium silicate**

sol·u·ble RNA *n.* = **transfer RNA**

so·lum /sṓləm/ (*plural* **-la** /-lə/ *or* **-lums**) *n.* the upper layers of a soil profile where the formation of new soil takes place and where most plant roots and soil animals are found [Mid-19thC. Via Modern Latin from Latin *solum* "ground, foundation."]

so·lus /sṓləss/ *adj.* used as a stage direction to indicate that a character appears alone on stage ○ *Enter Hector solus* [Late 16thC. From Latin, "alone."] —**solus** *adv.*

sol·ute /sól yòot/ *n.* **DISSOLVED SUBSTANCE** a substance dissolved in another substance ■ *adj.* **DISSOLVED** dissolved in a solution [15thC. From Latin *solutus,* past participle of *solvere* (see SOLUBLE).]

so·lu·tion /sə lòosh'n/ *n.* **1.** **WAY OF RESOLVING DIFFICULTY** a method of successfully dealing with a problem or difficulty **2.** **ANSWER TO A PUZZLE** the answer to a puzzle or question **3.** **FINDING OF A SOLUTION** the process of resolving a difficulty or finding the answer to a puzzle or question **4.** **FLUID WITH SUBSTANCE DISSOLVED IN IT** a substance consisting of two or more substances mixed together and uniformly dispersed, most commonly the result of dissolving a solid, fluid, or gas in a liquid. It is also, however, possible to form a solution by dissolving a gas or solid in a solid or one gas in another gas. **5.** **PROCESS OF FORMING A SOLUTION** the process of forming a solution or dissolving one substance in another, or the state of being dissolved in another substance **6.** MATH **VALUE SATISFYING AN EQUATION** a value for a variable that satisfies an equation **7.** LAW **TERMINATION OF A DISPUTE** the termination of a dispute or payment of a debt **8.** **ENDING OF SOMETHING** the act of ending, breaking, or separating something (*literary*) ■ *vt.* (**-tioned, -tion·ing, -tions**) **SOLVE** to find a solution to something [14thC. Via Old French from Latin *solutionem*, from *solvere* (see SOLVE).]

so·lu·tion set *n.* the set of values for a variable that satisfy an equation

So·lu·tre·an /sə lóotree ən/, **So·lu·tri·an** *adj.* belonging to a prehistoric culture that existed in Europe between 40,000 B.C. and 12,000 B.C., at the end of the Paleolithic period, in which people worked with leaf-shaped flint blades [Late 19thC. From French *solutréen*, from *Solutré*, a village in Saône-et-Loire, France, where relics were discovered.]

solv·a·ble /sólvəb'l/ *adj.* capable of being solved — **solv·a·ble·ness** *n.*

sol·vate /sól vàyt/ *vti.* (**-vat·ed, -vat·ing, -vates**) **BECOME OR CAUSE TO BECOME SOLUTION** to enter into solution with a solvent, or cause a solute to dissolve in solution with a solvent ■ *n.* **AGGREGATE OF SOLUTE AND SOLVENT** a compound consisting of an ion or molecule of solute combined with one or more of solvent [Early 20thC. Coined from SOLVENT + -ATE.]

sol·va·tion /sòl váysh'n/ *n.* the process by which molecules of a solvent develop a weak bond with molecules or ions of the solute

Sol·vay proc·ess /sól vay-/ *n.* an industrial process for producing sodium carbonate or washing soda from common salt. A solution of salt is saturated with ammonia and carbon dioxide is passed through it, which causes sodium hydrogen carbonate to precipitate; it is then heated to obtain sodium carbonate. [Late 19thC. Named for the Belgian chemist Ernest Solvay, 1838–1922.]

solve /solv/ (**solved, solv·ing, solves**) *vt.* **1. DEAL WITH A PROBLEM SUCCESSFULLY** to find a way of dealing successfully with a problem or difficulty **2. FIND ANSWER TO A PUZZLE** to find the answer to a question or puzzle **3.** MATH **FIND ANSWER TO MATH PROBLEM** to work out the solution to an equation or other mathematical problem [15thC. From Latin *solvere* "to loosen, dissolve."]

WORD KEY: ORIGIN

The Latin word *solvere*, from which ***solve*** is derived, is also the source of English *absolute*, *absolve*, *dissolve*, *resolve*, and *solution*.

sol·ven·cy /sólvənsee/ *n.* the position of having enough money to cover expenses and debts

sol·vent /sólvənt/ *adj.* **1. HAVING ENOUGH MONEY** having enough money to cover expenses and debts **2. DISSOLVING SOMETHING** able to dissolve substances ■ *n.* **SUBSTANCE THAT DISSOLVES THINGS** a substance in which other substances are dissolved, often a liquid [Early 17thC. Directly or via French from Latin *solventem*, present participle of *solvere* (see SOLVE).] —**sol·vent·ly** *adv.*

sol·vol·y·sis /sol vóllәsiss/ *n.* a chemical reaction in which the solute and solvent present in a solution combine to form a new compound

Farrar, Straus and Giroux, Inc.

Aleksandr Isayevich Solzhenitsyn

Sol·zhe·ni·tsyn /sòlzhə néetsin, səlzhə nyéetsin/, **Aleksandr Isayevich** (*b.* 1918) Russian writer. His imprisonment in the Soviet Union for political dissent (1945–53) inspired early novels such as *One Day in the Life of Ivan Denisovich* (1964). He was expelled after the publication of *The Gulag Archipelago* (1974–78), and lived in exile in the United States for 20 years, returning to Russia after the collapse of the Soviet Union. He won a Nobel Prize in literature (1970).

som /sōm/ (*plural* **som**) *n.* **1. KYRGYZ UNIT OF CURRENCY** the main unit of currency in Kyrgyzia, worth 100 tiyin. See table at **currency 2. som, soum UZBEK UNIT OF CURRENCY** the main unit of currency in Uzbekistan. See table at **currency 3. BILL WORTH A SOM** a bill worth a som

so·ma[1] /sómə/ (*plural* **-ma·ta** /-mətə/ *or* **-mas**) *n.* **1. ALL BODY CELLS EXCEPT GERM CELLS** all the cells and tissues in the body considered collectively, with the exception of germ cells **2. BODY AS DISTINCT FROM MIND** the body considered separately from the mind or soul [Mid-19thC. Via modern Latin from Greek *sôma* "body."]

so·ma[2] /sómə/ *n.* **1.** BEVERAGES **INTOXICATING DRINK IN HINDU SCRIPTURE** an intoxicating drink made from plant juice, mentioned in the Vedas, the most ancient sacred writings of Hinduism **2.** PLANTS **PLANT SOMA IS MADE FROM** the plant that soma is made from, thought to be ephedra, but not identified in the Vedas [Early 19thC. From Sanskrit.]

So·ma·li /sō maálee, sə-/ (*plural* **-li** *or* **-lis**), **So·ma·li·an** /sō maálee ən, sə-/ *n.* **1.** PEOPLES **MEMBER OF PEOPLE FROM SOMALIA** a member of an Islamic African people living mainly in Somalia **2.** LANG **SOMALI LANGUAGE** the national language of Somalia, also spoken in eastern Ethiopia. It belongs to the Cushitic branch of Afro-Asiatic languages. Somali is spoken by over five million people. [Early 19thC. From Somali.] —**So·ma·li** *adj.*

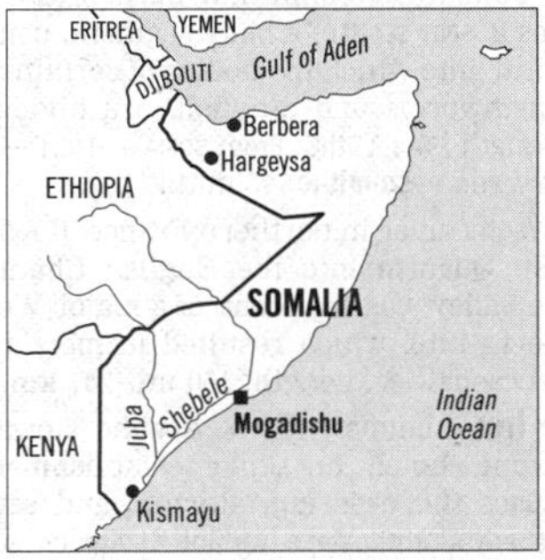

Somalia

So·ma·li·a /sō maálee ə, sə-/ republic in northeastern Africa. Language: Somali. Currency: Somali shilling. Capital: Mogadishu. Population: 6,802,000 (1996). Area: 246,201 sq. mi./637,657 sq. km. Official name **Somali Democratic Republic** —**So·ma·li** *adj.* — **So·ma·li·an** /sə maályen/ *adj.*

So·ma·li·an *n., adj.* = **Somali**

So·ma·li·land /sə maáli land/ region in northeastern Africa, comprising Somalia, Djibouti, and part of Ethiopia

somat- *prefix.* = **somato-** (*used before vowels*)

so·mat·ic /sō máttik/ *adj.* **1. AFFECTING BODY AS DISTINCT FROM MIND** relating to or affecting the body, especially the body as considered to be separate from the mind **2.** ANAT **RELATING TO OUTER WALLS OF BODY** relating to the outer walls of the body, not the inner organs **3. OF SOMATIC CELL** relating to a somatic cell [Late 18thC. From Greek *sōmatikós* "bodily," from *sôma* (see SOMA[1]).] — **so·mat·i·cal·ly** *adv.*

so·mat·ic cell *n.* any cell of the body with the exception of germ cells

so·ma·ti·cize /sō máttə sīz/ (**-cized, -ciz·ing, -cizes**) *vti.* to believe mistakenly that an emotional pain is a physical symptom

so·mat·ic nerv·ous sys·tem *n.* the part of the nervous system that serves the sense organs and muscles of the body wall and limbs, and brings about voluntary muscle activity. ◊ **autonomic nervous system**

somato- *prefix.* body ○ *somatotherapy* [From Greek *sōmat-*, the stem of *sōma*]

so·ma·tol·o·gy /sōmə tóləjee/ *n.* **1. PHYSIOLOGY AND ANATOMY** the study of both the physiology and anatomy of the body **2. ANTHROPOLOGICAL STUDY OF HUMAN ANATOMY** the branch of anthropology that studies human development through variation and change in physical characteristics —**so·ma·to·log·ic** /sōmətə lójjik/ *adj.* —**so·ma·to·log·i·cal** *adj.* — **so·ma·to·log·i·cal·ly** *adv.*

so·mat·o·me·din /sō màttə méed'n, sōmətə-/ *n.* a hormone produced in the liver that stimulates the growth of bone and muscle [Late 20thC. Coined from SOMATO- + INTERMEDIARY + -IN.]

so·mat·o·plasm /sō máttə plàzzəm, sómətə-/ *n.* the protoplasm of body cells as distinct from the protoplasm of germ cells —**so·mat·o·plas·tic** /sō màttə plástik, sōmətə-/ *adj.*

so·mat·o·pleure /sō máttə ploor, sō màttə-/ *n.* a fold of embryonic tissue in vertebrates formed by the fusion of ectoderm and mesoderm that gives rise to an embryo's inner and outer membranes — **so·mat·o·pleu·ral** /sōmətə ploórəl/ *adj.* — **so·mat·o·pleu·ric** *adj.*

so·mat·o·sen·so·ry /sə màttə sénssəree, sōmətə-/ *adj.* used to describe sensory stimuli coming from the skin and internal organs and the perception of these stimuli

so·mat·o·stat·in /sō màttə státt'n, sōmətə-/ *n.* a hormone produced in the hypothalamus that inhibits the release of growth hormone [Late 20thC. Coined from SOMATO- + *stat-*, from Latin *stare* "to stand" + -IN.]

so·mat·o·tro·pin /sə màttə trṓpin, sōmətə-/, **so·ma·to·tro·phin** /sə màttə trṓfin, sōmətə-/ *n.* = **growth hormone** [Mid-20thC. Coined from SOMATO- + -TROPIC + -IN.] —**so·mat·o·tro·pic** *adj.*

so·mat·o·type /sə máttə tīp, sómətə-/ *n.* the type of physical build that a person has

som·ber /sómbər/ *adj.* **1. DARK AND GLOOMY** lacking light or brightness and producing a dull, dark, or melancholy atmosphere **2. DARK IN COLOR** having a color or tone that is dark, dull, or suitable for a serious mood or occasion **3. SERIOUS AND MELANCHOLY** marked by or conveying strict seriousness combined with sadness or a troubled state of mind [Mid-18thC. Via French, "gloomy," from, ultimately, late Latin *subumbrare* "to shadow," from *sub* "under" + *umbra* "shade" (source of English *umbrage*).] —**som·ber·ly** *adv.* —**som·ber·ness** *n.*

som·bre *adj.* U.K. = **somber**

som·bre·ro /som brérrō/ (*plural* **-ros**) *n.* a straw or felt hat with a very wide upturned brim, originally worn by men in Mexico and some other Spanish-speaking countries [Late 16thC. Via Spanish, "hat," from *sombra* "shade," from Vulgar Latin *subombrare* (see SOMBER).]

som·brous /sómbrəss/ *adj.* somber (*archaic*) [Early 18thC. From French *sombre* (see SOMBER) + -OUS.]

some *stressed* /sum/; *unstressed* /səm/ CORE MEANING: a grammatical word used to indicate an unspecified or unknown quantity of people or things ○ (adj) *There is always some risk in any project.* ○ (pron) *There was plenty of food left over, so I took some.*

1. *adj., pron.* **A LITTLE** used to indicate an unspecified number, quantity, or proportion of a total, generally a fairly small to average or reasonable one ○ *I agree with you to some extent.* ○ *Some of you, I know, will disagree with me.* **2.** *adj.* **QUITE A FEW** used with a slight emphasis to indicate an unspecified but fairly large number or quantity ○ *We have been debating this problem for some months now.* **3.** *adj.* **PARTICULAR BUT UNSPECIFIED** used to indicate an unspecified single person or thing, often in a dismissive way ○ *He was reading some medical book.* **4.** *adj.* **USED FOR EMPHASIS** used to emphasize that somebody or something is impressive or remarkable in a certain way (*informal*) ○ *That was some performance you put on for us!* **5.** *adv.* **APPROXIMATELY** used to indicate that a number is approximate ○ *for some 30 years* **6.** *adv.* **TO A SMALL EXTENT** to a small extent or degree (*informal*) ○ *I do write some, but not as much as I'd like.* **7.** *adv.* **A GREAT DEAL** a great deal, at a considerable rate, or vigorously (*informal*) ○ *I'm going to have to study some to get through this exam.* [Old English *sum* "one, someone." Ultimately from an Indo-European word meaning "together with," which is also the ancestor of English *seem* and *similar.*] ◇ **and then some** used to emphasize that more, often considerably more, has been done than was suggested in a previous statement (*informal*)

-some *suffix.* **1.** characterized by a particular quality, condition, or thing ○ *troublesome* ○ *quarrelsome* **2.** a group containing a particular number of members ○ *foursome* [Old English *-sum*]

-some *suffix.* **1.** body ○ *cytosome* **2.** chromosome ○ *autosome* [From Greek *sōma* "body"]

some·bod·y /súm bòddee, súmbədee/, **some·one** /súm wùn/ *pron.* **SOME PERSON** some unspecified person ■ *pron., n.* (*plural* **-ies**) **IMPORTANT PERSON** an important or well-known person in society or in a particular place

some·day /súm dày/ *adv.* at some unknown, unspecified, and usually fairly distant time in the future

——WORD KEY: USAGE——

someday, someplace, sometime The adverbs ***someday*** and ***someplace*** are standard forms in American English: *Someday I'll take you away from all this. I must have left it someplace.* ***Sometime*** is written as one word as an adjective meaning "former" (*a sometime president of the Rotary Club*), and as an adverb meaning "at some time"(*I'll see you again sometime*).

some·how /sùm hów/ *adv.* **1. IN SOME WAY** in some unspecified or unknown way, often with great effort or difficulty ○ *He somehow managed to scramble back on board.* **2. FOR AN UNKNOWN REASON** for some unknown or inexplicable reason ○ *She somehow forgot to tell anyone where she was going.*

some·one *pron., n.* = **somebody**

some·place /súm plàyss/ *adv.* somewhere (*informal*)

——WORD KEY: USAGE——

See Usage note at ***someday.***

som·er·sault *n.* **1.** GYMNASTICS **ACROBATIC ROLLING OVER OF BODY** an acrobatic movement in which the body is rolled over, feet over head, either forward or backward, on the ground or in midair, finally returning to an upright position **2. REVERSAL OF OPINION OR DECISION** a complete change of mind or reversal of policy ■ *vi.* **(-sault·ed, -sault·ing, -saults)** GYMNASTICS **PERFORM SOMERSAULT** to perform an acrobatic somersault [Early 16thC. Via Middle French *sombresault*, a variant of *sobresault*, from Latin *super* SUPER + *saltus* "leap."]

Som·er·set /súmmər set/ city in southeastern Massachusetts, on the western bank of the Taunton River, across from Fall River. Population: 17,719 (1996).

Som·er·set Is·land island in Nunavut, Canada, in the Arctic Archipelago, north of the Boothia Peninsula. Area: 9,570 sq. mi./24,786 sq. km.

Som·er·ville /súmmər vil/ city in eastern Massachusetts, on the Mystic River. It is a northwestern suburb of Boston, and was founded in 1630. Population: 74,356 (1996).

some·thing /súm thing/ *pron.* **1. UNSPECIFIED THING** an unspecified or unidentified object, phenomenon, action, utterance, or feeling ○ *Don't just stand there, do something!* ○ *I had a feeling that there was something wrong.* ○ *Would you like something to eat?* **2. UNCERTAIN AMOUNT** an unspecified and approximate amount expressed in relation to a specific number or quantity ○ *something over 50* ○ *something between 20 and 30%* **3. SUGGESTING RESEMBLANCE** used to suggest that one thing or person resembles another to a certain extent or has some of the qualities of the other ○ *There's definitely something of the knight errant about him.* **4. RATHER** used to qualify a description of a thing or event and tone it down or make it sound more guarded ○ *It was something of a disappointment.* **5. SOMETHING IMPRESSIVE** an impressive or important person or thing ○ *He's really something!* ■ *adv.* **1. SOMEWHAT** slightly or to some degree ○ *It sounds something like what she might have said.* **2. TO AN EXTREME DEGREE** used to intensify the effect of an adjective, especially a strong adjective used as an adverb (*informal*) ○ *It hurts something awful.* **3. AND A BIT MORE** used to indicate that a number is slightly higher than the one mentioned (*informal*) ○ *She's thirty something.* ◇ **something else** somebody or something really special, remarkable, or extreme (*informal*) ◇ **have something to do with somebody** *or* **something** to be connected with or involve somebody or something

some·time /súm tìm/ *adv.* **1. AT SOME TIME** at some unspecified or unknown time ○ *They intend to marry sometime soon.* **2. FORMERLY** at one time in the past (*formal*) ○ *our speaker today, sometime a scholar of Lincoln College, Oxford* **3. OCCASIONALLY** occasionally or sporadically (*archaic*) ■ *adj.* **1. FORMER** who at one time in the past had the job, position, or status in question ○ *a sometime student of this university* **2. OCCASIONAL** occasional or sporadic ○ *an author and sometime lecturer*

——WORD KEY: USAGE——

See Usage note at ***someday.***

some·times /súm tìmz/ *adv.* **1. OCCASIONALLY** from time to time, not continually or every time ○ *We go to the theater sometimes.* **2. FORMERLY** at one time in the past (*archaic*) [Early 16thC. The *-s* is possessive (genitive) singular, not a plural.]

some·way /súm wày/, **some·ways** /-wàyz/ *adv.* using some means or method that is not yet known or not stated ○ *We'll figure it out someway.*

some·what /súm hwòt/ *adv.* to a certain extent or degree ○ *The hot night had cooled somewhat.*

some·where /súm hwàir/ *adv.* **1. IN SOME UNSPECIFIED PLACE** in, to, or at some unspecified place ○ *He lives somewhere in Scotland.* **2. APPROXIMATELY** used in giving approximate amounts, numbers, or times ○ *somewhere around three hundred* ○ *somewhere between three and four o'clock* ◇ **get somewhere** to make progress towards achieving something

some·wheres /súm hwàirz/ *adv.* somewhere (*nonstandard*)

some·wise /súm wìz/ *adv.* (*archaic*) **1. SOMEHOW** somehow **2. SOMEWHAT** somewhat

so·mite /sṓ mìt/ *n.* **1. EMBRYO CELL PAIR FORMING VERTEBRAE** one of a series of paired blocks of cells that develop along the back of a vertebrate embryo giving rise to the vertebral column and most of the skeletal muscles **2. BODY SEGMENT** a body segment, usually one of several, into which the bodies of certain animals, e.g., earthworms and crayfish, are divided along their length [Mid-19thC. From SOMA + -ITE.] —**so·mit·al** /sṓmət'l/ *adj.* —**so·mit·ic** /sō míttik/ *adj.*

Somme /som/ river in northern France, flowing from near St. Quentin into the English Channel. The Somme valley was the scene of a major World War I battle in 1916, which resulted in more than one million casualties. Length: 150 mi./241 km.

som·me·lier /sùmməl yáy/ *n.* a wine steward in a restaurant, hotel, or other establishment, who supervises the ordering, storing, and serving of wine [Early 20thC. Via a variant of French *sommerier*, *sommier*, "officer in charge of provisions," from somme "burden," from, ultimately, Greek *ságma*, "covering, packsaddle."]

som·mer *adv. S Africa* just, only, or somewhat (*informal*) [Mid-19thC. From Afrikaans *somaar, sommer.*]

somn- *prefix.* = **somni-** (*used before vowels*)

som·nam·bu·late /som námbyə làyt/ **(-lat·ed, -lat·ing, -lates)** *vi.* to sleepwalk (*technical*) —**som·nam·bu·lance** *n.* —**som·nam·bu·la·tion** /som nàmbyə láysh'n/ *n.* —**som·nam·bu·la·tor** /-námbyə làytər/ *n.*

som·nam·bu·lism /som námbyə lìzzəm/ *n.* sleepwalking (*technical*) —**somnambulist** *n.* —**som·nam·bu·lis·tic** /som nàmbyə lístik/ *adj.*

somni- *prefix.* sleep ○ *somnifacient* [From Latin *somnus*]

som·ni·fa·cient /sòmnə fáysh'nt/ *adj.* used to describe a drug designed to induce sleep

som·nif·er·ous /som níffərəss/ *adj.* making somebody, or designed to make somebody, feel sleepy —**som·nif·er·ous·ly** *adv.*

som·no·lent /sáwmnələnt/ *adj.* **1. SLEEPY** feeling sleepy or tending to fall asleep **2. LACKING ACTIVITY** quiet and with little or no activity **3. SLEEP-INDUCING** making somebody feel sleepy [15thC. Via Old French from Latin *somnulentus*, "sleepy," from *somnus* "sleep."] —**som·no·lence** *n.* —**som·no·lent·ly** *adv.*

So·mo·za /sə mṓzə/, **Anastasio** (1896–1956) Nicaraguan military and government leader. He was president of Nicaragua (1937–47, 1950–56), and the first of a dynasty of dictators ruling with U.S. support. After his assassination he was succeeded by his sons, Luis Somoza Debayle (1922–67) and Anastasio Somoza Debayle (1925–80). Full name **Anastasio Somoza García**

son /sun/ *n.* **1. MALE CHILD** a male child in relation to his parents **2. MALE DESCENDANT** a male descendant **3. MALE WITH CONNECTIONS WITH SOMETHING** a man or boy referred to in terms of his connection with a place, a time in history, or a sphere of interest ○ *the achievements of the sons of the Industrial Revolution* **4. TERM OF ADDRESS** an affectionate, or sometimes condescending, way of addressing a boy or man (*informal*) [Old English *sunu*. Ultimately from an Indo-European word meaning "to give birth."] —**son·less** *adj.* —**son·like** *adj.*

Son *n.* a title that Christians give to Jesus Christ, especially when referred to as the second person in the Holy Trinity

so·nant /sṓnənt/ *adj.* **1. HAVING SOUND** producing or possessing a sound (*formal*) **2. VOICED** made with vibration of the vocal cords **3. SYLLABIC** used to describe a consonant that is capable of forming a syllable on its own, without a vowel ■ *n.* **1. VOICED SOUND** a sound made with vibration of the vocal cords **2. SYLLABIC CONSONANT** a consonant capable of forming a syllable on its own, without a vowel [Mid-19thC. From Latin *sonans*, present participle of *sonare* "to sound."] —**so·nance** *n.* —**so·nan·tal** /sō nánt'l/ *adj.* —**so·nan·tic** *adj.*

so·nar /sṓ naar/ *n.* **1. SYSTEM FOR DETECTING UNDERWATER OBJECTS** a system that determines the position of unseen underwater objects by transmitting sound waves and measuring the time it takes for their echo to return after hitting the object. Many modern ships, especially warships, are equipped with sonar, as well as many large commercial fishing boats. **2. SONAR DEVICE** a device that uses sonar [Mid-20thC. Acronym from *sound navigation ranging.*]

so·na·ta /sə naatə/ *n.* **1. CLASSICAL COMPOSITION FOR A SOLO INSTRUMENT** a piece of classical music for a solo instrument or a small ensemble consisting of several movements, at least one of which is in sonata form **2. ONE-MOVEMENT BAROQUE KEYBOARD COMPOSITION** a piece of baroque keyboard music in a single movement [Late 17thC. Via Italian, from *sonare* "to sound," from Latin *sonare* (see SONANT).]

so·na·ta form *n.* an important musical form developed in the 18th century consisting of three sections, an exposition, development, and recapitulation, and used especially for the first movement of sonatas, concertos, and symphonies

son·a·ti·na /sònə teenə/ *n.* a short and usually less technically difficult sonata [Early 18thC. Via Italian, "little sonata," from *sonata* (see SONATA).]

son·dage /sawn daazh/ *n.* a deep trench dug in order to study the relative positions of human artifacts in horizontal layers [Mid-20thC. French, literally "sounding, bore hole" (see SOUND[1]).]

son·de /sond/ *n.* a collection of instruments that can be lowered down a borehole or carried into the upper atmosphere by balloon or rocket to transmit information relating to the conditions encountered [Early 20thC. From French, literally "plumb line, sound" (see SOUND[1]).]

Stephen Sondheim

Sond·heim /sónd hìm/, **Stephen** (*b.* 1930) U.S. composer and lyricist. His innovative musicals include the Pulitzer Prize-winning *Sunday in the Park with George* (1984). Full name **Stephen Joshua Sondheim**

sone /sōn/ *n.* a unit measuring the loudness of sound as subjectively perceived, equal to a tone of 1 kilohertz at 40 decibels above the threshold where sounds become audible to the listener [Mid-20thC. From Latin *sonus* "sound."]

son et lu·mière /sàwn ay loo myáir/ *n.* an outdoor nighttime spectacle that combines dramatic lighting effects with recorded sounds and music, usually staged at the site of a famous and historical building, often telling its history [French, literally "sound and light"]

song /sawng/ *n.* **1. SET OF WORDS SUNG** a usually relatively short musical composition consisting of words set to music and the music itself **2. SINGING** the art or practice of singing **3. INSTRUMENTAL WORK IN STYLE OF SONG** an instrumental work written in the style of a vocal song, or, in popular music, any musical work **4. CHARACTERISTIC SOUND OF BIRD OR INSECT** the characteristic sound that a bird or insect makes, usually either to attract a mate or to warn off competing members of its species **5. POETRY** poetry or verse (*literary*) **6. POEM** a poem, especially one that rhymes (*literary*) [Old English *sang*. Ultimately from an Indo-European word meaning "to sing."] —**song·like** *adj.* ◇ **for a song** very cheaply

Song *n.* = **Sung**

song and dance *n.* a long-winded attempt to explain or justify something (*informal*)

song·bird /sáwng bùrd/ *n.* a bird with a musical call, especially a perching bird belonging to the suborder that includes larks, finches, and thrushes. Suborder: Oscines.

song·book /sáwng bòòk/ *n.* a book containing the words and music for a collection of songs

song cy·cle *n.* a set of songs linked by a common subject or underlying musical theme or forming a narrative, often with words by a single poet and music by a classical composer

song·fest /sáwng fèst/ *n.* an informal gathering of people to sing folk or popular songs together

song·ful /sáwngf'l/ *adj.* resembling song, especially in having a pleasing melody —**song·ful·ly** *adv.* —**song·ful·ness** *n.*

Song·hai /sàwng hí, sòg gí/ (*plural* **-hai** *or* **-hais**), **Song·hay** (*plural* **-hay** *or* **-hays**) *n.* **1. MEMBER OF W AFRICAN PEOPLE** a member of a people living in West Africa, mainly in Mali and Niger. The Songhai established a powerful empire in this area during the 7th century A.D., and they remained the dominant ethnic group until the 16th century. **2. SONGHAI LANGUAGE** the Nilo-Saharan lanuage of the Songhai people. Songhai is spoken by about two million people.

Song of Sol·o·mon, **Song of Songs** *n.* a book of the Bible consisting of a set of love poems ascribed to King Solomon. See table at **Bible**

song·smith /sáwng smìth/ *n.* = **songwriter**

song spar·row *n.* a brown and white North American finch with a musical call. Latin name: *Melospiza melodia.*

song·ster /sáwngstər/ *n.* **1. SINGER** a singer, especially a talented one **2. SONGBIRD** a bird with a musical call **3. POET** a poet (*literary*)

song thrush *n.* a small common Eurasian bird with brown upper parts and a white breast speckled with brown that has a melodic whistling call. Latin name: *Turdus philomelos.*

song·writ·er /sáwng rìtər/ *n.* somebody who writes the words, music, or both for songs, especially popular songs

son·ic /sáwnik/ *adj.* **1. RELATING TO SOUND OR SOUND WAVES** relating to, using, or producing sound or sound waves **2. AUDIBLE TO HUMAN EAR** able to be heard by the human ear **3. RELATING TO SPEED OF SOUND** relating to or traveling at the speed of sound in air, approximately 760 mi. per hour/1,220 km per hour at sea level [Early 20thC. Coined from Latin *sonus* "sound" + -IC.]

son·ic bar·ri·er *n.* = **sound barrier**

son·ic boom *n.* a noise heard as a loud boom at ground level resulting from the shock waves created by an aircraft flying above the speed of sound

son·ics /sónwniks/ *n.* the study of sound or, more generally, elastic wave motion (*takes a singular verb*)

so·nif·er·ous /sə nífərəss/ *adj.* producing or transmitting sound [Early 18thC. Coined from Latin *sonus* "sound" + -IFEROUS.]

son-in-law (*plural* **sons-in-law**) *n.* the husband of somebody's daughter

son·net /sónnət/ *n.* a short poem with fourteen lines, usually ten-syllable rhyming lines, divided into two, three, or four sections. There are many rhyming patterns for sonnets, and they are usually written in iambic pentameter. [Mid-16thC. Via French and Italian *sonnetto* from Old Provençal *son* "poem," from Latin *sonus* "sound."]

son·net cy·cle *n.* = **sonnet sequence**

son·net·eer /sònnə téer/ *n.* **1. SONNET WRITER** a poet who writes sonnets **2. MEDIOCRE POET** a writer of mediocre poems

son·net se·quence *n.* a set of sonnets written by one poet and unified by a single theme or idea

son·ny /súnnee/ (*plural* **-nies**), **son·ny boy** *n.* an affectionate, or sometimes condescending, way of addressing a man or boy (*informal*)

so·no·buoy /sónnə bòò ee, -bòy, sáwnə bòòee, -bòy/ *n.* a buoy fitted with equipment for detecting underwater noises and transmitting them by radio [Mid-20thC. Coined from Latin *sonus* "sound" + BUOY.]

son of a bitch *n.* (*plural* **sons of bitch·es**) **1. OFFENSIVE TERM** an offensive term for somebody, usually a man, whom the speaker considers hateful, despicable, or intensely annoying (*slang insult*) **2. PERSON IN GENERAL** used, together with an adjective, as a familiar, humorous, and slightly vulgar term for a person, usually a man, who has the named characteristic (*slang*) ○ *He's a lucky son of a bitch.* ■ *interj.* **SWEARWORD** used as a swearword (*slang*)

son of a gun *n.* (*plural* **sons of guns**) **PERSON** a person, especially a man, and usually somebody affectionately or kindly regarded (*informal*) ■ *interj.* **EXCLAMATION** used to express mild annoyance or surprise (*informal*) [Perhaps originally for the illegitimate child of a soldier; also influenced by British argot *gun*, meaning "thief"]

son of God *n.* **1. ANGEL** a superhuman, angelic being **2. CHRISTIAN** a believer in the Christian faith

Son of God, **Son of Man** *n.* Jesus Christ, considered as the Messiah

son·o·gram /sónnə gràm, sṓnə-/ *n.* a graphical representation of sound, especially in the three dimensions of frequency, time, and intensity

So·no·ran De·sert /sə nàwrən-/ the largest desert in North America. It is situated in southwestern Arizona, southern California, and northwestern Mexico. Area: 120,000 sq. mi./310,000 sq. km.

so·nor·i·ty /sə náwrətee/ (*plural* **-ties**) *n.* **1. RESONANCE** a sonorous quality **2. RESOUNDING SOUND** a sound, especially a rich deep sound [Early 16thC. Via French *sonorité* from medieval Latin *sonoritas*, from Latin *sonorus* (see SONOROUS).]

so·no·rous /sə náwrəss, sónnərəss/ *adj.* **1. PRODUCING SOUND** producing or possessing sound **2. RESONANT** sounding with loud, deep, and clear tones **3. HAVING AN IMPRESSIVE MANNER OF SPEAKING** speaking, spoken, or expressed in a rich, full, and impressive manner [Early 17thC. From Latin *sonorus* "noisy, loud," from *sonor* "sound," from *sonare* "to make a sound."] —**so·no·rous·ly** *adv.* —**so·no·rous·ness** *n.*

Susan Sontag

Son·tag /són tag/, **Susan** (*b.* 1933) U.S. writer. She is best known for her social commentary such as the article "Notes on Camp" (1964) and *Illness as Metaphor* (1978). She has also written novels and short stories.

soon /soon/ *adv.* **1. AFTER A SHORT TIME** within or after a short time ○ *She soon realized that she had made a mistake.* **2. QUICKLY** quickly or without much delay ○ *How soon will you be ready?* ○ *I'll soon see about that!* **3. EARLY** before a reasonable or the desired length of time has elapsed ○ *Do you really have to go so soon?* ○ *It's a bit soon to be thinking of marriage, isn't it?* **4. WILLINGLY** used when expressing a preference for one alternative over another or an equal willingness to accept either, and often in the comparative form "sooner" ○ *I'd sooner stay in than go out.* ○ *I'd as soon stay in as go out.* [Old English *sōna*. Originally in the sense "immediately, at once," but current meanings developed in Old English.] ◇ **as soon as** immediately after ◇ **no sooner...than** immediately after one thing had happened, another took place ◇ **sooner or later** inevitably or certainly at some as yet unspecifiable time

soot /sòòt/ *n.* **BLACK DUST GIVEN OFF BY FIRE** a black powdery form of carbon produced when coal, wood, or oil is burned, which rises up in fine particles with the flames and smoke ■ *vt.* (**soot·ed, soot·ing, soots**) **COVER WITH SOOT** to sprinkle or cover something with soot [Old English *sōt*, literally "something that sits." Ultimately from a prehistoric Germanic word meaning "sit."]

sooth /sooth/ *n.* **TRUTH** truth (*archaic or literary*) ■ *adj.* (*archaic or literary*) **1. TRUE** true **2. SOFT** soft and soothing [Old English *sōþ* "true." Ultimately from an Indo-European word meaning "be," which is also the ancestor of English *is*.] —**sooth·ly** *adv.*

soothe /soo*th*/ (**soothed, sooth·ing, soothes**) *v.* **1.** *vt.* **EASE PAIN** to make pain or discomfort less severe **2.** *vti.* **CALM SOMEBODY DOWN** to make somebody less angry, anxious, or upset [Old English *sōþian* "to prove to be true, verify," from *sōþ* (see SOOTH). The modern meanings evolved from "prove true" via "support" and "encourage."] —**sooth·er** *n.* —**sooth·ing** *adj.* —**sooth·ing·ly** *adv.* —**sooth·ing·ness** *n.*

sooth·fast /sòòth fàst/ *adj.* (*archaic*) **1. TRUTHFUL** truthful **2. LOYAL** loyal

sooth·say /sòòth sày/ (**-said, -say·ing, -says** /-sèz/) *vi.* to predict the future [Early 17thC. Back-formation from SOOTHSAYER.] —**soothsaying** *n.*

sooth·say·er /sòòth sàyər/ *n.* somebody who attempts to predict the future

soot·y /sòòtee/ (**-i·er, -i·est**) *adj.* **1. SOOT-COVERED** covered in soot, or lined or blocked with soot **2. RESEMBLING SOOT** resembling soot in its blackness, dirtiness, or powdery texture

soot·y grouse *n.* = **blue grouse**

soot·y mold *n.* **1. FUNGAL PLANT DISEASE** a plant disease characterized by a black velvety fungus **2. FUNGUS** a fungus that causes sooty mold. Genus: *Meliola* and *Capnodium.*

soot·y shear·wa·ter *n.* a medium-sized dark-gray or brown seabird of the Atlantic and Pacific oceans that rolls its body from side to side as it skims the surface of the water. Latin name: *Puffinus griseus.*

soot·y tern *n.* a medium-sized jet-black seabird with white underparts that is found in tropical regions. Latin name: *Sterna fuscata.*

sop /sop/ *n.* **1. SOMETHING GIVEN TO SATISFY DISCONTENTED PERSON** something offered as a concession or gesture to pacify somebody who is angry or discontented **2.** FOOD **FOOD DIPPED IN LIQUID** a piece of food dipped or soaked in liquid before it is eaten **3. OFFENSIVE TERM** an offensive term that deliberately insults somebody's, especially a man's, courage (*dated informal insult*) ■ *vti.* (**sopped, sop·ping, sops**) **MAKE OR BECOME SOAKING WET** to make something, or become, thoroughly wet [Old English *sopp* "bread dipped in liquid," from *sūpan* "to swallow, taste." Ultimately from a prehistoric Germanic word meaning "to take liquid" (ancestor also of English *sip, soup*, and *supper*).]

sop up *vt.* to soak up a liquid with something absorbent

SOP *abbr.* standard operating procedure

sop. *abbr.* soprano

soph. *abbr.* sophomore

soph·ism /sóffìzzəm/ *n.* an argument or explanation that seems very clever or subtle on the surface but is actually flawed, misleading, or intended to deceive [14thC. Via Old French *sophisme* from, ultimately, Greek *sóphisma* "acquired skill, clever device," ultimately from *sophós* (see SOPHIST).]

soph·ist /sóffəst/ *n.* **1. soph·ist, Sophist** PHILOS **ANCIENT GREEK PHILOSOPHER** a member of a school of ancient Greek professional philosophers who were expert in and taught the skills of rhetoric, argument, and debate, but were criticized for specious reasoning. The sophists were active before and during the time of Socrates and Plato, who were their main critics. **2. SOMEBODY USING CLEVER TALK TO DECEIVE** somebody who deceives people with clever-sounding but flawed arguments or explanations [Mid-16thC. Via Latin from Greek *sophistḗs* "master of a craft, man clever in practical affairs," also "cheat," ultimately from *sophós* "skilled in a craft, clever, wise."]

so·phis·tic /sə fístik/, **sophistical** /-fístik'l/ *adj.* **1. CLEVER-SOUNDING BUT FLAWED** clever-sounding and plausible but based on shallow or dishonest thinking or flawed logic **2.** PHILOS **OF SOPHISTS** relating to sophists [Mid-16thC. Via Latin from Greek *sophistikós*, from *sophós* (see SOPHIST).] —**so·phis·ti·cal·ly** *adv.*

so·phis·ti·cate /sə fístə kàyt/ *v.* (**-cat·ed, -cat·ing, -cates**) **1.** *vt.* **MAKE SOMEBODY MORE CULTURED OR WORLDLY** to make somebody more cultured or worldly, especially by educating out or destroying his or her naturalness, naiveté, or innocence **2.** *vt.* **MAKE SOMETHING MORE COMPLEX** to make something more advanced or complex **3.** *vti.* **USE SOPHISTRY** to use sophistic arguments, or make reasoning or an argument sophistic **4.** *vt.* **CORRUPT** to make something impure, false, or adulterated ■ *n.* **SOMEBODY CULTURED OR WORDLY** somebody who is knowledgeable about the ways of the world and has cultured taste and refined manners [14thC. From medieval Latin *sophisticatus*, past participle of *sophisticare* "to deceive with words, disguise," from, ultimately, Greek *sophós* (see SOPHIST).] —**so·phis·ti·ca·tor** /sə fístə kàytər/ *n.*

so·phis·ti·cat·ed /sə fístə kàytəd/ *adj.* **1. KNOWLEDGEABLE AND CULTURED** knowledgeable about the ways of the world, self-confident, and not easily deceived **2. SUITABLE FOR SOPHISTICATED PEOPLE** appealing to or frequented by sophisticated people **3. ADVANCED** complex, advanced, and very up-to-date —**so·phis·ti·cat·ed·ly** *adv.*

so·phis·ti·ca·tion /sə fìstə káysh'n/ *n.* **1. KNOWLEDGEABLENESS AND REFINEMENT** a combination of worldly wisdom, self-confidence, and refinement in a person **2. TECHNICAL ADVANCEDNESS** technical advancedness and complexity **3. SOPHISTICATING** the process of sophisticating something or somebody

soph·is·try /sóffistree/ (*plural* **-tries**) *n.* **1. FLAWED METHOD OF ARGUMENTATION** a method of argumentation that seems clever but is actually flawed or dishonest **2.** = **sophism** [14thC. Via Old French *sophistrie* from Latin *sophistria* (see SOPHIST).]

Soph·o·cles /sóffə kleez/ (496?–406? B.C.) Greek dramatist. The seven tragedies of his 123 plays that survive in complete texts, including *Electra*, *Oedipus Rex*, and *Antigone*, demonstrate the powerful treatment of moral and religious themes that made him one of the greatest dramatists of all time.

soph·o·more /sóffə màwr/ *n.* **1. SECOND-YEAR STUDENT** a second-year student in a high school or college **2. SOMEBODY IN SECOND YEAR OF SOMETHING** somebody in the second year of a project or program [Late 17thC. Alteration of earlier *sophumer* (probably influenced by Greek *sophos* "wise" + *mōros* "dull"), from obsolete English *sophum* "sophism," a variant of SOPHISM.]

sophomoric /sòffə máwrik/ *adj.* **1. IMMATURE** showing the naive lack of judgement that accompanies immaturity **2. OF SOPHOMORES** relating to sophomores

-sophy *suffix.* wisdom, knowledge, science ○ *theosophy* [From Greek *sophia*, from *sophos* "wise"]

so·por /sṓpər/ *n.* an abnormally deep sleep or state of unconsciousness [Mid-17thC. From Latin, "sleep."]

sop·o·rif·ic /sòppə ríffik/ *adj.* **1. MAKING SOMEBODY SLEEPY** causing sleep or drowsiness **2. FEELING SLEEPY** experiencing sleepiness or drowsiness **3. TEDIOUS** dull and boring ■ *n.* **SLEEP-INDUCING DRUG** a drug or other substance that induces sleep —**sop·o·rif·i·cal·ly** *adv.*

sop·ping /sópping/, **sop·ping wet** *adj.* thoroughly wet

WORD KEY: SYNONYMS

See Synonyms at ***wet***.

sop·py /sóppee/ (**-pi·er, -pi·est**) *adj.* **1. OVERLY SENTIMENTAL OR AFFECTIONATE** affectionate or sentimental in an excessive way (*informal*) **2. SOAKING** thoroughly wet **3. RAINY** characterized by a lot of rain

so·pra·ni·no /sòpprə neénō/ (*plural* **-nos**) *n.* a musical instrument, usually a wind instrument, that has the highest pitch of all those in its family, being even higher than the soprano [Early 20thC. From Italian, "little soprano" (see SOPRANO).]

so·pran·o /sə práanō/ (*plural* **-os**) *n.* **1. WOMAN OR BOY WITH HIGHEST VOICE** a woman, girl, or a boy with the highest register of singing voice **2. HIGHEST SINGING VOICE** the highest register of singing voice a woman, girl, or boy can have **3. SINGING PART FOR SOPRANO VOICE** a singing part written for somebody with a soprano voice **4. MUSICAL INSTRUMENT WITH HIGH PITCH** a musical instrument, especially a wind instrument, with the highest pitch of the instruments in its family, or the second highest, if the family includes a sopranino [Early 18thC. From Italian, from *sopra* "above," from Latin *supra*.]

so·pran·o clef *n.* a C clef in which middle C is designated by the first line of the staff. It was formerly used for the soprano vocal line.

SOR, s.o.r. *abbr.* sale or return

so·ra /sáwrə/ *n.* a small grayish-brown North American bird that lives in bogs and swamps, and, though common, is seldom seen. Latin name: *Porzana carolina.* [Early 18thC. Origin unknown: possibly of Native North American origin.]

sorb /sawrb/ *n.* **1.** = **service tree 2. sorb, sorb ap·ple BERRY** the berry of the service tree [Early 16thC. Via French *sorbe* from Latin *sorbum* "service berry."] —**sor·bic** *adj.*

Sorb /sawrb/ *n.* = **Wend** [Mid-19thC. Via German *Sorbe*, ultimately from Lusatian *serbje*, related to, or a variant of, SERB.]

sor·bet /sáwrbət, -bay/ *n.* a frozen dessert, usually made with fruit syrup and sometimes egg whites, whisked until smooth [Late 16thC. Via French and Italian *sorbetto* from Turkish *şerbet* "cool drink" (see SHERBET).]

Sor·bi·an /sáwrbee ən/ *n., adj.* LANG, PEOPLES = **Wendish**

sor·bic ac·id /sàwrbik-/ *n.* a white crystalline solid acid obtained from the unripe berries of the mountain ash, or manufactured synthetically, and used as a food preservative and a fungicide. Formula: $C_6H_8O_2$.

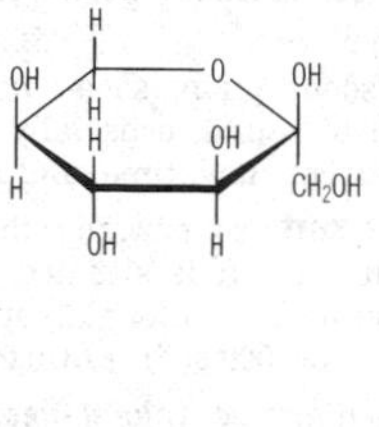

Sorbitol

sor·bi·tol /sáwrbə tàwl/ *n.* a white crystalline sweet alcohol extracted from the berries of the mountain ash tree, or manufactured synthetically, and used as a sweetener and in cosmetics, toiletries, and pharmaceuticals. Formula: $C_6H_{14}O_6$.

Sor·bonne /sawr bón/ *n.* a part of the University of Paris, founded in 1253, and containing the faculties of science and literature

sor·bose /sáwr bṑss/ *n.* a whitish crystalline sugar that is an isomer of fructose and a fermentation product of sorbitol, used in the preparation of vitamin C. Formula: $C_6H_{12}O_6$. [Late 19thC. From SORBITOL + -OSE.]

sor·cer·er /sáwrssərər/ *n.* somebody who is believed or claims to have magical powers [Early 16thC. Via French *sorcier* from, ultimately, Latin *sors* (see SORT).]

sor·cer·ess /sáwrsərəss/ *n.* a woman who is believed or claims to have magical powers

sor·cer·y /sáwrssəree/ *n.* the supposed use of magic —**sor·cer·ous** *adj.*

sor·did /sáwrdəd/ *adj.* **1. NASTY** demonstrating the worst aspects of human nature, e.g., immorality, selfishness, and greed **2. SQUALID** dirty and depressing [Late 16thC. Via French *sordide* and Latin *sordidus* from, ultimately, *sordes* "dirt."] —**sor·did·ly** *adv.* —**sor·did·ness** *n.*

sor·di·no /sawr deénō/ (*plural* **-ni** /-nee/) *n.* a device used to muffle or soften the tone of a musical instrument, e.g., a mute for a stringed or brass instrument or a damper on a piano [Late 16thC. From Italian, formed from *sordo* "unable to speak or hear," from Latin *surdus*.]

sore /sawr/ *adj.* (**sor·er, sor·est**) **1. PAINFUL** painful or tender because of an injury, infection, or unaccustomed exercise **2. ANNOYING** causing annoyance or embarrassment ○ *His dismissal has always been a sore point.* **3. OFFENDED** angry or irritated, especially because of something said or done by another person in the recent past (*informal*) ○ *He was still sore because I kidded him about his tie.* **4. URGENT** requiring urgent action to provide relief ○ *The survivors of the flood are in sore need of help.* **5. DISTRESSING** causing great worry or distress (*literary*) ○ *Her illness was a sore trial to her husband and children.* ■ *n.* MED **INFECTED SPOT** a painful open skin infection or wound ■ *adv.* **SORELY** sorely (*archaic*) [Old English *sār*. Ultimately from a prehistoric Germanic word that is also the ancestor of English *sorry*.] —**sore·ness** *n.*

sore·head /sáwr hèd/ *n.* somebody who is easily offended or angered (*informal*)

sore·ly /sáwrlee/ *adv.* to a great extent or degree (*formal*) ○ *I was sorely tempted to give him the money.*

sor·gho *n.* = **sorgo**

Sorghum

sor·ghum /sáwrgəm/ (*plural* **-ghums** *or* **-ghum**) *n.* **1.** PLANTS **CEREAL CROP** a cereal plant that is resistant to drought, widely cultivated in tropical and warm areas as a grain crop and for animal feed. Genus: *Sorghum.* **2.** FOOD **SYRUP FROM SORGHUM** a syrup made from the juice of some varieties of sorghum [Late 16thC. Via modern Latin from Italian *sorgo* (see SORGO).]

sor·go /sáwrgō/ (*plural* **-gos**), **sor·gho** (*plural* **-ghos**) *n.* any of several varieties of sorghum cultivated as a source of syrup [Mid-18thC. Via Italian from Vulgar Latin *syricum (granum)*, literally "Syrian (grain)."]

so·ri plural of **sorus**

so·ri·tes /sə rī́ teez/ (*plural* **-tes**) *n.* an argument consisting of a series of premises arranged so that the predicate of each premise forms the subject of the next. The conclusion unites the subject of the first premise with the predicate of the last. [Mid-16thC. Via Latin from Greek *sōreitēs*, from *sōros* "heap."]

Sor·op·ti·mist /sə róptimist/ *n.* a member of an international organization **(Soroptimist International)** of professional women and businesswomen that promotes public service. It was founded in California in 1921. [Early 20thC. A blend of Latin *soror* "sister" and OPTIMIST.]

so·ror·ate /sáwrə ràyt/ *n.* a custom in some societies in which a widower marries a younger sister of his deceased wife [Early 20thC. Formed from Latin *soror* "sister."]

so·ror·i·cide /sə ráwrə sīd/ *n.* **1. MURDER OF SISTER** the murder of a sister **2. KILLER OF SISTER** somebody who kills his or her sister [Mid-17thC. Coined from Latin *soror* "sister" + -CIDE.] —**so·ror·i·cid·al** /sə ràwrə sī́d'l/ *adj.*

so·ror·i·ty /sə ráwrətee/ (*plural* **-ties**) *n.* a social society for women students at a college or university, with a name made up of Greek letters. ◊ **fraternity** [Mid-16thC. From medieval Latin *sororitas*, from Latin *soror* "sister."]

sorp·tion /sáwrpsh'n/ *n.* the taking in or holding of something, either by absorption or adsorption [Early 20thC. Back-formation from ABSORPTION and ADSORPTION.]

sor·rel[1] /sáwrəl/ (*plural* **-rels** *or* **-rel**) *n.* a sharp-tasting plant of the dock family, used for salad greens and in medicines. Genus: *Rumex.* [14thC. From Old French *surele*, from *sur* "sour." Ultimately from a prehistoric Germanic word that is also the ancestor of English *sour*.]

sor·rel[2] /sáwrəl/ *adj.* COLORS **REDDISH BROWN** of a reddish-brown color ■ *n.* **1.** COLORS **BROWN WITH RED ADDED** a brown color with a suggestion of red **2.** ZOOL **REDDISH-BROWN ANIMAL** a sorrel horse or other animal [15thC. From Old French *sorel*, from *sor* "yellowish." Ultimately from a prehistoric Germanic word meaning "dry."]

sor·rel tree *n.* = **sourwood**

Sor·ren·to /sè réntō/ town and resort on the southern shore of the Bay of Naples, in Naples Province, Campania Region, in southern Italy. Population: 17,015 (1991).

sor·row /sáwrō, sórrō/ *n.* **1. GRIEF** a feeling of deep sadness caused by a loss or misfortune **2. SADDENING BURDEN** an unfortunate event, experience, or other cause of sorrow ■ *vi.* (**-rowed, -row·ing, -rows**) **GRIEVE** to feel or express deep sadness over something (*literary*) [Old English *sorg*. Ultimately from a prehistoric Germanic word meaning "care."] —**sor·row·er** *n.* ◇ **drown your sorrows** to take alcoholic drink in order to try to forget a source of sadness or disappointment

sor·row·ful /sáwrōf'l, sórrōf'l/ *adj.* **1. SAD** feeling or expressing sorrow **2. CAUSING SADNESS** characterized by or causing sorrow —**sor·row·ful·ly** *adv.* —**sor·row·ful·ness** *n.*

sor·ry /sáwree, sórree/ *adj.* (**-ri·er, -ri·est**) **1.** APOLOGETIC feeling or expressing regret for an action that has upset or inconvenienced somebody, or for a similar future action **2.** SYMPATHETIC feeling or expressing sympathy or empathy, especially because of something that has happened ○ *I'm sorry you're leaving.* **3.** PITIFUL pitifully bad or neglected **4.** VERY BAD pathetically or contemptibly unsatisfactory ○ *a sorry excuse for a car* ■ *interj.* **1.** APOLOGIZING FOR SOMETHING used as an apology for hurting, interrupting, or inconveniencing somebody ○ *Sorry – I didn't realize that was your foot.* **2.** ASKING SOMEBODY TO REPEAT SOMETHING used with an interrogative inflection to ask somebody to repeat something (*informal*) **3.** CORRECTING A REMARK used to introduce a correction in speech ○ *The company employs ten thousand – sorry, twelve thousand workers nationwide.* [Old English *sārig*, formed from *sār* (see SORE)] —**sor·ri·ly** *adv.* —**sor·ri·ness** *n.*

sort /sawrt/ *n.* **1.** CATEGORY a category of persons or things with shared attributes, to which somebody or something can be assigned ○ *What sort of instrument is that?* **2.** PARTICULAR TYPE a particular type of person (*informal*) ○ *She'll help – she's a good sort.* **3.** SIMILAR THING something similar to the thing specified ○ *It's a sort of play with dancing.* **4.** COMPUT SORTING OF DATA a process of arranging data in a set order **5.** PRINTING LETTER OR SYMBOL a particular character in a font of type (*often plural*) **6.** MANNER a manner of doing something (*archaic*) ■ *v.* (**sort·ed, sort·ing, sorts**) **1.** *vt.* PUT IN CATEGORIES to place people or things in categories according to shared attributes ○ *clothes sorted into piles* **2.** *vt.* COMPUT PUT IN SEQUENCE to arrange things in a set order, especially automatically as some computer programs do with data **3.** *vt.* = **sort out** *v.* 3 **4.** *vi.* BE COMPATIBLE to be compatible or in accord with something (*archaic*) **5.** *vi.* ASSOCIATE to associate with somebody (*archaic*) [14thC. Via French *sorte* and assumed Proto-Romance *sorta* "class, order" from Latin *sors* "lot, fortune" (source of English *sorcerer*).] —**sort·a·ble** *adj.* —**sort·er** *n.* ◇ **of a sort, of sorts** used to indicate that something is not very good ○ *We had a meal of sorts at the airport.* ◇ **out of sorts 1.** slightly unwell **2.** not in a very good mood ◇ **sort of** somewhat (*informal*) ○ *This place is sort of strange.*

WORD KEY: USAGE

See Usage note at ***kind***.

WORD KEY: SYNONYMS

See Synonyms at ***type***.

sort out *vt.* **1.** RESOLVE EFFECTIVELY to deal effectively with a problem ○ *I think we've sorted out our difficulties with the printer.* **2.** REACH CONCLUSION to think and come to a conclusion about a problem or difficulty **3.** PUT IN ORDER to put something into order, or disentangle something ○ *It took weeks to sort out the library.* **4.** SEPARATE to separate something from the mixture it exists in, or from another group of things

sor·ta·tion /sawr táysh'n/ *n.* the process of sorting items into categories or into a set order, especially when done by machine or computer

sor·tie /sáwrtee/ *n.* **1.** MIL ATTACK ON AN ENEMY an attack made by a small military force into enemy territory **2.** AIR AIRCRAFT MISSION a mission flown by a combat aircraft or group of combat aircraft **3.** SHORT TRIP a brief trip away from home, especially to an unfamiliar place (*humorous*) **4.** MIL PEOPLE ON SORTIE the personnel engaged in a military sortie ■ *vi.* (**-tied, -tie·ing, -ties**) MIL MAKE A SORTIE to make a sortie against an enemy position [Late 17thC. From French, the past participle of *sortir* "to go out," of uncertain origin: perhaps from, ultimately, Latin *sors* (see SORT).]

sor·ti·lege /sáwrt'lij/ *n.* **1.** PROPHECY BY DRAWING LOTS the supposed foretelling of the future by drawing lots **2.** MAGIC the supposed practice of magic or sorcery [14thC. Via French *sortilège* from, ultimately, Latin *sortilegus* "prophetic, soothsayer," from *sors* (see SORT) + *legere* "to read."]

so·rus /sáwrəss/ (*plural* **-ri** /-rī/) *n.* **1.** SPORE CASE CLUSTER a cluster of spore cases on the underside of some fern fronds **2.** SPORE-PRODUCING ORGAN a spore-producing organ in some algae, fungi, and lichens [Mid-19thC. Via modern Latin from Greek *sōros* "heap."]

SOS *n.* **1.** DISTRESS SIGNAL an international radio signal that ships or aircraft in serious distress can use to call for help. It consists of the letters "SOS" in Morse code (. . . – – – . . .), interpreted as meaning "save our souls." **2.** CALL FOR HELP a call or signal requesting help

so·sa·tie /sə saátee/ *n.* *S Africa* curried or spicy meat grilled on a skewer [Mid-19thC. Via Afrikaans from, ultimately, Malay *sesate*.]

so-so *adj.* NEITHER GOOD NOR BAD neither very good nor very bad (*informal*) ○ *The food was so-so, but the atmosphere was wonderful.* ■ *adv.* NEITHER WELL NOR BADLY neither very well nor very badly (*informal*) ○ *feeling so-so*

sos·te·nu·to /sòstə nóotō/ *adv.* WITH PROLONGED NOTES with notes sustained to or beyond the notated value (*used as a musical direction*) ■ *n.* (*plural* **so·ste·nu·tos**) SOSTENUTO PIECE OF MUSIC a piece of music, or a section of a piece, played sostenuto [Mid-18thC. From Italian, the past participle of *sostinere* "to sustain," from Latin *sustinere*.] —**so·ste·nu·to** *adj.*

sot /sot/ *n.* an offensive term for somebody who is nearly always drunk (*dated informal insult*) [Pre-12thC. Via Old French, "fool," from medieval Latin *sottus*.]

so·te·ri·ol·o·gy /sō tèeree óllǝjee/ *n.* the Christian doctrine that salvation has been brought about by Jesus Christ [Mid-18thC. Coined from Greek *sōtēria* "salvation" + -LOGY.] —**so·te·ri·o·log·ic** /sō tèeree ə lójjik/ *adj.*

So·thic cy·cle /sṓthik-, sòthik-/ *n.* CALENDAR a cycle of 1460 Sothic years in the ancient Egyptian calendar [Early 19thC. *Sothic* formed from Greek *Sōthis*, the star Sirius, used in calendar calculations.]

So·thic year *n.* CALENDAR a year of $365\frac{1}{4}$ days in the ancient Egyptian calendar, based on the first appearance of the dog star (**Sirius**) above the horizon [See SOTHIC CYCLE]

So·tho /sṓ tṑ, sóo tóo/ (*plural* **-tho** *or* **-thos**) *n.* **1.** PEOPLES MEMBER OF SOUTHERN AFRICAN PEOPLE a member of a large group of peoples who live in southern Africa, mainly in Botswana, Lesotho, and South Africa **2.** LANG SOTHO LANGUAGE the Bantu language of the Sotho, belonging to the Niger-Congo family. There are several languages in the group, including Tswana and Lesotho. —**So·tho** *adj.*

so·tol /sṓ tṑl/ *n.* **1.** PLANTS FLOWERING DESERT PLANT a desert plant of the southwestern United States and Mexico that has prickly leaves and dense clusters of whitish flowers. Genus: *Dasylirion*. **2.** BEVERAGES DRINK MADE FROM SOTOL an alcoholic drink made from the sap of the sotol plant [Late 19thC. Via American Spanish *sotole* from Nahuatl *tzotolli*.]

sot·tish /sóttish/ *adj.* **1.** DRUNKEN in the habit of drinking far too much alcohol **2.** DRUNK showing the effects of having drunk too much alcohol

sot·to vo·ce /sòttō vṓchee, -chày/ *adv.* in a soft voice, so as not to be overheard [Mid-18thC. From Italian, literally "under (the) voice."] —**sot·to vo·ce** *adj.*

sou /soo/ *n.* a French coin no longer in use, worth only a small amount [15thC. From French, back-formation from Old French *sous*, the plural of *sout* "sou," from Latin *solidus* (see SOLIDUS).]

sou·brette /soo brét/ *n.* **1.** MAIDSERVANT IN COMEDY a pretty, flirtatious woman's role in a comedy, especially one in which she plays a lady's maid involved in romantic intrigues **2.** ACTOR PLAYING SOUBRETTE an actor who often plays soubrettes **3.** DISMISSIVE TERM a dismissive term for a young woman whose behavior is interpreted as flirtatious (*dated*) [Mid-18thC. Via French, literally "maid," and Provençal *soubreto* "coy" from, ultimately, Latin *superare* "to surpass," from *super* "above."]

sou·bri·quet *n.* = **sobriquet**

sou·chong /soo cháwng, -chóng/ *n.* black China tea [Mid-18thC. From Cantonese *síu-chúng*, literally "small kind."]

sou·cou·yant /sóo koo yaán/ *n.* *Carib* somebody, usually a woman, who reportedly can shed her skin and change into a ball of fire and fly around by night, and who sucks people's blood. Local belief has it that she must return to her skin before daylight, and that salt and thorn-trees offer protection against her. [Mid-20thC. From a West Indian creole, of uncertain origin.]

souf·fle /sóoff'l/ *n.* a soft blowing sound inside somebody's chest, heard through a stethoscope and caused by blood flowing through blood vessels [Late 19thC. From French, literally "breath," formed from *souffler* (see SOUFFLÉ).]

souf·flé /soo fláy/ *n.* a baked or chilled dish that has been made light by adding whisked egg whites. Hot soufflés are usually based on a thick milk sauce and are baked, while cold soufflés are made with gelatin and set by chilling. [Early 19thC. From French, the past participle of *souffler* "to blow, to puff up," from Latin *sufflare*.] —**souf·flé** *adj.*

Sou·fri·ere Hills Vol·ca·no /sóofree àir-/ volcano on the island of Montserrat in the Caribbean Sea. It erupted in 1997, leaving large parts of the island uninhabitable. Height: 3,002 ft./915 m.

sough /sow, suf/ *vi.* (**soughed, sough·ing, soughs**) TO RUSTLE to make a soft rustling, sighing, or murmuring sound, like the wind in trees (*archaic or literary*) ■ *n.* SOUGHING SOUND a sound like that made by a gentle wind through trees (*archaic or literary*) [Old English *swōgan*, of prehistoric Germanic origin]

sought past tense, past participle of **seek**

sought-af·ter *adj.* in high demand because scarce ○ *Blue diamonds are among the most sought-after gems.*

souk /sook/, **suq** *n.* an open-air market in North Africa or the Middle East [Early 19thC. From Arabic *sūk*.]

souk·ous /sóo kóoss/ *n.* a style of dance music originally from the Congo, combining guitar, drums, and vocals [Late 20thC. Origin uncertain: probably via Lingala from French *secouer* "to shake."]

soul /sōl/ *n.* **1.** NONPHYSICAL ASPECT OF PERSON the complex of human attributes that manifests as consciousness, thought, feeling, and will, regarded as distinct from the physical body **2.** RELIG SPIRIT SURVIVING DEATH in some systems of religious belief, the spiritual part of a human being that is believed to continue to exist after the body dies. The soul is sometimes regarded as subject to future reward and punishment, and sometimes as able to take a form that allows it to remain on or return to earth. **3.** FEELINGS somebody's emotional and moral nature, where the most private thoughts and feelings are hidden ○ *Her soul was in turmoil.* **4.** ARTS SPIRITUAL DEPTH evidence of spiritual or emotional depth and sensitivity, either in a person or in something created by a person ○ *Though technically perfect, the drawing lacked soul.* **5.** ESSENCE the deepest and truest nature of a people or a nation, or what gives somebody or something a distinctive character ○ *In my travels I hoped to discover the soul of the Russian people.* **6.** TYPE OF PERSON somebody of a particular type, especially one regarded sympathetically or with familiarity ○ *Poor soul! What will he do now?* **7.** ANYONE anyone at all (*used in the negative*) ○ *You have to promise not to tell a soul.* **8.** INDIVIDUAL an individual person, especially when thought of as making up the number of a particular group (*usually plural*) ○ *a country of some 10 million souls* **9.** PERFECT EXAMPLE somebody who is a good example, or personification, of a positive quality ○ *The hotel manager was the soul of discretion.* **10.** SOMEBODY ESSENTIAL TO SOMETHING a leader or the most influential person in a group or movement **11.** AFRICAN AMERICAN SPIRIT the quality that characterizes African American culture, especially as manifested in somebody's natural sympathies and in social customs, speech, and music **12.** MUSIC = **soul music** [Old English *sāwol*. Ultimately from a prehistoric Germanic word that is also the ancestor of German *Seele* "soul."]

Soul /sōl/ *n.* the name for God in Christian Science

soul broth·er *n.* a man who is an African American like the person in question

soul food *n.* the traditional foods of African Americans of the South. Typical dishes are yams, chitterlings, black-eyed peas, and collard greens.

soul·ful /sṓlf'l/ *adj.* deeply or sincerely emotional —**soul·ful·ly** *adv.* —**soul·ful·ness** *n.*

soul kiss *n.* = **French kiss**

soul·less /sṓl ləss/ *adj.* **1.** LACKING FEELING lacking warmth, sensitivity, or feeling ○ *soulless bureaucrats* **2.** DEADENING lacking anything that might stimulate or engage the feelings —**soul·less·ly** *adv.* —**soul·less·ness** *n.*

soul mate *n.* somebody with whom somebody else naturally shares deep feelings and attitudes

soul mu·sic *n.* a style of African American popular music with a strong emotional quality, related to gospel music and rhythm and blues

soul-search·ing *n.* a thorough examination of personal thoughts and feelings, especially when faced with a difficult problem

soul sis·ter *n.* a woman who is an African American like the person in question (*dated*)

soum *n.* = **som**

sound[1] /sownd/ *n.* **1.** SOMETHING AUDIBLE something that can be heard ○ *not a sound in the whole house* ○ *the sound of gunfire* **2.** PHYS, ACOUSTICS VIBRATIONS SENSED BY THE EAR vibrations traveling through air, water, or some other medium, especially those within the range of frequencies that can be perceived by the human ear. At sea level and freezing point the speed of sound through the air is 760 mi./1,220 km per hour. **3.** SENSATION OF VIBRATIONS the sensation produced in the ear by vibrations traveling through air, water, or some other medium **4.** ELECTRON ENG REPRODUCED MUSIC OR SPEECH the music, speech, or other sounds heard through an electronic device such as a television, radio, or loudspeaker, especially with regard to volume or quality ○ *Please turn down the sound.* **5.** BROADCAST RECORDING MUSIC OR SPEECH the recording, editing, and replaying of music, speech, or sound effects in the broadcast or entertainment industry **6.** IMPLICATION an impression of somebody or something formed from limited but significant information, especially information lately received ○ *From the sound of it she's finally found a job she really likes.* **7.** NOISE meaningless noise ○ *I didn't care for the poetry – it had more sound than sense.* **8.** EARSHOT the distance or area within which something can be heard ○ *Our house was within sound of the church bells.* **9.** LING ELEMENT OF SPEECH AS HEARD a basic element of speech formed by the vocal tract and interpreted through the ear, or a combination of such sounds **10.** MUSIC TYPE OF MUSIC the distinctive quality that identifies bands or music from a particular place, area, or studio, or belonging to a particular movement or style ■ *v.* (**sound·ed, sound·ing, sounds**) **1.** *vi.* SEEM to give a particular impression when mentioned or described ○ *The party sounded awful.* **2.** *vi.* INDICATE STATUS to give a particular impression about physical or mental condition via speech or writing ○ *He sounded exhausted when I talked to him on the phone.* **3.** *vi.* HAVE PARTICULAR QUALITY WHEN HEARD to give a particular impression to a hearer about the quality of the noise or the identity of the source of the noise ○ *That sounds like the mailman.* **4.** *vti.* MAKE A NOISE to make a particular noise so as to be heard, or make something produce such a noise ○ *Somewhere down the corridor, an alarm sounded.* **5.** *vt.* ANNOUNCE SOMETHING to spread the news of or signal something by making a noise, or produce a similar effect by saying something ○ *She sounded a note of caution about the likely result of the reorganization.* **6.** *vt.* PHON ARTICULATE A SOUND to pronounce a specific letter or sound, especially in a context in which it might be silent ○ *You don't sound the "p" in "psychic."* **7.** *vt.* MED TEST BODILY CONDITION BY CAUSING SOUND to make an organ of the body emit a sound for testing or diagnostic purposes [13thC. Via Anglo-Norman *soun* and French *son* from Latin *sonus* (source of English *consonant, resonant,* and *sonnet*).]

sound off *vi.* **1.** SPEAK FORCEFULLY to express strong feelings through speech, or complain loudly about something (*informal*) ○ *always sounding off about high property taxes* **2.** MIL COUNT STEPS ALOUD to chant or count in turn while marching

sound out *vt.* to find out somebody's opinions about something before becoming committed to a course of action

sound[2] /sownd/ *adj.* **1.** NOT DAMAGED without any serious damage or decay **2.** HEALTHY free from injury, disease, or illness **3.** SENSIBLE based on good sense and valid reasoning ○ *a sound argument* **4.** COMPLETELY ACCEPTABLE worthy of approval, especially as agreeing with traditional views or conforming to conventional behavior **5.** DEEP AND PEACEFUL unbroken by waking and untroubled by dreams or discomfort ○ *She had a sound night's sleep.* **6.** COMPLETE including all necessary aspects and details ○ *sound knowledge of the subject* **7.** THOROUGH painful and thorough **8.** FIN WITH LITTLE FINANCIAL RISK financially secure and likely to make money **9.** LOGIC VALID WITH TRUE PREMISES having a true conclusion that follows from true premises **10.** LAW LEGALLY VALID legally valid [12thC. Shortening of Old English *gesund*. Ultimately from a prehistoric Germanic word that also produced German *gesund* "healthy."] — **sound·ly** *adv.* —**sound·ness** *n.* ◇ **sound asleep** sleeping with no waking or disturbance from dreams or discomfort

WORD KEY: SYNONYMS

See Synonyms at ***valid***.

sound[3] /sownd/ *v.* (**sound·ed, sound·ing, sounds**) **1.** *vti.* NAUT MEASURE DEPTH to measure the depth of water using a weighted line or sonar **2.** *vi.* ZOOL DIVE DOWN to dive suddenly and swiftly downward **3.** *vt.* MED EXAMINE WITH A PROBE to use a surgical probe to examine a bodily cavity or passage, e.g., the bladder, or to dilate an abnormal constriction ■ *n.* MED SURGICAL PROBE a surgical probe used to sound bodily cavities [14thC. Via French *sonder* from, ultimately, Vulgar Latin *subundare*, from Latin *sub* "under" + *unda* "wave" (source of English *undulate*).]

sound[4] /sownd/ *n.* **1.** GEOG WIDE CHANNEL a broad channel between two large bodies of water, or between an island and the mainland **2.** GEOG OCEAN INLET a long wide arm of the sea **3.** ZOOL AIR BLADDER a fish's air bladder [Old English *sund*. Ultimately from a prehistoric Germanic word that is also the ancestor of English *swim*. The current meaning evolved from "swimming," influenced by a related Scandinavian word.]

sound-a-like *n.* a performer whose voice or musical style closely resembles that of a particular well-known performer

sound bar·ri·er *n.* a sudden increase in the force of air opposing an aircraft or other moving body when it approaches the speed of sound, producing a sonic boom

sound bite *n.* a very short comment or phrase intended or suitable for broadcasting in a news program, especially one by a politician. Their use is often regarded as demonstrating superficiality and glibness.

sound·board /sównd bàwrd/, **sound·ing board** /sównding bàwrd/ *n.* a thin sheet of wood placed under or above the strings of a musical instrument to increase resonance. On a violin it is the top of the instrument.

sound bow *n.* the thick part of a bell, where the clapper strikes

sound·box /sównd bòks/ *n.* the hollow chamber in a stringed instrument that increases its resonance

sound card *n.* a computer circuit board that allows a personal computer to receive sound in digital form and reproduce it through speakers

sound ef·fect *n.* ARTS SOUND FOR A PERFORMANCE a recording or imitation of a particular sound used in a movie, radio or television program, play, or other theatrical performance ■ **sound ef·fects** *npl.* MOVIE SOUNDS all the sounds in a movie other than dialogue and music. They are generally added after shooting.

sound·er /sówndər/ *n.* a device for determining the depth of a body of water

sound hole *n.* an opening near the center of a hollow stringed instrument that increases resonance

sound·ing[1] /sównding/ *n.* **1.** NAUT DEPTH MEASUREMENT a measurement of the depth of water, taken using sonar or a weighted line **2.** METEOROL ATMOSPHERIC MEASUREMENT a measurement of the conditions in the atmosphere at a specific altitude ■ **sound·ings** *npl.* **1.** PRELIMINARY INQUIRY INTO OPINION a sampling of the views of a group of people taken before somebody becomes committed to a course of action ○ *taking soundings about the popularity of the council's plans* **2.** NAUT WATER WHERE SOUNDINGS ARE TAKEN a place where the water is shallow enough for a sounding line to be used to determine its depth

sound·ing[2] /sównding/ *adj.* having an impressive or resonant sound (*literary*) —**sound·ing·ly** *adv.*

sound·ing board *n.* **1.** MUSIC = **soundboard** **2.** SOMEBODY TO GIVE PRELIMINARY OPINION a person or group who gives feedback on preliminary ideas before they are considered for further development **3.** ACOUSTICS STRUCTURE THAT REFLECTS SOUND a rooflike structure built above a pulpit or platform to direct the speaker's voice to the audience

sound·ing line *n.* a weighted line with measurements marked on it, used for determining the depth of water

sound·ing rock·et *n.* a rocket used to make scientific observations within the earth's atmosphere

sound·less /sówndləss/ *adj.* not making any noise — **sound·less·ly** *adv.* —**sound·less·ness** *n.*

sound mix·er *n.* a person or machine that combines or balances sounds for a recording, broadcast, or movie soundtrack

sound pol·lu·tion *n.* = **noise pollution**

sound·post /sównd pòst/ *n.* a small piece of wood inside the body of a stringed instrument that supports the bridge and transmits the vibrations to the back

sound·proof /sównd proof/ *adj.* IMPENETRABLE TO NOISE constructed so that audible sound cannot enter or escape ■ *vt.* (**-proofed, -proof·ing, -proofs**) MAKE SOMETHING SOUNDPROOF to line or seal a room so that audible sound cannot enter or escape

sound rang·ing *n.* a method of locating the source of a sound by measuring the travel time of sound waves to a microphone at a fixed position

sound shift *n.* a systematic change over time in the pronunciation of a set of sounds in a language

sound spec·tro·graph *n.* an electronic instrument that makes a graphic representation of sound qualities

sound stage *n.* a large room or studio, usually soundproof, where movie scenes are shot

sound sys·tem *n.* electronic equipment for amplifying sound produced by recording, broadcasting, or live at public gatherings

sound·track /sównd tràk/ *n.* **1.** CINEMA, TV SOUND RECORDING FOR A MOVIE the recorded music, dialogue, and sound effects in a movie or video production **2.** CINEMA, VIDEO STRIP CARRYING MOVIE SOUND a thin strip at the edge of a movie reel or videotape on which sound or the soundtrack is recorded **3.** MUSIC MUSIC FROM MOVIE a commercially released recording of music that has been used in a particular movie

sound truck *n.* a truck with loudspeakers attached to the roof, used for broadcasting political messages or sales pitches

sound wave *n.* an audible pressure wave caused by a disturbance in water or air and carried forward in a ripple effect

soup /soop/ *n.* **1.** LIQUID FOOD a liquid food made by cooking meat, fish, vegetables, and other ingredients in water, milk, or stock **2.** SOMETHING THICK AND SWIRLING something with the consistency or appearance of soup, especially a swirling liquid or dense fog ○ *the primordial soup of hydrogen, oxygen, and other gases* **3.** EXPLOSIVE nitroglycerine or gelignite (*slang*) [Mid-17thC. Via French *soupe* from late Latin *suppa*, formed from assumed *suppare* "to soak." Ultimately from a prehistoric Germanic word that also produced English *sop* and *sup*.] ◇ **from soup to nuts** used to emphasize the variety or the wide range of something ◇ **in the soup** in difficulties or trouble (*informal*)

soup up *vt.* to make changes to a car, motorcycle, engine, or similar machine in order to make it more powerful (*informal*) [From the use of SOUP for "a drug injected into a horse to increase its speed"]

soup·çon /soop sáwN, so͝op sòn/ *n.* a very small amount of something [Mid-18thC. Via French, literally "suspicion," from, ultimately, the Latin stem *suspicion-* (see SUSPICION).]

soup du jour /so͝op də jo͝or/ (*plural* **soups du jour** /so͝op də jo͝or/) *n.* a soup featured by a restaurant on a particular day [Mid-20thC. From French *soupe du jour*.]

Souph·an·ou·vong /so͝o fanoo vóng/ (1909–95) Laotian prince and statesman. He fought for independence from French rule and helped to found the nationalist Pathet Lao in 1950. He was president of Laos (1975–86).

soup kitch·en *n.* a place that serves free meals to people who have no money

soup·spoon /so͝op spo͝on/ *n.* a large spoon for eating soup

soup·y /so͝opee/ (**-i·er, -i·est**) *adj.* **1.** LIKE SOUP like soup in appearance or consistency **2.** DAMP OR FOGGY unpleasantly damp or foggy (*informal*) **3.** SENTIMENTAL highly sentimental (*informal*)

sour /sowr/ *adj.* **1.** SHARP-TASTING having a tart or sharp taste that is acidic though not necessarily unpleasant, like the taste of vinegar, lemons, or unripe apples **2.** BAD THROUGH FERMENTATION unpleasantly rancid in taste or smell because of fermentation **3.** DISSATISFIED characterized by ill temper or feelings of bitterness or dissatisfaction ○ *a sour look* **4.** UNFRIENDLY unpleasant, unfriendly, or ill-disposed, having previously been harmonious, friendly, or approving **5.** UNPLEASANT causing distaste or discomfort **6.** AGRIC **LACKING LIME** acidic because of a shortage of lime, and so unfavorable to crops **7.** INDUST **SULFUROUS AND ACIDIC** acidic because of containing sulfur compounds. These make oil or gas foul-smelling, toxic, corrosive to metals, and poisonous to catalysts. ■ *vti.* (**soured, sour·ing, sours**) **1. BECOME OR MAKE SOMETHING SOUR** to become, or make something become, sour in taste, smell, or composition **2. BECOME OR MAKE SOMEBODY DISSATISFIED** to become, or make somebody become, ill-tempered, embittered, or dissatisfied **3. BECOME OR MAKE SOMEBODY UNFRIENDLY** to become, or make somebody or something become, unpleasant, unfriendly, or ill-disposed toward somebody or something, having previously been harmonious, friendly, or approving ○ *A breach of diplomacy soured relations between the countries.* ■ *n.* **1. SHARPNESS** sharpness or tartness of taste ○ *add some to tone down the sour* **2.** BEVERAGES **COCKTAIL WITH LEMON OR LIME** a cocktail made with whiskey, lemon or lime juice, and often sugar [Old English *sūr.* Ultimately from a prehistoric Germanic word that also produced English *sorrel*[1] and German *sauer* "sour" (source of English *sauerkraut*).] —**sour·ly** *adv.* —**sour·ness** *n.*

sour·ball /sówr bàwl/ *n.* a round hard piece of candy with a tart flavor

source /sawrss/ *n.* **1. ORIGIN** the place where something begins, the thing from which something is derived, or the person or group that initiated or created something **2. SOMEBODY OR SOMETHING PROVIDING INFORMATION** a person, organization, book, or other text that supplies information or evidence ○ *A reliable source* **3.** ARTS **WORK ON WHICH ANOTHER IS BASED** a creation such as a story or work of art that forms the basis of or inspiration for a later work **4.** GEOG **BEGINNING OF RIVER** the spring or fountain from which a river or stream first issues from the ground, or the area around this **5.** ELECTRON ENG **ELECTRODE REGION** a region of a transistor from which charge carriers flow ■ *v.* (**sourced, sourc·ing, sourc·es**) **1.** *vt.* **SPECIFY SOURCES OF SOMETHING WRITTEN** to list the people or materials used in researching a written work **2.** *vti.* MANUF **LOCATE SOMETHING FOR USE** to get or locate parts, materials, or information from elsewhere [14thC. Via Old French *sourse* "spring," from, ultimately, Latin *surgere* "to rise" (source of English *surge*).]

WORD KEY: SYNONYMS

See Synonyms at ***origin.***

source book, source·book *n.* a document or collection of documents that is the main source of information about a subject of study

source code *n.* computer code written in a recognized programming language that can be converted into machine code. ◊ **object code**

source lan·guage *n.* the language from which a translation is made

sour cher·ry *n.* **1.** TREES **FRUIT TREE** a Eurasian shrub or small tree with white flowers and edible fruit. Latin name: *Prunus cerasus.* **2.** FOOD **FRUIT OF THE SOUR CHERRY** the red or blackish fruit of the sour cherry tree. It has a sharp taste, and is used mainly in cooking and preserves.

sour cream *n.* a smooth thick cream that has been soured artificially, used in cooking and baking and as a topping

sour·dine /sóor deén, soor deén/ *n.* **1. OLD MUSICAL INSTRUMENT** a reed instrument with a soft tone similar to a bassoon. It is no longer in use. **2.** = **sordino 3. ORGAN STOP** a stop on an organ that produces a low muted tone [Early 17thC. Via French from Italian *sordina,* the feminine form of *sordino* (see SORDINO).]

sour grapes *n.* the scornful denial that something is attractive or desirable because it is unobtainable [In allusion to Aesop's fable *The Fox and the Grapes* where the fox disparages some grapes as sour when he cannot reach them]

sour gum *n.* a tree of the eastern United States that has glossy leaves and light wood. Latin name: *Nyssa sylvatica.*

sour mash *n.* **1. GRAIN MIXTURE FOR DISTILLING** a grain mash that is a mixture of new and old batches, used in distilling some kinds of whiskey **2. WHISKEY FROM SOUR MASH** whiskey distilled using sour mash

sour or·ange *n.* = **bitter orange**

sour·puss /sówr pòoss/ *n.* somebody who is gloomy or bad-tempered (*informal*)

sour·sop /sówr sòp/ (*plural* **-sops** *or* **-sop**) *n.* **1.** TREES **TROPICAL AMERICAN TREE** a tropical American tree with spicy fragrant leaves and spiny fruit. Latin name: *Annona muricata.* **2.** FOOD **FRUIT OF SOURSOP** the spiny fruit of the soursop tree with a tart fibrous pulp

sour·wood /sówr wòod/ (*plural* **-woods** *or* **-wood**) *n.* a tree of the eastern United States with thick bark, small white flowers, and sour-tasting leaves. Latin name: *Oxydendrum arboreum.*

Sou·sa /sóozə, -sə/, **John Philip** (1854–1932) U.S. military bandmaster and composer. His rousing patriotic compositions include "The Stars and Stripes Forever" (1897). Known as **the March King**

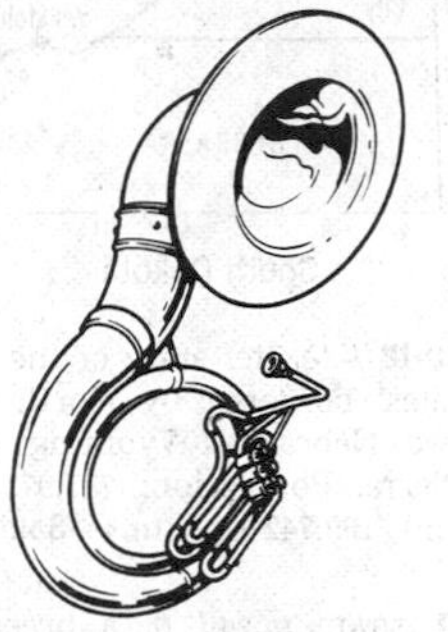

Sousaphone

sou·sa·phone /sóozə fōn/ *n.* a large brass instrument with a flaring bell, resembling a tuba. It is used in military marching bands. [Early 20thC. Named for its inventor, John Philip SOUSA.] —**sou·sa·phon·ist** *n.*

sous-chef /sóo-/ *n.* a head chef's assistant and deputy [Late 17thC. *Sous* via French, literally "under," from Latin *subtus.*]

souse /sowss/ *v.* (**soused, sous·ing, sous·es**) **1.** *vt.* **PICKLE SOMETHING** to steep something in vinegar or brine in order to preserve it (*often passive*) **2.** *vti.* **PLUNGE INTO LIQUID** to plunge, or plunge something, into a liquid **3.** *vti.* **SOAK** to make something soaking wet, or become soaking wet **4.** *vt.* **MAKE SOMEBODY INTOXICATED** to make somebody extremely intoxicated (*slang*) (*usually passive*) ■ *n.* **1. LIQUID USED IN PICKLING** the brine or vinegar used in pickling **2.** FOOD **PICKLED FOOD** pickled food, especially pork trimmings **3.** *Carib* FOOD **BROTH MADE WITH PORK** broth made with pig's snout, feet, and sometimes tail, boiled until tender along with sliced cucumbers and various seasonings such as onions, salt, lime, and pepper **4. HABITUAL ALCOHOL DRINKER** somebody who habitually consumes alcohol to excess (*slang*) **5. BINGE** a bout of heavy drinking (*slang*) [14thC. From Old French *sous.* Ultimately from a prehistoric Germanic word that is also the ancestor of English *salt* and German *Sülze* "aspic."]

sous·lik *n.* = **suslik**

sou-sou /sòo sòo/, **su·su** *n. Carib* an arrangement for saving money whereby participants pay a certain sum each month for a fixed period of time and take turns borrowing the total amount accumulated [Early 20th C. From Yoruba *eesu* or *esusu* "fund where several people pool their money, each paying a fixed sum and each drawing out the total in rotation," probably influenced by French *sou* "coin."]

Sousse /soos/ city and port in east central Tunisia. Population: 125,000 (1994).

sou·tache /soo tásh/ *n.* a narrow ornamental braid in a herringbone pattern, used for trimming garments [Mid-19thC. Via French from Hungarian *sujtás.*]

sou·tane /soo taán/ *n.* a priest's robe or cassock, especially one with buttons down the front [Mid-19thC. Via French from Italian *sottana,* from *sotto* "below," from Latin *subtus.*]

Sout·er /sóotər/, **David** (*b.* 1939) U.S. jurist. He was appointed to the Supreme Court (1990) and developed a reputation as a judicial centrist. Full name **David Hackett Souter**

sou·ter·rain /sóotə ráyn/ *n.* an ancient underground room or passage [Mid-18thC. From French, literally "underground."]

south /sowth/ *n.* **1. DIRECTION TO THE RIGHT FACING SUN** the direction that lies directly to the right of somebody facing the rising sun or that is located toward the bottom of a conventional map of the world. See table at **compass 2. COMPASS POINT OPPOSITE NORTH** the compass point that lies directly opposite north **3. south, South AREA IN THE SOUTH** the part of an area, country, or region that is situated in or toward the south **4. POSITION EQUIVALENT TO SOUTH** the position equivalent to south in any diagram consisting of four points at 90-degree intervals ■ *adj.* **1. IN THE SOUTH** situated in, facing, or coming from the south of a place, region, or country **2.** METEOROL **BLOWING FROM THE SOUTH** blowing from the south (*refers to winds*) ■ *adv.* **TOWARD THE SOUTH** in or toward the south [Old English *sūþ.* Ultimately from a prehistoric Germanic word that is probably also the ancestor of English *sun.*]

South /sowth/ *n.* **1. SOUTHERN STATES** the region of the United States that includes the states south of the Mason-Dixon Line **2. CONFEDERATE STATES** the states of the Confederacy during the Civil War

South Africa

South Af·ri·ca republic in southern Africa. It became a fully democratic republic in 1994. Language: Afrikaans, English. Currency: rand. Capital: Pretoria. Population: 42,327,458 (1997). Area: 472,731 sq. mi./1,224,691 sq. km. Official name **Republic of South Africa** —**South Af·ri·can** *n., adj.*

South Af·ri·can Dutch *n.* LANG = **Cape Dutch** *n.* (*not used in South Africa*)

South Af·ri·can Eng·lish *n.* a variety of English spoken in South Africa

WORD KEY: WORLD ENGLISH

The English language as used in the Republic of South Africa: since the early 19th century the mother tongue of settlers of British origin and a second language, in varying degrees, of indigenous Afrikaners, Africans, and Asians. Since 1994, the nation has had 11 official languages: English, Afrikaans, Ndebele, Sotho (Northern and Southern), Swati, Tsonga, Tswana, Venda, Xhosa, and Zulu. South African English is generally "non-rhotic" (i.e., "r" is not pronounced in words such as *art, door,* and *worker*), and, among Africans, tends to have full vowels in all syllables (e.g., *7* is pronounced "seh-ven" not "sevn"). In the speech of middle-class British South Africans distinctive usages are common: e.g., the vowels in *park* and *trap* are heard by outsiders as "pork" and "trep," and in *fair hair* as "fay hay." A curiosity of the grammar is the affirmative "*no,*" as in "How are you? – No, I'm fine," probably adopted from Afrikaans. With its parent Dutch, this language has provided the bulk of local borrowings: e.g., *Afrikaner* (South African Caucasian of Dutch or Huguenot origin), *apartheid* (separate racial development, now obsolete), *bakkie* (pickup truck), *braai* (barbecue), *drift* (ford), *kloof* (ravine), the now internationalized *trek* (journey), and *veld* (pronounced "felt") (open country), with its hybrid extensions *highveld* and *backveld.* Words from African languages include *impala, muti* (medicine), *sangoma* (diviner), and *tshwala* (sorghum beer). Distinctive English words are the now-archaic *bioscope* (movie), *location* (district set aside for a particular group), and *robot* (traffic light).

South A·mer·i·ca the fourth largest continent in the world, comprising Argentina, Bolivia, Brazil, Chile, Colombia, Ecuador, French Guiana, Guyana, Paraguay, Peru, Suriname, Uruguay, and Venezuela

South A·mer·i·can /sòwth ə mérrikən/ *adj.* relating to any of the countries of South America, or their peoples or cultures

South A·mer·i·can try·pan·o·so·mi·a·sis *n.* = **Chagas' disease**

South·amp·ton Is·land island in Nunavut, Canada, between Foxe Basin and Hudson Bay. Area: 15,913 sq. mi./41,214 sq. km.

South A·sia region comprising the countries of Bangladesh, Bhutan, India, the Maldives, Nepal, Pakistan, and Sri Lanka

South A·sian Eng·lish *n.* a variety of English spoken in South Asia

WORD KEY: WORLD ENGLISH

The English language as used since the 17th century in South Asia (the Indian Subcontinent), i.e., in Bangladesh, Bhutan, India, the Maldive Islands, Nepal, Pakistan, and Sri Lanka. Usage varies greatly from area to area, primarily because of the influence of local languages on pronunciation, grammar, and vocabulary, e.g.; Bengali in Bangladesh and the Indian state of Bengal, Hindi in northern India, Tamil in southern India and Sri Lanka, Urdu in Pakistan and India, and Sinhala in Sri Lanka. At the same time, however, there is considerable uniformity throughout the region as a consequence of British administrative, legal, and commercial usage and the presence of English-language media schools based on British models. South Asian English is "rhotic" (i.e., "r" is pronounced in words such as *art*, *door*, and *worker*). It tends to have full vowels in all syllables (e.g., *7* is pronounced "seh-ven" not *sevn*), and it is widely considered to have a "singsong" quality often compared with that of English speakers in Wales. Two widespread grammatical features are, first, *Wh*-questions without word-order inversion, as in "What you would like to buy, please? Where you are coming from? Why you are doing this?" Second is the end-of-sentence use of *only* for emphasis: "He is coming once a week only" meaning "He only comes once a week." Widely used in the region are adopted local expressions such as: *gherao* (in industrial actions, surrounding people so that they cannot leave a place; also used as a verb, e.g., "He was gheraoed yesterday"); *wallah* (man, used in compounds like *dhobiwallah* meaning "laundryman"; and the numbers *lakh* (one hundred thousand), e.g., "a lakh of rupees," and *crore* (ten million) in "They have crores of rupees." Hybridization of English with indigenous usages is common, as in *policewallah* (policeman), and *goondaism* (behaving like a *goonda* or thug, itself a South Asian word). See BANGLADESHI ENGLISH, INDIAN ENGLISH, PAKISTANI ENGLISH, SRI LANKAN ENGLISH.

South Aus·tra·lia state occupying the central part of southern Australia. Founded in 1834, it was the only Australian colony set up as a free settlement rather than a penal colony. Capital: Adelaide. Population: 1,474,000 (1996). Area: 380,070 sq. mi./984,377 sq. km. —**South Aus·tral·i·an** *n., adj.*

South Bend city in northern Indiana, on the Kankakee and St. Joseph rivers, southwest of Elkhart. Population: 102,100 (1996).

south·bound /sówth bòwnd/ *adj.* leading, going, or traveling toward the south

South·bridge /sówth brij/ town in south central Massachusetts, north of the Connecticut border, east of Springfield and southwest of Worcester. Population: 17,447 (1996).

south by east *n.* the direction or compass point midway between south and south-southeast. See table at **compass** —**south by east** *adj., adv.*

south by west *n.* the direction or compass point midway between south and south-southwest —**south by west** *adj., adv.*

South Carolina

South Car·o·li·na /-karə línə/ state of the southeastern United States, bordered by North Carolina, the Atlantic Ocean, and Georgia. One of the original 13 colonies, it was admitted as a state in 1788. Capital: Columbia. Population: 3,760,181 (1997). Area: 31,189 sq. mi./80,779 sq. km. —**South Car·o·lin·i·an** /-kàrrə línnee ən/ *n., adj.*

South Chi·na Sea part of the China Sea, surrounded by the Philippines, Borneo, Taiwan, southeastern China, and the Gulf of Thailand. Area: 895,400 sq. mi./2,319,086 sq. km.

South Dakota

South Da·ko·ta /-dəkṓtə/ state of the north central United States, bordered by North Dakota, Minnesota, Iowa, Nebraska, Wyoming, and Montana. Capital: Pierre. Population: 737,973 (1997). Area: 77,121 sq. mi./199,742 sq. km. —**South Da·ko·tan** *n., adj.*

South·down /sówth dòwn/ *n.* a breed of small-to-medium hornless English sheep with short dense wool, usually raised for mutton [Late 18thC. Named for the *South Downs*, where the breed originated.]

South Downs chalk ridge extending along the south coast of England, through Hampshire and Sussex

south·east /sowth éest/ *n.* **1.** COMPASS POINT BETWEEN S AND E the direction or compass point midway between south and east. See table at **compass** **2. south·east, South·east** AREA IN THE SOUTHEAST the part of an area, region, or country that is situated in or toward the southeast ■ *adj.* **1. south·east, South·east** IN THE SOUTHEAST situated in, facing, or lying toward the southeast of a region, place, or country **2.** METEOROL FROM THE SOUTHEAST blowing from the southeast (*refers to winds*) ■ *adv.* TOWARD THE SOUTHEAST in or toward the southeast [Old English]

South·east A·sia /sowth éest áyzhə/ region comprising the countries of Brunei, Cambodia, Indonesia, Laos, Malaysia, Myanmar, the Philippines, Singapore, Thailand, and Vietnam —**South·east A·sian** *n., adj.*

South·east A·sia Trea·ty Or·ga·ni·za·tion *n.* a former alliance of countries for economic cooperation and defense against communism in Southeast Asia and the South Pacific, formed in 1954 and disbanded in 1977. Its members were the United States, the United Kingdom, France, Australia, New Zealand, the Philippines, and Thailand.

south·east by east *n.* the direction or compass point midway between southeast and east-southeast. See table at **compass**

south·east by south *n.* the direction or compass point midway between southeast and south-southeast. See table at **compass**

south·east·er /sowth éestər/ *n.* a storm or wind that blows from the southeast

south·east·er·ly /sowth éestərlee/ *adj.* **1.** IN THE SOUTHEAST situated in or toward the southeast **2.** METEOROL BLOWING FROM THE SOUTHEAST blowing from the southeast (*refers to winds*) ■ *n.* (*plural* **-lies**) WIND FROM THE SOUTHEAST a wind blowing from the southeast

south·east·ern /sowth éestərn/ *adj.* **1.** IN THE SOUTHEAST situated in the southeast of a region or country **2.** FACING SOUTHEAST situated in or facing the southeast **3. south·east·ern, South·east·ern** OF THE SOUTHEAST typical of or native to the southeast of a region or country

south·east·ward /sowth éestwərd/ *adj.* IN THE SOUTHEAST toward or in the southeast ■ *n.* POINT IN THE SOUTHEAST a direction toward or a point in the southeast —**south·east·ward** *adv.* —**south·east·ward·ly** *adv., adj.* —**south·east·wards** *adv.*

south·er /sówthər/ *n.* a strong wind that blows from the south

south·er·ly /súthərlee/ *adj.* **1.** IN THE SOUTH situated in or toward the south **2.** METEOROL BLOWING FROM THE SOUTH blowing from the south (*refers to winds*) ■ *n.* (*plural* **-lies**) WIND FROM THE SOUTH a wind blowing from the south

south·ern /súthərn/ *adj.* **1.** IN THE SOUTH situated in the south of a region or country **2.** SOUTH OF EQUATOR lying south of the equator or south of the celestial equator **3.** FACING SOUTH situated in or facing the south **4. south·ern, South·ern** OF THE SOUTH typical of or native to the south of a region or country **5.** METEOROL FROM THE SOUTH blowing from the south (*refers to winds*) [Old English]

South·ern Cross *n.* a constellation near Centaurus in the sky of the southern hemisphere, with four bright stars placed as if at the points of a cross. The smallest of the 88 constellations, it contains the Coalsack, a dark cloud of dust obscuring the stars beyond it in the Milky Way.

South·ern Crown *n.* = **Corona Australis**

south·ern·er /súthərnər/, **South·ern·er** *n.* somebody who lives in or comes from the southern part of a country or region. The term applies especially to somebody from the southeastern United States.

south·ern hem·i·sphere *n.* **1.** GEOG SOUTHERN HALF OF EARTH the half of the earth that is south of the equator **2.** ASTRON SOUTHERN HALF OF THE CELESTIAL SPHERE the southern half of an imaginary sphere that contains the universe and is divided horizontally by the celestial equator

South·ern·ism /súthər nìzzəm/ *n.* **1.** LING EXPRESSION CHARACTERISTIC OF SOUTH an expression or pronunciation that is characteristic of the southern United States **2.** SOC SCI SOUTHERN BELIEF OR PRACTICE an attitude or custom that is characteristic of the South, especially in the United States

south·ern·most /súthərn mṑst/ *adj.* situated farthest south

South·ern Pai·ute *n.* **1.** PEOPLES MEMBER OF NATIVE N AMERICAN PEOPLE a member of a Native North American people who originally occupied lands in Utah, Nevada, Arizona, and California. Most Southern Paiute now live in Utah. **2.** LANG SOUTHERN PAIUTE LANGUAGE the Uto-Aztecan language of the Southern Paiute people —**South·ern Pai·ute** *adj.*

South·ern prick·ly ash *n.* = **Hercules' club** *n.* 2

south·ern·wood /súthərn wòd/ (*plural* **-woods** *or* **-wood**) *n.* a fragrant European shrub or plant that has cream-colored flowers and bitter-tasting leaves. Latin name: *Artemisia abrotanum.* [Old English]

South Geor·gia uninhabited mountainous island in the South Atlantic Ocean, southeast of the Falkland Islands. A dependency of the United Kingdom, it was first visited by Captain James Cook in 1775. Area: 1,450 sq. mi./3,755 sq. km.

South Had·ley /-hádlee/ town in south central Massachusetts, east of the Connecticut River and northeast of Holyoke. Mount Holyoke College is situated in the town. Population: 17,047 (1996).

South Hol·land province in the west central Netherlands. Capital: The Hague. Population: 3,313,193 (1994). Area: 1,287 sq. mi./3,333 sq. km.

south·ing /sówthing/ *n.* **1.** DISTANCE SOUTH FROM KNOWN LATITUDE how far south a point is from a reference latitude **2.** NAUTICAL PROGRESS TOWARD SOUTH the distance covered as a ship sails toward the south

South Is·land the larger and more southerly of the two main islands of New Zealand, in the southwestern Pacific Ocean. Population: 931,566 (1996). Area: 58,368 sq. mi./151,215 sq. km.

South Kings·town /-kíngstən/ town in southern Rhode Island comprising the villages of Wakefield, Kingstown, and West Kingstown. Population: 26,014 (1996).

South Ko·re·a ♦ **Korea, South**

South Ko·re·an SOMEBODY FROM SOUTH KOREA somebody who was born or raised in South Korea, or who has South Korean citizenship ■ *adj.* OF SOUTH KOREA relating to or typical of South Korea, or its people or culture

South·land /sówthlènd/ region of New Zealand, occupying the southernmost tip of the South Island. Population: 100,758 (1996). Area: 20,514 sq. mi./53,132 sq. km.

south·paw /sówth pàw/ *n.* a left-handed person, especially a left-handed baseball pitcher, a left-handed fiddler, or a boxer who leads with the left hand (*informal*) [Late 19thC. Originally used of left-handed baseball players, from the pitcher's orientation on the mound (since baseball diamonds are traditionally oriented to the same points of the compass).]

South Pole *n.* **1.** SOUTHERN END IN EARTH'S AXIS the southern end of the Earth's axis at the latitude of 90° S **2.** SOUTHERN AXIS INTERSECTION the point where the southern end of the Earth's axis intersects the celestial sphere

South Port·land city in southwestern Maine, on the southern shore of Casco Bay, southeast of Portland. Population: 22,985 (1996).

South·ron /sŭthrən/ *n.* **1.** *Southern U.S.* SOUTHERNER a Southerner (*dated*) **2.** *Scotland* ENGLISH PERSON somebody from England (*archaic or literary*) [15thC. Variant of SOUTHERN.]

South Sas·katch·e·wan /-sə skáchə wàan/ river rising in the Rocky Mountains and flowing north into Lake Winnipeg, Canada. Length: 865 mi./1,393 km.

South Sea Bub·ble *n.* frenzied speculation in the South Sea Company in early 18th-century Britain. In 1720 the company collapsed, ruining many banks and private investors. The company had taken over much of the national debt in return for sole trading rights in the area.

south-south·east *n.* COMPASS POINT BETWEEN S AND SE the direction or compass point midway between south and southeast. See table at **compass** ■ *adj., adv.* IN SOUTH-SOUTHEAST in, from, facing, or toward the south-southeast —**south-south·east·er·ly** *adv.*

south-south·west *n.* COMPASS POINT BETWEEN S AND SW the direction or compass point midway between south and southwest. See table at **compass** ■ *adj., adv.* IN SOUTH-SOUTHWEST in, from, facing, or toward the south-southwest —**south-south·west·er·ly** *adv.*

South Ta·ra·na·ki Bight /-tàrrə náki bīt/ gulf on the southwestern coast of the North Island, New Zealand. It extends from Otakeho in the west to Kakaramea in the east.

South Vi·et·nam /sòwth vee èt nám, sówth vyet nám, -vee èt nám/ former country in Southeast Asia between 1954 and 1976. It occupied the southern part of modern-day Vietnam. —**South Vi·et·nam·ese** /sòwth vee étnə meéz, -vyétnə meéz/ *n., adj.*

south·ward /sówthwərd/ *adv.* TOWARD THE SOUTH in a southerly direction ■ *n.* **south·ward** POINT IN THE SOUTH a direction toward or a point in the south [Old English] —**south·ward** *adj.* —**south·ward·ly** *adv., adj.*

WORD KEY: USAGE

southward or **southwards**? ***Southward*** is the only form available for the adverb: *In a southward direction* and in U.S. English is also more common than ***southwards*** for the adjective *The ship was moving slowly southward.*

south·west /sowth wést/ *n.* **1.** COMPASS POINT BETWEEN S AND W the direction or compass point midway between south and west. See table at **compass** **2.** **south·west, South·west** AREA IN THE SOUTHWEST the part of an area, region, or country that is situated in or toward the southwest ■ *adj.* IN THE SOUTHWEST situated in, facing, or lying toward the southwest of a region, place, or country ■ *adv.* TOWARD THE SOUTHWEST in or toward the southwest [Old English]

South·west /sowth wést/ *n.* the region of the United States that includes Texas, New Mexico, Arizona, Nevada, and California and, sometimes regarded as extending northward to Utah and Colorado

south·west by south *n.* the direction or compass point midway between southwest and south-southwest. See table at **compass**

south·west by west *n.* the direction or compass point midway between southwest and west-southwest. See table at **compass**

South·west Cape the southernmost point in New Zealand, situated at the southern tip of Stewart Island

south·west·er /sowth wéstər, sow-/ *n.* **1.** METEOROL STORM FROM SW a storm or wind that blows from the southwest **2.** CLOTHES = **sou'wester**

south·west·er·ly /sowth wéstərlee, sow-/ *adj.* **1.** IN THE SOUTHWEST situated in or toward the southwest **2.** METEOROL FROM THE SOUTHWEST blowing from the southwest (*refers to winds*) ■ *n.* (*plural* **-lies**) METEOROL WIND FROM THE SOUTHWEST a wind blowing from the southwest

south·west·ern /sowth wéstərn/ *adj.* **1.** IN THE SOUTHWEST situated in the southwest of a region or country **2.** FACING SOUTHWEST situated in or facing the southwest **3.** **south·west·ern, South·west·ern** OF THE SOUTHWEST typical of or native to the southwest of a region or country [Old English]

south·west·ward /sowth wéstwərd/ *adj.* IN THE SOUTHWEST toward or in the southwest ■ *n.* POINT IN THE SOUTHWEST a direction toward or a point in the southwest —**south·west·ward** *adv.* —**south·west·ward·ly** *adv., adj.* —**south·west·wards** *adv.*

Sou·van·na Phou·ma /soo vaànaa pòomaa/ (1901–84) Laotian prince and statesman. As prime minister of Laos for many of the years between 1951 and 1975, he negotiated the treaty of independence from French rule (1953). He was deposed in a coup in 1975.

sou·ve·nir /sòovə neér/ *n.* something bought or kept as a reminder of a particular place or occasion [Late 18thC. Via French, literally "memory," from, ultimately, Latin *subvenire* "to come into mind."]

sou·vlak·i·a /soov laákee ə/ *npl.* Greek kebabs consisting of pieces of meat, usually lamb, skewered and broiled. The meat is often marinated before cooking. [Mid-20thC. From modern Greek, literally "small skewers," from *souvla* "skewer."]

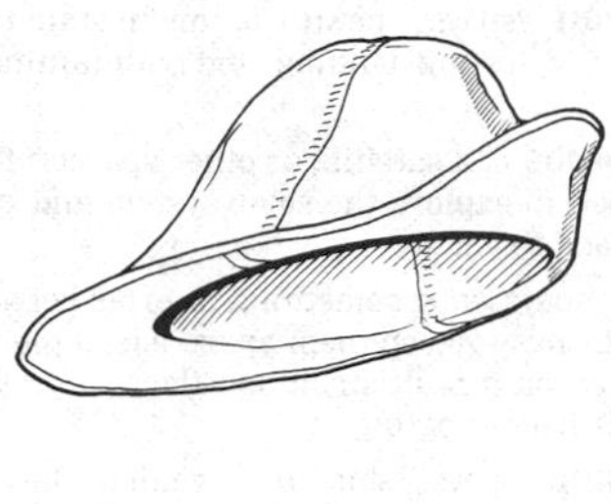

Sou'wester

sou'west·er /sow wéstər/ *n.* a waterproof hat with a broad brim covering the back of the neck, originally made of oilskin, now usually of rubber or plastic. Sou'westers were originally worn by sailors and fishermen. [Mid-19thC. Contraction of *southwester.*]

Sov. *abbr.* Soviet

sov·er·eign /sóvvrən/ *n.* **1.** POL MONARCH the ruler or permanent head of a state, especially a king or queen **2.** MONEY OLD BRITISH GOLD COIN a gold coin worth one pound, used in Britain between the early 17th century and the early 20th century ■ *adj.* **1.** INDEPENDENT self-governing and not ruled by any other state **2.** WITH COMPLETE POWER having supreme authority or power **3.** OUTSTANDING outstanding, e.g., in its excellence or effectiveness [13thC. Via Old French *souverein* from Vulgar Latin *superanus*, from Latin *super* "above."] —**sov·er·eign·ly** *adv.*

sov·er·eign·tist /sóvvrəntist/ *n.* *Can* a supporter of sovereignty for Quebec

sov·er·eign·ty /sóvvrəntee/ (*plural* **-ties**) *n.* **1.** TOP AUTHORITY supreme authority, especially over a state **2.** INDEPENDENCE freedom from outside interference and the right to self-government **3.** INDEPENDENT STATE a politically independent state

sov·er·eign·ty as·so·ci·a·tion *n.* *Can* a proposed type of economic and political association between a sovereign Quebec and the rest of Canada

so·vi·et /sṓvee ət, -èt/ *n.* HIST **1.** COMMUNIST COUNCIL one of the elected government councils that existed at local, regional, and national levels in the former Soviet Union. The highest was the Supreme Soviet. **2.** EARLY RUSSIAN REVOLUTIONARY COUNCIL a council in the early political organization of the Russian Revolution, based on the council of workers formed to seize city government in Petrograd in 1917 [Early 20thC. From Russian *sovet* "council."] —**so·vi·et·ism** *n.*

So·vi·et *adj.* TYPICAL OF U.S.S.R. relating to the former Soviet Union, or its people, culture, or political system ■ *n.* SOMEBODY FROM THE U.S.S.R. somebody who was born or raised in or was a citizen of the former Soviet Union ■ **So·vi·ets** *npl.* LEADERS OF THE SOVIET UNION the government of the former Soviet Union, or the leaders of the former Communist bloc

So·vi·et·ol·o·gist /sṑvee ə tólləjist/ *n.* a scholar who studies the Soviet Union, especially its government and political history

So·vi·et Un·ion *n.* a federation of Communist states in eastern Europe and northern and central Asia from 1922 until 1991. Moscow was its capital. Then the largest country in the world, the Soviet Union was the Communist superpower during the Cold War. Official name **Union of Soviet Socialist Republics**

sow[1] /sō/ (**sowed, sown** /sōn/ *or* **sowed, sow·ing, sows**) *v.* **1.** *vti.* PLANT SEED to scatter or plant seed on an area of land in order to grow crops **2.** *vt.* INTRODUCE AN IDEA to cause some feeling or belief to arise or become widespread, especially when negative or divisive ○ *Increased competition will only sow discord among the members of the company.* **3.** *vt.* SPREAD THICKLY to spread something thickly with something (*often passive*) ○ *a sky sown with stars* [Old English *sāwan*. Ultimately from an Indo-European word that is also the ancestor of English *season, seed,* and *semen.*] —**sow·a·ble** *adj.* —**sow·er** *n.*

sow[2] /sow/ *n.* **1.** ZOOL FEMALE HOG an adult female hog **2.** ZOOL ADULT FEMALE ANIMAL the adult female of several animals such as the bear, mink, badger, guinea pig, and hedgehog **3.** METALL CHANNEL FOR MOLTEN IRON a channel through which molten iron runs into a mold in the process of casting pig iron **4.** METALL HARDENED IRON a mass of iron that has hardened in a channel or mold in the process of casting pig iron [Old English *sugu*. Ultimately from an Indo-European word that is also the ancestor of English *swine* and Greek *hus* "hog" (source of English *hyena*).]

Sow. *abbr.* *S Asia* Sowbhagyawati

sow·back /sów bàk/ *n.* a long ridge of earth left by a glacier [Late 19thC. From sow[2].]

sow·bel·ly /sów bèllee/ *n.* fatty salt pork (*informal*)

Sow·bhag·ya·wa·ti /bàgee ə wóttee/ *n.* *S Asia* a title used in India before the name of a married woman whose husband is still alive, roughly equivalent to the English term "Mrs" [From Sanskrit]

sow·bread /sów brèd/ (*plural* **-breads** *or* **-bread**) *n.* a cyclamen, especially one of a southern European species with a single nodding flower. Genus: *Cyclamen.* [Mid-16thC. So-called because it is supposedly eaten by hogs.]

sow bug *n.* = **wood louse** [From its piglike shape]

So·we·to /sə wáytō, sè wéttō/ township in southern Johannesburg, Gauteng Province, South Africa. Population: 596,632 (1991).

sown past participle of **sow**[1]

sow this·tle *n.* a Eurasian plant with prickly leaves and yellow flowers. Genus: *Sonchus.* [Origin uncertain: perhaps by folk etymology from earlier *thowthistle*]

sox plural of **sock**[1] (*informal*)

soy /soy/, **soy·a** /sóy ə/ *n.* **1.** PLANTS SOYBEAN PLANT the soybean plant **2.** FOOD = **soy sauce** ■ *adj.* FROM SOYBEANS made or derived from soybeans ○ *soy inks* [Late 17thC. Via Dutch, Malay, and Japanese from Chinese *jiàngyoú*, literally "soybean oil."]

soy·a bean *n.* *U.K.* PLANTS = **soybean**

soy·bean /sóy beèn/ *n.* **1.** PLANTS PLANT WITH NUTRITIOUS SEEDS a southeastern Asian plant cultivated around the world for its nutritious seeds, for soil improvement, and to provide grazing for animals. Latin name: *Glycine max.* **2.** FOOD SEED OF SOYBEAN PLANT the edible seed of the soybean plant. It is rich in oil and protein.

soy·milk /sóy mìlk/ *n.* a milk substitute made from soybeans, often with vitamins and sugar added

soy sauce, **soy** *n.* a dark, salty liquid made by fermenting soybeans in brine, used to flavor foods

soz·zled /sózz'ld/ *adj.* extremely intoxicated (*informal*) [Late 19thC. Formed from English dialect *sozzle* "to splash," perhaps imitative of the sound.]

SP *abbr.* **1.** NAVY shore patrol **2.** ELEC single pole **3.** ARMY specialist **4.** NAVY submarine patrol

sp. *abbr.* **1.** special **2.** species **3.** specific **4.** specimen **5.** spelling

Sp. *abbr.* **1.** Spanish **2.** Spain **3.** Spaniard

s.p. *abbr.* without children [Latin, *sine prole*]

spa /spaa/ *n.* **1.** = **health spa** **2.** RESORT WITH BATHING AND MINERAL WATER a resort with mineral springs **3.** WHIRLPOOL BATH a tub with a device for aerating or swirling water [Early 17thC. Named for a resort town in eastern Belgium, famous for its mineral springs.]

SpA *abbr.* limited company (*used after the name of a company*) [Italian, *Società per Azioni*]

space /spayss/ *n.* **1.** REGION BEYOND EARTH'S ATMOSPHERE the region that lies beyond the Earth's atmosphere, and all that it contains **2.** REGION BETWEEN ALL CELESTIAL BODIES the region, usually of negligible density, between all celestial bodies in the universe **3.** THREE-DIMENSIONAL EXPANSE WHERE MATTER EXISTS the unbounded three-dimensional expanse in which all matter exists **4.** INTERVAL OF TIME a period or interval of time **5.** AREA SET APART an area set apart or available for use **6.** PRINTING BLANK AREA BETWEEN TYPE a blank area between characters, words, or lines of type, or an interval the width of a single character **7.** MUSIC INTERVAL BETWEEN LINES OF MUSICAL STAFF an interval between the lines of the musical staff **8.** COMMUNICATION TIME OR SPACE AVAILABLE FOR USE broadcast time or an area in a publication available for specific use, e.g., by advertisers **9.** MATH SET OF POINTS GOVERNED BY AXIOMS a collection of points that have geometric properties in that they obey set rules **(axioms)**, e.g., a Euclidian space that is governed by Euclidian geometry. Each non-Euclidian geometry, having its own axioms, has its own non-Euclidian space containing a collection of points governed by those axioms. **10.** PRINTING PIECE OF TYPE TO CREATE SPACE a piece of type used to create a blank interval in printing **11.** FREEDOM TO ASSERT IDENTITY the freedom or opportunity to assert a personal identity or fulfill personal needs (*informal*) ○ *I need my own personal space in order to live stress-free.* **12.** TECH INTERVAL IN TRANSMISSION OF TELEGRAPHIC MESSAGE an interval during the transmission of a telegraphic message when the key is not in contact ■ *v.* **(spaced, spac·ing, spac·es) 1.** *vt.* TO SET THINGS APART to set things some distance apart or arrange them with gaps between **2.** *vti.* BECOME INATTENTIVE to be or become distracted, forgetful, or inattentive (*slang*) [13thC. Via French *espace* from Latin *spatium* "space, distance."]

space age, Space Age *n.* the era marked by the exploration of space, often considered as beginning in 1957 when the Soviet Union launched Sputnik —**space-age** *adj.*

space·band /spáyss bànd/ *n.* a device used in printing to provide variable but even spacing between words in a justified line

space bar *n.* a horizontal bar at the bottom of a keyboard or typewriter that is pressed to introduce a space

space bi·ol·o·gy *n.* = **exobiology**

space blan·ket *n.* a plastic wrapping with aluminum foil coating that is used to restore body heat in people affected by exposure or exhaustion

space·borne /spáyss bàwrn/ *adj.* traveling or operating in outer space

space·bridge /spáyss brìj/ *n.* a way of communicating internationally by television, using transmissions from orbiting satellites

space ca·det *n.* somebody who behaves in a forgetful or dazed way, especially somebody who has taken hallucinogenic drugs (*slang*)

space cap·sule *n.* a vehicle or cabin designed to support life and used for transporting human beings or animals in outer space or at very high altitudes within Earth's atmosphere

space charge *n.* the net electric charge distributed in a given volume of space

space·craft /spáyss kràft/ (*plural* **-craft** *or* **-crafts**) *n.* a vehicle or device designed for travel or use in space

spaced-out *adj.* inattentive, dazed, confused, or lightheaded from or as if from drug use (*slang*)

space·far·ing /spáys fàiring/ *n.* the use of spacecraft for the exploration of outer space —**spacefaring** *adj.*

space·flight /spáyss flìt/ *n.* flight beyond Earth's atmosphere, or an instance of this

space heat·er *n.* a small portable appliance used to heat a small area

space·lab /spáyss làb/ *n.* a laboratory in space used to carry out scientific experiments

space lat·tice *n.* = **lattice** *n.* 4

space·less /spáyssliss/ *adj.* (*literary*) **1.** BOUNDLESS with no limits **2.** OCCUPYING NO SPACE not occupying any space

space·man /spáyss màn, -mən/ (*plural* **-men** /-men, -mən/) *n.* **1.** ASTRONAUT an astronaut or somebody who travels in space **2.** EXTRATERRESTRIAL a traveler to Earth from outer space, in science fiction

space med·i·cine *n.* a branch of medicine dealing with the effects of space flight on the human body

Space Needle

Space Nee·dle *n.* a tall tower in downtown Seattle, Washington, with a revolving restaurant and observation deck near the top. It was built for the 1962 World's Fair.

space o·pe·ra *n.* a science fiction drama involving space travel and, often, extraterrestrial beings

space plat·form *n.* = **space station**

space·port /spáyss pàwrt/ *n.* an installation for launching, testing, landing, and maintaining spacecraft

space probe *n.* a satellite or other spacecraft that is designed to explore the solar system and transmit data back to earth

spac·er /spàyssər/ *n.* something inserted between two other things to keep them apart, e.g., a pierced bar threaded on a multistring necklace to prevent the strands from tangling

space·ship /spáyss shìp/ *n.* a vehicle designed to transport people or materials through outer space

space shut·tle *n.* a reusable spacecraft designed to transport people and cargo between earth and space, with two solid rocket boosters and an external fuel tank that are jettisoned after takeoff

space sick·ness *n.* motion sickness experienced as a result of space flight

space sta·tion, space platform *n.* a spacecraft or satellite designed to be occupied by a crew for extended periods of time and used as a base for the exploration, observation, and research of space

Spacesuit: Astronaut Buzz Aldrin on the Moon

space·suit /spáyss sòot/ *n.* a sealed pressurized suit designed to support the wearer's life in space

space-time, space-time con·tin·u·um *n.* a four-dimensional system consisting of three spatial coordinates and one for time, in which it is possible to locate events

space·walk /spáyss wàwk/ *n.* ASTRONAUT'S EXCURSION OUT OF SPACECRAFT an excursion by an astronaut or cosmonaut outside the spacecraft ■ *vi.* **(-walked, -walk·ing, -walks)** LEAVE SPACECRAFT to go out of a spacecraft in order to perform a task or experiment —**space·walk·er** *n.*

space·ward /spáyssward/ *adv.* in the direction of outer space

space·wom·an /spáyss wòomən/ (*plural* **-en** /-wimmin/) *n.* **1.** WOMAN ASTRONAUT a woman astronaut or cosmonaut who travels in space **2.** FEMALE VISITOR TO EARTH a female who travels to Earth from outer space, in science fiction

space writ·er *n.* a writer paid according to the area of print taken up by what is written

spac·ey *adj.* = **spacy** (*informal*)

spa·cial /spáysh'l/ *adj.* = **spatial**

spac·ing *n.* **1.** SPACE OR ITS ARRANGEMENT the space, or the way this is arranged, between several things, e.g., between words or lines in type **2.** ARRANGING IN SPACES the act of arranging things in spaces

spa·cious /spáyshəss/ *adj.* **1.** CONTAINING GREAT SPACE roomy and containing ample space **2.** BROAD IN SCOPE expansive and broad in scope

Spack·le /spák'l/ *tdmk.* a trademark for a compound used in surfacing interior walls

spac·y /spáyssee/ **(-i·er, -i·est), spac·ey (-i·er, -i·est)** *adj.* spaced-out (*slang*)

spade[1] /spayd/ *n.* DIGGING TOOL a digging tool with a wide shallow blade flattened where it meets the shaft so it can be pushed into the ground with the foot ■ *vti.* **(spad·ed, spad·ing, spades)** DIG OR REMOVE SOMETHING WITH SPADE to dig or remove something using a spade [Old English *spadu*. Ultimately from an Indo-European word that is also the ancestor of English *spoon* and Greek *spathē* "broad blade" (source of English *spatula* and *spay*).] —**spad·er** *n.* ◇ **call a spade a spade** say plainly and bluntly what you mean without being euphemistic in any way

spade[2] /spayd/ *n.* **1.** SUIT WITH SPEAR-SHAPED SYMBOL one of the four suits used in cards, with a black figure shaped like a stylized spearhead as its symbol **2.** CARD OF SPADES SUIT a card of the suit of spades **3.** OFFENSIVE TERM an offensive term referring to somebody, especially a man, who is descended from an African people (*slang offensive*) [Late 16thC. Via Italian, the plural of *spada* "sword" (the sign used on Italian cards), and Latin *spatha* "broadsword" from Greek *spathē* (see SPADE[1]).] ◇ **in spades** to a very great degree (*informal*)

spade·fish /spáyd fìsh/ (*plural* **-fish** *or* **-fish·es**) *n.* a deep-bodied bony fish found in coastal waters of the Atlantic and used as a food fish. Family: Ephippidae. [Early 18thC. From its shape.]

spade·foot toad /spáyd fòot-/ *n.* a burrowing toad found in drier regions of the world, with a hardened edge on its hind feet that is used for excavating deep burrows. Family: Pelobatidae.

spade·work /spáyd wùrk/ *n.* **1.** WORK REQUIRING SPADE work done using a spade **2.** PRELIMINARY WORK preliminary work that is often hard drudgery

spa·di·ceous /spay díshəss, spə-/ *adj.* bearing or resembling a spadix [Mid-17thC. Formed from the Latin stem *spadic-* (see SPADIX).]

spa·di·ces plural of **spadix**

spa·dille /spə díl/ *n.* the highest trump card in some card games, e.g., ombre [Late 17thC. Via French and Spanish *espadilla*, literally "a small sword," from, ultimately, Latin *spatha* (see SPADE[2]).]

spa·dix /spáydiks/ (*plural* **-di·ces** /-di seez/) *n.* a fleshy or succulent plant spike bearing tiny flowers and usually enclosed in a leafy sheath **(spathe)** [Mid-18thC. Via Latin, literally "palm branch torn off with its fruit," from Greek, formed from *span* "to pull."]

spa·ghet·ti /spə géttee/ *n.* **1.** STRING-SHAPED PASTA pasta in the shape of long, thin strings **2.** COOKED STRING-SHAPED PASTA a dish of long thin strings of boiled pasta, usually served with a sauce **3.** ELEC TUBING FOR COVERING BARE WIRE insulating tubing used to cover bare wire [Mid-19thC. From Italian, literally "small strings," formed from *spago* "string," of unknown origin.]

spa·ghet·ti·ni /spàggə teénee/ *n.* a type of pasta that is thinner than spaghetti but thicker than vermicelli [Mid-20thC. From Italian, literally "small spaghetti" (see SPAGHETTI).]

spa·ghet·ti West·ern *n.* a Western made in Europe, usually Spain by an Italian film company, characterized by extreme and melodramatic violence

Spain /spayn/ monarchy in southwestern Europe on the Iberian Peninsula, east of Portugal. Language: Spanish. Currency: peseta. Capital: Madrid. Population: 39,181,114 (1996). Area: 194,897 sq. mi./504,782 sq. km. Official name **Kingdom of Spain**

spake past tense of **speak** (*archaic*)

spall /spawl/ *n.* SMALL CHIP OF STONE OR ORE a small fragment, splinter, or chip of stone or ore ■ *vti.* **(spalled, spall·ing, spalls)** BREAK INTO CHIPS to break up into small chips, flakes, or splinters [15thC. Origin unknown.]

Spain

spal·la·tion /spaw láysh'n/ *n.* **1.** NUCLEAR PHYS **EMISSION OF NUCLEAR PARTICLES BY BOMBARDMENT** a nuclear reaction in which several particles are emitted from the nucleus of an atom after bombardment with high-energy particles or radiation **2.** GEOL, ASTRON **REMOVAL OF ROCK SURFACE BY METEORITE** the removal of the surface layers of a rock by meteorite impact

spal·peen /spáwl peen/ *n. Ireland* **1. RASCAL** somebody who is mischievous and cunning **2. POOR FARM LABORER** an impoverished farm laborer [Late 18thC. From Irish *spailpín.*]

spam /spam/ *n.* **ELECTRONIC JUNK MAIL** an unsolicited often commercial message transmitted through the Internet as a mass mailing to a large number of recipients ■ *vti.* **(spammed, spam·ming, spams) POST MULTIPLE UNWANTED MESSAGES** to post a message many times to a newsgroup, an inappropriate message to multiple newsgroups, or to send an unsolicited message, often an advertisement, to many people [Late 20thC. Origin uncertain: perhaps from a Monty Python sketch in which *Spam* is served whether wanted or not.]

Spam /spam/ *tdmk.* a trademark for canned chopped meat, mainly of chopped pork, that is pressed into a loaf

span[1] /span/ *n.* **1. DISTANCE BETWEEN LIMITS** the distance or expanse between two extremes or limits **2. PERIOD FOR MAINTENANCE OF COGNITIVE FUNCTION** the period of time during which a mental function or act can be maintained ○ *a short attention span* **3.** CIV ENG **DISTANCE BETWEEN BRIDGE SUPPORTS** the extent or space between abutments or supports, e.g., on a bridge or arch, or a portion of the structure that is supported in this way **4.** AIR = **wingspan 5. PERIOD OF TIME** a period of time, especially the lifetime of an individual **6.** MEASURE **OLD MEASUREMENT** an old measurement based on the distance from the end of the thumb to the end of the little finger of a spread hand, approximately nine in./23 cm ■ *vt.* **(spanned, span·ning, spans) 1. EXTEND OVER OR ACROSS SOMETHING** to reach or extend over or across something **2. MEASURE SOMETHING WITH THE HAND** to measure something by or as if by the hand with fingers and thumb fully extended **3. ENCIRCLE SOMETHING WITH THE HANDS** to encircle or cover something with the hands, especially in order to estimate its size [Old English *spann.* Ultimately from a prehistoric Germanic word that also produced German *spannen* "to stretch" (source of English *spanner*).]

span[2] /span/ *vt.* **(spanned, span·ning, spans)** NAUT **TIE SOMETHING** to lash or tie something ■ *n.* **1.** NAUT **STRIP OF ROPE** a strip of rope that has been tied down at one end **2.** EQU **PAIR OF HORSES DRIVEN TOGETHER** a pair of horses or other animals harnessed and driven together [Mid-18thC. From Dutch, formed from *spannen* "to harness."]

span[3] past tense of **spin** (*archaic*)

Span. *abbr.* Spanish

spa·na·ko·pi·ta /spànnə kṓpeetə, -kə peétə/ *n.* a traditional Greek dish of spinach, feta cheese, and seasonings baked in phyllo dough [Mid-20thC. From modern Greek *spanakopēta,* literally "spinach pie."]

span·cel /spánss'l/ *n.* **ROPE USED TO HOBBLE ANIMAL** a rope with a noose used to hobble a horse, cow, or other animal ■ *vt.* **(-celed** *or* **-celled, -cel·ing** *or* **-cel·ling, -cels) HOBBLE ANIMAL WITH SPANCEL** to hobble a horse, cow, or other animal using a spancel [Early 17thC. From Dutch *spansel,* from *spannen* (see SPAN[2]).]

Span·dau /spán dow/ district of Berlin, Germany. It is home to a prison where Rudolf Hess was incarcerated after World War II. Population: 192,895 (1986).

span·dex /spán dèks/ *n.* a synthetic stretch fabric of fiber made from polyurethane [Mid-20thC. Coined from EXPAND.]

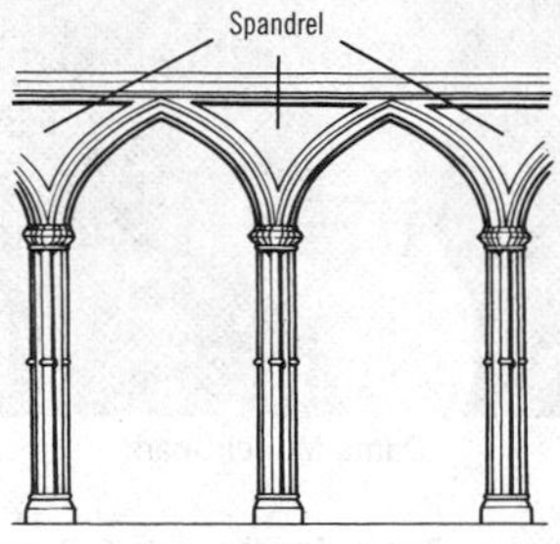

Spandrel

span·drel /spándrəl/, **span·dril** *n.* **1. SPACE BETWEEN ONE ARCH AND ANOTHER** the triangular space between the right or left exterior curve of an arch and the framework of another arch **2. SPACE BETWEEN TWO ARCHES AND CORNICE** the area between two arches and a horizontal cornice above them [15thC. Origin uncertain: perhaps via Anglo-Norman *spaundre* from Old French *espandre* (see SPAWN).]

spang /spang/ *adv.* completely, squarely, or exactly on target or in the middle of something (*informal*) [Mid-19thC. Origin uncertain: perhaps from a dialect verb meaning "to leap," or perhaps an alteration of *span-new.*]

span·gle /spáng g'l/ *n.* **1. SMALL SHINY DECORATION** a small shiny piece of metal or plastic used for decoration on clothing **2. SMALL SPARKLING OBJECT** a small sparkling spot or object ■ *v.* **(-gled, -gling, -gles) 1.** *vt.* **SPRINKLE SOMETHING WITH SPANGLES** to sprinkle or adorn something with spangles **2.** *vi.* **GLITTER WITH SPANGLES** to sparkle or glitter as if adorned with spangles [15thC. Formed from obsolete *spang* "glittering ornament," from Dutch *spange* "clasp."]

Spang·lish /spáng glish/ *n.* a variety of Spanish characterized by numerous borrowings from English. ◊ **Franglais** [Mid-20thC. A blend of SPANISH and ENGLISH.]

Span·iard /spánnyərd/ *n.* somebody who was born or raised in Spain, or who has Spanish citizenship [14thC. Via Old French *Espaignart* from, ultimately, Latin *Hispania* "Spain."]

Spaniel

span·iel /spánnyəl/ *n.* a small or medium-sized dog characterized by a long wavy silky coat, usually short legs, large drooping ears, and feathering on the legs and tail [14thC. Via Old French *espaigneul,* literally "Spanish," from, ultimately, Latin *Hispania* "Spain." From the breed's Spanish origin.]

Span·ish /spánnish/ *n.* LANG **ROMANCE LANGUAGE** one of the Romance languages, spoken in most of Spain and Central and South America ■ *npl.* PEOPLES **PEOPLE OF SPAIN** the people of Spain ■ *adj.* **1. RELATING TO SPAIN** relating to Spain, or its people or culture **2.** LANG **RELATING TO SPANISH LANGUAGE** relating to the Spanish language

Span·ish A·mer·i·ca parts of America that were colonized by the Spanish from the 16th century and where Spanish is still widely spoken. It includes much of Central and South America and some Caribbean islands.

Span·ish A·mer·i·can *n.* **1. U.S. CITIZEN OF SPANISH ORIGIN** a United States citizen of Spanish descent **2. SOMEBODY FROM SPANISH AMERICA** somebody who lives in or comes from Spanish America —**Span·ish-A·mer·i·can** *adj.*

Span·ish bay·o·net (*plural* **Span·ish bay·o·net** *or* **Span·ish bay·o·nets**) *n.* a plant with stiff pointed leaves, white flowers, and a long woody stem. Genus: *Yucca.* [From its swordlike leaves]

Span·ish ce·dar *n.* a tropical American tree with reddish fragrant wood, used for making cigar boxes. Genus: *Cedrela.*

Span·ish chest·nut *n.* = **chestnut** *n.* **1, chestnut** *n.* **2**

Span·ish fly *n.* **1.** INSECTS **EUROPEAN BEETLE** a green European blister beetle, used as a source of the stimulant and irritant cantharides. Latin name: *Lytta vesicatoria* and *Cantharis vesicatoria.* **2.** DRUGS **TOXIC PREPARATION USED AS APHRODISIAC** a toxic preparation made from the crushed dried bodies of the Spanish fly, used in the past as an aphrodisiac and to treat skin blisters

Span·ish gui·tar *n.* the classical six-stringed form of guitar

Span·ish In·qui·si·tion *n.* HIST an ecclesiastical tribunal of the Roman Catholic Church established in Spain in 1542, and finally suppressed in 1834, under which large numbers of supposed heretics were tortured and executed

Span·ish mack·er·el *n.* a large fish in the tuna family that is caught for food and sport, and is found along the Atlantic coast of North and South America. Latin name: *Scomberomorous maculatus.*

Span·ish Main /spànnish máyn/ **1.** region of 16th- and 17th-century Spanish America from the isthmus of Panama to the mouth of the Orinoco river **2.** section of the Caribbean Sea crossed by Spanish ships in colonial times

Span·ish moss *n.* a plant of the pineapple family that grows on trees in long drooping matted clusters of grayish-green filaments, from the southeastern United States to tropical South America. Latin name: *Tillandsia usneoides.*

Span·ish nee·dles *npl.* = **beggar's lice** (*takes a singular or plural verb*) [From its spiny fruit]

Span·ish om·e·let *n.* an omelet served with an often spicy sauce of tomato, green pepper, and onion [Because it contains ingredients typical in Spanish cuisine]

Span·ish on·ion *n.* an onion with yellow skin and a mild flavor. Latin name: *Allium fistulosum.*

Span·ish pa·pri·ka *n.* a fairly mild but spicy food seasoning made from red peppers

Span·ish rice *n.* rice cooked with onion, green pepper, tomato, and seasonings

Span·ish Sa·ha·ra former name for **Western Sahara**

spank[1] /spangk/ *vt.* **(spanked, spank·ing, spanks) SLAP THE BUTTOCKS** to strike somebody, usually on the buttocks with the open hand in punishment ■ *n.* **OPEN-HANDED SLAP** an open-handed slap on the buttocks [Early 18thC. Origin uncertain: probably an imitation of the sound.]

spank[2] /spangk/ *vi.* to move briskly, spiritedly, or smartly [Early 19thC. Origin uncertain: probably a back-formation from SPANKING.]

spank·er /spángkər/ *n.* the fore-and-aft sail on the sternmost mast of a square-rigged ship [Mid-17thC. Origin uncertain: perhaps formed from SPANK[2].]

spank·ing[1] /spángking/ *n.* a beating with the flat of the hand on somebody's buttocks, given as punishment

spank·ing[2] /spángking/ *adj.* **1. EXCEPTIONAL** with an unusual quality that makes something exceptional or remarkable of its kind **2. BRISK** lively, or moving briskly, especially a breeze ■ *adv.* **VERY** extremely or very [Mid-17thC. Origin uncertain: perhaps from a Scandinavian word.]

span·ner /spánnər/ *n.* **1.** *U.K.* = **wrench** *n.* **1 2. WRENCH WITH HOOK ON HEAD** a wrench with a hook or pin at one or both ends of the head for engaging corresponding notches or holes on the object to be turned [Mid-17thC. From German, formed from *spannen* (see SPAN[1]).]

span·worm /spán wùrm/ *n.* = **inchworm**

spar[1] /spaar/ *n.* **1.** NAUT **STOUT POLE SUPPORTING RIGGING** a stout pole used to support rigging on a ship **2.** AIR **LATERAL SUPPORT OF PLANE'S WING** one of the principal lateral members supporting the wing of an airplane **3.** MECH ENG **METAL POLE** a metal pole that is part of a machine for lifting or moving heavy objects ■ *vt.* **PROVIDE WITH SPARS** to provide something with spars [14thC. Origin uncertain: probably from Old French *esparre* or Old Norse *sperra.*]

spar[2] /spaar/ *vi.* **(sparred, spar·ring, spars) 1.** BOXING **TO BOX** to box, especially to fake a blow in order to draw an opponent or create an opening **2.** BOXING **USE LIGHT BLOWS** to engage in a practice or exhibition bout of boxing or martial arts using light blows **3. FIGHT USING FEET AND SPURS** to fight using the feet and spurs to strike an opponent (*refers to gamecocks*) **4. ARGUE** to engage in argument ■ *n.* BOXING **1. PRACTICE BOUT** a practice or exhibition bout of boxing **2. PARTICULAR MOTION IN BOXING** a motion in boxing for attack or defense [Late 16thC. Origin uncertain: perhaps an alteration of SPUR, or perhaps via Old French *esparer* "to kick" from, ultimately, Latin *parare* "to make ready."]

spar[3] /spaar/ *n.* a light-colored lustrous nonmetallic flaky mineral that cleaves easily, e.g., feldspar [Late 16thC. From Low German.]

SPAR /spaar/, **Spar** *n.* HIST, MIL a member of the woman's branch of the U.S. Coast Guard during World War II. The unit was disbanded in 1946.

spare /spair/ *v.* **(spared, spar·ing, spares) 1.** *vt.* **REFRAIN FROM HARMING SOMEBODY** to refrain from killing, punishing, or harming somebody **2.** *vt.* **TREAT SOMEBODY LENIENTLY** to treat leniently or refrain from treating somebody harshly **3.** *vt.* **SAVE SOMEBODY FROM DOING SOMETHING** to save or relieve somebody from the effort or trouble of doing something **4.** *vt.* **WITHHOLD SOMETHING** to withhold or avoid something **5.** *vt.* **USE SOMETHING FRUGALLY** to use or dispense something frugally **6.** *vt.* **AFFORD SOMETHING** to give up or be able to contribute something from one's resources, especially without inconvenience ○ *I can't spare any time to exercise.* **7.** *vt.* **REFRAIN FROM USING SOMETHING** to refrain from using something **8.** *vi.* **BE FRUGAL** to be frugal and thrifty (*archaic*) ■ *adj.* **1. KEPT IN RESERVE** kept in reserve for emergency use **2. SUPERFLUOUS** more than what is needed **3. LEAN** with a muscular physique and no excess fat **4. SCANTY** lacking in quantity or extent ■ *n.* **1. SOMETHING EXTRA** something extra that is kept in reserve **2. KNOCKING DOWN PINS IN TWO TRIES** in bowling, an instance of knocking down all the pins in two attempts **3. BOWLING SCORE** a score made in bowling by using two rolls to knock down all ten pins [Old English *sparian*. Ultimately from a prehistoric Germanic word that also produced German *sparen* "to save."] —**spar·er** *n.* —**spare·ly** *adv.* —**spare·ness** *n.* ◇ **to spare** more than what is needed

spare·rib /spáir rìb/ *n.* a rib of pork from which most of the meat has been removed, usually cooked in a barbecue or Chinese sauce [Late 16thC. By folk etymology from Low German *ribbesper* "pickled pork ribs roasted on a spit," by association with SPARE.]

spare tire *n.* **1.** AUTOMOT **EXTRA TIRE** an extra tire, mounted somewhere on a motor vehicle and carried in case of a flat tire **2. EXTRA FLESH** a roll of extra flesh around somebody's waist (*informal*)

spar·id /spárrəd/ (*plural* **-id** *or* **-ids**) *n.* a warm-water marine fish with a compressed body, large head, and sharp teeth. Porgies and breams are sparids. Family: Sparidae. [Late 20thC. Via modern Latin *Sparidae*, family name, from, ultimately, Greek *sparos* "sea bream."]

spar·ing /spáiring/ *adj.* **1. FRUGAL** showing careful restraint in the use of resources **2. SCANTY** limited or restricted in quantity **3. MERCIFUL** inclined to be lenient or merciful

spark[1] /spaark/ *n.* **1. FIERY PARTICLE** a small piece of a burning substance thrown off in combustion or produced in friction **2.** ELEC **ELECTRIC DISCHARGE** a quick bright discharge of electricity between two conductors **3. SOMETHING THAT ACTIVATES** a factor or device that sets off or acts as a stimulant, inspiration, or catalyst **4. SOMETHING CAPABLE OF DEVELOPMENT** a latent trace of something capable of development **5. sparks RADIO OPERATOR** the radio operator on a ship or aircraft (*informal*) (*takes a singular verb*) ■ *v.* **(sparked, spark·ing, sparks) 1.** *vi.* **THROW OFF SPARKS** to throw off sparks **2.** *vi.* ELEC **PRODUCE SPARKS** to have an electric ignition working properly so that it generates sparks **3.** *vt.* **STIMULATE OR INCITE SOMETHING** to stimulate or initiate a burst of activity [Old English *spærca*. Origin unknown.]

spark[2] /spaark/ *n.* **1. DANDY** a vain young man, especially one concerned with fashion and appearance (*archaic*) **2. BOYFRIEND** a male who courts a woman (*dated informal*) ■ *vti.* **(sparked, spark·ing, sparks) WOO** to try to persuade somebody to become romantically or sexually involved (*archaic*) [Early 16thC. Origin uncertain: probably from SPARK[1].]

Dame Muriel Spark

Spark /spaark/, **Dame Muriel** (*b.* 1918) British writer. She is best known for her novels, including *Memento Mori* (1959) and *The Prime of Miss Jean Brodie* (1961). Full name **Dame Muriel Sarah Spark**

spark cham·ber *n.* a device for tracking the path of a subatomic particle, consisting of charged plates that cause the particle to ionize the gas present and create sparks

spark coil *n.* the induction coil that produces the spark discharge to start combustion in an internal combustion engine

spark e·ro·sion *n.* a process for shaping metal, similar to conventional machining but using an electric arc from a moving electrode to remove metal

spark gap *n.* a space between two electrodes across which a discharge of electricity occurs, e.g., the gap between electrodes of a spark plug in an internal combustion engine

spark·ing plug *n.* U.K. = **spark plug** *n.* 1

spar·kle /spaárk'l/ *v.* **(-kled, -kling, -kles) 1.** *vi.* **THROW OFF SPARKS** to throw off sparks **2.** *vti.* **GLITTER** to give off or reflect light in brilliant, glittering flashes, or make something do this **3.** *vi.* **PERFORM VIVACIOUSLY** to perform brilliantly or be vivacious, witty, or enthusiastic **4.** *vi.* BEVERAGES **EFFERVESCE** to effervesce, especially a wine or other drink ■ *n.* **1. SHINING PARTICLE** a little spark or shining particle **2. ANIMATION** lively or brilliant animation and vivacity **3.** BEVERAGES **EFFERVESCENCE** effervescence in wine and other drinks [12thC. Formed from SPARK[1].] —**spark·ly** *adj.*

spar·kle·ber·ry /spaárk'l bèrree/ (*plural* **-ries**) *n.* = **farkleberry** [By folk etymology from FARKLEBERRY]

spar·kler /spaárklər/ *n.* **1. HANDHELD FIREWORK** a handheld firework that throws off sparks as it burns **2. SPARKLING GEM** a diamond or other sparkling gem (*informal*)

spar·kling wa·ter *n.* water charged with carbon dioxide to make it effervescent

spar·kling wine *n.* wine that is made effervescent naturally through a second fermentation or artificially through the introduction of carbon dioxide

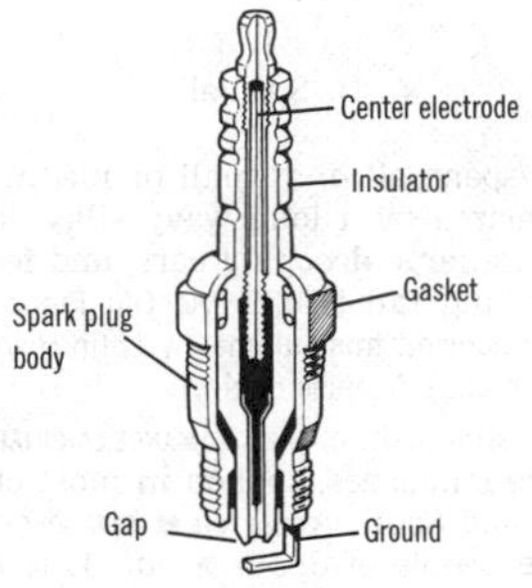

Spark plug

spark plug *n.* **1. DEVICE THAT IGNITES FUEL IN ENGINE** a device that ignites the fuel mixture in the cylinder in an internal-combustion engine by emitting a spark **2. SOMEBODY WHO ANIMATES** somebody who inspires enthusiasm for a project or task (*informal*)

spark trans·mit·ter *n.* an obsolete form of radio transmitter that used power generated from the discharge of a condenser across a spark gap

spark·y /spaárkee/ **(-i·er, -i·est)** *adj.* very lively and enthusiastic

spar·ling /spaárling/ (*plural* **-lings** *or* **-ling**) *n.* a herring that has not yet matured [14thC. From Old French *esperlinge*, of Germanic origin.]

spar·ring part·ner *n.* **1.** BOXING **SOMEBODY WHO SPARS WITH A BOXER** somebody who spars with a boxer to help in training **2. DEBATING PARTNER** somebody who is regularly involved in debates or arguments with somebody else

spar·row /spárrō/ *n.* **1. SMALL BROWNISH SONGBIRD** a small dull-colored songbird with a short stout bill for cracking seeds. Families: Passeridae and Emberizidae. **2. FINCH RESEMBLING SPARROW** a finch that resembles the true sparrow [Old English *spearwa*. Ultimately from a prehistoric Germanic word.]

spar·row·grass /spárrō gràss/ *n.* asparagus (*regional*) [Mid-17thC. By folk etymology from ASPARAGUS.]

spar·row hawk *n.* **1. N. AMERICAN KESTREL** a kestrel native to North America. Latin name: *Falco sparverius*. **2. EUROPEAN AND ASIAN HAWK** a small hawk of Europe and Asia that has short broad wings, a long tail, a dark gray to blackish back, and preys on smaller birds. Latin name: *Accipiter nisus*.

spar·ry /spaáree/ *adj.* relating to or resembling a mineral spar

sparse /spaarss/ *adj.* thinly spread, or occurring with many spaces in between [Early 18thC. From Latin *sparsus*, the past participle of *spargere* "to scatter" (source of English *aspersion* and *sparge*).]

Spar·ta·cist /spaártəssist/ *n.* a member of a German revolutionary group organized in 1918 and promoting an extreme socialistic agenda [Early 20thC. From German *Spartakist*, from *Spartakus* "Spartacus," adopted as pen name by the German socialist leader Karl Liebknecht.]

Spar·ta·cus /spaártəkəss/ (*d.* 71 B.C.) Roman enslaved laborer and rebel leader. He led an uprising that defeated several Roman armies before he was killed in battle against the Roman commander Crassus.

Spar·tan /spaárt'n/ *n.* **1.** PEOPLES **NATIVE OF SPARTA** a native or inhabitant of ancient Sparta **2. SOMEBODY WITH STRONG CHARACTER** somebody who has a strong character, marked by self-discipline, courage, and self-restraint ■ *adj.* **1.** HIST, GEOG **RELATING TO ANCIENT SPARTA** relating to the ancient Greek city of Sparta, its citizens, or its culture **2. MARKED BY DISCIPLINE AND AUSTERITY** marked by stern discipline, frugality, simplicity, or courage —**Spar·tan·ism** *n.*

Spar·tan·burg /spaártənbèrg/ city in northwestern South Carolina, in the foothills of the Blue Ridge Mountains, northeast of Greenville. Population: 42,136 (1996).

spar·te·ine /spaártə èen, -ee ìn/ *n.* a bitter thick poisonous liquid alkaloid obtained from the Scotch broom and used in medicine. Formula: $C_{15}H_{26}N_2$. [Mid-19thC. Formed from modern Latin *Spartium*, broom genus, from, ultimately, Greek *sparton* "esparto."]

spar var·nish *n.* a durable waterproof varnish for use on exterior wooden surfaces

spasm /spázsəm/ *n.* **1. INVOLUNTARY MUSCLE CONTRACTION** an involuntary sudden muscle contraction **2. SUDDEN BURST OF ACTIVITY** a sudden brief emotion, sensation, or action ○ *a spasm of pain* [14thC. Via French and Latin from Greek *spasmos*, from *span* "to pull."]

spas·mod·ic /spaz móddik/ *adj.* **1. AFFECTED BY SPASMS** affected or characterized by spasms **2. RESEMBLING SPASM** resembling a spasm in sudden brief intensity **3. INTERMITTENT** occurring at uneven intervals **4. EXCITABLE** prone to sudden outbursts of emotion [Late 17thC. Via modern Latin *spasmodicus* from Greek *spasmōdēs*, from *spasmos* (see SPASM).] —**spas·mod·i·cal·ly** *adv.*

spas·mo·lyt·ic /spàzmə líttik/ *n.*, *adj.* = **antispasmodic**

spas·tic /spástik/ *adj.* **1. AFFECTED BY SPASMS** relating to or affected by spasms **2. OFFENSIVE TERM** lacking physical coordination or the ability to perform competently (*slang offensive*) ■ *n.* **1. OFFENSIVE TERM** a highly offensive term referring to somebody affected by cerebral palsy (*dated insult*) **2. OFFENSIVE TERM** an offensive term that deliberately insults somebody's coordination or competence (*slang insult*) [Mid-18thC. Via Latin from Greek *spastikos*, from *span* (see SPASM).] —**spas·ti·cal·ly** *adv.*

spas·tic co·lon *n.* = **irritable bowel syndrome**

spat[1] /spat/ *n.* **1. PETTY QUARREL** a brief quarrel usually concerning petty matters **2. SLAP** a light blow or slap (*archaic*) 3. **SOUND OF RAINDROPS FALLING** the sound of raindrops falling ■ *v.* (**spat·ted, spat·ting, spats**) 1. *vi.* **QUARREL PETTILY** to engage in a petty, brief quarrel 2. *vt.* **SLAP SOMEBODY OR SOMETHING** to strike somebody or something with light force (*archaic*) 3. *vi.* **MAKE SPATTERING SOUND** to make the sound of rain falling in large spattering drops [Early 19thC. Origin unknown.]

spat² past tense, past participle of **spit**

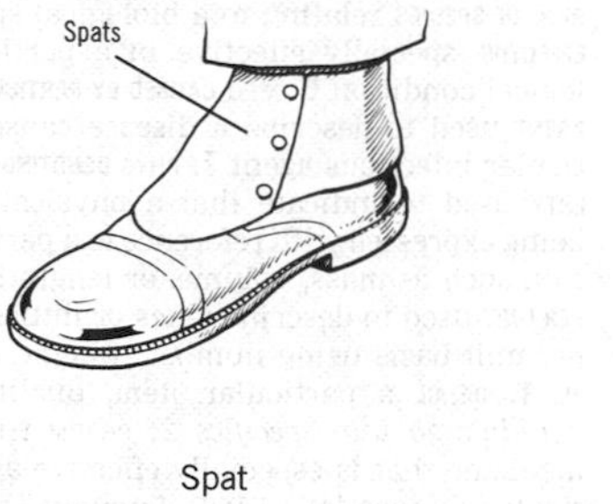

Spat

spat³ /spat/ *n.* a short cloth or leather gaiter, popular in the late 19th and early 20th centuries, worn over a shoe to cover the instep and the ankle [Early 19thC. Shortening of SPATTERDASH.]

spat⁴ /spat/ *n.* an immature bivalve mollusk, e.g., an oyster [Mid-17thC. From Anglo-Norman, of unknown origin.]

spatch·cock /spách kòk/ *n.* COOK **SPLIT BIRD FOR COOKING** a chicken or other fowl that is split, dressed, and broiled or roasted on a spit ■ *vt.* (**-cocked, -cock·ing, -cocks**) 1. COOK **PREPARE FOWL FOR ROASTING** to prepare a chicken or other fowl for roasting by splitting it open 2. **INSERT SOMETHING AWKWARDLY** to introduce or interpose something into a piece of writing, especially in a forced or inappropriate way [Late 18thC. Origin uncertain: perhaps an alteration of *spitchcock* "prepared eel," of unknown origin.]

spate /spayt/ *n.* 1. **FLOOD** a flood, or a river overflowing its banks ○ *After the heavy rain the river was in spate.* 2. **OUTBURST** a sudden strong outburst 3. **LARGE QUANTITY** a large quantity of something [15thC. Origin uncertain: perhaps via Old French *espoit* from Dutch *spuiten* "to flood."]

spathe /spayth/ (*plural* **spathes**) *n.* a leafy sheath (**bract**) that encloses the cluster of flowers (**spadix**) in some plants, e.g., the arum, and sometimes resembles a petal [Late 18thC. Via Latin *spatha* from Greek *spathē* (see SPADE¹).] —**spathed** /spaythd/ *adj.*

spath·ic /spáthik/ *adj.* resembling mineral spar, especially in being easy to split [Late 18thC. Formed from German *Spat(h)* "spar."]

spath·u·late /spáttyŏolət/ *n. U.K.* = **spatulate**

spa·tial, **spa·cial** *adj.* relating to, occupying, or happening in space [Mid-19thC. Formed from Latin *spatium* (see SPACE).] —**spa·ti·al·i·ty** /spàyshee állətee/ *n.* —**spa·tial·ly** /spásh'lee/ *adv.*

spa·ti·o·tem·po·ral /spàyshee ō témpərəl, -témprəl/ *adj.* 1. **RELATING TO SPACE AND TIME** relating to, existing in, or having the qualities of both space and time 2. **RELATING TO SPACE-TIME** relating to a four-dimensional space-time system [Early 20thC. Coined from Latin *spatium* (see SPACE) + TEMPORAL.] —**spa·ti·o·tem·po·ral·ly** *adv.*

spät·le·se /shpáyt làyzə/ (*plural* **-sen** /-làyz'n/ *or* **-ses**) *n.* a grade of high-quality German table wine made from late-picked grapes and typically medium sweet [Early 20thC. From German, literally "late vintage."]

spat·ter /spáttər/ *v.* (**-tered, -ter·ing, -ters**) 1. *vti.* **COME OUT IN DROPS** to expel something or come out in small scattered drops or splashes 2. *vt.* **SPLASH WITH LIQUID** to splash something with or as if with a liquid, especially if the liquid leaves a mark or residue 3. *vti.* **SCATTER IN DROPLETS** to splash or scatter in droplets 4. *vt.* **DEFAME** to defame or sully somebody's character ■ *n.* 1. **ACT OF SPATTERING** an act of spattering or being spattered 2. **SPATTERING SOUND** the sound of spattering 3. **DROPLET OF SOMETHING SPATTERED** a droplet or splash of something spattered 4. **SMALL AMOUNT** a small amount of something [Mid-16thC. Origin uncertain: perhaps an imitation of the sound.]

spat·ter·dock /spáttər dòk/ *n.* a North American water lily with globe-shaped yellow flowers. Latin name: *Nuphar advena.*

spat·u·la /spáchələ/ *n.* 1. COOK **FLAT UTENSIL WITH HANDLE** a flat flexible metal, plastic, or rubber utensil with a handle, used to scoop, lift, spread, or mix 2. MED **TONGUE DEPRESSOR** a flat wooden stick used to depress the tongue when the mouth or throat is being examined [Early 16thC. Via Latin, literally "a small broadsword," from, ultimately, Greek *spathē* (see SPADE¹).] —**spat·u·lar** *adj.*

spat·u·late /spáchələt/ *adj.* shaped like a spatula, with a narrow tapering base and a broad rounded tip

spav·in /spávvin/ *n.* an ailment of horses involving a swelling or enlargement of the hock joint [15thC. From Old French *espavin*, of uncertain origin: perhaps ultimately from a prehistoric Germanic word.]

spav·ined /spávvind/ *adj.* 1. **WITH SPAVIN** having or being lame with a spavin 2. **OLD AND WORN OUT** lacking health, vigor, and strength ○ *a spavined horse*

spawn /spawn/ *n.* 1. BIOL **EGG MASS** a mass of eggs of a fish, amphibian, or other aquatic animal 2. **OFFSPRING** progeny or offspring, especially if numerous 3. FUNGI **MYCELIUM** a mass of microscopic fungal threads (**mycelium**), especially when prepared on a growth medium for starting a new culture of the fungus 4. **SEED** a seed, germ, or the source of something ■ *v.* (**spawned, spawn·ing, spawns**) 1. *vi.* BIOL **DEPOSIT EGGS** to produce and deposit eggs 2. *vi.* **PRODUCE YOUNG** to produce offspring in large numbers 3. *vt.* **GIVE RISE TO SOMETHING** to generate or give rise to something 4. *vt.* **START NEW FUNGUS CULTURE** to start a new culture of a fungus using spawn [15thC. Via Anglo-Norman *espaundre* "to shed" and Old French *espandre* from Latin *expandere* "to spread out" (source of English *expand*).] —**spawn·er** *n.*

spay /spay/ (**spayed, spay·ing, spays**) *vt.* VET to surgically remove an animal's ovaries and adjacent parts of the uterus [15thC. From Old French *espeer*, literally "to cut with a sword," from *espee* "sword" (source of English *épée*), from, ultimately, Greek *spathē* (see SPADE¹).]

spa·za /spázə/ *n. S Africa* a small informal shop, often run from a home in a township

SPCA *n., abbr.* Society for the Prevention of Cruelty to Animals

SPCC *n., abbr.* Society for the Prevention of Cruelty to Children

speak /speek/ (**spoke** /spōk/, **spo·ken** /spṓkən/, **speak·ing, speaks**) *v.* 1. *vti.* **TALK** to utter words or articulate sounds with the voice 2. *vi.* **EXPRESS THOUGHTS AND OPINIONS** to communicate thoughts, opinions, or feelings by uttering with the voice 3. *vt.* **BE ABLE TO USE LANGUAGE** to know and be able to converse in a language 4. *vi.* **BE ON GOOD TERMS** to be on good and friendly terms with somebody ○ *It's sad, but they're not speaking anymore.* 5. *vi.* **DELIVER SPEECH TO AUDIENCE** to make a speech or deliver an address 6. *vti.* **EXPRESS IN WRITING** to express something or make a statement in writing 7. *vti.* **COMMUNICATE NONVERBALLY** to communicate by other than verbal means ○ *Actions speak louder than words.* 8. *vi.* **MAKE CHARACTERISTIC SOUND** to produce or make a sound typical of its kind ○ *The cannon spoke.* 9. *vt.* NAUT **COMMUNICATE WITH ANOTHER SEA-GOING VESSEL** to communicate with another vessel at sea 10. *vt.* **INDICATE SOMETHING** to hint at or indicate something ○ *Her poise spoke of self-esteem.* [Old English *specan, sprecan*. Ultimately from an Indo-European word that also produced German *sprechen* "to speak."] —**speak·a·ble** *adj.* ◇ **so to speak** used to indicate that you are expressing something in an unusual way, e.g., that you are being euphemistic ◇ **speak for itself** have an obvious meaning ◇ **to speak of** significant or worth mentioning

speak for *vt.* to act as an advocate for or speak on behalf of

speak out *vi.* 1. **TALK LOUDLY** to talk loudly or loudly enough to be heard 2. **SPEAK FRANKLY** to express opinions boldly, freely, and frankly

speak to *vt.* to address a particular issue in a speech or discussion (*formal*) ○ *a speech that spoke to the needs of international students*

speak up *vi.* 1. **TALK LOUDLY** to talk loudly enough to be heard 2. **TALK FRANKLY** to express opinions freely and frankly

speak·eas·y /spe͞ek e͞ezee/ (*plural* **-ies**) *n.* a place where alcoholic beverages are sold and consumed illegally, especially during Prohibition in the United States (*dated slang*) [Late 19thC. From the custom of speaking softly so as not to attract attention.]

speak·er /spe͞ekər/ *n.* 1. **SOMEBODY WHO SPEAKS** a person who speaks 2. **SOMEBODY WHO MAKES A SPEECH** somebody who makes a speech or gives a lecture or address 3. **SPOKESPERSON** somebody who represents or speaks for a group 4. = **loudspeaker**

Speak·er *n.* the presiding officer of a legislative body, e.g., the U.S. or the Australian House of Representatives or the British House of Commons

speak·er·phone /spe͞ekər fōn/ *n.* a telephone equipped with a loudspeaker and microphone

speak·ing /spe͞eking/ *adj.* 1. **INVOLVING SPEECH** involving speech or speaking 2. **ELOQUENT** capable of communicating in an eloquent or impressive way 3. **APPARENTLY REAL** resembling a real person or object ○ *the speaking image of her aunt* 4. **ABLE TO USE SPECIFIED LANGUAGE** able to speak a particular language (*usually used in combination*) ○ *French-speaking students*

speak·ing in tongues *n.* the making of utterances that are not recognizable as any known language and have no formal linguistic content. It is a normal aspect of worship in many Pentecostal and charismatic churches. ◊ **gift of tongues**

speak·ing tube *n.* a pipe connecting different parts of something, e.g., a ship or building, and through which conversation can be conducted

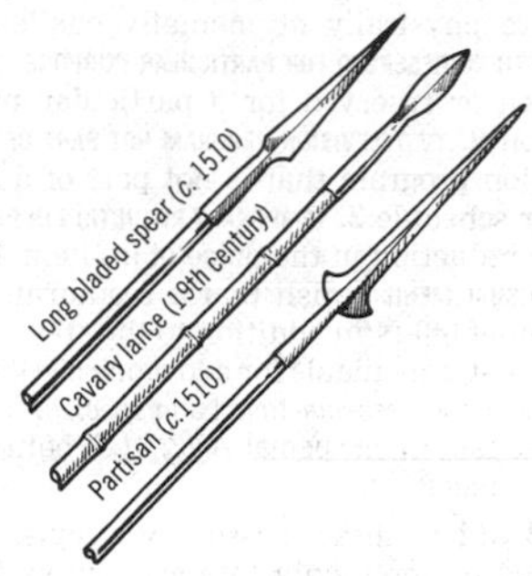

Spear

spear¹ /speer/ *n.* 1. **LONG-HANDLED WEAPON WITH BLADE** a weapon for throwing or thrusting that has a long handle and a blade or head with a sharpened point 2. **WEAPON FOR SPEARING FISH** a weapon with a sharp point and barbs used for catching fish by piercing them 3. = **spearman** ■ *v.* (**speared, spear·ing, spears**) 1. *vti.* **PIERCE SOMETHING WITH SPEAR** to stab, strike, pierce, or take somebody or something with or as though using a spear 2. *vt.* SPORTS **CATCH BALL WITH THRUST OF ARM** to catch a ball with an abrupt thrust of the arm [Old English *spere*. Ultimately from a prehistoric Germanic word that also produced German *Speer* "spear" and is.] —**spear·er** *n.*

spear² /speer/ *n.* BOT **YOUNG SHOOT** a young blade, shoot, or stalk of a plant such as asparagus or grass ■ *vi.* (**speared, spear·ing, spears**) **SEND UP SPEAR** to bear a spear or send one up through the soil [15thC. Alteration of SPIRE.]

spear car·ri·er *n.* 1. **MINOR MEMBER OF CAST** a minor member of a cast in a play or opera 2. **SOMEBODY WHOSE CONTRIBUTIONS ARE UNIMPORTANT** somebody who contributes little of importance or relevance (*informal*)

spear·fish /spe͞er fish/ *n.* (*plural* **-fish** *or* **-fish·es**) **LARGE MARINE FISH WITH SPEAR-SHAPED PROJECTION** a large marine billfish that is related to the marlin and sailfish and has a very long, pointed upper jaw. Genus: *Tetrapturus.* ■ *vi.* (**-fished, -fish·ing, -fish·es**) **FISH WITH SPEAR** to fish using a spear or spear gun

spear gun *n.* a gun designed to shoot a barbed spear underwater, used to catch fish

spear·head /spe͞er hèd/ *n.* 1. ARMS **POINTED HEAD OF SPEAR** the pointed head of a spear 2. MIL **LEADING FORCES IN MILITARY ATTACK** the leading forces in a military attack 3. **DRIVING FORCE IN EVENT** the leading or driving element or force in an undertaking ■ *vt.* (**-head·ed, -head·ing, -heads**) **ACT AS LEADER OF EVENT** to act as the leader or driving force of a military attack, or any event or undertaking

spear·man /spe͞ermən/ (*plural* **-men** /-mən/) *n.* a soldier or other person who is armed with a spear

spear·mint /spe͞er mìnt/ (*plural* **-mint** *or* **-mints**) *n.* a common mint, the leaves and essential oil of which are used for flavoring. Latin name: *Mentha* *spicata.* [Mid-16thC. From the stem's resemblance to a spear.]

spear·wort /spe͡er wùrt, -wàwrt/ (*plural* **-wort** *or* **-worts**) *n.* a buttercup with spear-shaped leaves and small yellow flowers that grows in Europe, Asia, and the eastern United States [Old English]

spec /spek/ *n.* DETAILED DESCRIPTION a detailed description of a particular thing, especially one detailed enough to provide somebody with the information needed to make that thing (*informal*) ■ *vt.* (**spec'd** *or* **specced, spec'·ing** *or* **spec·cing, specs**) WRITE SPECIFICATIONS FOR SOMETHING to write specifications for something (*informal*) [Late 18thC. Shortening.] ◇ **on spec 1.** *U.K.* with a chance of achieving something but no certainty of it (*informal*) **2.** without being sure of profit or being paid (*informal*)

spec. *abbr.* **1.** special **2.** specialist **3.** specification

spe·cial /spésh'l/ *adj.* **1.** UNUSUAL OR SUPERIOR distinct, different, unusual, or superior in comparison to others of the same kind **2.** PRIMARY of the greatest importance **3.** HELD IN ESTEEM regarded with particular esteem or affection **4.** RESERVED unique to or reserved for a specific person or thing **5.** MADE FOR PARTICULAR PURPOSE made or used for a particular purpose or occasion **6.** ARRANGED FOR SPECIFIC PURPOSE planned for a specific occasion **7.** ADDITIONAL in addition to or more than is usual **8.** RELATING TO EDUCATING SPECIAL-NEEDS CHILDREN designed or intended for educating children who are physically or mentally challenged ■ *n.* **1.** SOMETHING RESERVED FOR PARTICULAR PURPOSE something designed or reserved for a particular purpose or occasion **2.** TV TELEVISION PROGRAM NOT PART OF SCHEDULE a television program that is not part of a network's regular schedule **3.** TEMPORARY REDUCTION IN PRICE a temporary reduction in the price of an item **4.** FOOD DISH NOT ON USUAL MENU a dish that a restaurant or other food outlet offers in addition to the standard menu, or one that is available for a low price [12thC. Directly or via Old French *especial* from Latin *specialis*, from *species* (see SPECIES).] ◇ **on special** *ANZ, U.S.* being sold at a reduced price

spe·cial act *n.* an act passed by a legislative body intended to apply only to a specific individual or situation

Spe·cial Air Ser·vice *n.* full form of **SAS**

spe·cial as·sess·ment *n.* a specific local tax levied on private property to meet the cost of a public improvement that will result in an increase in the value of the property

spe·cial court-mar·tial *n.* a court-martial held to try offenses of an intermediate kind and presided over by three officers

spe·cial de·liv·er·y *n.* the delivery of mail more quickly than or outside normal delivery times for an extra fee

spe·cial draw·ing rights *n.* a method of settling international debts through the International Monetary Fund in order to stabilize exchange rates

spe·cial ed·u·ca·tion *n.* teaching modified to serve students with special educational needs

spe·cial ef·fects *npl.* extraordinary visual effects in a motion picture or television program achieved by technical means, either optically, digitally, or mechanically

Spe·cial Forc·es *npl.* a branch of the U.S. Army trained in guerrilla warfare and counterinsurgency tactics

spe·cial hand·ling *n.* the handling of fourth-class and parcel post mail as first-class mail for an additional fee

spe·cial-in·ter·est group *n.* a group seeking to influence government policy in favor of a particular interest or issue

spe·cial·ism /spésha lìzzəm/ *n.* **1.** CONCENTRATION IN FIELD OF STUDY concentration in a particular field of study ○ *There is a great deal of specialism in their education system.* **2.** = **specialty** *n.* 1

spe·cial·ist /spéshələst/ *n.* **1.** SOMEBODY SPECIALIZING IN PARTICULAR INTEREST somebody who is particularly interested in or good at an occupation, interest, or field of study **2.** MED TYPE OF PHYSICIAN a medical doctor who practices in a certain field, e.g., surgery, dermatology, or oncology **3.** MIL ENLISTED RANK IN U.S. ARMY an enlisted rank in the U.S. Army from corporal to sergeant first class, and denoting special technical skills —**spe·cial·is·tic** /spèshə lístik/ *adj.*

spe·ci·al·i·ty /spèshee állətee/ (*plural* **-ties**) *n.* an unusual, distinctive, or superior mark or quality

spe·cial·i·za·tion /spèshələ záysh'n/ *n.* **1.** ACT OF BECOMING SPECIALIZED the act or process of becoming specialized **2.** = **specialty** *n.* 1 **3.** BIOL ADAPTATION OF ORGANISM the adaptation of an organism or a part of an organism to a particular function or condition in response to environmental conditions **4.** BIOL ADAPTED BODY PART an organism or a part of an organism that has been adapted to a particular function or condition

spe·cial·ize /spéshə līz/ (**-ized, -iz·ing, -iz·es**) *v.* **1.** *vt.* SPECIFY SOMETHING to specify or make specific mention of something **2.** *vt.* ADAPT TO PARTICULAR PURPOSE to adapt something to suit a specific purpose **3.** *vi.* DEVOTE TIME TO PARTICULAR ACTIVITY to devote time exclusively to a particular interest, skill, or field of study **4.** *vi.* BECOME ADAPTED to become adapted to a particular function or condition

spe·cial ju·ry *n.* = **blue-ribbon jury**

special needs *npl.* the particular requirements, especially in education, that some people have because of physical challenges or learning difficulties

Spe·cial O·lym·pics *n.* an international athletic competition for athletes who are physically or mentally challenged (*takes a singular or plural verb*)

spe·cial plead·ing *n.* **1.** LAW PLEADING INTRODUCING NEW MATTER pleading that introduces new or special matter and that avoids allegations of matter pleaded by the opposite side, instead of direct denial of those allegations **2.** ARGUMENT PRESENTING ONLY ONE ASPECT an argument that presents only one aspect of an issue and avoids any unfavorable aspects

spe·cial rel·a·tiv·i·ty *n.* = **relativity** *n.* 1

spe·cial school *n.* a school catering to students who have special educational needs, e.g., because of learning difficulties or physical challenges

spe·cial ses·sion *n.* a session of a legislature, court, or council held in addition to and outside of regularly scheduled sessions

spe·cial team *n.* a group of football players who are on the field to perform only in particular situations, e.g., during a kickoff or punt

special theory of relativity *n.* = **relativity** *n.* 1

spe·cial·ty /spésh'ltee/ (*plural* **-ties**) *n.* **1.** SOMETHING SOMEBODY SPECIALIZES IN a skill, field of study, interest, or activity in which somebody specializes **2.** PRODUCT OF SPECIALIZATION the product or result of a specialization **3.** DISTINCTIVE MARK an unusual, distinctive, or superior mark or quality **4.** LAW LEGAL AGREEMENT UNDER SEAL a legal agreement made under seal

spe·ci·a·tion /spe͡eshee áysh'n, spe͡essee-/ *n.* the evolutionary formation of new biological species, usually by one species that divides into two or more species that are genetically unique [Early 20thC. Formed from SPECIES.] —**spe·ci·ate** /spe͡eshee-t, spe͡essee-t/ *vi.*

spe·cie /spe͡eshee, -ssee/ *n.* money in the form of coins [Mid-16thC. Shortening of Latin *in specie*, literally "in kind," from *species* (see SPECIES).] ◇ **in specie 1.** in the form of coins **2.** in a similar way or kind **3.** LAW in the form specified

spe·cies /spe͡eseez, spe͡esseez/ (*plural* **-cies**) *n.* **1.** BIOL TAXONOMIC GROUP a subdivision of a genus considered as a basic biological classification and containing individuals that resemble one another and that may interbreed **2.** BIOL ORGANISMS IN SPECIES the organisms belonging to a particular species **3.** KIND OR SORT a kind, sort, or variety of something **4.** HUMANKIND human beings or the human race **5.** CHEM ATOM CATEGORY a category of atomic nucleus, ion, molecule, or atom **6.** LOGIC SUBDIVISION OF GENUS a collection of objects or individuals that, on the basis of shared features, form a subdivision of a genus **7.** CHR BREAD AND WINE IN COMMUNION the two elements of the Communion, bread and wine, or their outward form after consecration [14thC. From Latin, "appearance, kind," (source also of English *spice*), formed from *specere* "to look" (source of English *spectator* and *spy*).]

WORD KEY: SYNONYMS

See Synonyms at ***type***.

spe·cies·ism /spe͡eshees ìzzəm, spe͡essees-/ *n.* the belief that the human race is superior to other species, and that exploitation of animals for the advantage of humans is justified

specif. *abbr.* **1.** specific **2.** specifically

spec·i·fi·a·ble /spéssə fī əb'l, spèssə fī əb'l/ *adj.* capable of being explicitly identified ○ *specifiable causes*

spe·cif·ic /spə síffik/ *adj.* **1.** PRECISE particular and detailed, avoiding vagueness ○ *specific instructions* **2.** RELATING TO PARTICULAR THING acting on or relating to a particular thing ○ *the instructions are specific to this task* **3.** DISTINCTIVE with individual qualities that allow a distinction to be made or make a distinction necessary ○ *discussing these specific problems* **4.** BIOL OF SPECIES relating to a biological species **5.** MED EFFECTIVE specially effective in a particular pathological condition **6.** MED CAUSED BY PARTICULAR INFECTIOUS AGENT used to describe a disease caused by a particular infectious agent **7.** PHYS DENOTING PHYSICAL PROPERTY used to indicate that a physical property is being expressed with reference to a particular quantity, such as mass, volume, or length **8.** COMM LEVIED PER UNIT used to describe taxes or duties levied on a per-unit basis using number, weight, or volume ■ *n.* **1.** DETAIL a particular item, quality, or detail ○ *didn't go into specifics* **2.** PHARM EFFECTIVE DRUG a medicine that is especially effective against a particular disease [Mid-17thC. From late Latin *specificus*, literally "making a kind," from Latin *species* "kind" (see SPECIES).] —**spe·cif·i·cal·ly** *adv.* —**spec·i·fic·i·ty** /spèssə físsətee/ *n.*

spec·i·fi·ca·tion /spèssəfə káysh'n/ *n.* **1.** DETAILED DESCRIPTION a detailed description of a particular thing, especially one detailed enough to provide somebody with the information needed to make that thing ○ *a look at the engine specification* **2.** DETAIL an item within a specification ○ *The machine's technical specifications are in Appendix A.* **3.** SPECIFYING the specifying of something **4.** COMM LAW INTELLECTUAL PROPERTY DESCRIPTION a detailed description of intellectual property, as required by law **5.** PUBL TYPOGRAPHICAL INSTRUCTIONS detailed instructions regarding information such as font, point size, and layout that are sent with material to be typeset and printed

spe·cif·ic charge *n.* the ratio of the electric charge of an elementary particle divided by its mass

spe·cif·ic grav·i·ty *n.* = **relative density** (*dated*)

spe·cif·ic heat *n.* the amount of heat needed to raise the temperature of one gram of a substance by one degree, usually measured in joules per kilogram per kelvin

spe·cif·ic heat ca·pac·i·ty *n.* *U.K.* = **specific heat**

spe·cif·ic per·form·ance *n.* LAW a court order compelling somebody to carry out an obligation, often something stated in a contract

spe·cif·ic re·sis·tance *n.* = **resistivity**

spec·i·fy /spéssə fī/ (**-fied, -fy·ing, -fies**) *vt.* **1.** STATE EXPLICITLY to state or identify something in detail or explicitly **2.** STIPULATE to state something or make it a condition ○ *The rules specify that pets cannot be kept here.* **3.** INCLUDE IN SPECIFICATION to include or state something in a specification [13thC. Via French *specifier* or directly from late Latin *specificare*, from *specificus* (see SPECIFIC).] —**spec·i·fi·a·ble** *adj.* —**spec·i·fi·ca·tive** /spéssəfə kaytiv, spə síffə-/ *adj.* —**spec·i·fi·er** /spéssə fī ər/ *n.*

spec·i·men /spéssəmən/ *n.* **1.** REPRESENTATIVE THING something that is representative because it is typical of its kind or of a whole, especially something that serves as an example (*often used before a noun*) ○ *a specimen of the candidate's handwriting* **2.** TYPE OF PERSON somebody who displays or seems to typify certain characteristics (*informal*) ○ *"turning away with disgust from the loathsome specimen of humanity before him"* (Baroness Orczy, *The Scarlet Pimpernel*; 1905) **3.** MED SAMPLE OF BODY MATERIAL a sample, e.g., of urine or blood used for testing and diagnosis **4.** SCI TYPICAL EXAMPLE an organism or one of its parts preserved as a typical example of its classification [Early 17thC. From Latin, where it was formed from *specere* "to look at" (source of English *expect*, *despise*, and *conspicuous*).]

spe·cious /spe͡eshəss/ *adj.* **1.** APPARENTLY TRUE BUT ACTUALLY FALSE appearing to be true but really false **2.** DECEPTIVELY ATTRACTIVE superficially attractive but actually of no real interest or value [14thC. From Latin *speciosus* "good-looking," from *species* "appearance" (see SPECIES). Originally in the meaning of "beautiful"; the modern meaning dates from the 17thC.] —**spe·cious·ly** *adv.* —**spe·cious·ness** *n.*

speck /spek/ *n.* 1. SMALL SPOT a very small mark or stain 2. PARTICLE a tiny particle of something solid ■ *vt.* (**specked, speck·ing, specks**) MARK WITH SPECKS to mark something with specks (*usually passive*) [Old English *specca*, of uncertain origin]

speck·le /spék'l/ *n.* SMALL COLORED SPOT a small spot or mark, often a small irregular patch of contrasting color, e.g., on plumage or an egg shell ■ *vt.* (**-led, -ling, -les**) MARK WITH SPECKLES to mark something with speckles (*usually passive*) [15thC. Origin uncertain: probably literally "little speck."]

speck·led /spék'ld/ *adj.* 1. WITH SMALL SPOTS with a pattern of many small spots or small irregular patches, often of a contrasting color 2. WITH CONTRASTS with parts that contrast distinctly with each other ○ *a speckled career* ○ *speckled shadows*

speck·led trout *n.* = **brook trout**

speck·le in·ter·fe·rom·e·try /-ìntərfeerómmətree/ *n.* a technique for reducing distortions in photographic images of celestial objects caused by atmospheric turbulence. A number of images of very short exposure are combined. The technique can also be used to measure the diameter of some stars.

specs /speks/ *npl.* (*informal*) 1. SPECTACLES eyeglasses 2. SPECIFICATIONS specifications

SPECT *abbr.* single photon emission computed tomography

spec·ta·cle /spéktək'l/ *n.* 1. SOMETHING REMARKABLE THAT CAN BE SEEN an object, phenomenon, or event that is seen or witnessed, especially one that is impressive, unusual, or disturbing 2. LAVISH DISPLAY an impressive performance or display, especially something staged as a form of entertainment 3. UNPLEASANT CENTER OF ATTENTION somebody or something that attracts attention by being unpleasant or ridiculous ○ *You are making a spectacle of yourself.* [14thC. Via French from Latin *spectaculum*, from *spectare* "to watch," from *specere* (see SPECIMEN).]

WORD KEY: ORIGIN

The Latin stem *spect-*, from which ***spectacle*** is derived, is also the source of English *aspect, circumspect, conspectus, expect, inspect, perspective, prospect, respect, retrospect, specter, spectrum,* and *suspect.*

spec·ta·cled /spéktək'ld/ *adj.* 1. WEARING SPECTACLES with eyeglasses on 2. ZOOL WITH MARKINGS LIKE SPECTACLES with markings on the face that encircle the eyes in a way that resembles spectacles

spec·ta·cled bear *n.* a rare South American bear found in the grasslands and forests of the Andes. It is black with white markings around the eyes and is threatened with extinction. Latin name: *Tremarcto ornatus.*

spec·ta·cles /spéktək'lz/ *npl.* a pair of glass or plastic lenses worn in a frame in front of the eyes to help correct imperfect vision [15thC. Plural of SPECTACLE. The word was earlier used for various implements of seeing, including windows and mirrors.]

spec·tac·u·lar /spek tákyələr/ *adj.* 1. VISUALLY IMPRESSIVE impressive or dramatic to look at or watch 2. REMARKABLE remarkably large, great, or speedy ■ *n.* EXTRAVAGANZA a lavish celebration or artistic production —**spec·tac·u·lar·ly** *adv.*

spec·tate /spék tàyt, spèk táyt/ (**-tat·ed, -tat·ing, -tates**) *vi.* to watch rather than participate [Early 18thC. Back-formation from SPECTATOR.]

spec·ta·tor /spék tàytər, spèk táytər/ *n.* 1. SOMEBODY WHO WATCHES somebody who watches or observes, especially somebody who watches an event 2. = **spectator shoe** [Late 16thC. Via French *spectateur* or directly from Latin *spectator*, from *spectare* "to watch" (see SPECTACLE).] —**spec·ta·to·ri·al** /spèktə táwree əl/ *adj.* —**spec·ta·tor·ship** /spék tàytər shìp, spek táytər shìp/ *n.*

spec·ta·tor·i·tis /spèk taytə rítəss, spek tàytə rítəss/ *n.* the tendency to watch leisure activities, whether live or on television, in preference to actively participating in them [Formed from SPECTATOR]

spec·ta·tor shoe, **spec·ta·tor** *n.* a shoe, especially one for women, in two contrasting colors of leather

spec·ta·tor sport *n.* a sport that attracts spectators in large numbers

spec·ter /spéktər/, **spec·tre** *n.* 1. GHOST a ghostly presence or apparition 2. UNPLEASANT PROSPECT a threat or prospect of something unpleasant ○ *the specter of my performance review* [Early 17thC. Via French or directly from Latin *spectrum* "image, apparition" (see SPECTRUM).]

spec·ti·no·my·cin /spèktinō míss'n/ *n.* an antibiotic used in the treatment of gonorrhea [Mid-20thC. Formed from modern Latin *spectabilis*, species name, from Latin, "visible," from *spectare* "to watch" (see SPECTACLE), modeled on *actinomycin*.]

spec·tra plural of **spectrum**

spec·tral /spéktrəl/ *adj.* 1. GHOSTLY relating to specters or in the form of a specter 2. OF SPECTRUM produced by a spectrum or relating to a spectrum —**spec·tral·i·ty** /spek trállətee/ *n.* —**spec·tral·ness** /spéktrəlnəss/ *n.* —**spec·tral·ly** /spéktrəlee/ *adv.*

spec·tral class *n.* = **spectral type**

spec·tral line *n.* any of the discrete bands of light in a spectrum associated with a specific wavelength. Characteristic spectral lines are emitted by atoms and molecules and may be used to identify substances.

spec·tral type, **spec·tral class** *n.* ASTRON a classification system for stars based on an analysis of the light they emit. This analysis also gives information on a star's temperature and chemical composition.

spec·tre *n.* = **specter**

spec·trin /spéktrin/ *n.* any of a group of fibrous proteins found especially in the membranes of red blood cells [Mid-20thC. Formed from SPECTER, because the material was first isolated from red blood cells lacking hemoglobin, called "ghosts."]

spectro- *prefix.* spectrum ○ *spectroscope* [From SPECTRUM]

spec·tro·gram /spéktrə gràm/ *n.* a photograph or representation of a spectrum

spec·tro·graph /spéktrə gràf/ *n.* an instrument consisting of a spectrometer and related equipment used to obtain a visual record of a spectrum —**spec·tro·graph·ic** /spèktrə gráffik/ *adj.* —**spec·tro·graph·i·cal·ly** /-gráffiklee/ *adv.* —**spec·trog·ra·phy** /spek tróggrəfee/ *n.*

spec·tro·he·li·o·gram /spèktrō he̅elee ə gràm/ *n.* an image of the sun produced using a narrow wavelength band of the radiation it emits

spec·tro·he·li·o·graph /spèktrō he̅elee ə gràf/ *n.* an instrument used to obtain images of the sun over a narrow band of wavelegths —**spec·tro·he·li·o·graph·ic** /spèktrō he̅elee ə gráffik/ *adj.* —**spec·tro·he·li·og·ra·phy** /spèktrō he̅elee óggrəfee/ *n.*

spec·tro·he·li·o·scope /spèktrō he̅elee ə skōp/ *n.* an instrument that is similar to a spectroheliograph but is used for viewing the sun's spectrum, as distinct from recording it —**spec·tro·he·li·o·scop·ic** /spèktrō he̅elee ə skóppik/ *adj.*

spec·trom·e·ter /spek trómmətər/ *n.* an instrument used to disperse radiant energy or particles into a spectrum and measure certain properties such as wavelength, mass, energy, or index of refraction —**spec·tro·met·ric** /spèktrə méttrik/ *adj.* —**spec·trom·e·try** /spèk trómmətree/ *n.*

spec·tro·pho·tom·e·ter /spèktrōfə tómmətər/ *n.* an instrument used to measure the relative intensities of wavelengths in a spectrum —**spec·tro·pho·to·met·ric** /spèktrō fōtə méttrik/ *adj.* —**spec·tro·pho·to·met·ri·cal·ly** /-méttriklee/ *adv.* —**spec·tro·pho·tom·e·try** /spèktrōfə tómmətree/ *n.*

spec·tro·scope /spéktrə skōp/ *n.* an instrument for dispersing light, usually light in the visible range, into a spectrum —**spec·tro·scop·ic** /spèktrə skóppik/ *adj.* —**spec·tro·scop·i·cal·ly** /-skóppiklee/ *adv.*

spec·tro·scop·ic a·nal·y·sis *n.* the use of spectroscopy to determine the chemical composition, energy levels, and molecular structure of substances

spec·tros·co·py /spek tróskəpee/ *n.* the study of spectra, especially to determine the chemical composition of substances and the physical properties of molecules, ions, and atoms —**spec·tros·co·pist** *n.*

spec·trum /spéktrəm/ (*plural* **-tra** /spéktrə/ *or* **-trums**) *n.* 1. PHYS DISTRIBUTION OF COLORED LIGHT a continuous distribution of colored light produced when a beam of white light is dispersed into its components, e.g., by a prism. ◊ **absorption spectrum, emission spectrum** 2. PHYS RADIATION FREQUENCY RANGE WITH SPECIFIED PROPERTY a range of radiation frequencies that have a specified property. ◊ **electromagnetic spectrum** 3. PHYS RECORD OF SUBSTANCE'S RADIATION DENSITY a visual record of the

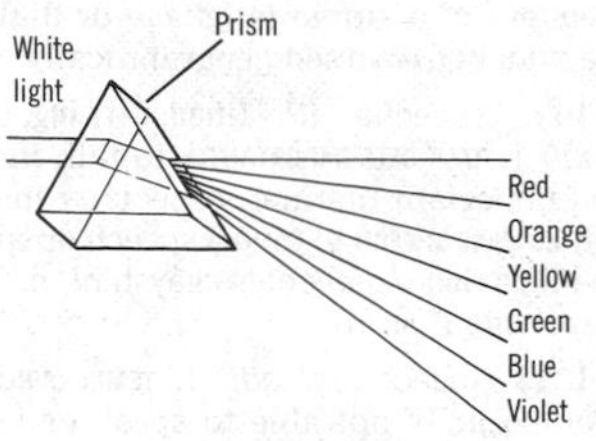

Spectrum

wavelengths of the radiation or particles emitted by a substance, used as a means of analyzing its physical properties, e.g., energy and mass. ◊ **mass spectrum** 4. ANY RANGE any range, especially one with opposite values at its limits ○ *a spectrum of opinions between the two extremes* 5. PHARM RANGE OF DRUG TARGETS the range of organisms that an antibiotic can kill [Late 19thC. From Latin, "image, apparition," from *specere* "to see" (see SPECIMEN).]

spec·u·la plural of **speculum**

spec·u·lar /spékyələr/ *adj.* 1. OPTICS OF OR LIKE MIRROR relating to mirrors or having the characteristics of a mirror 2. MED USING SPECULUM carried out using a speculum [Late 16thC. From Latin *specularis*, from *speculum* SPECULUM.]

spec·u·late /spékyə làyt/ (**-lat·ed, -lat·ing, -lates**) *v.* 1. *vti.* CONJECTURE to conjecture something based on incomplete facts or information 2. *vi.* CONSIDER SOMETHING to think over possibilities 3. *vi.* FIN MAKE RISKY DEALS FOR PROFIT to engage in financial transactions such as commodity trading that have an element of risk especially in the short term with the hope of making a profit 4. *vi.* TAKE RISKS to take risks in an attempt to achieve something or get some benefit [Late 16thC. From Latin *speculat-*, the past participle stem of *speculari* "to observe, spy out," from, ultimately, *specere* (see SPECIMEN).]

spec·u·la·tion /spèkyə láysh'n/ *n.* 1. OPINION BASED ON INCOMPLETE INFORMATION a conclusion, theory, or opinion based on incomplete information or evidence 2. REASONING BASED ON INCOMPLETE INFORMATION reasoning based on incomplete information or evidence 3. FIN RISKY TRANSACTION a financial transaction that involves risks but is potentially profitable 4. FIN MAKING RISKY TRANSACTIONS engaging in financial transactions that are risky but also potentially profitable

spec·u·la·tive /spékyə làytiv, -lətiv/ *adj.* 1. USING INCOMPLETE INFORMATION based on conjecture or incomplete information 2. FORMING CONCLUSIONS NOT BASED ON FACT given to forming conclusions or opinions that are not based on fact 3. FIN RISKY BUT POTENTIALLY PROFITABLE risky in nature but potentially profitable speculative investments ○ *speculative investments* —**spec·u·la·tive·ly** *adv.* —**spec·u·la·tive·ness** *n.*

spec·u·la·tor /spékyə làytər/ *n.* somebody who speculates, especially financially

spec·u·lum /spékyələm/ (*plural* **-la** /-lə/ *or* **-lums**) *n.* 1. OPTICS MIRROR a mirror or other reflective surface in an optical instrument such as a telescope 2. MED MEDICAL INSTRUMENT a medical instrument used to hold open a body passage, e.g., the anus or vagina, so that it can be examined 3. BIRDS COLORED PATCH ON BIRD'S WINGS a patch of color on the wings of ducks and certain other birds, helpful in identification [Late 16thC. From Latin, "mirror," formed from *specere* "to see" (see SPECIMEN).]

spec·u·lum met·al *n.* an alloy of copper and tin sometimes with other metals. It is hard, brittle, white, resistant to corrosion and, because it can be highly polished, is used for metal mirrors.

sped past tense, past participle of **speed**

speech /speech/ *n.* 1. SPEAKING ABILITY the ability to speak (*often used before a noun*) 2. COMMUNICATION BY SPEAKING the act of communicating by speaking 3. THINGS SAID things that are spoken ○ *recordings of human speech* 4. SPOKEN LANGUAGE spoken language especially as distinct from writing 5. ADDRESS a talk given to an audience 6. PARTICULAR WAY OF SPEAKING a particular way of speaking or using language, especially that of an individual or group 7. RUMOR

rumor or hearsay (*archaic*) [Old English *spǣc*, from *specan*, an earlier form of SPEAK]

speech com·mu·ni·ty *n.* a group that includes all the speakers of a single language or dialect. They may be widely dispersed geographically.

speech·i·fy /spéechə fī/ (**-fied, -fy·ing, -fies**) *vi.* (*informal*) **1.** TALK SELF-IMPORTANTLY to talk in a tedious and self-important manner, especially in giving an opinion **2.** MAKE SPEECH to give a speech or speeches —**speech·i·fi·ca·tion** /spèechəfə káysh'n/ *n.* —**speech·i·fi·er** /spéechə fī ər/ *n.*

speech·less /spéechləss/ *adj.* **1.** TEMPORARILY UNABLE TO SPEAK temporarily not able to speak or not able to think of something to say, e.g., because of surprise or fear **2.** UNABLE TO SPEAK lacking the power of speech **3.** REMAINING SILENT choosing not to say anything **4.** UNSPOKEN not expressed in words **5.** HARD TO EXPRESS difficult or impossible to put into words [Old English] —**speech·less·ly** *adv.* —**speech·less·ness** *n.*

speech·mak·er /spéech màykər/ *n.* somebody who makes a speech, often somebody regularly called upon to make speeches —**speech·mak·ing** *n.*

speech pa·thol·o·gy *n.* the study, diagnosis, and treatment of speech disorders, including failure of normal speech development in children and language disorders resulting from acquired brain dysfunction —**speech pa·thol·o·gist** *n.*

speech-read·ing *n.* = **lip-reading**

speech rec·og·ni·tion *n.* a system of computer input and control in which the computer can recognize spoken words and transform them into digitized commands or text. With such a system, a computer can be activated and controlled by voice commands or take dictation as input to a word processor or desktop publishing system.

speech syn·the·sis *n.* computer-generated audio output that resembles human speech

speech ther·a·py *n.* the treatment of speech disorders of all kinds —**speech ther·a·pist** *n.*

speech·writ·er /spéech rītər/ *n.* somebody who writes speeches for other people often professionally

speed /speed/ *n.* **1.** RATE OF MOVEMENT OR HAPPENING the rate at which something moves, happens, or functions **2.** RAPIDITY fast movement, progress, or operation **3.** RATE OF MOVEMENT IRRESPECTIVE OF DIRECTION rate of movement irrespective of direction. It is equal either to distance traveled divided by travel time, or to rate of change of distance with respect to time. **4.** DRUGS AMPHETAMINE an amphetamine drug (*slang*) **5.** SOMETHING SUITABLE something that matches somebody's tastes, abilities, or inclinations (*informal*) ○ *The intermediate course will be more my speed.* **6.** SUCCESS success or prosperity (*archaic*) **7.** MECH ENG GEAR RATIO a gear ratio in a motor, engine, or driving mechanism ○ *a ten-speed bicycle* ○ *operates at three different speeds* **8.** PHOTOGRAPHY PHOTOGRAPHIC FILM'S SENSITIVITY TO LIGHT a measure of the sensitivity of photographic film to light, expressed numerically according to any of various rating systems ■ *v.* (**sped** /sped/ *or* **speed·ed, sped** *or* **speed·ed, speed·ing, speeds**) **1.** *vti.* GO OR MOVE QUICKLY to go or move quickly, or to make something or somebody go or move quickly **2.** *vi.* DRIVE FAST to drive fast, especially exceeding the speed limit **3.** *vi.* PASS QUICKLY to pass or happen quickly or more quickly **4.** *vt.* HASTEN to make something happen sooner or more quickly **5.** *vi.* DRUGS USE AMPHETAMINES to be under the influence of amphetamines (*slang*) **6.** *vti.* MAKE OR BE PROSPEROUS to prosper or cause somebody or something to prosper (*archaic*) [Old English *spēd* "success, prosperity." Ultimately from an Indo-European base meaning "to prosper," which is also the ancestor of English *prosper* and *despair*.] ◇ **be** *or* **get up to speed 1.** to reach the maximum or desirable rate of movement or progress **2.** to be or become fully informed about the latest developments

speed·ball /spéed bàwl/ *n.* **1.** SPORTS GAME RESEMBLING SOCCER a team game similar to soccer. The ball can be passed forward with the hands and caught when in mid-air. **2.** DRUGS ILLEGAL DRUG MIXTURE a combination of illegal drugs such as cocaine and heroin taken by injection (*slang*)

speed·boat /spéed bōt/ *n.* a motorboat capable of traveling at high speeds

speed brake *n.* a flap on an aircraft wing used to decrease speed in flight before landing

speed bump *n.* a raised area or ridge on a road surface designed to limit traffic speeds

speed cam·er·a *n.* a roadside-mounted camera that automatically photographs a vehicle passing by it at excessive speed. It provides traffic police with concrete evidence of speeding offenses.

speed de·mon *n.* somebody who habitually drives too fast (*informal*)

speed di·al *n.* a function on a telephone that enables numbers to be stored in a memory so that they can be dialed by pressing a single button ○ *I have her number on speed dial.*

speed·er /spéedər/ *n.* a motorist who violates established speed limits

speed freak, speed·freak *n.* somebody who is addicted to amphetamines or somebody who habitually takes them

speed·ing /spéeding/ *n.* DRIVING VEHICLE ABOVE SPEED LIMIT the offense of driving a vehicle at a speed above the designated speed limit ■ *adj.* FAST-MOVING moving or working quickly

speed lim·it *n.* the maximum permitted speed, usually specified by law, at which a vehicle may travel on a particular stretch of road

speed mer·chant *n.* U.K. = **speed demon** (*informal*)

speed·om·e·ter /spə dómmətər/ *n.* an instrument that continuously measures a vehicle's speed and displays it either numerically or by means of a needle on a dial

speed-read /spéed reèd/ *vti.* to read something very fast using a learned technique of skimming the text

speed skate *n.* an ice skate designed for racing. It has a blade that is much longer than on a standard skate. —**speed skat·er** *n.*

speed skat·ing *n.* the sport of racing competitively on speed skates. Two skaters race against each other on a wide oval track divided into two lanes.

speed·ster /spéedstər/ *n.* (*dated slang*) **1.** FAST CAR a car that goes very fast **2.** HABITUAL SPEEDER somebody who habitually drives too fast [Early 20thC. Formed from SPEED, on the model of *roadster*.]

speed trap *n.* a stretch of road kept under hidden surveillance by police officers monitoring vehicle speeds, usually using radar equipment

speed·up /spéed up/ *n.* **1.** INCREASE IN SPEED an increase in rate or speed **2.** MORE WORK, SAME PAY a demanded increase in productivity from a workforce without a pay increase

speed walk·ing *n.* = **race walking**

speed·way /spéed wày/ *n.* **1.** MOTOR SPORTS RACETRACK FOR MOTOR VEHICLES a racetrack for cars or motorcycles **2.** TRANSP FAST ROAD a road on which vehicles are allowed to travel at high speeds

speed·well /spéed wèl/ *n.* a perennial European plant of the snapdragon family with opposite leaves and clusters of blue or pinkish flowers. Genus: *Veronica*. [Late 16thC. From SPEED (verb) + WELL.]

speed·writ·ing /spéed r-ting/ *n.* a system of shorthand writing that uses combinations of standard letters, as distinct from other systems that use symbols

speed·y /spéedee/ (**-i·er, -i·est**) *adj.* **1.** FAST accomplished or achieved quickly **2.** FAST-MOVING capable of moving very fast —**speed·i·ly** *adv.* —**speed·i·ness** *n.*

speed zone *n.* an area where a particular, usually reduced, speed limit is in effect

speiss /spīss/ *n.* a compound of arsenic or antimony formed during the smelting of certain ores such as iron, nickel, and copper [Late 18thC. From German *Speise* "food, speiss."]

spe·lae·an, spe·le·an *adj.* relating to caves, or found in caves [Mid-19thC. Via Latin *spelaeum* from Greek *spelaion* "cave."]

spe·le·ol·o·gy /spèelee ólləjee/ *n.* **1.** STUDY OF CAVES the scientific study or exploration of caves **2.** *U.K.* = **spelunking** —**spe·le·o·log·i·cal** /spèelee ə lójjik'l/ *adj.* —**spe·le·ol·o·gist** /spèelee óllәjist/ *n.*

spell[1] /spel/ (**spelled, spell·ing, spells**) *v.* **1.** *vti.* NAME OR WRITE LETTERS OF WORD to name or write in correct order the constituent letters of a word, part of a word, or group of words **2.** *vt.* FORM WORD to form a word when arranged in the correct order **3.** *vt.* SIGNIFY to be a sign or indication of something ○ *Increased interest rates could spell trouble for some corporate borrowers.* [13thC. Via Old French *espeller* from, ultimately, a prehistoric Germanic base that is also the ancestor of *spell*[2].]

spell out *vt.* **1.** MAKE COMPLETELY CLEAR to state something clearly, allowing no room for misunderstanding **2.** READ SLOWLY OR WITH DIFFICULTY to read something with difficulty or very slowly, especially by reading out words one letter at a time **3.** FIGURE OUT to figure something out by careful study or analysis

spell[2] /spel/ *n.* **1.** PARANORMAL WORDS WITH MAGICAL POWER a word or series of words believed to have magical power, spoken to invoke the magic **2.** SPELL'S INFLUENCE the influence that a spell has over somebody or something **3.** FASCINATION a compelling fascination or attraction ■ *vt.* (**spelled, spell·ing, spells**) INFLUENCE USING SPELL to put somebody or something under the influence of a spell [Old English, from a prehistoric Germanic base that is also the ancestor of English *spell*[1] and *gospel*. Originally in the meaning of "talk, speech."]

spell[3] /spel/ *n.* **1.** SHORT PERIOD a period of indeterminate but usually short duration (*informal*) ○ *Let's sit a spell.* **2.** PERIOD OF PARTICULAR WEATHER a period of weather of a particular type ○ *a warm spell* **3.** BOUT OF ILLNESS a period of illness ○ *a fainting spell* **4.** PERIOD OF WORK a period of work or purposeful activity **5.** TOUR OF DUTY somebody's turn to work or perform a particular duty **6.** SHORT DISTANCE a short but unspecified distance (*informal*) ○ *down the road a spell* ■ *v.* (**spelled, spell·ing, spells**) **1.** *vt. U.S., ANZ, Scotland* RELIEVE to relieve somebody of a task temporarily, especially in order to allow him or her to rest **2.** *vi.* TAKE TURNS to take turns working at a job [Late 16thC. The noun came from the verb, a variant of obsolete *spele* "to take the place of someone," from Old English *spelian*, of unknown origin.]

spell·bind·ing /spél bīnding/ *adj.* holding attention and interest completely, as if with the influence of a spell —**spell·bind** *vt.* —**spell·bind·er** *n.* —**spell·bind·ing·ly** *adv.*

spell·bound /spél bòwnd/ *adj.* with attention and interest held completely, as if under the influence of a spell [Late 18thC. Literally "bound by a spell," formed from SPELL[2].]

spell check·er *n.* a computer program usually associated with word processing software that compares words in a text to a file of correctly spelled words in order to detect misspellings —**spell-check** *vt.*

spell·down /spél dòwn/ *n.* = **spelling bee**

spell·er /spéllər/ *n.* **1.** SOMEBODY WHO SPELLS somebody who spells words, usually characterized with regard to accuracy **2.** EDUC BOOK FOR SPELLING a book for teaching or improving spelling

spell·ing /spélling/ *n.* **1.** ABILITY TO SPELL the ability to spell words correctly **2.** FORMING WORDS BY ORDERING LETTERS the forming of words with letters in a conventionally accepted order (*often used before a noun*) **3.** SPECIFIC EXAMPLE OF LETTER ORDER a specific example of how a word is actually spelled

spell·ing bee *n.* a competition in which the object is to see who can spell the most words correctly

spell·ing pro·nun·ci·a·tion *n.* a variant pronunciation of a word that differs from the standard pronunciation and is influenced by the way a word is spelled

spelt /spelt/ *n.* a hardy variety of wheat of inferior quality, sometimes grown in mountainous regions. Latin name: *Triticum spelta*. [Pre-12thC. From late Latin *spelta*, of uncertain origin: probably from Germanic.]

spel·ter /spéltər/ *n.* impure zinc often used as a cheap alternative for bronze in cast decorative items [Mid-17thC]

spe·lunk·ing /spə lúngking, spi-/ *n.* the sport or pastime of exploring caves [Mid-20thC. Formed from earlier *spelunk* "cave," via Old French *spelunque*, from Latin *spelunca*, from Greek *spelunx*.] —**spe·lunk·er** *n.*

spen·cer /spénssər/ *n.* **1.** SHORT BOYS' JACKET a short jacket worn by boys in the late 18th and early 19th centuries **2.** WOMEN'S JACKET a very short jacket worn by women over a high-waisted gown in the late 18th and early 19th centuries [Late 18thC. Named for George John *Spencer*, second Earl Spencer (1758–1834).]

Spen·cer /spénssər/, **Sir Stanley** (1891–1959) British painter. Many of his works, such as *The Resurrection, Cookham* (1923–27), place traditional biblical scenes in contemporary settings.

Sir Stanley Spencer

Spen·ce·ri·an /spen séerree ən, -sérree-/ *adj.* used to describe a style of handwriting with perfectly formed letters and ornamentation of capitals [Mid-19thC. Named for Platt Rogers *Spencer* (1800–64), a U.S. calligrapher.]

spend /spend/ (**spent** /spent/, **spent, spend·ing, spends**) *v.* **1.** *vti.* PAY MONEY to pay out money in exchange for goods or services **2.** *vt.* DEVOTE TIME OR EFFORT to devote time, energy, or thought to something ○ *spent a lot of time thinking about it* **3.** *vt.* PASS TIME to pass time in a specified place or way ○ *spend a week in Hawaii* **4.** *vt.* USE UP to deplete something totally **5.** *vt.* SACRIFICE SOMETHING to sacrifice something, especially for a cause ○ *spent her life working for reform* [Pre-12thC. From Latin *expendere* "to pay" (see EXPEND), but also in part from Old French *despendre* "to expend," from Latin *dispendere* "to distribute by weighing out" (see DISPENSE).]

spend·er /spéndər/ *n.* somebody who spends money, especially in a specified way

Spen·der /spéndər/, **Sir Stephen** (1909–95) British poet and editor. He was a prominent member of the left-wing British literary movement in the 1930s, and edited *Encounter* from 1953 to 1967. His works include *Collected Poems* (1986) and *Journals 1939–83* (1986). Full name **Sir Stephen Harold Spender**

spend·ing mon·ey *n.* cash used or available for personal expenses, especially expenditure on non-essential items

spend·thrift /spénd thrìft/ *n.* EXTRAVAGANT SPENDER somebody who spends money extravagantly and often recklessly ■ *adj.* WASTEFUL WITH MONEY tending to spend money extravagantly and wastefully [Late 16thC. From SPEND + THRIFT, in the archaic sense "savings, earnings."]

Spen·ser /spénssər/, **Edmund** (1552?–99) English poet. He wrote the epic romance *The Faerie Queene* (1590–96), a panoramic historical allegory and one of the classics of English Renaissance literature.

Spen·se·ri·an /spen séerree ən/ *adj.* relating to or characteristic of Edmund Spenser or his literary works —**Spen·se·ri·an** *n.*

Spen·se·ri·an son·net *n.* a sonnet with a rhyming scheme abab, bcbc, cdcd, ee, invented by Edmund Spenser

Spen·se·ri·an stan·za *n.* a stanza devised by Edmund Spenser. It contains eight lines of iambic pentameter and a ninth of iambic hexameter, using the rhyming scheme ababbcbcc. The scheme is used in *The Faerie Queene.*

spent /spent/ past tense, past participle of **spend** ■ *adj.* **1.** CONSUMED used or used up ○ *tossed the spent match into the fire* **2.** EXHAUSTED totally depleted of energy or strength ○ *felt totally spent by the end of the day* **3.** FINISHED at an end **4.** ZOOL EXHAUSTED OF SPAWN OR SPERM used to describe a female fish that has depositied all its spawn or a male fish that has used up all its sperm

sperm[1] /spurm/ (*plural* **sperm** *or* **sperms**) *n.* used popularly, but technically incorrectly, to refer to semen [14thC. Via late Latin *sperma* from Greek, "seed, semen." Ultimately "something scattered," from an Indo-European word meaning "to scatter," which is also the ancestor of English *spread* and *spore*.]

sperm[2] /spurm/ *n.* **1.** = **spermaceti 2.** = **sperm oil 3.** = **sperm whale** [Mid-19thC. Shortening.]

sper·ma·ce·ti /spùrmə séttee/ *n.* a white waxy solid obtained from oil in the head of sperm whales and other cetaceans, and used in cosmetics, candles, and ointments [Late 15thC. From medieval Latin, from late Latin *sperma* "semen" (see SPERM[1]) + Latin *ceti* "of a whale" (see CETUS). From its appearance (it serves no reproductive function).]

sper·ma·ry /spúrməree/ (*plural* **-ries**) *n.* an organ in which male reproductive cells are developed. The testes are spermaries.

spermat- *prefix.* = **spermato-** (*used before vowels*)

sper·ma·the·ca /spùrmə théekə/ *n.* a receptacle for storing sperm in the reproductive tracts of certain invertebrates such as insects [Early 19thC. Coined from late Latin *sperma* "seed, semen" (see SPERM) + THECA.] —**sper·ma·the·cal** *adj.*

sper·ma·ti·a plural of **spermatium**

sper·mat·ic /spur máttik/, **sper·mic** /spúrmik/ *adj.* **1.** OF SEMEN relating to, carrying, or containing semen **2.** OF SPERMARIES OR SPERMATIC CORDS relating to a spermary or to the spermatic cord —**sper·mat·i·cal·ly** *adv.*

sper·mat·ic cord *n.* a cord by which a testis is suspended in the scrotum. It contains the vas deferens as well as nerves, vessels, and veins.

sper·ma·tid /spúrmə tid/ *n.* any of the four cells that are formed from a spermatocyte and develop into spermatozoa

sper·ma·ti·um /spur máyshəm/ (*plural* **-a** /-máyshə/) *n.* a cell that functions as a male reproductive cell in certain algae, fungi, and lichens [Mid-19thC. Via modern Latin from Greek *spermation*, a diminutive of *sperma* (see SPERM[1]).]

spermato- *prefix.* **1.** sperm, spermatozoon ○ *spermatogenesis* **2.** seed ○ *spermatophyte* [From Greek *spermat-*, the stem of *sperma* (see SPERM[1])]

sper·mat·o·cide /spur máttə sīd/ *n.* = **spermicide** —**sper·mat·o·cid·al** /spùrmətə sīd'l/ *adj.*

sper·mat·o·cyte /spur máttə sīt/ *n.* a cell that develops from a spermatogonium. It divides into four spermatids by means of the kind of cell division known as meiosis.

sper·mat·o·gen·e·sis /spùrmətə jénnəssəss/ *n.* the formation and development of spermatozoa in the testes —**sper·mat·o·ge·net·ic** /spùrmətō jə néttik/ *adj.*

sper·mat·o·go·ni·um /spùrmətō gṓnee əm/ (*plural* **-a** /-nee ə/) *n.* a cell in the male testes that develops and divides to form spermatocytes. These subsequently divide to form spermatids, from which spermatozoa finally develop. —**sper·mat·o·go·ni·al** *adj.*

sper·mat·o·phore /spur máttə fawr/ *n.* a capsule or mass that encloses spermatozoa in insects and other lower animals and that is transferred to the female during insemination —**sper·ma·toph·o·ral** /spùrmə tóffərəl/ *adj.*

sper·mat·o·phyte /spur máttə fīt/ *n.* any plant that produces seeds, including angiosperms and gymnosperms —**sper·mat·o·phyt·ic** /spùrmətə fíttik/ *adj.*

sper·mat·or·rhe·a /spùrmətə rée ə/ *n.* the involuntary emission of semen without orgasm

sper·mat·o·zo·a plural of **spermatozoon**

sper·mat·o·zo·id /spùrmətə zṓ id, spúrmətə zṑ əd/ *n.* a male reproductive cell, resembling a ribbon, produced in algae, ferns, fungi, mosses, and some gymnosperms. It can move by means of flagella. [Mid-19thC. Coined from SPERMATOZOON + -ID.]

sper·mat·o·zo·on /spur màttə z-on, spùrmətə zṓ on/ (*plural* **-a** /spùrmətə zṓ ə/) *n.* CELL BIOL a male reproductive cell (**gamete**) that has an oval head with a nucleus, a short neck, and a tail by which it moves to find and fertilize an ovum —**sper·mat·o·zo·an** *adj.*

sperm bank *n.* a place that stores semen until it is required for use in artificial insemination

sperm count *n.* **1.** CONCENTRATION OF SPERM the concentration of sperm in a given volume of seminal fluid, taken as an index of male fertility **2.** TEST FOR NUMBER OF SPERM a test to determine a man's sperm count

spermi- *prefix.* = **spermo-**

sper·mic *adj.* = **spermatic**

sper·mi·cide /spúrmə sīd/ *n.* a pharmaceutical cream or gel used to kill spermatozoa, especially in conjunction with a birth-control device such as a condom or diaphragm —**sper·mi·cid·al** /spùrmə sīd'l/ *adj.*

sper·mi·o·gen·e·sis /spùrmee ō jénnəssəss/ *n.* th stage of spermatogenesis during which a spermatic is transformed into a spermatozoon —**sper·mi·o·ge·net·ic** /spùrmee ō jə néttik/ *adj.*

spermo- *prefix.* seed, sperm ○ *spermophyte* [From Greek *sperma* "seed"]

sperm oil, **sperm** *n.* a pale yellow oil obtained from the head of the sperm whale and used as an industrial lubricant in delicate mechanisms

sper·mo·phyte /spúrmə fīt/ *n.* = **spermatophyte**

sperm whale, **sperm** *n.* the largest of the toothed whales whose massive square head has a cavity filled with a mixture of sperm oil and spermaceti. Its intestines are the source of ambergris. [Shortening of *spermaceti whale*]

-spermy *suffix.* fertilization ○ *polyspermy* [From Greek *sperma* "seed" + -Y]

Sper·ry /spérree/, **Elmer Ambrose** (1860–1930) U.S. inventor and engineer. He invented the gyroscopic compass (1910) and ship and airplane stabilizers (1913). He held over 400 patents.

Sper·ry, Roger W. (1913–94) U.S. neurobiologist. He shared a Nobel Prize in physiology or medicine (1981) for his "split-brain" research. Full name **Roger Wolcott Sperry**

sper·ry·lite /spérri līt/ *n.* a silvery white mineral and ore of platinum consisting of white crystalline platinum arsenide [Early 20thC. Named for Francis L. *Sperry,* the Canadian chemist who identified the mineral.]

spes·sar·tine /spéssər tèen/, **spes·sar·tite** /spéssər tīt/ *n.* a yellow or reddish-brown garnet consisting of manganese aluminum silicate. It is used as a gemstone. [Mid-19thC. From French, named for *Spessart,* a district in Bavaria, Germany, where it is found.]

spew /spyoo/ *vti.* (**spewed, spew·ing, spews**) **1.** VOMIT SOMETHING to vomit something that has been eaten **2.** POUR OR FLOW OUT FORCEFULLY to flow out forcefully, or force something out in a stream ○ *a volcano spewing ash* **3.** SAY FORCEFULLY to utter something in an angry, forceful, or relentless way ■ *n.* VOMIT something ejected from the mouth, especially vomit [Old English *spīwan.* Ultimately from an Indo-European word meaning "to spit," an imitation of the sound, which is also the ancestor of English *spit, spout,* and *sputum.*] —**spew·er** *n.*

SPF *n.* the degree to which a sun cream, lotion, screen, or block provides protection for the skin against the sun. Abbr of **sun protection factor**

sp. gr. *abbr.* specific gravity

Spgs. *abbr.* Springs (*in place names*)

sphag·num /sfágnəm/ *n.* moss growing in wet, acid, temperate regions that decays and becomes compacted to form peat. Genus: *Sphagnum.* [Mid-18thC. Via modern Latin, genus name, from, ultimately, Greek *sphagnos,* a type of shrub.] —**sphag·nous** *adj.*

sphal·er·ite /sfállə rīt/ *n.* a yellow or brownish ore of zinc consisting of crystalline zinc sulfide [Mid-19thC. Formed from Greek *sphaleros* "slippery, uncertain," because the mineral is easily confused with galena.]

sphen- *prefix.* = **spheno-** (*used before vowels*)

sphene /sfeen/ *n.* a brown-black mineral composed of calcium titanium silicate that is widely found in low concentrations in coarse-grained igneous rocks [Early 19thC. Via French *sphène* from Greek *sphēn* "wedge."]

sphe·nic /sféenik/ *adj.* like a wedge in shape

spheno- *prefix.* wedge-shaped ○ *sphenogram* [From Greek *sphēn* "wedge"]

sphe·no·don /sféenə dòn/ *n.* = **tuatara** [Late 19thC. From modern Latin, genus name, literally "wedge-toothed," from Greek *sphēn* "wedge."]

sphe·no·gram /sféenə gràm/ *n.* any of the characters with wedge-shaped strokes used in the ancient writing systems known as cuneiform script

sphe·noid /sfée nòyd/ *adj.* **1.** WEDGE-SHAPED shaped like a wedge **2.** OF SPHENOID BONE relating to the sphenoid bone

sphe·noid bone, **sphe·noid** *n.* a bone with prominent wings at the base of the cranium. It forms part of the walls and roof of the nasal cavity.

spher- *prefix.* = **sphero-** (*used before vowels*)

spher·al /sféerəl/ *adj.* **1.** OF SPHERES relating to a sphere or to spheres in general **2.** SPHERE-SHAPED shaped like a sphere **3.** SYMMETRICAL forming a symmetrical or harmonious shape or whole

sphere /sfeer/ *n.* **1.** GLOBE any object similar in shape to a ball **2.** MATH THREE-DIMENSIONAL SURFACE a three-dimensional closed surface consisting of all points that are a given distance from a center **3.** MATH ROUND SOLID FIGURE the solid figure bounded by a sphere, or the volume it encloses **4.** FIELD OF KNOWLEDGE OR ACTIVITY a field of knowledge, interest, or activity **5.** AREA OF INFLUENCE an area of control or influence ○ *took no interest in matters beyond her sphere* **6.** GROUP IN SOCIETY a level or group within a society **7.** ASTRON ANY CELESTIAL OBJECT a celestial object, e.g., a planet, moon, or star (*literary*) **8.** ASTRON THE SKY the sky or the heavens (*literary*) **9.** ASTRON FORMER CONCEPT OF CELESTIAL LAYER any of the revolving concentric transparent shells on which, in early astronomy, the Sun, Moon, planets, and stars were thought to be fixed as they moved around the Earth ■ *vt.* (**sphered, spher·ing, spheres**) **1.** ENCIRCLE to surround, encircle, or enclose something (*literary*) **2.** PLACE IN HEAVEN to place in the sky or in heaven, among the celestial spheres (*literary*) **3.** FORM INTO BALL to form something into the shape of a ball [13thC. Via Old French *espere* from late Latin *sphera*, (which later influenced the English word), from Latin *sphaera*, from Greek *sphaira* "ball."] —**sphe·ric·i·ty** /sfe rɪ́ssətee/ *n.*

sphere of in·flu·ence *n.* a geographical region or area of activity in which a particular state, organization, or person is dominant

spher·i·cal /sfe͂erək'l, sfér-/, **spher·ic** /sfe͂erik, sfér-/ *adj.* **1.** ROUND shaped like a sphere **2.** OF SPHERES relating to a sphere, or to spheres in general **3.** ASTRON OF CELESTIAL BODIES relating to celestial objects **4.** ASTRON OF ANCIENT ASTRONOMY SPHERES relating to the spheres of ancient astronomy —**spher·i·cal·ly** *adv.* —**spher·i·cal·ness** *n.*

spher·i·cal ab·er·ra·tion *n.* a defect in a lens or curved mirror in which light passing through the edge has a different focal point from light passing through the center, resulting in blurred images

spher·i·cal an·gle *n.* an angle formed on a sphere at the point at which any two circles of maximum radius intersect

spher·i·cal co·or·di·nates *npl.* a set of coordinates used for locating a point in space representing its distance from some origin and two angles describing its orientation relative to perpendicular axes extending form that origin

spher·i·cal ge·om·e·try *n.* the geometry of figures formed on the surface of a sphere

spher·i·cal pol·y·gon *n.* a geometric figure formed on the surface of a sphere, bounded by three or more arcs of great circles

spher·i·cal tri·an·gle *n.* a spherical polygon that has three sides

spher·i·cal trig·o·nom·e·try *n.* trigonometry dealing with spherical triangles

spher·ics[1] /sfe͂eriks, sférriks/ *n.* **1.** = **spherical geometry** ((*takes a singular verb*)) **2.** = **spherical trigonometry**

spher·ics[2] /sfe͂eriks, sférriks/, **sfer·ics** *n.* the study of electromagnetic radiation emanating from natural sources in the atmosphere (*takes a singular verb*) [Mid-20thC. Shortening of ATMOSPHERICS.]

sphero- *prefix.* sphere, spherical ○ *spheroid* [Via Latin *sphaero-* from, ultimately, Greek *sphaira* "sphere"]

sphe·roid /sfe͂er oyd, sfé royd/ *n.* a three-dimensional object that is shaped like a sphere but is not perfectly round, e.g., an ellipsoid —**sphe·roi·dal** /sfi róydl'l, sfe-/ *adj.* —**sphe·roi·dal·ly** /-róydl'lee, -/ *adv.* —**sphe·roi·dic·i·ty** /sfe͂er oy dı́ssətee, sfè roy-/ *n.*

sphe·rom·e·ter /sfə ráwmətər/ *n.* an instrument used to measure the curvature of a surface

spher·o·plast /sfe͂erō plàst, sférō-/ *n.* a bacterium or yeast cell that has lost part of its cell wall and is as a result spherical in shape and more sensitive to osmosis

spher·ule /sfe͂er ool, sfé rool/ *n.* a minute sphere or globule [Mid-17thC. From late Latin *spherula*, literally "small sphere," from Latin *sphaera* (see SPHERE).] —**spher·u·lar** *adj.*

spher·u·lite /sfe͂eryə lìt, sférryə-/ *n.* a more or less spherical mass of radiating crystal fibers found in some kinds of volcanic rock, e.g., obsidian —**spher·u·lit·ic** /sfe͂e ryə lı́ttik, sfè rryə-/ *adj.*

spher·y /sfe͂eree/ *adj.* **1.** SPHERE-SHAPED in the shape of a sphere **2.** OF CELESTIAL BODIES relating to or resembling the planets, the stars, and other celestial bodies (*literary*)

sphinc·ter /sfı́ngktər/ *n.* a circular band of muscle that surrounds an opening or passage in the body and narrows or closes the opening by contracting [Late 16thC. Via Latin from Greek *sphigktēr*, from *sphiggein* "to bind tight."] —**sphinc·ter·al** *adj.*

sphin·ges plural of **sphinx**

sphin·go·sine /sfı́ng gə se͂en, -gəssən/ *n.* a long-chain amino glycol that is part of larger molecules found in nerve tissue, e.g., gangliosides, sphingomyelins, and cerebrosides. Formula: $C_{18}H_{37}O_2N$. [Late 19thC. Coined from Greek *sphiggos* "of a sphinx" (see SPHINX) + -INE. From the enigmatic character of the material.]

Sphinx, Giza, Egypt

sphinx /sfingks/ (*plural* **sphinx·es** *or* **sphin·ges** /sfı́n je͂ez/) *n.* **1.** GREEK COMPOSITE CREATURE in Greek mythology, a winged creature with a lion's body and a woman's head. It strangled all who could not answer its riddle, but killed itself when Oedipus answered correctly. **2.** EGYPTIAN COMPOSITE CREATURE in Egyptian mythology, a creature with a lion's body and the head of a man, ram, or bird **3.** SPHINX STATUE a statue of a sphinx **4.** MYSTERIOUS PERSON a mysterious or inscrutable person [Late 16thC. Via Latin from Greek *sphigx*, of uncertain origin: probably from *sphiggein* "to draw tight," because the sphinx that terrorized Thebes often took people by strangulation.]

sphinx·like /sfı́ngks lìk/ *adj.* difficult to understand or find out about

sphinx moth *n.* = **hawk moth** [*Sphinx* from its appearance, suggestive of a sphinx]

sphra·gis·tics /sfrə jı́stiks/ *n.* the study of seals and signet rings (*takes a singular verb*) [Mid-19thC. Directly or via French *sphragistique* from late Greek *sphragistikos* "of seals," from *sphragis* "seal."] —**sphra·gis·tic** *adj.*

sp ht *abbr.* specific heat

sphygm- *prefix.* = **sphygmo-** (*used before vowels*)

sphyg·mic /sfı́gmik/ *adj.* relating to the pulse [Early 18thC. From Greek *sphugmikos*, from *sphugmos* (see SPHYGMO-).]

sphygmo- *prefix.* pulse ○ *sphygmograph* [From Greek *sphugmos* "pulsation," from "sphug-," the stem of *spuzein* "to throb"]

sphyg·mo·graph /sfı́gmə gràf/ *n.* an apparatus used to make a graphical record (**sphygmogram**) of variations in blood pressure and pulse —**sphyg·mo·graph·ic** /sfìgmə gráffik/ *adj.* —**sphyg·mog·ra·phy** /sfig móggrəfee/ *n.*

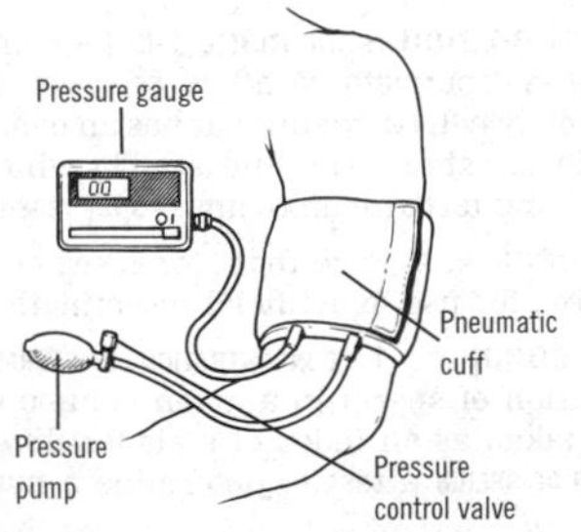

Sphygmomanometer

sphyg·mo·ma·nom·e·ter /sfìg mōmə nómmətər/ *n.* an instrument used to measure blood pressure in an artery. It consists of a pressure gauge, an inflatable cuff placed around the upper arm, and an inflater bulb or pressure pump.

spic /spik/ *n.* a highly offensive term referring to a Spanish-speaking person from Mexico or Central or South America (*slang taboo*) [Early 20thC. Shortening of *spiggoty*, of uncertain origin: perhaps from a nonstandard pronunciation of "(no) speak the (English)."]

spi·ca /spı́kə/ (*plural* **-cae** /-see/ *or* **-cas**) *n.* a bandage applied to a limb in an overlapping figure-eight pattern to immobilize it [14thC. From Latin, "ear of grain"; from its spiralling shape, which is reminiscent of an ear of grain.]

spic-and-span *adj.* = **spick-and-span**

spi·cate /spı́ kàyt/ *adj.* growing in the form of a spike, or with flowers growing in spikes [Mid-17thC. From Latin *spicatus*, the past participle of *spicare* "to furnish with sharp points," from *spica* "spike."]

spic·ca·to /spi kaátō/ *n.* (*plural* **-tos**) MUSICIAN'S BOWING TECHNIQUE a technique of playing staccato on stringed instruments, in which the bow is allowed to bounce on the string ■ *adj., adv.* USING SPICCATO BOWING played using a technique of allowing the bow to bounce on the string [Early 18thC. From Italian, the past participle of spiccare "to pick off, detach."]

spice /spīss/ *n.* **1.** AROMATIC PLANT SUBSTANCE USED AS FLAVORING any of various aromatic plant substances such as nutmeg and ginger used as flavorings **2.** FLAVORINGS FROM PLANTS food flavorings derived from the non leafy parts of plants (*often used before a noun*) **3.** EXCITING OR INTERESTING THING a source of excitement or interest **4.** STRONG SMELL a pungent odor or fragrance (*often used before a noun*) **5.** TRACE OF SOMETHING the tiniest amount of something ■ *vt.* (**spiced, spic·ing, spic·es**) **1.** SEASON WITH SPICE to season food or beverages with spice **2.** MAKE MORE EXCITING to introduce excitement or interest into something [13thC. Via Old French *espice* from Latin *species* "appearance, kind," in late Latin, in plural, "goods, wares" (see SPECIES).]

spice·ber·ry /spīss bèrree/ (*plural* **-ries**) *n.* **1.** BERRY-PRODUCING SHRUB a name given to various trees and shrubs that produce spicy orange, red, or black berries, e.g., the wintergreen **2.** SPICY BERRY a berry from a spiceberry plant

spice·bush /spīss bo͝osh/ *n.* a North American shrub that belongs to the laurel family. It has aromatic leaves and dense clusters of yellow flowers. Latin name: *Lindera benzoin.*

spice·y *adj.* = **spicy**

spick-and-span /spìk-/, **spic-and-span** *adj.* **1.** NEAT very clean and neat (*not hyphenated when used after a verb*) **2.** IN PERFECT CONDITION showing not the slightest sign of damage or wear and tear [Late 16thC. Shortening of *spick-and-span-new*, from obsolete *spick*, variant of SPIKE[1] + AND + *span-new*, from Old Norse *spánnyr*, literally "new chip," from *spán* "chip," related to English *spoon*.]

spic·ule /spı́kyool/ (*plural* **spic·ules** *or* **spiculum**) *n.* **1.** BIOL SMALL NEEDLE-SHAPED PART a small hard needle-shaped part, especially any of the calcium- or silicon-containing supporting parts of certain invertebrates such as sponges and corals **2.** ASTRON SOLAR PROMINENCE a slender column of relatively cool, high-density gas that rapidly erupts from the solar chromosphere and then falls back. There can be as many as 250,000 spicules rising above the solar surface at any moment. [Late 18thC. From modern Latin *spiculum*, literally "small spike," Latin *spica* "spike," ear of grain (see SPIKE[1]).] —**spic·u·lar** /spı́kyələr/ *adj.* —**spic·u·late** /spı́kyələt, spı́kyə làyt/ *adj.*

spic·y, **spice·y** (**spic·i·er, spic·i·est**) *adj.* **1.** SEASONED WITH SPICE smelling or tasting strongly of spices **2.** INVOLVING IMPROPRIETY arousing interest because of its scandalous nature, usually because it deals with sexual impropriety (*informal*) **3.** VIVACIOUS with a very lively personality **4.** BOT PRODUCING SPICES used to describe plants or plant parts from which spices are obtained —**spic·i·ly** *adv.* —**spic·i·ness** *n.*

spi·der /spı́dər/ *n.* **1.** BIOL EIGHT-LEGGED ANIMAL THAT SPINS WEBS a predatory animal with four pairs of legs and two or more abdominal organs (**spinnerets**) used for spinning webs that serve as nests and traps for prey. It is popularly thought to be an insect, although it is an arachnid. Order: Araneae. **2.** COOK FRYING PAN a cast-iron frying pan, originally one with legs or feet for cooking on a hearth (*regional dated*) **3.** TRIVET a trivet for supporting a pan on a hearth **4.** MECH ENG MECHANICAL DEVICE a mechanical device that has radiating arms, spokes, or other parts **5.** NAUT FRAME SECURING REDUNDANT ROPES a circular frame at the base of a ship's mast, used to secure ropes when

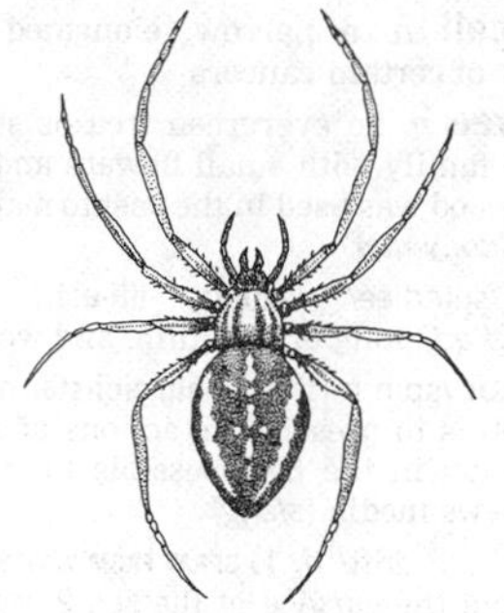

Spider

Steven Spielberg

sails are not in use **6.** COMPUT **PROGRAM SEARCHING INTERNET FOR INFORMATION** a computer program that searches the Internet for newly accessible information to be added to the index examined by a standard search tool **(search engine) 7.** CUE GAMES **CUE REST** a multi-position cue rest with wide legs designed to lift the cue tip over an intervening ball **8.** TRANSP = **spider phaeton 9.** *Aus* **ICE-CREAM SODA** an ice-cream soda (*informal*) [Old English *spīþra*, from *spinnan* "to spin." (see SPIN).]

WORD KEY: REGIONAL NOTE

Spider in the sense "frying pan" is an old-fashioned New England and Southern term that formerly competed with Midland *skillet.* Today, *frying pan* and *fry pan* are usual throughout the United States.

spi·der bee·tle *n.* a name given to various wingless beetles, many of which are pests to stored food in households and warehouses. Family: Ptinidae.

spi·der crab *n.* a marine crab with a small triangular body and long slender legs. Family: Majidae.

spi·der flow·er *n.* **1.** = **cleome 2. AUSTRALIAN FLOWER RESEMBLING SPIDER** a name given to various Australian flowering plants whose flowerheads resemble spiders. Genus: *Grevillea.*

spi·der hole *n.* a concealed sniper position (*informal*)

spi·der-hunt·ing wasp *n.* a large black or metallic-blue solitary wasp that preys on spiders. Family: Pepsidae.

spi·der lil·y *n.* = **crinum**

spi·der mite *n.* any tiny web-spinning mite. Some spider mites are garden and crop pests. Family: Tetranychidae.

spi·der mon·key *n.* a tree-dwelling monkey native to Central and South America. It has long slender limbs, a long prehensile tail, and a small head. Genus: *Ateles.*

spi·der phae·ton, spider *n.* a high-bodied lightweight fast horse carriage with large wheels

spi·der plant *n.* a plant of the lily family widely grown as a houseplant for its long narrow variegated leaves, white flowers, and clusters of plantlets. Latin name: *Chlorophytum variegatum.*

spi·der wasp *n.* = **spider-hunting wasp**

spi·der·web /spī́dər wèb/ *n.* a web that is constructed by a spider using silk produced from fluid from its abdominal glands, used especially to entrap prey

spi·der·wort /spī́dər wùrt, -wàwrt/ *n.* a plant widely grown as a houseplant for its pink, blue, or violet flowers. Genus: *Tradescantia.* ◊ **tradescantia** [*Spider* from the resemblance of the stamens to a spider's legs]

spi·der·y /spī́dəree/ *adj.* **1. THIN AND IRREGULAR** with thin lines or constituent parts that form irregular angles **2. SPIDER-INFESTED** infested with spiders **3. LIKE SPIDER** like a spider in shape or movement

spie·gel·ei·sen /spéeg'l ī̀z'n/, **spie·gel** /spéeg'l/ *n.* pig iron containing high concentrations of manganese and carbon. It is added to steel in the late stages of production to adjust the final composition. [Mid-19thC. From German, from *Spiegel* "mirror" (ultimately from Latin *speculum*; see SPECULUM) + *Eisen* "iron."]

spiel /speel, shpeel/ *n.* **SPEECH DESIGNED TO CONVINCE** an irritatingly long or predictably glib speech, e.g., a rambling apology or a prepared sales patter (*informal*) ■ *vi.* **(spieled, spiel·ing, spiels) GIVE SPIEL** to deliver a spiel (*informal*) [Late 19thC. From German, "play, game."]

spiel off *vt.* to say something very quickly or by rote ○ *spiel off a list of names*

Spiel·berg /spéel burg/, **Steven** (*b.* 1946) U.S. movie director and producer. His movies include *E.T.* (1982) and the Academy Award-winning *Schindler's List* (1993).

spi·er /spī́ ər/ *n.* somebody who spies or reconnoiters (*archaic*)

spiff·ing /spíffing/ *adj. U.K.* exceptionally good (*dated informal*) [Late 19thC. Origin unknown.]

spiff up /spìf úp/ **(spiffed up, spiff·ing up, spiffs up)** *vt.* to improve something by adding enhancing features (*informal*) [Late 19thC. Origin unknown.]

spiff·y /spíffee/ **(-i·er, -i·est)** *adj.* stylish or modern and attractive (*informal*) ○ *"a spiffy collection of supercomputers blinking away in a room of their own"* (Kathleen O'Gorman, *Detroit Free Press*; 1997) [Mid-19thC. Origin unknown.] —**spiffily** *adv.* —**spif·fi·ness** *n.*

spig·ot /spíggət/ *n.* **1. OUTDOOR FAUCET** faucet situated out of doors **2. INDOOR FAUCET** an indoor faucet (*regional*) **3. TAP FITTED TO CASK** a tap, usually wooden, that is fitted to a cask **4. PLUG FOR CASK HOLE** a plug for the vent hole of a cask [14thC. Origin uncertain: perhaps via Old French from Old Provençal *espiga* "ear of grain," from Latin *spica* (see SPIKE†).]

WORD KEY: REGIONAL NOTE

The word ***spigot*** spreads south and west out of Pennsylvania, where it yields to the New England term *faucet* in the northernmost counties. To the west, *faucet* and *tap* are usual in the Inland North. In the Upper Midwest and Western states, the form *spicket* reflects Midland and Southern influence.

spike[1] /spīk/ *n.* **1. POINTED METAL OR WOODEN PIECE** a sharply pointed piece of metal or wood, especially one of a number along the top of a railing, fence, or wall **2.** CONSTR **LARGE NAIL** a long heavy metal nail **3.** CLOTHES **METAL POINT ON RUNNING SHOE SOLE** a pointed metal stud, part of a set attached to the sole of an athlete's shoe to give better grip (*often used in the plural*) ◊ **cleat 4. SHARP POINT** narrow sharp point **5.** ZOOL **UNBRANCHED ANTLER OF DEER** the antler of a young deer, straight and without branches **6.** ELEC **VARIATION IN VOLTAGE** an abrupt temporary surge in the voltage or current in an electrical circuit. The change may be caused by turning off appliances, a lightning strike, or power being restored after an outage. **7. IMAGE OF PEAK AND FALL** a graphic representation of a sharp rise followed by a sharp fall, especially on a graph or as a reading on an instrument **8.** SPORTS **DOWNWARD SMASH OF VOLLEYBALL** a hard smash of a volleyball, hit close to the net and straight down into the opponent's court **9.** FOOTBALL **SIGN OF VICTORY AFTER TOUCHDOWN** a slamming of the ball to the ground in the end zone to signify triumph after a player has scored a touchdown **10.** *U.K.* **HOSTEL FOR PEOPLE WITHOUT HOMES** a hostel that houses people who have no place to live (*dated slang*) **11.** = **hypodermic needle** (*slang*) **12. METAL PART FOR GRIPPING AND CLIMBING** a sharp pointed metal projection strapped to a boot as an aid in gripping and climbing something **13. METAL ROD FOR LOOSE PAPERS** a pointed metal rod mounted on a base onto which loose papers are thrust, especially rejected news stories (*dated*) **14. SUDDEN BRIEF INCREASE** a sharp abrupt and brief rise in something **15.** ZOOL **MACKEREL** a young mackerel ■ **spikes** *npl.* **1.** SPORTS **PAIR OF SHOES WITH METAL STUDS** a pair of athletic shoes whose soles are equipped with pointed metal studs to give better traction **2.** CLOTHES **SPIKE HEEL SHOES** a pair of spike heel shoes (*informal*) ■ *v.* **(spiked, spik·ing, spikes) 1.** *vt.* **SNEAKILY ADD SOMETHING TO DRINK** to put alcohol, a drug, or a poison into another person's drink surreptitiously **2. FLAVOR PUNCH WITH ALCOHOL** to add alcohol, e.g., wine, to punch **3.** *vt.* SPORTS **CAUSE INJURY WITH SPIKES ON SHOE** to injure another player or competitor with the spikes of an athletic shoe **4.** *vi.* **RISE ABRUPTLY** to rise sharply and briefly **5.** *vt.* PRESS **DISCARD POTENTIAL NEWS STORY** to reject or decide not to use a news story (*slang*) **6.** *vt.* SPORTS **SMASH VOLLEYBALL DOWNWARD** to leap high close to the net and hit a volleyball straight down into an opponent's court **7.** *vt.* **RENDER USELESS** to make something useless or ineffective (*informal*) ○ *spike a rumor* **8.** *vt.* ARMS **DISABLE CANNON WITH SPIKE** to render a cannon useless by driving a spike into its vent [13thC. Origin uncertain: ultimately from an Indo-European base meaning "sharp point," which is also the ancestor of English *spit*[2], *spire*, and *spoke*.] —**spiked** *adj.*
◇ **hang up your spikes** to retire from a job, especially in a professional sport

spike[2] /spīk/ *n.* **1.** AGRIC **EAR OF GRAIN** an ear of grain such as wheat or barley **2.** PLANTS **FLOWER CLUSTER** a long cluster of flowers attached directly to a stem with the newest flowers at the tip. ◊ **inflorescence, raceme** [14thC. From Latin *spica* "ear of grain." Ultimately from an Indo-European base meaning "sharp point," which is also the ancestor of English *spine* and *spike*[1].]

spike heel *n.* a high pointed heel on a woman's shoe, or a shoe with such a heel

spike lav·en·der *n.* a European mint related to lavender that has light purple flowers and yields an oil used in paints. Latin name: *Lavandula latifolia.*

spike·let /spī́klət/ *n.* a small flower spike, especially any of the basic units of the flower cluster of a grass or sedge

spike·nard /spīk naàrd/ (*plural* **-nards** *or* **-nard**) *n.* **1. HIMALAYAN PLANT** a perennial aromatic Himalayan plant of the valerian family that has pinkish purple flowers. Latin name: *Nardostachys jatamansi.* **2. ANCIENT FRAGRANT OINTMENT** a fragrant ointment derived from spikenard, used in ancient times **3. PLANT WITH AROMATIC ROOT** a North American plant of the ginseng family that has small whitish flowers, purplish berries, and aromatic roots. Latin name: *Aralia racemosa.* [14thC. From medieval Latin *spica nardi*, literally "spike of nard" (translation of Greek *nardou stakhus*).]

spike-rush *n.* a perennial plant with narrow leaves and small flowers that grows in temperate regions. Genus: *Eleocharis.*

spik·y /spī́kee/ **(-i·er, -i·est)** *adj.* **1. WITH ONE OR SEVERAL SPIKES** with one or more narrow sharp points **2. IRRITABLE** easily made angry (*informal*) —**spik·i·ly** *adv.* —**spik·i·ness** *n.*

spile /spīl/ *n.* **1. HEAVY SUPPORTING POST** a heavy timber post driven into the ground as a foundation or support **2. WOODEN PEG** a wooden peg, especially used as a plug or stopper **3. TREE-TAPPING SPOUT** a tap for drawing sap from the sugar maple tree ■ *vt.* **(spiled, spil·ing, spiles) 1. SUPPORT WITH POST** to provide or support something with a heavy post driven into the ground **2. TAP TREE FOR SAP** to draw sap from a tree with a spout or spigot [Early 16thC. Via Dutch *spijl* from Middle Dutch or Middle Low German *spile* "splinter, wooden pin" (see SPILL[2]).]

spill[1] /spil/ *v.* **(spilled** *or* **spilt** /spilt/, **spilled** *or* **spilt, spill·ing, spills) 1.** *vti.* **FLOW FROM CONTAINER** to flow or allow something to flow from a container, especially accidentally and usually resulting in loss or waste **2.** *vi.* **COME OUT OF CONFINED SPACE** to come out from a building or other confined space in large numbers, often to the wrong place ○ *The fans spilled out onto the field* **3.** *vt.* **DIVULGE** to reveal or divulge something, often unintentionally (*informal*) ○ *spilled the news* **4.** *vti.* **FALL OFF SOMETHING** to fall off, or make somebody fall off, something onto the ground or floor, especially from a horse, bicycle, or motorbike (*informal*) **5.** *vt.* SAILING **LET WIND OUT OF SAIL** to let the wind escape from a sail ■ *n.* **1. ACT OF FALLING FROM SOMETHING** a tumble to the ground or floor, especially from a bicycle, motorbike, or horse (*informal*) **2. SOMETHING THAT RUNS OVER** a quantity of something that flows accidentally or unintentionally from a container or confined area, or an instance of this happening ○ *Workers fought hard to contain the spill.* **3.** = **spillway** [Old English *spillan* "to kill." The underlying meaning is "to shed blood."] —**spill·a·ble** *adj.* —**spill·er** *n.* ◇ **spill blood** wound or kill people ◇ **spill the beans** reveal a secret (*slang*) ◇ **spill your guts** tell or confess everything

spill over *vi.* **1. OVERFLOW** to overflow a container or an enclosed area **2. SPREAD OUT** to spread out from a confined space into a nearby area

spill[2] /spil/ *n.* **1.** SPLINTER OR PAPER USED FOR LIGHTING a splinter or twist of paper used to light something, e.g., a pipe or candle **2.** = **spile** *n.* 2 [14thC. From Middle Low German *spile* (source of English *spile*).]

spill·age /spíllij/ *n.* **1.** SPILLING OF SOMETHING the act of spilling something **2.** QUANTITY SPILLED a quantity of something that has been spilled

Spil·lane /spi láyn/, **Mickey** (*b.* 1918) U.S. writer. He specialized in crime fiction known for its raw energy and violence. Many of his stories featured the detective Mike Hammer. Real name **Frank Morrison Spillane**

spil·li·kin /spíllə kin/, **spi·li·kin** *n.* JACKSTRAW any of the thin pieces used in the game of jackstraws (*dated*) ■ **spil·li·kins, spi·likins** *npl.* JACKSTRAWS the game of jackstraws (*dated*) (*takes a singular verb*) [Mid-18thC. Formed from SPILL[2], literally "small spill."]

spill·o·ver /spíl ōvər/ *n.* **1.** = **spillage** *n.* 2 **2.** SPREAD any spread or expansion of something **3.** EFFECT an indirect effect of something

spill·way /spíl wày/ *n.* a channel for carrying away excess water, e.g., at a reservoir or dam

spilt past tense, past participle of **spill**

spilth /spilth/ *n.* = **spillage** [Early 17thC. Formed from SPILL[1].]

spin /spin/ *v.* (**spun** /spun/, **spun, spin·ning, spins**) **1.** *vti.* ROTATE QUICKLY to turn or make something turn round and round rapidly, as if on an axis ○ *He spun a coin.* ○ *watch the dancers spinning around the room* **2.** *vi.* FACE ABOUT QUICKLY to turn around rapidly to face in the opposite direction **3.** *vti.* TEXTILES CREATE YARN FROM RAW MATERIALS to twist raw fibers, e.g., of wool, silk, or cotton, so that they form a continuous yarn or thread **4.** *vti.* BIOL MAKE WEB OR COCOON to make a web or cocoon from filaments extruded from the body **5.** *vi.* ENG ROTATE FREELY to revolve or rotate rapidly around an axis ○ *Our wheels spun on the ice.* **6.** *vti.* SPORTS ROTATE RAPIDLY IN CHANGED DIRECTION to strike, throw, or kick something in a way that makes it revolve and change direction when it hits something, or to rotate and change direction in this way **7.** *vti.* AEROSP DIVE STEEPLY to go into a steep spiral dive, or make an aircraft do this **8.** *vt.* MUSIC PLAY RECORDING to play a piece of recorded music (*informal*) **9.** *vt.* INVENT LONG STORY to make up an extended story or a series of lies **10.** *vti.* SHAPE PUBLIC OPINION to cast somebody's remarks or relate a story in such a way as to influence public opinion in a desired way (*slang*) **11.** *vti.* DRY CLOTHES to remove most of the water from washed clothes in a washing machine by rotating them rapidly **12.** *vi.* BECOME DIZZY to feel dazed, as if whirling round ○ *my head is spinning* **13.** *vi.* DRIVE FAST AND WELL to drive smoothly and speedily **14.** *vi.* ANGLING FISH WITH RAPIDLY MOVING BAIT to fish with a rod, line, and reel, constantly drawing a revolving bait or lure through the water ■ *n.* **1.** ROTATION a quick rotating movement **2.** SPORTS ROTATION CAUSING CHANGED DIRECTION rotation given to a ball to make it change direction **3.** MARKETING INTERPRETATIVE POINT OF VIEW a viewpoint, bias, or interpretation, especially one that is presented to influence the public in a desired way (*slang*) ○ *There's no way the company can put a favorable spin on this disaster.* **4.** SPORTS ROTATION WHILE SKATING a stationary rotation during figure skating **5.** AEROSP SPIRALING DIVE a steep spiral dive in an aircraft **6.** SHORT JOURNEY IN VEHICLE a brief journey taken for pleasure in a motor vehicle **7.** DRYING OPERATION IN WASHING MACHINE the rapid rotation of washed clothes in a washing machine to remove most of the moisture from them **8.** DIZZY STATE a state of mental disorientation or dizziness **9.** PHYS ANGULAR MOMENTUM the intrinsic angular momentum of an elementary particle or system of such particles independent of its motion **10.** PHYS QUANTUM PROPERTY OF ANGULAR MOMENTUM the quantum property or number of an elementary particle that is a measure of its intrinsic angular momentum and magnetic moment [Old English *spinnan*. Ultimately from an Indo-European base meaning "to stretch, spin" that is also the ancestor of English *spider, spindle,* and *span.*] ◇ **spin your wheels** expend a lot of effort without making progress

spin off *v.* (*informal*) **1.** *vti.* COMM DERIVE SOMETHING INCIDENTALLY FROM SOMETHING ELSE to derive a new product, material, or service from something that already exists, or be derived in this way **2.** *vt.* FIN DIVEST A COMPANY OF A SUBSIDIARY to divest a company of a subsidiary by distributing the subsidiary's shares to shareholders in the parent corporation

spin out *v.* **1.** *vi.* LOSE CONTROL OF VEHICLE to skid out of control **2.** *vt.* MAKE SUPPLIES LAST to make something last longer than it ordinarily would, usually by careful management **3.** *vt.* PROLONG SOMETHING to make an activity last longer than it needs to, usually by adding something unnecessary

spi·na bif·i·da /spīnə bíffidə/ *n.* a congenital condition in which part of the spinal cord or meninges protrudes through a cleft in the spinal column, resulting in partial to total paralysis of the lower body. Spina bifida can sometimes be prevented by taking folic acid from the start of pregnancy. [From modern Latin, "spine split in two"]

spin·ach /spínich/ *n.* **1.** PLANT WITH EDIBLE LEAVES an annual plant with large, thick, dark-green, edible leaves. It is native to Asia and is widely cultivated in temperate regions. Latin name: *Spinacia oleracea.* **2.** EDIBLE LEAVES OF SPINACH PLANT the dark-green leaves of the spinach plant eaten cooked as a vegetable or raw in salads. They are rich in iron. [14thC. Via Old French *espinache* from, ultimately, Persian *aspānāk*.]

spi·nal /spīn'l/ *adj.* **1.** RELATING TO SPINE on, in, near, or relating to a spine, especially a backbone **2.** LIKE SPINE resembling a spine ■ *n.* MED SPINAL ANESTHETIC spinal anesthesia or a spinal anesthetic (*informal*) — **spi·nal·ly** *adv.*

spi·nal an·es·the·sia *n.* **1.** ANESTHESIA BY INJECTION INTO SPINE an anesthesia of the lower half of the body achieved by injecting an anesthetic into the fluid surrounding the spinal cord. ◊ **epidural** **2.** LOSS OF SENSATION FROM SPINAL INJURY the loss of sensation in part of the body caused by injury to the spine

spi·nal ca·nal *n.* a passage that runs through the opening in the middle of each vertebra of the spinal column and contains the spinal cord, the meninges, nerve roots, and blood vessels

spi·nal col·umn *n.* the axis of the skeleton of a vertebrate animal, extending from the head and consisting of a series of interconnected vertebrae that enclose and protect the spinal cord

spi·nal cord *n.* a thick whitish cord of nerve tissue extending from the bottom of the brain through the spinal column and giving rise to pairs of spinal nerves that supply the body. The spinal cord and brain together form the central nervous system.

spi·nal men·in·gi·tis *n.* inflammation of the membranes surrounding the spinal cord that particularly affects young children

spin con·trol *n.* the attempt to evoke a desired public response to something, especially a statement, policy, or action (*slang*)

spin cy·cle *n.* **1.** EXTRACTION OF WATER IN WASHING MACHINE a phase in which newly washed laundry is spun rapidly in the perforated drum of a washing machine in order to extract most of the water **2.** INSTANCE OF OPINION MANIPULATION an instance of, or the degree to which, public opinion is manipulated by efforts to control interpretation of something such as a leader's words (*slang*)

spin·dle /spínd'l/ *n.* **1.** TEXTILES SPECIALLY SHAPED ROD FOR SPINNING THREAD a handheld stick or rod with a notched end through which strands of natural fibers are drawn, then twisted into thread and wound around the rod **2.** TEXTILES THREAD-SPINNING ROD ON SPINNING WHEEL a device similar to the handheld spindle, attached to a spinning wheel **3.** MECHANICAL THREAD-SPINNING DEVICE a device on a spinning machine for spinning thread and winding it onto bobbins **4.** MECH ENG ROTATING ROD FOR DEVICE a rotating rod on a device such as a lathe, turntable, or door handle **5.** SPINDLE-SHAPED PIECE OF WOOD a long thin piece of wood such as a table leg or baluster that is shaped like a spindle **6.** BIOL SPINDLE-SHAPED CELL STRUCTURE a spindle-shaped structure along which chromosomes are distributed and drawn apart during meiosis and mitosis **7.** SPIKE FOR HOLDING PERSONAL PAPERS an upright spike fixed to a base, on which letters or bills are impaled **8.** INSECTS DRAGONFLY a dragonfly (*regional*) **9.** SHIPPING TOPPED METAL ROD USED AS WARNING a metal rod surmounted by a ball or lantern and fixed to a rock or shoal, used as a warning to approaching vessels ■ *v.* (**-dled, -dling, -dles**) **1.** *vti.* IMPALE SOMETHING ON SPINDLE to place on an upright spindle **2.** *vt.* MAKE WITH SPINDLE to form or equip something with a spindle **3.** *vi.* BOT RAPIDLY GROW TALL AND SLENDER to grow quickly into a high slender stalk or stem [Old English *spinel*. Ultimately from the same prehistoric Germanic base as *spin.*]

spin·dle cell *n.* a narrow, elongated cell characteristic of certain cancers

spin·dle tree *n.* an evergreen tree or shrub of the staff tree family with small flowers and red fruits. Its hard wood was used in the past to make spindles. Genus: *Euonymus.*

spin·dly /spíndlee/ (**-dli·er, -dli·est**), **spin·dling** /spíndling/ *adj.* long or tall, thin, and weak-looking

spin doc·tor /spín mīstər/, **spin·mei·ster** *n.* somebody whose job is to present the actions of a person or organization in the best possible light, especially via the news media (*slang*)

spin·drift /spín drìft/ *n.* **1.** SPRAY FROM WAVES spray that blows from the surface of the sea **2.** DRIVING SNOW OR SAND driving snow or sand in a storm [Early 17thC. Alteration (probably influenced by SPIN) of SPOONDRIFT.]

spin-dry (**spin-dried, spin-dry·ing, spin-dries**) *vt.* to remove most of the water from washed laundry by spinning it in a washing machine or a spin-dryer

spin-dry·er, **spin-dri·er** *n.* a machine that forces most of the water out of wet laundry by spinning it around rapidly in a perforated drum

spine /spīn/ *n.* **1.** ANAT = **spinal column** **2.** PRINTING VERTICAL BACK OF BOOK COVER the vertical back of a book's cover or a record's sleeve, usually printed with the title and the name of the author or performer **3.** ZOOL HARD SHARP PROJECTION ON ANIMAL'S BODY a sharp stiff projection on the body of an animal or a fish, e.g., the quill of a porcupine or the ray of a fish's fin **4.** BOT SHARP POINT ON PLANT a stiff sharp pointed plant part that is a modification of part of a leaf, e.g., in holly, or of an entire leaf, e.g., in cacti **5.** GEOG RIDGE IN MOUNTAINS a continuous ridge in a range of mountains or hills [14thC. Via Old French *espine* from Latin *spina* "thorn." Ultimately from an Indo-European base meaning "sharp point" that is also the ancestor of English *spike*[1] and *spike*[2].]

spine-chill·er *n.* something, especially a book, movie, or story, that is meant to frighten people — **spine-chill·ing** *adj.* —**spine-chill·ing·ly** *adv.*

spi·nel /spə nél/ *n.* a hard crystalline usually red mineral that consists of mixed oxides of magnesium, aluminum, and, in small amounts, iron or manganese. It is sometimes used as a gemstone. [Early 16thC. Via French *spinelle* from, ultimately, Latin *spina* (see SPINE); from its pointed crystals.]

spine·less /spínləss/ *adj.* **1.** WEAK AND COWARDLY lacking in willpower, courage, or strength of character **2.** WITHOUT SPINE lacking a vertebral column — **spine·less·ly** *adv.* —**spine·less·ness** *n.*

WORD KEY: SYNONYMS

See Synonyms at ***cowardly***.

spi·nes·cent /spī néss'nt/ *adj.* having or growing a spine or spines [Late 18thC. From Latin *spinescent-*, the present participle stem of *spinescere* "to become thorny," from *spina* (see SPINE).]

spin·et /spínnit/ *n.* **1.** SMALL KEYBOARD INSTRUMENT a small upright piano or electronic organ **2.** SMALL HARPSICHORD a small harpsichord, popular in the 18th century, that has the strings set at a slant to the keyboard [Mid-17thC. Via French *espinette* from Italian *spinetta*, of uncertain origin: probably formed from *spina* "quill," from Latin (see SPINE); from the original use of quills resembling thorns to pluck the strings.]

spine-tin·gling *adj.* causing nervous fear or excitement —**spine-tin·gling·ly** *adv.*

spi·nif·er·ous /spī níffərəss/ *adj.* having, producing, or bearing spines or needles [Mid-17thC. Coined from Latin *spina* (see SPINE) + -FEROUS.]

spi·ni·fex /spínə fèks/ (*plural* **-fex·es** *or* **-fex**) *n.* a perennial Australian grass that has sharp pointed leaves and grows in circular mounds in arid inland areas. Genera: *Plectrachne* and *Triodia.* [Early 19thC. From modern Latin, genus name, literally "thorn-maker."]

spin·mei·ster *n.* = **spin doctor**

spin·na·ker /spínnəkər/ *n.* a large triangular sail set at the front of a racing yacht for running before the wind [Mid-19thC. Origin uncertain: perhaps an alteration of *Sphinx's acre*, from *Sphinx*, the name of the first yacht to carry such a sail.]

spin·ner /spínnər/ *n.* **1.** SOMEBODY OR SOMETHING THAT SPINS a person, object, or device that spins **2.** ANGLING FISHING LURE an angling lure that spins in the water when the line is reeled in **3.** AIR COVER FOR AIRCRAFT PROPELLER a streamlined dome-shaped cap (**fairing**) that fits over the hub of the propeller of an aircraft

spin·ner·et /spìnnə rét, spínnə rèt/ *n.* **1.** BIOL **SILK-PRODUCING ORGAN** a tiny tubular structure, usually one of two pairs, that exudes the fluid produced by the abdominal glands of a silk-producing spider **2.** TEXTILES, INDUST **PERFORATED PLATE FOR MAKING SYNTHETIC FIBER** a device for making filaments of synthetic fiber, consisting of a finely perforated plate through which viscous liquid is extruded

spin·ney /spínnee/ (*plural* **-neys**) *n. U.K.* a small thicket or wood [Late 16thC. Via Old French *espinei* "thorny hedge" from Latin *spinetum*, from *spina* (see SPINE).]

spin·ning frame *n.* a machine that draws out fibers, twists them into yarn or thread, and winds them onto spindles

spin·ning jen·ny *n.* a spinning machine invented in the 18th century that was the first practical device to wind yarn onto more than one spindle. Because it allowed one person to spin several yarns at once the spinning jenny was a major invention of the Industrial Revolution.

spin·ning mule *n.* = **mule**[1] *n.* 5

spin·ning top *n.* = **top**[2] *n.*

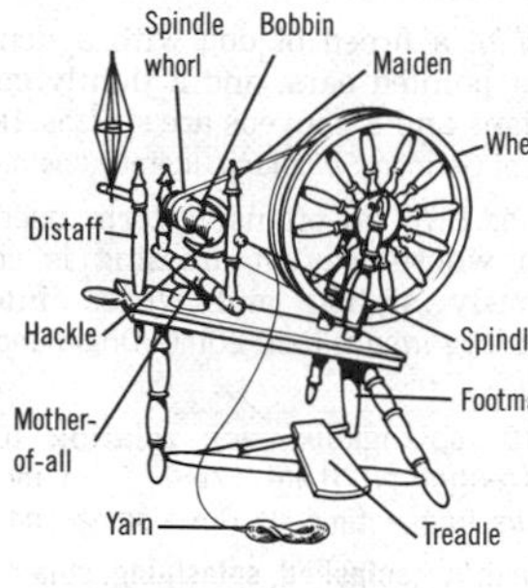

Spinning wheel

spin·ning wheel *n.* a machine used at home for twisting fibers into yarn or thread and winding it onto a spindle by means of a large wheel driven by hand or a treadle

spin·off /spín àwf/, **spin-off** *v.* (**-offed, -off·ing, -offs; spin-offed, spin-off·ing, spin-offs**) **PRODUCE AS BY-PRODUCT** to derive a new product, material, or service from something that already exists, or be derived in this way ■ *n.* **1. DERIVATIVE OF SOMETHING** a product, material, or service deriving from something that already exists **2.** BUSINESS **SUBSIDIARY DIVESTED BY DISTRIBUTING STOCK** a subsidiary of a company that is divested by means of a distribution of its shares of stock to shareholders of the parent corporation

spin·out /spín owt/, **spin-out** *n.* a skid, especially in a motor vehicle, that is out of control

Spi·no·za /spi nṓzə/, **Baruch** (1632–77) Dutch philosopher. Rejecting the Judaism of his cultural background, he developed a philosophy that combined rationalist and pantheistic elements. His major work was his *Ethics* (1674).

Spi·no·zism /spə nṓ zìzzəm/ *n.* the philosophical system developed by Baruch Spinoza, defining God as a unique impersonal deity with an infinite number of attributes and modes —**Spi·no·zist** *n.*

spin sta·bi·li·za·tion *n.* a method of steadying the flight of a projectile such as a bullet, shell, or rocket by spinning it about its long axis

spin·ster /spínstər/ *n.* **1. OFFENSIVE TERM** an offensive term for a woman, especially one who is no longer young or is of advanced years who has never married a man (*dated offensive*) **2.** LAW **UNMARRIED WOMAN IN LEGAL DOCUMENTS** in some legal documents, a woman who has never married a man **3. WOMAN SPINNER OF YARN** in former times, a woman whose livelihood was spinning yarn [14thC. Formed from SPIN.] —**spin·ster·hood** *n.*

spin·thar·i·scope /spin thérrə skōp/ *n.* an instrument used to detect ionizing radiation such as alpha particles that produces flashes of light on a phosphorescent screen [Early 20thC. Coined from Greek *spintharis* "spark" + -SCOPE.]

spin-the-bottle *n.* a game in which players in turn spin a bottle that is lying flat on the ground or floor, and then kiss the person it points at when it stops

spin·to /spín tō/ (*plural* **-tos**) *adj.* relating to an operatic voice that is both lyric and dramatic [Mid-20thC. From Italian, literally "pushed."]

spi·nule /spī́ nyool/ *n.* BOT a tiny spine or thorn — **spi·nu·lose** /spī́nyə lōss/ *adj.*

spin·y /spínee/ (**-i·er, -i·est**) *adj.* **1. WITH SPINES** with or covered with spines **2. THORNY** with thorns or prickles **3. LIKE SPINE** shaped like a spine —**spin·i·ness** *n.*

spin·y ant·eat·er *n.* = **echidna**

spin·y eel *n.* an African or Asian freshwater fish that resembles an eel and has a sensitive elongated snout with tubular nostrils and several sharp spines in front of the dorsal fin. Family: Mastacembelidae.

spin·y-head·ed worm *n.* a parasitic unsegmented worm that has a proboscis composed of rows of hooked spines, used for attachment to a vertebrate's intestinal wall. Phylum: Acanthocephala.

spin·y lob·ster *n.* a large edible crustacean that is like a lobster but has a spiny shell and lacks enlarged pincers. Family: Palinuridae.

spir·a·cle /spī́rək'l, spírrək'l/ *n.* **1.** GEOL **VENT IN LAVA FLOW** a small vent in a lava flow that allows the escape of built-up gases **2.** BIOL **BLOWHOLE** a blowhole (*technical*) **3.** INSECTS **SMALL APERTURE IN AN INSECT** a small paired aperture along the side of the thorax or abdomen of an insect or spider through which air enters and leaves **4.** ZOOL **SMALL GILL SLIT** a small gill slit or opening behind the eye area of some fishes, such as skates and rays [Early 17thC. Via Old French from Latin *spiraculum*, from *spirare* "to breathe" (see SPIRIT).] —**spi·rac·u·lar** /spə rákyələr, spī-/ *adj.*

spi·rae·a *n.* = **spirea**

spi·ral /spī́rəl/ *n.* **1.** GEOM **CONTINUOUS CIRCLING FLAT CURVE** a flat curve or series of curves that constantly increase or decrease in size in circling around a central point **2.** GEOM **HELIX** a helix **3. SOMETHING WITH CURVING CIRCULAR PATTERN** something that has a helical or spiral form **4.** AIR **FLIGHT MANEUVER** a maneuver in which an aircraft makes a continuous banking turn as it descends **5.** ECON **CHANGE IN ECONOMIC CYCLE** a continuous widening increase or decrease of prices, wages, or interest rates ■ *adj.* **1. CONTINUOUSLY CIRCLING WITH FLAT CURVES** with a flat curve or series of curves that constantly increase or decrease in size in circling around a central point **2. HELICAL** helical in shape ■ *v.* (**-raled** *or* **-ralled, -ral·ing** *or* **-ral·ling, -rals**) **1.** *vti.* **MOVE IN SPIRAL** to move or make something move in a spiral **2.** *vi.* ECON **CHANGE INCREASINGLY** to increase or decrease with ever increasing speed **3.** *vti.* **SHAPE SOMETHING LIKE SPIRAL** to take on or make something take on a spiral shape [Mid-16thC. From medieval Latin *spiralis* "coiled," from Latin *spira* (see SPIRE[2]).]

spi·ral bind·ing *n.* a binding, especially for a notebook or booklet, in which pages are fastened together with a spiral of wire or plastic that coils through a series of punched holes —**spi·ral-bound** *adj.*

spi·ral gal·ax·y *n.* a galaxy consisting of an older central nucleus of stars from which extend two spiral arms of gas, dust, and newer stars

spi·ral of Ar·chi·me·des *n.* MATH a spiral curve formed by a point moving at constant speed to or from a fixed point and along a line rotating, also at a constant speed, about the point [Mid-17thC. Named for ARCHIMEDES, who described it.]

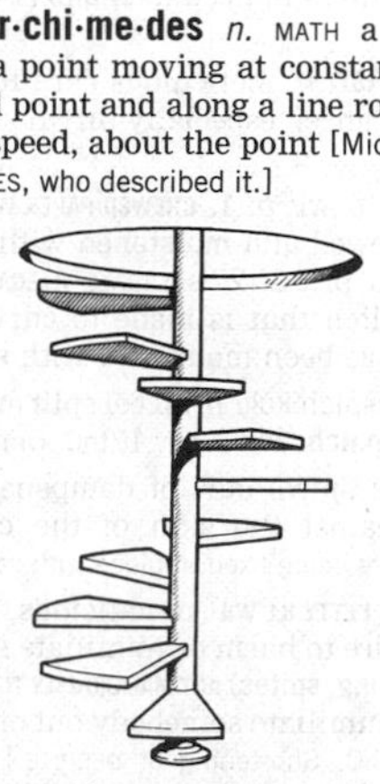
Spiral staircase

spi·ral stair·case *n.* a staircase that winds around a central axis, often made of stone or iron

spi·rant /spī́rənt/ *n., adj.* PHON = **fricative** [Mid-19thC. From Latin *spirant-*, the present participle stem of *spirare* "to breathe" (see SPIRIT).]

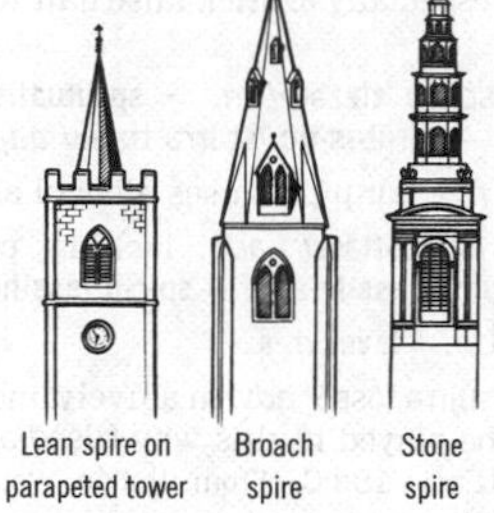

Spire

spire[1] /spīr/ *n.* **1.** ARCHIT **NARROW TAPERING STRUCTURE TOPPING SOMETHING** a tall narrow pointed structure on the top of a roof, tower, or steeple **2.** BOT **POINTED SHOOT OF PLANT** a slender, upward-pointing part of a plant such as a blade of grass or the top of a tree **3. UPWARD-FACING SPIKE** the top part of something narrow and pointed such as a mountain peak ■ *vi.* (**spired, spir·ing, spires**) **RISE TO POINT** to rise to a narrow point [Old English *spīr*. Ultimately from an Indo-European base meaning "sharp point" that is also the ancestor of English *spit*[2], *spike*[1], and *spine*.]

spire[2] /spīr/ *n.* **1. SPIRAL** a spiral or coil **2. CONVOLUTION OF SPIRAL** a convolution of a spiral or coil [Late 16thC. Via Latin *spira* "coil" from Greek *speira*.]

spi·re·a /spī rée ə/, **spi·rae·a** *n.* a shrub of the rose family that has dense clusters of small white or pink flowers. Genus: *Spiraea*. [Mid-17thC. Via modern Latin, genus name, from Greek *speiraia* "privet" (source of English *aspirin*), from *speira* "coil, twist."]

spi·ril·lum /spī ríIləm/ (*plural* **-la** /-lə/) *n.* a spiral-shaped or curved bacterium with a rigid body requiring oxygen for respiration. Genus: *Spirillum*. [Late 19thC. From modern Latin, genus name, literally "little spiral," from Latin *spira* (see SPIRE[2]).] —**spi·ril·lar** *adj.*

spir·it /spírrət/ *n.* **1. LIFE FORCE OF INDIVIDUAL** a vital force that characterizes a living being as being alive **2. WILL** somebody's will, sense of self, or enthusiasm for living **3. ENTHUSIASM** an enthusiasm and energy for living **4. DISPOSITION** somebody's personality or temperament ○ *She has a generous spirit.* **5. ATTITUDE** somebody's attitude or state of mind ○ *in the spirit of compromise* **6. GROUP LOYALTY** a sense of enthusiasm and loyalty that somebody feels through belonging to a group ○ *school spirit* **7. IMPORTANT INFLUENCE** somebody or something that is a divine, inspiring, or animating influence ○ *one of the guiding spirits of the Peace Movement* **8. REAL MEANING** the intention behind something such as a rule or decree, rather than its literal interpretation **9. SHARED OUTLOOK** a prevailing mood or outlook characteristic of a place or time **10.** PARANORMAL **SUPERNATURAL ENTITY** a supernatural being that does not have a physical body, e.g., a ghost, fairy, angel, or demon **11. PERSON** somebody who shows a specific quality **12. SOUL** somebody's soul, especially that of a dead person **13.** BEVERAGES **ALCOHOLIC DRINK** a strong alcoholic liquor made by distillation (*often used in the plural*) **14.** CHEM **DISTILLED LIQUID** any liquid produced by distillation, especially a distilled solution of ethanol and water (*often used in the plural*) **15.** CHEM **ALCOHOLIC SOLUTION** a solution of an essence or volatile substance in alcohol (*often used in the plural*) ■ **spir·its** *npl.* **MOOD** a particular frame of mind or mood ■ *vt.* (**-it·ed, -it·ing, -its**) **REMOVE SECRETLY** to take somebody or something away quickly in a secret or mysterious way ○ *spirited him out of the room* [13thC. Via Anglo-Norman from Latin *spiritus*, literally "breath," from *spirare* "to breathe," of unknown origin. The underlying idea is of the "breath" of life.] ◇ **out of spirits** sad or dejected

WORD KEY: ORIGIN

The Latin verb *spirare*, from which *spirit* is derived, is also the source of English *aspire, conspire, expire, inspire, perspire, respire*, and *transpire*.

Spir·it /spírrət/ *n.* in Christianity, the Holy Spirit

spir·it·ed /spírrətəd/ *adj.* **1. LIVELY** lively and vigorous **2. ANIMATED** with great animation **3. BEHAVING IN SPECIFIED WAY** behaving in a way that has a specified feeling, mood, or character (*usually used in combination*) ○ *low-spirited* —**spir·it·ed·ly** *adv.* —**spir·it·ed·ness** *n.*

spir·it gum *n.* a glue made from a solution of gum in ether, used especially to stick false hair to an actor's skin

spir·it·ism /spírrə tìzzəm/ *n.* = **spiritualism** *n.* 1 —**spir·it·ist** *n.* —**spir·it·is·tic** /spìrrə tístik/ *adj.*

spir·it lamp *n.* a lamp that uses alcohol as fuel

spir·it·less /spírrətləss/ *adj.* lacking courage or energy —**spir·it·less·ly** *adv.* —**spir·it·less·ness** *n.*

spir·it lev·el *n.* = **level** *n.* 8

spir·i·to·so /spìrrə tṓssō/ *adv.* in a lively and vivacious way, or to be played in this way (*used as a musical direction*) [Early 18thC. From Italian, "spirited."] —**spi·ri·to·so** *adj.*

spir·it·ous /spírrətəss/ *adj.* spirituous (*archaic*)

spir·its of am·mo·ni·a *n.* = **sal volatile**

spir·its of harts·horn *npl.* ammonium hydroxide (*archaic*) [So called because hart's horn was an early source of ammonia]

spir·its of tur·pen·tine *n.* = **turpentine** *n.* 3

spir·its of wine *n.* alcohol (*archaic*)

spir·i·tu·al /spírrichoo əl/ *adj.* 1. **OF THE SOUL** relating to the soul or spirit, usually in contrast to material things 2. RELIG **OF RELIGION** relating to religious or sacred things rather than worldly things 3. **TEMPERAMENTALLY OR INTELLECTUALLY AKIN** connected by an affinity of the mind, spirit, or temperament ○ *spiritual mother of the young artist* 4. **REFINED** showing great refinement and concern with the higher things in life ■ *n.* 1. MUSIC, CHR **FOLK HYMN** a religious song, especially one arising from African American culture 2. **THINGS OF THE SPIRIT** matters concerning the spirit ○ *He was deeply concerned with anything to do with the spiritual.* —**spir·i·tu·al·ly** *adv.* —**spir·i·tu·al·ness** *n.*

spir·i·tu·al bou·quet *n.* in the Roman Catholic Church, a promise of, or performance of, devotional acts, performed on behalf of another, e.g., in memory of somebody who has died

spir·i·tu·al·ism /spírrichoo ə lìzzəm/ *n.* 1. PARANORMAL **BELIEF IN COMMUNICATION WITH DEAD PEOPLE** the belief that the spirits of dead people can communicate with the living, especially through mediums 2. PARANORMAL **PRACTICES OF COMMUNICATING WITH DEAD PEOPLE** the practices used among people who believe that communication occurs between the dead and the living 3. RELIG **BELIEFS EMPHASIZING SPIRITUAL MATTERS** a system of belief that emphasizes the spiritual nature of existence 4. PHILOS **PHILOSOPHY EMPHASIZING SPIRITUAL NATURE OF REALITY** the philosophical doctrine that all reality is spiritual, not material 5. **SPIRITUAL STATE** the quality or state of being spiritual —**spir·i·tu·al·ist** *n.*

spir·i·tu·al·i·ty /spìrrichoo állətee/ (*plural* **-ties**) *n.* 1. **SPIRITUAL QUALITY** the quality or condition of being spiritual 2. CHR **CHURCH PROPERTY OR REVENUE** the property or revenue belonging to a church or church official (*often used in the plural*)

spir·i·tu·al·ize /spírrichoo ə lìz/ (**-ized, -iz·ing, -iz·es** /spírrichoo ə lìz/) *vt.* 1. **MAKE SPIRITUAL** to give something a spiritual content 2. **GIVE SPIRITUAL MEANING TO** to attribute a spiritual meaning to something —**spir·i·tu·al·i·za·tion** /spìrrichoo ələ záysh'n/ *n.* —**spir·i·tu·al·iz·er** /spírrichoo ə lìzər/ *n.*

spir·i·tu·al·ty /spìrrichoo àltee/ (*plural* **-ties**) *n.* CHR = **spirituality** *n.* 2

spir·i·tu·el /spìrrichoo él/, **spir·i·tu·elle** *adj.* showing a refined and graceful intellect [Late 17thC. SPIRITUEL from French (see SPIRITUAL), the masculine form; SPIRITUELLE from French, the feminine form.]

spir·i·tu·ous /spírrichoo əss/ *adj.* containing alcohol or made by distillation (*formal*) —**spir·i·tu·ous·ness** *n.*

spir·i·tus as·per /spírritəss áspər/ *n.* a rough breathing (*technical*) [From Latin, "rough breath"]

spir·i·tus le·nis /spìrritəss léenəss/ *n.* a smooth breathing (*technical*) [From Latin, "smooth breath"]

spir·it var·nish *n.* a varnish consisting of a resin dissolved in alcohol

spiro- *prefix.* breathing, respiration ○ *spirograph* [From Latin *spirare* "to breathe"]

spi·ro·chete /spírə kèet/ *n.* a coiled rod-shaped bacterium. The causative agents of syphilis and relapsing fever are spirochetes. Order: Spirochaetales. [Late 19thC. From modern Latin *Spirochaeta*, genus name, from Latin *spira* "coil" + *chaeta* "hair."]

spi·ro·che·to·sis /spìrōki tṓssəss/ (*plural* **-ses** /-sèez/) *n.* a disease caused by a spirochete

spi·ro·graph /spírə gràf/ *n.* an instrument that makes a record of the depth and rapidity of somebody's breathing [Late 19thC. Coined from Latin *spirare* "to breathe" + -GRAPH.] —**spi·ro·graph·ic** /spìrə gráffik/ *adj.* —**spi·ro·graph·i·cal·ly** /-gráffiklee/ *adv.* —**spi·rog·ra·phy** /spī róggrə fee/ *n.*

spi·ro·gy·ra /spìrə jírə/ *n.* a multicellular freshwater green alga. Genus: *Spirogyra.* [Late 19thC. From modern Latin, genus name, from Latin *spira* "coil" + Greek *guros* "round."]

spi·roid /spí royd/ *adj.* resembling a spiral in shape [Mid-19thC. Formed from Latin *spira* "coil" (see SPIRE[2]).]

spi·rom·e·ter /spī rommətər/ *n.* an instrument for measuring the capacity of the lungs [Mid-19thC. Coined from Latin *spirare* "to breathe" + -METER.] —**spi·ro·met·ric** /spìrə méttrik/ *adj.* —**spi·rom·e·try** /spī rómmətree/ *n.*

spi·ro·no·lac·tone /spìrənō láktōn/ *n.* a steroid used with other drugs in treating hypertension. Formula: $C_{24}H_{32}O_4S$. [Mid-20thC. Coined from *spirolactone*, name of a steroid derivative (from Latin *spira* "coil" + LACTONE) by inserting -ONE.]

spir·y *adj.* shaped like a spire (*literary*) [Early 17thC. Formed from SPIRE[1].]

spit[1] /spit/ *v.* (**spit** *or* **spat** /spat/, **spit** *or* **spat, spit·ting, spits**) 1. *vi.* **EJECT SALIVA** to expel saliva forcefully from the mouth 2. *vi.* **EXPEL SALIVA TO SHOW CONTEMPT** to show anger, contempt, or hatred by or as if by expelling saliva 3. *vt.* **EXPEL FROM YOUR MOUTH** to eject something harmful or unpleasant such as blood or food forcefully from the mouth 4. *vti.* **MAKE SOUND OF SPUTTERING** to make sputtering sounds, such as those made when a fire shoots out sparks 5. *vi.* **HISS LIKE CAT** to make a hissing explosive sound like an angry cat 6. *vti.* **RAIN OR SNOW LIGHTLY** to rain lightly or in scattered drops or flakes 7. *vt.* **UTTER ANGRILY** to utter something sharply and angrily ■ *n.* 1. **SPITTLE FROM MOUTH** saliva, especially when ejected from the mouth 2. **EXPULSION OF SOMETHING FROM THE MOUTH** a forceful ejection of saliva or something else from the mouth [Old English *spittan*. Ultimately from an Indo-European word that is also the ancestor of English *spew, spout,* and *sputum*.] ◇ **spit it out** to say something at once, especially something that has been withheld (*informal*) (*usually used as a command*)

spit up *vt.* to regurgitate or cough up something (*refers to babies*)

spit[2] /spit/ *n.* 1. COOK **THIN ROD FOR ROASTING SOMETHING** a thin rod on which something is impaled for roasting over a fire 2. GEOG **LAND PROJECTING FROM SHORE** an elongated point of land or shoal projecting into a body of water ■ *vt.* (**spit·ted, spit·ting, spits**) **IMPALE** to impale somebody or something on a roasting spit or on any long sharp pointed thing [Old English *spitu*. Ultimately from an Indo-European base meaning "sharp point" that is also the ancestor of English *spike*[1], *spire*[1], and *spine*.]

spit·al /spítt'l/ *n.* a hospital, especially for people with leprosy or others in need (*archaic*) [14thC. Shortening of HOSPITAL.]

spit and pol·ish *n.* meticulous care in presenting a neat appearance, especially in the armed forces (*informal*)

spit·ball /spít bàwl/ *n.* 1. **CHEWED PAPER WAD** a tiny wad of paper chewed and moistened with saliva that is thrown as a prank 2. BASEBALL **ILLEGAL BASEBALL PITCH** an illegal pitch that is made to curve deceptively because it has been moistened with saliva

spitch·cock /spích kòk/ *n.* an eel split and then grilled or fried. ◊ **spatchcock** [Early 17thC. Origin unknown.]

spit curl *n.* a spiral curl of dampened hair that is laid flat against the skin of the cheek or forehead [From its being fixed in place with saliva]

spite /spīt/ *n.* **PETTY ILL WILL** a malicious, usually small-minded desire to harm or humiliate somebody ■ *vt.* (**spit·ed, spit·ing, spites**) **ACT MALICIOUSLY TOWARDS** to harm, hinder, or humiliate somebody out of small-minded malice [13thC. Shortening of DESPITE.] ◇ **in spite of** notwithstanding, or without taking account of something

spite·ful /spítf'l/ *adj.* full of or showing petty maliciousness —**spite·ful·ly** *adv.* —**spite·ful·ness** *n.*

spit·fire /spít fìr/ *n.* somebody who is very quick-tempered [Late 17thC. The underlying meaning is "spitting out sparks."]

Spit·fire *n.* a British fighter plane used by the Royal Air Force during World War II

spit·ter /spíttər/ *n.* = **spitball** *n.* 1 [14thC. Formed from SPIT[1].]

spit·ting co·bra *n.* = **ringhals**

spit·ting dis·tance *n.* a short enough distance to seem within reach (*informal*)

spit·ting im·age *n.* an exact likeness of somebody (*informal*)

spit·tle /spítt'l/ *n.* 1. **SALIVA EJECTED FROM MOUTH** saliva, especially that has been or is about to be expelled from the mouth 2. **SOMETHING RESEMBLING FROTHY SALIVA** something that looks like frothy saliva, especially the secretions from spittlebugs deposited on plants (**cuckoo spit**) [15thC. Alteration (under the influence of SPIT[1]), of earlier *spattle*, from Old English *spātl* "spittle," from the same prehistoric Germanic base as *spit*[1].]

spit·tle·bug /spítt'l bùg/, **spit·tle in·sect** *n.* a small jumping plant-sucking insect whose larvae produce cuckoo spit

spit·toon /spi tóon/ *n.* a container for people to spit into. Spittoons, which used to be common in public places like bars, were especially used by men who chewed tobacco. [Mid-19thC. Formed from SPIT[1].]

spitz /spits/ *n.* a breed of dog with a dense heavy coat, erect pointed ears, and a tightly curled tail. Pomeranians and Samoyeds are spitzes. [Mid-19thC. Shortening of German *Spitzhund*, literally "pointed dog."]

spiv /spiv/ *n.* U.K. an offensive term used to refer to a man whose way of dressing is considered ostentatiously stylish and whose integrity is doubted (*slang insult*) [Mid-20thC. Origin uncertain.] —**spiv·vy** *adj.*

splanch·nic /splángknik/ *adj.* relating to the intestines (*technical*) [Late 17thC. From modern Latin *splanchnicus*, from, ultimately, Greek *splagkhna* "entrails."]

splash /splash/ *v.* (**splashed, splash·ing, splash·es**) 1. *vti.* **SPATTER LIQUID** to make a liquid scatter or fall in drops or larger amounts ○ *The children were splashing in the pool.* ○ *She splashed water over the side of the bath.* 2. *vi.* **BE SPATTERED ABOUT** to scatter or fly up in drops or larger amounts ○ *The waves splashed against the rocks.* 3. *vt.* **SPATTER DROPS OF LIQUID ON** to wet or dirty something by spattering it with liquid ○ *She splashed her blouse with the hot tea.* 4. *vti.* **MOVE WHILE SPLASHING** to make your way through water or another liquid, scattering it about ○ *They splashed through the puddles.* 5. *vt.* **ADD CONTRASTS TO** to apply contrasting color or light to something 6. *vt.* **DISPLAY PROMINENTLY** to display something such as a news headline, story, or photograph conspicuously (*usually passive*) ○ *The story was splashed across the front page.* ■ *n.* 1. **PROMINENT DISPLAY** a conspicuous display, e.g. a prominent news headline, story, or photograph 2. **NOISE OF WATER SCATTERING** an act or sound of splashing 3. **PATCH OF COLOR** an area of contrasting color or light, often irregular ○ *The dark forest was dappled with splashes of moonlight.* 4. **TINY AMOUNT OF LIQUID** a very small quantity of one liquid added to another (*informal*) ○ *Just a splash of milk in my coffee, please.* 5. **SOMETHING SPLASHED** something that is splashed 6. **MARK CAUSED BY SPLASH** a mark or stain made by something splashing or being splashed ○ *The backs of her legs were covered with splashes.* [Early 18thC. Origin uncertain: probably a variant of PLASH.] ◇ **make a splash** to attract a great deal of attention or publicity

splash down /splásh dòwn/ *vi.* AEROSP to land in the sea after a flight in space

splash·board /splásh bàwrd/ *n.* 1. NAUT **PROTECTIVE SCREEN ON BOAT** a screen for preventing water from splashing into a boat 2. AUTOMOT **PROTECTION AGAINST SPLASHES ON MOTOR VEHICLE** a protective guard that prevents mud or water from splashing the upper part of a motor vehicle and the people traveling in it

splash·down /splásh down/ *n.* the landing of a spacecraft or missile in the sea after a flight

splash·guard /splásh gaàrd/ *n.* AUTOMOT a flap attached behind the wheel of a vehicle to prevent mud or water from splashing up onto the vehicle, or onto the vehicles following

splash·y /spláshee/ (**-i·er, -i·est**) *adj.* 1. **ATTRACTING NOTICE** attracting a lot of attention (*informal*) 2. **COLORFUL** with lots of bright colors 3. **MAKING SPLASHES** with great splashing of liquid —**splash·i·ly** *adv.* —**splash·i·ness** *n.*

splat /splat/ *n.* WET SMACKING SOUND a sound made when something soft and wet hits something hard ■ *adv.* WITH SMACK with a wet smacking sound ■ *interj.* IMITATING IMPACT used to imitate the sound made when something soft and wet hits something hard [Late 19thC. An imitation of the sound.]

splat·ter /splátter/ *vti.* (**-tered, -ter·ing, -ters**) TO SPATTER to spatter or splash something, or to be spattered or splashed ■ *n.* A SPATTER a spatter or splash [Late 18thC. Origin uncertain: perhaps a blend of SPATTER and SPLASH.]

splat·ter·punk /splátter pùngk/ *n.* a form of narrative such as a story, movie, or comic strip that contains a lot of gory violence (*slang*)

splay /splay/ *vti.* (**splayed, splay·ing, splays**) **1.** SPREAD WIDE AND OUTWARD to spread out something such as the fingers or toes **2.** TURN OUT AWKWARDLY to turn something awkwardly outward **3.** ARCHIT MAKE SIDES OF SOMETHING SLANT to give something or have obliquely sloping edges, e.g., an opening in a wall that is bigger on one side than the other ■ *adj.* **1.** SPREAD FLAT AND OUTWARD sloping, turning, or spread flatly and outward **2.** TURNED AWKWARDLY OUTWARD turned awkwardly outward ■ *n.* ARCHIT SLANT TO SIDES OF OPENING an oblique slope given to the edges of something such as an opening in a wall, so that the opening is bigger on one side than the other [14thC. Shortening of DISPLAY.]

Splayd /splayd/ *tdmk.* *Aus* a trademark for a utensil shaped like a spoon with tines at the end like a fork and a sharp edge on one side like a knife

splay·foot /spláy fòot/ (*plural* **-feet** /-feet/) *n.* **1.** FLAT, OUTWARDLY TURNED FOOT a foot with fallen arches, often with widely spread toes, or the condition that causes this. ◊ **flatfoot 2.** OUTSPREAD FOOT a foot that is excessively turned outward, or the condition causing it —**splay·foot·ed** *adj.* —**splay·foot·ed·ly** *adv.*

spleen /spleen/ *n.* **1.** PHYSIOL ORGAN IN ABDOMEN a vascular ductless organ in the left upper abdomen of humans and other vertebrates that helps to destroy old red blood cells, form lymphocytes, and store blood **2.** BAD TEMPER anger or bad temper [13thC. Via Latin from Greek *splēn*.]

spleen·ful /spleénf'l/ *adj.* = **splenetic** *adj.* 1 —**spleen·ful·ly** *adv.*

spleen·wort /spleén wùrt, -wàwrt/ *n.* an evergreen fern of temperate and tropical regions that has feathery fronds. Genus: *Asplenium.* [Late 16thC. From the former belief that it cured illnesses of the spleen.]

splen·dent /spléndənt/ *adj.* (*literary*) **1.** LUSTROUS reflecting light so that it shines **2.** ILLUSTRIOUS distinguished in a particular field or endeavor [15thC. From Latin *splendere* "to shine."]

splen·did /spléndəd/ *adj.* **1.** MAGNIFICENT impressive because of quality or size **2.** RADIANT reflecting light brilliantly **3.** EXCELLENT excellent or highly enjoyable **4.** ACCLAIMED very well known and acclaimed [Early 17thC. From Latin *splendidus*, from *splendere* "to shine" (source also of English *splendor* and *resplendent*).] —**splen·did·ness** *n.*

splen·did·ly /spléndədlee/ *adv.* in a fine or admirable way ○ *a splendidly restored old castle*

splen·dif·er·ous /splen díffərəss/ *adj.* magnificent and wonderful (*humorous*) [Mid-19thC. Formed from SPLENDOR.] —**splen·dif·er·ous·ly** *adv.* —**splen·dif·er·ous·ness** *n.*

splen·dor /spléndər/ *n.* **1.** MAGNIFICENCE the condition of being magnificent, impressive, or brilliant **2.** SOMETHING SPLENDID something that is magnificent, impressive, or brilliant ○ *the splendors of Ancient Greece* [15thC. Directly and via Old French from Latin *splendor*, from *splendere* "to shine" (source also of English *splendid*).] —**splen·dor·ous** *adj.*

splen·dour *n.* U.K. = **splendor**

sple·nec·to·my /splə néktəmee/ (*plural* **-mies**) *n.* surgical removal of the spleen [Mid-19thC. Coined from Greek *splēn* "spleen" + -ECTOMY.]

sple·net·ic /splə néttik/ *adj.* **1.** BAD-TEMPERED extremely bad-tempered or spiteful **2.** OF SPLEEN relating to the spleen (*dated*) ■ *n.* SOMEBODY BAD-TEMPERED somebody who is bad-tempered or spiteful [Mid-16thC. From Latin *spleneticus*, from *splen* "spleen."] —**sple·net·i·cal·ly** *adv.*

splen·ic /spleénik, splénnik/ *adj.* relating to, in, or near the spleen [Early 17thC. Formed from Greek *splēn* "spleen."]

sple·ni·us /spleénee əss/ (*plural* **-i** /-ī/) *n.* either of two muscles on each side of the neck that reach from the base of the skull to the upper back and rotate and extend the head and neck [Mid-18thC. Via modern Latin from Greek *splēnion* "bandage, compress."] —**sple·ni·al** *adj.*

sple·no·meg·a·ly /splee nō méggəlee, splènnə-/ *n.* abnormal enlargement of the spleen [Early 20thC. Coined from Greek *splēn* "spleen" + the Greek stem *megal-* "great."]

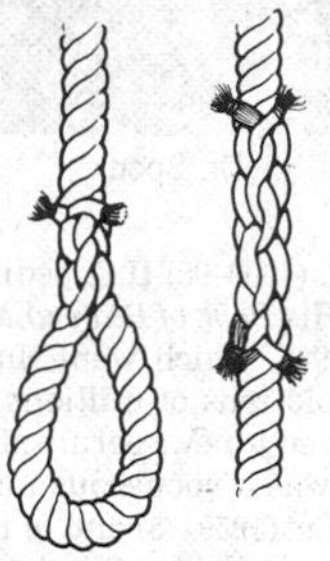

Splice

splice /splīss/ *vt.* (**spliced, splic·ing, splic·es**) **1.** SAILING, CONSTR INTERWEAVE STRANDS OF TWO ROPES to join two pieces of rope or wire by weaving the strands of each into the other **2.** CINEMA, RECORDING JOIN ENDS OF FILM OR TAPE to join the ends of two pieces of film or magnetic tape, e.g., in editing **3.** WOODWORK JOIN PIECES OF WOOD to join two pieces of wood together by overlapping them and bolting or otherwise attaching them **4.** GENETICS JOIN GENETIC MATERIAL to join together or insert pieces of genetic material when altering the genetic structure of something or when forming a new combination **5.** MARRY TWO PEOPLE to join a couple in marriage (*slang*) (*often passive*) ■ *n.* **1.** CONNECTION a join made by connecting two pieces of something **2.** JUNCTION OF SPLICING the junction where something has been spliced [Early 16thC. From Middle Dutch *splissen*. Ultimately from a prehistoric Germanic word meaning "to split" that is also the ancestor of English *split*, *splint*, and *splinter*.] —**splic·er** *n.*

spliff /splif/ *n.* a marijuana cigarette (*slang*) [Mid-20thC. Origin unknown.]

spline /splīn/ *n.* **1.** FLAT KEY FORMED IN SHAFT a flat, relatively narrow key that is integral to a shaft, produced by milling a longitudinal groove **2.** GUIDE FOR DRAWING CURVES a flat, flexible strip of something used in drawing curved lines **3.** = **slat** *n.* 1 **4.** CONNECTING STRIP a thin narrow piece of wood, metal, or plastic that fits onto or into the edges of tiles or boards and connects them together [Mid-18thC. Origin uncertain: perhaps related to SPLINTER.]

splint /splint/ *n.* **1.** MED DEVICE TO IMMOBILIZE BROKEN BONE a strip of rigid material used to keep a broken bone or other injured body part from moving **2.** CRAFT STRIP OF WOOD USED IN BASKETRY a thin strip of wood used to weave something such as a basket or chair seat **3.** = **splinter** *n.* 1 **4.** WOOD SLIVER FOR LIGHTING FIRES a sliver of wood used to carry a flame, e.g., to light a fire or a candle **5.** MIL, HIST METAL PLATE IN ARMOR any of the overlapping metal plates or strips used in making a suit of armor **6.** VET ENLARGEMENT OF HORSE'S LEG BONE a condition that occurs in young horses, consisting of painful bony outgrowths in or near the splint bones on the inner sides of the legs ■ *vt.* (**splint·ed, splint·ing, splints**) **1.** IMMOBILIZE INJURED PART to immobilize a broken bone or injured body part with a rigid support **2.** STRENGTHEN to give support or added strength to something [13thC. From Middle Low German or Middle Dutch *splinte*.]

splint bone *n.* either of a pair of thin bones on either side of the cannon bone in the lower legs of horses and other hoofed animals

splin·ter /splíntər/ *n.* **1.** THIN SHARP FRAGMENT a small thin sharp piece of wood, metal, stone, glass, or other material broken from a larger piece **2.** BOMB FRAGMENT a metal fragment thrown from an exploding bomb or shell **3.** = **splinter group** ■ *vti.* (**-tered, -ter·ing, -ters**) **1.** BREAK INTO SHARP FRAGMENTS to break something or be broken into thin sharp fragments **2.** DIVIDE GROUP to split a larger group into factions or independent groups, or to be split in this way [14thC. From Middle Dutch. Ultimately from the same base as *splint*.] —**splin·ter·y** *adj.*

splin·ter group *n.* a group formed by individuals who have dissociated themselves from a larger organization, usually because of disagreement

split /split/ *v.* (**split, split·ting, splits**) **1.** *vti.* DIVIDE LENGTHWISE to divide something or be divided lengthwise into two or more parts, usually by force **2.** *vti.* BURST to burst apart or rip something apart **3.** *vt.* AFFECT VIOLENTLY to disturb or disrupt something with a violently jarring presence **4.** *vti.* SEPARATE INTO PARTS to divide a whole into parts, or to be separated from the rest or from a whole **5.** *vt.* SEPARATE BY ADDING SOMETHING BETWEEN to separate a whole into its components by interposing something **6.** *vti.* DIVIDE INTO FACTIONS to separate from a main group, or make a group divide into factions, because of disagreement **7.** *vt.* SHARE to share something among a group **8.** *vt.* POL DIVIDE VOTE FOR CANDIDATES to divide a vote between candidates of different parties **9.** *vti.* DEPART to leave a place (*slang*) **10.** *vt.* SPORTS WIN HALF OF GAMES to win half the games of a series or one of a double-header **11.** *vt.* FIN DIVIDE SHARES OF STOCK to divide shares of stock so that shareholders receive more shares at a proportionately lower value, leaving the total value unchanged ■ *n.* **1.** ACT OF BREAKING APART the action of breaking or splitting something **2.** CRACK a crack or break in something, especially one that runs lengthways **3.** FRAGMENT a piece broken off from the whole **4.** DIVISION THROUGH DISAGREEMENT a breach in a group, caused by a disagreement between members **5.** PORTION a share, especially a share of money (*informal*) **6.** FOOD ICE CREAM DESSERT a dessert of fruit with ice cream and a topping of flavored syrup, nuts, and whipped cream **7.** CRAFT STRIP OF WOOD FOR BASKETRY a strip of flexible wood, usually willow, used for basketry **8.** LAYER OF ANIMAL HIDE a single thickness of animal hide other than the outermost layer **9.** INDUST LEATHER leather made from a single inner layer of animal hide **10.** BEVERAGES HALF-BOTTLE a half-bottle of alcohol or carbonated beverage **11.** BEVERAGES HALF-GLASS a half-glass of an alcoholic beverage **12.** WINE QUARTER-SIZE WINE BOTTLE a wine bottle holding 6 to 6.5 ounces/0.1875 liters **13.** SPORTS ARRANGEMENT OF STANDING BOWLING PINS in ten-pin bowling, a batch of remaining pins in which the pins are clustered into two groups with a large gap in between ■ **splits** *npl.* GYMNASTIC ACTION a gymnastic action in which the legs are fully extended in opposite directions until the body is sitting on or very close to the floor (*takes a singular verb*) ○ *do the splits* ■ *adj.* **1.** BROKEN broken, divided, or separated into parts **2.** DISUNITED divided because of disagreement **3.** FIN DIVIDED INTO SMALLER STOCK UNITS used to describe shares of stock that have been divided into smaller units [Late 16thC. From Dutch *splitten*.] —**split·ter** *n.*

split up *v.* **1.** *vi.* END RELATIONSHIP to end a relationship or a marriage **2.** *vti.* SEND PEOPLE DIFFERENT WAYS to go off in a different direction or send individuals off in different directions **3.** *vt.* DIVIDE INTO PARTS to divide something into separate parts

Split /split/ chief city and port of Dalmatia, southern Croatia, on the Adriatic Sea. Population: 189,388 (1991).

split brain *n.* a brain that has the corpus callosum surgically severed or missing from birth, so that the two hemispheres of the brain are not connected

split de·ci·sion *n.* BOXING in boxing, a win awarded by a majority of judges, rather than by a unanimous decision

split end *n.* **1.** FOOTBALL OFFENSIVE PLAYER a player at the end of an offensive line that lines up some distance outside the rest of the line **2.** HAIR HAIR STRAND WITH DAMAGED END a hair with a damaged end that has separated into strands

split in·fin·i·tive *n.* an infinitive in which the "to" and the verb are separated by another word, as in the phrase "to seriously think"

WORD KEY: USAGE

What is wrong with a split infinitive? The split infinitive is a stylistic issue that has been rationalized into a grammatical one. There is no grammatical basis for rejecting split infinitives, since to regard an infinitive with *to* as inseparable has no support in the typical structures of English grammar, which freely separates particles, auxiliary verbs, and other devices from the words to which they belong (e.g., *I have never been to Paris* separates *have* from *been*). The issue is one of style and not of grammar. If splitting an infinitive produces awkwardness, it is better to avoid it, but if the split is natural and supports or clarifies the meaning, there can be no objection to it. The adverb belongs closely with the verb in cases such as *They agreed to flatly forbid such actions* and *They were plotting to secretly copy the files* but can be moved to a more comfortable position in other cases such as *We expect to further modernize our services* (revise as: *... to modernize our services further*) and *I would like to briefly mention a few points* (revise to: *I would like briefly to ...*) It is usually advisable to avoid splitting the infinitive with an adverbial phrase (e.g., *They were trying to in some way improve the situation*). In some cases, however, even an adverbial phrase cannot be separated from its verb: *Prices are likely to more than double* (in which *more than double* is effectively regarded as a set verb phrase). The guiding principle, in sum, is that the split infinitive has a long history of use and is not a cardinal sin; it is acceptable when the rhythm and meaning of the sentence call for it or when its use is that of a set verb phrase. It should be avoided (either by repositioning or by rephrasing) when it seems stilted or awkward, or especially in formal writing where its inclusion may draw criticism.

---

split-lev·el *adj.* used to describe the floor of a room that is on different levels with steps between them —**split-lev·el** *n.*

split pea *n.* a pea that has been shelled, dried, and split in half, used especially in soup

split per·son·al·i·ty *n.* **1.** PSYCHIAT = **multiple personality** **2.** TENDENCY TO MOOD SWINGS a tendency toward erratic mood or temperament changes

split pin *n.* a two-pronged metal pin that holds things together when its prongs are passed through holes on both parts and then bent back

split rail *n.* a fence rail split lengthwise from a log

split ring *n.* a small steel ring with two spiral turns, often used as a key ring or as a means of fastening two parts together

split screen *n.* a movie or television screen frame divided into more than one image

split sec·ond *n.* an extremely brief amount of time

split-sec·ond *adj.* carried out instantly, or depending on instant skill or judgment

split shift *n.* a single work period that is divided into two or more sessions of work, separated by an interval that is longer than a normal rest or meal break

split stitch *n.* a back stitch in which each new stitch is made through the center of the previous one

split tick·et *n.* POL a ballot cast by a voter for candidates of more than one political party

split·ting /splítting/ *adj.* PAINFUL causing intense pain ○ *a splitting headache* ■ *n.* PSYCHIAT FREUDIAN DEFENSE MECHANISM a Freudian defense mechanism in which somebody separates something unpleasant such as an idea into parts that are each less threatening than the whole

split-up *n.* an instance or the act of separating, e.g., the ending of a relationship between two people

splotch /sploch/ *n.* LARGE SPOT a large irregular spot, stain, or discoloration ■ *vt.* (**splotched, splotch·ing, splotch·es**) STAIN SOMETHING to mark, stain, or discolor something with one or more large spots [Early 17thC. Origin uncertain: perhaps a blend of SPOT, BLOT, and BOTCH.]

splurge /splurj/ *v.* (**splurged, splurg·ing, splurg·es**) **1.** *vi.* INDULGE to indulge in something extravagant or expensive (*informal*) **2.** *vt.* SPEND MONEY EXTRAVAGANTLY to spend money in an extravagant or wasteful way ■ *n.* (*informal*) **1.** BOUT OF EXTRAVAGANCE a period of indulgence or extravagant spending **2.** GRAND DISPLAY a showy display of something such as wealth [Early 19thC. Origin uncertain: perhaps a blend of SPLASH and SURGE.]

splut·ter /splúttər/ *v.* (**-tered, -ter·ing, -ters**) **1.** *vi.* MAKE SPITTING SOUND to make a spitting or choking sound **2.** *vti.* SAY INCOHERENTLY to say something in a choking incoherent manner **3.** *vti.* SPIT SOMETHING OUT to scatter saliva, liquid, or particles of food from the mouth ■ *n.* **1.** INCOHERENT SPEECH a burst of choking incoherent speech **2.** CHOKING NOISE a spitting choking noise [Late 17thC. Origin uncertain: perhaps an alteration of SPUTTER.] —**splut·ter·er** *n.* —**splut·ter·ing** *n.*, *adj.*

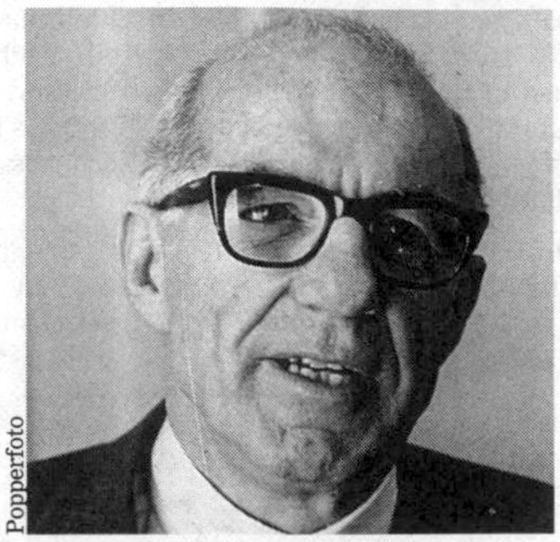
Popperfoto

Dr. Spock

Spock /spok/, **Dr.** (1903–98) U.S. pediatrician and political activist. His *Book of Baby and Child Care*, first published in 1946, which went through numerous editions and sold tens of millions of copies worldwide, popularized a new, permissive philosophy of parenting. He was a vociferous public opponent of the Vietnam War (1959–75) and of nuclear weapons. Full name **Benjamin McLane Spock**

Spode /spōd/ *tdmk.* a trademark for a high-quality porcelain or bone china

spod·u·mene /spójjə meen/ *n.* a grayish white, greenish, or lilac mineral, found as large translucent crystals, that consists of a silicate of lithium and aluminum and is the chief source of lithium. The green variety, (**hiddenite**), and the lilac variety, (**kunzite**), are used as gemstones. [Early 19thC. Via French from Greek *spodoumenos*, literally "burned to ashes," from *spodos* "ashes"; from its grayish color.]

spoil /spoyl/ *v.* (**spoiled** *or* **spoilt, spoiled** *or* **spoilt** /spoylt/, **spoil·ing, spoils**) **1.** *vt.* IMPAIR to damage or ruin something in such a way that a quality such as worth, beauty, or usefulness, is diminished **2.** *vt.* HARM BY OVERINDULGENCE to harm a person's character, especially a child's, by repeated overindulgence **3.** *vt.* TREAT INDULGENTLY to treat somebody with indulgence out of a desire to please ○ *The hotel staff really spoiled us.* **4.** *vt.* CAUSE TO SEEM UNSATISFACTORY to be so good by comparison with something else that what is usually offered no longer seems satisfactory ○ *All that sun spoils you for vacations in the far North.* **5.** *vi.* BECOME ROTTEN to become unfit to eat because of decay **6.** *vt.* TAKE PROPERTY FROM to take somebody's property by force or violence (*archaic*) ■ *n.* **1.** WASTE FROM EXCAVATION waste material removed from an excavation **2.** STEALING the act of plundering (*archaic*) ■ **spoils** *npl.* **1.** PROPERTY SEIZED BY VICTOR valuables or property seized by the victor in a conflict **2.** SOMETHING GAINED THROUGH EFFORT something valuable or desirable gained through effort, opportunism, or other means **3.** REWARDS AND BENEFITS OF WINNING the rewards and benefits considered by a winning political party to be its due [13thC. Via Old French *espoillier* "to plunder, despoil" from Latin *spoliare*, from *spolium* "booty."] ◇ **be spoiling for something** be eager for something, usually a conflict or confrontation ○ *spoiling for a victory after last year's losses*

spoil·age /spóylij/ *n.* **1.** DECAYING the process of decaying or becoming damaged, or such a condition **2.** WASTE waste arising from decay or damage **3.** AMOUNT WASTED the amount of something wasted because of decay or damage

spoiled /spoyld/ *adj.* **1.** RUINED severely or irrevocably impaired, e.g., by damage or decay **2.** OVERINDULGED willful or selfish because of having been overindulged

spoil·er /spóylər/ *n.* **1.** AIR AIRFOIL FOR CONTROLLING LIFT AND DRAG a narrow hinged airfoil attached lengthwise to the upper surface of an aircraft wing. It is raised to increase drag and reduce lift during banking and descent. **2.** AUTOMOT AUTOMOBILE AIR DEFLECTOR a fixed air deflector on the rear of an automobile, designed to keep it on the ground during high speeds **3.** SOMEBODY WHO CAN RUIN ANOTHER'S WIN a candidate for office, or a competitor in sports, who cannot win but can or does prevent an opponent from doing so **4.** SOMEBODY WHO WRECKS SOMETHING somebody or something that ruins or wrecks something **5.** ROBBER somebody or something that robs or pillages

spoil·sport /spóyl spàwrt/ *n.* somebody whose conduct spoils the plans or pleasure of others

spoils sys·tem *n.* the practice of a winning political party giving government jobs and public appointments to its supporters

spoilt *v.* past tense, past participle of **spoil**

Spo·kane /spō káyn/ **1.** river in the northwestern United States. It rises in Idaho and flows across Washington State into the Columbia River. Length: 120 mi./195 km. **2.** city in eastern Washington. Situated on the falls of the Spokane River, it is a commerical and manufacturing center. Population: 177,196 (1990).

Spoke

spoke[1] /spōk/ *n.* **1.** SUPPORTING ROD FOR WHEEL RIM any of the bars or rods that extend from the hub of a wheel to support or brace the rim **2.** KNOB ON SHIP'S WHEEL any of the knobs that stick out from the rim of a ship's wheel **3.** RUNG a rung of a ladder [Old English *spāca*. Ultimately from an Indo-European base meaning "pointed object" that is also the ancestor of English *spike* and *spine*.]

spoke[2] *v.* past tense of **speak**

spo·ken /spṓkən/ *v.* past participle of **speak** ■ *adj.* **1.** VOCAL expressed with the voice ○ *the spoken word* **2.** SPEAKING IN PARTICULAR WAY speaking in a stated way, e.g., with a particular voice quality, accent, command of the language, or attitude (*used in combination*) ○ *well-spoken* ◇ **be spoken for 1.** to be already owned or reserved by somebody **2.** to be already married, engaged or romantically committed to somebody (*dated*)

WORD KEY: SYNONYMS

See Synonyms at ***verbal***.

---

spokes·man /spṓksmən/ (*plural* **-men** /-mən/) *n.* somebody authorized to speak on behalf of another person or other people [Mid-16thC. Formed from SPOKE[2].]

spokes·per·son /spṓks pùrss'n/ (*plural* **-peo·ple** /-peep'l/) *n.* a spokesman or spokeswoman [Late 20thC. Modeled on SPOKESMAN.]

spokes·wom·an /spṓks wo͝omman/ (*plural* **-en** /-wìmmən/) *n.* a woman authorized to speak on behalf of another person or other people [Mid-17thC. Modeled on SPOKESMAN.]

spo·li·a·tion /spòlee áysh'n/ *n.* **1.** PLUNDERING the seizing of things by force **2.** SEIZURE OF SHIPS the seizure or plundering of neutral ships at sea by a belligerent power in time of war **3.** ALTERATION OF DOCUMENT the alteration or destruction of a document so as to make it invalid or unusable as evidence [15thC. From the Latin stem *spoliation-*, from *spoliare* (see SPOIL).] —**spo·li·a·tor·y** /spṓlee ə tàwree/ *adj.*

spon·da·ic /spon dáy ik/ *adj.* POETRY relating to spondees or written in spondees [Late 16thC. From French *spondaïque*, from, ultimately, Greek *spondeios* (see SPONDEE).]

spon·dee /spón dee/ *n.* POETRY a unit of rhythm in poetry (**foot**), consisting of two long or stressed syllables [14thC. Via French from, ultimately, Greek *spondeios*, literally "libational," from *spondē* "libation"; so called because the spondee was often used in songs accompanying libations.]

spon·dy·li·tis /spòndə lítiss/ *n.* inflammation of the vertebrae and the attached disks and ligaments [Mid-19thC. Formed from Latin *spondylus* "vertebra," from Greek *spondulos*, of unknown origin.]

sponge /spunj/ *n.* **1.** MARINE BIOL MARINE ANIMAL a chiefly marine invertebrate animal with a porous fibrous skeleton composed of calcium carbonate, silica, and spongin. Sponges live in colonies and attach themselves to underwater objects. Phylum: Porifera. **2.** HOUSEHOLD NATURAL MATERIAL USED FOR BATHING a lightweight

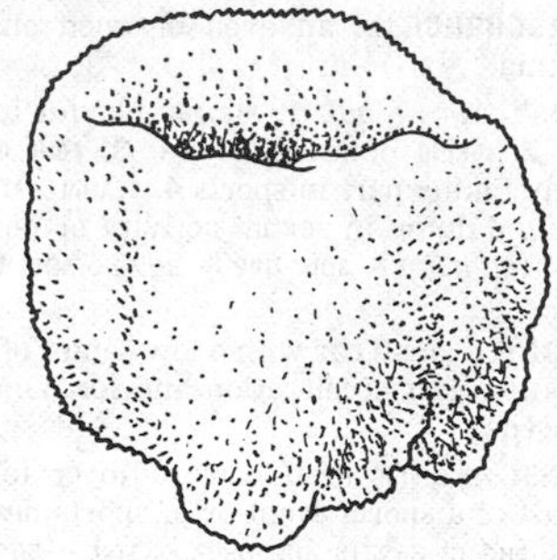

Sponge

porous absorbent piece of the skeleton of some sponges, used for bathing or cleaning **3.** HOUSEHOLD **SYNTHETIC MATERIAL USED FOR BATHING** a piece of cellulose or synthetic material resembling a true sponge, used for bathing and cleaning **4.** MED **GAUZE PAD** a folded gauze pad used in surgery or medicine to absorb discharges, to dress wounds, or to apply medications **5. CONTRACEPTIVE** an absorbent contraceptive device that contains a spermicide and is inserted into the vagina to cover the cervix **6.** = **sponger** *n.* 1 (*informal*) **7. HEAVY DRINKER** somebody who habitually drinks a lot of alcohol (*informal*) **8.** COOK **MASS OF RISING YEAST DOUGH** a small amount of yeast dough that is allowed to rise before being kneaded with the rest of the batch **9.** FOOD = **sponge cake 10. ACT OF CLEANING** the act of rubbing or bathing somebody or something with a wet sponge or cloth **11.** METALL **POROUS METAL** a porous metal capable of absorbing large quantities of gas, obtained by reduction without melting of a metal compound, or by electrolysis ■ *v.* (**sponged, spong·ing, spong·es**) **1.** *vt.* **CLEAN** to wipe something or clean somebody with a wet sponge or cloth **2.** *vt.* **REMOVE** to remove or destroy something by rubbing **3.** *vt.* **ABSORB** to absorb liquids with a sponge or with the efficiency of a sponge **4.** *vt.* **GET BY IMPOSING** to get something by imposing on the generosity of others **5.** *vi.* **LIVE OFF OTHERS** to live at the expense of others, repeatedly imposing on them and making no effort to live independently **6.** *vi.* **COLLECT SPONGES** to dive for sponges, especially under the sea [Pre-12thC. Via Latin *spongia* from, ultimately, Greek *sphoggos*. From a pre-Indo-European word that was probably also the source of Latin *fungus*.]

sponge bath *n.* a body cleansing just using a sponge and some water, without immersion, usually performed on somebody confined to bed

sponge cake *n.* a light open-textured cake made of flour, eggs, sugar, flavoring, but no shortening

sponge mush·room *n.* = **morel**

spong·er /spúnjər/ *n.* **1. SOMEBODY WHO LIVES OFF OTHERS** somebody who lives off others, habitually imposing on their generosity and making no effort to live independently (*informal*) **2. COLLECTOR OF SPONGES** somebody who dives for sponges, or a ship used for gathering sponges

spong·i·form en·ceph·a·lop·a·thy /spùnji fawrm en sèffə lóppəthee/ *n.* any of various brain diseases in humans and animals in which areas of the brain slowly degenerate and take on a spongy appearance

spon·gin /spúnjin/ *n.* a protein that forms the skeletal framework of sponges [Mid-19thC. Coined from SPONGE + -IN.]

spon·gi·o·blast /spúnjee ə blàst/ *n.* any of the embryonic cells in the brain and spinal cord that develop into supporting connective tissue (**glia**) [Early 20thC. Coined from Latin *spongia* "sponge" + -BLAST.] —**spon·gi·o·blas·tic** /spùnjee ə blástik/ *adj.*

spong·y /spúnjee/ (**-i·er, -i·est**) *adj.* **1. OPEN-TEXTURED** with a light open texture full of holes or cavities **2. ABSORBENT** absorbent and elastic **3. SOFT AND WET** soft and full of water

spong·y mes·o·phyll, **spong·y pa·ren·chy·ma** *n.* BOT a spongy tissue layer of irregularly shaped chlorophyll-bearing cells interspersed with air spaces, sandwiched between the upper and lower epidermal layers of a leaf

spon·son /spónss'n/ *n.* **1.** NAVY **SHIP'S GUN PLATFORM** a gun platform sticking out from the side of a ship. A gun can be mounted in such a way that it can fire both fore and aft. **2.** NAUT **AIR CHAMBER IN CANOE** an air chamber that runs along each side of a canoe to help keep it afloat **3.** AIR **STABILIZER FOR SEAPLANE** an air-filled structure or small wing projecting from the lower hull of a seaplane to stabilize it in water **4.** ARMY, HIST **GUN TURRET** a gun turret mounted on the side of an early tank **5.** NAUT **SUPPORT FOR PADDLE WHEEL** a structural support for a paddle wheel on a ship [Mid-19thC. Origin uncertain: perhaps an alteration of EXPANSION.]

spon·sor /spónssər/ *n.* **1. SOMEBODY RESPONSIBLE FOR ANOTHER** somebody who undertakes responsibility for another, especially during a period of education, apprenticeship, or probation **2.** BROADCAST **RADIO OR TELEVISION ADVERTISER** an individual or a business that pays for radio or television programming by buying advertising time **3.** FIN **CONTRIBUTOR TO EVENT'S FUNDING** a person or organization that provides or pledges money to help fund an event, especially an event run by another person or group **4.** FIN **CONTRIBUTOR TO CHARITY** a person or organization that donates money to a charity on the basis of the performance of a participant in an organized fundraising event **5.** POL **LEGISLATOR** a legislator who proposes and supports the passage of a bill **6. SUPPORTER** a country, organization, or group that supports or organizes an activity, or one who vouches for the acceptability of another **7.** CHR **SOMEBODY ANSWERING AT CHILD'S BAPTISM** somebody who answers for a child at baptism and assumes responsibility for the child's religious upbringing (*formal*) ■ *vt.* (**-sored, -sor·ing, -sors**) **ACT AS SPONSOR TO** to act as a sponsor to somebody or something [Mid-17thC. From late Latin, "baptismal sponsor," from Latin *spons-*, the past participle stem of *spondere* "to pledge."] —**spon·so·ri·al** /spon sáwree əl/ *adj.* —**spon·sor·ship** *n.*

WORD KEY: SYNONYMS

See Synonyms at ***backer***.

WORD KEY: ORIGIN

The Latin verb *spondere*, from which ***sponsor*** is derived, is also the source of English *despondent*, *respond*, *riposte*, and *spouse*.

spon·ta·ne·i·ty /spòntə née atee, -náy ətee/ *n.* **1. UNCONSTRAINED BEHAVIOR** behavior that is natural and unconstrained and is the result of impulse, not planning **2. GENERATION FROM WITHIN** the generating or provoking of activity from within, rather than as a result of external influences

spon·ta·ne·ous /spon táynee əss/ *adj.* **1. ARISING FROM INTERNAL CAUSE** resulting from internal or natural processes, with no apparent external influence **2. ARISING FROM IMPULSE** arising from natural impulse or inclination, rather than from planning or in response to suggestions from others **3. UNRESTRAINED** naturally unrestrained or uninhibited **4.** BOT **GROWING UNCULTIVATED** growing without cultivation [Mid-17thC. Formed from late Latin *spontaneus* "of one's own accord," from Latin *sponte*, of uncertain origin.] —**spon·ta·ne·ous·ly** *adv.* —**spon·ta·ne·ous·ness** *n.*

spon·ta·ne·ous a·bor·tion *n.* = **miscarriage** *n.* 1

spon·ta·ne·ous com·bus·tion *n.* the ignition of a combustible material such as hay as a result of internal heat generation usually caused by rapid oxidation

spon·ta·ne·ous gen·er·a·tion *n.* BIOL = **abiogenesis**

spon·ta·ne·ous ig·ni·tion *n.* = **spontaneous combustion**

spon·ta·ne·ous re·cov·er·y *n.* PSYCHOL the return of an extinguished conditioned response without reinforcement

spon·toon /spon tóon/ *n.* a short pike used by some infantry officers in the 18th century [Mid-18thC. Via obsolete French *sponton* from Italian *spontone* from, ultimately, *punto* "point," from Latin *punctum* (see POINT).]

spoof /spoof/ *n.* **1. HOAX** a good-humored hoax **2. AMUSING SATIRE** a light amusing satire ■ *vt.* (**spoofed, spoof·ing, spoofs**) **1. DECEIVE** to fool or deceive somebody **2. SATIRIZE** to satirize somebody or something good-naturedly [Late 19thC. Coined by the English comedian Arthur Roberts (1852–1933) as the name for a game of his creation involving hoaxing.] —**spoof·er** *n.*

spook /spook/ *n.* (*informal*) **1. GHOST** a ghost or a ghostly figure **2. SPY** a spy ■ *v.* (**spooked, spook·ing, spooks**) **1.** *vt.* **HAUNT** to haunt somebody as a ghost **2.** *vt.* **STARTLE SOMEBODY** to startle or make an animal or person feel uneasy **3.** *vi.* **BE FRIGHTENED** to feel frightened or uneasy [Early 19thC. From Dutch, of unknown origin.]

spook·y /spóokee/ (**-i·er, -i·est**) *adj.* **1. FRIGHTENINGLY SUGGESTIVE OF SUPERNATURAL INVOLVEMENT** frightening or unnerving because suggesting the presence of supernatural forces (*informal*) **2. AMAZING** strange or amazing, often because it seems that supernatural influences may have been at work (*informal*) **3. EASILY FRIGHTENED** easily frightened or startled —**spook·i·ly** *adv.* —**spook·i·ness** *n.*

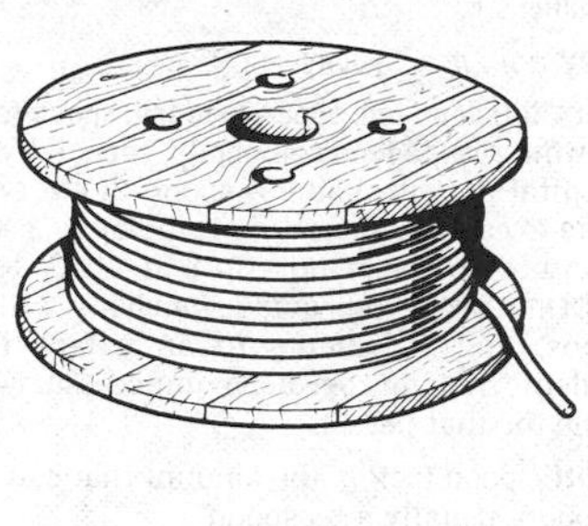

Spool

spool /spool/ *n.* **1. CYLINDER ON WHICH SOMETHING IS WOUND** a cylinder around which thread, tape, or film is wound. It has a central hole and a rim at each end. **2. AMOUNT ON SPOOL** the amount of something wound on a spool ■ *v.* (**spooled, spool·ing, spools**) **1.** *vti.* **WIND SOMETHING ON SPOOL** to wind something on a spool or on something similar to a spool such as a reel or bobbin **2.** *vi.* COMPUT **TRANSFER DATA TO STORE** to transfer data for printing into a memory store so that it can be printed later without slowing down the computer's operations [14thC. Directly and via Old French *espole* from Middle Dutch *spoele*.]

spool·ing /spóoling/ *n.* COMPUT the temporary storage of data in the memory of a computer to compensate for the slower operation of a peripheral device such as a printer while processing continues

spoon /spoon/ *n.* **1.** HOUSEHOLD **EATING UTENSIL** a utensil used for eating or preparing food, consisting of a shallow oval bowl attached to a handle **2.** ANGLING **SHINY FISHING LURE** a bright oval metal fishing lure with a hook attached **3.** GOLF **GOLF CLUB** a number three wood, used for hitting long high drives from the fairway (*dated*) **4.** DRUGS **QUANTITY OF DRUG** a quantity of hard drugs, especially a two-gram measure of heroin (*slang*) ■ *v.* (**spooned, spoon·ing, spoons**) **1.** *vt.* **EAT FOOD USING SPOON** to eat, scoop, or carry something with a spoon or with the action of somebody using a spoon **2.** *vt.* **HOLLOW OUT** to dig or scrape a hollow in something, or dig something out to leave a hollow **3.** *vt.* SPORTS **HIT BALL UP** to hit a ball upward with a scooping action, often as a result of an imperfect stroke **4.** *vi.* ANGLING **USE SPOON FISHING LURE** to fish with a spoon lure **5.** *vi.* **BE AMOROUS** to indulge in amorous behavior such as kissing and caressing (*dated slang*) [Old English *spōn* "wood chip." Ultimately from an Indo-European word meaning "flat piece of wood" that is also the ancestor of English *spade* and *spatula*.]

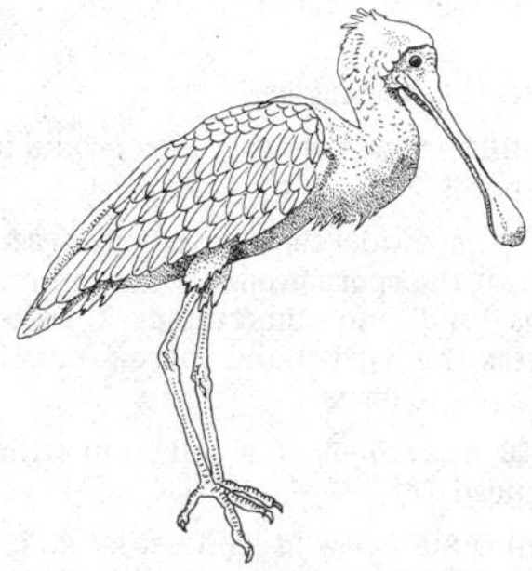

Spoonbill

spoon·bill /spóon bil/ *n.* **1. WADING BIRD** a long-legged wading bird found in tropical and warm regions. It is similar to the ibis but has a long flat bill shaped like a spoon. Family: Threskiornithidae. **2. BROADBILLED DUCK** a duck with a broad bill such as the shoveler

spoon bread *n.* *Southern U.S.* a soft moist bread made with cornmeal, eggs, milk, and shortening, baked in a bowl and eaten with a spoon

spoon·drift /spóon drìft/ *n.* = **spindrift** *n.* 2 [Mid-18thC. From obsolete *spoon* "to run before a sea" (of unknown origin) + DRIFT.]

spoon·er·ism /spóonə rìzzəm/ *n.* an accidental transposition of initial consonant sounds or parts of words, especially one that has an amusing result, e.g., "half-warmed fish" for "half-formed wish" [Early 20thC. Named for the British educator Reverend William *Spooner* 1844–1930, who was known for such transpositions.]

spoon·ey *adj., n.* = **spoony**

spoon-feed (**spoon-fed, spoon-feed·ing, spoon-feeds**) *vt.* **1. FEED WITH SPOON** to feed somebody, especially a child or hospital patient, using a spoon **2. GIVE EVERYTHING NEEDED TO** to cater to somebody completely, requiring him or her to make no effort at all **3. DEPRIVE OF INDEPENDENT THOUGHT** to provide somebody with ideas, opinions, and judgments to an extent that independent thought becomes unnecessary or impossible for that person

spoon·ful /spóon fòol/ *n.* the amount that can be held in a spoon, usually a teaspoon

spoon·y /spóonee/, **spoon·ey** *adj.* (**-i·er, -i·est**) **SENTIMENTAL** foolishly sentimental or amorous (*dated*) ■ *n.* (*plural* **-ies**) **SOMEBODY SENTIMENTAL** somebody foolishly sentimental or amorous (*archaic*)

spoor /spoor, spawr/ *n.* **ANIMAL TRAIL** the visible trail of an animal, especially an animal that is being hunted for sport ■ *vti.* (**spoored, spoor·ing, spoors**) **TRACK ANIMAL** to track an animal by following its trail [Early 19thC. Via Afrikaans from Middle Dutch. Ultimately from an Indo-European word meaning "ankle" that is also the ancestor of English *spur* and *spurn*.] —**spoor·er** *n.*

Spor·a·des /spórrədiz/ group of Greek islands in the Aegean Sea, north of the island of Euboea

spo·rad·ic /spə ráddik/ *adj.* **1. OCCURRING IRREGULARLY** occurring occasionally at intervals that have no apparent pattern **2.** MED **NOT EPIDEMIC** used to describe a disease that appears in scattered or isolated instances or locations [Late 17thC. Via medieval Latin from, ultimately, Greek *sporad-*, the stem of *sporas* "scattered."]

WORD KEY: SYNONYMS

See Synonyms at ***periodic***.

spo·ran·gi·um /spə ránjee əm/ (*plural* **-a** /-ə/) *n.* a hollow spore-producing organ in fungi, ferns, and some other plants [Early 19thC. From modern Latin, literally "spore-vessel," from Greek *spora* (see SPORE) + *aggeion* "small vessel" (see ANGIO-).]

spore /spawr/ *n.* BIOL **1. ASEXUAL REPRODUCTIVE STRUCTURE** a small, usually one-celled reproductive structure produced by seedless plants, algae, fungi, and some protozoans that is capable of developing into a new individual **2. DORMANT BACTERIUM** a dormant resistant form taken by some bacteria in response to adverse conditions ■ *vi.* (**spored, spor·ing, spores**) **PRODUCE SPORES** to produce or release spores [Mid-19thC. Via modern Latin from Greek *spora* "sowing, seed." Ultimately from an Indo-European base meaning "to scatter" that is also the ancestor of English *sprawl*, *sprout*, *sperm*, and *diaspora*.]

spore case *n.* = **sporangium**

spo·rif·er·ous /spaw ríffərəss/ *adj.* producing or releasing spores

spo·ro·carp /spáwrō kaarp/ *n.* BOT **1. SPORE-PRODUCING ORGAN OF ALGAE** the spore-producing organ in red algae and some fungi and slime molds **2. SPORE-PRODUCING ORGAN OF FERN** the hard round spore-producing organ of some aquatic ferns

spo·ro·cyte /spáwrō sìt/ *n.* a cell from which spores are produced

spo·ro·gen·e·sis /spàw rō jénnəssəss/ *n.* **1. SPORE PRODUCTION** the production or formation of spores **2. REPRODUCTION BY SPORES** reproduction by means of spores —**spo·rog·e·nous** /spaw rójjənəss/ *adj.*

spo·rog·o·ny /spə róggənee, spaw-/ *n.* the process in sporozoans by which sporozoites are formed from multiple fission of an encysted zygote

spo·ro·phore /spáwrə fàwr/ *n.* an organ in fungi that produces spores

spo·ro·phyll /spáwrə fil/, **spo·ro·phyl** *n.* a leaf or modified leaf that bears spore-producing organs, e.g., the fertile leaf of a fern or club moss

spo·ro·phyte /spáwrə fìt/ *n.* in plants that alternate between sexual and asexual phases, a plant in its asexual spore-producing phase —**spo·ro·phyt·ic** /spàwrə fíttik/ *adj.*

spo·ro·plasm /spáwrə plàzzəm/ *n.* an infective mass of protoplasm contained inside a spore that is injected into a host cell by various parasitic organisms

spo·ro·pol·len·in /spàwrə póllənin/ *n.* a polymer that forms the outer layer of pollen and some spores such as bacterial spores [Mid-20thC. Coined from SPORO- + POLLEN + -IN).]

spo·ro·tri·cho·sis /spàwrə tri kṓssiss/ *n.* a serious infectious disease caused by a fungus *Sporothrix schenckii* that enters the body from soil or wood via a skin wound. It typically produces skin ulcers and nodules on the lymph nodes. [Early 20thC. Formed from modern Latin *Sporotrichum*, former genus name of the fungus, from *spora* (see SPORE) + Greek *thrix* "hair."]

spo·ro·zo·an /spàwrə zṓ ən/ *n.* a parasitic single-celled organism (**protozoan**) that has alternating sexual and asexual generations and reproduces by means of spores. The malaria parasites are sporozoans. Class: Sporozoa. [Late 19thC. Formed from modern Latin *Sporozoa*, class name, from Greek *spora* (see SPORE) + *zōion* "animal."]

spo·ro·zo·ite /spàwrə zṓ ìt/ *n.* any of the small infectious motile individuals produced in sporozoans by sporogony usually within a host [Late 19thC. Formed from modern Latin *Sporozoa*, class name (see SPOROZOAN).]

spor·ran /spáwrən, spórrən/ *n.* a leather pouch, sometimes decorated with fur, worn hanging from a belt in front of the kilt in men's traditional Scottish Highland dress [Mid-18thC. Via Scottish Gaelic from Middle Irish *sporán*, of uncertain origin: probably from late Latin *bursa* (see BURSA).]

sport /spawrt/ *n.* **1. COMPETITIVE PHYSICAL ACTIVITY** an individual or group competitive activity involving physical exertion or skill, governed by rules, and sometimes engaged in professionally (*often used in the plural*) **2. PASTIME** an active pastime participated in for pleasure or exercise **3. SOMEBODY CHEERFUL** somebody who remains cheerful when losing or in an unpleasant situation (*informal*) **4. SOMEBODY WHO PLAYS FAIR** somebody noted for abiding by the rules in a game or for generally honorable behavior (*informal*) **5. GOOD COMPANION** somebody who is generally good-natured, easy-going, and good company (*informal*) **6. JOKING** good-natured joking (*formal*) ○ *a harmless prank done in sport* **7. DERISION** contemptuous mockery (*formal*) **8. OBJECT OF RIDICULE** an object of ridicule or mockery (*formal*) **9. SOMEBODY OR SOMETHING MANIPULATED BY OTHERS** somebody or something manipulated by external forces (*literary*) **10. GAMBLER** a gambler, especially somebody who gambles on sporting events (*informal*) **11.** *ANZ, U.S.* **FORM OF ADDRESS** a casual form of address, especially used between men or boys (*informal*) **12.** BIOL **MUTATED ORGANISM** a plant or animal that deviates markedly from its parent stock or type, usually as a result of mutation, especially mutation of somatic tissue **13.** BIOL **UNUSUAL CHARACTER** a mutant character of a mutated organism **14. AMOROUS BEHAVIOR** amorous behavior such as kissing or caressing (*archaic*) ■ *v.* (**sport·ed, sport·ing, sports**) **1.** *vt.* **WEAR** to wear or display something, usually proudly or with the intention of impressing others (*informal*) **2.** *vi.* **PLAY HAPPILY** to romp and play happily (*formal*) **3.** *vi.* **ENJOY YOURSELF** to enjoy yourself, especially by taking part in outdoor physical activity (*formal*) **4.** *vi.* **MAKE JOKES** to joke or trifle with somebody (*formal*) **5.** *vi.* BIOL **MUTATE** to produce or undergo a mutation **6.** *vi.* **RIDICULE** to ridicule somebody or something (*archaic*) ■ *adj.* **sports, sport 1. FOR SPORTING ACTIVITIES** relating to or used in physical or recreational activities ○ *sports equipment* **2.** CLOTHES **FOR INFORMAL WEAR** designed for informal or outdoor wear ○ *sports shirt* [14thC. Shortening of *disport* "diversion, amusement," from Old French *desport*, from *desporter* (see DISPORT).] —**sport·er** *n.* —**sport·ful** *adj.* —**sport·ful·ly** *adv.* —**sport·ful·ness** *n.*

sport·ing /spáwrting/ *adj.* **1. USED IN SPORTS** relating to or used in sports activities ○ *sporting dogs* **2. FAIR** in keeping with the principles of fair competition, respect for other competitors, and personal integrity **3.** GAMBLING **OF GAMBLING** relating to gambling, or taking an interest in gambling **4. RISKING** willing to take a risk

sport·ing chance *n.* an even or good chance of succeeding

spor·tive /spáwrtiv/ *adj.* **1. PLAYFUL** playful and frolicsome **2. JOKING** done as a joke **3. FOND OF SPORTS** regularly taking part in sports **4. SEXUALLY ACTIVE** frequently indulging in sexual activity or tending to enjoy it (*archaic*) —**spor·tive·ly** *adv.* —**spor·tive·ness** *n.*

sports car *n.* a small car with a low center of gravity designed for fast acceleration and for handling at high speeds

sports·cast /spáwrts kàst/ *n.* a radio or television broadcast of a sports event or of sports news [Mid-20thC. Blend of SPORTS and BROADCAST.] —**sports·cast·er** *n.*

sports drink *n.* a soft drink that is intended to quench thirst faster than water and replenish the sugar and minerals lost from the body during physical exercise

sports·man /spáwrtsmən/ (*plural* **-men** /-mən/) *n.* **1. MAN ENGAGING IN SPORTS** a man who participates in and gets pleasure from sports **2. SOMEBODY FAIR AND HONORABLE** somebody who behaves according to principles of fairness, and who observes rules, shows respect for others, and accepts defeat graciously —**sports·man·like** *adj.*

sports·man·ship /spáwrtsmən shìp/ *n.* **1. FAIR CONDUCT** conduct considered fitting for a sportsperson, including observance of the rules of fair play, respect for others, and graciousness in losing **2. TAKING PART IN SPORTS** participation in sports

sports med·i·cine *n.* the branch of medicine concerned with preventing and treating injuries resulting from sports

sports·per·son /spáwrts pùrss'n/ *n.* a sportsman or sportswoman

sports sup·ple·ment *n.* a dietry supplement used by athletes to enhance bursts of high performance [Late 20thC]

sports·wear /spáwrts wàir/ *n.* clothes appropriate for casual or informal occasions

sports·wom·an /spáwrts wòommən/ (*plural* **-en** /-wìmmən/) *n.* **1. WOMAN ENGAGING IN SPORTS** a woman who participates in and gets pleasure from sports **2. FAIR AND HONORABLE WOMAN** a woman who behaves according to principles of fairness, and who observes rules, shows respect for others, and accepts defeat graciously

sports·writ·er /spáwrts rìtər/ *n.* somebody who writes about sports, especially for a newspaper or magazine

sport-u·til·i·ty ve·hi·cle *n.* a four-wheel-drive vehicle used for everyday driving but suitable for rough terrain

sport·y /spáwrtee/ (**-i·er, -i·est**) *adj.* **1. FOR SPORTS** designed or appropriate for sports or leisure activities **2. ENTHUSIASTIC ABOUT SPORTS** enthusiastic about sports or outdoor activities and regularly taking part in them **3.** CARS **SIMILAR TO SPORTS CAR** with features resembling the style or performance of a sports car **4. SPORTING** in keeping with the principles of fair play, generosity, and honor **5. FLASHY** smart, bright, and expensive-looking, sometimes excessively so

spor·u·late /spáwrya làyt/ (**-lat·ed, -lat·ing, -lates**) *vi.* to produce spores [Late 19thC. Formed from modern Latin *sporula*, literally "small spore," from *spora* (see SPORE).] —**spor·u·la·tion** /spàwryə láysh'n/ *n.*

spot /spot/ *n.* **1. SMALL ROUND AREA** a small defined area that is different in color, material, or texture from the surrounding area, especially one that is more or less circular **2. STAIN** a dirty mark or stain **3. MARK ON SKIN** a mark or blemish on the skin, especially a pimple **4. CHARACTER BLEMISH** a blemish on somebody's character or reputation **5. PARTICULAR PLACE** a particular place or location ○ *find a weak spot in their defenses* **6. GEOGRAPHIC LOCATION** a geographic location or area ○ *a local spot of pristine beauty* **7.** BROADCAST **ANNOUNCEMENT OR ADVERTISEMENT** a brief announcement or advertisement inserted between regular radio or television programs **8.** ARTS **PERFORMER'S TIME SLOT** a performer's appearance in a variety show, or the scheduled or regular time for that appearance **9. AWKWARD SITUATION** an awkward or difficult situation (*informal*) **10. ENTERTAINMENT LOCALE** a place of entertainment (*informal*) ○ *a night spot* **11. POSITION** a position in a series or sequence **12. MONEY** a piece of paper money worth a certain amount (*informal*) (usually used in combination) ○ *She handed me a ten spot.* **13.** SMALL AMOUNT a small amount, e.g., of liquid to drink or of work to do **14.** ARTS = **spotlight** *n.* 1 **15.** ZOOL FOOD FISH OF N AMERICAN ATLANTIC a small edible marine fish in the croaker family, found in waters of the Atlantic coast of North America. It has a small spot near the gill on each side. **16.** CUE GAMES DOT ON BILLIARD TABLE any of the small black dots on the table in snooker and pool that mark where the balls should be placed **17.** CARDS SYMBOL ON PLAYING CARD one of the traditional symbols, heart, diamond, spade, or club, on a playing card **18.** CARDS PLAYING CARD any playing card from two to ten of any of the four suits ○ *a six spot* **19.** LEISURE DOT ON GAME PIECE one of the dots on a domino or dice **20.** ELECTRON ENG ILLUMINATED POINT ON CATHODE-RAY TUBE the point on the face of a cathode-ray tube at which the phosphor is illuminated by the impact of an electron beam ■ *adj.* **1.** AVAILABLE IMMEDIATELY used to describe goods or currencies that are paid for and delivered immediately after a sale **2.** BROADCAST ORIGINATING LOCALLY used to describe a news report that is broadcast from the place where it happens ■ *v.* **(spot·ted, spot·ting, spots) 1.** *vt.* SEE to see or detect something suddenly **2.** *vti.* MAKE OR BECOME STAINED to mark or dirty something with stains, or to become marked or dirtied with stains **3.** *vt.* BLEMISH SOMEBODY'S CHARACTER to blemish somebody's character or reputation **4.** *vt.* MARK WITH DOTS to mark something with dots **5.** *vt.* REMOVE STAINS FROM to remove stains from something **6.** *vt.* POSITION SOMEBODY OR SOMETHING to position somebody or something in a particular location **7.** *vt.* DISTRIBUTE AT INTERVALS to distribute people or things at intervals ○ *spotted the outfielders far into the stadium* **8.** *vti.* MIL ADJUST FIRE to adjust gunfire for accuracy by observation **9.** *vt.* GIVE SOMEBODY AN ADVANTAGE to concede an advantage or point margin to an opponent in a game or contest as a handicap (*informal*) **10.** *vt.* LEND TO OR BUY FOR SOMEBODY to give or lend money to somebody, or pay for something for somebody (*slang*) ○ *Will somebody spot me twenty bucks?* [12thC. Origin uncertain: perhaps from Middle Dutch *spotte*, or perhaps an alteration of Old English *splott* "spot." The sense "to see" comes from the idea of putting a spot on a criminal or suspected person.] ◇ **hit the high spots** to focus or touch on the most important points or things (*informal*) ◇ **hit the spot** to be absolutely what is required for total satisfaction, especially in terms of food or drink (*informal*) ◇ **in a spot** in a difficult or embarrassing position (*informal*) ◇ **on the spot 1.** in the exact place where something is happening **2.** immediately **3.** in a difficult situation or under pressure ◇ **put somebody on the spot** to put somebody in a difficult or embarrassing position, especially a position of having to make an instant judgment or decision

spot check *n.* a quick random inspection usually made without prior notice —**spot-check** *vt.*

spot·less /spótləss/ *adj.* **1.** IMMACULATE impeccably clean ○ *a spotless kitchen* **2.** UNBLEMISHED beyond reproach ○ *a spotless reputation* —**spotlessly** *adv.* —**spotlessness** *n.*

spot·light /spót lìt/ *n.* **1.** FOCUSED BEAM OF LIGHT a strong beam of light that can be directed to illuminate a small area, especially one focusing attention on a stage performer **2.** LAMP a lamp that produces a strong narrow beam of light that can be directed at will, e.g., one mounted on a police car **3.** FOCUS OF ATTENTION the focus of public attention ■ *vt.* **(-lit** /spót lìt/ *or* **-light·ed, -light·ing, -lights** /spót lìt/) **1.** ILLUMINATE WITH LIGHT BEAM to direct a beam of light on somebody or something **2.** FOCUS ATTENTION ON to focus public attention on somebody or something

spot mar·ket *n.* a market in which commodities, securities, or currencies are traded for immediate payment and delivery

spot price *n.* the market price for goods, currencies, or securities at a given time

spot·ted /spóttəd/ *adj.* **1.** WITH SPOTS with a pattern of spots **2.** STAINED stained or soiled with spots of something

spot·ted cranes·bill *n.* = **wild geranium**

spot·ted fe·ver *n.* any fever accompanied by skin eruptions, e.g., Rocky Mountain spotted fever, typhus, or epidemic cerebrospinal meningitis

spot·ted sal·a·man·der *n.* a common salamander of eastern North America. It has an irregular row of yellow or orange spots running down each side of its black back. Latin name: *Ambystoma maculatum.*

spot·ted sand·pi·per *n.* a small shore bird that is found near small lakes and streams in North America. It has spots on its white breast during the breeding season. Latin name: *Actitis macularia.*

spot·ter /spóttər/ *n.* **1.** SOMEBODY WHO MARKS SOMETHING somebody who puts marks or dots on something **2.** SOMEBODY WATCHING OUT somebody or something that watches for and locates something (*often used before a noun*) **3.** MIL LOCATER OF ENEMY POSITIONS a person or aircraft that locates and reports enemy positions **4.** SOMEBODY EMPLOYED TO SPY somebody employed to spy on fellow employees to check their honesty (*informal*) **5.** BROADCAST, SPORTS SPORTSCASTER ASSISTANT somebody who assists a sportscaster by identifying the players in the game **6.** SPORTS SPORTS ASSISTANT somebody whose job is to stand by and guard against injury during a sports practice, e.g., in gymnastics or water-skiing **7.** SOMEBODY LOOKING FOR TALENT somebody who watches for new talent or material **8.** SOMEBODY WHO REMOVES SPOTS somebody who removes spots, especially in dry cleaning

spot·ty /spóttee/ **(-ti·er, -ti·est)** *adj.* **1.** INCONSISTENT inconsistent in quality or character **2.** *U.K.* PIMPLY covered in pimples **3.** SPOTTED with a pattern of spots —**spot·ti·ly** *adv.* —**spot·ti·ness** *n.*

spot-weld *vt.* **(spot-weld·ed, spot-weld·ing, spot-welds)** WELD METAL IN SPOTS to join overlapping pieces of metal by making a series of small welds dotted about, rather than by making a large continuous weld. Spot-welding is used when the bond is subject to light temporary stresses but not to structural loads. ■ *n.* JOINT MADE BY SPOT-WELDING a joint between overlapping metal parts, formed using the technique of spot-welding —**spot-weld·er** *n.*

spou·sal /spówz'l/ *adj.* **1.** OF HUSBAND OR WIFE relating to somebody's husband or wife **2.** OF MARRIAGE relating to the institution or ceremony of marriage ■ *n.* WEDDING a wedding ceremony (*archaic*) (*often used in the plural*) [13thC. Via Old French *espousaille* "marriage" from, ultimately, Latin *sponsalia* "betrothal," from *spons-*, the past participle stem of *spondere* "to pledge" (see SPONSOR).] —**spou·sal·ly** *adv.*

spou·sal e·quiv·alent, spouse e·quiv·a·lent *n.* somebody who acts as or is regarded as the equivalent to a husband or wife, including a same-sex partner, especially for the purposes of tax, pension, or government benefits

spouse /spowss, spowz/ *n.* HUSBAND OR WIFE somebody's husband or wife ■ *vt.* **(spoused, spous·ing, spous·es)** MARRY to marry somebody (*archaic*) [12thC. Via Old French *spous* from Latin *sponsus*, literally "pledged," the past participle of *spondere* "to betroth."]

spouse e·quiv·a·lent *n.* = **spousal equivalent**

spout /spowt/ *vti.* **(spout·ed, spout·ing, spouts) 1.** DISCHARGE to discharge a substance forcibly in a jet or stream **2.** ZOOL DISCHARGE AIR FROM BLOWHOLE to discharge air and water through a blowhole (*refers to whales or dolphins*) **3.** TALK AT GREAT LENGTH to talk about something tediously and at great length, usually with no regard for the listener's interest ■ *n.* **1.** TUBE FOR POURING LIQUID a tube or pipe out of which a liquid is poured **2.** CHUTE FOR DISCHARGE OF SOLID SUBSTANCE a chute through which something solid such as grain is discharged **3.** STREAM OF LIQUID a continuous and forceful stream of liquid **4.** METEOROL = **waterspout** *n.* 2 **5.** ZOOL AIR AND WATER FROM BLOWHOLE a burst of air and water from a whale or other marine animal's blowhole [14thC. From Middle Dutch *spouten* "to spout." Ultimately from an Indo-European base, imitative of the sound of spitting that is also the ancestor of English *spew, spit,* and *sputum.*]

spout·ing /spówting/ *n. NZ, Northeast U.S.* the system of gutters and downspouts that carry rainwater from the roof of a building

spp. *abbr.* species (*plural*)

S.P.Q.R., SPQR *abbr.* the senate and people of Rome [Latin, *Senatus Populusque Romanus*]

sprain /sprayn/ *n.* INJURY TO LIGAMENTS a painful injury to the ligaments of a joint caused by wrenching or overstretching ■ *vt.* **(sprained, sprain·ing, sprains)** INJURE LIGAMENTS OF to injure a joint by a sudden wrenching of its ligaments [Early 17thC. Origin uncertain: perhaps, ultimately, from Latin *exprimere* (see EXPRESS).]

sprang *v.* past tense of **spring**

sprat /sprat/ *n.* **1.** (*plural* **sprats** *or* **sprat**) ZOOL SMALL EDIBLE FISH a small food fish of the herring family that lives in the northeast Atlantic Ocean and North Sea. Latin name: *Clupea sprattus.* **2.** ZOOL SMALL HERRING a small or young herring or similar fish such as an anchovy **3.** SOMEBODY YOUNG OR UNIMPORTANT somebody who is young, small, or dismissed as insignificant [Old English *sprot*]

sprawl /sprawl/ *vi.* **(sprawled, sprawl·ing, sprawls) 1.** LIE AWKWARDLY to sit or lie with the arms and legs spread awkwardly in different directions **2.** EXTEND DISORDERLY to extend over or across something in a disordered, awkward, or ugly way ○ *handwritten notes sprawled across the page* ■ *n.* **1.** AWKWARD SITTING OR LYING POSITION a sitting or lying position in which the arms and legs are spread out awkwardly **2.** UNCHECKED GROWTH OF URBAN AREA the scattered, unplanned, and unchecked expansion of a town or city into the surrounding countryside **3.** URBANIZED AREAS ON CITY'S EDGE the urbanized areas on the edge of a town or city that have developed as a result of unplanned and unchecked expansion [Old English *sprēawlian* "to move convulsively." Ultimately from an Indo-European base meaning "to strew" that is also the ancestor of English *spread* and *spray*[1].] —**sprawl·er** *n.* —**sprawl·ing** *adj.* —**spraw·ly** *adj.*

spray[1] /spray/ *n.* **1.** LIQUID PARTICLES a moving cloud or mist of water or other liquid particles **2.** JET OF LIQUID a jet of fine particles of liquid from an atomizer or pressurized container **3.** CONTAINER FOR RELEASING LIQUID an atomizer or pressurized container that releases fine particles of a liquid (*often used before a noun*) **4.** SOMETHING IN PRESSURIZED CONTAINER a liquid product such as a deodorant, paint, or insecticide that is packaged in an atomizer or pressurized container (*often used before a noun*) ■ *v.* **(sprayed, spray·ing, sprays) 1.** *vt.* PAINT WITH PAINT SPRAY to paint or mark something using a paint spray ○ *spray the car red* ○ *He sprayed his name on the wall.* **2.** *vi.* URINATE to put out a stream of urine, e.g., as a cat does when marking its territory [Early 17thC. From Middle Dutch *sprayen* "to sprinkle."]

spray[2] *n.* **1.** PLANT SPRIG a shoot or branch of a plant, with flowers, leaves, or berries on it **2.** FLOWER ARRANGEMENT a decorative arrangement of flowers and foliage **3.** DECORATION IMITATING FLOWERS AND FOLIAGE something decorative such as a brooch, made in imitation of a sprig of flowers and foliage [13thC. From assumed Old English *spræg*, probably related to sprig and Old English *spræc* "shoot, twig."]

spray can *n.* a small pressurized container used to disperse liquids in a fine mist

spray gun *n.* a device that uses pressure to apply atomized paint or other liquids, operated by means of a trigger

spread /spred/ *v.* **(spread, spread·ing, spreads) 1.** *vt.* OPEN FULLY to open or extend something to its fullest area **2.** *vti.* EXTEND WIDELY to extend, or cause something to extend, over a large area **3.** *vti.* EXTEND IN TIME to extend something over a period of time **4.** *vti.* EXTEND IN RANGE to extend over a wider range, or cause something to cover a wider range **5.** *vt.* SEPARATE THINGS BY STRETCHING to separate things by stretching or pulling, so that they become far apart **6.** *vti.* BECOME OR MAKE KNOWN to become widely known, or make something widely known **7.** *vt.* APPLY COATING TO to coat something with a layer of a substance, especially one smoothly applied **8.** *vti.* DISPERSE to disperse something over a wide area **9.** *vti.* SEND OUT IN ALL DIRECTIONS to send out something, or to be sent out, in all directions **10.** *vt.* DISPLAY to exhibit or display something in its fullest extent **11.** *vt.* GET TABLE READY FOR MEAL to prepare a table for a meal **12.** *vt.* PUT FOOD ON TABLE to lay out food or a meal on a table ■ *n.* **1.** EXTENSION OF SOMETHING the extension, diffusion, or distribution of something over an area, range, or time **2.** VARIETY a wide variety of things **3.** LIMIT OF EXTENSION the limit to which something can be extended **4.** DISTANCE BETWEEN THINGS the distance or range between two points or things **5.** EXPANSE OF LAND a large expanse of land (*regional*) **6.** RANCH a ranch (*regional*) **7.** BED OR TABLE COVER a covering for a bed or table **8.** FOOD SPREADABLE FOOD a food with a soft texture, designed to be spread on bread or crackers **9.** PUBL PAIR OF FACING PAGES two facing pages in a newspaper, magazine, or book, often with material printed across the fold **10.** PUBL EXTENSIVE STORY OR AD an advertisement or story that occupies two or more columns in a newspaper or magazine **11.** FOOD MEAL a large meal laid out on a table (*informal*) **12. WIDENING OF BODY** a widening of the hips and waist owing to weight gain (*informal*) **13.** AIR **PLANE'S WINGSPAN** the wingspan of an airplane (*informal*) **14.** FIN **DIFFERENCE BETWEEN BID AND OFFER** the difference between the asking price and the bid price of a security **15.** FIN **COMMODITIES MARKET TRANSACTION** a transaction in the commodities market in which the investor takes long and short positions in different commodities or different delivery dates in the same commodity **16. GEMSTONE SIZE** the size of a gemstone when viewed from above, expressed in carats ■ *adj.* **1. EXTENDED** extended or stretched out **2. SHALLOW** used to describe a gemstone that is shallow and flat **3.** PHON **WITH LIPS STRAIGHT** used to describe a speech sound that is pronounced with the lips forming a horizontal line [Old English *-sprǣdan*. Ultimately from an Indo-European base meaning "to strew" that is also the ancestor of English *sprawl*, *sprout*, and *spray*[1].] —**spread·able** *adj.*

spread ea·gle *n.* **1. SYMBOLIC IMAGE OF EAGLE** the image of an eagle with its wings and legs outstretched, especially when used as an emblem of the United States. The spread eagle appears on the Great Seal of the United States. **2.** ICE SKATING **SKATING FIGURE** in ice skating, a figure performed with the blades touching heel to heel **3. POSTURE WITH SPREAD LIMBS** a way of standing or lying with arms and legs spread apart

spread-ea·gle *v.* (**spread-ea·gled, spread-ea·gling, spread-ea·gles**) **1.** *vt.* **FORCE INTO SPREAD-OUT POSITION** to force somebody to stand or lie with arms and legs spread apart, especially when being arrested or searched **2.** *vi.* ICE SKATING **PERFORM SKATING FIGURE** in ice skating, to perform a spread eagle **3.** *vt.* **STRETCH BODY ACROSS** to stand or lie with limbs spread wide across a gap or an object **4.** *vi.* **ADOPT POSITION WITH SPREAD LIMBS** to stand or lie with arms and legs spread apart ■ *adj.* **1. OVERLY PATRIOTIC** boastful or chauvinistically patriotic about the United States (*slang*) **2. IN SPREAD-OUT POSITION** standing or lying with arms and legs spread apart

spread·er /spréddər/ *n.* **1. DEVICE FOR DISTRIBUTING SEED OR FERTILIZER** a machine used by farmers and gardeners to spread manure, fertilizer, seed, or similar material over the ground (*usually used in combination*) **2. IMPLEMENT FOR SPREADING** an implement such as a spatula, trowel, or broad-bladed knife, used for spreading soft substances (*usually used in combination*) **3. DEVICE FOR SEPARATING THINGS** a device such as a bar, used to hold things such as cables or wires apart

spread·ing fac·tor *n.* = **hyaluronidase**

spread·sheet /spréd shēet/ *n.* **1. COMPUTER PROGRAM FOR NUMERICAL DATA** a computer program that displays numerical data in cells in a simulated accountant's worksheet of rows and columns in which hidden formulas can perform calculations on the visible data. Changing the contents of one cell can cause automatic recalculation of other cells. **2. DISPLAY OR PRINTOUT OF SPREADSHEET** the display or printout of a spreadsheet, showing the many lines and columns of a ledger

sprech·ge·sang /shprékhgə zàng, shprék-/, **Sprech·ge·sang** *n.* a style of singing that blends elements of normal nonmusical speech into the voice [Early 20thC. From German, literally "speech song."]

sprech·stim·me /shprékh shtìmmə, shprék-/, **Sprech·stim·me** *n.* **1. VOICE SINGING SPRECHGESANG** the voice used to sing sprechgesang **2.** = **sprechgesang** [Early 20thC. From German, literally "speech voice."]

spree /sprēe/ *n.* **1. PERIOD OF EXTRAVAGANT ACTIVITY** a session of extravagant self-indulgent activity, especially of spending or drinking, but also of criminal activity **2. SOCIAL OUTING** a fun-filled sociable outing (*dated*) [Late 18thC. Origin unknown.]

spri·er /sprí'r/ comparative of **spry**

spri·est /sprí əst/ superlative of **spry**

sprig /sprig/ *n.* **1.** BOT **SMALL BRANCH** a shoot, stem, or twig cut or broken from a plant ○ *garnished with a sprig of parsley* **2.** CRAFT **DECORATION** an artistic representation of a sprig that is usually repeated in rows on fabric or wallpaper to produce a decorative pattern **3. YOUTH** a young man (*dated*) **4. SMALL NAIL** a small headless tack that tapers to a point ■ *vt.* (**sprigged, sprig·ging, sprigs**) **1.** CRAFT **PATTERN WITH SPRIGS** to decorate fabric, wallpaper, or pottery with a pattern of sprigs ○ *a dress of sprigged cotton* **2.** BOT **CUT TWIGS FROM PLANT** to cut small twigs or branches from a plant **3.** BUILDING, HOME MAINTENANCE **NAIL WITH TACKS** to nail something using brads or tacks [14thC. Origin uncertain: perhaps from Low German *sprick* "twig," and probably related to *spray*[2] and Old English *spræc* "shoot, twig."] —**sprig·ger** *n.* —**sprig·gy** *adj.*

spright·ful /sprítf'l/ *adj.* sprightly (*archaic*) [Late 16thC. See SPRIGHTLY.] —**spright·ful·ly** *adv.* —**spright·ful·ness** *n.*

spright·ly /sprítlee/ *adj.* (**-li·er, -li·est**) **VIGOROUS** full of life and vigor, especially with a light and springy step ■ *adv.* **VIGOROUSLY** in a lively and vigorous way [Early 16thC. Formed from an earlier variant of SPRITE.] —**spright·li·ness** *n.*

sprig·tail /sprig tàyl/ *n.* **1.** = **pintail 2.** = **ruddy duck**

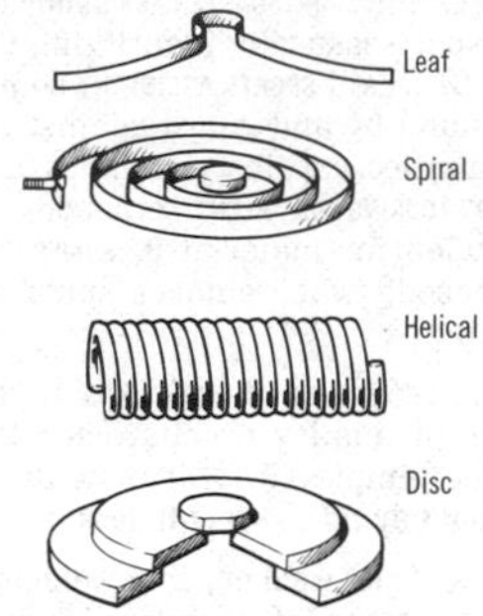

Spring

spring /spring/ *v.* (**sprang** /sprang/, **sprung** /sprung/, **spring·ing, springs**) **1.** *vi.* **MOVE SUDDENLY IN SINGLE MOVEMENT** to move rapidly upward or forward in a single movement or in a series of rapid movements ○ *He sprang to his feet.* **2.** *vt.* **LEAP OVER** to leap over a barrier **3.** *vi.* **RAPIDLY RESUME ORIGINAL POSITION** to move back rapidly to an original position after being forced in another direction **4.** *vi.* **EMERGE RAPIDLY** to appear or come into existence quickly ○ *new houses springing up* **5.** *vi.* **COME FROM SOMEBODY'S LIPS** to be uttered, especially as a sudden and almost involuntary reaction to something **6.** *vi.* **ORIGINATE FROM SOMETHING** to originate from a particular source ○ *reform that springs from discontent* **7.** *vi.* **BE DESCENDED** to be descended from a person or family **8.** *vt.* **SUDDENLY REVEAL TO SOMEBODY** to make something known to somebody unexpectedly or suddenly (*informal*) ○ *You can't just spring a decision like that on me!* **9.** *vi.* **PAY FOR SOMETHING** to pay for something, usually for another person (*slang*) ○ *I'll spring for lunch.* **10.** *vt.* **MAKE SOMETHING OPERATE** to operate a device or trap by releasing a mechanism that was held in check **11.** *vi.* **JUMP OUT OF PLACE** to move suddenly out of place or come suddenly loose within a mechanism **12.** *vt.* CRIMINOL **GET OUT OF PRISON** to release somebody from prison or help somebody escape from prison (*slang*) **13.** *vt.* HUNT **MOVE ANIMAL FROM COVER** to move an animal or bird out into the open during a hunting expedition **14.** *vti.* MIL **DETONATE MINE** to explode or detonate a mine, or be detonated **15.** *vti.* TECH **WARP OR SPLIT** to crack, split, or warp, or cause wood to do this **16.** *vi.* ARCHIT **EXTEND UPWARD** to extend upward from the topmost part of a column ■ *n.* **1.** MECH ENG **COIL OF METAL** a resilient metal coil used especially for cushioning and in clockwork **2. ABILITY TO REGAIN SHAPE** the ability of an object to revert rapidly to its original position after being extended, compressed, or under tension ○ *a mattress with a lot of spring left in it* **3. SEASON OF YEAR** the season of the year between winter and summer during which many plants bring forth leaves and flowers **4. ONWARD OR UPWARD LEAP** a rapid forward or upward movement **5. WATER EMERGING FROM UNDERGROUND** a source of water that flows out of the ground as a small stream or pool **6. SOURCE OF SOMETHING** the source of something such as a particular quality or state (*literary*) **7. FORCE CAUSING SOMETHING** a strong motivation that causes somebody to act in a particular way (*formal*) ○ *the springs of her ambition* **8. TIME OF RENEWAL** a time of new growth and regeneration **9.** TECH **WARPING OR BENDING** warping, cracking, or bending, especially when caused by great force **10.** METEOROL = **spring tide** *n.* 1 ■ *adj.* **1. HAPPENING IN SPRINGTIME** relating to, occurring in, or appropriate to the season of spring ○ *spring fashions* **2. GROWN IN SPRINGTIME** normally grown or growing in the season of spring ○ *spring flowers* **3. FULL OF SPRINGS** having or containing springs, especially for cushioning or as part of a clockwork mechanism **4. RECOILING** acting like a spring in being held back then quickly releasing energy [Old English *springan*. Ultimately from an Indo-European word meaning "rapid movement."]

WORD KEY: CULTURAL NOTE

The Rite of Spring, a ballet with music by the Russian composer Igor Stravinsky (1913). This one-act work is based on traditional dances performed at pagan festivals in Russia. Its use of dissonance and irregular pulsating rhythms combined with Nijinsky's unorthodox choreography outraged contemporary audiences, resulting in a famous riot at the first performance in Paris on May 29.

spring beau·ty *n.* a succulent herb of the purslane family of eastern North America that bears white or pinkish flowers in early spring. Genus: *Claytonia.*

spring·board /spring bàwrd/ *n.* **1.** SWIMMING **FLEXIBLE DIVING BOARD** a flexible board secured to a base at one end and projecting over the water at the other, used for diving **2.** GYMNASTICS **GYMNASTIC EQUIPMENT** a flexible board on which gymnasts bounce in order to gain height for vaulting **3. EVENT OR FACTOR HELPING ADVANCEMENT** an event, activity, or plan that helps to further somebody's career

Springbok

spring·bok /spring bòk/ (*plural* **-bok** *or* **-boks**) *n.* a small swift gazelle of the semiarid regions of southern Africa, noted for its ability to leap high in the air repeatedly when startled. Latin name: *Antidorcas marsupialis.* [Late 18thC. From Afrikaans, literally "leaping he-goat."]

spring break *n.* a vacation from school or college in the spring, usually lasting at least a week

spring·buck /spring bùk/ (*plural* **-buck** *or* **-bucks**) *n.* = **springbok**

spring chick·en *n.* a chicken less than ten months old, formerly available for eating only in spring ◇ **no spring chicken** no longer young, inexperienced, or agile

spring-clean (**spring-cleaned, spring-clean·ing, spring-cleans**) *vti.* to clean a house or room thoroughly, usually including all the contents and furnishings, at the end of the winter or during spring

spring-clean·ing *n.* the thorough cleaning of a house or room, traditionally carried out at the end of the winter

Spring·dale /spring dayl/ city in northwestern Arkansas, north of Fayetteville. Population: 38,576 (1996).

springe /sprinj/ *n.* a snare or trap for small animals, consisting of a noose attached to a branch under tension [13thC. From assumed Old English *sprencg.* Ultimately from a prehistoric Germanic word that is also the ancestor of English *spring.*]

spring·er /springər/ *n.* **1.** ARCHIT **WEDGE-SHAPED STONE** the first wedge-shaped stone (**voussoir**) of an arch resting on the top section of the arch's supporting pillar (**impost**) **2.** AGRIC **COW READY TO GIVE BIRTH** a cow that is on the point of giving birth to a calf **3.** ZOOL = **springer spaniel 4. SOMEBODY OR SOMETHING THAT LEAPS** a person or animal that springs or leaps

spring·er span·iel *n.* a hunting dog with a long wavy coat, short legs, and floppy ears, belonging to either an English or a Welsh breed

spring fe·ver *n.* a feeling of restlessness, yearning, lust, or sometimes laziness, believed to be brought on by the coming of spring

Spring·field /spring feeld/ **1.** city in central Illinois, on the southern bank of the Sangamon River, west of Decatur. President Abraham Lincoln lived in Springfield from 1844 until 1861 and is buried there. Population: 112,921 (1996). **2.** city in south central

Massachusetts, on the Connecticut River, north of the Connecticut border. It is home to the Basketball Hall of Fame. Population: 156,983 (1990).

Spring·field ri·fle /spring feeld-/ *n.* a bolt-action .30-caliber rifle developed at the federal arsenal in Springfield, Massachusetts, used by the U.S. Army in World War I.

spring·fish /spríng fish/ (*plural* **-fish** *or* **-fish·es**) *n.* a small North American freshwater fish associated with caves and underground passages in limestone formations, and related to cave fishes. Latin name: *Chlorogaster agassizi.*

spring·form pan /spríng fawrm-/ *n.* a cake pan with a detachable base that fastens to the rim with a spring or clamp

spring·haas /spring haàss/ (*plural* **-haas**) *n.* a large jumping mammal with hind legs like a kangaroo's and a long black-tufted tail, found in semiarid regions of southern Africa. It grows to approximately 16 in./41 cm in length excluding the tail. Latin name: *Pedestes capensis.* [Late 18thC. From Afrikaans, literally "leaping hare."]

spring·halt /spríng hàwlt/ *n.* = **stringhalt** [Early 17thC. Alteration of STRINGHALT.]

spring·head /spríng hèd/ *n.* **1.** STREAM SOURCE the source of a stream **2.** POINT OF ORIGIN the source of a particular way of thinking

spring·house /spríng hòwss/ (*plural* **-hous·es** /-hòwzəz/) *n.* a storehouse built over a spring, formerly used to keep meat and dairy products fresh and cool

spring·ing /spríngíng/ *n.* the point at which an arch, vault, or dome rises from its support

spring·let /springlət/ *n.* a small spring of water

spring line *n.* a rope by means of which a sailing vessel is made fast to an anchorage, usually one of two

spring-load·ed *adj.* fixed in place or controlled by a spring (*refers to a part of a mechanism*)

spring lock *n.* a lock that is bolted automatically by means of a spring

spring on·ion *n. U.K.* = **green onion**

spring peep·er *n.* a small brownish tree frog of eastern North America that has an X-shaped marking on its back and makes a shrill peeping call early in the spring. Latin name: *Hyla crucifer.*

spring roll *n.* a hot or cold pastry roll, especially one made with a meat and vegetable filling and often fried until crisp and golden [Translation of Chinese *chūn juǎn*]

Springs /springz/ town in Gauteng Province, South Africa, situated about 25 mi./40 km east of Johannesburg. Population: 170,000 (1991).

Spring·steen /spring steèn/, **Bruce** (*b.* 1949) U.S. singer and songwriter. His songs include "Born in the U.S.A." (1984). Full name **Bruce Frederick Joseph Springsteen**

spring·tail /spring tàyl/ *n.* a primitive wingless insect with a forked abdominal structure that helps it spring through the air. Order: Collembola.

spring tide *n.* **1.** TIDE AT NEW AND FULL MOON a tide that occurs near the times of the new moon and full moon and has a greater than average range **2.** RUSH OF EMOTION a great rush of emotion (*literary*)

spring·tide /spring tīd/ *n.* springtime (*literary*)

spring·time /spríng tīm/ *n.* **1.** SEASON OF SPRING the season of spring, between winter and summer **2.** EARLIEST AND BEST PART the earliest, freshest, and most pleasant stage of somebody's life, a relationship, or a period of time (*literary*)

spring·wood /spring wòod/ *n.* young relatively soft wood that develops just beneath the bark of trees in spring

spring·y /spríngee/ (**-i·er, -i·est**) *adj.* **1.** BOUNCING BACK INTO SHAPE springing back strongly to its original shape after being compressed or extended **2.** MAKING SPRINGING MOTIONS tending to make a lot of springing movements (*informal*) —**spring·i·ly** *adv.* —**spring·i·ness** *n.*

sprin·kle /spríngk'l/ *v.* (**-kled, -kling, -kles**) **1.** *vt.* DISTRIBUTE SMALL AMOUNTS OF to scatter small drops of a liquid or particles of a fine or powdery substance such as sugar, ashes, or flour over the surface of something **2.** *vi.* METEOROL RAIN VERY SLIGHTLY to rain very gently in fine drops, usually for a short period **3.** *vt.* SCATTER OR BE SCATTERED THROUGHOUT THINGS to scatter things in among other things, at random or as though at random, or be scattered among other things in this way ○ *fields sprinkled with poppies* **4.** *vt.* GIVE OUT IN SMALL AMOUNTS to distribute a substance, emotion, or commodity in small amounts ■ *n.* **1.** ACT OF SPRINKLING the action of scattering small drops of liquid or particles of a fine or powdery substance **2.** METEOROL LIGHT RAIN a light rain falling in fine or sporadic drops ■ **sprin·kles** *npl.* FOOD SUGAR PARTICLES FOR DECORATING CAKES small pieces of colored sugar or candy that are scattered over the surface of ice cream, cakes, or cookies as a decoration [14thC. Origin uncertain: perhaps from Dutch *sprenkelen* "to sprinkle."]

sprin·kler /spríngklər/ *n.* **1.** GARDENING WATERING APPARATUS a device that sends a moving spray of water onto a garden or lawn. A sprinkler may be attached to a movable hose or set permanently into a lawn or garden and remotely controlled. **2.** GARDENING NOZZLE a plastic or metal nozzle perforated with many small holes that fits onto a watering can or hose. It spreads the liquid being distributed so that it falls gently over a larger area. **3.** PERSON OR DEVICE THAT SPRINKLES somebody who or something that sprinkles small drops of liquid or particles of a solid on something

sprin·kler sys·tem *n.* **1.** ENG FIRE EXTINGUISHING SYSTEM a system for extinguishing fires, designed to release water from overhead nozzles that open automatically when a particular temperature is reached **2.** GARDENING GARDEN WATERING SYSTEM a system of sprinklers for watering a garden or lawn, operated by a single control

sprin·kling /spríngkling/ *n.* **1.** SMALL AMOUNT SCATTERED THINLY a small quantity of a fine or powdery substance such as sugar, snow, dust, or sand scattered on or throughout something **2.** MEAGER AMOUNT a small, thinly distributed amount of a particular emotion or quality ○ *a sprinkling of wit*

sprint /sprint/ *n.* **1.** SHORT SWIFT RACE a short race run or cycled at a very high speed **2.** FAST FINISHING RUN a burst of fast running or cycling during the last part of a longer race **3.** BURST OF ACTIVITY a sudden burst of activity or speed ■ *vi.* (**sprint·ed, sprint·ing, sprints**) GO AT TOP SPEED to run, swim, or cycle as rapidly as possible [Mid-16thC. From Old Norse *spretta* "to jump."]

sprit /sprit/ *n.* a pole that crosses a fore-and-aft sail diagonally [Old English *sprēot.* Ultimately from a prehistoric Germanic word that is also the ancestor of English *sprout.*]

sprite /sprīt/ *n.* **1.** SUPERNATURAL ELFIN CREATURE in folklore, a small supernatural being like an elf or a fairy, especially one associated with water **2.** SOMEBODY LIKE AN ELF a small or delicately built person who is likened to an elf or a fairy **3.** GHOST in folklore, a ghost or spirit **4.** COMPUT INDEPENDENT GRAPHIC OBJECT an independent graphic object that moves freely across a computer screen **5.** SOUL a soul (*archaic*) [14thC. Via Old French *esp(i)rit* from Latin *spiritus* (see SPIRIT).]

sprit·sail /sprít sàyl/; *nautical* /spríts'l/ *n.* a sail that is extended by being mounted on a sprit

spritz /sprits/ *vt.* (**spritzed, spritz·ing, spritz·es**) SPRAY LIQUID to spray a fine jet of liquid through a nozzle ■ *n.* FINE SPRAY OF LIQUID a fine spray of liquid squirted through a nozzle [Early 20thC. From German *spritzen* "to squirt."]

spritz·er /sprítsər/ *n.* a drink consisting of wine, generally white, diluted with sparkling water [Mid-20thC. From German, "splash."]

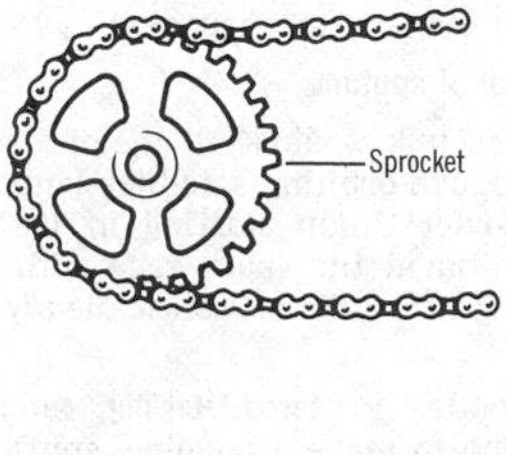

Sprocket

sprock·et /sprókət/ *n.* a projecting tooth on a wheel or cylinder that engages with the links of a chain or with perforations in film to make the chain or film move forward [Mid-16thC. Origin unknown.]

sprout /sprowt/ *v.* (**sprout·ed, sprout·ing, sprouts**) **1.** *vti.* BOT DEVELOP SHOOTS to develop buds or shoots **2.** *vi.* BOT GERMINATE to begin to grow from a seed **3.** *vti.* GROW to grow or cause something or somebody to grow **4.** *vti.* EMERGE to emerge and grow rapidly, or cause something to emerge and grow rapidly ■ *n.* **1.** BOT NEW GROWTH ON A PLANT a new growth on a plant, e.g., a bud or shoot **2.** SOMETHING LIKE A SPROUT somebody who or something that grows rapidly like a sprout **3.** = **Brussels sprout** ■ **sprouts** *npl.* FOOD EDIBLE SHOOTS OF PLANTS newly sprouted seeds or beans, eaten especially in sandwiches, salads, and stir-fries [Old English *-sprutan.* Ultimately from a prehistoric Germanic word that also produced German *sprießen* "to sprout."]

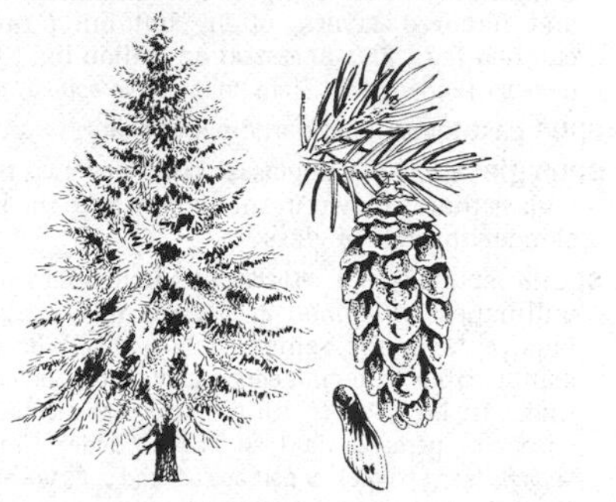

Spruce

spruce[1] /sprooss/ (*plural* **spruc·es** *or* **spruce**) *n.* **1.** EVERGREEN TREE an evergreen tree of the pine family with a pyramid shape, short needles, drooping cones, and soft light wood. Genus: *Picea.* **2.** SPRUCE WOOD the soft light wood of a spruce tree [Early 17thC. Shortening of *Spruce fir,* literally "Prussian fir"; *Spruce* an alteration of *Pruce,* from, ultimately, medieval Latin *Prussia.*]

spruce[2] /sprooss/ *vti.* (**spruced, spruc·ing, spruc·es**) MAKE NEAT to make something or somebody, usually yourself, clean and neat in appearance ■ *adj.* APPEARING NEAT AND TIDY having a clean and well-cared-for appearance ○ *a spruce young man* [Late 16thC. Origin uncertain: perhaps a shortening of *Spruce leather,* a type of fine leather first made in Prussia (see SPRUCE[1]).] —**spruce·ly** *adv.* —**spruce·ness** *n.*

spruce bud·worm *n.* a North American moth with destructive larvae that feed on the buds and branch tips of evergreen coniferous trees such as spruce and balsam. Latin name: *Choristoneura fumiferana.*

spruce grouse *n.* a common plump game bird of northern North American coniferous forests that has a black throat and breast. Latin name: *Dendragapus canadensis.*

spruce pine *n.* a tall pine of the southeastern United States with soft wood and needles in pairs. Latin name: *Pinus glabra.*

sprue[1] /sproo/ *n.* INDUST a vertical channel in a mold, used to pour in molten material [Early 19thC. Origin unknown.]

sprue[2] /sproo/ *n.* MED a tropical disease of unknown origin involving deficient absorption of nutrients from the intestine and marked by persistent diarrhea, weight loss, and anemia. Treatment with antibiotics and vitamin supplements is often effective. [Late 19thC. From Dutch *spruw* "the disease thrush."]

sprung past participle of **spring**

sprung rhythm *n.* a system of prosody that always places the accent on the first syllable of any foot in an effort to evoke the rhythms of ordinary speech. The term and practice were originated by the poet Gerard Manley Hopkins.

spry /sprī/ (**spry·er** *or* **spri·er, spry·est** *or* **spri·est**) *adj.* markedly brisk and active, especially at an advanced age [Mid-18thC. Origin uncertain: perhaps from a Scandinavian word, or perhaps a shortening of SPRIGHTLY.] —**spry·ly** *adv.* —**spry·ness** *n.*

spt. *abbr.* seaport

spud /spud/ *n.* **1.** FOOD POTATO a potato (*slang*) **2.** GARDENING GARDEN IMPLEMENT a spade with a sharp narrow blade, used for cutting through roots and digging up weeds **3.** FORESTRY TOOL FOR REMOVING BARK FROM TREES a tool resembling a chisel that is used to peel bark from trees ■ *v.* (**spud·ded, spud·ding, spuds**) **1.** *vi.*

INDUST **START DRILLING AN OIL WELL** to use a large bit to drill the upper part of the bore of a new oil well **2.** *vt.* FORESTRY **REMOVE BARK** to remove bark from trees by the use of a tool like a chisel **3.** *vt.* GARDENING **DIG WITH A SPUD** to use a spud to dig up weeds or cut through roots [15thC. Origin unknown. Originally in the meaning "dagger," its use for "potato" seems to have originated in New Zealand English.]

spume /spyoom/ *n.* **FOAM** a mass of fine bubbles on the surface of a liquid, especially on the ocean (*literary*) ■ *vi.* **(spumed, spum·ing, spumes) BE FOAMY** to produce or have a mass of fine bubbles on the surface (*literary*) [14thC. Directly or via Old French from Latin *spuma* "foam."] —**spu·mous** *adj.* —**spum·y** *adj.*

spu·mo·ni /spoo mṓnee/, **spu·mo·ne** *n.* **1. ICE CREAM** an Italian ice cream composed of differently colored and flavored layers, often containing nuts and candied fruit **2. LIGHT DESSERT** an Italian light mousse dessert [Early 20thC. From Italian, from *spuma* "foam."]

spun past tense, past participle of **spin**

spun glass *n.* **1.** = **fiberglass 2. GLASS WITH GLASS THREADS IN IT** glass that is blown in such a way as to incorporate slender threads of glass

spunk /spungk/ *n.* **1. PLUCKINESS** spiritedness or eager willingness (*informal*) **2. OFFENSIVE TERM** a highly offensive term for semen (*taboo slang*) **3. TINDER** a combustible material, especially soft wood or twigs, that can be used to kindle fires [Mid-16thC. Origin uncertain: perhaps via Irish *sponc* "tinder" from Latin *spongia* (see SPONGE), or perhaps a blend of SPARK and FUNK. Originally in the meaning "spark."]

spunk·y /spúngkee/ (**-i·er, -i·est**) *adj.* very lively, determined, and courageous (*informal*) —**spunk·i·ly** *adv.* —**spunk·i·ness** *n.*

spun silk *n.* inexpensive fabric or yarn made from short-fibered silk combined with silk waste

spun sug·ar *n.* FOOD = **cotton candy**

spun yarn *n.* rope or cord made from several light yarns twisted or spun together

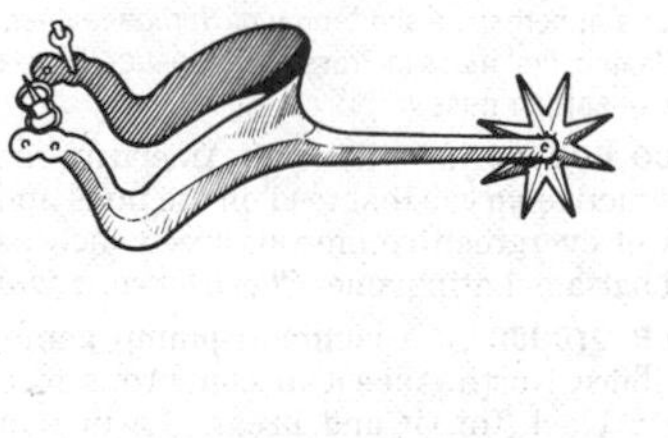

Spur

spur /spur/ *n.* **1.** RIDING **DEVICE ATTACHED TO A RIDER'S HEEL** a small spike or spiked wheel attached to the heel of a rider's boot that is nudged into the horse's sides to encourage it to go faster **2. INDUCEMENT** something such as the hope of a reward or the fear of punishment that encourages a person or organization to take action or to make a greater effort **3.** BOT **PROJECTING PLANT PART** a tubular extension from a flower part, e.g., that in larkspur and columbine **4.** BOT **SHORT BRANCH OR SHOOT** a short branch or lateral shoot from a stem or branch of a plant **5.** BIRDS **HORNY PROJECTION** a sharp horny projection on the legs of some male birds, e.g., roosters, above the claws **6.** RAIL **PART OF A RAILROAD** a short section of railroad track leading off a main line **7.** ZOOL **PROJECTING ANIMAL PART** a pointed extension or projecting part (**process**) on some animals, e.g., the stiff outgrowth on the legs of some insects and birds **8.** ANAT **SHORT BONY OUTGROWTH** a bony outgrowth, usually a normal part of the body but sometimes one that develops such as that on the bottom of the heel after an injury **9. SPIKE FASTENED TO THE LEG OF A GAMECOCK** a sharp metal spike attached to the leg of a gamecock **10.** BUILDING **PROP** a timber or masonry prop or support **11.** GEOG **MOUNTAIN RIDGE** a ridge that projects outward from a mountain range and descends toward a valley floor **12.** CIV ENG **SHORT JETTY** a small jetty extending from a shore to protect a beach against erosion or to trap shifting sands **13.** TRANSP **ROAD OFF A MAJOR ROAD** a short side road leading off a main road **14.** CERAMICS **CERAMIC SUPPORT IN A KILN** a small ceramic support placed beneath a pot in a kiln ■ *v.* **(spurred, spur·ring, spurs) 1.** *vt.* **ENCOURAGE SOMEBODY TO TRY HARDER** to stimulate a person or organization to take action or make greater efforts in the hope of a reward or in the fear of punishment ○ *"Public schools are spurred to perform better thanks to new reforms."* (*U.S. News & World Report*; December 1998) **2.** *vt.* RIDING **MAKE A HORSE GO FASTER** to encourage a horse to go faster by nudging spurs into its sides **3.** *vi.* RIDING **RIDE FAST** to ride fast, using spurs (*literary*) **4.** *vi.* **GO QUICKLY** to go or proceed hastily (*literary*) **5.** *vt.* RIDING **CAUSE INJURY TO A HORSE WITH SPURS** to injure a horse by using spurs too strongly and too frequently **6.** *vt.* **PUT SPURS ON SOMEBODY OR SOMETHING** to equip somebody or something with spurs [Old English *spura*. Ultimately from an Indo-European word meaning "to kick," which is also the ancestor of English *spoor* and *spurn*.] ◇ **win** *or* **gain your spurs 1.** to gain recognition and respect for the first time **2.** HIST in the past, to be given the rank of knight

WORD KEY: SYNONYMS

See Synonyms at ***motive***.

spurge /spurj/ *n.* a herb or shrub that has flowers without petals and a bitter milky juice. Genus: *Euphorbia.* [14thC. From Old French *espurge*, from *espurgier* "to purge," from Latin *expurgare* "to cleanse." From its purgative properties.]

spur gear *n.* a gear whose teeth are arranged along the rim parallel to its axis of rotation

spurge lau·rel *n.* a low-growing evergreen shrub of Europe and Asia with elongated glossy leaves and yellow flowers. Latin name: *Daphne laureola.*

spu·ri·ous /spyŏoree əs/ *adj.* **1. NOT GENUINE** being different from what it claims to be **2.** BOT **RESEMBLING A PLANT PART** having the outward appearance of another plant part but not its function or origin **3. BORN OUT OF WEDLOCK** born to parents not legally married to each other (*archaic*) [Late 16thC. Formed from Latin *spurius* "illegitimate child."] —**spu·ri·ous·ly** *adv.* —**spu·ri·ous·ness** *n.*

spurn /spurn/ *v.* **(spurned, spurn·ing, spurns) 1.** *vti.* **REJECT SOMEBODY OR SOMETHING WITH DISDAIN** to reject a person, offer, gift, or advances with scorn and contempt **2.** *vt.* **THRUST SOMETHING AWAY WITH THE FOOT** to reject something by pushing it away with the foot (*archaic*) ■ *n.* (*archaic*) **1. SCORNFUL REJECTION** a contemptuous or scornful rejection **2. KICK** a kick [Old English *spurnan*. Ultimately from an Indo-European word that is also the ancestor of English *spur* (see SPUR).] —**spurn·er** *n.*

spurred /spurd/ *adj.* **1.** RIDING **WEARING SPURS** having or wearing spurs **2.** BOT **WITH A PROJECTING PLANT PART** used to describe a flower or plant that has a tubular extension

spur·ry /spúr ee/ (*plural* **-ries**), **spur·rey** (*plural* **-reys**) *n.* a low-growing European plant of the pink family that has linear whorled leaves and small white flowers. Genus: *Spurgula.* [Late 16thC. From Dutch *spurrie*.]

spurt /spurt/ *n.* **1. JET OF LIQUID OR GAS** a sudden stream of liquid or gas, forced out under pressure **2. SUDDEN INCREASE** a short intense burst of energy, interest, action, or speed ○ *I had a spurt of energy as I was digging.* ■ *vt.* **(spurt·ed, spurt·ing, spurts) MAKE SOMETHING GUSH OUT** to cause a liquid or gas to gush out in a pressurized stream or jet ○ *The burst pipe was spurting water.* [Mid-16thC. Origin uncertain: perhaps ultimately from an Indo-European word thought to be imitative of the sound of spitting.]

spur·tle /spúrt'l/ *n.* *Scotland* a short turned stick, frequently with a decorative end, used for stirring porridge. Spurtles are now more frequently sold as tourist items, often with the decorative top in the design of a thistle. [Early 16thC. Origin unknown.]

spur wheel *n.* MECH ENG = **spur gear**

spu·ta plural of **sputum**

sput·nik /spŏotnik, spútnik/ *n.* one of a series of ten artificial Earth-orbiting satellites launched by the former Soviet Union starting in 1957. The first launch initiated the space race with the United States. [Mid-20thC. From Russian, literally "fellow traveler."]

sput·ter /spúttər/ *v.* **(-tered, -ter·ing, -ters) 1.** *vi.* **MAKE POPPING SOUND** to make a popping, spitting sound **2.** *vi.* **SPIT OUT FOOD AND SALIVA** to spray out drops of saliva or food particles, especially when talking or laughing while eating **3.** *vi.* **SPEAK EXPLOSIVELY** to make sounds or pronounce words in an explosive way, especially when angry or excited **4.** *vti.* PHYS **REMOVE SURFACE ATOMS BY ION BOMBARDMENT** to cause or experience the effect in which the atoms of a surface are removed through bombardment by ions, e.g., in cathode evaporation in a discharge tube **5.** *vti.* PHYS **USE A METAL TO COAT SOMETHING** to use a metal to coat something by the process of sputtering, or be coated in this way ■ *n.* **1. NOISE OF SPUTTERING** the noise of a person, fire, candle, or other object sputtering **2. INCOHERENT SPEECH** the confused or incoherent speech of somebody who is angry or excited **3. SOMETHING EMITTED WHILE SPUTTERING** drops of saliva or food particles sprayed out of the mouth while sputtering [Late 16thC. From Dutch *sputteren* "to spray," thought to suggest the action.] —**sput·ter·er** *n.*

spu·tum /spyŏotəm/ (*plural* **-ta** /-tə/) *n.* a substance such as saliva, phlegm, or mucus coughed up from the respiratory tract and usually ejected by mouth [Late 17thC. From Latin, "saliva," from *spuere* "to spit."]

spy /spī/ *n.* (*plural* **spies**) **1. SOMEBODY EMPLOYED TO OBTAIN SECRET INFORMATION** somebody who is employed by a government to obtain secret information, particularly regarding military matters, about other hostile countries (*often used before a noun*) ○ *a spy ring* **2. EMPLOYEE WHO OBTAINS INFORMATION ABOUT RIVALS** somebody who is employed by a company to obtain secret information about rival organizations **3. SECRET OBSERVER OF OTHERS** somebody who watches other people in secret **4. ACT OF A SPY** an instance of acting as a spy **5. CLOSE VIEW** a close view of something (*archaic*) ■ *v.* **(spied, spy·ing, spies) 1.** *vi.* **ACT AS A SPY** to work, operate, or function as a spy **2.** *vi.* **ENGAGE IN ESPIONAGE** to maintain a network of spies and gather intelligence in other clandestine ways **3.** *vi.* **OBSERVE IN SECRET** to observe somebody or something secretly ○ *Have you been spying on us again?* **4.** *vt.* **SEE SUDDENLY** to catch sight of somebody or something **5.** *vt.* **DISCOVER BY OBSERVATION** to discover something by close observation **6.** *vi.* **INVESTIGATE** to investigate something intensively [13thC. From Old French *espie*, from *espier* "to spy" (source of English *espy*), of prehistoric Germanic origin; related to Latin *specere* "to look" (source of English *spectator*).]

spy out *vt.* to discover something by close and discreet examination

spy·glass /spī glàss/ *n.* a telescope that is small enough to be held in the hand

spy·mas·ter /spī màstər/ *n.* the leader of espionage and intelligence-gathering activities for a country or organization, especially in fictional spy stories

sq. *abbr.* **1.** sequence **2.** sequens **3.** MEASURE square [Latin, "the one that follows"]

Sq. *abbr.* **1.** MAIL Square **2.** MIL Squadron

SQL *n.* a standardized language that approximates the structure of natural English for obtaining information from databases. Full form **structured query language**

Sqn. *abbr.* Squadron

sqq. *abbr.* sequentia [Latin, "those that follow"]

squab /skwob/ *n.* (*plural* **squabs** *or* **squab**) **1.** FOOD **YOUNG BIRD** a fledgling bird, especially a pigeon, sometimes cooked as a delicacy **2.** HOUSEHOLD **SOFA** a couch ■ *adj.* **(squab·ber, squab·best) 1. SHORT AND STOUT** short and somewhat stout **2.** BIRDS **NEWLY HATCHED** newly hatched and not flying yet [Late 17thC. Origin uncertain: perhaps from a Scandinavian word meaning "flabby."] —**squab·by** *adj.*

squab·ble /skwóbb'l/ *n.* **PETTY LOUD ARGUMENT** a noisy argument over a petty matter ■ *vi.* **(-bled, -bling, -bles) ARGUE NOISILY OVER SOMETHING UNIMPORTANT** to have a petty argument over a trivial matter [Early 17thC. An imitation of the sound.] —**squab·bler** *n.*

squad /skwod/ *n.* **1.** ARMY **GROUP OF SOLDIERS** any of three or four groups of soldiers that make up a platoon **2.** PUBLIC ADMIN **GROUP OF POLICE OFFICERS** a group of police officers, generally assigned to a particular task **3. TEAM OF PEOPLE** a small group of people engaged in the same activity, especially in a sport ○ *a squad of volunteers* **4.** MIL **MILITARY FORMATION** a small military formation, especially one that is doing a drill [Mid-17thC. Via French *escouade* and Italian *squadra* or Spanish *escuadra* from assumed Vulgar Latin *exquadra* (see SQUARE From the arrangement of troops in a square formation.]

squad car *n.* a police car linked by radio with police headquarters

squad·ron /skwóddrən/ *n.* **1.** NAVY **NAVAL UNIT** a naval unit containing two or more divisions of a fleet **2.** AIR FORCE **AIR FORCE UNIT** an element of a tactical air force belonging to a group and containing two or more flights **3.** MIL **CAVALRY UNIT** an armored cavalry unit belonging to a regiment and containing two or more troops **4. GROUP** an organized group of people, animals, or objects [Mid-16thC. From Italian *squadrone*, literally "large squad," from *squadra* (see SQUAD).]

squad·ron lead·er *n.* in the Royal Air Force, the commander of a squadron of military aircraft

squad room *n.* **1. ROOM IN A POLICE STATION** a room in a police station where officers are briefed **2.** ARMY **DORMITORY IN A BARRACKS** a room in a barracks where a number of soldiers are housed

squa·lene /skwáy leen/ *n.* a colorless hydrocarbon, found primarily in human sebum and shark-liver oil, that is a cholesterol precursor and is used as a bactericide and in the synthesis of some drugs. Formula: $C_{30}H_{50}$. [Early 20thC. Formed from modern Latin *Squalus*, shark genus, from Latin, "a sea fish."]

squal·id /skwóllәd/ *adj.* **1. NEGLECTED AND DIRTY** dirty and shabby because of neglect and lack of money **2. WITHOUT ANY FINE QUALITIES** lacking in honesty, dignity, and morals ○ *a squalid little scandal* [Late 16thC. From Latin *squalidus* "filthy, rough," from *squalere* "to be filthy," from *squalus* "filthy."] —**squal·id·ly** *adv.* —**squal·id·ness** *n.*

WORD KEY: SYNONYMS

See Synonyms at ***dirty***.

squall[1] /skwawl/ *n.* **1.** METEOROL **WINDSTORM** a sudden strong wind, often with heavy rain or snow **2. BRIEF DISTURBANCE** a short but noisy disturbance **3. SHOW OF TEMPER** a brief but intense outburst of temper ■ *vi.* **(squalled, squall·ing, squalls)** METEOROL **BLOW STRONGLY** to blow strongly and suddenly (*refers to the wind*) [Late 17thC. Origin uncertain: perhaps from a Scandinavian word.]

squall[2] /skwawl/ *vi.* **(squalled, squall·ing, squalls) YELL** to cry or yell hoarsely ■ *n.* **NOISY CRY** a noisy cry or yell [Mid-17thC. Origin uncertain: perhaps from a Scandinavian word imitative of the sound.] —**squall·er** *n.*

squall line *n.* a series of small storms that occur along a cold front

squall·y /skwáwlee/ **(-i·er, -i·est)** *adj.* **1.** METEOROL **STORMY** occurring in or characterized by strong gusts, often accompanied by rain or snow **2. INVOLVING ARGUMENTS** marked by sudden short noisy arguments

squal·or /skwóllәr/ *n.* **1. SHABBINESS** shabbiness and dirtiness resulting from poverty or neglect **2. MORAL DEGRADATION** a state of moral degradation [Early 17thC. From Latin, "dirtiness, roughness," from *squalere* (see SQUALID).]

squa·ma /skwáymә/ (*plural* **-mae** /-mee/) *n.* a scale, or a structure resembling a scale, of the type that make up the covering of fish, reptiles, and some mammals [Early 18thC. From Latin, "scale."]

squa·mate /skwáy màyt/ *n.* **LIZARD OR SNAKE** a reptile of the order that comprises all lizards and snakes and includes about 6,000 species. Order: Squamata. ■ *adj.* **WITH SCALES ON THE BODY** having scales or structures resembling scales of the type that make up the covering of fish, reptiles, and some mammals

squa·ma·tion /skwә máysh'n/ *n.* **1. STATE OF HAVING SCALES ON THE BODY** the state of having a body with scales or plates like scales **2. ARRANGEMENT OF SCALES ON THE BODY** the arrangement of scales on an animal's body

squa·mi·form /skwáymi fawrm/ *adj.* resembling a scale or scales of the type that make up the covering of fish, reptiles, and some mammals

squa·mo·sal /skway mṓss'l, skwә-/ *n.* a thin plate-shaped bone of the vertebrate skull that forms the forward and upper part of the temporal bone in humans [Mid-19thC. Formed from Latin *squamosus* "squamous."]

squa·mous /skwáymәss, skwáamәss/, **squa·mose** /skwá mṓss/ *adj.* **1.** BIOL **OF SCALES ON THE BODY** covered with, consisting of, or resembling scales or thin plates of the type that make up the covering of fish, reptiles, and some mammals **2.** BIOL **CONSISTING OF SCALE-SHAPED CELLS** used to describe a layer of skin **(epithelium)** made up of small scale-shaped cells **3.** ANAT **OF THE SKULL BONE** relating to the squamosal in the vertebrate skull —**squa·mous·ly** *adv.* —**squa·mous·ness** *n.*

squa·mous cell car·ci·no·ma *n.* a common type of cancer that usually develops in the epithelial layer of the skin but sometimes in various mucous membranes of the body. The cancerous cells often contain keratin, and sometimes intercellular bridges are formed.

squa·mu·lose /skwáymyә lṓss, skwámmyә-/ *adj.* having or consisting of tiny scales of the type that make up the covering of fish, reptiles, and some mammals [Mid-19thC. Formed from *squamule* "small scale," from Latin *squamula*, from *squama* "scale."]

squan·der /skwóndәr/ *v.* **(-dered, -der·ing, -ders) 1.** *vt.* **USE SOMETHING WASTEFULLY** to spend or use something precious in a wasteful and extravagant way **2.** *vti.* **STREW SOMETHING** to scatter something, or be scattered (*archaic*) ■ *n.* **EXTRAVAGANCE** extravagant spending [Late 16thC. Origin unknown.] —**squan·der·er** *n.*

Squan·to /skwóntō/ (1585?–1622) Wampanoag interpreter. He helped the Pilgrims of Plymouth Colony by interpreting for them and showing them how to fish and grow food in New England.

square /skwair/ *n.* **1.** GEOM **EQUILATERAL RECTANGLE** a geometric figure with four right angles and four equal sides **2. RECTANGULAR OBJECT** an object in the shape of a square or a rectangle that is nearly a square **3.** GAME **DIVISION OF A GAME BOARD** any of the four-sided divisions marked on the board used to play chess, checkers, or other games **4.** ARCHIT **OPEN SPACE IN A CITY** an open, usually four-sided area in a city or town where two or more streets meet, often containing trees, grass, and benches for recreational use **5.** ARCHIT **CITY BLOCK** a block of buildings surrounded by four streets **6.** MIL **MILITARY DRILL AREA** an open space within an army barracks where soldiers practice marching and handling weapons **7.** MATH **RESULT OF MULTIPLICATION** the product resulting from multiplying a number or term by itself ○ *The square of 7 is 49.* **8.** GEOM **DRAWING INSTRUMENT** an L- or T-shaped instrument made of plastic, wood, or metal, used for drawing or measuring right angles **9.** MIL **BODY OF SOLDIERS** formerly, a tactical formation of soldiers in a solid or hollow rectangle, with the soldiers on the sides facing outward **10. DULL UNFASHIONABLE PERSON** somebody who dresses and behaves in an unfashionable way and is out of touch with current popular culture (*slang dated*) **11. SQUARE MEAL** a square meal (*informal*) ■ *adj.* **1.** GEOM **SHAPED LIKE A SQUARE** having the shape of a square, with four more or less equal sides and angles **2.** GEOM **FORMING A RIGHT ANGLE** intersecting at, having, or making a right angle **3. CUBIC** in the shape of a cube ○ *a square block of stone* **4. VAGUELY SQUARE IN SHAPE** roughly square or angular in shape, and looking firm and solid **5.** MEASURE **OF THE MEASUREMENT OF SURFACE AREA** used to describe a measurement of area in which the specified unit refers to the length of each side of a square whose surface area constitutes the measurement. For example, one square meter is the surface area of a square all of whose sides are one meter long. ○ *One box contains enough tiles to cover 100 square feet.* **6.** MEASURE **WITH SIDES OF A SPECIFIED LENGTH** used to describe a square area with sides of a particular length ○ *a room ten feet square* **7. STRAIGHT OR LEVEL** adjusted or made to be perfectly straight, even, level, or lined up with something ○ *Make sure the picture is square on the wall.* **8. COMPLETELY FAIR** completely fair, honest, and direct ○ *a square deal* **9. BORING AND OLD-FASHIONED** dressing and behaving in an unfashionable way and out of touch with current popular culture (*slang dated*) **10. NOT OWING MONEY** with all outstanding debts paid up ○ *She paid me this morning – we're square now.* **11.** MUSIC **LACKING COMPLEXITY** in jazz and popular music, lacking swing or complexity ■ *v.* **(squared, squar·ing, squares) 1.** *vt.* **MAKE SOMETHING SQUARE** to make something into a square or rectangular shape **2.** *vt.* MATH **MULTIPLY A NUMBER BY ITSELF** to multiply a number or term by itself ○ *Seven squared equals 49.* **3.** *vt.* **DIVIDE SOMETHING INTO SQUARES** to divide a surface, sheet of paper, or other object into squares **4.** *vt.* **SET SOMETHING STRAIGHT** to move an object, item of clothing, or part of the body so that it is straight or level **5.** *vti.* **PUT OR BE AT RIGHT ANGLES** to adjust something or be adjusted so that it is at right angles to something else, or test something for this alignment **6.** *vt.* **SETTLE THINGS FAIRLY** to arrive at a fair and equal agreement with somebody about something, especially about paying off money owed ○ *He squared all his bills and left town.* **7.** *vt.* **BRIBE SOMEBODY** to bribe another person (*slang*) **8.** *vt.* SPORTS **BRING SCORES LEVEL** to level the scores, especially in a ballgame **9.** *vti.* **CONCUR OR MAKE SOMETHING AGREE** to agree with another person, fact, event, or idea, or make two facts, events, or ideas concur ○ *That doesn't square with what we know.* **10.** *vt.* **IMPROVE IMPRESSION** to try to improve the impression that somebody has of you ■ *adv.* **1. AT RIGHT ANGLES** so as to be even, straight, level, or at right angles to something **2. DIRECTLY** in a direct or forceful way (*informal*) ○ *She drove square into the wall.* **3. HONESTLY** in an honest and straightforward way (*informal*) [13thC. Via Old French *esquare* and assumed Vulgar Latin *exquadra* from, ultimately, Latin *quadrum*, from the Latin stem *quat-* "four" (source of English *quarter* and *squad*).] —**squar·er** *n.* —**square·ness** *n.* ◇ **all square 1.** SPORTS in which the scores are even **2.** in which all participants are on equal terms, especially because debts have been settled ◇ **on the square 1.** at right angles to something, or constructed with right angles **2.** in an honest and direct manner, or direct and honest **3.** done on equal terms, or being on equal terms with somebody ◇ **out of square 1.** not at right angles to something **2.** not in agreement with each other

square off *vi.* to take the proper stance for beginning to fight

square up *v.* **1.** *vi.* **SETTLE DEBTS** to pay bills, accounts, or other sums of money owed to somebody **2.** *vti.* **ARRANGE OR BE ARRANGED SATISFACTORILY** to arrange something or be arranged in an acceptable or pleasing way **3.** *vi.* **FACE SOMETHING UNPLEASANT** to confront something unpleasant or frightening **4.** *vi.* **ADOPT AN AGGRESSIVE POSTURE** to put up fists or adopt a similar posture that shows a readiness to fight **5.** *vt.* DESIGN **MAKE AN ENLARGEMENT USING A GRID OF SQUARES** to enlarge or transfer a drawing using a grid of squares

square brack·et *n.* = **bracket** *n.* **3**

square dance *n.* **1. COUNTRY DANCE** a country dance or style of country dancing featuring dancers in pairs or sets, lively music played on fiddles and other instruments, and a caller who announces the steps **2. DANCE WHERE FOUR COUPLES FORM SQUARES** a country dance in which four couples form a square —**square danc·ing** *n.*

square knot *n.* a symmetrical knot that will not slip after tying, made by passing one end of a rope over and around another first in one direction, then in the opposite direction. The usual formula for tying this knot is: left over right, then right over left.

square·ly /skwáirlee/ *adv.* **1. DIRECTLY** in a direct or forceful way ○ *She met my gaze squarely.* **2. HONESTLY** in an honest and straightforward way **3. AT RIGHT ANGLES** in or into a position that is at right angles to something else

square ma·trix *n.* a mathematical matrix that has equal numbers of rows and columns

square meal *n.* a filling and nourishing meal

square meas·ure *n.* a unit or system of units for measuring an area, e.g., a hectare or an acre

square-rigged *adj.* having principal sails that are at right angles to the length of the ship

square-rig·ger *n.* a sailing vessel equipped with square-shaped sails

$$\sqrt{81} = 9$$

$$9^2 = 81$$

Square root

square root *n.* a number or quantity that when multiplied by itself gives the stated number or quantity. For example, 4 or –4 is the square root of 16.

square sail *n.* a sail with four sides that is usually suspended horizontally on the mast

square shoot·er *n.* somebody who is straightforward and honest (*informal*)

square tim·ber *n.* *Can* logs that have been squared off for export

squar·rose /skwá ròss, skwáa-/ *adj.* with many scales or scabs (*dated*) [Mid-18thC. From Latin *squarrosus* "scurfy."]

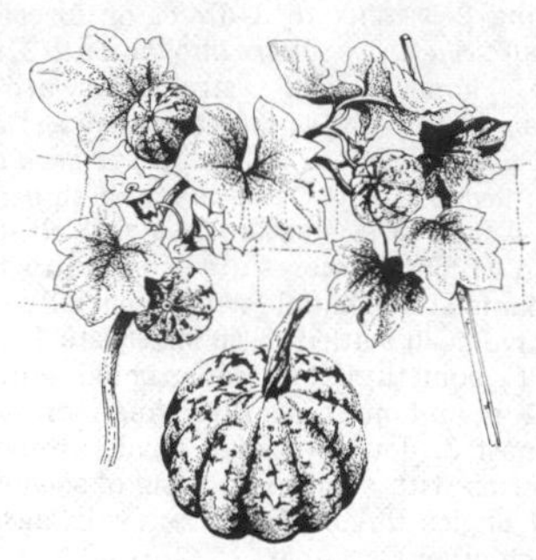

Squash

squash[1] /skwosh/ (*plural* **squash** *or* **squash·es**) *n.* **1.** FOOD **VEGETABLE OF THE GOURD FAMILY** the fruit of any plant of the gourd family, cooked and eaten as a vegetable. ◊ **summer squash, winter squash 2.** PLANTS **PLANT BEARING A GOURD** any plant yielding or cultivated for its edible gourds. Genus: *Cucurbita.* [Mid-17thC. Shortening of Narragansett *asquutasquash*, literally "green things that may be eaten raw."]

squash[2] /skwosh/ *v.* (**squashed, squash·ing, squash·es**) **1.** *vt.* **FLATTEN SOMETHING WITH PRESSURE** to apply pressure to something so that its shape is altered ○ *managed to squash it flat before packing it* **2.** *vti.* **ENTER OR PUT SOMETHING INTO A SMALL SPACE** to force your way into a confined space, or force something into a confined space ○ *people trying to squash into the elevator* **3.** *vt.* POL, MIL **PUT DOWN A REBELLION** to suppress a revolt or uprising completely by using force **4.** *vt.* **MAKE SOMEBODY FEEL SMALL** to silence somebody with a crushing answer **5.** *vi.* **BECOME FLAT** to become flat, often making a squelching sound ■ *n.* **1.** RACKET GAMES **BALLGAME IN A WALLED COURT** a game for two or four participants played in an enclosed court with long-handled rackets and a small ball that may be hit off any of the walls **2. MANY PEOPLE IN A SMALL SPACE** a situation in which a lot of people are crushed into a small space **3. ACTION OR NOISE OF SQUASHING** the action or noise that results when something is being squashed [Mid-16thC. Via Old French *esquasser* from assumed Vulgar Latin *exquassare*, from Latin *quassare* (see QUASH).] —**squash·er** *n.*

squash bug *n.* a large black North American bug that is destructive to plants of the gourd family such as squash and pumpkins. Latin name: *Anasa tristis.*

squash·y /skwóshee/ (**-i·er, -i·est**) *adj.* **1. EASILY SQUASHED** soft and easily squashed **2. OVERRIPE** overripe and full of juice **3. SOFT AND WET** soft and waterlogged **4. LOOKING SQUASHED** having a squashed appearance

squat /skwot/ *vi.* (**squat·ted, squat·ting, squats**) **1. CROUCH DOWN** to crouch down with the knees bent and the thighs resting on the calves **2. CROUCH DOWN LOW** to crouch close to the ground like an animal, especially in order to avoid being seen **3.** LAW **OCCUPY PROPERTY WITHOUT A LEGAL CLAIM** to occupy land or buildings without permission of the owner or other rights holder ■ *adj.* (**squat·ter, squat·test**) **1. SHORT AND SOLID** short and solidly built **2. IN A CROUCHED POSTURE** in a crouched position ■ *n.* **1. ACTION OF SQUATTING** the action of crouching down with the knees bent and the thighs resting on the calves **2. SQUATTING POSITION** a crouched posture with knees bent and thighs resting on calves **3.** SPORTS **WEIGHTLIFTING EXERCISE** an exercise in weightlifting in which the lifter raises a barbell while rising from a crouching position **4.** *U.K.* LAW **PROPERTY OCCUPIED BY SQUATTERS** a piece of property that is occupied by squatters **5.** ZOOL **HARE'S LAIR** the den of a hare [14thC. Via Old French *esquatir* "to crush," from, ultimately, Latin *coactus*, the past participle of *cogere* "to force together" (source of English *cogent*).] —**squat·ness** *n.*

squat·ly /skwóttlee/ *adv.* in a solid unyielding manner ○ *The piano stood squatly by the window.*

squat·ter /skwóttər/ *n.* **1.** LAW **ILLEGAL OCCUPANT OF LAND OR PROPERTY** somebody who occupies land or property illegally, especially somebody who takes over and lives in somebody else's empty house **2. SOMEBODY OR SOMETHING THAT CROUCHES** a person or animal that crouches down

squaw /skwaw/ *n.* **1. OFFENSIVE TERM** a highly offensive term for a Native North American woman or wife (*dated offensive*) **2. OFFENSIVE TERM** a highly offensive term for a woman or wife (*slang offensive*) [Mid-17thC. From Narragansett *squaws* "woman" or Massachusett *squa.*]

squaw·fish /skwáw fish/ (*plural* **-fish** *or* **-fish·es**) *n.* a freshwater fish of western North America that is large and slender and has soft fins. Genus: *Ptychocheilus.*

squawk /skwawk/ *v.* (**squawked, squawk·ing, squawks**) **1.** *vi.* **UTTER A HARSH CRY** to utter a loud harsh cry **2.** *vti.* **COMPLAIN LOUDLY** to complain or protest about something noisily and annoyingly (*informal*) **3.** *vi.* **CRY LOUDLY** to cry or wail loudly and annoyingly (*informal*) **4.** *vti.* **SAY SOMETHING LOUDLY AND SHRILLY** to say something in a loud harsh voice (*informal*) ■ *n.* **1. RAUCOUS CRY** a loud raucous cry **2. NOISY COMPLAINT** a noisy and annoying complaint or protest (*informal*) [Early 19thC. An imitation of the sound.] —**squawk·er** *n.*

squawk box *n.* a public-address system or one of its speakers, originally box-shaped (*dated slang*)

squaw man *n.* a highly offensive term for the husband of a Native North American woman who is himself not Native North American (*slang dated offensive*)

squaw·root /skwáw ròot/ *n.* a scaly herb of North America that has tube-shaped yellow flowers and lives as a parasite on the roots of trees such as oaks and hemlocks. Latin name: *Conophilis americana.* [Mid-19thC. From its use in traditional Native American medicine.]

squeak /skweek/ *v.* (**squeaked, squeak·ing, squeaks**) **1.** *vi.* **MAKE A HIGH-PITCHED SOUND** to make a short high-pitched sound or cry **2.** *vt.* **SAY SOMETHING SHRILLY** to say something in a high-pitched voice **3.** *vi.* **BARELY MANAGE SOMETHING** to barely manage to pass, win, or survive something (*informal*) ○ *squeaked through her final exams* **4.** *vi.* **BE AN INFORMER** to give information or evidence about somebody to the police (*slang disapproving*) ■ *n.* **HIGH-PITCHED CRY** a short high-pitched sound or cry [14thC. An imitation of the sound.] ◇ **a narrow** *or* **close** *or* **near squeak** an escape from something by an extremely narrow margin

squeak·er /skwéekər/ *n.* **1. SOMEBODY OR SOMETHING THAT SQUEAKS** a person, animal, or device that makes a short high-pitched sound or cry **2. NARROWLY WON VICTORY** a competition, election, race, or other event that is won by a very slight margin (*informal*) **3. INFORMANT** somebody who gives information about a criminal to the police (*slang disapproving*)

squeak·y /skwéekee/ (**-i·er, -i·est**) *adj.* **1. TENDING TO SQUEAK** having a tendency to squeak **2. DESIGNED TO SQUEAK** designed to make a squeaking noise when pressed —**squeak·i·ly** *adv.* —**squeak·i·ness** *n.*

squeak·y-clean *adj.* **1. EXTREMELY CLEAN** so clean that it squeaks when rubbed ○ *His hair was squeaky-clean.* **2. IRREPROACHABLY GOOD** appearing to be almost unnaturally free from general human shortcomings (*informal*)

squeal /skweel/ *n.* **1. SHRILL CRY** a short high cry expressing pain, excitement, delight, or other strong emotion **2. LOUD HIGH SOUND** the screaming sound made by tires when a vehicle brakes suddenly ■ *v.* (**squealed, squeal·ing, squeals**) **1.** *vti.* **GIVE A SHORT HIGH CRY** to speak or make a sound in a loud high-pitched tone **2.** *vi.* **BECOME AN INFORMER** to give information or evidence against somebody to the police (*slang disapproving*) [13thC. An imitation of the sound.] —**squeal·er** *n.*

squea·mish /skwéemish/ *adj.* **1. EASILY MADE TO FEEL SICK** easily sickened by such sights as blood or physical injuries **2. EASILY OFFENDED** easily shocked by such things as violence, the mention of bodily functions, or strong language **3. FASTIDIOUS** excessively scrupulous about manners or behavior [14thC. From Anglo-Norman *escoymous*, of unknown origin.] —**squea·mish·ly** *adv.* —**squea·mish·ness** *n.*

squee·gee /skwée jèe/ *n.* **1. IMPLEMENT FOR CLEANING WINDOWS** a T-shaped implement edged with plastic or rubber that is drawn across the surface of windows to remove water after washing **2.** PRINTING, PHOTOGRAPHY **IMPLEMENT TO ELIMINATE LIQUID** an implement, usually a rubber roller, that is used in printing and photography to remove excess water or ink ■ *vt.* (**-geed, -gee·ing, -gees**) **WIPE WITH A SQUEEGEE** to wipe or smooth a surface using a squeegee [Mid-19thC. Formed from obsolete *squeege* "to press," an alteration of SQUEEZE.]

squee·gee man *n.* a man or youth, typically one spending time on the streets, who enters stopped traffic without invitation, attempting to wash motorists' windshields for money (*slang*)

squeeze /skweez/ *v.* (**squeezed, squeez·ing, squeez·es**) **1.** *vt.* **PRESS SOMETHING FROM TWO SIDES** to press something hard in the hand or between two other objects, especially in order to reduce its size or alter its shape **2.** *vt.* **PRESS SOMEBODY ENCOURAGINGLY** to exert slight pressure on part of somebody's body such as the hand, knee, or shoulder, usually as a sign of affection and reassurance **3.** *vti.* **APPLY PRESSURE** to exert pressure on something ○ *Come on, squeeze harder!* **4.** *vt.* **HUG SOMEBODY** to hold somebody tightly in your arms **5.** *vt.* **PUSH A PERSON OR OBJECT INTO A GAP** to force a person, object, or part of the body into or through a small or narrow space **6.** *vi.* **PUSH INTO OR THROUGH SMALL SPACE** to push into or through a small, narrow, or crowded space ○ *I squeezed through a gap in the fence.* **7.** *vt.* **FIND TIME FOR** to find time or space for somebody or something in a busy schedule ○ *I could squeeze you in at 9:30.* **8.** *vt.* **PRESS FRUIT TO OBTAIN JUICE** to compress a piece of fruit, especially a citrus fruit, in order to extract its juice **9.** *vt.* **OBTAIN USING PHYSICAL PRESSURE** to extract something by exerting physical pressure on somebody or something **10.** *vt.* **EXTORT MONEY OR FAVORS** to obtain something such as money or favors from somebody by means of psychological pressure or threats **11.** *vt.* **DEMAND MONEY FROM** to make excessive financial demands on somebody, especially for rent and taxes **12.** *vt.* **PRODUCE WITH DIFFICULTY** to make an effort to produce something ○ *He managed to squeeze out a timid "thank you."* **13.** *vi.* **BARELY MANAGE** to barely succeed in winning, passing, or surviving something ○ *managed to squeeze through the exam with a D* **14.** *vt.* BASEBALL **BUNT THE BALL** in baseball, to bunt the ball attempting to bring in the runner from third base **15.** *vt.* CARDS **PLAY A CARD** to lead a card in bridge or whist that may force an opponent to discard a valuable card **16.** *vi.* **COLLAPSE** to condense or collapse under pressure **17.** *vi.* CRAFT **MAKE AN IMPRESSION OF** to make an impression or mold of an object using a soft material such as wax or plaster of Paris ■ *n.* **1. PHYSICAL PRESSING** a pressing action ○ *gave the sponge a quick squeeze* **2. SOMETHING PRESSED OUT** an amount pressed out of something ○ *Add a squeeze of lemon.* **3. HUG** a hug or close embrace **4. TOUCH THAT SHOWS AFFECTION** the action of briefly clasping somebody's hand, arm, knee, or other part of the body, usually as a sign of affection or reassurance **5. CROWD OF PEOPLE OR THINGS** a group of people or objects crowded together **6.** CARDS, BASEBALL **SQUEEZE PLAY** a squeeze play (*informal*) **7.** CRAFT **IMPRESSION OF AN OBJECT** an impression of an object made by using a soft material such as wax or plaster of Paris **8. SOMETHING EXTORTED** money or goods obtained from somebody as a result of threats or the use of force **9.** COMM **FINANCIAL PRESSURE TO ACT** an action by business competitors that influences or forces others to make some type of transaction [Mid-16thC. Alteration of obsolete *quease*, ultimately of unknown origin.] —**squeez·a·bil·i·ty** /skwèezə bíllətee/ *n.* —**squeez·a·ble** /skwéezəb'l/ *adj.* ◇ **put the squeeze on somebody 1.** to exert pressure on somebody by means of force and threats in order to extort money or goods or to obtain some other end, e.g., a confession (*slang*) **2.** to place somebody in a difficult situation, especially financially, or pressure somebody to do something (*slang*)

squeeze off *vi.* to fire a bullet from a gun

squeeze·box /skwéez bòks/ *n.* a concertina or small accordion (*informal*)

squeeze play *n.* **1.** BASEBALL **PLAY WHEN THE BATTER BUNTS** in baseball, a play in which the batter bunts the ball in an attempt to bring in a runner from third base **2.** CARDS **PLAY IN A GAME OF BRIDGE** a play in bridge or whist in which an opponent is forced to discard a valuable and potentially winning card

squelch /skwelch/ *v.* (**squelched, squelch·ing, squelch·es**) **1.** *vi.* **MAKE A SUCKING SOUND** to move with or make a sucking or gurgling sound like that of somebody walking on muddy ground **2.** *vt.* **CRUSH BY TRAMPLING** to crush something by trampling, or as if by trampling **3.** *vt.* **SILENCE SOMETHING** to silence something such as a rumor or an unwanted remark (*slang*) ■ *n.* **1. SUCKING SOUND** a sucking or gurgling sound like that of somebody walking on muddy ground **2.** CRUSHING RETORT an ingenious or cutting answer to something somebody has said (*slang*) **3.** ELECTRON ENG **ELECTRONIC CIRCUIT** an electronic circuit that automatically reduces the gain of a receiver in response to an input signal that exceeds a predetermined level [Early 17thC. An imitation of the sound.] —**squelch·er** *n.* —**squel·chy** *adj.*

sque·teague /skwə téeg/ (*plural* **-teague** *or* **-teagues**) *n.* any one of several large Atlantic fish of the croaker family, especially the Atlantic weakfish. Genus: *Cynoscion.* [Early 19thC. From southern New England *Algonquian.*]

squib /skwib/ *n.* **1.** SMALL FIRECRACKER a small firecracker **2.** DUD FIRECRACKER a faulty firecracker that burns without exploding **3.** LITERAT **PIECE OF SATIRE** a short satirical piece of writing or speech **4.** PRESS **SHORT JOURNALISTIC PIECE** a short humorous piece that acts as a filler in a newspaper **5.** AEROSP **DEVICE FOR FIRING A ROCKET ENGINE** a small device for firing a rocket engine **6.** SOMEBODY UNIMPORTANT somebody who is considered to be insignificant or mean-spirited (*archaic*) ■ *v.* (**squibbed, squib·bing, squibs**) **1.** *vt.* FOOTBALL **KICK A BALL LOW** in football, to kick the ball in such a way that it wobbles as it bounces along the ground **2.** *vt.* LITERAT **SATIRIZE SOMEBODY** to write a satirical squib about somebody **3.** *vi.* SET OFF A FIREWORK to set off a small firecracker [Early 16thC. Origin uncertain: perhaps an imitation of the sound made by a faulty firecracker.]

squib kick *n.* in football, a kick of the ball so that it wobbles as it bounces along the ground in order to make it hard to field and return

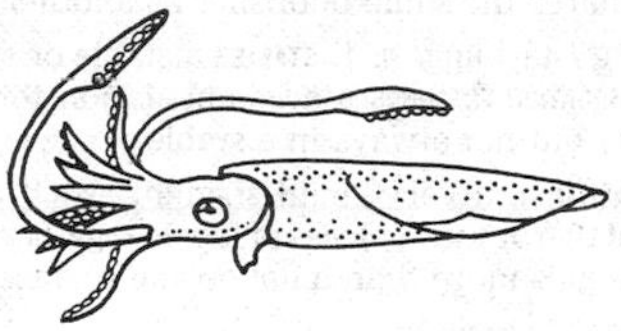

Squid

squid /skwid/ (*plural* **squid** *or* **squids**) *n.* **1.** MARINE BIOL **MOLLUSK WITH TEN ARMS** a marine cephalopod mollusk that has two long tentacles and eight shorter arms, a long tapered body, two triangular fins, and an internal shell. It is often cooked and eaten. Order: Teuthoidea. **2.** FOOD **SQUID AS FOOD** a dish of squid that has been prepared and cooked for eating [Late 16thC. Origin unknown.]

squig·gle /skwígg'l/ *n.* **1.** WAVY LINE a wavy or curly line or movement **2.** ILLEGIBLE WORD an illegible handwritten word or words ■ *vi.* (**-gled, -gling, -gles**) (*informal*) **1.** SQUIRM to twist, squirm, or wriggle **2.** DRAW SQUIGGLES to draw wavy or curly lines [Early 19thC. Origin uncertain: perhaps a blend of SQUIRM and WIGGLE or WRIGGLE.] —**squig·gler** *n.* —**squig·gly** *adj.*

squill /skwil/ *n.* **1.** PLANTS **PLANT WITH SMALL DROOPING FLOWERS** a bulbous plant native to Europe, Asia, and Africa that has small blue, white, pink, or purple drooping flowers. Genus: *Scilla* and *Pushkinia.* **2.** PLANTS = **sea onion 3.** MED **DRIED BULB OF A SEA ONION** the dried slices of a sea onion's bulb, used medicinally in the past as an expectorant and diuretic [14thC. Via Latin *squilla* "shrimp, squill" from Greek *skilla*, of unknown origin.]

squil·la /skwíllə/ *n.* a burrowing marine crustacean that has eyes on stalks and large grasping appendages. Genus: *Squilla.* [Early 16thC. From modern Latin, genus name, from Latin, "shrimp" (see SQUILL).]

squinch[1] /skwinch/ *n.* ARCHIT an arch, corbeling, or lintel built across the upper inside corner of a square tower to support the weight of a spire or other structure above [Mid-19thC. Alteration of *scuncheon*, from Old French *escoinson*, literally "corner out," from *coin* "corner" (see COIN).]

squinch[2] /skwinch/ (**squinched, squinch·ing, squinch·es**) *v.* **1.** *vt.* SCRUNCH UP THE FACE to scrunch up the eyes or face **2.** *vti.* CROUCH DOWN to crouch so as to take up less space [Early 19thC. Origin uncertain: probably a blend of SQUINT and PINCH.]

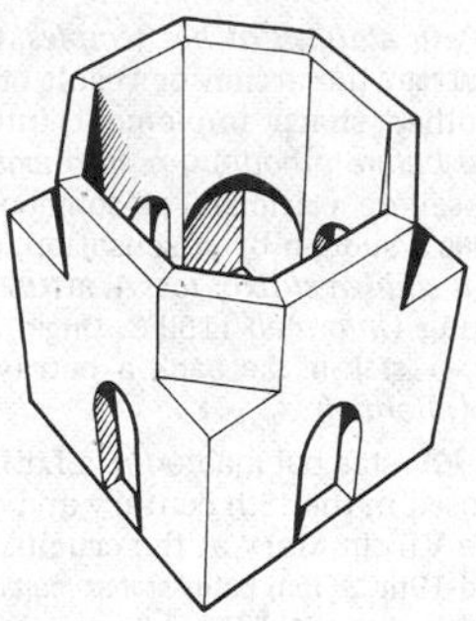

Squinch

squint /skwint/ *v.* (**squint·ed, squint·ing, squints**) **1.** *vi.* PARTLY CLOSE THE EYES to half- close the eyes so as to see better ○ *a photo of them squinting into the camera in bright sunlight* **2.** *vti.* HAVE EYES NOT LOOKING IN PARALLEL to have eyes that are not aligned in parallel **3.** *vi.* GLANCE ASIDE to glance or look at something sideways **4.** *vi.* LOOK ASKANCE to regard something with disapproval (*disapproving*) ○ *Congress clearly is squinting at the prospect of increased funding for the program.* ■ *n.* **1.** EYE CONDITION a condition in which the eyes are not aligned in parallel, causing a cross-eyed appearance. Technical name **strabismus 2.** QUICK GLIMPSE a quick look or glance at something, often to the side **3.** ACTION OF NARROWING EYES the act of narrowing the eyes to try to see better **4.** ARCHIT = **hagioscope** ■ *adj.* **1.** CROSS-EYED with a squint or a cross-eyed appearance **2.** ASKEW not level or properly aligned (*informal*) [Mid-16thC. Shortening of *asquint*, of uncertain origin: perhaps literally "on a slant," formed from Low German or Dutch.] —**squint·er** *n.* —**squint·y** *adj.* ◇ **have** *or* **take a squint at** to have a look at something (*informal*)

squint-eyed /skwínt íd/ *adj.* **1.** WITH SQUINT with one or both eyes looking slightly inward or outward rather than in parallel **2.** LOOKING WITH EYES PARTLY CLOSED looking with the eyes partly closed to see better **3.** ASKANCE looking askance or sidelong

squir·ar·chy /skwír aarkee/ *n.* = **squirearchy** [Late 18thC. Coined from SQUIRE + HIERARCHY.]

squire /skwír/ *n.* **1.** RURAL LANDOWNER a country landowner in England, often the main local landowner **2.** HIST **ATTENDANT TO A KNIGHT** a young apprentice knight who acted as an attendant to a knight in the Middle Ages **3.** MAN WHO ESCORTS A WOMAN a man who is escorting a woman or going out with her regularly (*dated*) **4.** TITLE GIVEN TO A RURAL DIGNITARY a title of respect given to a magistrate or local dignity, especially in a rural district (*dated*) ■ *vt.* (**squired, squir·ing, squires**) ESCORT SOMEBODY to escort or go out with a man or a woman (*dated*) (*often passive*) [13thC. From Old French *esquier* (see ESQUIRE).]

squire·ar·chy /skwír ə raarkee/ (*plural* **-chies**), **squir·ar·chy** (*plural* **-chies**) *n.* the main rural landowners collectively, especially the social, economic, or political class formed by such landed proprietors [Late 18thC. Coined from SQUIRE + HIERARCHY.] —**squire·ar·chal** *adj.* —**squire·ar·chic** *adj.*

squirm /skwurm/ *vi.* (**squirmed, squirm·ing, squirms**) **1.** WRIGGLE FROM DISCOMFORT to wriggle the body, especially because of discomfort or in an attempt to break free from being held **2.** FEEL EMOTIONAL DISTRESS to feel very uncomfortable, especially because of shame, embarrassment, or revulsion ○ *a tough question that made the press office squirm* ■ *n.* WRIGGLING MOVEMENT a wriggling movement, especially from discomfort or as an attempt to break free from being held [Late 17thC. Origin unknown.] —**squirm·er** *n.* —**squirm·y** *adj.*

squir·rel /skwúr rəl/ *n.* **1.** SMALL BUSHY-TAILED RODENT a small rodent that has a long bushy tail, lives in trees, and eats nuts and seeds. Family: Sciuridae. ◊ **gray squirrel, red squirrel 2.** RODENT LIKE A SQUIRREL a rodent related to or resembling the squirrel, e.g., the ground squirrel, flying squirrel, or chipmunk **3.** U.S. CRIMINAL SUSPECT a person who is a criminal or who is suspected of having committed a crime (*slang*) **4.** HOARDER somebody who hoards things (*informal*) ■ *vt.* (**-reled, -rel·ing, -rels**) HOARD SOMETHING to hoard or save things [14thC. Via Anglo-Norman *esquirel*, literally "little squirrel," from, ultimately, Greek *skiouros*, literally "shady-tail," from *skia* "shadow" + *oura* "tail."]

Squirrel

squir·rel cage *n.* **1.** ROTATING FRAMEWORK FOR AN ANIMAL a cage containing a cylindrical framework that goes around when a small pet rodent runs inside it **2.** DULL TASK a dull, repetitive, seemingly purposeless task **3.** MECH ENG **WINDING IN INDUCTION MOTORS** a rotor of an induction motor consisting of copper bars mounted in slots around the periphery

squir·rel corn *n.* a low-growing wild plant of the eastern United States that belongs to the fumitory family and has divided leaves, whitish-yellow flowers, and small tubers resembling grains of corn. Latin name: *Dicentra canadensis.*

squir·rel·fish /skwúr rəl fish/ (*plural* **-fish** *or* **-fish·es**) *n.* a brightly colored nocturnal fish that lives in the shallow waters of tropical reefs. Family: Holocentridae. [*Squirrel* possibly from their large round eyes and spiny dorsal fin, which is arched like a squirrel's tail]

squir·rel·ly /skwúr rəlee/ *adj.* **1.** VERY ECCENTRIC very eccentric or odd (*informal offensive*) **2.** CHARACTERISTIC OF SQUIRREL resembling or characteristic of a squirrel ["Eccentric" from the erratic movements of squirrels]

squir·rel mon·key *n.* a small long-tailed monkey of Central and South America that has soft yellowish-gray, brown, or reddish fur, a white face, and a black muzzle. Genus: *Saimiri.* [*Squirrel* perhaps from its long tail, which is used for balancing]

squirt /skwurt/ *v.* (**squirt·ed, squirt·ing, squirts**) **1.** *vti.* FORCE SOMETHING OUT FROM A NARROW OPENING to force something or be pushed out of a narrow opening in a strong quick stream ○ *The ketchup squirted all over the table.* ○ *managed to squirt the last of the toothpaste out of the tube* **2.** *vt.* SQUIRT LIQUID OVER SOMETHING to hit or cover somebody or something with liquid that is forced out of a narrow opening in a strong quick stream ○ *She squirted me with her water bottle.* ■ *n.* **1.** STREAM OF EJECTED LIQUID a small stream of liquid forced out of a narrow opening ○ *a squirt of body lotion* **2.** OFFENSIVE TERM an offensive term that deliberately insults somebody's young age or small size, especially in response to perceived impudence (*informal insult*) **3.** INSTRUMENT FOR SQUIRTING LIQUID an instrument such as a syringe that is used to dispense liquid in a thin quick stream [15thC. An imitation of the sound of something being squirted.]

squirt gun *n.* a toy gun that shoots a stream of water

squirt·ing cu·cum·ber /skwúrting-/ *n.* a Mediterranean vine of the gourd family with oblong fruit that burst when ripe, ejecting seeds and juice. Latin name: *Ecballium elaterium.*

squish /skwish/ *v.* (**squished, squish·ing, squish·es**) **1.** *vt.* SQUEEZE to squeeze or crush something soft **2.** *vi.* MAKE A SOFT SPLASHING NOISE to make a sucking or soft splashing sound when subjected to pressure, as when being walked on or squeezed ■ *n.* **1.** SOFT SPLASHING NOISE a sucking or soft splashing sound **2.** OFFENSIVE TERM an offensive term for somebody perceived as weak or cowardly (*slang insult*) [Mid-17thC. Origin uncertain: probably an alteration of SQUASH[2].]

squish·y /skwíshee/ (**-i·er, -i·est**) *adj.* **1.** SOFT soft and giving under pressure, like mud or a soft fruit **2.** OVERLY SENTIMENTAL overly sentimental or romantic (*disapproving*) **3.** WEAK lacking in courage or resolution (*slang*) ○ *a squishy foreign policy*

sr *symbol.* steradian

Sr *symbol.* strontium

Sr. *abbr.* **1. Sr., sr.** senior **2.** Señor **3.** Senhor **4.** Sir **5.** sister

Sra. *abbr.* **1.** Senhora **2.** Señora

srad·dhaa /sraádə/, **shrad·dh** /shraádə/ *n. S Asia* in the Indian subcontinent, a ceremonial offering of food and water to the dead [Late 18thC. From Sanskrit *śrāddha*, from *śraddhā* "faith, trust."]

SRAM *abbr.* static random access memory

Sra·nan·ton·go /sraánən tóng gō/, **Sra·nan** /sraánən/ *n.* a creole language based on English that is the lingua franca of Suriname [Mid-20thC. From Sranantongo, literally "Suriname tongue."]

S-R con·nec·tion *n.* the relationship between a stimulus and a response

Sreb·re·ni·ca /srèbbrə neétsə/ town in Bosnia-Herzegovina, southeastern Europe, situated between Sarajevo and Tuzla. During the Bosnian-Serbian-Croatian War, 1991 to 1995, it was declared a Muslim enclave. Population: 37,211 (1991).

Sri /sree, shree/ *n.* **1.** TITLE FOR A MAN a title of respect for a man in the Indian subcontinent, equivalent to "Mr" **2.** TITLE FOR A HINDU GOD OR HOLY MAN a title of respect for a Hindu deity or holy man **3.** = **Lakshmi** [Late 18thC. Via Hindi from Sanskrit *śrī* "lord," literally "beauty, wealth, majesty."]

Sri Lanka

Sri Lan·ka /shri láng kə/ island republic in southern Asia. It became independent from Britain in 1948. Language: Sinhala. Currency: Sri Lankan rupee. Capital: Colombo. Population: 18,318,000 (1996). Area: 25,326 sq. mi./65,610 sq. km. Official name **Democratic Socialist Republic of Sri Lanka**. Former name **Ceylon** —**Sri Lan·kan** *n., adj.*

Sri·man *n.* = **Sri** *n.* 1

Sri·na·gar /sri núggər, shrínnə gaar/, **Srī·na·ger** capital city of the state of Jammu and Kashmir, northwestern India. Population: 595,000 (1991).

sRNA *abbr.* soluble RNA

SRO *abbr.* **1.** single room occupancy **2.** standing room only

Srta. *abbr.* **1.** Senhorita **2.** Señorita

SS *abbr.* **1.** Social Security **2.** steamship **3.** Sunday school **4.** sworn statement [In sense 4, an abbreviation of German *Schutzstaffel*, literally "defense squadron"]

ss. *abbr.* **1.** sections **2.** scilicet

SS. *abbr.* Saints

SSA *abbr.* Social Security Administration

SSB *abbr.* single sideband (transmission)

SSE *abbr.* south-southeast

SSGT, **S., Sgt.** *abbr.* staff sergeant

SSI *abbr.* Supplemental Security Income

SSM *abbr.* surface-to-surface missile

ssp. (*plural* **sspp.**) *abbr.* subspecies

SSR *abbr.* HIST Soviet Socialist Republic

SST *abbr.* supersonic transport

SSW *abbr.* south-southwest

st *abbr.* short ton

ST *abbr.* standard time

st. *abbr.* **1.** stanza **2.** start **3.** state **4.** stet **5.** statute **6.** stitch **7.** strophe

St. *abbr.* **1.** Saint **2.** Strait **3.** Street

Sta *abbr.* Santa

sta. *abbr.* **1.** station **2.** stationary

stab /stab/ *v.* (**stabbed, stab·bing, stabs**) **1.** *vt.* THRUST A KNIFE INTO to thrust a knife or other sharp pointed instrument into somebody or something **2.** *vti.* JAB FINGER OR OBJECT AT to thrust a finger or an object sharply at something ○ *He stabbed his potato angrily with his fork.* **3.** *vi.* HURT LIKE A KNIFE WOUND to cause a sudden sharp hurting sensation, like that of a knife wound ○ *Pain stabbed at her temples.* ■ *n.* **1.** ACT OF STABBING SOMEBODY the action or result of thrusting a knife or other sharp implement into somebody (*often used before a noun*) ○ *a stab wound* **2.** SEVERE CRITICISM a severe criticism of somebody **3.** SUDDEN PAINFUL FEELING a sudden brief sensation, especially of pain ○ *felt a sudden stab of loss* **4.** ATTEMPT an attempt at something (*informal*) [15thC. Origin unknown.] —**stab·ber** *n.* ◇ **stab in the back** a betrayal or act of treachery (*informal*)

Sta·bat Ma·ter /staá bat maátər/ *n.* a Latin hymn that was composed in the 13th century and concerns the grief of the Virgin Mary at the crucifixion of Jesus Christ [Mid-19thC. From Latin *stabat mater dolorosa* "the mother stood, full of grief," the first words of the hymn.]

stab·bing /stábbing/ *n.* ACT OF THRUSTING A KNIFE INTO SOMEBODY an incident in which somebody is deliberately stabbed with a knife or sharp object ■ *adj.* WITH SUDDEN PAIN brief, sharp, and sudden, as if from the thrust of a knife ○ *a stabbing pain in the side*

sta·bile *n.* /stáy beel/ SCULPTURE SCULPTURE ATTACHED TO SOMETHING an abstract sculpture made of wire, metal, or other materials and attached to fixed supports. ◊ **mobile** ■ *adj.* /stáyb'l, stáy bīl/ **1.** STABLE in a fixed position **2.** CHEM NOT CHANGING CHEMICALLY not readily undergoing chemical change [Late 18thC. From Latin *stabilis* (see STABLE[1]).]

sta·bil·i·ty /stə bíllətee/ *n.* **1.** STABLE QUALITY the condition of being stable ○ *policies aimed at creating economic stability* **2.** MENTAL FIRMNESS mental or psychological firmness **3.** RESISTANCE TO CHANGE resistance to any sudden change or deterioration **4.** MECH ENG ABILITY TO ADJUST TO LOAD CHANGES a property of a transmission system that allows changes in load to be met without any reduction in performance **5.** METEOROL AIR MASS WITHOUT UPWARD MOVEMENT a condition of no upward movement in an air mass **6.** METEOROL RESISTANCE TO AIR CURRENTS a measure of the tendency of an air mass to be influenced by convection currents **7.** ECOL ABILITY TO MAINTAIN A BALANCE the ability of an ecological community to resist disturbance caused by changes in, e.g., climate, or the ability to return to its original state after disturbance **8.** AEROSP, SHIPPING RESISTANCE TO A CHANGED POSITION the capability of an aircraft, rocket, or ship to maintain a position and to return to it if displaced **9.** CHEM RESISTANCE TO A CHEMICAL CHANGE a resistance to chemical change **10.** PHYS MEASURE OF MAINTAINING EQUILIBRIUM a measure of the difficulty of displacing an object or system from equilibrium

sta·bi·li·za·tion /stàyb'lī záysh'n/ *n.* the act or process of stabilizing something

sta·bi·li·za·tion fund *n.* a reserve of money that a country uses to maintain its official exchange rate by buying and selling foreign exchange

sta·bi·lize /stáyb'l īz/ (**-lized, -liz·ing, -liz·es**) *v.* **1.** *vti.* MAKE OR BECOME STABLE to become stable, or make something stable ○ *The patient's condition has stabilized.* **2.** *vt.* MAINTAIN THE LEVEL OF SOMETHING to maintain an unfluctuating level of something

sta·bi·liz·er /stáybəlīzər/ *n.* **1.** AEROSP AIRFOIL THAT STABILIZES AN AIRCRAFT an airfoil or combination of airfoils, e.g., in the tail assembly of an airplane, that keeps an aircraft or missile aligned with the direction of flight. A vertical stabilizer controls yawing, or side-to-side motion, while a horizontal stabilizer controls pitching, or up-and-down motion. **2.** SHIPPING FINS TO CONTROL A SHIP'S ROLLING one or more pairs of submerged fins, often gyroscopically controlled, used to minimize the rolling of a ship in rough waters **3.** CHEM ADDITIVE THAT MAINTAINS CHEMICAL PROPERTIES a chemical compound added to another substance to make it resistant to chemical or physical change **4.** ELEC DEVICE TO PRODUCE A CONSTANT VOLTAGE a device used to maintain a constant voltage from a source of direct current **5.** INDUST SOMETHING ADDED TO DISPERSE PAINT a substance added to a fast-drying paint to improve the dispersion of pigment **6.** STABILIZING PERSON OR THING something that or somebody who acts to bring stability ■ **sta·bi·liz·ers** *npl. U.K.* = **training wheels**

sta·bi·liz·er bar *n.* AUTOMOT = **anti-roll bar**

sta·ble[1] /stáyb'l/ *adj.* **1.** NOT CHANGING steady and not liable to change ○ *Prices have remained stable.* **2.** NOT LIKELY TO MOVE steady or firm and not liable to move **3.** NOT EXCITABLE having a calm and steady temperament rather than being excitable or given to apparently irrational behavior **4.** CHEM NOT READILY UNDERGOING CHANGE not subject to changes in chemical or physical properties **5.** PHYS NOT NATURALLY RADIOACTIVE incapable of becoming a different isotope or element by radioactive decay [13thC. Via Anglo-Norman and Old French from Latin *stabilis* (source of English *establish*). Ultimately from an Indo-European word meaning "to stand" (see STABLE[2]).] —**sta·ble·ness** *n.* —**sta·bly** *adv.*

sta·ble[2] /stáyb'l/ *n.* **1.** AGRIC BUILDING FOR HORSES a building in which horses, and sometimes other large types of livestock, are kept **2.** EQU HORSES OWNED BY SOMEBODY the group of horses, especially racehorses, owned by one person or kept and trained at one establishment **3.** EQU PEOPLE WORKING IN A STABLE the people who work in a stable **4.** GROUP UNDER MANAGEMENT a group of people managed by the same person or organization ○ *a stable of bestselling authors* ■ *vti.* (**sta·bled, sta·bling, stables**) PUT OR LIVE IN A STABLE to keep or put a horse or other large animal in a particular building, or be kept in a particular building ○ *We stabled our horses in the barn.* [13thC. Via Old French *estable* from Latin *stabulum*. Ultimately from an Indo-European word meaning "to stand," which is also the ancestor of English *stand*, *stem*, and *static*.]

sta·ble door *n.* a door split into upper and lower sections that can be closed separately. In stables the opened top section allows a confined horse to see out.

sta·ble fly *n.* a biting bloodsucking fly like a housefly that attacks humans and domestic animals. Latin name: *Stomoxys calcitrans*.

sta·ble lad *n. U.K.* = **stableboy**

sta·ble·mate *n.* **1.** EQU HORSE FROM THE SAME STABLE a horse that belongs to the same owner or is kept and trained at the same racing stable as another **2.** PERSON ASSOCIATED WITH ANOTHER somebody who or something that is associated with another, e.g., an author who shares the same publisher as another author

sta·bling /stáybling/ *n.* **1.** STABLES a stable or stables **2.** ACCOMMODATION FOR HORSES accommodation for horses, usually but not always in a stable

stab stitch *n.* a very small straight stitch designed to hold two or more pieces of fabric together without showing as more than a dot on the surface

stacc. *abbr.* staccato

stac·ca·to /stə kaátō/ *adv.* MUSIC IN QUICK SEPARATE NOTES to be played, as rapid short detached notes (*used as a musical direction*) ■ *adj.* QUICK AND CLIPPED rapid, brief, and clipped in sound ■ *n.* (*plural* **-tos**) MUSIC STACCATO PASSAGE a staccato passage in music [Early 18thC. From Italian, literally "detached."]

sta·chys /stáykiss/ *n.* a plant with spiked whorls of purple, reddish, or white flowers such as lamb's ears or betony. Genus: *Stachys*. [Mid-16thC. Via modern Latin from Greek *stakhus* "ear of grain."]

stack /stak/ *n.* **1.** HEAPED PILE OF THINGS a pile of things more or less neatly arranged one on top of another ○ *a stack of chairs* **2.** AGRIC LARGE PILE OF SOMETHING STORED OUTDOORS a large pile of hay, straw, or grain often conical in shape, stored outdoors **3.** CHIMNEY OR CHIMNEYS a tall chimney or group of chimneys arranged together. ◊ **smokestack** **4.** LARGE NUMBER a large number or amount (*informal*) ○ *She has stacks of money.* **5.** AIR AIRCRAFT WAITING TO LAND a number of aircraft waiting a turn to land at an airport, circling at different heights **6.** GEOG ROCKY PILLAR RISING FROM COASTAL WATERS a steep-sided pillar of rock that has been isolated from nearby cliffs at the shoreline by the erosion of the waves **7.** COMPUT LIST IN A COMPUTER MEMORY an area in a computer memory where data can be stored temporarily in a list in which the last item entered is the first one removed. A control program uses a stack to save register information and return addresses temporarily so it can restore the environment upon returning from another procedure to which it has jumped. **8.** ARMS ARRANGEMENT OF FIREARMS a group of firearms formed in a pyramid, especially three rifles with their muzzles leaning against each other **9.** VERTICAL PIPE a vertical duct or waste pipe ■ **stacks** *npl.* BOOK STORAGE IN A LIBRARY an area of a library, usually not open to the public, where books are stored on shelves ■ *v.* (**stacked, stack·ing, stacks**) **1.** *vti.* PUT IN AN ORGANIZED PILE to put things one on top of another to form a pile, or to be arranged in this way **2.** *vt.* PUT THINGS ON A SHELF to arrange objects on a shelf **3.** *vi.* HEAP WITH PILES OF OBJECTS to load or heap something with large piles of articles or objects ○ *The bins were stacked with bargains.* **4.** *vt.* MANIPULATE A SITUATION UNETHICALLY to arrange something underhandedly to ensure a desired outcome **5.** *vti.*

AIR **KEEP AIRCRAFT WAITING IN A STACK** to keep aircraft waiting to land at an airport circling at different heights, or be kept in this position [13thC. From Old Norse *stakkr,* from a prehistoric Germanic word meaning "stick, pole," which is also the ancestor of English *stagger, stockade,* and *attack.*] —**stack·a·ble** *adj.* —**stack·er** *n.* ◇ **be stacked against** to amount to an unfair disadvantage ◇ **blow your stack** to become suddenly furious (*slang*) ◇ **stack the deck** *or* **cards 1.** CARDS to arrange playing cards in a deck for the purposes of cheating (*slang*) **2.** to arrange something dishonestly or unethically so as to gain an unfair advantage (*slang*)

stack up *v.* **1.** *vti.* **PUT IN A STACK** to put things, or be put, in a stack **2.** *vi.* **MEASURE UP TO** to be measurable against or comparable to something **3.** *vi. U.S., Aus* **ADD UP TO** to add up to a total

stacked /stakt/ *adj.* **1. OFFENSIVE TERM** an offensive term used to describe a woman in terms of her physical characteristics (*slang offensive*) **2. DISHONESTLY ARRANGED** unfairly or dishonestly manipulated or arranged **3.** AIR **DISPOSED AT DIFFERENT HEIGHTS** disposed at different heights prior to landing

stacked heel *n.* a wide high heel made of different colored layers of wood or material simulating wood

stack·up /sták ùp/ *n.* AIR = **stack** *n.* **5**

stac·te /stáktee/ *n.* a sweet spice mentioned in the Bible as being used by the ancient Jews in making incense [14thC. Via Latin from Greek *staktē*, from *staktos*, the past participle of *stazein* "to drip, ooze."]

stad·dle /stádd'l/ *n.* a supporting base to keep stored hay off the ground (*regional or archaic*) [Old English *staþol.* Ultimately from an Indo-European word meaning "to stand" (see STABLE[2]).]

stad·hold·er /stád hōldər/, **stadt·hold·er** *n.* **1. CHIEF MAGISTRATE OF A FORMER DUTCH REPUBLIC** the chief magistrate of the Dutch republic from the 16th to 18th centuries **2. GOVERNOR OF A FORMER DUTCH PROVINCE** in the past, a governor or viceroy of a province in the Netherlands [Mid-16thC. Partial translation of Dutch *stadhouder,* literally "place-holder."] —**stad·hold·er·ate** *n.* —**stad·hold·er·ship** *n.*

sta·di·a[1] plural of **stadium**

sta·di·a[2] /stáydee ə/ *n.* a method of measuring distances or differences in elevation using a telescopic instrument calibrated to correspond to distances from the surveyor [Mid-19thC. Directly or via Italian from Latin, plural of *stadium* (see STADIUM).]

sta·di·me·ter /stə dímmətər/ *n.* an optical instrument used for measuring distance from an object of known height such as a ship [Coined from STADIA[2] + METER]

sta·di·om·e·ter /stàydee ómmətər/ *n.* a device for measuring the length of a straight or curved line by tracing its path with a toothed wheel [Mid-19thC. Coined from Greek *stadion* STADIUM + -METER.]

sta·di·um /stáydee əm/ (*plural* **-ums** *or* **-a** /-dee ə/) *n.* **1. ARENA WITH TIERED SEATS** a place where people watch sports or other activities, usually a large enclosed flat area surrounded by tiers of seats for spectators **2.** HIST **ANCIENT GREEK RACETRACK** a racetrack for footraces in ancient Greece that had tiers of seats at each side and one end **3.** MEASURE **ANCIENT GREEK MEASUREMENT UNIT** a unit of linear measure in ancient Greece equal to about 607 ft./185 m [14thC. Via Latin from Greek *stadion* "racetrack, unit of measure."]

stadt·hold·er *n.* = **stadholder**

AKG London

Madame de Staël: Portrait (1808–9) by Elisabeth Vigee-Lebrun

Staël /staal/, **Madame de** (1766–1817) French writer. She is credited with disseminating the theories of romanticism in such works as *Germany* (1810). Full name **Baronne Anne Louise Germaine de Staël-Holstein.** Born **Anne Louise Germaine Necker**

staff[1] /staf/ *n.* **1. WORKERS** people who are employed by a company or individual **2. SPECIFIC BODY WITHIN A LARGER GROUP** a specific group of employees within a company, institution, or organization **3.** *U.K.* EDUC = **faculty 4. PEOPLE WHO WORK FOR A LEADER** a group of people who serve a leader or an executive of a company, organization, or institution **5.** MIL **GROUP OF AIDES TO A COMMANDER** a group of officers in the armed services who assist a commanding officer or work at headquarters as advisers or planners **6.** *Malaysia, Singapore* HOUSEHOLD, EDUC **MEMBER OF STAFF** a member of staff working for a company, organization, or school **7. LARGE HEAVY STICK** a stick, rod, or pole, such as a stick used as a support while walking, or a rod used as a symbol of authority in ceremonies **8.** = **flagpole** *n.* **9.** MUSIC **SET OF LINES FOR WRITING MUSIC** a set of five horizontal lines, together with the four spaces between them, on which the notes of music are written **10.** MEASURE **GRADUATED ROD USED FOR MEASURING** a graduated rod used for testing or measuring something, e.g., in surveying ■ *adj.* **1. EMPLOYED WITH SALARY** employed full-time, not on a freelance basis **2.** HOUSEHOLD **CONCERNED WITH STAFF** for or relating to the staff of a company, institution, or organization ■ *vt.* (**staffed, staff·ing, staffs**) **PROVIDE WITH WORKERS** to provide a place or organization with employees (*often passive*) [Old English *stæf* "stick, rod." Ultimately from an Indo-European word meaning "to support," which is also the ancestor of English *step, stampede,* and *stalag.*]

staff[2] /staf/ *n.* CONSTR a building material of plaster and fibrous material used as a temporary, especially decorative, finish on the outside of a structure [Late 19thC. Origin uncertain: perhaps from German *Stoff* "material."]

staff col·lege *n.* a school in which military officers are prepared for higher positions, e.g., as staff officers or commanders

staff·er /stáffhər/ *n.* somebody who belongs to the staff of an organization (*informal*) ○ *White House staffers*

staff of Aes·cu·la·pi·us /-èskyə lày pee əss/ *n.* a symbol for the medical profession consisting of a staff with a single snake entwined around it. ◊ **caduceus**

staff of·fi·cer *n.* a military officer who assists a commanding officer or works as a planner or adviser at a headquarters

staff of life *n.* bread, or sometimes another food, considered as an essential part of the human diet (*literary*) [*Staff* from STAFF[1], in the sense "staple, support"]

Staf·ford·shire bull ter·ri·er, **Staf·ford·shire ter·ri·er** *n.* a bull terrier belonging to a breed with a white coat and broad head and often marked or streaked with brown or black [Named for the county of *Staffordshire* in England where it was developed]

staff·room /stâf room, -rŏŏm/ *n. U.K.* a room used only by the teachers in a school, e.g., for relaxation between classes

staff ser·geant *n.* **1. U.S. ARMY RANK** a noncommissioned officer in the U.S. Army, ranking above sergeant and below sergeant first class **2. U.S. AIR FORCE RANK** a noncommissioned officer in the U.S. Air Force, ranking above sergeant and below technical sergeant **3. U.S. MARINE RANK** a noncommissioned officer in the U.S. Marines, ranking above sergeant and below gunnery sergeant **4. BRITISH ARMY RANK** a noncommissioned officer in the British Army, ranking above sergeant and below warrant officer

staff tree *n.* **SHRUBBY PLANT** a shrubby, usually climbing, plant of the staff tree family, including bittersweet ■ *adj.* **BELONGING TO A TWINING PLANT FAMILY** belonging to or used to describe a family of twining North American, Asian, or Australian trees and shrubs that have red seeds in pods, including khat and euonymus. Family: Celastraceae.

stag /stag/ *n.* **1.** ZOOL **MATURE MALE DEER** an adult male deer, especially a male red deer **2. UNACCOMPANIED MAN AT A SOCIAL EVENT** a man who goes to a social function without a partner (*informal*) **3.** AGRIC **CASTRATED ADULT ANIMAL** a male animal, e.g., a hog, castrated after it reaches maturity ■ *adj.* **RESTRICTED TO MEN** for men only, and usually involving activities that would not be appropriate in mixed company (*informal*) ■ *adv.* **WITHOUT A WOMAN DATE** without a woman companion on a social occasion (*informal*) ■ *vi.* (**stagged, stag·ging, stags**) **ATTEND AN EVENT WITHOUT A WOMAN DATE** to attend a social event without a woman companion (*informal*) [Old English (assumed) *stagga.* Ultimately from an Indo-European word meaning "pointed," which is also the ancestor of English *stochastic,* and probably of *sting.*]

stag bee·tle *n.* a large beetle, the male of which has long extended jaws (**mandibles**) shaped like a stag's antlers. Family: Lucanidae.

stage /stayj/ *n.* **1. PERIOD OR STEP DURING A PROCESS** a step, level, or period in the development or progress of something ○ *The project is still in its early stages.* **2. PLATFORM** a raised platform, e.g., in a hall or auditorium, where speeches are made and ceremonies are carried out **3.** THEATER **AREA IN A THEATER** the area in a theater where a performance takes place, especially a platform on which actors perform a play **4. SETTING IN WHICH SOMETHING HAPPENS** the scene of an event or series of events ○ *The summit marks her first appearance on the world stage.* **5. SIGNIFICANT PHASE** an important phase of cultural, economic, or social development **6.** TRANSP **PART OF JOURNEY** a distinct section of a journey, especially one after which a stop is made **7.** THEATER **DRAMATIC PROFESSION** the profession of acting, drama, or the theater **8.** AEROSP **DETACHABLE ROCKET UNIT** a separable unit of a rocket or spacecraft that contains fuel and can be jettisoned after the fuel is exhausted **9.** TRANSP = **stagecoach 10.** CONSTR **PLATFORM FOR WORKERS** a raised platform, especially a scaffolding for workers during the construction of a building **11. PLATFORM FOR DRYING SOMETHING** a platform used to dry fish or meat **12.** RECORDING = **sound stage 13.** BIOL **PERIOD OF DEVELOPMENT OF AN ORGANISM** a distinct period of development in the life of an organism when its form is different from earlier or later periods **14.** MEASURE **ELEVATION OF A RIVER SURFACE** a measure of how much the surface of a river or stream rises above a given point **15. PLATFORM FOR MOUNTING MICROSCOPIC SPECIMEN** the small platform of an optical microscope on which a specimen is placed for examination **16.** GEOL **PERIOD OF ROCK STRATA** a relatively short distinct period, a subdivision of a series, during which rock strata are deposited during an age of geologic time **17.** ELEC **UNIT OF ELECTRICAL COMPONENTS** a group of components that form part of an electronic or electrical system ■ *vt.* (**staged, stag·ing, stag·es**) **1. ORGANIZE A PERFORMANCE FOR THE PUBLIC** to put on a play, concert, exhibition, or similar event for an audience **2. ORGANIZE EVENT** to organize or carry out something, e.g., an event that will attract attention or publicity **3.** THEATER **SET PLAY IN PLACE OR TIME** to set a play in a particular place or time **4.** MED **CLASSIFY PHASES OF DISEASE** to classify the progress of a disease [13thC. Via Old French *estage* from assumed Vulgar Latin *staticum,* literally "standing place," from Latin *stat-,* past participle stem of *stare* "to stand" (see STATION).] —**stage·a·bil·i·ty** /stàyjə bíllətee/ *n.* —**stage·a·ble** /stày jəbəl/ *adj.* —**stage·a·bly** *adv.* ◇ **on stage** performing in something, especially as an actor ◇ **take center stage** to draw people's or public attention

stage brace *n.* a brace used to support upright pieces of scenery in a play

stage busi·ness *n.* THEATER = **business** *n.* **8**

Stagecoach

stage·coach /stáyj kōch/ *n.* a large four-wheeled horse-drawn coach used in the past to carry passengers and mail over a regular route

WORD KEY: CULTURAL NOTE

Stagecoach, a movie by John Ford (1939). Considered the first modern Western, it portrays an encounter between a diverse group of stagecoach passengers and an intimidating outlaw, the Ringo Kid (played by John Wayne). Its convincing and intriguing characters, magnificent desert setting, gripping narrative, and exciting climax made it a landmark in U.S. movie-making.

stage·craft /stáyj kràft/ *n.* the technique or art of writing, adapting, or putting plays on stage

stage di·rec·tion *n.* an instruction for an actor in the script of a play

stage door *n.* a door in the back or side of a theater that leads directly backstage and is usually used by performers

stage ef·fect *n.* a special visual or auditory effect created on a theatrical stage by lighting, scenery, or sound

stage fright *n.* fear or nervousness that somebody feels before going in front of an audience to speak or perform

stage·hand /stáyj hànd/ *n.* somebody who does physical work in a theater, e.g., setting up and removing stage sets

stage left *n.* the side of a stage that is to a performer's left when facing the audience. ◊ **stage right**

stage-man·age *v.* **1.** *vt.* **TIGHTLY CONTROL EVERY ASPECT OF EVENT** to control an organized event, especially in a way that is not public, so that it happens exactly as planned **2.** *vti.* THEATER **BE A STAGE MANAGER** to carry out the work of a stage manager, especially on a particular production

stage man·ag·er *n.* somebody who assists the director of a play by supervising all backstage activities

stag·er /stáyjər/ *n.* an actor (*archaic*) [Late 16thC. Origin uncertain: possibly a translation of Old French *estagier* "long-time resident," from *estage* "stage, dwelling" (see STAGE).]

stage right *n.* the part of a stage that is to the performer's right when facing the audience. ◊ **stage left**

stage-struck *adj.* loving theater and intensely wanting to be part of it, especially as a performer

stage wait *n.* an unintentional pause in the action of a play, especially one caused by an actor's missing a cue

stage whis·per *n.* **1.** THEATER **ACTOR'S LOUD WHISPER** something said on stage that for the purposes of the play is supposed to be a whisper but is intended to be heard by the audience **2. CONSPICUOUS WHISPER** a loud whisper intended to be overheard

stag·ey *adj.* = **stagy**

stag·fla·tion /stag fláysh'n/ *n.* a period of rising prices and unemployment but little growth in consumer demand and business activity [Mid-20thC. Blend of STAGNATION and INFLATION.] —**stag·fla·tion·ar·y** *adj.*

Stagg /stag/, **Amos Alonzo** (1862–1965) U.S. football coach. He coached at the University of Chicago (1892–1932) and College of the Pacific (1933–46), where he continued as an assistant until the age of 98.

stag·gard /stággərd/ *n.* a male red deer that is in its fourth year [14thC. Formed from STAG.]

stag·ger /stággər/ *v.* (**-gered, -ger·ing, -gers**) **1.** *vi.* **MOVE UNSTEADILY, NEARLY FALLING** to move or walk unsteadily, almost but not quite falling over **2.** *vt.* **MAKE PERSON OR ANIMAL STUMBLE** to make a person or animal stumble or nearly fall, especially by a blow **3.** *vt.* **ASTONISH SOMEBODY** to completely astonish or amaze somebody (*often passive*) **4.** *vt.* **ARRANGE ACTIVITIES FOR SEPARATE TIMES** to arrange activities so that they do not overlap **5.** *vt.* **MAKE INTO AN ALTERNATING OR ZIGZAG PATTERN** to arrange things so that they do not form a straight line, especially in an alternating or zigzag pattern (*often passive*) **6.** *vi.* **HESITATE** to hesitate or falter **7.** *vt.* AIR **ADJUST THE EDGE OF BIPLANE'S WING** to make the leading edge of one wing of a biplane project beyond the leading edge of the other wing ■ *n.* **1. STUMBLE NEARLY RESULTING IN A FALL** an unsteady movement in which a person or animal almost falls **2.** AIR **ARRANGEMENT OF BIPLANE WINGS** a design in which the leading edge of one wing of a biplane is ahead of that of the other wing [Mid-16thC. Alteration of obsolete *stacker*, from Old Norse *stakkra*, from *staka* "to push," from a prehistoric Germanic word meaning "pole" (see STACK).] —**stag·ger·er** *n.*

stag·ger·bush /stággər bo͝osh/ (*plural* **-bush·es** *or* **-bush**) *n.* a shrubby deciduous heath of the eastern United States that has clusters of white or pink flowers and leaves that are poisonous to livestock. Latin name: *Lyonia mariana.*

stag·gered /stággərd/ *adj.* **1. SHOCKED** shocked or astounded at something **2. ALTERNATING OR ZIGZAG** not arranged in sequence or in a straight line

stag·gered hours *npl.* an arrangement in a business in which employees arrive and leave at different times but work hours that overlap for part of the time

stag·ger·ing /stággəring/ *adj.* with the effect of shocking or astounding people —**stag·ger·ing·ly** *adv.*

stag·gers /stággərz/ *n.* (*takes a singular or plural verb*) **1.** VET = **blind staggers 2.** MED **VERTIGO LINKED TO DECOMPRESSION SICKNESS** a form of vertigo associated with decompression sickness, with symptoms including dizziness, weakness, and confusion

stag·horn /stág hàwrn/, **stag's horn** *n.* **1. PIECE OF STAG'S ANTLER** a stag's antler, or a piece of this used as material for carved objects **2.** = **staghorn fern 3.** = **staghorn moss 4.** = **staghorn sumac** ■ *adj.* **MADE FROM STAG'S ANTLER** made from a piece of a stag's antlers

stag·horn cor·al *n.* a form of stony coral branched like a deer's antlers. Genus: *Acropora.*

stag·horn fern *n.* a fern with broad leaves like antlers and smaller clinging leaves, often cultivated as a houseplant. Genus: *Platycerium.*

stag·horn moss *n.* a plant with creeping stems like antlers and tiny overlapping leaves. Latin name: *Lycopodium clavatum.*

stag·horn su·mac *n.* a sumac of the eastern United States whose compound leaves turn crimson or purple in fall. It has clusters of greenish flowers, red fruit, and its new branches are covered in soft hair until maturity. Latin name: *Rhus typhina.* [*Staghorn* from the resemblance of its branches to a deer's antlers in velvet]

stag·hound /stág hòwnd/ *n.* a hound like a large foxhound, used especially in the past in hunting stags

stag·ing /stáyjing/ *n.* **1.** THEATER **TECHNIQUE OF PRESENTING STAGE PLAY** the activity, process, or style of presenting a play on a stage **2.** CONSTR **SCAFFOLDING FOR BUILDING** a temporary structure of supports and platforms used in building or working on something **3.** AEROSP **TECHNIQUE FOR INCREASING SPACECRAFT'S VELOCITY** a technique to increase the velocity achieved by a spacecraft's launch vehicle by using multiple propulsive stages, each being jettisoned after use

stag·ing ar·e·a *n.* a place where soldiers and military equipment are gathered for final organization, outfitting, and training before deployment on an operation

stag·nant /stágnənt/ *adj.* **1. STILL AND UNMOVING** not flowing or moving **2. FOUL OR STALE** stale or impure from lack of motion **3. NOT DEVELOPING** not developing or making progress **4. INACTIVE** not active or lively ○ *a stagnant week on the stock market* [Mid-17thC. From Latin *stagnant-*, the present participle stem of *stagnare* (see STAGNATE).] —**stag·nan·cy** *n.* —**stag·nant·ly** *adv.*

stag·nate /stág nàyt/ (**-nat·ed, -nat·ing, -nates**) *vi.* **1. STOP FLOWING** to stop flowing or moving **2. BECOME FOUL** to become stale or impure through not flowing or moving **3. NOT DEVELOP OR MAKE PROGRESS** to fail to develop, progress, or make necessary changes **4. BECOME INACTIVE** to become listless and inactive [Mid-17thC. From Latin *stagnat-*, the past participle stem of *stagnare*, from *stagnum* "pool, swamp."] —**stag·na·to·ry** *adj.*

stag·na·tion /stag náysh'n/ *n.* a condition of no movement, activity, development, or progress, or the process of becoming like this

stag's horn *n.* = **staghorn** *n.* 1

stag·y /stáyjee/ (**-i·er, -i·est**), **stag·ey** (**-i·er, -i·est**) *adj.* exaggerated or artificial in manner, as if in a play (*disapproving*) —**stag·i·ly** *adv.* —**stag·i·ness** *n.*

staid /stayd/ *adj.* sedate and settled in habits or temperament, sometimes to the point of dullness [Mid-16thC. An obsolete past participle of STAY[1], literally "fixed, settled."] —**staid·ly** *adv.* —**staid·ness** *n.*

stain /stayn/ *n.* **1. DISCOLORED PATCH** a discolored mark made by something such as blood, wine, or ink **2. FINISH FOR COLORING SOMETHING** a liquid that is applied to something, especially wood, to darken it or change its color without hiding its texture or grain **3.** MICROBIOL **DYE USED TO COLOR MICROSCOPIC SPECIMENS** a dye used to color organic materials, e.g., tissues and cells, to make specimens more distinguishable under a microscope **4.** INDUST **DYE FOR TEXTILES OR LEATHER** a dye that is used in liquid form to color textiles or leather **5. CHARACTER BLEMISH** something that detracts from somebody's good reputation ■ *v.* (**stained, stain·ing, stains**) **1.** *vti.* **LEAVE MARK ON SOMETHING** to make a discolored mark on something (*often passive*) **2.** *vt.* **DYE SOMETHING** to dye something a different or deeper color using liquid or pigment that penetrates the surface **3.** *vt.* **TARNISH SOMETHING** to disgrace or detract from something **4.** *vt.* MICROBIOL **COLOR ORGANIC SPECIMENS** to color organic materials with dyes to make specimens more distinguishable under a microscope [15thC. Partly from Old Norse *steina* "to paint" (from *steinn* "stone, paint") and partly from Old French *desteindre*, literally "to discolor" (from Latin *tingere* "to dye"; see TINGE).] —**stain·a·bil·i·ty** /stàynə bíllətee/ *n.* —**stain·a·ble** *adj.* —**stain·er** /stáynər/ *n.*

stained glass *n.* glass that has been colored so that it can be used to make a mosaic picture, especially in a window. Stained glass may be made by enameling, burning pigments into the surface, or by fusing metallic oxides with it. (*hyphenated when used before a noun*)

stain·less /stáynləss/ *adj.* **1. ENTIRELY REPUTABLE** without any blemishes, especially of character or reputation **2. WITHOUT STAINS** without a stain or discolored mark **3. RESISTANT TO RUST** resisting rust or corrosion ■ *n.* = **stainless steel** —**stain·less·ly** *adv.*

stain·less steel *n.* a corrosion-resistant steel containing at least 12% chromium that has many domestic and industrial uses, e.g., cutlery, ball bearings, and turbine blades (*hyphenated when used before a noun*)

stair /stair/ *n.* **1. SINGLE STEP** a step in a series of steps leading from one floor or level to another **2. SERIES OF STEPS** a flight of steps leading from one floor or level to another ■ **stairs** *npl.* **SET OF STEPS** a set or several sets of steps leading from one floor or level to another [Old English *stǣger*. Ultimately from an Indo-European word meaning "to step, climb," which is also the ancestor of English *stile*[1] and *stirrup*.]

stair·case /stáir kàyss/ *n.* a set of stairs in a building, usually with banisters or handrails

stair·head /stáir hèd/ *n.* the landing at the top of a flight of stairs

Stair·Mas·ter *tdmk.* a trademark for exercise equipment

stair rod *n.* a rod laid to hold a carpet in place against the bottom of a riser in a staircase

stair·way /stáir wày/ *n.* a passageway from one floor or level of a building to another, consisting of stairs or a staircase

stair·well /stáir wèl/ *n.* the vertical space in a building where stairs are located

stake[1] /stayk/ *n.* **1. THIN POINTED POST IN THE GROUND** a thin wooden or metal post that is driven into the ground to mark or support something **2.** HIST **POST TO TIE AND BURN SOMEBODY** a wooden post used in an old form of execution to which the person was tied. Wood was then piled around its base and set alight. **3. FORM OF EXECUTION** the method of execution in which somebody was tied to a post and burnt **4.** TRANSP **POST TO RETAIN A LOAD** an independent upright post inserted into sockets of a flat wagon or truck to keep long loads such as logs in place **5.** RELIG **MORMON CHURCH DISTRICT** an administrative district in the Mormon Church that consists of wards, each governed by a president and two counselors ■ *v.* (**staked, stak·ing, stakes**) **1.** *vt.* **SUPPORT OR STRENGTHEN WITH STAKE** to support or strengthen something using a stake **2.** *vt.* **TIE OR TETHER TO STAKE** to tie or tether something to a stake **3.** *vi.* **MARK OR FENCE AREA WITH STAKES** to mark out, confine, or fence off an area using stakes driven into the ground around the boundary **4.** *vt.* **ASSERT RIGHTS OVER SOMETHING** to assert something, usually rights, over something such as an area of land [Old English *staca*, from a prehistoric Germanic word meaning "stick, pole" (see STACK)] ◇ **(pull) up stakes** to leave and move to another place ◇ **stake a claim** to claim something such as an area of land or a deposit of minerals

stake out *vt.* **1. WATCH CONTINUOUSLY** to watch a place continuously from a hidden vantage point (*informal*) **2. ESTABLISH BOUNDARIES** to establish the boundaries of an area intended to be used or controlled **3. ESTABLISH AND CLARIFY POSITION** to establish and clarify a personal position in a situation

stake[2] /stayk/ *n.* **1.** GAMBLING **MONEY RISKED IN GAMBLING** an amount of money risked in a bet or game **2. SHARE OR INTEREST IN SOMETHING** a share or interest in something, particularly through money risked in it **3. PERSONAL INVOLVEMENT** a personal or emotional interest, concern, or involvement ○ *We had a huge stake in his success.* **4.** = **grubstake** ■ **stakes** *npl.* **1. DEGREE OF RISK** the degree of hazard or danger involved in a situation **2. PRIZE AVAILABLE** the prize, reward, or success available in a gamble or competition **3.** GAMBLING **PRIZE MADE UP OF CONTRIBUTIONS** the total of bets made by players in a gambling game that is taken by the winner **4.** CARDS **AMOUNT OF BETS IN POKER** in poker, the cash values assigned to chips, bets, or raises ■ *vt.* **(staked, stak·ing, stakes) 1.** GAMBLING **WAGER SOMETHING** to bet something, especially money, on something **2. RISK THE LOSS OF SOMETHING** to risk the loss of something valuable **3. SUPPLY SOMEBODY WITH REQUIREMENTS** to give or lend somebody something needed or wanted **4.** FIN **INVEST IN SOMETHING** to put money into something, especially initial capital [Mid-16thC. Origin uncertain: perhaps from STAKE[1], from a supposed custom of placing a wagered object on a stake.] ◇ **at stake** at risk of being lost

stake·hold·er /stáyk hòldər/ *n.* **1. SOMEBODY OR SOMETHING WITH DIRECT INTEREST** a person or group with a direct interest, involvement, or investment in something, e.g., the employees, shareholders, and customers of a business concern ○ *"...demonstrating how to build powerful stakeholder relationships based on trust..."* (*Marketing Week*; December 1998) **2.** GAMBLING **HOLDER AND PAYER OF BETS** somebody who holds and pays out bets in a gambling game —**stake·hold·ing** *n.*

stake·out /stáyk òwt/ *n.* (*informal*) **1. POLICE SURVEILLANCE** hidden surveillance of somebody or something, especially by the police **2. PLACE FOR POLICE SURVEILLANCE** the place from which surveillance is carried out, especially by the police

stakes /stayks/ (*plural* **stakes**) *n.* a horserace in which a prize is offered, especially a sum of money made up of contributions from owners of horses that take part (*takes a singular verb*)

Sta·kha·nov·ite /stə káanə vìt/ *n.* **EFFECTIVE SOVIET WORKER** a worker in the former Soviet Union who received a reward for increasing production ■ *adj.* **REWARDING HARD WORK** rewarding people who work very hard, especially in the former Soviet Union [Mid-20thC. Named for the Soviet mine worker Aleksei Grigorevich *Stakhanov* (1906–77), who was held up as a model of productivity.]

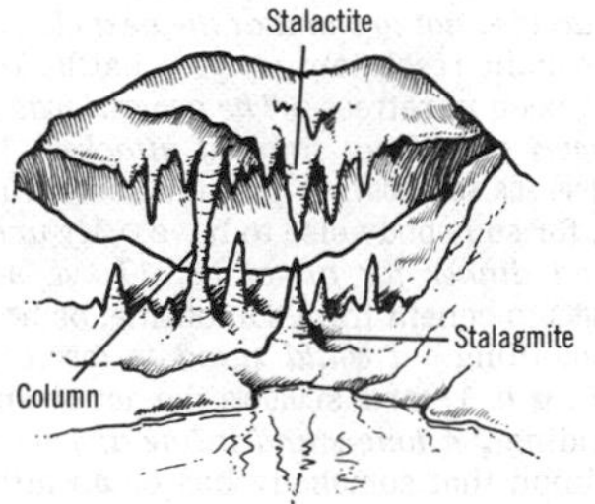

Stalactite and stalagmite

sta·lac·tite /stə lák tìt/ *n.* a conical hanging pillar in a limestone cave that has gradually built up as a deposit from ground water seeping through the cave's roof. ◊ **stalagmite** [Late 17thC. Via modern Latin *stalactites* from Greek *stalaktos* "dripping," from *stalak-*, the stem of *stalassein* "to drip," of unknown origin.] —**stal·ac·tit·ic** /stàllək títtik/ *adj.* —**stal·ac·tit·i·cal·ly** /-títtiklee/ *adv.*

sta·lag /stáa làag, stá làg/ *n.* a German prisoner of war camp in World War II for officers or lower ranks [Mid-20thC. From German, contraction of *Stammlager*, literally "main camp."]

sta·lag·mite /stə lág mìt/ *n.* a conical pillar in a limestone cave that is gradually built upward from the floor as a deposit from ground water seeping through and dripping from the cave's roof. ◊ **stalactite** [Late 17thC. Via modern Latin *stalagmites* from Greek *stalagmos* "something dropped," from *stalak-*, the stem of *stalassein* "to drip" (source also of English *stalactite*).] —**stal·ag·mit·ic** /stàlləg míttik/ *adj.* —**stal·ag·mit·i·cal·ly** /-míttiklee/ *adv.*

stale[1] /stayl/ *adj.* **(stal·er, stal·est) 1. KEPT TOO LONG** no longer fresh **2. LOW IN OXYGEN** stagnant and low in oxygen owing to lack of circulation or ventilation **3. FREQUENTLY HEARD AND BORING** heard too often before and no longer interesting or amusing **4. OUT OF CONDITION** ineffective, enervated, or bored because of doing too much of the same thing **5.** LAW **LEGALLY EXPIRED** having lost legal force through lack of use or elapse of time **6.** FIN **NOT NEGOTIABLE BECAUSE OF DELAY** used to describe financial statements or checks that are not negotiable by a bank because a time limit has expired ■ *vti.* **(staled, stal·ing, stales) 1. LOSE FRESHNESS** to become, or make something become, stale **2. LOSE EFFECTIVENESS** to lose effectiveness or energy **3. BECOME BORING** to become dull and uninteresting over time [13thC. From Old French *estale* "settled," literally "standing still," ultimately from *estal* "standing place," from prehistoric Germanic (see STALL[1]). Originally "wine or beer with settled sediment."]

stale[2] /stayl/ *vi.* **(staled, stal·ing, stales) URINATE** to urinate (*refers to livestock*) ■ *n.* **LIVESTOCK URINE** the urine of livestock, especially horses and cattle [14thC. Origin uncertain: perhaps from Old French *estaler* "to take up a position," from *estal* (see STALE[1]).]

stale·mate /stáyl màyt/ *n.* **1. SITUATION WITH NO POTENTIAL WINNERS** a situation in a contest in which neither side can make any further worthwhile action **2.** CHESS **CHESS SITUATION WITH NO WINNER** a situation in chess in which no winner is possible because neither player can move a piece without placing the king in check ■ *vt.* **(-mat·ed, -mat·ing, -mates) PUT INTO STALEMATE** to put somebody or something into a stalemate (*often passive*) [Mid-18thC. Coined from Anglo-Norman *estale* "fixed position" (from Old French *estaler* "to take up a position," from *estal*; see STALE[1]) + MATE[2].]

Joseph Stalin

Sta·lin /staálin/, **Joseph** (1879–1953) Georgian-born Soviet statesman. He was the general secretary of the Soviet Communist Party (1922–53). He ruled the Soviet Union as a dictator after 1930, eliminating political opponents in a series of purges and causing nationwide famine with his collectivist agricultural policy. After World War II, he extended Soviet control over most of eastern Europe. Real name **Iosif Vissarionovich Dzhugashvili**

Sta·lin·grad /staálin gràd/ former name for **Volgograd** (1925–61)

Sta·lin·ism /staálə nìzzəm/ *n.* the political principles and economic policies developed by Joseph Stalin from Marxist-Leninist thought, which included centralized autocratic rule and total suppression of dissent —**Sta·lin·ist** *n., adj.*

stalk[1] /stawk/ *n.* **1.** BOT **STEM OF PLANT** the main stem or axis of a plant that is fleshy rather than woody **2.** BOT **STEM OR STEMLIKE PART OF PLANT** a supporting part of a plant, e.g., a leaf stem (**petiole**) or flower stalk (**pedicel**) **3. SLENDER SUPPORTING PART** a thin cylindrical part of something that acts as a support, e.g., of a glass **4.** ZOOL **SLENDER STRUCTURAL PART OF ANIMAL** a slender supporting structure for an organ or body of an animal [14thC. Origin uncertain: probably an alteration of obsolete *stale* "stile of a ladder, handle," from Old English *stalu* "upright piece."] —**stalked** *adj.*

stalk[2] /stawk/ *v.* **(stalked, stalk·ing, stalks) 1.** *vt.* **FOLLOW STEALTHILY** to follow or try to get close to a person or animal unobtrusively **2.** *vi.* **WALK STIFFLY AND ANGRILY** to walk in a stiff, angry, or proud way **3.** *vt.* **PROCEED STEADILY AND MALEVOLENTLY** to proceed in a steady and sinister way **4.** *vt.* LAW **PERSISTENTLY HARASS SOMEBODY** to harass somebody by persistent and inappropriate attention, e.g., by constantly following, telephoning, or writing to him or her ■ *n.* **1. STEALTHY PURSUIT** a stealthy pursuit or hunt of something **2. STIFF WALK** a stiff, angry, or proud walk [Old English (assumed) *stealcian*, from a prehistoric Germanic base meaning "to steal," which is also the ancestor of English *steal* and *stealth*] —**stalk·a·ble** *adj.*

WORD KEY: SYNONYMS

See Synonyms at ***follow***.

stalk·er /stáwkər/ *n.* **1. STEALTHY PURSUER** somebody who follows or tries to approach somebody or something stealthily **2.** LAW **HARASSER** somebody who persistently and obsessively harasses somebody else with inappropriate attention

stalk-eyed *adj.* with the eyes located on stalks (**pedicels**), as, e.g., have some crustaceans and dipterans

stalk-eyed fly *n.* a fly mostly found in tropical regions, with eyes that project from the sides of its head on long stalks. Family: Diopsidae.

stalk·ing /stáwking/ *n.* **1. STEALTHY PURSUIT** the act or process of stealthily following or trying to approach somebody or something **2.** LAW **ACT OF STEADY HARASSMENT** the crime of harassing somebody with persistent and inappropriate attention —**stalk·ing·ly** *adv.*

stalk·ing horse *n.* **1. MEANS TO DISGUISE AN OBJECTIVE** something used as a means of disguising a real objective **2.** POL **DECEPTIVE CANDIDATE FOR ELECTION** a candidate who is in an election only to conceal the potential candidacy of somebody else, to divide the opposition, or to determine how strong the opposition is **3.** HUNT **FAKE HORSE** a horse or figure of a horse that is used as cover in the hunting of game

stalk·y /stáwkee/ **(-i·er, -i·est)** *adj.* **1. LONG AND THIN** long or tall and thin like a stalk **2. WITH STALKS** with stalks, especially a lot of stalks —**stalk·i·ly** *adv.* —**stalk·i·ness** *n.*

stall[1] /stawl/ *n.* **1.** COMM **SMALL AREA SELLING OR DISPENSING GOODS** a booth, table, counter, or compartment set up to display goods for sale or information to give out **2.** AGRIC **COMPARTMENT FOR A LARGE ANIMAL** a compartment in a building where a single large animal lives or is fed or milked **3.** AUTOMOT **SITUATION IN WHICH ENGINE HALTS** a situation in which an engine stops abruptly because of insufficient fuel, being braked too suddenly, or mechanical failure **4.** BUILDING **SMALL ROOM** a very small room, or partitioned area in a room, for a shower or toilet **5.** AIR **SUDDEN DIVE BY AN AIRCRAFT** a situation in which an aircraft suddenly dives because the airflow is so obstructed that lift is lost. The loss of airflow can be caused by insufficient airspeed or by an excessive angle of an airfoil when the aircraft is climbing. **6.** CHR **SEAT IN A CHURCH** a pew or enclosed seat in a church **7.** CARS **SPACE FOR PARKING** a space marked off for parking a motor vehicle in a garage or parking lot **8.** MED **SHEATH FOR FINGER** a protective covering for a finger or thumb ■ **stalls** *npl. U.K.* **SEATS CLOSEST TO STAGE** the seats in a theater or movie house on the ground floor nearest the stage or screen ■ *v.* **(stalled, stall·ing, stalls) 1.** *vti.* AUTOMOT **STOP OR MAKE AN ENGINE STOP** to stop working suddenly, or make an engine do this **2.** *vti.* AIR **PLUNGE OR CAUSE TO PLUNGE** to go into a sudden dive, or cause a sudden dive in an aircraft **3.** *vt.* AGRIC **PUT LARGE ANIMAL INTO STALL** to put a large animal into a compartment where it will live or be fed or milked **4.** *vti.* **BECOME STUCK** to cause something to get stuck, or become immovable ○ *stalled the project* ○ *a project that stalled* [Old English *steall* "standing place," from a prehistoric Germanic word that is also the ancestor of English *pedestal*, *stallion*, and *stale*]

stall[2] /stawl/ *v.* **(stalled, stall·ing, stalls) 1.** *vti.* **DELAY WITH HESITATION OR EVASION** to delay or obstruct somebody, or to use delaying tactics **2.** *vi.* **UNDULY PROLONG POSSESSION OF BALL** to prolong holding the ball when a football or basketball team is in the lead so as to use up time and prevent an opponent from scoring ■ *n.* **DECEPTIVE PRETEXT** a pretext or ruse used to delay or deceive somebody [Early 19thC. Alteration of obsolete *stale* "decoy, pickpocket's accomplice," from Anglo-Norman *estale*, literally "something set up."]

stall·age /stáwlij/ *n.* the right to use, or the rent paid for, a stall at a fair or market [14thC. Via Anglo-Norman *estalage* from Old French *estal* (see STALL[1]).]

stall an·gle *n.* AIR = **stalling angle**

stall-feed *vt.* to keep an animal in a stall while fattening it for slaughter

stall·ing an·gle *n.* the angle relative to the horizontal at which the flow of air around an airfoil changes abruptly, resulting in significant changes in the lift and drag of an aircraft

stal·lion /stállyən/ *n.* **1.** ZOOL **UNCASTRATED MALE HORSE** an uncastrated adult male horse, especially one kept for breeding. ◊ **gelding** **2. MAN WITH SUPPOSED SEXUAL PROWESS** a man with supposed great sexual prowess (*informal*) [14thC. From Anglo-Norman *estaloun*. Ultimately from a prehistoric Germanic word meaning "standing place," which is also the ancestor of English STALE[1]; perhaps because stallions were kept confined.]

Stal·lone /stə lṓn/, **Sylvester** (*b.* 1946) U.S. actor. He is best known for playing heroes in Hollywood action movies, most notably a boxer in the *Rocky* series (1976–90). Full name **Michael Sylvester Stallone**

stal·wart /stáwlwərt/ *adj.* **1. DEPENDABLE** dependable and loyal **2. STRONG** sturdy and strong ■ *n.* **HARD-WORKING LOYAL SUPPORTER** somebody who is faithful, dependable, and hard-working [15thC. Variant of *stealwurthe*, from Old English *stǣlwierþe* "good," literally "having a worthy foundation," from *staþol* "foundation" (see STADDLE) + *weorþ* (see WORTH).] —**stal·wart·ly** *adv.* —**stal·wart·ness** *n.*

sta·men /stáymən/ (*plural* **-mens** *or* **-mi·na** /stáymənə, stámmənə/) *n.* the male reproductive organ of a flower, typically consisting of a stalk (**filament**) bearing a pollen-producing anther at its tip [Mid-17thC. From Latin, "thread in the warp of a loom."] —**sta·mi·nal** *adj.* —**sta·mi·nif·e·rous** /stàmmə nífférəss/ *adj.*

Stam·ford /stámfərd/ city in southwestern Connecticut, founded in 1641. Population: 108,056 (1990).

stam·i·na /stámmənə/ *n.* enduring physical or mental energy and strength that allows somebody to do something for a long time [Early 18thC. From Latin, plural of *stamen* "thread in woven cloth" (see STAMEN). The meaning developed from "threads of a life," woven by the Fates, to "innate strength."] —**stam·i·nal** *adj.*

sta·mi·nate /stáymənət, stámmə-, -nàyt/ *adj.* used to describe plants that have stamens, especially flowers with stamens but without female parts (**carpels**)

stam·i·node /stáymə nṑd, stámmə-/, **stam·i·no·di·um** /stàymə nṓdee əm, stàmmə-/ (*plural* **-a** /-ə/) *n.* a sterile or vestigial stamen. It forms a conspicuous part of some flowers, e.g., in the iris. [Early 19thC. From modern Latin *staminodium*, from *stamen* "thread" (see STAMEN).]

sta·mi·no·dy /stáymə nṑdee, stámmə-/ *n.* the process by which other organs of a flower are changed into stamens

stam·mel /stámm'l/ *n.* **1.** TEXTILES **COARSE WOOLEN CLOTH** a coarse woolen cloth, usually red, used in medieval times to make undergarments **2.** COLORS **RED COLOR** a bright red color, like that of the stammel cloth of medieval times [Mid-16thC. Alteration of earlier *stamin*, via Old French *estamine* from, ultimately, Latin *stamineus* "consisting of threads," from *stamen* "thread" (see STAMEN).] —**stam·mel** *adj.*

stam·mer /stámmər/ *vti.* (**-mered, -mer·ing, -mers**) **SPEAK WITH HESITATIONS AND REPETITIONS** to speak, or say something, with many quick hesitations and repeated consonants or syllables because of a speech condition or a strong emotion ■ *n.* **SPEECH CONDITION** a speech condition that makes somebody speak with involuntary hesitations and repetition of consonants or syllables. Stammering will usually respond to treatment from a speech therapist. [Old English *stamerian*, from a prehistoric Germanic base meaning "to halt, stutter," which is also the ancestor of English *stumble* and *stem*[2]] —**stam·mer·er** *n.*

stamp /stamp/ *n.* **1.** MAIL **GUMMED PAPER PAYING FOR POSTAGE** a small piece of gummed paper that is stuck on an envelope or package to show that postage has been paid **2.** MAIL **CANCELLATION ACROSS A POSTAGE STAMP** a mark put across a postage stamp on an envelope or package to show that the stamp has been used **3.** PRINTING **SMALL BLOCK FOR PRINTING DESIGN** a small block with a raised design or lettering that can be printed onto paper by inking the block and pressing it to the paper **4. DESIGN PRINTED ONTO PAPER WITH A STAMP** a design printed onto paper using a stamp in order to show that a document has been read, canceled, or officially approved **5. GUMMED PAPER AS AN OFFICIAL MARK** a piece of printed gummed paper fixed to a document as an official sign of something, e.g., approval or validity **6. CHARACTERISTIC OF SOMETHING** a characteristic or distinguishing sign or impression **7. TYPE OF SOMETHING** a class or type of something **8.** COMM **WAY OF PAYING FOR SOMETHING** a piece of paper that can be purchased as a way of redeeming part or all of the amount charged for goods or a service. ◊ **trading stamp** **9. ACTION OF BANGING DOWN A FOOT** the action of bringing a foot down forcefully on a surface **10.** INDUST **MACHINE FOR CRUSHING ROCKS AND ORES** a machine that crushes rocks and ores, consisting of a freely falling weight lifted and dropped, or the weight in such a machine ■ *v.* (**stamped, stamp·ing, stamps**) **1.** *vt.* **PUT A STAMP ON A DOCUMENT** to press a stamp onto a document leaving a design or lettering on it in order to show that it has been seen, dated, canceled, or officially approved **2.** *vti.* **BANG A FOOT DOWN FORCIBLY** to bring a foot down forcefully on a surface **3.** *vt.* MAIL **STICK A POSTAGE STAMP ON SOMETHING** to stick a stamp on an envelope or package **4.** *vi.* **WALK FORCEFULLY** to walk by taking short forceful steps **5.** *vt.* **HAVE A LASTING EFFECT ON SOMEBODY** to have a lasting effect or influence on somebody **6.** *vt.* *U.K.* **SUPPRESS SOMETHING OR SOMEBODY** to suppress or eradicate something or somebody ○ *He stamped on any suggestion he should resign.* **7.** *vt.* INDUST **CRUSH ROCKS** to crush or pound rocks and ores [12thC. Origin uncertain: probably from assumed Old English *stampian* "to pound," from prehistoric Germanic.] —**stamp·a·ble** *adj.*

stamp out *vt.* **1. ERADICATE SOMETHING** to put an end to something **2. EXTINGUISH SOMETHING** to extinguish something by stamping on it with the feet **3. CUT SOMETHING OUT USING A SHARP TOOL** to cut out a shape or object by pressing a sharp-edged machine or tool onto a material

Stamp Act *n.* a law passed in the British parliament in 1765 introducing a tax on legal documents, commercial contracts, licenses, publications, and playing cards in the North American colonies. Because of colonial opposition the first Stamp Act was repealed in March 1766 but was later replaced by others.

stamp col·lect·ing *n.* the collecting of postage stamps as a hobby or investment. ◊ **philately** —**stamp col·lec·tor** *n.*

stamped /stampt/ *adj.* having or bearing a stamp

stam·pede /stam pééd/ *n.* **1. HEADLONG RUSH OF ANIMALS** an uncontrolled headlong rush of frightened animals **2. HEADLONG SURGE OF CROWD** an uncontrolled surging rush of a crowd of people **3. SUDDEN RUSH OF PEOPLE DOING SOMETHING** a sudden rush of many people all doing or wanting to do something at the same time ○ *There was a stampede to take advantage of the low prices.* **4. FESTIVAL INCLUDING A RODEO** a celebration in the western United States and especially in Canada, usually held annually, that includes a rodeo along with contests, exhibitions, dancing, and entertainment ■ *v.* (**-ped·ed, -ped·ing, -pedes**) **1.** *vti.* **RUSH FORWARD IN FRIGHTENED SURGE** to rush forward in a frightened headlong surge, or make animals or people surge forward **2.** *vt.* **FORCE SOMEBODY INTO DOING SOMETHING** to force somebody to do something before he or she is ready or has properly thought about it [Early 19thC. From Mexican Spanish *estampida*, from Spanish, "uproar." Ultimately from a prehistoric Germanic word that is also the ancestor of English *stamp*.] —**stam·ped·er** *n.*

stamp·er /stámpər/ *n.* **1. SOMEBODY OR SOMETHING THAT STAMPS** a person or device used for stamping **2.** INDUST **MACHINE FOR STAMPING SOMETHING** a tool or machine that stamps something, especially ore being pulverized **3.** RECORDING **MOLD FOR DISK RECORDINGS** a mold from which disk recordings are pressed

stamp·ing ground *n.* a place where somebody or a group of people is habitually found (*informal*)

stamp mill *n.* a machine in which ores and rocks are finely crushed, usually operated by hydraulic power, or a building housing one or more such machines

stance /stanss/ *n.* **1. ATTITUDE TOWARD SOMETHING** an attitude or view that somebody takes about something **2. WAY OF STANDING** the way a person or an animal stands **3.** SPORTS **POSITION OF PLAYER** the position in which a player holds the body in attempting to hit a ball, e.g., in baseball or golf **4.** MOUNTAINEERING **PLACE FOR PITCHING AND BELAYING** a place where a mountain climber can pitch and belay **5.** *Scotland* TRANSP **TRANSPORTATION WAITING PLACE** a place where buses or taxis wait for passengers [Mid-16thC. Via French, "position," from Italian *stanza* (see STANZA).]

stanch[1] /stawnch, stanch/ (**stanched, stanch·ing, stanch·es**), **staunch** /stáwnch/ (**staunched, staunch·ing, staunch·es**) *v.* **1.** *vti.* **STOP LIQUID FLOW** to stop the flow of a liquid, particularly blood, or be stopped from flowing **2.** *vt.* **STOP WOUND FROM BLEEDING** to stop a wound from bleeding or exuding pus **3.** *vt.* **ASSUAGE SOMETHING** to assuage or allay something that is bad (*archaic*) [14thC. Via Old French *estanchier* from assumed Vulgar Latin *stanticare*, literally "to cause to stand," from Latin *stant-*, present participle stem of *stare* (see STATION).] —**stanch·a·ble** *adj.* —**stanch·er** *n.*

WORD KEY: USAGE

See Usage note at ***staunch***.

stanch[2] *adj.* = **staunch**[1]

stan·chion /stánchən/ *n.* **1. UPRIGHT SUPPORTING POLE** a vertical pole, bar, or beam used to support something **2.** AGRIC **FRAME FOR CONFINING A COW** an upright frame in which the neck of a cow is loosely fitted, usually to confine the cow for milking ■ *vt.* (**-chioned, -chion·ing, -chions**) **SUPPORT SOMETHING WITH A POLE** to support something using a vertical pole, bar, or beam [15thC. From Old French *estanchon*, from *estance* "prop, support."]

stand /stand/ *v.* (**stood** /stŏŏd/, **stood, stand·ing, stands**) **1.** *vti.* **BE OR SET UPRIGHT** to be in an upright position, or put something in an upright position ○ *I was standing behind him.* ○ *Stand the box in the corner.* **2.** *vi.* **GET UP ON FEET** to get up into an upright position from a sitting or lying position ○ *The newborn foal tried to stand but only collapsed again.* **3.** *vi.* **BE IN PARTICULAR PLACE** to be situated or positioned in a particular place ○ *The castle stands on a headland.* **4.** *vi.* **MEASURE IN HEIGHT** to be of a particular height when upright ○ *He stood six feet tall.* **5.** *vi.* **BE IN PARTICULAR STATE** to be in a particular condition or state ○ *The old place stands in need of a few repairs.* ○ *The document can't be published as it stands.* **6.** *vi.* **REMAIN MOTIONLESS** to remain in a particular place without moving or being used ○ *The car stood outside the office all morning.* **7.** *vi.* **REMAIN VALID** to continue to be in effect or existence ○ *Her world record still stands.* **8.** *vi.* **STOP** to come to a halt ○ *I had to stand and catch my breath.* **9.** *vi.* **GATHER WITHOUT FLOWING AWAY** to gather somewhere and not flow away ○ *rainwater standing in pools* **10.** *vi.* **BE AT PARTICULAR POINT** to be at a particular point while subject to change or fluctuation ○ *The balance of the account stands at $400.* **11.** *vt.* **TOLERATE** to accept or put up with something ○ *He can't stand being kept waiting.* **12.** *vt.* **UNDERGO WITHOUT HARM** to resist or bear something without being harmed or damaged ○ *The mechanism is too delicate to stand rough handling.* **13.** *vt.* **SUBMIT TO SOMETHING** to submit or be subjected to something ○ *I am prepared to stand trial.* **14.** *vi.* POL **SEEK ELECTION** to enter an election as a candidate ○ *She decided not to stand at the next election.* **15.** *vi.* **FIGHT** to fight resolutely or give battle, often after having been in retreat ○ *The general was convinced the enemy would not stand if attacked.* **16.** *vt.* **BUY SOMETHING FOR SOMEBODY** to pay for something, e.g., a drink, for somebody else to have ○ *My uncle offered to stand dinner for all of us.* **17.** *vt.* **BENEFIT FROM SOMETHING** to benefit from something, or be no worse for something ○ *I could stand to lose a few more pounds.* ■ *n.* **1. ACT OF STANDING** the act or an example of standing ○ *a long stand in the airport* **2. ATTITUDE** an opinion that somebody has or an attitude that somebody adopts on a particular subject ○ *Management took a tough stand on absenteeism.* **3. SUPPORTING STRUCTURE** a framework or structure on which something is supported ○ *a music stand* **4.** FURNITURE **PIECE OF FURNITURE** a piece of furniture on which clothes or accessories are hung or supported (*often used in combination*) ○ *an umbrella stand* ○ *a hat stand* **5.** *U.K.* SPORTS = **stands** **6. STATIONARY CONDITION** a state of having stopped or being stationary ○ *The runaway vehicle came to a stand in a field.* **7.** COMM **PLACE WHERE SOMETHING IS SOLD** a booth or stall where something is sold or given out (*often used in combination*) ○ *a refreshment stand* **8. EXHIBITION AREA** one of several places in an exhibition where something is displayed **9.** BOT **AREA OF GROWING THINGS** a group of several plants, especially trees, growing together in one place ○ *a stand of trees* **10.** LAW **PLACE FOR WITNESSES IN COURT** a place in a court of law where witnesses are questioned ○ *take the stand* **11. HALT TO FIGHT** a halt made, especially by a force that has been retreating, to give battle ○ *Custer's last stand* **12.** TRANSP **PLACE FOR WAITING VEHICLES** a place where vehicles, especially taxis, wait to pick up passengers (*usually used in combination*) ○ *a taxi stand* **13.** ARTS **STOP FOR PERFORMANCE** a halt made to give a performance during a tour by a performer or theatrical company ○ *a* *three-week stand out of town* [Old English *standan*. Ultimately from an Indo-European word meaning "to stand," which is also the ancestor of English *stem*[1], *stead*, and *stud*.] ◇ **stand fast** to be resolute and refuse to give in ◇ **stand or fall by something** to succeed or fail depending on particular circumstances

stand by *vi.* **1.** REMAIN READY to wait in a state of readiness to act if required ○ *Stand by for further orders.* **2.** BE PRESENT WITHOUT ACTION to be present while something is happening but play no part in it ○ *I'm not prepared to stand by and let this go on.* **3.** SUPPORT to support or remain faithful to somebody ○ *Her friends all stood by her.* **4.** ADHERE TO SOMETHING to continue to assert or believe in something ○ *I stand by what I said yesterday.*

stand down *v.* **1.** *vi.* RESIGN to resign from office or withdraw from a contest **2.** *vi.* LAW END TESTIMONY to leave a witness stand after having been questioned **3.** *vti.* END DUTY to end somebody's period of duty, or to go off duty, especially military duty **4.** *vti.* MIL GO OFF ALERT to go off alert or be taken off alert or out of a combat zone

stand for *vt.* **1.** MEAN SOMETHING to mean or represent something else **2.** BELIEVE IN SOMETHING to believe in something strongly and fight for it ○ *To agree with this would go against everything I stand for.* **3.** BECOME A CANDIDATE FOR SOMETHING to enter an election as a candidate for a particular office **4.** PUT UP WITH to tolerate or put up with something ○ *She won't stand for any nonsense.* **5.** NAUT HEAD FOR A PLACE to set a course for a particular destination ○ *The fleet stood for home.*

stand in *vi.* to take the place of somebody or something else as a substitute ○ *Who's going to stand in while you're away?*

stand off *v.* **1.** *vti.* KEEP AWAY to keep at a distance from something, or to make somebody or something stay at a distance **2.** *vti.* NAUT SAIL AWAY to sail a vessel away from something such as a shore **3.** *vt.* SUSPEND FROM WORK to suspend somebody from work, usually temporarily

stand on *v.* **1.** *vt.* INSIST ON to insist on something or see it as being important ○ *We don't stand on ceremony in this house.* **2.** *vi.* NAUT MAINTAIN SAILING DIRECTION to continue sailing a vessel on a particular course

stand out *vi.* **1.** BE CONSPICUOUS to be conspicuous or prominent **2.** STICK OUT to project or protrude from something **3.** REFUSE TO ACCEPT SOMETHING to refuse to accept or comply with something, especially after others have done so

stand to *vti.* to take up position in readiness for military action, or to make somebody do this

stand up *v.* **1.** *vti.* RISE to rise to an upright position, or make something do this **2.** *vi.* RESIST SCRUTINY to be seen as still valid or right despite being closely examined or criticized ○ *I don't think her testimony will stand up in court.*

stand up for *vi.* to defend or act to protect the interests of somebody

stand up to *vi.* **1.** RESIST to resist or refuse to be cowed by somebody ○ *He'll back down if you stand up to him.* **2.** ENDURE to undergo something that is potentially damaging without being badly affected ○ *These cars won't stand up to being driven on rough terrain.*

stand up with *vi.* to act as best man or maid of honor for somebody who is getting married

stand-a·lone *adj.* able to operate as a self-contained unit independently of a computer network or system

stan·dard /stándərd/ *n.* **1.** LEVEL OF QUALITY OR EXCELLENCE the level of quality or excellence attained by somebody or something **2.** LEVEL OF QUALITY ACCEPTED AS NORM a level of quality or excellence that is accepted as the norm or by which actual attainments are judged (*often used in the plural*) **3.** MUSIC ITEM IN USUAL REPERTOIRE something, especially a song or other piece of music, that is very popular or is performed as part of the usual repertoire of somebody or something ○ *played all the old standards* **4.** FIN COMMODITY MONEY HAS VALUE BASED ON the commodity or commodities on which the value of a currency or monetary system is based **5.** AUTHORIZED MODEL OF UNIT OF MEASUREMENT an authorized model used to define a unit of measurement **6.** FLAG a flag with a distinctive design that is the emblem of, and often a focus of loyalty to, a particular nation, person, or group **7.** MIL DEVICE USED AS BATTLE RALLYING POINT a flag or other symbolic device attached to a pole and used as a rallying point for troops in battle **8.** COINS PROPORTION OF METAL IN COIN the proportion of gold or silver and of nonprecious metal that a coin is legally required to contain **9.** HERALDRY LONG TAPERING FLAG a long tapering flag ending in two points and with heraldic devices on it, used in heraldry as an emblem of a person or corporation. It was formerly carried on ceremonial occasions by or before the nobleman to whom it belonged. **10.** GARDENING PLANT WITH STRAIGHT BARE STEM a plant, especially a fruit tree or rose, trained so that its leaves and flowers grow at the top of a straight bare stem **11.** HOUSEHOLD SUPPORTING BASE a base or support for something such as a large tall vase **12.** BOT LARGE UPPER PETAL OF PEA the large upper petal in the flowers of plants of the pea family ■ **stan·dards** *npl.* PRINCIPLES principles or values that govern somebody's behavior ■ *adj.* **1.** NORMAL constituting or not differing from the norm for a particular thing **2.** WIDELY USED AND RESPECTED very widely used and generally regarded as authoritative ○ *the standard text in thermodynamics* **3.** GRAM GRAMMATICALLY CORRECT regarded as correct or acceptable by the majority of educated speakers of or authorities on a language **4.** GARDENING TRAINED TO GROW WITH STRAIGHT STEM trained in such a way that the leaves and flowers grow at the top of a straight bare stem [12thC. Via Anglo-Norman *estaundart* "flag to which troops rally" from Old French *estandart*, of uncertain origin: perhaps from prehistoric Germanic words.]

stan·dard a·men·i·ties *npl. U.K.* the sanitary equipment required as a basic minimum for all dwellings by British housing law, namely a bath or shower, washbasin, sink, and a flush toilet

stan·dard at·mos·phere *n.* MEASURE = **atmosphere** *n.* 6

stan·dard-bear·er *n.* **1.** LEADER a leader or prominent and inspiring representative of a movement, cause, or party **2.** SOMEBODY WHO CARRIES STANDARD somebody who carries a standard or flag, especially for a military unit

stan·dard·bred, **Stan·dard·Bred** *n.* a horse belonging to a North American breed specially bred for speed and stamina in harness races

stan·dard can·dle *n.* MEASURE = **candela**

stan·dard cell *n.* an electric cell that produces a constant known voltage and can be used to calibrate voltage-measuring equipment

stan·dard cost *n.* the budgeted expenditure of a regular manufacturing process against which the actual cost is measured

stan·dard de·vi·a·tion *n.* a statistical measure of the amount by which a set of values differs from the arithmetical mean, equal to the square root of the mean of the differences' squares

Stan·dard Eng·lish *n.* the variety of the English language used by educated speakers and regarded as representing correct usage in grammar, spelling, vocabulary, and punctuation, while taking into account some regional differences

stan·dard er·ror *n.* the standard deviation of the sample in a frequency distribution divided by the square root of the number of values in the sample. It is a measure of the variability that a constant would be expected to show during sampling.

stan·dard gauge *n.* the gauge used for most public railroad systems worldwide, the distance between the rails being 4 ft. $8\frac{1}{2}$ in./143.5 cm

Stan·dard Gen·er·al·ized Mark·up Lan·guage *n.* full form of **SGML**

stan·dard·ize /stándər dīz/ (**-ized, -iz·ing, -iz·es**) *v.* **1.** *vti.* MAKE STANDARD to remove variations and irregularities and make all types or examples of something the same or bring them into conformity with one another **2.** *vt.* ASSESS SOMETHING BY COMPARISON WITH STANDARD to assess something or determine its properties by comparing it with a standard — **stan·dard·iz·er** *n.*

stan·dard·ized test *n.* a test administered according to standardized procedures and that assesses a student's aptitude by comparison with a standard

stan·dard lamp *n. U.K.* = **floor lamp**

stan·dard of liv·ing *n.* the level of material comfort enjoyed by a person, group, or society

stan·dard op·er·at·ing pro·ce·dure *n.* a procedure that is usually followed when carrying out a particular operation or dealing with a particular situation

stan·dard time *n.* a system of measuring time in relation to the natural day usually based on the mean solar time at the central meridian of a particular time zone

stand·by /stánd bī/ *n.* **1.** PERSON OR THING READILY AVAILABLE something or somebody that can always be relied on to be available and useful, especially if needed as a substitute or in an emergency **2.** TRANSP UNRESERVED TICKET OR PASSENGER WITHOUT RESERVATION an unreserved ticket or a passenger having no prior reservation on a mode of public transportation such as an airline ■ *adj.* **1.** RESERVE able to be used as a replacement ○ *standby generator* **2.** TRANSP UNRESERVED AND SUBJECT TO AVAILABILITY made available, usually at a lower price, shortly before the departure of a flight when there are seats remaining unsold, or using a ticket made available in this way ■ *adv.* TRANSP ON STANDBY BASIS on the basis of standby ○ *flew standby from Washington to Amsterdam* [Late 18thC] ◇ **be on standby** to be available for use or service if necessary

stand-down, **stand·down** /stánd dòwn/ *n.* a return to normal status after being on alert, or the withdrawal of a military presence

stand·ee /stan dée/ *n.* somebody who stands, e.g., on a bus, usually because there are no seats available

stand-in *n.* **1.** TEMPORARY REPLACEMENT somebody or something that acts as a temporary replacement **2.** MOVIE ACTOR'S DOUBLE somebody who replaces an actor in a movie for preparatory or nonvital work on set or when dangerous stunts are being shot ■ *adj.* ACTING AS REPLACEMENT acting as a temporary replacement for somebody or something

stand·ing /stánding/ *n.* **1.** STATUS AND REPUTATION somebody's reputation or position, e.g., in society or business ○ *a person of some standing in computer electronics* **2.** DURATION the period over which something has been in existence ○ *a friend of long standing* ■ *adj.* **1.** UPRIGHT performed while standing rather than sitting or moving ○ *received a standing ovation* **2.** PERMANENT remaining permanently in existence or in force ○ *You have a standing invitation to visit us whenever you wish.* **3.** NOT FLOWING not flowing, or containing water that cannot flow or run away **4.** AGRIC NOT CUT DOWN growing where planted, having not been cut down

stand·ing ar·my *n.* a permanent professional military force maintained by a country in times of peace as well as war

stand·ing com·mit·tee *n.* a committee that remains in existence permanently in order to deal with a particular issue

stand·ing crop *n.* the total mass of living things of all kinds or of one particular kind found in a particular area at a particular time

stand·ing or·der *n.* an order or rule, especially one governing military procedures, that remains in force on all relevant occasions until it is specifically revoked

stand·ing rig·ging *n.* the wires and ropes holding the masts and spars of a sailing ship that are more or less permanently fixed in place

stand·ing room *n.* space where people can only stand, not sit

stand·ing wave *n.* a stationary wave characterized by points of zero vibration and points of maximum vibration, occurring when two waves of equal frequency and intensity traveling in opposite directions combine [Because the points of minimum and maximum vibration remain stationary]

stand·off /stánd àwf, -òf/ *n.* **1.** DEADLOCK a situation in which no result or conclusion can be reached because the two sides in a contest or dispute are equally matched or are equally intransigent **2.** SPORTS DRAW a draw or tie

stand·off in·su·la·tor *n.* an insulator that supports an electrical conductor and keeps it at a distance from other conducting elements. The insulators supporting power lines are examples of this.

stand·off·ish /stànd áwfish, -óffish/ *adj.* reluctant to show friendship or enter into conversation with other people

stand·off mis·sile *n.* a guided missile that can be fired from an aircraft at a sufficient distance from its target to be out of range of enemy defenses

stand oil *n.* a thick drying oil used in oil enamel paints, made by heating linseed or another oil to a high temperature [Translation of German *Standöl*; it was formerly prepared by allowing linseed oil to stand]

stand·out /stánd òwt/ *n.* somebody or something that is especially prominent or outstanding (*informal*) ○ *"Achieving cost-effective coverage and standout on TV is a problem ..."* (*Marketing Week*; December 1998)

stand·o·ver man /stánd òvər màn/ *n. Aus* somebody who intimidates people or threatens them with violence in order to extort money or obtain other services from them

stand·pat·ter /stánd pàttər/ *n.* somebody who resists change, especially in politics

stand·pipe /stánd pìp/ *n.* ENG a vertical, open-ended pipe attached to a pipeline to act as a pressure regulator, ensuring that the pressure head at that point cannot exceed the length of the pipe

stand·point /stánd pòynt/ *n.* the particular way an individual or a group thinks about or is affected by an event or an issue, usually as opposed to the way others view the same thing ○ *From the ecological standpoint, this is an utter disaster.*

stand·still /stánd stìl/ *n.* a situation in which all movement or activity ceases and further movement or activity is prevented ○ *Traffic is at a standstill.*

stand·still a·gree·ment *n.* an agreement that things should remain as they are, especially one between a creditor country and a debtor country that needs extra time to repay its debt

stand-up *adj.* **1.** ARTS **INVOLVING SOLO PERFORMANCE BY COMEDIAN** involving a performance by a comedian standing alone on stage telling jokes or stories to an audience ○ *stand-up comedy* **2. AT WHICH PEOPLE STAND** where or at which people stand, especially to eat or drink ○ *A large stand-up buffet was laid out for the reception.* **3. ERECT** standing erect and not folded down **4. TRUSTWORTHY** showing the qualities of honesty, loyalty, and dependability (*informal*) ■ *n.* **STANDING TO GET WORK** standing in a designated place to be hired for a day's work (*informal*) ○ *I'd get in early for the stand-ups*

Stan·field /stán feeld/, **Robert Lorne** (*b.* 1914) Canadian lawyer and statesman. He was prime minister of Nova Scotia (1956–67).

Stan·ford-Bi·net test /stànfərd bi náy-/ *n.* an intelligence test commonly given to children [Early 20thC. Named for *Stanford* University, California, + Alfred *Binet*, 1857–1911, a French psychologist who devised the original version.]

stan·hope /stán hòp/ *n.* a light open horse-drawn carriage with a single seat and two or four wheels [Early 19thC. Named for Fitzroy H. R. *Stanhope*, 1787–1864, an English clergyman for whom one was first made.]

Stan·i·slav·sky /stànni slaáv skee, -slaáf-, stənyi-/, **Konstantin Sergeyevich Alexeyev** (1863–1938) Russian actor and theater director. He helped to found the Moscow Arts Theater (1889), and there adopted methods of training actors that greatly influenced theater in the 20th century. — **Stan·i·slav·ski·an** *adj.*

Stan·i·slav·sky meth·od, Stan·i·slav·ski meth·od *n.* = **Method**

stank past tense of **stink**

Stan·ley /stánnlee/, **Sir H. M.** (1841–1904) British journalist and explorer. On his African expeditions he located David Livingstone at Ujiji on Lake Tanganyika (1871), traced the Lualaba and Congo rivers to the sea (1874–77), and helped to found the Congo Free State (1890–95). Full name **Sir Henry Morton Stanley**. Born **John Rowlands**

Stan·ley Pool former name for **Malebo Pool**

stann- *prefix.* tin ○ *stanniferous*

stan·nic /stánnik/ *adj.* containing or relating to tin, especially with a valence of four [Late 18thC. Formed from obsolete *stannum* (see STANN-).]

stan·nic sul·fide *n.* a solid compound of sulfur and tin that is usually found in the form of gold-colored crystals or a powder

stan·nif·er·ous /sta nífferəss/ *adj.* containing or yielding tin [Early 19thC. Formed from obsolete English *stannum* (see STANN-).]

stan·nite /stá nìt/ *n.* a gray mineral with a metallic luster that is a source of tin. Formula: Cu_2FeSn_4. [Mid-19thC. Formed form obsolete English *stannum* (see STANN-).]

stan·nous /stánnəss/ *adj.* containing or relating to tin, especially with a valence of two [Mid-19thC. Formed from obsolete English *stannum* (see STANN-).]

stan·nous fluor·ide *n.* a white crystalline powder with a bitter salty taste used to fluoridate toothpaste. Formula: SnF_2.

Stan·thorpe /stán thawrp/ town in southeastern Queensland, Australia. It is one of the highest towns in the state at 2,660 ft./811 m. Population: 4,154 (1996).

Stan·ton /stántən/, **Edwin McMasters** (1814–69) U.S. lawyer and statesman. He was attorney general (1860–61) and secretary of war under Presidents Lincoln and Andrew Johnson (1862–68). His expulsion from the cabinet became the cause of Johnson's impeachment.

Stan·ton, Elizabeth Cady (1815–1902) U.S. social reformer. She worked in the abolitionist and temperance movements, and after 1840 devoted herself to the campaign for women's suffrage and civil rights.

stan·za /stánzə/ *n.* a number of lines of verse forming a separate unit within a poem. In many poems each stanza has the same number of lines and the same rhythm and rhyme scheme. [Late 16thC. Via Italian from assumed Vulgar Latin *stantia* "a standing, stopping place," ultimately from Latin *stare* "to stand." From the idea of stopping after a section.] —**stan·za·ic** /stan záy ik/ *adj.*

sta·pe·dec·to·my /stàypi déktəmee/ (*plural* **-mies**) *n.* surgical removal of the stapes of the ear. It is performed in treating some forms of hearing loss. [Late 19thC. Formed from modern Latin *staped-*, stem of *stapes* (see STAPES).]

sta·pe·des plural of **stapes**

sta·pe·li·a /stə peélee ə/ (*plural* **-as** *or* **-a**) *n.* an African plant that resembles the cactus, has thick fleshy four-angled stems, no leaves, and bears large mottled flowers that give off a foul smell. Genus: *Stapelia.* [Late 18thC. Formed from modern Latin, genus name, named for Jan Bode van *Stapel*, died 1636, a Dutch botanist.]

sta·pes /stáy peez/ (*plural* **-pes** *or* **-pe·des** /stə peé deez/) *n.* a small stirrup-shaped bone in the middle ear of mammals, the innermost of the three small bones that transmit vibration to the inner ear [Mid-17thC. Via modern Latin from medieval Latin, "stirrup."] — **sta·pe·di·al** /stə peédee əl/ *adj.*

staph /staf/ *n.* a staphylococcus (*informal*) [Early 20thC. Shortening.]

staph·y·lo·coc·cus /stàffəlō kókəss/ (*plural* **-ci** /-sì/) *n.* a bacterium that typically occurs in clusters resembling grapes, normally inhabits the skin and mucous membranes, and may cause disease. These bacteria commonly infect the skin, eyes, and urinary tract, and some produce toxins responsible for septicemia and food poisoning. Genus: *Staphylococcus.* [Late 19thC. Via modern Latin, genus name, from Greek *staphulē* "bunch of grapes" + *kokkos* "berry."] — **staph·y·lo·coc·cal** *adj.*

sta·ple[1] /stáyp'l/ *n.* **1. BENT WIRE TO FASTEN PAPERS** a small thin piece of metal wire bent into the shape of a flattened U with square corners, used to fasten things together, especially sheets of paper. The staple is driven through the material by a device that also bends its two ends inward and flattens them so that they grip the material firmly. **2.** BUILDING **U-SHAPED FASTENER FOR WOOD OR MASONRY** a small U-shaped piece of strong metal wire with two sharp points, usually driven into a surface to hold something such as a bolt or cable in place ■ *vt.* **(-pled, -pling, -ples) FASTEN WITH STAPLES** to fasten something to something else or in position with staples [Old English *stapol* "post, pillar," of prehistoric Germanic origin. The underlying sense is perhaps of "something that supports or holds."]

sta·ple[2] /stáyp'l/ *n.* **1.** FOOD **BASIC INGREDIENT OF DIET** a food that forms the basis of the diet of the people of a particular country or region or of a particular animal **2. PRINCIPAL OR RECURRING INGREDIENT** a principal or continually recurring ingredient or feature of something ○ *Lurid stories are a staple of tabloid journalism.* **3.** COMM **MOST IMPORTANT ARTICLE OF TRADE** the commodity or product that is most important to the trade of a country, region, or organization **4. RAW MATERIAL** a raw material, especially the principal raw material produced or grown in a region **5.** MANUF **WOOL, COTTON, OR FLAX FIBER** the fiber of wool, cotton, or flax graded according to its length and fineness ■ *vt.* **(-pled, -pling, -ples)** MANUF **GRADE FIBERS** to grade the fibers of wool, cotton, or flax according to their length and fineness [14thC. Via Old French *estaple* from Middle Low German and Middle Dutch *stapel* "shop; pillar," from a prehistoric Germanic word that is also the ancestor of English *staple*[1].]

sta·ple gun *n.* a powerful device used to project heavy metal staples into wood or masonry

sta·pler /stáyplər/ *n.* a device that fastens paper and other materials together using staples, usually consisting of a flat metal base, a spring-loaded magazine of staples, and a top section

star /staar/ *n.* **1.** ASTRON **MASS OF GAS IN SPACE** a gaseous mass in space such as the Sun, ranging in size from that of a planet to larger than the Earth's orbit, which generates energy by thermonuclear reactions **2.** ASTRON **POINT OF LIGHT IN NIGHT SKY** a celestial body usually visible as a small bright point of light in the night sky **3. STAR SHAPE** a shape representing or based on that of a star as seen in the night sky, usually having five or more triangular points radiating from a center **4. STAR-SHAPED SYMBOL OF MERIT OR RANK** a star-shaped object or symbol used as a sign of merit, quality, or rank **5.** = **asterisk 6.** ARTS, SPORTS **POPULAR PERFORMER** a very famous, successful, and popular performer, especially in the field of entertainment or sports **7. MOST IMPORTANT OR PROFICIENT PERSON** somebody who is particularly good at some activity, or who is the most important or most skillful member of a group involved in a particular activity **8.** ZODIAC **CELESTIAL BODY IN RELATION TO FATE** a planet or constellation believed to influence somebody's character or fate on Earth ■ **stars** *npl.* ZODIAC **DESTINY** somebody's future, especially as supposedly revealed in a horoscope (*informal*) ■ *v.* **(starred, star·ring, stars) 1.** *vt.* THEATER **HAVE AS LEADING ACTOR** to have somebody as the leading performer or as one of the leading performers **2.** *vi.* THEATER **BE LEADING PERFORMER** to be the leading performer or one of the leading performers in something such as a movie or play **3.** *vt.* PRINTING **MARK SOMETHING WITH STAR** to mark something with an asterisk or a star-shaped symbol, especially to call attention to it **4.** *vt.* **COVER OR DECORATE SOMETHING WITH STARS** to cover or decorate something with stars, or with many brilliant or colorful objects so as to give an effect comparable to that of the stars in the night sky ■ *adj.* **OUTSTANDING** very or most important, skillful, or successful [Old English *steorra*. Ultimately from an Indo-European word that is also the ancestor of Latin *stella* (source of English *stellar*).] ◇ **see stars** see flashes of light, e.g., after receiving a hard blow to the head

star an·ise *n.* **1. CHINESE EVERGREEN TREE** a Chinese evergreen tree of the magnolia family that produces purple-red flowers and whose dried seeds and seed pods are used in Chinese cooking and medicine. Latin name: *Illicium verum.* **2. STAR ANISE SEED POD** the star-shaped aniseed-flavored dried seed and seed pod of the star anise tree, used in Chinese cooking and medicine

star ap·ple *n.* **1.** TREES **TROPICAL AMERICAN EVERGREEN TREE** a tropical American evergreen tree that bears purplish-white flowers and produces an apple-shaped fruit with a smooth greenish-purple skin. Latin name: *Chrysophyllum cainito.* **2.** FOOD **FRUIT OF THE STAR APPLE TREE** the fruit of the star apple tree, which is shaped like an apple and when cut open reveals an arrangement of seeds resembling a star

Sta·ra Za·go·ra /stàrrə zə górrə/ city in central Bulgaria, situated about 95 mi./153 km west of the Black Sea port of Burgas. Population: 151,218 (1995).

star bill·ing *n.* the fact of being advertised as the leading performer in something

star·board /staárbərd/ *n.* **RIGHT-HAND SIDE** the direction to the right of somebody facing the front of a ship or aircraft ■ *adj.* **ON RIGHT-HAND SIDE** on, toward, or from the right-hand side of somebody facing the front of a ship or aircraft ■ *adv.* **TOWARD STARBOARD** toward starboard or the starboard side of a ship or aircraft ■ *vt.* **(-board·ed, -board·ing, -boards) TURN TOWARD STARBOARD** to turn or move something, especially the helm, toward starboard [Old English *stēorbord*, from *stēor* "paddle" + *bord* "board." The modern meaning arose from the early Germanic custom of steering boats by means of a paddle on the right side.]

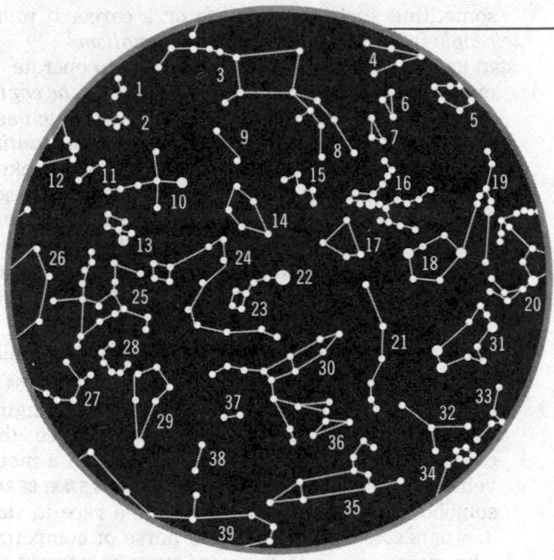

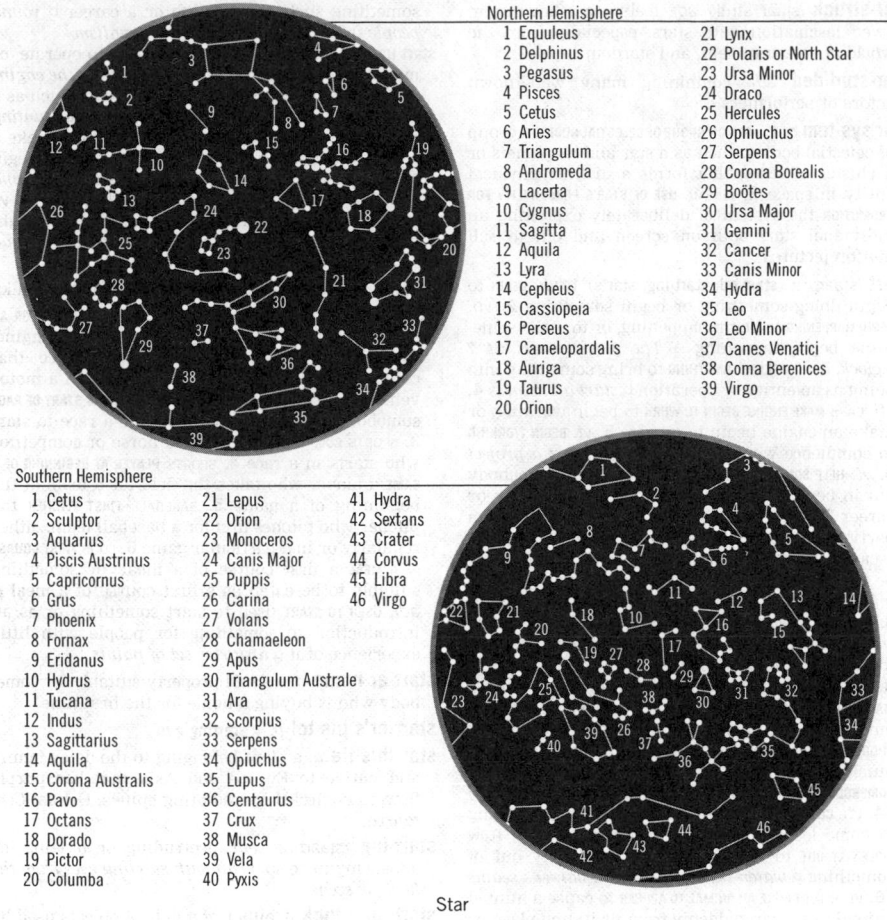

Northern Hemisphere

1 Equuleus
2 Delphinus
3 Pegasus
4 Pisces
5 Cetus
6 Aries
7 Triangulum
8 Andromeda
9 Lacerta
10 Cygnus
11 Sagitta
12 Aquila
13 Lyra
14 Cepheus
15 Cassiopeia
16 Perseus
17 Camelopardalis
18 Auriga
19 Taurus
20 Orion
21 Lynx
22 Polaris or North Star
23 Ursa Minor
24 Draco
25 Hercules
26 Ophiuchus
27 Serpens
28 Corona Borealis
29 Boötes
30 Ursa Major
31 Gemini
32 Cancer
33 Canis Minor
34 Hydra
35 Leo
36 Leo Minor
37 Canes Venatici
38 Coma Berenices
39 Virgo

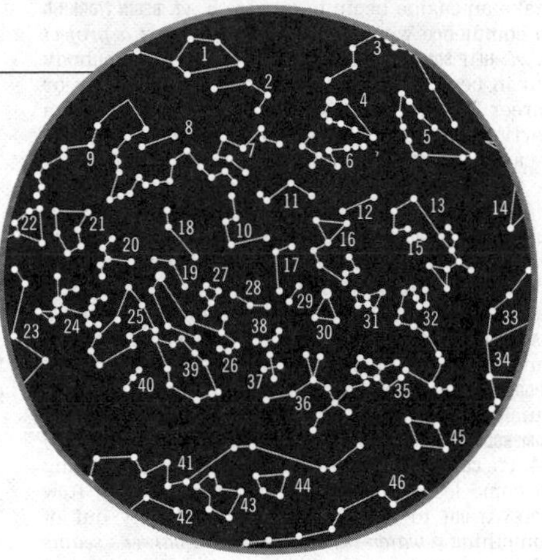

Southern Hemisphere

1 Cetus
2 Sculptor
3 Aquarius
4 Piscis Austrinus
5 Capricornus
6 Grus
7 Phoenix
8 Fornax
9 Eridanus
10 Hydrus
11 Tucana
12 Indus
13 Sagittarius
14 Aquila
15 Corona Australis
16 Pavo
17 Octans
18 Dorado
19 Pictor
20 Columba
21 Lepus
22 Orion
23 Monoceros
24 Canis Major
25 Puppis
26 Carina
27 Volans
28 Chamaeleon
29 Apus
30 Triangulum Australe
31 Ara
32 Scorpius
33 Serpens
34 Opiuchus
35 Lupus
36 Centaurus
37 Crux
38 Musca
39 Vela
40 Pyxis
41 Hydra
42 Sextans
43 Crater
44 Corvus
45 Libra
46 Virgo

Star

star·burst /staár bùrst/ *n.* a pattern of lines or light rays radiating outward from a center

star cac·tus *n.* a Mexican cactus with yellow flowers and spines arranged in clusters like stars. Genus: *Astrophytum.*

starch /staarch/ *n.* **1. CARBOHYDRATE SUBSTANCE** a carbohydrate substance manufactured by plants and stored in seeds, tubers, fruits, and stems and forming an important source of energy in the diet of human beings and animals. The two main components of starch are amylose and amylopectin. Formula: $(C_6H_{10}O_5)_n$. **2.** HOUSEHOLD **STIFFENING SUBSTANCE FOR FABRICS** a substance, especially natural starch in the form of a white powder extracted from potatoes and grain, used to stiffen the fabric of clothes before ironing **3.** FOOD **STARCHY FOODSTUFF** a foodstuff that contains a large amount of starch **4. STIFF AND FORMAL MANNER** behavior marked by a stiff manner and formality **5. COURAGE** great courage or energy ■ *vt.* **(starched, starch·ing, starch·es)** HOUSEHOLD **STIFFEN WITH STARCH** to stiffen fabric with starch [Old English (assumed) *stercan* "to stiffen," from a prehistoric Germanic base meaning "to be rigid," which is also the ancestor of English *stare*]

star cham·ber *n.* a court or tribunal noted for being harsh, arbitrary, and unaccountable in its proceedings

Star Cham·ber *n.* a court established by King Henry VII of England to try civil and criminal cases, especially those involving the security of the state, in secret. It was noted for its arbitrary proceedings and abolished in 1641. [*Star* because the ceiling of the original courtroom was decorated with stars]

starch syr·up *n.* a syrup created through the incomplete hydrolysis of glucose that contains dextrose, maltose, and dextrine

starch wheat *n.* = **emmer**

starch·y /staárchee/ **(-i·er, -i·est)** *adj.* **1. CONTAINING STARCH** containing a large amount of starch, or like starch, especially in consistency **2. FORMAL** very formal and unbending, and apparently lacking in warmth or a sense of humor

star con·nec·tion *n.* an electrical connection in a polyphase system in which the windings have one end connected to a common junction and the other ends connected to separate load points

star-crossed *adj.* believed to be destined by fate to be unhappy [From the belief in the influence of the stars over human lives]

star·dom /staárdəm/ *n.* **1. STAR STATUS** the status of a star performer in sports or entertainment, and the fame and prestige that go with it **2. STAR PERFORMERS** star performers considered as a group

star·dust /staár dùst/ *n.* **1. DREAMY ROMANTIC FEELING** a dreamy romantic sentimental feeling, or an imaginary substance, usually represented as starry and twinkling, that is supposed to induce this feeling **2.** ASTRON **FAR DISTANT STARS** far distant stars in a cluster or strewn like a cloud of bright dust in the night sky

stare /stair/ *v.* **(stared, star·ing, stares) 1.** *vti.* **LOOK FIXEDLY** to look directly at somebody or something for a long time without moving the eyes away, usually as a result of curiosity or surprise, or to express rudeness or defiance **2.** *vi.* **BE WIDE OPEN WITH SHOCK** to look wide open with shock, fear, or amazement (*refers to eyes*) **3.** *vi.* **BE OBVIOUS** to be obvious or blatant ○ *The answer was staring at you all the time; you just couldn't see it.* ■ *n.* **1. LONG CONCENTRATED LOOK** a long concentrated look at somebody or something, often full of curiosity or hostility **2. FACIAL EXPRESSION** a facial expression in which the eyes are wide open with shock or amazement and looking fixedly at somebody or something [Old English *starian*, from a prehistoric Germanic base meaning "to be rigid," which is also the ancestor of English *stern*. The underlying idea is of "something fixed."] —**star·er** *n.*

WORD KEY: SYNONYMS

See Synonyms at *gaze.*

stare down *vt.* **1. LOOK SOMEBODY DIRECTLY IN THE EYES** to look somebody directly in the eyes until he or she is forced to look away **2. CAUSE SOMEBODY TO BACK DOWN** to intimidate somebody or something into backing down ○ *two hostile nations trying to stare each other down*

stare out *vt. U.K.* = **stare down**

sta·rets /staá rèts/ (*plural* **star·tsy** /staártsee/) *n.* a religious teacher or spiritual adviser in the Eastern Orthodox Church, especially one who is a monk or holy man [Early 20thC. From Russian, "elderly man, elder."]

star fac·et *n.* one of the eight small triangular facets that surround the table of a gem cut in the brilliant style

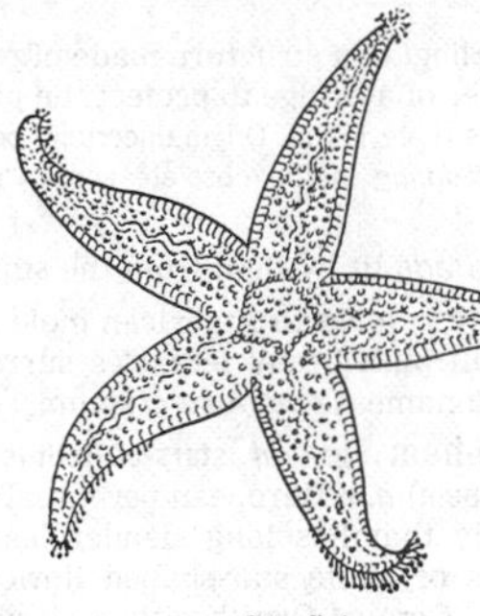

Starfish

star·fish /staár fish/ (*plural* **-fish** *or* **-fish·es**) *n.* a marine invertebrate animal **(echinoderm)** whose body consists of five or more arms radiating from a central disk. Starfish have a central mouth on the underside and feed on oysters and other mollusks on shores and the seabed. Class: Asteroidea.

star·fish flow·er *n.* = **stapelia**

star·flow·er /staár flòw ər/ *n.* a plant that has star-shaped flowers, e.g., the star-of-Bethlehem and some plants of northeastern North America

star fruit *n.* = **carambola**

star·gaze /staár gàyz/ **(-gazed, -gaz·ing, -gaz·es)** *vi.* **1. WATCH STARS AT NIGHT** to observe the stars at night **2. DAYDREAM** to engage in daydreaming

star·gaz·er /staár gàyzər/ *n.* **1. DAYDREAMER** somebody who daydreams **2.** ZOOL **TROPICAL MARINE FISH** a bottom-dwelling tropical marine fish that has eyes and mouth on the top of its head. Families: Uranoscopidae and Dactyloscopidae.

star grass *n.* a plant of the daffodil family found in tropical and temperate regions that has long leaves that look like grass and star-shaped white or yellow flowers. Genus: *Hypoxis.*

stark /staark/ *adj.* **1. FORBIDDINGLY BARE AND PLAIN** forbidding in its bareness and lack of any ornament, relieving feature, or pleasant prospect **2. UNAMBIGUOUS AND HARSH** presented in plain, unambiguous, and usually rather harsh terms ○ *confronting stark reality* **3. COMPLETE** having reached the fullest extent or degree of something **4. WITHOUT CLOTHES** completely unclothed and uncovered **5. RIGID** showing or affected by rigor mortis (*archaic*) ■ *adv.* **UTTERLY** to the utmost degree [Old English *stearc*, from a prehistoric Germanic base meaning "to be rigid," which is also the ancestor of English *stare* and *starve*] —**stark·ly** *adv.* —**stark·ness** *n.*

Hulton-Deutsch Collection/Corbis

Dame Freya Stark

Stark /staark/, **Dame Freya** (1893–1993) British writer. She wrote over 30 travel books describing aspects of the Middle East, especially life in the deserts. Full name **Dame Freya Madeline Stark**

stark-na·ked *adj.* completely unclothed and uncovered

star·let /staárlət/ *n.* a young woman actor billed as a possible major movie star of the future

star·light /staar līt/ *n.* the light that comes from the stars

star·ling[1] /staarling/ *n.* a common European bird with glossy greenish-black plumage, a short tail, and pointed wings. Starlings often gather in large noisy flocks to feed and roost. Latin name: *Sturnus vulgaris.* [Old English *stærlinc,* literally "little starling," from *stær* "starling." Ultimately from a prehistoric Germanic word.]

star·ling[2] /staarling/ *n.* a structure made of piles surrounding a pier of a bridge to protect the pier from floating debris [Late 17thC. Origin uncertain: perhaps an alteration of *staddling* in the obsolete sense "pier of a bridge."]

star·lit /staar lit/ *adj.* lit by light from the stars

star-nosed mole *n.* a North American mole that has a ring of small pink fleshy tentacles surrounding its nose. Latin name: *Condylura cristata.*

star-of-Beth·le·hem (*plural* **stars-of-Beth·le·hem** *or* **star-of-Beth·le·hem**) *n.* a European perennial plant of the lily family that has long slender leaves and bears clusters of white star-shaped flowers on a central stalk. Genus: *Ornithogalum.* [Late 16thC. From its abundance in Palestine.]

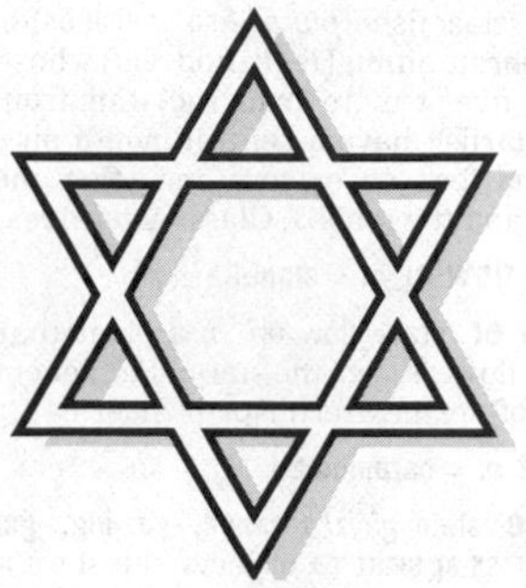

Star of David

Star of Da·vid *n.* a symbol of the Jewish faith and of the state of Israel consisting of two equilateral triangles superimposed on each other to form a six-pointed star

Starr /staar/, **Ringo** (*b.* 1940) British musician. He attained fame as the drummer of the Beatles (1962–70). Real name **Richard Starkey**

star ru·by *n.* a ruby with a crystalline structure that reflects light in a shape that resembles a star when it is cut with a convex surface

star·ry /staaree/ (**-ri·er, -ri·est**) *adj.* **1.** WITH MANY STARS SHINING bright with many shining stars **2.** COVERED WITH STARS covered or decorated with stars **3.** SIMILAR TO STAR relating to or similar in shape or brightness to a star

star·ry-eyed *adj.* having a happy and enthusiastic or romantic attitude that is naïve and unrealistic

Stars and Bars *n.* the first flag of the Confederacy during the Civil War, which had two red stripes and one white, and a circle of white stars representing the seceded states (*takes a singular or plural verb*)

Stars and Stripes *n.* the national flag of the United States, which has 13 alternating red and white stripes and one star for each state on a blue field (*takes a singular or plural verb*)

star sap·phire *n.* a sapphire with a crystalline structure that reflects light in a star shape when cut with a convex surface

star shell *n.* an artillery shell designed to burst in midair and release a flare or a shower of lights

star·ship /staar ship/ *n.* a spaceship designed to travel between stars or star systems, and as yet existing only in science fiction

star sign *n.* a sign of the zodiac, especially the sun sign under which somebody was born

star-span·gled *adj.* **1.** COVERED WITH STARS covered or decorated with stars **2.** FILLED WITH VIPS AND STARS attended by many important people, including politicians, CEOs, and movie stars ○ *The State Dinner was a star-spangled gathering unequaled in history.*

Star-Span·gled Ban·ner *n.* **1.** U.S. NATIONAL ANTHEM the national anthem of the United States **2.** NATIONAL FLAG OF U.S. the national flag of the United States

star·struck /staar strùk/ *adj.* feeling or showing an awed fascination with stars, especially from the world of entertainment, and stardom

star-stud·ded *adj.* containing many well-known actors or performers

star sys·tem *n.* **1.** ASTRON GROUP OF CELESTIAL BODIES a group of celestial bodies, such as a star and its planets or a cluster of stars, that forms a distinct physical entity in space **2.** CINEMA USE OF STAR'S PERSONALITY FOR PROMOTION the system of deliberately exploiting an individual star, both on screen and off, to sell motion pictures

start /staart/ *v.* (**start·ed, start·ing, starts**) **1.** *vti.* BEGIN to begin doing something or begin something **2.** *vti.* BEGIN HAPPENING to begin happening, or to make something begin happening ○ *The movie starts at 7 o'clock.* **3.** *vt.* CREATE SOMETHING to bring something into being as an entity or operation ○ *start a business* **4.** *vti.* CARS MAKE ENGINE BEGIN TO WORK to begin working, or make an engine begin to operate **5.** *vt.* BEGIN WORKING to commence work on something ○ *start a project* **6.** *vt.* HELP SOMEBODY BEGIN SOMETHING to help somebody out in beginning an activity such as a journey or career **7.** *vi.* GO FROM A PARTICULAR LEVEL to begin at a particular level ○ *Prices start at fifteen dollars.* **8.** *vti.* SPORTS PLAY FIRST IN A CONTEST to be or select somebody to be in a race or to play at the beginning of a game ○ *finally agreed to start the rookie in the next game* **9.** *vi.* BEGIN ARGUING to begin arguing or making a fuss (*informal*) ○ *Please don't start.* **10.** *vt.* RAISE SOMETHING to raise or care for something in the early stages of its growth ○ *start some plants in early spring* **11.** *vi.* MAKE SUDDEN MOVEMENT to make a sudden movement out of surprise, pain, fear, or anger **12.** *vti.* MOVE SUDDENLY to go or cause a person or animal to go very quickly from being still to moving **13.** *vt.* ALARM SOMEBODY to cause somebody to be alarmed (*archaic*) **14.** *vti.* COME LOOSE to come loose, or cause something to come loose, from its proper place **15.** *vi.* FLOW VIOLENTLY OUT to flow violently or suddenly out of something ○ *water starting from the barrel's seams* **16.** *vt.* HUNT CAUSE AN ANIMAL TO APPEAR to cause a hunted animal to appear suddenly from its hiding place or den ■ *n.* **1.** BEGINNING the first part of something that proceeds through time ○ *We missed the start of the play.* **2.** PLACE OR TIME OF START the place or time at which something starts ○ *The start of the race is scheduled for noon.* **3.** QUICK SUDDEN MOVEMENT a quick sudden movement from being still to moving **4.** SUDDEN INVOLUNTARY MOVEMENT a sudden involuntary movement caused by fear, pain, surprise, or anger **5.** SPORTS INSTANCE OF PARTICIPATING the fact or an instance of participating in a race or game ○ *winning three out of five starts* **6.** POSITION AHEAD OF OTHERS a position of being ahead of other competitors ○ *get a start on the rest* **7.** POSITION AT THE BEGINNING a set of circumstances at the beginning of something ○ *He needed a better start in life.* **8.** SIGNAL TO BEGIN the signal to begin something such as a race [12thC. Origin uncertain: probably ultimately from Old English *styrtan* "to jump," from prehistoric Germanic. The meaning "to begin" would have developed from "move suddenly" via "begin a journey."] ◇ **for a start, for starters** used in an argument to indicate that you are making the first point of many ◇ **to start with** at the beginning

start in *vi.* **1.** BEGIN to begin to do something (*informal*) ○ *Let's start in now so we can get this work done.* **2.** BEGIN TO SCOLD to begin to scold or criticize somebody ○ *Don't start on me again.*

start off *v.* **1.** *vti.* BEGIN to begin to do something, or cause or help somebody to begin to do something ○ *Let's start off by introducing ourselves.* **2.** *vi.* SET OFF to begin moving in a particular direction, or begin a journey ○ *She turned and started off up the hill.* **3.** *vt.* MAKE SOMEBODY START TALKING OR LAUGHING to do something that causes somebody else to start doing something such as talking, laughing, crying, or misbehaving (*informal*) ○ *Stop it, or you'll start her off again.*

start on *vt.* to begin to scold, criticize, or attack somebody (*informal*) ○ *Look, don't start on me. It's not my fault!*

start out *vi.* **1.** BEGIN JOURNEY to set off on a journey ○ *If we start out at about nine, we should be there in time for lunch.* **2.** BEGIN to do something at the beginning of a process ○ *He starts out trying to prove she's guilty and ends up convincing everyone she's innocent.* **3.** INTEND to intend to do something, or have something as an initial intention ○ *I didn't start out to cause a lot of trouble.* **4.** BEGIN STAGE OF LIFE to make a start in something such as adult life or a career ○ *young people who are starting out in journalism*

start up *v.* **1.** *vti.* BEGIN TO OPERATE to begin to operate, or make something begin to operate ○ *start the engine up* **2.** *vti.* OPEN BUSINESS to begin something such as a business venture ○ *started up her own accounting practice* **3.** *vi.* BEGIN TO MAKE SOUND to begin to make a sound, especially a characteristic sound, or begin to speak ○ *First a solitary blackbird started up, and soon the whole forest was alive with birdsong.* **4.** *vi.* RISE SUDDENLY to rise suddenly to a standing or upright position ○ *He started up from his chair at the loud sound and rushed to the window.*

START /staart/ *abbr.* Strategic Arms Reduction Talks

start·er /staartər/ *n.* **1.** MECH ENG STARTING DEVICE FOR AN ENGINE a device for starting a machine or engine, especially an electrically operated device that causes the internal-combustion engine in a motor vehicle to fire **2.** SPORTS SOMEBODY SIGNALING START OF RACE somebody who gives the signal for a race to start **3.** SPORTS COMPETITOR WHO STARTS a horse or competitor who starts in a race **4.** SPORTS PLAYER AT BEGINNING OF A GAME a player who takes the field for a team at the beginning of a game **5.** BASEBALL FIRST PITCHER the pitcher who pitches first for a baseball team, either regularly or in a particular game **6.** FOOD FIRST COURSE OF A MEAL a first course of a meal, or something suitable to be eaten as a first course of a meal ■ *adj.* USED TO START used to start something or as an introduction to something for people with little experience of it ○ *a starter set of paints*

start·er home *n.* a small property suitable for somebody who is buying a home for the first time

start·er's pis·tol *n.* = **starting gun**

star this·tle *n.* a plant belonging to the daisy family and native to Europe and Asia that has purple flowers encircled by radiating spines. Genus: *Centaurea.*

start·ing /staarting/ *adj.* protruding or bulging, or appearing to do so ○ *ran with starting eyes from the horrific scene*

start·ing block *n.* either of a pair of objects used by runners to brace their feet against at the start of a sprint race. The blocks are made up of a base that can be firmly placed onto the track and angled supports against which the runner places the feet.

start·ing gate *n.* **1.** STALLS HORSES LEAVE TO START A RACE a line of stalls into which racehorses are put at the start of a race that have gates at the front that spring open simultaneously when operated by the starter **2.** BARRIER CONNECTED TO TIMER a physical barrier or electronic beam that automatically starts a timing device when a competitor passes through it, e.g., at the start of a skiing race

start·ing grid *n.* a pattern of lines marked on an auto racing track, with numbered starting positions. The cars that recorded the fastest times in practice occupy the front positions.

start·ing gun *n.* a gun fired as the signal for a race to start

start·ing line *n.* a line marked across a racetrack to show runners where to start

star·tle /staart'l/ (**-tled, -tling, -tles**) *vt.* to disconcert or frighten a person or an animal into making an involuntary movement, or become disconcerted or frightened by a sudden shock [Old English *steartlian,* from a prehistoric Germanic base that is also the ancestor of English *start*] —**star·tler** *n.*

star·tle col·or *n.* a patch of bright color or a bold design on part of an animal's body that is normally hidden and is revealed to scare away predators

star·tling /staartling/ *adj.* provoking surprise, fright, wonder, or alarm —**star·tling·ly** *adv.*

star·tsy plural of **starets**

start-up /staart ùp/, **start-up** *n.* **1.** SOMETHING JUST BEGINNING something such as a company that is just beginning operations **2.** COMMENCEMENT OF SOMETHING the beginning of an activity such as the construction of a building

star·va·tion /staar váysh'n/ *n.* the state of having not enough food, or of losing strength or dying through lack of food

starve /staarv/ (**starved, starv·ing, starves**) *v.* **1.** *vti.* WEAKEN OR DIE BECAUSE OF HUNGER to weaken or die through lack of food, or cause somebody to do this ○ *The besieged city was starved into submission.* **2.** *vi.* BE HUNGRY to be very hungry (*informal*) ○ *I'm starving! What's for* *dinner?* **3.** *vt.* **DEPRIVE SOMEBODY** to deprive somebody or something of something vitally needed ○ *starved for affection* **4.** *vi.* **NEED** to feel deprived of something, or feel a great need or desire for something ○ *starving for a kind word* [Old English *steorfan* "to die," from a prehistoric Germanic base meaning "to be stiff"] —**starv·er** *n.*

starve out *vt.* to force an enemy to surrender by making necessary food and supplies inaccessible

starve·ling /stáarvling/ *n.* a very thin and hungry-looking person or animal (*archaic*)

star·wort /stáar wúrt, -wàwrt/ (*plural* **-worts** *or* **-wort**) *n.* = **water starwort**

stash /stash/ *n.* **1. HIDDEN STORE** a secret or hidden store of something such as money or valuables (*informal*) **2. HIDING PLACE** a secret hiding place (*informal*) **3. SECRET STORE OF DRUGS** a store of illegal drugs kept for personal consumption (*slang*) ■ *vt.* (**stashed, stash·ing, stash·es**) **1. HIDE SOMETHING** to put something into a secret hidden storage place (*informal*) **2. PUT SOMETHING AWAY** to put something somewhere, e.g., in a convenient place or where it belongs ○ *We'll eat after we've stashed our gear.* [Late 18thC. Origin unknown.]

sta·sis /stáyssiss/ *n.* **1. MOTIONLESS STATE** a state in which there is neither motion nor development, often resulting from opposing forces balancing each other **2.** MED **STOPPAGE OF FLOW OF BODY FLUIDS** a condition in which body fluids, such as blood or the contents of the bowel, are prevented from flowing normally through their channels **3.** BIOL **STATE OF NO CHANGE** a state in which there is little or no apparent change in a species of organism over a long period of time. It is most evident in so-called living fossils, such as the coelacanth, which have remained unchanged for many millions of years. [Mid-18thC. Via modern Latin from Greek, "standing, stoppage." Ultimately from an Indo-European word that is also the ancestor of English *stand*.]

stat[1] /stat/ *n.* a statistic (*informal*) [Mid-20thC. Shortening.]

stat[2] /stat/ *adv.* MED **IMMEDIATELY** used in prescriptions to indicate that a drug is to be given immediately ■ *adj.* MED **URGENT** urgent ○ *The doctor received a stat page while on call.* [Late 19thC. Shortening of Latin *statim* "immediately."]

stat. *abbr.* **1.** statue **2.** statute **3.** stationary

-stat *suffix.* **1.** device for stabilizing or regulating ○ *humidistat* ○ *rheostat* **2.** a device for focusing something in a single direction ○ *siderostat* **3.** a substance or device that inhibits the growth or flow of something ○ *fungistat* ○ *haemostat* [Via modern Latin *-stata* from Greek *statos* "standing" and *statēs* "one that causes to stand"]

state /stayt/ *n.* **1. CONDITION** the condition that something or somebody is in at a particular time **2. PHYSICAL STAGE** a growth or developmental stage of an animal or plant ○ *the larval state* **3.** POL **MOSTLY AUTONOMOUS REGION OF FEDERAL COUNTRY** an area forming part of a federal country such as the United States or Australia with its own government and legislature and control over most of its own internal affairs **4.** POL **COUNTRY** a country or nation with its own sovereign independent government **5.** POL **GOVERNMENT** a country's government and those government-controlled institutions that are responsible for its internal administration and its relationships with other countries ○ *a corporation owned and run by the state* **6. NERVOUS, UPSET, OR EXCITED CONDITION** a very nervous, upset, or excited frame of mind or manner of behaving (*informal*) ○ *Don't get into a state worrying about money.* **7. CEREMONIOUS STYLE** a very formal, dignified or grand way of doing something in which all the appropriate ceremonies are observed ○ *The senator will lie in state in the Capitol rotunda.* **8.** PHYS **FORM OR ENERGY LEVEL** any of the various forms such as solid or liquid or quantifiable conditions such as energy levels that a physical substance can be in depending on its temperature and other circumstances **9. BAD PHYSICAL CONDITION** a very messy or disreputable condition (*informal*) ○ *The house is in such a state that we'll never get it clean.* ■ *adj.* **1.** POL **RELATING TO GOVERNMENT** involving or relating to a state or to its government **2.** POL **HELD OR RUN BY A STATE** owned, operated, or financed by a state **3. DONE WITH FULL CEREMONY** involving many grand rituals and ceremonies, especially those appropriate to a head of state ○ *worn only on state occasions* ■ *vt.* (**stat·ed, stat·ing, states**) **1. EXPRESS IN WORDS** to express something in spoken or written words, especially to announce something publicly in a deliberate formal way ○ *I have already stated my position on this issue.* **2.** LAW **DECLARE WITH FORCE OF LAW** to declare something officially so that it has the force of a law or regulation ○ *It is expressly stated in your contract that you must not work for another employer.* **3.** MUSIC **PLAY MUSICAL THEME FOR FIRST TIME** to play a particular musical theme or motif for the first time before it is repeated and developed within a piece of music [12thC. Directly or via Old French *estat* from Latin *status* "way of standing, condition" (as in *status rei publicae* "condition of the republic").]

state bank *n.* a bank that receives its charter from, and operates under the laws of, a state of the United States

state cap·i·tal·ism *n.* an economic system in which the state controls the use of capital and the means of production

state·craft /stáyt kràft/ *n.* the art of governing or managing the affairs of a country well

stat·ed /stáytəd/ *adj.* **1. OFFICIALLY LAID DOWN** laid down by an official agreement or in a legal document **2. PREVIOUSLY ANNOUNCED** announced previously, especially in a public medium

State De·part·ment *n.* the department of the United States government that deals with foreign affairs and is headed by a Cabinet secretary and staffed by career foreign service officers

state·hood /stáyt hòòd/ *n.* the status of a state in a federal union, especially in the United States, as opposed to that of a territory or dependency

state·hood·er /stáyt hòòdər/ *n.* a person who advocates full U.S. state status for, e.g., a territory or commonwealth

state·house /stáyt hòwss/ (*plural* **-hous·es** /-hòwzəz/), **state house, State·house** (*plural* **-hous·es**) *n.* a building in which a state legislature convenes in any of the U.S. state capitals

state·less /stáytləss/ *adj.* not being a citizen of any country and having no nationality

state·less so·ci·e·ty *n.* a society, e.g., one in Africa, organized around kinship or other forms of obligation and lacking the concentration of political power and authority associated with states

state·ly /stáytlee/ (**-li·er, -li·est**) *adj.* **1. IMPRESSIVELY WEIGHTY AND DIGNIFIED** characterized by an impressively weighty and dignified but graceful manner **2. GRAND AND IMPOSING** grand and imposing in appearance

state·ment /stáytmənt/ *n.* **1. EXPRESSION IN WORDS** the expression in spoken or written words of something such as a fact, intention, or policy, or an instance of this **2. SOMETHING SAID** something that somebody says that is not a question or an exclamation and that expresses an idea or facts in definite terms ○ *We were unable to verify the truth of that statement.* **3. SPECIALLY PREPARED PUBLIC ANNOUNCEMENT** a specially prepared announcement or reply that is made public ○ *Has she made a statement to the press?* **4.** CRIMINOL **ACCOUNT OF FACTS** an account of the facts relating to a crime or case given to the police or in a court of law usually for use as evidence **5.** ARTS **WORDLESS EXPRESSION OF IDEA** a bold or conspicuous expression of an idea, opinion, or concept made in a nonverbal way ○ *Her art is a powerful statement of her political beliefs.* **6.** FIN **PRINTED RECORD OF BANK ACCOUNT** a printed record of all transactions that have taken place over a period of time in a bank account and of the amount of the holder's current credit or debt **7.** FIN **CUSTOMER'S ACCOUNT** an account issued to a customer showing charges made, payments received, and any balance owing **8.** MUSIC **FIRST PRESENTATION OF MUSICAL THEME** the first presentation of a theme or idea that is to be developed later in a piece of music **9.** COMPUT **COMPUTER INSTRUCTION** a computer instruction written in a source language

Sta·ten Is·land /státt'n-/ one of the five boroughs of New York. It has a regular ferry service to Manhattan and is mainly residential. Population: 378,977 (1990).

state of the art *n.* **MOST ADVANCED LEVEL OF TECHNOLOGY** the most advanced level of knowledge and technology currently achieved in any field at any given time ■ *adj.* **state-of-the-art MOST ADVANCED** representing the most advanced level of knowledge or technology currently achieved in any field at any given time

state of war *n.* **1. ACTUAL HOSTILITIES** armed conflict between states or other groups, with or without a formal declaration of war **2. LEGAL SITUATION OF DECLARATION OF WAR** the situation brought about by a declaration of war, with or without the commencement of actual armed conflict, in which special internationally agreed-on laws apply

state pris·on *n.* a prison run by a state of the United States in which prisoners convicted of serious crimes are held

stat·er[1] /stáytər/, **Stat·er** *n.* somebody who comes from a particular state, especially of the United States, or from a particular type of state (*usually used in combination*) ○ *Bay Staters are from Massachusetts.*

sta·ter[2] /stáytər/ *n.* any of various ancient Greek coins in gold or silver [14thC. Via late Latin from Greek *statēr*, from the base of *histanai* "to weigh."]

state·room /stáyt ròòm, -ròòm/ *n.* a large and luxuriously furnished private cabin on a ship or a private sleeping compartment on a train

state room *n.* a large imposing room in a palace or government building, used for large-scale functions and entertaining important guests

States /stayts/ *npl.* the United States of America (*informal*)

state's at·tor·ney, state at·tor·ney *n.* an attorney who acts as prosecutor in court cases on behalf of a state

state school *n.* an institution, usually a prison for delinquent minors, that is controlled and financed by a state government (*informal*)

state se·cret *n.* a piece of information, usually considered important to national security, that is supposed to be known only to certain people authorized by the state

state's ev·i·dence *n.* evidence given for the prosecution in a criminal trial in the United States and certain other nations, sometimes by one of the accused or by an accomplice to the crime, or the person who agrees to give such evidence ○ *His accomplice turned state's evidence in exchange for a reduced sentence.*

States-Gen·er·al *npl.* the legislative body in France before 1789, consisting of representatives of the three estates of the realm

state·side /stáyt sīd/ *adv.* **IN OR TOWARD UNITED STATES** in or toward the continental United States ■ *adj.* **RELATING TO UNITED STATES** relating to, in, or toward the continental United States

states·man /stáytsmən/ (*plural* **-men** /-mən/) *n.* **1. LEADING POLITICIAN** a senior politician who plays an important role in government or in international affairs **2. RESPECTED IMPARTIAL SENIOR MALE POLITICIAN** a senior politician who is widely respected for integrity and impartial concern for the public good —**states·man·like** *adj.* —**states·man·ship** *n.*

state so·cial·ism *n.* a political and economic system in which the state controls major industries and banks and plans its economic and social welfare programs in order to bring about an egalitarian society —**state so·cial·ist** *n.*

states' rights *npl.* **1. POWERS AND RIGHTS OF U.S. STATES** the powers and rights not granted by the U.S. Constitution to the federal government and not forbidden to the states by the Constitution **2. U.S. ANTIFEDERAL POLITICAL DOCTRINE** a political doctrine that advocates the reduction of federal rights and powers and a maximization of those of the U.S. states —**states' right·er** *n.*

states·wo·man /stáyts wòòmmən/ (*plural* **-men** /-wimmin/) *n.* **1. LEADING WOMAN POLITICIAN** a senior politician who plays an important role in government or in international affairs **2. RESPECTED IMPARTIAL SENIOR WOMAN POLITICIAN** a senior woman politician who is widely respected for integrity and impartial concern for the public good

state troop·er *n.* a member of the highway patrol police of a state

state·wide /stáyt wīd, -wīd/ *adj.* **AFFECTING ENTIRE STATE** affecting or happening throughout an entire state ○ *a statewide search for the escaped prisoner* ■ *adv.* **THROUGHOUT STATE** throughout an entire state

stat·ic /státtik/ *adj.* **1. MOTIONLESS** not moving or changing, or fixed in position **2.** PHYS **OF FORCES NOT CAUSING MOVEMENT** relating to forces, weight, or pressures that act without causing movement **3.** PHYS **INVOLVING STATICS** relating to, involving, or characteristic of statics

4. ELEC **INVOLVING STATIONARY ELECTRIC CHARGES** relating to, involving, or characteristic of stationary electric charges **5.** BROADCAST **CAUSED BY ELECTRICAL INTERFERENCE** relating to or caused by electrical interference in a radio or television broadcast **6.** COMPUT **NOT NEEDING TO BE REFRESHED** retaining its contents without having to be refreshed by the central processor (*refers to a random-access-memory computer chip*) ■ *n.* **1.** BROADCAST **ELECTRICAL INTERFERENCE** electrical interference in a radio or television broadcast, causing a random crackling noise or disruption of a picture **2.** ELEC = **static electricity 3. OPPOSITION OR INTERFERENCE** criticism, opposition, or unwanted interference by somebody else (*informal*) ○ *getting a lot of static from the boss* [Mid-19thC. Via modern Latin from Greek *statikos* "causing to stand," from *statos* "standing" (see STATO-).] —**stat·i·cal·ly** *adv.*

stat·i·ce /státtəssee/ *n.* = **sea lavender** [Mid-18thC. Via modern Latin, former genus name, from, ultimately, Greek *statikos* "causing to stand or stop" (see STATIC), because it stops the flow of blood.]

stat·ic e·lec·tric·i·ty *n.* a stationary electric charge that builds up on an insulated object, e.g., on a capacitor or a thundercloud

stat·ic line *n.* a rope attached to an aircraft and a parachutist's parachute. When the parachutist jumps from the aircraft the line opens the parachute automatically.

stat·ic pres·sure *n.* pressure not caused by motion at a point on the surface of an object moving freely in a flowing fluid

stat·ics /státtiks/ *n.* a branch of mechanics that deals with forces and systems in equilibrium (*takes a singular verb*)

stat·ic tube *n.* a tube used to measure the static pressure present in a moving fluid

sta·tion /stáysh'n/ *n.* **1. STOP ON RAILROAD OR BUS ROUTE** a place along a train or bus route where passengers are picked up or set down, often with amenities such as ticket offices, waiting rooms, refreshments, toilets, and facilities for goods and parcels **2. LOCAL BRANCH OF AN ORGANIZATION** a local branch or headquarters of an official organization such as the police force, fire department, or ambulance service **3. SPECIALLY EQUIPPED BUILDING** a building or group of buildings that provides a particular function or service ○ *a pumping station* **4.** BROADCAST **BROADCASTING BUILDING** a place equipped to make and broadcast radio or television programs **5.** BROADCAST **BROADCASTING CHANNEL** a television or radio channel **6. USUAL PLACE** the place or position where somebody or something is usually to be found or is supposed to be found **7. POSITION FOR PERFORMING TASK** a position where somebody performs a task, e.g., in a factory, or the equipment used in performing a task **8. RANK** the position somebody holds in society or in an organization in terms of rank **9.** MIL **MILITARY POSTING** a place where military personnel are sent to carry out duties **10.** SHIPPING **PLACE ON SHIP FOR CREW MEMBER** a place on board a ship where a crew member carries out duties **11.** NAVY **PLACE WHERE SHIP IS SENT** a place where a naval ship or fleet is sent for a period of duty **12.** *ANZ* **SHEEP OR CATTLE FARM** a large farm in Australia or New Zealand where sheep or cattle are raised **13.** CIV ENG **SURVEYOR'S REFERENCE POINT** a fixed point used by surveyors as a reference **14.** CHR **STATION OF THE CROSS** one of the Stations of the Cross **15.** *U.K.* **MILITARY OR GOVERNMENT SETTLEMENT IN INDIA** a place where military officers or government officials lived in India while it was under British rule ■ *vt.* **(-tioned, -tion·ing, -tions) PUT IN OR SEND TO A PLACE** to assign somebody to a particular place, or put something in a particular place (*often passive*) [Mid-16thC. Via Old French from the Latin stem *station-* "standing still," from *stare* "to stand" (source of English *stage* and *obstacle*).]

sta·tion·ar·y /stáyshə nèrree/ *adj.* **1. NOT MOVING** not moving, especially at a standstill after being in motion **2. IMMOBILE** fixed in position and not able to be moved **3. UNCHANGING** not changing **4. STAYING IN ONE PLACE** showing a tendency to remain in the same place [15thC. Directly or via French *stationnaire* "motionless" from medieval Latin *stationarius*, from Latin, "of a military station," from the stem *station-* (see STATION).]

WORD KEY: USAGE

stationary or **stationery**? The two words are distantly related but have quite different meanings. ***Stationary*** is an adjective meaning "not moving" (normally used of vehicles), whereas ***stationery*** is a noun meaning "writing materials." Confusion can be avoided by remembering the connection between ***stationery*** and *stationer*, a seller of ***stationery***.

sta·tion·ar·y bi·cy·cle *n.* = **exercise bike**

sta·tion·ar·y front *n.* a weather condition in which the boundary between a cold air mass and a warm air mass is stationary

sta·tion·ar·y or·bit *n.* an orbit around a celestial body that has the same period as one revolution of the celestial body. An object in such an orbit appears stationary above the surface.

sta·tion·ar·y wave *n.* = **standing wave**

sta·tion break *n.* a time when a radio or television program is interrupted by an announcement giving the name, and sometimes other details, of the company that is broadcasting the program

sta·tion·er /stáysh'nər/ *n.* **1. SELLER OF STATIONERY** a person or store that sells stationery **2.** PUBL **BOOK PUBLISHER** a person or company that publishes or sells books (*archaic*)

WORD KEY: ORIGIN

In medieval Latin a *stationarius* was originally a "trader who kept a permanent stall" (as opposed to an itinerant seller) — the word's source, the Latin stem *station-* (see STATION), meant literally "standing, keeping still." Such permanent stores were comparatively rare in the Middle Ages. Of those that did exist, the commonest were bookstores, licensed by the universities, and so English adopted the Latin term. It has since come down in the world somewhat to "seller of paper, pens, etc." (a sense first recorded in the mid 17th century).

sta·tion·er·y /stáyshə nèrree/ *n.* paper, envelopes, pens, pencils, and other things used in writing

WORD KEY: USAGE

See Usage note at ***stationary***.

sta·tion house *n.* a building housing a police department or precinct office, or a fire department

sta·tion·mas·ter /stáysh'n màstər/ *n.* somebody whose job is to oversee the running of a railroad station

Sta·tions of the Cross *npl.* **1. SERIES OF 14 IMAGES** a series of 14 images around the inside of a Roman Catholic church, each representing a stage in Jesus Christ's road to Calvary **2. SERIES OF 14 PRAYERS** a Roman Catholic devotion in which a prayer is said before each of the Stations of the Cross

sta·tion-to-sta·tion *adj.* **CHARGED FROM TIME OF ANSWER** charged from the time somebody answers the telephone (*dated*) ■ *adv.* **BY STATION-TO-STATION CALL** by a station-to-station call

sta·tion wag·on *n. U.S., Can, ANZ* an automobile with an extended area behind the rear seats that provides extra seating or carrying capacity, usually with a tailgate [Originally a covered carriage for transporting passengers to and from train stations]

stat·ism /stáy tìzəm/ *n.* the theory, or its practice, that economic and political power should be controlled by a central government leaving regional government and the individual with relatively little say in political matters [Early 17thC. Formed from STATE.] —**stat·ist** *n.*

sta·tis·tic /stə tístik/ *n.* **1. ELEMENT OF DATA** a single element of data from a collection **2. NUMERICAL VALUE OR FUNCTION** a numerical value or function, such as a mean or standard deviation, used to describe a sample or population **3. PIECE OF INFORMATION** somebody or something treated as a piece of data or information [Late 18thC. Back-formation from STATISTICS.] —**sta·tis·ti·cal** *adj.* —**sta·tis·ti·cal·ly** *adv.*

sta·tis·ti·cal me·chan·ics *n.* the branch of physics that analyzes macroscopic systems by applying statistical principles to their microscopic constituents (*takes a singular verb*)

stat·is·ti·cian /stàttə stísh'n/ *n.* somebody who is skilled in statistics, or who compiles and works with statistics

sta·tis·tics /stə tístiks/ *n.* **BRANCH OF MATHEMATICS** a branch of mathematics that deals with the analysis and interpretation of numerical data in terms of samples and populations (*takes a singular verb*) ■ *npl.* **COLLECTION OF NUMERICAL DATA** a collection of numerical data ○ *this month's sales statistics* [Late 18thC. Via German *Statistik* from, ultimately, Latin *status* (see STATE). The underlying meaning is "the study of data relating to the state."]

sta·tive /stáytiv/ *adj.* **DEALING WITH STATES, NOT ACTIONS** used to describe a verb, e.g., "know" or "own," that deals with states, as opposed to one, e.g., "listen," "talk," or "go," that deals with actions ■ *n.* **STATIVE VERB** a verb dealing with states not actions [Mid-17thC. From Latin *stativus*, from *stat-*, past participle stem of *stare* (see STATION).]

stato- *prefix.* **1.** balance, equilibrium ○ *statoscope* **2.** resting ○ *statoblast* [From Greek *statos* "standing." Ultimately from an Indo-European base meaning "to stand," which is also the ancestor of English *stand*, *station*, and *status*.]

stat·o·blast /státtə blàst/ *n.* a chitin-encased body that serves as a means of asexual reproduction for freshwater bryozoans. It can withstand climatic extremes and prolonged dormancy.

stat·o·cyst /státtə sìst/ *n.* a fluid-filled organ of balance in some invertebrates such as the lobster containing suspended bony granules that, along with sensory cells, help it to determine its position

stat·o·lith /státtə lìth/ *n.* **1.** ZOOL **GRANULES WITHIN A STATOCYST** any of the tiny bony granules that are suspended in fluid within a statocyst and whose movement is detected by sensory hairs that determine an invertebrate's position **2.** BOT **STARCH GRAIN** a starch grain or other particle inside plant cells that moves in response to gravity, and is thought to influence the way shoots or other organs grow —**stat·o·lith·ic** /stàttə líthik/ *adj.*

sta·tor /stáytər/ *n.* a stationary part in a machine, such as a motor or generator, around which or in which a rotor rotates [Late 19thC. From modern Latin, literally "one that stands," from Latin *stat-*, the past participle stem of *stare* (see STATION).]

stat·o·scope /státtə skōp/ *n.* a sensitive aneroid barometer used to detect small changes in atmospheric pressure, often used in aircraft to determine changes in altitude

stat·u·ar·y /stáchoo èrree/ *n.* **1. STATUES CONSIDERED TOGETHER** statues considered collectively **2. ART OF MAKING STATUES** the art and techniques of making statues ■ *adj.* **ABOUT STATUES** relating to, belonging to, typical of, or for statues [Mid-16thC. From Latin *statuarius* "of a statue," from *statua* (see STATUE).]

stat·ue /stáchoo/ *n.* a three-dimensional image of a human being or animal that is sculpted, modeled, cast, or carved [14thC. Via Old French from Latin *statua*, from *statuere* "to set up" (see STATUTE).]

Barnaby's

Statue of Liberty

Stat·ue of Lib·er·ty *n.* a huge statue of a woman holding a torch and a book inscribed "July 4, 1776." It stands in New York Harbor. At 152 ft./46 m high, it is one of the tallest statues in the world. A gift from France to the United States, it was unveiled in 1886.

stat·u·esque /stàchoo ésk/ *adj.* like a statue, especially in having classical beauty, elegance, or proportions —**stat·u·esque·ly** *adv.*

stat·u·ette /stàchoo ét/ *n.* a small usually portable statue

stat·ure /stáchər/ *n.* **1. HEIGHT** the standing height of somebody or something **2. INDIVIDUAL'S STANDING** somebody's standing or level of achievement [13thC. Via Old French from *statura*, Latin from *stat-*, the past participle stem of *stare* (see STATION).]

sta·tus /stáytəss, státtəss/ *n.* **1. RANK** the relative position or standing of somebody or something in a society or other group **2. PRESTIGE** high rank or standing, especially in a community, workforce, or organization **3. CONDITION** a condition that is subject to change ○ *What's the current status of the in-*

vestigation? **4.** LAW **LEGAL STANDING** somebody's standing in terms of the law [Late 18thC. From Latin (see STATE).]

Sta·tus In·di·an, sta·tus In·di·an *n. Can* a member of an indigenous people whom the federal government recognizes as having special rights and privileges, especially residence on a reserve

sta·tus quo /-kwṓ/ *n.* the condition or state of affairs that currently exists [From Latin, literally "the state in which"]

sta·tus sym·bol *n.* a possession that is a sign of wealth or prestige

stat·u·ta·ble /stáchətəb'l/ *adj.* **1. STATUTORY** regulated or imposed by statute **2. COVERED BY STATUTE** covered by a statute, and subject to the penalty laid down by that statute —**stat·u·ta·bly** *adv.*

stat·ute /stáchoot/ *n.* **1.** LAW **LAW ENACTED BY LEGISLATURE** a law established by a legislative body **2.** BUSINESS **ESTABLISHED RULE** a permanent established rule or law, especially one involved in the running of a company or other organization [13thC. Via Old French from late Latin *statutum*, literally "something set up," from Latin *statuere* "to set up," from *status* "position" (see STATE).]

stat·ute book *n.* a record of the acts that have been passed by a legislature and remain in force

stat·ute law *n.* the body of law that has been enacted by a legislature, or a specific law so enacted

stat·ute mile *n.* = **mile** *n.* 1 [From the fact that it is fixed by law]

stat·ute of lim·i·ta·tions *n.* a statute that lays down the time within which legal proceedings must be started

stat·u·to·ry /stáchə tàwree/ *adj.* **1. OF A STATUTE** relating to a statute **2. CONTROLLED BY STATUTE** regulated or imposed by statute **3. SUBJECT TO PENALTY** covered by a statute, and subject to the penalty laid down by that statute —**stat·u·to·ri·ly** *adv.*

stat·u·to·ry dec·la·ra·tion *n.* a declaration that somebody makes on oath according to statute

stat·u·to·ry rape *n.* the offense under U.S. law of having sexual relations with somebody who has not reached the legal age of consent

staunch[1] /stawnch/, **stanch** /stawnch, stanch/ *adj.* **1. LOYAL** showing loyalty, dependability, and enthusiasm **2. STURDY** solidly built or substantial [15thC. Via Anglo-Norman *estaunche* from, ultimately, Old French *estanchier* "to stop" (see STANCH[1]).] —**staunch·ly** *adv.* —**staunch·ness** *n.*

WORD KEY: USAGE

stanch or **staunch**? There are two words spelled ***staunch*** and two others spelled ***stanch***. The adjective ***staunch*** is the most commonly used form in the meaning "loyal, trustworthy," although ***stanch*** is also used to mean the same thing. Conversely, ***stanch*** is more common as a verb meaning "to stop the flow of," though ***staunch*** can also occur in this meaning: *The government is trying to staunch the outflow of money.*

staunch[2] *vt.* = **stanch**[1]

stau·ro·lite /stàwrə lìt/ *n.* a reddish-brown or black mineral of iron and magnesium that occurs as prismatic crystals in metamorphic rocks, often in a cross shape. It is used as a gemstone. [Late 18thC. Coined from Greek *stauros* "cross" (because it often forms twin crystals in the shape of a cross) + -LITE.] —**stau·ro·lit·ic** /stàwrə líttik/ *adj.*

Sta·vang·er /staa vaángər/ city and port in southwestern Norway. Population: 103,590 (1995).

stave /stayv/ *n.* **1. BAND OF WOOD** a long thin piece of wood, one of several sealed together to make the hull of a boat, or the body of a container such as a barrel **2. RUNG OR BAR OF WOOD** a bar or strip of wood or other material, especially one that forms a rung in a ladder or a crosspiece between the legs of a chair **3.** = **staff**[1] *n.* 7 **4.** MUSIC = **staff**[1] *n.* 6 **5.** LITERAT **POETRY STANZA** a stanza of poetry ■ *v.* (**staved** *or* **stove** /stōv/, **stav·ing, staves**) **1.** *vti.* **BREAK STAVES** to break a barrel, a tub, or a boat's hull by smashing its staves in, or to break by having the staves smashed in **2.** *vti.* **BREAK A HOLE IN AN OBJECT** to smash a hole in the side of a boat or a barrel **3.** *vt.* **BREAK INWARD** to strike something such as a door or a rib making it break inward **4.** *vt.* **FIT A STAVE TO** to fit a stave to something such as a chair or a ladder [14thC. Back-formation from *staves*, the plural of STAFF.]

staves·a·cre /stáyvz àykər/ *n.* a delphinium with purple flowers that grows in Europe and Asia. Its poisonous seeds were once used as a cathartic and an emetic. Latin name: *Delphinium staphisagria.* [14thC. Alteration of earlier *staphisagre*, which came via Latin from Greek *staphis agria*, literally "wild raisin."]

stay[1] /stay/ *v.* (**stayed** *or* **staid, stayed, stay·ing, stays**) **1.** *vi.* **REMAIN** to continue to be in the same place, condition, or state **2.** *vi.* **RESIDE FOR A SHORT TIME** to spend some time or live temporarily in a specified place **3.** *vti.* **PASS SOME TIME** to spend a specified length of time at a place or in doing something **4.** *vi.* **REMAIN IN CONTENTION** to keep up with somebody or something, especially by going along with the leader or leaders of a race **5.** *vi.* **PERSEVERE** to continue to do something, especially to support something, e.g., an idea, plan, or project ○ *stay the course until the task is completed* **6.** *vt.* **UNDERGO** to endure, put up with, or survive something, especially something trying, difficult, or unpleasant ○ *The runner had trouble staying the final mile.* **7.** *vi.* **BE AROUND FOR SOMETHING** to be present long enough to take part in something, especially a meal **8.** *vi.* **LINGER** to linger or wait somewhere ○ *Stay a moment.* **9.** *vt.* **STOP** to put a stop to something **10.** *vt.* **POSTPONE OR HINDER** to postpone, hinder, or delay something ○ *stay a trip untl the weather improves* **11.** *vt.* **ALLEVIATE IN THE SHORT TERM** to relieve or ease something temporarily, e.g., hunger, thirst, or other physical need **12.** *vt.* **RESTRAIN** to hold something back or in check **13.** *vt.* LAW **SUSPEND LEGAL PROCESS TEMPORARILY** to suspend a judgment or proceedings temporarily **14.** *vi. Scotland* **RESIDE** to live permanently in a place **15.** *vi.* GAMBLING **STAKE SAME AMOUNT** to stake the same amount of money on a poker hand as the person who last raised the stake **16.** *vt.* **CRUSH OR STIFLE** to suppress something unwelcome, such as an uprising or criticism (*archaic*) ■ *n.* **1. A VISIT** a short spell of being away from home ○ *a weekend stay in the country* **2. CURB OR CHECK** something that acts to stop or delay something negative happening **3.** LAW **TEMPORARY HALT** a temporary halt in legal proceedings, or a period during which a judgment may not be carried out [15thC. Via Old French *ester* from Latin *stare* "to stand" (source of English *stance, stage, distant*, and *constant*).] ◇ **stay put** to remain in a place or position

stay on *vi.* to remain somewhere after others have left or after the expected time of leaving

stay out *vi.* to be away from home, usually for or until a specified time

stay up *vi.* to remain awake and not go to bed at the normal time

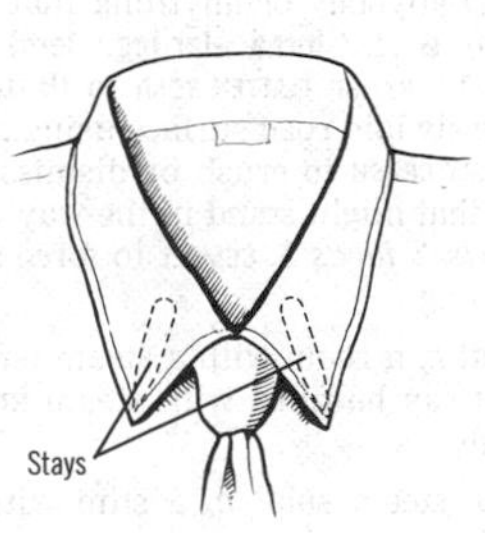

Stay

stay[2] /stay/ *n.* CLOTHES **1. A SUPPORT** something that gives extra support to something else, e.g., a brace, prop, or buttress **2. CORSET BONE** a small bone or piece of metal or plastic used as a stiffener in corsets and girdles ■ **stays** *npl.* CLOTHES **STIFFENED CORSET** a corset that is stiffened with strips of whalebone, metal, or other material ■ *vt.* (**stayed, stay·ing, stays**) **1. SUPPORT** to support something (*archaic*) **2. COMFORT** to give somebody comfort or strength (*formal*) [Early 16thC. From Old French *estaye*, of prehistoric Germanic origin.]

stay[3] /stay/ *n.* **1.** SAILING **ROPE SUPPORTING MAST** a rope or cable used to support a mast **2.** BUILDING **STEADYING ROPE** a rope used for steadying or guiding something, especially on a chimney or flagpole ■ *vti.* (**stayed, stay·ing, stays**) SAILING **TURN ONTO OTHER TACK** to turn onto the other tack, or make a vessel turn [Old English *stæg*. Ultimately from an Indo-European base meaning "to make stand," which is also the ancestor of English *stay*[2] and *steel*.]

stay·er /stáy ər/ *n.* **1. SOMEBODY WHO STAYS** somebody or something that stays **2. SOMEBODY PERSISTENT** somebody who has plenty of stamina and shows persistence **3. HORSE OR DOG THAT RACES PERSISTENTLY** a racehorse or greyhound that has stamina and competes to the end of a race, even under difficult conditions

stay·ing pow·er *n.* the ability to keep doing something or keep trying, especially over long periods of time

stay·sail /stáy sàyl/; *nautical* /stáyss'l/ *n.* an extra sail hoisted on one of the stays of a sailing vessel

stay stitch·ing *n.* an extra line of stitches reinforcing a seam, used to prevent stretching and fraying

stbd. *abbr.* starboard

STD *abbr.* MED sexually transmitted disease

std. *abbr.* standard

Ste. *abbr.* Sainte [French, "(female) Saint"]

stead /sted/ *n.* the position or role of somebody or something else [Old English *stede* "place." Ultimately from an Indo-European base meaning "to stand," which is also the ancestor of English *stand, stud*, and *station*.] ◇ **stand somebody in good stead** to be useful to somebody, especially at a later time

stead·fast /stéd fàst/, **sted·fast** *adj.* **1. FIRM** firm and unwavering in purpose, loyalty, or resolve **2. FIXED** firmly fixed or constant [Old English *stedefæst*, literally "fixed in place"] —**stead·fast·ly** *adv.* —**stead·fast·ness** *n.*

stead·y /stéddee/ *adj.* (**-i·er, -i·est**) **1. STABLE** fixed, stable, or not easily moved **2. STAYING THE SAME** showing no tendency to change or fluctuate **3. CONSTANT OR CONTINUOUS** coming in a regular nonstop flow **4. REGULAR OR ORDINARY** reliable, but often rather dull or routine **5. UNRUFFLED** not easily upset or excited **6. STAID OR SERIOUS** having a serious and calm attitude or character **7. REGULAR OR INDUSTRIOUS** regular, habitual, or industrious ■ *adv.* (**-i·er, -i·est**) **STEADILY** in a steady way ■ *vti.* (**-ied, -y·ing, -ies**) **MAKE OR BECOME STEADY** to become steady or make something steady ■ *n.* (*plural* **-ies**) **SOMEBODY DATED REGULARLY** the person with whom somebody regularly goes on dates (*informal*) ■ *interj.* **1. BE CAREFUL** used to tell somebody to be careful or be calm **2.** SAILING **KEEP TO PRESENT COURSE** used to tell somebody steering a ship or boat to keep to the present course [Mid-13thC. Formed from STEAD. The underlying idea is of being fixed in place.] —**stead·i·er** *n.* —**stead·i·ly** *adv.* —**stead·i·ness** *n.* ◇ **go steady** to go out together regularly as a couple (*informal*)

stead·y state *n.* a condition of stability or equilibrium in a system, e.g., in the energy levels of an atom, in which there is little or no change over time

stead·y-state the·o·ry *n.* a theory in astronomy that the universe has always existed at a uniform density that is maintained because new matter is created continuously as the universe expands

steak /stayk/ *n.* **1. CUT OF BEEF** a thick slice of beef from a lean part of a cow **2. PIECE OF MEAT OR FISH** a piece of meat other than beef, e.g., pork, ham, venison, or veal, or of a large fish, e.g., cod, salmon, or tuna **3. SERVING OF GROUND MEAT** ground meat formed into a solid shape, usually a flat roundish shape, and served broiled, fried, or barbecued [15thC. From Old Norse *steik* "meat roasted on a spit." Ultimately from an Indo-European word meaning "pointed," which is also the ancestor of English *stick, instigate*, and *instinct*.]

steak·house /stáyk howss/ (*plural* **-hous·es** /-hòwzez/) *n.* a restaurant that specializes in serving beef steaks

steak knife *n.* a table knife with a sharp usually serrated blade, suitable for cutting steak

steak tar·tare *n.* freshly ground beef that is served uncooked with raw egg, chopped onions, and seasonings [*Tartare* from French, "Tartar"]

steal /steel/ *v.* (**stole** /stōl/, **sto·len** /stṓlən/, **steal·ing, steals**) **1.** *vti.* **TAKE UNLAWFULLY** to take something that belongs to somebody else, illegally or without the owner's permission **2.** *vt.* **TAKE FURTIVELY** to take or get something secretly, surreptitiously, or through trickery ○ *steal a glance* **3.** *vi.* **SNEAK** to move quietly, especially in the hope of not been seen or caught **4.** *vt.* **TAKE AND USE ANOTHER'S IDEAS** to take something that another person has created, especially ideas, theories, or a piece of writing, and present it as one's own **5.** *vi.* **PASS UNNOTICED** to pass or move without being noticed (*literary*) ○ *Dawn was stealing over the mountaintops.* **6.** *vti.* BASEBALL **GAIN A BASE WITHOUT HIT** to gain a base by running without the ball being hit by the batter and in the absence of an error by the fielding team **7.** *vt.* **SUCCEED AT UNEXPECTEDLY** to win or succeed at something unexpectedly, luckily, or dishonestly at the expense of another or others (*informal*) ■ *n.* **1.** ACT OF STEALING an act of stealing **2.** BARGAIN something that does not cost very much or that costs a lot less than would be expected (*informal*) [Old English *stelan*, from a prehistoric Germanic base that is also the ancestor of English *stalk*] —**steal·er** *n.*

WORD KEY: SYNONYMS

steal, pinch, filch, purloin, pilfer, embezzle, misappropriate

CORE MEANING: the taking of property unlawfully

steal a general word meaning to take unlawfully another person's property or money; **pinch** an informal word meaning the same as "steal"; **filch** a formal word meaning the same as "pinch," often suggesting quick casual theft of something of little value; **purloin** a formal or humorous word meaning the same as "steal"; **pilfer** meaning to steal things of little value and usually in small amounts, especially when done repeatedly; **embezzle** meaning to take money unlawfully when it has been entrusted to the perpetrator; **misappropriate** a formal word meaning the same as "embezzle" or "steal".

stealth /stelth/ *n.* **1.** ACTION TO AVOID DETECTION the action of doing something slowly, quietly, and covertly, in order to avoid detection **2.** FURTIVENESS secretive, dishonest, or cunning behavior or actions ■ *adj.* MIL VIRTUALLY UNDETECTABLE BY RADAR designed or constructed in such a way and using requisite technology and materials so as to be invisible to enemy radar ○ *stealth bombers* [13thC. from assumed Old English *stælþ*, from a prehistoric Germanic base that is also the ancestor of English *steal*.] —**stealth·ful** *adj.*

stealth tow·er *n.* an ecologically friendly and aesthetic, camouflaged wireless telecommunicaitons tower, e.g., one configured as a pine tree, intended to soften the environmental and visual impact of proliferating antenna sites (*informal*)

stealth·y /stélthee/ (**-i·er, -i·est**) *adj.* **1.** DONE CAREFULLY done in a deliberately slow, careful, and quiet way **2.** FURTIVE secretive, furtive, or cunning —**stealth·i·ly** *adv.* —**stealth·i·ness** *n.*

WORD KEY: SYNONYMS

See Synonyms at ***secret***.

steam /steem/ *n.* **1.** VAPORIZED WATER the vapor that is formed when water is boiled **2.** MIST OF WATER VAPOR the visible mist that forms when water vapor condenses in the air **3.** VAPOR any visible form of vapor **4.** POWER stamina, strength, or speed (*informal*) ○ *running out of steam* ■ *adj.* **1.** DRIVEN BY STEAM driven or powered by steam **2.** USING STEAM using steam to do something ■ *v.* (**steamed, steam·ing, steams**) **1.** *vi.* PRODUCE STEAM to produce or be produced as steam **2.** *vi.* MOVE BY STEAM to move or be powered by steam **3.** *vti.* COOK IN STEAM to cook something or be cooked in the steam of boiling water **4.** *vi.* MOVE FAST to move very quickly and energetically (*informal*) **5.** *vi.* GENERATE STEAM to generate steam (*refers especially to boilers*) [Old English *stēam*] ◇ **get up steam** to gather together enough energy and speed to do something (*informal*)

steam up *vti.* to become, or make something become, clouded with condensation

steam bath *n.* a steam-filled room or compartment that people go into to relax and refresh themselves through sweating. A steam bath is often used as a way of temporarily losing weight through sweat loss, especially by boxers and jockeys who need to reach target weights.

steam·boat /steém bōt/ *n.* a boat with an engine powered by steam

steam chest *n.* a compartment in a steam engine from which steam is supplied to the valve of the engine

steam en·gine *n.* an engine powered by steam, typically incorporating a flywheel attached to a reciprocating piston that in turn is driven by the expansive action of steam generated in a boiler

steam·er /steémər/ *n.* **1.** SHIPPING BOAT POWERED BY STEAM a boat or ship that is powered by a steam engine or engines **2.** COOK PAN FOR STEAMING FOOD a covered pan in which food is cooked by steam. It has a perforated base and fits on top of a saucepan in which water is boiled to produce steam. **3.** CONSTR CONTAINER FOR STEAMING WOOD a container in which wood is treated with steam to make it pliable **4.** FOOD SOFT-SHELL CLAM a soft-shell clam, especially when steamed and eaten

steam·er rug *n.* a warm blanket that people can put over their knees and legs for warmth, especially when sitting on the deck of a ship

steam·er trunk *n.* a traveler's trunk, especially one that is shallow enough to fit underneath a bunk on a ship

steam·fit·ter /steém fittər/ *n.* somebody whose job is to install and repair pipes and accessories that carry steam

steam-gen·er·at·ing heav·y-wa·ter re·ac·tor *n.* a nuclear reactor that uses ordinary water as the coolant, which produces steam, and heavy water as the moderator

steam·ing /steéming/ *adj.* very angry or upset (*informal*)

steam i·ron *n.* an electric iron with a chamber for water. As the iron heats up steam is produced and channelled through holes in the face of the iron to dampen the laundry.

steam jack·et *n.* a covering or casing surrounding the cylinders and heads of a steam engine to keep the surfaces hot and dry

steam or·gan *n.* *U.K.* = **calliope**

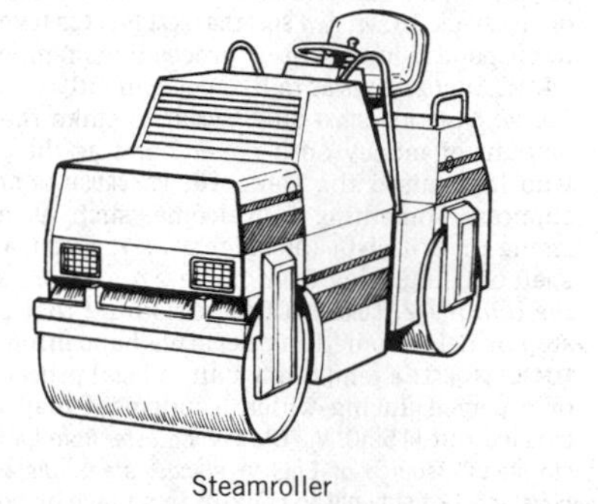

Steamroller

steam·rol·ler /steém rōlər/ *n.* **1.** TRANSP VEHICLE FOR FLATTENING ROADS a specialized vehicle, originally steam-powered, with large heavy rollers for wheels, designed to flatten and compress newly laid road surfaces **2.** CRUSHING FORCE somebody or something that is a powerful driving force, often crushing or dismissing anybody or anything that might stand in the way ■ *vt.* (**-lered, -ler·ing, -lers**) **steam·rol·ler, steam·roll** **1.** TRANSP FLATTEN ROAD to flatten and compress a newly laid road surface using a steamroller **2.** RUTHLESSLY CRUSH to crush or dismiss anybody or anything that might stand in the way ○ *steamroller everyone else's ideas* **3.** COMPEL to force somebody to do something

steam room *n.* a room with a steam bath in it, or a room that can be filled with steam and used as a steam bath

steam·ship /steém ship/ *n.* a ship with an engine powered by steam

steam shov·el *n.* a large steam-powered excavating machine, especially an earthmover that has a bucket on a boom fixed to a jib that can be rotated

steam ta·ble *n.* a table used for keeping cooked food hot. The food sits in containers in the table and hot water or steam circulates underneath the containers.

steam tur·bine *n.* a turbine that uses the heat energy of steam to generate the power for mechanical rotation

steam whis·tle *n.* a large whistle blown by forcing steam through it. Steam whistles were used in the past on steam locomotives, or in factories to signal the end of the working day.

steam·y /steémee/ (**-i·er, -i·est**) *adj.* **1.** FULL OF STEAM covered with, full of, affected by, or like steam **2.** HOT AND CLAMMY unbearably or uncomfortably hot and humid **3.** OVERTLY SEXUAL with an exaggerated emphasis on sexual relations or sexuality (*informal*) —**steam·i·ly** *adv.* —**steam·i·ness** *n.*

ste·ap·sin /stee áps'n/ *n.* an enzyme in pancreatic juice that catalyses the hydrolysis of fats [Late 19thC. Blend of Greek *stear* "fat" (because it helps to break down fats) and PEPSIN.]

ste·a·rate /steér àyt/ *n.* a salt or ester of stearic acid [Mid-19thC. Coined from Greek *stear* (see STEATO-) + -ATE.]

ste·ar·ic /stee érrik, stéarik/ *adj.* **1.** CONTAINING STEARIN OR FAT relating to, containing, or typical of stearin or fat **2.** DERIVED FROM STEARIC ACID about, derived from, or containing stearic acid [Mid-19thC. Formed from Greek *stear* (see STEATO-).]

ste·ar·ic ac·id *n.* a colorless odorless waxy crystalline fatty acid that occurs naturally in animal and vegetable oils and is used in candles, cosmetics, soaps, lubricants, and medicines. Formula: $C_{18}H_{36}O_2$.

ste·a·rin /steé ərin, steérin/, **ste·a·rine** /steé ə reén, steérin/ *n.* **1.** ESTER OF GLYCEROL AND STEARIC ACID a colorless ester of glycerol and stearic acid used in making soap, candles, and adhesives **2.** = **stearic acid** **3.** SOLID FORM OF FAT the solid form of fat [Early 19thC. Coined from Greek *stear* (see STEATO-) + -IN.]

ste·a·tite /steé ətīt/ *n.* = **soapstone** [Mid-18thC. Via Latin from Greek *steatitis (lithos)* "tallow-like (stone)," from *stear* (see STEATO-).] —**ste·a·tit·ic** /steé ə títtik/ *adj.*

steato- *prefix.* fat ○ *steatopygia* [From Greek *steat-*, the stem of *stear* "solid fat, tallow"]

ste·at·o·pyg·i·a /stee àtta píjjee ə, -pījee ə/ *n.* an accumulation of fat on the buttocks [Early 19thC. Coined from STEATO- + Greek *pugē* "buttocks," of unknown origin.] —**ste·a·to·py·gous** /steé ətə pīgəss/ *adj.*

ste·at·or·rhe·a /steé ətə reé ə/ *n.* an unusual condition in which an excess of fat is present in stools

ste·at·or·rhoe·a *n.* U.K. = **steatorrhea**

sted·fast *adj.* = **steadfast**

steed /steed/ *n.* a horse, especially a lively spirited one [Old English *stēda* "stallion." Ultimately from the same prehistoric Germanic base that produced *stud*.]

steel /steel/ *n.* **1.** STRONG ALLOY OF IRON AND CARBON a strong alloy of iron containing up to 1.5% carbon along with small amounts of other elements such as manganese, chromium, and nickel. A wide range of mechanical properties can be produced by varying the composition and treatment. **2.** SOMETHING MADE OF STEEL something made of steel, e.g., a weapon **3.** KNIFE SHARPENER a steel rod, often with a handle, that knives are drawn back and forward along in order to sharpen them **4.** TOUGHNESS determination, toughness, or great strength of character ■ *adj.* STRONG OR HARD like steel, especially in strength or hardness ■ *vt.* (**steeled, steel·ing, steels**) **1.** TREAT WITH STEEL to coat, plate, edge, or point something with steel **2.** PREPARE BY HARDENING to make somebody unfeeling, or tough enough to withstand a setback or trial ○ *steeled myself for the news* [Old English *stēli*. Ultimately from an Indo-European base denoting "to stand, be solid," which is also the ancestor of English *stay*[2] and *stay*[3].]

steel band *n.* a group of musicians who play steel drums and often specialize in calypsos

steel blue *adj.* of a cold grayish-blue color

steel drum, **steel pan** *n.* a Caribbean percussion instrument made by hammering an oil drum into a concave shape with flattened areas that make musical notes when struck

Steele, Mount /steel/ peak in the Saint Elias Range, in southwestern Yukon Territory, Canada. Height: 16,644 ft./5,073 m.

steel en·grav·ing *n.* **1.** ENGRAVING ON STEEL PLATE the art, technique, or process of engraving on a steel plate **2.** PRINT FROM STEEL PLATE a print made from an engraved steel plate

steel gray *adj.* of a dark gray color with a bluish tinge

steel gui·tar *n.* a fretless guitar played on a horizontal stand with a plectrum and a movable metal slide. ◊ **pedal steel guitar**

steel·head /steél hèd/ (*plural* **-heads** *or* **-head**) *n.* a rainbow trout that has matured in the North Pacific Ocean and acquired a silver coloration, popular for sport fishing

steel pan *n.* = **steel drum**

steel-trap *adj.* very quick and keen [From the expression "a mind like a steel trap," that is, quick to grasp things]

steel wool *n.* thin strands of steel tangled together to form an abrasive mass, used for cleaning and polishing

steel·work /steél wùrk/ *n.* something made from steel, especially a structural framework

steel·work·er /steél wùrkər/ *n.* somebody who works at making steel

steel·works /steel wùrks/ *n.* a factory where steel is made

steel·y /steélee/ *adj.* **1. LIKE STEEL** like steel, especially in color or in being tough or determined **2. MADE OF STEEL** made of steel (*dated or literary*) —**steel·i·ness** *n.*

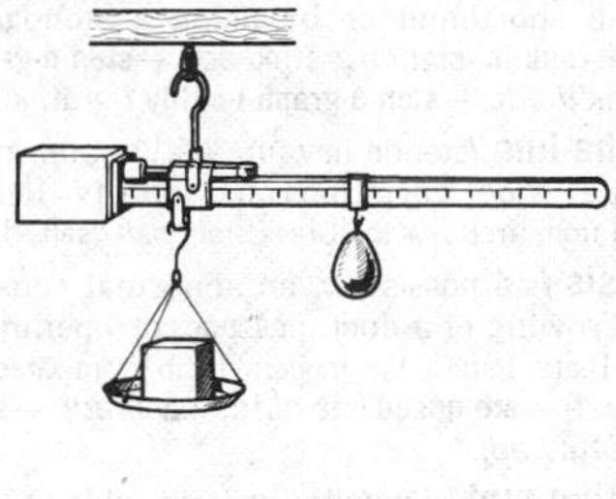

Steelyard

steel·yard /steél yaárd/ *n.* a portable balance for weighing objects. The object is hung on a hook and a counterweight is moved along a scaled arm to find the weight. [Mid-17thC. From YARD "rod, spar."]

steen·bok /steén bòk/ (*plural* **-boks** *or* **-bok**), **steinbok** /stīn bàk/ *n.* a small slender antelope that lives on the grasslands of southern Africa. It has short straight horns, long legs, and a reddish-brown coat. Latin name: *Raphicerus campestris.* [Late 18thC. Via Afrikaans from Middle Dutch *steenboc*, literally "stone buck."]

steep[1] /steep/ *adj.* **1. ALMOST VERTICAL** sloping very sharply, often to the extent of being almost vertical **2. EXCESSIVE** unreasonably or excessively high, especially in cost (*informal*) **3. RAPID OR HUGE** faster or greater than is usual, or might be expected ○ *There's been a steep decline in the number of people out of work.* **4. TAXING** very ambitious or difficult ■ *n.* **SOMETHING STEEP** something such as a slope that is steep [Old English *stēap* "high." Ultimately from a prehistoric Germanic base meaning "lofty, deep," which is also the ancestor of English *steeple* and *stoop*.] —**steep·ly** *adv.* —**steep·ness** *n.*

steep[2] /steep/ *v.* (**steeped, steep·ing, steeps**) **1.** *vti.* **IMMERSE IN LIQUID** to soak something, or be soaked, in a liquid, especially for cleaning or softening, or in order to extract something **2.** *vt.* **PERMEATE** to permeate somebody or something with a substance or quality, usually over a long period (*usually passive*) ○ *steeped in tradition* ■ *n.* **1. A SOAKING** an act or the process of steeping something in a liquid **2. LIQUID FOR SOAKING** a liquid that something is or can be steeped in [14thC. From assumed Old English *stiepan*, from a prehistoric Germanic base that is also the ancestor of English *stoup*.] —**steep·er** *n.*

steep·en /steépən/ (**-ened, -en·ing, -ens**) *vti.* to become, or make something become, steep or steeper

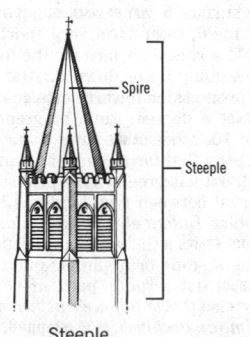

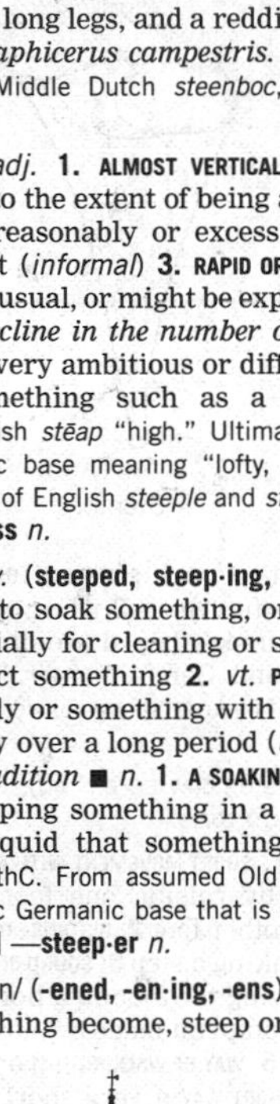

Steeple

stee·ple /steép'l/ *n.* **1. CHURCH TOWER** a tall ornamental structure, usually a tapering tower with a spire on top of it, found on the roofs of churches and temples **2. SPIRE** a spire [Old English *stēpel*, from a prehistoric Germanic base meaning "lofty, deep" (see STEEP[1])] —**stee·pled** *adj.*

stee·ple·bush /steép'l bŏŏsh/ *n.* = **hardhack** [Mid-19thC. *Steeple* of uncertain origin: probably from the shape of the flower clusters.]

stee·ple·chase /steép'l chàyss/ *n.* **1.** HORSERACING **HORSERACE WITH JUMPS ON TRACK** a horserace run over a course that has obstacles, e.g., hedges, ditches, and water jumps, that the horses must jump over. ◊ **flat race 2.** SPORT **TRACK EVENT WITH WATER JUMP** a track event in which the runners must jump over a water jump as well as hurdles **3.** HORSERACING **HORSERACE WITH JUMPS IN OPEN COUNTRY** a cross-country horserace that has natural obstacles such as hedges and ditches for the horses to jump over (*archaic*) ■ *vi.* (**-chased, -chas·ing, -chas·es**) **RUN A STEEPLECHASE** to compete in a steeplechase [Late 18thC. From the fact that a church steeple was originally the competitors' goal.] —**stee·ple·chas·er** *n.*

stee·ple·jack /steép'l jàk/ *n.* somebody who builds, works on, or repairs high structures, especially steeples and tall chimneys

steer[1] /steer/ *v.* (**steered, steer·ing, steers**) **1.** *vti.* TRANSP **DIRECT** to guide something such as a motor vehicle or ship in a direction using a steering wheel, rudder, or other device **2.** *vt.* **INFLUENCE DIRECTION** to try to influence people to follow a particular course of action by unobtrusively guiding them toward it **3.** *vi.* **FOLLOW PARTICULAR COURSE** to follow a specified course **4.** *vi.* TRANSP **MANEUVER IN A CERTAIN WAY** to go or move in a specified way or direction when being driven or propelled ○ *This car steers to the left.* ■ *n.* **PIECE OF ADVICE** a piece of information or advice (*informal*) [Old English *stīeran*, from a prehistoric Germanic base meaning "to steer," which is also the ancestor of English *stern* and *starboard*] —**steer·a·ble** *adj.* —**steer·er** *n.*

WORD KEY: SYNONYMS

See Synonyms at ***guide***.

steer[2] /steer/ *n.* a male of the cattle family that has been castrated before reaching sexual maturity and is raised for beef, especially a young bull [Old English *stēor*]

steer·age /steérij/ *n.* **1.** SHIPPING **INEXPENSIVE ACCOMMODATIONS ON SHIPS** the cheapest passenger accommodations on board a ship, usually in the area near the rudder and steering gear **2.** NAUT **STEERING** the act or process of steering a boat

steer·age·way /steérij wày/ *n.* a rate of forward movement that is fast enough to allow a boat to be steered from the helm

steer·ing col·umn *n.* the part in a motor vehicle that connects the steering wheel, or the handlebars on a motorcycle, with the steering gear

steer·ing com·mit·tee *n.* a group of selected people who decide agendas and topics for discussion, and prioritize urgent business, especially one acting for a legislative body or other assembly

steer·ing gear *n.* the mechanism in a vehicle or ship that allows it to be steered

steer·ing wheel *n.* a wheel in a vehicle or ship that is connected by way of the steering column to the steering gear and is turned to change direction

steers·man /steérzmən/ (*plural* **-men** /-mən/) *n.* somebody who steers a boat or ship [Old English *stēoresman*, literally "man for steering," from *stēor* "steering"]

steeve[1] /steev/ *n.* SHIPPING **CARGO-STOWING AID** a spar with a pulley block at one end that is used for stowing cargo on a boat or ship ■ *vt.* (**steeved, steev·ing, steeves**) SHIPPING **PUT CARGO ON BOARD** to stow cargo in the hold of a boat or ship and make it secure [Mid-19thC. Origin uncertain: perhaps via Spanish *estibar* or Catalan *stivar* "to stow cargo" from Latin *stipare* "to stuff" (source of English *stevedore* and *constipate*).]

steeve[2] /steev/ *vti.* (**steeved, steev·ing, steeves**) SAILING **INCLINE UPWARD** to incline upward, or make a bowsprit incline upward ■ *n.* SAILING **ANGLE OF INCLINATION OF BOWSPRIT** the angle at which a bowsprit inclines upward from the horizontal [Mid-17thC. Origin unknown.]

Stef·fens /stéff'nz/, **Lincoln** (1866–1936) U.S. journalist. The author of articles exposing business and political corruption, he was a leader of the so-called muckraking school of journalism. Full name **Joseph Lincoln Steffens**

Steg·ner /stégnər/, **Wallace** (1909–93) U.S. writer. He wrote fiction and nonfiction, both often set in the American West, and won a Pulitzer Prize for *Angle of Repose* (1972). Full name **Wallace Earle Stegner**

steg·o·saur /stéggə sàwr/, **steg·o·sau·rus** /stèggə sáwrəss/ *n.* a plant-eating dinosaur that lived in the Jurassic and Early Cretaceous periods and had tough bony dorsal plates and spikes. Genus: *Stegosauria.* [Early 20thC. From modern Latin *Stegosaurus*, genus name, from Greek *stegos* "plate" + *sauros* "lizard."]

Steich·en /stík'n/, **Edward** (1879–1973) Luxembourg-born U.S. photographer. His works did much to establish photography as an art form. He headed the photography department of New York City's Museum of Modern Art (1947–62). Full name **Edward Jean Steichen**

stein /stīn/ *n.* **1. EARTHENWARE BEER MUG** a large beer mug, especially a German earthenware or pewter one, often with a hinged lid **2. QUANTITY OF BEER** the amount of beer or other liquid that a stein holds [Mid-19thC. From German, shortening of *Steinkrug* "stoneware mug."]

Gertrude Stein: Photographed by Man Ray (1930)

Stein /stīn/, **Gertrude** (1874–1946) U.S. writer. Her novels and works of fiction are characterized by experimentation with language and style.

John Steinbeck

Stein·beck /stín bek/, **John** (1902–68) U.S. writer. His fiction includes *Of Mice and Men* (1937) and *The Grapes of Wrath* (1939), and is notable for its social realism. He won a Nobel Prize in literature in 1962. Full name **John Ernst Steinbeck**

stein·bok *n.* = **steenbok**

Gloria Steinem

Stein·em /stínəm/, **Gloria** (*b.* 1934) U.S. feminist. A leading member of the women's movement, she was one of the founders of *Ms.* magazine (1972).

Stein·er /stínər, shtínər/, **Rudolf** (1861–1925) Austrian philosopher. He founded the Anthroposophical Society (1912) to promote his intellectually-based spirituality. The Waldorf School movement is based on his work.

ste·la /steélə/ (*plural* **-lae** /steé lee/) *n.* = **stele** *n.* 1 [Late 18thC. Via Latin from Greek *stēlē* (see STELE).]

ste·le /steel, steélee/ (*plural* **-lae** /stee lī/) *n.* **1.** ARCHEOL **ANCIENT STONE SLAB** an ancient stone slab or pillar, usually engraved, inscribed, or painted, and set upright. Found among the ruins of civilizations as diverse as China, Greece, and Mexico, they are believed to have had religious significance. **2.** BOT **CENTRAL PART OF STEMS AND ROOTS** the cylindrical core of the stem and roots of a plant that contains the sap-conducting vascular tissues and varying amounts of packing tissue **(pith)** [Early 19thC. From Greek *stēlē* "standing stone." Ultimately from an Indo-European word meaning "post," which is also the ancestor of English *stultify*.] —**ste·lar** *adj.*

Stel·la /stéllə/, **Frank** (*b.* 1936) U.S. artist. His abstract geometric forms are often painted on irregularly shaped canvases. Full name **Frank Philip Stella**

stel·lar /stéllər/ *adj.* **1.** ASTRON **INVOLVING STARS** relating to, consisting of, or like a star or stars **2. EXCEPTIONAL** exceptionally good **3. INVOLVING FAMOUS PEOPLE** about, involving, typical of, or full of famous people, especially those in the movie or entertainment industries [Mid-17thC. From late Latin *stellaris*, from Latin *stella* "star" (source of English *constellation*). Ultimately from the Indo-European word for "star," which is also the ancestor of English *star* and *disaster*.]

stel·lar wind *n.* a stream of ionized particles ejected from the surface of a star. ◊ **solar wind**

stel·late /stéllət, sté làyt/, **stel·lat·ed** /stéllətəd, sté làytid/ *adj.* **1. STAR-SHAPED** shaped like a star **2. HAVING PARTS RADIATING FROM CENTER** having a central part with smaller parts radiating out from it, like a starfish, some flower heads, and some crystal formations [Mid-17thC. Formed from Latin *stella* (see STELLAR).] —**stel·late·ly** *adv.*

Stel·ler's jay /stèllərz-/ *n.* a gregarious bird of western North America that has a black high-crested head and blue and black plumage. Latin name: *Cyanocitta stelleri.* [Named for the German naturalist and explorer Georg Wilhelm *Steller* (1709–46)]

stel·li·form /stéllə fàwrm/ *adj.* shaped like a star [Late 18thC. Coined from Latin *stella* (see STELLAR) + -FORM.]

stel·lu·lar /stéllyələr/ *adj.* **1. FULL OF LITTLE STARS** full of or covered in little stars **2. LIKE LITTLE STAR** like a little star [Late 18thC. Formed from Latin *stellula*, literally "small star," from *stella* (see STELLAR).] —**stel·lu·lar·ly** *adv.*

stem[1] /stem/ *n.* **1.** BOT **MAIN AXIS OF PLANT** the main axis of a plant that bears buds and shoots. It is usually above ground, although some plants have underground stems **(rhizomes)**. **2.** BOT **SECONDARY PLANT BRANCH** a slender part of a plant other than its main axis that supports a leaf, flower, or fruit **3. NARROW CONNECTING PART** any long slim part of an object, e.g., the part that connects the base of a wine glass to its bowl, or the hollow tube on a smoker's pipe **4. GENEALOGICAL LINE** the major line of descent in a family tree **5. CYLINDRICAL WATCH PART** a short rod, usually with an expanded crown at the end of it, that is used in winding a watch **6.** LANG **BASE OF A WORD** the base of a word, to which affixes are added **7. VERTICAL LETTER PART** an upright stroke, especially the main one, in a letter or character **8.** MUSIC **VERTICAL PART OF MUSIC NOTE** the vertical part that extends from the head of a written musical note **9.** SAILING **UPRIGHT BOW TIMBER** the main upright timber at the bow of a ship ■ *v.* **(stemmed, stem·ming, stems) 1.** *vi.* **ORIGINATE** to derive, originate, or be caused by something **2.** *vt.* **REMOVE STEM OF** to take off the stem or part of the stem from something, especially a flower, fruit, or vegetable **3.** *vt.* **GIVE STEM TO** to give something a stem, e.g., a smoker's pipe or a wineglass **4.** *vt.* SAILING **MAKE HEADWAY** to make headway in a ship or boat against a tide or wind [Old English *stefn.* Ultimately from an Indo-European base meaning "to stand" (see STATO-).] —**stem·mer** *n.* ◇ **from stem to stern** through the whole of a place, especially a ship

stem[2] /stem/ *v.* **(stemmed, stem·ming, stems) 1.** *vt.* **PREVENT FROM FLOWING** to hinder, obstruct, or stop something from flowing, especially by creating a dam or plug **2.** *vt.* **STOP UP** to plug something such as a blast or drill hole by packing it **3.** *vti.* SKIING **TURN SKI IN** to turn the tip of a ski or skis inward in order to turn or slow down ■ *n.* **stem, stem turn** SKIING **TURNING IN OF SKI** an act or the technique of turning the tip of a ski or skis inward to turn or slow down [13thC. From Old Norse *stemma*, from a prehistoric Germanic base meaning "to halt, stammer," which is also the ancestor of English *stammer* and *stumble*.]

stem cell *n.* an undifferentiated cell from which specialized cells, e.g., blood cells, develop

stem chris·tie /stèm krístee/ *n.* a skiing turn performed by stemming one ski and then bringing the other parallel to it during the turn [*Stem* from STEM[2]; *christie* a shortening and alteration of CHRISTIANIA]

stem gin·ger *n.* round portions of the underground stem of a ginger plant, cooked until tender and preserved in syrup

stem·ma /stémmə/ (*plural* **-ma·ta** /-mətə/) *n.* **1. FAMILY TREE** a family tree **2.** LITERAT **DIAGRAM OF TEXTS OF LITERARY WORK** a diagram like a family tree, showing the relationships between different texts of a literary work **3.** ZOOL **EYE OF ARTHROPOD** a simple eye or facet of a compound eye of some arthropods [Mid-17thC. Via Latin from Greek, "garland"; from the ancient Roman practice of placing garlands on images of their ancestors.]

stemmed /stemd/ *adj.* **1. HAVING A STEM** having a stem, often of a specified kind (*often used in combination*) ○ *long-stemmed lilies* **2. WITHOUT A STEM** having the stem or stems removed

stem rust *n.* a fungal disease of plants in which streaks of dark pustules appear, especially on the stem

stem·son /stémss'n/ *n.* a timber attached to the stem and keelson in the bow of a wooden ship [Mid-18thC. Formed from STEM[1], on the model of KEELSON.]

stem turn *n.* = **stem**[2] *n.* ["Stem" from STEM[2]]

stem·ware /stém wàir/ *n.* glasses, goblets, and other glass vessels that have stems

stench /stench/ *n.* a really disgusting smell, especially a strong lingering one [Old English *stenc* "odor," from a prehistoric Germanic base that is also the ancestor of English *stink*]

WORD KEY: SYNONYMS

See Synonyms at ***smell***.

Stencil

sten·cil /sténss'l/ *n.* **1. PLATE WITH CUTOUT DESIGN** a thin sheet of material with a shape cut out of it that is marked on a surface when paint or ink is applied **2. PATTERN** the design, lettering, or other characters marked using a stencil ■ *vt.* **(-ciled** *or* **-cilled, -cil·ing** *or* **-cil·ling, -cils) 1. MAKE PATTERN USING STENCIL** to apply a design, lettering, or other characters to a surface using a stencil **2. DECORATE USING STENCIL** to decorate or mark a surface, e.g., a wall or paper, using a stencil [Early 18thC. Via Old French *estenceler* "to decorate with bright colors" from, ultimately, Latin *scintilla* "spark" (source of English *scintillate* and *tinsel*).] —**sten·cil·er** *n.*

Sten gun /stén-/ *n.* a light, cheaply manufactured submachine gun used in the past by the British Army, especially in World War II [*Sten* coined from the first letters of R. V. *Shepherd* and H. J. *Turpin*, who designed it + the district of *Enfield* in Greater London, where it was made (modeled on BREN GUN).]

sten·o /sténnō/ (*plural* **-os**) *n.* (*informal*) **1. STENOGRAPHER** a stenographer **2. STENOGRAPHY** stenography [Early 20thC. Shortening.]

steno- *prefix.* narrow, small ○ *stenothermal* [From Greek *stenos*]

sten·o·bath·ic /stènnə báthik/ *adj.* able to live only within a narrow range of depth of water [Early 20thC. Coined from STENO- + Greek *bathos* "depth."] —**sten·o·bath** /sté nə bàth/ *n.*

sten·o·graph /sténnə graaf/ *n.* **1. SHORTHAND TYPEWRITER** a machine like a small typewriter with keys for shorthand characters **2. SHORTHAND CHARACTER** a character in a system of shorthand writing ■ *vt.* **(-graphed, -graph·ing, -graphs) WRITE OR TYPE IN SHORTHAND** to record something in shorthand by writing or using a stenograph

ste·nog·ra·pher /stə nóggrəfər/ *n.* **1. SOMEBODY USING STENOGRAPH** somebody who uses a stenograph **2. WRITER OR TYPIST USING SHORTHAND** somebody who is skilled at or whose job involves writing shorthand and typing up reports and letters from shorthand copy

ste·nog·ra·phy /stə nóggrəfee/ (*plural* **-phies**) *n.* **1. SHORTHAND WRITING OR TYPING** the act, process, or skill of recording something in shorthand by writing or by using a stenograph **2. SOMETHING WRITTEN OR TYPED IN SHORTHAND** something that has been recorded in written shorthand or by using a stenograph —**sten·o·graph·ic** /stènnə gráffik/ *adj.* —**sten·o·graph·i·cal** /-gráffik'l/ *adj.* —**sten·o·graph·i·cal·ly** /-gráffik'lee/ *adv.*

sten·o·ha·line /stènnō háy līn, -há līn/ *adj.* unable to tolerate wide variations in salinity [Mid-20thC. Coined from STENO- + the Greek stem *hal-* "salt."]

ste·no·sis /stə nṓssiss/ *n.* an abnormal constriction or narrowing of a duct, passage, or opening in the body [Late 19thC. Via modern Latin from Greek *stenos* "narrow."] —**ste·nosed** /stə nṓzd, -nṓst/ *adj.* —**ste·not·ic** /stə nóttik/ *adj.*

sten·o·ther·mal /stènnə thúrm'l/ *adj.* able to live only within a narrow temperature range

sten·o·type /stènnə tīp/ *n.* a machine whose keyboard is used to record speech by means of phonetic shorthand

sten·o·typ·y /sténnə tīpee/ *n.* a form of phonetic shorthand that uses combinations of letters to represent sounds and short words —**sten·o·typ·ic** /stènnə típpik/ *adj.* —**sten·o·typ·ist** /sténnə tīpist/ *n.*

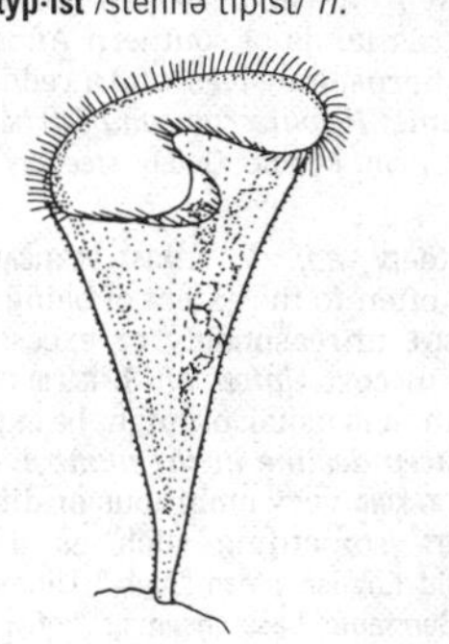

Stentor

sten·tor /stén tàwr/ *n.* **1. SOMEBODY LOUD** somebody with a loud powerful voice **2.** ZOOL **TRUMPET-SHAPED MICROORGANISM** a trumpet-shaped protozoan with a mouth at the broad end. Genus: *Stentor.* [Early 17thC. Named for *Stentor*, a famously strong-voiced Greek herald in the Trojan war.]

sten·to·ri·an /sten táwree ən/ *adj.* loud, powerful, or declamatory in tone

step /step/ *n.* **1. SHORT MOVEMENT WITH FOOT** a short movement made by raising one foot and lowering it ahead of the other foot **2. DISTANCE OF STEP** the distance traveled in taking a step **3. SOUND OF FOOTFALL** the sound made by moving the foot on a horizontal surface **4. FOOTPRINT** the footprint made by putting down the foot on a surface **5. WAY OF WALKING** a particular manner of walking **6. SHORT WAY** a very short distance **7. RAISED SURFACE** a raised surface for the foot, especially in a series going up or down **8. STAGE IN PROGRESS** a stage in a progression toward some goal or target **9. DEGREE OR GRADE** a degree, rank, or grade, especially on a scale **10.** DANCE **DANCE MOVES** a movement of the feet and body that forms part of a dance **11.** MUSIC **DEGREE OR INTERVAL** a degree of a musical staff or scale, or the interval between two degrees **12. STEP AEROBICS** step aerobics (*informal*) ○ *a step class* ■ **steps** *npl.* **1. OUTDOOR STAIRS** a flight of stairs, usually outdoors, and made of stone or a similar material **2. PATH MADE BY SOMEBODY ELSE** a route, path, or course set by somebody else ○ *She followed in her mother's steps and became an architect.* ■ *v.* **(stepped, step·ping, steps) 1.** *vti.* **MOVE FOOT** to move a foot on top of something or in a particular direction ○ *Please step aside.* **2.** *vi.* **WALK A FEW STEPS** to walk a short distance or to a specific place **3.** *vi.* **TO MOVE FORWARD WITH FOOT** to move forward by raising one foot and setting it down in front of the other **4.** *vi.* DANCE **MOVE IN REGULAR RHYTHM** to move at a measured pace, e.g., in a dance **5.** *vi.* **TREAT SOMEBODY WITHOUT RESPECT** to show or treat somebody with arrogant disregard and unkindness ○ *She is stepping on other people's feelings constantly.* **6.** *vi.* **EASILY WALK INTO SITUATION** to come into a new situation with ease or with little preparation **7.** *vt.* **ARRANGE IN STEPS** to arrange or organize something in steps, or to furnish something with steps **8.** *vt.* **MEASURE BY STEPS** to measure something by walking or pacing its length [Old English *stæpe*, from a prehistoric Germanic base meaning "to tread," which is also the ancestor of English *stamp*, *stump*, and *stoop*²] —**stepped** *adj.* —**step·per** *n.* ◇ **be in** *or* **out of step (with somebody** *or* **something) 1.** to agree or disagree with somebody or something in your attitudes or opinions **2.** to move in unison with other people, or at a different pace and rhythm ◇ **step by step** gradually ◇ **step on it** to hurry (*slang*) ◇ **take steps** to take action ◇ **watch your step 1.** to be careful and cautious **2.** to tread carefully

step down *v.* **1.** *vi.* **WITHDRAW FROM POSITION** to resign, retire, or withdraw from a position **2.** *vti.* **DECREASE IN STAGES** to lower or decrease in stages

step in *vi.* to intervene or become involved in something

step out *vi.* **1. LEAVE BRIEFLY** to leave a place for a brief period **2. WALK WITH LONG STRIDES** to walk fast, with longer strides than usual **3. DATE SOMEBODY** to go on a date or to a social gathering with somebody (*informal*) **4. WITHDRAW FROM AN ACTIVITY** to withdraw from some activity (*informal*) **5. TO BE UNFAITHFUL** to be unfaithful to a spouse or partner (*informal*)

step up *v.* **1.** *vt.* **RAISE IN STAGES** to raise or increase something in stages **2.** *vt.* **RAISE VOLTAGE** to raise voltage using a transformer **3.** *vi.* **TO COME FORWARD** to come forward, e.g., to stand for something or to take responsibility for something

step- *prefix.* related because of remarriage, not by blood ○ *stepson* [Old English *stēop-*]

step aer·o·bics *n.* an exercise program done to music that involves performing different movements with the arms and legs while stepping onto and off a small portable platform (*takes a singular or plural verb*)

step·broth·er /stép brùthər/ *n.* a boy or man who has brothers or sisters through the remarriage of a parent to somebody who has children

step·child /stép chīld/ (*plural* **-chil·dren** /-chìldrən/) *n.* the son or daughter of a stepparent

step dance *n.* DANCE a dance in which feet and leg movements, rather than body or arm movements, are most important. It is often performed with the dancer remaining in one place.

step·daugh·ter /stép dàwtər/ *n.* the daughter of somebody's spouse by a previous marriage

step-down *adj.* **1. DECREASING** decreasing in quantity, size, or status, especially in stages **2.** ELEC **LOWERING VOLTAGE** serving to lower voltage —**step-down** *n.*

step·fam·i·ly /stép fàmməlee/ (*plural* **-lies**) *n.* a family in which there is a stepparent

step·fa·ther /stép faathər/ *n.* a man who has married somebody's mother after the death of or divorce from the person's father

step func·tion *n.* a mathematical function such as a waveform that remains constant in value over a given interval but changes abruptly in value from one interval to the next

steph·a·no·tis /stèffə nṓtiss/ (*plural* **-tis·es** *or* **-tis**) *n.* a vine or shrub grown for its fragrant white waxy flowers and leathery leaves. Genus: *Stephanotis.* [Mid-19thC. From Greek *stephanōtis* "fit for a crown," from *stephanos* "crown, wreath," from *stephein* "to crown."]

Ste·phen /steevən/, **St.** (*d.* 36) Christian martyr. Condemned to death on a charge of blasphemy, he was the first Christian martyr. Known as **the Protomartyr**

Ste·phen I, St., King of Hungary (975?–1038). He founded the Hungarian state and established Christianity in Hungary. He is the country's patron saint.

Ste·phens /steevənz/, **Alexander** (1812–83) U.S. statesman. He was vice president of the Confederacy (1861–65) and served in the House of Representatives (1843–59 and 1874–83).

step-in *adj.* **PUT ON BY BEING STEPPED INTO** without fastenings and put on by stepping into it ■ **step-ins** *npl.* **CLOTHING STEPPED INTO** a step-in article of clothing, especially panties with wide legs worn by women in the 1920s and 1930s (*dated*)

step·lad·der /stép làddər/ *n.* a folding ladder that has flat broad steps and a hinged supporting frame

step·moth·er /stép mùthər/ *n.* a woman who has married somebody's father after the death of or divorce from the person's mother

step·par·ent /stép pàirənt, -pàrrənt/ *n.* a stepfather or a stepmother —**step·par·ent·ing** *n.*

steppe /step/ *n.* GEOG an extensive, usually treeless plain, often semiarid and grass-covered [Late 17thC. Via German from Russian *step.*]

Steppes /steps/ *n.* the vast grassy plains of Russia and the Ukraine

step·ping stone, step·ping·stone *n.* **1. STONE OVER WET AREA** one of a series of stones on which somebody is able to step, e.g., to cross shallow water **2. STEP TOWARD GOAL** a stage or step that helps achieve a goal

step rock·et *n.* = **multistage rocket**

step·sis·ter /stép sìstər/ *n.* a girl or woman who has brothers or sisters through the remarriage of a parent to somebody who has children

step·son /stép sùn/ *n.* the son of somebody's spouse by a previous marriage

step stool *n.* a stool with hinged steps that can be folded

step turn *n.* a turn in which a skier lifts one ski in a desired direction, brings it down, and then aligns the other ski with it

step-up *adj.* **1. INCREASING** increasing in quantity, size, or status, usually in stages **2.** ELEC **RAISING VOLTAGE** serving to raise voltage —**stepped-up** *adj.* —**step-up** *n.*

step·wise /stép wīz/ *adj.* **1. ARRANGED IN STEPS** arranged in or resembling steps **2. MOVING TO NEXT TONE** moving from one adjacent tone to another in intervals of a second

ster. *abbr.* sterling

-ster *suffix.* **1.** somebody who is associated with, or does or makes a particular thing ○ *gangster* ○ *punster* **2.** somebody who has a particular characteristic ○ *youngster* [Old English *-estre*, originally a feminine suffix]

ste·ra·di·an /stə ráydee ən/ *n.* the basic International System unit of measurement of a solid angle in a sphere. One steradian is the solid angle made at the center of a sphere by an area on the surface of the sphere equal to the square of the sphere's radius. Symbol **sr** [Late 19thC. Coined from STEREO- + RADIAN.]

ster·co·ra·ceous /stùrkə ráyshəss/ *adj.* consisting of or resembling dung or feces [Mid-18thC. Formed from the Latin stem *stercor-* "dung." Ultimately from an Indo-European word that is also the ancestor of English *dreck* and *scatology.*]

stere /steer/ *n.* a cubic meter, equal to 35.32 cubic ft [Late 18thC. Via French *stère* from Greek *stereos* (see STEREO-).]

stere- *prefix.* = **stereo-** (*used before vowels*)

ster·e·o /stéree ō, steer-/ (*plural* **-os**) *n.* **1. DEVICE PRODUCING STEREOPHONIC SOUND** an audio system or device that reproduces stereophonic sound **2. STEREOPHONIC REPRODUCTION** stereophonic sound reproduction **3. STEREOSCOPIC PHOTOGRAPHY** photography using stereoscopy **4.** PRINTING = **stereotype** *n.* 3 [Late 19thC. Shortening.]

stereo- *prefix.* **1.** three-dimensional ○ *stereology* **2.** solid ○ *stereotaxy* [From Greek *stereos* "solid" (source of English *cholesterol*). Ultimately from an Indo-European word meaning "stiff," which is also the ancestor of *stern*¹, *stare*, *strut*, and *torpid.*]

ster·e·o·bate /stérree ō-, steer-/ *n.* **1. SUPPORTING PLATFORM** a masonry platform that supports a building **2.** = **stylobate** [Mid-19thC. From Latin *stereobates*, from Greek *stereos* "solid" + *-batēs* "walker."]

ster·e·o·chem·is·try /stèrree ō kémmistree, steer-/ *n.* the study of the spatial distribution of atoms in a chemical compound and their effects on the compound's properties

ster·e·o·chrome /stérree ə krōm, steeree/ *n.* a wall painting that uses water glass as a medium or preservative [Mid-19thC. From German *Stereochrom*, from Greek *stereos* "solid" + *khroma* "color."] —**ster·e·o·chro·my** *n.*

ster·e·o·gram /stérree ə gràm, steeree ə-/ *n.* **1.** PHOTOGRAPHY = **stereograph 2.** ARTS **DIAGRAM GIVING THREE-DIMENSIONAL IMPRESSION** a diagram or picture that shows objects as though in relief

ster·e·o·graph /stérree ə gràf, steeree ə-/ *n.* a picture with two superimposed images or two almost identical pictures placed side-by-side which when viewed through special glasses or a stereoscope produce a three-dimensional image

ster·e·og·ra·phy /stèrree óggrəfee, steeree-/ *n.* **1. ILLUSTRATING THREE-DIMENSIONAL FIGURE ON FLAT SURFACE** the technique or art of depicting or drawing a three-dimensional object on a flat surface **2.** GEOM **STUDY OF SOLID GEOMETRIC OBJECTS** the study and construction of defined geometric objects —**ster·e·o·graph·ic** /stèrree ə gráffik, steeree-/ *adj.* —**ster·e·o·graph·i·cal·ly** /-gráffiklee/ *adv.*

ster·e·o·i·so·mer /stèrree ō ī́ssəmər, steeri ō-/ *n.* one molecule in a group of molecules in which the atoms in the molecules are connected in the same order but have different spatial arrangements

ster·e·o·i·som·er·ism /stèrree ō ī sómmə rìzzəm, steeree/ *n.* isomerism in which the atoms in the molecules are connected in the same order but have different spatial arrangements —**ster·e·o·i·so·mer·ic** /stèrrree ō ī̀ssə mérrik/ *adj.*

ster·e·ol·o·gy /stèrree óllәjee, steeree-/ *n.* the study of the properties of three-dimensional structures and objects based on two-dimensional views of them —**ster·e·o·log·i·cal** *adj.*

ster·e·o·phon·ic /stèrree ə fónnik, steeree/ *adj.* using an audio system based on two or more soundtracks to make recorded sound seem more natural when reproduced —**ster·e·o·phon·i·cal·ly** *adv.* —**ster·e·oph·on·y** /stèrree óffənee, steeree-/ *n.*

ster·e·op·sis /stèrree ópsiss, steeree-/ *n.* three-dimensional vision

ster·e·op·ti·con /stèrree ópti kòn, steeree-/ *n.* a type of slide projector able to allow one image to gradually replace another [Mid-19thC. From modern Latin, from Greek *stereos* "solid" + *optikos* "optic."]

ster·e·o·scope /stérree ə skōp, steeree/ *n.* a device resembling a pair of binoculars in which two-dimensional pictures of a scene taken at slightly different angles are viewed concurrently, one with each eye, creating the illusion of three dimensions —**ster·e·o·scop·i·cal·ly** /-skóppikəlee/ *adv.*

ster·e·o·scop·ic /stèrree ə skóppik, steeree-/ *adj.* **1. PRODUCING THREE-DIMENSIONAL EFFECT WHEN SEEN** involving, producing, or resembling the effects of seeing something as three dimensional **2. RELATING TO STEREOSCOPE** produced by or relating to a stereoscope —**ster·e·o·scop·i·cal·ly** *adv.*

ster·e·os·co·py /stèrree óskəpee, steeree-/ *n.* the visual perception of objects as being three dimensional

ste·re·o·spe·cif·ic /stèrree ō spə síffik, steeree/ *adj.* relating to a process in which atoms are in a fixed spatial position

ster·e·o·tax·is /stèrree o táksiss, steeree o-/ *n.* **1.** BIOL **MOVEMENT IN RESPONSE TO SOLID OBJECT** the movement of an entire organism in response to contact with a solid object **2.** MED **TECHNIQUE IN BRAIN SURGERY** neurological surgery involving the insertion of delicate instruments that are guided to a specific area by the use of three-dimensional scanning techniques —**ster·e·o·tac·tic** /-táktik/ *adj.* —**ster·e·o·tac·ti·cal·ly** /-táktikəlee/ *adv.* —**ster·e·o·tax·ic** /-táksik/ *adj.* —**ster·e·o·tax·i·cal·ly** /-táksikəlee/ *adv.*

ster·e·ot·ro·pism /stèrree óttrə pìzzəm, steeree-/ *n.* = **thigmotropism** —**ster·e·o·trop·ic** /stèrree ə tróppik, steeree-/ *adj.*

ster·e·o·type /stérree ə tīp, steeree-/ *n.* **1. OVERSIMPLIFIED CONCEPTION** an oversimplified standardized image or idea held by one person or group of another **2.** PSYCHOL = **stereotypy** *n.* 1 **3.** PRINTING **METAL PRINTING PLATE** a metal printing plate cast from a mold in another material such as papier-mâché ■ *vt.* (**-typed, -typ·ing, -types**) **1. REDUCE TO OVERSIMPLIFIED CATEGORIES** to categorize individuals or groups according to an oversimplified standardized image or idea **2.** PRINTING **USE STEREOTYPE IN PRINTING** to cast or print using a stereotype [Late 18thC. From French *stéréotype* "solid-block printing."] —**ster·e·o·typ·er** *n.* —**ster·e·o·typ·ist** *n.* —**ster·e·o·typ·i·cal** /stèrree ə típpik'l, steeree-/ *adj.*

ster·e·o·ty·py /stérree ə tīpee, steeree-/ *n.* **1. ster·e·o·ty·py, ster·e·o·type** PSYCHOL **PERSISTENT INFLEXIBLE BEHAVIOR PATTERN** a pattern of persistent, fixed, and repeated speech or movement that is apparently meaningless and is characteristic of some mental conditions **2. PRINTING STEREOTYPES** the process of casting or printing stereotypes

ster·ic /stérrik, steér-/ *adj.* related to the way atoms are spatially arranged [Late 19thC. Coined from STEREO-.] —**ster·i·cal·ly** *adv.*

ste·rig·ma /stə rígmə/ (*plural* **-ma·ta** /-mətə/ *or* **-mas**) *n.* a tiny stalk that bears a spore or spores in a fungus [Mid-19thC. Via modern Latin from Greek, "support," from *sterizein* "to support."]

ster·il·ant /stérrələnt/ *n.* MED a substance used to sterilize [Mid-20thC. Formed from STERILE.]

ster·ile /stérrəl, -īl/ *adj.* **1.** ECOL **BARREN** incapable of supporting vegetation **2.** BIOL **INFERTILE** incapable of becoming pregnant or of inducing pregnancy **3.** BIOL **NOT PRODUCING SEEDS** not producing seeds, fruit, or spores **4.** MED **FREE FROM INFECTIVE ORGANISMS** free from living bacteria and other microorganisms **5. DULL AND UNCREATIVE** unstimulating, uncreative, and lacking in ideas that will lead to any useful outcome [15thC. Via Old French from Latin *sterilis.*] —**ster·ile·ly** *adv.* —**ste·ril·i·ty** /stə ríllətee/ *n.*

ster·il·i·za·tion /stèrrələ záysh'n/ *n.* **1.** MED **DESTRUCTION OF MICROORGANISMS** the destruction of living microorganisms to prevent infection **2.** MED, ZOOL **SURGICAL OPERATION PREVENTING REPRODUCTION** a surgical procedure that prevents reproduction by total or partial removal of the reproductive organs

ster·il·ize /stérrə līz/ (**-ized, -iz·ing, -iz·es**) *vt.* **1.** MED **DESTROY MICROORGANISMS** to kill all living microorganisms in order to make something incapable of causing infection **2.** ZOOL, MED **MAKE INFERTILE** to stop a person or animal from reproducing, e.g., by surgical removal or alteration of reproductive organs —**ster·il·iz·a·ble** *adj.* —**ster·il·iz·er** *n.*

ster·let /stúrlət/ (*plural* **-lets** *or* **-let**) *n.* a small caviar-bearing sturgeon of the Black and Caspian Seas. Latin name: *Acipenser ruthenus.* [Late 16thC. From Russian *sterlyad*, ultimately of prehistoric Germanic origin.]

ster·ling /stúrling/ *n.* **1.** = **sterling silver 2.** MONEY **BRITISH CURRENCY** British money **3. BRITISH STANDARD FOR COIN METAL PURITY** the official standard of purity in terms of precious metal content for gold and silver coins in Britain, being 91.666% (22 carat) or 74.999% (18 carat) for gold and 92.5% for silver ■ *adj.* **1. OF STERLING SILVER** made of sterling silver **2. ADMIRABLE** admirable or valuable [13thC. Origin uncertain: probably literally "small star," from an earlier form of STAR. So called because some early Norman pennies bore such a design.]

ster·ling sil·ver, **ster·ling** *n.* an alloy containing at least 92.5% silver with the remainder usually copper, or objects made from this

stern[1] /sturn/ *adj.* **1. STRICT** rigid, strict, and uncompromising **2. SEVERE** severe and allowing no leeway **3. FORBIDDING** grim, austere, or forbidding in appearance [Old English *styrne.* Ultimately from an Indo-European word meaning "stiff," which is also the ancestor of English *starch* and *stare.*]

stern[2] *n.* **1.** NAUT **REAR OF SHIP** the rear part of a vessel **2. BACK PART** the rear part of something ■ *adj.* **IN REAR** located at or resembling the stern [13thC. Origin uncertain: probably from Old Norse *stjórn* "rudder," from the same prehistoric Germanic base that produced English *steer.*]

Stern /sturn/, **Isaac** (*b.* 1920) Russian-born U.S. violinist. He achieved international acclaim and recorded many of the works in the classical repertoire.

Stern, Otto (1888–1969) German-born U.S. physicist. He won a Nobel Prize in physics (1943) for his research into the magnetic properties of atoms.

ster·na plural of **sternum**

stern-chas·er, **stern chas·er** *n.* a cannon mounted at the stern of a vessel for firing to the rear

Sterne /sturn/, **Laurence** (1713–58) British novelist. His comic masterpiece, *The Life and Opinions of Tristram Shandy* (1759–67), anticipated many of the techniques of the modern novel.

ster·nite /stúr nīt/ *n.* a ventral shield or cover on the underside of a segment of an arthropod, especially the chitinous sternum of an insect [Mid-19thC. Coined from STERNUM + -ITE.]

Sterno *tdmk.* a trademark for canned liquid cooking fuel

sterno- *prefix.* the sternum ○ *sternotomy* [From Greek *sternon* (see STERNUM)]

ster·no·cla·vic·u·lar /stùrnō klə víkyələr/ *adj.* relating to or connecting the sternum and clavicle

ster·no·cos·tal /stùrnō kóst'l/ *adj.* situated between or relating to the sternum and ribs [Late 18thC. Coined from STERNO- + Latin *costa* "rib."]

stern·post /stérn pōst/ *n.* the main upright timber in the stern of a vessel

stern·sheets /stúrn sheets/ *npl.* the space at the rear of an open boat that is behind the rowers' bench [Mid-17thC. From SHEET[2] "forward or after section of a boat."]

stern·son /stúrnss'n/ *n.* a reinforcing timber at the joint of a sternpost and keelson at the stern of a wooden vessel [Mid-19thC. Formed from STERN[2], on the model of KEELSON.]

ster·num /stúrnəm/ (*plural* **-nums** *or* **-na** /-nə/) *n.* **1.** ANAT **BREASTBONE** the breastbone (*technical*) **2.** ZOOL **ARTHROPOD'S ABDOMINAL COVERING** the chitinous ventral plate covering the abdomen of an arthropod [Mid-17thC. Via modern Latin from Greek *sternon* "breastbone." Ultimately from an Indo-European word meaning "to spread," which is also the ancestor of English *stratus* and *street.*] —**ster·nal** *adj.*

ster·nu·ta·tion /stùrnyə táysh'n/ *n.* the act of sneezing, or a sneeze (*formal*) [Mid-16thC. From the Latin stem *sternutation-*, from *sternutare*, literally "to keep sneezing," from *sternuere* "to sneeze."]

ster·nu·ta·to·ry /stur nyōōtə tàwree/ *adj.* **CAUSING SNEEZING** causing or resulting in sneezing ■ *n.* (*plural* **-ries**) **SOMETHING THAT CAUSES SNEEZING** any substance that causes sneezing [Early 17thC]

stern·ward /stúrnwərd/, **stern·wards** /-wərdz/ *adv.* in the direction of the stern

stern·way /stúrn wày/ *n.* any backward movement of a vessel

stern-wheel·er /stúrn hweelər/ *n.* a boat propelled by a large paddle wheel at the rear, especially a river boat

ster·oid /steer òyd, sté ròyd/ *n.* an organic fat-soluble compound composed of four joined carbon rings formed naturally or synthetically, and including bile acids, adrenocortical and sex hormones, sterols, and vitamin D [Mid-20thC. Coined from STEROL + -OID.] —**ste·roid·al** /steeróyd'l, steróyd'l/ *adj.*

ster·ol /steer òl, sté ròl/ *n.* a waxy colorless organic solid such as cholesterol or ergosterol, containing an alcohol group and found in animal and plant lipids [Early 20thC. Shortening of CHOLESTEROL.]

-sterone *suffix.* steroid hormone ○ *androsterone* [From STEROL + -ONE]

ster·tor /stúrtər/ *n.* noisy or laborious snoring, heard when somebody is deeply unconscious or when there are obstructed air passages [Early 19thC. From modern Latin, formed from Latin *stertere* "to snore." Ultimately, from an Indo-European base that was originally an imitation of the sound of sneezing or snoring.] —**ster·to·rous** *adj.* —**ster·to·rous·ly** *adv.* —**ster·to·rous·ness** *n.*

stet /stet/ *vti.* (**stet·ted, stet·ting, stets**) **RESTORE DELETED TEXT** to restore or direct somebody to restore something that has previously been deleted from a printed or written text ■ *n.* **INSTRUCTION TO RESTORE DELETED TEXT** a word or mark indicating that previously deleted printed or written matter should be restored [Mid-18thC. From Latin, "let it stand."]

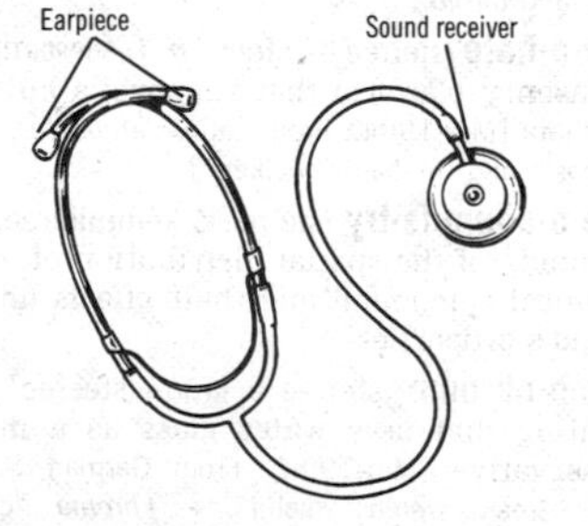

Stethoscope

steth·o·scope /stéthə skōp/ *n.* a medical instrument used for listening to breathing, heartbeats, and other sounds made by the body [Early 19thC. Coined from Greek *stēthos* "chest" + -SCOPE.] —**steth·o·scop·ic** /stèthə skóppik/ *adj.* —**ste·thos·co·py** /ste thóskəpee/ *n.*

Stet·son /stéts'n/ *tdmk.* a trademark for hats having wide brims and high crowns

ste·ve·dore /steévə dàwr/ *n.* **DOCKWORKER** somebody whose job is to load and unload ships ■ *vti.* (**-dored, -dor·ing, -dores**) **DO STEVEDORE WORK** to work as a dockworker, loading and unloading ships [Late 18thC. Via Spanish *estibador* or Portuguese *estivador* from, ultimately, Latin *stipare* (see STEEVE[1]).]

ste·ve·dore's knot *n.* a knot that forms a lump to prevent a line from passing through a hole

Ste·vens /steévənz/, **John** (1749–1838) U.S. inventor and engineer. He pioneered steam power, patenting a boiler (1803) and building the world's first ocean-going steamboat (1809).

Ste·vens, John Paul (*b.* 1920) U.S. jurist. He was appointed an associate justice of the Supreme Court (1975), where he became known as a moderate.

Ste·vens, Thaddeus (1792–1868) U.S. statesman. He twice served as a congressman (1849–53 and 1859–68), opposed slavery, and led the move to impeach President Andrew Johnson.

Wallace Stevens

Ste·vens, Wallace (1879–1955) U.S. poet. His poems have a strongly philosophical bent. He won a Pulitzer Prize for his *Collected Poems* (1954).

Ste·vens-John·son syndrome /steévənz jónss'n-/ *n.* a severe inflammation of the skin and mucous membranes, often after a respiratory infection or as an allergic reaction to drugs [Mid-20thC. Named for Albert Mason *Stevens* (1884–1945) and Frank Chambliss *Johnson* (1894–1934), U.S. pediatricians, who identified the disease.]

Ste·ven·son /steévənssən/, **Adlai** (1900–65) U.S. statesman. He helped found the United Nations in 1945 and was a popular Democratic governor of Illinois (1949–53) before losing two presidential elections to Dwight D. Eisenhower (1952, 1956).

Ste·ven·son /steévənss'n/, **Robert Louis** (1850–94) Scottish writer. He lived in Europe, the United States, and, after 1889, in Samoa. Among his many books of travel, autobiography, and verse, he is best remembered for classic adventure tales such as *Treasure Island* (1883) and *Kidnapped* (1886). Full name **Robert Louis Balfour Stevenson**

stew[1] /stoo/ *n.* **1.** COOK **SIMMERED DISH** a dish of meat, fish, or vegetables, or a combination of them, that is cooked by slow simmering **2. MIXTURE** any widely assorted mixture **3. BROTHEL** a brothel (*archaic*) ■ *v.* (**stewed, stew·ing, stews**) **1.** *vti.* COOK **COOK BY SIMMERING** to cook something by long slow simmering **2.** *vi.* **BE UPSET** to be deeply troubled or agitated **3.** *vi.* **BE VERY HOT** to swelter or become uncomfortably hot [14thC. Via Old French *estuve* "steam bath" from assumed vulgar Latin *extufa* (see STOVE).] ◇ **be** *or* **get in a stew** to be in a difficult situation or to become agitated or anxious (*informal*)

stew[2] *n.* flight attendant (*dated slang*)

stew·ard /stōō ərd/ *n.* **1.** TRANSP **PLANE OR SHIP ATTENDANT** somebody who attends to the passengers on an aircraft or ship, or handles food provisions and dining arrangements on a ship **2.** = **shop steward 3. HOTEL OR CLUB MANAGER** somebody who manages the domestic affairs of a hotel, club, college, or other establishment that provides meals or lodging **4. PROPERTY MANAGER** somebody who manages the property, finances, or household of another **5. OFFICIAL AT PUBLIC EVENT** somebody who acts as a marshal or official at a large public event ■ *vti.* (**-ard·ed, -ard·ing,**

-ards) **WORK AS STEWARD** to work as a steward [Old English *stigweard*, from *stig* "house, hall" (source of English *sty*[1]) + *weard* "keeper" (see WARD)]

stew·ard·ess /stóo ərdəss/ *n.* a woman who attends to the passengers on an aircraft (*dated*)

Jimmy Stewart

Stew·art /stóo ərt, styóo-/, **Jimmy** (1908–97) U.S. actor. He was an appealing, drawling presence in dozens of movies, and was most closely identified with his roles in *Mr. Smith Goes to Washington* (1939) and *It's a Wonderful Life* (1946). Full name **James Maitland Stewart**

Stew·art, Potter (1915–85) U.S. jurist. He was an associate justice of the U.S. Supreme Court (1958–81).

Stew·art Is·land island in New Zealand, situated off the south coast of the South Island. Population: 417 (1996). Area: 670 sq. mi./1,735 sq. km.

stewed /stood, styood/ *adj.* **1.** COOK **SIMMERED** cooked by slow simmering **2. INTOXICATED** very intoxicated (*slang*)

St. Ex. *abbr.* Stock Exchange

stg. *abbr.* sterling

stge. *abbr.* storage

Sth. *abbr.* South

sthe·ni·a /sthə ní ə, sthéenee-/ *n.* great strength or vitality (*archaic or formal*) [Late 18thC. Formed from Greek *sthenos* "strength," of unknown origin.] —**sthen·ic** *adj.*

stib·ine /stíbbeen, -in/ *n.* a foul-smelling poisonous gas produced by the action of hydrochloric acid on an alloy of antimony and zinc. Formula: SbH_3. [Mid-19thC. Coined from Greek *stibi* "antimony" + -INE.]

stib·nite /stíb nìt/ *n.* MINERALS a soft grayish crystalline mineral that is the chief ore of antimony [Mid-19thC. Coined from STIBINE + -ITE.]

stich /stik/ *n.* a line of poetry [Early 18thC. From Greek *stikhos* "row, rank, line of verse."]

Stich /stik, stikh/, **Michael** (*b.* 1968) German tennis player. He won both the Wimbledon Men's Singles (1991) and Men's Doubles (1992), and the ATP World Championship (1993).

sti·cho·myth·i·a /stìkə míthee ə/ *n.* a form of dramatic dialogue in which characters speak single lines alternately [Mid-19thC. From Greek *stikhomuthia*, literally "speaking in lines."] —**stich·o·myth·ic** *adj.*

stick[1] /stik/ *n.* **1.** TREES **THIN BRANCH** a thin branch or shoot cut or broken from a tree **2. WOOD USED FOR FUEL OR CONSTRUCTION** wood pieces used as fuel for a fire or as construction material **3. SPECIALLY SHAPED WOOD** a shaped piece of wood used for a specified purpose ○ *a hockey stick* **4. ROD** a rod, wand, or baton **5. CANE** a cane, club, or cudgel **6. SHORT THIN THING** a short slender part or piece ○ *a stick of celery* **7. SOMETHING USED TO SECURE COMPLIANCE** something used to intimidate or coerce somebody into compliant behavior ○ *carrot and stick* **8.** NAUT **SHIP'S MAST** a mast or spar on a ship **9.** ARMS **BOMBS FALLING ON TARGET AT INTERVALS** a group of bombs that are arranged to fall on a target at regular intervals **10.** AIR **PARACHUTISTS JUMPING TOGETHER** a group of parachutists all jumping at the same time **11.** *U.K.* **CRITICISM** strong adverse criticism (*informal*) **12.** FURNITURE **FURNITURE** a piece of furniture (*informal*) ○ *We need a few sticks to furnish the apartment* **13.** PRINTING = **composing stick 14. BORING PERSON** somebody who is dull or very formal and conventional in manner (*informal*) **15.** DRUGS **CANNABIS CIGARETTE** a marijuana cigarette (*dated slang*) ■ **sticks** *npl.* **REMOTE PLACE** a rural or remote place or district, especially one that is unsophisticated or unfashionable (*informal*) ○ *living out in the sticks* ■ *vt.* (**sticked, stick·ing, sticks**) **1.** GARDENING **SUPPORT PLANT WITH STICK** to support a plant with a stake or stick **2.** PRINTING **USE COMPOSING STICK** to set type using a composing stick (*dated*) [Old English *sticca* "peg." Ultimately from an Indo-European base meaning "to stick, stab," which is also the ancestor of English *stitch, stick*†, *steak, stigma*, and *instigate*.]

stick[2] /stik/ (**stuck** /stuk/, **stick·ing, sticks**) *v.* **1.** *vti.* **PENETRATE** to pierce, stab, or puncture something, or be pierced, stabbed, or punctured **2.** *vt.* **FASTEN WITH POINTED OBJECT** to fasten something in position by thrusting a pointed object such as a pin or nail through something **3.** *vti.* **FASTEN WITH ADHESIVE** to fasten or fix something, or remain attached, by means of an adhesive **4.** *vti.* **PROTRUDE** to protrude or cause something to protrude ○ *She stuck out her hand.* **5.** *vt.* **PUT SOMEWHERE** to place or put something in a location or position (*informal*) ○ *Stick it on the shelf.* **6.** *vti.* **BE UNABLE TO MOVE** to be at or cause to be at a standstill or unable to move or proceed ○ *be stuck in traffic* **7.** *vt.* **PUZZLE** to bewilder or perplex (*usually passive*) ○ *stuck for an answer* **8.** *vi.* **STAY IN THE MIND** to remain in the mind ○ *He told me all the facts but they didn't stick.* **9.** *vi.* COMPUT **RETURN TO WEBSITE** to return often to a particular site on the World Wide Web (*informal*) **10.** *vt.* **USE SOMEBODY** to impose on or exploit somebody (*usually passive*) ○ *stuck with the boring jobs* **11.** *vt.* **KILL ANIMAL** to kill an animal by stabbing ○ *stick a pig* [Old English *stician*. Ultimately from the same Indo-European base as *stick*[1].] ◇ **stick it to** to exploit somebody or treat somebody unfairly (*informal*) ◇ **stick your neck out** to take a risk or make yourself vulnerable (*informal*) ◇ **stick in your craw** *or* **throat** to be extremely distasteful or objectionable (*informal*) ◇ **stick to your guns** to stand firm or maintain an opinion ◇ **stick to your ribs** to be substantial, nourishing, or hearty as a meal (*informal*) ◇ **be stuck on somebody** to be infatuated with somebody (*slang*) ◇ **stick it out** to persist with something to the end, even when doing so is difficult

stick around *vti.* to linger or wait for somebody or something (*informal*)

stick at *vt.* to persist at something ○ *stick at a job until it's done*

stick by *vt.* to remain loyal to something or somebody ○ *I'll stick by you no matter what.*

stick out *vt.* **1. EXTEND SOMETHING** to make something protrude **2. PUT UP WITH** to endure something disagreeable ○ *stick out a long wait*

stick to *v.* **1.** *vti.* **ADHERE TO** to adhere to something, or make something adhere to something **2.** *vt.* **BE LOYAL TO** to be loyal or close to somebody or something **3.** *vt.* **PERSIST WITH** to persist with something **4.** *vt.* **CONTINUE WITH** to keep to without digression

stick together *vi.* to stay close physically or to remain unified ○ *stuck together through thick and thin*

stick up *v.* **1.** *vti.* **BE UPRIGHT** to protrude or point upward, or to make something protrude or point upward **2.** *vt.* **ROB SOMEBODY WITH GUNS** to carry out an armed robbery on somebody (*informal*)

stick up for *vt.* to defend a belief or a person

stick with *vt.* **1. PERSIST WITH** to continue an enterprise rather than succumb to the temptation to cease **2. STAY LOYAL TO** to remain loyal or faithful to somebody or something

stick·ball /stík bàwl/ *n.* a game using baseball rules and played with a rubber ball and a broomstick or other stick

stick·er /stíkər/ *n.* **1. SOMETHING WITH ADHESIVE** an adhesive label, poster, or paper **2. SOMETHING THAT STICKS** something that or somebody who sticks, especially a barbed part of a plant **3. SOMEBODY PERSISTENT** somebody who perseveres

stick·er price *n.* = **list**

stick-fight·ing *n.* *Carib* a highly stylized form of fighting in which two chanting combatants attempt to score points by striking each other with sticks

stick fig·ure *n.* a simple or crude drawing of a person or animal with single lines for the torso, arms, and legs, and a circle for the head

stick·ful /stík fòol/ *n.* the amount of type a composing stick will hold

stick·han·dle /stík hànd'l/ (**-dled, -dling, -dles**) *vt.* to control and maneuver a ball or puck using a lacrosse or ice hockey stick —**stick·han·dler** *n.* —**stick·han·dling** *n.*

stick·ie /stíkee/ *n.* a self-sticking slip of paper sold in pads

stick·ing point *n.* an issue, detail, or item likely to cause difficulty or prevent progress from being made, e.g., in a negotiation

Stick insect

stick in·sect *n.* a long brown or green insect that resembles a twig. Family: Phasmidae.

stick-in-the-mud *n.* somebody who resists new ideas (*informal*)

stick·le /stík'l/ (**-led, -ling, -les**) *vi.* to dispute stubbornly about trivial matters (*archaic*) [Early 17thC. Alteration of obsolete *stightle*, literally "to keep trying to control things," from Old English *stihtian* "to arrange, settle."]

stick·le·back /stík'l bàk/ (*plural* **-backs** *or* **-back**) *n.* a small spiny-backed fish found in both salt and fresh water that has distinctive nest-building and courtship behavior. Family: Gasterosteidae. [15thC. *stickle*, from Old English *sticel* "thorn, sting."]

stick·ler /stíklər/ *n.* **1. SOMEBODY FUSSY ABOUT DETAILS** somebody who insists on every detail being right **2. PUZZLE** a puzzling or perplexing problem [Mid-16thC. Formed from STICKLE.]

stick pin *n.* an ornamental pin with a long shaft and a decoration or design at one end

stick·seed /stík seèd/ *n.* a plant found in Europe, Asia, and North America with prickly seeds that can stick to clothing. Genus: *Lappula.*

stick shift *n.* a manually operated transmission in a motor vehicle, the gearshift that operates it, or a motor vehicle with a manual transmission

stick tack·le *n.* an illegal challenge in field hockey when a player hits another player's stick instead of the ball

stick·tight /stík tìt/ *n.* a plant with barbed fruits that can stick to clothing or fur

stick-to-it-ive·ness /stik tóo itivnəss/ *n.* tenaciousness or perseverance

stick·um /stíkəm/ *n.* any glue or other adhesive substance

stick·up, stick-up *n.* an armed robbery (*informal*)

stick·weed /stík weèd/ (*plural* **-weeds** *or* **-weed**) *n.* a North American plant that has clinging seeds, especially ragweed

stick·y /stíkee/ (**-i·er, -i·est**) *adj.* **1. COVERED IN GLUEY STUFF** covered in something gluey or viscous **2. ADHESIVE** having adhesive qualities **3. HUMID AND HOT** uncomfortably warm and humid ○ *sticky weather* **4. SENTIMENTAL** cloying or excessively sentimental (*informal*) **5.** COMPUT **ATTRACTING VIEWERS** relating to a site on the World Wide Web that attracts users, especially for long periods (*informal*) —**stick·i·ly** *adv.* —**stick·i·ness** *n.*

stick·y·beak /stíki beèk/ *n.* *ANZ* (*informal*) **1. SOMEBODY NOSY** somebody who pries or snoops into the affairs of others **2. NOSY LOOK** an inquisitive look ■ *vi.* (**-beaked, -beak·ing, -beaks**) *ANZ* **SNOOP** to pry or snoop into the affairs of others (*informal*)

stick·y wick·et *n.* an awkward or difficult situation (*informal*)

Stieg·litz /steéglits/, **Alfred** (1864–1946) U.S. photographer. A promoter of photography as an art form, he was known for portraiture and wrote extensively on photographic technique. He was the husband of Georgia O'Keeffe.

stiff /stif/ *adj.* **1. RIGID** rigid, inflexible, or hard to move **2. NOT SUPPLE** painful and not supple ○ *stiff muscles* **3. SEVERE** very harsh or severe ○ *a stiff punishment* **4. TAXING** difficult or demanding ○ *stiff competition* **5. FORCEFUL** having force or power ○ *a stiff breeze* **6. STRONG** strong or potent to the taste or in effect on the body **7. RESOLUTE** showing determination and resolve ○ *stiff resistance* **8. TOO HIGH** higher than is justified or normal ○ *stiff prices* **9. FORMAL** rigidly formal or distant in manner ○ *a stiff manner* **10.** SAILING **NOT LIKELY TO CAPSIZE** relatively stable in the water **11. INTOXICATED** having had too much alcohol to drink (*slang*) ■ *adv.* **1. TOTALLY** totally or utterly ○ *bored stiff* **2. IN A STIFF WAY** in a stiff way or manner ■ *n.* **1. PERSON** a person, especially somebody of a particular type (*slang*) ○ *a lucky stiff* **2. OFFENSIVE TERM** an offensive term referring to somebody regarded as unpleasant or overly formal (*slang insult*) **3. OFFENSIVE TERM** an offensive term referring to somebody who leaves insufficient tips (*slang insult*) **4. CORPSE** a dead body (*slang*) **5. FLOP** something that is an utter failure (*slang*) ■ *vt.* (**stiffed, stiff·ing, stiffs**) **RENEGE** to fail to pay somebody an amount due or expected (*slang*) ○ *He stiffed me on the tip.* [Old English *stīf*. Ultimately, from an Indo-European word meaning "to compress, pack," which is also the ancestor of English *constipate* and *stevedore*).] —**stiff·ish** *adj.* —**stiff·ly** *adv.* —**stiff·ness** *n.*

stiff-arm *adj.* = **straight-arm**

stiff·en /stíff'n/ (**-ened, -en·ing, -ens**) *vti.* **1. BECOME INFLEXIBLE** to become or make something rigid or inflexible **2. STRENGTHEN SOMETHING** to make something stronger or more effective or to become stronger or more effective ○ *stiffen regulations*

stiff-necked *adj.* extremely obstinate and arrogant

sti·fle[1] /stīf'l/ (**-fled, -fling, -fles**) *v.* **1.** *vti.* **SUFFOCATE** to impair somebody's breathing or find it hard to breathe **2.** *vt.* **CHECK OR REPRESS** to curb, repress, or prevent the development of something ○ *stifled the spreading discontent* **3.** *vt.* **REPRESS PHYSICAL ACT** to cut off a physical act, e.g., a yawn or laugh, before it develops [14thC. Origin uncertain: probably an alteration of Old French *estouffer* "to smother" (influenced by Old Norse *stífla* "to stop up"), perhaps of prehistoric Germanic origin.] —**sti·fler** *n.*

sti·fle[2] /stīf'l/ *n.* the joint, corresponding to the human knee, in the hind leg of a four-legged animal [14thC. Origin uncertain: perhaps via Old French *estivel* "leg" from, ultimately, Latin *stipes* "stick, post."]

sti·fling /stīfling/ *adj.* **1. TOO HOT** uncomfortably hot and stuffy **2. REPRESSIVE** repressive in not allowing full expression —**sti·fling·ly** *adv.*

stig·ma /stígmə/ *n.* **1. SIGN OF SOCIAL UNACCEPTABILITY** the shame or disgrace attached to something regarded as socially unacceptable **2.** BOT **PLANT PART** the part of a flower's female reproductive organ (**carpel**) that receives the male pollen grains. It is generally located at the tip of a slender projecting style. **3. stig·ma** (*plural* **-ma·ta**) **MARK ON SKIN** a mark on the skin indicating, e.g., a medical condition **4.** ZOOL **SPOT ON BUTTERFLIES** a colored mark or spot, often resembling an eye, found on certain protozoans and invertebrates, especially butterflies and other lepidoptera [Late 16thC. Via Latin from Greek, "mark on the skin," from *stig-*, the stem of *stizein* "to prick." Ultimately from an Indo-European base that is also the ancestor of English *stick*[1] and *instigate*.]

stig·mas·ter·ol /stig mástə ràwl/ *n.* a sterol found in soybeans and calabar beans, used in making progesterone. Formula: $C_{29}H_{48}O$. [Early 20thC. Coined from a shortening of *Physostigma* genus name of calabar bean + STEROL.]

stig·ma·ta /stig maátə, stígmətə/ *npl.* marks on the hands and feet resembling the wounds from Jesus Christ's crucifixion [Mid-17thC. From Greek, the plural of stigma (see STIGMA).]

stig·mat·ic /stig máttik/ *adj.* **1. SOCIALLY UNACCEPTABLE** socially unacceptable **2.** OPTICS = **anastigmatic** ■ *n.* CHR **SOMEBODY WITH STIGMATA** somebody who bears stigmata [Late 16thC. Formed from Greek *stigmat-*, the stem of *stigma* (see STIGMA). In sense 2, back-formation from ASTIGMATIC.]

stig·ma·tism /stìgmə tìzzəm/ *n.* **1.** OPHTHALMOL **PROPERTIES OF AN ANASTIGMATIC LENS** the properties of an anastigmatic lens **2.** MED **BEING ANASTIGMATIC** the condition in which the eye focuses normally **3.** CHR **HAVING STIGMATA** the condition of having stigmata [Mid-19thC. In senses 1 and 2, back-formation from ASTIGMATISM.]

stig·ma·tist /stígmətist/ *n.* = **stigmatic**

stig·ma·tize /stígmə tīz/ (**-tized, -tiz·ing, -tiz·es**) *v.* **1.** *vt.* **LABEL AS SOCIALLY UNDESIRABLE** to label somebody or something as socially undesirable **2.** *vti.* **MARK WITH STIGMA** to mark somebody or be marked with a stigma or stigmata —**stig·ma·ti·za·tion** /stìgmətə záysh'n/ *n.* —**stig·ma·tiz·er** /stígmə tīzər/ *n.*

stilb /stilb/ *n.* a unit of luminescence equal to 1 candela per square centimeter [Mid-20thC. Via French from Greek *stilbein* "to glitter," of unknown origin.]

stil·bene /stíl been/ *n.* a crystalline solid used in making dyes. Formula: $C_{14}H_{12}$. [Mid-19thC. Coined from Greek *stilbein* "to glitter" + -ENE.]

stil·bes·trol /stil béstrawl/ *n.* = **diethylstilbestrol** [Mid-20thC. Coined from STILBENE + ESTRUS + -OL.]

stil·bite /stíl bīt/ *n.* a white or yellow mineral consisting of a silicate of aluminum, calcium, and sodium chemically combined with water [Early 19thC. Coined from Greek *stilbein* "to glitter" + -ITE; from its lustrous crystals.]

stile[1] /stīl/ *n.* **1. STEPS IN FENCE** a step or rung that enables people to climb over a fence or wall **2.** = **turnstile** [Old English *stigel*. Ultimately from an Indo-European base meaning "to step, climb," which is also the ancestor of English *stair* and *stirrup*.]

stile[2] /stīl/ *n.* a vertical piece in a door, frame, or panel [Late 17thC. Origin uncertain: probably via Dutch *stijl* "prop, doorpost" from, ultimately, Latin *stilus* "column, post" (see STYLUS).]

sti·let /stílət/ *n.* **1. WIRE IN CATHETER** a wire inserted in a catheter to give it rigidity **2. WIRE USED AS PROBE** a fine wire used as a probe in surgery [Late 17thC. Via French from Italian *stiletto* (see STILETTO).]

sti·let·to /sti léttō/ *n.* (*plural* **sti·let·tos** *or* **sti·let·toes**) **1.** ARMS **SMALL DAGGER** a small dagger with a narrow tapering blade **2. POINTED TOOL** a pointed tool for making holes in fabric or leather **3.** CLOTHES = **stiletto heel** ■ *vt.* (**sti·let·toed, sti·let·to·ing, sti·let·tos**) **TO STAB WITH A STILETTO** to stab somebody with a stiletto [Early 17thC. From Italian, literally "small dagger," from *stilo* "dagger," from Latin *stilus* (see STYLUS).]

sti·let·to heel *n.* a high pointed heel on a woman's shoe, or a shoe with such a heel

still[1] /stil/ *adj.* **1. NOT MOVING** motionless and undisturbed **2.** BEVERAGES **NOT CARBONATED** not sparkling or bubbly **3. QUIET** subdued, gentle, or quiet **4.** PHOTOGRAPHY **TAKING STATIC PHOTOGRAPHS** designed for, or relating to the process of, taking photographs as opposed to making movies ■ *adv.* **SILENTLY OR WITHOUT MOTION** without sound or movement ■ *n.* **1. PEACE** silence or peace (*literary*) **2.** CINEMA **SCENE FROM A MOTION PICTURE** a photographic print, either made from a single frame of a motion-picture film or shot independently with a still camera during production ■ *v.* (**stilled, still·ing, stills**) **1.** *vti.* **MAKE CALM** to make somebody or cause somebody to become quiet, calm, soundless, or immobile **2.** *vt.* **RELIEVE** to allay or relieve ○ *stilled our fears* [Old English *stille*. Ultimately from an Indo-European base meaning "to stay put," which is also the ancestor of English *stall*[2], *stele*, and *apostle*.]

WORD KEY: SYNONYMS

See Synonyms at ***calm***.

still[2] /stil/ *adv.* **1. EXISTING NOW** an adverb used to indicate that a situation that used to exist has continued, and exists now ○ *The original is still my favorite.* ○ *I still believe it's a mistake.* ○ *It was still light.* **2. EVEN AT THIS TIME** used to emphasize that something is the case even up to the point mentioned ○ *Her birthday is still a month away.* ○ *He may still be around.* ○ *Still to come...* **3. EVEN MORE** used to emphasize that there is even more of a quality or quantity (*often used with a comparative*) ○ *Profits next year will be larger still.* ○ *The market for flour is equal to almost any in the West, and it will be still better.* **4. NEVERTHELESS** used to emphasize that something remains the case in spite of the situation mentioned ○ *How am I going to do your work and still have time to do my own?* **5. ALWAYS** always or constantly (*archaic or literary*) [13thC. From STILL[1]. The present-day meanings evolved via "constantly" from "motionlessly."]

still[3] /stil/ *n.* **1. APPARATUS FOR DISTILLING** an apparatus for distilling liquids, especially alcohol **2.** = **distillery** [Mid-16thC. Shortening of DISTILL.]

Still /stil/, **Clyfford** (1904–80) U.S. painter. He painted vast abstract expressionist works with dominant jagged areas of intense color.

still a·larm *n.* an alarm given by telephone in which the warning signal is not heard in the place where it is set off

still and all *adv.* nonetheless or notwithstanding

still·birth /stíl bùrth/ *n.* the birth of a dead fetus after the 28th week of pregnancy

still·born /stíl bàwrn/ *adj.* **1.** MED **BORN DEAD** dead at birth **2. INEFFECTUAL** useless or ineffectual from the start [Mid-16thC. Formed from STILL[1] in the obsolete meaning "dead."]

still frame *n.* a single frame from a motion-picture or television program displayed as a photograph

still hunt *n.* a hunt in which game is stalked or ambushed

still-hunt *vt.* to hunt game by stalking or ambushing

Still life: *Still life with Dessert and Bouquet* (1632) by Georg Flegel

still life (*plural* **still lifes**) *n.* **1. PORTRAYAL OF SOMETHING INANIMATE** a representation of inanimate objects, e.g., fruit, flowers, or food, often in a domestic setting, in paintings, pictures, and photographs (*hyphenated when used before a noun*) ○ *a still-life class* **2. STYLE OF STILL LIFE PORTRAYALS** the style or genre of still life used in the various arts such as painting and photography

Still·son /stílss'n/ *tdmk.* trademark for a monkey wrench whose serrated jaws tighten when pressure is applied to the wrench handle

stilt /stilt/ *n.* **1. POLE FOR WALKING** either of two poles with footrests high off the ground on which somebody balances and walks **2.** CONSTR **SUPPORTING POST** a tall post or column that supports a structure above land or water **3.** BIRDS **LONG-LEGGED WADING BIRD** a three-toed, straight-billed, black-and-white shore bird that lives near ponds and marshes. Genera: *Himantopus* and *Cladorhynchus*. ■ *vt.* (**stilt·ed, stilt·ing, stilts**) **RAISE ON STILTS** to place or raise something up on stilts [14thC. Origin uncertain: probably from Low German; ultimately from an Indo-European base meaning "to set up," which is also the ancestor of English *stout*, *stalk*[1], and *still*[1].]

stilt·ed /stíltəd/ *adj.* **1. NOT FLUENT** lacking fluency in being halting or unnatural in flow **2. FORMAL** pompous or unduly formal **3.** BUILDING **RESTING ON VERTICAL PIECES OF STONE** used to describe an arch that is joined to its supporting impost by vertical pieces of stone [Early 17thC. Originally, "having stilts." The sense "not fluent" evolved via the idea of being unnaturally elevated, hence, "restrained."]

Stil·ton[1] /stíltən/ *n.* either of two strong-flavored British white cheeses made from whole milk, one veined with blue mold, the other plain [Mid-18thC. Named after the village of STILTON in Cambridgeshire, England, where the cheese was originally sold.]

Stil·ton[2] /stíltən/ village near Peterborough, in eastern England. It gave its name to Stilton cheese, made in the surrounding areas. Population: 2,219 (1991).

Stil·well /stíl wel, stíllwəl/, **Joseph** (1883–1946) U.S. army general. He commanded U.S. forces in China, Burma, and India during World War II. Full name **Joseph Warren Stilwell**. Known as **Vinegar Joe**

Stim·son /stímsən/, **Henry** (1867–1950) U.S. statesman. He was U.S. secretary of state (1929–33) and secretary of war (1940–45). Full name **Henry Lewis Stimson**

stim·u·lant /stímmyələnt/ *n.* **1. SOURCE OF STIMULUS** something that provides a stimulus, incentive, or quickening **2.** MED **AGENT PRODUCING INCREASE IN FUNCTIONAL ACTIVITY** a drug or other agent that produces a temporary increase in functional activity of a body organ or part ■ *adj.* **INCREASING ACTIVITY** increasing bodily activity or acting as a stimulus or incentive

stim·u·late /stímmyə làyt/ (**-lat·ed, -lat·ing, -lates**) *v.* **1.** *vt.* **ENCOURAGE** to encourage something, e.g., an activity or a process, so that it will begin, increase, or develop **2.** *vt.* **MAKE INTERESTED** to cause somebody to become interested in or excited about something **3.** *vt.* **CAUSE TO RESPOND** to cause physical activity in something such as a nerve or an organ **4.** *vti.* **MAKE MORE ALERT** to cause somebody to become more alert or active, as by the use of caffeine or a drug [Early 16thC. From Latin *stimulat-*, the past participle stem of *stimulare*, literally "to goad," from *stimulus* (see STIMULUS).] —**stim·u·la·ble** *adj.* —**stim·u·lat·ing** *adj.* —**stim·u·lat·ing·ly** *adv.* —**stim·u·la·tion** /stìmmyə láysh'n/ *n.* —**stim·u·la·tive** /stímmyə làytiv, stímmyələtiv/ *adj.* —**stim·u·la·tor** /stímmyə làytər/ *n.* —**stim·u·la·to·ry** /stímmyələ tàwree/ *adj.*

stim·u·lus /stímmyələss/ (*plural* **-li** /-lī/) *n.* **1. INCENTIVE** something that encourages an activity or a process to begin, increase, or develop **2. SOMETHING AROUSING INTEREST** an agent or factor that provokes interest, enthusiasm, or excitement **3. CAUSE OF A RESPONSE** something, e.g., a drug or an electrical impulse, that causes a physical response in an organism [Late 17thC. From Latin, "goad, stake," of uncertain origin.] —**stim·u·lant** *adj.*

sting /sting/ *v.* (**stung** /stung/, **sting·ing, stings**) **1.** *vti.* **INJECT WITH TOXIN** to prick the skin and inject a small quantity of a poisonous or irritant substance, causing a sharp pain often followed by itchiness and swelling **2.** *vti.* **PRODUCE SHARP PAIN** to feel, or cause somebody to feel, a sharp pain, usually only for a short period of time ○ *His eyes were stinging from the onions.* **3.** *vt.* **UPSET** to make somebody feel upset, hurt, or annoyed ○ *I was stung by her harsh criticisms.* **4.** *vt.* **GOAD** to urge somebody on, usually with criticism ○ *words that stung them into action* ■ *n.* **1. WOUND CAUSED BY STING** a skin wound that may hurt, swell up, and itch, caused by an insect, plant, or animal piercing the skin and injecting a small quantity of poison **2.** = **stinger**[1] *n.* 2 **3. SHARP PAIN** a short sharp pain, e.g., that caused by the application of an antiseptic to a fresh wound **4. HURTFULNESS** the hurtful nature of something, e.g., criticism **5. POWER TO UPSET** the power to inflict mental or emotional discomfort ○ *threats that have lost their sting* **6.** = **stinging hair 7. UNDERCOVER OPERATION** a complex undercover operation to catch criminals (*slang*) (*often used before a noun*) **8. TRICK** an underhanded scheme, especially a carefully planned and orchestrated swindle (*slang*) [Old English *stingan*] —**sting·ing·ly** *adv.*

Sting /sting/ (*b.* 1952) British singer, songwriter, and actor. He formed the group The Police (1978–84), and later pursued a solo singing and acting career. Real name **Gordon Sumner**

sting·a·ree /stíngə rèe, stìngə rée/ (*plural* **-rees** *or* **-ree**) *n. U.S., Can, ANZ* = **stingray**

sting·er[1] /stíngər/ *n.* **1. SOMETHING STINGING** something that stings, especially a hurtful or critical comment **2. POISON-INJECTING ORGAN** the sharp organ through which an insect or other animal injects poison to immobilize its prey or for defense **3. BLOW** a sharp blow or slap that causes a smarting pain (*informal*) **4. UNDERCOVER OFFICER** a law enforcement officer who is taking part in an undercover operation (*informal*)

sting·er[2] /stíngər/ *n.* BEVERAGES **1. COCKTAIL** a cocktail consisting of crème de menthe and brandy **2.** *U.K.* **WHISKEY DRINK** a whiskey and soda with crushed ice [Early 20thC. Alteration of *stengah*.]

sting·ing cell *n.* = **cnidoblast**

sting·ing hair *n.* a glandular plant hair, e.g., on a stinging nettle, that releases an irritant chemical when touched

sting·ing net·tle *n.* = **nettle** *n.* 1

sting·less bee *n.* a social bee that has no functional stinger, but may bite. Subfamily: Meliponinae.

sting·ray /stíng rày/ (*plural* **-rays** *or* **-ray**) *n.* a ray with a flexible tail shaped like a whip with poisonous spines. There are several species, mainly found in shallow warm waters. Family: Dasyatidae.

stin·gy /stínjee/ (**-gi·er, -gi·est**) *adj.* **1. UNGENEROUS** not generous in giving or spending money **2. SMALL OR INADEQUATE** ungenerously small or inadequate ○ *a stingy tip* [Mid-17thC. Origin uncertain: perhaps formed from a variant of STING, with an underlying meaning "irritable, bad-tempered."] —**stin·gi·ly** *adv.* —**stin·gi·ness** *n.*

stink /stingk/ *vi.* (**stank** /stangk/ *or* **stunk** /stungk/, **stunk, stink·ing, stinks**) **1. SMELL HORRIBLE** to have a very strong and extremely unpleasant smell **2. BE WORTHLESS** to be loathsomely bad or worthless (*informal*) ○ *This

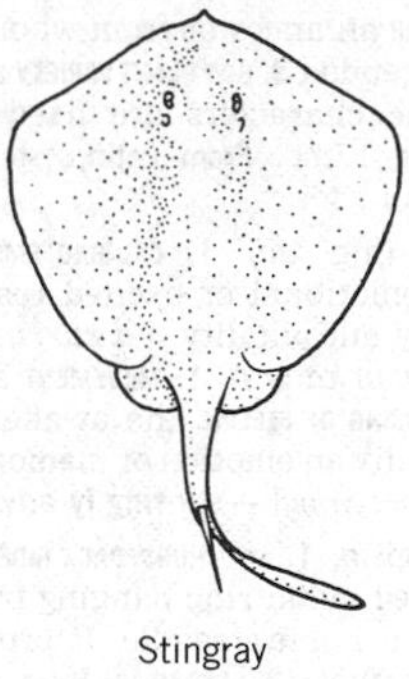

Stingray

poetry is so bad it stinks.* **3. BE CORRUPT** to be despicably corrupt or dishonest (*informal*) ○ *The whole admissions process stinks.* **4. HAVE TOO MUCH** to have, or be suspected of having, been assisted by improper influence (*informal*) ○ *a career that stinks of nepotism* ■ *n.* **1. TERRIBLE SMELL** a very strong and unpleasant smell **2. SCANDAL** a scandalous revelation (*informal*) ○ *"even if there was a stink, he had plenty good friends in San Francisco"* (Robert Louis Stevenson, *The Wrecker*; 1896) [Old English *stincan* "to smell"] —**stink·i·ly** *adv.* —**stink·y** *adj.* ◇ **make a stink, raise a stink** to cause trouble, especially by protesting (*informal*)

WORD KEY: SYNONYMS

See Synonyms at ***smell***.

stink up *vt.* to give something a very strong and unpleasant smell ○ *The smell of rotting potatoes stank the whole place up.*

stinkaroo *n.* = **stinkeroo** (*slang*)

stink·ball /stíngk bàwl/ *n.* = **stinkpot** *n.* 4

stink bomb *n.* a practical joker's toy in the form of a small glass or plastic capsule that, when smashed, emits a horrible smell

stink·bug /stíngk bùg/ *n.* an insect that emits foul-smelling secretions. It typically has a flattish body, and is often camouflaged to blend with its surroundings. Family: Pentatomidae.

stink·er /stíngkər/ *n.* (*informal*) **1. SOMETHING UNPLEASANT** something that is very difficult or unpleasant ○ *That last exam was a real stinker.* **2. BAD BEHAVER** somebody who behaves in an obnoxious or hateful way **3.** BIRDS **SPITTING SEABIRD** a fulmar or petrel that spits a foul-smelling oil at aggressors. They feed on offal and carrion.

stink·er·oo /stingkə ró͞o, stíngkə ró͞o/ (*plural* **-oos**), **stink·a·roo** (*plural* **-roos**) *n.* an irritating, loathsome, or otherwise unpleasant person (*slang*) [Mid-20thC. Formed from STINK.]

stink·horn /stíngk hàwrn/ *n.* a fungus with a thick white stalk and a thimble-shaped foul-smelling cap containing spores. The smell attracts flies, which disperse the spores. Order: Phallales.

stink·ing /stíngking/ *adj.* **1. SMELLY** having or giving off a very strong and unpleasant smell **2. EXTREMELY BAD** used to describe an action or behavior regarded as unpleasant or contemptible (*informal*) ○ *"This was, of course, a stinking lie."* (Richard Kadrey, *Metrophage*; 1995) **3. INTOXICATED** very intoxicated (*slang*) ■ *adv.* **USED FOR EMPHASIS** used to emphasize the contemptible extent of something (*informal*) —**stink·ing·ly** *adv.* —**stink·ing·ness** *n.*

stink·ing ash *n.* a deciduous tree with fragrant greenish white flowers, native to eastern North America. Its fruits have a flavor similar to hops and are used in brewing beer. Latin name: *Ptelea trifoliata.*

stink·ing ce·dar *n.* = **California nutmeg** [From its foul-smelling leaves and wood]

stink·ing cham·o·mile *n.* an annual plant, similar to a daisy, with foul-smelling leaves. It grows as a weed on cultivated and waste ground throughout Europe. Latin name: *Anthemis cotula.*

stink·o /stíngkō/ *adj.* **1. INTOXICATED** very intoxicated (*dated slang*) **2. POOR-QUALITY** of the poorest quality (*informal*) ○ *a stinko bowl of stew*

stink·pot /stíngk pòt/ *n.* **1. SOMETHING WITH HORRIBLE SMELL** somebody or something that smells horrible (*informal*) **2. OFFENSIVE TERM** an offensive term referring to somebody considered very unpleasant or unpopular (*slang insult*) **3.** ZOOL **SMALL N AMERICAN TURTLE** a small species of musk turtle found in ponds and sluggish streams in the United States. It emits a foul-smelling secretion from its cloacal glands. Latin name: *Sternotherus odoratus.* **4.** ARMS **STINKING WEAPON** a military weapon used in former times, consisting of an earthenware pot that released a suffocating vapor when thrown into an enemy position or onto an enemy ship

stink·stone /stíngk stōn/ *n.* rock, especially limestone, that gives off a highly unpleasant odor when rubbed or struck [Early 20thC. Translation of German *Stinkstein*.]

stink·weed /stíngk wèed/ (*plural* **-weeds** *or* **-weed**) *n.* **1.** = **wall rocket 2. FOUL-SMELLING PLANT** a plant with unpleasant-smelling flowers or foliage, e.g., mayweed or pennycress

stink·wood /stíngk wo͝od/ (*plural* **-woods** *or* **-wood**) *n.* **1. TREE WITH FOUL-SMELLING WOOD** a tree with unpleasant-smelling wood, in particular a South African deciduous tree whose hard wood is used for making furniture **2. WOOD** the hard durable wood of any of the stinkwood trees [Mid-18thC. Translation of Dutch *stinkhout*.]

stint[1] /stint/ *v.* (**stint·ed, stint·ing, stints**) **1.** *vi.* **BE MISERLY** to be ungenerous in offering, providing, or giving ○ *For a really good mousse, you can't stint on the chocolate.* **2.** *vt.* **DENY** to deny somebody something out of miserliness, or deny something of the self, usually in an act of sacrifice ○ *"your mother and me economizing and stinting ourselves to give you a University education"* (Thomas Hardy, *Tess of the d'Urbervilles*; 1891) **3.** *vi.* **STOP** to stop or halt (*archaic*) ■ *n.* **1. ALLOTTED TIME** a fixed period of time spent on a particular task or job ○ *do a two-year stint as an apprentice* **2. LIMITATION** limitation or restriction, especially one of time or amount ○ *"I gave him time and thought without stint"* (Willa Cather, *The Professor's House*; 1925) **3. STOPPAGE** a pause or stoppage (*archaic*) [Old English *styntan* "to blunt," later reinforced by Old Norse *stytta* "to shorten"] —**stint·er** *n.*

stint[2] /stint/ (*plural* **stints** *or* **stint**) *n.* BIRDS any one of various sandpipers [15thC. Origin unknown.]

stip. *abbr.* **1.** stipend **2.** stipulation

stipe /stīp/ *n.* **1.** BOT **FUNGUS OR FERN STALK** the stalk of a mushroom or fern **2.** ZOOL = **stipes** *n.* 1 [Late 18thC. Via French from Latin *stipes* (see STIPES).]

sti·pel /stīp'l/ *n.* a structure shaped like a tiny leaf or scale located at the base of a leaflet of a compound leaf [Early 19thC. Via French from modern Latin *stipella*, literally "small stipule," from *stipula* (see STIPULE).] —**sti·pel·late** /stī péllət, sti péllət, stīpə làyt/ *adj.*

sti·pend /stī pènd, stīpənd/ *n.* a fixed amount of money paid at regular intervals as a salary or to cover living expenses [15thC. Directly or via Old French from Latin *stipendium* "soldier's pay," from *stips* "payment" + *pendere* "to weigh out" (see PENSIVE).]

WORD KEY: SYNONYMS

See Synonyms at ***wage***.

sti·pen·di·ar·y /stī péndee èrree/ *adj.* **1. PROVIDED WITH ALLOWANCE** receiving a fixed amount of money on a regular basis as a salary or to cover living expenses **2. WITH STIPEND** paying a stipend or paid for by a stipend ■ *n.* (*plural* **-ies**) **SOMEBODY RECEIVING STIPEND** somebody who receives a fixed amount of money on a regular basis as a salary or to cover living expenses, e.g., a graduate student

sti·pes /stī pèez/ (*plural* **stip·i·tes** /stíppi tèez/) *n.* **1.** ZOOL **MOUTHPART** the second or bottom mouthpart of some insects and crustaceans **2.** ZOOL **EYESTALK** the eyestalk of a crayfish or crab **3.** BOT = **stipe** *n.* 1 [Mid-18thC. Via modern Latin from Latin, "post."] —**sti·pi·form** /stíppiə fàwrm/ *adj.*

stip·i·tate /stíppi tàyt/ *adj.* BOT having or supported by a stipe [Late 18thC. From modern Latin *stipitatus*, from *stipit-*, the stem of *stipes* (see STIPES).]

stip·i·tes plural of **stipes**

stip·ple /stípp'l/ *vt.* (**-pled, -pling, -ples**) **1. PAINT BY DABBING** to paint, draw, or engrave something using dots or short dabbing strokes **2. APPLY WITH DABBING STROKES** to apply paint or any other substance in dots or short dabbing strokes **3. MAKE SURFACE MATERIAL APPEAR GRAINY** to give something, e.g., wet paint or plaster, a rough grainy texture with dabbing strokes **4. DAPPLE** to mark something with dots or speckles (*literary; usually passive*) ○ *its lime-green clapboard stippled with sunlight* ■ *n.* **1.** PAINTING **ARTISTIC TECHNIQUE** the technique of painting, engraving, or drawing using dots or short dabbing strokes **2.** CONSTR **DABBED FINISH** an irregular or grainy finish in paint or wet plaster, produced using dabbing strokes [Mid-18thC. From Dutch *stippelen*, literally "to keep pricking," from, ultimately, *stip* "point, dot."] —**stip·pler** *n.* —**stip·pling** *n.*

stip·u·late[1] /stíppyə lày̆t/ (**-lat·ed, -lat·ing, -lates**) *v.* **1.** *vt.* **SPECIFY** to specify something such as a condition when making an agreement or an offer ○ *The contract stipulates which expenses will be covered.* **2.** *vti.* **DEMAND** to make a specific demand for something, usually as a condition in an agreement ○ *stipulate a price* **3.** *vt.* **MAKE FORMAL PROMISE** to promise something formally or legally **4.** *vi.* LAW **AGREE** to agree, in terms of the conduct of a legal proceeding ○ *We will stipulate to our receipt of all pertinent discovery documents, Your Honor.* **5.** *vt.* LAW **ADMIT FACT** to confess, admit, or agree to a fact rather than require the opposition to prove that fact ○ *Will the defendant stipulate her presence at the scene of the crime?* [Early 17thC. From Latin *stipulat-*, the past participle stem of *stipulari* "to demand, bargain," of uncertain origin.] —**stip·u·la·ble** /stíppyələb'l/ *adj.* —**stip·u·la·tion** /stìppyə láysh'n/ *n.* —**stip·u·la·tor** /stíppyə làytər/ *n.* —**stip·u·la·to·ry** /stíppyələ tàwree/ *adj.*

stip·u·late[2] /stíppyə lit/ *adj.* used to describe a stem or stalk that has a pair of growths resembling leaves (**stipules**) at the base [Late 18thC. Formed from STIPULE.]

stip·ule /stíppyool/ *n.* either of a pair of small growths at the base of a leaf stalk or stem that resemble leaves [Late 18thC. Directly or via French from Latin *stipula* "straw, stalk" (source of English *stubble*), of uncertain origin.] —**stip·u·lar** /stíppyələr/ *adj.*

stir[1] /stur/ *v.* (**stirred, stir·ring, stirs**) **1.** *vt.* **MIX INGREDIENTS** to move a spoon, stick, or some other implement through a liquid in order to mix or cool the contents ○ *Slowly stir the cream into the soup.* **2.** *vi.* **BE ABLE TO BE STIRRED** to be of a consistency that allows a spoon or other implement to be moved around **3.** *vti.* **MOVE** to move gently or cause something to move gently **4.** *vi.* **LEAVE** to move or leave, especially from a favorite or usual place ○ *The guards were told not to stir from their posts.* **5.** *vi.* **MOVE AFTER RESTING** to get up and move about, especially after a rest ○ *anyone stirring at this early hour* **6.** *vt.* **GOAD INTO ACTION** to rouse somebody into action **7.** *vt.* **AROUSE FEELING** to arouse something, e.g., an emotion or a memory (*formal*) **8.** *vi.* **BE FELT** to begin to be experienced as an emotion (*formal*) ○ *Deep-seated bitterness began to stir within him.* **9.** *vti.* **MAKE EMOTIONAL** to arouse strong emotions in somebody ○ *music that never fails to stir me* **10.** *vi.* **HAPPEN** to happen or be current (*informal*) ○ *What's stirring this week on Capitol Hill?* ■ *n.* **1.** **ACT OF STIRRING** an act or instance of stirring a liquid **2.** **COMMOTION** a fervent reaction, usually either excitement or controversy **3.** **SLIGHT MOVEMENT** a gentle movement **4.** *Aus* **TROUBLE** trouble (*informal*) [Old English *styrian* "to agitate." Ultimately from an Indo-European word meaning "to whirl," which is also the ancestor of English *storm*, *turbine*, and *disturb*.] —**stir·ra·ble** *adj.* —**stir·rer** *n.*

stir up *vt.* **1.** **CAUSE TROUBLE** to cause trouble or a confrontation deliberately **2.** **AGITATE** to cause something such as dust to rise and swirl around

stir[2] /stur/ *n.* prison (*slang*) [Mid-19thC. Origin uncertain: perhaps from Romany *sturbin* "jail."]

stir-cra·zy *adj.* mentally unsettled as a result of spending a long time in a confined space, e.g., a prison cell (*informal or humorous*) [From STIR[2]]

stir-fry *vt.* **FRY FOOD RAPIDLY** to fry small tender pieces of food rapidly in a small amount of oil over high heat, stirring continuously. This method is used extensively in Chinese cooking. ■ *n.* **STIR-FRIED DISH** a dish of food prepared by stir-frying

Stir·ling en·gine /stúrling-/ *n.* an external-combustion engine in which heat generated on the outside of the cylinders causes either air or an inert gas within the cylinders to expand and drive the pistons [Mid-19thC. Named for the Scottish minister and engineer Rev. Robert *Stirling* (1790–1878), who invented it.]

Stir·ling's for·mu·la /stúrlingz-/ *n.* a mathematical formula used to calculate the approximate value of the factorial of a very large number [Mid-20thC. Named for the Scottish mathematician James *Stirling* (1692–1770), who devised the formula.]

stirps /sturps/ (*plural* **stir·pes** /stúr peez/) *n.* **1.** HERALDRY **STOCK** a line of descendants from a common ancestor **2.** LAW **ANCESTOR** an ancestor from whom a particular family is descended **3.** BOT **PLANT VARIETY** a plant variety in which the characters are fixed through cultivation [Late 17thC. From Latin, "stem, lineage," of unknown origin.]

stir·ring /stúr ring/ *adj.* **1.** **CAUSING EMOTIONAL REACTION** causing an emotional or excited reaction **2.** **LIVELY** full of energy and vitality ○ *a stirring rendition of a Chopin mazurka* ■ *n.* **1.** **MOVEMENT** a slight movement **2.** **AROUSING OF FEELING** the awakening of something, especially an emotion or memory (*formal*) [Old English *styrend, styring*] —**stir·ring·ly** *adv.*

stir·rup /stúr əp/ *n.* **1.** EQU **HORSEBACK RIDER'S FOOT SUPPORT** a flat-bottomed metal ring hanging from a strap on each side of a horse's saddle. It provides support for a rider's foot. **2.** **STRAP** a loop or strap that supports a foot or passes under a foot, such as the straps supporting a woman's feet in childbirth **3.** NAUT **SHIP'S ROPE** one of a set of ropes hanging from a sail-supporting spar (**yard**) on a ship. Loops at the bottom allow another rope for standing on to be threaded through. [Old English *stigrāp*, literally "rope for getting up," from *stīgan* "to go up" (see STY) + *rāp* "rope"]

stir·rup bone *n.* the stapes [From its shape]

stir·rup cup *n.* a farewell drink of alcohol, originally one shared with a departing horseback rider

stir·rup i·ron *n.* the metal ring of a riding stirrup

stir·rup leath·er *n.* a leather strap that attaches a stirrup to the saddle

stir·rup pants *npl.* women's stretch pants with straps attached that pass under the feet

stir·rup pump *n.* a portable hand-operated pump, held on the ground with the feet, which draws water from a bucket, and sprays it out. It is used to fight small fires. [From the shape of the foot-piece used to hold the pump in place]

stish·ov·ite /stíshə vīt/ *n.* a rare crystalline form of quartz found in meteor craters. It is formed from common quartz by the tremendous pressure produced on impact. [Mid-20thC. Named for the 20th-century Russian mineralogist S. M. *Stishov*, who first synthesized it.]

stitch /stich/ *n.* **1.** SEW **LENGTH OF THREAD IN MATERIAL** a short length of thread that has been passed through one or more pieces of material, either for decoration or to join pieces together **2.** SURG **SURGICAL THREAD** a single loop of surgical thread used to close up a wound **3.** KNITTING **LOOP OF WOOL** a single loop of wool or similar material, passed around a knitting needle or a crochet hook **4.** CRAFT **STYLE OF NEEDLEWORK** a specified style of sewing or knitting ○ *lock stitch* **5.** **ACHING PAIN** a cramp in the side of the abdomen caused, e.g., by exercising or laughing **6.** **ARTICLE OF CLOTHING** a single article of clothing (*informal*) ○ *didn't have a stitch on* **7.** AGRIC **RIDGE BETWEEN FURROWS** the ridge between two adjacent furrows in a field ■ *vt.* (**stitched, stitch·ing, stitch·es**) **1.** SEW **SEW** to join, finish, or decorate something with stitches **2.** SURG **CLOSE WOUND** to close a wound with one or more stitches **3.** PRINTING **BIND PAGES** to bind the pages of a book, pamphlet, or other publication with thread or staples [Old English *stice* "prick." Ultimately from Indo-European, meaning "to jab" (ancestor also of English *stick*). Sense 7, "ridge," probably from the same source, the underlying idea being "cut, divided land."] —**stitch·er** *n.* ◇ **in stitches** laughing a great deal

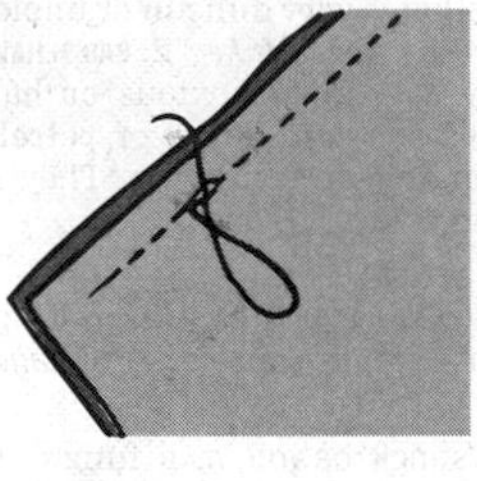

Running stitch

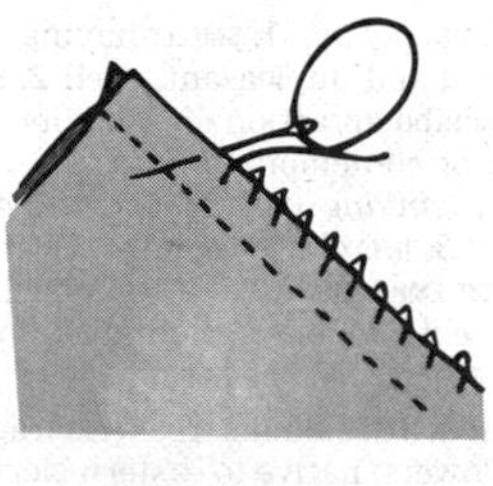

Overcast stitch

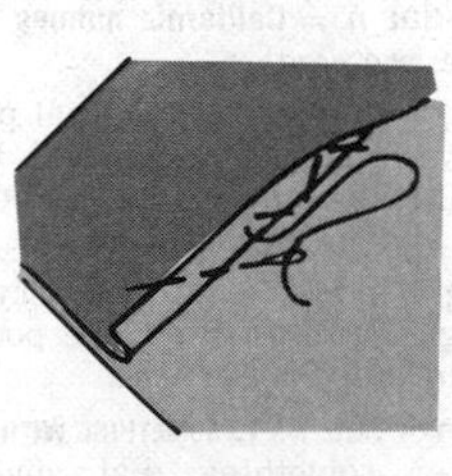

Blindstitch

Stitch

stitch·er·y /stíchəree/ *n.* needlework, especially when it is functional rather than decorative [Early 17thC. Probably coined by Shakespeare.]

stitch·wort /stích wùrt, stích wàwrt/ (*plural* **-worts** *or* **-wort**) *n.* a low-growing herbaceous plant with small white star-shaped flowers. There are several species. Genus: *Stellaria*. [Old English *sticwyrt*; from its former use to cure sharp pains in the side]

stith·y /stíthee, stíthee/ *n.* (*plural* **-ies**) (*archaic*) **1.** **ANVIL** an anvil **2.** **FORGE OR SMITHY** a place where metalwork is done ■ *vt.* (**-ied, -y·ing, -ies**) **FORGE SOMETHING** to forge something on an anvil (*archaic*) [13thC. From Old Norse *steði*. Ultimately from an Indo-European word meaning "to stand," which is also the ancestor of English *stand* and *stead*.]

sti·ver /stívər/ *n.* **1.** **OLD DUTCH COIN** a Dutch coin, no longer in circulation, worth one-twentieth of a guilder **2.** **SOMETHING TRIFLING** something of very little value, especially the least or smallest amount of money (*archaic*) [Early 16thC. From Dutch *stuiver*. Ultimately from a prehistoric Germanic word meaning "small piece," which is also the ancestor of English *stub*.]

stk. *abbr.* stock

S.T.M. *abbr.* Master of Sacred Theology [Shortening of latin *Sacrae Theologiae Magister*]

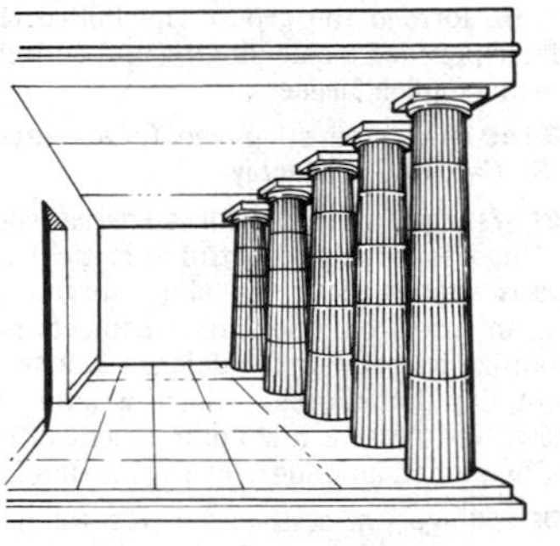

Stoa

sto·a /stṓ ə/ (*plural* **-as** *or* **-ae** /stṓ ee/) *n.* in ancient Greece, a covered walkway, usually with a row of columns on one side and a wall on the other [Early 17thC. From Greek (source also of English *stoic*).]

stoat /stōt/ (*plural* **stoats** *or* **stoat**) *n.* = **ermine** [15thC. Origin unknown.]

stob /stob/ *n.* *U.K., Southern U.S.* a stake or stump (*regional*) [14thC. Origin uncertain: probably a variant of STUB.]

sto·chas·tic /stə kástik/ *adj.* **1.** **RANDOM** involving or showing random behavior **2.** **INVOLVING PROBABILITY** involving or subject to probabilistic behavior **3.** **INVOLVING GUESSWORK** involving guesswork or conjecture (*formal*) [Mid-20thC. From Greek *stokhastikos*, from *stokhos* "target, aim," literally "pointed stake." Ultimately from an Indo-European word that is also the ancestor of English *stag*.] —**sto·chas·ti·cal·ly** *adv.*

stock /stok/ *n.* **1.** COMM **SUPPLY OF SALABLE GOODS** a supply of goods for sale, kept on the premises by a store or business **2.** **SUPPLY** a supply held in reserve for future use **3.** **AVAILABLE AMOUNT** the amount of something, e.g., a natural resource or a service, available in a particular area ○ *an alarming fall in North*

Atlantic fish stocks **4.** *U.K.* FIN = **capital stock** **5.** FIN **INVESTOR'S CAPITAL SHARE** the share of capital held by an individual investor (*often used in the plural*) **6.** FIN **TOTAL SHARES ISSUED** the total number of shares issued by a company or sector **7.** **SOMEBODY'S REPUTATION** somebody's standing or reputation ○ *Her stock is high in terms of public opinion because of her aid work.* **8.** AGRIC = **livestock** **9.** **DESCENT** ancestry, usually with reference to race, ethnic group, region, or profession **10.** **ORIGINAL VARIETY** the original variety from which other similar plants, animals, or languages are descended **11.** BIOL **RELATED ORGANISMS** a race, family, breed, or other related group of animals or plants **12.** LING **RELATED LANGUAGES** a group of related languages **13.** COOK **BROTH** a liquid made by simmering meat, fish, bones, or vegetables with herbs in water, used in soups, stews, and sauces **14.** BOT **TRUNK** the trunk of a tree or the main stem of a plant **15.** BOT **PLANT RECEIVING GRAFT** a plant or plant stem onto which a shoot or bud is grafted **16.** BOT **PLANT USED FOR CUTTINGS** a plant or part of a plant from which cuttings are taken **17.** AGRIC **ANIMAL PEN** a small pen or frame where a single animal can be confined, e.g., for veterinary examination or treatment (*often used in the plural*) **18.** ARMS **PART OF FIREARM** the part of a firearm to which the barrel and firing mechanism are attached. It is held in the hand or rested against the shoulder. **19.** ARMS **PART OF GUN CARRIAGE** the long beam on a field artillery carriage that extends behind it. When placed on the ground, it becomes the piece's third point of contact, along with the two wheels. **20.** AGRIC, HIST **PART OF PLOW** the frame of a horse-drawn plow **21.** **HANDLE** a handle, e.g., the handle of a fishing rod, whip, or carpentry tool **22.** **WOODEN BLOCK** a block of wood, especially the block from which a bell is hung **23.** **SUPPORTING PART** any upright supporting part **24.** NAUT **ANCHOR PART** the crosspiece on certain types of anchor **25.** **RAW MATERIAL** the basic material from which anything is manufactured **26.** CINEMA **UNEXPOSED FILM** movie film that has not yet been exposed **27.** METALL **PIECE OF METAL** a piece of cut metal ready to be processed, especially by forging **28.** (*plural* **stocks** *or* **stock**) **FLOWERING PLANT** a plant with clusters of fragrant, brightly colored flowers. There are several varieties, some of which are widely grown as ornamentals. They are native chiefly to Europe and Asia. Genus: *Matthiola*. **29.** (*plural* **stocks** *or* **stock**) = **Virginia stock** **30.** EQU **RIDING NECKCLOTH** a white neckcloth now only worn as part of formal riding dress. In the 18th century it was part of general male attire. **31.** CHR **CLERICAL SHIRT FRONT** a broad piece of cloth worn on the chest below a clerical collar by members of the clergy in some denominations of the Christian Church **32.** GAME **UNDISTRIBUTED CARDS OR COUNTERS** a pile of cards or counters not dealt out at the start of a game, but picked up during it **33.** THEATER **SYSTEM OF PRESENTING PLAYS** a system by which a permanent theater company presents a set of works during a season, usually in its own theater **34.** THEATER **REPERTOIRE OF PLAYS** a theater company's repertoire of plays **35.** THEATER = **stock company** *n.* 2 **36.** *U.K.* **HUB** the hub of a wheel **37.** GEOL **ROCK MASS** a roughly circular mass of exposed igneous rock **38.** RAIL = **rolling stock** **39.** CLOTHES **SOCK** a sock or stocking (*archaic*) ■ **stocks** *npl.* **1.** **PUNISHMENT DEVICE** a wooden frame in which, in former times, an offender was secured by the hands and feet or head and hands and left in public to be ridiculed or abused **2.** NAUT **CONSTRUCTION STAND** a frame that supports a boat or ship while it is being built ■ *v.* (**stocked, stock·ing, stocks**) **1.** *vt.* **HAVE PRODUCT IN STOCK** to have an item available for sale **2.** *vt.* **FILL WITH SUPPLY OF SOMETHING** to fill something with goods **3.** *vt.* **FILL UP** to fill with a plentiful supply of something ○ *We've stocked the refrigerator with cold cuts for the big game.* **4.** *vt.* **SUPPLY FARM WITH LIVESTOCK** to supply a farm with livestock **5.** *vi.* BOT **SPROUT** to sprout new shoots **6.** *vt.* **PUNISH SOMEBODY IN STOCKS** to punish somebody by putting him or her in the stocks ■ *adj.* **UNORIGINAL** typical or familiar and therefore lacking originality ○ *When pushed for an answer, he gave the stock response.* [Old English *stocc* "tree trunk." In sense 27, shortening of earlier *stock-gillyflower.*] —**stock·er** *n.* ◇ **take stock 1.** to think carefully about something so that you can form an opinion about it **2.** COMM make an inventory of the stock, especially at the end of a season in a store or business

stock up *vti.* to collect a large supply for future use

stock·ade /sto kάyd/ *n.* **1.** **DEFENSIVE BARRIER** a tall fence or enclosure made of wooden posts driven into the ground side by side, to keep out enemies or intruders **2.** **AREA INSIDE STOCKADE** an area surrounded by a stockade **3.** **MILITARY PRISON** a prison on a military base ■ *vt.* (**-ad·ed, -ad·ing, -ades**) **SURROUND AREA WITH STOCKADE** to enclose an area with a stockade [Early 17thC. Via obsolete French *estocade* from Spanish *estacada*, from *estaca* "stake," of prehistoric Germanic origin.]

stock·breed·er /stók breedər/ *n.* somebody who breeds and raises farm animals for a living —**stock·breed·ing** *n.*

stock·bro·ker /stók brōkər/ *n.* somebody who buys and sells stocks, shares, and other securities for clients on a commission basis —**stock·bro·ker·age** *n.* —**stock·bro·ker·ing** *n.*

stock·bro·ker belt *n. U.K.* an affluent residential area outside a city, typically inhabited by middle-class professional people who commute to the city to work

stock car *n.* **1.** MOTOR SPORTS **KIND OF RACING CAR** a standard passenger car that has been modified for professional racing **2.** RAIL **RAILROAD CAR FOR LIVESTOCK** a railroad car used for transporting livestock

stock cer·tif·i·cate *n.* a certificate specifying the number of shares owned by an individual or a company in a corporation's stock

stock com·pa·ny *n.* **1.** BUSINESS **COMPANY ISSUING TRADABLE SHARES** a company that has its capital divided into shares that are freely tradable **2.** THEATER **THEATER COMPANY PERFORMING CYCLE OF PLAYS** a permanent theater company that puts on a repertoire of plays, usually in its own theater

stock cu·be *n. U.K.* = **bouillon cube**

stock dove *n.* a grayish dove that is native to Europe. It is slightly smaller than a wood pigeon, and it nests in holes in trees and cliffs. Latin name: *Columba oenas.* [Origin uncertain: probably from STOCK "tree trunk," from its nesting in trees]

stock ex·change *n.* **1.** = **stock market** *n.* 1 **2.** **BUILDING** a building in which a stock exchange is sited

stock farm *n.* a farm on which animals, e.g., cattle, sheep, and hogs, are bred and raised

stock·fish /stók fish/ (*plural* **-fish** *or* **-fish·es**) *n.* fish, usually cod or haddock, that has been cured by being split and air-dried without the addition of salt [13thC. Translation of Low German and Middle Dutch *stokvisch*, from *stok* "stick, tree trunk" + *visch* "fish." The reason for the name is unknown.]

Stock·haus·en /shtók howz'n, stók-/, **Karlheinz** (*b.* 1928) German composer. He was a major figure in the musical avant-garde from the late 1950s, and his work incorporates serialism, random elements, and electronic sound.

stock·hold·er /stók hōldər/ *n.* FIN somebody who owns one or more shares of a company's stock —**stock·hold·ing** *n.*

Stock·holm /stók hōm/ capital city of Sweden, on the eastern coast of the country. Population: 711,119 (1996).

Stock·holm syn·drome *n.* a condition experienced by people who have been held as hostages for some time in which they begin to identify with and feel sympathetic toward their captors [Late 20thC. Named for STOCKHOLM, Sweden, where a bank employee taken hostage in a robbery became attached to one of her captors.]

stock·i·nette /stòki nét, stóki nèt/, **stock·i·net** *n.* a stretchy knitted fabric formerly used to make stockings and undergarments, now used for bandages and dishcloths [Late 18thC. Origin uncertain: probably an alteration of *stocking net*.]

stock·i·nette stitch *n.* a pattern in knitting that alternates rows of plain and purl stitches

stock·ing /stóking/ *n.* **1.** **COVERING FOR WOMAN'S LEG** either of a pair of tightly fitting leg coverings for women, made of silk, nylon, or wool (*often used in the plural*) **2.** **SOCK** a sock (*dated or formal*) **3.** **CHRISTMAS STOCKING** a Christmas stocking (*informal*) **4.** **DIFFERENTLY COLORED PART OF ANIMAL'S LEG** a differently colored part of the lower leg of an animal, especially a horse [Late 16thC. From STOCK in the obsolete sense "stocking," of uncertain origin.] —**stock·inged** *adj.*

WORD KEY: ORIGIN

The use of ***stocking*** to mean leg coverings may have arisen in the 15th century from the blackly humorous comparison of the stocks in which one's legs were restrained as punishment with "leggings, hose." Until comparatively recently ***stocking*** was a unisex term (as it still is in the expression "in one's stockinged feet"); the restriction to women's hose is a 20th-century development.

stock·ing cap *n.* a tightly fitting, cone-shaped knitted cap with a tapering tail that often has a tassel on the end

stock·ing fil·ler *n. U.K.* = **stocking stuffer**

stock·ing mask *n.* a nylon stocking pulled over the head to disguise the features, usually worn by somebody committing a crime

stock·ing stitch *n. U.K.* = **stockinette stitch**

stock·ing stuff·er *n.* a small and usually inexpensive Christmas gift, especially one put into a child's Christmas stocking

stock-in-trade *n.* **1.** **BASIC RESOURCE** a resource that somebody needs and regularly makes use of, especially at work ○ *Courtesy and composure are the receptionist's stock-in-trade.* **2.** **GOODS AND EQUIPMENT** the goods and equipment that need to be kept on the premises for a business or store to run

stock·job·ber /stók jòbbər/ *n.* **1.** **STOCKBROKER** a stockbroker, especially an unscrupulous dealer trading worthless securities (*dated*) **2.** *U.K.* **DEALER TRADING WITH BROKERS ONLY** formerly, a dealer on the London stock exchange who dealt only with brokers, not with members of the public —**stock·job·ber·y** *n.* —**stock·job·bing** *n.*

stock·man /stókmən, -màn/ (*plural* **-men** /-mən, -mèn/) *n.* **1.** **BREEDER OF FARM ANIMALS** a man who owns or breeds farm animals, especially cattle **2.** **MAN TENDING LIVESTOCK** a man who takes care of the livestock on a farm or ranch **3.** **MAN WORKING IN WAREHOUSE** a man who works in a warehouse or stockroom

stock mar·ket *n.* **1.** **FINANCIAL MARKET** an organized market where brokers meet to buy and sell stocks and shares **2.** **FINANCIAL TRADING** the activity of buying and selling stocks and shares, or the global market for stocks and shares (*hyphenated when used before a noun*)

stock·pile /stók pīl/ *vti.* (**-piled, -pil·ing, -piles**) **AMASS** to accumulate large quantities of something, e.g., food or weapons ■ *n.* **LARGE SUPPLY** a large supply of something, e.g., food or weapons, often accumulated in anticipation of future difficulties —**stock·pil·er** *n.*

WORD KEY: SYNONYMS

See Synonyms at ***collect***.

stock·pot /stók pòt/ *n.* a large pot for cooking stock

stock·room /stók ro͞om, -ro͝om/ *n.* a room where merchandise or supplies are stored in a store, office, or factory

stock·route /stók ro͞ot, stók ròwt/ *n. ANZ* a road or track that cattle are herded along

stock sad·dle *n.* a large and heavy saddle for a horse with a raised pommel. It was originally used on ranches in the western and southwestern United States. [Originally a Scottish phrase meaning "saddle with a wooden tree"]

stock-still *adv.* absolutely motionless

stock·tak·ing /stók tàyking/ *n.* **1.** **ASSESSING OF SITUATION** evaluating a personal situation, or that of somebody else **2.** = **inventory**

Stock·ton /stóktən/ city and inland port in central California, on the San Joaquin River, south of Sacramento. Population: 210,943 (1990).

Stock·ton, Frank (1834–1902) U.S. writer. His whimsical short stories include "The Lady or the Tiger?" (1882). Real name **Francis Richard Stockton**

Stock·ton, Richard Nathaniel (1730–81) American patriot. A New Jersey delegate to the Continental Congress (1775–78), he signed the Declaration of Independence (1776).

stock·wo·man /stók wo͝omən/ (*plural* **-men** /-wìmmin/) *n.* **1.** **WOMAN BREEDER OF FARM ANIMALS** a woman who owns or breeds farm animals, especially cattle **2.** **WOMAN TENDING LIVESTOCK** a woman who takes care of the livestock on a farm or ranch **3.** **WOMAN WORKING IN WAREHOUSE** a woman who works in a warehouse or stockroom

stock·y /stókee/ (**-i·er, -i·est**) *adj.* **1.** **BROAD AND STRONG-LOOKING** having a broad strong-looking physique, and usually short in stature **2.** **OVERWEIGHT** somewhat overweight [Early 17thC. The underlying idea is "having the form of a tree stump or lump of wood."] —**stock·i·ly** *adv.* —**stock·i·ness** *n.*

stock·yard /stók yaard/ *n.* a large enclosed yard with pens or covered stables where livestock is kept before being sold, slaughtered, or shipped

stodg·y /stójjee/ (**-i·er, -i·est**) *adj.* **1. UNIMAGINATIVE** lacking originality, flair, or imagination (*informal*) ○ *another stack of stodgy poems* **2. FORMAL OR POMPOUS** boringly or laughably conventional, formal, or pompous (*informal*) ○ *another of his stodgy dinner parties* **3. FILLING** heavy, filling, and usually fairly tasteless (*informal*) **4. HEAVY AND PLODDING** heavy, bulky, and plodding —**stodg·i·ly** *adv.* —**stodg·i·ness** *n.*

stoep /stoop/ *n. S Africa* a porch or veranda [Late 18thC. Via Afrikaans from Dutch (see STOOP[2]).]

sto·gy /stṓgee/ (*plural* **-gies**), **sto·gie, sto·gey** (*plural* **-geys**) *n.* **1. CHEAP CIGAR** a long slim inexpensive cigar **2. HEAVY BOOT OR SHOE** a heavy boot or shoe that is not well made [Mid-19thC. Shortening of *Conestoga*, supposedly because drivers of Conestoga wagons used such cigars and shoes.]

sto·ic /stṓ ik/ *n.* **SOMEBODY IMPASSIVE** somebody who appears unaffected by emotions, especially somebody admired for showing patience and endurance in the face of adversity ■ *adj.* **sto·ic, sto·i·cal IMPASSIVE** tending to remain unemotional, especially showing admirable patience and endurance in the face of adversity [Late 16thC. From STOIC.] —**sto·i·cal·ly** *adv.*

WORD KEY: SYNONYMS

See Synonyms at ***impassive***.

Sto·ic /stṓ ik/ *n.* **ANCIENT PHILOSOPHER** a member of an ancient Greek school of philosophy that asserted that happiness can only be achieved by accepting life's ups and downs as the products of unalterable destiny. It was founded around 308 B.C. by Zeno. ■ *adj.* **OF THE STOICS** relating to the philosophy of the Stoics [14thC. From Latin *Stoicus*, from, ultimately, Greek *stoa* "porch," referring to the Painted Porch in Athens, where Zeno taught.]

sto·i·cal, **sto·ic** *adj.* = **stoic**

stoi·chi·ol·o·gy /stòykee óllajee/ *n.* the study of the elements or principles of any discipline, especially the chemical principles underlying cell and tissue physiology [Mid-19thC. Coined from Greek *stoikheion* "element" on the model of German *Stöchiologie*.] —**stoi·chi·o·log·i·cal** /stòykee ə lójjik'l/ *adj.*

stoi·chi·om·e·try /stòykee ómmətree/ *n.* **1. BRANCH OF CHEMISTRY** the branch of chemistry concerned with measuring the proportions of elements that combine when chemical reactions take place **2. MEASURE** a measure of the relative proportions of the chemical elements that take part in a chemical reaction [Mid-19thC. Coined from Greek *stoikheion* "element" on the model of German *Stöchiometrie*.] —**stoi·chi·o·met·ric** /stòykee ō méttrik/ *adj.* —**stoi·chi·o·met·ri·cal·ly** /-méttrikəlee/ *adv.*

sto·i·cism /stṓ i sìzzəm/ *n.* emotional indifference, especially admirable patience and endurance shown in the face of adversity

Sto·i·cism /stṓ i sìzzəm/ *n.* an ancient Greek school of philosophy that asserted that happiness can only be achieved by accepting life's ups and downs as the products of unalterable destiny. It was founded around 308 B.C. by Zeno.

stoke /stōk/ (**stoked, stok·ing, stokes**) *vti.* **1. ADD FUEL** to add fuel to a fire and stir it up to make it burn more intensely **2. TEND BOILER** to be responsible for adding fuel to and tending the boiler of a furnace [Mid-17thC. Back-formation from STOKER.]

stoke up *v.* **1.** *vt.* **ADD FUEL TO FIRE** to add fuel to a fire or a furnace and stir it up so that it burns more intensely **2.** *vt.* **INTENSIFY EMOTION** to cause an emotion, e.g., anger or fear, to be felt more strongly **3.** *vi.* **EAT IN BULK** to eat food in large quantities, because or as if food may not be had (*informal*)

stoked /stōkt/ *adj.* in an excited or euphoric state, especially from having taken drugs

stoke·hold /stṓk hōld/ *n.* NAUT the boiler room of a steamship

stoke·hole /stṓk hōl/ *n.* **1. MOUTH OF FURNACE** the opening through which fuel is added to a boiler or furnace **2.** NAUT = **stokehold** [Mid-17thC. Translation of Dutch *stookgat*.]

stok·er /stṓkər/ *n.* **1. TENDER OF FURNACE** somebody whose job it is to add fuel to and tend a furnace or boiler, e.g., on a steamship **2. DEVICE FEEDING FURNACE** a mechanical device for adding fuel to a furnace [Mid-17thC. From Dutch, from, ultimately, Middle Dutch *stoken* "to poke with a stick."]

Stokes-Ad·ams syn·drome /stōks áddəms-/ *n.* episodes of temporary dizziness or fainting, due to disruption or extreme slowing of the heartbeat and consequent brief stoppage of blood flow [Early 20thC. Named for the Irish physicians William *Stokes* 1804–75 and Robert *Adams* 1791–1875.]

Stok·ow·ski /stə kówf skee, -ków-/, **Leopold** (1882–1977) British-born U.S. conductor. He brought the Philadelphia Orchestra international recognition as its principal conductor (1912–38). Full name **Leopold Antoni Stanislaw Boleslawowicz Stokowski**

STOL /stawl, stol/ *n.* **1. FLYING SYSTEM** a flying system that gives an aircraft the ability to take off and land on a very short runway. Abbr of **short takeoff and landing 2. AIRCRAFT** an aircraft fitted with the STOL system

stole[1] past tense of **steal**

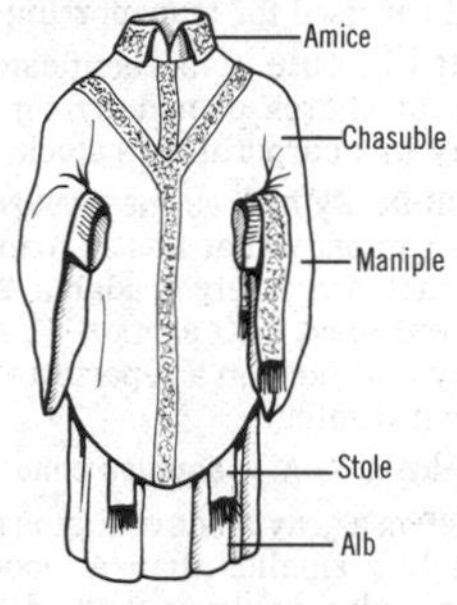

Stole

stole[2] /stōl/ *n.* **1.** CLOTHES **WOMAN'S SCARF** a woman's scarf or shawl often made of fur or worn as part of evening wear **2.** CHR **ECCLESIASTICAL SCARF** a long, narrow, and usually embroidered scarf made of silk or linen, worn by various members of the clergy **3.** HIST **ROMAN ROBE** a draped robe worn by women of high standing in ancient Rome [Pre-12thC. Via Latin from Greek *stolē* "robe, equipment."]

sto·len past participle of **steal**

stol·id /stóllәd/ *adj.* solemn and showing little or no emotion [Late 16thC. Directly or via French from Latin *stolidus* "dense, stupid." Ultimately from an Indo-European word meaning "standing object, post," which is also the ancestor of English *stele*.] —**sto·lid·i·ty** /stə líddətee/ *n.* —**stol·id·ly** /stóllədlee/ *adv.* —**stol·id·ness** /stóllədnəss/ *n.*

WORD KEY: SYNONYMS

See Synonyms at ***impassive***.

stol·len /stṓlən, shtṓlən/ (*plural* **-len** *or* **-lens**) *n.* a rich sweet German fruit bread made with nuts, raisins, and other dried fruits. It is traditionally served at Christmas. [Early 20thC. Via German from Old High German *stollo* "post, support."]

sto·lon /stṓ lòn, stṓlən/ *n.* **1.** BOT **PLANT SHOOT** a long stem or shoot that arises from the central rosette of a plant and droops to the ground. It may form new plantlets where it touches the soil. **2.** ZOOL **ORGANISM'S ANCHORING PART** a budding of the body wall in simple organisms, especially an extension of certain colonial organisms, e.g., hydroids, that anchors the colony to a rock or other substrate [Early 17thC. From the Latin stem *stolon-*. Ultimately from an Indo-European word meaning "something standing up," which is also the ancestor of English *stalk*[1].] —**sto·lon·ate** /stṓlə nàyt/ *adj.* —**sto·lon·if·er·ous** /stṓlə nífférəss/ *adj.*

sto·ma /stṓmə/ (*plural* **-ma·ta** /-mətə/) *n.* **1.** BOT **PLANT PORE** a tiny pore in the outer layer (**epidermis**) of a plant leaf or other stem that controls the passing of water vapor and other gases into and out of the plant **2.** ZOOL **MOUTH OR SIMILAR STRUCTURE** a mouth, or an opening that acts as or is shaped like a mouth **3.** SURG **SURGICAL OPENING** an artificial opening made in an organ, especially an opening in the colon or ileum made via the abdomen [Late 17thC. Via modern Latin from Greek, "mouth" (source also of English *stomach*).]

stom·ach /stúmmək/ *n.* (*plural* **-achs**) **1.** BIOL **VERTEBRATES' DIGESTIVE ORGAN** an organ resembling a sac in which food is mixed and partially digested. It forms part of the digestive tract of vertebrates and is situated between the esophagus and the small intestine. **2.** = **abdomen** (*informal*) **3.** ZOOL **INVERTEBRATES' DIGESTIVE ORGAN** a digestive organ in some invertebrate animals in which food is mixed, stored, and partially digested **4. COMPARTMENT OF ANIMAL'S STOMACH** any of the four digestive chambers that make up the stomach in ruminant animals (*informal*) **5. SEAT OF UNPLEASANT FEELINGS** the part of the body in which disgust, nausea, and fear are experienced ○ *The very idea makes me sick to my stomach.* **6. RESISTANCE TO UNPLEASANTNESS** the ability to withstand disgust, nausea, or fear ○ *This is not a job for someone with a weak stomach.* ■ *vt.* (**-ached, -ach·ing, -achs**) **TOLERATE** to put up with something ○ *I find their gloating hard to stomach.* [14thC. Via Old French *stomaque* from, ultimately, Greek *stomakhos* "throat, gullet," from *stoma* "mouth."]

stom·ach·ache /stúmmək àyk/ *n.* a pain in the abdominal region, caused, e.g., by indigestion or an infection

stom·ach crunch *n.* an exercise in which you lie flat on your back with your legs bent and then raise the upper part of your body a few inches off the ground without using your hands

stom·ach·er /stúmməkər/ *n.* a stiff panel of material, often decorated with embroidery or jewels, worn over the chest and abdomen by women in the 17th and 18th centuries, and earlier by both sexes

sto·mach·ic /stə mákik/ *adj.* **sto·mach·ic, sto·mach·i·cal 1. RELATING TO THE STOMACH** associated with the stomach **2. BENEFICIAL FOR STOMACH** good for the stomach, especially in stimulating digestion (*archaic*) ■ *n.* **STOMACH MEDICINE** a medicinal preparation that stimulates gastric activity or improves appetite (*archaic*) —**sto·mach·i·cal·ly** *adv.*

stom·ach pump *n.* a popular name for the equipment, consisting of a simple tube, funnel, and bucket, used to flush out the stomach contents of somebody who has, e.g., ingested a poison (*informal*)

stom·ach tooth *n.* either of the first canine teeth in the lower jaw of humans, whose appearance is popularly believed to be hastened by stomach upsets in infants

stom·ach worm *n.* a parasitic nematode worm that lives in the stomachs of mammals, especially one of those that infest cattle and sheep

sto·mal /stṓm'l/ *adj.* relating to a surgical stoma, or occurring in or near a surgical stoma

stomat- *prefix.* = **stomato-** (*used before vowels*)

sto·ma·ta plural of **stoma**

sto·ma·tal /stṓmət'l, stómmət'l/ *adj.* relating to a stoma, especially in plants and animals [Mid-19thC. Formed from Greek *stomat-*, the stem of *stoma* (see STOMA).]

sto·ma·ti·tis /stòmə títiss/ *n.* inflammation of the mucous tissue lining the mouth [Mid-19thC. Coined from Greek *stomat-* (see STOMATAL) + -ITIS.] —**sto·ma·tit·ic** /stòmə títtik/ *adj.*

sto·ma·tol·o·gy /stòmə tólləjee/ *n.* the branch of medicine or dentistry that is concerned with the study of the mouth and diseases of the mouth —**sto·ma·to·log·ic** /stòmətə lójjik/ *adj.* —**sto·ma·to·log·i·cal** /-lójjik'l/ *adj.* —**sto·ma·tol·o·gist** /stòmə tólləjist/ *n.*

sto·mat·o·pod /stṓmətə pòd, stō máttə pòd/ *n.* shellfish with abdominal gills and a second pair of claws. They include the squilla. Order: Stomatopoda.

sto·ma·tous /stṓmətəss/ *adj.* resembling a stoma in shape or function

-stome *suffix.* mouth, stoma ○ *peristome* [From Greek *stoma* "mouth"] —**-stomous** *suffix.*

sto·mo·de·um /stòmə dée əm/ (*plural* **-a** /-dée ə/), **sto·mo·dae·um** (*plural* **-a**) *n.* a depression in the surface of an early embryo that develops into the mouth [Late 19thC. From modern Latin, from Greek *stoma* "mouth" + *hodaios* "on the way, becoming" (formed from *hodos* "way, road").] —**sto·mo·de·al** *adj.*

stomp /stomp/ *v.* (**stomped, stomp·ing, stomps**) **1.** *vti.* **WALK WITH HEAVY STEPS** to tread heavily and noisily, often in anger **2.** *vt.* **TREAD HEAVILY ON SOMETHING** to bring a foot down heavily on something or somebody with the intention of causing damage or injury (*informal*) ■ *n.* **1.** DANCE **JAZZ DANCE** a kind of jazz dance with stamping foot movements **2.** MUSIC **JAZZ MUSIC** jazz music accompanying the stomp [Early 19thC. Variant of STAMP.] —**stomp·er** *n.* —**stomp·ing·ly** *adv.*

stom·pie /stómpee/ *n. S Africa* a cigarette or cigarette butt (*informal*) [Mid-20thC. From Afrikaans, literally "little stump," from *stomp* "stump."]

-stomy *suffix.* a surgical operation that creates an artificial opening ○ *gastrostomy* [Coined from Greek *stoma* "mouth, opening" + -Y]

stone /stōn/ *n.* **1.** HARD NONMETALLIC MATERIAL the hard solid nonmetallic substance that rocks are made of. It is used as a building material. **2.** ROCK FRAGMENT a small piece of rock of any shape **3.** SHAPED ROCK FRAGMENT a piece of rock that has been shaped for a particular purpose, e.g., a gravestone (*often used in combination*) **4.** SMALL HARD MASS a small hard mass, e.g., a hailstone (*usually used in combination*) **5.** = **gemstone 6.** HARD MASS INSIDE FRUIT the hard central part of certain fruits, such as cherries, plums, olives, and peaches, that contains the seed **7.** (*plural* **stone** *or* **stones**) *U.K.* MEASURE UNIT OF WEIGHT in the United Kingdom, a unit of weight equivalent to 14lb./6.35 kg. It is used especially for expressing somebody's weight. ○ *He's trying to get down to 12 stone.* **8.** MED MINERAL MASS INSIDE ORGAN a small hard mass of mineral material formed in an organ, e.g., the kidney or gall bladder. Technical name **calculus 9.** COLORS LIGHT GRAY OR BEIGE a dull light color between light gray and beige **10.** PRINTING PRINTER'S TABLE a very smooth flat table that is used for arranging printing type **11.** SPORTS CURLING BLOCK the shaped and polished mass of granite or iron that is slid along the ice in the game of curling **12.** = **testicle** (*archaic slang*) ■ *adj.* **1.** STONEWARE made of stoneware **2.** COLORS LIGHT GRAY TO BEIGE IN COLOR of a dull light color between light gray and beige ■ *adv.* **1.** USED FOR EMPHASIS used to emphasize the degree of a quality, usually a quality associated with stone, such as coldness, stillness, or lifelessness **2.** USED FOR EMPHASIS used to emphasize the degree of a quality (*slang*) ○ *stone fine* ○ *stone tired* ■ *vt.* (**stoned, ston·ing, stones**) **1.** THROW STONES AT SOMEBODY to throw stones at somebody or something, especially as a form of punishment, execution, or vandalism **2.** REMOVE STONE FROM FRUIT to remove the hard central part from a piece of fruit, e.g., a plum **3.** RUB WITH STONE to polish or sharpen something on a stone or with a stone [Old English *stān.* Ultimately from an Indo-European word that is also the ancestor of English *tungsten.*] —**stone·less** *adj.* —**stone·like** *adj.* ◇ **be carved** *or* **set** *or* **cast in stone, be carved** *or* **set** *or* **cast in tablets of stone** be so firmly established as to make changes impossible or unthinkable ◇ **cast** *or* **throw the first stone** to be the first person to accuse, criticize, or quarrel with somebody else ◇ **leave no stone unturned** to be very thorough in making a search or in carrying out a task

Stone /stōn/, **Edward Durell** (1902–78) U.S. architect. His most prestigious commission was the Kennedy Center for the Performing Arts in Washington, D.C. (1964).

Stone, Harlan Fiske (1872–1946) U.S. jurist. He was associate justice of the U.S. Supreme Court (1925–41), and served as U.S. chief justice (1941–46).

Stone, Lucy (1818–93) U.S. feminist and abolitionist. She organized the first U.S. Woman's Rights Convention (1850) and founded the *Women's Journal* (1870).

Stone, Oliver (*b.* 1946) U.S. movie director. His movies, which include the Academy Award-winning *Platoon* (1986), deal with contemporary issues, often controversially.

Stone, Thomas (1743–87) American patriot. A Maryland delegate to the Continental Congress (1775–78), he signed the Declaration of Independence (1776).

Stone Age *n.* the earliest period of human history, in which tools and weapons were made of stone rather than metal. It is divided into the Paleolithic, Mesolithic, and Neolithic periods. It extends from around 2.5 million years ago to around 2400 B.C.

Stone-Age /stṓn àyj/ *adj.* **1.** FROM STONE AGE dating from the Stone Age, the earliest period of human history **2. Stone-Age, stone-age** VERY OLD-FASHIONED hopelessly behind the times

stone bass *n.* a large dark brown and yellow fish found in Atlantic and Mediterranean waters. It belongs to the perch family and tends to inhabit offshore wreckage. Latin name: *Polyprion americanus.* [From its inhabiting rocky ledges and wrecks]

stone-blind *adj.* an offensive term meaning completely unable to see (*offensive*) —**stone-blind·ness** *n.*

stone-broke *adj.* having no money at all (*informal*)

stone ca·nal *n.* ZOOL a narrow calcareous tube found in starfish and other echinoderms that connects the ring canal surrounding the mouth with an external pore (**madreporite**)

stone·cat /stṓn kàt/ (*plural* **-cats** *or* **-cat**) *n.* a slender yellowish-brown North American catfish that inhabits the beds of streams, rivers, and lakes, typically under stones. It has poisonous pectoral spines. Latin name: *Noturus flavus.*

stone cell *n.* BOT a short squat plant cell that performs a strengthening function. It occurs in large numbers in fruits such as the quince and the pear.

stone·chat /stṓn chàt/ (*plural* **-chats** *or* **-chat**) *n.* a small songbird found in the grassy regions and dry plains of Europe and North Africa. Males have a black head, brown back, chestnut breast, and white rump. Latin name: *Saxicola torquata.* [Late 18thC. *Stone* from the resemblance of the bird's call to colliding stones.]

stone-cold *adj.* COMPLETELY COLD completely cold, especially too cold to be palatable ■ *adv.* ABSOLUTELY completely and utterly (*informal*) ○ *stone-cold sober*

stone crab *n.* a large crab native to shores of the southern United States. It lays several million eggs and can be a serious pest of oyster beds. Latin name: *Menippe mercenaria.*

stone·crop /stṓn kròp/ (*plural* **-crops** *or* **-crop**) *n.* **1.** PLANT WITH FLESHY LEAVES an annual or perennial flowering plant with fleshy leaves, native mainly to northern temperate regions. Many varieties are grown as ornamentals. Genus: *Sedum.* **2.** PLANT SIMILAR TO STONECROP a plant related or similar to the stonecrop [Old English *stāncropp*, from an earlier form of STONE (because the plant grows on rocks) + CROP in the obsolete sense "flower cluster, ear of grain"]

stone cur·lew *n.* a brownish, mostly nocturnal wading bird that inhabits an open dry stony habitat. It has a large head and eyes, and thick knee joints. Family: Burhinidae.

stone·cut·ter /stṓn kùttər/ *n.* **1.** SOMEBODY WHO CUTS STONE somebody who is skilled at cutting and carving stone **2.** MACHINE FOR CUTTING STONE a machine that is used to cut stone and concrete, especially a handheld power tool with a circular blade —**stone·cut·ting** *n.*

stoned /stōnd/ *adj.* **1.** UNDER THE INFLUENCE OF DRUGS relaxed, excited, or euphoric from taking illegal drugs, especially marijuana (*slang*) **2.** INTOXICATED very intoxicated (*informal*)

stone-dead *adj.* definitely or completely lifeless

stone-deaf *adj.* an offensive term meaning completely unable to hear (*offensive*)

stone-faced *adj.* = **stony-faced**

stone·fish /stṓn fish/ (*plural* **-fish·es** *or* **-fish**) *n.* a tropical marine fish whose mottled and knobbly body serves as camouflage in its rocky habitat. It has dorsal spines that can eject poison. Genus: *Synanceja.*

stone·fly /stṓn flī/ (*plural* **-flies** *or* **-fly**) *n.* an insect that, in its wingless juvenile stage, lives among stones in rivers and streams. The adults have long antennae and usually two pairs of wings. Both larvae and adults are used as fishing bait. Order: Plecoptera.

stone fruit *n.* = **drupe**

stone·ground /stṑn grównd/ *adj.* ground in the traditional way with millstones rather than with metal rollers

stone·heart·ed *adj.* = **stony-hearted**

Barnaby's

Stonehenge

Stone·henge /stōn hénj/ prehistoric monument on Salisbury Plain, southern England, consisting of two concentric circles of large standing stones. It was built between 2800 and 1500 B.C. and is thought to have been an astronomical calendar or a temple to the sun.

stone lil·y *n.* a fossil of a sea lily

stone mar·ten *n.* **1.** MARTEN OF EUROPE AND ASIA a marten found in the woods of Europe and Asia. It has dark brown fur with a lighter throat and undersides. It hunts rats and mice. Latin name: *Martes foina.* **2.** FUR the fur of the stone marten [From its inhabiting rocky inlets and crevices]

stone·ma·son /stṓn màyss'n/ *n.* somebody who shapes and prepares stone for use in building work and who is often also skilled at building with stone and repairing stone structures —**stone·ma·son·ry** *n.*

stone mint *n.* an aromatic plant of the mint family found in the dry woodlands and grasslands of eastern North America. It has clusters of small, tubular, purplish or white flowers. It was once used as a remedy for snakebite and fever. Latin name: *Cunila origanoides.* [So called because it grows in rocky places]

Stone Moun·tain /stṑn-/ massive granite outcropping near Atlanta, northern Georgia, United States. A monumental memorial to the Confederacy is carved on its northern face. Height: 700 ft./213 m.

stone·roll·er /stṓn rōlər/ (*plural* **-ers** *or* **-er**) *n.* a small brown freshwater minnow found in eastern North America. In the breeding season, males turn orange and dig nests in the stream bed. Latin name: *Campostoma anomalum.* [Late 19thC. From the minnow's practice of moving stones as it feeds.]

stone's throw *n.* not very far away at all

stone·wall /stṓn wàwl/ (**-walled, -wall·ing, -walls**) *v.* **1.** *vti.* REFUSE TO COOPERATE to refuse to cooperate with somebody by avoiding answering questions or providing information (*informal*) ○ *All reporters' questions were steadfastly stonewalled.* **2.** *vi.* DELIBERATELY CREATE DELAY to create obstructions or employ delaying tactics [Late 19thC. The underlying meaning is "to put up an immovable barrier."] —**stone·wall·er** *n.*

stone·ware /stṓn wàir/ *n.* dense opaque nonporous pottery that is fired at a very high temperature

stone·washed /stṓn wòsht/ *adj.* washed with small pumice pebbles to give a worn faded look

stone·work /stṓn wùrk/ *n.* **1.** STONE PARTS OF BUILDING the parts of a building or other structure that are made of stone **2.** BUILDING WITH STONE using stone as a building material —**stone·work·er** *n.*

stone·wort /stṓn wùrt, -wàwrt/ (*plural* **-wort** *or* **-worts**) *n.* green algae that grow in fresh or slightly salty water. They have jointed branches, often encrusted with lime. Genus: *Chara.*

ston·y /stṓnee/ (**-i·er, -i·est**), **ston·ey** (**-i·er, -i·est**) *adj.* **1.** COVERED WITH STONES covered with or having a great many stones **2.** OF OR LIKE STONE made of stone or similar to stone in appearance, texture, or color **3.** EMOTIONLESS expressing no emotion, especially no friendliness or pity —**ston·i·ly** *adv.* —**ston·i·ness** *n.*

ston·y cor·al *n.* a coral with a robust external calcium-based skeleton. It forms reefs and islands. Order: Scleractinia and Madreporaria.

ston·y-faced, stone-faced *adj.* showing not the slightest emotion, especially no sign of friendliness

ston·y-heart·ed, stone·heart·ed /stṑn náartəd/ *adj.* having or showing no compassion or kindness —**ston·y·heart·ed·ness** *n.*

ston·y-iron me·te·or·ite *n.* a meteorite consisting of metal and stony material

ston·y me·te·or·ite *n.* a meteorite that is composed mainly of rock-forming silicate minerals, especially olivine, plagioclase, and pyroxine

stood past tense, past participle of **stand**

stooge /stooj/ *n.* **1.** COMIC LOSER a comic actor, usually part of a double act, who acts as the butt of most of the jokes **2.** SOMEBODY EXPLOITED somebody whom others take advantage of, especially somebody used by criminals in perpetrating their crimes (*slang insult*) **3.** = **stool pigeon** *n.* 1 (*slang*) ■ *vi.* (**stooged, stoog·ing, stoog·es**) BE TAKEN ADVANTAGE OF to be taken advantage of by another (*informal*) [Early 20thC. Origin unknown.]

stool /stool/ *n.* **1.** SIMPLE SEAT a simple seat with three or four legs and no back or armrests **2.** MED EXCREMENT a piece of excrement **3.** BOT PLANT BASE the base of a plant, from which shoots or suckers sprout **4.** BOT CLUMP OF SHOOTS a clump of shoots or suckers sprouting from the base of a plant **5.** HUNT **HUNTER'S DECOY** a real or artificial bird used by hunters as a decoy **6.** **AFRICAN CHIEF'S THRONE** in West Africa, a chief's throne **7.** **TOILET** a toilet or toilet seat (*slang*) ■ *vi.* **(stooled, stool·ing, stools) 1.** **SPROUT SHOOTS** to sprout shoots or suckers from a stool **2.** **EVACUATE BOWELS** to evacuate the bowels **3.** HUNT **BE DECOY OR HUNT WITH DECOY** to be a decoy for a hunter of wildfowl, or to hunt wildfowl using decoys **4.** **BE STOOL PIGEON** to provide information to law enforcement agencies about criminals (*slang*) [Old English *stōl* "chair." Ultimately from an Indo-European base meaning "to stand," which is also the ancestor of English *stand* and *stead*. In sense 2, from the idea of sitting to defecate.]

stool pi·geon *n.* **1.** **POLICE INFORMER** somebody who provides information to law enforcement agencies about criminals or their activities (*slang*) **2.** **DECOY CRIMINAL** a criminal working as a decoy for a gang of criminals, with the job of distracting attention or throwing the police off the scent (*slang*) **3.** HUNT **HUNTER'S DECOY PIGEON** a pigeon, or a dummy of a pigeon, used by a hunter as a decoy [From the fact that such decoys were originally tied to a wooden platform]

stoop[1] /stoop/ *v.* **(stooped, stoop·ing, stoops) 1.** *vti.* **BEND BODY** to bend the top half of the body forward and downward **2.** *vi.* **WALK OR STAND BENT OVER** to walk or stand with the head and shoulders bent forward and downward **3.** *vi.* **BEHAVE UNETHICALLY** to act in an unethical or self-degrading way ○ *I never imagined you would stoop so low.* **4.** *vi.* **CONDESCEND** to do something reluctantly and with the attitude of somebody who does not normally do something that is so unworthy ○ *"He could not stoop to love; No lady in the land had power His frozen heart to move"*; (Sir Walter Scott, *Waverley*; 1814) **5.** *vi.* **SWOOP DOWN** to swoop down with wings folded, e.g., when attacking prey (*refers to birds*) **6.** *vi.* **ADMIT DEFEAT** to admit defeat (*archaic*) ○ *"as befits mine honor To stoop in such a case"* (William Shakespeare, *Anthony & Cleopatra*; 1606) ■ *n.* **1.** **BENT POSTURE** a posture in which the head and shoulders are bent forward and downward **2.** BIRDS **BIRD'S DOWNWARD SWOOP** the downward swoop of a bird of prey [Old English *stūpian*] —**stoop·ing** *adj.* —**stoop·ing·ly** *adv.*

stoop[2] /stoop/ *n.* a small porch or veranda at the entrance to a house [Mid-18thC. From Dutch *stoep*. Ultimately from a prehistoric Germanic word meaning "firm support," which is also the ancestor of English *step* and *staple*.]

stoop[3] *n.* CHR = **stoup**

stoop·ball /stoop bàwl/ *n.* a game based on baseball in which a player throws a ball against a stoop or wall, with the number of bounces representing the number of bases reached [Mid-20thC. Formed from STOOP[2].]

stoop·er /stoopər/ *n.* **1.** **SOMEBODY WHO STOOPS** somebody who has a stooping posture **2.** **SEEKER OF DISCARDED TICKETS** somebody who looks for winning pari-mutuel tickets accidently thown away by others at a racetrack (*slang*)

stoor *n. Scotland* = **stour**

stop /stop/ *v.* **(stopped, stop·ping, stops) 1.** *vti.* **DISCONTINUE** to cease doing something or make somebody cease doing something ○ *She's trying to stop smoking.* **2.** *vti.* **CEASE MOVING** to come to a standstill or bring something to a standstill ○ *Stop the car! I feel sick.* **3.** *vti.* **END** to come to an end or bring something to an end ○ *The snow has stopped.* **4.** *vt.* **PREVENT FROM HAPPENING** to prevent something from happening or continuing ○ *We couldn't stop the roof from caving in.* **5.** *vt.* **PREVENT AN ACTION** to prevent somebody or something from doing something ○ *a way of stopping the children from climbing the fence* **6.** *vi.* **PAUSE** to pause in order to do something before continuing ○ *I urge you to stop and think before deciding.* **7.** *vi.* **INTERRUPT TRIP** to interrupt a trip in order to make a brief visit somewhere ○ *Stop at the post office on the way into town.* **8.** *vt.* **FILL HOLE** to fill or block a hole ○ *We need to stop the cracks in the wall.* **9.** *vt.* **BLOCK** to block or plug something, e.g., a pipe or a wound, so that nothing can pass through it ○ *grease stopping up the drain* **10.** *vt.* FIN **INTERDICT CHECK** to instruct a bank not to honor a check **11.** *vt.* MUSIC **PRESS MUSICAL STRING** to press a string on a stringed instrument in order to produce a particular note **12.** *vt.* MUSIC **COVER HOLE ON INSTRUMENT** to use a finger to close a hole on a wind instrument in order to produce a particular note **13.** *vt.* MUSIC **PUT HAND INSIDE FRENCH HORN** to alter the tone and pitch of a French horn by putting a hand inside the bell **14.** *vt.* BOXING **KNOCK OUT** to defeat an opponent by a knockout **15.** *vti.* CARDS **BLOCK BRIDGE SUIT** to block the winning of a suit in bridge **16.** *vt.* **BE HIT BY SOMETHING** to be hit by something, usually a punch or a bullet (*informal*) **17.** *vt.* **DEFEAT SOMEBODY OR SOMETHING** to defeat an opponent or competitor or overcome an obstacle (*informal*) ○ *Nothing's going to stop us now.* ■ *n.* **1.** **STANDSTILL** a complete end or lack of movement **2.** **BREAK IN TRIP** a short break in a trip, e.g., to rest or to visit somebody **3.** **PLACE VISITED ON THE WAY** a place visited while on a trip **4.** **PAUSE ON ROUTE** a place where a bus or a train regularly pauses on its route ○ *Is this your stop?* **5.** **BLOCKAGE** a blockage or obstruction **6.** **PLUG** something, e.g., a plug or a stopper, that is used to block the flow or passage of something **7.** **DEVICE PREVENTING MOVEMENT** a device or control that prevents movement (*often used in combination*) **8.** FIN **ORDER INTERDICTING CHECK** an order to a bank not to honor a check ○ *had to put a stop on the lost check* **9.** MUSIC **STOPPING ON MUSICAL INSTRUMENT** an act of stopping a string or a hole on a musical instrument **10.** MUSIC **SUBSET OF ORGAN PIPES** a subset of organ pipes or harpsichord strings with a common tone color that can be played in isolation by silencing the remaining pipes or strings **11.** MUSIC **ORGAN CONTROL** a knob or lever on an organ or harpsichord that isolates a subset of pipes or strings **12.** PHOTOGRAPHY **CAMERA'S APERTURE SETTING** one of the graded settings for the size of the aperture of a camera lens **13.** PHOTOGRAPHY **CAMERA'S DIAPHRAGM** the diaphragm of a camera **14.** SAILING **SHORT ROPE** a short length of line used to tie up something, e.g., a sail **15.** PHON **SPEECH SOUND** a consonant sound made by closing the passage of air through the mouth and then suddenly opening it again. ◊ **continuant 16.** ZOOL **PART OF ANIMAL'S FACE** the area between the nose and the forehead of a cat or a dog **17.** FENCING **COUNTERTHRUST** a swift counterthrust made at the time of an opponent's thrust that seeks to make contact first **18.** ARCHIT **CARVING** a carving that finishes the end of a molding [Old English *-stoppian* "to block up." Via prehistoric Germanic from assumed Vulgar Latin *stuppare* "to plug up" (source of English *stuff*), from Latin *stuppa* "plug, stopper," from Greek *stuppē*.] —**stop·pa·ble** *adj.* ◇ **pull out all the stops** to make every possible effort in order to accomplish something ◇ **put a stop to something** to bring something to an end, usually quickly and permanently

stop down *vti.* to make the aperture of a camera lens smaller

stop off *vi.* to interrupt a trip briefly in order to do something or see somebody ○ *We stopped off at the supermarket on the way home.*

stop bath *n.* PHOTOGRAPHY an acid solution in which a negative or print is immersed in order to halt the developing process

stop·cock /stóp kòk/ *n.* a valve or faucet used to turn on, turn off, or regulate the flow of a fluid in a pipe

stope /stōp/ *n.* **STEP-SHAPED EXCAVATION** an excavation that resembles steps, used especially in the mining of ore ■ *vti.* **(stoped, stop·ing, stopes)** **MAKE STEP-SHAPED EXCAVATIONS** to make stopes in a mine, or to extract ore in this way [Mid-18thC. Origin uncertain: possibly from Low German.]

Popperfoto

Marie Stopes

Stopes /stōps/, **Marie** (1880–1958) Scottish pioneer advocate of birth control and writer. She wrote prolifically promoting scientific methodology of birth control, and established the first birth control clinic in Britain (1921). Full name **Marie Charlotte Carmichael Stopes**

stop·gap /stóp gàp/ *n.* **TEMPORARY SUBSTITUTE** something used as a temporary substitute for something that is really needed ■ *adj.* **MAKESHIFT** used as a temporary substitute for something that is really needed ○ *a stopgap spending bill*

stop·light /stóp lìt/ *n.* **1.** = **traffic light 2.** **VEHICLE REAR LIGHT ACTIVATED BY BRAKE** a red light on the rear of a motor vehicle that lights up when the vehicle's brakes are applied

stop-off *n.* = **stopover**

stop or·der *n.* an order to a stock broker to buy or sell a stock when it has risen or fallen to a specified price

stop·o·ver /stóp ōvər/ *n.* **1.** **STOP MADE DURING A TRIP** a usually brief halt on a journey **2.** **PLACE STOPPED AT** a place where somebody makes a brief halt on a trip

stop·page /stóppij/ *n.* **1.** **ACT OF STOPPING** the act of stopping the movement of something **2.** **SITUATION WHERE THINGS ARE STOPPED** a situation in which something has been stopped or blocked ○ *a work stoppage*

Popperfoto

Sir Tom Stoppard

Stop·pard /stóppərd, stóp aard/, **Sir Tom** (*b.* 1937) Czech-born British dramatist. He had instant success with *Rosencrantz and Guildenstern Are Dead* (1966). Later plays include *Arcadia* (1993). Born **Tom Straussler**

stop pay·ment *n.* an order by a person or organization to a bank telling it that a particular check is not to be paid

stop·per /stóppər/ *n.* **1.** **CORK OR PLUG** something that is put into an opening in order to close it **2.** **SOMEBODY OR SOMETHING THAT STOPS SOMETHING** a person or thing that brings something to a stop **3.** CARDS **CARD THAT PREVENTS TAKING OF SUIT** a card held by somebody that will prevent the opponents from taking all the tricks in that card's suit during a hand of bridge **4.** BASEBALL **ACE RELIEF PITCHER** the most effective relief pitcher who is brought on to win important games (*informal*) ■ *vt.* **(-pered, -per·ing, -pers)** **CLOSE WITH STOPPER** to close or secure something with a stopper

stop·ple /stópp'l/ *n.* = **stopper** *n.* 1 [15thC. Formed from STOP.] —**stop·ple** *vt.*

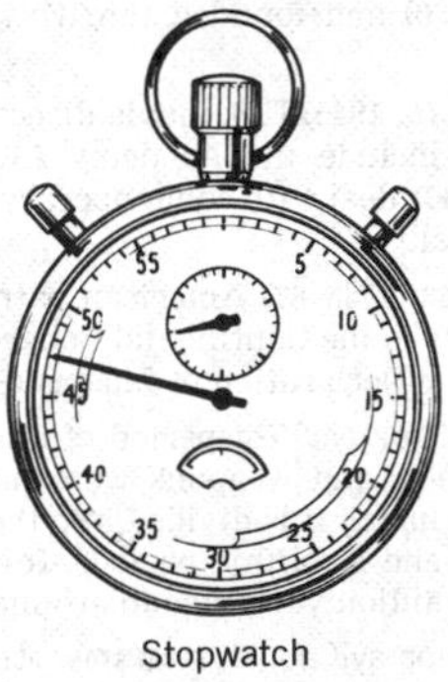

Stopwatch

stop·watch /stópp wòch/ (*plural* **-watch·es**) *n.* a special watch that can be started and stopped instantly and is used to measure the amount of time somebody or something takes, e.g., a runner in a race

stor·age /stáwrij/ *n.* **1.** **STORING OR BEING STORED** the act of storing something, or the condition of being stored **2.** **SPACE FOR STORING** space in which to store things, especially the amount of such space **3.** COMPUT **MEDIUM FOR STORING DATA** any primary or secondary device or medium used to store data and programs for use by a computer **4.** FIN **PRICE FOR STORING** the price charged for storing something **5.** ELEC **RECHARGING OF BATTERY** the recharging of a battery

stor·age bat·ter·y *n.* a rechargeable battery consisting of one or more cells for producing electrical energy from stored chemical energy

stor·age cell *n.* = **secondary cell**

sto·rax /stáwr àks/ *n.* **1.** SUBTROPICAL TREE WITH WHITE FLOWERS any of various related tropical or subtropical trees or shrubs with hairy leaves and long clusters of drooping white flowers. Genus: *Styrax.* **2.** VANILLA-SCENTED BALSAM a vanilla-scented balsam obtained from a storax tree and used in the past in medicine and perfumery, and as incense. Latin name: *Styrax officinalis.* **3.** FRAGRANT BALSAM a liquid fragrant balsam used as an expectorant and in perfumery, obtained from the bark of an Asian tree. Latin name: *Liquidambar orientalis.* [14thC. From Latin, an alteration of *styrax.*]

store /stawr/ *v.* (**stored, stor·ing, stores**) **1.** *vt.* PUT AWAY to put something away for use in the future **2.** *vt.* PUT SOMETHING INTO SAFEKEEPING to put or hold something somewhere for safekeeping, e.g., in a warehouse **3.** *vt.* HOLD SOMETHING FOR SAFEKEEPING to hold something for safekeeping, e.g., in a warehouse **4.** *vi.* SURVIVE STORAGE to survive or stay fresh while being kept in storage ○ *Apples will store well in a cool, humid building.* **5.** *vt.* STOCK ITEMS to fill or provide something with other things **6.** *vt.* COMPUT HOLD DATA to enter or save data or programs into a computer memory ■ *n.* **1.** COMM PLACE SELLING GOODS a place where merchandise is offered for retail sale to customers **2.** QUANTITY SAVED FOR FUTURE USE a quantity or collection put away for future use ○ *a store of grain in a silo* **3.** PLACE WHERE GOODS ARE KEPT a place where merchandise is kept in quantity, e.g., a warehouse **4.** GREAT QUANTITY a great quantity or large collection ○ *a rich store of memories* ■ **stores** *npl.* SUPPLIES items or materials needed for something, e.g., a business, expedition, or vessel ■ *adj.* COMMERCIALLY BOUGHT purchased from a retail store [13thC. Via Old French *estorer* "to build, supply" from Latin *instaurare.* Ultimately from an Indo-European word meaning "to set up," which is also the ancestor of English *restore* and *stow.*] —**stor·a·ble** *adj.* ◇ **in store 1.** about to happen in the future ○ *She has a surprise in store for you.* **2.** in a large amount ○ *He has come back with money in store.* ◇ **mind the store** to be in charge of running something, usually in the temporary absence of the person who is normally in charge (*informal*) ◇ **set** *or* **lay** *or* **put great store by something** to consider something to be important, valuable, or worthwhile

store-bought *adj.* bought already made from a retail store rather than being homemade

store cheese *n.* = **cheddar** [Perhaps so called because it is commonly stocked in stores, or because it keeps well]

store·front /stáwr frùnt/ *n.* **1.** ENTRANCE SIDE OF STORE the side of a store that faces the street or parking lot and includes the main entrance, usually having one or more large windows that display the store's goods **2.** ROOM OR BUILDING WITH STOREFRONT a room, suite of rooms, or building that has a storefront ■ *adj.* **1.** LOCATED ON STOREFRONT located on or near the side of the store where the main entrance is **2.** BASED IN STOREFRONT working or based in a storefront rather than in a more professional or expensive location ○ *a storefront clinic*

store·house /stáwr hòwss/ (*plural* **-hous·es** /-hòwzəz/) *n.* **1.** BUILDING WHERE THINGS ARE STORED a place where things are stored **2.** COLLECTION an abundant source, collection, or supply ○ *She's a storehouse of information on local history.*

store·keep·er /stáwr keepər/ *n.* **1.** RETAIL STORE OWNER somebody who runs a retail store or shop, usually the owner of a small store **2.** SOMEBODY IN CHARGE OF SUPPLIES somebody who is responsible for overseeing the supplies or stores of a military unit, ship, or organization

store·room /stáwr ro͝om, stáwr ro͞om/ *n.* a room or enclosed space where things are stored

store·wide /stáwr wīd/ *adj.* applying to or involving all of a department store or another retail store or its merchandise

sto·rey *n. U.K.* = **story**[2]

sto·reyed *adj. U.K.* = **storied**[2]

sto·ried[1] /stáwreed/ *adj.* **1.** INTERESTING OR CELEBRATED interesting, famous, or celebrated in stories and books (*literary*) ○ *the storied outlaw Robin Hood* **2.** DECORATED WITH HISTORICAL SCENES decorated with images of scenes from history or legend [14thC. Formed from STORY[1].]

sto·ried[2] /stáwreed/ *adj.* with stories, usually of a given number (*often used in combination*) ○ *a multistoried shopping mall* [Early 17thC. Formed from STORY[2].]

Stork

stork /stawrk/ (*plural* **storks** *or* **stork**) *n.* large wading bird that is related to heron and ibis and has long legs, a long neck, a long straight bill, and black-and-white plumage. Family: Ciconiidae. [Old English *storc.* Ultimately from an Indo-European base meaning "stiff," which is also the ancestor of English *strut* and *stark.*]

storks·bill /stáwrks bìl/ *n.* any of various plants of the geranium family that have lobed leaves, clusters of pink or purple flowers, and fruits with a beak-shaped tip. Genus: *Erodium.*

storm /stawrm/ *n.* **1.** METEOROL VIOLENT WEATHER a disturbance in the air above the earth, with strong winds and usually also with rain, snow, sleet, or hail and sometimes lightning and thunder **2.** METEOROL HEAVY RAIN OR SNOW a heavy fall of rain, snow, or sleet, often occurring with strong winds **3.** METEOROL STRONG WIND a gale that has a speed of 64 to 72 mi./103 to 106 km per hour **4.** RAIN OF OBJECTS a heavy bombardment of solid objects **5.** OUTBURST OF FEELING a sudden strong outpouring of feeling in reaction to something, e.g., of protest or laughter ○ *a storm of anger* **6.** BUILDING STORM WINDOW a storm window (*informal*) (*often used in the plural*) **7.** MIL SUDDEN STRONG ATTACK a sudden strong attack on a defended place or position ■ *v.* (**stormed, storm·ing, storms**) **1.** *vti.* ATTACK VIOLENTLY to attack or capture a place, especially a well defended one, suddenly and with great force ○ *stormed the barricades* **2.** *vti.* BE ANGRY to be violently and noisily angry **3.** *vi.* RUSH WITH VIOLENCE OR ANGER to go somewhere in a rush, violently or angrily ○ *stormed out of the room in a huff* **4.** *vi.* METEOROL BLOW WITH OR WITHOUT PRECIPITATION to blow strongly, to drop large amounts of rain, snow, or sleet, or to do both together [Old English. Ultimately from an Indo-European base meaning "to whirl," which is also the ancestor of English *stir*[1] and *disturb.*] ◇ **take somebody** *or* **something by storm 1.** to capture a place or overwhelm a body of enemies suddenly and with great force **2.** to make a great and immediate impression on somebody or something ◇ **up a storm** with great energy and enthusiasm or skill (*informal*) ○ *danced up a storm at the party*

storm·bound /stáwrm bòwnd/ *adj.* unable to leave, go out, or get in touch with anyone because of a strong storm

storm cel·lar *n.* a shelter underground used as a refuge during a windstorm

storm cen·ter *n.* **1.** METEOROL CENTRAL AREA OF LOW PRESSURE the central region of a cyclonic storm, with a low barometric pressure and relatively calm conditions **2.** FOCUS OF DISTURBANCE a focus of trouble, disturbance, or controversy

storm cloud *n.* **1.** METEOROL CLOUD INDICATING BAD WEATHER a large dark cloud that is a sign of approaching heavy rain or a storm **2.** SIGN OF WAR a sign that violence, especially war, is soon to break out

storm door *n.* a door added outside the main door of a house to provide additional protection against extremes of weather

storm drain *n.* = **storm sewer**

storm pet·rel, stormy petrel *n.* any of various small seabirds that have black or brown plumage with a white rump, especially a variety that lives in the northern Atlantic and Mediterranean. Latin name: *Hydrobates pelagicus.* [So called because the bird's appearance was thought to forebode a storm]

storm·proof /stáwrm pro͞of/ *adj.* able to withstand the wind, rain, or other elements of a storm, or providing protection from them

storm sew·er *n.* a large drain built to carry away excess water from a road during heavy rain

storm-tossed *adj.* subjected to or disturbed by storms

storm troop·er *n.* **1.** MEMBER OF NAZI MILITIA a member of the SA, a private militia of the Nazi party that used tactics of violence and brutality **2.** SOLDIER OF ATTACK FORCE a member of a military shock force specially trained to carry out attacks **3.** SOMEBODY LIKE NAZI STORM TROOPER somebody who acts like a Nazi storm trooper in terms of cruelty, brutality and ruthlessness [Formed from *storm troop*, a translation of German *Sturmabteilung*]

storm win·dow *n.* a window added outside an ordinary house window to provide additional protection against extremes of weather

storm·y /stáwrmee/ (**-i·er, -i·est**) *adj.* **1.** AFFECTED BY OR SUBJECT TO STORMS affected by or experiencing a storm or frequent storms **2.** STRONGLY EMOTIONAL dominated by or subject to strong emotions or disturbances —**storm·i·ly** *adv.* —**storm·i·ness** *n.*

storm·y pet·rel *n.* **1.** BIRDS = **storm petrel** **2.** SOMEBODY CAUSING TROUBLE somebody who causes trouble or whose appearance is usually followed by trouble

Storn·o·way /stáwrnə wày/ *n. Can* the name of the house that is the official residence of the leader of the political opposition in Canada

sto·ry[1] /stáwree/ *n.* (*plural* **-ries**) **1.** FACTUAL OR FICTIONAL NARRATIVE a factual or fictional account of an event or series of events **2.** LITERAT SHORT FICTIONAL PROSE PIECE a work of fiction in prose that is shorter than a novel **3.** LITERAT, THEATER PLOT OF FICTION OR DRAMA the plot of a novel, play, motion picture, or other fictional narrative work **4.** ACCOUNT OF FACTS what somebody says has happened ○ *changed her story several times* **5.** FALSEHOOD something that one person tells another that is not true (*informal*) ○ *Don't give me any stories.* **6.** PRESS NEWS REPORT a report in the news of something that has happened **7.** SUBJECT FOR REPORT a subject or material for a news report **8.** LITERAT LEGEND OR ROMANCE traditional tales and legends, or the literature based on such tales ■ *vt.* (**-ried, -ry·ing, -ries**) **1.** DECORATE WITH LEGENDARY SCENES to decorate something with images of scenes from history or legend **2.** TELL SOMETHING AS STORY to tell something as or in a story (*archaic*) [13thC. Via Anglo-Norman *estorie* from Latin *historia* (see HISTORY).] ◇ **a likely story** something that is probably untrue (*informal ironic*) ◇ **the same old story** what always happens or is said (*informal*) ◇ **to make** *or* **cut a long story short** to say something in a brief rather than a longer and more detailed way

sto·ry[2] /stáwree/ (*plural* **-ries**) *n.* **1.** FLOOR IN BUILDING any of the different floors or levels in a building **2.** ROOMS ON ONE BUILDING LEVEL a set of rooms, or space, on a particular floor of a building [14thC. Via Anglo-Latin *historia* from Latin (see HISTORY), perhaps because historical scenes were often painted on the façades of medieval buildings.]

Sto·ry /stáwree/, **Joseph** (1779–1845) U.S. jurist. He served as associate justice of the U.S. Supreme Court (1812–45) and wrote extensively on law.

sto·ry·board /stáwri bàwrd/ *n.* a set of sketches, arranged in sequence on panels, outlining the scenes that will make up something to be filmed, e.g., a motion picture, television show, or advertisement

sto·ry·book /stáwri bo͝ok/ *n.* BOOK OF CHILDREN'S STORIES a book of stories for children ■ *adj.* LIKE CHILDREN'S STORIES typical of or like something found in children's stories rather than the real world

sto·ry line *n.* = **story**[1] *n.* 3

sto·ry·tell·er /stáwri tèllər/ *n.* **1.** TELLER OR WRITER OF STORIES somebody who tells or writes stories **2.** SOMEBODY WHO FIBS somebody who tells lies (*informal*) —**sto·ry·tell·ing** *n.*

stoss /stoss, stawss, shtōss/ *adj.* used to describe a mountain, hill, or slope that faces the direction of an oncoming glacier [Late 19thC. From German, "thrust, push."]

sto·tin /sto teén/ *n.* a subunit of currency in Slovenia, worth one hundredth of a tolar. See table at **currency** [From Slovene, literally "hundredth"]

sto·tin·ka /stō tíngkə/ (*plural* **-ki** /-kee/) *n.* **1.** BULGARIAN SUBUNIT OF CURENCY a subunit of currency in Bulgaria, worth one hundredth of a lev. See table at **currency**

2. COIN WORTH A STOTINKA a coin worth a stotinka [Late 19thC. From Bulgarian, literally "hundredth," from *sto* "hundred." Ultimately from an Indo-European word that is also the ancestor of English *hundred, cent, hecto-,* and *satem.*]

Stough·ton /stṓwtən/ town in eastern Massachusetts, south of Boston and northwest of Brockton. Population: 27,481 (1996).

stoup /stoop/, **stoop** *n.* a basin for holy water in a church [14thC. From Old Norse *staup* "drinking vessel."]

stour /stoor/, **stoor** *n. U.K.* confusion, turmoil, or uproar (*regional*) [15thC. Origin uncertain: perhaps from Anglo-Norman *estur* "tumult."]

stout /stowt/ *adj.* **1. THICKSET OR HEAVY** thicker and heavier in body than an average person of the same height **2. COURAGEOUS AND DETERMINED** possessing or showing courage and determination **3. STRONG** strong and substantial **4. STRONG IN STRUCTURE** strong and substantial in structure ■ *n.* **1.** BEVERAGES **DARK STRONG BEER** a strong, very dark, almost black beer made from roasted malted barley **2.** CLOTHES **SIZE OR GARMENT FOR LARGE PERSON** a size of clothing that fits a person who is heavier than average, or a garment in such a size **3. STOUT PERSON** somebody who is thicker-waisted and heavier than average for a certain height [13thC. From Anglo-Norman, of prehistoric Germanic origin.] —**stout·ish** *adj.* —**stout·ly** *adv.* —**stout·ness** *n.*

stout·en /stówt'n/ (**-ened, -en·ing, -ens**) *vti.* to become, or make somebody or something, stout or stouter

stout·heart·ed /stòwt haártəd/ *adj.* having or showing courage and resolution —**stout·heart·ed·ly** *adv.* —**stout·heart·ed·ness** *n.*

stove[1] /stōv/ *n.* **1. APPLIANCE FOR COOKING OR HEATING** an appliance that uses electricity or burns a fuel to produce heat for cooking or for heating **2. HEAT-PRODUCING CHAMBER OR DEVICE** a device or chamber that is used to heat or dry something, e.g., a kiln ■ *vt.* (**stoved, stoving, stoves**) INDUST **HEAT IN A STOVE** to treat something by heating it in a stove in order to coat it with a surface such as enamel [15thC. Origin uncertain: probably from Middle Dutch or Middle Low German, "heated room."]

stove[2] past tense, past participle of **stave**

stove·pipe /stṓv pìp/ *n.* **1. PIPE FOR STOVES** a pipe used as a chimney for a fuel-burning stove, usually made of sheet steel formed into a tube **2.** = **stovepipe hat**

stove·pipe hat *n.* a tall tube-shaped silk hat for a man

sto·ver /stṓvər/ *n.* leaves and stalks of corn that are left in a field after harvesting and are dried for use as fodder [Mid-17thC. From Anglo-Norman *estover,* a variant of Old French *estoveir* "to be necessary," from Latin *est opus* "it is necessary."]

stov·ies /stṓviz/ *npl. Scotland* a dish of sliced potatoes and onions stewed together, sometimes with a little meat

stow /stō/ (**stowed, stow·ing, stows**) *vt.* **1. PUT SOMETHING AWAY NEATLY** to pack something or put something away, especially when the result is neat and orderly **2. FILL SOMETHING WITH TIGHTLY PACKED THINGS** to fill something with other things, especially things packed tightly ○ *to stow a boat's hold with cargo* **3. STORE SOMETHING FOR LATER USE** to store something for use in the future **4. HOLD SOMETHING** to be capable of containing something **5. STOP SOMETHING** to stop doing something (*slang*) ○ *Stow this silly chatter.* **6. LODGE SOMEBODY TEMPORARILY** to find a room or a place for somebody to stay, often for only a short time [14thC. Formed from Old English *stōw* "place." Ultimately from an Indo-European word meaning "to stand," which is also the ancestor of English *stand, stead,* and *store.*]

stow away *vi.* to hide on a ship or aircraft in the hope of being taken somewhere without having to pay

stow·age /stṓ ij/ *n.* **1. STOWING OF THINGS** a loading, packing, or storing of something, or a way of doing this **2. SITUATION OR ARRANGEMENT OF THINGS PACKED** the condition of being stowed, or the way this has been done **3. THINGS STOWED** something that is stowed somewhere or is to be stowed **4. PLACE OR SPACE FOR STOWING** a place, container, or space for stowing things **5. FEE FOR STOWING** a fee or fees for stowing something

stow·a·way /stṓ ə wày/ *n.* somebody who hides on a ship or aircraft in the hope of being taken somewhere without having to pay

Stowe /stō/, **Emily Howard** (1831–1903) Canadian doctor. She was the first Canadian woman to practice medicine in Canada. She founded Woman's Medical College in Toronto (1883). Born **Emily Jennings**

Library of Congress

Harriet Beecher Stowe

Stowe, Harriet Beecher (1811–96) U.S. writer and abolitionist. She is best known for her antislavery novel *Uncle Tom's Cabin* (1852). Born **Harriet Elizabeth Beecher**

STP[1] *abbr.* standard temperature and pressure

STP[2] *tdmk.* a trademark for a fuel additive designed to improve the performance of internal-combustion engines

STR *abbr.* synchronous transmitter receiver

str. *abbr.* **1. str., Str.** strait **2.** steamer **3.** POETRY strophe **4.** stroke **5.** MUSIC stringed **6.** MUSIC strings

stra·bis·mus /strə bízməss/ *n.* a squint (*technical*) [Late 17thC. Via modern Latin from, ultimately, Greek *strabizein* "to squint," from *strabos* "squinting."] —**stra·bis·mal** *adj.* —**stra·bis·mic** *adj.* —**stra·bis·mi·cal** *adj.*

Stra·chey /stráykee/, **Lytton** (1880–1932) British writer. A member of the Bloomsbury Group, he wrote *Eminent Victorians* (1918) and other biographies known for illuminating the personality of their subjects. Full name **Giles Lytton Strachey**

Strad /strad/ *n.* a Stradivarius violin (*informal*) [Late 19thC. Shortening.]

strad·dle /strádd'l/ *v.* (**-dled, -dling, -dles**) **1.** *vt.* **SIT OR STAND WITH LEGS ASTRIDE SOMETHING** to sit or stand so that one leg is on one side and the other leg is on the other side of something or somebody **2.** *vt.* **BE OVER OR ACROSS SOMETHING** to be on both sides of something ○ *The city straddles the river.* **3.** *vt.* **APPLY TO MORE THAN ONE THING** to exist in, belong to, or apply to more than one situation or category ○ *The rule of the dynasty straddled the end of one century and the beginning of the next.* **4.** *vti.* **FAVOR BOTH SIDES** to appear to favor both sides of an issue, or resist committing to one side or the other **5.** *vt.* **SPREAD LEGS APART** to spread the legs apart, usually so that each leg is on one side of something **6.** *vt.* **STRIKE AND NARROWLY MISS TARGET** to strike a target as well as miss it on either side **7.** *vi.* **SIT OR WALK WITH LEGS APART** to sit, stand, or walk with the legs spread apart or on both sides of something **8.** *vt.* MIL **FIRE SHELLS FOR RANGE** to fire artillery shells in front of and behind a target to find the correct range ■ *n.* **1. POSITION ACROSS OR OVER SOMETHING** a position in which something is over or across something else, or somebody's legs are apart or on both sides of something **2. ACT OF STRADDLING** the act of putting one leg on either side of something **3. NONCOMMITAL POSITION** a position on an issue that seems to favor both sides or resists committing to one side or the other **4.** FIN **STOCK TRANSACTION** the simultaneous holding of options to buy and sell a commodity at a set price during a specific period of time. This ensures a profit for the holder, irrespective of any rises or falls in value. [Mid-16thC. Origin uncertain: probably a variant of obsolete *stridlen,* literally "to keep striding," from an earlier form of STRIDE.] —**strad·dler** *n.*

Stra·di·va·ri /stràddə váiree, -vaáree/, **Antonio** (1644–1737) Italian violin maker. The instruments that he produced, including violas and cellos, are among the most highly prized in the world.

Strad·i·var·i·us /stràddə váiree əss/ *n.* a violin or other stringed instrument that was made by the Italian violinmaker Antonio Stradivari or his sons [Mid-19thC. Latinized form of STRADIVARI.]

strafe /strayf/ *vt.* (**strafed, straf·ing, strafes**) **ATTACK SOMETHING WITH GUNFIRE** to attack a position or troops on the ground with machine gun or cannon fire from a low-flying aircraft ■ *n.* **AIR ATTACK** a machine gun or cannon attack by low-flying aircraft on a ground target [Early 20thC. From German *strafen* "to punish."] —**straf·er** *n.*

strag·gle /strágg'l/ *vi.* (**-gled, -gling, -gles**) **1. STRAY FROM PATH** to stray from a path, or wander away from or become separated from a group **2. MOVE OR BECOME SPREAD OUT** to move or become spread out over a large area **3. COME OR GO IRREGULARLY** to come or go in an irregular or disorganized way **4. GROW UNTIDILY** to grow or hang in an untidy or irregular way ■ *n.* **STRAGGLED GROUP OR ARRANGEMENT** a group or arrangement that lacks order, is spread out, or is untidy [15thC. Origin uncertain.] —**strag·gly** *adj.*

strag·gler /strágg'lər/ *n.* a person or animal that wanders or becomes separated from a group, especially a soldier who falls behind in a march ○ *fell behind to wait for the stragglers*

straight /strayt/ *adj.* **1. NOT CURVED** without bends, curves, irregularities, or deviations **2. LEVEL** level, even, or properly positioned ○ *Your tie isn't straight.* **3. ACCURATE** accurate or correct ○ *You can rely on her for the straight figures.* **4. CANDID** making no attempt to deceive or soften the truth ○ *Give a straight answer.* **5. HONESTLY STRAIGHTFORWARD** honest, fair and upright ○ *straight dealings* **6. CONSECUTIVE** following one after another, without interruption ○ *The team celebrated its tenth straight win.* **7.** BEVERAGES **NOT DILUTED** not diluted or mixed with any other drink **8. NEAT AND TIDY** neat and tidy, or in order **9. NOT FUNNY** not intended to be funny or unconventional ○ *playing both straight and comic roles* **10. CONSISTENT** not leaving or differing from a principle or political party ○ *the straight party line* **11. DELIVERED WITH UNBENT ARM** delivered with the arm unbent ○ *a straight left to the body* **12. HETEROSEXUAL** heterosexual (*slang*) **13. CONVENTIONAL** unremarkable or conventional in outlook, style, or way of life (*slang*) ○ *gave up being a rock musician and got a straight job* **14.** DRUGS **NOT USING DRUGS** not using or addicted to drugs (*slang*) **15. LACKING DISCOUNT** attracting no discount, no matter how many are bought ■ *adv.* **1. WITHOUT BENDING** without bending, curving, or diverging from a course **2. IMMEDIATELY** without delay or detour ○ *She went straight home.* **3. IN A LEVEL POSITION** in a level, even, or proper position ○ *Put your hat on straight.* **4. CANDIDLY** without any attempt to deceive or soften the truth ○ *Give it to me straight.* **5. WITH NO INTERRUPTION** one after another, without interruption ○ *three nights straight* **6. UNDILUTED** without being diluted or mixed with any other drink **7. INTO NEAT CONDITION** in or into a neat, tidy, or orderly condition ○ *We'll have to put the place straight after the party.* **8. WITHOUT BEING FUNNY** without trying to be funny or unconventional ■ *n.* **1. SOMETHING STRAIGHT** something that is straight, e.g., a line **2.** CARDS **FIVE CARDS IN SEQUENCE** a poker hand in which the cards form a continuous sequence but are not all of the same suit **3.** *U.K.* = **straightaway** *n.* **4. HETEROSEXUAL PERSON** a heterosexual person (*slang*) **5. CONVENTIONAL PERSON** somebody who is conventional in outlook, style, or way of life (*slang*) **6. CIGARETTE WITHOUT FILTER** a cigarette with no filter [14thC. Originally the past participle of STRETCH.] —**straight·ish** *adj.* —**straight·ly** *adv.* —**straight·ness** *n.*

straight-a·head *adj.* showing very little variation from what is usual or typical ○ *straight-ahead Italian opera*

straight and nar·row *n.* the orthodox and law-abiding way to live life (*informal*)

straight an·gle *n.* an angle of 180 degrees

straight-arm, *vt.* (**straight-armed, straight-arm·ing, straight-arms**) **1. PUSH OPPONENT AWAY WITH OUTSTRETCHED ARM** in football, to push an opponent away with the arm stretched fully out and the hand upturned and stiff **2. WARD OFF OR TURN ASIDE** to ward somebody off or turn somebody aside using, or as if you were using, a push or thrust from a straightened arm ■ *n.* **ACT OF STRAIGHT-ARMING SOMEBODY** an act or instance of straight-arming somebody

straight ar·row *n.* somebody who is conventionally moral and upright in dealing with others (*informal*) —**straight-ar·row** *adj.*

straight·a·way /stráyt ə wày/ *adv.* **AT ONCE** immediately and without hesitation ■ *n.* **STRAIGHT TRACK** a part of a racing track that does not bend ■ *adj.* **WITHOUT CURVES** following a straight course, without any turns or curves

straight chain *n.* an open chain of atoms in a molecule that has no side branches

straight·edge /stráyt ej/ *n.* a rigid strip of wood, metal, or plastic that is used in drawing a straight line or checking for straightness

straight·en /stráyt'n/ (**-ened, -en·ing, -ens**) *vti.* to make something straight, or become straight —**straight·en·er** *n.*

straighten out *vti.* **1.** MAKE OR BECOME STRAIGHT to make something straight, or become straight **2.** MAKE OR BECOME CLEAR OR SATISFACTORY to become, or make something, clear, satisfactory, or less complicated

straighten up *vti.* to become, or make something, upright or in line

straight face *n.* a serious expression on somebody's face that does not betray the fact that he or she really wants to laugh —**straight-faced** *adj.* —**straight-fac·ed·ly** /stràyt fáystlee, -fáyssədlee/ *adv.*

straight flush *n.* a poker hand in which all the cards are of the same suit and form a continuous sequence

straight·for·ward /stràyt fáwrwərd/ *adj.* **1.** FRANK truthful and to the point, rather than evasive **2.** EASY not complicated, difficult, or hard to understand **3.** STRAIGHT OR DIRECT following a straight or direct path ■ *adv.* IN STRAIGHTFORWARD WAY in a straightforward way or direction —**straight·for·ward·ly** *adv.* —**straight·for·ward·ness** *n.*

straight·jack·et *n., vt.* = **straitjacket**

straight-line *adj.* **1.** HAPPENING IN STRAIGHT LINE happening in or along a straight line, or following a straight path **2.** MADE USING STRAIGHT LINES made using a straight line or lines **3.** LAID OUT IN STRAIGHT LINES laid out or set up in straight lines or so that something will follow a direct path **4.** MOVING IN STRAIGHT LINE with components that are designed to move or make something move in a straight line, or are arranged in a straight line

straight man *n.* a comedian whose role is to say or do things that allow another comedian to deliver a punch line or make witty or humorous comments in response

straight off *adv.* right away or at once (*informal*)

straight-out *adj.* (*informal*) **1.** BLUNT OR UNRESTRAINED showing directness or bluntness rather than restraint ○ *a straight-out refusal* **2.** COMPLETE AND TOTAL complete and thoroughgoing, without mitigation ○ *a straight-out jerk*

straight pok·er *n.* a way of playing poker in which each player is dealt five cards and no more cards can be drawn

straight ra·zor *n.* a razor with a single straight blade that is attached to a handle by a hinge and that is stored by folding it edge-first into a slot in the handle

straight shoot·er *n.* somebody who is honest, speaks frankly, and behaves ethically (*informal*)

straight stitch *n.* a simple stitch that forms a straight line on the surface of the fabric

straight tick·et *n.* a ballot where all the candidates selected by the voter are from the same political party

straight up *adv.* used to describe a cocktail that is served without any ice

straight·way /stráyt wày/ *adv.* **1.** IMMEDIATELY at once and without delay **2.** BY DIRECT ROUTE by a direct route

strain[1] /strayn/ *v.* (**strained, strain·ing, strains**) **1.** *vti.* PULL OR STRETCH TIGHT to pull or stretch something until it is tight, or be pulled or stretched until tight **2.** *vi.* WORK VERY HARD to work extremely hard or exert yourself to the limit of your power **3.** *vt.* USE SOMETHING TO THE UTMOST to make the greatest possible use of or demands on something **4.** *vt.* INJURE SOMETHING to damage a part of the body through using it too hard or too much **5.** *vti.* BE OR MAKE SOMETHING TENSE to put something or somebody under stress, or be put under stress **6.** *vti.* PASS SOMETHING THROUGH STRAINER to pass something through a filter in order to remove some of its contents, or be passed through a filter **7.** *vt.* REMOVE SOMETHING USING STRAINER to remove part of something from the rest of it with a filter **8.** *vt.* HUG SOMEBODY to hold somebody closely and tightly **9.** *vt.* PHYS DEFORM STRUCTURE to deform a body or material by applying an external force to it **10.** *vt.* COMPEL SOMEBODY OR SOMETHING to compel or constrain somebody or something (*archaic*) ○ *"The quality of mercy is not strain'd"* (William Shakespeare, *The Merchant of Venice*; 1596) ■ *n.* **1.** STRAINING an act of straining something ○ *Give the sauce a thorough strain.* **2.** BEING STRAINED the state of being strained **3.** FORCE THAT STRAINS SOMETHING a pulling or stretching force **4.** MENTAL OR PHYSICAL STRESS mental or physical stress caused by an intense or extreme pressure or demand **5.** DEMAND THAT CAUSES STRESS an intense or extreme demand or pressure that causes mental or physical stress **6.** GREAT EXERTION a great, taxing, or extreme exertion or effort **7.** MED PHYSICAL INJURY an injury to a part of the body caused by excessive use or by a twisting or stretching of muscles or tendons beyond their normal range **8.** PHYS DEFORMATION OF STRUCTURE the deformation of a body or material caused by applying an external force to it [14thC. Via Old French *estreindre* "to draw tight" from Latin *stringere* (see STRINGENT).]

strain[2] /strayn/ *n.* **1.** LINE OF ANCESTRY a line of ancestry or a group of descendants from a common ancestor **2.** ZOOL VARIETY OF ORGANISM a subgroup of a species of organism that shows particular characteristics, sometimes developed by breeders for those characteristics **3.** INHERITED QUALITY OR TRAIT an inherited tendency, character, or trait **4.** TRACE a trace, or small amount of something mixed in with something else **5.** CHARACTER OR MOOD the style, character, mood, or theme of something **6.** MUSIC MUSICAL THEME a musical theme or melody **7.** ELOQUENT LANGUAGE OR WORDS language that is eloquent, passionate, poetic, or otherwise heightened [Old English *strēon* "offspring," originally "gain." Ultimately from an Indo-European base meaning "to spread flat," which is also the ancestor of English *strew* and *construct*.]

strained /straynd/ *adj.* **1.** PASSED THROUGH STRAINER having been passed through a strainer to remove part of its content **2.** NOT NATURAL not natural or spontaneous but produced by an effort **3.** TENSE full of tension and often on the verge of hostility

strain·er /stráynər/ *n.* **1.** DEVICE FOR REMOVING SOMETHING a device for removing part of the content of something, especially lumps or solids from a liquid **2.** DEVICE FOR TIGHTENING a device that is used to tighten or stretch something

strain gauge *n.* **1.** DEVICE FOR MEASURING STRESS a device that measures pressure or stress, using the change of electrical resistance in a wire that is subjected to the same stress as the object being measured **2.** = **extensometer**

strain·ing beam, strain·ing piece *n.* a horizontal beam that connects the tops of two vertical posts (**queen posts**) in a roof truss

strait /strayt/ *n.* (*often used in the plural*) **1.** GEOG CHANNEL JOINING TWO SEAS a narrow body of water that joins two larger bodies of water, usually a body of salt water **2.** DIFFICULT SITUATION a situation that is difficult or involves hardship ■ *adj.* (*archaic*) **1.** DISTRESSED OR TRYING distressed, difficult, or trying **2.** NARROW OR CONFINED narrow or with very little room **3.** STRICT OR RIGID very strict or severe [14thC. Via Old French *estreit* from Latin *strictus* "narrow," the past participle of *stringere* "to draw tight" (see STRINGENT).] —**strait·ly** *adv.* —**strait·ness** *n.*

strait·ened /stráyt'nd/ *adj.* made very difficult, restricted, or narrow ○ *had lost all their money and were living in straitened circumstances*

strait·jack·et /stráyt jàkət/, **straight·jack·et** *n.* **1.** CONFINING JACKET-SHAPED GARMENT a jacket-shaped garment with long sleeves that can be tied, used to restrict the arm movements of a resisting person, e.g., a prisoner **2.** THING THAT RESTRICTS something that limits somebody's freedom of action or initiative ○ *a bureaucratic straitjacket of regulations* ■ *vt.* (**-et·ed, -et·ing, -ets**) **1.** PUT SOMEBODY INTO STRAITJACKET to put a resisting person into a straitjacket **2.** RESTRICT SOMEBODY to limit somebody's freedom of action or initiative

strait-laced *adj.* **1.** EXCESSIVELY STRICT prudish, or very strict in morals **2.** LACED TIGHTLY fitting tightly when laces are pulled and tied, or wearing a garment like this —**strait-lac·ed·ly** /stràyt láyssədlee, -láystlee/ *adv.* —**strait-lac·ed·ness** /-láyssədnəss/ *n.*

strake /strayk/ *n.* a continuous band of wooden planks or metal plates along the hull of a boat or ship [15thC. From assumed Old English *straca*; ultimately related to STRETCH.]

stra·mo·ni·um /strə mṓnee əm/ *n.* a preparation of dried leaves and flowers of the jimsonweed containing alkaloids and formerly used as medicine [Mid-17thC. From modern Latin, of uncertain origin: perhaps ultimately related to Russian *durman*.]

strand[1] /strand/ *n.* LAND AT WATER'S EDGE a strip of land along the edge of a body of water ■ *v.* (**strand·ed, strand·ing, strands**) **1.** *vti.* RUN ASHORE OR AGROUND to leave or run a ship or aquatic animal aground, or be left or driven aground **2.** *vt.* LEAVE SOMEBODY IN DIFFICULTY to leave somebody in a strange place without the capability or resources to get out of it (*often passive*) ○ *stranded without any means of getting home* **3.** *vt.* BASEBALL LEAVE SOMEBODY ON BASE to leave a base runner on a base at the end of an inning in a baseball game [Old English, of uncertain origin]

strand[2] /strand/ *n.* **1.** FIBER, THREAD, WIRE, OR FILAMENT any of the fibers, threads, wires, or other filaments that are twisted or braided together to form a rope, cable, or yarn **2.** LONG THIN PIECE a single length of something long and thin such as wire, string, rope, or wool **3.** HUMAN HAIR OR HAIRS a human hair, or a tress of hair **4.** LENGTH OF TISSUE RESEMBLING THREAD a length of animal, plant, or mineral fiber or tissue that resembles a thread **5.** ACCESSORIES STRING OF BEADS a length of strung pearls or beads, especially when twisted into a ropelike form **6.** ELEMENT OF WHOLE any of the elements that together make up a larger complex whole ■ *vt.* (**strand·ed, strand·ing, strands**) MAKE SOMETHING BY TWISTING to make something such as a rope or cable by braiding or twisting threads, wires, or other filaments together ○ *to strand a rope* [15thC. Origin unknown.]

strand·line /stránd lìn/, **strand line** *n.* a shoreline, usually one that the sea, a lake, or a river had at an earlier point in time and that is higher than the present shoreline

strange /straynj/ *adj.* (**strang·er, strang·est**) **1.** UNEXPECTED OR EXTRAORDINARY not expected, normal, or ordinary **2.** UNFAMILIAR not known or experienced previously **3.** HARD TO EXPLAIN difficult to explain or understand **4.** EXOTIC coming from a different place or environment, or belonging to a different kind **5.** UNACCUSTOMED not yet used to or familiar with something ○ *strange to these new surroundings* **6.** RESERVED reserved or shy, often because of being unfamiliar with people **7.** ILL AT EASE uncomfortable, embarrassed, or slightly ill ○ *I've been feeling a little strange since I took the medicine.* **8.** PHYS SHOWING QUANTUM CHARACTERISTIC OF STRANGENESS showing or having the quantum characteristic of strangeness ■ *adv.* IN UNUSUAL WAY in a strange way (*nonstandard*) [13thC. Via Old French *estrange* from Latin *extraneus* "foreign," from *extra*, feminine of *exter* "outside" (see EXTERIOR).]

strange·ly /stráynjlee/ *adv.* **1.** IN UNUSUAL WAY in an unusual or puzzling way **2.** ODDLY it is odd or puzzling that ○ *Strangely, they seemed to have no firm plan of action.*

strange·ness /stráynjnəss/ *n.* **1.** CONDITION OF BEING STRANGE the condition or quality of being strange **2.** PHYS QUANTUM CHARACTERISTIC a quantum characteristic of some elementary particles that is conserved in strong and electromagnetic, but not weak, interactions and has a value (**strangeness number**) of zero for most particles

strange·ness num·ber *n.* the value of the quantum characteristic of strangeness, equal to the hypercharge minus the baryon number

strange par·ti·cle *n.* an elementary particle having a strangeness number other than zero [From the fact that such particles' long lifetimes were hard to explain]

strange quark *n.* a quark that has an electric charge equal to $\frac{1}{3}$ that of the electron and a strangeness number of –1

strang·er /stráynjər/ *n.* **1.** UNFAMILIAR PERSON a person whom somebody does not know **2.** NEWCOMER somebody who is new to a particular place **3.** OUTSIDER somebody who is not a member of a particular organization or group **4.** VISITOR OR GUEST somebody who does not live in a particular house or community but is present as a visitor or guest **5.** PERSON UNACCUSTOMED TO SOMETHING somebody who is not accustomed to or acquainted with something specified ○ *Being a stranger to hard physical work, he found the job exhausting.* **6.** ALIENATED PERSON somebody who has become distanced or alienated from another, others, or something ○ *She is a stranger to her former colleagues.* **7.** PERSON NOT PRIVY TO TRANSACTION somebody who is neither privy nor party to a transaction [14thC. From Old French *estrangier*, from *estrange* "foreign" (see STRANGE).]

WORD KEY: CULTURAL NOTE

The Stranger, a novel by French writer Albert Camus (1942). This classic existentialist work is also known as *The Outsider*. It is set in Algiers and recounts how a young man's extreme sense of alienation leads him to commit murder. During his trial, however, the absurdities of the judicial process compel him to acknowledge the value of human life.

stran·gle /stráng g'l/ (**-gled, -gling, -gles**) *vti.* **1. KILL OR DIE BY CHOKING** to kill a person or an animal by squeezing the throat so that air cannot pass through it into the lungs, or die in this way **2. SUPPRESS UTTERANCE** to suppress suddenly a sound that is being uttered, or be suppressed suddenly ○ *I managed to strangle my giggles.* **3. STIFLE OR BE STIFLED IN DEVELOPMENT** to hinder or stop the growth or development of something, or be hindered or stopped [13thC. Via Old French *estrangler* from Latin *strangulare* (see STRANGULATE).] —**stran·gler** *n.*

stran·gle·hold /stráng g'l hòld/ *n.* **1. COMPLETE POWER** power over something or somebody that is complete and prevents any movement or change **2.** WRESTLING **CHOKING WRESTLING HOLD** an illegal hold in wrestling that chokes an opponent

stran·gler fig *n.* an evergreen tree that grows in the West Indies and Florida and has yellow fruit. Latin name: *Ficus aurea.* [From the fact that it eventually envelops the host tree on which it grows]

stran·gles /stráng g'lz/ *n.* an infectious disease of horses in which they experience inflammation and abscesses of the mucous membranes of the respiratory tract, causing strangling. It is caused by the bacterium *Streptococcus equi.* (*takes a singular verb*)

stran·gu·late /stráng gyə làyt/ (**-lat·ed, -lat·ing, -lates**) *v.* **1.** *vt.* **STRANGLE** to strangle a person or animal **2.** *vti.* MED **OBSTRUCT OR BE OBSTRUCTED** to constrict a part of the body, or become constricted, until the natural flow of blood or air is prevented [Mid-17thC. Via Latin *strangulare* from Greek *straggalan*, from *straggalē* "halter, cord." Perhaps ultimately from an Indo-European word.] —**stran·gu·la·tion** /stràng gyə láysh'n/ *n.*

stran·gu·ry /stráng gyəree/ *n.* painful and slow urination caused by spasms that make urine come out drop by drop [14thC. Via Latin from Greek *straggouria*, from *stragx* "drop" + *ouron* "urine."]

strap /strap/ *n.* **1. FLEXIBLE STRIP USED FOR BINDING** a narrow flexible strip of leather, nylon webbing, plastic, metal, or other material used to bind or secure something **2. LOOP OF MATERIAL USED AS HANDLE** a loop of flexible material attached to something so that it can be grasped or slung over a shoulder and used in lifting or carrying something **3.** TRANSP **LOOP TO HANG ON TO** a loop of leather, rubber, or plastic suspended from the roof inside a bus or train for standing passengers to hold for support **4. RAZOR STROP** a strop for a razor **5. LEATHER STRIP FOR FLOGGING** a long narrow strip of leather used for flogging or beating ■ *vt.* (**strapped, strap·ping, straps**) **1. SECURE WITH STRAP** to secure or bind somebody or something with a strap **2. FASTEN STRAPS OF** to secure the straps that are used to fasten something ○ *stood up without strapping her shoes* **3. BEAT WITH STRAP** to beat or flog somebody with a strap **4. SHARPEN WITH STROP** to sharpen something, e.g., a razor, with a strop [Early 17thC. Originally a Scottish dialect form of STROP.]

strap·hang·er /stráp hàngər/ *n.* (*informal*) **1. STANDING RIDER** a passenger who stands while riding a bus or train and holds onto a strap that is suspended from the roof **2. RIDER OF PUBLIC TRANSPORTATION** somebody who rides or commutes on a bus, subway, or another form of public transportation

strap hinge *n.* a hinge with a flap fastened to the exposed surface of a door, lid, or gate

strap·less /stráppləss/ *adj.* **NOT HAVING STRAPS** without straps, other supports, or covering over the shoulders ■ *n.* **WOMAN'S GARMENT WITHOUT SHOULDER STRAPS** a woman's garment that does not have straps, other support, or covering over the shoulders

strap·pa·do /strə páydō, -paádō/ (*plural* **-does**) *n.* **1. FORM OF TORTURE** a form of torture in which somebody is hoisted by a rope around the wrists, which are bound behind the back, and then dropped, but not to the ground **2. APPARATUS USED FOR TORTURE** an apparatus or machine that is used to deliver a strappado [Mid-16thC. Alteration of French *(e)strapade*, from Italian *strappata*, from *strappare*, of uncertain origin.]

strapped /strapt/ *adj.* very short of or in need of something, especially money (*informal*)

strap·per /stráppər/ *n.* somebody who is big and powerfully built (*informal*)

strap·ping /strápping/ *adj.* **ROBUST** tall and powerfully built (*informal*) ■ *n.* **1. STRAPS** straps in general, or a set of straps **2. MATERIAL FOR STRAPS** material for making straps or for use as straps

strap·py /stráppee/ (**-pi·er, -pi·est**) *adj.* with straps, especially when they are an important part of the look or design of something (*informal*) ○ *strappy sandals*

strap work *n.* decorative work in the form of crossing or interlaced bands on the outside of a building, especially in Tudor architecture

Stras·berg /stráss burg/, **Lee** (1901–82) Austro-Hungarian-born U.S. actor and teacher. Following the theories of Stanislavsky, he developed and taught the influential Method Acting technique. Real name **Israel Strassberg**

Stras·bourg /stráz burg/ capital city of Bas-Rhin Department, Alsace Region, northeastern France. It is the site of the headquarters of the European Parliament and the Council of Europe. Population: 252,338 (1990).

strass /strass/ *n.* = **paste**[1] *n.* 4 [Early 19thC. From German, named for the 18thC. German jeweler Joseph *Strasser*, who invented it.]

stra·ta plural of **stratum**

strat·a·gem /stráttəjəm/ *n.* **1.** MIL **RUSE FOR DECEIVING ENEMY** a military tactic or maneuver that is designed to deceive an enemy **2. CLEVER SCHEME** clever ruse or scheme that is designed to deceive others or achieve something **3. USE OF CLEVER SCHEMES** the use of stratagems to deceive an enemy or others, or skill in using stratagems [15thC. Via French *stratagème* from, ultimately, Greek *stratēgēma*, from *stratēgos* "general" (see STRATEGY).]

stra·ta ti·tle /straáttə-/ *n. Aus* a system of ownership of space within an apartment building. Titles are issued for each apartment and for common property, which is managed by a committee of unit owners.

stra·ta u·nit *n. Aus* an apartment whose ownership is registered according to strata title

stra·te·gic /strə teéjik/, **stra·te·gi·cal** /-teéjik'l/ *adj.* **1. TYPICAL OF STRATEGY** relating to involving, or typical of strategy or a strategy ○ *strategic planning* **2. DONE FOR REASONS OF STRATEGY** necessary to a strategy, or done because a strategy requires it ○ *a strategic retreat* **3. DISPLAYING SOUND STRATEGY** displaying a sound strategy or plan of action ○ *showing strategic timing in selling a stock short* **4.** MIL **DESTROYING ENEMY'S FIGHTING CAPACITY** done to destroy, or having the capability to destroy, an enemy's ability to fight a war ○ *strategic bombing* **5.** MIL **NECESSARY FOR FIGHTING WAR** necessary for fighting a war, or essential to the military forces fighting a war ○ *strategic metals* ○ *strategic air bases*

stra·te·gi·cal·ly /strə teéjikəlee/ *adv.* **1. AS PART OF STRATEGY** as part of, or in a way useful to, a strategy **2. IN USEFUL WAY** in a clever or useful way

stra·te·gics /strə teéjiks/ *n.* the science or art of military strategy (*takes a singular verb*)

strat·e·gist /stráttəjist/ *n.* somebody who can develop and execute an effective strategy, especially for winning a war

strat·e·gize /stráttə jìz/ (**-gized, -giz·ing, -giz·es**) *vi.* to plan or decide on a strategy

strat·e·gy /stráttəjee/ (*plural* **-gies**) *n.* **1.** MIL **PLANNING OF WAR** the science or art of planning and conducting a war or a military campaign **2. PLANNING IN ANY FIELD** a carefully devised plan of action to achieve a goal, or the art of developing or carrying out such a plan **3.** BIOL **ADAPTATION IMPORTANT TO EVOLUTIONARY SUCCESS** in evolutionary theory, a behavior, structure, or other adaptation that improves viability [Early 19thC. Via French *stratégie* from Greek *stratēgia* "generalship," from *stratēgos* "general," from *stratos* "army" + *agein* "to lead."]

stra·ti plural of **stratus**

strati- *prefix.* stratum, layer ○ *stratigraphy* [From STRATUM]

stra·tic·u·late /strə tíkyələt/ *adj.* used to describe a rock formation that is made up of thin layers [Late 19thC. Formed from STRATUM, on the model of *particulate.*] —**stra·tic·u·la·tion** /strə tìkyə láysh'n/ *n.*

strat·i·fi·ca·tion /stràttəfə káysh'n/ *n.* **1.** GEOL **FORMATION OF ROCK LAYERS** the formation of layers in sedimentary rocks through biological, chemical, or physical changes in the sediments forming them **2. FORMATION OF LAYERS** the formation of layers, castes, classes, or other types of strata **3. SITUATION WHERE THINGS ARE STRATIFIED** a situation or condition where something is arranged in several strata **4.** GEOL **LAYERED ARRANGEMENT OR APPEARANCE** a layered arrangement or appearance of successive rock strata **5.** AGRIC **SEED STORAGE IN CHILLED MOIST ENVIRONMENT** the storing of seeds in a chilled moist environment or material in order to induce germination or to preserve them — **strat·i·fi·ca·tion·al** *adj.*

strat·i·fi·ca·tion·al gram·mar *n.* a form of grammar in which language is analyzed in terms of layers linked to one another by rules

strat·i·fied charge en·gine *n.* an internal combustion engine with two layers of fuel density within the cylinder. A rich mixture is adjacent to the spark plug whose combustion assists in the ignition of a lean mixture in the remainder of the cylinder.

strat·i·form /stráttə fàwrm/ *adj.* **1. COMPOSED OF LAYERS** composed of layers, or with a layered appearance or arrangement **2. FORMED AS LAYER** forming or formed as a layer **3.** METEOROL **LIKE STRATUS CLOUD** like or having the form of a stratus cloud

strat·i·fy /stráttə fì/ (**-fied, -fy·ing, -fies**) *v.* **1.** *vti.* **FORM INTO LAYERS** to form something into a layer or layers, or become formed into a layer or layers **2.** *vti.* SOC SCI **FORM INTO STATUS GROUPS** to form or be formed into castes, classes, or other groups based on status **3.** *vt.* AGRIC **STORE SEEDS IN CHILLED MOIST ENVIRONMENT** to store seeds in chilled moist sand, peat moss, or other material in order to induce germination or preserve the seeds

strat·i·graph·ic /stràttə gráffik/, **strat·i·graph·i·cal** /-gráffik'l/ *adj.* relating to stratigraphy — **strat·i·graph·i·cal·ly** *adv.*

strat·i·graph·ic col·umn *n.* a succession of rocks laid down over a particular period of geologic time

strat·i·graph·ic u·nit *n.* a body of rock defined by its fossil record, physical appearance, or time span

stra·tig·ra·phy /strə tíggrəfee/ (*plural* **-phies**) *n.* **1.** GEOL **STUDY OF ROCK STRATA** the study of the origin, composition, and development of rock strata **2.** ARCHEOL **VERTICAL SECTION THROUGH GROUND** a section cut vertically through the earth showing its different layers and allowing artefacts to be dated according to the layers in which they are found **3.** GEOL **DISPOSITION OF ROCK STRATA** the way in which rock strata are arranged, and the chronology of their formation — **stra·tig·ra·pher** *n.* —**strat·i·graph·ist** *n.*

stra·toc·ra·cy /strə tókrəssee/ (*plural* **-cies**) *n.* government by armed forces (*formal*) [Mid-17thC. Coined from Greek *stratos* "army" (originally "crowd, people spread out") + -CRACY.] —**strat·o·crat** /stráttə kràt/ *n.* — **strat·o·crat·ic** /stràttə kráttik/ *adj.*

stra·to·cu·mu·lus /stráytō kyoómyələss, stràttō-/ (*plural* **-li** /-lì/) *n.* a cloud formation in a low-lying extensive layer with large dark round or rolling masses

strat·o·pause /stráttə pàwz/ *n.* the boundary layer between the stratosphere and the mesosphere, at around 30 mi./50 km above the Earth's surface [Mid-20thC. From STRATOSPHERE, modeled on *tropopause.*]

strat·o·sphere /stráttə sfeer/ *n.* **1. REGION OF THE ATMOSPHERE** the region of the Earth's atmosphere between the troposphere and mesosphere, from 6 mi./10 km to 30 mi./50 km above the Earth's surface. It has no clouds and is marked by gradual temperature increase. ◊ **ionosphere, mesosphere, troposphere 2. VERY HIGH OR HIGHEST POSITION** a very high or the highest level or position [Early 20thC. Coined from STRATUM + -SPHERE.]

strat·o·spher·ic /stràttə sféerik, -sférrik/ *adj.* **1. RELATING TO STRATOSPHERE** relating or belonging to the stratosphere **2. VERY HIGH** very or excessively high — **strat·o·spher·i·cal·ly** *adv.*

strat·o·vol·ca·no /stràytō vol káynō, stràttō-/ (*plural* **-noes** *or* **-nos**) *n.* a volcano consisting of layers of lava alternating with ash or cinder

stra·tum /stráytəm, strát-/ (*plural* **-ta** /-tə/) *n.* **1. LAYER** any of several parallel layers or levels of something (*formal*) ○ *We found several strata of archeological material on the site.* **2.** GEOL = **bed** *n.* 12 **3. LAYER OF**

ATMOSPHERE OR SEA a layer of the atmosphere or the sea **4.** BIOL **LAYER OF CELLS** a layer of living cells **5.** SOC SCI **LAYER OF SOCIETY** a social class or level of society consisting of people of similar cultural, economic, or educational status **6.** **LEVEL WITHIN SYSTEM** a layer or level within an ordered system ○ *the various strata of meaning within the text* [Late 16thC. From modern Latin, from Latin, literally "something thrown down," from, ultimately, *sternere* (see STREW).] —**stra·tal** *adj.*

stra·tus /stráytəss, strát-/ (*plural* **-ti** /-tee/) *n.* a low-lying flat gray cloud formation [Early 19thC. From modern Latin, which evolved from Latin, the past participle of *sternere* (see STREW).]

Strauss /strowss, shtrowss/, **Johann** (1804–49) Austrian conductor and composer. His compositions include many waltzes and marches. Known as **Johann Strauss the Elder**

Strauss, Johann (1825–99) Austrian composer. The son of Johann Strauss the Elder, he wrote operettas including *Die Fledermaus* (1874) and waltzes and other dance pieces including *The Blue Danube* (1867). Known as **Johann Strauss the Younger**

Strauss, Richard (1864–1949) German conductor and composer. His late romantic symphonic poems and operas such as *Der Rosenkavalier* (1911) develop the ideas of Richard Wagner and are characterized by rich harmonization.

AKG London

Igor Stravinsky

Stra·vin·sky /strə vín skee/, **Igor** (1882–1971) Russian-born U.S. composer. A major figure in 20th-century music, he experimented widely with musical styles and forms and wrote the music for Sergei Diaghilev's ballets *The Firebird* (1910), *Petrushka* (1911), and *The Rite of Spring* (1913). Full name **Igor Fyodorovich Stravinsky**

straw /straw/ *n.* **1.** **STALKS OF THRESHED CEREAL CROPS** the stalks of threshed cereal crops such as wheat or barley. It is used as bedding and food for animals, for weaving into objects such as baskets or mats, and for thatching. **2.** **THIN TUBE FOR SUCKING UP DRINK** a long thin tube, often made of paper or plastic, used for sucking up a drink **3.** BOT **DRIED GRASS STALK** a single dried stalk of a cereal crop or grass **4.** CRAFT **ITEM MADE OF STRAW** something made of straw, e.g., a hat or basket **5.** **SOMETHING WORTHLESS** anything of little or no importance or value **6.** COLORS = **straw color** ■ *adj.* **1.** **WORTHLESS** worthless or of little value **2.** **ACTING AS A FRONT** acting as a front for somebody else's activities or to show an adversary up **3.** COLORS **OF STRAW COLOR** of the pale browish-yellow color of straw [Old English *strēaw.* Ultimately from an Indo-European word meaning "to spread," which is also the ancestor of English *strew.* The underlying idea is of something strewn.] —**straw·y** *adj.* ◇ **a straw in the wind** a relatively minor incident or thing that gives some indication of what is likely to happen in the future ◇ **clutch** *or* **grasp at straws** to be willing to try anything that may help in a situation that is unlikely to succeed ◇ **draw the short straw** to be chosen from a group of people to do a difficult or unpleasant task

straw·ber·ry /stráw bèrree/ (*plural* **-ries**) *n.* **1.** PLANTS **PLANT WITH EDIBLE RED FRUIT** a trailing plant of the rose family that has white flowers and is cultivated for its edible red fruit. Genus: *Fragaria.* **2.** FOOD **EDIBLE PART OF STRAWBERRY PLANT** a small soft sweet part of the strawberry plant, approximately heart-shaped, with tiny single-seeded fruits on its surface. It may be eaten raw or processed to flavor other foods. ["Straw" perhaps in the obsolete sense "small piece of chaff" (referring to the external seeds), or perhaps because the plant's runners resemble straws]

Strawberry

straw·ber·ry blond *adj.* **REDDISH BLOND** used to describe hair that is very pale in color with a reddish or pinkish tinge ■ *n.* **SOMEBODY WITH STRAWBERRY BLOND HAIR** somebody who has strawberry blond hair

straw·ber·ry bush *n.* a shrub or small tree of eastern North America with tiny flowers and scarlet pods and seeds. Latin name: *Euonymus americanus.*

straw·ber·ry mark *n.* a raised red birthmark, often found on the scalp or face, containing small blood vessels

straw·ber·ry roan *n.* a horse that has coat of reddish hairs mixed with white

straw·ber·ry shrub *n.* = **Carolina allspice**

straw·ber·ry to·ma·to *n.* **1.** PLANTS **TROPICAL PLANT WITH EDIBLE FRUIT** a hairy tropical plant of the nightshade family bearing edible yellow fruit. Genus: *Physalis.* **2.** FOOD **FRUIT OF STRAWBERRY TOMATO PLANT** the round yellow edible fruit of the strawberry tomato plant

straw·ber·ry tree *n.* a small evergreen tree of the heath family, native to southern Europe, that has white or pink flowers and small berries resembling strawberries. Latin name: *Arbutus unedo.*

straw·board /stráw bàwrd/ *n.* a coarse cardboard made of straw pulp and used in making packaging materials and book covers

straw boss *n.* a worker who also supervises a small work crew, acting as an assistant to the foreman (*informal*) [From U.S. farms, where the second in command was formerly responsible for straw coming out of the thresher]

straw col·or *n.* a pale brownish yellow color —**straw-col·ored** *adj.*

straw·flow·er /stráw flòwr/ *n.* an Australian plant with flower heads that remain colorful when dried. Latin name: *Helichrysum bracteatum.*

straw-hat *adj.* used to describe or relating to a theater that operates only in the summer [From the relatively rustic beginnings of these theaters, whose productions were often staged in a converted barn or town hall]

straw man *n.* **1.** **FRONT FOR SOMEBODY** somebody who acts as a front for somebody else's questionable or illegal activities **2.** **UNIMPORTANT ISSUE OR PERSON** an issue or person of little importance or relevance, brought up to be shown as an easily defeatable idea or adversary **3.** **FIGURE MADE OF STRAW** a straw figure made to resemble a human being

straw mush·room *n.* a small brown or pale-colored edible mushroom used in Chinese cooking. It has a delicate flavor and a slightly gelatinous texture. Latin name: *Volvariella volvacea.*

straw poll, **straw vote** *n.* an unofficial poll or vote used to discover the likely result of an election or the trend of opinion regarding a particular issue

straw wine *n.* a type of sweet wine made from grapes that have been partially dried in the sun, especially on a bed of straw

straw·worm /stráw wùrm/ *n.* = **caddis worm** [*Straw* because it infests stalks of grain]

stray /stray/ *vi.* (**strayed, stray·ing, strays**) **1.** **WANDER AWAY** to leave the correct course or wander away from the correct place, often unintentionally **2.** **BECOME SEPARATED FROM GROUP** to move away from or become separated from a flock or group **3.** **WANDER ABOUT AIMLESSLY** to roam or wander without a particular aim or destination **4.** **DIGRESS FROM SUBJECT** to digress or become diverted from the main subject **5.** **DEPART FROM ACCEPTED STANDARDS** to depart from traditional or accepted standards of behavior **6.** **MEANDER** to take an indirect course ■ *adj.* **1.** **LOST OR HOMELESS** homeless, lost, or wandering **2.** **SCATTERED OR SEPARATED** scattered, separated, or happening accidentally or randomly ■ *n.* **1.** **SOMEBODY LOST** somebody, especially a child, who is lost **2.** AGRIC **LOST OR HOMELESS DOMESTIC ANIMAL** a domestic animal that is lost, has been turned loose, or has wandered away from the place where it lives ■ **strays** *npl.* ELECTRON ENG **ELECTRICAL INTERFERENCE** electrical interference in a radio or television broadcast, causing a random crackling noise or disruption of a picture [13thC. Shortening of *astray,* from Old French *estraier,* of uncertain origin: perhaps ultimately from Latin *extra vagari* "to wander outside" (source of English *extravagant*).] —**stray·er** *n.*

streak /streek/ *n.* **1.** **THIN STRIPE OF CONTRASTING COLOR** a long thin stripe or band that is a different color from its background or surroundings **2.** **SHORT PERIOD OR UNBROKEN RUN** a short period or unbroken run, especially of good or bad luck ○ *The team is finally having a winning streak.* **3.** **CONTRASTING CHARACTERISTIC** a characteristic of somebody or something, especially one that is only occasionally evident or that contrasts with other characteristics ○ *a happy-go-lucky streak* **4.** **LAYER OF SOMETHING** a layer or strip of something **5.** **LIGHTNING FLASH** a flash of lightning **6.** MINERALS **MARK OF MINERAL POWDER** the colored mark that a mineral makes when scratched on an unglazed porcelain tile. This mark is used to identify the mineral. **7.** BOT **VIRAL PLANT DISEASE** a viral disease of plants such as potatoes or tomatoes that produces discolored markings on stems and leaves **8.** MICROBIOL **LINEAR GROWTH OF BACTERIA** a linear growth of bacteria on the surface of a culture medium, produced by drawing a contaminated needle across the medium ■ *v.* (**streaked, streak·ing, streaks**) **1.** *vt.* **MARK WITH STREAKS** to mark or cover something with streaks **2.** *vt.* HAIR **LIGHTEN HAIR** to lighten strands or sections of hair with a bleach or dye **3.** *vi.* **BECOME STREAKED** to become streaked or form streaks **4.** *vi.* **DASH OR RUSH** to move at great speed **5.** *vi.* **RUN NAKED THROUGH PUBLIC PLACE** to run across or through a public place with no clothes on, usually as a joke or publicity stunt (*informal*) [Old English *strica.* Ultimately from a prehistoric Germanic word meaning "to touch lightly," which is also the ancestor of English *strike.*] —**streaked** *adj.* ◇ **talk a blue streak** to talk in a fast and animated way

streak·er /streékər/ *n.* somebody who runs through a public place with no clothes on, usually as a joke or publicity stunt (*informal*)

streak·y /streékee/ (**-i·er, -i·est**) *adj.* **1.** **MARKED WITH STREAKS** covered or marked with streaks ○ *I cleaned the windows twice but they still looked streaky.* **2.** **OCCURING AS STREAKS** occurring in the form of streaks **3.** **INCONSISTENT** variable and uneven in quality ○ *Her work's a bit streaky.* —**streak·i·ly** *adv.* —**streak·i·ness** *n.*

stream /streem/ *n.* **1.** **SMALL RIVER** a narrow and shallow river **2.** **CONSTANT FLOW** a constant flow of liquid or gas **3.** **AIR OR WATER CURRENT** a current of air or water **4.** **CONTINUOUS SERIES** a continuous series or procession of people, things, or events, usually moving in a line or in a certain direction **5.** **QUICK OR UNBROKEN FLOW** a quick or uninterrupted burst, flow, or succession ○ *a stream of questions* **6.** **PREVAILING ATTITUDE** a general or prevailing attitude, drift, or trend **7.** **BEAM OF LIGHT** a steady ray or beam of light **8.** *U.K.* EDUC **GROUP OF PUPILS OF SIMILAR ABILITY** a group or level in which pupils of similar ability are placed and taught together ■ *v.* (**streamed, stream·ing, streams**) **1.** *vi.* **FLOW IN LARGE QUANTITIES** to flow continuously or quickly in large quantities **2.** *vi.* **MOVE IN QUANTITY IN SAME DIRECTION** to move continuously in large numbers in the same direction **3.** *vti.* **PRODUCE FLOW OF LIQUID** to emit or produce liquid in a continuous flow ○ *His eyes streamed tears.* **4.** *vti.* **FLOAT FREELY** to float or trail freely in air, wind, or water, or cause something to do this ○ *an advertising banner streaming behind the airplane* **5.** *vi.* **POUR OUT IN TRAIL OR BEAM** to issue in a beam or move forward leaving a trail **6.** *vti. U.K.* EDUC **PUT PUPILS IN ABILITY GROUPS** to place pupils in groups according to their ability [Old English *strēam.* Ultimately from an Indo-European word meaning "to flow," which is also the ancestor of English *rhythm, hemorrhoid,* and *maelstrom.*]

stream·bed /streém bèd/ *n.* a channel through which a stream flows or used to flow

stream·er /streémər/ *n.* **1.** **NARROW FLAG** a long narrow flag or banner **2.** **DECORATIVE PAPER STRIP** a long narrow strip of colored paper or other material that is used for decoration **3.** ASTRON **LUMINOUS STREAK IN SKY** any one of the luminous streaks that make up the aurora borealis and the aurora australis **4.** PRESS **HEADLINE RUNNING ACROSS A FULL PAGE** a large headline that extends the entire width of a newspaper page

stream·ing /stréeming/ *n.* CELL BIOL = **cyclosis**

stream·let /stréemlət/ *n.* a small stream

stream·line /stréem līn/ *vt.* (**-lined, -lin·ing, -lines**) **1. DESIGN OR BUILD WITH SMOOTH SHAPE** to design or build something with a smooth shape so that it moves with minimum resistance through air or water **2. MAKE SOMETHING MORE EFFICIENT** to make something such as a business, organization, or manufacturing process more efficient, especially by simplifying or modernizing it ■ *n.* **1. CONTOUR DESIGNED TO MINIMIZE RESISTANCE** a contour of a body, e.g., of a car, boat, or airplane, designed to minimize resistance when moving through air or water **2.** PHYS **LINE IN FLUID** a line in a fluid indicating the direction of the velocity of a particle —**stream·lined** *adj.* —**stream·lin·ing** *n.*

stream·line flow *n.* a flow of fluid in which the particles follow continuous paths and the fluid velocity at a particular point either remains constant or varies regularly with time. ◊ **turbulent flow**

stream of con·scious·ness *n.* **1.** LITERAT **LITERARY STYLE** a literary style that presents a character's continuous random flow of thoughts as they arise (*hyphenated when used before a noun*) **2.** PSYCHOL **FLOW OF THOUGHTS** the continuous uninterrupted flow of thoughts and feelings through somebody's mind

stream·y /stréemee/ (**-i·er, -i·est**) *adj.* **1. HAVING MANY STREAMS** covered with or rich in streams (*literary*) **2. FLOWING** flowing in a steady stream —**stream·i·ness** *n.*

Streep /streep/, **Meryl** (*b.* 1949) U.S. actor. She won Academy Awards for *Kramer vs. Kramer* (1979) and *Sophie's Choice* (1982). Real name **Mary Louise Streep**

street /street/ *n.* **1. PUBLIC ROAD IN TOWN** a public road, especially in a town or city, usually lined with buildings **2. BUILDINGS ON STREET** the buildings on a particular street **3. PART OF ROAD BETWEEN SIDEWALKS** the part of a road that lies between the sidewalks and is used by vehicles **4. WORKERS LOCATED ON STREET** the people who work or live on a particular street ■ *adj.* **RELATED TO MODERN URBAN SOCIETY** widely found or used in a modern urban environment or fashionable in its culture, especially among young people or the underworld ○ *Street language has worked its way into the mainstream language.* [Old English *strǣt*. Via prehistoric West Germanic from late Latin *strata* "paved road," from, ultimately, Latin *sternere* "to pave, throw down" (source of English *strew*).] ◇ **be on the street** to have no place to live ◇ **be right up somebody's street** to be exactly suitable or appropriate for somebody ◇ **go on the streets** to become a prostitute ◇ **the man** *or* **person** *or* **woman in the street** the average person

street Ar·ab, **street ar·ab** *n.* an offensive term for a child who has run way from home and lives on the streets (*dated offensive*) [From the perception of Arabs as nomadic]

street·car /stréet kaar/ *n.* a public transport vehicle that runs through city streets on metal rails built into the road surface

street cred·i·bil·i·ty *n.* popularity and acceptance among fashionable urban people, especially the young —**street-cred·i·ble** *adj.*

street door *n.* the door of a house or other building that opens onto the street

street fight·er *n.* **1. SOMEBODY WHO LEARNED FIGHTING ON STREETS** somebody whose fighting skills were learned on the streets rather than through formal training as a boxer **2. SOMEBODY CUNNING** somebody who is tough, cunning, and aggressive (*informal*)

street·light /stréet līt/, **street·lamp** /-làmp/ *n.* a light, normally attached to the top of a tall post and one of a series, that illuminates a road or street at night

street·scape /stréet skàyp/ *n.* an artistic portrayal of a street and its activities, especially a busy city street

street-smart *adj.* = **streetwise**

street smarts *npl.* the ability to survive in a hostile or dangerous urban environment

street the·a·ter *n.* dramatic entertainment usually performed outdoors, e.g., in a park or shopping mall

street val·ue *n.* the price that something illegal would be worth if sold to a customer

street vi·rus *n.* the natural virulent strain of a virus as distinguished from a less virulent strain of the same organism that has been grown or treated in a laboratory

street·walk·er /stréet wàwkər/ *n.* a prostitute who solicits in the streets (*informal*) —**street·walk·ing** *n.*

street·wise /stréet wīz/ *adj.* shrewd and experienced enough to be able to survive in the often difficult and dangerous environment of a modern city (*informal*)

Streis·and /strī sand/, **Barbra** (*b.* 1942) U.S. singer, actor, and movie director. The star of musicals, comedies, and dramas, she won an Academy Award for her acting debut in *Funny Girl* (1968). Born **Barbara Joan Streisand**

Strelitzia

stre·lit·zi·a /strə lítsee ə/ (*plural* **-as** *or* **-a**) *n.* a perennial plant of southern Africa that is widely cultivated for its showy flowers that are often unusual or irregular in shape. Genus: *Strelitzia.* [Late 18thC. Named for Charlotte of Mecklenburg-*Strelitz*, queen of George III.]

strength /strength/ *n.* **1. PHYSICAL OR MENTAL POWER** the physical or mental power that makes somebody or something strong **2. RESISTANCE** the ability to withstand force, pressure, or stress **3. DEFENSIVE ABILITY** the ability to resist attack **4. DEGREE OF INTENSITY** degree of intensity, e.g., of color, light, smell, or sound **5. FORCE OF FEELING** degree of force or effectiveness, e.g., of beliefs or feelings **6. PERSUASIVE POWER** power to convince or persuade, e.g., by argument or suggestion **7. INTENSITY OF EXPRESSION** the intensity of the way somebody expresses ideas or feelings **8. POTENCY** the potency of something such as an alcoholic drink or a drug **9. NUMBER OF PEOPLE NEEDED FOR SOMETHING** the number of people required to make something such as an army, team, or workforce complete, used as a measure of capability **10. ASSET OR QUALITY** an extremely valuable or useful ability, asset, or quality ○ *One of the strengths of this system is its adaptability.* **11.** FIN **MAINTENANCE OF PRICES** tendency of stock or overall market prices to be stable or rise due to sufficient demand at current prices [Old English *strengþu*. Ultimately from a prehistoric Germanic base meaning "strong," which is also the ancestor of English *strong*.] ◇ **go from strength to strength** to go on from one success or achievement to another and get progressively better ◇ **in strength** in large numbers ◇ **on the strength of something** on the basis of something

strength·en /stréngth'n/ (**-ened, -en·ing, -ens**) *vti.* to make something stronger or more powerful, or increase in strength or force —**strength·en·er** *n.*

stren·u·ous /strénnyoo əss/ *adj.* **1. TAXING** requiring great effort, energy, stamina, or strength **2. FORCEFUL** active, energetic, or determined [Early 17thC. Formed from Latin *strenuus* "brisk, active," of unknown origin.] —**stren·u·os·i·ty** /strènnyoo óssətee/ *n.* —**stren·u·ous·ly** /strénnyoo əsslee/ *adv.* —**stren·u·ous·ness** /strénnyoo əssnəss/ *n.*

WORD KEY: SYNONYMS

See Synonyms at ***hard***.

strep /strep/ *n.* **STREPTOCOCCUS** a streptococcus (*informal*) ■ *adj.* **STREPTOCOCCAL** streptococcal (*informal*)

strep throat *n.* an acute sore throat caused by the bacterium *Streptococcus pyogenes* and accompanied by fever and inflammation

strepto- *prefix.* **1.** streptococcus ○ *streptokinase* **2.** twisted chain ○ *streptococcus* **3.** streptomyces ○ *streptothricin* [From Greek *streptos* "twisted," from *strephein* "to turn"]

strep·to·ba·cil·lus /strèptō bə síllǝss/ (*plural* **-li** /-lī/) *n.* a rod-shaped bacterium that often causes disease, e.g., rat-bite fever. Individual cells join to form structures resembling chains. Genus: *Streptobacillus.*

strep·to·car·pus /strèptə kaárpəss/ *n.* a subtropical plant with brightly colored tubular flowers and often only one large leaf. Genus: *Streptocarpus.* [Early 19thC. Via modern Latin, genus name, from Greek *streptos* "twisted" + *karpos* "fruit," because its fruit is spirally twisted.]

strep·to·coc·cus /strèptə kókəss/ (*plural* **-ci** /-sī, -kī/) *n.* a spherical bacterium that often causes disease, e.g., scarlet fever or pneumonia. The bacteria link together in pairs or chains. Genus: *Streptococcus.* [Late 19thC. Via modern Latin, genus name, literally "twisted berry," from Greek *streptos* "twisted" (because the chains are usually twisted) + *coccus* "berry."] —**strep·to·coc·cal** *adj.* —**strep·to·coc·cic** /strèptə kóksik, -kókik/ *adj.*

strep·to·dor·nase /strèptə dáwr nàyss, -nàyz/ *n.* an enzyme derived from streptococci and used with streptokinase to liquefy and drain blood clots and purulent discharges, especially during surgery [Mid-20thC. Coined from STREPTOCOCCUS + contraction of *deoxyribonuclease*.]

strep·to·kin·ase /strèptō kí nàyss, -kī-, -nàyz/ *n.* an enzyme produced by streptococci that dissolves blood clots [Mid-20thC. Coined from STREPTOCOCCAL + KINASE.]

strep·to·ly·sin /strèptə líssin/ *n.* a substance that breaks down red blood cells and is produced by streptococci

strep·to·my·ces /strèptə mī seez/ (*plural* **-ces**) *n.* an aerobic soil bacterium. Some streptomyces produce antibiotics. Genus: *Streptomyces.* [Mid-20thC. From modern Latin, genus name, coined from Greek *strepto-* "twisted" + *mukēs* "fungus," because it forms twisted chains and resembles mold.]

strep·to·my·cin /strèptə míssən/ *n.* an antibiotic produced by a soil bacterium that is used to treat infections caused by certain bacteria, e.g., tuberculosis. Formula: $C_{21}H_{39}N_7O_{12}$.

strep·to·thri·cin /strèptə thríssən/ *n.* an antibiotic produced by a soil bacterium that is used against bacteria and certain fungi [Mid-20thC. Coined from modern Latin *Streptothric-*, stem of *Streptothrix*, former genus name, coined from Greek *strepto-* "twisted" + *thrix* "hair," because it grows in hairlike filaments.]

stress /stress/ *n.* **1. STRAIN FELT BY SOMEBODY** mental, emotional, or physical strain caused, e.g., by anxiety or overwork. It may cause such symptoms as raised blood pressure or depression. **2. CAUSE OF STRAIN** something that causes mental or emotional strain **3. SPECIAL IMPORTANCE** special emphasis, importance, or significance attached to something **4.** PHON **EMPHASIS ON SYLLABLE** the emphasis placed on a particular sound or syllable by pronouncing it more loudly or forcefully than those surrounding it in the same word or phrase **5.** POETRY **EMPHASIS IN POETRY** the emphasis placed on a particular syllable or word as part of the rhythm of a poem or line **6.** MUSIC **ACCENT IN MUSIC** the emphasis placed on a particular note as part of the rhythm of a piece of music, or a mark representing this **7.** PHYS **FORCE DEFORMING A BODY** a force or system of forces exerted on a body and resulting in deformation or strain ■ *vt.* (**stressed, stress·ing, stress·es**) **1. EMPHASIZE SOMETHING** to place emphasis on or attach importance to something **2.** PHON **PRONOUNCE FORCEFULLY** to pronounce a word or syllable more loudly or forcefully than those surrounding it **3.** LANGUAGE = **accent** *n.* 3 **4. SUBJECT TO STRESS** to cause somebody or something to experience mental or physical stress [14thC. Partly a shortening of DISTRESS, and partly via Old French *estresse* "narrowness," from Latin *strictus* "compressed" (source of English *strict*).] —**stressed** *adj.*

WORD KEY: SYNONYMS

See Synonyms at ***worry***.

stress out *vti.* to affect somebody with emotional, mental, or physical stress, or be so affected

STRESS /stress/ *abbr.* structural engineering system solver

stressed out *adj.* unable to relax or function properly as the result of experiencing mental or emotional stress (*informal*) (*hyphenated when used before a noun*)

stress frac·ture *n.* a small fracture of a bone caused by repeated physical strain, sometimes experienced, e.g., by gymnasts, long-distance runners, or marching soldiers

stress·ful /strésf'l/ *adj.* causing or involving mental or physical stress —**stress·ful·ly** *adv.* —**stress·ful·ness** *n.*

stress mark *n.* a mark placed before, on, or after a syllable that is to be stressed when the word containing it is pronounced

stres·sor /stréssər/ *n.* an activity, experience, or other situation that causes stress, e.g., lack of water to a plant or overwork to a person

stretch /strech/ *v.* (**stretched, stretch·ing, stretch·es**) **1.** *vti.* EXTEND OR BECOME EXTENDED to lengthen, widen, or extend something, or become lengthened, widened, or extended, especially by force **2.** *vi.* EXPAND AND REGAIN ORIGINAL SHAPE to be capable of expanding and returning to its original shape afterward **3.** *vti.* EXTEND OR BE EXTENDED EXCESSIVELY to extend something or be extended excessively so that the shape is permanently altered ○ *The sleeves of this sweater have stretched.* **4.** *vti.* EXTEND BODY TO FULL LENGTH to straighten or extend the body or part of it, especially the limbs, to full length ○ *She woke up, yawned, and stretched.* **5.** *vt.* STRAIN BODY PART to strain a part of the body such as a muscle **6.** *vti.* MAKE SOMETHING TAUT to make something taut or tight, or become taut or tight **7.** *vt.* SUSPEND SOMETHING BETWEEN TWO POINTS to suspend something, or make something reach, between two points **8.** *vi.* EXTEND IN SPACE to spread out or extend over an area or in a particular direction **9.** *vti.* EXTEND SOMETHING OVER TIME to last or continue over a period of time, or prolong something **10.** *vt.* MAKE SMALL AMOUNT GO FURTHER to make limited supplies or resources go further than usual, planned, or expected **11.** *vi.* BE ENOUGH to be sufficient to allow something ○ *Will the budget stretch to hiring a temporary assistant?* **12.** *vt.* EXCEED LIMIT OR BREAK RULE to exceed a limit or break a rule that would usually prohibit something **13.** *vt.* PUSH SOMETHING TO LIMIT to strain or push something to the limit ○ *You're stretching my patience.* **14.** *vt.* PUSH SOMEBODY TO LIMIT OF ABILITY to cause somebody to make full use of abilities or intellect, e.g., with challenging or demanding work **15.** *vt.* EXAGGERATE to make something sound better or worse than it really is, especially in order to make it seem more impressive (*informal*) ○ *To call his house a mansion is stretching it a bit.* **16.** *vt.* KNOCK SOMEBODY DOWN to knock somebody down with a blow (*informal*) **17.** *vti.* HANG SOMEBODY to hang or be hanged from a noose (*archaic*) ■ *n.* **1.** STRETCHING EXERCISE the straightening and extending of a part of the body, e.g., as an exercise **2.** EXPANSE a large expanse of something, especially land or water **3.** PERIOD OF TIME an uninterrupted period of time **4.** PRISON TERM a term of imprisonment (*slang*) **5.** ELASTICITY the ability to expand and return to the original shape afterward **6.** CHALLENGE something that is difficult to achieve (*informal*) **7.** HORSERACING, MOTOR SPORTS, SPORT STRAIGHT PART OF RACETRACK the straight part of a racetrack, especially the final section approaching the finishing line **8.** FINAL STAGE the final stage of an event, task, process, or period of time, especially one that has been difficult or challenging **9.** BASEBALL POSITION BY PITCHER the position taken by a pitcher in order to hold a runner close to a base ○ *He had so many base runners that he was pitching from the stretch all day.* ■ *adj.* EXTENDED TO PROVIDE EXTRA SPACE extended or enlarged in order to prove extra space, e.g., for additional seating [Old English *streccan*, of uncertain origin. Probably ultimately from a prehistoric Germanic base meaning "rigid" (hence "taut, stretched"), which is also the ancestor of English *starch*.] —**stretch·a·bil·i·ty** /strèchə bíllətee/ *n.* —**stretch·a·ble** /stréchəb'l/ *adj.* ◇ **at a stretch 1.** continuously ○ *worked five hours at a stretch* **2.** with great difficulty or effort ○ *could get there by six at a stretch* ◇ **at full stretch** using all the energy or resources available

stretch·er /stréchər/ *n.* **1.** MED DEVICE FOR CARRYING SOMEBODY LYING DOWN a device consisting of a sheet of material such as canvas stretched over a frame, used to carry somebody in a lying position who is sick, injured, or dead **2.** *ANZ* CAMPING CAMP BED a camp bed consisting of a folding tubular metal frame and a canvas covering **3.** PAINTING FRAME FOR ARTIST'S CANVAS a wooden frame over which a canvas for an oil painting is stretched **4.** FURNITURE BAR BRACING FURNITURE LEGS a bar that joins and braces the legs of a chair, table, or other piece of furniture **5.** BUILDING STRONG BEAM USED AS BRACE a strong, usually horizontal beam or bar that is used as a brace in the framework of a structure **6.** BUILDING STONE WITH LONG EDGE FACING OUT a brick or stone laid in a wall so that its longer edge forms part of the face of the wall. ◊ **header 7.** EXAGGERATED STORY an exaggerated story or a lie based partly on the truth (*slang*)

stretch·er-bear·er *n.* somebody who helps carry a stretcher, especially a soldier given the task in wartime

stretch knit *n.* knitted fabric that can stretch and return to its original shape afterward (*hyphenated when used before a noun*)

stretch mark *n.* a mark left on the skin of the abdomen, breasts, buttocks, or thighs after pregnancy or weight loss (*often used in the plural*)

stretch-out *n.* **1.** INDUST EXTENDING TIME TO MEET PRODUCTION QUOTA changing a production schedule so that the same amount of goods can be produced over a longer period of time **2.** FIN LENGTHENING OF TIME FOR DEBT REPAYMENT a restructuring of a debt payment schedule so that the debt can be paid back over a longer period of time **3.** INDUST ADDITIONAL WORK WITHOUT ADDITIONAL PAY an industrial practice in which workers are required to do more work with little or no additional compensation

stretch·y /stréchee/ (**-i·er, -i·est**) *adj.* capable of being stretched, usually returning to its original shape afterward, or tending to stretch —**stretch·i·ness** *n.*

stret·to /stréttō/ (*plural* **-tos** *or* **-ti** /-tee/) *n.* **1.** OVERLAPPING PASSAGES IN FUGUE in a fugue or similar work, the successive statements of the theme very close together in time **2.** FAST PASSAGE the speeding up of a piece of music at a climactic moment [Mid-18thC. Via Italian, literally "narrow, tight," from Latin *strictus* (see STRICT).]

streu·sel /stro͝os'l, stròyz-/ *n.* a crumbly topping for cakes and quick breads. It is made of sugar, flour, butter, cinnamon, and often chopped nuts. [Early 20thC. From German, from *streuen* "to sprinkle."]

strew /stroo/ (**strewed, strewn** /stroon/ *or* **strewed, strew·ing, strews**) *v.* **1.** *vt.* SCATTER SOMETHING to scatter something, especially carelessly or untidily ○ *Clothes were strewn all over the floor.* **2.** *vti.* SPREAD OVER AREA to spread or become spread over a large area ○ *areas strewn with landmines* [Old English *strewian*. Ultimately from an Indo-European word that is also the ancestor of English *straw* and *stratum*.] —**strew·er** *n.*

stri·a /strī́ ə/ (*plural* **-ae** /-ee/) *n.* **1.** GROOVE OR SCRATCH a thin narrow groove or channel in the surface of something, e.g., a decorative feature on a column **2.** STRIPE OR BAND a stripe, streak, or narrow band, e.g., a band of nerve fibers or stretch marks seen in pregnancy (**striae gravidarum**) **3.** GEOL = **striation** *n.* 3 [Mid-16thC. From Latin, "furrow, channel" (originally "something grazed"). Ultimately from an Indo-European word that is also the ancestor of English *strike*.]

stri·ate /strī́ àyt/ *vt.* (**-at·ed, -at·ing, -ates**) MARK WITH STRIAE to mark something with parallel grooves, ridges, stripes, or narrow bands ■ *adj.* = **striated** [Late 17thC. From Latin *striare*, from *stria* (see STRIA).]

stri·at·ed /strī́ àytəd/ *adj.* marked with parallel grooves, ridges, stripes, or narrow bands

stri·at·ed mus·cle *n.* a muscle or muscle tissue, e.g., cardiac muscle or the muscles attached to the skeleton, that shows light and dark bands within the muscle fibers

stri·a·tion /strī áysh'n/ *n.* **1.** STRIPY PATTERN patterning or marking with parallel grooves or narrow bands **2.** ANAT BANDING OR BAND WITHIN MUSCLE FIBER the striped pattern of striated muscle, or any of the light and dark bands that make up this effect **3.** GEOL GROOVE OR SCRATCH a narrow groove or scratch on an exposed rock face, caused by abrasion by hard rock fragments embedded in a moving glacier

strick·en /stríkən/ past participle of **strike** ■ *adj.* **1.** DEEPLY OR BADLY AFFECTED BY SOMETHING deeply or very badly affected by something such as grief, misfortune, or trouble **2.** AFFECTED BY ILLNESS experiencing severe physical symptoms caused by illness or injury **3.** HIT BY MISSILE injured, struck, or wounded, e.g., by a missile —**strick·en·ly** *adv.*

strick·le /strík'l/ *n.* **1.** BOARD FOR LEVELING OFF EXCESS MATERIAL a board used to level off excess grain or other material in a container or measuring device **2.** TOOL FOR SHAPING MOLD SURFACE a tool used to shape the surface of a mold ■ *vt.* (**-led, -ling, -les**) USE STRICKLE ON SOMETHING to level or shape something with a strickle [Old English *stricel*. Ultimately from a prehistoric Germanic base that is also the ancestor of English *strike*.]

strict /strikt/ *adj.* **1.** SEVERE IN MAINTAINING DISCIPLINE severe in maintaining discipline or rigorous in ensuring that rules are obeyed **2.** ENFORCED RIGOROUSLY needing to be closely obeyed **3.** PRECISE exact, precise, or narrowly interpreted **4.** FAITHFUL closely observing rules, principles, or practices **5.** ABSOLUTE complete, utter, or absolute **6.** BOT GROWING UPRIGHT growing upward at or very close to the vertical [15thC. From Latin *strictus*, past participle of *stringere* "to draw tight."] —**strict·ly** *adv.* —**strict·ness** *n.*

WORD KEY: ORIGIN

The Latin word Latin *stringere*, from which ***strict*** is derived, is also the source of English *constrain, constrict, distress, district, prestige, restrain, restrict, strain, stress,* and *stringent.*

stric·ture /stríkchər/ *n.* **1.** SEVERE CRITICISM a severe criticism or strongly critical remark (*formal*) **2.** LIMIT OR RESTRICTION a limit or restriction, especially one that seems unfair or too harsh (*formal*) **3.** MED CONSTRICTION OF BODY PASSAGE an abnormal constriction or narrowing of a body passage [14thC. From Latin *strictura*, from, ultimately, *stringere* "to draw tight."] —**stric·tured** *adj.*

stride /strīd/ *v.* (**strode** /strōd/, **strid·den** /strídd'n/, **strid·ing, strides**) **1.** *vi.* WALK WITH LONG REGULAR STEPS to walk with long regular steps, often briskly or energetically **2.** *vti.* TAKE LONG STEP OVER SOMETHING to cross or step over something with a long step **3.** *vti.* STRADDLE to sit or stand astride something (*archaic or literary*) ■ *n.* **1.** LONG STEP a long step, especially one taken briskly or energetically **2.** DISTANCE COVERED BY LONG STEP the distance covered when somebody or something takes a long step **3.** ADVANCE TOWARD IMPROVING SOMETHING an advance or step toward improving or developing something **4.** WAY OF WALKING a way of walking or running in long regular steps, often taken briskly or energetically **5.** ZOOL COORDINATED FORWARD MOVEMENT BY ANIMAL an act of forward motion by a four-legged animal consisting of a coordinated cycle of movements that brings the legs back to their original positions **6.** MUSIC = **stride piano** ■ **strides** *npl. Aus* TROUSERS a pair of trousers (*informal*) [Old English *strīdan* "to straddle," of uncertain origin. Perhaps ultimately from a prehistoric Germanic word meaning "to diverge," which may also be the ancestor of English *strife* and *strive*.] —**strid·er** *n.* ◇ **hit** *or* **reach your stride** to become familiar with and at ease with something so that you can do it easily and well ◇ **take something in (your) stride** to accept something without being unduly upset or worried about it

stri·dent /strī́d'nt/ *adj.* **1.** LOUD harsh, loud, grating, or shrill **2.** STRONGLY EXPRESSED loudly, strongly, or urgently expressed [Mid-17thC. From Latin, the present participle stem of *stridere* "to creak" (source of English *stridulate*).] —**stri·dence** *n.* —**stri·den·cy** *n.* —**stri·dent·ly** *adv.*

stride pi·an·o *n.* a style of jazz piano playing in which the right hand plays the melody while the left hand alternates between playing a single note and playing a related chord [*Stride* in the sense "to straddle," from the movements of the left hand]

stri·dor /strī́dər/ *n.* **1.** HARSH NOISE a harsh, grating, or creaking noise **2.** PATHOL HARSH HIGH-PITCHED WHEEZE a harsh high-pitched wheezing sound made when breathing in or out, caused by obstruction of the air passages [Mid-17thC. From Latin, from *stridere* (see STRIDENT).]

strid·u·lant *adj.* = **stridulous**

strid·u·late /stríjjə làyt/ (**-lat·ed, -lat·ing, -lates**) *vi.* to make a chirping or grating sound by rubbing certain parts of the body together, as, e.g., male crickets and grasshoppers do [Mid-19thC. Via French *striduler* from, ultimately, Latin *stridere* (see STRIDENT).] —**strid·u·la·tion** /strìjjə láysh'n/ *n.* —**strid·u·la·tor** /stríjjə làytər/ *n.* —**strid·u·la·to·ry** /-lə tàwree/ *adj.*

strid·u·lous /stríjjələss/, **strid·u·lant** /-lənt/ *adj.* **1.** MAKING A GRATING SOUND having or making a shrill, harsh, or grating sound **2.** PATHOL OF OBSTRUCTED BREATHING relating to, affected by, or characteristic of stridor [Early 17thC. Formed from Latin *stridulus* "creaking," from *stridere* (see STRIDENT).] —**strid·u·lous·ly** *adv.* —**strid·u·lous·ness** *n.*

strife /strīf/ *n.* **1.** BITTER CONFLICT OR RIVALRY bitter and sometimes violent conflict, struggle, or rivalry **2.** STRIVING hard work to get or achieve something (*archaic*) [12thC. From Old French *estrif*, of uncertain origin: perhaps ultimately from Old High German *strīt* "quarrel."] —**strife·less** *adj.*

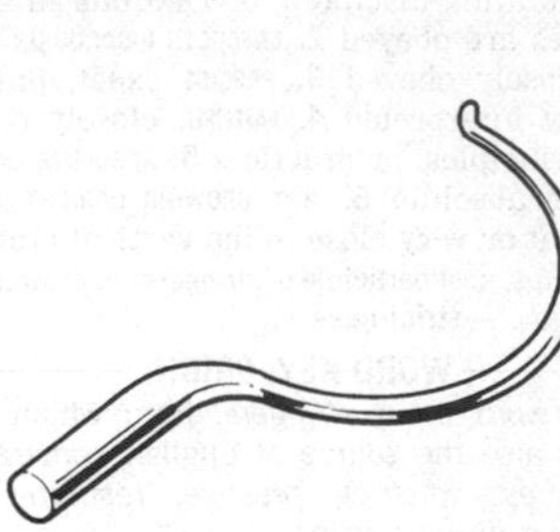
Strigil

strig·il /stríjjəl/ *n.* an instrument with a curved blade used in ancient Greece and Rome to scrape dirt and sweat from the skin after bathing or exercising [Late 16thC. From Latin *strigilis*.]

stri·gose /strī gōss/ *adj.* **1.** BOT SCALY OR BRISTLY covered with fine scales or short bristles **2.** ZOOL RIDGED with thin, closely spaced grooves or ridges [Late 18thC. From modern Latin *strigosus*, from Latin *striga* "row."]

strike /strīk/ *v.* (**struck** /struk/, **struck** *or* **strick·en, strik·ing, strikes**) **1.** *vti.* HIT SOMEBODY OR SOMETHING to hit somebody or something, e.g., with a hand, tool, or weapon ○ *She was struck on the arm by a piece of falling masonry.* **2.** *vti.* DELIVER BLOW to deliver or inflict something such as a blow or punch **3.** *vti.* COLLIDE WITH SOMEBODY OR SOMETHING to crash into, knock hard against, or collide with somebody or something ○ *The car swerved and struck a tree.* **4.** *vti.* PENETRATE SOMETHING to penetrate or seem to go right through something ○ *The pain struck deep into my shoulder blade.* **5.** *vti.* MAKE AN ATTACK to make an attack on somebody or something ○ *The enemy struck under cover of darkness.* **6.** *vi.* INDUST STOP WORKING AS PROTEST to stop working as a collective form of protest against an employer **7.** *vti.* DAMAGE SOMEBODY OR SOMETHING to hit and damage or injure something or somebody **8.** *vt.* INDUST STOP WORKING FOR SOMEBODY to take part in a strike against an employer ○ *They're striking the auto plant.* **9.** *vt.* KNOCK AWAY to remove something with a blow ○ *She struck the wasp from the child's head.* **10.** (*past participle* **strick·en** *or* **struck**) *vti.* AFFECT SOMEBODY SUDDENLY to affect somebody suddenly or unexpectedly ○ *The illness can strike at any age.* **11.** *vti.* PRODUCE FIRE to produce fire by friction, or be produced by friction **12.** *vti.* FIND OR DISCOVER SOMETHING to come across, find, or discover something, especially suddenly or unexpectedly **13.** *vti.* LIGHT MATCH to cause a match to light or to be lit by friction ○ *The matches won't strike if they get damp.* **14.** *vt.* OPERATE SOMETHING BY PRESSING KEY to operate, produce, or play something by pressing a key or touching a string, e.g., on a musical instrument or a typewriter **15.** *vt.* AGREE TO TERMS to agree on the terms of something ○ *struck a deal* **16.** *vti.* INDICATE TIME BY MAKING SOUND to indicate the time by making a sound such as chiming **17.** *vt.* METALL MAKE SOMETHING BY STAMPING to make or form something such as a coin by stamping or punching ○ *Moonbeams struck the placid water on the lake.* **18.** *vti.* SHINE ON SOMETHING to fall or shine on something ○ *Moonbeams struck the placid water on the lake.* **19.** *vt.* BE NOTICED BY SOMEBODY to catch somebody's attention, or be noticed by somebody or something **20.** *vt.* BE PERCEIVED BY SOMEBODY to be perceived by or become audible to somebody **21.** *vt.* MAKE CERTAIN IMPRESSION ON SOMEBODY to have a certain effect on or make a certain impression on somebody **22.** *vt.* ENTER SOMEBODY'S MIND to enter somebody's mind or occur to somebody, especially suddenly **23.** *vt.* AFFECT SOMEBODY WITH EMOTION to affect somebody or cause somebody to be affected with an emotion in a deep, painful, or sudden way **24.** *vi.* BITE OR STING SUDDENLY to deliver a sudden, fast bite or sting, typically resulting in injury to the one bitten or stung ○ *Suddenly the snake struck.* **25.** *vti.* HAPPEN SUDDENLY to happen to somebody or something suddenly or unexpectedly **26.** *vt.* CROSS SOMETHING OUT to cancel, delete, or cross something out ○ *The judge ordered that the preceding remark be stricken from the record.* **27.** *vt.* ACHIEVE SOMETHING BY CAREFUL CONSIDERATION to achieve something such as a balance or a compromise by careful consideration or calculation **28.** *vt.* ADOPT POSE to adopt or assume something such as a pose or attitude **29.** *vti.* ANGLING TAKE BAIT to take or attempt to take a bait ○ *The fish are striking today.* **30.** *vti.* BOT GROW ROOTS to send out and establish roots **31.** *vt.* DISMANTLE SOMETHING to dismantle something such as a tent or stage set **32.** *vt.* NAUT LOWER MAST OR SAIL to lower a mast or sail **33.** *vt.* NAUT LOWER SOMETHING IN RESPECT OR SURRENDER to lower something such as a flag or sail as a sign of respect or surrender **34.** *vt.* SHIPPING LOWER SOMETHING INTO SHIP'S HOLD to lower something into the hold of a ship **35.** *vi.* NAVY ATTEMPT TECHNICAL RATING IN U.S. NAVY to work hard with the aim of achieving a certain technical rating in the U.S. Navy **36.** *vt.* = **strickle** ■ *n.* **1.** HIT OR BLOW DELIVERED a blow delivered by striking **2.** SOUND OF HIT a sound produced by striking somebody or something **3.** INDUST WORK STOPPAGE a work stoppage by employees as a protest against an employer **4.** REFUSAL TO DO SOMETHING AS PROTEST a refusal to carry out a regular action or activity, e.g., eating or paying rent, as a form of protest **5.** MIL MILITARY ATTACK USING AIRCRAFT a military attack, especially one using aircraft **6.** SUCCESS IN FINDING SOMETHING a success in finding or discovering something, especially a valuable mineral source such as gold or oil **7.** BOWLING KNOCKING DOWN OF BOWLING PINS the knocking down of all the pins with the first ball in a session of bowling **8.** BASEBALL MISSED PITCH a pitch in baseball that is swung at and missed or is in the strike zone and not hit **9.** COINS COINS STRUCK AT SAME TIME the number of coins or medals struck at the same time **10.** GEOL DIRECTION OF GEOLOGIC FORMATION the compass direction of a horizontal line on a sloping rock surface, used to define geologic features such as bedding or faults **11.** = **strickle** *n.* 1 **12.** VET ANIMAL DISEASE CAUSED BY FLIES an animal disease caused by an infestation of flies or fly eggs in open wounds or moist areas of the skin **13.** ANGLING PULL ON FISHING LINE BY FISH a pull on a fishing line indicating that a fish has taken the bait **14.** BOT SENDING OUT OF PLANT ROOTS the establishment of roots by a plant cutting or seedling [Old English *strīcan*. Ultimately from a prehistoric Germanic base meaning "to touch lightly," which is also the ancestor of English *stroke* and *streak*.] ◇ **strike it rich** to be extremely lucky or successful, particularly in money matters

strike down *vt.* **1.** CAUSE TO FALL to cause somebody or something to fall by hitting **2.** CAUSE SOMEBODY TO BECOME VERY ILL to affect somebody or cause somebody to become seriously ill, especially suddenly **3.** KILL SOMEBODY to cause somebody to die, especially suddenly **4.** CAUSE SOMETHING TO BECOME INEFFECTIVE to cause something to be no longer in effect or valid

strike off *vt.* **1.** DELETE SOMETHING to cancel or remove something from a list, record, or register by crossing it out ○ *A steward struck off the names of the passengers as they boarded the plane.* **2.** PRINTING PRINT to print something

strike out *v.* **1.** *vi.* FAIL to be unsuccessful (*informal*) ○ *I tried three times to get that job, but struck out completely.* **2.** *vti.* BASEBALL HAVE THREE STRIKES to put a batter out, or to be made out, with three strikes **3.** *vt.* SET OUT ENERGETICALLY to set out energetically, especially for a particular destination or in a particular direction ○ *We struck out at sunrise, determined to get there by nightfall.* **4.** *vi.* ATTACK SOMEBODY OR SOMETHING to attack somebody or something, either physically or verbally **5.** *vt.* DRAW LINE THROUGH SOMETHING to draw a line through something in order to cancel or delete it **6.** *vi.* BEGIN SOMETHING to begin doing something, especially independently

strike up *v.* **1.** *vti.* BEGIN TO PLAY to begin playing or singing something ○ *struck up the band and played a waltz* **2.** *vt.* BEGIN SOMETHING to begin something, or cause something to begin

strike·bound /strīk bòwnd/ *adj.* closed or unable to operate because people have stopped work as a form of protest

strike·break·er /strīk bràykər/ *n.* **1.** SOMEBODY WHO WORKS WHILE OTHERS STRIKE somebody who continues to work for an employer while other employees are on strike **2.** SOMEBODY HIRED TO REPLACE STRIKER somebody hired to do the work of somebody who is on strike

strike·break·ing /strīk bràyking/ *n.* **1.** ACTION OF STRIKEBREAKER the act of working for an employer while other employees are on strike **2.** BREAKING UP OF STRIKE action intended to break up a workers' strike

strike fault *n.* a fault with a strike parallel to the rock strata

strike-out *n.* an out made in baseball by a batter charged with three strikes

strike·o·ver /strīk ōvər/ *n.* **1.** TYPING OVER ALREADY TYPED CHARACTER the typing of one character over another already typed without erasing the first one **2.** SOMETHING TYPED OVER a character or word that has been typed over by something else

strike pay *n.* money paid by a trade union to members who are on strike

strik·er /strīkər/ *n.* **1.** INDUST SOMEBODY ON STRIKE somebody who has stopped working or taken other action as a form of protest **2.** SOCCER ATTACKING PLAYER IN SOCCER TEAM an attacking player in a soccer team whose main role is to score goals **3.** DEVICE THAT STRIKES TO TELL TIME a device that strikes to tell the time, e.g., a hammer in a clock or a clapper in a bell **4.** ARMS MECHANISM THAT DRIVES FIRING PIN FORWARD the mechanical part of a firearm that drives the firing pin forward **5.** NAVY SAILOR WORKING TO GET TECHNICAL RATING somebody enlisted in the U.S. Navy who is working hard toward a technical rating

strike-slip fault *n.* a geological fault that moves in a direction parallel to its strike

strike zone *n.* in baseball, the area above homeplate, between the batter's armpits and knees, through which the ball must travel in order to be called a strike

strik·ing /strīking/ *adj.* **1.** CONSPICUOUS conspicuous, marked, or noticeable **2.** ATTRACTIVE OR IMPRESSIVE attracting attention, especially in an impressive or unusual way **3.** INDUST ON STRIKE not working as a form of protest —**strik·ing·ly** *adv.* —**strik·ing·ness** *n.*

strik·ing dis·tance *n.* closeness to something or to achieving something

strik·ing price *n.* the price at which the holder of stock options or warrants has the right to buy or sell

AKG London
August Strindberg

Strind·berg /strínd burg, strín-/, **August** (1849–1912) Swedish dramatist. Often considered the greatest figure in Swedish literature, he greatly influenced European and U.S. dramatists with his naturalistic novels and plays, notably *The Ghost Sonata* (1908). Full name **Johan August Strindberg** —**Strind·berg·i·an** /strind búrgee ən/ *adj.*

Strine /strīn/, **strine** *n.* Australian English, especially a humorous representation in writing of Australian pronunciation, e.g., "Emma Chisit" for "How much is it?" (*humorous*) [Mid-20thC. An imitation of the supposed Australian pronunciation of AUSTRALIAN, first used in the books of Alistair Morrison under the pseudonym Afferbeck Lauder, Strine for "alphabetical order."]

string /string/ *n.* **1.** THIN CORD a thin cord or twine, usually made of twisted fibers, used for binding, fastening, hanging, or tying **2.** SOMETHING RESEMBLING STRING something that resembles string in form or texture **3.** SUCCESSION OF ITEMS a series of similar or connected acts, events, or things **4.** LINE OF THINGS a series of things forming or arranged in a line, usually one behind another **5.** GROUP OF ASSOCIATED THINGS a group of similar things belonging to, managed by, or connected with a single person or a set of people **6.** SEQUENCE OF SIMILAR ELEMENTS a sequence of elements of the same nature, e.g., letters, numbers, symbols, binary digits, sounds, or words **7.** OBJECTS THREADED TOGETHER a set of objects connected with a single thread **8.** MUSIC LONG CORD STRETCHED ACROSS MUSICAL INSTRUMENT a cord made of nylon, wire, or gut that is stretched across a musical instrument and plucked, bowed, or otherwise vibrated in order to produce sound **9.** RACKET GAMES **THIN CORD STRETCHED ACROSS SPORTS RACKET** any of the thin cords that are tightly stretched across the face of a sports racket and interwoven to form a mesh **10.** ARCHERY **CORD STRETCHED ACROSS ARCHER'S BOW** the cord stretched between the ends of a bow in archery **11. PLANT FIBER** a tough chewy fiber in a fruit or vegetable **12. TENDON** a tendon or ligament of an animal (*archaic*) **13.** BUILDING = **stringboard 14.** BUILDING = **stringcourse 15.** SPORTS **PERSON CHOSEN AND RANKED ON ABILITY** a person or group of people chosen, especially for a sports team, and ranked at a specified level on the basis of their ability **16.** CUE GAMES **HIT DETERMINING PLAYING ORDER IN BILLIARDS** an act of hitting the cue ball in billiards toward the head cushion (**lag**) to determine who will play first **17.** CUE GAMES = **balkline** *n.* 1 **18.** BOWLING **TEN FRAMES OF BOWLING** a game of bowling consisting of ten frames **19.** PHYS, ASTRON **HYPOTHETICAL ONE-DIMENSIONAL ENTITY** a hypothetical one-dimensional entity that vibrates as it moves through space and is held to be a fundamental component of matter. ◊ **cosmic string, superstring** ■ **strings** *npl.* MUSIC **1. MUSICIANS PLAYING STRINGED INSTRUMENTS** the section of an orchestra consisting of musicians who play stringed instruments **2. STRINGED INSTRUMENTS OF ORCHESTRA** the stringed instruments of an orchestra or other musical ensemble considered as a group ■ *v.* (**strung** /strung/, **strung, string·ing, strings**) **1.** *vt.* **THREAD ONTO STRING** to thread things onto a string **2.** *vt.* **HANG SOMETHING BETWEEN TWO POINTS** to hang or stretch something between two points **3.** *vt.* **ARRANGE OR EXTEND SOMETHING IN LINE** to arrange or extend something in a line or series **4.** *vt.* **PROVIDE SOMETHING WITH STRING OR STRINGS** to provide something, e.g., a sports racket or musical instrument, with a string or strings **5.** *vt.* **FASTEN OR TIE SOMETHING WITH STRING** to bind, fasten, hang, or tie something with a string or strings **6.** *vt.* COOK **REMOVE FIBERS** to remove the stringy fibers from vegetables **7.** *vi.* **BECOME STRINGY** to form strings or become stringy **8.** *vti.* CUE GAMES **DETERMINE PLAYING ORDER IN BILLIARDS** to hit the cue ball in billiards toward the head cushion (**lag**) to determine who will play first ■ *adj.* **MADE OF STRING** made of a mesh of string or similar material [Old English *streng*. Ultimately from a prehistoric Germanic base meaning "stiff" (ancestor also of English *strong*), the underlying idea being of something twisted until stiff.] —**string·less** *adj.* ◇ **have somebody on a string** to be able to control somebody easily ◇ **pull strings** to use influence to try to gain an advantage ◇ **pull the strings** to be in control, although not obviously so ◇ **with no strings (attached)** without any conditions or restrictions being made

string along *v.* (*informal*) **1.** *vt.* **DECEIVE OVER A LONG TIME** to deceive or fool somebody over an extended period of time, especially by keeping him or her in a state of false hope **2.** *vi.* **ACCOMPANY OR STAY WITH** to accompany or stay with somebody, often in a casual manner ○ *She wanted to string along with us when we went to the shops.* **3.** *vi.* **AGREE WITH** to agree or go along with another or another person's idea or suggestion

string band *n.* a group of musicians who play folk or country music on stringed instruments

string bass *n.* = **double bass**

string bean *n.* **1.** PLANTS **CULTIVATED BEAN PLANT** a climbing or bushy bean plant with slim green pods and white or purplish flowers. Latin name: *Phaseolus vulgaris*. **2.** FOOD **POD OF STRING BEAN** the long green pod of the string bean plant, containing edible seeds **3. TALL AND THIN PERSON** somebody who is tall and thin (*informal*)

string·board /stríng bàwrd/ *n.* a board that covers the ends of the steps on a staircase [Because the board "strings" the steps together]

string·course /stríng kàwrss/ *n.* a decorative feature on a building in the form of a horizontal band or molding

stringed in·stru·ment, string in·stru·ment *n.* a musical instrument in which sound is produced by the vibration of a string or strings tightly stretched across a soundboard. Most stringed instruments, e.g., the violin, cello, guitar, and lute, are played by bowing or plucking the strings.

strin·gen·do /strin jéndō/ *adv.* at an accelerating tempo (*used as a musical direction*) [Mid-19thC. Via Italian, present participle of *stringere* "to press, squeeze," from Latin, "to draw tight" (source of English *strict*).] —**strin·gen·do** *adj.*

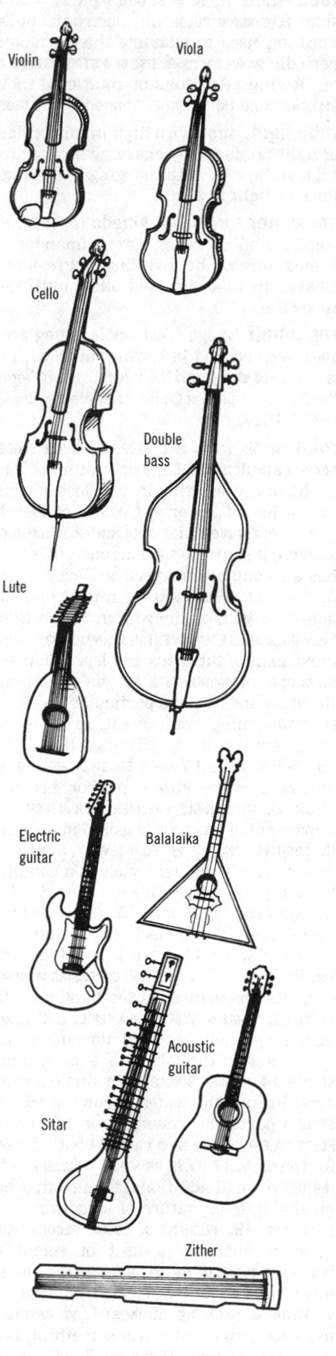

Stringed instruments

strin·gent /strínjənt/ *adj.* strictly controlled or enforced [Early 17thC. From Latin, present participle stem of *stringere* "to draw tight, bind" (source of English *strict*).] —**strin·gen·cy** *n.* —**strin·gent·ly** *adv.*

string·er /stríngər/ *n.* **1.** PRESS **FREELANCE OR PART-TIME JOURNALIST** a journalist, often covering a particular geographic area, who works on a freelance or part-time basis for a newspaper, network, or news agency **2.** BUILDING **HORIZONTAL TIMBER** a heavy horizontal timber used for structural purposes **3.** BUILDING = **stringboard 4.** AEROSP **AUXILIARY MEMBER OF WING** a light auxiliary part parallel with the main structural members of a wing or fuselage, used mainly for bracing and stabilizing **5.** SPORTS **PLAYER OF SPECIFIED ABILITY** a member of a team who is ranked according to excellence or skill (*usually used in combination*) **6.** GEOL **NARROW MINERAL VEIN** a narrow or discontinuous linear vein of ore mineral

string·halt /stríng hàwlt/ *n.* a condition of horses marked by sudden lifting of and lameness in the hind legs, caused by muscle spasms [Early 16thC. From STRING in the sense "tendon" + HALT "to limp."] —**string·halt·ed** *adj.*

string in·stru·ment *n.* = **stringed instrument**

string line *n.* CUE GAMES = **balkline**

string or·ches·tra *n.* a small orchestra of stringed instruments including violins, violas, cellos, and double basses

string·piece /stríng peess/ *n.* a beam of wood placed horizontally to support a framework

string quar·tet *n.* **1. GROUP OF FOUR STRING PLAYERS** a group of four musicians playing stringed instruments, traditionally two violins, a cello, and a viola **2. MUSIC FOR FOUR STRING PLAYERS** a piece of music composed for four stringed instruments, traditionally two violins, a cello, and a viola

string the·o·ry *n.* a mathematical theory that provides a unified structure to explain the properties and behavior of elementary particles and fundamental forces

string tie *n.* **1. NARROW NECKTIE IN A BOW** a narrow necktie made of ribbon, tied in a bow, briefly popular in the 1890s **2. NARROW NECKTIE FASTENED WITH SLIDING CLIP** a narrow thong held by a sliding clip, worn as a necktie, especially by cowboys

string·y /stríngee/ (**-i·er, -i·est**) *adj.* **1. FIBROUS** containing strands of fiber and unpleasant to chew **2. UNATTRACTIVELY THIN** unattractively thin, with bones or muscles showing beneath the skin **3. RESEMBLING STRINGS** looking like strings or hanging in long thin strands ○ *a stringy beard* **4. FORMING STRANDS** forming long sticky threads

strip[1] /strip/ *v.* (**stripped, strip·ping, strips**) **1.** *vi.* **GET UNDRESSED** to remove your clothes, either completely or to a particular extent **2.** *vt.* **UNDRESS SOMEBODY** to remove somebody's clothes, either completely or to a particular extent **3.** *vi.* **DO STRIPTEASE** to do a striptease, or be a striptease artist **4.** *vt.* **REMOVE COVERING** to take off a covering, or take the covering off something ○ *strip the wallpaper* **5.** *vt.* **REMOVE PAINT OR VARNISH FROM SURFACE** to remove old paint or varnish from a surface by scraping or burning it or by using a chemical **6.** *vt.* **REMOVE CONTENTS** to remove all the contents from a room, building, or similar place **7.** *vt.* GARDENING **REMOVE ALL LEAVES OR PLANTS** to remove all the leaves or flowers from a plant, or remove all the plants from an area **8.** *vt.* **DEPRIVE OF STATUS OR POSSESSIONS** to take status or possessions away from somebody ○ *stripped him of his rank* **9.** *vt.* **TAKE SOMETHING APART** to break down a machine, engine, or weapon into pieces in order to clean or repair it **10.** *vti.* MECH ENG **DAMAGE SCREW THREAD OR GEAR TEETH** to damage a screw or gearwheel by breaking the thread or teeth, or undergo this damage **11.** *vt.* CHEM **REMOVE VOLATILE CONTENT** to separate one or more components, especially a volatile one, from a solution or mixture, e.g., by distillation or evaporation **12.** *vt.* PRINTING, PHOTOGRAPHY **MAKE INTO PRINTING PLATE** to put pieces of photographic film or paper together to make a plate for printing ■ *n.* **ACT OF STRIPPING** the performance of a striptease [Old English *-strȳpan*, from prehistoric Germanic]

strip[2] /strip/ *n.* **1. LONG FLAT PIECE** a long flat narrow piece of something **2.** AIR = **airstrip 3.** PUBL = **comic strip 4.** COMM **ROAD LINED WITH BUSINESSES** a road lined with stores, shopping centers, restaurants, and other businesses ■ *vt.* (**stripped, strip·ping, strips**) **DIVIDE INTO STRIPS** to cut, tear, or divide something into strips [15thC. Origin uncertain: probably from Low German *strippe* "strap, thong."]

strip[3] /strip/ (**stripped, strip·ping, strips**) *vt.* to remove the last remaining milk from the udder of a cow or goat by hand after machine-milking [Early 17thC. Origin uncertain.]

strip club *n.* a club or bar where people can watch striptease acts

strip crop·ping *n.* the growing of different crops in an arrangement of lines or bands to prevent soil erosion

stripe[1] /strīp/ *n.* **1. LONG NARROW BAND** a long narrow band that differs in color, composition, or texture from the surrounding surface or background **2. PATTERN** a pattern of stripes **3.** TEXTILES **FABRIC** a fabric with a pattern of stripes **4.** MIL **INDICATION OF RANK** a narrow band or V-shaped piece of fabric, sewn on to a uniform as a symbol of rank **5. TYPE OF PERSON** a recognizable type of person with a particular character or set of opinions ○ *This is a tyrant of a very different stripe.* **6. SET OF CHARACTERISTICS** a particular set of characteristics ○ *"...portals of all stripes face a* *challenging future...*" (*Washington Post*; November 1998) ■ *vt.* (**striped, strip·ing, stripes**) **MARK WITH STRIPES** to put stripes on something [15thC. Origin uncertain: probably from Middle Dutch or Middle Low German *strīpe*.]

stripe[2] /strīp/ *n.* a blow from a whip, lash, cane, or belt [15thC. Origin uncertain: probably from Low German or Dutch.]

striped /strīpt/ *adj.* patterned or marked with stripes

striped bass /-báss/ *n.* a large fish found along the coasts of the United States that travels up rivers to breed, has black stripes, and is a food and game fish. Latin name: *Morone saxatilus.*

striped ma·ple *n.* a maple of the northeastern United States and southeastern Canada with green bark marked with white stripes. Latin name: *Acer pennsylvanicum.*

striped mar·lin *n.* a large game and food fish of the Pacific with dark blue vertical stripes on the sides. Latin name: *Makaira audax.*

striped mus·cle *n.* = **striated muscle**

striped skunk *n.* a common North American skunk that has a white cap on its head and white stripes down either side of the spine. Latin name: *Mephitis mephitis.*

strip·er /strīpər/ *n.* **1.** MIL **SOMEBODY WITH STRIPES INDICATING RANK** a member of the armed forces whose stripes on the uniform indicate rank or length of service (*slang; usually used in combination*) ○ *a three-striper* **2.** ZOOL = **striped bass**

strip-graz·ing *n.* a system in which cattle or other livestock are periodically allocated a fresh strip of pasture to graze by moving an electrified fence across the field

strip joint *n.* a strip club (*informal*)

strip·light *n.* a row of shaded lamps used to light a theater stage

strip·ling /strípplinɡ/ *n.* a boy in his early teenage years, who has not yet grown to his full size [14thC. Origin uncertain: probably formed from STRIP[2], with the underlying meaning "thin as a strip."]

strip mall *n.* a long building next to a road divided into separate stores and businesses with parking spaces in front

strip mine *n.* a mine where mineral seams near the surface of the ground are exposed by stripping away soil and land —**strip min·ing** *n.*

stripped-down *adj.* deprived of all but the most essential or simple features

strip·per[1] /strípper/ *n.* **1.** **STRIPTEASE ARTIST** somebody who performs striptease acts **2.** **PAINT OR WALLPAPER REMOVER** a tool or substance used for removing paint, varnish, wallpaper, or other substances from a surface **3.** **SOMEBODY WHO STRIPS SOMETHING** somebody whose job is to strip something

strip·per[2] /strípper/, **strip·per well** *n.* a small oil or gas well with limited production capacity [Formed from STRIP[3]; the word originally meant "a cow that no longer gives much milk"]

strip pok·er *n.* a variety of the card game poker in which, at each round, players who lose have to remove an item of their clothing

strip·py /stríppee/ *n.* **TYPE OF PATCHWORK** a type of patchwork in which broad strips of fabric are pieced together in vertical bands, then quilted ■ *adj.* **OF STRIPS** consisting of strips

strip-search (**strip-searched, strip-search·ing, strip-search·es**) *vti.* to compel somebody to undress completely while searching for concealed drugs, weapons, or contraband —**strip search** *n.*

strip steak *n.* a boneless steak from the upper part of the loin [From its long narrow shape]

strip·tease /stríp teez, strip téez/ *n.* an entertainment in which the performer slowly undresses in an erotic way, usually with music as an accompaniment —**strip·teas·er** *n.*

strip·y /strīpee/ (**-i·er, -i·est**) *adj.* decorated with, marked with, or in the form of stripes

strive /strīv/ (**strove** /strōv/ *or* **strived, striv·en** /strívv'n/ *or* **strived, striv·ing, strives**) *vi.* **1.** **TRY HARD** to try hard to achieve or get something **2.** **OPPOSE** to fight in opposition to something **3.** **COMPETE** to compete resolutely against somebody or something [12thC. From Old French *estriver* "to contend," from *estrif* (see STRIFE).] —**striv·er** *n.*

strobe /strōb/ *n.* **1.** = **strobe light** **2.** = **stroboscope** **3.** **SHORT ELECTRONIC PULSE** an electronic pulse of short duration used to examine the characteristics of a periodic waveform **4.** **USE OF A STROBOSCOPE** the process of viewing vibrations or rotational motion with a stroboscope [Mid-20thC. Shortening of STROBOSCOPE.]

strobe light, **strobe** *n.* a high intensity flashing beam of light produced by charging a capacitor to a very high voltage then discharging it as a high-intensity flash of light in a tube

Stroess·ner /stréssnər/, **Alfredo** (*b.* 1912) Paraguayan soldier and dictator. As commander in chief of armed forces, he overthrew President Federico Chavez in 1954 and held office until he was overthrown in 1989.

strog·a·noff /strógə nàwf, -nòf/, **Strog·a·noff** *adj.* **WITH SOUR CREAM** cooked in a wine sauce with sour cream ■ *n.* = **beef stroganoff** [Mid-20thC. From French, named for the Russian diplomat Count Pavel Aleksandrovich *Stroganov* (1772–1817).]

stroke /strōk/ *n.* **1.** MED **STOPPAGE OF THE BLOOD FLOW TO THE BRAIN** a sudden blockage or rupture of a blood vessel in the brain resulting in, e.g., loss of consciousness, partial loss of movement, or loss of speech. Technical name **cerebrovascular accident** **2.** **SUDDEN OCCURRENCE** a sudden instance or occurrence of something that has a strong or unexpected effect ○ *a stroke of luck* **3.** SPORTS **HITTING OF A BALL** the hitting of a ball in racket games or golf, or the way in which this is done **4.** SWIMMING **SINGLE MOVEMENT IN SWIMMING** a single complete movement of the arms and legs when swimming **5.** SWIMMING **SWIMMING STYLE** a style of swimming, using the arms and legs in a particular way **6.** ENG **MOVEMENT OF A PISTON** a single movement, up or down, of a piston in an engine or the distance that it travels in a single movement **7.** ARTS **BRUSH OR PEN LINE** a single line or mark made with a pen or brush ○ *a brush stroke* **8.** ARTS **SINGLE MOVEMENT OF A PEN OR BRUSH** a single movement of a pen or brush to make a line or mark **9.** **POSITIVE WORD OF ENCOURAGEMENT** a usually positive comment or statement such as a compliment made by one person to another ○ *I need all the positive strokes I can right now.* **10.** **STRIKING OF A CLOCK** a single sound made by a clock that is striking ○ *at the stroke of seven* **11.** **HIT** a hit or blow made by the hand, a cane, or a tool **12.** **CARESSING MOVEMENT** a gentle caressing movement of the hand over fur, hair, or skin **13.** **SINGLE MOVEMENT IN A SERIES** a single movement forming part of a series of movements, e.g., the beat of a wing or the swing of a pendulum ○ *a wing stroke* **14.** ROWING **SINGLE PULL** a single movement of the oars through the water in rowing **15.** ROWING **ROWING STYLE** a particular rowing style **16.** ROWING **ROWER WHO KEEPS TIME** a rower in a racing boat who sets the pace for the crew **17.** *U.K.* PRINTING = **slash** *n.* 5 **18.** **ADDITIONAL FEATURE** a small additional feature that has an effect on the style or nature of something ○ *a stroke of sarcasm* **19.** **ELEMENT OF SOCIAL RECOGNITION** in transactional analysis, a unit of social recognition between two or more people that, in its simplest form, can be a one-word greeting such as "hello" ■ *v.* (**stroked, strok·ing, strokes**) **1.** *vt.* **CARESS SOMETHING** to move the hand gently over something as if caressing it ○ *stroked the cat gently* **2.** *vt.* SPORTS **HIT A BALL SMOOTHLY** to hit or kick a ball smoothly in various sports **3.** *vt.* **COMPLIMENT SOMEBODY** to behave encouragingly or solicitously toward somebody as a way of persuading or eliciting cooperation **4.** *vi.* ROWING **MOVE OARS** to row at a particular speed or rate of the oars **5.** *vt.* ROWING **SET THE ROWING PACE FOR SOMEBODY** to be the rower who sets the pace for the crew **6.** *vt.* **PUSH GENTLY** to push something somewhere gently with a light movement of the hand **7.** *vt.* **CROSS SOMETHING OUT** to draw a line through something ■ *adj.* **PORNOGRAPHIC** pornographic (*slang*) [Old English *strācian*. Ultimately from an Indo-European base meaning "to rub, press," which is also the ancestor of English *strike, streak,* and *stringent*.] ◇ **different strokes for different folks** used to emphasize that people are all individuals and that what suits one will not necessarily suit another

stroke play *n.* GOLF = **medal play**

stroll /strōl/ *v.* (**strolled, stroll·ing, strolls**) **1.** *vti.* **WALK UNHURRIEDLY** to walk along somewhere in a slow unhurried way, especially for enjoyment **2.** *vi.* **DO EFFORTLESSLY** to do, obtain, or achieve something in a casual effortless way ○ *she strolled through the exam* ■ *n.* **LEISURELY WALK** a slow leisurely walk for pleasure ○ *went for a stroll in the park* [Early 17thC. Origin uncertain: probably from German *strollen* "to wander," a variant of *strolchen*, from *Strolch* "vagabond, fortuneteller," perhaps via Italian from, ultimately, Greek *astrologos* "astronomer."]

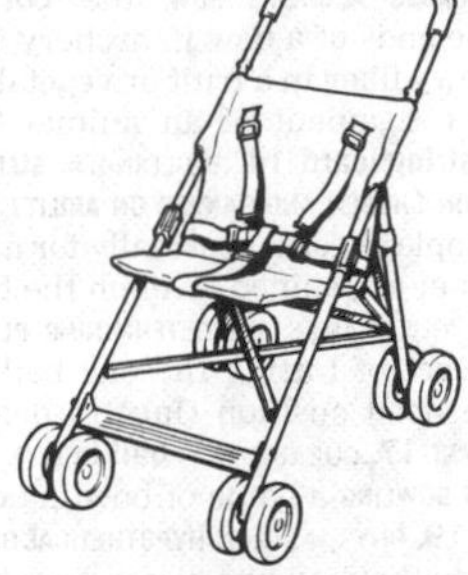
Stroller

stroll·er /strōlər/ *n.* **1.** *U.S., Can, Aus* **BABY TRANSPORT** a light chair with wheels in which a young child can be pushed around **2.** **WALKER** somebody who is walking in a slow leisurely way for pleasure **3.** THEATER **TRAVELING PERFORMER** an actor or performer who travels from place to place (*archaic*) **4.** **VAGRANT** a man who has no regular home and so wanders from place to place (*archaic*)

stroll·ing /strōling/ *adj.* going from place to place to earn a living, especially by entertaining ○ *strolling minstrels*

stro·ma /strōmə/ (*plural* **-ma·ta** /-mətə/) *n.* **1.** ANAT **CONNECTIVE TISSUE** the connective tissue that provides the framework of an organ or other anatomical structure rather than carrying out its functions **2.** BOT **INTERIOR OF A CHLOROPLAST** the fluid-filled interior of a chloroplast containing enzymes and other components required for photosynthesis, including the light-trapping components [Mid-19thC. Via modern Latin from Greek *strōma* "bed, cushion." Ultimately from an Indo-European base meaning "to spread," which is also the ancestor of English *strew, straw,* and *stratum*.] —**stro·mat·ic** /strō máttik/ *adj.*

stro·mat·o·lite /strō mátt'l īt/ *n.* a very old fossil formed in sedimentary rock by marine blue-green algae and consisting of a rounded or columnar calcium-containing mass of many layers [Mid-20thC. Coined from late Latin *stromat-*, the stem of *stroma* "bed-covering" + -LITE.] —**stro·mat·o·lit·ic** /strō màttə líttik/ *adj.*

Strom·bo·li /strómbə lee, strom bólee/ volcanic island in the Italian Lipari Islands in the Adriatic Sea, north of Sicily. Area: 5 sq. mi./13 sq. km.

strong /strong/ *adj.* **1.** **PHYSICALLY POWERFUL** having the physical strength needed to exert considerable force, e.g., in lifting, pulling, or pushing something **2.** **USING FORCE** using great physical force **3.** **ROBUST AND STURDY** sturdy, well made, and not easily damaged or broken **4.** **WITH INNER STRENGTH** having emotional strength that gives the ability to cope with stress, grief, loss, risk, and other difficulties **5.** **HEALTHY AND WELL** in good health, especially after an illness ○ *getting stronger every day* **6.** **THRIVING** thriving, developing well, and likely to continue so ○ *a strong economy* **7.** **LIKELY TO SUCCEED** very likely to succeed, win, or come to be something ○ *a strong candidate for the job.* **8.** **CONVINCING** supported by facts or good evidence and likely to be correct or effective ○ *a strong argument* **9.** **KNOWLEDGEABLE** very skillful or knowledgeable in a particular subject or area ○ *Physics was never one of my strongest subjects!* **10.** **EXERTING INFLUENCE** influential or authoritative by virtue of having or holding power **11.** **EFFECTIVE** having a powerful effect ○ *strong painkillers* **12.** **FELT OR EXPRESSED POWERFULLY** felt or expressed with a powerful effect ○ *She has strong views on the subject.* **13.** **DISTINCTIVE** bold, clearly defined, and prominent ○ *strong features* **14.** **EXTREME** unusually severe of its kind ○ *Strong measures were taken to prevent a riot.* **15.** **INTENSE IN IMPRESSION** having an intense, powerful, or vivid effect on the senses ○ *a strong smell of garlic* **16.** **EASY TO DETECT** easy to detect or receive ○ *The signal gets stronger as you get closer.* **17.** **CONCENTRATED** containing a lot of the main ingredient and not diluted or watery ○ *strong black coffee* **18.** **ALCOHOLIC** containing much alcohol **19.** **FAST MOVING** flowing or blowing at high speed ○ *a strong current* **20.** CHEM **FULLY IONIZED** producing ions freely in solution

21. MIL **WELL DEFENDED** well defended and difficult to defeat ○ *a strong fortress* **22. WITH SPECIFIED NUMBER** having a particular number of members ○ *a force 50,000 strong* **23.** OPTICS **WITH HIGH MAGNIFICATION** having a powerful magnifying or corrective ability ○ *a strong lens* **24.** COMM **WITH HIGH PRICES** characterized by high or rising prices ○ *a strong currency* **25.** GRAM **WITH A CHANGED VOWEL** used to describe an irregular verb that changes the vowel in the stem in its different forms, e.g., "ring," "rang," "rung" [Old English *strang*. Of prehistoric Germanic origin.] —**strong·ly** *adv.* ◇ **come on strong 1.** to behave or express something aggressively (*slang*) **2.** to begin to have a vivid or powerful effect (*slang*) ◇ **going strong** thriving and doing well

strong-arm *adj.* **USING FORCE** using or prepared to use coercion or physical force (*informal*) ○ *ready to use strong-arm tactics* ■ *vt.* (**strong-armed, strong-arm·ing, strong-arms**) **USE FORCE AGAINST SOMEBODY** to use coercion against somebody to induce cooperation (*informal*)

strong·box /stróng bòks/ *n.* a secure metal box or safe where money or valuables can be kept

strong breeze *n.* a wind with a speed between 25 and 31 mi./40 and 50 km per hour

strong force *n.* PHYS = **strong interaction**

strong gale *n.* a wind with a speed between 47 and 54 mi./76 and 87 km per hour

strong·hold /stróng hòld/ *n.* **1.** MIL **DEFENSIBLE PLACE** a place that is fortified or that can easily be defended **2. CONCENTRATED AREA** a place where a particular group, activity, or set of opinions is concentrated

strong in·ter·ac·tion, strong force *n.* a fundamental force between elementary particles that is responsible for binding protons and neutrons together in an atomic nucleus and other interactions between elementary particles (**hadrons**). Mediated by gluons, the interaction is the most powerful force known and is responsible for the particle creation that occurs when high-energy particles collide.

strong lan·guage *n.* language that expresses something in a forceful way, especially with abusive words or swearing

strong·man /stróng màn/ (*plural* **strong·men** /-mèn/) *n.* **1. POWERFUL LEADER** a powerful, typically dictatorial, leader who rules by force **2. PERFORMER SHOWING STRENGTH** a performer of feats of strength, e.g., at a fair or circus

strong-mind·ed *adj.* **1. DETERMINED** determined and persevering in the face of difficulty **2. MENTALLY STRONG** confident, intelligent, and independent in thought —**strong-mind·ed·ly** *adv.* —**strong-mind·ed·ness** *n.*

strong point, strong suit *n.* a particular area for which somebody has a talent ○ *Tact was never his strong point.*

strong·room /stróng ròom, -ròom/ *n.* a reinforced room designed to withstand fire or theft and used for the storage of valuables

strong side *n.* in football, the side of the offensive formation with more players and the tight end

strong suit *n.* **1.** = **strong point 2.** CARDS **SUIT WITH MOST CARDS** in various card games, the suit in which a player or team holds the most cards or the most face cards. ◊ **long suit**

strong-willed *adj.* determined to prevail in the face of difficulty or opposition

stron·gyle /strón jīl/, **stron·gyl** *n.* a parasitic nematode worm related to the hookworms that infests the intestinal tract of mammals. Superfamily: Strongyloidea. [Mid-19thC. Anglicization of modern Latin *Strongylus*, genus name, from Greek *stroggulos* "round, compact," of unknown origin.]

stron·gy·loi·di·a·sis /stròn jə loy dī́ əssiss/ *n.* intestinal infection in mammals by strongyles, producing various severe and sometimes fatal intestinal disorders, especially in individuals with weakened immune systems [Mid-20thC. Formed from modern Latin *Strongyloidea*, superfamily name, from *Strongylus* (see STRONGYLE).]

stron·gy·lo·sis /stròn jə lóssiss/ *n.* an illness, usually of horses, caused by infection with strongyles

stron·tia /strónshee ə, -tee ə/ *n.* = **strontium monoxide** [Early 19thC. Back-formation from STRONTIAN.]

stron·ti·an /strónshee ən, -tee-/ *n.* **1.** MINERALS = **strontianite 2.** CHEM = **strontium monoxide 3.** CHEM = **strontium** [Late 18thC. Shortening of *Strontian earth*; named for the parish of *Strontian* in Scotland, where the mineral was discovered in lead mines.]

stron·ti·an·ite /strónshee ə nīt, -tee-/ *n.* a variously colored mineral consisting of strontium carbonate, a major source of strontium. Formula: $SrCO_3$. [Late 18thC. Formed from STRONTIAN.]

stron·ti·um /strónshee əm, -tee-/ *n.* a soft yellow or silvery-white metallic chemical element of the alkaline-earth group, found only in combination with other substances. It is used in fireworks and flares to produce red flames, and in alloys. Symbol **Sr** [Early 19thC. Coined from STRONTIA.]

stron·ti·um 90 *n.* a radioactive isotope of strontium with a mass number of 90, present in nuclear fallout and assimilated like calcium in bone formation

stron·ti·um mon·ox·ide *n.* a white insoluble solid resembling quicklime. It is used in the purification of sugar. Formula: SrO.

stron·ti·um u·nit *n.* a unit of measurement of the amount of strontium 90 in an organic substance such as soil or bone, in relation to the concentration of calcium in the same substance

Stroop ef·fect /stròop-/ *n.* difficulty identifying the colors in which names of colors are written. For example, if the word "red" is printed in green ink, people are likely to say "red" when asked the color of the printed word. [Mid-20thC. Named for J.R. *Stroop*, who first published a study of the effect in English.]

strop /strop/ *n.* **1. LEATHER STRAP FOR SHARPENING** a leather strap used for sharpening a straight razor **2.** NAUT **STRAP FOR CARGO** a strap of leather or rope used for lifting cargo ■ *vt.* (**stropped, strop·ping, strops**) **SHARPEN RAZOR** to sharpen a straight razor on a strop [Assumed Old English *strop* "band, cord," via Latin *stroppus* from Greek *strophos* (see STROPHOID)]

stro·phe /strṓfee/ *n.* ◊ **antistrophe 1.** POETRY **FIRST METRICAL FORM IN A POEM** the first type of metrical form in a poem that alternates two contrasting metrical forms **2.** LITERAT **MOVEMENT IN ANCIENT GREEK DRAMA** the first of two movements made by the chorus in a classical Greek drama, or the part of an ode sung during this [Early 17thC. From Greek *strophē*, literally "turning" (source of English *catastrophe*). Ultimately from an Indo-European base meaning "to turn," which is also the ancestor of *strepto-* and *stroboscope*.] —**stro·phic** /stróffik, strṓfik/ *adj.*

stro·phoid /strṓ fòyd/ *n.* a plane curve symmetric to the x-axis, generated by a point whose distance from the y-axis along a straight line is equal to the y-intercept [Late 19thC. Formed from Greek *strophos* "twisted cord." Ultimately from an Indo-European base meaning "to turn," which is also the ancestor of English *strophe*, *stroboscope*, and *strepto-*.]

stroph·u·lus /stróffyələss/ *n.* a skin eruption seen in children and infants, e.g., hives or heat rash (*dated*) [Early 19thC. From modern Latin, of uncertain origin.]

strop·py /stróppee/ (**-pi·er, -pi·est**) *adj. U.K.* bad-tempered and uncooperative (*informal*) [Mid-20thC. Origin uncertain: perhaps an alteration of OBSTREPEROUS.]

stroud /strowd/ *n.* a rough woolen fabric used originally by British traders in trade with Native North Americans [Late 17thC. Origin uncertain.]

strove past tense of **strive**

struck /struk/ past tense, past participle of **strike** ■ *adj.* **AFFECTED BY STRIKES** closed temporarily or working at reduced output because of a labor dispute

struck ju·ry *n.* a jury reduced to the proper number when lawyers for the two sides have eliminated names from a list of candidates

struck meas·ure *n.* a quantity of something such as grain, measured by leveling the substance with the top of a container

struc·tur·al /strúkchərəl/ *adj.* **1. RELATING TO STRUCTURE** relating to the way that the parts of something are put together or how they work together **2. RESULTING FROM STRUCTURE** resulting from the interrelationship of constituent parts, e.g., in a political or economic system **3. BASIC TO A STRUCTURE** constituting an important or essential part of a structure **4. USED IN CONSTRUCTION** suitable for use in construction ○ *structural fiberglass* **5.** CHEM **CAUSED BY ATOMIC ARRANGEMENT** relating to or caused by the arrangement of atoms in a molecule **6.** GEOG **OF ROCK STRUCTURE** relating to or caused by movement of the earth's surface —**struc·tur·al·ly** *adv.*

struc·tur·al for·mu·la *n.* the expanded form of a chemical formula representing the arrangement of atoms and bonds within a molecule

struc·tur·al gene *n.* a gene that codes for a sequence of amino acids that form a polypeptide or protein

struc·tur·al·ism /strúkchərə lìzzəm/ *n.* **1.** SOC SCI **SOCIOLOGICAL METHOD** a method of sociological analysis based on the notion of human society as a network of interrelated elements whose patterns and significance can be analyzed **2.** PSYCHOL = **structural psychology 3.** LING = **structural linguistics** —**struc·tur·al·ist** *n., adj.*

struc·tur·al·ize /strúkchərə līz/ (**-ized, -iz·ing, -iz·es**) *vt.* to arrange or organize something so that it has a structure

struc·tur·al lin·guis·tics *n.* a branch of linguistics that emphasizes the significance of the interrelations between the elements that constitute a linguistic system (*takes a singular verb*) —**struc·tur·al lin·guist** *n.*

struc·tur·al psy·chol·o·gy *n.* a school of psychology of the early part of the 20th century that sought to organize the components of subjective experience in a hierarchy from simplest to most complex —**struc·tur·al psy·chol·o·gist** *n.*

struc·tur·al steel *n.* strong steel shaped and suitable for use in construction

struc·ture /strúkchər/ *n.* **1. SOMETHING BUILT OR ERECTED** a building, bridge, framework, or other object that has been put together from many different parts **2. ORDERLY SYSTEM OF PARTS** a system or organization made up of interrelated parts functioning as an orderly whole **3. WAY THAT PARTS LINK OR FUNCTION** the way in which the different parts of something link or work together, or the fact of being linked together ○ *the structure of local government* ○ *The essay is interesting, but it lacks structure.* **4.** BIOL **ORGANIC FEATURE** a part of a body or organism, e.g., an organ or tissue, identifiable by its shape and other properties **5.** CHEM **ARRANGEMENT OF ATOMS** the specific arrangement of atoms in a molecule **6.** GEOL **COMPONENT PARTS OF ROCKS** the physical disposition of a rock mass, e.g., its folding and faulting, or the disposition of its mineral components, e.g., its texture ■ *vt.* (**-tured, -tur·ing, -tures**) **GIVE STRUCTURE TO** to organize or arrange something so that it works as a cohesive whole [15thC. Directly or via French from Latin *structura*, from *struct-*, the past participle stem of *struere* "to build."]

WORD KEY: ORIGIN

The Latin word *struere*, from which ***structure*** is derived, is also the source of English *construct*, *construe*, *destroy*, *instruct*, and *obstruct*.

struc·tured /strúkchərd/ *adj.* **1. ORGANIZED** planned, organized, and controlled **2. DEFINED** with a definite shape, form, or pattern ○ *For business wear, suits need a more structured look.*

struc·tured pro·gram·ming *n.* a style of computer programming in which a program consists of a hierarchy of simple subroutines

struc·tured que·ry lan·guage *n.* full form of **SQL**

struc·tur·i·zer /strúkchər īzər/ *n.* a hair conditioner designed to strengthen and restructure the hair shaft

stru·del /stròod'l/ *n.* a pastry made with very thin pastry rolled and baked with a filling, usually of chopped apples, raisins, and sugar [Late 19thC. Via German from Middle High German, "whirlpool."]

strug·gle /strúgg'l/ *vi.* (**-gled, -gling, -gles**) **1. TRY TO OVERCOME A PROBLEM** to try very hard to deal with a challenge, problem, or difficulty ○ *he was struggling with his math homework* **2. MAKE A GREAT PHYSICAL EFFORT** to make a great physical effort to achieve or obtain something ○ *A rescue party struggled to reach the stranded climbers.* **3. FIGHT BY WRESTLING** to fight with somebody by grappling and wrestling **4. WRITHE TO ESCAPE** to move and wriggle forcefully in an attempt to escape **5. MOVE WITH DIFFICULTY** to move with great effort ○ *so weak I just managed to struggle out of bed* ■ *n.* **1. GREAT EFFORT TO OVERCOME DIFFICULTIES** a great effort made over a period of time to overcome difficulties or achieve something **2. FIGHT** a prolonged fight or conflict **3. HARD TASK** a strenuous physical or mental effort, or something requiring this [14thC. Origin uncertain.] —**strug·gler** *n.*

strug·gle for ex·is·tence *n.* the ongoing effort to survive and reproduce in an environment of competing organisms

strum /strum/ *v.* **(strummed, strum·ming, strums) 1.** *vti.* **PLAY AN INSTRUMENT BY BRUSHING THE STRINGS** to play a guitar or other stringed instrument by brushing the strings with the fingers or a plectrum **2.** *vt.* **PLAY TUNE** to play a tune by strumming an instrument ■ *n.* **SOUND OF STRUMMING** the sound of somebody strumming an instrument [Late 18thC. An imitation of the sound.] —**strum·mer** *n.*

stru·ma /stroómə/ (*plural* **-mae** /-mee/ *or* **-mas**) *n.* **1.** BOT **SWELLING ON MOSS** a swelling at the base of a moss capsule **2.** MED = **goiter 3.** MED **SCROFULA** scrofula (*archaic*) [Mid-16thC. Via modern Latin from Latin, "scrofulous tumor," of unknown origin.] —**stru·mat·ic** /stroo máttik/ *adj.* —**stru·mose** /stroó mōss/ *adj.* —**stru·mous** /stroóməss/ *adj.*

strum·pet /strúmpət/ *n.* an offensive term for a prostitute or woman regarded as too sexually active (*archaic insult*) [14thC. Origin uncertain.]

strung past tense, past participle of **string** ■ *adj.* **OVERWROUGHT** very tired, tense, and overwrought

strung out *adj.* **1.** DRUGS **DRUGGED** under the influence of a drug, especially a narcotic drug (*slang*) **2.** DRUGS **WEAKENED** debilitated by long-term drug use (*slang*) **3.** **OVERWROUGHT** tired, tense, or overwrought (*informal*)

strut /strut/ *v.* **(strut·ted, strut·ting, struts) 1.** *vi.* **WALK IN A STIFF ARROGANT WAY** to walk in a conspicuously stiff or proud way, suggesting arrogance or pomposity **2.** *vt.* **SHOW SOMETHING OFF** to show something off to other people in an ostentatious way **3.** *vt.* CONSTR **SUPPORT WITH PLANKS** to prop something up with supporting planks or boards ■ *n.* **1.** CONSTR **SUPPORTING MEMBER** a long rigid plank, board, or other structural member used as a support in building **2. PROUD WALKING** a stiff, proud, pompous way of walking [Old English *strūtian* "to protrude stiffly." Ultimately from Indo-European, meaning "stiff" (ancestor also of English *starch*). Senses relating to "support" of uncertain origin: probably from, ultimately, the same Indo-European source.]

stru·thi·ous /strúthee əss, strúth-/ *adj.* relating to flightless birds, especially the ostrich [Late 18thC. Formed from late Latin *struthio* "ostrich," via late Greek *strouthiōn* from Greek *strouthos*.]

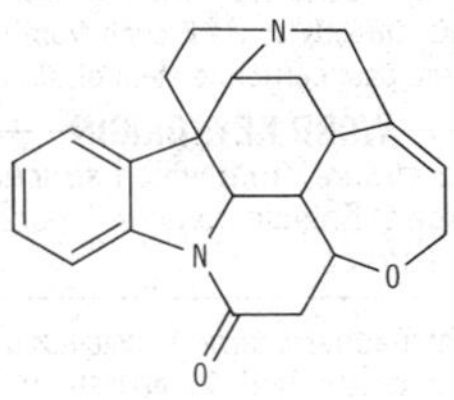

Strychnine

strych·nine /strík nīn, -neen/ *n.* a bitter white poisonous alkaloid obtained from nux vomica and related plants, used as a poison for rodents and medicinally as a stimulant for the central nervous system. Formula: $C_{21}H_{22}N_2O_2$. [Early 19thC. From French, formed from modern Latin *Strychnos*, genus name, via Latin *strychnon* "nightshade" from Greek *strukhnos*, of unknown origin.] —**strych·nic** /stríknik/ *adj.*

Strze·leck·i Range /strez léki-/ range of hills in southern Victoria, Australia. Highest peak: 1,640 ft./500 m.

Stu·art /stoó ərt, styoó-/, **Charles Edward** (1720–88) British prince and claimant to the British throne. The son of James Francis Edward Stuart, he led the Jacobite uprising in Scotland in 1745 and after its failure lived in exile in Europe. Known as **Bonnie Prince Charlie, the Young Pretender**

Stu·art /styoó ərt/, **Gilbert** (1755–1828) U.S. artist. Of the many portraits he painted, the best known are of George Washington. Full name **Gilbert Charles Stuart**

Stu·art, James Francis Edward (1688–1766) British prince and claimant to the British throne. The son of James II, he was supported in his claim to the British throne by France and by the Jacobites in their unsuccessful rising in Scotland (1715). After 1719 he lived in Rome. Known as **the Old Pretender**

stub /stub/ *n.* **1. SHORT REMAINING PART** a short part of something that is left after the main part has been removed or used **2. SMALL SECTION OF A TICKET OR CHECK** a small detachable section of a ticket, check, or voucher, retained as a record of a transaction **3. STUMP OF A TREE OR PLANT** the stump of a tree or plant **4. SMALL PROJECTION** a small projection from a surface ■ *vt.* **(stubbed, stub·bing, stubs) 1. BANG THE TOE** to bang your toe against something accidentally **2.** GARDENING **DIG UP BY THE ROOTS** to dig up a plant or tree by the roots **3.** AGRIC **CLEAR LAND OF STUMPS** to clear land of tree stumps [Old English *stubb* "tree stump," of prehistoric Germanic origin]

stub out *vt.* to put out a cigarette or cigar by pushing the burning end against something

stub·ble /stúbb'l/ *n.* **1. SHORT BEARD GROWTH** the short spiky growth of beard on a man's face when he has not shaved **2.** AGRIC **SHORT STALKS IN A FIELD** short stalks left in the ground after a grain crop has been harvested [13thC. Via Old French *estuble* from Latin *stupula* "straw," an alteration of *stipula* (see STIPULE).] —**stub·bly** *adj.*

stub·born /stúbbərn/ *adj.* **1. UNREASONABLY DETERMINED** unreasonably and obstructively determined to persevere or prevail **2. DOGGED** carried out in a determined, persistent way ○ *met with stubborn resistance* **3. HARD TO REMOVE** difficult to remove or deal with ○ *a stubborn stain* [14thC. Origin uncertain.] —**stub·born·ly** *adv.* —**stub·born·ness** *n.*

stub·by /stúbbee/ *adj.* **1. SHORT AND STOUT** short and stout in build **2. SHORT AND THICK** short and thick, broad, or blunt ○ *stubby fingers* **3. WITH MANY STUBS** with projecting stubs or short bristles ■ *n. Aus* **BEER BOTTLE** a small squat bottle of beer (*informal*)

stub nail *n.* a short thick nail

stuc·co /stúkō/ *n.* **1. WALL PLASTER** plaster used for surfacing interior or exterior walls, often used in association with classical moldings **2. DECORATIVE PLASTER WORK** decorative work molded from stucco ■ *vt.* **(-coed, -co·ing, -coes** *or* **stuc·cos) COVER WITH STUCCO** to apply a coating of stucco to a wall [Late 16thC. From Italian, of Germanic origin.] —**stuc·co·er** *n.*

stuc·co·work /stúkō wùrk/ *n.* = **stucco** *n.* 2

stuck /stuk/ past tense, past participle of **stick**[2] ■ *adj.* **1. JAMMED OR CAUGHT** jammed, caught, or held in a position from which it is impossible to move ○ *the drawer was stuck fast* **2. UNABLE TO FIND A SOLUTION** not able to find a solution or way out of a situation **3. PIERCED** pierced by a sharp object ◇ **stuck on** infatuated with somebody or something (*informal*)

stuck-up *adj.* snobbish and conceited (*informal*)

stud[1] /stud/ *n.* **1.** EQU **BREEDING STALLION** a male animal, especially a stallion, used for breeding **2. SEXUALLY ACTIVE MAN** a man considered to be sexually active or good at sex (*informal*) **3.** CARDS = **stud poker 4.** EQU **ESTABLISHMENT WITH STALLIONS** a stable or farm where male animals, especially stallions, are kept for breeding **5.** EQU **GROUP OF STALLIONS** a group of male animals, especially stallions, used for breeding [Old English *stōd*, literally "standing place"] ◇ **at stud** available for breeding with female animals, especially mares

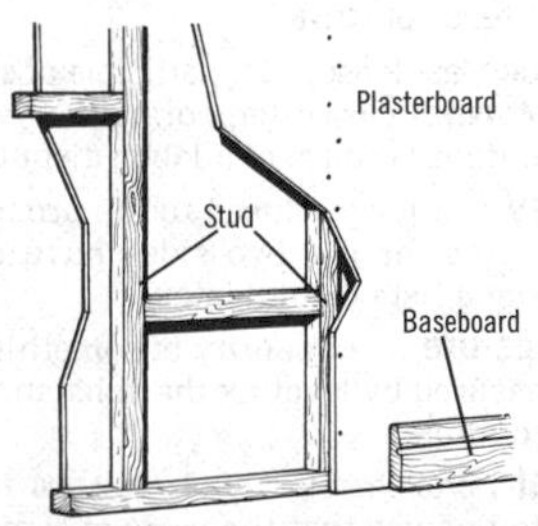

Stud

stud[2] /stud/ *n.* **1.** ACCESSORIES **FASTENER FOR A SHIRT** a fastener for dress shirts or collars consisting of a small disk attached to a short rod **2.** CARS **PROJECTION ON A TIRE** a small metal point embedded in the surface of a tire for better traction on snow and ice **3.** ACCESSORIES **EARRING** an earring for pierced ears that has a simple rounded head or is set with a single gemstone **4.** BUILDING **VERTICAL SUPPORT** a vertical post that is one of the uprights supporting a timber wall or partition **5. METAL KNOB** a small metal knob or the head of a nail protruding slightly from a surface, especially for decorative effect **6.** *U.K.* SPORTS = **cleat** *n.* 1 **7. HEADLESS BOLT** a headless bolt with threads on both ends separated by a threadless section **8.** ENG **PROJECTION ON A MACHINE** a short rod or other projection on a machine serving as support for something else ■ *vt.* **(stud·ded, stud·ding, studs) 1. OCCUR THROUGHOUT SOMETHING** to be present or visible in all parts of something ○ *a star-studded cast* **2. SUPPLY WITH STUDS** to fit or decorate something with studs ○ *a studded leather jacket* [Old English *studu*. Ultimately from an Indo-European base meaning "to stand," which is also the ancestor of English *stand, stead,* and *static*.] ◇ **studded with** scattered or dotted with something

stud·book /stúd bòòk/ *n.* a book containing a record of the parentage of purebred animals, especially horses or dogs

stud·ding·sail /stúnss'l, stúdding sàyl/ *n.* an additional sail on an extra yard and boom at either side of a square sail, for use in light winds [Mid-16thC. *Studding* of uncertain origin: perhaps from Middle Low German or Middle Dutch *stōtinge* "thrusting," from *stōten* "to thrust."]

stu·dent /stoód'nt/ *n.* **1. PERSON STUDYING** somebody who is studying at a school, college, or university **2. KNOWLEDGEABLE OR INTERESTED PERSON** somebody who has studied or takes a great interest in a particular subject ○ *a student of human foibles* ■ *adj.* **IN TRAINING FOR A JOB** studying as part of the training for a job or profession ○ *student pilots* [15thC. Alteration of Old French *estudiant*, from Latin *student-*, the present participle stem of *studere* (see STUDY).]

stu·dent bod·y *n.* the students of a school collectively

stu·dent coun·cil *n.* an elected group of students with consultative powers in school administration, especially in a high school

stu·dent gov·ern·ment *n.* a representative assembly of college or university students with consultative powers

stu·dent lamp *n.* a desk lamp with a flexible stalk allowing the light to be moved into different positions

stu·dent loan *n.* a loan taken by a student to pay for educational expenses, usually at a favorable rate of interest that is subsidized by the government

stu·dent·ship /stoód-t ship/ *n.* = **scholarship** *n.* 1

Stu·dent's t-test *n.* = **t-test** [Named for *Student*, the pen name of W. S. Gosset (1876–1937), the British statistician who invented it.]

stu·dents' un·ion *n. U.K.* = **student union**

stu·dent teach·er *n.* a student enrolled in a teacher preparation program who is doing practice teaching under supervision

stu·dent un·ion *n.* a building or area at a college or university used primarily for the social or recreational activities of students, with food and beverage services

stud·horse /stúd hàwrss/ *n.* a stallion used for breeding [Old English *stod hors*]

stud·ied /stúddeed/ *adj.* thought about or planned in advance rather than being spontaneous ○ *an air of studied nonchalance*

stu·di·o /stoódee ō/ *n.* (*plural* **stu·di·os**) **1. RECORDING PRODUCTION ROOM** a room or building equipped for making movies, television or radio productions, or musical recordings **2. SMALL APARTMENT** a one-room apartment **3.** CINEMA **MOVIE COMPANY** a commercial movie production company **4. ARTIST'S WORKPLACE** a place where an artist, photographer, or musician works **5.** DANCE **DANCE SCHOOL** a place where dance is taught or where dancers can practice ■ **stu·di·os** *npl.* CINEMA **MOVIE PRODUCTION BUILDINGS** all the buildings connected with a movie production company, used for shooting and producing movies [Early 19thC. Via Italian from Latin *studium* (see STUDY).]

stu·di·o a·part·ment *n.* = **studio** *n.* 2

stu·di·o couch *n.* a usually backless sofa that can be converted into a double bed by sliding out a frame from underneath

stu·di·o flat *n. U.K.* = **studio** *n.* 2

stu·di·o sys·tem *n.* the process for making a large number of movies economically, efficiently, and simultaneously, as used by the major Hollywood studios from the silent era into the 1950s. Each studio was a self-contained factory with separate departments for each aspect of production and had a number of actors under contract.

stu·di·ous /stoodee əss/ *adj.* **1.** INCLINED TO STUDY having a thoughtful nature and given to studying **2.** CAREFUL AND PAINSTAKING careful and painstaking, with considerable attention to detail ○ *a studious investigation* [14thC. From Latin *studiosus*, from *studium* (see STUDY).] —**stu·di·ous·ly** *adv.* —**stu·di·ous·ness** *n.*

stud·muf·fin /stúd mùfin/ *n.* a man regarded as being physically attractive (*slang*)

stud pok·er, **stud** *n.* a variety of the card game poker in which all but the first card are dealt face up, allowing players to see one another's hands. A round of betting follows each round of dealing. [Mid-19thC. Probably a shortening of earlier *studhorse poker*, of uncertain origin: perhaps in reference to the exchange of money involved in horse breeding and horseracing.]

stud·work /stúd wùrk/ *n.* **1.** BUILDING STUD ARRANGEMENT the arrangement of studs in a building framework **2.** STUD DECORATION the decoration of something with studs

stud·y /stúddee/ *v.* (**-ied, -y·ing, -ies**) **1.** *vti.* LEARN ABOUT SOMETHING to learn about a particular subject by reading and researching **2.** *vti.* TAKE AN EDUCATIONAL COURSE to take a course at a college or university **3.** *vt.* INVESTIGATE to discover facts about something by doing research or experiments ○ *a team of researchers studying the effects of sleep deprivation* **4.** *vt.* LOOK AT AND CONSIDER to look at or read something and think about it carefully ○ *He studied the map, frowning.* **5.** *vt.* THEATER LEARN LINES to learn the lines spoken by a character in a play ■ *n.* (*plural* **-ies**) **1.** PROCESS OF LEARNING the process of learning about a subject by reading, thought, intuition, or research ○ *devoted the afternoons to study* **2.** INVESTIGATION an investigation or research project designed to discover facts about something **3.** REPORT ON RESEARCH a report or book describing an investigation or piece of research **4.** ROOM FOR STUDYING a room used for work that involves reading, thinking, or writing **5.** ARTS SMALL PREPARATORY WORK OF ART a small drawing or sculpture done as preparation for a larger work **6.** MUSIC INSTRUMENTAL WORK an instrumental work intended for teaching or practice **7.** THEATER ACTOR LEARNING LINES somebody who learns something, especially a role in a play, considered in terms of the particular amount of time this takes ○ *she's a quick study* ■ **stud·ies** *npl.* EDUC SUBJECT OF STUDY a particular subject of study, especially as an educational course or academic specialization ○ *social studies* [12thC. Via Old French *estudier* (verb) and *estudie* (noun) from, ultimately, Latin *studium* "zeal, care," from *studere* "to be diligent."]

stud·y hall *n.* **1.** STUDY TIME IN SCHOOL a period during the school day assigned for study rather than classroom instruction **2.** ROOM FOR STUDY a schoolroom used for independent study rather than instruction

stuff /stuf/ *vt.* (**stuffed, stuff·ing, stuffs**) **1.** FILL to fill something by pushing things into it ○ *What are you stuffing the cushions with?* **2.** PUSH THINGS INTO CONTAINER to push things into a container, often hurriedly or forcefully **3.** PUT HURRIEDLY to put something somewhere in a quick careless way ○ *stuffed it under the pillow, out of sight* **4.** EAT TOO MUCH to eat or feed somebody a lot of food **5.** COOK FILL FOOD WITH STUFFING to put stuffing or filling into food such as pasta, meat, or vegetables **6.** RESTORE THE SHAPE OF A DEAD ANIMAL to fill a dead animal's skin with material to make it look lifelike and suitable for display **7.** POL SUBMIT INVALID VOTES to put invalid ballots into a ballot box to rig an election **8.** OFFENSIVE TERM a highly offensive term used typically by men meaning to have sex with a woman (*slang taboo*) **9.** INDUST TREAT LEATHER to treat leather with chemicals that preserve and soften it ■ *n.* **1.** THINGS material things generally, especially when unidentified, worthless, or unwanted ○ *What's all this stuff doing in my office?* **2.** WORDS OR ACTION action, speech, or writing of a particular kind ○ *all that stuff in the news about changing weather patterns* ○ *I really like her stuff.* **3.** POSSESSIONS personal possessions ○ *called by to collect her stuff* **4.** PERSONAL QUALITIES personal qualities of a particular kind ○ *She's got the stuff heroes are made of.* **5.** SPORTS SPIN spin given to a ball ○ *Ryan really had his stuff yesterday.* **6.** SPECIALTY something that somebody does uniquely or very well **7.** DRUGS a drug, especially heroin (*informal*) **8.** FOOLISH WORDS OR ACTION foolish or blameworthy action, speech, or writing **9.** MONEY money (*slang*) **10.** TEXTILES WOOLEN FABRIC woolen fabric, especially as distinguished from fabric made from other natural fibers ■ *interj.* USED TO DISMISS SOMETHING used, often with "it," to dismiss something angrily or carelessly (*slang*) [14thC. From Old French *estoffer* "to equip," of prehistoric Germanic origin.] —**stuff·er** *n.* ◇ **do your stuff** to do what is required or expected ◇ **strut your stuff** to do something impressively, suggesting talent for it or thorough preparation (*slang*)

WORD KEY: CULTURAL NOTE

The Right Stuff, a book by Tom Wolfe (1979). This imaginative account of the early years of the U.S. space program contrasts the media's manipulation of the story and the public's hunger for heroes with the real-life experiences of the astronauts. It was made into a movie by Philip Kaufman in 1983. Subsequent to the novel, *right stuff* entered the general language, meaning "the complex of courage, self-worth, technical know-how, emotional stability, and dependability needed for a person to accomplish great things in any profession or field."

stuffed /stuft/ *adj.* **1.** FOOD WITH FILLING filled with stuffing or some other filling **2.** COMPLETELY FULL completely full, especially after eating too much (*informal*)

stuffed shirt *n.* somebody who behaves in a formal self-important way (*informal*) [Origin uncertain: perhaps from the image of a puffed-up man in a tight-fitting, starched shirt; perhaps also from the implied absence of ideas]

stuff·ing /stúffing/ *n.* **1.** FOOD WELL-FLAVORED FILLING FOR FOOD a mixture of well-flavored or highly seasoned ingredients used to stuff meat or vegetables. Stuffings often have a breadcrumb or rice base and may include herbs, spices, fruit, or vegetables. **2.** INDUST FILLING FOR CUSHIONS feathers, fabric, or artificial fiber used to fill cushions or pillows ◇ **knock the stuffing out of somebody** to have a sudden or immediate weakening effect on somebody (*informal*)

stuff·ing box *n.* an enclosure containing compressed packing that is used to prevent leakage around a moving part such as a piston rod

stuff·y /stúffee/ (**-i·er, -i·est**) *adj.* **1.** AIRLESS without any fresh air, and often too warm **2.** STRAIT-LACED too old-fashioned, strict, or conventional **3.** BLOCKED WITH MUCUS blocked up with mucus, making breathing difficult ○ *a stuffy nose* —**stuff·i·ly** *adv.* —**stuff·i·ness** *n.*

stull /stul, stool/ *n.* a supporting timber in a mine or mineshaft [Late 18thC. Origin uncertain: perhaps from German *Stollen* "support, prop" (source of English *stollen*).]

stul·ti·fy /stúlti fì/ (**-fied, -fy·ing, -fies**) *vt.* **1.** DIMINISH INTEREST to diminish somebody's interest and liveliness of mind by being repetitive, tedious, and boring **2.** MAKE SOMEBODY SEEM STUPID to cause somebody or something to seem unintelligent or silly **3.** RENDER USELESS to render something useless or ineffectual **4.** LAW PROVE SOMEBODY INCAPABLE OF LEGAL RESPONSIBILITY to show or allege somebody to be not legally responsible because of a psychiatric disorder or instability [Mid-18thC. From late Latin *stultificare*, literally "to make foolish," from Latin *stultus* "foolish," literally "immovable."] —**stul·ti·fi·ca·tion** /stùltəfə káysh'n/ *n.* —**stul·ti·fi·er** /stúlti fì ər/ *n.*

stum /stum/ *n.* WINE = **must**[2] ■ *vt.* (**stummed, stum·ming, stums**) ADD STUM to ferment wine by adding stum to it while it is in a cask or vat [Mid-17thC. From Dutch *stom*, literally "dumb," a translation of French *muet*.]

stum·ble /stúmb'l/ *vi.* (**-bled, -bling, -bles**) **1.** TRIP OVER to trip when walking or running **2.** WALK UNSTEADILY to walk unsteadily, as if intoxicated **3.** SPEAK OR ACT HESITATINGLY to speak or act hesitatingly, confusedly, or incompetently ○ *spoke the verse without stumbling* **4.** FIND BY CHANCE to find or come across something by chance ○ *I stumbled across the note while I was cleaning the closet.* ■ *n.* **1.** ACT OF TRIPPING an instance of tripping over something **2.** MISTAKE a mistake or hesitation [14thC. Origin uncertain: probably from assumed Old Norse *stumla*, a variant of *stumra* "to walk unsteadily," from a prehistoric Germanic word that is also the ancestor of English *stammer*.] —**stum·bler** *n.*

WORD KEY: SYNONYMS

See Synonyms at ***hesitate***.

stum·ble·bum /stúmb'l bùm/ *n.* **1.** OFFENSIVE TERM an offensive term for somebody who does things in a blundering unskillful way (*slang insult*) **2.** LOSING BOXER a losing prizefighter

stum·bling block *n.* something that stands in the way of achieving a goal or of understanding something [Early 16thC. Translation of Greek *proskomma*, literally "something you stumble against."]

stump /stump/ *n.* **1.** BASE OF A TREE the base of a tree trunk and its roots after the tree has been felled **2.** REMAINING SMALL PART the part of something such as a limb that is left after the main part has been cut off or removed **3.** DRAWING CYLINDRICAL IMPLEMENT USED IN DRAWING a short cylindrical piece of rolled paper, cork, rubber, or leather with ends formed into a point, used in drawing especially to soften lines and in representing shade and shadow **4.** HEAVY FOOTSTEP the sound of a heavy footstep ■ **stumps** *npl.* LEGS somebody's legs (*slang*) ■ *v.* (**stumped, stump·ing, stumps**) **1.** *vt.* BAFFLE SOMEBODY to baffle somebody by presenting a problem that seems impossible to solve **2.** *vi.* POL CAMPAIGN to campaign for elective office (*informal*) **3.** *vi.* WALK HEAVILY to walk heavily and often angrily **4.** *vt.* LOP to lop the top off a tree, leaving a stump **5.** *vt.* REMOVE STUMPS to clear an area of land of tree stumps **6.** *vt.* STUB THE TOE to stub your toe against something accidentally (*regional*) [13thC. From Middle Low German, of prehistoric Germanic origin.] —**stump·er** *n.* ◇ **on the stump** engaged in making political speeches to win office

stump·age /stúmpij/ *n.* standing timber, or the amount of money it would bring if felled

stump·work /stúmp wùrk/ *n.* raised embroidery, with small decorative stitches made over pieces of padding [Early 20thC. Because the designs are raised upon stumps of wood.]

stump·y /stúmpee/ (**-i·er, -i·est**) *adj.* short, thick, and unattractive —**stump·i·ness** *n.*

stun /stun/ (**stunned, stun·ning, stuns**) *vt.* **1.** MAKE UNCONSCIOUS to make a person or animal unconscious for a short time with a blow or by using a drug **2.** SHOCK to shock, upset, or amaze somebody ○ *a tragedy that left the nation stunned and bewildered* **3.** OVERWHELM to overwhelm one of the senses, e.g., with loud noise or very bright light [14thC. Via Anglo-Norman *estuner* from assumed Vulgar Latin *extonare*, from Latin *tonare* "to thunder" (source of English *astonish*, *detonate*, and *tornado*).]

stung past tense, past participle of **sting**

stun gun *n.* a gun used for stunning animals or people for a short while without causing injury

stunk past tense, past participle of **stink**

stun·ner /stúnnər/ *n.* **1.** IMPRESSIVE PERSON OR THING somebody who or something that is extraordinarily impressive or beautiful (*informal*) **2.** ARMS = **stun gun**

stun·ning /stúnning/ *adj.* strikingly impressive or attractive in appearance ○ *They looked stunning at the reception.* —**stun·ning·ly** *adv.*

stun·sail /stúnss'l/ *n.* NAUT = **studdingsail** [Mid-18thC. Contraction of STUDDINGSAIL.]

stunt[1] /stunt/ *n.* **1.** DANGEROUS FEAT something dangerous that is done as a challenge or to entertain people **2.** SOMETHING UNDERHANDED DONE FOR ATTENTION something underhanded, silly, or unusual that is done to gain unfair advantage or to attract attention ○ *a publicity stunt* ■ *vi.* (**stunt·ed, stunt·ing, stunts**) **1.** FOOTBALL SHIFT DEFENSIVE LINEMEN to shift the positions of defensive linemen in football to improve their chances of avoiding offensive linemen's blocks **2.** PERFORM STUNTS to perform dangerous feats as a challenge or to entertain people [Late 19thC. Origin unknown. Originally college athletics slang.]

stunt[2] /stunt/ *vt.* (**stunt·ed, stunt·ing, stunts**) RESTRICT THE GROWTH OF to restrict the growth of something so that it does not develop to its normal size ■ *n.* **1.** SOMETHING NOT FULLY DEVELOPED something that has not grown to its normal size because its growth has been restricted **2.** BOT PLANT DISEASE a plant disease resulting in retarded growth [Old English, "unintelligent, dull," from a prehistoric Germanic base that may also be the ancestor of English *stump*. The meaning was influenced by the related Old Norse *stuttr* "short, dwarf."]

stunt·man /stúnt màn/ (*plural* **-men** /-mèn/) *n.* a man whose job is to take the place of a movie actor in a scene involving danger or requiring acrobatic skill

stunt·wom·an /stúnt wòommən/ (*plural* **-en** /-wìmmin/) *n.* a woman whose job is to take the place of a movie actor in a scene involving danger or requiring acrobatic skill

stu·pa /sto͝opə/ *n.* a Buddhist shrine, temple, or pagoda that houses a relic or marks the location of an auspicious event [Late 19thC. From Sanskrit *stūpaḥ* (source of English *tope*).]

stupe[1] /stoop/ *n.* a hot, damp, sometimes medicated, cloth or sponge applied in former times to the skin as a compress or a counterirritant to relieve pain [14thC. Via Latin *stuppa* "tow" from Greek *stuppē*; from the use of tow in making compresses.]

stupe[2] /stoop/ *n.* an offensive term referring to somebody regarded as unintelligent (*slang insult*) [Mid-18thC. Shortening of STUPID.]

stu·pe·fa·cient /sto͝opə fáysh'nt/ *adj.* STUPEFYING causing stupor ■ *n.* STUPEFYING DRUG a drug or other agent that causes stupor [Mid-17thC. From Latin *stupefacient-*, the present participle stem of *stupefacere* (see STUPEFY).]

stu·pe·fac·tion /sto͝opə fáksh'n/ *n.* **1.** AMAZEMENT great amazement or astonishment (*literary*) **2.** INABILITY TO THINK CLEARLY the inability to think clearly because of boredom, tiredness, or amazement [15thC. Via French, from, ultimately, Latin *stupefacere* (see STUPEFY).]

stu·pe·fy /sto͝opə fī/ (**-fied, -fy·ing, -fies**) *vt.* **1.** AMAZE to amaze or astonish somebody **2.** MAKE SOMEBODY UNABLE TO THINK CLEARLY to make somebody unable to think clearly because of boredom, tiredness, or amazement [15thC. Via French *stupéfier* from Latin *stupefacere*, from *stupere* "to be stunned" (see STUPID) + *facere* "to make."] —**stu·pe·fi·er** *n.* —**stu·pe·fy·ing·ly** *adv.*

stu·pen·dous /stoo péndəss/ *adj.* impressively large, excellent, or great in extent or degree ○ *a stupendous achievement* [Mid-17thC. Formed from Latin *stupendus*, the gerundive of *stupere* "to be stunned," source of English *stupor*.] —**stu·pen·dous·ly** *adv.* —**stu·pen·dous·ness** *n.*

stu·pid /sto͝opəd/ *adj.* **1.** UNINTELLIGENT thought to show a lack of intelligence, perception, or common sense ○ *a stupid mistake* **2.** SILLY irritatingly silly or time-wasting ○ *had us playing stupid games* **3.** EXPRESSING IRRITATION used to express anger, annoyance, or frustration (*informal*) ○ *I can't get the stupid thing to work!* **4.** DAZED in a dazed state, e.g., from shock, fatigue, or from the effects of drugs or alcohol ○ *almost stupid with tiredness* [Mid-16thC. From Latin *stupidus*, from *stupere* "to be stunned."]

stu·pid·i·ty /stoo píddətee/ (*plural* **-ties**) *n.* **1.** LACK OF INTELLIGENCE lack of intelligence, perception, or common sense **2.** RASHNESS OR THOUGHTLESSNESS extremely rash or thoughtless behavior **3.** RASH OR THOUGHTLESS ACTION extremely rash or thoughtless behavior

stu·pid·ly /sto͝opədlee/ *adv.* **1.** IN UNINTELLIGENT WAY in a way that demonstrates lack of intelligence, perception, or common sense ○ *I had stupidly forgotten to note down the date I mailed it.* **2.** IN BEWILDERMENT in a way that suggests diminished ability to perceive or reason ○ *He gazed stupidly after her.*

stu·por /sto͝opər/ *n.* **1.** DAZED STATE an acute lack of mental alertness brought on, e.g., by shock or lack of sleep **2.** UNCONSCIOUSNESS a state of near-unconsciousness induced by, e.g., drugs or alcohol [14thC. From Latin, formed from *stupere* "to be stunned."] —**stu·por·ous** *adj.*

stur·dy /stúrdee/ (**-di·er, -di·est**) *adj.* **1.** WELL MADE solidly made and likely to withstand prolonged use **2.** WITH A STRONG BUILD having a well-developed strong-looking body and limbs **3.** RESOLUTE having or displaying decisiveness, resoluteness, or firmness of purpose ○ *sturdy defenders of the right to free speech* [13thC. Via Old French *estourdir* "dazed" from, ultimately, Latin *turdus* "thrush," formerly associated with drunkenness. The earliest sense was "recklessly violent."] —**stur·di·ly** *adv.* —**stur·di·ness** *n.*

stur·geon /stúrj'n/ (*plural* **-geons** *or* **-geon**) *n.* a large bottom-feeding fish with a long snout and tough bony-plated skin, found in northern rivers and coastal waters. It is important as a source of caviar and isinglass. Family: Acipenseridae. [13thC. From Old French *esturgeon*, of Germanic origin.]

Sturm und Drang /shto͝orm o͝ond dráang/ *n.* **1.** LITERAT GERMAN LITERARY MOVEMENT a movement in late 18th-century German literature whose works typically portray the tortured emotions of a central character who violently rejects society **2.** EMOTIONAL TURMOIL a state of extreme emotional upheaval (*literary*) ○ *movies that explore his own personal Sturm und Drang* [Late 18thC. From German, literally "storm and stress."]

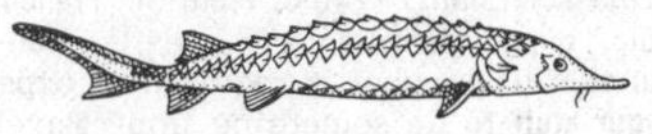

Sturgeon

stut·ter /stúttər/ *v.* (**-tered, -ter·ing, -ters**) **1.** *vti.* SAY OR SPEAK WITH STAMMER to say something haltingly, repeating sounds frequently when attempting to pronounce them, either from nervousness or as the result of a speech disorder ○ *managed to stutter an apology* **2.** *vi.* MAKE SHORT NOISES to make repeated short noises that suggest mechanical inefficiency or failure ○ *The motor stuttered briefly and then died again.* ■ *n.* **1.** STAMMERING AS A SPEECH DISORDER a speech disorder that makes the speaker repeat certain speech sounds that are found difficult to pronounce ○ *has a slight stutter* **2.** BURST OF REPEATED SOUNDS a burst of repeated short sounds [Early 16thC. Alteration of obsolete *stut*, of Germanic origin.] —**stut·ter·er** *n.* —**stut·ter·ing** *adj.* —**stut·ter·ing·ly** *adv.*

Stutt·gart /sto͝ot gaart/ capital of Baden-Württemberg State, in southwestern Germany. Population: 592,000 (1994).

Stuy·ve·sant /stívisənt/, **Peter** (1610?–72) Dutch colonial administrator. He was the last Dutch governor of New Netherland in present-day New York (1647–64), which he was forced to surrender to English troops.

STV *abbr.* subscription television

sty[1] /stī/ *n.* (*plural* **sties**) AGRIC HOG'S ENCLOSURE an enclosure in which hogs are kept ■ *vt.* (**stied, sty·ing, sties**) AGRIC HOUSE A HOG to put or keep a hog in a sty [Old English *stī* "pen." Variant of stig (see STEWARD).]

sty[2] /stī/ (*plural* **sties**), **stye** *n.* MED a temporary swelling on an eyelid at the base of an eyelash [Early 17thC. By folk etymology from obsolete *styanye*, as if "sty-on-eye." From Old English *stīgend* "rising" + *ye* "eye."]

Styg·i·an /stíjjee ən/ *adj.* **1.** PITCH-BLACK unremittingly dark and frightening, as hell is imagined to be (*literary*) **2.** MYTHOL OF THE STYX relating to the Styx, the river in Greek mythology that the souls of the dead were ferried across into Hades **3.** BINDING eternally binding, as were promises sworn on the banks of the river Styx in Greek mythology (*literary*) [Mid-16thC. Via Latin *Stygius* from Greek *Stugios*, from *Stux* (see STYX).]

styl- *prefix.* = **stylo-** (*used before vowels*)

sty·lar /stílər/ *adj.* relating to or using a stylus

style /stīl/ *n.* **1.** ARTS DISTINCTIVE FORM a distinctive and identifiable form in an artistic medium such as music, architecture, or literature ○ *a facade in the neoclassical style* ○ *a different style of jazz* **2.** WAY OF DOING SOMETHING a way of doing something, especially a way regarded as expressing a particular attitude or typifying a particular period (*often used in combination*) ○ *a hands-on management style* ○ *old-style politics* ○ *Confrontation just isn't his style.* **3.** WAY OF WRITING OR PERFORMING the way in which something is written or performed as distinct from the content of the writing or performance **4.** FLAIR impressive flair in the way something is done, especially a quality that suggests a self-confident willingness to exhibit skill or good taste ○ *furnished with impeccable style* **5.** FASHIONABLE STATUS fashionable status or quality ○ *a look that has gone out of style* **6.** FASHION an example of cut or shape of garment or way of wearing the hair ○ *dressed in all the latest styles* ○ *That style really suits you.* **7.** LUXURIOUSNESS extravagance or lavishness ○ *dining in style* **8.** PUBL PUBLISHING CONVENTIONS the ways in which written material is presented, usually in a particular publication or by a particular publisher ○ *editing text into the publisher's house style* **9.** SUNDIAL POINTER the pointer on a sundial **10.** BOT FLOWER PART an extension of a flower's ovary, shaped like a stalk, that supports the stigma **11.** ZOOL = **stylet** *n.* 2 **12.** = **stylus** *n.* 3 **13.** TITLE a name or title, especially one that is official or legally correct (*formal*) ■ *vt.* (**styled, styl·ing, styles**) **1.** SHAPE SOMETHING to give something a particular shape or design ○ *hair styled in the most up-to-date fashion* **2.** CAUSE TO CONFORM to bring something into conformity with a particular style **3.** NAME SOMEBODY to give somebody or something a name or title (*formal*) [13thC. Via Old French from Latin *stilus* "writing instrument, style."] —**styl·er** *n.* ◇ **cramp somebody's style** to limit what somebody is able to do, often by limiting the person's capacity to impress others (*informal*)

style·book /stíl bo͝ok/ *n.* a publishing company's gathered conventions in presenting printed material, used as a guide by writers and editors

sty·let /stílət/ *n.* **1.** MED WIRE PREVENTING BLOCKAGE IN A NEEDLE a fine wire inserted into a catheter or hollow needle to prevent it from becoming blocked when not in use **2.** ZOOL PART SHAPED LIKE A BRISTLE a thin long organ or appendage shaped like a bristle, e.g., any of the mouthparts of some insects **3.** LONG POINTED INSTRUMENT any long thin pointed instrument (*formal*) [Late 17thC. Via French from Italian *stiletto* (see STILETTO).]

sty·li plural of **stylus**

styli- *prefix.* = **stylo-**

sty·li·form /stī́lə fàwrm/ *adj.* long, thin, and pointed, like a bristle (*formal*) [Late 16thC. From modern Latin *stiliformis*, from Latin *stilus* "style" + *forma* "form."]

styling /stī́ling/ *n.* **1.** SHAPING OF THE HAIR the act or an instance of giving a particular shape or design to somebody's hair (*often used before a noun*) ○ *styling mousse* **2.** INSTANCE OF CREATING SOMETHING an instance of creating something, especially something artistic, in a particular or idiosyncratic way (*informal*) ○ *the zany comedy stylings of the country's favorite stand-up*

styl·ish /stī́lish/ *adj.* **1.** SOPHISTICATED AND FASHIONABLE having confident good taste and appreciation of what is fashionable **2.** IMPRESSIVE having or showing impressive skill or accomplishment ○ *the most stylish player in the team* —**styl·ish·ly** *adv.* —**styl·ish·ness** *n.*

styl·ist /stī́list/ *n.* **1.** HAIR HAIRDRESSER a hairdresser, especially a more senior hairdresser in a salon **2.** ARTS, LITERAT ACCOMPLISHED ARTIST somebody whose creative work shows a distinctive and accomplished style **3.** COMM DESIGNER a designer who is consulted on matters of style, especially somebody responsible for creating a distinctive visual image for a product or company

sty·lis·tic /stī lístik/ *adj.* relating to matters of style, especially in literature and the arts ○ *stylistic brilliance compromised by a certain thinness of content* —**sty·lis·ti·cal·ly** *adv.*

stylis·tics /stī lístiks/ *n.* the branch of linguistics that deals with determining which features of written or spoken language characterize particular groups or contexts, especially particular literary genres or works (*takes a singular verb*)

sty·lite /stī́ līt/ *n.* a Christian ascetic in ancient times who lived alone on top of a tall pillar [Mid-17thC. From late Greek *stulitēs*, from Greek *stulos* "pillar."] —**sty·lit·ic** /stī líttik/ *adj.*

styl·ize /stī́ līz/ (**-ized, -iz·ing, -iz·es**) *vt.* to give something a distinctive, often artificial artistic style —**styl·i·za·tion** /stīlə záysh'n/ *n.* —**styl·iz·er** /stī́ līzər/ *n.*

styl·ized /stī́ līzd/ *adj.* created or performed according to distinctive established styles, usually in order to achieve a particular artistic effect, often at the expense of naturalness or spontaneity ○ *a highly stylized backhand stroke*

stylo- *prefix.* style, column ○ *stylograph* ○ *styloid* [From Latin *stylus* (see STYLUS)]

sty·lo·bate /stī́lə bàyt/ *n.* a continuous raised platform of masonry supporting a row of columns [Mid-16thC. Via Latin *stylobata* from Greek *stulobatēs*, literally "column step."]

sty·lo·graph /stī́lə gràf/ *n.* a fountain pen that has a thin hollow tube as its writing point instead of the traditional nib

sty·log·ra·phy /stī lóggrəfee/ *n.* the art of drawing or engraving using a stylus —**sty·lo·graph·ic** /stīlə gráffik/ *adj.* —**sty·lo·graph·i·cal·ly** /-gráffiklee/ *adv.*

sty·loid /stī́ lòyd/ *adj.* ANAT used to describe a bony protuberance (**process**) that is long and thin

sty·lo·lite /stī́lə lìt/ *n.* a join between two layers of limestone that in cross section looks like a row of interlocking pegs —**sty·lo·lit·ic** /stī̀lə líttik/ *adj.*

sty·lo·po·di·um /stī̀lə pṓdee əm/ (*plural* **-a** /-dee ə/) *n.* the typically broad base of the style of flowers in plants of the carrot family

Stylus

sty·lus /stī́ləss/ (*plural* **-li** /-lī/) *n.* **1.** RECORDING **PHONOGRAPH NEEDLE** the jewel-tipped needle of a phonograph that rests in the grooves of a record as it revolves. It transmits vibrations to the cartridge. **2.** ELECTRON ENG **MACHINE'S TRACING PEN** the tracing pen on an electronic device such as a seismograph or polygraph that converts an electrical signal into a written record **3.** **ENGRAVING TOOL** a pointed instrument used for engraving, especially one used in ancient times for writing on clay or wax tablets [Early 18thC. From Latin, a spelling variant of *stilus*, "stake, pointed writing instrument," influenced by Greek *stulos*, "pillar."]

sty·mie /stī́mee/, **sty·my** *vt.* (**-mied, -mie·ing, -mies; -mied, -my·ing, -mies**) **1.** **HINDER THE PROGRESS OF** to prevent somebody or something from making further progress **2.** GOLF **BLOCK AN OPPONENT'S LINE** to obstruct the line between a golf opponent's ball and the hole (*dated*) ■ *n.* (*plural* **-mies**) **1.** **PROBLEM SITUATION** a situation in which obstacles hinder progress **2.** GOLF **OBSTRUCTION OF AN OPPONENT'S BALL** a situation in which one golf player's ball blocks another's. In the modern game, the obstructing ball is lifted and replaced by a marker. (*dated*) [Mid-19thC. Origin unknown.]

styp·sis /stípsiss/ *n.* the use of a styptic substance, or its antibleeding effect [Late 19thC. Via late Latin from Greek *stupsis*, from *stuphein* "to contract."]

styp·tic /stíptik/ *adj.* **ABLE TO STOP BLEEDING** slowing down the rate of bleeding or stopping bleeding altogether, whether by causing the blood vessels to contract or by accelerating clotting ■ *n.* **STYPTIC SUBSTANCE** a styptic drug, cream, or lotion [14thC. Via late Latin *stypticus* from Greek *stuptikos*, from *stuphein* "to contract."]

styp·tic pen·cil *n.* an astringent substance in solid form in a small cylindrical container that is applied to stop bleeding in small cuts, e.g., after shaving

sty·rax *n.* = **storax** *n.* **3**

sty·rene /stī́ reen/ *n.* a colorless flammable liquid hydrocarbon used in the manufacture of synthetic rubber and plastic. Formula: C_8H_8. [Late 19thC. Coined from Latin *styrax* (see STORAX) + -ENE.]

Sty·ro·foam /stī́rə fōm/ *tdmk.* a trademark for a light plastic material used to make disposable items, insulation, and packing materials

William Styron

Sty·ron /stī́rən/, **William** (*b.* 1925) U.S. writer. His novel *The Confessions of Nat Turner* (1967) won a Pulitzer Prize. Full name **William Clark Styron, Jr.**

Styx /stiks/ *n.* in Greek mythology, the river across which the souls of the dead were ferried into the underworld [14thC. Via Latin from Greek *Stux*.]

su·a·ble /sóo əb'l/ *adj.* able or liable to be made the subject of a lawsuit —**su·a·bil·i·ty** /sòo ə bíllətee/ *n.*

sua·sion /swáyzh'n/ *n.* the art of persuasion or an instance of persuading (*formal*) [14thC.Via Old French or directly from Latin *suasion-*, the stem of *suasio*, from, ultimately, *suadere*, "to advise."] —**sua·sive** /swáyssiv, swáyziv/ *adj.*

suave /swaav/ (**suav·er, suav·est**) *adj.* **1.** **CHARMING** polite and charming, especially in a way that seems affected or insincere **2.** **PLEASINGLY DRESSED** well groomed and pleasingly dressed (*dated*) [Early 16thC. Via French or directly from Latin *suavis* "sweet, agreeable," from, ultimately, an Indo-European base that is also the ancestor of English *sweet*.] —**suave·ly** *adv.* —**suave·ness** *n.* —**suav·i·ty** *n.*

sub[1] /sub/ *n.* (*informal*) **1.** **A SUBSTITUTE** a substitute, especially a substitute player in a game **2.** **SUBTITLE** a subtitle to a document or printed matter ■ *v.* (**subbed, sub·bing, subs**) (*informal*) **1.** *vi.* **REPLACE** to take the place of somebody temporarily, usually in a work situation **2.** *vti.* **SUBCONTRACT** to subcontract work, or work as a subcontractor **3.** *vt.* **SUBTITLE SOMETHING** to add subtitles to something [Late 17thC. Shortening.]

sub[2] /sub/ *n.* (*informal*) **1.** NAVY **SUBMARINE** a submarine **2.** FOOD **SANDWICH** a sandwich made with a long roll cut horizontally

sub. *abbr.* **1.** subito **2.** suburb **3.** suburban

sub- *prefix.* **1.** under, below, beneath ○ *subcutaneous* ○ *subfloor* **2.** subordinate, secondary ○ *subparagraph* **3.** less than completely ○ *subliterate* **4.** subdivision ○ *subkingdom* ○ *subcontinent* **5.** bordering on ○ *subequatorial* **6.** smaller or younger than ○ *subcompact* ○ *subteen* **7.** nearly, partly, somewhat ○ *subfossil* **8.** containing less than the normal amount of an element ○ *suboxide* [From Latin *sub* "under"]

sub·ac·id /sùb ássid/ *adj.* **1.** **SLIGHTLY SOUR** moderately sour in flavor (*archaic*) **2.** **SOMEWHAT CRITICAL** mildly unkind or critical in tone (*literary*) —**sub·a·cid·i·ty** /sùbbə síddətee/ *n.* —**sub·ac·id·ly** /sùb ássidlee/ *adv.*

sub·a·cute /sùbbə kyóot/ *adj.* used to describe a medical condition that develops less rapidly and with less severity than an acute condition —**sub·a·cute·ly** *adv.*

sub·a·cute scle·ros·ing pan·en·ceph·a·li·tis /-pàn en sèffə lī́təss/ *n.* a severe, usually fatal, inflammatory disease of the brain, chiefly affecting children and linked to infection from measles

sub·ad·ar /sóobə daar/, **sub·ah·dar** *n.* the chief Indian officer in a company of Indian soldiers in the former British Indian army [Late 17thC. From Urdu and Persian *ṣūbahdār*, literally "subah holder" (see SUBAH).]

sub·aer·i·al /sub áiree əl/ *adj.* formed or situated on or just below the surface of the soil ○ *a plant with subaerial roots*

su·bah /sóobə/ *n.* **1.** HIST **MOGUL PROVINCE** any of the provinces of the Mogul empire **2.** MIL = **subadar** [Mid-18thC. Via Urdu and Persian *ṣūbah* from Arabic, "heap."]

sub·ah·dar *n.* MIL = **subadar**

sub·al·pine /sub ál pīn/ *adj.* relating to or growing naturally on the lower slopes of mountains, especially the areas below the tree line

sub·al·tern /sə báwltərn, súbbəl tùrn/ *n.* **1.** MIL **JUNIOR OFFICER** a junior officer in some armies, e.g., a commissioned officer below the rank of captain in the British army **2.** **SUBORDINATE PERSON** somebody who holds a subordinate or inferior position **3.** LOGIC **IMPLIED PROPOSITION** a particular proposition that is implied by a universal proposition ■ *adj.* **1.** **SUBORDINATE** in a subordinate or inferior position **2.** LOGIC **IMPLIED** implied as a particular proposition by a universal proposition [Late 16thC. From late Latin *subalternus*, from Latin *alternus* "alternate" (see ALTERNATE).]

sub·al·ter·nate /sub áwltərnət/ *adj.* **1.** BOT **WITH LEAFLETS NOT FULLY ALTERNATE** used to describe a leaf whose leaflets are arranged in semistaggered rows, neither fully alternate nor fully opposite **2.** **SUBORDINATE** in a subordinate or inferior position —**sub·al·ter·na·tion** /sub àwltər náysh'n/ *n.*

sub·ant·arc·tic /sùb an taarktik/ *adj.* relating to the area between the Antarctic Circle and the South Pole

sub·ap·os·tol·ic /sùb appə stóllik/ *adj.* belonging to the period in the history of the Christian Church that immediately followed the time of the Apostles

sub·aq·ua /sùb aakwə/ *adj.* relating to or providing facilities for underwater sports such as scuba diving [Mid-20thC. Coined from SUB- + Latin *aqua* "water."]

sub·a·quat·ic /sùbbə kwaatik/ *adj.* **1.** BIOL **IN WATER AND ON LAND** existing or able to exist partly in water and partly on land **2.** **RELATING TO UNDERWATER REGIONS** relating or belonging to underwater regions

sub·a·que·ous /sub áykwee əss, -ák-/ *adj.* living, found, or formed under water

sub·a·rach·noid /sùbbə rák nòyd/ *adj.* situated beneath the middle of the three membranes (**arachnoids**) that cover the brain and spinal cord

sub·arc·tic /sùb aarktik/ *adj.* **1.** **SOUTH OF THE ARCTIC CIRCLE** relating to the area bordering the Arctic Circle to the south **2.** **LIKE THE BORDERS OF THE ARCTIC** similar to the regions that border the Arctic Circle, e.g., in landscape or weather conditions

sub·ar·id /sùb érrid/ *adj.* having a climate in which there is very little rainfall but not as little as in arid regions

sub·as·sem·bly /sùbbə sémblee/ (*plural* **-blies**) *n.* a group of pieces assembled separately and incorporated into a larger assembled structure

sub·a·tom·ic /sùbbə tómmik/ *adj.* **1.** PHYS **PART OF OR SMALLER THAN AN ATOM** occurring as part of an atom, or smaller than an atom **2.** SCI **ON A SMALLER-THAN-ATOM SCALE** on a scale smaller than the atom, or involving phenomena at this level

sub·au·di·tion /sùb aw dísh'n/ *n.* **1.** **IMPLICATION** the act of understanding a word or thought that is implied but not actually expressed in speech or writing **2.** **IMPLIED WORD OR IDEA** a word, idea, or thought understood by a hearer or reader that is implied but not expressed [Mid-17thC. From late Latin *subaudition-*, the stem of *subauditio*, from, ultimately, Latin *audire* "to hear."]

sub·ax·il·lar·y /sùb áksə lèrree/ *adj.* **1.** ZOOL, ANAT **BELOW THE ARMPIT** located beneath the armpit **2.** BOT **BELOW THE AXIL** growing beneath the axil in plants

sub·base /súb bàyss/ *n.* **1.** BUILDING **BOTTOM STRUCTURAL LAYER** a deep layer of large stones that forms the lowest level of a roadbed or of the foundation of a building **2.** **BOTTOM OF A BASE** the lowest section of any base or foundation, e.g., the bottom part of a pedestal

sub·base·ment /súb bàyssmənt/ *n.* a story below the basement in a building

sub·cal·i·ber /sub kállibər/ *adj.* used to describe ammunition whose caliber is smaller than that of the gun from which it is fired. Smaller ammunition is often used for practice because it is cheaper.

sub·car·ti·lag·i·nous /sùb kaart'l ájjənəss/ *adj.* **1.** **BENEATH CARTILAGE** lying beneath cartilage or a body part composed of cartilage **2.** **PARTLY OF CARTILAGE** made up partly of cartilage

sub·cat·e·go·ry /sùb káttə gàwree, súb kàttə gàwree/ (*plural* **-ries**) *n.* any one of the smaller sections into which a main category is divided

sub·ce·les·tial /sùb sə léschəl/ *adj.* belonging to the earth, not to the heavens or the stars (*literary*)

sub·cel·lu·lar /sub séllyələr/ *adj.* **1.** BIOL **INSIDE A CELL** existing inside a cell, or relating to the component parts of cells **2.** SCI **ON A SMALLER-THAN-CELL SCALE** on a scale smaller than a cell, or involving phenomena at this level

sub·cen·tral /sub séntrəl/ *adj.* at a level below the main or central one ○ *subcentral governments* —**sub·cen·tral·ly** *adv.*

sub·chas·er /súb chàyssər/ *n.* NAVY a submarine chaser (*informal*)

sub·class /súb klàss/ *n.* **1.** **SUBORDINATE CLASS** any of the smaller groups into which a main class is divided **2.** BIOL **BIOLOGICAL CLASS** a subdivision of a class in the classification of plants and animals **3.** MATH = **subset**

sub·cla·vi·an /sub kláyvee ən/ *adj.* located under the collarbone (**clavicle**) [Mid-17thC. Formed from modern Latin *subclavius*, from Latin *clavis* "key" (source of English *clavicle*).]

sub·clin·i·cal /sub klínnik'l/ *adj.* used to describe an early stage or mild form of a medical condition, no symptoms of which are detectable —**sub·clin·i·cal·ly** *adv.*

sub·com·mit·tee /súbkə mìttee/ *n.* a committee set up by and consisting of members of an existing committee to deal with a particular issue

sub·com·pact /sub kóm pàkt/ *n.* a small car, usually the smallest and lightest model in a manufacturer's range

sub·con·scious /sub kónshəss/ *adj.* EXISTING UNKNOWN IN THE MIND present in your mind without you being aware of it ■ *n.* UNCONSCIOUS PART OF THE MIND mental activity not directly perceived by your consciousness, from which memories, feelings, or thoughts can influence your behavior without you realizing it —**sub·con·scious·ly** *adv.* —**sub·con·scious·ness** *n.*

sub·con·ti·nent /sub kónt'nənt/, **Sub·con·ti·nent** *n.* a large area that is an identifiably separate part of a continent, especially the area encompassing the countries of India, Pakistan, and Bangladesh regarded as a distinct part of Asia —**sub·con·ti·nen·tal** /sùb kont'n ént'l/ *adj., n.*

sub·con·tract /sub kón tràkt, súb kòn trakt/ *n.* SECONDARY CONTRACT a secondary contract in which the person or company originally hired in turn hires somebody else to do all or part of the work ■ *v.* (**-tract·ed, -tract·ing, -tracts**) 1. *vt.* GIVE WORK UNDER A SUBCONTRACT to pass on work to a second person or company under the terms of a subcontract 2. *vi.* TAKE ON WORK FROM A CONTRACTOR to work on contract with a person or company who is a contractor to somebody else —**sub·con·trac·tor** *n.*

sub·con·trar·y /sub kóntrəree/ *adj.* NOT FALSE TOGETHER used to describe logical propositions that are related to each other in such a way that both cannot be false at the same time, although both may be true ■ *n.* (*plural* **-ies**) SUBCONTRARY PROPOSITION a subcontrary logical proposition [Early 17thC. From late Latin *subcontrarius*, a translation of Greek *hupenantios* "contrary."]

sub·cor·tex /sub káwr tèks/ (*plural* **-ti·ces** /-káwrtə seez/) *n.* the parts of the brain that lie immediately beneath the cerebral cortex —**sub·cor·ti·cal** /-káwrtik'l/ *adj.*

sub·cra·ni·al /sub kráynee əl/ *adj.* located beneath the dome of the skull

sub·cul·ture /súb kùlchər/ *n.* 1. SOCIOL SEPARATE SOCIAL GROUP an identifiably separate social group within a larger culture, especially one regarded as existing outside mainstream society 2. BIOL SECONDARY BIOLOGICAL CULTURE a bacterial culture that is grown from another culture —**sub·cul·tur·al** /sùb kúlchərəl/ *adj.*

sub·cu·ta·ne·ous /sùbkyə táynee əss/ *adj.* located, living, or made beneath the skin —**sub·cu·ta·ne·ous·ly** *adv.*

sub·dea·con /sub deekən/ *n.* 1. DEACON'S ASSISTANT a member of the Roman Catholic clergy who acts as a deacon's assistant, e.g., by preparing the vessels that are to be used in celebrating Mass 2. CLERIC ABOVE LECTOR a cleric ranking just above a lector in an Eastern Church

sub·di·ac·o·nate /sùb dī ákənət/ *n.* the position or term of office of a subdeacon —**sub·di·ac·o·nal** *adj.*

sub·di·rec·to·ry /sùbdi réktəree, sùb dī-/ (*plural* **-ries**) *n.* a division of a directory on a magnetic storage device such as a hard disk

sub·di·vide /sùbdi vīd/ (**-vid·ed, -vid·ing, -vides**) *v.* 1. *vt.* DIVIDE FURTHER to divide a section, or all the sections of something into sections that are smaller still 2. *vi.* BE DIVIDED FURTHER to be divided, or be able to be divided, into sections that are smaller still —**sub·di·vid·er** *n.*

sub·di·vi·sion /sùb di vízh'n, súbdi vìzh'n/ *n.* 1. SUBDIVIDING OF SOMETHING the dividing of a divided part into units that are smaller still 2. SUBSIDIARY SECTION a section of something that is itself a division of a larger thing 3. BUILDING DEVELOPMENT SITE an area of land divided up into building lots —**sub·di·vi·sion·al** /sùbdi vízh'nəl/ *adj.*

sub·dom·i·nant /sub dómminənt/ *n.* 1. FOURTH NOTE IN A SCALE the fourth note in a major or minor scale 2. SUBDOMINANT HARMONY a key, chord, or harmony based on a subdominant

sub·duct /səb dúkt/ (**-duct·ed, -duct·ing, -ducts**) *vi.* to be carried under the edge of an adjoining continental or oceanic plate, causing tensions in the Earth's crust that can produce earthquakes or volcanic eruptions [Late 16thC. From Latin *subduct-*, the past participle stem of *subducere* "to draw up," from *ducere* "to lead."] —**sub·duc·tion** /səb dúksh'n/ *n.*

sub·due /səb dóo/ (**-dued, -du·ing, -dues**) *vt.* 1. BRING UNDER FORCIBLE CONTROL to bring a person or group of people under control using force 2. SOFTEN to soften something or make it less intense ○ *idealism subdued by experience* 3. REPRESS to repress or control feelings or emotions ○ *worked hard to subdue her irritation* [14thC. Via Old French *souduire* "to seduce" from Latin *subducere* "to draw up" (see SUBDUCT).] —**sub·du·a·ble** *adj.* —**sub·du·er** *n.*

sub·dued /səb dóod/ *adj.* 1. NOT HARSH not bright, loud, or intense, or made less bright, loud, or intense ○ *subdued lighting* 2. VERY QUIET sad or in low spirits 3. QUIET quiet and restrained ○ *speaking in subdued tones*

sub·dur·al /sùb dóorəl/ *adj.* beneath the dura mater that covers the brain and spinal cord

sub·ed·it /sub éddət/ (**-it·ed, -it·ing, -its**) *vt.* *U.K.* = **copyedit** [Mid-19thC. Back-formation from SUBEDITOR.]

sub·ed·i·tor /sub éddətər/ *n.* 1. ASSISTANT EDITOR an assistant editor helping to prepare material for publication 2. *U.K.* = **copyreader**

sub·e·qua·to·ri·al /sùb ekwə táwree əl/ *adj.* relating to or situated in the regions that lie just north and south of the equator

su·ber·in /sóobərən/ *n.* a fatty substance found in the cell walls of many plants, especially in cork tissue where it provides resistance to water and decay [Early 19thC. From French *subérine*, from Latin *suber* "cork."]

su·ber·ize /sóobə rīz/ (**-ized, -iz·ing, -iz·es**) *vt.* to deposit suberin in plant cell walls during their conversion to cork tissue [Late 19thC. Coined from Latin *suber* "cork" + -IZE.]

su·ber·ose /sóobə rōss, -rōz/ *adj.* relating to cork, or similar to cork in appearance or texture [Mid-19thC. From modern Latin *suberosus*, from Latin *suber* "cork."]

sub·fam·i·ly /súb fàmməlee/ (*plural* **-lies**) *n.* 1. BIOL BIOLOGICAL CLASSIFICATION a subdivision of a family in the classification of plants and animals 2. LING LINGUISTIC CATEGORIZATION a smaller group of related languages within a language family

sub·field /súb feeld/ *n.* a mathematical field that is a subset of another field

sub·floor /súb flàwr/ *n.* an underlying layer of rough or unfinished material supporting a finished floor —**sub·floor·ing** *n.*

sub·fos·sil /súb fòss'l/ *adj.* PARTLY FOSSILIZED partially fossilized ■ *n.* SUBFOSSIL ORGANISM a partially fossilized organism

sub·freez·ing /sub freezing/ *adj.* lower than 0° Celsius or 32° Fahrenheit

sub·ge·nus /súb jeenəss/ (*plural* **-gen·e·ra** /-jènnərə/) *n.* a category in the classification of plants and animals that is larger than a species but smaller than a genus

sub·gla·cial /sub gláysh'l/ *adj.* formed below or at the bottom of a glacier —**sub·gla·cial·ly** *adv.*

sub·grade /súb gràyd/ *n.* the bed of ground on which the foundations of a road, railroad, or building are laid

sub·group /súb gròop/ *n.* 1. DIVISION OF GROUP a smaller group distinguished in some way from the larger group of which it is a part 2. MATH MATHEMATICAL GROUP a mathematical group whose members are also members of a larger group

sub·gum /súb gùm/ *n.* a Chinese dish with a base of mixed vegetables [Mid-20thC. From Chinese (Cantonese) *shâp kám*, literally "mixed brocade."]

sub·head /súb hèd/, **sub·head·ing** /súb hèdding/ *n.* PRINTING a heading or title subordinate to the main one

sub·hu·man /sub hyóomən, -yóomən/ *adj.* 1. LESS THAN HUMAN relating to or displaying behavior that is distastefully inferior in sophistication, moral standards, or intelligence to what is regarded as normal for human beings ○ *a subhuman thug* 2. BIOL NEARLY HUMAN at the level of development that is considered just below humans

sub·i·ma·go /sùbbi máygō, -maágō/ (*plural* **sub·i·ma·goes** *or* **sub·i·mag·ines** /-máygə neez, -maágə neez/) *n.* a mayfly or related insect in a metamorphic stage in which functional wings are present but not all adult features have developed fully

sub·in·dex /sub ín dèks/ (*plural* **-dex·es** *or* **-di·ces** /-di seez/) *n.* 1. INDEX OF SUBSECTION an index to a section of a main classification 2. MATH = **subscript**

sub·in·feu·da·tion /sùb ìnfyoo dáysh'n/ *n.* 1. SUBDIVIDING OF FEUDAL LAND in the feudal system, the leasing of a portion of the land held by a feudal lord's servant (**vassal**) to somebody else who became the servant's servant in turn 2. LAND GRANTED a portion of land granted to a feudal servant under the terms of subinfeudation —**sub·in·feu·date** /sùbbin fyóo dàyt/ *vt.*

sub·ir·ri·gate /sub írri gàyt/ (**-gat·ed, -gat·ing, -gates**) *vt.* to irrigate land from below the surface of the ground, e.g., with porous pipes laid underground —**sub·ir·ri·ga·tion** /sùb irri gáysh'n/ *n.*

su·bi·to /sóobitō/ *adv.* suddenly or abruptly (*used as a musical direction*) [Early 18thC. Via Italian from, ultimately, Latin *subire* "to come over."]

subj. *abbr.* 1. GRAM subject 2. subjective 3. GRAM subjunctive

sub·ja·cent /sùb jáyss'nt/ *adj.* (*formal*) 1. UNDERLYING lying under or just below something 2. LOWER next to something and at a lower level than it ○ *"in the damper tracts of subjacent country and along the river-courses"* (Thomas Hardy, *Jude the Obscure*; 1895) [Late 16thC. From Latin *subjacent-*, the present participle stem of *subjacere* "to lie under."] —**sub·ja·cen·cy** *n.* —**sub·ja·cent·ly** *adv.*

sub·ject *n.* /súb jèkt/ 1. TOPIC a matter that is being discussed, examined, studied, or otherwise dealt with 2. EDUC COURSE OF STUDY a branch of learning that forms a course of study (*often used in the plural*) 3. SOMEBODY TREATED OR ACTED UPON somebody who undergoes treatment or who is the focus of an activity ○ *not an appropriate subject for hypnosis* 4. RULED PERSON somebody who is under the rule of a king, queen, or other authority 5. ARTS THING REPRESENTED BY AN ARTIST somebody who or something that a painter, sculptor, or photographer represents in a piece of work 6. LITERAT SOMEBODY FEATURED IN A BIOGRAPHY the main person written about in a biography 7. GRAM GRAMMATICAL PERFORMER OF A VERB'S ACTION the part of a sentence or utterance, a noun, noun phrase, or equivalent, that the rest of the sentence asserts something about and that agrees with the verb. The subject typically performs the action expressed by the verb. "She" and "The dog" are the subjects of "She gave me the book" and "The dog was found asleep" respectively. 8. MUSIC MUSICAL THEME the principal theme or melodic phrase that is developed in the course of a musical composition ■ *adj.* 1. PRONE TO likely to be affected by or with a tendency to be affected by a particular thing ○ *areas subject to flooding* ○ *a child subject to mood swings* 2. RULED under the control of somebody or something such as a ruler or a law, and obliged to obey ○ *a subject nation* ○ *not subject to the laws that apply in this country* ■ *adv.* DEPENDING depending on or conditional on somebody or something ○ *The plans have been drawn up, subject to your final approval.* ■ *vt.* /səb jékt/ (**-ject·ed, -ject·ing, -jects**) 1. CAUSE TO HAVE AN UNPLEASANT EXPERIENCE to cause somebody to undergo something unpleasant ○ *recruits subjected to rigorous physical training* 2. SUBMIT TO TREATMENT to make something undergo treatment of a particular kind ○ *proposals subjected to detailed scrutiny* 3. OVERPOWER to bring a person or group under the power or influence of another person or group ○ *a nation subjected to rule from overseas* [14thC. Via Old French from Latin *subjectus*, from, ultimately, *subicere* "to place under," from *jacere* "to throw."]

WORD KEY: SYNONYMS

subject, topic, subject matter, matter, theme, burden

CORE MEANING: what is under discussion

subject a general word that describes what is under discussion or investigation; **topic** an item selected for discussion; **subject matter** a fairly formal term meaning the same as *subject*. It is sometimes used when drawing a distinction with the style or form of a piece of writing; **matter** a formal word used in the same way as *subject matter*; **theme** an important unifying idea in something such as a piece of writing, a painting, or a movie; **burden** a formal or literary word used to mean the main argument or recurrent theme of something such as a piece of writing.

sub·jec·tion /səb jéksh'n/ *n.* 1. DOMINATION the bringing of a person or people under the control of another, usually by force 2. ACT OF SUBJECTING the subjecting of somebody to something

sub·jec·tive /səb jéktiv/ *adj.* **1. NOT IMPARTIAL** based on somebody's opinions or feelings rather than on facts or evidence ○ *Of course, that's only my subjective impression.* **2.** PHILOSOPHY **EXISTING BY PERCEPTION** existing only in the mind and not independently of it **3.** MED **OBSERVED ONLY BY THE PATIENT** used to describe a medical condition that is perceived to exist only by the patient and is not recognizable to anyone else **4.** GRAM **RELATING TO THE SUBJECT OF VERB** relating to or forming the subject of a verb —**subjectively** *adv.* —**sub·jec·tive·ness** *n.*

sub·jec·tive i·de·al·ism *n.* a philosophical theory arguing that the external world only exists because it is perceived to exist, and does not have existence of its own

sub·jec·tiv·ism /səb jékti vìzzəm/ *n.* **1.** PHILOS **THEORY OF THE VALIDITY OF KNOWLEDGE** a theory stating that people can only have knowledge of what they experience directly **2.** PHILOS **THEORY OF THE VALIDITY OF MORAL STANDARDS** a theory stating that the only valid moral standard is the one imposed by somebody's own conscience, and therefore that society's moral codes are invalid **3. EMPHASIS ON PERSONAL INTERPRETATION** emphasis on personal feelings or responses as opposed to external facts or evidence —**sub·jec·tiv·ist** *adj.* —**sub·jec·tiv·is·tic** /səb jèkti vístik/ *adj.* —**sub·jec·tiv·is·ti·cal·ly** /-vístikəlee/ *adv.*

sub·jec·tiv·i·ty /sùb jek tívvətee/ *n.* **1. PERSONAL INTERPRETATION** interpretation based on personal opinions or feelings rather than on external facts or evidence **2.** ARTS **PERSONAL VISION** concentration on personal, individual responses in artistic expression

sub·ject mat·ter *n.* the matter dealt with in a book, movie, discussion, or other pursuit ○ *contains subject matter unsuitable for children*

WORD KEY: SYNONYMS

See Synonyms at ***subject.***

sub·join /sub jóyn/ (**-joined, -join·ing, -joins**) *vt.* to add something at the end of what has already been written or said (*formal*)

sub ju·di·ce /sub jóodəssee, -yóodə kày/ *adj.* currently under consideration by a judge or a court of law and therefore not to be commented upon publicly [Early 17thC. From Latin, literally "under a judge."]

sub·ju·gate /súbjə gàyt/ (**-gat·ed, -gat·ing, -gates**) *vt.* to bring somebody, especially a people or nation, under the control of another, e.g., by military conquest [15thC. From Latin *subjugat-*, the past participle stem of *subjugare*, from, ultimately, *jugum* "yoke."] —**sub·ju·ga·ble** *adj.* —**sub·ju·ga·tor** /-gàytər/ *n.*

sub·junc·tive /səb júngktiv/ *n.* **1. GRAMMATICAL MOOD** a grammatical mood that expresses doubts, wishes, and possibilities. The verb "were" is in the subjunctive in the phrase "if I were you." **2. SUBJUNCTIVE VERB** a verb or form in the subjunctive ■ *adj.* **RELATING TO THE SUBJUNCTIVE** in or relating to the subjunctive [Mid-16thC. Via late Latin *subjunctivus* from, ultimately, Latin *subjungere* "to subordinate," from *jungere* "to join."] —**sub·junc·tive·ly** *adv.*

WORD KEY: USAGE

Use of the subjunctive in English: Most people associate the subjunctive with Latin and Greek, and are sometimes surprised to realize that they are using it themselves as a regular (if now limited) feature of English grammar. The subjunctive is distinguishable from the regular form of verbs (called the *indicative*) only in the third person singular present tense, which omits the final *-s* (as in *make* rather than *makes*), and in the forms *be* and *were* of the verb *to be.* A typical use of the subjunctive is in clauses introduced by *that* expressing a wish or suggestion, of the type *I suggested to her that she drop by for a drink before the concert. They demanded that he answer their questions.* The form *were* is used in clauses introduced by *if, as if, as though,* or *supposing*, as in: *If you were to go, you might regret it. It's not as though he were an expert. Supposing I were to meet you outside the theater.* The subjunctive also occurs in fixed expressions such as *as it were, be that as it may, come what may,* and *far be it from me.*

sub·king·dom /súb kìngdəm/ *n.* a category in the classification of plants and animals that is smaller than a kingdom and larger than a phylum

sub·lease *n.* /súb lèess/ **LEASE TO RENT FROM A TENANT** an arrangement to rent a property from somebody who is already renting it from somebody else ■ *vt.* /sub lèess/ (**-leased, -leas·ing, -leas·es**) = **sublet** —**sub·les·see** /sùb le sée/ *n.* —**sub·les·sor** /sub lé sàwr/ *n.*

sub·let /sùb lét/ *vti.* (**-let, -let·ting, -lets**) **RENT PROPERTY UNDER A SUBLEASE** to rent a property to or as a subsidiary tenant ■ *n.* **PROPERTY RENTED UNDER A SUBLEASE** a property, especially an apartment, that is rented from somebody who is renting it from somebody else

sub·li·mate /súbbli màyt/ *v.* (**-mat·ed, -mat·ing, -mates**) **1.** *vt.* PSYCHOL **REDIRECT** to channel impulses or energies regarded as unacceptable, especially sexual desires, toward an activity that is more socially acceptable, often a creative activity **2.** *vti.* CHEM = **sublime** *v.* 1 ■ *n.* CHEM **SUBSTANCE FORMED FROM SUBLIMATION** a chemical substance formed as a result of sublimation [15thC. From Latin *sublimat-*, the past participle stem of *sublimare* "to elevate," from *sublimis* "elevated."]

sub·li·ma·tion /sùbbli máysh'n/ *n.* **1.** CHEM **CHEMICAL CONVERSION** a chemical process in which a solid substance is converted into a gas directly, without passing through an intermediate liquid phase **2.** PSYCHOL **REDIRECTING OF UNACCEPTABLE IMPULSES** the channeling of impulses or energies regarded as unacceptable, especially sexual desires, toward activities regarded as more socially acceptable, often creative activities

sub·lime /sə blím/ *adj.* (**-lim·er, -lim·est**) **1. BEAUTIFUL** so awe-inspiringly beautiful as to seem almost heavenly ○ *Monteverdi at his most sublime* **2. MORALLY WORTHY** of the highest moral or spiritual value **3. EXCELLENT** excellent or particularly impressive (*informal*) ○ *a sublime pasta creation* **4. COMPLETE** complete or utter ○ *in sublime ignorance* ■ *n.* **SOMETHING SUBLIME** something that is sublime ○ *going from the sublime to the ridiculous* ■ *v.* (**-limed, -lim·ing, -limes**) **1.** *vti.* CHEM **CONVERT A SOLID SUBSTANCE TO GAS** to convert a solid substance directly into a gas without there being an intermediate liquid phase, or to undergo this process **2.** *vti.* CHEM **CONVERT THEN RECONVERT** to convert a solid directly into a gas and then back to a solid again without an intermediate liquid phase, or to undergo this process **3.** *vt.* **MAKE PURE** to make something such as an emotion finer or purer [14thC. From Latin *sublimis* "elevated."] —**sub·lime·ly** *adv.* —**sub·lime·ness** *n.* —**sub·lim·i·ty** /sə blímmətee/ *n.*

Sub·lime Porte *n.* HIST = **Porte** [Early 17thC. From French, literally "High Gate," a translation of Turkish *Babiâli*, referring to the palace gate where justice was administered.]

sub·lim·i·nal /sub límmin'l/ *adj.* entering, existing in, or affecting the mind without conscious awareness ○ *subliminal messages* [Late 19thC. Coined from SUB- + Latin *limin-*, the stem of *limen* "threshhold."]

sub·lim·i·nal ad·ver·tis·ing *n.* advertising in the form of images flashed onto the screen during a movie or television show that are too brief to be noticed but long enough to be registered subconsciously

sub·lin·gual /sub líng gwəl/ *adj.* **1.** ANAT **UNDER THE TONGUE** situated under the tongue **2.** MED **PLACED UNDER THE TONGUE** used to describe medicines that are administered by being placed under the tongue to dissolve —**sub·lin·gual·ly** *adv.*

sub·lit·er·ate /sub líttərət/ *adj.* having or demonstrating a level of language competency that is below the level regarded as literate

sub·lit·er·a·ture /sub líttrəchər, -líttrə chòor/ *n.* popular literature such as crime novels, and romances

sub·lit·to·ral /sub líttərəl/ *adj.* **RELATING TO SHALLOW COASTAL WATERS** relating to, living near, or located in the shallow water near a shoreline ■ *n.* **COASTAL PART OF A SEA** the area of a sea that lies between the shore and the continental shelf

sub·lu·na·ry /sub lóonəree/ *adj.* **1.** ASTRON **BETWEEN MOON AND EARTH** relating to or found in the area of space that lies between the Moon and the Earth **2. WORLDLY OR MUNDANE** belonging to the material world rather than to the spiritual or intellectual world (*archaic or literary*)

sub·lux·a·tion /sùb luk sáysh'n/ *n.* a partial dislocation of bones that leaves them misaligned but still in some contact with each other

sub·ma·chine gun /sùbmə shéen-/ *n.* a lightweight portable machine gun fired from the hip or the shoulder. It can fire either in single rounds or continuous bursts.

sub·man·dib·u·lar /sùb man díbbyələr/ *adj.* relating to or located under the lower jaw

sub·mar·gin·al /sub maárjin'l/ *adj.* falling below a necessary minimum, especially the minimum conditions necessary for profitability —**sub·mar·gin·al·ly** *adv.*

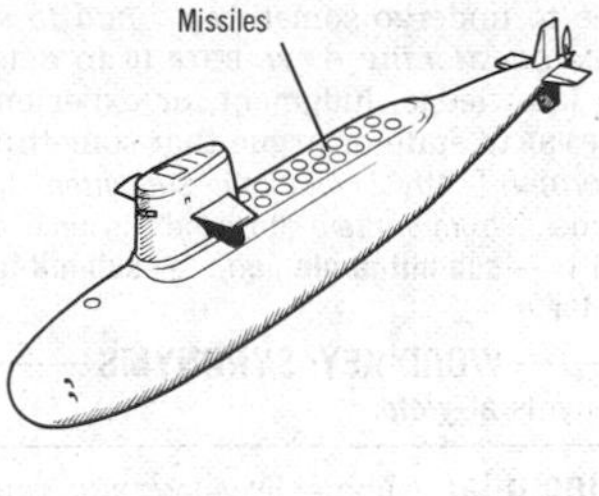

Submarine

sub·ma·rine /súbmə rèen/ *n.* **1.** NAUT **UNDERWATER BOAT** a boat built to operate and travel for long periods underwater **2.** FOOD **LONG SANDWICH** a sandwich made with a long roll cut horizontally ■ *adj.* **UNDERWATER** taking place or growing underwater, especially in the sea ○ *submarine research* [Mid-17thC. Originally, "underwater."]

sub·ma·rine chas·er *n.* a small maneuverable ship designed for pursuing and attacking submarines (*informal*)

sub·ma·rin·er /sùb mə réenər, sùb mérrinər/ *n.* a crew member on a submarine

sub·max·il·lar·y /sub máksə lèrree/ *adj.* = **submandibular**

sub·me·di·ant /sub méedee ənt/ *n.* **1. SIXTH NOTE IN A SCALE** the sixth note in a major or minor scale **2. SUBMEDIANT HARMONY** a key, chord, or harmony based on a submediant

sub·merge /səb múrj/ (**-merged, -mer·ging, -mer·ges**) *v.* **1.** *vt.* **PLUNGE IN LIQUID** to put something into water or some other liquid so that all of it is under the surface **2.** *vi.* **GO UNDER WATER** to go under the surface of water or another liquid **3.** *vt.* **SUPPRESS** to keep something such as feelings or a secret hidden from others [Early 17thC. From Latin *submergere*, from *mergere* "to dip."] —**sub·merged** *adj.* —**sub·mer·gence** /səb múrjənss/ *n.*

sub·merse /səb múrss/ (**-mersed, -mers·ing, -mers·es**) *vt.* = **submerge** [Early 18thC. From Latin *submers-*, the past participle stem of *submergere* (see SUBMERGE).]

sub·mers·i·ble /səb múrssəb'l/ *adj.* **1. FOR UNDERWATER USE** designed for use under water **2. NOT DAMAGED UNDERWATER** capable of being put underwater without being damaged ■ *n.* **UNDERWATER BOAT** an underwater vessel, especially a small craft designed for use at deep levels

sub·mi·cro·scop·ic /sùb mìkrə skóppik/ *adj.* too small to be seen with an optical microscope —**sub·mi·cro·scop·i·cal·ly** *adv.*

sub·min·i·a·ture /sub mínnee əchər, -mínnee ə chòor, -mínnichər/ *adj.* **SMALLER THAN MINIATURE** smaller in size than miniature ■ *n.* **sub·min·i·a·ture, sub·min·i·a·ture cam·er·a VERY SMALL CAMERA** a camera substantially smaller than a compact camera, using film smaller than the 35mm miniature format

sub·min·i·a·tur·ize (**-ized, -iz·ing, -iz·es**) *vt.* to manufacture something that is very small in scale —**sub·min·i·a·tur·i·za·tion** /sùb mìnnee əchərə záysh'n, sùb mìnnəchərə záysh'n/ *n.*

sub·mis·sion /səb mísh'n/ *n.* **1. YIELDING, OR READINESS TO YIELD** a willingness to yield or surrender to somebody, or the act of doing so ○ *demanded nothing less than total submission to his authority* **2. IDEA SUBMITTED** something put forward for consideration or approval, e.g., a suggestion, proposal, or plan **3. ACT OF SUBMITTING SOMETHING** the act of submitting or handing in something, e.g., a proposal to be considered or written work to be judged **4.** LAW **AGREEMENT TO ARBITRATE** an agreement between parties in a dispute to have a contested matter arbitrated **5.** WRESTLING **WITHDRAWAL FROM WRESTLING BOUT** an acknowledgment by a wrestler that he or she cannot continue a bout because of pain

sub·mis·sive /səb míssiv/ *adj.* giving in or tending to give in to the demands or the authority of others —**sub·mis·sive·ly** *adv.* —**sub·mis·sive·ness** *n.*

sub·mit /səb mít/ (**-mit·ted, -mit·ting, -mits**) *v.* **1.** *vt.* PROPOSE OR HAND IN SOMETHING to hand something in or put something forward for consideration, approval, or judgment ○ *Applications must be submitted in triplicate.* **2.** *vi.* YIELD TO SOMEBODY to give in to somebody's authority, control, or demands **3.** *vi.* AGREE TO to agree to undergo something ○ *had to submit to intensive questioning* **4.** *vi.* DEFER TO to defer to another's knowledge, judgment, or experience **5.** *vt.* ARGUE A POINT to state or argue that something is the case (*formal*) [14thC. From Latin *submittere,* literally "to send under," from *mittere* "to send" (source of English *mission*).] —**sub·mit·ta·ble** *adj.* —**sub·mit·tal** *n.* —**sub·mit·ter** *n.*

WORD KEY: SYNONYMS

See Synonyms at ***yield.***

sub·mo·lec·u·lar /sùbmə lékyələr/ *adj.* relating to, consisting of, or involving a particle smaller than a molecule

sub·mon·tane /sùb món tàyn/ *adj.* **1.** ON LOWER PART OF A MOUNTAIN relating to or found in the foothills or on the lower slopes of a mountain **2.** PASSING UNDER A MOUNTAIN passing under or through a mountain —**sub·mon·tane·ly** *adv.*

sub·mu·co·sa /sùb myoo kṓzə/ *n.* a layer of loosely meshed microscopic fibers and associated cells occurring beneath a mucous membrane, e.g., in the small intestine [Late 19thC. From modern Latin, from Latin *mucosa* "mucous," the feminine of *mucosus,* from *mucus.*]

sub·mul·ti·ple /sub múltip'l/ *n.* EXACTLY DIVISIBLE NUMBER a number that can be divided into another an exact number of times and leave no remainder. For example, 7 is a submultiple of 35. ■ *adj.* EXACTLY DIVISIBLE INTO ANOTHER NUMBER able to be divided into another number an exact number of times without leaving a remainder [Late 17thC. From late Latin *submultiplus,* from *multiplus* (see MULTIPLE).]

sub·nor·mal /sub náwrm'l/ *adj.* lower or less than normal or average —**sub·nor·mal·i·ty** /sùb nawr mállətee/ *n.* —**sub·nor·mal·ly** /sub náwrm'lee/ *adv.*

sub·o·ce·an·ic /sùb ōshee ánnik/ *adj.* found, formed, or occurring beneath the sea or the sea bed

sub·or·bi·tal /sub áwrbət'l/ *adj.* **1.** BELOW THE EYE SOCKET relating to the region below the eye socket (**orbit**) **2.** ASTRON NOT MAKING A FULL ORBIT OF A PLANET not designed to make a complete orbit of the Earth or another celestial body

sub·or·der /súb àwrdər/ *n.* a taxonomic category that is a subdivision of an order and usually contains several similar families

sub·or·di·nar·y /sə báwrd'n èrree/ (*plural* **-ies**) *n.* a small shape or design such as a lozenge that can appear on a coat of arms and is smaller than the most prominent shape (**ordinary**)

sub·or·din·ate *adj.* /sə báwrd'nət/ **1.** LOWER IN RANK lower than somebody in rank or status **2.** OF SECONDARY IMPORTANCE secondary in importance **3.** GRAM MODIFYING acting as a modifying noun, adjective, or adverb within a sentence ■ *n.* /sə báwrd'nət/ SOMEBODY IN A JUNIOR POSITION somebody who is junior in rank or status ■ *vt.* /sə báwrd'n àyt/ (**-at·ed, -at·ing, -ates**) **1.** MAKE SOMETHING SECONDARY to treat something as less important and allow something else to dominate or take priority ○ *had increasingly subordinated her research to the demands of her busy work schedule* **2.** PLACE IN A LOWER RANK to give or regard somebody as having a more junior rank or status [15thC. From medieval Latin *subordinare,* literally "to place below," from Latin *ordinare* "to place" (source of English *ordain*), from, ultimately, *ordo* (see ORDER).] —**sub·or·di·nate·ly** /sə báwd'nətlee/ *adv.* —**sub·or·di·nate·ness** /sə báwrd'nətnəss/ *n.*

sub·or·di·nate clause *n.* a clause that cannot stand alone as a separate sentence since its meaning depends on the meaning of the main clause and simply gives additional information. In the sentence "We had to run because we were late," the clause "because we were late" is the subordinate clause and "We had to run" is the main clause.

sub·or·di·nate con·junc·tion, sub·or·di·nat·ing con·junc·tion *n.* a conjunction that introduces a subordinate clause, either one word such as "although," "because," or "since," or a group of words such as "in order that" or "as long as"

sub·or·di·na·tion /sə bàwrd'n áysh'n/ *n.* **1.** RELEGATION TO A SECONDARY POSITION the assignment of somebody or something to a position of secondary importance, status, or rank **2.** STATUS OF SUBORDINATE CLAUSE the position of a subordinate clause within a sentence

sub·or·di·na·tion·ism /sə bàwrd'n áysh'n ìzzəm/ *n.* the theological doctrine that the first person of the Holy Trinity is superior to the second, and the second to the third —**sub·or·di·na·tion·ist** *n.*

sub·or·di·na·tor /sə báwrd'n àytər/ *n.* GRAM = **subordinate conjunction**

sub·orn /sə báwrn/ (**-orned, -orn·ing, -orns**) *vt.* to persuade somebody to commit a crime or other wrongdoing, e.g., to bribe another party to tell lies in court [Early 16thC. From Latin *subornare,* literally "to equip secretly," from *ornare* (see ORNATE).] —**sub·or·na·tion** /sù bawr náysh'n/ *n.* —**sub·or·na·tive** /sə báwrnətiv/ *adj.* —**sub·orn·er** /-báwrnər/ *n.*

sub·ox·ide /sub ók sīd/ *n.* an oxide that contains less oxygen than the normal oxide formed by a particular element

sub·par·a·graph /súb pèrrə gràf, sub pérrə gràf/ *n.* a section of a paragraph, especially a numbered section of a paragraph in a legal document

sub·pe·na *n., vt.* = **subpoena**

sub·per·i·os·te·al /sùb perree óstee əl/ *adj.* relating to the region immediately underlying the connective tissue that surrounds bones (**periosteum**)

sub·phy·lum /sub fīləm/ (*plural* **-la** /-lə/) *n.* a subcategory of a phylum, used in the classification of animals and containing one or more similar classes. ◊ **subdivision** [Mid-20thC. From modern Latin, from *phylum* "phylum."] —**sub·phy·lar** *adj.*

sub·plot /súb plòt/ *n.* **1.** STORY SECONDARY TO MAIN STORY a second and less prominent story within a book, play, or movie **2.** SMALLER SECTION OF PLOT OF LAND a division of a plot of land, used especially for crop husbandry experiments

sub·poe·na /sə péenə/, **sub·pena** *n.* LEGAL ORDER DEMANDING EVIDENCE a written legal order summoning a witness or requiring evidence to be submitted to a court or similar deliberative body ■ *vt.* (**-naed, -na·ing, -nas; sub·pe·naed, sub·pe·na·ing, sub·pe·nas**) SUMMON TO GIVE EVIDENCE to issue a written legal order summoning a witness or requiring something to be submitted in evidence to a court or other deliberative body [15thC. From Latin *sub poena* "under penalty" (the first words of the writ), from *sub* "under" + *poena* "penalty."] —**sub·poe·naed** *adj.*

sub·po·lar /sub pṓlər/ *adj.* **1.** NEAR THE POLAR REGIONS being near the Arctic or the Antarctic polar region **2.** FOUND IN AREAS NEAR POLAR REGIONS relating to, belonging to, or found in the areas that border the Arctic and Antarctic

sub·pop·u·la·tion /sùb poppyə láysh'n/ *n.* a section of a statistical population that is identifiably separate or distinctive

sub·prin·ci·pal /sub prínssəp'l/ *n.* an assistant principal of a school

sub·re·gion /súb rèejən/ *n.* a part of a region, especially an ecological or zoogeographical division —**sub·re·gion·al** *adj.*

sub·rep·tion /səb répsh'n/ *n.* the deliberate concealment or distortion of the truth in order to gain some benefit, or the benefit gained by doing this (*archaic*) [Early 17thC. Via the Latin stem *subreption-* from, ultimately, *subripere* "to snatch secretly," from *rapere* (see RAPE[1]).] —**sub·rep·ti·tious** /sùb rep tíshəss/ *adj.*

sub·ring /súb rìng/ *n.* a ring that is a subset of a larger ring

sub·ro·gate /súbbrə gàyt/ (**-gat·ed, -gat·ing, -gates**) *vt.* to substitute one person for another, especially in transferring a right or claim [15thC. From Latin *subrogare* (see SURROGATE).]

sub·ro·ga·tion /sùbbrə gáysh'n/ *n.* the substitution of one claim for another, especially the transfer of the right to receive payment of a debt to somebody other than the original creditor

sub ro·sa /-rṓzə/ *adv.* in a secret or private way (*formal*) [Mid-17thC. From Latin, literally "under the rose," because the rose was an emblem of confidentiality hung above council tables to remind those present of the need for secrecy.]

sub·rou·tine /súbroo tèen/ *n.* COMPUT a sequence of programming statements that performs a single task and can be used repeatedly

subs. *abbr.* subscription

sub·scap·u·lar /sub skáppyələr/ *adj.* situated underneath, or on the underside of, the shoulder blade (**scapula**)

sub·scribe /səb skríb/ (**-scribed, -scrib·ing, -scribes**) *v.* **1.** *vi.* MAKE ADVANCE PAYMENT FOR SOMETHING to agree to pay for and receive something over a particular period of time, e.g., a periodical, series of books, or set of tickets to musical or dramatic performances **2.** *vti.* PROMISE TO GIVE MONEY REGULARLY to pledge to make regular donations to something, especially a charity **3.** *vti.* GUARANTEE TO INVEST IN SOMETHING to promise to pay for something when it will occur, e.g., the financing of a new business or a new issue of stock **4.** *vi.* SUPPORT VIEW to support or believe in a theory or view **5.** *vt.* LAW SIGN NAME ON LEGAL DOCUMENT to sign a legal document to indicate agreement or approval of its terms (*formal*) [15thC. From Latin *subscribere* "to write underneath," from *scribere* (see SCRIBE).] —**sub·scrib·er** *n.*

sub·script /súb skrìpt/ *n.* CHARACTER PRINTED ON LOWER LEVEL a character that is printed on a level lower than the rest of the characters on the line, e.g., the "2" in the chemical formula "H_2O." ◊ **superscript** ■ *adj.* PRINTED BELOW CHARACTER printed below a character in a line of type. ◊ **superscript** [Early 18thC. From Latin *subscript,* the past participle stem of *subscribere* (see SUBSCRIBE). Originally, "writing at the end of a document."]

sub·scrip·tion /səb skrípsh'n/ *n.* **1.** ADVANCE PAYMENT FOR SOMETHING an agreement to pay for and receive something over a particular period of time, e.g. a periodical, series of books, or set of tickets to musical or dramatic performances ○ *a subscription movie channel* **2.** PLEDGE TO PAY FOR SOMETHING a promise to pay for something when it will occur, e.g., the financing of a new business or a new issue of stock **3.** LAW SIGNING OF DOCUMENT OR SIGNATURE the process of signing, or a signature on, a legal document as an indication of approval of its terms (*formal*) **4.** TOTAL AGREEMENT OR APPROVAL a full agreement with or approval of something (*literary*) **5.** *U.K.* MEMBERSHIP FEE a fee paid for membership in a club or society [15thC. Originally in the sense "writing at the end of a document."]

sub·sel·lium /səb séllee əm/ (*plural* **-lia** /-lee ə/) *n.* = **misericord** [Early 18thC. From Latin, literally "low seat," from *sella* "seat." Originally used for "seat in an amphitheater."]

sub·se·quence[1] /súbsəkwənss/ *n.* something that happens after something else, or the occurrence of something after something else

sub·se·quence[2] /súb sèekwənss/ *n.* a sequence within another mathematical sequence

sub·se·quent /súbsəkwənt/ *adj.* happening or existing after something [15thC. Directly or via French *subséquent* from Latin *subsequent-,* the present participle stem of *subsequi* "to follow closely," from *sequi* (see SEQUENCE).]

sub·se·quent·ly /súbsəkwəntlee/ *adv.* occurring or happening after something else

sub·sere /súb sèer/ *n.* a secondary development of natural plant and animal communities after these have been destroyed by fire, flood, or human action [Early 20thC. Coined from SUB- + SERE[2].]

sub·serve /səb súrv/ (**-served, -serv·ing, -serves**) *vt.* to help to further, promote, or bring something about [Early 17thC. From Latin *subservire,* literally "to serve under," from *servire* (see SERVE).]

sub·ser·vi·ent /səb súrvee ənt/ *adj.* **1.** TOO EAGER TO OBEY too eager to follow the wishes or orders of others **2.** SECONDARY IN IMPORTANCE in a position of secondary importance **3.** INSTRUMENTAL IN SOMETHING helping to achieve or bring something about [Mid-17thC. From Latin *subservire,* literally "to serve under," from *servire* (see SERVE).] —**sub·ser·vi·ence** *n.* —**sub·ser·vi·ent·ly** *adv.*

sub·set /súb sèt/ *n.* MATH a mathematical set whose elements are contained in another set

sub·shrub /súb shrùb/ *n.* a low-growing plant with woody stems and main branches and nonwoody tips that die back each year [Mid-19thC. Translation of modern Latin *suffrutex,* from Latin *frutex* "shrub."] —**sub·shrub·by** *adj.*

sub·side /səb sīd/ (**-sid·ed, -sid·ing, -sides**) *vi.* **1.** DIMINISH IN INTENSITY to become less active or intense **2.** DROP TO LOWER LEVEL to sink to a low or lower level **3.** SINK TO BOTTOM OF LIQUID to sink to the bottom of a liquid **4.** GRADUALLY SIT OR LIE DOWN to sink into a sitting or lying position, e.g., out of exhaustion (*formal*) [Mid-17thC. From Latin *subsidere*, literally "to settle down," from *sidere* "to settle."] —**sub·sid·er** *n.*

sub·si·dence /səb sīd'nss, súbsədənss/ *n.* **1. SINKING OF LAND LEVEL** the sinking down of land resulting from natural shifts or human activity, frequently causing structural damage to buildings **2. DECREASING OF SOMETHING** the waning or lessening of something

sub·sid·i·ar·i·ty /səb sìddee érrətee/ *n.* **1. ASSIGNMENT OF POWER TO SMALL UNITS** the principle that political power should be exercised by the smallest possible unit of government **2. QUALITY OF BEING SUBSIDIARY** the fact or quality of being subsidiary [Mid-20thC. Translation of German *Subsidiarität*.]

sub·sid·i·ar·y /səb síddee èrree/ *adj.* **1. SECONDARY IN IMPORTANCE** having secondary importance or occupying a subordinate position **2. HELPING OR SUPPORTING** serving to aid, supplement, or support **3. AS SUBSIDY** in the form of a subsidy ■ *n.* (*plural* **-a·ries**) **1. SOMEBODY OR SOMETHING AUXILIARY** somebody or something that occupies a secondary or subordinate position **2. COMPANY CONTROLLED BY LARGER ONE** a company controlled or owned by a larger one —**sub·sid·i·ar·i·ly** *adv.* —**sub·sid·i·ar·i·ness** *n.*

sub·sid·i·ar·y com·pa·ny *n.* = **subsidiary** *n.* 2

sub·si·dize /súbssə dīz/ (**-dized, -diz·ing, -diz·es**) *vt.* to contribute money to somebody or something, especially in the form of a government grant to a private company, organization, or charity to help it to continue to function —**sub·si·diz·a·ble** *adj.* —**sub·si·di·za·tion** /sùbssədə záysh'n/ *n.* —**sub·si·diz·er** /súbssə dīzər/ *n.*

sub·si·dy /súbsədee/ (*plural* **-dies**) *n.* **1.** FIN, ECON **MONEY GIVEN BY GOVERNMENT** a grant or gift of money from a government to a private company, organization, or charity to help it to continue to function **2.** FIN **HELP WITH EXPENSES** a monetary gift or contribution to somebody or something, especially to pay expenses [14thC. Via Anglo-Norman from Latin *subsidium* "reserve troops," from, ultimately, *sedere* (see SEDENTARY).]

sub·sist /səb síst/ (**-sist·ed, -sist·ing, -sists**) *v.* **1.** *vi.* **MANAGE TO LIVE** to remain alive or viable, especially with the help of something **2.** *vt.* **MAINTAIN SOMEBODY OR SOMETHING** to support or maintain somebody by providing something that is needed, e.g., by supplying troops with food or businesses with capital (*formal*) **3.** *vi.* **BE ATTRIBUTABLE TO SOMETHING** to have something as its reason or origin (*formal*) **4.** *vi.* **INHERE IN SOMETHING** to reside in or consist of something (*formal*) **5.** *vi.* PHILOS, MATH **HAVE ABSTRACT EXISTENCE** to have a timeless conceptual existence (*refers to numbers or mathematical sets*) [Mid-16thC. Directly or via French *subsister* from Latin *subsistere*, literally "to stand up to," from *sistere* (see ASSIST).] —**sub·sis·tent** *adj.* —**sub·sist·er** *n.*

sub·sis·tence /səb sístənss/ *n.* **1. CONDITION OF MANAGING TO STAY ALIVE** the condition of being or managing to stay alive, especially when there is barely enough food or money for survival **2. CONTINUING TO EXIST** the condition of continuing to exist **3.** MATH, PHILOS **QUALITY OF ABSTRACT EXISTENCE** the quality that something possesses of existing independently, timelessly, or by virtue of its essence

sub·sis·tence al·low·ance *n.* **1. MONEY COVERING SPECIAL EXPENSES** a sum of money given to an employee to cover special expenses incurred in the performance of his or her work **2. ADVANCE ON SOMEBODY'S FIRST WAGE** an advance paid to a new employee or soldier to help to meet living costs until wages begin to be paid

sub·sis·tence farm·ing *n.* farming that generates only enough produce to feed the farmer's family, with little or nothing left over to sell —**sub·sis·tence farm·er** *n.*

sub·sis·tence wage *n.* a wage so low that it is barely enough to live on

sub·so·cial /sub sṓsh'l/ *adj.* used to describe insects that associate with others but without any fixed or organized social structure —**sub·so·cial·ly** *adv.*

sub·soil /súb sòyl/ *n.* **SOIL BENEATH TOPSOIL** the compacted soil beneath the topsoil ■ *vt.* (**-soiled, -soil·ing, -soils**) **TURN LOWER LAYER OF SOIL** to turn, break, or stir the compacted soil beneath the topsoil

sub·soil·er /súb sòylər/ *n.* **1. PLOW FOR BREAKING UP SUBSOIL** a farm implement consisting of a frame with long stout vertical tines. It is drawn through the soil to break up compacted subsoil in order to improve drainage and aeration. **2. SOMEBODY OPERATING SUBSOILER** somebody who operates a subsoiler

sub·so·lar /sub sṓlər/ *adj.* **1. DIRECTLY BENEATH SUN** located directly below the Sun on the Earth's surface when the Sun is at its highest point **2. LOCATED BETWEEN TROPICS** located in the equatorial region that lies between the Tropics of Cancer and Capricorn

sub·song /súb sòng/ *n.* an unstructured birdsong that is quieter and lower-pitched than full birdsong and is often performed by young adult birds

sub·son·ic /sub sónnik/ *adj.* **1. SLOWER THAN SPEED OF SOUND** slower than 760 mph/1,220 kmph, the speed at which sound travels in air **2. FLYING SLOWER THAN SOUND** flying at speeds slower than the speed of sound, especially not designed to fly above the speed of sound **3.** PHON = **infrasonic** —**sub·son·i·cal·ly** *adv.*

sub·spe·cial·ize /sub spéshə līz/ (**-ized, -iz·ing, -iz·es**) *vi.* to work in a very narrow field or area of study within an existing specialty

sub·spe·cial·ty /sub spésh'ltee/ (*plural* **-ties**) *n.* a very narrow or specialized field of study, within an existing specialty

sub·spe·cies /súb spēesheez, -seez/ (*plural* **-cies**) *n.* a category used to classify plants and animals whose populations are distinct, e.g., in distribution, appearance, or feeding habits, but can still interbreed —**sub·spe·cif·ic** /sùb spə síffik/ *adj.* —**sub·spe·cif·i·cal·ly** *adv.*

subst. *abbr.* **1.** substantive **2.** substitute

sub·stage /súb stàyj/ *n.* a component assembly in a microscope that contains the condenser, mirror, or other accessories and is located below the stage

sub·stance /súbstənss/ *n.* **1. MATERIAL** a particular kind of matter or material **2. TANGIBLE PHYSICAL MATTER** physical reality that can be touched and felt **3. PRACTICAL VALUE** real or practical value or importance ○ *There was nothing of substance in the document.* **4. MATERIAL WEALTH** wealth in the form of money and possessions **5. GIST OF MEANING** the actual meaning of something said or written ○ *the substance of their argument* **6.** PHILOS **UNCHANGING ESSENCE** the unchanging essence of something **7.** PHILOS **SOMETHING INDIVIDUAL AND CAUSED** something that is individual and caused [13thC. Via French from Latin *substantia* "essence" (a translation of Greek *hupostasis*), from, ultimately, Latin *substare*, literally "to stand under," from *stare* (see STAND).]

sub·stance a·buse *n.* the excessive consumption or misuse of any substance for the sake of its nontherapeutic effects on the mind or body, especially drugs or alcohol

sub·stance P *n.* a peptide found in body tissues, especially nervous tissue, that is involved in the transmission of pain and in inflammation

sub·stan·dard /sub stándərd/ *adj.* below the expected or required standard of quality

sub·stan·tial /səb stánsh'l/ *adj.* **1. CONSIDERABLE** considerable in amount, extent, value, or importance **2. SOLID OR STURDY** solidly built **3. FILLING** providing a lot of nourishment **4. RICH** wealthy and prosperous **5. REAL AND TANGIBLE** actual and real in a palpable way **6.** PHILOS **CONSISTING OF SUBSTANCE** consisting of or involving substance ■ *n.* **IMPORTANT PART** an important or essential part [14thC. Directly or via French *substantiel* from Christian Latin *substantialis* "having substance" (a translation of Greek *hupostatikos*), from, ultimately, *substare*, literally "to stand under," formed from *stare* (see STAND).] —**sub·stan·ti·al·i·ty** /səb stànshee állətee/ *n.* —**sub·stan·tial·ness** *n.*

sub·stan·tial·ism /səb stánsh'l ìzzəm/ *n.* the philosophical doctrine that beings or entities of substantial reality underlie all phenomena —**sub·stan·tial·ist** *n.*

sub·stan·tial·ize /səb stánsh'l īz/ (**-ized, -iz·ing, -izes**) *vti.* to make something that is imaginary, theoretical, or spiritual become palpable, or to become palpable

sub·stan·tial·ly /səb stánsh'lee/ *adv.* **1. CONSIDERABLY** in an extensive, substantial, or ample way **2. ESSENTIALLY** generally or in essence

sub·stan·ti·ate /səb stánshee àyt/ (**-at·ed, -at·ing, -ates**) *vt.* **1. PROVE OR SUPPORT SOMETHING** to confirm that something is true or valid **2. MAKE SOMETHING ACTUAL** to give something an actual physical existence [Mid-17thC. From medieval Latin *substantiare*, literally "to give substance to," from Latin *substantia* "substance," from, ultimately, *stare* (see STAND).] —**sub·stan·ti·a·tive** *adj.* —**sub·stan·ti·a·ble** *adj.* —**sub·stan·ti·a·tion** /səb stànshee áysh'n/ *n.* —**sub·stan·ti·a·tor** *n.*

sub·stan·ti·val /sùbstən tīv'l/ *adj.* = **substantive** *adj.* 3 —**sub·stan·ti·val·ly** *adv.*

sub·stan·tive *n.* /súbstəntiv, səb stántiv/ GRAM **NOUN** a noun, or a word or group of words used like a noun ■ *adj.* /súb stəntiv/ **1. WITH PRACTICAL IMPORTANCE** with practical importance, value, or effect ○ *a substantive agreement* **2. ESSENTIAL** relating to the substance of something **3.** GRAM **USED LIKE NOUN** relating to or used like a noun **4.** GRAM **EXPRESSING EXISTENCE** expressing existence, as e.g., the verb "to be" **5. INDEPENDENT** continuing independently **6. SUBSTANTIAL** substantial in amount or quantity ○ *a substantive meal* **7.** LAW **RELATING TO LEGAL PRINCIPLES NOT PROCEDURE** relating to the essential principles that a court applies in its work, not to the rules of procedure and practice. ◊ **adjective** **8. DIRECTLY ATTACHING AS DYE COLOR** attaching as a color directly to a material being dyed without the use of a fixing substance **9.** MIL **PERMANENT** used to describe a rank or appointment that is permanent —**sub·stan·tive·ly** *adv.*

sub·stan·tive right *n.* a basic human right such as the right to life or liberty that is regarded as existing naturally and indispensably

sub·stan·ti·vize /səb stánti vīz/ (**-vized, -viz·ing, -viz·es**) *vt.* to make a word or words function like a noun —**sub·stan·ti·v·i·za·tion** /səb stàntəvə záysh'n/ *n.*

sub·sta·tion /súb stàysh'n/ *n.* **1.** ELEC **BRANCH OF POWER STATION** a branch of a main electrical power station where electrical current is converted, redistributed, or modified in strength **2.** MAIL **SUBSIDIARY POST OFFICE OR STATION** any office, building, or installation that is a branch of something larger, especially a branch of a post office

sub·stit·u·ent /səb stíchoo ənt/ *n.* an atom or group of atoms that replaces another atom or group in a molecule [Late 19thC. From Latin *substituere*, literally "to set up under," from *statuere* (see STATUE).]

sub·sti·tut·a·ble /súbstə to͞otəb'l/ *adj.* capable of replacing or taking the place of another —**sub·sti·tut·a·bil·it·y** /sùbstə tootə bíllətee/ *n.*

sub·sti·tute /súbstə to͞ot/ *v.* (**-tut·ed, -tut·ing, -tutes**) **1.** *vti.* **REPLACE OR TAKE PLACE OF** to put somebody or something in place of another, or to take the place of another (*often passive*) **2.** *vt.* CHEM **REPLACE ATOM OR ATOMS IN MOLECULE** to replace an atom or group of atoms in a molecule with another atom or group **3.** *vt.* MATH **REPLACE MATHEMATICAL ELEMENT WITH EQUIVALENT** to replace one mathematical element with another of equal value ■ *n.* **1. SOMEBODY OR SOMETHING REPLACING ANOTHER** somebody or something that takes the place of another, e.g., a team member in a game who is ready to replace another on the field **2.** GRAM **GRAMMATICALLY REPLACEABLE WORD** a word that can take the place of another grammatically, such as "did" for "yelled" in the sentence "I yelled and he did, too" [15thC. From Latin *substitutus*, the past participle of *substituere*, literally "to set up under," from *statuere* (see STATUE).] —**sub·sti·tu·ter** *n.*

WORD KEY: USAGE

substitute or **replace**? The constructions used by these two words are different, although the resulting meaning is usually the same. You ***substitute*** item A *for* item B, but ***replace*** item B *with* (or less often *by*) item A.

sub·sti·tute teach·er *n.* a teacher who takes the place of another temporarily

sub·sti·tu·tion /sùbstə to͞osh'n/ *n.* **1. ACT OF REPLACING** the replacement of somebody or something with another, especially one team member with another **2. SOMEBODY OR SOMETHING THAT REPLACES** somebody or something that replaces another, especially one team member who replaces another **3.** MATH **MATHEMATICAL ELEMENT REPLACING EQUIVALENT** the replacement of one mathematical element with another of equal value **4.** LOGIC **REPLACEMENT OF LOGICAL EXPRESSION** the replacement of one logical expression with another, or the expression so replaced —**sub·sti·tu·tion·al** *adj.* —**sub·sti·tu·tion·al·ly** *adv.*

sub·sti·tu·tive /súbstə to͞otiv/ *adj.* acting or usable as a substitute [Early 17thC. Partly formed from SUBSTITUTE, partly from Latin *substitutivus*, from the past participle stem of *substituere* (see SUBSTITUTE).] —**sub·sti·tu·tive·ly** *adv.* —**sub·sti·tu·tiv·i·ty** /sùbstə too tívvətee/ *n.*

sub·strate /súb stràyt/ *n.* **1.** CHEM **SOMETHING ACTED UPON IN BIOCHEMICAL REACTION** a substance that is acted upon, especially by an enzyme, in a biochemical reaction

2. ELECTRON ENG **SEMICONDUCTOR CRYSTAL USED AS BASE** a single crystal of a semiconductor used as the basis for an integrated circuit or transistor **3.** BIOL = **substratum** *n.* **6** **4.** SCI = **medium** *n.* **8** [Early 19thC. Anglicization of SUBSTRATUM.]

sub·strat·o·sphere /sub stráttə sfeer/ *n.* the lowest layer of the Earth's atmosphere, at a height of about 12 mi./20 km above the Earth. ◊ **exosphere, ionosphere, stratosphere**

sub·stra·tum /súb strāytəm, -stràttəm/ (*plural* **-ta** /-tə/) *n.* **1. UNDERLYING BASE** an underlying base, layer, or element **2.** AGRIC = **subsoil** **3.** GEOL = **bedrock** **4.** PHOTOGRAPHY **BASE FOR EMULSION** a layer of a substance placed on a film or plate as a foundation for an emulsion **5.** LING **SET OF RETAINED INDIGENOUS LINGUISTIC FEATURES** a set of linguistic features retained from the speech of an indigenous culture, especially one that influences the language of a colonizer. ◊ **superstratum** **6.** BIOL **NONLIVING FOUNDATION FOR GROWING ORGANISM** the nonliving material or base on which an organism lives or grows **7.** PHILOS **ESSENTIAL SUBSTANCE** the essential substance of something [Mid-17thC. From modern Latin, a noun use of the neuter past participle of Latin *substernere* "to spread underneath," from *sternere* (see STRATUM).] —**sub·stra·tal** *adj.* —**sub·stra·tive** *adj.*

sub·struc·ture /súb strùkchər/ *n.* **1.** BUILDING **FOUNDATION OF BUILDING** the foundation of an erected structure **2. UNDERLYING STRUCTURE** any underlying structure that supports or gives strength to something —**sub·struc·tur·al** /sub strukchərəl/ *adj.*

sub·sume /səb so͞om/ (**-sumed, -sum·ing, -sumes**) *vt.* **1. INCLUDE SOMETHING** to include or incorporate something into a larger order, category, or classification **2. MAKE SUBJECT TO RULE** to show that a rule applies to something [Mid-16thC. From medieval Latin *subsumere*, literally "to take up so as to include," from Latin *sumere* (see SUMPTUOUS). Originally, "to make one point within another."] —**sub·sum·a·ble** *adj.*

sub·sump·tion /səb súmpsh'n/ *n.* **1. ACT OF SUBSUMING** the act of subsuming or the fact of being subsumed **2. SOMETHING SUBSUMED** something that is subsumed [Mid-17thC. From the medieval Latin stem *subsumption-*, from, ultimately, *subsumere* (see SUBSUME).] —**sub·sump·tive** *adj.*

sub·sur·face /súb sùrfəss/ *adj.* **LOCATED BELOW SURFACE OF SOMETHING** relating to or located in an area that lies just below the surface of something, especially of the Earth or a body of water ■ *n.* **MATERIAL BELOW SURFACE** material that is located just below the surface of something, especially of the Earth or a body of water

sub·sys·tem /súb sìstəm/ *n.* a system that forms part of a larger system

sub·tan·gent /súb tànjənt/ *n.* the part of the x-axis included by the ordinate of a given point on a curve and the tangent at that point

sub·teen /súb teen/ *n.* = **preteen** [Mid-20thC]

sub·tem·per·ate /sub témpərət/ *adj.* relating to or occurring in the colder areas of the Temperate Zone

sub·ten·ant /sub ténnənt/ *n.* somebody who rents property from a tenant who in turn rents it from the owner —**sub·ten·an·cy** *n.*

sub·tend /səb ténd/ (**-tend·ed, -tend·ing, -tends**) *vt.* **1.** GEOM **EXTEND OPPOSITE** to extend from one side to the other, opposite an angle or side of a geometric figure **2.** BOT **ENCLOSE A PART** to lie underneath something so as to surround or enclose it [Late 16thC. From Latin *subtendere* "to stretch underneath," from *tendere* (see TEND[1]).]

sub·ter·fuge /súbtər fyo͞oj/ *n.* a plan, action, or device designed to hide a real objective, or the process of hiding a real objective [Late 16thC. Directly or via French from late Latin *subterfugium*, from Latin *subterfugere* "to flee secretly," from *fugere* (see FUGITIVE).]

sub·ter·mi·nal /sub túrmən'l/ *adj.* positioned very near the end of something

sub·ter·ra·ne·an /sùb tə ráynee ən/, **sub·ter·ra·ne·ous** /sùb tə ráynee əss/ *adj.* **1. UNDERGROUND** existing or situated below ground level **2. SECRET** existing or carried on in secret [Early 17thC. Formed from Latin *subterraneus* "underground," from *terra* (see TERRACE).] —**sub·ter·ra·ne·an·ly** *adv.*

sub·text /súb tèkst/ *n.* an underlying meaning or message —**sub·tex·tu·al** /sub tékschoo əl/ *adj.*

sub·thresh·old /sub thréshōld/ *adj.* used to describe a stimulus that is not strong or large enough to have an effect

sub·tile /sútt'l/ *adj.* subtle (*archaic*) [14thC. Via French *subtil* from Latin *subtilis* (see SUBTLE).]

sub·til·i·sin /sub tílləssin/ *n.* an enzyme that breaks down proteins and peptides and is derived from a bacterium [Mid-20thC. Formed from modern Latin *subtilis* "subtle," from Latin (see SUBTLE).]

sub·til·ize /sútt'l īz, súbtə līz/ (**-ized, -iz·ing, -iz·es**) *v.* **1.** *vti.* **BE SUBTLE IN DISCUSSING** to make or use subtle distinctions in discussing something **2.** *vt.* **REFINE SOMETHING** to make something increasingly refined —**sub·til·i·za·tion** /sùtt'lə záysh'n, sùbtələ-/ *n.* —**sub·til·iz·er** /sútt'l īzər, súbtə līzər/ *n.*

sub·ti·tle /súb tīt'l/ *n.* **1. CAPTION FOR FOREIGN-LANGUAGE MOVIE** a printed translation of the dialogue in a foreign-language film, usually appearing at the bottom of the screen. ◊ **supertitle, surtitle** **2. CAPTION IN SILENT MOVIE** a caption for the action or dialogue of a silent movie, appearing at intervals as a full-screen panel **3.** = **closed caption** (*often used in the plural*) **4. LESSER TITLE** a second and subsidiary title for something such as a book ■ *vt.* (**-tled, -tling, -tles**) **1. PROVIDE SUBTITLES FOR** to provide subtitles for a movie **2.** to give a subtitle to something such as a book —**sub·tit·u·lar** /sub tíchələr/ *adj.*

sub·tle /sútt'l/ *adj.* **1. SLIGHT** slight and not obvious **2. PLEASANTLY UNDERSTATED** pleasantly delicate and understated **3. ABLE TO MAKE REFINED JUDGMENTS** intelligent, experienced, or sensitive enough to make refined judgments and distinctions **4. INGENIOUS** cleverly indirect and ingenious [14thC. Via Old French *sutil* from Latin *subtilis* "fine, thin," from, ultimately, *sub tela*, literally "beneath the weaving," from *sub* "beneath" + *tela* "weaving." The underlying idea is "finely woven."] —**sub·tly** *adv.* —**sub·tle·ness** *n.*

sub·tle·ty /sútt'ltee/ (*plural* **-ties**) *n.* **1. QUALITY OF BEING SUBTLE** the quality or state of being subtle **2. FINE DISTINCTION** a distinction that is difficult to make but is important (*often used in the plural*)

sub·tor·rid /sub táwrid/ *adj.* = **subtropical**

sub·to·tal /súb tōt'l/ *n.* **TOTAL OF PARTIAL SET OF FIGURES** a sum or total of part of a set of figures ■ *vt.* (**-taled, -tal·ing, -tals**) **CALCULATE SUBTOTAL OF** to calculate the total of part of a set of figures

sub·tract /səb trákt/ (**-tract·ed, -tract·ing, -tracts**) *v.* **1.** *vti.* ARITH **DEDUCT ARITHMETICALLY** to perform the arithmetical calculation of deducting one number or quantity from another **2.** *vt.* **REMOVE SOMETHING FROM SOMETHING LARGER** to withdraw or take away something from a larger unit [Mid-16thC. From Latin *subtract-*, the past participle stem of *subtrahere* "to pull away," from *trahere* (see TRACTOR).] —**sub·tract·er** *n.*

sub·trac·tion /səb tráksh'n/ *n.* **1.** ARITH **DEDUCTION OF NUMBER** the act or process of deducting one number or quantity from another. Symbol **-** **2. REMOVAL FROM SOMETHING LARGER** a withdrawal or deduction of something from a larger whole **3.** LAW **WITHDRAWAL OF BENEFIT** the withdrawal or withholding of a benefit

sub·trac·tive /səb tráktiv/ *adj.* **1.** ARITH **ABLE TO SUBTRACT** with the power to subtract something **2.** ARITH **INDICATING SUBTRACTION** indicating or needing subtraction **3.** PHYS **REMAINING AFTER ABSORPTION BY TINTED FILTERS** used to describe the color that remains after all other components of the visible spectrum have been absorbed by tinted filters

sub·tra·hend /súbtrə hènd/ *n.* ARITH a number that is to be deducted from another number. ◊ **minuend** [Late 17thC. From Latin *subtrahendus*, literally "to be subracted," a form of *subtrahere* "to pull away," from *trahere* (see TRACTOR).]

sub·tribe /súb trīb/ *n.* a subdivision of a tribe

sub·trop·i·cal /sub tróppik'l/ *adj.* relating to or found in areas between tropical and temperate regions, and experiencing tropical conditions at some times of the year or nearly tropical conditions all year round

sub·type /súb tīp/ *n.* a type that is a subdivision of a larger type —**sub·typ·i·cal** /sub típpik'l/ *adj.*

su·bu·late /súbbyə lāyt, -lət/ *adj.* used to describe a plant part that is long and thin and tapers to a point [Mid-18thC. From modern Latin *subulatus*, from Latin *subula* "awl."]

sub·um·brel·la /súb um brèllə/ *n.* the inwardly curving underside of a jellyfish

sub·u·nit /súb yo͞onit/ *n.* **1. SUBSIDIARY UNIT** a unit that forms part of a larger unit **2.** CHEM **SEPARABLE PART OF MOLECULE** a part of a large molecule or complex that can be dissociated from the whole without rupture of covalent chemical bonds

sub·u·nit vac·cine *n.* a vaccine that creates a bodily immunity to a virus or bacterium from whose DNA the vaccine is made

sub·urb /sú bùrb/ *n.* a district, especially a residential one, on the edge of a city or large town [14thC. Directly or via French *suburbe* from Latin *suburbium*, literally "near a city," from *urbs* (see URBAN).]

sub·ur·ban /sə búrbən/ *adj.* **1. RELATING TO SUBURB** relating to, belonging to, or located in a suburb **2. RESEMBLING SUBURB** resembling a suburb or its residents

sub·ur·ban·ite /sə búrbə nīt/ *n.* somebody who lives in the suburbs

sub·ur·ban·ize /sə búrbə nīz/ (**-ized, -iz·ing, -izes**) *vt.* to give something an appearance or character typical of the suburbs —**sub·ur·ban·i·za·tion** /sə bùrbənə záysh'n/ *n.*

sub·ur·bi·a /sə búrbee ə/ *n.* suburbs collectively, or the people who live in them

sub·vene /səb veen/ (**-vened, -ven·ing, -venes**) *vi.* to happen or appear in a helpful way, especially in avoiding or preventing something (*formal*) [Mid-18thC. From Latin *subvenire*, literally "to come from below," from *venire* (see VENUE).]

sub·ven·tion /səb vénsh'n/ *n.* (*formal*) **1. GRANT OR SUBSIDY** a sum of money given by an official body such as a government, especially to an institution of learning, study, or research **2. AID OR SUPPORT** the giving of help or support, especially financial —**sub·ven·tion·ar·y** *adj.*

sub·ver·sion /səb vúrzh'n, -vúrsh'n/ *n.* **1. ACTIVITY UNDERMINING GOVERNMENT** an action, plan, or activity intended to undermine or overthrow a government or other institution **2. OVERTHROW OF SOMETHING** the destruction or ruining of something [14thC. Directly or via French from the late Latin stem *subversion-*, from, ultimately, *subvertere* (see SUBVERT).]

sub·ver·sive /səb vúrssiv/ *adj.* **DESIGNED TO OVERTHROW GOVERNMENT** intended or likely to undermine or overthrow a government or other institution ■ *n.* **SOMEBODY INVOLVED IN SUBVERSIVE ACTIVITIES** somebody involved in activities intended to undermine or overthrow a government or other institution —**sub·ver·sive·ly** *adv.* —**sub·ver·sive·ness** *n.*

sub·vert /səb vúrt/ (**-vert·ed, -vert·ing, -verts**) *vt.* to undermine or overthrow a government or other institution [14thC. Directly or via Old French *subvertir* from Latin *subvertere*, literally "to turn from below," from *vertere* (see VERSE).] —**sub·vert·er** *n.*

sub·vi·rus /sub vīrəss/ *n.* an infective agent such as a prion that is structurally more primitive than a virus —**sub·vi·ral** *adj.*

sub·vo·cal /sub vōk'l/ *adj.* LING mouthed or mentally pictured but not sounded out loud —**sub·vo·cal·ly** *adv.*

sub·vo·cal·ize /sub vōkə līz/ (**-ized, -iz·ing, -izes**) *vti.* LING to mouth words or other speech sounds without saying them out loud —**sub·vo·cal·i·za·tion** /sub vōkələ záysh'n/ *n.*

sub·way /súb wāy/ *n.* **1. UNDERGROUND RAILROAD** an underground railroad, especially one powered by electricity **2.** *U.K.* **UNDERGROUND PASSAGE** a passage under a road or railroad for pedestrians to get to the other side

sub·ze·ro /sùb zeerō/ *adj.* being below zero degrees in temperature

suc·cah *n.* = **sukkah**

suc·ceed /sək seed/ (**-ceed·ed, -ceed·ing, -ceeds**) *v.* **1.** *vi.* **ACHIEVE INTENTION** to manage to do what is planned or attempted ○ *We succeeded in persuading them to change their decision.* **2.** *vi.* **GAIN FAME, WEALTH, OR POWER** to realize a goal, especially to gain fame, wealth, or power **3.** *vi.* **MAKE SIGNIFICANT PROGRESS** to do well in an activity, making admirable progress or recording impressive achievements ○ *She was one of the first women to succeed in the sciences.* **4.** *vi.* **PROSPER** to thrive or prosper **5.** *vti.* **BE NEXT AFTER SOMEBODY** to follow somebody occupying a post or position ○ *Mary succeeded him as president over a year ago.* **6.** *vt.* **FOLLOW IN TIME** to come after something in time (*often passive*) **7.** *vi.* **BE INHERITED BY SOMEBODY** to pass to somebody as an inheritance (*formal*) [14thC. Directly or via

French *succéder* from Latin *succedere*, literally "to go after," from *cedere* (see CEDE).] —**suc·ceed·a·ble** *adj.* —**suc·ceed·er** *n.*

suc·cen·tor /sək séntər/ *n.* CHR a deputy to a precentor [Mid-17thC. From late Latin, from Latin *succinere* "to sing to," from *canere* (see CANT²).] —**suc·cen·tor·ship** *n.*

suc·cès de scan·dale /sük sày də skaaN dáal/ (*plural* **suc·cès de scan·dale**) *n.* something such as a book, movie, or play that is successful because it is controversial, or the success that is gained as a result of controversy (*literary*) [From French, literally "success of scandal"]

suc·cès d'es·time /sük sày dəs teém/ (*plural* **suc·cès d'es·time**) *n.* something such as a book, movie, or play that is successful with the critics but not with the public, or the success that is gained through critical acclaim (*literary*) [From French, literally "success of esteem"]

suc·cès fou /sük sày fóo/ (*plural* **suc·cès fous**) *n.* an overwhelming success (*literary*) [From French, literally "mad success"]

suc·cess /sək séss/ *n.* **1.** ACHIEVEMENT OF DESIRED AIM the achievement of something planned or attempted **2.** ATTAINMENT OF FAME, WEALTH, OR POWER impressive achievement, especially the attainment of fame, wealth, or power **3.** SOMETHING THAT TURNS OUT WELL something that turns out as planned or intended **4.** SOMEBODY WHO HAS SIGNIFICANT ACHIEVEMENTS somebody who has a record of achievement, especially in gaining wealth, fame, or power [Mid-16thC. From Latin *successus*, from *success-*, the past participle stem of *succedere* (see SUCCEED). The original English sense was "result, outcome."]

suc·cess·ful /sək séssf'l/ *adj.* **1.** TURNING OUT WELL having the intended result **2.** POPULAR popular and making a lot of money **3.** WITH RECORD OF SIGNIFICANT ACHIEVEMENTS having achieved or gained much, especially wealth, fame, or power —**suc·cess·ful·ly** *adv.* —**suc·cess·ful·ness** *n.*

suc·ces·sion /sək sésh'n/ *n.* **1.** SERIES IN TIME a sequence of people or things coming one after the other in time ○ *rented a succession of dingy apartments around town* **2.** FOLLOWING the following of one thing after another ○ *three wins in succession.* **3.** TAKING UP OF TITLE OR POSITION the assumption of a position or title, the right to take it up, or the order in which it is taken up **4.** DEVELOPMENT OF PLANT AND ANIMAL COMMUNITY the series of changes that create a full-fledged plant and animal community, e.g., from the colonization of bare rock to the establishment of a forest —**suc·ces·sion·al** *adj.* —**suc·ces·sion·al·ly** *adv.*

suc·ces·sion crop *n.* a crop that follows another crop as a successive planting, or a crop of a variety with a different rate of growth

suc·ces·sive /sək séssiv/ *adj.* following in an uninterrupted sequence —**suc·ces·sive·ly** *adv.* —**suc·ces·sive·ness** *n.*

suc·ces·sor /sək séssər/ *n.* somebody or something that follows another and takes up the same position —**suc·ces·so·ral** *adj.*

suc·cess sto·ry *n.* somebody or something that is very successful

suc·ci·nate /súksə nàyt/ *n.* a salt or ester of succinic acid [Late 18thC. Formed from SUCCINIC.]

suc·cinct /sək síngkt, -síngt/ *adj.* **1.** BRIEF AND TO THE POINT showing or expressed with brevity and clarity, with no wasted words **2.** ENCLOSED OR RESTRICTED confined tightly by something such as a belt or girdle (*archaic*) [15thC. Directly or via French from Latin *succinctus*, the past participle of *succingere*, literally "to encompass from below," from *cingere* (see PRECINCT).] —**suc·cinct·ly** *adv.* —**suc·cinct·ness** *n.*

suc·cin·ic /sək sínnik/ *adj.* **1.** RELATING TO SUCCINIC ACID relating to or containing succinic acid or succinate **2.** RELATING TO AMBER relating to or obtained from amber [Late 18thC. Formed from Latin *succinum* "amber," from *succus* (see SUCCUS).]

suc·cin·ic ac·id *n.* a colorless odorless acid synthesized or derived from amber and the tissues of plants and animals. It is used in making lacquers, perfumes, and pharmaceuticals. Formula: $C_4H_6O_4$.

suc·cin·yl·cho·line /sùksən'l kō leen, sùksənil-/ *n.* a drug used to induce relaxation of muscles during surgery under general anesthesia, electroconvulsive therapy, or other procedures [Mid-20thC. Coined from SUCCINIC (ACID) + -YL + CHOLINE.]

suc·cor /súkər/ *n.* (*literary*) **1.** HELP FOR SOMEBODY OR SOMETHING help or relief for somebody or something **2.** SOMEBODY OR SOMETHING GIVING HELP somebody or something that provides help or relief ■ *vt.* (**-cored, -cor·ing, -cors**) GIVE HELP TO to provide help or relief to somebody or something (*literary*) [13thC. Via Old French *socorre* from Latin *succurrere*, literally "to run under," formed from *currere* "to run" (source of English *current*). The underlying idea is "running to someone's assistance."] —**suc·cor·a·ble** *adj.* —**suc·cor·er** *n.* —**suc·cor·less** *adj.*

suc·co·ry /súkəree/ *n.* = **chicory** [Mid-16thC. Alteration of obsolete French *cicorée* (see CHICORY) on the model of Middle Low German *suckerie* and Middle Dutch *sūkerie.*]

suc·co·tash /súkə tàsh/ *n.* kernels of corn and lima beans cooked together, often with tomatoes [Mid-18thC. From Narragansett *msiquatash*, literally "boiled corn or maize and beans."]

Suc·coth, Suc·cot *n.* = **Sukkoth**

suc·cour /súkər/ *n., vt.* U.K. = **succor**

suc·cu·bus /súkyəbəss/ (*plural* **-bi** /-bì/ *or* **-bus·es**) *n.* a woman demon that was believed in medieval times to have sexual intercourse with men while they were asleep. ◊ **incubus** [14thC. From medieval Latin, an alteration (modeled on English *incubus*) of late Latin *succuba*, literally "one who lies under another," from, ultimately, *cubare* "to lie."]

suc·cu·lent /súkyələnt/ *adj.* **1.** JUICY AND TASTY juicy and pleasant to the taste **2.** WITH FLESHY WATER-STORING PARTS with thick fleshy leaves and stems that can store water **3.** INTERESTING exciting and interesting (*informal*) ■ *n.* SUCCULENT PLANT a plant with thick fleshy leaves and stems that can store water. Succulents such as cacti and aloes typically grow in hot, arid conditions or in salty soils. [Early 17thC. Directly or via French from Latin *succulentus*, from *succus* (see SUCCUS).] —**suc·cu·lence** *n.* —**suc·cu·lent·ly** *adv.*

suc·cumb /sə kúm/ (**-cumbed, -cumb·ing, -cumbs**) *vi.* **1.** GIVE IN to yield to somebody or something powerful **2.** DIE FROM SOMETHING to die from an illness or injury [15thC. Directly or via French *succomber* from Latin *succumbere*, literally "to lie under," from *cumbere* "to lie" (source of English *incumbent*).] —**suc·cum·ber** *n.*

WORD KEY: SYNONYMS

See Synonyms at ***yield.***

suc·cus /súkəss/ (*plural* **-ci** /-kì/) *n.* a fluid, especially a secretion, of plant or animal origin [Late 18thC. From Latin, "juice, moisture, sap" (source of English *succulent*).]

suc·cuss /sə kúss/ (**-cussed, -cus·sing, -cuss·es**) *vt.* MED to shake a patient in order to detect the abnormal presence of air or fluid in a body cavity, especially the space between the lungs and the chest wall [Mid-19thC. Back-formation from succussion.] —**suc·cus·sion** *n.* —**suc·cus·sive** *adj.*

such /such/ *adj.* **1.** OF PARTICULAR KIND of a particular kind ○ *I've never heard such nonsense.* **2.** SO MUCH to so great an extent or degree ○ *Don't be such a fool.* ■ *adv.* VERY extremely or to a great degree ○ *I had never seen such lovely flowers.* ■ *n.* THIS this, or something of this kind ○ *Such was his fate.* [Old English *swilc, swelc, swylc.* Ultimately from a prehistoric Germanic compound word meaning literally "so formed," from the ancestors of SO + LIKE.] ◇ **as such** being what has been specified ◇ **such as 1.** for example **2.** resembling something ◇ **such as it is** being what it is and no more

WORD KEY: USAGE

We are such stuff as dreams are made on (Shakespeare, *The Tempest* Act 4, scene 1, modernized spelling) In sentences of this type ***such*** is followed by *as* and not by a relative pronoun *that, who,* etc.: *the new law affects only such people as (not: that) are eligible for supplementary benefits.* However, the construction *such ... that ...* is used to indicate the consequence of a stated circumstance: *The country faces such hardship that it will need a great deal of foreign aid.*

such and such *adj.* UNSPECIFIED not specified or named ■ *pron.* SOMETHING UNSPECIFIED something that is not specified or named

such·like /súch lìk/ *pron.* OTHERS OF THE SAME KIND others of the same kind as those just mentioned (*informal*) ■ *adj.* SIMILAR TO THOSE JUST MENTIONED similar to the kind just mentioned

such·ness /súchnəss/ *n.* PHILOS an essential quality or condition [Old English *swilcnes*]

suck /suk/ *v.* (**sucked, suck·ing, sucks**) **1.** *vti.* DRAW LIQUID OUT WITH MOUTH to draw the liquid out of something with the mouth ○ *The baby sucked on her bottle.* **2.** *vti.* MAKE PULLING MOUTH MOVEMENTS ON SOMETHING to hold something in the mouth and make movements with the tongue and lips as if drawing liquid out of it ○ *sucked his thumb* **3.** *vti.* MAKE SOMETHING DISSOLVE IN MOUTH to consume something by making it slowly dissolve in the mouth, rolling the tongue around it and making pulling movements with the cheeks and lips ○ *sucking lozenges for a sore throat* **4.** *vt.* EXTRACT SOMETHING to draw something out of a container (*often passive*) ○ *Fuel is sucked into the cylinder.* **5.** *vt.* PULL IRRESISTIBLY to pull or draw something somewhere with a powerful or irresistible force ○ *The swirling currents suck swimmers under.* **6.** *vi.* BE VERY BAD to be very bad or inferior (*slang*) ○ *The movie really sucked, so we walked out.* ■ *n.* ACT OF SUCKING SOMETHING an act of sucking something [Old English *sūcan.* Ultimately from an Indo-European base meaning "to take liquid" that is also the ancestor of Latin *sugere* "to suck" (source of English *suction*) and of English *soak.*]

suck back *vt.* to drink something in gulps

suck in *v.* **1.** *vti.* BREATHE IN to breathe in sharply **2.** *vt.* INVOLVE SOMEBODY IN SOMETHING to make somebody become more and more involved in something in a way that he or she is unable to prevent **3.** *vt.* DECEIVE SOMEBODY to trick or deceive somebody (*slang*)

suck off *vt.* an offensive term meaning to perform fellatio or cunnilingus on somebody (*offensive taboo*)

suck up to *vt.* to try to please or win the favor of somebody important by being extremely flattering or helpful (*informal*)

suck·er /súkər/ *n.* **1.** SOMEBODY EASILY FOOLED somebody who can be easily fooled or tricked (*informal*) **2.** SOMEBODY WHO GIVES IN EASILY somebody who finds it very hard to resist, or who is easily influenced by, some particular thing (*informal*) ○ *He's a real sucker for flattery.* **3.** ANY PERSON OR THING used to refer, usually with emphasis or some degree of irritation, to any person or thing somebody happens to be dealing with (*slang*) ○ *Let's see if we can get this sucker to work.* **4.** *U.K.* = **suction cup 5.** LOLLIPOP a lollipop (*informal*) **6.** ZOOL ORGAN THAT CLINGS BY SUCTION a muscular organ, found, e.g., on the tentacles of octopuses and similar sea animals, used to cling to or hold things such as prey **7.** ZOOL ORGAN FOR SUCKING IN FOOD the mouth of an animal such as the leech or lamprey that is adapted for sucking in food **8.** BOT SHOOT GROWING FROM ROOT a shoot that grows from the underground root or stem of a plant, and that is often able to produce its own roots and grow into a new plant **9.** ZOOL ANIMAL LIVING ON MOTHER'S MILK a young animal such as a young pig or whale that is still taking milk from its mother **10.** SUCTION PUMP PISTON the piston of a suction pump, or the valve of the piston in a suction pump **11.** SUCTION PIPE a pipe that a liquid is drawn through by means of suction **12.** ZOOL FRESHWATER FISH WITH A SUCKING MOUTH a bony bottom-feeding freshwater fish found mostly in North America that has a downward facing sucking mouth without teeth and resembles the carp. Family: Catostomidae. ■ *v.* (**-ered, -er·ing, -ers**) **1.** *vt.* TRICK SOMEBODY to take advantage of somebody's ignorance, innocence, or foolishness to trick him or her (*informal*) ○ *got suckered into the scheme* **2.** *vi.* BOT PRODUCE SUCKERS to produce or form suckers **3.** *vt.* BOT REMOVE SUCKERS to remove the suckers from a plant

suck·er·fish /súkər fish/ (*plural* **-fish** *or* **-fish·es**) *n.* = **remora**

suck·er punch *n.* a blow delivered when somebody is not expecting it

suck·er-punch (**suck·er-punched, suck·er-punch·ing, suck·er-punch·es**) *vt.* to hit somebody with a sucker punch

suck·ing /súking/ *adj.* still feeding on its mother's milk and not yet weaned ○ *sucking pig* [Old English *sūcende*]

suck·ing louse *n.* a wingless primitive parasitic insect with mouth parts specially adapted for sucking body fluids, e.g., the head louse and pubic louse that infest human beings. Suborder: Siphunculata.

suck·le /súk'l/ (**-led, -ling, -les**) *v.* **1.** *vti.* **FEED FROM BREAST, TEAT, OR UDDER** to take milk from a mother's breast, teat, or udder, or to allow a young child or animal to feed on milk from the breast, teat, or udder **2.** *vt.* **NOURISH** to nourish somebody or something (*literary*) [14thC. Origin uncertain: probably a back-formation from SUCKLING.] —**suck·ler** *n.*

suck·ling /súkling/ *n.* a human baby or young animal such as a calf or pig that is still feeding on its mother's milk [13thC. Formed from SUCK, probably on the model of Middle Dutch *sūgeling*.]

su·crase /so͝o krayss, -krayz/ *n.* = **invertase** [Early 20thC. Formed from SUCROSE + -ASE.]

su·cre /so͝o kray/ *n.* **1. ECUADOREAN UNIT OF CURRENCY** the main unit of currency in Ecuador, worth 100 centavos. See table at **currency 2. BILL WORTH ONE SUCRE** a bill worth one sucre [Late 19thC. Named for Antonio José de SUCRE.]

Su·cre /so͝ok ray/, **Antonio José de** (1795–1830) Venezuelan-born South American soldier and statesman. After helping to liberate Ecuador and Bolivia from Spain, he became the first president of Bolivia (1826–29).

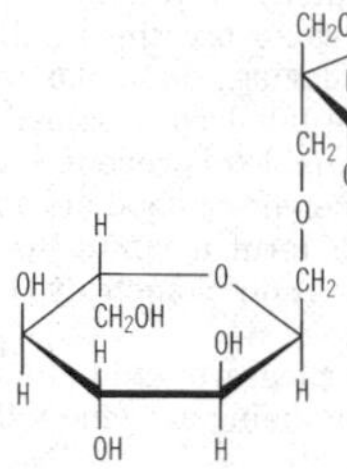

Sucrose

su·crose /so͝o krōss, -krōz/ *n.* a white water-soluble crystalline carbohydrate, found naturally in many plants and extracted from sugar cane and sugar beets to make common sugar. Formula: $C_{12}H_{22}O_{11}$. [Mid-19thC. Formed from French *sucre* "sugar," from Old French *sukere* (see SUGAR).]

suc·tion /súksh'n/ *n.* **1. SUCKING** the act or process of sucking **2. FORCE CREATED BY PRESSURE DIFFERENCE** physical force created by a difference in pressure such as that caused by sucking a liquid through a straw [Early 17thC. From the late Latin stem *suction-*, from Latin *suct-*, the past participle stem of *sugere* "to suck."] —**suc·tion·al** *adj.*

suc·tion cup *n.* a round, slightly cupped piece of plastic or rubber that when pressed onto a flat surface sticks to it by suction

suc·tion pump *n.* a pump that works by means of the suction created when a piston is moved up and down inside a cylinder. One example of a suction pump is the type of pump used to raise water from an underground source by moving a handle up and down.

suc·tion stop *n.* PHON a click (*technical*)

suc·to·ri·al /suk táwree əl/ *adj.* **1.** ZOOL **USED FOR ADHERING AND SUCKING** specially adapted for sucking or for clinging on by suction **2. WITH SUCKERS** having one or more suckers for feeding or for clinging on to something [Mid-19thC. Formed from modern Latin *suctorius*, from Latin *suct-*, the past participle stem of *sugere* (see SUCTION).]

Su·dan /soo dán/ **1.** republic in northeastern Africa,

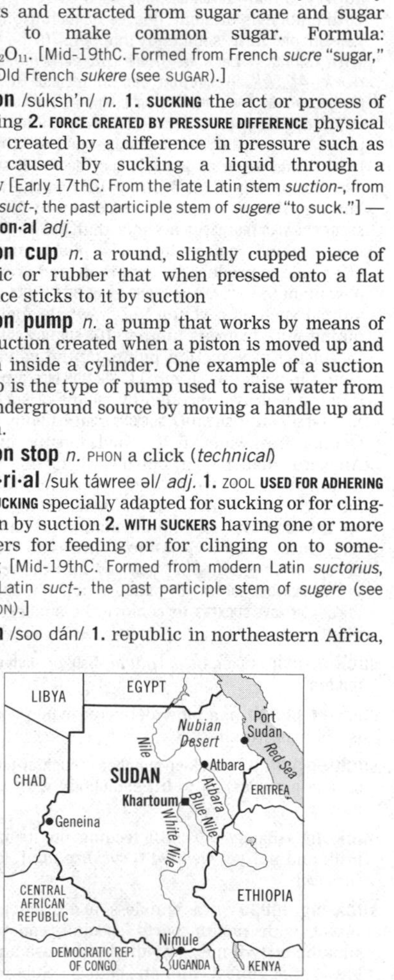

Sudan

and the continent's largest country. Language: Arabic. Currency: dinar. Capital: Khartoum. Population: 31,065,000 (1996). Area: 967,500 sq. mi./2,505,813 sq. km. Official name **Republic of the Sudan 2.** region of savanna and dry grassland in western Africa, between the Sahara and the tropical forest belt —**Su·da·nese** *n., adj.*

Su·dan·ic /soo dánnik/ *n.* **GROUP OF LANGUAGES SPOKEN IN SUDAN** a group of languages belonging to the Chari-Nile branch of the Nilo-Saharan family of languages, spoken by peoples in some areas of Sudan ■ *adj.* **1. RELATING TO SUDANIC LANGUAGES** relating to the Sudanic group of languages **2. RELATING TO SUDAN** relating to or typical of Sudan, its people, or culture

su·da·to·ri·um /so͝odə táwree əm/ (*plural* **su·da·to·ri·a** /-ree ə/) *n.* a room, especially in an ancient Roman bathhouse, in which people are made to sweat by hot air or steam [Mid-18thC. From Latin, a noun use of the neuter singular of *sudatorius* (see SUDATORY).]

su·da·to·ry /so͝odə tàwree/ *n.* (*plural* **su·da·to·ries**) **1.** = **sudorific** *n.* **2.** = **sudatorium** ■ *adj.* = **sudorific** *adj.* [Early 17thC. From Latin *sudatorius* "for sweating," from, ultimately, *sudare* "to sweat" (source of English *exude*).]

Sud·bur·y /súdbəree, -bree/ city north of Georgian Bay in east central Ontario, Canada. Population: 160,488 (1996).

sudd /sud/ *n.* a floating mass of reeds and weeds that obstructs some tropical rivers, especially the White Nile [Late 19thC. From Arabic, literally "obstruction," from *sadda* "to obstruct."]

sud·den /súdd'n/ *adj.* done or happening quickly, unexpectedly, and often without warning [13thC. Via Anglo-Norman *sudein* from, ultimately, Latin *subitaneus*, itself from, ultimately, *subire*, literally "to go secretly" (hence "taking by surprise"), from *ire* "to go."] —**sud·den·ly** *adv.* —**sud·den·ness** *n.* ◇ **all of a sudden** in a sudden and unexpected way

sud·den death *n.* the continuation of play in a tied sports contest until one team or player scores, that team or player being declared the winner

sud·den in·fant death syn·drome *n.* crib death (*technical*)

Su·de·ten·land /soo dáyt'n land/ region in the northern Czech Republic, in the Sudetes Mountains Range. It was annexed by Germany in 1938 and returned to Czechoslovakia in 1945.

su·dor·if·er·ous /so͝odə ríffərəss/ *adj.* producing sweat (*formal*) [Late 16thC. Formed from late Latin *sudorifer* "sudorific" (the original sense in English), from Latin *sudor* "sweat."] —**su·dor·if·er·ous·ness** *n.*

su·dor·if·ic /so͝odə ríffik/ *adj.* **CAUSING PRODUCTION OF SWEAT** causing the production of sweat ■ *n.* **DRUG CAUSING SWEATING** a drug or other agent that causes sweating [Early 17thC. From modern Latin *sudorificus*, from late Latin *sudorifer* (see SUDORIFEROUS).]

Su·dra /so͝odrə/ *n.* **1. LOWEST HINDU CASTE** the lowest of the four main Hindu castes, traditionally comprising artisans and laborers and their families. There is a wide range of subgroups within the Sudra caste, however, some being landowners. **2. MEMBER OF SUDRA** a member of the Sudra caste [Mid-17thC. From Sanskrit *śūdra*.]

suds /sudz/ *npl.* **BUBBLES** a froth of bubbles on the surface of soapy water ■ *n.* **BEER** beer (*slang*) [Mid-16thC. Origin uncertain: probably from Middle Dutch *sudse* "marsh, bog." Originally used for "dregs, muck."] —**suds·y** *adj.*

sue /soo/ (**sued, su·ing, sues**) *v.* **1.** *vti.* **UNDERTAKE LEGAL PROCEEDINGS** to take legal action against somebody in order to obtain something, usually compensation for a wrong **2.** *vi.* **BEG FOR SOMETHING** to make a humble, earnest, or begging request for something (*formal*) ○ *After three humiliating defeats, they were forced to sue for peace.* [12thC. Via Anglo-Norman *suer* "to follow" (the original English sense), from, ultimately, Latin *sequi* (source of English *pursue*). The underlying idea is of "following up" a matter.] —**su·er** *n.*

suede /swayd/ *n.* **1. LEATHER WITH VELVETY SURFACE** leather with the flesh side outward and rubbed up to make a velvety nap **2. FABRIC LIKE SUEDE** a woven fabric that looks like suede ■ *vti.* (**sued·ed, sued·ing, suedes**) **GIVE LEATHER A VELVETY NAP** to give leather a velvety nap [Mid-17thC. From French *gants de Suède* "gloves of Sweden," from *Suède* "Sweden," where it originated.]

su·et /so͝o ət/ *n.* a hard white fat found on the kidneys and loins of sheep and cattle, used in cooking and as a source of tallow [14thC. Origin uncertain: probably from Anglo-Norman, literally "small suet," from *sue, seu* "tallow, suet," from Latin *sebum* (source of English *sebaceous*).] —**suety** /so͝o ətee/ *adj.*

Sue·to·ni·us /swee tónee əss/, **Gaius Tranquillus** (*b.* 69?–70? AD) Roman biographer and historian. His works include biographies of eleven Roman emperors.

Su·ez /so͝o əz/ city and port at the head of the Gulf of Suez and at the southern end of the Suez Canal, northeastern Egypt. Population: 388,000 (1992).

Su·ez Ca·nal canal in Egypt, connecting the Mediterranean and Red seas. It was opened in 1869. Length: 101 mi./163 km.

suff. *abbr.* **1. suff., suf.** suffix **2.** sufficient

suf·fer /súffər/ (**-fered, -fer·ing, -fers**) *v.* **1.** *vti.* **FEEL PAIN** to feel pain or great discomfort in body or mind **2.** *vti.* **UNDERGO SOMETHING UNPLEASANT** to experience or undergo something unpleasant or undesirable **3.** *vti.* **ENDURE** to endure or put up with something painful or unpleasant ○ *I do not suffer fools gladly.* **4.** *vi.* **HAVE AN ILLNESS** to have a disease or a physical or psychological condition **5.** *vi.* **HAVE AS WEAKNESS** to have as a bad quality, weakness, or flaw ○ *Their whole manifesto suffers from a lack of vision.* **6.** *vi.* **APPEAR TO BE LESS GOOD** to become or appear to be less good **7.** *vi.* **BE ADVERSELY AFFECTED** to be adversely affected by something ○ *The business suffered when the partnership was dissolved.* **8.** *vt.* **ALLOW** to allow somebody to do something (*archaic or literary*) [12thC. Via Anglo-Norman *suffrir* from, ultimately, Latin *sufferre*, literally "to carry up from underneath," hence "to sustain," from *ferre* "to carry" (source of English *fertile*).] —**suf·fer·er** *n.*

suf·fer·a·ble /súffərəb'l/ *adj.* able to be endured or tolerated

suf·fer·ance /súffərənss/ *n.* **1. TOLERANCE OF SOMETHING PROHIBITED** tacit permission for or tolerance of something, because no action is taken to prevent it **2. ENDURANCE OF DIFFICULTY OR PAIN** the capacity to withstand difficulty or pain **3. PATIENT ENDURANCE** the fact of enduring hardship patiently (*archaic*) ◇ **on sufferance** as a result of permission or consent given reluctantly and liable to be withdrawn

suf·fer·ing /súffəring/ *n.* physical or psychological pain and distress, or an experience of it

suf·fice /sə físs/ (**-ficed, -fic·ing, -fic·es**) *vti.* to be enough for somebody or something (*formal*) [14thC. From Old French *suffic-*, from, ultimately, Latin *sufficere*, literally "to make up to," hence "to be enough," which was formed from *facere* "to make" (source of English *fact*).]

suf·fi·cien·cy /sə físh'nsee/ (*plural* **-cies**) *n.* **1. SUFFICIENT AMOUNT** an amount of something that is enough for somebody or something **2. STATE OF BEING SUFFICIENT** the fact or state of being enough

suf·fi·cient /sə físh'nt/ *adj.* as much as is needed [14thC. Directly or via Old French from Latin *sufficient-*, the present participle stem of *sufficere* (see SUFFICE).] —**suf·fi·cient·ly** *adv.*

suf·fi·cient rea·son *n.* PHILOS the philosophical principle that nothing happens by chance and that an explanation must be available for everything

suf·fix *n.* /súffiks/ **ELEMENT ADDED AT END OF WORD** a letter or group of letters added at the end of a word or word part to form another word, e.g., "-ly" in "quickly" or "-ing" in "talking" ■ *vt.* /súffiks, sə fíks/ (**-fixed, -fix·ing, -fix·es**) **ADD AS SUFFIX** to add something as a suffix [Early 17thC. Via modern Latin *suffixum* from, ultimately, Latin *suffigere*, literally "to fasten underneath," from *figere* (see FIX).] —**suf·fix·al** /súffiks'l, sə fíks'l/ *adj.* —**suf·fix·a·tion** /suffik sáysh'n/ *n.*

suf·fo·cate /súffə kàyt/ (**-cat·ed, -cat·ing, -cates**) *vti.* **1. STOP BREATHING** to deprive somebody of air or prevent somebody from breathing, or to be unable to breathe **2. DIE FROM LACK OF AIR** to die from lack of air or kill somebody by stopping him or her from breathing **3. MAKE OR FEEL TOO WARM** to feel uncomfortable or make somebody feel uncomfortable through excessive heat and lack of fresh air **4. NOT ALLOW TO DEVELOP** to confine and restrict somebody or something with adverse effects, or be or feel confined and restricted in development or self-expression [15thC. From Latin *suffocat-*, the past participle stem of *suffocare*, literally "to narrow up," from the stem *fauc-* "throat, narrow entrance."] —**suf·fo·cat·ing** *adj.* —**suf·fo·cat·ing·ly** *adv.* —**suf·fo·ca·tion** /sùffə káysh'n/ *n.* —**suf·fo·ca·tive** *adj.*

Suf·folk[1] /súffək/ county in East Anglia, eastern England. It is largely agricultural. Ipswich is the county town. Population: 648,000 (1992). Area: 1,467 sq. mi./3,800 sq. km.

Suf·folk[2] /súffək/ *n.* a large black-faced hornless sheep belonging to a breed originating in England and bred for meat [Mid-19thC. Named for the county of SUFFOLK, England.]

Suf·folk punch *n.* a powerful horse with short legs and a chestnut brown coat, belonging to a breed originating in England, used for pulling loads such as plows or carts [*Punch* from English dialect, "stocky draught horse" (originally "short overweight person"), a shortening of PUNCHINELLO]

suf·fra·gan /súffrəgən/ *n.* **1. ASSISTANT BISHOP** a bishop appointed to assist the main bishop in a diocese **2. BISHOP AS ASSISTANT TO ARCHBISHOP** the bishop of a diocese who is an assistant to the archbishop of the province to which the diocese belongs [14thC. Via Anglo-Norman and Old French from medieval Latin *suffraganeus* "assisting," from Latin *suffragium* (see SUFFRAGE).] —**suf·fra·gan** *adj.* —**suf·fra·gan·ship** *n.*

suf·frage /súffrij/ *n.* **1. RIGHT TO VOTE** the right to vote in public elections **2. ACT OF VOTING** a vote or the act of voting (*literary*) **3. SHORT PRAYER** a short prayer on behalf of somebody, especially a prayer said as part of a litany [14thC. Directly and partly via French from Latin *suffragium* "support, vote."]

suf·fra·gette /sùffrə jét/ *n.* a woman campaigning for the right of women to vote in elections, especially one who took part in militant protests in the United Kingdom in the early 20th century. Among the leaders of the suffragette movement in the United States was Susan B. Anthony. —**suf·fra·get·tism** *n.*

suf·fra·gist /súffrəjist/ *n.* a supporter of the extension of the right to vote to a particular group, especially to women, or to all people above a particular age —**suf·fra·gism** *n.*

suf·fuse /sə fyóoz/ (**-fused, -fus·ing, -fus·es**) *vt.* to spread over or through something (*usually passive*) ○ *A blush suffused his face with color.* [Late 16thC. From Latin *suffus-*, the past participle stem of *suffundere*, literally "to pour from below," from *fundere* "to pour" (source of English *fuse*).] —**suf·fu·sion** /sə fyóozh'n/ *n.* —**suf·fu·sive** /sə fyóossiv, -ziv/ *adj.*

Su·fi /sóofee/ (*plural* **-fis**) *n.* a Muslim mystic [Mid-17thC. From Arabic *ṣūfī*, literally "woolen" (because of their woolen garments).] —**Su·fi** *adj.* —**Su·fic** *adj.* —**Su·fism** *n.* —**Su·fis·tic** /soo fístik/ *adj.*

sug·ar /shóoggər/ *n.* **1. SWEET-TASTING SUBSTANCE** a sweet-tasting substance, usually in the form of tiny hard white or brown grains, obtained commercially from sugar cane and sugar beets, and used to sweeten food and drinks. Different types of sugar, e.g., granulated sugar, brown sugar, or confectioner's sugar, are made at different processing levels. **2. PORTION OF SUGAR** a spoonful, lump, cube, or other portion of sugar ○ *likes his coffee black with two sugars* **3. SWEET CARBOHYDRATE** any of a group of simple carbohydrates found in many plants that are sweet-tasting, crystalline, and soluble in water **4. TERM OF ENDEARMENT** used as a term of endearment (*informal*) **5. WAY OF MAKING SOMETHING MORE AGREEABLE** something used as a means of persuasion or to make a difficult or unpleasant thing seem less so **6. STRONG DRUG** a strong drug such as heroin or LSD (*dated slang*) ■ *v.* (**-ared, -ar·ing, -ars**) **1.** *vt.* **ADD SUGAR TO SOMETHING** to add sugar to food or a drink **2.** *vt.* **TRY TO MAKE SOMETHING MORE AGREEABLE** to try to make something more appealing or flattering or to make something unpleasant seem less so **3.** *vi.* **MAKE SUGAR** to make sugar or form sugar crystals [13thC. Via Old French *çukre*, *sukere* (source of English *sucrose*) from medieval Latin *succarum*, which came via Arabic *sukkar* from, ultimately, Sanskrit *śarkarā* "grit, ground sugar" (source of English *saccharin*).]

sugar off *vi.* to boil maple sap to make maple syrup and maple sugar

sug·ar ap·ple *n.* = **sweetsop**

sug·ar beans *npl.* *S Africa* dried beans that are reddish or brown speckled

sug·ar beet *n.* a variety of beet with a large whitish conical root that is an important commercial source of sugar. Latin name: *Beta vulgaris*.

sug·ar·ber·ry /shóoggər bèrree/ (*plural* **-ries**) *n.* = **hackberry**

sug·ar·bird *n.* either of two African nectar-eating birds with dull brownish plumage, a long curved bill, and a very long drooping tail. Genus: *Promerops*.

sug·ar bush *n.* a wood or group of trees consisting mainly of sugar maples

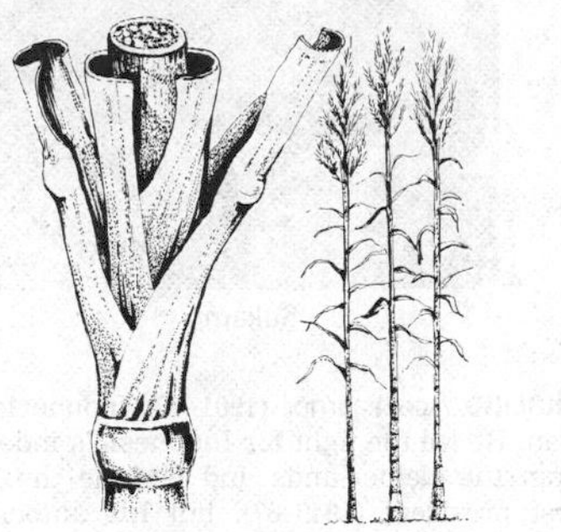

Sugar cane

sug·ar cane *n.* a tall tough-stemmed species of grass grown in warm regions throughout the world as a source of sugar, which is obtained from its sweet sap. Latin name: *Saccharum officinarum*. (*hyphenated when used before a noun*)

sug·ar·coat /shóoggər kōt/ (**-coat·ed, -coat·ing, -coats**) *vt.* **1. MAKE SOMETHING SEEM LESS UNPLEASANT** to make something unpleasant seem less so **2. COAT WITH SUGAR** to enclose something in a hard sugar shell or coat something with sugar

sug·ar corn *n.* = **sweet corn**

sug·ar-cured *adj.* cured in a mixture of sugar, salt, and a nitrate or nitrite

sug·ar dad·dy *n.* a rich man who gives money and gifts to a younger partner in a relationship (*informal*)

sug·ared /shóoggərd/ *adj.* **1. COATED WITH SUGAR** covered or coated in a layer of sugar **2. SWEETENED** sweetened with sugar **3. MADE MORE APPEALING** marked by an attempt to make somebody or something seem more pleasant, appealing, or acceptable

sug·ar gum *n.* a small eucalyptus tree that has smooth bark, barrel-shaped fruit, and sweet-tasting leaves that are often eaten by cattle. Latin name: *Eucalyptus cladocalyx*.

sug·ar·house /shóoggər hòwss/ (*plural* **-houses** /-hòwzəz/) *n.* a refinery where sugar is processed, especially one in which maple sap is boiled to produce maple syrup and maple sugar

sug·ar loaf *n.* **1. CONE-SHAPED MASS OF SUGAR** a solid cone-shaped mass of refined sugar **2. SOMETHING SHAPED LIKE SUGAR LOAF** something that has a conical shape like a cone of sugar, e.g., a hill

Barnaby's

Sugarloaf Mountain

Sug·ar·loaf Moun·tain /shóoggər lōf-/ peak on the edge of Rio de Janeiro, Brazil, that provides a panoramic view of the city. Height: 1,296 ft./395 m.

sug·ar ma·ple *n.* a North American maple that produces a sweet sap from which maple sugar and maple syrup are made. Latin name: *Acer saccharum*.

sug·ar of lead *n.* = **lead acetate**

sug·ar pea *n.* a variety of garden pea that has an edible thin flat pod. Latin name: *Pisum sativum*.

sug·ar pine *n.* a tall pine tree native to the west coast of North America that has a sugary resin and large cones. Latin name: *Pinus lambertiana*.

sug·ar·plum /shóoggər plùm/ *n.* a small round candy made of boiled and flavored sugar

sug·ar shack *n.* = **sugarhouse**

sug·ar·y /shóoggəree/ *adj.* **1. CONTAINING SUGAR** containing a great deal of sugar **2. LIKE SUGAR** looking or tasting like sugar **3. EXAGGERATEDLY PLEASANT** exaggeratedly and often insincerely pleasant or amiable **4. SENTIMENTAL** cloyingly sentimental —**sug·ar·i·ness** *n.*

sug·gest /sə jést, səg jést/ (**-gest·ed, -gest·ing, -gests**) *vt.* **1. PROPOSE FOR CONSIDERATION** to state or refer to somebody or something as a possible choice, plan, or course of action for somebody else to consider **2. REMIND SOMEBODY OF SOMETHING** to remind somebody of something or make somebody think of something **3. IMPLY** to imply or hint at something **4. INDICATE AS LIKELY** to indicate that something is likely [Early 16thC. Back-formation from SUGGESTION.] —**sug·gest·er** *n.*

WORD KEY: SYNONYMS

See Synonyms at ***recommend***.

sug·gest·i·bil·i·ty /sə jèstə bíllətee, səg jèstə-/ *n.* **1. SUSCEPTIBILITY TO SUGGESTIONS** the condition of being easily influenced by other people's suggestions **2.** PSYCHOL **MENTAL STATE OF HEIGHTENED ACCEPTANCE** a mental state in which somebody accepts without question the ideas, attitudes, or instructions of others, usually occurring under hypnosis

sug·gest·i·ble /sə jéstəb'l, səg jést-/ *adj.* **1. EASILY INFLUENCED** easily influenced by other people **2. ABLE TO BE SUGGESTED** capable of being suggested —**sug·gest·i·ble·ness** *n.* —**sug·gest·i·bly** *adv.*

sug·ges·tion /sə jéstshən, səg jést-/ *n.* **1. IDEA OR PROPOSAL** an idea or proposal put forward for consideration **2. SLIGHT TRACE** a slight trace, indication, or hint of something **3. ACT OF SUGGESTING** the act or process of suggesting something **4. ABILITY TO CONJURE UP ASSOCIATIONS** the ability of words or images to conjure up ideas or feelings, the process by which they do this, or a particular idea or image conjured up by something **5. PUTTING IDEAS INTO SOMEBODY'S MIND** the deliberate introduction into somebody's mind of an opinion, belief, or instruction, e.g., through hypnosis or advertising, so that it is accepted or acted on as that person's own idea ○ *The power of suggestion is used in TV commercials to make us want a product.* [14thC. Directly or via French from the Latin stem *suggestion-*, from, ultimately, *suggerere*, literally "to bring up," from *gerere* "to bring" (source of English *digest*).]

sug·ges·tive /sə jéstiv, səg-/ *adj.* **1. CONJURING UP IDEAS OR IMAGES** able to conjure up ideas or images in the mind or start a train of thought **2. IMPROPER** implying or hinting at something rude or improper, especially something of a sexual nature —**sug·ges·tive·ly** *adv.* —**sug·ges·tive·ness** *n.*

Su·har·to /sə háartō, sōo-/ (*b.* 1921) Indonesian statesman. As president of Indonesia (1967–98), he developed a petroleum-based economy. He was forced to resign as the economy declined and his regime was accused of corruption.

Sui /sway/ *n.* a Chinese dynasty lasting from A.D. 581 to A.D. 618 that succeeded the Han dynasty, united all of northern China, and reconquered southern China

su·i·cid·al /sòo i sīd'l/ *adj.* **1. WANTING TO COMMIT SUICIDE** intending or wishing to commit suicide **2. RELATING TO SUICIDE** produced by or involving a wish to commit suicide **3. EXTREMELY DANGEROUS** likely to lead to death, destruction, or ruin, or very much against somebody's own best interests **4. VERY UNHAPPY** deeply unhappy or frustrated (*informal*) —**su·i·cid·al·ly** *adv.*

su·i·cide /sóo i sīd/ *n.* **1. KILLING YOURSELF** the act of deliberately killing yourself. ◊ **parasuicide 2. SOMEBODY WHO COMMITS SUICIDE** somebody who deliberately kills himself or herself. ◊ **parasuicide 3. DOING SOMETHING AGAINST OWN BEST INTERESTS** the act of doing something that seems contrary to your own best interests and likely to lead to a disaster such as financial ruin or loss of position or reputation [Mid-17thC. From modern Latin *suicidium* "killing of yourself" and *suicida* "somebody who kills himself or herself," both formed from Latin *sui* "of yourself."]

su·i·cide bomb·ing *n.* a bomb attack in which the person carrying out the attack deliberately allows himself or herself to be killed in the process of attempting to destroy something or kill somebody —**su·i·cide bomb·er** *n.*

su·i·cide pact *n.* an agreement between two or more people that they will kill themselves at the same time

su·i·cide watch *n.* the regular checking by prison guards of the cells of prisoners who are thought likely to commit suicide

su·i ge·ne·ris /sóo ī jénnəriss, sóo i-/ *adj.* unique, or in a class of its own [From Latin, literally "of its own kind"]

sui ju·ris /sóo ī jóoriss, sóo i-/ *adj.* competent to assume legal responsibility for his or her own affairs [From Latin, literally "of its own right"]

su·int /sóo int, swint/ *n.* the grease found in sheep's wool, formed from dried perspiration [Late 18thC. From French, from *suer* "to sweat," from Latin *sudare* (see SUDATORY).]

suit /soot/ *n.* **1.** CLOTHES **CLOTHES MADE OF SAME MATERIAL** a set of clothes made from the same material, consisting of a jacket and trousers or a skirt, sometimes together with a vest **2.** CLOTHES **CLOTHES FOR PARTICULAR PURPOSE** a piece of clothing or set of clothes worn for a particular purpose (*often used in combination*) ○ *a diving suit* **3.** CARDS **SET OF PLAYING CARDS** one of the four different sets of playing cards in a pack **4.** LAW **LEGAL PROCEEDINGS** a case brought to a law court **5. PETITION** a petition, especially to somebody in authority (*formal*) **6. BUSINESS EXECUTIVE** a business executive, especially when seen as an anonymous bureaucrat (*slang*) **7. SET OF SAILS OR TOOLS** a set of sails or tools **8. WOOING OF WOMAN** a man's wooing of a woman and attempts to persuade her to marry him (*archaic*) ■ *v.* (**suit·ed, suit·ing, suits**) **1.** *vti.* **BE RIGHT FOR SOMETHING OR SOMEBODY** to be appropriate to or the right thing for somebody or something **2.** *vt.* **BE SATISFYING TO SOMEBODY** to be something that a person likes or enjoys **3.** *vti.* **BE CONVENIENT TO SOMEBODY** to be convenient or acceptable to somebody **4.** *vt.* **LOOK GOOD ON SOMEBODY** to look good on somebody or go well with something ○ *The color suits you.* **5.** *vt.* **MAKE SUITABLE** to adapt something in order to meet requirements or circumstances **6.** *vr.* **PLEASE YOURSELF** to do what you prefer [13thC. Via Anglo-Norman *siute* from, ultimately, assumed Vulgar Latin *sequere* "to follow," alteration of Latin *sequi* (source of English *persecute*). Originally, "body of followers," later "set of things generally."] ◇ **be somebody's strong suit** to be something at which somebody is particularly good ◇ **follow suit 1.** to do the same as somebody else has done **2.** to play a card of the same suit as a card led to a trick or played before

suit·a·ble /sóotəb'l/ *adj.* of the right type or quality for a particular purpose or occasion [Late 16thC. Originally in the sense "matching."] —**suit·a·bil·i·ty** /sòotə bíllətee/ *n.* —**suit·a·ble·ness** /sóotəb'lnəss/ *n.*

suit·a·bly /sóotəblee/ *adv.* **1. APPROPRIATELY** in a way that is right for a particular purpose or occasion **2. TO AN APPROPRIATE DEGREE** to an appropriate or the expected extent

suit·case /sóot kàyss/ *n.* a rectangular case used for carrying clothes and other belongings during travel

suite /sweet/ *n.* **1. SET OF ROOMS** a set of rooms, e.g., in a hotel **2. SET OF MATCHING FURNITURE** a set of matching furniture for a room, e.g., a bed, end tables, and a dresser for a bedroom **3.** MUSIC **SET OF INSTRUMENTAL WORKS PERFORMED TOGETHER** a set of instrumental pieces, especially dances, intended to be performed together. This type of composition was especially popular in the Baroque period. **4. PEOPLE WITH SOMEBODY IMPORTANT** a group of followers, servants, or advisers accompanying somebody important **5.** COMPUT **COLLECTION OF INTEGRATED SOFTWARE** a collection of integrated application programs functioning as a single program, each of which can incorporate data from the others, eliminating the need for re-entry or transfer of data. A typical suite includes word processing, spreadsheet, database management, and electronic mail programs, and additionally such functions as presentation graphics, address book, and appointment calendar. [Late 17thC. Via French from, ultimately, assumed Vulgar Latin *sequere* (see SUIT).]

suit·ing /sóoting/ *n.* CLOTHES material for making suits

suit·or /sóotər/ *n.* **1. MAN WOOING WOMAN** a man who is trying to persuade a woman to marry him (*dated*) **2.** BUSINESS **SOMEBODY TAKING OVER BUSINESS** somebody who wants to buy or tries to take over a business **3.** LAW **SOMEBODY WHO BRINGS LAWSUIT** somebody on whose behalf a case is brought to a law court [13thC. Via Anglo-Norman *seutor, suitour* from Latin *secutor* "follower," from, ultimately, *sequi* (see SUIT).]

Popperfoto

Sukarno

Su·kar·no /soo kàarnō/ (1901–70) Indonesian statesman. He led the fight for Indonesia's independence from the Netherlands and became the country's first president (1949–67), but his autocratic rule eventually led to his forced resignation.

su·ki·ya·ki /sòoki yàakee/ *n.* a Japanese dish consisting of thin slices of beef or other meat, vegetables, bean curd, and noodles, cooked quickly in a sweet soy sauce, usually at the table [Early 20thC. From Japanese, literally "slice-grill."]

suk·kah /sóokə, -kàa/, **suc·cah** *n.* a temporary light shelter with a roof of branches built in Jewish homes, yards, or temples for the festival of Sukkoth. The shelters are built in memory of the huts or tents the Israelites lived in during the time they were wandering in the desert after leaving Egypt. [Late 19thC. From Hebrew *sukkāh*, literally "hut."]

Suk·koth /sóo kōt, -kōth, -kōss, sóokəss/, **Suc·coth, Suk·kot** *n.* CALENDAR an eight-day Jewish autumn harvest festival beginning on the eve of the 15th day of Tishri [Late 19thC. From Hebrew *sukkōt*, the plural of *sukkāh* (see SUKKAH).]

Suk·kur /súkər/ city and district in Sind Province, Pakistan, on the banks of the Indus. Population: 190,551 (1981).

Su·lay·man I (the Magnificent) /sóolli maan, sóoli-, sóol ay-/, **Su·lei·man I** (1494–1566) Ottoman sultan. He ruled from 1520 to 1566, extending the Ottoman Empire throughout the Balkans, the Middle East, and northern Africa, and encouraging artistic and scientific endeavors.

sul·cus /súlkəss/ (*plural* **-ci** /-kī/) *n.* a shallow groove or depression, especially any of those separating the convolutions of the surface of the brain [Mid-17thC. From Latin, "furrow, trench."]

Su·lei·man I /sóolay màan, sóolə-/ = **Sulayman I**

sulf- *prefix.* sulfur ○ *sulfite* [From SULFUR]

sul·fa·di·a·zine /sùlfə dī ə zèen, sùlfə dī əzin/ *n.* a sulfa drug used to fight bacterial infections, especially in patients weakened by other conditions. Formula: $C_{10}H_{10}N_4O_2S$. [Mid-20thC. Coined from *sulfa-* (see SULFA DRUG) + DIAZINE.]

sul·fa·di·mi·dine /sùlfə dímmə dèen/ *n.* = **sulfamethazine**

sul·fa drug /súflə-/ *n.* a drug synthesized from sulfonamide, once used to treat a range of bacterial infections. Sulfa drugs are now restricted because of their toxicity and increased bacterial resistance to them. [*Sulfa* shortening of SULFANILAMIDE]

sul·fa·meth·a·zine /sùlfə méthə zèen/ *n.* a sulfonamide used together with other sulfonamides or with antibiotics to treat bacterial infections. Formula: $C_{12}H_{14}N_4O_2S$. [Mid-20thC. Coined from *sulfa-* (see SULFA DRUG) + METH- + AZINE.]

sul·fa·nil·a·mide /sùlfə nìllə mīd/ *n.* the first of the sulfa drugs, once used to treat bacterial infections, including gonorrhea and urinary tract infections. Formula: $C_6H_8N_2O_2S$. [Mid-20thC. Coined from SULF- + ANILINE + AMIDE.]

sul·fa·tase /sùlfə tàyss, -tàyz/ *n.* an enzyme found in animal tissue and some microorganisms that accelerates the decomposition of sulfuric esters

sul·fate /súl fàyt/ *n.* **SULFURIC ACID SALT OR ESTER** a salt or ester of sulfuric acid ■ *v.* (**-fat·ed, -fat·ing, -fates**) **1.** *vti.* **MAKE LAYER OF LEAD SULFATE** to make a layer of lead sulfate form on the plates of a battery, or become covered with lead sulfate **2.** *vt.* **TREAT SOMETHING WITH SULFUR** to treat something with sulfur, sulfuric acid, or a sulfate **3.** *vt.* **CONVERT TO SULFATE** to convert something to a sulfate —**sul·fa·tion** /sul fáysh'n/ *n.*

sul·fide /súl fīd/ *n.* a chemical compound containing sulfur and one or more other elements

sul·fite /súl fīt/ *n.* a salt or ester of sulfurous acid —**sul·fit·ic** /sul fíttik/ *adj.*

sulfon- *prefix.* sulfonic ○ *sulfonyl* [From SULFONE]

sul·fon·a·mide /sul fónnə mīd/ *n.* a substance that is responsible for the antibacterial action of sulfa drugs. Sulfanamides work by depriving bacteria of the ability to synthesize the essential nutrient folic acid. [Late 19thC. From SULFONE + AMIDE.]

sul·fo·nate /súlfə nàyt/ *n.* **SULFONIC ACID SALT OR ESTER** a salt or ester of sulfonic acid ■ *vt.* **TREAT WITH SULFURIC ACID** to treat an organic substance with sulfuric acid [Late 19thC. Formed from SULFONIC.] —**sul·fo·na·tion** /sùlfə náysh'n/ *n.*

sul·fone /súl fōn/ *n.* a compound containing the sulfonyl group in which sulfur is attached to two carbon atoms [Late 19thC. From German *Sulfon*, from *Sulfur* "sulfur."]

sul·fon·ic /sul fónnik/ *adj.* relating to, containing, or derived from the acid group SO_2OH [Late 19thC. Formed from German *Sulfon* (see SULFONE).]

sul·fon·ic ac·id *n.* an organic acid used in the making of dyes and drugs

sul·fo·ni·um /sul fōnee əm/ *n.* an ion or radical containing sulfur with a valence of three [Late 19thC. Formed from SULFUR.]

sul·fon·meth·ane /sùl fōn mé thàyn/ *n.* a hypnotic and potentially addictive drug used in medicine. Formula: $C_7H_{16}O_4S_2$.

sul·fo·nyl /súlfə nìl/ *n.* the bivalent chemical group SO_2 [Early 20thC. Formed from SULFONIC.]

sul·fo·nyl·ur·e·a /sùlfənil yóoree ə/ *n.* a drug given orally to lower blood sugar in diabetic patients

sul·fur /súlfər/, **sul·phur** *n.* **1. YELLOW NONMETALLIC ELEMENT** a nonmetallic yellow chemical element that occurs alone in nature or combined in sulfide and sulfate minerals and is used to make sulfuric acid, matches, fungicides, and gunpowder. Symbol **S 2. YELLOWISH-GREEN COLOR** a yellowish-green color [14thC. Via Anglo-Norman *sulf(e)re*, from, ultimately, Latin *sulfur, sulphur*.] —**sul·fur** *adj.* —**sul·fur·y** *adj.*

sul·fu·rate /súlfə ràyt, súlfyə-/ (**-rat·ed, -rat·ing, -rates**) *vt.* to treat or combine something with sulfur —**sul·fu·ra·tion** /sùlfə ráysh'n, sùlfyə-/ *n.*

sul·fur bac·te·ri·um *n.* a bacterium that is capable of metabolizing sulfur or inorganic sulfur compounds. Genus: *Thiobacillus*.

sul·fur di·ox·ide *n.* a colorless pungent toxic gas used in making sulfuric acid and as a preservative, fumigant, and bleaching agent. It is formed by burning sulfur and constitutes a major component of air pollution in industrial regions. Formula: SO_2.

sul·fur·e·ous *adj.* = **sulfurous** *adj.* 1 —**sul·fur·e·ous·ly** *adv.* —**sul·fure·ous·ness** *n.*

sul·fu·ric /sul fyóorik/ *adj.* relating to or containing sulfur, especially with a higher valence than in sulfurous compounds

sul·fu·ric ac·id *n.* a strong colorless oily corrosive acid that is used in batteries and in the manufacture of many products such as fertilizers, explosives, detergents, dyes, and chemicals. Formula: H_2SO_4.

sul·fur·ize /súlfyə rīz/ (**-ized, -iz·ing, -iz·es**) *vt.* to treat or combine something with sulfur or a sulfur compound —**sul·fur·i·za·tion** /sùlfərə záysh'n/ *n.*

sul·fur·ous /súlfərəss, súlfyə-/, **sul·fur·e·ous** /sul fyóoree əss/ *adj.* **1. CONTAINING SULFUR** relating to or containing sulfur, especially with a valence of 4 **2. SIMILAR TO BURNING SULFUR** with the color or acrid smell of burning sulfur **3. RELATING TO HELL** relating to hell or hellfire (*literary*) **4. FIERY** fiery, especially in having or showing a violent temper or in being emotionally charged and containing many swearwords or blasphemies (*literary*) [15thC. Formed from Latin *sulphurosus*, or from SULFUR.] —**sul·fur·ous·ly** *adv.* —**sul·fur·ous·ness** *n.*

sul·fur·ous ac·id *n.* a weak colorless acid that is a solution of sulfur dioxide in water and is used as a disinfectant, food preservative, and bleaching agent. Formula: H_2SO_3.

sul·fur spring *n.* a spring with significant amounts of sulfur compounds in the water

sul·fur·yl /súlfə rìl, súlfyə-/ *n.* = **sulfonyl** [Mid-19thC. Coined from SULFUR + -YL.]

sulk /sulk/ *vi.* (**sulked, sulk·ing, sulks**) BE ANGRILY SILENT to refuse to talk to or associate with others as a show of resentment for a real or imagined grievance ■ *n.* **1.** BAD-TEMPERED SILENCE a period, state, or show of resentfulness and refusal to communicate **2.** SOMEBODY WHO SULKS somebody who tends to sulk [Late 18thC. Back-formation from SULKY.] —**sulk·er** *n.*

sulk·y /súlkee/ *adj.* (**-i·er, -i·est**) ANGRILY SILENT in a bad mood and refusing to communicate because of resentment for a real or imagined grievance ■ *n.* (*plural* **-ies**) HORSE-DRAWN VEHICLE FOR ONE PERSON a light open two-wheeled vehicle for one person, pulled by one horse. Sulkies are today used mostly for racing. [Mid-18thC. Origin uncertain: perhaps an alteration of earlier *sulke* "sluggish," from, perhaps, Old English *āsolcen*, an adjectival use of the past participle of *āseolcan* "to become sluggish." In the noun sense, perhaps from its having room for only one person.] —**sulk·i·ly** *adv.* —**sulk·i·ness** *n.*

sul·lage /súllij/ *n.* **1.** WASTE MATERIAL sewage or any other form of waste or refuse **2.** SILT solid material deposited by flowing water, e.g., by a river [Mid-16thC. Origin uncertain: perhaps from Anglo-Norman *suillage*, from Old French *soill(i)er* "to soil" (see SOIL).]

sul·len /súllən/ *adj.* **1.** HOSTILELY SILENT showing bad temper or hostility by a refusal to talk, behave sociably, or cooperate cheerfully **2.** CLOUDY AND DULL dull and gray because of clouds, fog, or haze (*literary*) **3.** SLOW-MOVING moving slowly (*literary*) ○ *a sullen stream* [14thC. From Anglo-Norman *sulein* "alone," from *sol* "sole, single" (the original English sense), from Latin *solus* (see SOLE).] —**sul·len·ly** *adv.* —**sul·len·ness** *n.*

Sul·li·van /súllәvәn/, **Sir Arthur** (1842–1900) British composer. He is best known for his 14 popular comic operas, containing much musical parody, to librettos by Sir William S. Gilbert. Full name **Sir Arthur Seymour Sullivan**

Sul·li·van, Harry Stack (1892–1949) U.S. psychiatrist. He developed the influential theory that personality and psychiatric disorders are formed by the interaction of personal and social forces.

Sul·li·van, John L. (1858–1918) U.S. boxer. He was the last bare-knuckled heavyweight champion of the world (1882–92). Full name **John Lawrence Sullivan**

Sul·li·van, Louis (1856–1924) U.S. architect. His tall steel-framed buildings, built mostly in Chicago, were the world's first skyscrapers. Full name **Louis Henri Sullivan**

sul·ly /súllee/ (**-lied, -ly·ing, -lies**) *v.* **1.** *vti.* SPOIL to spoil or detract from something, especially somebody's reputation, that has previously been pure and honorable, or to become spoiled or tarnished **2.** *vt.* MAKE DIRTY to make something dirty (*literary*) [Late 16thC. Origin uncertain: perhaps from French *souiller* "to soil," from Old French *soill(i)er* (see SOIL).] —**sul·lied** *adj.*

Sul·ly /súllee/, **Thomas** (1783–1872) British-born U.S. artist. He is known for his colorful romantic portraits, including several of U.S. presidents.

sul·pha·di·mi·dine /sùlfə dímmə deen/ *n. U.K.* = **sulfamethazine** [Mid-20thC. Coined from SULPH- + DI- + *pyrimidine*.]

sul·phur *n.* = **sulfur**

Sul·phur /súlfər/ city in southwestern Louisiana, northeast of Port Arthur, Texas, and northwest of Lake Charles. Population: 20,883 (1996).

sul·tan /súltən/ *n.* **1.** MUSLIM RULER the sovereign ruler of a Muslim country, especially in the past and especially the head of the Ottoman Empire. Only three countries now have sultans as their head of state: Brunei, Oman, and Malaysia. **2.** POWERFUL AND DOMINEERING MAN a man who is powerful in some sphere of activity, especially one who behaves in a domineering or tyrannical fashion (*literary*) [Mid-16thC. Directly or via French from medieval Latin *sultanus*, from Arabic *sulṭān* "ruler, power" from Aramaic *salīṭa* "to rule."] —**sul·tan·ic** /sul tánnik/ *adj.* —**sul·tan·ship** /súltən shìp/ *n.*

sul·tan·a /sul tánnə/ *n.* **1.** DRIED GRAPE a small dried seedless white grape **2.** SULTAN'S WOMAN RELATIVE a wife, mother, sister, daughter, or mistress of a sultan [Late 16thC. From Italian, the feminine of *sultano* "sultan," from, ultimately, Arabic *sulṭān* (see SULTAN).]

sul·tan·ate /súltənət, súltə nàyt/ *n.* **1.** COUNTRY RULED BY SULTAN a country ruled by a sultan **2.** RANK OF SULTAN the rank or position of sultan **3.** SULTAN'S REIGN the period of a particular sultan's reign

sul·try /súltree/ *adj.* **1.** HOT AND DAMP oppressively hot and damp **2.** SENSUAL giving a suggestion of underlying passion and sensuality [Late 16thC. Formed from earlier *sulter* "to swelter," of uncertain origin: perhaps an alteration of SWELTER.] —**sul·tri·ly** *adv.* —**sul·tri·ness** *n.*

sum /sum/ *n.* **1.** TOTAL the total amount resulting when two or more numbers or quantities are added together **2.** AMOUNT OF MONEY an amount of money **3.** ARITHMETICAL CALCULATION a mathematical problem involving adding, subtracting, multiplying, or dividing numbers, especially one given to students to solve **4.** COMBINED TOTAL the combined total amount of anything **5.** GIST the essential point of something that somebody has said or written (*literary*) **6.** MATH LIMIT OF SUM OF SERIES the limit, as n increases indefinitely, of the sum of the first n terms of an infinite series ■ *vt.* (**summed, sum·ming, sums**) ADD UP to add together two or more amounts to find their total (*formal*) [13thC. Via Old French *summe* from Latin *summa* "sum, substance" (literally "highest (thing)"), a noun use of the feminine of *summus* "highest" (source of English *consummate, summary,* and *summit*), from, ultimately, *super* "above" (source of English *super*) from Latin *summa* "sum."] ◇ **in sum** in short or as a summary

WORD KEY: ORIGIN

The semantic development of ***sum*** from "highest" to "sum total" resulted from the Roman practice of counting columns of figures from the bottom upwards, the total being written at the top.

su·mac /sóò màk, shóò-/, **su·mach** *n.* **1.** TREE OF CASHEW FAMILY a tree or shrub of the cashew family that has clusters of green flowers, red hairy fruit, and feathery leaves. Genus: *Rhus.* ◊ **poison sumach 2.** GROUND AND DRIED SUMAC LEAVES the ground dried leaves of one species of sumac, used in tanning and dyeing [14thC. Directly or via French *sumac* from medieval Latin *sumac(h)*, from Arabic *summāḳ*.]

Su·ma·tra /sòò maátrə/ island in western Indonesia, in the Indian Ocean, separated from the Malay Peninsula by the Strait of Malacca. It is the westernmost of the Sundra Islands. Population: 36,881 (1990). Area: 164,150 sq. mi./425,150 sq. km. —**Su·ma·tran** *n., adj.*

Su·mer /sóòmər/ ancient country of western Asia in southern Mesopotamia, in present-day Iraq. Archeological discoveries reveal the area to have been first settled in the 5th millennium B.C. It became prosperous and powerful from about 3000 B.C., and fell into decline from about 1760 B.C., when it was absorbed into Babylonia and Assyria.

Su·me·ri·an /soo mérree ən, soo meeree ən/ *n.* **1.** PEOPLES MEMBER OF ANCIENT BABYLONIAN PEOPLE a member of an ancient people that built the flourishing civilization of Sumer **2.** LANG SUMERIAN LANGUAGE the language spoken in ancient Sumer. It is not related to any other known language. Sumerian is the oldest language preserved in writing, its cuneiform tablets dating from about 3000 B.C. —**Su·me·ri·an** *adj.*

sum·ma /súmmə, sóòmmə, sóòmə/ (*plural* **sum·mae** /-mì, -mee/) *n.* a summary of what is known of a subject, especially a medieval treatise on theology, philosophy, canon law, or alchemy [15thC. From Latin, "main thing, substance, gist," a noun use of the feminine of *summus* (see SUM). The original English meaning was "sum total."]

sum·ma cum lau·de /sòòmmə kòòm lów dày, sòòmə koom-, -lówdee/ *adv.* achieving the highest academic honors at graduation, usually awarded on the basis of the candidates' cumulative grade point average. ◊ **cum laude, magna cum laude** [From Latin, literally "with highest praise"] —**sum·ma cum lau·de** *adj.*

sum·mae plural of **summa**

sum·mand /sú mànd, sə mánd/ *n.* any of the numbers or quantities in a sum [Mid-19thC. From medieval Latin *summandus*, literally "for adding," a form of *summare* "to add," from *summa* (see SUM).]

sum·mar·i·ly /sə mérrəlee, súmmərəlee/ *adv.* immediately and without discussion or attention to formalities [Early 16thC. Originally in the sense "briefly."]

sum·ma·rize /súmmə rìz/ (**-rized, -riz·ing, -riz·es**) *vti.* to make or give a shortened version of something that has been said or written, stating its main points —**sum·mar·ist** *n.* —**sum·ma·riz·a·ble** *adj.* —**sum·ma·ri·za·tion** /sùmmərə záysh'n/ *n.* —**sum·ma·riz·er** /súmmə rìzər/ *n.*

sum·ma·ry /súmmaree/ *n.* (*plural* **-ries**) SHORT VERSION CONTAINING GIST OF SOMETHING a shortened version of something that has been said or written, containing only the main points ■ *adj.* **1.** IMMEDIATE done immediately and with little discussion or attention to formalities ○ *summary execution* **2.** GIVING ONLY MAIN POINTS shortened and giving only the main points of something **3.** LAW RELATING TO LOWER COURTS relating to, dealt with, or given by lower courts operating without the formality of full proceedings [15thC. From Latin *summarium*, from *summa* (see SUM).] —**sum·ma·ri·ness** *n.*

sum·mate /sú màyt/ (**-mat·ed, -mat·ing, -mates**) *vti.* to summarize what has been said before, especially to make a final summary of a case in a court of law (*formal*) [Early 20thC. Back-formation from SUMMATION.]

sum·ma·tion /su máysh'n/ *n.* **1.** LAW FINAL ARGUMENT IN COURT the final summing-up of an argument in a court of law **2.** SUMMARY OF SOMETHING SAID a summary of something that has been said or written **3.** TOTAL a total amount or aggregate **4.** ADDITION the process of adding something up to find a total [Mid-18thC. From the modern Latin stem *summation-*, from medieval Latin *summare* (see SUMMAND).] —**sum·ma·tion·al** *adj.* —**sum·ma·tive** /súmmətiv/ *adj.*

sum·mer[1] /súmmər/ *n.* **1.** WARMEST SEASON the warmest season of the year, falling between spring and autumn, and reckoned astronomically from the summer solstice to the autumn equinox **2.** WARM WEATHER the warm weather associated with the summer season **3.** PERIOD OF GREAT HAPPINESS a period of greatest happiness, success, or fulfillment in the life of somebody or something **4.** YEAR a year, especially of somebody's age (*literary*) ■ *v.* (**-mered, -mer·ing, -mers**) **1.** *vi.* SPEND SUMMER to spend the summer ○ *They summer at the lake.* **2.** *vt.* PASTURE FOR SUMMER to keep cattle or other animals on a particular pasture during the summer [Old English *sumor, sumer.* Ultimately from a prehistoric Germanic word that is also the ancestor of Dutch *zomer* and German *Sommer.*] —**sum·mer·y** *adj.*

sum·mer[2] /súmmər/ *n.* **1.** PRINCIPAL FLOOR BEAM a principal horizontal beam in a building used to support floor joists **2.** STONE SUPPORTING ARCH ON COLUMN a stone that lies atop a pier, column, or wall and supports one or more arches **3.** = **lintel** [13thC. Via Anglo-Norman *sumer*, Old French *som(i)er* "main beam" (originally "pack horse") from, ultimately, late Latin *sagmarius* "pack horse," from *sagma* "pack-saddle," from Greek. The semantic development resulted from analogy between a burdened pack horse and a main supporting beam in a structure.]

sum·mer camp *n.* a place, usually residential, offering outdoor recreational activities and skill development for children during the summer

sum·mer cy·press *n.* a plant of the goosefoot family that has leaves that turn red in the fall. Latin name: *Kochia scoparia.*

sum·mer·house /súmmər hòwss/ (*plural* **sum·mer·hous·es** /-hòwzəz/) *n.* **1.** **sum·mer house** HOUSE FOR SUMMER VACATION a house, e.g., in the mountains or by the shore, used during summer vacations **2.** LIGHT SHELTER IN GARDEN OR PARK a small building or structure in a garden or park to give seating and shade during the summer [Old English *sumerhūs*]

sum·mer·sault *n., vi.* = **somersault**

sum·mer sa·vor·y *n.* = **savory**[2]

sum·mer school *n.* a course of study held during the summer vacation, usually an extra course for high school or college students, especially for those with fewer than the standard number of credits for their standing

sum·mer squash *n.* a squash grown as a vegetable. It must be used shortly after picking. Latin name: *Cucurbita pepo melopepo.*

sum·mer stock *n.* productions of plays and musicals by stock companies in the summer

sum·mer·time /súmmər tìm/ *n.* the season of summer

sum·mer·tree /súmmər trèe/ *n.* = **summer**[2] *n.* 1

sum·mer·wood /súmmər wòòd/ *n.* the part of a tree's annual wood growth produced late in the growing season that is harder and less porous than its earlier growth (**springwood**)

sum·mit /súmmit/ *n.* **1.** HIGHEST POINT OF MOUNTAIN the highest point or top of something, especially a mountain **2.** TOP-LEVEL DIPLOMATIC CONFERENCE a meeting between heads of government or other high-ranking officials to discuss a matter of great importance **3.**

HIGHEST POINT OF SOMETHING the highest point, level, or degree of something such as a career [14thC. From Old French *som(m)ete, sumet,* literally "small top," from *som, sum* "top," from Latin *summum,* the neuter of *summus* (see SUM).] —**sum·mi·tal** *adj.*

sum·mit·eer /sùmmi tēer/ *n.* somebody who takes part in a summit conference

sum·mit·ry /súmmitree/ *n.* the practice of holding, or deciding matters of international importance through, summit conferences

sum·mon /súmmən/ (**-moned, -mon·ing, -mons**) *v.* **1.** *vt.* CALL INTO COURT to order somebody to appear in court by serving a summons **2.** *vt.* SEND FOR SOMEBODY to send or be a signal for somebody to come ○ *We were summoned to his presence.* **3.** *vt.* CONVENE GROUP to call together a formal or official body ○ *They summoned a meeting to debate the issue.* **4.** *vt.* CALL UPON SOMEBODY to request or require somebody to do something ○ *She summoned him to help her.* **5.** *vi.* MANAGE TO GET SOMETHING to gather the resources, especially courage or strength, to cope with or do something ○ *trying to summon up the courage to tell him the news* [13thC. Via Old French *sumondre* from, ultimately, Latin *summonere,* literally "to remind secretly," from *sub-* "under" + *monere* "to warn" (see MONISH).]

sum·mons /súmmənz/ *n.* **1.** COURT ORDER TO DEFENDANT a written order to somebody to appear in court to answer a complaint **2.** COURT ORDER TO WITNESS a written order to a witness or juror to appear in court **3.** ORDER BY AUTHORITY TO APPEAR an authoritative demand to appear at a particular place for a particular purpose ■ *vt.* (**-monsed, -mons·ing, -mons·es**) SERVE SOMEBODY WITH SUMMONS to serve somebody with a summons to appear in court [13thC. From Old French *somonse,* the feminine past participle of *somondre* (see SUMMON).]

Sumo

Barnaby's

su·mo /sōō mō/ *n.* traditional Japanese wrestling in which each contestant tries to force the other outside a circle or to touch the ground other than with the soles of his feet [Late 19thC. From Japanese *sumō.*]

sump /sump/ *n.* **1.** RESERVOIR FOR LIQUID a low area such as a pit or reservoir into which a liquid drains **2.** = **cesspool 3.** *U.K.* AUTOMOT = **oil pan 4.** MINING DRAINAGE RESERVOIR IN MINE an area at the bottom of a mineshaft into which water drains and is then pumped away **5.** CIV ENG ADVANCE EXCAVATION an excavation ahead of the main excavation of a mineshaft or tunnel [15thC. From Middle Dutch *somp* or Middle Low German *sump.* Ultimately from a prehistoric Germanic word meaning "spongy" that is also the ancestor of English *swamp.*]

sump pump *n.* a pump used to remove liquid from a sump, especially water that has accumulated in a basement

sump·ter /súmptər/ *n.* a packhorse, mule, or other pack animal (*archaic*) [Late 16thC. Via Old French *sommetier* "pack-horse driver" from assumed Vulgar Latin *saumatarius,* from Latin *sagma* "packsaddle," from Greek, from *sattein* "to pack," of unknown origin.]

sump·tu·ar·y /súmpchoo èrree/ *adj.* **1.** REGULATING EXPENDITURE relating to or controlling personal spending **2.** REGULATING BEHAVIOR intended to regulate personal behavior on moral or religious grounds [Early 17thC. From Latin *sumptuarius,* from *sumptus* "expense," the past participle of *sumere* "to spend," literally "to take up," from *emere* (see EXAMPLE).]

sump·tu·ous /súmpchoo əss/ *adj.* **1.** SPLENDID magnificent or grand in appearance **2.** EXTRAVAGANT entailing great expense [15thC. Via Old French *somptueux* from Latin *sumptuosus,* from *sumptus* "expense" (see SUMPTUARY).] —**sump·tu·ous·ly** *adv.* —**sump·tu·ous·ness** *n.*

Sum·ter /súmptər/ city in South Carolina. It is southwest of Florence and east of Columbia. Population: 38,565 (1996).

sum to·tal *n.* **1.** EVERYTHING PUT TOGETHER a combined total of separate elements ○ *The sum total of his belongings is the clothes on his back.* **2.** FINAL TOTAL a numerical amount obtained by adding sums

sum-up *n.* a concise presentation of the main points or substance of something

sun /sun/ *n.* **1. Sun, sun** ASTRON STAR AROUND WHICH EARTH REVOLVES the star at the center of our solar system around which the Earth and the eight other planets orbit. It provides us with heat and light. **2.** STAR any star or bright celestial body, especially one around which planets orbit **3.** ASTRON SUN'S RADIATION the light or heat emitted by the Sun **4.** SOMEBODY LIKE THE SUN somebody or something thought to resemble the Sun in radiance, glory, or warmth, or in being the center of a society (*literary*) **5.** DAY OR YEAR a day or year (*literary*) **6.** SUNRISE OR SUNSET the rising or setting of the Sun (*archaic*) ○ *working from sun to sun* ■ *v.* (**sunned, sun·ning, suns**) **1.** *vr.* BASK IN THE SUN to expose the body to the sun's rays for warmth or for a suntan ○ *The cat lay sunning herself on the lawn.* **2.** *vt.* WARM OR DRY IN THE SUN to expose something to the sun's rays for warmth or drying [Old English *sunne.* Ultimately from an Indo-European word that is also the ancestor of English *south, solar,* and *helium.*] ◇ **take the sun** to go out in the sunshine, especially with the aim of gaining some benefit to your health or well-being ◇ **under the sun** in the whole world

Sun. *abbr.* CALENDAR Sunday

sun·bake /sún bàyk/ *vi.* (**-baked, -baked, -bakes**) *Aus* SUNBATHE to sunbathe ■ *n. Aus* SUNBATH a sunbath

sun·baked /sún bàykt/ *adj.* **1.** HARDENED BY THE SUN hard and dry from prolonged exposure to the sun **2.** BAKED IN THE SUN baked by a process of exposure to the sun

sun·bath /sún bàth/ *n.* an act or period of exposing the body to the sun or a sun lamp, especially in order to get a tan

sun·bathe /sún bàyth/ (**-bathed, -bath·ing, -bathes**) *vi.* to expose the body to sun or a sun lamp, especially in order to get a tan —**sun·bath·er** *n.*

sun·beam /sún bēem/ *n.* a ray of light emitted by the sun —**sun·beam·y** *adj.*

sun bear *n.* a small bear of forests of southeastern Asia with sleek black fur, a light-colored muzzle, and a yellowish breast marking. Latin name: *Helarctos malayanus.*

sun·bed /sún bèd/ *n. U.K.* = **tanning bed**

sun·bird /sún bùrd/ *n.* a small brightly colored singing bird native to southern and southeastern Asia, Africa, and Australia. It has a long thin curved bill and feeds on insects and nectar. Family: Nectariniidae.

sun bit·tern *n.* a semiarboreal solitary wading bird of tropical Central and South America that has mottled brownish plumage featuring a chestnut marking like a sunburst when its wings are spread. Latin name: *Eurypyga helius.*

sun·block /sún blòk/ *n.* a substance that is applied to the skin as a cream or lotion to protect it from the sun's harmful ultraviolet rays

sun·bon·net /sún bònnət/ *n.* a bonnet with a wide brim and a flap at the back, worn by babies and, in the past, by women to protect the face and neck from sun

sun·bow /sún bō/ *n.* a spectrum of colors similar to a rainbow produced by sunlight refracting through spray, mist, or water vapor, e.g., above a waterfall [Modeled on "rainbow"]

sun·burn /sún bùrn/ *n.* BURNED SKIN FROM OVEREXPOSURE TO SUN an inflammation and sometimes blistering of the skin caused by overexposure to ultraviolet radiation from the sun ■ *vi.* (**-burned** *or* **-burnt** /-bùrnt/, **-burned** *or* **-burnt, -burn·ing, -burns**) BURN SKIN IN SUN to cause the skin to become inflamed and sometimes blistered as a result of overexposure to ultraviolet radiation from the sun

sun·burned /sún bùrnd/, **sun·burnt** /-bùrnt/ *adj.* affected by sunburn

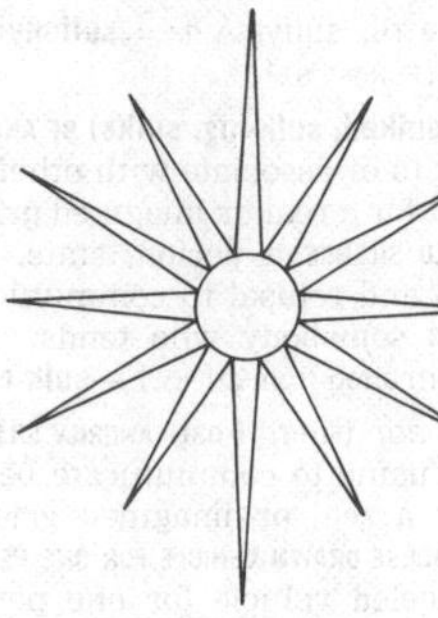

Sunburst

sun·burst /sún bùrst/ *n.* **1.** SUDDEN BURST OF SUNSHINE a sudden appearance of the sun from behind clouds **2.** SUN-SHAPED DESIGN a design meant to resemble the sun, consisting of a series of rays extending outward from a central circle **3.** SUN-SHAPED BROOCH a brooch or other ornament designed as a sunburst

Sun·bur·y /súnbree/ town in southern Victoria, Australia, a residential and agricultural center. Population: 22,126 (1996).

sun·choke /sún chōk/ *n.* = **Jerusalem artichoke** [Late 20thC. Coined from *sunflower* + *artichoke.*]

sun cream *n. U.K.* = **suntan lotion**

sun·dae /sún dày/ *n.* an ice-cream dessert served with toppings such as whipped cream, fruit, nuts, and flavored syrup [Late 19thC. Alteration of SUNDAY.]

Sun·da Is·lands /sùndə-/ island group of the Malay Archipelago between the South China Sea and the Indian Ocean. It consists of two groups, the Greater Sunda Islands, which include Sumatra, Java and Borneo, and the Lesser Sunda Islands, which include Bali and Timor.

sun dance *n.* an important ceremonial dance of Native North American peoples living on prairies, held annually in honor of the sun

Sun·day /sún dày, súndee/ *n.* CALENDAR **1.** 1ST DAY OF WEEK the day of the week after Saturday and before Monday **2.** CHRISTIAN SABBATH DAY in Christian tradition, the day set aside for the Sabbath ■ *adj.* **1.** OF SUNDAY relating to or occupying a Sunday **2.** FOR SPECIAL OCCASIONS worn or used for special occasions **3.** ONLY AT WEEKENDS OR AS HOBBY lacking experience, efficiency, or professional skill ○ *These Sunday drivers are a menace on the roads.* [Old English *sunnandæg,* literally "day of the sun," a translation of Latin *dies solis*]

Sun·day-go-to-meet·ing *adj.* suitable for attending a church service (*informal*)

Sun·day punch *n.* **1.** KNOCKOUT PUNCH a boxer's most powerful punch, especially a knockout blow **2.** EFFECTIVE WEAPON a means of delivering a devastating blow to an opponent

Sun·days /sún dàyz, súndeez/ *adv.* every Sunday

Sun·day school *n.* a school or class offering children religious education or activities on Sundays

sun deck *n.* **1.** NAUT SHIP'S DECK an open upper deck on a passenger ship **2.** *U.S., ANZ* PLACE TO SUNBATHE a balcony, terrace, or platform attached to a building, used for sunbathing

sun·der /súndər/ (**-dered, -der·ing, -ders**) *vti.* to separate or make something separate into parts, especially with force (*archaic or literary*) [Old English *sundrian,* from *sundor* "apart." Ultimately from an Indo-European base that is also the ancestor of Latin *sine* "without."] —**sun·der·er** *n.*

sun·dew /sún dōō, sún dyōō/ *n.* a plant that produces a rosette of hairy sticky leaves that are used to trap and digest insects. Sundews occur worldwide, but especially in Australia and New Zealand. Family: Droseraceae. [Translation of Latin *ros solis;* so called because the drops of juice the plant secretes resemble dew]

sun·di·al /sún dī əl/ *n.* an instrument that shows the time of day by the position of a sun-generated shadow cast by a fixed arm (**gnomon**) onto a graduated plate or surface

sun disk *n.* an ancient Egyptian sun-god symbol, consisting of a disk with wings and two serpents

sun·dog /sún dòg/ *n.* **1.** = **parhelion 2.** SMALL RAINBOW NEAR SUN a small spectrum of light occasionally visible in the sky at the same altitude as the sun, either to

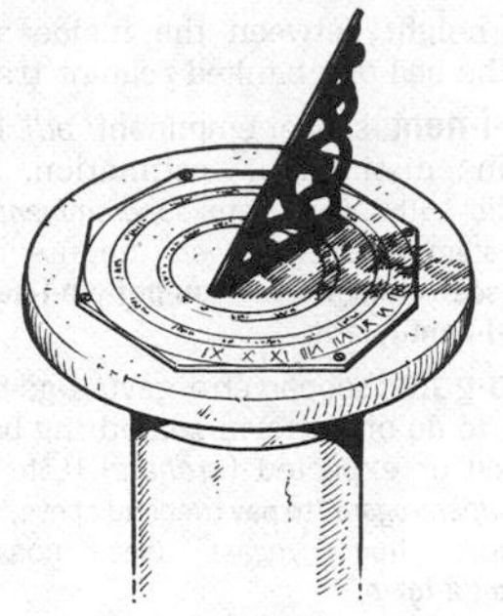

Sundial

the left or right of the sun and sometimes on both sides simultaneously

sun·down /sún dòwn/ *n.* the time when the sun sets

sun·down·er /sún dòwnər/ *n. U.K., S Africa* an alcoholic drink taken early in the evening, around sunset (*informal*)

sun·dress /sún drèss/ *n.* a light sleeveless summer dress with a low bodice that exposes the shoulders, back, and arms to the sun

sun-dried *adj.* dried out naturally by the sun, not by applying artificial heat

sun·dries /súndreez/ *npl.* small miscellaneous items, often of too little value to be enumerated

sun·drops /sún dròps/ (*plural* **-drops**) *n.* = **evening primrose**

sun·dry /súndree/ *adj.* assorted but, perhaps for convenience, being considered as a single category or group ○ *and other sundry items.* ◊ **sundries** [Old English *syndrig* "separate"] ◇ **all and sundry** everyone without exception (*takes a plural verb*)

Sunds·vall /sŏŏndz vaal/ town and port on the Gulf of Bothnia, Sweden, situated about 250 mi./400 km north of Stockholm. Population: 94,531 (1995).

sun·fish /sún fish/ (*plural* **-fish** *or* **-fish·es**) *n.* **1. N AMERICAN FRESHWATER FISH** a small to medium sized spiny-finned North American freshwater fish, often with iridescent colors. The family includes several game fish. Examples are the smallmouth bass, the largemouth bass, the black-and-white crappie, the bluegill, and the pumpkinseed. **2.** *U.K.* = **ocean sunfish**

sun·flow·er /sún flòwr/ *n.* **1. TALL PLANT WITH YELLOW-RAYED FLOWERS** a tall annual plant with large yellow-rayed flowers and edible seeds that yield an oil. It is grown for ornament and as a farm crop for sunflower oil. Latin name: *Helianthus annus.* **2. PLANT RELATED TO COMMERCIALLY-GROWN SUNFLOWER** any of several plants related to the seed- and oil-giving sunflower. Genus: *Helianthus.* [Mid-16thC. Translation of modern Latin *flos solis* and Greek *helianthos.* So called from its yellow-rayed flowers and because it turns to follow the sun throughout the day.]

WORD KEY: CULTURAL NOTE

Sunflowers, a series of paintings by Dutch artist Vincent Van Gogh (1888). These simple still lifes constitute one of Van Gogh's most successful attempts to transform everyday objects into powerful poetic symbols. Their intense colors and ragged, writhing forms suggest the life forces inherent in nature as well as the energy of the artist, but also hint at an underlying sense of anxiety and despair.

sung past participle of **sing**

Sung /sŏŏng/, **Song** *n.* a Chinese imperial dynasty lasting from A.D. 960–1279, under which science, philosophy, and the arts thrived [Late 17thC. From Chinese *Song.*]

sun·gaz·er /sún gàyzər/ *n.* a lizard of southern Africa that grows to about 14 in./355 cm and is known for its habit of basking in the sun. Latin name: *Cordylus giganteus.*

sun·glass /sún glàss/ *n.* **LENS TO FOCUS SUN'S RAYS** a convex lens used to focus the sun's rays to produce heat, especially in order to start a fire ■ **sun·glass·es** *npl.* **GLASSES THAT SHIELD EYES FROM GLARE** eyeglasses with tinted or darkened lenses to protect the eyes from sunlight or its glare

sun·glow /sún glṓ/ *n.* a pale pink or yellow glow seen in the sky just before sunrise or just after sunset

sun god, **sun-god** *n.* **1. SUN AS GOD** the sun worshiped as a god **2. GOD OF THE SUN** a god that personifies or is seen as controlling the sun

sun-grebe *n.* a diving bird that lives along rivers and lakes of tropical America, Africa, and Asia. It has brownish plumage and lobed toes and feeds on aquatic invertebrates. Family: Heliornithidae.

sun·hat /sún hàt/ *n.* a hat with a broad brim that is designed to keep the sun off the face and neck

su·ni /sŏŏnee/ (*plural* **-nis** *or* **-ni**) *n.* a small southern African antelope, growing to only about 14 in./355 cm long, that has small straight horns and a strong musky odor from facial glands. Latin name: *Neotragus moschatus.* [Late 19thC. Of Bantu origin.]

sunk /sungk/ past participle, past tense of **sink** ■ *adj.* **DOOMED TO FAILURE** without hope of success (*informal*)

WORD KEY: USAGE

See Usage note at ***sink***.

sunk·en /súngkən/ *adj.* **1. SUBMERGED** having sunk beneath the surface of something **2. HOLLOW-LOOKING** appearing hollow or concave ○ *sunken cheeks* **3. SUNK LOWER** having settled to a lower level **4. AT LOWER ELEVATION** at a lower level than something adjoining

WORD KEY: USAGE

See Usage note at ***sink***.

sunk fence *n.* a ditch containing a fence or wall that separates lands without marring the appearance of the landscape

sun·lamp /sún làmp/ *n.* **1. LAMP USED FOR TANNING** a lamp that emits ultraviolet light, used to get a suntan or for therapeutic purposes **2. PHOTOGRAPHER'S LAMP** a lamp with parabolic mirrors that are directed to focus light, used in cinema photography

sun·less /súnnləss/ *adj.* **1. WITHOUT SUNLIGHT** deprived of or lacking sunlight **2. JOYLESS** without joy or happiness

sun·light /sún lìt/ *n.* light emitted by the sun —**sun·lit** /sún lìt/ *adj.*

sun lo·tion *n.* = **suntan lotion**

sun lounge *n. U.K.* = **sunroom**

sunn /sun/ *n.* **1.** PLANTS **TROPICAL ASIAN LEGUMINOUS PLANT** a plant of the pea family that has thin branches and clusters of yellow flowers and grows in tropical Asia and Australia. Latin name: *Crotalaria juncea.* **2.** INDUST **FIBER FROM SUNN PLANT** strong light fiber obtained from the inner bark of the sunn plant, used for such things as rope and sacks [Late 18thC. Via Hindustani *san* from Sanskrit *śāṇa-* "hempen."]

Sun·na /sŏŏnnə, súnnə/, **Sun·nah** *n.* one of the basic sources of Islamic law based on Muhammad's words and deeds as recorded in the Hadith. The Sunna compliments and often explains the Koran. [Early 18thC. From Arabic, "rule, custom."]

Sun·ni /sŏŏnnee/ (*plural* **-ni** *or* **-nis**) *n.* **1. BRANCH OF ISLAM** the largest branch of Islam, which believes in the traditions of the Sunna and accepts the first four caliphs as rightful successors to Muhammad **2. SUNNI MUSLIM** a member of the Sunni branch of Islam [Late 16thC. From Arabic, "lawful," from *sunna* "rule, custom."]

sun·nies /súnniz/ *npl. ANZ* sunglasses (*informal*)

Sun·nite /sŏŏ nìt, sú-/ *n.* = **Sunni** *n.* 2

sun·ny /súnnee/ (**-ni·er, -ni·est**) *adj.* **1. FULL OF SUNSHINE** with a lot of sunshine **2. FULL OF SUNLIGHT** bright with or exposed to sunlight **3. CHEERFUL** characterized by or showing happiness or cheerfulness —**sun·ni·ly** *adv.* —**sun·ni·ness** *n.*

sun·ny-side up *adj.* used to describe fried eggs that are not turned over in cooking and so have a visible yellow yolk uppermost

sun par·lor *n.* = **sunroom**

sun pro·tec·tion fac·tor *n.* full form of **SPF**

sun·rise /sún rìz/ *n.* **1. COMING UP OF SUN** the rising of the sun above the eastern horizon each morning **2. GLOW FROM RISING SUN** an atmospheric glow and coloring near the horizon as the sun rises **3. TIME SUN RISES** the time at which the sun rises above the horizon in the morning

sun·roof /sún ròof/ *n.* a small panel in the roof of a car that can be raised or slid back to let in air and light

sun·room /sún ròom, -rŏŏm/ *n. U.S., ANZ* a room with large windows designed to receive the maximum sunlight

sun·screen /sún skrēen/ *n.* a cosmetic cream, lotion, or oil, or an ingredient of one, intended to protect the skin from burning without preventing tanning

sun·set /sún sèt/ *n.* **1. GOING DOWN OF SUN** the setting of the sun below the western horizon in the evening **2. GLOW FROM SETTING SUN** an atmospheric glow and coloring near the horizon as the sun sets **3. TIME SUN SETS** the time at which the sun sets below the horizon in the evening **4. LAST PART** the period during which something is declining or coming to an end

WORD KEY: CULTURAL NOTE

Sunset Boulevard, a movie by Billy Wilder (1950). Wilder uses the story of the relationship between an out-of-favor screenwriter and a faded and eccentric silent-movie star to create one of the cinema's most savage satires on the cynicism and ruthlessness of the Hollywood system. The performances, camerawork, and direction all reinforce the powerful atmosphere of corruption and decay.

sun·shade /sún shàyd/ *n.* something, e.g., an awning or parasol, under which somebody is protected from the sun

sun·shine /sún shìn/ *n.* **1. DIRECT SUNLIGHT** direct rays of the sun, producing heat and light ○ *a ray of sunshine* **2. SUNNY PLACE** a place where the sun's rays are falling ○ *Let's sit in the sunshine.* **3. SOURCE OF GOOD FEELINGS** somebody or something producing joy, happiness, or warmth ○ *bringing a little bit of sunshine into people's lives* ■ *adj.* **GIVING ACCESS TO THE PUBLIC** used to describe a law or legislation requiring that meetings and records of some governmental bodies be open to the public —**sun·shin·y** *adj.*

Sun·shine Coast region in southeastern Queensland, Australia, consisting of the 28 mi./45 km stretch of coastline between Noosa Heads and Caloundra. It is a popular tourist destination.

sun·spot /sún spòt/ *n.* one of the relatively cool dark patches that appear in cycles on the Sun's surface and possess a powerful magnetic field

sun·stone /sún stṑn/ *n.* = **aventurine** [Translation of Latin *gemma solis*]

sun·stroke /sún strṑk/ *n.* a condition caused by prolonged and excessive exposure to the sun and characterized by feverishness, faintness, convulsions, and coma. It results when the temperature becomes too extreme to be handled by the body's heat-regulating mechanism. Technical name **insolation**

sun·suit /sún sòot/ *n.* a child's one-piece garment usually consisting of shorts and a bib top with shoulder straps, worn in hot weather

sun·tan /sún tàn/ *n.* = **tan**[1] *n.* 1 —**sun·tanned** *adj.*

sun·tan lo·tion *n.* a cosmetic lotion used to protect the skin from the sun and usually also to help somebody develop a suntan

sun·trap /sún tràp/ *n. U.K.* a sheltered area with bright sunlight and little or no wind

sun·up /sún ùp/ *n.* = **sunrise** *n.* 3

Sun Val·ley city in central Idaho, in the Sawtooth Mountains, east of Boise. It is a popular ski resort. Population: 1,011 (1996).

sun·ward /súnnwərd/ *adj.* **FACING THE SUN** turned toward or in the direction of the sun ■ *adv.* **sun·ward, sun·wards TOWARD THE SUN** in the direction of the sun

Sun Yat-sen /sŏŏn yátsén/ (1866–1925) Chinese statesman. He developed his democratic political philosophy during years of foreign travel, and returned to China to lead the overthrow of the Manchu dynasty (1911). He founded the nationalist Kuomintang Party (1923) and headed an opposition government in Guangzhou (1917–25), but failed to establish a national republican government.

sup[1] /sup/ *vti.* (**supped, sup·ping, sups**) **1. SIP LIQUID** to drink small amounts of liquid at one time **2. EAT BY THE SPOONFUL** to eat something that is swallowed directly, e.g., soup or oatmeal, with a spoon ■ *n.* **SIP OF LIQUID** a small amount or mouthful of liquid [Old English *sūpan.* Ultimately from a prehistoric Germanic base that is also the ancestor of English *sip, soup,* and *sup*[2].]

sup[2] /sup/ *vi.* (**supped, sup·ping, sups**) **HAVE SUPPER** to eat the evening meal (*archaic*) ■ *n.* **SUPPER** the evening meal (*archaic*) [14thC. From Old French *souper,* from *soupe* (see SOUP).]

sup. *abbr.* **1.** supra **2.** GRAM superlative **3.** GRAM supine **4.** supplement **5.** supplementary **6.** supply **7.** superior

su·pa·ri /soo pa̋aree/ *n. S Asia* areca palm nuts chewed with betel leaves, especially after meals as a digestive [Mid-17thC. From Hindi *supārī*.]

Sup. Ct. *abbr.* **1.** Supreme Court **2.** Superior Court

Supdt. *abbr.* PUBLIC ADMIN Superintendent

su·per /so͞opər/ *adj.* **1. EXCELLENT** with outstanding or excellent qualities (*informal*) ○ *a super idea* **2. VERY GREAT** exceptionally large or powerful (*informal*) **3. EXCESSIVE** greater than what is normal ■ *adv.* **ESPECIALLY** to or in a high or extreme degree (*informal*) ○ *Everyone has been super helpful.* ■ *n.* **1. BUILDING SUPERINTENDENT** a superintendent, especially of an apartment building (*informal*) **2. SUPERVISOR** a supervisor (*informal*) **3. SOMETHING BIGGER OR BETTER** something superior in grade or quality or large in size **4.** THEATER **ACTOR EMPLOYED AS WALK-ON** a supernumerary, especially an actor with a walk-on part (*informal*) **5. HIGH-OCTANE GASOLINE** high-octane gasoline **6.** AGRIC **TOP OF BEEHIVE WITH HONEY** a removable upper part of a beehive in which the bees store honey **7.** CRAFT **OPEN-WEAVE FABRIC FOR BOOK BINDINGS** a starched cotton gauze fabric used for reinforcing book bindings ■ *interj.* **GREAT!** used to express enthusiasm, approval, or agreement (*informal*) [Mid-19thC. From SUPER-, or a shortening of various words beginning with SUPER-.]

super. *abbr.* **1.** superfine **2.** superior

super- *prefix.* **1.** something larger, stronger, or faster than others of its kind ○ *superstore* **2.** over, above, on ○ *supernatant* ○ *superstructure* **3.** exceeding the usual or normal limits ○ *superheat* **4.** a more inclusive group or category ○ *superclass* **5.** in addition to, over and above ○ *superfetation* **6.** greater in size, quality, number, or degree, superior ○ *superhuman* [From Latin *super* "over, above" (source of English *supreme* and *sovereign*). Ultimately from an Indo-European base that is also the ancestor of *over* and *hyper-*.]

su·per·a·ble /so͞opərəb'l/ *adj.* capable of being overcome [Early 17thC. From Latin *superabilis*, from *superare* "to overcome," from *super* (see SUPER-).] —**su·per·a·bil·i·ty** /so͞opərə bíllətee/ *n.* —**su·per·a·ble·ness** /so͞opərəb'l nəss/ *n.* —**su·per·a·bly** *adv.*

su·per·a·bound /so͞opərə bównd/ (**-bound·ed, -bound·ing, -bounds**) *vi.* to be too numerous or abundant [14thC. From late Latin *superabundare*, from *abundare* (see ABOUND).]

su·per·a·bun·dant /so͞opərə búndənt/ *adj.* present in excess of what is sufficient [15thC. From late Latin *superabundant-*, the present participle stem of *superabundare* (see SUPERABOUND).] —**su·per·a·bun·dance** *n.* —**su·per·a·bun·dant·ly** *adv.*

su·per·add /so͞opərə ád/ (**-add·ed, -add·ing, -adds**) *vt.* to add something onto what has already been added [15thC. From Latin *superaddere*, from *addere* (see ADD).] —**su·per·ad·di·tion** /so͞opərə dísh'n/ *n.* —**su·per·ad·di·tion·al** /-díshən'l/ *adj.*

su·per·al·loy /so͞opər á lòy/ *n.* a heat-resistant alloy with superior mechanical properties, often having aerospace applications

su·per·an·nu·ate /so͞opər ánnyoo àyt/ (**-at·ed, -at·ing, -ates**) *v.* **1.** *vti.* **RETIRE WITH A PENSION** to become retired or retire somebody with a pension **2.** *vt.* **GET RID OF SOMETHING** to reject something or cause something to be rejected because of obsolescence [Mid-17thC. Back-formation from SUPERANNUATED.] —**su·per·an·nu·a·tion** /so͞opər ànnyoo áysh'n/ *n.*

su·per·an·nu·at·ed /so͞opər ánnyoo àytəd/ *adj.* **1. RETIRED** having been retired with a pension **2. TOO WORN** too much used for more useful service **3. OUT-OF-DATE** no longer in fashion [Mid-17thC. From medieval Latin *superannuatus* "more than a year old," from *annus* "year."]

su·perb /soo púrb, sə-/ *adj.* **1. EXCELLENT** of the highest quality **2. GRAND** impressive in size or appearance **3. SUMPTUOUS** rich and sumptuous in appearance or detail [Mid-16thC. Via French from Latin *superbus* "proud, superior," from *super* (see SUPER-).] —**su·perb·ly** *adv.* —**su·perb·ness** *n.*

Su·per Bowl *tdmk.* a trademark for the championship game of the National Football League played each year between the champions of the National Football Conference and the American Football Conference

su·per·bug /so͞opər bùg/ *n.* a bacterium that has become resistant to the antibiotics normally used to treat it

su·per·cal·en·der /so͞opər kàlləndər/ *n.* **MACHINE FOR FINISHING PAPER** a machine with an extra large number of rollers to give a glossy finish to paper ■ *vt.* (**-dered, -der·ing, -ders**) **GIVE PAPER A SHEEN** to produce a glossy finish on paper using a supercalender

su·per·car·go /so͞opər ka̋argō/ (*plural* **-gos**) *n.* an officer who is in charge of the cargo and commercial matters aboard a merchant ship [Late 17thC. Alteration (influenced by SUPER-) of earlier *supracargo*, an alteration (influenced by SUPRA-) of Spanish *sobrecargo*, from *sobre-* "over" (from Latin *super-*) + Spanish *cargo* (see CARGO).]

su·per·cen·ter *n.* a supermarket with other departments such as a pharmacy, banking center, or clothing department (*often used with retail trade names*)

su·per·charge /so͞opər cha̋arj/ (**-charged, -charg·ing, -charg·es**) *vt.* **1.** AUTOMOT **INCREASE ENGINE'S POWER** to increase the power of an internal-combustion engine by means of a supercharger **2. FILL SOMETHING WITH TOO MUCH FEELING** to charge something, e.g., the atmosphere or a remark, with excessive emotion or energy

su·per·charg·er /so͞opər cha̋arjər/ *n.* a device that supplies air to an internal-combustion engine at a pressure greater than the ambient atmospheric pressure in order to increase its power. The blower or air pump on an engine's intake system could be a supercharger.

su·per·cil·i·ar·y /so͞opər síllee èrree/ *adj.* **1. OF THE EYEBROW** relating to or in the region of the eyebrow **2. ABOVE THE EYE** used to describe markings above an animal's eye [Mid-18thC. Formed from Latin *supercilium* "eyebrow" (see SUPERCILIOUS).]

su·per·cil·i·ous /so͞opər síllee əss/ *adj.* full of contempt and arrogance [Early 16thC. From Latin *superciliosus*, from *supercilium* "eyebrow," from *super* "above" + *cilium* "eyelid," referring to raised eyebrows as a sign of haughty disdain.]

su·per·class /so͞opər klàss/ *n.* a taxonomic category of related organisms ranking below a phylum and above a class

su·per·clus·ter /so͞opər klùstər/ *n.* an association of clusters of galaxies

su·per·col·lid·er /so͞opər kə lī̀dər/ *n.* a very large high-energy particle accelerator

su·per·com·put·er /so͞opər kəm pyo͞otər/ *n.* a state-of-the-art computer with the highest processing speeds technologically possible at a given time, used for solving complex scientific and engineering problems

su·per·con·duc·tiv·i·ty /so͞opər kòndək tívvətee/ *n.* the ability of some metals, alloys, and ceramics to conduct electric current with negligible internal resistance at temperatures near absolute zero and, in some cases, at higher temperatures. Scientists have developed superconductors that function at temperatures up to 100 degrees above absolute zero. —**su·per·con·duct·ing** /so͞opər kən dúkting/ *adj.* —**su·per·con·duc·tion** /-dúksh'n/ *n.* —**su·per·con·duc·tive** /-dúktiv/ *adj.* —**su·per·con·duc·tor** /-dúktər/ *n.*

su·per·con·ti·nent /so͞opər kònt'nənt/ *n.* one of the large continental masses believed to have broken into several parts that drifted apart to form the present continents. These land masses included Pangaea, Gondwana, and Laurasia.

su·per·cool /so͞opər ko͞ol/ *vti.* (**-cooled, -cool·ing, -cools**) **COOL BELOW FREEZING POINT WITHOUT SOLIDIFYING** to cool a liquid, or become cooled, to a temperature below freezing point without change to a solid ■ *adj.* **TOTALLY MODERN** extremely fashionable in attitude or image (*informal*)

su·per-dup·er /so͞opər do͞opər/ *adj.* of the greatest excellence, size, or efficiency (*informal*) (*often used ironically*) [Doubling of SUPER]

su·per·e·go /so͞opər éegō, so͞opər éegō/ (*plural* **-gos**) *n.* according to Freudian theory, the part of the mind that acts as a conscience to the ego, developing moral standards and rules through contact with parents and society [Early 20thC. Translation of German *Über-Ich*, coined by Sigmund Freud.]

su·per·el·e·va·tion /so͞opər èllə váysh'n/ *n.* the distance in height between the inside and outside edges of the bed of a banked road or track

su·per·em·i·nent /so͞opər émminənt/ *adj.* higher than others in distinction, estimation, or prominence [Mid-16thC. From Latin *supereminent-*, the present participle stem of *supereminere* "to rise above," from *eminere* (see EMINENT).] —**su·per·em·i·nence** *n.* —**su·per·em·i·nent·ly** *adv.*

su·per·er·o·gate /so͞opər érrə gàyt/ (**-ga·ted, -ga·ting, -gates**) *vi.* to do or perform something beyond what is required or expected (*archaic*) [Late 16thC. From late Latin *supererogare* "to pay over and above," from *erogare* "to spend," from *rogare* (see ROGATION).] —**su·per·er·o·ga·tor** *n.*

su·per·er·o·ga·tion /so͞opər èrrə gáysh'n/ *n.* the performance of work beyond what is required or expected [Early 16thC. From the medieval Latin stem of *supererogatio*, from *supererogare* (see SUPEREROGATE).]

su·per·e·rog·a·to·ry /so͞opərə róggə tàwree/ *adj.* **1. BEYOND THE CALL OF DUTY** performed to an extent beyond what is required or expected **2. SUPERFLUOUS** beyond what is sufficient or necessary, and not wanted —**su·per·er·o·ga·to·ri·ly** *adv.*

su·per·fam·i·ly /so͞opər fàmmalee/ (*plural* **-lies**) *n.* a taxonomic category of related organisms ranking below an order and above a family

su·per·fec·ta /so͞opər fèktə/ *n.* a type of bet, especially in horseracing, in which the bettor, in order to win, must pick the first four finishers in the correct sequence [Late 20thC. Blend of SUPER and PERFECTA.]

su·per·fe·cun·da·tion /so͞opər fèkən dáysh'n/ *n.* **1. SEPARATE FERTILIZATION OF OVA** the fertilization of two or more ova at different times during one menstrual cycle by sperm from the same or different males **2. FERTILIZATION OF MANY OVA** the fertilization of an unusually large number of ova at the same time

su·per·fe·ta·tion /so͞opər fi táysh'n/ *n.* the fertilization of a second ovum after the start of pregnancy, resulting in the presence of two fetuses at different stages of development in the same uterus. It is a normal occurrence in some animal species. [Early 17thC. Via French from, ultimately, modern Latin *superfetare* "to conceive a second time," from Latin *foetus* (see FETUS).]

su·per·fi·cial /so͞oopər físh'l/ *adj.* **1. NOT PROFOUND** concerned with or understanding only the obvious ○ *a superficial knowledge of the text* **2. RELATING TO THE SURFACE** on, near, relating to, or affecting the surface of something ○ *a superficial wound* **3. WITHOUT DEPTH OF CHARACTER** shallow in character or attitude ○ *I find her quite superficial.* **4. CURSORY** swift and not thorough ○ *after a superficial examination of the injury* **5. ONLY APPARENTLY SO** only seeming to be real or the case ○ *The picture bears a superficial resemblance, nothing more.* **6. INSIGNIFICANT** with little significance or substance ○ *superficial changes to the policy* [14thC. Formed from Latin *superficies* (see SUPERFICIES).] —**su·per·fi·ci·al·i·ty** /so͞opər fishee állətee/ *n.* —**su·per·fi·cial·ly** /so͞opər físh'lee/ *adv.*

su·per·fi·cies /so͞opər físhiz/ (*plural* **-cies**) *n.* **1. OUTER SURFACE** an outer surface or area of something **2. OUTWARD APPEARANCE** the outward appearance or form of something [Mid-16thC. From Latin, from *super* "above" + *facies* (see FACE).]

su·per·fine /so͞opər fī̀n, so͞opər fī́n/ *adj.* **1. FINEST IN TEXTURE** of extremely fine grain or texture **2. FINEST IN QUALITY** of the highest quality or grade **3. AFFECTEDLY REFINED** excessively refined in manner —**su·per·fine·ness** *n.*

su·per·flu·id /so͞opər flo͞o id/ *n.* **FLUID FLOWING FREELY AT LOW TEMPERATURES** a fluid characterized by the absence of viscosity at temperatures near absolute zero. The only known example is liquid helium. ■ *adj.* **BEHAVING LIKE SUPERFLUID** relating to or exhibiting the properties of a superfluid —**su·per·flu·id·i·ty** /so͞opər floo íddətee/ *n.*

su·per·flu·i·ty /so͞opər flo͞o ətee/ (*plural* **-ties**) *n.* **1. SOMETHING INESSENTIAL** something beyond what is necessary **2. EXCESSIVE QUANTITY** an excessive or overabundant supply of something

su·per·flu·ous /sə púrfloo əss/ *adj.* **1. MORE THAN NECESSARY** that is in excess of what is needed ○ *a lot of superfluous detail* **2. INESSENTIAL** not essential ○ *superfluous to the discussion* **3. EXTRAVAGANT** extravagant in living or spending (*archaic*) [14thC. Directly or via Old French *superflueux* from Latin *superfluus*, from *superfluere* "to overflow," from *fluere* (see FLUENT).] —**su·per·flu·ous·ly** *adv.* —**su·per·flu·ous·ness** *n.*

su·per·gene /sŏŏpər jeen/ *n.* a group of genes that lie close together on a chromosome, function as a unit, and are rarely separated

su·per·gi·ant /sŏŏpər jī ənt/ *n.* an extremely large brilliant star with a luminosity thousands of times greater than that of the Sun. The stars Rigel and Betelgeuse are examples.

su·per·glue /sŏŏpər gloo/ *n.* a fast-acting glue that forms a strong bond by polymerization

su·per·graph·ics /sŏŏpər gràffiks/ *n.* simple brightly colored graphic designs of very large proportions (*takes a singular or plural verb*)

su·per·grav·i·ty /sŏŏpər grávvətee/ *n.* a theory in physics that encompasses all known fundamental interactions, using hypothetical particles (**gravitons**) to carry the gravitational force. It has largely been supplanted by superstring theory.

su·per·group /sŏŏpər groop/ *n.* a rock music group whose performers are already famous from having performed individually or in other groups

su·per·heat /sŏŏpər heet/ *vt.* (**-heat·ed, -heat·ing, -heats**) **1. HEAT LIQUID WITHOUT VAPORIZATION** to heat a liquid above its pressure-related boiling point without causing it to vaporize **2. HEAT VAPOR TO SATURATION** to heat a vapor not in contact with its liquid to the point at which a lowering of temperature or increase in pressure will not change it to a liquid **3. GET SOMETHING VERY HOT** to heat something to an extremely high temperature ■ *n.* **HEAT FOR SUPERHEATING** the heat used to superheat a vapor —**su·per·heat·er** *n.*

su·per·heav·y·weight /sŏŏpər hévvee wàyt/ *n.* an athlete, especially a boxer, wrestler, or weightlifter, who competes in the heaviest weight division —**su·per·heav·y·weight** *adj.*

su·per·he·lix /sŏŏpər heeliks/ (*plural* **-hel·i·ces** /-hèlli seez, -heeli-/) *n.* a molecule with a helical structure formed by another helical molecule, e.g., a nucleosome formed of DNA

su·per·he·ro /sŏŏpər heerō/ (*plural* **-roes**) *n.* a fictional character, e.g., from a cartoon, who has superhuman powers and uses them to fight crime or evil

su·per·het·er·o·dyne /sŏŏpər héttərə dīn/ *adj.* **WITH MIXING OF RADIO FREQUENCIES** relating to a method of receiving radio signals in which the incoming signal is mixed with a frequency generated by the receiver. The resulting intermediate frequency is amplified then decoded. ■ *n.* **SUPERHETERODYNE RECEIVER** a radio receiver that operates using the superheterodyne method of receiving signals [Early 20thC. Formed from SUPERSONIC + HETERODYNE, because the incoming signals are outside the range of sound.]

su·per·high fre·quen·cy /sŏŏpər hī-/ *n.* a radio frequency between 3,000 and 30,000 megahertz

su·per·high·way /sŏŏpər hī wày/ *n.* **1. HIGHWAY** a highway or expressway designed for high-speed traffic, with several lanes in each direction **2.** = **information superhighway**

su·per·hu·man /sŏŏpər hyŏŏmən, -yŏŏmən/ *adj.* **1. BEYOND HUMAN CAPABILITY** beyond ordinary human capability **2. SUPERNATURAL** with higher or greater powers than those within human experience ○ *a superhuman being* [Early 17thC. From late Latin *superhumanus*, from *humanus* (see HUMAN).] —**su·per·hu·man·i·ty** /sŏŏpər hyoo mánnətee, -yoo-/ *n.* —**su·per·hu·man·ly** /sŏŏpər hyŏŏmənlee, -yŏŏmənlee/ *adv.* —**su·per·hu·man·ness** /-hyŏŏmən nəss, -yŏŏmən-/ *n.*

su·per·im·pose /sŏŏpərim pṓz/ (**-posed, -pos·ing, -pos·es**) *vt.* **1. LAY SOMETHING OVER SOMETHING** to place something, e.g., a transparent image, on or over something else, often with the result that both things appear simultaneously, although one may partially obscure the other **2. ADD ONTO SOMETHING** to add a feature or element without incorporating it ○ *superimpose one culture on another* —**su·per·im·po·si·tion** /sŏŏpərimpə zísh'n/ *n.*

su·per·in·cum·bent /sŏŏpərin kúmbənt/ *adj.* lying or resting on or above something [Mid-17thC. From Latin *superincumbere* "to lie on top of," from *incumbere* (see INCUMBENT).] —**su·per·in·cum·bence** *n.* —**su·per·in·cum·ben·cy** *n.* —**su·per·in·cum·bent·ly** *adv.*

su·per·in·duce /sŏŏpərin dŏŏss/ (**-duced, -duc·ing, -duc·es**) *vt.* to introduce somebody or something additional [Mid-16thC. From Latin *superinducere*, literally "to bring in upon," from *inducere* (see INDUCE).] —**su·per·in·duc·tion** /sŏŏpərin dúksh'n/ *n.*

su·per·in·fec·tion /sŏŏpərin féksh'n/ *n.* an infection that develops during drug treatment for another infection, caused by a different microorganism that is resistant to the treatment used for the first infection —**su·per·in·fect** /sŏŏpərin fékt/ *vt.*

su·per·in·tend /sŏŏpərin ténd/ (**-tend·ed, -tend·ing, -tends**) *vt.* to be responsible for and supervise something, e.g., a project or job [Early 17thC. Back-formation from SUPERINTENDENT.]

su·per·in·ten·dence /sŏŏpərin téndənss/ *n.* = **superintendency** *n.* 2

su·per·in·ten·den·cy /sŏŏpərin téndənssee/ (*plural* **-cies**) *n.* **1. JOB OF SUPERINTENDENT** the office, position, authority, or administrative district of a superintendent **2. MANAGEMENT** supervision or administration by a superintendent

su·per·in·ten·dent /sŏŏpərin téndənt/ *n.* **1. SOMEBODY IN CHARGE** an administrator or manager of something, e.g., an office or school system **2. JANITOR** somebody in charge of the maintenance of a building **3. HIGH-RANKING POLICE OFFICER** in the United Kingdom, a police officer ranking higher than an inspector ■ *adj.* **IN CHARGE** acting in an administrative or supervisory capacity [Mid-16thC. Formed from ecclesiastical Latin *superintendere* "to oversee," from *intendere* (see INTEND), as a translation of Greek *episkopos* "overseer."]

su·pe·ri·or /sə peeree ər/ *adj.* **1. HIGHER IN QUALITY** above average or better than another in quality or grade **2. BETTER THAN OTHERS** surpassing others in something, e.g., intellect, achievement, or ability **3. HIGHER IN RANK** higher in rank, position, or authority than another **4. HIGHER** upper, or situated higher up **5. CONDESCENDING** adopting or showing an attitude of condescension toward others ○ *He gave a superior smile.* **6. LARGER** greater in number or amount ○ *a quantity superior to our needs* **7. UNCONCERNED** above being affected or influenced by something ○ *She considered herself superior to such taunts.* **8.** ANAT **NEARER THE HEAD** nearer the head than another body part **9.** BOT **ABOVE OTHER FLOWER PARTS** used to describe an ovary of a flower whose stamens, petals, and sepals arise either beside or below it **10.** PRINTING = **superscript** *adj.* ■ *n.* **1. SOMEBODY OR SOMETHING HIGHER OR BETTER** somebody or something higher in rank, position, authority, or quality than another ○ *Don't argue with your superiors.* **2.** PRINTING = **superscript** *n.* **3.** RELIG **SOMEBODY IN CHARGE OF RELIGIOUS ORDER** a head of a religious order or institution [14thC. Via Old French from Latin, literally "higher," from *superus* "above," from *super* (see SUPER-).] —**su·pe·ri·or·i·ty** /sə peeree áwrətee/ *n.* —**su·pe·ri·or·ly** /sə peeree ərlee/ *adv.*

Su·pe·ri·or, Lake lake in North America. The northernmost and westernmost of the Great Lakes, it is also the world's largest freshwater lake. Area: 31,700 sq. mi./82,100 sq. km. Depth: 1,333 ft./406 m. Length: 350 mi./563 km.

su·pe·ri·or con·junc·tion *n.* a position of a celestial body in which it is opposite the Earth on the far side of the Sun

su·pe·ri·or court *n.* a court in some states of the United States that is higher than an inferior court but lower than an appellate court

su·pe·ri·or·i·ty com·plex *n.* an exaggerated sense of being better than other people

su·pe·ri·or plan·et *n.* a planet whose distance from the Sun is greater than that of the Earth. The superior planets are Mars, Jupiter, Saturn, Uranus, Neptune, and Pluto.

su·per·ja·cent /sŏŏpər jáyss'nt/ *adj.* lying on or above something [Late 16thC. Formed from Latin *superjacere*, literally "to lie above," from *jacere* "to lie, throw" (see JET[2]).]

su·per·jet /sŏŏpər jèt/ *n.* a large supersonic jet plane

su·per·la·tive /soo púrlətiv/ *adj.* **1. EXCELLENT** of the highest quality or degree **2.** GRAM **HIGHEST IN DEGREE OF COMPARISON** expressing the highest degree of grammatical comparison of an adjective or adverb ○ *The superlative form of an adjective or adverb typically has the ending "-est."* ■ *n.* **1.** GRAM **GRAMMATICAL FORM** the grammatical form expressing the highest degree of comparison ○ *Put "tiny" into the superlative and you get "tiniest."* **2.** GRAM **SUPERLATIVE ADJECTIVE OR ADVERB** a superlative form of an adjective or adverb ○ *the difference between a comparative and a superlative* **3. SOMEBODY OR SOMETHING SUPERLATIVE** somebody or something of the highest quality **4. EXAGGERATED PRAISE** an exaggerated description or way of referring to somebody or something, usually expressing admiration ○ *heaping superlatives on their performance* [14thC. Via Old French from Latin *superlativus*, from *superlat-*, the past participle stem of *superferre*, literally "to carry above."] —**su·per·la·tive·ly** *adv.* —**su·per·la·tive·ness** *n.*

su·per·lin·er /sŏŏpər līnər/ *n.* a large luxurious ocean-going passenger ship

su·per·lu·na·ry /sŏŏpər lŏŏnəree/, **su·per·lu·nar** /-lŏŏnər/ *adj.* **1.** ASTRON **BEYOND THE MOON** located beyond the Moon **2.** RELIG **CELESTIAL** belonging to a higher world or celestial plane [Early 17thC. Modeled on SUBLUNARY.]

su·per·man /sŏŏpər màn/ (*plural* **-men** /-mèn/) *n.* **1. EXCEPTIONAL MAN** a man possessing exceptional or superhuman strength, abilities, or powers **2. NIETZSCHE'S IDEAL MAN** according to the philosophy of Nietzsche, an ideal man who through creativity and integrity is able to transcend good and evil and is the goal of human evolution [Early 20thC. Coined by George Bernard Shaw as a translation of German *Übermensch*, which was coined by Friedrich Nietzsche.]

WORD KEY: CULTURAL NOTE

Superman, a comic strip created by U.S. writer Jerry Siegal and drawn by U.S. artist Joseph Shuster which first appeared in 1938. The alter ego of "mild-mannered reporter" Clark Kent, Superman is an almost invincible, crime-fighting superhero in a red cape who was originally sent to Earth as a child from the doomed planet Krypton. The story has been made into radio shows, musicals, television series, and feature movies.

su·per·mar·ket /sŏŏpər maarkət/ *n.* a large self-service retail store selling food and household goods

sup·er·max /sóopər màks/ *n.* protected or made secure by the most extensive and elaborate security arrangements that are available or in current use ○ *a supermax penitentiary*

su·per·mod·el /sŏŏpər mòdd'l/ *n.* one of an elite group of fashion models who are very well paid and in high demand by fashion designers and photographers

su·per·mom /sŏŏpər mòm/ *n.* a woman who cares for a home and family, is involved in children's and community activities, and often also may be employed full-time (*informal*)

su·per·nal /soo púrn'l/ *adj.* (*literary*) **1. IN THE SKY** coming from or located in the heavens **2. HEAVENLY** suited to or characteristic of the heavens [15thC. Via Old French from, ultimately, Latin *supernus* "heavenly," from *super* (see SUPER-).] —**su·per·nal·ly** *adv.*

su·per·na·tant /sŏŏpər náyt'nt/ *n.* **LIQUID ON THE SURFACE** a usually clear liquid above material deposited by precipitation, centrifugation, or sedimentation ■ *adj.* **ON THE SURFACE** lying or floating on the surface of a liquid after precipitation, centrifugation, or sedimentation [Mid-17thC. From Latin *supernatant-*, the present participle stem of *supernatare*, literally "to float above," from *natare* (see NATANT).]

su·per·na·tion·al /sŏŏpər náshən'l/ *adj.* = **supranational**

su·per·nat·u·ral /sŏŏpər náchərəl/ *adj.* **1. NOT OF NATURAL WORLD** relating or attributed to phenomena that cannot be explained by natural laws **2. RELATING TO A DEITY** relating or attributed to a deity **3. MAGICAL** relating or attributed to magic or the occult ■ *n.* **1. SUPERNATURAL THINGS** supernatural beings or phenomena **2. WORLD OF SUPERNATURAL THINGS** the realm of supernatural beings or phenomena —**su·per·nat·u·ral·ly** *adv.* —**su·per·nat·u·ral·ness** *n.*

su·per·nat·u·ral·ism /sŏŏpər náchərə lìzzəm/ *n.* **1. STATE OF BEING SUPERNATURAL** the quality or condition of being supernatural **2. BELIEF IN SUPERNATURAL** the belief that supernatural or divine beings and phenomena intervene in human events —**su·per·nat·u·ral·ist** *n.*, *adj.* —**su·per·nat·u·ral·is·tic** /sŏŏpər nàchərə lístik/ *adj.*

su·per·nor·mal /sŏŏpər náwrm'l/ *adj.* **1. BEYOND WHAT IS NORMAL** exceeding what is normal or usual **2.** = **paranormal** —**su·per·nor·mal·i·ty** /sŏŏpər nawr mállətee/ *n.* —**su·per·nor·mal·ly** /sŏŏpər náwrməlee/ *adv.*

su·per·no·va /sŏŏpər nṓvə, sŏŏpər nṓvə/ (*plural* **-vae** /-vee/ *or* **-vas**) *n.* a catastrophic explosion of a large star in the latter stages of stellar evolution, with a resulting short-lived luminosity from 10 to 100 million times that of the Sun

su·per·nu·mer·ar·y /sŏŏpər nŏŏmə rèrree/ *adj.* **1. EXTRA** exceeding the usual number **2.** HR **SUBSTITUTING** employed as a substitute or extra worker ■ *n.* (*plural*

-ies) 1. SOMEBODY OR SOMETHING EXTRA somebody or something in addition to the usual number 2. THEATER WALK-ON ACTOR an actor who appears on stage but has no lines to speak 3. HR SUBSTITUTE EMPLOYEE somebody employed as a substitute or extra worker [Early 17thC. From late Latin *supernumerarius*, from Latin *super* "above" + *numerus* "number."]

su·per·or·der /sóopər àwrdər/ *n.* a taxonomic category of related organisms ranking below a class and above an order

su·per·or·di·nate /sóopər áwrd'nət/ *n.* 1. LING UMBRELLA TERM a word whose meaning encompasses the meaning of another more specific word. "Animal" is a superordinate of "cat." ◊ **hyponym** 2. SOMEBODY OR SOMETHING SUPERIOR somebody or something of superior rank, status, or class [Early 17thC. Coined from SUPER- + SUBORDINATE.] —**su·per·or·di·nate** *adj.*

su·per·or·gan·ism /sóopər áwrgə nìzzəm/ *n.* a group of organisms functioning as a social unit. An insect colony is an example of a superorganism.

su·per·o·vu·la·tion /sóopər òvvyə láysh'n/ *n.* increased frequency of ovulation or production of a large number of ova at one time. It is often caused by the administration of gonadotropin hormones, which are prescribed to induce ovulation in infertility. —**su·per·o·vu·late** /sóopər óvvyə làyt/ *vi.*

su·per·plas·tic /sóopər plástik/ *adj.* used to describe alloys that are capable of being easily deformed and molded at high temperatures without fracturing —**su·per·plas·tic·i·ty** /sóopər pla stíssətee/ *n.*

su·per·pose /sóopər pṓz/ (**-posed, -pos·ing, -pos·es**) *vt.* 1. PLACE ON TOP OF ANOTHER to place or lay one object on top of or above another 2. GEOM MAKE GEOMETRIC FIGURES COINCIDE to move one geometric figure so that it coincides exactly with another [Early 19thC. Origin uncertain: probably from French *superposer*, a back-formation from *superposition* "superposition," from, ultimately, Latin *superponere* "to place over," from *super-* (see SUPER-) + *ponere* "to place."] —**su·per·pos·a·ble** *adj.* —**su·per·posed** *adj.* —**su·per·po·si·tion** /sóopərpə zísh'n/ *n.*

su·per·pow·er /sóopər pòwr/ *n.* 1. POL POWERFUL NATION an extremely powerful nation with greater political, economic, or military power than most other nations, or with all three 2. PHYS EXTREMELY HIGH POWER extremely high electrical or mechanical power —**su·per·pow·ered** *adj.*

su·per·sat·u·rat·ed /sóopər sáchə ràytəd/ *adj.* 1. CONTAINING MORE SOLUTE THAN NORMAL used to describe a chemical solution containing a greater amount of solute than normally possible at a given temperature and pressure, often as a result of cooling 2. CONTAINING MORE GASEOUS MATERIAL THAN NORMAL used to describe a vapor containing more gaseous material than normally possible at a given temperature and pressure —**su·per·sat·u·ra·tion** /sóopər sachə ráysh'n/ *n.*

su·per·scribe /sóopər skrīb/ (**-scribed, -scrib·ing, -scribes**) *vt.* to write or print something such as a name or address above, outside, or on the surface of something else

su·per·script /sóopər skrìpt/ *n.* SOMETHING WRITTEN ABOVE ANOTHER CHARACTER a letter, character, or symbol that is written above, or above and to the right or left of, another character ■ *adj.* WRITTEN ABOVE ANOTHER CHARACTER written or printed as a superscript

su·per·scrip·tion /sóopər skrípsh'n/ *n.* 1. SOMETHING WRITTEN ABOVE SOMETHING ELSE something that is written, printed, or engraved above, outside, or on the surface of something else 2. ACT OF SUPERSCRIBING SOMETHING the act of writing or printing something above, outside, or on the surface of something else

su·per·sede /sóopər seéd/ (**-sed·ed, -sed·ing, -sedes**) *vt.* 1. REPLACE SOMETHING LESS EFFICIENT to take the place or position of something that is less efficient, less modern, or less appropriate, or cause something to do this 2. SUCCEED SOMEBODY OR SOMETHING to succeed somebody or something in a particular role, office, or function (*formal*) [15thC. Via Old French *superceder* "to refrain from," from Latin *supersedere* "to be superior to," from *super-* (see SUPER-) + *sedere* "to sit."] —**su·per·sed·a·ble** *adj.* —**su·per·sed·ence** *n.* —**su·per·sed·er** *n.*

WORD KEY: USAGE

Spelling trap: Note that this word is correctly spelt *-sede* and not *-cede*. It is derived not from the Latin verb *cedere* "to go" (as *intercede* and *precede* are) but from *sedere* "to sit."

su·per·sen·si·ble /sóopər sénssəb'l/, **su·per·sen·so·ry** /-sénssəree/ *adj.* above or beyond the perception of the senses —**su·per·sen·si·bly** *adv.*

su·per·sen·si·tive /sóopər sénssətiv/ *adj.* = **hypersensitive** —**su·per·sen·si·tive·ly** *adv.* —**su·per·sen·si·tiv·i·ty** /sóopər sènssə tívvətee/ *n.*

su·per·sen·so·ry *adj.* = **supersensible**

su·per·serv·er /sóopər sùrvər/ *n.* an extremely powerful computer that controls a network or networks of other computers

su·per·son·ic /sóopər sónnik/ *adj.* produced by, capable of reaching, or relating to a speed that is faster than the speed at which sound travels through the air [Early 20thC. Coined from SUPER- + Latin *sonus* "sound."] —**su·per·son·i·cal·ly** *adv.*

su·per·son·ics /sóopər sónniks/ *n.* the science or study of supersonic motion or phenomena (*takes a singular verb*)

su·per·son·ic trans·port *n.* a transport aircraft that travels at supersonic speed

su·per·star /sóopər staar/ *n.* somebody who is extremely famous or successful, especially in sports or entertainment, and who has great public appeal —**su·per·star·dom** *n.*

su·per·sta·tion /sóopər stàysh'n/ *n.* a television channel broadcast nationally or internationally through satellite and cable

su·per·sti·tion /sóopər stísh'n/ *n.* 1. IRRATIONAL BELIEF an irrational but usually deep-seated belief in the magical effects of a particular action or ritual, especially in the likelihood that good or bad luck will result from performing it 2. IRRATIONAL BELIEFS irrational and often quasi-religious belief in and reverence for the magical effects of certain actions and rituals or the magical powers of certain objects [15thC. Via Old French from the Latin stem *superstition-*, from *superstes* "standing over" (in awe), from *stare* "to stand" (see STATION).]

su·per·sti·tious /sóopər stíshəss/ *adj.* 1. BELIEVING IN SUPERSTITIONS convinced that performing or not performing certain actions brings good or bad luck, that certain events or phenomena are omens, and, generally, fearfully believing in a supernatural dimension to events 2. BASED ON IRRATIONAL BELIEF based on a false or irrational belief in, or fear of, the supernatural

su·per·store /sóopər stàwr/ *n.* 1. VERY LARGE SUPERMARKET a very large supermarket or store offering a wider and more varied range of consumer goods than other stores of the same type 2. SPECIALIST RETAILER a retail chain or single store that specializes in a range of related products offered at discount prices ○ *a computer superstore*

su·per·stra·tum /sóopər stràytəm, -stràttəm/ (*plural* **-ta** /-stràytə, -stràttə/) *n.* 1. OVERLYING LAYER a layer, especially of rock or sedimentation, on top of another one 2. LING ELEMENTS OF CONQUERING LANGUAGE the language of an invading or colonizing population in relation to the language of an indigenous population that it changes or influences

su·per·string /sóopər strìng/ *n.* a hypothetical one-dimensional entity (**string**) of extremely short length held to be a fundamental component of matter in some theories of elementary particles involving supersymmetry

su·per·struc·ture /sóopər strùkchər/ *n.* 1. NAUT UPPER PART OF SHIP the part of a ship above the main deck 2. CONSTR VISIBLE PART OF BUILDING the part of a building above its foundations 3. PART DEVELOPED ON BASE any physical or intellectual structure built on or developed from a fundamental form, base, or concept 4. POL INSTITUTIONS ASSOCIATED WITH TYPE OF ECONOMY in Marxist theory, the complex of social, legal, and political institutions that are an extension and reflection of the type of economy operating in a given society —**su·per·struc·tural** /sóopər strúkchərəl/ *adj.*

su·per·sym·me·try /sóopər símmətree/ *n.* a theory in physics proposing a type of symmetry that would apply to all elementary particles, both bosons and fermions

su·per·tank·er /sóopər tàngkər/ *n.* a very large tanker ship, usually with a capacity of 300,000 tons/275,000 tonnes or more

su·per·tax /sóopər tàks/ *n.* = **surtax** *n.* 2

su·per·ti·tle /sóopər tīt'l/ *n.* a translation of words being spoken or sung in a foreign language during the performance of a play or opera, projected on a screen above the stage [Late 20thC. Modeled on *subtitle*.]

su·per·ton·ic /sóopər tònnik/ *n.* the note one step above the tonic in a major or minor scale, or the harmony built upon this note

Su·per Tues·day *n.* a Tuesday in a presidential election year on which many states hold primary elections, the results of which provide the basis for choosing the parties' presidential candidates

su·per·vene /sóopər veén/ (**-vened, -ven·ing, -venes**) *vi.* (*formal*) 1. FOLLOW UNEXPECTEDLY to follow or come about unexpectedly, usually interrupting or changing what is going on 2. FOLLOW IMMEDIATELY to follow immediately after something [Mid-17thC. From Latin *supervenire*, literally "to come above," from *venire* "to come" (see VENUE).] —**su·per·ven·tion** /sóopər vénsh'n/ *n.*

su·per·ven·ient /sóopər veénee ənt/ *adj.* existing only as a result of the presence or combination of other characteristics or qualities [Late 16thC. From Latin *supervenient-*, the present participle stem of *supervenire* (see SUPERVENE).] —**su·per·ven·ience** *n.*

su·per·vise /sóopər vīz/ (**-vised, -vis·ing, -vis·es**) *vti.* 1. OVERSEE ACTIVITY to watch over a particular activity or task being carried out by other people and ensure that it is carried out correctly 2. OVERSEE PEOPLE to be in charge of a group of people engaged in some activity and to keep order or ensure that they carry out a task adequately [Late 16thC. From medieval Latin *supervis-*, the past participle stem of *supervidere* "to look over, oversee," from Latin *videre* "to see" (see VISION).] —**su·per·vis·ion** /sóopər vízh'n/ *n.*

su·per·vi·sor /sóopər vīzər/ *n.* 1. BOSS somebody whose job is to oversee and guide the work or activities of a group of other people 2. EDUC MAIN TEACHER OF SUBJECT a teacher or other school official who oversees the teaching and teachers of a single subject area 3. PUBLIC ADMIN ELECTED OFFICIAL an elected official in various local authorities such as townships and counties 4. *U.K.* UNIV TUTOR FOR A GRADUATE in some British universities, a teacher assigned to supervise the work of an individual student, especially research done by a graduate student —**su·per·vi·sor·ship** *n.* —**su·per·vi·so·ry** /sóopər vīzəree, sóopər vīzəree/ *adj.*

su·per·wom·an /sóopər wòommən/ (*plural* **-en** /-wìmmən/) *n.* 1. HIGH ACHIEVER a woman who succeeds triumphantly in combining several roles, e.g., as worker, wife, mother, and homemaker, and does it all with apparent ease (*informal*) 2. SUPERHUMAN WOMAN an imaginary or fictional woman with superhuman powers

su·pi·nate /sóopə nàyt/ (**-nat·ed, -nat·ing, -nates**) *v.* 1. *vti.* TURN PALM UPWARD to turn the hand so that the palm faces upward, or be turned in this way 2. *vti.* TURN SOLE UPWARD to turn the foot so that the sole is facing upward, or be turned in this way 3. *vi.* LIE FACING UPWARD to turn the face upward, or lie in a supine position with the face upward [Mid-19thC. From Latin *supinat-*, the past participle stem of *supinare* "to turn backward," from *supinus* "backward" (see SUPINE).] —**su·pi·na·tion** /sóopə náysh'n/ *n.*

su·pi·na·tor /sóopə nàytər/ *n.* a muscle, especially of the forearm, that brings about supination

su·pine /sóo pīn/ *adj.* 1. LYING ON THE BACK lying on the back and with the face upward 2. PALM UPWARD with the palm of the hand facing upward or away from the body 3. LETHARGIC utterly passive or inactive, especially in a situation where a vigorous reaction is called for ■ *n.* GRAM TYPE OF LATIN NOUN a Latin noun formed from a past participle stem and having only accusative and ablative inflections [15thC. From Latin *supinus* "lying on the back." Ultimately from an Indo-European word meaning "under, up," which is also the ancestor of English *up*, *above*, and *subterfuge*.]

supp. *abbr.* 1. supplement 2. supplementary

sup·per /súppər/ *n.* 1. EVENING MEAL a light meal eaten in the evening 2. MAIN EVENING MEAL the main meal of the day when taken in the evening 3. SOCIAL EVENT an evening social event that includes a meal [13thC. From Old French *soper* "to eat supper," from *soupe* "sop, broth" (see SOUP).] ◇ **sing for your supper** to work or do something in exchange for your food and board, or for something that you want

WORD KEY: USAGE

See Usage note at ***dinner***.

WORD KEY: CULTURAL NOTE

The Last Supper, a painting by Italian artist Leonardo da Vinci (1495–97). Painted directly onto a wall in the monastery of Santa Maria delle Grazie in Milan, it depicts the moment when Jesus Christ declares that one of his companions will betray him. It is noted for its magnificent composition and powerful depiction of the outrage of the disciples, the serenity of Jesus Christ, and the guilt of Judas.

sup·per club *n.* **1. RESTAURANT** a restaurant serving fancy evening meals and sometimes featuring entertainment **2. GROUP THAT DINES IN RESTAURANT** a group of people who get together periodically to dine in restaurants

sup·per·time /súppər tìm/ *n.* the time at which supper is served or eaten

suppl. *abbr.* **1.** supplement **2.** supplementary

sup·plant /sə plánt/ (**-plant·ed, -plant·ing, -plants**) *vt.* **1. OUST SOMEBODY** to take somebody's place or position by force or intrigue **2. REPLACE** to take the place of something, especially something much used, inferior, outmoded, or irrelevant [13thC. Directly or via French from Latin *supplantare* "to trip up, overthrow," from *sub-* "up from beneath" + *planta* "sole of the foot" (see PLANT).] —**sup·plan·ta·tion** /sùpplan táysh'n/ *n.* —**sup·plant·er** /sə plántər/ *n.*

sup·ple /súpp'l/ (**-pler, -plest**) *adj.* **1. FLEXIBLE** flexible and elastic **2. MOVING EASILY** capable of bending, stretching, and moving with ease, fluidity, and grace **3. ADAPTABLE** adaptable and responsive in grappling with problems or dealing with new challenges **4. COMPLIANT** excessively compliant and agreeable (*literary*) [13thC. Via French from, ultimately, Latin *supplex* "submissive," literally "bending under," from *-plex* "fold" (source of English *duplex*).] —**sup·ple·ly** *adv.* —**sup·ple·ness** *n.*

sup·ple·jack /súpp'l jàk/ (*plural* **-jacks** *or* **-jack**) *n.* **1. WOODY VINE** a woody vine of the southeastern United States with tiny white flowers and bluish fruits. Latin name: *Berchemia scandens.* **2. TROPICAL VINE** a tropical American vine whose wood is used for walking sticks. Latin name: *Paullinia curvassica.* [*Supple* from its pliant stem]

sup·ple·ment *n.* /súppləmənt/ **1. ADDITION** an addition to something to increase its size or make up for a deficiency ○ *a useful supplement to the family income* **2.** PUBL **PUBLICATION** a publication that amplifies or corrects one already published **3.** PRESS **PERIODICAL PART** an additional section included in or sold with a magazine or newspaper, especially an additional section that appears regularly **4.** FOOD **FOOD** a substance with a particular nutritional value taken to make up for a real or supposed deficiency in diet **5.** COMM **EXTRA CHARGE** a charge payable in addition to the basic charge for a special service or under certain conditions **6.** MATH **ANGLE OR ARC** an angle or arc that, when added to another, makes 180° or a semicircle ■ *vt.* /súpplə mént/ (**-ment·ed, -ment·ing, -ments**) **1. MAKE ADDITION TO SOMETHING** to increase, extend, or improve something by adding something to it ○ *supplemented their meager diet with vitamins* **2. BE ADDITIONAL PART** to be a supplement to something ○ *Her remarks supplemented the report.* [14thC. From Latin *supplementum*, from *supplere* "to fill out, complete" (see SUPPLY).] —**sup·ple·men·tal** /sùpplə mént'l/ *adj.* —**sup·ple·men·tal·ly** /-mént'lee/ *adv.* —**sup·ple·men·ta·tion** /sùpplə men táysh'n/ *n.* —**sup·ple·ment·er** /súpplə mèntər/ *n.*

sup·ple·men·ta·ry /sùpplə méntəree/ *adj.* **1. ADDITIONAL** additional to an existing one, or to the normal number or amount **2. COMPLETING** making up for something that is lacking ■ *n.* (*plural* **-ries**) **SOMETHING ADDITIONAL** an additional thing, person, or question —**sup·ple·men·tar·i·ly** /sùpplə men térrəlee/ *adv.*

sup·ple·men·ta·ry an·gle *n.* an angle that when added to another angle makes up 180°

sup·ple·tion /sə pleésh'n/ *n.* the use of an unrelated word to fill the gap when some inflected or derived forms of a word are missing, as "was" forms the past tense of "to be" —**sup·ple·tive** /sə pleétiv, súppletiv/ *adj.*

sup·pli·ant /súpplee ənt/ *adj.* **ENTREATING** expressing a humble but heart-felt appeal to somebody who has the power to grant a request (*formal*) ■ *n.* = **supplicant** *n.* [15thC. From French, present participle of *supplier* "to supplicate," from Latin *supplicare*, literally "to bend under," from *supplex* (see SUPPLE).] —**sup·pli·ance** *n.* —**sup·pli·ant·ly** *adv.*

sup·pli·cant /súppləkənt/ *n.* **HUMBLE PETITIONER** somebody who addresses a humble but heart-felt appeal to somebody who has the power to grant his or her request (*formal*) ■ *adj.* = **suppliant** *adj.* [Late 16thC. From Latin *supplicant-*, present participle stem of *supplicare* (see SUPPLIANT).] —**sup·pli·ca·to·ry** /súppləkə tàwree/ *adj.*

sup·pli·ca·tion /sùpplə káysh'n/ *n.* (*formal*) **1. APPEAL MADE TO SOMEBODY IN AUTHORITY** a humble appeal to somebody who has the power to grant a request **2. ADDRESSING OF REQUESTS** the addressing of humble requests and prayers to somebody with the power to grant them —**sup·pli·cate** /súpplə kàyt/ *vti.*

sup·ply /sə plí/ *vt.* (**-plied, -ply·ing, -plies**) **1. PROVIDE** to give, sell, or make available something that is wanted or needed by somebody or something ○ *supplied equipment for the expedition* **2. SATISFY A NEED** to satisfy a need or requirement (*formal*) **3. MAKE UP FOR A LACK** to make up for a deficiency, loss, or lack (*formal*) **4. SERVE AS A SUBSTITUTE** to act as a substitute for somebody, especially in a church (*formal*) ■ *n.* (*plural* **-plies**) **1. AVAILABLE AMOUNT** an amount or quantity of something available for use ○ *a plentiful supply of food and drink* **2. PROVISION** the act or business of bringing something needed to the people or things that need it, or the system that brings something needed ○ *the supply of electric power to villages in the mountains* **3.** ECON **QUANTITY AVAILABLE IN A MARKET** the quantity of a type of goods or services available in a market at a given time **4. SUBSTITUTE** somebody who acts as a substitute, especially for a preacher (*formal*) ■ **sup·plies** *npl.* **NEEDED THINGS** the things, especially food and equipment, that a group of people need to survive and operate, or that are needed to carry out a particular task or activity ○ *Our supplies were running very low.* [14thC. Via Old French *supplier* "to meet a deficiency" from Latin *supplere*, literally "to fill up," from *plere* "to fill" (source of English *complete* and *deplete*).] —**sup·pli·a·ble** *adj.* —**sup·pli·er** *n.* ◇ **in short supply** present or available only in small or insufficient quantities

sup·ply and de·mand *n.* the relationship between the availability of a good or service and the need or desire for it among consumers

sup·ply-side ec·o·nom·ics *n.* economic policies that promote conditions favoring the producers of goods and services (*takes a singular or plural verb*)

sup·port /sə páwrt/ *vt.* (**-port·ed, -port·ing, -ports**) **1. KEEP FROM FALLING** to keep something or somebody upright or in place, or prevent something or somebody from falling ○ *Those pillars support the roof.* **2. BEAR CERTAIN WEIGHT** to be strong enough to hold a particular object or weight in place without breaking or giving way ○ *Are you sure the ice is thick enough to support the weight?* **3. SUSTAIN FINANCIALLY** to provide somebody with money and the other necessities of life over a period of time ○ *She succeeds in supporting her family on what she earns in a part-time job.* **4. GIVE ACTIVE HELP AND ENCOURAGEMENT** to give active help, encouragement, or money to somebody or something ○ *We support the charity through voluntary work.* **5. BE IN FAVOR OF SOMETHING** to be in favor of something such as a cause, policy, or organization, and wish to see it succeed **6. BE PRESENT AND GIVE ENCOURAGEMENT** to give encouragement to somebody or something by being present at an event **7. GIVE ASSISTANCE OR COMFORT** to give assistance or comfort to somebody in difficulty or distress ○ *He supported me throughout my crisis.* **8. CORROBORATE** to give something greater credibility by being consistent with it or providing further evidence for it ○ *There is further evidence that supports the defendant's claim.* **9.** ARTS **PLAY SMALL ROLE ALONGSIDE SOMEBODY** to play a subsidiary role in a play or movie alongside another actor with a leading part **10. TOLERATE SOMETHING** to put up with something unpleasant (*literary*) ■ *n.* **1. SOMETHING THAT SUPPORTS** a means of holding something upright or in place, or of preventing it from falling ○ *If you remove those supports the plank will fall down.* **2. REINFORCEMENT TO HOLD THINGS IN PLACE** physical force or reinforcement used to hold things steady or in place ○ *Stakes give the plant extra support.* **3. ACTIVE ASSISTANCE OR ENCOURAGEMENT** active assistance and encouragement to, or an approving and encouraging attitude toward, somebody or something ○ *Support for the cause continues to rise.* **4. HELP IN CRISIS** the encouragement and help somebody gets from others, e.g., friends, family, and charitable organizations, especially during times of crisis and change. It may be emotional, moral, or practical. **5. SUPPORTIVE PERSON** somebody who provides assistance, money, encouragement, or comfort **6. SUPPORTERS** the supporters of an organization such as a political party, or of an individual, considered as a group ○ *His support is drawn mainly from the rural areas.* **7.** ARTS **SUPPORTING BANDS OR ENTERTAINERS** the other band or bands, or the other entertainers, appearing in a program along with the main attraction [14thC. Via French from Latin *supportare*, literally "to bear up," from *portare* "to carry" (see PORT[1]).] —**sup·port·a·bil·i·ty** /sə pàwrtə bíllətee/ *n.* —**sup·port·a·ble** /sə páwrtəb'l/ *adj.* —**sup·port·a·bly** *adv.* ◇ **in support of** in order to support somebody or something

sup·port ar·e·a *n.* an area with a supply of military material and personnel standing ready for use

sup·port·er /sə páwrtər/ *n.* **1. SOMEBODY WHO SUPPORTS SOMETHING** somebody who supports a cause, person, idea, course of action, or political party ○ *greeted by a crowd of supporters* **2.** CLOTHES **SUPPORTING GARMENT** a garment that supports or protects a part of the body, especially one used by male athletes to protect the genitals **3.** HERALDRY **STANDING FIGURE** either of a pair of standing figures on either side of a shield in a coat of arms

sup·port group *n.* a group of people with a problem or concern in common who meet regularly to discuss it and support one another

sup·port hose *npl.* elasticized stockings that support the veins in the lower legs, used by people with varicose veins or bad circulation

sup·port·ing /sə páwrting/ *adj.* **1. SECONDARY** accompanying and assisting, but secondary to, the main action or the main participants in something ○ *a supporting role* **2.** ARTS **APPEARING OR SHOWN WITH MAIN ATTRACTION** appearing in the same movie, play, or program as the main star or attraction

sup·por·tive /sə páwrtiv/ *adj.* giving support, especially moral or emotional support —**sup·por·tive·ness** *n.*

sup·port lev·el *n.* the price at which a security whose price has been falling begins to attract investors again because of its intrinsic worth

sup·port sys·tem *n.* the group of friends, colleagues, or professionals available to help a person or organization when required

sup·pos·a·ble /sə pṓzəb'l/ *adj.* considered to be possible ○ *a supposable scenario* —**sup·pos·a·bly** *adv.*

sup·pose /sə pṓz/ (**-posed, -pos·ing, -pos·es**) *v.* **1.** *vti.* **BELIEVE TO BE TRUE** to believe or imagine something to be the case ○ *I suppose you haven't heard the news.* **2.** *vi.* **IMAGINE AS POSSIBLE** to consider or imagine something to be a possibility ○ *Suppose that he doesn't know about your plan.* **3.** *vt.* **TAKE AS PRECONDITION** to require something as a precondition ○ *Your plan supposes that there are enough presents to go around.* **4.** *vt.* **BE REQUIRED TO DO SOMETHING** to be expected to do something as the result of a previous agreement or arrangement or an obligation (*usually passive*) ○ *You're supposed to leave tomorrow.* **5.** *vt.* **BE EXPECTED TO DO SOMETHING** to be expected to do something as a consequence of a particular action or set of conditions (*usually passive*) ○ *The light's supposed to come on when the tank is almost empty.* **6.** *vti.* **AGREE TO SOMETHING RELUCTANTLY** used when agreeing to do something or that something is the case, reluctantly, uncertainly, or noncommitally ○ *I suppose we'd better get going.* [14thC. Via French from, ultimately, Latin *supponere*, literally "to place under," from *ponere* "to place" (see POSITION). The meaning was influenced by Greek *hypothesis* "supposition."] —**sup·pos·er** *n.*

sup·posed /sə pṓzd, -pṓzəd/ *adj.* accepted, at least by some, as correct, real, or having a particular quality, but on slender or uncertain evidence ○ *Frankly, I'm very dubious about this supposed brilliant idea of his.*

sup·pos·ed·ly /sə pṓzədlee/ *adv.* as some people believe, or as people were led to believe ○ *He was supposedly going to pick us up after work.* ○ *a supposedly instant remedy*

sup·pos·ing /sə pṓzing/ *conj.* imagining or assuming something to be the case ○ *Supposing she comes, will you let her in?*

sup·po·si·tion /sùppə zísh'n/ *n.* **1. HYPOTHESIS** something that it is suggested might be true, or that is accepted as true, on the basis of some evidence but without proof **2. MENTAL ACT OF SUPPOSING** the mental act of supposing something to be the case, or ideas that result from supposing, especially as opposed to ideas based on firm evidence ○ *All this is mere supposition.* [Late 16thC. Directly and via French from the Latin stem *supposition-*, from *supposit-*, the past participle stem of *supponere* (see SUPPOSE). Translation of Greek *hupothesis*.] —**sup·po·si·tion·al** *adj.* —**sup·po·si·tion·al·ly** *adv.*

sup·po·si·tious /sùppə zíshəss/ *adj.* based on some evidence but without proof (*formal*)

sup·pos·i·ti·tious /sə pòzzə tíshəss/ *adj.* substituted for something else in order to deceive (*formal*) [Early 17thC. From Latin *supposititius*, from *suppositus*, the past participle of *supponere* (see SUPPOSE).] —**sup·pos·i·ti·tious·ly** *adv.*

sup·pos·i·tive /sə pózzətiv/ *adj.* **EXPRESSING SUPPOSITION** expressing or relating to supposition, or introducing a clause expressing a supposition ■ *n.* **SUPPOSITIVE CONJUNCTION** a conjunction such as "if," "provided that," or "supposing" that introduces a clause expressing a supposition

sup·pos·i·to·ry /sə pózzə tàwree/ (*plural* **-ries**) *n.* a medicated solid preparation, usually in the form of a cylinder or cone, that melts at body temperature and is designed to be inserted into the rectum, vagina, or urethra. The drug or active ingredient is incorporated in an inert base, commonly cocoa butter, glycerinated gelatin, or polyethylene glycol. [14thC. From medieval Latin *suppositorium*, from Latin *supposit-*, the past participle stem of *supponere* "to place under" (see SUPPOSE).]

sup·press /sə préss/ (**-pressed, -press·ing, -press·es**) *vt.* **1. PUT AN END TO SOMETHING** to put an end to something, especially something perceived as a threat, by the use of force or a prohibition ○ *suppressed all complaints with a gag order* **2. PREVENT SOMETHING** to prevent something from happening, operating, or becoming apparent, or restrain something and limit its effects **3. STOP SPREAD OR PUBLICATION OF SOMETHING** to prevent information or evidence from becoming known, or written material from being published ○ *The report was suppressed for political reasons.* **4.** PSYCHOL **RESIST SOMETHING CONSCIOUSLY** to resist particular thoughts or feelings consciously as they arise, and try to banish them from the mind ○ *Try to suppress your anger.* **5.** ELECTRON ENG **DIMINISH OSCILLATION** to reduce unwanted noise or oscillation in a circuit or unwanted frequencies in a signal **6.** BIOL **REDUCE BODILY FUNCTION** to cause or undergo the reduction or cessation of a normal bodily function, e.g., menstruation or growth **7.** GENETICS **INHIBIT GENE EFFECT** to cancel or reverse the effects of a gene [14thC. From Latin *suppress-*, the past participle stem of *supprimere*, literally "to push down," from *premere* "to press" (see PRESS).] —**sup·pres·ser** *n.* —**sup·press·i·bil·i·ty** /sə prèssə bíllətee/ *n.* —**sup·press·i·ble** /sə préssəb'l/ *adj.*

sup·pres·sant *n.* a substance, medication, or activity that restrains or limits the effects of something (*often used in combination*) ○ *an appetite suppressant*

sup·pres·sion /sə présh'n/ *n.* **1. FORCEFUL PREVENTION** conscious and forceful action to put an end to something, destroy it, or prevent it from becoming known **2. STATE OF CONSTRAINT** the state of being forcefully restrained or held back **3.** PSYCHOL **AVOIDANCE OF THOUGHTS AND FEELINGS** conscious avoidance or inhibition of particular memories, desires, or thoughts **4.** ELECTRON ENG **DIMINISHING OF OSCILLATION** reduction of unwanted noise or oscillation in a circuit or of unwanted frequencies in a signal **5.** BIOL **DEVELOPMENTAL FAILURE** the failure of an organ, tissue, or part to develop **6.** PHYSIOL **CESSATION OF BODILY FUNCTION** the reduction or stoppage of a normal bodily function, e.g., secretion or excretion. ◊ **immunosuppression 7.** MED **REMOVAL OF SYMPTOMS** the lessening or abolition of a symptom or the outward signs of a disease **8.** GENETICS **REVERSAL OF MUTATION** the cancellation or reversal of the effect of a gene, especially of one genetic mutation by another

sup·pres·sive /sə préssiv/ *adj.* having the effect of suppressing something —**sup·pres·sive·ly** *adv.*

sup·pres·sor /sə préssər/ *n.* **1.** GENETICS **SUPPRESSING GENE** a gene that prevents the expression of another gene **2.** ELECTRON ENG **SUPPRESSING DEVICE** a device that reduces unwanted interference or current in a circuit

sup·pres·sor T cell, sup·pres·sor cell *n.* a T cell that diminishes or suppresses the immune response to an antigen of B cells and other T cells

sup·pu·rate /súppyə ràyt/ (**-rat·ed, -rat·ing, -rates**) *vi.* to produce or discharge pus as a result of an injury or infection [Mid-16thC. From Latin *suppurat-*, the past participle stem of *suppurare*, from *pus* (see PUS).] —**sup·pu·ra·tion** /sùppyə ráysh'n/ *n.* —**sup·pu·ra·tive** /súppyə ràytiv/ *adj.*

su·pra /so͞oprə/ *adv.* used in formal writing to refer the reader back to something at an earlier point in the same text (*formal*) [Early 16thC. From Latin, "above."]

supra- *prefix.* **1.** over, on top of ○ *suprarenal* **2.** transcending ○ *supranational* [From Latin *supra* "above, beyond" (source of English *soprano*). Related to *super* "above, over" (see SUPER-).]

su·pra·lap·sar·i·an /so͞oprə lap sérree ən/ *n.* somebody who believes in or expounds the Calvinist view that God preordained the Fall, and had preordained the salvation of some souls in advance of it [Mid-17thC. Coined from SUPRA- + Latin *lapsus* "sin, fall" (see LAPSE).] —**su·pra·lap·sar·i·an·ism** *n.*

su·pra·lim·i·nal /so͞oprə límmən'l/ *adj.* at or above the threshold of consciousness —**su·pra·lim·i·nal·ly** *adv.*

su·pra·mo·lec·u·lar /so͞oprə mə lékyələr/ *adj.* **1. MORE COMPLEX THAN A MOLECULE** more complex in form than a molecule **2. COMPOSED OF MOLECULES** composed of more than one molecule

su·pra·na·tion·al /so͞oprə násh'n'l/ *adj.* not limited by the concerns or boundaries of a single nation —**su·pra·na·tion·al·ism** *n.* —**su·pra·na·tion·al·ly** *adv.*

su·pra·or·bi·tal /so͞oprə áwrbət'l/ *adj.* located above the bony socket (**orbit**) of the eye

su·pra·re·nal /so͞oprə re͞en'l/ *adj.* located above the kidneys

su·pra·seg·men·tal /so͞oprə seg mént'l/ *adj.* connected with features of speech such as pitch and stress that accompany rather than constitute phonemes —**su·pra·seg·men·tal·ly** *adv.*

su·prem·a·cist /sə prémməssəst, soo-/ *n.* somebody who holds the view that a particular group is innately superior to others and therefore is entitled to dominate them (*usually used in combination*)

su·prem·a·cy /sə prémməssee, soo-/ *n.* a position of superiority or authority over all others [Mid-16thC. Formed from SUPREME, on the model of *primacy*.]

su·prem·a·tism /sə prémmə tìzzəm, soo-/ *n.* a school of cubist painting from early 20th-century Russia [Mid-20thC. From Russian *suprematizm*, from French *suprématie* "supremacy."] —**su·prem·a·tist** *n.*

su·preme /sə pre͞em, soo-/ *adj.* **1. ABOVE ALL OTHERS** above all others in power, authority, rank, status, or skill ○ *holding supreme authority* **2. HIGHEST IN DEGREE** of the greatest or most admirable kind ○ *a supreme example of the architect's skill* **3. ULTIMATE** greater than any that have gone before, or the greatest possible ○ *the supreme sacrifice* **4. IN THE HIGHEST DEGREE** in the highest degree or of the most unmitigated kind ○ *viewed them with supreme contempt* [15thC. From Latin *supremus*, literally "uppermost," from *superus* "upper," from *super* "above" (see SUPER-).]

su·prême /sə prém, soo-/ *adj.* served with a suprême sauce ○ *chicken suprême* [Early 19thC. From French, "supreme."]

Su·preme Be·ing *n.* God

su·preme com·man·der *n.* the highest ranking and controlling military officer in a theater of war

Su·preme Court *n.* **1. HIGHEST COURT** the highest federal court, consisting of nine justices appointed by the president and making decisions solely on consitutional matters **2. HIGHEST STATE COURT** the highest appellate court in many states of the United States **3. HIGHEST COURT IN COUNTRY** the highest court in a country, or in a state or territory of a federation

su·prême sauce *n.* a rich sauce made of chicken or veal stock with added cream and egg yolks

Su·preme So·vi·et *n.* the two-chamber national legislature of the former Soviet Union, or a similar legislature in any of the former individual Soviet republics

supt., Supt. *abbr.* superintendent

supvr. *abbr.* supervisor

suq *n.* = souk

Su·qua·mish /sə kwáamish, skwáamish/ (*plural* **-mish·es** *or* **-mish**) *n.* **1.** PEOPLES **MEMBER OF NATIVE N AMERICAN PEOPLE** a member of a Native North American people who originally lived in lands along the Puget Sound in Washington State and many of whom still live in that area **2.** LANG **SUQUAMISH LANGUAGE** the Salish language of the Suquamish people [Mid-19thC. From a Salish language.]

sur. *abbr.* **1.** surplus **2.** surface

Sur. *abbr.* Suriname

sur- *prefix.* **1.** over, above, on top of ○ *surprint* **2.** additional, extra ○ *surcharge* [Via French from Latin *super* (see SUPER-)]

su·ra /so͞orə/ *n.* a chapter of the Koran [Early 17thC. From Arabic *sūra*, of uncertain origin: probably from Syriac *ṣūrṭā* "scripture."]

Su·ra·ba·ya /so͞orə bī́ ə/ city on northeastern Java Island, Indonesia. Population: 2,473,272 (1990).

su·rah /so͞orə/ *n.* a twilled silk or rayon fabric, used in making women's clothing [Late 19thC. Anglicization of French *surat* "Surat," the town in India where it was first produced.]

su·ral /so͞orəl/ *adj.* relating to the calf of the leg (*technical*) [Early 17thC. Formed from Latin *sura* "calf of the leg," of unknown origin.]

su·rat /so͞o rat/ *n.* a coarse cotton fabric formerly produced in and around the town of Surat in India

sur·base /súr bàyss/ *n.* an architectural molding at the top of a base such as a pedestal or baseboard —**sur·base·ment** /sur báyssmənt/ *n.*

sur·based[1] /súr bàyst/ *adj.* featuring an architectural molding at the top of a base

sur·based[2] /sùr báyst/ *adj.* used to describe an arch with a rise of less than half its span [Mid-18thC. From French *surbaissé*, the past participle of *surbaisser* "to flatten," from *baisser* "to lower," ultimately from medieval Latin *bassus* "low."]

sur·cease /sər se͞ess, súr se͞ess/ *vti.* (**-ceased, -ceas·ing, -ceas·es**) **STOP DOING SOMETHING** to cease, or bring something to an end or stop doing it (*formal*) ■ *n.* **STOPPAGE** a cessation, especially a temporary one (*literary*) [15thC. Via Anglo-Norman *surseser* (influenced by CEASE) from, ultimately, Latin *supersedere* "to refrain" (see SUPERSEDE).]

sur·charge /súr chaarj/ *v.* (**-charged, -charg·ing, -charg·es**) **1.** *vti.* **CHARGE EXTRA** to add an additional charge to the amount somebody has to pay **2.** *vti.* **OVERCHARGE** to charge somebody too much for something **3.** *vt.* **MAKE SOMEBODY PERSONALLY RESPONSIBLE FOR REPAYMENT** to make somebody repay from personal funds any losses stemming from negligent or intentional mismanagement of a fiduciary responsibility **4.** *vt.* STAMPS **RAISE STAMP VALUE BY OVERPRINTING** to overprint an existing postage stamp so as to increase its face value **5.** *vt.* **OVERBURDEN** to overburden somebody or something, or overload something such as a ship (*literary*) ■ *n.* **1. EXTRA CHARGE** an excess or extra charge **2.** STAMPS **MARK ON STAMP** a mark on a postage stamp increasing its face value [15thC. From Old French *surcharger*, from *chargier* "to charge" (see CHARGE).] —**sur·charg·er** *n.*

sur·cin·gle /súr sìng g'l/ *n.* **1.** EQU **STRAP AROUND HORSE** a broad band fastened around the body of a horse to hold a rug or pack in place **2.** CLOTHES **BELT FOR CASSOCK** a belt worn around a priest's cassock (*archaic*) [14thC. From Old French *surcengle*, literally "belt over," from *cengle* "belt, girdle," from Latin *cingulum* (see CINGULUM).]

sur·coat /súr kōt/ *n.* **1. TUNIC WORN OVER ARMOR** a short

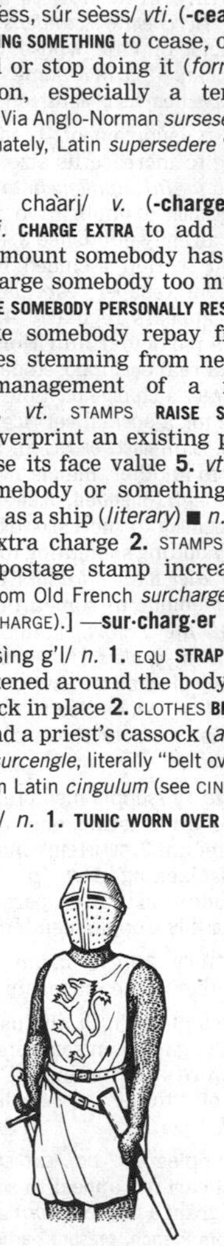

Surcoat

tunic worn over armor in medieval times **2. SLEEVELESS CEREMONIAL GARMENT** a short sleeveless garment worn as part of the ceremonial costume of an order of knighthood [14thC. From Old French *surcote*, literally "overcoat," from *cote* "coat" (see COAT).]

surd /surd/ *n.* **1.** MATH **IRRATIONAL ROOT OR NUMBER** an irrational root or irrational number, or an expression containing one or the other **2.** PHON **VOICELESS SOUND** a consonant pronounced without vibration of the vocal cords [Mid-16thC. From Latin *surdus* "unable to hear or speak."]

sure /shoor/ *adj.* **1. DEFINITELY TRUE** unquestionably true or real and not in doubt ○ *One thing is sure, we'll never make the same mistake again!* **2. FIRMLY BELIEVING** believing strongly and for a good reason, or knowing for a fact that something is true or the case ○ *Are you sure that she understood you?* **3. BOUND TO** inevitably going to do something or to happen, or confidently expected to be going to do something or to happen ○ *He's sure to notice something's missing.* **4. CERTAIN TO OBTAIN SOMETHING** definitely able to or definitely going to obtain or achieve something ○ *Many people book early in order to be sure of getting the best seats.* **5. VERY CONFIDENT** very confident about something, especially personal beliefs or abilities ○ *It was her self-confidence that made her so sure of her answer.* **6. ALWAYS EFFECTIVE** effective, accurate, and reliable at all times ○ *His aggressive manner is a sure sign that he is frightened.* **7. FIRM AND SECURE** firm, secure, and steady ○ *The fashion had gained a sure hold on every boy.* **8. UNERRING** showing both confidence and competence ○ *a sure grasp of the complexities of the situation* **9. DEPENDABLE** able to be safely relied on ○ *a sure friend in time of trouble* ■ *adv.* (*informal*) **1. UNDOUBTEDLY** used to give emphasis to something that somebody is saying and to indicate that somebody does not expect anyone to disagree with it ○ *This sure tastes good.* **2. YES** used to indicate emphatic or enthusiastic assent ○ *I asked him if he'd like to come and he said, "Sure!"* [14thC. Via Old French from Latin *securus* (see SECURE).] —**sure·ness** *n.* ◇ **be sure and** *or* **to do something** used to tell somebody to remember to do something ○ *Be sure and remember to introduce us.* ◇ **for sure 1.** without a doubt, or inevitably (*informal*) **2.** definitely and precisely ◇ **make sure (that) 1.** to take the necessary action to have something done or make something happen **2.** to check that something is the case, or that something has been done as instructed or requested ◇ **sure enough** as was expected ◇ **to be sure** used when admitting or agreeing that something is true, even though it may not agree with most of what you are saying

WORD KEY: USAGE

We sure are glad to see you! The use of ***sure*** as an intensifying adverb is characteristic of informal American usage. Note that it does not mean the same as *surely*, which is more judgmental in tone: *They surely don't want us to pay for this?*

sure-fire *adj.* always successful or effective (*informal*)

sure-foot·ed *adj.* **1. UNLIKELY TO STUMBLE OR FALL** skilled and confident in moving or climbing, and so unlikely to stumble or fall **2. CONFIDENT** confident and competent, and so unlikely to err —**sure·foot·ed·ly** *adv.* —**sure·foot·ed·ness** *n.*

sure·ly /shŏŏrlee/ *adv.* **1. USED TO INVITE A RESPONSE** used as a means of getting somebody to confirm, deny, agree, or disagree with something being said, by adding in an element of challenging self-assurance or considerable hesitancy ○ *Surely you've met before.* **2. WITHOUT FAIL** definitely or unavoidably ○ *slowly but surely* **3. WITHOUT DOUBT** without a doubt or without fail ○ *Did he get his message across? He surely did.* **4.** *Southern U.S.* **YES** used to show ready agreement

sure thing *n.* **SOMETHING CERTAIN** something that can be relied on to happen or to be successful (*informal*) ■ *adv.* **YES OF COURSE** used to express assent, agreement, or willingness to do something (*informal*)

sur·e·ty /shŏŏrətee/ (*plural* **-ties**) *n.* **1. GUARANTOR** somebody who assumes responsibility for another's obligations in case of default, particularly by giving a guarantee **2. CERTAINTY** the condition or quality of being sure (*formal*) [14thC. Via Old French *surete* from Latin *securitas*, from *securus* "secure" (see SECURE).] —**sur·e·ty·ship** *n.*

Surf: A surfer rides a wave at La Jolla Beach, California

surf /surf/ *n.* **FOAMY WAVES** the lines of foamy waves that break on a seashore or reef ○ *play in the surf* ■ *v.* (**surfed, surf·ing, surfs**) **1.** *vi.* **USE A SURFBOARD** to ride waves on a surfboard **2.** *vt.* **RIDE WAVES IN A PARTICULAR AREA** to go surfing in a particular place ○ *Have you surfed Waikiki?* **3.** *vti.* COMPUT **SEARCH MEDIUM FOR ENTERTAINMENT** to go on the Internet or watch television for recreation, frequently changing the site or channel [Late 17thC. Origin unknown.] —**surf·a·ble** *adj.* —**surf·er** *n.* —**surf·ing** *n.* —**surf·y** *adj.*

sur·face /súrfəss/ *n.* (*plural* **-fac·es**) **1. OUTER PART** the outermost or uppermost part of a thing, the one that is usually presented to the outside world, and can be seen and touched **2. UPPER PART OF EARTH, SEA, WATER** the part of the earth, the sea, or any water that meets the atmosphere **3. SOLID FLAT AREA** a solid flat area, e.g., on top of a fitment or piece of furniture, especially an area on which it is suitable to work **4. THIN APPLIED OUTER LAYER** a relatively thin outer layer or coating applied to something, usually to give it a smooth finish ○ *a nonstick surface* **5. SUPERFICIAL PART** the superficial parts or aspects of something, especially when contrasted with the essence of the thing **6.** GEOM **TWO-DIMENSIONAL EXTENT** a flat or curved continuous area definable in two dimensions ○ *the surface of a sphere* ■ *adj.* **1. USED ON SURFACE** occurring or used on, or relating to, the surface of something ○ *surface lubricants* **2. SUPERFICIAL** applying only to the outermost or uppermost part **3. APPARENT** put on for effect and not natural, deep-seated, or deeply felt **4. ON LAND OR SEA** operating or transported over land or sea but not in the air ■ *v.* (**-faced, -fac·ing, -fac·es**) **1.** *vi.* **COME TO THE TOP** to come to or appear at the surface, especially of water ○ *She surfaced after a dive of 20 minutes.* **2.** *vi.* **APPEAR** to reappear after being hidden or out of reach for a time ○ *She surfaced in Berlin after the war.* **3.** *vi.* **BECOME KNOWN** to become apparent or known ○ *The information surfaced during a routine investigation.* **4.** *vt.* **GIVE A SURFACE TO SOMETHING** to provide something with a surface, especially with a smooth outer layer ○ *surfacing the road* **5.** *vt.* **TREAT A SURFACE** to treat a surface, especially in order to smooth or perfect it **6.** *vi.* MINING **WORK NEAR THE TOP** to mine at or near the earth's surface [Early 17thC. From French, formed from *sur-* "upon" and *face* (see FACE), on the model of Latin *superficies* "surface" (see SUPERFICIES).] —**sur·face·less** *adj.* —**sur·fac·er** *n.* ◇ **on the surface** to outward appearances or when examined superficially ○ *appears cool and collected on the surface* ◇ **scratch the surface** to deal with only a very small or relatively unimportant part of something

sur·face-ac·tive *adj.* having the property of reducing the surface tension of a liquid so that the liquid spreads out, rather than collecting in droplets

sur·face lift *n.* a type of ski lift that carries skiers uphill while they are standing on their skis

sur·face mail *n.* mail that is transported by sea or land, as opposed to by air

sur·face noise *n.* noise produced as a phonograph stylus travels over a revolving record, caused by friction, dust, scratches, or static electricity on the record

sur·face run·off *n.* the flow of water over the surface of the ground occurring when rainfall is not absorbed into the soil or evaporated

sur·face struc·ture *n.* in certain types of grammar, a representation of the sequence of syntactic elements that constitute an actual phrase or sentence. ◊ **deep structure**

sur·face ten·sion *n.* the property of liquids that gives their surfaces a slightly elastic quality and enables them to form into separate drops. It is caused by the interaction of molecules at or near the surface that tend to cohere and contract the surface into the smallest possible area. Symbol γ, σ

sur·face-to-air *adj.* launched from a ship or from the ground against a target in the air ○ *surface-to-air missiles*

sur·face-to-sur·face *adj.* launched from a ship or from the ground against another ship or a target on the ground ○ *a surface-to-surface missile*

sur·fac·tant /sur fáktənt/ *n.* **1. SUBSTANCE REDUCING SURFACE TENSION OF LIQUIDS** an agent, e.g., a detergent or a drug, that reduces the surface tension of liquids so that the liquid spreads out, rather than collecting in droplets **2.** PHYSIOL **SUBSTANCE SECRETED IN LUNGS** a surface-active lipoprotein substance secreted naturally in the lungs, lack of which causes respiratory problems especially in premature babies [Mid-20thC. Coined from SURFACE + ACTIVE + -ANT.]

surf and turf *n. U.S., Aus* a meal, menu, or dish including both seafood and meat, especially steak and lobster [*Surf* in reference to the seafood; *turf* in reference to the beef, cattle being land-dwelling animals]

surf·bird /súrf bùrd/ *n.* a winter shorebird of the American Pacific coast that has dark spotted plumage and a black-and-white tail. It breeds in Alaska and the Yukon. Latin name: *Aphriza virgata.* [*Surf* from its being found among wave-washed rocks along the shoreline]

surf·board /súrf bàwrd/ *n.* a long narrow board, with a rounded or pointed front end, on which a surfer stands while riding waves —**surf·board·er** *n.* —**surf·board·ing** *n.*

surf·boat /súrf bṑt/ *n.* a light sturdy boat, often with a raised prow and stern and bouyancy chambers, suitable for use in high surf

surf·cast·ing /súrf kàsting/ *n.* a method of fishing in which a baited line is tossed into the surf from the shore or a boat —**surf·cast·er** *n.*

surf clam *n.* a large edible clam inhabiting the surf of coastal waters. Family: Mactridae.

surf duck *n.* = **surf scoter**

sur·feit /súrfət/ *n.* **1. EXCESSIVE NUMBER** an excessive number or quantity of something, especially so much of it that people become sickened, repelled, or bored by it **2. OVERINDULGENCE** overindulgence, or a bout of overindulgence, in something, especially food or drink **3. DISGUST OR REVULSION** disgust or revulsion resulting from overindulgence (*literary*) ■ *vt.* (**-feit·ed, -feit·ing, -feits**) **GIVE SOMEBODY SURFEIT** to give somebody a surfeit of something [13thC. From Old French, the past participle of *surfaire*, literally "to overdo," from *faire* "to do" (see AFFAIR).] —**sur·feit·er** *n.*

Surf·ers Par·a·dise /sùrferz párrə dīss/ coastal town in southeastern Queensland, Australia. It is a major tourist resort, and the center of the Gold Coast region. Population: 24,033 (1996).

surf fish *n.* = **surfperch**

sur·fi·cial /sur físh'l/ *adj.* relating to or occurring on a surface, especially the surface of the earth [Late 19thC. Blend of SURFACE and SUPERFICIAL.]

sur·fie /súrfee/ *n. ANZ* somebody whose main interest is surfing (*informal*)

surf-life·sav·er *n. Aus* somebody, usually a volunteer, who patrols a beach and assists swimmers or surfers who get into difficulties in the water

surf·perch /súrf pùrch/ (*plural* **-perch·es** *or* **-perch**) *n.* a bony fish living in shallow Pacific waters off North America and resembling a perch. Family: Embiotocidae.

surf sco·ter *n.* a large marine duck of North America, the male of which is mostly black with white patches on its head. Latin name: *Melanitta perspicillata.*

surg. *abbr.* **1.** surgical **2.** surgery **3.** surgeon

surge /surj/ *vi.* (**surged, surg·ing, surg·es**) **1. MOVE LIKE WAVES** to move in or like a wave, rising up and subsiding and sweeping forward or back ○ *The boat surged in the rising swell.* **2. MAKE CONCERTED RUSH** to move in a body with a sudden rush in a particular direction **3. INCREASE SUDDENLY** to increase strongly and suddenly **4.** NAUT **SLIP** to slip while being turned on a capstan or windlass (*refers to ropes and cables*) ■

n. **1. LARGE MOTION** a powerful rising and falling, or forward rushing movement, like that of the sea **2. SUDDEN INCREASE** a sudden increase in something, especially one that seems to rush through somebody or something like a wave **3.** ELEC **POWER INCREASE** a sudden and temporary increase in electrical current or voltage **4.** ASTRON **ENERGETIC SOLAR PROMINENCE** an energetic solar prominence lasting for several minutes, which accompanies a solar flare **5.** NAUT **SLIP OF ROPE** a sudden slipping or slackening of a rope or cable on a boat or ship [Early 16thC. From French *surgir* "to rise up" and *sourge-*, the stem of *sourdre* "to spring up," both ultimately from Latin *surgere*, literally "to rise up from below."] —**surg·er** *n.*

sur·geon /súrjən/ *n.* **1.** MED **DOCTOR SPECIALIZING IN SURGERY** a doctor specializing in operations that involve gaining access to the patient's body, e.g., by making incisions into it, in order to correct defects, repair injuries, or treat diseases **2.** MIL **FORCES' MEDICAL OFFICER** a medical officer in the armed services or on board a ship [14thC. Via Anglo-Norman from Old French *cirurgien*, from *cirurgie* (see SURGERY).]

sur·geon·cy /súrjənssee/ *n.* the position, profession, or office of a surgeon

sur·geon·fish /súrjən fìsh/ (*plural* **-fish** *or* **-fish·es**) *n.* a tropical fish that is often brightly colored and has spines at the base of its tail that it uses to inflict wounds. Family: Acanthuridae. [*Surgeon* from an imagined resemblance of its spines to a surgeon's needle]

sur·geon gen·er·al (*plural* **sur·geons gen·er·al**) *n.* **1.** MIL **MILITARY DOCTOR** the chief medical officer in many branches of the military service **2.** POL **PUBLIC HEALTH CHIEF** the cabinet-level chief public health officer of the United States, or the chief public health officer of some individual states

sur·geon's knot *n.* a surgical knot of a type that can be relied on to remain tight

sur·ger·y /súrjəree/ (*plural* **-ies**) *n.* **1. MEDICAL PROCEDURES INVOLVING OPERATIONS** medical treatment that involves operations or manipulations on the patient's body and, usually, cutting the body open to perform these **2. BRANCH OF MEDICINE** the branch of medicine that deals with diseases and conditions treated by operation or manipulation, or the range of diseases treated in this way **3. SURGEON'S ART OR ACTIVITY** the art or activity of performing surgery **4. OPERATING ROOM** a hospital or clinic room where surgery is performed **5.** *U.K.* **DOCTOR'S OFFICE** a doctor's, dentist's, or veterinarian's office [14thC. Via Old French *cirurgerie* from, ultimately, Greek *kheirourgia*, literally "working with the hands," from *kheir* "hand" + *ergon* "work."]

sur·gi·cal /súrjik'l/ *adj.* **1. OF SURGERY** relating to or accomplished by surgery **2. RESULTING FROM SURGERY** due to or as a consequence of surgery **3. PRECISE** like surgery in requiring or being characterized by great skill or great precision [Late 18thC. Alteration (under the influence of SURGEON) of French *cirurgical*, from *cirurgien* "surgeon" (see SURGERY).] —**sur·gi·cal·ly** *adv.*

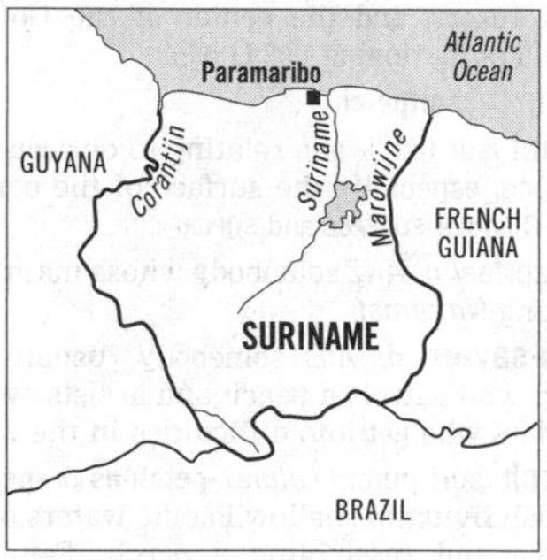

Suriname

Suriname /sŏŏr' naàm, -nàm/ republic in northeastern South America, north of Brazil, on the Atlantic Ocean. Language: Dutch. Currency: Suriname guilder. Capital: Paramaribo. Population: 436,418 (1996). Area: 63,037 sq. mi./163,265 sq. km. Official name **Republic of Suriname**. Former name **Netherlands Guiana** —**Su·ri·na·mese** /sŏŏrənə meéz, -meéss/ *n., adj.*

Su·ri·name toad *n.* ZOOL = **pipa**

sur·jec·tion /sur jéksh'n/ *n.* a mathematical function for which each element of a set is the image of at least one element of another set [Mid-20thC. Formed from SUR-, on the model of INJECTION.] —**sur·jec·tive** *adj.*

sur·ly /súrlee/ (**-li·er, -li·est**) *adj.* bad-tempered, unfriendly, rude, and somewhat threatening ○ *a person with a surly manner* [Late 16thC. Alteration of obsolete *sirly* "lordly, imperious," from SIR.]

sur·mise /sur míz/ *vti.* (**-mised, -mis·ing, -mis·es**) **MAKE GUESS ABOUT SOMETHING** to conclude that something is the case on the basis of only limited evidence or intuitive feeling ■ *n.* **GUESSWORK** a conclusion drawn on only limited evidence or intuitive feeling [Early 16thC. From Anglo-Norman *surmis*, past participle of *surmettre* "to accuse," literally "to put over," ultimately from Latin *mittere* "to send" (source of English *mission*).] —**sur·mis·a·ble** *adj.* —**sur·mis·er** *n.*

sur·mount /sur mównt/ (**-mount·ed, -mount·ing, -mounts**) *vt.* **1. OVERCOME DIFFICULTY** to deal with a difficulty successfully **2. GET TO TOP OF SOMETHING** to get over the top of a physical obstacle (*formal*) **3. BE PLACED ON TOP OF SOMETHING** to be positioned on top of something or rise above it (*formal*) ○ *the statues surmounting the parapet* **4. PUT SOMETHING ON TOP OF SOMETHING** to place something on top of or above something (*formal*) ○ *surmount the parapet with a row of statues* [14thC. From French *surmonter*, literally "to climb over," from *monter* "to mount" (see MOUNT[1]).] —**sur·mount·a·bil·i·ty** /sur mòwntə bíllətee/ *n.* —**sur·mount·a·ble** /sur mówntəb'l/ *adj.* —**sur·mount·er** /-mówntər/ *n.*

sur·mul·let /sur múllət/ (*plural* **-lets** *or* **-let**) *n.* = **goatfish** [Late 17thC. From French *surmulet*, from Old French *sor* "red, brown" + *mulet* "mullet" (see MULLET).]

sur·name /súr nàym/ *n.* **1. SOMEBODY'S FAMILY NAME** the name that identifies somebody as belonging to a particular family and that he or she has in common with other members of the family **2. DESCRIPTIVE ADDITION TO NAME** a descriptive addition to somebody's name e.g., "the Great" in "Catherine the Great" (*archaic*) ■ *vt.* (**-named, -nam·ing, -names**) **GIVE SOMEBODY A SURNAME** to give or transmit a surname to somebody (*usually passive*) [14thC. Translation of Old French *surnom*, literally "name above," from *nom* "name."] —**sur·nam·er** *n.*

sur·pass /sur páss/ (**-passed, -pass·ing, -pass·es**) *vt.* **1. EXCEED EXPECTATIONS** to go beyond what was expected or hoped for, usually by being bigger, better, or greater **2. DO BETTER THAN SOMEBODY OR SOMETHING** to be bigger, greater, better, or worse than somebody or something else **3. BE BEYOND SOMEBODY'S ABILITY** to be beyond somebody's ability to deal with or understand (*formal*) [Mid-16thC. From French *surpasser* "to transgress," literally "to pass beyond," from *passer* "to pass" (see PASS).] —**sur·pass·a·ble** *adj.*

sur·pass·ing /sur pássing/ *adj.* of a quality far superior to others (*literary*) ○ *a view of surpassing beauty* —**sur·pass·ing·ly** *adv.*

sur·plice /súrpləss/ *n.* a white ecclesiastical outer garment like a smock, with wide, often flared sleeves, and varying in length [13thC. Via Anglo-Norman *surpliz* from medieval Latin *superpellicium*, literally "(vestment worn) over a fur garment," from *pellicium* "fur coat."]

sur·plus /súrpləss/ *n.* **1. EXCESS AMOUNT** an amount remaining after the original purpose has been served or the original requirement met **2.** FIN **EXCESS MONEY** an amount of money remaining after all liabilities have been met ○ *The government is predicting a trade surplus this year.* **3.** ACCT **EXTRA WORTH** the amount by which the net worth of a company's assets exceed the value of its owned stock ■ *adj.* **ADDITIONAL TO REQUIREMENTS** not required to meet existing needs, or left over after these have been met ○ *be surplus to requirements* [14thC. Via Anglo-Norman from medieval Latin *superplus*, literally "more beyond," from Latin *plus* "more" (source of English *plus*).]

sur·plus·age /súrplәssij/ *n.* **1.** LAW **IRREVELANT MATTER** an irrelevant matter introduced into legal proceedings **2. VERBIAGE** redundant words or arguments (*formal*) **3. SURPLUS** an excess of something (*formal*)

sur·plus val·ue *n.* in Marxist economic theory, the difference between the price of a product produced by labor and the value of labor itself in terms of the wages paid to workers

sur·print /súr prìnt/ *vt.* (**-print·ed, -print·ing, -prints**) = **overprint** *v.* ■ *n.* = **overprint** *n.* 1

sur·prise /sər príz/ *vt.* (**-prised, -pris·ing, -pris·es**) **1. MAKE SOMEBODY AMAZED** to cause somebody to feel sudden wonder or amazement, especially because of something unexpected **2. TAKE SOMEBODY OR SOMETHING UNAWARE** to attack, come upon, or catch somebody or something unexpectedly **3. GIVE SOMEBODY SOMETHING UNEXPECTEDLY** to make an unexpected gift to somebody ○ *surprised me with flowers* **4. TRICK SOMEBODY** to cause somebody to do something unexpected by trickery or deceit **5. ELICIT SOMETHING FROM SOMEBODY** to cause somebody to admit something unexpectedly by trickery or deceit ■ *n.* **1. AMAZING EVENT** the act or an instance of causing somebody to feel unexpected wonder or delight **2. SOMETHING UNEXPECTED** an unexpected gift or event **3. AMAZEMENT** a feeling of unexpected amazement or delight [15thC. From French, the feminine past participle of *surprendre*, literally "to overtake," from *sur-* "over" + Latin *prehendere* (see PREHENSION).] —**sur·pris·er** *n.* —**sur·pris·ing** *adj.* —**sur·pris·ing·ly** *adv.* ◇ **take somebody by surprise** to happen unexpectedly to somebody ○ *Their arrival took everybody by suprise.*

surr. *abbr.* surrender

sur·ra /sŏŏrə, súrrə/ *n.* a tropical disease similar to sleeping sickness that affects camels and horses, and occasionally cattle and dogs. It is caused by a protozoan but transmitted by biting flies. [Late 19thC. From Marathi *sūra*, literally "air breathed through the nostrils."]

sur·re·al /sə reé əl/ *adj.* **DREAMLIKE** suggesting or having qualities associated with surrealism, e.g., bizarre landscapes and distorted objects ■ *n.* **DREAMLIKE QUALITIES OR CHARACTER** the bizarre or unreal qualities associated with surrealism [Mid-20thC. Back-formation from SURREALISM.]

sur·re·al·ism /sə reé ə lìzzəm/ *n.* **1. ART MOVEMENT** an early 20th-century movement in art and literature that tried to represent the subconscious mind by creating fantastic imagery and juxtaposing elements that seem to contradict each other **2. TYPE OF ART** surreal art or literature [Early 20thC. From French *surréalisme*, literally "beyond realism."] —**sur·re·al·ist** *n., adj.* —**sur·re·al·is·tic** /sə reè ə lístik/ *adj.* —**sur·re·al·is·ti·cal·ly** /-lístiklee/ *adv.*

sur·re·join·der /sùrri jóyndər/ *n.* in a civil court action, the second reply of the person bringing the action (**plaintiff**), in response to the defendant's second statement (**rejoinder**)

sur·ren·der /sə réndər/ *v.* (**-dered, -der·ing, -ders**) **1.** *vi.* MIL **STOP FIGHTING BECAUSE UNABLE TO WIN** to declare to an opponent that he or she has won and that fighting can cease **2.** *vt.* **GIVE UP POSSESSION OF SOMETHING** to relinquish possession or control of something because of coercion or force **3.** *vt.* **GIVE SOMETHING OUT OF COURTESY** to give somebody a seat, position, or office as a courtesy or as a gesture of goodwill **4.** *vt.* **GIVE SOMETHING UP** to give up or abandon something such as an idea or intention **5.** *vi.* **GIVE SELF UP TO SOMETHING** to yield to a strong emotion, influence, or temptation **6.** *vt.* LAW **ABANDON RIGHTS TO SOMETHING** to give up or abandon rights to something, especially to give up a lease before it has expired ■ *n.* **1.** MIL **GIVING UP A FIGHT** an act of declaring defeat at the hands of an opponent ○ *The French demanded an unconditional surrender.* **2. GIVING UP CONTROL** a relinquishment of control to somebody or something **3. DELIVERY INTO LEGAL CUSTODY** the delivery of a prisoner or fugitive into legal custody **4.** LAW **ABANDONMENT OF LEGAL RIGHTS** the abandonment of legal rights, especially the giving up of a lease or an insurance policy before it has expired **5. GIVING SELF UP TO AUTHORITIES** an act of willing submission to authorities [15thC. From Anglo-Norman, literally "to give over," from *render* "to give (back)," a variant of Old French *rendre* (see RENDER).] —**sur·ren·der·er** *n.*

WORD KEY: SYNONYMS

See Synonyms at ***yield***.

sur·rep·ti·tious /sùrrəp tíshəss/ *adj.* **1. SECRET** done, made, or acquired by secret or sneaky methods **2. STEALTHY** operating with or characterized by stealth [15thC. Via Latin *surreptitius* from, ultimately, *surripere* "to seize secretly," literally "to seize from beneath," from *rapere* (see RAPE[1]).] —**sur·rep·ti·tious·ly** *adv.* —**sur·rep·ti·tious·ness** *n.*

WORD KEY: SYNONYMS

See Synonyms at ***secret***.

sur·rey /súrree/ (*plural* **-reys**) *n.* a late 19th-century horse-drawn four-wheeled carriage with two or four seats, used for short pleasure trips [Late 19thC. Named for *Surrey*, a county in SE England, where it was originally manufactured.]

sur·ro·ga·cy /súrrəgəssee/ (*plural* **-cies**) *n.* **1. CONDITION OR ACT OF BEING SUBSTITUTE** the condition or act of being a substitute, especially a surrogate mother **2.** LAW **TYPE OF JUDGESHIP** in some jurisdictions, the position or office of a judge who probates wills and settles estates (**surrogate**)

sur·ro·gate *adj.* /súrrəgət/ **TAKING PLACE OF SOMEBODY OR SOMETHING** taking the place of somebody or something else ■ *n.* /súrrəgət/ **1. SUBSTITUTE** somebody who takes the place or fills the role of somebody else **2.** MED **WOMAN WHO GIVES BIRTH FOR ANOTHER** a woman who bears a child for a couple, with the intention of handing it over at birth. She usually either is artificially inseminated by the man or implanted with a fertilized egg from the woman. **3.** LAW **KIND OF JUDGE** a judge in some states, e.g., New York, who probates wills and settles estates **4.** PSYCHOL **SUBSTITUTE AUTHORITY FIGURE** a respected person, e.g., a teacher or older sibling, who replaces a lost or nonexistent parent in somebody's unconscious ■ *vt.* /súrrə gàyt/ (**-gat·ed, -gat·ing, -gates**) **APPOINT AS A STAND-IN** to put somebody in somebody else's place [Mid-16thC. From Latin *surrogatus*, the past participle of *surrogare*, literally "to ask for in place of," from *rogare* (see ROGATION).] —**sur·ro·gate·ship** /súrrəgət shìp/ *n.* —**sur·ro·ga·tion** /sùrrə gáysh'n/ *n.*

sur·round /sə równd/ *vt.* (**-round·ed, -round·ing, -rounds**) **1. ENCLOSE** to occupy the space all around something **2. CLOSE OFF MEANS OF ESCAPE** to encircle something completely, especially an enemy's military position **3. BE AROUND SOMEBODY** to associate closely with somebody ■ *n.* **1. AREA AROUND** an area or border around a specific thing or place **2. SURROUNDINGS** the immediate environment of something or somebody (*often plural*) **3. METHOD OF HUNTING** a method of hunting in which animals are driven into a place from which they cannot escape [Early 17thC. Via Old French *suronder* "to overflow" from late Latin *superundare*, from Latin *unda* "wave" (see UNDULATE).]

WORD KEY: USAGE

Risk of redundancy ***Surround*** and its synonyms such as *encircle* and *enclose* do not occur by degrees. Thus a spit of land, for example, should not be said to be *partly surrounded* (or *partly encircled* or *partly enclosed*) by water; it is *almost surrounded* (etc.). By the same token, *completely surrounded* may be excusable as emphatic, but it is redundant.

sur·round·ings /sə równdingz/ *npl.* the immediate environment of somebody or something, including events, circumstances, scenery, conditions, people, and objects

sur·round sound *n.* a system of recording and reproducing sound that uses three or more channels and speakers in order to create the effect of the listener being surrounded by sound sources

sur·sum cor·da /súrssəm káwrdə, sŏŏrsəm-/ *n.* **1.** CHR **PART OF MASS** in the Roman Catholic church, a short sentence (**versicle**) spoken by a priest during Mass, just before the preface **2. EXHORTATION** a cry or exhortation, especially of hope (*literary*) [From late Latin, literally "(lift) up (your) hearts," the versicle's opening words]

sur·tax /súr tàks/ *n.* **1. ANOTHER TAX** a tax that is charged in addition to other taxes **2. HIGHER TAX** a higher level or levels of tax imposed on individuals and corporations when income or profits exceed a certain amount ■ *vt.* (**-taxed, -tax·ing, -tax·es**) **CHARGE SOMEBODY SURTAX** to charge somebody with an additional or higher tax [Late 19thC. From French *surtaxe*, literally "over tax," from *taxe* "tax," from *taxer* (see TAX).]

sur·ti·tle /súr tìt'l/ *n.* = **supertitle** (*often used in the plural*)

sur·veil·lance /sər váylənss/ *n.* continual observation of a person or group, especially one suspected of doing something illegal [Early 19thC. From French, formed from *surveiller* "to watch over," from *veiller* "to keep watch," from Latin *vigilare* (see VIGILANT).] —**sur·veil·lant** *adj., n.*

sur·vey *vt.* /sər váy/ (**-veyed, -vey·ing, -veys**) **1. CONSIDER SOMETHING GENERALLY** to look at or consider something in a general or very broad way **2. LOOK AT SOMETHING CAREFULLY** to look at or consider somebody or something closely, especially in order to form an opinion **3.** GEOG **PLOT A MAP OF SOMEWHERE** to make a detailed map of an area of land, including its boundaries, area, and elevation, using geometry and trigonometry to measure angles and distances **4.** STATS **QUESTION PEOPLE IN A POLL** to do a statistical study of a sample population by asking questions about age, income, opinions, buying preferences, and other aspects of people's lives **5. GAZE AT SOMETHING** to look at or over something in a casual or leisurely way **6.** *U.K.* BUILDING **INSPECT A BUILDING** to inspect a building in order to determine its structural soundness or assess its value ■ *n.* /súr vày/ (*plural* **-veys**) **1. GENERAL VIEW** a very broad or general view of a subject or situation **2. CRITICAL INSPECTION** a very detailed, critical examination of something such as a situation or event **3. ACT OF MEASURING LAND** an act of taking detailed measurements of an area of land **4. GROUP DOING A SURVEY** a team of surveyors working together **5. REPORT ON LAND MEASUREMENT** a report that shows the results of a survey **6.** GEOG **AREA SURVEYED** an area of land that is being or has been surveyed **7.** STATS **ANALYSIS OF POLL SAMPLE** a statistical analysis of answers to a poll of a sample of a population, e.g., to determine opinions, preferences, or knowledge [15thC. Via Anglo-Norman *surveier* from medieval Latin *supervidere* "to oversee" (source of English *supervise*), from Latin *videre* (see VISION).] —**sur·vey·a·ble** /sər váyəb'l/ *adj.*

sur·vey·or /sər váyər/ *n.* somebody whose occupation is taking accurate measurements of land areas in order to determine boundaries, elevations, and dimensions

sur·vey·or's chain *n.* a unit of for measuring length equal to 22 yd. (about 20 m)

sur·vey·or's lev·el *n.* an instrument with a telescope and a level attached, mounted on a tripod and rotating around the vertical axis, used for measuring elevations of land

sur·vey·or's meas·ure *n.* a system of measurement based on the unit the surveyor's chain, 22 yd. (about 20 m)

sur·viv·al /sər vív'l/ *n.* **1. STAYING ALIVE** continuation in life or existence **2. FACT OF LIVING THROUGH SOMETHING** the fact of having managed to live through something **3. SOMETHING FROM THE PAST** a custom, idea, or belief that remains when other similar things have been lost or forgotten

sur·vi·val·ist /sər vívəlist/ *n.* somebody who is determined to survive a perceived coming disaster by hoarding weapons and food, and often going off to live alone or with a like-minded group —**sur·viv·al·ism** *n.*

sur·vive /sər vív/ (**-vived, -viv·ing, -vives**) *v.* **1.** *vi.* **REMAIN ALIVE OR IN EXISTENCE** to manage to stay alive or continue to exist, especially in difficult situations **2.** *vt.* **STAY ALIVE LONGER THAN SOMEBODY** to remain alive after the death of somebody else **3.** *vt.* **LIVE THROUGH SOMETHING** to remain alive or in existence after something such as an accident or war that threatens life [15thC. Via Anglo-Norman *survivre* from Latin *supervivere*, literally "to live beyond," from *vivere* (see VIVID).] —**sur·viv·a·bil·i·ty** /sər vīvə bíllətee/ *n.* —**sur·viv·a·ble** /sər vívəb'l/ *adj.*

Jacqueline Susann

Su·sann /soo zán/, **Jacqueline** (1926–74) U.S. writer. Her first novel, *Valley of the Dolls* (1968), was a best seller.

Su·san·na /soo zánnə/ *n.* in the Apocrypha, a woman of Babylon who was saved by the prophet Daniel after being falsely accused of adultery

sus·cep·ti·bil·i·ty /sə sèptə bíllətee/ (*plural* **-ties**) *n.* **1. LIKELIHOOD OF BEING AFFECTED** the likelihood of being affected by something **2. SENSITIVITY** the ability to be affected by strong feelings and emotions **3. FEELINGS** somebody's feelings, especially those of somebody who easily becomes upset **4.** PHYS = **magnetic susceptibility 5.** ELEC = **electric susceptibility**

sus·cep·ti·ble /sə séptəb'l/ *adj.* **1. EASILY AFFECTED** easily influenced or affected by something **2. LIKELY TO BE AFFECTED** liable to being affected by something ○ *susceptible to hay fever and other allergies* **3. EMOTIONAL** easily affected emotionally **4. CAPABLE OF SOMETHING** capable or permitting of something [Early 17thC. Directly or via French from, ultimately, Latin *suscipere*, literally "to take up," from *capere* (see CAPTURE).] —**sus·cep·ti·ble·ness** *n.* —**sus·cep·ti·bly** *adv.*

sus·cep·tive /sə séptiv/ *adj.* **1. SUSCEPTIBLE** easily affected by something **2. RECEPTIVE** open to new ideas and suggestions [Mid-15thC. Formed from Latin *suscept-*, the past participle stem of *suscipere* (see SUSCEPTIBLE).] —**sus·cep·tive·ness** *n.* —**sus·cep·tiv·i·ty** /sə sèp tívvətee/ *n.*

su·shi /sóoshee, sŏŏ-/ *n.* small cakes of cold boiled rice, shaped by hand or wrapped in seaweed and topped with pieces of raw or cooked fish, vegetables, or egg [Late 19thC. From Japanese.]

Su·si·an /sóozee ən/ *n.* LANG = **Elamite** *n.* 2 [Mid-16thC. Via Latin *Susianus* from, ultimately, Greek *Sousa* "Susa," where Elamite was spoken.] —**Su·si·an** *adj.*

Su·sit·na /soo sítnə/ river in Alaska, flowing from the Alaska Range into the Pacific Ocean at Cook Inlet. Length: 300 mi./483 km.

sus·lik /sússlik/ (*plural* **-liks** *or* **-lik**), **sous·lik** /sóosslik/ (*plural* **-liks** *or* **-lik**) *n.* a ground squirrel of Europe and Asia with large eyes and small ears that lives in dry open areas. Latin name: *Citellus citellus.* [Late 18thC. From Russian.]

sus·pect *v.* /sə spékt/ (**-pect·ed, -pect·ing, -pects**) **1.** *vt.* **BELIEVE SOMEBODY IS GUILTY** to believe that somebody may have committed a crime or wrongdoing without having any proof **2.** *vt.* **DOUBT SOMETHING** to doubt the truth or validity of something **3.** *vt.* **BELIEVE SOMETHING TO BE SO** to think that something is probable or likely **4.** *vti.* **HAVE SUSPICIONS** to be suspicious about something ■ *n.* /súss pèkt/ **SOMEBODY WHO MIGHT BE GUILTY** somebody who is thought to be possibly guilty of wrongdoing or doing something illegal ■ *adj.* **1. SUSPICIOUS** thought or likely to be false or untrustworthy ○ *All his claims about the wealth of his family are rather suspect.* **2. LIKELY TO CONTAIN SOMETHING ILLEGAL** looking likely to contain something dangerous or illegal [14thC. From Latin *suspect-*, the past participle stem of *suspicere*, literally "to look up at," from *specere* (see SPECTACLE).]

WORD KEY: USAGE

Suspect as it is used in criminal contexts denotes somebody who has been or may be charged with a crime, and who is entitled to seek to prove his or her innocence, as opposed to someone who has been already found guilty. But unless the word is referring to a specific individual, its refusal to affirm guilt may be beside the point, as it is in *The day after the burglary the police began searching for suspects.* And when guilt is evident, even though ***suspect*** serves to acknowledge that a legal defense may yet be possible, it may seem foolish: *After the jewels were found in his house and he confessed to the burglary, the suspect was remanded for trial.*

sus·pend /sə spénd/ (**-pend·ed, -pend·ing, -pends**) *v.* **1.** *vt.* **HANG SOMETHING FROM ABOVE** to hang something from above, especially so that it can swing freely **2.** *vt.* **STOP SOMETHING FOR A PERIOD** to stop something or make something ineffective, usually for a short time **3.** *vt.* **BAR SOMEBODY FOR A PERIOD** to bar somebody from a privilege, a position, or an organization, usually when under suspicion of wrongdoing **4.** *vt.* **POSTPONE SOMETHING** to delay or defer action on a decision or a judgment until more of the facts are known **5.** *vt.* **HANG ABOVE** to hang over or above something **6.** *vt.* CHEM **DISPERSE SOMETHING IN LIQUID** to cause particles to be dispersed in a liquid **7.** *vt.* MUSIC **SUSTAIN A NOTE** to hold a note until the next note or chord is sounded, so that they are heard together **8.** *vi.* FIN **STOP MAKING PAYMENTS** to cease payment on something, especially because of an inability to meet financial obligations [13thC. Directly or via French *suspendre* from Latin *suspendere*, literally "to hang up," from *pendere* (see PENDANT).] —**sus·pend·i·bil·i·ty** /sə spèndə bíllətee/ *n.* —**sus·pend·i·ble** /sə spéndəb'l/ *adj.*

sus·pend·ed an·i·ma·tion *n.* **1.** BIOL **TEMPORARY SLOWING OF LIFE FUNCTIONS** the stopping or slowing of the vital functions of an organism for some period of time, especially by freezing **2.** PHYSIOL **STATE LIKE DEATH** a state, often caused by asphyxia, in which an organism loses consciousness and stops breathing so that it appears to be dead

sus·pend·ed sen·tence *n.* a sentence imposed on somebody found guilty of a crime that need not be served as long as the individual commits no other crime during the term of the sentence

sus·pend·er /sə spéndər/ *n.* **1.** STRAP FOR HOLDING UP PANTS a strap, usually made of elastic, worn over the shoulders and with a clip at either end to attach to pants so that they do not fall down (*usually plural*) **2.** SOMETHING THAT LETS SOMETHING HANG something that allows something else to hang, e.g., one of the cables on a suspension bridge **3.** *U.K.* = **garter**

sus·pend·er belt *n. U.K.* = **garter belt**

sus·pense /sə spénss/ *n.* **1.** UNCERTAINTY the state or condition of being unsure or in doubt about something **2.** ENJOYABLE TENSION a feeling of tense excitement about how something such as a mystery novel or movie will end **3.** ANXIETY a state of anxiety or intense worry about something [15thC. Via Anglo-Norman from Latin *suspensus*, the past participle of *suspendere* (see SUSPEND).] —**sus·pense·ful** *adj.*

sus·pense ac·count *n.* an account in which entries are made temporarily, until it is determined where they belong

sus·pen·sion /sə spénsh'n/ *n.* **1.** TEMPORARY STOP OF SOMETHING an interruption of something for a period of time **2.** LAW POSTPONEMENT OF A SENTENCE a delay in the carrying out of a sentence or the making of a decision or judgment **3.** TEMPORARY REMOVAL OF SOMEBODY the temporary removal of somebody from a team, position, school, or organization, especially as punishment **4.** TRANSP SYSTEM REDUCING VEHICLE'S VIBRATION a system of springs and shock absorbers on a wheeled vehicle that reduces the impact of bumps and uneven running surfaces on the occupants and gives the wheels better contact **5.** FIN END TO REPAYING DEBTS an end to the repayment of financial obligations because of a lack of money **6.** CHEM DISPERSION OF PARTICLES a dispersion of fine solid particles in a liquid **7.** MUSIC TECHNIQUE FOR CREATING DISSONANCE a technique in which a note of the first chord is held into the second chord, the dissonance created being resolved by moving a step lower in the third chord

sus·pen·sion bridge *n.* a bridge that has the roadway suspended from cables that are anchored by towers at either end and, sometimes, with supporting structures for the cables placed at regular intervals

sus·pen·sion point *n.* one of a series of dots, usually three, used in printed and written material to indicate an omission from text being reproduced or an incomplete phrase (*often used in the plural*)

sus·pen·sive /sə spénssiv/ *adj.* **1.** STOPPING SOMETHING causing or tending to cause something to stop or be deferred **2.** CAUSING TENSION causing, arousing, or relating to a feeling of doubt or anxious excitement **3.** UNDECIDED ABOUT SOMETHING inclined to delay making a decision or judgment —**sus·pen·sive·ly** *adv.* —**sus·pen·sive·ness** *n.*

sus·pen·soid /sə spén sòyd/ *n.* a solution made up of solid particles dispersed throughout a liquid [Early 20thC. Formed from SUSPENSION.]

sus·pen·so·ry /sə spénssəree/ *n.* (*plural* **-ries**) **1.** ANAT LIGAMENT OR MUSCLE a ligament or muscle from which a structure or part is suspended **2.** MED BANDAGE OR SLING something such as a bandage or a sling that holds part of the body in position while it heals ■ *adj.* TEMPORARILY STOPPING SOMETHING temporarily interrupting or delaying the completion of something

sus·pen·so·ry lig·a·ment *n.* a ligament that provides support for an organ or another body part, especially a fibrous membrane that holds the lens of the eye in place

sus·pi·cion /sə spísh'n/ *n.* **1.** FEELING OF SOMETHING WRONG an unsubstantiated belief that something is the case, especially a belief that something wrong has happened or that somebody may have committed a crime ○ *a sneaking suspicion that she was the one who ate the last cookie* **2.** MISTRUST a feeling of mistrust or doubt, especially because something wrong has happened and has not been explained ○ *an atmosphere of suspicion* **3.** CONDITION OF BEING SUSPECTED the condition of being suspected of something, especially wrongdoing ○ *under suspicion* **4.** SMALL AMOUNT OF SOMETHING a tiny amount of something, e.g., a color or flavor [13thC. Via Anglo-Norman *suspeciun* from, ultimately, Latin *suspicere* (see SUSPECT).] —**sus·pi·cion·al** *adj.*

sus·pi·cious /sə spíshəss/ *adj.* **1.** AROUSING SUSPICION creating or liable to create suspicion **2.** TENDING TO SUSPECT inclined or tending to believe that something is wrong ○ *a suspicious nature* **3.** SUGGESTING DOUBT showing or indicating suspicion —**sus·pi·cious·ly** *adv.* —**sus·pi·cious·ness** *n.*

sus·pire /sə spír/ (**-pired, -pir·ing, -pires**) *vi.* (*dated literary*) **1.** BREATHE IN to draw in breath **2.** SIGH to give a sigh [15thC. From Latin *suspirare*, literally "to breathe up," from *spirare* (see SPIRIT).] —**sus·pi·ra·tion** /sùspi ráysh'n/ *n.*

Sus·que·han·na[1] *n.* = **Susquehannock**

Sus·que·han·na[2] /sùskwə hánnə/ river that rises in central New York, flowing across Pennsylvania before emptying into Chesapeake Bay in Maryland. Length: 444 mi./715 km.

Sus·que·han·nock /sùskwə hánnək/ (*plural* **-nock** *or* **-nocks**), **Sus·que·han·na** /-hánnə/ (*plural* **-na** *or* **-nas**) *n.* a member of a Native North American people who occupied lands along the Susquehanna River in New York, Pennsylvania, and Maryland. The Susquehannock were extinct by around 1768. [Early 17thC. Of Algonquian origin.]

Sus·sex Drive, 24 Sus·sex Drive *n.* the address of the official residence of the Prime Minister of Canada

Sus·sex span·iel /Sùssəks spánny əl/ *n.* a breed of short-legged spaniel with long ears and a golden silky coat, or a dog of this breed [Mid-19thC. Named for *Sussex*, the county in SE England where it was developed.]

sus·tain /sə stáyn/ *vt.* (**-tained, -tain·ing, -tains**) **1.** WITHSTAND SOMETHING to manage to withstand something and continue doing something in spite of it **2.** BE AFFECTED BY SOMETHING to experience a setback, injury, damage, loss, or defeat ○ *The child who fell sustained no more than several broken bones.* **3.** MAINTAIN to make something continue to exist **4.** NOURISH to provide somebody with nourishment or the necessities of life **5.** SUPPORT FROM BELOW to keep something in position by holding it from below ○ *The floor will not sustain the weight of a grand piano.* **6.** PROVIDE WITH MORAL SUPPORT to keep somebody going with emotional or moral support **7.** LAW VALIDATE SOMETHING to decide that a statement or objection is valid or justified **8.** CONFIRM SOMETHING to confirm that something is true or valid **9.** KEEP A PRETENSE GOING to maintain a pretense successfully ■ *n.* MUSIC PROLONGED NOTE a note that is prolonged [13thC. Via Anglo-Norman *sustein-*, the stem of *sustenir*, from Latin *sustinere*, literally "to hold up," from *tenere* (see TENANT).] —**sus·tain·a·bil·i·ty** /sə stàynə bílləteeˌ/ *n.* —**sus·tain·ment** /sə stáynmənt/ *n.*

sus·tain·a·ble *adj.* **1.** ABLE TO BE MAINTAINED able tobe maintained **2.** ECOL MAINTAINING ECOLOGICAL BALANCE used to describe a system of exploiting natural resources without destroying the ecological balance of a particular area

sus·tain·a·ble de·vel·op·ment *n.* economic development maintained within acceptable levels of global resource depletion and environmental pollution

sus·tained yield *n.* **1.** CONSISTENT RESOURCE the ongoing supply of a natural resource, e.g., timber, by scheduled harvesting **2.** AMOUNT HARVESTED the amount of a natural resource obtained by scheduled harvesting

sus·tain·ing ped·al *n.* the right pedal of a piano, which is used to keep the dampers off the strings so that they can vibrate freely

sus·tain·ing pro·gram *n.* a radio or television program that does not have commercials because the station or network on which it is broadcast supports it

sus·te·nance /sústənanss/ *n.* **1.** NOURISHMENT something, especially food, that supports life ○ *There isn't much sustenance in a small chocolate bar.* **2.** LIVELIHOOD a means of supporting somebody financially **3.** CONDITION OF BEING SUSTAINED the condition of being supported ○ *"I have hardly a penny in the world – I am staying with my aunt for my bare sustenance."* (Thomas Hardy, *Far from the Madding Crowd*; 1874) [13thC. From Anglo-Norman *sustenaunce*, from *sustenir* (see SUSTAIN).]

sus·ten·tac·u·lar /sùstən tákyələr/ *adj.* used to describe cells or fibers that serve as a support and have no other function [Late 19thC. Formed from modern Latin *sustentaculum* "support," from Latin *sustentare* (see SUSTENTATION).]

sus·ten·ta·tion /sùstən táysh'n/ *n.* (*formal*) **1.** SUPPORT something that supports or sustains something **2.** MEANS OF SUPPORT a means of support [14thC. Via French from, ultimately, Latin *sustentare*, literally "to keep holding up," from *sustinere* (see SUSTAIN).] —**sus·ten·ta·tive** /sústən tàytiv, sə stén tətiv/ *adj.*

su·su *n.* = **sou-sou**

Su·su /sóo sóo/ (*plural* **-su** *or* **-sus**) *n.* **1.** PEOPLES W AFRICAN PEOPLE a member of a people who live in West Africa, mainly in Guinea, Sierra Leone, and Sudan **2.** LANG W AFRICAN LANGUAGE the language of the Susu people, belonging to the Mande group of Niger-Congo languages. Susu is spoken by about 700,000 people. [Late 18thC. From Susu.] —**Su·su** *adj.*

su·sur·rate /sóossə ràyt/ (**-rat·ed, -rat·ing, -rates**) *vi.* to whisper or rustle softly [Early 17thC. Back-formation from *susurration*, from Latin *susurrare*, from *susurrus* "whisper," ultimately an imitation of the sound.] —**su·sur·rant** *adj.* —**su·sur·ra·tion** /sóossə ráysh'n/ *n.*

su·sur·rus /sə súrrəss/ *n.* a whispering or murmuring sound (*literary*) [15thC. From Latin (see SUSURRATE).]

Suth·er·land /súthərlənd/, **Donald** (*b.* 1934) Canadian-born U.S. actor. His many movies include *M.A.S.H.* (1970) and *Ordinary People* (1980).

Dame Joan Sutherland: Performing in *Lucia di Lammermoor*

Suth·er·land, Dame Joan (*b.* 1926) Australian singer. In a career stretching from 1947 to 1990, she became an opera singer of international renown, noted especially for her coloratura roles in Italian opera.

Su·ther·land Falls falls on the South Island, New Zealand. It is one of the highest in the world. Height: 1,904 ft./580 m.

Sut·lej /súttlij/ river in southern Asia, flowing through Tibet, India, and Pakistan. Length: 850 mi./933 km.

sut·ler /súttlər/ *n.* somebody who follows an army and sells merchandise to the soldiers (*archaic*) [Late 16thC. From obsolete Dutch *soeteler*, from *soetelen* "to befoul, do menial work."] —**sut·ler·ship** *n.*

su·tra /sóotrə/ *n.* **1.** INDIAN RELIG SUMMARY OF HINDU TEACHING a short aphoristic summary of the teachings of Hinduism, created to be memorized and later incorporated into Hindu literature **2. sutra, sutta** BUDDHISM BUDDHIST TEXT a classic religious text of Buddhism, especially one regarded as a discourse of the Buddha [Early 19thC. From Sanskrit *sūtram* "aphorism," literally "thread." Ultimately from an Indo-European base meaning "to sew," which is also the ancestor of English *sew, seam,* and *suture*.]

sut·tee /sə tée, sú tèe/, **sa·ti** *n.* **1.** SUICIDE ON HUSBAND'S FUNERAL PYRE in the Indian subcontinent, the practice, now illegal, of a widow throwing herself on her husband's funeral pyre **2.** WIDOW COMMITTING SUICIDE ON FUNERAL PYRE a Hindu widow who throws herself on her husband's funeral pyre [Late 18thC. From Sanskrit *satī*, literally "good woman," the feminine present participle of *as-* "to be." Ultimately from an Indo-European base that is ancestor also of English *is* and *sooth*.] —**sut·tee·ism** *n.*

Sut·ter /súttər/, **John Augustus** (1803–80) German-born U.S. pioneer. He founded a colony in Mexican California (1839), and discovered gold there (1848), initiating the Gold Rush. Sutter lost everything and spent the rest of his life vainly seeking compensation for his discovery.

Sut·ton /sútt'n/, **Henry** (1856–1912) Australian inventor. He was a pioneer of aviation, telecommunications, and color photography, and in 1885 designed a prototype television.

su·ture /sóochər/ *n.* **1.** SURG MATERIAL FOR SURGICAL STITCHING a piece of material, e.g., catgut, thread, or wire, used to close a wound or connect tissues **2.** SURG SURGICAL SEAM the line formed where a wound has been closed or tissues have been joined **3.** SEAM any seam or line at which two edges have been joined

4. ANAT **IMMOVABLE JOINT** a type of joint, found especially in the skull, in which the bones are tightly bound together by fibrous connective tissue, permitting no movement between them **5.** ZOOL **LINE AT POINT OF JUNCTURE** a distinguishable line at the junction of adjacent structures, e.g., between the chambers of a mollusk shell or between the exoskeletal plates of an insect **6.** BOT **LINE ON SEED POD OR FRUIT** a line along which a seed pod or fruit will split to release its seeds ■ *vt.* (**-tured, -tur·ing, -tures**) SURG **CLOSE A WOUND** to close a wound by joining the edges [15thC. From Latin *sutura*, from *sut-*, the past participle stem of *suere* "to sew."] —**su·tur·al** *adj.* —**su·tur·al·ly** *adv.*

SUV *abbr.* sport-utility vehicle

Su·va /sóovə/ capital and largest city of Fiji. Situated on the southeastern coast of Viti Levu Island, it is Fiji's main seaport. Population: 69,665 (1986).

Su·wan·nee /soo wónnee/ river in the southeastern United States. It rises in southern Georgia and flows 190 mi./306 km through Florida into the Gulf of Mexico.

su·ze·rain /sóozərən, syóozə ràyn/ *n.* a nation that controls a dependent nation's international affairs but otherwise allows it to control its internal affairs [Early 19thC. From Old French *suserain*, of uncertain origin: probably formed from *sus* "up" (from Latin *su(r)sum*) on the model of *souverain* (see SOVEREIGN).] —**su·ze·rain·ty** *n.*

Su·zhou /soo jṓ/ city on the Grand Canal in southern Jiangsu Province, eastern China. Population: 706,459 (1990).

Su·zu·ki /soo zóoki/, **Harunobu** (1725–70) Japanese artist. He is noted for his color prints and woodcuts, many of which were used to illustrate books.

Sv *symbol.* sievert

SV *abbr.* **1.** RELIG Holy Virgin **2.** RELIG Your Holiness **3.** SAILING sailing vessel

s.v. *abbr.* under the word or term

SV40 *n.* a virus that causes cancer in monkeys and is widely used in genetic and medical research [SV from *simian virus*]

Sval·bard /svál baard/ Norwegian archipelago in the Arctic Ocean. Population: 2,864 (1996). Area: 23,958 sq. mi./62,050 sq. km.

SVC, **svc.** *abbr.* service

svelte /svelt, sfelt/ *adj.* graceful and slender in figure or contour [Early 19thC. Via French from Italian *svelto* "stretched," the past participle of *svellere* "to pluck out," from assumed Vulgar Latin *exvellere*, from Latin *vellere* "to pull" (source of English *convulse*).]

Sven·ga·li /sven gáalee, sfen-/ *n.* somebody who controls and manipulates somebody else, usually for evil puposes [Early 20thC. From the name of a villainous hypnotist in the novel *Trilby* (1894), by George du Maurier.]

Sver·drup Is·lands /sfáirdrəp-/ island group in Nunavut, Canada, within the Queen Elizabeth Islands, comprising Axel Heiberg, Ellef Ringnes, and Amund Ringnes

SW *abbr.* **1.** COMPASS southwest **2.** COMPASS southwestern **3.** RADIO short wave

Sw. *abbr.* **1.** GEOG Sweden **2.** LANG Swedish

SWA *abbr.* Namibia (*international vehicle registration*)

swab /swob/ *n.* **1.** SURG **SOFT MATERIAL FOR MOPPING UP BLOOD** a small piece of gauze, cotton, or other soft material, used to mop up blood during surgery **2.** MED **SMALL STICK WITH COTTON** a small stick, wire, or plastic wand with cotton attached to one or both ends, often used to clean wounds, apply medicine, or obtain a specimen of something **3.** MED **SPECIMEN** a specimen of mucus or another secretion obtained by using a swab **4.** ARMS **PIECE OF MATERIAL FOR CLEANING GUN** a small piece of absorbent material that is used to clean the bore of a firearm **5. MOP** a mop used to clean decks or floors **6. SOMEBODY WHO MOPS** somebody who uses a mop to clean, especially on a ship **7. SAILOR** a sailor (*slang*) **8. WORTHLESS PERSON** somebody who is regarded as uncouth or worthless (*archaic slang*) ■ *vt.* (**swabbed, swab·bing, swabs**) **1.** MED **CLEAN WITH A SWAB** to clean out or apply medicine to a wound with a soft piece of material **2. MOP SOMETHING** to clean something such as a floor or a deck with a mop **3. CLEAN SOMETHING UP** to clean up something such as a spill [Mid-17thC. Back-formation from obsolete *swabber* "deck mop," from assumed Dutch *zwabber*, from obsolete Dutch *zwabben* "to mop."]

swab·bie /swóbbee/ *n.* = **swab** *n.* 7 (*slang*)

swad·dle /swódd'l/ (**-dled, -dling, -dles**) *vt.* **1. WRAP SOMEBODY IN SOMETHING** to wrap or bandage somebody or something with something **2. WRAP BABY UP TIGHTLY** to wrap a baby tightly in soft material **3. SMOTHER** to restrain somebody or something with a complete wrapping [15thC. Origin uncertain: probably a back-formation from Middle English *swadling band*, ultimately from an earlier form of SWATHE.]

swad·dling clothes *npl.* **1. WRAPPING FOR A BABY** long strips of linen or some other soft material, used in some cultures to wrap babies in order to keep them still and calm **2. LIMITATIONS** restrictions or limitations placed on those who are not adults

Swa·de·shi /swaa dáyshee, swaa déshee/ *adj. S Asia* **PRODUCED WITHIN INDIA** used in India to describe goods produced within the country of India ■ *n. S Asia* HIST **FAVORING OF INDIAN PRODUCTS** the practice of favoring domestic products and refusing to buy imported goods as part of the struggle for independence in India [Early 20thC. Via Hindi *svadeśī* from, ultimately, Sanskrit *svadeśaḥ* "your own country."]

swag /swag/ *n.* **1.** DOMESTIC **CURTAIN** an ornamental drapery or curtain that hangs in a curve between two points **2. FESTOON** an ornamental draping of fruit or flowers **3. LOOT** stolen property (*slang*) **4.** *Aus* **PACK** a pack or rolled-up blanket containing the personal belongings of a wanderer **5. LURCHING MOVEMENT** a lurching or swaying movement ■ *vi.* (**swagged, swag·ging, swags**) **MOVE WITH LURCH** to move with a lurching or swaying movement [Early 16thC. Origin uncertain: probably from a Scandinavian source.]

swag·bel·ly /swág bèllee/ *n.* a large overhanging stomach (*informal*) —**swag·bel·lied** /swág bèllid, swàg béllid/ *adj.*

swage /swayj/ *n.* **1. TOOL USED TO SHAPE COLD METAL** a tool or die used to shape cold metal by hammering or applying pressure **2.** = **swage block** ■ *vt.* (**swaged, swag·ing, swag·es**) **SHAPE METAL** to bend or shape metal with a swage [14thC. From Old French *souage* "decorative molding," of unknown origin.] —**swag·er** *n.*

swage block *n.* a metal block with holes or grooves used to work cold metal

swag·ger /swággər/ *vi.* (**-gered, -ger·ing, -gers**) **1. STRUT AROUND** to walk in an arrogant or proud way **2. BRAG** to talk boastfully about personal accomplishments ■ *n.* **ARROGANT WALK** an arrogant way of walking or behaving [Early 16thC. Origin uncertain: probably formed from SWAG.]

swag·ger stick *n.* a short stick often carried by army officers

swag·man /swág màn/ (*plural* **-men** /-mèn/) *n. Aus* a tramp or itinerant worker who carries his belongings in a pack or rolled-up blanket (*informal*)

Swa·hi·li /swaa heélee, swə-/ (*plural* **-li** *or* **-lis**) *n.* **1.** PEOPLES **MEMBER OF E AFRICAN PEOPLE** a member of a people who live mainly along the eastern coasts of Central and Southern Africa, and on the islands lying off these regions **2.** LANG **LANGUAGE OF SWAHILI PEOPLE** the national language of Tanzania and Kenya, widely used in Uganda, Congo, and neighboring countries. Swahili belongs to the Bantu group of Benue-Congo languages, spoken as a native language by around 2 million speakers, but used as a lingua franca by over 20 million people. [Early 19thC. Via Kiswahili from Arabic *sawāḥilīy* "of the coasts," from *sāḥil* "coast."] —**Swa·hi·li** *adj.*

swain /swayn/ *n.* (*archaic or literary*) **1. YOUNG COUNTRYMAN** a young man who lives in the country **2. WOMAN'S ADMIRER** a woman's male admirer or lover [Late 16thC. From Old Norse *sveinn* "boy, servant," ultimately from a prehistoric Germanic word meaning "your own."]

SWAK /swak/ *abbr.* sealed with a kiss

swale /swayl/ *n.* **1. SMALL VALLEY** a depression between slopes that provides for drainage **2. LOW AREA OF MOIST LAND** a low area of land, especially one that is moist or marshy [Early 16thC. Origin uncertain.]

swal·low[1] /swóllō/ *v.* (**-lowed, -low·ing, -lows**) **1.** *vti.* **TAKE IN FOOD** to take in food or liquid through the mouth and pass it down the throat into the stomach **2.** *vi.* **GULP** to perform the act of swallowing, usually as an emotional response to something ○ *swallowing hard to hold back the tears* **3.** *vt.* **DESTROY SOMETHING** to engulf or destroy something **4.** *vt.* **SUPPRESS FEELINGS** to refrain from expressing thoughts or feelings ○ *Swallow your pride and apologize.* **5.** *vt.* **BELIEVE SOMETHING** to accept something as true without questioning it (*informal*) ○ *They'll never swallow anything so far-fetched.* **6.** *vt.* **ENDURE SOMETHING** to put up with something unpleasant without saying or doing anything to stop it **7.** *vt.* **RETRACT A REMARK** to withdraw a statement or remark as false or unjustified ■ *n.* **1. ACT OF TAKING SOMETHING DOWN THROAT** the act of taking something in through the mouth and down the throat **2. AMOUNT PASSED DOWN THROAT** an amount taken into the mouth and passed down the throat [Old English *swelgan*; of prehistoric Germanic origin]

Swallow

swal·low[2] /swólō/ *n.* a small graceful swift-flying migratory songbird, with long pointed wings and a notched or forked tail. It eats insects that it catches in flight. Family: Hirundinida. [Old English *swealwe*, of prehistoric Germanic origin]

swal·low dive *n. U.K.* = **swan dive** [From the resemblance of the diving position to the shape of a swallow in flight]

swal·low·tail /swólōtàyl/ (*plural* **-tails** *or* **-tail**) *n.* **1.** ZOOL **BUTTERFLY** a colorful butterfly distinguished by the small tails that extend from the ends of its hind wings. Family: Papilionidae. **2.** BIOL **TAIL OF A SWALLOW** the tail of a swallow or similar bird —**swal·low-tailed** *adj.*

swal·low-tailed coat *n.* a man's evening tailcoat with a split rounded tail

swam past tense of **swim**

swa·mi /swaámee/ *n.* a title of respect for a Hindu saint or religious teacher [Late 18thC. Via Hindi from Sanskrit *svāmin-* "being your own master." Ultimately from an Indo-European word meaning "self," which is also the ancestor of English *suicide*.]

swamp /swomp/ *n.* **WETLAND** an area of land, usually fairly large that is always wet and is overgrown with various shrubs and trees ■ *v.* (**swamped, swamp·ing, swamps**) **1.** *vt.* **OVERBURDEN SOMEBODY** to overwhelm somebody by being too much or too many to cope with (*usually passive*) **2.** *vt.* **INUNDATE AN AREA** to submerge an area in water **3.** *vti.* NAUT **SINK A BOAT** to cause a boat to fill with water and sink, or become full of water and sink [Early 17thC. Origin uncertain.] —**swamp·y** *adj.*

swamp boat *n.* a flat-bottomed boat used to travel in swamps and shallow water. It is powered by an airplane propeller.

swamp bug·gy *n.* a light vehicle used to travel in areas with swamps and shallow lakes

swamp cy·press *n.* TREES = **bald cypress**

swamp·er /swómpər/ *n.* **1. SWAMP DWELLER OR WORKER** somebody who works or lives in a swamp, especially in the South **2. SOMEBODY WHO CLEARS SWAMP** somebody who works clearing a swamp of trees and undergrowth or who clears a path through a forest so that logs can be moved **3. TRUCK DRIVER'S ASSISTANT** an assistant to a truck driver **4. HELPER IN RESTAURANT** a helper in a restaurant

swamp fe·ver *n.* **1.** MED **DISEASE PREVALENT IN SWAMPS** any disease such as malaria or leptospirosis that is liable to be contracted by people in swampy areas **2.** VET **HORSE DISEASE** equine infectious anemia (*dated*)

swamp·land /swómp lànd/ *n.* an area of land that is always moist or that has many swamps in it

swamp pink *n.* an orchid found in the northeastern United States, with rose-colored flowers marked with purple. Genus: *Arethusa*.

Swan

swan /swon/ *n.* **LARGE LONG-NECKED AQUATIC BIRD** a large graceful aquatic bird with webbed feet and a long slender neck and usually with white plumage. Family: Anatidae. ■ *vi.* **(swanned, swan·ning, swans)** *U.K.* **WANDER ABOUT IDLY** to wander around in a relaxed way, especially one regarded as irresponsible or selfish (*informal*) [Old English, literally "singer." Ultimately from an Indo-European base meaning "to make a sound," which is also the ancestor of English *sound*.]

WORD KEY: CULTURAL NOTE

Swan Lake, a ballet by Russian composer Pyotr Ilyich Tchaikovsky (1876). Tchaikovsky's first ballet is the romantic tale of Prince Siegfried, who falls in love with Odette, one of a group of swans he has seen metamorphose into beautiful maidens. When he is tricked into declaring his love for another swan-maiden, Siegfried rushes to Odette and the two drown themselves in the Lake of Tears.

Swan /swon/ river in southwestern Western Australia, flowing through the city of Perth. Length: 240 mi./386 km.

swan dive *n.* a dive performed with the back arched, the legs held together straight, and the arms outstretched

swank /swangk/ *adj.* **1. GRAND** extremely elegant or fashionable (*informal*) **2. VERY SHOWY** extremely pretentious and ornate ■ *n.* **ELEGANCE** the quality of being very chic or smart in style or appearance ■ *vi.* **(swanked, swank·ing, swanks) SHOW OFF** to behave or swagger in a pretentious way (*dated slang*) [Early 19thC; of uncertain origin; originally a dialect word]

swank·y /swángkee/ *adj.* very stylish and expensive (*informal*) —**swank·i·ly** *adv.* —**swank·i·ness** *n.*

swan·ner·y /swónnəree/ (*plural* **-ies**) *n.* a place where swans are bred and raised

swan·ny /swónee/ *interj. Southern U.S.* used to express pleasant surprise (*informal*) [Mid-19thC. Origin uncertain: probably from an English dialect pronunciation of *(I) shall warrant ye*.]

swans·down /swónz dòwn/, **swan's-down** *n.* **1. SWAN FEATHERS** the soft down feathers of a swan **2. SOFT FABRIC** a soft woolen fabric often used to make baby clothes **3.** = **flannelette**

swan·skin /swón skìn/ *n.* any of several cotton or woolen fabrics that are very soft to the touch

swan song *n.* **1. FINAL PUBLIC ACT** a final appearance, performance, or work, as a farewell to a career or profession **2. DYING SONG** a song of legendary beauty said to be sung only once by a swan during its lifetime, when it is dying

swap, swop *vti.* **(swapped, swap·ping, swaps; swopped, swop·ping, swops) TRADE SOMETHING** to trade or exchange one thing or person for another (*informal*) ■ *n.* **1. AN EXCHANGE** a trade or exchange (*informal*) **2. SOMETHING EXCHANGED** somebody or something that is traded or exchanged (*informal*) **3.** FIN **CONTRACT** a contract in which the parties exchange liabilities on outstanding debts, often exchanging fixed-rate interest for debts with floating-rate interest, either as a means of managing debt or in the business of trading [14thC. Origin uncertain: probably from an earlier meaning "to strike" (ultimately an imitation of the sound), from the practice of striking hands together to seal an agreement.]

swap meet *n.* **1. FLEA MARKET** a flea market where new, used, and sometimes rare or specialty items are sold **2. GATHERING** a gathering that people, especially hobbyists, attend for the purpose of exchanging things

swap·tion /swópsh'n/ *n.* an option giving the holder the right to enter into a swap [Contraction of *swap option*]

sward /swawrd/ *n.* **AREA OF GRASS** an area of turf or grass ■ *vti.* **(sward·ed, sward·ing, swards) COVER OR BECOME COVERED WITH GRASS** to cover or become covered with turf or grass [Old English *sweard* "hairy skin, rind," of prehistoric Germanic origin]

swarf /swawrf/ *n.* **1. ORBITING DEBRIS** debris, especially from disintegrating satellites, orbiting the Earth (*informal*) **2. GRINDINGS** the fine metallic shavings removed by grinding or cutting tools [Mid-16thC. Origin uncertain: possibly from a Scandinavian source.]

swarm¹ /swawrm/ *n.* **1. GROUP OF INSECTS** a large group of insects, especially bees or gnats, in flight **2. LARGE MASS** a large crowd or group of people or animals moving in a confused or disorderly way ■ *v.* **(swarmed, swarm·ing, swarms) 1.** *vi.* **FORM A FLYING GROUP** to form a flying group, especially to found a new colony ○ *Do bees swarm often?* **2.** *vi.* **MOVE IN A MASS** to move or gather in a large crowd ○ *people swarmed all over the road* **3.** *vi.* **BE OVERRUN** to be overrun with a large mass or group ○ *swarming with people* **4.** *vt.* **CAUSE SOMETHING TO SWARM** to cause something to swarm, or produce a swarm [Old English *swearm*. Ultimately from a prehistoric Germanic word that was an imitation of the sound of buzzing.]

swarm² /swawrm/ **(swarmed, swarm·ing, swarms)** *vi.* to climb up somewhere using the arms and legs [Mid-16thC. Origin unknown.]

swarm cell, swarm spore *n.* = **zoospore**

swart /swawrt/ *adj.* swarthy (*archaic or literary*) [Old English *sweart*. Ultimately from an Indo-European base meaning "dirty, black," which is also the ancestor of English *sordid*.]

swarth·y /swáwrthee/ **(-i·er, -i·est)** *adj.* with a dark and often weather-beaten complexion [Late 16thC. Alteration of obsolete *swarty*, from SWART.] —**swar·thi·ly** *adv.* —**swar·thi·ness** *n.*

swash /swosh/ *n.* **1.** GEOG **CHANNEL** a narrow channel through which tides flow **2.** GEOG **SANDBAR** a sandbar that is washed over by waves **3. SPLASH** the motion or sound of the motion of water splashing or washing over something **4. ARROGANCE** boastful or arrogant behavior (*archaic*) **5.** = **swashbuckler** ■ *v.* **(swashed, swash·ing, swash·es) 1.** *vi.* **WASH OVER** to strike or move with a splashing sound **2.** *vt.* **SPLASH SOMETHING** to throw a liquid at or on something, especially with a splashing sound **3.** *vi.* **STRUT** to move in a swaggering, pretentious way (*dated*) [Early 16thC. Origin uncertain: probably an imitation of the sound of splashing liquid or of a blow.]

swash·buck·ler /swósh bùklər/ *n.* **1. ADVENTURER** a bold and swaggering swordsman or adventurer **2.** LITERAT, CINEMA **NOVEL OR MOVIE ABOUT ADVENTURER** a play, novel, or movie about an adventurer [Mid-16thC. From SWASH + BUCKLER, from the sound of swords striking shields.] —**swash·buck·ling** *adj.*

swash let·ter *n.* an ornate italic letter with elaborate flourishes and tails [Origin unknown]

swas·ti·ka /swóstikə/ *n.* **1.** POL **NAZI SYMBOL** a Nazi and fascist symbol formed by a Greek cross with the four ends of the arms bent in a clockwise direction. It became the official symbol of Nazi Germany in 1935. **2.** RELIG **RELIGIOUS SYMBOL** an ancient religious symbol formed by a Greek cross, usually with the four ends of the arms bent at right angles in a clockwise or counterclockwise direction [Late 19thC. From Sanskrit *svastikaḥ* "good-luck sign," from *svasti* "good luck," literally "well-being."]

swat /swot/ *vti.* **(swat·ted, swat·ting, swats) STRIKE OR SLAP SOMETHING** to strike or slap somebody or something sharply ■ *n.* **1. SHARP BLOW** a sharp blow or slap **2. ATTEMPT** a try at doing something [Early 17thC. Alteration of SQUAT, in the obsolete meaning "to crush, flatten."]

SWAT /swot/ *n.* a police unit that is trained in the use of military weapons and tactics. Abbr of **Special Weapons and Tactics**

swatch /swoch/ *n.* a piece cut from a material, e.g., fabric or carpeting, used as a sample [Early 16thC. Originally a northern English dialect word meaning "counterfoil," later "tally attached to cloth sent for dyeing," of unknown origin.]

swath /swoth/, **swathe** /swayth/ *n.* **1. WIDTH CUT** the width cut by a single passage of a scythe or mowing machine **2. PATH CUT** the path through a crop made during a single passage of a scythe or mowing machine **3. AMOUNT CUT** the amount of grass or grain left in the path made by a single passage of a scythe or mowing machine [Old English *swæþ* "track," of prehistoric Germanic origin] ◇ **cut a swath through something** to destroy or use up a large part of something

swathe¹ /swayth/ *vt.* **(swathed, swath·ing, swathes) 1. WRAP COMPLETELY** to wrap or cover somebody or something completely with bandages or as if with bandages **2. ENFOLD** to envelop somebody or something ■ *n.* **WRAPPING** a bandage, wrapping, or other binding [Old English *swaþian* "to wrap up": of uncertain origin]

swathe² *n.* = **swath**

swat·ter /swóttər/ *n.* **1. FLAT TOOL FOR KILLING INSECTS** a flat meshed flexible piece of metal or plastic attached to a long handle, used to kill insects, especially flies **2.** BASEBALL **GOOD BATTER** a baseball player who frequently makes extra-base hits, especially home runs

sway /sway/ *v.* **(swayed, sway·ing, sways) 1.** *vti.* **SWING** to swing or cause something to swing back and forth **2.** *vi.* **LEAN OVER** to lean or bend to one side or in different directions in turn **3.** *vti.* **WAVER BETWEEN OPINIONS** to go back and forth or cause somebody to go back and forth between two or more opinions **4.** *vt.* **INFLUENCE** to persuade or influence somebody to believe or do something (*usually passive*) ○ *Don't let yourself be swayed.* **5.** *vi.* **MOVE GRACEFULLY** to move back and froth in a graceful way **6.** *vi.* **STAGGER** to move from side to side in a clumsy and unsteady way **7.** *vt.* SAILING **HOIST SOMETHING** to hoist a yard, mast, or other spar (*technical*) ■ *n.* **1. SWINGING MOTION** the act of swinging back and forth **2. CONTROL OVER SOMEBODY** influence or control over a person, groups or country [13thC. Origin uncertain: probably from a Scandinavian source.] —**sway·a·ble** *adj.* —**sway·er** *n.*

sway·back /swáy bàk/ *n.* an extreme inward or downward curving of the spine in horses and human beings

sway bar *n.* = **anti-roll bar**

Swa·zi /swaázee/ (*plural* **-zi** *or* **-zis**) *n.* **1.** PEOPLES **MEMBER OF AFRICAN PEOPLE** a member of an African people who live in Swaziland and parts of Transvaal in South Africa **2.** LANG **SWAZI LANGUAGE** an official language of Swaziland, along with English. It belongs to the Benue-Congo family of languages. Swazi is spoken by around two million people. [Late 19thC. Alteration of Nguni *Mswati*, the name of a former Swazi king.] —**swazi** *adj.*

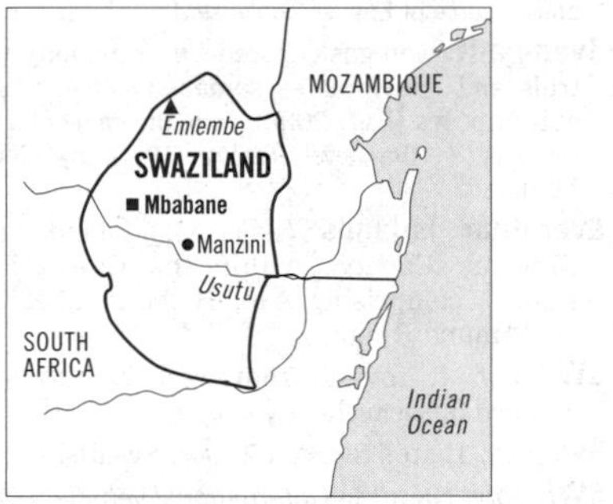

Swaziland

Swa·zi·land /swaázi lànd/ landlocked monarchy in southern Africa. It became independent from Britain in 1968. Language: Swazi, English. Currency: lilangeni. Capital: Mbabane. Population: 934,000 (1996). Area: 6704 sq. mi./17,363 sq. km. Official name **Kingdom of Swaziland**

swbd, swbd. *abbr.* switchboard

SWbS *abbr.* southwest by south

SWbW *abbr.* southwest by west

swear /swair/ **(swore** /swawr/, **sworn** /swawrn/, **swear·ing, swears)** *v.* **1.** *vti.* **AFFIRM TRUTH OF SOMETHING** to declare solemnly or forcefully that what is said is true, sometimes calling somebody or something thought to be sacred as a witness ○ *She swore on her mother's grave that she had done as she had been asked.* **2.** *vti.* **SOLEMNLY PROMISE** to promise something very solemnly ○ *He swore that he would serve humanity.* **3.** *vi.* **SAY SOMETHING OFFENSIVE** to use blasphemous or obscene language, usually as an expression of strong feelings or with the intention of giving offense **4.** *vti.* TAKE AN OATH to make a formal promise in a court of law or when taking up an official position **5.** *vti.* DECLARE SOMETHING ON OATH to make a solemn statement under oath, especially in a court of law, or cause somebody to make such a statement **6.** *vt.* MAKE SOMEBODY PROMISE SOLEMNLY to cause somebody to take an oath or make a promise [Old English *swerian.* Ultimately, from an Indo-European base that is also the ancestor of English *sermon* and *answer.*] —**swear·er** *n.*

swear by *vt.* **1.** TRUST SOMETHING OR SOMEBODY to have great faith or complete confidence in the effectiveness of something or the ability of somebody for a particular purpose or task **2.** CALL ON SOMEBODY AS WITNESS to use the name of a person or thing thought to be sacred to reinforce a solemn declaration or promise

swear in *vt.* to cause somebody to make a formal promise in a court of law or when taking up an official position

swear off *vt.* to make a solemn promise to give something up, especially a bad habit

swear out *vt.* LAW to issue a warrant for arrest by making a charge or accusation under a formal oath

swear·word /swáir wùrd/ *n.* a word or phrase that is considered unacceptable in polite language, especially one that is blasphemous or obscene, used to express strong feelings or give offense

sweat /swet/ *n.* **1.** MOISTURE ON SKIN the clear salty liquid that passes to the surface of the skin when somebody is hot or as a result of strenuous activity, fear, anxiety, or illness **2.** STATE OF HAVING SWEAT ON SKIN the production or secretion of sweat, e.g., during strenuous activity or illness, or a state of fear or anxiety that causes this **3.** SCI MOISTURE CONDENSED ON SURFACE drops of liquid that appear on the surface of something, usually by condensation of water vapor from the surrounding warmer air **4.** SCI LIQUID EXUDED TO THE SURFACE drops of liquid that ooze through and collect on the surface of something, e.g., sap on a tree **5.** HARD OR BORING WORK hard, unpleasant, or tedious work **6.** HORSERACING RUN BEFORE RACE a run that a horse has before a race, as exercise ■ **sweats** *npl.* CLOTHES TWO-PIECE SPORTS OUTFIT a sweatshirt and sweatpants made of matching fabric and worn together for sport or casual activities ■ *v.* (**sweat·ed, sweat·ing, sweats**) **1.** *vt.* MAKE SOMEBODY SWEAT to make somebody sweat, e.g., as a medical treatment, **2.** *vt.* WET OR MARK WITH SWEAT to make something damp or stained with sweat **3.** *vti.* SCI FORM OR APPEAR AS MOISTURE to produce or form as moisture on the surface of something, usually by condensation of water vapor from the surrounding warmer air **4.** *vti.* SCI EXUDE LIQUID AT THE SURFACE to produce or form as liquid beads by oozing through the surface of something and collecting there **5.** *vti.* AGRIC REMOVE MOISTURE to remove moisture, e.g., when fermenting fruits or tobacco or when curing animal hides **6.** *vti.* COOK COOK SOMETHING IN OWN JUICES to cook something in a covered pan in its own juices until tender **7.** *vt.* HEAT SOLDER UNTIL IT MELTS to heat solder until it melts and runs between surfaces to bond them **8.** *vi.* WORK HARD to work very hard or overwork (*informal*) **9.** *vt.* OVERWORK OR UNDERPAY EMPLOYEES to make somebody work very hard, often in poor conditions or for low wages (*informal*) **10.** *vt.* EXTORT INFORMATION FROM SOMEBODY to force somebody to give up information, especially by relentless interrogation or physical violence (*informal*) **11.** *vi.* BE UNDER STRESS to be very anxious, impatient, or afraid (*informal*) ○ *He left them sweating in the corridor while he made up his mind.* **12.** *vi.* SUFFER FOR WRONGDOING to suffer physically or mentally, especially as a punishment (*informal*) [Old English *swāt.* Ultimately from an Indo-European base that is also the ancestor of Latin *sudor* (source of English *exude*).] —**sweat·less** *adj.* ◇ **no sweat** used to say that something can be done with ease and without foreseeable problems (*slang*)

sweat off *vt.* to get rid of excess weight by sweating, e.g., in a sauna or through strenuous activity

sweat out *vt.* **1.** MED GET RID OF ILLNESS BY SWEATING to relieve the symptoms of an illness by maintaining a raised body temperature, and hence cause profuse sweating **2.** ENDURE SOMETHING TO THE END to carry on doing something difficult or put up with something unpleasant until it is over (*informal*) **3.** WAIT FOR SOMETHING ANXIOUSLY to wait for something in a state of anxiety (*informal*)

sweat·band /swét bànd/ *n.* **1.** SPORTS BAND WORN TO ABSORB SWEAT a strip of terry cloth or other fabric worn around the head or wrists to stop sweat running into the eyes or onto the hands while playing sports **2.** CLOTHES BAND PROTECTING HAT FROM SWEAT a strip of fabric or leather sewn inside a hat to protect it from damage by sweat

sweat·box /swét bòks/ *n.* **1.** DEVICE FOR REMOVING WATER FROM HIDES a device in which hides or some fruits are placed to remove water **2.** CONFINED PLACE a very small room, especially a narrow cell where a prisoner is confined for punishment (*informal*) **3.** PLACE WHERE SOMEBODY SWEATS a place where somebody is made to sweat through heat or fear (*informal*)

sweat eq·ui·ty *n.* **1.** EQUITY FROM CONTRIBUTED LABOR equity in property earned by virtue of carrying out manual work to improve the property or make it habitable **2.** LABOR FOR EQUITY manual labor contributed in restoring a property with a view to gaining some equity in it

sweat·er /swéttər/ *n.* **1.** CLOTHES KNITTED GARMENT a warm knitted piece of clothing, usually with long sleeves, worn on the upper part of the body **2.** SOMEBODY WHO IS SWEATING somebody who is sweating visibly, or who sweats to a specified degree [The meaning "knitted garment" developed from "clothes worn to produce sweat and reduce weight"]

sweat gland *n.* any of numerous small tube-shaped glands in the skin of most parts of the body from which sweat is released

sweat lodge *n.* a hut, cavern, or building heated by steam from water poured over hot rocks and used, especially by Native Americans, for therapeutic or ritual sweating

sweat·pants /swét pànts/ *npl.* long pants made of a soft knitted fabric that has fleece on the inside, often with elastic at the waist and ankles, worn casually or for exercising

sweat·shirt /swét shùrt/ *n.* a long-sleeved pullover or zipped jacket made of soft knitted fabric with fleece on the inside, worn casually or for sport

sweat·shop /swét shòp/ *n.* a small factory or other establishment where employees are made to work very hard in poor conditions for low wages

sweat suit *n.* a sweatshirt and sweatpants made of matching fabric and worn together for sport or casual activities

sweat·y /swéttee/ (**-i·er, -i·est**) *adj.* **1.** DAMP WITH SWEAT damp with or smelling of sweat **2.** CAUSING SWEAT making somebody sweat **3.** SCI WITH MOISTURE ON SURFACE with drops of exuded or condensed liquid on the surface —**sweat·i·ly** *adv.* —**sweat·i·ness** *n.*

Swed, Swed. *abbr.* Sweden

swede /sweed/ *n. U.K.* PLANTS = **rutabaga** [Early 19thC. From SWEDE, from its introduction (into Scotland) from Sweden.]

Swede /sweed/ *n.* somebody who was born or raised in Sweden, or who has Swedish citizenship [Early 17thC. From Middle Low German or Middle Dutch *Swēde*, of uncertain origin: probably, ultimately, from Old Norse *Svíar* (plural) "Swedes" + *þjóð* "people."]

Sweden

Swe·den /swéed'n/ kingdom in Scandinavia, in northwestern Europe. Language: Swedish. Currency: krona. Capital: Stockholm. Population: 8,858,000 (1996). Area: 173,732 sq. mi./449,964 sq. km. Official name **Kingdom of Sweden**

Swed·ish /swéedish/ *n.* OFFICIAL LANGUAGE OF SWEDEN the official language of Sweden and one of the two official languages of Finland. Swedish belongs to the North Germanic branch of the Indo-European family of languages. It is spoken by about 8.5 million people. ■ *adj.* **1.** OF SWEDEN relating to Sweden, or its people or culture **2.** OF SWEDISH relating to the Swedish language [Early 17thC. Formed from either SWEDEN or SWEDE.]

Swed·ish mas·sage *n.* a system of massage employing both active and passive exercising of the muscles and joints [*Swedish* from the system of massage having originated in Sweden]

Swed·ish mile *n.* a unit of measure used in Sweden equal to 6.2 mi./10 km

sweep /sweep/ *v.* (**swept** /swept/, **swept, sweep·ing, sweeps**) **1.** *vti.* CLEAN A PLACE WITH A BROOM to remove something such as dust, dirt, debris, or snow from the floor or ground with a broom, brush, or similar implement **2.** *vt.* CLEAR A CHIMNEY to remove soot from the inside of a chimney with a long-handled brush **3.** *vt.* MOVE SOMETHING WITH A HORIZONTAL STROKE to move something with a long smooth stroke or a quick brushing stroke ○ *I swept the papers off the desk.* **4.** *vti.* BRUSH AGAINST THE GROUND to brush against a horizontal surface such as the floor or the ground **5.** *vi.* MOVE WITH SPEED AND FORCE to move quickly, smoothly, and forcefully, often in a large body or group ○ *the crowd swept across the bridge* **6.** *vi.* MOVE WITH DIGNITY to move quickly and smoothly with a proud, majestic, or self-important air ○ *swept angrily out of the room* **7.** *vti.* MOVE ACROSS A PLACE to move quickly and forcefully across an area ○ *the gales that are sweeping the country* **8.** *vti.* SPREAD THROUGH A PLACE to pass or spread quickly through a place ○ *the news swept through the city* **9.** *vt.* CARRY SOMEBODY OR SOMETHING ALONG to carry somebody or something quickly and forcefully in the same direction ○ *swept along by the current* **10.** *vt.* GET RID OF SOMETHING to remove, dismiss, or destroy something quickly, forcefully, and completely ○ *All her illusions were swept away.* **11.** *vt.* STRONGLY INFLUENCE SOMEBODY to strongly influence or overwhelm somebody (*often passive*) ○ *We were swept along by their enthusiasm.* **12.** *vti.* WIN SOMETHING OVERWHELMINGLY to win something easily and overwhelmingly, or win all the games in a series or set of games for a championship ○ *watched them sweep to victory* **13.** *vi.* STRETCH OUT IN AN ARC to extend in a long smooth graceful curve or a wide circle ○ *plains sweeping down to the coast* **14.** *vti.* EXTEND OVER A WIDE AREA to be directed over a wide range or the entire area of something ○ *Her eyes swept around the room.* **15.** *vti.* SEARCH A PLACE FOR SOMETHING to search a place for something, e.g., an area of water for mines or a room for hidden recording devices ■ *n.* **1.** BOUT OF CLEANING WITH A BRUSH a cleaning of something with a brush, broom, or similar implement **2.** BRUSHING STROKE a quick brushing stroke **3.** LONG SMOOTH MOVEMENT a long smooth curved movement ○ *with a sweep of her arm* **4.** LONG SMOOTH CURVE a long smooth graceful curve ○ *the sweep of the coastline* **5.** WIDE EXPANSE a wide expanse or extent ○ *the sweep of the horizon* **6.** CURVED RANGE the range over which something is directed, usually a wide arc or circle ○ *stay out of the sweep of the searchlights* **7.** BROAD RANGE the broad range or comprehensive nature of something ○ *the sweep of history* **8.** SEARCH a thorough search ○ *a sweep of the neighborhood* **9.** OVERWHELMING VICTORY an overwhelming or absolute victory ○ *their sweep to power* **10.** = **chimney sweep** **11.** ROWING OAR FOR PROPELLING A BOAT a long oar that is used to propel small boats or sometimes act as a rudder **12.** ELECTRON ENG ELECTRON BEAM MOTION IN CATHODE-RAY TUBE the steady movement of the electron beam across the fluorescent surface of a cathode-ray tube. The motion may be straight, as with television screens, or circular, as with radar screens. **13.** WINDMILL SAIL a sail of a windmill **14.** POLE FOR LIFTING A BUCKET IN A WELL a long pole used as a lever to raise or lower a bucket in a well **15. sweeps** SWEEPSTAKES sweepstakes (*informal*) (*takes a singular or plural verb*) ■ **sweeps** *npl.* TELEVISION RATINGS IN A PARTICULAR PERIOD a periodic survey of television ratings that is used to determine advertising rates, or the period when these ratings are done [13thC. Origin uncertain: probably from the past tense of Old English *swāpan* "to sweep," from a prehistoric Germanic base meaning "to swing" (see SWIFT).] —**sweep·y** *adj.* ◇ **make a clean sweep (of something) 1.** to have a complete change by getting rid of everything or everyone unwanted or unnecessary **2.** to win everything ◇ **sweep somebody off his** *or* **her feet** to attract somebody with a sudden and intense romantic passion ○ *I wanted to be swept off my feet by a mysterious lover.*

sweep up *vti.* to remove dust, dirt, or debris from the floor or ground with a brush or similar implement

sweep·back /swēep bȧk/ *n.* an aircraft wing that slants backward toward the tail assembly, forming an acute angle with the fuselage

sweep·er /swēepər/ *n.* **1.** SOMEBODY WHO SWEEPS somebody whose job involves sweeping something, usually floors or roads **2.** SOMETHING THAT SWEEPS a device or machine, usually fitted with brushes, that sweeps something such as a floor or a road **3.** SOCCER ROVING DEFENSIVE PLAYER in soccer, a defensive player who is not assigned to cover an attacking player but plays across the field in the space between other defenders and the goalkeeper

sweep·ing /swēeping/ *adj.* **1.** ON A LARGE SCALE wide-ranging and comprehensive, and usually affecting a large number of things or people ○ *sweeping reforms* **2.** TOO GENERAL failing to take specific exceptions or details into consideration ○ *a sweeping condemnation of modern youth* **3.** OVERWHELMING complete, overwhelming, or decisive ○ *a sweeping victory* **4.** WITH BROAD EXTENT covering a large area, usually a wide arc or circle ○ *included in her sweeping glance* ■ *n.* ACT OF USING A BROOM the action of somebody who sweeps with a broom or brush —**sweep·ing·ly** *adv.* —**sweep·ing·ness** *n.*

sweep·ings /swēepingz/ *npl.* dirt and refuse swept up

sweep·stakes /swēep stȧyks/ (*plural* **-stakes**) *n.* a lottery in which the payout is determined by the amount paid in and the winner determined by the outcome of a horserace, or the prize itself [Formed from the obsolete meaning "person who takes (sweeps) all the stakes in a game"]

sweet /sweet/ *adj.* **1.** TASTING OR SMELLING OF SUGAR tasting or smelling of sugar or a similar substance **2.** CONTAINING OR RETAINING SUGAR containing a relatively large amount of sugar, or retaining some natural sugars ○ *sweet cider* **3.** PHYSIOL NOT SALT, BITTER, OR SOUR associated with the basic taste sensation that is not bitter, salt, or sour **4.** FRESH not stale, rancid, or soured ○ *sweet water* **5.** NOT SALTY not salty or saline ○ *sweet butter* **6.** PLEASING TO THE SENSES pleasing to any of the senses ○ *the sweet strains of the violin* **7.** SATISFYING desirable, gratifying, or satisfying ○ *Revenge turned out not to be sweet after all.* **8.** KIND kind, thoughtful, or generous ○ *He's so sweet, he never forgets my birthday.* **9.** VERY PLEASING TO LOOK AT having an appearance that is charming or endearing ○ *a sweet little cottage by the lake* **10.** AGRIC NOT ACIDIC used to describe land that contains no acid or corrosive substances **11.** ENERGY CONTAINING LITTLE OR NO SULFUR used to describe gasoline or oil that contains little or no sulfur **12.** RESPECTED dear, respected, or beloved (*archaic*) ○ *Indeed, my sweet lord.* ■ *adv.* PLEASANTLY in a pleasant manner ○ *sing sweet* ■ *n.* **1.** FOOD = **candy 2.** *U.K.* FOOD DESSERT a course or dish of sweet food served at or near the end of a meal **3.** SWEET FOOD any item of sweet food **4.** SWEET POTATO a sweet potato (*informal*) **5.** SENSATION OF SWEETNESS a sweet taste or smell **6.** SOMETHING PLEASANT a pleasant thing or experience (*literary*) ○ *squander the sweets of life* **7.** DEAR used as a term of endearment ○ *Come to me, my sweet.* **8.** INDUST SULFUR-FREE NATURAL GAS OR OIL a natural gas or crude oil that is essentially free from acidic or odorous sulfur compounds [Old English *swēte*. Ultimately from an Indo-European word that is also the ancestor of English *assuage* and *suave*.] —**sweet·ly** *adv.* —**sweet·ness** *n.* ◇ **be sweet on somebody** to be in love with somebody (*dated*)

sweet a·ca·cia *n.* = **huisache**

sweet a·lys·sum *n.* a perennial European plant widely cultivated for its clusters of low-growing fragrant white, pink, or purple flowers. Latin name: *Lobularia maritima.*

sweet-and-sour *adj.* cooked in or served with a sauce that has sugar and vinegar among the ingredients

sweet bas·il *n.* an herb with aromatic leaves used for seasoning. Latin name: *Ocimum basilicum.*

sweet bay *n.* **1.** N AMERICAN MAGNOLIA a small magnolia bush or tree of the eastern United States that has large fragrant white flowers, yellow-green leaves, and red fruit. Latin name: *Magnolia virginia.* **2.** = **laurel** *n.* 1

sweet birch *n.* **1.** TREES N AMERICAN BIRCH TREE a birch of the eastern United States with smooth blackish-brown bark, hard dark wood, and aromatic stems that are a source of methyl salicylate. Latin name: *Betula lenta.* **2.** INDUST WOOD OF THE SWEET BIRCH the wood from the sweet birch tree

sweet·bread /swēet brĕd/ *n.* the pancreas or thymus of a calf, lamb, or other young animal soaked, fried, and eaten as food [*Bread* probably from Old English *brǣd* "flesh"]

sweet·bri·ar /swēet brīr/ (*plural* **-ars** *or* **-ar**), **sweet·bri·er** (*plural* **-ers** *or* **-er**) *n.* a rose of Europe and Asia that has a long stem with prickles, fragrant leaves, and rosy pink or white single flowers. Latin name: *Rosa rubiginosa.*

sweet cher·ry *n.* **1.** TREES CHERRY TREE a large cherry tree of Europe and Asia that has reddish bark and white flowers and is widely grown for its sweet edible fruit. Latin name: *Prunius avium.* **2.** FOOD FRUIT OF THE SWEET CHERRY the fruit of the sweet cherry tree

sweet cic·e·ly /-síss'lee/ (*plural* **sweet cic·e·ly**) *n.* **1.** HERB WITH AROMATIC ROOTS an herb of the carrot family that is native to America and Asia, with aromatic fleshy roots and clusters of small white flowers. Genus: *Osmorhiza.* **2.** EUROPEAN HERB a perennial European herb that has umbels of small white flowers and aromatic compound leaves. Latin name: *Myrrhis odorata.*

sweet ci·der *n.* = **cider**

sweet clo·ver *n.* = **melilot**

sweet corn *n.* **1.** PLANTS EDIBLE CORN a variety of corn with kernels that contain a high concentration of sugar and are yellowish in color. Latin name: *Zea mays rugosa.* **2.** FOOD CORN KERNELS AS FOOD the sweet yellowish kernels of some varieties of corn plant, cooked and eaten as a vegetable

sweet·en /swēet'n/ (**-ened, -en·ing, -ens**) *v.* **1.** *vti.* INCREASE IN SWEETNESS to make something taste sweet or sweeter by adding sugar or some other natural or artificial substance, or to become sweet or sweeter in flavor **2.** *vt.* IMPROVE THE TASTE OR SMELL OF SOMETHING to make something taste or smell more pleasant **3.** *vt.* MAKE SOMETHING MORE DESIRABLE to make something more attractive, agreeable, or acceptable ○ *sweeten the offer* **4.** *vt.* SOFTEN OR PERSUADE SOMEBODY to make somebody kinder, gentler, friendlier, or calmer, or persuade somebody by flattery, cajolery, or bribery to accept or agree to something ○ *might sweeten his temper* **5.** *vti.* CHEM ENG IMPROVE THE PROPERTIES OF SOMETHING to improve a product by making it less corrosive, its odor less offensive, or its color more acceptable. Petroleum products are sweetened during refining by the removal of sulfides or the conversion of them into disulfides. **6.** *vt.* AGRIC, GARDENING LESSEN THE ACIDITY OF to make something less acidic by adding a chemical preparation to it ○ *He spread some lime in the garden to sweeten the soil.* **7.** *vt.* FIN INCREASE THE VALUE OF COLLATERAL to add securities to collateral so that its value is increased **8.** *vt.* CARDS INCREASE VALUE OF A POT in poker, to add stakes to a pot remaining from a previous deal (*informal*)

sweet·en·er /swēet'nər/ *n.* **1.** FOOD SUBSTANCE MAKING SOMETHING SWEETER a natural or artificial substance that is added to food or drink to make it sweet or sweeter, especially a synthetic substance used in place of sugar **2.** EXTRA PAYMENT OR GIFT something given as a bribe, incentive, or means of persuading somebody to accept or agree to something (*informal*)

sweet·en·ing /swēet'ning/ *n.* **1.** FOOD SUBSTANCE MAKING SOMETHING SWEETER a substance that makes food or drink sweet or sweeter, especially an artificial additive **2.** ACT OF MAKING SOMETHING SWEET the act of making something sweet or sweeter

sweet FA, sweet Fanny Adams *n.* nothing at all (*slang*)

sweet fern *n.* an eastern North American shrub of the wax myrtle family that has heads of small brownish flowers and aromatic leaves similar to those of a fern. Latin name: *Comptonia peregrina.*

sweet flag *n.* a perennial marsh herb that has narrow sword-shaped leaves, tiny greenish flowers, and an aromatic rootstock. Latin name: *Acorus calamus.*

sweet gale *n.* a shrub of the bayberry family that is native to marshy regions of North America, Asia, and Europe and has aromatic lance-shaped leaves. Latin name: *Myrica gale.*

sweet gum *n.* **1.** N AMERICAN TREE WITH HARD WOOD a North American tree of the witch hazel family that has lobed leaves, hard wood, and round prickly fruit clusters. Latin name: *Liquidambar styraciflua.* **2.** AROMATIC RESIN the amber aromatic resin of the sweet gum tree

sweet·heart /swēet haart/ *n.* **1.** BOYFRIEND OR GIRLFRIEND somebody who is a boyfriend, girlfriend, or lover (*dated*) **2.** AFFECTIONATE TERM OF ADDRESS used as a term of endearment, usually addressed to a lover or child **3.** KIND PERSON a kind or obliging person ○ *Be a sweetheart and make me a cup of coffee, will you?* **4.** SOMETHING CHERISHED something cherished for its fine qualities and often considered one of a kind

sweet·heart a·gree·ment *n.* an arrangement arrived at secretly to benefit some at the expense of the rest, especially an industrial agreement between union and management representatives that is not in the workers' best interest [*Sweetheart* from the privileged treatment of one party]

sweet·heart neck·line *n.* on women's clothing, a low-cut neckline with two curves over the bust, making the bodice look heart-shaped

sweet·ie /swēetee/ *n.* (*informal*) **1.** TERM OF ENDEARMENT used as a term of endearment **2.** ENDEARING PERSON OR ANIMAL a likable or lovable person or animal

sweet·ie pie *n.* a lovable or likable person (*informal*)

sweet·ing /swēeting/ *n.* an eating apple with sweet flesh

sweet mar·jo·ram *n.* a Mediterranean herb that has small purple flowers and aromatic leaves used as a seasoning in cookery and salads. Latin name: *Origanum majorana.*

sweet·meat /swēet meet/ *n.* a superior type of candy or confectionery served at the end of a meal or with tea (*archaic*)

sweet·ness and light *n.* pleasantness and friendliness or peace and harmony, especially in contrast to normal behavior or circumstances ○ *He has a vile temper, but when he gets his way, he's all sweetness and light.*

sweet noth·ings *npl.* romantic words and phrases

sweet pea *n.* a climbing plant of the legume family, native to Italy and widely cultivated for its sweet-scented butterfly-shaped flowers. Latin name: *Lathyrus odoratus.*

sweet pep·per *n.* **1.** PLANTS PEPPER PLANT a variety of pepper plant with large bell-shaped fruits. Latin name: *Capsicum frutescens grossum.* **2.** FOOD PEPPER USED AS A VEGETABLE the fruit of the sweet pepper plant, eaten raw or cooked as a vegetable

sweet po·ta·to *n.* **1.** PLANTS PLANT PRODUCING FLESHY EDIBLE TUBERS a tropical American vine with funnel-shaped purplish flowers, cultivated for its fleshy yellow tuberous root. The tuber is similar to that of the yam, but the plants are unrelated. Latin name: *Ipomoea batatas.* **2.** FOOD SWEET POTATO ROOT USED AS A VEGETABLE the fleshy orange root of the sweet potato plant, cooked and eaten as a vegetable **3.** MUSIC OCARINA an ocarina (*informal*)

sweet·shop /swēet shŏp/ *n. U.K.* = **candy store**

sweet·sop /swēet sŏp/ (*plural* **-sops** *or* **-sop**) *n.* **1.** PLANTS TROPICAL AMERICAN EVERGREEN SHRUB a tropical evergreen shrub that is native to America and is grown for its edible fruit. Latin name: *Annona squamosa.* **2.** FOOD FRUIT OF THE SWEETSOP the fruit of the sweetsop, which has a hard green rind and a sweet edible pulp [From the sweet pulp of its fruit]

sweet sor·ghum *n.* = **sorgo**

sweet spot *n.* the most effective place to hit the ball on a racket, bat, club, or other piece of sports equipment [*Sweet* in the sense of "desirable"]

sweet sul·tan (*plural* **sweet sul·tans** *or* **sweet sul·tan**) *n.* a shrub native to the countries of the eastern Mediterranean that is noted for its large varicolored flowers. Latin name: *Centaurea moschata.* [Ultimately from *sultan's flower*]

sweet talk *n.* flattering or pleasing words used to persuade somebody (*informal*)

sweet-talk *vti.* to use flattering or pleasing words to persuade somebody to do something (*informal*)

sweet tooth *n.* a particular fondness for sweet food

sweet wil·liam /-wíllyəm/ (*plural* **sweet wil·liams** *or* **sweet wil·liam**) *n.* a plant of Europe and Asia widely grown for its flat clusters of white, pink, red, or purple flowers with banded or mottled patterns. Latin name: *Dianthus barbatus.* [*William* from the first name *William*]

sweet wood·ruff *n.* = **woodruff**

swell /swel/ *v.* (**swelled, swelled** *or* **swol·len** /swṓlən/, **swell·ing, swells**) **1.** *vti.* **INCREASE IN SIZE** to make something larger, fuller, or rounder, or to expand in size or shape, usually as a result of pressure from within ○ *the wind swelled the sails* **2.** *vi.* MED **BECOME LARGER THAN NORMAL** to increase in size temporarily, typically as a result of injury, infection, or other medical condition ○ *my ankles had swelled in the heat* **3.** *vti.* **INCREASE IN QUANTITY** to increase something in number or amount, usually by adding to it, or to increase in this way ○ *new members to swell the ranks of the Party* **4.** *vti.* **INCREASE IN DEGREE** to make something stronger or more intense, or become stronger or more intense ○ *could feel indignation swelling inside her* **5.** *vti.* MUSIC **INCREASE AND DECREASE IN LOUDNESS** in music, to alternate in growing gradually louder and softer, or alternately increase and decrease in volume **6.** *vti.* **FILL WITH EMOTION** to be filled, or cause somebody's heart or soul to be filled, with a strong feeling or emotion ○ *His heart swelled with pride.* **7.** *vi.* **UNDULATE ON A SURFACE** to rise and fall in long large waves ■ *n.* **1. UNDULATION OF THE SEA SURFACE** the rising and falling movement of a large area of the sea as a long wave travels through it without breaking ○ *There's quite a swell out there today.* **2. ROUND SHAPE** the full, round shape of something **3. BULGE** a bulge or protuberance **4. INCREASING OF SIZE** an increase in size, fullness, or roundness **5. INCREASING OF NUMBER** an increase in number, amount, or degree **6.** MUSIC **CRESCENDO THEN DIMINUENDO** a gradual increase in the loudness of music followed by a gradual decrease, or the sign indicating this **7.** MUSIC = **swell box 8. GENTLE SLOPE** a low hill or gentle slope **9. FASHIONABLE PERSON** a fashionably and expensively dressed person (*dated informal*) **10. SOMEBODY OF HIGH STATUS** a very important person, especially in society or politics (*dated informal*) ■ *adj.* (*dated informal*) **1. GOOD** very good **2. GRAND** grand, stylish, or fashionable [Old English *swellan*, from prehistoric Germanic. The meaning "fashionable person," which gave rise to the adjective, probably evolved from "(showing) swollen, pompous behavior."]

swell box *n.* a device on an organ, usually an enclosed box with pipes, that permits crescendo and diminuendo, a characteristic otherwise lacking on this instrument [*Swell* from the part of the organ housed in the box]

swelled head *n.* a feeling of exaggerated self-importance, usually stimulated by personal success or by praise received from others

swell·fish /swél fìsh/ (*plural* **-fish** *or* **-fish·es**) *n.* ZOOL a puffer fish [*Swell* from its ability to inflate by swallowing air]

swell·head /swél hèd/ *n.* somebody who is conceited and arrogant (*informal*) —**swell·head·ed** /swél hèddəd/ *adj.* —**swell·head·ed·ness** /-hèddədnəss/ *n.*

swell·ing /swélling/ *n.* **1.** MED **ENLARGEMENT** an increase in size of part of the body, typically as a result of injury, infection, or other medical condition ○ *The swelling should go down in a couple of days.* **2. LUMP OR PROTUBERANCE** a bulge or protuberance caused by swelling

swel·ter /swéltər/ *v.* (**-tered, -ter·ing, -ters**) **1.** *vi.* **BE OPPRESSED BY HEAT** to feel uncomfortable hot ○ *We had been sweltering in a hot car all afternoon.* **2.** *vt.* **EXUDE SOMETHING** to exude something such as venom (*archaic*) ○ *"Toad, that under cold stone Days and nights has thirty-one Swelter'd venom sleeping got, Boil thou first i' the charmed pot."* (William Shakespeare, *Macbeth*; 1623) ■ *n.* **UNPLEASANT HEAT OR SENSATION OF HOTNESS** excessive or oppressive heat, or the uncomfortable feeling it produces [15thC. Literally "to faint repeatedly," formed from *swelten* "to faint," from Old English *sweltan* "to die," from a prehistoric Germanic base meaning "to burn."]

swel·ter·ing /swéltəring/ *adj.* **1. OPPRESSIVELY HOT** oppressively hot **2. FEELING VERY HOT** feeling uncomfortably hot —**swel·ter·ing·ly** *adv.*

swept past tense, past participle of **sweep**

swept·back /swépt bàk, swèpt bák/ *adj.* used to describe a wing that is angled backward toward the aircraft's tail

swept·wing /swépt wìng/ *adj.* used to describe an aircraft or missile that has sweptback wings

swerve /swurv/ *vti.* (**swerved, swerv·ing, swerves**) **TURN AWAY FROM A DIRECT COURSE** to make a sudden change in direction, often to avoid a collision, or make something change direction suddenly ○ *had to swerve to avoid a pedestrian* ■ *n.* **ABRUPT CHANGE IN DIRECTION** a sudden change in direction [Old English *sweorfan* "to file, scour, turn aside." Ultimately from an Indo-European word meaning "to turn."] —**swerv·er** *n.*

swid·den /swídd'n/ *n.* a place temporarily cleared for agriculture by cutting back and burning off previous growth [Late 18thC. Variant of *swithen* "to burn," from Old Norse *sviðna* "to be singed."]

Swift

swift /swift/ *adj.* **1. HAPPENING FAST** happening or done very quickly or suddenly ○ *issued a swift denial* **2. ACTING FAST** acting very quickly or promptly ○ *they were swift to respond* **3. MOVING FAST** moving or able to move very quickly ■ *adv.* **QUICKLY** very quickly ○ *a swift-flowing river* ■ *n.* **1.** (*plural* **swift** *or* **swifts**) BIRDS **SMALL BIRD RESEMBLING SWALLOW** a small dark bird related to the hummingbirds and resembling a swallow, that has long narrow wings. Swifts are noted for their rapid flight. Family: Apodidae. **2.** ZOOL **SMALL FAST LIZARD** a small fast-running North American lizard. Genera: *Sceloporus* and *Uta*. **3.** TEXTILES **REEL OR CYLINDER ON A MACHINE** the reel on which yarn is placed while it is wound off, or the cylinder on a machine that cards flax [Old English, "quick, moving along a course," from a prehistoric Germanic base meaning "to swing, bend," which is also the ancestor of English *sweep, swivel*, and *swoop*] —**swift·ly** *adv.* —**swift·ness** *n.*

Swift /swift/, **Jonathan, Dean** (1667–1745) Irish author and clergyman. The dean of St Patrick's, Dublin, he was the leading satirist of his age. He wrote *Gulliver's Travels* (1726) and *A Tale of a Tub* (1704). —**Swift·ian** *adj.*

Swift Cur·rent /swìft kúr ənt/ town and railroad hub 152 mi./245 km west of Regina in southwestern Saskatchewan, Canada. Population: 16,437 (1996).

swift fox *n.* a small western North American fox with large ears. Latin name: *Vulpes velox*.

swift·let /swíftlət/ *n.* a small cave-dwelling Asian swift whose nest is used in making birds' nest soup. Genus: *Collocalia*.

swig /swig/ *vti.* (**swigged, swig·ging, swigs**) **DRINK IN LARGE GULPS** to drink something in large gulps (*informal*) ■ *n.* **LARGE GULP OF DRINK** a large gulp of drink (*informal*) [Mid-16thC. Origin unknown.] —**swig·ger** *n.*

swill /swil/ *v.* (**swilled, swill·ing, swills**) **1.** *vt.* **WASH SOMETHING WITH WATER** to wash or rinse something by flooding or filling it with water **2.** *vti.* **MOVE LIQUID AROUND IN SOMETHING** to make liquid move around or over something, or move in this way ○ *He swilled the water around in the bucket.* **3.** *vti.* **DRINK A LOT OF SOMETHING** to drink large amounts of something (*disapproving*) **4.** *vt.* AGRIC **FEED HOGS WITH WATERY FEED** to feed animals, especially hogs, with a watery feed typically containing kitchen waste or food by-products ■ *n.* **1.** AGRIC **HOG FEED** a watery feed for livestock, especially hogs, typically containing kitchen waste or food byproducts **2. KITCHEN WASTE** kitchen waste or general refuse **3. LARGE DRINK** a large drink or mouthful of drink **4. INFERIOR FOOD OR DRINK** inferior or unpleasant food or drink **5. SLOPPY LIQUID MIXTURE** a sloppy liquid mixture or mess **6. NONSENSE** talk or writing that is utter nonsense (*informal*) [Old English *swillan*. Ultimately from an Indo-European base that is also the ancestor of English *swallow*. Originally in the meaning "to wash, gargle."] —**swill·er** *n.*

swim /swim/ *v.* (**swam** /swam/, **swum** /swum/, **swim·ming, swims**) **1.** *vi.* **MOVE THROUGH WATER** to move or propel yourself unsupported through water using natural means of propulsion such as legs, tails, or fins **2.** *vt.* **TRAVEL A DISTANCE BY SWIMMING** to cross a particular stretch of water or travel a particular distance by swimming **3.** *vt.* **COMPETE IN A SWIMMING RACE** to take part as a competitor in a swimming race **4.** *vt.* **SWIM WITH A PARTICULAR STROKE** to swim using a particular stroke **5.** *vi.* **BE DIZZY** to be dizzy or confused ○ *The noise made my head swim.* **6.** *vi.* **SEEM TO MOVE OR SPIN** to appear to move, whirl, or sway ○ *words swimming on the page* **7.** *vi.* **FLOAT ON THE SURFACE** to float on the surface of a liquid ○ *oil swimming on the water* **8.** *vi.* **BE COVERED IN LIQUID** to be surrounded or covered with a large quantity of liquid ○ *mushrooms swimming with garlic butter* **9.** *vi.* **HAVE PLENTY** to have a large amount of something ○ *not exactly swimming in offers* ■ *n.* **1. SPELL OF SWIMMING** a period of time spent swimming, usually for pleasure or exercise (*often used beofre a noun*) ○ *went for her morning swim* ○ *a swim club* **2. SMOOTH MOVEMENT** a smooth gliding movement **3. DIZZINESS** dizziness or confusion ○ *with my head in a swim* **4.** ANGLING **PLACE WITH MANY FISH** a place where fish are found in abundance [Old English *swimman*, from a prehistoric Germanic base that also produced Old Norse *sund* "swimming" (source of English *sound* "channel")] —**swim·ma·ble** *adj.* —**swim·mer** *n.* ◇ **be in the swim** to be involved with the latest fashions or trends (*informal*)

swim blad·der *n.* ZOOL = **air bladder**

swim·mer·et /swìmmə rét, swímmə rèt/ *n.* an abdominal appendage of shrimp, lobsters, and some other crustaceans that is adapted for swimming and, in females, for carrying eggs

swim·mer's itch *n.* an inflammation of the skin caused by the larvae of some schistosomes that penetrate the skin and cause itching. It often occurs after swimming in infested waters.

swim·ming /swímming/ *n.* the action or activity of making progress unsupported through water using the arms and legs, usually for pleasure, exercise, or sport

swim·ming·ly /swímminglee/ *adv.* very smoothly, easily, and successfully ○ *The whole evening went swimmingly.*

swim·ming pool *n.* a water-filled structure in which people can swim, usually set into the ground outdoors or the floor indoors, or a building that houses such a structure

swim·ming trunks *npl.* a piece of clothing worn by men and boys for swimming. Swimming trunks may be brief, like close-fitting underpants, or larger and looser, like shorts.

swim·suit /swím sòot/ *n.* a piece of clothing worn for swimming

swim·wear /swím wàir/ *n.* any type of clothing worn for swimming

swin·dle /swínd'l/ *vt.* (**-dled, -dling, -dles**) **CHEAT SOMEBODY OF SOMETHING** to obtain something from somebody, especially money, by deception or fraud ○ *I've been swindled!* ■ *n.* **FRAUDULENT TRANSACTION** a transaction in which one person or organization obtains something from another by deception or fraud [Late 18thC. Back-formation from *swindler*, from German *Schwindler* "cheat," from *schwindeln* "to be dizzy," literally "to vanish repeatedly," ultimately, from Old High German *swintan* "to vanish."] —**swin·dler** *n.*

swine /swīn/ (*plural* **swine**) *n.* **1.** AGRIC **HOG** a hog, boar, or similar animal **2. OFFENSIVE TERM** an offensive term that deliberately insults somebody's manners or behavior (*insult*) [Old English *swīn*. Ultimately, from an Indo-European word that is also the ancestor of English *hyena* and *sow* "female hog."] —**swin·ish** *adj.* —**swin·ishly** *adv.*

swine fe·ver *n.* *U.K.* = **hog cholera**

swine·herd /swīn hùrd/ *n.* somebody who looks after hogs (*archaic or literary*)

swine·pox /swīn pòks/ *n.* an infectious viral disease of hogs marked by lesions of the skin

swing /swing/ *v.* (**swung, swung** /swung/, **swing·ing, swings**) **1.** *vti.* **MOVE TO AND FRO** to move freely from side to side or backward and forward, usually hanging from a fixed point, or make something move in this way **2.** *vti.* **PIVOT OR ROTATE** to move or turn in a circle or an arc, usually pivoting around a fixed point, or make something move or turn in this way ○ *The door door swung open.* **3.** *vti.* **SUSPEND OR HANG SOMETHING** to fix something so that it can swing, or be fixed in this way **4.** *vti.* **MOVE IN A CURVE** to move in a smooth curve, or make something move in this way ○ *The limousine swung into the drive.* **5.** *vi.* **WALK WITH A SWAYING MOTION** to walk with a swaying motion in a relaxed or easy manner **6.** *vti.* **STRIKE WITH A SWEEPING BLOW** to hit or attempt to hit somebody or something with a sweeping blow or stroke ○ *swing at the ball wildly* **7.** *vti.* **RIDE ON A SWINGING SEAT** to move backward and forward on a swinging seat, or make somebody move in such a way by pushing the person or the seat **8.** *vti.* **FLUCTUATE OR VACILLATE** to change from one feeling or condition to another, sometimes quickly or suddenly, or make something or somebody change in this way ○ *Their mood swung between elation and gloom.* **9.** *vt.* **ARRANGE OR MANIPULATE SOMETHING** to achieve a desired change or result by using influence, persuasion, or other means (*informal*) ○ *You want the job? I can swing it for you.* **10.** *vi.* **BE HANGED FOR SOMETHING** to be hanged as punishment for something (*informal*) **11.** *vi.* **SWAP SEXUAL PARTNERS** to have a number of sexual partners, especially by exchanging them within a group (*slang*) **12.** *vi.* **BE LIVELY** to be lively or animated (*informal*) ○ *The party was really swinging by the time we arrived.* **13.** *vi.* **BE MODERN AND FASHIONABLE** to be interested in and involved in modern or fashionable trends (*informal*) **14.** *vti.* MUSIC **PLAY JAZZ** to play in a style of big-band jazz music suitable for dancing ■ *n.* **1. HANGING SEAT** a seat hung from a frame or branch for somebody to sit on and move backward and forward, especially one on which children play **2. SWINGING MOVEMENT** the process of swinging, or a swinging movement **3. RANGE OF MOVEMENT** the curve or distance covered by something as it swings **4. SWEEPING STROKE OR BLOW** a sweeping stroke, blow, or punch ○ *took a swing at the ball* **5. RELAXED SWINGING MOTION** a relaxed or graceful swaying motion **6.** SPORTS **WAY SOMEBODY SWINGS SOMETHING** the manner of movement used to swing a bat or club or bowl a ball ○ *practicing her golf swing* **7. SHIFT OR FLUCTUATION** a sudden or significant change, especially in the way people think or act ○ *frequent mood swings* ○ *a massive swing in popularity toward the younger candidate* **8. UP-AND-DOWN CYCLICAL CHANGES** the up-and-down cycles of something, e.g., business profits, economic growth, or stock prices **9. STEADY PROGRESSION** a steady progression or advance across territory, or through a process, activity, or phase **10.** MUSIC **STYLE OF JAZZ MUSIC** a style of jazz music suitable for dancing, popular especially in the 1930s and 1940s and generally played by big bands (*often used before a noun*) ○ *swing dance* **11. A CIRCULAR TOUR** a tour or course that finishes where it began, e.g., as part of a political campaign **12. FREEDOM OF ACTION** complete freedom to act or take decisions [Old English *swingan* "to flog, rush," from a prehistoric Germanic base meaning "violent circulatory movement," which also produced English *swinge* and *swink*] —**swing·y** *adj.* ◇ **be in full swing** to be in vigorous progress ◇ **get into the swing of things** to get back into your normal rhythm or routine ◇ **go with a swing** to be lively and animated ○ *The evening really went with a swing.*

swing around *vi.* **1. TURN AROUND QUICKLY** to turn around quickly or suddenly **2. CHANGE DIRECTION QUICKLY** to change direction quickly or suddenly

swing bridge *n.* a low movable bridge that pivots horizontally on a pier in midstream and is swung parallel to the stream to allow a ship to pass

swing-by *n.* a deliberate change in the course of an interplanetary vehicle brought about by moving through the gravitational field of a celestial body, especially that of a planet

swing door *n. U.K.* = **swinging door**

swinge /swinj/ (**swinged, swinge·ing, swing·es**) *vt.* to punish somebody severely, especially by beating or flogging (*archaic*) [Mid-16thC. Ultimately from a prehistoric Germanic base that is also the ancestor of English *swing*.]

swinge·ing /swínjing/ *adj. U.K.* causing great harm or hardship ○ *swingeing cuts in spending*

swing·er /swíngər/ *n.* somebody who lives a somewhat unconventional and hedonistic life, especially somebody who exchanges sexual partners with others (*slang*)

swing·ing /swínging/ *adj.* **1. FASHIONABLE** lively and fashionable (*dated*) **2. LIVELY** lively and animated **3. OFTEN CHANGING SEXUAL PARTNERS** frequently changing or exchanging sexual partners (*slang*)

swing·ing door *n.* a door that can be opened by pushing from either side, especially one that swings shut automatically

swing·ing vot·er *n. ANZ* somebody who does not consistently vote for the same political party in elections

swin·gle·tree /swíng g'l treé/ *n. U.K.* = **whiffletree**

swing·man /swíngmən/ (*plural* **-men** /-mən/) *n.* a player who is able to play in two different positions, especially a basketball player who can play both forward and guard [Mid-20thC. *Swing* from the player's shifting positions.]

swing shift *n.* **1. SHIFT BETWEEN DAY AND NIGHT SHIFTS** a period of work beginning in the afternoon and ending at night. It overlaps between the day shift and the night shift. **2. WORKERS ON A SWING SHIFT** a group of employees working on a swing shift

swing vot·er *n.* somebody who does not consistently vote for the same political party in elections

swing-wing *adj.* **WITH MOVABLE WINGS** used to describe an aircraft whose wings are constructed to allow them to move backward and forward relative to the fuselage during flight. The rearward configuration improves streamlining at high speeds, while the forward configuration improves lifting qualities during takeoff and landing. ■ *n.* **AIRPLANE WITH MOVABLE WINGS** an airplane with variable-sweep wings

swipe /swīp/ *v.* (**swiped, swip·ing, swipes**) **1.** *vti.* **HIT SOMEBODY OR SOMETHING HARD** to strike or attempt to strike somebody or something with a forceful swinging or sweeping blow **2.** *vt.* **STEAL SOMETHING** to steal something, often with a snatching movement (*informal*) **3.** *vt.* **PUT A CARD THROUGH MACHINE** to pass a card on which data has been stored magnetically through an electronic reading device, e.g., to gain access to a building or to initiate a banking transaction, or to be read successfully by such a device ○ *the card won't swipe through the machine* ■ *n.* **1. SWINGING BLOW** a forceful swinging or sweeping blow ○ *took a swipe at me but missed* **2. CRITICAL ATTACK** a critical remark or attack (*informal*) **3. PIVOTED POLE** a long pole used as a lever to raise or lower a bucket in a well [Early 19thC. Partly from a Scottish variant of SWEEP and partly from obsolete English *swip* "stroke, blow," from SWEEP.] —**swip·er** *n.*

swipe card *n.* a plastic card such as a credit card on which data have been stored magnetically and that can be passed through and read by an electronic reading device and decoded

swirl /swurl/ *v.* (**swirled, swirl·ing, swirls**) **1.** *vti.* **TURN WITH A CIRCULAR MOTION** to turn around and around with a twisting or spiraling movement, or to make something move in this way ○ *caught up in a swirling throng of dancers and musicians* **2.** *vi.* **BE DIZZY** to be dizzy or confused ■ *n.* **1. CIRCULAR MOTION** a turning, twisting, spiraling movement, or something that moves in this way **2. SPIRAL** a curl, twist, or spiral ○ *the water swirled and eddied around us* ○ *a carpet with black swirls on a red background* **3. CONFUSION** dizziness or confusion [15thC. Originally "whirlpool," of uncertain origin: perhaps from a Low German or Scandinavian word, thought to be an imitation of the sound of whirling water.] —**swirl·y** *adj.*

swish /swish/ *v.* (**swished, swish·ing, swish·es**) **1.** *vi.* **MAKE OR MOVE WITH A WHISTLING SOUND** to make the soft smooth whistling or rustling sound of something moving quickly through the air, or to move with such a sound **2.** *vt.* **MOVE SOMETHING WITH A WHISTLING SOUND** to cause something to make or move with a swishing sound ○ *swishing a sword* **3.** *vt.* **CUT WITH A SWIFT SHARP BLOW** to cut or strike something or somebody with a swift sharp swishing blow ■ *n.* **1. SWISHING SOUND OR MOVEMENT** a soft smooth whistling or rustling sound, or a movement that makes such a sound ○ *the angry swish swish of its tail* **2. STICK OR STROKE** a rod used to beat or flog a person or animal, or a blow from such a rod **3. OFFENSIVE TERM** an offensive term for a homosexual man that deliberately insults his manner or behavior as being more typical of a woman (*insult*) ■ *adj.* **1.** *U.K.* **ELEGANT** elegant and fashionable (*informal*) **2. OFFENSIVE TERM** an offensive term that deliberately insults a homosexual man whose manner or behavior is regarded as more typical of a woman (*insult*) [Mid-18thC. Origin uncertain: probably an imitation of the sound made when moving through or brushing against something.] —**swish·er** *n.* —**swish·y** *adj.*

Swiss /swiss/ *n.* (*plural* **Swiss**) **1. SOMEBODY FROM SWITZERLAND** somebody who was born or raised in Switzerland, or who has Swiss citizenship **2. DIALECT SPOKEN IN SWITZERLAND** any of the dialects of German, French, and Italian spoken in Switzerland ■ *adj.* **OF SWITZERLAND** relating to Switzerland, or its people or culture [Early 16thC. From French *Suisse*, ultimately, from Middle High German *Swīz* "Switzerland."]

Swiss ar·my knife *n.* a pocketknife with a number of additional items that fold into the handle, e.g., a corkscrew, nail file, bottle opener, and scissors

Swiss chard, chard *n.* a variety of beet with large edible leaves and stems that are similar to spinach, cooked and eaten as a vegetable. Latin name: *Beta vulgaris cicla.*

Swiss Guard *n.* a group of Swiss-born soldiers employed to protect the pope at the Vatican, or a member of this group

swiss mus·lin *n.* a fine cotton fabric, often with a raised pattern, used to make light clothes or curtains

swiss roll, Swiss roll *n. U.K.* = **jelly roll**

Swiss steak, swiss steak *n.* a piece of meat, usually a cut of beef such as round steak, braised with vegetables

switch /swich/ *n.* **1.** ELEC ENG **BUTTON OR LEVER CONTROLLING AN ELECTRICAL CIRCUIT** a mechanical or electronic device that opens, closes, or changes the connections in an electrical circuit, e.g., one used to turn a light or machine on or off **2. SUDDEN CHANGE** a quick or sudden change **3. SUBSTITUTION** an exchange or substitution **4. THIN ROD OR CANE** a thin flexible stick, especially one used for punishment, or a blow or beating with such a stick **5.** HAIR **PONYTAIL HAIRPIECE** a hairpiece in the form of a false ponytail **6.** ZOOL **TIP OF AN ANIMAL'S TAIL** a tuft of hair at the end of the tail of a cow or other animal **7.** CARDS **CARD GAME** any card game in which the suit can be changed during play **8.** RAIL **DEVICE FOR SHIFTING TRAINS BETWEEN TRACKS** a device enabling trains to transfer from one track to another, usually including movable rails **9.** RAIL **RAILROAD SIDING** a railroad siding onto which trains can be detoured **10.** UTIL **ROUTING DEVICE USED WITHIN TELEPHONE EXCHANGES** a device used within a telephone exchange to route transmissions between network nodes **11.** COMPUT **TECHNIQUE FOR CONTROLLING A PROGRAM'S LOGIC** a programmed technique for indicating which alternative path to take at a decision point in a program's logic ■ *v.* (**switched, switch·ing, switch·es**) **1.** *vti.* **CHANGE, SHIFT, OR TRANSFER** to change from one time, activity, or situation to another, often quickly or suddenly, or to cause somebody or something to make such a change ○ *The dancing class has been switched from Friday afternoon to Saturday morning.* **2.** *vti.* **MAKE AN EXCHANGE OR SUBSTITUTION** to exchange two similar or related things, or put one in the place of the other, sometimes secretly or surreptitiously **3.** *vti.* ELEC **CHANGE AN ELECTRICAL FUNCTION** to make an electrical device do something different by operating a switch to cause current to stop or start flowing or change its path ○ *He switched the radio to a different station.* **4.** *vti.* RAIL **MOVE A TRAIN BETWEEN TRACKS** to move a locomotive or train from one track to another **5.** *vti.* **FLICK OR SWING TO AND FRO** to move quickly from side to side or backward and forward, or make something move in this way **6.** *vt.* **BEAT SOMEBODY WITH SWITCH** to beat somebody with a switch, especially as a punishment [Late 16thC. Origin uncertain: probably from Middle Dutch *swijch* "twig." The verb originally meant "to beat with a switch," hence "to bend like a flexible stick, divert, exchange."] —**switch·a·ble** *adj.* —**switch·er** *n.*

switch off *vti.* to stop paying attention, lose interest, or stop thinking about something, or make somebody do this (*informal*)

switch·back /swích bàk/ *n.* **1. TWISTY ROAD WITH MANY HILLS** a road or track with many steep uphill and downhill slopes and sharp bends **2. SHARP BEND ON A STEEP SLOPE** a sharp bend on a road or track going steeply uphill or downhill **3.** *U.K.* LEISURE = **roller coaster** [Mid-19thC. Originally a zigzag railroad track used on steep slopes, where the individual tracks were connected by switches at each of which the train was reversed in direction.]

switch·blade /swích blàyd/, **switch·blade knife** *n.* a pocketknife with a blade that springs out of the handle automatically when a button is pressed

switch·board /swích bàwrd/ *n.* **1.** UTIL **MANUAL DEVICE FOR CONNECTING TELEPHONE LINES** a manually operated device for interconnecting telephone lines and routing telephone calls, usually within a telephone exchange or in a workplace, hotel, or other large building **2.** ELEC ENG **CONTROL PANEL CONTAINING ELECTRICAL DEVICES** one or more insulating panels containing the electrical devices and instruments, e.g., switches, circuit breakers, fuses, and meters, required to operate electrical equipment

switch·er·oo /swìchə ro͞o/ (*plural* **-oos** *informal*) *n.* a sudden unexpected change, reversal, or switching of something (*slang*) [Mid-20thC. Imaginative formation from SWITCH.]

switch-hit·ter *n.* **1.** BASEBALL **RIGHT-HANDED AND LEFT-HANDED BASEBALL BATTER** in baseball, a batter who hits both left-handed and right-handed with equal skill **2. BISEXUAL PERSON** somebody who is bisexual (*slang*) [Switch from switching the batting arm]

switch·man /swíchmən/ (*plural* **-men** /-mən/) *n.* somebody who operates a rail junction and is responsible for the switching of trains to the proper track

switch·yard /swích yaàrd/ *n.* a railroad yard or terminal in which railroad cars are moved between tracks and trains are assembled and disassembled

swith·er /swíthər/ (**-ered, -er·ing, -ers**) *vi. Scotland* to hesitate or be indecisive [Early 16thC. Origin unknown.]

Switz. *abbr.* Switzerland

Swit·zer /swítsər/ *n.* **1. SWISS PERSON** a Swiss person (*archaic*) **2. SWISS GUARD** a member of the Swiss Guard [Mid-16thC. From Middle High German *Swītzer*, from *Swīz* "Switzerland."]

Switzerland

Swit·zer·land /swítsər lànd/ federal republic consisting of 23 cantons in west central Europe. It has been neutral since 1515. Language: French, German, Italian. Currency: Swiss Franc. Capital: Bern. Population: 7,207,060 (1996). Area: 15,940 sq. mi./41,284 sq. km. Official name **Swiss Confederation**

swiv·el /swívv'l/ *v.* (**-eled, -el·ing, -els**) **1.** *vti.* **PIVOT OR ROTATE** to turn freely or horizontally in a circle, or make something turn in this way **2.** *vt.* **PROVIDE SOMETHING WITH A PIVOTING JOINT** to fit, attach, or support something with a joint that allows complete freedom of movement ■ *n.* **1. DEVICE ALLOWING PARTS TO TURN** a joint or fastening that allows something attached to it to turn freely **2. SUPPORT ALLOWING SOMETHING TO PIVOT** a pivoting support that allows something such as a gun, chair, or camera to turn from side to side or up and down, sometimes in a full circle **3.** ARMS **PIVOTING GUN** a gun that can be turned from side to side horizontally because of the pivoting mount supporting it [14thC. From Old English *swīfan* "to sweep." Ultimately from a prehistoric Germanic base that is also the ancestor of English *swift*.]

swiv·el chair *n.* a chair, generally an office chair, mounted on a central support with a device that enables it to turn horizontally in a circle

swiv·el-hipped *adj.* moving with loosely swinging hips, usually in an exaggerated manner

swiv·et /swívvət/ *n.* a flustered or agitated state (*informal*) [Late 19thC. Origin unknown.]

swiz·zle /swízz'l/ *n.* **MIXED ALCOHOLIC DRINK** an iced cocktail, usually containing rum, that is stirred to make it frothy or to frost the glass ■ *vt.* (**-zled, -zling, -zles**) **STIR DRINK WITH A SWIZZLE STICK** to stir a drink with a swizzle stick to mix the ingredients, make it frothy, or reduce its effervescence [Early 19thC. Origin uncertain: perhaps an alteration of earlier *switchel* "drink of molasses and water," of unknown origin.]

swiz·zle stick *n.* a small thin plastic rod used for stirring a drink to mix the ingredients, make it frothy, or reduce its effervescence

swob /swob/ *n.* **SWAB** a swab (*archaic*) ■ *vt.* (**swob, swobbed, swob·bing, swobs**) **SWAB SOMETHING** to swab somebody or something (*archaic*)

swol·len past participle of **swell**

swol·len head *n. U.K.* = **swelled head** —**swol·len-head·ed·ness** *n.*

swoon /swoon/ *vi.* (**swooned, swoon·ing, swoons**) **1. FEEL FAINT WITH JOY** to be overwhelmed by happiness, excitement, adoration, or infatuation **2. FALL IN A FAINT** to experience a sudden and usually brief loss of consciousness ■ *n.* **LOSS OF CONSCIOUSNESS** a sudden and usually brief loss of consciousness [13thC. Origin uncertain: probably from Old English *iswowen* "in a swoon," from *geswōgen*, past participle of assumed *swōgan* "to suffocate," of unknown origin.]

swoop /swoop/ *v.* (**swooped, swoop·ing, swoops**) **1.** *vi.* **MAKE SWEEPING DESCENT** to descend quickly and suddenly with a sweeping movement, usually from the air **2.** *vi.* **POUNCE** to make a sudden swift attack or raid on something or somebody ○ *The police swooped in on the terrorists.* **3.** *vt.* **SEIZE QUICKLY OR SUDDENLY** to seize or snatch something in a sudden swift attack ■ *n.* **1. SUDDEN DESCENT** a quick sudden sweeping descent **2. SUDDEN ATTACK** a sudden swift attack or raid [Mid-16thC. Origin uncertain: probably from a variant of Old English *swāpan*, an earlier form of SWEEP.]

swoosh /swoosh, swo͝osh/ *v.* (**swooshed, swoosh·ing, swoosh·es**) **1.** *vi.* **MAKE OR MOVE WITH RUSHING SOUND** to make the rushing or swirling sound of fast-moving water or air, or move with such a sound **2.** *vt.* **MOVE SOMETHING WITH RUSHING SOUND** to cause something to make or move with a swooshing sound ■ *n.* **SWOOSHING SOUND** a swooshing sound or movement [Mid-19thC. An imitation of the sound.]

swop *vti., n.* = **swap**

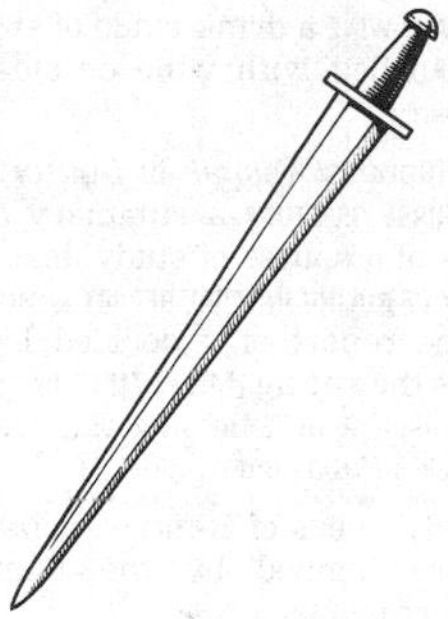
Sword

sword /sawrd/ *n.* **1. LONG-BLADED WEAPON** a hand-held weapon with a long blade that is sharp on one or both edges and sometimes slightly curved. It is used for cutting and thrusting. **2. USE OF FORCE** the use of force, violence, or military power ○ *The pen is mightier than the sword.* [Old English *sweord*. Ultimately from a prehistoric Germanic word that also produced German *Schwert* "sword."] —**sword·less** *adj.* ◇ **cross swords (with somebody)** to argue or come into conflict with somebody ◇ **put somebody to the sword** to kill somebody violently, especially in war (*literary*)

sword and sor·cer·y *adj.* set in a fantasy place or time with a technology that has not advanced beyond bladed weapons and in which magic is important (*informal*)

sword bay·o·net *n.* a type of bayonet with a very long blade

sword·bear·er /sáwrd bàirər/ *n.* an official who carries a sword that is a symbol of somebody's authority, e.g., a sovereign's sword

sword·bill /sáwrd bìl/ *n.* a South American hummingbird that has a bill longer than its body. Latin name: *Ensifera ensifera.*

sword cane *n.* a hollow cane or walking stick whose handle is also the handle of a narrow sword hidden inside the cane

sword·craft /sáwrd kràft/ *n.* = **swordsmanship**

sword dance *n.* a dance in which swords are used, especially a traditional Scottish Highland dance in which somebody dances over swords crossed on the ground

sword fern *n.* a fern with long fronds shaped like swords, e.g., the variety from which the Boston fern was developed. Latin name: *Nephrolepis exaltata.*

sword·fish /sáwrd fìsh/ (*plural* **-fish** *or* **-fish·es**) *n.* a large ocean fish with an upper jaw that extends into a long point. It is caught for food and sport. Latin name: *Xiphias gladius.*

sword grass *n.* a type of grass with leaves that have very sharp edges

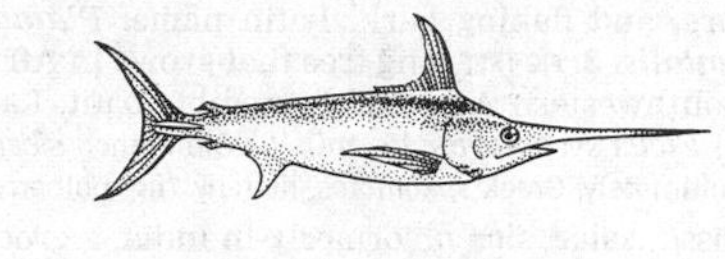
Swordfish

sword knot *n.* a decorative ribbon or tassel on the hilt of a sword

sword lil·y *n.* = **gladiolus** [From its sword-shaped leaves]

Sword of Dam·o·cles *n.* something that threatens to bring imminent disaster [(See DAMOCLES)]

sword·play /sáwrd plày/ *n.* fighting with a sword, especially when done with skill

swords·man /sáwrdzmən/ (*plural* **-men** /-mən/) *n.* somebody who fights with a sword with a particular degree of skill

swords·man·ship /sáwrdzmən shìp/ *n.* the skill of fighting with a sword

sword·swal·low·er *n.* a performer who passes or creates an illusion of passing a sword down his or her throat to its hilt

swords·wom·an /sáwrdz wo͝omman/ (*plural* **-en** /-wìmmin/) *n.* a woman who fights with a sword with a particular degree of skill

sword·tail /sáwrd tàyl/ *n.* a small brightly colored freshwater fish of Central America that has a long sword-shaped tail and is popular as an aquarium fish. Latin name: *Xiphophorus helleri.*

swore past tense of **swear**

sworn past participle of **swear**

swot *vti.* = **swat**

swot·ter *n.* = **swatter**

SWPA *abbr.* South-West Pacific Area

swum past participle of **swim**

swung past participle, past tense of **swing**

swung dash *n.* a character (~) used in printing to represent all or part of a word previously spelled out

syb·a·rite /síbbə rìt/ *n.* somebody devoted to luxury and the gratification of sensual desires [Mid-16thC. Via Latin *Sybarita* from, ultimately, Greek *Subaris* "Sybaris," an ancient Greek city in southern Italy known as a place of luxury and indulgence.] —**syb·a·rit·ic** /sìbbə ríttik/ *adj.* —**syb·a·rit·i·cal** /-ttik'l/ *adj.* —**syb·a·rit·i·cal·ly** /-ríttikalee/ *adv.* —**syb·a·rit·ism** /síbbə rìt ìzzəm/ *n.*

Syb·a·rite /síbbə rìt/ *n.* somebody who was born in or was a citizen of Sybaris, an ancient Greek city in southern Italy —**Syb·a·rit·ic** /sìbbə ríttik/ *adj.*

syc·a·mine /síkə mìn, -min/ *n.* a tree that is mentioned in the Bible and is thought to be the black mulberry [Early 16thC. Via Greek *sukaminon* from Hebrew *šiḳmāh*.]

Sycamore

syc·a·more /síkə màwr/ (*plural* **-mores** *or* **-more**) *n.* **1. TYPE OF MAPLE TREE** a maple tree with five-lobed leaves, hanging clusters of greenish-yellow flowers, and two-winged fruits. Originally grown in central and southern Europe and Asia, it has been naturalized in North America. Latin name: *Acer pseudoplatanus.* **2.** LARGE SPREADING PLANE TREE a large spreading plane tree that grows in eastern and central North America and has lobed leaves, round spiked fruit clusters, and flaking bark. Latin name: *Platanus occidentalis.* **3.** FIG TREE a fig tree that grows in Africa and southwestern Asia and has edible fruit. Latin name: *Ficus sycomorus.* [14thC. Via Old French *sicamor* from, ultimately, Greek *sukomoros*, literally "fig-mulberry."]

syce /sīss/, **saice, sice** *n.* formerly in India, a groom, stable hand, or other attendant [Mid-17thC. Via Persian and Urdu *sā'is* from Arabic, formed from *sūs* "to tend a horse."]

sy·co·ni·um /sī kṓnee əm/ (*plural* **-a** /-ə/) *n.* a type of fleshy fruit, e.g., a fig, in which numerous seeds are borne inside the enlarged hollow tip of the flower stalk [Mid-19thC. Via modern Latin from Greek *sukon* "fig."]

syc·o·phan·cy /síkəfənsee, -fànssee, sī́kəfənsee, -fàns see/ *n.* servility, obsequious flattery, and other fawning behavior

syc·o·phant /síkəfənt, -fànt, sī́kəfənt, -fànt/ *n.* somebody who servilely or obsequiously flatters a powerful person for personal gain [Mid-16thC. Via Latin *sycophanta* from Greek *sukophantēs* "informer," from *sukon* "fig, obscene gesture" + *-phantes* "shower" (formed from *phanein* "to show").] —**syc·o·phan·tic** /sìkə fántik, sī́kə-/ *adj.* —**syc·o·phan·ti·cal·ly** /-fántikəlee/ *adv.*

sy·co·sis /sī kṓssiss/ *n.* inflammation of hair follicles, especially of the beard, caused by bacterial infection and marked by pustules and encrustations [Late 16thC. Via modern Latin from Greek *sukōsis*, from *sukon* "fig." From the pustule's resemblance to a fig.]

Syd·en·ham's cho·re·a /sídd'nəmz-, sī́d'n hàmz-/ *n.* a neurological disease of children and pregnant women, sometimes following rheumatic fever, in which those affected experience involuntary jerking movements of the body [Late 19thC. Named for the English physician Thomas *Sydenham* (1624–89), who first described it.]

Syd·ney /sídnee/ city on the southeastern coast of Australia. Founded in 1788, it is the capital of the state of New South Wales. Population: 3,276,207 (1996).

AKG London

Sydney Opera House

Syd·ney O·pera House *n.* an arts center in Sydney Harbor, Australia, that was designed by Jörn Utzon and completed in 1973. Its unusual sail-shaped towers make it Australia's best-known building.

sy·e·nite /sī́ ə nìt/ *n.* a light-colored coarse-grained igneous rock consisting mainly of feldspar [Late 18thC. From Latin *syenites (lapis)*, literally "(stone of) Syene." Named for Syene (Aswan), where it was mined.]

syl. *abbr.* **1.** syllable **2.** syllabus

Syl·het /sil hét/ city and administrative headquarters of Sylhet District, Chittagong Division, in northeastern Bangladesh. Population: 114,284 (1991).

syll. *abbr.* **1.** syllable **2.** syllabus

syl·la·bar·y /síllə bàiree/ (*plural* **-ies**) *n.* a list or set of written characters in which each character represents a single syllable e.g., the Japanese kana

syl·la·bi plural of **syllabus**

syl·lab·ic /si lábbik/ *adj.* **1.** INVOLVING SYLLABLES relating to, involving, or typical of a syllable or syllables **2.** BEING A SYLLABLE WITHOUT A VOWEL used to describe a consonant that acts as a syllable without a vowel, as does the "l" in "bottle" **3.** MARKED BY CLEAR ENUNCIATION clearly enunciated with every syllable distinct **4.** POETRY BASED ON THE NUMBER OF SYLLABLES used to describe verse in which the rhythm is set by the number of syllables rather than accents, stresses, or vowel strengths ■ *n.* SYLLABIC CONSONANT OR SOUND a syllabic consonant, character, or sound

syl·lab·i·fy /si lábbə fī/ (**-fied, -fy·ing, -fies**), **syl·lab·i·cate** /-kàyt/ (**-cat·ed, -cat·ing, -cates**) *vt.* to break a word down into syllables, in speech or writing [Early 20thC. Back-formation from *syllabification*, from Latin *syllaba* "syllable."] —**syl·lab·i·ca·tion** /si làbbə káysh'n/ *n.* —**syl·lab·i·fi·ca·tion** /si làbbəfə káysh'n/ *n.*

syl·la·bism /síllə bìzzəm/ *n.* **1.** USE OF SYLLABIC CHARACTERS the use of characters that stand for individual syllables in writing **2.** DIVISION INTO SYLLABLES the breaking down of words into syllables, in speech or writing

syl·la·ble /sílləb'l/ *n.* **1.** UNIT OF SPOKEN LANGUAGE a unit of spoken language that consists of one or more vowel sounds alone, a syllabic consonant alone, or any of these with one or more consonant sounds **2.** LETTERS CORRESPONDING TO SPOKEN SYLLABLE one or more letters in a word that roughly correspond to a syllable of spoken language **3.** MENTION the slightest mention of something (*usually used in negative statements*) ■ *vt.* (**-bled, -bling, -bles**) PRONOUNCE SOMETHING CLEARLY to pronounce something in distinct or separate syllables [14thC. Via Anglo-Norman *sillable* and Old French *sillabe* from, ultimately, Greek *sullabē*, from *sullambanein* "to bring together," from *lambanein* "to take."]

syl·la·bub /síllə bùb/, **sil·la·bub** *n.* **1.** FOOD DESSERT OF CREAM WHIPPED WITH BRANDY a light soft cold dessert made from cream whipped with brandy, wine or sherry, lemon juice, and a little sugar **2.** BEVERAGES DRINK OF MILK AND WINE a drink made of sweetened milk or cream curdled with wine or cider [Mid-16thC. Origin unknown.]

syl·la·bus /síllәbəss/ (*plural* **-bi** /-bī/ *or* **-bus·es**) *n.* **1.** OUTLINE OF COURSE OF STUDY a summary or list of the main topics of a course of study, text, or lecture **2.** LAW SUMMARY OF RULING IN LEGAL REPORT a short note that precedes the report of a decided legal case and summarizes the ruling [Mid-17thC. From modern Latin, originally a misprint of Latin *sittybas* "indexes," from, ultimately, Greek *sittuba* "index, label."]

Syl·la·bus, **Syl·la·bus of Er·rors** *n.* a list of religious doctrines condemned by the Roman Catholic Church as erroneous

syl·lep·sis /si lépsiss/ (*plural* **-ses** /-seez/) *n.* **1.** GRAMMATICAL AGREEMENT WITH ONLY ONE ELEMENT the use of a word that relates to, qualifies, or governs two or more other words but agrees in number, gender, or case with only one of them. "Neither Fred nor I want to," is an example of syllepsis where "want" agrees with "I" but not "Fred." **2.** DIFFERENT SEMANTIC RELATIONSHIP the use of a word that relates to, qualifies, or governs two or more other words but has a different meaning in relation to each, as in the example "He picked up his hat and a taxi" [Late 16thC. Via late Latin and Greek *sullēpsis*, literally "a taking together," from, ultimately, *lambanein* (see SYLLABLE).]

syl·lo·gism /síllə jìzzəm/ *n.* **1.** ARGUMENT INVOLVING THREE PROPOSITIONS a formal deductive argument made up of a major premise, a minor premise, and a conclusion. An example is "all birds have feathers, penguins are birds, therefore penguins have feathers." **2.** DEDUCTIVE REASONING reasoning from the general to the specific, or an example of this **3.** SPECIOUS ARGUMENT a subtle piece of reasoning, or one that seems true but is actually false or deceptive [14thC. Via Latin from Greek *sullogismos*, from *sullogizesthai* "to infer," from, ultimately, *logos* "reason" (source of English *logic*).]

syl·lo·gis·tic /sìllə jístik/ *adj.* relating to, using, or typical of syllogisms [Mid-17thC. Via Latin from Greek *sullogistikos*, from *sullogizesthai* (see SYLLOGISM).] —**syl·lo·gis·ti·cal·ly** *adv.*

syl·lo·gize /síllə jīz/ (**-gized, -giz·ing, -giz·es**) *vti.* to reason or infer something by means of syllogisms [15thC. Via late Latin *syllogizare* from Greek *sullogizesthai* (see SYLLOGISM).] —**syl·lo·gi·za·tion** /sìlləjə záysh'n/ *n.* —**syl·lo·giz·er** /síllə jīzər/ *n.*

sylph /silf/ *n.* **1.** SLIM AND GRACEFUL GIRL a woman or girl who is slight and graceful **2.** MYTHOL FEMALE CREATURE THAT INHABITS THE AIR an elemental soulless female being imagined to inhabit the air [Mid-17thC. From modern Latin *sylpha*, of uncertain origin: perhaps a blend of Latin *sylvestris* "of the forest" and *nympha* "nymph."] —**sylph·ic** *adj.* —**sylph·ish** *adj.*

sylph·like /sílf lìk/ *adj.* slight and graceful as a female figure

syl·va *n.* = **silva**

syl·van /sílvən/ *adj.* **1.** OF A FOREST relating to, typical of, or found in a forest (*literary*) **2.** WOODED covered in or full of trees (*literary*) **3.** RURAL typical of the countryside, especially in an idyllic way ■ *n.* INHABITANT OF A FOREST a person, animal, or spirit that lives in a forest

syl·van·ite /sílvə nìt/ *n.* a mixed telluride mineral containing gold and silver, occurring in long striated crystals. Formula: $(Au, Ag)Te_2$. [Late 18thC. Named for TRANSYLVANIA, where tellurium, to which the word was originally applied, was found.]

syl·vat·ic /sil váttik/ *adj.* **1.** OF WILD ANIMALS affecting wild animals ○ *sylvatic plague* **2.** WOODED covered in or full of trees

syl·vi·cul·ture *n.* = **silviculture**

syl·vite /síl vìt/, **syl·vine** /-veen, -vin/ *n.* a colorless transparent mineral form of potassium chloride, used as a source of potassium [Mid-19thC. Formed from modern Latin *(sal digestivus) Silvii* "(digestive salt) of Silvius." Named for François de la Boë *Sylvius* (1614–72), Flemish physician who first discovered its medicinal use.]

sym. *abbr.* **1.** symbol **2.** symptom **3.** symphony **4.** CHEM symmetrical

sym- *prefix.* = **syn-** (*used before b, m, and p*)

sym·bi·ont /sím bi ònt, -bī-/ *n.* an animal or plant living in close and often mutually beneficial association with another of a different species [Late 19thC. Formed from Greek *bioun* "to live," from *bios* (see SYMBIOSIS).] —**sym·bi·on·tic** /sím bi òntik, -bī-/ *adj.* —**sym·bi·on·ti·cal·ly** /-óntikəlee/ *adv.*

sym·bi·o·sis /sìm bī óssiss, -bee óssiss/ (*plural* **-ses** /-seez/) *n.* **1.** ZOOL CLOSE ASSOCIATION OF ANIMALS OR PLANTS a close association of animals or plants of different species that is often, but not always, of mutual benefit. The relationship between a small fish and a larger fish on which it eats parasites is an example of symbiosis. **2.** MUTUALLY BENEFICIAL RELATIONSHIP a cooperative, mutually beneficial relationship between two people or groups [Early 17thC. Via modern Latin and Greek *sumbiōsis*, literally "a living together," from, ultimately, *bios* "life."] —**sym·bi·ot·ic** /sìmm bī óttik, -bee óttik/ *adj.* —**sym·bi·ot·i·cal** /-óttik'l/ *adj.* —**sym·bi·ot·i·cal·ly** /-óttikəlee/ *adv.*

sym·bol /símb'l/ *n.* **1.** SOMETHING THAT REPRESENTS SOMETHING ELSE something that stands for or represents something else, especially an object representing an abstraction **2.** SIGN WITH SPECIFIC MEANING a written or printed sign or character that represents something in a particular context, e.g., an operation or quantity in mathematics or music **3.** PSYCHOANAL OBJECT REPRESENTING SOMETHING REPRESSED IN UNCONSCIOUS an object or act that represents an impulse or wish in the unconscious mind that has been repressed [15thC. Via Latin from Greek *sumbolon* "mark," from *sumballein* "to compare," from *ballein* "to throw" (source of English *problem*).]

sym·bol·ic /sim bóllik/, **sym·bol·i·cal** /-bóllik'l/ *adj.* **1.** OF SYMBOLS relating to or typical of symbols **2.** USING SYMBOLS using a symbol or symbols to represent something else **3.** REPRESENTING SOMETHING ELSE acting as a symbol ○ *a gesture symbolic of repentance* **4.** INVOLVING USE OF SYMBOLS characterized by or involving the use of symbols or symbolism ○ *symbolic art* —**sym·bol·i·cal·ly** *adv.*

sym·bol·ic lan·guage *n.* **1.** ARTIFICIAL LANGUAGE USING SYMBOLS EXTENSIVELY an artificially constructed language with many symbols, used for precise formulations, e.g., in symbolic logic or mathematics **2.** COMPUT PROGRAMMING LANGUAGE a computer programming language that expresses memory addresses and operation codes in symbols recognizable to the programmer rather than in machine language

sym·bol·ic log·ic *n.* the branch of formal logic that studies the meaning and relationships of statements through precise mathematical methods and a standardized system of symbols and rules of inference

sym·bol·ism /símbə lìzzəm/ *n.* **1.** USE OF SYMBOLS the use of symbols to invest things with a representative meaning or to represent something abstract by something concrete **2.** SYSTEM OF SYMBOLS a set or system of symbols **3.** SYMBOLIC MEANING symbolic meaning or quality **4.** ARTS ARTISTIC USE OF SYMBOLS the artistic method of revealing ideas or truths through the use of symbols **5. sym·bol·ism, Sym·bol·ism** ARTS 19THC LITERARY AND ARTISTIC MOVEMENT a 19th century

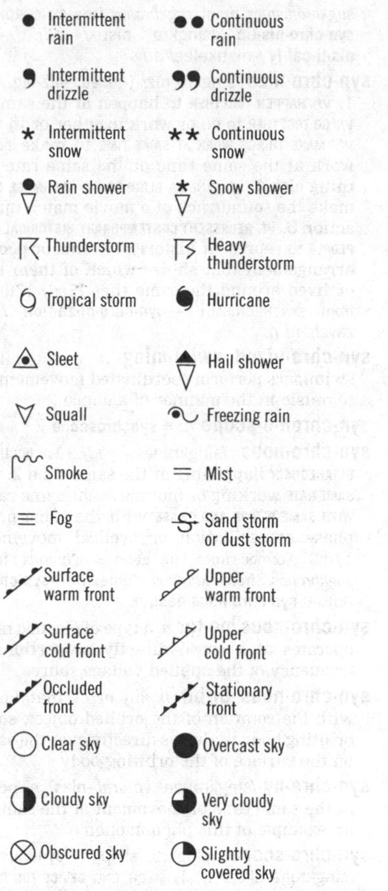

Symbol: Weather symbols

literary and artistic movement that sought to evoke, rather than describe, ideas or feelings through the use of symbolic images **6.** CHR **BELIEF IN SYMBOLIC NATURE OF EUCHARIST** the belief that the bread and wine used in the Eucharist are symbols and not literally the flesh and blood of Jesus Christ

sym·bol·ist /símbəlist/ *n.* **1. SOMEBODY USING SYMBOLS** somebody who uses symbols or symbolism **2. SOMEBODY SKILLED AT INTERPRETING SYMBOLS** somebody skilled in the study or interpretation of symbols **3. sym·bol·ist, Sym·bol·ist** ARTS **SOMEBODY INVOLVED IN 19C ARTISTIC SYMBOLISM** a writer or artist involved in or associated with the 19th century movement of symbolism **4.** CHR **SOMEBODY BELIEVING EUCHARIST USES SYMBOLS** somebody who believes that the bread and wine used in the Eucharist are symbols and not literally the flesh and blood of Jesus Christ ■ *adj.* **1. OF OR USING SYMBOLS** relating to, involving, or using symbols **2. sym·bol·ist, Sym·bol·ist** ARTS **ASSOCIATED WITH 19C ARTISTIC SYMBOLISM** involved in, associated with, or typical of the 19th century movement of symbolism —**sym·bol·is·tic** /sìmbə lístik/ *adj.* —**sym·bol·is·ti·cal·ly** /-lístikəlee/ *adv.*

sym·bol·ize /símbə lìz/ (**-ized, -iz·ing, -iz·es**) *v.* **1.** *vt.* **BE SYMBOL OF SOMETHING** to serve as or be understood as a symbol of something **2.** *vt.* **REPRESENT SOMETHING** to represent something by means of a symbol **3.** *vi.* **USE SYMBOLS** to use symbols or symbolism —**sym·bol·i·za·tion** /sìmbələ záysh'n/ *n.*

sym·bol·o·gy /sim bóllәjee/ *n.* **1. STUDY OF SYMBOLS** the study or interpretation of symbols **2. USE OF SYMBOLS** the use of symbols to represent things —**sym·bo·log·i·cal** /sìmbə lójjik'l/ *adj.* —**sym·bol·o·gist** /sim bóllәjist/ *n.*

sym·met·al·lism /sim métt'l ìzzəm/ *n.* a system of coinage in which the unit of currency consists of a combination of two or more metals in fixed relative proportions

sym·met·ri·cal /si méttrik'l/, **sym·met·ric** /-rik/ *adj.* **1. EXHIBITING SYMMETRY** having both sides of a central dividing line correspond or be identical to each other **2. BALANCED** relating to or having balanced proportions, especially in two halves of a whole **3.** MATH **WITH PARTICULAR PAIRS OF POINTS** used to describe two points that can be joined by a line bisected by a given point or perpendicular, or a shape that has such pairs of points **4.** MATH **WITH INTERCHANGEABLE TERMS** used to describe an equation or function in which terms or variables may be interchanged without altering its value or form **5.** CHEM **WITH SYMMETRICAL MOLECULAR STRUCTURE** with atoms or groups that display symmetry about a plane in a chemical structure **6.** ANAT **ON OPPOSITE SIDES** used to describe body parts that have the same function but are situated on opposite sides, either of the same organ or the same body

sym·met·ric ma·trix *n.* a square matrix that is identical to the matrix formed by transposing its rows and columns

sym·me·trize /símmə trìz/ (**-trized, -triz·ing, -triz·es**) *vt.* to give symmetry to something —**sym·me·tri·za·tion** /sìmmətrə záysh'n/ *n.*

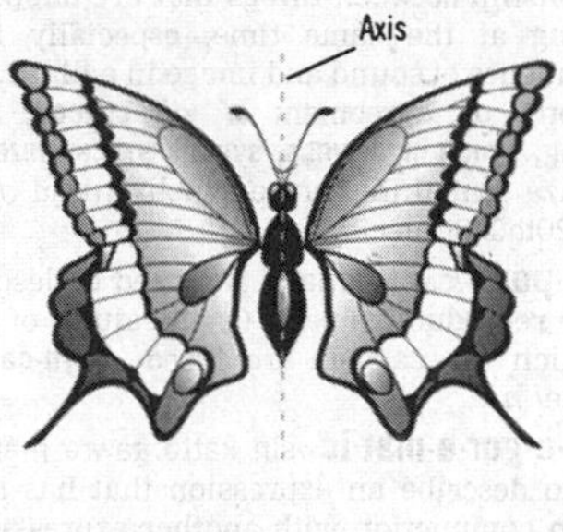

Symmetry

sym·me·try /símmətree/ (*plural* **-tries**) *n.* **1. PROPERTY OF SAMENESS** the property of being the same or corresponding on both sides of a central dividing line **2. BALANCED PROPORTIONS** harmony or beauty of form that results from balanced proportions **3.** MATH **EXACT CORRESPONDENCE IN POSITION** a correspondence in the position of pairs of points of a geometric object that are equally positioned about a point, line, or plane that bisects the object **4.** PHYS **STATE OF INVARIANCE** a state of invariance shown by some phenomena when changes of orientation, charge, or parity are made [Mid-16thC. Via Latin and Greek *summetria*, literally "similar measure," from, ultimately, *metron* "measure" (source of English *meter*).]

sym·pa·thec·to·my /sìmpə théktəmee/ (*plural* **-mies**) *n.* the surgical interruption of a pathway in the sympathetic nervous system, e.g., by cutting out a nerve segment. The operation was formerly common, especially to improve the blood supply to a limb, but is now rarely if ever performed. [Early 20thC. Coined from SYMPATHETIC + -ECTOMY.]

sym·pa·thet·ic /sìmpə théttik/ *adj.* **1. FEELING OR SHOWING SYMPATHY** showing, having, or resulting from shared feelings, pity, or compassion **2. APPROVING** showing favor, agreement, or approval **3. PROVOKING SYMPATHY** provoking sympathy, interest, or compassion **4. SUITED** agreeably suited to somebody's tastes or mood **5.** ACOUSTICS **PRODUCED BY OTHER SOUNDS** used to describe vibrations such as musical tones that are produced in something as a result of similar vibrations at the same frequency from something else **6.** ANAT **OF SYMPATHETIC NERVOUS SYSTEM** relating or belonging to the sympathetic nervous system or one of its components [Mid-17thC. Formed from SYMPATHY on the model of PATHETIC.] —**sym·pa·thet·i·cal·ly** *adv.*

sym·pa·thet·ic mag·ic *n.* magic based on the belief that somebody or something can be supernaturally affected by something done to an object representing the person or thing

sym·pa·thet·ic nerv·ous sys·tem *n.* the part of the autonomic nervous system that is active during stress or danger and is involved in regulating pulse and blood pressure, dilating pupils, and changing muscle tone

sym·pa·thet·ic string *n.* a string on some musical instruments that is not played but is made to vibrate by the vibrations of the bowed or plucked strings

sym·pa·thize /símpə thìz/ (**-thized, -thiz·ing, -thiz·es**) *vi.* **1. FEEL OR SHOW SYMPATHY** to share the feelings of somebody else or show pity or compassion for another ○ *I can sympathize; the same thing happened to me.* **2. BE OF SAME OPINION** to share the ideas or ideals of another person or group —**sym·pa·thiz·er** *n.*

sym·pa·tho·lyt·ic /sìmpəthō líttik/ *adj.* **ACTING AGAINST NERVE IMPULSES** used to describe a drug that opposes or blocks the effects of the sympathetic nervous system ■ *n.* **SYMPATHOLYTIC DRUG** a drug or agent that acts against the sympathetic nervous system [Mid-20thC. Coined from SYMPATHETIC + -LYTE.]

sym·pa·tho·mi·met·ic /sìmpəthō mi méttik/ *adj.* **STIMULATING SYMPATHETIC NERVOUS SYSTEM** used to describe a drug that stimulates the sympathetic nervous system or produces similar effects ■ *n.* **SYMPATHOMIMETIC DRUG** a drug or agent that stimulates or initiates the sympathetic nervous system [Early 20thC. Coined from SYMPATHETIC + MIMETIC.]

sym·pa·thy /símpəthee/ (*plural* **-thies**) *n.* **1. CAPACITY TO SHARE FEELINGS** the ability to enter into, understand, or share somebody else's feelings **2. FEELINGS CAUSED BY SYMPATHY** the feelings of somebody who enters into or shares another's feelings **3. SORROW FOR ANOTHER'S PAIN** the feeling or expression of pity or sorrow for the pain or distress of somebody else ○ *We extended our sympathies to the widow.* **4. INCLINATION TO FEEL ALIKE** the inclination to think or feel the same as somebody else **5. AGREEMENT** agreement or harmony with something or somebody else **6. ALLEGIANCE OR LOYALTY** allegiance or loyalty to a group or cause (*often used in the plural*) ○ *nationalist sympathies* [Late 16thC. Via Latin from Greek *sumpatheia*, from *sumpathēs*, literally "feeling with," from *pathos* "feeling" (source of English *pathetic* and *pathology*).]

sym·pa·thy strike *n.* a strike by workers demonstrating their support for another group of strikers rather than against their own employer

sym·pa·thy vote *n.* a vote that people give to somebody for whom they feel pity or affection

sym·pat·ric /sim páttrik/ *adj.* used to describe species that occupy roughly the same area of land but do not interbreed [Early 20thC. Formed from Greek *patra* "fatherland," from *patēr* "father."] —**sym·pat·ri·cal·ly** *adv.*

sym·phon·ic /sim fónnik/ *adj.* **1. OF OR LIKE MUSICAL SYMPHONY** relating to, involving, or typical of a musical symphony, or resembling one in form or content **2. HARMONIOUS** harmonious in sound, color, or composition

sym·phon·ic po·em *n.* an extended piece of music for a symphony orchestra that is based on a literary, artistic, or ideological theme, e.g., a folktale or landscape

sym·pho·ni·ous /sim fōnee əss/ *adj.* in agreement or harmony, especially in sound (*literary*) —**sym·pho·ni·ous·ly** *adv.*

sym·pho·nist /símfənist/ *n.* somebody who composes symphonies or other musical works for symphony orchestra

sym·pho·ny /símfənee/ (*plural* **-nies**) *n.* **1. COMPLEX MUSICAL COMPOSITION** a major work for an orchestra, including wind, string, and percussion instruments, usually composed in four movements, at least one of which is in sonata form **2.** = **symphony orchestra 3. CONCERT BY SYMPHONY ORCHESTRA** a concert performed by a symphony orchestra **4. HARMONIOUS COMPOSITION OR ARRANGEMENT** something that is harmoniously composed of various elements ○ *The color scheme was a symphony of blues, greens, and yellows.* **5. HARMONY OF SOUNDS OR COLORS** harmony or agreement of sounds or colors (*archaic*) [13thC. Via Latin and Greek *sumphōnia* "harmony," literally "sounding together," from, ultimately, *phōnē* "sound." Originally used for any of several medieval musical instruments.]

sym·pho·ny or·ches·tra *n.* a large orchestra that includes wind, string, and percussion instruments and plays symphonies and other works scored for these instruments

sym·phy·sis /símfəssiss/ (*plural* **-ses** /-seez/) *n.* **1.** ANAT **GROWING TOGETHER OF BONES OR PARTS** the natural merging of two or more separate bones or parts of the body, or a point where this occurs **2.** MED **ABNORMAL CONDITION** an abnormal condition in which two or more separate bones or parts of the body have merged **3.** ANAT **JOINT WITH LITTLE MOVEMENT** a joint in which the bones are connected by tough cartilage (**fibrocartilage**) and there is very little movement between them, e.g., between adjacent vertebrae in the spinal column **4.** BOT **FUSION OF PLANT PARTS** a fusion of two similar organs or parts of a plant, or a line marking such a fusion [Late 16thC. Via modern Latin from Greek *sumphusis* "growing together," from *phusis* "growth."] —**sym·phy·se·al** /sim fízzee əl/ *adj.* —

sym·phys·tic /sim fístik/ *adj.* —**sym·phy·tic** /sim fíttik/ *adj.*

sym·po·di·um /sim pṓdee əm/ (*plural* **-a** /-ə/) *n.* a main plant stem, e.g., the stem of a grapevine, that develops from a series of lateral branches, often in a zigzag pattern [Mid-19thC. From modern Latin, formed from the Greek stem *pod-* "foot."] —**sym·po·di·al** *adj.* —**sym·po·di·al·ly** *adv.*

sym·po·si·a plural of **symposium**

sym·po·si·arch /sim pṓzee aàrk/ *n.* somebody who is in overall charge of a symposium [Early 17thC. From Greek *sumposiarkhos*, from *sumposion* (see SYMPOSIUM).]

sym·po·si·ast /sim pṓzee àst/ *n.* somebody who takes part in a symposium (*formal*) [Mid-17thC. Formed from Greek *sumposiazein* "to drink together," from *sumposion* (see SYMPOSIUM).]

sym·po·si·um /sim pṓzee əm/ (*plural* **-ums** *or* **-a** /-ə/) *n.* **1.** FORMAL MEETING FOR DISCUSSION OF SUBJECT a formal meeting held for the discussion of a particular subject and during which individuals may make presentations **2.** PUBL PUBLISHED COLLECTION OF OPINIONS a published collection of opinions or writings on a subject, often in a periodical **3.** HIST DRINKING PARTY IN ANCIENT GREECE a drinking party in ancient Greece, usually with music and philosophical conversation [Late 16thC. Via Latin from Greek *sumposion* "drinking party," from *sumpotēs* "fellow drinker," from *potēs* "drinker."] —**sym·po·si·ac** *adj.*

symp·tom /símptəm/ *n.* **1.** MED INDICATION OF ILLNESS FELT BY PATIENT an indication of some disease or other disorder, especially one experienced by the patient, e.g., pain, dizziness, or itching, as opposed to one observed by the doctor (**sign**) **2.** SIGN OF SOMETHING ELSE a sign or indication of the existence of something, especially something undesirable [Mid-16thC. Via late Latin from Greek *sumptōma* "occurrence," from *sumpiptein*, literally "to fall together," from *piptein* "to fall."] —**symp·tom·less** *adj.*

symp·to·mat·ic /sìmptə máttik/ *adj.* **1.** MED INDICATING ILLNESS indicating or typical of a specific illness **2.** CHARACTERISTIC typical or indicative of something, especially something undesirable ○ *symptomatic of the breakdown in communication between children and parents* **3.** MED OF SYMPTOMS relating to, affecting, or based on a symptom or symptoms of bodily disorder ○ *Only symptomatic relief is available for the common cold.* [Late 17thC. From late Latin *symptomaticus*, ultimately from Greek *sumptoma* (see SYMPTOM).] —**symp·to·mat·i·cal·ly** *adv.*

symp·to·ma·tol·o·gy /sìmptəmə tólləjee/ (*plural* **-gies**) *n.* **1.** STUDY OF SYMPTOMS the study of the relationships between symptoms and diseases **2.** SET OF SYMPTOMS the set of symptoms that are associated with a particular disease or that affect a patient [Late 18thC. Coined from Greek *sumptōmat-* stem of *sumptōma* (see SYMPTOM) + -LOGY.]

symp·tom·ize /símptəmìz/ (**-ized, -iz·ing, -iz·es**) *vt.* to be an indication of the existence of something

syn. *abbr.* **1.** synonym **2.** synonymous

syn- *prefix.* together, together with, united ○ *syncarpous* [From Greek *sun* "together"]

syn·aer·e·sis *n.* = **syneresis**

syn·aes·the·sia *n.* = **synesthesia**

syn·a·gogue /sínnə gòg/ *n.* **1.** HOUSE OF WORSHIP FOR JEWISH CONGREGATION the place of worship and communal center of a Jewish congregation **2.** JEWISH CONGREGATION a body of followers of Judaism who worship together [12thC. Via French and late Latin *synagoga* from Greek *sunagōgē* "assembly," from *sunagein* "to bring together," from *agein* "to lead."] —**syn·a·gog·al** /sínnə gógg'l/ *adj.* —**syn·a·gog·i·cal** /-gójjik'l/ *adj.*

syn·a·le·pha /sìnnə léefə/, **syn·a·loe·pha** *n.* the blending of two adjacent vowels into one, e.g., when a word ending in a vowel is immediately followed by a word beginning with a vowel [Mid-16thC. Via late Latin from Greek *sunaloiphē*, from *sunaleiphein* "to smear together," from *aleiphein* "to smear."]

syn·apse /sí nàps, sə náps/ *n.* GAP BETWEEN NERVE ENDS a junction between two nerve cells, where the club-shaped tip of a nerve fiber almost touches another cell in order to transmit signals ■ *vi.* (**-apsed, -aps·ing, -aps·es**) FORM SYNAPSE to form a synapse between nerve cells [Late 19thC. Anglicization of SYNAPSIS.]

syn·ap·sis /sə nápsiss/ (*plural* **-ses** /-seez/) *n.* the pairing of homologous chromosomes from each parent during the initial phase (**prophase**) of cell division [Mid-17thC. Via modern Latin and Greek *sunapsis* "connection" from, ultimately, *haptein* "to join."]

syn·ap·tic /sə náptik/ *adj.* **1.** ANAT OF SYNAPSE relating to or involving a junction between nerve cells **2.** BIOL OF SYNAPSIS relating to, involving, or typical of synapsis [Late 19thC. Formed from SYNAPSIS or SYNAPSE on the model of Greek *sunaptikos* "connective."]

syn·ar·chy /sínnərkee, sí naàrkee/ (*plural* **-chies**) *n.* joint rule over something [Mid-18thC. From Greek *sunarkhia*.]

syn·ar·thro·sis /sìn aar thrṓssiss/ (*plural* **-ses** /-seez/) *n.* a rigid joint formed by the union of two bones and connected by fibrous tissue —**syn·ar·thro·di·al** /-thrṓdee əl/ *adj.* —**syn·ar·thro·di·al·ly** /-thrṓdee əlee/ *adv.*

sync /singk/, **synch** *n.* (*informal*) **1.** SYNCHRONIZATION the relationship between things that are happening or working at the same time, especially the correspondence of sound and image in a film **2.** HARMONY harmony or agreement ■ *vti.* **synced, synched, sync·ing, synch·ing, syncs, synchs** SYNCHRONIZE to synchronize something, or be synchronized (*informal*) [Early 20thC. Shortening.]

syn·car·pous /sin kaárpəss/ *adj.* used to describe the female reproductive parts (**gynoecium**) of a flower in which the carpels are fused —**syn·car·py** /sín kaàrpee/ *n.*

syn·cat·e·gor·e·mat·ic /sìn kattə gàwrə máttik/ *adj.* used to describe an expression that has meaning only in conjunction with another expression [Early 19thC. Via medieval Latin *syncategorematicus* and Greek *sugkatēgorēmatikos*, literally "predicating jointly," from, ultimately, *katēgorein* "to predicate" (source of English *category*).]

synch *n.*, *vti.* = **sync** (*informal*)

syn·chon·dro·sis /sìngkən drṓssiss/ (*plural* **-ses** /-seez/) *n.* **1.** JOINT WITH BONES LINKED BY CARTILAGE a type of joint in which there is slight movement between bones that are held together by cartilage, e.g., between the ribs and the breastbone **2.** JOINT WITH CARTILAGE CONVERTING TO BONE a type of joint in which the cartilage linking two bones in childhood is replaced by bone as development progresses [Late 16thC. Via modern Latin from late Greek *sugkhondrōsis*, from *khondros* "cartilage."]

syn·chro /síngkrō/ (*plural* **-chros**) *n.* ELEC ENG = **selsyn** [Mid-20thC. Shortening of *synchronizing* (see SELSYN).]

synchro- *prefix.* synchronous, synchronized ○ *synchroscope* [From SYNCHRONOUS]

syn·chro·cy·clo·tron /sìngkrō sīklə tròn/ *n.* a particle accelerator that compensates for increases in the relativistic mass of accelerated particles, and so achieves greater energies, by using the synchronizing effects of a frequency-modulated electric field

syn·chro·flash /síngkrō flàsh/ *n.* a mechanism in a camera that opens the shutter at the moment when the light from the flashbulb or electronic flash is brightest

syn·chro·mesh /síngkrō mèsh/ *n.* a gear system in which the speeds of the driving and driven parts are synchronized before they engage, making gear changes smoother —**syn·chro·mesh** *adj.*

syn·chro·nal /síngkrən'l/ *adj.* happening at the same time [Mid-17thC. Formed from late Latin *synchronus* (see SYNCHRONOUS).]

syn·chron·ic /sin krónnik/ *adj.* relating to or studying something, especially a language, as it exists at a certain point in time, without considering its historical development. ◊ **diachronic** [Mid-19thC. Formed from late Latin *synchronus* (see SYNCHRONOUS).] —**syn·chron·i·cal·ly** *adv.*

syn·chro·nic·i·ty /sìngkrə nissətee/ *n.* **1.** = **synchronism** *n.* 1 **2.** COINCIDENCE OF EVENTS THAT SEEM RELATED the coincidence of events that seem related but are not obviously caused one by the other. The term was first used in this sense in the work of the psychologist Carl Jung.

syn·chro·nism /síngkrə nìzzəm/ *n.* **1.** OCCURRENCE AT SAME TIME the simultaneous occurrence of two or more things **2.** ARRANGEMENT OF CONTEMPORARY EVENTS AND PEOPLE an arrangement in chronological order showing historical events that happened or people who were alive around the same time [Late 16thC. From Greek *sugkhronismos*, from *sugkhronos* (see SYNCHRONOUS).] —**syn·chro·nis·tic** /sìngkrə nístik/ *adj.* —**syn·chro·nis·ti·cal·ly** /-nístikəlee/ *adv.*

syn·chro·nize /síngkrə nìz/ (**-nized, -niz·ing, -niz·es**) *v.* **1.** *vi.* HAPPEN TOGETHER to happen at the same time **2.** *vi.* GO TOGETHER to go or work together or in unison **3.** *vt.* MAKE THINGS WORK AT SAME TIME to make something work at the same time or the same rate as something else **4.** *vt.* CINEMA ALIGN SOUND AND IMAGE OF MOVIE to make the soundtrack of a movie match up with the action **5.** *vt.* REPRESENT CONTEMPORARY HISTORICAL EVENTS AND PEOPLE to represent historical events or people in an arrangement that shows which of them happened or lived around the same time [Early 17thC. Formed from SYNCHRONISM.] —**syn·chro·ni·za·tion** /sìngkrənə záyshən/ *n.*

syn·chro·nized swim·ming *n.* a sport in which swimmers perform coordinated movements in time to music in the manner of a dance

syn·chron·o·scope *n.* = **synchroscope**

syn·chro·nous /síngkrənəss/ *adj.* **1.** OCCURRING SIMULTANEOUSLY happening at the same time **2.** WORKING AT SAME RATE working or moving at the same rate **3.** PHYS WITH SAME PERIOD AND PHASE with the same period and phase of oscillation or cyclical movement [Mid-17thC. Formed from late Latin *synchronus*, from Greek *sugkhronos*, from *khronos* "time."] —**syn·chro·nous·ly** *adv.* —**syn·chro·nous·ness** *n.*

syn·chro·nous mo·tor *n.* a type of electric motor that operates at a speed directly proportional to the frequency of the applied voltage source

syn·chro·nous or·bit *n.* an orbit that keeps time with the rotation of the orbited object, so that the orbiting body is always directly over the same point on the surface of the orbiting body

syn·chro·ny /síngkrənee/ (*plural* **-nies**) *n.* occurrence at the same time or movement at the same rate, or an example of this phenomenon

syn·chro·scope /síngkrə skōp/, **syn·chro·no·scope** /síngkronə skōp/ *n.* **1.** MECH ENG DEVICE FOR DETERMINING SYNCHRONICITY an instrument used to find whether or not two things such as moving machine parts are synchronous **2.** ELEC ENG INSTRUMENT INDICATING FREQUENCY DIFFERENCE an instrument used to indicate the difference in frequency between two alternating current supplies

syn·chro·tron /síngkrə tròn/ *n.* a very high-energy circular particle accelerator that operates by using a high-frequency electric field and a magnetic field in synchrony with the movement of the particles. The particles are guided around inside a large hollow ring by strategically placed electromagnets while being accelerated by the electric field.

syn·chro·tron ra·di·a·tion *n.* the electromagnetic radiation emitted by charged particles, usually electrons, moving in curved paths in a magnetic field at speeds approaching that of light. Such radiation is emitted from synchrotrons, supernova remnants, and radio galaxies.

syn·cline /sín klìn/ *n.* a fold in a rock formation that is shaped like a basin or trough and contains younger rocks in its core —**syn·cli·nal** /sin klín'l/ *adj.*

Syn·com /sín kòm/ *n.* a communications satellite that is in synchronous orbit over Earth [Late 20thC. Contraction of *synchronous communications*.]

syn·co·pate /síngkə pàyt/ (**-pat·ed, -pat·ing, -pates**) *vt.* **1.** MUSIC MODIFY RHYTHM BY ACCENTING WEAK BEAT to modify a musical rhythm by shifting the accent to a weak beat of the bar **2.** PHON SHORTEN WORD BY LOSS OF SOUNDS to shorten a word by the loss of one or more sounds or letters from the middle —**syn·co·pa·tor** *n.*

syn·co·pa·tion /sìngkə páysh'n/ *n.* **1.** MUSIC PLACING OF ACCENT ON WEAK BEAT a rhythmic technique in music in which the accent is shifted to a weak beat of the bar **2.** PHON = **syncope** *n.* 2

syn·co·pe /síngkəpee/ *n.* **1.** MED FAINTING EPISODE a loss of consciousness due to lack of oxygen to the brain (*technical*) **2.** PHON LOSS OF SOUNDS FROM WORD the shortening of a word by the loss of sounds or letters from its middle [Mid-16thC. Via late Latin from Greek *sugkopē*, from *sugkoptein* "to cut short," from *koptein* "to cut."] —**syn·co·pal** *adj.* —**syn·cop·ic** /sing kóppik/ *adj.*

syn·cre·tism /síngkrə tìzzəm/ *n.* **1.** RELIG, PHILOS COMBINATION OF DIFFERENT BELIEFS the attempted combination of different systems of philosophical or religious belief or practice **2.** GRAM MERGING OF DIFFERENT INFLECTIONAL FORMS the use of a single inflectional form of a word to cover functions previously covered by two separate forms, e.g., "spun" in English, now used for both the past tense and the past participle although the past tense used to be "span" [Early 17thC. Via modern Latin *syncretismus* from Greek *sugkrētismos* "union," from *sugkrētizein* (see SYNCRETIZE).] —**syn·cretic** /sing kréttik/ *adj.* —**syn·cre·tist** /síngkrətist/ *n.* —**syn·cre·tis·tic** /-tístik/ *adj.*

syn·cre·tize /síngkrə tīz/ (**-tized, -tiz·ing, -tiz·es**) *vti.* to combine, or try to combine, elements from different systems of philosophical or religious belief or practice [Late 17thC. From Greek *sugkrētizein* "to unite (against a common enemy)," of unknown origin.] —**syn·cre·ti·za·tion** /sìngkrətə záyshən/ *n.*

syn·cy·ti·um /sin síshəm, -shee əm/ (*plural* **-a** /-shə, -shee ə/) *n.* a mass of cytoplasm within a cell membrane that contains multiple nuclei and is often the result of cellular fusion, e.g., in certain slime molds [Late 19thC. Formed from Greek *kutos* (see -CYTE).] —**syn·cy·ti·al** /sin sísh'l/ *adj.*

synd. *abbr.* syndicate

syn·dac·tyl /sin dákt'l/ *adj.* having two or more fingers or toes joined together. This may be a natural condition, as in certain animals, or a congenital abnormality, as in people with webbed toes. —**syn·dac·tyl** *n.* —**syn·dac·tyl·ism** *n.* —**syn·dac·ty·ly** *n.*

syn·de·sis /síndəssiss/ *n.* the use in grammar of constructions in which clauses are joined by conjunctions [Early 20thC. From German, formed from Greek *desis* "binding," from, ultimately, *dein* (see SYNDETIC).]

syn·des·mo·sis /sìndəss mṓssiss/ (*plural* **-ses** /-seez/) *n.* a type of immovable joint in which the bones are held firmly by fibrous tissue but are not very close together, e.g., at the lower ends of the tibia and fibula [Late 16thC. Formed from Greek *sundesmos* "ligament," from *sundein* (see SYNDETIC).] —**syn·des·mot·ic** /sìndəs móttik/ *adj.*

syn·det·ic /sin déttik/ *adj.* used to describe a construction in grammar in which two clauses are joined by a conjunction [Early 17thC. From Greek *sundetikos*, from *sundein* "to bind together," from *dein* "to bind."] —**syn·det·i·cal·ly** *adv.*

syn·det·on /síndə tòn, síndətən/ *n.* a grammatical construction in which two clauses are joined by a conjunction [Mid-20thC. Back-formation from ASYNDETON and POLYSYNDETON.]

syn·dic /síndik/ *n.* **1.** BUSINESS **BUSINESS AGENT** somebody appointed to represent an organization, e.g., a corporation or a university, in business transactions **2.** POL **EUROPEAN OFFICIAL** a government official, especially a civil magistrate, in some European countries [Early 17thC. Via French, "delegate," from, ultimately, Greek *sundikos* "defendant's advocate," from *dikē* "judgment."] —**syn·di·cal** *adj.* —**syn·dic·ship** *n.*

syn·di·cal·ism /síndikə lìzzəm/ *n.* **1. REVOLUTIONARY POLITICAL DOCTRINE** a revolutionary political doctrine that advocates the seizure of the means of production by workers organized in trade unions **2. WORKERS' CONTROL OF MEANS OF PRODUCTION** a system of government in which workers organized in trade unions control the means of production [Early 20thC. Via French *syndicalisme* from, ultimately, *syndic* (see SYNDIC).] —**syn·di·cal** *adj.* —**syn·di·cal·ist** *n.* —**syn·di·cal·is·tic** /sìndikə lístik/ *adj.*

syn·di·cate *n.* /síndəkət/ **1.** BUSINESS **GROUP OF BUSINESSES** an association of businesses jointly contributing capital to a major project **2.** COMMUNICATION **BUSINESS THAT SELLS NEWS MATERIALS** a business or agency that sells news stories or photographs to the media **3.** PRESS **GROUP OF NEWSPAPERS UNDER SAME OWNER** a group of newspapers that have the same owner **4. GROUP OF PEOPLE** a group of people who combine to carry out a business, enterprise, or some other common purpose **5.** CRIMINOL **ASSOCIATION OF GANGSTERS** an association of gangsters that controls a particular area of organized crime **6.** POL **COUNCIL OR JURISDICTION OF CIVIL MAGISTRATE** a council or body of syndics, or the office or jurisdiction of a government official, especially a civil magistrate, in some European countries ■ *v.* /síndə kàyt/ (**-cat·ed, -cat·ing, -cates**) **1.** *vt.* PUBL **SELL SOMETHING FOR MULTIPLE PUBLICATION** to sell something, e.g., an article or a cartoon strip, for publication in a number of newspapers or magazines simultaneously **2.** *vt.* TV **SELL TV PROGRAMS TO INDEPENDENT STATIONS** to sell television or radio programs directly to independent stations **3.** *vt.* **CONTROL SOMETHING AS SYNDICATE** to control or manage something as a syndicate **4.** *vi.* **COME TOGETHER AS SYNDICATE** to come together to form a syndicate

syn·drome /sín drōm/ *n.* **1.** MED **GROUP OF IDENTIFYING SIGNS AND SYMPTOMS** a group of signs and symptoms that together are characteristic or indicative of a specific disease or other disorder **2. THINGS THAT FORM PATTERN** a group of things or events that form a recognizable pattern, especially of something undesirable [Mid-16thC. Via modern Latin and Greek *sundromē*, literally "running together," from, ultimately, *dramein* "to run."]

syne /sīn/ *adv. Scotland* since then [14thC. Contraction of *sithen* (see SINCE).]

syn·ec·do·che /si nékdəkee/ *n.* a figure of speech in which the word for part of something is used to mean the whole, e.g., "sail" for "boat," or vice versa [14thC. Via Latin from Greek *sunekdokhē*, from *sunekdekhesthai* "to take on a share of," from *ekdekhesthai* "to take."] —**syn·ec·doch·ic** /si nèk dókik, sìnnək-/ *adj.* —**syn·ec·doch·i·cal** /-ik'l/; /sìnnək dókik'l/ *adj.* —**syn·ec·doch·i·cal·ly** /-ikəlee/; /sìnnək dókikəlee/ *adv.*

syn·e·cious /si néeshəss/, **syn·oe·cious** *adj.* with male and female organs on the same flower or other structure [Mid-19thC. Formed from Greek *oikos* "house."]

syn·e·col·o·gy /sìnni kólləjee/ *n.* a branch of ecology dealing with the structure and development of entire ecological communities and the interrelationships of the plants and animals within them —**syn·e·co·log·ic** /sìnnikə lójjik/ *adj.* —**syn·e·co·log·i·cal** /-ik'l/ *adj.* —**syn·e·co·log·i·cal·ly** /-ikəlee/ *adv.*

syn·ec·tics /si néktiks/ *n.* an approach to solving problems based on the creative thinking of a group of people from different areas of experience and knowledge (*takes a singular verb*) [Mid-20thC. Formed from late Latin *synecticus* "producing an effect immediately," via Greek *sunektikos* from, ultimately, *ekhein* "to hold."]

syn·er·e·sis /si nérrəssiss, -néerəssiss/, **syn·aer·e·sis** *n.* **1. LIQUID SEPARATION IN GEL** the process by which a liquid is separated from a gel owing to further coagulation **2. MERGING OF VOWELS INTO DIPHTHONG** the merging of two vowels into a diphthong **3. MERGING OF VOWELS INTO ONE SYLLABLE** the merging of two vowels into one syllable without making it into a diphthong [Late 16thC. Via late Latin and Greek *sunairesis*, literally "contraction," from, ultimately, *hairein* "to take."]

syn·er·gism /sínnər jìzzəm/ *n.* **1.** = **synergy 2.** CHR **CHRISTIAN THEOLOGICAL DOCTRINE** the doctrine in Christian theology that the human will and the Holy Spirit work together to bring about spiritual regeneration or salvation [Mid-18thC (see SYNERGY)] —**syn·er·gis·tic** /sìnnər jístik/ *adj.* —**syn·er·gis·ti·cal·ly** /-ikəlee/ *adv.*

syn·er·gist /sínnərjist/ *n.* something that works in combination with something else to increase its effect, e.g., a drug that increases the effect of another drug

syn·er·gy /sínnərjee/ (*plural* **-gies**) *n.* **1. COMBINED EFFORT BEING GREATER THAN PARTS** the working together of two or more things, people, or organizations, especially when the result is greater than the sum of their individual effects or capabilities **2.** MED **COMBINED ACTION OF DRUGS OR MUSCLES** the phenomenon in which the combined action of two things, e.g., drugs or muscles, is greater than the sum of their effects individually. In the case of drugs, the result may be dangerous to the patient. [Mid-17thC. Via Latin from Greek *sunergia*, from *sunergein* "to work together," from, ultimately, *ergos* "work."] —**syn·er·get·ic** /sìnnər jéttik/ *adj.* —**syn·er·get·i·cal·ly** /-ikəlee/ *adv.* —**syn·er·gic** /si núrjik/ *adj.*

syn·e·sis /sínnississ/ *n.* grammatical agreement according to meaning rather than strict syntax, e.g., the use of a plural form of a verb or a plural pronoun with a collective noun. Synesis is shown, e.g., in "The team are playing badly so we have stopped supporting them," with "are" and "them" rather than "is" and "it." [Late 19thC. Via modern Latin from Greek *sunesis* "union," from *sunienai* "to bring together," from *hienai* "to send."]

syn·es·the·sia /sìnnəss théezhə/, **synaesthesia** *n.* **1.** PHYSIOL **SENSATION FELT ELSEWHERE IN BODY** the feeling of sensation in one part of the body when another part is stimulated **2.** PSYCHOL **STIMULATION OF ONE SENSE ALONGSIDE ANOTHER** the evocation of one kind of sense impression when another sense is stimulated, e.g., the sensation of color when a sound is heard **3.** LITERAT **RHETORICAL DEVICE** in literature, the description of one kind of sense perception using words that describe another kind of sense perception, as in the phrase "shining metallic words" (*literary*) [Late 19thC. From modern Latin, which was coined from *syn-* (see SYN-) + the stem of Greek *aisthēsis* "sensation," modeled on anesthesia.] —**syn·es·thet·ic** /-théttik/ *adj.*

syn·fu·el /sín fyoo əl/ *n.* a liquid fuel synthesized from a nonpetroleum source such as coal, oil shale, or waste plastics, and used as a substitute for a petroleum product [Late 20thC. A blend of SYNTHETIC and FUEL.]

syn·ga·my /síng gəmee/ *n.* sexual reproduction through the fusion of gametes [Early 20thC. Coined from SYN- + Greek *gamos* "marriage."] —**syn·gam·ic** /sing gámmik/ *adj.* —**syn·ga·mous** /síng gəməss/ *adj.*

J. M. Synge: Portrait by John B. Yeats

Synge /sing/, **J. M.** (1871–1909) Irish dramatist. A dominant figure of the Irish Renaissance, he wrote the controversial masterpiece, *The Playboy of the Western World* (1907). Full name **John Millington Synge**

syn·ge·ne·ic /sìnjə née ik/ *adj.* having an identical or closely similar genetic makeup, especially one that will allow the transplantation of tissue without provoking an immune response [Mid-20thC. Formed from Greek *sungeneia* "kinship," from *genos* "kind."] —**syn·ge·ne·i·cal·ly** *adv.*

syn·gen·e·sis /sin jénnəssiss/ *n.* reproduction involving fusion of male and female genetic material —**syn·ge·net·ic** /sìnjə néttik/ *adj.*

syn·kar·y·on /sin kárree on/ *n.* a cell nucleus formed through the fusion of male and female nuclei [Early 20thC. Formed from Greek *karuon* "seed."] —**syn·kar·y·on·ic** /sìn karree ónnik/ *adj.*

syn·ki·ne·sis /sìngkə néessiss/, **syn·ki·ne·sia** /sìngkə néezhə/ *n.* the performing of an unintended movement when making a voluntary one —**syn·ki·net·ic** /sìngkə néttik/ *adj.*

syn·od /sínnəd/ *n.* **1. CHURCH COUNCIL** a special council of church members that holds regular meetings to discuss religious issues **2. ASSEMBLY OR COUNCIL** an assembly or council held for the discussion of issues (*formal*) [14thC. Via late Latin from Greek *sunodos* "meeting," from *hodos* "way."] —**syn·od·al** /sínnəd'l, si nódd'l/ *adj.*

syn·od·ic /si nóddik/, **syn·od·i·cal** /-ik'l/ *adj.* **1.** ASTRON **OF ALIGNMENT OF SAME CELESTIAL BODIES** relating to the alignment of celestial bodies, or the interval between occasions when the same celestial bodies are aligned **2.** CHR **OF CHURCH SYNOD** relating to or having the character of a church synod —**syn·od·i·cal·ly** *adv.*

syn·od·ic month *n.* = **lunar month**

syn·oe·cious *adj.* = **synecious**

syn·o·nym /sínnə nìm/ *n.* **1. WORD MEANING SAME AS ANOTHER** a word that means the same, or almost the same, as another word in the same language, either in all of its uses or in a particular context. Examples of synonyms in this sense are "environment" and "surroundings" and the verbs "tear" and "rip." **2. ALTERNATIVE NAME** a word or expression that is used as another name for something in certain styles of speaking or writing or to emphasize a particular aspect or association. Examples of synonyms in this sense are "Gotham" and "New York." **3.** BIOL **REJECTED DUPLICATE TAXONOMIC NAME** a duplicate taxonomic name that has been rejected or replaced [15thC. Via Latin *synonymum* from, ultimately, Greek *sunōnumos* "synonymous," from *onuma* "name."] —**syn·o·nym·ic** /sìnnə nímmik/ *adj.* —**syn·o·nym·i·ty** /-nímmətee/ *n.*

syn·on·y·mize /si nónnə mīz/ (**-mized, -miz·ing, -miz·es**) *vt.* to provide an analysis or listing of the synonyms of a word or expression

syn·on·y·mous /si nónnəməss/ *adj.* **1. HAVING SAME MEANING** meaning the same, or almost the same, as another word in the same language, or being an alternative name for somebody or something **2. HAVING SIMILAR CONNOTATION** having an implication similar to the idea expressed by another word ○ *Andy Warhol is synonymous with pop art.* —**syn·on·y·mous·ly** *adv.* —**syn·on·y·mous·ness** *n.*

syn·on·y·my /si nónnəmee/ (*plural* **-mies**) *n.* **1. EQUIVALENCE OF MEANING** the state or quality of being synonymous **2. STUDY OF SYNONYMS** the study, classification, and distinguishing of synonyms **3. ANNOTATED LIST OF SYNONYMS** a list or book of synonyms, with emphasis on the discrimination of meanings **4.** BIOL **LIST OF TAXONOMIC NAMES** a record of scientific names, often chronological, that have been applied to a particular taxonomic group

syn·op·sis /si nópsiss/ (*plural* **-ses** /-seez/) *n.* **1. SUMMARY OF TEXT** a condensed version of a text, e.g., a summary of the plot of a book, movie, or television show **2. SUMMARY OF SUBJECT** a concise outline or survey of a subject [Early 17thC. Via late Latin from Greek *sunopsis* "general view," from *opsis* "view."]

syn·op·size /si nóp sīz/ (**-sized, -siz·ing, -siz·es**) *vt.* to summarize or make a synopsis of something

syn·op·tic /si nóptik/ *adj.* **1. PERTAINING TO SYNOPSIS** constituting a general view of the whole of a subject **2.** METEOROL **DISPLAYING WIDESPREAD WEATHER** pertaining to or showing simultaneous weather conditions over a large area **3. Syn·op·tic, syn·op·tic** BIBLE **SHARING VIEWS OF JESUS CHRIST'S LIFE** used to describe the gospels of Matthew, Mark, and Luke that tell the story of Jesus Christ's life and ministry from a similar point of view and are similar in structure ■ *n.* **1. Syn·op·tic, syn·op·tic SYNOPTIC GOSPEL** any one of the Synoptic gospels of Matthew, Mark, or Luke **2. Syn·op·tic** = **synoptist** [Early 17thC. Via modern Latin from Greek *sunoptikos*, from *sunopsis* (see SYNOPSIS).] —**syn·op·ti·cal** *adj.* —**syn·op·ti·cal·ly** *adv.*

syn·op·tist /si nóptist/, **synoptic** /si nóptik/ *n.* an author of one of the Synoptic gospels

syn·os·to·sis /sìn oss tṓssiss/ (*plural* **-ses** /-seez/) *n.* the formation of a single bone from the fusion of two adjacent bones —**syn·os·tot·ic** /-tóttik/ *adj.*

syn·o·vi·a /sī nṓvee ə/ *n.* a clear viscous fluid that lubricates the linings of joints and the sheaths of tendons [Mid-17thC. From modern Latin *sinovia*, of uncertain origin: probably coined by Philippus *Paracelsus*.] —**syn·o·vi·al** /sī n'vee əl/ *adj.*

sy·no·vi·tis /sīnō vítəss/ *n.* inflammation of the synovial membrane of a joint —**syn·o·vit·ic** /-víttik/ *adj.*

syn·sep·al·ous /sin séppələss/ *adj.* BOT = **gamosepalous** [Mid-19thC. Coined from SYNTHETIC + SEPAL + -OUS.]

syn·tac·tic /sin táktik/, **syn·tac·ti·cal** /-ik'l/ *adj.* **1. OF SYNTAX** relating to the rules or patterns of syntax **2. CONFORMING TO RULES OF SYNTAX** correctly formed according to the rules or accepted structures of syntax [Early 19thC. Via Latin from Greek *suntaktikos*, from *suntassein* (see SYNTAX).] —**syn·tac·ti·cal·ly** *adv.*

syn·tag·ma /sin tágmə/ (*plural* **-ma·ta** /-mətə/ *or* **-mas**), **syn·tagm** /sín tam/ *n.* linguistic units made up of sets of phonemes, words, or phrases that are arranged sequentially [Mid-17thC. Via late Latin from Greek *suntagma*, from *suntassein* (see SYNTAX).] —**syn·tag·mat·ic** /sìn tag máttik/ *adj.*

syn·tax /sín tàks/ *n.* **1. ORGANIZATION OF WORDS IN SENTENCES** the ordering of and relationship between the words and other structural elements in phrases and sentences. The syntax may be of a whole language, a particular phrase or sentence, or of a particular speaker. **2. BRANCH OF GRAMMAR** the branch of grammar that studies syntax **3. RULES OF SYNTAX** an exposition of or set of rules for producing grammatical structures according to the syntax of a language **4.** LOGIC **RULES FOR DERIVING LOGICAL FORMULAS** the part of logic that gives the rules that define which combinations of expressions in the logical system yield well-formed formulas **5.** COMPUT **RULES GOVERNING PROGRAM STRUCTURE** the rules governing which statements and combinations of statements in a programming language will be acceptable to a compiler for that language **6. RULE-BASED ARRANGEMENT** the arrangement of any group of elements in a systematic or rule-based manner [Late 16thC. Via French or late Latin from Greek *suntaxis*, from *suntassein* "to put in order," from *tassein* "to arrange."]

synth /sinth/ *n.* a synthesizer (*informal*)

syn·the·sis /sínthəssiss/ (*plural* **-ses** /-seez/) *n.* **1. RESULT OF COMBINING DIFFERENT ELEMENTS** a new unified whole resulting from the combination of different ideas, influences, or objects **2. COMBINING OF DIFFERENT ELEMENTS INTO WHOLE** the process of combining different ideas, influences, or objects into a new whole (*formal*) **3.** CHEM **FORMATION OF CHEMICAL COMPOUNDS** the process of forming a complex compound through a series of one or more chemical reactions involving simpler substances **4.** MUSIC **PRODUCING OF SOUND WITH SYNTHESIZER** the production of music or speech using an electronic synthesizer **5.** LING **USE OF INFLECTIONS** the expression of syntactic relationships by means of inflections rather than word order or prepositions and other function words **6.** PHILOS **IDEA RESOLVING CONTRADICTIONS** in Hegelian philosophy, the new idea that resolves the conflict between the initial proposition (**thesis**) and its negation (**antithesis**) **7.** PHILOS **DEDUCTIVE REASONING** the process of deductive reasoning from first principles to a conclusion [15thC. Via Latin, literally "collection," from Greek *sunthesis*, from *suntithenai* "to put together," from *tithenai* "to put."] —**syn·the·sist** *n.*

syn·the·sis gas *n.* a mixture of carbon monoxide and hydrogen, derived from the breakdown of carbon- and hydrogen-containing materials, used as a raw material for many chemical products. It is used as a source of hydrogen for the manufacture of ammonia and other products.

syn·the·size /sínthə sīz/ (**-sized, -siz·ing, -siz·es**) *v.* **1.** *vti.* **COMBINE DIFFERENT ELEMENTS INTO NEW WHOLE** to combine different ideas, influences, or objects into a new whole, or be combined in this way **2.** *vt.* SCI **PRODUCE SUBSTANCE BY CHEMICAL PROCESS** to produce a substance or material by chemical or biological synthesis —**syn·the·si·za·tion** /sìnthəssə záysh'n/ *n.*

syn·the·siz·er /sínthə sīzər/ *n.* **1.** MUSIC **ELECTRONIC MUSICAL INSTRUMENT** an electronic device capable of generating and modifying sounds electronically, often one designed as a musical instrument **2.** SCI **MANUFACTURER OF SYNTHETIC SUBSTANCES** somebody or something involved in the synthesis of substances or materials **3. SOMEBODY WHO COMBINES DIFFERENT ELEMENTS** somebody who combines different ideas, influences, or objects into a new whole

syn·thet·ic /sin théttik/ *adj.* **1.** CHEM **MADE BY A CHEMICAL PROCESS** made artificially by a chemical process of synthesis, especially so as to resemble a natural product **2. INSINCERE** not genuine, especially expressed but not genuinely felt ○ *synthetic expressions of sympathy* **3.** PHILOSOPHY **WITH TRUTH DEPENDING ON FACTS** used to describe a proposition whose truth or falsity is a matter of facts and not merely a matter of the meaning of the words in the sentence **4.** LING **USING INFLECTIONS TO EXPRESS SYNTAX** used to describe a language that expresses syntactic relationships by means of inflections rather than word order or prepositions and other function words ■ *n.* CHEM **CHEMICALLY PRODUCED SUBSTANCE OR MATERIAL** a substance or material produced by chemical processes rather than occurring naturally [Late 17thC. Via French or modern Latin from Greek *sunthetikos* "component," from *sunthetos* "combined," from *suntithenai* (see SYNTHESIS).] —**syn·thet·i·cal** *adj.* —**syn·thet·i·cal·ly** *adv.*

syn·thet·ic res·in *n.* a resin produced by polymerization of simple molecules rather than obtained directly from plant substances

syn·thet·ic rub·ber *n.* a compound synthesized from unsaturated hydrocarbons that resembles rubber

syn·ton·ic /sin tónnik/ *adj.* **1. EMOTIONALLY RESPONSIVE TO SURROUNDINGS** used to describe somebody who is normally attuned to the environment **2. ACCORDING WITH BELIEFS** in ego psychology, used to describe behavior that does not conflict with somebody's basic attitudes and beliefs and, therefore, is not anxiety-provoking (*used in combination*) ○ *ego-syntonic* [Late 19thC. Formed from Greek *suntonos* "attuned," from *sunteinein* "to draw tight."] —**syn·ton·i·cal·ly** *adv.*

sy·pher /sífər/ (**-phered, -pher·ing, -phers**) *vt.* to join planks with chamfered edges so as to form a flush surface [Mid-19thC. Variant of CIPHER.]

syph·i·lis /síffəliss/ *n.* a serious sexually transmitted disease caused by the spirally twisted bacterium *Treponema pallidum* that affects many body organs and parts, including the genitals, brain, skin, and nervous tissue [Early 18thC. From modern Latin the name of the person allegedly first affected according to a poem *Syphilis sive morbus Gallicus* (Syphilis or the French Disease) (1530) by Girolamo Fracastoro, 1483–1553, a physician from Verona.]

syph·i·lit·ic /sìffə líttik/ *adj.* **OF SYPHILIS** relating to, caused by, or affected by syphilis ■ *n.* **SOMEBODY WITH SYPHILIS** somebody who has been infected with the spirochete that causes syphilis (*offensive*) [Late 18thC. From modern Latin *syphiliticus*, from SYPHILIS.] —**syph·i·lit·i·cal·ly** *adv.*

syph·i·loid /síffə lòyd/ *adj.* resembling syphilis or having similar characteristics

sy·phon *n., vt.* = **siphon**

Syr·a·cuse /sírrə kyooz/ **1.** capital city and port of Syracuse Province, Sicily, situated about 35 mi./56 km south of Catania. Population: 126,800 (1992). **2.** city in New York beside Onondaga Lake, west of Utica, and east of Rochester. Population: 155,865 (1996).

syr·ah /sírrə/ *n.* **1. BLACK GRAPE GROWN FOR WINE** a black grape grown mainly in the Rhône valley of France but also in California and Australia, and used to make wine **2. SYRAH WINE** a typically strong full-bodied wine made from the syrah grape variety [Early 19thC. Alteration of SHIRAZ, where the grape is supposed to have originated.]

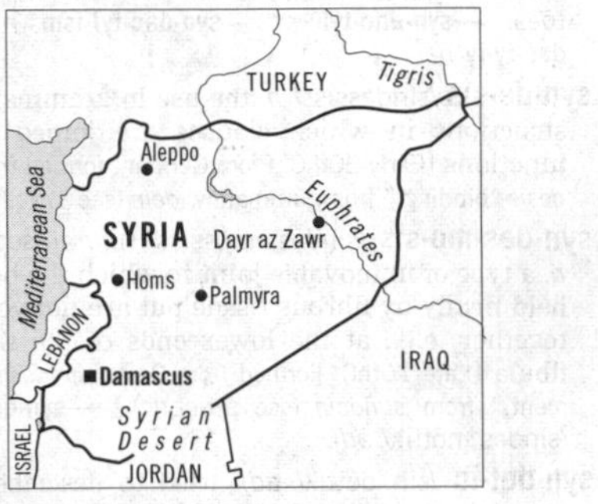

Syria

Sy·ria /sírree ə/ republic in the Middle East, bordered by Turkey, Iraq, Jordan, Israel, Lebanon, and the Mediterranean Sea. Language: Arabic. Currency: Syrian pound. Capital: Damascus. Population: 14,798,000 (1996). Area: 71,498 sq. mi./185,050 sq. km. Official name **Syrian Arab Republic** —**Syr·i·an** *n., adj.*

Syr·i·ac /sírree àk/ *n.* a form of Aramaic used in the 3rd to 13th centuries that survives in some Eastern Orthodox churches —**Syr·i·ac** *adj.*

sy·rin·ga /si ríng gə/ *n.* **1.** = **mock orange** *n.* 1 **2. LILAC FLOWER OR TREE** a lilac flower or shrub. Genus: *Syringa*. [Mid-17thC. Modern Latin from Greek *surigx* "panpipe." From the former use of lilac stems for making pipes.]

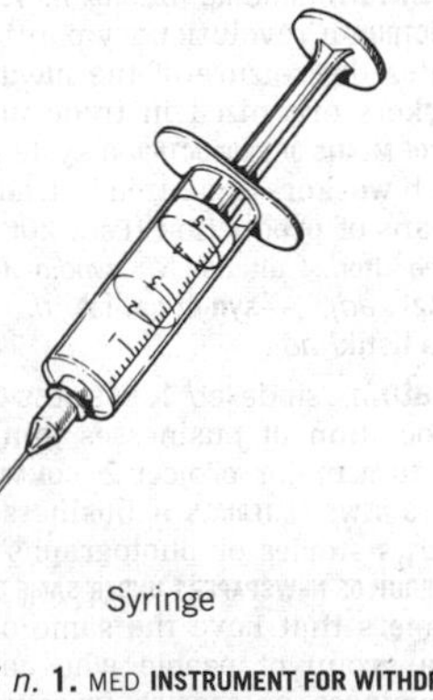
Syringe

sy·ringe /si rínj/ *n.* **1.** MED **INSTRUMENT FOR WITHDRAWING AND EJECTING FLUIDS** an instrument consisting of a piston in a small tube, used in conjunction with a hollow needle or tube for the withdrawal and ejection of fluids and for cleaning wounds. ◊ **hypodermic syringe 2. DEVICE FOR PUMPING AND SPRAYING LIQUIDS** a device similar to a medical syringe that is used for spraying or extracting fluids by means of pressure or suction ■ *vt.* (**-ringed, -ring·ing, -rin·ges**) **USE SYRINGE ON SOMETHING** to clean, spray, or inject something using a syringe [15thC. Via medieval Latin *syringa* from, ultimately, Greek *surigx* "panpipe." From its shape.]

sy·rin·ges plural of **syrinx**

sy·rin·go·my·e·li·a /si rìng gō mī éelee ə/ *n.* a chronic progressive disease of the spinal cord in which tubular fluid-filled cavities form in the nerve tissue, causing sensory disturbances and, eventually, paralysis [Late 19thC. Coined from SYRINGE + MYEL- + -IA.] —**sy·rin·go·my·el·ic** *adj.*

syr·inx /sírringks/ (*plural* **syr·inx·es** *or* **sy·rin·ges** /sə ríng geéz, sə rín jeéz/) *n.* **1.** MUSIC **PANPIPE** a panpipe or set of panpipes **2.** BIRDS **VOCAL ORGAN OF BIRDS** the vocal organ of a bird, usually situated near the junction between the trachea and bronchi **3.** ARCHEOL **CORRIDOR IN EGYPTIAN TOMB** a narrow corridor or gallery in an ancient Egyptian tomb **4.** MED **CAVITY IN SPINAL CORD** one of the tubular fluid-filled cavities formed in the nerve tissue of the spinal cord in cases of syringomyelia [Early 17thC. Via Latin from Greek *surigx* (see SYRINGE).] —**sy·rin·ge·al** /sə ríng gee əl, sə rínjee əl/ *adj.*

syr·phid /súrfid/ *n.* a dipteran fly that hovers and darts, feeds on nectar and pollen, and has coloration mimicking that of a bee or wasp. Family: Syrphidae. [Late 19thC. From modern Latin *Syrphidae*, family name, from *Syrphus* (see SYRPHUS FLY).] —**syr·phid** *adj.*

Syr·tis Ma·jor /sùrtiss máyjər/ *n.* a highly conspicuous wedge-shaped dark area on the surface of Mars in the equatorial region, first observed in 1659

syr·up /sírrəp/, **sir·up** *n.* **1. SWEET LIQUID** a liquid made of sugar dissolved in water by heating, widely used in sweet cookery. Syrups vary in density and strength, and can be boiled down to form caramel. **2. FLAVORED SWEET LIQUID** a flavored thick sweet liquid **3.** PHARM **PHARMACEUTICAL LIQUID** a thick sweet liquid used as vehicle for various medicinals **4. MAPLE SYRUP** maple syrup **5. CORN SYRUP** corn syrup [14thC. Via French *sirop* or medieval Latin *siropus* from Arabic *šarāb* "drink."]

syr·up·y /sírrəpee/ (**-i·er, -i·est**) *adj.* **1. RESEMBLING SYRUP** resembling syrup in taste, quality, or consistency **2. MAWKISH** excessively sentimental in a cloying saccharine fashion

sys·op /síss op/ *n.* a system operator (*informal*) [Late 20thC. Contraction.]

syst. *abbr.* system

sys·tal·tic /si stáltik/ *adj.* used to describe an organ such as the heart that undergoes alternating rhythmic contraction and dilation [Late 17thC. Via late Latin from Greek *sustaltikos*, from *sustellein* (see SYSTOLE).]

sys·tem /sístəm/ *n.* **1. COMPLEX BODY** a combination of related elements organized into a complex whole **2. SET OF PRINCIPLES** a scheme of ideas or principles, e.g., for classification or for forms of government or religion **3. WAY OF PROCEEDING** a method or set of procedures for achieving something **4.** TRANSP **TRANSPORT NETWORK** a physical network of roads, railways, and other routes for travel, transport, or communication **5.** PHYSIOL **GROUP OF RELATED BODY PARTS** a set of organs or structures in the body that have a common function ○ *the nervous system* **6.** PHYSIOL **WHOLE BODY** the human or animal body as a unit ○ *My grandmother used to insist that licorice was good for the system.* **7.** ENG **ASSEMBLY OF COMPONENTS** an assembly of mechanical or electronic components that function together as a unit **8.** COMPUT **SET OF COMPUTER COMPONENTS** an assembly of computer hardware, software, and peripherals functioning together ○ *A turnkey system has all the hardware and software installed and is ready to run.* **9. ORDERLINESS** the use or result of careful planning and organization of elements **10.** ASTRON **GROUP OF CELESTIAL BODIES** a group of celestial bodies or other gravitationally linked objects **11.** MINERALS **MINERAL CLASSIFICATION** any of various divisions used to classify minerals according to their crystal structures **12.** GEOL **STRATIGRAPHIC UNIT OF ROCK** a stratigraphic division of rocks larger than a series but smaller than a stage, used to distinguish formations of a specific era or period **13.** SCI **ASSEMBLY OF SUBSTANCES IN EQUILIBRIUM** an assembly of substances in chemical or physical equilibrium **14.** MUSIC **GROUP OF MUSICAL STAVES** a number of musical staves that are grouped together by a line or brace in a score and are played simultaneously **15. sys·tem, Sys·tem THE WAY THINGS ARE** the established order, especially regarded as thwarting the individual [Early 17thC. Via French or late Latin from Greek *sustēma*, from *sunistanai* "to combine," from *histanai* "to set up."] —**sys·tem·less** *adj.* ◇ **all systems go** used to indicate that everything is functioning and an operation or activity can start

sys·tem·at·ic /sìstə máttik/, **sys·tem·at·ic·al** /sìstə máttik'l/ *adj.* **1. DONE METHODICALLY** carried out in a methodical and organized manner **2. WELL ORGANIZED** habitually using a method or system for organization **3. METHODICAL** deliberate and regular in a methodical manner **4. BASED ON SYSTEM** constituting, based on, or resembling a system **5.** BIOL **PERTAINING TO TAXONOMIC CLASSIFICATION** in accordance with a system of taxonomic classification (**systematics**) [Mid-17thC. Via late Latin from Greek *sustēmatikos*, from *sustēma* (see SYSTEM).] —**sys·tem·at·i·cal·ly** *adv.*

WORD KEY: USAGE

systematic or **systemic** These two words are distinct. The former means, essentially, "according to a system or plan." The latter means "within or throughout a system," the system in question here often being a biological one. Thus, *a systematic effort to defraud; systemic poison.*

sys·tem·at·ic de·sen·si·ti·za·tion *n.* a therapy for phobias and other anxiety disorders in which patients are gradually given longer and longer exposures to the object of their fears

sys·tem·at·ics /sìstə máttiks/ *n.* the study of systems and classification, especially the science of classifying organisms

sys·tem·a·tism /sístəmə tìzzəm/ *n.* the practice of classifying information in a systematic manner

sys·tem·a·tist /sístəmətist/ *n.* **1. SOMEBODY WHO CONSTRUCTS SYSTEMS** somebody engaged in constructing a system or systems **2.** BIOL **SOMEBODY WHO CLASSIFIES ORGANISMS** somebody engaged in classifying organisms according to a taxonomic system **3. SOMEBODY ADHERING TO SYSTEM** somebody who conforms to a method or system

sys·tem·a·tize /sístəmə tīz/ (**-tized, -tiz·ing, -tiz·es**), **sys·tem·ize** /sístə mīz/ (**-ized, -iz·ing, -iz·es**) *vti.* to arrange something, or be arranged, according to a system [Mid-18thC. Formed from the Greek stem *sustēmat-* (see SYSTEM).] —**sys·tem·a·ti·za·tion** /sìstəmətə záysh'n/ *n.* —**sys·tem·a·tiz·er** /sístəmə tīzər/ *n.*

sys·tem·ic /si stémmik/ *adj.* **1. OF A SYSTEM** affecting or relating to a system as a whole **2.** PHYSIOL **AFFECTING WHOLE BODY** affecting the whole body as distinct from having a local effect ○ *a systemic infection* **3.** AGRIC **AFFECTING WHOLE PLANT** used to describe an herbicide or other chemical that works by spreading through all the tissues of a plant rather than just staying on the surface ■ *n.* AGRIC **SYSTEMIC CHEMICAL** a systemic herbicide, pesticide, or other chemical —**sys·tem·i·cal·ly** *adv.*

WORD KEY: USAGE

See Usage note at ***systematic***.

sys·tem·ic cir·cu·la·tion *n.* the main part of the blood circulation as distinct from the pulmonary circulation

sys·tem·ic lu·pus er·y·the·ma·to·sus /-lóopəss èrr thèemə tóssiss/ *n.* a chronic inflammatory autoimmune disease of connective tissue that occurs especially in women, marked by fever, muscle pain, arthritis, anemia, skin eruptions, pleurisy, and kidney disease

sys·tem·ize *vt.* = **systematize** —**sys·tem·i·za·tion** *n.* —**sys·tem·iz·er** *n.*

sys·tem op·er·a·tor *n.* somebody who manages an online bulletin board or maintains a small computer network

sys·tems a·nal·y·sis *n.* the determination of the data-processing requirements of a company, project, procedure, or task, and the designing of computer systems to fulfill them —**sys·tems an·a·lyst** *n.*

sys·tems en·gi·neer·ing *n.* the design and implementation of production systems that require the integration of diverse and complex tasks, e.g., automobile assembly lines —**sys·tems en·gi·neer** *n.*

sys·tem soft·ware *n.* the operating system and utility programs used to operate and maintain a computer system and provide resources for application programs such as word processors and spreadsheets

sys·to·le /sístəlee/ *n.* the contraction of the heart, during which blood is pumped into the arteries [Mid-16thC. Via late Latin from Greek *sustolē*, from *sustellein* "to contract," from *stellein* "to put."] —**sys·tol·ic** /si stóllik/ *adj.*

syz·y·gy /sízzəjee/ (*plural* **-gies**) *n.* **1.** ASTRON **CONJUNCTION OF THREE CELESTIAL BODIES** the straight-line conjunction or opposition of three celestial bodies, e.g., the Sun, Earth, and Moon **2. TWO CONNECTED THINGS** a pair of related things that are either similar or opposite (*formal*) **3.** POETRY **TWO METRICAL FEET** a metrical unit of two feet in classical Greek and Latin verse [Early 17thC. Via late Latin from Greek *suzugia*, from *suzugos* "paired," from *zugon* "yoke."] —**syz·y·get·ic** /sìzzə jéttik/ *adj.* —**syz·y·get·i·cal·ly** /-jéttikəlee/ *adv.* —**sy·zyg·i·al** /si zíjjee əl/ *adj.*

Szcze·cin /shtét shin/ capital city and port of Szczecin Province, in northwestern Poland. Population: 419,300 (1995).

Sze·chuan pep·per /sèch waan-/, **Sze·chwan pep·per** *n.* a pepper with a hot aniseed flavor, one of the spices used in Chinese five spice powder [Mid-20thC. Named for Szechuan (now Sichuan).]

Sze·ged /sé ged/ city and river port in southeastern Hungary. Population: 178,878 (1994).

Szell /sel, zel/, **George** (1897–1970) Hungarian-born U.S. conductor. As the musical director of the Cleveland Orchestra from 1946 to 1970, he established the orchestra as one of the finest in the world.

Szi·lard /zíllərd, zə laárd/, **Leo** (1898–1964) Hungarian-born U.S. biophysicist. He worked on uranium fission and contributed to the development of the atomic bomb, but later advocated only peaceful uses of atomic energy.

Tt

t[1] /tee/ (*plural* **t's**), **T** (*plural* **T's** *or* **Ts**) *n.* **1. 20TH LETTER OF ENGLISH ALPHABET** the 20th letter of the modern English alphabet **2. SPEECH SOUND CORRESPONDING TO LETTER "T"** the speech sound that corresponds to the letter "T" **3. LETTER "T" WRITTEN** a written representation of the letter "T" **4. SOMETHING "T"-SHAPED** something shaped like a "T" ◇ **to a T** exactly

t[2] *symbol.* **1.** time **2.** troy

T[1] *symbol.* **1.** absolute temperature **2.** kinetic energy **3.** PHYS period **4.** surface tension **5.** temperature **6.** tesla **7.** tritium

T[2] *abbr.* tera-

t. *abbr.* **1.** tare **2.** teaspoon **3.** teaspoonful **4.** tempo **5.** tempore **6.** tenor **7.** tense **8.** ton **9.** tons **10.** transitive

T. *abbr.* **1.** tablespoon **2.** tablespoonful **3.** Tuesday

Ta *symbol.* tantalum

TA *abbr.* **1.** teaching assistant **2.** transactional analysis

Taal /taal/ *n. S Africa* LANG the Afrikaans language [Late 19thC. Via Afrikaans from Dutch *taal* "language."]

tab[1] /tab/ *n.* **1. FLAP FOR HOLDING** a small strip, loop, or other attachment to something, used for lifting, moving, hanging, opening, or closing **2.** CLOTHES **FLAP ON GARMENT** a small strip or square of fabric attached to a garment for decoration **3.** *U.S., Can, Aus* **RESTAURANT CHECK** the check for a meal or drinks in a restaurant or bar (*informal*) **4. TAG OR LABEL** a small piece of paper, cloth, or plastic attached to something and containing information about the object **5.** AEROSP **AUXILIARY AIRFOIL** a small auxiliary airfoil on a control surface such as an aileron or rudder, used to stabilize an aircraft **6.** = **pull-tab** ■ *vt.* **(tabbed, tab·bing, tabs) ATTACH TAB TO** to attach a tab to something [Early 17thC. Origin unknown.] ◇ **keep tabs on somebody** *or* **something** to watch somebody or something closely (*informal*) ◇ **pick up the tab** *U.S., Can, Aus* to pay the bill (*informal*)

tab[2] /tab/ *n.* a key on a computer keyboard, or a device or key on a typewriter, that advances the next character to a predetermined position, used to align lines or columns. Full form **tabulator** [Early 20thC. Shortening of TABULATOR.]

tab[3] /tab/ *n.* a tablet or piece of paper containing a drug, especially one that is illegal [Mid-20thC. Shortening of TABLET.]

tab[4] /tab/ *n.* = **tableau curtain** [Early 20thC. Shortening.]

TAB /tab/ *abbr.* **1.** paratyphoid A **2.** paratyphoid B (vaccine) **3.** typhoid

tab. *abbr.* table

ta·ban·ca /tə bángkə/ *n. Carib* a state of sadness resulting from unrequited or lost love (*slang*) [Late 19thC. Origin uncertain: probably from a Cariban language, possibly Macusi *tabangke* "wonder."]

ta·ba·nid /tə báynid, tə bánnid, tábbənid/ *n.* a stout-bodied bloodsucking fly such as a horsefly. Family: Tabanidae. [Late 19thC. Formed from Latin *tabanus* "horsefly."]

tab·ard /tábbərd/ *n.* **1. SLEEVELESS OVERGARMENT** a sleeveless tunic with slits at the sides, worn by women and girls **2. HERALD'S COAT** an official coat worn by a herald, bearing the sovereign's coat of arms **3.** HIST **KNIGHT'S JACKET** a sleeveless or short-sleeved garment worn by a knight over his armor [13thC. From Old French *tabart*, of unknown origin.]

tab·a·ret /tábbə rèt/ *n.* a hard-wearing fabric with alternate satin and watered-silk stripes, used for upholstery [Late 18thC. Origin uncertain: probably from TABBY.]

Tabard

Ta·bas·co /tə báskō/ *tdmk.* a trademark for a hot-tasting sauce made from peppers, vinegar, and spices

tab·bou·leh /tə bóolee/, **ta·boo·li** *n.* a Middle Eastern salad made with bulgur wheat, tomatoes, mint, olive oil, and parsley, served finely ground with lettuce leaves for scooping it up [Mid-20thC. From Arabic *tabbūla*.]

tab·by /tábbee/ *n.* (*plural* **-bies**) **1. tabby, tabby cat STRIPED CAT** a brown or gray cat with a striped or mottled coat **2. PET FEMALE CAT** a domestic cat, especially a female one **3. OFFENSIVE TERM** an offensive term that deliberately insults a woman who is thought to be gossiping, spiteful, and interfering (*informal insult*) **4.** TEXTILES **SILK WITH STRIPED PATTERN** watered silk or taffeta with a striped or wavy pattern **5.** TEXTILES **PLAIN WEAVE FABRIC** a plain-woven fabric ■ *adj.* **1. HAVING STRIPED COAT** having a brown or gray coat with a striped or mottled pattern **2. STRIPED OR BRINDLED** having a striped or wavy pattern **3.** TEXTILES **RESEMBLING TABBY** resembling or made of tabby [Late 16thC. Via French *tabis* from Arabic *'attābī*. Named for *al-'Attābiyya*, a quarter in Baghdad, Iraq, where the (originally striped) fabric was made.]

WORD KEY: ORIGIN

It was the stripes on the fabric called ***tabby*** that led to the application of the word to brindled cats. The usage is first recorded in the 1660s.

tab·er·na·cle /tábbər nàk'l/ *n.* **1. tab·er·na·cle, Tab·er·na·cle** RELIG **TENT FOR CARRYING ARK OF COVENANT** a portable tent used as a sanctuary for the Ark of the Covenant by the Israelites during the Exodus **2. tab·er·na·cle, Tab·er·na·cle** JUDAISM **JEWISH TEMPLE** the Jewish Temple, regarded as representing the presence of God **3.** JUDAISM = **sukkah 4.** RELIG **EVANGELICAL PLACE OF WORSHIP** a place of worship, especially in some evangelical Christian denominations **5.** CHR **CONTAINER FOR HOLY BREAD AND WINE** a box or case in which the consecrated elements of Communion are kept **6.** ARCHIT **NICHE FOR ICON** a canopied recess or niche for an icon **7. HUMAN BODY** the human body considered as a place temporarily housing the soul or principle of life (*literary*) **8.** NAUT **SOCKET FOR MAST** a support for the foot of a mast [13thC. Directly or via French from Latin *tabernaculum* "tent," from *taberna* "hut" (source of English *tavern*).] —**tab·er·nac·u·lar** /tàbbər nákyələr/ *adj.*

Tab·er·na·cles /tábbər nak'lz/ *n.* CALENDAR = **Sukkoth**

ta·bes /táybeez/ (*plural* **-bes**) *n.* **1. PROGRESSIVE EMACIATION** progressive wasting of the body, usually as a result of a chronic disease **2.** MED = **tabes dorsalis** [Late 16thC. From Latin, "wasting away."] —**ta·bet·ic** /tə béttik/ *adj.*

ta·bes dor·sa·lis /-dawr sáyliss/, **ta·bes** *n.* a disorder of the nervous system characteristic of late-stage syphilis and marked by degeneration of nerve fibers, wasting, pain, and inability to move the leg muscles. Tabes dorsalis is now rare because syphilis can be effectively treated at a much earlier stage. [From late Latin, literally "dorsal tabes"]

tab·la /taáblə, túbblə/ *n.* an Indian musical instrument consisting of a pair of small drums played with the hands [Mid-19thC. Via Persian and Hindi from Arabic *ṭabl* "drum."]

tab·la·ture /tábblə chŏor/ *n.* **1.** MUSIC **SPECIAL MUSICAL NOTATION** a special kind of musical notation in which the notes themselves are not represented but rather the hand positions required to play them. It is used especially in early lute and modern popular guitar music. **2.** ARTS **ENGRAVED TABLET** a tablet or other flat surface that has been engraved or painted [Late 16thC. Via French from, ultimately, *tavolare* "to set to music," from *tavola* "table."]

ta·ble /táyb'l/ *n.* **1. ITEM OF FURNITURE WITH FLAT TOP** a piece of furniture with a flat top and one or more legs, used for placing things on or doing things at **2. TABLE FOR FOOD** a table at which people sit to eat meals, or a similar structure provided outdoors at which birds may feed **3. FLAT SURFACE FOR PARTICULAR PURPOSE** a raised flat surface with a nondomestic or office use, e.g., one at which a surgeon operates or one on which a piece of machinery rests **4. FOOD SERVED** the food provided in a household or restaurant in terms of its quality or quantity **5. PEOPLE SITTING AT TABLE** a group of people sitting at a table, especially for a meal ○ *The whole table erupted in laughter.* **6. ARRANGEMENT OF INFORMATION IN COLUMNS** an arrangement of information or data into columns and rows or a condensed list **7.** GEOG = **tableland 8.** ARCHIT **BAND OR PANEL ON WALL** a band of masonry or a rectangular panel on a wall either raised or depressed and with ornamentation or inscriptions **9. FLAT SURFACE OF GEM** the upper horizontal surface of a cut gem **10. SLAB FOR INSCRIPTION** a slab of wood, stone, or metal for inscription **11.** BACKGAMMON **PART OF BACKGAMMON BOARD** either one of the two hinged halves of a backgammon board **12.** MUSIC **FRONT PART OF STRINGED INSTRUMENT** the part of the body of a stringed instrument that acts as a sounding board **13.** ANAT **PLATE OF BONE** a flat layer of bone, especially either one of the inner or outer surfaces of the skull that are separated by a more spongy bone (**diploë**) **14. AREA ON PALM** an area on the palm defined by four lines, regarded as significant in palmistry ■ **ta·bles** *npl.* HIST **ANCIENT TABLETS WITH LAWS INSCRIBED** tablets on which certain ancient Greek, Roman, and Hebrew laws were inscribed, or the laws themselves ■ *vt.* **(-bled, -bling, -bles) 1. POSTPONE DISCUSSION OF SOMETHING** to postpone discussion of a bill or motion for a later time **2. ENTER INFORMATION INTO TABLE** to enter information in a tabular form **3. PUT SOMETHING ON TABLE** to place or lay something on a table **4.** *U.K.* **PROPOSE SOMETHING** to put forward a bill or proposal for discussion at a meeting [Pre-12thC. Directly or via French from Latin *tabula* "board, slab."] —**table·ful** *n.* ◇ **on the table 1.** put forward for discussion at a meeting **2.** postponed for discussion at a later time ◇ **turn the tables (on somebody)** to reverse a situation and gain the advantage from somebody who had previously held it ◇ **under the table** secretly and often illegally, in the form of a bribe ○ *He paid under the table for his rent-stabilized apartment.*

tab·leau /tá blō, ta blṓ/ (*plural* **-leaux** /tá blōz, ta blṓz/ *or* **-leaus**) *n.* **1. PICTURESQUE DISPLAY** a vivid and wide-ranging description or display **2. STRIKING VISUAL SCENE**

a visually dramatic scene or situation that suddenly arises **3.** THEATER = **tableau vivant** [Late 17thC. Via French from Old French *tablel*, literally "a small table" (see TABLE).]

tab·leau cur·tain *n.* either one of a pair of stage curtains that are drawn to each side and upward by a cord

tab·leau vi·vant (*plural* **tab·leaux vi·vants**) *n.* a representation of a scene by a group in appropriate costume posing silent and motionless [From French, literally "living picture"]

Ta·ble Bay /tàyb'l-/ inlet of the Atlantic Ocean, overlooked by Table Mountain, southwestern South Africa. Length: 12 mi./19 km.

ta·ble·cloth /táyb'l klàwth/ *n.* a cloth for covering a table, especially before it is set for a meal

ta·ble d'hôte /taàb'l dṓt, taàblə-/ *n.* a restaurant meal or menu offering a series of courses at a fixed price [Early 17thC. From French, literally "host's table."]

ta·ble-hop (**ta·ble-hopped, ta·ble-hop·ping, ta·ble-hops**) *vi.* to circulate among tables in a restaurant or nightclub in a sociable way (*informal*) —**ta·ble-hop·per** *n.*

ta·ble·land /táyb'l lànd/ *n.* an extensive elevated region of flat land

ta·ble·mate /táyb'l màyt/ *n.* somebody sitting at the same table as another, especially for a meal

Ta·ble Moun·tain /tàyb'l mówntin/ flat-topped mountain overlooking Cape Town, southwestern South Africa. Height: 3,563 ft./1,086 m.

ta·ble·spoon /táyb'l spo͞on/ *n.* **1.** SERVING SPOON a large serving spoon a size larger than a dessertspoon **2. tablespoon, tablespoonful** MEASURE MEASURE BASED ON CAPACITY OF TABLESPOON a unit of capacity used in recipes, equal to half a fluid ounce/15 ml or three teaspoons **3.** AMOUNT HELD BY TABLESPOON the amount of food or liquid that a tablespoon can hold

tab·let /tábblət/ *n.* **1.** COMPRESSED POWDERED DRUG FOR SWALLOWING a small shaped cake of a fixed amount of a compressed powdered drug, usually intended to be swallowed whole **2.** SMALL FLAT CAKE OF SOMETHING a small compressed cake of a substance such as soap **3.** INSCRIBED STONE OR WOODEN SLAB a slab of stone, wood, or metal used for inscription or engraving **4.** SHEETS OF PAPER FASTENED TOGETHER a number of sheets of paper for writing or drawing, fastened together along one edge **5.** SHEET OF MATERIAL TO WRITE ON a thin stiff sheet of wood, slate, or ivory on which somebody writes **6.** ARCHIT = **table** *n.* 8 [14thC. From Old French, literally "little table," from *table* (see TABLE). Sense 1 evolved via the idea of something "flat," hence "compressed."]

ta·ble talk *n.* **1.** INFORMAL CONVERSATION informal conversation on subjects considered suitable during a meal **2.** BRIDGE IMPROPER DISCUSSION OF STRATEGY IN BRIDGE in bridge, the discussion of bidding and strategy across the table with a partner, which is not permitted

ta·ble ten·nis *n.* a game that resembles tennis and is played with small paddles and a light hollow ball on a table divided by a net

ta·ble·ware /táyb'l wàir/ *n.* dishes, plates, glasses, flatware, and other articles used at meals

ta·ble wine *n.* an unfortified wine for drinking with meals

tab·loid /táb lòyd/ *n.* **1. tabloid, tabloid newspaper** SMALL NEWSPAPER WITH SHORT ARTICLES a small-format popular newspaper with a simple style, many photographs, and sometimes an emphasis on sensational stories **2.** CONDENSED PIECE OF WRITING a piece of writing, especially a news story, in a condensed form ■ *adj.* SENSATIONALIST relating to or characteristic of tabloid newspapers, especially in having a popular sensationalist style [Late 19thC. Originally a proprietary name for tablets of condensed medicine; the underlying idea is of condensed writing.]

WORD KEY: ORIGIN

Tabloid was registered as a proprietary name for a brand of tablet in 1884 by Burroughs, Wellcome, and Company. It was the underlying notion of "compression" or "condensation" that led to its application to newspapers of small page size and "condensed" versions of news stories, which emerged at the beginning of the 20th century.

ta·boo /tə bo͞o/, **ta·bu** *adj.* **1.** SOCIALLY OR CULTURALLY PROSCRIBED forbidden to be used, mentioned, or approached because of social or cultural rather than legal prohibitions **2.** RELIG SACRED AND PROHIBITED set apart as sacred and at the same time forbidden to be used ■ *n.* **1.** PROHIBITION a prohibition or rejection of particular types of behavior or language because they are considered socially unacceptable **2.** FORBIDDEN BEHAVIOR a type of behavior or a subject that is forbidden or disapproved of because it is considered socially unacceptable **3.** RELIG PROHIBITION ON GROUNDS OF BEING SACRED the practice, especially in some Polynesian societies, of regarding particular things, people, or types of behavior as sacred and therefore forbidden to be used, made contact with, or engaged in ■ *vt.* (**-booed, -boo·ing, -boos; -bued, -bu·ing, -bus**) **1.** FORBID OR DISCOURAGE SOMETHING to prohibit or disapprove of particular types of behavior or language because they are considered socially unacceptable **2.** RELIG PROHIBIT SOMETHING BECAUSE SACRED to regard particular things, people, or types of behavior as sacred and therefore forbidden to be used, made contact with, or engaged in [Late 18thC. From Tongan *tabu*, allegedly introduced into English by Captain James COOK.]

ta·boo·li *n.* = **tabbouleh**

ta·bor /táybər/, **ta·bour** *n.* a small drum played with one hand while the other hand plays a pipe. Tabors were used especially in the Middle Ages. [13thC. From Old French *tabour*, of uncertain origin: probably from Persian *tabīr* "drum" (source of English *tambourine*).] —**ta·bor·er** *n.*

Ta·bor, Mount /táyb ər-/ peak in northern Israel, east of Nazareth. In the Christian Bible, it is the site of the transfiguration of Jesus Christ. Height: 1,929 ft./588 m.

Ta·bo·ra /ta báwrə/ capital city of Tabora Region, west-central Tanzania, situated about 220 mi./354 km northwest of Dodoma. Population: 214,000 (1986).

tab·o·ret /tàbbə rét, tàbbə ráy/, **tab·ou·ret** *n.* **1.** FURNITURE LOW CYLINDRICAL STOOL a low solid seat without arms or a back **2.** SEW = **tambour** *n.* 1 **3.** MUSIC SMALL TABOR a small tabor or tambourine [Mid-17thC. From French, literally "small tabor" (see TABOR).]

ta·bour *n.* = **tabor**

tab·ou·ret *n.* = **taboret**

ta·bu *adj.*, *n.*, *vt.* = **taboo**

tab·u·lar /tábbyələr/ *adj.* **1.** ARRANGED IN TABLE arranged in a table or in columns and rows **2.** HAVING FLAT SURFACE having a flat surface that resembles a table **3.** CRYSTALS BROAD AND FLAT used to describe crystals that are broad and flat **4.** GEOL SPLITTING INTO THIN PLATES made up of and splitting into thin horizontal plates **5.** MATH COMPUTED USING TABLE calculated with or making use of a table, e.g., of logarithms [Mid-17thC. From Latin *tabularis*, from *tabula* (see TABLE).] —**tab·u·lar·ly** *adv.*

tab·u·la ra·sa /tàbbyələ raàssə, -raàzə/ (*plural* **tab·u·lae ra·sae** /-raàssee, -raàzee/) *n.* **1.** PHILOSOPHY MIND PRIOR TO EXPERIENCES the mind at birth, regarded as having no innate conceptions **2.** CHANCE TO START AFRESH an opportunity to make a clean break or a fresh start [Mid-16thC. From Latin, literally "scraped table."]

tab·u·lar·ize /tábbyələ rīz/ (**-ized, -iz·ing, -iz·es**) *vt.* = **tabulate** *v.* 1 —**tab·u·lar·i·za·tion** /tàbbyələ rəzáysh'n/ *n.*

tab·u·late *vt.* /tábbyoo làyt/ (**-lat·ed, -lat·ing, -lates**) **1.** ARRANGE INFORMATION IN TABLE to arrange information systematically in a table or in columns and rows **2.** MAKE SOMETHING FLAT to give a flat top or upper surface to something (*usually passive*) ■ *adj.* /tábbyə lit, -làyt/ FLAT with a flat surface that resembles a table [Late 16thC. Via late Latin *tabulatus* from, ultimately, Latin *tabula* (see TABLE).] —**tab·u·la·ble** *adj.* —**tab·u·la·tion** /tàbbyə láysh'n/ *n.*

tab·u·la·tor /tàbbyə láytər/ *n.* **1.** SOMEBODY OR SOMETHING TABULATING DATA a person or device that tabulates information **2.** COMM, COMPUT full form of **tab**[2] *n.*

tab·un /taà bo͞on/ *n.* an organic phosphorus compound used in chemical warfare. Formula: $C_5H_{11}N_2O_2P$. [Mid-20thC. From German, of unknown origin.]

TAC *abbr.* Tactical Air Command

tac·a·ma·hac /tákəmə hàk/, **tac·ma·hack** /tákmə-/ *n.* **1.** STRONG-SMELLING RESINOUS SUBSTANCE a resinous gum obtained from particular trees and used to make ointments and incense **2.** TREE YIELDING TACAMAHAC RESIN a tree from which tacamahac resin is obtained, especially the balsam poplar [Late 16thC. Via obsolete Spanish *tacamahaca* from Aztec *tecomahiyac*.]

Tac·an /tá kàn/ *n.* an aircraft navigation system using ultrahigh-frequency signals emitted from a transmitting station to determine distance and bearing [Mid-20thC. Acronym formed from TACTICAL + AIR + NAVIGATION.]

ta·cet /tássət, tάyssət, taá kèt/ *n.* a musical direction instructing a musician not to play or sing a certain passage [Early 18thC. From Latin, literally "(it) is silent," formed from *tacere* (see TACIT).]

tach /tak/ *n.* a tachometer (*informal*) [Mid-20thC. Shortening.]

Ta·ché /taa sháy/, **Sir Etienne-Paschal** (1795–1865) Canadian politician. A local and federal officeholder, he chaired the conference (1864) that paved the way for the unification of Canada.

tach·e·om·e·ter *n.* = **tachymeter**

tach·e·om·e·try /tàkee ómmətree/ *n.* = **tachymetry** —**tach·e·o·met·ric** /tàkee ə métrik/ *adj.* —**tach·e·o·met·ri·cal·ly** /-métrik'lee/ *adv.*

tach·i·na fly /tákənə-/ *n.* a bristly fly whose larvae live as parasites on other insects. They are sometimes used to control harmful insect species. Family: Tachinidae. [*Tachina* via modern Latin, genus name, from, ultimately, Greek *takhinos* "swift"]

tach·i·nid /tákənid/ *n.* = **tachina fly** ■ *adj.* RELATING TO TACHINA FLY relating to the family of insects that the tachina fly belongs to [Late 19thC. From modern Latin *Takhinidae*, family name, from *Takhina* (see TACHINA FLY).]

tach·ism /tá shìzzəm/, **tach·isme** *n.* a type of action painting in which random blotches of color are used as a method of instinctive expression [Mid-20thC. From French *tachisme*, from *tache* "spot."] —**tach·ist** *n.*, *adj.*

ta·chis·to·scope /tə kístə skṓp/ *n.* an instrument for displaying visual images very briefly, used to test perception and memory [Late 19thC. Coined from Greek *takhistos* "swiftest" (formed from *takhus* "swift") + -SCOPE.] —**ta·chis·to·scop·ic** /tə kìstə skóppik/ *adj.* —**ta·chis·to·scop·i·cal·ly** /-skóppikəlee/ *adv.*

tach·o·gram /tákə gràm/ *n.* a record in graph form produced by a tachograph

tach·o·graph /tákə gràf/ *n.* an instrument that produces a record of the use and readings of a tachometer, especially one in a commercial vehicle or bus recording speeds and distances traveled. In effect, a tachograph records the hours worked by a driver.

ta·chom·e·ter /ta kómmətər/ *n.* a device used to determine speed of rotation, typically of a vehicle's crankshaft and usually in revolutions per minute —**tach·o·met·ric** /tàkə méttrik/ *adj.* —**tach·o·met·ri·cal·ly** /-méttrikəlee/ *adv.* —**ta·chom·e·try** /ta kómmətree/ *n.*

tachy- *prefix.* accelerated, rapid ○ *tachygraphy* [From Greek *takhus* "swift"]

tach·y·ar·rhyth·mi·a /tàkee ə ríthmee ə/ *n.* a medical condition in which the heartbeat is fast and irregular

tach·y·car·di·a /tàki kaárdee ə/ *n.* an excessively rapid heartbeat, typically regarded as a heart rate exceeding 100 beats per minute in a resting adult [Late 19thC. Coined from TACHY- + Greek *kardia* "heart" (see CARDIA).] —**tach·y·car·di·ac** *adj.*

ta·chyg·ra·phy /ta kíggrəfee/ *n.* **1.** ANCIENT SHORTHAND the shorthand system used by the ancient Greeks and Romans **2.** ABBREVIATED MEDIEVAL WRITING the abbreviated cursive writing used in medieval times for Latin and Greek —**ta·chyg·ra·pher** *n.* —**tach·y·graph·ic** /tàki gráffik/ *adj.* —**tach·y·graph·i·cal·ly** /-gráffikəlee/ *adv.*

tach·y·lite /tákə līt/, **tach·y·lyte** *n.* black volcanic glass formed by the chilling of basaltic magma [Mid-19thC. Via German *Tachylyt*, which was coined from Greek *takhu-* "quickly" (see TACHY-), from its rapid decomposition in acids, + *lutos* "soluble."] —**tach·y·lit·ic** /tàki líttik/ *adj.*

ta·chym·e·ter /ta kímmətər/, **tach·e·om·e·ter** /tàkee ómmətər/ *n.* an instrument used in surveying to work out distances, elevations, and directions at speed

ta·chym·e·try /ta kímmətree/, **tach·e·om·e·try** /tàkee ómmətree/ *n.* the measurement of distances, elevations, and directions using a tachymeter —**tach·y·met·ric** /tàki méttrik/ *adj.* —**tach·y·met·ri·cal·ly** /-méttrikəlee/ *adv.*

tach·y·on /tákee òn/ *n.* a hypothetical elementary particle that always travels faster than the speed of light

tac·it /tássit/ *adj.* **1. IMPLIED BUT NOT EXPRESSED** understood or implied without being stated openly **2. SILENT** not spoken (*archaic*) [Early 17thC. From Latin *tacitus*, the past participle of *tacere* "to be silent."] —**tac·it·ly** *adv.* —**tac·it·ness** *n.*

tac·i·turn /tássi tùrn/ *adj.* habitually uncommunicative or reserved in speech and manner [Late 18thC. Via French *taciturne* from Latin *taciturnus*, from *tacitus* (see TACIT).] —**tac·i·tur·ni·ty** /tàssi túrnətee/ *n.* —**tac·i·turn·ly** /tássi tùrnlee/ *adv.*

WORD KEY: SYNONYMS

See Synonyms at ***silent***.

tack[1] /tak/ *n.* **1.** JOINERY, HOME MAINTENANCE **SMALL NAIL** a small sharp nail with a broad head **2.** = **thumbtack 3. COURSE OF ACTION** a course of action or method of approach intended to achieve something, especially one adopted after another has failed **4.** SAILING **CHANGE IN DIRECTION OF SAILING** a change in the direction of movement of a sailing ship or sailboat made in order to maximize the benefit from the wind **5.** SAILING **PART OF ZIGZAG SAILING COURSE** a stage or series of stages in the zigzag movement of a sailing ship or sailboat that is changing direction in order to maximize the benefit from the wind **6.** SAILING **DIRECTION OF SAILING** the direction of movement of a sailing ship or sailboat in relation to the side from which the wind is blowing, effected by the position of its sails **7. SLIGHT STICKINESS** slight stickiness, e.g., of glue or paint that has not yet dried **8.** SAILING **ROPE HOLDING DOWN SAIL** a rope holding down the corner of some sails, or the corner that is held down **9.** SEW **TEMPORARY STITCH** a long loose temporary stitch, often used to align seams in preparation for final sewing ■ *v.* (**tacked, tack·ing, tacks**) **1.** *vt.* JOINERY, HOME MAINTENANCE **FASTEN SOMETHING WITH TACKS** to attach something with small sharp broad-headed nails **2.** *vt.* **ATTACH SOMETHING WITH THUMBTACK** to attach something light to a board or wall with a thumbtack **3.** *vt.* **PUT THINGS TOGETHER ARBITRARILY** to bring different things together to form an arbitrary or illusory whole **4.** *vi.* **CHANGE APPROACH** to take a different course of action or use a different method **5.** *vt.* SEW **SEW SOMETHING TEMPORARILY** to sew something with long loose temporary stitches **6.** *vti.* SAILING **CHANGE DIRECTION OF SAILING SHIP** to change the direction or course of a sailing ship or sailboat, or to steer it on alternate tacks [14thC. From Old Northern French *taque* "fastening," of Germanic origin.] ◇ **tack on** *vt.* add something to something else either as a supplement or an afterthought

tack[2] /tak/ *n.* saddles, bridles, and other parts of a horse's harness [Late 18thC. Shortening of TACKLE.]

tack[3] /tak/ *n.* goods that are tasteless and vulgar or cheap and shoddy (*informal*) [Late 20thC. Back-formation from TACKY.]

tack[4] /tak/ *n.* foodstuff, especially of the poor quality fed to a ship's crew in the days of sailing ships (*slang*) ◊ **hardtack** [Late 16thC. Origin unknown.]

tack·board /ták bàwrd/ *n.* a bulletin board (*informal*)

tack·le /ták'l/ *n.* **1.** SPORTS **ATTEMPT TO STOP OPPONENT'S PROGRESS** a physical challenge against an opposing player who has the ball, puck, or other object of possession in football, hockey, and some other games. A tackle is made by seizing and forcing the opponent to the ground in football, by using the foot in soccer, and with the stick in hockey. **2. SPORTS EQUIPMENT** the equipment used for a particular activity such as fishing, angling, or rock climbing **3.** MECH ENG **ROPES AND PULLEYS** equipment consisting of ropes and pulleys used for lifting heavy weights through increased mechanical advantage **4.** NAUT **SHIP'S RIGGING** the gear and rigging of a ship **5.** FOOTBALL **LINEMAN NEXT TO END** a lineman positioned between a guard and an end, or the position of such a player ■ *vt.* (**-led, -ling, -les**) **1. EMBARK ON DOING SOMETHING** to undertake or deal with something that requires effort **2. CONFRONT SOMEBODY** to open a conversation or discussion on a difficult issue with somebody who would prefer to avoid it **3.** SPORTS **MAKE TACKLE ON SOMEBODY** to make a physical challenge on an opposing player **4. HARNESS AN ANIMAL** to put a harness on an animal, especially a horse [13thC. Origin uncertain: probably from Low German *takel* "ship's rigging," from *taken* "to seize."] —**tack·ler** *n.*

tack on *vt.* to add something on as a supplement or an afterthought (*informal*)

tack weld·ing *n.* the welding of two metals by individual welds at isolated points

tack·y[1] /tákee/ (**-i·er, -i·est**) *adj.* slightly sticky to the touch [Late 18thC. Formed from TACK[1].] —**tack·i·ly** *adv.* —**tack·i·ness** *n.*

tack·y[2] /tákee/ (**-i·er, -i·est**) *adj.* (*informal*) **1. IN BAD TASTE** perceived of as vulgar, lacking in taste, or no longer fashionable **2. SHABBY** appearing to be cheaply made or in need of repair [Early 19thC. Origin unknown. Originally in the meaning "inferior horse."] —**tack·i·ly** *adv.* —**tack·i·ness** *n.*

tac·ma·hack *n.* = **tacamahac**

ta·co /taá kō/ (*plural* **-cos**) *n.* a crisp fried corn tortilla usually filled with meat, lettuce, tomatoes, cheese, and hot sauce [Mid-20thC. Via American Spanish from Spanish, "wad."]

Ta·co·ma /tə kṓmə/ city in western Washington State, a deepwater port on Commencement Bay, an arm of Puget Sound. Population: 183,060 (1994).

tac·o·nite /tákə nìt/ *n.* a banded iron formation consisting of layers of the iron oxides magnetite and hematite that may be extracted from ground-up rock using a magnet [Early 20thC. Named for *Taconic*, a mountain range in New York State where it was first found.]

tact /takt/ *n.* **1. ABILITY TO AVOID GIVING OFFENSE** skill in situations in which other people's feelings have to be considered **2. DISCRETION** an intuitive sense of what is right or appropriate [Early 17thC. Via French from Latin *tactus* "(sense of) touch," from *tangere* "to touch."]

tact·ful /táktfəl/ *adj.* having or showing concern about upsetting or offending people —**tact·ful·ly** *adv.* —**tact·ful·ness** *n.*

tac·tic /táktik/ *n.* a method used or a course of action followed in order to achieve an immediate or short-term aim [Mid-17thC. Via modern Latin from Greek *taktikos* "of arrangement," from *taktos* "arranged," from *tassein* "to arrange."]

tac·ti·cal /táktik'l/ *adj.* **1. OF TACTICS** relating to or involving tactics **2. AS MEANS TO END** done or made for the purpose of trying to achieve an immediate or short-term aim **3. SHOWING SKILLFUL PLANNING** showing skillful planning in order to accomplish something **4.** MIL **WITH LIMITED MILITARY OBJECTIVE** used or made to support limited military operations **5.** MIL **SUPPORTING OTHER MILITARY OBJECTIVE** undertaken or for use in support of other military and naval operations —**tac·ti·cal·ly** *adv.*

tac·ti·cian /tak tísh'n/ *n.* somebody who is skilled at using tactics or responsible for tactics, or somebody with a particular kind of tactical ability

tac·tics /táktiks/ *n.* (*takes a singular verb*) **1.** MIL **DIRECTION OF FORCES IN BATTLE** the science of organizing and maneuvering forces in battle to achieve a limited or immediate aim **2. FINDING MEANS TO END** the art of finding and implementing means to achieve particular immediate or short-term aims

tac·tile /tákt'l/ *adj.* **1. OF TOUCH** relating to or used for the sense of touch **2. TANGIBLE** capable of perception by the sense of touch **3. HABITUALLY TOUCHING PEOPLE** inclined to touch people a lot, e.g., while talking to them **4.** ARTS **APPARENTLY THREE-DIMENSIONAL** giving an illusion of physical solidity and tangibility **5. PLEASANT TO TOUCH** pleasing or interesting to the sense of touch [Early 17thC. Directly or via French from Latin *tactilis*, from *tactus* (see TACT).] —**tac·tile·ly** *adv.* —**tac·til·i·ty** /tak tíllətee/ *n.*

tac·tile cor·pus·cle, **tac·tile bud** *n.* a tiny egg-shaped touch receptor that responds to light pressure and is found in the skin of the palms, lips, soles, and other hairless sensitive areas

tact·less /táktləss/ *adj.* lacking or showing a lack of concern about upsetting or offending people —**tact·less·ly** *adv.* —**tact·less·ness** *n.*

tac·tu·al /tákchoo əl/ *adj.* relating to the sense of touch or imparting the sensation of contact [Mid-17thC. Formed from Latin *tactus* (see TACT).] —**tac·tu·al·ly** *adv.*

tad /tad/ *n.* (*informal*) **1. SMALL AMOUNT** a very slight amount or degree of something **2. SMALL BOY** a small child, especially a boy [Late 19thC. Origin uncertain: perhaps a shortening of TADPOLE.]

tad·pole /tád pòl/ *n.* the aquatic larva of a frog, toad, or salamander that has a limbless round body, gills, and a tail [15thC. From earlier forms of TOAD + POLL.]

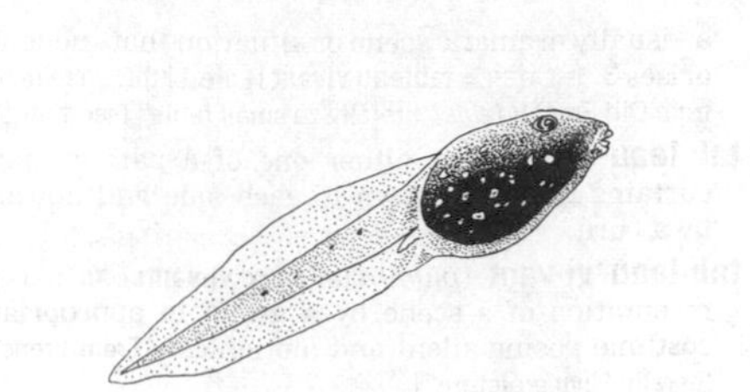

Tadpole

Ta·dzhik, **Ta·dzhik·i** *n.* PEOPLES, LANG = **Tajik**

Ta·dzhik·i·stan = **Tajikistan**

tae kwon do /tì kwon dṓ/ *n.* a Korean martial art resembling karate but also employing a wide range of kicking moves [Mid-20thC. From Korean, literally "art of hand and foot fighting."]

tael /tayl/ *n.* **1.** MEASURE **E ASIAN UNIT OF WEIGHT** a varying unit of weight used in East Asia, usually around 1.75 oz/38 g **2.** MONEY **OLD UNIT OF CHINESE CURRENCY** a silver coin that was a unit of currency in China between 1889 and 1912, equivalent to a tael of silver [Late 16thC. Via Portuguese from Malay *tahil*, unit of weight.]

ta'en *v.* taken (*archaic or literary*)

tae·ni·a /téenee ə/ (*plural* **-ae** *or* **-as**), **te·ni·a** (*plural* **-ae** /téenee ee/ *or* **-as**) *n.* **1.** ANAT **PART SHAPED LIKE RIBBON** a body part that resembles a ribbon, especially muscle or nervous tissue **2.** ARCHIT **HORIZONTAL BAND IN DORIC ARCHITECTURE** in the Doric order of ancient Greek architecture, a narrow band (**fillet**) between the main beam (**architrave**) across the top of the columns and the frieze above **3.** ZOOL **PARASITIC TAPEWORM** a large parasitic tapeworm. Genus: *Taenia*. **4.** CLOTHES, HISTORY **NARROW HEADBAND** a fillet or headband worn in ancient Greece [Mid-16thC. Via Latin from Greek *tainia* "band."]

tae·ni·a·cide /téenee ə sìd/, **te·ni·a·cide** *n.* a substance for killing tapeworms

tae·ni·a·fuge /téenee ə fyooj/, **te·ni·a·fuge** *n.* a drug or other agent that expels tapeworms from the body

tae·ni·a·sis /tee nī́ əssis/, **te·ni·a·sis** *n.* infestation with adult tapeworms, usually following the eating of raw or undercooked meat containing tapeworm larvae

taf·fe·ta /táffətə/ *n.* a stiff lustrous silk or a silky fabric with a slight rib, usually used for women's clothes [14thC. Via medieval Latin or Old French *taffetas* from, ultimately, Persian *tāftah*, from *tāftan* "to shine."]

taff·rail /táf ràyl/ *n.* NAUT **1. STERN RAIL** the rail around the stern of a ship **2. TOP PART OF STERN** the upper flat and often carved part of a ship's stern [Early 19thC. From Dutch *taffereel*, literally "a small table," from *tafel* (see TABLE).]

taf·fy /táffee/ (*plural* **-fies**) *n.* **1. CHEWY CANDY** a chewy candy made of sugar or molasses boiled down and pulled until glossy and light in color **2. INSINCERE FLATTERY** flattery of an insincere kind (*informal dated*) [Early 19thC. Origin uncertain: probably originally a dialect form of TOFFEE.]

Taft /taft/, **Robert A.** (1889–1953) U.S. statesman. A conservative Republican senator from Ohio (1938–53), he led the opposition to the Democratic administrations of Franklin D. Roosevelt and Harry S. Truman. He was cosponsor of the Taft-Hartley Act (1947), which tightened restrictions on labor unions. Full name **Robert Alphonso Taft**. Known as **Mr. Republican**

Taft, William Howard (1857–1930) U.S. statesman and

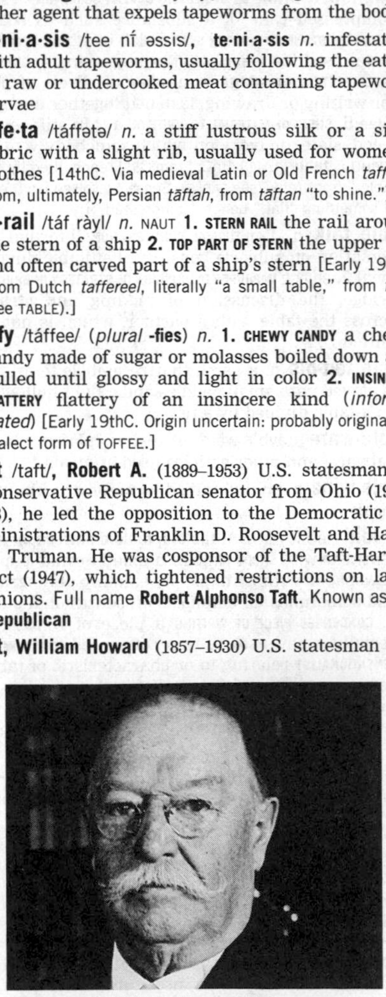

William Howard Taft

27th president of the United States. A Republican, he was president from 1909 to 1913 and chief justice of the Supreme Court from 1921 to 1930.

tag[1] /tag/ *n.* **1.** LABEL a small piece or strip of cloth, paper, plastic, or other material attached to something, especially by one end, or hung on it as a label or means of identification **2.** CRIMINOL **ELECTRONIC DEVICE WORN BY OFFENDER** an electronic device worn, usually on the ankle or wrist, by a convicted offender serving a sentence in the community to allow his or her movements to be monitored **3.** COMPUT **CLASSIFYING LABEL FOR DATA** a label that classifies a piece of data, e.g., by its type, to facilitate later retrieval **4.** **TIP AT END OF SHOELACE** a plastic or metal tip attached to the end of shoelace or cord to prevent it from fraying **5.** ZOOL **TIP OF ANIMAL'S TAIL** the tip of an animal's tail, especially if in a contrasting color with the rest of the tail **6.** **SMALL LOOSE OR RAGGED PIECE** a small piece of a material hanging loosely or raggedly from the main piece **7.** AGRIC, ZOOL **MATTED LOCK OF WOOL** a dirty matted lock of wool or hair in an animal's fleece or coat **8.** ANGLING **ATTACHMENT TO ARTIFICIAL FLY** a piece of usually brightly colored material tied around the shank of the hook in the body of an artificial fly **9.** LANG **WELL-KNOWN QUOTATION** a well-known or hackneyed quotation, often in Latin, usually intended to add dignity or weight to a speech or piece of writing **10.** LANG **EPITHET** a descriptive word or phrase used, especially frequently, about somebody or something **11.** LANG **ENDING FOR PIECE OF WRITING** an ending or added endpiece for a piece of writing, e.g., a refrain, the cue line ending an actor's speech, or a final speech addressed to the audience **12.** LING = **tag question** **13.** **GRAFFITI ARTIST'S SIGNATURE** a signature or identifying symbol used by a graffiti artist ■ *v.* (**tagged, tag·ging, tags**) **1.** *vt.* **LABEL WITH TAG** to attach a tag to something or label something with a tag **2.** *vt.* **ADD SOMETHING AT END** to add an additional piece or section to the end of something, especially a piece of writing ○ *tagged on a couple of extra lines at the end* **3.** *vt.* LANG **ATTACH EPITHET TO** to give somebody a nickname or assign a verbal label to somebody **4.** *vt.* CRIMINOL **ATTACH ELECTRONIC TAG TO OFFENDER** to make an offender wear an electronic tag **5.** *vt.* LAW **TICKET CAR** to attach a ticket to a vehicle to notify the driver that a traffic or parking offense has been committed **6.** *vt.* LAW **CHARGE SOMEBODY WITH CRIME** to charge somebody with a crime (*often passive*) ○ *tagged for theft* **7.** *vt.* LANG **ATTACH RHYMES TO SOMETHING** to put unrhymed verse or prose into rhyme **8.** *vt.* AGRIC **REMOVE TAGS FROM WOOL** to remove tags from an animal's fleece or hair **9.** *vti.* **FOLLOW CLOSELY** to follow along close behind somebody [From Middle English *tagge* "dangling section of garment," of unknown origin]

tag along *vi.* to accompany or follow somebody, often when your presence is unwanted

tag[2] /tag/ *n.* **1.** GAME **CHILDREN'S CHASING AND TOUCHING GAME** a children's game in which one player is chosen to chase the others and try to touch one of them. Anyone touched then becomes "it" and is then the player who does the chasing. **2.** BASEBALL **INSTANCE OF TAGGING RUNNER OUT** an instance of tagging a runner out in baseball **3.** WRESTLING = **tag wrestling** **4.** WRESTLING **INSTANCE OF TAGGING IN WRESTLING** an instance of tagging a partner in wrestling ■ *vt.* (**tagged, tag·ging, tags**) **1.** **CATCH PLAYER IN GAME OF TAG** to touch a player in the children's game of tag, making that player "it" **2.** BASEBALL **TOUCH RUNNER WITH BALL** to get a runner out in baseball by touching him or her with the ball before he or she reaches the base **3.** WRESTLING **TOUCH PARTNER'S HAND IN WRESTLING** to touch the hand of a partner in tag-team wrestling in order to switch places [Mid-18thC. Origin uncertain: perhaps a variant of Scots *tig* "touch," ultimately from TICK in the obsolete sense "to touch lightly."] ◇ **tag up** *vi.* in baseball, to touch a base before running to the next one after a fly ball is caught

Ta·ga·log /tə gaáləg, tə gaá lòg/ (*plural* **-log** *or* **-logs**) *n.* **1.** PEOPLES **MEMBER OF FILIPINO PEOPLE** a member of a people who originally lived in the Manila area of the Philippines **2.** LANG **TAGALOG LANGUAGE** the Austronesian language of the Tagalog people. Tagalog is the basis of Filipino, the national language of the Philippines. It is spoken by about 17 million people. [Early 19thC. From Tagalog *tagá* "native" + *ilog* "river."] —**Tagalog** *adj.*

tag·a·long /tággə lòng/ *n.* somebody or something that persistently follows another, especially somebody whose attentions are unwelcome

tag day *n.* a day when people collect money for charity and give donors a tag to wear

tag end *n.* **1.** **LAST BIT** the very last or last remaining part of something **2.** **LOOSE PIECE** a loose or detached piece of something

tag·et·es /tàjjə teéz, tə jétteez/ *n.* a marigold, especially an African or French marigold. Latin name: *Tagetes.* [Late 18thC. From modern Latin *Tagetes*, genus name, from Latin *Tages*, name of an Etruscan god.]

tag·ger /tággər/ *n.* a graffiti artist who spray-paints his or her name or symbol on a public structure (*slang*) [Mid-20thC]

tag·gers /tággərz/ *npl.* iron or steel in thin sheets coated with tin [Mid-19thC. Perhaps because such sheets were used to make shoelace tags.]

tag·li·a·tel·le /tàllyə tél/ *n.* pasta in the form of long narrow ribbons [Late 19thC. From Italian, formed from *tagliare* "to cut into strips."]

tag line *n.* **1.** **PUNCH LINE** the final line of a joke, story, or drama, delivering a humorous or dramatic point **2.** **SLOGAN** a phrase repeatedly used in connection with a person, organization, or product, especially in publicity

tag·ma /tágmə/ (*plural* **-ma·ta** /tágmətə/) *n.* a distinct functional region of the body of an arthropod, e.g., the thorax [Early 20thC. From Greek, "something arranged," from *tag-*, the stem of *tassein* "to arrange" (see TAXIS).]

tag·meme /tág meém/ *n.* any one of the various positions in the structure of a sentence into which a word or phrase of a particular grammatical type can fit [Mid-20thC. Formed from Greek *tagma* "something arranged."] —**tag·mem·ic** /tag meémik/ *adj.*

tag·mem·ics /tag meémiks/ *n.* a grammatical analysis of language based on the way in which the different elements that make up a sentence are arranged within it (*takes a singular verb*)

Rabindranath Tagore

Ta·gore /tə gáwr/, **Rabindranath** (1861–1941) Indian writer. A prolific author of poetry, plays, short stories, and novels, he revolutionized Bengali poetry by using colloquial language and new verse forms, and translated his own works into English. He was awarded the Nobel Prize in literature in 1913.

tag ques·tion *n.* a short clause added on to a statement to turn it into a question, e.g., "don't you?" or "isn't it?", or a statement with a question clause attached. The main function of a tag question is to cue a response from the listener or obtain his or her agreement to the original statement.

tag team *n.* a team of two wrestlers, only one of whom may wrestle at a time. Wrestlers change places only after touching hands.

tag·uan /taá gwaán/ *n.* a large nocturnal East Indian flying squirrel that leaps from tree to tree with the help of skin flaps that stretch between its limbs. Latin name: *Petaurista petaurista.* [Early 19thC. Origin uncertain: probably from a local name in the Philippines.]

Ta·gus /táygəs/ the longest river of the Iberian Peninsula, in southwestern Europe. It enters the Atlantic Ocean at Lisbon, Portugal. Length: 626 mi./1,007 km.

tag wrestling *n.* a form of wrestling in which wrestlers compete in teams of two or more, taking it in turns to enter the ring, a touch of hands being required for a changeover

ta·hi·ni /tə heénee/, **tahina** /tə heénə/ *n.* an oily paste made from crushed sesame seeds, used as seasoning [Mid-20thC. From Arabic *ṭaḥīnā*, from *ṭaḥana* "to grind."]

Ta·hi·ti /tə heétee/ island of French Polynesia, the largest of the Society Islands, in the southern Pacific Ocean. Population: 115,820 (1998). Area: 400 sq. mi./1,036 sq. km. —**Ta·hi·tian** *n., adj.*

Ta·hoe, Lake /taáhō/ lake in the western United States, lying on the border between Nevada and California. Area: 193 sq. mi./500 sq. km.

tahr /taar/ *n.* a ruminant mammal similar to a goat, with a shaggy coat and curved horns, that is native to mountainous regions in southern Asia. Genus: *Hemitragus.* [Mid-19thC. From Nepalese *thār.*]

tah·sil /taa seél/ *n.* an administrative district in some states of India [Mid-19thC. Via Urdu and Persian from *taḥṣīl* "revenue," from Arabic *ḥaṣala* "to collect."]

tah·sil·dar /taá seel daár/ *n.* in India, a government official in charge of collecting taxes and other revenues in a tahsil [Late 18thC. Via Urdu *taḥṣīldār* from Persian, literally "revenue-holder," from *taḥṣīl* (see TAHSIL).]

Tai /tī/ (*plural* **Tai** *or* **Tais**) *n.* LANG a group of tonal languages spoken in Southeast Asia, including Thai and Lao. Tai is sometimes considered to be related to the Sino-Tibetan language family. —**Tai** *adj.*

ta·ia·ha /tí ə haá, taá ee ə haá/ *n.* *NZ* a carved Maori staff, formerly used as a weapon, now carried by speakers at public ceremonies [Mid-19thC. From Maori.]

tai chi /tī cheé/, **Tai Chi, T'ai Chi, tai chi chuan** /tī chee chwaán/, **Tai Chi Chuan, T'ai Chi Ch'uan** *n.* a Chinese form of physical exercise characterized by a series of very slow and deliberate balletic body movements

tai·ga /tígə/ *n.* the subarctic coniferous forests of North America, northern Europe, and Asia located south of tundra [Late 19thC. From Russian, of Altaic origin.]

tail /tayl/ *n.* **1.** ZOOL **REAR PART OF ANIMAL'S BODY** the flexible rear part, or a movable extension to the rear part, of a vertebrate animal's body, that begins above the anus and often contains the terminal vertebrae **2.** **REAR PART OF SOMETHING** the rear, last, or lowest part of something ○ *the tail of the procession* **3.** AIR **REAR OF AIRCRAFT** the rear part of an aircraft together with horizontal and vertical stabilizing surfaces attached to it **4.** **BUTTOCKS** the buttocks (*informal*) **5.** ASTRON **STREAM OF GAS FROM COMET** the luminous stream of gas and dust particles driven by the solar wind from a comet as it approaches and then recedes from the sun **6.** **OFFENSIVE TERM** an offensive term used by some men to refer to sexual intercourse with a woman (*taboo offensive*) **7.** **OFFENSIVE TERM** an offensive term used by some men to refer to a woman perceived only as a potential partner for sexual intercourse (*taboo offensive*) **8.** **OFFENSIVE TERM** an offensive term used to refer to a woman's genitals (*taboo offensive*) **9.** **SOMEBODY FOLLOWING ANOTHER** somebody who secretly follows or observes another (*informal*) ○ *The police put a round-the-clock tail on the suspect.* **10.** **TRAIL** somebody's trail, especially when he or she is being followed or pursued (*informal*) **11.** HAIR **LONG LOCK OR BRAID OF HAIR** a long lock or braid of hair **12.** ARMS **REAR OF MISSILE** the rear part of a missile or bomb, including structures for controlling the angle of the trajectory **13.** PRINTING **BOTTOM OF PAGE** the bottom of a printed page, or the margin between the bottom of the page and the lowest line of type **14.** **PEOPLE IN A LINE** a line of people or things **15.** HIST = **horsetail** *n.* 2 ■ **tails** *npl.* **1.** CLOTHES **MAN'S FORMAL COAT WITH TAILS** a formal, usually black coat for a man, cut short at the front and with two long tails at the back **2.** CLOTHES **MAN'S EVENING CLOTHES** full evening clothes for a man **3.** **REVERSE OF COIN** the reverse side of a coin ■ *v.* (**tailed, tail·ing, tails**) **1.** *vt.* **FOLLOW SOMEBODY SECRETLY** to follow somebody secretly in order to keep watch on him or her (*informal*) ○ *Someone must have tailed you back to the house.* **2.** *vi.* **FOLLOW** to follow behind somebody or something ○ *She strode out purposefully, leaving the rest of the party to tail along behind.* **3.** *vi.* **FORM LINE** to form a long line when moving, especially a long spread-out line **4.** *vt.* **REMOVE STALK FROM FRUIT** to remove the stalk from something such as a piece of fruit **5.** *vt.* VET, AGRIC **REMOVE TAIL OF ANIMAL** to remove or cut short the tail of an animal **6.** *vt.* **JOIN THINGS END TO END** to join two or more things end to end **7.** *vti.* CONSTR **BUILD SOMETHING INTO WALL** to build one end of something such as a joist, beam, or brick, into a wall, or to be fixed into a wall at one end **8.** *vi.* NAUT **LIE WITH STERN**

IN PARTICULAR DIRECTION to lie with the stern pointing in a particular direction when moored [Old English *tægel*, from prehistoric Germanic] —**tail·less** *adj.* —**tail·less·ness** *n.* ◇ **turn tail** turn and walk or run away ◇ **with your tail between your legs** in an abject, ashamed manner

WORD KEY: SYNONYMS
See Synonyms at ***follow.***

tail off *vi.* to grow less, smaller, or fainter, usually gradually

tail·back /táyl bàk/ *n.* the offensive back positioned farthest behind the line of scrimmage in a football game

tail beam *n.* = **tailpiece**

tail·bone /táyl bōn/ *n.* = **coccyx**

tail·coat /táyl kōt/ *n.* a formal, usually black coat for a man, cut short at the front and with two long tails at the back

tail cov·ert *n.* any one of the small feathers on a bird's tail that cover the bases of the tail feathers

tail end *n.* **1.** LAST PART the last or hindmost part of something **2.** BUTTOCKS the buttocks (*informal*)

tail·en·der /tayl éndər/ *n.* somebody or something that comes at or toward the end of something or in last place (*informal*)

tail fan *n.* a fan-shaped structure at the rear end of some crustaceans such as the lobster

tail·gate /táyl gàyt/ *n.* **1.** GATE AT BACK OF VEHICLE a gate at the back of a truck or utility vehicle that can be laid flat or dropped down during loading or unloading **2.** GATE IN WATERWAY a gate controlling the flow of water at the lower end of a lock in a waterway ■ *v.* (**-gat·ed, -gat·ing, -gates**) **1.** *vti.* DRIVE CLOSE BEHIND to drive very close behind another vehicle **2.** *vi.* HAVE TAILGATE PARTY to have a tailgate party —**tail·gat·er** *n.*

tail·gate party *n.* a social gathering before a sports event game held in a parking lot outside the stadium. Spectators park close together and use their vehicles and the adjoining space for picnicking, barbecuing, and other activities.

tail·ing /táyling/ *n.* BUILT-IN END the end of something such as a beam that is built into a wall during construction ■ **tail·ings** *npl.* WASTE LEFT AFTER ORE PROCESSING the waste left after ore has been extracted from rock

tail lamp *n.* = **taillight**

taille /tī, tayl/ *n.* a tax levied by the French monarch on his subjects before the French Revolution [Mid-16thC. From French, "tax," literally "a cut."]

tail·light /táyl lìt/ *n.* a red light, usually one of two, mounted at the rear of a vehicle

tai·lor /táylər/ *n.* CLOTHES MAKER somebody who makes, alters, or repairs clothes ■ *v.* (**-lored, -lor·ing, -lors**) **1.** *vti.* MAKE CLOTHES FOR PARTICULAR NEED to make clothes to meet a particular need or for a particular person **2.** *vt.* ADAPT SOMETHING to adapt something to make it suitable for a particular purpose **3.** *vi.* WORK AS TAILOR to work as a tailor [13thC. Via Anglo-Norman *taillour* from Old French *tailleur* "cutter," from *taillier* "to cut," from late Latin *taliare*, from Latin *talea* "twig, cutting."]

tai·lor·bird /táylər bùrd/ *n.* a tropical Asian warbler that makes a nest by sewing leaves together with plant fibers. Genus: *Orthotomus.*

tai·lored /táylərd/ *adj.* **1.** CLOTHES MADE TO FIT NEATLY marked by a neat fit with trim lines and a clean and formal or severe look **2.** CLOTHES MADE BY TAILOR made by a tailor **3.** MADE FOR PARTICULAR PURPOSE made or adapted for a particular purpose

tai·lor-made *adj.* **1.** IDEAL FOR SOMEBODY OR SOMETHING perfectly suited to somebody or for a particular purpose **2.** MADE BY TAILOR made by a tailor rather than in a factory ■ *n.* SOMETHING MADE BY TAILOR a garment made by a tailor

tai·lor's chalk *n.* a chalk used by tailors to mark out the positions of cuts or alterations on material

tail·piece /táyl peess/ *n.* **1.** END something that forms an end or is added at the end of something **2.** PRINTING DECORATION AT BOTTOM OF PAGE a decoration at the bottom of a page, e.g., at the end of a chapter **3.** MUSIC PART OF STRINGED INSTRUMENT a piece of wood or metal at the lower end of a stringed instrument such as a violin, to which the strings are attached **4.** BEAM EMBEDDED IN WALL a beam that has one end embedded in a wall

tail·pipe /táyl pìp/ *n.* a pipe through which exhaust gases are expelled from an internal-combustion engine, e.g., in a motor vehicle or aircraft

tail·plane /táyl plàyn/ *n.* the horizontal part of the tail of an aircraft, designed to give stability

tail·race /táyl ràyss/ *n.* **1.** CHANNEL CARRYING WATER AWAY FROM MILL a channel that carries water that has passed through a mill wheel or turbine **2.** CHANNEL CARRYING AWAY MINE TAILINGS a channel that carries away mine tailings in water

tail rotor *n.* a small propeller on the tail of a helicopter that counteracts the main rotor, preventing the body of the helicopter from rotating in the opposite direction to it

tail·skid /táyl skìd/ *n.* **1.** SUPPORT UNDER AIRCRAFT TAIL a support or runner on the underside of the tail of an aircraft **2.** REAR WHEEL SKID a skidding of the rear wheels of a motor vehicle

tail·spin /táyl spìn/ *n.* **1.** SPIRAL DESCENT a rapid spiral descent of an aircraft **2.** STATE OF PANIC a state of great confusion or distress (*informal*)

tail·stock /táyl stòk/ *n.* a movable part of a lathe, used to support the free end of the workpiece and permitting it to rotate freely

tail·wind /táyl wìnd/ *n.* a wind that blowing in the same direction that a ship or aircraft is traveling. A tailwind adds to an aircraft's effective speed.

Tai·no /tī nō/ (*plural* **-no** *or* **-nos**) *n.* PEOPLES a member of a Native Central American people that formerly lived on the Caribbean islands of the Greater Antilles and the Bahamas and died out during the 16th century [Mid-19thC. From Taino.]

taint /taynt/ *v.* (**taint·ed, taint·ing, taints**) **1.** *vt.* POLLUTE SOMETHING to pollute or contaminate something with something undesirable or dangerous **2.** *vt.* CORRUPT SOMEBODY MORALLY to corrupt somebody morally or detract from somebody's reputation by associating him or her with something reprehensible **3.** *vt.* FLAVOR SOMETHING to give a scent or flavor of one thing to another **4.** *vi.* SPOIL to spoil or become rotten ■ *n.* **1.** IMPERFECTION DETRACTING FROM QUALITY an imperfection that detracts from the quality of somebody or something ○ *a taint on her reputation* **2.** SOMETHING DETRACTING FROM PURITY OF SOMETHING something that detracts from the purity or cleanliness of something [Late 16thC. Partly via Anglo-Norman *teint*, literally "colored, dyed," from Latin *tingere* (see TINGE), and partly from Old French *ataint* "convicted," the past participle of *ateindre* (see ATTAIN).] —**taint·less** *adj.*

'tain't /taynt/ *contr.* it ain't (*nonstandard*)

tai·pan[1] /tī pàn/ *n.* a foreigner in charge of a business or trading operation in China, especially a powerful business tycoon [Mid-19thC. From Chinese (Cantonese) *daaihbāan.*]

tai·pan[2] /tī pàn/ *n.* a large, rare, and highly venomous snake found in northern Australia, brown in color with a lighter brown belly, that can grow to 11 ft./3.3 m in length. Latin name: *Oxyuranus scutellatus.* [Mid-20thC. Of Australian Aboriginal origin.]

Tai·pei /tī páy, -báy/, **T'ai·pei** capital city of Taiwan. The largest city in the country, it is officially regarded as its temporary capital. Population: 2,702,678 (1994).

Tai·ping /tī píng/ *n.* somebody who supported or took part in the Taiping rebellion against the Manchu dynasty in China between 1850 and 1864 [Mid-19thC. From Chinese *tài píng*, literally "great peace."]

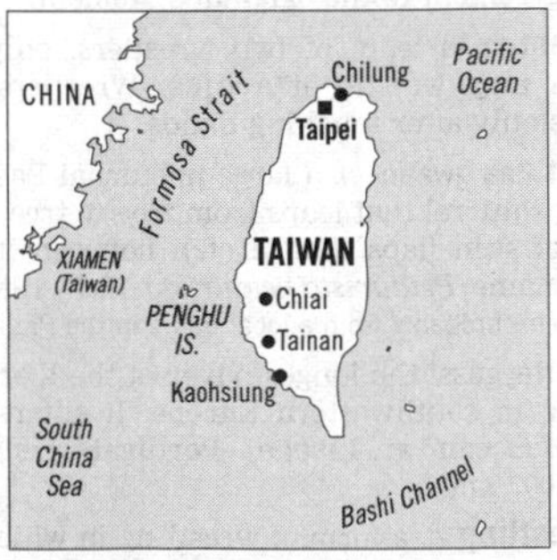

Taiwan

Tai·wan /tī wáan/ country occupying the island of Taiwan and neighboring small islands, administered separately since 1949 by the Chinese Nationalist government after its retreat from mainland China. It is claimed as a province by the People's Republic of China. Language: Mandarin Chinese. Currency: New Taiwan dollar. Capital: Taipei. Population: 21,703,304 (1997). Area: 13,900 sq. mi./36,000 sq. km. Official name **Republic of Taiwan** —**Tai·wan·ese** *n., adj.*

Tai·yu·an /tī ywán, tī yoo án/ capital city of Shanxi Province in northern China, southwest of Beijing. Population: 1,960,000 (1990).

taj /taaj/ *n.* a tall brimless conical cap, often richly decorated, worn by Muslims as a mark of distinction [Late 19thC. Via Arabic from Persian *tāj* "crown." Ultimately from an Indo-European word meaning "to cover" that is also the ancestor of English *tegument* and *tile.*]

Ta·jik /taa jík/ (*plural* **-jiks** *or* **-jik** /taa jeek/), **Ta·dzhik** (*plural* **-dzhiks** *or* **-dzhik**) *n.* **1.** PEOPLES SOMEBODY FROM TAJIKISTAN somebody who was born and raised in Tajikistan, or who has Tajik citizenship **2. Ta·jik, Ta·dzhik, Ta·jik·i, Ta·dzhik·i** LANG OFFICIAL LANGUAGE OF TAJIKISTAN the official language of Tajikistan. It belongs to the Iranian group of Indo-European languages. Tajik is spoken by about 4.5 million people. [Early 19thC. From Persian.] —**Ta·jik** *adj.*

Ta·jik·i /taa jíkee/, **Ta·dzhik·i** *n.* LANG = **Tajik** *n.* **2** ■ *adj.* PEOPLES RELATING TO TAJIKS relating to the Tajiks or their culture

Tajikistan

Ta·jik·i·stan /taa jíkee stàn, -staàn/, **Ta·dzhik·i·stan** republic in southeastern Central Asia, bordered by Kyrgyzstan, Uzbekistan, China, and Afghanistan. It was part of the Soviet Union until 1991. Language: Tajik. Currency: Tajik ruble. Capital: Dushanbe. Population: 5,945,903 (1997). Area: 55,250 sq. mi./143,100 sq. km. Official name **Republic of Tajikistan**

Barnaby's

Taj Mahal

Taj Ma·hal /taaj mə haal/ *n.* a white marble mausoleum in Agra, northern India, completed in 1643 in memory of Mumtaz Mahal, the wife of Mughal emperor Shah Jahan. It is considered the greatest example of Mughal architcture.

ta·ka /taakə/ *n.* **1.** UNIT OF BANGLADESHI CURRENCY a unit of currency in Bangladesh, worth 100 paisas. See table at **currency 2.** COIN OR BILL WORTH ONE TAKA a coin or bill worth one taka [Late 20thC. Via Bengali *ṭākā* from Sanskrit *ṭaṅkaḥ* "stamped coin."]

Takakkaw Falls /tá kək aw-/ Canada's highest falls, located in Yoho National Park, British Columbia. Height: 1,650 ft./503 m.

take /tayk/ *v.* (**took** /tòok/, **tak·en** /táykən/, **tak·ing, takes**) **1.** *vt.* REMOVE SOMETHING to remove or steal something belonging to somebody else ○ *I wish you wouldn't take things without asking.* **2.** *vt.* GET A HOLD OF SOMEBODY to get a hold of something or somebody using a hand, or receive something into your hand ○ *She took him by the arm and steered him out of the room.*

3. *vt.* **CARRY SOMETHING** to carry, bring, or transport something or somebody from one place to another ○ *We'll need to take plenty of warm clothing.* **4.** *vt.* **WIN SOMETHING** to capture or gain possession of a place, area, or object, or win something in a contest or competition ○ *took the town after a long siege* ○ *took first prize in the competition.* **5.** *vt.* **SELECT SOMETHING OR SOMEBODY** to choose an individual object or person from a number available ○ *Here, take a chocolate.* **6.** *vt.* **GET INTO OR ONTO SOMETHING** to place yourself in something, or start to occupy something ○ *Please take a seat.* **7.** *vt.* **CLAIM OR ASSUME SOMETHING** to obtain something, especially credit, glory, or blame, or accept or maintain that this is deserved ○ *He doesn't mind taking the credit for the party's recent successes.* **8.** *vt.* **REGULARLY RECEIVE SOMETHING** to buy, consume, or perform something as a regular habit ○ *We take the Sunday paper.* ○ *I've stopped taking lunch breaks.* **9.** *vt.* **LEAD SOMEBODY SOMEWHERE** to enable somebody to go toward a particular place or in a specified direction, or go along something that leads to a particular place ○ *Will this road take us to the beach?* ○ *Take the first road on the left.* **10.** *vt.* **AGREE TO PERFORM SOMETHING** to agree to perform or assume the duties associated with something ○ *I decided to take the job.* **11.** *vt.* **BE WILLING TO ACCEPT SOMETHING** to be prepared to accept something as valid, true, or satisfactory ○ *The machine refused to take my card.* **12.** *vt.* **BE ABLE TO BEAR SOMETHING** to endure, deal with, accept, or put up with something, especially when it is unpleasant or unavoidable ○ *She cannot take criticism.* **13.** *vt.* **REACT TO SOMETHING** to behave, feel, or act in response to being told or finding out about something ○ *I don't know how they will take the news.* **14.** *vt.* **HAVE STRENGTH TO HOLD UP SOMETHING** to be capable of supporting something physically, without collapsing or breaking ○ *Will the shelf take the weight of all those books?* **15.** *vt.* **TRAVEL BY MEANS OF SOMETHING** to use a particular means of transport to make a journey ○ *Let's take a taxi.* **16.** *vt.* **HAVE ROOM FOR SOMETHING** to be capable of containing a specified amount or quantity of something ○ *The tank takes 20 gallons.* **17.** *vt.* **WRITE SOMETHING** to record something in a written form ○ *Do you mind if I take notes?* **18.** *vt.* PHOTOGRAPHY **CAPTURE SOMETHING ON CAMERA** to use a camera to make a photograph ○ *Let's take a few photos to record the event.* **19.** *vt.* EDUC **STUDY SOMETHING** to study something on a formal basis ○ *I took physics in my senior year.* **20.** *vt.* **START TO DO SOMETHING** to start to perform or occupy something ○ *The new treasurer takes office next month.* **21.** *vt.* **CARRY OUT SOMETHING** to perform or carry out something ○ *I'll take action on this immediately.* **22.** *vt.* **TRAVEL OVER OR AROUND SOMETHING** to travel over or around something, especially in a vehicle or on a motorcycle or horse and in a particular way ○ *He took the bend too fast.* **23.** *vt.* **DERIVE FROM SOMETHING OR SOMEBODY** to copy or derive something from a particular text or author (*often passive*) ○ *That quote is taken from Shakespeare.* **24.** *vt.* **CONSIDER SOMETHING** to use somebody or something as an example or as a subject for consideration or discussion ○ *Let's take your last point first.* **25.** *vt.* **REQUIRE PARTICULAR LENGTH OF TIME** to need a particular amount of time to be completed or performed ○ *The trip usually takes about three hours.* **26.** *vt.* **NEED SOMETHING IN ORDER TO FUNCTION** to need a particular thing in order to operate ○ *This cassette recorder takes four size C batteries.* **27.** *vt.* **REQUIRE SOMETHING** to require something, especially a particular quality or characteristic, for something to be achieved ○ *It took a lot of courage to admit that you were wrong.* **28.** *vt.* **EXPERIENCE EMOTION OR HAVE VIEW** to experience a particular emotion, have a particular reaction, or adopt a particular opinion with regard to something ○ *They looked so pathetic I took pity on them.* **29.** *vt.* **INTERPRET SOMETHING IN PARTICULAR WAY** to interpret, recognize, or understand something, especially somebody's words or actions, in a particular way ○ *I took her silence as a rejection.* **30.** *vt.* **ASSUME SOMETHING** to make an assumption, usually a mistaken one, about somebody's identity or about the nature of a thing or a situation ○ *I took you for her sister.* **31.** *vt.* **CONSUME SOMETHING** to swallow or receive something into the body or system ○ *He refuses to take his medicine.* **32.** *vt.* **EXPOSE BODY TO ELEMENTS** to go or sit out in the sun, or expose the body to other elements ○ *She was lying on the beach, taking the sun.* **33.** *vi.* **WORK OR BE SUCCESSFUL** to work or have an effect in the intended way ○ *The flu shot didn't take.* **34.** *vi.* BOT **START TO GROW** to start to grow by producing roots ○ *The cutting has taken nicely.* **35.** *vt.* **MEASURE SOMETHING** to measure something in an accurate way using a special instrument or procedure ○ *His temperature was normal when I took it this morning.* **36.** *vi.* **BECOME ILL** to become noticeably or suddenly unwell or more unwell ○ *The whole family took sick.* **37.** *vt.* MATH **SUBTRACT NUMBER** to subtract a number or quantity from something ○ *Take 19 from 36 and you get 17.* **38.** *vt.* **ASSUME CHARGE OF SOMETHING** to assume control of something as a person who holds authority or has the attention of others ○ *She took the chair at the meeting.* **39.** *vt.* **HAVE SEX WITH SOMEBODY** to penetrate somebody in an act of sexual intercourse, especially perfunctorily or without the person's consent **40.** *vti.* ANGLING **BITE** to bite the hook or fly at the end of an angler's line or the bait containing the hook ○ *The fish just weren't taking that morning.* **41.** *vt.* **CHEAT SOMEBODY** to cheat or swindle somebody, especially out of a particular amount of money ■ *n.* **1.** COMM **MONEY OBTAINED IN BUSINESS TRANSACTIONS** the amount of money received from customers or clients during a specified period of time ○ *What was the take last week?* **2.** CINEMA **CAMERA SHOT** a single uninterrupted recording of a piece of the action in a movie by a camera ○ *This is the 15th take of this scene.* **3.** MUSIC **SINGLE UNINTERRUPTED SOUND RECORDING** a single uninterrupted session in which a work or section of a work is recorded by audio recording equipment **4.** ANGLING **GRABBING OF BAIT** the action of a fish in picking up or grabbing a bait or lure **5.** **IMPRESSION** a personal impression or opinion of something ○ *What's your take on his presentation?* [Pre-12thC. From Old Norse *taka*.] —**tak·a·ble** *adj.* ◇ **be taken aback** be startled or disconcerted ◇ **be taken with somebody or something** to find somebody or something pleasing or attractive ◇ **on the take** taking or willing to take bribes (*informal*) ◇ **take it 1.** to be able to tolerate a situation, usually one involving hardship, punishment, or criticism **2.** to assume that something is true ○ *I take it that you want some breakfast* ◇ **take it or leave it 1.** used to indicate that somebody can either accept or refuse something, but cannot alter the conditions **2.** to be able either to accept or do something, or decline or not do something ◇ **take part** to be actively involved in something, usually as a member of a group

take after *vt.* **1.** **RESEMBLE SOMEBODY** to look or behave like somebody else, especially within the same family **2.** **BEGIN CHASING SOMEBODY** to begin to pursue somebody

take apart *vt.* **1.** **DISMANTLE SOMETHING** to reduce something whole to its individual parts or pieces **2.** **CRITICIZE SOMETHING** to criticize somebody or something in a severe and detailed way (*informal*) **3.** **BEAT SOMEBODY SEVERELY** to give somebody a severe beating or inflict a heavy defeat on somebody (*informal*)

take away *vt.* **1.** **REMOVE SOMETHING** to remove or take something or somebody elsewhere **2.** **SUBTRACT A NUMBER** to subtract a number or quantity

take back *vt.* **1.** **WITHDRAW SOMETHING** to withdraw something said or written **2.** **REGAIN POSSESSION OF SOMETHING** to gain possession of something previously held but lost or given up **3.** COMM **RETURN SOMETHING BOUGHT AS UNACCEPTABLE** to return an unwanted or unsatisfactory article to the place where it was bought for a refund or exchange **4.** COMM **ACCEPT GOODS BACK** to accept an article returned as unwanted or unsatisfactory and offer a refund or exchange **5.** **REACCEPT SOMEBODY** to reaccept somebody into a relationship or home **6.** **REMIND SOMEBODY OF PAST** to remind somebody of an earlier time

take down *vt.* **1.** **LOWER IN POSITION** to move something from a higher position to a lower one **2.** **DISMANTLE SOMETHING** to dismantle or demolish something **3.** **HUMILIATE SOMEBODY** to make somebody less arrogant or powerful ○ *That public criticism sure took him down a peg or two!* **4.** **WRITE SOMETHING DOWN** to make a note of something in writing ○ *take down the names and addresses of the witnesses* **5.** WRESTLING **FORCE OPPONENT TO FALL** to force an opponent to the mat during a wrestling match

take for *vt.* to think of somebody or something as being of a particular description, often mistakenly ○ *Do you take me for a fool?*

take in *vt.* **1.** **DECEIVE SOMEBODY** to deceive somebody by presenting a false appearance ○ *We were all taken in by her plausible manner.* **2.** **INCLUDE SOMETHING** to include something within its scope ○ *The study takes in the whole postwar period.* **3.** **ACCEPT PEOPLE AS PAYING GUESTS** to accept people as paying guests into a home **4.** **GIVE SOMEBODY SHELTER** to give somebody shelter in your home **5.** SEW **MAKE GARMENT NARROWER** to alter a garment to make it narrower **6.** **GO AND SEE** to go and see some kind of entertainment or sport ○ *take in a movie* **7.** **UNDERSTAND SOMETHING** to understand and remember something ○ *Children can't be expected to take in so much new information in one lesson.* **8.** **BRING SOMEBODY TO POLICE STATION** to bring somebody as a prisoner or witness to a police station **9.** BUSINESS **WORK ON SOMETHING AT HOME** to do paid work on something at home ○ *takes in ironing twice a week* **10.** **ACCEPT SOMETHING AS REAL** to accept something as real or true ○ *The news was such a shock that we still haven't taken it in.*

take off *v.* **1.** *vi.* **BEGIN FLYING** to leave the ground and begin flying **2.** *vt.* **HAVE AS A BREAK FROM WORK** to spend a particular amount of time not working ○ *I took a day off for the wedding.* **3.** *vt.* **REMOVE A GARMENT** to remove something you are wearing **4.** *vt.* **DEDUCT AN AMOUNT** to deduct an amount from a price or sum **5.** *vi.* **SUCCEED** to begin suddenly to be very successful or popular (*informal*) **6.** *vi.* **JUMP** to leave the ground at the beginning of a jump **7.** *vi.* **DEPART** to leave, especially in a hurry or on short notice (*informal*) **8.** *vt.* **IMITATE SOMEBODY** to imitate somebody or something, especially for comic effect (*informal*) **9.** *vt.* **RELEASE SOMETHING** to remove the restraining effect of something ○ *Take the brake off.* **10.** *vt.* **STOP SOMETHING OPERATING** to end the operation of something ○ *took off regular flights to the island*

WORD KEY: SYNONYMS

See Synonyms at ***imitate***.

take on *v.* **1.** *vt.* **UNDERTAKE** to begin doing something or accept responsibility for something ○ *I can't take on any more projects at the moment.* **2.** *vt.* **OPPOSE SOMEBODY OR SOMETHING** to oppose somebody or something in a competition or fight ○ *took on the city council* **3.** *vt.* TRANSP **TAKE PEOPLE OR THINGS ON BOARD** to have people or things loaded on board a vessel or vehicle **4.** *vt.* **ADOPT SOMETHING** to acquire or display a different character ○ *Her voice took on a kindlier tone.* **5.** *vt.* **HIRE SOMEBODY** to hire additional people to do work **6.** *vi.* **BE UPSET** to show extreme feelings, especially grief (*dated informal*) **7.** *vti.* *Carib* **WORRY ABOUT SOMETHING** to pay attention to or worry about somebody or something (*slang*)

take out *v.* **1.** *vt.* **HAVE SOMEBODY AS COMPANION AT SOMETHING** to take somebody as a companion or guest to a social event or function **2.** *vt.* **OBTAIN SOMETHING** to obtain something such as a permit, mortgage, or insurance by applying for it **3.** *vt.* **DIRECT ANGER AT SOMEBODY OR SOMETHING** to express or relieve a strong feeling such as anger or frustration by directing it against somebody or something that is not the actual cause of it ○ *Don't take it out on me because you didn't get the job.* **4.** *vt.* **DESTROY SOMETHING** to destroy, kill, or neutralize somebody or something took out enemy artillery (*slang*) ○ *took out enemy artillery* **5.** *vt.* **REMOVE SOMETHING** to remove or extract something from another substance **6.** *vt.* **BRING SOMETHING INTO OPEN** to bring something into the open from a place where it was contained or concealed **7.** *vt.* *Aus* **WIN** to win something, especially a sports event (*informal*) ○ *They took out this year's premiership.* **8.** *vi.* **BEGIN JOURNEY** to start out on a journey ○ *took out for the frontier*

take over *vti.* **1.** **TAKE CONTROL** to obtain or assume control of something, or gain control of something from somebody else ○ *taken over by a larger company* **2.** **TAKE SOMEBODY'S PLACE** to begin to do something or operate something in place of somebody else ○ *She takes over when I finish my shift.*

take to *vt.* **1.** **FORM LIKING FOR SOMEBODY** to develop a liking for somebody or something, especially quickly **2.** **START DOING OR USING SOMETHING** to start doing or using something as a habit, especially for help or consolation ○ *I've taken to checking that all the windows are locked before I leave the house.* **3.** **ADAPT YOURSELF** to adapt yourself to something or become comfortable with something new ○ *quickly took to the new procedure* **4.** **GO TO A PLACE** to go to a place, especially for safety ○ *The slightest cough or sneeze would make him take to his bed.* ○ *took to their cars and fled*

take up *vt.* **1.** **BEGIN DOING SOMETHING REGULARLY** to begin doing something regularly either as an occupation or a hobby **2.** **BEGIN DOING SOMETHING AGAIN** to begin doing something again after a break ○ *take up where you left off* **3.** **USE SOMETHING WASTEFULLY** to make use of or occupy something, especially in a wasteful or unwelcome way ○ *I don't want to take up too much of your time.* **4.** **ABSORB SOMETHING** to absorb a liquid **5.** SEW **SHORTEN GARMENT** to raise the hem of a garment such as a skirt to make the garment shorter **6.** **LIFT**

SOMEBODY OR SOMETHING to lift or raise something or somebody **7.** ACCEPT to accept something offered ○ *took up his offer to stay for another year* **8.** PAY OFF to pay off a debt, e.g., a mortgage

take up on *vt.* to accept somebody's offer or wager ○ *I'll take you up on that sometime.*

take up with *vt.* **1.** RAISE SOMETHING FOR DISCUSSION WITH SOMEBODY to raise a matter for discussion with somebody **2.** BEGIN ASSOCIATING WITH SOMEBODY to begin associating with a particular person or people

take·a·way[1] /táyk ə wày/, **take-a·way** *n., adj. U.K.* a football play in which the defensive team gains control of the ball from the offensive team by recovering a fumble or intercepting a pass. = **takeout**

take·a·way[2] /táyk ə wày/ *adj. U.K.* = **takeout** ■ *n. U.K.* = **takeout**

take·down /táyk dòwn/ *n.* **1.** SPORTS WRESTLING MOVE FORCING OPPONENT TO GROUND a move in wrestling or martial arts that forces an opponent to the ground **2.** INSTANCE OF HUMILIATION an instance of making somebody less arrogant or powerful **3.** ARMS EASILY DISASSEMBLED FIREARM a firearm designed to be disassembled easily and quickly ■ *adj.* EASILY DISASSEMBLED capable of being disassembled quickly

take-home pay *n.* the amount of pay left to an employee after all deductions, e.g., for tax, have been made

tak·en past participle of **take**

take-no-pris·on·ers *adj.* persistent in an assertive way

take·off /táyk àwf, -òf/ *n.* **1.** BEGINNING OF FLIGHT the process of leaving the ground and beginning to fly **2.** IMITATION an imitation of somebody or something, especially for comic effect (*informal*) **3.** POINT OF RAPID GROWTH a point at which substantial success or economic expansion is achieved and the prospect of further success or growth seems assured **4.** BEGINNING OF JUMP the act or point of leaving the ground at the beginning of a jump

take·out /táyk òwt/ *adj.* **1.** FOR EATING ELSEWHERE bought ready-made and taken away to be eaten elsewhere ○ *selling takeout food* **2.** selling ready-made food for eating elsewhere ■ *n.* **1.** PREPARED FOOD BOUGHT FOR EATING ELSEWHERE a meal bought ready-made for eating elsewhere. **2.** SHOP SELLING FOOD FOR EATING ELSEWHERE a restaurant or shop that sells ready-made food for eating elsewhere

take·o·ver /táyk ōvər/ *n.* an assumption or seizure of control of something, especially of a corporation, political entity, or organization ○ *The conglomerate's takeover of the small manufacturer stunned investors.*

tak·er /táykər/ *n.* somebody who accepts something, especially a wager or an offer (*often plural*) ○ *He offered the painting at auction, but there were no takers.*

take-up *n.* **1.** WINDING PART OF MECHANISM a part of a mechanism onto which something passing through it, e.g., tape, is wound **2.** LEVEL OF ACCEPTANCE the degree to which something offered or made available is accepted or made use of by people

ta·kin /taá keen/ *n.* a large ruminant mammal of mountainous regions of southern Asia with a heavy build, shaggy coat, and heavy horns that curve back. Latin name: *Budorcas taxicolor.* [Mid-19thC. Origin uncertain: probably from a local Tibeto-Burman name.]

tak·ing /táyking/ *adj.* **1.** CHARMING displaying a charming or fascinating appeal **2.** CATCHING infectious (*informal*)

tak·ings /táykingz/ *npl. U.K.* money received through sales by a business

taki-taki /taàkee taákee/ *n.* LANG = **Sranantongo** [alteration of *talk*]

Ta·ko·ma Park /tə kṓmə-/ city in central Maryland, a northeastern suburb of Washington, D.C. Population: 17,792 (1996).

ta·la /taálə/ (*plural* **-la** *or* **-las**) *n.* **1.** SAMOAN UNIT OF CURRENCY a unit of currency in Samoa, worth 100 sene. See table at **currency 2.** COIN OR BILL WORTH A TALA coin or bill worth one tala

tal·a·poin /tállə pòyn, -pwàn/ *n.* **1.** GUENON MONKEY a small olive-green guenon monkey that lives in swampy forests, often near villages, in western equatorial Africa. Latin name: *Cercopithecus talapoin* and *Miopithecus talapoin.* **2.** BUDDHIST MONK in Myanmar and Thailand, a Buddhist monk [Late 16thC. Via French and Portuguese from, ultimately, Mon *tala pói*, literally "lord of merit." "Guenon monkey" from the imagined resemblance of its fur to a Buddhist monk's robes.]

ta·lar·i·a /tə láiree ə/ *npl.* winged sandals worn by characters in Greek myth, especially by Hermes [Late 16thC. From Latin, the plural of *talaris* "of the ankles," from *talus* "ankle" (source of English *talon*).]

Tal·bot /tálbət, táwl-/ *n.* a dog belonging to an extinct breed of large hounds with long ears and a white or pale coat [15thC. Origin uncertain: probably from the English name *Talbot*, because hounds of this type are one of the family's traditional heraldic emblems.]

talc /talk/ *n.* **1.** SOFT HYDRATED MINERAL a soft mineral consisting of hydrated magnesium silicate, found in igneous and metamorphic rocks and used especially in making talcum powder **2.** TALCUM POWDER talcum powder (*informal*) ■ *vt.* (**talcked** *or* **talced, talck·ing** *or* **talc·ing, talcs**) APPLY TALC to put talc onto something [Late 16thC. Via French *talc* and medieval Latin *talcum* from, ultimately, Persian *ṭalḳ*.] —**talc·ose** /tál kṓss/ *adj.*

tal·ca·rie *n. Carib* a dish of curried meat or vegetables served with roti, popular in Trinidad, Guyana, and Surinam

tal·cum pow·der /tálkəm-/ *n.* a powder made from purified talc, often scented, that is put onto the skin to perfume it and absorb moisture

tale /tayl/ *n.* **1.** NARRATIVE a narrative or account of events **2.** SHORT PIECE OF FICTION a short piece of fiction, often one of a connected series **3.** PIECE OF GOSSIP an item of gossip or a malicious rumor **4.** FALSEHOOD a story or report that is untrue [Old English *talu*, from a prehistoric Germanic base meaning "to count or recount," which is also the ancestor of English *tell* and *talk*] ◇ **tell tales, tell tales out of school** to report acts of wrongdoing to somebody in authority

tale·bear·er /táyl bàirər/ *n.* somebody who informs against other people or spreads malicious rumors —**tale·bear·ing** *n.*

tal·ent /tállənt/ *n.* **1.** ABILITY a natural ability to do something well **2.** SOMEBODY WITH AN EXCEPTIONAL ABILITY a person or people with an exceptional ability **3.** *U.K.* POSSIBLE ROMANTIC PARTNERS people considered collectively as possible romantic or sexual partners (*slang*) **4.** ANCIENT UNIT any of various ancient units of weight and money [14thC. Via Old French "mental inclination" (the original sense in English), from Latin *talentum* "balance, sum of money" (from the idea of desiring things), from Greek *talanton*.]

WORD KEY: SYNONYMS

talent, gift, aptitude, flair, bent, knack, genius

CORE MEANING: the ability to do something well

talent a great natural ability to do something well that can be developed into an even greater skill; **gift** a more informal word meaning the same as *talent.* It is used especially to talk about creative or artistic abilities; **aptitude** a natural ability to do something or to learn something; **flair** a natural ability to do something, especially something creative or artistic; **bent** an inclination toward or liking for doing something, especially when this is accompanied by ability; **knack** a fairly informal word for an intuitive ability to do something well; **genius** truly exceptional talent and skill, especially when this is accompanied by original thinking.

---

tal·ent con·test *n.* = **talent show**

tal·ent scout *n.* somebody whose job is to search for people who have exceptional abilities in some field, e.g., entertainment or sports, and recruit them for professional work

tal·ent show *n.* a public performance made up of acts by amateur entertainers who compete for a prize and are sometimes given professional opportunities

tales /taylz, táy leèz/, **ta·les** *n.* (*plural* **tales;** *plural* **-les**) SUMMONS TO JURY DUTY a writ used to summon people to court to fill vacancies on a jury (*takes a singular verb*) ■ *npl.* PEOPLE FILLING JURY VACANCIES a group of people summoned to court to fill vacancies on a jury [15thC. From Latin *tales de circumstantibus* "such of the bystanders," a phrase in the writ.]

tales·man /táylzmən, táy leèzmən/ (*plural* **-men** /-mən/) *n.* somebody selected from a group to fill a vacant seat in a jury

tale·tell·er /táyl tèllər/ *n.* **1.** SOMEBODY WHO INFORMS AGAINST OTHER PEOPLE somebody who informs against other people or spreads malicious rumors **2.** STORYTELLER somebody who tells stories —**tale·tell·ing** *n.*

ta·li plural of **talus**[1]

tal·i·on /tállee ən/ *n.* a punishment that has the same nature as the crime, e.g., the death penalty for murder [15thC. Via Anglo-Norman from the Latin stem *talion-* (source of English *retaliate*).]

tal·i·pes /tállə peèz/ *n.* clubfoot (*technical*) [Mid-19thC. From modern Latin, formed from Latin *talus* "ankle" + *pes* "foot."]

tal·i·pot /tállə pòt/ *n.* a palm tree of Southeast Asia with large fan-shaped leaves. Latin name: *Corypha umbraculifera.* [Late 17thC. Via Malayalam from, ultimately, Sanskrit *tālī* "fan palm" + *patra* "leaf."]

tal·is·man /tállissmən, tállizmən/ *n.* **1.** MAGICAL OBJECT an object, e.g., a stone or jewel, believed to give magical powers to somebody who carries or wears it **2.** SOMETHING WITH MAGIC POWER anything believed to have magical properties [Mid-17thC. Via French or Spanish from, ultimately, Greek *telesma* "something consecrated," from *telein* "to complete, consecrate," from *telos* "result."] —**tal·is·man·ic** /tàlliss mánnik, tàlliz-/ *adj.*

talk /tawk/ *v.* (**talked, talk·ing, talks**) **1.** *vti.* EXPRESS SOMETHING BY SPEAKING to speak, or to express something using speech **2.** *vi.* HAVE CONVERSATION ABOUT SOMETHING to address spoken words to somebody or have a conversation with somebody **3.** *vt.* DISCUSS SUBJECT to discuss a particular subject ○ *talk business* **4.** *vi.* COMMUNICATE to communicate in a way other than by speaking ○ *talk in sign language* **5.** *vti.* SPEAK IN SPECIFIED LANGUAGE to use, or be able to use, a particular language to communicate with people ○ *talks Italian with his grandmother* **6.** *vi.* REVEAL INFORMATION to reveal information, especially when being pressured to do so ○ *They interrogated her for hours but she wouldn't talk.* **7.** *vi.* GOSSIP to discuss the affairs of others, or to spread rumors ○ *People are starting to talk.* **8.** *vi.* MAKE SOUNDS LIKE SPEECH to imitate the sounds of speech ○ *The baby is beginning to talk.* **9.** *vi.* BE PERSUASIVE to have the power to influence or persuade people (*informal*) ○ *Money talks!* **10.** *vi.* LECTURE to give a speech or lecture on a subject **11.** *vt.* SPEAK IN TERMS OF SOMETHING PARTICULAR to have to do or deal with something when discussing a particular topic (*informal*) ○ *You're talking big money for a job like that.* **12.** *vi.* BE FRIENDLY WITH SOMEBODY to be on sufficiently friendly terms with somebody to be able to have a conversation (*informal*) ○ *Don't bother asking me how she is, because we're not talking.* ■ *n.* **1.** CONVERSATION a conversation or exchange of ideas or information between two or more people **2.** THINGS SAID the things said by somebody or by a group of people in conversation ○ *The talk after dinner was mostly about politics.* **3.** SPEECH ON PARTICULAR SUBJECT a speech or lecture on a particular subject, given before an audience **4.** GOSSIP ABOUT AFFAIRS OF OTHERS idle or malicious conversation about the affairs of others **5.** EMPTY SPEECH speech about something without any intention of taking action ○ *He's all talk; he won't do anything!* **6.** THING TALKED ABOUT a subject of discussion or gossip among a group of people ○ *the talk of the town* **7.** WAY OF SPEAKING a particular way of speaking ○ *baby talk* ■ **talks** *npl.* NEGOTIATIONS formal discussions among parties to bring about a resolution to a problem ■ *adj.* BROADCAST USING INFORMAL INTERVIEWS made up mainly of informal interviews with guests or telephone calls from viewers or listeners ○ *talk radio* [13thC. Ultimately from a prehistoric Germanic base.] —**talk·er** *n.*

talk at *vt.* to speak to somebody without showing any interest in listening to the person's reply

talk back *vi.* to make an impudent reply

talk down *v.* **1.** *vi.* SPEAK PATRONIZINGLY to speak to somebody in a superior or condescending way **2.** *vt.* PREVENT SOMEBODY FROM SPEAKING to prevent somebody from speaking by speaking loudly and ignoring attempts to interrupt **3.** *vt.* TELL SOMEBODY HOW TO LAND AIRCRAFT to give radio guidance to somebody on how to land an aircraft

talk into *vt.* to persuade somebody to do something by talking to him or her ○ *We talked her into staying for dinner.*

talk out *vt.* **1.** RESOLVE SOMETHING BY TALKING to settle a difference of opinion through discussion **2.** *U.K.* BLOCK LEGISLATION BY DISCUSSION to prevent the passage of a piece of legislation, especially a bill in Parliament, by prolonging the discussion of it until it is too late to vote on it

talk out of *vt.* **1.** DISSUADE SOMEBODY to dissuade somebody from doing something by talking to him or her ○ *talked him out of buying a car* **2.** **GAIN SOMETHING BY DECEIT** to use words to convince somebody to give you something

talk over *vt.* **1.** **DISCUSS SOMETHING** to discuss something at length or thoroughly **2.** **PERSUADE SOMEBODY TO AGREE** to persuade somebody to agree with an opinion or point of view ○ *talked them over to our side*

talk up *vt.* to praise something in the hope of making it popular or successful

talk·a·thon /táwkə thòn/ *n.* a long period of discussion [Mid-20thC. Coined from TALK + MARATHON.]

talk·a·tive /táwkətiv/ *adj.* tending to talk readily and at length —**talk·a·tive·ly** *adv.* —**talk·a·tive·ness** *n.*

WORD KEY: SYNONYMS

talkative, chatty, gossipy, loquacious

CORE MEANING: for somebody who talks a lot

talkative a general and fairly neutral word for somebody who talks a lot, especially as a matter of disposition; **chatty** a fairly informal word for somebody who talks a lot in a friendly way, especially on a particular occasion; **gossipy** a fairly informal word used disapprovingly of somebody who talks a lot about other people and their lives; **garrulous** a formal word used disapprovingly of somebody who talks too much or at great length, especially as a matter of disposition; **loquacious** a formal word for somebody who talks a great deal but who is exceptionally articulate.

talk·back /táwk bàk/ *n.* a system of communication in a broadcasting studio that enables the staff to speak to each other without the speech being broadcast

talk·fest /táwk fèst/ *n.* a long period of discussion or conversation

talk·ie /táwkee/ *n.* an early film with a soundtrack (*dated*) [Early 20thC. Shortening of *talking picture*, on the model of "movie."]

talk·ing head *n.* somebody such as a newscaster who talks at length into a camera in a television broadcast, usually shown only from the shoulders up

talk·ing point *n.* **1.** **INTERESTING ITEM FOR DISCUSSION** a topic, or aspect of something, that provokes a lot of discussion **2.** **SOMETHING SUPPORTING AN ARGUMENT** something that supports an argument, e.g., a particularly convincing point **3.** **PUBLICITY POINT** a claim made about a product in publicity material that is considered particularly interesting or persuasive to potential customers

talk·ing-to *n.* a scolding given to somebody, especially by somebody in authority (*informal*)

talk show *n.* **1.** **PROGRAM WITH INTERVIEWS** a television or radio program made up mainly of interviews with guests, especially famous people **2.** **DISCUSSION PROGRAM** a television or radio program in which ordinary people discuss aspects of their lives or current social issues

talk·y /táwkee/ (-i·er, -i·est) *adj.* **1.** **TALKATIVE** tending to talk a great deal **2.** **CONTAINING TOO MUCH DIALOGUE** containing too much dialogue and not enough action ○ *a talky and dull movie*

tall /tawl/ *adj.* **1.** **VERY HIGH** reaching or having grown to a considerable or above-average height ○ *tall trees* **2.** **CERTAIN HEIGHT** having reached a particular height ○ *five feet tall* **3.** **LARGE** substantial, demanding, or difficult to deal with ○ *a tall order* **4.** **INCREDIBLE** exaggerating the events of something beyond the bounds of probability ○ *a tall tale* **5.** **POMPOUS** having an excessively grand or boastful style **6.** **GOOD** fine or admirable, especially by being brave and good (*archaic*) ■ *adv.* **PROUDLY** in a proud or courageous way ○ *There are times when you must stand tall and defend your beliefs.* ■ *n.* CLOTHES **SIZE FOR TALL PEOPLE** a clothing size for tall people, or a garment in this size [Old English *getæl* "quick, ready," from a prehistoric Germanic base meaning "to count," which is also the ancestor of English *tell* and *talk*] —**tall·ish** *adj.* —**tall·ness** *n.*

Tal·la·de·ga /tàllə dáygə, -déegə/ city in eastern Alabama, west of Talladega National Forest and east of Birmingham. Population: 18,246 (1996).

tal·lage /tállij/ *n.* **1.** **ROYAL TAX** a tax levied by the Norman and Angevin kings of England on royal lands and towns **2.** **TAX LEVIED BY LORD** in feudal times, a tax levied by a lord on his vassals or tenants ■ *vt.* (-laged, -lag·ing, -lag·es) **LEVY TAX ON SOMEBODY OR SOMETHING** to levy a tax, especially a tallage, on somebody or something [13thC. From Old French *taillage*, from *taillier* "to cut."]

Tal·la·has·see /tàllə hássee/ capital city of Florida, situated in the northern part of the state. Population: 133,718 (1994).

tall·boy /táwl bòy/ *n. U.K.* **1.** = **highboy** **2.** **PART OF CHIMNEY** a narrow fitting at the top of a chimney to prevent smoke being carried back down

Tall·chief /táwl chèef/, **Maria** (*b.* 1925) U.S. ballerina. She was the prima ballerina with the New York City Ballet (1948–65). Born **Betty Marie Tallchief**

Tal·ley·rand /tàale ràaN/, **Charles Maurice de** (1754–1838) French statesman. His long career spanned the French Revolution and the Napoleonic period. As foreign minister, he represented France at the Congress of Vienna (1814–15). Full name **Charles Maurice de Talleyrand-Périgord**

Tal·linn /tállin, ta lín, -leen/ capital city of Estonia. A major port, it is situated on the Bay of Tallinn, an inlet of the Gulf of Finland, opposite Helsinki, Finland. Population: 490,000 (1994).

tal·lis *n.* = **tallith**

Tal·lis /tálləs/, **Thomas** (1510?–85) English composer. He was a major composer of religious choral works.

tal·lith /taaliss, taalith, taa leet/ (*plural* **-lith·im** /taalə seem, taalə theem/ *or* **-liths**), **tal·lis** /taaliss/ (*plural* **-li·sim**) *n.* a Jewish four-cornered fringed prayer shawl of white material with a black, blue, or purple stripe, worn at morning prayers [Early 17thC. From Rabbinical Hebrew *ṭallīṯ*, from biblical Hebrew *ṭillel* "to cover."]

tall oil *n.* an oily liquid produced as a by-product of a chemical process in the manufacture of wood pulp and used in making soaps and emulsions [Early 20thC. Partial translation of German *Tallöl*, from Swedish *tallolja*, from *tall* "pine" + *olja* "oil."]

tal·low /tállō/ *n.* **1.** **FATTY SUBSTANCE USED TO MAKE CANDLES** a hard fatty substance extracted from the fat of sheep and cattle and used to make candles and soap **2.** **SUBSTANCE MADE FROM VEGETABLE MATTER** a substance similar to tallow, made from vegetable matter ■ *vt.* (-lowed, -low·ing, -lows) **COVER SOMETHING WITH TALLOW** to cover or grease something with tallow [13thC. From Low German.] —**tal·low·y** *adj.*

tall pop·py (*plural* **tall pop·pies**) *n. Aus* somebody who, through achievements or wealth, has become a prominent member of society (*informal*)

tall pop·py syn·drome *n. Aus* a tendency among the media and the public to denigrate the achievements of prominent members of society

tall ship *n.* a square-rigged sailing ship [*Tall* from the lofty masts carried on full-rigged ships]

tal·ly /tállee/ *v.* (-lied, -ly·ing, -lies) **1.** *vti.* **AGREE OR CAUSE THINGS TO AGREE** to agree, correspond, or come to the same amount, or to cause two or more things to agree **2.** *vti.* SPORTS, GAME **MAKE A SCORE** to gain a point, run, goal, or other score in a contest **3.** *vi.* **KEEP SCORE** to keep a record of a score or account **4.** *vt.* **COUNT SOMETHING** to count or reckon something **5.** *vt.* **REGISTER SOMETHING IN AN ACCOUNT** to register something in an account of items **6.** *vt.* **PUT LABEL OR TAG ON SOMETHING** to put an identifying label or tag on something ■ *n.* (*plural* **-lies**) **1.** **RECORD** a record or account of items, e.g., things bought or points scored ○ *keep a tally* **2.** SPORTS, GAME **SINGLE SCORE** a single score, e.g., a run or a touchdown, in a contest **3.** **IDENTIFYING LABEL OR MARK** something, e.g., a label or mark, that identifies something **4.** **COUNTERPART** something that corresponds to or is the counterpart of something else **5.** **NOTCHED STICK** a stick with notches cut into it as a record of something, e.g., loans made or items bought on credit **6.** **NOTCH CUT INTO STICK AS RECORD** any of the notches cut into a tally as a record **7.** **MARK REPRESENTING NUMBER** a mark or marks representing a number, especially a set of four short vertical lines crossed by a diagonal fifth line used for numbering things in fives [15thC. Via Anglo-Norman from, ultimately, Latin *talea* "twig, cutting."] —**tal·li·er** *n.*

WORD KEY: ORIGIN

The Latin word *talea*, from which **tally** is derived, is also the source of English *detail, entail, retail*, and *tailor.*

tal·ly·ho /tállee hō/ *interj.* **EXCLAMATION THAT FOX HAS BEEN SIGHTED** used by a participant in a fox hunt to let others know that a fox has been sighted ■ *n.* (*plural* **-hos**) **1.** **FOX HUNTER'S CRY** a cry by a participant in a fox hunt to let others know that a fox has been sighted **2.** = **four-in-hand** *n.* 1 ■ *vi.* (-hoed, -ho·ing, -hos) **SHOUT "TALLYHO"** to give a shout of "tallyho" [Late 18thC. Origin uncertain: probably an alteration of French *taïaut*.]

tal·ly·man /tálleemən/ (*plural* **-men**) *n.* **1.** **RECORD KEEPER** somebody who keeps a record or account of something, e.g., items bought on credit or points scored **2.** *U.K.* **TRAVELING SALES REPRESENTATIVE** a traveling sales representative who sells goods to be paid for in installments

Tal·mud /taal mōōd, tálməd/ *n.* the collection of ancient Jewish writings that makes up the basis of Jewish religious law, consisting of the early scriptural interpretations (**Mishnah**) and the later commentaries on them (**Gemara**) [Mid-16thC. From post-biblical Hebrew *talmūḏ*, literally "instruction," from Hebrew *lāmaḏ* "to learn."] —**Tal·mu·dic** /taal mōōdik, tal-/ *adj.* —**Tal·mu·di·cal** /-mōōdik'l/ *adj.* —**Tal·mud·ism** /taal mōō dìzzəm, tálmə dìzzəm/ *n.* —**Tal·mud·ist** /taal mōōdist, tálmədist/ *n.*

tal·on /tállən/ *n.* **1.** **HOOKED CLAW** a hooked claw, especially of a bird of prey **2.** **SOMETHING LIKE A CLAW** something that looks like a claw, e.g., a curled human finger **3.** **PART OF A LOCK** the part of a lock that the key is pressed against when turned and that causes the bolt to slide out **4.** ARCHIT = **ogee** *n.* 1 **5.** CARDS **UNDEALT CARDS** the remainder of the deck of cards after a deal in particular games, e.g., in solitaire [14thC. Via French from the assumed Vulgar Latin stem *talon-* "heel, spur," from Latin *talus* "ankle."] —**tal·oned** *adj.*

Tal·on /ta lóN/, **Jean Baptiste, Comte d'Orsainville** (1625?–94) French colonial administrator. As the second-in-command of New France (now Canada) (1665–68 and 1669–72), he promoted agriculture and industry and the immigration to maintain them.

ta·luk /taa lōōk/ (*plural* **-lu·ka** *or* **-loo·ka** /taa lōōkə/) *n. S Asia* **1.** **SUBDIVISION OF DISTRICT** a subdivision of a district in India **2.** **PIECE OF HEREDITARY LAND** a piece of hereditary land in India [Late 18thC. Via Urdu and Persian *ta'alluḳ* "estate" from, ultimately, Arabic *ta'allaḳa* "to be attached."]

ta·lus[1] /táyləss/ (*plural* **-li** /táy lī/) *n.* the bone in the ankle that connects with the lower leg bones to form the ankle joint [Late 16thC. From Latin, "ankle," of uncertain origin: possibly from Celtic.]

ta·lus[2] /táyləss/ *n.* **1.** MIL **AREA OF RUBBLE** a sloping area of rock rubble **2.** **ROCK RUBBLE** rock rubble, e.g., at the base of a cliff **3.** MIL **BASE OF FORTIFICATION** the sloping base of a fortification [Mid-17thC. Origin unknown.]

tal·weg *n.* = **thalweg**

tam /tam/ *n.* a tam-o'-shanter (*informal*) [Shortening]

ta·ma·le /tə maalee/ *n.* a Mexican dish made by mixing fried chopped meat with peppers and seasonings, rolling the mixture in cornmeal dough, wrapping it in corn husks, and then steaming it [Late 17thC. Back-formation from American Spanish *tamales*, the plural of *tamal*, from Nahuatl *tamalli*.]

ta·man·du·a /tə mándoo ə/, **ta·man·du** /tə mándoo/ *n.* a small tree-living toothless anteater of Central and South America with a long prehensile tail. Latin name: *Tamandua tetradactyla* and *Tamandua mexicana*. [Early 17thC. Via Portuguese from Tupi *tamanduá*, literally "ant hunter."]

Ta·mar /táym ər/ river in northern Tasmania, Australia, formed by the confluence of the North and South Esk rivers. Length: 40 mi./65 km.

tam·a·rack /támmə ràk/ *n.* **1.** TREES **N AMERICAN LARCH** a deciduous North American larch with bluish-green needles and oval cones. Latin name: *Larix laricina*. **2.** INDUST **WOOD OF TAMARACK** the wood of the tamarack tree [Early 19thC. From Canadian French *tamarac*, of uncertain origin: probably of Algonquian origin.]

tam·a·rau /támmə rów/ (*plural* **-raus**), **tam·a·rao** (*plural* **-raos**) *n.* a small rare buffalo that lives in swamps of the island of Mindoro in the Philippines. Latin name: *Bubalus mindorensis*. [Late 19thC. From Tagalog.]

ta·ma·ri /tə maaree/ *n.* a rich Japanese soy sauce [Late 20thC. From Japanese.]

ta·ma·ril·lo /támmə rillō/ (*plural* **-los**) *n.* **1.** TREES **PERUVIAN TREE** a tree or shrub originally from the Peruvian Andes but cultivated elsewhere for its edible fruit. Latin name: *Cyphomandra betacea*. **2.** FOOD **FRUIT OF PERUVIAN TREE** the edible fruit of the tamarillo tree, similar to the plum [Mid-20thC. Alteration of TOMATILLO.]

tam·a·rin /támmərin/ *n.* a small South American monkey that has a long tail and is highly vocal. Genus: *Saguinus.* [Late 18thC. Via French from Galibi.]

tam·a·rind /támmərind/ *n.* **1.** TREES **TROPICAL TREE** a tropical evergreen tree that has yellow flowers with red streaks and pods containing an edible acid pulp. Latin name: *Tamarindus indica.* **2.** FOOD **FRUIT OF TAMARIND TREE** the edible acid fruit of the tamarind tree, used in making preserves, drinks, and medicines **3.** INDUST **WOOD FROM TAMARIND** the wood of the tamarind tree [Mid-16thC. Via Old French from Arabic *tamr hindī*, literally "Indian date."]

tam·a·risk /támmərisk/ *n.* a tree or shrub with leaves resembling scales and masses of small flowers that grows in Europe, Asia, and Africa. Genus: *Tamarix.* [14thC. From late Latin *tamariscus*, a variant of Latin *tamarix*, of unknown origin.]

Ta·ma·tave /taámaa taáv/ former name for **Toamasina**

Ta·ma·yo /taa maá yō/, **Rufino** (1899–1991) Mexican artist. His abstract paintings are influenced by folk themes, pre-Columbian art, and European styles such as cubism and fauvism.

tam·bac *n.* = **tombac**

tam·ba·la /taàm baálə/ (*plural* **-la** *or* **-las**) *n.* **1. SUBUNIT OF MALAWIAN CURRENCY** a subunit of currency in Malawi, 100 of which are worth one kwacha. See table at **currency 2. COIN WORTH A TAMBALA** a coin worth one tambala

tam·bour /tám boor/ *n.* **1.** SEW **EMBROIDERY FRAME** a round frame on which material is stretched while it is being embroidered **2.** SEW, FURNITURE **EMBROIDERY** embroidery done on a tambour **3. FLEXIBLE ROLLING TOP OF DESK** a flexible rolling top of a desk or sliding front of a cabinet made of thin strips of wood attached to canvas **4.** MUSIC, MIL **DRUM** a drum, especially a snare drum **5.** ARCHIT **CIRCULAR WALL** a circular wall, especially one supporting a dome ■ *vti.* (**-boured, -bour·ing, -bours**) SEW **EMBROIDER DESIGN USING TAMBOUR** to embroider using a tambour, or embroider a design onto material using a tambour [15thC. Via Old French from, ultimately, Persian *tabīra* "drum," perhaps influenced by Arabic *ṭunbūr* "lute."]

tam·bou·ra /tam boorə/ *n.* a fretless stringed Asian instrument resembling a lute, played to produce a harmonic drone [Late 16thC. Via Arabic and Persian from Persian *dunbara*, literally "lamb's tail."]

tam·bou·rin /támbərin/ *n.* **1.** DANCE **DANCE** an 18th-century Provençal dance in a two-beat rhythm, usually accompanied by a drum **2.** MUSIC **MUSIC FOR TAMBOURIN** a piece of music composed for or in the rhythm of a tambourin **3.** MUSIC **DRUM** a small Provençal drum [Late 18thC. From French, literally "small drum," from *tambour* (see TAMBOUR).]

tam·bou·rine /tàmbə reén/ *n.* a shallow single-headed drum with jingling metallic disks in its frame, held in one hand and played by shaking it or striking it with the free hand [Late 16thC. From French, literally "small drum," from *tambour* (see TAMBOUR).] —**tam·bou·rin·ist** *n.*

tam·bu·bam·bu band /tàmboo bámboo bánd/ *n. Carib* a small band of musicians using bamboo sticks as instruments and parading through the streets during Carnival, especially in Trinidad. The forerunners of the modern steel bands, they are rarely seen nowadays. (*dated*)

Tam·bur·laine /támbə layn/ = **Tamerlane**

tame /taym/ *adj.* (**tam·er, tam·est**) **1. NO LONGER WILD** changed from a wild or uncultivated state to one suitable for domestic use or life **2. FRIENDLY TOWARD PEOPLE** unafraid of human contact **3. WITHOUT SPIRIT** lacking in spirit or vigor **4. BLAND** showing little of the qualities that make something interesting, e.g., imagination, adventurousness, or inspiration ○ *Considering the controversial nature of his other movies, this latest one is very tame.* **5. SLOW-MOVING** with very little current ○ *a tame stretch of river* ■ *vt.* (**tamed, tam·ing, tames**) **1. DOMESTICATE SOMETHING** to make a wild animal or uncultivated land suitable for domestic life or use **2. SUBDUE SOMEBODY** to remove the wildness, spirit, or energy from somebody or something **3. MODERATE SOMETHING** to make something much less harsh or extreme **4. BRING SOMETHING UNDER HUMAN CONTROL** to bring a natural force under human control ○ *a series of dams to tame the raging river* [Old English *tam*. Ultimately from an Indo-European word meaning "to constrain," which is also the ancestor of English *daunt, indomitable,* and *diamond.*] —**tam·a·ble** *adj.* —**tam·a·ble·ness** *n.* —**tame·ly** *adv.* —**tame·ness** *n.* —**tam·er** *n.*

Tam·er·lane /támmər làyn/, **Tam·bur·laine** /támbər làyn/ (1336–1405) Turkic ruler and conqueror. His conquests established an empire that extended from India to the Mediterranean Sea. He died whilst trying to invade China, and was buried in his capital, Samarkand. Born **Timur**

Tam·il /támm'l, taám'l/ (*plural* **-ils** *or* **-il**) *n.* **1.** PEOPLES **MEMBER OF S ASIAN PEOPLE** a member of a people who live in southern India and northern Sri Lanka **2.** LANG **TAMIL LANGUAGE** the Dravidian language of the Tamil people. Tamil has an ancient literary tradition and is spoken by over 50 million people. [Mid-18thC. From Tamil *Tamiḻ*.] —**Tam·il** *adj.*

Tam·il Na·du /tàmmil naa doo/ state in southern India. Capital: Chennai. Population: 58,840,000 (1994). Area: 50,215 sq. mi./130,058 sq. km.

tam·is /támmee/ (*plural* **-is** /tamis/) *n.* = **tammy**[2] [Early 17thC. Via French from medieval Latin *tamisium*, ultimately from prehistoric Germanic.]

Tam·man·y Hall /támmənee-/ *n.* a political organization formed as a fraternal society in New York in 1789 but mainly known for political corruption in the early 20th century [Mid-19thC. Named for the headquarters of the *Tammany* Society.] —**Tam·man·y·ism** *n.* —**Tam·man·y·ite** *n.*

Tam·muz /taá mooz, taa mooz/ *n.* CALENDAR in the Jewish calendar, the tenth month of the civil year and the fourth month of the religious year. It is 29 days long. [Mid-16thC. Via Hebrew *Tammūz* from Babylonian *Du'uzu*, the name of a deity.]

tam·my[1] /támmee/ *n.* a tam-o'-shanter (*informal*) [Late 19thC. Formed from TAM.]

tam·my[2] /támmee/ *n.* (*plural* **tam·mies**) **tam·my, tam·my cloth STRAINING CLOTH** a fine strainer made of woolen cloth ■ *vt.* (**tam·mied, tam·my·ing, tam·mies**) **STRAIN SOMETHING** to strain something such as a sauce using a tammy [Mid-18thC. Origin uncertain: probably from French *tamis* (source of English *tamis*).]

tam-o'-shan·ter /tàmmə shántər/ *n.* a brimless Scottish wool hat, usually with a bobble at the center of the crown [Mid-19thC. From *Tam o' Shanter*, the eponymous hero of a poem by Robert Burns.]

ta·mox·i·fen /tə móksəfin/ *n.* a drug used to treat breast cancer by inhibiting the actions of estrogen. It is also used in treating some types of infertility. Formula: $C_{26}H_{29}NO$. [Late 20thC. Alteration of form coined from TRANS- + AMINE + OXY- + PHENOL.]

tamp /tamp/ *vt.* (**tamped, tamp·ing, tamps**) **1. PACK SOMETHING DOWN** to pack or push something down, especially by tapping it repeatedly **2. FILL DRILL HOLE WITH SUBSTANCE** to pack a substance such as sand or dirt into a drill hole above an explosive ■ *n.* **TAMPING DEVICE** a device for pushing tobacco down into the bowl of a pipe [Early 19thC. Origin uncertain: perhaps a back-formation from *tampin*, variant of TAMPION, taken as "tamping"; perhaps influenced by STAMP.]

Tam·pa /támpə/ industrial city, seaport, and tourist resort on the western coast of Florida, at the mouth of the Hillsborough River. Population: 285,523 (1994).

Tam·pax /tám pàks/ *tdmk.* a trademark for a tampon for use during menstruation

tam·per[1] /támpər/ (**-pered, -per·ing, -pers**) *vi.* **1. INTERFERE WITH AND DAMAGE SOMETHING** to interfere with something in a way that damages it or has harmful results **2. INFLUENCE SOMETHING CORRUPTLY** to try to corrupt or influence somebody or affect the outcome of something [Mid-16thC. Origin uncertain: probably a variant of TEMPER; the current meaning "interfere" developed from the earlier "work in, mix thoroughly," used of clay.] —**tam·per·er** *n.*

tam·per[2] /támpər/ *n.* **1. SOMEBODY OR SOMETHING THAT TAMPS SOMETHING** somebody or something that packs something down with repeated blows **2.** *U.K.* = **tamp** *n.* **3.** MIL **CASING ON NUCLEAR WEAPON** the casing around the core of a nuclear weapon that reflects neutrons back into the core, slowing the expansion of the nuclear reaction and increasing the weapon's power

Tam·pe·re /támpərə, -e ray/ city in Häma Province, southwestern Finland, situated about 105 mi./169 km northwest of Helsinki. Population: 182,742 (1995).

Tam·pi·co /tam peékō/ seaport in eastern Mexico, situated on the Pánuco River close to the Gulf of Mexico. Population: 262,690 (1990).

tam·pi·on /támpee ən/, **tom·pi·on** *n.* a plug or cover for the muzzle of a gun to keep out moisture and dust when it is not in use [15thC. From French *tampon* (see TAMPON).]

tam·pon /tám pòn/ *n.* **1. PLUG OF MATERIAL USED DURING MENSTRUATION** a cylindrical plug of soft material inserted in the vagina during menstruation to absorb blood **2. PAD TO CHECK BLEEDING** a pad of cotton or other absorbent fabric that is used for plugging wounds or for controlling blood flow in body cavities, especially during surgery ■ *vt.* (**-poned, -pon·ing, -pons**) **CONTROL BLOOD FLOW** to use a tampon to plug a wound or to control blood flow in a body cavity, especially during surgery [Mid-19thC. From French *tampon* "plug, bung," variant of *tapon* "piece of cloth to stop a hole," from assumed Frankish *tappo* "stopper."]

tam·pon·ade /tàmpə náyd/ *n.* the insertion of a tampon during surgery to check bleeding

tam-tam /túm tùm, tám tàm/ *n.* **1. LARGE GONG** a large gong **2.** = **tom-tom** [Mid-19thC. Origin uncertain: perhaps from Hindi *ṭam-ṭam* "tom-tom."]

Tam·worth[1] /tám wùrth/ *n.* a reddish-gold pig with a long snout belonging to a hardy breed developed in the British Midlands and traditionally reared for pork. It is now regarded as a rare breed in its native region, but herds have been created in North America, Australia, and elsewhere. [Mid-19thC. Named for the town of *Tamworth*, Staffordshire, England.]

Tam·worth[2] /tám wùrth, támmwərth/ city in northeastern New South Wales, Australia, an agricultural center and site of an annual country music festival. Population: 31,865 (1996).

tan[1] /tan/ *n.* **1. SUNTAN** the brownish color that the skin takes on after being exposed to ultraviolet light, especially from the sun or a sunlamp **2.** COLORS **LIGHT BROWN COLOR** a light brown color tinged with orange **3.** = **tanbark** *n.* **1 4.** = **tannin** ■ *v.* (**tanned, tan·ning, tans**) **1.** *vti.* **GET OR GIVE SOMEBODY A SUNTAN** to give somebody's skin a brownish color, or take on such a color **2.** *vt.* MANUF **CONVERT HIDE TO LEATHER** to convert an animal skin or hide into leather by treating it with something such as tannin **3.** *vt.* **BEAT SOMEBODY** to give a beating to somebody (*informal*) ■ *adj.* (**tan·ner, tan·nest**) **1. OF LIGHT BROWN COLOR** of a light brown color tinged with orange **2. SUN-BRONZED** bronzed by the sun or some other source of ultraviolet light **3.** MANUF **OF PROCESS OF TANNING HIDES** relating to or used in the process of tanning animal skins and hides [Pre-12thC. From medieval Latin *tannare* "to tan, dye a tawny color," from *tannum* "tanbark" (source of English *tannin*), of uncertain origin: probably from Celtic.] —**tan·na·ble** *adj.* —**tan·nish** *adj.*

tan[2] /tan/ *abbr.* tangent

Tan /tann/, **Amy** (*b.* 1952) U.S. writer. She came to prominence with her first novel, *The Joy Luck Club* (1989), which deals with the relationships between Chinese-born women and their U.S.-born daughters.

tan·a /taánə/ *n.* **1. SMALL MADAGASCAN LEMUR** a small Madagascan lemur with a gray-brown back, whitish underparts, and a dark stripe that runs along the back and encircles each eye. Latin name: *Phaner furcifer.* **2. ASIAN TREE SHREW** a mainly ground-dwelling tree shrew that is native to Borneo and Sumatra and has a brownish coat with a black stripe along the back. Genus: *Lyongale.* [Early 19thC. Via modern Latin from Malay *tūpai tāna* "ground squirrel" (source of English *tupaia*).]

Ta·na, Lake /taánə/ the largest lake in Ethiopia, situated on the northern central plateau of the Ethiopian highlands. Area: 1,219 sq. mi./2,156 sq. km.

Tan·a·ba·ta /taá naa baá taa/ *n.* CALENDAR an annual festival celebrated in Japan on or around July 7. It originated in a Chinese legend about two lovers who were allowed to meet only once a year, on the seventh night of the seventh month. [Early 20thC. From Japanese.]

Tan·ach /taa naákh/, **Tan·akh** *n.* the sacred book of Judaism consisting of the Torah, Prophets, and Hagiographa [Mid-20thC. From Hebrew *tĕnak*, an acronym formed from *tōrāh* "law" + *nĕbī'īm* "prophets" + *kĕṯūbīm* "hagiographa."]

tan·a·ger /tánnəjər/ *n.* a songbird found in the forests of North and South America that is usually fairly small and brightly colored in bold patterns with a conical bill. Tanagers feed on insects and fruit, and some are popular as cage birds. Family: Thraupidae. [Early 17thC. From modern Latin *Tanagra*, genus name, ultimately an alteration of Tupi *tangará*.]

Tan·akh *n.* = **Tanach**

tan·bark /tán baàrk/ *n.* **1.** MANUF **TREE BARK USED AS TANNIN** the bark of some kinds of tree, especially oak and hemlock, used as a source of tannin **2.** INDUST **BARK FOR GROUND COVERAGE** tree bark with the tannin removed, used as a ground covering, especially in circus arenas, racetracks, and other places where animals are kept **3.** ARTS **CIRCUS RING** the part of a circus arena that is covered with tanbark **4.** TREES = **tan oak**

tan·dem /tándəm/ *n.* **1.** = **tandem bicycle 2. HORSE-DRAWN CARRIAGE** a two-wheeled carriage drawn by two horses harnessed one behind the other **3. HORSE TEAM HARNESSED IN SINGLE FILE** a team of two horses harnessed one behind the other **4. ARRANGEMENT IN SINGLE FILE** a setup in which two things are arranged one behind the other **5. VEHICLE WITH AXLES CLOSE TOGETHER** a vehicle with two axles close together ■ *adv.* **ONE BEHIND ANOTHER** with one behind the other ○ *We'll ride tandem.* [Late 18thC. From Latin *tandem* "at length" (from *tam* "so" + demonstrative suffix *-dem*), humorously interpreted as "in a straight line"; originally "carriage drawn by two horses one behind the other."]

tan·dem bi·cy·cle *n.* a bicycle that has two seats and two sets of handlebars and pedals, one behind the other, so that it can be ridden by two people at the same time

tan·door /tan dóor/ *n.* a clay oven used especially in the cuisine of or derived from the north of the Indian subcontinent for cooking food quickly at high temperature. It is traditionally fueled by charcoal or wood, which gives the food a distinctive smoky flavor, although it can also now be fueled by gas. [Mid-19thC. Via Urdu *tandūr*, Persian *tanūr* from, ultimately, Arabic *tannūr* "oven, furnace."]

tan·door·i /tan dóoree/ *adj.* baked or cooked in a tandoor. In the cuisine of or derived from the north of the Indian subcontinent, meat or seafood is generally cooked in this way after being marinated in a mixture of yogurt and spices. [Mid-20thC. From Persian and Urdu, formed from Urdu *tandūr* and Persian *tanūr* (see TANDOOR).]

Tan·dy /tándee/, **Jessica** (1909–94) British-born U.S. actress. She acted in the first production of *A Streetcar Named Desire* (1947) and won an Academy Award for *Driving Miss Daisy* (1989).

Ta·ney /táwnee/, **Roger** (1777–1864) U.S. jurist. He was chief justice of the Supreme Court (1836–64), and is best known for a legal decision that asserted the legitimacy of slavery. Full name **Roger Brooke Taney**

tang[1] /tang/ *n.* **1. STRONG TASTE** a distinctively sharp strong taste **2. PUNGENT SMELL** a smell that has a sharp biting quality **3. SUGGESTION** a slight hint or flavor of a particular thing ○ *a cake with a tang of lemon* **4. SHARP END GOING INTO HANDLE** the sharp part at one end of a chisel, knife blade, or other similar tool that secures it to the handle or shaft ■ *vt.* (**tanged, tang·ing, tangs**) **1. SUPPLY WITH TANG** to put a tang on something such as a knife or chisel **2. GIVE TANG TO SOMETHING** to mark something with a sharp distinctive smell or taste ○ *mountain breezes tanged with the scent of pine* [14thC. From a Scandinavian word.]

tang[2] /tang/ *n.* **RINGING SOUND** a loud, often harsh, ringing noise ■ *vti.* (**tanged, tang·ing, tangs**) **MAKE RINGING SOUND** to make or cause something to make a loud, often harsh, ringing noise [Early 17thC. An imitation of the sound.]

Tang /taang/, **T'ang** *n.* **CHINESE DYNASTY** a wealthy Chinese dynasty that lasted from A.D. 618–907 and was renowned for its encouragement and patronage of the arts, especially poetry and ceramics, and the development of printing ■ *adj.* **OF TANG DYNASTY** relating to or characteristic of the Tang dynasty or the literature, pottery, and other arts and crafts that flourished in China during this period [Mid-17thC. From Chinese *táng*.]

tan·ga /təng gaá/ *n.* an undergarment or the lower part of a bikini made of two small triangles of fabric fastened with ties [Early 20thC. Via Portuguese, in which the word denoted a triangular loincloth worn in tropical America, from Bantu.]

Tan·ga /táng gə, taáng-/ town in northeastern Tanzania, on the Indian Ocean. Population: 188,000 (1994).

Tan·gan·yi·ka /tàng gən yeékə/ former country in East Africa constituting the mainland part of what is now Tanzania —**Tan·gan·yi·kan** *n., adj.*

Tan·gan·yi·ka, Lake /taàng gən yeékə-/ the second largest lake in Africa, located in the eastern central part of the continent, with shorelines in Burundi, Tanzania, Zambia, and the Democratic Republic of the Congo. Area: 12,700 sq. mi./32,900 sq. km. Length: 420 mi./680 km.

tan·ga·ta whe·nu·a /tàngutta fénnoo ə/ *npl. NZ* the Maori people of a particular area

Tan·ge Ken·zo /taàng gay kénnzō/ (*b.* 1913) Japanese architect. He is often considered Japan's greatest modern architect. His works include the Peace Center at Hiroshima (1955).

tan·ge·lo /tánjə lō/ (*plural* **-los**) *n.* **1.** TREES **HYBRID CITRUS TREE** a hybrid citrus tree produced by crossing a tangerine tree with a grapefruit tree **2.** FOOD **FRUIT OF TANGELO TREE** the fruit of the tangelo, bigger than an orange and with smooth easily peeled skin and sharp-tasting orange flesh [Early 20thC. Blend of TANGERINE and POMELO, sometimes used to refer to grapefruit.]

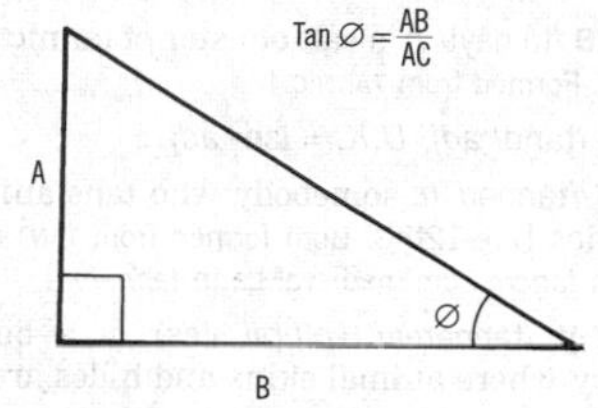

Tangent

tan·gent /tánjənt/ *n.* **1. LINE OR SURFACE THAT TOUCHES ANOTHER** a line, curve, or surface that touches another curve or surface but does not cross or intersect it **2.** MATH **TRIGONOMETRIC FUNCTION** for a given angle in a right-angled triangle, a trigonometric function equal to the length of the side opposite the angle divided by the length of the adjacent side. ◊ **cosine, sine 3. PART OF SURVEY LINE** the part of a survey line that is straight **4.** MUSIC **PART OF CLAVICHORD** a part of the clavichord that resembles a small hammer and strikes the strings ■ *adj.* **1.** = **tangential** *adj.* 2 **2. AWAY FROM THE POINT** not relevant to the subject currently under consideration **3. TOUCHING AT A SINGLE POINT** touching only at a single point **4. TOUCHING BUT NOT CROSSING** in contact, but not crossing or intersecting [Late 16thC. From Latin *tangent-*, present participle stem of *tangere* "to touch." Originally "line touching a circle."] —**tan·gen·cy** *n.* ◇ **go off at** *or* **on a tangent** to change quickly and suddenly to a different subject or line of thought

WORD KEY: ORIGIN

The Latin word *tangere*, from which ***tangent*** is derived, is also the source of English *contact, intact, tact, taste,* and *tax.*

tan·gent gal·va·nom·e·ter *n.* a device with a compass needle suspended horizontally in a vertical coil through which a direct current is passed, causing deflection of the needle proportional to the current size. It can be used to calculate the strength of the Earth's magnetic field.

tan·gen·tial /tan jénshəl/ *adj.* **1. ALMOST IRRELEVANT** with only slight relevance to the current subject **2. OF TANGENT** relating to or involving a tangent —**tan·gen·ti·al·i·ty** /tan jènshee állətee/ *n.* —**tan·gen·tial·ly** /tan jénshəlee/ *adv.*

tan·ger·ine /tànjə reén, tánjə reén/ *n.* **1.** FOOD **CITRUS FRUIT** an edible citrus fruit with an orange skin that is easily peeled and sweet-tasting flesh **2.** TREES **WIDELY CULTIVATED CITRUS TREE** a citrus tree native to Southeast Asia but widely cultivated in tropical and warm regions for its fruit. Many varieties and hybrids have been produced, including the clementine, satsuma, and tangelo. Latin name: *Citrus reticulata.* **3.** COLORS **BRIGHT ORANGE COLOR** a bright orange color like that of a tangerine ■ *adj.* COLORS **OF BRIGHT ORANGE COLOR** of a bright orange color like a tangerine [Early 17thC. Origin uncertain: probably modeled on Spanish *Tangerino* "of or from Tangier," the current senses via *Tangerine orange.*]

Tan·ger·ine /tànjə reén, tánjə reén/ *adj.* relating to the Moroccan port of Tangier, or its people or culture

tan·gi /táng gee, taáng gee/ (*plural* **-gis**) *n. NZ* a Maori funeral ceremony and the feast that accompanies it [Mid-19thC. From Maori, "lament, action of crying."]

tan·gi·ble /tánjəb'l/ *adj.* **1. ABLE TO BE TOUCHED** able to be touched or perceived through the sense of touch ○ *a tangible coldness* **2. ACTUAL** capable of being understood and evaluated, and therefore regarded as real ○ *There is no tangible evidence to support this claim.* **3. ABLE TO BE REALIZED** capable of being given a physical existence ○ *some very tangible financial benefits* ■ *n.* **SOMETHING TANGIBLE** something that has a physical form, especially a financial asset (*often used in the plural*) [Late 16thC. Directly or via French from late Latin *tangibilis* "that may be touched," from Latin *tangere* (see TANGENT).] —**tan·gi·bil·i·ty** /tànjə bíllətee/ *n.* —**tan·gi·ble·ness** /tánjəb'lnəss/ *n.* —**tan·gi·bly** /tánjəblee/ *adv.*

Tan·gier /tàn jeér/ port city in northern Morocco. Population: 307,000 (1993).

tan·gle[1] /táng g'l/ *v.* (**-gled, -gling, -gles**) **1.** *vti.* **BECOME TWISTED** to become or make something become twisted together into a jumbled mass **2.** *vt.* **CATCH AND HOLD SOMETHING** to catch and entwine somebody or something in something that is difficult to get out of, e.g., a net or trap ○ *I got my jacket tangled in the branches.* **3.** *vt.* **TRAP SOMEBODY IN DIFFICULT SITUATION** to trap somebody in a complicated, awkward, or dangerous situation ○ *tangled in a web of controversy* **4.** *vi.* **COME INTO CONFLICT** to become involved in a confrontation or disagreement with somebody, especially somebody powerful or important ○ *You'll regret it if you tangle with them.* ■ *n.* **1. JUMBLED MASS** a mass of fibers, lines, or other things twisted together **2. DIFFICULTY** a complicated situation or problem **3. STATE OF MENTAL UPSET** a state of mental or emotional confusion or upset [14thC. Earlier *tangilen*, variant of *tagilen* "to involve in an embarrassing situation," of uncertain origin: probably from Scandinavian.] —**tan·gle·ment** *n.* —**tan·gler** *n.* —**tan·gly** *adj.*

tan·gle[2] /táng g'l/, **tan·gle weed** *n.* a large brown seaweed, various kinds of which grow on shores at or below the level of low tide [Mid-16thC. Origin uncertain: probably from Norwegian *tångel*, from Old Norse *þongull*, from *þang* "bladderwrack."]

Popperfoto

Tango

tan·go /táng gō/ *n.* (*plural* **tan·gos**) **1.** DANCE **DANCE OF LATIN AMERICAN ORIGIN** a highly stylized ballroom dance of Latin American origin in 2/4 time in which the steps are punctuated by glides and sudden pauses **2.** MUSIC **MUSIC FOR TANGO** a piece of music that is suitable for a tango ■ *vi.* (**tan·goed, tan·go·ing, tan·gos**) DANCE **DANCE TANGO** to dance a tango [Late 19thC. From Argentine Spanish *tango*, originally a dance to the sound of drums, of uncertain origin: probably from a Niger-Congo language.] —**tan·go·ist** *n.*

Tan·go *n.* a word used to represent the letter "T" in radio communications

tan·gram /tán gràm/ *n.* a puzzle of Chinese origin that involves putting together seven pieces, usually a square, a parallelogram, and five triangles, to form different shapes. The seven pieces can also be put together to form a square. [Mid-19thC. Origin uncertain: perhaps coined from Chinese *t'ang* "Chinese" + -GRAM.]

Tang·shan /tàng shán/ city in Hebei Province, northern China, southeast of Beijing. Population: 1,500,000 (1991).

Tan·guy /taang geé, tang-/, **Yves** (1900–55) French-born U.S. artist. He is known for his surrealist paintings of organic forms in dreamlike landscapes.

tang·y /tángee/ (**-ier, -i·est**) *adj.* with a strong sharp taste or smell

Tang Yin /taàng yínn/ (1470–1523) Chinese painter and poet. He is noted for his paintings of beautiful and elegant women.

Ta·ni /taánee/, **Buncho** (1763–1840) Japanese artist. A noted book illustrator, he was responsible for introducing Western style to Japanese painting.

tan·ist·ry /tánnistree/ *n.* the process of selecting an heir apparent to a Celtic chieftain while the current chieftain is still alive

tani·wha /tún ee faà/ *n. NZ* a Maori water spirit that inspires fear [Mid-19thC. From Maori.]

Tan·i·za·ki Jun·i·chi·ro /taàni zaáki jòoni chéerō/ (1886–1965) Japanese writer. His novels present the conflict between modern Western-influenced realities and traditional values.

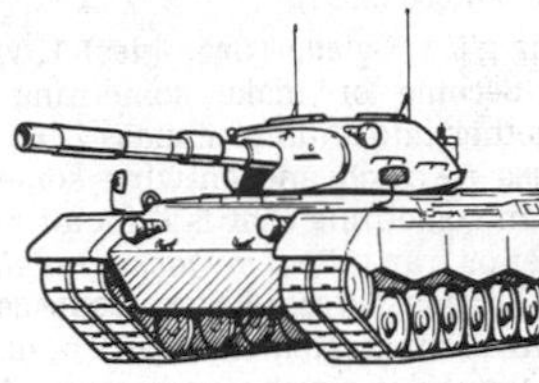

Tank

tank /tangk/ *n.* **1.** LARGE CONTAINER FOR LIQUIDS OR GASES a large container for storing liquids or gases **2.** AMOUNT HELD BY TANK the amount of liquid or gas that a particular tank holds ○ *We should get there and back on a couple of tanks of gas.* **3.** MIL ARMORED VEHICLE a large armored combat vehicle with Caterpillar™ treads and a rotating turret **4.** JAIL prison or a prison cell (*informal*) **5.** POND OR RESERVOIR a fairly small body of water, especially one used for water storage (*regional*) **6.** PHOTOGRAPHY CONTAINER FOR DEVELOPING FILM a lightproof container for developing film, designed so that processing chemicals can be poured in and out without light entering **7.** PHOTOGRAPHY TRAY FOR PROCESSING SHEETS OF FILM a large tray or container for processing a number of sheets of film together **8.** CLOTHES = **tank top** ■ *vt.* (**tanked, tank·ing, tanks**) **1.** PUT SOMETHING IN A TANK to put or keep something in a tank **2.** STOP TRYING TO WIN A COMPETITION to make no effort to win, especially in a sports competition (*informal*) ○ *He tanked the second set.* [Early 17thC. From Gujarati *tāṅkū* and Marathi *ṭāṅkē* "pond, cistern," perhaps with influence from Portuguese *tangue* (from Latin *stagnum* "pond").]

tank up *v.* **1.** *vti.* FILL UP WITH FUEL to fill the fuel tank of a motor vehicle (*informal*) **2.** *vi.* GET DRUNK to drink enough alcohol to become drunk (*slang*)

tan·ka /taáng kaà/ (*plural* **-kas** *or* **-ka**) *n.* **1.** JAPANESE VERSE FORM a five-line Japanese verse form in which the first and third lines have five syllables each and the other lines have seven syllables each. ◊ **haiku 2.** JAPANESE POEM a poem with a tanka verse structure [Late 19thC. From Japanese, from *tan* "short" + *ka* "song."]

tank·age /tángkij/ *n.* **1.** TANK CAPACITY the amount that can be held by a tank or tanks **2.** STORAGE IN TANK the storage of something in a tank, or the cost of this **3.** AGRIC FERTILIZER a by-product of the slaughter of livestock consisting of carcass trimmings cooked to reduce moisture and drained of surplus fat, used as a feed supplement or fertilizer

tank·ard /tángkərd/ *n.* **1.** BIG BEER MUG a large mug with a handle and sometimes a hinged lid, made of glass, pewter, or silver plate, typically used for drinking beer **2.** AMOUNT HELD IN TANKARD the amount of liquid that a tankard holds

tank car *n.* a railroad car that has a large tank for transporting liquids, semiliquids, or gases in bulk

tank de·stroy·er *n.* an armored military vehicle or aircraft mounted with antitank guns and designed to destroy tanks

tanked /tangkt/, **tanked-up** *adj.* extremely drunk (*slang*)

tank en·gine, tank lo·co·mo·tive *n.* a steam engine that carries its water supply in tanks at the sides of the boiler instead of carrying it in a tender

tank·er /tángkər/ *n.* a ship, truck, or airplane designed to carry large quantities of liquid or gas

tank farm *n.* a site with several large storage tanks, especially ones containing oil

tank farm·ing *n.* = **hydroponics**

tank·ful /tángk fòol/ *n.* the amount a tank can hold

tank lo·co·mo·tive *n.* = **tank engine**

tank suit *n.* a one-piece swimsuit with a scoop neck and wide shoulder straps [So called because they were worn in swimming pools, which were also called "swimming tanks"]

tank top *n.* a sleeveless garment with a scoop- or V-neck [Because it resembles either the top half of a tank suit, or a garment worn by the crews of armored tanks]

tank town *n.* a small town [*Tank* from the fact that originally trains stopped at such towns only to take on water]

tank trap *n.* something such as a concrete block designed to stop or slow the movement of military tanks

tank wag·on *n. U.K.* = **tank car**

tan·nage /tánnij/ *n.* **1.** HIDE TANNING the tanning of animal hides or skins **2.** TANNED HIDE an animal skin or hide that has been tanned [Mid-17thC. Formed from TAN[1]; perhaps also from French *tannage*.]

tan·nate /tá nàyt/ *n.* a salt or ester of tannic acid [Early 19thC. Formed from TANNIC.]

tanned /tand/ *adj. U.K.* = **tan**[1] *adj.* 2

tan·ner /tánnər/ *n.* somebody who tans animal skins or hides [Pre-12thC. Both formed from TAN[1] and via Old French *tanere* from medieval Latin *tannator*.]

tan·ner·y /tánnəree/ (*plural* **-ies**) *n.* a building or factory where animal skins and hides are tanned

tan·nic /tánnik/ *adj.* relating to, containing, or derived from tannin [Mid-19thC. From French *tannique*, from *tanin* (see TANNIN).]

tan·nic ac·id *n.* = **tannin**

tan·nin /tánnin/ *n.* a brownish or yellowish substance found in plants and used in tanning, dyeing, and as an astringent [Early 19thC. From French *tanin*, from *tan* "tanbark," from medieval Latin *tannum* (see TAN[1]).]

tan·ning /tánning/ *n.* **1.** CONVERSION OF ANIMAL SKIN INTO LEATHER the conversion of animal skins and hides into leather **2.** BROWNING OF SKIN the browning of skin when it is exposed to the sun or some other ultraviolet light source **3.** SOUND BEATING a sound beating or whipping

tanning bed *n.* an apparatus resembling a bed with a special canopy that emits rays of ultraviolet light so that the person lying on it develops a tan

tan oak *n.* a large evergreen hardwood tree native to California and Oregon and belonging to the beech family, the bark of which is used for tanning. Latin name: *Lithocarpus densiflora.*

Ta·no·an /taánō ən/ *n.* a group of languages spoken mainly in New Mexico and Arizona. Tanoan languages are spoken by about 3,000 people. [From Spanish *Tano* "Tewa"]

tan·rec *n.* = **tenrec**

tan·sy /tánzee/ (*plural* **-sies**) *n.* **1.** PLANT WITH YELLOW FLOWERS an aromatic perennial European and Asian plant of the daisy family with leaves divided into toothed leaflets and flat-topped clusters of yellow flower heads. The leaves were traditionally used as a piquant culinary flavoring, as a rodent repellent, and as a medicine. Latin name: *Tanacetum vulgare.* **2.** PLANT RESEMBLING TANSY any plant similar to the tansy, e.g., the ragwort [13thC. Origin uncertain: perhaps from Old French *tanesie*, ultimately from late Latin *tanacetum* "wormwood"; or from medieval Latin *athanasia*, from Greek, "immortality."]

tan·sy rag·wort *n.* a plant native to Europe, Asia, and Africa with yellow flowers resembling daisies. It is poisonous to livestock. Latin name: *Senecio jacobaea.*

Tan·ta /tóntə/ city in the Nile delta, northeastern Egypt, capital of Gharbiyah Governorate. Population: 380,000 (1992).

tan·tal·ic /tan tállik/ *adj.* relating to tantalum, especially when it has a valence of five

tan·ta·lite /tánt'l ìt/ *n.* a reddish-black mineral that is an ore of tantalum and also contains iron and manganese. It occurs in granites and pegmatites. Formula: $(Fe,Mn)Ta_2O_6$.

tan·ta·lize /tánt'l ìz/ (**-lized, -liz·ing, -liz·es**) *vt.* to tease or torment people by letting them see, but not have, something they desire [Late 16thC. Formed from Latin *Tantalus* (see TANTALUS).] —**tan·ta·li·za·tion** /tànt'li záysh'n/ *n.* —**tan·ta·liz·er** /tánt'l ìzər/ *n.*

tan·ta·liz·ing /tánt'l ìzing/ *adj.* tempting but unavailable or unattainable ○ *a really tantalizing offer* —**tan·ta·liz·ing·ly** *adv.*

tan·ta·lum /tánt'ləm/ *n.* a dense blue-gray metallic chemical element used in making electronic components, alloys, and in plates and pins for orthopedic surgery. Symbol **Ta** [Early 19thC. Via modern Latin from Latin *Tantalus* (see TANTALUS), because of its inability to absorb acid even when it is immersed in it.]

tan·ta·lus /tánt'ləss/ *n.* a lockable stand or case for decanters of alcoholic drinks, especially spirits. The decanters are visible but without the key the contents cannot be reached. [Late 19thC. Ultimately from Latin *Tantalus* (see TANTALUS).]

Tan·ta·lus /tánt'ləss/ *n.* in Greek mythology, a king who was condemned to stand in water under a fruit tree. Whenever he tried to drink or eat, the water or fruit receded beyond his reach. [Mid-18thC. Via Latin from Greek.]

tan·ta·mount /tántə mòwnt/ *adj.* equivalent to a particular thing in effect, outcome, or value, especially something unpleasant ○ *an answer that was tantamount to a refusal* [Mid-17thC. Ultimately from Anglo-French *tant amunter* "to amount to as much," from Old French *tant* "as much" + *amonter* "to amount" (source of English *amount*).]

tan·ta·ra /tan térrə, tan taárə, tántərə/ *n.* a fanfare or blast on a horn, or a sound that resembles this, especially when used to announce something important [Mid-16thC. An imitation of the sound.]

tant·ie /tántee/, **Tant·ie** *n. Carib* an older aunt, or any older woman [Late 19thC. From French Creole, a blend of French *tante* and AUNTIE.]

tan·tiv·y /tan tívvee/ *n.* (*plural* **-ies**), *interj.* HUNTER'S SHOUT a hunting cry, especially one given by a hunter riding a horse at full gallop ■ *n.* (*plural* **-ies**) FAST MOVEMENT a fast ride, especially on a horse going at full gallop ■ *adj.* SPEEDY moving very fast, especially when on a horse going at full gallop ■ *adv.* SPEEDILY in a very fast way, especially at full gallop [Mid-17thC. Origin uncertain: probably an imitation of the sound of galloping horses, with influence from TANTARA.]

Tan·tra /túntrə, tántrə/ *n.* the sacred books of Tantrism. They were written between the 7th and 17th centuries A.D. and mostly consist of a dialogue between Shiva and his wife Shakti. [Late 18thC. From Sanskrit, "loom, warp, groundwork, system, doctrine."]

Tan·trism /tún trìzzəm, tán trìzzəm/ *n.* a movement in Hinduism and Buddhism, especially a variety based on yoga and intended to release energy through sexual intercourse in which the orgasm is withheld or delayed —**Tan·tric** *adj.* —**Tan·trist** *n.*

tan·trum /tántrəm/ *n.* an outburst of anger, especially a childish display of rage or bad temper [Early 18thC. Origin unknown.]

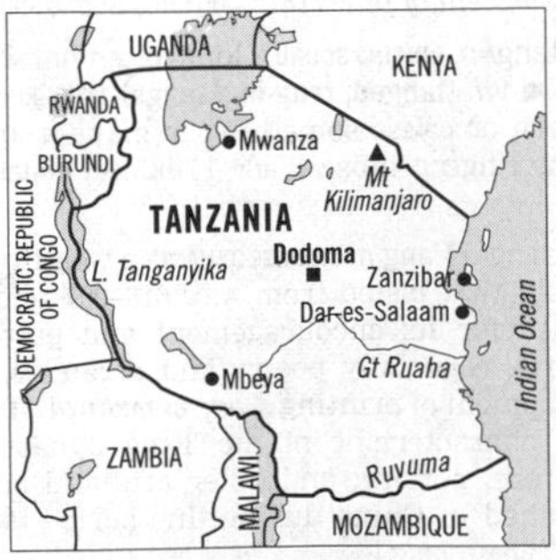

Tanzania

Tan·za·ni·a /tànzə née ə/ republic in southeastern Africa, including the islands of Zanzibar and Pemba. Language: Swahili, English. Currency: Tanzanian shilling. Capital: Dodoma. Population: 29,898,774 (1997). Area: 364,900 sq. mi./945,100 sq.

km. Official name **United Republic of Tanzania** — **Tan·za·ni·an** *n., adj.*

Tao /tow, dow/ *n.* **1.** ULTIMATE REALITY in Taoist philosophy, the ultimate reality in which all things are located or happen **2. Tao, tao** UNIVERSAL ENERGY the universal energy that makes and maintains everything that exists **3.** RELATIONSHIP BETWEEN INDIVIDUAL AND UNIVERSE the order and wisdom of individual life, and the way that this harmonizes with the universe as a whole [Mid-18thC. From Chinese *dào* "way, path, right way (of life), reason."]

Taoi·seach /theeshək/ *n.* the prime minister of the Republic of Ireland [Mid-20thC. From Irish, literally "chief, leader."]

Tao·ism /tów ìzzəm, dów-/ *n.* **1.** PHILOSOPHY OF SIMPLICITY AND NONINTERFERENCE a Chinese philosophy that advocates a simple life and a policy of noninterference with the natural course of things. It was founded in the 6th century B.C. by the mystic and philosopher Lao Tzu. **2.** RELIGION BASED ON TAOISM a popular Chinese religion that seeks harmony and long life through the philosophy of Taoism combined with pantheism and magical practices —**Tao·ist** *n., adj.* — **Tao·is·tic** /tow ístik, dow-/ *adj.*

ta·on·ga /taa áwng gə/ *n. NZ* something that should be cherished and is considered very valuable

Ta·or·mi·na /towr meénə/ winter resort town in Messina Province, eastern Sicily, situated about 28 mi./45 km north of Catania. Population: 9,979 (1991).

Tao Te Ching /tòw tə chíng, dòw-/ *n.* the most important Taoist text, a collection of 81 poems by the mystic and philosopher Lao Tzu, the founder of Taoism [Literally, "the Book of the Way"]

tap[1] /tap/ *v.* (**tapped, tap·ping, taps**) **1.** *vti.* HIT SOMETHING LIGHTLY to hit something or somebody lightly, especially more than once **2.** *vt.* HIT OBJECT AGAINST SOMETHING ELSE to hit an object lightly against something else **3.** *vt.* MAKE SOUND to produce something such as a noise or rhythm by tapping **4.** *vi.* MOVE MAKING LIGHT SOUNDS to move making a series of light noises **5.** *vi.* TAP-DANCE to tap-dance **6.** *vt.* REINFORCE SHOE to attach a small piece of leather or metal to the toe or heel of a shoe to cover worn parts or to protect against wear **7.** *vt.* GIVE POSITION TO SOMEBODY to select and appoint somebody for a particular role or office (*usually passive*) ○ *"The coal industry was tapped to lead the way for reform"* (*U.S. News & World Report*; December 1998) ■ *n.* **1.** LIGHT BLOW a light blow, especially one that produces a noise **2.** SOUND OF BLOW the sound made by a light blow **3.** REINFORCEMENT FOR SHOE a small piece of leather or metal attached to the toe or heel of a shoe to cover a worn part or to protect against wear **4.** METAL PART ON TAP-DANCING SHOE a metal tip attached to the toe or heel of a tap-dancing shoe so that it can produce a noise **5.** TAP-DANCING tap-dancing (*informal*) **6.** PHON TOUCH OF TONGUE TO MOUTH TOP the production of a speech sound made when any flexible speech organ hits any hard part of the mouth, such as when the tongue is brought into contact with the hard palate [12thC. Origin uncertain: perhaps an imitation of the sound, or via French *taper* "tap, strike," from Gallo-Romance, Germanic, or Scandinavian.] —**tap·pa·ble** *adj.* —**tap·per** *n.*

tap[2] /tap/ *n.* **1.** = **faucet 2.** BARREL PLUG a stopper in a cask or barrel, used to seal in the contents and also to allow liquid to be drawn off at a controlled rate **3.** BEER FROM CASK liquid, especially beer, that has been drawn from a tap in a cask or barrel and is regarded as having particular qualities because of this **4.** = **taproom 5.** TELECOM LISTENING DEVICE a device put into a telephone or other telecommunication equipment in order to secretly listen to or record other people's conversations **6.** SURG SURGICAL FLUID EXTRACTION a surgical procedure that involves drawing off a body fluid using a hollow needle or tube **7.** TECH TOOL FOR MAKING INTERNAL SCREW THREADS a tool used to make an internal screw thread. ◊ **die 8.** ELEC TEMPORARY CONNECTION IN CIRCUIT a point in a circuit where a temporary connection may be made **9.** STOCK EXCH SECURITY ON MARKET AT PREDETERMINED PRICE a government security made available gradually on the stock market when its price reaches a predetermined level ■ *v.* (**tapped, tap·ping, taps**) **1.** *vt.* TELECOM PLACE LISTENING DEVICE ON PHONE LINE to fit a device into a telephone or other telecommunication equipment in order to secretly listen to or record other people's conversations **2.** *vt.* ATTACH TAP to attach a tap to something in order to draw off or control the flow of liquid **3.** *vt.* DRAW LIQUID FROM BARREL to draw off liquid, e.g., wine or beer, from a barrel by means of a tap **4.** *vt.* SURG DRAW FLUID FROM BODY to surgically draw off fluid from a part of the body **5.** *vt.* FORESTRY OBTAIN SAP to cut into a tree in order to draw off sap or resin **6.** *vt.* ELEC ENG GET INTO POWER SUPPLY to connect to a power supply and divert energy from it, usually illegally **7.** *vti.* PUT RESOURCE TO USE to make use of a resource or supply of something (*informal*) ○ *tapping into the reserves of goodwill that exist in the community* **8.** *vt.* BORROW MONEY to borrow a sum of money from somebody (*informal*) ○ *She tapped me for 20 bucks.* **9.** *vt.* TECH MAKE INTERNAL SCREW THREAD to cut an internal screw thread into something [Old English *tæppa* (noun) and *tæppian* (verb), from prehistoric Germanic] —**tap·pa·ble** *adj.* —**tap·per** *n.* ◇ **on tap 1.** available for immediate use (*informal*) **2.** available to be drawn from a container (*informal*)

ta·pa /taápə, táppə/ *n.* **1.** TREE BARK the inner bark of the paper mulberry tree **2.** FABRIC MADE FROM TAPA a strong fabric made from the inner bark of the paper mulberry tree [Early 19thC. From Polynesian.]

ta·pas /taá paàs/ *npl.* small savory snacks that are often served as an appetizer along with alcoholic drinks, originally in Spain [Mid-20thC. Plural of Spanish *tapa* "cover, lid."]

tap dance *n.* a step dance performed by a dancer wearing shoes with metal tips at the toes and heels to make a rhythmic sound as they hit the floor —**tap danc·er** *n.*

tap-dance *vi.* to perform a dance or dances wearing shoes with metal tips at the toes and heels to make a rhythmic sound —**tap-danc·ing** *n.*

tape /tayp/ *n.* **1.** STRIP OF STICKY MATERIAL a long strip of plastic or cloth with adhesive on one or both sides, usually on a roll **2.** VIDEO OR AUDIO CASSETTE a cassette used for audio or video recording or playback ○ *Put the tape in the player.* **3.** LONG NARROW STRIP OF MATERIAL a long narrow strip of material such as paper, fabric, or plastic used to secure or tie something **4.** = **tape recording 5.** MAGNETIC TAPE magnetic tape used in cassettes and some computers **6.** SPORTS FINISH LINE MARKER a long strip of material that marks the finish line in a race **7.** TAPE MEASURE a tape measure ■ *v.* (**taped, tap·ing, tapes**) **1.** *vti.* RECORD SOMETHING to record something, especially music or a television program on magnetic tape **2.** *vt.* FIX SOMETHING USING TAPE to secure, fasten, or strengthen something using tape **3.** *vt.* MEASURE SOMETHING USING TAPE MEASURE to measure something using a tape measure [Old English *tæppe* "narrow strip of cloth," of uncertain origin]

tape deck *n.* an electrical device that plays and records tapes, especially audio cassettes

tape grass *n.* a perennial grass that grows largely submerged in fresh water, forming tufts of long narrow leaves and bearing inconspicuous pinkish-white flowers. Latin name: *Vallisneria spiralis.*

tape·line /táyp līn/ *n.* = **tape measure**

tape ma·chine *n. U.K.* STOCK EXCH = **ticker**

tape meas·ure *n.* a long roll or strip of fabric, plastic, paper, or thin metal that is marked off in inches or centimeters and used for measuring

ta·pe·nade /taápə naád/ *n.* a paste, originally from Provence in France, made from puréed black olives, capers, and anchovies [From French Provençal *tapeno* "caper"]

ta·per /táypər/ *vti.* (**-pered, -per·ing, -pers**) **1.** GET OR MAKE NARROWER to become or make something narrower at one end, especially gradually **2.** REDUCE GRADUALLY to become or make something smaller in size or amount, or less important, especially gradually ○ *Sales of the first album are beginning to taper off.* ■ *n.* **1.** SLIM CANDLE a slim candle that is narrower at the top than at the bottom **2.** STRIP FOR TRANSFERRING FLAME a strip of wood or waxed paper used for taking a flame to light something else **3.** NARROWING OF SHAPE a gradual narrowing in the shape of something ○ *a spire with a pronounced taper* **4.** DIM LIGHT a faint source of light, e.g., from a small candle [Pre-12thC. Originally "candle" (hence "get narrower"); alteration of Latin *papyrus* "papyrus" (source of English *paper*), whose pith was used for candle wicks.] —**ta·per·ing** *adj.* — **ta·per·ing·ly** *adv.*

tape-re·cord *vt.* to record something, especially sound, on a magnetic tape

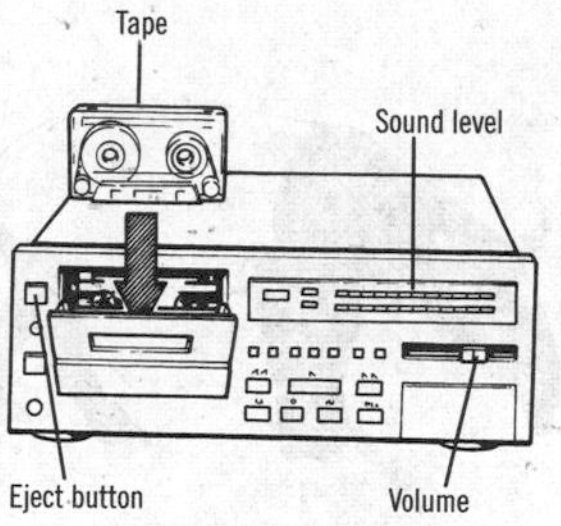

Tape recorder

tape re·cord·er *n.* a machine that can record and play cassette or reel-to-reel tapes, especially one with its own speaker

tape re·cord·ing *n.* a recording made on magnetic tape, especially an audio recording

tap·es·tried /táppəstreed/ *adj.* **1.** COVERED WITH TAPESTRY covered with tapestry or tapestries **2.** SHOWN IN TAPESTRY depicted in tapestry (*archaic or literary*)

tap·es·try /táppəstree/ (*plural* **-tries**) *n.* **1.** FABRIC WITH WOVEN DESIGN a heavy fabric with a woven pattern or picture, used as a wall hanging or for upholstery **2.** EMBROIDERY RESEMBLING TAPESTRY embroidery stitched on canvas to resemble tapestry **3.** SOMETHING VARIED AND INTRICATE something that is considered to be rich, varied, or intricately interwoven ○ *the rich tapestry of life* [14thC. Via French *tapisserie* from, ultimately, *tapis* "carpet," ultimately from Greek *tapēt-*, of uncertain origin: probably from Iranian.]

WORD KEY: CULTURAL NOTE

The Bayeux Tapestry, a large embroidery found at Bayeux in northern France (1092). A remarkable work of art and an important historical document, it consists of a band of linen measuring 231 ft./70 m by 20 in./50 cm, embroidered with vivid scenes that depict the Norman conquest of England. Its existence was first recorded in 1476 at Bayeux, where it was used to decorate the nave of the cathedral.

tap·es·try moth *n.* a moth whose caterpillars eat fabrics made from wool and other natural fibers. The adults are brown with white-tipped forewings and prefer damp conditions. Latin name: *Trichophaga tapetzella.*

ta·pe·tum /tə peétəm/ (*plural* **-ta** /-tə/) *n.* **1.** BIOL LAYER OF CELLS a specialized membrane or layer of cells **2.** ANAT REFLECTIVE LAYER IN EYE a layer of cells in the wall of the eye that reflects light back onto the retina, enhancing visual sensitivity in dim light. It occurs in nocturnal and deep-sea animals. Light reflected by this layer is responsible for the shining eyes of cats seen when they are illuminated at night. [Early 18thC. Via late Latin from Latin *tapete*, and ultimately from Greek *tapēt-* (see TAPESTRY).] —**ta·pe·tal** *adj.*

tape·worm /táyp wùrm/ *n.* a flatworm with a long ribbon-shaped segmented body that exists in many varieties and lives mainly as a parasite in the gut of vertebrate animals. Infestation is common among domestic animals, and humans can also become infested, especially by eating undercooked meat containing tapeworm larvae. Class: Cestoda. Technical name **cestode**

tap·hole /táyp hōl/ *n.* a hole at the bottom of a furnace for drawing off molten metal or slag

ta·phon·o·my /tə fónnəmee/ *n.* the scientific study of fossilization [Mid-20thC. Formed from Greek *taphos* "grave."] —**taph·o·nom·ic** /tàffə nómmik/ *adj.* — **ta·phon·o·mist** /tə fónnəmist/ *n.*

tap·house /táp hòwss/ (*plural* **-houses** /-hòwzəz/) *n.* an inn, bar, or other place where alcohol is served (*archaic*)

tap-in *n.* **1.** = **tip-in** *n.* 1 **2.** SHORT PUTT in golf, a short putt to put the ball in the hole

tap·i·o·ca /tàpee ókə/ *n.* a starch obtained from the roots of the cassava plant. It comes in the form of small hard beads and is used in making puddings and for thickening sauces. [Mid-17thC. Via Portuguese or Spanish from Tupi *tipioca*, from *tipi* "residue, dregs" + *ok* "to squeeze out."]

Tapir

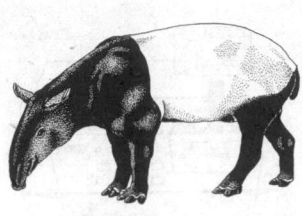

ta·pir /táypər/ (*plural* **-pirs** *or* **-pir**) *n.* a nocturnal hoofed forest-dwelling mammal of Central and South America and Southeast Asia. Tapirs have short limbs and a fleshy snout and feed on fruit and vegetation. They are related to rhinoceroses and horses. Family: Tapiridae. [Late 18thC. Ultimately from Tupi *tapira*.]

tap·is /táppee, táppiss, ta peé/ (*plural* **-is**) *n.* a heavy tapestry used as a wall covering, curtain, carpet, or tablecloth (*archaic*) [15thC. Via French from, ultimately, Greek *tapēt-* (see TAPESTRY).] ◇ **on the tapis** currently being considered or discussed

tap-off *n.* = **tip-off**[2] *n.*

Tap·pan /táppən/, **Arthur** (1786–1865) U.S. philanthropist. He cofounded the American Anti-Slavery Society (1833) and the American and Foreign Anti-Slavery Society (1840).

Tap·pan, Lewis (1788–1873) U.S. philanthropist. The brother of Arthur Tappan, he founded the first U.S. credit-rating service (1841), and shared his brother's abolitionist commitment and activities.

tap·pet /táppit/ *n.* a lever, arm, or other machine part that transfers motion from a cam to a part such as a valve or push rod [Mid-18thC. Formed from TAP[1].]

tap·ping /tápping/ *n. U.K.* ELEC = **tap**[2] *n.* **8**

tap·room /táp ro͝om, -ro͞om/ *n. U.K.* a bar in a place such as a hotel

tap·root /táp ro͞ot/ *n.* a prominent and often bulky root that extends downward below the stem of some plants and has fine lateral roots. It often serves as a food storage organ, e.g., in the carrot. [Early 17thC. *Tap* from TAP[2].]

taps /taps/ *n.* (*takes a singular or plural verb*) **1. SIGNAL AT FUNERAL** a bugle call or other signal given at a funeral or memorial service, especially a military one **2. SIGNAL FOR LIGHTS OUT** a bugle call or other signal given at the end of the day, especially in a military camp, as an order that lights should be put out [Early 19thC. Origin uncertain: either formed from TAP[1] or an alteration of *taptoo*, variant of TATTOO.]

tap·ster /tápstər/ *n.* somebody who serves drinks in a bar (*archaic*) [Old English *tæpestre*, originally feminine of *tapper*, from TAP[2]]

tap·stress /tápstrəss/ *n.* a woman who serves drinks in a bar (*archaic*)

tap·u /taá po͞o/ *adj. NZ* taboo [Mid-19thC. Variant of TABOO.]

tap wa·ter *n.* water that comes out of the faucet, as opposed to water from some other source, e.g., mineral water or rainwater

tar[1] /taar/ *n.* **1. THICK BLACK LIQUID** a thick black liquid obtained through the destructive distillation of an organic substance such as wood or coal **2. RESIDUE FROM TOBACCO SMOKE** the residue from tobacco smoke ■ *vt.* (**tarred, tar·ring, tars**) **COVER WITH TAR** to coat or cover something, especially a road surface, with tar [Old English *teoru*. Ultimately from an Indo-European word that is also the ancestor of English *tree*. The original application was probably to trees' tarry resins.]

tar[2] /taar/ *n.* a sailor (*archaic informal*) [Late 17thC. Origin uncertain: perhaps from TAR[1], or a shortening of TARPAULIN, used to refer to sailors in the mid-17thC.]

tar·a·did·dle *n.* = **tarradiddle**

Ta·ra·hu·ma·ra /taárə hoo maárə, tèrrə-/ (*plural* **-ra** *or* **-ras**) *n.* **1.** PEOPLES **MEMBER OF NATIVE N AMERICAN PEOPLE** a member of a Native North American people who live in northern Mexico **2.** LANG **TARAHUMARA LANGUAGE** the Uto-Azecan language of the Tarahumara people [Late 19thC. From Spanish, with ultimate origin unknown.]

ta·ra·ma·sa·la·ta /taà raa maa sə laátə/ *n.* a light creamy pink or beige paste of Greek origin, made from smoked fish roe, olive oil, lemon juice, and garlic. It is usually served in the form of a pâté or dip as an appetizer or snack. [Early 20thC. From modern Greek, from *taramas* "preserved roe" (from Turkish *tarama* "preparation of soft roe or red caviar") + *salata* "salad."]

Ta·ra·na·ki /tàrrə naákee/ administrative region of New Zealand, located in the southwestern part of the North Island and including the city of New Plymouth. Population: 106,570 (1996). Area: 4,880 sq. mi./12,640 sq. km.

Ta·ra·na·ki, Mount dormant volcano near the western coast of the North Island, New Zealand. Height: 8,260 ft./2,518 m.

tar·an·tass /taàrən taáss/ *n.* a large Russian horse-drawn carriage with four wheels and no springs [Mid-19thC. From Russian *tarantas*.]

tar·an·tel·la /tèrrən téllə/ *n.* **1. ITALIAN RURAL DANCE** a fast whirling dance from southern Italy in 6/8 time **2. MUSIC FOR TARANTELLA** music in 6/8 time that is suitable for a tarantella [Late 18thC. From Italian, from *Taranto*, a town in southern Italy (source of English *tarantism* and *tarantula*).]

Popperfoto

Quentin Tarantino

Ta·ran·ti·no /tàrrən teénō/, **Quentin** (*b.* 1963) U.S. movie director and screenwriter. His first movie, *Reservoir Dogs* (1992), was followed by *Pulp Fiction* (1994), establishing him as an important but controversial moviemaker. He has often been accused of glamorizing violence.

tar·an·tism /térrən tìzzəm/ *n.* a nervous condition characterized by uncontrollable body movements, common during the 15th through 17th centuries in southern Italy and believed to be caused by the bite of the tarantula [Mid-17thC. From Italian *tarantismo*, from *Taranto* (see TARANTELLA).]

Ta·ran·to /taà rəntō/ city, port, and administrative center of Taranto Province, Apulia Region, southern Italy. Population: 230,207 (1992).

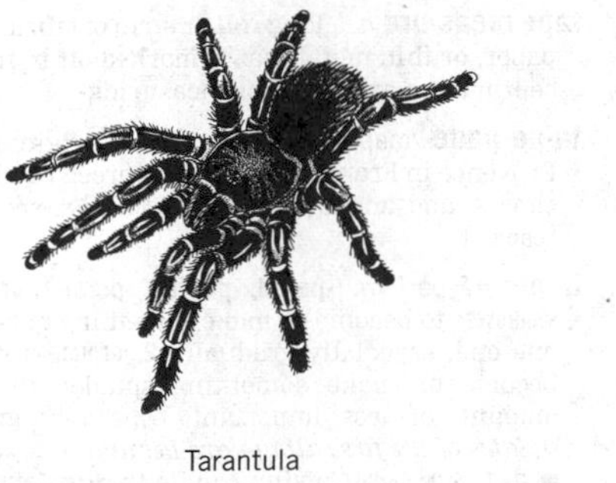

Tarantula

ta·ran·tu·la /tə ránchələ/ (*plural* **-las** *or* **-lae** /tə ránchəlee/) *n.* **1. LARGE HAIRY AMERICAN SPIDER** a large tropical or subtropical American spider that has a hairy body and legs. Tarantulas are typically nocturnal and feed on invertebrates, toads, small reptiles, and young birds. Some can inflict a painful bite if handled. Family: Theraphosidae. **2. WOLF SPIDER** a European wolf spider formerly believed to cause tarantism with its bite. Latin name: *Lycosa tarentula*. [Mid-16thC. Via medieval Latin from Italian *tarantola*, from *Taranto* (see TARANTELLA), near where such spiders are found.]

Tararua Range /tàrrə ro͞o ə-/ mountain range in the southern part of the North Island, New Zealand, north of Wellington. Its highest point is Mitre Peak, 5,154 ft./1,571 m.

tar·ax·a·cum /taáraksəkəm/ *n.* **1. PLANT SUCH AS THE DANDELION** a plant such as the dandelion that produces flower heads made up of numerous florets and with seeds attached to whitish hairs. Genus: *Taraxacum*. **2. PREPARATION OF DANDELION ROOTS OR LEAVES** an herbal remedy extracted from dandelion roots or leaves, used as a mild laxative, liver tonic, and diuretic [Early 18thC. Via medieval Latin *altaraxacon* from Arabic and Persian *ṭarakšakūn* "dandelion, wild endive," ultimately from Persian *talk* "bitter" + *čakūk* "purslane."]

tar ba·by *n.* a very troublesome situation, especially one that is difficult or impossible to get out of (*dated*) [Early 20thC. From the Uncle Remus story *Brer Rabbit and the Tar Baby* by J. C. Harris, after the doll smeared in tar used by Brer Fox to catch Brer Rabbit.]

Tar·bell /taár bel/, **Ida** (1857–1944) U.S. journalist. One of the "muckrakers," she is known for *The History of the Standard Oil Company* (1904). Full name **Ida Minerva Tarbell**

tar·boosh /taar bo͞osh/, **tar·bush** *n.* a brimless usually red felt hat, similar to a fez, that has a silk tassel and is worn by Muslim men by itself or with a turban [Early 18thC. Via Egyptian Arabic *ṭarbūš* from Ottoman Turkish *terpōş* and Turkish *tarbuş*, from Persian *sarpūš*, from *sar* "head" + *pūš* "cover."]

tar cam·phor *n.* = **naphthalene**

tar·di·grade /taárdi gràyd/ *n.* **TINY WATER CREATURE** a tiny aquatic invertebrate animal with a short body and four pairs of stubby legs. Phylum: Tardigrada. ■ *adj.* **1. RELATING TO TARDIGRADES** relating or belonging to the tardigrades **2. SLUGGISH** sluggish or slow moving [Early 17thC. Directly or via French from Latin *tardigradus*, literally "walking slowly," from *tardus* "slow" (source of English *tardy*).]

tar·dive dys·ki·ne·sia /taàrdiv-/ *n.* a condition marked by involuntary movements of the tongue and facial muscles, especially after prolonged treatment with phenothiazine tranquilizers and similar drugs [*Tardive* from French *tardif* (see TARDY)]

tar·dy /taárdee/ *adj.* **1. LATE** later than the expected or usual time **2. SLUGGISH** slow to move or react (*archaic or literary*) ■ *n.* **INSTANCE OF LATENESS** an instance of being late, especially for school or work, that is noted down as a misdemeanor ○ *Just one more tardy and you'll be staying after school.* [Mid-16thC. Alteration of *tardyve*, from French *tardif*, from, ultimately, Latin *tardus* "slow, sluggish" (source of English *bustard*).] —**tar·di·ly** *adv.* —**tar·di·ness** *n.*

tare[1] /tair/ *n.* **1. VETCH PLANT** a trailing or scrambling vetch plant of Europe and North Africa that has compound leaves with paired leaflets and tendrils, and spikes of bluish or purplish flowers. Genus: *Vicia*. **2. VETCH SEED** the seed of a vetch or tare **3. PROBLEMATIC WEED** in the Bible, a weed found growing among crops, usually considered to be the darnel [13thC. Origin uncertain.]

tare[2] /tair/ *n.* **1. WEIGHT OF PACKAGING** the weight of a container or packaging used to wrap goods **2. ALLOWANCE FOR WEIGHT OF PACKAGING** an allowance for the packaging around goods, deducted from the total weight and not included in transportation costs **3. VEHICLE'S UNLADEN WEIGHT** the weight of a motor vehicle without fuel, cargo, passengers, or equipment **4. CONTAINER OF KNOWN WEIGHT** a container of known weight that is used as a counterbalance when calculating the net weight of a cargo ■ *vt.* (**tared, tar·ing, tares**) **WEIGH PACKAGING** to weigh packaging in order to calculate the amount of tare to be deducted from a particular cargo [15thC. Via French *tāre* "waste in goods, deficiency" from, ultimately, Arabic *ṭarḥ* "that which is deducted," from *ṭaraḥa* "to reject, subtract."]

targe /taarj/ *n.* a round shield, especially used by Scottish Highlanders (*archaic*) [Pre-12thC. Origin uncertain: probably from Old Norse *targa* "shield"; later reinforced by Old French *targe* "light shield."]

tar·get /taárgət/ *n.* **1. OBJECT AIMED AT IN SHOOTING** a round object or surface marked with concentric circles that is aimed at in archery, rifle shooting, and similar sports **2. SOMETHING AIMED AT** an area, surface, object, or person aimed at ○ *The bird's bright plumage makes it an easy target.* **3. GOAL** a goal or objective toward which effort is directed ○ *Our target is to raise $20,000 for cancer research.* **4. SOMEBODY OR SOMETHING ON RECEIVING END** somebody or something that is the focus or object of the behavior or actions of others ○ *the target of her anger* **5.** CIV ENG **MARKER FOR TAKING LEVELS** a sliding weight on a surveyor's leveling rod that is used to help determine proper levels **6.** PHYS **SOMETHING HIT BY PARTICLE ACCELERATOR BEAM** a substance that is hit by a beam of electrons or other elementary particles or ions from a particle accelerator in order to start a nuclear reaction **7.** PHYS **SURFACE HIT BY ELECTRONS** a surface or electrode, often luminescent, that is hit by an electron beam to produce an output signal, e.g., in an X-ray tube or a television camera tube **8. SMALL SHIELD** a small round shield (*archaic*) ■ *vt.* **(-get·ed, -get·ing, -gets) 1. MAKE SOMEBODY OR SOMETHING TARGET** to make a particular person or thing the focus or object of something ○ *A campaign that targets under-35s.* **2. AIM SOMETHING** to aim something at or direct something toward a particular person, group, or thing ○ *The missiles were targeted on the enemy capital.* [13thC. Formed from TARGE, and originally meaning "small targe."]

tar·get date *n.* a date by which it is expected that something such as a project or piece of work will be completed

tar·get lan·guage *n.* **1. TRANSLATION LANGUAGE** the language into which a particular text is to be translated **2. LANGUAGE BEING LEARNED** a foreign language that is being learned **3.** COMPUT **LANGUAGE INTO WHICH SOURCE CODE COMPILED** the computer language into which a source code is to be compiled

tar·get man *n.* a soccer forward whose role is to receive high passes and crosses, especially in front of the goal

Tar·gum /taár goŏm, -goōm/ *n.* a translation of part of the Bible in Aramaic [Late 16thC. Via Hebrew from Aramaic *targūm* "interpretation," from *targēm* "to interpret."] —**Tar·gu·mic** /taar goómik/ *adj.* —**Tar·gu·mist** /taar goŏmist/ *n.*

Tar Heel, Tar·heel *n.* somebody who comes from or lives in North Carolina [Mid-19thC. Origin uncertain; perhaps from the resin, turpentine, and tar that were once major products of the state.]

tar·iff /térrif/ *n.* **1. DUTY LEVIED ON GOODS** a duty or duties levied by a government on imported or sometimes exported goods **2. LIST OF TARIFFS** a list or system of tariffs **3. LIST OF COSTS** a list of fees, fares, or other prices charged by a business ■ *vt.* **(-iffed, -iff·ing, -iffs) SET COST** to fix a specified tariff or price on something [Late 16thC. Via Italian *tariffa* from Arabic *ta'rif* "notification, inventory of fees to be paid," from *'arrafa* "to notify."]

Tar·king·ton /taárkingtən/, **Booth** (1869–1946) U.S. writer. His novels include the Pulitzer Prize-winning *The Magnificent Ambersons* (1918). Full name **Newton Booth Tarkington**

tar·la·tan /taárlət'n/ *n.* an open-weave transparent highly starched cotton muslin, used for stiffening collars and other parts of clothes [Early 18thC. From French *tarlatane*, an alteration of *tarnatane*, of uncertain origin: probably of Indian origin.]

tar·mac /taár màk/ *n.* a material used for surfacing roads

tarn /taarn/ *n.* a small mountain lake, especially one formed by the action of glaciers [14thC. From Scandinavian.]

tar·na·tion /taar náysh'n/ *interj.* used to express anger and annoyance (*regional*) [Late 18thC. Alteration of *darnation* (formed from DARN) or DAMNATION.]

tar·nish /taárnish/ *vti.* **(-nished, -nish·ing, -nish·es) 1. BECOME DULL AND DISCOLORED** to lose or make something lose its shine and become dull because of oxidation or rust **2. DAMAGE SOMEBODY'S REPUTATION** to damage somebody's reputation or good name, or to become damaged ■ *n.* **1. DISCOLORATION** the dullness or discoloration of metal affected by oxidation or rust **2. FILM OF DISCOLORATION ON METAL** the film of discoloration that forms on metal **3. SULLIED CONDITION** the damaged condition of somebody's reputation or good name [15thC. From French *terniss-*, stem of *ternir* "make dull," of uncertain origin: probably formed from *terne* "dull, dark," ultimately from Frankish.] —**tar·nish·a·ble** *adj.*

ta·ro /taárō, térrō/ (*plural* **-ros**) *n.* a perennial plant of Southeast Asia that is cultivated in tropical regions for its edible starchy tubers and is also widely grown as an ornamental plant. Latin name: *Colocasia esculenta.* [Mid-18thC. From Polynesian.]

tar·ok /térrək/ *n.* a card game developed in medieval times that uses a pack of cards consisting of 56 cards equivalent to modern cards, plus 22 tarot cards [Early 17thC. From Italian *tarocchi*, plural of *tarocco*, which is of unknown origin.]

Tarot

tar·ot /térrō, tə rṓ/ *n.* **1. FORTUNE-TELLING WITH CARDS** a system of fortune-telling using a special pack of 78 cards that consists of 4 suits of 14 cards together with 22 picture cards **2. tar·ot, tar·ot card CARD USED FOR FORTUNE-TELLING** any of the cards used in tarot [Late 19thC. From French, from Italian *tarocchi*, plural of *tarocco*, of unknown origin.]

tarp /taarp/ *n.* a tarpaulin (*informal*) [Early 20thC. Shortening.]

tar·pan /taar pán/ *n.* a small gray-brown horse with a short thick neck, erect mane, and a stripe along the back. It lived wild in southern Russia and Poland until the mid-19th century. Animals similar to the tarpan have been bred from related horses such as Przewalski's horse and reintroduced to parts of their ancestral habitat. [Mid-19thC. From Turkic.]

tar·pa·per /taár pàypər/ *n.* a heavy paper coated with tar and used in building for waterproofing

tar·pau·lin /taar páwlin, taárpəlin/ *n.* **1. WATERPROOF MATERIAL** a heavy waterproof material, especially treated canvas, used as a covering and to protect things from moisture **2. SHEET OF TARPAULIN** a sheet of tarpaulin [Early 17thC. Origin uncertain: probably from TAR[1] + PALL[2] + -ING[2], from the fact that the canvas is sometimes made waterproof with a coating of tar.]

Tar·pei·an Rock /taar peé yən-/ *n.* a rock on the Capitoline Hill in ancient Rome, from which traitors were hurled to their death [Early 17thC. Named for *Tarpeia*, legendary daughter of the commander of the citadel, which she betrayed to the Sabines; she was reputedly buried at the foot of the rock.]

tar pit *n.* an area where tar or asphalt naturally accumulates, trapping animals and preserving their bones

tar·pon /taárpən/ (*plural* **-pon** *or* **-pons**) *n.* a tropical or subtropical marine fish with a streamlined body and thick silvery scales. Genus: *Megalops.* [Late 17thC. Origin uncertain: probably from Dutch *tarpoen*, perhaps ultimately from a Central American language.]

tar·ra·did·dle /tèrrə díd'l/, **tar·a·did·dle** *n.* (*informal*) **1. IDLE TALK** nonsense or idle talk **2. LIE** a small lie [Late 18thC. Origin uncertain: probably thought to suggest unintelligible speech; the second part is perhaps from DIDDLE[1].]

Tarragon

tar·ra·gon /térrəgən/ *n.* an aromatic perennial herb native to temperate Asia that is widely cultivated for its leaves, that are used in cooking. It bears clusters of small greenish-white flowerheads. Latin name: *Artemisia dracunculus.* [Mid-16thC. From medieval Latin *tragonia* and *tarchon*, of uncertain origin: perhaps via Arabic *ṭarkūn* from, ultimately, Greek *drakont-* "dragon," associated with *drakontion* "dragonwort."]

Tar·ra·go·na /tàrrə gṓnə/ city, port, and administrative center of Tarragona Province, northeastern Spain. It has extensive Roman remains. Population: 114,931 (1995).

tar·ri·ance /tárree əns/ *n.* a short stay or visit (*archaic*)

tar·ry[1] /térree/ *vi.* **(-ried, -ry·ing, -ries) 1. REMAIN** to stay temporarily at a place **2. LINGER** to delay a departure or arrival, especially in an idle way **3. WAIT** to wait ■ *n.* (*plural* **-ries**) **SHORT STAY** a short stay or visit (*archaic or literary*) [13thC. Origin unknown.] —**tar·ri·er** *n.*

tar·ry[2] /taáree/ (**-ri·er, -ri·est**) *adj.* similar to or covered with tar [Mid-16thC] —**tar·ri·ness** *n.*

tar·si·er /taársee ər, taársee ày/ *n.* a small tree-living nocturnal animal that has large eyes and delicate grasping fingers and toes ending in pads. It is found in the Philippines, Indonesia, and neighboring islands. It is able to swivel its head around almost 360 degrees. Genus: *Tarsius.* [Late 18thC. From French, from *tarse* "tarsus"; from the animal's long tarsal bones.]

tar·so·met·a·tar·sus /taársō mettə taársəss/ (*plural* **-si** /-sī, -seè/) *n.* the bone in the lower leg of birds that connects to the toes [Mid-19thC. Formed from TARSUS + METATARSUS.]

tar·sus /taársəss/ (*plural* **-si** /taár sī, taár seè/) *n.* **1. ANKLE BONES** the group of bones that forms the ankle joint in vertebrates, located between the inner bone of the lower leg (**tibia**) and the main skeleton of the foot (**metatarsus**) **2. PART OF EYELID** the small section of connective tissue along the edge of the eyelid **3.** = **tarsometatarsus 4. PART OF ARTHROPOD LEG** the part of the leg of an arthropod that is furthest from the tibia [Late 17thC. Via modern Latin from Greek *tarsos* "eyelid, flat part of the foot."]

Tar·sus /taársəss/ city in southern Turkey, near the Mediterranean Sea. During Roman rule in the 1st century B.C. it was one of the most prominent cities of Asia Minor. Population: 146,502 (1985).

tart[1] /taart/ *adj.* **1. SHARP-TASTING** with a sharp and sour but usually pleasant flavor **2. SHARPLY CRITICAL** sharp, cutting, or critical [14thC. From Old English *teart* "painful, severe," of uncertain origin: perhaps literally "tearing."] —**tart·ness** *n.*

tart[2] /taart/ *n.* a pie that has no top crust and is usually filled with something sweet such as fruit or custard [14thC. From Old French *tarte*, of uncertain origin: perhaps ultimately from late Latin *torta* "round loaf of bread."]

tart[3] /taart/ *n.* an offensive term referring to a woman thought to be a prostitute or to behave like one (*slang insult*) [Mid-19thC. Origin uncertain: probably a shortening of SWEETHEART. Originally a term of endearment for a girl or woman.]

tar·tan[1] /taárt'n/ *n.* **1. WOOL FABRIC** a Scottish wool or worsted fabric woven in a wide range of checked or plaid patterns, many of which are associated with particular Scottish clans. The association between clans and tartan has no historical basis and arose in the 19th century. **2. PATTERN OF TARTAN** a particular pattern of tartan, officially registered and associated with a particular clan, regiment, or other organization **3. FABRIC WITH TARTAN DESIGN** fabric, especially wool fabric, with a tartan design **4. TARTAN GARMENT** a piece of clothing made of tartan **5.** *Scotland* **TRADITIONAL HIGHLAND DRESS** the traditional dress of the Scottish Highlands ○ *wearing the tartan with pride* [15thC. Origin uncertain: perhaps from French *tiretaine* "linen and wool fabric," from *tiret*, a kind of cloth, ultimately from medieval Latin *tyrius* "cloth from Tyre," named for *Tyre*, Phoenician capital.]

tar·tan[2] /taárt'n/ *n.* a Mediterranean sailing ship with a single mast and a lateen sail [Early 17thC. Via French *tartane* from, ultimately, Old Provençal *tartana* "buzzard," thought to imitate the sound of a buzzard.]

tar·tar /taártər/ *n.* **1.** DENT **HARD DEPOSIT ON TEETH** a hard deposit consisting mostly of organic material that forms on the teeth at the gum line. Failure to remove it regularly contributes to dental decay. **2.** BEVERAGES **SUBSTANCE DEPOSITED IN WINE CASKS** a substance found on the inner surface of wine casks and consisting mostly of potassium bitartrate. It is deposited during the fermentation process. [14thC. Via medieval Latin *tartarum* from medieval Greek *tartaron*, of unknown origin.]

Tar·tar /taártər/ *n.* **1.** PEOPLES, LANG = **Tatar 2. tar·tar, Tar·tar** FEARSOME PERSON a fearsome or ferocious person (*offensive in some contexts*) [14thC. Directly or via French from medieval Latin *Tartarus* (influenced by TARTARUS in Latin), an alteration of a Turkish word.] —**Tar·tar·ian** /taar térree ən/ *adj.* —**Tar·tar·ic** /taar térrik/ *adj.*

tar·tare sauce *n.* = **tartar sauce**

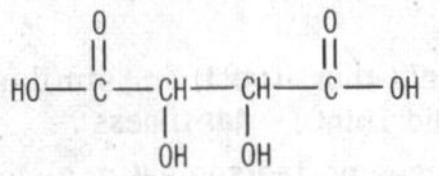

Tartaric acid

tar·tar·ic ac·id /taar tàrrik-/ *n.* a white crystalline organic acid obtained from tartar in wine vats and used in the food industry. Formula: $(CHOH)_2(COOH)_2$.

tar·tar·ous /taártərəss/ *adj.* containing or resembling tartar

tar·tar sauce, tar·tare sauce *n.* mayonnaise mixed with capers, chopped pickles, olives, onion, and herbs, often served as an accompaniment to fish [*Tartare* from French (see TARTAR)]

tar·tar steak *n.* = **steak tartare**

Tar·ta·rus /taártərəss/ *n.* MYTHOL **1.** LOWEST PART OF UNDERWORLD in Greek mythology, the lowest part of the underworld where the worst evildoers were imprisoned **2.** THE UNDERWORLD in Greek mythology, Hades or the underworld in general [Mid-16thC. Via Latin from Greek *Tartaros.*]

tart·let /taártlət/ *n.* a miniature tart, usually intended to serve one person [15thC. From French *tartelette,* a diminutive of *tarte* (see TART).]

tart·ly /taártlee/ *adv.* in a tone of voice or with words conveying strong but tight-lipped disapproval or annoyance

tar·trate /taár tràyt/ *n.* a salt or ester of tartaric acid [Late 18thC. From French, from *tartre* (see TARTAR).]

tar·trat·ed /taár tràytəd/ *adj.* in the form of a tartrate

Tar·tu /taártoo/ city in eastern Estonia, on the Emajogi River. Population: 101,901 (1997).

Tar·tuffe /taar tóof, taar tóof/, **Tar·tufe** *n.* somebody who hypocritically affects religious piety —**Tar·tuf·fi·an** *adj.*

tart·y /taártee/ (-i·er, -i·est) *adj.* an offensive term that deliberately insults a woman's appearance (*slang insult*) [Old English]

tar·weed /taár weèd/ *n.* a resinous strong-smelling plant of western North America and Chile with yellow flower heads resembling daisies. Genus: *Madia.*

TAS *abbr.* **1.** TELECOM telephone answering system **2.** AEROSP true airspeed

Tas. *abbr.* Tasmania

Tash·kent /taash ként/ capital city of Uzbekistan, situated in the eastern part of the country. Population: 2,100,000 (1994).

task /task/ *n.* **1.** JOB ASSIGNED a particular piece of work that is assigned, especially one that is unpleasant or difficult **2.** DIFFICULT JOB an unpleasant or difficult job or mission **3.** ANY ASSIGNMENT a piece of work or assignment, especially one that is important ■ *vt.* **(tasked, task·ing, tasks) 1.** BURDEN SOMEBODY to burden somebody excessively with work or duties **2.** ASSIGN WORK to assign a task to somebody [13thC. Via Old North French *tasque* "duty, tax" from medieval Latin *tasca,* from, ultimately, Latin *taxare* "to censure, assess" (see TAX).] ◇ **take somebody to task** to scold or criticize somebody

task force *n.* **1.** MIL TEMPORARY MILITARY GROUP a formation of military units put together on a temporary basis to accomplish a specific mission **2.** TEMPORARY GROUP FOR PERFORMING TASK a group of people and resources temporarily brought together for a specific purpose

task·mas·ter /task màstər/ *n.* **1.** PERSON WHO SUPERVISES WORK DEMANDINGLY a person who assigns and supervises work, especially in a demanding way **2.** A DEMANDING RESPONSIBILITY a responsibility or discipline that is very demanding or requires a lot of hard work

task·mis·tress /task mìstrəss/ *n.* a woman who assigns and supervises work, especially in a demanding way

task·work /task wùrk/ *n.* unpleasant, hard, or difficult work

Tas·ma·ni·a /taz máynee ə/ **1.** island in the Tasman Sea, separated from the southeastern coast of Australia by the Bass Strait. Area: 26,383 sq. mi./68,331 sq. km. **2.** state of southeastern Australia, occupying the island of Tasmania. First settled by the British in 1803, it became a separate colony in 1825. Capital: Hobart. Population: 475,000 (1996). Former name **Van Diemen's Land** —**Tas·ma·ni·an** *n., adj.*

Tasmanian devil

Tas·ma·ni·an dev·il *n.* a burrowing carnivorous marsupial characterized by a black coat with white markings and large powerful jaws, once ranging all over Australia but now confined to remote regions of Tasmania. Latin name: *Sarcophilus harrisii.*

Tas·ma·ni·an wolf *n.* = **thylacine**

tasse /tass/ *n.* any of the overlapping metal plates attached to and hanging below an armored breastplate in a suit of armor to protect the lower part of the trunk and the thighs [Mid-16thC. Origin uncertain: perhaps from Old French, "purse," via Middle High German *tasche* "pouch, pocket" from, ultimately, medieval Latin *tasca* "assessment."]

tas·sel /táss'l/ *n.* **1.** DECORATION MADE OF BUNCHED LOOSE THREADS a bunch of loose parallel threads that are tied together at one end and used as a decoration, e.g., on curtains, cushions, or clothes **2.** AGRIC TUFT AT END OF CORN something resembling a tassel, especially the tuft of male flowers at the top of the main stem of a corn plant ■ *v.* **(-seled** *or* **-selled, -sel·ing** *or* **-sel·ling, -sels) 1.** *vt.* DECORATE SOMETHING WITH TASSELS to decorate or fringe something with tassels **2.** *vi.* AGRIC PRODUCE A TUFT ON CORN to produce a tuft of stamens at the end of a flower cluster, especially as seen on an ear of corn **3.** *vt.* AGRIC REMOVE TASSEL FROM CORN to remove the tassel from an ear of corn [14thC. From Old French "clasp," of uncertain origin: perhaps from, ultimately, Latin *talus* "knuckle-bone."] —**tas·sel·ly** *adj.*

tas·set /tássət/ *n.* = **tasse** [Mid-19thC. From French *tassette,* from *tasse* "pouch," of uncertain origin: perhaps ultimately from Latin *tasca* (see TASK).]

taste /tayst/ *n.* **1.** PHYSIOL SENSE THAT IDENTIFIES FLAVORS the sense that perceives the particular qualities of something such as a food by means of the sensory organs in the tongue **(taste buds) 2.** PHYSIOL SENSATION STIMULATED IN TASTE BUDS the sensation stimulated in the taste buds when food, drink, or other substances are in contact with them. Sweetness, saltiness, bitterness, and sourness are considered the four basic taste sensations, and all flavors combine these in various ways with the sense of smell. **3.** ACT OF TASTING an act of tasting something **4.** SMALL QUANTITY TASTED a very small quantity of something eaten, drunk, or tasted ○ *Can I have a taste of that?* **5.** FIRST EXPERIENCE a brief sample, preview, or first experience of something ○ *a taste of freedom* **6.** LIKING FOR SOMETHING a tendency to like or enjoy a particular thing or type of thing ○ *She has a taste for modern art.* **7.** QUALITY the distinctive quality of something **8.** ABILITY TO JUDGE AESTHETICALLY the faculty of making discerning judgments in aesthetic matters ○ *He has good taste.* **9.** SENSE OF THE SOCIALLY ACCEPTABLE a sense of what is proper or acceptable socially ○ *The remark was in bad taste.* ■ *v.* **(tast·ed, tast·ing, tastes) 1.** *vt.* PHYSIOL DISCERN FLAVOR to discern the flavor of a substance by means of the taste buds **2.** *vt.* TEST SOMETHING FOR FLAVOR to put a small amount of food or drink into the mouth in order to try it or to test its flavor ○ *Taste this for salt.* **3.** *vti.* EXPERIENCE SOMETHING to experience something, especially for the first time or only briefly ○ *He had tasted success.* **4.** *vt.* HAVE PARTICULAR FLAVOR to have a particular flavor ○ *This tastes horrible.* **5.** *vt.* ENJOY SOMETHING to enjoy something very much (*archaic*) [13thC. From Old French *taster* "to touch," of uncertain origin: possibly from, ultimately, Latin *tangere* (see TAX). Originally also in the meaning of "touch."] —**tast·a·ble** *adj.*

taste bud *n.* a sensory receptor on the surface of the tongue or in the mouth that sends signals to the brain when stimulated by certain chemicals, producing the sense of taste. Taste buds are classified according to the type of substance they respond to: sweet, salty, bitter, or sour.

taste·ful /táystfəl/ *adj.* **1.** SHOWING GOOD TASTE having or exhibiting good aesthetic taste **2.** NICE TASTING having a pleasant flavor —**taste·ful·ly** *adv.* —**taste·ful·ness** *n.*

taste·less /táystləss/ *adj.* **1.** WITHOUT FLAVOR having little or no flavor **2.** SHOWING LACK OF GOOD TASTE showing a lack of taste or judgment in aesthetic or social matters —**taste·less·ly** *adv.* —**taste·less·ness** *n.*

taste·mak·er /táyst màykər/ *n.* somebody who is influential in deciding what is tasteful, stylish, or worthwhile, e.g., in fashion or the arts

tast·er /táystər/ *n.* **1.** JUDGE OF FOOD OR DRINK QUALITY a specialist who tastes food or drink to judge its quality **2.** DEVICE USED FOR TASTING a device or container used for tasting, e.g., a small cup for tasting wine **3.** PERSON TESTING FOR POISON somebody engaged, especially in the past, to test an important person's food or drink by sampling it first in case it contains poison

tast·y /táystee/ (-i·er, -i·est) *adj.* **1.** HAVING PLEASANT FLAVOR having a pleasant or full flavor **2.** TASTEFUL in good taste —**tast·i·ly** *adv.* —**tast·i·ness** *n.*

tat /tat/ **(tat·ted, tat·ting, tats)** *vti.* to work at or produce tatting [Late 19thC. Back-formation from TATTING.]

TAT *n., abbr.* thematic apperception test

ta·ta *interj.* used as a childish or familiar way of saying goodbye (*informal*) [Early 19thC. Origin unknown.]

ta·ta·mi /tə taámee, taa-/ (*plural* **-mi** *or* **-mis**) *n.* a straw mat, used especially in Japanese homes as a floor covering [Early 17thC. From Japanese.]

Ta·tar /taátər/, **Tar·tar** /taártər/ *n.* **1.** PEOPLES MEMBER OF HISTORICAL CENTRAL ASIAN PEOPLE a member of a people that originally came from eastern Central Asia and who established a huge empire stretching into Serbia, Russia, and Ukraine. The Tatars joined with the Monguls and their combined empire flourished until the 16th century, when they were defeated by the Russians and the Ottoman Turks. **2.** PEOPLES DESCENDANT OF TATARS a descendant of the Tatar people. Most now live in an area of European Russia between the Volga River and the Ural Mountains, with communities in Crimea and Siberia. **3.** LANG TATAR LANGUAGE The Turkic language of the Tatar people. Tatar is spoken by about 6 million people. ■ *adj.* OF TATAR PEOPLE relating to the Tatar people, their empire, or their culture [Early 17thC. From Turkish.] —**Ta·tar·i·an** /taa táiree ən/ *adj.* —**Ta·tar·ic** /taa térrik/ *adj.*

Tate /tayt/, **Allen** (1899–1979) U.S. writer. His poems include "Ode to the Confederate Dead" (1926). Full name **John Orley Allen Tate**

ta·ter /táytər/ *n.* a potato (*regional*) [Mid-18thC. Alteration of POTATO.]

Tat·lin /tátlin/, **Vladimir** (1885–1953) Russian sculptor and painter. He founded constructivism in the early 20th century with his abstract sculptures made from different industrial materials.

Ta·tra Moun·tains /taátrə, táttrə/ the highest range of the Carpathian Mountains of central Europe, extending along the border between Poland and Slovakia. The highest peak is Gerlachovka, 8,711 ft./2,655 m.

tat·ter /táttər/ *n.* **1.** TORN OR RAGGED PIECE OF CLOTH a torn or ragged piece of cloth **2.** RUINED STATE a ruined or damaged state (*usually used in the plural*) ○ *The policy was in tatters.* ■ *vti.* **(-tered, -ter·ing, -ters)** BECOME RAGGED OR MAKE SOMETHING RAGGED to become ragged or make something ragged or torn to shreds [15thC. From Old Norse *totrar* (plural) "rags."]

tat·ter·de·mal·ion /tàttərdə máylyən, -máylee ən/ *adj.* DRESSED IN RAGS raggedly dressed and unkempt ■ *n.* RAGGEDLY CLOTHED PERSON somebody wearing ragged clothes [Early 17thC. *Tatter* from TATTERED; *-demalion* of unknown origin.]

tat·tered /táttərd/ *adj.* **1.** RAGGED ragged or torn to shreds **2.** DRESSED IN RAGS dressed in ragged clothes **3.** SHABBY shabby and rundown [15thC. Formed from TATTER.]

tat·ter·sall /táttər sàwl, táttərssəl/ *n.* **1.** DESIGN PATTERN OF SQUARES OR CHECKS a pattern of squares or checks formed by dark lines on a light or brightly colored background **2.** TEXTILES TATTERSALL-PATTERNED CLOTH cloth with a tattersall pattern [Late 19thC. Named for *Tattersall's* horse market, London, England, named for Richard *Tattersall* (1724–95), English auctioneer; referring to the traditional design of horse blankets.]

tat·ting /tátting/ *n.* **1.** TYPE OF LACE a form of lace made with a shuttle **2.** PROCESS OF MAKING TATTING the process or craft of making tatting [Mid-19thC. Origin unknown.] —**tat·ter** *n.*

tat·tle /tátt'l/ *v.* (**-tled, -tling, -tles**) **1.** *vi.* GOSSIP to gossip about the personal secrets or plans of others **2.** *vti.* DISCLOSE SECRET to disclose somebody's personal or private information **3.** *vi.* TALK IDLY to talk or chatter idly ■ *n.* **1.** SOMEBODY WHO GOSSIPS a gossip or informer **2.** IDLE GOSSIP idle talk, chatter, or gossip [15thC. Origin uncertain: probably from Middle Flemish *tatelen*, an imitation of the sound.]

tat·tler /táttlər/ *n.* **1.** PERSON WHO TATTLES somebody who gossips, reveals secrets, or talks idly **2.** SHOREBIRD WITH LOUD CRY a long-legged shorebird that is related to the sandpipers and is noted for its loud cries. Genus: *Heteroscelus*.

tat·tle·tale /tátt'l tàyl/ *n.* SOMEBODY REVEALING SECRET somebody who reveals the secrets or misdeeds of others (*often used by or to children*) ■ *adj.* REVEALING inadvertently revealing ○ *a tattletale sign of the times*

tat·tle·tale gray *adj.* of a white color with a gray tinge —**tattle·tale gray** *n.*

tat·too[1] /ta to͞o, tə-/ *n.* (*plural* **-toos**) PERMANENT PICTURE OR DESIGN ON SKIN a permanent picture, design, or other markings made on the skin by pricking it and staining it with an indelible dye ■ *vt.* (**-tooed, -too·ing, -toos**) MAKE TATTOO to mark the skin with a tattoo, or to form a tattoo on the skin [Mid-18thC. Of Polynesian origin.] —**tat·too·er** *n.* —**tat·too·ist** *n.*

tat·too[2] /ta to͞o, tə-/ *n.* (*plural* **-toos**) **1.** CALL TO RETURN TO QUARTERS a bugle or drum call that tells soldiers to return to their quarters in the evening **2.** MIL EVENING MILITARY DISPLAY FOR ENTERTAINMENT a military display, often with a variety of items, performed as an entertainment, usually in the evening **3.** REGULAR BEATING ON SURFACE a steady rhythmical beating made on a surface such as a drum ■ *vti.* (**-tooed, -too·ing, -toos**) BEAT ON SOMETHING WITH STEADY RHYTHM to beat a steady rhythm, or to beat rhythmically on something such as a drum [Mid-17thC. From Dutch *taptoe*, literally "shut the tap (of the beer barrel)," a signal at closing time in the taverns. Originally "signal for soldiers to return to quarters."]

tat·ty /táttee/ (**-ti·er, -ti·est**) *adj.* shabby, rundown, or in poor condition [Mid-20thC. Formed from *tat* "rag," of uncertain origin.] —**tat·ti·ly** *adv.* —**tat·ti·ness** *n.*

Ta·tum /táytəm/, **Edward Lawrie** (1909–75) U.S. geneticist. His work with Joshua Lederberg and George W. Beadle on genetic mutations earned them a Nobel Prize in physiology or medicine (1958).

tau /tow, taw/ *n.* the 19th letter of the Greek alphabet, represented in the English alphabet as "t." See table at **alphabet** [14thC. From Greek.]

Taube /tawb, towb/, **Henry** (*b.* 1915) Canadian-born U.S. inorganic chemist. His study of electron transfer reactions won him a Nobel Prize (1983).

tau cross *n.* a cross shaped like a T

taught past tense, past participle of **teach**

tau neu·tri·no *n.* a subatomic particle of the lepton family with no electric charge and a mass less than 69 times that of an electron, created during the decay of a tauon

taunt[1] /tawnt/ *vt.* (**taunt·ed, taunt·ing, taunts**) **1.** PROVOKE OR RIDICULE SOMEBODY to provoke, ridicule, or tease somebody in a hurtful or mocking way **2.** TO TANTALIZE SOMEBODY to tantalize somebody, e.g., by refusing to disclose a secret ■ *n.* **1.** HURTFUL REMARK a hurtfully mocking or provocative remark **2.** OBJECT OF TAUNTS somebody at whom a taunt is directed (*archaic*) [Early 16thC. From French *tant (pour tant)* "so much (for so much)," from Latin *tantus* "so great." In English, anglicized as "taunt for taunt" and used for "sarcastic rejoinder."] —**taunt·er** *n.* —**taunt·ing** *adj.* —**taunt·ing·ly** *adv.*

taunt[2] /tawnt/ *adj.* used to describe a mast that is taller than normal [Early 17thC. Origin unknown.]

Taun·ton /táwntən/ **1.** town and administrative center of Somerset, southwestern England. Population: 60,300 (1993). **2.** city in southeastern Massachusetts, on the Taunton River, southeast of Attleboro and north of Fall River. Population: 51,937 (1996).

Tau·nus /táwnəss, tównəss/ mountain range in west central Germany, extending northeastward from the eastern bank of the Rhine River. Height: 2,887 ft./880 m.

tau·on /táw òn/ *n.* an unusually massive subatomic particle of the lepton family with the same charge as an electron but nearly 3,500 times its mass [Late 20thC. Formed from TAU.]

taupe /tōp/ *n.* a dark gray color tinged with brown ■ *adj.* DARK BROWNISH-GRAY of a dark gray color tinged with brown, like moleskin [Early 20thC. Via French from Latin *talpa* "mole."]

Tau·re·an *n.* = **Taurus** *n.* 3 —**Tau·re·an** *adj.*

tau·rine[1] /táw rīn/ *adj.* relating to or resembling a bull [Early 17thC. From Latin *taurinus*, from *taurus* (see TAURUS).]

tau·rine[2] /táw reen, táwrin/ *n.* a crystalline derivative of cysteine found in the bile, nervous tissue, and muscle juices of many animals. Formula: $C_2H_7NO_3S$. [Mid-19thC. Formed from TAUROCHOLIC ACID.]

tau·ro·chol·ic ac·id /tawrə kòllik-/ *n.* a crystalline bile acid that is found as a sodium salt in humans and other carnivores and in certain herbivores. Formula: $C_{26}H_{45}NO_7$. [Mid-19thC. Coined from TAURO- + CHOLE-.]

Tau·rus /táwrəss/ (*plural* **-rus·es** *or* **-ri** /táw rī/) *n.* **1.** ASTRON CONSTELLATION IN THE NORTHERN HEMISPHERE a constellation in the northern hemisphere located between Aries and Gemini and containing the bright star Aldebaran, the Pleiades and Hyades, and the Crab Nebula **2.** ZODIAC SIGN OF THE ZODIAC the second sign of the zodiac, represented by a bull and lasting from approximately April 20 to May 20. Taurus is classified as an earth sign, and its ruling planet is Venus. **3.** ZODIAC SOMEBODY BORN UNDER TAURUS somebody whose birthday falls between April 20 and May 20 [14thC. From Latin *taurus* "bull." Ultimately from an Indo-European word meaning "bull," which is also the ancestor of English *toreador*.] —**Tau·rus** *adj.*

Tau·rus Moun·tains /tàwrəss-/ mountain range in southern Turkey, parallel to the Mediterranean coast. Its highest point is Aladag, 12,251 ft./3,734 m.

Taus·sig /tówsig/, **Helen** (1898–1986) U.S. pediatrician. She studied and treated blue babies and played a major role in exposing the dangers of thalidomide to the developing fetus. Born **Helen Brooke**

taut /tawt/ *adj.* **1.** STRETCHED TIGHTLY pulled or stretched tightly **2.** PHYSIOL FIRM AND FLEXED flexed and working, as opposed to being in a relaxed state ○ *taut muscles* **3.** STRESSED stressed, tense, or anxious **4.** CONCISE concise and efficient in its use of language or reasoning **5.** KEPT IN GOOD ORDER trim, tidy, and well-run ○ *a taut ship* [13thC. Origin uncertain.] —**taut·ly** *adv.* —**taut·ness** *n.*

taut- *prefix.* = **tauto-** (*used before vowels*)

taut·en /táwt'n/ (**-ened, -en·ing, -ens**) *vti.* to become tightly stretched, or to pull something, such as a rope, tight [Early 19thC]

tau·tog /táw tàwg, taw táwg/ *n.* a large dark-colored edible fish of the wrasse family, found along the Atlantic coast of North America, growing to 3 ft./1 m in length. Latin name: *Tautoga onitis*. [Mid-17thC. From Narragansett *tautauog*.]

tau·tol·o·gize /taw tóllə jīz/ (**-gized, -giz·ing, -giz·es**) *vi.* to use tautology —**tau·tol·o·gist** *n.*

tau·tol·o·gy /taw tóllәjee/ (*plural* **-gies**) *n.* **1.** LING REDUNDANCY a redundant repetition of a meaning in a sentence or idea using different words **2.** INSTANCE OF TAUTOLOGY an instance of redundant repetition **3.** LOGIC LOGICAL TRUE PROPOSITIONAL a proposition or statement that, in itself, is logically true —**tau·tol·o·gize** *vi.* —

tau·to·log·i·cal /tàwtə lójjik'l/ *adj.* —**tau·to·log·i·cal·ly** /-lójjikəlee/ *adv.*

tau·to·mer /táwtəmər/ *n.* a compound exhibiting tautomerism [Early 20thC. Coined from TAUTO- + ISOMER.]

tau·tom·er·ism /taw tómmə rìzzəm/ *n.* the property of a compound that permits it to exist as a mixture of two isomers that are interconvertible and thus exist in equilibrium —**tau·to·mer·ic** /tàwtə mérrik/ *adj.*

tau·to·nym /táwtə nìm/ *n.* a species name in which the epithet for the species is the same as that of the genus, e.g., the name of the filarial worm *Loa loa*. This kind of name is used for animal but not plant species. —**tau·to·nym·ic** /tàwtə nímmik/ *adj.* —**tau·ton·y·my** /taw tónnəmee/ *n.*

tav /taaf, tawf/ *n.* the 23rd and final letter of the Hebrew alphabet, represented in the English alphabet as "t." See table at **alphabet** [Mid-17thC. From Hebrew *tāw*.]

Tav·el /taa vél/ *n.* a dry rosé wine produced in the Rhone region of France [Late 19thC. Named for the locale in France where the wine is produced.]

tav·ern /távvərn/ *n.* **1.** ESTABLISHMENT WHERE ALCOHOL SOLD AND DRUNK a place where alcohol is sold to be consumed on the premises **2.** CAFÉ a café, bar, or inn (*dated*) [13thC. Via French *taverne* from Latin *taberna* "hut, inn."] —**tav·ern·er** *n.*

ta·ver·na /tə vúrnə, taa váirnə/ *n.* **1.** RESTAURANT IN GREECE a small restaurant or café in Greece **2.** GREEK GUESTHOUSE WITH BAR a guesthouse in Greece that has a bar [Early 20thC. Via modern Greek from Latin *taberna* "hut, inn."]

taw[1] /taw/ (**tawed, taw·ing, taws**) *vt.* to whiten animal skins by applying alum or other mineral salts [Old English *tawian*, from a prehistoric Germanic base meaning "to make," which is also the ancestor of English *tool* and *heriot*] —**taw·er** *n.*

taw[2] /taw/ *n.* **1.** MARBLE USED AS A SHOOTER a fancy marble used as a shooter **2.** LINE FROM WHICH PLAYER SHOOTS MARBLES in a game of marbles, the line from which a player must shoot **3.** GAME PLAYED WITH MARBLES a game of marbles in which the object is to shoot as many marbles as possible out of a circular area where they have been placed [Early 18thC. Origin unknown.]

ta·wa /taáwə/ *n.* a tall tree of the laurel family that grows in New Zealand and has edible purple fruit. Latin name: *Beilschmiedia tawa*. [Mid-19thC. From Maori.]

taw·dry /táwdree/ *adj.* (**-dri·er, -dri·est**) **1.** GAUDY AND POOR QUALITY gaudy, cheap in appearance, and of inferior quality **2.** MEAN-SPIRITED mean-spirited and lacking in human decency ■ *n.* CHEAP GAUDY FINERY gaudy finery of inferior quality [Early 17thC. Shortening of *tawdry lace*, an alteration of *St. Audrey's lace*.] —**taw·dri·ly** *adv.* —**taw·dri·ness** *n.*

WORD KEY: ORIGIN

Anna, Anglo-Saxon king of East Anglia, had a daughter called Etheldreda, who became queen of Northumbria. She had an inordinate fondness in her youth for fine lace neckerchiefs, and when she later developed a fatal tumor of the neck, she regarded it as divine retribution for her former extravagance. After her death in 679 she was canonized and made patron saint of Ely. In the Middle Ages fairs were held in her memory, known as "St. Audrey's fairs" (*Audrey* is a conflated form of *Etheldreda*) at which lace neckties were sold. These were often made from cheap gaudy material, and by the 17th century the eroded form *tawdry* was being used generally for "cheap and gaudy."

taw·ny /táwnee/ (**-ni·er, -ni·est**) *adj.* **1.** ORANGY BROWN of an orange-brown color tinged with gold **2.** BEVERAGES MATURED FOR TEN YEARS PLUS used to describe port wine that has matured for at least ten years in the barrel before bottling, and is therefore paler than ruby port [14thC. Via Anglo-Norman *tauné* from Old French *tané* "tan" (see TAN).] —**taw·ni·ness** *n.*

taw·ny owl *n.* a common round headed owl with brown or gray plumage, black eyes, and tawny markings found in woodlands from Europe to China. Latin name: *Strix aluco*.

tax /taks/ *n.* **1.** ECON MONEY PAID TO A GOVERNMENT an amount of money levied by a government on its citizens and used to run the government and the country or state **2.** FIN CHARGE PAID BY MEMBERS an amount charged to members of a club or organization to be used for expenses **3.** STRAIN a strain or heavy demand ■ *vt.* (**taxed, tax·ing, tax·es**) **1.** ECON CHARGE TAX to charge a tax on something such as a company's or individual's income **2. STRAIN OR MAKE HEAVY DEMANDS ON** to strain or make heavy demands on something or somebody ○ *You're starting to tax my patience.* **3. ACCUSE OR CHARGE** to accuse or charge somebody **4.** LAW **DETERMINE COSTS OF LITIGATION** to determine the costs of litigation and the total amount of costs payable at the end of a trial [13thC. Via French *taxer* from Latin *taxare* "to censure, assess," literally "to touch repeatedly," from *tangere* "to touch" (source of English *tact* and *attain*).] —**tax·er** *n.* —**tax·less** *adj.*

tax- *prefix.* = **taxo-** (*used before vowels*)

ta·xa plural of **taxon**

tax·a·ble /táksəb'l/ *adj.* **SUBJECT TO A TAX** subject to a tax ○ *taxable income* ■ *n.* **SOMEBODY OR SOMETHING SUBJECT TO TAX** somebody or something that is subject to taxation —**tax·a·bil·i·ty** /táksə bíllətee/ *n.* —**tax·a·ble·ness** *n.* —**tax·a·bly** /táksəblee/ *adv.*

tax·a·tion /tak sáysh'n/ *n.* **1. SYSTEM OF LEVYING TAXES** the system whereby taxes are levied upon certain types of income, earnings, or purchases **2. MONEY COLLECTED IN TAXES** the amount of money raised by collecting taxes **3. TAX ON SOMETHING** an amount levied as a tax on something —**tax·a·tion·al** *adj.*

tax-de·duct·i·ble *adj.* used to describe an expenditure that can be deducted from taxable income to lower the amount of tax owed by an individual or business

tax-deferred *adj.* not taxable until a later time, often after retirement

tax·eme /ták seem/ *n.* a small linguistic feature such as selection, order, or phonetic modification [Mid-20thC. Coined from TAXIS + -EME.] —**tax·e·mic** /tak séemik/ *adj.*

tax e·va·sion *n.* an illegal activity in which a taxpayer seeks to hide taxable income or claim unauthorized tax deductions

tax-ex·empt *adj.* legally exempt from taxation

tax-free *adj.* not subject to taxation

tax ha·ven *n.* a country with favorable tax rates

tax hol·i·day *n.* a period during which a company is exempt from state taxation, e.g., when just starting out in business

tax·i /táksee/ *n.* (*plural* **-is** *or* **-ies**) TRANSP **CAR TAKING PAYING PASSENGERS** a car, usually with a taximeter, whose driver is paid to transport passengers, typically for short distances ■ *vti.* (**-ied, -i·ing** *or* **-y·ing, -is** *or* **-ies**) **1.** AIR **MOVE AIRCRAFT ON GROUND** to make an aircraft move under its own power on the ground, typically before takeoff or after landing, or to move on the ground in this way **2.** TRANSP **TRAVEL IN TAXI** to transport somebody or something in a taxi, or to travel in a taxi **3. TRANSPORT SOMEBODY OR BE TRANSPORTED** to transport somebody or something or be transported, especially in a car (*informal*) ○ *taxi the children to school* [Early 20thC. Shortening of *taximeter cab* (see TAXIMETER).]

taxi- *prefix.* = **taxo-**

tax·i danc·er *n.* somebody who is paid, dance by dance, to dance with patrons of a nightclub or dance hall —**tax·i danc·ing** *n.*

tax·i·der·my /táksi dùrmee/ *n.* the art or skill of preparing, stuffing, and presenting dead animal skins so that they appear lifelike [Early 19thC. Coined from Greek *taxis* "arrangement" (see TAXIS) + -DERM.] —**tax·i·der·mal** /táksi dúrm'l/ *adj.* —**tax·i·der·mist** /táksi dùrmist/ *n.*

tax·i·me·ter /táksee meetər/ *n.* a device installed in a taxi that automatically computes the fare, which is usually based on time, distance traveled, or a combination of both [Late 19thC. From French *taximètre*, from *taxe* "charge, tariff."]

tax·i·met·rics /táksə méttriks/ *n.* = **numerical taxonomy**

tax·ing /táksing/ *adj.* placing numerous or severe demands on somebody —**tax·ing·ly** *adv.*

tax·is /táksiss/ *n.* **1.** BIOL **MOVEMENT OF CELL** movement of a cell or microorganism toward or away from the source of a stimulus **2.** SURG **REPOSITIONING OF ORGAN** the manipulating of a displaced body part such as in a hernia to return it to its normal position [Late 16thC. From Greek, "arrangement," formed from the stem of *tassein* "to arrange" (source of English *tactics*).]

-taxis *suffix.* **1.** movement in response to a stimulus ○ *hydrotaxis* **2.** arrangement, order of parts ○ *phyllotaxis* [From Greek *taxis* "order, arrangement" (see TAXIS]

tax·i squad *n.* FOOTBALL in professional football, a group of players who practice with the team but are not allowed to play in official games [Mid-20thC. From the use by a football team owner of his reserve players as taxi drivers when their services were not required on the football field.]

tax·i stand *n.* an area reserved for parked taxicabs awaiting customers

tax·i truck *n. Aus* a truck and driver for rental, often used for moving house

tax·i·way /táksee wày/ *n.* a path used by aircraft when taxiing to and from a runway or other ground facility

tax loss *n.* a transaction that results in a reduced tax liability, even though it may not be associated with an actual cash loss, the loss associated with depreciation expenses

taxo- *prefix.* order, arrangement ○ *taxonomy* [From Greek *taxis* (see TAXIS)]

tax·on /ták sòn/ (*plural* **ta·xa** /-sə/ *or* **tax·ons**) *n.* any of the groups to which organisms are assigned according to the principles of taxonomy, including species, genus, family, order, class, and phylum [Early 20thC. Back-formation from TAXONOMY.]

tax·on·o·my /tak sónnəmee/ (*plural* **-mies**) *n.* **1. GROUPING OF ORGANISMS** the science of classifying plants, animals, and microorganisms into increasingly broader categories based on shared features. Traditionally, organisms were grouped by physical resemblances, but in recent times other criteria such as genetic matching have also been used. **2. PRINCIPLES OF CLASSIFICATION** the practice or principles of classification **3. STUDY OF CLASSIFICATION** the study of the rules and practice of classifying living organisms [Early 19thC. From French *taxonomie*, from Greek *taxis* "arrangement" (see TAXIS).] —**tax·o·nom·ic** /tàksə nómmik/ *adj.* —**tax·o·nom·i·cal·ly** /-nómmikəlee/ *adv.* —**tax·on·o·mist** /tak sónnəmist/ *n.*

tax·pay·er /táks pày ər/ *n.* somebody who pays tax, especially income tax —**tax·pay·ing** *adj.*

tax rate *n.* the percentage of income paid in income taxes

tax re·turn *n.* the collection of government forms on which earnings and expenses are recorded in order to calculate the tax liability of an individual or business

tax shel·ter *n.* an investment activity that tends to reduce income tax liability —**tax-shel·tered** *adj.*

-taxy *suffix.* order, arrangement ○ *epitaxy* [From Greek *-taxia*, from *tag-*, the stem of *tassein* (see TAXIS)]

Elizabeth Taylor

Tay·lor /táylər/, **Elizabeth** (*b.* 1932) British-born U.S. actor. She became a star in her early film *National Velvet* (1944). She continued in the public eye both as an actor and as a celebrity. Full name **Elizabeth Rosemond Taylor**

Tay·lor, Frederick Winslow (1856–1915) U.S. industrial engineer. He contributed to industrial efficiency by applying "scientific management," based upon time-and-motion studies.

Tay·lor, George (1716–81) American patriot. He signed the Declaration of Independence (1776) as Pennsylvania delegate to the Continental Congress (1776–77).

Tay·lor, Joseph, Jr. (*b.* 1941) U.S. physicist. He shared a Nobel Prize with Russell A. Hulse (1993) for researching binary pulsars. Full name **Joseph Hooton Taylor, Jr.**

Tay·lor, Maxwell D. (1901–87) U.S. soldier. A hero of World War II and the Korean War, he chaired the U.S. Joint Chiefs of Staff (1962–64) and contributed to the U.S. escalation of the war in Vietnam. Full name **Maxwell Davenport Taylor**

Library of Congress

Zachary Taylor

Tay·lor, Zachary (1785–1850) U.S. soldier and 12th president of the United States. He was a hero of the Mexican War (1846–47) prior to becoming president (1849–50). Known as **Old Rough and Ready**

Tay·lor's se·ries *n.* a basic theorem of calculus relating an approximation of the value of a continuous function at a point to the successive derivatives of the function evaluated at the point [Early 19thC. Named for the English mathematician Brook *Taylor* (1685–1731).]

Tay·my·ri·a /tày mírее ə/ autonomous region in north central Siberia, Russia. Area: 332,850 sq. mi./862,100 sq. km.

tay·ra /tírə/ *n.* an agile South American weasel similar to the marten, with a brown coat and a buff patch on the throat. Latin name: *Eira barbara.* [Mid-19thC. Via Portuguese or Spanish *taira* from Tupi.]

Tay-Sachs dis·ease *n.* a genetic disease that principally affects Jewish people of eastern European ancestry. Marked by accumulation of lipids in the brain and nerves, it results in loss of sight and brain functions. [Early 20thC. Named for Warren *Tay* (1843–1927), an English ophthalmologist, and Bernard *Sachs* (1858–1944), a U.S. neurologist.]

taz·za /taátsə/ *n.* an ornamental vessel that has a shallow bowl, usually mounted on a pedestal [Early 19thC. Via Italian from Arabic *ṭasa* (see TASS).]

Tb *symbol.* terbium

TB *abbr.* **1.** torpedo boat **2. TB, T.B.** tuberculosis **3. TB, t.b.** ACCT trial balance

TBA, tba *abbr.* to be announced

T-ball *n.* a children's version of baseball without pitching in which the batter hits a ball placed on a tee

T-bar *n.* **1. METAL BAR T-SHAPED IN CROSS SECTION** a metal bar that is T-shaped in cross section **2.** SKIING **SKI TOW FOR TWO PEOPLE** a ski tow for two people, shaped like an inverted T. Skiers rest against a horizontal bar on either side of a central shaft that pulls them along with their skis on the ground.

TBD *abbr.* to be discussed (*used in e-mail communications*)

Tbi·li·si /təbə leé see/ capital city of Georgia, in the east central part of the country, on the Kura River. Population: 1,268,000 (1990).

T-bill *n.* = **Treasury bill**

T-bone steak *n.* a large thick steak containing a T-shaped bone

tbs., tbsp. *abbr.* tablespoon

Tc *symbol.* technetium

T cell *n.* a type of white blood cell (**lymphocyte**) that matures in the thymus and is essential for various aspects of immunity, especially in combating virus infections and cancers. ◊ **cytotoxic T cell, helper T cell, suppressor T cell** [*T* is a shortening of *thymus-derived*]

Tchai·kov·sky /chī káwfskee/, **Peter Ilich** (1840–93) Russian composer. A major composer of the romantic era, his works include symphonies, piano concertos, and ballet scores such as *Swan Lake* (1876).

tchotch·ke /chóchkə/ *n.* a trinket or piece of bric-a-brac

TCP/IP *abbr.* transmission control protocol/Internet protocol

Peter Ilich Tchaikovsky

TD *abbr.* **1.** tank destroyer **2.** FOOTBALL touchdown **3. TD, T.D.** treasury department

TDD *abbr.* telecommunications device for the deaf

TDM *abbr.* time-division multiplexing

TDY *abbr.* MIL temporary duty

te *n.* = **ti**

Te *symbol.* tellurium

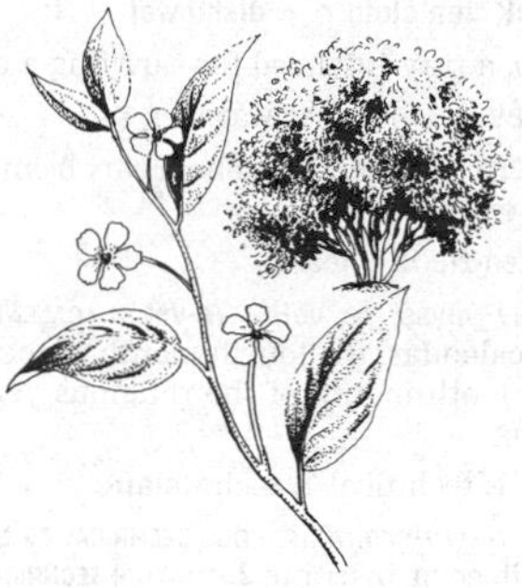
Tea

tea /tee/ *n.* **1.** PLANTS **ASIAN EVERGREEN SHRUB** an evergreen shrub of the Theaceae family, native to Asia, with toothed leathery leaves and fragrant cup-shaped flowers. Latin name: *Camellia sinensis.* **2.** BEVERAGES **PLANT'S DRIED LEAVES FOR MAKING DRINK** the dried leaves of the tea plant, often shredded, used to make a drink by adding boiling water **3. TEA DRINK** a tea drink, usually served hot but sometimes with ice **4.** BEVERAGES **DRINK MADE BY INFUSION** any drink made by infusion of particular plant leaves, or the dried leaves used as the basis of a drink **5.** PLANTS **PLANT USED FOR INFUSED DRINK** a plant other than the tea plant used to make an infused beverage **6.** FOOD **AFTERNOON MEAL OF CAKES AND TEA** a light meal taken in the afternoon, usually consisting of cake, sandwiches, and tea or other nonalcoholic drinks, or an afternoon social event at which this meal is eaten **7.** *U.K., Aus, NZ, Scotland* FOOD **MAIN MEAL OF DAY** the main meal of the day when it is eaten early in the evening **8. BREAKFAST IN GUYANA** in Guyana, the first meal of the day **9.** DRUGS **MARIJUANA** marijuana (*dated slang*) [Mid-17thC. Origin uncertain: probably via earlier Dutch *tee* from, ultimately, Chinese (Amoy dialect) *te*.]

WORD KEY: USAGE

See Usage note at *dinner.*

tea bag *n.* a small bag made of permeable paper or cloth containing tea leaves that is placed in boiling water to make one serving of tea

tea ball *n.* a small perforated metal ball for holding tea leaves that is placed in boiling water to make tea

tea·ber·ry /teé bèree/ (*plural* **-ries**) *n.* **1.** = **wintergreen 2.** = **withe rod** [Late 18thC. *Tea* from the fact that its leaves can be used as a substitute for tea.]

tea cad·dy *n.* a small container, usually with a tight-fitting lid, for holding tea leaves

tea·cake /teé kàyk/ *n.* a plain cookie, cake, or biscuit served with tea

tea cart *n.* = **tea wagon**

tea cer·e·mo·ny *n.* a Japanese ritual in which tea is prepared, served, and drunk in a prescribed manner

teach /teech/ (**taught, taught** /tawt/, **teach·ing, teach·es**) *v.* **1.** *vt.* **IMPART KNOWLEDGE OR SKILL** to impart knowledge or skill to somebody by instruction or example **2.** *vti.* **GIVE LESSONS** to give lessons in a subject, or to give lessons to a person or animal **3.** *vt.* **MAKE UNDERSTAND BY EXPERIENCE** to bring understanding to somebody, especially through an experience ○ *The episode taught me a lesson I'll never forget.* **4.** *vt.* **TEACH REGULARLY** to engage in imparting knowledge or instruction for a period of time in a particular place ○ *teaches college* **5.** *vt.* **ADVOCATE OR PREACH SOMETHING** to advocate or preach something [Old English *tǣcan*. Ultimately from an Indo-European base meaning "to show," which is also the ancestor of English *token, digit,* and *deictic*.]

WORD KEY: SYNONYMS

teach, educate, train, instruct, coach, tutor, school, drill

CORE MEANING: to cause to acquire knowledge or skill in something

teach to impart information to somebody or show somebody how to do something; **educate** to teach somebody generally, for example, in a school or college, especially when taking into account all that a person learns over a period of time; **train** to teach somebody how to do something by means of instruction, observation, and practice. Used especially in relation to jobs; **instruct** a formal word meaning the same as *teach*; **coach** to teach a specific subject or skill to one person or a very small group of people, especially in preparation for an exam. It is used especially to talk about specialized sports instruction; **tutor** to give somebody individual tuition on a particular subject or in a particular skill; **school** a fairly formal word used to talk about teaching somebody a particular skill or area of expertise in a thorough and detailed way; **drill** to teach something by means of repeated exercises and practice. Used especially when this seems rigorous or severe.

teach·a·ble /teéchəb'l/ *adj.* **1. WILLING TO LEARN** willing and able to learn **2. ABLE TO BE TAUGHT** relating to something such as a skill or subject that can be taught —**teach·a·bly** *adv.*

teach·er /teéchər/ *n.* **1. SOMEBODY WHO TEACHES** somebody who teaches, especially as a profession **2. ANYTHING THAT TEACHES** anything from which something may be learned ○ *Experience is a great teacher.* —**teach·er·less** *adj.* —**teach·er·ly** *adj.*

teach·er bird *n.* = **ovenbird** [*Teacher* is an imitation of the sound made by the bird]

teach·ers col·lege, **teach·ers' col·lege** *n.* a college for the training of teachers

teach·er's pet *n.* **1. TEACHER'S FAVORITE STUDENT** a student who is especially favored by a teacher (*insult*) **2. SOMEBODY FAVORED BY AUTHORITY FIGURE** somebody who is in special favor with a figure in authority

teach-in *n.* an extended period of speeches, lectures, and discussions, usually held at a college or university as part of a political or social protest

teach·ing /teéching/ *n.* **1. PRACTICE OR PROFESSION OF A TEACHER** the profession or practice of being a teacher **2. SOMETHING TAUGHT** something that is taught, e.g., a point of doctrine (*often used in the plural*) ■ *adj.* **1. USED FOR TEACHING** used for or in teaching **2. THAT TEACHES** being a person or establishment that teaches

teach·ing a·ssis·tant, **teach·ing fel·low** *n.* a graduate student in a college or university who teaches, especially undergraduates, in return for tuition and usually a small stipend —**teach·ing a·ssis·tant·ship** *n.*

teach·ing fel·low *n.* = **teaching assistant** —**teach·ing fel·low·ship** *n.*

teach·ing hos·pi·tal *n.* a hospital that provides supervised practical training for medical students, student nurses, or other health-care professionals, often in conjunction with a medical school

tea co·zy *n.* a soft, padded cover for keeping a teapot warm

tea·cup /teé kùp/ *n.* **1. CUP FOR TEA** a small to medium-sized cup, usually used with a saucer, especially for serving tea **2. tea·cup, tea·cup·ful AMOUNT IN TEACUP** the amount a teacup holds

tea dance *n.* an afternoon social event at which tea is often served and people do ballroom or other partner dancing

tea gar·den *n.* **1. GARDEN WHERE TEA IS SERVED** a garden or outdoor restaurant where tea and light refreshments are served to the public **2.** AGRIC **TEA PLANTATION** a plantation where tea is grown

tea gown *n.* a loose, usually waistless, dress of light thin fabric trimmed with lace, worn by women in the late 19th century for afternoon social occasions at which men would not be present

tea·house /teé hòwss/ (*plural* **-hous·es** /-hòwzəz/) *n.* a restaurant, especially in China or Japan, that serves tea and light refreshments

teak /teek/ *n.* **1.** TREES **TALL EAST INDIAN TREE** a tall East Indian tree of the vervain family, valued for its wood. Latin name: *Tectona grandis.* **2. teak, teak·wood** INDUST **WOOD OF THE TEAK TREE** the wood of the teak tree, used for making furniture and in shipbuilding **3.** TREES **TREE OR WOOD SIMILAR TO TEAK** a tree or wood that is similar to teak **4.** COLORS **YELLOWISH-BROWN COLOR** a yellowish-brown color ■ *adj.* COLORS **YELLOWISH-BROWN** of a yellowish-brown color like teak [Late 17thC. Via Portuguese *teca* from Tamil or Malayalam *tēkku*.]

tea·ket·tle /teé kètt'l/ *n.* a kettle used for boiling water for making tea

teal /teel/ *n.* (*plural* **teal** *or* **teals**) **1.** BIRDS **SMALL DUCK** a small freshwater surface-feeding duck with bright iridescent blue or green patches on the wings. Genus: *Anas.* **2.** COLORS **GREENISH-BLUE COLOR** a greenish-blue color ■ *adj.* COLORS **OF A GREENISH-BLUE COLOR** of a greenish-blue color [13thC. Origin unknown.]

tea leaf *n.* **1.** PLANTS **DRIED LEAF OF TEA PLANT** a dried leaf or shredded part of the dried leaf of the tea plant, used to make tea **2.** BEVERAGES **TEA LEAF AFTER INFUSION** a tea leaf, or part of a leaf, after it has been infused (*often used in the plural*)

team /teem/ *n.* **1.** SPORTS **GROUP FORMING SIDE IN SPORTS COMPETITION** a group of people forming one side in a sports competition **2. COOPERATIVELY FUNCTIONING GROUP** a number of people organized to function cooperatively as a group **3. ANIMALS WORKED TOGETHER** two or more animals worked together, especially to pull a vehicle or agricultural equipment **4. TEAM OF ANIMALS WITH VEHICLE** a team of animals and the vehicle harnessed to them **5. ANIMALS PERFORMING TOGETHER** a group of animals that perform or are shown together **6. GROUPING OF ANIMALS** a grouping of animals such as a flock, brood, or herd (*regional*) ■ *v.* (**teamed, team·ing, teams**) **1.** *vti.* **FORM OR FORM INTO A TEAM** to form a team, or to form people or animals into a team **2.** *vt.* **TRANSPORT BY A TEAM** to transport something using a team of animals **3.** *vi.* **DRIVE A TEAM** to drive a team of farm animals or a truck [Old English *tēam*. Ultimately from an Indo-European base meaning "to lead," which is also the ancestor of English *tug* and *duct*.]

team·mate /teém màyt/ *n.* a player on the same team

team play·er *n.* somebody who is willing to work cooperatively with others and to subordinate personal interests in order to achieve a common goal

team spir·it *n.* an enthusiastic attitude toward working productively with a team or work group

team·ster /teémstər/ *n.* **1. TRUCK DRIVER** somebody who drives a truck that is used commercially for hauling loads, especially as an occupation **2. SOMEBODY WHO DRIVES A TEAM OF ANIMALS** somebody who drives a team of animals used for hauling **3. MEMBER OF THE TEAMSTERS UNION** a member of the Teamsters Union

Team·sters Un·ion *n.* a labor union whose members are mainly truck drivers. Full form **International Brotherhood of Teamsters, Chauffeurs, Warehousemen, and Helpers of America**

team teach·ing *n.* an instructional program involving two or more subjects that are taught in a coordinated way by specialist teachers

team·work /teém wùrk/ *n.* **1. COOPERATIVE WORK BY A GROUP** a cooperative effort by a group or team **2. WORK PRODUCED BY A GROUP** work produced by a group or team

tea par·ty *n.* an afternoon social event at which tea is served

tea·pot /teé pòt/ *n.* a covered container with a spout and handle, used for making and serving tea

tea·poy /teé pòy/ *n.* **1. SMALL TABLE** a small three-legged ornamental table or stand **2. SMALL TABLE USED FOR TEA** a small table used to hold a tea caddy and tea service [Early 19thC. By folk etymology (from TEA) from Hindi *tipāī*, an alteration of Persian *si-pāya*, literally "three-footed."]

tear[1] /tair/ *v.* (**tore** /tawr/, **torn** /tawrn/, **tear·ing, tears**) **1.** *vti.* **PULL OR COME APART** to pull something such as paper or cloth into pieces, or to come apart or rip ○ *She tore open the package.* **2.** *vt.* **SEPARATE SOMETHING USING FORCE** to remove or separate something using force **3.** *vi.* **MOVE OR ACT QUICKLY OR CARELESSLY** to move or act with great or careless speed ○ *He went tearing off down the road.* **4.** *vt.* DIVIDE SOMETHING to divide or fragment something ○ *an organization torn by internal conflict* **5.** *vt.* MAKE A HOLE IN SOMETHING to make a hole or opening in something such as a garment ○ *tore her skirt on a nail* **6.** *vt.* CUT SOMETHING LEAVING JAGGED EDGES to cut something, especially flesh, leaving jagged edges **7.** *vt.* MED SPRAIN to injure a muscle or ligament so that some of the tissue is pulled apart and separated **8.** *vti.* UPSET OR DISTRESS to upset or distress somebody ○ *the memory tore at his heart* ■ *n.* **1.** ACT OF TEARING an act of tearing **2.** SPLIT CAUSED BY TEARING a hole or split caused by tearing **3.** A HURRY a hurry or rush **4.** SPREE an unrestrained activity or indulgence [Old English *teran.* Ultimately from an Indo-European base meaning "to split," which is also the ancestor of English *turd* and probably *tart.*] —**tear·a·ble** *adj.* —**tear·er** *n.*

WORD KEY: SYNONYMS

tear, rend, rip, split

CORE MEANING: to pull apart forcibly

tear a general word for pulling something apart forcibly, either by accident or on purpose; **rend** a formal or literary word suggesting tearing with extreme strength or violence, most often now used figuratively; **rip** to tear something with one rapid uninterrupted movement, either by accident or on purpose; **split** to divide something into two parts with a single movement usually with the blade of a tool or weapon.

tear apart *vt.* **1.** FRAGMENT to cause division, separation or conflict in a group or organisation ○ *a family torn apart by war* **2.** DISTRESS SOMEBODY to cause somebody distress or emotional conflict ○ *the strain of separation was tearing us apart* **3.** SEARCH to search a place thoroughly, often causing disruptions and mess ○ *The police tore apart looking for the weapon.*

tear away *vt.* to force or persuade yourself or somebody else to leave a place or object

tear down *vt.* to demolish, destroy, or dismantle something such as a building

tear into *vt.* to attack somebody or something vigorously, either physically or verbally

tear off *vt.* **1.** REMOVE CLOTHES QUICKLY to remove clothes quickly and carelessly **2.** PRODUCE SOMETHING QUICKLY to produce something quickly and carelessly

tear up *vt.* to tear something into small pieces, e.g., in order to destroy it

tear[2] /teer/ *n.* **1.** PHYSIOL SINGLE DROP OF FLUID FROM THE EYE a single drop of salty fluid secreted by the lacrimal gland of the eye **2.** DROP OF LIQUID a drop of liquid or hardened fluid, epecially one with a round base and narrower top ■ **tears** *npl.* **1.** CRYING weeping accompanied by intense emotion **2.** PHYSIOL LIQUID BATHING THE EYE the salty liquid secreted by the lacrimal gland that moistens and protects the surface of the eye and its surrounding tissue **3.** EXCESS OF LIQUID IN THE EYES a greater than usual amount of liquid produced by the eye or eyes, often accompanying intense emotions, or caused by irritation of the eye ■ *vi.* **(teared, tear·ing, tears)** PRODUCE TEARS to produce tears, especially in excessive amounts ○ *My eyes tear a lot during the allergy season.* [Old English *tēar.* Ultimately from an Indo-European word meaning "tear," which is also the ancestor of English *lachrymose.*] —**tear·less** *adj.*

tear·drop /teér dròp/ *n.* **1.** = **tear**[2] *n.* 1 **2.** SHAPE RESEMBLING A TEAR a shape that resembles a tear, or something having this shape

tear duct /teér-/ *n.* a passage that conveys tears, especially the duct that drains tears from the inner corner of the eye into the nasal cavity

tear·ful /teérfəl/ *adj.* **1.** CRYING crying, about to cry, or feeling like crying, usually because of an emotion such as great sadness **2.** LIKELY TO CAUSE TEARS sad enough to cause weeping ○ *a tearful occasion* —**tear·ful·ly** *adv.* —**tear·ful·ness** *n.*

tear gas /teér-/ *n.* a chemical agent, delivered by a grenade or other means, that incapacitates a person by irritating the eyes

tear-gas /teér gàss/ **(tear-gassed, tear-gas·sing, tear-gas·es)** *vt.* to spray somebody with tear gas

tear·ing /táiring/ *adj.* violent or frenzied ○ *in a tearing hurry*

tear·jerk·er /teér jùrkər/ *n.* a story or artistic work that is excessively sentimental (*informal*) —**tear-jerk·ing** *adj.*

tear-off /táir àwf/ *adj.* produced in a block of paper in sheet form, or perforated, so that individual pieces can be removed easily

tea·room /teé ròom, -ròom/ *n.* **1.** RESTAURANT SERVING TEA a restaurant or café serving tea and other beverages, as well as light refreshments (*often used in the plural*) **2.** *S Africa* SMALL SHOP SELLING VARIETY OF GOODS a small shop in which some staple groceries, newspapers, and small consumer goods are sold

tea rose *n.* any of one several varieties of a bush rose native to China that grows large tea-scented pink or yellow flowers. Latin name: *Rosa odorata.*

tear sheet /táir-/ *n.* a single page taken from a magazine or other periodical, often used to prove to an advertiser that an advertisement has been published

tear·stain /teér stàyn/ *n.* a mark or track left by tears —**tear-stained** *adj.*

tear·y /teéree/ **(-i·er, -i·est)** *adj.* **1.** WET WITH TEARS wet with or full of tears **2.** ABOUT TO CRY seeming to be about to cry **3.** CAUSING WEEPING causing or sad enough to cause weeping **4.** LIKE TEARS resembling tears —**tear·i·ly** *adv.* —**tear·i·ness** *n.*

tear·y-eyed *adj.* **1.** WITH TEARS IN THE EYES with tears in the eyes, especially if caused by emotion **2.** CHARACTERIZED BY WEEPING characterized by weeping, especially when caused by sadness

tease /teez/ *v.* **(teased, teas·ing, teas·es) 1.** *vti.* DELIBERATELY ANNOY OR IRRITATE to deliberately annoy or irritate a person or an animal **2.** *vti.* MAKE FUN OF SOMEBODY to make fun of somebody, either playfully or maliciously **3.** *vt.* PERSUADE BY COAXING to urge somebody, especially to do something, by continual coaxing **4.** *vt.* AROUSE PHYSICAL DESIRE WITHOUT GIVING SATISFACTION to arouse hope, curiosity, or especially physical desire in somebody with no intention of giving satisfaction **5.** *vt.* HAIR MAKE HAIR LOOK THICKER to comb the hair with quick short movements toward the roots so that it stands up away from the head **6.** *vt.* TEXTILES PULL FIBERS APART to pull fibers apart by combing or carding **7.** *vt.* TEXTILES RAISE A NAP BY COMBING to raise the nap on cloth by combing it with a wire brush **8.** *vt.* BIOL SEPARATE TISSUE to separate the parts of a tissue specimen gently with a needle in preparation for examination under a microscope ■ *n.* **1.** SOMEBODY WHO TEASES a person who has a tendency to tease others **2.** PERSON WHO TEASES SEXUALLY a person who teases somebody else sexually **3.** PROVOCATIVE OPENING REMARK an opening remark or action intended to stimulate curiosity or interest **4.** ACT OF TEASING an act of teasing [Old English *t_æsan.* Originally "to separate the fibers of wool" (with the prickly "teasel" flower), hence "irritate," later "make fun of."] —**teas·ing** *adj.* —**teas·ing·ly** *adv.*

tease out *vt.* **1.** GRADUALLY SEPARATE SOMETHING to gradually separate things that are tangled up, or gradually separate something from an object with which it is entangled **2.** EXTRACT THE TRUTH to extract something gradually, e.g., the truth or information

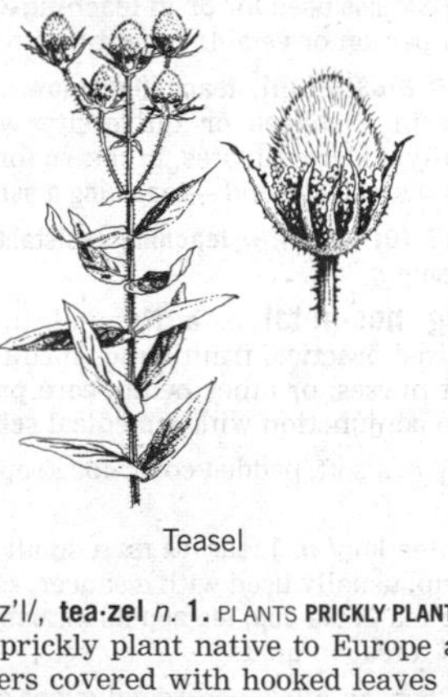

Teasel

tea·sel /teéz'l/, **tea·zel** *n.* **1.** PLANTS PRICKLY PLANT OF EUROPE AND ASIA a prickly plant native to Europe and Asia with flowers covered with hooked leaves (**bracts**). Genus: *Dipsacus.* **2.** TEXTILES TEASEL FLOWER HEADS the flower heads of the teasel, used in the textile industry to raise the nap on fabric **3.** IMPLEMENT USED TO RAISE NAP an industrial implement or device used to raise the nap on fabric [Old English *tæsel*] —**tea·sel·ler** *n.*

teas·er /teézər/ *n.* **1.** = **tease** *n.* 1 **2.** TRICKY PROBLEM a tricky or difficult problem or question **3.** MARKETING ADVERTISEMENT OFFERING A GIFT an advertisement offering something for free such as a bonus or gift **4.** TV PREVIEW OF A TV SHOW, BOOK, OR MOVIE a preview intended to arouse curiosity and interest in a forthcoming broadcast or publication (*informal*) **5.** TEXTILES IMPLEMENT FOR TEASING WOOL an implement for teasing fibers, especially wool

tea ser·vice, tea set *n.* a set of matching articles such as cups, saucers, and a teapot, used for serving tea

tea·shop /teé shop/ *n.* = **tearoom** [Mid-19thC]

tea·spoon /teé spòon/ *n.* **1.** SMALL SPOON a small spoon, used especially for stirring tea and other beverages and for eating desserts **2. tea·spoon, tea·spoon·ful** AMOUNT HELD BY A TEASPOON the amount held by a teaspoon **3.** ONE THIRD OF A TABLESPOON a standard household measure equal to one-third of a tablespoon or 5 ml

teat /teet, tit/ *n.* **1.** ANAT, ZOOL BODY PART FOR PRODUCING MILK a protuberance on the breast or udder of a female mammal through which milk is excreted for the nourishment of young **2.** *U.K.* = **nipple** *n.* 2 [12thC. From Old French *tete,* of Germanic origin.] —**teat·ed** *adj.*

tea ta·ble *n.* a small table at which tea is served

tea·time /teé tīm/ *n.* the usual time at which tea is served, typically mid- or late afternoon

tea tow·el, tea cloth *n.* = **dishtowel**

tea tray *n.* a tray intended for carrying a tea service

tea trol·ley *n. U.K.* = **tea wagon**

tea wag·on *n.* a small household cart from which tea can be served

tea·zel, tea·zle *n.* = **teasel**

Te·bet /táy vàyss, te vét/, **Te·vet** *n.* CALENDAR in the Jewish calendar, the fourth month of the civil year and the tenth month of the religious year. It is 29 days long.

tec. *abbr.* **1.** technical **2.** technician

tech /tek/ *n.* (*informal*) **1.** EDUC TECHNICAL COLLEGE a technical college or institute **2.** THEATER TECHNICAL REHEARSAL a technical rehearsal [Early 20thC.]

tech. *abbr.* **1.** technician **2.** technology **3.** technical

tech cit·y (*plural* **tech cit·ies**) *n.* a town or city that has a lot of advanced technology industries, especially connected with computing and electronic engineering

teched /techt/ *adj.* = **tetched**

tech·ie /tékee/, **tek·kie** *n.* somebody who is interested in, adept at, or studying a technical discipline, especially one that is based on computing or electronics (*informal*) [Mid-20thC. Formed from TECH.]

tech·ne·ti·um /tek neéshee əm/ *n.* a silvery-gray radioactive metallic element found only in the fission products of uranium or made artificially by the particle bombardment of molybdenum. Symbol **Tc** [Mid-20thC. From modern Latin, formed from Greek *tekhnētos* "artificial," from *tekhnē* (see TECHNICAL).]

tech·ne·tron·ic /tèknə trónnik/ *adj.* associated with or marked by the changes brought about by modern technology and electronics [Mid-20thC. Blend of Greek *tekhnē* "art, skill" (see TECHNICAL) and ELECTRONIC.]

tech·nic /téknik/ *n.* **1.** INDUST = **technics** (*takes a singular or plural verb*) **2.** TECHNIQUE the way in which the basics of something are treated or skill in handling a technique (*dated*) [Early 17thC. From Greek *tekhnikos* "of art" (see TECHNICAL).]

tech·ni·cal /téknik'l/ *adj.* **1.** RELATING TO INDUSTRY OR APPLIED SCIENCE relating to or specializing in industrial techniques or subjects or applied science **2.** SKILLED IN PRACTICAL SUBJECTS skilled in practical or scientific subjects **3.** BELONGING TO PARTICULAR SUBJECT OR PROFESSION belonging to or involving a particular subject, field, or profession ○ *technical glossaries* **4.** EXHIBITING TECHNIQUE exhibiting or deriving from technique or the use of technique ○ *a high level of technical expertise* **5.** STRICTLY INTERPRETED according to a strict interpretation of rules or words **6.** FIN ANALYZING PRICES AND MARKET INDICATORS used to describe a type of security analysis based on past prices and volume levels as well as other market indicators **7.** CLOTHES HIGH-TECH used to describe outdoor clothing that has been made using state-of-the-art materials and techniques ○ *Our technical fleece jacket has advanced dual construction.* ■ *n.* BASKETBALL = **technical foul** [Early 17thC. Formed from Greek *tekhnikos* "of art," from *tekhnē* "art, skill." Ultimately from an Indo-European base meaning "to weave," which is also the ancestor of

English *text* and *tectonic*.] —**tech·ni·cal·ly** *adv.* —**tech·ni·cal·ness** *n.*

tech·ni·cal draw·ing *n.* a precise scale drawing of something, usually prepared by a draftsman for architectural, engineering, or industrial purposes, showing dimensions or quantities. Computer-assisted design programs have automated many of the drafting functions and made it possible to reduce significantly the time from concept to finished product.

tech·ni·cal foul *n.* in basketball, a foul against a player or coach for unsporting behavior or language rather than for physical contact with an opponent

tech·ni·cal·i·ty /tèkni kállətee/ (*plural* **-ties**) *n.* **1.** INFORMATION UNDERSTOOD ONLY BY SPECIALISTS information such as a detail or a term that is understood by or relevant only to a specialist **2.** TRIVIAL POINT FROM STRICTLY APPLYING RULES a minor point arising from a rigorous interpretation of laws or rules ○ *the case was dismissed on a legal technicality* **3.** QUALITY OR STATE OF BEING TECHNICAL the quality or state of being technical

tech·ni·cal knock·out *n.* a decision in boxing that ends a match because one of the participants is too badly injured to continue fighting

tech·ni·cal re·hears·al *n.* a rehearsal of a play or other theatrical presentation for the purpose of making sure that lights, sound, and any other technical effects are cued correctly and in working order

tech·ni·cal ser·geant *n.* a noncommissioned rank in the U.S. Air Force higher than staff sergeant and lower than master sergeant

tech·ni·cal sup·port *n.* a repair or advice service offered to customers by some computer hardware and software manufacturers, usually by telephone, fax, or e-mail

tech·ni·cian /tek nísh'n/ *n.* **1.** SPECIALIST IN INDUSTRIAL TECHNIQUES a person who is skilled in specific industrial techniques **2.** LABORATORY EMPLOYEE somebody employed to do practical work in a laboratory **3.** SOMEBODY SKILLED RATHER THAN EXPERT somebody who has skills but lacks originality or flair

tech·ni·col·or /tékni kùllər/, **tech·ni·col·ored** *adj.* brightly, vividly, or garishly colored [Mid-20thC. From TECHNICOLOR.]

Tech·ni·col·or /tékni kùllər/ *tdmk.* a trademark for an early color process for making motion pictures that used three-color separation negatives and a dye transfer process with three matrices made from the negatives

tech·nics /tékniks/, **tech·nic** *n.* the science or rules of a particular field of knowledge, especially a technical one (*takes a singular or plural verb*) [Mid-19thC. Plural of TECHNIC.]

tech·nique /tek neék/ *n.* **1.** PROCEDURE OR SKILL USED IN A TASK the procedure, skill, or art used in a particular task **2.** WAY IN WHICH THE BASICS ARE TREATED the way in which the basics of something, e.g., an artistic work or a sport, are treated **3.** SKILL IN HANDLING THE TECHNIQUE OF SOMETHING skill or expertise in handling the technique of something ○ *a pianist with superb technique* **4.** SPECIAL ABILITY a special ability or knack [Early 19thC. Via French from Greek *tekhnikos* "of art" (see TECHNICAL).]

techno- *prefix.* technology, technological ○ *technophobia* [From TECHNOLOGY]

tech·no·bab·ble /téknō bàbb'l/ *n.* language in which technical jargon or terms are overused, with the effect of making straightforward information difficult or impossible to understand

tech·noc·ra·cy /tek nókrəssee/ (*plural* **-cies**) *n.* **1.** GOVERNMENT BY TECHNICIANS a social system in which scientists, engineers, and technicians have high social standing and political power **2.** PHILOSOPHY PROMOTING TECHNOCRACY a philosophy that advocates the enlistment of a bureaucracy of highly trained engineers, scientists, or technicians to run the government and society

tech·no·crat /téknə kràt/ *n.* **1.** ENGINEER OR ECONOMIST AS BUREAUCRAT a bureaucrat who is intensively trained in engineering, economics, or some form of technology **2.** ADHERENT OF TECHNOCRACY a proponent of government by technicians —**tech·no·crat·ic** /tèknə kráttik/ *adj.*

tech·no·freak /téknə freék/ *n.* somebody who is a technical expert in, or obsessively enthusiastic about, information systems (*informal*) [Late 20thC]

technol. *abbr.* technology

tech·nol·o·gize /tek nóllə jīz/ (**-gized, -giz·ing, -giz·es**) *vti.* to modify or modernize something by introducing technology —**tech·nol·o·gi·za·tion** /tek nòlləji záysh'n/ *n.*

tech·nol·o·gy /tek nólləjee/ (*plural* **-gies**) *n.* **1.** APPLICATION OF TOOLS AND METHODS the study, development, and application of devices, machines, and techniques for manufacturing and productive processes ○ *recent developments in seismographic technology* **2.** METHOD OF APPLYING TECHNICAL KNOWLEDGE a method or methodology that applies technical knowledge or tools ○ *a new technology for accelerating incubation* ○ *"...Maryland-based firm uses database and Internet technology to track a company's consumption of printed goods..."* (*Forbes Global Business and Finance*; November 1998) **3.** ANTHROP SUM OF A SOCIETY'S OR CULTURE'S KNOWLEDGE the sum of a society's or culture's practical knowledge, especially with reference to its material culture [Early 17thC. From Greek *tekhnologia*, literally "systematic treatment," literally "science of craft," from *tekhnē* "art, craft."] —**tech·no·log·ic** /tèknə lójjik/ *adj.* —**tech·no·log·i·cal** /-lójjik'l/ *adj.* —**tech·nol·o·gist** /tek nólləjist/ *n.* —**tech·no·log·i·cal·ly** /tèknə lójjiklee/ *adv.*

tech·no·phile /téknə fīl/ *n.* somebody who is comfortable with and adapts readily to new technology or computerization

tech·no·phobe /téknə fōb/ *n.* somebody who is intimidated and confused by new techology and computerization

tech·no·pho·bi·a /tèknə fōbee ə/ *n.* fear of or resistance to new technology and computerization —**tech·no·phobe** /téknə fōb/ *n.*

tech·no·struc·ture /téknə strùkchər/ *n.* a network of controlling technocrats in an organization or society

tech·no·thril·ler /téknə thrìllər/ *n.* a suspenseful book or movie in which the plot turns on seemingly plausible technological wonders

tech·y *adj.* = **tetchy** —**tech·i·ly** *adv.* —**tech·i·ness** *n.*

tec·ta plural of **tectum**

tec·ton·ic /tek tónnik/ *adj.* **1.** GEOL OF THE DEFORMATION OF ROCKS relating to the forces that produce movement and deformation of the Earth's crust **2.** CONSTR OF CONSTRUCTION relating to construction and architecture [Mid-17thC. Via late Latin from Greek *tektonikos*, from *tekton* "builder, carpenter" (source of English *architect*).] —**tec·ton·i·cal·ly** *adv.*

tec·ton·ic plate *n.* a segment of the earth's crust that moves relative to other plates and is characterized by volcanic and seismic activity around its margins

tec·ton·ics /tek tónniks/ *n.* **1.** GEOL STUDY OF THE EARTH'S CRUST the study of the mechanisms and results of large-scale movement of the Earth's crust, such as that producing mountain ranges and extensive fault systems (*takes a singular verb*) ◊ **plate tectonics 2.** BUILDING SCIENCE OF BUILDING the science or practice of building construction

tec·trix /téktriks/ (*plural* **-tri·ces** /-seēz/) *n.* ZOOL = **covert** *n.* 3 [Late 19thC. From modern Latin, from Latin *tect-*, past participle stem of *tegere* (see TECTUM).] —**tec·tri·cial** /tek trísh'l/ *adj.*

tec·tum /téktəm/ (*plural* **-ta** /-tə/) *n.* a part in the body that forms a covering or is arranged like a roof [Early 20thC. From Latin, "roof," from *tegere* "to cover" (source of English *detect* and *protect*).] —**tec·tal** *adj.*

Te·cum·seh /tə kúmssə/ (1768?–1813) Native North American leader. As leader of the Shawnee people he attempted to form an alliance of Native American tribes to fight against U.S. expansion into the Midwest. He was killed in battle fighting on the British side in the War of 1812.

ted /ted/ (**ted·ded, ted·ding, teds**) *vt.* to spread or shake up mown grass in order to dry it when making hay [15thC. From Old Norse *teðja* "to spread (manure)."] —**ted·der** *n.*

ted·der /téddər/ *n.* a machine or person that spreads or shakes mown grass so that it can dry during hay making

ted·dy /téddee/ (*plural* **-dies**) *n.* **1.** = **teddy bear 2.** CLOTHES WOMAN'S UNDERWEAR a woman's one-piece undergarment serving as both bra and panties [Early 20thC. Origin of sense 2 uncertain: probably from sense 1, perhaps because the loose-fitting, all-in-one shape was thought to resemble a teddy bear.]

ted·dy bear, **ted·dy** *n.* a furry stuffed toy in the shape of a stylized bear cub [Early 20thC. Named for *Theodore ("Teddy")* ROOSEVELT, who was fond of bear-hunting.]

WORD KEY: ORIGIN

President Theodore Roosevelt was fond of bear-hunting. His nickname "Teddy," was used in a humorous poem in the *New York Times* about the adventures of two bears. Their names (Teddy B and Teddy G) were then appropriated to two bears in the Bronx Zoo whose popularity caused toy manufacturers to market toy bears as ***teddy bears***.

ted·dy boy, **Teddy boy** *n.* a young man in Britain in the 1950s and early 1960s who followed the fashion of dressing in neo-Edwardian style with tight narrow trousers, pointed shoes, and long sideburns [Mid-20thC. *Teddy* from the nickname for *Edward*, alluding to EDWARD VII.]

Te De·um /tay dáy əm, tee deé əm/ (*plural* **Te De·ums**) *n.* **1.** CHRISTIAN HYMN an ancient Christian hymn praising God that is sung or recited at matins in the Roman Catholic Church or at morning prayers in the Church of England **2.** CHRISTIAN SERVICE OF THANKSGIVING a Christian service of thanksgiving that uses the Te Deum [Pre-12thC. From Latin *Te Deum laudamus* "Thee God, we praise," the first words of the hymn.]

te·di·ous /teédee əss/ *adj.* boring because of being long, monotonous, or repetitive —**te·di·ous·ly** *adv.* —**te·di·ous·ness** *n.*

WORD KEY: SYNONYMS

See Synonyms at ***boring***.

te·di·um /teédee əm/ *n.* the quality of being boring, monotonous, too long, or repetitive [Mid-17thC. From Latin *taedium* "weariness, disgust," from *taedere* "to be wearisome."]

tee[1] /tee/ *n.* **1.** LETTER T the letter T **2.** CLOTHES T-SHIRT a T-shirt (*informal*) **3.** T-SHAPED THING something with the shape or form of a capital T, e.g., two pipes joined to form this shape **4.** SPORTS TARGET the mark aimed at in curling, quoits, and some other games [15thC. The sense "target" is of uncertain origin: perhaps from the meaning "T-shaped thing," from the shape of the marks that were originally used.]

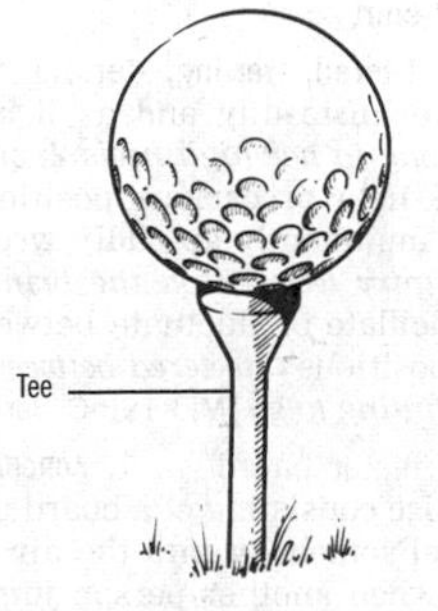

Tee

tee[2] /tee/ *n.* **1.** GOLF PEG a small wooden or plastic peg with one pointed and one cupped end, inserted in the ground to hold a golf ball **2.** GOLF STARTING AREA an area on a golf course where play for a new hole begins **3.** FOOTBALL, RUGBY BALL STAND a plastic device that supports a football or rugby ball on the ground in kicking position ■ *vti.* (**teed, tee·ing, tees**) GOLF POSITION THE BALL to place a ball on a tee ready for striking [Late 17thC. Originally Scottish dialect, of uncertain origin: perhaps a back-formation from earlier *teaz* (taken as plural), of unknown origin.]

tee off *vi.* **1.** GOLF START PLAY to hit the ball from a tee at the start of a hole of golf **2.** START SOMETHING NEW to start a new activity (*informal*)

teed off *adj.* angry, especially because of something that somebody has done (*informal*) [Origin uncertain: probably an alteration of *peed (pissed) off*]

tee-hee, **te-hee** *interj.* EXPRESSING LAUGHTER used to indicate brief, especially mocking or gloating laughter ■ *vi.* (**tee-heed, tee-hee·ing, tee-hees; te-heed, te-hee·ing, te-hees**) LAUGH to laugh or chuckle [14thC. An imitation of the sound.]

teem[1] /teem/ (**teemed, teem·ing, teems**) *vi.* to have an extremely large number of people or animals in a place ○ *streets teeming with people* [Old English *tēman*, from a prehistoric Germanic word, which is also the ancestor of English *team*. The meaning "abound" evolved from "give birth" via "produce offspring prolifically."]

teem[2] /teem/ (**teemed, teem·ing, teems**) *v.* **1.** *vt.* DISCHARGE SOMETHING to pour out or empty something **2.** *vi.* RAIN HEAVILY to rain very hard [14thC. From Old Norse *tœma* "to empty," from *tómr* "empty."]

teen[1] /teen/ *adj.* TEENAGE teenage (*informal*) ■ *n.* TEENAGER a teenager (*informal*) [Early 19thC. Shortening.]

teen[2] /teen/ *n.* a feeling of misery or pain (*archaic*) [Old English *tēona*. Ultimately from an Indo-European word meaning "misfortune, suffering."]

teen·age /teé nàyj/, **teen-age, teen·aged** /teén àyjd/, **teen-aged** *adj.* **1.** BETWEEN 13 AND 19 aged between 13 and 19 ○ *teenage girls* **2.** OF TEENAGERS relating to teenagers ○ *teenage styles*

teen·ag·er /teé nàyjər/ *n.* a boy or girl between the ages of 13 and 19

WORD KEY: SYNONYMS

See Synonyms at *youth*.

teens /teenz/ *npl.* **1.** 13 TO 19 the numbers ending in "-teen" **2.** YEARS BETWEEN 13 AND 19 the years in somebody's life between the ages of 13 and 19, or the years between 13 and 19 in a century [Late 16thC. Formed from -TEEN.]

teen·sy /teénsee/ (**-si·er, -si·est**) *adj.* = **teeny** (*informal*) [Late 19thC. Origin uncertain: probably formed from TEENY.]

teen·sy-ween·sy *adj.* = **teeny-weeny** (*informal*) [Modeled on TEENY-WEENY]

tee·ny /teénee/ (**-ni·er, -ni·est**) *adj.* very small (*informal*) [Early 19thC. Variant of TINY, modeled on WEENY.]

teen·y·bop·per /teénee bòppər/ *n.* a young teenager, usually a young girl, who follows the latest fads in fashion and music (*informal insult*) [Mid-20thC. An allusion to the teenager's preoccupation with dancing and pop music.]

tee·ny-wee·ny *adj.* very small (*informal*)

tee·pee *n.* = **tepee**

tee-piece *n.* = **T-piece**

Tees /teez/ river of northeastern England, flowing into the North Sea at Teesmouth. Length: 80 mi./128 km.

tee shirt *n.* = **T-shirt**

tee·ter /teétər/ (**-tered, -ter·ing, -ters**) *vi.* **1.** TOTTER to walk or move unsteadily and as if about to fall ○ *teetering along in her high heels* **2.** BE IN PRECARIOUS POSITION to be in a precarious position in which things could imminently go badly wrong ○ *For 24 hours the country teetered on the brink of war.* **3.** VACILLATE to vacillate or fluctuate between different attitudes or positions ○ *teetered between wanting to go and not wanting to go* [Mid-19thC. Variant of TITTER.]

tee·ter·board /teétər bàwrd/ *n.* **1.** ACROBAT'S DEVICE an acrobat's device consisting of a board on a fulcrum used to propel somebody into the air standing on the low end when another person jumps onto the high end **2.** *Northeast U.S.* SEESAW a seesaw

tee·ter-tot·ter *n.* = **seesaw** *n.* 1

teeth plural of **tooth**

teethe /teeth/ (**teethed, teeth·ing, teethes**) *vi.* to grow baby teeth [15thC. Formed from TEETH.]

teeth·ing ring *n.* a ring of hard rubber or plastic on which a baby can bite when teething

tee·to·tal /teé tōt'l/ *adj.* **1.** RESOLVED TO ABSTAIN completely abstaining from alcoholic beverages **2.** TOTAL complete and absolute [Mid-19thC. Formed from the initial letter of TOTAL + TOTAL. Allegedly coined by the Englishman Richard Turner in a speech calling for abstinence from all alcohol, including beer.] —**tee·to·tal·er** *n.* —**tee·to·tal·ism** *n.* —**tee·to·tal·ly** *adv.*

tee·to·tum /tee tōtəm/ *n.* a top spun with the fingers, once used in a game of chance [Early 18thC. Formed from Latin *totum* "all" + its initial letter "T," which is inscribed on one side of the toy.]

teff /tef/, **tef** *n.* an annual North African grass cultivated for its seed, which is used as a grain. Latin name: *Eragrostis tef.* [Late 18thC. From Amharic *têf.*]

te·fil·lin /tə fíllin/ *npl.* the small leather boxes containing Hebrew texts ritually worn by orthodox Jewish men. ◊ **phylactery** [Early 17thC. From Aramaic *tĕpillīn* "prayers."]

TEFL /téff'l/ *abbr.* Teaching (of) English as a Foreign Language

Tef·lon /téf lòn/ *tdmk.* a trademark for a plastic material with nonstick properties that is used as a coating, e.g., for cookware

teg·men /tégmən/, **teg·men·tum** /teg méntəm/ (*plural* **-mi·na** /tégmənə/ *or* **-men·ta** /teg méntə/) *n.* **1.** BOT INNER LAYER IN A SEED the inner layer of a seed's coat **2.** INSECTS INSECT FOREWING the forewing of a primitive insect such as the cockroach **3.** BIOL COVERING PART a covering part in a plant or animal [Early 19thC. Ultimately from Latin *tegere* (see TECTUM).] —**teg·mi·nal** *adj.*

te·gu /tə goó/ (*plural* **-gus** *or* **-gu**) *n.* a fast-running lizard of Central and South America that grows up to 4 feet long. Genus: *Tupinambis.* [Mid-20thC. Shortening of *teguexin*, from Aztec *tecoixin* "lizard."]

Te·gu·ci·gal·pa /te goósee gálpə/ capital city of Honduras, in the Central District in the south central section of the country. It is the nation's largest city. Population: 738,500 (1993).

teg·u·lar /téggyələr/, **teg·u·lat·ed** /téggyə láytəd/ *adj.* relating to or resembling tiles [Early 19thC. Ultimately from Latin *tegula* "tile" (source of English *tile*), from Latin *tegere* (see TECTUM).] —**teg·u·lar·ly** *adv.*

teg·u·ment /téggyəmənt/ *n.* an integument [15thC. From Latin *tegumentum* "covering," from *tegere* (see TECTUM).] —**teg·u·men·tal** /tèggyə mént'l/ *adj.* —**teg·u·men·ta·ry** /-méntəree, -méntree/ *adj.*

te-hee *interj., vi.* = **tee-hee**

Teh·ran /te rán, -raán/, **Teh·rān** capital city of Iran, located in the northern part of the country. Population: 6,475,527 (1991).

Teide, Pico de /táydə, táythə/ the highest mountain in Spain, on the island of Tenerife. Height: 12,188 ft./3,715 m.

te ig·i·tur /tay íggi toór, tay íjji toór/ *n.* the first prayer of the Roman Catholic mass, beginning "te igitur clementissime Pater" [Early 19thC. From Latin, "thee, therefore."]

teig·lach /táygləkh, tíglәkh/ *npl.* a Jewish or German confection made from spiced dough shaped into small balls and simmered in honey, nuts, and spices. When cold, the cooked balls can be packed in a syrup made from the remains of cooking honey. (*takes singular or plural verb*) [Early 20thC. From Yiddish *teyglekh*, from *teyg* "dough," ultimately from Old High German *teic.*]

tei·id /teé id/ *adj.* relating to or used to describe a member of an American reptile family of large tropical carnivorous lizards with forked tongues. Family: Teiidae. [Mid-20thC. From modern Latin *Teiidae*, family name, ultimately via Portuguese *teiu* "lizard" from Tupi *tejú*.]

Teil·hard de Char·din /te jaárd də shaár dén/, **Pierre** (1881–1955) French priest, paleontologist, and theologian. He was one of the discoverers of Peking Man, and in his major work, *The Phenomenon of Man* (1955), he argued that scientific evolutionary theory is compatible with Christian doctrine.

Te Ka·na·wa /tə kaánəwə, tay-/, **Dame Kiri** (*b.* 1944) New Zealand opera singer. She made her debut as a soprano at Covent Garden in 1970 and went on to perform at major opera houses worldwide. Full name **Kiri Janette Te Kanawa**

Te·ka·po, Lake /tékəpō/ lake in the center of the South Island, New Zealand. Area: 32 sq. mi./83 sq. km.

tek·kie *n.* = **techie** (*informal*)

tek·tite /ték tīt/ *n.* a small dark-colored glassy object, possibly resulting from meteoric impact, found in groups at various locations throughout the world [Early 20thC. Formed from Greek *tēktos* "molten," from *tēkein* "to melt."]

tel. *abbr.* **1.** telegram **2.** telegraph **3.** telegraphic **4.** telephone

tel·a /teélə/ (*plural* **-ae** /-lee/) *n.* a delicate part or tissue in the body with a fine or intricate pattern like a web [Early 20thC. From Latin, "web."]

tel·aes·the·sia *n.* = **telesthesia**

tel·a·mon /téllə mòn, téllәmәn/ (*plural* **-mon·es** /-mṓ neez/) *n.* ARCHIT = **atlas** *n.* 3 [Early 17thC. Ultimately from Greek *Telamon*, the name of a Greek mythical hero.]

tel·an·gi·ec·ta·sia /te lànjee ek táyzhə/, **tel·an·gi·ec·ta·sis** /-ek táyssiss/ *n.* permanent dilation of the capillaries and small blood vessels, especially in the face and thighs, producing dark red blotches [Mid-19thC. Ultimately from Greek *telos* "end" + *aggeion* "vessel" + *ektasis* "extension."] —**tel·an·gi·ec·tat·ic** /te lànjee ek táttik/ *adj.*

Tel A·viv /tèl ə veév/, **Tel A·viv-Jaf·fa** /tèl ə veév jáffə/ city in Israel on the Mediterranean Sea. It comprises the historic Arab town of Jaffa and modern Tel Aviv. Population: 353,100 (1997).

tele- *prefix.* **2.** to, at, or over a distance ○ *telekinesis* ○ *telemeter* **2.** telephone ○ *telecommuting* **3.** television ○ *telecast* ○ *telegenic* [From Greek, formed from *tēle* "far off"]

tel·e·bank·ing /téllə bàngking/ *n.* a system of transacting business with a bank by telephone

tel·e·cam·er·a /téllə kàmmərə, -kàmmrə/ *n.* a television camera

tel·e·cast /téllə kàst/ *n.* TV BROADCAST a television broadcast ■ *vti.* (**-cast** *or* **-cast·ed, -cast·ing, -casts**) BROADCAST A TV PROGRAM to broadcast a program on television —**tel·e·cast·er** *n.*

tel·e·com /téllə kòm/ *n.* telecommunication (*informal*) [Mid-20thC. Shortening.]

tel·e·com·mu·ni·ca·tion /tèllə kə myooni káysh'n/ *n.* the transmission of encoded sound, pictures, or data over significant distances, using radio signals or electrical or optical lines

tel·e·com·mu·ni·ca·tions /tèllə kə myooni káysh'nz/ *n.* the science and technology of transmitting information electronically by means of wires or radio signals with integrated encoding and decoding equipment (*takes a singular or plural verb*)

tel·e·com·mute /téllə kə myoót/ (**-c·om·mut·ed, -e·com·mut·ed, -e·com·mut·ing, -e·com·mutes**) *vi.* to work from home on a computer linked to the workplace via modem —**tel·e·com·mut·er** *n.*

tel·e·com·mut·ing /tèllə kə myoóting/ *n.* the process of working at home while transmitting data and documents to and from a nominal workplace over telephone lines using a telephone, fax machine, and modem-equipped computer

tel·e·coms /téllə kòmz/ *n.* telecommunications (*informal*) (*takes a singular or plural verb*) [Contraction of TELECOMMUNICATIONS]

tel·e·con·fer·ence /téllə kònfərəns, -kònfrəns/ *n.* MEETING VIA TELECOMMUNICATIONS EQUIPMENT a meeting held among people in different places by means of telecommunications equipment ■ *vi.* (**-enced, -enc·ing, -enc·es**) TAKE PART IN A TELECONFERENCE to hold a teleconference, or take part in one

tel·e·con·fer·enc·ing /téllə kònfərənsing, -kònfrəns ing/ *n.* a system of video-conferencing that uses a restricted band of frequencies and allows participants to be connected by telephone lines

Tel·e·cop·i·er /téllə kòppee ər/ *tdmk.* a trademark for a device used for sending copies of documents electronically over a telephone line

tel·e·course /téllə kàwrs/ *n.* a course of televised lectures offered by an educational institution

tel·e·dra·ma /téllə draámə, -drámmə/ *n.* a drama filmed to be broadcast on television

tel·e·du /téllə doó/ (*plural* **-dus** *or* **-du**) *n.* a Southeast Asian carnivorous mammal of the weasel family with a dark coat and a white stripe down its back. It emits a foul-smelling secretion from anal glands when provoked. Latin name: *Mydaus javanensis.* [Early 19thC. From Javanese.]

tel·e·film /téllə film/ *n.* a movie made for television

teleg. *abbr.* **1.** telegraph **2.** telegraphic **3.** telegraphy **4.** telegram

tel·e·gen·ic /tèllə jénnik/ *adj.* pleasant and attractive when viewed on television —**tel·e·gen·i·cal·ly** *adv.*

te·leg·o·ny /tə léggənee/ *n.* the now discredited idea that characteristics from the sire of a female's earlier pregnancy can be inherited by offspring from a subsequent sire —**tel·e·gon·ic** /tèllə gónnik/ *adj.* —**te·leg·o·nous** /tə léggənəss/ *adj.*

tel·e·gram /téllə gràm/ *n.* a message sent by telegraph [Mid-19thC. Coined on the model of TELEGRAPH.] —**tel·e·gram·mat·ic** /tèllәgrə máttik/ *adj.* —**tel·e·gram·mic** /tèllə grámmik/ *adj.*

tel·e·graph /téllə gràf/ *n.* **1.** LONG DISTANCE COMMUNICATION METHOD THROUGH WIRES a method of long-distance communicating by coded electric impulses transmitted through wires **2.** = **telegram** ■ *v.* (**-graphed, -graph·ing, -graphs**) **1.** *vti.* SEND BY WIRE to send a message to somebody by telegraph **2.** *vt.* **INDICATE** to communicate a thought or feeling indirectly or nonverbally **3.** *vt.* **SHOW INTENTION** to give advance notice of intentions, especially unwittingly, to an audience or opponent [Early 18thC. From French *télégraphe,* literally "something that writes far," from *-graphe* (see -GRAPH).] —**te·leg·ra·pher** /tə léggrəfər/ *n.* —**te·leg·ra·phist** /tə léggrəfist/ *n.*

tel·e·graph·ese /tèllə gra féez, -féess/ *n.* language reduced to its essential elements without regard to elegance or grammar, as typically found in telegrams

tel·e·graph·ic /tèllə gráffik/ *adj.* **1. RELATING TO TELEGRAMS** relating to telegraphy or telegrams **2. CONCISE** concise or elliptical in spoken or written expression —**tel·e·graph·i·cal·ly** *adv.*

tel·e·graph plant *n.* a tropical Asian shrub of the legume family, with small leaflets that jerk spasmodically under solar radiation. Latin name: *Desmodium gyrans.* [*Telegraph* from the movement of its leaves, suggesting the movement of semaphore signals]

te·leg·ra·phy /tə léggrəfee/ *n.* the system, study, or operation of telegraph communications

Tel·e·gu *n., adj.* = **Telugu**

tel·e·ki·ne·sis /tèllə ki neéssiss, -kī neéssiss/ *n.* the supposed psychic power to move or deform inanimate objects without the use of physical force —**tel·e·ki·net·ic** /tèllə ki néttik, -kī néttik/ *adj.* —**tel·e·ki·net·i·cal·ly** *adv.*

Te·lem·a·chus /tə lémmakəss/ *n.* in Greek mythology, the son of Odysseus, who waited with his mother, Penelope, for his father's return after the Trojan War

Te·le·mann /táylə maan/, **Georg Philipp** (1681–1767) German composer. A prolific composer, he bridged the baroque and early classical periods in works that include 40 operas and numerous orchestral suites and chamber pieces.

tel·e·mark /téllə maark/ *n.* a turn in cross-country skiing accomplished by putting the outside ski forward and turning it slowly inward [Early 20thC. Named for *Telemark,* a region in Norway where it originated.]

tel·e·mar·ket·ing /téllə maarkəting/ *n.* selling or promoting goods and services by telephone —**tel·e·mar·ket·er** *n.*

tel·e·med·i·cine /téllə mèddissin/ *n.* the use of video links, e-mail, telephone, or another telecommunications system to transmit medical information, e.g., in consultations between a doctor and patient or supervision of medical staff

tel·e·me·ter /téllə meetər, tə lémmətər/ *n.* **1. REMOTE MEASURING DEVICE** a device used to record information about a remote object or event and transmit it to an observer **2. DEVICE FOR MEASURING DISTANCES DIRECTLY** a device used for measuring distances directly that does not use rods or chains across the distance to be measured ■ *vt.* **(-tered, -ter·ing, -ters) TRANSMIT DATA** to collect and transmit data about a remote object, especially using a satellite —**tel·e·met·ric** /tèllə méttrik/ *adj.* —**tel·e·met·ri·cal** /-méttrik'l/ *adj.* —**tel·e·met·ri·cal·ly** /-méttrikəlee/ *adv.*

te·lem·e·try /tə lémmətree/ *n.* **1. SCIENCE OF REMOTE MEASUREMENT** the science or activity of gathering data about remote objects and transmitting the data electronically **2. MEASUREMENT OF DISTANCES** measurement of distances using a tellurometer

tel·en·ceph·a·lon /tèll en séffəlon, tèll en séffə lòn/ *n.* the frontmost part of the brain, consisting of the cerebral hemispheres —**tel·en·ce·phal·ic** /tèl ensə fállik/ *adj.*

tel·e·o·log·i·cal ar·gu·ment *n.* an argument for God's existence from the existence of order and design in the universe

tel·e·ol·o·gy /tèllee óllajee/ *n.* **1. STUDY OF CAUSES** the study of ultimate causes in nature **2. APPROACH TO ETHICS** an approach to ethics that studies actions in relations to their ends or utility **3. GOAL-DIRECTED ACTIVITY** any activity that tends towards the achievement of a goal [Mid-18thC. From modern Latin *teleologia,* literally "science of ends," from Greek *telos* "end."] —**tele·ol·o·gism** *n.* —**tel·e·ol·o·gist** *n.*

tel·e·ost /téllee òst/, **tel·e·os·te·an** *n.* any bony fish with rayed fins in a suborder that includes most living species, numbering around 20,000, but excluding sturgeons, gars, sharks, rays, and related fish. Subclass: Teleostei. [Mid-19thC. Coined from Greek *telos* "end" + *osteon* "bone."]

tel·e·path /téllə pàth/ *n.* somebody who is believed or who claims to communicate by telepathy

tel·e·pa·thize /tə léppə thīz/ **(-thized, -thiz·ing, -thiz·es)** *vi.* to claim or be believed to communicate by telepathy

te·lep·a·thy /tə léppəthee/ *n.* supposed communication directly from one person's mind to another's without speech, writing, or other signs or symbols —**tel·e·path·ic** /tèllə páthik/ *adj.*

Telephone

tel·e·phone /téllə fōn/ *n.* **1. ELECTRONIC COMMUNICATION DEVICE** an electronic apparatus containing a receiver and transmitter that is connected to a telecommunications system, enabling the user to speak to and hear others with similar equipment **2. COMMUNICATION USING TELEPHONES** a system of communications using telephones ○ *a telephone company* ■ *vti.* **(-phoned, -phon·ing, -phones) 1. USE TELEPHONE** to contact and speak to somebody using the telephone **2. CONVEY SOMETHING BY TELEPHONE** to send a message by telephone ○ *Bob couldn't come to the party and telephoned his regrets.* —**tel·e·phon·er** *n.* —**tel·e·phon·ic** /tèllə fónnik/ *adj.* —**tel·e·phon·i·cal·ly** *adv.*

tel·e·phone an·swer·ing ma·chine *n.* an answering machine

tel·e·phone book *n.* an alphabetical listing of individuals or businesses who have telephones, along with their addresses and telephone numbers

tel·e·phone booth *n.* an enclosed or partly enclosed space with a pay telephone in it

tel·e·phone ex·change *n.* a center that houses equipment used for interconnecting telephone lines

tel·e·phone pole *n.* a high wooden pole for supporting telephone wires

tel·e·phone tag *n.* a situation in which two people repeatedly return each other's telephone calls and leave messages without succeeding in speaking directly to each other (*informal*)

te·leph·o·ny /tə léffənee/ *n.* the science, technology, or system of communication by telephone

tel·e·pho·to /téllə fō tō/ *adj.* **MAGNIFYING A DISTANT OBJECT** producing a large image of a distant object ■ *n.* (*plural* **-tos**) **1.** = **telephoto lens 2. PHOTO TAKEN WITH TELEPHOTO LENS** a photograph taken using a telephoto lens [Early 20thC. Shortening.]

tel·e·pho·tog·ra·phy /tèllə fə tóggrəfee/ *n.* the photographing of distant objects with the use of special lenses or electronic equipment —**tel·e·pho·to·graph·ic** /tèllə fōtə gráffik/ *adj.*

tel·e·pho·to lens *n.* a camera lens that integrates a telescope

tel·e·play /téllə plày/ *n.* a treatment or script for a play written for presentation on television

tel·e·port /téllə pàwrt/ **(-port·ed, -port·ing, -ports)** *v.* **1.** *vt.* **MOVE SOMETHING USING MENTAL POWER** to move an object supposedly using telekinesis **2.** *vi.* **MOVE SOMEWHERE WITHOUT TRAVELING** in science fiction and fantasy, to move instantly from one place to another by some paranormal or magical means [Mid-20thC. Coined from TELE- + Latin *portare* "to carry."] —**tel·e·por·ta·tion** /tèllə pawr táysh'n/ *n.*

tel·e·print·er /téllə prìntər/ *n.* = **teletypewriter**

tel·e·proc·ess·ing /téllə pró sèssing/ *n.* the use of computer terminals in different locations, connected to a main computer, to process data

Tel·e·PrompT·er /téllə pròmptər/ *tdmk.* a trademark for a device showing text for somebody speaking on television to read

Tel·e·ran /téllə ràn/ *tdmk.* trademark for a radar system that gathers information about the airspace surrounding an airport and relays it to local air traffic via television

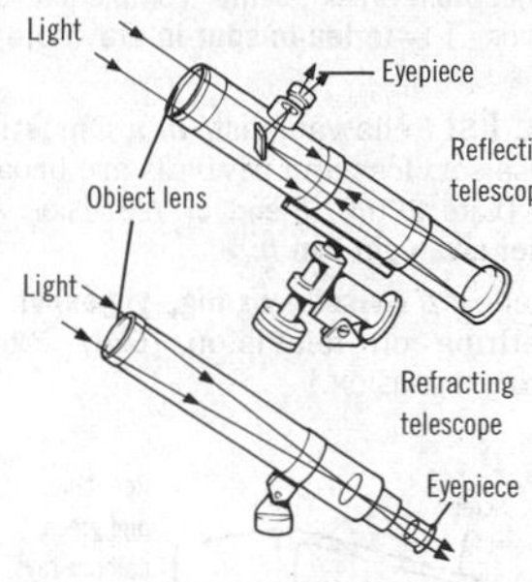

Telescope

tel·e·scope /téllə skōp/ *n.* **1. DEVICE FOR LOOKING AT DISTANT OBJECTS** a device for making distant objects appear nearer and larger by means of compound lenses or concave mirrors **2.** = **radio telescope** ■ *v.* **(-scoped, -scop·ing, -scopes) 1.** *vi.* **COLLAPSE NEATLY** to slide neatly one inside another like the sections of a telescope **2.** *vt.* **CONDENSE SOMETHING** to make something shorter in time or length ○ *telescoped his adventure into a one-hour talk* [Mid-17thC. From Italian *telescopio* or modern Latin *telescopium,* both literally "looking far," from, ultimately, Greek *skopein* "to look" (source of English *scope* and *bishop*).]

tel·e·scop·ic /tèllə skóppik/ *adj.* **1. OF TELESCOPES** relating to or visible only by using a telescope **2. ENLARGING** with the ability to make something distant seem nearer or larger ○ *a telescopic lens* **3. ABLE TO SEE FAR** able to see great distances ○ *telescopic vision* **4. COLLAPSIBLE** consisting of parts that slide one inside another ○ *a tripod with telescopic legs* —**tel·e·scop·i·cal·ly** *adv.*

tel·e·scop·ic sight *n.* a telescope mounted on a rifle and used for sighting, especially on distant targets

Tel·e·sco·pi·um /tèllə skṓpee əm/ *n.* a constellation in the sky of the southern hemisphere between Sagittarius and Pavo

te·les·co·py /tə léskəpee/ *n.* the science and technology of making and using telescopes

tel·e·shop·ping /téllə shòpping/ *n.* the practice or activity of ordering goods advertised on television by phone or computer

tel·e·ster·e·o·scope /tèllə stérree ə skōp/ *n.* a binocular telescope or telescopic stereoscope adapted to provide a three-dimensional view of distant objects or landscapes

tel·es·the·sia /tèlləs theézhə/, **tel·aes·the·sia** *n.* the supposed perception of phenomena or events considered beyond the range of normal senses [Late 19thC. Literally "perception from afar," formed from Greek *aisthēsis* "perception."] —**tel·es·thet·ic** /tèlləs théttik/ *adj.*

tel·e·stich /tə léstik, téllə stìk/ *n.* an acrostic or poem in which the last letters in each line spell a word [Mid-17thC. From Greek *telos* "end" + *stikhos* "row, line of verse" (see ACROSTIC).]

Te·les·to /tə lèstó/ *n.* a very small natural satellite of Saturn, discovered in 1980. It is irregular in shape with a maximum dimension of 19 mi./30 km, and occupies an intermediate orbit.

tel·e·text /téllə tèkst/ *n.* a system of broadcasting news and other information in written form that can be viewed on specially equipped television sets, superimposed on, or in place of, the picture

tel·e·the·a·ter /téllə theè ətər/ *n.* a viewing area, e.g., in an off-track betting parlor, where horseraces are broadcast live on video screens

tel·e·thon /téllə thòn/ *n.* a lengthy television broadcast that combines entertainment with appeals to donate to a particular charity [Mid-20thC. Blend of TELE- and MARATHON.]

tel·e·tran·scrip·tion /tèllə tran skrípshən/ *n.* the transcription of a television programme by the use of videotape

Tel·e·type /téllə tīp/ *tdmk.* a trademark for a teletypewriter

tel·e·type·writ·er /tèllə típ rìtər/ *n.* a telegraphic communication device similar to a typewriter used for data input and output

te·leu·to·spore /tə loótə spàwr/ *n.* BIOL = **teliospore** [Late 19thC. Formed from Greek *teleutē* "completion" (from *telos* "end") + SPORE.] —**te·leu·to·spor·ic** /tə loótə spáwrik/ *adj.*

tel·e·van·ge·list /tèllə vánjəlist/ *n.* a Christian evangelist whose services and revivals are broadcast on television [Late 20thC. Blend of TELEVISION and EVANGELIST.] —**tel·e·van·gel·ism** *n.*

tel·e·vise /téllə vìz/ (**-vised, -vis·ing, -vis·es**) *vt.* to broadcast something on television [Early 20thC. Back-formation from TELEVISION.]

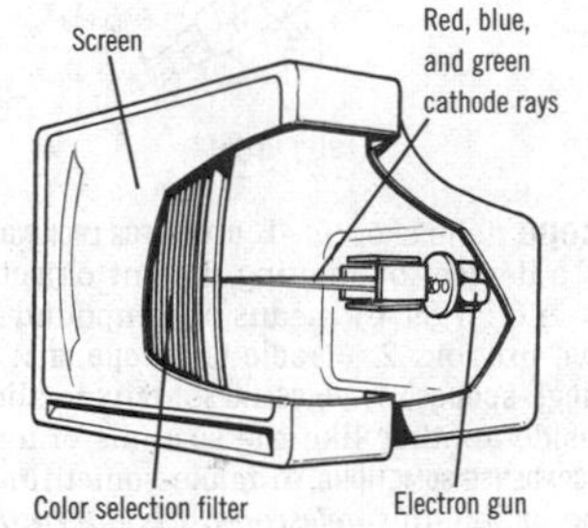

Television set

tel·e·vi·sion /téllə vìzh'n/ *n.* **1. VIDEO BROADCASTING SYSTEM** a system of capturing images and sounds, broadcasting these via a combined electronic audio and video signal, and reproducing them to be viewed and listened to **2. TV SET** an electronic device for receiving and reproducing the images and sounds of a television signal **3. TV INDUSTRY** the television industry ○ *works in television* **4. BROADCAST CONTENT** the image, sound, or content of a television broadcast ○ *appearing on television for the first time* —**tel·e·vi·sion·al** *adj.* —**tel·e·vi·sion·al·ly** *adv.* —**tel·e·vi·sion·a·ry** *adj.*

tel·e·vi·sion set *n.* = **television** *n.* 2

tel·e·vi·sion tube *n.* = **tube** *n.* 7

tel·ex /té lèks/ *n.* **1. COMMUNICATIONS SYSTEM** a communications system using teletypewriters that communicate via telephone lines **2. MESSAGE** a message sent or received by telex ■ *vti.* (**-exed, -ex·ing, -ex·es**) **SEND BY TELEX** to send a message to somebody by telex [Mid-20thC. Blend of TELEPRINTER and EXCHANGE.]

tel·fer *n.* = **telpher**

tel·fer·age *n.* = **telpherage**

te·li·a plural of **telium**

tel·ic /téllik, téelik/ *adj.* directed toward a definite end or purpose [Mid-19thC. From Greek *telikos* "final," from *telos* "end."]

Tel·i·don /téllə dòn/ *tdmk.* a trademark for a Canadian system that sends information by computer and telephone, allowing people to buy tickets or shop from home

te·li·o·log·i·cal /téllə ə lójjik'l, téelee ə lójjik'l/, **te·li·o·log·ic** /-lójjik/ *adj.* relating to the study of ultimate causes in nature or of actions in relation to their ends or utility —**te·li·o·log·i·cal·ly** *adv.*

te·li·o·spore /téelee ə spàwr/ *n.* a resting spore that develops in rust and smut fungi in the fall and germinates in the spring [Early 20thC. Formed from TELIUM + SPORE.] —**te·le·o·spor·ic** /téelee ə spáwrik/ *adj.*

te·li·um /téelee əm/ (*plural* **-a** /-ə/) *n.* the spore case of a rust or smut fungus that bears teliospores [Early 20thC. Formed from Greek *telos* "end."] —**te·li·al** *adj.*

tell /tel/ *v.* (**told, tell·ing, tells**) **1.** *vt.* **RELATE EVENTS OR FACTS** to give an account in speech or writing of events or facts ○ *tell a story* **2.** *vt.* **EXPRESS SOMETHING** to speak, expressing a particular thing ○ *tell a lie* **3.** *vt.* **INFORM SOMEBODY** to inform somebody, or inform somebody of something ○ *Who told you?* ○ *Jim told us the news.* **4.** *vti.* **EXPRESS IN WORDS** to express thoughts or feelings to somebody in words **5.** *vt.* **ORDER SOMEBODY** to command or order somebody to do something **6. DISTINGUISH** to be able to distinguish things ○ *couldn't tell one from the other* **7.** *vt.* **REVEAL THE FUTURE** to purport to reveal future events ○ *tell your fortune* **8.** *vt.* **COUNT THINGS** to count things, e.g., votes cast or beads as part of a prayer ○ *tell a rosary* **9.** *vi.* **REVEAL A SECRET** to reveal secret or damaging information, especially to an authority ■ *n.* **REVEALING ACTION** an action that unconsciously reveals secret information [Old English *tellan*, from a prehistoric Germanic word meaning "put in order" (both in narration and counting), which is also the ancestor of English *tale* and *talk*] —**tell·a·ble** *adj.* ◇ **all told** altogether, or when everything else is taken into consideration ◇ **tell it like it is** to give a complete and accurate account of something (*informal*) ◇ **tell me about it! 1.** used to indicate heartfelt agreement (*informal*) **2.** used to indicate that you have experienced what somebody is talking about (*informal*) ◇ **you're telling me!** used to indicate agreement with an observation (*informal*)

tell apart *vt.* to distinguish two or more similar things or people

tell off *vt.* to scold or rebuke somebody, especially in anger (*informal*)

tell on *vt.* **1. AFFECT ADVERSELY** to have an adverse effect on somebody or something **2. REPORT TO AUTHORITY** to report damaging or incriminating information to an authority

Tell, William /tel/ in Swiss legend, a patriot who liberated Switzerland from Austrian rule in the 14th century. He was forced by an Austrian governor to shoot an arrow through an apple on his son's head, and later killed the governor.

tell-all *adj.* not witholding any information, even what may be considered secret, private, or unsuitable

tel·ler /téllər/ *n.* **1. SOMEBODY WHO TELLS** somebody who tells something ○ *a teller of tales* **2.** BANKING **BANK EMPLOYEE** an employee in a bank or savings institution who receives and pays out money **3. COUNTER OF VOTES** somebody who counts votes in an election or legislature

Tel·ler /téllər/, **Edward** (*b.* 1908) Hungarian-born U.S. physicist. He helped construct the first atomic bomb (1945) and was the principal architect of the hydrogen bomb, first tested in 1952.

tel·lin /téllin/ (*plural* **-lins** *or* **-lin**) *n.* a marine bivalve mollusk that lives in intertidal sand. Genus: *Tellina.* [Early 18thC. Via Latin from Greek *tellinē* "type of shellfish."]

tell·ing /télling/ *adj.* **1. REVEALING** revealing information inadvertently or indirectly ○ *a telling glance* **2. EFFECTIVE** very effective or expressive ○ *a telling indictment* —**tell·ing·ly** *adv.*

tell·tale /tél tàyl/ *adj.* **CLEARLY SHOWING SOMETHING** clearly showing or indicating something that is secret or hidden ○ *telltale signs* ■ *n.* **1. DEVICE** a device or signal intended to monitor a machine or system **2.** RAIL **SIGN OF A HAZARD** vertical strips suspended above a railroad track to warn of an imminent low bridge or tunnel **3.** SAILING **WIND STRIPS** strips of ribbon hung aloft on a sailboat to show apparent wind direction **4.** *U.K.* = **tattletale** (*informal*) **5.** RACKET GAMES **METAL STRIP** a horizontal metal strip across the front wall of a squash or racketball court, above which the ball must be bounced

tel·lu·rate /téllyə ràyt/ *n.* a salt or ester of telluric acid [Early 19thC. Formed from TELLURIUM.]

tel·lu·ri·an /tə lóoree ən, te-/ *adj.* **RELATING TO EARTH** relating to the Earth or life on Earth ■ *n.* **EARTHLING** an inhabitant of the Earth, as described in science fiction [Mid-19thC. Formed from Latin *tellus* "earth."]

tel·lu·ric[1] /tə lóorik, te-/ *adj.* **1. FROM EARTH** originating or proceeding from the Earth or its atmosphere **2.** = **tellurian** *adj.* [Mid-19thC. Formed from Latin *tellus* "earth."]

tel·lu·ric[2] /tə lóorik, te-/ *adj.* containing or relating to tellurium, especially in a high valence [Early 19thC. Formed from TELLURIUM.]

tel·lu·ric ac·id *n.* a white crystalline inorganic acid produced by the action of hydrogen peroxide on tellurium. Formula: H_6TeO_6. [From TELLURIC[2]]

tel·lu·ride /téllyə rìd/ *n.* a binary compound of tellurium with an electropositive element or group [Mid-19thC. Formed from TELLURIUM.]

tel·lu·ri·on /tə lóoree ən, te-/ *n.* a model that shows how day and night and the seasons result from the Earth's orbit and its tilted axis in relation to the Sun [Mid-19thC. Formed from Latin *tellus* "earth."]

tel·lu·ri·um /tə lóoree əm, te-/ *n.* a semimetallic element that occurs naturally, both in a native state and in mineral ores, and is used in alloys and various manufacturing processes. Symbol **Te** [Early 19thC. Formed from Latin *tellus* "earth," on the model of URANIUM.]

tel·lur·ize /téllyə rìz/ (**-ized, -iz·ing, -iz·es**) *vt.* to cause something to combine with tellurium

tel·lu·rom·e·ter /tèllyə rómmətər/ *n.* a device that measures distances from the travel time of microwaves or radiowaves trasmitted across the distance to be measured [Mid-20thC. Formed from Latin *tellus* "earth."]

tel·lu·rous /téllyərəss, tə lóorəss, te-/ *adj.* containing or relating to tellurium, especially in a low valence [Mid-19thC. Formed from TELLURIUM, on the model of FERROUS.]

Tel·lus /tálləss/ *n.* in Roman mythology, the goddess of the earth and of fertility [From Latin, literally "earth"]

tel·ly /téllee/ (*plural* **-lies**) *n. U.K.* television, or a television set (*informal*) [Mid-20thC. Shortening.]

TELNET /tél nèt/, **Telnet** *n.* a terminal emulation program that allows computer users to connect interactively to a server and access remote sites, e.g., on the Internet [Late 20thC. Coined from TELETYPE + NETWORK.]

telo- *prefix.* end ○ *telophase* [Formed from Greek *telos* "end"]

tel·o·cen·tric /téelə séntrik, tèllə-/ *adj.* used to describe a chromosome whose centromere is located at or near one end. ◊ **acentric, acrocentric**

tel·o·lec·i·thal /téelə léssithəl, tèllə-/ *adj.* used to describe reptile, shark, or bird eggs in which the yolk is concentrated at one end [Late 19thC. Coined from TELO- + Greek *lekithos* "egg yolk."]

tel·o·mere /téelə meer, téllə-/ *n.* a region of DNA at the end of a chromosome that protects the start of the genetic coding sequence against shortening during successive replications

tel·o·phase /téelə fàyz, téllə-/ *n.* the final stage of cell division, in which daughter cell nuclei form around chromosomes at opposite ends of the dividing mother cell. ◊ **anaphase, metaphase, prophase** —**tel·o·phas·ic** /téelə fáyzik, tèllə-/ *adj.*

tel·o·tax·is /téelō táksiss, tèllō-/ *n.* an organism's movement toward or away from a particular stimulus while maintaining a constant angle to that stimulus. This behavior is seen in some insects.

tel·pher /télfər/, **tel·fer** *n.* **CABLE CAR** a car or other carrying unit suspended from a cable in a telpherage ■ *vt.* (**-phered, -pher·ing, -phers; -fered, -fer·ing, -fers**) **TAKE BY TELPHER** to transport something in a container suspended from cables [Late 19thC. Contraction of *telephore*, from TELE- + -PHORE.] —**tel·pher·ic** *adj.*

tel·pher·age /télfərij/, **tel·fer·age** *n.* a transportation system in which cargoes or passengers are carried in containers suspended from cables

tel·son /télsən/ *n.* the terminal segment of an arthropod or arachnid body, e.g., the stinger of a scorpion [Mid-19thC. From Greek, literally "limit."] —**tel·son·ic** /tel sónnik/ *adj.*

Tel·star /tél staar/ *n.* a communication satellite used for transmitting television programs and telephone messages. Two of these were launched by the United States in 1962 and 1963. [Mid-20thC. Blend of TELE- and STAR.]

Tel·u·gu /téllə goo/ (*plural* **-gu** *or* **-gus**), **Tel·e·gu** (*plural* **-gu** *or* **-gus**) *n.* **1.** LANG **INDIAN LANGUAGE** a language spoken in southeastern and central India. Telugu is a member of the Dravidian family of languages. **2.** PEOPLES **SOMEBODY WHO SPEAKS TELUGU** a member of the Dravidian people who speak Telugu [Late 18thC. From Kannada and Tamil.] —**Te·lu·gu** *adj.*

Te·ma /téemə/ city in southeastern Ghana, on the Gulf of Guinea, near Accra. Population: 180,600 (1990).

tem·blor /témblər, -blàwr/ *n.* an earthquake or tremor [Late 19thC. From American Spanish, literally "trembling," from, ultimately, Vulgar Latin *tremulare* "to tremble" (source of English *tremble*).]

te·mer·i·ty /tə mérrətee/ *n.* reckless confidence that might be offensive [15thC. From Latin *temeritas* "rashness," ultimately from assumed *temus* "darkness." The underlying idea is of "acting in the dark."] —**tem·er·ar·i·ous** /tèmmə ráiree əss/ *adj.*

tem·mok·u /témmō kòo/ *n.* a Japanese iron glaze that is black in color but breaks into rust where the glaze coat is thin [Late 19thC. Via Japanese from Chinese *tiān mù* "eye of heaven."]

Tem·ne /témnee/ (*plural* **-nes** *or* **-ne**) *n.* **1.** PEOPLES **MEMBER OF PEOPLE OF SIERRA LEONE** a member of a people who live in Sierra Leone, where they are one of the dominant ethnic groups **2.** LANG **TEMNE LANGUAGE** the language of the Temne people, belonging to the Niger-Congo family of languages. About one million people speak Temne. [Late 18thC. From Temne.] —**Tem·ne** *adj.*

temp /temp/ *n.* **TEMPORARY WORKER** a temporary worker, especially one hired from an agency ■ *vi.* (**temped, temp·ing, temps**) **WORK TEMPORARILY** to do temporary work, especially through an agency [Early 20thC. Shortening.]

temp. *abbr.* **1.** temperance **2.** temperature **3.** template **4.** temporal **5.** temporary **6.** temperate

tem·pe *n.* = **tempeh**

Tem·pe /témpee/ city in central Arizona, on the Salt River. Population: 162,701 (1996).

tem·peh /tém pày/, **tem·pe** *n.* fermented soy beans popular as a health food and in some Asian cuisines [Mid-20thC. From Indonesian *tempe.*]

tem·per /témpər/ *n.* **1. EMOTIONAL CONDITION** an emotional condition or predisposition of a particular kind ○ *an even temper* **2.** (*plural* **-pers** *or* **-per**) **TENDENCY TO ANGER** a tendency to get angry easily and suddenly ○ *has quite a temper* **3. ANGRY STATE** a state of anger or ill temper ○ *got himself into a terrible temper* **4. CALM STATE** a state of calm and balance ○ *lost your temper* **5.** METALL **HARDNESS OF METAL** the degree of hardness of a metal **6. ADDITIVE** something added to improve the consistency or strength of something ■ *vt.* (**-pered, -per·ing, -pers**) **1. SOFTEN** to make something less harsh or unacceptable, especially by adding something to it ○ *temper criticism with kindness* **2. MAKE SOMEBODY STRONGER** to make somebody stronger through exposure to hardship ○ *tempered by combat duty* **3.** METALL **HARDEN METAL** to harden metal by heating it to very high temperatures and then cooling ○ *temper steel* **4.** MUSIC **TUNE EARLY KEYBOARD INSTRUMENT** to tune a baroque keyboard instrument so that consistent harmonic intervals are achieved throughout its range [Pre-12thC. From Latin *temperare* "to mix, restrain yourself," from *tempus* "time" (see TEMPORAL[1]). Originally "mixture," which led to "emotional condition" and finally "angry state."] —**tem·per·a·bil·i·ty** /tèmpərə bílləteе, tèmprə-/ *n.* —**tem·per·a·ble** /témpərəb'l, témprəb'l/ *adj.* —**tem·per·er** /témpərər/ *n.*

tem·per·a /témpərə/ *n.* **1. PAINTING TECHNIQUE** a technique of painting with colors made from powdered pigments mixed with water and egg yolk, size, or casein **2. TEMPERA PAINTING** a painting done in tempera [Mid-19thC. Via Italian, from, ultimately, Latin *temperare* (see TEMPER).]

tem·per·a·ment /témprəmənt, témpərə-/ *n.* **1. QUALITY OF MIND** a prevailing or dominant quality of mind that characterizes somebody **2. MOODINESS** excessive moodiness, irritability, or sensitivity **3.** HIST **MEDIEVAL PHYSIOLOGICAL CLASSIFICATION** in medieval physiology, the quality of mind resulting from various proportions of the four cardinal humors in an individual **4.** MUSIC **NOTE INTERVAL SETTING** the subtle relationship of the pitches of notes of keyboard instruments, and the consequences this has on harmony

tem·per·a·men·tal /tèmprə mént'l, tèmpərə-/ *adj.* **1. EASILY UPSET** easily upset or irritated **2. UNPREDICTABLE** unpredictable and erratic in behavior **3. OF TEMPERAMENT** relating to temperament —**tem·per·a·men·tal·ly** *adv.*

tem·per·ance /témprəns, -pərəns/ *n.* **1. ABSTINENCE FROM ALCOHOL** total abstinence from alcoholic drink **2. RESTRAINT** self-restraint in the face of temptation or desire

tem·per·ate /témprət, -pərət/ *adj.* **1. MILD** mild or restrained in behavior or attitude **2.** METEOROL **WITHOUT EXTREMES** used to describe a climate that has a range of temperatures within moderate limits **3.** MICROBIOL **NOT SPREADING** used to describe viruses that exist in host cells but do not cause lysis —**tem·per·ate·ly** *adv.* —**tem·per·ate·ness** *n.*

Tem·per·ate Zone *n.* the parts of the earth that lie between the tropics and the polar circles and have generally hot summers, cold winters, and intermediate autumns and springs

tem·per·a·ture /témpərə choor, -chər, témprə-/ *n.* **1. DEGREE OF HEAT** the degree of heat as an inherent quality of objects expressed as hotness or coldness relative to something else **2. RELATIVE DEGREE OF HEAT** the heat of something measured on a particular scale such as the Fahrenheit or Celsius scale. Symbol *T, t* **3. BODY HEAT** the degree of heat in a living organism **4. FEVER** human body heat in excess of 98.6° F/37.0° C or somebody's normal body heat ○ *running a temperature* [15thC. The meaning evolved from "mixture" via "mild (well balanced) weather."]

tem·per·a·ture gra·di·ent *n.* the rate of change in air temperature over distance, especially elevation

tem·per·a·ture-hu·mid·i·ty in·dex *n.* a measure of ambient humidity relative to heat as it affects human comfort

tem·per·a·ture in·ver·sion *n.* METEOROL = **inversion** *n.* 4

tem·pered /témpərd/ *adj.* **1. WITH A PARTICULAR TEMPER** with a temper or temperament of a particular quality (*usually used in combination*) ○ *even-tempered* **2. WELL PROPORTIONED** with elements combined in balanced and suitable proportion **3.** INDUST **HARDENED** hardened through a tempering process ○ *tempered steel* **4.** MUSIC **TUNED TO A TEMPERAMENT** tuned to a particular temperament, especially equal temperament

tem·pest /témpəst/ *n.* **1. STORM** a severe storm with very high winds and often rain, hail, or snow (*literary*) **2. EMOTIONAL UPHEAVAL** a severe commotion or disturbance, especially an emotional upheaval [13thC. Via Old French from, ultimately, Latin *tempestas*, from *tempus* "time." The Latin word originally meant "period of time," which evolved into "weather" and, finally, "storm."] ◇ **tempest in a teapot** commotion raised about an unimportant matter

WORD KEY: CULTURAL NOTE

The Tempest, a play by English dramatist William Shakespeare (1611). An elaborate blend of comedy, drama, and fantasy, it is set on an enchanted island where Prospero, rightful duke of Milan, has lived since being usurped by his brother Antonio. Using his magical powers, Prospero conjures up a storm that forces Antonio and his companions onto the island, paving the way for an ingenious reconciliation. The word *sea-change*, meaning a change caused by the sea, and figuratively, a major transformation, comes from Act I, scene ii of this play: "Nothing of him that doth fade,/ But doth suffer a sea-change/ Into something rich and strange.".

tem·pes·tu·ous /tem péschoo əss/ *adj.* **1. WITH STORMS** having or affected by frequent or violent storms ○ *tempestuous seas* **2. EMOTIONALLY TURBULENT** frequently turbulent and giving rise to many emotions ○ *a tempestuous relationship* —**tem·pes·tu·ous·ly** *adv.* —**tem·pes·tu·ous·ness** *n.*

tem·pi plural of **tempo**

Tem·plar /témplər/ *n.* = **Knight Templar** [13thC. From the place in Jerusalem (*Temple of Solomon*), where the medieval order had its headquarters.]

tem·plate /témplət/ *n.* **1. MASTER** something that serves as a master or pattern from which other similar things can be made **2.** ENG **PATTERN** a mechanical pattern or mold with one or more shapes used to guide the manufacture or drawing of objects with a similar shape **3.** BUILDING **SHORT BEAM** a short beam of metal, wood, or stone, used to distribute weight or pressure in a structure **4.** BIOCHEM **MASTER MOLECULE** a molecule that provides a pattern for the synthesis of other molecules in biochemical reactions [Late 17thC. Alteration of earlier TEMPLET, on the model of PLATE.]

tem·ple[1] /témp'l/ *n.* **1.** RELIG **BUILDING FOR WORSHIP** a building used as a place of worship **2. SPECIAL PLACE** an institution or building considered as a guardian of, or reservation for, a particular activity ○ *a temple of learning* **3. MEETING PLACE** a building where a fraternal order holds meetings and rites **4.** RELIG **HOLY DWELLING** a place where something holy or divine is thought to dwell, e.g., the body of a holy person **5.** JUDAISM **SYNAGOGUE** a synagogue **6.** JUDAISM **BIBLICAL PLACE OF WORSHIP IN JERUSALEM** either of the two places of worship in Jerusalem, Solomon's Temple and Herod's Temple, built in biblical times **7.** CHR **MORMON CHURCH** a Mormon place of worship where sacred ordinances such as marriage are executed [Pre-12thC. From Latin *templum* "sacred place, place marked out for worship," of uncertain origin: perhaps ultimately from an Indo-European word meaning "cut" (source of English *-tomy*).]

tem·ple[2] /témp'l/ *n.* **1.** ANAT **PART OF THE HEAD** the part of either side of the head between the eye and the ear **2.** OPHTHALMOL **GLASSES PART** either of the stemlike pieces on a pair of glasses that are connected to the frame and rest on the ears [14thC. Via Old French from, ultimately, Latin *tempora*, plural of *tempus* "temple, time" (see TEMPORAL). The meaning evolved via "right time" and "right place (for dealing a fatal blow)."]

tem·ple[3] /témp'l/ *n.* the part of a loom that keeps the cloth being woven stretched to the proper width [15thC. From French, of uncertain origin: probably from Latin *templum* (see TEMPLE[1]) in its secondary meaning "plank, raft."]

Tem·ple[1] *n.* either of two groups of buildings in Paris and London built on sites that once belonged to the Knights Templar. The London site is now the home of two of the Inns of Court.

Tem·ple[2] *n.* either of two successive temples in Jerusalem. The First Temple, built by Solomon in 957 B.C., was destroyed by Nebuchadnezzar in 586 B.C. The Second Temple was destroyed by the Romans in A.D. 70.

Shirley Temple

Tem·ple /témp'l/, **Shirley** (*b.* 1928) U.S. actor. She made 25 movies from 1934 as an internationally popular child star. She was later U.S. ambassador to the United Nations, under her married name of Shirley Temple Black.

tem·plet /témplət/ *n.* a template (*archaic*) [Formed from TEMPLE[3]]

tem·ple tree *n.* a frangipani tree [*Temple* from the fact that the tree is commonly planted on graves]

tem·po /témpō/ (*plural* **-pi** /témpee/ *or* **-pos**) *n.* **1.** MUSIC **MUSIC'S SPEED** the speed at which a musical composition or passage is performed **2. PACE** the pace or rate of something ○ *the tempo of urban life* [Mid-17thC. Via Italian from Latin *tempus* (see TEMPORAL[1]).]

tem·po·la·bile /tèmpō láy bīl, -b'l/ *adj.* changing at an uneven rate [Mid-20thC. From Latin *tempus* "time" + *labilis*, from *labi* "to slip."]

tem·po·ral[1] /témprəl, témpərəl/ *adj.* **1. RELATING TO TIME** relating to measured time **2.** CHR **RELATING TO LAITY** relating to the laity rather than the clergy in the Christian church **3.** RELIG **OF THIS WORLD** connected with life in the world, rather than spiritual life **4. BRIEF** lasting only a short time **5.** GRAM **RELATING TO TENSES** relating to grammatical tenses or the expression of time in a language [14thC. Directly or via French from Latin *temporalis*, from *tempus* "time," of uncertain origin: perhaps ultimately from an Indo-European word meaning "stretch" (ancestor of English *thin*).] —**tem·po·ral·ly** *adv.*

tem·po·ral[2] /témprəl, témpərəl/ *adj.* relating to or in the region of the temples on the head [Late 16thC. From late Latin *temporalis*, ultimately from Latin *tempus* (see TEMPLE[2]).]

tem·po·ral bone *n.* either of a pair of bones that form part of the sides and base of the skull and contain the middle and inner ears

tem·po·ral·i·ty /tèmpə rállətee/ *n.* **BEING TEMPORAL** the quality or state of being connected with time or the world ■ **tem·po·ral·i·ties** *npl.* CHR **CHURCH ASSETS** the secular property and assets of a church

tem·por·al·ize /témprə līz, témpərə-/ (**-ized, -iz·ing, -iz·es**) *vt.* to make something temporal or secular

tem·po·ral lobe *n.* either of two lobes of the brain, located on the side of each cerebral hemisphere, that contain the auditory centers responsible for hearing

tem·po·rar·y /témpə rèrree/ *adj.* **HAVING A LIMITED DURATION** lasting for or relating to a limited time ■ *n.* (*plural* **-ies**) **WORKER HIRED FOR LIMITED TIME** somebody who is hired to work in an office or other workplace for a limited time only —**tem·po·rar·i·ly** /tèmpə rérrəlee/ *adv.* —**tem·po·rar·i·ness** /témpə rèrreenəss/ *n.*

WORD KEY: SYNONYMS

temporary, fleeting, passing, transitory, ephemeral, evanescent

CORE MEANING: lasting only a short time

temporary lasting for a short time, usually because this is what is intended. It is often used to suggest that something is makeshift or not ideal; **fleeting** very short-lived or brief in duration, especially when it does not seem long enough; **passing** describes something such as an interest, feeling, or fashion that is not permanent; **transitory** a fairly formal word used to suggest that something, by its very nature, is bound to come to an end; **ephemeral** a formal or literary word used to describe something that lasts for only a very short time, especially when it is something that also seems unimportant; **evanescent** a literary word used to describe something that lasts for only a very short time or is soon forgotten.

tem·po·ro·man·dib·u·lar joint /tempərō man dìbbyələr-/ *n.* either of the joints connecting the lower part of the jaw (**mandible**) with the temporal bone on each side of the head. Both joints act together when the jaw is moved. ["Temporomandibular" formed from TEMPORAL[2] + MANDIBLE]

tem·po·ro·man·dib·u·lar syn·drome *n.* a painful condition involving the temporomandibular joint and the muscles used for chewing, sometimes causing clicking sounds and restricted jaw movement. It is usually associated with a faulty dental bite.

tempt /tempt/ *vt.* **1. INCITE DESIRE** to cause desire or craving to arise in somebody ○ *tempted by that chocolate cake* **2. INCITE TO TRANSGRESSION** to persuade or attempt to persuade somebody to do something considered wrong **3. INVITE** to invite or attract somebody ○ *The sightseeing tour tempted us.* **4. RISK** to risk the possible destructive powers of something ○ *tempt the gods* —**tempt·able** *adj.* —**tempt·er** *n.*

temp·ta·tion /tèmp táyshən/ *n.* **1. FEELING** a craving or desire for something, especially something thought wrong ○ *yield to temptation* **2. ENTICING ACT** the enticing of desire or craving in somebody **3. ENTICING THING** something that or somebody who tempts somebody ○ *too many temptations for me here*

Tempt·er /témp tər/ *n.* RELIG Satan

tempt·ing /témp ting/ *adj.* causing craving or desire to arise ○ *a tempting offer* —**tempt·ing·ly** *adv.* —**tempt·ing·ness** *n.*

temp·tress /tèmp tríss/ *n.* an offensive term for a woman that deliberately insults her sexuality and public behavior

tem·pu·ra *n.* a Japanese dish of vegetables or seafood coated in light batter and deep-fried

tempus fugit /tèmpoŏs fyoōjit/ time flies

ten /ten/ *n.* **1. NUMBER 10** the number 10 **2. SOMETHING WITH VALUE OF 10** something in a numbered series, e.g., a playing card, with a value of ten ○ *the ten of clubs* ○ *to play the ten* **3. GROUP OF TEN** a group of ten objects or people

ten·a·ble /ténnəb'l/ *adj.* **1. WITH REASONABLE ARGUMENTS TO SUPPORT IT** justified in a fair or rational way and able to be defended because there is sufficient evidence or reason behind it **2. ABLE TO BE OCCUPIED** capable of being occupied or held, usually by a particular person or for a particular period of time (*formal*) **3.** MIL **CAPABLE OF BEING DEFENDED IN BATTLE** able to be held successfully against an enemy attack [Late 16thC. From French *tenir* "to hold."] —**ten·a·bil·i·ty** /tènnə bíllətee/ *n.* —**ten·a·ble·ness** /ténnəb'lnəss/ *n.* —**ten·a·bly** *adv.*

ten·ace /té nàyss, ténnəss/ *n.* a combination of two high cards in the same suit that do not form a sequence, e.g., a jack and king [Mid-17thC. Via French from Spanish *tenaza*, literally "pincers, tongs," the underlying idea being "holding."]

te·na·cious /tə náyshəss/ *adj.* **1. VERY DETERMINED OR STUBBORN** tending to stick firmly to any decision, plan, or opinion without changing or doubting it **2. TIGHTLY HELD** difficult to loosen, shake off, or pull away from **3. ABLE TO REMEMBER MANY THINGS** capable of absorbing and retaining a large store of information and of recalling details accurately **4. STICKY OR CLINGING** sticking or clinging to something else, especially a surface **5. NOT EASILY DISCONNECTED** holding together tightly or fused solidly [Early 17thC. Formed from Latin *tenax* "holding fast," from *tenere* "to hold."] —**te·na·cious·ly** *adv.* —**te·na·cious·ness** *n.*

te·nac·u·lum /tə nákyələm/ (*plural* **-la** /-lə/ *or* **-lums**) *n.* a long-handled instrument with a slender sharp hook, used especially in surgery to grasp and hold arteries or other bodily parts [Late 17thC. From Latin, "holder," from *tenere* "to hold."]

ten·an·cy /ténnənsee/ (*plural* **-cies**) *n.* **1. OCCUPATION OF PROPERTY FOR RENT** exclusive possession of property or land owned by somebody else for a fixed period, in return for an agreed rent. This is usually under the terms of a lease or some similar legal entitlement or agreement. **2. TIME OF SOMEBODY'S TENANCY** a period of time when a piece of property, e.g., a house or farm, is legally occupied and used by somebody paying an agreed rent **3. PLACE LIVED IN BY A TENANT** a piece of property that somebody is entitled to use or occupy on condition that an agreed rent is paid to the owner [15thC. Formed from TENANT.]

ten·ant /ténnənt/ *n.* **1. RENTER OF PROPERTY** somebody who rents a building, house, apartment, plot of land, or some other piece of property for a fixed period of time. This arrangement is usually under the terms of a lease or some similar legal entitlement or agreement. **2. OCCUPIER OF A PLACE** somebody living in or on a particular piece of property ■ *vti.* (**-ant·ed, -ant·ing, -ants**) **PAY RENT TO OCCUPY PROPERTY** to live in or on another person's property as a tenant [14thC. Via Anglo-Norman *tenaunt* from Old French *tenant*, from *tenir* "to hold," from Latin *tenere* "to hold, keep."] —**ten·ant·a·ble** *adj.* —**ten·ant·ed** *adj.* —**ten·ant·less** *adj.*

WORD KEY: ORIGIN

The Latin word *tenere*, from which ***tenant*** is derived, is also the source of English *abstain, contain, continent, continue, countenance, detain, maintain, obtain, retain, sustain, tenacious, tenement, tenet, tennis, tenon, tenor,* and *tenure.*

ten·ant far·mer *n.* a farmer who rents a farm, plot, or agricultural land, and pays the owner in cash or with produce

ten·ant·ry /ténnəntree/ *n.* **1. PEOPLE OCCUPYING RENTED PROPERTY** all tenants or tenant farmers, especially all those renting property from a particular landowner (*formal*) **2. TENANCY** tenancy (*dated*)

ten-cent store *n.* COMM = **five-and-dime**

tench /tench/ (*plural* **tench** *or* **tench·es**) *n.* a European freshwater food and game fish related to the carp, with a heavy greenish body, small scales, and a barbel on each side of its mouth. Latin name: *Tinca tinca.* [14thC. Via Old French *tenche* from late Latin *tinca.*]

Ten Com·mand·ments *npl.* the ten laws given by God to Moses, according to the Bible. They summarize human obligations to each other and to God.

tend[1] /tend/ (**tend·ed, tend·ing, tends**) *vi.* **1. BE GENERALLY INCLINED OR LIKELY** to be generally inclined or likely to react or behave in a particular way, or be in the habit of doing something **2. MOVE GRADUALLY OR SLIGHTLY TOWARD SOMETHING** to make a gentle steady movement in a particular direction [14thC. Via Old French *tendre* "to move toward," from Latin *tendere* "to stretch, extend."]

WORD KEY: ORIGIN

The Latin word *tendere*, from which ***tend*** is derived, is also the source of English *attend, contend, détente, distend, extend, intend, ostensible, portend, pretend, standard, tense,* and *tent.*

tend[2] /tend/ (**tend·ed, tend·ing, tends**) *v.* **1.** *vt.* **TAKE CARE OF SOMETHING OR SOMEBODY** to do or provide the things that a person, animal, or plant needs, or a group of them need, for their health, comfort, and welfare **2.** *vt.* **BE IN CHARGE OF SOMETHING** to manage something, especially something that needs constant supervision **3.** *vi.* **GIVE ATTENTION TO SOMEBODY OR SOMETHING** to give your attention to a particular person or task **4.** *vti.* **SERVE SOMEBODY** to be somebody's attendant, waiter, or servant (*archaic*) [12thC. Shortening of ATTEND.]

ten·dance /téndəns/ *n.* the act of looking after or attending to something (*archaic or formal*) [Late 16thC. Either a shortening of ATTENDANCE, or formed from TEND[2] "to take care of."]

ten·den·cious *adj.* = **tendentious**

ten·den·cy /téndənsee/ (*plural* **-cies**) *n.* **1. GENERAL INCLINATION OR LIKELIHOOD** a way that somebody or something typically behaves or is likely to react or behave **2. PREDISPOSITION TOWARD SOMETHING** a character or quality that makes it likely that something will happen ○ *My ankle has a tendency to twist.* **3. MOVEMENT TOWARD SOMETHING** a gradual but steady progress, development, or shift of opinion in a particular direction ○ *a tendency toward greater assertiveness* [Early 17thC. From medieval Latin *tendentia*, from, ultimately, Latin *tendere* "to tend, be inclined to."]

ten·den·tious /ten dénshəss/, **ten·den·cious** *adj.* written or spoken by somebody who obviously wants to promote a particular cause or who supports a particular viewpoint [Early 20thC. Formed from TENDENCY.] —**ten·den·tious·ly** *adv.* —**ten·den·tious·ness** *n.*

ten·der[1] /téndər/ *adj.* **1. PHYSICALLY PAINFUL** hurting or unusually sensitive when touched or pressed **2. WITH GENTLE FEELING** showing care, gentleness, and feeling **3. KIND AND SYMPATHETIC** sensitive and caring toward others and often feeling emotions intensely **4. FOOD PLEASANTLY SOFT FOR EATING** soft enough for the teeth to go through easily without much chewing **5.** BOT, AGRIC **NEEDING PROTECTION FROM HARSH WEATHER** easily damaged or killed by unsuitable weather or conditions, especially frost and cold **6. YOUNG AND DEFENSELESS** vulnerably or pitifully young, weak, and inexperienced **7. FRAGILE** so delicate, soft, or weak as to be hurt, crushed, or broken easily [13thC. Via French *tendre* from Latin *tener* "delicate, tender" (source also of English *tendril*).] —**ten·der·ly** *adv.* —**ten·der·ness** *n.*

WORD KEY: CULTURAL NOTE

Tender is the Night, a novel by F. Scott Fitzgerald (1934). Set on the French Riviera in the 1930s, it focuses on a group of glamorous American expatriates. Psychologist Richard Diver's attempts to nurse his wife and former patient, Nicole, and his involvement with a visiting woman actor lead to his mental collapse. A powerful depiction of human frailty, it is also admired for the elegance of its prose.

ten·der[2] /téndər/ *v.* (**-dered, -der·ing, -ders**) **1.** *vt.* **OFFER SOMETHING FORMALLY IN WRITING** to present something formal or official, in the form of a document ○ *tender a resignation* **2.** *vi.* COMM **OFFER TO SUPPLY SOMETHING** to offer to undertake a job or supply particular goods ○ *tender for a contract* **3.** *vt.* LAW **OFFER A SUM IN SETTLEMENT** to offer to pay money or goods as a way of settling a debt or claim ■ *n.* **1.** COMM **OFFER TO UNDERTAKE A JOB** a formal offer to undertake a job or supply particular goods ○ *Their tender was accepted because it was the lowest.* **2.** COMM **ACT OF TENDERING** the act of tendering for a contract **3.** LAW **OFFER MADE TO SETTLE SOMETHING** a formal offer to settle legal proceedings on payment of an amount of damages [Mid-16thC. Via Old French *tendre* from Latin *tendere* "to hold out, stretch" (source also of English *tendency*).] —**ten·der·a·ble** *adj.* —**ten·der·er** *n.*

tend·er[3] /téndər/ *n.* **1. SOMEBODY WHO TENDS** somebody who tends something or somebody **2.** SHIPPING **SMALL BOAT FERRYING TO LARGE BOAT** a small boat used to go to and from a larger one such as a yacht **3.** RAIL **VEHICLE CARRYING STEAM ENGINE'S SUPPLIES** the permanently coupled rear part of a large steam locomotive, which carries its coal and water [15thC. Either a shortening of *attender* (from ATTEND), or formed from TEND[2].]

ten·der·foot /téndər foŏt/ (*plural* **-feet** /-feet/ *or* **-foots**) *n.* **1. BEGINNER AT SOMETHING** somebody just starting to do or try something, with little or no previous experience of it (*informal*) **2. SOMEBODY UNUSED TO TOUGH OUTDOOR LIFE** a new arrival at a place where the work and conditions are rough, e.g., on a ranch or mine **3. LOWEST RANK IN THE SCOUTS** a member of the lowest rank of a Boy or Girl Scout troop (*dated*)

ten·der·heart·ed /tèndər haártəd/ *adj.* quick to show compassion and sympathy to other people —**ten·der·heart·ed·ly** *adv.* —**ten·der·heart·ed·ness** *n.*

ten·der·ize /téndə rīz/ (**-ized, -iz·ing, -iz·es**) *vt.* to make meat tender, usually by beating it, soaking it in a marinade, or sprinkling it with a special substance (**tenderizer**) that breaks down the fibers in the meat —**ten·der·i·za·tion** /tèndəri záysh'n/ *n.*

ten·der·iz·er /téndə rīzər/ *n.* **1. SUBSTANCE FOR MAKING MEAT TENDER** a commercial preparation containing enzymes that break down fibrous tissue in meat **2. HAMMER FOR POUNDING MEAT** a wooden or metal mallet used to tenderize meat. It has a short handle and a fairly broad head with a hammering surface covered in shallow bumps.

ten·der·loin /téndər lòyn/ *n.* **1. FILLET STEAK** a prime cut of lean tender beef, pork, or lamb taken from the curve of the ribs at the backbone **2. RED-LIGHT OR CRIMINAL DISTRICT OF TOWN** a part of a city where prostitution, vice, and extortion are common (*informal*)

ten·di·ni·tis /tèndə nítiss/, **ten·do·ni·tis** *n.* inflammation of a tendon. It is often painful, usually occurs after excessive use, as in a sports injury, and is generally cured by rest. [Early 20thC. From modern Latin *tendin-*, the stem of *tendo* "tendon."]

ten·di·nous /téndənəss/ *adj.* relating to, consisting of, or resembling a tendon or tendons [Mid-17thC. Via French *tendineux*, from, ultimately, the medieval Latin stem *tendon-* (see TENDON).]

ten·don /téndən/ *n.* an inelastic cord or band of tough white fibrous connective tissue that attaches a muscle to a bone or other part [Mid-16thC. Directly and via French from medieval Latin *tendon-*, stem of *tendo*, a translation of Greek *tenōn* "sinew," from, ultimately, *teinein* "to stretch."]

ten·don ham·mer *n.* = **plexor**

ten·do·ni·tis *n.* = **tendinitis**

ten·dril /téndril/ *n.* **1.** BOT **THREADLIKE PLANT PART ATTACHED TO SUPPORT** a modified stem, leaf, or other part of a climbing plant, usually in the form of a thread, that coils around and attaches the plant to supporting objects **2. DELICATE TWIST OR COIL** a slim, wispy, curling, or winding piece of something, especially hair (*literary*) [Mid-16thC. Via Middle French *tendrillon*, literally "little shoot, little cartilage," from *tendron*, "shoot, cartilage," from Old French *tendre* (see TENDER[1]).]

Ten·e·brae /ténnə brày, -bree/ *n.* in the Roman Catholic Church, the office of matins and lauds for the last three days of Holy Week (*takes a singular or plural verb*) [Mid-17thC. From Latin, literally "darkness," because candles are extinguished during the service in memory of the darkness at the crucifixion.]

te·neb·ri·o·nid /tə nébbree ə nìd, ténnə brí ə nìd/ (*plural* **-nids** *or* **-nid**) *n.* = **darkling beetle** [Early 20thC. From modern Latin.]

te·neb·ri·ous *adj.* = **tenebrous**

ten·e·brism /ténnə brìzzəm/, **Te·ne·brism** *n.* a style of painting, popular in 17th-century Naples and Spain and largely associated with Caravaggio, that uses large areas of shadow and dark colors, sometimes with a shaft of light [Mid-20thC. Formed from Italian *tenebroso*, literally "dark," a term for one of a group of 17thC Italian painters.] —**tene·brist** *n.*

ten·e·brous /ténnəbrəss/, **te·neb·ri·ous** /tə nébbree əss/ *adj.* dark, murky, or obscured by shadows (*literary*) [15thC. Via Old French *tenebrus* from, ultimately, Latin *tenebrae* "darkness."] —**ten·e·bros·i·ty** /ténnə bróssətee/ *n.* —**ten·e·brous·ness** /ténnəbrəssnəss/ *n.*

ten-eight·y, 1080 *n.* a poisonous preparation of sodium fluoroacetate, used as a pesticide and for killing rodents [From its laboratory serial number]

ten·e·ment /ténnəmənt/ *n.* **1. URBAN APARTMENT BUILDING** a large residential building in a city, usually of three or more stories and with only basic amenities, where a large number of people live in self-contained rented apartments **2.** LAW **ITEM OF RENTED PROPERTY** a piece of property such as land or houses held by one person but owned by another [14thC. Via Old French, "tenure," the original sense in English, from, ultimately, Latin *tenere* "to hold."]

Ten·er·ife /tènnə rééf/, **Ten·er·iffe** the largest of the Canary Islands, in Santa Cruz de Tenerife Province, Spain. Population: 759,388 (1986). Area: 795 sq. mi./2,059 sq. km.

te·nes·mus /tə nézməss/ *n.* an urgent, painful, and unsuccessful attempt to defecate or urinate [Early 16thC. Via medieval Latin from, ultimately, Greek *tēnesmos*, from *teinein* "to stretch, strain."]

ten·et /ténnət/ *n.* any of a set of established and fundamental beliefs, especially one relating to religion or politics (*formal*) ○ *a tenet of Christianity* [Late 16thC. From Latin, literally "he or she holds," the 3rd person present singular form of *tenere* "to hold."]

ten·fold /tén fòld/ *adj.* **1. WITH TEN PARTS** made up of ten parts **2. TIMES TEN** multiplied by ten ■ *adv.* **TEN TIMES OVER** to ten times the amount or number, or multiplied by or up to that amount or number

ten-four, 10–4 *interj.* used to express affirmation or confirmation [From a code originally used by police in the sense "message received"]

ten-gal·lon hat *n.* a cowboy hat with a high round uncreased crown and a wide brim

ten·ge /téngày/ (*plural* **-ge**) *n.* **1. UNIT OF KAZAKH CURRENCY** a unit of currency in Kazakhstan. See table at **currency 2. BILL WORTH ONE TENGE** a bill worth one tenge **3. ten·ge** (*plural* **-ga**) **MINOR UNIT OF TURKMEN CURRENCY** a minor unit of currency in Turkmenistan, 100 of which are worth one manat

te·ni·a *n.* = **taenia**

te·ni·a·cide *n.* = **taeniacide**

te·ni·a·fuge *n.* = **taeniafuge**

te·ni·a·sis *n.* = **taeniasis**

Tenn. *abbr.* Tennessee

Ten·nent /ténnənt/, **Gilbert** (1703–64) Irish-born American clergyman. His fiery preaching helped to create the religious revival known as the Great Awakening in the North American Middle Colonies in the 1730s.

Ten·nent, William (1673–1745) Irish-born American clergyman. Many of the students at his "Log College" in Pennsylvania, including his son Gilbert, became important figures in the Great Awakening of the 1730s.

ten·ner /ténnər/ *n.* (*informal*) **1.** *U.S., ANZ, Can* **TEN DOLLARS** ten dollars, either as cash or as a sum **2.** *U.K.* **TEN POUNDS** ten pounds sterling, either as cash or as a sum

Tennessee

Ten·nes·see /tènnə séé/ **1.** state in the eastern central United States, bordered by Kentucky, Virginia, North Carolina, Georgia, Alabama, Mississippi, Arkansas, and Missouri. Capital: Nashville. Population: 5,368,198 (1997). Area: 42,146 sq. mi./109,158 sq. km. **2.** river of the southeastern United States, formed by the confluence of the Holston and French Broad rivers and flowing into the Ohio River. Length: 652 mi./1,050 km. —**Ten·nes·se·an** *n., adj.*

Ten·nes·see walk·ing horse, Ten·nes·see walk·er *n.* any of a breed of easy-gaited saddle horses developed in Tennessee from standardbred and Morgan stock

Ten·niel /ténnyəl/, **Sir John** (1820–1914) British illustrator. He contributed more than 2,300 cartoons to the British satirical magazine *Punch* from 1851 to 1901. His illustrations for *Alice's Adventures in Wonderland* (1865) and *Through the Looking-Glass* (1871) fixed the images of Lewis Carroll's characters for generations of children.

ten·nis /ténniss/ *n.* a game played on a rectangular court by two, or two pairs of, players with rackets who hit a ball back and forth over a net. ◊ **lawn tennis, court tennis, paddle tennis, table tennis** [14thC. Origin uncertain: probably from Old French *tenez* "hold!", a plural form of *tenir* "to hold," hence, "to receive," presumably shouted by the serving player to the opponent.]

ten·nis ball *n.* a white or yellow fuzzy cloth-surfaced hollow rubber ball about 3 in./7.5 cm in diameter, used in tennis. In lawn tennis the ball is pressurized, and in paddle tennis it is punctured.

ten·nis brace·let *n.* a slim chain-style bracelet made with small diamonds or other precious stones

ten·nis el·bow *n.* painful inflammation of the tendon in the outer elbow region caused by excessive and repetitive strain from overuse, e.g., as a result of playing tennis and similar sports. It may be treated with rest, massage, and steroid drugs.

ten·nis shoe *n.* CLOTHES = **sneaker**

ten·nis skirt *n.* a short skirt, traditionally white, worn by some women tennis players

Ten·ny·son /ténniss'n/, **Alfred, 1st Baron Tennyson of Freshwater and Aldworth** (1809–92) British poet. His many works include "The Lady of Shalott" (1832), *In Memoriam* (1850), and "The Charge of the Light Brigade" (1854). He was poet laureate from 1850. —**Ten·ny·so·ni·an** /ténn is ṓn ee ən/ *n., adj.*

ten·on /ténnən/ *n.* **PROJECTION ON WOOD FOR MAKING JOINT** a projection made on the end of one piece of wood that fits into a mortise on another piece, making a joint ■ *vt.* (**-oned, -on·ing, -ons**) **1. MAKE A TENON** to make a tenon on a piece of wood **2. JOIN PIECES OF WOOD USING TENON** to join two pieces of wood using a tenon [Early 17thC. From French, from *tenir* "to hold."] —**ten·on·er** *n.*

ten·on saw *n.* a small thin saw with a strong back, used especially for cutting tenons

ten·or /ténnər/ *n.* **1.** MUSIC **HIGH MALE VOICE** the highest natural male singing voice, or an adult whose voice is in this register **2.** MUSIC **HIGH OR FAIRLY HIGH INSTRUMENT** an instrument with a range similar to a tenor voice (*often used before a noun*) **3. WAY SOMETHING IS PROGRESSING** the direction in which something is steadily moving (*formal*) **4. WHAT SOMETHING IS MAINLY ABOUT** the overall nature, pattern, or meaning of something, especially a written or spoken statement (*formal*) **5.** LAW **EXACT WORDS OF DEED** the exact wording of a document, rather than its effect **6.** LAW **EXACT COPY** an exact copy or transcript of a document [13thC. Via Anglo-Norman *tenur* and Old French *tenour* from Latin *tenor* "continuous course," from *tenere* "to hold," the underlying idea being "something that is held to."]

ten·or clef *n.* one of the C clefs, in which middle C is represented by the second highest line on the staff, used in the past to notate the tenor voice

ten·or·ite /ténnə rìt/ *n.* a black mineral form of copper oxide, occurring with copper ores or near volcanoes [Mid-19thC. Named for Michelo *Tenore* (1781–1861), president of the Naples Academy of Sciences in Italy.]

ten·o·syn·o·vi·tis /tènnō sīnə vítiss, tènnō sinnə vítiss/ *n.* inflammation of a tendon sheath, usually in the wrist, with swelling and audible creaking on movement. It often results from repetitive movements as in typing or some sports. [Late 19thC. From modern Latin, from Greek *tenōn*, "tendon," and SYNOVITIS.]

te·not·o·my /tə nóttəmee/ (*plural* **-mies**) *n.* the surgical cutting of a tendon

ten·pen·ny /tén pènnee/ *adj.* costing or worth ten cents (*dated*)

ten·pen·ny nail *n.* a nail 3 in./7.6 cm long (*dated*)

ten·pin /tén pìn/ *n.* one of the ten pins used in tenpin bowling

ten·pin bowl·ing /tén pìnz/, **ten·pins** *n.* = **bowling** *n.* **1**

ten·pound·er /tèn pówndər/ *n.* = **ladyfish** *n.* **1**

ten·rec /tén rèk/ (*plural* **-recs** *or* **-rec**), **tan·rec** /tán-/ (*plural* **-recs** *or* **-rec**) *n.* a small to medium-sized insect-eating mammal with a long pointed snout, native to Madagascar and the Comoro Islands. Some have spines and some fur. Family: Tenrecidae. [Late 18thC. Via French *tanrec* from Malagasay *tàndraka, tràndraka*.]

TENS /tenz/ *n.* a method of treating chronic pain by applying electrodes to the skin and passing small electric currents through sensory nerves and the spinal cord, thus suppressing the transmission of pain signals. Full form **transcutaneous electrical nerve stimulation**

tense[1] /tenss/ *adj.* (**tens·er, tens·est**) **1. WORRIED AND NERVOUS** affected by anxious feelings or mental strain, so that it is impossible to behave in a natural relaxed way **2. RESTRAINED AND UNNATURAL** making people feel unusually anxious, nervous, and uncertain, so that they do not talk or behave in a natural relaxed way **3. TIGHT AND STIFF** stretched or held tight and stiff **4.** PHON **PRONOUNCED WITH TAUT MUSCLES** used to describe a speech sound that is pronounced with muscular effort, is relatively long in duration, and is accurate in articulation ■ *vti.* (**tensed, tens·ing, tens·es**) **BECOME OR MAKE TENSE** to become tense or make something tense [Late 17thC. From Latin *tensus* "stretched," the past participle of *tendere* "to stretch" (source also of English *tent*).] —**tense·ly** *adv.* —**tense·ness** *n.*

tense up *vti.* = **tense[1]** *v.*

tense[2] /tenss/ *n.* the facet of a verb that expresses the different times at which action takes place relative to the speaker or writer, e.g., the present, past, or future [14thC. Via Old French *tens*, "time," from Latin *tempus*.] —**tense·less** *adj.*

ten·sile /ténss'l, tén sìl/ *adj.* **1. RELATING TO TENSION** relating to or involving tension **2. STRETCHABLE** capable of being stretched or pulled out of shape [Early 17thC. From medieval Latin *tensilis* from, ultimately, Latin *tendere* (see TENSE[1]).] —**ten·sile·ly** *adv.* —**ten·sile·ness** *n.* —**ten·sil·i·ty** /ten sílletee/ *n.*

ten·sile strength *n.* the maximum stretching force that a material, e.g., wire, can withstand before breaking

ten·sim·e·ter /ten símmətər/ *n.* an instrument used to measure differences in vapor pressure [Early 20thC. Coined from TENSION + -METER.]

ten·si·om·e·ter /tènsee ómmətər/ *n.* **1.** INSTRUMENT FOR MEASURING TENSILE STRESS an instrument used to measure tensile stress **2.** INSTRUMENT FOR MEASURING SURFACE TENSION an instrument used to measure the surface tension of liquids **3.** GEOL INSTRUMENT FOR MEASURING SOIL MOISTURE an instrument used to measure the moisture content of soils [Early 20thC. Coined from TENSION + -METER.]

ten·sion /ténshən/ *n.* **1.** ANXIOUS FEELINGS mental worry or emotional strain that makes natural relaxed behavior impossible **2.** UNEASY FEELING IN RELATIONSHIP a state of wariness, mistrust, controlled hostility, or fear of hostility felt by countries, groups, or individuals in their dealings with one another (*often used in the plural*) **3.** LITERAT SENSE OF DIFFERENT ELEMENTS CONFLICTING the way that opposing elements or characters clash or interact interestingly with each other in a literary work **4.** LITERAT BUILDUP OF SUSPENSE the buildup of suspense in a fictional work, leading to the dénouement **5.** TAUTNESS how tightly something such as wire, string, thread, or a muscle is stretched **6.** SEW DEVICE CONTROLLING TIGHTNESS OF THREAD a device on a sewing machine or a loom that regulates how tight the thread is **7.** PHYS PULLING FORCE a force that pulls or stretches something **8.** PHYS STRESS FROM TENSION the stress resulting from a force of tension, or a measure of it **9.** ELEC VOLTAGE voltage or electromotive force (*often used in combination*) [Mid-16thC. Directly or via French from Latin *tension-* "stretching," from, ultimately, *tendere*, "to stretch" (source also of English *tent*).] —**ten·sion·al** *adj.*

ten·si·ty /ténsətee/ *n.* the state or quality of being tense

ten·sive /ténsiv/ *adj.* causing or relating to tension [Early 18thC. Via French *tensif* from, ultimately, Latin *tendere* (see TENSE[1]).]

ten·som·e·ter *n.* = **tensiometer** *n.* 1, **tensiometer** *n.* 2

ten·sor /ténsər, tén sàwr/ *n.* **1.** ANAT STRETCHING MUSCLE a muscle that tenses or stretches a part of the body **2.** MATH GENERALIZATION OF A VECTOR the generalization of a vector, a mathematical entity specified with respect to a given coordinate system and able to undergo transformation to other coordinate systems [Early 18thC. From modern Latin, from Latin *tendere* (see TENSE[1]).] —**ten·so·ri·al** /ten sáwree əl/ *adj.*

ten-speed *adj.* WITH TEN DIFFERENT GEARS with ten different gears controlling the speed ■ *n.* BICYCLE a ten-speed bicycle

ten-strike *n.* **1.** BOWLING BOWLING STRIKE a strike in tenpin bowling **2.** SOMETHING REALLY SUCCESSFUL a great achievement, result, or action (*informal*)

tent[1] /tent/ *n.* **1.** COLLAPSIBLE SHELTER a collapsible movable shelter consisting of a tough fabric or plastic cover held up by poles and kept in place by ropes and pegs **2.** TENT-SHAPED OBJECT something that looks like a tent, is constructed in a similar way, or serves a similar purpose ○ *an oxygen tent* ■ *v.* (**tent·ed, tent·ing, tents**) **1.** *vt.* COVER SOMETHING AS A TENT DOES to form a raised nonrigid cover over something ○ *Tent the roast with aluminum foil.* **2.** *vi.* CAMP to live or camp in a tent **3.** *vt.* SUPPLY A TENT FOR SOMEBODY to accommodate a person or group of people in tents, or provide somebody or something with tents [13thC. Via Old French *tente* from Latin *tenta*, "tent," from *tendere*, "to stretch." Because a tent consists of a cover stretched over a framework.]

tent[2] /tent/ *n.* PLUG FOR WOUND a cone-shaped expandable plug of soft material, e.g., gauze, used to keep a wound or orifice open ■ *vt.* (**tent·ed, tent·ing, tents**) INSERT A TENT to open or expand a wound or orifice with a tent [14thC. Via French *tente* from, ultimately, Latin *temptare*, "to feel, try."]

ten·ta·cle /téntək'l/ *n.* **1.** ZOOL LONG FLEXIBLE ORGAN a long flexible organ around the mouth or on the head of some animals, especially invertebrates such as squid, and used in holding, grasping, feeling, or moving **2.** PLANTS HAIR ON A PLANT LEAF a sticky glandular hairy projection from the leaf of an insect-eating plant such as the sundew, whose secretions trap and digest prey **3.** SOMETHING FAR-REACHING something that gradually or unnoticeably insinuates its way into and around things and takes hold of them firmly or has a definite presence or effect (*literary*) [Mid-18thC. Anglicization of modern Latin *tentaculum* from, ultimately, Latin *temptare*, "to feel, try" (source also of English *tempt*).] —**ten·ta·cled** *adj.* —**ten·tac·u·lar** /ten tákyələr/ *adj.*

tent·age /téntij/ *n.* tents in general or as a group

ten·ta·tive /téntətiv/ *adj.* **1.** UNCERTAIN said or done in a slow, hesitant, and careful way, revealing a lack of confidence **2.** ROUGH OR PROVISIONAL likely to have many later changes before it becomes final and complete [Late 16thC. From medieval Latin *tentativus*, from, ultimately, Latin *tentare*, a variant of *temptare*, "to feel, try" (source of English *tempt*).] —**ten·ta·tive·ly** *adv.* —**ten·ta·tive·ness** *n.*

tent cat·er·pil·lar *n.* a destructive caterpillar that builds large tent-shaped communal webs in the branches of trees. Genus: *Malacosoma.*

tent dress *n.* a dress made so that the fabric hangs in a full loose shape from the shoulders

tent·ed /téntəd/ *adj.* **1.** WITH TENT SHAPE constructed or shaped like a tent **2.** WITH TENTS covered in tents (*literary*) **3.** CAMPED IN TENTS staying in tents, or supplied with tents as shelter

ten·ter /téntər/ *n.* FRAME FOR CLOTH a frame on which cloth is held taut during various phases of its manufacture, especially while it dries ■ *vt.* (**-tered, -ter·ing, -ters**) STRETCH ON TENTER to stretch cloth on a tenter [13thC. From medieval Latin *tentorium* from, ultimately, Latin *tendere* "to stretch."]

ten·ter·hook /téntər ho͝ok/ *n.* any one of the hooks used to hold cloth taut on a frame during manufacture, especially while it dries ◇ **be on tenterhooks** to be anxious or in suspense

tenth /tenth/ *n.* **1.** ONE OF TEN PARTS OF SOMETHING one of ten equal parts of something **2.** ORDINAL NUMBER CORRESPONDING TO 10 the ordinal number assigned to item number 10 in a series **3.** MUSIC MUSICAL INTERVAL an interval equal to an octave plus a third [Old English *teogoþa, tēoþa*, from an earlier form of TEN] —**tenth** *adj., adv.*

tent stitch *n.* a type of short parallel diagonal stitch used to fill in an area in needlepoint or embroidery, or a single stitch of this kind

ten·u·is /ténnyoo iss/ (*plural* **-es** /-èez/) *n.* LING a voiceless stop consonant in classical Greek grammar [Mid-17thC. Formed from Latin, "thin, fine," a translation of Greek *psilon* "bare, smooth."]

ten·u·ous /ténnyoo əss/ *adj.* **1.** WEAK AND UNCONVINCING not based on anything significant or substantial, and so liable to break down easily when challenged ○ *That's an extremely tenuous argument.* **2.** EXTREMELY DELICATE AND FINE thin and fine and so easily broken (*literary*) **3.** SCI DILUTED thin or diluted in consistency [Late 16thC. Formed by alteration from Latin *tenuis* (see TENUIS).] —**te·nu·i·ty** /te no͞o itee/ *n.* —**ten·u·ous·ly** /ténnyoo əsslee/ *adv.* —**ten·u·ous·ness** /ténnyoo əssnəss/ *n.*

ten·ure /ténnyər/ *n.* **1.** APPOINTMENT OR PERIOD OF APPOINTMENT the occupation of an official position, or the length of time a position is occupied (*formal*) ○ *her tenure as president* **2.** PROPERTY-HOLDING the rights of a tenant to hold property, or the holding of property as a tenant **3.** EDUC, HR PERMANENT STATUS the position of having a formal secure appointment until retirement, especially at an educational institution after working on a temporary or provisional basis [15thC. Via Old French "tenure, estate," from, ultimately, Latin *tenere* "to hold."]

ten·ured /ténnyərd/ *adj.* **1.** HR PERMANENTLY HELD formally granted to somebody to possess or occupy until retirement, especially in an educational institution ○ *a tenured position at a good university* **2.** EDUC HAVING PERMANENT STATUS formally granted the right to hold an academic job until retirement ○ *She's a tenured professor.* **3.** LAW HAVING TENURE subject to a guaranteed period of time during which rights cannot be withdrawn

ten·ure-track *adj.* guaranteed consideration for tenure in the U.S. and Canadian system of academic employment ○ *offered a tenure-track position at the university*

te·nu·to /tay no͞otō, tə-/ *adv., adj.* indicating that a musical note should be held for its full value (*used as a musical direction*) [Mid-18thC. Via Italian, the past participle of *tenere*, "to hold," from Latin, "to hold."]

te·o·cal·li /tèe ə kállee, tày ə kaálee/ *n.* a temple in ancient Mexico or Central America, or the pyramidal mound on which one was built [Early 17thC. Via American Spanish from Nahuatl *teokalli*, literally "deity's house."]

te·o·sin·te /tày ō síntee, tèe ə-/ *n.* a tall annual grass of Mexico and Central America, related to, and perhaps the ancestor of, corn, and grown as forage. Latin name: *Zea mexicana.* [Late 19thC. Via French *téosinté* from Nahuatl *teocintli*, perhaps literally "dried corn ear of a deity."]

te·pa /téepə/ *n.* a crystalline compound used in the sterilization of insects, treatment of some cancers, and fireproofing of textiles. Formula: $C_6H_{12}N_3OP$. [Mid-20thC. Acronym formed from TRI- + ETHYLENE+ PHOSPH- + AMIDE-.]

te·pal /téep'l, tépp'l/ *n.* any of the parts that form the outer whorl (**perianth**) of flowers such as in the tulip, in which there is no differentiation into petals and sepals [Mid-19thC. From French, a blend of *sépale* "sepal," and *pétale* "petal."]

tep·a·ry bean /téppəree-/ *n.* an annual twining bean of the southwestern United States and Mexico, grown for its round edible seeds. Latin name: *Phaseolus acutifolius latifolius.* [*Tepary* of unknown origin]

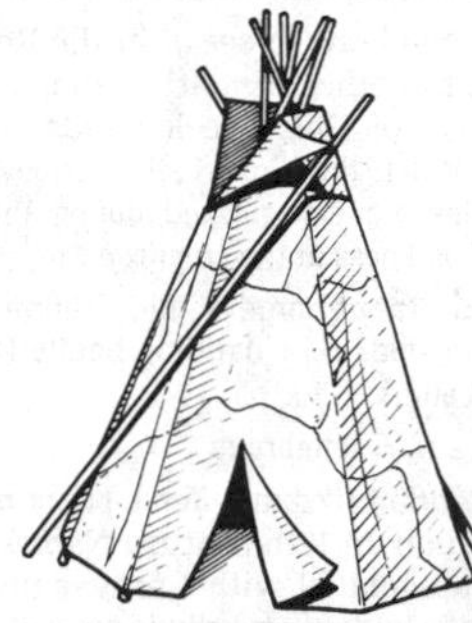

Tepee

te·pee /tée pee/, **tee·pee, ti·pi** *n.* a conical tent built around several long branches or wooden poles that meet and cross at the top. A tepee is traditionally made of animal hide and used as a dwelling by Plains Indians and some other Native North American people. [Mid-18thC. From Sioux *típi* "dwelling."]

teph·ra /téffrə/ *n.* solid material ejected explosively from a volcano, e.g., ash, dust, and bolders [Mid-20thC. From Greek, "ashes."]

tep·id /téppid/ *adj.* **1.** LUKEWARM slightly warm **2.** UNENTHUSIASTIC showing little enthusiasm or warmth ○ *tepid applause* [14thC. From Latin *tepidus*, from *tepere*, "to be warm."] —**te·pid·i·ty** /tə píddətee/ *n.* —**tep·id·ly** /téppidlee/ *adv.* —**tep·id·ness** /téppidnəss/ *n.*

TEPP /tep/ *n.* a crystalline compound used as an insecticide and in medicine as a stimulant of the parasympathetic nervous system. Formula: $C_8H_{20}O_7P_2$. Full form **tetraethyl pyrophosphate**

te·qui·la /tə kéelə/ *n.* a strong Mexican liquor made by redistilling the fermented juice of the agave plant (**mescal**). It is drunk neat or used as a base for cocktails. [Mid-19thC. From Mexican Spanish, named for *Tequila*, a town in Central Mexico where the drink is produced.]

te·qui·la sun·rise *n.* a cocktail based on tequila that also contains orange juice and grenadine

ter. *abbr.* **1.** territory **2.** territorial **3.** terrace

Ter. *abbr.* Terrace (*used in street names and addresses*)

tera- *prefix.* one trillion (10^{12}). Symbol **T** [Formed from Greek *teras* "monster"]

ter·a·byte /térrə bìt/ *n.* an information unit of one trillion bytes

ter·a·flop /térrə flòp/ *n.* one trillion floating-point operations per second, a measure of computer speed [Late 20thC. Coined from TERA- and an acronym formed from *floating-point operations per second.*]

ter·a·hertz /térrə hùrts/ (*plural* **-hertz**) *n.* a unit of frequency equal to one trillion hertz

te·rai /tə rí/, **te·rai hat** *n.* a wide-brimmed felt hat with a double crown, once widely worn in the subtropics [Late 19thC. Named for the *Terai* region of the Himalayas, where such a hat would have been worn.]

a at; aa father; aw all; ay day; air hair; ə about, edible, item, common, circus; e egg; ee eel; hw when; i it; ī ice; 'l apple; 'm rhythm; 'n fashion; o odd; ō open; o͝o good; oo pool; ow owl; oy oil; th thin; th this; u up; ur urge;

ter·aph /térrəf/ (*plural* **-a·phim** /térrəfim/) *n.* an image or idol worshiped by ancient Semitic peoples [Early 19thC. Back-formation from 14thC *teraphim*, via late Latin *theraphim* and Greek *theraphin* from Hebrew *tĕrāpīm*.]

terato- *prefix.* irregular form ○ *teratology* [From Greek *terat-*, stem of *teras* "monster"]

ter·a·to·car·ci·no·ma /tèrrə tō kaárs'n ṓmə/ (*plural* **-mas** *or* **-ma·ta** /-ṓmətə/) *n.* a malignant teratoma, most often occurring in the testes

te·rat·o·gen /tə ráttəjən, térrətəjən/ *n.* an agent, e.g., a chemical, virus, or ionizing radiation, that interrupts or alters the normal development of a fetus, with results that are evident at birth —**ter·a·to·gen·ic** /tèrrətə jénnik/ *adj.*

ter·a·to·gen·e·sis /tèrrətə jénnəssiss/ *n.* the process of interrupting or altering normal development, especially of a fetus, with results that are evident at birth

ter·a·toid /térrə tòyd/ *adj.* affected by a visible condition caused by the interruption or alteration of normal development

ter·a·tol·o·gy /tèrrə tólləjee/ *n.* the scientific study of visible conditions caused by the interruption or alteration of normal development —**ter·a·to·log·ic** /tèrrətə lójjik/ *adj.* —**ter·a·tol·o·gist** /tèrrə tólləjist/ *n.*

ter·a·to·ma /tèrrə tṓmə/ *n.* a tumor composed of various tissues, e.g., bone, hair, and teeth, not normally found together at the site of origin, and probably derived from embryonic remnants. They most often occur in the ovary, where they are benign, and in the testis, where they are malignant. —**ter·a·to·ma·tous** /tèrrə tṓmətəss/ *adj.*

ter·bi·um /túrbee əm/ *n.* a silvery gray metallic chemical element of the rare-earth group that is used in lasers and X-ray and television tubes. Symbol **Tb** [Mid-19thC. Named for *Ytterby,* the village in Sweden where it was discovered.] —**ter·bic** *adj.*

terce /turs/ *n.* in the Roman Catholic Church, the third of the seven prayer times (**canonical hours**) when specific prayers are said [14thC. Via Old French, a variant of *tierce* (see TIERCE).]

Ter·cei·ra /tər sáyrə, tər sírə/ the second largest island in the Azores archipelago, in the North Atlantic Ocean. Population: 55,800 (1987). Area: 153 sq. mi./397 sq. km.

ter·cel /túrs'l/ (*plural* **-cels** *or* **-cel**), **tier·cel** /teérs'l/ (*plural* **-cels** *or* **-cel**) *n.* a male falcon or hawk used in falconry [14thC. Via Old French *terçuel* from, ultimately, Latin *tertius* "third," because it is about a third smaller than the female, or from the belief that the third egg hatched was male.]

ter·cen·ten·a·ry /tùrs'n ténnəree, tùr séntə nèrree/, **ter·cen·ten·ni·al** /-ténnee əl/ *n.* (*plural* **-ries**) **300TH ANNIVERSARY** a year, or an exact day, 300 years after a specific thing happened, usually something of special historic significance ■ *adj.* **MARKING 300 YEARS SINCE SOMETHING HAPPENED** coinciding with the 300th anniversary of a particular event, and often celebrating or commemorating this [Mid-19thC. Coined from Latin *ter* "three times"+ CENTENARY or CENTENNIAL.]

ter·cet /túrsət/ *n.* a group of three lines of verse that rhyme with each other or with another group of three [Late 16thC. Via French from Italian *terzetto,* from, ultimately, Latin *tertius* "third."]

ter·e·binth /térrə bìnth/ (*plural* **-binths** *or* **-binth**) *n.* a small Mediterranean tree of the cashew family that has clusters of small flowers and yields a turpentine. Latin name: *Pistacia terebinthus.* [14thC. Directly and via Old French *t(h)erebinte* from Latin *terebinthus,* from Greek *terebinthos.*]

ter·e·bin·thine /tèrrə bínthin, -bín thīn/ *adj.* **1.** BOT **OF TEREBINTH TREE** relating to the terebinth tree **2.** CHEM **LIKE TURPENTINE** like or consisting of turpentine [Early 16thC. From Latin *terebinthinus,* from *terebinthus* (see TEREBINTH).]

te·re·do /tə reé dō, -ráy-/ (*plural* **-dos** *or* **-do**) *n.* = **shipworm** [14thC. Via Latin from Greek *terēdōn,* from the base of *teirein* "to rub hard, wear away, bore."]

Ter·ence /térrənss/ (185–159 B.C.) Roman playwright. His six surviving comedies, based on Greek originals, are forerunners of the modern comedy of manners. Full name **Publius Terentius Afer**

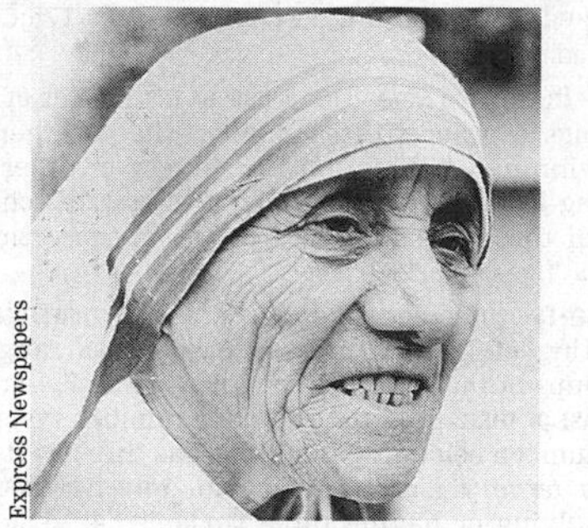

Mother Teresa

Te·re·sa (of Calcutta) /tə reéssə-/, **Mother** (1910–97) Albanian-born nun. From 1948 she devoted her life to helping the poor and the sick of Calcutta. She founded the Missionaries of Charity (1950) and opened a shelter for dying people (1952). Real name **Agnes Gonxha Bojaxhiu**

Te·resh·ko·va /tə resh kṓvə/, **Valentina** (*b.* 1937) Soviet cosmonaut. She was the first woman to fly in space (June 16–19, 1963).

te·rete /tə reét/ *adj.* used to describe a plant part that is smooth, cylindrical, and tapering, e.g., a grass stem [Early 17thC. From Latin *teret-,* the stem of *teres* "rounded."]

ter·ga plural of **tergum**

ter·giv·er·sate /tər jívvər sàyt, túrjivər-, tùrji vúr-/ (**-sat·ed, -sat·ing, -sates**) *vi.* (*formal*) **1. CHANGE SIDES** to change sides or opinions **2. BE EVASIVE** to use evasions or subterfuges [Mid-17thC. From Latin *tergiversare* "to turn your back," from *tergum* "back" + *vertere* "to turn."] —**ter·gi·ver·sant** /tùrji vúrs'nt, tər jívvərs'nt/ *n.* —**ter·gi·ver·sa·tor** /tər jívvər sàytər, túrjivər-, tùrji vúr-/ *n.* —**ter·gi·ver·sa·tor·y** /tùr ji vúrsə tàwree, tər jívvərsə-/ *adj.*

ter·gum /túrgəm/ (*plural* **-ga** /túrgə/) *n.* a thick plate covering the dorsal surface of a body segment of an arthropod, or the movable segments of a barnacle's shell [Early 19thC. From Latin, "back."] —**ter·gal** *adj.*

ter·i·ya·ki /tèrree yaákee/ *n.* a Japanese dish consisting of broiled shellfish or meat brushed with a marinade of soy sauce, sugar, and rice wine [Mid-20thC. From Japanese, literally "glaze grill."]

term /turm/ *n.* **1. NAME OR WORD FOR SOMETHING** a particular word or combination of words, especially one used to mean something very specific or one used in a specialized area of knowledge or work ○ *The correct legal term is easement.* **2. PERIOD OF TIME SOMETHING LASTS** the length of time that something lasts, with a fixed or specified beginning and end, often a period during which somebody holds a specific appointment or office (*formal*) **3. PERIOD OF TIME BODY CONTINUES MEETING** a length of time over which a political or legal body, e.g., a legislature or court of law, regularly assembles and carries out its formal duties **4.** EDUC **DIVISION OF ACADEMIC YEAR** one of the sections of the academic year during which students attend a school, college, or university and receive regular instruction **5.** GYN **EXPECTED TIME FOR BIRTH OF CHILD** the time at the end of a woman's pregnancy when the baby is expected to be born ○ *came to term* **6.** LOGIC **SUBJECT OR PREDICATE OF PROPOSITION** in traditional Aristotelian logic, the subject or the predicate of a categorical proposition **7.** LOGIC **NAME OR INDIVIDUAL VARIABLE** in modern logic, a name or individual variable **8.** MATH **MATHEMATICAL EXPRESSION** a mathematical expression that forms part of a fraction or proportion, is part of a series, or is associated with another by a plus or minus sign **9.** SCULPTURE **SCULPTURED PILLAR** a sculptured pillar, especially one with an armless bust, or an animal portrait, on top of a square post **10.** LAW **ESTATE RUNNING FOR LIMITED PERIOD** an estate limited to a prescribed period ■ **terms** *npl.* **1. WAY PEOPLE GET ALONG TOGETHER** the treatment given by one person, nation, or power to another, or the opinions or attitudes they have or express toward each other ○ *on good terms with the neighbors* **2. PARTS THAT MAKE UP AN AGREEMENT** the particular requirements laid down formally in an agreement or contract, or proposed by one side when negotiating an agreement **3. LANGUAGE** the words that somebody uses, or specifically chooses to use, when speaking or writing ■ *vt.* (**termed, term·ing, terms**) **USE A PARTICULAR WORD FOR SOMETHING** to describe or refer to something using a particular name or expression ○ *His followers were termed "Roundheads."* [13thC. Via French *terme* "limit of time or space" (the original sense in English), from Latin *terminus* (see TERMINUS).] ◇ **come to terms (with something)** to reach a state of acceptance or agreement about something ◇ **in terms of something** in relation to something ◇ **not be on speaking terms (with somebody)** to have had a quarrel or disagreement with somebody, so that neither will speak to the other

term. *abbr.* **1.** termination **2.** terminal

ter·ma·gant /túrməgənt/ *n.* an offensive term that deliberately insults a woman's temperament and supposed propensity for arguing, criticizing, and quarreling (*literary*) [13thC. Via Old French *Tervagant,* the name of an overbearing non-Christian deity in medieval mystery plays (the original sense in English), from Italian *Trivigante.*] —**ter·ma·gan·cy** *n.*

-termer /túrmər/ *suffix.* somebody who is serving a particular term as a political appointee or in a prison ○ *a second-termer*

ter·mi·na·ble /túrmənəb'l/ *adj.* **1. CAPABLE OF TERMINATION** able to be terminated (*formal*) ○ *The contract is terminable at any time.* **2.** INSUR **WITH A FIXED END POINT** ending or capable of being ended after a certain period or on a particular date ○ *a terminable annuity* [15thC. Formed from earlier *termine* "to terminate," via French *terminer* from Latin *terminare.*] —**ter·mi·na·bil·i·ty** /tùrmənə bílləteel/ *n.* —**ter·mi·na·bly** /túrmənəblee/ *adv.*

ter·mi·nal /túrmən'l/ *adj.* **1. CAUSING DEATH** inevitably, but often gradually, leading to the death of the person affected by the condition ○ *a terminal illness* **2. DYING** affected by a fatal illness or condition that is approaching its final stages **3. RELATING TO DYING PATIENTS** for or concerned with patients with a terminal condition ○ *terminal care* **4. AT THE VERY END** forming or found at the extreme point or limit of something, or relating to the very end of something ○ *the terminal moraine of the glacier* **5. ENDING A SERIES** constituting the end of a series of things ○ *the terminal performance of the Mostly Mozart concerts* **6. OF FIXED DURATION** lasting for a certain period or term (*formal*) **7.** BOT **AT END OF STEM** at the end of a stem, stalk, or branch ■ *n.* **1. END PART** a section or point that forms the end of something **2.** TRANSP **STATION AT END OF TRANSPORTATION ROUTE** a building or complex containing facilities needed by transportation operators and passengers at either end of a travel or shipping route by air, rail, road, or sea **3.** ELEC **ELECTRICAL CONDUCTOR** a conductor attached at the point where electricity enters or leaves a circuit, e.g., on a battery **4.** COMPUT **DEVICE LINKED TO COMPUTER** a remote input or output device linked to a computer, or a combination of such devices, e.g., a keyboard and video display **5.** TRANSP = **terminus** *n.* 1 **6.** ARCHIT **ORNAMENTAL CARVING** an ornamental carving or figure at the end of a larger structure [15thC. From Latin *terminalis,* from *terminus* "end, boundary, limit."] —**ter·mi·nal·ly** *adv.*

WORD KEY: SYNONYMS

See Synonyms at ***deadly.***

ter·mi·nal ve·loc·i·ty *n.* the constant speed that a falling object reaches when the downward gravitational force equals the frictional resistance of the medium through which it is falling, usually air. This is the maximum speed that a freely falling body can reach under particular conditions.

ter·mi·nate /túrmə nàyt/ (**-nat·ed, -nat·ing, -nates**) *v.* **1.** *vti.* **FINISH** to come to an end, or bring something to an end (*formal*) **2.** *vt.* **FIRE SOMEBODY** to discontinue somebody's or a group's employment ○ *He was terminated after 20 years in the job.* [Late 16thC. From Latin *terminare,* from *terminus* "end, boundary, limit."] —**ter·mi·na·tive** *adj.* —**ter·mi·na·tor·y** /túrmənə tàwree/ *adj.*

ter·mi·nat·ing dec·i·mal *n.* a decimal fraction with a finite number of digits

ter·mi·na·tion /tùrmə náysh'n/ *n.* **1. ENDING OF SOMETHING** the process of bringing something to an end or of being brought to an end, or an individual example of this (*formal*) **2.** LING **WORD ENDING** a word ending such as a suffix or an inflection **3. TIP OR EDGE** something that forms the end or final limit of something (*formal*) **4. FINAL OUTCOME** something that happens or is produced as a result of something else (*formal*) [14thC. Directly or via French from Latin, from *terminare* (see TERMINATE).] —**ter·mi·na·tion·al** *adj.*

ter·mi·na·tor /túrmə nàytər/ *n.* **1.** **SOMEBODY WHO OR SOMETHING THAT TERMINATES SOMETHING** somebody who or something that puts an end to something (*formal*) **2.** ASTRON **LINE BETWEEN MOON'S LIGHT AND DARK** the boundary between the part of the moon or a planet that is illuminated and that which is dark

ter·min·a·tor gene *n.* a gene inserted into genetically modified plants that makes them unable to produce seed after one season

ter·mi·nol·o·gy /tùrmə nólləjee/ (*plural* **-gies**) *n.* **1.** **SPECIALIZED VOCABULARY** the expressions and words, or a set of expressions and words, used by people involved in a specialized activity or field of work **2.** LING **STUDY OF NAMES AND TERMS** the systematic study of names and terms [Early 19thC. Via German *Terminologie*, from medieval Latin *terminus* "term."] —**ter·mi·no·log·i·cal** /tùrminə lójjək'l/ *adj.* —**ter·mi·no·log·i·cal·ly** /tùrmənə lójjiklee/ *adv.* —**ter·mi·nol·o·gist** /tùrmə nólləjist/ *n.*

term in·sur·ance *n.* life insurance that pays a sum of money only if the person who is covered has a loss within a particular period of time

ter·mi·nus /túrmənəss/ (*plural* **-ni** /-nī/ *or* **-nus·es**) *n.* **1.** TRANSP **PLACE WHERE TRANSPORTATION ROUTE ENDS** a town, city, or location at the end or beginning of a fixed transport route such as a railroad or bus route **2.** **VERY LAST POINT** a point where something stops or reaches its end **3.** SCULPTURE = **term** [Mid-16thC. From Latin "end, boundary, limit."]

ter·mi·nus ad quem /-ad kwém/ *n.* the aim or finishing point of something [From Latin, literally "end to which"]

ter·mi·nus a quo /-aa kwṓ/ *n.* the starting point of something [From Latin, literally "end from which"]

Termitarium: Queensland, Australia

ter·mi·tar·i·um /-əm/ (*plural* **-a** /-térree ə/) *n.* a nest, sometimes extremely large, made by a group of termites [Mid-19thC. Coined from TERMITE + -ARIUM.]

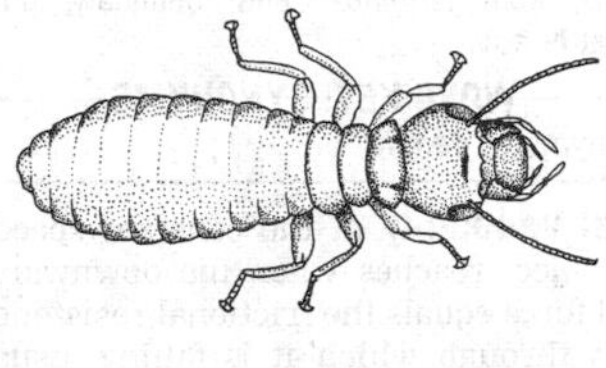
Termite

ter·mite /túr mīt/ *n.* a light-colored social insect that forms large colonies. Many species live in warm or tropical regions, feed on wood, and are highly destructive to trees and wooden structures. Order: Isoptera. [Late 18thC. From Latin *termit-*, the stem of *termes* "woodworm," an alteration of *tarmes*, perhaps influenced by *terere* "to rub."] —**ter·mit·ic** /tər míttik/ *adj.*

term·less /túrmləss/ *adj.* **1.** **ENDLESS** having no end or limit (*literary*) **2.** **UNCONDITIONAL** not depending on any particular terms and conditions (*formal*)

term pa·per *n.* a long essay required of a student during an academic term

tern[1] /túrn/ (*plural* **terns** *or* **tern**) *n.* a seabird, typically black and white, related to the gulls but with a more slender body and wings, a pointed bill, and a forked tail. Subfamily: Sterninae. [Late 17thC. From Scandinavian.]

tern[2] /túrn/ *n.* **1.** GAMBLING **GROUP OF THREE** a set of three things, especially three numbers that together form a winning combination in a lottery or other gambling game **2.** NAUT **THREE-MASTED SCHOONER** a schooner with three masts [14thC. Via French *terne* from Latin *terni* "three each."]

ter·na·ry /túrnəree/ (*plural* **-ries**) *adj.* **1.** **THREEFOLD** consisting of three things or parts, or arranged in groups of three (*formal*) ○ *ternary form* **2.** MATH **WITH A BASE OF THREE** used to describe a number system, or a number belonging to it, that has three as its base ○ *a ternary logarithm* **3.** MATH **WITH THREE VARIABLES** involving or having three variables **4.** METALL **WITH THREE COMPONENTS** used to describe an alloy that consists of three components **5.** CHEM **WITH THREE ATOMS OR MOLECULES** used to describe a chemical compound that consists of three active elements, e.g., three atoms, molecules, or radicals [15thC. From Latin *ternarius*, from *terni*, "three at a time," from *ter* "three times."]

ter·na·ry sys·tem, **ternary number system** *n.* the number system that has 3 as its base. Decimal numbers are expressed as sequences of the digits 0, 1, and 2.

ter·nate /túr nàyt, túrnət/ *adj.* used to describe a compound leaf that is divided into three more or less equal parts [Mid-18thC. From modern Latin *ternatus*, from medieval Latin, the past participle of *ternare* "to make threefold."] —**ter·nate·ly** *adv.*

terne /turn/ *n.* **1.** **METAL ALLOY** an alloy of lead and tin with antimony, used as a coating **2.** = **terneplate** [Mid-19thC. Origin uncertain: probably from French, "dull, tarnished."]

terne·plate /túrn plàyt/ *n.* a steel or iron plate coated with terne

Ter·ni /túrnee/ capital of Terni Province, Umbria Region, central Italy. Population: 108,150 (1992).

ter·pene /túr peen/ *n.* any of a class of hydrocarbons obtained from the essential oils of plants such as conifers and used in organic synthesis. Formula: $C_{10}H_{16}$. [Late 19thC. Formed from German *Terpentin* "turpentine."] —**ter·pe·nic** /tur peénik/ *adj.*

ter·pin·e·ol /tur pínnee àwl/ *n.* a combustible colorless derivative of pine oil, usually found as one of three isomers with a lilac or hyacinth aroma, used in flavorings and perfumes, and as a solvent. Formula: $C_{10}H_{17}OH$. [Late 19thC. Coined from earlier *terpin*, from TERPENE.]

ter·pol·y·mer /tur póllәmər/ *n.* a polymer consisting of three monomers [Mid-20thC. Coined from Latin *ter* "three times" POLYMER.]

Terp·sich·o·re /turp síkəree/ *n.* the Muse of choral songs and dance in Greek mythology

terp·si·cho·real /tùrp sìkə reé əl, tùrpsəkə-/ *adj.* = **terpsichorean** *adj.* (*formal humorous*)

terp·si·cho·re·an /tùrp sìkə reé ən, tùrpsəkə-/ *adj.* **RELATING TO DANCE** relating to or like dance (*formal humorous*) ■ *n.* **DANCER** a dancer (*formal humorous*) [Early 19thC. Formed from Greek *Terpsikhorē*, literally "delighting in dance," from *terpein* "delight" + *khoros* "dance."]

terr. *abbr.* **1.** territory **2.** territorial **3.** terrace

ter·ra /térrə/ (*plural* **ter·rae** /térree/) *n.* any of the light-colored highland or mountainous areas of the moon or of a planet [Early 17thC. Directly or via Italian from Latin, "earth, land."]

ter·ra al·ba /tèrrə álbə/ *n.* a white substance such as kaolin or gypsum, used in the making of paints and paper [From Latin, literally "white earth"]

ter·race /térrəss/ *n.* **1.** **BALCONY** a level outdoor surface that extends from one of the upper floors of an apartment or house **2.** ARCHIT **PORCH OR WALKWAY WITH PILLARS** a promenade or portico, usually with columns or a balustrade along the side or sides **3.** AGRIC **STRIP OF AGRICULTURAL LAND ON HILLSIDE** a flat, fairly narrow, level strip of ground, bounded by a vertical or steep slope and constructed on a hillside so that the land can be cultivated **4.** GEOG **AREA OF NATURAL GROUND ALONG COAST** a flat raised strip of beach or ground that has been formed naturally along the coast, beside a river or lake, or along the side of a valley by erosion or the changing sea level **5.** **ROW OF IDENTICAL HOUSES JOINED TOGETHER** a long row of houses built together in the same style, separated only by shared dividing side walls **6.** CIV ENG **CONSTRUCTED BANK OF GROUND** a raised bank of ground, artificially constructed **7.** **ROOFTOP PATIO** a flat roof used as living space **8.** **FLAT AREA BESIDE A BUILDING** a paved or grassy area immediately outside and on a level with a building, used for sitting or eating outdoors **9.** **BUILDINGS SET ON RAISED GROUND** a row of houses facing down from a raised position on or along the top of a piece of sloping ground, or built on a raised bank of ground **10.** **STREET SET ON A HILL** a street constructed along a piece of raised or sloping ground ■ *vt.* (**-raced, -rac·ing, -rac·es**) **FORM TERRACE ON LAND** to convert land into a terrace or terraces [Early 16thC. Via Old French, "rubble, platform" from, ultimately, Latin *terra* (see TERRA).]

ter·raced house, **ter·race house** *n. U.K.* = **row house**

ter·rac·ing /térrəssing/ *n.* **1.** **STRIPS OF AGRICULTURAL LAND IN STEPS** a series of level, fairly narrow strips of ground constructed on a hillside that would otherwise be too steep for cultivation **2.** **MAKING OF TERRACES** the act or process of creating a terrace or terraces

ter·ra cot·ta /tèrrə kóttə/ *n.* **1.** CERAMICS **REDDISH-BROWN POTTERY CLAY** unglazed reddish-brown hard-baked clay, often used to make pottery objects **2.** CRAFT **SOMETHING MADE OF TERRA COTTA** a work of art or craft modeled in terra cotta, or terra cotta items generally **3.** COLORS **BROWNISH-RED COLOR** a brownish-red color, like that of terra cotta [Early 18thC. From Italian, literally "baked earth."]

ter·ra-cot·ta *adj.* of a brownish-red color, like terra cotta

ter·rae, **ter·rae in·cog·ni·tae** plural of **terra, terra incognita**

ter·ra fir·ma /-fúrmə/ *n.* solid ground, in contrast to water or air [From Latin, literally "firm land"]

ter·rain /tə ráyn/ (*plural* **-rains** *or* **-rain**) *n.* **1.** GEOG, MIL **LAND OR COUNTRYSIDE** ground or a piece of land seen in terms of its surface features or general physical character, especially when crossing it or using it for military purposes **2.** GEOL = **terrane** [Early 18thC. Via French from, ultimately, Latin *terrenum* "land, ground," from *terrenus* "of the earth," from *terra* (see TERRA).]

ter·ra in·cog·ni·ta /-in kog neétə, -in kógnitə/ (*plural* **ter·rae in·cog·ni·tae** /tèrree in kog neétee, -in kógnitee/) *n.* **1.** **UNEXPLORED REGION** a country or region that is unknown or has not been explored **2.** **UNEXPLORED SUBJECT** a subject or area of knowledge that has not been explored and about which nothing is known [From Latin, "unknown land"]

Ter·ra·my·cin /tèrrə mīss'n/ *tdmk.* a trademark for oxytetracycline

ter·rane /tə ráyn, té ràyn/ *n.* a section of the Earth's crust that is defined by clear fault boundaries, with stratigraphic and structural properties that distinguish it from adjacent rocks [Early 18thC. Via French from, ultimately, Latin *terrenus*, from *terra* "earth."]

Ter·ra No·va Na·tion·al Park /tèrrə nṓvə-/ national park and wildlife preserve on eastern Newfoundland Island, Canada. Area: 154 sq. mi./400 sq. km.

ter·ra nul·li·us /-nə leé əss, -noólee əss/ *n.* in Australia, the idea and legal concept that when the first Europeans arrived in Australia the land was owned by no one and therefore open to settlement. It has been judged not to be legally valid.

ter·ra·pin /térrəpin/ (*plural* **-pins** *or* **-pin**) *n.* **1.** **N AMERICAN TURTLE** a moderate-sized turtle found in brackish water in eastern North America. Numbers have been severely reduced by overharvesting. Latin name: *Malaclemys terrapin.* **2.** **SMALL FRESHWATER TURTLE** a turtle with four webbed feet, a shell like that of a tortoise, and a retractable head. They are usually smaller than tortoises, live in fresh water and on land, and are carnivorous. Family: Emydidae. **3.** **TORTOISE** a tortoise (*regional*) [Early 17thC. Formed from an alteration of an Algonquian word, perhaps *torope*, + "-in," of unknown origin.]

WORD KEY: REGIONAL NOTE

Terrapin in the sense "tortoise" is a common term throughout the Middle Atlantic and Southern states. A variant is *dry-land terrapin*.

ter·ra·que·ous /te ráykwee əss, te rák-/ *adj.* consisting of areas of water and areas of dry land (*archaic or literary*) [Mid-17thC. Coined from Latin *terra* "earth" + AQUEOUS.]

ter·rar·i·um /tə ráiree əm/ (*plural* **-ums** *or* **-a** /-ree ə/) *n.* **1. ENCLOSURE FOR SMALL ANIMALS** an enclosure that is used for keeping or observing small land animals such as lizards in a simulated natural environment **2. CONTAINER FOR PLANTS** a sealed glass container often in the shape of a globe that is used for growing ornamental plants that require a high level of humidity [Late 19thC. From medieval Latin, from Latin *terra* "earth" (modeled on AQUARIUM), because it was designed for land animals.]

ter·raz·zo /tə rázzō, te raátsō/ *n.* a type of mosaic used as a floor or wall covering that is made by laying marble or stone chips in mortar and grinding them to a polished level surface [Early 20thC. From Italian, "terrace," of uncertain origin: perhaps from Old Provençal *terrassa*.]

Ter·re Haute /tèrrə hṓt/ city in western Indiana, on the eastern bank of the Wabash River, northwest of Bloomington and southwest of Indianapolis. Population: 54,585 (1996).

ter·rene /te réen, tə-/ *adj.* (*archaic or literary*) **1. WORLDLY OR EARTHLY** worldly or earthly as opposed to heavenly or spiritual **2. EARTHY** consisting of or like earth ■ *n.* **LAND** a land or territory, or the entire earth (*archaic or literary*) [14thC. Via Anglo-Norman from, ultimately, Latin *terra* "earth."] —**ter·rene·ly** *adv.*

ter·re·plein /térrə plàyn/ *n.* a raised embankment or platform behind a parapet where heavy guns are positioned [Late 16thC. Via French from, ultimately, Italian *terrapienare* "to fill with earth," from *terra* "earth" + *pieno* "full" (from Latin *plenus*).]

ter·res·tri·al /tə réstree əl/ *adj.* **1. RELATING TO EARTH** relating to Earth rather than other planets **2. BELONGING TO THE LAND** belonging to the land rather than the sea or air **3.** BIOL **LIVING OR GROWING ON LAND** living or growing on land rather than in the sea or the air **4.** BROADCAST **BROADCAST BY A LAND-BASED TRANSMITTER** broadcast by a land-based transmitter rather than by satellite **5. WORLDLY OR MUNDANE** worldly or mundane as opposed to heavenly ■ *n.* **DWELLER ON PLANET EARTH** a person or creature who lives on the Earth, especially in science fiction [14thC. Formed from Latin *terrestris*, from *terra* "earth" (source of English *terrier*).] —**ter·res·tri·al·ly** *adv.* —**ter·res·tri·al·ness** *n.*

ter·res·tri·al guid·ance *n.* a missile or rocket guidance system in which the missile is given precise details of its flight path, enabling it to follow a predetermined route. Data given include gravitational field, magnetic field, and atmospheric pressure. ◊ **inertial guidance**

ter·res·tri·al plan·et *n.* any of the four planets, Mars, Venus, Mercury, and Earth, that are nearest the Sun and are similar in density and composition

ter·res·tri·al ra·di·a·tion *n.* electromagnetic radiation in the form of heat emitted by the earth as it cools down at night, especially when the air is dry and there are no clouds

ter·res·tri·al tel·e·scope *n.* a telescope used for viewing objects on Earth rather than in space. It has an objective and a four-lens eyepiece that give an upright image.

ter·ret /térrət/ *n.* **1. METAL RING ATTACHED TO HARNESS PAD** either of two metal rings attached to the driving harness of a horse, through which the reins are passed to prevent them from slipping around the horse's flanks **2. METAL RING ON DOG'S COLLAR** a metal ring on a dog's collar to which a leash can be attached [Late 15thC. From Old French *toret* "little ring," from *tour* (see TOUR).]

terre verte /tair vúrt/ *n.* a grayish green pigment of powdered glauconite that is used in paints [From French, "green earth"]

ter·ri·ble /térrəb'l/ *adj.* **1. EXTREME** very serious or severe ○ *a terrible cold* **2. VERY UNPLEASANT** very unpleasant or harrowing ○ *The past few days have been a terrible time.* **3. EXTREMELY LOW IN QUALITY** of a very low standard or quality ○ *My cooking isn't that great, but it's not terrible.* **4. ILL OR UNHAPPY** unwell, or extremely unhappy ○ *You look terrible. Are you ill?* **5. TROUBLING** causing considerable fear or anxiety ○ *a terrible shock* ○ *a terrible sight* **6. FORMIDABLE** causing awe or dread ○ *a terrible responsibility* [14thC. Via Old French from Latin *terribilis*, from *terrere* "to frighten" (source also of English *terror*).] —**ter·ri·ble·ness** *n.*

ter·ri·bly /térrəblee/ *adv.* **1. EXTREMELY** to an extreme degree ○ *I'm terribly pleased that you can come.* **2. IN PAINFUL WAY** in a way that is extremely difficult or painful ○ *affected terribly by the news*

ter·ric·o·lous /te ríkələss, tə-/ *adj.* living in or on the soil [Mid-19thC. Formed from Latin *terricola*, literally "earth-dweller," from *terra* "earth."]

Terrier

ter·ri·er /térree ər/ *n.* any of several types of small lively dog that were initially bred to hunt animals living in underground burrows, but are now common as pets. They include the Airedale, cairn, fox, Scottish, and West Highland terriers, and the schnauzer. [15thC. From Old French *(chien) terrier* "terrier (dog)," from, ultimately, Latin *terra* "earth," because it pursues animals into their burrows.]

ter·rif·ic /tə ríffik/ *adj.* **1. VERY GOOD** exceptionally good in a way that inspires enthusiasm (*informal*) **2. VERY GREAT** very great in size, force, or degree ○ *terrific speed* **3. VERY FRIGHTENING** inspiring a sense of terror (*archaic*) [Mid-17thC. From Latin *terrificus* "frightening," from *terrere* "to frighten." "Very good" evolved from "frightening" via "very great" in a way similar to, for example, AWFUL.]

ter·rif·i·cal·ly /tə ríffikəlee/ *adv.* to a very high degree or very great extent

ter·ri·fy /térrə fī/ (**-fied, -fy·ing, -fies**) *vt.* **1. MAKE SOMEBODY VERY FRIGHTENED** to make somebody feel very frightened or alarmed **2. INTIMIDATE SOMEBODY** to coerce somebody to do something by using threats ○ *terrified into naming the members* [Late 16thC. From Latin *terrificare*, from *terrificus* (see TERRIFIC).] —**ter·ri·fi·er** *n.* —**ter·ri·fy·ing** *adj.* —**ter·ri·fy·ing·ly** *adv.*

ter·rig·e·nous /te ríjjənəss, tə-/ *adj.* relating to a sediment derived from land erosion that may be formed or deposited on the land or found underwater in shallow ocean areas [Late 17thC. Formed from Latin *terrigenus* "earth-born," from *terra* "earth."]

ter·rine /te réen, tə-/ *n.* **1.** HOUSEHOLD **COOKING DISH** a small dish with a tight-fitting lid that is used for cooking and serving food, especially cooked pâtés **2.** FOOD **FOOD COOKED IN TERRINE** the food that is cooked and served in a terrine dish, often a coarse pâté **3.** HOUSEHOLD = **tureen** [Early 18thC. From French, the feminine of Old French *terrin* "earthen," from Latin *terra* "earth."]

ter·ri·to·ri·al /tèrrə táwree əl/ *adj.* **1. RELATING TO OWNED LAND** relating to land or water owned or claimed by an entity, especially a government **2.** ZOOL **ASSERTING OWNERSHIP OF AN AREA** having a tendency to appropriate an area or territory and to protect that area or territory against intruders of the same species, particularly other males **3.** MIL **RELATING TO RESERVE ARMY** relating to a reserve army that has been trained for use in emergencies —**ter·ri·to·ri·al·ly** *adv.*

Ter·ri·to·ri·al *n.* a member of a reserve army that has been trained for use in emergencies

ter·ri·to·ri·al court *n.* a court in an administrative territory of the United States that has local and federal jurisdiction

ter·ri·to·ri·al·ism /tèrrə táwree ə lìzzəm/ *n.* **1. SYSTEM WITH LANDOWNERS HOLDING POWER** a social system in which the landowners hold or control most of the positions of power and authority **2. STATE REGULATION OF RELIGIOUS PRACTICES** a system of civil government in which the citizens of a territory are penalized unless they adopt the same religion as their civil ruler. Historically it is associated particularly with the Lutheran Church in Germany. —**ter·ri·to·ri·al·ist** *n.*

ter·ri·to·ri·al·i·ty /tèrrə tawree állətee/ *n.* **1.** POL **RANKING OF REGION AS TERRITORY** the ranking of a region as a territory **2.** ZOOL **ANIMAL DEFENSE OF TERRITORY** a pattern of animal behavior marked by the establishment, demarcation, and defense of an area that can support the growth and activity of an animal or group of animals

ter·ri·to·ri·al·ize /tèrrə táwree ə līz/ (**-ized, -iz·ing, -iz·es**) *vt.* **1. ORGANIZE INTO TERRITORIES** to organize something on a territorial basis **2.** POL **ENLARGE A COUNTRY BY ADDING TERRITORY** to enlarge a country by adding more territory or territories to it —**ter·ri·to·ri·al·i·za·tion** /tèrrə tawree əli záysh'n/ *n.*

ter·ri·to·ri·al wa·ters *npl.* the area of sea around a country's coast recognized as being under that country's jurisdiction

ter·ri·to·ry /térrə tàwree/ (*plural* **-ries**) *n.* **1.** GEOG **LAND** land, or an area of land **2.** POL **GOVERNED GEOGRAPHIC AREA** a geographic area that is owned and controlled by a particular government or country **3. ter·ri·to·ry, Ter·ri·to·ry** POL **AREA OF COUNTRY WITH SEPARATE GOVERNMENT** an area of a country or empire such as the United States, Canada, or Australia that is not a state or province but has a separate organized government **4. FIELD OF INQUIRY** a field of knowledge, investigation, or experience **5.** ZOOL **AREA THAT ANIMAL CONSIDERS ITS OWN** an area that an animal considers as its own and that it defends against intruders of the same species **6.** COMM **DISTRICT THAT AGENT COVERS** the district that an agent, especially a sales representative, is responsible for **7.** SPORTS **AREA DEFENDED BY TEAM** the area of a playing field defended by a team [14thC. From Latin *territorium* from *terra* "earth"), modeled on, for example, DORMITORY from Latin *dormitorium*.] ◇ **come** *or* **go with the territory** to be an inseparable part of or accompaniment to something else

ter·ror /térrər/ *n.* **1. INTENSE FEAR** intense or overwhelming fear **2. TERRORISM** violence or the threat of violence carried out for political purposes **3. SOMETHING CAUSING FEAR** something such as an event or situation that causes intense fear ○ *Her anger was the terror of the earth.* **4. ANNOYING PERSON** an annoying, difficult, or unpleasant person, particularly a naughty child (*informal*) [14thC. Via Old French from Latin, from *terrere* "to frighten" (source also of English *deter*).]

Ter·ror *n.* = **Reign of Terror**

ter·ror·ism /térrə rìzzəm/ *n.* violence or the threat of violence, especially bombing, kidnapping, and assassination, carried out for political purposes

ter·ror·ist /térrərist/ *n.* somebody who uses violence or the threat of violence, especially bombing, kidnapping, and assassination, to intimidate, often for political purposes —**ter·ror·is·tic** /tèrrə rístik/ *adj.*

ter·ror·ize /térrə rīz/ (**-ized, -iz·ing, -iz·es**) *vt.* **1. MOTIVATE SOMEBODY BY VIOLENCE** to intimidate or coerce somebody with violence or the threat of violence **2. MAKE SOMEBODY VERY FEARFUL** to fill somebody with feelings of intense fear over a period of time —**ter·ror·i·za·tion** /tèrrəri záysh'n/ *n.* —**ter·ror·iz·er** /térrə rīzər/ *n.*

ter·ror-strick·en, ter·ror-struck *adj.* filled with a feeling of intense fear

ter·ry /térree/ (*plural* **-ries**) *n.* **1. UNCUT LOOP OF THREAD** an uncut loop of thread in the pile of a fabric that consists of such loops **2. TYPE OF FABRIC** a type of fabric used for towels, bath mats, and bathrobes that has uncut loops of thread on both sides [Late 18thC. Origin uncertain: perhaps an alteration of French *tiré* "drawn," ultimately from *tirer* "to draw out."]

Ter·ry /térree/, **Dame Ellen** (1847–1928) English actor. A noted Shakespearean actor, she maintained a stage partnership with Sir Henry Irving that lasted 24 years. Full name **Dame Ellen Alicia Terry**

ter·ry cloth *n.* = **terry** *n.* 2

terse /turs/ (**ters·er, ters·est**) *adj.* **1. ABRUPT** brief and unfriendly, often conveying annoyance ○ *a terse exchange between the two delegates* **2. CONCISE** concise and economically phrased [Early 17thC. From Latin *tersus* "wiped off, clean," the past participle of *tergere* "to wipe." The modern meanings evolved via the sense "polished, smooth."] —**terse·ly** *adv.* —**terse·ness** *n.*

ter·tial /túrsh'l/ *adj., n.* BIRDS = **tertiary** *adj.* 3, **tertial** [Mid-19thC. Formed from Latin *tertius* (see TERTIARY).]

ter·tian /túrsh'n/ *adj.* **APPEARING EVERY OTHER DAY** used to describe a fever, especially a malarial fever, with symptoms that appear every other day ■ *n.* **TERTIAN FEVER** a tertian fever or set of symptoms [14thC. From Latin *(febris) tertiana* "(fever) of the third (day)," from *tertius* (see TERTIARY).]

ter·ti·ar·y /túrshee èrree, -sharee/ *adj.* **1. THIRD** third in degree, order, place, or importance (*formal*) **2.** BIRDS **RELATING TO BIRD'S SHORT FLIGHT FEATHERS** relating to the short flight feathers nearest the body on the rear edge of a bird's wing, so named because they make up the third row of feathers **3.** FROM EARLY CENOZOIC ERA formed in, occurring in, or relating to the first period of the Cenozoic era during which mammals became dominant and modern plants evolved **4.** CHEM CHARACTERIZED BY REPLACEMENT IN THIRD DEGREE characterized by replacement in the third degree, particularly replacement of three of the hydrogens present in a methyl group or ammonia by three organic groups ■ *n.* (*plural* **-ies**) **1.** BIRDS BIRD'S SHORT FLIGHT FEATHER a bird's tertiary feather, on the rear edge of a bird's wing **2.** FIRST PERIOD OF CENOZOIC ERA the first period of the Cenozoic era during which mammals became dominant and modern plants evolved, 65 million to 1.6 million years ago. It is divided into the Paleocene, Eocene, Oligocene, Miocene, and Pliocene epochs. **3. ter·ti·ar·y, Ter·ti·a·ry** CHR MEMBER OF LAY GROUP in the Roman Catholic Church, a member of a group of the laity associated with a religious order [Mid-16thC. From Latin *tertiarius* "of the third part or rank," from *tertius* "third." Ultimately from an Indo-European word that is also the ancestor of English *third*.]

ter·ti·ar·y col·or *n.* a color made by mixing two secondary colors together or by mixing a primary color with the secondary color closest to it

ter·ti·ar·y in·dus·try *n.* the field of industry that provides services, e.g., transportation or finance, rather than manufacturing or extracting raw materials

ter·ti·ar·y syph·i·lis *n.* the final stage of syphilis in which the disease spreads throughout the body, affecting the brain, spinal cord, heart, skin, bones, and joints

ter·ti·um quid /tùrshəm-, tùrshee əm-/ *n.* an unknown or indefinite thing or factor that is related to but cannot be classified as belonging to either of two other areas or categories (*formal*) [From late Latin, literally "some third thing"]

Ter·tul·lian /tər túllyən/ (160?–225?) Roman theologian. The first important theological writer in Latin, his often impassioned works greatly influenced his successors.

ter·va·lent /tùr váylənt/ *adj.* = **trivalent** —**ter·va·len·cy** *n.*

ter·za ri·ma /tèrtsə reemə/ (*plural* **ter·ze rime** /tèrtse reeme/) *n.* a rhyming verse form of Italian origin, consisting of three-line, 11-syllable verses (**tercets**), with the middle line of one verse rhyming with the first and third lines of the next [From Italian, "third rhyme"]

ter·zet·to /turt séttō/ (*plural* **-tos** *or* **-ti** /-tee/) *n.* a musical trio for instruments or voices [Early 18thC. From Italian (see TERCET).]

TESL /téss'l/ *abbr.* Teaching (of) English as a Second Language

tes·la /tésslə/ *n.* the derived unit of magnetic flux density in the SI system, equal to a flux of one weber in an area of one square meter. Symbol **T** [Late 19thC. Named for Nikola TESLA.]

Tes·la /tésslə/, **Nikola** (1856–1943) Croatian-born U.S. electrical engineer. He is credited with many inventions, and was a pioneer of alternating-current systems.

tes·la coil *n.* an air-core transformer that is used to produce high voltages at high frequencies, e.g., in X-ray tubes [Named for Nikola TESLA, its inventor]

TESOL /té sòl, tee sòl/ *abbr.* **1.** Teaching (of) English to Speakers of Other Languages **2.** Teachers of English to Speakers of Other Languages

tes·sel·late /téssə làyt/ (**-lat·ed, -lat·ing, -lates**) *v.* **1.** *vt.* ARCHIT DECORATE SOMETHING WITH MOSAIC EFFECT to construct, pave, or decorate something with small pieces of stone or glass to give a mosaic effect **2.** *vi.* GEOM FIT TOGETHER EXACTLY to fit together without leaving any spaces (*refers to geometric shapes*) [Late 18thC. From Latin *tessellatus* "made of small square stones," ultimately from *tessera* (see TESSERA).] —**tes·sel·la·tion** /tèssə láysh'n/ *n.*

tes·ser·a /téssərə/ (*plural* **-ae** /-ree/) *n.* **1.** MOSAIC PIECE a small square of stone, tile, or glass piece used as a die or token that is used to make a mosaic **2.** DIE a piece of bone or wood that was used in ancient Greece and Rome as a die, tally, or ticket [Mid-17thC. Via Latin from, ultimately, Greek *tesseres*, a variant of *tessares* "four," from the sides of the square.] —**tes·ser·al** *adj.*

tes·ser·act /téssə ràkt/ *n.* the four-dimensional extension of a cube [Late 19thC. Formed from Greek *tessera-*, from *tesseres* (see TESSERA) + Greek *aktis* "ray."]

tes·si·tu·ra /tèssi tóorə/ (*plural* **-tu·ras** *or* **-ture** /-tóor ày/) *n.* the pitch range that predominates in a particular piece of music [Late 19thC. Via Italian from Latin *textura* "web, structure" (source also of English *texture*).]

test[1] /test/ *n.* **1.** EDUC EXAMINATION a series of questions, problems, or practical tasks to gauge somebody's knowledge, ability, or experience **2.** TRIAL RUN-THROUGH OF A PROCESS a trial run-through of a process or on equipment to find out if it works **3.** BASIS FOR EVALUATION a basis for evaluating or judging something or somebody **4.** DIFFICULT SITUATION an often difficult situation or event that will provide information about somebody or something **5.** MED EXAMINATION OF PART OF THE BODY an examination of part of the body or of a bodily fluid or specimen in order to find something out, e.g., whether it is functioning properly or is infected ○ *a pregnancy test* **6.** CHEM PROCEDURE TO DETECT PRESENCE OF SOMETHING a procedure to ascertain the presence of or the properties of a particular substance ○ *a test for nitrates in drinking water* **7.** CHEM REACTIVE SUBSTANCE a substance or a reagent that reacts in a particular way to show the presence of a particular substance **8.** CHEM RESULT OF A PROCEDURE a result of a procedure to ascertain the presence of a specific substance ○ *Your test hasn't come back yet.* **9.** OATH a declaration, demonstration, or oath of conformity or loyalty, especially to the Anglican Church (*archaic*) ■ *v.* (**test·ed, test·ing, tests**) **1.** *vt.* TRY SOMETHING OUT to try something out, e.g., by touching, operating, or experiencing it, in order to find out what it is like, how well it works, or what it feels like **2.** *vt.* EVALUATE SOMETHING to use something on a trial basis in order to evaluate it **3.** *vt.* ASK SOMEBODY QUESTIONS to ask somebody questions or make somebody do a practical activity in order to gauge knowledge, skill, or experience **4.** *vt.* MED CARRY OUT A MEDICAL TEST to carry out a test on part of the body or on a bodily specimen **5.** *vti.* EXAMINE SOMETHING TO DETECT A PRESENCE to examine something in order to ascertain the presence of or the properties of a particular substance ○ *test for bacteria* **6.** *vi.* ACHIEVE PARTICULAR TEST RESULT to achieve a particular result on a test ○ *She tested positive for rubella immunity.* **7.** *vi.* EDUC ACHIEVE ACADEMIC RATING to achieve a rating in academic examination ○ *tested poorly in math skills* **8.** *vt.* MAKE DEMANDS ON SOMEBODY to make considerable demands on somebody, particularly somebody's skills or abilities [14thC. Via Old French, "pot," from Latin *testum* "earthenware pot." The main modern meaning evolved from "pot in which metals are heated" via "examination of properties or qualities."] —**test·a·bil·i·ty** /tèstə bíllətee/ *n.* —**test·a·ble** *adj.*

test[2] /test/ *n.* the hard outer covering or shell of some invertebrates such as mollusks and crustaceans [Mid-16thC. From Latin *testa* "tile, shell."]

test. *abbr.* **1.** LAW testator **2.** LAW testatrix **3.** BIBLE testimony

Test. *abbr.* BIBLE Testament

tes·ta /téstə/ (*plural* **-tae** /-tee/) *n.* the protective covering of a seed from a flowering plant [Late 18thC. From Latin (see TEST[2]).]

tes·ta·ceous /te stáyshəss/ *adj.* **1.** SHELL OF OR HAVING A SHELL made of shell, or having a shell or other hard covering **2.** BROWNISH-RED of a brownish-red color like a brick or a terracotta tile (*technical*)

tes·ta·cy /téstəssee/ *n.* the condition of having made a legally valid will [Mid-19thC. Formed from TESTATE on the model of *intestacy*.]

tes·tae plural of **testa**

tes·ta·ment *n.* **1.** PROOF something that shows that something else exists or is true ○ *His remarkable recovery is a testament to the doctor's skill.* **2.** FORMAL STATEMENT OF BELIEFS a formal statement or speech outlining beliefs (*formal*) **3.** LAW A WILL an old word for a legal will, used most often in the phrase "last will and testament" (*archaic*) **4.** JUD-CHR COVENANT BETWEEN GOD AND HUMANKIND a covenant made between God and humankind (*archaic or formal*) [13thC. From Latin *testamentum* "will," from, ultimately, *testis* "witness," the underlying idea being of a "witnessed" document.] —**tes·ta·men·tal** /tèstə mént'l/ *adj.*

WORD KEY: ORIGIN

The Latin word *testis*, from which ***testament*** is derived, is also the source of English *attest, contest, detest, intestate, protest, testicle, testify*, and *testimony*.

Tes·ta·ment *n.* **1.** EITHER HALF OF BIBLE either of the two major divisions of the Bible, known as the Old Testament and the New Testament **2.** COPY OF NEW TESTAMENT a printed copy of the New Testament [13thC. Mistranslation of Greek *diathēkē* "covenant," as well as "will, testament." Originally intended to apply to the "covenant" between God and human beings.]

tes·ta·men·tar·y /tèstə méntəree, -méntree/ *adj.* **1.** RELATING TO WILLS relating to a will (*formal*) **2.** STATED IN A WILL bequeathed or set out in a will

tes·tate /té stàyt, téstàt/ *adj.* HAVING MADE A WILL having made a legally valid will ■ *n.* SOMEBODY HAVING MADE A WILL somebody who has made a legally valid will [15thC. From Latin *testatus*, the past participle of *testari* "to bear witness, make your will," from *testis* (see TESTAMENT).]

tes·ta·tor /té stàytər, te stáytər/ *n.* somebody, especially a man, who has made a legally valid will [14thC. Via Anglo-Norman from Latin, from *testari* (see TESTATE).]

tes·ta·trix /té stày triks, te stáy trìks/ (*plural* **-tri·ces** /te stáytrə seez, tèstə trī seez/) *n.* a woman who has made a legally valid will [Late 16thC. From late Latin, the feminine of *testator* (see TESTATOR).]

test ban *n.* an agreement between nations to suspend testing of some or all nuclear weapons

test bed *n.* a facility designed and equipped to test engines and machinery under circumstances as close to actual operating conditions as possible

test case *n.* **1.** GROUND-BREAKING LEGAL CASE an important legal case that establishes a precedent referred to in future cases **2.** LAW CASE INTENDED TO TEST CONSTITUTIONALITY a case brought with the intention of challenging the constitutionality of a statute **3.** TELLING EVENT an event that provides an opportunity to prove or disprove a hypothesis

test·cross /tést kràwss/ *n.* **1.** GENETIC CROSS TECHNIQUE a procedure used especially in plant breeding whereby an individual's genetic constitution is inferred by examining the progeny resulting from crossing it with another individual of known genetic makeup **2.** RESULT OF TESTCROSS an organism produced by a testcross ■ *vt.* (**-crossed, -cross·ing, -cross·es**) SUBJECT ORGANISM TO TESTCROSS to subject an organism to a testcross

test drive *n.* a short drive in a car or other motor vehicle in order to see what it is like, usually with a view to buying it

test-drive *vt.* to drive a car or other motor vehicle for a short period in order to see what it is like, usually with a view to buying it

test·er[1] /téstər/ *n.* **1.** SOMEBODY WHO TESTS NEW PRODUCTS somebody whose job it is to try out new products **2.** SAMPLE OF PRODUCT a sample of a product, especially a cosmetic **3.** EQUIPMENT TO CHECK PROPER FUNCTIONING a piece of equipment that tests if a machine or device is working properly **4.** SMALL STICK a small stick inserted into something that is baking to determine if it is done **5.** SOMEBODY WHO TESTS somebody who administers or carries out tests ○ *a water tester*

tes·ter[2] /téstər/ *n.* a canopy, especially one over a four-poster bed or a pulpit [14thC. Via medieval Latin *testerium* from late Latin *testa* "head," from Latin, "tile, shell."]

tes·tes plural of **testis**

tes·ti·cle /téstik'l/ *n.* the male gonad or sperm-producing gland (**testis**) usually with its surrounding membranes, particularly in humans or other higher vertebrates [15thC. From Latin *testiculus*, literally "small testis," from *testis* (see TESTIS).] —**tes·tic·u·lar** /te stíkyələr/ *adj.*

tes·ti·fy /téstə fī/ (**-fied, -fy·ing, -fies**) *vi.* **1.** MAKE FACTUAL STATEMENT BASED ON EXPERIENCE to make a factual statement based on personal experience or to declare something to be true from personal experience **2.** DECLARE SOMETHING UNDER OATH IN COURT to declare something that can be taken as evidence under oath in a court of law **3.** PROVE OR DEMONSTRATE to be clear evidence of something (*formal*) **4.** CHR TALK ABOUT EXPERIENCE AS A CHRISTIAN to talk to an audience or group of listeners about personal experience as a Christian [14thC. From Latin *testificari*, literally "to make yourself a witness," from *testis* "witness" (source also of English *testament*).] —**tes·ti·fi·ca·tion** /tèstəfi káysh'n/ *n.* — **tes·ti·fi·er** /téstə fìr/ *n.*

tes·ti·mo·ni·al /tèstə mónee əl/ *n.* **1.** RECOMMENDATION a favorable report on the qualities and virtues of somebody or something **2.** STATEMENT BACKING UP CLAIM a statement backing up a claim or supporting a fact **3.** TRIBUTE something given, held, or done in order to honor or thank somebody ■ *adj.* RELATING TO TESTIMONY OR TESTIMONIAL relating to or consisting of testimony or a testimonial

tes·ti·mo·ny /téstə mònee/ (*plural* **-nies**) *n.* **1.** EVIDENCE GIVEN BY WITNESS IN COURT evidence that a witness gives to a court of law. It may take the form of a written or oral statement detailing what the witness has seen or knows about a particular case. **2.** PROOF something that supports a fact or a claim ○ *This win is testimony to the tactical skill of the coach.* **3.** BIBLE TEN COMMANDMENTS the Ten Commandments inscribed on two stone tablets, or the Ark of the Covenant in which the tablets were stored **4.** CHR PUBLIC AVOWAL a public profession of Christian faith or religious experience [14thC. From Latin *testimonium*, from *testis* "a witness" (source also of English *testament*).]

test·ing /tésting/ *adj.* subjecting somebody or something to challenging difficulties ○ *A testing time lies ahead for the new administration.*

tes·tis /téstiss/ (*plural* **-tes** /-steez/) *n.* either of the paired male reproductive glands, roundish in shape, that produce sperm and male sex hormones, and hang in a small sac (**scrotum**) [Early 18thC. From Latin, "a witness," because it "bears witness" to a man's virility.]

test mar·ket·ing *n.* the use of a sample of a larger market to try out a particular marketing strategy or product

tes·tos·ter·one /te stóstə ròn/ *n.* a male steroid hormone produced in the testicles and responsible for the development of secondary sex characteristics. It can also be made synthetically and used to treat androgen deficiency. Formula: $C_{19}H_{28}O_2$. [Mid-20thC. Coined from TESTIS + *-sterone* (a blend of STEROL and KETONE).]

test pa·per *n.* a small piece of paper soaked in a particular chemical or reagent, e.g., litmus, that is used to show the presence or properties of a particular substance

test pat·tern *n.* a geometric pattern transmitted by a television broadcaster to help viewers to tune in their television sets and obtain optimum reception

test pi·lot *n.* a pilot who flies new aircraft in order to assess their performance

test-screen·ing *n.* a screening of a provisional version of a movie to test audience reaction

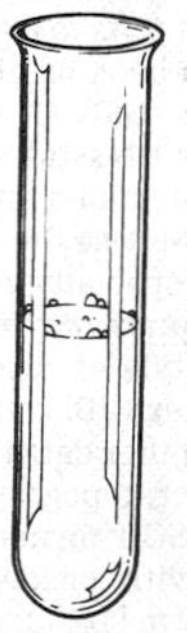

Test tube

test tube *n.* GLASS TUBE a small glass tube-shaped container that is closed and rounded at one end and open at the other, used to mix, heat, and store chemicals in laboratories ■ *adj.* **test-tube** ARTIFICIAL made in a test tube or by other artificial means, rather than occurring or arising naturally

test-tube ba·by *n.* a baby that has been conceived by fertilizing a woman's egg in a laboratory (**in vitro fertilization**) and then inserting it in her womb to develop normally for the remainder of the pregnancy (*informal*)

tes·tu·di·nal /te stóod'nəl/, **tes·tu·di·nar·y** /-èrree/ *adj.* resembling a tortoise or the shell of a tortoise

tes·tu·do /te stóodō/ (*plural* **-dines** /-stóod'n eez/) *n.* a type of shelter against missiles from above used by the ancient Roman army in siege warfare. It was either a single structure that could be carried or was made by soldiers holding their shields above their heads to form a protective roof. [14thC. From Latin, "tortoise-shell, shelter," from *testa* "pot, shell."]

tes·ty /téstee/ (**-ti·er, -ti·est**) *adj.* impatient and easily upset or annoyed (*informal*) [14thC. Via Anglo-Norman *testif*, ultimately from Latin *testa* "tile, pot," and later used humorously in the sense "head." The modern meaning evolved from the sense "headstrong, impetuous."] — **tes·ti·ly** *adv.* —**tes·ti·ness** *n.*

Tet /tet/ *n.* CALENDAR a festival held in Vietnam over three days to celebrate the lunar New Year [Late 19thC. From Vietnamese.]

te·tan·ic /te tánnik/ *adj.* **1.** RELATING TO TETANUS relating to tetanus or to the sustained contraction of the muscles that is characteristic of tetanus **2.** SPASM-PRODUCING capable of producing muscle spasms such as are seen in tetanus [Early 18thC. Via Latin *tetanicus* from, ultimately, Greek *tetanos* (see TETANUS).] — **te·tan·i·cal·ly** *adv.*

tet·a·nize /tétt'n ìz/ (**-nized, -niz·ing, -niz·es**) *vt.* to cause tetanic spasms in a muscle —**tet·a·ni·za·tion** /tètt'ni záysh'n/ *n.*

tet·a·nus /tétt'nəss/ *n.* **1.** INFECTIOUS DISEASE an acute infectious disease, usually contracted through a penetrating wound, that causes severe muscular spasms and contractions, especially around the neck and jaw. The spasms are caused by a toxin released by the bacterium. Latin name: *Clostridium tetani.* **2.** MUSCLE CONTRACTION sustained muscle contraction, e.g., induced by electrical stimulation [14thC. Via Latin from Greek *tetanos* "muscular spasm," from *teinein* "to stretch" (source also of English *hypotenuse*).] —**tet·a·nal** *adj.* —**tet·a·noid** *adj.*

tet·a·ny /tétt'nee/ *n.* repeated prolonged contraction of muscles, especially of the face and limbs, caused by low blood calcium arising from, e.g., an underactive parathyroid gland or vitamin D deficiency [Late 19thC. Via French, "intermittent tetanus," from Latin *tetanus* (see TETANUS).]

tetched /techt/, **teched** *adj.* unable to function in a logical or reasonable way (*informal*) [Mid-20thC. Alteration of TOUCHED.]

tetch·y /téchee/ (**-i·er, -i·est**), **techy** (**tech·i·er, tech·i·est**) *adj.* oversensitive and easily upset or annoyed (*informal*) [Late 16thC. Origin uncertain: probably formed from *tache* in the obsolete sense of "blemish, defect."] — **tetch·i·ly** *adv.* —**tetch·i·ness** *n.*

tête-à-tête /tàytə táyt/ *n.* **1.** INTIMATE CONVERSATION FOR TWO a private conversation between two people **2.** TYPE OF SOFA a two-seater sofa shaped like an S, allowing those seated to face each other ■ *adv.* INTIMATELY in private with only two people present [From French, literally "head-to-head"]

tête-bêche /tàyt bésh/ *adj.* used to describe a pair of stamps, one of which is printed right side up and the other upside-down [From French, literally "(sleeping) head to foot"]

teth /tayt, tayth, tet, teth/ *n.* the ninth letter of the Hebrew alphabet [Early 19thC. From Hebrew.]

teth·er /té*th*ər/ *n.* ROPE ATTACHED TO AN ANIMAL a rope or chain attached to an animal and attached to something at the other end, thus restricting the animal's movement ■ *vt.* (**-ered, -er·ing, -ers**) TIE ANIMAL WITH TETHER to tie something, especially an animal with a rope or chain in order to restrict its movement [14thC. From Old Norse *tjóðr*, from a prehistoric Germanic base meaning "to fasten."] ◇ **at the end of your tether** having reached the limit of your patience, strength, or endurance

teth·er·ball /té*th*ər bàwl/ *n.* a game for two players who use their hands to hit in opposite directions a ball that is on a length of rope attached to the top of a pole. The object of the game is to wind the rope completely around the pole.

Te·thys /téethiss/ *n.* **1.** MYTHOL TITAN a Titan in Greek mythology who was the wife of Oceanus and the mother of thousands of sea and river gods and nymphs **2.** ASTRON SATELLITE OF SATURN the third moon of the planet Saturn to be discovered. It has a diameter of 651 mi./1,050 km and is Saturn's ninth most distant satellite, orbiting at a distance of 182,900 mi./295,000 km. **3.** GEOL ANCIENT SEA an ancient sea that is thought to have separated Laurasia and Gondwanaland, surviving vestigially today as the Mediterranean [Late 19thC. Via Latin from Greek *Tēthus*.]

Tet·ley /tétlee/, **Glen** (*b.* 1926) U.S.-born Canadian dancer and choreographer. He danced with internationally known companies including those of Robert Joffrey, Martha Graham, and the American Ballet Theatre, and was associated with the National Ballet of Canada from 1987. He created works including *Tagore* (1989).

Te·ton[1] /tée tòn, tée t'n/ (*plural* **-ton** *or* **-tons**), **Teton Da·ko·ta** *n.* **1.** PEOPLES NATIVE N AMERICAN a member of a group of Native North American peoples that originally occupied western parts of the Great Plains, and whose members now live mainly in North and South Dakota. Included in this group are the Oglala, Hunkpapa, Brulé, and Miniconjou peoples. **2.** LANG TETON LANGUAGE the Siouan language of the Teton people. Teton is spoken by about 6,000 people. [Early 19thC. From Dakota *thíthuwa*, literally "dwellers on the prairie."]

Te·ton[2] /tée tòn/ range of the Rocky Mountains in northwestern Wyoming and southwestern Idaho. The highest peak is Grand Teton, 13,770 ft./4,197 m.

tet·ra /téttrə/ (*plural* **-ras** *or* **-ra**) *n.* a brightly-colored freshwater fish that lives in tropical regions and is a popular aquarium fish. Family: Characidae. [Mid-20thC. Shortening of modern Latin *Tetragonopterus*, the former name of the genus, from late Latin *tetragonum* (see TETRAGON) + Greek *pteron* "wing."]

tet·ra·ba·sic /tèttrə báyssik/ *adj.* containing four atoms of replaceable hydrogen in a molecule (*refers to acids*) [Mid-19thC. Coined from TETRA- + BASIC.] — **tet·ra·ba·sic·i·ty** /tèttrə bay síssətee/ *n.*

tet·ra·brach /téttrə bràk/ *n.* a word consisting of four short syllables in Latin or classical Greek literature [From Greek *tetrabrakhus*, literally "four short," from *brakhus* "short"]

tet·ra·caine /téttrə kàyn/ *n.* a crystalline compound related chemically to procaine and used in the form of its hydrochloride as a local anesthetic. Formula: $C_{15}H_{24}N_2O_2$. [Mid-20thC. Coined from TETRA- + -CAINE.]

tet·ra·chlo·ride /tèttrə kláw rìd/ *n.* a compound that has four chlorine atoms in each molecule

tet·ra·chlo·ro·me·thane /tèttrə kláwrə mé thàyn/ *n.* = **carbon tetrachloride** [Early 20thC. Coined from TETRA- + CHLOROMETHANE.]

tet·ra·chord /téttrə kàwrd/ *n.* a group of four notes, the first and last of which form a perfect fourth, used principally in ancient Greek music [Early 17thC. Coined from TETRA- + CHORD.] —**tet·ra·chor·dal** /tèttrə káwrd'l/ *adj.*

te·trac·id /te trássid/ *n.* **1.** BASE NEEDING FOUR MOLECULES TO REACT a base that can react with four molecules of a monobasic acid to form a salt **2.** ALCOHOL WITH FOUR OH GROUPS an alcohol with four OH groups per molecule [Coined from TETRA- + ACID]

tet·ra·cy·clic /tèttrə síklik/ *adj.* containing four rings in its molecular structure [Late 19thC. Coined from TETRA- + CYCLIC.]

tet·ra·cy·cline /tèttrə sí kleen/ *n.* a broad-spectrum antibiotic made from chlortetracycline or derived from some microorganisms of the genus *Streptomyces.* Tetracycline is used in the treatment of acne and for treating general infections. Formula: $C_{22}H_{24}N_2O_8$. [Mid-20thC. Coined from TETRACYCLIC + -INE.]

tet·rad /té tràd/ *n.* **1.** SERIES OF FOUR a group or series of four things or people **2.** GENETICS GROUP OF FOUR CHROMOSOMES a group of four chromosomes in a diploid cell that is about to undergo the cell division (**meiosis**) that produces sex cells **3.** BIOL GROUP OF FOUR CELLS a group of four cells produced by the division (**meiosis**) of a single parent cell, e.g., as it occurs in the formation of pollen and spores **4.** CHEM ATOM WITH VALENCE OF FOUR an atom or chemical group with a valence of four [Mid-17thC. From Greek *tetrad-*, the stem of *tetras* "a group of four, the number four."]

tet·ra·dac·tyl /tèttrə dákt'l/ *adj.* *U.K.* = **tetradactylous** ■ *n.* FOUR-TOED ANIMAL an animal that has four toes on each foot [Mid-19thC. Coined from TETRA- + DACTYL.]

te·trad·y·mite /te tráddi mìt/ *n.* a gray metallic ore of tellurium, found in veins with quartz and gold. Formula: Bi_2Te_2S. [Mid-19thC. Via German from Greek *tetradumos* "fourfold," from the double twin crystals in which it is usually found.]

tet·ra·dy·na·mous /tèttrə dínəməss/ *adj.* with four long stamens and two short stamens, e.g., in flowers of the mustard family [Early 20thC. Coined from TETRA- + Greek *dynamis* "strength" (see DYNAMIC) + -OUS.]

tet·ra·eth·yl lead /tèttrə eéth'l-/ *n.* a colorless extremely poisonous oily liquid that used to be added to gasoline as an antiknock agent. Use of tetraethyl lead has declined because it poisons the catalysts in catalytic converters. Formula: $Pb(C_2H_5)_4$. [*Tetraethyl* coined from TETRA- + ETHYL]

tet·ra·gon /téttrə gòn/ *n.* a geometric figure with four sides and four angles [Early 17thC. Via late Latin *tetragonum* from, ultimately, Greek *tetragōnos*, literally "four-angled," from *gōnos* "angled."]

te·trag·o·nal /te trággən'l/ *adj.* relating to the crystal system characterized by three axes at right angles to each other of which only the two horizontal axes are usually equal. Zircon crystals are tetragonal. —**te·trag·o·nal·ly** *adv.*

tet·ra·gram /téttrə gràm/ *n.* a word that has four letters

Tet·ra·gram·ma·ton /tèttrə grámmə tòn/ *n.* a four-letter Hebrew name for God, usually written YHVH or YHWH, and revealed to Moses (Exodus 3:13–14). Orthodox Jews regard this name as too sacred to be pronounced. [14thC. From Greek *Tetragrammaton*, the neuter of *tetragrammatos*, literally "having four letters," from *gramma* "letter."]

tet·ra·he·drite /tèttrə heé drīt/ *n.* a gray to black metallic sulfide of copper, iron, and antimony. It is often found as tetrahedral crystals and is an important ore of copper and other metals. [Mid-19thC. Formed either from *tetrahedron* or from Greek *tetraedron* (see TETRAHEDRON).]

tet·ra·he·dron /tèttrə heédrən/ (*plural* **-drons** *or* **-dra** /-heédrə/) *n.* a solid figure that has four faces [Late 16thC. From Greek *tetraedron*, the neuter of *tetraedros* "four-sided," from *hedra* "face."] —**tet·ra·he·dral** *adj.* —**tet·ra·he·dral·ly** *adv.*

tet·ra·hy·dro·can·nab·i·nol /tèttrə hī drō kə nábbə nòl/ *n.* full form of **THC** [Mid-20thC. Coined from TETRA- + HYDRO- + *cannabinol*.]

tet·ra·hy·drox·y /tèttrə hī dróksee/ *adj.* with four hydroxyl groups in a molecule

te·tral·o·gy /te trálləjee, -tróllәjee/ (*plural* **-gies**) *n.* a series of four related literary, dramatic, artistic, or musical works [Mid-17thC. From Greek *tetralogia*, literally "four dramas," from *-logia* "discourse."]

tet·ra·mer /téttrəmər/ *n.* a polymer that is formed from four identical monomers —**tet·ra·mer·ic** /tèttrə mérrik/ *adj.*

te·tram·er·ous /te trámmərəss/ *adj.* with four parts, or with parts arranged in multiples of four —**te·tram·er·ism** *n.*

te·tram·e·ter /te trámmətər/ *n.* POETRY **1. VERSE LINE WITH FOUR FEET** a line of verse that has four metrical feet **2. LINE WITH FOUR PAIRS OF FEET** in classical poetry, a line of verse made up of four pairs of feet **3. VERSE IN TETRAMETER** verse written in tetrameters [Early 17thC. Via late Latin from Greek *tetrametron*, a form of *tetrametros*, literally "having four measures," from *metron* "measure."]

tet·ra·ploid /téttrə plòyd/ *adj.* **WITH FOUR SETS OF CHROMOSOMES** possessing four matched sets of chromosomes in the cell nucleus ■ *n.* **TETRAPLOID CELL OR ORGANISM** a tetraploid cell, nucleus, or organism —**tet·ra·ploi·dy** *n.*

tet·ra·pod /téttrə pòd/ *n.* **1. VERTEBRATE WITH FOUR LEGS** a vertebrate animal that has four limbs or legs **2. DEVICE FORMING TRIPOD** a device comprising four arms projecting from a central point at 120° to each other, making a tripod with the fourth arm projecting vertically upward [Early 19thC. Via modern Latin *tetrapodus* from, ultimately, the Greek stem *tetrapod-*, literally "four-footed," from *pous* "foot."]

tet·ra·po·dy /te tráppədee/ (*plural* **-dies**) *n.* a poetic measure of four feet —**tet·ra·po·dic** /tèttrə póddik/ *adj.*

te·trap·ter·ous /te tráptərəss/ *adj.* used to describe insects that have four wings

tet·rarch /té traàrk/ *n.* **1. RULER OF QUARTER OF COUNTRY** the ruler of a quarter of a country or a province **2. JOINT RULER** one of four joint rulers **3. SUBORDINATE PRINCE** a ruler of a subordinate principality, especially in the eastern provinces of the Roman Empire **4. PHALANX COMMANDER** the commander of a subdivision of a Macedonian phalanx in ancient Greece [Pre-12thC. Via late Latin *tetrarcha* from, ultimately, Greek *tetrarkhēs*, literally "four ruling," from *arkhēs* "ruler."] —**te·trar·chic** /te traàrkik/ *adj.*

tet·rar·chy /té traàrkee/ (*plural* **-chies**), **tet·rar·chate** /-kayt, té traàrkət/ *n.* **1. GOVERNMENT OF TETRARCHS** government by four rulers **2. DOMAIN OF TETRARCH** the rule or domain of one of four joint rulers

tet·ra·spore /téttrə spàwr/ *n.* an asexual spore that occurs after cell division (**meiosis**), usually in groups of four, in red algae —**tet·ra·spor·ic** /tèttrə spáwrik/ *adj.*

tet·ra·stich /téttrə stìk/ *n.* a poem, verse, or strophe that has four lines [Late 16thC. Via Latin *tetrastichon* from, ultimately, Greek *tetrastikhos*, literally "containing four rows," from *stikhos* "row, line of verse."] —**tet·ra·stich·ic** /tèttrə stíkik/ *adj.*

tet·ra·syl·la·ble /tèttrə sílləb'l/ *n.* a word with four syllables —**tet·ra·syl·lab·ic** /tèttrə si lábbik/ *adj.*

tet·ra·tom·ic /tèttrə tómmik/ *adj.* **1. WITH FOUR ATOMS** with four atoms per molecule **2. WITH FOUR REPLACEABLE ATOMS** with four replaceable atoms or radicals

tet·ra·va·lent /tèttrə váylənt/ *adj.* with a valence of four —**tet·ra·va·lence** *n.*

tet·raz·zi·ni /tèttrə zeénee/, **Tet·raz·zi·ni** *adj.* made with noodles, mushrooms, and almonds in a cream sauce, topped with parmesan cheese and oven-browned [Mid-20thC. Named for Luisa Tetrazzini (1874–1940), Italian opera singer, for whom it was first made.]

tet·rode /té trōd/ *n.* a four-element electron tube containing an anode, a cathode, a control grid, and an additional electrode or screen grid

tet·ro·do·tox·in /tèttrədō tóksin/ *n.* a potent neurotoxin that is found in puffer fish and some newts and causes a general loss of the ability to move in humans who ingest it. Formula: $C_{11}H_{17}N_3O_8$.

te·trox·ide /te trók sīd/, **te·trox·id** /te trók sìd/ *n.* a chemical compound that has four oxygen atoms per molecule [Mid-19thC. Coined from TETRA- + OXIDE.]

tet·ryl /téttril/ *n.* a yellow crystalline compound that is used as a detonator in explosives. Formula: $C_7H_5N_5O_8$.

Teut. *abbr.* Teutonic

Teu·to·burg For·est /tòytə burg-/, **Teu·to·bur·ger Wald** /tòytə burgər váwld/ ridge of wooded hills in northwestern Germany, scene of a major Roman defeat by Germans in A.D. 9

Teu·ton /to͞ot'n/ *n.* **1.** PEOPLES **ANCIENT GERMAN** a member of an ancient Germanic people that originally came from Jutland. During the second century B.C. they invaded Gaul but were wiped out by the Romans in 102 B.C. **2. GERMAN SPEAKER** somebody from a German-speaking culture, especially from Germany, Switzerland, or Austria [Early 18thC. From Latin *Teutoni* or *Teutones* (plural) "the Teutons." Ultimately from an Indo-European word meaning "tribe," which is also the ancestor of English *Dutch*.]

Teu·ton·ic /too tónnik/ *adj.* **1. RELATING TO GERMANIC PEOPLES** relating to German-speaking cultures or people **2. RELATING TO TEUTONS** relating to the ancient Teuton people, or their culture —**Teu·ton·i·cal·ly** *adv.*

Teu·ton·ic Knights *npl.* a German religious and military order that was founded as a charitable order in Palestine in 1190 during the Third Crusade but became a military organization operating in Eastern Europe. In the 13th century it conquered Prussia where it introduced Christianity through killing many of the native inhabitants and colonizing it with Germans.

Teu·ton·ism /to͞ot'n ìzzəm/ *n.* **1. SOMETHING TYPICALLY GERMAN** a German characteristic, custom, or idiom **2. GERMAN WAY OF LIFE** German society or civilization **3.** = **Germanism** —**Teu·ton·ist** *n.*

Teu·ton·ize /to͞ot'n īz/ (**-ized, -iz·ing, -iz·es**) *vti.* to become German or to make something German —**Teu·ton·i·za·tion** /to͞ot'ni záysh'n/ *n.*

Te·vet /táy vàyss, te vét/ *n.* CALENDAR = **Tebet**

Te·wa /táywə/ (*plural* **-was** *or* **-wa**) *n.* **1.** PEOPLES **MEMBER OF NATIVE N AMERICAN PEOPLE** a member of a group of Native North American Pueblo peoples that originally occupied lands in New Mexico, and whose members now live mainly in the north of the state **2. Te·wa** LANG **TEWA LANGUAGE** the Tanoan language of the Tewa people [Mid-19thC. From Tewa *téwa* "moccasins."]

Tewks·bur·y /to͞oksbəree/ town in northeastern Massachusetts, northeast of Billerica and southeast of Lowell. Population: 28,644 (1996).

Tex. *abbr.* **1.** Texas **2.** Texan

Tex·ar·kan·a /tèks aar kánə, tèks aàrkənə/ two cities forming a single community on either side of the Texas-Arkansas border, one in southwestern Arkansas, the other in northeastern Texas. Population: 54,287 (1990).

Texas

Tex·as /téks iss/ state of the southwestern United States, bordered by Oklahoma, Arkansas, Louisiana, the Gulf of Mexico, Mexico, and New Mexico. Capital: Austin. Population: 19,439,337 (1997). Area: 266,873 sq. mi./691,201 sq. km. —**Tex·an** /téksən/ *n., adj.*

Tex·as fe·ver *n.* an infectious disease of cattle characterized by high fever, anemia, and severe weight loss, that is transmitted by tick bites and caused by a protozoan [Mid-19thC. Named for TEXAS, because it was first identified there.]

Tex·as leagu·er *n.* in baseball, a fly ball that drops between infielders and outfielders, resulting in a base hit [Formed from *Texas League*, a minor league in baseball]

Tex·as Rang·er *n.* a member of the Texas state police

Tex·as tow·er *n.* an offshore radar tower that is built on a base that resembles an offshore oil platform [Mid-20thC. Named for TEXAS, from its resemblance to a Texan oil rig.]

Tex-Mex /téks mèks/ *adj.* showing a blend of Texan and Mexican cultures or cuisines [Shortening]

text /tekst/ *n.* **1. MAIN BODY OF BOOK** the main body of a book or other printed material as distinct from the introduction, index, illustrations, and headings **2. WRITTEN MATERIAL** words that have been written down, typed, or printed **3. WRITTEN VERSION OF SOMETHING** a complete written, typed, or printed version of something such as a speech or a statement ○ *the full text of the president's speech* **4. EDITION** one among the extant forms or versions of a written work ○ *compared various texts to arrive at this reading* **5.** EDUC **BOOK FOR STUDY** a book or piece of writing that is used for academic study or discussion **6.** EDUC = **textbook 7.** BIBLE **BIBLE PASSAGE** a short passage from the Bible that is read aloud and on which a sermon is based **8. ORIGINAL WORDING** the original wording of a piece of writing, especially the Bible, as opposed to a translation, summary, or revision **9.** PRINTING **TYPEFACE FOR TEXT** a style of type that is suitable for printing running text **10.** COMPUT **WORDS APPEARING ON COMPUTER SCREEN** computer data that represents words, numbers, and other typographic characters, typically stored in ASCII format ■ *adj.* COMPUT **USING WORDS** associated with or designed for use with words in written form [14thC. Via Old French from Latin *textus* "woven material," hence "literary composition," from the past participle stem of *texere* "to weave" (source also of English *tissue*).]

WORD KEY: ORIGIN

The Latin word *texere*, from which ***text*** is derived, is also the source of English *context, pretext, texture,* and *tissue*.

text·book /tékst bo͝ok/ *n.* EDUC **BOOK FOR STUDY** a book that treats a subject comprehensively and is used by students as a basis for study ■ *adj.* **TYPICAL** typical overall and in detail, and thus a suitable example for study ○ *a textbook case of superpower aggression*

text e·di·tion *n.* **1.** PUBL **PRINTED VERSION** the printed version of something that is published in some other form such as CD-ROM or on the Internet **2.** EDUC **SCHOOL BOOK** an edition of a book designed for use in education

text ed·i·tor *n.* COMPUT a program that permits the creation and editing of stored text

text file *n.* COMPUT a file consisting of alphanumeric characters exclusive of transmission characters

tex·tile /ték stīl/ *n.* **1. FABRIC** cloth or fabric that is woven, knitted, or otherwise manufactured **2. RAW MATERIAL USED FOR MAKING FABRICS** raw material such as fiber or yarn that is used for making fabrics [Early 17thC. From Latin *textilis*, from the past participle stem of *texere* "to weave" (source also of English *text*).]

text proc·ess·ing *n.* the use of a computer to create, store, edit, and print or display text

tex·tu·al /tékschoo əl/ *adj.* **1. CONCERNING THE WAY SOMETHING IS WRITTEN** relating to the way a book or piece of writing is written **2. CONSISTING OF WORDS** consisting of words or text [14thC. From medieval Latin *textualis*, from *textus* (see TEXT).] —**tex·tu·al·ly** *adv.*

tex·tu·al crit·i·cism *n.* **1. STUDY OF MANUSCRIPTS** the study of a group of manuscripts, especially of the Bible or works of literature, in order to determine which is the original or most authentic one **2. LITERARY ANALYSIS** the critical study of a work of literature involving a detailed analysis of the way in which it was written, e.g., its context, use of language, and principal themes —**tex·tu·al crit·ic** *n.*

tex·tu·al·ism /tékschoo ə lìzzəm/ *n.* **1. STRICT ADHERENCE TO TEXT** unswerving adherence to a text, especially a text from the Bible **2. DETAILED ANALYSIS OF TEXT** detailed and critical analysis of a text —**tex·tu·al·ist** *n.*

tex·tu·ar·y /tékschoo èrree/ *adj.* **TEXTUAL** textual (*formal*) ■ *n.* (*plural* **-ies**) **BIBLE STUDENT** somebody who has studied the Bible extensively and systematically (*archaic*) [Early 17thC. From medieval Latin *textuarius*, from *textus* (see TEXT).]

tex·ture /tékschər/ *n.* **1. FEEL OF A SURFACE** the feel and appearance of a surface, especially how rough or smooth it is **2. STRUCTURE OF SOMETHING** the structure of a substance or material such as soil or food, especially how it feels when touched or chewed **3. ROUGH QUALITY** the rough quality of a surface or fabric ○ *a fabric that has a lot of texture* **4. DISTINCTIVE CHARACTER** the typical and distinctive character of something complex ○ *The book captures the texture of 1950s provincial England.* **5. WAY AN ARTIST DEPICTS A SURFACE** the way in which an artist depicts the quality or appearance of a surface **6. EFFECT OF DIFFERENT COMPONENTS OF MUSIC** the effect of the different components of a piece of music, e.g., melody, harmony, rhythm, or the use of different instruments ■ *vt.* (**-tured, -tur·ing, -tures**) **GIVE A SURFACE A PARTICULAR FEEL** to give a surface a particular feel, usually one that is rough and grainy [15thC. Via Old French from Latin *textura* "a weaving," from the past participle stem of *texere* "to weave" (source also of English *text*).] —**tex·tur·al** *adj.* —**tex·tur·al·ly** *adv.*

tex·tured /tékschərd/ *adj.* with a distinctive texture or surface ○ *textured rice paper*

tex·tured veg·e·ta·ble pro·tein *n.* full form of **TVP**

T-for·ma·tion *n.* in football, an offensive formation in which the center, quarterback, and fullback are in a straight line with the halfbacks on either side of and sometimes slightly behind the fullback, roughly forming a T

TG *abbr.* transformational grammar

TGIF, **T.G.I.F.** *abbr.* Thank God It's Friday *or* Thank Goodness It's Friday (*informal*)

T-group *n.* a therapy group that meets to discuss the way members of the group communicate with each other in order to increase sensitivity toward others and improve leadership skills (*dated*) [From "training group"]

TGV *n.* in France and some other countries, a very high-speed train [From French, from *t(rain) (à) g(rande) v(itesse)* "high-speed train"]

Th *symbol.* thorium

Th. *abbr.* **1.** BIBLE Thessalonians **2.** CALENDAR Thursday

Thack·er·ay /thákə rày/, **William Makepeace** (1811–63) British novelist. Serialization of his novel *Vanity Fair* (1847–48) established him as a major literary figure. He is remembered for his humorous and moralizing portraits of middle- and upper-class life in Britain.

Thad·dae·us /tháddee əss, thə dée əss/ *n.* in the New Testament, one of the 12 apostles. He is traditionally identified with St. Jude (Mark 3:16–19) (Matthew 10:2–4).

Thai /tī/ *n.* (*plural* **Thais** *or* **Thai**) **1.** PEOPLES **SOMEBODY FROM THAILAND** somebody who was born or raised in Thailand, or who has Thai citizenship **2.** LANG **OFFICIAL LANGUAGE OF THAILAND** the official language of Thailand. It belongs to the Tai language group. Thai is spoken by about 25 million people. ■ *adj.* PEOPLES **RELATING TO THAILAND** relating to Thailand, or its people or culture [Early 19thC. From Thai, "free."]

Thailand

Thai·land /-tī land, -tīlənd/ kingdom in Southeast Asia bordered by Myanmar, Laos, Cambodia, the Gulf of Thailand, Malaysia, and the Andaman Sea. Language: Thai. Currency: baht. Capital: Bangkok. Population: 59,450,818 (1997). Area: 198,115 sq. mi./513,115 sq. km. Official name **Kingdom of Thailand**. Former name **Siam**

Thai·land, Gulf of wide inlet of the South China Sea separating Vietnam, Cambodia, and eastern Thailand from the Malay Peninsula. Length: 500 mi./800 km. Former name **Gulf of Siam**

thal·a·mus /thálləməss/ (*plural* **-mi** /-mī/) *n.* **1. BRAIN PART** either of a pair of egg-shaped masses of gray matter lying beneath each cerebral hemisphere in the brain. They relay sensory information to the cerebral cortex and are concerned with awareness of all the main senses except for smell. **2.** BOT = **receptacle** *n.* **2** [Late 17thC. Via Latin, "inner chamber," from Greek *thalamos*.] —**tha·lam·ic** /thə lámmik/ *adj.* —**tha·lam·i·cal·ly** /-lámmikəlee/ *adv.*

Tha·las·sa /thə lássə/ *n.* a small inner natural satellite of Neptune, discovered in 1989 by the space probe Voyager 2. It is approximately 50 mi./80 km in diameter.

thal·as·se·mi·a /thàllə séemee ə/ *n.* a hereditary form of anemia, particularly prevalent around the Mediterranean, that is caused by a dysfunction in the synthesis of the red blood pigment hemoglobin [Mid-20thC. Formed from Greek *thalassa* "sea" (from its discovery in Mediterannean countries) + *haima* "blood."] —**thal·as·se·mic** *adj.*

tha·las·sic /thə lássik/ *adj.* **1. LIVING IN THE SEA** living in or growing in the sea **2. RELATING TO THE SEA** relating to a sea or ocean, especially a smaller inland sea [Mid-19thC. From French, from Greek *thalassa* "sea."]

thal·as·soc·ra·cy /thàllə sókrəssee/ (*plural* **-cies**), **tha·lat·toc·ra·cy** /-tókrəssee/ (*plural* **-cies**) *n.* naval or commercial supremacy over a large area of sea or ocean [Mid-19thC. From Greek *thalassokratia*, literally "authority over the sea," from *thalassa* "sea."] —**tha·las·so·crat** /thə lássə kràt/ *n.*

tha·las·so·ther·a·py /thàlləssō thérrəpee/ *n.* a therapeutic treatment that involves bathing in sea water [Late 19thC. Coined from Greek *thalassa* "sea" + THERAPY.]

tha·ler /taalər/ (*plural* **-ler** *or* **-lers**), **ta·ler** (*plural* **-ler** *or* **-lers**) *n.* any of several silver coins that were used as currency in Germany, Austria, and Switzerland between the 15th and 19th centuries [Late 18thC. From archaic German (now *Taler*).]

Tha·li·a /thə lī ə, tháylee ə, tháylyə/ *n.* **1.** MYTHOL **GREEK MUSE** the muse of comedy in Greek mythology. ◊ **Muse 2. ONE OF THE THREE GRACES** one of the three Graces in Greek mythology who lived on Mount Olympus and tended the goddess Aphrodite. ◊ **Grace**

tha·lid·o·mide /thə líddə mīd/ *n.* a synthetic sedative and hypnotic drug that has caused physical defects, including limb malformation, in fetuses when taken by women in the first three months of pregnancy [Mid-20thC. Coined from an alteration of phthalic acid (shortening of *naphthalic*, from NAPHTHALENE) + (IM)ID(E) + (IM)IDE, elements of its chemical name.]

thal·lic /thállik/ *adj.* made of or containing thallium, especially with a valence of three

thal·li·um /thállee əm/ *n.* a soft highly toxic white metallic element that in the past was used in pesticides and insecticides. It is used in the manufacture of low-melting glass, photocells, and infrared detectors, and several of its isotopes are members of the uranium, actinium, neptunium, and thorium radioactive series. Symbol **Tl** [Mid-19thC. Formed from Greek *thallos* "green shoot" (because its spectrum is marked by a green band).]

thal·lo·phyte /thállə fīt/ *n.* a plant that has no stem, roots, or leaves, e.g., algae, lichens, and fungi [Mid-19thC. Formed from modern Latin *Thallophyta*, group name, from Greek *thallos* (see THALLIUM) + *phuton* "plant."] —**thal·lo·phyt·ic** /thàllə fíttik/ *adj.*

thal·lous /thálləss/ *adj.* made of or containing thallium, especially with a valence of one

thal·lus /-lləss/ (*plural* **-li** /thá lī/ *or* **-lus·es**) *n.* the body of a plant such as an alga or liverwort that is not differentiated into leaves, stems, and roots [Early 19thC. From Greek *thallos* "a green shoot," from *thallein* "to bloom."] —**thal·loid** /thá lòyd/ *adj.*

thal·weg /tól vèg/, **tal·weg** *n.* GEOG a line connecting the lowest points of successive cross sections through a river channel or valley [Mid-19thC. From German, from obsolete *thal* "valley" (now *Tal*) + *weg* "path."]

than /than, thən/ CORE MEANING: used after a comparative adjective or adverb in order to introduce the second element of a comparison ○ (prep) *paying more than $490 a year in fees* ○ (prep) *The hole was no deeper than 12 ft.* ○ (conj) *The risk may be higher than the figures indicate.*

conj. **1. STATING A PREFERENCE** used to introduce a rejected alternative in a contrast between two alternatives, in order to state a preference ○ *more a state of mind than a physical condition* **2. WHEN** used especially after inverted constructions to say when something happened ○ *Barely had she opened the door than the phone started to ring.* [Old English *þanne*, *þonne*, *þænne*, and *þan*; ultimately the same word as English *then*]

WORD KEY: USAGE

older than he or **older than him**? Because ***than*** is a preposition as well as a conjunction, either construction is possible, as is the fuller form *older than he is*. The form *older than him* is generally considered to be more informal, although it is usually more natural in any context.

than·a·tol·o·gy /thànnə tólləjee/ *n.* the study of the medical, psychological, and sociological aspects of death and the ways in which people deal with it [Mid-19thC. Coined from Greek *thanatos* "death" + -LOGY.] —**than·a·to·log·i·cal** /thànnət'l ójjik'l/ *adj.* —**than·a·tol·o·gist** /thànnə tólləjist/ *n.*

than·a·top·sis /thànnə tópsiss/ (*plural* **-ses** /-tóp seez/) *n.* an expression of somebody's thoughts about death, e.g., in a poem (*literary*) [Early 19thC. Coined from Greek *thanatos* "death" + *-opsis* "sight" see -OPSY).]

Than·a·tos /thánnə tòss/ *n.* **1.** MYTHOL **PERSONIFICATION OF DEATH** in Greek mythology, the personification of death and the son of Nyx, goddess of the night. Roman equivalent **Mors 2.** PSYCHOL **DEATH INSTINCT** the universal death instinct theorized by Sigmund Freud [Mid-20thC. From Greek, "death."]

thane /thayn/ *n.* **1. RETAINER OF ANGLO-SAXON LORD** an Anglo-Saxon nobleman of low rank who held lands in return for military service to a lord **2. FEUDAL BARON IN SCOTLAND** a baron in feudal Scotland, or a hereditary tenant of the Scottish crown [Old English *þegn*. Ultimately from a prehistoric Germanic word meaning "boy, man."] —**than·age** *n.* —**thane·ship** *n.*

thank /thangk/ (**thanked, thank·ing, thanks**) *vt.* **1. EXPRESS GRATITUDE** express feelings of gratitude to somebody **2. BLAME SOMEBODY FOR SOMETHING** to blame somebody or hold somebody responsible for something ○ *You have only yourself to thank for this situation.* **3. BE GRATEFUL** to be grateful to somebody or something because of something that has happened ○ *Thank goodness you got here in time.* [Old English *þancian*. Ultimately from an Indo-European word that is also the ancestor of English *think* and *thought*.] ◇ **I'll thank you (not) to** used in an ironic or angry way to ask somebody to do or not do something ○ *I'll thank you not to mention that again.*

thank·ful /thángkfəl/ *adj.* **1.** FEELING GRATITUDE feeling or expressing gratitude ○ *We must be thankful for small mercies.* **2.** GLAD ABOUT SOMETHING glad or relieved about something —**thank·ful·ness** *n.*

thank·ful·ly /thángkfəlee/ *adv.* **1.** WITH GRATITUDE with feelings or expressions of gratitude ○ *They thankfully accepted her offer of a room for the night.* **2.** USED TO EXPRESS RELIEF used to express approval or relief about a situation (*informal*) ○ *Thankfully, it didn't rain until the game was over.*

WORD KEY: USAGE

Sentence adverb The adverb ***thankfully*** is used in two ways: as a conventional adverb of manner (*They received the good news thankfully*), and as a sentence adverb (*Thankfully, the news was good*). Some people dislike the second use, although the objection is not as strong as that to *hopefully* used in a corresponding way.

thank·less /thángkləss/ *adj.* **1.** UNAPPRECIATED not likely to be appreciated or rewarded ○ *a thankless task* **2.** UNGRATEFUL not showing or feeling gratitude —**thank·less·ly** *adv.* —**thank·less·ness** *n.*

thanks /thangks/ *npl.* **1.** GRATITUDE FOR SOMETHING gratitude or appreciation for something **2.** EXPRESSION OF GRATITUDE an expression of gratitude for something ○ *Many thanks for your help yesterday.* ■ *interj.* USED TO EXPRESS GRATITUDE used to express gratitude to somebody ○ *Goodbye, and thanks!* ◇ **no thanks to somebody** *or* **something** despite somebody or something or without somebody's assistance ◇ **thanks a lot** used to express great gratitude, sometimes ironically (*informal*) ○ *Thanks a lot for coming over.* ○ *You took my glass? Thanks a lot!* ◇ **thanks to somebody** *or* **something** because of somebody or something

WORD KEY: USAGE

Thanks much This expression is not standard English but is, rather, a jocular formation, somewhat like *Who'd of thunk?* It is unclear whether the ***thanks*** in *thanks much* is a plural noun (as in *I offer you my thanks*) or whether the expression is a shortened form of *I thank you very much*. Regardless, *Many thanks* or *Thanks very much* are the proper expressions.

thanks·giv·ing /thàngks gívving, thángks gìvving/ *n.* **1.** RELIG PRAYER OF THANKS a prayer that offers thanks to God **2.** GIVING OF THANKS an expression or an act of giving thanks **3.** RELIG PUBLIC ACKNOWLEDGMENT OF DIVINE GOODNESS a public acknowledgment or celebration of divine goodness

Thanks·giv·ing Day, Thanks·giv·ing *n.* CALENDAR **1.** LEGAL HOLIDAY IN UNITED STATES the fourth Thursday in November observed as a legal holiday in the United States to commemorate the feast given in thanks for the harvest by the Pilgrim colonists in 1621 **2.** *Can* LEGAL HOLIDAY IN CANADA the second Monday in October, observed in Canada as a legal holiday and day of giving thanks for the harvest and other good things received

thank-you *n.* EXPRESSION OF GRATITUDE an expression of gratitude to somebody ○ *a big thank-you to all our readers* ■ *adj.* EXPRESSING GRATITUDE expressing gratitude to somebody for something ○ *Send a thank-you note promptly.*

Thant /thaant, thant/, **U** (1909–74) Burmese statesman. Following a series of senior government posts, he became secretary general of the United Nations (1961–71).

thar /t͟haar/ *adv.* there (*regional regional or nonstandard*)

Thar Des·ert /taar-/ desert in northwestern India, in the state of Rajasthan, extending across the border into Pakistan. Area: 77,000 sq. mi./199,429 sq. km.

Tharp /thaarp/, **Twyla** (*b.* 1941) U.S. dancer and choreographer. Her individualistic dance style combines ballet, tap, and jazz.

Thar·sis /thaársiss/ *n.* an extensive shallow bulge on the surface of Mars in the northern hemisphere about 1200 mi./2000 km across and 5 mi./8 km high, supporting several volcanoes

Thá·sos /táss oss/ island in northeastern Greece, in the Aegean Sea, about 5 mi./8 km from the mainland. Population: 13,111 (1981). Area: 146 sq. mi./378 sq. km.

that /t͟hat/; (*unstressed*) /t͟hət/ CORE MEANING: a grammatical word used to indicate somebody or something that has already been mentioned or identified or something that is understood by both the speaker and hearer ○ (adj) *Do you remember that discussion we had?* ○ (adj) *Later that week I saw her again.* ○ (pron) *Is that why you're here?* ○ (pron) *Don't touch that!*

1. *adj., pron.* INDICATING DISTANCE FROM THE SPEAKER indicating somebody or something a distance away from you, or further away from another, referred to as "this" ○ (adj) *You see that girl over there?* ○ (adj) *That bag looks more spacious than this one.* ○ (pron) *What's that you're doing?* ○ (pron) *That looks much nicer than this.* **2.** *adj., pron.* INDICATING A FAMILIAR PERSON OR THING used to refer to somebody or something not described, but familiar to the speaker and hearer and not requiring identification ○ (adj) *Did you read that e-mail I sent?* ○ (adj) *that woman we met yesterday* ○ (pron) *That was a great year.* **3.** *adj.* INDICATING A TYPE used to characterize a particular type, person, or thing ○ *I really want a sleep that goes on forever.* **4.** *pron.* IDENTIFYING SOMEBODY OR SOMETHING used to introduce a clause giving more information to identify the person or thing mentioned ○ *the committee that deals with such matters* ○ *Take the road that forks to the left.* ○ *on the day that he left* **5.** *conj.* EXPRESSING A COMMENT OR FACT used to introduce a noun clause expressing a comment on a situation or a supposed or real fact ○ *It was clear that she wanted to see the concert.* ○ *The report stated that sales were improving.* **6.** *conj.* EXPRESSING A RESULT used to introduce a clause expressing result or effect ○ *It made such a noise that we had to cover our ears.* **7.** *conj.* EXPRESSING A CAUSE used to introduce a clause expressing the cause of a feeling ○ *I feel hurt that you should think such a thing.* ○ *He's sorry that he told her now.* **8.** *conj.* EXPRESSING PURPOSE used to introduce a clause expressing purpose ○ *We continue to give, that others will receive and live.* **9.** *conj.* EXPRESSING DESIRE OR AMAZEMENT used after an understood but unspoken statement such as "I wish" or "If only" to introduce a clause expressing desire, amazement, or indignation ○ *Oh that I had never set eyes on her!* ○ *That you could think such a thing!* **10.** *adv.* TO THE STATED DEGREE used to specify the extent of something ○ *I came that close to hitting the car in front.* **11.** *adv.* SO VERY used before adjectives to emphasize the quality they are describing (*informal*) ○ *I didn't think she'd be that upset.* [Old English *þæt*. Ultimately from an Indo-European demonstrative base (see THE).] ◇ **and (all) that** and everything else that is similar or included (*informal*) ○ *I've painted the doors and window frames and all that.* ◇ **at that 1.** in addition ○ *It was a coincidence, and a happy one at that.* **2.** nevertheless, or in spite of something else ○ *It just might work at that.* **3.** at a specific point or place ○ *I think we'll leave it at that for today.* ◇ **just like that** without great effort, trouble, or inconvenience ○ *I can't move to another country just like that.* ◇ **that is** in other words, or to be specific ○ *You need a further qualification, that is, a Ph.D.* ◇ **that's that 1.** used to say that something is finished or dealt with **2.** used to say that something has been settled and there will be no more discussion on it ◇ **with that** immediately after saying or doing something specified ○ *With that she turned to go.*

WORD KEY: USAGE

that or **which**? As relative pronouns the two words are often interchangeable: *The house that/which stands on the corner is up for sale. The school that/which they go to is several miles away.* (When ***that*** or ***which*** is the object of a following verb, it can be omitted altogether, as in *The school they go to . . . .*) When the relative clause adds incidental information rather than identifying the noun it follows, ***which*** is used and is preceded by a comma: *The house, which stands on the corner, is up for sale.*

WORD KEY: USAGE

That in reference to people For centuries ***that*** has been used to refer to people as well as things. Sometimes this usage can be clumsy: *He's the one that did it.* But it is not incorrect, and occasionally ***that*** is the most artful possible choice of relative pronoun: *Anything or anyone that helps me is my friend.*

that·a·way /t͟hátta wày/ *adv.* in that direction, or over there (*regional humorous*) ○ *The masked man went thataway, Sheriff.* [Mid-19thC. Alteration of *that way.*]

thatch /thach/ *n.* **1.** BUILDING PLANT MATERIAL USED FOR A ROOF a plant material such as straw or rushes used as roofing on a house **2.** BUILDING ROOF OF THATCH a roof made of thatch **3.** HAIR ON SOMEBODY'S HEAD the hair on somebody's head, especially when it is thick ○ *The child had an unmistakable thatch of red hair.* **4.** GARDENING LAYER OF DEAD MATERIAL IN GRASS a matted layer of dead plant material that builds up next to the soil at the base of lawn grasses ■ *vti.* (**thatched, thatch·ing, thatch·es**) BUILDING ROOF BUILDING WITH THATCH to put a roof of thatch on a building, or to work at doing this [Old English *þeccan*. Ultimately from an Indo-European word meaning "to cover," which is also the ancestor of English *deck, protect,* and *tile*.] —**thatch·er** *n.*

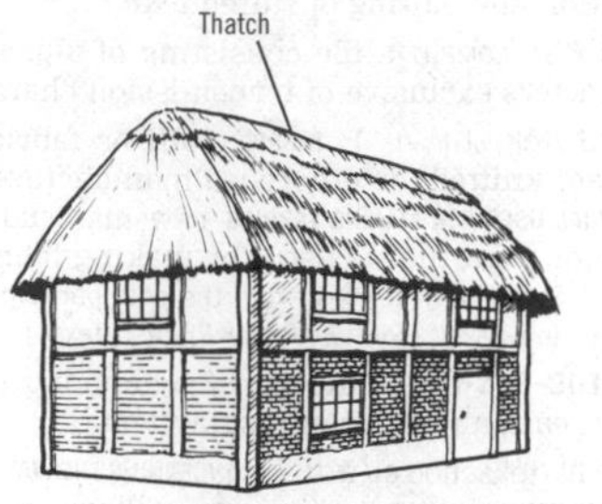

Thatch

thatched /thacht/ *adj.* made of thatch, or with a roof made of thatch ○ *an old-fashioned thatched cottage*

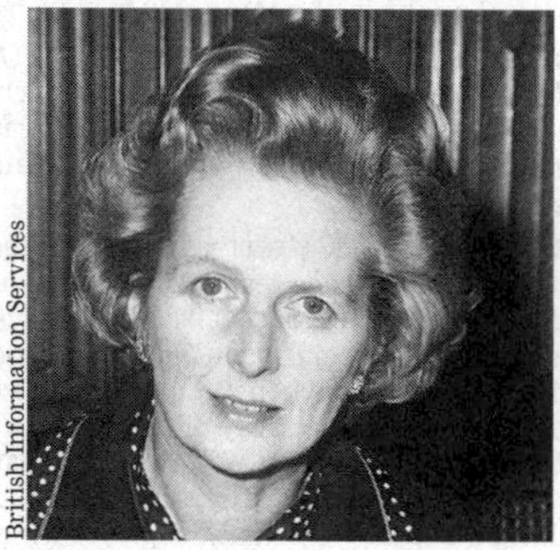

Margaret Thatcher

Thatch·er /tháchər/, **Margaret, Baroness Thatcher of Kesteven** (*b.* 1925) British political leader. Leader of the Conservative Party from 1975, and first woman prime minister (1979–90), she pursued policies of privatization and economic deregulation. Born **Margaret Hilda Roberts**

thatch·ing /tháching/ *n.* **1.** CRAFT OF MAKING THATCHED ROOVES the craft or process of constructing or repairing thatched rooves **2.** = **thatch** *n.* 1

thau·ma·tol·o·gy /thàwmə tólləjee/ *n.* the study or description of miracles [Mid-19thC. Coined from Greek *thauma* "wonder" + -LOGY.]

thau·ma·trope /tháwmə trōp/ *n.* a card with different pictures on either side so that when the card is rapidly twirled, the images appear to combine [Early 19thC. Coined from Greek *thauma* "wonder" + *tropos* "turning."] —**thau·ma·trop·i·cal** /thàwmə tróppik'l/ *adj.*

thau·ma·turge /tháwmə tùrj/, **thau·ma·tur·gist** *n.* somebody who performs magic or miracles [Early 18thC. Via medieval Latin from Greek *thaumatourgos*, from *thauma* "wonder" + *-ergos* "working."]

thau·ma·tur·gy /tháwmə tùrjee/ *n.* the performance of miracles or magic —**thau·ma·tur·gic** *adj.*

thaw /thaw/ *v.* (**thawed, thaw·ing, thaws**) **1.** *vti.* MELT to melt or make something melt **2.** *vti.* FOOD DEFROST to defrost frozen food or become defrosted ○ *Leave the cake out to thaw.* **3.** *vi.* BECOME LESS COLD to become less cold or numb through exposure to heat ○ *Come thaw out by the fire.* **4.** *vi.* METEOROL BE WARM ENOUGH TO MELT ICE to be warm enough that snow and ice will melt **5.** *vi.* BECOME LESS HOSTILE to become less hostile, tense, or aloof ○ *The atmosphere thawed.* ■ *n.* **1.** PROCESS OF THAWING the action or process of thawing **2.** METEOROL WARMER WEATHER a period of weather warm enough to melt snow and ice **3.** LESSENING OF HOSTILITY a lessening of hostility, tension, or aloofness [Old English *þawian*. Ultimately from a prehistoric Germanic word that also produced German *tauen* "to thaw."]

Thay·er /tháy ər, thair/, **Sylvanus** (1785–1872) U.S. soldier and educator. As the long-term superintendent (1817–33) of the U.S. Military Academy at West Point, he is credited with transforming it into a fully effective institution. Known as **Father of West Point**

Th.B. *abbr.* Bachelor of Theology [Latin, *Theologiae Baccalaureus*]

THC *n.* the main active chemical constituent of cannabis. Full form **tetrahydrocannabinol**

Th.D. *abbr.* Doctor of Theology [Latin, *Theologiae Doctor*]

the *(stressed/emphatic)* /thee/; *(unstressed)(before a vowel)* /thee/; *(unstressed)(before a consonant)* /thə/ CORE MEANING: an adjective, the definite article, used before somebody or something that has already been mentioned or identified, or something that is understood by both the speaker and hearer, as distinct from "a" or "an" ○ *The movie ended with the hero riding off into the desert.* ○ *The food was excellent but the service was poor.*

1. **INDICATING ONE AS DISTINCT FROM ANOTHER** used to refer to a particular one of a number of things or people, identified as distinct from all others by the use of some kind of modifier ○ *Put them in the small bag.* ○ *the door on the left* ○ *the girl who answered the phone* ○ *the right to vote* ○ *the points made earlier.* ◊ **a, an** 2. **INDICATING GENERIC CLASS** used to refer to a person or thing considered generically or universally ○ *Exercise is good for the heart.* ○ *she played the violin* ○ *The dog is a loyal pet.* 3. **INDICATING SHARED EXPERIENCE** used to refer to objects and concepts associated with the shared experience of a culture, society, or community ○ *go to the hospital* ○ *thinking about the future* ○ *lying in the sun* 4. **ALL PEOPLE OF A PARTICULAR TYPE** used before adjectives to refer generically to people of a particular type or class ○ *new measures to help the unemployed* ○ *They say the good always die young.* 5. **TITLES AND NAMES** used before titles and some names, e.g., place names ○ *the King of Spain* ○ *the Times newspaper* ○ *the President of the United States* 6. **QUALIFYING NAMES AND TITLES** used in names and titles before adjectives and nouns that distinguish somebody from others of the same name or title ○ *Ivan the Terrible* ○ *Henry the Fifth* 7. **INDICATING PARTS OF THE BODY** used instead of "my," "your," etc. to refer to a part of somebody's body. ○ *patted him on the head* ○ *took her by the hand* 8. **INDICATING MOST FAMOUS OR IMPORTANT** the best, only, or most outstanding ○ *It's* THE *place to be.* 9. **EXPRESSING RATES AND RATIOS** used to indicate how many units apply to the particular items being measured ○ *ordered in at $60 the ton* 10. **INDICATING A FAMILY RELATIONSHIP** used instead of "your," "my," etc. to refer to somebody having a particular family relationship. (*informal*) ○ *Give my regards to the family.* ○ *How's the wife?* 11. **PERIOD OF TIME** used to refer to a specified period of time, especially a decade or an era ○ *living in the sixties* 12. *adj.* **TO THAT EXTENT** used adverbially to emphasize that somebody or something is true to a particular extent (*used before comparatives*) ○ *She looks the better for her holiday.* ○ *the worse for wear* 13. *adv.* **BY HOW MUCH OR BY THAT MUCH** used adverbially to indicate how one amount or quality changes in relation to another (*used before each of two comparative adjectives or adverbs*) ○ *the cheaper the better* ○ *The more you exercise, the fitter you'll feel.* [Old English *þe*, alteration of earlier *se*. Ultimately from an Indo-European demonstrative base that is also the ancestor of English *that, then, there , they,* and *this.*]

WORD KEY: USAGE

Pronunciation: It is a curious fact that one of the English words used most often, consisting of one syllable and spelled with three letters, has two distinct pronunciations, according to context. Before a word beginning with a consonant sound the vowel in ***the*** is pronounced as a schwa, as in *thuh mare, thuh gray mare*, but before a word beginning with a vowel sound it is pronounced with a long *e*, as in *thee old gray mare.*

the- *prefix.* = **theo-** (*used before vowels*)

the·an·thro·pism /thee ánthrə pìzzəm/ *n.* 1. **ASSIGNMENT OF HUMAN CHARACTERISTICS TO GOD** the assigning of human characteristics to a god or gods 2. **CHRISTIAN DOCTRINE** the Christian doctrine that the human and the divine are united in Jesus Christ [Early 19thC. Formed from Greek *theanthrōpos* "god-man," from *theos* "god" + *anthrōpos* "man."] —**the·an·throp·ic** /thee ən thróppik/ *adj.* —**the·an·thro·pist** /thee ánthrəpist/ *n.*

the·ar·chy /thee aarkee/ (*plural* **-chies**) *n.* 1. **RULE BY GOD** rule by God, by a god, or by priests 2. **COMMUNITY UNDER DIVINE RULE** a community that is ruled by God, by a god, or by priests 3. **HIERARCHY OF GODS** a hierarchy or system of gods [Mid-17thC. From Greek *thearkhia*, from *theos* "god."] —**the·arch·ic** *adj.*

theat. *abbr.* 1. theater 2. theatrical

the·a·ter /theé ətər/, **the·a·tre** *n.* 1. THEATER **PLACE FOR PLAYS** a building, room, or other setting where plays or other dramatic presentations are performed 2. CINEMA **PLACE WHERE MOVIES ARE SHOWN** a building, room, or other setting where movies are shown 3. MED **OPERATING THEATER** an operating theater (*informal*) 4. **ROOM WITH TIERS OF SEATS** a room with rising tiers of seats, used for lectures, demonstrations, or assemblies 5. THEATER **PLAYS** plays or other dramatic literature 6. THEATER **DRAMA AS ART OR PROFESSION** dramatic performance as an art, profession, or way of life ○ *She decided to make the theater her life.* 7. THEATER **DRAMATIC QUALITY** dramatic or theatrical quality or effectiveness ○ *As a public speaker he has a great sense of theater.* 8. **PLACE OF SIGNIFICANT EVENTS** the place or realm where significant actions or events take place ○ *the political theater* 9. GEOG **LAND THAT RISES IN STEPS** a natural land formation that rises by steps or gradations ■ *adj.* **FOR USE IN THEATER OF OPERATIONS** relating to or for use in a military theater of operations [14thC. Via Old French and Latin from Greek *theatron*, from *theasthai* "to watch."]

the·a·ter·go·ing *n.* **PRACTICE OF GOING TO THEATER** the practice of going to the theater, especially regularly ■ *adj.* **ATTENDING THE THEATER** attending the theater, especially regularly ○ *The theatergoing public is being shortchanged by plays of this standard.* —**the·a·ter·go·er** *n.*

the·a·ter-in-the-round (*plural* **the·a·ters-in-the-round**) *n.* 1. **THEATER WITH STAGE IN THE CENTER** a theater in which the stage is in the center with the seats surrounding on all sides 2. **DRAMA FOR THEATER-IN-THE-ROUND** drama or the style of drama written for performance in a theater-in-the-round

the·a·ter of cru·el·ty *n.* a form of surrealist drama emphasizing that human beings live in a threatening world with precarious moral values. It was originated by Antonin Artaud in the early 1930s.

the·a·ter of op·er·a·tions *n.* an area where fighting takes place during a war

the·a·ter of the ab·surd *n.* a form of drama that represents the absurdity of human life in a meaningless universe by deliberately unrealistic means and by ignoring or distorting conventions of plot and characterization

the·a·ter of war *n.* a large area of land, sea, and air in which warfare may take place. ◊ **theater of operations**

the·a·tre *n.* = **theater**

the·at·ri·cal /thee áttrik'l/ *adj.* 1. THEATER **RELATING TO THEATER** relating to or typical of the theater or dramatic performance 2. **MARKED BY ARTIFICIAL EMOTION** full of exaggerated or false emotion ■ *n.* THEATER **ACTOR** a professional actor —**the·at·ri·cal·ism** *n.* —**the·at·ri·cal·i·ty** /thee àttri kállətee/ *n.* —**the·at·ri·cal·ly** /-áttrikəlee/ *adv.* —**the·at·ri·cal·ness** /-áttrik'lnəss/ *n.*

the·at·ri·cals /thee áttrək'lz/, **the·at·rics** /-áttriks/ *npl.* 1. **PERFORMANCE OF PLAYS** the performance of plays, often by amateurs 2. **DRAMATIC BEHAVIOR** showy dramatic gestures and actions

the·ba·ine /theébə een, thi báy in/ *n.* a poisonous alkaloid component of opium that causes convulsions similar to those caused by strychnine and that was once used medicinally. Formula: $C_{19}H_{21}NO_3$. [Mid-19thC. Formed from Greek *Thēbai* "Thebes" (in Egypt) because Upper Egypt was an important source of opium.]

the·be /tébbe/ (*plural* **-be**) *n.* 1. **SUBUNIT OF BOTSWANAN CURRENCY** a subunit of currency in Botswana, 100 of which are worth one pula. See table at **currency** 2. **COIN WORTH A THEBE** a coin worth one thebe

The·be /th-b-/ *n.* the fourteenth moon of the planet Jupiter to be discovered, with a diameter of 60 mi./100 km. It is Jupiter's fourth most distant satellite, orbiting at a distance of 138,000 mi./222,000 km. [Mid-18thC. Via Latin, name of the nymph who was daughter of the river god Asopus, from Greek.]

Thebes /theebz/ 1. city of ancient Greece, in Boethia, northwest of present-day Athens. A celebrated city in Greek myth, it was the most important city in Boethia from the beginning of the 6th century B.C., and was destroyed by Alexander the Great in 335 B.C. 2. capital city of ancient Egypt, situated on both sides of the Nile River, south of present-day Cairo. It first appeared in Egyptian records in the middle of the 3rd millennium B.C., and served as the capital of Egypt until 1085 B.C. It is the site of the tombs of the pharaohs in the Valley of the Kings. —**The·ban** *n., adj.*

the·ca /theékə/ (*plural* **-cae** /theé seè, -keè/) *n.* an enclosing organ, capsule, or sheath, e.g., the spore case of a moss or the horny covering of the pupa of an insect [Early 17thC. Via Latin from Greek *thēkē* "case."] —**the·cal** *adj.* —**the·cate** /theé kàyt/ *adj.*

the·co·dont /theékə dònt/ *adj.* **WITH TEETH IN SOCKETS** used to describe animals whose teeth are set in sockets ■ *n.* 1. **EXTINCT PREHISTORIC REPTILE** any of an order of extinct reptiles that lived in the Triassic period, had teeth set in sockets, and were the ancestors of the dinosaurs. Order: Thecodontia. 2. **THECODONT REPTILE** a thecodont reptile [Mid-19thC. Coined from Latin *theca* (see THECA) + -ODONT.]

thé dan·sant /tày daaN saaN/ (*plural* **thés dan·sants** /tày daaN saaN/) *n.* a tea dance (*dated*) [From French, literally "dancing tea"]

thee /thee/ *pron.* 1. **OBJECTIVE OF "THOU"** the objective form of "thou" used as the object of a verb or preposition to mean "you" (*archaic*) 2. **"THOU" AS USED BY QUAKERS** a subjective form of "thou" as used by members of the Christian denomination, the Society of Friends ○ *See that thee keepest silence.* [Old English *þē*, the objective form of *þū* (see THOU)]

theft /theft/ *n.* 1. **STEALING OF PROPERTY** the stealing of somebody else's property 2. **SOMETHING STOLEN** something that has been stolen (*archaic*) [Old English *þēoft*. Ultimately from a prehistoric Germanic word that is also the ancestor of English *thief.*]

WORD KEY: SYNONYMS

theft, robbery, burglary, hold-up, mugging, shoplifting, embezzlement, larceny

CORE MEANING: taking property unlawfully

theft a general word used to talk about the unlawful taking of somebody else's property or money; **robbery** theft that involves force or violence, or the threat of it; **burglary** the act of illegally entering a building in order to commit a felony, usually in order to steal; **hold-up** a robbery involving the threat or use of guns; **mugging** an informal word used to describe an attack on somebody when the attacker's motive is to steal from that person; **shoplifting** stealing goods from stores; **embezzlement** the unlawful taking of money by somebody who has been placed in a position of trust, especially taking money from an employer; **larceny** a formal or legal word meaning the same as *theft.*

theine /theé een, -in/ *n.* caffeine, particularly as found in tea [Mid-19thC. Formed from modern Latin *Thea*, former genus name of the tea plant, from Dutch *thee* (see TEA).]

their /thair/ *adj.* **BELONGING TO THEM** belonging to or relating to a particular group of people or things ○ *They have sold their house and moved to Arizona.* ■ **BELONGING TO AN INDIVIDUAL** belonging to an individual person (*informal*) ○ *Everyone should make their own way home.* [12thC. From Old Norse *þeirra* "theirs."]

WORD KEY: USAGE

See Usage note at ***they.***

theirs /thairz/ *pron.* 1. **BELONGING TO THEM** belonging to a particular group of people or things ○ *Theirs was the biggest house in the town.* 2. **BELONGING TO AN INDIVIDUAL** belonging to an individual person (*informal*) ○ *I have spare copies of the agenda if anyone has forgotten theirs.*

the·ism /theé ìzzəm/ *n.* 1. **BELIEF IN GOD** belief that one God created and rules humans and the world, not necessarily accompanied by belief in divine revelation such as through the Bible 2. **BELIEF IN GOD OR GODS** belief in the existence of a god or gods [Late 17thC. Formed from Greek *theos* (see THEO-).] —**the·ist** *n.* —**the·is·tic** /-ístik/ *adj.* —**the·is·ti·cal** *adj.* —**the·is·ti·cal·ly** /-ístikəlee/ *adv.*

them /them/; *(unstressed)* /thəm/ *pron.* 1. **OBJECTIVE FORM OF "THEY"** used to refer to a group of people or things other than the speaker or people addressed ○ *I'll put them in a box for you.* 2. **HIM OR HER** used instead of "him" or "her" to refer to a person without specifying gender (*informal*) ○ *If anyone is looking for me, tell them I'll be back soon.* 3. **THOSE** a dialect form of "those" (*regional or nonstandard*) ○ *Give me one of them oranges.* 4. **THEMSELVES** used instead of "themselves" when the object of a verb refers to the same people or things as the subject of the verb (*regional nonstandard*) ○ *They got them a new car.* [12thC. From Old Norse *þeim.*]

the·mat·ic /thə máttik/ *adj.* **1. RELATING TO THEME** relating to or being a theme **2.** LING **RELATING TO WORD STEM** relating to the stem of a word **3.** LING **LAST BEFORE INFLECTION** being the last part of a word stem before the inflectional ending [Late 17thC. From Greek *thematikos*, from *thema* (see THEME).] —**the·mat·i·cal·ly** *adv.*

the·mat·ic ap·per·cep·tion test *n.* a test for exploring aspects of personality in which somebody is shown pictures of people in various situations and asked to describe what is happening. The presumption is that emotions, prejudices, and other psychological states of the subject will be projected onto the figures in the picture.

theme /theem/ *n.* **1. SUBJECT OF DISCUSSION OR COMPOSITION** a subject of a discourse, discussion, piece of writing, or artistic composition **2. DISTINCT AND UNIFYING IDEA** a distinct, recurring, and unifying quality or idea ○ *Efficiency will be the theme of this organization.* **3.** MUSIC **REPEATED MELODY** a melody that is repeated, often with variations, throughout a piece of music ○ *one of the themes of the concerto* **4. MUSIC IN FILM** a song or tune that is played at the beginning or end of, or during, a film or television program, and is identified with it ○ *the theme from "The Magnificent Seven"* **5. ESSAY OR WRITTEN EXERCISE** a short essay or written exercise for a student **6.** GRAM = **stem**[1] *n.* **6** ■ *adj.* **WITH DISTINCT SUBJECT** with one distinct and recurring subject, organizational principle, or idea ○ *We ate at a Wild West theme restaurant.* ■ *vt.* **(themed, them·ing, themes) GIVE SOMETHING DISTINCT CHARACTER** to give something a single distinct character or subject ○ *The local bar has been themed as an Irish pub.* [13thC. Via Old French and Latin from Greek *thema* "proposition."]

WORD KEY: SYNONYMS

See Synonyms at ***subject.***

theme park *n.* an amusement park in which all of the entertainments and facilities are designed around a particular subject or idea

The·mis·toc·les /thə místə kleez/ (527?–460? B.C.) Greek general and statesman. He built up the Athenian navy and led it to victory over the Persians at the battle of Salamis (480 B.C.), laying the foundations for Athenian domination of Greece.

them·selves /thəm sélvz, them sélvz/ *pron.* **1. REFLEXIVE OF "THEY" OR "THEM"** used to refer to a group of people or things when the object of a verb is the same as the subject ○ *They all made themselves at home.* **2. THEIR NORMAL SELVES** their real or normal selves (*usually used in negative constructions*) ○ *They haven't been themselves since the accident.* **3. EMPHASIZING** used to emphasize the people or things being referred to ○ *They themselves would rather have gone to a movie.* **4. HIMSELF OR HERSELF** used to refer to an individual person without using "himself" or "herself" (*informal*) ○ *Everyone needs to take care of themselves.*

then /then/ CORE MEANING: an adverb used to indicate a particular time in the past or future ○ *We were much happier then.* ○ *Until then, he'll be staying with me.*

1. *adv.* **AFTER THAT** after that or subsequently in time, order, or position ○ *Fry the onions and garlic, then the vegetables.* ○ *We went for a walk, then came home.* **2.** *adv.* **THEREFORE** that being the case, or in that case ○ *Then why don't you go back?* **3.** *adv.* **IN ADDITION** in addition to something else, or besides what has been mentioned ○ *I have to pay the money, then a penalty on top of that!* **4.** *adj.* **BEING AT THAT TIME** being at that time, or existing or belonging to the time mentioned ○ *the then governor* [Old English *þænne.* Ultimately from an Indo-European demonstrative base (see THE).] ◇ **but then again** used to introduce a contrasting and additional fact that has to be taken into account ○ *It was a brave thing to do, but then I would have expected no less of her.* ◇ **then and there** immediately and in that very place (*informal*) ○ *Did you expect me to hand over the money then and there?*

the·nar /thee naar/ *n.* **1. PALM OF HAND** the palm of the hand (*technical*) **2. BASE OF THUMB** the fleshy area at the base of the thumb ■ *adj.* **IN PALM OR BALL OF THUMB** relating to or in the palm of the hand or the fleshy area at the base of the thumb [Mid-17thC. From Greek, "palm of the hand."]

Thé·nard /tay naar/, **Louis Jacques, Baron** (1777–1857) French chemist. He discovered sodium peroxide and potassium peroxide, as well as a pigment used to color porcelain and known as Thénard's blue. He wrote a once-standard treatise on chemistry.

thence /thenss/ *adv.* (*formal or literary*) **1. FROM THERE** from that place ○ *We went by boat to Rotterdam and thence to Amsterdam.* **2. THEREFORE** from that fact, or therefore **3. THEREAFTER** from that time, or thereafter [13thC. Formed from earlier *thenne.* Ultimately from an Indo-European demonstrative base (see THE).]

thence·forth /thenss fáwrth/ *adv.* from that time on

thence·for·ward /thens fáwrwərd/ *adv.* from that place or time on or forward

the·o·bro·mine /thee ō brṓ meen/ *n.* a white powder derived from the cacao bean that has effects similar to caffeine and has been used as a diuretic and in treating cardiovascular disorders. Formula: $C_7H_8N_4O_2$. [Mid-19thC. Formed from modern Latin *Theobroma*, genus name of the cacao tree, literally "food of the gods," from Greek *brōma* "food."]

the·o·cen·tric /thee ə séntrik/ *adj.* with God, a god, or gods as the focal point —**the·o·cen·tri·cism** *n.* —**the·o·cen·tric·i·ty** /thee ə sen tríssətee/ *n.* —**the·o·cen·trism** /-sén trìzzəm/ *n.*

the·oc·ra·cy /thee ókrəssee/ (*plural* **-cies**) *n.* **1. GOVERNMENT BY GOD** government by a god or by priests **2. COMMUNITY GOVERNED BY GOD** a community governed by a god or priests [Early 17thC. From Greek *theokratia*, literally "rule of the gods."] —**the·o·crat** /thee ə kràt/ *n.* —**the·o·crat·ic** /thee ə kráttik/ *adj.* —**the·o·crat·i·cal** /-kráttik'l/ *adj.* —**the·o·crat·i·cal·ly** /-kráttikəly/ *adv.*

The·oc·ri·tus /thee ókrətəss/ (310?–250? B.C.) Greek poet. His graceful lyrics were the foundation of European pastoral poetry.

the·od·i·cy /thee óddissee/ (*plural* **-cies**) *n.* argument in defense of God's goodness despite the existence of evil [Late 18thC. Anglicization of French *Théodicée*, the title of a book by Gottfried Leibniz, literally "justice of the gods," from Greek *dikē* "justice."] —**the·od·i·ce·an** /thee òddi see ən/ *adj.*

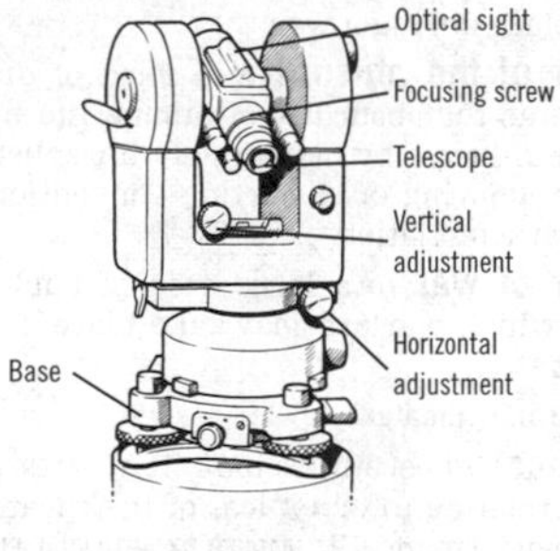

Theodolite

the·od·o·lite /thee óddə līt/ *n.* an optical instrument consisting of a rotating telescopic sight used by a surveyor to measure horizontal and vertical angles [Late 16thC. From modern Latin *theodelitus*, of unknown origin.] —**the·od·o·lit·ic** /thee òddə líttik/ *adj.*

The·o·do·ra /thèe ə dáwrə/ (508?–548) Byzantium empress. She was the wife of Justinian I, with whom she shared power. She acted to save the throne during the Nika riots (532).

The·o·dore Roo·se·velt Na·tion·al Park national park in western North Dakota, established in 1978 near the Little Missouri River. Area: 70,447 acres/28,509 hectares.

The·o·dor·ic /thee óddə rìk/, **King of the Ostrogoths** (*d.* 526?). King from 474, he invaded Italy in 488 and became its leader in 493, making Ravenna the capital and bringing a period of peace to Italy. Known as **Theodoric the Great**

the·og·o·ny /thee óggənee/ (*plural* **-nies**) *n.* the origin and descent of the gods, or an account of this [Early 17thC. From Greek *theogonia*, literally "birth of the gods."] —**the·o·gon·ic** /thee ə gónnik/ *adj.* —**the·og·o·nist** /thee óggənist/ *n.*

theol. *abbr.* **1.** theologian **2.** theological **3.** theology

the·o·lo·gi·an /thee ə lṓjən/ *n.* somebody who is an expert in or a student of theology

the·o·log·i·cal /thee ə lójjik'l/, **the·o·log·ic** /-lójjik/ *adj.* about, using, engaged in, or typical of theology —**the·o·log·i·cal·ly** *adv.*

the·o·log·i·cal vir·tues *npl.* faith, hope, and charity, the three spiritual graces that according to Christian theology are given directly by God

the·ol·o·gize /thee óllə jīz/ (**-gized, -giz·ing, -giz·es**) *v.* **1.** *vt.* **TREAT THEOLOGICALLY** to give a theological or religious significance to something **2.** *vi.* **SPECULATE ON RELIGIOUS TOPICS** to theorize, speculate, or discourse on religious topics —**the·ol·o·giz·er** *n.*

the·ol·o·gy /thee óllajee/ (*plural* **-gies**) *n.* **1. STUDY OF RELIGION** the study of religion, especially the Christian faith and God's relation to the world **2. RELIGIOUS THEORY** a religious theory, school of thought, or system of belief **3. COURSE OF RELIGIOUS TRAINING** a course of specialized religious training, especially one intended to lead students to a vocation in the Christian Church [14thC. Via French and Latin from Greek *theologia*, literally "study of divine things."] —**the·ol·o·gist** *n.*

the·o·mor·phic /thee ə máwrfik/ *adj.* in the form or likeness of a deity [Late 19thC. Formed from Greek *theomorphos*, literally "of divine form."] —**the·o·mor·phism** *n.*

the·on·o·my /thee ónnəmee/ *n.* the state of being governed by God, a god, or priests [Late 19thC. Coined from THEO- + -NOMY on the model of German *Theonomie.*] —**the·on·o·mous** *adj.*

the·oph·a·ny /thee óffənee/ (*plural* **-nies**) *n.* the appearance of a god in a visible form to a human being [Mid-17thC. Via medieval Latin from Greek *theophaneia*, literally "appearance of the gods."] —**the·o·phan·ic** /thee ə fánnik/ *adj.*

The·oph·i·lus /thee óffələss/ *n.* ASTRON a crater on the Moon northwest of Mare Nectaris. It is approximately 60 mi./100 km in diameter and has a central mountain 7200 ft./2200 m in height.

the·oph·yl·line /thee óffəlin, thee ō fí leen/ *n.* an alkaloid substance extracted from tea leaves or made synthetically, used medicinally as a vasodilator, smooth muscle relaxant, and diuretic, and in treating bronchial asthma. Formula: $C_7H_8N_4O_2.H_2O$. [Late 19thC. Coined from modern Latin *Thea* (see THEINE) + PHYLLO- + -INE.]

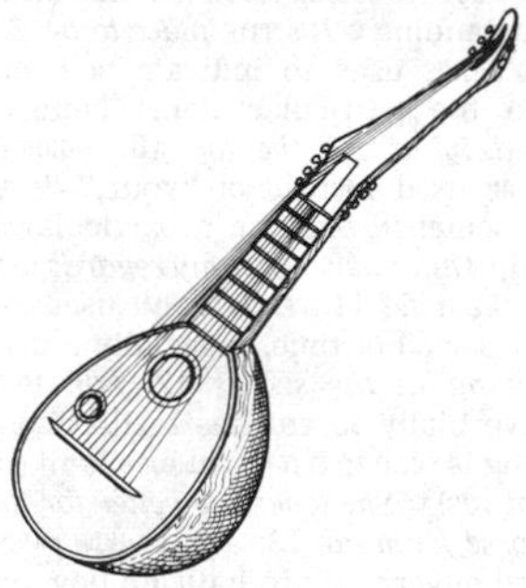

Theorbo

the·or·bo /thee áwr bō/ *n.* a stringed instrument from the 17th century similar to the lute except larger and with an extra set of bass strings longer than the main set [Early 17thC. Via Italian *tiorba* from, ultimately, Turkish *torba* "bag."] —**the·or·bist** *n.*

the·o·rem /thee ərəm, theerəm/ *n.* **1.** LOGIC, MATH **PROVABLE PROPOSITION OR FORMULA** a proposition or formula in mathematics or logic provable from a set of axioms and basic assumptions **2. IDEA ACCEPTED AS TRUE** an idea accepted or proposed as true [Mid-16thC. Via late Latin from Greek *theōrēma* "speculation," from *theōrein* "to look at," from *theōros* (see THEORY).] —**the·o·re·mat·ic** /thee ərə máttik, theerə máttik/ *adj.* —**the·o·re·mat·i·cal·ly** /thee ərə máttikalee, theerə-/ *adv.*

the·o·ret·i·cal /thee ə réttik'l/, **the·o·ret·ic** /thee ə réttik/ *adj.* **1. BASED ON THEORY** about, involving, or based on theory **2. DEALING WITH THEORY** dealing with theory or speculation rather than practical applications **3. SPECULATIVE** inclined to or skilled in speculative contemplation or theorizing **4. HYPOTHETICAL** existing only in theory [Early 17thC. Formed from late Latin *theoreticus*, from Greek *theōretikos*, from *theōrētos* "observable," from *theorein* "to look at."] —**the·o·ret·i·cal·ly** *adv.*

the·o·re·ti·cian /thee ərə tísh'n, theerə-/ *n.* somebody who is inclined to or skilled in speculative contemplation or theorizing, or is learned in the theoretical aspect of a subject

the·o·ret·ics /thee̍ ə réttiks/ *n.* the theoretical or speculative aspect of a subject (*takes a singular verb*)

the·o·rist *n.* somebody who holds or expounds a theory

the·o·rize /thee̍ ə rīz, thír īz/ (**-rized, -riz·ing, -riz·es**) *v.* **1.** *vi.* SPECULATE to speculate or form a theory about something **2.** *vt.* CONCEIVE OF THEORETICALLY to conceive of something in a theoretical way ○ *Research scientists were able to theorize the existence of the particle before it was actually discovered.* —**the·o·ri·za·tion** /thee̍ əri záysh'n, thee̍ri-/ *n.* —**the·o·riz·er** /thee̍ ə rīzər, thí rīzər/ *n.*

the·o·ry /thee̍ əree, thee̍ree/ (*plural* **-ries**) *n.* **1.** RULES AND TECHNIQUES the body of rules, ideas, principles, and techniques that applies to a particular subject, especially when seen as distinct from actual practice ○ *economic theories* **2.** SPECULATION abstract thought or contemplation **3.** IDEA FORMED BY SPECULATION an idea of or belief about something arrived at through speculation or conjecture ○ *She believed in the theory that you catch more flies with honey than with vinegar.* **4.** HYPOTHETICAL CIRCUMSTANCES a set of circumstances or principles that is hypothetical ○ *That's the theory, but it may not work out in practice.* **5.** SCIENTIFIC PRINCIPLE TO EXPLAIN PHENOMENA a set of facts, propositions, or principles analyzed in their relation to one another and used, especially in science, to explain phenomena [Late 16thC. Via late Latin from Greek *theōria* "contemplation, theory," from *theōros* "spectator."] ◇ **in theory** under hypothetical or ideal circumstances but perhaps not in reality

the·o·ry of games *n.* = **game theory**

the·o·ry of mind *n.* the way somebody conceives of mental activity in others, including how children conceptualize mental activity in others and how they attribute intention to and predict the behavior of others

theos. *abbr.* **1.** theosophical **2.** theosophy

the·os·o·phy /thee óssəfee/ (*plural* **-phies**) *n.* any religious philosophy based on intuitive insight into the nature of God [Mid-17thC. Via medieval Latin from late Greek *theosophia*, literally "knowledge of the gods."] —**the·o·soph·ic** /thee̍ ə sóffik/ *adj.* —**the·o·soph·i·cal** /-sóffik'l/ *adj.* —**the·o·soph·i·cal·ly** /-sóffikəlee/ *adv.* —**the·os·o·phism** /thee óssə fizzəm/ *n.* —**the·os·o·phist** /-óssəfist/ *n.*

The·os·o·phy /thee óssəfee/ *n.* the teachings of the Theosophical Society, a religious movement founded in New York in 1875, incorporating chiefly Buddhist and Brahmanic theories such as reincarnation and karma —**The·o·soph·i·cal** /thee̍ ə sóffik'l/ *adj.* —**The·o·so·phist** /thee óssəfist/ *n.*

The·ra /thee̍rə/ island and tourist center in the Cyclades group, Greece, north of Crete. Destroyed by a volcanic eruption in 1500 B.C., it is sometimes claimed as the origin of the Atlantis legend. Population: 10,000 (1994). Area: 29 sq. mi./76 sq. km.

therap. *abbr.* **1.** therapeutic **2.** therapeutics

ther·a·peu·tic /thèrrə pyóotik/ *adj.* **1.** USED IN TREATING DISEASE about, involving, or used in the treatment of disease or disorders **2.** RESTORING OR MAINTAINING HEALTH working or done to restore or maintain somebody's health [Mid-16thC. Via French *therapeutique* or late Latin *therapeutica* from, ultimately, Greek *therapeutēs* "one who treats," from *therapeuein* (see THERAPY).] —**ther·a·peu·ti·cal·ly** *adv.*

ther·a·peu·tic in·dex *n.* a ratio that indicates the relative efficiency of a drug, calculated by dividing the dose of the drug that causes cell damage by the dose needed to produce results

ther·a·peu·tics /thèrrə pyóotiks/ *n.* the branch of medicine that deals with methods of treatment and healing, especially the use of drugs to treat diseases (*takes a singular verb*)

ther·a·pist /thérrəpist/ *n.* **1.** SOMEBODY TRAINED IN THERAPY somebody trained to treat disease, disorders, or injuries, especially one who uses methods other than drugs and surgery **2.** PSYCHOL PSYCHOTHERAPIST a psychoanalyst or a professional from another school of psychotherapy who is trained to treat mental and emotional problems with psychological methods

the·rap·sid /thə rápsid/ *n.* any extinct reptile of an order that lived during the Permian and Triassic periods. Many of them are thought to be ancestors of the mammals. Order: Therapsida. [Early 20thC. From modern Latin *Therapsida*, order name, from Greek *thēr* "wild animal" + *hapsis* "vault." From the opening at the base of its skull.]

ther·a·py /thérrəpee/ (*plural* **-pies**) *n.* **1.** TREATMENT TO CURE treatment of physical, mental, or behavioral problems that is meant to cure or rehabilitate somebody (*often used in combination*) ○ *radiation therapy* **2.** PSYCHOL PSYCHOTHERAPY psychoanalysis or techniques from another school of psychotherapy intended to treat mental and emotional problems with psychological methods [Mid-19thC. Via modern Latin from Greek *therapeia*, from *therapeuein* "to treat medically," from *theraps* "attendant."]

Ther·a·va·da /thèrrə vaádə/ *n.* the doctrines of the Hinayana Buddhists [Late 19thC. From Pali, literally "doctrine of the elders."]

there /thair/; *unstressed* /thər/ CORE MEANING: an adverb used to indicate a place, either one that has already been mentioned or is understood, or one indicated by pointing or looking ○ *I don't know how to get there by car.* ○ *May I sit there?*

1. *adv.* AT THAT POINT used to refer to a point reached in an activity or process ○ *I suggest we pause there and have coffee.* ○ *And there we end our news bulletin.* **2.** *adv.* ON THAT MATTER on that matter, or with respect to that ○ *I can't agree with you there.* **3.** *adv.* AT A SUCCESSFUL POINT used to indicate that something has reached a final or successful point or stage ○ *We're not the best yet, but we're getting there.* **4.** USED TO IDENTIFY used to identify somebody or something emphatically ○ *They ran into that house there.* **5.** *pron.* INTRODUCING A SENTENCE used to introduce a sentence stating that something exists, develops, or can be seen ○ *There's a stain on this sweater.* ○ *There remain several important issues to be discussed.* **6.** *interj.* USED TO EXPRESS FEELINGS used to express strong feelings such as anger, satisfaction, relief, finality, or reassurance ○ *There! I told you she would make it.* [Old English *þær*. Ultimately from an Indo-European demonstrative base (see THE).] ◇ **be there for somebody** to be ready to give your support, sympathy, or friendship to somebody ◇ **not all there** not fully conscious, rational, or aware of something ◇ **so there** used to express defiance, triumph, or finality ◇ **there and then** immediately and in that very place ◇ **there, there** used to console, soothe, or comfort somebody ○ *There, there. Don't cry.* ◇ **there you are** **1.** used when giving somebody something **2.** used to express triumph at having been seen to be right **3.** used to express resignation or sorrow at something that has happened

there·a·bouts /-bówts/, **there·a·bout** /-bówt/ *adv.* near that place, amount, number, or time ○ *We're expecting twenty guests or thereabouts.*

there·af·ter /thair áftər/ *adv.* after that time or from that time on ○ *She graduated from college, and shortly thereafter found a good job.*

there·at /thair át/ *adv.* (*archaic*) **1.** AT THAT TIME at that time or place **2.** FOR THAT REASON because of that

there·by /thair bī/ *adv.* **1.** BY MEANS OF THAT by means of or because of that ○ *Interest rates may fall, thereby discouraging investment.* **2.** IN CONNECTION WITH THAT in connection with or with reference to that ○ *Thereby hangs a tale.*

there·for /thair fáwr/ *adv.* for this, that, or it (*archaic*)

there·fore /thair fawr/ *adv.* **1.** AND SO and so, or because of that ○ *This statement is true; therefore that statement must be false.* **2.** ACCORDINGLY accordingly, or to that purpose ○ *We were forbidden to attend and therefore stayed at home.*

there·from /thair fróm/ *adv.* from that place or thing (*archaic or formal*)

there·in /thair ín/ *adv.* in that matter, respect, or detail ○ *Therein lies the problem.*

there·in·af·ter /thàir in áftər/ *adv.* from then on in something, especially a legal document (*formal*)

there·in·to /thàir in tóo/ *adv.* into that place or thing (*archaic*)

ther·e·min /thérrəmin/ *n.* an early electronic musical instrument producing a tremulous sound whose pitch and volume is controlled by the distance between two antennae and the player's hands [Early 20thC. Named for its inventor, the Russian engineer Leo *Theremin* (1896–1993).]

there·of /thair úv, -óv/ *adv.* (*formal*) **1.** OF THAT of or about that ○ *a levy of $50 per annum or part thereof* **2.** FROM THAT CAUSE from that as a reason or cause

there·on /thair ón/ *adv.* **1.** ON THAT on the place or surface just mentioned (*formal*) ○ *a metal plate with an inscription thereon* **2.** ON THAT POINT regarding the point just mentioned (*archaic*) ○ *income and capital expense, including tax thereon*

The·re·sa of Li·sieux /tə réessə əv lee zyő/ (1873–97) French nun. She is the author of *The Story of a Soul* (1898), in which she described the "little way," the simple path to Christianity. With Joan of Arc, she is a patron saint of France.

there·to /thair tóo/ *adv.* to that thing just mentioned (*formal*)

there·to·fore /thàirtə fáwr/ *adv.* before or up to that time (*formal*)

there·un·der /thair úndər/ *adv.* **1.** BELOW THAT below that, or after that, especially in a legal document (*formal*) **2.** UNDER THAT under that place or thing mentioned (*archaic*)

there·up·on /thàirə pón/ *adv.* **1.** AT THAT POINT at that point in time (*archaic*) ○ *She was found to have leaked information to a rival firm, and he thereupon insisted on her dismissal.* **2.** UPON THAT POINT upon or concerning that point (*formal*)

there·with /thair wíth, -wíth/, **there·with·al** /-with áwl, -with-/ *adv.* **1.** WITH THAT with that, or as well as that (*formal*) **2.** AT THAT POINT at that point, or immediately

the·ri·an·throp·ic /thee̍ree ən thróppik, -an-/ *adj.* MYTHOL used to describe a mythological creature such as a centaur that is partly human and partly animal [Late 19thC. Coined from Greek *thērion* "small wild animal" + anthrōpos (see ANTHROPO-) + -IC.] —**the·ri·an·throp·ism** /thee̍ree ánthrə pìzzəm/ *n.*

the·ri·o·mor·phic /thee̍ree ə máwrfik/ *adj.* in the form of an animal, or thought of as being in animal form [Late 19thC. Coined from Greek *thērion* (see THERIANTHROPIC) + -MORPHIC.]

therm /thurm/ *n.* a unit of heat equal to 100,000 British thermal units or 1.055×10^8 joules [Early 20thC. From Greek *thermē* "heat."]

therm. *abbr.* thermometer

therm- *prefix.* = **thermo-** (*used before vowels*)

ther·mae /thúrmee/ *npl.* hot springs or baths, especially the public baths of ancient Rome [Mid-16thC. Via Latin from Greek *thermai*, from *thermē* "heat."]

ther·mal /thúrm'l/, **ther·mic** /thúrmik/ *adj.* **1.** INVOLVING HEAT about, involving, affected by, or producing heat ○ *thermal energy* **2.** HOT OR WARM hot or warm, especially because of the presence of hot springs ○ *thermal baths* **3.** MANUF USING HEAT FOR PRODUCTION using heat to produce something **4.** CLOTHES FOR RETENTION OF BODY HEAT designed to retain body heat ○ *thermal underwear* ■ *n.* METEOROL AIR COLUMN a current of warm air rising through cooler surrounding air ○ *watching hawks ride thermals* ■ **ther·mals** *npl. U.K.* THERMAL CLOTHING thermal clothing, especially underwear (*informal*) [Mid-18thC. From French, formed from Greek *thermē* "heat."] —**ther·mal·ly** *adv.*

ther·mal bar·ri·er *n.* the problematic heating effect caused by air friction on an aircraft flying at high speed

ther·mal con·duc·tiv·i·ty *n.* the rate at which heat flows through a material between points at different temperatures, measured in watts per meter per degree. Symbol λ, k

ther·mal ef·fi·cien·cy *n.* the work done by a heat engine divided by the thermal energy required to operate it

ther·mal im·ag·ing *n.* the use of a device that detects the different levels of infrared energy given off by areas of different temperatures and displays these as a pattern on a screen

ther·mal·ize /thúrm'l īz/ (**-ized, -iz·ing, -iz·es**) *vt.* to slow neutrons in a nuclear reactor to give them thermal energy and thus produce fission —**ther·mal·i·za·tion** /thùrm'li záysh'n/ *n.*

ther·mal neu·tron *n.* = **slow neutron**

ther·mal noise *n.* noise in an electronic circuit, e.g., an amplifier, caused by electrons in conducting elements that are agitated by the absorption of heat

ther·mal pol·lu·tion *n.* the discharge into a natural body of water of heated water or other liquid that is hot enough to harm aquatic life

ther·mal print·er *n.* **1.** PRINTING DEVICE USING HEAT a printing device that uses heat to print characters onto specially coated paper **2.** COMPUT COMPUTER OUTPUT DEVICE an output device that produces visible characters by moving heated wires over specially treated heat-sensitive paper

ther·mic *adj.* = **thermal** —**ther·mi·cal·ly** *adv.*

Ther·mi·dor /thúrmə dàwr/ *n.* CALENDAR the 11th month of the year in the French Revolutionary calendar, corresponding to July 20 to August 18 in the Gregorian calendar [Early 19thC. From French, formed from Greek *thermē* "heat" + *dōron* "gift." From the fact that it is the hottest time of year.]

therm·i·on /thúr mī̀ ən/ *n.* a positive ion or electron given off by a very hot material such as a hot cathode —**therm·i·on·ic** /thùrmee ónnik/ *adj.*

therm·i·on·ic cur·rent *n.* an electric current generated by the flow of electrons leaving a heated cathode and flowing to other electrodes

therm·i·on·ics /thùrmee ónniks/ *n.* a branch of electronics that deals with the emission of electrons from hot bodies (*takes a singular verb*)

therm·i·on·ic tube *n.* an electronic component that consists of an evacuated glass tube containing a heated cathode that emits electrons, an anode that collects the electrons, and other electrodes

therm·i·on·ic valve *n. U.K.* = **thermionic tube**

therm·is·tor /thúr mìstər/ *n.* a semiconductor device with a resistance that is very sensitive to temperature, resistance decreasing as the temperature increases [Mid-20thC. Contraction of *thermal resistor*.]

Ther·mit /thúrmit/, **Ther·mite** /thúr mīt/ *tdmk.* a trademark for a mixture of aluminum powder and metal oxide, usually of iron, that gives off great heat when ignited. It is used in welding and in incendiary bombs.

ther·mo·ba·rom·e·ter /thùr mō bə rómmətər/ *n.* an instrument that measures both air temperature and pressure

ther·mo·cau·ter·y /thùr mō káwtəree/ *n.* the use of a heated instrument, e.g., a hot wire, to destroy tissue, especially in cauterizing wounds

ther·mo·chem·is·try /thùr mō kémmistree/ *n.* a branch of chemistry concerned with the relationship between chemical action and heat —**ther·mo·chem·i·cal** /thùr mō kémmik'l/ *adj.* —**ther·mo·chem·i·cal·ly** /-kémmikəlee/ *adv.* —**ther·mo·chem·ist** /-kémmist/ *n.*

ther·mo·cline /thúr mō klīn/ *n.* a layer of water, e.g., in a lake, where there is an abrupt change in temperature that separates the warmer surface water from the colder deep water

ther·mo·cou·ple /thúr mō kùpp'l/ *n.* a device for measuring temperature in which two wires of different metals are joined. The potential difference between the wires is a measure of the temperature of something they touch.

ther·mo·dur·ic /thùr mō dóorik/ *adj.* used to describe a microorganism that is capable of surviving high temperatures or pasteurization [Early 20thC. Coined from THERMO- + Latin *durare* "to endure" + -IC.]

ther·mo·dy·nam·ic /thùr mō dī námmik/, **ther·mo·dy·nam·i·cal** /-námmik'l/ *adj.* **1.** OF THERMODYNAMICS about or involving thermodynamics **2.** OBEYING THE LAWS OF THERMODYNAMICS obeying or affected by the laws of thermodynamics —**ther·mo·dy·nam·i·cal·ly** *adv.*

ther·mo·dy·nam·ics /thùr mō dī námmiks/ *n.* PHYSICS OF ENERGY AND MECHANICAL ACTIONS the branch of physics that deals with the conversions from one to another of various forms of energy and how these affect temperature, pressure, volume, mechanical action, and work (*takes a singular verb*) ■ *npl.* PROCESSES OF THERMODYNAMICS thermodynamic processes or phenomena —**ther·mo·dy·nam·i·cist** *n.*

ther·mo·e·lec·tric /thùrmō i léktrik/, **ther·mo·e·lec·tri·cal** /-trik'l/ *adj.* involving a direct relationship between temperature of materials and electricity —**ther·mo·e·lec·tri·cal·ly** *adv.*

ther·mo·e·lec·tric·i·ty /thùrmō i lek tríssətee/ *n.* electricity produced by maintaining a temperature difference at the point where two different materials come into contact, e.g., in a thermocouple

ther·mo·e·lec·tron /thùrmō i lék tròn/ *n.* an electron emitted by a material that is at high temperature

ther·mo·form /thúrmə fàwrm/ (**-formed, -form·ing, -forms**) *vt.* to shape plastic using heat and pressure —**ther·mo·form·a·ble** /thùrmə fáwrməb'l/ *adj.*

ther·mo·gen·e·sis /thùrmō jénnəssiss/ *n.* the production of heat in a person's or animal's body by physiological processes, especially metabolic processes —**ther·mo·ge·net·ic** /thùrmō jə néttik/ *adj.*

ther·mo·gram /thúrmə gràm/ *n.* **1.** MED IMAGE FROM THERMOGRAPHY an image or record of the heat radiating from the body, made by thermography **2.** PHYS TEMPERATURE RECORD a record of temperatures made by a thermograph

ther·mo·graph /thúrmə gràf/ *n.* **1.** RECORDING THERMOMETER an instrument that continuously records temperature readings **2.** MED DEVICE SHOWING BODY HEAT a device that show patterns of heat radiated from a person's or an animal's body, used in diagnostic thermography

ther·mog·ra·phy /thər mógrəfee/ (*plural* **-phies**) *n.* **1.** MED RECORDING IMAGE OF BODY HEAT the recording of a visual image of the heat that bodies emit as infrared radiation. The technique is used to diagnose disease and tumors, especially breast tumors. **2.** PRINTING PRINTING PROCESS USING HEAT the process of producing a raised image on a printed suface by using heat to fuse a resinous powder and wet ink to the surface —**ther·mog·ra·pher** *n.* —**ther·mo·graph·ic** /thùrmə gráffik/ *adj.* —**ther·mo·graph·i·cal·ly** /-gráffikəlee/ *adv.*

ther·mo·junc·tion /thùrmō júngkshən/ *n.* a point at which two dissimilar metals of differing temperatures come into contact, producing a thermoelectric current

ther·mo·la·bile /thùrmə láyb'l, thùrmə láy bīl/ *adj.* used to describe substances such as some enzymes that are easily destroyed or altered by heat

ther·mo·lu·mi·nes·cence /thùrmō loomi néss'ns/ *n.* phosphorescence released by certain previously irradiated substances when they are heated. The process is used by geologists and archeologists to date rocks and pottery. —**ther·mo·lu·mi·nes·cent** *adj.*

ther·mol·y·sis /thər mólləssiss/ *n.* **1.** PHYSIOL HEAT LOSS loss of heat from the body, e.g., by sweating **2.** CHEM DECOMPOSITION BY HEAT the breaking down of a substance by heat —**ther·mo·lyt·ic** /thùrmə líttik/ *adj.*

ther·mo·mag·net·ic /thùrmō mag néttik/ *adj.* relating to the relationship between heat and magnetism, and especially the effects of heat upon the magnetic properties of a substance

ther·mom·e·ter /thər mómmətər/ *n.* an instrument for measuring temperature, e.g., an instrument with a graduated glass tube and a bulb containing mercury or alcohol that rises in the tube when the temperature increases [Mid-17thC. From French *thermomètre*, from Greek *thermos* "warm" (see THERM) + *-mètre* "-meter."]

ther·mom·e·try /thər mómmətree/ *n.* temperature measurement and the branch of physics concerned with measuring temperature —**ther·mo·met·ric** /-méttrik/ *adj.* —**ther·mo·met·ri·cal** /-méttrik'l/ *adj.* —**ther·mo·met·ri·cal·ly** /-méttrikəlee/ *adv.*

ther·mo·nu·cle·ar /thùrmō nóoklee ər/ *adj.* **1.** NUCLEAR PHYS, INDUST OF NUCLEAR FUSION relating to nuclear fusion or making use of nuclear fusion ○ *thermonuclear energy* **2.** ARMS BASED ON FUSION making use of nuclear fusion ○ *thermonuclear war*

ther·mo·pe·ri·od·ism /thùrmō péeree ə dìzzəm/, **ther·mo·pe·ri·o·dic·i·ty** /-peeree ə díssətee/ *n.* the response of a plant to cycles of temperature, e.g., the regular cycles of day and night —**ther·mo·pe·ri·od·ic** /thùrmō peeree óddik/ *adj.*

ther·mo·phile /thúrmə fīl/ *n.* an organism that thrives in a warm environment, e.g., a bacterium —**ther·mo·phile** *adj.* —**ther·mo·phil·ic** /thùrmə fíllik/ *adj.* —**ther·mo·phil·ous** /thər móffələss/ *adj.*

ther·mo·pile /thúrmə pīl/ *n.* a set of thermocouples, either joined in series for increased voltage or in parallel for increased current, used to measure radiant energy or to convert radiant energy into electric current

ther·mo·plas·tic /thùrmə plástik/ *n.* a substance that becomes soft and pliable when heated, without a change in its intrinsic properties. Polystyrene and polyethylene are thermoplastics. —**ther·mo·plas·tic** *adj.* —**ther·mo·plas·tic·i·ty** /thùrmō pla stíssətee/ *n.*

Ther·mop·y·lae /thər móppəl-/ pass in ancient Greece, northwest of Athens, that controlled entry to central Greece. It was the site of the battle of 480 B.C. fought by Leonidas I and thousands of his troops, all of whom were killed by the Persian army, led by Xerxes.

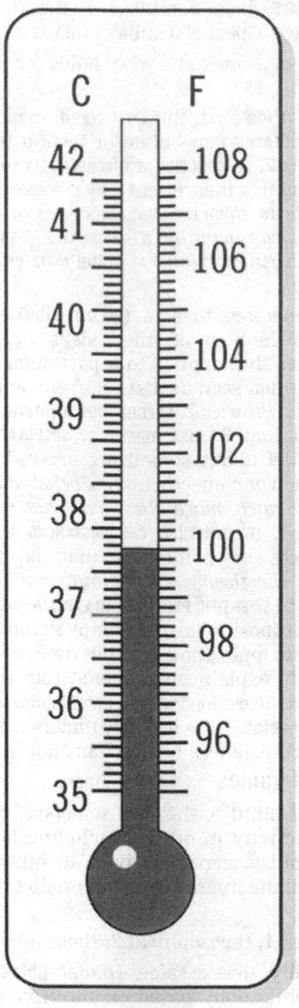

Thermometer

ther·mo·re·cep·tor /thùrmō ri séptər/ *n.* a sensory receptor, usually a nerve ending in the skin, that is stimulated by heat or cold

ther·mo·reg·u·la·tion /thùrmō reggyə láysh'n/ *n.* the maintenance of a particular body temperature regardless of changes in the environment —**ther·mo·reg·u·la·tor** /thùrmō réggyə làytər/ *n.* —**ther·mo·reg·u·late** /-làytə/ *vi.*

Ther·mos /thúrməss/ *tdmk.* a trademark for an insulated or vacuum container used to hold a liquid and maintain it at a constant temperature

ther·mo·scope /thúrmə skōp/ *n.* an instrument that measures changes in temperature by their effects on a substance, e.g., the change in volume of a gas —**ther·mo·scop·ic** /thùrmə skóppik/ *adj.* —**ther·mo·scop·i·cal** /-skóppik'l/ *adj.* —**ther·mo·scop·i·cal·ly** /-skóppikəlee/ *adv.*

ther·mo·set·ting /thúrmō sètting/ *adj.* used to describe a plastic that sets permanently when heated

ther·mo·sphere /thúrmə sfeer/ *n.* the region of the atmosphere above the mesosphere in which temperature steadily increases with height, beginning at about 53 mi./85 km above the earth's surface

ther·mo·sta·ble /thùrmō stáyb'l/ *adj.* used to describe substances such as some toxins that are able to withstand heat without being destroyed or altered —**ther·mo·sta·bil·i·ty** /thùrmō stə bíllətee/ *n.*

ther·mo·stat /thúrmə stàt/ *n.* **1.** TEMPERATURE REGULATOR a device that regulates temperature by means of a temperature sensor, e.g., a bimetallic strip. Thermostats are used in vehicle engines and domestic heating systems. **2.** DEVICE TRIGGERED BY TEMPERATURE CHANGE a device that activates a mechanism or system, e.g., a fire alarm or a sprinkler system, in response to a change in temperature [Mid-19thC. Coined from THERMO- + -STAT "instrument holding constant value," from, ultimately, Greek *statikos* "causing to stand."] —**ther·mo·stat·ic** /thùrmə státtik/ *adj.* —**ther·mo·stat·i·cal·ly** /-státtikəlee/ *adv.*

ther·mo·tax·is /thùrmə táksiss/ *n.* movement of a living organism toward or away from a heat source —**ther·mo·tac·tic** /thùrmə táktik/ *adj.* —**ther·mo·tax·ic** /-táksik/ *adj.*

ther·mo·ther·a·py /thùrmō thérrəpee/ (*plural* **-pies**) *n.* the use of heat to alleviate pain and stiffness, especially in joints and muscles, and to increase circulation

ther·mot·ro·pism /thər móttrə pìzzəm/ *n.* the movement of a plant part toward or away from a source of heat —**ther·mo·trop·ic** /thùrmə tróppik/ *adj.*

-thermy *suffix.* heat ○ *diathermy* [Via modern Latin *-thermia* from, ultimately, Greek *thermē* "heat" (see THERM)]

the·ro·pod /theérə pòd/ *n.* any carnivorous dinosaur with strong hind legs and short front limbs. Tyrannosaurs and megalosaurs are theropods. Suborder: Theropoda. [Early 20thC. From modern Latin *Theropoda*, suborder name, from Greek *thēr* "wild animal" (see TREACLE) + POD- "foot."] —**the·rop·o·dan** /thi róppədən/ *adj.*

The·roux /thə ro͞o/, **Paul** (*b.* 1941) U.S. writer. He is known for his travel books such as *The Great Railway Bazaar* (1975) and his novels such as *The Mosquito Coast* (1981). Full name **Paul Edward Theroux**

the·sau·rus /thə sáwrəss/ (*plural* **-ri** /-rī/ *or* **-rus·es**) *n.* **1. BOOK OF WORD GROUPS** a book that lists words related to each other in meaning, usually giving synonyms and antonyms **2. BOOK OF SPECIALIST VOCABULARY** a dictionary of words relating to a particular subject **3. TREASURY** a place in which valuable things are stored [Early 19thC. Via Latin, "treasury," from Greek *thēsauros* "storehouse" (source also of English *treasure*).]

these /theez/ *pron., adj.* the form of "this" used before a plural noun or with a multiple referent ○ (pron) *These are the people I was telling you about.* ○ (adj) *These delays, along with the paperwork demanded by government, can be costly for banks.* [Old English *þæs*, *þās*, plural of *þes* (see THIS)]

The·se·us /theésee əss, theéss yo͞oss/ *n.* in Greek mythology, a great hero who performed many brave deeds, including slaying the Minotaur, defeating the Amazons, and descending into Hades to rescue Persephone

the·sis /theéssiss/ (*plural* **-ses** /-seez/) *n.* **1. PROPOSITION** a proposition advanced as an argument **2. ESSAY SUBJECT** a subject for an essay **3. LENGTHY ACADEMIC PAPER** a dissertation based on original research, especially as work toward an academic degree **4. STATEMENT** an unproved statement, especially one serving as a premise in an argument **5.** MUSIC **DOWNBEAT** the downbeat of a bar of music **6.** POETRY **STRESSED SYLLABLE** a long syllable, on which the stress naturally falls, in classical Greek and Latin poetry. ◊ **arsis** *n.* 1 **7.** POETRY **UNSTRESSED SYLLABLE** a short unstressed syllable in modern accentual poetry. ◊ **arsis** *n.* 2 **8.** PHILOS **FIRST STAGE OF DIALECTIC** the first of three stages in Hegelian dialectic [14thC. Via Latin from Greek, "proposition, stressed beat." Ultimately from an Indo-European base that is also the ancestor of English *do* and *fact*.]

thes·pi·an /théspee ən/ *n.* **ACTOR** an actor or actress ■ *adj.* **1. thes·pi·an, Thes·pi·an OF THE THEATER** relating to the theater or the profession of acting (*literary*) **2. OF THESPIS** relating to the ancient Greek poet Thespis [Early 19thC. Formed from *Thespis*, the name of the Greek poet (6thC B.C.) who was the father of Greek tragedy.]

Thess. *abbr.* BIBLE Thessalonians

Thes·sa·lo·ni·an /thèssə lṓnee ən/ *n.* PEOPLES **SOMEBODY FROM THESSALONICA** somebody who was born in or lived in the ancient Greek city of Thessalonica ■ **Thes·sa·lo·ni·ans** *npl.* BIBLE **BOOK OF BIBLE** either of two letters written to the Christians of Thessalonica by the Apostle Paul, included as books of the Christian Bible (*takes a singular verb*) —**Thes·sa·lo·ni·an** *adj.*

Thes·sa·lo·ní·ki /thè saa law neékee/ capital city of the department of Thessaloníki, northeastern Greece. Population: 377,951 (1991).

Thes·sa·ly /théssəlee/ region in north central Greece, consisting mainly of a broad plain. Area: 5,000 sq. mi./13,000 sq. km. —**Thes·sa·li·an** *n., adj.*

the·ta /tháytə, theétə/ *n.* the eighth letter of the Greek alphabet, represented in the English alphabet as "th." See table at **alphabet** [Early 17thC. From Greek, of Phoenician origin.]

the·ta rhythm, **the·ta wave** *n.* a pattern of brain waves with a frequency between 4 and 7 Hz seen on an electroencephalogram. The pattern is normal in children under the age of 12 but in adults may be a sign of stress or mental disorder.

thet·ic /théttik/, **thet·i·cal** *adj.* **1. OF STRESS IN POETRY** relating to or having stress in classical poetry **2. ARBITRARY** imposed arbitrarily [Late 17thC. From Greek *thetikos*, from *thetos* "placed, stressed," from *tithenai* "to place."] —**thet·i·cal·ly** *adv.*

the·ur·gy /theé ərjee/ *n.* **1. SUPERNATURAL OR DIVINE INTERVENTION** intervention of supernatural or divine powers in human affairs **2. PERSUADING THE SUPERNATURAL TO INTERVENE** the art of securing the intervention of supernatural or divine powers in human affairs **3. MAGIC PERFORMED FOR GOOD** magic with the help of benevolent spirits, as practiced by Neo-Platonists [Mid-16thC. Via late Latin *theurgia* from Greek *theourgia* "ritual, mystery," from *theos* "god" + *ergon* "work."] —**the·ur·gic** /thee úrjik/ *adj.* —**the·ur·gi·cal·ly** /-úrjikəlee/ *adv.* —**the·ur·gist** /-arjist/ *n.*

thew /thyoo/ *n.* muscle or muscular strength (*literary*) (*often used in the plural*) [Old English *þēaw* "custom, habit," literally "observance." Ultimately from an Indo-European base meaning "to watch," (ancestor also of English *tutor*). The underlying meaning is "good habit, virtue, strength."] —**thew·y** *adj.*

they /thay/ *pron.* **1. PEOPLE IN GENERAL** used to refer to people in general when making statements about the things people do, think, or say ○ *As people and businesses move out of inner cities, bank branches follow, they say.* **2. HE OR SHE** used instead of "he" or "she" to refer to a person without specifying gender (*informal*) ○ *A friend phoned the other day and they told me what you had said.* **3. THOSE** an archaic word for "those" (*archaic*) [12thC. Old Norse *þeir*. Ultimately from an Indo-European word meaning "the, that," which is also the ancestor of English *the*, *this*, *that*, and *there*.]

WORD KEY: USAGE

Everyone taking the test should do the best they can Because English is deficient in that it lacks a gender-neutral third person singular pronoun, ***they***, together with associated words such as *their*, is often used in this role and is a revival of an older use that was once well established in English. In more formal contexts, and when the individuality of the subject is significant, it is necessary to use *he or she*, but this phrase is too cumbersome to provide a solution in informal conversational usage such as that given in the example.

they'd /thayd/ *contr.* **1. THEY HAD** a short form of "they had" **2. THEY WOULD** a short form of "they would"

they'll /thayl/ *contr.* **1. THEY WILL** a short form of "they will" **2. THEY SHALL** a short form of "they shall"

they're /thair/ *contr.* a short form of "they are"

they've /thayv/ *contr.* a short form of "they have"

THI *abbr.* temperature-humidity index

thi- *prefix.* = **thio-** (*used before vowels*)

thi·a·ben·da·zole /thī ə béndə zōl/ *n.* a white compound used as a drug to destroy a wide variety of parasitic worms and as an antifungal agent. Formula: $C_{10}H_7N_3S$. [Mid-20thC. Contraction of THIAZOLE + BENZENE + IMIDAZOLE.]

thi·a·mine /thī ámmin, thī ə meen, -əmin/, **thi·a·min** /thī əmin/ *n.* one of the group of B vitamins, found in grains, meat, and yeast. It metabolizes carbohydrates and has been found to prevent beriberi and diseases of the nervous system. Formula: $C_{12}H_{17}ClN_4OS$. [Mid-20thC. Coined from THIO- + AMINE.]

thi·a·zide /thī ə zīd, thī əzid/ *n.* one of a group of compounds used to treat high blood pressure and as a diuretic. These compounds work by inhibiting the reabsorption of sodium and increasing the release of calcium by the kidneys, causing greater excretion of water. [Mid-20thC. Coined from THIO- + AZINE + OXIDE.]

thi·a·zine /thī ə zeen/ *n.* one of a group of organic compounds containing a ring of four carbon atoms, a sulfur atom, and a nitrogen atom. Some are used as dyes and others as tranquilizers. [Early 20thC. Coined from THIO- + AZINE.]

thi·a·zole /thī ə zōl/, **thi·a·zol** /thī ə zawl/ *n.* **1. LIQUID CHEMICAL COMPOUND** a volatile colorless liquid with a sharp odor. Formula: C_3H_3NS. **2. DERIVATIVE OF THIAZOLE** one of a group of compounds derived from thiazole. Some are used as dyes, others as fungicides or in chemical reactions as accelerators. [Late 19thC. Coined from THIO- + AZOLE.]

thick /thik/ *adj.* **1. DEEP OR BROAD** of relatively large extent from surface to surface or side to side ○ *a thick carpet* ○ *The child wrote her name in thick capital letters.* **2. LARGE IN DIAMETER** having a large diameter ○ *a thick cable* **3. OF STATED DEPTH OR BREADTH** having a specified depth or breadth ○ *a wall two feet thick* **4. FILLED** densely covered or filled ○ *The air was thick with mosquitoes.* **5. HARD TO SEE THROUGH** permitting little or no light to enter ○ *a thick mist* **6. NOT CLEAR** not articulating words clearly ○ *a voice thick with emotion* **7. DENSE** composed of many densely packed objects ○ *a thick forest* ○ *thick hair* **8. VISCOUS** having a liquid consistency that is not free-flowing ○ *thick paint* **9. PRONOUNCED** readily noticeable or distinct ○ *I found her thick southern accent charming.* **10. UNINTELLIGENT** slow to learn or understand (*insult*) **11. OF HEAVY FABRIC** made of thick material ○ *thick socks* **12. FRIENDLY** allied in a close relationship (*informal*) ○ *They seem very thick with each other.* ■ *adv.* **MAKING DEEP LAYER** in a way that produces something deep, broad, or dense ■ *n.* **1. MOST ACTIVE PART** the most intense, crowded, or busiest part of something ○ *in the thick of the battle* **2. DENSEST PART** the part of something with the greatest depth, density, or breadth ○ *in the thick of the jungle* [Old English *þicce*] —**thick·ly** *adv.* ◇ **thick and fast** in large numbers and with great frequency ◇ **through thick and thin** no matter what might happen

thick·en /thíkən/ (**-ened, -en·ing, -ens**) *v.* **1.** *vti.* **MAKE OR BECOME THICKER** to become thick or thicker or to make something thick or thicker **2.** *vi.* **BECOME MORE COMPLEX** to become more complicated or puzzling —**thick·en·er** *n.* —**thick·en·ing** *n.*

thick·et /thíkit/ *n.* a dense or tangled growth of small trees or bushes [Old English *þiccet*, from *þicce* "thick"]

thick-film tech·nol·o·gy *n.* a method of fabricating electronic circuitry in which a glaze is printed onto a glass or ceramic support. Wiring and components such as microchips are then added. ◊ **thinfilm technology**

thick·head /thík hèd/ *n.* an offensive term that deliberately insults somebody's intelligence (*informal insult*) —**thick·head·ed** *adj.* —**thick·head·ed·ness** *n.*

thick·ness /thíknəss/ *n.* **1. THICK QUALITY** the quality or state of being thick **2. DIMENSION** the dimension between two surfaces of an object, especially the shortest dimension as opposed to the width or the length **3. LAYER** an individual layer **4. THICK PART** a part of something that is thick

thick·set /thík sèt/ *adj.* **1. OF STOCKY BUILD** with a stocky physique **2. DENSE** growing closely together

thick-skinned *adj.* **1. UNSYMPATHETIC** insensitive to other people's feelings or circumstances **2. IMPERVIOUS TO CRITICISM** not easily offended by criticism or insults

thick-wit·ted *adj.* lacking intelligence (*insult*) —**thick-wit·ted·ly** *adv.* —**thick-wit·ted·ness** *n.*

thief /theef/ (*plural* **thieves** /theevz/) *n.* somebody who steals something, especially with the intention of escaping notice [Old English *þēof*] —**thiev·ish** /theévish/ *adj.* —**thiev·ish·ly** /theévishlee/ *adv.* —**thiev·ish·ness** /-nəss/ *n.*

thief ant *n.* any small ant that pillages the colonies of other ants, taking food stores and even the young of the colony

thieve /theev/ (**thieved, thiev·ing, thieves**) *vti.* to steal things [Old English *þēofian*, from *þēof* "thief"] —**thiev·e·ry** (*plural* **-ries**) *n.*

thigh /thī/ *n.* **1. TOP PART OF LEG** the top of the leg between the knee and the hip **2. UPPER PART OF ANIMAL'S LEG** the part of an animal's leg that corresponds to a human thigh [Old English *þēoh*. Ultimately from an Indo-European base meaning "to swell," which is also the ancestor of English *thumb*, *tumor*, and *thousand*.]

thigh·bone /thī bōn/ *n.* = **femur** *n.* 1

thig·mo·tax·is /thìgmə táksiss/ *n.* BIOL = **stereotaxis** [Early 20thC. Coined from Greek *thigma* "touch" + -TAXIS.] —**thig·mo·tac·tic** *adj.* —**thig·mo·tac·ti·cal·ly** /-táktikəlee/ *adv.*

thig·mot·ro·pism /thig móttrə pìzzəm/ *n.* a directional growth movement (**tropism**) of a plant part, especially a tendril, in response to physical contact with a surface [Early 20thC. Coined from Greek *thigma* "touch" + TROPISM.] —**thig·mo·trop·ic** *adj.*

thill /thil/ *n.* one of the two shafts of a carriage or wagon [15thC. Origin uncertain: perhaps from Old English *þille* "plank."]

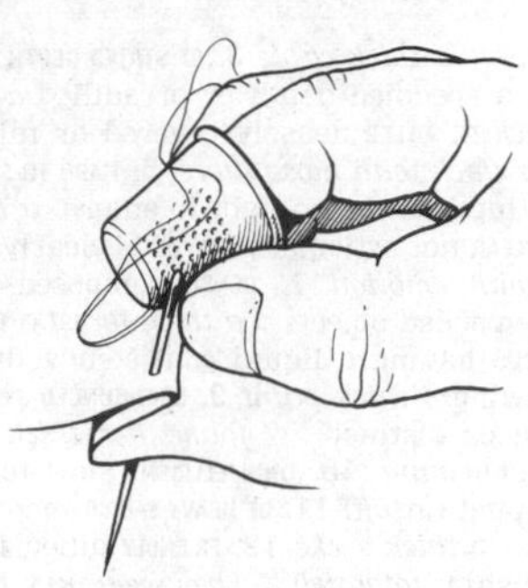

Thimble

thim·ble /thímb'l/ *n.* **1. COVER FOR FINGER WHEN SEWING** a small protective cap for a finger, used to push a needle through fabric **2.** NAUT **RING PROTECTING LOOP FROM WEAR** a metal ring, concave on the outside, that fits into a loop in a rope or an eye in a sail **3.** MECH ENG **METAL SLEEVE** any small metal tube or sleeve used in machinery [Old English *þȳmel* "leather thumb protector," from *þūma* (see THUMB)]

thim·ble·ber·ry /thímb'l bèrree/ (*plural* **-ries**) *n.* a North American raspberry with red or dark-purple thimble-shaped fruit. Latin name: *Rubus parviflorus* and *Rubus occidentalis* and *Rubus odoratus.*

thim·ble·ful /thímb'l fòol/ *n.* a very small amount of liquid

thim·ble·rig /thímb'l rìg/ *n.* **1. GUESSING GAME USING TRICKERY** a trick in which a participant guesses which of three cups covers an object after somebody has moved them about, using sleight of hand to change the object's location **2. SOMEBODY MOVING CUP** somebody moving the cup in thimblerig ■ *vt.* (**-rigged, -rig·ging, -rigs**) **SWINDLE** to cheat or swindle somebody [Early 19thC. From THIMBLE + RIG².] —**thim·ble·rig·ger** *n.*

thim·ble·weed /thímb'l weed/ *n.* a North American plant of the buttercup family with white flowers and a thimble-shaped fruiting head. Latin name: *Anemone virginiana* and *Anemone cylindrica.*

thi·mer·o·sal /thī mérrə sàl/ *n.* a cream-colored mercury compound used as a local antiseptic. Formula: $C_9H_9HgNaO_2S$. [Mid-20thC. Origin uncertain: probably a contraction of THIO- + MERCURY + SALICYLATE.]

Thim·phu /thímfoo/, **Thim·bu** /thímboo/ capital city of Bhutan, situated in the western part of the country at an altitude of 7,770 ft./2,368 m. Population: 30,340 (1993).

thin /thin/ *adj.* (**thin·ner, thin·nest**) **1. SHALLOW OR NARROW** of relatively small extent from surface to surface or side to side ○ *A thin layer of snow covered the path.* ○ *Draw a thin line.* **2. OF SMALL DIAMETER** having a small diameter ○ *thin wire* **3. SLIM** with little body fat **4. SPARSE** composed of few things widely spaced ○ *thin hair* ○ *a thin forest* **5. WATERY** with a free-flowing consistency similar to that of water ○ *a thin soup* ○ *thin paint* **6. LIGHTWEIGHT** made of light or flimsy material ○ *a thin summer dress* ○ *thin cotton socks* **7. EASY TO SEE THROUGH** permitting light to enter or pass through ○ *thin mist* **8. QUIET** lacking volume or resonance ○ *a thin sound* **9. WEAK** lacking intensity or color **10. UNCONVINCING** lacking credibility or adequacy ○ *a thin excuse* **11.** PHOTOGRAPHY **LACKING CONTRAST** of a photographic negative, lacking density or contrast ■ *adv.* **MAKING THIN LAYER** in a way that produces something shallow, narrow, or sparse ○ *Spread the paint thin.* ■ *vti.* (**thinned, thin·ning, thins**) **MAKE OR BECOME THINNER** to reduce something in thickness or number or to become reduced in thickness or number ○ *You can thin down the paint before you use it.* ○ *The crowd started to thin out in the evening.* [Old English *þynne.* Ultimately from an Indo-European base meaning "to stretch," which is also the ancestor of English *tense, tenuous,* and *tone.*] —**thin·ly** *adv.* —**thin·ness** *n.*

WORD KEY: SYNONYMS

thin, lean, slim, slender, emaciated, scrawny, skinny, scraggy

CORE MEANING: without much flesh, the opposite of fat

thin a general word used to describe somebody with little or no spare flesh on his or her body. It can also be used to describe animals. It can be used fairly neutrally, but is often seen as implying disapproval; **lean** used showing approval to describe a person or animal that is muscular and fit-looking without excess fat; **slim** used showing approval to describe somebody who is not at all fat; **slender** used showing approval to describe somebody who is not at all fat, especially somebody who appears graceful and fragile as a result; **emaciated** a fairly formal word used to describe a person or animal who is unhealthily thin, usually because of illness or starvation; **scrawny** describes a person or animal who is so thin as to appear undernourished; **skinny** an informal word meaning extremely thin; **scraggy** used with the same meaning as "scrawny."

thine /thīn/ *pron., adj.* belonging to or associated with you, when "you" is singular (*archaic*) (*used before a vowel*) ○ (pron) *Thine is the womb where our riches have birth.* ○ (adj) *Know thine enemy.* [Old English *þīn,* a possessive form of *þū* (see THOU)]

thin-film tech·nol·o·gy *n.* a method of fabricating electronic circuitry in which a thin layer of semiconductor is applied to a glass or ceramic support. Wiring and passive components, e.g., resistors, are then added. ◊ **thickfilm technology**

thing /thing/ *n.* **1. OBJECT** an inanimate object ○ *What's that thing over there?* **2. UNSPECIFIED ITEM** an unnamed or unspecified object ○ *I need a few things in town.* **3. OCCURRENCE** something that occurs or something that is done ○ *The fire was a terrible thing.* **4. WORD OR THOUGHT** a thought or an utterance ○ *Don't say another thing!* **5. DETAIL** a piece of information ○ *You forgot one important thing.* **6. AIM** the objective of an action ○ *The thing is to win.* **7. CONCERN** a matter of responsibility or concern ○ *I have several things to do.* **8. DEED** an act or deed ○ *She promises to do great things.* **9. LIVING CREATURE** a person or animal, often spoken of affectionately ○ *The poor thing was soaked to the bone.* **10. GARMENT** an article of clothing ○ *This old thing?* **11. PREFERRED ACTIVITY** a favorite activity or special interest (*informal*) ○ *Golf's not really my thing.* **12. WHAT CAN BE POSSESSED** an object or right that can be possessed or owned **13. FASHION** the fashion (*informal*) ○ *When we were young, we considered it the latest thing.* **14. STRONG LIKE OR DISLIKE** a particularly strong feeling of attraction or repulsion (*informal*) ○ *He's got a thing about spiders.* **15. IDEAL** what is needed or desirable (*informal*) ○ *Iced tea would be just the thing.* ■ **things** *npl.* **1. BELONGINGS** personal items owned or carried ○ *You can leave your things in my room.* **2. APPARATUS** equipment for a particular activity ○ *a drawer for all my writing things* **3. AFFAIRS** general matters or circumstances ○ *How are things today?* [Old English *þing* "assembly." From a prehistoric Germanic word meaning "time" (from the idea of an "appointed time"). The sense "unspecified object" evolved via "matter for discussion" and "matter."] ◇ **be on to a good thing** to know something advantageous, or know about something that will give you an advantage ◇ **first thing 1.** very early in the morning **2.** before doing anything else ◇ **it comes to the same thing** it has the same result ◇ **make a (big) thing of something** to exaggerate the importance of something and make a fuss about it

WORD KEY: ORIGIN

The long-lost ancestral meaning of ***thing*** is "time" (the related Gothic *theihs,* for example, meant "time"). Its prehistoric Germanic precursor evolved semantically via "appointed time" to "judicial or legislative assembly." This was the meaning it originally had in English, and it survives in other Germanic languages (the Icelandic parliament is known as the *Althing,* literally "general assembly"). In English, however, the word moved on through "subject for discussion in such an assembly" to "subject in general, affair, matter" and finally "entity, object."

thing·a·ma·jig /thíngəmə jìg/, **thing·um·a·jig, thing·a·ma·bob** /thíngəmə bòb/, **thingumabob** /thíngəmee/, **thing·um·my** (*plural* **-mies**) *n.* a word used when the proper word for something is not known or does not come to mind (*informal*) [Early 19thC. Formed from obsolete *thingum* (see THINGUMMY) + JIG.]

thing-in-it·self (*plural* **things-in-them·selves**) *n.* an object that exists even though we have no experience or perception of it [Translation of German *Ding an sich*]

thing·ness /thíngnəss/ *n.* status as a material thing, as distinct from something that is abstract

thing·um·a·bob *n.* = **thingamajig** (*informal*)

thing·um·a·jig *n.* = **thingamajig** (*informal*)

thing·um·my *n.* = **thingamajig** (*informal*) [Late 18thC. Alteration of obsolete *thingum,* from THING.]

think *regional* /thingk/ *v.* (**thought** *or* **thunk, thought** /thawt/ *or* **thunk** /thungk/, **think·ing, thinks**) **1.** *vti.* **FORM THOUGHTS** to use the mind to consider ideas and make judgments ○ *Think carefully before you start writing.* **2.** *vt.* **HAVE AS AN OPINION** to believe something or have something as an opinion ○ *I don't think it will rain today.* ○ *She seems to think she's a good dancer.* **3.** *vti.* **COMPREHEND SOMETHING** to imagine or understand something or the possibility of something ○ *I can't think of letting you leave so soon.* **4.** *vti.* **HAVE IN MIND** to bring something to mind ○ *I can't think what the date is today.* ○ *I hadn't thought about him for months.* **5.** *vt.* **CONCENTRATE ON** to focus the attention on something ○ *He thinks golf day and night.* **6.** *vi.* **HAVE REGARD** to regard somebody with care or concern ○ *You need to think of your family.* **7.** *vt.* **VIEW IN CERTAIN WAY** to regard somebody or something in a specified way ○ *Don't think me unkind.* **8.** *vti.* **INTEND** to have something as a plan ○ *She thought she'd go out after dinner.* **9.** *vt.* **FORESEE** to anticipate something happening ○ *I didn't think he'd actually do it.* **10.** *vt.* **BE HEEDFUL OF** to be attentive or considerate enough to do something ○ *Didn't you think to ask about her mother?* **11.** *vi.* **CHOOSE** to make a mental choice ○ *Think of a card and I'll try to guess what it is.* **12.** *vt.* **INFLUENCE WITH THE MIND** to bring something to a particular condition using the mind ○ *Try to think the pain away.* ■ *n.* **SPELL OF THINKING** an act of thinking or a period of time spent thinking (*informal*) ○ *She sat down to have a think.* [Old English *þencan*] —**think·er** *n.* ◇ **have got another think coming** used to say that somebody is mistaken (*informal*) ○ *If he thinks I'm going to help him he's got another think coming.* ◇ **not think much of somebody** *or* **something** to regard somebody or something as not being very good ◇ **think better of something** to change an opinion about something after consideration ○ *She was about to speak her mind, but then thought better of it.* ◇ **think nothing of something** to regard something as not being unusual ○ *She thinks nothing of working all night to finish a project.* ◇ **think twice** to consider something very carefully ○ *You should think twice about lending them so much money.*

think over *vt.* to reflect on something ○ *Maybe you'd like to think it over before you sign.*

think through *vt.* to consider or reflect on something carefully, especially in order to reach a decision ○ *I needed some time to think it through.*

think up *vt.* to invent or devise something ○ *I've thought up an easy way to do it.*

think·a·ble /thíngkəb'l/ *adj.* **1. UNDERSTANDABLE** capable of being understood **2. FEASIBLE** capable of happening —**think·a·bly** *adv.*

think·ing /thíngking/ *adj.* **RATIONAL** capable of using the mind to reason or reflect ○ *the thinking person's choice* ■ *n.* **1. FORMING OF THOUGHTS** use of the mind to form thoughts ○ *There's a lot of thinking to do before we make that decision.* **2. JUDGMENT** opinions or conclusions arrived at ○ *What's your thinking on the political situation?*

think·ing cap ◇ **put your thinking cap on** to think carefully about something, especially to find a solution to a problem

think piece *n.* an article giving somebody's analysis or opinion of a situation or event, written to provoke thought

think tank *n.* a committee of experts that undertakes research or gives advice, especially to a government

thin·ner /thínnər/ *n.* a liquid used to dilute paint or varnish. Turpentine is a thinner.

thin-skinned *adj.* **1. SENSITIVE TO CRITICISM** easily offended by criticism or insults **2. WITH THIN PEEL** covered in a thin peel or rind

thi·o·car·ba·mide /thī ō kaárbə mīd/ *n.* = **thiourea**

thi·o·cy·a·nate /thī ō sī́ ə nàyt/ *n.* a salt or ester of thiocyanic acid

thi·o·cy·an·ic ac·id /thī ō sī ànnik-/ *n.* a colorless liquid used in the form of salts or esters in insecticides. Formula: HSCN.

Thi·o·kol /thī́ ə kàwl/ *tdmk.* a trademark for a polysulfide polymer available in various formulations and used in coatings, sealants, hoses for gasoline and oil, and in other industrial applications

thi·ol /thī́ àwl/ *n.* an organic compound similar to an alcohol but in which the oxygen atom has been replaced by a sulfur atom. Thiols are liquids with penetrating unpleasant smells. [Late 19thC. Coined from THIO- + -OL.]

thi·on·ic /thī ónnik/ *adj.* relating to, derived from, or containing sulfur [Late 19thC. Formed from Greek *theion* "sulfur."]

thi·o·nyl /thī́ ə nìl/ *n.* containing the chemical group SO [Mid-19thC. Coined from THIO- + -IN + -YL.]

thi·o·pen·tal so·di·um /thī ə pent'l-/ *n.* a substance used intravenously as a general anesthetic and in psychotherapy as a hypnotic. Formula: $C_{11}H_{17}N_2O_2SNa$.

thi·o·pen·tone so·di·um /thī ō pèn tōn-/ *n.* U.K. = **thiopental sodium**

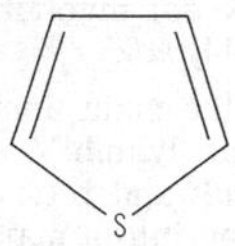

Thiophen

thi·o·phen /thī́ əfən, -ə fèn/, **thi·o·phene** /thī́ ə fe͞en/ *n.* a colorless liquid used as a solvent and to make dyes, pharmaceuticals, and resins. Formula: C_4H_4S. [Late 19thC. Coined from THIO- + PHENO-.]

thi·o·sul·fate /thī ō súl fàyt/ *n.* a salt or ester of thiosulfuric acid

thi·o·sul·fu·ric ac·id /thī ō sul fyo͝orik-/ *n.* an acid known in the form of salts or esters or in solution. Formula: $H_2S_2O_3$.

thi·o·te·pa /thee ō te͞epə/ *n.* a compound used in the treatment of malignant tumors. Formula: $C_6H_{12}N_3PS$. [Mid-20thC. Coined from THIO- + tepa, name of a compound, an acronym formed from TRI-, ETHYLENE, PHOSPHORUS and AMIDE.]

thi·o·ur·a·cil /thī ō yo͝orə sìl/ *n.* a white bitter-tasting substance used in the treatment of hyperthyroidism. Formula: $C_4H_4N_2OS$.

thi·o·u·re·a /thī ō yo͝oree ə/ *n.* a crystalline substance used to make resins and in photographic fixing. Formula: $CS(NH_2)_2$.

third /thurd/ *n.* **1.** ONE OF THREE PARTS one of three equal parts of something **2.** ORDINAL NUMBER CORRESPONDING TO 3 the ordinal number assigned to item number 3 in a series **3.** ONE AFTER SECOND IN IMPORTANCE somebody or something ranking next after second in authority or precedence **4.** VEHICLE GEAR in a motor vehicle, the forward gear between second and fourth **5.** = **third base 6.** MUSIC MUSICAL INTERVAL in a standard musical scale, the interval between one note and another that lies two notes above or below it. In the scale of C major, C and E form a third. **7.** MUSIC NOTE A THIRD AWAY FROM ANOTHER in a standard musical scale, a note that is a third away from another note **8.** MUSIC HARMONIC a harmonic of a combination of two tones a third apart **9.** EDUC UNIVERSITY DEGREE the lowest class of honors degree awarded by a British university **10.** BALLET = **third position** [Old English *thirdda, thridda.* Ultimately from an Indo-European base meaning "three," which is also the ancestor of English *three.*] —**third** *adj., adv.*

WORD KEY: CULTURAL NOTE

The Third Man, a movie by British director Sir Carol Reed (1949). Set in Vienna immediately after World War II, this stylish and gripping movie noir recounts American writer Holly Martins's attempts to discover the truth behind the mysterious death of his old friend Harry Lime. It is made particularly memorable by its dramatic war-ravaged setting, innovative lighting and editing, and haunting zither theme.

third base *n.* **1.** THIRD OF FOUR BASES IN BASEBALL the base to the batter's left that is the third of four bases on the baseball diamond and that must be touched safely to score a run **2.** FIELDER'S POSITION the position played by the fielder playing nearest to third base —**third base·man** *n.*

third class *n.* **1.** THIRD IN A CLASSIFICATION SYSTEM the next below second in grade or category **2.** CHEAPEST ACCOMMODATION the least expensive and least luxurious accommodation on a ship or train **3.** MAIL CLASS a class of mail in the United States and Canada for unsealed printed matter —**third-class** *adj., adv.*

third de·gree *n.* intensive interrogation, often also implying rough treatment (*informal*) ○ *The interrogators gave the suspects the third degree.* [From the interrogation required to reach the "third degree," the highest rank in Freemasonry]

WORD KEY: SYNONYMS

See Synonyms at ***question***.

third-de·gree burn *n.* a burn of the most serious kind, in which the skin and the tissues beneath it are severely damaged

third di·men·sion *n.* **1.** DEPTH the added dimension of depth that distinguishes a solid object from one that is two-dimensional or planar **2.** ENHANCING QUALITY a quality that makes something more vivid —**third-di·men·sion·al** *adj.*

third es·tate *n.* the third social class, traditionally the commons, in a society divided into estates

third eye·lid *n.* = **nictitating membrane**

third force *n.* a group that mediates between two opposing political groups or parties

third·hand /thurd hánd/ *adj., adv.* **1.** TWICE PREVIOUSLY OWNED used by, or after having been used by, two previous owners **2.** TWICE PREVIOUSLY COMMUNICATED from or through two intermediate sources [Mid-16thC. Modeled on SECONDHAND.]

third·ly /thúrdlee/ *adv.* used to introduce the third point in an argument or discussion

third mar·ket *n.* the over-the-counter trading of securities listed on a stock exchange

third par·ty *n.* **1.** SOMEBODY INVOLVED BY CHANCE somebody who is involved in a legal matter incidentally, as distinct from the principal parties ○ *The signatures need to be witnessed by a third party.* **2.** THIRD MAJOR POLITICAL PARTY a major political party that operates for a limited time in opposition to the two parties usually operating in a state or nation with a two-party system

third per·son *n.* **1.** GRAM VERB OR PRONOUN FORM the form of a verb or a pronoun indicating somebody or something being spoken about. In English, the third-person subject pronouns are "he," "she," "it," "one," and "they." **2.** GRAM SET OF GRAMMATICAL FORMS the grammatical set containing the forms indicating the third person **3.** WRITING IN THIRD-PERSON a style of writing using third-person forms ○ *Write your account in the third person.*

third po·si·tion *n.* a position in ballet in which the feet are turned outward with the heel of the front foot touching the instep of the back foot

third rail *n.* a rail from which some electrically powered trains pick up current

third-rate *adj.* of a low or the lowest quality

third read·ing *n.* the third presentation of a bill to a legislative assembly. In the U.K. Parliament, it is to discuss a committee's report. In the U.S. Congress, it is the final presentation before a vote.

Third Reich *n.* the Nazi regime in Germany between 1933 and 1945

Third Re·pub·lic *n.* the French system of government set up after Napoleon III's reign. It lasted until 1940.

third-stream *n.* music that draws from both classical music and jazz [Mid-20thC. Modeled on MAINSTREAM.] —**third-stream** *adj.*

Third World, **third world** *n.* the nations outside the capitalist industrial nations of the First World and the industrialized Communist nations of the Second World, generally less economically advanced but with varied economies (*hyphenated when used before a noun*) [Translation of French *tiers monde*] —**Third World·er** *n.*

Thirl·mere, Lake /thúrl meer/ lake in Cumbria, in northwestern England, that serves as a main reservoir for Manchester. Length: 3.25 mi./5 km.

thirst /thurst/ *n.* NEED FOR LIQUID a desire or need to drink a liquid, or the feeling of dryness in the mouth and throat caused by a need for a liquid ■ *vi.* (**thirst·ed, thirst·ing, thirsts**) EXPERIENCE THIRST to feel a thirst for a liquid ■ *n.* CRAVING a strong desire for something ○ *a thirst for knowledge* ■ *vi.* (**thirst·ed, thirst·ing, thirsts**) TO DESIRE to desire something strongly ○ *thirsted for news of home* [Old English *þurst.* Ultimately from an Indo-European base meaning "to be dry," which is also the ancestor of English *terrain* and *toast.*] —**thirst·er** *n.*

thirst·y /thúrstee/ (**-i·er, -i·est**) *adj.* **1.** NEEDING LIQUID feeling the need to drink a liquid ○ *Gardening always makes me thirsty.* **2.** LACKING WATER having insufficient water, especially in the form of irrigation ○ *The land was thirsty for rain.* **3.** DESIRING having a strong desire or craving ○ *thirsty for companionship* **4.** CAUSING THIRST causing the need to drink a liquid (*informal*) ○ *thirsty work* —**thirst·i·ly** *adv.* —**thirst·i·ness** *n.*

thir·teen /thər te͞en/ *n.* **1.** NUMBER 13 the number 13 **2.** SOMETHING WITH VALUE OF THIRTEEN something in a numbered series with a value of thirteen **3.** GROUP OF THIRTEEN a group of thirteen objects or people [Old English *þrēotīne*, from *þrēo* "three" (see THREE) + *-tīne* "ten"]

thir·teenth /thər te͞enth/ *n.* **1.** ONE OF 13 PARTS one of thirteen equal parts of something **2.** ORDINAL NUMBER CORRESPONDING TO 13 the ordinal number assigned to item number thirteen in a series **3.** MUSIC MUSICAL NOTE the note an octave and a sixth above the principal note in a musical scale —**thir·teenth** *adj., adv.*

thir·ti·eth /thúrtee ith/ *n.* **1.** ONE OF 30 PARTS OF SOMETHING one of thirty equal parts of something **2.** ORDINAL NUMBER CORRESPONDING TO 30 the ordinal number assigned to item number thirty in a series —**thir·ti·eth** *adj., adv.*

thir·ty /thúrtee/ *n.* (*plural* **-ties**) **1.** NUMBER 30 the number 30 **2.** GROUP OF 30 a group of thirty objects or people **3.** TENNIS SCORE IN TENNIS in a game of tennis, the score awarded to a player with a score of fifteen on winning a further point ■ **thir·ties** *npl.* **1.** NUMBERS 30 TO 39 the numbers 30 to 39, particularly as a range of temperature ○ *in the low thirties* **2.** YEARS 1930 TO 1939 the years 1930 to 1939 **3.** PERIOD FROM AGE 30 TO 39 the period of somebody's life from the age of 30 to 39 [Old English *þritig.* Ultimately from the Indo-European word for "three."]

thir·ty-eight *n.* a handgun with a .38 caliber.

thir·ty-sec·ond note *n.* MUSIC a note with the time value of one thirty-second of a whole note

thir·ty-thir·ty *n.* a rifle that fires a .30 caliber cartridge with a 30-grain powder charge, usually written .30-.30.

thir·ty-three *n.* MUSIC a long-playing record (*dated*) [From its playing speed of $33\frac{1}{3}$ rpm]

thir·ty-two·mo /thùrtee to͞o mṑ/ (*plural* **thir·ty-two·mos**) *n.* PRINTING **1.** PAPER SIZE a size of page that is formed when a standard printing sheet is cut or folded into 32 leaves or 64 pages **2.** BOOK WITH THIRTY-TWOMO PAGES a book made with thirty-twomo pages [Late 18thC. Pronunciation of the printer's abbreviation *32mo.*]

this /thiss/ (*plural* **these**) CORE MEANING: a grammatical word used to indicate somebody or something that has already been mentioned or identified or something that is understood by both the speaker and hearer ○ (adj) *This book is brilliant* ○ (adj) *This holiday — how much is it going to cost?* ○ (pron) *Is this why you've been so happy lately?* ○ (pron) *I first encountered this while traveling abroad*

1. *adj., pron.* CLOSE BY indicating somebody or something present or close by, especially as distinct from somebody or something further away, referred to as "that" ○ (adj) *I much prefer this painting to that one* ○ (pron) *What's this?* **2.** *adj., pron.* INDICATING WORDS TO FOLLOW used to indicate a phrase or statement about to be said ○ (adj) *All I can say is this — he hadn't called by the time I left.* ○ (pron) *Hey, listen to this!* **3.** *pron., adj.* A STATED TIME used to refer to a particular time in the past or present ○ (pron) *I expected him back before this.* ○ (adj) *At this particular moment she felt she'd never experience such happiness again.* **4.** *adj.* NOT PREVIOUSLY MENTIONED used to indicate somebody or something not previously mentioned, especially when telling a story to give a sense of immediacy (*informal*) ○ (adj) *Then this woman came running up to me, shouting at the top of her voice.* **5.** *adv.* TO THIS DEGREE used to emphasis the degree of a feeling or quality ○ *I was this close to quitting* [Old English *þis, þes*] ◇ **this and that** miscellaneous unimportant things

this·a·way /thíssə wày/ *adv.* this way (*regional*)

This·be *n.* MYTHOL ➧ **Pyramus and Thisbe**

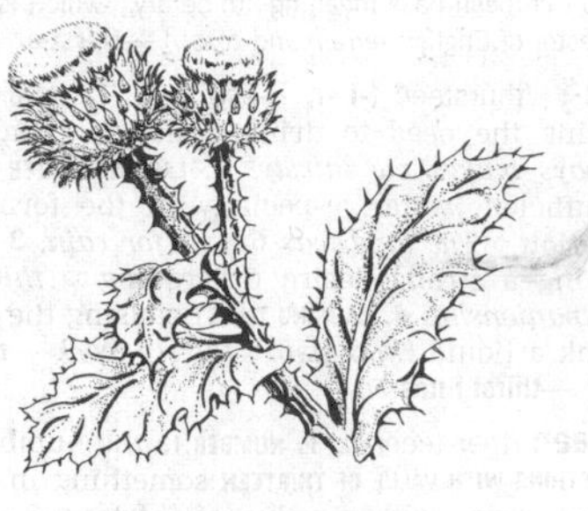

Thistle

this·tle /thíss'l/ *n.* **1. PRICKLY WEED** a prickly composite plant with dense, usually purple, flower heads surrounded by thorny bracts. Genera: *Carduus* and *Cirsium* and *Onopordum.* **2. PLANT RESEMBLING THISTLE** any of various prickly plants similar to a thistle [Old English *þistel*]

this·tle but·ter·fly *n.* = **painted lady** [So called because its larvae live on thistles]

this·tle·down /thíss'l dòwn/ *n.* **1. FLUFFY SEED MASS** the fluffy mass of hairs attached to the seeds of the mature flower head of a thistle **2. LIGHT FINE SILKY SUBSTANCE** anything fine and silky that resembles thistledown, e.g., a baby's hair or a delicate fabric

thist·ly /thíss'lee/ (**-li·er, -li·est**) *adj.* **1. FULL OF THISTLES** full or consisting of thistles **2. AWKWARD** difficult to deal with

thith·er /thíthər/ *adv.* **IN THAT DIRECTION** to or in the direction of that place (*archaic formal*) ○ *"I will set thee on thy way to Benares, if thou goest thither, and tell thee what must be known by us."* (Rudyard Kipling, *Kim*; 1901) ■ *adj.* **MORE DISTANT** farther or on the more distant side (*archaic formal*) [Old English *þider*, an alteration (under the influence of *hider* "hither") of *þæder*, literally "to that place"]

thith·er·to /thìthər tóo, thíthər too/ *adv.* until that time (*archaic formal*) [15thC. Modeled on HITHERTO.]

thith·er·ward /thíthərwərd/ *adv.* = **thither**

thix·o·trop·ic /thìksə tróppik/ *adj.* becoming fluid when shaken or stirred and returning to a gel state when allowed to stand [Early 20thC. Coined from Greek *thixis* "touch" + -TROPIC, literally "changing at a touch."] —**thix·o·trope** /thíksə trōp/ *n.* —**thix·ot·ro·py** /thik sóttrəpee/ *n.*

Th.M. *abbr.* Master of Theology [Latin, Theologiae Magister]

tho /thō/ *adv., conj.* though (*informal*)

thole[1] /thōl/ *n.* = **tholepin** [Old English *þol*. Ultimately from an Indo-European base meaning "to stick out," which is also the ancestor of English *tumor* and *tuber*.]

thole[2] /thōl/ *vt. Scotland, N England* to experience or bear something such as pain or grief patiently or uncomplainingly [Old English *þolian*. Ultimately from an Indo-European base meaning "to support, lift up," which is also the ancestor of English *tolerate* and *extol*.]

thole·pin /thṓl pìn/ *n.* a small upright wooden peg in the gunwale of a boat, usually provided in pairs to support an oar and act as a pivot when the oar is used

tho·los /thṓ lòss/ (*plural* **-loi** /-lòy/) *n.* an ancient Greek circular domed building, especially a Mycenaean drystone tomb [Mid-17thC. From Greek.]

Thom·as /tómməss/ *n.* in the New Testament, one of the 12 apostles of Jesus Christ. His reluctance to recognize Jesus Christ's resurrection until he had seen and touched his wounds gave rise to the phrase "doubting Thomas" (John 14:1–7, John 20:19–29).

Thom·as /tómməss/, **Clarence** (*b.* 1948) U.S. Supreme Court justice. A prominent African American conservative who opposed minority preference programs, he became associate justice of the U.S. Supreme Court (1991).

Thom·as, Dylan (1914–53) Welsh poet. His best known work includes the poem "Fern Hill" and the radio play *Under Milk Wood* (1954).

Tho·mism /tṓ mìzzəm/ *n.* the philosophical and theological doctrines of Thomas Aquinas, which formed the basis of medieval scholasticism [Early 18thC. Formed from the name of St. THOMAS.] —**Tho·mist** *n., adj.* —**Tho·mis·tic** /tō místik/ *adj.*

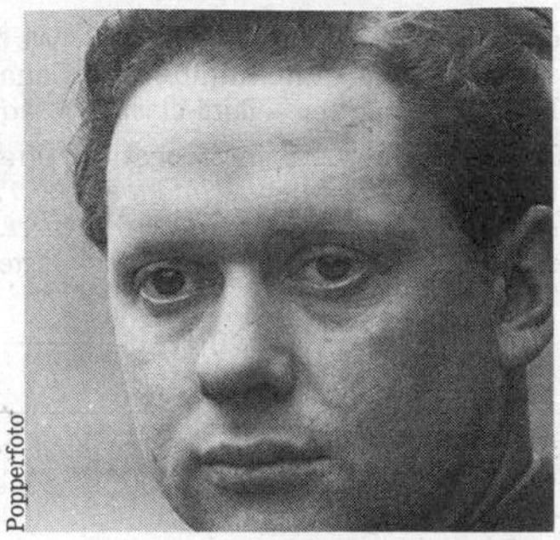

Popperfoto

Dylan Thomas

Thomp·son /tómps'n/ **1.** the main tributary of the Fraser River in southern British Columbia, Canada. Length: 304 mi./489 km. **2.** city in central Manitoba, Canada, on the Burntwood River. Population: 14,385 (1996).

Thomp·son, Daley (*b.* 1958) British athlete. In the decathlon he was Olympic gold medalist (1980 and 1984) and world champion (1983). Real name **Francis Morgan Thompson**

Thomp·son, David (1770–1857) British-born Canadian explorer. He was the first to map comprehensively Canada's western territories.

Thomp·son, Hunter S. (*b.* 1939) U.S. journalist. An iconoclastic commentator on American culture, his *Fear and Loathing in Las Vegas* (1972) exemplifies the style of writing dubbed New Journalism. Full name **Hunter Stockton Thompson**

Thomp·son, Sir John Sparrow David (1845–94) Canadian lawyer and statesman. He was prime minister of Canada from 1892 to 1894.

Thomp·son sub·ma·chine-gun /tómsən-/ *n.* a relatively lightweight submachine-gun introduced in 1915. It was intended as an infantry weapon. [Early 20thC. Named for U.S. army officer John T. *Thompson* (1860–1940), whose company manufactured it.]

Thom·son /tómsən/, **Charles Edward Poulett, 1st Baron of Sydenham** (1799–1841) British colonial administrator. He was governor general of Canada (1839–41) and worked to unite Upper and Lower Canada (1840).

Thom·son, Virgil (1896–1989) U.S. composer and critic. His symphonies, ballets, and musical "portraits" draw on American folk tunes, and include the Pulitzer Prize-winning score for the documentary movie *Louisiana Story* (1948). Full name **Virgil Garnett Thomson**

Thom·son ef·fect /tómsən-/ *n.* the phenomenon of temperature differences within a conductor or semiconductor causing an electric potential gradient [Late 19thC. Named for William *Thomson* (William KELVIN), who described the phenomenon.]

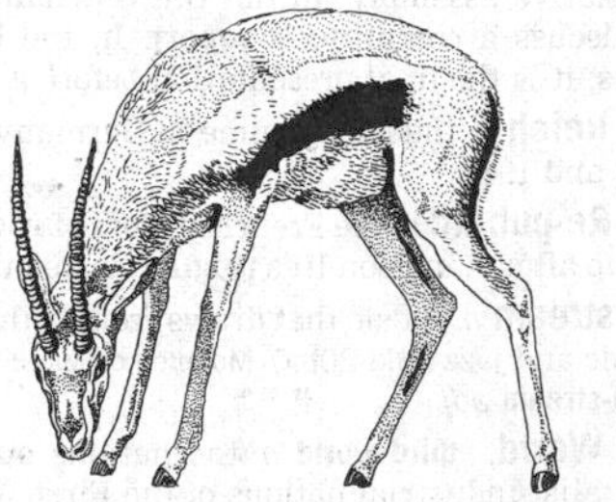

Thomson's gazelle

Thom·son's ga·zelle *n.* a small gazelle that has a broad black stripe on its side and is found in the grasslands and dry woodlands of Africa. Latin name: *Gazella thomsoni.* [Late 19thC. Named for the Scottish explorer Joseph *Thomson* (1858–94).]

-thon *suffix.* a long session devoted to a single activity ○ *talkathon* [From MARATHON]

thong /thong/ *n.* **1. LONG THIN PIECE OF LEATHER** a thin strip of something, especially leather, used for fastening or supporting things **2. WHIP** a whip made of braided leather, cord, or some other material **3. CLOTHES LIGHT SANDAL** a light sandal held on by strips of material that join the sole of the sandal at either side of the foot and between the first and second toes **4. BIKINI OR UNDERWEAR BOTTOM** a narrow piece of cloth or leather that goes between the legs and is attached to a band around the hips, worn as a bikini bottom or as underwear [Old English *þwong*]

Thor /thawr/ *n.* in Norse mythology, the god of thunder and eldest son of Odin. Thursday is named for him.

tho·ra·cen·te·sis /thàwrə sen teéssiss/ (*plural* **-ses** /-seez/) *n.* a surgical procedure in which a needle is inserted through the chest wall in order to withdraw fluid, blood, or air [Mid-19thC. Coined from THORACO- + Greek *kentēsis* "pricking" (from *kentein* "to prick"; source of English *center*).]

tho·ra·ces plural of **thorax**

tho·rac·ic /thə rássik/ *adj.* involving or located in the chest —**tho·rac·i·cal·ly** *adv.*

tho·rac·ic duct *n.* the main duct of the lymphatic system that drains lymph from smaller lymph vessels in the trunk and returns it to the bloodstream by emptying into a major vein. In human beings, it ascends in front of the spinal column and discharges into the left subclavian vein at the base of the neck.

thoraco- *prefix.* chest, thorax ○ *thoracolumbar* [From Greek *thōrak-*, the stem of *thōrax* (see THORAX)]

tho·ra·co·lum·bar /thàwrəkō lúmbər/ *adj.* used to describe the thoracic and lumbar areas of the body

tho·ra·cot·o·my /thàwrə kóttəmee/ (*plural* **-mies**) *n.* a surgical incision made in the chest wall

tho·rax /tháw ràks/ (*plural* **-rax·es** *or* **-ra·ces** /thə ráy seez, tháwrə-/) *n.* **1.** ANAT **UPPER PART OF TORSO** the part of the human body between the neck and abdomen, enclosed by the ribs and containing the heart and lungs **2.** ZOOL **UPPER PART OF ANIMAL'S BODY** the area corresponding to the human thorax in other vertebrates **3.** ZOOL **PART BETWEEN HEAD AND ABDOMEN** the middle division of the body of an insect, crustacean, or arachnid [14thC. Via Latin from Greek *thōrax* "chest, breastplate," of unknown origin.]

Tho·ra·zine /tháwrə zeen/ *tdmk.* a trademark for chlorpromazine

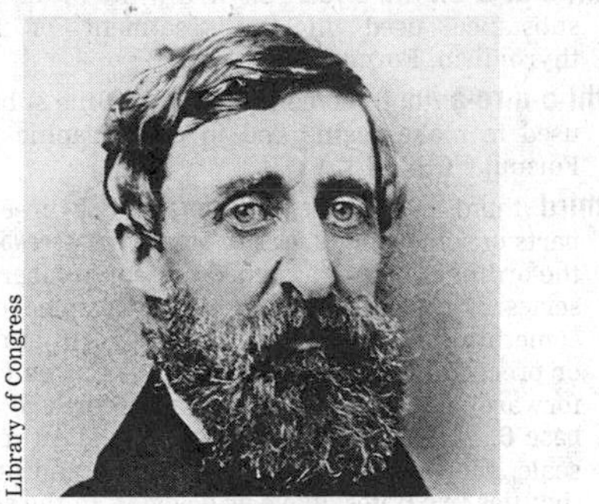

Library of Congress

Henry David Thoreau

Tho·reau /thə rṓ, thaw-, tháw rō/, **Henry David** (1817–62) U.S. essayist and philosopher. He was a leading transcendentalist and libertarian. His works include "Civil Disobedience" (1849) and *Walden* (1854), in which he describes a life lived simply and close to nature. Born **David Henry Thoreau**

tho·ri·a /tháwree ə/ *n.* = **thorium dioxide** [Mid-19thC. Formed from THORIUM, on the model of MAGNESIA.]

tho·ri·an·ite /tháwree ə nīt/ *n.* a rare black radioactive mineral that is an oxide of thorium mixed with rare-earth metals. It is used as a source of thorium and uranium. Formula: $ThO_2U_3O_8$. [Early 20thC. Coined from THORIA + -ITE.]

tho·rite /tháw rīt/ *n.* a rare brown, black, or yellow radioactive mineral that is a silicate of thorium. It is used as a source of thorium. Formula: $ThSiO_4$. [Mid-19thC. Coined from THOR + -ITE.]

tho·ri·um /tháwree əm/ *n.* a soft silvery-white radioactive metallic chemical element that is found in thorite, thorianite, and monzanite. It is used in alloys and as a source of nuclear energy. Symbol **Th** [Mid-19thC. Coined from THOR + -IUM.] —**tho·ric** *adj.*

tho·ri·um di·ox·ide *n.* a white powder that is an oxide of thorium, used in incandescent mantles, refractories, ceramics, and optical glass and as a catalyst. Formula: ThO_2.

tho·ri·um se·ries *n.* one of the natural radioactive decay series that shows how the unstable isotope thorium-232 changes by stages into the stable isotope lead-208

thorn /thawrn/ *n.* **1. SHARP POINT ON A PLANT STEM** a sharply pointed woody growth projecting from the stem of some trees, shrubs, and woody plants **2. PLANT WITH THORNS** a tree, shrub, or woody plant that has thorns **3. WOOD OF TREE WITH THORNS** the wood of a tree or shrub with thorns **4. RUNIC LETTER** a runic letter used to represent both of the "th" sounds, as in "this" and "thick," in Old English and Middle English. It also represents the voiceless sound, as in "thick," in Old Norse and Icelandic and was formerly used as a phonetic symbol. [Old English *þorn.* From a prehistoric Germanic word that is also the ancestor of Dutch *doorn* and German *Dorn.*] —**thorned** *adj.* —**thorn·less** *adj.* —**thorn·like** *adj.* ◇ **be a thorn in somebody's flesh or side** to be a source of constant irritation to somebody

thorn ap·ple *n.* **1.** *U.K.* = **jimsonweed 2. FRUIT OF HAWTHORN** the fruit of a hawthorn

thorn·back /tháwrn bàk/ (*plural* **-backs** *or* **-back**) *n.* a ray with one to three rows of large hooked spines on its back. Latin name: *Raja clavata* and *Platyrhinoidis triseriatis.*

thorn·bill /tháwrn bìl/ (*plural* **-bills** *or* **-bill**) *n.* **1. AUSTRALIAN WARBLER** a small Australian bird of the warbler family that has a short sharp bill. Genus: *Acanthiza.* **2. S AMERICAN HUMMINGBIRD** a South American hummingbird with a bill that resembles a thorn. Latin name: *Ramphomicron microrhynchum.*

Barnaby's

Dame Sybil Thorndike

Thorn·dike /tháwrn dìk/, **Dame Sybil** (1882–1976) British actor. A member of the Old Vic Theater, London, she played the title role in George Bernard Shaw's *St. Joan* more than 2,000 times after he wrote the part for her in 1924. Full name **Dame Agnes Sybil Thorndike**

Thorn·ton /tháwrnt'n/, **Matthew** (1714–1803) American patriot. He signed the Declaration of Independence (1776) as a delegate from New Hampshire.

thorn·y /tháwrnee/ (**-i·er, -i·est**) *adj.* **1. PROBLEMATIC** complicated and difficult to resolve **2. PRICKLY WITH THORNS** covered in or full of thorns —**thorn·i·ly** *adv.* —**thorn·i·ness** *n.*

tho·ron /tháw ròn/ *n.* a radioactive isotope of radon with a half-life of 55 seconds, formed by the radioactive decay of thorium [Early 20thC. Formed from THORIUM, on the model of RADON.]

thor·ough /thúrrō/ *adj.* **1. EXTREMELY CAREFUL** extremely careful and accurate in doing something ○ *She's very thorough in her research methods.* **2. DONE FULLY** complete in every detail and carried out with care ○ *The doctor gave me a thorough examination.* **3. ABSOLUTE** that is so to the fullest extent or in the truest sense of the word ○ *a thorough bore.* ■ *prep.* **THROUGH** through (*archaic*) [Old English *þuruh* "from end to end," a variant of *þurh* (see THROUGH)] —**thor·ough·ly** *adv.* —**thor·ough·ness** *n.*

WORD KEY: SYNONYMS

See Synonyms at ***careful.***

thor·ough·bass /thúrrə bàyss, thúrrə-/ *n.* = **continuo** [Mid-17thC. From THOROUGH in the obsolete sense "all the way through."]

thor·ough brace *n.* a strong leather strap running underneath a carriage from front to back, forming, with several other such straps, the carriage's support and springs [From THOROUGH in the obsolete meaning "from end to end"] —**thor·ough-braced** /thúrrə bràyst/ *adj.*

thor·ough·bred /thúrrə brèd/ *n.* **1. PUREBRED ANIMAL** a purebred animal, especially a horse **2. WELL-BRED PERSON** somebody who is has been brought up to be refined and well-mannered ■ *adj.* **1. PUREBRED** bred from pure stock **2. WELL-BRED** brought up to be refined and well-mannered [Early 18thC. From THOROUGH in the obsolete meaning "all the way through."]

Thor·ough·bred *n.* **BREED OF RACEHORSE** a pure breed of horse descended from English mares and Arabian stallions, originally bred in Britain and most often used for racing ■ *adj.* **BRED FROM THOROUGHBRED STOCK** bred from Thoroughbred stock or characteristic of it —**Thor·ough·bred** *adj.*

thor·ough·fare /thúrrə fàir/ *n.* **1. PUBLIC ROAD** a public highway that passes through a place ○ *a truck blocking a busy thoroughfare* **2. MEANS OF ACCESS** a way or passage from one place to another **3. RIGHT OF PASSAGE** the right to go from one place to another along a certain route **4. HEAVILY USED ROUTE** a stretch of road or water, or a pathway between two places, that is used by many people [14thC. From THOROUGH in the obsolete meaning "from end to end" + obsolete fare "way, journey."]

thor·ough·go·ing /thùrrō gṓ ing, thùrrə-/ *adj.* **1. THOROUGHLY DONE** carried out in an extremely careful and thorough way ○ *not very thoroughgoing when it comes to housework* **2. ABSOLUTE** that is so to the fullest extent or in the truest sense of the word ○ *a thoroughgoing pragmatist* [Early 19thC. From THOROUGH in the obsolete meaning "all the way through."]

thor·ough·paced /thùrrō páyst, thùrrə-/ *adj.* **1. TRAINED TO PERFORM ALL PACES** thoroughly trained so as to be able to perform all paces well (*refers to horses*) **2. THOROUGHGOING** thoroughgoing (*archaic*)

thor·ough·pin /thúrrō pin, thúrrə-/ *n.* inflammation and swelling above the hock joint on both sides of a horse's leg, affecting the flexor tendon and causing lameness [Late 18thC. From THOROUGH in the obsolete meaning "all the way through"; from the appearance of the swelling, like a pin passing through the tendon.]

thor·ough·wort /thúrrō wùrt, -wàwrt, thúrrə-/ (*plural* **-worts** *or* **-wort**) *n.* PLANTS = **boneset** [Late 16thC. From THOROUGH in the obsolete meaning "through," because the plant's stem appears to grow through its leaves.]

thorp /thawrp/, **thorpe** *n.* a small village (*archaic*) (*often used in place names*) [Old English *þorp* (related to Dutch *dorp* and German *Dorf*)]

Thorpe /thawrp/, **Jim** (1888–1953) U.S. athlete. One of the outstanding athletes of the 20th century, he won Olympic gold medals for the pentathlon and decathlon (1912) and played professional baseball (1913–19) and football (1917–29). Full name **James Francis Thorpe**

those /t͟hōz/ *pron., adj.* the form of "that" used before a plural noun or with a multiple referent ○ *Those are the ones I prefer.* ○ *Do you remember those outings to the seaside?* [Old English *þās* (see THESE)]

Thoth /thōth, tōt/, **Thot** *n.* in ancient Egyptian mythology, the god of the moon, associated with writing and wisdom. He is usually depicted as a man with the head of an ibis, or as a baboon. ➧ **Hermes Trismegistus**

thou[1] /thow/ (*plural* **thous** *or* **thou**) *n.* a thousand, especially when referring to money (*slang*) [Mid-19thC. Shortening of THOUSAND.]

thou[2] /t͟how/ *pron.* **1. YOU** you (*archaic or regional*) (*used in familiar address*) **2. thou, Thou YOU, GOD** used to address God, e.g., in prayers and hymns ■ *vt.* **ADDRESS SOMEBODY AS "THOU"** to address as "thou" (*archaic or regional*) [Old English *þū.* Ultimately from an Indo-European word that is also the ancestor of Latin *tu.*]

though /t͟hō/ *conj.* **ALTHOUGH** in spite of the fact that ○ *He didn't receive any special treatment, even though he is a close friend of the chairman.* ○ *Though she served as president of the student government in her senior year, she was attracted to journalism rather than politics.* ■ *adv.* **1. AND YET** indicating a statement that modifies a statement just made ○ *The weather has improved a lot, though it still doesn't feel like spring.* **2. NEVERTHELESS** follows a statement modifying the statement that preceded it [13thC. Partly from Old English *þeah* and partly Old Norse *þó.* Ultimately from an Indo-European base meaning "that," which is also the ancestor of English *the, this,* and *thus.*] ◇ **as though** as if ○ *It seems as though every week we hear about some incredible new development.*

WORD KEY: USAGE

See Usage note at ***although.***

thought[1] /thawt/ *n.* **1. THINKING** the activity or process of thinking ○ *deep in thought* **2. IDEA PRODUCED BY MENTAL ACTIVITY** an idea, plan, conception, or opinion produced by mental activity ○ *The thought had crossed my mind.* **3. SET OF IDEAS** the intellectual, scientific, and philosophical ideas associated with a particular place, time, or group ○ *medieval religious thought* **4. REASONING POWER** the ability to think and reason ○ *felt incapable of rational thought* **5. PROCESS OF CONSIDERING** the process of applying the mind to thinking about a particular person or subject ○ *I didn't give it another thought.* **6. INTENTION** an intention of doing something ○ *I had no thought of offending anybody.* **7. EXPECTATION** an expectation or hope that something will happen ○ *entertained no thoughts of failure* **8. COMPASSIONATE CONSIDERATION** a feeling of respect, affection, or consideration for somebody or something ○ *no thought for other people* **9. SMALL AMOUNT** a small amount on a comparative scale ○ *Could you be a thought quieter, please?* [Old English *þōht.* From a prehistoric Germanic base that is also the ancestor of English *think* and *thank.*] ◇ **perish the thought!** used to indicate, often humorously, that something is too terrible to be thought of

thought[2] past participle, past tense of **think**

thought·ful /tháwtfəl/ *adj.* **1. CONSIDERATE** treating people in a kind and considerate way, especially by anticipating their wants or needs **2. PENSIVE** appearing to be deep in thought **3. CAREFULLY THOUGHT OUT** showing the application of careful thought —**thought·ful·ly** *adv.* —**thought·ful·ness** *n.*

thought·less /tháwtləss/ *adj.* **1. INCONSIDERATE** showing a lack of consideration for other people or for consequences **2. DONE WITHOUT THOUGHT** showing a lack of planning or forethought **3. UNABLE TO THINK** not having or using the faculty of thought —**thought·less·ly** *adv.* —**thought·less·ness** *n.*

thought-out *adj.* showing evidence of careful planning (*usually used in combination*)

thou·sand /thówz'nd/ *n.* (*plural* **-sand** *or* **-sands**) **1. NUMBER 1,000** the number 1,000 **2. FOURTH DIGIT FROM RIGHT** the fourth digit to the left of the decimal point in the decimal number system **3. LARGE NUMBER** a very large number or amount (*informal*) ○ *must have told him a thousand times* ■ **thou·sands** *npl.* **VERY MANY** a very large but unspecified number ○ *sold thousands of copies* [Old English *þūsend.* From a prehistoric Germanic word meaning "swollen hundred"; ultimately from an Indo-European base meaning "to swell," which is also the ancestor of English *thigh, thumb,* and *tumor.*]

Thou·sand Is·land dress·ing *n.* a salmon-pink salad dressing containing mayonnaise, tomato sauce, chopped gherkins, onions, and spices [Early 20thC. Origin uncertain: perhaps named for the THOUSAND ISLANDS.]

Thou·sand Is·lands group of more than 1,000 small islands in southeastern Ontario and northern New York, in the St. Lawrence River.

thou·sandth /thówz'nth/ *n.* one of a thousand equal parts of something

thp, t.hp. *abbr.* thrust horsepower

Thrace /thráyss/ region in southeastern Europe, forming part of present-day Greece, Bulgaria, and Turkey. Area: 3,312 sq. mi./8578 sq. km.

Thra·cian /thráysh'n/ *n.* **1.** PEOPLES **SOMEBODY FROM THRACE** a member of an ancient people who inhabited Thrace **2.** LANG **ANCIENT THRACIAN LANGUAGE** the language of the ancient Thracians, which belonged to the Indo-European family ■ *adj.* PEOPLES **OF THRACE** relating to Thrace, its ancient people or culture, or their extinct language

Thra·co-Phryg·i·an /thràykō fríjjee ən/ *n.* LANG a branch of the Indo-European family of languages of which all members are now extinct with the exception of Armenian

thral·dom *n.* = **thralldom**

thrall /thrawl/ *n.* **1. SOMEBODY WHOSE LIFE IS CONTROLLED** somebody whose life is completely controlled by a more powerful person or a moral or intellectual force **2. SOMEBODY CONTROLLED BY SOMETHING** somebody who is completely controlled by a particular physical or mental need **3. DOMINATION** a condition of being controlled by a more powerful person or force (*literary*) ■ *vt.* (**thralled, thrall·ing, thralls**) **DOMINATE SOMEBODY** to control somebody completely (*archaic*) [Old English *þræl*, from Old Norse *þræll*. Ultimately from a prehistoric Germanic word meaning "to run."]

thrall·dom /thráwldəm/, **thral·dom** *n.* = **thrall** *n.* 3

thrash /thrash/ *v.* (**thrashed, thrash·ing, thrash·es**) **1.** *vt.* BEAT PERSON OR ANIMAL to beat a person or animal with a whip or stick **2.** *vt.* SPORTS DEFEAT PERSON OR TEAM DECISIVELY to defeat a person or team decisively, especially in a sporting competition ○ *The home team was thrashed in the playoffs.* **3.** *vti.* TOSS ABOUT to toss or move the body and limbs about in an uncontrolled or restless way ○ *thrashed around unable to sleep* **4.** *vi.* PADDLE WITH LEGS to move the legs up and down in the water while performing a swimming stroke **5.** *vti.* = **thresh** *v.* 1 **6.** *vti.* SAILING SAIL BOAT AGAINST TIDE OR WIND to sail a boat so that it is forcing its way against the direction of the tide or wind ■ *n.* **1.** BEATING a blow or beating with a whip or stick **2.** SOCIAL PARTY a party or celebration (*dated informal*) **3.** = **thrash metal** [Late 16thC. Variant of THRESH.]

WORD KEY: SYNONYMS

See Synonyms at ***defeat***.

thrash out *vt. U.K.* = **hash out**

thrash·er /thráshər/ *n.* **1.** BIRD WITH DOWNWARD-CURVED BILL a long-tailed brownish North American bird that has a downward-curved bill and a speckled breast. It is related to the mockingbird. Genus: *Toxostoma.* **2.** = **thresher** *n.* 3 **3.** AGRIC THRESHER OF CROPS a person or machine that threshes crops

thrash·ing /thráshing/ *n.* **1.** PHYSICAL BEATING a physical beating, e.g., with a whip or stick **2.** SPORTING DEFEAT a decisive defeat in a sporting competition

thrash met·al *n.* a very fast, often discordant, type of heavy metal music, strongly influenced by punk

thra·son·i·cal /thray sónnik'l/ *adj.* boastful (*literary*) [Mid-16thC. Formed from Greek *Thrasō*, name of an arrogant character in Terence's play *Eunuchus*.] — **thra·son·i·cal·ly** *adv.*

thread /thred/ *n.* **1.** FINE TWISTED CORD fine cord made of two or more twisted fibers, used in sewing and weaving **2.** PIECE OF THREAD a length of thread **3.** VERY THIN LINE OF SOMETHING a fine strand of solid material, trickle of liquid, or wisp of gas **4.** MECH ENG RIDGE ON SCREW the continuous helical ridge on a screw or pipe **5.** ZOOL FILAMENT OF SPIDER'S WEB one of the filaments of a spider's web **6.** SOMETHING CONNECTING ELEMENTS a continuous unifying element running through a story, argument, discussion, or series of events **7.** COMPUT ELEMENT OF DISCUSSION ON INTERNET one of a series of messages in an Internet discussion group (**forum**), commenting on or replying to a previous message **8.** HUMAN LIFE the course of human life, believed by the ancient Greeks to be spun, measured out, and cut by the Fates **9.** MINING VEIN OF ORE a thin seam of ore or coal ■ **threads** *npl.* CLOTHES CLOTHING what somebody wears (*slang*) ■ *v.* (**thread·ed, thread·ing, threads**) **1.** *vt.* PASS THROUGH SOMETHING to pass something such as thread, photographic film, magnetic tape, or ribbon through a hole or gap in something else **2.** *vt.* STRING ON THREAD to string beads or pearls on a thread **3.** *vti.* GO CAREFULLY to move along carefully, following a winding route **4.** *vt.* MECH ENG PRODUCE SCREW THREAD to produce a thread on a screw or bolt, or within a material into which a bolt or screw may be inserted **5.** *vt.* INTERSPERSE WITH SOMETHING to distribute something at intervals in something else ○ *hair threaded with gray* **6.** *vi.* COOK FORM THREAD to form a fine thread when dropped from a spoon (*refers to sugar syrup*) [Old English *þræd* "twisted cord." Ultimately from an Indo-European word meaning "to turn, twist," which is also the ancestor of English *throw*.]

thread·bare /thréd bàir/ *adj.* **1.** WORN AWAY TO REVEAL THREADS so heavily used that the soft part of the fabric has been worn away to reveal the threads beneath **2.** OVERUSED SO NO LONGER CONVINCING having been used so often so as to be no longer convincing ○ *the same old threadbare excuses* **3.** MEAGER not large, varied, or substantial enough to be satisfactory ○ *eked out a threadbare existence* **4.** SHABBILY DRESSED wearing worn-out shabby clothes —**thread·bare·ness** *n.*

thread·er /thréddər/ *n.* a device for threading a needle, consisting of a loop of extremely fine wire attached to a flat metal disk that is held between the thumb and forefinger. The loop is passed through the eye of the needle, the thread is passed through the loop, and the loop is withdrawn through the eye, taking the thread with it.

thread·fin /thréd fìn/ (*plural* **-fins** *or* **-fin**) *n.* a tropical marine fish with long rays resembling threads on the lower part of its pectoral fin and a small mouth on the underside of its head. Family: Polynemidae.

thread·worm /thréd wùrm/ *n.* a long nematode worm, such as a pinworm

thread·y /thréddee/ (**-i·er, -i·est**) *adj.* **1.** MED ONLY JUST PERCEPTIBLE used to describe a weak and barely perceptible pulse **2.** SOUNDING WEAK sounding thin and lacking in power and tone **3.** THREADLIKE resembling thread **4.** HAVING MANY THREADS consisting of or containing many threads, especially loose or visible ones **5.** COOK FORMING THREADS thick and sticky enough to form threads when dropped from a spoon or other utensil —**thread·i·ness** *n.*

threat /thret/ *n.* **1.** DECLARATION OF INTENT TO CAUSE HARM the expression of a deliberate intention to cause harm or pain **2.** INDICATION OF SOMETHING BAD a sign or danger that something undesirable is going to happen ○ *a threat of severe thunderstorms* **3.** SOMEBODY OR SOMETHING LIKELY TO CAUSE HARM a person, animal, or thing likely to cause harm or pain ○ *The dog is no threat.* ■ *vt.* (**threat·ed, threat·ing, threats**) THREATEN to threaten somebody or something (*archaic*) [Old English *þrēat* "crowd, menace." Ultimately from an Indo-European word meaning "to press in," which is also the ancestor of English *thrust* and *protrude*.]

threat·en /thrétt'n/ (**-ened, -en·ing, -ens**) *v.* **1.** *vti.* EXPRESS A THREAT TO SOMEBODY to express a deliberate intention to harm or hurt somebody unless the person does what is demanded **2.** *vti.* ENDANGER WELL-BEING to be a threat to the well-being, safety, or happiness of somebody or something **3.** *vti.* SIGNIFY SOMETHING BAD HAPPENING to signify that something bad is going to happen, especially that bad weather is going to arrive **4.** *vt.* SUGGEST IN A THREAT to suggest or announce something by means of a threat [Old English *þrēatnian*, literally "to press in on," from *þrēat* (see THREAT)] —**threat·en·er** *n.*

threat·ened /thrétt'nd/ *adj.* used to describe an organism or species that is in danger of becoming extinct (*refers to a species or organism*)

threat·en·ing /thrétt'ning/ *adj.* **1.** EXPRESSING A THREAT expressing an intention to cause somebody deliberate harm or pain **2.** likely to bring rain or severe weather ○ *a threatening sky* **3.** MAKING SOMEBODY FEEL ANXIOUS OR FEARFUL causing somebody to feel anxious, fearful, and unconfident —**threat·en·ing·ly** *adv.*

Thred·bo /thrédbō/ ski resort in the Australian Alps, New South Wales, Australia. Population: 2,100 (1996).

three /three/ *n.* **1.** MATH NUMBER 3 the number 3 **2.** SOMETHING WITH VALUE OF 3 something in a numbered series, e.g., a playing card, with a value of 3 ○ *the three of clubs* ○ *to throw a three* **3.** GROUP OF THREE a group of three objects or people [Old English *þrēotīne*. Ultimately from the Indo-European word for "three," which is also the ancestor of English *triple, triad, troika,* and *testament*.]

three-bag·ger *n.* BASEBALL a triple (*slang*)

three-base hit *n.* BASEBALL = **triple**

three-card mon·te *n.* a game in which three cards are dealt face up and then turned face down and moved around. The bettor must then guess the position of a particular card.

three-col·or *adj.* using, produced by, or relating to a color printing process in which the print is produced by superimposing separate plates for the colors yellow, magenta, and cyan

three-D, 3-D *n.* THREE DIMENSIONS a three-dimensional effect ■ *adj.* = **three-dimensional** *adj.* 1, **three-dimensional** *adj.* 2 (*informal*)

three-deck·er *n.* **1.** SOMETHING WITH THREE LEVELS a vehicle, building, or other construction with three levels or floors **2.** SHIP WITH THREE DECKS a warship with three decks set with guns, or any ship with three decks **3.** SANDWICH WITH THREE SLICES OF BREAD a sandwich consisting of two layers of filling between three slices of bread

three-di·men·sion·al *adj.* **1.** WITH THREE DIMENSIONS possessing or appearing to possess the dimensions of height, width, and depth **2.** APPEARING TO HAVE DEPTH creating the illusion of depth behind a flat surface **3.** BELIEVABLE represented with sufficient complexity to be convincing

three-field sys·tem *n.* a system of crop rotation that was in operation in western Europe by the 9th century. One-third of land was left fallow, one-third planted in spring grains, and one-third in the season's crops such as barley and vegetables.

three·fold /three fōld/ *adj.* **1.** CONSISTING OF THREE made up of three parts or elements **2.** THREE TIMES AS MANY OR MUCH being or having three times as many or as much ■ *adv.* BY THREE TIMES by three times as many or as much

three-gait·ed *adj.* able to perform the standard three paces, the walk, the trot, and the canter (*refers to horses*)

Three Kings Is·lands /three kíngz īləndz/ group of uninhabited islands 31 mi./50 km northwest of the North Island, New Zealand. The islands are a wildlife refuge. Area: 3 sq. mi./8 sq. km.

three-leg·ged race *n.* a race in which pairs of runners compete with their adjacent legs bound together

Three Mile Is·land island in the Susquehanna River, near Harrisburg, southeastern Pennsylvania. An accidental release of radiocativity at the nuclear plant on the island in 1979 led to stricter regulation of the U.S. nuclear industry.

three-mile lim·it *n.* the outer limit of a country's territorial waters, three nautical miles from shore

three·pence /thréppəns, thrúppəns/, **thrup·pence** /thrúppəns/ *n.* **1.** FORMER BRITISH COIN a coin used in the U.K. from the sixteenth century until 1971, worth three old pennies **2.** THREE PENNIES a sum of three pennies, especially old pence (*dated*) (*takes a singular verb*)

three·pen·ny /thréppənee, thrúppənee/, **thrup·pen·ny** /thrúppənee/ *adj.* (*dated*) **1.** WORTH THREE PENNIES worth or costing three pennies, especially old pence **2.** OF LITTLE VALUE worth or costing very little

three-phase *adj.* **1.** IN THREE PHASES consisting of three separate phases **2.** ELEC USING THREE ALTERNATING VOLTAGES used to describe an electrical system or circuit of three alternating voltages that have the same frequency but are separated by one third of a cycle

three-piece *adj.* IN THREE MATCHING PIECES consisting of three matching or coordinated pieces ■ *n.* SUIT OF THREE MATCHING GARMENTS a suit consisting of matching trousers or skirt, vest or blouse, and jacket

three-ply *adj.* **1.** WITH THREE LAYERS consisting of three layers or laminations **2.** WITH THREE STRANDS made up of three twisted strands ■ *n.* THREE-PLY KNITTING YARN knitting yarn made up of three twisted strands

three-point land·ing *n.* an aircraft landing in which the two main wheels of the landing gear and the nose or tail wheel touch the ground at the same time

three-quar·ter *adj.* **1.** BEING THREE FOURTHS OF SOMETHING being three fourths of something measurable or countable, e.g., length, an area, or a time interval **2.** BEING THREE QUARTERS OF FULL LENGTH being three quarters of the full or usual length **3.** ARTS WITH FACE SLIGHTLY TURNED showing the subject's face turned slightly to one side (*refers to a portrait*)

three-quar·ter bind·ing *n.* a type of binding in which the spine and most of the sides of a book are covered in the same material

three-ring cir·cus *n.* **1.** CIRCUS WITH THREE RINGS a circus in which performances take place simultaneously in three separate rings **2.** HECTIC SITUATION a situation full of activity and confusion (*informal*)

three Rs, 3 Rs *npl.* the skills of reading, writing, and arithmetic, considered as the basis of elementary education [Presumed to have originated with a toast proposed by Sir William Curtis (1752–1829), illiterate Lord Mayor of London]

three·score /three skáwr/ *adj., n.* sixty (*archaic*) ○ *threescore years and ten*

three·some /threessəm/ *n.* **1.** GROUP OF THREE a group of three people **2.** ACTIVITY FOR THREE a game or activity for three people **3.** SEXUAL EXPERIENCE a sexual experience involving three people **4.** TYPE OF GOLF GAME a golf game involving three players, one playing one ball and the other two taking alternate shots to play another ball

three-spine stick·le·back, three-spined stick·le·back *n.* a small stickleback of temperate fresh and salt water that has three dorsal spines and is found throughout the northern hemisphere. Latin name: *Gasterosteus aculeatus.*

three-square *adj.* shaped like an equilateral triangle when viewed in cross section

three strikes and you're out *n.* a law that requires mandatory life sentences for criminals convicted three times for major capital offenses

three-toed sloth *n.* a slow tree-dwelling mammal of the sloth family that has three long-clawed toes on each forefoot. Genus: *Bradypus.*

three-toed wood·peck·er *n.* either of two kinds of North American woodpeckers with three toes on each foot. Latin name: *Picoides tridactylus* and *Picoides arcticus.*

three-way *adj.* **1. WITH THREE PARTICIPANTS** involving three participating people or things **2. WITH THREE ROUTES** providing routes to three different places from one point ○ *a three-way junction*

three-wheel·er *n.* a vehicle with three wheels such as a small car or a tricycle

Three Wise Men *n.* = **Magi**

threm·ma·tol·o·gy /thrèmmə tóllǝjee/ *n.* the science of breeding domesticated plants and animals [Late 19thC. Coined from the Greek stem *thremmat-* "nursling" + -LOGY.]

thren·o·dy /thrénnədee/ (*plural* **-dies**), **thren·ode** /threé nōd, thré nōd/ *n.* a song, poem, or speech of lament for the dead [Mid-17thC. From Greek *thrēnōidia,* from *thrēnos* "lament" + *ōidē* "song" (see ODE).] —**thre·no·di·al** /thrə nṓdee əl/ *adj.* —**thre·nod·ic** /thrə nóddik/ *adj.* —**thren·o·dist** /thrénnədist/ *n.*

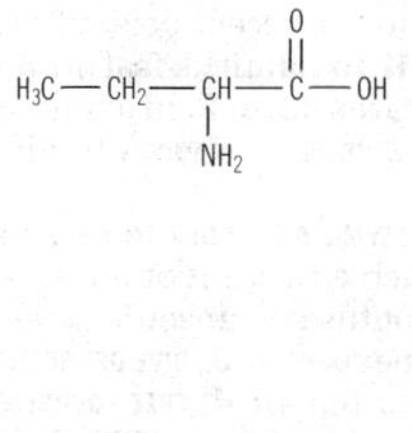

Threonine

thre·o·nine /threé ə neèn, threé ənin/ *n.* a colorless crystalline essential amino acid obtained from the hydrolysis of some proteins. Formula: $C_4H_9NO_3$. [Mid-20thC. Coined from *threose,* a kind of sugar + -INE.]

thresh /thresh/ *v.* (**threshed, thresh·ing, thresh·es**) **1.** *vti.* AGRIC **SEPARATE SEEDS FROM PLANT** to use a machine, flail, or other implement to separate the seeds of a harvested plant from the straw and chaff, husks, or other residue **2.** *vt.* **BEAT** to beat a person, animal, or object **3.** *vt.* **EXAMINE EXHAUSTIVELY** to examine something such as an issue or a proposal, exhaustively **4.** *vi.* **FLAIL ABOUT** move the body and limbs about in an uncontrolled or restless way ■ *n.* AGRIC **THRESHING** an act of threshing a harvested crop [Old English *þerscan.* Ultimately from an Indo-European base meaning "to rub," which is also the ancestor of English *attrition* and *threshold.*]

thresh·er /thréshər/ *n.* **1. SOMEBODY WHO THRESHES PLANTS** somebody who threshes a harvested crop with a machine, flail, or other implement **2.** = **threshing machine 3. thresh·er, thresh·er shark SHARK WITH LONG TAIL** a large, widely distributed shark that has a curved elongated upper lobe on the tail with which it agitates or threshes the water. Family: Alopiidae.

thresh·ing ma·chine *n.* a static power-driven agricultural machine formerly widely used to beat or rub harvested plants in order to separate the seeds from the rest of the plant

thresh·old /thré shōld/ *n.* **1. WOOD OR STONE BELOW DOOR** a piece of stone or hardwood that forms the bottom of a doorway **2. DOORWAY** a doorway or entrance **3. STARTING POINT** the point where a new era or experience begins ○ *on the threshold of maturity* **4. LEVEL AT WHICH AN EFFECT STARTS** the level at which a psychological or physiological effect or state starts ○ *the threshold of consciousness* [Old English *þerscold.* Ultimately from a prehistoric Germanic word whose first element (related to English *thresh*) meant "tread."]

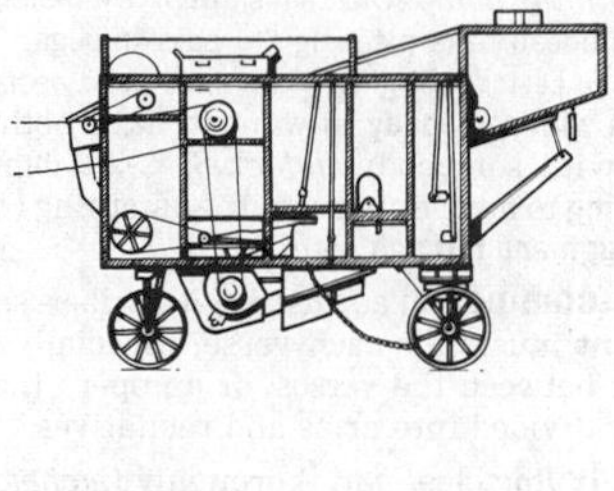

Threshing machine

threw past tense of **throw**

thrice /thrīss/ *adv.* **1. THREE TIMES** three times over (*archaic or literary*) **2. THREEFOLD** by three times as many or as much (*archaic or literary*) **3. GREATLY** to a high degree (*archaic*) [12thC. Alteration of *thries,* from obsolete *thrie* "three times," from Old English *þriga,* from *þrī* (see THREE).]

thrift /thrift/ *n.* **1. PRUDENT USE OF MONEY AND GOODS** the sensible and cautious management of money and goods in order to waste as little as possible and obtain maximum value **2.** BANKING **SAVINGS AND LOAN ASSOCIATION** a savings and loan association or sometimes a savings bank **3.** PLANTS **PLANT WITH PINK OR WHITE FLOWERS** a perennial evergreen plant of the plumbago family with pointed leaves and dense round pink or white flower heads. Genus: *Armeria.* **4.** ZOOL **STRONG GROWTH** vigorous and healthy growth of living things such as plants **5. PROSPERITY** the enjoyment of wealth and a good standard of living (*archaic*) [13thC. From Old Norse *þrift* "prosperity," from *þrífask* (see THRIVE).]

thrift in·sti·tu·tion *n.* = **thrift** *n.* **2**

thrift·less /thríftləss/ *adj.* **1. WASTING MONEY AND RESOURCES** showing carelessness and wastefulness in the handling of money and other resources **2.** having little value or usefulness (*archaic*) —**thrift·less·ly** *adv.* —**thrift·less·ness** *n.*

thrift shop *n.* a store that sells used goods, particularly clothing, usually for charity

thrift·y /thríftee/ (**-i·er, -i·est**) *adj.* **1. CAREFUL WITH MONEY AND RESOURCES** managing money and resources in a cautious and sensible way so as to waste as little as possible **2. PROSPEROUS** prosperous and thriving (*archaic*) **3. GROWING WELL** growing healthily and vigorously —**thrift·i·ly** *adv.* —**thrift·i·ness** *n.*

thrill /thril/ *vti.* (**thrilled, thrill·ing, thrills**) **1. BE OR MAKE SOMEBODY VERY EXCITED** to feel or make somebody experience intense excitement ○ *The children were thrilled by the amusement park.* **2. BE PLEASURABLE** to feel or make somebody feel great pleasure ○ *It thrilled me to see my old friends.* **3. VIBRATE OR CAUSE TO VIBRATE** to vibrate or make something or somebody quiver or vibrate ■ *n.* **1. CAUSE OF GREAT EXCITEMENT** a source or cause of great excitement, and often pleasure **2. FEELING OF EXCITEMENT** a feeling of great excitement, which may be experienced as a quivering or trembling sensation **3. TREMOR ASSOCIATED WITH HEART-VALVE DEFECTS** a slight vibration of the chest wall often associated with some types of heart-valve defects [Old English *þyrlian* "to go through," from *þyrel* "hole" (source of English *nostril*)]

thrill·er /thríllər/ *n.* **1. SOMETHING WITH EXCITING PLOT** a book, play, or movie that has an exciting plot involving crime, mystery, or espionage **2. PROVIDER OF THRILLS** somebody or something that thrills people

thrill·ing /thrílling/ *adj.* **1. VERY EXCITING** causing intense excitement **2. VIBRATING** characterized by trembling or vibrating —**thrill·ing·ly** *adv.*

thrips /thrips/ (*plural* **thrips**) *n.* a tiny sucking insect with four long thin wings fringed with hairs. It feeds on the sap of plants. Order: Thysanoptera. [Late 18thC. Via Latin from Greek, "woodworm," of unknown origin.]

thrive /thrīv/ (**thrived** *or* **throve** /thrōv/, **thrived** *or* **thriv·en** /thrívv'n/, **thriv·ing, thrives**) *vi.* **1. GROW WELL** to grow vigorously and healthily **2. DO WELL** to be successful and often profitable [13thC. From Old Norse *þrífask,* literally "to grasp for oneself," from *þrífa* "to seize," of unknown origin.] —**thriv·er** *n.*

thrive on *vt.* to enjoy and be stimulated by something generally considered difficult or undesirable

thro' /throo/, **thro** *prep., adv.* through (*informal or literary*) [15thC. From an earlier form of THROUGH.]

throat /thrōt/ *n.* **1.** ANAT **DIGESTIVE AND BREATHING PASSAGE** the part of the airway and digestive tract between the mouth and both the esophagus and the windpipe **2.** ANAT **FRONT OF NECK** the front part of the neck of an animal or human being **3. NARROW PART** a narrow part or passage that resembles a human's or animal's throat in shape or function **4.** BOT **OPENING OF TUBULAR ORGAN OF FLOWER** the opening of a tubular organ of a flower, e.g., of a corolla ■ *vt.* (**throat·ed, throat·ing, throats**) **UTTER SOMETHING IN DEEP TONES** to speak or sing in a deep or hoarse voice [Old English *þrote* (source also of English *throttle*)] ◇ **jump down somebody's throat** to speak angrily and impatiently to somebody ◇ **ram** *or* **force something down somebody's throat** to make repeated and emphatic attempts to get somebody to listen to or accept a view or belief ◇ **stick in your throat** to be extremely difficult to accept

throat·latch /thrṓt làch/ *n.* the strap that passes under a horse's jaw to hold its bridle in place

throat mi·cro·phone, throat mike *informal n.* a microphone that is placed in contact with the throat to pick up the vibrations produced by speech

throat·y /thrṓtee/ (**-i·er, -i·est**) *adj.* **1. HUSKY-SOUNDING** sounding deep and husky **2. DEEP OR ROUGH IN TONE** deep or rough in tone, as though having been produced in the throat —**throat·i·ly** *adv.* —**throat·i·ness** *n.*

throb /throb/ *vi.* (**throbbed, throb·bing, throbs**) **1. BEAT RAPIDLY AND FORCEFULLY** to beat or pulsate in a rapid forceful way ○ *My head is throbbing.* **2. BEAT REGULARLY** to have a regular rhythmical beat ■ *n.* **1. SINGLE BEAT** a single beat or pulsation **2. REGULAR BEAT** a regular beat or pulsation ○ *a heart throb* [14thC. Origin uncertain: probably an imitation of pulsating.] —**throb·bing** *adj.* —**throb·bing·ly** *adv.*

throe /thrō/ *n.* **PANG** a spasm of pain ■ **throes** *npl.* **1. EFFECTS OF PANGS** the effects of severe physical pain **2. EFFECTS OF UPHEAVAL** the effects of an upheaval or struggle [12thC. Origin uncertain: perhaps an alteration of Old English *þrawu,* from *þrēah* "pain," of unknown origin.] ◇ **in the throes of something** in the process of doing something, usually something difficult or unpleasant

thromb- *prefix.* = **thrombo-** (*used before vowels*)

throm·bi plural of **thrombus**

throm·bin /thrómbin/ *n.* an enzyme in blood that causes clotting by catalyzing the conversion of fibrinogen to fibrin [Late 19thC. Coined from THROMBO- + -IN.]

throm·bo·cyte /thrómbə sīt/ *n.* = **platelet** —**throm·bo·cyt·ic** /thròmbə síttik/ *adj.*

throm·bo·cy·to·pe·ni·a /thròmbə sītə peénee ə/ *n.* the state of having fewer than the normal number of blood platelets per unit volume of blood, often associated with hemorrhaging [Early 20thC. Coined from THROMBOCYTE + Greek *penia* "poverty."] —**throm·bo·cy·to·pe·nic** *adj.*

throm·bo·em·bo·lism /thròmbō émbə lìzzəm/ *n.* the blockage of a blood vessel by a blood clot (**thrombus**) that has broken away from its site of origin —**throm·bo·em·bol·ic** /thròmbō em bóllik/ *adj.* —**throm·bo·em·bo·lit·ic** /thròmbō embə líttik/ *adj.*

throm·bo·ki·nase /thrómbō kī nàyss, -nàyz/ *n.* = **thromboplastin**

throm·bol·y·sis /throm bólləssiss/ *n.* the breaking down of a blood clot by infusion of a specific enzyme into the blood —**throm·bo·lyt·ic** /thròmbə líttik/ *adj.*

throm·bo·phle·bi·tis /thròmbō flə bī́tiss/ *n.* inflammation of a vein with the formation of a blood clot

throm·bo·plas·tic /thròmbō plástik/ *adj.* causing or increasing blood clot formation —**throm·bo·plas·ti·cal·ly** *adv.*

throm·bo·plas·tin /thròmbō plástin/ *n.* an enzyme found in blood platelets that converts prothrombin to thrombin during the process of blood clotting

throm·bose /thróm bōz/ (**-bosed, -bos·ing, -bos·es**) *vti.* to affect something such as a coronary artery, with thrombosis or to be affected by thrombosis

throm·bo·sis /throm bṓssiss/ (*plural* **-ses** /throm bṓ seez/) *n.* the formation or presence of one or more blood clots that may partially or completely block an artery, e.g., flowing to the heart or brain, or a vein [Early 18thC. Via modern Latin from, ultimately, Greek *thrombos* "clot."] —**throm·bot·ic** /throm bóttik/ *adj.*

throm·box·ane /throm bók sàyn/ *n.* a substance that is formed in platelets and that causes blood clotting and constriction of blood vessels

throm·bus /thrómbəss/ (*plural* **-bi** /-bī/) *n.* a blood clot that forms in a blood vessel and remains at the site of formation. ◊ **embolism** [Late 17thC. Via modern Latin from Greek *thrombos* "clot."]

throne /thrōn/ *n.* **1.** CHAIR OF MONARCH OR BISHOP an ornate chair, often raised on a platform and covered by a canopy, occupied by a monarch or bishop on ceremonial occasions **2.** PERSON ON THRONE somebody who has the status to occupy a throne **3.** POWER OF ROYAL PERSON the power, rank, and privileges of a monarch ■ **thrones** *npl.* CHR ORDER OF ANGELS the third group of angels, ranking after the Seraphim and Cherubim, in the first circle of the traditional Christian hierarchy (*literary*) ■ *v.* (**throned, thron·ing, thrones**) **1.** *vti.* PUT SOMEBODY ON THRONE to place somebody or be placed on a throne **2.** *vi.* SIT ON A THRONE to be seated on a throne [12thC. Via Old French *trone* from, ultimately, Greek *thronos*. Ultimately from an Indo-European word meaning "to support," which is also the ancestor of English *firm*.] —**throne·less** *adj.*

throng /thrawng/ *n.* CROWD a large crowd of people or objects ■ *v.* (**thronged, throng·ing, throngs**) **1.** *vt.* CROWD INTO PLACE to crowd into or fill a place **2.** *vi.* MOVE IN CROWD to move or gather in a throng **3.** *vt.* CROWD AROUND SOMEBODY to surround and push against somebody [Old English *geþrang*. Ultimately from a prehistoric Germanic word meaning "to press, crowd."]

thros·tle /thróss'l/ *n.* **1.** SONG THRUSH a thrush, especially a song thrush (*literary*) **2.** OLD SPINNING MACHINE a machine formerly used for the continuous spinning of cotton or wool fibers [Old English *þrostle*. Ultimately from an Indo-European word that is also the ancestor of English *thrush*, *ostrich*, and *sturdy*.]

throt·tle /thrótt'l/ *n.* MECH ENG **1.** VALVE CONTROLLING FLUID FLOW a valve used to control the flow of a fluid, especially the amount of fuel and air entering the cylinders of an internal-combustion engine **2.** CONTROL FOR THROTTLE a pedal or lever for controlling a throttle valve ■ *vt.* (**-tled, -tling, -tles**) **1.** MECH ENG REGULATE FUEL FLOW USING THROTTLE to regulate the amount of fuel entering an engine using a throttle **2.** MECH ENG REGULATE ENGINE SPEED to regulate the speed of an engine by using a throttle **3.** KILL PERSON OR ANIMAL BY CHOKING to kill or injure a person or animal by squeezing the throat **4.** SILENCE OR SUPPRESS SOMEBODY OR SOMETHING to prevent somebody or something from expressing an opinion freely or from engaging in an activity [14thC. Formed from THROAT.] —**throt·tler** *n.*

throt·tle·hold /thrótt'l hōld/ *n.* = **stranglehold**

through /throo/ CORE MEANING: a grammatical word used to indicate movement from one side or end of something to or past the other side or end

1. *prep., adv.* TRAVELING ACROSS traveling across or to various places in a town, country, or area ○ *He spent the summer traveling through Europe.* ○ *We're not stopping long; we're just passing through.* **2.** *prep., adv.* AMONG in the midst of, or having things or people all around or on either side of ○ *She wandered through the crowds milling around outside the cathedral.* ○ *Massage the conditioner through to the ends of the hair.* **3.** *prep., adv.* PAST A BARRIER past the limitations or difficulties of something such as a barrier or a problem ○ *the problems involved in wading through acres of bureaucracy* ○ *The road has been narrowed to prevent larger vehicles getting through.* **4.** *prep., adv.* FROM BEGINNING TO END from the beginning until the end or conclusion of ○ *Martin and Johanson's works will be on view through June.* ○ *I can't come I'm afraid; I'm working through.* **5.** *adv., prep.* TO CONCLUSION to a successful conclusion ○ *We've been trying to get through all morning but the lines are busy.* ○ *The bill will never get through Congress.* **6.** *prep.* VIA by way or means of ○ *How the marketing is done, through a branch or telemarketing or a future service, is up to each bank.* **7.** *prep.* OVER THE EXTENT OF happening or existing over the entire extent of or affecting all of ○ *A flu of epidemic proportions swept through the town.* **8.** *prep.* BECAUSE OF as a result of ○ *Through his mishandling of our affairs, we'll be lucky to have any credit at all this year.* **9.** *prep.* UP TO AND INCLUDING up to and including that time ○ *Museum hours are 2–4:30 p.m. Tuesdays through Fridays.* **10.** *adv.* THOROUGHLY completely and in every part **11.** *prep.* by means of ○ *Through joint ventures, bankers have lent hundreds of millions of dollars to inner-city projects.* **12.** *adj.* GOING DIRECTLY going directly without stopping or requiring a change ○ *The through train leaves on the hour.* [Old English *þurh*. Ultimately from an Indo-European base meaning "to pass through," which is also the ancestor of English *thrill*, *trans-*, and *nectar*.] ◇ **be through with somebody** to want to have nothing else to do with somebody (*informal*) ◇ **be through with something** to have finished with something (*informal*) ◇ **through and through** completely

through-com·posed *adj.* used to describe a song with different music for each verse, especially without pauses between the verses, or an opera that is not clearly divided into arias and recitatives

through·ly /thróolee/ *adv.* thoroughly (*archaic*)

through·out /throo ówt/ *prep., adv.* **1.** THROUGH THE WHOLE OF through or during the whole of ○ *Societies throughout history believed they had reached the frontiers of human accomplishment.* ○ *Throughout, they maintained their dignity.* **2.** IN ALL PARTS OF happening or existing in all parts of ○ *The group is seeking out experts of any age throughout the area.* ○ *The house is carpeted throughout.*

through·put /thróo pòot/ *n.* the amount of something such as data or raw material that is processed over a given period [Modeled on INPUT and OUTPUT]

through·way /thróo wày/, **thru·way** *n.* = **expressway**

throve past tense of **thrive**

throw /thrō/ *vt.* (**threw** /throo/, **thrown** /thrōn/, **throw·ing, throws**) **1.** PROPEL SOMETHING FROM THE HAND to make something move relatively quickly from the hand and through the air **2.** DROP SOMETHING CARELESSLY to put or drop something somewhere without paying proper attention to where it is left ○ *throws magazines all over the place* **3.** FORCE SOMEBODY OR SOMETHING SOMEWHERE to move somebody or something forcefully or suddenly into a particular position or in a particular direction **4.** PUT SOMEBODY OR SOMETHING IN DIFFERENT CIRCUMSTANCES to bring somebody or something suddenly or unexpectedly into a particular state, especially an undesirable one ○ *thrown out of a job* **5.** HURL SOMEBODY TO THE GROUND to make a movement that causes somebody, e.g., an opponent in wrestling or judo or a horseback rider, to fall to the ground **6.** PROJECT LIGHT to send out light to illuminate a particular place, or create a shadow by blocking light **7.** CAST DOUBT OR SUSPICION to cause doubt or suspicion in people's minds by saying or doing something **8.** DIRECT THE EYES to direct a look or glance quickly or suddenly in a particular direction ○ *She threw me a warning look.* **9.** DISCONCERT SOMEBODY to take somebody by surprise to the extent that he or she does not know how to react (*informal*) ○ *His unexpected arrival threw me.* **10.** MOVE AN OPERATING SWITCH OR LEVER to move something, usually a switch or lever, to make a machine or system operate or to connect up a system **11.** HAVE AN EXTREME REACTION to be affected by a sudden outburst of strong emotion such as anger or ill-temper ○ *throw a tantrum* **12.** SEND SOMETHING ACROSS to make something that extends from one point to another, especially hastily ○ *The enemy threw a bridge across the moat.* **13.** DELIVER A PUNCH to deliver a punch or blow with a movement of the arm **14.** ARTS MAKE AN OBJECT ON POTTER'S WHEEL to produce a ceramic object by turning clay on a potter's wheel **15.** TURN MATERIAL ON LATHE to turn wood or metal on a lathe **16.** HOST A PARTY to organize and be the host at a party **17.** LOSE SOMETHING INTENTIONALLY to lose a fight, race, or contest deliberately, e.g., by not trying or by committing a foul **18.** MAKE MATERIAL INTO YARN to make silk or filaments into thread by twisting or spinning **19.** PROJECT VOICE project a vocal sound so that it seems to be coming from elsewhere **20.** ROLL DICE to tip or roll dice onto a flat surface to obtain a score, or score a particular number in this way **21.** GIVE BIRTH TO YOUNG to give birth to young (*refers especially to cows*) **22.** *Malaysia, Singapore* THROW AWAY to throw something away ○ *Once you get your new card you can throw the old one.* ■ *n.* **1.** ACT OF THROWING an act of throwing something, e.g., a ball or missile, or dice in a game **2.** DISTANCE THROWN the distance that something is thrown or can be thrown **3.** WAY OF THROWING an act of being thrown, or a way of throwing an opponent, in wrestling or judo **4.** SCORE THROWN the score obtained by throwing something, e.g., dice or darts, in a game **5.** EACH each item or attempt (*informal*) ○ *I didn't buy any; they were ten dollars a throw.* **6.** HOUSEHOLD COVER FOR FURNITURE a light cover or rug to cover furniture **7.** MECH ENG MOVEMENT OF MACHINE PART the maximum movement in a single direction of a machine part driven by a crank, cam, or eccentric **8.** PHYS DEFLECTION OF MEASURING INSTRUMENT the distance moved by the tip of the needle of a measuring instrument **9.** GEOL VERTICAL DISPLACEMENT ALONG GEOLOGICAL FAULT the vertical displacement up or down produced by movement along a geological fault [Old English *þrāwan* "to twist, hurl." Ultimately from an Indo-European base meaning "to twist," which is also the ancestor of English *thread*.] —**throw·er** *n.* ◇ **throw yourself into something** to start doing something with great energy and commitment

WORD KEY: SYNONYMS

throw, chuck, fling, heave, hurl, toss, cast

CORE MEANING: to send something through the air

throw to cause something to go through the air using a physical movement; **chuck** to throw something with force and often in a reckless or aimless way; **fling** an informal word that means to throw something in a casual or careless way; **heave** to throw something with effort, for example, because it is large or heavy; **hurl** to throw something with great force; **toss** to throw something small or light in a casual or careless way; **cast** a literary word that means to throw something to a particular place or into a particular thing. It is also used with the meaning to throw a fishing line or net.

throw around *vt.* to spend money in an extravagant, ostentatious way

throw away *vt.* **1.** DISCARD SOMETHING to get rid of something no longer wanted **2.** WASTE SOMETHING to fail to take advantage of an opportunity to do something **3.** SAY SOMETHING IN OFFHAND MANNER to say a line in a play in a way that makes it seem unimportant, even though it may be crucial to the plot **4.** in a card game, to discard a card

throw in *vt.* **1.** ADD SOMETHING TO DISCUSSION to contribute a comment to a conversation or discussion **2.** ADD SOMETHING AS EXTRA to add something as an extra, especially another item at no extra cost when selling something ◇ **throw in the towel, throw in the sponge** to admit or accept defeat (*informal*) ◇ **throw in your hand 1.** to admit defeat in a card game by laying your cards down **2.** to admit or accept defeat ◇ **throw in the sponge** *or* **towel** to give up or admit defeat

throw off *vt.* **1.** STYMIE A PURSUER to make a pursuer lose something such as a scent or a trail **2.** MAKE SOMEBODY FLUSTERED to confuse or unsettle somebody by doing something unexpected **3.** GIVE OFF SOMETHING to emit a substance into the air **4.** FREE YOURSELF FROM SOMETHING to get rid of something troublesome or oppressive **5.** TAKE CLOTHES OFF HASTILY to remove an item of clothing in a hurried or careless way **6.** SAY SOMETHING IN OFFHAND WAY to say or write something in a casual manner

throw on *vt.* to put an item of clothing on in a hurried or careless way

throw out *vt.* **1.** DISCARD SOMETHING to get rid of something no longer wanted, especially something that has been kept for a while **2.** EJECT SOMEBODY to eject somebody forcibly from a place **3.** DISMISS SOMEBODY to expel somebody from membership of an organization **4.** SUGGEST SOMETHING to make a suggestion, proposal, or hint, especially in an informal way **5.** BASEBALL PUT BASEBALL PLAYER OUT in baseball, to throw the ball to a teammate who puts the runner out **6.** REJECT LAWSUIT to reject a lawsuit so that the defendant does not have to stand trial **7.** GIVE OFF SOMETHING to emit a substance into the air **8.** DISCONCERT SOMEBODY to confuse or unsettle somebody by doing something unexpected

throw over *vt.* to end a romantic or sexual relationship with somebody (*informal*)

throw together *vt.* (*informal*) **1.** MAKE SOMETHING HASTILY to make something in a hurry or carelessly **2.** BRING PEOPLE INTO CONTACT to cause people to meet and become acquainted with each other in a casual or unplanned way

throw up *v.* **1.** *vti.* VOMIT to vomit the contents of the stomach (*informal*) **2.** *vt.* BUILD SOMETHING HASTILY to erect a building or structure quickly **3.** *vt.* ABANDON SOMETHING to give something up, especially something important or valuable (*informal*)

throw·a·way /thrṓ ə wày/ *n.* **1.** SOMETHING TO BE DISCARDED an object designed to be thrown away after use **2.** ADVERTISING LEAFLET OR HANDBILL an advertising leaflet or handbill that is discarded after being read **3.** ABANDONED CHILD OR YOUNG PERSON a child or young person thrown out by parents or guardians and living on the streets ■ *adj.* **1.** OFFHAND said or written in an apparently offhand manner **2.** DISPOSABLE designed to be thrown away after use **3.** ABANDONED BY PARENTS OR

GUARDIANS having been thrown out by parents or guardians and living on the streets **4.** WASTEFUL tending to discard things too readily ○ *a throwaway society*

throw·back /thrṓ bàk/ *n.* **1.** ORGANISM REPRESENTING REVERSION TO EARLIER TYPE an organism with the characteristics of an earlier type **2.** REVERSION TO EARLIER TYPE reversion to an earlier ancestral type **3.** ANIMAL OR PERSON RESEMBLING ANCESTOR an animal or person bearing a striking resemblance to an ancestor **4.** SOMETHING BELONGING TO THE PAST something contemporary that seems to belong to the past

throw-in *n.* **1.** SOCCER RETURN OF SOCCER BALL TO PLAY an act of returning a soccer ball to play from the sideline by propelling it from behind the head with both hands **2.** BASEBALL RETURN OF BALL FROM OUTFIELD an act of returning a baseball after it has been hit to the outfield **3.** BASKETBALL RETURN OF BASKETBALL TO PLAY an act of returning a basketball to play by passing it onto the court **4.** BRIDGE STRATAGEM AT BRIDGE a surrender of at trick at bridge to an opponent who must then make a lead that will cost one or more tricks

throw·ing stick *n.* **1.** DEVICE FOR THROWING A SPEAR a grooved rod used for throwing a spear with greater leverage **2.** STICK USED AS HUNTING WEAPON a stick, often with a handgrip, used by hunters in preliterate societies as a weapon to hurl at birds or small game

thrown past participle of **throw**

throw pil·low *n.* a small decorative pillow placed on a couch or an armchair

throw rug *n.* = **scatter rug**

throw·ster /thrṓstər/ *n.* somebody who twists filaments into thread

throw weight *n.* the total weight of a missile's payload, including the warhead and guidance system but not the rocket

thru /throo/ *prep., adv., adj.* through (*informal*)

thrum[1] /thrum/ *v.* (**thrummed, thrum·ming, thrums**) **1.** *vti.* STRUM to strum on a stringed instrument **2.** *vi.* TAP STEADILY to drum on something, especially with the fingers **3.** *vti.* SAY OR SPEAK MONOTONOUSLY to say something or talk monotonously ■ *n.* MONOTONOUS BEAT a low monotonous beating sound [Late 16thC. An imitation of the sound.] —**thrum·mer** *n.*

thrum[2] /thrum/ *n.* **1.** THREAD END LEFT ON LOOM an unwoven end or row of ends from warp threads that are left on a loom after the web has been cut off **2.** FRINGE a short fringe or thread end ■ **thrums** *npl.* YARN PIECES ADDED TO CANVAS short pieces of yarn inserted in canvas in order to create a rough surface and prevent chafing or leaks ■ *vt.* (**thrummed, thrum·ming, thrums**) **1.** ADD FRINGES TO SOMETHING to put fringes on something **2.** INSERT YARN PIECES IN CANVAS to insert pieces of yarn in canvas in order to create a rough surface and prevent chafing or leaks [Old English]

thrup·pence *npl.* = **threepence**

thrup·pen·ny *adj.* = **threepenny**

Thrush

thrush[1] /thrush/ (*plural* **thrush·es** *or* **thrush**) *n.* **1.** SLENDER-BILLED SONGBIRD a small to medium-sized songbird with a slender bill and often melodious song. The robin, wood thrush, and hermit thrush are thrushes. Family: Turdidae. **2.** BIRD RESEMBLING TRUE THRUSH a bird that resembles a thrush, e.g., the North American water thrush [Old English *þrysce*]

thrush[2] /thrush/ *n.* **1.** FUNGAL DISEASE OF MOUTH a fungal infection of the mouth characterized by white patches **2.** FUNGAL INFECTION OF VAGINA a fungal infection of the vagina characterized by a white discharge and itching **3.** DISEASE OF HORSE'S HOOF infection of the fleshy part of a horse's foot (**frog**), causing softening of the horn and a foul-smelling discharge [Mid-17thC. Origin uncertain.]

thrust /thrust/ *v.* (**thrust, thrust·ing, thrusts**) **1.** *vt.* PUSH SOMEBODY OR SOMETHING FORCEFULLY to push somebody or something with great force **2.** *vt.* FORCE SOMEBODY INTO SOMETHING to force somebody to accept or deal with something ○ *He was thrust into the limelight.* **3.** *vti.* STRETCH OR EXTEND to stretch or extend something, or be stretched or extended ○ *towers thrusting skyward* **4.** *vti.* ATTACK BY STABBING to attack somebody with a piercing or stabbing movement with a weapon **5.** *vti.* FORCE WAY to force a way **6.** *vt.* INSERT SOMETHING to add or insert material, usually inappropriately, into a context ■ *n.* **1.** FORCEFUL PUSH a forceful push or shove **2.** FORWARD MOVEMENT a forward movement or impetus **3.** STABBING ACTION a piercing or stabbing action **4.** AIR REACTIVE FORCE OF EXPELLED GASES the reactive force of expelled gases, e.g., those generated by a rocket ship or jet engine **5.** MILITARY ATTACK a military assault or offensive **6.** ENG FORCE OF PROPELLER a propulsive force produced by a rotating propeller, e.g., on a ship or aircraft **7.** GIST OR AIM OF SOMETHING the chief meaning, direction, or purpose of something **8.** GEOL FORCE IN EARTH'S CRUST a force in the earth's crust that results in recumbent folding of rock strata **9.** GEOL = **thrust fault 10.** CIV ENG FORCE EXERTED BY STRUCTURE the continuous force exerted sideways or downward by one structure on another, e.g., by an arch on an abutment or a rafter against a wall [12thC. From Old Norse.] —**thrust·ful** *adj.*

thrust bear·ing *n.* a bearing designed to withstand axial loading and to prevent movement along the axis of a loaded shaft

thrust·er /thrústər/ *n.* **1.** SPACE TECH ROCKET THAT CONTROLS ALTITUDE a rocket on a spacecraft or high-altitude aircraft that controls an altitude or flight path **2.** INDUST MANEUVERING DEVICE ON OIL-DRILLING VESSEL a jet or propeller on an oil-drilling ship or offshore rig, used to maneuver it into position **3.** SPORTS SURFBOARD OR SAILBOARD WITH EXTRA FIN a surfboard or sailboard equipped with one or more extra fins designed to give it greater speed or maneuverability

thrust fault *n.* an inclined fault in which rocks on the lower side of the slope are displaced downward

thrust stage *n.* a stage surrounded on three sides by the audience

thru·way /thróo wày/ *n.* = **throughway**

Thu, Thu. *abbr.* CALENDAR Thursday

Thu·cyd·i·des /thoo síddi dèez/ (460?–400? B.C.) Athenian historian. A major figure in the development of historical writing, he is known for his *History of the Peloponnesian War*, a conflict in which he himself had fought.

thud /thud/ *n.* **1.** DULL HEAVY SOUND a loud dull sound made by a heavy object impacting with a surface **2.** DULL HEAVY BLOW a blow that makes a dull heavy sound ■ *vi.* (**thud·ded, thud·ding, thuds**) MAKE A THUD to make a dull heavy sound [Early 16thC. Origin uncertain: probably from Old English *þyddan* "to thrust."]

thug /thug/ *n.* **1.** BRUTAL PERSON somebody, especially a criminal, who is brutal and violent **2. thug, Thug** HIST INDIAN ROBBER a member of a former secret organization of robbers in India, worshippers of the goddess Kali, who strangled their victims [Early 19thC. Via Hindi *ṭhag*, literally "swindler, cheat, robber," from, ultimately, Sanskrit *sthagayati* "covers, conceals."] —**thug·ger·y** *n.* —**thug·gish** *adj.*

thug·gee /thúggee/ *n.* the method of robbery and murder by strangulation characteristic of the former thugs of India [Mid-19thC. From Hindi *ṭhagī*, from *ṭhag* (see THUG).]

thu·ja /thóojə, -yə/ (*plural* **-jas** *or* **-ja**), **thu·ya** /thóoyə/ (*plural* **-yas** *or* **-ya**) *n.* TREES = **arborvitae** [Mid-18thC. Via modern Latin *Thuja*, genus name, from medieval Latin *thuia* "cedar," from Greek.]

thu·li·um /thóolee əm/ *n.* a very rare soft bright silvery-gray metallic element belonging to the lanthanide series. Symbol **Tm** [Late 19thC. Named for THUL; from the fact that it was first found in Norway.]

thumb /thum/ *n.* **1.** ANAT THICKEST DIGIT ON HUMAN HAND the shortest thickest digit of the human hand, located next to the forefinger. Since it is opposable, it can be moved to face and touch the other fingers so that objects can be grasped. **2.** ZOOL ANIMAL'S DIGIT RESEMBLING HUMAN THUMB a short thick digit in some animals, e.g., many primates, that is adapted for grasping and corresponds to the human thumb **3.** CLOTHES SECTION OF GLOVE FOR THUMB the part of a glove or mitten that covers the thumb **4.** ARCHIT = **ovolo** ■ *v.* (**thumbed, thumb·ing, thumbs**) **1.** *vti.* HITCH RIDE to obtain or try to obtain a ride by signaling with the thumb to passing drivers **2.** *vt.* MAKE SOMETHING DIRTY BY USE to soil or cause wear on something, especially a book, by repeated handling (*often passive*) ○ *a well-thumbed book* **3.** *vti.* FLIP THROUGH PRINTED MATTER to glance through pages of a book or magazine [Old English *þúma*] —**thumb·less** *adj.* ◇ **all thumbs** extremely awkward or clumsy ◇ **stick out like a sore thumb** to be completely obvious, or conspicuously out of place ◇ **thumb your nose at somebody** *or* **something** to express defiance or contempt, especially by putting the thumb to the nose and extending the fingers ◇ **twiddle your thumbs** to be idle or unoccupied, especially involuntarily ◇ **under somebody's thumb** under the influence and control of somebody

Thumb /thum/, **"General" Tom** (1838–83) U.S. entertainer. Three feet four inches tall, he starred in various exhibitions and circuses (1842–82). Real name **Charles Sherwood Stratton**

thumb·hole /thúm hṑl/ *n.* **1.** HOLE TO ALLOW THUMB TO GRIP a hole in something such as a bowling ball into which a thumb can be inserted in order to provide a grip **2.** HOLE FOR THUMB IN WIND INSTRUMENT a hole in a wind instrument that is covered and uncovered by the thumb to produce notes

thumb in·dex *n.* a series of labeled indentations cut into the pages of a book down the edge opposite the binding to facilitate quick location of divisions or sections —**thumb-in·dex** *vt.*

thumb knot *n.* = **overhand knot**

thumb·nail /thúm nàyl/ *n.* NAIL OF THUMB the hard growing plate of keratin on the back surface of the tip of the thumb ■ *adj.* CONCISE covering the salient points concisely ○ *a thumbnail sketch*

thumb·nut /thúm nùt/ *n.* = **wing nut**

thumb pi·an·o *n.* a box-shaped African musical instrument consisting of a row of tuned metal or wooden strips that vibrate when plucked by the thumb

thumb·print /thúm prìnt/ *n.* an impression of the fleshy pad near the tip of the thumb, often used to identify people

thumb·screw /thúm skròo/ *n.* **1.** TORTURE DEVICE FOR CRUSHING THUMBS an instrument of torture used to crush the thumbs **2.** FLAT-HEADED SCREW a screw with a flat head to be turned with the thumb and forefinger

thumbs down *n.* an indication of disapproval or rejection (*informal*) [From the custom of pointing the thumbs downwards to signify rejection, perhaps originating in the arenas of ancient Rome, where it indicated that a gladiator should be put to death]

thumb·stall /thúm stàwl/ *n.* a sheath of rubber, leather, or fabric used to protect the thumb, e.g., by covering a dressing on an injured thumb

thumbs up *n.* an indication of approval or acceptance (*informal*) [From the custom of pointing the thumbs upwards to signify acceptance, perhaps originating in the arenas of ancient Rome, where it indicated that a gladiator should be permitted to live]

thumb·tack /thúm tàk/ *n.* TACK FOR PINNING UP PAPERS a short pin with a large flat head used for attaching papers or cards to a board by pressing into the board with the thumb ■ *vt.* (**-tacked, -tack·ing, -tacks**) AFFIX SOMETHING WITH THUMBTACK to affix papers or cards with one or more thumbtacks

Thum·mim *n.* ➧ **Urim and Thummim** [Mid-16thC. From Hebrew *tummīm*, plural of *tōm* "completeness."]

thump /thump/ *v.* (**thumped, thump·ing, thumps**) **1.** *vti.* STRIKE HEAVILY to strike somebody or something heavily with the fist or an object **2.** *vi.* PALPITATE OR POUND to beat very fast or loudly because of fear or excitement (*refers to the heart*) **3.** *vi.* MAKE DULL HEAVY SOUND to make the loud dull sound that a heavy object makes when it impacts with a surface **4.** *vti.* DEFEAT CONVINCINGLY to inflict a humiliating defeat upon somebody (*informal*) (*often passive*) ○ *Our team was thumped 9–0.* ■ *n.* **1.** HEAVY BLOW a heavy blow struck with the fist or an object **2.** DULL HEAVY SOUND the loud dull sound made by a heavy object impacting with a surface ○ *I heard a loud thump from next door.* [Mid-16thC. An imitation of the sound.] —**thump·er** *n.*

thump·ing /thúmping/ *adj.* LARGE huge, resounding, or impressive (*informal*) ○ *won by a thumping majority*

■ *adv.* VERY extremely or exceptionally (*informal*) ○ *a thumping good read* —**thump·ing·ly** *adv.*

Thun /toon/ town in the canton of Bern, central Switzerland. Population: 39,253 (1996).

thun·ber·gia /thùn búrjə, -jee ə/ *n.* an African and southern Asian plant of the acanthus family with opposite pairs of simple leaves and five-lobed tubular flowers. It is widely cultivated as an ornamental. Genus: *Thunbergia.* [Late 18thC. From modern Latin *Thunbergia,* genus name, named for C. P. *Thunberg* (1743–1822), a Swedish botanist.]

thun·der /thúndər/ *n.* **1.** LOUD NOISE FOLLOWING LIGHTNING a loud rumbling noise caused by the rapid expansion of air suddenly heated by lightning **2.** NOISE RESEMBLING THUNDER a loud deep rumbling noise resembling thunder **3.** THREATENING OR VEHEMENT UTTERANCE a manifestation of somebody's anger in an explosion of strong words ■ *v.* (**-dered, -der·ing, -ders**) **1.** *vi.* MAKE LOUD NOISE FOLLOWING LIGHTNING to make a loud rumbling noise caused by the rapid expansion of air suddenly heated by lightning **2.** *vi.* RUMBLE LOUDLY LIKE THUNDER to make a loud deep rumbling noise resembling thunder **3.** *vti.* SHOUT VEHEMENTLY to shout something loudly and angrily [Old English *þunor* and *þunrian*] ◇ **steal somebody's thunder** to prevent somebody from receiving acclaim for doing something by doing it or something similar first

thun·der·a·tion /thùndə ráysh'n/ *n.* used as an expression of annoyance or surprise (*humorous*)

Thun·der Bay city in northwestern Ontario, Canada, on Thunder Bay, an arm of Lake Superior. Population: 125,562 (1996).

The Purcell Team/Corbis

Thunderbird: Totem pole, Stanley Park, Vancouver, Canada

thun·der·bird /thúndər bùrd/ *n.* in Native North American mythology, a bird that produces thunder

thun·der·bolt /thúndər bōlt/ *n.* **1.** FLASH OF LIGHTNING WITH THUNDER a flash of lightning accompanied by a crash of thunder **2.** STARTLING OCCURRENCE a sudden shocking action, occurrence, pronouncement, or piece of news **3.** MYTHOLOGICAL WEAPON WIELDED BY GODS in mythology, a destructive missile hurled to earth by a god in a flash of lightning **4.** SOMEBODY OR SOMETHING FORMIDABLE somebody who or something that seems to resemble a thunderbolt, especially in energy and destructive power

thun·der·clap /thúndər klàp/ *n.* **1.** CRASH OF THUNDER a loud crashing noise produced by thunder **2.** STARTLING OCCURRENCE a sudden shocking occurrence or piece of news **3.** NOISE RESEMBLING THUNDER a sudden loud sound resembling thunder

thun·der·cloud /thúndər klòwd/ *n.* a large dark cumulonimbus cloud that produces thunder and lightning

thun·der·head /thúndər hèd/ *n.* the upper rounded mass of a cumulonimbus cloud associated with the development of a thunderstorm

thun·der·ing /thúndəring/ *adj. U.K.* GREAT very great (*dated informal*) ■ *adv. U.K.* VERY extremely or exceptionally (*dated informal*) —**thun·der·ing·ly** *adv.*

thun·der·ous /thúndərəss, -drəss/ *adj.* **1.** VERY LOUD resembling thunder in its loudness ○ *thunderous applause* **2.** THREATENING angry and threatening —**thun·der·ous·ly** *adv.*

thun·der run *n.* formerly, either of two inclined wooden troughs down which iron balls were rolled offstage to simulate thunder as a theatrical sound effect

thun·der sheet *n.* a large sheet of metal shaken to simulate thunder as a theatrical sound effect

thun·der·show·er /thúndər shòwər/ *n.* a shower of rain during a thunderstorm

thun·der·stone /thúndər stōn/ *n.* **1.** LONG TAPERING ROCK a naturally occurring long tapering piece of rock, formerly believed to be a thunderbolt **2.** THUNDERBOLT a thunderbolt (*archaic*)

thun·der·storm /thúndər stàwrm/ *n.* a storm with thunder, lightning, heavy rain, and sometimes hail

thun·der·strick·en /thúndər strìkən/ *adj.* thunderstruck (*literary*)

thun·der·struck /thúndər strùk/ *adj.* **1.** EXTREMELY SURPRISED OR INCREDULOUS so surprised, incredulous, or startled as to be in a state of shock **2.** HIT BY LIGHTNING struck by lightning (*archaic*)

thun·der·y /thúndəree/ *adj.* **1.** CAUSING OR HERALDING THUNDER causing or indicating the onset of thunder or a thunderstorm **2.** SOUNDING LIKE THUNDER resembling thunder in sound

thunk[1] /thungk/ *n.* THUD a thud (*informal*) ■ *vi.* MAKE A THUD to make a thud (*informal*) [Mid-20thC. An imitation of the sound.]

thunk[2] *v.* past tense, past participle of **think** (*regional*)

Thur. *abbr.* CALENDAR Thursday

Thur·ber /thúrbər/, **James** (1894–1961) U.S. writer and cartoonist. He is known for his humorous and poignant portrayals of the frustrations and absurd situations of modern life. Full name **James Grover Thurber**

thu·ri·ble /thóorəb'l/ *n.* = **censer** [15thC. Directly or via French from Latin *t(h)uribulum,* from, ultimately, Greek *thuos* "sacrifice, incense."]

thu·ri·fer /thóorəfər/ *n.* somebody who carries the censer in religious ceremonies [Mid-19thC. Via late Latin from, ultimately, Greek *thuos* "sacrifice, incense."]

Thurs. *abbr.* CALENDAR Thursday

Thurs·day /thúrz dày, -dee/ *n.* CALENDAR the fourth day of the week, coming after Wednesday and before Friday [Old English *u(n)resdæg,* literally "day of thunder," translation of late Latin *Jovis dies* "day of Jupiter (the god of thunder)"]

Thurs·day Is·land /th/ island in the Torres Strait, off the northeastern coast of Australia. Area: 1.4 sq. mi./3.6 sq. km.

Thurs·days /thúrz dàyz, -deez/ *adv.* CALENDAR every Thursday

Thur·so /thúrssō/ town and seaport on the northern coast of Scotland. It is the northernmost town on the mainland of Great Britain. Population: 8,488 (1991).

thus /thuss/ *adv.* **1.** CONSEQUENTLY as a result (*formal*) **2.** LIKE THIS in this way (*formal*) **3.** TO THIS DEGREE to this degree or extent [Old English]

thus·ly /thússlee/ *adv.* thus (*humorous*)

Thut·mo·se III /thoot mṓsə/ (*d.* 1450 B.C.) Egyptian pharaoh. He became pharaoh in 1504 B.C. Through military conquest, he extended the Egyptian empire eastward as far as the Euphrates River, and with the vast wealth of his Asian territories erected great temples and other imperial buildings in Egypt.

thu·ya *n.* = **thuja**

thwack /thwak/ *vt.* (**thwacked, thwack·ing, thwacks**) SMACK SOMEBODY OR SOMETHING to strike somebody or something with a flat object such as the flat of the hand ■ *n.* SHARP BLOW WITH FLAT OBJECT a sharp smacking blow with a flat object [Early 16thC. An imitation of the sound of the blow.] —**thwack·er** *n.*

thwart /thwawrt/ *v.* (**thwart·ed, thwart·ing, thwarts**) **1.** *vt.* FRUSTRATE SOMETHING to prevent somebody or somebody's plan from being successful **2.** *vti.* CROSS to place one thing across another or be placed across something (*archaic*) ■ *adj.* EXTENDING ACROSS situated or extending across something ■ *n.* CROSSWISE SEAT IN BOAT a crosswise seat or transverse member on a rowboat, canoe or similar small boat ■ *prep.* ATHWART athwart (*archaic*) ■ *adv.* ATHWART athwart (*archaic*) [13thC. From Old Norse.] —**thwart·ed·ly** /thwáwrtədlee/ *adv.* —**thwart·er** *n.*

thy /thī/ *adj.* belonging or relating to you, the second person singular possessive corresponding to "thou" (*archaic*) [12thC. Shortening of an earlier form of THINE.]

Thy·es·tes /thī ésteez/ *n.* in Greek mythology, the brother of Atreus and king of Mycenae. After usurping the throne from his brother, he was tricked into eating the flesh of his own sons. —**Thy·es·te·an** *adj.*

thy·la·cine /thílə sìn, thíləssin/ *n.* a large carnivorous marsupial of Tasmania that resembles a dog and has brownish fur and black stripes across the back. It was once widespread through Australia but is thought to be extinct. Latin name: *Thylacinus cynocephalus.* [Mid-19thC. From modern Latin *Thylacinus,* genus name, from Greek *thulakos* "pouch."]

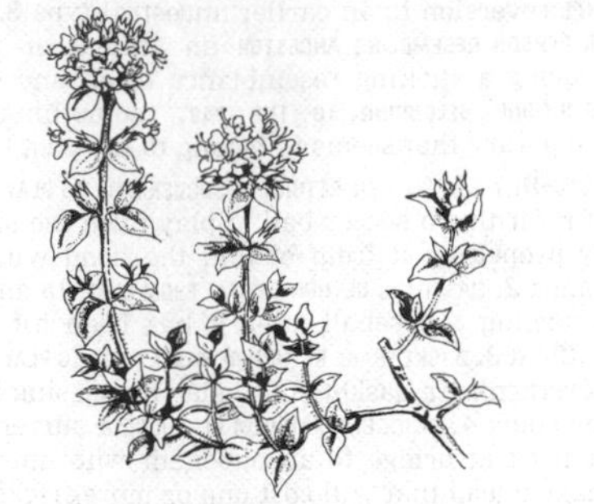

Thyme

thyme /tīm/ *n.* **1.** FOOD CULINARY HERB the tiny leaves of an aromatic shrub, used fresh or dried as a flavoring in cooking **2.** PLANTS AROMATIC SHRUB a small low shrub of the mint family with narrow leaves yielding thyme and white, pink, or red flowers. It also yields an aromatic essential oil containing thymol. Genus: *Thymus.* [15thC. Via Old French *thym* from, ultimately, Greek *thumon,* from *thuein* "to burn, sacrifice," from its use as incense.] —**thym·y** *adj.*

thy·mec·to·my /thī méktəmee/ (*plural* **-mies**) *n.* surgical removal of the thymus gland [Early 20thC. Coined from THYMUS + -ECTOMY.]

thy·mi plural of **thymus**

-thymia *suffix.* condition or state of mind ○ *dysthymia* [Via modern Latin from, ultimately, Greek *thumos* "mind"]

thy·mic[1] /thímik/ *adj.* relating to the thymus

thy·mic[2] /tímik, thímik/ *adj.* relating to thyme

thy·mi·dine /thímə deen/ *n.* a nucleoside that is one of the principal components of DNA, consisting of one molecule of thymine linked to one molecule of the sugar, deoxyribose. Formula: $C_{10}H_{14}N_2O_5$. [Early 20thC. Coined from THYMINE + -IDINE.]

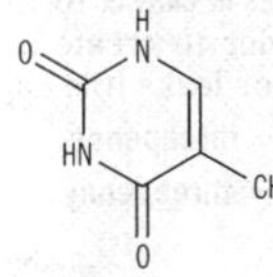

Thymine

thy·mine /thí meen, thímin/ *n.* a component of nucleic acid that pairs with adenine to carry hereditary information in DNA in cells. Chemically, it is a pyrimidine derivative. Formula: $C_5H_6N_2O_2$. Symbol **T** [Late 19thC. Coined from THYMIC[1] + -INE.]

thy·mo·cyte /thímə sìt/ *n.* a type of small white blood cell (**lymphocyte**) occurring in the thymus that is a precursor of a T-cell

thy·mol /thí màwl/ *n.* a colorless crystalline phenol with an aromatic odor, obtained from thyme oil or made synthetically. It is used as a fungicide and preservative, and in making perfumes. Formula: $C_{10}H_{14}O$. [Mid-19thC. Coined from Greek *thumon* (see THYME) + -OL.]

thy·mo·ma /thī mṓmə/ (*plural* **-mas** *or* **-ma·ta** /-mətə/) *n.* a tumor of the thymus [Early 20thC. Coined from THYMO- + -OMA.]

thy·mo·sin /thímәssin/ *n.* a hormone that influences the development and differentiation of T-cells in the thymus [Mid-20thC. Coined from Greek *thumos* (see THYMUS) + -IN.]

thy·mus /thímәss/ (*plural* **-mus·es** *or* **-mi** /-mī/), **thy·mus gland** *n.* an organ, located at the base of the neck, that is involved in development of cells of the immune system, particularly T-cells. It is prominent in the young but shrinks after puberty. [Late 16thC. Via modern Latin from Greek *thumos* "warty growth resembling a bunch of thyme."]

thy·ra·tron /thírә tròn/ *n.* a gas-filled hot-cathode tube that acts as an electronic switch or relay in which a signal applied to the control grid initiates anode current but does not limit it [Early 20thC. Coined from Greek *thura* (see THYROID) + -TRON.]

thy·ris·tor /thī rístәr/ *n.* a semiconductor device that has two stable switches used for conductive and nonconductive modes [Mid-20thC. Blend of THYRATRON and TRANSISTOR.]

thyro- *prefix.* thyroid ○ *thyrotropin* [From THYROID]

thy·ro·cal·ci·to·nin /thírō kàlsә tṓnin/ *n.* = **calcitonin**

thy·roid /thí ròyd/ *n.* **1.** = **thyroid gland 2.** = **thyroid cartilage 3. MEDICINE OBTAINED FROM ANIMAL THYROID GLAND** a preparation obtained from the thyroid gland of certain animals that is used in treating conditions of the thyroid gland ■ *adj.* **1. thy·roid, thy·roi·dal OF THYROID GLAND** relating to, situated in, supplying, or secreted by the thyroid gland **2. thy·roid, thy·roid·al OF THYROID CARTILAGE** relating to the thyroid cartilage [Early 18thC. Via obsolete French from, ultimately, Greek *thura* "door," from the oblong shape of the cartilage in front of the throat.]

thy·roid car·ti·lage *n.* the largest cartilage of the larynx, forming the projection called the Adam's apple

thy·roid·ec·to·my /thì roy déktәmee/ (*plural* **-mies**) *n.* surgical removal of the thyroid gland or part of it

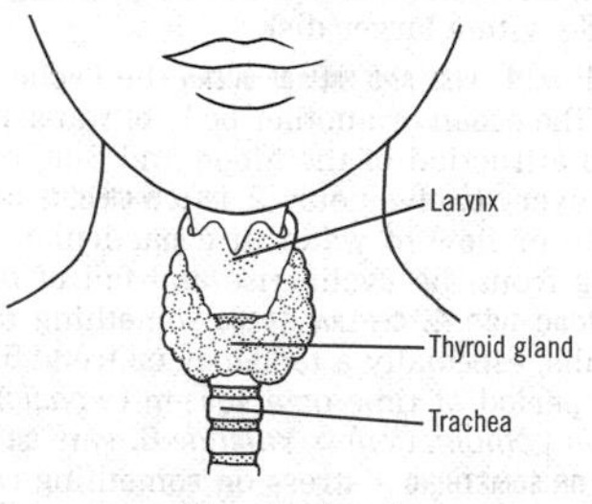

Thyroid gland

thy·roid gland *n.* an endocrine gland located in the neck of human beings and other vertebrate animals that secretes the hormones responsible for controlling metabolism and growth. Excessive action of the thyroid gland can cause Graves' disease, while underactivity can cause myxedema.

thy·roid hor·mone *n.* either of the two hormones, thyroxine and triiodothyronine, that are secreted by the thyroid gland and regulate body metabolism and growth

thy·roid·i·tis /thì roy dítiss/ *n.* inflammation of the thryoid gland. This may be acute, as a result of bacterial infection, or chronic, as a result of an autoimmune response in which lymphocytes invade the gland.

thy·roid-stim·u·lat·ing hor·mone *n.* = **thyrotropin**

thy·ro·tox·i·co·sis /thírō tòksә kṓssiss/ *n.* = **hyperthyroidism**

thy·ro·tro·pin /thìrә trṓpin/, **thy·ro·tro·phin** /-trṓfin/ *n.* a hormone that is secreted by the anterior lobe of the pituitary gland and stimulates release of hormones by the thyroid gland [Mid-20thC. Coined from THYRO- + -TROPIC + -IN.]

thy·ro·tro·pin-re·leas·ing hor·mone *n.* a peptide hormone that is produced by the hypothalamus and controls the release of thyrotropin by the pituitary gland

thy·rox·ine /thī rók seen/, **thy·rox·in** /-róksin/ *n.* the principal hormone secreted by the thyroid gland. It stimulates metabolism and is essential for normal growth and development. A synthetic form is used to treat hypothyroidism. [Early 20thC. Coined from THYRO- + OXY- + INDOLE (from a misunderstanding of its chemical structure), altered on the model of -INE.]

thyrse /thurs/ *n.* a flower head, e.g., in lilacs, that consists of numerous branching clusters of individual flowers arising from a single main stem [Early 17thC. Via French from Latin *thyrsus* (see THYRSUS).] —**thyr·soid** *adj.*

thyr·sus /thúrsәss/ (*plural* **-si** /-sī/) *n.* **1.** MYTHOL **STAFF CARRIED BY DIONYSUS** in Greek mythology and art, a staff tipped with a pine cone, carried by the Greek god Dionysus and his followers **2.** BOT = **thyrse** [Late 16thC. Via Latin from Greek *thursos* "stalk of a plant, staff carried by Dionysus," of unknown origin.]

thy·sa·nu·ran /thìssә nóorәn/ *n.* = **bristletail** [Mid-19thC. Formed from modern Latin *Thysanura*, order name, from Greek *thusanos* "tassel, fringe" + *oura* "tail."] — **thy·sa·nu·rous** *adj.*

thy·self /thī sélf/ *pron.* (*archaic*) **1. FORM OF "THY"** the form of "thy" used to refer to the same individual who is being addressed and is the subject of the verb **2. USED FOR EMPHASIS** used to emphasize that the individual being addressed is also being referred to [Old English. Originally from THEE + SELF (as an adjective), but interpreted as being from THY + SELF (as a noun).]

THz *abbr.* terahertz

ti[1] /tee/ *n.* a syllable that represents the seventh note in a scale, used for singing solfeggio. In fixed solfeggio it represents the note B, the seventh note in the scale of C, while in solfeggio with movable do it is used to represent the seventh note of the key being sung. [Mid-19thC. Alteration of SI.]

ti[2] /tee/ (*plural* **tis**) *n.* a woody Polynesian and Australian plant of the agave family with leaves used for thatching, garments, and fodder and with roots used as food and for making beverages. Genus: *Cordyline.* [Mid-19thC. From Tahitian and Maori.]

Ti *symbol.* titanium

Tian·an·men Square /tyaan aan mèn-/ *n.* a large square in central Beijing, China, that is a traditional site for festivals, rallies, and demonstrations. In 1989 it was the scene of a prodemocracy demonstration led by students in which hundreds were killed when troops were ordered to clear the square.

Tian Shan /tyèn shán/ = **Tien Shan**

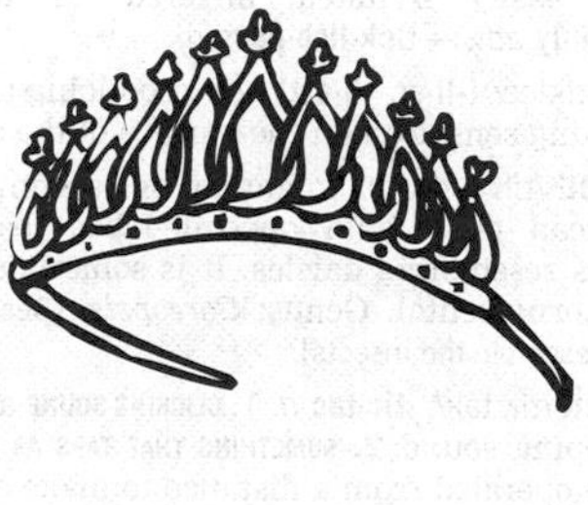
Tiara

ti·ar·a /tee áarә, -érrә/ *n.* **1. WOMAN'S JEWELED CORONET** a small jeweled semicircular headdress worn by a woman on formal occasions **2. POPE'S CROWN** a headdress consisting of three coronets with an orb and a cross on top, worn by the pope or carried before him on ceremonial occasions **3. PERSIAN KING'S CROWN** a high headdress worn by an ancient Persian king [Mid-16thC. Directly and via Italian from Latin, from Greek *tiara(s)*, probably from a language of southwestern Asia.] —**ti·ar·aed** *adj.*

Ti·ber /tíbәr/ river of central Italy. Rising in the Apennines, it flows through Rome and empties into the Tyrrhenian Sea. Length: 252 mi./405 km.

Ti·be·ri·us /tī beeree әss/ (42 B.C.–A.D. 37) Roman emperor. His reign (A.D. 14–37) was marked by revolts and conspiracies. Full name **Tiberius Julius Caesar Augustus**

Ti·bet /tә bét/ country north of the Himalayas, since 1965 a province-level administrative region of China. With an average elevation of more than 12,000 ft./4,000 m, it is the highest region on earth. Capital: Lhasa. Population: 2,196,010 (1990). Area: 472,000 sq. mi./1,222,000 sq. km. Official name **Tibet Autonomous Region**

Ti·bet·an /ti bétt'n/ *n.* **1.** PEOPLES **SOMEBODY FROM TIBET** somebody who was born or raised in Tibet, or who is of Tibetan descent **2.** LANG **LANGUAGE OF TIBET** the language of Tibet, spoken also in neighboring parts of China, Nepal, and India. It belongs to the Tibeto-Burman branch of the Sino-Tibetan family of languages. Tibetan is spoken by about six million people. —**Ti·bet·an** *adj.*

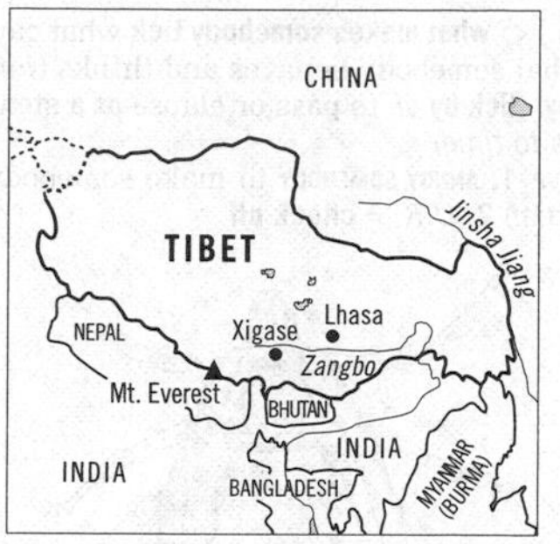

Tibet

Ti·bet·an Bud·dhism *n.* = **Lamaism**

Ti·bet·an span·iel *n.* a small dog with a long thick coat, a plumed tail curled over the back, and drooping ears, belonging to a breed that originated in Tibet. It was traditionally a sacred breed, confined to monasteries and palaces.

Ti·bet·an ter·ri·er *n.* a small terrier with a long shaggy coat that falls over its eyes and a backcurling tail, belonging to a breed that originated in Tibet

Ti·bet·o-Bur·man /tә bèttō búrmәn/ *n.* LANG a branch of the Sino-Tibetan family of languages that comprises Tibetan, Burmese, and many other languages of Southern and Southeast Asia [Mid-20thC. Coined from *Tibeto-* (from TIBETAN) + BURMAN.] —**Ti·bet·o-Bur·man** *adj.*

tib·i·a /tíbbee ә/ (*plural* **-ae** /-èe/ *or* **-as**) *n.* **1.** ANAT **INNER BONE OF LOWER LEG** the inner and larger of the two bones in the lower leg, extending from the knee to the ankle bone alongside the fibula **2.** ZOOL **BONE IN ANIMAL'S LEG** a bone in the lower leg of vertebrates corresponding to the human tibia **3.** INSECTS **PART OF INSECT'S LEG** the fourth segment of an insect's leg, between the femur and the tarsus **4.** BIRDS **PART OF BIRD'S LEG** the lower feathered segment or drumstick of a bird's leg **5.** MUSIC **ANCIENT WIND INSTRUMENT** an ancient flute, originally made from an animal's tibia [Late 17thC. From Latin, "shinbone," earlier "pipe," of unknown origin.] —**tib·i·al** *adj.*

tib·i·o·fib·u·lar /tìbbee ō fíbbyәlәr/ *adj.* relating to the tibia and fibula, the bones of the lower leg

tib·i·o·tar·sus /tìbbee ō taarsәss/ (*plural* **-si** /-sī/) *n.* the main bone of a bird's lower leg, formed by a fusion of the tibia and some of the bones of the tarsus

tic /tik/ *n.* **1. MUSCLE TWITCH** a sudden involuntary spasmodic muscular contraction, especially of facial, neck, or shoulder muscles, which may become more pronounced when somebody is stressed **2. QUIRK OF BEHAVIOR** a distinctive behavioral trait or quirk [Early 19thC. Via French from Italian *ticchio.*]

tic·al /ti kaal, tík'l/ (*plural* **-als** *or* **-al**) *n.* **1. OLD UNIT OF THAI CURRENCY** a silver coin that was a unit of currency in Thailand between 1909 and 1950 **2. OLD UNIT OF WEIGHT IN THAILAND** a former unit of weight in Thailand, equal to about half an ounce/14 grams [Mid-17thC. From Portuguese, of uncertain origin: probably from Marathi *ṭakā* or Bengali *ṭākā* "coin."]

tic dou·lou·reux /tìk doolә roo, -rú/ *n.* = **trigeminal neuralgia** [From French, literally "painful tic"]

Ti·ci·no /ti cheenō/ river in western Europe, a tributary of the Po River. Length: 154 mi./248 km.

tick[1] /tik/ *n.* **1. RECURRING CLICK** a slight quiet recurring clicking sound, especially one made by a clock or watch. ◊ **tock 2. DEGREE ON SCALE** an increment on a scale, especially the smallest amount by which a security may rise or fall in a stock or bond market **3.** *U.K.* **VERY SHORT TIME** a very short time (*informal*) ○ *I'll be back in a tick.* **4.** *U.K.* = **check** *n.* 8 ■ *v.* **(ticked, tick·ing, ticks) 1.** *vi.* **MAKE RECURRING CLICKING SOUND** to make a slight quiet recurring clicking sound **2.** *vi.* **REGISTER TAXI FARE BY CLICKING** to make a clicking sound while registering the progressive increase of a taxi fare **3.** *vt.* **CHECK OFF SOMETHING** to put a mark, check, or electronic signal beside an item as a record or reminder **4.** *vi.* **FUNCTION PROPERLY** to function well or in the specified way (*informal*) [13thC. Origin uncertain.] ◇ **what makes somebody tick** what causes the way that somebody behaves and thinks (*informal*)

tick away, tick by *vi.* to pass or elapse at a steady pace (*refers to time*)

tick off *vt.* **1. ANNOY SOMEBODY** to make somebody angry (*informal*) **2.** *U.K.* = **check off**

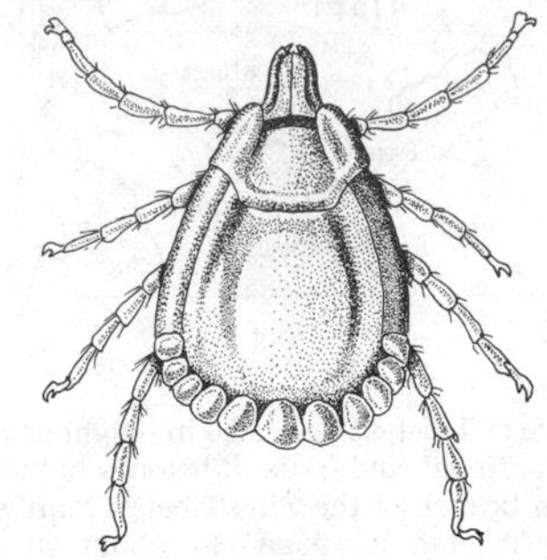

Tick

tick[2] /tik/ *n.* **1. TINY PARASITIC INSECT** a small wingless bloodsucking insect that lives on the skin of humans and warm-blooded animals and may transmit diseases. Families: Argasidae and Ioxidae. **2. BLOODSUCKING FLY** a parasitic fly that lives on the skin of sheep, cattle, horses, and other animals [Old English *ticia*. Ultimately of prehistoric Germanic origin.]

tick[3] /tik/ *n.* the cloth case or covering that is filled with cotton, feathers, or other materials to form a pillow or mattress [15thC. Via Middle Dutch *tēke* from, ultimately, Greek *thēkē* "cover, case."]

tick[4] /tik/ *n. U.K.* the system of owing somebody money for goods that are acquired (*dated informal*) ○ *bought it on tick* [Mid-17thC. Shortening of TICKET in the obsolete sense "note of goods received on credit."]

tick·bird /tík bùrd/ *n.* a bird that feeds on ticks, e.g., the oxpecker

tick-borne *adj.* used to describe a disease in which the causative microorganism is transmitted by the bite of a tick, e.g., Lyme disease or many forms of encephalitis

tick·er /tíkər/ *n.* **1. HEART** somebody's heart (*informal*) **2.** STOCK EXCH **MACHINE DISPLAYING STOCK PRICES** an electronic device that displays the prices of securities, formerly a telegraphic receiving instrument that automatically printed stock quotations on ticker tape **3. WATCH** a small portable timepiece (*dated informal*)

tick·er tape *n.* formerly, a continuous paper ribbon on which a ticker automatically printed stock quotations

tick·er-tape ma·chine *n.* STOCK EXCH = **ticker** *n.* 1

tick·er-tape pa·rade *n.* a parade honoring a visiting celebrity who is showered with shredded paper or confetti, formerly ticker tape, from buildings while being driven through the streets

tick·et /tíkit/ *n.* **1.** TRANSP **TRAVEL PASS** a printed piece of cardboard or paper showing that the holder is entitled to be traveling on a means of transport **2.** LEISURE **PASS FOR ENTERTAINMENT** a printed piece of cardboard or paper showing that the holder is entitled to admission to a place of public entertainment or a sports facility **3.** PUBLIC ADMIN **NOTIFICATION OF TRAFFIC OFFENSE** a printed notice that a traffic or parking offense has been committed and a fine must be paid **4.** COMM **LABEL OR TAG** a small piece of card attached to an article, showing the price or other details **5.** POL **GROUP OF CANDIDATES RUNNING TOGETHER** a list of candidates put forward by one party or group in an election **6. PRECISELY WHAT IS NEEDED** the right, just, desired, or appropriate thing (*informal*) ○ *A month in Europe would be just the ticket.* **7.** TRANSP **QUALIFICATION OF PILOT OR SHIP'S OFFICER** a certificate of qualification as a ship's captain or an aircraft pilot ■ *vt.* (**-et·ed, -et·ing, -ets**) **1.** PUBLIC ADMIN **GIVE SOMEBODY A PARKING TICKET** to issue a motor vehicle or its driver with a ticket for a traffic or parking violation **2.** COMM **ATTACH A TICKET TO AN ARTICLE** to attach a ticket to an article, showing the price or other details **3.** LEISURE **ISSUE A PASS TO SOMETHING** to issue a ticket for admission to something **4. CATEGORIZE SOMEBODY OR SOMETHING** to assign somebody to a particular category, or designate something for a particular purpose [Early 16thC. Via obsolete French *étiquet* "ticket, label" (source of English *etiquette*), from, ultimately, Old French *estiquier* "to stick"; from the idea of sticking on a label.] ◇ **have tickets on yourself** *Aus* to have an inflated opinion of yourself (*informal*)

tick·et·y-boo *adj. U.K., Can* perfectly fine (*dated informal*) [Origin uncertain: perhaps from Hindi *ṭhīk hai* "all right"]

tick fe·ver *n.* an acute infectious disease transmitted by the bite of a tick, e.g., Rocky Mountain spotted fever or Texas fever

tick·ing /tíking/ *n.* a strong cotton fabric, often twilled, that is used to cover mattresses and pillows [Mid-17thC. Formed from TICK[4].]

tick·le /tík'l/ *v.* (**-led, -ling, -les**) **1.** *vt.* **MAKE SOMEBODY LAUGH AND TWITCH** to touch, prod, stroke, or caress lightly a sensitive part of somebody's body, usually so as to produce involuntary laughter and wriggling **2.** *vti.* **CAUSE ITCHINESS** to cause an itchy or scratchy feeling by light touching of a sensitive part of the body ○ *This feather boa tickles.* **3.** *vt.* **PLEASE OR AMUSE SOMEBODY** to make somebody pleased, or appeal to somebody's sense of humor (*often passive*) ■ *n.* **1. TOUCH THAT MAKES SOMEBODY LAUGH** a light touch, prod, stroke, or caress applied to a sensitive part of somebody's body, usually so as to produce involuntary laughter and wriggling **2. ITCHY FEELING** an itchy or scratchy feeling caused when a sensitive part of the body is touched lightly by something, especially material [14thC. Origin uncertain: probably formed from TICK[1] in the obsolete sense "to touch lightly," in which case its original literal sense would have been "to keep on touching lightly."] ◇ **tickled pink, tickled silly, tickled to death** extremely pleased (*informal*) ◇ **tickle somebody's fancy** to please or entertain somebody (*informal*)

tick·ler /tíklər/ *n.* **1.** = **tickler file** **2.** ACCT **ACCOUNTING JOURNAL** a single-entry journal in which obligations are entered chronologically **3.** ELEC ENG = **tickler coil**

tick·ler coil *n.* a small coil connected in series with a radio vacuum tube's plate circuit and inductively coupled to a coil located in a grid circuit to provide regenerative feedback

tick·ler file *n.* a file consisting of reminders of matters that must be dealt with

tick·lish /tíklish/ *adj.* **1. SENSITIVE TO TICKLING** sensitive to being tickled **2. PROBLEMATIC** requiring careful or delicate handling because of its risk or difficulty **3. TOUCHY** easily irritated, angered, or upset — **tick·lish·ly** *adv.* —**tick·lish·ness** *n.*

tick·ly /tíklee/ (**-li·er, -li·est**) *adj.* producing a tickling or itching sensation on the surface of the skin

tick·seed /tík seèd/ *n.* an annual or perennial North American plant with opposite-lobed leaves and flowers resembling daisies. It is sometimes grown as an ornamental. Genus: *Coreopsis.* [Because their seeds resemble the insects]

tick·tack /tík tàk/, **tic·tac** *n.* **1. CLICKING SOUND** a clicking or tapping sound **2. SOMETHING THAT TAPS AS A PRANK** a device operated from a distance to make a tapping sound on a window or door as a practical joke [Mid-16thC. An imitation of the sound.]

tick-tack-toe, tic-tac-toe *n.* a game played by two players who alternately mark squares in a grid with O's or X's, the winner being the first to get three marks in a row [Origin uncertain: probably imitative of the sound of an earlier game in which players brought pencils down on slates with their eyes closed]

tick·tock /tík tòk/ *n.* **TICKING OF TIMEPIECE** the clicking sound made by a clock or watch ■ *vi.* (**-tocked, -tock·ing, -tocks**) **MAKE TICKING NOISE** to make a quiet recurring clicking sound (*refers to a timepiece*) [Mid-19thC. An imitation of the sound.]

tick tre·foil *n.* a leguminous tropical or subtropical plant with trifoliate leaves and jointed seed pods that cling to fur or clothing. Some varieties are cultivated as livestock forage. Genus: *Desmodium.* [Because the joints of the pods stick to things as ticks cling to the fur of animals]

tick·y-tack·y /tìki tákee/, **tick·y-tack** /tìki ták/ *adj.* **DULL AND SHODDY** dull, unimaginative, and often of uniform quality or design (*informal*) ■ *n.* **SOMETHING DULL AND SHODDY** dull, unimaginative, or inferior materials, or something made from them (*informal*) [*Ticky* alteration of TACKY "shoddy"]

Ti·con·de·ro·ga /tì kondə rṓgə/ village in northeastern New York, on the La Chute River. It is the site of Fort Ticonderoga, an important strategic fortification in the French and Indian War (1754–63) and the Revolution (1775–83). Population: 2,770 (1990).

tic·tac *n.* = **ticktack**

tic-tac-toe *n.* = **tick-tack-toe**

t.i.d. *abbr.* three times a day (*used in doctors' prescriptions*) [Latin *ter in die*]

tid·al /tíd'l/ *adj.* **1. OF TIDES** relating to or affected by tides **2. DEPENDENT ON TIDE** having a time of departure dependent on the phase of a tide ○ *a tidal ferry* **3. DEFINED BY TIDE LEVEL** changing in character or accessibility according to the level of the tide **4. FLUCTUATING** not constant but fluctuating between periods of intense activity and periods of little activity — **tid·al·ly** *adv.*

tid·al air *n.* the volume of air that passes in and out of the body during normal breathing [*Tidal* from its obsolete sense "periodic, intermittent"]

tid·al ba·sin *n.* an artificial basin cut in rock that fills up at high tide

tid·al pow·er, tid·al en·er·gy *n.* the generation of electricity using the force created by the rise and fall of ocean tides

tid·al wave *n.* **1. HUGE OCEAN WAVE** an enormous and destructive ocean wave caused by extremely strong winds or seaquakes. ◊ **tsunami** **2. OVERWHELMING SURGE** a powerful widespread expression or surge of something ○ *a tidal wave of public emotion*

tid·bit /tíd bìt/ *n.* **1. SMALL MORSEL** a small, usually bite-sized, piece of delicious food **2. PIECE OF GOSSIP** a small piece of interesting information or gossip [Mid-17thC. *Tid* perhaps from obsolete English dialect, "tender."]

tid·dly·wink /tíddlee wìngk/, **tid·dle·dy·wink** /tíddlee-, tídd'ldee-/ *n.* a plastic disk used in the game of tiddlywinks [Mid-19thC. Origin uncertain.]

tid·dly·winks /tíddlee wìngks/, **tid·dle·dy·winks** /tíddlee-, tídd'ldee-/ *n.* a game in which players try to flip plastic disks into a cup by pressing them on the side with a larger disk

tide /tīd/ *n.* **1. RISE AND FALL OF OCEAN** the cyclic rise and fall of the ocean or another body of water produced by the attraction of the Moon and Sun, occurring about every twelve hours **2. INFLOW OR OUTFLOW OF WATER** the ebb or flow of water at a particular place resulting from the cyclic rise and fall of the ocean **3.** = **flood tide** **4. GENERAL TREND** something that rises and falls, especially a tendency or trend **5. PERIOD OF TIME** a period of time or a season (*archaic*) (*usually used in combination*) ○ *Yuletide* **6.** PHYS **GRAVITATIONAL STRESS ON SOMETHING** a stress on something caused by a gravitational attraction, e.g., in the atmosphere or on a celestial body **7. CRUCIAL POINT** an extreme or critical point or position **8. APPROPRIATE TIME** an appropriate time for something (*archaic*) ■ *v.* (**tid·ed, tid·ing, tides**) **1.** *vti.* **CARRY ALONG ON TIDE** to carry somebody or something along on the tide, or be carried along in this way **2.** *vi.* **EBB AND FLOW** to ebb and flow like the tide [Old English *tīd* "time." Ultimately from an Indo-European base meaning "to divide," the underlying idea being of a "portion of time."] —**tide·less** *adj.* ◇ **swim against the tide** to have an opinion or take a stance that is different from or opposite to that taken by others ◇ **swim with the tide** to follow the opinions and attitudes of other people ◇ **turn the tide** to reverse the way things happen

tide over *vt.* to help somebody through a difficult time, especially with a loan or gift of money

tide gauge *n.* a gauge used to measure the level of tidal movement

tide·land /tīd lànd, -lənd/ *n.* **1. LAND SUBMERGED AT HIGH TIDE** land that is covered by water at high tide **2. TERRITORIAL LAND** land submerged beneath territorial waters (*often used in the plural*)

tide·mark /tīd maàrk/ *n.* **1. MARK LEFT BY TIDE** a mark made by the highest or lowest point of a tide **2. MARKER INDICATING LEVELS OF TIDES** a marker indicating the highest or lowest point of a tide **3. POINT MARKING RISE OR FALL** a point that somebody or something has reached, risen above, or fallen below

tide race *n.* a fast tidal current

tide-rip *n.* = **rip tide**

tide ta·ble *n.* a table showing the expected times and levels of tides at a particular place

tide·wa·ter /tīd wàwtər, -wòttər/ *n.* **1. WATER AFFECTED BY TIDES** water whose movement or level is affected by tides **2. WATER COVERING LAND AT HIGH TIDE** water at high tide covering land that is dry at low tide **3. SEACOAST**

a coastal region, especially that of eastern Virginia

Tide·wa·ter *n.* an English dialect spoken in eastern Virginia

tide·way /tīd wày/ *n.* **1.** TIDAL CHANNEL a channel in which a tide runs **2.** TIDAL CURRENT a current in a tidal channel

tid·ings /tīdingz/ *npl.* news or information (*literary*) ○ *I bring you glad tidings.* [Old English *tīdung*, an alteration of Old Norse *tíðendi* "events"]

ti·dy /tīdee/ *adj.* (**-di·er, -di·est**) **1.** NEAT IN APPEARANCE having a neat orderly appearance **2.** METHODICAL tending to perform tasks in a systematic way **3.** CONSIDERABLE considerable and significant (*informal*) ○ *cost a tidy sum* **4.** *NZ, U.S.* SATISFACTORY adequate or satisfactory, especially when circumstances are taken into account (*informal*) ○ *negotiated a tidy redundancy package* ■ *vti.* (**-died, -dy·ing, -dies**) MAKE SOMEBODY OR SOMETHING TIDY to make somebody or something neat and orderly ■ *n.* (*plural* **-dies**) **1.** HOUSEHOLD COVERING FOR BACK OF CHAIR an ornamental protective covering for the back of a chair or sofa **2.** BOX FOR HOLDING SMALL OBJECTS a box for holding small objects that would otherwise be messily unsorted ○ *a desk tidy* [13thC. Formed from TIDE in the obsolete sense "time." The main modern meaning evolved via the senses "timely, at an appropriate time" and "good."] —**ti·di·ly** *adv.* —**ti·di·ness** *n.*

ti·dy·tips /tīdi tips/ (*plural* **-tips**) *n.* an annual plant with yellow white-tipped flowers resembling daisies, native to the western United States and cultivated as an ornamental. Latin name: *Layia platyglossa.*

tie /tī/ *v.* (**tied, ty·ing, ties**) **1.** *vt.* FASTEN THINGS WITH ROPE to fasten things together with a rope, string, or cord **2.** *vt.* FASTEN SOMETHING BY KNOTTING to fasten something with a knot or bow **3.** *vt.* MAKE A KNOT to make a knot or bow with rope, string, or cord **4.** *vt.* CONNECT THINGS to make a connection or link between people or things **5.** *vt.* RESTRICT to restrict somebody to certain conditions **6.** *vi.* SPORTS, LEISURE HAVE AN EQUAL SCORE to achieve the same score or place as somebody else in a game, race, or competition **7.** *vt.* MUSIC SUSTAIN A MUSICAL NOTE to hold a note from one bar to the next, thereby extending its value **8.** *vt.* MUSIC CONNECT NOTES WITH A CURVED LINE in musical notation, to connect two notes with a curved line ■ *n.* (*plural* **ties**) **1.** ACCESSORIES STRIP OF FABRIC WORN AROUND NECK a long tapering piece of fabric worn around the neck, under a shirt collar, and tied at the front so that the ends hang down the front of the shirt. ◊ **bow tie, bolo tie** **2.** SOMETHING USED FOR ATTACHING a long thin piece of something such as rope or wire used to fasten or close something else ○ *Where are the twist ties for the garbage bags?* **3.** SOMETHING THAT FORMS A CONNECTION something that links or unites people or things **4.** SPORTS, LEISURE EQUAL OUTCOME OF A CONTEST an equal score or result in a game, race, or competition **5.** RAIL WOODEN BEAM SUPPORTING A RAIL a wooden beam laid across a railroad track to support the rails **6.** SOMETHING THAT RESTRICTS something that restricts or confines somebody or something **7.** CONSTR STRENGTHENING BEAM a connecting, strengthening, or supporting beam or rod **8.** MUSIC CURVED LINE INDICATING EXTENSION OF NOTES a curved line shown above or below two notes of the same pitch, indicating that they are to be sounded without a break for their combined duration **9.** CIV ENG SURVEYING MEASUREMENT either of two measurements on a survey line used to fix the position of a reference point ■ *adj.* SPORTS MADE EQUAL having an equal outcome [Old English *tīgan*. Ultimately from a prehistoric Germanic base meaning "to pull" (also the ancestor of English *tug*).] ◇ **fit to be tied** extremely angry or exasperated (*informal*)

tie down *vt.* prevent somebody from acting freely

tie up *v.* **1.** *vt.* BIND to fasten or bind something using rope or string **2.** *vti.* NAUT DOCK A BOAT to moor a boat or ship by securing lines, or be moored in this way **3.** *vt.* OCCUPY SOMEBODY OR SOMETHING to keep somebody or something busy **4.** *vt.* COMPLETE SOMETHING to complete the work needed for something **5.** *vti.* STOP to bring something to a halt, or come to a halt **6.** *vt.* FIN INVEST MONEY WITH RESTRICTIONS to invest money in such a way that it cannot be used for other purposes **7.** *vt.* LAW PLACE RESTRICTIONS ON PROPERTY to place legal restrictions on the selling or alienation of property

tie·back /tī bak/ *n.* a length of cord or fabric used to hold a curtain to one side

tie beam *n.* a beam such as the bottom horizontal member of a roof truss that pulls together a structure and stops it spreading outward

tie·break·er /tī bràykər/, **tie-break** *n.* a means of deciding the winner of a game or competition when there is a tie

tie·break·ing /tī bràyking/ *adj.* deciding the winner of a game or competition when there is a tie ○ *the tiebreaking question*

tie clip, tie clasp *n.* an ornamental clip that holds a necktie in place

tied /tīd/ *adj.* loaned on condition of being spent only on goods or services supplied by the lender

tie-dye *vt.* DYE DESIGNS USING BUNCHED CLOTH to dye designs on cloth by tightly tying portions of it with waxed thread so that the dye only affects the exposed areas ■ *n.* **1.** FABRIC WITH TIE-DYED DESIGNS a piece of fabric whose designs are made by tie-dyeing (*informal*) **2.** = **tie-dyeing**

tie-dye·ing *n.* a method of dyeing textiles to produce patterns by tightly tying waxed thread around sections of the fabric so that they will not become impregnated with the dye

tie-in *n.* **1.** LINK a link or relationship with something **2.** JOINT PROMOTION OF PRODUCTS an arrangement by which related products are sold, promoted, or marketed together, e.g., a book or toy along with a movie **3.** RELATED PRODUCT a product that is sold, promoted, or marketed in close connection with another **4.** SALE REQUIRING DUAL PURCHASES a sale in which items are advertised or sold with the stipulation that they must be purchased together, or a product sold in this way

tie line *n.* a telephone line that connects two private exchanges

tie·man·nite /teemə nīt/ *n.* a dark gray mineral form of mercury selenide [Mid-19thC. From German *Tiemannit*, named for the German scientist J. C. W. F. *Tiemann* (1848–99).]

Tien Shan /tyèn sháan/ mountain range in Central Asia, stretching about 1,500 mi./2,400 km from Kyrgyzstan in the west through northwestern China to Mongolia in the east. The highest point is Victory Peak, 24,406 ft./7,439 m.

tie·pin /tī pìn/ *n.* = **tie tack**

tier /teer/ *n.* **1.** ROW OF SEATS IN RISING SERIES any of a series of rows placed one above and behind another, e.g., seats in a theater **2.** LAYER any of a series of layers or levels placed one above the other (*often used in combination*) ○ *a three-tier cake* **3.** LEVEL IN HIERARCHY a hierarchical level in an organization (*often used in combination*) ■ *vt.* (**tiered, tier·ing, tiers**) ARRANGE SOMETHING IN RISING ROWS to arrange something in rows rising one above the other [15thC. From French *tire* "rank, sequence, order," from *tirer* "to draw out, elongate."]

tierce /teers/ *n.* **1.** CHR = **terce** **2.** CARDS THREE CARDS OF THE SAME SUIT a sequence of three cards of the same suit **3.** THIRD PART a third or third part (*archaic*) **4.** FENCING PARRYING POSITION the third of eight positions from which a fencing parry can be made **5.** MEASURE FORMER MEASURE OF CAPACITY a former measure of capacity equal to 42 wine gallons [15thC. Via Old French from Latin *tertia*, a form of *tertius* "third."]

tier·cel *n.* = **tercel**

tiered /teerd/ *adj.* arranged in layers or levels placed one above the other (*often used in combination*)

tie rod *n.* a metal rod that joins or supports two parts such as one used as a linkage in the steering mechanism of a motor vehicle. Tie rods are also used to keep trusses and arches from spreading.

Ti·er·ra del Fue·go /tee èrrə del fwáygō/ archipelago off the southern tip of South America. Separated from the mainland by the Strait of Magellan, and bounded by the Atlantic, the Antarctic, and the Pacific oceans, the islands belong partly to Argentina and partly to Chile.

tie tack, tie tac *n.* an ornamental pin used to fasten a necktie to the front of a shirt

tie-up *n.* **1.** CONNECTION something that connects one thing with another **2.** DELAY a temporary delay or obstruction, e.g., in the flow of traffic **3.** NAUT DOCKING PLACE a mooring place for a boat or ship

tiff /tif/ *n.* **1.** QUARREL a minor quarrel **2.** ILL HUMOR a brief period of bad temper ■ *vi.* (**tiffed, tiff·ing, tiffs**) ARGUE to have a minor quarrel with somebody [Early 18thC. Origin uncertain: probably originally a dialect word; thought to suggest the sound of a "burst" of escaping gas.]

TIFF *abbr.* COMPUT tagged image file format

tif·fa·ny /tíffənee/ (*plural* **-nies**) *n.* a fine gauzy fabric [Early 17thC. Via Old French *tifanie* from, ultimately, Greek *theophaneia*, literally "vision of God," perhaps because the body is visible through the material.]

Tif·fa·ny /tíffənee/, **Charles Lewis** (1812–1902) U.S. jeweler and retailer. He introduced the British standard of sterling silver in the United States, and founded Tiffany and Company (1853).

Tif·fa·ny, Louis Comfort (1848–1933) U.S. glassmaker and interior designer. He is known for the stained glass, vases, and lamps produced by his Tiffany Studios (1902–32). He patented the iridescent glass used in his flowing art nouveau pieces.

TIFF file, TIF file *n.* a graphic file in a format often used for storing bitmapped images

tif·fin /tíffin/ *n.* **1.** *S Asia* LIGHT MEAL a light midday meal or snack **2.** = **tiffin carrier** [Early 19thC. Variant of *tiffing*, literally "drinking," from obsolete *tiff* "to drink," of unknown origin.]

tif·fin car·ri·er *n.* *S Asia* a carrier consisting of several metal containers stacked one on top of another, used to carry prepared food

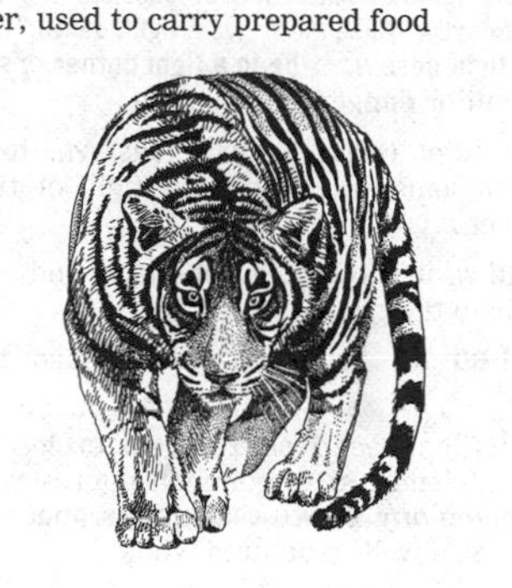

Tiger

ti·ger /tīgər/ (*plural* **-gers** *or* **-ger**) *n.* **1.** LARGE STRIPED FELINE a carnivorous Asian cat, the largest member of the cat family, that has a tawny coat and black stripes. Latin name: *Panthera tigris.* **2.** SOMEBODY FIERCE somebody who is fierce, brave, or forceful [13thC. Via Old French *tigre* from, ultimately, Greek *tigris*, of uncertain origin: perhaps from Iranian.]

ti·ger bee·tle *n.* a fast-running predatory beetle that lives in warm regions. It has strong sharp jaws for digging and brightly colored patterned wing covers. Family: Cicindelidae. [*Tiger* from its predatory habits]

ti·ger cat *n.* **1.** SMALL CAT WITH MARKINGS RESEMBLING A TIGER'S a small striped or spotted cat such as the margay, serval, or ocelot **2.** TABBY CAT a domestic cat with blotched or striped markings resembling those of a tiger

ti·ger·eye /tīgər ī/ *n.* = **tiger's-eye**

ti·ger lil·y *n.* **1.** ASIAN PLANT an Asian lily that has red or orange flowers with dark purple or brown spots. Latin name: *Lilium lancifolium* and *Lilium tigrinum.* **2.** LILY RESEMBLING THE ASIAN TIGER LILY any lily that resembles the Asian tiger lily [*Tiger* from its coloring]

ti·ger moth *n.* a moth that has bold black and yellow or orange markings, especially on its wings. Family: Arctiidae.

ti·ger sal·a·man·der *n.* a black North American salamander with yellow or green stripes. It is among the largest of the terrestrial salamanders, growing to 13 in./33 cm. Latin name: *Ambystoma tigrinum.* [*Tiger* from its stripes]

ti·ger's-eye *n.* a striped yellow-brown rock composed of bands of quartz and fibrous silicate crocidolite used as a gemstone

ti·ger shark *n.* a large striped or spotted shark that lives mainly in tropical seas and has a voracious and indiscriminate appetite. Latin name: *Galeocerdo cuvieri.*

ti·ger swal·low·tail *n.* a large North American butterfly with a deeply forked tail and yellow wings with black stripes. Latin name: *Palilio glaucus* and *Palilio rutilus.*

tight /tīt/ *adj.* **1. SNUG** fitting the body very closely ○ *a tight sweater* **2. TAUT** stretched so that there is no slack ○ *pulled the rope tight* **3. FIXED** firmly secured or held ○ *a tight knot* **4. SEALED** sealed against gas or liquid leaks ○ *An air lock must have a tight seal.* **5. STRICT** strictly controlled or administered ○ *security was tight for the conference* **6. CRAMPED** lacking sufficient space to move freely ○ *It's going to be tight in the back seat.* **7. HAVING NO EXTRA TIME** allowing no time beyond what is needed to do something ○ *a tight schedule* **8. HAVING NO EXTRA MONEY** allowing no money beyond what is required ○ *working to a tight budget* **9. MISERLY** excessively frugal with money **10. HARD TO GET OUT OF** difficult or dangerous to handle ○ *We're in a tight fix now.* **11. WITH CLOSE RIVALS** characterized by well-matched competitors or teams ○ *a tight race* **12. DRUNK** intoxicated with alcohol (*slang*) **13. WELL DONE** arranged or performed with style and precision ○ *a tight performance by the whole team* **14. SUCCINCT** characterized by clear concise expression ○ *tight prose* **15. INTIMATE** having a very close relationship with somebody (*informal*) ○ *He's tight with his boss.* **16. HARD TO GET** characterized by conditions in which demand exceeds supply, often with concomitant rising prices ○ *a tight economy* ■ *adv.* **FIRMLY** in a firm, close, snug, or secure way ○ *hold on tight* [14thC. Alteration of obsolete *thight* "dense, thick," from Old Norse *théttr* "watertight, dense."] —**tight·ly** *adv.* —**tight·ness** *n.* ◇ **be in a tight corner** *or* **spot** be in a difficult or dangerous situation

tight·en /tīt'n/ (**-ened, -en·ing, -ens**) *vti.* to become or cause something to become tight or tighter —**tight·en·er** *n.*

tight end *n.* in football, an offensive end who lines up near to the tackle

tight·fist·ed /tīt fístəd/ *adj.* disinclined to spend money

tight·knit /tīt nít/ *adj.* **1. CLOSELY CONNECTED** closely united by love, friendship, or common interests ○ *a tight-knit community* **2. WELL-ORGANIZED** arranged or functioning as a well-structured whole

tight-lipped *adj.* **1. RELUCTANT TO TALK** unwilling to communicate ○ *He is remaining tight-lipped in the face of intense press speculation.* **2. HAVING THE LIPS TOGETHER** having the lips firmly closed, e.g., in anger or pain

tight·rope /tīt rōp/ *n.* a rope or wire stretched taut and suspended above the ground, on which somebody walks or performs a balancing act ◇ **walk a tightrope** to have to deal cautiously with a precarious situation, often one involving a choice or compromise

tights /tīts/ *npl.* **1. THICK ONE-PIECE GARMENT** a one-piece close-fitting garment made of opaque colored wool or cotton, covering the body from the waist to the feet and worn by women and girls for warmth and casual wear **2. DANCER'S ONE-PIECE GARMENT** a one-piece close-fitting garment covering the body from the neck or waist to the feet, worn by men and women dancers and acrobats **3.** *U.K.* = **pantyhose**

tight·wad /tīt wòd/ *n.* somebody who dislikes spending money (*informal insult*)

Tig·lath-pi·le·ser I /tìglath pī léezər/ (*b.* 1115?-1077? B.C.) Assyrian king. He expanded his kingdom by conquering Babylonia and recovering Armenia from invaders.

tig·lic ac·id /tìgglik-/ *n.* a viscous poisonous colorless liquid derived from croton oil, used in the pharmaceutical industry and perfumery. Formula: $C_5H_8O_2$. [*Tiglic* formed from modern Latin *(Croton) tiglium*, scientific name of the tree from whose seeds croton oil is obtained, from medieval Latin]

ti·glon /tíglən/, **ti·gon** /tígən/ *n.* the offspring of a male tiger and a female lion [Mid-20thC. Blend of TIGER and LION.]

ti·gress /tígrəss/ *n.* **1. FEMALE TIGER** a female tiger **2. FIERCE WOMAN** a fierce, brave, or passionate woman [Late 16thC. Formed from TIGER on the model of French *tigresse* "tigress."]

Ti·gri·nya /tə greényə/ *n.* LANG a Semitic language of northern Ethiopia that belongs to the Afro-Asiatic family of languages [Mid-19thC. From Tigrinya.]

Tig·ris /tígriss/ river in southeastern Asia. It rises in southeastern Turkey, flows through Iraq, and joins the Euphrates to form the Shatt Al-Arab, which empties into the Persian Gulf. Length: 1,150 mi./1,850 km.

Ti·jua·na /ti wàanə, -hwàanə/ city in northwestern Mexico, just south of the United States border. It is an industrial and tourist center. Population: 747,381 (1990).

tike *n.* = **tyke**

ti·ki /téekee/ *n.* **1. MAORI AMULET** a small carved human fetal figure, especially in greenstone, representing an ancestor and worn as an amulet by some Maori and Polynesian peoples **2. IMAGE OF A POLYNESIAN GOD** a stone or wooden representation of a Polynesian god [Late 18thC. From Maori.]

tik·ka /tíkə/ *adj.* an Indian dish of skewered meat that is marinated and then roasted in an oven [Mid-20thC. From Punjabi *ṭikkā*.]

til /til/ *n.* = **sesame** *n.* 2 [Mid-19thC. From Sanskrit *tila*.]

'til /til/, **til, 'till** *contr.* until. See Usage note at **till** [Mid-20thC. Shortening.]

ti·la·pi·a /tə làapee ə, tə láypee ə/ (*plural* **-as** *or* **-a**) *n.* a tropical African freshwater fish of the cichlid family, some species of which are important food fish and have been introduced and cultivated worldwide. Genus: *Tilapia*. [Mid-19thC. From modern Latin, the genus name.]

Til·burg /tíl bùrg/ industrial city in North Brabant Province, southern Netherlands. Population: 163,383 (1994).

til·de /tíldə/ *n.* a mark (~) placed over a letter to show that the pronunciation is nasalized, e.g., over "n" in Spanish, and over "a" or "o" in Portuguese [Mid-19thC. Via Spanish, from Latin *titulus* "heading," with the sounds in the middle transposed.]

Til·den /tíldən/, **Bill** (1893–1953) U.S. tennis player. He won many singles and doubles titles, including seven in the U.S. Open and three at Wimbledon. Full name **William Tatem Tilden II**

Til·den, Samuel Jones (1814–86) U.S. politician. He was governor of New York (1875–77). He ran for U.S. president and won the popular vote but lost in the electoral college to Rutherford B. Hayes (1876).

tile /tīl/ *n.* **1.** BUILDING **COVERING FOR FLOORS, ROOFS, OR WALLS** a thin flat or curved piece of baked, sometimes glazed clay or synthetic material used to cover roofs, floors, and walls, or for decoration **2.** BUILDING **SHORT PIPE IN A DRAIN** a short pipe of baked clay, concrete, or plastic used in making a drain **3.** BUILDING **HOLLOW BLOCK** a hollow block of baked clay, concrete, or gypsum used as a building material for walls or floors **4.** BUILDING **TILES COLLECTIVELY** tiles considered collectively **5.** GAME **PLAYING PIECE** a rectangular playing piece in various games such as mahjong **6.** CLOTHES **HAT** a hat (*dated informal*) ■ *v.* (**tiled, til·ing, tiles**) **1.** *vt.* **LAY TILES ON SOMETHING** to cover a surface with tiles **2.** *vt.* **FIT SOMETHING WITH DRAINAGE TILES** to put drainage tiles in something **3.** *vti.* COMPUT **ARRANGE WINDOWS** to arrange the windows on a computer screen side by side so that all are visible [Pre-12thC. From Latin *tegula*. Ultimately from an Indo-European base meaning "to cover" that is also the ancestor of English *thatch*.] —**til·er** *n.*

tile·fish /tīl fìsh/ (*plural* **-fish** *or* **-fish·es**) *n.* a long blue fish with yellow spots on its upper body, found in deep waters of the Atlantic off the coast of North America. Latin name: *Lopholatilus chamaeleonticeps*. [Late 19thC. *Tile* from the genus Lopholatilus, and perhaps also from the bright coloring resembling ornamental tiles.]

til·ing /tīling/ *n.* **1. LAID TILES** tiles that have been laid **2. LAYING OF TILES** the laying of tiles on a wall or floor **3. TILES** tiles collectively

till[1] /til/ *conj., prep.* until [Old English *til* "up to a particular point," from a prehistoric Germanic word meaning "aim, goal"]

WORD KEY: USAGE

till or **until**? Both words have the same meaning and function (preposition and conjunction), and are largely interchangeable. In practice, however, ***till*** is more informal than ***until*** and is more likely to be heard in speech: *Just wait till we get home!* ***Until*** is more usual at the beginning of a sentence: *Until last week there was no one here that we knew.* The spellings *'til* and *'till* reflect the commonly held belief that ***till*** is a shortened form of ***until*** but ***till*** is in fact the older form.

till[2] /til/ *n.* **1. CONTAINER FOR MONEY** a box, drawer, or tray, e.g., in a cash register, in which money is kept **2. MONEY** available cash [15thC. Origin uncertain: perhaps via Anglo-Norman *tylle* from Old French *tille* "compartment, shelter on a ship," from Scandinavian.]

till[3] /til/ (**tilled, till·ing, tills**) *vt.* to prepare land for the growing of crops by plowing or harrowing [Old English *tilian* "to cultivate," earlier "to strive to obtain something." Ultimately from a prehistoric Germanic word meaning "an aim, purpose."] —**till·a·ble** *adj.* —**til·ler** *n.*

till[4] /til/ *n.* GEOG sediment of various particle sizes deposited by the direct action of ice [Late 17thC. Origin unknown.]

till·age /tíllij/ *n.* **1. TILLING OF LAND** the plowing or harrowing of land in preparation for growing crops **2. TILLED LAND** land that has been tilled

til·land·si·a /ti lándzee ə/ *n.* an epiphytic plant of the pineapple family such as Spanish moss that grows in tropical or subtropical America. Genus: *Tillandsia*. [Mid-18thC. From modern Latin, the genus name, from the name of Elias *Tillands* (1640–93), a Swedish botanist.]

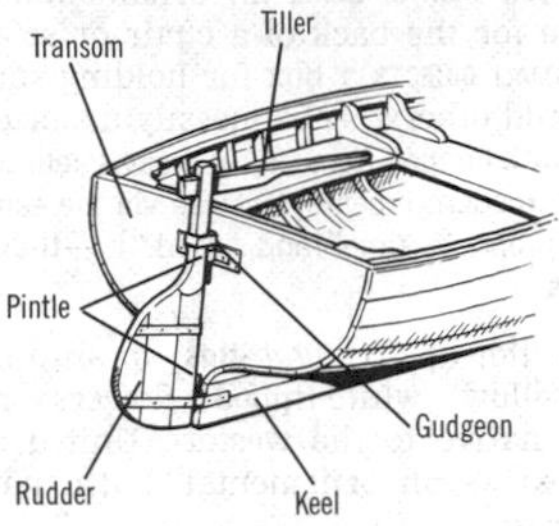

Tiller

til·ler[1] /tíllər/ *n.* NAUT the means by which a small boat is steered, consisting of a handle attached to the rudder [14thC. Via Anglo-Norman *telier* "weaver's beam," from, ultimately, Latin *tela* "web." The modern meaning evolved via "the beam of a crossbow."]

til·ler[2] /tíllər/ *n.* AGRIC a person or machine that plows or cultivates the soil

til·ler[3] /tíllər/ *n.* BOT a shoot growing from the base of a stem, especially the stem of a grass [Mid-17thC. Origin uncertain: probably from Old English *telgor* "extended," from *telga* "branch."]

til·ler·man /tíllərman/ (*plural* **-men** /-mən/) *n.* somebody who handles the tiller and steers a boat

Til·ley /tíllee/, **Sir Samuel Leonard** (1818–96) Canadian statesman. He was a provincial and federal official who advocated confederation and the development of Canadian railroads.

Til·lich /tíllik, tíllikh/, **Paul** (1886–1965) German-born U.S. philosopher and theologian. He emigrated to the United States in 1933. His scholarly and popular books sought to reconcile existential philosophy and contemporary secular culture with Christian faith, and included *The Courage to Be* (1952) and *Systematic Theology* (1951–63). Full name **Paul Johannes Tillich**

tilt[1] /tilt/ *v.* (**tilt·ed, tilt·ing, tilts**) **1.** *vti.* **SLOPE** to slant or cause something to slant ○ *She tilted her head as she listened.* **2.** *vi.* **HAVE AS A PREFERENCE** to tend toward favoring a particular opinion, course of action, or side in a dispute **3.** *vi.* **CRITICIZE** to make a spoken or written attack on somebody or something **4.** *vi.* **COMBAT** to combat or struggle against somebody or something **5.** *vti.* HIST **CHARGE WITH A LANCE** to attack an opponent using a lance **6.** *vi.* HIST **JOUST WITH SOMEBODY** to take part in a joust against somebody **7.** *vi.* HIST **POINT A LANCE** to hold a lance ready for combat in a joust **8.** *vt.* **USE A TILT HAMMER ON SOMETHING** to work on something using a tilt hammer ■ *n.* **1. ACT OF TILTING** an act of tilting or of causing something to tilt **2. INCLINE** a slanted surface or position ○ *his hat was at a rakish tilt* **3. CRITICISM** a spoken or written attack on somebody or something **4. PREFERENCE** a tendency to favor a particular opinion, course of action, or side in a dispute **5.** HIST **JOUST** a jousting contest **6.** HIST **LANCE THRUST** a thrust made with a lance in a jousting contest **7.** = **tilt hammer** [14thC. Origin uncertain: probably from assumed Old English *tyltan* "to fall over," from a prehistoric Germanic word meaning "unsteady."] —**tilt·er** *n.* ◇ **(at) full tilt** at full speed

tilt[2] /tilt/ *n.* a canvas cover or canopy used to cover an otherwise open boat, booth, or trailer of a truck [15thC. From Old English *teld*, perhaps influenced by TENT.]

tilth /tilth/ *n.* **1.** TILLING OF LAND the plowing of land in preparation for growing crops **2.** TILLED LAND land under cultivation **3.** CONDITION OF LAND the condition of a piece of tilled land, in terms of its cultivation history and suitability for crops **4.** DEGREE OF FINENESS OF SOIL the degree of fineness of soil particles in the topmost soil layer [Old English *tilþ(e)*, from *tilian*, an earlier form of TILL[3]]

tilt ham·mer *n.* a heavy drop hammer used to forge metal, pivoted by a lever [*Tilt* because it can be tilted]

tilt·yard /tílt yaard/ *n.* a place, usually enclosed, where a jousting contest was held

Tim. *abbr.* BIBLE Timothy

Ti·ma·ru /tímmərooˈ/ city on the east central coast of the South Island, New Zealand. Population: 27,521 (1996).

tim·bal /tímb'l/, **tym·bal** *n.* a kettledrum (*archaic*) [Late 17thC. From French *timbal*, alteration (modeled on *cymbale* "cymbal") of obsolete *tamballe*, from (influenced by *tambour* "drum") Spanish *atabal*, from Arabic *aṭ -ṭabl*, literally "the drum."]

tim·bale /tímb'l, tim baal/ *n.* **1.** DISH MADE IN A MOLD a dish consisting of a mixture of ingredients, often set with eggs, made in a mold and served hot or cold **2.** COOKING MOLD a small deep or tall mold in which a timbale dish is made [Early 19thC. From French (see TIMBAL), from its shape.]

tim·ber /tímbər/ *n.* **1.** GROWING TREES standing trees or their wood, especially when suitable for sawing into building materials **2.** WOODED LAND land covered with trees **3.** *U.K.* = **lumber 4.** BUILDING LARGE WOODEN BUILDING SUPPORT a large piece of wood, usually squared, used in a building, e.g., as a beam **5.** PART OF THE FRAMEWORK OF A SHIP a large piece of wood used in the framework of a wooden ship **6.** SOMEBODY AS SUITABLE MATERIAL FOR POSITION somebody who is characterized as being suitable material for a position ○ *She's definitely of congressional timber.* ■ *adj.* MADE OF TIMBERS constructed of timbers ■ *interj.* WARNING OF A FALLING TREE used by a lumberjack to warn others that a tree has been cut and is about to fall ■ *vt.* **(-bered, -ber·ing, -bers)** PROVIDE SOMETHING WITH TIMBERS to build, cover, or support something with timbers [Old English, "a building." Ultimately from an Indo-European base meaning "to build" that is also the ancestor of English *domestic*. The modern meaning evolved via the sense "building material."]

tim·bered /tímbərd/ *adj.* **1.** BUILDING CONSTRUCTED OF TIMBERS made of timber or having exposed timbers (*often used in combination*) ○ *a half-timbered house* **2.** WOODED covered with growing trees

tim·ber·head /tímbər hèd/ *n.* the top of a timber of a ship that projects above the deck and is used as a tall post (**bollard**) for securing the ship to a wharf or dock

tim·ber hitch *n.* a knot used to tie a rope around a spar or log that is to be hoisted or hauled

tim·ber·ing /tímbəring/ *n.* timber or objects made of timber

tim·ber·land /tímbər lànd/ *n.* an area of wooded land, especially one with trees that have commercial value as lumber

tim·ber·line /tímbər līn/ *n.* the altitude or latitude above which trees will not grow

tim·ber rat·tle·snake *n.* a poisonous rattlesnake of the eastern United States that is yellow-brown with wide dark bands and feeds on small mammals. Latin name: *Crotalus horridus.*

tim·ber wolf *n.* = **gray wolf**

tim·ber·work /tímbər wùrk/ *n.* something constructed of timbers, or the timber parts of something

tim·bre /támbər, taaNbrə/ *n.* **1.** PHON SPEECH SOUND QUALITY the quality of a speech sound that comes from its tone rather than its pitch or volume **2.** MUSIC MUSICAL TONE QUALITY the quality or color of tone of an instrument or voice [Mid-19thC. Via French, originally "drum, bell hit with a hammer," from, ultimately, Greek *tumpanon* "drum" (source of English *timpani*).]

tim·brel /tímbrəl/ *n.* in the Bible, a tambourine or small hand drum [Early 16thC. Origin uncertain: perhaps literally "little drum," formed from obsolete *timbre* "drum," from French (see TIMBRE).]

Tim·buk·tu[1] /tìm buk tóo, tim búk tóo/ *n.* a place that is far away or extremely remote (*informal*)

Tim·buk·tu[2] city in central Mali, on the southern edge of the Sahara Desert. Population: 19,165 (1976).

time /tīm/ *n.* **1.** SYSTEM OF DISTINGUISHING EVENTS a dimension that enables two identical events occurring at the same point in space to be distinguished, measured by the interval between the events. Symbol *t* **2.** PERIOD WITH LIMITS a limited period during which an action, process, or condition exists or takes place ○ *elapsed time* **3.** METHOD OF MEASURING INTERVALS a system for measuring intervals of time ○ *sidereal time* ○ *Central Daylight Time* **4.** MINUTE OR HOUR the minute or hour as indicated by a clock ○ *What time is it?* **5.** TIME AS A CAUSATIVE FORCE time conceived as a force capable of acting on people and objects ○ *time's ravages* **6.** MOMENT SOMETHING OCCURS a moment or period at which something takes place ○ *at the time of her 90th birthday* **7.** SUITABLE MOMENT a moment or period chosen as appropriate for something to be done or to take place ○ *The times for the games will be announced.* **8.** UNALLOCATED PERIOD a period that is not allocated for a particular purpose ○ *I had time on my hands* **9.** PERIOD NEEDED a period required, allocated, or taken to complete an activity ○ *How much time?* **10.** PERIOD WITH A PARTICULAR QUALITY a period, activity, or occasion that has a particular quality or characteristic (*often used in the plural*) ○ *They've been through some rough times.* ○ *We had an interesting time there.* **11.** APPOINTED MOMENT a designated or customary moment or period at which something is done or takes place ○ *It's time to get up.* **12.** *U.K.* CLOSING TIME the time at which a pub or bar is legally required to close **13.** CERTAIN INTERVAL a limited but unspecified period ○ *We stayed for a time.* **14.** HISTORICAL PERIOD a period in history, often characterized by a particular event or person (*often used in the plural*) ○ *in Shakespeare's time* ○ *ancient times* **15.** NOW the present as distinguished from the past or future (*often used in the plural*) ○ *technology that is ahead of the times* **16.** GEOL GEOLOGIC DIVISION a chronological division of geologic history **17.** ANTICIPATED MOMENT a moment in which some important event such as a birth or death is expected to happen ○ *He knew his time had come.* **18.** SOMEBODY'S LIFETIME a period during which somebody is alive, especially the most active or productive period in somebody's life ○ *She'd been a well-known athlete in her time.* ○ *We didn't worry about such trifles in my time.* **19.** APPRENTICESHIP PERIOD a period during which somebody is an apprentice ○ *had served his time* **20.** PRISON TERM a term in prison (*informal*) ○ *serve time for robbery* **21.** MILITARY SERVICE a term of military service **22.** SEASON a period during which particular climatic conditions prevail ○ *the rainy times of the year* **23.** INSTANCE a separate occasion of a recurring event ○ *I told you three times.* **24.** MUSIC TEMPO OF MUSIC the relative speed at which a musical composition is played **25.** MUSIC MUSICAL BEAT the number of beats per measure of a musical composition **26.** PERIOD WORKED the period during a day or week that somebody works ○ *working half time* **27.** PAY a rate of pay ○ *paid double time* **28.** SPORTS PLAYING PERIOD a period of play in a game **29.** SPORTS = **timeout** *n.* 1 ■ *v.* **(timed, tim·ing, times) 1.** *vt.* MEASURE HOW LONG SOMETHING TAKES to measure or record the duration, speed, or rate of something **2.** *vt.* SCHEDULE SOMETHING to plan the moment or occasion for something, especially in order to achieve the best result or effect ○ *time an entrance* **3.** *vt.* SET THE TIME OF SOMETHING to regulate or set the time of something such as a clock or a train's schedule **4.** *vi.* STAY IN RHYTHM to keep time to a rhythmical or musical beat [Old English *tīma* "period of time," from a prehistoric Germanic base meaning "to extend," which is also the ancestor of English *tide*] ◇ **all in good time** no sooner than is appropriate ◇ **all the time** continuously ◇ **at one time 1.** at a time in the past **2.** simultaneously ◇ **at the same time 1.** simultaneously **2.** nevertheless ◇ **at times** sometimes ◇ **behind the times** out of touch with modern fashions, methods, or attitudes ◇ **for the time being** for a short period of time starting from now ◇ **from time to time** occasionally ◇ **have no time for somebody** *or* **something** to regard somebody or something with dislike or contempt ◇ **have the time of your life** to have a very enjoyable experience ◇ **in good time 1.** early enough ○ *got there in good time so we could find a parking space* **2.** quickly ◇ **in (less than) no time** in a very short period of time ◇ **in time 1.** early enough ○ *we were in time for the concert* **2.** after some time has passed ○ *He'll understand in time that you were trying to help him.* **3.** in the correct rhythm ○ *clapping in time to the music* ◇ **in your own time** at a speed or pace that feels natural and comfortable ◇ **keep time 1.** to show the time accurately **2.** to do something in the correct rhythm, or in the same rhythm as somebody or something else ◇ **live on borrowed time** to enjoy an unexpected extension of life ◇ **make time with somebody** to pursue somebody as a sexual partner (*informal*) ◇ **on time** at the scheduled time ◇ **on your own time** not during working hours ◇ **pass the time of day (with somebody)** to engage in casual conversation with somebody ◇ **take your time 1.** to take whatever time is necessary **2.** to do something unacceptably slowly ◇ **time after time, time and (time) again** repeatedly ◇ **time out of mind** for an extremely long time ◇ **time was** there was a time in the past

time and a half *n.* a rate of pay equal to one and a half times the normal rate, usually paid for overtime work

time and mo·tion stud·y *n.* an analysis of the working practices of, e.g., a person, department, or factory, done with the aim of finding ways to increase efficiency

time bomb *n.* **1.** BOMB EXPLODING AT A FIXED TIME a bomb with a timing mechanism that allows it to explode at a specified time **2.** FUTURE DANGER something that is not dangerous or harmful at the moment but is likely to become so

time cap·sule *n.* a container of articles representative of the present, placed in a building's foundation or buried for a future generation to find and learn about the period it represents

time·card /tīm kaard/ *n.* a card that an employee has stamped by a time clock when starting and finishing work

time clock *n.* a clock with a mechanism for stamping employees' timecards when they start and finish work

time-con·sum·ing *adj.* taking up or wasting a great deal of time

time de·pos·it *n.* a bank deposit from which a withdrawal can be made only after a specified period of time or after giving notice

time di·la·tion, time dil·a·ta·tion *n.* the principle that time elapsed is relative to motion, such that time passes more slowly for a system in motion than for one at rest relative to an outside observer. Further, as predicted by Einstein's Special Theory of Relativity, time passes increasingly slowly as the motion relative to the observer approaches the speed of light.

timed-re·lease, time-re·lease *adj.* formulated with a drug that releases its active ingredient gradually to prolong its effect

time ex·po·sure *n.* **1.** RELATIVELY LONG EXPOSURE the exposure of photographic film for an unusually long time to achieve a desired effect **2.** PHOTOGRAPH WITH A RELATIVELY LONG EXPOSURE a photograph taken by time exposure

time frame *n.* a period of time during which something takes place or is planned to take place ○ *What's the time frame for the project?*

time-hon·ored *adj.* respected or continued because of having been the custom for a long time

time im·me·mo·ri·al *n.* **1.** DISTANT PAST time so distant in the past as to be beyond memory or record **2.** LAW TIME BEFORE LEGAL RECORDS the time prior to a date fixed as the start of the keeping of official legal records, before which no claims or rights are valid

time·keep·er /tīm keepər/ *n.* **1.** SPORTS SOMEBODY RECORDING THE TIME ELAPSED somebody who keeps a record of the time elapsed during a sporting event **2.** SOMEBODY RECORDING THE TIME WORKED somebody who keeps a record of the time worked by employees **3.** WATCH OR CLOCK an instrument for recording or showing the time such as a watch or clock —**time·keep·ing** *n.*

time lag *n.* an amount of time that passes between two connected events

time-lapse pho·tog·ra·phy *n.* a method of filming a slow process such as the opening of a flower by taking a series of single exposures, then showing them at higher speed to simulate continuous action

time·less /tímləss/ *adj.* **1.** UNCHANGED remaining invariable throughout time ○ *fiction that has a timeless appeal* **2.** ETERNAL having no beginning or end — **time·less·ly** *adv.* —**time·less·ness** *n.*

time lim·it *n.* a period of time within which something must be done or is effective

time line *n.* a linear representation of significant events in a subject area shown in chronological order, e.g., the history of art

time loan *n.* a loan that has to be repaid by or on a given date. ◊ **call loan**

time lock *n.* a lock on a device such as a safe or bank vault with a timing mechanism that sets it to open only at set times

time·ly /tímlee/ (**-li·er, -li·est**) *adj.* **1.** OCCURRING AT A GOOD TIME happening or done at the right time or an appropriate time ○ *a timely invention* **2.** EARLY early (*archaic*) —**time·ly** *adv.* —**time·li·ness** *n.*

time ma·chine *n.* a fictional or hypothetical machine that can be used to travel backward or forward in time

time note *n.* a legal document such as a promissory note that specifies a date for repayment

Time of Trou·bles *n.* the period between the death of Tsar Ivan IV, when the Boyars attempted to regain control of Russia, and the selection of Michael Romanov as tsar in 1613

time·out /tím òwt/ *n.* **1.** SPORTS TIME DURING WHICH GAME STOPS a break taken to allow players to rest, confer, or be substituted **2.** COMPUT LACK OF RESPONSE FROM A COMPUTER DEVICE an interruption in the operation of a computer when a device such as a printer or disk drive does not respond to a command in a predetermined amount of time. A timeout usually results in a message to the user giving the option of retrying or canceling the command. ■ *interj.* REQUEST FOR A BREAK used to ask for or suggest a break in a game or an activity

time out *n.* a short break or rest from work or other activities ○ *took time out from her studies to travel for a year*

time·piece /tím peèss/ *n.* an instrument for recording or showing the time such as a watch or clock, especially one that does not strike or chime

tim·er /tímər/ *n.* **1.** TIME-SETTING DEVICE a device that can be preset to start or stop something at a given time or that sounds after a set period of time **2.** TIME-RECORDING DEVICE a device for recording, showing, or measuring time such as a stopwatch **3.** SOMEBODY TRACKING TIME somebody who measures or records elapsed time **4.** AUTOMOT DEVICE CONTROLLING IGNITION a device in an internal-combustion engine that controls the timing of the spark in the cylinders

time-re·lease *adj.* = **timed-release**

times /tīmz/ *prep.* used to indicate that a number is to be multiplied by another ○ *Three times two is six.*

time·sav·ing /tím sàyving/ *adj.* designed to reduce the length of time taken to do something —**time·sav·er** *n.*

time·scale /tím skàyl/ *n.* **1.** PERIOD OF TIME a period of time scheduled for something to be completed **2.** TIME MEASURED RELATIVE TO MAJOR EVENTS a measurement of time relative to the time in which a typical event occurs, e.g., in geologic or cosmic time

time se·ries *n.* a sequence of data gathered at uniformly spaced intervals of time

time·serv·er /tím sùrvər/, **time-server** *n.* somebody whose opinions and behavior change to suit the times and circumstances without regard for principle —**time·serv·ing** *n., adj.*

time·share /tím shàir/ (**-shared, -shar·ing, -shares**) *n.* **1.** = **time-sharing** *n.* 1 **2.** LEISURE JOINTLY OWNED PROPERTY a property, usually an apartment in a resort area, that is jointly owned by people who use it at different times

time-share /tím shàir/ (**time-shared, time-shar·ing, time-shares**) *vti.* **1.** COMPUT USE A COMPUTER SIMULTANEOUSLY to use a main computer according to a system in which a number of individuals work from remote work stations **2.** JOINTLY OWN PROPERTY to own a property jointly with others who share its use —**time-shar·er** *n.*

time-shar·ing *n.* **1.** LEISURE JOINT OWNERSHIP the joint ownership of a property such as an apartment in a resort area in which each owner may occupy the property for a specific time during the year **2.** COMPUT SIMULTANEOUS COMPUTER USE a technique for the concurrent use of a computer by many people working at remote terminals, each apparently operating as the only user of the computer's resources. The apparent simultaneous use is possible because the computer's processing speed is extremely fast in comparison with any individual's typing speed at a keyboard.

time sheet *n.* a sheet or card on which the hours worked by an employee are recorded

time sig·na·ture *n.* a sign used in music to show meter, represented by a fraction in which the upper figure shows beats per measure and the lower figure shows each beat's time value

times sign *n.* a multiplication sign

times ta·ble *n.* a multiplication table (*informal; often used in combination*)

time stud·y *n.* = **time and motion study**

time·ta·ble /tím tàyb'l/ *n.* = **schedule** *n.* 4

time-test·ed *adj.* proven to be effective over a long period

time tri·al *n.* a race in which competitors compete individually for the fastest time

time warp *n.* a hypothetical distortion in the continuum of space-time, popular in science fiction, allowing time to stand still or people to travel from one time to another

time·work /tím wùrk/ *n.* work paid according to the time it takes, especially by the hour or the day — **time·work·er** *n.*

time·worn /tím wàwrn/ *adj.* **1.** HAVING DETERIORATED THROUGH LONG USE showing the effects of having been used for a long period of time **2.** HACKNEYED having lost effectiveness through overuse ○ *a timeworn phrase*

time zone *n.* any of the 24 longitudinal areas into which the world is divided and within which the same standard time is used

tim·id /tímmid/ *adj.* demonstrating a lack of courage or self-assurance [Mid-16thC. Directly or via French from Latin *timidus* "fearful," from *timere* "to fear."] —**ti·mid·i·ty** /ti míddətee/ *n.* —**tim·id·ly** /tímmidlee/ *adv.*

tim·ing /tíming/ *n.* **1.** JUDGMENT OF WHEN TO ACT the ability to choose or the choice of the best moment to do or say something, e.g., in performing music or comedy or in sports ○ *a comedian with an immaculate sense of timing* ○ *split-second timing* **2.** RECORDING OF TIME the measurement and recording of the time taken to do something **3.** AUTOMOT ADJUSTMENT OF VALVES OF ENGINE the adjustment of the sequence and relative position of the valves and crankshaft of an automobile engine such that maximum output power is achieved

Ti·mi·şoa·ra /teémmee shwaárə/ capital city of Timiş County, western Romania. Population: 327,830 (1994).

Tim·mins /tímminz/ mining city in eastern Ontario, Canada. Population: 47,499 (1996).

ti·moc·ra·cy /ti mókrəssee/ (*plural* **-cies**) *n.* **1.** GOVERNMENT BY THE PROPERTIED CLASS government in which the possession of property is a qualification for holding office **2.** GOVERNMENT BY PEOPLE OF HONOR a form of government in which honor is the guiding principle [15thC. Via French *timocratie* from, ultimately, Greek *timokratia*, from *timē* "honor, value."] —**ti·mo·crat·ic** /tìmmə kráttik/ *adj.*

Ti·mor /teé mawr, tee máwr/ island in the Malay Archipelago. It is the largest and easternmost of the Lesser Sunda Islands, bordered on the north by the Savu and Banda seas and on the south by the Timor Sea. Population: 1,382,207 (1980). Area: 11,900 sq. mi./30,820 sq. km.

tim·or·ous /tímmərəss/ *adj.* showing fear or hesitancy [15thC. Via Old French *temoreus* from medieval Latin *timorosus*, from, ultimately, Latin *timere* "to fear" (source of English *timid*).] —**tim·or·ous·ly** *adv.* —**tim·or·ous·ness** *n.*

Ti·mor Sea arm of the Indian Ocean separating the island of Timor from northern Australia. Area: 175,000 sq. mi./450,000 sq. km.

tim·o·thy /tímməthee/, **tim·o·thy grass** *n.* a perennial grass that grows in temperate regions, has a cylindrical flower spike, and is widely cultivated for hay and pasture. Latin name: *Phleum pratense.* [Mid-18thC. Named for *Timothy* Hanson, an American farmer who introduced the grass from New York to the Carolinas around 1720.]

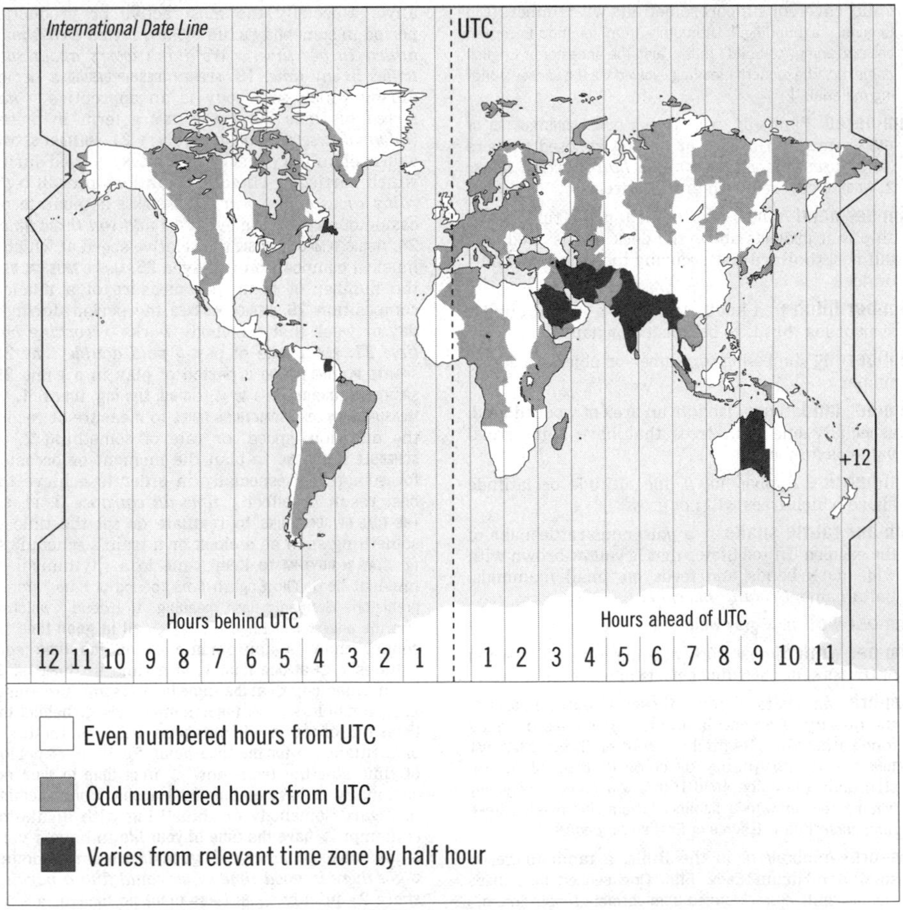

Time zone

Tim·o·thy *n.* two books in the Bible, in the form of epistles addressed to Timothy, traditionally believed to be from St. Paul. They are concerned with the organization of Christian doctrine and codes of Christian behavior. See table at **Bible**

Timothy, St. /tímməthee/ *n.* in the Bible, an early Christian missionary, and friend and disciple of St. Paul.

tim·pa·ni /tímpənee/, **tym·pa·ni** *npl.* a set of two or more kettledrums, usually played as part of an orchestra (*takes a singular or plural verb*) [Late 19thC. From Italian, plural of *timpano* "kettledrum," ultimately from Greek *tumpanon* "drum" (source of English *timbre*).] — **tim·pa·nist** *n.*

tin /tin/ *n.* **METALLIC ELEMENT** a silvery, easily shaped metallic element extracted from its oxide ore. It is used extensively in alloys such as solder, bronze, and pewter and as a protective coating for steel. Symbol **Sn** ■ *vt.* **(tinned, tin·ning, tins) COAT SOMETHING WITH TIN** to coat or plate something with tin ■ *n.* **1.** *U.K.* = **can 2. SHEET-METAL CONTAINER** a lidded container made of thin sheet metal and often decorated **3. CORRUGATED IRON** corrugated or galvanized iron ■ *adj.* **1. MADE OF TIN** made from thin sheet metal coated with tin **2. MADE OF CORRUGATED IRON** made of corrugated or galvanized iron ■ *vt.* **(tinned, tin·ning, tins)** *U.K.* = **can** [Old English. Ultimately of prehistoric Germanic origin.]

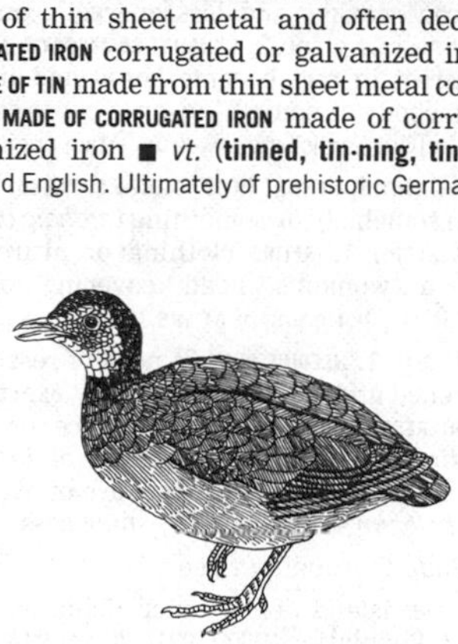

Tinamou

tin·a·mou /tínnə moo/ (*plural* **-mous** *or* **-mou**) *n.* a short round-bodied ground-dwelling bird of grassy and jungle areas of Central and South America. Family: Tinamidae. [Late 18thC. Via French from Carib *tinamu*.]

tin·cal /tíngk'l/ *n.* a sodium borate mineral formed by the weathering of borax [Mid-17thC. Origin uncertain: probably from Portugese *tincal*, from Persian and Urdu *tinkār*, ultimately from Sanskrit *ṭaṅkaṇa*.]

tin can *n.* **1. CONTAINER** a container made of tin or aluminum, especially one used for food **2. NAVAL DESTROYER** a naval destroyer (*informal*)

tinct /tingkt/ *n.* **TINT** a tint (*archaic*) ■ *vti.* **(tinct·ed, tinct·ing, tincts) TINT** to tint (*archaic*) ■ *adj.* **TINTED** tinted or colored (*literary*) [15thC. From Latin *tinctus* "a dyeing" (see TINT).]

tinct. *abbr.* tincture

tinc·ture /tíngkchər/ *n.* **1. ALCOHOL SOLUTION** a solution of a plant product or chemical substance in alcohol ○ *tincture of iodine* **2. TINGE OR COLOR** a tint or slight coloration **3. TINY AMOUNT OF SOMETHING** a hint or small amount of something **4.** HERALDRY **HERALDIC COLOR** a color, metal, or fur used in heraldry **5. DYE** a dye or stain (*archaic*) ■ *vt.* **(-tured, -tur·ing, -tures) 1. ADD A TINT TO** to give something a hint of color **2. IMBUE WITH** to suffuse something with a quality or property ○ *praise tinctured with criticism* [14thC. From Latin *tinctura* "dyeing," from the past participle stem of *tingere* "to dye" (source of English *tinge*).]

tin·der /tíndər/ *n.* material such as dry sticks that is easily combustible and can be used for lighting a fire [Old English *tynder*, from a prehistoric Germanic base meaning "to ignite, kindle"]

tin·der·box /tíndər bòks/ *n.* **1.** HIST **BOX CONTAINING TINDER** a metal box containing tinder, often fitted with a flint and steel, formerly used for lighting fires **2. SOMEBODY OR SOMETHING POTENTIALLY VIOLENT** a person, place, or situation that is likely to become violent

tine /tīn/ *n.* **1. PRONG** a thin pointed projection of a utensil or implement such as a fork or pitchfork **2.** ZOOL **ANTLER'S BRANCH** a pointed branch of a deer's antler [Old English *tind*] —**tined** *adj.*

tin·e·a /tínnee ə/ *n.* an infection of the skin caused by any of several species of fungi that live as parasites on the outer layer of the skin, nails, or hair [14thC. From Latin, "gnawing worm, moth."] — **tin·e·al** *adj.*

tin·e·a bar·bae /-baárbee/ *n.* barber's itch (*technical*) [From Latin, literally "tinea of the beard"]

tin·e·a cru·ris /-kroóriss/ *n.* jock itch (*technical*) [From Latin, literally "tinea of the leg"]

tin·e·a ped·is /-péddiss/ *n.* athlete's foot (*technical*) [From Latin, literally "tinea of the foot"]

tin ear *n.* an inability to perceive differences in musical sounds or subtleties in speech (*informal*) [From the idea of metal as incapable of sensation]

tin·e·id /tínnee id/ *n.* a very small moth found throughout the world whose larvae either eat fabrics of animal origin or are scavengers. Family: Tineidae. [Mid-19thC. From modern Latin *Tineidae* (plural), family name, ultimately from Latin *tinea* "moth."]

tin·foil /tín fòyl/ *n.* **1. THIN ALUMINUM SHEET** aluminum in a very thin sheet, used to wrap food **2. THIN TIN SHEET** tin, or an alloy of tin and lead, in a very thin sheet

ting /ting/ *n.* **LIGHT RINGING SOUND** a light high-pitched ringing sound, like that of a small bell ■ *vti.* **(tinged, ting·ing, tings) RING LIGHTLY** to produce or cause something to produce a light high-pitched ringing sound [Early 17thC. An imitation of the sound.]

ting-a-ling /tíngə lìng/ *n.* a tinkling sound resembling that made by a small bell [An imitation of the sound]

tinge /tinj/ *n.* **1. SLIGHT ADDED COLOR** a slight amount of a color added to something **2. SLIGHT ADDED ELEMENT** a slight amount of something, e.g., an emotion or a flavor ○ *with a tinge of regret in her voice* ■ *vt.* **(tinged, tinge·ing** *or* **ting·ing, ting·es) 1. ADD COLOR TO SOMETHING** to add a slight amount of color to something **2. MIX IN AN ELEMENT OF SOMETHING** to mix a slight amount of something with something else ○ *celebrations tinged with sadness* [15thC. From Latin *tingere* "to moisten," hence "to dye" (via the sense "to dip into liquid dye") (source of English *taint* and *tint*).]

tin·gle /tíng g'l/ *vti.* **(-gled, -gling, -gles) STING OR PRICKLE SOMEBODY** to feel or to cause somebody to feel a sensation of stinging, pricking, or vibration, e.g., from cold or a slight electric shock ○ *The frost made our faces tingle* ■ *n.* **STINGING OR PRICKLY FEELING** a sensation of stinging, pricking, or vibration [14thC. Variant of an earlier form of TINKLE.] —**tin·gler** *n.* — **tin·gling·ly** *adv.* —**tin·gly** *adj.*

tin god *n.* somebody, often in a position of minor authority, who behaves in a self-important, overbearing way [In reference to tin as a base metal]

tin hat *n.* a steel helmet (*informal*)

tin·horn /tín hàwrn/ *n.* somebody relatively insignificant who pretends to be wealthy, influential or important, especially a gambler (*informal*) [Late 19thC. From the horn-shaped metal can used to shake the dice in the game of chuck-a-luck.]

tin·ker /tíngkər/ *n.* **1. TRAVELING POT MENDER** formerly, somebody who traveled from place to place mending metal household items such as pots and pans **2. UNSKILLFUL WORKER** somebody who works clumsily or unskillfully, especially at repair work **3. ACT OF FIDDLING WITH SOMETHING** an act of fiddling with something in an attempt to repair it **4. SOMEBODY GOOD AT MANY TASKS** somebody able to do many different kinds of work successfully **5.** ZOOL **YOUNG MACKEREL** a mackerel that is not fully grown ■ *vi.* **(-kered, -ker·ing, -kers) 1. FIDDLE WITH** to fiddle with something in an attempt to repair it ○ *had been tinkering with the car all morning* **2. HANDLE SOMETHING UNSKILLFULLY** to handle something clumsily or unskillfully **3. BE TRAVELING POT MENDER** to work as a traveling pot mender [13thC. Origin uncertain: perhaps from obsolete English *tink* "to tinkle," an imitation of the sounds made by tinkers repairing pots.] —**tin·ker·er** *n.*

tin·ker's damn, **tin·ker's dam** *n.* the slightest possible amount of care, heed, or value (*informal*) (*used in negative statements*) ○ *This car isn't worth a tinker's damn.* [Origin uncertain: probably from the reputation of tinkers for cursing]

Tin·ker·toy /tíngkər tòy/ *tdmk.* a trademark for a construction toy consisting of pieces such as rods and wheels that can be fitted together

tin·kle /tíngk'l/ *v.* **(-kled, -kling, -kles) 1.** *vti.* **JINGLE** to make or cause something to make light metallic ringing sounds **2.** *vi.* **URINATE** to urinate (*informal*) ■ *n.* **1. JINGLING SOUND** a series of light metallic ringing sounds **2. ACT OF URINATING** an act of urinating (*informal*) [14thC. Literally "to keep on making a faint metallic sound," formed from obsolete English *tink* "to make a faint metallic sound," of uncertain origin: perhaps an imitation of the sound.] —**tin·kly** *adj.*

Tin·ley Park /tínnlee-/ village in northeastern Illinois, northeast of Joliet, a southwestern suburb of Chicago. Population: 43,310 (1996).

tin liz·zie /-lízzee/ *n.* a cheap, old, or dilapidated car (*informal*) [From *Tin Lizzie*, nickname for the Model T Ford automobile]

tinned /tind/ *adj.* *U.K.* = **canned** *adj.* 1

tin·ner /tínnər/ *n.* **1. TIN MINER** somebody who works in a tin mine **2.** = **tinsmith**

tin·nie /tínnee/, **tin·ny** (*plural* **-nies**) *n.* *Aus* a can of beer (*informal*)

tin·ni·tus /ti nītəss, tínnitəss/ *n.* a continual noise in the ear such as a ringing or roaring, usually caused by damage to the hair cells of the inner ear [Mid-19thC. From Latin, from *tinnire* "to ring, tinkle," an imitation of the sound.]

tin·ny /tínnee/ *adj.* **(-ni·er, -ni·est) 1. HAVING A THIN METALLIC SOUND** lacking a full resonant sound ○ *banging out tunes on a tinny old piano* **2. CONSISTING OF TIN** yielding, containing, or having the characteristics of tin **3. TASTING OF METAL** having a metallic taste **4. INFERIOR IN QUALITY** cheaply or shoddily made **5.** *ANZ* **LUCKY** lucky (*informal*) ■ *n.* *Aus* = **tinnie** (*informal*) —**tin·ni·ly** *adv.* — **tin·ni·ness** *n.*

tin-o·pen·er *n.* *U.K.* = **can opener**

Tin Pan Al·ley *n.* (*dated*) **1. POPULAR MUSIC DISTRICT** a city district in which the business of composing and publishing popular music is carried on **2. COMPOSERS AND PUBLISHERS** popular music composers and publishers considered collectively [*Tin pan* in the sense of "tinny piano," from the cheap pianos associated with music publishers' offices]

tin plate *n.* steel or iron in thin sheets coated with tin

tin-plate **(tin-plat·ed, tin-plat·ing, tin-plates)** *vt.* to coat sheet iron or steel with tin —**tin-plat·er** *n.*

tin-pot *adj.* inferior in quality or importance (*informal insult*) [In reference to tin as a base metal]

tin·sel /tínsəl/ *n.* **1. GLITTERING MATERIAL** a thin strip of glittering metal foil, paper, or plastic, used for decoration **2. SOMETHING SHOWY** something worthless that appears glamorous ■ *vt.* **(-seled** *or* **-selled, -sel·ing** *or* **-sel·ling, -sels) 1. DECORATE WITH TINSEL** to decorate something with tinsel or other glittering material **2. MAKE SHOWY** to give something a gaudy, flashy quality ■ *adj.* **1. MADE OF TINSEL** made of or decorated with tinsel **2. GAUDY** appearing glamorous but in fact worthless [15thC. Via French *étincelé* "sparkling" (particularly used of fabric with metallic thread woven through it), from Old French *estincele* "spark," from Latin *scintilla* (source of English *scintillate*).] —**tin·sel·ly** *adj.*

Tin·sel·town /tínsəl tŏn/ *n.* a disapproving nickname for Hollywood and the U.S. movie as a place of substantial glamour (*informal*) [From its perception as superficially glamourous]

tin·smith /tín smìth/ *n.* somebody who makes or repairs objects made of tin or other easily worked metals

tin snips *npl.* shears used for cutting sheet metal

tin·stone /tín stŏn/ *n.* MINERALS = **cassiterite**

tint /tint/ *n.* **1. PALE SHADE** a shade of a color, especially a pale one **2. COLOR WITH WHITE ADDED** a color mixed with white to give low saturation and high lightness **3. TRACE OF COLOR** a slight amount of a color **4. HAIR DYE** a dye for the hair **5. HINT OF SOMETHING** a barely noticeable addition of something **6.** PRINTING **BACKGROUND COLOR** a pale color printed as a background onto which another color is printed **7.** ARTS **SHADING IN ENGRAVING** a shading effect in engraving, produced by a series of parallel lines ■ *vti.* **(tint·ed, tint·ing, tints) GIVE A TINT TO SOMETHING** to color or shade something with a tint, or to acquire a tint [Early 18thC. Variant of TINCT, from the past participle of Latin *tingere* "to soak," later "to dye" (source of English *tinge*) from the idea of "dipping into liquid dye."] —**tint·er** *n.*

Tin·tag·el /tin tájjəl/ coastal village in Cornwall, southwestern England, said to be the birthplace of the legendary King Arthur

tin·tin·nab·u·la·tion /tìntə nabbyə láysh'n/ *n.* the ringing of bells [Mid-19thC. Formed from Latin *tintinnabulum* (see TINTINNABULUM).] —**tin·tin·nab·u·lar** /tìntə nábbyələr/ *adj.*

tin·tin·nab·u·lum /tìntə nábbyələm/ (*plural* **-la** /-lə/) *n.* a small bell with a high clear ring [Late 16thC. From Latin, "bell," from *tintinnare*, literally "to ring repeatedly," from *tinnire* "to ring," an imitation of the sound.]

Tin·to·ret·to /tìntə réttō/ (1518?–94) Italian painter. Based in Venice, he painted large murals in the mannerist style, using free brush strokes and dramatic foreshortened perspectives. Real name **Jacopo Robusti**

tin·type /tín tīp/ *n.* PHOTOGRAPHY = **ferrotype**

tin·ware /tín wàir/ *n.* objects made of tin plate, especially utensils

tin·work /tín wùrk/ *n.* things made of tin

tin·works /tín wùrks/ (*plural* **-works**) *n.* a place where tin is smelted and rolled (*takes a singular or a plural verb*)

ti·ny /tínee/ *adj.* (**-ni·er, -ni·est**) **SMALL** extremely small ■ *n.* (*plural* **-nies**) **YOUNG CHILD** a very young child (*informal*) [Late 16thC. Formed from obsolete English *tine* "very small," of unknown origin.] —**ti·ni·ly** *adv.* —**ti·ni·ness** *n.*

-tion *suffix.* an action or process, or the result of it ○ *pollution*

tip[1] /tip/ *n.* **1. POINTED END** the end of an object, especially a narrow or pointed end ○ *a pencil with a sharp tip* **2. PART FITTED ON AN END** a piece fitted to the end of something else ■ *vt.* (**tipped, tip·ping, tips**) **1. PROVIDE OR BE END** to provide something with an end or form the end of something **2. COVER THE END OF SOMETHING** to cover or decorate the end of something ○ *shoes with steel-tipped toes* **3. TAKE THE END OFF SOMETHING** to remove the end from something [15thC. Origin uncertain: probably from Old Norse *typpi*, from a prehistoric Germanic word meaning "upper extremity" that is also the ancestor of English *top* and *toupee*.] ◇ **the tip of the iceberg** the small visible or obvious part of a largely unseen problem or difficulty ◇ **on the tip of somebody's tongue 1.** nearly, but not quite, brought to mind **2.** on the verge of being said but remaining unsaid

tip[2] /tip/ *v.* (**tipped, tip·ping, tips**) **1.** *vti.* **TILT SOMETHING** to cause something to slant or to become slanted ○ *sitting with his chair tipped back* **2.** *vti.* **KNOCK SOMETHING OVER** to turn something on its side or upside down or become turned on the side or upside down ○ *high winds caused the truck to tip over on its side* **3.** *vti. U.K.* **DUMP GARBAGE** to dispose of refuse **4.** *vt.* **TAKE OFF YOUR HAT** to touch or lift a hat as a greeting ■ *n.* **1. ACT OF TIPPING** an act of tipping something **2. TILT** an incline from vertical or horizontal **3.** *U.K.* **GARBAGE DUMP** a place to dump refuse [14thC. Origin uncertain: perhaps from Scandinavian.] —**tip·pa·ble** *adj.*

tip[3] /tip/ *n.* **1. GRATUITY** a gift of money for a service, especially as an amount above what is owed **2. WARNING OR INFORMATION** an item of advance, inside, or confidential information given, e.g., to warn of something about to occur or to help in solving a crime **3. HELPFUL HINT** a useful suggestion or idea for doing something ○ *cooking tips* ■ *vti.* (**tipped, tip·ping, tips**) **1. GIVE A GRATUITY** to give somebody a gift of money in return for a service, especially in addition to what is owed **2. INFORM SOMEBODY** to give somebody advance, inside, or confidential information [Early 17thC. Origin uncertain: perhaps from TIP[4].] —**tip·pa·ble** *adj.*

tip off *vt.* to give somebody a warning or some useful advance information ○ *the police had been tipped off about their whereabouts*

tip[4] /tip/ *n.* **1. LIGHT HIT** a light glancing blow **2.** BASEBALL **DEFLECTED BASEBALL** a baseball struck so that it glances off the bat ■ *v.* (**tipped, tip·ping, tips**) **1.** *vt.* **HIT SOMEBODY LIGHTLY** to strike somebody or something with a light glancing blow **2.** *vt.* BASEBALL **DEFLECT BASEBALL WITH BAT** to strike a baseball so that it glances off the bat **3.** *vi. Southern U.S.* **TIPTOE** to walk quietly on tiptoe [15thC. Origin uncertain: perhaps from Low German *tippen*, or from TIP[1], from the idea of touching something with the "tip" of something else.]

tip·cart /típ kaàrt/ *n.* a type of cart whose load is emptied by tilting its body

ti·pi *n.* = **tepee**

tip-in *n.* **1.** BASKETBALL **BASKETBALL GOAL** in basketball, a goal scored by lightly pushing a rebound into the basket with the fingertips **2.** HOCKEY **HOCKEY GOAL** in hockey, a goal scored at very close range by giving a short stroke with the stick

tip-off[1] *n.* (*informal*) **1. WARNING** advance information or a warning given in an effort to help **2. SIGN OF SOMETHING** a sign or indication of something, or that something is likely to happen

tip-off[2] *n.* BASKETBALL in basketball, the start of a period of play in which two players try to tap a jump ball to one of their teammates

tip·per /típpər/ *n.* somebody who leaves a tip or gratuity

Tip·per·ar·y /tìppə ráiree/ former county in Munster Province, southern Republic of Ireland. It now comprises the counties of Tipperary North Riding and Tipperary South Riding.

tip·per truck, **tip·per lor·ry** *n. U.K.* = **dump truck**

tip·pet /típpit/ *n.* **1.** CLOTHES **STOLE WITH HANGING ENDS** a stole or cape, often made of fur, with long ends that hang down the front **2.** CHR **STOLE OF ANGLICAN CLERGY** the long stole worn around the shoulders and over the robes of Anglican clergy during services **3.** CLOTHES **HANGING END OF A GARMENT** a long hanging end worn attached to a sleeve, hood, or cape up to the 16th century **4.** BIRDS **BIRD'S RUFF** the ruff of a bird **5.** ANGLING **PART TO WHICH A FLY IS TIED** in angling, the thin end section of a leader to which a fly is tied [14thC. Origin uncertain: probably formed from TIP[1].]

tip·ple[1] /típp'l/ *v.* (**-pled, -pling, -ples**) **1.** *vi.* **DRINK ALCOHOL HABITUALLY** to drink alcoholic liquor habitually or excessively **2.** *vti.* **DRINK ALCOHOL REPEATEDLY** to drink alcoholic liquor repeatedly a little at a time ■ *n.* **ALCOHOLIC DRINK** an alcoholic drink (*informal*) [Mid-16thC. Origin uncertain: probably a back-formation from *tippler* "ale seller," of Scandinavian origin.]

tip·ple[2] /típp'l/ (**-pled, -pling, -ples**) *n.* **1. DEVICE FOR UNLOADING ORE CARS** a device for tipping coal or ore cars to unload them **2. PLACE FOR UNLOADING ORE** a place where ore or coal cars are unloaded **3. PLACE FOR SCREENING COAL** a place where coal is screened and loaded into trucks or railroad cars [Mid-19thC. Literally "to keep on unloading," formed from TIP[2].]

tippler[1] *n.* somebody who is a habitual drinker of alcohol

tip·pler[2] /típplər/ *n.* a breed of domestic pigeon bred for flight or show [Mid-19thC. Formed from TIPPLE[2], so called because it often turns over backward in flight.]

tip·py /típpee/ (**-pi·er, -pi·est**) *adj.* not stable and likely to tilt or tip over

tip·staff /típ stàf/ (*plural* **-staves** /-stàyvz/ *or* **-staffs**) *n.* **1. METAL-TIPPED STAFF** a metal-tipped staff carried as a sign of official authority **2.** LAW **COURT OFFICIAL** a court official who once carried a staff, e.g., a bailiff or constable

tip·ster /típstər/ *n.* somebody who provides or sells information to people who bet on horseraces or to speculators in financial markets [Mid-19thC. Formed from TIP[3].]

tip·sy /típsee/ (**-si·er, -si·est**) *adj.* **1. DRUNK** slightly drunk **2. LIKELY TO TIP** inclined to tilt or tip —**tip·si·ly** *adv.* —**tip·si·ness** *n.*

tip·toe /típ tō/ *vi.* (**-toed, -toe·ing, -toes**) **1. WALK WITH HEELS RAISED** to walk on the toes and the balls of the feet with the heels off the ground **2. MOVE CAUTIOUSLY** to move or proceed quietly or cautiously ■ *n.* **POSITION WITH HEELS RAISED** a standing position in which the heels are raised off the ground and the weight is on the front part of the feet, with the body often also stretched up to gain extra height ○ *walking on tiptoe* ■ *adj.* **1. WALKING ON THE TOES** walking or standing on the toes or balls of the feet **2. CAUTIOUS** proceeding with caution or stealth ■ *adv.* **ON THE TIPS OF TOES** on the toes or the balls of the feet [14thC. Formed from TIP[1] + TOE.]

tip·top /típ tòp/ *adj.* **TOP QUALITY** of the highest quality or rank (*informal*) ■ *adv.* **WELL** exceptionally well (*informal*) ■ *n.* (*informal*) **1. HIGHEST POINT** the highest point **2. HIGHEST IN QUALITY** the highest degree of quality or excellence [Early 18thC. Doubling of TOP, under the influence of TIP[1].]

tip-up *adj.* designed to tilt upward or fold up (*dated*)

ti·rade /tī ràyd, tī ráyd/ *n.* a long angry speech, usually of criticism or denunciation [Early 19thC. From French, "volley," from *tirer* "to draw," from assumed Vulgar Latin *tirare*.]

ti·ra·mi·su /teèrə meè sō, teèrə mi sōō/ *n.* an Italian dessert made with layers of sponge cake soaked in coffee, especially espresso, marsala or other alcohol, mascarpone cheese, and chocolate [Late 20thC. From Italian *tira mi sù* "pick me up."]

Ti·ra·na /ti raánə/ capital city of Albania, in the central part of the country, situated 17 mi./27 km from the Adriatic coast. Population: 251,000 (1991).

tire[1] /tīr/ *n.* **1. HOLLOW RUBBER EDGING** a circular hollow band of rubber fitted around the edge of a vehicle's wheel to ease movement and help absorb bumps in road surfaces. It is filled with compressed air. **2. SOLID RUBBER EDGING** a circular solid band of rubber fitted to a wheel's edge, e.g., on baby carrieages and children's bicycles **3. METAL EDGING** a band of metal fitted for reinforcement to the rims of wheels on various vehicles, e.g., handcarts and railroad cars

tire[1] /tīr/ (**tired, tir·ing, tires**) *vti.* **1. GROW OR MAKE SOMEBODY TIRED** to make somebody feel in need of rest or sleep, or to grow weaker and less energetic and feel a need for rest or sleep **2. EXHAUST SOMEBODY'S INTEREST** to lose interest in and become bored and impatient with somebody or something, or to cause somebody to do this [Old English *tyrian*, of uncertain origin]

tire[2] /tīr/ *vt.* (**tired, tir·ing, tires**) **CLOTHE SOMEBODY** to attire or adorn somebody or something (*archaic or literary*) ■ *n.* (*archaic*) **1. ATTIRE** clothing or attire **2. HEAD COVERING** a woman's head covering or ornament [14thC. Shortening of ATTIRE.]

tired /tīrd/ *adj.* **1. NEEDING REST** in need of rest or sleep, or weakened and made less active by exertion **2. NO LONGER INTERESTED** having lost patience or interest ○ *grew tired of hearing the same complaints* **3. OVERUSED** no longer new or fresh because of overuse ○ *a tired old slogan* —**tired·ly** *adv.* —**tired·ness** *n.*

tired out *adj.* thoroughly tired

Ti·ree /tī reé/ island of the Inner Hebrides, western Scotland. Population: 950 (1991). Area: 29 sq. mi./76 sq. km.

tire·less /tīrləss/ *adj.* never slackening or stopping, and apparently immune to tiredness or fatigue —**tire·less·ly** *adv.* —**tire·less·ness** *n.*

Ti·re·si·as /tī reèsee əss/ *n.* in Greek mythology, a seer from Thebes who often delivered prophecies to Oedipus. In the most common version of the myth, Athena struck him sightless after he saw her bathing, but gave him the power of prophecy.

tire·some /tīrsəm/ *adj.* causing weariness, annoyance, or boredom —**tire·some·ly** *adv.* —**tire·some·ness** *n.*

Tîr·gu Mu·res /tùrgoo moòr esh/ capital city of Mures County in central Romania. Population: 166,315 (1994).

tir·ing /tīring/ *adj.* causing somebody to feel tired, usually because requiring great physical or mental exertion

Tír na n-Óg /teèr na nòg/ *n.* in Irish legend, a land of eternal youth [Late 19thC. From Irish *tír na n-óg* "land of the young."]

ti·ro (*plural* **-ros**) *n.* = **tyro**

Ti·ros /tī ròss/ (*plural* **-ros**) *n.* a satellite with infrared and television equipment for transmitting weather data to Earth [Late 20thC. An acronym formed from *television infrared observational satellite*.]

Tir·so de Mo·li·na /teèrsō the mō leénaa/ (1571?–1648) Spanish playwright and theologian. He is the author of several hundred plays, including the comedy *The Trickster of Seville* (1630), which has the first literary presentation of Don Juan. Pseudonym of **Gabriel Téllez**

Tir·than·ka·ra /teer thúngkərə/ *n.* a traditional holy man of Jainism, belonging to a group who have attained personal immortality through enlightenment and by their teaching have made a path for others to follow [Mid-19thC. From Sanskrit *tīrthaṁkaraḥ*, literally "ford maker," from *tīrtham* "ford, passage" + *kṛ-* "to make" (source of English *karma*).]

Ti·ruch·chi·rap·pal·li /tìrrə chìrə púllee, ti roòchi raápəlee/ city in southern India, Tamil Nadu State, capital of the Tiruchchirappalli District. Population: 387,223 (1991). Former name **Trichinopoly**

Ti·ru·nel·ve·li /tìrroō nélvəlee/ town in Tirunelveli District, Tamil Nadu State, southern India. Population: 135,762 (1991).

Tir·yns /tírrinz/ ancient city in Argolis Department in the Peloponnesus, southern Greece, situated between Naplion and Mycenae

'tis /tiz/ *contr.* it is (*archaic or literary*)

ti·sane /ti zán/, **ptis·an** *n.* an infusion of leaves or flowers used as a beverage, e.g., an herbal tea [14thC. Via French from, ultimately, Greek *ptisanē* "barley water" (see PTISAN).]

Tish·a b'Av /tìshə ba̋av/ *n.* in Judaism, a fast on the ninth day of the month of Av to commemorate the destruction of the First and Second Temples [From Hebrew *tišāh bĕāḇ* "ninth of Av"]

Tish·ri /tíshree/ *n.* in the Jewish calendar, the first month of the religious year and the seventh month of the civil year, 30 days long and falling in September and October [Mid-17thC. From Hebrew *tišrî*, of uncertain origin.]

Ti·siph·o·ne /ti síffənee/ *n.* in Greek mythology, one of the three Furies. The others were Alecto and Megaera.

tis·sue /tíshoo/ *n.* **1.** PIECE OF ABSORBENT PAPER a piece of soft absorbent paper that can be used as a handkerchief or a towel **2.** = **tissue paper 3.** CELL BIOL GROUP OF CELLS IN AN ORGANISM organic body material in animals and plants made up of large numbers of cells that are similar in form and function and their related intercellular substances. The four basic types of tissue are nerve, muscle, epidermal, and connective. **4.** INTRICATE SERIES an intricate interrelated series of things ○ *a tissue of lies* **5.** TEXTILES GAUZY FABRIC a thin, finely woven fabric with a gauzy texture [14thC. From Old French *tissu*, from the past participle of *tistre* "to weave," from Latin *texere* (see TEXT).]

tis·sue cul·ture *n.* **1.** GROWTH OF TISSUE the growth of tissue outside an organism in a nutrient medium, or the techniques involved in the process **2.** TISSUE the tissue grown in a culture medium

tis·sue pa·per *n.* a thin soft paper used for wrapping and protecting delicate items

tis·sue plas·min·o·gen ac·ti·va·tor *n.* an anticlotting enzyme that is produced naturally in blood vessel linings and is genetically engineered for use in treating heart attacks, to dissolve blood clots, and to prevent heart muscle damage

tis·sue type *n.* the chemical characteristics of the body tissue of an individual that determine whether or not the tissue is immunologically compatible with the tissue of another individual —**tis·sue type** *vti.*

Ti·sza /tíss aw/ major tributary of the Danube River in eastern Europe. Length: 600 mi./970 km.

tit[1] /tit/ *n.* **1.** OFFENSIVE TERM an offensive term for a woman's breast (*slang offensive*) **2.** TEAT a teat [Old English *titt*; ultimately from prehistoric Germanic]

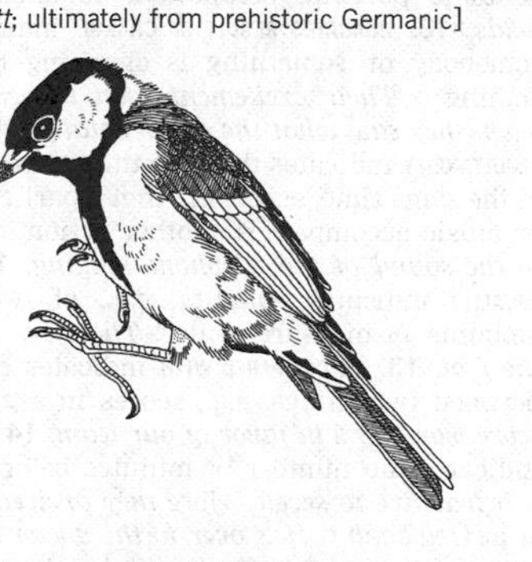

Tit: Great tit

tit[2] /tit/ *n.* a small active songbird of the northern hemisphere with a short bill and strong feet, e.g., the bluetit, crested tit, or great tit [Early 18thC. Shortening of TITMOUSE.]

Tit. *abbr.* Titus

ti·tan /tít'n/ *n.* somebody whose power, achievement, intellect, or physical size is extraordinarily impressive [Early 19thC. Via Latin from Greek, "Titan."]

Ti·tan[1] *n.* MYTHOL in Greek mythology, one of the twelve children of Uranus and Gaia, supreme rulers of the universe until they were overthrown by Zeus [Mid-17thC. Via Latin from Greek.]

Ti·tan[2] *n.* ASTRON the largest natural satellite of Saturn, discovered in 1655. It is 3,198 mi./5,150 km in diameter and has a significant atmosphere that is composed mainly of nitrogen. [15thC. From Latin, used for the sun god Helios (the original sense in English), from Greek.]

ti·tan·ate /tít'n àyt/ *n.* a chemical compound that is a salt or an ester of titanic acid

Ti·ta·ni·a /tī táynee ə, ti-/ *n.* **1.** QUEEN OF FAIRIES in medieval folklore, the wife of Oberon and queen of the fairies **2.** ASTRON SATELLITE OF URANUS the largest moon of the planet Uranus, the fourth most distant satellite observable from the Earth, orbiting at a distance of 262,000 mi./436,000 km with a diameter of 947 mi./1578 km. Although it was one of the first two satellites of Uranus to be discovered in 1787, Oberon being the other, Titania is officially designated as Uranus III.

ti·tan·ic /tī tánnik/ *adj.* **1.** VERY LARGE OR STRONG having extraordinary physical strength or size **2.** POWERFUL of extraordinary power, scope, or impressiveness **3.** CHEM ELEM OF TITANIUM relating to or containing titanium —**ti·tan·i·cal·ly** *adv.*

Ti·tan·ic *adj.* MYTHOL relating to or like the Titans of mythology

ti·tan·ic ox·ide *n.* = **titanium dioxide**

ti·tan·if·er·ous /tít'n íffərəss/ *adj.* yielding or containing titanium [Early 19thC. Coined from TITANIUM + -FEROUS.]

Ti·tan·ism /tít'n ìzzəm/ *n.* the spirit of defiance of authority, conventional society, and the established order

ti·tan·ite /tít'n ìt/ *n.* MINERALS = **sphene** [Mid-19thC. Formed from TITANIUM.]

ti·ta·ni·um /tī táynee əm/ *n.* a corrosion-resistant silvery metallic chemical element that occurs in rutile and ilmenite and whose strength and light weight make it useful in the manufacture of alloys for the aerospace industry. Symbol **Ti** [Late 18thC. Formed from TITAN, on the model of URANIUM.]

ti·ta·ni·um di·ox·ide *n.* a white crystalline compound that occurs naturally in rutile and other minerals and is used as a pigment in paint for its durability and its ability to cover surfaces. Formula: TiO_2.

ti·ta·ni·um white *n.* **1.** = **titanium dioxide 2.** WHITE PAINT PIGMENT a brilliant white paint pigment consisting primarily of titanium dioxide

ti·tan·o·saur /tī tánnə sàwr, tít'nə-/ *n.* a huge herbivorous sauropod dinosaur of the Cretaceous and Jurassic periods, found especially in South America. Genus: *Titanosaurus.* [Late 19thC. From modern Latin *Titanosaurus*, genus name, from Greek *Titan* "Titan" + *sauros* "lizard."]

ti·tan·o·there /tī tánnə theer, tít'nə-/ *n.* a large mammal similar to a rhinoceros that lived in North America during the Tertiary Period [Mid-20thC. From modern Latin *Titanotherium*, genus name, from Greek *Titan* "Titan" + *therion* "wild beast."]

ti·tan·ous /tít'nəss/ *adj.* relating to or containing titanium with a valence of three

titbit /tít bìt/ *n.* = **tidbit**

ti·ter /títər/ *n.* **1.** CHEM SUBSTANCE CONCENTRATION the concentration of a substance in solution as determined by titration **2.** BIOCHEM ANTIBODY CONCENTRATION the concentration of an antibody determined by how much it is diluted before it no longer reacts positively to an antigen [Mid-19thC. From French *titre* "qualification, quality (of gold or silver alloy)," a variant of *title* (see TITLE).]

tit for tat *n.* the process or act of repaying a wrong or injury suffered by inflicting equivalent harm on the doer (*hyphenated before a noun*) ○ *tit-for-tat strikes* [Mid-16thC. Origin uncertain: perhaps an alteration of *tip for tap.*]

tith·a·ble /títhəb'l/ *adj.* required to pay or subject to the payment of tithes

tithe /tīth/ *n.* **1.** CHR INDIVIDUAL'S FINANCIAL SUPPORT FOR A CHURCH one tenth of somebody's income or produce paid voluntarily or as a tax for the support of a church or its clergy **2.** CHR OBLIGATION OF SUPPORTING A CHURCH FINANCIALLY the obligation to pay a tithe to a church or its clergy **3.** ASSESSMENT OR CONTRIBUTION any voluntary contribution or tax payment, especially when it constitutes one tenth of somebody's income **4.** SMALL PART OF SOMETHING one tenth or a small part of anything ■ *v.* **(tithed, tith·ing, tithes) 1.** *vti.* PAY ONE TENTH OF INCOME to contribute or pay one tenth of your income or produce, especially to support a church **2.** *vt.* COLLECT ONE TENTH OF SOMEBODY'S INCOME to assess or collect the payment of one tenth of somebody's income [Old English *tēoþa* "tenth"] —**tith·er** *n.*

tith·ing /tīthing/ *n.* **1.** CHR PAYING OF TITHES the assessing or paying of tithes **2.** ONE TENTH one tenth part of anything [Old English *tēoþung*]

ti·ti[1] /tee teé, teé teé/ (*plural* **-tis**) *n.* ZOOL a tropical South American arboreal monkey with a round face, thick soft fur, and a long tail. Genus: *Callicebus.* [Mid-18thC. Via Spanish *tití* from Aymara.]

ti·ti[2] /tí tī, teé tee/ *n.* BOT **1.** EVERGREEN SHRUB WITH FRAGRANT FLOWERS an evergreen shrub or small tree of the southeastern United States that has glossy leathery leaves and fragrant white or pinkish flowers. Latin name: *Cliftonia monophylla.* **2.** EVERGREEN TREE a small American evergreen tree or shrub with leathery leaves and yellow fruit. Latin name: *Cyrilla racemiflora.* [Early 19thC. Origin unknown.]

ti·tian /tísh'n/, **Ti·tian** *adj.* of a bright auburn color tinged with gold ○ *titian hair* [Late 19thC. Named for TITIAN, who used the color frequently.]

AKG London

Titian: Self-portrait (1555)

Ti·tian /tíshən/ (1477?–1576) Italian painter. The foremost Venetian painter of the Renaissance, he painted portraits and religious and mythological scenes that are noted for their rich coloration. Real name **Tiziano Vecellio**

Ti·ti·ca·ca, Lake /tìtti ka̋akə/ lake in east central South America, extending from southeastern Peru to western Bolivia. It is the largest lake on the continent and the highest navigable lake in the world, about 12,500 ft./3,810 m above sea level. Area: 3,200 sq. mi./8,288 sq. km.

tit·il·late /títti làyt/ **(-lat·ed, -lat·ing, -lates)** *v.* **1.** *vti.* EXCITE SOMEBODY to excite or stimulate somebody pleasurably, usually in a mildly sexual way **2.** *vt.* CAUSE SOMEBODY TO TINGLE to cause a tingling sensation in somebody by touching him or her lightly [Early 17thC. From Latin *titillare* "to tickle."] —**tit·il·lat·ing** *adj.* —**tit·il·lat·ing·ly** *adv.* —**tit·il·la·tion** /tìtti láysh'n/ *n.* —**tit·il·la·tive** /títti làytiv/ *adj.*

tit·lark /tít laark/ *n.* BIRDS = **pipit** [Mid-17thC. Formed from TIT[2] + LARK[1].]

ti·tle /tít'l/ *n.* **1.** NAME a name that identifies a book, movie, play, painting, musical composition, or other literary or artistic work **2.** DESCRIPTIVE HEADING a descriptive heading for something such as a book chapter, a magazine article, or a speech **3.** DESIGNATION ADDED TO A NAME a word such as "Mr," "Ms," "Dr," or "Lord" added to and usually preceding somebody's name to indicate his or her rank, social status, or profession, or as a courtesy **4.** NAME DESCRIBING A POSITION a name that describes somebody's job or position in a company or organization ○ *a job title* **5.** SPORTS CHAMPIONSHIP the status of champion in a sport or competition ○ *a title fight* **6.** LAW RIGHT OR PROOF OF IT any legitimate right or anything providing proof or justification for that claim **7.** PUBL PUBLISHED WORK a work published or recorded by a company ○ *this spring's new titles* **8.** LAW DOCUMENT a document giving the legal right to property **9.** LAW EVIDENCE OF PROPERTY RIGHTS the evidence of legal right to property **10.** PUBL = **title page 11.** LAW CLAIM BASED ON A RIGHT a claim based on a legitimate right **12.** LAW RIGHT TO POSSESS PROPERTY a legal right to possess and dispose of property **13.** LAW DIVISION a division of a law, statute, or law book **14.** LAW LAW HEADING a heading for a lawsuit or legal action, or one that names a document or statute **15.** CHR REQUIREMENT OF ORDINATION a source of income or office in the church required of a candidate by the Church of England before ordination **16.** CHR ROMAN CATHOLIC CHURCH IN ROME a Roman Catholic church in or near Rome that has a bishop or cardinal as its nominal head ■ **ti·tles** *npl.* CINEMA, TV **CREDITS OR SUBTITLES ON SCREEN** the written presentation on the screen of credits, narration, or subtitles in a movie or television program ■ *vt.* (**-tled, -tling, -tles**) **1. NAME SOMETHING** to give a name or title to somebody or something **2. CALL SOMEBODY BY A TITLE** to call somebody by a title [14thC. From Old English *titul* and Old French *title*, both from Latin *titulus* "inscription."]

ti·tled /tī́t'ld/ *adj.* having a title, especially of nobility

ti·tle deed *n.* LAW a deed or document that is evidence of somebody's legal right to property

ti·tle·hold·er /tī́t'l hòldər/ *n.* **1.** SPORTS **HOLDER OF A CHAMPIONSHIP TITLE** somebody who holds a sports championship title **2.** LAW **SOMEBODY WITH TITLE TO PROPERTY** somebody who holds legal title to property — **ti·tle·hold·ing** *n.*

ti·tle page *n.* PUBL a page at the beginning of a book that gives its title and the name of the author and publisher

ti·tle role *n.* CINEMA, THEATER the role in a play or movie that gives the work its name

ti·tlist /tī́t'list/ *n.* SPORTS = **titleholder** *n.* 1

tit·man /títmən/ (*plural* **-men** /títmən/) *n. Northeast U.S.* **1. RUNT** the runt of a litter, especially of hogs **2. OFFENSIVE TERM** a very small person (*offensive*) [Early 19thC. Formed from obsolete *tit* "something small, runt" (of uncertain origin: probably from Scandinavian) + MAN.]

tit·mouse /tít mòwss/ (*plural* **-mice** /-mīss/) *n.* a small bird widespread in North America, Asia, Africa, and Europe. Genus: *Parus*. [14thC. Alteration (influenced by *mouse*) of *titmose*, from obsolete *tit* "something small, runt" (of uncertain origin: probably from Scandinavian) + *mose* "titmouse" (from Old English *māse*).]

AKG London

Tito

Ti·to /teétō/ (1892–1980) Yugoslavian statesman. After leading partisan forces against the Germans in World War II, as president of Yugoslavia (1942–77) he established a Communist state independent of the Soviet Union. Known as **Marshal Tito**. Real name **Josip Broz**

Ti·to·ism /teé tō ìzzəm/ *n.* the form of Communism associated with Tito and practiced by him in Yugoslavia, especially involving the pursuit of national interests independent of the then Soviet Union and its satellites —**Ti·to·ist** *n., adj.*

ti·trant /tī́trənt/ *n.* a reagent, e.g., a solution of known concentration, that is added in titration [Mid-20thC. Formed from TITRATE.]

ti·trate /tī́ tràyt/ (**-trat·ed, -trat·ing, -trates**) *vt.* to measure the concentration of a solution by titration [Late 19thC. From French *titrer*, from *titre* (see TITER).] — **ti·trat·a·ble** /tī́ tràytəb'l/ *adj.*

ti·tra·tion /tī tráysh'n/ *n.* a method of calculating the concentration of a dissolved substance by adding quantities of a reagent of known concentration to a known volume of test solution until a reaction occurs

ti·tre /tī́tər/ *n.* U.K. = **titer**

ti·tri·met·ric /tītrə méttrik/ *adj.* using or calculated by titration [Late 19thC. Coined from TITRATION + -METRIC.] — **ti·tri·met·ri·cal·ly** *adv.*

tit·ter /títtər/ *vi.* (**-tered, -ter·ing, -ters**) **LAUGH NERVOUSLY** to laugh in a nervous self-conscious way ■ *n.* **NERVOUS GIGGLE** a short high-pitched nervous laugh or giggle [Early 17thC. An imitation of the sound.] —**tit·ter·er** *n.* —**tit·ter·ing** *n.* —**tit·ter·ing·ly** *adv.*

tit·tle /títt'l/ *n.* **1. TINY BIT** the tiniest bit **2.** PRINTING **MARK USED IN PRINTING** a small mark used in printing and writing such as an accent, punctuation, or diacritical mark [14thC. From medieval Latin *titulus*, literally "small superscript mark," from Latin, "title."]

tit·tle-tat·tle *n.* **GOSSIP** idle gossip ■ *vi.* (**tit·tle-tat·tled, tit·tle-tat·tling, tit·tle-tat·tles**) **TO GOSSIP** to gossip or chatter idly [Early 16thC. Doubling of TATTLE.] —**tit·tle-tat·tler** *n.*

tit·tup /títtəp/ *vi.* (**-tuped** *or* **-tupped, -tup·ing** *or* **-tup·ping, -tups**) **PRANCE** to move in a lively prancing way ■ *n.* **PRANCING MOVEMENT** a sometimes exaggerated lively prancing movement [Late 17thC. Origin uncertain: perhaps an imitation of the sound of horse's hoofs.]

tit·u·ba·tion /tìchə báysh'n/ *n.* an unsteady or stumbling gait or a head tremor, often caused by a disorder of the cerebellum [Mid-17thC. From Latin *titubare* "to stagger," of unknown origin.]

tit·u·lar /tíchələr/ *adj.* **1. IN NAME ONLY** having a particular title, rank, or position but not possessing the power or exercising the functions usually associated with it **2. WITH A TITLE OF RANK** holding a title of rank **3. FROM A TITLE** derived from or figuring in the title of a work such as a book or movie **4.** CHR **FROM AN INACTIVE SEE** bearing the title of a see or monastery that is no longer active ■ *n.* **1. SOMEBODY WITH A TITLE OF RANK** somebody who holds a title of rank **2. HOLDER OF A NOMINAL TITLE** somebody who holds a title in name only [Late 16thC. Formed from Latin *titulus* "title."] — **tit·u·lar·ly** *adv.* —**tit·u·lar·y** *n.*

Ti·tus[1] /tītəss/ *n.* in the Bible, an early Christian leader, and a disciple of St. Paul.

Ti·tus[2] *n.* in the Bible, a letter addressed to Titus, traditionally believed to be from St. Paul. It contains advice on the organization of the Christian Church. See table at **Bible**

Ti·tus /tī́təss/ (39–81) Roman general and emperor. He captured and destroyed Jerusalem in A.D.70. As emperor (79–81) he was noted for his leniency and generosity, and he also completed the Colosseum in Rome. Full name **Titus Flavius Sabinus Vespasianus**

Tiv /tiv/ (*plural* **Tivs** *or* **Tiv**) *n.* **1.** PEOPLES **MEMBER OF A W AFRICAN PEOPLE** a member of a people living in West Africa, mainly in southern Nigeria and neighboring Cameroon **2.** LANG **TIV LANGUAGE** the language of the Tiv people, belonging to the Benne-Congo family of languages. It is spoken by around 1.5 million people. [Mid-20thC. Of Bantu origin.]

Ti·vo·li /tívvəlee/ town in central Italy, near Rome, location of the Renaissance-period Tivoli Gardens and the ruined villa of the emperor Hadrian. Population: 54,352 (1990).

Ti·wa /teéwə/ (*plural* **-was** *or* **-wa**) *n.* **1.** PEOPLES **MEMBER OF NATIVE N AMERICAN PEOPLE** a member of a group of Native North American Pueblo peoples who originally occupied lands in New Mexico, and whose members now live mainly in Texas and northern New Mexico **2. TIWA LANGUAGE** the language of the Tiwa people. It belongs to the Tanoan family of languages and is spoken by fewer than 5,000 people. [Early 18thC. From Tiwa.]

Tiz·ard /tíz aard/, **Dame Cath** (*b.* 1931) New Zealand politician. She was the first woman to become governor-general of New Zealand (1990–96). Full name **Dame Catherine Anne Tizard**

tiz·zy /tízzee/ *n.* a nervous agitated state (*informal*) [Mid-20thC. Origin unknown.]

T-joint, **tee-joint** *n.* a joint in wood or other material forming the letter T

tk. *abbr.* truck

TKO *abbr.* BOXING technical knockout

tkt. *abbr.* ticket

Tl *symbol.* thallium

t.l. *abbr.* INSUR total loss

Tlax·cala /tlaaks kaálə, -kállə/ capital city of Tlaxcala State in east central Mexico. It is the site of the Church of San Francisco, the oldest church in North America (1521). Population: 50,631 (1990).

TLC *abbr.* tender loving care (*informal*)

Tlem·cen /tlem sén/ town in northwestern Algeria. Population: 126,882 (1987).

Tlin·git /tlíng git, tlíngit/ (*plural* **-gits** *or* **-git**) *n.* **1.** PEOPLES **MEMBER OF NATIVE N AMERICAN PEOPLE** a member of a group of Native North American peoples that originally occupied coastal lands in southeastern Alaska, and whose members continue to live mainly there and in British Columbia **2.** LANG **TLINGIT LANGUAGE** the Na-Dené language of the Tlingit people. It is spoken by about 2,000 people. [Mid-19thC. From Tlingit, "person."]

t.l.o. *abbr.* INSUR total loss only

T lym·pho·cyte *n.* = **T cell**

Tm *symbol.* thulium

TM *abbr.* trademark

T.M. *abbr.* transcendental meditation

T-man (*plural* **T-men**) *n.* a special investigator of the Department of the Treasury (*informal*)

tme·sis /tmeés is, meéssiss, tə meéssiss/ *n.* the separation of the parts of a word by inserting a word or words between them [Mid-16thC. From Greek *tmēsis* "cutting," from *temnein* "to cut."]

TMJ syn·drome *n., abbr.* temporomandibular joint syndrome

TMOT *abbr.* trust me on this (*used in e-mail messages*)

TN *abbr.* Tennessee

tng. *abbr.* training

tnpk., **Tnpk.** *abbr.* turnpike

TNT *n.* a yellow flammable crystalline compound used as an explosive and in making dyestuffs. Formula: $C_7H_5N_3O_6$. Full form **trinitrotoluene**

to (*strong*) /too/; (*weak*) /tŏŏ, tə/ CORE MEANING: a preposition or adverb indicating the direction, destination, or position of somebody or something ○ *I met him on his way to school.* ○ *She climbed all the way to the top.* ○ *You'll see a supermarket to your left.*

1. INDICATES DIRECTION indicates the direction or destination of somebody or something ○ *He was on his way to the party.* **2. INDICATES POSITION** indicates the position of somebody or something ○ *To the right of the door is a bulletin board.* **3. FORMS INFINITIVE** used before the base form of a verb to make the infinitive of that verb ○ *I want to leave now.* **4. INDICATES PURPOSE** used with the base form of a verb to indicate the intention or purpose of an action ○ *The news agency is used to distribute information.* **5. INDICATES RECIPIENT** indicates the recipient of something (*used with a noun phrase to form the indirect object*) ○ *Give it to me.* ○ *mail sent to another user on the same computer* **6. INDICATES DIRECTION OF FEELING OR ACTION** indicates who or what a particular feeling or action is directed toward ○ *I was very grateful to her for everything she did for me.* **7. INDICATES ATTACHMENT** indicates that two things are joined together ○ *Each triangle consists of three square faces joined to one another along two edges.* **8. UNTIL** indicates that something goes on until a certain time or until it reaches a certain amount ○ *He closes the store on Mondays and opens from Tuesday to Saturday.* **9. INDICATES RANGE** indicates a range of things or topics ○ *Medical studies have explored everything from alcohol to pesticides to genetics to parental occupations to electromagnetic fields.* **10. INDICATES RESULT OF CHANGE** indicates what somebody or something is changing into or becoming ○ *Their excitement soon turned to gloom when they saw what the climb entailed.* **11. INDICATES SIMULTANEITY** indicates that two things are happening at the same time, especially that a particular sound or music accompanies another action ○ *I woke up to the sound of the telephone ringing.* **12. INDICATES EQUALITY** indicates equality, e.g., of two weights, amounts, or measurements ○ *There are 12 inches to the foot.* **13. AS COMPARED WITH** indicates comparison between two things, e.g., scores in a game ○ *The score was 5 to 3 in favor of our team.* **14. BEFORE HOUR** indicates the number of minutes before the hour ○ *It was five to seven before they arrived home.* **15. AT** at (*regional*) ○ *He's over to the doctor's.* ■ *adv.* **1. SHUT OR ALMOST SHUT** indicates that a door is shut or across the opening but not completely or firmly shut ○ *He pulled the door to after him.* **2. CONSCIOUS AGAIN** into a returned state of lucidity and consciousness ○ *came to in the recovery room* ○ *brought the patient to* **3.** NAUT **INTO WIND** into the direction from which the wind is blowing ○ *turned the yacht to* [Old English *tō*. From a prehistoric Germanic word that is also the ancestor of English *too* and *tattoo*.]

TO, **T/O** *abbr.* turnover

toad /tōd/ *n.* **1. TERRESTRIAL AMPHIBIAN SIMILAR TO FROG** a small squat tailless amphibian distributed nearly worldwide. It is similar to a frog but has dry warty skin and, except for breeding in water, lives mostly on land. Family: Bufonidae. **2. AMPHIBIAN THAT RESEMBLES TOAD** an amphibian similar to a toad such as the horned toad but belonging to a different taxonomic family **3. OFFENSIVE TERM** an offensive term used to

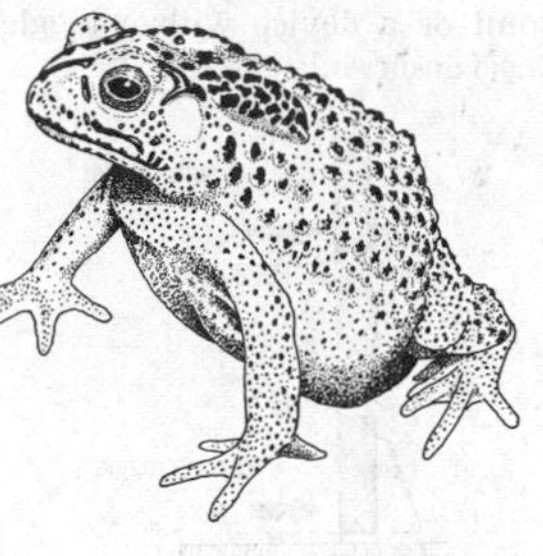

Toad

refer to somebody considered loathsome or disgusting (*insult*) [Old English *tādige*, of unknown origin] —**toad·ish** *adj.*

toad·eat·er /tṓd ēetər/ *n.* a toady (*archaic*)

WORD KEY: ORIGIN

The term ***toadeater*** originated in the dubious selling methods of itinerant doctors. They employed an assistant who pretended to eat a toad (toads were thought to be poisonous), so that the doctor could appear to effect a miraculous cure with his medicine.

toad·fish /tṓd fish/ (*plural* **-fish** *or* **-fish·es**) *n.* a scaleless spiny bottom-feeding fish that lives in tropical and temperate seas and has a broad flattened head and wide mouth. Family: Batrachoididae.

toad·flax /tṓd flàks/ (*plural* **-flax·es** *or* **-flax**) *n.* **1.** **PLANT WITH ORANGE-AND-YELLOW FLOWERS** a plant native to Europe but widespread in North America, with narrow leaves and spurred two-lipped orange-and-yellow flowers similar to those of a snapdragon. Latin name: *Linaria vulgaris.* **2.** **PLANT RELATED TO COMMON TOADFLAX** a plant related to the common toadflax and similar to it, but usually with lilac-colored flowers. Genus: *Linaria.*

toad spit, **toad spit·tle** *n.* = **cuckoo spit**

toad·stone /tṓd stṑn/ *n.* a stone or similar object believed to have formed in the head or body of a toad, formerly worn around the neck as a charm against evil and disease

toad·stool /tṓd stool/ *n.* a poisonous umbrella-shaped fungus with a spore-producing round flat cap on a stalk [14thC. So called because it resembles a small stool and grows in environments where toads are found.]

toad·y /tṓdee/ *n.* (*plural* **-ies**) **SOMEBODY SERVILE AND INGRATIATING** a self-serving person who behaves in a servile sycophantic manner, flattering and fawning on people with power or influence ■ *vi.* (**-ied, -y·ing, -ies**) **BEHAVE INGRATIATINGLY** to behave in an obsequious and ingratiating manner [Early 19thC. Shortening of TOADEATER.] —**toad·y·ish** *adj.* —**toad·y·ism** *n.*

Toa·ma·si·na /twaamə seenə/ city and major port on the Indian Ocean, in eastern Madagascar, situated about 130 mi./209 km northeast of Antananarivo. Population: 127,441 (1993). Former name **Tamatave**

to and fro *adv.* **1.** **BACK AND FORTH** moving backward and forward **2.** **HERE AND THERE** moving about here and there —**to-and-fro** *adj.* —**to-and-fro** *n.* —**to·ing and fro·ing** *n.*

toast /tōst/ *n.* **1.** FOOD **BREAD BROWNED WITH HEAT** sliced bread that has been browned on both sides with heat, under a grill, in a toaster, or in front of an open fire **2.** **CALL TO HONOR SOMEBODY OR SOMETHING** a call to a gathering to honor somebody or something by raising glasses and drinking **3.** **RAISING OF GLASSES TO HONOR SOMEBODY** an act of raising a glass and drinking in honor of somebody or something **4.** **SOMEBODY OR SOMETHING HONORED** somebody or something honored by a toast **5.** **ADMIRED PERSON** somebody who is the object of much attention or admiration ○ *the toast of Hollywood* ■ *v.* (**toast·ed, toast·ing, toasts**) **1.** *vti.* FOOD **HEAT AND BROWN FOOD** to heat and brown bread or other food, or to become browned, on a grill, over an open fire, or in a toaster **2.** *vt.* **WARM BODY** to warm the body or a part of the body near a source of heat **3.** *vti.* **DRINK IN SOMEBODY'S HONOR** to drink or propose a drink in honor of somebody or something [14thC. Via Old French *toster* "to roast" from, ultimately, Latin *tost-*, the past participle stem of *torrere* "to scorch."] ◇ **be toast** to be in serious trouble (*informal*) ○ *Do that again and you're toast!*

toast·er /tṓstər/ *n.* a small electrical appliance for making toast that works by exposing the bread to heated electrical coils [Late 16thC. Originally used for "someone that toasts things."]

toast·er ov·en *n.* an electrical device that is portable and can work both as a toaster and as a small oven

toast·mas·ter /tṓst màstər/ *n.* somebody who proposes toasts and introduces speakers at a banquet or reception

toast·mis·tress /tṓst mìstrəss/ *n.* a woman who proposes toasts and introduces speakers at a banquet or reception

toast rack *n.* a stand that holds slices of toast on end and separate from each other

Tob. *abbr.* BIBLE Tobit

to·bac·co /tə bákō/ (*plural* **-cos** *or* **-co**) *n.* **1.** **DRIED PROCESSED LEAVES** the dried leaves of a plant of the nightshade family, processed primarily for smoking **2.** **PLANT WHOSE LEAVES ARE SMOKED** a plant native to tropical America and cultivated for tobacco. Genus: *Nicotiana.* **3.** **PRODUCT MADE FROM TOBACCO LEAVES** any of the products made from tobacco leaves, e.g., cigarettes **4.** **HABIT OF USING TOBACCO** the habit of using tobacco products **5.** **CROP OF TOBACCO** a crop of tobacco referred to collectively [Late 16thC. From Spanish *tabaco*, of uncertain origin: possibly from Taino "roll of tobacco, or pipe, for smoking" or perhaps from Arabic *ṭabbāk* "herbs."]

to·bac·co bud·worm *n.* a destructive rust-colored moth caterpillar that feeds on the leaves and buds of tobacco plants. Latin name: *Heliothis virescens.*

to·bac·co horn·worm *n.* the larva of a large hawk moth of North America and the West Indies that feeds on the leaves of tobacco plants. Latin name: *Manduca sexta.*

to·bac·co mo·sa·ic *n.* a viral disease that affects tobacco and nightshade and is caused by the tobacco mosaic virus

to·bac·co mo·sa·ic vi·rus *n.* a retrovirus that causes mosaic disease in tobacco and other plants belonging to the nightshade family

to·bac·co moth *n.* a drab gray scavenger moth that infests tobacco and is a pest in tobacco storage facilities. Latin name: *Ephestia elutella.*

to·bac·co·nist /tə bákənist/ *n.* a person or shop that specializes in selling tobacco products and supplies such as cigarettes, tobacco, and pipes [Mid-17thC. Formed from TOBACCO + -IST.]

to·bac·co road *n.* a shabby poverty-stricken rural community [Mid-20thC. From the title of a novel by Erskine Caldwell.]

to·bac·co worm *n.* = **tobacco hornworm**

To·ba·go /tə báygō/ island in the West Indies, a constituent part of Trinidad and Tobago. Population: 50,282 (1990). Area: 116 sq. mi./300 sq. km.

To·ba So·jo /tṑbaa sṓjō/ (1053–1140) Japanese artist and Buddhist high priest. He is noted for his Buddhist icons and humorous paintings.

To·bey /tṓbee/, **Mark** (1890–1976) U.S. artist. He is noted for the "white writing" calligraphic technique used in his abstract paintings.

To·bit /tṓbit/ *n.* **1.** **BIBLICAL CHARACTER** in the Bible, a pious Israelite living in Nineveh at the end of the 8th century B.C. **2.** **BOOK IN BIBLE** book in the Roman Catholic Bible and the Protestant Apocrypha. It tells the story of Tobit. See table at **Bible**

to·bog·gan /tə bóggən/ *n.* **LONG NARROW RUNNERLESS SLED** a long narrow sled without runners, made of strips of wood running lengthwise and curled up at the front, used for coasting downhill on snow ■ *vi.* (**-ganed, -gan·ing, -gans**) **1.** **RIDE A TOBOGGAN** to ride on a toboggan **2.** **FALL RAPIDLY** to fall or decline rapidly (*informal*) [Early 19thC. Via Canadian French *tabagane* from Micmac *topağan* "sled."] —**to·bog·gan·er** *n.* —**to·bog·gan·ist** *n.*

To·bruk /tə brook/ city and port in northeastern Libya, on the Mediterranean Sea. British forces were besieged there during World War II. Population: 94,006 (1984).

to·by jug /tṓbee/, **to·by** (*plural* **-bies**), **To·by** (*plural* **-bies**) *n.* a beer mug or jug in the shape of a stout man wearing a three-cornered hat [Mid-19thC. From *Toby* (nickname for *Tobias*), a common 19th-century male name.]

toc·ca·ta /tə kaátə/ (*plural* **-tas**) *n.* a composition for a keyboard instrument written in a free style that includes full chords and elaborate runs and is intended to show off the player's technique [Early 18thC. From Italian, from the feminine past participle of *toccare* "to touch," from assumed Vulgar Latin *toccare.*]

To·char·i·an /tō kérree ən/, **To·khar·i·an** *n.* **1.** PEOPLES **MEMBER OF EARLY CHINESE PEOPLE** a member of a people that lived in the Tarim Pendi in western China before being defeated by the Uigurs during the 9th century A.D. They are believed to have spread into China from Eastern Europe. **2.** LANG **TOCHARIAN LANGUAGE** the extinct Indo-European language of the Tocharian people. It forms a separate branch of the Indo-European family and shows close resemblances to some western branches of the family. [Early 20thC. Formed from Latin *Tochari*, from Greek *Tokharoi* "the Tocharians."] —**Tocharian** *adj.*

to·coph·er·ol /tō kóffə ràwl/ *n.* a fat-soluble oily compound with vitamin-E properties, present in vegetable oils, leafy greens, and milk, and required for normal growth in most vertebrates [Mid-20thC. Coined from Greek *tokos* "childbirth" + *pherein* "to bear" + -OL.]

Tocque·ville /tṓk vìl/, **Alexis de** (1805–59) French historian and political writer. After visiting the United States, he wrote the influential *Democracy in America* (1833), his most famous work. Full name **Alexis Charles Henri Maurice Clérel de Tocqueville**

toc·sin /tóksin/ *n.* **1.** **ALARM** an alarm sounded by means of a bell **2.** **BELL** a bell that sounds an alarm **3.** **WARNING** any warning signal [Late 16thC. Via French from, ultimately, Old Provençal *tocasenh*, from *tocar* "to strike" (from assumed Vulgar Latin *toccare*) + *senh* "bell" (from Latin *signum* "signal").]

to·day /tə dáy/ *n.* **1.** **THIS DAY** this day, as distinct from yesterday or tomorrow **2.** **PRESENT AGE** the present time or age ○ *the fashions of today* ■ *adj.* **MODERN** modern or of the present day ○ *a today look* ■ *adv.* **1.** **ON THIS DAY** on or during this day ○ *She is working today.* **2.** **IN PRESENT TIME** during the present time or age ○ *Children today have far more sophisticated toys than we ever had.* [Old English *tō dæge*, literally "to (this) day"]

tod·dle /tódd'l/ *vi.* (**-dled, -dling, -dles**) **1.** **TAKE SHORT UNSTEADY STEPS** to walk with short unsteady steps, as a child does when learning to walk **2.** **WALK UNHURRIEDLY** to walk at a leisurely pace (*informal*) ■ *n.* **1.** **UNSTEADY STEPS** an unsteady, tottering gait **2.** **UNHURRIED WALK** a leisurely walk (*informal*) [Late 16thC. Origin unknown.]

tod·dler /tóddlər/ *n.* **1.** **YOUNG CHILD** a young child who is learning to walk **2.** **STANDARD SIZES OF CHILDREN'S CLOTHING** any of the standard sizes of clothing for children between the ages of one and three

tod·dy /tóddee/ (*plural* **-dies**) *n.* **1.** **HOT ALCOHOLIC DRINK** a drink made with alcoholic liquor, hot water, sugar, and sometimes spices **2.** **PALM TREE SAP** the sweet sap of a variety of Asian palm tree used as a beverage, either fresh or fermented [Late 18thC. Via Hindi *tāṛī* "palm sap" from, ultimately, Sanskrit *tālaḥ* "palm," probably of Dravidian origin.]

tod·dy cat *n.* = **palm civet**

to-do (*plural* **to-dos**) *n.* a fuss, especially an angry complaint or protest (*informal*)

to·dy /tṓdee/ (*plural* **-dies**) *n.* a small Caribbean bird similar to a kingfisher with a short tail and round wings, a bright green back, red throat, and a long straight beak. Family: Todidae. [Late 18thC. Origin uncertain: probably via French *todier* from, ultimately, Latin *todus*, a small bird.]

toe /tō/ *n.* **1.** ANAT **FOOT PART** any one of the digits of the foot, equivalent to the fingers and thumb of the hand **2.** ZOOL **VERTEBRATE'S FOOT PART** a part corresponding to the human toe in other vertebrates **3.** ZOOL **PART OF HOOF** the forepart of an animal's hoof **4.** CLOTHES **PART OF SHOE OR SOCK** the part of a shoe, boot, sock, or stocking that covers the toes and the front part of the foot **5.** GOLF **PART OF GOLF CLUB** the end of the head of a golf club **6.** **PART RESEMBLING TOE** a part that resembles the front part of a foot in form or position ○ *the toe of Italy* **7.** MECH ENG **LOWER END OF SHAFT** the lower end of a vertical shaft that turns in a bearing **8.** GEOG **BASE OF EMBANKMENT** the base of an embankment, cliff, wall, or dam ■ *v.* (**toed, toe·ing, toes**) **1.** *vi.* **STAND WITH TOES POINTED** to stand or move with the toes pointed in a particular direction **2.** *vt.* **TOUCH SOMETHING WITH TOES** to touch, kick, reach, or mark something with the toes or the front part of the foot **3.** *vt.* GOLF **STRIKE GOLF BALL** to strike a golf ball with the front part of the head of the club **4.** *vt.* BUILDING **DRIVE NAIL AT ANGLE**

to drive in a nail or spike at an angle **5.** *vt.* BUILDING **FASTEN SOMETHING WITH ANGLED NAIL** to fasten something with a nail or spike driven in at an angle [Old English *tā*. Ultimately from an Indo-European base meaning "to point" that is also the ancestor of English *digit* and *index*.] ◇ **on your toes** alert and ready for action ◇ **step, tread on somebody's toes** to offend or upset somebody by interfering with something considered to be that person's own responsibility ◇ **turn up your toes** to die (*informal*)

toe·a /tóy ə/ (*plural* **-a** *or* **-as**) *n.* **1. SUBUNIT OF PAPUA NEW GUINEAN CURRENCY** a subunit of currency in Papua New Guinea, 100 of which are worth one kina. See table at **currency 2. COIN WORTH A TOEA** a coin worth a toea [Late 20thC. From Motu, literally "conical shell," used as currency.]

toe and heel *n.* MOTOR SPORTS a technique used by race drivers for operating the brake and accelerator simultaneously with the right foot, using the heel for one pedal and the toe for the other

toe·cap /tṓ kàp/ *n.* a metal or leather covering reinforcing the toe of a shoe or boot

toed /tōd/ *adj.* **1.** ANAT, ZOOL **HAVING TOES** having toes of a particular kind or number (*usually used in combination*) ○ *three-toed* **2.** BUILDING **DRIVEN IN AT AN ANGLE** used to describe nails driven in at an angle, or something fastened by nails or spikes driven in at an angle

toe dance *n.* **DANCE ON TOES** a dance performed on the toes ■ *vi.* **DO TOE DANCE** to perform a toe dance —**toe danc·er** *n.*

TOEFL /tṓf'l/ *n.* a test of English for speakers of other languages that is an entrance requirement for study at a U.S. university. Full form **Test of English as a Foreign Language**

toe·hold /tṓ hṑld/ *n.* **1.** CLIMBING **SMALL RECESS IN ROCK** a small recess or ledge in a rock giving support for the toes **2. SMALL ADVANTAGE** a small advantage or gain that can be used to get a larger one later **3.** WRESTLING **HOLD ON FOOT** a wrestling hold in which one competitor holds the foot and twists the leg of the other

toe-in *n.* the alignment of a motor vehicle's front wheels so that the front edges are slightly closer together that the rear edges to improve its steering capabilities and reduce tire wear

toe loop *n.* a jump in which an ice skater, skating backward, takes off from one skate, makes one rotation in the air, and lands on the outer edge of the same skate

toe·na·der·ing /tṓ nàddəring/ *n. S Africa* a getting together or rapprochement between political parties (*informal*) [Early 20thC. Via Afrikaans from Dutch, from *toe* "to" + *nadering* "approach" (translation of French *rapprochement*).]

toe·nail /tṓ nàyl/ *n.* **1.** ANAT, ZOOL **NAIL ON TOE** the nail of a toe **2.** BUILDING **NAIL DRIVEN IN AT ANGLE** a nail driven in at an angle, e.g., to join intersecting structural parts ■ *vt.* (**-nailed, -nail·ing, -nails**) BUILDING **JOIN WITH ANGLED NAILS** to join parts of a structure with nails driven in at an angle

toe ring *n.* a ring worn on the toe, particularly a silver ring worn by married Hindu women

toe-to-toe *adj.* **OPPOSING** being in direct opposition ■ *adv.* **IN DIRECT OPPOSITION** in direct opposition as if in close combat

toff /tof/ *n. U.K.* somebody who is rich or upper-class, especially somebody who is also smartly dressed (*informal*) [Mid-19thC. Origin uncertain: probably a variant of *tuft*, a golden plume worn by titled students at Oxford and Cambridge.]

tof·fee /tóffee/ *n.* a candy that can be soft and chewy or hard and brittle, made by boiling brown sugar or molasses with butter and sometimes flavorings or nuts [Early 19thC. Variant of TAFFY.]

tof·fee ap·ple *n. U.K.* = **candy apple**

toft /toft/ *n. U.K.* (*archaic*) **1. HOUSE AND BUILDINGS** a house with its adjoining buildings and land **2. ENTIRE HOLDING** an entire holding including a homestead and all additional land [Old English. From Old Norse *topt*.]

to·fu /tṓ fo͝o/ *n.* a soft food with no particular flavor made from coagulated soybean extract pressed into a cake [Late 18thC. Via Japanese from Chinese *dòufǔ*, literally "fermented beans."]

tog /tog/ *npl.* **togs CLOTHES** clothes of any kind (*informal*) ■ *vti.* (**togged, tog·ging, togs**) **DRESS UP** to dress up, or dress somebody up, usually in smart clothing (*informal*) [Late 18thC. Shortening of obsolete slang *togeman*, from obsolete French *togue* "cloak," from Latin *toga* (see TOGA).]

to·ga /tṓgə/ *n.* **1. GARMENT WORN BY ROMAN CITIZENS** an outer garment worn by the citizens of ancient Rome, consisting of a semicircular piece of cloth draped around the body **2. ROBE OF OFFICE** a robe of office [Early 17thC. From Latin. Ultimately from an Indo-European base meaning "to cover" that is also the ancestor of English *deck*, *thatch*, and *tile*.] —**to·gaed** *adj.*

to·ga prae·tex·ta /-pri tékstə/ (*plural* **to·gae prae·tex·tae** /tōgee pri tékstee/) *n.* a toga with a purple border worn in ancient Rome by some magistrates and priests and by boys before the age of puberty [From Latin, "bordered toga"]

to·ga vi·ri·lis /-veérilәss/ (*plural* **to·gae vi·ri·les**) *n.* a white toga worn by boys in ancient Rome from the age of 14 or 15 as a sign of manhood and citizenship [From Latin, "men's toga"]

to·geth·er /tə géṯhər/ CORE MEANING: an adverb indicating that people are with each other, or that something is done with another person or other people, or by joint effort ○ *My brother and I always walked to school together.*

1. WITH OTHERS in company with others in a group or in a place ○ *Spawning cod come together near the sea floor in huge schools.* **2. INTERACTING WITH ONE ANOTHER** interacting, communicating, or in a relationship with one another ○ *They spend all their time together talking in low voices.* ○ *They get on well together.* **3. BY JOINT EFFORT** cooperating with one another or by joint or combined effort ○ *The only way we'll get anywhere is if we work together on this one.* **4. INTO CONTACT** indicates that two or more things are put into contact with one another, or unite to form a single whole ○ *The mummy wore moccasins made of three kinds of animal skin, sewn together with two types of stitching.* ○ *Mix together mustard, lime, salt and pepper, cayenne pepper, and jalapeño.* **5. COLLECTIVELY** considered collectively or as a whole ○ *Taken together, these developments add up to a significant change in policy.* ○ *He earns more than all the others together.* **6. IN INTEGRATED COHERENT STRUCTURE** in or into a unified structure or a coherent integrated whole ○ *If you understand how something is put together, you will use it better.* **7. INTO ORDERLY CONDITION OR STATE** into an orderly condition or a stable and effective emotional state (*informal*) ○ *"I'm just trying to get my life together," he said quietly.* **8. IN AGREEMENT** in or into agreement or harmony ○ *They can't seem to get together on anything.* **9. UNINTERRUPTEDLY** without interruption ○ *It has been raining four days together.* **10. IN A COUPLE** indicates that two people are married, having a sexual relationship, or form an established and recognized couple (*informal*) ○ *got back together again after a trial separation* ■ *adj.* **STABLE AND SELF-CONFIDENT** emotionally stable, self-confident, and well-organized (*informal*) ○ *She's a very together person.* [Old English *tōgædere*, from *to* "to" + a prehistoric Germanic word meaning "joined together"] ◇ **get it together** *vr.* to become organized and calm so as to perform efficiently (*slang*) ◇ **together with** as well as or in addition to

WORD KEY: USAGE

This remark, together with earlier comments of the same kind, was not well received When ***together*** with forms an addition to the grammatical subject of a verb, the verb agrees with the subject proper, in this case *remark*.

to·geth·er·ness /tə géṯhərnəss/ *n.* a feeling of closeness in being with others

tog·ger·y /tóggəree/ *n.* (*informal*) **1. CLOTHES** clothes **2. CLOTHING STORE** a place to buy clothes, such as a clothing or specialty shop [Early 19thC. Formed from TOG.]

tog·gle /tógg'l/ *v.* (**-gled, -gling, -gles**) **1.** *vti.* COMPUT **SWITCH BETWEEN OPERATIONS WITH ONE KEY** to switch back and forth between two computer operations using the same key or command **2.** *vt.* **SUPPLY OR FASTEN SOMETHING WITH TOGGLES** to supply or fasten something with a toggle or toggles ■ *n.* **1.** COMPUT **KEY FOR SWITCHING BETWEEN OPERATIONS** a key or command that switches back and forth between computer operations each time it is used **2. PEG INSERTED IN LOOP** a peg or rod that is inserted crosswise into a loop at the end of a rope, chain, or strap to hold or fasten something **3.** CLOTHES **FASTENER ON CLOTHES** a small peg sewn on clothes or on a bag, inserted crosswise into a loop or buttonhole and used as a fastener **4.** NAUT **PIN INSERTED INTO KNOT** a pin inserted into a nautical knot to keep it from coming undone **5. SOMETHING WITH TOGGLE JOINT** a toggle joint or a device with a toggle joint [Late 18thC. Origin unknown.] —**tog·gler** *n.*

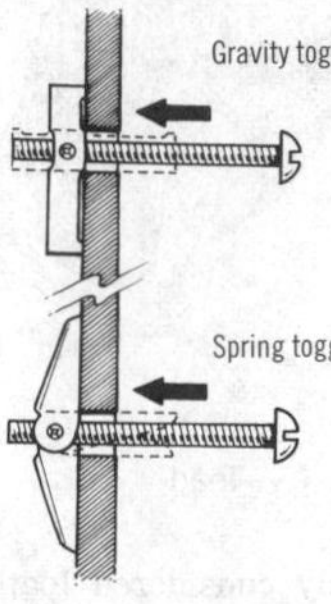

Toggle bolt

tog·gle bolt *n.* a threaded bolt that has a nut with spring-loaded hinged wings attached and is used especially for securing things to hollow walls. When the bolt is inserted into a hole in the wall, the wings spread open inside, pressing back against the wall's inner surface and allowing the bolt to be tightened.

tog·gle iron, **tog·gle har·poon** *n.* a whaling harpoon with a pivoting barb that keeps the whale from freeing itself

tog·gle joint *n.* a device with two arms hinged together so that pressure applied at the pivot point to straighten the device exerts force along the two arms

tog·gle switch *n.* **1.** ENG **SWITCH FOR ELECTRICAL CIRCUITS** a small spring-loaded mechanical switch that opens and closes an electric circuit by manual operation **2.** COMPUT = **toggle** *n.* 1

To·gliat·ti /tōl yaátee/ industrial city on the Volga River in southern European Russia. Population: 642,000 (1990).

Togo

To·go /tṓgō/ republic in West Africa, bordered by Burkina Faso, Benin, the Gulf of Guinea, and Ghana. Language: French. Currency: franc. Capital: Lomé. Population: 4,735,610 (1997). Area: 21,925 sq. mi./56,785 sq. km. Official name **Togolese Republic** —**To·go·lese** /tōgə leéz/ *n., adj.*

To·go·land /tṓgō land/ former German protectorate in western Africa, divided between British and French administration in 1922. British Togoland was incorporated into Ghana (1956), and French Togoland became independent as Togo (1960).

togue /tōg/ (*plural* **togue** *or* **togues**) *n.* = **lake trout** [Late 19thC. Via Canadian French from Micmac *atoǥwa:su*.]

to·he·ro·a /tṑ ə rṓ ə/ (*plural* **-a** *or* **-as**) *n.* **1.** MARINE BIOL **LARGE EDIBLE MOLLUSK OF NEW ZEALAND** a large edible mollusk with a hinged shell found along the coasts of New Zealand. Latin name: *Amphidesma ventricosum*. **2. TOHEROA SOUP** a greenish soup made from the toheroa [Late 19thC. From Maori.]

To·ho·no O'O·dham /tōhṓ nō ṑdaam/ *n.* PEOPLES, LANGUAGE = **Papago**

toil[1] /toyl/ *n.* **1. HARD WORK** hard exhausting work or effort **2. STRIFE** strife or struggle (*archaic*) ■ *v.* (**toiled, toil·ing, toils**) **1.** *vi.* **WORK HARD** to work long and hard **2.** *vi.* **PROGRESS SLOWLY** to progress slowly and with difficulty **3.** *vt.* **ACHIEVE SOMETHING BY EFFORT** to achieve something by hard work (*archaic*) [13thC. Via Anglo-Norman *toiler* "to drag around" from, ultimately, Latin *tudicula* "machine for bruising olives," from *tudes* "hammer."]

WORD KEY: SYNONYMS

See Synonyms at *work*.

toil[2] /toyl/ *n.* a net, snare, or other thing that entraps or entangles (*archaic or literary*) (*often used in the plural*)

toile /twaal/ *n.* **1.** SHEER FABRIC a sheer cotton or linen fabric **2.** PROTOTYPE OF DESIGNER GARMENT a prototype of a designer garment made up in a cheap fabric so that alterations can be made [Late 18thC. Via French from, ultimately, Latin *tela* "web." Ultimately from an Indo-European base meaning "to weave" that is also the ancestor of English *subtle* and *text*.]

toile de Jouy /twa̍al də zhwe̍e/ *n.* a fabric with a white or light-colored background and a floral or pastoral print usually in one color only, used for curtains and upholstery [Mid-18thC. From French, named for *Jouy*-en-Josas, the French town near Paris where the fabric was made.]

toi·let /tóylət/ *n.* **1.** FIXTURE FOR DISPOSING OF BODILY WASTE a bowl-shaped fixture with a waste drain and a flushing device connected to a water supply, used for defecating and urinating **2.** ROOM WITH TOILET a room with a toilet and usually a sink **3.** OUTDOOR TOILET an outdoor room or building with facilities for defecation and urination **4.** WASHING AND DRESSING the process of attending to your personal appearance and making it presentable, e.g. by washing, dressing, shaving, and fixing your hair (*formal*) **5.** MED CLEANSING ASSOCIATED WITH A SURGICAL PROCEDURE a cleansing of part of the body after a medical or surgical procedure, often in preparation for applying dressings or bandages **6.** DRESSING TABLE a dressing table (*archaic*) [Late 17thC. From French *toilette* "bag for clothing," from Old French *tellette*, from *teile* "cloth," from Latin *tela* "web."]

toi·let pa·per *n.* a usually soft absorbent paper, especially in a roll, used for cleaning the body after defecating or urinating

toi·let roll *n.* a length of toilet paper wound around a cardboard cylinder, or the cardboard cylinder on which the paper is wound

toi·let·ry /tóylətree/ (*plural* **-ries**) *n.* an article such as shampoo, deodorant, or soap, used in washing or caring for the appearance (*usually used in the plural*)

toi·lette /twaa lét/ *n.* the process of attending to your personal appearance and making it presentable (*literary*) [Mid-16thC. From French (see TOILET).]

toi·let tis·sue *n.* = **toilet paper**

toi·let train·ing *n.* the process of teaching a young child to control bladder and bowel movements and to use the toilet

toi·let wa·ter *n.* a lightly perfumed liquid used to freshen or scent the skin

toil·some /tóylsəm/ *adj.* requiring long hard work (*literary*) —**toil·some·ly** *adv.* —**toil·some·ness** *n.*

toil·worn /tóyl wàwrn/ *adj.* worn, damaged, or exhausted from hard work

toi·toi /tóy tòy/ (*plural* **-tois**) *n.* a tall grass with feathery fronds that grows in New Zealand. Genus: *Cortederia*. [Mid-19thC. From Maori.]

To·jo Hi·de·ki /tṑjō he̍edekì/ (1884–1948) Japanese general and statesman. During World War II, he was minister of war (1940–41) and then premier (1941–44). He was tried and hanged for war crimes (1948).

To·kaj /tō káy, to-, -kí/ town in northeastern Hungary. Tokay wines are produced in the surrounding region. Population: 5,371 (1990).

to·ka·mak /tókə màk/ *n.* an experimental doughnut-shaped nuclear reactor for producing fusion using an electric current and a magnetic field to heat and contain a gaseous plasma [Mid-20thC. From Russian, a contraction of *toroidal'naya kamera s aksial'nym magnitnym polem* "toroidal chamber with axial magnetic field."]

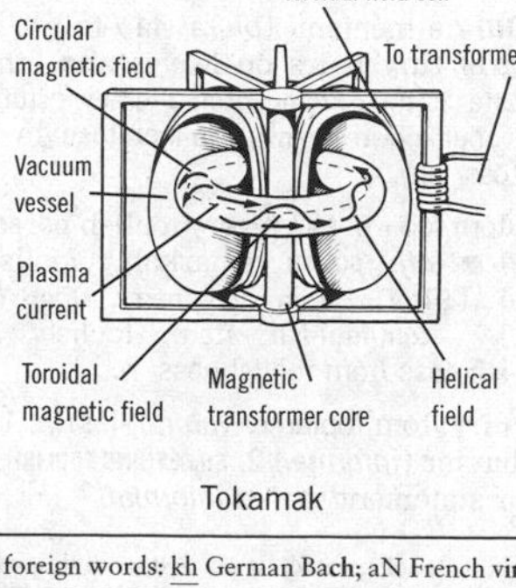

Tokamak

to·kay /tō káy/ *n.* a small lizard of southern and Southeast Asia that has a retractile claw at the tip of each digit. Latin name: *Gekko gecko*. [Mid-18thC. Via Malay dialect *toke'* from Javanese *tekèk*, ultimately an imitation of the animal's call.]

To·kay *n.* **1.** WINE SWEET WINE a sweet wine made near Tokaj, Hungary, or a similar sweet wine produced elsewhere **2.** PLANTS LARGE SWEET GRAPE OF HUNGARY a large sweet variety of grape originally grown near Tokaj, Hungary that is the source of Tokay [Early 18thC. Named for TOKAJ (Tokay), where the wine is made.]

toke /tōk/ *n.* PUFF OF MARIJUANA a puff on a cigarette or pipe containing marijuana (*slang*) ■ *vti.* (**toked, tok·ing, tokes**) PUFF MARIJUANA to puff on a cigarette or pipe containing marijuana (*slang*) [Mid-20thC. Origin uncertain: perhaps from Spanish *toque* "a hit," from *tocar* "to touch."]

to·ken /tṓkən/ *n.* **1.** SOMETHING REPRESENTING SOMETHING ELSE something that represents, expresses, or is a symbol of something else ○ *Please accept this gift as a token of our appreciation.* **2.** DISK USED LIKE MONEY a disk of metal or plastic used instead of money, e.g., in slot machines **3.** KEEPSAKE an object kept in memory of something **4.** LING INSTANCE OF EXPRESSION a particular instance of a word or expression **5.** LING CONCRETE EXAMPLE a written or spoken expression considered as a concrete example ■ *adj.* EXISTING AS GESTURE ONLY made, given, or existing merely because expected or required, not because sincere or serving a real purpose ○ *the token student on the committee* [Old English *tācen*. Ultimately from an Indo-European word meaning "to point, show" that is also the ancestor of English *teach* and *digit*.]

to·ken·ism /tṓkə nìzzəm/ *n.* the practice of making only a symbolic effort at something, especially in order to meet the minimum requirements of the law —**to·ken·is·tic** /tōkə nístik/ *adj.*

To·khar·i·an *n., adj.* PEOPLES, LANG = **Tocharian**

tok·o·loshe /tòko lósh, -lóshee/ *n.* a small mischievous evil spirit or water sprite in African folklore that takes on human or animal appearance [Mid-19thC. Of Nguni origin.]

to·ko·no·ma /tṑkə nṓmə/ *n.* an alcove in the living room of a Japanese house where a decoration such as flowers or an ornament is displayed [Early 18thC. From Japanese.]

To·ko·ro·a /tṑkō rṓ ə/ town in the northwestern part of the North Island, New Zealand, that services the paper and timber mills at nearby Kinleith. Population: 15,528 (1996).

Tok Pis·in /tòk píssin/ *n.* LANG a creole, originating as a Pidgin based on English, that is widely spoken in Papua New Guinea. Tok Pisin is spoken by over 2 million people. [Mid-20thC. From Pidgin English, "to talk pidgin."]

To·ky·o /tṓkee ō/ capital city of Japan, located on Tokyo Bay on the eastern coast of Honshu Island. Population: 8,019,938 (1995).

to·la /tṓlə/ *n.* an Indian unit of weight equal to 180 grains troy weight or 11.7 grams [Early 17thC. Via Hindi *tolā* from Sanskrit *tulā* "weight." Ultimately from an Indo-European base meaning "to lift up, weigh," which is also the ancestor of English *toll*[1] and *tolerate*.]

to·lar /tólaar/ *n.* **1.** UNIT OF SLOVENIAN CURRENCY a unit of currency in Slovenia, worth 100 stotins. See table at **currency** **2.** COIN OR BILL WORTH A TOLAR a coin or bill worth one tolar [From Slovene, from German *Taler* (see THALER)]

tol·booth /tṓl bo͞oth/ *n.* **1.** *Scotland* TOWN HALL OR PRISON a town hall or a prison, or a building that performed both functions (*archaic*) **2.** *U.K.* = **tollbooth**

tol·bu·ta·mide /tol byo͞otə mìd/ *n.* a drug used in the treatment of adult-onset diabetes to lower blood-glucose levels by stimulating the islets in the pancreas to produce more insulin. Formula: $C_{12}H_{18}N_2O_3S$. [Mid-20thC. Contraction of TOLUENE + BUTYL + AMIDE.]

told past tense, past participle of **tell**

tole[1] /tōl/ *n.* lacquered or enameled metal used to make decorative objects, usually brightly painted or gilded or both, or objects made of this kind of decorated metal [Mid-20thC. Via French *tôle* "sheet iron" from, ultimately, Latin *tabula* "board" (source of English *table*).]

tole[2] *vt.* = **toll**[2] *v.* 3

To·le·do[1] /tə le̍edō/ (*plural* **-dos**) *n.* a sword or sword blade of highly tempered steel, made in Toledo, Spain

To·le·do[2] /to le̍edō/ **1.** city and major river port in northwestern Ohio, located close to Lake Erie. Population: 613,000 (1995). **2.** historic city in central Spain, the administrative center of Toledo Province. Population: 63,561 (1991).

tol·er·a·ble /tóllərəb'l/ *adj.* **1.** CAPABLE OF BEING TOLERATED not too unpleasant or severe to put up with **2.** FAIRLY GOOD moderately good, but not outstanding —**tol·er·a·bil·i·ty** /tòllərə bíllətee/ *n.* —**tol·er·a·ble·ness** /tóllərəb'lnəss/ *n.* —**tol·er·a·bly** /tóllərəblee/ *adv.*

tol·er·ance /tóllərənss/ *n.* **1.** ACCEPTANCE OF DIFFERENT VIEWS the accepting of the differing views of other people, e.g., in religious or political matters, and fairness toward the people who hold these different views **2.** TOLERATING OF SOMETHING the act of putting up with something or somebody irritating or otherwise unpleasant **3.** ABILITY TO ENDURE HARDSHIP the ability to put up with harsh or difficult conditions **4.** MED ABILITY TO REMAIN UNAFFECTED the loss of or reduction in the normal response to a drug or other agent, following use or exposure over a prolonged period **5.** ENG ALLOWANCE MADE FOR DEVIATION allowance made for something to deviate in size from a standard, or the limit within which it is allowed to deviate **6.** BIOL ABILITY TO WITHSTAND EXTREMES the ability of an organism to survive in extreme conditions

tol·er·ant /tóllərənt/ *adj.* **1.** ACCEPTING DIFFERENT VIEWS accepting the differing views of others, e.g., different religious or political beliefs **2.** WITHSTANDING HARSH TREATMENT able to put up with harsh conditions or treatment **3.** MED NOT AFFECTED BY A DRUG no longer responding to a drug that has been taken over a prolonged period, or suffering no ill effects from exposure to a harmful substance —**tol·er·ant·ly** *adv.*

tol·er·ate /tóllə ràyt/ (**-at·ed, -at·ing, -ates**) *vt.* **1.** PERMIT SOMETHING to be willing to allow something to happen or exist **2.** ENDURE SOMETHING to withstand the unpleasant effects of something **3.** ACCEPT EXISTENCE OF DIFFERENT VIEWS to recognize other people's right to have different beliefs or practices without an attempt to suppress them **4.** MED BE UNAFFECTED BY A DRUG to fail to respond to a drug because the body has built up a resistance to it, or suffer no ill effects from being exposed to a harmful substance [Early 16thC. From Latin *tolerare*. Ultimately from an Indo-European base meaning "to support," which is also the ancestor of English *toll*[1] and *talent*.] —**tol·er·a·tive** *adj.* —**tol·er·a·tor** *n.*

tol·er·a·tion /tòllə ráysh'n/ *n.* **1.** OFFICIAL ACCEPTANCE OF DIFFERENT RELIGIONS official acceptance by a government of religious beliefs and practices that are different from those it upholds **2.** TOLERATING OF SOMETHING the act of tolerating something —**tol·er·a·tion·ism** *n.* —**tol·er·a·tion·ist** *n., adj.*

tol·i·dine /tóllə de̍en/ *n.* an isomeric derivative of toluene used in making dyes. Formula: $C_{14}H_{16}N_2$. [Late 19thC. Coined from TOLYL + *benzidine*.]

Tol·kien /tṓl ke̍en, tól-/, **J. R. R.** (1892–1973) South African-born British scholar and writer. A philologist at Oxford University, he wrote *The Hobbit* (1937) and its large-scale sequel *The Lord of the Rings* (1954–55). Full name **John Ronald Reuel Tolkien**

toll[1] /tōl/ *n.* **1.** TRANSP FEE FOR USING A ROAD a fee charged for a privilege, usually crossing a bridge or using a road **2.** TRANSP BOOTH a tollbooth, where tolls are paid (*often used in the plural*) **3.** DAMAGE SUSTAINED the damage done by an accident or disaster in terms of, e.g., people killed, property destroyed, or financial loss ○ *The toll on the environment was significant.* **4.** FIN FEE FOR SERVICES a fee charged for services, e.g., transportation **5.** TELECOM CHARGE FOR A TELEPHONE CALL a charge for a long-distance telephone call ■ *vti.* (**tolled, toll·ing, tolls**) TRANSP CHARGE A TOLL ON A ROAD to charge a toll for the use of a road or bridge [Old English *toll, toln*. Via medieval Latin *toloneum*, from, ultimately, Greek *telōnion* "toll house," from *telos* "tax" (source of English *philately*).]

toll[2] /tōl/ *v.* (**tolled, toll·ing, tolls**) **1.** *vti.* RING SLOWLY AND REPEATEDLY to ring a bell, repeatedly and with long pauses between each ring, especially to announce a death, or be rung in this way ○ *"never send to* *know for whom the bell tolls; it tolls for thee"* (John Donne, *Devotions*; 1624) **2.** *vt.* **ANNOUNCE SOMETHING WITH A BELL** to announce something or call somebody with the repeated slow ringing of a bell ○ *bells tolling the death of the king* **3. toll (tol·ling), tole (toled, tol·ing, toles)** *vt.* **LURE FISH OR GAME** to lure fish or game into being caught ■ *n.* **ACT OR SOUND OF BELL TOLLING** the act of ringing a bell slowly and repeatedly, or the sound so made [15thC. Origin uncertain: probably from Old English *-tyllan* "to pull"; the underlying meaning is "to pull on a bell rope."] —**toll·er** *n.*

toll·booth /tṓl bo͝oth/ *n.* a booth on a road or bridge where tolls for use of the road or bridge are collected

toll bridge *n.* a bridge where a toll is charged for crossing

toll call *n. U.S., NZ* a long-distance telephone call charged at a higher rate than a local call

toll·gate /tṓl gàyt/ *n.* a gate barring the way on a road or bridge where a toll must be paid to proceed

toll·house /tṓl hòwss/ (*plural* **-hous·es** /-hòwzəz/) *n.* a shelter or kiosk for a toll collector at a tollgate

Toll-House *tdmk.* a trademark for a cookie made with flour, brown sugar, chocolate chips, and often chopped nuts

toll·house cookie *n.* a cookie made with flour, brown sugar, chocolate chips, and often chopped nuts

AKG London

Count Leo Nikolayevich Tolstoy

Tol·stoy /táwl stòy/, **Count Leo Nikolayevich** (1828–1910) Russian writer. He wrote the epic novels *War and Peace* (1865–69) and *Anna Karenina* (1875–77). A profound social thinker and moralist, he was excommunicated from the Russian Orthodox Church for his radical views on Church authority.

Tol·tec /tṓl tèk, tól-/ (*plural* **Toltec** *or* **Toltecs**) *n.* PEOPLES a member of a Native Central American people who formerly occupied lands in central Mexico. They dominated the area from around the 10th to the 12th centuries A.D., when they were defeated by the Chichimecs and their lands were later taken over by the Aztecs. [Late 18thC. Via Spanish *tolteca* from Nahuatl *toltecatl*, literally "someone from Tula," an ancient Toltec city.] —**Tol·tec** *adj.*

to·lu /tə ló͞o, tō-/ *n.* an aromatic resin obtained from a South American tree, used in cough medicine [Late 17thC. From Spanish *tolú*, named for the town of Santiago de *Tolú* in Colombia, from which it was exported.]

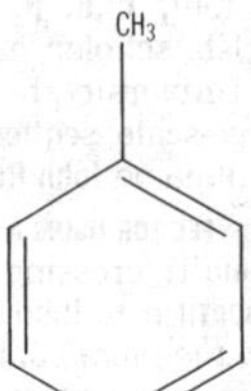

Toluene

tol·u·ene /tóllyoo ēen/ *n.* a colorless liquid aromatic hydrocarbon resembling benzene but less flammable, used in high-octane fuels and organic synthesis. Formula: C_7H_8. [Late 19thC. Formed from TOLU, from which it was originally obtained.]

to·lu·i·dine /tə ló͞o i dèen/ *n.* any of three isomeric derivatives of toluene used in making dyes. Formula: C_7H_9N.

tol·u·ol /tóllyoo òl/ *n.* = **toluene**

tol·yl /tó lìl/ *n.* any of three chemical groups derived from toluene. Formula: C_7H_7.

tom /tom/ *n.* the male of various animals, especially the domestic cat [14thC. From the name *Tom*.]

Tom (Tommed, Tom·ming, Toms) *n.* = **Uncle Tom** (*slang offensive*)

Tomahawk

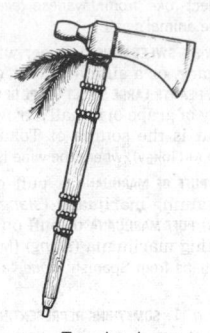

tom·a·hawk /tómmə hàwk/ *n.* **1. NATIVE N AMERICAN WEAPON** a small ax, formerly used as a weapon by some Native North American peoples. It could be thrown like a knife and used as a hand weapon in close combat. **2.** *ANZ* **SMALL AX** a small short-handled ax ■ *vt.* **(-hawked, -hawk·ing, -hawks) ATTACK SOMEBODY WITH TOMAHAWK** to attack or kill somebody with a tomahawk [Early 17thC. From Virginia Algonquian *tamahaac*.]

to·mal·ley /tə mállee, tó màllee/ *n.* a soft green part of the insides of a cooked lobster, often called the liver but technically an organ called the hepatopancreas, eaten as a delicacy [Mid-17thC. Via French *taumalin* from Carib *taumali*.]

to·man /tə maán/ *n.* **1. IRANIAN COIN** an Iranian coin worth ten rials **2. OLD UNIT OF PERSIAN CURRENCY** a gold coin that was a unit of currency in Persia between 1600 and 1912 [Mid-16thC. Via Persian *tūmān* from, ultimately, western Tocharian *tmān*, of uncertain origin.]

Tom and Jer·ry (*plural* **Tom and Jer·ries**) *n.* a hot drink containing rum, brandy, nutmeg, and egg, to which milk is sometimes added [Named for Corinthian *Tom* and *Jerry* Hawthorne, two characters in the novel *Life in London* (1821) by Pierce Egan]

to·ma·til·lo /tōmə tée yō/ (*plural* **-los**) *n.* **1.** FOOD **MEXICAN FRUIT** a purplish sticky edible fruit that grows on a Mexican ground cherry **2.** PLANTS **PLANT BEARING TOMATILLOS** the ground cherry plant that bears tomatillos. Latin name: *Physalis ixocarpa*. [Early 20thC. From Spanish, literally "small tomato," from *tomate* (see TOMATO).]

Tomato

to·ma·to /tə máytō, -maátō/ (*plural* **-toes**) *n.* **1.** FOOD **RED VEGETABLE** a round vegetable with bright-red, occasionally yellow, skin and pulpy seedy flesh. It grows like fruit on climbing plants and is widely eaten cooked or raw. **2.** PLANTS **TOMATO PLANT** a climbing plant that yields tomatoes and is native to South America but is grown as an annual throughout the world, in northern regions usually in greenhouses. Genus: *Lycopersicon*. **3. OFFENSIVE TERM** an offensive term for a woman who is considered sexually desirable (*slang offensive*) [Early 17thC. Alteration of Spanish *tomate*, from Nahuatl *tomatl*.]

to·ma·to fruit·worm *n.* the larva of a moth native to the United States that is destructive to corn, cotton, tomatoes, and other crops. Latin name: *Heliothis zea*.

to·ma·to horn·worm *n.* the larva of a North American hawk moth that feeds on the leaves of tomato plants. Latin name: *Manduca quinquemaculata*.

to·ma·to sphinx *n.* the adult form of a tomato hornworm

tomb /to͞om/ *n.* **1. GRAVE** a grave or other place for burying a dead person **2. BURIAL CHAMBER** a cave or chamber used for burial of a dead person **3. MONUMENT** a monument to a dead person, often built over the place where he or she is buried **4. DEATH** death (*literary*) ○ *go to the tomb unrepentant* **5. HARDENED ENCLOSURE** a hardened enclosure for a closed nuclear reactor, designed to contain radioactive emissions [12thC. Via French *tombe* from, ultimately, Greek *tumbos* "mound, tomb."] —**tomb·less** *adj.*

Tom·ba /táwmbaa/, **Alberto** (*b.* 1966) Italian skier. In 1988 he won the first of many medals, including Olympic gold medals and World Cups in slalom and giant slalom events.

tom·bac /tóm bàk/, **tam·bac** /tám bàk/ *n.* an alloy of copper and zinc, often with tin and arsenic, originally used in Eastern countries to make gongs and bells and now used worldwide to make inexpensive jewelry [Early 17thC. Via French from, ultimately, Malay *tembaga* "copper, brass."]

tom·bo·lo /tómbəlō/ (*plural* **-los**) *n.* a narrow strip of sand or shingle that links one island to another or to the mainland [Late 19thC. Via Italian, literally "sand dune," from Latin *tumulus* (see TUMULUS.]

Tom·bouc·tou /tòmb ok to͞o/ = **Timbuktu**

tom·boy /tóm bòy/ *n.* a girl who dresses or behaves in a way regarded as boyish, especially a girl who enjoys rough boisterous play [Mid-16thC. From the name *Tom* (short for *Thomas*). The word originally referred to a boisterous or unruly boy.] —**tom·boy·ish** *adj.* —**tom·boy·ish·ly** *adv.* —**tom·boy·ish·ness** *n.*

tomb·stone /to͞om stōn/ *n.* an ornamental stone on or at the site of a grave, often with the dead person's name and dates of birth and death engraved on it

Tomb·stone /to͞omstōn/ city in southeastern Arizona. Its history as a lawless mining town has made it a popular tourist center. Population: 1,414 (1996).

tom·cat /tóm kàt/ *n.* **1. MALE CAT** a male domestic cat **2. OFFENSIVE TERM** an offensive term for a man who seeks many sexual partners, or who has casual sex with many partners (*slang insult*) ■ *vi.* **(-cat·ted, -cat·ting, -cats) OFFENSIVE TERM** an offensive term meaning to seek many sexual partners, or have casual sex with many partners (*slang*) (*refers to a man*)

tom·cod /tóm kòd/ *n.* either one of two small sea fishes of the cod family, one of North American Atlantic waters and the other of northern Pacific waters. Both are valued as food fish. Latin name: *Microgradus tomcod* and *Microgradus proximus*.

Tom Col·lins /-kóllinz/ *n.* **1.** an alcoholic cocktail consisting of gin, lemon or lime juice, soda water, and sugar **2.** anyone at all [Late 19thC. Origin uncertain: said to have been named for a London bartender.]

tome /tōm/ *n.* **1. LARGE BOOK** a book, especially a large heavy book on a serious subject (*formal or humorous*) **2. SINGLE VOLUME** a single volume of a book made up of several volumes [Early 16thC. Via French from, ultimately, Greek *tomos* "section, volume." Ultimately from an Indo-European base meaning "to cut," which is also the ancestor of English *atom* and *anatomy*.]

-tome *suffix.* **1.** segment, part ○ *myotome* **2.** cutting instrument ○ *microtome* [Via modern Latin *-tomus* from, ultimately, Greek *tomos* "cutting" (see TOME)]

to·men·tum /tə méntəm/ (*plural* **-ta** /-tə/) *n.* a downy covering of tiny hairs on leaves and other plant parts [Late 17thC. From Latin, literally "stuffing for a cushion," of unknown origin.] —**to·men·tose** /tə mén tōss, tṓ men tōss/ *adj.*

tom·fool /tòm fo͞ol/ *n.* **FOOL** a very foolish person (*dated informal*) ■ *adj.* **FOOLISH** remarkably foolish (*dated informal*) [14thC. From the name *Tom* (short for *Thomas*).] —**tom·fool·ish** /tom fo͞olish/ *adj.* —**tom·fool·ish·ness** /tom fo͞olishnəss/ *n.*

tom·fool·er·y /tom fo͞olərее/ (*plural* **-ies**) *n.* **1. SILLINESS** silly behavior (*informal*) **2. SOMETHING FOOLISH** a foolish action or statement (*dated informal*)

tom·my /tómmee/ (*plural* **-mies**), **Tom·my At·kins** /-átkinz/ *n. U.K.* a private in the British army (*dated slang*) [Late 19thC. From *Thomas Atkins*, a fictitious name used on sample forms in the British army.]

Tom·my gun *n.* a hand-held machine gun, especially a Thompson submachine gun (*informal*)

tom·my·rot /tómmee ròt/ *n.* complete nonsense (*dated informal*) [Late 19thC. *Tommy* from the use of *Tommy* (short for *Thomas*) as a name for somebody foolish.]

tom·my·to (*plural* **-toes**) *n. Southern U.S.* a cherry tomato

WORD KEY: REGIONAL NOTE

This is a term with high incidence in the middle, interior South, from the western Carolinas to Arkansas and occurring in diminishing numbers in every section of the Gulf states except lower Texas, where it is absent.

to·mo·gram /tṓmə gràm/ *n.* an image, especially one of the body, made using tomography

to·mog·ra·phy /tə móggrəfee/ *n.* the technique of using ultrasound, gamma rays, or X-rays to produce a focused image of the structures across a certain depth within the body, while blurring details at other depths. A series of such images can be combined, e.g., by computer, to give a high-definition three-dimensional image. [Mid-20thC. Coined from Greek *tomos* (see TOME) + -GRAPH + -Y.]

to·mor·row /tə máwrō/ *n.* **1.** THE NEXT DAY the day after today **2.** THE FUTURE a future time, or the future in general ○ *the leaders of tomorrow* ■ *adv.* **1.** ON THE NEXT DAY on the day after today **2.** IN FUTURE in the future, or at some time in the future [Old English *tō morgenne*, literally "in the morning"] ◇ **like** *or* **as if there was** *or* **were no tomorrow** used to emphasize the degree of speed, intensity, or carelessness with which somebody is doing something (*informal*) ○ *ran from the fire like there was no tomorrow*

tom·pi·on *n.* = **tampion**

toms /tomz/ *npl.* = **tom-tom** *n.* 2 [Early 20thC. Shortening.]

Tomsk /tomsk/ city and port on the Tom River in southern Siberian Russia. Population: 502,000 (1990).

Tom Thumb *n.* a character in English folklore who was no taller than his father's thumb

tom·tit /tóm tìt/ *n.* a bird of the tit family, especially the blue tit (*informal*) [Early 18thC. *Tom* from the name *Tom* (short for *Thomas*).]

tom-tom /tóm tòm/, **tam-tam** /tám tàm/ *n.* **1.** DRUM HIT WITH THE HANDS a drum hit with the hands, especially a drum with a long narrow shell and a small head, first used by Native North Americans and other peoples as a signaling instrument **2.** DEEP-SIDED DRUM IN MODERN DRUM KIT a deep-sided drum that forms part of a modern drum kit, deeper in tone than a snare drum but not as deep as a bass drum **3.** SOUND OF BEATING DRUM the sound of a drum being repeatedly beaten, especially slowly and monotonously [Late 17thC. From Telugu *ṭamaṭama* or Hindi *ṭam ṭam*, ultimately an imitation of the drum's sound.]

-tomy *suffix.* cutting, incision ○ *lobotomy* [Via modern Latin *-tomia* from, ultimately, Greek *tomos* "cutting" (see TOME)]

ton[1] /tun/ *n.* **1.** U.S. UNIT OF WEIGHT an imperial unit of weight, equal to 2,000 lb. in the United States **2.** U.K. UNIT OF WEIGHT an imperial unit of weight, equal to 2,240 lb./1016 kg in the United Kingdom **3.** = **metric ton 4.** = **displacement ton 5.** UNIT MEASURING SHIP'S INTERNAL CAPACITY a unit used to measure the capacity of the inside of a ship, equal to 100 cu.ft./28.3 c. m **6.** = **freight ton 7.** LARGE AMOUNT a very great number of things or of something (*informal*) (*often used in the plural*) ○ *tons of things to do* ■ *adv.* **tons** A GREAT DEAL to a great degree or extent [13thC. Variant of TUN.] ◇ **come down on somebody like a ton of bricks** to scold or punish somebody severely (*informal*)

ton[2] /toN/ *n.* the current trend in fashion, or the group of people who like to stay at the cutting edge of fashion [Mid-18thC. From French, literally "tone."]

to·nal /tṓn'l/ *adj.* **1.** RELATING TO TONE relating to tone or tonality **2.** RELATING TO HARMONIC MUSIC relating to music written in a harmonic system in which there is a key. ◊ **atonal** —**to·nal·ly** *adv.*

to·nal·i·ty /tō nállətee/ *n.* **1.** QUALITY OF TONE the quality of tone, especially that of an instrument or voice **2.** MUSIC SYSTEM OF MUSICAL TONES the relationship between the notes and chords of a passage or work that tends to establish a central note or harmony as its focal point. ◊ **atonality 3.** ARTS ARRANGEMENT OF COLORS the scheme connecting the color tones in a work of art such as a painting

ton·do /tóndō/ (*plural* **-dos**) *n.* a circular painting or relief carving [Late 19thC. From Italian, a shortening of *rotondo* "round," from Latin *rotundus* (see ROTUND).]

tone /tōn/ *n.* **1.** PARTICULAR KIND OF SOUND a sound with a particular quality ○ *The first bell has a clearer tone.* **2.** WAY OF SPEAKING the way somebody says something as an indicator of what that person is feeling or thinking ○ *a defiant tone in her voice* **3.** GENERAL QUALITY the general quality or character of something as an indicator of the attitude or view of the person who produced it ○ *the optimistic tone of the report* **4.** MACHINE SOUND a sound, especially one produced by a machine **5.** PREVAILING CHARACTER the characteristic style that something has, particularly in relation to elegance or standing ○ *neon signs that lower the tone of the place* **6.** COLORS SHADE OF COLOR any of the possible shades of a particular color ○ *a green with a more vibrant tone* **7.** ARTS COMBINATIONS OF COLOR AND SHADING the overall blend of color and light and shade in a painting or photograph **8.** PHYSIOL FIRMNESS OF MUSCLES the natural firmness of muscles when they are not being flexed, or of the body generally **9.** PHON INTONATION the way a syllable of a word is spoken in terms of pitch ○ *the rising tone signifying a question* **10.** MUSIC TIMBRE the quality of a sound that makes it distinctive to a particular source, e.g., a voice or musical instrument **11.** MUSIC = **whole tone 12.** MUSIC PLAINSONG a melody used in singing plainsong, e.g., in singing psalms **13.** MUSIC = **note** *n.* 3 ■ *v.* (**toned, ton·ing, tones**) **1.** *vi.* BLEND IN WITH SOMETHING to be similar to something else, especially in color or brightness, and fit well with it **2.** *vti.* PHOTOGRAPHY CHANGE COLOR OF PHOTOGRAPH to develop the color image of a silver negative in making a photograph **3.** *vt.* PHON SAY SOMETHING WITH PARTICULAR PITCH to say a syllable or word with a particular pitch [13thC. Via French *ton* from, ultimately, Greek *tonos* "tension, tone." Ultimately from an Indo-European base meaning "to stretch" that is also the ancestor of English *thin, tenuous,* and *tendon.*]

tone down *vt.* **1.** MAKE SOMETHING LESS INTENSE to make something less intense or extreme, usually in order to make it less offensive or controversial **2.** MAKE SOMETHING LESS BRIGHT to make something less intense, bright, or loud

tone up *vt.* to make muscles, or the body in general, firmer and stronger

tone arm, **tone·arm** *n.* a record player's pivoting, or sometimes sliding, arm with a stylus on its end

tone clus·ter *n.* a group of adjacent notes played together and forming a chord, usually resulting in a dissonant sound

tone col·or *n.* = **timbre** *n.* 2

tone con·trol *n.* a control on a radio, record player, or other piece of audio equipment that adjusts the tone it produces, accentuating the higher or lower sound frequencies

tone-deaf *adj.* unable to hear the differences between musical notes —**tone-deaf·ness** *n.*

tone lan·guage *n.* a language in which the meaning of a fixed sequence of sounds depends on the pitch in which it is pronounced, different tones identifying different words. Tone languages include the Bantu languages of Africa and Mandarin Chinese.

tone·less /tṓnləss/ *adj.* **1.** EXPRESSIONLESS lacking expression in speech **2.** LIFELESS lacking brightness or vitality —**tone·less·ly** *adv.* —**tone·less·ness** *n.*

ton·eme /tṓ neem/ *n.* a phoneme in a tone language in which the distinctive feature is a tone [Early 20thC. Modeled on *phoneme.*] —**to·ne·mic** /tō neémik/ *adj.*

tone po·em *n.* MUSIC = **symphonic poem**

ton·er /tṓnər/ *n.* **1.** COSMETICS SKIN COSMETIC a lotion or light astringent used to improve the look or feel of the skin, especially of the face **2.** PRINTING INK ink in powder or liquid form for a photocopier or computer printer **3.** PHOTOGRAPHY PHOTOGRAPHIC CHEMICAL a chemical solution used in photograph development

tone row, **tone se·ries** *n.* a sequence of notes that is the basis of a piece of serial music, especially a series of 12 notes

to·net·ic /tō néttik/ *adj.* relating to a language in which changes in pitch distinguish meaning [Early 20thC. Modeled on *phonetic.*] —**to·net·i·cal·ly** *adv.*

tong[1] /tong/ (**tonged, tong·ing, tongs**) *vt.* to lift or move something with tongs

tong[2] /tong/ *n.* a Chinese secret society thought to be involved in criminal activity [Late 19thC. From Chinese (Cantonese) *t'ōng* "hall, meeting place."]

ton·ga /tóng gə/ *n.* a light horse-drawn carriage in southern and central India [Late 19thC. From Hindi *tāgā.*]

Ton·ga[1] /tóng gə/ (*plural* **-gas** *or* **-ga**) *n.* **1.** PEOPLES MEMBER OF CENTRAL AFRICAN PEOPLE a member of a people living in southern central Africa, mainly in southwestern Zambia and northwestern Zimbabwe **2.** LANG TONGA LANGUAGE the language of the Tonga people. It belongs to the Bantu group of Benue-Congo languages. [Mid-19thC. From Tonga.]

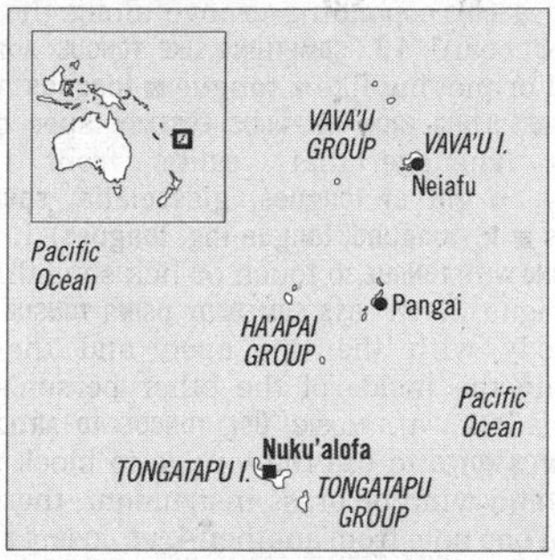

Tonga

Ton·ga[2] /tóng gə/ independent island nation consisting of more than 150 islands in the southern Pacific Ocean. Language: English, Tongan. Currency: pa'anga. Capital: Nuku'alofa. Population: 107,335 (1997). Area: 290 sq. mi./750 sq. km. Official name **Kingdom of Tonga** —**Ton·gan** *n., adj.*

Ton·ga·ri·ro, Mount /tòngə reérō/ active volcano in New Zealand, in the central part of the North Island. It last erupted in 1926. Height: 6,453 ft./1,967 m.

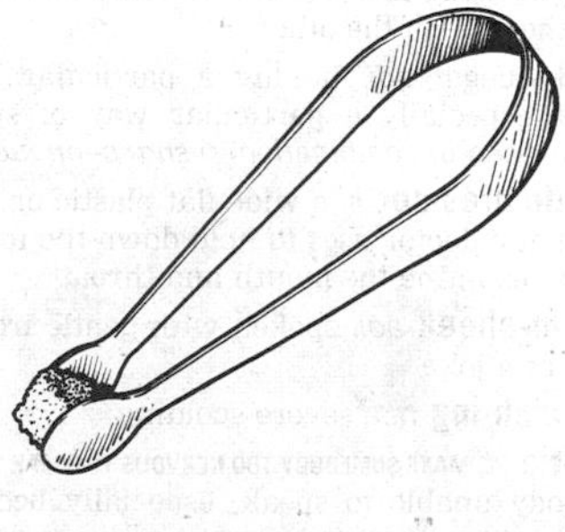
Tongs

tongs /tongz/ *npl.* a utensil for handling things that consists of two hinged or sprung arms that press together in a pinching movement around the object to be lifted [Old English *tang.* Ultimately from an Indo-European word meaning "to bite" that is also the ancestor of English *tang*[1] and *tough.*]

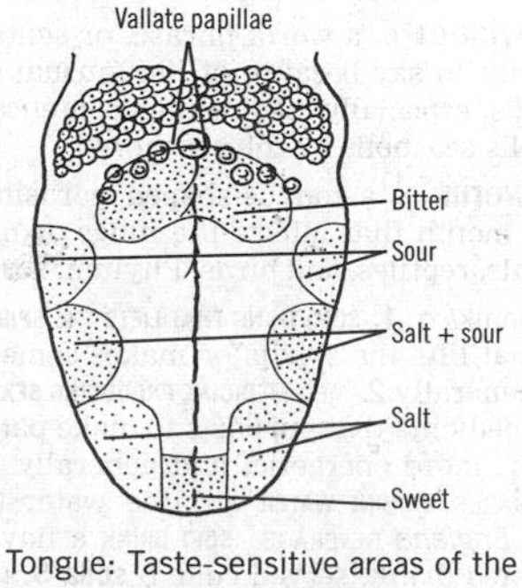

Tongue: Taste-sensitive areas of the human tongue

tongue /tung/ *n.* **1.** FLESHY ORGAN INSIDE MOUTH the movable fleshy organ attached to the bottom of the inside of the mouth of humans and most animals, used for tasting, licking, swallowing, and, in humans, speech. Technical name **glossa 2.** FOOD ANIMAL'S TONGUE USED AS FOOD the tongue of an animal, especially a cow, used as food **3.** LANGUAGE **a language or dialect** **4.** **WAY OF SPEAKING** somebody's manner of speaking (*formal*) **5.** **ABILITY TO SPEAK** the power of speech ○ *She found that her tongue had deserted her.* **6.** CLOTHES **FLAP IN SHOE** the middle flap in the opening of a shoe or boot **7.** **PIN IN BUCKLE** the pivoting pin in a buckle **8.** **CLAPPER IN BELL** the small swinging hammer inside a bell that hits against the inside of the bell to make the sound **9.** GEOG **STRIP OF LAND** a narrow strip of land sticking out into a sea, a lake, or river **10.** MUSIC **VIBRATING END OF MUSICAL REED** the vibrating end of a reed in a wind instrument **11.** TRANSP **POLE ON CARRIAGE** the pole at the front of a coach or carriage to which the horses' harnesses are fastened **12.** CONSTR **PROJECTING STRIP FITTING INTO GROOVE** a strip that sticks out along the edge of a wooden board and is designed to fit into a corresponding groove along the edge of another board **13.** **SOMETHING LIKE TONGUE** something shaped or moving like a tongue ■ **tongues** *npl.* RELIG **SPEECH RESULTING FROM RELIGIOUS ECSTASY** speech in no known language that results from religious ecstasy. = **gift of tongues, glossolalia, speaking in tongues** ■ *v.* (**tongued, tongue·ing, tongues**) **1.** *vt.* **TOUCH SOMETHING WITH TONGUE** to touch or lick something with the tongue **2.** *vt.* **KISS SOMEBODY USING TONGUE** to kiss somebody with the lips open and the tongue touching the inside of the other person's mouth (*informal*) **3.** *vti.* MUSIC **USE TONGUE TO ARTICULATE INSTRUMENT'S NOTES** to use the tongue to block the flow of air on a wind or brass instrument, thereby separating one note from another **4.** *vt.* CONSTR **CUT TONGUE ALONG BOARD'S EDGE** to cut a tongue along the edge of a wooden board, to make one half of a tongue-and-groove joint [Old English *tunge.* Ultimately from the Indo-European word for "tongue" that is also the ancestor of English *lingual* and *language.*] —**tongue·less** *adj.* ◇ **hold your tongue** to keep silent ◇ **(with) tongue in cheek** with gentle irony and as a joke

WORD KEY: SYNONYMS

See Synonyms at ***language.***

tongue-and-groove joint *n.* a joint made between two wooden boards consisting of a projecting strip or tongue along the edge of one board and a groove along the edge of the other

tongued /tungd/ *adj.* having a particular kind of tongue, especially a particular way of speaking (*usually used in combination*) ○ *sharp-tongued*

tongue de·pres·sor *n.* a wide flat plastic or wooden stick that a doctor uses to hold down the tongue in order to examine the mouth and throat

tongue-in-cheek *adj.* spoken with gentle irony and meant as a joke

tongue-lash·ing *n.* a severe scolding

tongue-tie *vt.* **MAKE SOMEBODY TOO NERVOUS TO SPEAK** to make somebody unable to speak, especially because of awe, shyness, or embarrassment ■ *n.* MED **INABILITY TO MOVE TONGUE FREELY** the inability to move the tongue with the normal amount of freedom, because the small membrane (**frenulum**) that attaches the tongue to the floor of the mouth is unusually short

tongue-tied *adj.* **1.** **SPEECHLESS THROUGH NERVOUSNESS** unable to speak because of awe, shyness, or embarrassment **2.** MED **AFFECTED BY TONGUE-TIE** unable to move the tongue freely because of tongue-tie

tongue twist·er *n.* a word, phrase, or sentence that is difficult to say because of its unusual sequence of sounds, especially an invented sentence such as "She sells seashells by the seashore"

tongue worm *n.* a tongue-shaped parasite with a hooked mouth that infests the lungs or nostrils of mammals, reptiles, and birds. Phylum: Arthropoda.

ton·ic /tónnik/ *n.* **1.** **SOMETHING THAT LIFTS THE SPIRITS** something that lifts the spirits or makes somebody feel better generally **2.** MED **MEDICINE PRODUCING SENSE OF WELL-BEING** a medicine that purports to make patients feel stronger, more energetic, and generally healthier **3.** BEVERAGES **QUININE WATER** quinine water (*informal*) **4.** *New England* BEVERAGES **SOFT DRINK** a flavored and carbonated drink, served cold. ◊ **soda** **5.** MUSIC **FIRST NOTE OF SCALE** the first note in a scale and the harmony built on this note **6.** PHON **STRESSED SYLLABLE** the syllable that has the main stress in a word ■ *adj.* **1.** **LIFTING THE SPIRITS** lifting the spirits and generally creating a feeling of well-being **2.** **BOOSTING ENERGY** designed or serving to boost energy and generally create a feeling of strength and health **3.** PHYSIOL **RELATING TO MUSCLE TONE** relating to or affecting muscular tone or contraction **4.** MUSIC **RELATING TO FIRST NOTE** based on the first note of a scale **5.** PHON **OF A STRESSED SYLLABLE** constituting or relating to the main stressed syllable in a word **6.** LING = **tonetic** [Mid-17thC. Via French *tonique* from Greek *tonikos* "of stretching," from *tonos.*] —**ton·i·cal·ly** *adv.*

WORD KEY: REGIONAL NOTE

Tonic in the sense "soft drink" is an old Boston word that extended north, west, and south into New England according to the Boston truck routes. Other regional synonyms include *pop* (Inland North and West), *soda* (Northeast), and *cold drink* (Lower South).

ton·ic ac·cent *n.* **1.** MUSIC **MUSICAL ACCENT PRODUCED BY HIGHER PITCH** a musical accent produced by higher pitch rather than by stress **2.** PHON **SYLLABLE STRESS CREATED BY HIGHER PITCH** stress on a syllable created through a change in pitch

to·nic·i·ty /tō níssətee/ *n.* **1.** **BEING TONIC** the state or quality of being tonic **2.** PHYSIOL **STATE OF SLIGHT MUSCLE CONTRACTION** the state or quality of muscles being slightly contracted or ready to contract

ton·ic sol-fa *n.* a system of using syllables to denote degrees of a musical scale, and in which the syllables are movable depending on the key of the piece

ton·ic wa·ter *n.* = **quinine water** [So called because it was originally drunk to stimulate the appetite or digestion]

to·night /tə nít/ *n.* **NIGHT OF PRESENT DAY** the night or evening of the present day ■ *adv.* **ON PRESENT DAY'S NIGHT** on or during the night or evening of the present day [Old English *tō niht*, literally "at night"]

ton·ka bean /tóngkə-/ *n.* **1.** **FRAGRANT BLACK SEED USED IN PERFUME** the fragrant black almond-shaped seed of a tropical American tree used to make perfumes and to perfume tobacco and snuff **2.** **TROPICAL AMERICAN TREE** a tall tropical American tree that produces tonka beans. Latin name: *Dipteryx odorata.* [Origin uncertain: possibly from Tupi or Galibi *tonka*]

Ton·kin, Gulf of /tón kín, tóng kín/ northwestern arm of the South China Sea, bounded by Vietnam, mainland China, and the Chinese island of Hainan

Ton·le Sap /tòn lay sáp/ the largest lake in Southeast Asia, in western Cambodia, linked to the Mekong River by the Tonle Sap River. A shallow lake, it swells from 1,000 sq. mi./2,600 sq. km in the dry season to 4,020 sq. mi./10,400 sq. km in the monsoon season.

ton·nage /túnnij/ *n.* **1.** MEASURE **WEIGHT IN TONS** weight measured in imperial or metric tons **2.** **SHIP'S SIZE OR CAPACITY** the size of a ship measured in tons or cubic feet or meters of seawater displaced, or the capacity of a ship measured in cubic feet or meters **3.** SHIPPING **WEIGHT OF SHIP'S CARGO** the weight of a ship's cargo, measured in tons **4.** SHIPPING **DUTY CHARGED ON SHIP'S CARGO** the duty charged at a rate per ton on a ship's cargo **5.** SHIPPING **SIZE OF FLEET OF SHIPS** the size of a fleet of ships, e.g., a merchant company's fleet or a nation's warships, calculated as the combined weights or carrying capacities of all ships [15thC. Formed from TON[1].]

tonne /tun/ *n.* = **metric ton** [Late 19thC. Via French from medieval Latin *tunna*, of uncertain origin: probably from Celtic.]

WORD KEY: USAGE

tonne, ton, or **tun**? All three words are pronounced the same way (tun), although ***tonne*** is sometimes pronounced *ton* to distinguish it from ***ton.*** A ***ton*** is a nonmetric unit and differs in value in British and American usage (see ***ton***). A ***tonne*** is a metric unit equal to 1000 kilograms. A ***tun*** is a large beer cask or a unit of liquid capacity equal to 252 gallons.

ton·neau /tə nṓ, tónnō/ (*plural* **-neaus**) *n.* the back-seat compartment of an open-top vintage car, or a flexible cloth cover protecting it when it is not being used [Late 18thC. From French, literally "barrel" (so called because of its shape), from *tonne* (see TONNE).]

to·nom·e·ter /tō nómmətər/ *n.* **1.** PHYS **INSTRUMENT MEASURING SOUND'S PITCH** an instrument, often one fitted with a range of tuning forks, that measures the exact pitch of a sound **2.** MED **INSTRUMENT MEASURING PRESSURE IN BODY PART** an instrument that measures pressure in a part of the body such as the blood vessels, or the eyeball as a test for glaucoma [Early 18thC. Coined from Greek *tonos* (see TONE) + -METER.] —**to·no·met·ric** /tṑnə méttrik/ *adj.* —**to·nom·e·try** /tō nómmətree/ *n.*

to·no·plast /tṓnə plàst/ *n.* the semipermeable membrane separating a fluid-filled internal cavity (**vacuole**) from the surrounding cytoplasm inside a plant cell [Late 19thC. Coined from Greek *tonos* (see TONE) + -PLAST.]

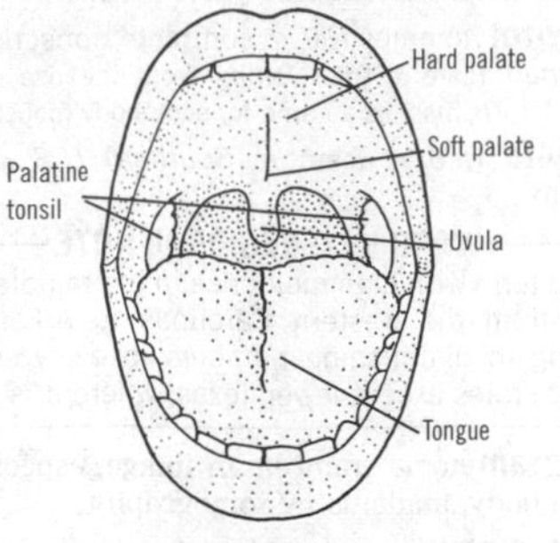

Tonsil

ton·sil /tónsəl/ *n.* **1.** **OVAL TISSUE MASS IN THE MOUTH** either of two small oval masses of tissue, one on each side of the back of the mouth, that are important for the body's immune system **2.** **TONSIL-SHAPED LUMP OF TISSUE ELSEWHERE** any of various lumps of tissue shaped like the tonsils of the mouth, e.g., either of two small lumps in the brain (**tonsils of the cerebellum**) [Late 16thC. From Latin *tonsillae* "tonsils," of uncertain origin.] —**ton·sil·lar** *adj.* —**ton·sil·lar·y** *adj.*

ton·sil·lec·to·my /tònsə léktəmee/ (*plural* **-mies**) *n.* a surgical procedure to remove the tonsils of the mouth

ton·sil·li·tis /tònsə lítiss/ *n.* inflammation of the tonsils of the mouth, caused either by bacteria or a virus, which makes the throat very sore and can lead to fever and earache —**ton·sil·lit·ic** /tònsə líttik/ *adj.*

ton·so·ri·al /ton sáwree əl/ *adj.* relating to barbers or their work (*formal or humorous*) [Early 19thC. Formed from Latin *tonsorius*, from *tonsor* "barber," from *tondere* "to clip" (source of English *tonsure*).]

ton·sure /tónshər/ *n.* **PARTIALLY SHAVED HEAD** a shaved patch on the crown of the heads of priests and monks in some religious orders, or the shaving of the head in this way ■ *vt.* (**-sured, -sur·ing, -sures**) **PARTIALLY SHAVE THE HEAD** to shave the crown of the head [14thC. Directly or via French from, ultimately, Latin *tondere* "to clip."]

ton·tine /tón teen, ton teen/ *n.* an investment or insurance scheme in which contributors pay equal amounts into a common fund and receive equal dividends and benefits from it, with the final surviving contributor receiving everything [Mid-18thC. From French, named for a Neapolitan banker, Lorenzo *Tonti* (1630–95), who started such a scheme.]

ton·to /tón tō/ *adj.* an offensive term used to describe somebody who is thought to be psychologically challenged (*slang insult*) [Late 20thC. From Spanish.]

to·nus /tṓnəss/ *n.* the normal state of a healthy muscle when resting in a state of slight contraction [Late 19thC. Via Latin from Greek *tonos* (see TONE).]

ton·y /tṓnee/ *adj.* having an aristocratic, expensive, or stylish presentation (*informal*)

To·ny /tṓnee/ (*plural* **-nys**) *n.* an award made annually in the United States for achievement in the theater [Mid-20thC. From *Tony*, nickname of the U.S. actor and producer Antoinette Perry (1888–1946).]

too /too/ *adv.* **1.** **AS WELL** used to indicate that a person, thing, or aspect of a situation applies in addition to the one just mentioned ○ *Can cats be affected by it too?* ○ *You ought to see a doctor, and quickly too!* ◊ **also** **2.** **MORE THAN IS DESIRABLE** more of an amount or degree of something than is desirable, necessary, or fitting ○ *He's a little too conservative for me.* **3.** **EXTREMELY** used to emphasize a quality ○ *She's only too aware of how this will affect her career.* **4.** **VERY** used to modify the force of a negative statement in order to sound polite or cautious ○ *It didn't look too good.* **5.** **INDEED** used to emphasize the force of a statement or command ○ *"I didn't touch it." – "You did too!"* [Old English *tō* (see TO), in the sense "in addition, furthermore"] ◇ **only too right** used to express emphatic agreement with a statement that has just been made ○ *You are only too right in saying that*

too·dle-oo /to͝od'l o͞o/ *interj.* farewell (*dated informal or humorous*) [Early 20thC. Origin uncertain: possibly an alteration of French *à tout à l'heure* "see you later."]

took past tense of **take**

tool /to͞ol/ *n.* **1.** MECH ENG **DEVICE FOR DOING WORK** an object designed to do a particular kind of work, e.g., cutting or chopping, by directing manually applied force or by means of a motor **2.** MECH ENG **CUTTING PART OF MACHINE** the cutting or shaping part of a power-driven device, e.g., the blade on a lathe **3.** CRAFT **BOOKBINDER'S IMPLEMENT** any of the implements that a bookbinder uses to make a design on leather, or the design made by such an implement **4. MEANS TO AN END** something used as a means of achieving something **5. SOMETHING USED FOR A JOB** an item people use in the course of their everyday work ○ *Words are the poet's tool.* **6. SOMEBODY MANIPULATED BY ANOTHER** somebody who is manipulated by somebody else, especially one person who carries out the unsavory or dishonest tasks the other person does not want to do **7. OFFENSIVE TERM** an offensive term for a human penis (*slang offensive*) ■ *v.* (**tooled, tool·ing, tools**) **1.** *vt.* CRAFT **WORK SOMETHING USING HAND TOOLS** to cut, shape, or form something, especially to press a design into the leather cover of a book, using hand tools **2.** *vt.* INDUST **GIVE SOMEBODY OR SOMETHING TOOLS** to equip somebody or something with tools **3.** *vti.* CARS **DRIVE A CAR** to drive a car in a particular way, especially at high speeds (*slang*) ○ *tooling along at a cool 65* [Old English *tōl*. Ultimately from a prehistoric Germanic base meaning "to manufacture."] —**tool·er** *n.* —**tool·less** *adj.*

tool up *vti.* INDUST on a large scale, to provide a factory or an industry with the equipment needed to manufacture many things ○ *tooled up the automotive industry for the war effort*

tool·bar /to͞ol bàar/ *n.* a row of icons on a computer screen that are clicked on to perform certain frequently used functions

tool·ing /to͞oling/ *n.* any kind of decorative work done with hand tools, especially the carving of stone or the pressing or stamping of designs onto leather

tool·mak·er /to͞ol màykər/ *n.* somebody who makes or repairs precision tools, especially the cutting or shaping parts of industrial machines —**tool·mak·ing** *n.*

tool push·er *n.* somebody who supervises drilling operations on a drill rig (*informal*)

tool·room /to͞ol ro͞om, -ro͝om/ *n.* a room in a machine shop where tools are stored, maintained, or made

tool·shed /to͞ol shèd/ *n.* a small outbuilding where tools are kept, especially one in a yard used for storing gardening tools

tool steel *n.* hard steel used to make the cutting or shaping parts of hand tools and power tools

toon[1] /to͞on/ *n.* **1.** TREES **RED-FLOWERED TREE** a tree of the mahogany family native to Australia and tropical Asia. It has fragrant hard wood and red flowers that are used to make dye. Latin name: *Cedrela toona.* **2.** INDUST **REDDISH HARDWOOD** the fragrant reddish wood of the toon tree, whose exceptional hardness makes it a highly prized wood for furniture and top-quality joinery [Early 19thC. Via Hindi *tūn* from Sanskrit *tunnaḥ*.]

toon[2] *n.* any kind of cartoon or cartoon chracter, or the whole of the cartoon-making industry

too·nie /to͞onee/ *n. Can* a coin worth two Canadian dollars [Blend of TWO and LOONIE]

too·rie /to͞oree/ *n. Scotland* a soft flat cap, with or without a brim, that has a pompon on its top, or a pompon on such a hat (*informal*) [Early 19thC. Originally in the sense "little tower," formed from *tour*, a variant of TOWER.]

toot[1] /to͞ot/ *n.* **SOUND OF VEHICLE HORN** the high-pitched hooting sound that a vehicle's horn makes, or a similar sound ■ *v.* (**toot·ed, toot·ing, toots**) **1.** *vti.* **MAKE SHORT HOOTING SOUND** to make, or cause the horn of a vehicle to make, a short high-pitched hooting sound **2.** *vi.* **PASS GAS** to pass gas noisily (*slang*) [Early 16thC. An imitation of the sound.] —**toot·er** *n.*

toot[2] /to͞ot/ *n.* (*slang*) **1. DRINKING BOUT** a bout of heavy drinking **2. INHALED ILLEGAL SUBSTANCE** a quantity of an illegal drug, especially cocaine, taken by inhaling through the nose ■ *vti.* (**toot·ed, toot·ing, toots**) **INHALE ILLEGAL SUBSTANCE** to inhale an illegal drug, especially cocaine (*slang*) [Late 17thC. Origin unknown.]

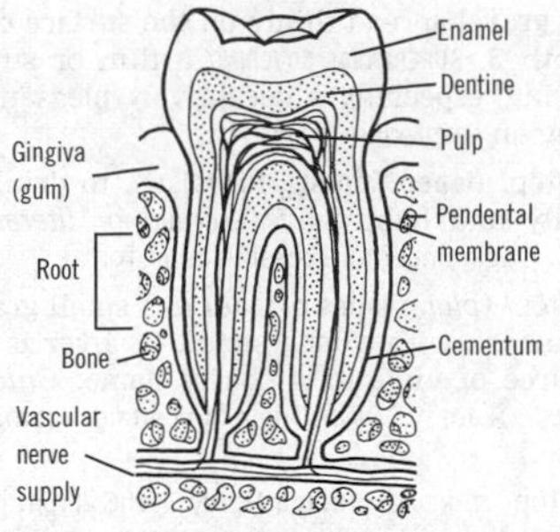

Tooth: Cross section of a human tooth

tooth /to͞oth/ *n.* (*plural* **teeth** /teeth/) **1.** PHYSIOL **WHITISH BONY OBJECT IN THE MOUTH** any of the hard whitish bony objects arranged in two arched rows inside a human or vertebrate animal's mouth and used for biting and chewing food **2.** ZOOL **INVERTEBRATE PART RESEMBLING A TOOTH** a sharp part on an invertebrate made of horny, calcareous, or chitinous material and functioning like or resembling a vertebrate tooth **3. INDENTATION** an object resembling the shape of or performing the function of a tooth, e.g., one of the jagged indentations along the edge of a saw or a leaf **4.** MECH ENG **PART STICKING OUT ON GEAR WHEEL** any of a set of parts that stick out from the edge of a gear wheel or sprocket, designed to interlock with another set **5. SURFACE ROUGHNESS ALLOWING SUBSTANCE TO ADHERE** the roughness of a surface, especially the surface of paper, which allows paints, glues, and other substances to stick to it **6. SOMETHING DESTRUCTIVE** something that has the power to destroy (*usually used in the plural*) ○ *the teeth of the gale* **7. TASTE FOR SOMETHING** a liking for the taste of something ○ *a sweet tooth* ■ **teeth** *npl.* **EFFECTIVE POWER** the power or ability to accomplish something ○ *Sanctions without teeth won't do any good.* ■ *v.* (**toothed, tooth·ing, tooths**) **1.** *vt.* MECH ENG **PUT TEETH ON SOMETHING** to give something teeth, especially to cut teeth into a saw blade or around the edge of a gear wheel or sprocket **2.** *vti.* **FIT TOGETHER WITH INTERLOCKING TEETH** to interlock by means of teeth that fit one set inside the other [Old English *tōþ*. Ultimately from the Indo-European word for "tooth," which is also the ancestor of English *tusk*, *dental*, and *mastodon*.] ◇ **armed to the teeth (with something)** extremely well armed or equipped with something (*informal*) ◇ **cut your teeth (on something)** to learn how to do something and gain experience from it ◇ **get your teeth into something** to start doing something that will be challenging and satisfying ◇ **in the teeth of** against oppostion or contradiction from ◇ **set your teeth on edge** to irritate ◇ **show your teeth** to indicate that you have power and intend to use it

tooth·ache /to͞oth àyk/ *n.* pain in or around a tooth, especially because the tooth is decaying

tooth·ache tree *n.* either of two prickly-branched North American varieties of ash that have a fragrant bark that was formerly chewed as a cure for toothache. Latin name: *Zanthoxylum americanum* and *Zanthoxylum clava-herculis.* ◊ **prickly ash**

tooth and nail *adv.* very aggressively or with every available means

tooth·brush /to͞oth brùsh/ *n.* a small brush for cleaning the teeth, with a long handle and a comparatively small head —**tooth·brush·ing** *n.*

toothed /tootht/ *adj.* having a particular number or kind of teeth (*often used in combination*)

toothed whale *n.* a smallish whale that has teeth and feeds on fish and mollusks. Suborder: Odontoceti.

tooth fair·y *n.* a fairy who, in children's folklore, takes away the baby tooth that a child leaves under the pillow and replaces it with a coin or small gift

tooth·less /to͞othləss/ *adj.* **1. LACKING TEETH** lacking teeth, especially because the teeth have decayed and fallen out **2. LACKING POWER** lacking power, authority, or a forceful manner

tooth·less whale *n.* a whale without teeth but with thin horny plates hanging from the upper jaw through which it filters plankton. Toothless whales are larger than toothed ones. ◊ **toothed whale**

tooth·paste /to͞oth pàyst/ *n.* paste brushed onto the teeth to clean them and protect them from decay

tooth·pick /to͞oth pìk/ *n.* a thin pointed stick of wood or plastic used to remove pieces of food from between the teeth

tooth pow·der *n.* powder that is mixed to a lather with a damp toothbrush and used to clean the teeth and protect them from decay

tooth shell *n.* a mollusk with a tapering shell, or the shell of such a mollusk. Class: Scaphopoda.

tooth·some /to͞othsəm/ *adj.* **1. DELICIOUS** having a pleasing smell, taste, and appearance **2. ATTRACTIVE** attractive, especially sexually (*dated informal*) (*offensive in some contexts*) —**tooth·some·ly** *adv.* —**tooth·some·ness** *n.*

tooth·wort /to͞oth wùrt, -wàwrt/ (*plural* **-worts** *or* **-wort**) *n.* **1. N AMERICAN PLANT WITH SCALY ROOTS** a North American flowering plant with scaly rhizomes and often showy pink or purple flowers. Latin name: *Cardamine bulbifera.* **2. EUROPEAN PLANT WITH SCALY ROOTS** a leafless European plant that grows on tree roots and has pinkish flowers and horizontal underground stems (**rhizomes**) that are covered with scales resembling teeth. Latin name: *Lathraea squamaria.*

tooth·y /to͞othee/ (**-i·er, -i·est**) *adj.* having or showing a lot of teeth, large teeth, or protruding teeth —**tooth·i·ly** *adv.* —**tooth·i·ness** *n.*

too·tle /to͞ot'l/ *v.* (**-tled, -tling, -tles**) (*informal*) **1.** *vi.* **DRIVE SLOWLY** to proceed slowly or aimlessly, especially in a car **2.** *vti.* **MAKE HOOTING SOUND** to make or cause something to make repeated high-pitched tooting sounds ■ *n.* **REPEATED SOUND** a gentle repeated tooting sound (*informal*) [Early 19thC. Formed from TOOT[1].] —**too·tler** *n.*

too-too *adj.* exaggeratedly and artificially refined or elegant (*informal humorous*)

toots /to͝ots/ *n.* an affectionate or patronizing way of addressing somebody, especially a woman (*dated informal*) (*offensive in some contexts*) [Mid-20thC. Origin unknown.]

toot·sie *n.* **1. PROSTITUTE** a prostitute (*slang*) **2.** = **tootsy** *n.* 1 (*slang*) **3.** = **toots** (*dated informal*) (*offensive in some contexts*) [Mid-20thC. Origin unknown.]

toot·sy (*plural* **-sies**) *n.* **1. FOOT OR TOE** a child's word for foot or toe (*slang*) **2.** = **toots** (*dated informal*) (*offensive in some contexts*) [Mid-19thC. Alteration of FOOTSIE.]

top[1] /top/ *n.* **1. HIGHEST PART** the highest part or point (*often used in combination*) ○ *snow on the mountain tops* **2. UPPER SURFACE** the upper side or surface ○ *dust on the top of the cupboard* **3. LID OR COVER** the part covering and sealing the open upper side of an object or an opening on the upper side (*often used in combination*) ○ *bottle tops* **4.** CLOTHES **GARMENT COVERING UPPER BODY** a piece of clothing, especially women's clothing, covering the upper body **5. MOST IMPORTANT POSITION OR PERSON** the most important position or most senior rank, or the person occupying it ○ *at the top of her profession* **6. BEST PART** the best part or section ○ *They only take the top of the group.* **7. MOST EXCELLENT LEVEL** the level of highest excellence ○ *not at the top of his game* **8. MOST INTENSE LEVEL** the level of greatest intensity, power, or force ○ *at the top of her voice* **9. BEGINNING OR EARLIEST PART** the beginning or the first or earliest section ○ *Take it from the top.* **10. CROWN OF HEAD** the crown of the head ○ *from top to toe* **11.** AUTOMOT **CAR ROOF** the roof of a car, especially a convertible **12.** *U.K.* AUTOMOT = **high** *n.* 7 (*informal*) **13.** SPORTS **TOPSPIN** topspin (*informal*) **14.** SPORTS **STROKE HITTING BALL ABOVE CENTER** a stroke that puts topspin on a ball by hitting the ball above its center **15.** BASEBALL **FIRST HALF OF BASEBALL INNING** the first half of an inning in a baseball game **16.** CARDS **PLAYER'S BEST CARD OR CARDS** the best card or group of cards in a player's hand **17.** ACOUSTICS **HIGH-FREQUENCY PART OF SOUND** the high-frequency element of any sound **18.** CHEM **VOLATILE PART OF A SOLUTION** the part of a distilled solution that volatizes first **19.** SAILING **PLATFORM ON A MAST** a platform around the head of a lower mast on a sailing ship, used to stand on or to support rigging ■ **tops** *npl.* **ROOT VEGETABLE'S VISIBLE PARTS** the parts of a root vegetable that are visible above the ground when it is growing (*often used in combination*) ■ *adj.* **1. UPPERMOST OR HIGHEST** situated at the top, or higher than all others ○ *the top shirt on the pile* **2. LEADING OR MOST SUCCESSFUL** most important, senior, successful, or respected ○ *a convention of top academics* **3. OF BEST QUALITY** of the finest quality available ○ *one of the city's top hotels* **4. MAXIMUM** being at the highest level or degree ○ *at top speed* ■ *vt.* (**topped, top·ping, tops**) **1. ADD TOPPING TO SOMETHING** to put a topping on something (*often passive*) ○ *topped with a layer of melted cheese* **2.** **CUT TOP OFF SOMETHING** to cut the top off something, especially a vegetable prior to cooking ○ *First top the carrots.* **3.** **OUTRANK ALL OTHERS IN SOMETHING** to be at the head of something such as a list or hierarchy ○ *They've topped the music charts for the fifth week in a row.* **4.** **EXCEED OR BETTER SOMETHING** to do better than something, or be greater than something ○ *profits topping $500 million* **5.** **REACH APEX OF SOMETHING** to reach or go over the top of something, e.g., a mountain **6.** SPORTS **PUT TOPSPIN ON BALL** to hit a ball above its center, putting topspin on it **7.** GOLF **HIT GOLF BALL ABOVE CENTER** to hit a golf ball too far above its center, so that it runs along the ground instead of rising into the air **8.** CHEM **DISTILL VOLATILE PART OF SOLUTION** to take the most volatile part of a solution through distillation [Old English *topp.* Ultimately from a prehistoric Germanic word meaning "tuft, crest," which is also the ancestor of English *tip*[1], *tuft,* and *toupee.*] ◇ **blow your top** to lose your temper and fly into a rage (*informal*) ◇ **off the top of your head** without thinking deeply, checking, or planning something

top up *vt.* **1.** **FILL CONTAINER** to fill or refill a container that is partly empty **2.** FIN **INCREASE SUM BY ADDING MONEY** to give extra money to augment a sum or fund of money, especially in order to bring it up to a required or desirable level

top[2] /top/ *n.* a toy that spins around on a rounded or pointed base, traditionally a conical wooden toy that is set spinning by pulling a string wrapped around it [Pre-12thC. Origin unknown.]

top- *prefix.* = **topo-** (*used before vowels*)

to·paz /tṓ pàz/ *n.* **1.** MINERALS **TRANSPARENT BROWN GEMSTONE** a mineral found in granites and pegmatites that occasionally occurs as well-formed crystals in a variety of colors including brown and pink that are valued as gemstones **2.** MINERALS **YELLOWISH GEMSTONE** a yellowish gemstone, especially yellow sapphire or a yellow variety of quartz **3.** BIRDS **HUMMINGBIRD WITH YELLOWISH THROAT** either of two vividly-colored yellowish-throated hummingbirds of the South American rainforest. Latin name: *Topaza pyra* and *Topaza pella.* **4.** COLORS **YELLOWISH-BROWN COLOR** a light-brown color tinged with yellow ■ *adj.* COLORS **OF YELLOWISH-BROWN COLOR** of a light brown color tinged with yellow [13thC. Via Old French *topace* from, ultimately, Greek *topazos,* of unknown origin.]

to·paz·o·lite /tō pázzə lìt/ *n.* a yellowish-green variety of garnet used as a gemstone [Early 19thC. Coined from TOPAZ + -LITE.]

top ba·nan·a *n.* (*slang*) **1.** **LEADER** the main person in a group **2.** ARTS **LEADING COMEDIAN** the leading comedian in a comedy show, especially a vaudeville show

top bil·ling *n.* **1.** ARTS **STATUS AS STAR PERFORMER** a performer's status as the star attraction in a show with his or her name appearing first in any list of performers or promotional material **2.** **PROMINENCE** the position of greatest prominence in something

top boot *n.* a knee-length boot with a band of differently colored leather around the top

top brass *n.* the highest-ranking officers or officials (*informal*)

top·coat /tóp kṑt/ *n.* **1.** **FINAL COAT OF PAINT** a finishing coat of paint, applied over an undercoat **2.** CLOTHES **OVERCOAT** a lightweight coat for outdoor wear

top dead-cen·ter *n.* the position of a piston in an engine or pump when it is at the top of its stroke

top dog *n.* the most important or powerful person, often somebody who has beaten all other competitors (*informal*)

top dol·lar *n.* a high price, or the highest price (*informal*)

top-down *adj.* **1.** **CONTROLLED BY THE MOST SENIOR PEOPLE** having all control in the hands of the people at the most senior levels **2.** **WORKING FROM GENERAL TO SPECIFIC** starting at the most general level and working toward details or specifics ○ *a top-down approach*

top draw·er *n.* **1.** **THE BEST** the highest level of excellence, or the people at this level **2.** **UPPER CLASS** the upper class or highest class in society —**top-draw·er** *adj.*

top-dress *vt.* to spread a thin layer of something on the ground, especially fertilizer on the surface of soil, a growing crop, or a lawn

top dress·ing *n.* **1.** AGRIC **SURFACE FERTILIZER** fertilizer spread thinly on the surface of soil, a growing crop, or on a lawn **2.** TRANSP **LOOSE GRAVEL AS A ROAD SURFACE** loose gravel spread thinly on the surface of a road or path **3.** **SUPERFICIAL COVERING** a thin or superficial covering, especially a deceptively pleasant facade hiding an unpleasant reality

tope[1] /tōp/ (**toped, top·ing, topes**) *vti.* to drink liquor heavily and habitually (*archaic or literary*) [Mid-17thC. Origin uncertain: possibly from TOP[1].]

tope[2] /tōp/ (*plural* **topes** *or* **tope**) *n.* a small gray European shark with a long snout. Its liver is used as a source of vitamin A. Latin name: *Galeorhinus galeus.* [Late 17thC. Origin uncertain: perhaps from Cornish.]

tope[3] /tōp/ *n.* RELIG = **stupa** [Early 19thC. From Hindi *top,* of uncertain origin: probably from Prakrit *thūpo.*]

to·pee /tṓpee/, **to·pi** *n.* = **pith helmet** [Mid-19thC. From Hindi *ṭopī* "hat."]

To·pe·ka /tō peékə/ capital city of Kansas, in the northeastern part of the state, on the Kansas River, east of Manhattan and west of Kansas City. Population: 119,658 (1996).

top·er /tṓpər/ *n.* somebody who drinks liquor heavily and habitually (*archaic literary or informal*) [From TOPE[1]]

top·flight /tóp flìt/ *adj.* of the highest quality or status

top·gal·lant /top gállənt, tóp gàl-/; (*nautical use*) /tə gál-/ *n.* **1.** **topgallant mast, topgallant SHIP'S MAST** a ship's mast that is taller than a topmast or is an extension of a topmast **2.** **topgallant sail, topgallant SAIL SET ON TOPGALLANT** a sail set on a topgallant mast [Early 16thC. The underlying idea is that the extension of the top mast presents a gallant display above the other masts.]

top gear *n.* *U.K.* = **high gear**

top gun *n.* somebody who is the very best in his or her field (*informal*)

WORD KEY: CULTURAL NOTE

Top Gun, a movie by English director Tony Scott (1986). A drama about U.S. Navy fighter pilots in training, it centers on two outstanding pilots in the class competing for the much coveted title of "Top Gun." An encounter with enemy aircraft provides them with an opportunity to prove their worth. The movie is memorable for its spectacular, high-speed dog-fights. The term "top gun" promptly moved into the general language, meaning "somebody who is the very best in his or her field."

top-ham·per *n.* the uppermost sails, spars, and other equipment on a sailing ship, especially when regarded as weight to be minimized or monitored because of the destabilizing effect it can have [From HAMPER[1]]

top hat *n.* a man's tall cylindrical hat with a flat top and a narrow brim. It is usually black, is often made of silk, and is worn as part of formal dress.

top-heav·y *adj.* **1.** **UNBALANCED BECAUSE TOO HEAVY AT TOP** unbalanced or unstable owing to excessive weight at the top **2.** BUSINESS **OVERBURDENED WITH EXECUTIVES** with too many executives or managers in proportion to the numbers of staff at junior levels —**top-heav·i·ly** *adv.* —**top-heav·i·ness** *n.*

To·phet /tṓfət, tṓ fèt/, **To·pheth** *n.* **1.** BIBLE **PLACE OF PUNISHMENT AFTER DEATH** according to the Bible, a place of torment and punishment where the wicked are sent after death **2.** **TERRIBLE SITUATION** an extremely unpleasant situation or condition (*archaic or literary*) [14thC. From Hebrew *Tōpeṯ,* an area near Jerusalem associated first with primitive religious worship and later with the burning of trash and, by extension, Hell.]

to·phus /tṓfəss/ (*plural* **-phi** /-fì/) *n.* a hard deposit of crystalline uric acid and its salts in cartilage, joints, or skin. It is a characteristic of gout. [Mid-16thC. From Latin, "tufa."] —**to·pha·ceous** /tə fáyshəss/ *adj.*

to·pi[1] /tṓpee/ (*plural* **-pis** *or* **-pi**) *n.* an African antelope that has curved horns, a long muzzle, and bluish-black and yellow markings. It is said to be the fastest of all the antelopes. Latin name: *Damaliscus lunatus.* [Late 19thC. Origin uncertain.]

to·pi[2] *n.* = **pith helmet**

to·pi·ar·y /tṓpee èrree/ (*plural* **-ies**) *n.* **1.** **ART OF SHAPING BUSHES** the art of trimming bushes, hedges, and trees into decorative shapes **2.** **SHAPED BUSH** a bush, hedge, or tree trimmed into a decorative shape **3.** **TOPIARY GARDEN** a garden in which topiaries feature prominently [Late 16thC. Via French from Latin *topiarius* from, ultimately, Greek *topos* "place."] —**to·pi·ar·ist** /tṓpee ərist/ *n.*

Topi

top·ic /tóppik/ *n.* **1.** **SUBJECT** a subject written or spoken about **2.** LOGIC **ARGUMENTS USED IN REASONING** a class of arguments used as a source of proofs in formal reasoning [15thC. Formed from *Topics,* title of Aristotle's treatise on rhetorical commonplaces, from Latin *Topica,* from, ultimately, Greek *topos* "place."]

WORD KEY: SYNONYMS

See Synonyms at ***subject.***

top·i·cal /tóppik'l/ *adj.* **1.** **OF CURRENT INTEREST** relating to something that is of particular interest at the moment **2.** **OF TOPICS** relating to topics or in the form of topics **3.** **LOCAL** relating to, or situated in, a particular place or part **4.** MED **APPLIED EXTERNALLY** used to describe drugs or medications that are applied directly to the surface of the part of the body being treated —**top·i·cal·ly** *adv.*

top·i·cal·i·ty /tòppi kállətee/ *n.* relevance to matters that are of interest at the moment

top·ic sen·tence *n.* a sentence that states the main idea of a paragraph or larger section of writing, usually placed at or near the beginning

top·knot /tóp nòt/ *n.* **1.** HAIR **HAIR DECORATION** a decorative arrangement of hair, or of hairbands or bows, worn on top of the head **2.** BIRDS **BIRD'S CREST** a small tuft of feathers on the head of some birds, e.g., the quail

top·less /tópləss/ *adj.* **1.** **WITH NOTHING COVERING BREASTS** wearing no covering over the breasts or upper torso **2.** **WHERE WOMEN SHOW BREASTS** where women can or do expose their breasts in public ○ *a topless beach* **3.** **WITH NO TOP PART** with no covering for the upper torso **4.** **MISSING A TOP** without or missing a top **5.** **ELEVATED** very high, either physically or in rank or importance (*archaic or literary*) —**top·less·ness** *n.*

top-lev·el *adj.* **1.** **INVOLVING IMPORTANT PEOPLE** involving the most senior or influential people **2.** **AT MOST SENIOR LEVEL** at the highest level of influence or authority

top·loft·y /tóp lòftee/ (**-i·er, -i·est**) *adj.* haughty, pretentious, or condescending (*informal*) —**top·loft·i·ly** *adv.* —**top·loft·i·ness** *n.*

top·mast /tóp màst/ *n.* a mast that is taller than the lowest mast and is usually the tallest mast on a ship whose sails run fore-and-aft. It is the next tallest after the topgallant mast on a ship whose sails are square-rigged.

top·min·now /tóp mìnnō/ (*plural* **-nows** *or* **-now**) *n.* a small freshwater fish that swims near the surface in warmer waters and has an upturned mouth for catching prey. Guppies and mollies are topminnows. Families: Cyprinodontidae and Poeciliidae and Goodeidae.

top·most /tóp mṑst/ *adj.* highest or uppermost

top·notch /tóp nòch, top nóch/ *adj.* meeting the highest standards of excellence and quality (*informal*) —**top·notch·er** *n.*

topo- *prefix.* place, region ○ *topotype* [From Greek *topos* "place"]

topog. *abbr.* topography

to·pog·ra·phy /tə póggrəfee/ (*plural* **-phies**) *n.* **1.** GEOG **MAPPING OF SURFACE FEATURES** the study and mapping of the features on the surface of land, including natural features such as mountains and rivers and constructed features such as highways and railroads **2.** **AREA'S FEATURES** the features on the surface of a particular area of land **3.** **DESCRIPTION OF STRUCTURE** a study or detailed description of the various features of any object or entity and the relationships between them —**to·pog·ra·pher** *n.* —**top·o·graph·ic** /tòppə gráffik/ *adj.* —**top·o·graph·i·cal** /-gráffik'l/ *adj.* —**top·o·graph·i·cal·ly** /-gráffikəlee/ *adv.*

to·poi plural of **topos**

to·pol·o·gy /tə póllәjee/ *n.* **1.** GEOM **STUDY OF GEOMETRIC PROPERTIES** the study of the properties of figures that are independent of size or shape and are not changed by stretching, bending, knotting, or twisting **2.** MATH **FAMILY OF SUBSETS** the family of all open subsets of a mathematical set, including the set itself and the empty set, which is closed under set union and finite intersection **3.** ANAT **ANATOMY OF BODY PART** the anatomy of a specific part of the body **4. STUDY LINKING TOPOGRAPHY AND TIME** the study of changes in topography that occur over time and, in particular, of how such changes taking place in a particular area affect the history of that area **5. RELATIONSHIPS BETWEEN LINKED ELEMENTS** the relationships between elements linked together in a system, e.g., a computer network (*formal*) —**top·o·log·ic** /tòppә lójjik/ *adj.* —**top·o·log·i·cal** /-lójjik'l/ *adj.* —**top·o·log·i·cal·ly** /-lójjikәlee/ *adv.* —**to·pol·o·gist** /tә póllәjist/ *n.*

top·o·nym /tóppә nìm/ *n.* (*formal*) **1. PLACE NAME** a name given to a place **2. NAME DERIVED FROM A PLACE NAME** a name, e.g., a personal name, that is derived from the name of a place [Late 19thC. Coined from TOPO- on the model of SYNONYM.]

to·pon·y·my /tә pónnәmee/ *n.* the study of the place names of a particular region or language —**top·o·nym·ic** /tòppә nímmik/ *adj.* —**top·o·nym·i·cal** /-nímmik'l/ *adj.*

to·pos /tő pòss, tő pòss/ (*plural* **-poi** /tő pòy/) *n.* a traditional theme, especially one developed in literature or rhetoric [Mid-20thC. From Greek, "place, rhetorical commonplace."]

top·o·type /tóppә tìp/ *n.* a biological specimen taken from its typical habitat

top·per /tóppәr/ *n.* **1.** CLOTHES **TOP HAT** a top hat (*informal*) **2.** CLOTHES **WOMAN'S COAT** a woman's short, loose-fitting coat or jacket **3. SOMEBODY OR SOMETHING DEALING WITH TOPS** a person or machine that removes or adds tops **4. CROWNING COMMENT** a remark or joke that improves on or triumphs over a preceding one (*informal*) **5.** *U.K.* **BEST OF ITS KIND** something that surpasses all others of its kind (*dated slang*)

top·ping /tópping/ *n.* something put on top of food, especially a sauce or garnish

top·ple /tópp'l/ (**-pled, -pling, -ples**) *v.* **1.** *vti.* **FALL OR MAKE SOMETHING FALL OVER** to fall forward or tip over, or make something fall forward or tip over **2.** *vi.* **TOTTER** to lean or sway precariously, as if about to fall over **3.** *vt.* **OVERTHROW SOMEBODY OR SOMETHING** to overthrow somebody or something from a position of authority [Mid-16thC. Literally in the sense "to keep on falling over" (as if top-heavy), from TOP[1].]

top-rank·ing *adj.* of a senior rank or the highest rank

top round *n.* a lean boneless cut of beef from the outer thigh

tops /tops/ *adj.* **RANKED HIGHEST** ranked highest in quality, degree, or esteem (*informal*) ○ *She's tops in her field.* ■ *adv.* **AT MOST** at the most (*informal*) [Mid-20thC. From plural of TOP[1].]

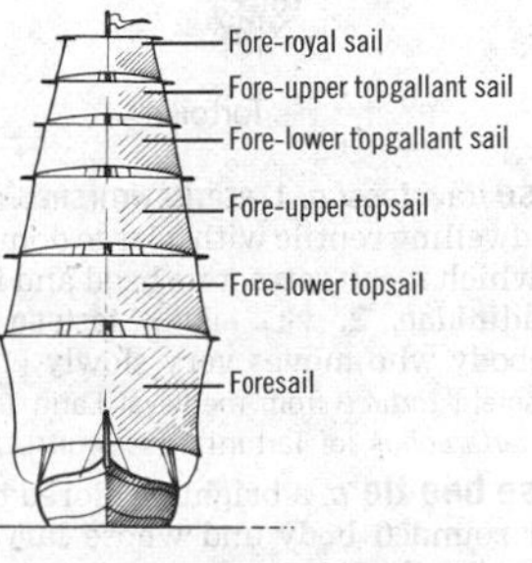

Topsail: Topsails on a square-rigged ship

top·sail /tóps'l, -sàyl/ *n.* a sail set above the lowermost sail on a mast on a square-rigged sailing vessel, or above the gaff on a fore-and-aft-rigged vessel

top-se·cret *adj.* requiring complete secrecy or containing information that must be kept completely secret, especially because its disclosure would pose the gravest danger to national security

top ser·geant *n.* a first sergeant in the United States Army

top·side /tóp sìd/ *n.* **1. UPPER SIDE** the uppermost side of something **2.** NAUT **UPPER HULL** the part of a ship's hull that lies above the water **3. HIGHEST RANK** the highest office or position **4.** *U.K., NZ* FOOD = **top round** ■ *adj.* **1.** NAUT **ON THE TOPSIDE OF A SHIP** relating to or situated on the topside of a ship **2. HIGH IN RANK** of the highest position or rank ■ *adv.* **top·side, top·sides** SAILING **TO A SHIP'S DECK** up on or to the deck of a ship

Top·Sid·er /tóp sìdәr/ *tdmk.* a trademark for soft leather or canvas deck shoes

top·soil /tóp sòyl/ *n.* **SOIL'S TOP LAYER** the upper fertile layer of soil, from which plant roots take nutrients ■ *vt.* (**-soiled, -soil·ing, -soils**) **1. SPREAD WITH TOPSOIL** to spread topsoil onto farming or gardening land to improve fertility **2. REMOVE TOPSOIL** to remove the top layer of soil from farming or gardening land

top·spin /tóp spìn/ *n.* forward spin given to a ball by hitting it on its upper half, making it arc more sharply in the air or bounce higher on impact

top·stitch /tóp stìch/ *n.* **ROW OF STITCHING ON OUTSIDE** a row of stitching on the outer or upper side of a garment, near the seam ■ *vt.* (**-stitched, -stitch·ing, -stitch·es**) **SEW TOPSTITCH ON SOMETHING** to sew a topstitch on a garment —**top·stitch·ing** *n.*

top·sy-tur·vy /tòpsee túrvee/ *adj., adv.* **1. UPSIDE DOWN** with the bottom at the top and the top at the bottom **2. IN OR INTO CONFUSION** in or into a confused or chaotic state, especially one in which the natural order or arrangement of things is inverted ■ *n.* **DISORDER OR CONFUSION** a state of complete disorder or confusion [Early 16thC. Origin uncertain: perhaps formed from TOP[1] + obsolete English *terve* "to turn over."] —**top·sy-tur·vi·ly** *adv.* —**top·sy-tur·vi·ness** *n.*

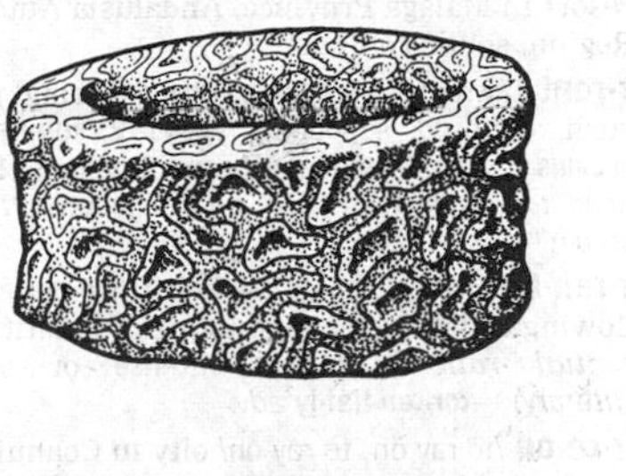

Toque

toque /tōk/ *n.* **1. BRIMLESS HAT** a close-fitting, brimless hat worn by women **2. CHEF'S HAT** a tall white hat worn by chefs **3. HAT WORN IN THE PAST** a velvet hat with a narrow brim and pouched crown, popular in the 16th century with men and women **4.** *Can* ACCESSORIES = **tuque** [Early 16thC. From French, of uncertain origin: perhaps from Spanish *toca*, which in turn may be of Arabic origin.]

tor /tawr/ *n.* a rocky peak of a hill or mountain, specifically one exposed by the weathering of surrounding rock (*often used in place names*) [Old English *torr*. Origin uncertain: perhaps from Celtic.]

To·rah /táwrә/ *n.* **1. FIVE BOOKS OF MOSES** the Jewish Pentateuch, or a parchment scroll on which the Pentateuch is written for use in services in synagogues **2. JEWISH SCRIPTURE** the collective body of Jewish teaching embodied in the Hebrew Bible and the Talmud [Late 16thC. From Hebrew *tôrāh* "law."]

tor·bern·ite /táwrbәr nìt/ *n.* a green mineral that is an ore of uranium. It occurs in platelike crystals in places where uranium and copper minerals have been altered. [Mid-19thC. Named for the Swedish chemist *Torbern* Olof Bergman (1735–84).]

torch /tawrch/ *n.* **1. BURNING STICK** a stick of wood dipped in wax or with one end wrapped in combustible material, set on fire and carried, especially in the past, as a source of light **2.** *U.K.* = **flashlight 3. DEVICE EMITTING FLAME** a portable device that emits an extremely hot flame, e.g., one used in welding or for stripping paint **4. SOURCE OF ENLIGHTENMENT** a source of guidance or enlightenment (*literary*) ■ *vt.* (**torched, torch·ing, torch·es**) **SET ON FIRE** to set fire to something, especially as an act of arson or terrorism (*slang*) [13thC. Via French *torche* from, ultimately, Latin *torques* "torque," from *torquere* "to twist." The French word earlier denoted a twist for burning.] ◇ **carry a torch for somebody** to be in love with somebody, especially when this feeling is secret or unrequited (*informal*)

torch·bear·er /táwrch bàirәr/ *n.* **1. SOMEBODY WHO CARRIES A TORCH** somebody who carries a torch, usually in a procession or ceremony **2. SOMEBODY WHO LEADS OR INSPIRES** somebody who provides leadership or inspiration (*literary*)

tor·chère *n.* a tall decorated stand for holding a candle or candelabrum [Early 20thC. From French, formed from *torche* "torch" (see TORCH).]

tor·chier /tawr sháir/, **tor·chiere** /tawr sheér/ *n.* a tall floor lamp that gives indirect upward lighting [Early 20thC. Variant of TORCHÈRE.]

torch·light /táwrch lìt/ *n.* **1. LIGHT OF TORCH** the light from a torch or torches **2.** = **torch** *n.* 1

tor·chon lace /táwr shòn-/ *n.* lace made from coarse linen or cotton, with a simple open pattern

torch song *n.* a popular sentimental song about unrequited love [From the idea of the torch as a symbol of unrequited love] —**torch sing·er** *n.*

torch·wood /táwrch wòòd/ *n.* **1.** TREES **RESINOUS FLORIDA TREE** a tree found in Florida and the West Indies whose resinous wood was once used to make torches. Genus: *Amyris*. **2.** INDUST **RESINOUS WOOD** the resinous wood of the torchwood tree

torch·y /táwrchee/ (**-i·er, -i·est**) *adj.* typical or reminiscent of popular sentimental songs about unrequited love (**torch songs**) (*informal*)

tore[1] past tense of **tear**

tore[2] /tawr/ *n.* ARCHIT = **torus** *n.* 2 [Mid-17thC. Via French from Latin *torus* "bulge."]

tor·e·a·dor /táwree ә dàwr/ *n.* a bullfighter, especially one on horseback [Early 17thC. From Spanish, formed from *torear* "to fight bulls," from *toro* "bull" (see TORERO).]

to·re·ro /tә rérrō/ (*plural* **-ros**) *n.* a bullfighter, especially one on foot [Early 18thC. From Spanish, formed from *toro* "bull," from Latin *taurus*.]

to·reu·tics /tә ròòtiks/ *n.* the art of making detailed reliefs in metal using the techniques of embossing and engraving (*takes a singular verb*) [Mid-19thC. Via Greek *toreutikos* from, ultimately, *toreus* "boring tool."] —**to·reu·tic** *adj.*

to·ri plural of **torus**

tor·ic /táwrik/ *adj.* ring- or doughnut-shaped like a torus, or relating to tori

tor·ic lens *n.* an eyeglass lens used to correct the vision of somebody with astigmatism. It is curved in such a way as to have a different focal length along each axis.

to·ri·i /táwree ee/ (*plural* **-i**) *n.* a form of gateway to a Japanese Shinto temple that has two posts and two crosspieces [Early 18thC. From Japanese, literally "bird's perch."]

tor·ment *vt.* /tawr mént/ (**-ment·ed, -ment·ing, -ments**) **1. INFLICT PAIN ON SOMEBODY OR SOMETHING** to inflict torture, pain, or anguish on somebody or something **2. TEASE SOMEBODY** to tease a person or an animal persistently **3. TWIST SOMETHING** to severely distort, twist, or wrench something (*archaic or literary*) ■ *n.* /táwr mènt/ **1. TORTURE** severe mental anguish or physical pain **2. CAUSE OF ANGUISH** a source of severe mental anguish or physical pain **3. CAUSE OF ANNOYANCE** a source of annoyance or anxiety [13thC. Via Old French from Latin *tormentum* "catapult, torment," from *torquere* "to twist."] —**tor·ment·ed·ly** /tawr méntәdlee/ *adv.* —**tor·ment·ing·ly** /tawr méntinglee/ *adv.*

tor·ment·er *n.* = **tormentor**

tor·men·til /táwrmәn tìl/ (*plural* **-tils** *or* **-til**) *n.* a downy plant of the rose family that has yellow flowers and an astringent root used in medicine, tanning, and dyeing. Latin name: *Potentilla erecta*. [14thC. Via French *tormentille* from, ultimately, Latin *tormentum* "torment" (see TORMENT).]

tor·men·tor /tawr méntәr/, **tor·ment·er** *n.* **1. CAUSE OF TORMENT** somebody who or something that causes somebody mental anguish, physical pain, annoyance, or anxiety **2.** THEATER **CURTAIN MASKING STAGE WINGS** a curtain or screen at either side of a theater stage that hides the wings from the audience **3.** CINEMA **ECHO-REDUCING DEVICE IN FILMING** a panel of sound-absorbent material used to eliminate echo on a movie set [13thC. Via Anglo-Norman *tormentour* and Old French *tormenteor* from, ultimately, Latin *tormentum* "to torment" (see TORMENT).]

torn past participle of **tear** ■ *adj.* UNDECIDED favoring or tending toward both options and therefore unable to choose between them

tor·na·do /tawr náydō/ (*plural* **-dos** *or* **-does**) *n.* **1.** COLUMN OF SWIRLING WIND an extremely destructive funnel-shaped rotating column of air that passes in a narrow path over land **2.** AFRICAN WIND a short-lived but severe windstorm, especially one that occurs on the West African coast **3.** FRANTIC PERSON OR STATE a state of frenzied activity or intense emotion, or somebody in such a state (*informal*) [Mid-16thC. Origin uncertain: probably an alteration of Spanish *tronada* "thunderstorm" from, ultimately, Latin *tonare* "to thunder."] —**tor·nad·ic** /tawr náydik, -náddik/ *adj.*

torn·il·lo /tawr neé yō, tàwr neélō/ (*plural* **-los**) *n.* = **screw bean** [Mid-19thC. Via American Spanish from Spanish, "screw," from, ultimately, Latin *tornus* "lathe" (see TURN).]

to·roid /táwr òyd, tṓr-/ *n.* GEOM = **torus** *n.* 1

To·ron·to /tə róntō/ capital city of Ontario Province, Canada, located on the northwestern shore of Lake Ontario. Population: 4,263,757 (1996). —**To·ron·to·ni·an** /tə ròn tṓnee ən, tàwrən-/ *n.*

to·rose /táw rṑss/, **to·rous** /táwr əss, tṓr-/ *adj.* cylindrical and knotted or bulging [Mid-18thC. From Latin *torosus* "brawny," from *torus* "bulge."] —**to·ros·i·ty** /taw róssətee/ *n.*

tor·pe·do /tawr peédō/ *n.* (*plural* **-does**) **1.** NAVY SELF-PROPELLED UNDERWATER WEAPON a cylindrical self-propelled missile that is launched from an aircraft, ship, or submarine and travels underwater to hit its target **2.** NAVY UNDERWATER MINE an underwater explosive mine (*dated*) **3.** FIREWORK a gravel-filled firework that explodes when thrown against a hard surface **4.** RAIL RAILROAD DANGER SIGNAL a detonating device placed on a railroad track that acts as a danger signal to the crew of a train that runs over it **5.** INDUST EXPLOSIVE FOR OIL WELLS an explosive device used to release the oil from an oil well **6.** FOOD SANDWICH a sandwich with a long roll cut horizontally **7.** ZOOL = **electric ray 8.** CRIMINOL PROFESSIONAL KILLER a hired thug or assassin (*slang*) ■ *vt.* (**-doed, -do·ing, -does**) **1.** NAVY HIT WITH TORPEDO to hit or destroy a ship with a torpedo **2.** DESTROY to spoil, thwart, or destroy something completely (*informal*) [Early 16thC. From Latin, "numbness," from *torpere* "to be stiff."]

tor·pe·do boat *n.* a small light fast boat used to launch torpedoes

tor·pe·do bomb·er *n.* an aircraft that carries and launches torpedoes

tor·pe·do tube *n.* a tube from which torpedoes are fired from submarines or ships

tor·pid /táwrpid/ *adj.* **1.** SLUGGISH lacking physical or mental energy **2.** BIOL DORMANT in a dormant state, especially when hibernating **3.** MED NUMB used to describe a part of the body that has lost the ability to move or feel [Early 17thC. From Latin *torpidus*, from *torpere* "to be stiff."] —**tor·pid·i·ty** /tawr píddətee/ *n.* —**tor·pid·ly** /táwrpidlee/ *adv.*

tor·por /táwrpər/ *n.* **1.** LACK OF ENERGY lack of mental or physical energy **2.** BIOL DORMANCY dormancy, especially in hibernation **3.** MED NUMBNESS absence of the ability to move or feel [13thC. From Latin, formed from *torpere* "to be stiff."] —**tor·por·if·ic** /tàwrpə ríffik/ *adj.*

torque[1] /tawrk/ *n.* **1.** PHYS ROTATING FORCE force that causes rotation, twisting, or turning, e.g., the force generated by an internal-combustion engine to turn a vehicle's drive shaft **2.** MECH ENG ABILITY TO OVERCOME RESISTANCE the measurement of the ability of a rotating gear or shaft to overcome turning resistance ■ *vt.* (**torqued, torquing, torques**) TURN SOMETHING UP to turn something, e.g., heat or air conditioning, up (*slang*) ○ *Can you torque up the heater? I'm freezing.* [Late 19thC. Formed from Latin *torquere* "to twist" (source of English *torture* and *torment*).]

torque[2] /tawrk/ *n.* a metal collar or armband worn by the ancient Gauls and Britons [Mid-19thC. Via French from Latin *torques* (see TORCH).]

torque con·vert·er *n.* a hydraulic coupling designed to change the mechanical advantage or torque speed between an input and an output shaft

Tor·que·ma·da /tàwrkay maáthaa, tàwrkə maádə/, **Tomás de** (1420–98) Spanish monk. As grand inquisitor for Spain (1483–98), he was notorious for his cruelty. He was largely responsible for the expulsion of the Jews from Spain (1492).

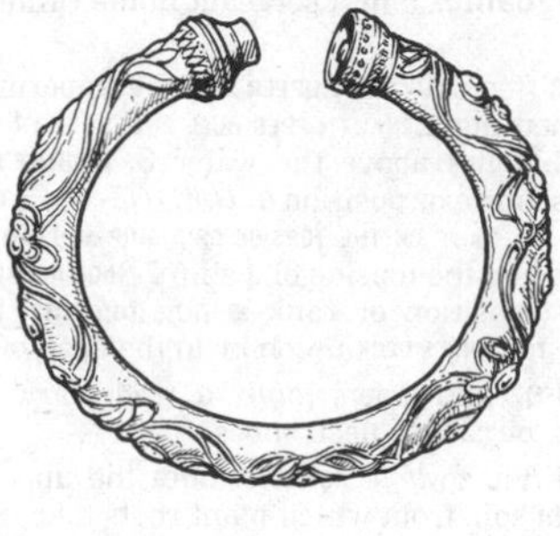

Torque

torques /tawrks/ (*plural* **torques**) *n.* a ring of color, hair, or feathers around the neck of an animal [Mid-16thC. From Latin *torques* "torque, collar" (see TORCH).]

torque wrench *n.* a wrench with a gauge attached for regulating the amount of torque applied to a bolt

torr /tawr/ (*plural* **torr**) *n.* a unit of pressure equal to about 133.3 pascals or one millimeter of mercury supported in a column [Mid-20thC. Named for Evangelista TORRICELLI.]

Tor·re del Gre·co /tòr ay del grékō/ coastal city near Naples, southern Italy, at the base of Mount Vesuvius. Population: 100,688 (1992).

tor·re·fy /táwrə fì/ (**-fied, -fy·ing, -fies**) *vt.* to subject something to intense heat, especially an ore or a chemical, for the purpose of removing excess water [Early 17thC. Via French *torréfier* from, ultimately, Latin *torrere* "to scorch."] —**tor·re·fac·tion** /tàwrə fákshən/ *n.*

Tor·re·mo·li·nos /tòr ay mə leén ōss/ major seaside resort in Malaga Province, Andalusia Autonomous Region, southern Spain

tor·rent /táwrənt/ *n.* **1.** RUSH OF LIQUID a fast and powerful rush of liquid, especially water **2.** TUMULTUOUS OUTPOURING a violent or tumultuous flow [Late 16thC. Via Latin *torrens* "hot, rushing" from, ultimately, *torrere* "to scorch."]

tor·ren·tial /taw rénshəl, tə-/ *adj.* **1.** FLOWING POWERFULLY flowing or falling fast and in great quantities ○ *torrential rain* **2.** INTENSE intense or abundant (*literary*) —**tor·ren·tial·ly** *adv.*

Tor·re·ón /tó ray òn, tò ray ón/ city in Coahuila State, northern Mexico, on the Nazas River. Population: 439,436 (1990).

Tor·ri·cel·li /tàwri chéllee/, **Evangelista** (1608–47) Italian mathematician and physicist. He invented the barometer and defined atmospheric pressure. A unit of pressure, the torr, is named for him.

tor·rid /táwrid/ *adj.* **1.** FULL OF PASSION full of passion, especially sexual passion **2.** SCORCHING HOT used to describe weather that is hot and dry enough to scorch land **3.** SCORCHED used to describe land that has been scorched by extremely hot and dry weather [Late 16thC. Via French *torride* or directly from Latin *torridus*, from *torrere* "to scorch."] —**tor·rid·i·ty** /taw ríddətee/ *n.* —**tor·rid·ly** /táwrədlee/ *adv.* —**tor·rid·ness** /táwrədnəss/ *n.*

Tor·rid Zone *n.* the region of the earth that lies between the Tropics of Cancer and Capricorn

Tor·ri·jos Her·re·ra /taw reéhawss er rérraa/, **Omar** (1929–81) Panamanian general and statesman. He headed a dictatorship (1968–81) that promoted the interests of less-privileged classes.

tor·sade /tawr saád, -sáyd/ *n.* a decorative twist of beads, cord, or fabric [Late 19thC. Via French from, ultimately, an alteration of Latin *tortus* "twisted" (see TORSION).]

Tórs·hav·n /táwrz haav'n/ town and administrative center of the Faroe Islands, Denmark, situated on the island of Streymoy. Population: 15,272 (1995).

tor·si plural of **torso**

tor·si·bil·i·ty /tàwrsə bíllətee/ *n.* the ability to undergo or resist twisting [Mid-19thC. Formed from TORSION + -IBILITY.]

tor·sion /táwrsh'n/ *n.* **1.** TWISTING OF AN OBJECT the twisting of an object by applying equal and opposite torques to its ends **2.** MECHANICAL STRESS the stress placed on an object that has been twisted **3.** TWISTING the twisting of something, or a twisted state (*technical*) [15thC. Via French from, ultimately, Latin *tortus*, the past participle of *torquere* "to twist."]—**tor·sion·al** *adj.* —**tor·sion·al·ly** *adv.*

tor·sion bal·ance *n.* an instrument that measures small electric or magnetic forces by the degree of twist they produce in a filament

tor·sion bar *n.* a metal bar that acts as a spring when subjected to torsion, e.g., in a motor vehicle's suspension system

torsk /tawrsk/ (*plural* **torsks** *or* **torsk**) *n.* *U.K.* ZOOL = **cusk** [Early 18thC. Via Norwegian from Old Norse *þorskr.*]

tor·so /táwrsō/ (*plural* **-sos** *or* **-si** /táwrsee/) *n.* **1.** ANAT UPPER BODY the upper part of the human body, not including the head and arms **2.** SCULPTURE SCULPTURE a sculpture of a torso, or a broken statue of a human figure, with the head, arms, and legs missing **3.** SOMETHING WITH PARTS MISSING something that has parts missing, either because it has been mutilated or because it has not been completed (*literary*) [Late 18thC. Via Italian, "trunk of a statue," from Latin *thyrsus* (see THYRSUS).]

tort /tawrt/ *n.* in civil law, a wrongful act for which damages can be sought by the injured party [14thC. Via Old French from medieval Latin *tortum* from, ultimately, Latin *torquere* "to twist."]

torte /tawrt/ *n.* a very rich cake consisting of layers sandwiched together with a cream filling [Mid-18thC. Via German *Torte* from Italian *torta* "cake" from late Latin, a type of bread.]

tor·tel·li·ni /tàwrtə leénee/ *npl.* small filled pasta that is shaped into rings, boiled, and served in a soup or sauce [Mid-20thC. From Italian, the plural of *tortellino*, literally "little cake," from *torta* "cake."]

tor·ti·col·lis /tàwrtə kólliss/ *n.* a twisting of the neck to one side, resulting in the head being tilted. It can be temporary, caused by muscle spasm, or a permanent result of a structural condition, e.g., a short neck muscle. [Early 19thC. From modern Latin, formed from Latin *tortus* "twisted" (see TORSION) + *collum* "neck."] —**tor·ti·col·lar** *adj.*

tor·til·la /tawr teéyə/ (*plural* **-las**) *n.* a thin flat Mexican bread made with either corn meal or wheat flour, cooked on a hot griddle and eaten folded, with a filling of beans, cheese, or ground meat [Late 17thC. From Spanish, formed from *torta* "cake," from late Latin, a type of bread.]

tor·til·la chip *n.* a thin crunchy chip made of corn meal, often served with dips, e.g., salsa or guacamole

tor·tious /táwrshəss/ *adj.* involving or constituting a tort in civil law —**tor·tious·ly** *adv.*

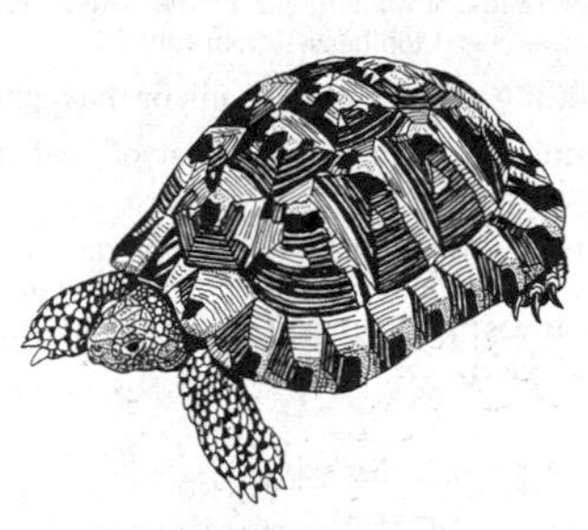

Tortoise

tor·toise /táwrtəss/ *n.* **1.** REPTILE WITH SHELL a slow-moving land-dwelling reptile with a large dome-shaped shell into which it can retract its head and limbs. Family: Testudinidae. **2.** MIL, HIST = **testudo 3.** SLOW MOVER somebody who moves very slowly [15thC. Alteration of obsolete *tortuce* from medieval Latin *tortuca* from late Latin *tartaruchus* "of Tarturus" (see TURTLE).]

tor·toise bee·tle *n.* a brightly colored beetle that has a flat rounded body and whose larvae eat leaves. Subfamily: Cassidinae.

tor·toise·shell /táwrtəss shèl/, **tor·toise shell** *n.* **1.** ZOOL OUTER PART OF TURTLE SHELL the hard mottled outer layer of the shell of a hawksbill turtle, used to make combs, ornaments, and jewelry **2.** INDUST SYNTHETIC TORTOISESHELL a synthetic substance made to resemble tortoiseshell **3.** ZOOL TYPE OF CAT a type of domestic cat with black, cream, and brownish markings **4.** INSECTS ORANGE-BROWN BUTTERFLY a butterfly that has jagged orange-brown wings with black markings. Family: Nymphalidae. **5.** ZOOL = **hawksbill** ■ *adj.*

tor·toise·shell, tor·toise-shell COLORS **MOTTLED YELLOW AND BROWN** with mottled yellow and brown markings

tor·to·ni /tawr tṓnee/ *n.* rich Italian ice cream often flavored with sherry or rum and chopped cherries or almonds [Early 20thC. Origin uncertain: probably named for an Italian café-owner of 18thC Paris.]

tor·tri·cid /táwrtrəssid/ *n.* any of a family of small moths whose larvae live in coiled leaves and are often destructive to plants. Family: Tortricidae. [Late 19thC. Coined from modern Latin *tortrix*, genus name (from Latin *tortus* "twisted"; see TORSION) + -ID.]

Tor·tu·ga Is·land /tawr to͝ogə-/ island in northern Haiti, in the West Indies. Population: 22,880 (1982). Area: 70 sq. mi./180 sq. km.

tor·tu·os·i·ty /tàwrchoo óssətee/ (*plural* **-ties**) *n.* **1. TWISTEDNESS** the state of being twisted or crooked **2. BEND** a twist or turn

tor·tu·ous /táwrchoo əss/ *adj.* **1. TWISTING AND WINDING** with many turns or bends **2. INTRICATE** extremely complex or intricate **3. DEVIOUS** devious or deceitful [14thC. Via Anglo-Norman from Latin *tortuosus* from, ultimately, *torquere* "to twist."] —**tor·tu·ous·ly** *adv.* —**tor·tu·ous·ness** *n.*

WORD KEY: USAGE

tortuous or **torturous**? Even though both words come ultimately from a Latin word meaning "twist," their meanings diverge in English. A mountain pass is ***tortuous*** ("twisting, winding"), and by figurative extension, a legal argument can be ***tortuous*** ("circuitous, devious") as well. A severe illness is ***torturous*** ("agonizing, painful"), and by figurative extension, a ***torturous*** decision is one that is highly painful, even agonizing, to make.

tor·ture /táwrchər/ *n.* **1. INFLICTING OF PAIN** the inflicting of severe physical pain on somebody, e.g., as punishment or to persuade somebody to confess or recant something **2. METHODS OF INFLICTING PAIN** the methods used to inflict physical pain on people **3. ANGUISH** mental or physical anguish ■ *vt.* (**-tured, -tur·ing, -tures**) **1. INFLICT PAIN ON SOMEBODY** to inflict extreme pain or physical punishment on people **2. CAUSE SOMEBODY ANGUISH** to cause somebody mental or physical anguish ○ *This headache is torturing me.* **3. DISTORT SOMETHING** to twist or distort something into an unnatural form [Mid-16thC. Via French from, ultimately, Latin *tortus* "twisted" (see TORSION).] —**tor·tur·er** *n.* —**tor·tur·ing·ly** *adv.*

tor·tur·ous /táwrchərəss/ *adj.* **1. INFLICTING PAIN** inflicting, or designed to inflict, severe physical pain, e.g., as punishment **2. CAUSING ANGUISH** causing great physical or mental anguish [15thC. Via Anglo-Norman, from *torture* "torture," from, ultimately, Latin *torquere* "to twist."] —**tor·tur·ous·ly** *adv.*

WORD KEY: USAGE

See Usage note at ***tortuous***.

tor·u·la /táwryələ, táwrələ/ (*plural* **-lae** /táwryə lèe, -lī, táwrə-/ *or* **-las**) *n.* **1. tor·u·la, tor·u·la yeast NUTRITIOUS YEAST** an edible yeast that is cultivated for use as a medicine and food additive. Latin name: *Candida utilis.* **2. FUNGUS** a yeast fungus that does not have sexual spores. Many of them grow on dead vegetation and fermented sugars. Genus: *Torula.* [Mid-19thC. From modern Latin, genus name, formed from Latin *torus* "bulge."]

to·rus /táwrəss/ (*plural* **-ri** /-rī/) *n.* **1.** GEOM **RING-SHAPED SURFACE** a doughnut-shaped geometric surface generated by rotating a circle about a line in the same plane as the circle but not intersecting it **2.** ARCHIT **MOLDING** a large convex molding, especially at the base of a classical column **3.** ANAT **RIDGED BODY PART** a body part in the shape of a rounded ridge or bulge, e.g., the bony ridge below an eyebrow **4.** BOT **FLOWER PART** the receptacle of a flower [Mid-16thC. From Latin, "bulge."]

To·ry /táwree/ (*plural* **-ries**) *n.* **1. AMERICAN SUPPORTER OF BRITAIN** a resident of the American colonies who supported Britain during the American Revolution **2. BRITISH CONSERVATIVE** in Britain, a member of the Conservative and Unionist Party **3. CANADIAN CONSERVATIVE** in Canada, a member of the Progressive Conservative Party **4. ENGLISH ROYALIST** a member of an English political party, active from the late 17th century until the 1830s, that supported the social order represented by the monarchy and the Church of England **5. To·ry, to·ry SUPPORTER OF CONSERVATIVE PRINCIPLES** somebody who holds politically conservative or reactionary views **6. 17THC IRISH OUTLAW** in 17th century Ireland, any of the Irish people who became outlaws harrying the English settlers who had displaced and dispossessed them [Mid-17thC. Via Irish *tóraidhe* "highwayman," from Old Irish *tóir* "chase."] —**To·ry** *adj.* —**To·ry·ism** *n.*

WORD KEY: ORIGIN

In English ***Tory*** originally denoted an Irish guerrilla, one of a group of Irishmen who in the 1640s were thrown off their property by the British and took to a life of harrying and plundering the British occupiers. In the 1670s it was applied as a term of abuse to Irish Catholic royalists, and then more generally to supporters of the Catholic James II, and after 1689 it came to be used for the members of the British political party that had at first opposed the removal of James and his replacement with the Protestants William and Mary.

To·sa Mit·su·no·bu /tṓsaa mìtsoo nṓboo/ (1434–1525) Japanese artist. Founder of a school of painting, he is known for his portrait of Emperor En-yu (1492).

Tos·ca·ni·ni /tòskə néenee/, **Arturo** (1867–1957) Italian-born conductor. He was conductor at La Scala opera house, Milan, and the Metropolitan Opera, New York, and also conducted the NBC Symphony Orchestra (1937–57).

toss /toss/ *v.* (**tossed, toss·ing, toss·es**) **1.** *vt.* **LIGHTLY THROW SOMETHING** to lightly throw something, especially with the palm of the hand upward ○ *tossed the letter on the table* **2.** *vti.* **THROW OR BE THROWN UP AND DOWN** to be thrown, or throw something, repeatedly sup and down or to and fro ○ *tossed by the waves* **3.** *vti.* **THROW COIN** to throw a coin upward, usually spinning it with the thumb on the way, the side it falls on being a way of deciding between two options **4.** *vt.* **MIX SOMETHING** to mix something, especially a salad with its dressing, by lifting and turning its parts rather than by stirring **5.** *vt.* EQU **THROW RIDER** to throw the rider of a horse or other animal off its back **6.** *vt.* **HURL UPWARD** to hurl somebody or something upward with apparent ease **7.** *vt.* **JERK HEAD UPWARD** to jerk the head upward, e.g., in a gesture of anger or impatience **8.** *vi.* **MOVE RESTLESSLY** to move about restlessly, especially in sleep ■ *n.* **1. THROWING** an act of throwing somebody or something **2. HEAD JERK** an abrupt jerk of the head **3. DECIDING THROW OF COIN** a spinning of a coin in the air as a method of deciding between two options [Early 16thC. Origin unknown.] ◇ **toss your cookies** to vomit (*slang*)

WORD KEY: SYNONYMS

See Synonyms at ***throw***.

toss off *vt.* **1. DO SOMETHING QUICKLY** to do something quickly and easily **2. toss off, toss down DRINK SOMETHING QUICKLY** to drink something quickly, often in one gulp

toss·pot /tóss pòt/ *n.* a drunken person (*archaic or literary*)

toss-up /tóss ùp/ *n.* **1. DECIDING THROW OF A COIN** a throw of a coin into the air that decides, by which side it falls on, between two options **2. EVEN CHANCE** an even risk or chance

tos·ta·da /tō staádə/, **tos·ta·do** /tō staádō/ *n.* a crisply fried Mexican-style tortilla, usually served with several meat and vegetable toppings [Mid-20thC. From Spanish, formed from the past participle of *tostar* "to toast."]

tot /tot/ *n.* **1. LITTLE CHILD** a small child (*informal*) **2. SMALL AMOUNT** a small amount of something, especially liquor [Early 18thC. Origin unknown.]

to·tal /tṓt'l/ *n.* **SUM** the sum of several amounts added or considered together ■ *adj.* **1. USED FOR EMPHASIS** used to emphasize how good, bad, or complete something is ○ *a total success* **2. OVERALL** with all elements added or considered together ○ *the total price* ■ *vt.* (**-taled, -tal·ing, -tals**) **1. ADD TOGETHER** to add several amounts together to arrive at a total **2. AMOUNT TO TOTAL** to amount to a total when added or considered together ○ *The numbers totaled in the hundreds.* **3. KILL OR DESTROY** to kill, destroy, wreck, or demolish somebody or something (*slang*) [14thC. Via Old French from medieval Latin *totalis*, from Latin *totus* "entire."]

to·tal e·clipse *n.* an eclipse in which the entire surface of a celestial body, e.g., the Sun or the Moon, is obscured

to·tal heat *n.* PHYS = **enthalpy**

to·tal in·ter·nal re·flec·tion *n.* the complete reflection of a light ray at the boundary of the medium in which it is traveling, when the angle of incidence exceeds the critical angle

to·tal·i·tar·i·an /tō tàllə táiree ən/ *adj.* **CENTRALIZED AND DICTATORIAL** relating to or operating a centralized government system in which a single party without opposition rules over political, economic, social, and cultural life ■ *n.* **SUPPORTER OF A TOTALITARIAN SYSTEM** somebody who advocates or operates a totalitarian system [Early 20thC. Formed from TOTALITY on the model of AUTHORITARIAN.] —**to·tal·i·tar·i·an·ism** *n.*

to·tal·i·ty /tō tállətee/ (*plural* **-ties**) *n.* **1. COMPLETENESS** the state of being complete or total **2. TOTAL AMOUNT** the sum or total amount of something **3.** ASTRON **FULLNESS OF ECLIPSE** the stage of an eclipse at which light is completely obscured

to·tal·i·za·tor /tṓt'lə zàytər/ *n.* a machine that records and calculates totals, especially one that records bets, odds, and totals, and calculates winnings in the pari-mutuel betting system [Late 19thC. Formed from TOTALIZE + -ATOR, modeled on French *totalisateur.*]

to·tal·ize /tṓt'l ìz/ (**-ized, -iz·ing, -iz·es**) *vt.* to add several amounts to make a total —**to·tal·i·za·tion** /tṓt'li záysh'n/ *n.*

to·tal·iz·er /tṓt'l ìzər/ *n.* = **totalizator**

to·tal·ly /tṓt'lee/ *adv.* **1. COMPLETELY** in a complete or utter way **2. USED FOR EMPHASIS** used to emphasize how good, bad, or complete something is (*informal*) ○ *I totally hate this!*

to·tal re·call *n.* the ability to remember accurately in every detail

to·tal re·flec·tion *n.* = **total internal reflection**

to·ta·quine /tṓtə kween/ *n.* a mixture of quinine and other alkaloids from cinchona bark, used to treat malaria [Mid-20thC. From modern Latin *totaquina*, from Latin *totus* "whole" + Spanish *quina* "cinchona bark," because all the essential alkaloids are contained in the bark.]

tote[1] /tōt/ *vt.* (**tot·ed, tot·ing, totes**) (*informal*) **1. CARRY** to carry or haul something, especially something heavy **2. HAVE ON YOUR PERSON** to carry something, especially a gun, on your person ■ *n.* **HEAVY LOAD** a heavy load that is hauled or carried [Late 17thC. Origin uncertain: perhaps originally a dialect form of Gullah *tot* "to carry," probably from a West African language.] —**tot·er** *n.*

WORD KEY: REGIONAL NOTE

Tote in the sense "to carry" is a general currency term throughout the Southern states. Probably of West African origin, the form extends across the South Midland region as well, including western reflexes, or similar forms, in the Rocky Mountain states.

tote[2] /tōt/ *n.* = **pari-mutuel** (*informal*) [Late 19thC. Shortening of TOTALIZATOR.]

tote[3] /tōt/ (**tot·ed, tot·ing, totes**) *vt.* to add things up (*informal*) [Late 19thC. Shortening of TOTAL.]

tote bag *n.* a soft open bag with handles, often made of canvas, leather, plastic, or straw

tote board *n.* a large electronically operated board displaying statistics, e.g., betting odds or voting results

to·tem /tṓtəm/ *n.* **1. IMPORTANT TRIBAL OBJECT** an object, animal, plant, or other natural phenomenon revered as a symbol of a tribe and often used in rituals among some tribal or other traditional groups of people **2. CARVING** a carving or other representation of a totem **3. SYMBOLIC THING** something regarded as a symbol, especially something treated with the kind of respect normally reserved for religious icons [Mid-18thC. From Ojibwa *nindoodem* "my totem."] —**to·tem·ic** /tō témmik/ *adj.*

to·tem·ism /tṓtə mìzzəm/ *n.* **1. USE OF TOTEMS** the use of totems as symbols of kinship **2. SOCIAL ORGANIZATION** the organizing of societies into groups whose members share a common totem —**to·tem·ist** *n.* —**to·tem·is·tic** /tōtə místik/ *adj.*

to·tem pole *n.* **1. CARVED POLE** among some Native North American peoples, a tall wooden pole carved with totems that symbolize family and historical relationships **2. HIERARCHY** a hierarchy, e.g., in a company or organization (*informal*)

toth·er /tú*th*ər/, **t'oth·er** *adj., pron.* the other or that other (*regional*) [14thC. Contraction of *the other.*]

to·ti·pal·mate /tṓti pál màyt/ *adj.* used to describe birds that have all four toes webbed, e.g., pelicans and gannets [Late 19thC. Coined from Latin *totus* "whole" + PALMATE.] —**to·ti·pal·ma·tion** /tṓti pal máysh'n/ *n.*

Totem pole

to·tip·o·tent /tō típpətənt/ *adj.* used to describe a cell, e.g., a fertilized ovum, that is capable of generating new tissue, organs, or individuals [Early 20thC. Coined from Latin *totus* "whole" + POTENT.] —**to·tip·o·ten·cy** *n.*

tot·siens *interj.* *S Africa* used as a friendly farewell greeting (*informal*) [Mid-20thC. From Afrikaans, literally "till seeing."]

tot·ter /tóttər/ *vi.* (**-tered, -ter·ing, -ters**) **1. WALK UNSTEADILY** to move or walk unsteadily **2. WOBBLE** to sway or wobble as if about to fall **3. BE UNSTABLE** to be unstable or on the point of collapse ○ *an economic system tottering on the brink of collapse* ■ *n.* **WOBBLING GAIT** a wavering or wobbling gait [13thC. Origin uncertain; perhaps from Scandinavian.] —**tot·ter·er** *n.* —**tot·ter·ing·ly** *adv.* —**tot·ter·y** *adj.*

Toucan

tou·can /to͞o kàn/ (*plural* **-cans** *or* **-can**) *n.* a fruit-eating bird with bright plumage and a very large curved beak. It is native to the tropics of Central and South America. Family: Ramphastidae. [Mid-16thC. Via French from Portuguese *tucano*, from, ultimately, Tupi *tucan*, of uncertain origin: probably an imitation of the bird's call.]

touch /tuch/ *v.* (**touched, touch·ing, touch·es**) **1.** *vti.* **PUT THE BODY IN CONTACT WITH SOMETHING** to put a part of the body, especially the fingertips, in contact with something so as to feel it **2.** *vti.* **BE OR PUT IN CONTACT** to be in, or bring something into, physical contact with an object ○ *so that the ends are just touching* **3.** *vt.* **PRESS SOMETHING LIGHTLY** to apply the slightest pressure to something ○ *You only have to touch the brake.* **4.** *vt.* **INTERFERE WITH SOMETHING** to interfere with or disturb something by handling it ○ *told the kids not to touch anything on my desk* **5.** *vt.* **HAVE AN EFFECT ON** to have an effect or influence on somebody or something ○ *events that touched all our lives* **6.** *vt.* **AFFECT SOMEBODY EMOTIONALLY** to affect somebody emotionally, usually arousing gratitude, affection, pity, or compassion ○ *Your concern for my welfare touches me greatly.* **7.** *vt.* **CONSUME SOMETHING** to consume something, especially food or drink, or otherwise make use of something ○ *You've hardly touched your meal.* **8.** *vt.* **HAVE DEALINGS WITH SOMETHING** to have dealings or become involved with something ○ *Don't touch that issue; it's very controversial.* **9.** *vt.* **MATCH SOMEBODY OR SOMETHING** to come close to somebody or something in level of excellence ○ *Others may have more technique, but nobody can touch her style.* **10.** *vt.* **APPROACH A LEVEL** to approach or reach a level ○ *profits touching 2 billion* **11.** *vt.* **APPROACH SOMEBODY FOR MONEY** to ask somebody for a loan or gift of money (*slang*) ■ *n.* **1. FEELING SENSE** the sense by which the texture, shape, and other qualities of objects are felt through contact with parts of the body, especially the fingertips ○ *the sense of touch* **2. FELT QUALITIES** the quality or combination of qualities experienced through the sensation of touch **3. CONTACT MADE** a coming into contact with a part of the body ○ *felt the touch of her hand on my face* **4. LIGHT STROKE** a light pushing or pressing stroke **5. SMALL AMOUNT** a small but noticeable amount ○ *a touch of malice in her voice* **6. DISTINCTIVE STYLE** a distinctive style or general facility in doing something ○ *a sure touch* **7. DETAIL** a detail that adds to or completes something **8. ATTACK OF ILLNESS** a mild attack of an illness or disease ○ *a touch of bronchitis* **9. COMMUNICATION** the fact of getting into communication, or the state of being in communication ○ *I completely lost touch with my brother.* ○ *Keep in touch.* **10. LENDER OF MONEY** somebody considered in terms of his or her willingness to lend money (*slang*) ○ *He's always been a soft touch.* **11. REQUEST FOR MONEY** an act of asking for money or a sum of money given (*slang*) **12.** SPORTS **AREA OUT OF PLAY** in some team sports, the area beyond the touchlines in which the ball is out of play **13.** FENCING **FENCING SCORE** in competitive fencing, a scoring hit delivered to a specified part of an opponent's body [13thC. Via Old French *to(u)chier* from assumed Vulgar Latin *toccare* "to strike," originally "to make a sound by striking" (the probable source of English *toccata*), perhaps of imitative origin.] —**touch·a·bil·i·ty** /tùchə bíllətee/ *n.* —**touch·a·ble** /túchəb'l/ *adj.* —**touch·a·ble·ness** /túchəb'lnəss/ *n.* —**touch·er** /túchər/ *n.* ◇ **be touch and go** to be highly uncertain or precarious

touch down *vi.* to land in an aircraft or spacecraft

touch off *vt.* **1. MAKE SOMETHING EXPLODE** to make something explode, especially by touching it with a flame or smoldering match **2. INITIATE SOMETHING** to make something begin, especially something that is difficult to control ○ *touched off a bitter disagreement between them*

touch up *vt.* **1. IMPROVE SOMETHING** to make slight improvements to something, e.g., with paint **2. FALSIFY SOMETHING** to make changes to something, especially a photograph, so that it is no longer an accurate representation (*disapproving*)

touch-and-go *adj.* highly uncertain or unpredictable (*not hyphenated when used after a verb*) ○ *a touch-and-go situation*

touch·back /túch bàk/ *n.* a play in football in which the defense recovers and downs a ball that has been kicked or passed into its end zone

touch·down /túch dòwn/ *n.* **1.** FOOTBALL **SCORING PLAY** in football, a scoring of six points achieved by being in possession of the ball behind an opponent's goal line **2.** AEROSP **LANDING** a landing made by an aircraft or spacecraft, or the precise moment when it lands

tou·ché /too sháy/ *interj.* **1.** FENCING **ACKNOWLEDGMENT OF A SCORING HIT** a word used to acknowledge that an opponent has made a scoring hit **2. ACKNOWLEDGMENT OF A TELLING REMARK** a word used to acknowledge that somebody has made an especially witty, penetrating, or cogent remark, usually in retaliation [Early 20thC. From French *touché*, past participle of *toucher* "to touch," from Old French *touchier* (see TOUCH).]

touched /tucht/ *adj.* **1. AFFECTED EMOTIONALLY** affected emotionally, usually with gratitude, affection, pity, or compassion **2. MODIFIED BY SOMETHING** slightly marked or modified by something (*literary*) ○ *blond hair touched with gray*

touch foot·ball *n.* an informal noncompetitive version of football in which touching replaces tackling

touch·hole /túch hòl/ *n.* the opening in the breech of an early cannon or gun where a flame or smoldering material was applied to set off the gunpowder

touch·ing /túching/ *adj.* **CAUSING EMOTIONS** giving rise to feelings of sympathy, tenderness, or tearfulness ■ *prep.* **ABOUT** concerning or relating to something (*archaic or literary*) —**touch·ing·ly** *adv.* —**touch·ing·ness** *n.*

touch·line /túch lìn/ *n.* either of the lines that mark the side boundaries of a playing area, especially in soccer

touch·mark /túch maàrk/ *n.* a mark stamped on something made of pewter that identifies the maker

touch-me-not *n.* **1.** = **jewelweed 2.** = **sensitive plant** *n.* 1 [Late 16thC. Translated from Latin *noli me tangere*.]

touch pad *n.* an electronic device, e.g., an input device in a computer system or a control panel on a microwave oven, on which somebody can choose options by touching the display

touch screen *n.* a computer screen that displays options that a user can choose by touching it with a finger

touch·stone /túch stōn/ *n.* **1. EXCELLENT EXAMPLE** a standard by which something is judged **2.** METALL **STONE USED TO TEST GOLD** a hard black stone formerly used to test the purity of gold and silver according to the color of the streak left when the metal was rubbed against it [Translation of Old French *touchepierre*]

touch sys·tem *n.* a method of typing in which the typist finds the keys with his or her fingers without looking at the keyboard

touch-tone, touch·tone /túch tōn/ *adj.* used to describe a type of telephone with keys that produce tones when pressed, each of which is decoded as a number at the telephone exchange

touch-type *vi.* to type without having to look at the keyboard —**touch-typ·ist** *n.*

touch-up /túch ùp/ *n.* **1. IMPROVEMENT** an improvement to something such as makeup or paintwork **2. ALTERATION** an alteration, especially one made to cover up or repair a flaw

touch·wood /túch wo͝od/ *n.* dry decayed wood that can be used as tinder

touch·y /túchee/ (**-i·er, -i·est**) *adj.* **1. EASILY UPSET** liable to become, or make somebody, angry or upset ○ *a touchy subject* **2. TRICKY** needing care or tact to prevent an undesirable outcome **3. FLAMMABLE** easily catching fire **4. SENSITIVE TO TOUCH** very sensitive to being touched —**touch·i·ly** *adv.* —**touch·i·ness** *n.*

touch·y-feel·y /tùchee féelee/ *adj.* (*informal*) **1. DEMONSTRATIVE** physically and emotionally demonstrative, e.g., in hugging other people or crying openly, often in a way that is considered excessive **2. ENCOURAGING DEMONSTRATIVENESS** encouraging demonstrativeness, especially in losing inhibitions about touching other people and the free expression of emotions

tough /tuf/ *adj.* **1. DURABLE** able to withstand much use, strain, or wear without breaking, tearing, or other damage ○ *boots made of tough leather* **2.** FOOD **HARD TO CHEW OR CUT** not easily chewed or cut ○ *This steak is pretty tough.* **3. VERY STRONG** physically or mentally strong and possessing great endurance ○ *Is he tough enough to make the climb?* **4. THREATENING** characterized by antisocial behavior, crime, and social deprivation ○ *a tough neighborhood* **5. RESOLUTE** having or showing firm resolve ○ *She's a tough person to negotiate with.* **6. DIFFICULT** difficult to do or deal with, or needing great effort to do ○ *That's a tough question.* **7. SEVERE** involving or inflicting severe punishment or strict rules ○ *the police policy of being tough on drink-driving* **8. HARD TO ENDURE** unfortunate or hard to bear (*informal*) ○ *a tough break* **9. GREAT** perceived as being the best or most wonderful (*dated slang*) ○ *an album with some tough sounds* ■ *n.* **THUG** an aggressive or antisocial person ■ *adv.* **AGGRESSIVELY** in an aggressive way that makes the person appear to be strong, forceful, and unafraid (*informal*) ○ *act tough* ■ *interj.* **BAD LUCK!** used to comment that something is unfortunate but cannot be helped, and often that the speaker does not really care that this is so [Old English *tōh*, of prehistoric Germanic origin] —**tough·ly** *adv.* ◇ **tough it out** to be strong and hold out during a time of difficulty (*informal*)

WORD KEY: SYNONYMS

See Synonyms at ***hard***.

tough·en /túff'n/ (**-ened, -en·ing, -ens**) *vti.* **1. MAKE OR BECOME TOUGHER** to become, or make something, less easy to cut or chew or less liable to wear or damage **2. MAKE OR BECOME STRONGER** to become, or make somebody, more resolute, hardier, or physically or emotionally stronger **3. MAKE OR BECOME MORE SEVERE** to become, or make somebody or something, stricter or more severe —**tough·en·er** *n.*

tough·ie /túffee/ *n.* (*informal*) **1. SOMETHING DIFFICULT** something that is difficult to deal with **2. TOUGH PERSON** a tough person, especially a child, regarded with some affection or amusement because he or she is rather self-assertive and resilient

tough love *n.* a caring but strict attitude adopted toward a friend or loved one with a problem, as distinct from an attitude of indulgence

tough-mind·ed *adj.* able to face hardship and misfortunes in a realistic, determined, and unsentimental way —**tough-mind·ed·ly** *adv.* —**tough-mind·ed·ness** *n.*

tough·ness /túfnəss/ *n.* **1. STATE OF BEING TOUGH** the fact or quality of being tough **2.** METALL **RESISTANCE OF A METAL TO STRESS** the resistance of a metal to breaking under repeated twisting and bending forces, measured in kilojoules

Tou·lon /too lóN/ city, port, and naval base in southeastern France, on the Mediterranean Sea. Population: 170,167 (1990).

Tou·louse /too lo͞oz/ capital city of Haute-Garonne Department, Languedoc-Roussillon Region, southern France. Population: 365,933 (1990).

Henri de Toulouse-Lautrec

Tou·louse-Lau·trec /too lo͞oz lō trék/, **Henri de** (1864–1901) French artist. He is noted especially for his portraits, paintings of Paris nightlife, and posters advertising Parisian artists. Full name **Henri Marie Raymond de Toulouse-Lautrec-Monta**

tou·pee /too páy/ *n.* **1. WIG** a wig or partial wig worn to cover a bald area **2. TUFT ON A WIG** a prominent lock or tuft on a wig (*archaic*) [Early 18thC. Alteration of French *toupet* "tuft of hair," from, ultimately, a prehistoric Germanic word meaning "topknot."]

tour /toor/ *n.* **1.** LEISURE **PLEASURE TRIP** a journey visiting several places, usually taken for pleasure, e.g., on vacation **2.** ARTS **PERFORMING TRIP** a long series of performances in different places, e.g., by a rock band or a theater company **3.** SPORTS **PLAYING TRIP** a series of games or tournaments played by the same team in different places, often overseas **4. BRIEF TRIP TO SEE SOMETHING** a short trip, especially for the purpose of viewing or inspecting different items **5. PERIOD OF DUTY** a period of duty, especially in a particular place or for a specific length of time ■ *vti.* (**toured, tour·ing, tours**) **TAKE PART IN A TOUR** to take part in a tour, for some purpose or of a specified place [14thC. Via Old French from Latin *tornus* "lathe"; the underlying meaning is "circular movement."]

tou·ra·co /to͝orə kō/ (*plural* **-cos**), **tu·ra·co** (*plural* **-cos**) *n.* an African bird resembling the cuckoo that has brightly colored feathers and a long tail. Touracos are found in dense forest. They are weak flyers and hop around branches. Family: Musophagidae. [Mid-18thC. Via French *touraco* from a West African language.]

tour de force /to͝or də fáwrss/ (*plural* **tours de force** /to͝or də fáwrss/) *n.* something done with supreme skill or brilliance [Early 19thC. From French, "feat of strength."]

tour·er /to͝orər/ *n.* = **touring car**

Tou·rette syn·drome /to͞o rét-/, **Tou·rette's syn·drome** *n.* a condition in which somebody experiences multiple tics and twitches, and utters involuntary vocal grunts and obscene speech [Late 19thC. Named for Gilles de la *Tourette* (1857–1904), the French neurologist who identified the condition.]

tour·ing car *n.* a convertible car, popular in the 1920s, designed for long-distance leisure driving

tour·ing com·pa·ny *n.* a theater company that takes part in performing tours rather than performing solely in one venue

tour·ism /to͝or ìzzəm/ *n.* **1.** LEISURE **TRAVEL FOR PLEASURE** the visiting of places away from home for pleasure **2.** BUSINESS **TRAVEL BUSINESS** the business of organizing travel and services for people traveling for pleasure

tour·ist /to͝orist/ *n.* somebody who visits places away from home for pleasure —**tour·is·tic** /toor ístik/ *adj.* —**tour·ist·y** /to͝oristee/ *adj.*

tour·ist class, **tour·ist** *n.* the cheapest class of accommodation on an aircraft or ship

tour·ma·line /to͝orməlin, -leen/ *n.* a hard crystalline borosilicate mineral with a range of compositions, used in electrical and optical devices and, in green, pink, blue, and black varieties, as semiprecious gemstones [Mid-18thC. From, ultimately, Sinhalese *toramalli* "cornelian."] —**tour·ma·lin·ic** /to͝ormə línnik/ *adj.*

Tour·nai /toor náy/ city in Hainault Province, southwestern Belgium. Population: 67,939 (1996).

tour·na·ment /to͝ornəmənt, túrnəmənt/ *n.* **1.** SPORTS **SERIES OF GAMES** a sports event made up of a series of games, rounds, or contests **2.** HIST **MOCK FIGHTING** a sporting contest popular in the Middle Ages in which knights took part in jousting or combat, generally with blunted weapons [12thC. From Old French *torneiement*, literally "act of jousting," from *torneier* (see TOURNEY). The sense "series of games" came into use in the mid-18thC.]

tour·ne·dos /to͝ornə dō/ (*plural* **-dos**) *n.* a small round cut of fillet steak [Late 19thC. From French, from *tourner* "to turn" + *dos* "back."]

tour·ney /túrnee/ *n.* (*plural* **-neys**) = **tournament** ■ *vi.* (**-neyed, -ney·ing, -neys**) **COMPETE IN A TOURNAMENT** to take part in a tournament [13thC. Via Old French *torneier* "to joust, tilt," from, ultimately, Latin *tornare* "to turn."] —**tour·ney·er** *n.*

tour·ni·quet /túrnikət/ *n.* a tight encircling band applied around an arm or leg in an emergency to stop severe arterial bleeding that cannot be controlled in any other way [Late 17thC. From French, of uncertain origin: possibly from Old French *tournicle* "coat of mail," literally "small tunic," ultimately from Latin *tunica* "tunic"; influenced by *tourner* "to turn."]

tour of du·ty *n.* = **tour** *n.* **5**

Tours /toor, toorz/ capital city of Indre-et-Loire Department, Centre Region, western central France. Population: 133,403 (1990).

tou·sle /tówz'l/ *vt.* (**-sled, -sling, -sles**) **TANGLE HAIR** to make hair or fur tangled or ruffled ■ *n.* **TANGLED MASS** a tangled mass of something, especially hair or fur [15thC. Literally "to pull repeatedly," formed from *touse* "to pull, handle roughly," ultimately from a prehistoric Germanic base that is also the ancestor of English *tease.*] —**tousled** *adj.*

Tous·saint L'Ou·ver·ture /too sáN loover tür/, **François Dominique** (1743?–1803) Haitian soldier and statesman. Born into slavery, he was active in the movement that led to its abolition in Haiti (1791). The effective ruler of Haiti from 1797, he was captured by the French in 1802. Born **François Dominique Toussaint**

tout /towt/ *v.* (**tout·ed, tout·ing, touts**) **1.** *vi.* **ATTRACT CUSTOMERS** to try to attract customers or support, especially in an aggressive or persistent way ○ *street traders touting for business* **2.** *vt.* **OFFER OR ADVERTISE SOMETHING** to claim to have something available or on hand, or offer something for sale **3.** *vt.* **PRAISE SOMEBODY OR SOMETHING** to praise or recommend somebody or something enthusiastically (*usually passive*) ○ *was touted as the next champion* **4.** *vi.* **SPY ON RACEHORSES** to spy on racehorses in training to gain information useful to people who bet on horseraces **5.** *vti.* **SELL INFORMATION ABOUT RACEHORSES** to sell information about racehorses to potential gamblers ■ *n.* **1. SOMEBODY WHO SELLS INFORMATION ABOUT RACEHORSES** somebody who spies on racehorses in training to obtain information and then sells it to people who bet on horseraces **2. AGGRESSIVE SELLER** somebody who tries to attract customers or sell things aggressively [14thC. Ultimately from a prehistoric Germanic base meaning "to poke out, project." The original English meaning was "to peek," which became "to spy on" and, later, "to look for business."] —**tout·er** *n.*

tout en·sem·ble /to͞ot aan saámb'l/ *n.* the total appearance or effect of something [Early 18thC. From French, "all together."]

to·va·rish /tə vaárich, -rish/ (*plural* **-rish·es**), **to·va·rich** (*plural* **-rich·es**), **to·va·risch** (*plural* **-risch·es**) *n.* a friend or comrade, often used as a term of address, especially in the former Soviet Union [Early 20thC. From Russian *tovarishch*, of uncertain origin: possibly from a Tatar word.]

tow[1] /tō/ *vt.* (**towed, tow·ing, tows**) **PULL SOMETHING** to pull something such as a barge or a broken-down car along by a rope or chain attached to it ■ *n.* **1. ACT OF PULLING SOMETHING ALONG** the act of pulling something along by a rope or chain attached to it **2. STATE OF BEING PULLED ALONG** the state of being towed by a rope or chain **3. ROPE** a rope or chain used for towing something **4. SOMETHING THAT PULLS** something that tows something else [Old English *togian.* Ultimately from an Indo-European word meaning "to lead," which is also the ancestor of English *education* and *team.*] —**tow·a·ble** *adj.* —**tow·er** *n.* ◇ **have** *or* **take somebody in tow 1.** to follow or accompany somebody **2.** to act as a protector or guide for somebody

WORD KEY: SYNONYMS

See Synonyms at ***pull***.

tow[2] /tō/ *n.* fibers of flax, hemp, or jute, or of a synthetic material such as rayon [Old English *tow-*, from prehistoric Germanic]

tow·age /tṓ ij/ *n.* **1. ACT OF TOWING OR BEING TOWED** the act or process of towing somebody or something, or the state of being towed **2. CHARGE FOR TOWING** a charge made for towing something

to·ward /tawrd, tə wáwrd/, **to·wards** /tawrdz, tə wáwrdz/ *prep.* **1. IN A PARTICULAR DIRECTION** used to indicate that some person or thing is moving or facing in the direction of another person or thing ○ *They headed off toward town.* **2. SHORTLY BEFORE** shortly before a particular time ○ *toward midnight* **3. WITH SPECIFIC AUDIENCE INTENDED** with a particular target group in mind ○ *remarks slanted toward those sitting in the front row* **4. REGARDING** concerning or with regard to ○ *his attitude toward her* **5. CONTRIBUTING TO** as a contribution to or means of achieving something ○ *a grant toward the cost of refurbishment* [Old English *tōweardes* (-*es*, adverbial ending)]

WORD KEY: USAGE

See Usage note at ***toward***.

tow-a-way zone *n.* an area where parking is restricted or not allowed and from which parked vehicles are likely to be towed away

tow·bar /tṓ baar/ *n.* a rigid metal bar or frame attached to the back of a vehicle and used for towing other vehicles

tow·boat /tṓ bōt/ *n.* **1.** = **tugboat 2. BARGE-PUSHING BOAT** a powerful boat with a broad bow, designed for pushing barges on rivers or canals

tow-col·ored *adj.* having a pale yellow color like hemp or flax

tow·el /tówəl/ *n.* **1. ABSORBENT CLOTH** a usually rectangular piece of absorbent cloth or paper, used to dry the body **2. DISHTOWEL** a towel used in the kitchen to dry dishes ■ *vti.* (**-eled** *or* **-elled, -el·ing** *or* **-el·ling, -els**) **DRY SOMEBODY WITH TOWEL** to use a towel to dry somebody or something [13thC. Via Old French *toaille*, from a prehistoric Germanic base meaning "to wash."] ◇ **throw in the towel** to give up doing something that is proving difficult, or give in to somebody (*informal*)

tow·el·ette /tòwə lét/ *n.* a small moistened piece of paper or cloth used for cleaning the hands and face

tow·el·ing /tówəling/, **tow·el·ling** *n.* a soft absorbent, usually looped cotton fabric, used to make towels and bathrobes

tow·er[1] /tówər/ *n.* **1.** ARCHIT **TALL BUILDING** a tall structure, sometimes the upper part or a tall part of a building or structure and sometimes a separate building **2.** MIL **FORTRESS** a building designed to withstand attack **3.** HOUSEHOLD **CD SHELF** a tall wooden, plastic, or metal case in which to store CDs or videos ■ *vi.* (**-ered, -er·ing, -ers**) **1. BE TALL** to be very high or tall, or much higher or taller than somebody or something else **2. BE SUPERIOR** to be considerably superior to somebody or something [12thC. Via Latin *turris* from Greek.] ◇ **a tower of strength** somebody who is reliable and supportive (*informal*)

tow·er[2] /tṓwər/ *n.* somebody or something, e.g., a vehicle, that tows something by a rope or chain. ◆ **tow**

tow·er·ing /tówəring/ *adj.* **1. HIGH OR TALL** rising very high or standing very tall **2. OUTSTANDING** being of the highest quality or importance **3. INTENSE** characterized by extreme or intense emotion or pain ○ *a towering rage* —**tow·er·ing·ly** *adv.*

tow·head /tṓ hèd/ *n.* **1.** HAIR **SOMEBODY WITH BLOND HAIR** somebody with fair or tousled hair **2.** HAIR **HEAD OF WHITE-BLOND HAIR** a head that is covered with light blond hair **3.** GEOG **LOW ISLAND** a low alluvial island in a river, especially one with a stand of trees [From TOW[2]] —**tow·head·ed** *adj.*

tow·hee /tṓ hèe, tō hée/ *n.* a large long-tailed North American sparrow, typically a ground feeder. Genera: *Pipilo* and *Chlorura.* [Mid-18thC. An imitation of the call of the bird.]

tow·line /tṓ lìn/ *n.* = **towrope**

town /town/ *n.* **1.** LARGE AREA OF BUILDINGS a densely populated area with many buildings, larger than a village and smaller than a city **2.** URBAN AREA a large urban area, either a town, a city, or a borough **3.** POL UNIT OF LOCAL GOVERNMENT in certain parts of the United States, a unit of local government that is smaller than a county or city **4.** LOCAL TOWN the nearest large town or city, or the town or city in which somebody lives ○ *moving into town* **5.** CENTER OF SETTLED AREA the center of a town or city **6.** POPULATION OF SETTLED AREA the people who live in a town ○ *The whole town's talking about it.* **7.** NONACADEMIC POPULATION the permanent residents of a town that has a university, as opposed to the staff and students of the university ○ *town and gown* **8.** ZOOL PRAIRIE DOG BURROWS a group of prairie dog burrows [Old English *tūn* "yard, buildings within an enclosure." The term came to mean "cluster of dwellings" and, by the 12thC, its main present meaning was in use.] —**town·ish** *adj.* ◇ **go to town (on somebody or something)** to do something with great enthusiasm or thoroughness (*informal*) ◇ **on the town** spending time enjoying the entertainment available in a town or city, especially if a lot of money is spent (*informal*) ◇ **paint the town red** to go out and celebrate, especially by spending a lot of money for entertainment (*informal*)

WORD KEY: SYNONYMS

See Synonyms at ***city.***

town-and-gown *adj.* relating to a town that has a large population of students in higher education

town clerk *n.* a public official responsible for such things as keeping the records of a town and issuing licenses

town coun·cil *n.* the people elected or appointed to govern a town

town cri·er *n.* **1.** GOSSIP somebody who makes public information about other people's lives (*informal*) **2.** SOMEBODY WHO MAKES PUBLIC ANNOUNCEMENTS somebody employed by a town, especially formerly, to make public announcements in the streets

town hall *n.* a building that houses the offices of the local administration and often has a public hall that can be used for meetings

town house *n.* **1.** HOUSE IN TOWN a house in a town or city, especially one that belongs to somebody who also has a house in the country **2.** ARCHIT = **row house 3.** *U.K.* ARCHIT ROW HOUSE a row house in a town or city, especially one in a fashionable area **4.** *ANZ* ARCHIT MODERN TOWN DWELLING in New Zealand, a modern, usually two-story town dwelling of superior quality, in a block of two, three, or four and with limited garden space

town·ie /tównee/, **town·y** (*plural* **-ies**) *n.* **1.** TOWN DWELLER somebody who lives permanently in a town, as opposed to somebody who lives in the country (*informal*) **2.** NONACADEMIC RESIDENT a nonacademic town resident as opposed to a student or member of staff at a university in the town

town man·ag·er *n.* an official in charge of the administrative activities of a town

town meet·ing *n.* **1.** MEETING OF INHABITANTS a public meeting involving all of the inhabitants of a town **2.** *New England* MEETING OF VOTERS a public meeting involving all of the voters of a town, with the authority to make legislative decisions **3.** POL, TV TELEVISED GATHERING a television program centering on an issue of national interest, in which people from a particular area ask questions of debaters or speakers ○ *a televised national town meeting on the role of the military in global peacekeeping*

town plan·ning *n. U.K.* = **urban planning**

town·scape /tówn skàyp/ *n.* **1.** VISIBLE AREA OF TOWN the part of a town within the sight of somebody looking at it **2.** PICTURE OF TOWN a painting or photograph of an urban scene

towns·folk /tównz fṑk/ *npl.* = **townspeople**

town·ship /tówn shìp/ *n.* **1.** POL SUBDIVISION OF A COUNTY a subdivision of a county, often serving as a unit of local government **2.** POL AREA GOVERNED BY TOWN MEETING in some parts of the United States, an area governed by a town meeting **3.** MEASURE 36 SQUARE MILES an area of surveyed public land equal to 36 sections or 36 square miles **4.** *S Africa* HIST URBAN SETTLEMENT FOR BLACK PEOPLE an urban settlement planned for Black people only, usually implying inferior facilities and services [Old EnglishThe meaning "subdivision of a county" is found in the late 17thC]

towns·man /tównzmən/ (*plural* **-men** /-mən/) *n.* **1.** TOWN DWELLER a man who lives in a town **2.** MAN LIVING IN SAME TOWN a man who lives in the same town as somebody else

towns·peo·ple /tównz pèep'l/ *npl.* the people who live in a town or who have lived in a town and are used to the ways of town life

Towns·ville /tównzvil/ city on the eastern coast of Queensland, Australia. It is a commercial and industrial center. Population: 101,398 (1996).

towns·wom·an /tównz wòomən/ (*plural* **-en** /-wìmmən/) *n.* **1.** TOWN DWELLER a woman who lives in a town **2.** WOMAN LIVING IN SAME TOWN a woman who lives in the same town as somebody else

town·y *n.* = **townie**

tow·path /tṓ pàth/ (*plural* **-paths** /-pàthz, -pàths/) *n.* a path beside a canal or river for people or animals to walk along, originally as they pulled a barge or boat

tow·rope /tṓ rṑp/, **tow·line** *n.* a rope used to tow something, e.g., a boat or a broken-down car

tow truck *n.* = **wrecker** *n.* 1

tox. *abbr.* toxicology

tox- *prefix.* = **toxi-** (*used before vowels*)

tox·al·bu·min /toks álbyəmin/ *n.* a toxic albumin protein found in some plants such as toadstools and in bacteria and snake venom

tox·a·phene /tóksə fèen/ *n.* a waxy amber-colored poisonous compound that smells of pine and is used as an insecticide. Formula: $C_{10}H_{10}Cl_8$. [Mid-20thC. Coined from TOXI- + a shortening of *chlorinated camphene.*]

tox·e·mi·a *n.* a condition produced by the presence of bacterial toxins in the blood, usually with tissue or organ damage, fever, and severe intestinal upset [Mid-19thC. Coined from TOX- + Greek *haima* "blood" + -IA.] —**tox·e·mic** *adj.*

toxi- *prefix.* poison, poisonous ○ *toxigenic* [From TOXIC]

tox·ic /tóksik/ *adj.* **1.** INVOLVING SOMETHING POISONOUS relating to or containing a poison or toxin **2.** DEADLY causing serious harm or death ■ *n.* POISONOUS SUBSTANCE a toxic substance [Mid-17thC. Via medieval Latin *toxicus* "poisoned" from, ultimately, Greek *toxikos* "of the bow" (Greek *toxikon pharmakon* meant "poison for smearing arrows").] —**tox·i·cal·ly** *adv.*

tox·i·cant /tóksikənt/ *n.* a toxic substance, especially one used as a pesticide

tox·ic·i·ty /tok síssətee/ (*plural* **-ties**) *n.* **1.** DEGREE OF POISONOUSNESS the degree to which something is poisonous **2.** CAPABILITY TO POISON SOMEBODY the state of being poisonous to somebody or something

toxico- *prefix.* poison ○ *toxicogenic* [From Latin *toxicum* (see TOXIC)]

tox·i·co·gen·ic /tòksikō jénnik/ *adj.* = **toxigenic**

tox·i·col·o·gy /tàwksi kóllәjee/ *n.* the scientific study of poisons, especially their effects on the body and their antidotes —**tox·i·co·log·ic** /tòksikə lójjik/ *adj.* —**tox·i·co·log·i·cal·ly** /-lójjәkəlee/ *adv.* —**tox·o·col·o·gist** /tòksi kóllәjist/ *n.*

tox·i·co·sis /tòksi kṓssiss/ (*plural* **-ses** /-kṓ sèez/) *n.* the harmful effects of a poison, including any disease caused by toxins

tox·ic shock syn·drome *n.* acute, potentially fatal circulatory failure, commonly associated with the use of vaginal tampons, which can create conditions promoting the growth of a toxin-producing staphylococcal bacterium

tox·i·gen·ic /tòksi jénnik/ *adj.* **1.** POISON-PRODUCING producing poisonous substances **2.** PRODUCED BY TOXIN caused or produced by a toxin —**tox·i·ge·nic·i·ty** /tòksijә níssətee/ *n.*

tox·in /tóksin/ *n.* **1.** POISON FROM A LIVING CREATURE a poison produced by a living organism, especially bacteria, capable of causing disease and also of stimulating the production within the body of antibodies to counter their effects **2.** any substance said to accumulate in the body that is considered to be harmful or poisonous to the system ○ *drinking plenty of water to eliminate toxins* [Late 19thC. Coined from TOXIC + -IN.]

tox·in-an·ti·tox·in *n.* a mixture of a toxin and its antitoxin in which the toxin is in slight excess, formerly used as a vaccine, e.g., for diphtheria

tox·o·car·i·a·sis /tòksi kə rī́ əssiss/ *n.* an infestation of the larvae of a kind of roundworm in human beings, from worm eggs picked up from contaminated soil or domestic pets [Mid-20thC. Coined from TOX- + Greek *kara* "head" + -IASIS.]

tox·oid /tók sòyd/ *n.* a preparation of a toxin produced by infectious agents, largely rendered harmless by chemical treatment but still capable of stimulating antibodies and used as a vaccine [Early 20thC. Coined from shortening of TOXIN + -OID.]

tox·oph·i·lite /tok sóffə lìt/ *n.* an archer or archery enthusiast (*literary or humorous*) [Late 18thC. Formed from *Toxophilus,* "lover of the bow," which was coined by Roger ASCHAM (1545) (from TOXO- + Greek *philos* "friend").] —**tox·oph·i·ly** *n.*

tox·o·plas·ma /tòksə plázzəmə/ *n.* a microscopic protozoan organism that lives as a parasite in the organs of vertebrates, especially birds and mammals, and can cause disease. Genus: *Toxoplasma.* [Early 20thC. From modern Latin, coined from toxo-, a variant of TOXI- + PLASMA.] —**tox·o·plas·mic** *adj.*

tox·o·plas·mo·sis /tòksō plaz mṓssiss/ (*plural* **-ses** /-sèez/) *n.* a disease of mammals caused by a toxoplasma transmitted to humans via undercooked meat or through contact with infectious animals, especially cats

toy /toy/ *n.* **1.** THING TO PLAY WITH something meant to be played with, especially by children **2.** REPLICA a replica of a real object, meant to be played with or used as an ornament **3.** MINIATURE BREED an animal, especially a dog, that is a miniature version of another animal ○ *a toy poodle* **4.** SOMETHING UNIMPORTANT something of little value or importance **5.** SOMEBODY WHOSE EMOTIONS ARE PLAYED WITH somebody whose feelings and emotions are treated as unimportant (*informal*) **6.** *Southern U.S.* SHOOTER MARBLE a marble used as a shooter ■ *adj.* EASILY DISMISSED used pejoratively to belittle somebody or something or make somebody or something deemed irrelevant or of inferior quality appear insignificant (*insult*) [14thC. Origin unknown. Its original meaning was "amorous dalliance," and the sense "plaything" came into use in late 16thC.] —**toy·er** *n.*

toy with *vt.* **1.** PLAY WITH SOMETHING to play or fiddle with something, especially because of a lack of real interest in it or preoccupation with something else **2.** THINK ABOUT SOMETHING to consider doing something **3.** TREAT SOMEBODY OR SOMETHING CRUELLY to behave in a cruelly insincere or offhand way toward somebody or something **4.** TREAT SOMEBODY INSINCERELY to treat somebody in an insincere or flirtatious way, merely for amusement

toy boy *n.* an offensive term for a young man who is the lover of somebody who is older (*slang insult*)

to·yi-to·yi /tóy toy/ *n. S Africa* a militant dance performed by a circular group of protestors, with high steps, accompanied by chanting of slogans and singing [Late 20thC. From an African language, perhaps Xhosa.]

Toyn·bee /tóyn bèe/, **Arnold** (1889–1975) British historian. His masterwork, the 12-volume *Study of History* (1934–61), treated history as a succession of civilizations rather than of nations. Full name **Arnold Joseph Toynbee**

toy·on /tóy òn/ *n.* an evergreen Californian shrub with white flowers and red berrylike fruit. Latin name: *Heteromeles arbutifolia.* [Mid-19thC. From Mexican Spanish *tollón.*]

To·yo·to·mi Hi·dey·o·shi /tṑyō tṓmee hìdde yṓshee/ (1537–98) Japanese politician. He united Japan in 1590 and coordinated two unsuccessful invasions of Korea (1592 and 1597).

tp, Tp *abbr.* **1.** toilet paper (*slang*) **2.** township **3.** troop

t.p. *abbr.* PUBL title page

TPA *abbr.* tissue plasminogen activator

tpk, Tpk *abbr.* turnpike

TPN *abbr.* triphosphopyridine nucleotide

Tpr *abbr.* Trooper

TQM *abbr.* BUSINESS total quality management

TR *abbr.* TELECOM transmit-receive

tr. *abbr.* **1.** GRAM transitive **2.** LANG, BUSINESS translator **3.** PRINTING transpose **4.** PRINTING transposition **5.** FIN treasurer **6.** MUSIC trill **7.** troop **8.** FIN trust **9.** FIN trustee

tra·be·at·ed /tráybee àytəd/, **tra·be·ate** /tráybee àyt, tráybee ət/ *adj.* ARCHIT built using horizontal beams rather than arches [Mid-16thC. Formed from the Latin stem trab- "beam."] —**tra·be·a·tion** /tràybee áysh'n/ *n.*

tra·bec·u·la /trə békyələ/ (*plural* **-lae** /-lèe/ *or* **-las**) *n.* **1.** ANAT **ROD-SHAPED SUPPORT IN AN ORGAN** a rod-shaped body part that forms an internal support of an organ and divides it into separate chambers **2.** ANAT **BAR OF BONY TISSUE** any of the thin bars of bony tissue in spongy bone that form a meshwork with interconnecting spaces that contain bone marrow **3.** BOT **ROD-SHAPED CELL** a rod-shaped cell or structure that bridges a cavity, e.g., between cells [Mid-19thC. From Latin, literally "small beam," from the stem *trab-* "beam."] —**tra·bec·u·lar** *adj.* —**tra·bec·u·late** *adj.*

trace[1] /trayss/ *n.* **1. REMAINING SIGN** a sign that remains to show the former presence of a person or thing no longer there **2. TINY QUANTITY** a tiny amount or the slightest amount **3.** CHEM **JUST DETECTABLE AMOUNT** an amount of something that is detectable but too small to be quantified **4. FOOTPRINT** a footprint or physical sign of the passage of a person or animal **5. PATH** a path or track left by people or animals regularly passing **6. LINE MARKING SOMETHING** a line made by a recording instrument, e.g., one drawn by a seismograph or one formed on the screen of a cathode ray tube, or the record made in this way **7. DRAWING** a drawing, especially one made using tracing paper **8. ATTEMPT TO FIND ANOTHER** an attempt to find or follow somebody or something **9.** PSYCHOL = **engram 10.** GEOM **INTERSECTION** the point of intersection of a line or plane with the surface of a coordinate plane **11.** MATH **SUM OF DIAGONAL ENTRIES** the sum of the diagonal entries of a square matrix **12.** METEOROL **AMOUNT OF PRECIPITATION** an amount of precipitation that is too small to be recorded by instruments, or the record of such an amount ■ *v.* **(traced, trac·ing, trac·es) 1.** *vt.* **FIND SOMEBODY OR SOMETHING** to find out where somebody or something is or who or what somebody or something was **2.** *vti.* **FOLLOW OR BE FOLLOWED** to follow or show a course or series of developments, or be able to be followed back in time or to a source **3.** *vti.* **COPY SOMETHING** to copy writing, a design, or drawing by putting translucent paper on top of it and drawing the visible outlines on this paper **4.** *vt.* **DRAW SOMETHING CAREFULLY** to draw or write something with great care **5.** *vt.* **OUTLINE SOMETHING** to give an outline or brief description of something **6.** *vt.* ARCHIT **DECORATE SOMETHING** to decorate something with tracery **7.** *vi.* **SEARCH SOMETHING** to search through something [13thC. Via Old French *tracier* "to make one's way" from, ultimately, Latin *trahere* "to pull."] —**trace·a·bil·i·ty** /tràyssə bíllətee/ *n.* —**trace·a·ble** *adj.* —**trace·a·ble·ness** *n.* —**trace·a·bly** *adv.* —**trace·less** *adj.* —**trace·less·ly** *adv.*

WORD KEY: ORIGIN

See Origin note at *trace*[2].

trace[2] /trayss/ *n.* **1.** EQU **HORSE'S PULLING STRAPS** either of the two straps or chains connected to a horse's harness by means of which it pulls something such as a cart (*often used in the plural*) **2.** MECH ENG **BAR TRANSFERRING MOTION** a hinged bar that enables motion to be transferred from one part of a machine to another [14thC. From Old French *trais*, plural of *trait* "strap for harnessing," from Latin *tractus* "drawing" (see TRACTOR).] ◇ **kick over the traces** reject restrictions and controls to do something unconventional (*informal*)

WORD KEY: ORIGIN

The Latin word *tractus*, from which ***trace*** is derived, passed into Old French as *trait* "pulling, draft," hence "harness strap" (source of English *trait*). Its plural *trais* was borrowed into English in the 14th century as ***trace*** "harness-strap." It also formed the basis of a Vulgar Latin verb that evolved into Old French *tracier*, from which English in the 14th century got the verb ***trace***. A noun ***trace*** was also derived from *tracier*, and this too was acquired by English as ***trace***, in the 13th century. At first it denoted a "path" or "track"; the modern sense "visible sign" did not develop until the 17th century.

trace el·e·ment *n.* **1.** CHEM **ELEMENT PRESENT IN TINY AMOUNT** a chemical element present in minute but detectable amounts, much less than one percent, in something such as a metal or ore **2.** BIOL **ELEMENT ESSENTIAL FOR HEALTH** an element such as zinc, iodine, or manganese that is required in minute amounts for normal growth and development and the functioning of vital enzyme systems **3. MINUSCULE AMOUNT** a very tiny amount ○ *only a trace element of truth to that statement*

trace fos·sil *n.* a feature in sedimentary rocks that resulted from the activity of an animal, e.g., a worm cast or footprint

trac·er /tráyssər/ *n.* **1.** = **tracer bullet 2. AMMUNITION ACTING AS TRACERS** ammunition that has been treated to act as tracers ○ *a gun loaded with tracer* **3.** MED = **tracer element 4. INVESTIGATION OR INVESTIGATOR** an investigation into the whereabouts of something missing, e.g., an item of mail or a cargo shipment, or somebody who carries out such an investigation **5. SOMEBODY OR SOMETHING THAT MAKES TRACINGS** somebody or something that makes tracings **6.** a device that gives out a signal that can be tracked and followed when attached to a vehicle or person

trac·er bul·let, **trac·er** *n.* a bullet that has been treated with chemicals to make it leave a glowing or smoky trail as it flies

trac·er el·e·ment, **trac·er** *n.* MED a radioactive element used in experiments so that its movements can be monitored

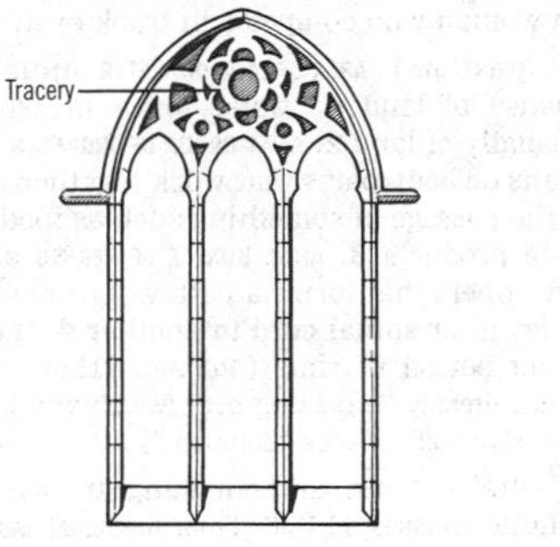

Tracery

trac·er·y /tráyssəree/ (*plural* **-ies**) *n.* **1.** ARCHIT **WINDOW ORNAMENTATION** decorative ribs in windows, especially medieval church windows, and screens **2.** DRAWING **INTERLACED PATTERN** a decorative pattern of interlaced lines, especially one that resembles the form or patterns found in church windows —**trac·er·ied** *adj.*

tra·che·a /tráykee ə/ (*plural* **-ae** /-èe/ *or* **-as**) *n.* **1.** ANAT **WINDPIPE** the tube in air-breathing vertebrates that conducts air from the throat to the bronchi, strengthened by incomplete rings of cartilage **2.** ZOOL **BREATHING TUBE** a tube in insects and related air-breathing animals through which air is drawn into the body by the pumping action of the abdominal muscles **3.** BOT **TUBE OF PLANT CELLS** a tubular part of water-conducting plant tissue that provides mechanical support and transport of water and nutrients [14thC. From medieval Latin, ultimately from Greek (*artēria*) *trakheia* "rough (artery)." From its rings of cartilage.] —**tra·che·al** *adj.* —**tra·che·ate** /tráykee ət, tráykee àyt/ *adj.*

tra·che·id /tráykee id/ *n.* BOT a cell in the trachea of conifers and other gymnosperm plants, with bands of lignin thickening the cell walls and adding structural support [Late 19thC. From German *Tracheïde*, literally "something belonging to the trachea."] —**tra·che·i·dal** /tray kée id'l, tray kéed'l/ *adj.*

tra·che·i·tis /tràykee ítiss/ *n.* inflammation of the trachea

tracheo- *prefix.* trachea ○ *tracheostomy*

tra·che·o·bron·chi·al /tràykee ō bróngkee əl/ *adj.* relating to or in both the trachea and the bronchi

tra·che·o·e·soph·a·ge·al /tràykee ō i sóffə jée əl/ *adj.* relating to or in both the trachea and the esophagus

tra·che·ole /tráykee ōl/ *n.* any of the fine channels that branch off from an insect's trachea and carry oxygen to its tissues [Early 20thC. Literally "small trachea."]

tra·che·o·phyte /tráykee ō fīt/ *n.* a plant that has a system of vascular tissues for conducting water and nutrients through it [Mid-20thC. Coined from TRACHEA- + Greek *phuton* "plant."]

tra·che·os·co·py /tràykee óskəpee/ (*plural* **-pies**) *n.* the examination of the inside of the trachea, e.g., using a laryngoscope —**tra·che·o·scop·ic** /tràykee ə skóppik/ *adj.*

tra·che·os·to·my /tràykee óstəmee/ (*plural* **-mies**) *n.* **1. HOLE IN THE TRACHEA** a hole cut in the trachea, e.g., to ensure the airway is unblocked and to suck out secretions **2. CUTTING INTO THE TRACHEA** an operation to cut a hole in the trachea

tra·che·ot·o·my /tràykee óttəmee/ (*plural* **-mies**) *n.* the making of an incision through the neck into the trachea to assist breathing when the upper airways are blocked

tra·cho·ma /trə kṓmə/ *n.* a contagious bacterial eye disease in which scar tissue forms inside the eyelid, eventually causing it to curve inward and the eyelashes to scrape the eye, often leading to infection [Late 17thC. From Greek *trakhōma* "roughness."] —**tra·cho·ma·tous** *adj.*

tra·chyte /trá kīt, tráy-/ *n.* fine-grained volcanic rock, characterized by the presence of alkaline feldspar minerals [Early 19thC. Formed from Greek *trakhus* "rough" + -ITE.] —**tra·chy·toid** /tráka tòyd, tráykee-/ *adj.*

tra·chyt·ic /trə kíttik/ *adj.* used to describe igneous rocks in which the crystals are arranged in parallel and show the flow of the molten lava from which they were formed

trac·ing /tráyssing/ *n.* **1. TRACED COPY** a copy of something made by tracing it onto a sheet of translucent paper laid on top of it **2. INSTRUMENT RECORD** a graphic record made by an instrument such as a seismograph

trac·ing pa·per *n.* a type of paper through which it is possible to see what is underneath, and on which it is possible to draw a copy of something underneath

track /trak/ *n.* **1. MARK LEFT** a mark left by a moving person, animal, or thing, e.g., a footprint, an animal's paw print, or the mark of a wheel **2. PATH** a path or road, especially one made by the continual passing of people or animals or one specially created for some purpose **3.** RAIL **RAIL STRUCTURE** a rail or pair of parallel rails on which a vehicle, especially a train, runs, along with the supporting structures such as crossties **4. COURSE OF TRAVEL** the path taken by somebody or something while traveling **5. LINE OF ACTION OR THOUGHT** a line of thought or investigation, or course of action ○ *realized our research was on the wrong track* **6.** SPORTS **RACE COURSE** a course laid out for racing **7.** SPORTS **SPORTS TAKING PLACE ON SPORTS TRACK** a collective term for all sports that take place on a sports track **8.** SPORTS = **track and field 9.** RECORDING **SEPARATE RECORDING OF MUSIC** a separate piece of music or song on a disc, tape, or record **10.** RECORDING **PATH FOR RECORDING** a separate section of a magnetic tape where the input of a single channel is recorded **11.** RECORDING **RECORDED INPUT** a recording on separate tracks of a magnetic tape that are combined to give a final version, e.g., of a piece of recorded music or a film **12.** RECORDING = **soundtrack** *n.* 1 **13.** COMPUT **SECTION OF COMPUTER DISK** a path on the surface of a storage medium such as a diskette or CD-ROM on which information is recorded and from which recorded information is read. The path is a series of concentric rings on floppy disks and hard files and a spiral on videodisks and CD-ROMs. **14.** CINEMA = **tracking shot 15.** AUTOMOT **TREADS OF A TANK OR BULLDOZER** a continuous loop of rubber or metal plates driven by wheels, giving great traction over soft or rough ground, used especially on bulldozers and heavy military vehicles such as tanks **16.** EDUC **COURSE OF STUDY** a course of study that is tailored to the relative abilities or needs of students **17.** BUSINESS **CAREER PATH** the course or projected course of a career **18.** INDUST **MOVING ASSEMBLY LINE** a moving belt carrying things along a factory assembly line **19.** HOUSEHOLD **SUPPORTING RAIL** a usually grooved rail along which something moves, e.g., a lighting fixture or the supporting hooks of a curtain **20.** PHYS **PATH OF A PARTICLE** the path taken by a particle of ionizing radiation in a cloud chamber, bubble chamber, or photographic emulsion **21.** ENG **DISTANCE BETWEEN WHEELS** the distance between a pair of wheels, e.g., the front wheels of a motor vehicle ■ **tracks** *npl.* **NEEDLE MARKS** marks or scars on the body of a drug user caused by frequent injections (*slang*) ■ *v.* **(tracked, track·ing, tracks) 1.** *vti.* **FOLLOW A TRAIL** to follow a trail made by somebody or something, or to try to find somebody or something by following a trail left behind **2.** *vt.* ELEC ENG **FOLLOW THE FLIGHT PATH** to follow the flight path of a vehicle such as a spacecraft using electronic equipment or radar **3.** *vt.* **FOLLOW PROGRESS** to follow the progress or development of something

4. *vti.* **FOLLOW A PATH** to follow a path through a place 5. *vti.* CINEMA **FOLLOW A MOVING OBJECT** to film a moving person or object with a mobile camera 6. *vi.* ENG **ALIGN** to be in alignment or the correct distance apart, especially wheels on a motor vehicle 7. *vi.* RECORDING **FOLLOW THE GROOVE ON A RECORD** to follow the groove on a phonograph record 8. *vi.* **TRAVEL** to travel, especially on a long or laborious journey (*informal*) 9. *vt.* **BRING AND LEAVE DIRT** to carry something, especially mud, on the shoes or feet and leave some of it on a floor 10. *vt.* **SUPPLY SOMETHING WITH TRACKS** to supply something, especially a railroad line, with tracks 11. *vt.* EDUC **ASSIGN SOMEBODY TO A TRACK** to assign a student to an educational track [15thC. From French *trac* "footprint, mark," of uncertain origin: perhaps from Middle Dutch *trek* "pulling" (source of English *trek*).] —**track·a·bil·i·ty** /tràkə bíllətee/ *n.* —**track·a·ble** *adj.* ◇ **cover your tracks** remove all signs of having been somewhere or done something (*informal*) ◇ **from the wrong side of the tracks** from the less affluent and socially advantaged part of a town or area (*informal insult*) ◇ **in your tracks** 1. suddenly and immediately, just where somebody or something is or in the middle of what somebody or something is doing (*informal*) 2. as somebody or something is going along (*informal*) ◇ **keep track (of)** to follow, pay attention to, or keep a check on the position or progress of ◇ **lose track (of)** to fail to follow or pay attention, or fail to keep an adequate check on the position or progress of ◇ **make tracks** to leave (*informal*) ◇ **off the beaten track** away from main roads and busy populated areas, and perhaps difficult to find or gain access to as a result (*informal*) ○ *The cottage is lovely but it's off the beaten track.* ◇ **on track** on the correct or desired path or schedule

track down *vt.* to find a person, animal, or object by searching or following a trail

track·age /trákij/ *n.* 1. **RAILROAD TRACKS** railroad tracks collectively 2. **RIGHT TO USE TRACKS** the right of one railroad company to use tracks belonging to another company 3. **CHARGE FOR USING TRACKS** a fee charged by one railroad company to another for use of its tracks

track and field *n.* athletic sports carried out on a running track and an adjacent field, e.g., hurdling or javelin throwing —**track-and-field** *adj.*

track·ball /trák bàwl/ *n.* a freely rotating ball moved by the fingers to control a cursor on a computer screen

tracked /trakt/ *adj.* moving on tracks, as a military tank or bulldozer does, or along a fixed track, as a dockside crane does

tracked ve·hi·cle *n.* a vehicle such as a military tank or a bulldozer that is propelled by tracks instead of wheels

track·er /trákər/ *n.* somebody who follows another person's or an animal's trail, especially somebody who is particularly skilled at doing this in order to guide others, e.g., police, soldiers, or hunters

track e·vent *n.* a sports competition that takes place on a running track

track·ing /tráking/ *n.* 1. **FOLLOWING OF A TRAIL** the act or process of following the trail of a person or animal 2. VIDEO **FINDING BEST PICTURE** the finding by a video player of the best quality picture 3. ELEC ENG **LEAKING OF CURRENT** the leaking of current between two insulated points, e.g., caused by damp or dirt 4. EDUC **GROUPING OF STUDENTS** the assigning of students to particular courses that will suit their abilities or needs

track·ing poll *n.* an opinion poll in which the same people are asked questions periodically to give an indication of changes in opinion

track·ing shot *n.* a camera shot filmed from a moving dolly, following the movement of somebody or something

track·ing sta·tion *n.* a place from which the movement of something such as a launched missile or a space vehicle can be followed using radar or radio signals

track·less /trákləss/ *adj.* 1. **LACKING PATHS** so isolated that there are no trails or paths 2. **LEAVING NO TRAIL** leaving no track or trail 3. RAIL **RUNNING WITHOUT RAILS** not needing rails on which to run —**track·less·ly** *adv.* —**track·less·ness** *n.*

track light *n.* an electric light that can be moved and repositioned anywhere along the length of an electrified track mounted on a wall or ceiling — **track light·ing** *n.*

track·man /trákmən/ (*plural* **-men** /-mən/) *n.* 1. **PERSON WHO MAINTAINS RAILROAD TRACK** somebody whose job is to lay and maintain rails 2. SPORTS **TRACK ATHLETE** a man who competes in track events

track meet *n.* an athletic competition in which teams from several places participate in track events

track rec·ord *n.* 1. **PAST PERFORMANCE** a record of the past performance of a person, organization, or thing (*informal*) 2. SPORTS **SPORTS ARENA RECORD** a record for a particular sports arena, as opposed to a national or international record

track shoe *n.* either of a pair of lightweight spiked running shoes

track·side /trák sīd/ *n.* the area immediately beside a running track or racetrack

track·suit /trák soot/ *n.* a loose-fitting long-sleeved top and matching pants in knitted nylon or cotton, worn by athletes over their sports clothes and by other people as casual wear

track·walk·er /trák wàwkər/ *n.* somebody employed to inspect railroad track

track·wom·an /trák wòommən/ (*plural* **-en** /-wìmmin/) *n.* a woman who competes in track events

tract[1] /trakt/ *n.* 1. **AREA OF LAND OR WATER** an unmeasured expanse of land or water, or a measured area, especially of land 2. ANAT **GROUP OF ORGANS** a system of organs or body parts that work together to provide for the passage of something such as food or bodily waste products 3. ANAT **BUNDLE OF NERVES** a group of nerve fibers that forms a pathway from one part of the brain or spinal cord to another 4. **LENGTH OF TIME** a long period of time (*archaic*) [15thC. From Latin *tractus*, literally "a drawing out" (which was formed from *trahere* "to pull"), hence "duration."]

tract[2] /trakt/ *n.* an anthem sung in some Roman Catholic masses [14thC. From medieval Latin *tractus*, from Latin (see TRACT[1]).]

tract[3] /trakt/ *n.* a pamphlet that sets out a position or an analysis, especially one dealing with a political or religious issue [Pre-12thC. From Latin *tractatus*, ultimately from *tractare* "to handle," literally "to draw repeatedly," from *trahere* (see TRACT[1]).]

trac·ta·ble /tráktəb'l/ *adj.* 1. **DOCILE** being very easy to control or persuade 2. **MALLEABLE** being very easy to bend or work with [15thC. From Latin *tractabilis*, from *tractare* (see TRACT[3]).] —**trac·ta·bil·i·ty** /tràktə bíllətee/ *n.* —**trac·ta·bly** /tráktəblee/ *adv.*

Trac·tar·i·an·ism /trak térree ən ìzzəm/ *n.* CHR = **Oxford Movement** [Mid-19thC. So called because of the tracts distributed.] —**Trac·tar·i·an** *n.*, *adj.*

trac·tate /trák tàyt/ *n.* a short essay on a particular subject (*formal*) [15thC. From Latin *tractatus* (see TRACT[3]).]

tract house *n.* one of many similar houses built on a tract of land —**tract hous·ing** *n.*

trac·tile /trákt'l/ *adj.* able to be stretched into another shape without breaking [Mid-19thC. Formed from Latin *tract-*, past participle stem of *trahere* (see TRACT[1]).] — **trac·til·i·ty** /trak tíllətee/ *n.*

trac·tion /trákshən/ *n.* 1. MED **APPLICATION OF WEIGHTS** application of a pulling force for surgical purposes, e.g., to reduce a fracture, maintain bone alignment, relieve pain, or prevent spinal injury 2. MECH ENG **FRICTION ALLOWING MOVEMENT** the adhesive friction between a moving object and the surface on which it is moving, e.g., between a tire and the ground, without which the object cannot move 3. ENG **PULLING** the act or process of pulling something, especially by means of a motor, or the fact or state of being pulled along 4. AUTOMOT **WAY TO MOVE VEHICLES** a means of moving vehicles 5. **WAY TO ACHIEVE PROGRESS** a means by which, or the degree to which, progress can be made ○ *could not get any traction in trying to push through the legislation* [Early 17thC. From either French *traction* or medieval Latin *traction-*, formed from Latin *tract-*, past participle stem of *trahere* (see TRACT[1]).] —**trac·tion·al** *adj.*

trac·tor /tráktər/ *n.* 1. AGRIC **FARM VEHICLE** a motor vehicle used for pulling heavy loads, especially on farms, where its typically large deep-treaded rear wheels enable it to move in fields 2. TRANSP **FRONT PART OF A HEAVY TRUCK** a large vehicle, the front section of a truck used to haul heavy loads, with a driving cab, engine, and coupling for trailers 3. AIR **AIRCRAFT WITH**

Tractor

THE PROPELLER IN FRONT an aircraft that has its propeller in front of the engine, exerting a pull through the air rather than a pushing force 4. AIR **PROPELLER** a propeller at the front of an aircraft engine 5. PRINTING = **tractor feed** [Late 18thC. Formed from Latin *tract-*, past participle stem of *trahere* "to draw" (see TRACT[1]).]

WORD KEY: ORIGIN

The Latin word *trahere*, from which ***tractor*** is derived, is also the source of English *abstract, attract, contract, detract, distract, extract, retract, retreat, subtract, trace, train, trait, treat, treatise*, and *treaty*.

trac·tor feed, **tractor** *n.* a mechanism for feeding paper into a printer, using toothed wheels to mesh with the perforations in continuous paper

trac·tor-trail·er *n.* a truck for pulling heavy loads, consisting of a tractor attached to a trailer or semi-trailer

Barnaby's

Spencer Tracy

Tra·cy /tráyssee/, **Spencer** (1900–67) U.S. actor. He won Academy Awards for his movies *Captains Courageous* (1937) and *Boy's Town* (1938).

trad. /trad/ *abbr.* traditional [Mid-20thC. Shortening.]

trade /trayd/ *n.* 1. **AREA OF BUSINESS OR INDUSTRY** a particular area of business or industry ○ *the book trade* 2. **OCCUPATION** somebody's particular occupation, especially one that involves a skill ○ *learn a trade* 3. **PEOPLE IN BUSINESS** the people who work in a particular area of business or industry ○ *You'll never convince the trade that this tax is fair.* 4. **BUYING AND SELLING** the activity of buying and selling, or sometimes bartering, goods ○ *a suspension of trade between the two countries* 5. **WORK IN COMMERCE** work in commerce as opposed to a profession ○ *graduates going into trade* 6. **CUSTOMERS** customers or business generated by customers ○ *losing trade to their competitors* 7. **COMMERCIAL CUSTOMERS** customers in business and industry, as opposed to the general public, who purchase products related to their business or industry ○ *This counter is for the trade only.* 8. **EXCHANGE** an exchange of somebody or something for another ○ *If neither of you likes your room, why don't you do a trade?* 9. METEOROL **TRADE WIND** a trade wind ○ *the southern trades* 10. **BUSINESS PUBLICATION** a publication meant for people in a particular line of business ○ *advertising in all the trades* 11. **DEAL** a deal or transaction ■ *v.* (**trad·ed, trad·ing, trades**) 1. *vi.* **BUY AND SELL GOODS** to take part in buying and selling goods for trade 2. *vt.* **EXCHANGE SOMETHING** to give and receive something alternately with somebody else ○ *trading punches* 3. *vt.* **DEAL IN SOMETHING** to buy and sell a particular commodity 4. *vti.* **MAKE AN EXCHANGE** to make an exchange, or exchange somebody or something for another ○ *Each had something the other wanted and they were happy to trade.* 5. *vi.* **SHOP OR BUY REGULARLY FROM BUSINESS** to shop or buy something regularly at a particular place of business [14thC. From Middle Low German, "track," which became used to denote "regular path (of business) pursued by someone" and hence, in the 16thC, "buying and selling."] —**trad·a·ble** *adj.* —**trade·less** *adj.*

trade down *vi.* to sell something large or expensive and buy something smaller or less expensive

trade in *vt.* to give an old or used item, especially a car, in part payment for a new one

trade on *vt.* to take advantage of a personal quality or situation, often unfairly or excessively

trade up *vi.* to sell something small or inexpensive and buy something larger and more expensive

trade ac·cep·tance *n.* a bill of exchange for the amount of a purchase drawn by the seller on the buyer, signed by the buyer and often specifying the place and date of payment

trade a·gree·ment *n.* a treaty between two or more countries to regulate trade between them

trade as·so·ci·a·tion *n.* an organization formed to represent the collective interests of a number of businesses in the same trade

trade book, trade e·di·tion *n.* a standard edition of a book, meant for sale to the general public, as opposed to a deluxe or book-club edition

trade cy·cle *n. U.K.* = **business cycle**

trade def·i·cit *n.* the difference, measured in monetary value, between a nation's imports and its exports when the exports exceed the imports

trade dis·count *n.* a reduction in the standard price of something, offered by one business to another, e.g., by a manufacturer to a retailer, especially within the same trade

trad·ed op·tion *n.* a stock option that is marketable

trade e·di·tion *n.* = **trade book**

trade-in *n.* **1. ITEM USED IN PARTIAL PAYMENT** a used item such as a car that is used as partial payment for something new **2. ACT OF TRADING SOMETHING IN** a transaction in which an old or used item serves as partial payment for something new

trade jour·nal *n.* a periodical devoted to news and features relating to a particular trade or profession

trade lan·guage *n.* a language used between native speakers of different languages to allow them to communicate so that they can trade with each other. ◊ **lingua franca, pidgin**

trade-last *n.* an exchange in which somebody repeats an overheard compliment to the complimented person if that person will first offer an overheard compliment about the other (*informal*)

trade·mark /tráyd maàrk/ *n.* **1. COMPANY SYMBOL** a name or symbol used to show that a product is made by a particular company and legally registered so that no other manufacturer can use it **2. DISTINCTIVE CHARACTERISTIC** a distinctive characteristic associated with a particular person ○ *Quick exits are her trademark.* ■ *vt.* (**-marked, -mark·ing, -marks**) **1. REGISTER SOMETHING AS A TRADEMARK** to register a name or symbol as a trademark **2. LABEL PRODUCT WITH A TRADEMARK** to place a trademark on a product

trade name *n.* **1. PRODUCT NAME** a name given by a manufacturer to a product or service **2. NAME USED IN A TRADE** a name for something that is usually only known to or used by people working in a particular trade **3. COMPANY NAME** a name under which a company or business operates

trade·off /tráyd òf/, **trade-off** *n.* a situation in which somebody is prepared to compromise by giving up all or part of one thing in exchange for another ○ *a tradeoff between quality and price*

trade pa·per·back *n.* a paperback edition of a book that is superior in production quality to a mass-market paperback edition and is similar to a hardback in size

trad·er /tráydər/ *n.* **1. SOMEBODY TRADING IN GOODS** somebody who buys and sells retail goods **2.** STOCK EXCH **SOMEBODY TRADING IN STOCKS** somebody who deals in stocks and shares, especially a person who tries to profit by making frequent deals, each netting a small profit **3.** SHIPPING **SHIP** a merchant ship

trade ref·er·ence *n.* a person or company that furnishes a report concerning somebody's credit standing in response to an inquiry by somebody else in the same trade, especially a supplier

trade route *n.* a route used by merchant ships or trading vehicles

trad·es·can·tia /tràddə skánshə, -skánshee ə/ (*plural* **-tias** *or* **-tia**) *n.* a plant grown for its striped leaves and blue, white, or pink flowers. Genus: *Tradescantia.* ◊ **spiderwort** [Early 18thC. From modern Latin, named for John TRADESCANT or his son.]

trade school *n.* a school that gives instruction in a particular trade or that offers vocational courses in general

trade se·cret *n.* **1. COMPANY'S SECRET** a secret formula or technique that is used to make a product, known only to the company that manufactures it **2. SECRET** any secret (*informal*) ○ *Which shampoo do you use – or is it a trade secret?*

trades·man /tráydzmən/ (*plural* **-men** /-mən/) *n.* **1. SKILLED WORKER** a man who works in a skilled trade, especially a job related to the construction industry such as plumbing and carpentry **2. STOREKEEPER** a man involved in trade, especially a storekeeper (*dated*)

trades·peo·ple /tráydz peèp'l/ *npl.* people employed in trade, especially storekeepers (*dated*)

trades un·ion *n.* = **labor union**

trades·wom·an /tráydz wòommən/ (*plural* **-en** /-wìmmin/) *n.* a woman who works in a skilled trade, especially a job related to the construction industry such as plumbing and carpentry

trade un·ion *n.* = **labor union** —**trade un·ion·ism** *n.* —**trade un·ion·ist** *n.*

trade wind *n.* a prevailing tropical wind blowing toward the equator from the northeast in the northern hemisphere or from the southeast in the southern hemisphere. The trade winds are major components of the global weather system. [From *blow trade* "to blow in a constant direction," which was based on obsolete *trade* "course"]

trad·ing card *n.* a card with a picture or information on it that is one of a set designed to be collected. Trading cards often feature pictures of popular sports figures.

trad·ing post *n.* **1. STORE IN REMOTE AREA** especially formerly, a store in a remote area, where local products can be bartered for supplies **2.** STOCK EXCH **LOCATION IN STOCK EXCHANGE** a location where a particular security is traded on the floor of a stock exchange

trad·ing stamp *n.* a stamp that can be exchanged for goods, given by a store to customers each time they spend a certain amount of money

tra·di·tion /trə dísh'n/ *n.* **1. CUSTOM OR BELIEF** a long-established custom or belief, often one that has been handed down from generation to generation **2. BODY OF CUSTOMS** a body of long-established customs and beliefs viewed as a set of precedents **3. HANDING DOWN OF CUSTOMS** the handing down of customs, practices, and beliefs that are valued by a particular culture **4.** CHR **ACCEPTED UNWRITTEN CHRISTIAN DOCTRINES** the body of Christian doctrines that are accepted as the teachings of Jesus Christ and the apostles without written evidence **5.** ISLAM **TEACHINGS SUPPLEMENTING KORAN** the body of Islamic beliefs and customs that are not written in the Koran, e.g., the words of Muhammad **6.** LAW **TRANSFER OF OWNERSHIP** especially in Roman and Scots law, the formal transfer of ownership of movable property [14thC. Via Old French from, ultimately, Latin *tradere* "to hand over, betray" (source also of English *traitor*), from *trans-* "across, over" + *dare* "to give."] —**tra·di·tion·less** *adj.*

WORD KEY: SYNONYMS

See Synonyms at ***habit***.

tra·di·tion·al /trə díshən'l, -díshnəl/ *adj.* **1. OF TRADITION** based on or relating to tradition **2.** MUSIC **IN OLDER JAZZ STYLE** used to describe older styles of jazz, usually played by small ensembles featuring clarinet, trumpet, trombone, and rhythm sections. Traditional jazz flourished in New Orleans, Chicago, and Kansas City in the early 20th century. —**tra·di·tion·al·i·ty** /trə dìsh'n állətee/ *n.* —**tra·di·tion·al·ize** /trə díshən'l ìz, -díshnə l ìz/ *vt.* —**tra·di·tion·al·ly** /trə díshən'lee, -díshnəlee/ *adv.*

tra·di·tion·al·ism /trə díshən'l ìzzəm, -díshnə lìzzəm/ *n.* **1. RESPECT FOR TRADITION** deep respect for tradition, especially cultural or religious practices **2.** RELIG **BELIEF IN TRANSMISSION OF DIVINE REVELATION** the idea that all knowledge comes from divine revelation and is passed on by tradition —**tra·di·tion·al·ist** *n.* —**tra·di·tion·al·is·tic** /trə dìshən'l ístik, -dìshnə lístik/ *adj.*

trad·i·tor /trádditər/ (*plural* **-to·res** /-táwreez/) *n.* an early Christian who betrayed other Christians during the Roman persecutions [14thC. From Latin (See TRAITOR).]

tra·duce /trə dóoss/ (**-duced, -duc·ing, -duc·es**) *vt.* to say very critical or disparaging things about somebody [Late 16thC. From Latin *traducere* "to convert, transfer," also "to scorn, disgrace," from *trans-* "across, over" + *ducere* "to lead."] —**tra·duce·ment** *n.* —**tra·duc·er** *n.* —**tra·duc·i·ble** *adj.*

tra·du·cian·ism /trə dóosh'n ìzzəm/ *n.* the belief that a child inherits a soul as well as its bodily characteristics from its parents [Mid-18thC. Formed from late Latin *traducianus* "believer in traducianism," from Latin *tradux* "inheritance, transmission," from *traducere* (see TRADUCE).] —**tra·du·cian** *n., adj.* —**tra·du·cian·ist** *n., adj.* —**tra·du·cian·is·tic** /trə dòosh'n ístik/ *adj.*

traf·fic /tráffik/ *n.* **1.** TRANSP **MOVEMENT OF VEHICLES** the movement of vehicles along the roads in a particular area **2.** TRANSP **SEA OR AIR TRANSPORT** the movement of ships, trains, or aircraft between two places, or the volume of passengers or goods transported by sea, rail, or air **3.** COMM **BUSINESS OF TRANSPORTATION** the business of transporting goods or people **4.** CRIMINOL **TRADE** illegal trade in goods such as drugs or weapons **5.** COMMUNICATION **FLOW OF COMMUNICATIONS** the volume or flow of messages carried by a communications system in a particular period **6. NEGOTIATIONS** dealings or negotiations between people ■ *v.* (**-ficked, -fick·ing, -fics**) **1.** *vi.* CRIMINOL **TRADE ILLEGALLY** to engage in illegal trading **2.** *vi.* **HAVE DEALINGS** to have dealings with somebody or something **3.** *vt.* **TRADE SOMETHING** to trade or exchange anything ○ *We spent the afternoon trafficking gossip.* [Early 16thC. Via obsolete French *trafique* from Old Italian *traffico*, from *trafficare* "to carry on trade," of uncertain origin.]

traf·fic cir·cle *n.* a road junction consisting of a circular island around which traffic can flow continuously

traf·fic cone *n.* a marker in the shape of a cone, usually made of orange plastic, used to separate lines of traffic during road repairs or to prevent vehicles from entering an area

traf·fic cop *n.* a police officer who directs the flow of traffic, especially at an intersection (*informal*)

traf·fic court *n.* a court that deals with people who have committed traffic violations

traf·fic en·gi·neer·ing *n.* the design and planning of roads and walkways, considering such factors as pedestrian and vehicular capacity and means for controlling traffic

traf·fic is·land *n.* a raised area in the center of a street to separate lanes of traffic and allow pedestrians to wait safely until they can cross

traf·fic jam *n.* a line of traffic that cannot move or moves very slowly or spasmodically because of overcrowding or an obstruction

traf·fic light *n.* a signal that uses red, green, and amber lights to control traffic, especially at an intersection

traf·fic pat·tern *n.* the pattern of routes to which an aircraft is restricted when approaching or circling an airport

traf·fic sig·nal *n.* = **traffic light**

traf·fic war·den *n. U.K.* a uniformed public official who enforces parking restrictions on the highway and may also direct traffic

trag·a·canth /trájjə kànth, trággə-/ *n.* **1. NATURAL GUM** a gum used in the manufacture of pills and adhesives, in textile printing, and as a stabilizer and thickener in sauces **2. PLANT YIELDING TRAGACANTH** a plant from which tragacanth gum is obtained, especially a spiny Asian plant with white, yellow, or purple flowers. Genus: *Astragalus.* [Late 16thC. Via French *tragacanthe* from, ultimately, Greek *tragakantha*, literally "goat's thorn," from *tragos* "goat" + *akantha* "thorn" (see ACANTHUS).]

tra·ge·di·an /trə jeèdee ən/ *n.* **1. ACTOR IN TRAGEDIES** an actor who plays tragic roles **2. SOMEBODY WHO WRITES TRAGEDIES** a playwright who specializes in tragedies

tra·ge·di·enne /trə jeèdee én/ *n.* a woman actor who performs tragic roles (*dated*) [Mid-19thC. From French, formed from *tragédie* (see TRAGEDY).]

trag·e·dy /trájjədee/ (*plural* **-dies**) *n.* **1. VERY SAD EVENT** an event in life that evokes feelings of sorrow or grief **2. DISASTROUS EVENT** a disastrous circumstance or event such as serious illness, financial ruin, or fatality **3.** THEATER, LITERAT **TRAGIC PLAY** a serious play with a tragic theme, often involving a heroic struggle and the downfall of the main character **4.** LITERAT **TRAGIC PIECE OF LITERATURE** a literary work that deals with a tragic theme **5.** THEATER, LITERAT **TRAGEDIES AS A GENRE** the genre of plays or other literary works that deals with tragic themes [14thC. Via French *tragédie* from, ultimately, Greek *tragōidia*, literally "goat's song," from *tragos* "goat" + *aeidein* "to sing" (source of English *ode*).]

tra·gi /tray gī, tray jī/ plural of **tragus**

trag·ic /trájjik/, **trag·i·cal** /-ik'l/ *adj.* **1. DEEPLY SAD** provoking deep sadness, distress, or grief **2.** THEATER, LITERAT **OF TRAGEDY** relating to tragedies as a genre [Mid-16thC. Via Latin from Greek *tragikos* "of tragedy," from *tragos* "goat" (see TRAGEDY).] —**trag·i·cal·ly** *adv.*

trag·ic flaw *n.* a character flaw that causes the downfall of the protagonist in a tragedy

trag·ic i·ro·ny *n.* the revealing to an audience of a tragic event or consequence that remains unknown to the character concerned. It is a kind of dramatic irony.

trag·i·com·e·dy /tràjji kómmədee/ (*plural* **-dies**) *n.* **1.** THEATER, LITERAT **WORK COMBINING TRAGEDY AND COMEDY** a play or other literary work that combines elements of tragedy and comedy **2.** THEATER, LITERAT **TRAGICOMIC PLAYS AS A GENRE** tragicomic plays or literary works considered as a genre **3. EVENT MIXING TRAGEDY AND COMEDY** an event or situation that has both tragic and comical aspects [Late 16thC. Via French *tragicomédie* from late Latin *tragicomoedia*, a shortening of *tragicocomoedia*, from *tragicus* "tragic" (see TRAGIC) + *comoedia* "comedy" (see COMEDY).] —**trag·i·com·ic** *adj.* —**trag·i·com·i·cal** *adj.* —**trag·i·com·i·cal·ly** *adv.*

Tragopan

trag·o·pan /trággə pàn/ *n.* a brightly colored pheasant native to Asia. The male has a bright blue bare throat and fleshy appendages on its head that look like horns. Latin name: *Tragopan temminckii.* [Early 17thC. Via Latin from Greek, type of hornbill, from *tragos* "goat" + *pan* "Pan," the horned god of flocks and fields.]

tra·gus /tráygəss/ (*plural* **-gi** /-gī, -jī/) *n.* **1. PART OF OUTER EAR** the pointed flap of cartilage that lies above the earlobe and partly covers the entrance to the ear passage **2. HAIR INSIDE EAR PASSAGE** a hair growing just inside the opening of the ear passage [Late 17thC. Via modern Latin from Greek *tragos* "goat," also "hairy part of the ear."] —**tra·gal** *adj.*

trail /trayl/ *v.* (**trailed, trail·ing, trails**) **1.** *vt.* **FOLLOW SOMEBODY SECRETLY** to follow a person or animal either by staying close but out of sight or by looking for signs of movement left behind, e.g., footprints or scent **2.** *vti.* SPORTS **FALL BEHIND IN ATHLETIC COMPETITION** to be losing in a race, match, or competition **3.** *vi.* **LAG** to walk slowly, usually from tiredness or boredom **4.** *vti.* **DRAG SOMETHING OR BE DRAGGED** to be pulled or dragged along, or pull or drag something along **5.** *vi.* **DRAPE** to hang, grow, or float loosely ○ *Her curly hair trailed along her shoulders and down her back.* **6.** *vt.* **TOW SOMETHING** to tow something such as a trailer behind a vehicle **7.** *vt.* CERAMICS **DECORATE SOMETHING BY DRIZZLING LIQUID CLAY** to decorate ceramics with liquid clay (**slip**) that is drizzled or sprayed on **8.** *vt.* **CARRY WEAPON IN LOW POSITION** to carry a weapon horizontally or with the butt near to the ground **9.** *vti.* **MAKE TRACK** to make a track through a place ■ *n.* **1. ROUTE THROUGH COUNTRYSIDE** a route through the countryside that links paths and points of interest ○ *a nature trail* **2. MARKS WHERE SOMEBODY OR SOMETHING MOVED** a sequence of marks left by somebody or something moving along a surface **3.** HUNT **SCENT FOLLOWED** a scent or track that is followed in a hunt **4. PATH** a path or track, especially one that has been beaten through a wild area **5.** ARMS **BOTTOM OF GUN CARRIAGE** the part of a gun carriage that rests on the ground [14thC. Via Old French *trailler* "to tow" from, ultimately, Latin *tragula* "dragnet, sledge," which was probably formed from *trahere* "to pull."]

WORD KEY: SYNONYMS

See Synonyms at ***follow.***

trail away, trail off *vi.* to become quieter or fainter in sound and gradually fade away

trail bike *n.* a lightweight motorcycle for use on rough terrain

trail·blaz·er /tráyl blàyzər/, **trailbreaker** *n.* **1. PIONEER** a pioneer or innovator in a particular field **2. CREATOR OF ROUTE** somebody who makes a new path through a wilderness —**trail·blaz·ing** *adj.*, *n.*

trail·er /tráylər/ *n.* **1. TOWED VEHICLE** a vehicle that is towed by another vehicle, e.g., a small open cart or a platform used for transporting a boat **2. PART OF TRUCK** a large van that is pulled by a truck, used especially for hauling freight **3. MOBILE HOME** a mobile home **4.** CINEMA, TV **ADVERTISEMENT FOR MOVIE** an advertisement for a movie consisting of extracts from it, shown on television or in a movie theater **5.** PHOTOGRAPHY **END OF REEL OF FILM** a blank piece of film at the end of a reel **6. SOMEBODY OR SOMETHING THAT TRAILS** somebody who or something that trails, especially somebody who lags behind others **7.** BOT **PLANT** a trailing plant ■ *v.* (**-ered, -er·ing, -ers**) **1.** *vt.* TRANSP **MOVE SOMETHING BY TRAILER** to transport something using a trailer **2.** *vi.* **LIVE IN TRAILER** to live or travel in a trailer **3.** *vi.* **GO IN TRAILER** to be capable of being transported by trailer

trail·er park *n.* a site where people can park and live in mobile homes

trail·head /tráyl hèd/ *n.* the start of a trail for walkers, sometimes with an information kiosk

trail·ing ar·bu·tus *n.* a trailing evergreen shrub with leathery leaves and clusters of fragrant pink-and-white flowers. It is native to eastern North America. Latin name: *Epigaea repens.*

trail·ing edge *n.* **1. REAR EDGE OF WING** the rear edge of a wing, airfoil, or propeller blade **2.** PHYS **PART OF PULSED SIGNAL** the part of a pulsed signal during which its amplitude decreases

trail mix *n.* a snack containing nuts, dried fruit, and seeds [From its use by walkers]

trail rope *n.* **1.** AEROSP **BALLOON ANCHOR** a rope that hangs from a balloon or airship and is used for mooring or as a brake **2.** ARMS **ROPE TO GUN CARRIAGE** a long rope attached to the trail of a gun carriage

trail·side /tráyl sīd/ *adj.* situated beside or relating to the area beside a trail

train /trayn/ *n.* **1.** RAIL **LINKED RAILROAD CARS** a number of railroad cars pulled by a locomotive (*often used before a noun*) **2.** CLOTHES **TRAILING PART OF GOWN** a long part at the back of a gown or robe that trails on the ground **3. LONG MOVING LINE** a long moving line of people or animals **4.** MIL **ARMY FOLLOWERS** the people and military vehicles supporting or supplying an army unit **5. SEQUENCE OF EVENTS** a series or sequence of events, actions, or things ○ *interrupting her train of thought.* **6.** MECH ENG **MECHANICAL SERIES** a series of connected wheels or other mechanical parts **7. LINE OF GUNPOWDER** a line of gunpowder or other combustible material **8. ENTOURAGE** a retinue or group of followers **9. SOMETHING DRAGGED BEHIND** something that is pulled or dragged along or that follows something else ■ *v.* (**trained, train·ing, trains**) **1.** *vti.* **LEARN OR TEACH SKILLS** to learn or teach somebody the skills necessary to do a particular job, especially through practical experience **2.** *vt.* **DOMESTICATE ANIMAL** to teach an animal to behave in ways acceptable to people, especially by repetition or practice **3.** *vti.* SPORTS **PREPARE FOR SPORTING COMPETITION** to prepare or prepare somebody for a sporting competition, usually with a planned program of appropriate physical exercises **4.** *vt.* GARDENING **MAKE PLANT GROW AS WANTED** to make a plant, bush, or tree grow in a particular way, e.g., by pruning or tying it **5.** *vt.* HAIR **SHAPE HAIR TO ENCOURAGE PARTICULAR GROWTH** to comb or otherwise arrange hair to encourage it to grow in a particular direction **6.** *vt.* **AIM SOMETHING** to aim something such as a weapon or a camera at somebody or something **7.** *vt.* **PRODUCE IMPROVEMENT** to improve something, especially the mind, with discipline **8.** *vi.* RAIL **TRAVEL BY TRAIN** to make a journey by train (*informal*) [Mid-15thC. From Old French *traïn* "something that drags or trails behind," from *traïner* "to draw, pull," of uncertain origin: perhaps via assumed Vulgar Latin *traginare* from Latin *trahere* "to pull, draw."]

WORD KEY: SYNONYMS

See Synonyms at ***teach.***

train·band /tráyn bànd/ *n.* a company of trained civilian militia operating in England and North America from the 16th to the 18th centuries [Mid-17thC. Contraction of *trained band.*]

train·bear·er /tráyn bàirər/ *n.* an attendant who holds up the train of somebody walking in a procession or other ceremony

train·ee /tray née/ *n.* somebody who is being trained to do a job (*often used after or before a noun*) ○ *a hairdresser trainee*

WORD KEY: SYNONYMS

See Synonyms at ***beginner.***

train·er /tráynər/ *n.* **1. SOMEBODY WHO TRAINS ANIMALS OR PEOPLE** somebody who trains animals or people, especially racehorses or athletes **2. TRAINING APPARATUS** an apparatus or device used in training, especially a simulation cockpit in which pilots train **3.** *U.K.* = **sneaker**

train·ing /tráyning/ *n.* **1. ACQUIRING OF SKILL** the process of teaching or learning a skill or job (*often used before a noun*) ○ *a training program* **2. IMPROVING OF FITNESS** the process of improving physical fitness by exercise and diet

train·ing school *n.* **1. VOCATIONAL SCHOOL** a vocational or technical school **2. CORRECTIONAL FACILITY FOR JUVENILES** a residential correctional facility where juvenile offenders are taught a trade

train·ing ta·ble *n.* a table in a dining hall, e.g., in a college dormitory, at which athletes in training eat special meals that are part of their regimen

train·ing wheels *npl.* **1. EXTRA WHEELS TO BALANCE BICYCLE** a pair of small wheels fitted to the back wheel of a bicycle to help balance it while somebody is learning to ride **2. HELP FOR BEGINNERS** things provided to help beginners use something (*informal*) ○ *The PC comes with training wheels for new users.*

train·load /tráyn lṑd/ *n.* the number of people or the amount of cargo that a train can carry ○ *a trainload of tourists*

train·man /tráynmən/ (*plural* **-men** /-mən/) *n.* a man who is a member of a train crew, especially a brakeman, who works to assist the conductor

train oil *n.* oil from the blubber of a whale or other marine animal. It is used, e.g., in the manufacture of soap and margarine, as a lubricant, and to dress leather. [*Train* from Low German *trān* or Middle Dutch *traen* "train oil"]

traipse /trayps/ (**traipsed, traips·ing, traips·es**) *vi.* to walk around casually or without a specific destination ○ *Don't come traipsing in here late again.* [Late 16thC. Origin uncertain: perhaps from Old French *trapasser* "to pass over, beyond" (source of English *trespass*).]

trait /trayt/ *n.* **1. INDIVIDUAL CHARACTERISTIC** a particular characteristic or quality that distinguishes somebody **2.** GENETICS **INHERITED CHARACTERISTIC** a quality or characteristic that is genetically determined **3. INDICATION** a hint or trace of something (*literary*) [Late 16thC. Via French, literally "act of pulling or drawing," hence "line drawn, feature," from Latin *tractus.*]

trai·tor /tráytər/ *n.* somebody who behaves in a disloyal or treacherous manner [13thC. Via Old French from Latin *traditor* "betrayer," from *tradere* (see TRADITION).]

trai·tor·ous /tráytərəss/ *adj.* **1. TREACHEROUS** behaving in a disloyal or treacherous way **2. TREASONABLE** constituting treason —**trai·tor·ous·ly** *adv.* —**trai·tor·ous·ness** *n.*

tra·ject /trə jékt/ (**-ject·ed, -ject·ing, -jects**) *vt.* to transmit or convey something, especially something abstract such as a quality (*literary*) [Mid-17thC. From Latin *traject-*, the past participle stem of *trajicere* "to throw across, pass through," from *trans-* "across, over" + *jacere* "to throw" (source of English *jet* and *adjacent*).] —**tra·jec·tion** *n.*

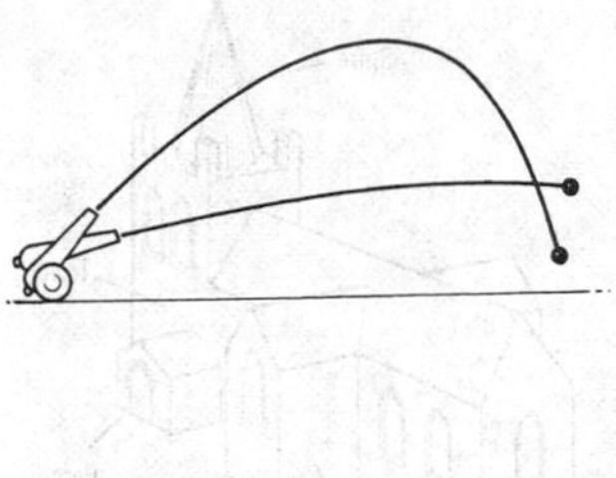

Trajectory

tra·jec·to·ry /trə jéktəree/ (*plural* **-ries**) *n.* **1.** AEROSP **PATH OF FLYING OBJECT** the path a projectile makes through space under the action of given forces such as thrust, wind, and gravity **2.** GEOM **CURVE INTERSECTING AT CONSTANT ANGLE** a curve or surface that intersects all of a family of curves or surfaces at a constant angle [Late 17thC. From medieval Latin *trajectorius* "relating to throwing across," from Latin *traject-* (see TRAJECT).]

tram[1] /tram/ *n.* **1.** *U.K.* TRANSP = **streetcar 2. CABLE CAR** a cable car **3.** MINING **VEHICLE IN COAL MINE** a small vehicle on rails used to carry coal and other materials in a coal mine [Early 16thC. Originally a Scottish dialect word meaning "(shaft of) wheelbarrow," of uncertain origin: perhaps from Middle Flemish *tram* "beam."]

tram[2] /tram/ (**trammed, tram·ming, trams**) *vt.* to adjust or align mechanical parts accurately [Late 19thC. From *tram-staff* "straight edge used by millwrights to adjust the millstone spindle," from *tram* "instrument for drawing ellipses," shortening of TRAMMEL.]

tram[3] /tram/ *n.* heavy silk thread used for the horizontal weave in velvet or silk [Late 17thC. Via French *trame* from Latin *trama* "woof of a web."]

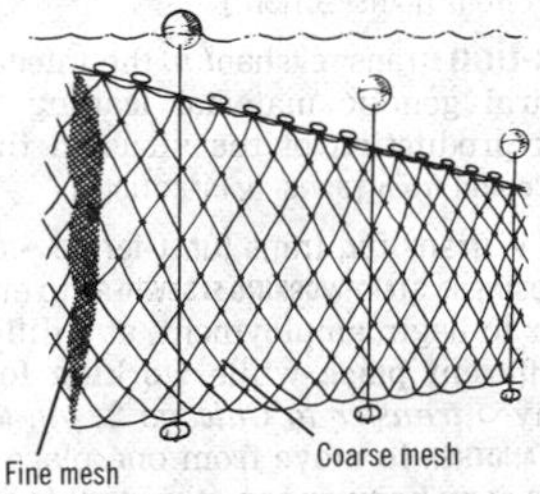

Trammel

tram·mel /trámm'l/ *n.* **LIMITATION TO FREEDOM** something that limits a person's freedom ■ *vt.* (**-meled, -mel·ing, -mels**) **ENSNARE SOMETHING** to catch or entangle somebody or something ■ *n.* **1.** ZOOL **FISHING NET** a fishing net consisting of a fine net between two layers of coarse mesh **2. SHACKLE** a shackle used to teach a horse to amble **3. DRAWING INSTRUMENT** an instrument used to draw ellipses **4.** HOUSEHOLD **FIREPLACE HOOK** a hook in a fireplace on which a kettle or pot can be hung and raised or lowered ■ *vt.* (**-meled, -mel·ing, -mels**) **1. CONFINE SOMEBODY** to restrain somebody or something **2.** MECH ENG = **tram**[2] *v.* [14thC. Via Old French *tramail* from late Latin *tremaculum*, from Latin *tres* "three" + *macula* "mesh."]

tra·mon·ta·na /traa mawn taanə/ *n.* a cold dry wind that blows down from mountains, especially a north wind that blows into Italy from the Alps [Late 18thC. Via Italian, "north wind," from, ultimately, Latin *transmontanus* "beyond the mountains," which was coined from *trans-* "trans-" + *mont-*, the stem of *mons* (see MOUNTAIN).]

tra·mon·tane /trə món tàyn, trámmən-/ *adj.* **1. BEYOND MOUNTAINS** living or situated on the far side of the mountains, especially the Alps as seen from Italy **2. FOREIGN** foreign and uncivilized, originally from an Italian point of view ■ *n.* **1.** METEOROL = **tramontana 2. FOREIGNER** somebody who lives or comes from beyond the mountains, especially from beyond the Alps as seen from Italy [Late 16thC. Via Italian *tramontano* from Latin *transmontanus* (see TRANSMONTANE.]

tramp /tramp/ *n.* **1. VAGRANT** somebody who has no home and travels on foot, often begging for a living **2. OFFENSIVE TERM** an offensive term that deliberately insults a woman who is considered sexually promiscuous or who works as a prostitute (*slang insult*) **3. SOUND OF FEET** the sound of heavy footsteps or horses' hooves **4.** *U.K.* **LONG JOURNEY ON FOOT** a long journey on foot, e.g., as part of a walking tour **5. HEAVY STEP** a heavy step or tread **6. METAL PLATE ON BOOT** a metal plate that protects the sole of a boot when the wearer is digging **7.** GARDENING **PART OF SPADE FOR FOOT** the part of a spade on which the digger's foot presses ■ *v.* (**tramped, tramp·ing, tramps**) **1.** *vi.* **TREAD HEAVILY** to tread heavily or noisily **2.** *vi.* **WALK** to walk, especially a long way **3.** *vt.* **COVER DISTANCE ON FOOT** to traverse an area, especially wearily, or cover a distance in a steady weary way **4.** *vt.* **CRUSH SOMETHING UNDERFOOT** to crush something by treading on it **5.** *vi.* **LIVE AS VAGRANT** to live or wander aimlessly as a vagrant **6.** *vi.* *NZ* **HIKE IN BUSH** to go hiking in the country for recreation [14thC. From Middle Low German *trampen* "to stamp." Ultimately from a prehistoric Germanic word that is also the ancestor of English *trap*. The noun is first recorded in the mid-17thC.] —**tramp·er** *n.* —**tramp·ing** *n.* —**tramp·ish** *adj.*

tram·ple /trámpəl/ (**-pled, -pling, -ples**) *vti.* **1. TREAD ON SOMETHING** to tread heavily, or to tread heavily on something or somebody so as to cause damage or injury **2. TREAT SOMEBODY ARROGANTLY** to behave in an insulting contemptuous way or to treat somebody in a hurtful insulting way [14thC. Formed from TRAMP.] —**tram·pler** *n.*

tram·po·line /trámpə leen/ *n.* a strong sheet, usually of canvas, that is stretched tightly on a horizontal frame to which it is connected by springs. It is used for jumping and tumbling. [Late 18thC. From Italian *trampolino* "springboard," from *trampoli* "stilts."] —**tram·po·line** *vi.* —**tram·po·lin·er** *n.* —**tram·po·lin·ist** *n.*

tramp steam·er *n.* a merchant ship that carries cargo but does not follow a fixed route

tram·road /trám ròd/ *n.* a small railroad used for moving freight, especially in a quarry

tram·way /trám wày/ *n.* **1. CABLES FOR CABLE CAR** a cable or the cables for a cable car **2.** *U.K.* **STREETCAR LINE** a streetcar line **3.** = **tramroad**

trance /trans/ *n.* **1. DAZED STATE** a state in which somebody is dazed or stunned or in some other way unaware of the environment and unable to respond to stimuli **2. HYPNOTIC STATE** a hypnotic or cataleptic state **3. RAPTUROUS STATE** a state of rapture or exaltation in which somebody loses consciousness **4. SPIRITUAL MEDIUM'S STATE** the state of apparent semi-unconsciousness that a spiritual medium enters into, allegedly in an attempt to communicate with the dead **5.** MUSIC **HYPNOTIC ELECTRONIC DANCE MUSIC** a type of electronic dance music with a repetitive hypnotic beat. It is a kind of techno. ■ *vt.* (**tranced, tranc·ing, tranc·es**) **ENTRANCE SOMEBODY** to put somebody in a trance (*literary*) [14thC. From Old French *transe*, from *transir* "to be numb with fear," originally "to die," from Latin *transire* (see TRANSIENT).]

trance chan·nel·ing *n.* = **channeling**

tranche /traansh/ *n.* a portion or section, often a division of something in financial terms, such as a single repayment of a loan or an individual class of securities [Mid-20thC. From French, literally "slice," from Old French *trenchier* "to cut" (source of English *trench*).]

tran·quil /trángkwəl, tránkwəl/ *adj.* **1. FREE FROM COMMOTION** free of any disturbance or commotion ○ *a tranquil morning* **2. COMPOSED** free from or showing no signs of anxiety or agitation [Mid-15thC. Via French *tranquille* from Latin *tranquillus*, which may have been formed from the same base as *quies* "quiet" (source of English *coy* and *quiet*).] —**tran·quil·ly** *adv.* —**tran·quil·ness** *n.*

WORD KEY: SYNONYMS

See Synonyms at ***calm***.

tran·quil·i·ty *n.* = **tranquillity**

tran·quil·ize /trángkwə lìz, tránkwə-/ (**-ized, -iz·ing, -iz·es**), **tran·quil·lize** *v.* **1.** *vt.* **MAKE SOMEBODY CALM** to induce calmness in a person or an animal, usually with medication **2.** *vi.* **BECOME CALM** to become calm or calmer **3.** *vi.* **HAVE CALMING EFFECT** to have a calming effect —**tran·quil·i·za·tion** /tràngkwəli záysh'n, tránkwəli-/ *n.*

tran·quil·iz·er /trángkwə lìzər, tránkwə-/ *n.* **1. CALMING DRUG** a medication that reduces anxiety and tension. Major tranquilizers are used to treat such psychoses as schizophrenia, while minor tranquilizers such as diazepam treat anxiety and other lesser conditions. **2. SOMETHING MAKING PERSON OR ANIMAL CALM** anything that renders a person or animal calm

tran·quil·li·ty /trang kwíllətee, tran-/, **tran·quil·i·ty** *n.* a state of peace and calm [14thC. Via Old French *tranquillité* from Latin *tranquillitas* "quietness," from, ultimately, *quies* "quiet" (source of English *coy* and *quiet*).]

tran·quil·lize *vt.* = **tranquilize**

trans. *abbr.* **1.** transaction **2.** transferred **3.** GRAM transitive **4.** translated **5.** translation **6.** transportation **7.** transpose **8.** transverse

trans- *prefix.* **1.** across, on the other side of, beyond ○ *transcontinental* ○ *transfinite* **2.** through ○ *transdermal* **3.** indicating change, transfer, or conversion ○ *transliterate* [From Latin *trans* "across, over, through"]

trans·act /tran zákt, tran sákt/ (**-act·ed, -act·ing, -acts**) *vti.* to conduct or carry out something such as business [Late 16thC. Back-formation from TRANSACTION.] —**trans·ac·tor** *n.*

trans·ac·tin·ide /tran záktə nìd, -sáktə-/ *n.* an element with an atomic number greater than 103 (*often used before a noun*) [Late 20thC. Coined from TRANS- + ACTINIDE by Dr Glenn T. Seaborg, modeled on transuranium, which he discovered.]

trans·ac·tion /tran zákshən, -sákshən/ *n.* **1.** BUSINESS **BUSINESS** a business deal that is being negotiated or has been settled **2. INTERACTION** a communication or activity between two or more people that influences and affects all of them (*formal*) **3.** BUSINESS **ACT OF NEGOTIATING** the act of negotiating something or carrying out a business deal **4.** COMPUT **ADDITION TO DATABASE** an action that adds, removes, or changes data in a database or other computer program ■ **trans·ac·tions** *npl.* **PROCEEDINGS** the published records of a learned society [Mid-15thC. Via French from, ultimately, Latin *transigere* "to drive through, accomplish," from *agere* "to drive, do" (see AGENT).] —**trans·ac·tion·al** *adj.* —**trans·ac·tion·al·ly** *adv.*

trans·ac·tion·al a·nal·y·sis *n.* a form of psychotherapy that emphasizes the interactions within and between individuals and classifies these interactions as "adult," "parent," or "child"

trans·ac·tion·al im·mu·ni·ty *n.* immunity from prosecution granted to a witness in any offense to which his or her testimony relates

trans·ac·ti·va·tion /tran zàkti váysh'n, -sàkti-/ *n.* the process whereby an infecting virus activates another virus's genes that are already integrated into the chromosome of the host bacterium, inducing the host cell to replicate the initial virus

trans·al·pine /tran zál pìn, -sál-/ *adj.* **1. BEYOND THE ALPS** relating to or found in the area beyond the Alps, especially as seen from Italy **2. CROSSING ALPS** relating to or engaged in crossing the Alps ■ *n.* **SOMEBODY FROM BEYOND THE ALPS** somebody who comes from or lives beyond the Alps, especially as seen from Italy [Late 16thC. From Latin *transalpinus*, from *alpes* "the Alps."]

trans·am·i·nase /tran zámmi nàyss, -nàyz, -sámmi-/ *n.* an enzyme that catalyzes the transfer of an amino group in the process of transamination

trans·am·i·na·tion /tran zàmmi náysh'n, -sàmmi-/ *n.* a process in the metabolism of amino acids and in the synthesis of proteins in the body in which one amino acid is formed from another

trans·at·lan·tic /trànzət lántik, trànsət-/ *adj.* **1. CROSSING ATLANTIC** relating to or engaged in crossing the Atlantic **2. BEYOND THE ATLANTIC** situated on or coming from the other side of the Atlantic

trans·ax·le /tran záksəl, -sáksəl/ *n.* a combined front axle and transmission in a motor vehicle with front-wheel drive [Mid-20thC. Coined from TRANSMISSION + AXLE.]

trans·bor·der /tranz báwrdər, trans-/ *adj.* crossing national borders, especially electronically

trans·bound·a·ry /tranz bówndree, trans-/ *adj.* crossing or existing across national boundaries

Trans·cau·ca·sia /trànss kaw káyzhə, -káyzee ə/ region in southeastern Europe, south of the Caucasus Mountains, between the Black and Caspian seas, forming the southern part of Caucasia. It consists of the republics of Georgia, Armenia, and Azerbaijan. —**Trans·cau·ca·sian** *adj.*

trans·ceiv·er /trans séevər, tran-/ *n.* **1.** RADIO **COMBINED RADIO TRANSMITTER AND RECEIVER** a radio transmitter and receiver combined in a single, often portable unit **2.** COMPUT **DATA TRANSMITTER AND RECEIVER** a device that can receive and transmit data, e.g., a modem [Mid-20thC. A blend of TRANSMITTER and RECEIVER.]

tran·scend /tran sénd/ (**-scend·ed, -scend·ing, -scends**) *vt.* **1. GO BEYOND LIMIT** to go beyond a limit or range, e.g., of thought or belief **2. SURPASS SOMETHING** to go beyond something in quality or achievement **3. BE INDEPENDENT OF WORLD** to exist above and apart from the material world [14thC. Via Old French from Latin *transcendere* "to climb over, beyond," from *scandere* "to climb, mount."]

tran·scen·dence /tran séndənss/, **tran·scen·den·cy** /-séndənsee/ *n.* **1. INDEPENDENCE FROM WORLD** existence above and apart from the material world **2. GREATER STATUS** the quality or state of exceeding or surpassing something

tran·scen·dent /tran séndənt/ *adj.* **1. BETTER** superior in quality or achievement **2.** PHILOS **BEYOND LIMITS OF EXPERIENCE** in Kant's philosophical system, exceeding the limits of experience and therefore unknowable except hypothetically **3.** PHILOS **BEYOND CATEGORIES** above or outside all known categories **4.** RELIG **INDEPENDENT OF THE WORLD** existing outside the material universe and so not limited by it ■ *n.* **SOMETHING OR SOMEBODY TRANSCENDENT** something that or somebody who is or appears to be transcendent —**tran·scen·dent·ly** *adv.* —**tran·scen·dent·ness** *n.*

tran·scen·den·tal /tràn sen dént'l/ *adj.* **1.** = **transcendent** *adj.* 1 **2.** PHILOS **NOT EXPERIENCED BUT KNOWABLE** independent of human experience of phenomena but within the range of knowledge **3.** RELIG **MYSTICAL** relating to mystical or supernatural experience and therefore beyond the material world **4.** MATH **NOT ALGEBRAIC** used to describe a number or function that is not algebraic and is not the root of an algebraic equation ■ *n.* MATH **NUMBER IMPOSSIBLE TO EXPRESS AS INTEGER** a number that cannot be expressed as an integer, e.g., a nonrepeating decimal such as pi [Early 17thC. From late Latin *transcendentalis* "transcending the bounds of all categories," from *transcendere* (see TRANSCEND).] —**tran·scen·den·tal·i·ty** /tràn sen den tállətee/ *n.* —**tran·scen·den·tal·ly** /tràn sen dént'lee/ *adv.*

tran·scen·den·tal·ism /tràn sen dént'l ìzzəm/ *n.* **1.** PHILOS **PHILOSOPHY EMPHASIZING REASONING** a system of philosophy, especially that of Kant, that regards the processes of reasoning as the key to knowledge of reality **2.** PHILOS **PHILOSOPHY EMPHASIZING DIVINE** a system of philosophy, especially that associated with Ralph Waldo Emerson and other New England writers, that emphasizes intuition or the divine **3. TRANSCENDENTAL THOUGHT** transcendental thought or language **4. TRANSCENDENTAL NATURE** the state or quality of being transcendental —**tran·scen·den·tal·ist** *n., adj.*

tran·scen·den·tal med·i·ta·tion *n.* a form of meditation in which a mantra is repeated silently. It is based on Hindu traditions.

trans·con·ti·nen·tal /tràns kontə nént'l/ *adj.* **1. ACROSS CONTINENT** extending across a continent **2. BEYOND CONTINENT** situated on or coming from the other side of a continent ■ *n.* TRANSP **TRAIN CROSSING CONTINENT** a train or railroad that crosses a continent —**trans·con·ti·nen·tal·ly** *adv.*

tran·scribe /tran skríb/ (**-scribed, -scrib·ing, -scribes**) *vt.* **1. COPY SOMETHING** to write out an exact copy of something **2. EXPAND SOMETHING IN WRITING** to write something out in full from notes or shorthand **3.** PHON **WRITE SOUNDS PHONETICALLY** to write speech sounds phonetically **4. TRANSLATE SOMETHING** to translate or transliterate something **5.** MUSIC **REARRANGE MUSIC** to arrange a piece of music for a different instrument, voice, or combination **6.** BROADCAST **RECORD SOMETHING FOR LATER BROADCASTING** to record something so that it can be broadcast at a later time **7.** BROADCAST **BROADCAST SOMETHING TRANSCRIBED** to broadcast something that has been transcribed earlier **8.** COMPUT **TRANSFER SOMETHING TO OTHER STORAGE FORMAT** to transfer information from one way of storing it on computer to another, or from a computer to an external storage device **9.** GENETICS **CONVERT CODE FOR TRANSMISSION TO RNA** to convert the genetic code carried by DNA into an equivalent form carried by a molecule of messenger RNA **10.** GENETICS **CONVERT GENETIC CODE INTO DNA MOLECULE** to convert the genetic code carried by the RNA of a retrovirus into a molecule of DNA [Mid-16thC. From Latin *transcribere* "to copy, convey," literally "to write across," from *scribere* "to write."] —**tran·scrib·a·ble** *adj.* —**tran·scrib·er** *n.*

tran·script /trán skrìpt/ *n.* **1. WRITTEN RECORD** a written record of something, e.g., a copy of the script of a broadcast program or a record of court proceedings **2. STUDENT'S ACADEMIC HISTORY** an official document showing the educational work of a student in a school or college **3. COPY** any copy or record **4.** GENETICS **RNA WITH TRANSCRIBED CODE** a molecule of messenger RNA that carries coded genetic information converted from the genetic code held by the DNA during the process of transcription in living cells **5.** GENETICS **DNA CARRYING CODED RETROVIRUS** the DNA that carries the coded information of a retrovirus, converted from the genetic code held by the virus's RNA during transcription following the infection of a living cell [Mid-15thC. From Latin *transcriptum*, from the past participle of *transcribere* (see TRANSCRIBE).]

tran·scrip·tase /tran skríp tàyss, -tàyz/ *n.* an enzyme that catalyzes the synthesis of messenger RNA from a DNA template during transcription

tran·scrip·tion /tran skrípshən/ *n.* **1. TRANSCRIBING** the act or process of transcribing something **2. TRANSCRIPT** something that has been transcribed **3.** PHON **PHONETIC REPRESENTATION** a phonetic representation of speech using special symbols **4.** GENETICS **TRANSFER OF GENETIC CODE** the first step in carrying out genetic instructions in living cells, in which the genetic code is transferred from DNA to molecules of messenger RNA, which subsequently direct protein manufacture **5.** GENETICS **TRANSFER OF GENETIC INFORMATION** the first step in the replication of a retrovirus following its infection of a living cell, in which its genetic code is transferred from RNA to a molecule of RNA

tran·scrip·tion·al /tran skrípshən'l, -skrípshnəl/ *adj.* relating to transcripts, or to the transcribing of things —**tran·scrip·tion·al·ly** *adv.*

tran·scrip·tive /tran skríptiv/ *adj.* used for transcribing or in the form of a transcript —**tran·scrip·tive·ly** *adv.*

trans·cul·tur·al /trans kúlchərəl/ *adj.* extending across cultures or involving more than one culture

trans·cul·tu·ra·tion /tràns kúlchə ráysh'n/ *n.* the change in a culture brought about by the diffusion within it of elements from other cultures

trans·cur·rent /trans kúr ənt/ *adj.* running across something, especially perpendicular to an expected direction or flow [Early 17thC. From Latin, from the present participle stem of *transcurrere* "to run across, traverse," from *currere* "to run" (see CURRENT).]

trans·cu·ta·ne·ous /tràns kyoo táynee əss/ *adj.* = **transdermal**

trans·cu·ta·ne·ous e·lec·tri·cal nerve stim·u·la·tion *n.* MED full form of **TENS**

trans·der·mal /tranz dúrm'l, trans-/ *adj.* used to describe something, especially a drug, that is introduced into the body through the skin

trans·der·mal patch *n.* a patch applied to the skin as a way of releasing a preset dose of medication into the body in a controlled manner

trans·duce /tranz dóoss, trans-/ (**-duced, -duc·ing, -duc·es**) *vt.* **1.** PHYS **CONVERT INTO DIFFERENT ENERGY** to change one type of energy into another type **2.** GENETICS **TRANSFER GENETIC MATERIAL** to effect the transfer of genetic material from one bacterium to another using a bacteriophage [Mid-20thC. Back-formation from TRANSDUCER.]

trans·duc·er /tranz dóossər, trans-/ *n.* **1.** PHYS **DEVICE THAT CONVERTS ENERGY** a device that transforms one type of energy into another, e.g., a microphone, a photoelectric cell, or an automobile horn **2.** BIOL **BIOLOGICAL CONVERTER OF ENERGY** a biological entity that converts energy in one form to another, e.g., the rods and cones of the eye or the hair cells of the ear [Early 20thC. Formed from Latin *transducere* "to lead across, transfer" (see TRADUCE).]

trans·duc·tion /tranz dúksh'n, trans-/ *n.* **1.** GENETICS **TRANSFER OF GENETIC MATERIAL** the transfer of genetic material from one bacterium to another using a bacteriophage **2.** PHYSIOL **TRANSPORTATION OF STIMULI TO NERVOUS SYSTEM** the conversion of stimuli detected in receptor cells to electrical impulses that are then transported by the nervous system, as occurs when the ear converts sound waves into nerve impulses —**trans·duc·tion·al** *adj.*

tran·sect /tran sékt/ *vt.* (**-sect·ed, -sect·ing, -sects**) **CUT ACROSS SOMETHING** to divide something by running or cutting across it ■ *n.* ECOL **LINE FOR ECOLOGICAL MEASUREMENTS** a strip of ground along which ecological measurements, e.g., the number of organisms, are made at regular intervals [Mid-17thC. Coined from TRANS- + INTERSECT.] —**tran·sec·tion** /tran séksh'n/ *n.*

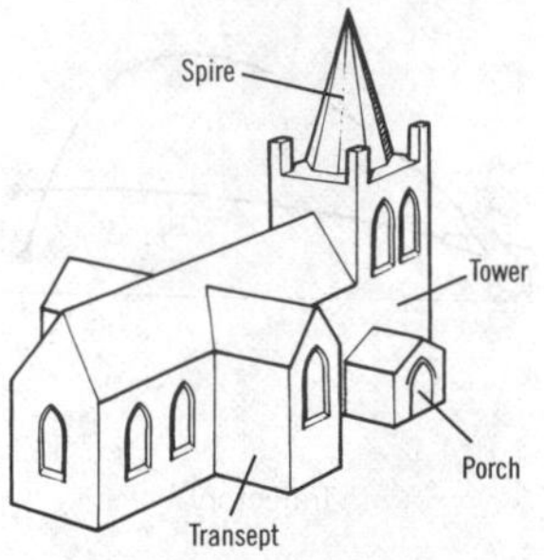

Transept

tran·sept /trán sèpt/ *n.* **1. WINGS OF CHURCH** a portion of a cross-shaped church that runs at right angles to the long central part (**nave**) **2. ARM OF TRANSEPT** either of the two arms of a transept [Mid-16thC. From modern Latin *transeptum*, literally "across enclosure," from Latin *saeptum* "enclosure, wall, fence."] —**tran·sep·tal** /tran sépt'l/ *adj.*

tran·se·unt /tránsee ənt/, **tran·sient** /tránshənt, tránzhənt, tránzee ənt/ *adj.* that produces effects outside the mind

transf. *abbr.* transferred

trans·fat·ty ac·id /tràns fátti-/, **trans-fat** /tránss fàt/ *n.* a potentially harmful unsaturated fat produced when a liquid vegetable oil is solidified by the process of hydrogenation, especially in the manufacture of low-fat spreads. Trans-fatty acids are viewed as a health risk because they raise cholesterol levels.

trans·fect /trans fékt/ (**-fect·ed, -fect·ing, -fects**) *vt.* to infect a cell with viral nucleic acid or DNA from a source other than the cell itself [Mid-20thC. Back-formation from TRANSFECTION.]

trans·fec·tion /trans fékshən/ *n.* the infection of a cell with viral genetic material leading to the subsequent production of the virus in the cell [Mid-20thC. Coined from TRANS- + INFECTION.]

trans·fer *v.* /trans fúr, tráns fúr/ (**-ferred, -fer·ring, -fers**) **1.** *vti.* BUSINESS **START WORKING ELSEWHERE** to employ somebody, or to begin employment, at a different job or in a different place while working for the same company ○ *transfer to Chicago* **2.** *vti.* **MOVE FROM ONE PLACE TO ANOTHER** to move from one place to another, or cause somebody or something to do so **3.** *vti.* **PASS FROM ONE PERSON TO ANOTHER** to pass from one person, group, or organization to another, or cause something to be passed from one person, group, or organization to another **4.** *vti.* TRANSP **CHANGE VEHICLES** to change from one vehicle or method of transportation to another, or cause somebody to do this **5.** *vti.* EDUC **CHANGE SCHOOLS OR SUBJECTS** to move from one school or university to another, or change from one course to another **6.** *vt.* LAW **GIVE OWNERSHIP OF** to pass ownership rights in something to somebody else ○ *transfer a deed* **7.** *vt.* **PUT IMAGE ON ANOTHER SURFACE** to copy a design or image from a piece of paper onto a different material ■ *n.* /tráns fùr/ **1. CHANGE OF PLACE** the conveying of somebody or something from one place, e.g., one department of an organization, to another **2.** TRANSP **TICKET ALLOWING PASSENGER TO TRANSFER** a ticket that allows a passenger to change from one vehicle to another on a journey, or the place where this is done **3. SOMEBODY TRANSFERRED** somebody who is transferred, e.g., a student **4.** LAW **CONVEYANCE** the passing of rights or property from one person to another, or a document that conveys rights or property between persons **5. DESIGN APPLIED TO SURFACE** an image on a piece of film or paper that is specially designed to be lifted off by heat or pressure and applied permanently to the surface of a material **6.** FIN **RECORDING OF SALE** the recording of a change of ownership of shares or bonds in the books of the issuer [14thC. From Latin *transferre* "to carry across," from *ferre* "to carry" (see FERTILE).]

trans·fer·a·ble /trans fúr əb'l/, **trans·fer·ra·ble** *adj.* able to be transferred, especially to somebody else's ownership —**trans·fer·a·bil·i·ty** /trans fùr ə bíllətee, trànsfərə-/ *n.*

transferal /trans fúr əl/ *n.* = **transference** *n.* 1

trans·fer·ase /tránsfə ràyss, -ràyz/ *n.* any enzyme that catalyzes the transfer of a chemical group from one molecule to another

trans·fer char·ac·ter·is·tic *n.* a graphical illustration of the relationship between the input and output of an electronic system

trans·fer·ee /transfə reé/ *n.* **1.** SOMEBODY TRANSFERRED somebody who has been transferred, e.g., to a new department or organization **2.** LAW SOMEBODY TO WHOM SOMETHING IS TRANSFERRED somebody to whom a right or property is transferred by law

trans·fer·ence /trans fúr əns/ *n.* **1.** ACT OF TRANSFERRING the transferring of something from one place or person to another **2.** PROCESS OF BEING TRANSFERRED the change from one person or place to another that happens when something is transferred **3.** PSYCHOL REDIRECTION OF FEELING the process in psychoanalysis or other psychotherapy whereby somebody unconsciously redirects feelings, fears, or emotions onto a new object, often the analyst or therapist —**trans·fer·en·tial** /transfə rénshəl/ *adj.*

trans·fer fac·tor *n.* a polypeptide that is produced by white blood cells and can transfer immunity from one cell to another or from one person to another

trans·fer·or /tránsfə ràwr/, **trans·fer·rer** /tránsfərər/ *n.* somebody who transfers a title, right, or property to another person

trans·fer pay·ment *n.* an item of personal income that comes from the state or a financial institution and is not included in calculating the national income

trans·fer·ra·ble *adj.* = **transferable**

trans·fer·ral *n.* = **transferal**

trans·fer·rer *n.* = **transferor**

trans·fer·rin /trans férrin/ *n.* a protein in blood serum that binds to iron and transports it to the bone marrow where it is used in the production of red blood cells [Mid-20thC. Coined from TRANS- + Latin *ferrum* "iron" + -IN.]

trans·fer RNA *n.* a type of RNA that attaches amino acids to a ribosome to allow protein to be produced in living cells

trans·fig·u·ra·tion /trans figgyə ráysh'n/ *n.* **1.** CHANGE IN APPEARANCE a dramatic change in appearance, especially one that glorifies or exalts somebody **2.** TRANSFIGURED STATE the transfiguring of somebody or something, or the changed state that results

Trans·fig·u·ra·tion /trans figgyə ráysh'n/ *n.* **1.** RADIANT APPEARANCE OF JESUS CHRIST the radiant appearance of Jesus Christ on the mountaintop before three of his disciples, as recorded in the Bible **2.** FESTIVAL OF THE TRANSFIGURATION the Christian festival that commemorates the Transfiguration, held on August 6 or, in the Eastern Orthodox Church, on August 19

trans·fig·ure /trans fíggyər/ (**-ured, -ur·ing, -ures**) *vt.* to transform the appearance of somebody or something, revealing great beauty, spirituality, or magnificence [14thC. From Latin *transfigurare* "to change the shape of," literally "to (put) across the shape," from *figura* "shape" (see FIGURE).] —**trans·fig·ure·ment** *n.*

trans·fi·nite /trans fí nìt/ *adj.* used to describe a mathematical entity such as a number, group, or quantity that extends beyond infinity [Early 20thC. From German *transfinit*, from Latin *trans-* "across, over" + *finitus* "finite, limited."]

trans·fi·nite num·ber *n.* a system of cardinal and ordinal numbers, used in the comparison of infinite sets, to which several types of infinity can be assigned concurrently

trans·fix /trans fíks/ (**-fixed, -fix·ing, -fix·es**) *vt.* **1.** MAKE SOMEBODY IMMOBILE WITH SHOCK to shock or terrify somebody so much as to induce a momentary inability to move **2.** PIERCE THROUGH SOMEBODY to pierce somebody or something through with a weapon or other sharp object **3.** MED CUT COMPLETELY THROUGH LIMB to cut through a part of the body completely, e.g., when amputating a limb [Late 16thC. Directly or via Old French *transfixer* from Latin *transfix-*, the past participle stem of *transfigere* "to pierce, run through," literally "to fix through," from *figere* "to fix" (see FIX).] —**trans·fix·ion** /trans fíkshən/ *n.*

trans·form[1] (**-formed, -form·ing, -forms**) *v.* /trans fáwrm/ **1.** *vt.* CHANGE SOMETHING DRAMATICALLY to change people or things completely, especially improving their appearance or usefulness **2.** *vi.* UNDERGO TOTAL CHANGE to change completely for the better **3.** *vt.* PHYS CONVERT SOMETHING TO DIFFERENT ENERGY to convert one form of energy to another **4.** *vt.* ELEC ENG CHANGE ELECTRICAL CURRENT BY TRANSFORMER to increase or decrease current or voltage by means of a transformer **5.** *vt.* MATH CHANGE MATHEMATICAL EXPRESSION BY OPERATOR to change the form of a mathematical expression in keeping with a mathematical rule, especially by the substitution of variables or the change of coordinates **6.** *vt.* LING CHANGE CONSTRUCTION BY LINGUISTIC TRANSFORMATION to apply transformational rules to a linguistic construction [14thC. Directly or via French *transformer* from Latin *transformare*, literally "to form across," from *formare* "to form" (see FORM).] —**trans·form·a·ble** *adj.* —**trans·form·a·tive** *adj.*

WORD KEY: SYNONYMS

See Synonyms at ***change***.

trans·form[2] /tráns fàwrm/ *n.* **1.** LING = **transformation** *n.* 7 **2.** MATH RESULT OF MATHEMATICAL TRANSFORMATION a process or rule by which one mathematical entity such as a line or expression can be derived from another

trans·for·ma·tion /trànsfər máysh'n/ *n.* **1.** COMPLETE CHANGE a complete change, usually into something with an improved appearance or usefulness **2.** TRANSFORMING the act or process of transforming somebody or something **3.** MATH SUBSTITUTION OF VARIABLES the mathematical conversion of an expression, equation, or function into another equivalent entity, e.g., by the substitution of one set of variables with another **4.** BIOL CELL MODIFICATION the conversion of a normal cell into a malignant cell brought about by the action of a carcinogen or virus **5.** MATH CHANGE IN POSITION OF AXIS a change in the position or direction of the axes of a mathematical coordinate system without changing their relative angles **6.** PHYS CHANGE IN ATOMIC NUCLEUS the change of one type of atom to another, resulting from a nuclear reaction **7.** LING CHANGE OF GRAMMATICAL STRUCTURE in transformational grammar, the process of converting one linguistic construction or structure to another, following the rules that convert deep structure to surface structure **8.** LING STAGE IN TRANSFORMATIONAL PROCESS in transformational grammar, a construction or structure generated by using the rules that convert deep structure into surface structure **9.** THEATER SUDDEN SET CHANGE a sudden changing of a stage set that takes place in sight of the audience **10.** GENETICS GENETIC CHANGE a permanent change in the genetic makeup of a cell when it acquires foreign DNA

trans·for·ma·tion·al gram·mar *n.* a kind of grammar that is based on the theory that language has a deep structure and that there are rules that transform the deep structure into the surface structure. It uses transformational rules to describe a language.

trans·for·ma·tion·al rule *n.* **1.** LING RULE CHANGING UNDERLYING GRAMMATICAL STRUCTURE in transformational grammar, a rule that generates one stage from another in the conversion of deep structure into surface structure **2.** LOGIC RULE FOR DERIVING THEOREMS in logic, a rule for deriving theorems from axioms

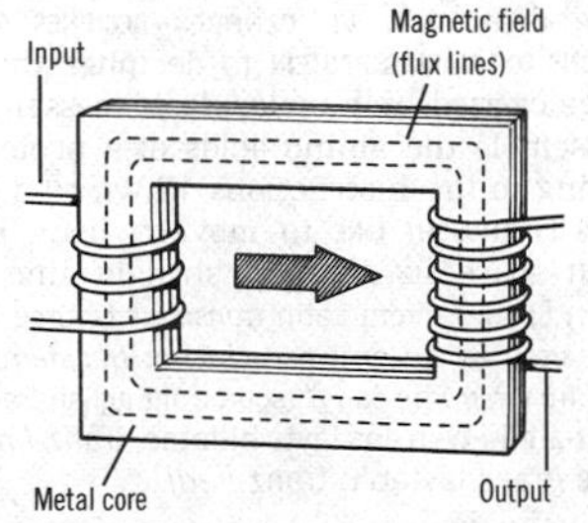

Transformer

trans·form·er /trans fáwrmər/ *n.* **1.** ELEC DEVICE FOR CHANGING ELECTRICAL ENERGY a device that transfers electrical energy from one alternating circuit to another with a change in voltage, current, phase, or impedance **2.** SOMEBODY OR SOMETHING THAT TRANSFORMS somebody who or something that effects a transformation

trans·fuse /trans fyóoz/ (**-fused, -fus·ing, -fus·es**) *vt.* **1.** MED GIVE BLOOD TO SOMEBODY to administer blood obtained from one person into the bloodstream of another person **2.** MED PUT FLUID INTO BLOODSTREAM OF to administer a fluid such as saline or plasma into somebody's bloodstream **3.** TRANSFER SOMETHING BY POURING to pour something from one container into another (*formal or technical*) **4.** SPREAD THROUGHOUT SOMETHING to spread throughout something and affect every part of it [Early 15thC. From Latin *transfus-*, the past participle stem of *transfundere* "to decant, transfer," literally "to pour across (into another vessel)," from *fundere* "to pour" (see FUSE).] —**trans·fus·a·ble** *adj.* —**trans·fus·er** *n.* —**trans·fu·sive** *adj.*

trans·fu·sion /trans fyóozh'n/ *n.* **1.** MED GIVING OF BLOOD the transfer of whole blood, blood components, or bone marrow from a healthy donor into the bloodstream of somebody who has lost blood or who has a blood disorder **2.** TRANSFUSING the act or process of transfusing something

trans·gen·ic /tranz jénnik, trans-/ *adj.* GENETICS **1.** WITH GENES FROM DIFFERENT SPECIES used to describe an animal or plant that contains genes from a different species, transferred using genetic engineering techniques. Using such techniques can, e.g., induce disease resistance in plants and modify animals so that their organs can be used in human transplants. **2.** INVOLVING TRANSFER OF GENETIC MATERIAL used to describe the technique of transferring genetic material from one organism into the DNA of another —**trans·gen·i·cal·ly** *adv.*

trans·gress /tranz gréss/ (**-gressed, -gress·ing, -gress·es**) *v.* **1.** *vi.* DO WRONG to commit a crime or do wrong by disobeying a law, command, or moral code ○ *He transgressed against the organization's code of conduct.* **2.** *vt.* BREAK LAW to break a law, rule, or moral code ○ *transgress the law* **3.** *vt.* OVERSTEP PROPER LIMIT to go beyond a limit, usually in a blameworthy way ○ *She'd transgressed the bounds of civil behavior.* [15thC. Directly or via French *transgresser* from Latin *transgress-*, the past participle stem of *transgredi* "to step across, go over," from *gradi* "to step, go."] —**trans·gres·sive** *adj.* —**trans·gres·sive·ly** *adv.* —**trans·gres·sor** *n.*

trans·gres·sion /tranz grésh'n/ *n.* **1.** ACTION VIOLATING LAW OR CODE a crime or any act that violates a law, command, or moral code **2.** COMMISSION OF WRONGS the committing of acts that violate a law, command, or moral code **3.** OVERSTEPPING A LIMIT an act or the process of overstepping a limit

trans·gres·sive fic·tion *n.* a literary genre traceable to such writers as the Marquis de Sade and William Burroughs, characterized by graphic exploration of taboo topics. It is based on the belief that knowledge is to be found at the very edge of human experience.

tran·ship *vti.* = **transship**

trans·hu·mance /trans hyóomənss/ *n.* the practice of moving livestock between different grazing lands according to season, especially up to mountain pastures in summer and back down into the valleys in winter [Early 20thC. From French, from *transhumer*, literally "to go across ground," ultimately from Latin *humus* "ground."] —**trans·hu·mant** *adj.*

tran·sient /tránshənt, tránzhənt, tránzee ənt/ *adj.* **1.** SHORT IN DURATION lasting for only a short time and quickly coming to an end, disappearing, or changing ○ *a transient emotion* ○ *transient sunlight on an otherwise cloudy day* **2.** NOT PERMANENTLY SETTLED IN PLACE staying in a place for only a short period of time ○ *transient workers* **3.** PHILOS = **transeunt** ■ *n.* **1.** SOMEBODY STAYING BRIEFLY somebody who stays in a place for only a short time, e.g., a migrant laborer or hotel guest **2.** ELEC ENG BRIEF DISTURBANCE IN ELECTRICAL CIRCUIT an oscillation or brief disturbance in a system, e.g., a sudden pulse of current or voltage in an electrical circuit [Late 16thC. Alteration of Latin *transiens* (stem *transeunt-*), the present participle of *transire* "to pass away, go across," from *ire* "to go."] —**tran·sience** *n.* —**tran·sien·cy** *n.* —**tran·sient·ly** *adv.*

trans·il·lu·mi·nate /trànzi lóomə nàyt/ (**-nat·ed, -nat·ing, -nates**) *vt.* to shine a bright light through a body organ or cavity to detect disease or other abnormality —**trans·il·lu·mi·na·tion** /tranzi lóomə náysh'n/ *n.* —**trans·il·lu·mi·na·tor** /trànzə lóomə nàytər/ *n.*

tran·sis·tor /tran zístər/ *n.* **1.** ELECTRON ENG SOLID-STATE ELECTRONIC DEVICE a small low-powered solid-state electronic device consisting of a semiconductor and at least three electrodes, used as an amplifier and rectifier and frequently incorporated into integrated circuit chips **2.** RADIO a transistor radio [Mid-20thC. Blend of TRANSFER and RESISTOR (from its transference of electrical current across a resistor).]

tran·sis·tor·ize /tran zístə rīz/ (**-ized, -iz·ing, -iz·es**) *vt.* to equip a device or circuit with transistors

tran·sis·tor ra·di·o *n.* a small portable radio using transistors in its circuits

tran·sit /tránzit/ *n.* **1.** ACT OF TRAVEL ACROSS SOMETHING the act of traveling or being transported through or across an area, over a distance, or from one place to another ○ *a transit permit* **2.** TRANSP PUBLIC TRANSPORTATION the transportation of passengers by means of a local public transportation system ○ *traveled by rapid transit* **3.** PUBLIC TRANSPORT SYSTEM a local public transportation system ○ *city transit* **4.** ASTRON PLANET'S CROSSING OF SUN the movement of Venus or Mercury across the face of the Sun, or of a moon or its shadow across the face of a planet, as seen from Earth **5.** ASTRON PASSAGE OF STAR ACROSS MERIDIAN the apparent movement of a star or planet across the meridian from which it is being observed, caused by the Earth's rotation **6.** ZODIAC PLANET'S CROSSING OF ZODIAC the passing of a planet across a particular point on the zodiac **7.** TRANSITION a transition or passing, e.g., from life to a supposed spiritual existence after death **8.** CIV ENG SURVEYING INSTRUMENT a surveying instrument surmounted by a telescope that can be rotated completely around its horizontal axis, used for measuring vertical and horizontal angles ■ *v.* (**-sit·ed, -sit·ing, -sits**) **1.** *vti.* PASS THROUGH to pass through or over something ○ *They transited the area on foot.* **2.** *vti.* ASTRON MAKE A TRANSIT to make a transit across the face of the Sun or a planet, or across a meridian **3.** *vt.* CIV ENG REVERSE DIRECTION OF SURVEYING TELESCOPE to rotate the telescope of a surveying instrument horizontally through 180 degrees, thus reversing its direction [15thC. From Latin *transitus* "passage," from *transire* "to go across," from *ire* "to go."] —**tran·sit·a·ble** *adj.* ◇ **in transit** in the process of traveling or being transported from one place to another

tran·sit cir·cle *n.* an astronomical telescope that moves in a north-south plane enabling it to be used to determine the exact time a star, planet, or other celestial object passes most nearly overhead

tran·sit in·stru·ment *n.* a telescopic instrument that can move only in the plane of a meridian, used to determine the exact time a star, planet, or other celestial object crosses that meridian

tran·si·tion /tran zísh'n/ *n.* **1.** PROCESS OF CHANGE a process or period in which something undergoes a change and passes from one state, stage, form, or activity to another **2.** MUSIC MUSICAL PASSAGE a passage connecting two sections of a musical composition **3.** MUSIC CHANGE OF KEY a progression from one key to another in a piece of music **4.** GRAM LINKING WORD OR PHRASE a word, phrase, or passage that links one subject or idea to another in speech or writing **5.** PHYS, CHEM CHANGE BETWEEN PHASES a change between phases such as solid to liquid or liquid to gas **6.** ARCHIT STYLE BETWEEN ROMANESQUE AND GOTHIC a style of architecture in many buildings dating from the 12th century in western Europe, in which elements of the Romanesque and Gothic styles are combined **7.** NUCLEAR PHYS CHANGE IN AN ATOMIC NUCLEUS a change in the energy level or state of an atomic nucleus in which a single quantum of electromagnetic radiation is either lost or gained ■ *vti.* (**-tioned, -tion·ing, -tions**) CAUSE TO CHANGE to undergo a change of status or condition, or to cause somebody or something to undergo a change (*informal*) ○ *"We must transition Social Security from a pay-as-you-go fund to a true pension fund."* (*Speech by H. Ross Perot, Asbury Park Press; 1996*) [15thC. From the Latin stem *transition-*, from *transire* (see TRANSIT).]

tran·si·tion·al /tran zíshən'l, tran zíshnəl/ *adj.* **1.** DURING TRANSITION marked by or during a transition from one state or condition to another ○ *The détente was a transitional period in international relations.* **2.** ARCHIT CHARACTERISTIC OF TRANSITION characteristic of a period of architectural transition, combining elements of the earlier and later forms or styles between which something is progressing ○ *a transitional style* —**tran·si·tion·al·ly** *adv.*

transitionary *adj.* = **transitional** (*literary*)

tran·si·tion el·e·ment, **tran·si·tion met·al** *n.* any of the metallic elements that have an incomplete penultimate electron shell, variable valences, and typically form colored compounds. Copper, chromium, and gold are transition elements.

tran·si·tion point *n.* = **transition temperature**

tran·si·tive /tránzitiv/ *adj.* **1.** GRAM REQUIRING DIRECT OBJECT needing or usually taking a direct object ○ *a transitive verb* **2.** LOGIC, MATH INVOLVING SAME RELATION BETWEEN TERMS used to describe a given relation such that if it exists between "a" and "b" and between "b" and "c" then it also exists between "a" and "c." Typical transitive relationships include "is greater than," "is equal to," and "is similar to." —**tran·si·tive·ly** *adv.* —**tran·si·tive·ness** *n.* —**tran·si·tiv·i·ty** /trànzi tívvətee/ *n.*

tran·sit lounge *n.* a waiting room at an international airport used mainly by passengers transferring from one flight to another without presenting themselves to customs or immigration officials

tran·si·to·ry /tránzə tàwree/ *adj.* not permanent or lasting, but existing only for a short time ○ *a transitory infatuation* —**tran·si·to·ri·ly** /trànzə táwrilee/ *adv.* —**tran·si·to·ri·ness** /tránzə tàwreenəss/ *n.*

tran·sit pas·sen·ger *n.* a passenger at an airport who is there simply to change flights

Trans·kei /tránss kī/ former homeland in South Africa, now part of Eastern Cape Province

transl. *abbr.* **1.** translator **2.** translation **3.** translated

trans·late /trans láyt, tranz-/ (**-lat·ed, -lat·ing, -lates**) *v.* **1.** *vti.* TURN WORDS INTO DIFFERENT LANGUAGE to give an equivalent in another language for a particular word or phrase, or reproduce a written or spoken text in a different language while retaining the original meaning ○ *Can you translate that phrase?* **2.** *vi.* BE CAPABLE OF BEING TRANSLATED to be capable of being translated, or have an equivalent in another language ○ *The idiom doesn't translate well.* **3.** *vt.* COMPUT CONVERT CODE to convert data to a different form following an algorithm ○ *translate the program into machine code* **4.** *vt.* SAY SOMETHING IN UNDERSTANDABLE TERMS to say or explain something in terms that are easier to understand ○ *What he really means is "We don't know what happened to your car."* **5.** *vt.* INTERPRET MEANING to explain the meaning of something not expressed in words, e.g., an action, gesture, or look ○ *I translated his silence as approval.* **6.** *vti.* CHANGE FORM OF SOMETHING to change something, or be changed, from one form or effect into another ○ *"Microchips controlled by software now translate the flick of a pilot's wrist into the movement of a wing flap"* (Evan I. Schwartz, *Trust Me, I'm Your Software, Discover Magazine; May 1996*) **7.** *vt.* MOVE SOMEBODY OR SOMETHING to move or carry somebody or something from one place to another, usually involving a complete change of condition or scene ○ *She was translated from her small country home to a high-rise city apartment* **8.** *vt.* CHR TRANSFER CLERGY to transfer a member of the clergy to another office, especially to transfer a bishop to another see **9.** *vt.* CHR MOVE SAINT'S REMAINS to move the remains or relics of a saint from one place to another **10.** *vt.* RELIG CONVEY SOMEBODY TO HEAVEN to convey somebody to heaven, especially in a way that is believed not to involve death **11.** *vt.* GENETICS DECIPHER GENETIC INSTRUCTIONS FOR MAKING PROTEIN to decipher the genetic message carried by a molecule of messenger RNA and assemble the amino acids of a protein chain according to the instructions **12.** *vt.* PHYS MOVE BODY SIDEWAYS IN STRAIGHT LINE to move a body sideways through space in a direct straight line without rotation [14thC. From Latin *translatus* (source of English *elation*), used as the past participle of *transferre* "to carry across," from *ferre* "to carry" (source of English *transfer*).] —**trans·lat·a·bil·i·ty** /trans làytə bíllətee, tranz-/ *n.* —**trans·lat·a·ble** /trans láytəb'l, tranz-/ *adj.*

trans·la·tion /trans láysh'n, tranz-/ *n.* **1.** VERSION IN ANOTHER LANGUAGE a word, phrase, or version in another language that has a meaning equivalent to that of the original **2.** EXPRESSING OF SOMETHING IN A DIFFERENT LANGUAGE the rendering of something written or spoken in one language in words of a different language ○ *She read the novel in translation.* **3.** CHANGE OR TRANSFERENCE a change in form or state, or transference to a different place, office, or sphere **4.** GENETICS PROCESS DETERMINING AMINO ACID SEQUENCE the process by which information in messenger RNA directs the sequence of amino acids assembled by a ribosome during protein synthesis **5.** PHYS MOTION IN STRAIGHT LINE the movement of a body in a straight line so that every point on the body follows a parallel path and no rotation takes place —**trans·la·tion·al** *adj.*

trans·la·tor /trans láytər, tranz-/ *n.* **1.** SOMEBODY WHO TRANSLATES somebody or something that translates, in writing or speech, from one language into another **2.** RADIO TRANSMITTER THAT ALTERS SIGNAL FREQUENCY a radio transmitter that receives a signal on one frequency and retransmits it on another **3.** COMPUT CONVERTING COMPUTER PROGRAM a computer program that converts other programs from one computer language into another —**trans·la·to·ri·al** /trànslə táwree əl, trànzlə-/ *adj.*

trans·lit·er·ate /trans líttə ràyt, tranz-/ (**-at·ed, -at·ing, -ates**) *vt.* to represent a letter or word written in one alphabet using the corresponding letter or letters of another, so that the sound of the letter or word remains approximately the same [Mid-19thC. Formed from TRANS- + Latin *litera* "letter" (see LETTER) + -ATE.] —**trans·lit·er·a·tion** /trans lìttə ráysh'n, tranz-/ *n.* —**trans·lit·er·a·tor** /trans líttə ràytər, tranz-/ *n.*

trans·lo·cate /trans lō káyt, tranz-/ (**-cat·ed, -cat·ing, -cates**) *vt.* to move somebody or something from one place or position to another

trans·lo·ca·tion /trans lō káysh'n, tranz-/ *n.* **1.** MOVEMENT FROM ONE PLACE TO ANOTHER movement, or the act of moving something or somebody, from one place or position to another **2.** BOT MOVEMENT OF FOOD IN PLANTS the movement of soluble materials within a plant. Common examples are the movement of food materials from the leaves to storage organs, and the movement of dissolved minerals upward from the roots. **3.** GENETICS TRANSFER OF PART OF CHROMOSOME the transfer of part of a chromosome to a new position on the same or on a different chromosome with resultant rearrangement of the genes

trans·lu·cent /trans lóos'nt, tranz-/ *adj.* **1.** LETTING LIGHT THROUGH DIFFUSELY allowing light to pass through, but only diffusely, so that objects on the other side cannot be clearly distinguished ○ *a translucent membrane* **2.** GLOWING having a glowing appearance, as if light were coming through ○ *translucent skin* [15thC. From Latin *translucent-*, the present participle stem of *translucere* "to shine through," from *lucere* "to shine" (see LUCID).] —**trans·lu·cence** *n.* —**trans·lu·cen·cy** *n.* —**trans·lu·cent·ly** *adv.*

trans·lu·nar /trans lóonər, tranz-/, **trans·lu·nar·y** /trans lóonəree, tranz-/ *adj.* situated or coming from beyond the Moon or its orbit around the Earth

trans·ma·rine /trànzmə réen/ *adj.* **1.** CROSSING THE SEA involving crossing a sea or ocean **2.** FROM ACROSS THE SEA situated or coming from across a sea or ocean [Late 16thC. From Latin *transmarinus*, from *marinus* "relating to the sea" (see MARINE).]

trans·mi·grant /tranz mīgrənt/ *n.* SOMEBODY PASSING THROUGH somebody passing through a country on the way to another country in which he or she intends to settle ■ *adj.* BEING IN TRANSIT passing through a country or place on the way to somewhere else, or through a transitional stage in a process of development [Mid-17thC. From Latin *transmigrant-*, the present participle stem of *transmigrare* "to transmigrate," from *migrare* "to migrate" (see MIGRATE).]

trans·mi·grate /tranz mī gràyt/ (**-grat·ed, -grat·ing, -grates**) *vi.* **1.** MOVE FROM ONE PLACE TO ANOTHER to move from one place or country to another **2.** INDIAN RELIG PASS TO ANOTHER BODY in some religions, to pass into another body at or after death (*refers to the soul*) [15thC. From Latin *transmigrat-*, the past participle stem of *transmigrare*, from *migrare* "to migrate" (see MIGRATE).] —**trans·mi·gra·tion** /trànz mī gráysh'n/ *n.* —**trans·mi·gra·tion·al** /trànz mī gráyshən'l, -gráyshnəl/ *adj.* —**trans·mi·gra·tive** /-mígrətiv/ *adj.* —**trans·mi·gra·tor** /tranz mī gràytər/ *n.* —**trans·mi·gra·to·ry** /tranz mīgrə tàwree/ *adj.*

trans·mis·si·ble spong·i·form en·ceph·a·lop·a·thy /tranz mìssəb'l spawnji fawrm ensəfə láwpəthee/ *n.* full form of **TSE**

trans·mis·sion /tranz mísh'n/ *n.* **1.** ACT OF TRANSMITTING the act or process of transmitting something, especially radio signals, radio or television broadcasts, data, or a disease **2.** SOMETHING TRANSMITTED something transmitted, e.g., a radio or signal **3.** BROADCAST RADIO OR TV BROADCAST a radio or television broadcast **4.** AUTOMOT MECHANISM TRANSFERRING POWER TO WHEELS the mechanical system, including gears and shafts, by which power is transmitted from the engine of a motor vehicle to the drive wheels **5.** AUTOMOT SET OF GEARS a set of gears and the protective casing that covers this in a vehicle or engine **6.** PHYS ABILITY TO LET RADIATION THROUGH the ability of a material to let incoming radiation pass completely through it [Early 17thC. Directly or via French from the Latin stem *transmission-*, from *missio* "a letting go, release" (see MISSION).] —**trans·mis·si·bil·i·ty** /tranz mìssə bíllətee/ *n.* —**trans·mis·si·ble** /tranz míssib'l/ *adj.* —**trans·mis·sive** /tranz míssiv/ *adj.* —**trans·mis·sive·ly** *adv.* —**trans·mis·sive·ness** *n.*

trans·mis·sion line *n.* a conductor such as a coaxial cable that carries electricity or other electromagnetic waves, usually over long distances

trans·mit /tranz mít/ (**-mit·ted, -mit·ting, -mits**) *v.* **1.** *vt.* **SEND SOMETHING** to send something, pass something on, or cause something to spread, from one person, thing, or place to another ○ *The disease is transmitted by droplet infection.* **2.** *vt.* **COMMUNICATE INFORMATION** to communicate a message, information, or news ○ *Data was quickly transmitted.* **3.** *vti.* TELECOM, RADIO **SEND A SIGNAL** to send a signal by radio waves, satellite, or wire **4.** *vti.* BROADCAST **BROADCAST A PROGRAM** to broadcast a radio or television program **5.** *vt.* PHYS **MAKE RADIATION PASS THROUGH SOMETHING** to make heat, sound, light, or other radiation pass or spread through space or a medium **6.** *vt.* PHYS **ALLOW RADIATION THROUGH** to allow heat, sound, or light or other radiation to pass through **7.** *vt.* MECH ENG **TRANSFER POWER** to transfer power, force, or movement from one part of a mechanism to another [14thC. From Latin *transmittere*, literally "to send across," from *mittere* "to send."] —**trans·mit·ta·ble** *adj.* —**trans·mit·tal** *n.*

trans·mit·tance /tranz mítt'ns/ *n.* **1. ACT OF TRANSMITTING SOMETHING** the act or process of transmitting something **2.** PHYS **ABILITY TO LET RADIATION THROUGH** the ability of a material to let incoming radiation pass completely through it, measured as the ratio of incident radiation to transmitted radiation

trans·mit·ter /tranz míttər/ *n.* **1. AGENT OR MEANS OF TRANSMISSION** somebody or something that transmits something **2.** BROADCAST **PART OF BROADCASTING EQUIPMENT** a piece of broadcasting equipment that generates a radio-frequency wave, modulates it so that it carries a meaningful signal, and sends it out from an antenna **3.** TELECOM **TELEPHONE PART** the part of a telephone that converts sound waves to electrical impulses

trans·mog·ri·fy /tranz máwgrə fī/ (**-fied, -fy·ing, -fies**) *vt.* to change the appearance or form of something, especially in a grotesque or bizarre way [Mid-17thC. Origin uncertain: perhaps an alteration of TRANSMIGRATE modeled on verbs ending in -FY.] —**trans·mog·ri·fi·ca·tion** /tranz màwgrəfi káysh'n/ *n.*

trans·mon·tane /tranz máwn tayn/ *adj., n.* = **tramontane** *adj.* 1, **tramontane** *adj.* 2, **tramontane** *n.* 2

trans·mun·dane /tranz mún dàyn/ *adj.* not belonging to this material world and its concerns, or extending beyond them (*literary*)

trans·mu·ta·tion /trànzmyoo táysh'n/ *n.* **1. CHANGE** a change, or the process of changing, from one form, substance, nature, or state to another **2.** PHYS **CHANGE OF ONE ELEMENT INTO ANOTHER** the transformation of the atom of one chemical element into the atom of another by disintegration or nuclear bombardment **3.** HIST **CONVERSION TO GOLD** the supposed conversion of base metals into gold or silver by alchemy — **trans·mu·ta·tion·al** *adj.*

trans·mute /tranz myoot/ (**-mut·ed, -mut·ing, -mutes**) *vti.* **1. CHANGE** to change something, or be changed, from one form, nature, substance, or state to another **2.** PHYS **CHANGE FROM ONE ELEMENT TO ANOTHER** to change one element into another through disintegration or nuclear bombardment, or undergo a change of this kind **3.** HIST **CONVERT BASE METAL TO GOLD** to convert a base metal into gold or silver by alchemy, or be converted in this way [14thC. From Latin *transmutare*, literally "to change thoroughly," from *mutare* "to change." Perhaps also partly a back-formation from TRANSMUTATION.] —**trans·mut·a·bil·i·ty** /tranz myootə bíllətee/ *n.* —**trans·mut·a·ble** /tranz myootəb'l/ *adj.* — **trans·mut·a·bly** /tranz myootəblee/ *adv.* —**trans·mut·a·tive** /tranz myootər/ *adj.* —**trans·mut·er** *n.*

WORD KEY: SYNONYMS

See Synonyms at ***change***.

trans·na·tion·al /tranz náshən'l, -náshnəl/ *adj.* **NOT CONFINED TO SINGLE NATION** not confined to a single nation or state, but including, extending over, or operating within several of them ■ *n.* **TRANSNATIONAL ENTITY** a company or organization that does business or owns corporations in more than one nation

trans·o·ce·an·ic /tranz ōshee ánnik/ *adj.* **1. CROSSING AN OCEAN** involving crossing an ocean **2. FROM ACROSS AN OCEAN** situated or coming from across an ocean

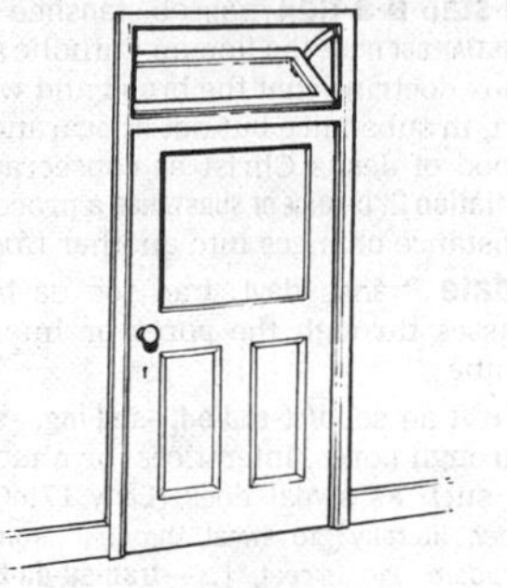

Transom

tran·som /tránsəm/ *n.* **1.** BUILDING **STRUCTURAL BEAM ABOVE A WINDOW** a horizontal beam or stone above a window that supports the structure above **2.** BUILDING **CROSSPIECE ABOVE DOOR** a crosspiece over a door or between the top of a door and a window above **3.** BUILDING **WINDOW ABOVE DOOR** a small rectangular window over a door **4.** BUILDING **CROSSBAR THAT DIVIDES WINDOW** a crossbar of wood or stone that divides a window horizontally **5.** NAUT **BEAM FOR STRENGTHENING STERN** any of several transverse beams for strengthening the stern of a ship **6.** NAUT **PLANKING AT SHIP'S STERN** the planking forming a flat surface across the stern of a ship **7. HORIZONTAL BEAM OF CROSS OR GALLOWS** the horizontal beam of a cross or gallows [14thC. Origin uncertain: probably an alteration of Latin *transtrum* "crossbeam" (source of English *trestle*), from *trans* "across."]

tran·son·ic /tran sónnik/ *adj.* relating to speeds close to the speed of sound or conditions encountered when traveling at those speeds [Mid-20thC. Formed from TRANS- + SONIC on the model of SUPERSONIC and ULTRASONIC.]

tran·son·ic bar·ri·er *n.* the sound barrier (*technical*)

transp. *abbr.* **1.** transport **2.** transportation

trans·pa·cif·ic /trànspə síffik/ *adj.* **1. CROSSING THE PACIFIC** involving crossing the Pacific Ocean **2. FROM ACROSS THE PACIFIC** situated or coming from across the Pacific Ocean

trans·pa·dane /tránspə dàyn, trans páy dàyn/ *adj.* from or on the north side of the Po River in northern Italy [Early 17thC. From Latin *transpadanus*, from *padanus* "of the Padus (River Po)."]

trans·par·en·cy /trans pérrənsee/ (*plural* **-cies**) *n.* **1. STATE OF BEING TRANSPARENT** the quality or state of being transparent **2.** PHOTOGRAPHY **SEE-THROUGH PHOTOGRAPH OR PICTURE** a positive photographic image on a transparent material, especially film or a slide, that can be viewed when light is shone through it. Transparencies are generally viewed using a projector, a light table, or a handheld viewer. [Late 16thC. From medieval Latin *transparentia*, from the stem *transparent-* (see TRANSPARENT).]

trans·par·ent /trans pérrənt/ *adj.* **1. EASILY SEEN THROUGH** allowing light to pass through with little or no interruption or distortion so that objects on the other side can be clearly seen ○ *transparent plastic* **2. FINE ENOUGH TO SEE THROUGH** thin or fine enough in texture to see through ○ *transparent fabric* **3. OBVIOUS AND EASY TO RECOGNIZE** clearly recognizable as what it, he, or she really is ○ *a transparent motive* **4. FRANK** completely open and frank about things ○ *was grateful for the transparent honesty of the reply* **5.** PHYS **LETTING RADIATION THROUGH** allowing electromagnetic radiation of specified wavelengths to pass through [15thC. Directly or via French from medieval Latin *transparent-*, the present participle stem of *transparere* "to shine through," from Latin *parere* "to appear."] — **trans·par·ent·ly** *adv.* —**trans·par·ent·ness** *n.*

trans·par·ent con·text *n.* in logic, an expression in which the truth-value is not changed when any term is replaced by another with the same reference

tran·spic·u·ous /tran spíkyoo əss/ *adj.* easily understood or seen through (*literary*) [Mid-17thC. Formed from modern Latin *transpicuus*, from Latin *transpicere* "to look through," from *specere* "to look."] —**tran·spic·u·ous·ly** *adv.*

trans·pierce /trans péers/ (**-pierced, -pierc·ing, -pierc·es**) *vt.* to pierce through something (*literary*)

tran·spire /trans pír/ (**-spired, -spir·ing, -spires**) *v.* **1.** *vt.* **COME TO LIGHT** to become known or be disclosed ○ *It later transpired that they had been furious at what had happened* **2.** *vi.* **HAPPEN** to take place ○ *What transpired after they left remains a secret.* **3.** *vti.* PHYSIOL **GIVE OFF VAPOR THROUGH SKIN** to give off water vapor through the pores of the skin. ◊ **sweat 4.** *vti.* BOT **LOSE WATER VAPOR** to lose water vapor from a plant's surface, especially through minute surface pores (**stomata**) [15thC. Directly or via French *transpirer* from medieval Latin *transpirare*, literally "to breathe through," from Latin *spirare* "to breathe."] —**tran·spir·a·ble** *adj.* — **tran·spi·ra·tion** /trànspi ráysh'n/ *n.* —**tran·spi·ra·to·ry** /trans pírə tàwree/ *adj.*

WORD KEY: USAGE

Tell me what transpired at the meeting. This use of ***transpire*** to mean "to happen" is sometimes objected to, although it has been in common use for several centuries and conveys something of the sense inherent in its other (uncontroversial) meaning "to become known, come to light": *It transpired that the President had known about the plan all along.*

trans·plant *v.* /transs plánt/ (**-plant·ed, -plant·ing, -plants**) **1.** *vt.* GARDENING **RELOCATE PLANT** to remove a plant from the place where it is growing and replant it somewhere else **2.** *vt.* **MOVE SOMEBODY TO ANOTHER PLACE** to move somebody or something to another place or position **3.** *vt.* SURG **TRANSFER BODY ORGAN** to transfer an organ or tissue from one body to another, or from one place in somebody's body to another **4.** *vi.* **BE CAPABLE OF BEING MOVED** to be capable of being transplanted ○ *Poppies do not transplant well.* ■ *n.* /tránss plànt/ **1.** SURG **SURGICAL PROCEDURE** a surgical operation or procedure to transplant an organ or tissue **2.** SURG **TRANSPLANTED ORGAN OR TISSUE** an organ or tissue that has been transplanted **3.** GARDENING **TRANSPLANTED PLANT** a plant that has been transplanted **4. RESIDENT FROM ELSEWHERE** somebody who has moved from one place and become a permanent resident in another [15thC. Directly or via French *transplanter* from late Latin *transplantare*, literally "to plant across," from Latin *plantare* "to plant" (see PLANT).] —**trans·plant·a·ble** /trans plántəb'l/ *adj.* —**trans·plan·ta·tion** /trans plàn táysh'n/ *n.* —**trans·plant·er** /trans plántər/ *n.*

trans·po·lar /trans pṓlər/ *adj.* crossing or extending across either of the polar regions

tran·spond·er /trans póndər/, **tran·spon·dor** *n.* **1.** RADIO **RADIO OR RADAR TRANSCEIVER** a radio or radar transceiver that automatically transmits a signal of its own when it receives a predetermined signal from elsewhere, used especially for locating and identifying objects **2.** TELECOM **SATELLITE RECEIVER AND TRANSMITTER** a receiving and transmitting device in a communication or broadcast satellite that relays the signals it receives back to Earth [Mid-20thC. Formed from TRANSMIT + RESPOND + -ER.]

trans·pon·tine /trans pón tīn/ *adj.* on or from the other side of a bridge (*formal*) [Mid-19thC. Formed from Latin *pont-*, the stem of *pons* "bridge" (see PONS).]

trans·port *vt.* /trans páwrt/ (**-port·ed, -port·ing, -ports**) **1.** TRANSP **CARRY SOMEBODY OR SOMETHING** to carry people or goods from one place to another, usually in a vehicle **2. MAKE SOMEBODY IMAGINE BEING ELSEWHERE** to take somebody on a mental or imaginative journey to another place or time ○ *The sounds of the game transported him back to his youth.* **3. AFFECT SOMEBODY WITH STRONG EMOTION** to put somebody in a state of intense or uncontrollable emotion, especially joy ○ *She was transported with joy.* **4.** HIST **SEND SOMEBODY TO PENAL COLONY** to exile somebody to a penal colony ■ *n.* /tráns pàwrt/ **1.** TRANSP **CONVEYANCE OF SOMEBODY OR SOMETHING** the act or business of carrying people or goods from one place to another, especially in vehicles **2.** *U.K.* TRANSP = **transportation 3.** MIL **A CRAFT CARRYING PEOPLE OR FREIGHT** a ship or aircraft for carrying passengers, especially military personnel, or freight **4. EXPERIENCE OR DISPLAY OF INTENSE EMOTION** an experience or display of intense and uncontrollable emotion, especially joy (*often used in the plural*) ○ *in transports of delight* **5.** HIST **SOMEBODY SENT TO PENAL COLONY** somebody exiled to a penal colony [14thC. Directly or via French *transporter* from Latin *transportare* "to carry across," from *portare* "to carry."] —**trans·port·a·bil·i·ty** /trans pàwrtə bíllətee/ *n.* —**trans·port·a·ble** /trans páwrtəb'l/ *adj.* — **trans·por·tive** *adj.*

trans·por·ta·tion /trànspər táysh'n/ *n.* **1. CONVEYANCE OF SOMEBODY OR SOMETHING** the act or business of carrying people or goods from one place to another, especially in vehicles **2. MEANS OF TRAVELLING** a means of traveling, or of carrying people or goods, from one place to another **3. CHARGE** the fare paid or charge made for traveling in a bus, train, or other public vehicle **4.** HIST **PENAL EXILE** exile to a penal colony

trans·port café *n. U.K.* = **truck stop**

trans·port·er /trans páwrtər/ *n.* **1. SOMEBODY OR SOMETHING THAT TRANSPORTS** somebody or something that transports something **2.** AUTOMOT **LARGE VEHICLE** a large vehicle used to carry heavy loads, often other vehicles

trans·port·er bridge *n.* a bridge consisting of a high overarching framework from which a moving platform is suspended on cables. The platform goes back and forth carrying vehicles across a body of water.

trans·pose /trans pṓz/ *v.* **(-posed, -pos·ing, -pos·es) 1.** *vt.* **REVERSE ORDER** to make two things change places or reverse their normal order, e.g., to reverse the order of two letters in a word **2.** *vt.* **MOVE SOMETHING TO DIFFERENT POSITION** to move something to a different position, especially in a sequence ○ *transposed that section to the end of the essay* **3.** *vt.* **CHANGE SETTING OF SOMETHING** to take something such as a story, incident, or play out of its usual setting or time and relocate it in another ○ *transposing the action from Shakespeare's time to the present* **4.** *vti.* MUSIC **CHANGE MUSIC TO A DIFFERENT KEY** to rewrite or play a musical composition in a key or at a pitch other than the one in which it was originally written or in which it is usually performed **5.** *vt.* MATH **MOVE TERM IN EQUATION** to transfer a term from one side of an equation to the other, reversing its sign ■ *n.* MATH **TYPE OF MATRIX** a matrix created by interchanging the rows and columns of a previously given matrix [14thC. From French *transposer*, an alteration (by association with *poser* "to place") of Latin *transponere*, literally "to place across," from *ponere* "to place" (see POSITION).] —**trans·pos·a·bil·i·ty** /trans pṓzə bíllətee/ *n.* —**trans·pos·a·ble** /trans pṓzəb'l/ *adj.* —**trans·pos·al** *n.* —**trans·pos·er** *n.* —**transpositive** *adj.*

trans·pos·ing in·stru·ment /trans pṓzing-/ *n.* a musical instrument such as a horn or clarinet that plays in a key other than C major, and whose part must therefore be written transposed to be in tune with other instruments

trans·po·si·tion /trànspə zísh'n/ *n.* **1. REVERSAL OF ORDER** a reversal or alteration of the positions or order in which things stand **2. RECASTING** a placing of something in a different setting, or its recasting in a different language, style, or medium **3.** MUSIC **PUTTING IN DIFFERENT KEY** a rewriting or playing of a piece of music in a key or at a pitch other than the original or usual one **4.** MATH **TRANSFER OF TERM IN EQUATION** a transfer of a term from one side of an equation to another, reversing the sign **5.** GENETICS **DNA TRANSFER** a transfer of a DNA segment to a new position on the same or another chromosome —**trans·po·si·tion·al** *adj.*

trans·po·son /trans pṓ zòn/ *n.* a segment of DNA that can move to a new position on the same or another chromosome, often modifying the action of neighboring genes [Late 20thC. Formed from TRANSPOSITION + -ON.]

trans·put·er /trans pyṓotər/ *n.* a powerful microchip with the functions of a microprocessor, having its own memory and the ability to carry out parallel processing

trans·sex·u·al /trans sékshoo əl/ *n.* **1. SOMEBODY WHOSE SEX IS SURGICALLY CHANGED** somebody who has undergone surgical and hormonal treatment to change his or her anatomical sex **2. SOMEBODY WHO IDENTIFIES WITH OPPOSITE SEX** somebody who identifies himself or herself as and wants to become a member of the opposite sex —**trans·sex·u·al** *adj.* —**trans·sex·u·al·ism** *n.*

trans·ship /trans shíp/ **(-shipped, -ship·ping, -ships)**, **tran·ship (-shipped, -ship·ping, -ships)** *vti.* to transfer goods, or be transferred, from one means of transportation to another —**trans·ship·ment** *n.*

tran·sub·stan·ti·ate /trànsəb stánshee àyt/ **(-at·ed, -at·ing, -ates)** *v.* **1.** *vi.* CHR **CHANGE SUBSTANCE** in the belief of some Christian churches, to undergo a change in substance, from bread and wine to the body and blood of Jesus Christ during Communion **2.** *vti.* **CHANGE SUBSTANCE** to change, or change something, from one substance into another (*formal*) [15thC. From medieval Latin *transubstantiat-*, the past participle stem of *transubstantiare*, literally "to change the substance of thoroughly," from Latin *substantia* (see SUBSTANCE).] —**tran·sub·stan·tial** *adj.* —**tran·sub·stan·ti·al·ly** *adv.*

tran·sub·stan·ti·a·tion /trànsəb stanshee áysh'n/ *n.* **1.** CHR **CHRISTIAN DOCTRINE** the Roman Catholic and Eastern Orthodox doctrine that the bread and wine of Communion, in substance but not appearance, the body and blood of Jesus Christ at consecration. ◊ **consubstantiation 2. CHANGE OF SUBSTANCE** a process whereby one substance changes into another (*formal*)

tran·su·date /tránsə dàyt, tran sṓo dàyt/ *n.* a fluid that passes through the pores or interstices of a membrane

tran·sude /tran sṓod/ **(-sud·ed, -sud·ing, -sudes)** *vi.* to pass through pores, interstices, or a membrane, as a fluid such as sweat does [Early 17thC. Via French *transsuder*, literally "to sweat through" from, ultimately, Latin *sudare* "to sweat."] —**tran·su·da·tion** /trànsə dáysh'n/ *n.* —**tran·su·da·to·ry** /tran sṓodə tàwree/ *adj.*

trans·u·ran·ic /trànzyə ránnik/, **trans·u·ra·ni·an** /-ráynee ən/, **trans·u·ra·ni·um** /-ráynee əm/ *adj.* having a higher atomic number than uranium

Trans·vaal /tránz vaàl/ former province of South Africa, situated in the northeastern part of the country

trans·val·ue /tranz vál yoo, trans-/ **(-ued, -u·ing, -ues)** *vt.* to reevaluate something using a different standard, especially one that differs from conventional or accepted standards and results in a very different assessment of the worth of something —**trans·val·u·a·tion** /tranz vàl yoo áysh'n/ *n.* —**trans·val·u·er** /tranz vál yoo ər/ *n.*

trans·ver·sal /tranz vúrsəl/ *n.* **LINE INTERSECTING OTHER LINES** a line that intersects two or more other lines ■ *adj.* = **transverse** *adj.* 1, **transverse** *adj.* 2 —**trans·ver·sal·ly** *adv.*

trans·verse /tranz vúrs/ *adj.* **1. CROSSWISE** lying or going crosswise or at right angles to something **2.** GEOM **PASSING THROUGH THE FOCI OF A HYPERBOLA** passing through a hyperbola's foci ■ *n.* **CROSSWISE THING** something lying or extending crosswise [14thC. From Latin *transversus*, the past participle of *transvertere* "to turn across," from *vertere* "to turn."] —**trans·verse·ly** *adv.* —**trans·verse·ness** *n.*

trans·verse co·lon *n.* the part of the colon that passes from right to left across the upper abdominal cavity just beneath the liver and stomach

trans·verse flute *n.* a flute with the mouth hole on top of the barrel near one end, so that the player blows across the hole while holding the flute in a sideways position. The modern flute used to be known as the transverse flute in order to distinguish it from an end-blown flute such as a recorder.

trans·verse proc·ess *n.* ANAT either of the two bony projections on the sides of a vertebra

trans·verse wave *n.* PHYS a wave that makes the medium through which it travels vibrate in a direction at right angles to the direction of its travel

trans·ves·tite /tranz vés tìt/ *n.* somebody who habitually or frequently adopts the dress and often the behavior of the opposite sex [Early 20thC. From German *Transvestit*, literally "cross-dresser," from Latin *vestire* "to clothe, dress" (see VEST).] —**trans·ves·tism** /tranz vés tìzzəm/ *n.* —**trans·ves·ti·tism** /tranz vésti tìzzəm/ *n.*

Tran·syl·va·nia /trànssil váyn yə/ historic region in eastern Europe that now forms the central and northwestern parts of Romania. Area: 24,000 sq. mi./62,000 sq. km. —**Tran·syl·va·ni·an** *adj.*

Tran·syl·va·ni·an Alps /trànssil váyn yən-/ mountain range in the Carpathian Mountains, running east to west through south central Romania

trap[1] /trap/ *n.* **1. SOMETHING DESIGNED TO CATCH ANIMALS** a device designed to catch an animal and kill it or prevent it escaping, e.g., a concealed pit or a mechanical device that springs shut **2. PLAN TO TRICK SOMEBODY** an ambush, scheme, or trick intended to catch somebody unawares and put the person at a disadvantage or in somebody else's power **3. CONFINING SITUATION** a situation from which it is difficult to escape and in which somebody feels confined, restricted, or in another person's power ○ *wanted to avoid the trap of being typecast in the same roles* **4.** CONSTR **SECTION OF DRAINPIPE BLOCKING GAS** a curved section of a drainpipe that holds a quantity of water to act as a barrier to prevent sewer gas from rising up the pipe **5.** CONSTR **DEVICE PREVENTING THE PASSAGE OF GAS**

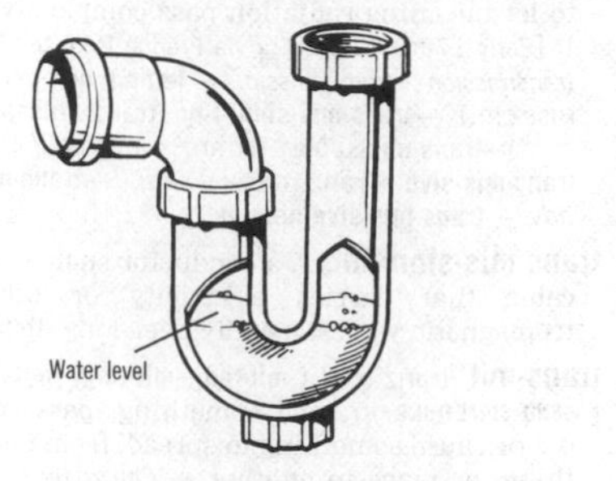

Trap

any device designed to prevent gas, vapor, or other substances passing through or escaping from something **6.** = **trap door 7. MOUTH** the mouth (*informal*) ○ *If the cops ask questions, keep your trap shut.* **8.** SPORTS **DEVICE USED IN TRAPSHOOTING** a device that throws clay pigeons into the air for trapshooting **9.** GOLF **GOLF BUNKER** a hazard, especially a bunker, on a golf course **10.** SPORTS **STARTING STALL FOR A GREYHOUND** one of the set of stalls from which greyhounds are released at the start of a race **11.** TRANSP **CARRIAGE** a light horse-drawn carriage with two wheels ■ **traps** *npl.* **1.** MOTOR SPORTS **LENGTH OF RACETRACK WHERE VEHICLES ARE TIMED** a measured stretch of track over which electronic timers register the speeds of racing vehicles, especially in drag racing **2.** MUSIC **PERCUSSION INSTRUMENT** a set of percussion instruments, especially the drum set used in a dance orchestra or jazz band (*informal*) ■ *v.* **(trapped, trap·ping, traps) 1.** *vt.* **CATCH IN TRAP** to catch an animal in a trap so that it is killed or unable to escape **2.** *vi.* HUNT **SET TRAPS FOR ANIMALS** to set traps for animals or make a living by catching animals in traps **3.** *vt.* **HOLD SOMETHING IN A TIGHT GRIP** to catch or hold something in a tight grip or narrow space so that it cannot be moved or is painfully squeezed ○ *I trapped my finger in the door.* **4.** *vt.* **PLACE SOMEBODY IN A CONFINING SITUATION** to put somebody in a situation from which it is difficult or impossible to escape ○ *They were trapped inside the burning building.* ○ *felt trapped in a deadend job* **5.** *vt.* **TAKE SOMEBODY BY SURPRISE** to put somebody at a disadvantage by means of an ambush, surprise, clever plan, or trick ○ *She was trapped into admitting the truth.* **6.** *vt.* SOCCER **CONTROL A BALL** to bring a moving ball quickly under control using a part of the body **7.** *vt.* CRIMINOL **CATCH AN OFFENDER** to identify or catch an offender by means of a speed trap or a security device **8.** *vt.* **PREVENT AIR FROM ESCAPING** to prevent air, gas, heat, or a fluid from escaping **9.** *vt.* CONSTR **EQUIP SOMETHING WITH A TRAP** to put a trap into a drainpipe [Old English *træppe* (in *coltetræppe*, a plant name) and *treppe* "trap, snare," from a prehistoric Germanic base. The etymological sense is perhaps "something that is trodden on."]

trap[2] /trap/ *n.* MINERALS = **traprock** [Late 18thC. From Swedish *trapp*, from *trappa* "stair" (from the rock's common appearance).]

trap[3] /trap/ *n.* **TRAPPINGS** trappings ■ *vt.* **(trapped, trap·ping, traps) PROVIDE SOMETHING WITH TRAPPINGS** to provide somebody or something with trappings or adornments ○ *they were all trapped out in the gaudiest of clothes* [14thC. Alteration of French *drap* "cloth" (source of English *drape*), from late Latin *drappus*, of uncertain origin: perhaps from a Celtic source.]

Tra·pa·ni /traa paánee/ seaport and capital city of Trapani Province, northwestern Sicily. Population: 69,497 (1996).

trap door *n.* a hatch covering a horizontal or sloping opening in a floor, ceiling, or roof

trap·door spi·der *n.* a spider found in warm regions that constructs a tubular silk-lined burrow with a hinged lid like a trap door. Family: Ctenizidae.

tra·peze /trə peéz/ *n.* a horizontal bar attached to the ends of two ropes hanging parallel to each other, used for gymnastics or for acrobatics, especially in a circus [Mid-19thC. Via French *trapèze* from late Latin *trapezium* (see TRAPEZIUM), from the quadrilateral shape formed by the trapeze's crossbar and ropes and the roof.]

tra·pe·zi·a plural of **trapezium**

tra·pe·zi·form /trə peézi fàwrm/ *adj.* shaped like a trapezium

tra·pe·zi·i plural of **trapezius**

tra·pe·zi·um /trə péezee əm/ (*plural* **-ums** *or* **-a** /-péezee ə/) *n.* **1.** GEOM **QUADRILATERAL WITH NO PARALLEL SIDES** a quadrilateral that has no parallel sides **2.** *U.K.* GEOM = **trapezoid** *n.* 1 **3.** ANAT **WRIST BONE** a small bone in the wrist at the base of the thumb [Late 16thC. Via late Latin (source of English *trapeze*) from Greek *trapezion*, literally "small table," from *trapeza* "table," literally "with four feet," from *peza* "foot."] —**tra·pe·zi·al** *adj.*

tra·pe·zi·us /trə péezee əss/ (*plural* **-us·es** *or* **-i** /-péezee ī/) *n.* either of the two large flat triangular muscles that run from the back of the neck and cover each shoulder. They help to move the shoulder blades and draw the head backward. [Early 18thC. From modern Latin, from late Latin *trapezium* (see TRAPEZIUM), from the pair together forming a trapezium.]

tra·pe·zo·he·dron /trə pèe zō hée drən/ (*plural* **-drons** *or* **-dra** /-héedrə/) *n.* a form of crystal with faces that are all trapezoids in shape [Early 19thC. Coined from TRAPEZIUM + -HEDRON on the model of, for example, TETRAHEDRON.] —**tra·pe·zo·he·dral** *adj.*

trap·e·zoid /tráppə zòyd/ *n.* **1.** GEOM **QUADRILATERAL WITH TWO PARALLEL SIDES** a quadrilateral that has two parallel sides **2.** *U.K.* GEOM = **trapezium** *n.* 1 **3.** ANAT **WRIST BONE** a small bone in the wrist near the metatarsal bone that connects with the index finger —**tra·pe·zoid·al** *adj.*

trap·per /tráppər/ *n.* somebody who makes a living by trapping animals for their fur or hides

trap·pings /tráppingz/ *npl.* **1. ACCESSORIES AND OUTWARD SIGNS** the dress, accessories, insignia, and other outward signs associated with an office, position, or status ○ *the trappings of power* **2.** EQU **ORNAMENTAL HARNESS FOR A HORSE** an ornamental or ceremonial rig for a horse, including a decorated harness, saddle, and cloth covering

Trap·pist /tráppist/ *n.* a member of the main reformed branch of the Cistercian order of Christian monks, established in 1664 at La Trappe monastery in Normandy and noted for its vow of silence [Early 19thC. From French *trappiste*, from *La Trappe*, name of the monastery in Normandy, France.]

trap·rock /tráp ròk/ *n.* a dark, fine-grained igneous rock such as basalt, used in road construction

trap·shoot·ing /tráp shòoting/ *n.* the sport of shooting at clay pigeons thrown by a trap —**trap·shoot** *n.* —**trap·shoot·er** *n.*

tra·pun·to /trə póon tō/ *n.* quilting in which only the design, which is outlined with parallel lines of stitches, is padded to give it a raised look [Early 20thC. From Italian, past participle of *trapungere* "to embroider" (literally "to prick across"), from Latin *pungere* "to prick" (see PUNGENT).]

trash /trash/ *n.* **1. DISCARDED MATERIAL** discarded, unwanted, or worthless material or objects **2. NONSENSE** something spoken or written that is viewed as meaningless or absurd ○ *You're talking trash!* **3. POOR QUALITY LITERATURE OR ART** literature or art considered worthless or offensive ○ *How can you read such trash?* **4. OFFENSIVE TERM** an offensive term that deliberately insults somebody's social position or morals **5.** AGRIC **TRIMMINGS FROM PLANTS** twigs, branches, or leaves that have fallen or been trimmed from trees and plants **6.** INDUST **SUGAR CANE REFUSE** the dry refuse of sugar cane after it has been crushed for the juice, often used as fuel ■ *vt.* (**trashed, trash·ing, trash·es**) **1. DESTROY SOMETHING** to destroy, severely damage, or vandalize something deliberately (*informal*) ○ *wondered whether rock stars still trashed their hotel rooms* ○ *"The storm trashed bridges in Honduras and Central America."* (*U.S. News & World Report*; December 1998) **2. DISCARD SOMETHING** to throw away or discard something (*informal*) **3. CRITICIZE SOMEBODY SAVAGELY** to criticize something or somebody savagely, or condemn something or somebody as worthless (*informal*) **4.** AGRIC **REMOVE TWIGS AND BRANCHES** to remove twigs, branches, or leaves from plants **5.** INDUST **STRIP LEAVES FROM SUGAR CANE** to strip the outer leaves from sugar cane [14thC. Origin uncertain: probably from a Scandinavian source (compare Norwegian dialect *trask* "rubbish" and Old Norse *tros* "fallen leaves and twigs, rubbish").] ◇ **talk trash** to try to intimidate somebody, especially a rival or an opponent in a sporting contest, by being boastful or insulting (*slang*)

trash can *n.* a garbage can (*informal*)

trash fish *n.* **1.** = **rough fish** *n.* **2. FISH NOT EATEN BY HUMANS** a fish that is not marketable as human food but is used in animal feeds, fertilizers, and paints **3. FISH ABLE TO BE EATEN BY HUMANS** a fish such as skate or monkfish formerly thought of as unfit for human consumption but now valued for its quality

trash·man /trásh màn/ (*plural* **-men** /-mèn/) *n.* a garbage man (*informal*)

trash·mov·er *n.* a storm whose violent winds or heavy rains spread debris about (*regional*)

WORD KEY: REGIONAL NOTE

This is common in folk speech across the rural South with other descriptive terms such as *chunk floater, frog strangle, gully washer, lighter(d)-knot floater, pourdown,* and *toad strangler*.

trash·y /tráshee/ (**-i·er, -i·est**) *adj.* cheap or of very little worth or merit ○ *a trashy novel* —**trash·i·ly** *adv.* —**trash·i·ness** *n.*

Tra·si·me·no, Lake /tràzzə méenō/ lake in central Italy, and the largest lake in the Italian peninsula. Area: 49 sq. mi./128 sq. km.

trat·to·ri·a /traàtə rée ə/ (*plural* **-as** *or* **-e** /-rée èe/) *n.* an Italian restaurant, especially one that is simple in style [Early 19thC. From Italian, from *trattore* "restaurateur," from, ultimately, Latin *tractare* "to drag, manage," from *trahere* "to pull" (source of English *tractor*).]

trau·ma /trówmə, tráwmə/ (*plural* **-mas** *or* **-ma·ta** /trówmətə, tráwmətə/) *n.* **1.** PSYCHOL **EMOTIONAL SHOCK** an extremely distressing experience that causes severe emotional shock and may have long-lasting psychological effects **2.** MED **BODILY INJURY** a physical injury or wound to the body [Late 17thC. From Greek, "wound."]

trau·mat·ic /trow máttik, traw-/ *adj.* **1. EXTREMELY DISTRESSING** extremely distressing, frightening, or shocking, and sometimes having long-term psychological effects **2.** PSYCHOL **RELATING TO TRAUMA** relating to or caused by psychological trauma **3.** MED **RELATING TO INJURIES** relating to wounds or injuries [Mid 17thC. Via late Latin *traumaticus* from Greek *traumatikos*, from *traumat-*, the stem of *trauma* "wound."] —**trau·mat·i·cal·ly** *adv.*

trau·ma·tism /trówmə tìzzəm, tráwmə-/ *n.* the condition resulting from a physical injury or wound or from an emotional shock [Mid-19thC. Formed from Greek *traumat-* (see TRAUMATIC).]

trau·ma·tize /trówmə tīz, tráwmə-/ (**-tized, -tiz·ing, -tiz·es**) *vt.* **1.** PSYCHOL **CAUSE EMOTIONAL SHOCK TO** to cause somebody to experience severe emotional shock or distress, often resulting in long-lasting psychological damage **2.** MED **INJURE** to cause physical injury to somebody or something [Early 20thC. Formed from Greek *traumat-* (see TRAUMATIC).] —**trau·ma·ti·za·tion** /tròwməti záysh'n, tràwməti-/ *n.*

trau·ma·tol·o·gy /tròwmə tóllajee, tràwmə-/ *n.* the branch of medicine that deals with serious injuries and wounds and their long-term consequences [Late 19thC. Coined from Greek *traumat-* (see TRAUMATIC + -LOGY).] —**trau·ma·tol·o·gist** *n.*

tra·vail /trə váyl, trá vàyl/ *n.* **1. HARD WORK** work, especially work that involves hard physical effort over a long period **2.** CHILDBIRTH labor pains (*archaic*) ■ *vi.* (**-vailed, -vail·ing, -vails**) **1. WORK LONG AND HARD** to work long and hard (*literary*) **2. BE IN LABOR** to be in labor (*archaic*) (*refers to a woman*) [13thC. From French, "pain," and its source *travailler* "to toil," ultimately from assumed Vulgar Latin *tripalium* "instrument of torture," from Latin *tripalis* "having three stakes," from *palus* "stake."]

trave /trayv/ *n.* **1.** BUILDING = **crossbeam** **2.** BUILDING **SOMETHING FORMED BY CROSSBEAMS** a section of a building, e.g., in a ceiling, formed by crossbeams **3.** EQU **FRAME FOR A DIFFICULT HORSE** a frame to restrain a difficult horse while it is being shod [14thC. Via Old French, "beam," from Latin *trab-*, the stem of *trabs* (source of English *architrave* and *trabeated*).]

trav·el /trávv'l/ *v.* (**trav·eled, trav·el·ing, trav·els**) **1.** *vi.* **GO ON A JOURNEY** to go on a journey to a particular place, usually using some form of transportation **2.** *vi.* **GO FROM PLACE TO PLACE** to go from place to place or visit various places and countries for business or pleasure ○ *We hope to travel more when we retire.* **3.** *vt.* **JOURNEY THROUGH AN AREA** to go on journeys through, around, or within a particular area ○ *They liked to travel the countryside stopping at places of interest.* **4.** *vt.* **COVER A PARTICULAR DISTANCE** to go or cover a particular distance ○ *travel 10 kilometers* **5.** *vi.* **GO AT A PARTICULAR SPEED** to move at a particular speed or in a particular way ○ *The train was traveling at 90 mph when it had to stop.* **6.** *vi.* **MOVE FAST** to move swiftly (*informal*) ○ *With the new engine this car can really travel.* **7.** *vi.* COMMUNICATION **GO TO DIFFERENT PLACES TO DO BUSINESS** to go from place to place as a salesperson or as part of a business ○ *After five years traveling, she wanted an office job.* **8.** *vi.* **TOLERATE BEING TRANSPORTED** to retain its quality or freshness while being transported ○ *Snakes do not travel well.* **9.** *vi.* **BE TRANSMITTED** to be transmitted or communicated ○ *News traveled fast.* **10.** *vi.* **SCAN** to scan an object or scene in the process of observing or filming it **11.** *vi.* MECH ENG **MOVE IN A FIXED PATH** to move in a fixed path while operating (*refers to a machine part*) **12.** *vi.* **ASSOCIATE WITH A SPECIFIC GROUP** to associate with a particular person or group ○ *They've been traveling with a new crowd.* **13.** *vi.* BASKETBALL **TAKE AN ILLEGAL NUMBER OF STEPS** to take more steps while holding the ball than the rules of basketball allow ■ *n.* **1. ACTIVITY OF TRAVELING** the activity of going on journeys, often using a particular form of transportation, or visiting different places ○ *air travel* **2.** MECH ENG **TOTAL DISTANCE A MECHANICAL PART MOVES** the total distance that a mechanical part such as a piston inside a cylinder moves **3. TRAFFIC** the amount of traffic at a given place along a route ■ **trav·els** *npl.* **1. SERIES OF JOURNEYS** a series of journeys undertaken by a particular person or group ○ *She's off on her travels again.* **2.** LITERAT **ACCOUNT OF SOMEBODY'S JOURNEYS** an account of the journeys undertaken by a particular person or group ■ *adj.* **FOR TRAVELERS** designed for use by travelers, especially by being lightweight and smaller than usual ○ *a travel kettle* [14thC. Variant of TRAVAIL (the underlying notion perhaps being "wearisome journey").]

trav·el a·gen·cy *n.* a business that arranges transportation, accommodations, and tours for travelers —**trav·el a·gent** *n.*

trav·el bu·reau *n.* = **travel agency**

trav·eled /trávv'ld/ *adj.* **1. EXPERIENCED IN TRAVEL** having been on many journeys, or being experienced as a traveler **2. MUCH USED** used by many travelers ○ *Keep to the traveled roads.*

trav·e·ler /trávv'lər/ *n.* **1. SOMEBODY ON A JOURNEY** somebody who is on a journey to a particular place or who uses a particular form of transportation **2. SOMEBODY WHO HAS TRAVELED** somebody who has traveled or travels extensively ○ *an experienced traveler* **3.** MECH ENG **MOVING PART** a part of a mechanism that is designed to move in a fixed path **4.** NAUT **RING ON A ROPE** a metal ring that moves freely on a rope, spar, or rod **5.** NAUT **ROPE** a rope, spar, or rod on which a metal ring moves

trav·e·ler's check *n.* an internationally accepted check for a sum in a particular currency that can be exchanged elsewhere for local currency or for goods and is usually guaranteed against loss or theft

trav·e·ler's joy *n.* a European climbing plant of the buttercup family that has white flowers and feathery fruits. Latin name: *Clematis vitalba*.

trav·e·ler's tale *n.* a fantastic, unlikely, or obviously untrue account of something, as given by a traveler to people who do not travel

trav·el·ing sales·man /trávv'ling/ *n.* a salesperson whose work consists of traveling around calling on potential customers within a territory

traveling saleswoman *n.* a woman salesperson whose work consists of traveling around calling on potential customers within a territory

trav·el·ing wave *n.* PHYS a wave that continuously carries energy away from its source

trav·el·ler *n.* U.K. = **traveler**

trav·e·logue /trávvə lòg/, **trav·e·log** *n.* a film, videotape, or piece of writing, or a lecture accompanied by pictures, video or film, about travel, especially to interesting or remote places, or about somebody's travels in particular

trav·el sick·ness *n.* = **motion sickness** —**trav·el-sick** *adj.*

Trav·ers, Mount /trávvərz/ mountain in the north of the South Island, New Zealand, situated in the northern part of the Southern Alps. Height: 7,671 ft./2,338 m.

tra·verse *v.* /trə vúrss/ (**-versed, -vers·ing, -vers·es**) **1.** *vt.* **MOVE ACROSS AN AREA** to travel or move across, over, or through an area or a place ○ *traverse the countryside* **2.** *vti.* **MOVE BACK AND FORTH** to move backward and forward across something ○ *volunteers traversed the field looking for clues* **3.** *vt.* **REACH ACROSS SOMETHING** to extend or reach across something ○ *traverse the river* **4.** *vti.* MOUNTAINEERING **MOVE AT AN ANGLE** to move at an angle across a rock face while ascending or descending it **5.** *vti.* SKIING **FOLLOW A ZIGZAG COURSE** to ski in diagonal runs following a zigzag course down a slope **6.** *vti.* **SWIVEL A GUN** to swivel something, especially a gun, from side to side on a pivot **7.** *vi.* FENCING **SLIDE A BLADE TOWARD AN OPPONENT'S HILT** to slide the blade of a sword toward an opponent's hilt while at the same time applying pressure to his or her blade **8.** *vt.* **THWART SOMEBODY** to thwart somebody or something (*literary*) **9.** *vt.* LAW **DENY ALLEGATIONS** to deny the opposing party's allegations as set out in the pleading in a lawsuit, formally and, usually, in their entirety **10.** *vt.* LAW **JOIN ISSUE** to join issue with somebody on an indictment ■ *n.* /trá vərss, trə vúrss/ **1. JOURNEY** a movement or journey across, over, or through something **2. ROUTE** a route or way across or over something **3.** MOUNTAINEERING **MOVEMENT ACROSS A ROCK FACE** a horizontal or oblique movement across a rock face in climbing **4.** SKIING **DIAGONAL RUN** a diagonal zigzag skiing run down a ski slope **5.** BUILDING **CROSS-BEAM** something that is fixed across a gap or lies crosswise such as a structural member of a building **6.** BUILDING **GALLERY** a gallery or loft that crosses from side to side inside a building **7.** BUILDING **BARRIER WITHIN A BUILDING** a railing, curtain, screen, or partition forming a barrier **8.** MIL **BARRIER ACROSS A TRENCH** a defensive barrier of earth across a trench **9. OBSTRUCTION** something that thwarts or obstructs (*literary*) **10.** GEOM = **transversal** *n.* **11.** NAUT **ZIGZAG COURSE** the zigzag course of a sailing vessel in contrary winds **12.** MECH ENG **LATERAL MOVEMENT** the horizontal movement of a machine part such as a lathe or grinding tool as it moves across the work piece **13.** LAW **DENIAL OF ALLEGATIONS** a formal denial of the opposing party's allegations as set out in their pleading in a lawsuit **14.** CIV ENG **TYPE OF SURVEY** a survey made using a series of intersecting straight lines of known length whose angles of intersection are measured for recording on a map or in a table of data ■ *adj.* /trá vərss, trə vúrss/ **CROSSWISE** lying across something [14thC. Via French *traverser* from late Latin *tra(ns)versare*, from Latin *transversus*, the past participle of *transvertere* "to turn across," from *vertere* "to turn" (see VERTICAL).] —**tra·vers·a·ble** *adj.* —**tra·vers·al** *n.* —**tra·vers·er** *n.*

tra·verse rod *n.* a rod with a mechanism that allows attached curtains or draperies to be opened and closed with a pull cord

trav·er·tine /trávvər teen/, **trav·er·tin** *n.* a hard semi-crystalline white or light-colored limestone precipitated in hot springs and caves and used as a facing material in building [Late 18thC. Via Italian *travertino* from, ultimately, Latin *(lapis) tiburtinus* "(stone) of Tibur (Tivoli, a town in Italy)."]

trav·es·ty /trávvəstee/ *n.* (*plural* **-ties**) **1. FALSE REPRESENTATION** a distorted or debased version of something ○ *it was a kangaroo court, a travesty of justice* **2.** ARTS **GROTESQUE IMITATION** a literary or artistic work, usually meant as a parody, that ridicules something serious by imitating it in a grotesque or distorted manner ■ *vt.* (**-tied, -ty·ing, -ties**) **MAKE A TRAVESTY OF SOMETHING** to imitate or mock something in a grotesque or distorted manner [Mid-17thC. From French *travesti*, "dressed in disguise," from *travestir*, "to disguise, ridicule," and Italian *travestire*, from Latin *tra-*, "trans-," + *vestire*, "to clothe."]

Trav·is /trávviss/, **William Barret** (1809–36) U.S. soldier. He commanded Texan forces against Santa Anna's Mexican army at the Alamo and was killed when it was taken (1836).

tra·vois /trə vóy, trávvoy/ (*plural* **-vois** /trə vóyz, trávvoyz/ *or* **-vois·es**) *n.* a sled made of two poles connected by a frame and pulled by an animal, used in the past by Native North Americans of the Great Plains [Mid-19thC. From French, from *travail*, from Latin *trabs*, "beam."]

Tra·vol·ta /trə vṓltə/, **John** (*b.* 1954) U.S. actor. His movies include *Saturday Night Fever* (1977), *Grease* (1978), and *Pulp Fiction* (1994).

trawl /trawl/ *n.* **1. FISHING NET** a large net that is dragged along the sea bottom behind a commercial fishing boat **2. SUSPENDED FISHING LINE** a long fishing line suspended between buoys that has several shorter lines with baited hooks attached ■ *vti.* (**trawled, trawl·ing, trawls**) **FISH WITH A TRAWL** to use or put out a trawl or setline to catch fish [Mid-16thC. From Middle Dutch *traghelen*, "to drag," from *traghel*, "trawl net," from Latin *tragula*, from *trahere*, "to pull" (source of English *tractor*).]

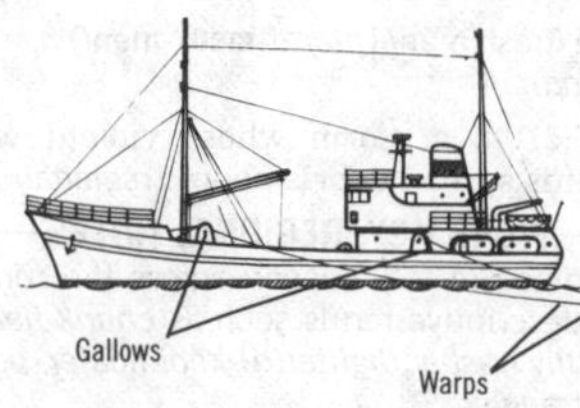

Trawler

trawl·er /tráwlər/ *n.* **1. FISHING BOAT** a boat that is used in trawling for fish **2. SOMEBODY WHO TRAWLS** somebody who fishes by trawling

trawl·er·man /tráwlərmən/ (*plural* **-men**) *n.* a fisherman who works on a trawler

trawl line *n.* = **trawl** *n.* 2

trawl net *n.* = **trawl** *n.* 1

tray /tray/ *n.* **1. FLAT CARRIER FOR SMALL OBJECTS** a flat piece of plastic, wood, or metal with a raised edge, used for carrying or displaying light objects **2. TRAY AND THINGS IT CARRIES** a tray and the objects on it ○ *dropped a tray of dishes* **3. CONTAINER IN WHICH TO ORGANIZE THINGS** a shallow container, sometimes part of a desk drawer or cabinet, in which to keep items such as stationery or jewelry [Old English *trīg*. Ultimately from an Indo-European word that is also the ancestor of English *tree* and *trough*.]

tray ta·ble *n.* **1. SMALL FOLDAWAY TABLE IN AIRCRAFT** a small table that folds down from the back of the seat in front of you in a plane or train **2. TRAY WITH LEGS** a tray with folding legs, used especially for eating meals in bed

treach·er·ous /tréchərəss/ *adj.* **1. TRAITOROUS** betraying or ready to betray somebody's trust, confidence, or faith **2. PERILOUS** involving hidden dangers or hazards ○ *treacherous seas* [14thC. From Old French *trecheros* "deceitfulness," from *trechier* (see TREACHERY).] —**treach·er·ous·ly** *adv.* —**treach·er·ous·ness** *n.*

treach·er·y /tréchəree/ (*plural* **-ies**) *n.* **1. BETRAYAL** betrayal or deceit **2. ACT OF BETRAYAL** an act or instance of betrayal or deceit [12thC. From Old French *trecherie*, from *trechier, trichier* (see TRICK).]

trea·cle /tréek'l/ *n.* **1. SOMETHING CLOYING** something cloying or excessively sentimental **2. FORMER ANTIDOTE TO POISON** a preparation used in the past as an antidote to poison **3.** *U.K.* = **molasses** [14thC. Via Old French *triacle* and Latin *theriaca* from Greek *thēriakē (antidotos)*, "(antidote to) poisonous animals," from *thērion*, "wild or poisonous animal," from *thēr*, "wild."]

WORD KEY: ORIGIN

Treacle retained its original meaning of "antidote" when it came into English, but it later gradually broadened out into "medicine," and the practice of disguising the unpleasant taste of medicine with sugar syrup led in the 17th century to its application to "syrup."

trea·cly /tréeklee/ *adj.* cloying or excessively sentimental —**trea·cli·ness** *n.*

tread /tred/ *v.* (**trod** /trod/ *or* **tread·ed, trod·den** /tródd'n/ *or* **trod, tread·ing, treads**) **1.** *vi.* **TRAMPLE SOMETHING** to step or put a foot on something, especially so as to crush or damage it **2.** *vti.* **WALK OR STEP ON SOMETHING** to take a step or steps, or walk or step on, across, or along something **3.** *vt.* **FORM A PATH** to form something such as a path by trampling or walking **4.** *vt.* **DANCE STEPS** to perform the steps of a dance (*dated*) **5.** *vi.* **ACT IN STATED WAY** to proceed or behave in a particular way ○ *tread carefully* **6.** *vi.* **CRUSH** to repress or treat somebody or something harshly ■ *n.* **1. WAY OF TREADING** a way or sound of walking or stepping ○ *heard the heavy tread of marching feet* **2. ACT OF TREADING** an act of walking or of trampling something **3. HORIZONTAL PART OF A STEP** the horizontal part of a step in a staircase **4. WIDTH OF A STEP** the width of the horizontal part of a step, measured from front to back **5.** AUTOMOT **OUTER SURFACE OF A TIRE** the part of the surface of a tire or wheel that comes in contact with a road or rail **6. DEPTH OF GROOVES ON A TIRE SURFACE** the depth of grooves on the surface of a tire **7.** CLOTHES **PART OF SHOE THAT TOUCHES THE GROUND** the part of the sole of a shoe that touches the ground [Old English *tredan*, from a prehistoric Germanic word that is also the ancestor of English *trade* and *trot*] —**tread·er** *n.*

tread·le /trédd'l/ *n.* **FOOT-OPERATED PEDAL** a lever pushed repeatedly by the foot to provide drive for a machine such as a sewing machine or potter's wheel ■ *vti.* (**-led, -ling, -les**) **POWER MACHINE WITH A TREADLE** to operate a treadle, or operate a machine by using a treadle [Old English *tredel*, from *tredan* (see TREAD). The modern meaning, "foot lever," evolved from "step, stair."] —**tread·ler** *n.*

tread·mill /tréd mìl/ *n.* **1.** MECH ENG **CYLINDER PROVIDING POWER** a continuous belt or series of steps kept moving by people or animals walking on it that is used to provide power to a machine, e.g., to grind grain or raise water from a well **2.** FITNESS **EXERCISE MACHINE** a machine with an endless belt on which somebody can walk, jog, or run, used for exercise and stress testing **3. NEVER-ENDING ROUTINE** a monotonous and seemingly endless task, job, or routine

treas. *abbr.* **1.** treasurer **2.** treasury

trea·son /tréez'n/ *n.* **1. BETRAYAL OF COUNTRY** violation of the allegiance owed by a person to his or her own country, e.g., by aiding an enemy. ◊ **high treason 2. TREACHERY** betrayal or disloyalty **3. ACT OF BETRAYAL** an act of betrayal or disloyalty [12thC. Via Anglo-Norman *treisoun*, "treacherous handing over, betrayal," from the Latin stem *tradition-*, from *tradere*, "to hand over" (source of English *traitor, betrayal*, and *tradition*).]

trea·son·a·ble /tréez'nəb'l/, **trea·son·ous** /tréez'nəss/ *adj.* involving, being, or punishable as treason —**trea·son·a·ble·ness** *n.* —**trea·son·a·bly** *adv.*

treas·ure /trézhər/ *n.* **1. JEWELS AND PRECIOUS OBJECTS AS WEALTH** wealth, especially in the form of jewels and precious objects, often accumulated or hoarded **2. SOMETHING VALUABLE** something of great value or worth **3. SOMEBODY HIGHLY VALUED** somebody who is highly valued or loved ○ *an actor considered as one of our national treasures* ■ *vt.* (**-ured, -ur·ing, -ures**) **1. REGARD AS VERY VALUABLE** to prize somebody or something as being of great value or worth ○ *treasured the memory of that day* **2. ACCUMULATE AND STORE SOMETHING VALUABLE** to accumulate and store something regarded as valuable [12thC. Via French *trésor* from Latin *thesaurus*, from Greek *thēsauros*, "treasure."] —**treas·ur·a·ble** *adj.*

WORD KEY: CULTURAL NOTE

Treasure Island, a novel by Scottish writer Robert Louis Stevenson (1883). This classic romance recounts young Jim Hawkins' adventures with a treacherous band of pirates searching for lost treasure on a distant island. The book's most memorable character is one-legged pirate Long John Silver, who carries a pet parrot given to shrieking "Pieces of eight!".

treas·ure house *n.* **1. STORE OF VALUABLE THINGS** a place or collection in which many valuable things are located **2. TREASURY** a building in which treasure is kept

treas·ure hunt *n.* a game in which competitors attempt to follow a series of clues that lead to a hidden prize

trea·sur·er /trézhərər/ *n.* a manager of the finances of a government, organization, or corporation, usually the chief financial officer —**treas·ur·er·ship** *n.*

treas·ure-trove *n.* **1. DISCOVERED UNCLAIMED WEALTH** silver or gold coins or bullion found buried in the earth and for which there is no known owner **2. SOMETHING FOUND OF VALUE** something discovered that is valuable or the source of something valuable ○ *The new store is a treasure-trove of antiques.* [Mid-16thC. *Trove* from Anglo-Norman *tresor trove*, from Old French *tresor* "treasure" + *trove*, the past participle of *trover* "to find."]

treas·ur·y /trézhəree/ (*plural* **-ies**) *n.* **1.** BUSINESS **STORE OF MONEY** the funds or revenues of a government, organization, or corporation, or the place in which they are deposited and disbursed **2. PLACE FOR THINGS OF VALUE** a place in which treasure or other valuable items are stored and preserved **3. COLLECTION OF VALUABLE THINGS** a source or collection of valuable things, e.g., literary or artistic works [13thC. Via Old French *tresorie* from *trésor* (see TREASURE).]

Treas·ur·y (*plural* **Treas·ur·ies**) *n.* **1. GOVERNMENT FINANCE DEPARTMENT** in many countries, the government department in charge of collecting and managing public revenue **2. GOVERNMENT SECURITY** a security issued by the U.S. Treasury

Trea·sur·y bill *n.* a short-term obligation issued by the U.S. government, sold at a discount from its face value and redeemed at its face value upon maturity

Treas·ur·y bond *n.* an interest-bearing debt security issued by the U.S. government, with an initial life of between ten and thirty years

Treas·ur·y note *n.* an intermediate-term, interest-paying debt instrument issued by the U.S. government, with an initial life of between one and ten years

treat /treet/ *v.* (**treat·ed, treat·ing, treats**) **1.** *vt.* **REGARD SOMEBODY IN A PARTICULAR WAY** to behave toward or think of somebody or something in a particular way ○ *They treated us practically like family.* **2.** *vt.* MED **UNDERTAKE TO CURE SOMEBODY** to give medical aid to somebody or apply medical techniques to a disease or symptom in order to provide a cure **3.** *vt.* TECH **SUBJECT TO A PROCESS OR AGENT** to subject something to a physical, chemical, or biological process or agent such as a chemical reaction or the application of a coating **4.** *vt.* **PAY FOR SOMEBODY ELSE** to pay for somebody else's food, drink, entertainment, or gifts ○ *I'll treat you to lunch at the hotel.* **5.** *vt.* **PROVIDE SOMEBODY WITH SOMETHING PLEASURABLE** to give somebody or yourself something enjoyable ○ *They treated their mother to breakfast in bed.* **6.** *vt.* **DEAL WITH SOMETHING IN A PARTICULAR WAY** to present or handle a subject, especially in art or literature, in a particular way ○ *treat a delicate subject with great sensitivity* **7.** *vi.* **DISCUSS A TOPIC** to discuss or deal with a topic in writing or speech ○ *a play that treats of greed and revenge* **8.** *vi.* **NEGOTIATE TERMS** to negotiate, especially in order to reach a settlement (*formal*) ○ *refusing to treat with the enemy* ■ *n.* **1. ENTERTAINMENT PAID FOR BY SOMEBODY ELSE** something such as food, entertainment, or a gift that is given to somebody and paid for by somebody else **2. ACT OF PAYING FOR SOMEBODY ELSE** an act of paying for something such as food, entertainment, or a gift, for somebody else **3. SOMETHING ENJOYABLE** something enjoyable, especially when a surprise ○ *It's a treat to see a smile on his face again.* [13thC. Via Old French *traitier*, "to bargain with, negotiate," from Latin *tractare*, "to handle," literally "to drag about," from *trahere*, "to pull" (source of English *contract*).] —**treat·a·ble** *adj.* —**treat·er** *n.*

trea·tise /tréetiss/ *n.* a formal written work that deals with a subject systematically and usually extensively [14thC. Via Anglo-Norman *tretiz* from Old French *traitier* (see TREAT).]

treat·ment /tréetmənt/ *n.* **1.** MED **PROVISION OF MEDICAL CARE** the application of medical care to cure disease, heal injuries, or ease symptoms **2.** MED **MEDICAL CARE** a particular remedy, procedure, or technique for curing or alleviating a disease, injury, or condition ○ *a new treatment for asthma* **3. WAY OF HANDLING SOMEBODY OR SOMETHING** the particular way in which somebody or something is dealt with or handled ○ *had pretty rough treatment* **4.** ARTS **PRESENTATION OF A SUBJECT** the way of presenting or handling a subject, especially in art or literature **5.** CINEMA **SCHEMATIC VERSION OF A MOVIE** a schematic version of a movie script, generally without dialogue and individual shots, indicating how the story is to be dealt with in a screenplay **6.** TECH **TREATING SOMETHING WITH AGENT** an act of subjecting something to a physical, chemical, or biological process or agent **7. USUAL ACTIONS TAKEN** the usual way of dealing with somebody or something in a particular situation (*informal*) ○ *As guests of the government we got the full VIP treatment.*

trea·ty /tréetee/ (*plural* **-ties**) *n.* **1.** POL **AGREEMENT BETWEEN STATES** a formal contract or agreement negotiated between countries or other political entities **2. PACT** an agreement or contract between two or more parties [14thC. Via Old French *traité*, "assembly, agreement, treaty," from Latin *tractatus*, from *tractare* (see TREAT).]

trea·ty In·di·an *n. Can* = **status Indian**

trea·ty port *n.* in the past, a port where foreign trade was allowed by a treaty, especially in China, Japan, and Korea

treb·le /trébb'l/ *adj.* **1. TRIPLE** three times as many or much **2.** MUSIC **OF OR FOR THE HIGHEST MUSICAL RANGE** relating to or intended for a soprano voice or a high-pitched instrument **3. HIGH-PITCHED** high-pitched or shrill ■ *n.* **1.** MUSIC **HIGH-PITCHED INSTRUMENT OR VOICE** a treble voice, singer, instrument, or part **2. HIGH-PITCHED SOUND** a high-pitched or shrill sound **3.** RECORDING **AUDIO FREQUENCY RANGE** the higher audio frequencies electronically reproduced by a radio, recording, or sound system **4.** RECORDING **CONTROL FOR HIGH-FREQUENCY AUDIO RESPONSE** a control for increasing or decreasing the high-frequency response on a radio or audio amplifier **5. SOMETHING TRIPLED** something three times as many or as much ■ *vti.* (**-led, -ling, -les**) **TRIPLE SOMETHING** to become or make something become three times as many or as much ○ *output has trebled over the past year* [13thC. Via Old French from Latin *triplus*, "triple." In the sense "high-pitched," from early contrapuntal music, in which the highest voice part was the third part (after tenor and alto).] —**treb·le·ness** *n.* —**treb·ly** *adv.*

treb·le clef *n.* a clef that puts G above middle C on the second line of the staff, used for soprano and alto voices, high-pitched instruments, and the right hand of keyboard instruments

Tre·blin·ka /tre blínkə/ site of two Nazi concentration camps in eastern Poland, situated near Malkinia, about 60 mi./97 km northeast of Warsaw

treb·u·chet /trèbbyə shét/, **treb·uc·ket** /trèbbyə két/ *n.* a medieval siege engine with a sling attached to a wooden arm for hurling large stones [14thC. From French *trébuchet*, from *trébucher*, "to overturn," of uncertain origin: perhaps ultimately from Latin *trans-* "across" + Old French *buc* "trunk (of the body)," from prehistoric Germanic.]

tre·cen·to /tray chéntō/ *n.* the 14th century, used especially in referring to Italian art and literature [Mid-19thC. From Italian, shortening of *mil trecento* "one thousand three hundred."] —**tre·cen·tist** *n.*

tree /tree/ *n.* **1.** PLANTS **LARGE PERENNIAL WOODY PLANT** a woody perennial plant that grows to a height of several feet and typically has a single erect main stem with side branches **2.** PLANTS **PLANT RESEMBLING A TREE** a large shrub or nonwoody plant that resembles a tree such as a palm tree or tree fern **3. SOMETHING BRANCHED LIKE A TREE** something that has branches or pegs on which to hang things ○ *a hat tree* **4.** CONSTR **WOODEN SUPPORT** a wooden beam, bar, or post that supports or is part of a structure **5. DIAGRAM OF A HIERARCHICAL STRUCTURE** a diagram of a hierarchical structure that shows the relationships between components as branches **6.** COMPUT **HIERARCHICAL DATA STRUCTURE** a hierarchical data structure in which each element contains data and may be linked by branches to two or more other elements. Every element has only a single predecessor, except for the first, which is called the root and has no predecessor. **7.** CRYSTALS **CRYSTALLINE GROWTH** a branching growth of crystals, particularly of a metal **8. GALLOWS** a gallows (*archaic*) **9.** CHR **CROSS JESUS CHRIST DIED ON** in Christianity, the cross on which Jesus Christ was crucified (*archaic*) ■ *vt.* (**treed, tree·ing, trees**) **1. FORCE UP A TREE** to chase or force an animal or person to climb a tree **2. PUT IN A DIFFICULT SITUATION** to force somebody into a position of difficulty or disadvantage (*informal*) **3. STRETCH ON A SHOETREE** to stretch or shape a shoe or a boot on a shoetree [Old English *trēo(w)*. Ultimately from an Indo-European word meaning "oak tree," which is also the ancestor of English *druid*, *tray*, and *trough*.] —**tree·less** *adj.* —**tree·less·ness** *n.* ◇ **be barking up the wrong tree** to be mistaken, especially as regards the best way to achieve something ◇ **out of your tree** behaving irrationally (*slang*) ◇ **up a tree** in a position of difficulty or disadvantage (*informal*)

tree di·a·gram *n.* = **tree** *n.* 5

tree farm *n.* an area where trees are grown commercially for their wood products

tree fern *n.* a tropical fern that grows to the height of a tree and has a crown of fronds. Family: Cyatheaceae and Marattiaceae.

tree frog *n.* a small frog, found mainly in America, Asia, and Australia, that has long digits with adhesive disks that allow it to climb trees. Family: Hylidae.

tree·hop·per /trée hòppər/ *n.* a small tree-dwelling insect that feeds on the sap of trees. Many species have grotesque projections on their backs. Family: Membracidae.

tree house *n.* a platform, often with a roof and walls, built among the branches of a tree, especially for children to play in

tree line *n.* **1.** = **timberline 2. FOREST EDGE** the edge of a wood or forest

tre·en /treen/ *n.* **WOODEN UTENSILS** tableware and other household utensils made of wood ■ *adj.* **WOODEN** made of wood (*archaic*) [Old English *trēowen*, "made of wood," from TREE. "Wooden tableware" dates from the early 20thC.]

tree·nail /trée nàyl, trénn'l, trúnn'l/, **tre·nail, trun·nel** /trúnn'l/ *n.* a large cylindrical peg made of dry wood that expands to give a tight fit when it is wet and is used to fasten timbers together, e.g., in ships

tree-of-heav·en (*plural* **trees-of-heav·en**) *n.* a deciduous tree, originally Chinese but now cultivated elsewhere, that grows rapidly and has foul-smelling flowers. Latin name: *Ailanthus altissima* and *Ailanthus glandulosa*.

tree of knowl·edge *n.* in the Bible, the tree that grew in the Garden of Eden and produced the fruit that was forbidden to Adam and Eve (Genesis 2:9, 3)

tree of life *n.* in the Bible, the tree that grew in the Garden of Eden and produced a fruit that gave eternal life to somebody who ate it (Genesis 3:22–24)

tree ring *n.* BOT = **growth ring**

tree shrew *n.* a small mammal resembling a squirrel with a long snout that lives in the forests of Southeast Asia and eats insects. Family: Tupaiidae.

tree spar·row *n.* **1. LARGE N AMERICAN SPARROW** a large North American sparrow with a chestnut cap and a gray breast with a single dark chest spot. Latin name: *Spizella arborea*. **2. SMALL EURASIAN SPARROW** a small sparrow of Europe and Asia that differs from the house sparrow in having a black spot near its ear and a chestnut crown. It does not normally nest in towns. Latin name: *Passer montanus*.

tree sur·geon *n.* somebody trained in pruning trees or treating diseased or damaged trees, e.g., by cutting off branches or filling cavities —**tree sur·ger·y** *n.*

tree toad *n.* = **tree frog**

tree to·ma·to *n. U.K.* = **tamarillo**

tree·top /trée tòp/ *n.* the highest branches of a tree

tref /trayf/ *adj.* not kosher and hence forbidden to Jews under dietary laws. ◊ **kosher** [Mid-19thC. From Hebrew *ṭĕrēpāh* "flesh from an animal that has been torn," from *ṭārap* "to tear, rend."]

tre·foil /trée fòyl, tré-/ *n.* **1.** PLANTS **PLANT WITH THREE-LOBED LEAVES** a plant of the pea family that has three-lobed leaves, especially clover **2.** BOT **THREE-LOBED LEAF OR PART** a leaf or other plant part with three lobes **3. THREE-LOBED SHAPE OR OBJECT** an object or design with three lobes or connected parts, such as an emblem used in heraldry **4.** ARCHIT **ORNAMENT IN THE SHAPE OF A CLOVER LEAF** an architectural ornament or form resembling a clover leaf [14thC. Via Anglo-Norman *trifoil* from Latin *trifolium*, literally "with three leaves," from *folium* "leaf" (source of English *foil*).]

tre·ha·la /tri haálə/ *n.* an edible sugary substance that comes from the pupal case of an Asian beetle [Mid-19thC. Via Turkish *tigale* from Persian *tīgāl*.]

tre·ha·lase /tri haá làyss, -làyz/ *n.* an enzyme found in yeast and molds that catalyzes the breakdown of the sugar trehalose [Late 19thC. Coined from TREHALA + -ASE.]

tre·ha·lose /tri haá lòss, -lòz/ *n.* a sugar found in yeast, some fungi, bacteria, and the blood of many insects. Formula: $C_{12}H_{22}O_{11}$. [Mid-19thC. Coined from TREHALA + -OSE.]

treil·lage /tray aázh, tráylij/ *n.* a trellis or latticework [Late 17thC. From French, from *treille*, from Latin *trichila* "bower, arbor."]

trek /trek/ *vi.* (**trekked, trek·king, treks**) **1. MAKE A LONG DIFFICULT JOURNEY** to make a long difficult journey, especially on foot and often over rough or mountainous terrain **2. GO SLOWLY OR LABORIOUSLY** to go somewhere slowly or with difficulty ○ *I had to trek across town to the other bookstore* **3.** *S Africa* **GO BY OX WAGON** to travel in a wagon pulled by an ox ■ *n.* **1. LONG DIFFICULT JOURNEY** a long difficult journey, especially on foot and often over rough or mountainous terrain **2.** *S Africa* **OX WAGON JOURNEY** a journey or migration by ox wagon [Mid-19thC. Via Afrikaans from Dutch, "to draw, pull, travel." The modern meaning "to travel cross-country by foot" evolved from "to travel by ox wagon."] —**trek·ker** *n.*

WORD KEY: CULTURAL NOTE

Star Trek, a television series created in 1966 by U.S. writer and producer Gene Roddenberry (1921–91). The adventures of the Starship Enterprise, a 23rd-century spacecraft on a mission "to boldly go where no man has gone before," initially ran for 79 episodes. The popularity of the series later gave rise to numerous movie spinoffs, the follow-up television series *Star Trek: The Next Generation, Star Trek: Voyager* and *Star Trek: Deep Space Nine*, and a worldwide network of dedicated fans known as Trekkies.

Trek·kie /trékee/ *n.* a fan of the science-fiction television series "Star Trek" (*informal*)

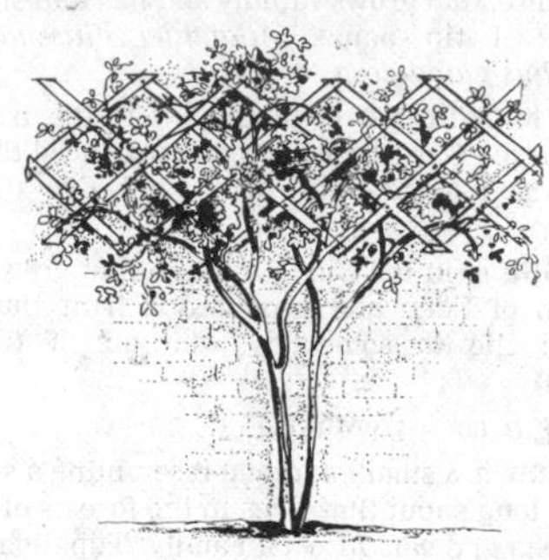

Trellis

trel·lis /trélliss/ *n.* **1.** LATTICE FOR SUPPORTING A PLANT a lattice of wood, metal, or plastic used to support plants, usually fixed to a wall **2.** LATTICEWORK STRUCTURE a structure made of latticework, especially an arch ■ *vt.* **(-lised, -lis·ing, -lis·es) 1.** TRAIN A PLANT ON A LATTICE to support or train a plant such as a vine on a trellis **2.** MAKE SOMETHING INTO A TRELLIS to interweave pieces of wood, metal, or plastic to make a trellis [14thC. Via Old French *trelis* from Latin *trilix*, literally "three threads," from *licium* "thread of a warp."]

trel·lis·work /trélliss wùrk/ *n.* latticework, usually for supporting plants

trem·a·tode /trémmə tōd/ *n.* a flatworm that lives as a parasite in the liver, gut, lungs, or blood vessels of vertebrates, attaching itself by suckers or hooks and sometimes causing serious disease. Class: Trematoda. [Mid-19thC. Via modern Latin *Trematoda* from Greek *trēmatōdēs* "perforated" (because many worms of this class have perforated skins), from *trēma* "hole, orifice."]

trem·ble /trémb'l/ *vi.* **(-bled, -bling, -bles) 1.** SHAKE SLIGHTLY BUT UNCONTROLLABLY to shake with slight movements, continuously and uncontrollably, e.g., from fear, cold or anger **2.** VIBRATE to shake or vibrate as a result of an external force ○ *We felt the house tremble as the train passed.* **3.** BE AFRAID to be afraid or anxious about something ■ *n.* QUIVERING a shaking, vibration, or quivering [14thC. Via Old French *trembler* from medieval Latin *tremulare* "to shake," from *tremulus* "shaking," from *tremere* "to shake" (source of English *tremulous*).] —**trem·bling** *adj.* —**trem·bling·ly** *adv.* —**trem·bly** *adj.*

trem·bles /trémb'lz/ *n.* poisoning in sheep and cattle that have fed on white snakeroot or rayless goldenrod. Affected animals tremble and become weak. (*takes a singular verb*)

tre·men·dous /trə méndəss/ *adj.* **1.** VERY GREAT extremely large, powerful, or great ○ *There was a tremendous clap of thunder.* **2.** VERY GOOD extremely good, successful, or impressive ○ *a tremendous improvement* **3.** FRIGHTENING causing fear or horror (*archaic*) [Mid-17thC. Formed from Latin *tremendus* "fearful," literally "to be trembled at," from *tremere* (see TREMBLE).] —**tre·men·dous·ly** *adv.* —**tre·men·dous·ness** *n.*

trem·o·lite /trémmə lìt/ *n.* a white, gray, or pale green mineral silicate of calcium and magnesium with traces of iron, found in metamorphic rocks and used as a substitute for asbestos [Late 18thC. Named for *Tremola*, a valley in Switzerland where it was discovered.]

trem·o·lo /trémmə lō/ (*plural* **-los**) *n.* **1.** TREMULOUS SOUND IN MUSIC the rapid repetition of a tone or the rapid alternation between two tones in singing or playing a musical instrument, which produces a quavering effect **2.** DEVICE FOR PRODUCING A TREMOLO a device in an organ for producing tremolo [Mid-18thC. Via Italian from Latin *tremulus* (see TREMBLE).]

trem·or /trémmər/ *n.* **1.** SEISMOL MINOR EARTHQUAKE a quivering or vibration caused by slippage of the Earth's crust at a fault, especially before or after a major earthquake **2.** MED TREMBLING a slight shaking or trembling movement **3.** SHUDDER a quiver or shudder, e.g., from fear, illness, or nervousness **4.** SUDDEN SENSATION a sudden and usually brief feeling of excitement, nervousness, or anticipation **5.** WAVERING SOUND OR LIGHT a fluctuation in a sound or light [14thC. Directly or via Old French *tremour* from Latin *tremor* "trembling, terror," from *tremere* "to shake."] —**trem·or·ous** *adj.*

trem·u·lant /trémmyələnt/ *adj.* shaking or trembling [15thC. Coined from TREMULOUS + -ANT.]

trem·u·lous /trémmyələss/ *adj.* **1.** TREMBLING shaking, trembling, or quavering, e.g., from fear or nervousness ○ *in a tremulous voice* **2.** FEARFUL showing fear or nervousness about something [Early 17thC. Formed from Latin *tremulus*, from *tremere* (see TREMBLE).] —**trem·u·lous·ly** *adv.* —**trem·u·lous·ness** *n.*

tre·nail *n.* = **treenail**

trench /trench/ *n.* **1.** DITCH WITH STEEP SIDES a long deep hole dug in the ground, usually with steep or vertical sides **2.** MIL PROTECTION AGAINST ENEMY FIRE a long excavation, often with the excavated earth banked up in front, used as a defense against enemy fire ○ *warfare conducted in the trenches* **3.** OCEANOG VALLEY ON THE OCEAN FLOOR a long narrow valley on an ocean or sea floor ■ *v.* **(trenched, trench·ing, trench·es) 1.** *vti.* DIG A TRENCH IN SOMETHING to dig a long deep hole in or through something **2.** *vt.* MIL FORTIFY SOMETHING WITH TRENCHES to fortify a position with trenches as a defense against enemy fire **3.** *vt.* PUT SOMETHING IN A TRENCH to place something such as a pipe in a trench [14thC. From Old French *trenche* "ditch, cutting, slice," from *trenchier* "to cut," from Latin *truncare* "to cut (off)," from *truncus* "tree trunk."]

trench·ant /trénchənt/ *adj.* **1.** INCISIVE direct, incisive, and deliberately hurtful ○ *trenchant criticism* **2.** ENERGETIC effective and relevant in the pursuit or achievement of a goal ○ *trenchant opinions* [14thC. From Old French, "cutting," formed from *trenchier* (see TRENCH).] —**trench·an·cy** *n.* —**trench·ant·ly** *adv.*

trench coat *n.* a belted double-breasted raincoat, originally modeled on a military coat of World War I

trench·er[1] /trénchər/ *n.* in the past, a wooden platter used to serve or cut food (*archaic*) [14thC. Via Anglo-Norman *trenchour* from Old French *trenchoir*, from *trenchier* (see TRENCH).]

trench·er[2] /trénchər/ *n.* somebody or something that digs trenches, especially a machine that cuts a furrow or ditch in which to lay cables or pipes

trench·er·man /trénchərmən/ (*plural* **-men**) *n.* somebody who eats heartily and enjoys food

trench fe·ver *n.* a contagious illness whose symptoms include fever, headaches, and muscle aches, common among soldiers fighting in trenches in World War I and caused by the bacterium *Rochalimaea quintana*

trench foot *n.* a painful condition of the feet caused by prolonged exposure of the feet to cold and wet. It results in loss of sensation, tissue damage, and sometimes gangrene.

trench mor·tar *n.* a small cannon capable of firing shells at high trajectories over short distances, often used in trench warfare

trench mouth *n.* MED = **Vincent's angina**

trench war·fare *n.* **1.** MIL WARFARE BETWEEN ENTRENCHED ARMIES a form of warfare in which armies conduct attacks on each other from opposing positions in fortified trenches **2.** LONG-STANDING DISAGREEMENT long-standing and bitter conflict in which opposing parties continually attack each other

trend /trend/ *n.* **1.** TENDENCY a general tendency, movement, or direction ○ *a report documenting recent such trends* **2.** PREVAILING STYLE a current fashion or mode ○ *the latest trends in designer kitchens* ■ *vi.* **(trend·ed, trend·ing, trends)** TEND OR MOVE to show a tendency or movement toward something or in a particular direction ○ *public opinion trending toward reunification* [Late 16thC. From Old English *trendan* "to revolve" (hence "to turn," "to turn in a particular direction"), from a prehistoric Germanic word meaning "roundness."]

trend·set·ter /trénd sèttər/ *n.* somebody or something that starts or popularizes a new trend or fashion —**trend·set·ting** *adj.*

trend·y /tréndee/ *adj.* **(trend·i·er, trend·i·est)** (*informal*) **1.** CURRENTLY FASHIONABLE relating to or exemplifying the latest fashion ○ *a trendy restaurant* **2.** REFLECTING THE LATEST FAD deliberately reflecting or adopting fashionable, often faddish, ideas or tastes ■ *n.* (*plural* **trend·ies**) SOMEBODY FOLLOWING CURRENT FASHION somebody who follows the latest trends or fashions, often slavishly (*informal*) —**trend·i·ly** *adv.* —**trend·i·ness** *n.*

trente et qua·rante /traaNt ay ka raaNt/ *n.* GAMBLING = **rouge et noir** [Late 17thC. From French, literally "thirty-and-forty"; because thirty and forty are respectively winning and losing numbers.]

Tren·ton /trént'n/ capital city of New Jersey, in the west central part of the state, 28 mi./45 km northeast of Philadelphia. Population: 88,675 (1990).

tre·pan[1] /trə pán/ *n.* **1.** SURG EARLY TYPE OF TREPHINE an early cylindrical surgical instrument (**trephine**) used especially to cut a hole in the skull **2.** MECH ENG TOOL FOR CUTTING DISK OR CYLINDER a machine tool used to remove a circular disk from a metal sheet or a shallow cylindrical core from a metal ingot or block. The hole is made by removing a concentric ring of material as opposed to disintegrating the material originally within the hole, as with drilling and boring. **3.** MINING ROCK-BORING TOOL a tool for boring holes in rock ■ *vt.* **(tre·panned, tre·pan·ning, tre·pans) 1.** SURG = **trephine 2.** MECH ENG CUT SOMETHING OUT USING A TREPAN to cut a disk or cylindrical core from something using a trepan **3.** MINING BORE HOLE IN ROCK WITH TREPAN to bore a hole in rock using a trepan [14thC. Via medieval Latin *trepanum* "rotary saw," from Greek *trupanon* "borer," from *trupan* "to pierce," from *trupē* "hole."] —**trep·a·na·tion** *n.* —**tre·pan·ner** *n.*

tre·pan[2] /trə pán/, **tra·pan** *vt.* **(-panned, -pan·ning, -pans)** LURE SOMEBODY OR SOMETHING to trap or ensnare somebody or something (*archaic*) ■ *n.* SOMEBODY OR SOMETHING THAT LURES OTHERS somebody or something that entraps or ensnares others (*archaic*) [Mid-17thC. From earlier *trapan*. Probably a variant of TRAP.]

tre·pang /trə páng/ *n.* a large sea cucumber that lives in the southern Pacific and Indian oceans. It is eaten in soups, especially in China and Indonesia. Genera: *Holothuria* and *Actinopyga*. [Late 18thC. From Malay *teripang*.]

tre·phine /trə fín, treé fìn/ *n.* SURGICAL INSTRUMENT a cylindrical sharp or sawtooth-edged surgical instrument used especially to cut a hole in the skull. It is also used in corneal grafting to remove an opaque disk from a cornea so that it can be replaced with a clear disk. ■ *vt.* **(-phined, -phin·ing, -phines)** REMOVE A CIRCLE OF BONE OR TISSUE to remove a circular section from a bone, especially the skull, or from corneal tissue with a trephine [Early 17thC. From Latin *tres fines* "three ends," partly modeled on TREPAN.] —**treph·i·na·tion** /trèffi náysh'n/ *n.*

trep·i·da·tion /trèppi dáysh'n/ *n.* **1.** APPREHENSION fear or uneasiness about the future or a future event **2.** TREMBLING an involuntary trembling (*archaic*) [15thC. From the Latin stem *trepidation-*, from *trepidare* "to startle, be agitated."]

trep·o·ne·ma /trèppə neémə/ (*plural* **-ma·ta** /-neémətə/ *or* **-mas**), **trep·o·neme** /tréppə neem/ *n.* a spirochete bacterium that lives as a parasite in warm-blooded animals. One species causes syphilis in humans. Genus: *Treponema*. [Early 20thC. From modern Latin, from Greek *trepein* "to turn," + *nēma* "thread."] —**trep·o·ne·mal** *adj.*

tres·pass /tréspəss, tréss pàss/ *vi.* **(-passed, -pass·ing, -pass·es) 1.** LAW ENTER SOMEBODY ELSE'S LAND UNLAWFULLY to go onto somebody else's land or enter somebody else's property without permission **2.** LAW CAUSE INJURY TO to cause injury to the person, property, or rights of another **3.** ENCROACH ON SOMEBODY to intrude on somebody's privacy or time **4.** BREAK A MORAL OR SOCIAL LAW to commit a sin or break a social law (*archaic*) ■ *n.* **1.** UNLAWFUL ENTRY ONTO SOMEBODY ELSE'S LAND the act or an instance of going onto somebody else's land or entering somebody else's property without permission **2.** ENCROACHMENT an intrusion into somebody's privacy or time **3.** SIN a sin or act of wrongdoing (*archaic*) [14thC. From Old French *trespas* "transgression," from *trespasser* "to pass beyond or across," from medieval Latin *transpassare*.] —**tres·pass·er** *n.*

tress /tress/ *n.* **1.** LOCK OF HAIR a lock of long hair, especially a woman's hair **2.** BRAID OF WOMAN'S HAIR a braid of hair, especially a woman's hair (*archaic*) ■ **tress·es** *npl.* HAIR somebody's hair, especially a woman's long hair [13thC. From Old French *tresse*, of uncertain origin: perhaps ultimately from Greek *trikhia* "rope," from *thrix* "hair."]

tres·tle /tréss'l/ *n.* **1.** SUPPORTING FRAMEWORK a supporting framework consisting of a horizontal beam held up by a pair of splayed legs at each end **2.** CONSTR TOWER FOR SUPPORTING A BRIDGE any of a series of timber, steel, or reinforced concrete towers that supports a bridge **3.** CONSTR **BRIDGE SUPPORTED BY TOWERS** a bridge consisting of multiple short spans supported by braced towers [14thC. From Old French *trestel*, literally "small beam," from Latin *transtrum* "beam, crossbar."]

Trestle table

tres·tle ta·ble *n.* a table whose top is supported on trestles

tres·tle·tree /tréss'l treè/ *n.* either of two horizontal beams fixed to the masthead to support the crosstrees

tres·tle·work /tréss'l wùrk/ *n.* a system of supporting trestles, e.g., one that supports a bridge

tret·i·noin /trétti nòyn/ *n.* a drug related chemically to vitamin A and applied to the skin to treat acne and other skin disorders [Late 20thC. Coined from TRANS- + *retinoic (acid)* (coined from RETINO- + -IC) + -IN.]

tre·val·ly /trə vállee/ (*plural* **-lies**) *n.* an Australian marine food fish with a slender body and sharply forked tail. Family: Carangidae. [Late 19thC. Alteration of *cavally* (see CAVALLA).]

Tre·vi·no /trə veénō/, **Lee** (*b.* 1939) U.S. golfer. He won 27 Professional Golfers' Association (PGA) titles, including six major tournaments. Full name **Lee Buck Trevino**

Tre·vi·so /tre veéssō/ capital city of Treviso Province, Veneto Region, northeastern Italy. Population: 84,100 (1990).

trews /trooz/ *npl.* close-fitting pants, usually made of plaid cloth, worn by some Scottish army regiments [Mid-16thC. From Irish *triús* or Gaelic *triubhas* "close-fitting shorts" (also the sources of English *trousers*).]

trey /tray/ (*plural* **treys**) *n.* a card, or the face of a die or domino, with three pips [14thC. Via Old French *trei(s)* from Latin *tres* "three."]

T.R.H. *abbr.* thyrotropin-releasing hormone

tri- *prefix.* three, third ○ *trilateral* [From Latin and Greek. Ultimately from the Indo-European word for "three," which is also the ancestor of English *three*.]

tri·a·ble /trī́ əb'l/ *adj.* **1.** LAW **SUBJECT TO COURT TRIAL** subject to or fit for trial in a court of law **2. CAPABLE OF BEING TESTED** able to be tested or tried [15thC. From Anglo-Norman, from TRY + -ABLE.] —**tri·a·ble·ness** *n.*

tri·ac·id /trī àssid/ *adj.* **1. REACTING WITH 3 HYDROGEN ATOMS** used to describe a base capable of reacting with three hydrogen atoms per molecule, so that one molecule of the base can react with three molecules of a monobasic acid **2. CONTAINING 3 REPLACEABLE HYDROGEN ATOMS** used to describe an acid or a salt that contains three replaceable hydrogen atoms [Mid-19thC. Coined from TRI- + ACID.]

tri·ad /trī́ àd, -əd/ *n.* **1. SET OF 3** a group of three people or things **2.** MUSIC **MUSICAL CHORD** a musical chord consisting of three notes, especially a chord made up of a tonic, a third, and a fifth **3.** CHEM **ATOM WITH VALENCE OF 3** an atom or chemical group with a valence of three **4.** MIL **U.S. STRATEGIC MISSILE FORCE** a U.S. strategic missile force made up of bombers, land-based ballistic missiles, and submarine-launched ballistic missiles **5.** LITERAT **WELSH LITERARY FORM** a form of composition in ancient Welsh literature in which subjects or statements are arranged in groups of three [Mid-16thC. Via French *triade* or the late Latin stem *triad-* from Greek *triados* "of three."] —**tri·ad·ic** /trī áddik/ *adj.*

tri·age /tree aázh, treè aázh/ *n.* the process of prioritizing sick or injured people for treatment according to the seriousness of the condition or injury [Early 18thC. From French, from *trier* (see TRY).]

tri·al /trī́ əl, trīl/ *n.* **1.** LAW **FORMAL LEGAL PROCESS** a formal examination of the facts and law in a civil or criminal action before a court of law in order to determine an issue **2.** LAW **USE OF A COURT TRIAL** the use of a court trial to determine an issue or somebody's guilt or innocence ○ *standing trial for fraud* **3. TEST** a test or experiment to determine the quality, safety, performance, usefulness, or public acceptance of something ○ *a drug currently undergoing clinical trials* **4. PAINFUL EXPERIENCE** an instance of trouble or hardship, especially one that tests somebody's ability to endure **5. SOMEBODY OR SOMETHING TROUBLESOME** somebody or something that causes trouble or annoyance to somebody ○ *He's such a trial!* **6. EFFORT** an earnest attempt to do something (*formal*) ○ *a trial to circle the globe in a hot-air balloon* **7.** SPORTS **PRELIMINARY COMPETITION** a sports competition or preliminary test to select candidates for a later competition ■ *adj.* **1. EXPERIMENTAL** done as a test or experiment ○ *a trial separation* **2.** LAW **OF A COURT TRIAL** relating to or used in a court trial ○ *a trial judge* [Mid-15thC. Via Anglo-Norman, or medieval Latin *triallum*, from Old French *trier* (see TRY).]

WORD KEY: CULTURAL NOTE

The Trial, a novel (1925) by Austrian writer Franz Kafka. It is the story of Josef K, a young bank clerk who is abruptly arrested for an unspecified misdemeanor. After a long, unsuccessful attempt to discover the nature of his crime, Josef is executed. This enigmatic work is seen as a disturbing allegory of the human condition.

tri·al and er·ror *n.* a method of finding a satisfactory solution or means of doing something by experimenting with alternatives and eliminating failures

tri·al bal·ance *n.* a statement used to check that the debits and credits in a double-entry bookkeeping ledger are equal

tri·al bal·loon *n.* a tentative suggestion, proposal, or plan put forward to test opinion or reaction

tri·al by fire *n.* a thorough test of somebody's abilities or character under pressure

tri·al court *n.* a court in which a case is first decided, as opposed to a court of appeals

tri·al law·yer *n.* a lawyer who practices in a trial court as opposed to a court of appeals

tri·a·logue /trī́ ə lòg/, **tri·a·log** *n.* discussion involving three people or groups [Mid-16thC. Blend of TRI- and DIALOGUE.]

tri·al run *n.* a test of something new or untried, especially to assess its performance

tri·am·cin·o·lone /trì am sínnə lòn/ *n.* a synthetic drug (**corticosteroid**) used to treat inflammation of the mouth, gums, skin, and joints. Formula: $C_{21}H_{27}FO_6$. [Mid-20thC. Coined from TRI- + *amyl* + *cinene* + *prednisolone*.]

tri·an·gle /trī́ àng g'l/ *n.* **1. 3-SIDED PLANE POLYGON** a plane figure that has three sides and three angles. The triangle is a fundamental figure of plane geometry, since it is the polygon with the fewest sides and any other polygon can be subdivided into triangles. **2. OBJECT WITH 3 SIDES** something shaped like a triangle **3. DRAFTING INSTRUMENT FOR RULING LINES** any thin, flat, three-sided instrument used as a drawing and drafting guide to rule straight lines at specific angles or for determining the angle of ruled lines. Typically the instruments have angles of 90°, 45°, 60°, and 30°. **4.** MUSIC **PERCUSSION INSTRUMENT** a metal bar bent into the shape of a triangle with one angle open, used as a percussion instrument **5. 3-PERSON RELATIONSHIP** an emotional relationship involving three people. ◊ **eternal triangle** [14thC. Via Old French or directly from Latin *triangulum*, from *triangulus* "three-cornered" (source of English *angle*).]

tri·an·gu·lar /trī áng gyələr/ *adj.* **1. OF A TRIANGLE** relating to or in the shape of a triangle **2. WITH A TRIANGULAR BASE** having a base in the shape of a triangle **3. HAVING 3 ELEMENTS** consisting of or involving three parts or people [14thC. From late Latin *triangularis*, from *triangulum* (see TRIANGLE).] —**tri·an·gu·lar·i·ty** /trī àng gyə lérrətee/ *n.* —**tri·an·gu·lar·ly** /trī áng gyələrlee/ *adv.*

tri·an·gu·late *vt.* /trī áng gyə làyt/ (**-lat·ed, -lat·ing, -lates**) **1. MEASURE SOMETHING USING TRIGONOMETRIC RELATIONSHIPS** to measure something using the trigonometric relationships between pairs of the sides and angles of triangles **2. SURVEY OR MAP SOMETHING BY TRIANGULATION** to survey or map an area by the process of triangulation **3. SPLIT SOMETHING INTO TRIANGLES** to divide a surface into triangles **4. MAKE SOMETHING TRIANGULAR** to make something into the shape of a triangle ■ *adj.* /trī áng gyələt, trī áng gyə làyt/ **MADE UP OF TRIANGLES** shaped like a triangle or made up of triangles [15thC. Formed from Latin *triangulum* (see TRIANGLE). The adjective came via medieval Latin *triangulatus*.] —**tri·an·gu·late·ly** *adv.*

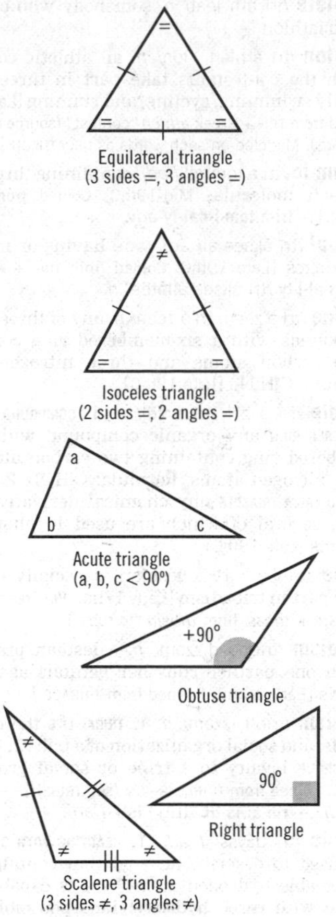

Triangle

tri·an·gu·la·tion /trī àng gyə láysh'n/ *n.* **1.** NAVIG **METHOD FOR DETERMINING LOCATION TRIGONOMETRICALLY** a navigation technique that uses the trigonometric properties of triangles to determine a location or course by means of compass bearings from two points a known distance apart. Space-age global positioning systems enable people to triangulate their location relative to the known positions of Earth-orbiting satellites. **2. DIVIDING OF AN AREA INTO TRIANGLES FOR SURVEYING** the division of a large area into adjacent triangles for survey purposes using trigonometric relationships to calculate the dimensions of an area bounded by each triangle. One side (**baseline**) and the angles to the third point of each adjacent triangle are measured, enabling the lengths of the other sides to be calculated. **3.** NAVIG **SYSTEM OF TRIANGLES USED IN TRIANGULATION** the system of triangles laid out in triangulation [Early 19thC. Coined from the verb TRIANGULATE and -ATION.]

Tri·an·gu·lum /trī áng gyələm/ *n.* a small constellation in the northern hemisphere near Aries and Perseus

Tri·an·gu·lum Aus·tra·le /-aw stráylee/ *n.* a small constellation in the southern hemisphere near the Southern Cross

tri·ar·chy /trī́ aarkee/ (*plural* **-chies**) *n.* **1. RULE BY 3 LEADERS** a system in which a country is ruled by three leaders **2. COUNTRY WITH 3 RULERS** a country ruled by three leaders [Early 17thC. Either from Greek *triarkhia* "triumvirate," or coined from TRI- + -ARCH.]

Tri·as·sic /trī ássik/ *n.* the period of geologic time when reptiles flourished and dinosaurs, modern corals, and coniferous forests first appeared, 245 to 208 million years ago [Mid-19thC. Coined from German *Trias*, from Latin, "three, triad," from Greek, + -IC. From there being three subdivisions to this period.] —**Tri·as·sic** *adj.*

tri·ath·lete /trī áth leet/ *n.* somebody who competes in a triathlon

tri·ath·lon /trī áthlən, -lòn/ *n.* an athletic contest in which the contestants take part in three events, usually swimming, cycling, and running [Late 20thC. Coined from TRI- + Greek *athlon* "contest" (source of English *athletics*). Modeled on such words as DECATHLON.]

tri·a·tom·ic /trī ə tómmik/ *adj.* containing three atoms in each molecule [Mid-19thC. Coined from TRI- + ATOMIC.] —**tri·a·tom·i·cal·ly** *adv.*

tri·ax·i·al /trī áksee əl/ *adj.* MATH having or involving three axes [Late 19thC. Coined from TRI- + AXIAL.] —**tri·ax·i·al·i·ty** /trī àksee állətee/ *n.*

tri·a·zine /trí ə zeen, trī á zeen/ *n.* any of three organic compounds with a six-membered ring containing three carbon atoms and three nitrogen atoms. Formula: $C_3H_3N_3$. [Late 19thC]

tri·a·zole /trí ə zōl, trī á zōl/ *n.* **1.** COMPOUND WITH A 5-MEMBERED RING any organic compound with a five-membered ring containing two carbon atoms and three nitrogen atoms. Formula: $C_2H_3N_3$. **2.** CHEMICAL DERIVED FROM TRIAZOLE any chemical derivative of triazole, several of which are used in photocopying systems [Late 19thC]

trib·ade /tríbbəd/ *n.* a lesbian, especially one who takes part in tribadism [Early 17thC. Via French or Latin from Greek *tribas*, from *tribein* "to rub."]

trib·a·dism /tríbbə dìzzəm/ *n.* a lesbian practice in which one partner rubs her genitals against the other's [Early 19thC. Formed from TRIBADE.]

trib·al·ism /tríb'l ìzzəm/ *n.* **1.** TRIBAL LIFE the customs, beliefs, and social organization of a tribe **2.** ALLEGIANCE TO A GROUP loyalty to a tribe or social group [Late 19thC. Coined from TRIBAL + -ISM (see TRIBE).] —**trib·al·ist** *n., adj.* —**trib·al·is·tic** /trìb'l ístik/ *adj.*

tri·ba·sic /trī báyssik/ *adj.* **1.** REACTING WITH 3 HYDROXYL IONS used to describe an acid that contains three replaceable hydrogen atoms and is capable of reacting with three hydroxyl ions per molecule **2.** CONTAINING 3 UNIVALENT METAL ATOMS used to describe a compound that contains three univalent metal atoms or groups in each molecule [Mid-19thC. Coined from TRI- + BASIC.]

tribe /trīb/ *n.* **1.** SOCIAL DIVISION OF PEOPLE a society or division of a society whose members have ancestry, customs, beliefs, and leadership in common **2.** FAMILY a large family (*informal*) **3.** GROUP WITH SOMETHING IN COMMON a group of people who have something in common such as an occupation, social background, or political viewpoint (*disapproving*) ○ *rebelled against the whole tribe of earnest policy works* **4.** BIOL TAXONOMIC DIVISION a division in the scientific classification of animals and plants, between a subfamily and a genus **5.** HIST ANCIENT ROMAN SOCIAL GROUP any of the three groups, Latins, Sabines, and Etruscans, into which ancient Roman society was divided [13thC. Via Old French *tribu* from Latin *tribus* "one of three ethnic divisions of the Roman people," from *tri-* "three" (source of English *tribune* and *contribution*).] —**trib·al** *adj.* —**trib·al·ly** *adv.*

tribes·man /tríbzmən/ (*plural* **-men** /-mən/) *n.* a man who is a member of a tribe

tribes·peo·ple /tríbz peep'l/ *npl.* people who belong to a tribe

tribes·wom·an /tríbz wòommən/ (*plural* **-en** /-wìmmin/) *n.* a woman who belongs to a tribe

tribo- *prefix.* friction ○ *triboelectricity* [From Greek *tribos* "rubbing," from *tribein* "to rub" (source also of English *diatribe*)]

tri·bo·e·lec·tric·i·ty /trìbō i lek tríssətee, -ée lek-, tribbō-/ *n.* an electric charge generated by friction, e.g., by rubbing materials together —**tri·bo·e·lec·tric** /trìbō i léktrik, trìbbō-/ *adj.*

tri·bol·o·gy /trī bólləjee, tri-/ *n.* the science and technology of interacting surfaces in relative motion, including the study of friction, lubrication, and wear [Mid-20thC. Coined from TRIBO- + -LOGY.] —**tri·bo·log·i·cal** /trìbə lójjik'l, trìbbə-/ *adj.* —**tri·bol·o·gist** /trī bólləjist, tri-/ *n.*

tri·bo·lu·mi·nes·cence /trìbō loomi néss'nss, trìbbō-/ *n.* luminescence caused by friction [Late 19thC. Coined from TRIBO- + LUMINESCENCE.] —**tri·bo·lu·mi·nes·cent** *adj.*

tri·brach /trí bràk/ (*plural* **-brachs**) *n.* a metrical foot made up of three short syllables [Late 16thC. Via Latin *tribrachys* from Greek *tribrakhus*, from *tri-* "three" + *brakhus* "short."] —**tri·brach·ic** /trī brákik/ *adj.*

tri·bro·mo·eth·a·nol /trī brōmō éthə nàwl/ *n.* a white crystalline organic compound used as a general anesthetic. Formula: CBr_3CH_2OH. [Early 20thC. Coined from TRI- + BROMO- + ETHANOL.]

trib·u·la·tion /trìbbyə láysh'n/ *n.* **1.** HARDSHIP great difficulty, affliction, or distress **2.** CAUSE OF SUFFERING something such as an ordeal that causes difficulty, affliction, or distress ○ *the trials and tribulations of the struggling author* [13thC. Via Old French *tribulation* from, ultimately, Latin *tribulare* "to afflict, press," from *tribulum* "threshing tool" (board with sharp points), from *terere* "to rub" (source of English *attrition*).]

tri·bu·nal /trī byōon'l, tri-/ *n.* **1.** LAW COURT a court of justice **2.** JUDGING BODY a body that is appointed to make a judgment or inquiry ○ *an industrial tribunal* **3.** RAISED SEAT a bench or seat on a platform where a judge or magistrate sits [15thC. Directly and via Old French from Latin *tribunal* "platform for magistrates," from *tribunus* (see TRIBUNE[1]).]

trib·u·nate /tríbbyə nàyt, tri byōonət/ *n.* the office, rank, or authority of a tribune in ancient Rome [Mid-16thC. From Latin *tribunatus*, from *tribunus* (see TRIBUNE[1]).]

trib·une[1] /tríb byoon, tri byōon/ *n.* **1.** HIST REPRESENTATIVE ELECTED BY THE ROMAN COMMON PEOPLE a representative of the common people in the ancient Roman republic, elected annually **2.** DEFENDER OF PUBLIC RIGHTS a person or institution that defends the rights of the people [14thC. Via Old French *tribun* from Latin *tribunus* "magistrate," literally "head of a tribe," from *tribus* (see TRIBE).] —**trib·u·nar·y** /tríbbyənèree/ *adj.* —**trib·une·ship** /tríb byoon ship, tri byōon ship/ *n.*

trib·une[2] /tríb byōon, tri byōon/ *n.* **1.** PLATFORM a raised platform for a speaker **2.** ARCHIT BISHOP'S THRONE OR SITE OF IT a bishop's throne, or an apse of a Christian basilica containing the throne **3.** ARCHIT CHURCH GALLERY a gallery in a Christian church [Mid-18thC. From French and Italian *tribuna* "raised platform," alteration of Latin *tribunal*, from *tribunus* (see TRIBUNE[1]).]

trib·u·tar·y /tríbbyə tèrree/ *n.* (*plural* **-ies**) **1.** STREAM FEEDING A LARGER BODY OF WATER a stream, river, or glacier that joins a larger stream, river, or glacier, or a lake **2.** HIST PAYER OF TRIBUTE a person or nation that pays a monetary tribute to another ■ *adj.* **1.** FLOWING INTO A LARGER BODY OF WATER joining a larger stream, river, or glacier, or a lake **2.** HIST PAID AS TRIBUTE paid or owed as a tribute **3.** PAYING TRIBUTE paying tribute in praise, money, or goods [14thC. From Latin *tributarius* "liable to tax or tribute," from *tributum* (see TRIBUTE).]

trib·ute /tríbbyoot/ *n.* **1.** EXPRESSION OF GRATITUDE OR PRAISE something said or given to show gratitude, praise, or admiration **2.** EVIDENCE OF GOOD something that is indicative of a value, benefit, or good quality in somebody or something ○ *His success is a tribute to his determination.* **3.** HIST PAYMENT BY ONE RULER TO ANOTHER a payment made by one ruler or state to another as a sign of submission **4.** EXTORTED MONEY payment exacted or extorted for protection **5.** HIST PAYMENT TO A FEUDAL LORD in medieval society, a payment made by a vassal to a lord, or an obligation for such payment [14thC. Via Old French *tribut*, or directly from Latin *tributum*, from *tribuere* "to give out among the tribes," from *tribus* (see TRIBE).]

tri·car·box·yl·ic ac·id cy·cle /trī kaarbok sìllik-/ *n.* = **Krebs cycle**

trice[1] /trīss/ *n.* a very short period of time [15thC. From TRICE[2]. The meaning evolved from "resulting from a single pull or tug," via "taking a short time."]

trice[2] /trīss/ (**triced, tric·ing, tric·es**) *vt.* to haul up or fasten something, especially with a rope [14thC. From middle Dutch *trīsen* "to pull," from *trīse* "pulley."]

tri·cen·ten·a·ry /trī sen ténnəree, trī sént'n èrree/ *adj., n.* = **tercentenary**

tri·cen·ten·ni·al *adj., n.* = **tercentenary**

tri·ceps /trí sèpss/ (*plural* **-ceps·es** *or* **-ceps**) *n.* a muscle that has three points of anchorage, especially the large muscle running along the back of the upper arm that straightens the elbow [Late 16thC. From Latin *triceps* "three-headed," from *caput* "head."]

tri·cer·a·tops /trī sérrə tòpss/ (*plural* **-tops** *or* **-tops·es**) *n.* a plant-eating dinosaur of the Cretaceous Period, somewhat similar in appearance to a rhinoceros, with a bony crest on the back of its neck and three horns. Genus: *Triceratops.* [Late 19thC. From modern Latin, formed from Greek *trikeratos* "three-horned" + *ōps* "face."]

trich- *prefix.* = **tricho-** (*used before vowels*)

tri·chi·a·sis /tri kí əssiss/ *n.* the inward growth of hair around a body opening, especially inward growth of the eyelashes, causing irritation of the eyeball [Mid-17thC. Via late Latin from, ultimately, Greek *trikhian* "to be hairy."]

tri·chi·na /tri kínə/ (*plural* **-nae** /tri kínee/ *or* **-nas**) *n.* a small slender nematode worm that infests the intestines of meat-eating mammals, and whose larvae form cysts in skeletal muscle. Infection may derive from undercooked meat. Symptoms include diarrhea, nausea, and fever. Latin name: *Trichinella spiralis.* [Mid-19thC. Via modern Latin from, ultimately, Greek *trikhinos* "hairy," from *thrix* "hair."] —**trich·i·nal** *adj.* —**trich·i·nous** *adj.*

trich·i·nize /tríkə nīz/ (**-nized, -niz·ing, -niz·es**) *vt.* to infest a person, an animal, or meat with trichinae (*often passive*) [Mid-19thC. Coined from TRICHINA + -IZE.] —**trich·i·nized** *adj.* —**trich·i·ni·za·tion** /trìkəni záysh'n/ *n.*

Trich·i·no·po·ly /trìnchin óppəlee/ former name for **Tiruchchirappalli**

trich·i·no·sis /trìkə nōssiss/ *n.* a disease caused by infestation with trichinae and marked by fever, muscle pain, and diarrhea, often resulting from eating undercooked pork infected with the larvae

trich·ite /trí kīt/ *n.* a dark needle-shaped crystal found in volcanic rock —**tri·chit·ic** /tri kíttik/ *adj.*

tri·chlor·eth·yl·ene *n.* = **trichloroethylene**

tri·chlor·fon /trī kláwr fòn/, **tri·chlor·phon** *n.* an organophosphorus insecticide used typically in agricultural sheep dips and in household ant killer. Formula: $C_4H_8Cl_3O_4P$. [Mid-20thC. Coined from TRI- + CHLORO- + *-fon*, a shortening of *phosphonate*.]

tri·chlo·ride /trī kláw rīd/, **tri·chlo·rid** /-kláwrid/ *n.* any compound with three chloride atoms per molecule

tri·chlo·ro·a·ce·tic ac·id /trī klawrō ə séetik-/ *n.* a corrosive toxic acid used in weed control and as an astringent and antiseptic. Formula: $C_2Cl_3HO_2$. [Late 19thC]

tri·chlo·ro·e·thane /trī klawrō ée thàyn/ *n.* a volatile colorless nonflammable liquid used in industry as a solvent, especially for cleaning electrical equipment. Formula: $C_2H_3Cl_3$. [Early 20thC. Coined from TRI- + CHLORO- + ETHANE.]

tri·chlo·ro·eth·yl·ene /trī klawrō éth'l een/, **tri·chlor·eth·yl·ene** /trī klawr éth'l een/ *n.* a volatile colorless nonflammable liquid used as a solvent and degreaser, and as an anesthetic. Formula: C_2HCl_3.

tri·chlor·phon *n.* CHEM = **trichlorfon**

tricho- *prefix.* hair, filament, thread ○ *trichoid* [From Greek *trikh-*, the stem of *thrix* "hair" (source of English *tress* and *trichina*)]

trich·o·cyst /tríkə sìst/ *n.* a stinging or grasping organ resembling a thread that protrudes from minute cavities on the surface of some protozoans, especially ciliates, ejected from minute cavities —**trich·o·cys·tic** /trìkə sístik/ *adj.*

trich·o·gyne /tríkə jīn, -gīn/ *n.* a projection resembling a hair on the female sex organ of some fungi, lichens, and algae that attracts and receives the male sex cell prior to fertilization —**tri·cho·gyn·i·al** /trìkə jínee əl, -gínnee əl/ *adj.* —**tri·cho·gyn·ic** /trìkə jínik, -gínnik/ *adj.*

trich·oid /trí kòyd/ *adj.* resembling hair or a hair

tri·chol·o·gy /tri kólləjee/ *n.* the study and treatment of hair and its diseases —**tri·cho·log·i·cal** /trìkə lójjik'l/ *adj.* —**tri·chol·o·gist** /tri kólləjist/ *n.*

trich·ome /trí-, trí kōm/ *n.* **1.** PLANT OUTGROWTH an outgrowth of a plant's outer cell layer (**epidermis**). Trichomes have various shapes and functions, and include root hairs. **2.** SLENDER CHAIN OF CELLS a filamentous chain of bacterial or cyanobacterial cells [Late 19thC. Formed from Greek *trikhōma* "growth of hair," from, ultimately, *thrix* "hair."] —**tri·chom·ic** /tri kómmik, trī kómmik/ *adj.*

trich·o·mo·nad /trìkə mó nàd/ *n.* a flagellated protozoan that lives as a parasite in the digestive and reproductive tracts of humans and animals. Genus: *Trichomonas.* —**trich·o·mo·nad·al** /trìkə mónnəd'l/ *adj.* —**trich·o·mon·al** /trìkə mónn'l, tri kómmən'l/ *adj.*

trich·o·mo·ni·a·sis /trikəmə ní əssiss/ *n.* **1.** MED SEXUALLY TRANSMITTED DISEASE a sexually transmitted infection, especially of the vagina, marked by persistent discharge and intense itching. It is caused by a protozoan parasite *Trichomonas vaginalis.* **2.** VET **INFECTION OF ANIMALS** an infection of animals caused by parasitic protozoans (**trichomonads**). In cattle, this condition can lead to spontaneous abortion or sterility. [Early 20thC. Coined from TRICHOMONAD + -IASIS.]

tri·chop·ter·an /trī kaáptərən/ *n.* = **caddis fly** [Mid-19thC. From modern Latin *Trichoptera*, order name, from Greek *trikho-* (see TRICHO-) + *ptera*, plural of *pteron* "wing."]

tri·chot·o·my /trī kóttəmee/ (*plural* **-mies**) *n.* **1. DIVISION INTO 3 SECTIONS** the division of something into three categories, classes, elements, or parts (*formal*) **2. TRIPARTITE DIVISION OF HUMAN NATURE** the division of human nature into body, soul, and spirit [Early 17thC. From modern Latin *trichotomia*, from Greek *trikha* "in three parts" + -TOMY.] —**trich·o·tom·ic** /trìkə tómmik/ *adj.* —**tri·chot·o·mous** /trī kóttəməss/ *adj.* —**tri·chot·o·mous·ly** /-kóttəməsslee/ *adv.*

tri·chro·ism /trī krō ìzzəm/ *n.* the property possessed by some crystals of showing three different colors when viewed along each of their three axes [Mid-19thC. Formed from Greek *trikhroos*, literally "three-colored."] —**tri·chro·ic** /trī krṓ ik/ *adj.*

tri·chro·mat /trī krō màt/ *n.* somebody who has normal color vision and is able to perceive red, green, and blue [Early 20thC. Back-formation from TRICHROMATIC.]

tri·chro·mat·ic /trī krō máttik/, **tri·chrome** /trī krṓm/, **tri·chro·mic** /trī-/ *adj.* **1. 3-COLOR** relating to, involving, or using three colors **2. COMBINING PRIMARY COLORS** involving the combination of the three primary colors to produce the other colors **3. RELATING TO NORMAL COLOR VISION** relating to normal color vision, which is able to perceive red, green, and blue —**tri·chro·ma·tism** /trī krṓmə tìzzəm/ *n.*

trich·u·ri·a·sis /trìkyə rī́ əsiss/ *n.* intestinal infection with nematodes of the genus *Trichuris*. It usually produces no symptoms, but may cause diarrhea and bleeding in severely infected children. [Early 20thC. Formed from modern Latin *Trichuris*, genus name, from TRICH- + Greek *oura* "tail."]

trick /trik/ *n.* **1. CUNNING DECEPTION** a cunning action or plan that is intended to cheat or deceive **2. PRANK** a prank, joke, or mischievous action or plan ○ *played a trick on his sister* **3. SPECIAL SKILL** a special, effective, or ingenious knack, skill, or technique ○ *taught me the tricks of the trade* **4. SKILLFUL ACT DESIGNED TO AMUSE** a skillful act or feat, designed to amuse or entertain ○ *taught the dog to do tricks* **5. ACT OF MAGIC** an act of magic or illusion, especially one involving sleight of hand, designed to puzzle or entertain ○ *a conjuring trick* **6. DECEPTIVE EFFECT OF LIGHT** an illusion, especially one caused by the light **7. PECULIAR HABIT** a peculiar characteristic, habit, mannerism, or way of behaving ○ *He has this trick of scratching his ear when he's being evasive.* **8. UNFORESEEN EVENT** a strange event or development that was not anticipated or that seems unfair or sad ○ *a cruel trick of fate* **9. CHILDISH ACT** a childish, disgraceful, or unacceptable action (*informal*) ○ *Up to your usual tricks, are you?* **10.** CARDS **CARDS FROM EACH PLAYER IN A ROUND** the cards played by all the players participating in one round of a card game and won by an individual player **11. PERIOD OF DUTY** a period of duty, e.g., at the helm of a ship **12. PROSTITUTE'S CUSTOMER** somebody who hires a prostitute (*slang*) **13. SEX WITH SOMEBODY FOR MONEY** an individual engagement between a prostitute and a client (*slang*) **14. PRISON TERM** a period of imprisonment (*slang*) ■ *vti.* (**tricked, trick·ing, tricks**) **CHEAT** to cheat or deceive somebody ○ *Hundreds of readers were tricked into sending them money.* ■ *adj.* **1. OF TRICKS** involving or intended to be used for tricks or trickery ○ *trick photography* **2. PERFORMING TRICKS** skilled at doing tricks **3. MADE AS AN IMITATION FOR A JOKE** made as an imitation of something so that it can be used to play a joke on somebody **4.** MED **OCCASIONALLY SYMPTOMATIC** displaying symptoms of injury from time to time (*informal*) ○ *a trick ankle* [15thC. From Old North French *trique*, of uncertain origin: probably from, ultimately, Latin *tricae* "complications, trifles."] —**trick·er** *n.* —**trick·less** *adj.* ◇ **do** *or* **turn the trick** to be effective and do what is needed (*informal*) ◇ **never** *or* **not miss a trick** to notice everything that is happening, or any opportunity that is advantageous (*informal*) ◇ **show somebody a trick or two** to demonstrate more skill than somebody who is watching

trick out, trick up *vt.* to decorate or dress somebody or something up, especially in a fancy or garish way (*literary*) [15thC. Origin uncertain: probably from the underlying sense of "deception" in the verb, easily extended to denote "adornment." Perhaps influenced by the obsolete French *s'estriquer* "to deck oneself, adorn."]

trick·er·y /tríkəree/ (*plural* **-ies**) *n.* a trick, or the use of tricks, especially in order to cheat or deceive

trick·le /trík'l/ *v.* (**-led, -ling, -les**) **1.** *vti.* **FLOW SLOWLY IN A THIN STREAM** to flow or cause something to flow in a thin stream or in drops ○ *sweat trickled down his face* **2.** *vi.* **MOVE SLOWLY OR GRADUALLY** to move, come, or go slowly or gradually ○ *The crowd trickled slowly away and the park emptied.* ■ *n.* **1. THIN SLOW FLOW** a thin slow flow, movement, or stream ○ *a trickle of blood* **2. ACT OF FLOWING IN THIN STREAM** an act of flowing or of causing a liquid to flow in a thin stream [14thC. Origin uncertain: perhaps an imitation of the sound.]

trick·le charg·er *n.* a small low-current device used to recharge batteries slowly and maintain them in a fully charged state —**trick·le charge** *n.*

trick·le-down the·o·ry *n.* the economic theory that financial and other benefits received by big businesses gradually spread to benefit the rest of society

trick or treat *n.* **CHILDREN'S HALLOWEEN CUSTOM** a Halloween custom in which children call at neighbors' houses and threaten to play a trick unless they are given a treat such as candy ■ *interj.* **GREETING WHEN TRICK-OR-TREATING** used as a greeting by children when they call on a house in order to ask for candy on Halloween

trick-or-treat (**trick-or-treat·ed, trick-or-treat·ing, trick-or-treats**) *vi.* to go to neighbors' houses and ask for candy on Halloween

trick·ster /tríkstər/ *n.* somebody who deceives, swindles, or plays tricks

trick·sy /tríksee/ *adj.* **1. MISCHIEVOUS** mischievous, playful, or inclined to play tricks **2. NOT STRAIGHTFORWARD** intricate, complicated, or over elaborate **3. DECEITFUL** employing craft, cunning, or deceit (*archaic*) **4. DAPPER** sprucely or smartly dressed (*archaic*) —**trick·si·ness** *n.*

trick·y /tríkee/ (**-i·er, -i·est**) *adj.* **1. PROBLEMATIC** difficult to do or deal with and requiring skill, caution, or tact ○ *a tricky maneuver* ○ *a tricky situation* **2. CRAFTY OR SLY** likely to cheat or outwit somebody —**trick·i·ly** *adv.* —**trick·i·ness** *n.*

tri·clad /trī́ klàd/ *n.* a flatworm with an intestine that is divided into three sections. Order: Tricladida. [Late 19thC. Shortening of modern Latin *Tricladida*, from Greek *tri-* "three" + *klados* "branch."]

tri·clin·ic /trī klínnik/ *adj.* used to describe a crystal that has three unequal axes, none of which is perpendicular to another [Mid-19thC. From -CLINIC.]

tri·clin·i·um /trī klínnee əm/ (*plural* **-a** /trī klínnee ə/) *n.* **1. COUCH** a couch arranged around three sides of a table and used by ancient Romans to recline on at meals **2. ROMAN DINING ROOM** an ancient Roman dining room, especially one containing a triclinium [Mid-17thC. Via Latin from Greek *triklinion*, from *triklinos* "room with three couches," from *klinē* "couch."]

tri·col·or /trī́ kùllər/ *n.* **1. 3-COLORED FLAG** a flag with three colors **2. tri·col·or, Tri·col·or FRENCH NATIONAL FLAG** the French national flag, consisting of three equal vertical bands of blue, white, and red **3.** ZOOL **3-COLORED DOG** a black, tan, and white dog ■ *adj.* **tri·col·or, tri·col·ored 1. 3-COLORED** with, involving, or using three colors **2.** ZOOL **PIEBALD** having a coat of black, tan, and white

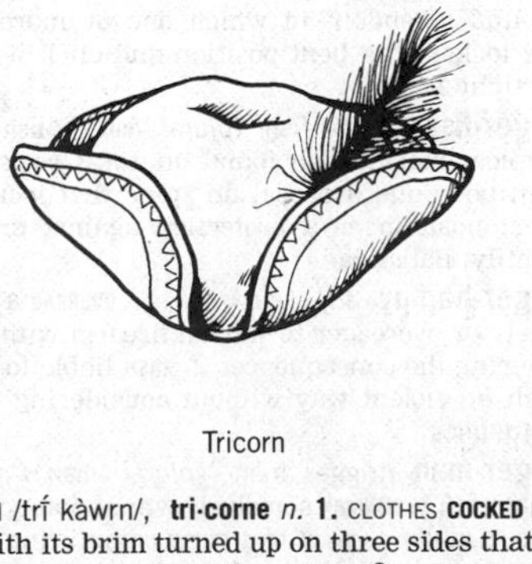

Tricorn

tri·corn /trī́ kàwrn/, **tri·corne** *n.* **1.** CLOTHES **COCKED HAT** a hat with its brim turned up on three sides that was worn by men in the 18th century **2.** MYTHOL **MYTHICAL ANIMAL** an imaginary animal with three horns ■ *adj.* **3-HORNED** having three horns or corners [Mid-18thC. Via French *tricorne* or directly from Latin *tricornis* "three-horned," which was formed from *cornu* "horn."]

tri·cor·nered /trī́ kàwrnərd/ *adj.* having three corners

tri·cot /treé kō/ *n.* **1. CLOSE-KNIT FABRIC** a plain close-knit fabric of natural or artificial fiber, used particularly for underwear **2. RIBBED DRESS FABRIC** a soft ribbed dress fabric made of wool or a wool and cotton mix [Late 18thC. From French *tricoter* "to knit," of Germanic origin.]

tric·o·tine /trìkə teén, treékə-/ *n.* a strong woolen fabric woven with a double twill [Early 20thC]

tri·cus·pid /trī kúspid/ *adj.* **tri·cus·pid, tri·cus·pi·dal, tri·cus·pi·date 1. 3-POINTED** having three cusps or points **2. OF A TRICUSPID VALVE OR TOOTH** relating to a tricuspid valve or tooth ■ *n.* **PART WITH THREE CUSPS** something such as a tooth, valve, or leaf that has three cusps

tri·cus·pid valve *n.* a heart valve consisting of three flaps that prevents blood from flowing back into the right atrium when the right ventricle contracts

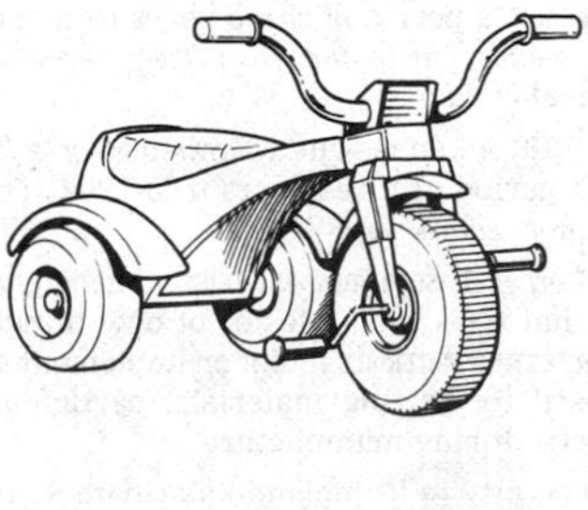

Tricycle

tri·cy·cle /trī́ssik'l/ *n.* **PEDAL-DRIVEN 3-WHEELED VEHICLE** a pedal-driven vehicle with two wheels at the back and one at the front, ridden now especially by young children ■ *vi.* (**-cled, -cling, -cles**) **RIDE A TRICYCLE** to ride a tricycle —**tri·cy·clist** *n.*

tri·cy·clic /trī sī́klik/ *adj.* CHEM **WITH 3 RINGS** having a molecular structure containing three rings ■ *n.* PHARM **ANTIDEPRESSANT DRUG** a tricyclic drug used to treat depression

tri·dac·tyl /trī dákt'l/, **tri·dac·ty·lous** /-dáktələss/ *adj.* ZOOL having three claws, fingers, or toes on each limb

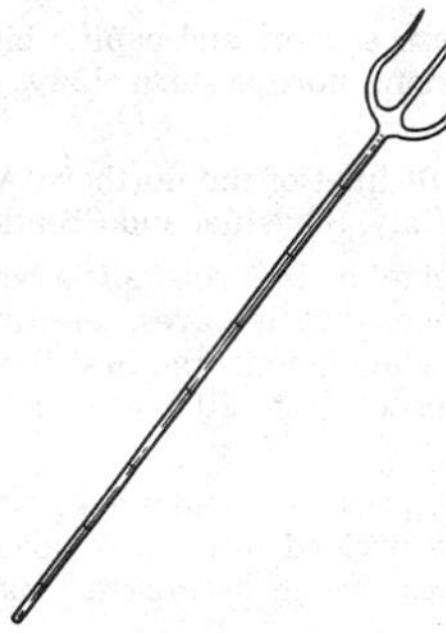

Trident

tri·dent /trī́d'nt/ *n.* **1. 3-PRONGED SPEAR** an instrument, spear, or weapon with three prongs **2.** MYTHOL **3-PRONGED SPEAR OF POSEIDON OR NEPTUNE** in classical mythology, the three-pronged spear carried by the Greek sea god, Poseidon, or his Roman equivalent, Neptune ■ *adj.* **tri·dent, tri·den·tal, tri·den·tate 3-PRONGED** having three prongs, points, or teeth [15thC. From Latin *trident-*, the stem of *tridens*, from *dens* "tooth."]

Tri·dent *n.* a U.S.-manufactured ballistic missile system fired from nuclear submarines and in service with the U.S. Navy and the British Royal Navy

Tri·den·tine /trī dén tīn, -teén/ *adj.* **OF THE COUNCIL OF TRENT** relating to the Council of Trent or its decrees, in which the traditional doctrines of Roman Catholicism were reasserted and the Counter Reformation was begun ■ *n.* **TRADITIONALIST ROMAN CATHOLIC** a Roman Catholic who adheres to doctrines laid down by the Council of Trent, especially in opposition to the reforms of the Second Vatican

Council [Mid-16thC. Via medieval Latin *Tridentinus* from, ultimately, Latin *Tridentum* "Trent."]

tri·di·men·sion·al /trī di ménshən'l, -dī-/ *adj.* SCI having three dimensions —**tri·di·men·sion·al·i·ty** /trī di ménshə náIlətee, -dī-/ *n.* —**tri·di·men·sion·al·ly** /-ménshən'lee/ *adv.*

tried /trīd/ past tense, past participle of **try** ■ *adj.* (*often used in combination*) **1.** **PROVED TO BE GOOD** proved through experience or testing to be good, effective, or reliable ○ *a tried and tested formula for successful game shows* **2.** **HARRIED** subjected to considerable strain, stress, or worry ○ *the sorely tried teacher of a class of noisy students*

tried and true *adj.* proved through experience or extensive testing to be good, effective, or reliable ○ *a tried and true method of instruction*

tri·ene /trī́ een/ *n.* any chemical compound that has three double bonds

tri·en·ni·al /trī énnee əl/ *adj.* **1.** **HAPPENING EVERY 3 YEARS** taking place once every three years **2.** **LASTING 3 YEARS** lasting for a period of three years ■ *n.* **1.** **THIRD ANNIVERSARY** a third anniversary of an event **2.** **TRIENNIAL** an event that takes place every three years **3.** **3-YEAR PERIOD** a period of three years [Mid-16thC. From Latin *triennis*, from *triennium* (see TRIENNIUM).] —**tri·en·ni·al·ly** *adv.*

tri·en·ni·um /trī énnee əm/ (*plural* **-ums** *or* **-a** /trī énnee ə/) *n.* a period of three years [Mid-19thC. From Latin, formed from *annus* "year."]

tri·er /trī́ ər/ *n.* **1.** **SOMEBODY WHO TRIES** somebody or something that tries, e.g., a tester of new things **2.** TECH **TOOL FOR TESTING MATERIALS** a tool or implement designed and used for testing materials, particularly food products, during manufacture

Trier /treer/ city in Rhineland-Palatinate State, southwestern Germany, in the center of a wine-growing region. Population: 98,900 (1992).

tri·er·arch /trī́ ə raark/ (*plural* **-archs**) *n.* **1.** **TRIREME CAPTAIN** the captain of a trireme in ancient Greece **2.** **OUTFITTER OF A TRIREME** in ancient Greece, a citizen commissioned to outfit a trireme for the use of a city-state [Mid-17thC. Via Latin *trierarchus* or directly from Greek *triērarkhos*, literally "trireme commander."]

tri·er·ar·chy /trī́ ə raarkee/ (*plural* **-chies**) *n.* **1.** **SYSTEM FOR SUPPORTING THE ANCIENT GREEK NAVY** in ancient Greece, the system that required citizens to subsidize triremes **2.** **OFFICE OF TRIERARCH** the authority, office, or position of a trierarch **3.** **TRIERARCHS** trierarchs as a group [Mid-19thC. From Greek *triērarkhia*, from *triērarkhos* (see TRIERARCH).]

Tri·este /tree ést/ seaport and capital city of Friuli-Venezia Region, northeastern Italy. Population: 228,398 (1992).

Tri·este, Gulf of inlet of the northern Adriatic Sea, bordered by Italy, Slovenia, and Croatia

tri·fec·ta /trī féktə/ *n.* *U.S. Australia* a bet, especially on a horserace, that involves selecting the competitors that will come in the first three places in the correct order [Late 20 century. Blend of TRI- + PERFECTA.]

tri·fid /trī́ fid/ *adj.* BIOL used to describe a tail or organ that is deeply divided into three parts [Mid-18thC. Via Latin *trifidus* "having three clefts" from, ultimately, *findere* "to split."]

tri·fle /trī́f'l/ *n.* **1.** **SOMETHING TRIVIAL** something that has little or no importance, significance, or value ○ *dismissed the complaint as a mere trifle* **2.** **SMALL QUANTITY** a small amount of something ○ *What he'd earned seemed a trifle beside his mountain of debts.* **3.** COOK **COLD DESSERT** a cold dessert typically consisting of sponge cake soaked in sherry or fruit juice, spread with jam, jelly, or fruit, and topped with custard or whipped cream or sometimes both **4.** METALL **MEDIUM-HARD PEWTER** pewter of medium hardness ■ **tri·fles** *npl.* HOUSEHOLD **PEWTER UTENSILS** objects or utensils made of trifle [13thC. From Old French *trufle*, a variant of *truffe*, "deception," of unknown origin.] —**tri·fler** *n.* ◇ **a trifle** slightly or somewhat (*formal or humorous*)

trifle with *vt.* to treat or take advantage of somebody or something thoughtlessly or without due respect or consideration ○ *had trifled with her affections*

tri·fling /trī́fling/ *adj.* **1.** **INSIGNIFICANT** insignificant, trivial, or of little value **2.** **FRIVOLOUS** concerned with matters of little importance ○ *"He is not a trifling, silly young man"* (Jane Austen, *Emma*; 1816) —**tri·fling·ly** *adv.*

tri·fo·cal /trī fṓk'l/ *adj.* **WITH THREE FOCAL POINTS** used to describe a lens that has three different sections, each with a different focal point ■ **tri·fo·cals** *npl.* **EYEGLASSES WITH TRIFOCAL LENSES** eyeglasses with trifocal lenses whose three sections correct separately for near, medium, and distant vision

tri·fold /trī́ fṑld/ *adj.* consisting of three parts

tri·fo·li·ate /trī fṓlee ət/, **tri·fo·li·at·ed** /trī fṓlee àytəd/ *adj.* **1.** **tri·fo·li·ate, tri·fo·li·at·ed, tri·fo·li·o·ate** BOT **WITH 3 LEAFLETS** used to describe a compound leaf consisting of three leaflets that arise from the same point, e.g., a clover leaf **2.** **WITH OR SHAPED LIKE 3-PART LEAVES** with leaves composed of three leaflets or shaped like such a leaf

tri·fo·ri·um /trī fáwree əm/ (*plural* **-a** /-fáwree ə/) *n.* an arcaded story in a church between the nave arches and the clerestory [13thC. From Anglo-Latin, of uncertain origin: perhaps an alteration of TRIFOLIUM.] —**tri·fo·ri·al** *adj.*

tri·form /trī́ fàwrm/, **tri·formed** *adj.* having or consisting of three different forms or parts

tri·fur·cate *adj.* /trī fúrkət, trī fúr kàyt, trī́fər-/ **tri·fur·cate, tri·fur·cat·ed** **THREE-BRANCHED** divided into three branches or forks ■ *vi.* /trī fúr kàyt, trī́fər kàyt/ (**-cat·ed, -cat·ing, -cates**) **DIVIDE INTO THREE** to divide into three branches or forks [Early 18thC. From Latin *trifurcus*, from *furca* "fork."] —**tri·fur·ca·tion** /trī fur káysh'n, trī́fər-/ *n.*

trig[1] /trig/ *n.* trigonometry, especially as a school subject (*informal*) [Mid-19thC. Shortening.]

trig[2] /trig/ *n.* **CHOCK** a brake or supporting block used to stop something from rolling (*regional*) ■ *vt.* (**trigged, trig·ging, trigs**) (*regional*) **1.** **HOLD IN POSITION WITH A BLOCK** to stop something from moving with a block or wedge **2.** **PROP OR SUPPORT SOMETHING** to prop or support something, e.g., with a wedge [Late 16thC. Origin uncertain: perhaps from Old Norse *tryggja* "to secure."]

trig. *abbr.* **1.** trigonometric **2.** trigonometry

tri·gem·i·nal /trī jémmin'l/ *adj.* relating to or involving the trigeminal nerve [Mid-19thC. Formed from modern Latin *trigeminus*, literally "three twins," from Latin *geminus* "twin."]

tri·gem·i·nal nerve, **tri·gem·i·nal** *n.* either of the fifth pair of cranial nerves that provide the jaw, face, and nasal cavity with motor and sensory functions

tri·gem·i·nal neu·ral·gia *n.* a condition involving recurring sudden sharp pain in the face along the branches of the trigeminal nerve

trig·ger /tríggər/ *n.* **1.** ARMS **ASMALL LEVER THAT FIRES A GUN** a small lever that is pressed with a finger to fire a gun **2.** MECH ENG **LEVER THAT OPERATES A MECHANISM** a small lever or device that is pressed or squeezed to operate a mechanism by, e.g., releasing a spring **3.** **STIMULUS FOR SOMETHING** a stimulus that sets off an action, process, or series of events **4.** ENG **SIGNAL FOR STARTING AN OPERATION** an automatic or manual pulse or signal for an operation to start ■ *vt.* (**-gered, -ger·ing, -gers**) **1.** **MAKE SOMETHING HAPPEN** to set something off, bring something about, or make something happen ○ *memories triggered by the sight of old photos* **2.** ARMS **FIRE A WEAPON BY PULLING A TRIGGER** to fire a weapon or initiate an explosion by operating a trigger **3.** ENG **SET SOMETHING IN MOTION** to initiate electrical or mechanical activity that will then allow a device to function for a time under its own control [Early 17thC. From Dutch *trekker*, formed from *trekken* "to pull."]

trig·ger fin·ger *n.* **1.** **FOREFINGER** the finger used to pull the trigger on a gun, usually the right-hand forefinger **2.** MED **BENT-FINGER DISORDER** a disorder, caused by inflammation of the fibrous sheath around a tendon, in which one or more fingers are locked in a bent position and click if forcibly straightened

trig·ger·fish /tríggər fish/ (*plural* **-fish** *or* **-fish·es**) *n.* a tropical marine fish found on coral reefs with a thin body and a dorsal fin spine that locks in an erect position as a protection against predators. Family: Balistidae.

trig·ger-hap·py *adj.* (*informal*) **1.** **OVEREAGER TO SHOOT** likely or overeager to shoot a firearm without considering the consequences **2.** **RASH** liable to act in a rash or violent way without considering the consequences

trig·ger·man /tríggər màn/ (*plural* **-men** /-mèn/) *n.* (*informal*) **1.** **GUNMAN** somebody who shoots somebody else, usually as part of a gang committing a crime **2.** **BODYGUARD** a bodyguard, especially one working for a gangster [Mid-20thC. Coined during the height of Prohibition in the United States, an era of violent criminal activity, especially shootings.]

tri·glyc·er·ide /trī glíssə rīd/ *n.* a chemical compound (**ester**) formed from a molecule of the alcohol glycerol and three molecules of fatty acids. Triglycerides constitute many of the fats and oils of animal and vegetable tissues and, like cholesterol, may have an adverse effect on human health in excessive amounts.

tri·glyph /trī́ glif/ *n.* in classical architecture, a block carved with three vertical groves that separates the square panels (**metopes**) in a Doric frieze [Mid-16thC. Via Latin from Greek *trigluphos*, from tri- "three" + glupē "carving."] —**tri·glyph·ic** /trī glíffik/ *adj.*

tri·gon /trī́ gòn/ *n.* **1.** MUSIC **ANCIENT TRIANGULAR HARP OR LYRE** a triangular harp or lyre of ancient Greece and Rome **2.** ZODIAC = **triplicity** *n.* **3** [Mid-16thC. Via Latin *trigonum* from Greek *trigōnon* "triangle," from, ultimately, *gōnia* "angle."]

trigon. *abbr.* **1.** trigonometric **2.** trigonometry

trig·o·nal /tríggən'l/ *adj.* **1.** **TRIANGULAR** in the shape of a triangle **2.** CRYSTALS **WITH THREEFOLD SYMMETRY** used to describe a crystal that has threefold symmetry [Late 16thC] —**trig·o·nal·ly** *adv.*

trig·o·no·met·ric func·tion *n.* any of a group of functions of an angle or arc expressed as a ratio of the two sides of a right triangle containing the angle. The trigonometric functions are sine, cosine, tangent, cotangent, secant, and cosecant.

trig·o·nom·e·try /trìggə nómmətree/ *n.* a branch of mathematics dealing with properties of trigonometric functions and their applications, e.g., in surveying —**trig·o·no·met·ric** /trìggənə méttrik/ *adj.* —**trig·o·no·met·ri·cal** /-méttrik'l/ *adj.* —**trig·o·no·met·ri·cal·ly** /-méttrikəlee/ *adv.*

trig·o·nous /tríggənəss/ *adj.* BOT used to describe a stem or other plant part that is triangular in cross section

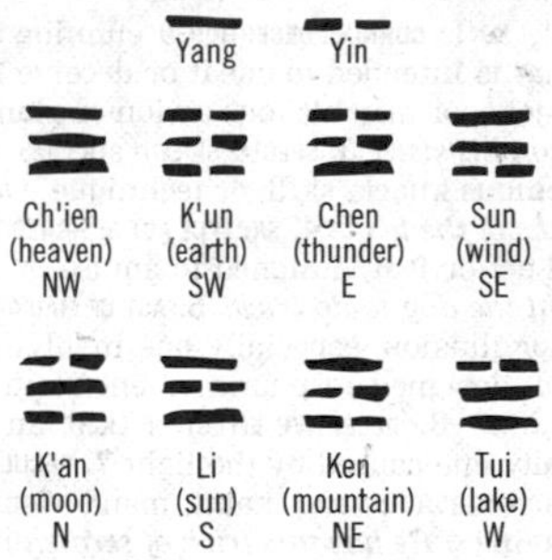

Trigram

tri·gram /trī́ gràm/ *n.* **1.** **GROUP OF 3 LETTERS** a group of any three alphabet letters **2.** **DESIGN OF 3 LINES** one of the eight combinations of three solid or broken lines that are joined in pairs to form the hexagrams of the I Ching, the Chinese system of divination —**tri·gram·mat·ic** /trī grə máttik/ *adj.* —**tri·gram·mat·i·cal·ly** /-máttikəlee/ *adv.*

tri·graph /trī́ gràf/ *n.* a group of three successive letters, especially one representing a single sound such as "igh" in "might" —**tri·graph·ic** /trī gráffik/ *adj.* —**tri·graph·i·cal·ly** /-gráffikəlee/ *adv.*

tri·he·dral /trī heédrəl/ *adj.* **3-FACED** having three plane faces ■ *n.* = **trihedron**

tri·he·dron /trī heédrən/ (*plural* **-drons** *or* **-dra** /-heédrə/), **tri·he·dral** /trī heédrəl/ *n.* GEOM a figure formed by the intersection of three planes

tri·i·o·do·thy·ro·nine /trī ī ōdō thīrə neen/ *n.* an iodine-containing amino acid with activity similar to thyroxine but more potent, used to treat hypothyroidism. Formula: $C_{15}H_{12}I_3NO_4$. [Mid-20thC. Coined from TRI- + IODO- + THYRONINE.]

tri·jet /trī́ jèt/ *n.* an airplane propelled by three jet engines

trike /trīk/ *n.* a child's tricycle (*informal*) [Late 19thC. Shortening and alteration of TRICYCLE.]

tri·lat·er·al /trī láttərəl, -láttrəl/ *adj.* **1.** **3-SIDED** used to describe a geometric figure that has three sides **2.** **TRIPARTITE** involving three countries or parties ■ *n.* **3-SIDED FIGURE** a geometric figure with three sides —**tri·lat·er·al·ly** *adv.*

tri·lat·er·al·ism /trī láttərə lìzzəm, -láttrə-/ *n.* three-sided relations or discussions between nations, areas, or groups —**tri·lat·er·al·ist** *n.*

tri·lin·e·ar /trī línnee ər/ *adj.* consisting of, contained by, or involving three lines

tri·lin·gual /trī líng gwəl/ *adj.* **1. KNOWING 3 LANGUAGES** able to speak or use three languages, especially fluently **2. IN 3 LANGUAGES** relating to or expressed in three languages. ◊ **bilingual, monolingual** ■ *n.* **TRILINGUAL PERSON** somebody who speaks three languages well or to an equal extent —**tri·lin·gual·ism** *n.* —**tri·lin·gual·ly** *adv.*

tri·lit·er·al /trī líttərəl/ *adj.* **1. 3-LETTERED** consisting of three alphabetic letters **2. WITH 3 CONSONANTS** consisting of three consonants ■ *n.* **TRILITERAL WORD OR ROOT** a root or word consisting of three alphabetic letters or consonants. Roots in Semitic languages are triliterals.

AKG London

Trilithon

tri·lith·on /trī lí thòn, tríli thòn/, **tri·lith** /trī lith/ *n.* a prehistoric structure consisting of two large vertical stones supporting a horizontal stone laid on top of them [Mid-18thC. Via Greek, from, ultimately, *lithos* "stone."] —**tri·lith·ic** /trī líthik/ *adj.*

trill /tril/ *n.* **1. WARBLING SOUND** a high-pitched warbling sound, especially one made by a bird **2.** MUSIC **MELODIC ORNAMENT** a musical ornament consisting of rapid alternation between two adjacent notes. The interval between the notes of a trill can vary but is usually a semitone or major second. **3.** PHON **SOUND MADE BY VIBRATING VOCAL ORGANS** a sound or consonant made by two vocal organs vibrating rapidly against each other, e.g., the tip of the tongue vibrating against the ridge behind the front teeth ■ *vti.* (**trilled, trilling, trills**) **UTTER SOMETHING WITH A TRILL** to play, sing, pronounce, or utter something with a trill or sound resembling a trill [Mid-17thC. From Italian *trillare*, of uncertain origin: perhaps an imitation of the sound.]

tril·lion /tríllyən/ (*plural* **-lion** *or* **-lions**) *n.* **1. 1 FOLLOWED BY 12 ZEROS** the number equal to 10^{12}, written as 1 followed by 12 zeros **2.** *U.K.* **1 FOLLOWED BY 18 ZEROS** the number equal to 10^{18}, written as 1 followed by 18 zeros (*dated*) **3. LARGE NUMBER OF SOMETHING** an exceptionally large but unspecified number or amount of something (*informal; often used in the plural*) ○ *had trillions of fans wanting to meet her* [Late 17thC. From French, modeled on *million*.] —**tril·lion** *adj.*

WORD KEY: USAGE

See Usage note at ***billion***.

tril·lionth /tríllyənth/ *n.* one of a trillion equal parts of something —**tril·lionth** *adj., adv.*

tril·li·um /tríllyəm/ *n.* a North American or Asian plant with a cluster of three leaves at the top of the stem and a single large white, pink, or purple three-petaled flower [Mid-19thC. From modern Latin, of uncertain origin: probably an alteration of Swedish *trilling* "triplet," referring to the triplets of leaves and petals in the plant.]

tri·lo·bate /trī lṓ bàyt/, **tri·lo·bat·ed** /trī lṓ bàytəd/, **tri·lobed** /trī lōbd/ *adj.* BOT used to describe a leaf that has three lobes

tri·lo·bite /trīlə bīt/ *n.* an extinct Paleozoic marine arthropod with a flat oval body and a dorsal exoskeleton divided into three vertical sections. Class: Trilobita. [Mid-19thC. Via modern Latin *Trilobites* from, ultimately, Greek *lobos* "lobe."] —**tri·lo·bit·ic** /trīlə bíttik/ *adj.*

tri·loc·u·lar /trī lókyələr/ *adj.* having or consisting of three cavities, cells, or chambers [Mid-19thC. Coined from TRI- + Latin *loculus* "a little place," from *locus* "place."]

tril·o·gy /trílləjee/ (*plural* **-gies**) *n.* **1. SET OF 3 RELATED WORKS** a group or series of three related works, especially of literature or music **2. SET OF THREE** a set of three related things [Mid-17thC. From Greek *trilogia*, from *logos* "word" (see -LOGY).]

trim /trim/ *v.* (**trimmed, trim·ming, trims**) **1.** *vt.* **MAKE SOMETHING TIDY BY CUTTING** to make something neat and tidy by clipping, cutting, or pruning **2.** *vt.* **CUT TO THE REQUIRED SIZE** to reduce something by cutting it to the required shape or size ○ *The editor said I needed to trim the manuscript down to 40,000 words.* **3.** *vt.* **REMOVE EXCESS BY CUTTING** to reduce or remove something, especially something excess, by cutting ○ *We had to trim the budget.* **4.** *vt.* **DECORATE** to decorate or embellish something ○ *He trimmed the hat with fur.* **5.** *vt.* CINEMA **EDIT A FILM** to cut pieces from a film during editing **6.** *vti.* SAILING **CHANGE THE ARRANGEMENT OF SAILS** to change the position or arrangement of the sails so that a ship is ready to set sail **7.** *vti.* SHIPPING **CHANGE THE DISTRIBUTION OF CARGO** to improve, alter, or maintain a vessel's balance by changing the way the ballast or cargo is distributed **8.** *vi.* NAUT **BE BALANCED IN THE WATER** to be or become well-balanced in the water (*refers to a vessel*) **9.** *vt.* AIR **MAKE ADJUSTMENTS TO IMPROVE AIRCRAFT STABILITY** to improve the stability of an aircraft, especially by adjustment of the controls during flight **10.** *vti.* **ALTER AN OPINION TO SUIT CIRCUMSTANCES** to alter opinions or behavior to suit the circumstances of a particular time as an expedient means of gaining an advantage **11.** *vi.* **ADOPT A NEUTRAL POSITION** to adopt a neutral position between two parties that are in dispute **12.** *vt.* **BEAT THOROUGHLY** to beat or overwhelm somebody completely (*informal*) ○ *got trimmed regularly at tennis by her partner* **13.** *vt.* **SCOLD** to reprimand or scold somebody (*informal*) **14.** *vt.* **DEFEAT** to inflict a heavy defeat on somebody or something (*informal*) **15.** *vt.* **CHEAT** to cheat or deceive somebody (*informal*) ■ *adj.* (**trim·mer, trim·mest**) **1. FIT** fit, healthy, slim, or in good physical condition ○ *had a trim figure* **2. NEAT AND TIDY** neat and tidy, compact, or in good order **3. READY FOR USE** fitted out or made ready for use ■ *n.* **1. ACT OF CUTTING** the cutting of something in order to make it neater or tidier ○ *gave the hedge a trim* **2.** HAIR **HAIRCUT** a haircut that tidies rather than changes a hairstyle **3. SOMETHING USED AS DECORATION** something used for decoration such as contrasting material attached to a piece of clothing **4.** CARS **DECORATIVE PARTS OF A VEHICLE** the accessories and decorative parts added to the interior or exterior of a vehicle **5.** CONSTR **DECORATIVE ADDITIONS TO A BUILDING** the nonstructural decorative additions to a building, especially moldings around doorways, windows, and walls **6.** COMM **WINDOW DRESSING** the goods, props, and other items placed in a store window **7. SOMETHING TRIMMED OFF** a piece of something removed by trimming **8.** CINEMA **FILM CUT DURING EDITING** a piece of film eliminated from a shot during editing **9.** AIR **ADJUSTMENT OF AN AIRCRAFT FOR STABILITY** adjustment of the controls of an aircraft to give stability **10.** AIR **FLIGHT POSITION** the position of an aircraft in flight relative to the horizon **11.** NAUT **APPEARANCE OF A VESSEL** the way a vessel appears when it is fitted out and prepared for sailing **12.** NAUT **RELATION BETWEEN A SAIL AND A DIRECTION** the relation between the plane of a sail and the direction in which the vessel is pointing **13.** NAUT **POSITION OF A VESSEL** the position of a ship or boat, especially with reference to the horizontal and to the difference between the depth in water at the front and back of the vessel **14.** NAUT **BUOYANCY** the relative buoyancy of a submarine [Old English *trymman* "to strengthen." Ultimately from an Indo-European base meaning "to be solid" that is also the ancestor of English *tree*.] —**trim** *adv.* —**trim·ly** *adv.* —**trim·ness** *n.*

tri·ma·ran /trīmə ràn/ *n.* a sailboat with three hulls arranged side by side [Mid-20thC. Blend of TRI- and CATAMARAN.]

tri·mer /trīmər/ *n.* a polymer formed by combining three identical molecules [Mid-20thC. Coined from TRI- + -MER.] —**tri·mer·ic** /trī mérrik/ *adj.*

trim·er·ous /trímmərəss/ *adj.* **1. WITH 3 PARTS** having or consisting of three similar parts or segments **2.** BOT **WITH PARTS IN THREES** used to describe a flower with parts arranged in groups of three [Early 19thC. Formed from Greek *trimerēs*, from *meros* "part."]

tri·mes·ter /trī méstər/ *n.* **1. PERIOD OF 3 MONTHS** a period of three months, especially one of the three three-month periods into which human pregnancy is divided for medical purposes **2.** EDUC **1 OF 3 COLLEGE**

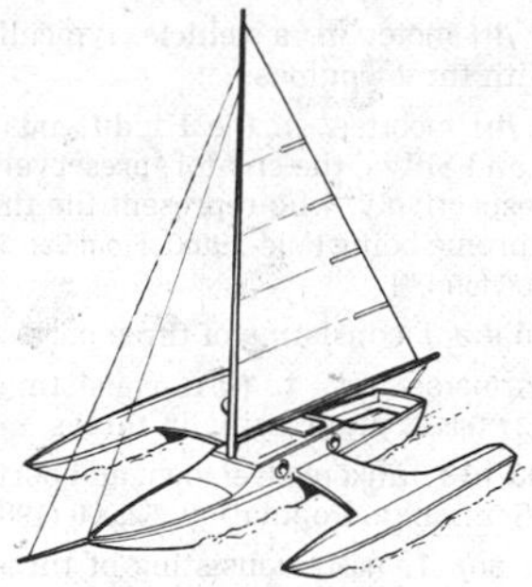

Trimaran

TERMS one of the three terms into which the academic year is divided by some U.S. colleges, schools, and universities [Early 19thC. Via French *trimestre* from Latin *trimestris* "of three months," from mensis "month."] —**tri·mes·tral** /trī méstrəl/ *adj.* —**tri·mes·tri·al** /trī méstree əl/ *adj.*

trim·e·ter /trímmətər/ *n.* a line of verse made up of three metrical feet [Mid-16thC]

tri·meth·a·di·one /trī methə dī ōn/ *n.* a bitter white crystalline compound with an odor similar to camphor, used as an anticonvulsant in the treatment of epilepsy. Formula: $C_6H_9NO_3$. [Contraction of TRI- + METHYL + DI- + -ONE]

tri·meth·o·prim /trī méthə prìm/ *n.* a synthetic drug used as an antibacterial and in the treatment of malaria [Mid-20thC. Contraction of TRI- + METHYL + OXY- + PYRIMIDINE.]

tri·met·ric /trī méttrik/, **tri·met·ri·cal** /-méttrik'l/ *adj.* **1.** POETRY **IN TRIMETERS** consisting of one or more trimeters **2.** CRYSTALS = **orthorhombic**

tri·met·ro·gon /trī méttrə gòn/ *n.* a technique in which three aerial photographs are taken at the same time, one vertical and two at oblique angles, in order to obtain more topographical detail [Mid-20thC. Coined from TRI- + *Metrogon*, the name of a commercial lens.]

trim·mer /trímmər/ *n.* **1. SOMEBODY OR SOMETHING THAT TRIMS** somebody or something that trims such as a machine for trimming hedges, lawns, or timber **2. SOMEBODY ALTERING AN OPINION ACCORDING TO CIRCUMSTANCES** somebody whose opinions or behavior change to suit the circumstances of a particular time in order to gain an advantage (*disapproving*) **3.** ELECTRON ENG **VARIABLE CAPACITOR** a small variable capacitor used, usually in parallel with a larger capacitor, to adjust the overall capacitance of the combination **4.** CONSTR **CROSSWISE JOIST** a joist or beam that is set crosswise and has the ends of the joists running lengthwise fitted into it **5.** SHIPPING **SOMEBODY WHO STOWS CARGO** somebody who stows the cargo on a ship to ensure good stability

trim·ming /trímming/ *n.* **1. SOMETHING ATTACHED AS DECORATION** a piece of material used as a decoration on clothing or furnishings, e.g., a strip of lace, fur, or braid along the edge of a piece of clothing **2. ACT OF SOMETHING THAT TRIMS** the act of somebody or something that trims **3. BEATING** a vigorous beating or thrashing (*informal*) ■ **trim·mings** *npl.* **1.** COOK **FOOD ACCOMPANYING A MAIN DISH** the items of food traditionally served as accompaniments to a main dish **2. EXTRAS** things added to something as accessories or extras **3. PIECES CUT OFF DURING TRIMMING** the parts or pieces cut off when something is trimmed

tri·mo·lec·u·lar /trīmə lékyələr/ *adj.* relating to or consisting of three molecules

tri·month·ly /trī múnthlee/ *adj.* occurring or done every three months —**tri·month·ly** *adv.*

tri·morph /trī màwrf/ *n.* **1. MULTIFORM MINERAL** a substance, especially a mineral, that occurs in three distinct crystalline forms **2. FORM OF TRIMORPH** one of the crystalline forms in which a trimorph exists

tri·mor·phism /trī mawr fizzəm/ *n.* **1.** CRYSTALS **CONDITION OF HAVING 3 CRYSTAL FORMS** the property of existing in three different crystalline forms **2.** BIOL **ADOPTION OF 3 FORMS** the adoption of three successive forms during a life cycle, e.g., the forms of larva, pupa, and adult in some insects [Mid-19thC. Formed from Greek *trimorphos*, from *morphē* "form."] —**tri·mor·phic** /trī máwrfik/ *adj.* —**tri·mor·phous** /-máwrfəss/ *adj.* —**tri·mor·phi·cal·ly** /-máwrfikəlee/ *adv.*

tri·mo·tor /trī̍ mṑtər/ *n.* a vehicle, typically an airplane, with three engines

Tri·mur·ti /tri mo͝ortee/ *n.* the Hindu gods Brahma, Vishnu, and Shiva, the creator, preserver, and destroyer respectively, who represent the three forms of the supreme being [Mid-19thC. From Sanskrit, formed from *murti* "form."]

tri·nal /trī́n'l/ *adj.* consisting of three parts

tri·na·ry /trī́nəree/ *adj.* **1.** TRIPLE consisting of three parts **2.** BY THREES progressing in threes

Trin·co·ma·lee /trìnkōmə lée/ town and port in northeastern Sri Lanka. Population: 52,000 (1986).

trine /trīn/ *adj.* **1.** TRIPLE consisting of three parts **2.** ZODIAC 120° APART AS SEEN FROM EARTH used in astrology to describe two planets or celestial bodies separated by an angle of 120° as seen from the Earth ■ *n.* **1.** GROUP OF 3 a group of three, or something consisting of three parts **2.** ZODIAC ASPECT OF 120° BETWEEN TWO PLANETS in astrology, an aspect of 120° between two planets or celestial bodies as seen from the Earth [14thC. Via Old French from Latin *trinus*, the singular of *trini* "in threes."]

Trin·i·dad /trínni dàd/ island in the West Indies, a constituent part of Trinidad and Tobago. Population: 1,184,106 (1990). Area: 1,864 sq. mi./4,828 sq. km. —**Trin·i·dad·i·an** /trìnni dádee ən/ *n., adj.*

Trinidad and Tobago

Trin·i·dad and To·ba·go /trìnni dàd ənd tə báy gō/ republic comprising the two southernmost of the Caribbean Islands, situated off the northeastern coast of Venezuela. Language: English. Currency: Trinidad and Tobago dollar. Capital: Port-of-Spain. Population: 1,130,337 (1997). Area: 1,980 sq. mi./5,128 sq. km. Official name **Republic of Trinidad and Tobago**

Trin·i·tar·i·an /trìnni térree ən/ *n.* somebody who believes in the Christian doctrine of the Trinity — **Trin·i·tar·i·an** *adj.* —**Trin·i·tar·i·an·ism** *n.*

tri·ni·tro·ben·zene /trī nītrō bén zeen/ *n.* an explosive yellow crystalline compound. Formula: $C_6H_3(N_3O_2)_3$.

tri·ni·tro·tol·u·ene /trī́ nītrō tólyoo èen/, **tri·ni·tro·tol·u·ol** /-tólyoo òl/ *n.* full form of **TNT**

trin·i·ty /trínnitee/ (*plural* **-ties**) *n.* **1.** THREE a group of three **2.** THREENESS the condition of existing as three persons or things [13thC. Via Old French *trinité*, from Latin *trinitas*, from *trinus* "threefold" (see TRINE).]

Trin·i·ty *n.* CHR **1.** FATHER, SON, AND HOLY SPIRIT the union of the three persons of the Christian God, the Father, Jesus Christ, the Son, and the Holy Spirit, in a single Godhead **2.** = **Trinity Sunday**

Trin·i·ty Sun·day, **Trin·i·ty** *n.* the Sunday eight weeks after Easter when Christians celebrate the doctrine of the Trinity. It marks an important division in the Christian liturgical calendar.

trin·ket /tríngkit/ *n.* **1.** SMALL ITEM OF LITTLE VALUE a small article of little value such as an ornament or piece of jewelry **2.** SOMETHING TRIVIAL something trivial or unimportant [Mid-16thC. Origin uncertain.]

tri·no·mi·al /trī nṓmee əl/ *adj.* **1.** MATH HAVING 3 MATHEMATICAL EXPRESSIONS consisting of three mathematical terms or expressions **2.** BIOL HAVING 3 NAMES relating to or consisting of three taxonomic names, denoting the genus, species, and subspecies or variety of an organism ■ *n.* MATH POLYNOMIAL WITH 3 TERMS a polynomial made up of three terms linked by plus or minus signs [Late 17thC. A blend of TRI- and BINOMIAL.] — **tri·no·mi·al·ly** *adv.*

tri·nu·cle·o·tide /trī nóoklee ə tīd/ *n.* a chemical compound consisting of three linked mononucleotides

tri·o /trée ō/ (*plural* **-os**) *n.* **1.** GROUP OF 3 a group or set of three **2.** MUSIC GROUP OF 3 MUSICIANS a group of three musicians who perform together **3.** MUSIC MUSIC FOR 3 MUSICIANS a piece of music composed for a group of three musicians **4.** MUSIC MIDDLE SECTION OF A MUSICAL PIECE the middle section of a minuet, march, or other piece of music, composed in a contrasting style and originally written for three instruments **5.** CARDS SET OF 3 CARDS a set of three equal-ranking cards, e.g., in piquet [Early 18thC. From Italian, formed from *tri-* on the model of *duo* "duet."]

tri·ode /trī́ ōd/ *n.* an electron tube that has an anode, a cathode, and a grid that controls electron flow between the two

tri·ol /trī́ àwl/ *n.* a chemical compound that has three hydroxyl groups

tri·o·let /trée ələt, trī́-, trée ə láy/ *n.* a poem consisting of eight lines with a rhyme scheme of abaaabab in which the first, fourth, and seventh lines are the same, as are the second and eighth lines [Mid-17thC. From French, literally "small trio."]

tri·ose /trī́ ōss/ *n.* a simple sugar containing three carbon atoms

tri·ox·ide /trī ók sīd/ *n.* an oxide containing three oxygen atoms per molecule

trip /trip/ *n.* **1.** JOURNEY a journey of relatively short duration, especially to a place and back again, usually for a specific purpose such as a vacation or business meeting **2.** FALL CAUSED BY CATCHING THE FOOT a fall or stumble caused by catching the foot on something **3.** ACTION THAT CAUSES A FALL an action that causes somebody to fall or stumble **4.** LIGHT STEP a light or nimble skip, step, or tread **5.** ERROR a blunder, error, or mistake **6.** TECH SOMETHING ACTING AS A SWITCH a catch or switch that activates a mechanism **7.** DRUGS DRUG-INDUCED HALLUCINATION the experience produced by taking a hallucinogenic drug (*slang*) **8.** STIMULATING EXPERIENCE an intense, emotional, or stimulating experience (*slang*) ○ *a nostalgia trip* **9.** INTENSE INTEREST an obsessive and often short-lived interest in something (*slang*) **10.** UNUSUAL OR AMUSING THING something such as an experience, event, or person that somebody enjoys or takes pleasure in (*slang*) ○ *living abroad may not be your trip* ■ *v.* (**tripped, trip·ping, trips**) **1.** *vti.* STUMBLE OR CAUSE SOMEBODY TO STUMBLE to stumble or fall as a result of catching the foot on something, or to cause somebody to stumble or fall by making the person's foot catch on something ○ *I tripped and fell.* **2.** *vt.* CATCH SOMEBODY IN A MISTAKE to detect or catch somebody in a mistake **3.** *vti.* MAKE A MISTAKE to make or cause somebody to make a mistake **4.** *vi.* MOVE WITH RAPID LIGHT STEPS to move, run, walk, or dance with rapid light steps ○ *went tripping off down the road* **5.** *vt.* TECH CAUSE A DEVICE TO OPERATE to operate or to cause a device or system to operate **6.** *vi.* DRUGS EXPERIENCE DRUG EFFECTS to experience the effects of a hallucinogenic drug (*slang*) **7.** *vi.* GO ON A JOURNEY to go on a journey, tour, or excursion **8.** *vt.* NAUT FREE AN ANCHOR to free an anchor from the sea bed so that it hangs loose on the end of its rope or chain **9.** *vt.* SAILING TIP UP A YARD to tilt or tip up a yard or mast so that it can be lowered **10.** *vt.* SAILING RAISE AN UPPER MAST to raise one of the upper masts of a sailing ship to remove the bar (**fid**) that supports it so that it can be lowered [14thC. From Old French *tripper*, of Germanic origin.] —**trip·ping·ly** *adv.*

tri·pal·mi·tin /trī pálmitin/ *n.* = **palmitin**

tri·par·tite /trī paar tīt/ *adj.* **1.** INVOLVING 3 PARTIES involving, made between, or ratified by three parties, groups, or nations ○ *a tripartite agreement* **2.** IN 3 PARTS divided into or made up of three parts **3.** BOT WITH 3 LOBES used to describe a leaf that has three deeply divided lobes [15thC] —**tri·par·tite·ly** *adv.*

tri·par·ti·tion /trī paar tísh'n/ *n.* a division of something into three parts or among three parties

tripe /trīp/ *n.* **1.** STOMACH LINING OF A COW OR SHEEP the stomach lining of a ruminant such as a cow or sheep, used as food **2.** NONSENSE something absurd, untrue, or worthless (*informal*) [14thC. From Old French, of unknown origin.]

trip ham·mer /tríp hàmmər/, **trip·ham·mer** *n.* a power hammer with a massive head raised by a cam

tri·phen·yl·meth·ane /trī fèen'l méth àyn, -fènn'l-/ *n.* a colorless crystalline hydrocarbon used in the preparation of dyes. Formula: $CH(C_6H_5)_3$.

tri·phib·i·an /trī fíbbee ən/ *n.* **1.** TRANSP ALL-PURPOSE CRAFT a craft that can operate on water, on land, and in the air **2.** SPORTS TRIATHLETE a competitor in a triathlon ■ *adj.* = **triphibious** [Mid-20thC. A blend of TRI- and AMPHIBIAN.]

tri·phib·i·ous /trī fíbbee əss/, **tri·phib·i·an** *adj.* operating or occurring in the water, on the land, and in the air [Mid-20thC. A blend of TRI- and AMPHIBIOUS.]

tri·phos·phate /trī fóss fàyt/ *n.* a salt or ester with three phosphate groups

tri·phos·pho·py·ri·dine nu·cle·o·tide /trī fòsfō pìrrə deen-/ *n.* = **NADP**

triph·thong /tríf thòng, tríp-/ *n.* **1.** VOWEL SOUND WITH 3 ELEMENTS a vowel sound that combines three elements in one syllable. ◊ **diphthong 2.** = **trigraph** [Mid-16thC. Via French *triphtongue* from, ultimately, medieval Greek *triphthongos*, from Greek *phthongos* "sound."] — **triph·thon·gal** /trif thóng g'l, trip-/ *adj.*

tri·pin·nate /trī pínnət/ *adj.* used to describe a leaf in which the main stalk bears opposite pairs of leaflets that themselves have a similar arrangement of secondary leaflets that are also similarly subdivided — **tri·pin·nate·ly** *adv.*

tripl. *abbr.* triplicate

tri·plane /trī́ plàyn/ *n.* an airplane with three main wings positioned above one another

tri·ple /trípp'l/ *adj.* **1.** HAVING 3 PARTS consisting of three parts, members, or units **2.** 3 TIMES AS MUCH three times as great, as much, or as many **3.** DONE 3 TIMES done or occurring three times **4.** POETRY WITH 3 SIMILAR SYLLABLES having three similar or corresponding syllables in a verse **5.** MUSIC WITH 3 BEATS having three musical beats in a measure ■ *v.* (**-pled, -pling, -ples**) **1.** *vti.* MAKE 3 TIMES AS MUCH to become or cause something to become three times as great, as much, or as many **2.** *vi.* BASEBALL MAKE A HIT IN BASEBALL to make a hit in baseball that allows the batter to reach third base **3.** *vt.* BASEBALL SEND A BASE RUNNER HOME WITH A HIT to advance a runner in baseball by hitting a triple ■ *n.* **1.** SOMETHING 3 TIMES GREATER a number or amount that is three times greater than another or than usual **2.** BEVERAGES TREBLE MEASURE a measure, usually of an alcoholic beverage, containing three times the amount of a single measure **3.** SET OF 3 a group, series, or set of three things **4.** BASEBALL HIT WITH THREE BASES a hit in baseball that allows a batter to reach third base **5.** HORSERACING = **trifecta** [14thC. Via French or directly from Latin *triplus*, from Greek *triplous*.]

tri·ple bond *n.* a chemical bond having three covalent bonds between two atoms

Tri·ple Crown *n.* **1.** HORSERACING VICTORY IN 3 MAJOR HORSE-RACES in horseracing, victory in the Belmont Stakes, Kentucky Derby, and Preakness Stakes in the same season **2.** BASEBALL BATTING, HOME-RUN, AND RBI TITLES the accomplishment of leading a baseball league in batting average, runs batted in, and home runs in a single season

tri·ple-deck·er *n.* something such as a building or sandwich with three levels or layers

tri·ple-head·er *n.* a program of sports contests, e.g., in baseball, in which three games follow one after the other

tri·ple jump *n.* an event requiring an athlete to perform a short run and three consecutive jumps, landing first on one foot, then the opposite foot, and finally both feet, in continuous motion

tri·ple meas·ure *n.* = **triple time**

tri·ple-nerved *adj.* used to describe a leaf that has three main veins

tri·ple play *n.* a play in baseball in which three outs are made

tri·ple point *n.* CHEM the temperature and pressure at which the solid, liquid, and gaseous phases of a substance exist in equilibrium

tri·ple rhyme *n.* a rhyme in which three syllables rhyme with another three, e.g., "snobbery" and "robbery"

tri·ple sec *n.* a sweet colorless liqueur that is orange-flavored

trip·let /tríplət/ *n.* **1.** GROUP OF 3 three things that are connected or related to each other in some way **2.** ONE OF 3 OFFSPRING one of three children or animals that are delivered by the same mother during one birth **3.** GENETICS = **codon 4.** PHYS GROUP OF 3 ELEMENTARY PARTICLES a group of three elementary particles with similar characteristics that differ only in their charge **5.** CHEM CHEMICAL UNIT WITH 2 UNPAIRED ELECTRONS an atom, molecule, or radical with two unpaired electrons **6.** MUSIC GROUP OF 3 NOTES a group of three notes played in the time usually taken by two notes of the same value **7.** POETRY **VERSE OF 3 LINES** a poetic stanza of three lines, usually with a single rhyme and sometimes sharing the same metrical pattern [Mid-17thC. Formed from TRIPLE, on the model of *doublet.*]

tri·ple·tail /trípp'l tàyl/ *n.* a large bony marine fish found mainly in tropical waters whose long dorsal, anal, and caudal fins together resemble a three-lobed tail. Latin name: *Lobotes surinamensis.* [Early 19thC]

tri·ple time *n.* a musical meter or time signature with three beats to the bar ○ *a waltz in triple time*

tri·ple-tongue *vti.* to produce a rapid series of articulated notes in a wind instrument such as a trumpet by repeating articulated syllables with the tongue. ◊ **single-tongue, double-tongue**

tri·ple witch·ing hour *n.* a time when stock options, stock index futures, and options on such futures all mature at once. Triple witching hours occur quarterly and are usually marked by highly volatile trading.

tri·plex /trí plèks, trī́-/ *n.* a building divided into three apartments on three separate floors, or a single apartment that occupies three floors [Early 17thC. From Latin, "threefold."]

trip·li·cate *adj.* /trípplikət/ **THREEFOLD** triple or tripled ■ *n.* /trípplikət/ **WITH 3 IDENTICAL PARTS** something that has three identical parts to it or that exists in three identical copies ■ *v.* /tríppli kàyt/ (**-cat·ed, -cat·ing, -cates**) **1.** *vt.* **MAKE 3 COPIES OF SOMETHING** to make three identical copies of something **2.** *vti.* **MULTIPLY SOMETHING BY 3** to multiply, or cause something to be multiplied, by three [15thC. From Latin *triplicat-*, the past participle stem of *triplicare* "to triple," from *triplex* (see TRIPLEX).] —**trip·li·ca·tion** /trìppli káysh'n/ *n.*

tri·plic·i·ty /tri plíssətee, trī-/ (*plural* **-ties**) *n.* **1. EXISTENCE OF 3 IDENTICAL COPIES** the condition of existing in three identical copies **2. GROUP OF 3** a group or combination of three **3.** ZODIAC **ZODIACAL DIVISION** one of the four groups that the zodiac is traditionally divided into, each separated from the other by 120° and consisting of three astrological signs [14thC. From late Latin *triplicitas*, from Latin *triplex* (see TRIPLEX). Originally only in the meaning "group of three star signs."]

trip·lo·blas·tic /trìpplō blástik/ *adj.* used to describe a multicellular animal that has three primary germ layers (**ectoderm, endoderm, mesoderm**) during embryonic development. This is typical of all multicellular animals except coelenterates. ◊ **diploblastic** [Late 19thC. Coined from Greek *triploos* "threefold" + *-blastic* (see -BLAST).]

trip·loid /trí plòyd/ *adj.* **WITH 3 OF EACH CHROMOSOME** possessing three representatives of each chromosome ■ *n.* **TRIPLOID CELL OR ORGANISM** a triploid cell, nucleus, or organism —**trip·loi·dy** *n.*

trip·ly /trípplee/ *adv.* threefold or in a triple number, measure, or degree

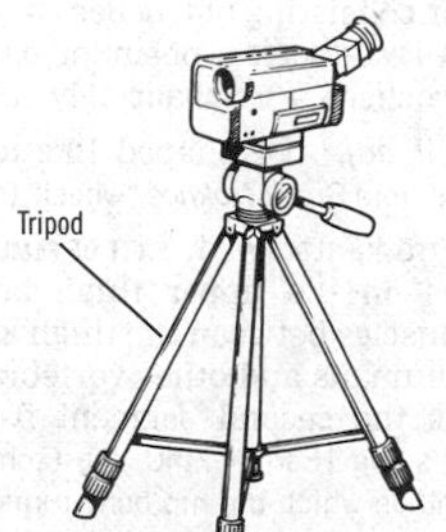

Tripod

tri·pod /trí pòd/ *n.* **1. 3-LEGGED SUPPORT** a frame or stand with three legs that are usually collapsible, used for supporting something such as a camera, compass, theodolite, or other piece of equipment **2. 3-LEGGED HOUSEHOLD OBJECT** a piece of furniture such as a pot, cauldron, stool, or table with three legs [Early 17thC. From Latin *tripod-*, the stem of *tripus*, from Greek *tripous*, literally "three-footed," from *pous* "foot."] —**trip·o·dal** /tríppəd'l, trí pòdd'l/ *adj.*

trip·o·li /tríppəlee/ *n.* a light porous siliceous sedimentary rock containing schist or shells of diatoms and used in powdered form for polishing [Early 17thC. From French; named for Tripoli, either the city in Lebanon or that in Libya.]

Trip·o·li /tríppəlee/ **1.** capital city of Libya, situated on the Mediterranean Sea, in the northwestern part of the country. Population: 1,500,000 (1994). **2.** city in northwestern Lebanon, on the Mediterranean Sea. Population: 500,000 (1985).

Trip·o·li·ta·ni·a /tri pòlli táynee ə, trī pəlli-/ ancient region surrounding Tripoli in northwestern Libya. Founded as a Phoenician colony in the 7th century B.C., it was captured by the Turks in the 16th century, and occupied by Italy between 1912 and 1941. —**Trip·lo·ta·ni·an** *n., adj.*

tri·pos /trí pòss/ (*plural* **-pos·es**) *n. U.K.* a final honors examination for the B.A. degree at Cambridge University in England [Late 16thC. Alteration of Latin *tripus* "tripod" (see TRIPOD). From the stool occupied by the speaker at commencement, and later his humorous speech, on the reverse of which was printed the honors list.]

trip·per /tríppər/ *n.* **1.** *U.K.* **SOMEBODY ON A TRIP** somebody who is on a journey or outing, especially one taken for pleasure (*informal*) **2.** DRUGS **SOMEBODY TAKING LSD** somebody who takes, or is taking, a hallucinogenic drug such as LSD (*slang*)

trip·pet /tríppət/ *n.* a mechanism that strikes another part at regular intervals or is struck by it [15thC. Formed from TRIP.]

trip·ping·ly /tríppinglee/ *adv.* in a manner that is nimble, lively, or fluent

trip·py /tríppee/ (**-pi·er, -pi·est**) *adj.* accompanied by or producing distorted visual or sound effects similar to those associated with psychedelic drugs, especially LSD (*slang*)

trip switch *n.* an electric switch designed to interrupt a circuit, or the power to a machine, quickly

trip·tane /tríp tàyn/ *n.* a colorless liquid alkane used for its antiknock properties in aviation fuel. Formula: C_7H_{16}. [Mid-20thC. Contraction of *trimethylbutane.*]

trip·tych /tríptik/ *n.* **1. WORK OF ART IN 3 PIECES** a painting or carving consisting of three panels, often made as an altarpiece hinged together so that when the smaller outer panels are folded the middle part is entirely covered **2. 3 CONNECTED WRITING TABLETS** in ancient times, a set of three writing tablets hinged or tied together [Mid-18thC. From Greek *triptukhos* "threefold," from *ptux* "fold."]

trip·wire /tríp wìr/ *n.* **1. WIRE THAT ACTIVATES EQUIPMENT** a wire that is attached to a trap, mine, weapon, alarm, camera, or other device in such a way that it will set the device off if disturbed **2. HIDDEN WIRE FOR TRIPPING PEOPLE** a concealed length of wire or rope stretched across a piece of land at ground level in such a way that an enemy or intruder will likely trip over it **3. SOMETHING THAT TRIGGERS GREATER ACTION** something that activates something greater such as a small military operation that could activate the use of a larger force

tri·que·tral bone /trī kweetrəl-, -kwèttrəl-/, **tri·que·tral** *n.* a pyramid-shaped bone in the wrist that connects with the inner bone of the forearm (**ulna**) on the side of the little finger [Mid-17thC. Formed from Latin *triquetrus* "three-cornered."]

tri·que·trous /trī kweetrəss, -kwét-/ *adj.* triangular, especially in a cross section of something [Mid-17thC. Formed from Latin *triquetrus* "three-cornered."]

tri·ra·di·ate /trī ráydee ət/ *adj.* having three rays or radiating branches —**tri·ra·di·ate·ly** *adv.*

Tri·rat·na /tree rátnə, -rútnə/ *n.* the three principal components of Buddhism, namely the Buddha or teacher, the teaching, and the priesthood [From Sanskrit, "three jewels," formed from *ratna* "jewel"]

tri·reme /trí reem/ *n.* a galley, originally used by the ancient Greeks as a warship and later adopted by the Romans, that had three rows of oars on each side, arranged one above the other [Early 17thC. Directly or via French *trirème* from Latin *triremis*, literally "having three banks of oars," from *remus* "oar."]

tri·sac·cha·ride /trī sákə rīd/ *n.* a sugar that has three linked monosaccharide units

tri·sect /trī sèkt, trī sékt/ (**-sect·ed, -sect·ing, -sects**) *vt.* to divide something into three parts, especially equal parts —**tri·sec·tion** /trī sèkshən, trī sékshən/ *n.* —**tri·sec·tor** /trī sèktər, trī séktər/ *n.*

tri·sep·al·ous /trī séppələss/ *adj.* used to describe the outer whorl (**calyx**) of a flower with three sepals

tri·shaw /trí shàw/ *n.* = **rickshaw**

tris·kai·dek·a·pho·bi·a /trìs kī dékə fóbee ə/ *n.* an irrational or obsessive fear of the number 13 [Early 20thC. Coined from Greek *triskaideka* "thirteen" + -PHOBIA.] —**tris·kai·dek·a·phobe** /trìs kī dékə fōb/ *n.* —**tris·kai·dek·a·pho·bic** /-dekə fóbik/ *adj.*

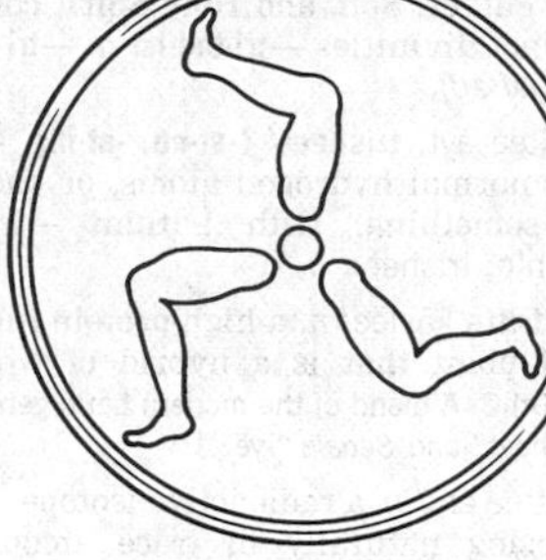

Triskelion

tri·skel·i·on /trī skéllee ən, tri-/ (*plural* **-a** /-ə/), **tri·skele** /trī skeel, trí-/ *n.* a symbol in the form of three bent or curved lines or limbs radiating from a common center. It is sometimes a representation of three human limbs. [Mid-19thC. Via modern Latin from Greek *triskelēs* "three-legged," from *skelos* "leg."]

tris·mus /trízməss/ *n.* a sustained spasm of the jaw muscles, characteristic of the early stages of tetanus (*technical*) [Late 17thC. Via modern Latin from Greek *trismos* "grinding."] —**tris·mic** *adj.*

tris·oc·ta·he·dron /tri sòktə heedrən/ (*plural* **-drons** *or* **-dra** /-drə/) *n.* a solid with 24 identical triangular faces, each triplet of which rests on a face of an underlying octahedron [Mid-19thC. Coined from Greek *tris* "thrice" + OCTAHEDRON.] —**tris·oc·ta·he·dral** *adj.*

tri·so·di·um /trī sódee əm/ *adj.* containing three sodium atoms in a molecule

tri·so·my /trí sòmee, trī sómee/ *n.* the genetic condition of having one or more sets of three chromosomes instead of the usual two chromosomes. Trisomy is usually followed by the number of the affected chromosome pair. For example, Down syndrome is trisomy 21. —**tri·so·mic** /trī sómmik/ *adj.*

Tris·tan and Iseult /trístən ənd i sóolt, trì stan-/, **Tris·tram and Isolde** /trìstrəm ənd i sóldə, -zóldə/ *n.* a pair of lovers in medieval legend. Tristan was a knight who fell in love with Iseult, his uncle's bride, after drinking a love potion.

Tris·tan da Cunha /trìstən də kóonə/ group of volcanic islands in the South Atlantic Ocean, part of the British dependency of St. Helena. Population: 313 (1988). Area: 78 sq. mi./202 sq. km.

tri·state /trí stàyt/ *adj.* GEOG relating to three adjacent states of the United States or the adjoining parts of them

triste /treest/ *adj.* with a sad, melancholy, or mournful quality (*literary*) [15thC. Via French from Latin *tristis* "sad."]

tri·ste·a·rin /trī stée ərin, -steerin/ *n.* = **stearin**

tris·tich /trístik/ *n.* a poem, stanza, refrain, or other division of poetry that consists of three lines [Early 19thC. Modeled on *distich.*] —**tris·tich·ic** /tri stíkik, trī-/ *adj.*

tris·tich·ous /trístikəss/ *adj.* used to describe an arrangement of leaves in which successive leaves arise one-third of the way around the stem from the previous leaf, thus forming three rows up the stem [Mid-19thC]

tri·stim·u·lus val·ues /trī stímmyələss-/ *npl.* the three values representing the amounts of red, green, and blue light that in combination match a particular color

Tris·tram *n.* ◆ **Tristan and Iseult**

tri·sul·fide /trī súl fīd/ *n.* a sulfide that has 3 sulfur molecules per atom

tri·syl·la·ble /trī sílləb'l/ *n.* a word of three syllables, e.g., "enormous" —**tri·syl·lab·ic** /trìssi lábbik/ *adj.* —**tri·syl·lab·i·cal·ly** /-lábbikəlee/ *adv.*

tri·tan·o·pi·a /trìt'n ópee ə/ *n.* a rare condition in which perception of blue and green becomes confused. It is due to the absence of blue-sensitive pigment in the cone cells of the retina. [Early 20thC. Coined from Greek *tritos* "third" + *anōpia* "blindness." From not seeing a third of the color spectrum.]

trite /trīt/ *adj.* overused and consequently lacking in interest or originality [Mid-16thC. From Latin *tritus*, the past participle of *terere* "to wear out" (source of English *attrition* and *contrite*).] —**trite·ly** *adv.* —**trite·ness** *n.*

tri·the·ism /trīthee ìzzəm/ *n.* belief in three gods, especially the belief or doctrine that the Christian Trinity of Father, Son, and Holy Spirit consists of three distinct divinities —**tri·the·ist** *n.* —**tri·the·is·tic** /trì thee ístik/ *adj.*

tri·ti·ate /trítee àyt, tríshee-/ (**-at·ed, -at·ing, -ates**) *vt.* to replace normal hydrogen atoms, or chemically combine something, with tritium —**tri·ti·a·tion** /trìttee áysh'n, trìshee-/ *n.*

trit·i·ca·le /trìttə káylee/ *n.* a high-protein high-yielding cereal plant that is a hybrid of wheat and rye [Mid-20thC. A blend of the modern Latin genus names *Triticum* "wheat" and *Secale* "rye."]

trit·i·um /tríttee əm/ *n.* a radioactive isotope of hydrogen occurring naturally in trace amounts and having atomic mass 3 and a half-life of 12.3 years. Although rare in nature it can be produced artificially and is used in tracers and hydrogen bombs. Symbol **T** [Mid-20thC. Via modern Latin from Greek *tritos* "third." So named from its atomic weight of 3.]

tri·ton[1] /trít'n/ *n.* a large tropical marine gastropod mollusk with a heavy multicolored spiral shell. Family: Cymatiidae. [Late 18thC. Via the modern Latin genus name *Triton*, from Latin *Triton* (see TRITON). From representations of the sea god holding a conch shell.]

tri·ton[2] /trí tòn/ *n.* the nucleus of a tritium atom, consisting of one proton and two neutrons [Mid-20thC. Formed from TRITIUM.]

Tri·ton[1] /trít'n/ *n.* a god of the sea in Greek mythology, the son of Poseidon and Amphitrite, represented as having the tail of a fish and the upper body of a man [Late 16thC. Via Latin from Greek *Tritōn*.]

Tri·ton[2] *n.* the largest moon of the planet Neptune, about 1,680 mi./2,700 km in diameter, and revolving in a direction counter to that of the planet [From its dependence on the planet Neptune, in allusion to the demigod Triton's dependence on the sea god Neptune]

tri·tone /trí tōn/ *n.* a dissonant musical interval composed of three whole tones

trit·u·rate *vt.* /tríchə ràyt/ (**-rat·ed, -rat·ing, -rates**) **MAKE SOMETHING INTO POWDER** to grind or rub a substance into a fine powder ■ *n.* /tríchərət/ **FINELY GROUND POWDER** a finely ground powder, especially a drug [Mid-18thC. From late Latin *triturat-*, the past participle stem of *triturare* "to thresh," from, ultimately, Latin *terere* "to rub."] —**trit·u·ra·ble** *adj.* —**trit·u·ra·tor** *n.*

trit·u·ra·tion /trìchə ráysh'n/ *n.* **1. PROCESS OF GRINDING SOMETHING INTO POWDER** the process of grinding or rubbing a substance into a fine powder **2. BEING A FINE POWDER** the condition of having been ground or rubbed into a fine powder **3.** PHARM **POWDERED DRUG MIXTURE** a mixture of powdered drugs prepared pharmaceutically, especially one containing lactose **4.** DENT **MIXING OF AMALGAM** the mixing of an amalgam, usually of silver and mercury, for use in filling cavities in teeth

tri·umph /trí əmf/ *n.* **1. SUCCESS** an act or occasion of winning, being victorious, or overcoming something **2. JOY ABOUT SUCCESS** the happiness, pride, or feeling of elation that comes from winning, being victorious, or overcoming something **3. OUTSTANDING SUCCESS** something that is notable for its exceptional quality or for being a great achievement ○ *The reviews hailed the company's new production of Hamlet as a triumph.* **4. ROMAN VICTORY PARADE** in ancient Rome, a procession through the streets of Rome to the Capitoline Hill to mark a general's victory over a foreign army **5. CELEBRATORY SPECTACLE** a public display or parade, especially one held as a festival or celebration (*archaic*) ■ *vi.* (**-umphed, -umph·ing, -umphs**) **1. WIN OR ACHIEVE SUCCESS** to be successful, especially against an adversary or in combating the odds against success **2. BECOME EXULTED** to experience the happiness, pride, or feeling of elation that comes from winning, being victorious, or overcoming something [14thC. Via Old French *triumphe* from Latin *triumphus*, of uncertain origin: probably via Etruscan from Greek *thriambos* "hymn to Dionysus."]

tri·um·phal /trī úmfəl/ *adj.* celebrating or commemorating a victory ○ *a triumphal procession* —**tri·umph·al·ism** *n.*

WORD KEY: USAGE

triumphal or **triumphant**? ***Triumphal*** is a neutral word that classifies something as being connected with a success or victory, usually of a military kind: *There is a triumphal arch in the center of the city. The band will play a triumphal march.* ***Triumphant*** is a more judgmental word describing the feelings that follow a success: *The winning team returned home triumphant. She told us of her win with a triumphant look on her face.*

tri·um·phal arch *n.* a monument, usually in the form of an ornamental free-standing arch spanning a street, built to commemorate something, especially an outstanding military victory

tri·um·phant /trī úmfənt/ *adj.* **1. FULL OF PRIDE AT VICTORY** displaying or feeling great pride in having achieved a victory **2. VERY IMPRESSIVE** outstandingly successful ○ *made a triumphant reappearance in the role he made famous* **3. TRIUMPHAL** triumphal (*archaic*) [15thC] —**tri·um·phant·ly** *adv.*

WORD KEY: USAGE

See Usage note at ***triumphal***.

tri·um·vir /trī úmvər/ (*plural* **-virs** *or* **-vi·ri** /-və rī/) *n.* **1. MEMBER OF A TRIUMVIRATE** one of the three people who made up a triumvirate, especially in ancient Rome **2. SOMEBODY SHARING POWER WITH 2 OTHERS** somebody who has an equal share in a position of authority with two other people (*formal*) [Late 16thC. From Latin, a back-formation from *triumviri* "board of three men," from *trium virum* "of three men."] —**tri·um·vi·ral** *adj.*

tri·um·vi·rate /trī úmvərət, -úmvə ràyt/ *n.* **1. ROMAN COMMITEE OF 3 RULERS** a group of three men who together were responsible for public administration or civil authority in the government system of ancient Rome **2. 3 SHARING AUTHORITY** a group of three people who jointly share some responsibility, authority, or power **3. POSITION OF SHARING POWER** the position of being one of three who exercise power or authority **4. TERM OF OFFICE OF SHARED POWER** the duration of the term of office for somebody who shares power or authority with two others **5. RULE BY A GROUP OF 3** government or rule by a group of three [Late 16thC. From Latin *triumviratus*, from *triumviri* (see TRIUMVIR).]

tri·une /trí yoon/, **Tri·une** *adj.* **THREE IN ONE** consisting of or being three in one, e.g., in the Christian Trinity ■ *n.* **GROUP OF THREE** a group consisting of three members, especially the Christian Trinity [Early 17thC. Coined from TRI- + Latin *unus* "one."]

tri·u·ni·ty /trī yóonətee/ (*plural* **-ties**) *n.* = **trinity**

tri·va·lent /trī váylənt/, **ter·va·lent** /tur váylənt/ *adj.* **1. WITH VALENCE OF 3** having a chemical valence of three **2. WITH 3 VALENCES** with three chemical valences **3. FORMED BY 3 CHROMOSOMES** formed by three homologous chromosomes that lie close together or appear to join during the first division of meiosis —**tri·va·len·cy** *n.*

Tri·van·drum /tri vándrəm/ port and capital city of Kerala State, southern India. Population: 523,723 (1991).

triv·et /trívvit/ *n.* **1. 3-LEGGED STAND** a stand or support, usually metal with three legs, for hot pans and dishes **2. 3-LEGGED SUPPORT FOR PAN** a device, usually metal with three legs, that fits over the grate of a fire to support a pan or kettle [15thC. Origin uncertain: probably an alteration of the Latin *triped-*, the stem of *tripes* "three-footed," from *pes* "foot."]

triv·i·a[1] /trívvee ə/ *npl.* a collection of insignificant or obscure items, details, or information (*takes a singular or plural verb*) [Early 20thC. Latinized back-formation from TRIVIAL.]

triv·i·a[2] plural of **trivium**

triv·i·al /trívvee əl/ *adj.* **1. HAVING LITTLE VALUE** lacking in seriousness, importance, significance, or value **2. COMMONPLACE** lacking any qualities that are unique or interesting **3. CONCERNED WITH TRIVIA** relating to or concerned with trivia **4.** MATH **WITH ZERO VALUES** used to describe the simplest possible case mathematically, especially with all mathematical variables equal to zero [15thC. From Latin *trivialis* "relating to the trivium division of subjects," hence "commonplace" (because the trivium was considered to incorporate the less important subjects), from *trivium* (see TRIVIUM).] —**triv·i·al·ly** *adv.* —**triv·i·al·ness** *n.*

WORD KEY: ORIGIN

Medieval teachers and scholars recognized seven liberal arts: the lower three, grammar, logic, and rhetoric, were known as the *trivium*, and the upper four, arithmetic, astronomy, geometry, and music, were known as the *quadrivium*. The notion of "less important subjects" led in the 16th century to the use of the derived adjective ***trivial*** for "commonplace, of little importance."

triv·i·al·i·ty /trìvvee állətee/, **triv·i·al·ism** /trívvee ə lìzzəm/ *n.* **1. UNIMPORTANCE** the condition or quality of having little importance or seriousness **2. SOMETHING UNIMPORTANT** something that is considered to lack importance or seriousness

triv·i·al·ize /trívvee ə līz/ (**-ized, -iz·ing, -iz·es**) *vt.* to treat something as, or make it appear, less important, significant, or valuable than it really is —**triv·i·al·i·za·tion** /trìvvee əli záysh'n/ *n.*

triv·i·al name *n.* **1.** CHEM **POPULAR NAME FOR A SUBSTANCE** a common or popular name for a substance that does not describe its exact chemical composition **2.** BIOL = **specific epithet**

Triv·ial Pur·suit *tdmk.* a trademark for a board game that tests the players' knowledge of trivia

triv·i·um /trívvee əm/ (*plural* **-a** /-ə/) *n.* grammar, rhetoric, and logic, three of the seven liberal arts that formed the basis of medieval university study, traditionally considered to be less important than the other four. ◊ **quadrivium** [Early 19thC. From medieval Latin, a variant sense of Latin *trivium* "place where three roads cross" (see TRIVIAL.]

tri·week·ly /trī wéeklee/ *adj.* **1. APPEARING OR DONE EVERY 3 WEEKS** occurring, published, or performed once every three weeks **2. APPEARING OR DONE 3 TIMES WEEKLY** occurring, published, or performed three times each week ■ *adv.* **1. EVERY 3 WEEKS** once every three weeks **2. 3 TIMES A WEEK** three times each week ■ *n.* (*plural* **-lies**) **1. 3-WEEKLY PUBLICATION** a publication that comes out every three weeks **2. PUBLICATION 3 TIMES A WEEK** a publication that comes out three times each week

-trix *suffix.* **1.** a woman who performs a particular function ○ *administratrix* **2.** a geometric element that performs a particular function ○ *directrix* [From Latin, the feminine form of *-tor*]

t-RNA *abbr.* transfer RNA

TRO *abbr.* temporary restraining order

Tro·bri·and Is·lands /trō bree ànd-, -àand-/ island group of Papua New Guinea in the Solomon Sea, east of New Guinea. Area: 170 sq. mi./440 sq. km.

tro·car /trō kaar/ *n.* a sharply pointed steel rod sheathed with a tight-fitting cylindrical tube (**cannula**), used together to drain or extract fluid from a body cavity. The whole instrument is inserted then the trocar is removed, leaving the cannula in place. [Early 18thC. From French *trocart*, from carre "side of an instrument," from, ultimately, Latin *quadrum* "square."]

tro·cha·ic /trō káy ik/ *adj.* **OF TROCHEES** relating to, belonging to, or consisting of trochees ■ *n.* **1.** = **trochee** **2. POEM WRITTEN IN TROCHEES** a poem, or part of a poem, written in trochees —**tro·cha·ic·al·ly** *adv.*

tro·chal /trók'l/ *adj.* ZOOL shaped like a wheel [Mid-19thC. Formed from Greek *trokhos* "wheel" (see TROCHOID).]

tro·chan·ter /trō kántər/ *n.* **1. PART OF FEMUR** one of two rough knobs on the upper thigh bone (**femur**), where the muscles between the thigh and pelvis are attached in humans and other vertebrates **2. PART OF AN INSECT'S LEG** the second segment from the base of an insect's leg [Early 17thC. Via French from Greek *trokhantēr* "ball on which the hip bone turns in its socket," from *trekhein* "to run."]

tro·che /trókee/ *n.* a medicinal lozenge [Late 16thC. Alteration of earlier *trochisk*, from, ultimately, Greek *trokhiskos* "small wheel," from *trokhos* "wheel" (see TROCHOID).]

tro·chee /trókee/ *n.* a metrical foot that consists of one stressed syllable followed by an unstressed syllable, e.g., the word "human." ◊ **iamb** [Late 16thC. Via Latin *trochaeus* from Greek *trokhaios* "running," from, ultimately, *trekhein* "to run." From the rhythmic pattern that resembles a gallop.]

troch·le·a /tróklee ə/ *n.* an anatomical part or structure with a grooved surface that resembles a pulley, especially the surface of a bone over which a tendon passes [Late 17thC. Via Latin from Greek *trokhileia* "pulley."]

troch·le·ar /tróklee ər/ *adj.* relating to, situated near, or resembling a trochlea or trochlear nerve [Late 17thC]

troch·le·ar nerve *n.* either of the fourth pair of cranial nerves serving the muscle that is used to rotate the eyeball outward and downward

tro·choid /trṓ kòyd/ *n.* GEOM **CURVE FORMED BY POINT ON RADIUS** a curve formed by a point on the radius of a circle, or on the extended radius, as the circle rolls along a straight line ■ *adj.* **tro·choid, tro·choi·dal** **1.** MATH **ROTATING ABOUT CENTRAL AXIS** rotating, showing rotation, or able to rotate about a central axis **2.** ANAT **RESEMBLING PIVOT** resembling or functioning in the body like a pivot or pulley [Early 18thC. From Greek *trokhoeidēs* "wheel-like," from *trokhos* "wheel," from *trekhein* "to run."] —**tro·choi·dal·ly** /trō kóyd'lee/ *adv.*

troch·o·phore /trókə fàwr/, **troch·o·sphere** /-sfeer/ *n.* a free-swimming ciliated larval form of certain invertebrates such as mollusks and rotifers [Late 19thC. Coined from Greek *trokhos* "wheel" + -PHORE.]

trod past tense, past participle of **tread**

trod·den past participle of **tread**

trode past tense of **tread** (*archaic*)

trof·fer /tróffər/ *n.* an inverted recess in a ceiling that acts as a support and reflector for a fluorescent light [Mid-20thC. A blend of TROUGH and COFFER.]

trog·lo·dyte /trógglə dīt/ *n.* **1.** **CAVE DWELLER** somebody who lives in a cave, especially somebody who belonged to a prehistoric cave-dwelling community **2.** **SOMEBODY LIVING IN SECLUSION** somebody who lives alone and has little to do with other people, especially somebody considered to be antisocial or unconventional [Late 15thC. Via Latin *Troglodyta* from, ultimately, Greek *Trōglodutai*, literally "ones who enter a hole," an alteration of *Trōgodutai*, an Ethiopian tribe.] —**trog·lo·dyt·ic** /trògglə díttik/ *adj.*

tro·gon /trṓ gòn/ *n.* a tropical or subtropical tree-dwelling bird with a short hooked bill, long tail, and brightly colored plumage. Family: Trogonidae. ◊ **quetzal** [Late 18thC. Via modern Latin from, ultimately, Greek *trōgein* "to gnaw."]

troi·ka /tróykə/ *n.* **1.** TRANSP **HORSE-DRAWN RUSSIAN VEHICLE** a carriage of Russian origin drawn by three horses harnessed abreast of each other **2.** TRANSP **3 HORSES HARNESSED TOGETHER** a team of three horses harnessed abreast of each other **3.** = **triumvirate** *n.* 2 [Mid-19thC. From Russian, formed from *troe* "group of three."]

tro·i·lite /tróy līt/ *n.* a variety of iron sulfide that is found in some meteorites [Mid-19thC. Named for Domenico *Troili*, the 18th-century Italian who described a meteorite containing this mineral.]

Troi·lus /tróyləss/ *n.* in Greek mythology, the son of the Trojan king Priam. He was killed during the Trojan War by the Greek warrior Achilles. In medieval legend he is depicted as the betrayed lover of Cressida.

Trois-Ri·vières /twraà reev yáir/ city on the St. Lawrence River between Quebec City and Montreal, in southern Quebec Province, Canada. Population: 48,419 (1996).

Tro·jan /trṓjən/ *n.* **1.** PEOPLES **CITIZEN OF ANCIENT TROY** somebody who was born in or was a citizen of ancient Troy **2.** **DEDICATED WORKER** somebody who does something with great dedication, determination, stamina, or courage —**Tro·jan** *adj.*

Tro·jan horse *n.* **1.** MYTHOL **HOLLOW HORSE CONCEALING GREEKS** in Greek legends, a hollow wooden horse that hid Greek soldiers, left at the gates of Troy. The Trojans were convinced it was a gift to Athena and dragged it inside. **2.** **CONCEALED STRATAGEM** somebody or something that is meant to disrupt, undermine, subvert, or destroy an enemy or rival, especially somebody or something that operates while concealed within an organization **3.** COMPUT **DESTRUCTIVE COMPUTER PROGRAM** a computer program that appears to be useful but that actually does damage. ◊ **virus**

troll[1] /trōl/ *v.* (**trolled, troll·ing, trolls**) **1.** *vti.* ANGLING **DRAG BAITED LINE THROUGH WATER** to drag a baited line through water, often from the back of a boat moving slowly **2.** *vti.* ANGLING **TROLL IN ONE AREA** to troll a particular area **3.** *vti.* ANGLING **TROLL FOR PARTICULAR FISH** to try to catch a particular kind of fish by trolling **4.** *vi.* **AMBLE ABOUT** to walk casually about **5.** *vti.* **WANDER AROUND SEARCHING FOR SOMEBODY** to wander around a particular area or place, especially in search of a sexual partner (*slang*) **6.** *vti.* MUSIC **SING LOUDLY OR ENTHUSIASTICALLY** to sing or be sung loudly and with vigor, especially in a round, refrain, or chorus (*archaic*) **7.** *vti.* **ROLL OR CAUSE SOMETHING TO ROLL** to roll or rotate, or cause something to roll or rotate ■ *n.* **1.** **LURE USED IN FISHING** a lure or bait used for trolling **2.** ANGLING **ACTIVITY OF DRAGGING BAITED FISHING LINE** the act or process of fishing by trolling [14thC. Origin uncertain: perhaps from Old French *troller* "to wander," probably of Germanic origin.] —**troll·er** *n.*

troll[2] /trōl/ *n.* a supernatural being in Scandinavian legends depicted as either a dwarf or giant and living in caves or under bridges [Early 17thC. Via Swedish or Norwegian from Old Norse, "demon."]

trol·ley /tróllee/ *n.* (*plural* **-leys**) **1.** = **trolley car 2.** ELEC **DEVICE COLLECTING POWER FROM AN OVERHEAD WIRE** a device such as a wheel or pulley carried at the end of a pole that collects current from an overhead electric wire in order to power a vehicle **3.** *Canada U.K.* FOOD **WHEELED TABLE** a small wheeled table used for serving or moving food and drinks **4.** TRANSP **WAGON ON RAILS FOR MOVING THINGS** a small open cart that runs on rails and carries materials, especially goods in a factory or coal or other minerals in a mine or quarry **5.** *Canada U.K.* **WHEELED CART PUSHED BY HAND** a wheeled cart that is pushed by hand, and used for transporting things, especially luggage at an airport or railroad station or goods in a supermarket **6.** TRANSP = **trolley bus 7.** TRANSP **SUSPENDED TRUCK** a small cart or basket suspended from an overhead rail and used, especially in factories and mines, for transporting loads **8.** *U.K.* MED = **gurney** ■ *vti.* (**-leyed, -ley·ing, -leys**) **MOVE BY TROLLEY** to travel by or transport something using a wheeled cart on a track or a vehicle powered by electrical current from overhead wires [Early 19thC. Origin uncertain: probably from TROLL[1], in the sense of "to roll."]

trol·ley bus, **trol·ley** *n.* an electric bus that takes its power from overhead wires by means of a trolley pole

trol·ley car, **trol·ley** *n.* a streetcar

trol·lop /tróllәp/ *n.* **1.** **OFFENSIVE TERM** an offensive term referring to a woman who is a prostitute or who is reputed to be too active sexually (*offensive*) **2.** **OFFENSIVE TERM** an offensive term that deliberately insults a girl's or a woman's appearance or her indifference to household chores (*insult*) [Early 17thC. Origin uncertain: perhaps from TROLL[1].] —**trol·lop·y** *adj.*

Trol·lope /tróllәp/, **Anthony** (1815–82) British novelist. He is best known for two sequences of novels, the Barsetshire novels (1855–67), which have a clerical setting, and the political Palliser novels (1865–80). —**Trol·lop·i·an** /trə lóppee ən/ *adj.*

trom·bic·u·li·a·sis /trom bìkyə lī́ əssiss/, **trom·bi·di·a·sis** /tròmbə dī́ əssiss/ *n.* infestation with mite larvae (**chiggers**) that often causes severe rickettsial disease or viral disease [Early 20thC. Coined from modern Latin *Trombicula* (a genus of mites) + -IASIS.]

trom·bone /trom bṓn, trəm bṓn, tróm bṑn/ *n.* **1.** **BRASS MUSICAL INSTRUMENT** a brass wind instrument of varying size with valves resembling those of a trumpet or a U-shaped slide that is moved to produce different pitches **2.** **TROMBONE PLAYER** somebody who plays the trombone in an orchestra or brass band [Early 18thC. Directly or via French from Italian, literally "big trumpet," from *tromba* "trumpet," of Germanic origin.]

trom·mel /trómm'l/ *n.* a rotating sieve for sizing or screening crushed rock or ore [Late 19thC. From German *Trommel*, "drum."]

tromp /tromp/ (**tromped, tromp·ing, tromps**) *v.* **1.** *vt.* = **tramp** *v.* 4 **2.** *vt.* **DEFEAT OR BEAT SOMEBODY** to defeat somebody completely or beat somebody physically **3.** *vi.* **WALK HEAVILY** to tramp or walk with a heavy tread **4.** *vi.* **STAMP ON SOMETHING** to stamp or apply heavy pressure with the feet [Late 19thC. Alteration of TRAMP.]

trompe /tromp/ *n.* a device formerly used for supplying air in a forge by means of a thin column of falling water [From French, "trumpet"]

trompe l'oeil /tràwmp lóy/ (*plural* **trompe l'oeils** /tràwmp lóy/) *n.* **1.** **3-D PAINTING TECHNIQUE** a technique used in realistic paintings to trick the eye, especially through the use of perspective to create an illusion of three-dimensionality **2.** **ARTISTIC WORK THAT TRICKS THE EYE** a painting or other artistic object that uses trompe l'oeil [Late 19thC. From French, literally "deceives the eye."]

Trompe l'oeil: Fresco (1561?) by Paolo Veronese at the Villa Barbaro, Maser, Italy

Trom·sø /trómssō/ town and fishing port in northern Norway, located on the offshore island of Tromsøy. Population: 51,218 (1990).

-tron *suffix.* **1.** a device for manipulating atoms or subatomic particles, accelerator ○ *cyclotron* **2.** a vacuum tube ○ *klystron*

tro·na /trṓnə/ *n.* a grayish-white or yellowish mineral consisting of a hydrated sodium carbonate found in salt deposits [Late 18thC. From Swedish, of uncertain origin: probably from a dialect variant of Arabic *naṭrūn* (see NATRON).]

Trond·heim /trón hàym/ city and port in central Norway. It is situated on Trondheim Fjord, which opens onto the Norwegian Sea. Population: 140,718 (1993).

Troon /troon/ coastal resort on the Firth of Clyde, southwestern Scotland, known for its golf course. Population: 15,231 (1991).

troop /troop/ *n.* **1.** **BIG GROUP** a large group of similar people, animals, or things **2.** MIL **MILITARY UNIT** a unit of soldiers that forms a subdivision of a cavalry or armored cavalry squadron (*often used before a noun*) ○ *troop movements in the area* **3.** SCOUTING **SCOUTING UNIT** a unit of Boy Scouts or Girl Scouts under an adult leader and usually subdivided into several patrols. ◊ **company 4.** ZOOL **COLLECTIVE NAME FOR SOME ANIMALS** a collective name for some animals, especially monkeys and kangaroos ■ **troops** *npl.* **1.** MIL **MILITARY GROUP** a body of soldiers ○ *Order was restored by flooding the area with troops.* **2.** **LARGE NUMBER OF PEOPLE OR THINGS** a large number of people or things ■ *vi.* (**trooped, troop·ing, troops**) **1.** **GO AS A LARGE ORDERLY GROUP** to move or gather together as a large orderly group **2.** **GO AS IF MARCHING** to walk somewhere in a deliberate or heavy-footed way, as if marching ○ *After breakfast the family trooped off to church.* **3.** **CONSORT WITH SOMEBODY** to associate with somebody (*archaic*) [Mid-16thC. From French *troupe*, of uncertain origin: probably from Germanic.]

troop·er /troópər/ *n.* **1.** **MEMBER OF A CAVALRY UNIT** a member of a cavalry unit **2.** **CAVALRY HORSE** a cavalry horse **3.** **MOUNTED POLICE OFFICER** a member of a mounted police unit **4.** **STATE TROOPER** a state trooper

troop·ship /troóp ship/ *n.* a ship, sometimes one originally in the merchant navy, used for transporting military personnel

troost·ite /troó stīt/ *n.* a grayish or reddish form of the mineral willemite in which zinc is partly replaced by manganese [Mid-19thC. Named for the U.S. geologist Gerard *Troost* (1776–1850), who discovered it.]

trop. *abbr.* **1.** tropical **2.** tropic

trop- *prefix.* = **tropo-** (*used before vowels*)

trope /trōp/ *n.* **1.** LANG **FIGURE OF SPEECH** a word, phrase, expression, or image that is used in a figurative way, usually for rhetorical effect **2.** CHR **MEDIEVAL RELIGIOUS TEXT** in the medieval Christian church, a phrase or text interpolated into the service of the Mass [Mid-16thC. Via Latin *tropus* from Greek *tropos* "turn." Ultimately from an Indo-European base meaning "to turn" which is also the ancestor of English *contrive*.]

troph- *prefix.* = **tropho-** (*used before vowels*)

troph·al·lax·is /tròffə láksiss/ (*plural* **-es** /-lák seez/) *n.* an exchange of food between organisms, especially the liquid secretions exchanged by social insects such as the adults or larvae of termites and ants [Early 20thC. Coined from TROPH- + Greek *allaxis* "exchange."] —**troph·al·lac·tic** *adj.*

troph·ic /tróffik/ *adj.* relating to the nutritive value of food [Late 19thC] —**troph·i·cal·ly** *adv.*

-trophic *suffix.* **1.** needing or pertaining to a particular kind of food or nutrition ○ *autotrophic* **2.** = **-tropic** [Formed from Greek *trophē* (see TROPHO-)]

troph·ic lev·el *n.* a stage in a food chain that reflects the number of times energy has been transferred through feeding, e.g., when plants are eaten by animals that are in turn eaten by predators. Plants and plant-eating animals occupy the first two levels, followed by carnivores, usually to a maximum of six levels.

tropho- *prefix.* nutrition, feeding ○ *trophoblast* [From Greek *trophē* "food, nutrition," from *trephein* "to nourish"]

tro·pho·blast /tróffə blàst/ *n.* a thin outer layer (**ectoderm**) that encloses the embryo of mammals, attaches the fertilized ovum to the wall of the womb, and absorbs nutrients —**tro·pho·blas·tic** /tròffə blástik/ *adj.*

tro·pho·derm /tróffə dùrm/ *n.* a trophoblast and its underlying layer (**mesoderm**)

tro·pho·zo·ite /tròffə zṓ ìt/ *n.* the active or feeding form of a protozoan, especially a parasite, as opposed to the resting or reproductive form

tro·phy /trṓfee/ *n.* (*plural* **-phies**) **1. TOKEN OF VICTORY** a cup, shield, plaque, medal, or other award given in acknowledgment of a victory, success, or some other achievement, especially in a sporting contest **2. HUNTING OR WAR SOUVENIR** a memento that symbolizes victory or success, e.g., the head of an animal killed during a hunting expedition or something taken from an enemy killed in battle **3. MEMENTO OF SUCCESS** something that symbolizes a personal victory or achievement **4.** HIST **GREEK OR ROMAN VICTORY MEMORIAL** in ancient Greece or Rome, a victory memorial in a public place or near a battlefield, originally a display of enemy weapons **5.** HIST **GREEK OR ROMAN BATTLE COMMEMORATION** a representation of a Greek or Roman battle trophy, e.g., on a commemorative medal, plaque, or monument **6.** ARCHIT **DECORATIVE CARVING OF WEAPONS** a decorative casting or carving showing weapons or armor on a square or circular base ■ *adj.* **OFFENSIVE TERM** an offensive term used to refer to a person or thing that is considered to improve the status of somebody (*offensive*) [Early 16thC. Via French *trophée* from Latin *tropaeum* "monument to victory" from Greek *tropaion* from, ultimately, *tropē* "a turning."]

-trophy *suffix.* **1.** nutrition, food ○ *dystrophy* **2.** growth ○ *hypertrophy* [From Greek *-trophia*, from *trophē* (see TROPHO-)]

trop·ic[1] /tróppik/ *n.* **1. LINE OF LATITUDE** a line of latitude on the Earth's globe either 23° 26' north of the equator (**tropic of Cancer**) or 23° 26' south (**tropic of Capricorn**) **2.** ASTRON **CIRCLE ON THE CELESTIAL SPHERE** either of two circles on the celestial sphere that have the same latitudes and mark the limits of the apparent north-and-south movement of the Sun. The tropics lie in the same planes as the tropic of Cancer and the tropic of Capricorn. ■ **trop·ics, Trop·ics** *npl.* **AREA BETWEEN THE TROPICS** the area between or near the tropic of Cancer and the tropic of Capricorn ■ *adj.* **TROPICAL** tropical [Early 16thC. Via Old French *tropique* from Latin *tropicus* from, ultimately, Greek *tropē* "a turning," from the ancient belief that the sun "turned back" at the tropics of Cancer and Capricorn.]

WORD KEY: CULTURAL NOTE

Tropic of Cancer, a novel (1934) by Henry Miller. It is an autobiographical account of a struggling American writer's sojourn in 1930s Paris. Its focus on the protagonist's erotic encounters gained it notoriety and led to it being banned in both the United States and Britain until the 1960s, but its openness was an inspiration for many contemporary writers.

trop·ic[2] /trṓ pik/ *adj.* BIOL relating to or showing tropism

-tropic *suffix.* **1.** turning, changing, or reacting in a particular way ○ *dexiotropic* **2.** attracted to, having an affinity for, or moving toward a particular thing ○ *neurotropic* **3.** acting on something in a particular way ○ *vagotropic* [Formed from Greek *tropē* "turning" (see TROPIC)]

trop·i·cal /tróppik'l/ *adj.* **1. TYPICAL OF THE TROPICS** relating to or characteristic of the tropics **2. HOT AND SULTRY** very hot and often combined with a high degree of humidity —**trop·i·cal·i·ty** /tròppi kállətee/ *n.* —**trop·i·cal·ly** /tróppikəlee/ *adv.*

trop·i·cal cy·clone *n.* a cyclone that develops over tropical oceans and has winds up to hurricane force

trop·i·cal fish *n.* a fish, usually small, that is native to warm waters and is frequently kept in aquariums because of its often brightly colored appearance

trop·i·cal·ize /tróppikə lìz/ (**-ized, -iz·ing, -iz·es**) *vt.* to make or adapt something so that it becomes tropical in character or appearance or can be used under tropical conditons —**trop·i·cal·i·za·tion** /tròppikəli záysh'n/ *n.*

trop·i·cal storm *n.* a severe storm that develops offshore over tropical seas with less than hurricane force winds but with the ability to develop into a hurricane

trop·i·cal year *n.* = **solar year** [From calculating the time from solstice to solstice]

trop·ic·bird /tróppik bùrd/ *n.* a tropical aquatic web-footed bird, found in the tropics and related to the pelicans, that has long slender tail feathers, small legs, and white plumage with black markings. Family: Phaethontidae.

trop·ic of Can·cer *n.* a line of latitude that is about 23.5 ° north of the equator [From the constellation that its celestial projection intersects]

trop·ic of Cap·ri·corn *n.* a line of latitude that is about 23.5° south of the equator [From the constellation that its celestial projection intersects]

tro·pine /trṓ peen, trṓpin/, **tro·pin** /trṓpin/ *n.* a colorless crystalline alkaloid formed by heating atropine with barium hydroxide. Formula: $C_8H_{15}NO$. [Mid-19thC. Shortening of ATROPINE.]

tro·pism /trṓ pìzzəm/ *n.* BIOL the involuntary response of an organism or one of its parts toward or away from a stimulus such as heat or light [Late 19thC. From -TROPISM.] —**tro·pis·tic** /trō pístik/ *adj.* —**tro·pis·ti·cal·ly** /-pístikəlee/ *adv.*

tropo- *prefix.* **1.** turning, change ○ *tropopause* **2.** tropism ○ *tropotactic* [From Greek *tropē*]

tro·pol·o·gy /trō póllәjee/ (*plural* **-gies**) *n.* **1. USE OF FIGURATIVE LANGUAGE** the use of figurative language in speaking or writing **2. TREATISE ON FIGURATIVE LANGUAGE** a piece of discursive writing on the use of figurative language **3.** CHR **METHOD OF INTERPRETING THE BIBLE** a method of interpreting the moral teaching of the Bible through its use of figurative language [Early 16thC. From TROPE.] —**tro·po·log·ic** /tròppə lójjik/ *adj.* —**tro·po·log·i·cal·ly** /-lójjikəlee/ *adv.*

tro·po·my·o·sin /tròpə mí əssin, tròppə-/ *n.* a protein in muscle that acts with troponin to regulate the interaction of actin and myosin in muscle contraction

tro·po·nin /trṓpənin, tróppənin/ *n.* a muscle protein that binds with calcium ions to bring about muscular contraction and acts with tropomyosin to control the interaction of actin and myosin [Mid-20thC. Coined from TROPOMYOSIN + -IN, with arbitrary insertion of *n*.]

tro·po·pause /trṓpə pàwz, tróppə-/ *n.* the transitional region of the atmosphere between the troposphere and stratosphere, 10 mi./16 km above the equator and 6 mi./9 km above polar regions [Early 20thC. A blend of TROPOSPHERE and PAUSE.]

tro·po·phyte /trṓpə fìt, tróppə-/ *n.* a plant that is adapted to living through seasonal changes in heat, cold, dryness, or moisture, e.g., by shedding leaves during a dry season —**tro·po·phyt·ic** /trȍpə fíttik, tròppə-/ *adj.*

tro·po·sphere /trṓpə sfeer, tróppə-/ *n.* the lowest and most dense layer of the atmosphere, extending 6 to 12 mi./10 to 20 km, in which temperature decreases with rising altitude and most weather occurs —**tro·po·spher·ic** /trȍppə sféerik, trȍppə-, tròppə-/ *adj.*

tro·po·tax·is /trȍppə táksiss, tròppə-/ *n.* the movement of an organism toward or away from a stimulus as a result of comparing sensory input received from paired receptors on both sides of the body —**tro·po·tac·tic** /trȍppə táktik, tròppə-/ *adj.* —**tro·po·tac·ti·cal·ly** /-táktikəlee/ *adv.*

-tropous *suffix.* turning or growing in a particular way ○ *anatropous* ○ *orthotropous* [Formed from Greek *tropos* "turning, changing," from *trepein* "to turn"]

trop·po /tróppō/ *adv.* excessively or too much (*used in musical directions*) ◊ **non troppo** [From Italian, "too much"]

-tropy *suffix.* the condition of taking a particular molecular form ○ *allotropy* [From Greek *-tropia*, from *tropos* (see -TROPOUS)]

trot /trot/ *v.* (**trot·ted, trot·ting, trots**) **1.** *vti.* RIDING **MOVE AT PACE SLOWER THAN CANTERING** to move or cause a four-legged animal such as a horse to move at a rate that is faster than walking but slower than cantering, and in which diagonal pairs of feet are off the ground alternately. ◊ **pace 2.** *vi.* **MOVE AT A JOGGING PACE** to move at a jogging pace that is faster than walking but not as fast as running ○ *The team trotted onto the field.* ■ *n.* **1. PACE FASTER THAN A WALK** the forward movement of a four-legged animal, especially a horse, in which it trots **2.** RIDING **RIDE AT A RATE FASTER THAN A WALK** a ride on a horse in which it trots **3. JOGGING PACE** a jogging pace that is faster than a walk but slower than a run **4.** HORSERACING **TROTTERS' RACE** a race for horses who run in harness **5.** ANGLING = **trotline 6.** = **pony** *n.* **6** (*informal*) ■ **trots** *npl.* (*informal*) **1.** MED **DIARRHEA** a prolonged bout of diarrhea **2.** *ANZ* HORSERACING **TROTTER RACES** races for trotters in harness [13thC. Via Old French *troter* from, ultimately, a prehistoric Germanic base that is also the ancestor of English *tread*.] ◇ **on the trot 1.** *U.K.* = **in a row 2.** *U.K., Can* busy, especially doing something that involves walking about a lot

trot out *vt.* to bring something out or display something repeatedly, especially in the expectation of gaining admiration or approval (*informal*) ○ *He trots out the same old excuses every time he's late.*

troth /trōth/ *n.* **1. SOLEMN VOW** a solemn pledge, especially the promise to remain faithful exchanged by a bride and groom or an engaged couple (*formal*) **2. BETROTHAL** a betrothal (*archaic*) [13thC. Variant of TRUTH.]

trot·line /trót lìn/ *n.* a long fishing line with shorter baited lines attached, used in streams or near the shore [Mid-19thC. Origin uncertain: perhaps from TROT.]

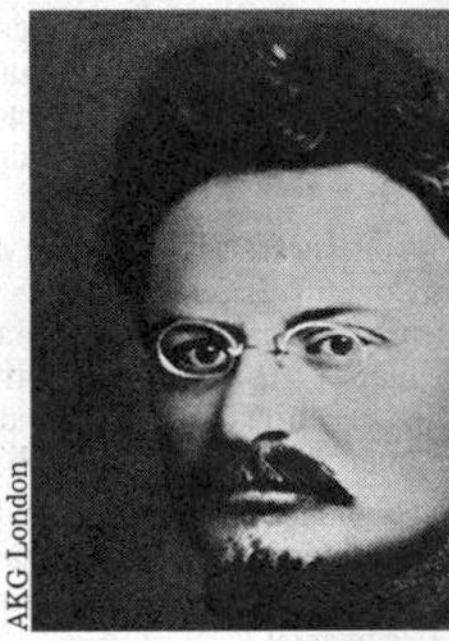

AKG London

Leon Trotsky

Trot·sky /trótskee/, **Leon** (1879–1940) Russian revolutionary leader. With Lenin he played a major part in the Bolshevik Revolution of 1917 in Russia. He is credited with creating and directing the Red Army, but failed to take power on Lenin's death and was murdered in exile by one of Stalin's agents. Born **Lev Davidovich Bronstein**

Trots·ky·ism /trótskee ìzzəm/ *n.* an interpretation of socialism advanced by Leon Trotsky, asserting that fully developed Marxist principles and practices would culminate in a world revolution by the proletariat. ◊ **Leninism, Stalinism** —**Trots·ky·ist** *n., adj.* —**Trots·ky·ite** *n., adj.*

trot·ter /tróttər/ *n.* **1.** FOOD **PIG OR SHEEP FOOT** the foot of an animal, especially that of a pig or sheep, when used as food **2.** HORSERACING **TROTTING PERSON OR ANIMAL** somebody who or something that trots, especially a horse that has been specially trained to trot in harness. ◊ **pacer**

trot·ting race *n.* *ANZ* a harness race

trou·ba·dour /tróobə dàwr, -dòor/ *n.* **1. MEDIEVAL POET OR SINGER** a writer or singer of lyric verses about courtly love, especially in parts of Europe during the 11th to the 13th centuries **2. LOVE POET OR SINGER** a writer or singer of love poems or songs **3. SINGER** somebody who sings while strolling around an area such as a restaurant [Early 18thC. Via French from Old Provençal *trobador*, from *trobar* "to compose," of uncertain origin: perhaps from, ultimately, Latin *tropus* "trope" (see TROPE).]

trou·ble /trúbb'l/ *n.* **1. CONDITION OF DISTRESS** a condition of distress, anxiety, or danger ○ *When the bills started to come in they realized they were in serious trouble.* **2. SOMEBODY OR SOMETHING UPSETTING** a source or cause of worry, distress, or concern ○ *This car* *has been nothing but trouble.* **3. SOURCE OF DIFFICULTY** something that is extremely difficult or presents a problem ○ *Sorry I'm late – I had trouble getting the car to start.* **4. REAL OR APPARENT WEAKNESS** an actual or perceived failing or drawback ○ *Your trouble is that you give up too easily.* **5.** MED **MEDICAL PROBLEMS** an illness or physical condition involving a particular body part that is not functioning as it should ○ *off work with back trouble* **6. EFFORT** the effort or exertion involved in doing something ○ *I hope you like your CD —I went to a lot of trouble to find it.* **7. DISORDER OR UNREST** disorder or unruly behavior in a public place **8. MALFUNCTIONING** a condition in which something mechanical or electronic is not functioning or operating as it should ○ *My car has engine trouble.* ■ *v.* **(-bled, -bling, -bles) 1.** *vt.* **WORRY OR UPSET SOMEBODY** to cause worry, distress, or concern to somebody or something ○ *I'm troubled by the fact that she hasn't been in touch.* **2.** *vt.* **PHYSICALLY AFFECT SOMEBODY** to cause pain or discomfort to somebody or something ○ *My arthritis troubles me from time to time.* **3.** *vt.* **IMPOSE ON SOMEBODY** to put somebody to the inconvenience of doing something ○ *Could I trouble you to open the window?* **4.** *vti.* **TO MAKE AN EFFORT** to make an effort to do something or take pains in doing it ○ *He hadn't troubled to check the figures.* **5.** *vt.* **MAKE WATER ROUGH** to agitate or disturb something, especially the surface of water (*often passive*) [13thC. Via Old French *troubler* from, ultimately, late Latin *turbidare*, from Latin *turbidus* "confused, muddy" (source of English *turbid*).] —**trou·bler** *n.* —**trou·bling** *adj.* —**trou·bling·ly** *adv.* ◇ **in trouble 1.** discovered in wrongdoing and liable to be punished **2.** pregnant and unmarried (*dated informal; used euphemistically*)

WORD KEY: SYNONYMS

See Synonyms at ***bother***.

trou·bled /trúbb'ld/ *adj.* **1. ANXIOUS OR UPSET** experiencing worry or distress **2. MARKED BY PROBLEMS** characterized by difficulties or adversity ○ *The bill has had a troubled passage through the Senate.* **3. LACKING INNER CALM** experiencing or prone to emotional conflict or psychological difficulties

trou·ble·mak·er /trúbb'l màykər/ *n.* somebody who deliberately and frequently tries to make difficulties

Trou·bles /trúbb'lz/ *npl.* the political and civil unrest in Northern Ireland during the period from 1919 to 1923 and after 1969

trou·ble·shoot /trúbb'l shoot/ (**-shot, -shot** /trúbb'l shòt/, **-shoot·ing, -shoots**) *vti.* to act or operate as somebody who finds and eliminates problems [Mid-20thC. Back-formation from TROUBLESHOOTER.]

trou·ble·shoot·er /trúbb'l shootər/ *n.* **1. SOMEBODY WHO FINDS AND SOLVES PROBLEMS** somebody who has the task of finding problems, difficulties, or faults and then eliminating them **2. MEDIATOR** somebody who is called upon to settle political, industrial, or diplomatic disagreements

trou·ble·shoot·ing /trúbb'l shooting/ *n.* **1. FINDING AND ELIMINATING OF PROBLEMS** the act or process of identifying and eliminating problems, difficulties, or faults, especially in electronic or computer equipment **2. MEDIATION** the act or process of mediating in political, industrial, or diplomatic disagreements **3. OCCUPATION OF FINDING AND SOLVING PROBLEMS** the occupation of finding and eliminating problems, e.g., in an organization

trou·ble·some /trúbb'lsəm/ *adj.* **1. DIFFICULT TO DO OR WORK OUT** causing difficulties or taking a great deal of time ○ *Fixing the bug in the program proved more troublesome than I thought.* **2. WORRYING OR IRRITATING** producing annoyance, discomfort, or anxiety, especially in a recurrent way ○ *a troublesome knee injury* —**trou·ble·some·ly** *adv.* —**trou·ble·some·ness** *n.*

trou·ble spot *n.* **1. SITE OF TROUBLE** a place where trouble occurs, especially a place that is notorious for disruption to civil order or a lack of political control **2. PLACE WHERE A FAULT OCCURS** a location where a fault, flaw, or problem occurs

trou·blous /trúbbləss/ *adj.* **1. VERY DIFFICULT** fraught with difficulty or many problems (*archaic or literary*) **2. UNEASY** full of uneasiness or anxiety (*archaic or literary*) **3. TROUBLESOME** troublesome (*archaic*) [15thC] —**trou·blous·ly** *adv.* —**trou·blous·ness** *n.*

trough /trawf/ *n.* **1.** AGRIC **CONTAINER FOR ANIMAL FOOD OR WATER** a long low narrow open container that holds feed or water for animals **2.** INDUST **INDUSTRIAL CONTAINER** a long, low, narrow, open container used in industry, e.g., in washing, kneading, or mixing substances **3. CHANNEL FOR LIQUID** a narrow channel, gully, or gutter in which liquid passes, especially one under the eaves of a roof for catching rainwater **4.** METEOROL **AREA OF LOW PRESSURE** an elongated area of low atmospheric pressure that may be associated with a front. ◊ **ridge 5. SUNKEN AREA** a long hollow area in the surface of the ground or the sea bed, or between waves **6. LOW POINT** any low or negative point, especially a temporary one **7.** ECON **LOWEST POINT OF AN ECONOMIC CYCLE** the lowest point or period of an economic cycle. ◊ **peak 8.** PHYS **LOW PART OF A WAVE OR SIGNAL** the low or negative half of the amplitude in the cycle of a periodic wave or alternating signal [Old English *trog.* Ultimately from an Indo-European base meaning "wood, tree," which is also the ancestor of English *tree.*]

trounce /trownss/ (**trounced, trounc·ing, trounc·es**) *vt.* **1. BEAT SOMEBODY OR SOMETHING DECISIVELY** to defeat an opponent or team convincingly **2. BEAT UP SOMEBODY OR SOMETHING** to beat somebody or something severely (*dated*) [Mid-16thC. Origin unknown.]

WORD KEY: SYNONYMS

See Synonyms at ***defeat***.

troupe /troop/ *n.* **GROUP OF TRAVELING PERFORMERS** a group of actors, circus people, or other entertainers, especially one that travels around ■ *vi.* (**trouped, troup·ing, troupes**) **TRAVEL OR PERFORM WITH A TROUPE** to travel as or perform in a troupe of actors or entertainers [Early 19thC. From French (see TROOP).]

troup·er /troopər/ *n.* **1. MEMBER OF A TROUPE** somebody who is a member of a group of traveling entertainers **2. SOMEBODY RELIABLE AND DEDICATED** somebody who is conscientious, dependable, and selfless **3. VETERAN THEATRICAL PERFORMER** somebody who has been involved in the theater for many years, especially an actor or entertainer

trou·pi·al /troopee əl/ *n.* **1. LARGE S AMERICAN ORIOLE** a large oriole of South America with bright black-and-orange plumage. Latin name: *Icterus icterus.* **2. GREGARIOUS BIRD** a member of a family of gregarious birds in the Americas that includes the bobolinks, blackbirds, and orioles. Family: Icteridae. [Early 19thC. From French *troupiale*, an alteration (influenced by *troupe* "flock") of American Spanish *turpial*, of Caribbean origin.]

trou·ser /trówzər/ *adj.* **ASSOCIATED WITH TROUSERS** belonging to, concerning, suitable for, or part of trousers ○ *a trouser pocket* ■ *n.* **TROUSERS** a pair of trousers, especially one suitable for a smart or formal occasion [Mid-19thC. Back-formation from TROUSERS.] —**trou·sered** *adj.*

trou·sers /trówzərz/, **trow·sers** *npl.* a garment for the lower body that covers the area from the waist to the ankles and has separate tube-shaped sections for each leg [Early 17thC. From, ultimately, Gaelic *triubhas*, of uncertain origin.]

trou·ser suit *n. U.K.* = **pantsuit**

trous·seau /troo sō, troo sṓ/ (*plural* **-seaus** *or* **-seaux** /troo sōz, troo sṓz/) *n.* a bride's clothes and linen, especially items such as nightgowns, underwear, blankets, and sheets, that she has collected during the period of her engagement [Early 19thC. From French, literally "little bundle," from, ultimately, *trousser* "to truss" (source of English *truss*).]

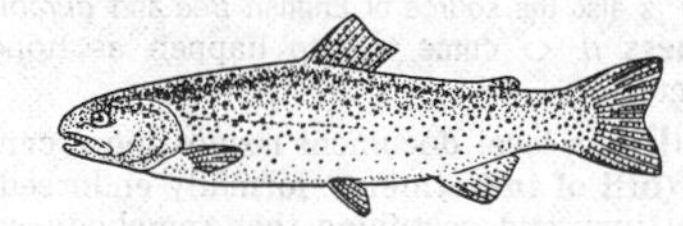

Trout

trout /trowt/ (*plural* **trouts** *or* **trout**) *n.* ZOOL **1. FRESHWATER FISH SIMILAR TO A SALMON** a freshwater fish that is typically smaller than the related salmon and has a speckled body, small scales, and soft fins. Genus: *Salmo.* **2. GAME FISH OF THE SALMON FAMILY** a game fish of the salmon family such as the sea trout. Genus: *Salvelinus.* **3. FISH UNRELATED TO THE TROUT** a fish similar to but unrelated to, the trout such as the trout-perch [Pre-12thC. From late Latin *tructa*, of uncertain origin: perhaps from Greek *trōktēs*, a type of sea fish, from *trōgein* "to nibble."]

trout lil·y *n.* = **dogtooth violet** [Probably from its speckled leaves]

trout·perch /trówt pùrch/ (*plural* **-perch**) *n.* a small North American freshwater fish that has a spotted body, an adipose fin, and rough scales. Family: Percopsidae.

trou·vaille /troo vī/ *n.* something interesting, amusing, or beneficial discovered by chance ○ *The anecdote was one of her many literary trouvailles.* [From French, "a find"]

trou·vère /troo váir/ *n.* a poet-musician of northern France during the 12th and 13th centuries who wrote poems and songs of courtly love, as well as narrative and satirical works [Late 18thC. Via French from Old French *trovere* from, ultimately, *trover* "to compose" (see TROVER).]

trove /trōv/ *n.* **1. COLLECTION OF VALUABLES** a collection of discovered valuable items **2. VALUABLE DISCOVERY** a discovery of great importance or monetary value [Late 19thC. Shortening.]

tro·ver /trṓvər/ *n.* a common law action to recover goods that have been wrongly appropriated by somebody else (*archaic*) [Late 16thC. Via Anglo-Norman from Old French, "to find," of uncertain origin.]

trow /trō/ (**trowed, trow·ing, trows**) *vti.* to think, believe, or suppose that something is the case (*archaic*) [Old English *trēowian.* From a prehistoric Germanic base that is also the ancestor of English *true, betroth,* and *truce.*]

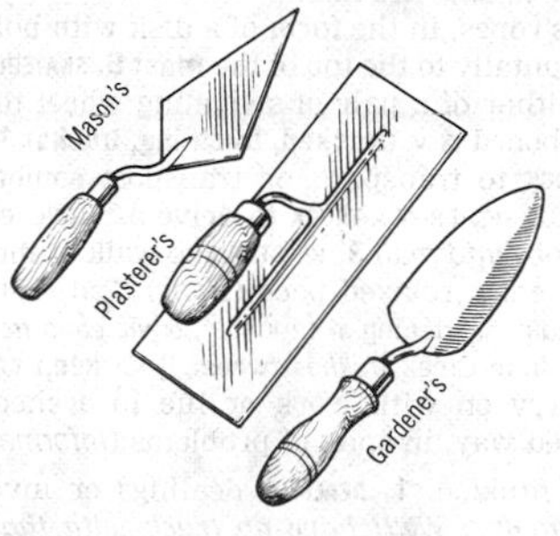

Trowel

trow·el /trów əl/ *n.* **1. FLAT-BLADED HAND TOOL** a small hand tool with a short handle and a flat, usually pointed, blade used for spreading, shaping, and smoothing plaster, cement, or mortar **2.** GARDENING **GARDENER'S SHORT-HANDLED TOOL** a hand tool with a short handle and a curved tapering blade, used for making holes to put plants and seedlings in and for other light digging work ■ *vt.* (**trow·eled** *or* **trow·elled, trow·el·ing** *or* **trow·el·ling, trow·els**) **WORK MATERIAL WITH A TROWEL** to dig, spread, or level something such as earth or mortar using a trowel [14thC. Via Old French *troele* from late Latin *truella* "dipper," from Latin *trua* "ladle."] —**trow·el·er** *n.* ◇ **lay it on with a trowel** to exaggerate, especially in order to flatter somebody (*informal*)

troy /troy/ *adj.* measured in or using the troy weight system [14thC. Origin uncertain: probably from *Troyes*, a city in France with a fair at which this weight was used.]

Troy /troy/ **1.** city in eastern New York, east of the Massachusetts border and northeast of Albany. Population: 52,518 (1996). **2.** city of ancient Greece on the Aegean sea coast, in present-day Turkey. Site of the ten-year Trojan War described in the epic poems of Homer, the city, also called Ilium, was thought to be purely legendary until ruins were discovered by the archeologist Heinrich Schliemann in 1870. It is now believed to have been founded during the Bronze Age in 3000 B.C.

Troyes /trwaa/ capital of Aube Department, in Champagne, northeastern France. Population: 60,755 (1990).

troy weight *n.* a system of weights used for precious metals and gemstones, based on a 12-ounce pound, a 20-pennyweight ounce, and a 24-grain pennyweight

trp. *abbr.* troop

trs. *abbr.* PRINTING transpose

tru·an·cy /tro͝o ənsee/ (*plural* **-cies**) *n.* **1. ABSENTEEISM** absence from school without permission **2. OCCASION OF BEING ABSENT** a single occasion on which a student is absent from school without permission

tru·ant /tro͝o ənt/ *n.* **1. SOMEBODY ABSENT FROM SCHOOL** somebody who is absent without permission or good reason, especially from school **2. SHIRKER** somebody who avoids work or shirks responsibilities (*dated*) ■ *adj.* **1. ABSENT** absent without permission **2. LAZY** preferring to idle away time rather than attend to work or responsibilities (*dated*) ■ *vi.* (**-ant·ed, -ant·ing, -ants**) **1. BE ABSENT** to be absent without permission, especially from school **2. BE LAZY** to idle away time, especially in preference to attending to work or responsibilities (*dated*) [14thC. From Old French, "beggar, vagabond," of Celtic origin.]

truce /trooss/ *n.* **1.** MIL **AGREED BREAK IN FIGHTING** a cessation of military hostilities that both sides agree to hold to, usually for a fixed period ○ *Both sides called a truce.* **2.** MIL **AGREEMENT TO STOP FIGHTING** an agreement to suspend military hostilities **3. AGREED BREAK IN ARGUING** an agreed break in any kind of dispute or feud, or the agreement to stop arguing [14thC. Variant of earlier *trewes*, the plural of *trewe* "treaty, pledge," from Old English *trēow*.]

Tru·cial States /tro͝oshəl-/ former name for **United Arab Emirates** (until 1971)

truck[1] /truk/ *n.* **1. LARGE GOODS VEHICLE** a large vehicle for transporting goods by road **2. CART PUSHED BY HAND** any kind of cart or barrow with two or more wheels that is pushed by hand and is used for moving heavy objects **3.** *U.K.* RAIL **RAILROAD CAR FOR FREIGHT** an open railroad car that carries freight **4.** RAIL **TRAIN'S WHEEL UNIT** a swiveling frame that the wheels and springs are mounted on at either end of a railroad car **5.** SAILING **ROPE GUIDE ON A SHIP'S MAST** a guide for a ship's ropes, in the form of a disk with holes, fitted horizontally to the top of the mast **6. SKATEBOARD WHEEL UNIT** either of a pair of swiveling wheel units on a skateboard ■ *v.* (**trucked, truck·ing, trucks**) **1.** *vti.* **TAKE BY TRUCK** to transport, or transport something, by truck **2.** *vi.* **DRIVE A TRUCK** to drive a truck, especially as a job (*informal*) **3.** *vi.* **STROLL** to walk or move along at an easy, relaxed pace (*slang*) [Early 17thC. Origin uncertain: shortening of TRUCKLE[2], or via Latin *trochus* "iron hoop" from Greek *trokhos* "wheel."] ◇ **keep on trucking** to carry on with work or life in a cheerful and relaxed way, in spite of problems (*informal*)

truck[2] /truk/ *n.* **1. DEALINGS** dealings or involvement (*informal*) ○ *We'll have no truck with that kind of behavior.* **2.** AGRIC **MARKET PRODUCE** vegetables and fruit grown for market **3.** COMM **GOODS** traded goods of any kind **4.** COMM **TRADE** the buying, selling, or bartering of goods **5. STUFF** miscellaneous items (*informal*) ○ *"Now I wanted thirty dollars' worth of artist truck, for I was always sketching in the woods."* (Robert Louis Stevenson, *The Wrecker*; 1896) **6. PAYMENT IN KIND** payment in goods rather than with money ■ *vti.* (**trucked, truck·ing, trucks**) **1. EXCHANGE SOMETHING** to exchange or barter something, or take part in the business of bartering **2. BE INVOLVED WITH SOMEBODY** to have dealings with somebody, especially secret or dishonest dealings [12thC. From Old French dialect *troquer* "to barter," of unknown origin.]

truck·age /trúkij/ *n.* **1. TRANSPORTATION BY TRUCK** the carrying of freight by truck **2. CHARGE FOR TRUCK TRANSPORTATION** a charge made for transporting goods by truck

truck·er[1] /trúkər/ *n.* **1. TRUCK DRIVER** somebody who drives a truck, especially somebody whose job is transporting goods by truck **2. TRANSPORTATION MANAGER** somebody who owns or manages a truck transportation company

truck·er[2] /trúkər/ *n.* **1.** = **truck farmer 2. BARTERER** somebody who barters

truck farm *n.* a farm producing vegetables for sale commercially —**truck farm·ing** *n.*

truck farm·er *n.* a farmer who produces fruit and vegetables for commercial sale

truck·ing /trúking/ *n.* the carrying of freight on roads in trucks

truck·le[1] /trúk'l/ (**-led, -ling, -les**) *vi.* to behave in a weak or servile way [Early 17thC. Shortening of TRUCKLE BED, from the use of such beds by servants.] —**truck·ler** *n.*

truck·le[2] /trúk'l/ *n.* **1. CASTER** a small wheel on which something runs **2.** FOOD **SMALL CHEESE** a small cylindrical cheese [14thC. Via Anglo-Norman *trocle* from, ultimately, Greek *trokhileia* "system of pulleys," from *trokhos* "wheel."]

truck·le bed *n.* = **trundle bed**

truck·load /trúk lōd/ *n.* the quantity carried by a truck, or a quanitity large enough to fill a truck

truck stop *n.* a roadside station that sells fuel for trucks and has a restaurant for truck drivers

truc·u·lence /trúkyələnss/, **truc·u·len·cy** /-lənsee/ *n.* **1. AGGRESSIVE DEFIANCE** aggressive or sullen uncooperativeness **2. FEROCITY** extreme anger or aggression

truc·u·lent /trúkyələnt/ *adj.* **1. AGGRESSIVELY DEFIANT** aggressively or sullenly refusing to accept something or do what is asked **2. FIERCE** displaying great anger or aggression [Mid-16thC. From Latin *truculentus*, from *trux* "fierce."] —**truc·u·lent·ly** *adv.*

Tru·deau /troo dṓ/, **Garry B.** (*b.* 1948) U.S. cartoonist. His long-running political comic strip *Doonesbury*, first syndicated in 1970 and awarded a Pulitzer Prize in 1974, frequently provoked controversy with its sharp satire.

Tru·deau, Pierre (*b.* 1919) Canadian statesman. He was Liberal prime minister of Canada (1968–79 and 1980–84). Full name **Pierre Elliott Trudeau**

trudge /truj/ *vti.* (**trudged, trudg·ing, trudg·es**) **WALK WEARILY** to walk, or walk a particular path or distance, with slow heavy weary steps ■ *n.* **LONG WALK** a long and exhausting walk [Mid-16thC. Origin unknown.] —**trudg·er** *n.*

true /troo/ *adj.* (**tru·er, tru·est**) **1. REAL OR CORRECT** conforming with reality or fact **2. GENUINE** genuine, not pretended, insincere, or artificial **3. PERSONALLY FAITHFUL** showing loyalty to another person ○ *a true friend* **4. COMMITTED** faithful to a cause, purpose, or religious belief ○ *a true believer* **5. CONFORMING TO A STANDARD OR MEASURE** conforming to a standard, measure, or pattern ○ *a true fit* **6. RIGHTFUL** conforming to the way things should be by right ○ *returned to the true owners* **7.** GEOG **IN RELATION TO EARTH'S POLES** measured in relation to geographic points on the earth's surface, rather than to points of magnetic attraction ○ *true north* **8. CONFORMING TO INCLUSION CRITERIA** meeting the criteria for inclusion in a particular category, in contrast to being given the same name because of superficial resemblance to members of that category ○ *A shooting star is not a true star.* **9.** PHYS **NOT RELATIVE** not relative as a value and corrected for all error factors, e.g., the difference between true time and mean time **10.** MUSIC **IN TUNE** perfectly in tune ○ *The orchestra maintained true pitch throughout.* ■ *adv.* **1. SO AS TO CORRESPOND WITH REALITY** in a way that corresponds with reality or fact ○ *His explanations just didn't ring true.* **2. ACCURATELY** so as to arrive at the precise position aimed for ○ *The arrow flew straight and true.* **3. HONESTLY** in a frank and open way that seeks to hide nothing ○ *Tell me true.* **4. CERTAINLY** used to admit the validity or accuracy of a statement, often in a discussion or when considering the advantages and disadvantages of something ○ *True, it does rain a lot here.* **5.** AGRIC **WITHOUT LOSS OF ANCESTRAL FEATURES** without variation from the ancestral form, or producing offspring with the same hereditary characteristics ○ *breed true* ■ *vt.* (**trued, tru·ing** *or* **true·ing, trues**) **ADJUST POSITION OF SOMETHING** to adjust something to make it straight or level or put it in any other required position ■ *n.* **1. ALIGNMENT** a correct position, especially a position in relation to the horizontal or vertical **2. REALITY** the absolute truth [Old English *trēowe* "trustworthy." Ultimately from an Indo-European word meaning "to be solid," which is also the source of English *tree* and *durable*.] —**true·ness** *n.* ◇ **come true** to happen as hoped or expected

true bill *n.* a legal document requesting a criminal trial (**bill of indictment**), formally endorsed by a grand jury and certifying that somebody can be brought to trial

true-blue *adj.* completely loyal or faithful ○ *a true-blue pal* [Because *blue* is often taken to represent constancy, perhaps originating in the fact that it is the normal color of the sky]

true·born /tro͝o bàwrn/ *adj.* having one's true social position or nationality beyond doubt, because it was established at birth ○ *a trueborn French aristocrat*

true bug *n.* ZOOL = **bug** *n.* **1**

true-false test *n.* a test in which statements are given that must be marked as either true or false

true-life *adj.* presenting matters, especially human relationships, as they are or have been in reality ○ *a true-life adventure story*

true·love /tro͝o lùv/ *n.* somebody who is deeply loved by another

true lov·ers' knot, true·love knot *n.* a complicated bow-knot that is difficult to untie, symbolizing lovers' faithfulness

true·pen·ny /tro͝o pènnee/ (*plural* **-nies**) *n.* an honest, loyal, or trustworthy person (*dated*) [From the name given to a coin of genuine metal]

true rib *n.* a rib that is attached to the breastbone (**sternum**) by cartilage. The seven uppermost ribs in the human body are true ribs.

true seal *n.* ZOOL = **earless seal**

François Truffaut

Truf·faut /troofṓ/, **François** (1932–84) French movie director and critic. His first movie, the semi-autobiographical *The 400 Blows* (1959), was one of the first movies of the French New Wave movement. Other movies include *Shoot the Piano Player* (1960) and *Jules et Jim* (1961).

truf·fle /trúff'l/ *n.* **1. FLESHY FUNGUS EATEN AS DELICACY** an underground fungus whose fleshy edible fruiting body is highly valued as a delicacy. Pigs and dogs are often used to sniff out truffles. Genus: *Tuber*. **2. CHOCOLATE CANDY** a rich ball-shaped chocolate with a center of soft chocolate [Late 16thC. Alteration of French *trufe*, via Provençal *trufa* from, ultimately, Latin *tuber* (see TUBER).]

trug /trug/ *n.* *U.K.* a shallow rectangular basket made from curved strips of wood, used especially for carrying garden produce [14thC. Origin uncertain: perhaps a dialectal variant of TROUGH.]

tru·ism /tro͝o ìzzəm/ *n.* a statement that is so obviously true and so often repeated that people find it trite or meaningless —**tru·is·tic** /troo ístik/ *adj.*

Tru·ji·llo /troo khèe yō, -hèe-/, **Rafael Leonidas** (1891–1961) Dominican soldier and national leader. Elected president in 1930, he remained the army generalissimo and dictator of the Dominican Republic until his assassination by the army. Full name **Rafael Leonidas Trujillo Molina**

trull /trul/ *n.* a prostitute (*archaic*) [Early 16thC. From Middle High German *trulle*.]

tru·ly /tro͝olee/ *adv.* **1. SINCERELY** honestly, without affectation or pretense ○ *feel truly sorry* **2. USED FOR EMPHASIS** used to emphasize the extent or degree of something ○ *a truly remarkable achievement* **3. COMPLETELY** to the fullest extent or in the fullest degree ○ *Only she can truly appreciate how happy I feel.* **4. USED TO SIGN A LETTER** used alone or with "yours" as a way to sign a letter ◇ **yours truly** used to refer to yourself (*humorous*) ○ *Doubtless they're expecting yours truly to pick them up from the airport.*

Tru·man /tro͝omən/, **Bess** (1885–1982) U.S. first lady. She married Harry S. Truman, a childhood sweetheart, in 1919, and during his presidency (1945–53) was one of his most trusted advisers. Born **Elizabeth Virginia Wallace**

Tru·man, Harry S. (1884–1972) U.S. statesman and 33rd president of the United States. A Democrat, he became president on the death of F. D. Roosevelt (1945), serving until 1953. He actively opposed Communism overseas, notably in Korea (1950–53).

Trum·bull /trúmbəl/, **John** (1750–1831) U.S. lawyer and poet. One of the "Connecticut Wits," he is known for the comic epic *"M'Fingal"* (1776–82), satirizing British Loyalists during the Revolution.

Harry S. Truman Library

Harry S. Truman

Trum·bull, Jonathan (1710–85) American political leader. He served as Connecticut's colonial governor (1769–84) and was a leader in the Revolution.

tru·meau /troo mṓ/ (*plural* **-meaux** /-mṓz/) *n.* a pillar or a section of wall that separates two doors or two sections of a door [Late 19thC. From French, literally "calf of the leg."]

trump[1] /trump/ *n.* **1.** CARDS **CARD FROM HIGHEST SUIT** in card games, a card from a suit declared to be higher in value than any other suit, or the suit itself **2. KEY RESOURCE** a highly valuable resource or advantage, especially one held in reserve for future use **3. FINE PERSON** an admirable or reliable person (*informal*) ■ *vt.* **(trumped, trump·ing, trumps) 1.** CARDS **DEFEAT BY PLAYING A TRUMP** in card games, to beat an opponent or an opponent's card by playing a trump **2. OUTDO** to defeat or outdo a competitor by bringing a valuable resource or advantage into play [Early 16thC. Alteration of TRIUMPH.]

trump up *vt.* to invent false accusations or false evidence in order to incriminate somebody wrongly

trump[2] /trump/ *n.* a trumpet, or the sound of a trumpet (*literary*) [13thC. From Old French *trompe* (see TRUMPET).]

trump card *n.* = **trump**[1] *n.* 1, **trump**[1] *n.* 2 ◇ **play your trump card** to make use of a highly valuable resource or advantage that has been held in reserve

trumped-up *adj.* false and deliberately invented, usually in order to incriminate somebody wrongly ○ *trumped-up charges* [*Trumped* formed from TRUMP[1] in the obsolete sense "to fabricate, invent," the underlying idea being "to deceive"]

trump·er·y /trúmpəree/ (*plural* **-ies**) *n.* (*archaic or literary*) **1. WORTHLESS THING** something worthless or useless, often something showy that seems appealing at first glance **2. NONSENSE** empty or ridiculous talk **3. DECEPTION** the deceiving of somebody, or schemes conceived for the purpose of deceiving [15thC. From French *tromperie* "trickery," from *tromper* "to deceive," of unknown origin.]

trum·pet /trúmpət/ *n.* **1.** MUSIC **BRASS INSTRUMENT** a brass musical instrument, either straight or coiled, with three valves and a flared bell. It has a brilliant tone and a middle to high register. **2. SOMETHING SHAPED LIKE A TRUMPET** something shaped like the flared bell of a trumpet **3. SOUND LIKE TRUMPET'S** a loud high sound made by a trumpet, or a similarly strident sound such as the call of an elephant **4. EAR TRUMPET** an ear trumpet **5.** MUSIC **ORGAN STOP** a solo organ stop that imitates the sound of a trumpet ■ *v.* **(-pet·ed, -pet·ing, -pets) 1.** *vti.* **ANNOUNCE SOMETHING** to announce something loudly, proudly, or with great ceremony **2.** *vt.* **SPEAK PROUDLY OF SOMEBODY OR SOMETHING** to speak of somebody or something with ostentatious admiration or pride **3.** *vi.* **MAKE ELEPHANT'S CALL** to make an elephant's characteristically high-pitched, penetrating call **4.** *vt.* **EXPRESS BY TRUMPETING** to convey something with a trumpeting call ○ *The elephant trumpeted a warning.* [14thC. From Old French *trompette*, literally "small horn," from *trompe* "horn," of prehistoric Germanic origin; probably ultimately an imitation of the sound of a horn.]

trum·pet creep·er, **trum·pet vine** *n.* a woody deciduous North American vine with compound leaves and large red trumpet-shaped flowers. Latin name: *Campsis radicans.*

trum·pet·er /trúmpətər/ *n.* **1.** MUSIC **TRUMPET PLAYER** a musician who plays the trumpet **2.** BIRDS **TROPICAL BIRD WITH A LOUD CALL** a medium-sized South American bird that rarely flies and has long legs, a short stout bill, dark glossy plumage, and a loud call. Family: Psophidae. **3.** BIRDS **PIGEON** a domestic pigeon that has a long ruff, heavily feathered feet, and a loud call

trum·pet·er swan *n.* a large white swan with a black bill and a loud call, found in western Canada and Alaska. Latin name: *Cygnus buccinator.*

trum·pet·fish /trúmpət fish/ (*plural* **-fish·es** *or* **-fish**) *n.* a name given to various tropical reef fish with long bodies and tubular snouts. Family: Aulostomidae.

trum·pet flow·er *n.* **1. PLANT WITH TRUMPET-SHAPED FLOWERS** a plant with trumpet-shaped flowers, e.g., the trumpet creeper **2. FLOWER** the flower of a trumpet flower

trum·pet hon·ey·suck·le *n.* a North American variety of honeysuckle plant with scarlet or orange trumpet-shaped flowers. Latin name: *Lonicera sempervirens.*

trum·pet vine *n.* = **trumpet creeper**

trumps /trumps/ *npl.* in card games, the suit that is chosen at the outset to be the highest in value (*takes a singular or plural verb*) ○ *Diamonds are trumps.*

trun·cate /trúng kàyt/ *vt.* **(-ca·ted, -cat·ing, -cates) 1. SHORTEN SOMETHING BY REMOVING PART** to shorten something by cutting off or removing a part **2.** MATH **SHORTEN DECIMAL NUMBER** to restrict the precision of a decimal number by limiting the digits to the right of the decimal point without rounding ■ *adj.* **1.** = **truncated** *adj.* 1 **2.** BOT **NOT POINTED** used to describe a leaf that has a blunt end, giving the impression that a part has been cut off [15thC. From Latin *truncare* "to cut short, mutilate," from *truncus* (see TRUNK).] —**trun·cate·ly** *adv.* —**trun·ca·tion** /trung káysh'n/ *n.*

trun·ca·ted /trúng kàytəd/ *adj.* **1. WITH END REMOVED** shortened by having a part cut off or removed **2.** GEOM **WITH END REPLACED BY PLANE** used to describe a geometric figure that has the apex or an end removed and replaced with a plane section, often parallel to the base **3.** CRYSTALS **HAVING INCOMPLETE CORNERS** used to describe a crystal lacking the fully formed corners or faces that would be present in a simple form of the crystal **4.** POETRY **WITH ONE SYLLABLE FEWER** used to describe a line of poetry that has one syllable fewer in one of its feet than in others in the line

trun·cheon /trúnchən/ *n.* **1.** ARMS **POLICE OFFICER'S CLUB** a short heavy stick carried by a police officer **2. SYMBOLIC STICK** a baton carried as a symbol of rank or authority **3.** ARMS **SPEAR'S SHAFT** the shaft of a spear **4.** ARMS **CLUB** any short heavy stick used as a weapon of attack (*archaic*) ■ *vt.* **(-cheoned, -cheon·ing, -cheons) HIT SOMEBODY WITH A TRUNCHEON** to hit somebody or something with a truncheon [13thC. Via Old Northern French *tronchon* from, ultimately, Latin *truncus* (see TRUNK).]

trun·dle /trúnd'l/ *v.* **(-dled, -dling, -dles) 1.** *vti.* **MOVE HEAVILY ON WHEELS** to move, or move something, slowly and heavily, especially on wheels or rollers **2.** *vt.* **ROTATE SOMETHING** to turn something around and around repeatedly (*archaic*) ■ *n.* **1. WHEEL** a small wheel or roller by which something is moved along **2. ROLLING MOVEMENT** a slow heavy movement, especially a rolling movement **3. CART WITH WHEELS** a trolley or cart with small wheels **4.** HOUSEHOLD = **trundle bed** [Mid-16thC. Variant of *trendle* "wheel," from Old English *trendel* "circle."]

trun·dle bed, **trundle** *n.* a low bed on casters that can be stowed away under another bed

trun·dler /trúndlər/ *n. NZ* **1. GOLF CART** a cart for pulling a golf bag along by hand **2. TROLLEY** a shopping trolley **3. PUSHCHAIR** a child's pushchair

trunk /trungk/ *n.* **1.** TREES **TREE'S MAIN STEM** the main stem of a tree, excluding branches and roots **2.** CARS **AUTOMOBILE'S STORAGE COMPARTMENT** an enclosed storage compartment in an automobile, usually at the rear **3. LARGE TRAVELING CASE** a large strong traveling case or box with a hinged lid that is bigger, more rigid, and less portable than a suitcase **4.** ANAT, ZOOL **UPPER BODY** the main part of the body of a human being or an animal, excluding the head, neck, and limbs **5.** ZOOL **ELEPHANT'S NOSE** the long muscular proboscis of an elephant, used for grasping, feeding, and drinking **6. MAIN PART** the main part of something that has branches or subsidiary parts leading off it, e.g., a transportation network or an electrical or communications network **7.** ANAT **STEM OF BLOOD VESSEL** the main stem of a blood vessel or nerve, with branches leading off it **8.** NAUT **PART OF CABIN ABOVE DECK** the part of a boat's cabin that sits above the deck **9.** BUILDING **DUCT** any kind of duct in a building, e.g., a ventilation duct or a duct carrying electrical wires **10.** ARCHIT **PART OF COLUMN** the shaft of an architectural column, excluding the base and the capital ■ **trunks** *npl.* CLOTHES **MEN'S SWIMWEAR** men's shorts worn for sports, especially swimming [15thC. Via French *tronc* "tree trunk, alms box" from Latin *truncus*, literally "something cut off" (source of English *truncate* and *trench*).]

trunk·fish /trúngk fish/ (*plural* **-fish·es** *or* **-fish**) *n.* a brightly colored tropical fish that has a body covered in bony plates. Family: Ostraciidae.

trunk hose *n.* short puffed-out breeches worn by men in the late 16th and early 17th centuries. They extended from the waist to the upper or mid thigh.

trunk·ing /trúngking/ *n.* casing used to anchor, conceal, and protect cables and small pipes

trun·nion /trúnnyən/ *n.* either of a pair of pivots, especially the cylindrical knobs on the side of a cannon's barrel that allow it to pivot on the gun carriage [Early 17thC. From French *trognon* "fruit core, tree stump," of uncertain origin.] —**trun·nioned** *adj.*

Tru·ro /tróōrō/ town on Cobequid Bay in central Nova Scotia, Canada. Population: 11,938 (1996).

truss /truss/ *vt.* **(trussed, truss·ing, truss·es) 1. BIND SOMETHING** to tie something or somebody tightly **2.** COOK **TIE SOMETHING FOR COOKING** to prepare meat for roasting by tying it into a neat shape. Birds such as chickens and turkeys are trussed to keep wings and legs close to the body. **3.** CIV ENG **SUPPORT SOMETHING WITH LOAD-BEARING MEMBERS** to support or strengthen a roof, bridge, or other elevated structure with a network of beams and bars **4.** MED **SUPPORT A HERNIA** to support a hernia with a specially designed device ■ *n.* **1.** MED **SUPPORT FOR A HERNIA** a device designed to apply pressure to a hernia to stop it from enlarging or protruding **2.** BOT **FRUIT CLUSTER** a cluster of flowers or fruit on a single branching stem, e.g., on a tomato plant **3.** SAILING **MAST FITTING** a metal fitting used to attach a ship's beam **(yard)** to a mast **4. BUNDLE** a bundle, especially a bundle of hay of varying weight [12thC. From Old French *trousse*, from *trousser* "to truss," of uncertain origin: perhaps via assumed Vulgar Latin *torsare* from, ultimately, Latin *torquere* "to twist" (see TORQUE[1]).] —**truss·er** *n.*

truss bridge *n.* a bridge whose supporting structure consists of a network of beams in a series of triangular sections

truss·ing /trússing/ *n.* a framework of beams arranged in triangular sections and supporting a roof, bridge, or other structure, or the beams themselves

trust /trust/ *n.* **1. RELIANCE** confidence in and reliance on good qualities, especially fairness, truth, honor, or ability **2. CARE** responsibility for taking good care of somebody or something ○ *We put our children in the trust of a good daycare center.* **3. POSITION OF OBLIGATION** the position of somebody who is expected by others to behave responsibly or honorably ○ *breached the public trust* **4. SOMETHING IN WHICH CONFIDENCE IS PLACED** somebody who or something that people place confidence or faith in (*archaic or literary*) **5. HOPE FOR THE FUTURE** hopeful reliance on what will happen in the future **6. RESPONSIBILITY THAT SOMEBODY HAS** something entrusted to somebody to be responsible for ○ *accepted his responsibilities as a sacred trust* **7.** LAW **HOLDING OF ANOTHER'S PROPERTY** the legal holding and managing of money or property belonging to somebody else, e.g., that of a minor **8.** LAW **ARRANGEMENT TO MANAGE ANOTHER'S PROPERTY** a legal arrangement by which one person **(trustee)** holds and manages money or property belonging to somebody else **9.** COMM **CREDIT** credit given to somebody on purchases made ○ *let me have it on trust* **10.** COMM **CARTEL** a combination of corporations with the purpose of reducing competition and controlling prices ■ *v.* **(trust·ed, trust·ing, trusts) 1.** *vti.* **RELY ON SOMETHING** to place confidence in somebody's good qualities, especially fairness, truth, honor, or ability **2.** *vt.* **CONFIDENTLY ALLOW SOMEBODY TO HAVE SOMETHING** to allow somebody to do or use something in confidence that the person will behave responsibly or properly ○ *I trust you to do the right thing.* **3.** *vt.* **PLACE SOMETHING IN SOMEBODY'S CARE** to place somebody or something in the care of another person ○ *You could certainly trust him with such an important job.* **4.** *vt.* **SUPPOSE** to hope or suppose something ○ *I trust you had a good vacation.* **5.** *vt. Carib* **GIVE CREDIT TO SOMEBODY** to give somebody credit on a purchase ○ *wouldn't even trust me a carton of milk* [12thC. From Old Norse *traust* "confidence" and *treysta* "to trust." Ultimately from an Indo-European base meaning "to be solid," which is also the ancestor of English *true, tryst,* and *tree.*] —**trust·a·bil·i·ty** /trùstə bíllətee/ *n.* —**trust·a·ble** /trústəb'l/ *adj.* —**trust·er** *n.*

trust·bust·er /trúst bùstər/ *n.* a government official who carries out investigations into commercial cartels and works to break them up —**trust·bust·ing** *n.*

trust com·pa·ny *n.* a bank or other commercial organization that sets up and operates trusts for private individuals and businesses

trus·tee /tru steé/ *n.* **1.** LAW **MANAGER OF ANOTHER'S PROPERTY** somebody who is given the legal authority to manage money or property on behalf of somebody else **2.** FIN **FINANCE MANAGER** a member of a group of people responsible for managing the financial affairs of an institution or organization **3.** POL **COUNTRY SUPERVISING TRUST TERRITORY** a country responsible for administering a trust territory ■ *vti.* (**-teed, -tee·ing, -tees**) **ENTRUST SOMETHING TO A TRUSTEE** to entrust something to a trustee, or act as a trustee

trus·tee·ship /tru steé shìp/ *n.* **1.** LAW, FIN **TRUSTEE'S POSITION** the status or responsibilities of a trustee, or the period of time for which a trustee holds office **2.** POL **GOVERNMENT UNDER UNITED NATIONS' TERMS** the administration of a country that is not self-governing by a foreign country under terms laid down by the United Nations

trust·ful /trústfəl/ *adj.* = **trusting** —**trust·ful·ly** *adv.* —**trust·ful·ness** *n.*

trust fund *n.* an investment fund managed on behalf of somebody, particularly a minor, by one or more people given legal authority to do so

trust·ing /trústing/, **trustful** /trústfəl/ *adj.* willing or tending to trust people —**trust·ing·ly** *adv.* —**trust·ing·ness** *n.*

trust·less /trústləss/ *adj.* (*archaic or literary*) **1. UNTRUSTWORTHY** not worthy of being trusted **2. SUSPICIOUS** tending not to trust others —**trust·less·ly** *adv.* —**trust·less·ness** *n.*

trust ter·ri·to·ry *n.* a country that does not have its own government but is run by a foreign country under terms laid down by the United Nations

trust·wor·thy /trúst wùrthee/ *adj.* deserving trust, or able to be trusted —**trust·wor·thi·ly** *adv.* —**trust·wor·thi·ness** *n.*

trust·y /trústee/ *adj.* (**-i·er, -i·est**) **RELIABLE** able to be relied on ■ *n.* (*plural* **-ies**) **1. TRUSTED PERSON** somebody who is trusted by others **2. TRUSTED PRISONER** a prisoner regarded by the prison authorities as trustworthy and given special privileges —**trust·i·ly** *adv.* —**trust·i·ness** *n.*

truth /trooth/ *n.* **1. TRUE QUALITY** correspondence to fact or reality **2. SOMETHING FACTUAL** something that corresponds to fact or reality ○ *spoke the truth* **3. TRUE STATEMENT** a statement that corresponds to fact or reality **4. OBVIOUS FACT** something that is so clearly true that it hardly needs to be stated **5. SOMETHING GENERALLY BELIEVED** a statement that is generally believed to be true ○ *a religious truth* **6. HONESTY** honesty, sincerity, or integrity **7. DESCRIPTIVE ACCURACY** accuracy in description or portrayal ○ *a criticism that had an element of truth in it* **8. CONFORMITY** adherence to a standard or law **9. LOYALTY** faithfulness to a person or a cause (*dated*) **10.** *U.K.* **ACCURACY** accuracy of alignment, setting, position, or shape (*dated*) [Old English *trēowth* "faithfulness" (source also of TROTH)]

Truth *n.* in Christian Science, the word used to refer to God

Truth /trooth/, **Sojourner** (1797?–1883) U.S. abolitionist. Freed from enslavement, she campaigned for the rights of African Americans and women. Born **Isabella Van Wagener**

truth-con·di·tion *n.* the condition that must apply if a given philosophical proposition is to be true

truth drug *n.* = **truth serum**

truth·ful /troóthfəl/ *adj.* **1. HONEST** telling the truth, or tending to tell the truth **2. ACCURATE** corresponding to fact or reality —**truth·ful·ness** *n.*

truth·ful·ly /troóthfəlee/ *adv.* **1. SO AS TO EXPRESS TRUTH** in a way that corresponds to fact or reality or that expresses the truth **2. EMPHASIZING TRUTH** used to reinforce the truth of what has just been said or is about to be said ○ *Truthfully, I did not know she was there.*

truth se·rum *n.* a drug supposed to make the person taking it tell the truth, e.g., by reducing inhibitions or causing hypnosis

truth set *n.* a set of all the values that make a given mathematical or logic statement true when substituted in the statement

truth ta·ble *n.* **1.** LOGIC **TABLE USED IN LOGIC** a table used to work out the truth or falsity of a compound statement in logic **2.** ELECTRON ENG **TABLE USED IN TRANSISTOR TECHNOLOGY** in electronics and computing, a table used to indicate the value of the output signal from a logic circuit or device for every possible input

truth-val·ue *n.* in logic, the truth or falsity of a proposition or of a compound statement consisting of two or more propositions

try /trī/ *v.* (**tried, try·ing, tries**) **1.** *vti.* **MAKE AN EFFORT** to make an effort or an attempt to do or achieve something **2.** *vt.* **TEST SOMETHING FOR PURPOSE OF ASSESSMENT** to test, sample, or experiment with something in order to assess its usefulness, worth, or quality ○ *You get to try the software out at home.* **3.** *vt.* **STRAIN OR VEX SOMEBODY** to subject somebody or something to great strain ○ *The long wait tried her patience.* **4.** *vt.* LAW **SUBJECT SOMEBODY TO LEGAL TRIAL** to carry out the trial in court of somebody accused of a crime or offense **5.** *vt.* LAW **CONDUCT A CASE IN COURT** to conduct a legal case in court ○ *asked when the case would be tried* **6.** *vt.* FOOD = **render** *v.* **8** ■ *n.* (*plural* **tries**) **1. EFFORT** an attempt made to do or achieve something **2.** RUGBY **SCORE IN RUGBY** a score achieved by touching the ball on the ground behind the line of the opponent's posts (**goal line**). In Rugby Union, five points are scored, while the score is three points in Rugby League. [13thC. Via Old French *trier* "to sift out" from assumed Vulgar Latin *triare*, of unknown origin.]

WORD KEY: USAGE

try and or **try to**? The two expressions are often interchangeable (*We'll try and come* or *We'll try to come*), although ***try and*** is somewhat more informal. In the past tense and in negative and continuous constructions, however, ***try to*** is needed: *They tried to deliver the package on Friday. We are not trying to be funny. Are you trying to tell me something?*

WORD KEY: SYNONYMS

try, attempt, endeavor, strive

CORE MEANING: to make an effort to do something

try to make an effort to do or achieve something; **attempt** used in a similar way to "try," but often used to suggest that the task is difficult and so the chances of success are not high; **endeavor** a fairly formal word meaning to try to do or achieve something that involves great exertion or effort; **strive** like "endeavour," but often with the implication of persistence.

try on *vt.* to put on an item of clothing to test its fit or suitability

try out *vi.* to undergo a competitive test of suitability, especially for a place on a sports team or for a part as an actor ○ *plans to try out for the play*

try·ing /trī ing/ *adj.* placing great strain on somebody's patience, composure, or good nature, and often physically exhausting as a result —**try·ing·ly** *adv.*

try·out /trī òwt/ *n.* **1. TEST OF SUITABILITY** a trial to test somebody's suitability, especially to play on a sports team or play a specific role as an actor **2. PERFORMANCE BEFORE OFFICIAL OPENING** a performance of a play staged prior to its official opening ○ *changes made to the script following the out-of-town tryout*

try·pan blue /tríppən-, trí pàn-/ *n.* a blue dye used to distinguish live cells from dead cells. Only dead cells turn blue in the presence of trypan blue. [Shortening of TRYPANOSOME]

try·pan·o·some /tri pánnə sòm, tríppənə-/ *n.* a simple microscopic organism (**protozoan**) that lives as a parasite in the blood of certain vertebrates, including human beings. It is transmitted by insect bites and causes serious diseases. Genus: *Trypanosoma.* [Early 20thC. From modern Latin, genus name, from Greek *trupanon* "borer" + *sōma* "body."] —**try·pan·o·so·mal** /tri pànnə sóm'l, trìppənə-/ *adj.*

try·pan·o·so·mi·a·sis /tri pànnə sō mī əssis, trìppənə sō-/ *n.* a disorder caused by infestation with a microscopic organism that lives as a parasite in the blood, especially sleeping sickness

tryp·sin /trípsin/ *n.* an enzyme in pancreatic juice that acts as a catalyst for breaking proteins down into peptides [Late 19thC. Origin uncertain: probably formed from Greek *tripsis* "rubbing," because it was first obtained by rubbing a pancreas with glycerin.] —**tryp·tic** *adj.*

tryp·sin·o·gen /trip sínnəjən/ *n.* the inactive substance secreted in the juices of the pancreas and converted into trypsin

tryp·ta·mine /tríptə meén/ *n.* a crystalline amine found in plant and animal tissue, formed synthetically or by the decomposition of the amino acid tryptophan. Formula: $C_{10}H_{12}N_2$. [Early 20thC. Coined from TRYPTOPHAN + -AMINE.]

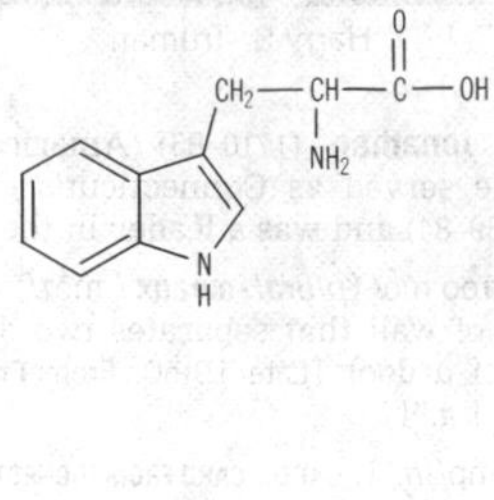

Tryptophan

tryp·to·phan /tríptə fàn/ *n.* an essential amino acid found in proteins such as casein and fibrin. Formula: $C_{11}H_{12}O_2N_2$. [Late 19thC. Coined from *tryptic* "of trypsin" + -PHANE.]

try·sail /trīss'l, trī sàyl/ *n.* a strong sail used in stormy weather that is either square or triangular and is set to run parallel to the length of the ship (**fore-and-aft**) [Mid-18thC. From *a-try* "hove to."]

try square *n.* a woodworking tool used to test and mark out right angles, consisting of a rectangular handle with a thin flat rectangular metal blade fitted perpendicular to it

tryst /trist/ *n.* **1. ARRANGEMENT TO MEET** an arrangement to meet, especially one made privately or secretly by lovers **2. SECRET MEETING** a secret meeting, or place of meeting, especially between lovers ■ *vi.* (**tryst·ed, tryst·ing, trysts**) **MEET OR ARRANGE TO MEET** to arrange a meeting with somebody or keep an arrangement to meet, especially secretly with a lover [14thC. From Old French *triste* "place to lie in wait," of prehistoric Germanic origin.] —**tryst·er** *n.*

T.S., t.s. *abbr.* tensile strength

tsad·dik *n.* = **tzaddik**

tsar /zaar, tsaar/, **tzar, czar** *n.* an emperor of Russia, before 1917 —**tsar·dom** *n.*

tsare·vitch /zaárə vìch, tsaárə-/, **czare·vitch** *n.* a son of a Russian emperor, especially the eldest son [Early 18thC. From Russian *tsarevich*, from *tsar'* (see TSAR).]

tsar·ev·na /zaa révnə, tsaa-/, **czar·ev·na** *n.* **1. TSAREVITCH'S WIFE** the wife of a tsarevitch **2. TSAR'S DAUGHTER** the daughter of a tsar [Late 19thC. From Russian *tsarevna*, from *tsar'* (see TSAR).]

tsa·rina /zaa reénə, tsaa reénə/, **tsaritsa, cza·rina, cza·rit·za** *n.* **1. RUSSIAN EMPRESS** an empress of Russia, before 1917 **2. TSAR'S WIFE OR WIDOW** the wife or widow of a tsar [Early 18thC. From Italian or Spanish *zarina*, feminine of *zar*, from Russian *tsar'* (see TSAR).]

tsar·ism /zaá rìzzəm/ *n.* **1. RULE BY TSAR** government by an emperor who has absolute power **2. DICTATORSHIP** absolute rule of any kind, especially the cruel abuse of absolute power by a despot

tsar·it·sa *n.* HIST = **tsarina** [Late 17thC. From Russian.]

tsats·ke /tsaátskə, chaáchkə/ *n.* = **chachka**

Tsa·vo Na·tion·al Park /saa vō-/ national park and game reserve in Kenya, established in 1948. Area: 8,000 sq. mi./20,700 sq. km.

TSE *n.* a disease that affects the nervous system and can be transmitted from one species to another. Full form **transmissible spongiform encephalopathy**

tset·se fly /tsétsee-, sétsee-/, **tzet·ze fly** *n.* a two-winged biting fly found in central Africa that feeds on the blood of humans and animals and is responsible for transmitting several diseases, including sleeping sickness. Genus: *Glossina.* [Mid-19thC. Via Afrikaans from Setswana.]

T.Sgt. *abbr.* Technical Sergeant

TSH *abbr.* thyroid-stimulating hormone

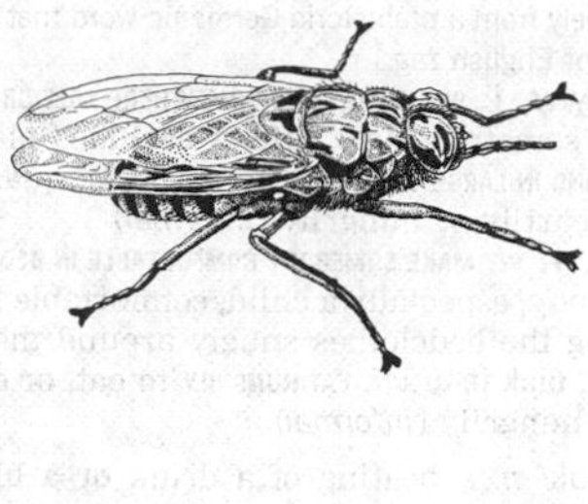

Tsetse fly

T-shirt, **tee-shirt** *n.* **1.** **COLLARLESS SHORT-SLEEVED SHIRT** a collarless buttonless, often short-sleeved, knit shirt, usually made of cotton and worn for leisure and sports. T-shirts are often printed with designs and slogans. **2.** **UNDERSHIRT** a man's short-sleeved undershirt [Early 20thC. From its T-shape when spread out.]

Tshom·be /cháwmbay/, **Moise** (1919–69) Congolese statesman. He was president of the secessionist state of Katanga (1960–63) and prime minister of the Democratic Republic of the Congo (1964–65). Full name **Moise Kapenda Tshombe**

tshwa·la /chwaálə/ *n. S Africa* thick home-brewed beer made from sorghum millet, corn, or other grain that is a traditional drink in South Africa [From Zulu *utshwala*]

tsim·mes *n.* = **tzimmes**

Tsim·shi·an /chímshee ən, tsímshee ən/ (*plural* **-an** *or* **-ans**) *n.* **1.** PEOPLES **MEMBER OF NATIVE N AMERICAN PEOPLE** a member of a Native North American people who originally occupied coastal lands in southeastern Alaska and British Columbia, and whose members mainly continue to live in the same area **2.** LANG **TSIMSHIAN LANGUAGE** the language of the Tsimshian and other Native North American peoples. It is spoken by about 1,500 people. [Mid-19thC. From Tsimshian *čamsián*, literally "inside the Skeena River."] —**Tsim·shi·an** *adj.*

tsk /tisk/ *interj.* **SOUND EXPRESSING DISAPPOINTMENT** a word used in writing to represent a sucking or clicking sound that people make to express disappointment, disgust, or sympathy ■ *vti.* (**tsked, tsk·ing, tsks**) **SAY "TSK"** to scold somebody or express disappointment, sympathy, or disgust by making a sucking or clicking sound [Mid-20thC. An imitation of the sound.]

Tson·ga /tsáwng gə/ (*plural* **-ga** *or* **-gas**) *n.* **1.** PEOPLES **MEMBER OF SOUTHERN AFRICAN PEOPLE** a member of a people who live in southern Africa, mainly in Mozambique, Swaziland, and South Africa **2.** LANG **TSONGA LANGUAGE** the language of the Tsonga people. It belongs to the Bantu group of Benue-Congo languages. Tsonga is spoken by about 4 million people. [Early 20thC. Of Bantu origin.] —**Tson·ga** *adj.*

tsot·si /tsótsee/ *n. S Africa* a young Black man who belongs to a gang involved in criminal activities of various kinds, especially one that operates in townships (*informal*) [Mid-20thC. Origin uncertain: perhaps from Nguni *-tsotsa* "to dress in exaggerated clothing," from the type of clothing such members wear.]

tsp. *abbr.* teaspoon

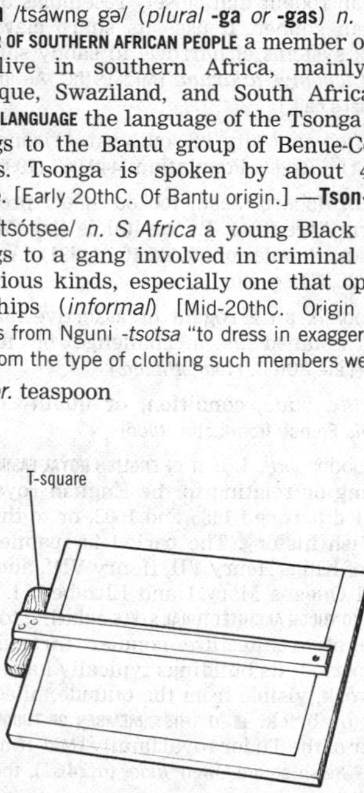

T-square

T-square, **T square** *n.* a drawing-board ruler consisting of a rectangular handle with a straight-sided wooden or plastic blade attached perpendicular to it, to form a T shape. The handle sits against the board's edge.

TSS *abbr.* toxic shock syndrome

tsu·na·mi /tsoo naámee, soo-/ (*plural* **-mis**) *n.* a large destructive ocean wave caused by an underwater earthquake or some other movement of the earth's surface [Late 19thC. From Japanese, literally "harbor wave."] —**tsu·na·mic** /tsoo naámik, soo-, -námmik/ *adj.*

tsu·ris /tsóoriss, tsúr iss, sóoriss, súr iss/, **tzu·ris** *n.* problems or difficulties (*informal*) [Early 20thC. Via Yiddish *tsores* "troubles" from, ultimately, Hebrew *ṣārāh* "trouble."]

Tsu·shi·ma /tsoo shéemə, tsóo shee maá/ island group in the Korea Strait, southwestern Japan. Population: 48,875 (1985). Area: 271 sq. mi./702 sq. km.

tsut·su·ga·mu·shi dis·ease /tsóotsəgə móoshi-, sóotsə-/ *n.* = **scrub typhus** [Early 20thC. From Japanese, literally "disease tick."]

Tswa·na /tswaánə, swaánə/ (*plural* **-na** *or* **-nas**) *n.* **1.** PEOPLES **MEMBER OF SOUTHERN AFRICAN PEOPLE** a member of a people living in southern Africa, mainly in Botswana, where they form the largest ethnic group **2.** LANG **TSWANA LANGUAGE** the language of the Tswana people belonging to the Sotho group of Benue-Congo languages [Mid-20thC. Of Bantu origin.]

TT *abbr.* **1.** teetotal **2.** BANKING telegraphic transfer **3.** teletypewriter **4.** transit time **5.** trust territory **6.** tuberculin-tested

t-test *n.* a test of whether a sample of observations comes from a larger sample with a normal distribution of statistical properties

TTL[1] *n.* a method of constructing electronic logic circuits. Full form **transistor transistor logic**

TTL[2] *abbr.* through-the-lens

TTY *abbr.* teletypewriter

TTYTT *abbr.* to tell you the truth (*used in e-mail messages*)

Tu. *abbr.* CALENDAR Tuesday

T.U. *abbr.* **1.** trade union **2.** TELECOM transmission unit

tuan /twaan/ *n.* in Malay-speaking countries, a respectful form of address for a man [Early 18thC. From Malay.]

Tua·reg /twaá règ/ (*plural* **-reg** *or* **-regs**) *n.* **1.** PEOPLES **AFRICAN PEOPLE** a member of a nomadic people who live in northwestern Africa, mainly in the Sahara and Sahel regions **2.** LANG **TUAREG LANGUAGE** the Berber language of the Tuareg people. It belongs to the Afro-Asiatic family of languages. [Early 19thC. From Berber.]

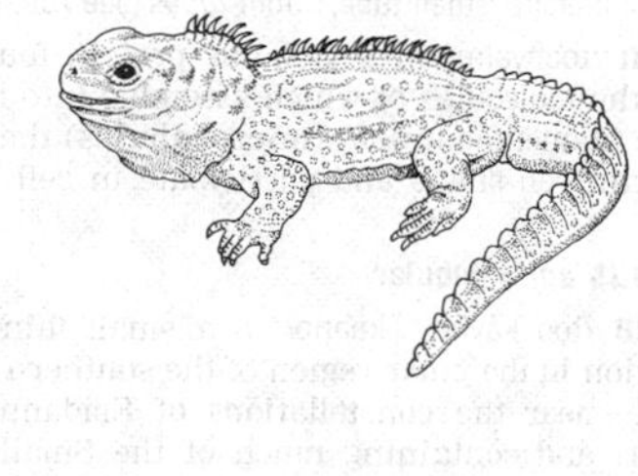

Tuatara

tu·a·ta·ra /tóo ə taárə/ *n.* a large spiny greenish-gray reptile that looks like an iguana but does not belong to the iguana family. It is found only on islands off New Zealand. Latin name: *Sphenodon punctatum.* [Late 19thC. From Maori, literally "with spines on its back."]

tub /tub/ *n.* **1.** **LOW OPEN CONTAINER** a low open, often round, container of any size that is used for purposes such as storage and washing **2.** **ROUND CONTAINER FOR LIQUIDS** a small, often round, plastic or cardboard container for liquid, semi-liquid, or soft substances such as ice cream or margarine **3.** **AMOUNT HELD BY TUB** the contents of a tub **4.** **BATHTUB** a bathtub **5.** **BATH** an instance of bathing in a bathtub (*informal*) ○ *You'll feel better after a tub and a hot meal.* **6.** NAUT **POOR QUALITY BOAT** a slow unreliable boat (*informal*) **7.** MINING **MINE VEHICLE** an open-top vehicle on rails used to transport coal and other excavated minerals in a mine ■ *v.* (**tubbed, tub·bing, tubs**) **1.** *vt.* **STORE SOMETHING IN TUB** to store or package something in a tub **2.** *vti.* **BATHE** to wash, or wash something or yourself, in a bathtub (*informal*) [14thC. From Middle Low German or Middle Dutch.]

tu·ba /tóobə/ *n.* a low-pitched brass musical instrument held vertically with the bell pointing upward and the mouthpiece set horizontally. It has three to five valves. [Mid-19thC. Via French or Italian from Latin, "large war trumpet."]

tu·bal /tóob'l/ *adj.* **1.** **OF TUBES** relating to or in the form of a tube or tubes **2.** ANAT **OF FALLOPIAN TUBE** relating to or developing in a fallopian tube

tu·bal li·ga·tion *n.* a sterilization technique in which a woman's fallopian tubes are tied to prevent ova entering the uterus. It is usually performed using endoscopic surgery.

tu·bate /tóo bàyt/ *adj.* tubular in shape

tub·by /túbbee/ (**-bi·er, -bi·est**) *adj.* **1.** **OFFENSIVE TERM** an offensive term referring to somebody regarded as being overweight (*informal insult*) **2.** **TUB-SHAPED** like a tub in shape **3.** MUSIC **LACKING RESONANCE** used to describe a violin or other string instrument that lacks resonance —**tub·bi·ness** *n.*

tube /toob/ *n.* **1.** **CYLINDER FOR TRANSPORTING OR STORING LIQUIDS** any long hollow cylinder used to transport or store liquids **2.** ANAT **CYLINDRICAL BODY ORGAN** any hollow cylindrical organ that transports liquids or gases around the body **3.** **COLLAPSIBLE CONTAINER WITH CAP** a collapsible, generally cylindrical, container sealed at one end and closed with a cap at the other. It is used for packaging semi-liquid substances such as toothpaste. **4.** RAIL **UNDERGROUND RAILWAY** the underground railway system in London (*informal*) **5.** *U.K.* RAIL **UNDERGROUND TRAIN** a train on an underground railway system **6.** **INNER TUBE** an inner tube of a pneumatic tire **7.** TV **CATHODE RAY TUBE IN TV** a cathode ray tube used to reproduce television images **8.** TV = **boob tube**[2] *n.* **9.** BOT **CHANNEL IN PLANT** any narrow enclosed channel in a plant such as the organ in a germinating pollen grain that conveys the male gametes to the ovule **10.** BOT **FLOWER PART** a roughly cylindrical fusion of the petals of a flower such as a daffodil **11.** ELECTRON ENG **VACUUM TUBE** a vacuum tube (*informal*) **12.** MUSIC **BODY OF WIND INSTRUMENT** the hollow cylinder that forms the main body of a wind instrument, through which the player's breath passes **13.** **PART OF A WAVE** the tunnel formed when a large rolling wave prepares to break ■ *vt.* (**tubed, tub·ing, tubes**) **1.** **FIT WITH TUBE** to supply or fit something with a tube **2.** **ENCLOSE IN TUBE** to put something in a tube [Early 17thC. Via French from Latin *tubus*, of uncertain origin.]

tu·bec·to·my /too béktəmee/ (*plural* **-mies**) *n.* the surgical removal of a fallopian tube (*informal*)

tube foot *n.* an outgrowth of the body wall of marine invertebrates of the sea urchin family (**echinoderms**), used for feeding, moving around, or performing other functions depending on the species

tube·less tire /tóobləss-/ *n.* a pneumatic tire that does not require an inner tube because the casing and wheel rim form an airtight seal

tube-mouthed fish *n.* any fish with a long tubular snout such as the orse, shrimpfish or cornetfish. Order: Solenichthys.

tube·nose /tóob nōz/ *adj.* **HAVING HORNY TUBE ON BILL** used to describe seabirds with horny tubes that extend their nostrils onto their bills. The albatross is an example of a tubenose bird. Order: Procellariiformes. ■ *n.* **SMALL PACIFIC FISH** a small marine fish found in the eastern Pacific that is related to the stickleback and has its ribs fused to lateral bony plates. Latin name: *Aulorhynchus flavidum.*

tube pan *n.* a round cooking pan with a hollow cylinder or cone in the middle, used for baking or molding foods in a ring shape

tu·ber /tóobər/ *n.* **1.** BOT **FLESHY UNDERGROUND PLANT PART** a fleshy swollen part of a root, e.g., a dahlia root, or of an underground stem, e.g., a potato, that stores food over winter and produces new growth in spring. A stem tuber has buds, popularly called eyes, unlike a root tuber. **2.** ANAT **SMALL BULGE ON BODY** a small raised area or swelling on the body [Mid-17thC. From Latin, "swelling" (source of English *truffle*). Ultimately from an Indo-European base meaning "to swell" that is also the ancestor of *thumb* and *tumor.*]

tu·ber·cle /tóobərk'l/ *n.* **1.** BOT, ZOOL **NODULE** a small raised area on a plant or animal part **2.** MED **SMALL LESION** a small rounded swelling on the skin or on a mucous membrane, caused by a disease, especially a nodule in the lungs that is the characteristic symptom of tuberculosis [Late 16thC. From Latin *tuberculum*, literally "small swelling," from *tuber* (see TUBER).]

tu·ber·cle ba·cil·lus *n.* a rod-shaped bacterium that causes tuberculosis. Latin name: *Mycobacterium tuberculosis.*

tu·ber·cu·lar /tə búrkyələr, too-/, **tu·ber·cu·lous** /tə búrkyələss, too-/ *adj.* **1. OF TUBERCULOSIS** relating to, characteristic of, or affected by tuberculosis **2. CAUSED BY TUBERCLE BACILLUS** caused by the tubercle bacillus ○ *tubercular meningitis* **3. NODULE-SHAPED** taking the form of a small rounded swelling or nodule [Late 18thC. Formed from Latin *tuberculum* (see TUBERCLE).]

tu·ber·cu·late /tə búrkyələt, too-/ *adj.* covered with small rounded swellings or nodules **(tubercles)** [Late 18thC. Formed from Latin *tuberculum* (see TUBERCLE).] —**tu·ber·cu·late·ly** *adv.* —**tu·ber·cu·la·tion** /tə bùrkyə láysh'n, too-/ *n.*

tu·ber·cu·lin /tə búrkyəlin, too-/ *n.* a sterile liquid obtained from cultures of the tubercle bacillus and used in a scratch test to establish whether somebody has or has had tuberculosis [Late 19thC. Formed from Latin *tuberculum* (see TUBERCLE).]

tu·ber·cu·lin-test·ed *adj.* used to describe a dairy herd that has been certified as not having tuberculosis, or to describe milk from such a herd (*dated*)

tu·ber·cu·loid /tə búrkyə lòyd, too-/ *adj.* producing symptoms that resemble those produced by tuberculosis ○ *tuberculoid leprosy* [Late 19thC. Formed from Latin *tuberculum* (see TUBERCLE).]

tu·ber·cu·lo·sis /tə bùrkyə lṓssiss, too-/ *n.* an infectious disease that causes small rounded swellings **(tubercles)** to form on mucous membranes, especially a disease **(pulmonary tuberculosis)** that affects the lungs [Mid-19thC. Formed from Latin *tuberculum* (see TUBERCLE).]

tu·ber·cu·lous *adj.* = **tubercular** [Mid-18thC. Formed from Latin *tuberculum* (see TUBERCLE).]

Tuberose

tu·be·rose[1] /tóo brṑz, tóobə rṑz/ *n.* a perennial Mexican plant with blade-shaped leaves and spikes of fragrant white flowers. It is a kind of agave. Latin name: *Polianthes tuberosa.* [Mid-17thC. From modern Latin *tuberosa*, species name, from Latin *tuberosus*, from *tuber* (see TUBER).]

tu·ber·ose[2] /tóobə rṑss/ *adj.* = **tuberous**

tu·ber·os·i·ty /tòobə róssətee/ (*plural* **-ties**) *n.* a rounded protruberance, especially at a point on a bone where muscles or ligaments are attached

tu·ber·ous /tóobərəss/, **tu·ber·ose** *adj.* **1. OF TUBERS** relating to tubers or in the form of tubers **2. HAVING WARTS** producing or covered with knobbly growths [Mid-17thC. From Latin *tuberosus* (see TUBEROSE[1]).]

tube steak *n.* a hot dog (*slang*)

tube top *n.* a short strapless stretchy top for women

tube worm *n.* a worm that builds itself a tube-shaped shelter that sticks out of the soil

tu·bi·fex /tóobə fèks/ *n.* a thin reddish freshwater worm that builds a tube-shaped shelter in the sand of riverbeds. Such worms are often used as food for aquarium fish. Genus: *Tubifex.* [Mid-20thC. From modern Latin, genus name, from Latin *tubus* "tube" + *-fex* "maker."]

tub·ing /tóobing/ *n.* **1. SYSTEM OF TUBES** a system or series of tubes **2. MATERIAL USED FOR TUBES** the hollow, cylindrical material that tubes are made of **3.** = **piping**

Tü·bing·en /tóobingən/ city in Baden-Württemberg State, southwestern Germany. Population: 82,900 (1992).

Library of Congress/Corbis

Harriet Tubman

Tub·man /túbmən/, **Harriet** (1830–1913) U.S. abolitionist. Escaping from slavery (1849), she helped other enslaved laborers escape to freedom along the clandestine route known as the Underground Railroad.

tu·bo·cu·ra·rine /tòobō kōō ráarin, -rèen/ *n.* **1. ACTIVE CONSTITUENT OF CURARE** a toxic substance that is an alkaloid and the active constituent of curare, used as a muscle relaxant **2. HYDROCHLORIDE SALT OF TUBOCURARINE** the hydrochloride salt of tubocurarine [Late 19thC. Coined from TUBE (from the fact that it is shipped in bamboo tubes) + CURARE + -INE.]

tu·bo·plas·ty /tóobō plàstee/ (*plural* **-ties**) *n.* the surgical repair of one or both fallopian tubes, especially when these have been cut and tied for contraceptive reasons

tub-thump (**tub-thumped, tub-thump·ing, tub-thumps**) *vi.* to speak out in favor of somebody or something in a passionate or aggressive way (*informal*) —**tub-thump·er** *n.* —**tub-thump·ing** *adj.*

tu·bu·lar /tóobyələr/, **tu·bu·late** /tóobyələt/, **tu·bu·lous** /tóobyələss/ *adj.* **1. TUBE-SHAPED** shaped like a tube **2. HAVING TUBES** having a tube or tubes [Late 17thC. Formed from Latin *tubulus* (see TUBULE).]

tu·bu·lar bells *npl.* a set of tuned metal tubes, usually arranged in a scale and hung from a frame that are struck with a mallet

tu·bu·late *adj.* = **tubular** [Mid-18thC. From Latin *tubulatus*, from *tubulus* (see TUBULE).]

tu·bule /tóo byool/ *n.* a very small tubular part in a plant or animal organism [Late 17thC. From Latin *tubulus*, literally "small tube," from *tubus* (see TUBE).]

tu·bu·lin /tóobyəlin/ *n.* a globular protein found in cells, the molecules of which assemble into microscopic filamentous tubes **(microtubules)** that help maintain cell shape and participate in cell movement

tu·bu·lous *adj.* = **tubular**

Tu·ca·na /too káynə, -kaánə/ *n.* a small faint constellation in the polar region of the southern hemisphere, near the constellations of Eridanus and Hydrus and containing much of the Small Magellanic Cloud

tu·chun /too chóon, doo jóon/ *n.* formerly, the military leader of a Chinese province [Early 20thC. From Chinese *dūjūn*, from *dū* "to govern" + *jūn* "military."]

tuck[1] /tuk/ *v.* (**tucked, tuck·ing, tucks**) **1.** *vt.* **FOLD SOMETHING INTO POSITION** to push, fold, or bend something such as a flap of material into a particular place or position **2.** *vti.* **DRAW SOMETHING TOGETHER** to pull or draw something together, or be pulled or drawn together **3.** *vt.* SEW **SEW FOLD INTO FABRIC** to sew a fold into fabric, e.g., to reduce its length or for decoration **4.** *vt.* SURG **TIGHTEN SKIN WITH SURGERY** to perform a surgical operation to remove loose or wrinkled skin, usually for cosmetic reasons ■ *n.* **1. TUCKED PART** any part that is tucked safely or neatly into position **2.** SEW **PLEAT** a fold sewn into a piece of fabric, e.g., to reduce its length or for decoration **3.** SURG **SURGICAL REMOVAL OF LOOSE SKIN** a surgical operation to remove loose or wrinkled skin, especially one performed for cosmetic reasons **4.** SPORTS **BODY POSITION** a compact body position with the knees drawn up to the chest, the hands around the shins, and the chin held on the chest. It is adopted in various sports such as diving and gymnastics. **5. PART OF SHIP'S STERN** the part of a ship's hull where the side planks or plates join the spar or spars forming the stern [15thC. Origin uncertain: probably from Middle Dutch *tucken* "to draw up." Ultimately from a prehistoric Germanic word that is also the source of English *tug.*]

tuck away *vt.* **1. PUT SOMETHING SOMEWHERE SAFE OR CONCEALED** to put something in a safe or secluded place **2. EAT SOMETHING IN LARGE QUANTITIES** to eat large quantities of food heartily or hungrily (*informal*)

tuck in *v.* **1.** *vt.* **MAKE SOMEBODY COMFORTABLE IN BED** to make somebody, especially a child, comfortable in bed by tucking the bedclothes snugly around the body **2. tuck in, tuck in·to** *vti.* **EAT HUNGRILY** to eat, or eat something, hungrily (*informal*)

tuck[2] /tuk/ *n.* a beating of a drum or a blast on a trumpet as a flourish [15thC. Via Old North French *toquer* "to strike" from assumed Vulgar Latin *toccare* (see TOUCH).]

tuck[3] /tuk/ *n.* strength or vigor (*archaic*) [Late 19thC. Origin uncertain: possibly from TUCK[1].]

tuck[4] /tuk/ *n.* a rapier (*archaic*) [Early 16thC. Origin uncertain: probably via a dialect form of Old French *estoc*, of prehistoric Germanic origin.]

tuck·a·hoe /túkə hṑ/ *n.* **1. PLANT WITH EDIBLE ROOT** any of various North American plants with arrow-shaped leaves and edible rootstocks. They are species of arum and were traditionally used as food by Native North Americans. **2. EDIBLE FUNGUS** the large edible food storage body of a fungus that grows underground on the roots of trees. It is found in the southern United States. Latin name: *Poria cocos.* [Early 17thC. From Virginia Algonquian *tockawhoughe.*]

tuck·er[1] /túkər/ *n.* **1.** *ANZ* **FOOD** food (*informal*) (*often used before a noun*) **2.** SEW **SEWING-MACHINE ATTACHMENT** an attachment for a sewing machine, used to sew tucks **3.** CLOTHES **DETACHABLE PART OF DRESS** a detachable lace or linen cover for the neck and chest, formerly worn by women under a low-cut dress [13thC. Formed from TUCK[1].]

tuck·er[2] /túkər/ (**-ered, -er·ing, -ers**) *vt.* to tire a person or animal out completely (*informal*) [Mid-19thC. Origin uncertain: perhaps from TUCK[1].]

tuck·et /túkit/ *n.* a fanfare played on a trumpet (*archaic*) [Late 16thC. Formed from TUCK[2].]

tuck-point (**tuck-point·ed, tuck-point·ing, tuck-points**) *vt.* to finish a wall by sealing the facing joints between the bricks or stones **(pointing)** with a thin line of putty or very fine lime-based mortar

tu·co·tu·co /tòokō tóokō/ (*plural* **-cos**) *n.* a South American rodent that closely resembles the North American gopher. It uses its sharp claws to dig complex systems of burrows in sandy soils. Latin name: *Ctenomys talarum.* [Mid-19thC. An imitation of the animal's call.]

Tuc·son /tóo son/ city in southern Arizona, on the Santa Cruz River. Population: 449,002 (1996).

Tu·cu·man /tòokoo maan, tòokoo máan/ province in northern Argentina. Its capital is San Miguel de Tucuman. Population: 1,142,105 (1991). Area: 8,694 sq. mi./22,524 sq. km.

'tude /tood/ *n.* an arrogant or assertive manner or stance assumed as a challenge or for effect (*slang*) [Late 20thC. From *attitude.*]

-tude *suffix.* state, condition, or quality ○ *decrepitude* [Via French from Latin *-tudo*]

Tu·dor /tóodər/ *adj.* **1.** HIST **OF ENGLISH ROYAL FAMILY OR REIGN** belonging or relating to the English royal family that ruled between 1485 and 1603, or to this period of English history. The period is spanned by the reigns of Kings Henry VII, Henry VIII, and Edward VI, and Queens Mary I and Elizabeth I. **2.** ARCHIT **RELATING TO TUDOR ARCHITECTURAL STYLE** relating to or being a style of architecture popular throughout the Tudor period. Its buildings typically have a timber framework, visible from the outside, filled in with plaster or brick. ■ *n.* HIST **MEMBER OF TUDOR FAMILY** a member of the Tudor royal family [Mid-18thC. Named after the Welsh squire Owen *Tudor* (d.1461), the father of Henry VII.]

Tue., Tues. *abbr.* CALENDAR Tuesday

Tues·day /tóoz dày, tóozdee/ *n.* CALENDAR the second day of the week, coming after Monday and before Wednesday [Old English *Tīwesdæg* "Tiu's day," from *Tīw*, the Germanic god of war (a translation of Latin *Martis dies* "Mars' day")]

Tues·days /to͞oz dàyz, to͞ozdeez/ *adv.* CALENDAR every Tuesday

tu·fa /to͞ofə/ *n.* porous rock that has a spongy appearance and is often used as a medium in which to grow alpine plants. It is a calcium carbonate deposit that is found naturally in areas near salty springs. [Late 18thC. Via obsolete Italian from Late Latin *tofus* "porous rock," of unknown origin.] —**tu·fa·ceous** /too fáyshəss/ *adj.*

tuff /tuf/ *n.* rock made up of very small volcanic fragments compacted together [Mid-16thC. Via French from, ultimately, Latin *tofus* (source of English *tufa*).] —**tuff·a·ceous** /tu fáyshəss/ *adj.*

tuf·fet /túffət/ *n.* **1.** **GRASSY MOUND** a small mound or clump of grass **2.** **SEAT** a low seat or stool [Mid-16thC. Alteration of TUFT.]

tuft /tuft/ *n.* **1.** **BUNCH OF FIBERS OR GRASS** a small bunch of hair, grass, feathers, or fibers held or growing together at the base **2.** **CLUMP OF PLANTS** a small clump of plants or trees **3.** **BUNCH OF THREADS DRAWN THROUGH UPHOLSTERY** a group of threads drawn through fabric and tied to secure it to material beneath ■ *v.* (**tuft·ed, tuft·ing, tufts**) **1.** *vti.* **FORM INTO TUFTS** to grow in tufts, or form something into tufts **2.** *vt.* SEW **SEW TUFTS IN SOMETHING** to sew tufts in fabric, either for decoration or to secure one surface to another [14thC. Alteration of Old French *toffe*, of uncertain origin: possibly from late Latin *tufa* "helmet crest," or from Germanic.] —**tuft·ed** *adj.* —**tuft·y** *adj.*

tuft·ed duck *n.* a common diving duck found in Europe and Asia. Males are black with white flanks and bellies and have feathery crests dangling over the back of the neck. Latin name: *Aythya fuligula.*

tuft·ed tit·mouse *n.* a common small crested songbird found in eastern North America. It is gray with a white breast. Latin name: *Parus bicolor.*

Tu Fu /do͞o fo͞o/ (710?–770) Chinese poet. He is often considered to be the greatest of all Chinese poets.

tug /tug/ *v.* (**tugged, tug·ging, tugs**) **1.** *vti.* **PULL AT OR MOVE SOMETHING** to pull at or haul something with a sharp forceful movement **2.** *vt.* SHIPPING **TOW SHIP** to tow a ship with a tugboat **3.** *vi.* **MAKE LABORIOUS EFFORT** to work hard or struggle to do something ■ *n.* **1.** **STRONG PULL** a quick sharp or forceful pull ○ *gave it a tug* **2.** **STRUGGLE OR CONTEST** a struggle or strenuous contest between opposing forces or individuals **3.** SHIPPING = **tugboat** **4.** TRANSP **VEHICLE THAT PULLS ANOTHER** any type of vehicle, whether land, sea, air, or space, that is used to pull another **5.** **CHAIN OR STRAP FOR HAULING** a chain, rope, or strap that is used for hauling or pulling something [13thC. Ultimately from an Indo-European word meaning "to pull" that is also the ancestor of English *tie* and *tow*.] —**tug·ger** *n.*

WORD KEY: SYNONYMS

See Synonyms at ***pull***.

tug·boat /túg bòt/ *n.* a small powerful boat used to tow ships and barges

Tu·ge·la /too gáylə/ river in eastern South Africa, flowing into the Indian Ocean. Length: 312 mi./502 km.

Tu·ge·la Falls /too gáylə-/ series of waterfalls on the Tugela River, KwaZulu-Natal Province, South Africa. Height: 3,110 ft./948 m.

tu·ghrik *n.* = **tugrik**

tug of war *n.* **1.** SPORTS **CONTEST OF STRENGTH** an athletic contest in which two teams pull at opposite ends of a rope, the winner being the one who drags the other across a specified line **2.** **STRUGGLE** any struggle between two evenly matched people, parties, or influences

tu·grik /to͞ogrik/ (*plural* **-grik** *or* **-griks**), **tu·ghrik** (*plural* **-ghrik** *or* **-ghriks**) *n.* **1.** **UNIT OF MONGOLIAN CURRENCY** the main unit of currency in Mongolia, worth 100 mongo. See table at **currency** **2.** **COIN WORTH ONE TUGRIK** a coin worth one tugrik [Mid-20thC. From Mongolian *dughurik*, literally "round thing."]

Tug·well /túgwəl/, **Rexford** (1891–1979) U.S. economist and political scientist. He joined Franklin D. Roosevelt's "Brain Trust" (1932), headed the Resettlement Commission (1935–36), and was governor of Puerto Rico (1941–46). Full name **Rexford Guy Tugwell**

tu·i /to͞o ee/ *n.* a common New Zealand bird that has iridescent dark blue-green plumage, white tufts at the throat, and white spots on the wings. It feeds on nectar, insects, and fruit. Latin name: *Prosthemadera novaeseelandiae.* [Mid-19thC. From Maori.]

tu·i·tion /too ísh'n/ *n.* **1.** FIN **FEE FOR INSTRUCTION** a sum charged for instruction at a school or university **2.** EDUC **TEACHING** instruction or teaching, especially instruction given individually or in a small group [15thC. Via Old French from Latin *tuitio* "support," from *tueri* "to protect."] —**tu·i·tion·al** *adj.*

tu·la·re·mi·a /to͞olə réemee ə/ *n.* an acute infectious disease of rabbits and rodents caused by the bacterium *Francisella tularensis* that can be spread to other animals and humans by insect bites, animal contact, or water. Symptoms include enlarged lymph nodes, headaches, muscular pain, and weight loss. [Early 20thC. Coined from *Francisella tularensis*, species name of the causative bacterium (named for *Tulare* County, California) + -EMIA.] —**tu·la·re·mic** *adj.*

tu·le /to͞olee/ *n.* (*plural* **-les** *or* **-le**) **BULRUSH OF SOUTHWESTERN N AMERICA** either of two bulrushes found in marshes and flooded land in California and adjacent areas of southwestern North America. Latin name: *Scirpus californicus* and *Scirpus acutus.* ■ **tu·les** *npl.* **SWAMPY LAND IN N CALIFORNIA** land in Northern California that is swampy or marshy [Mid-19thC. Via American Spanish from Nahuatl *tullin*.]

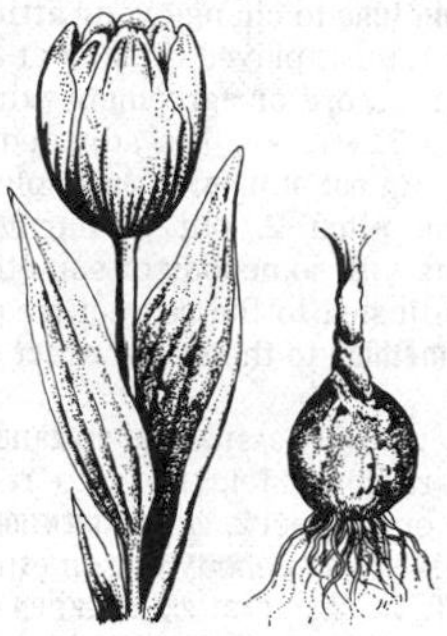

Tulip

tu·lip /to͞olip/ *n.* **1.** **PLANT WITH CUP-SHAPED FLOWERS** a plant that has lance-shaped leaves and a large, usually single, variously colored flower shaped like a bell or cup. Growing from bulbs, they are originally native to western Asia. Genus: *Tulipa.* **2.** **TULIP FLOWER OR BULB** the flower or bulb of a tulip plant [Late 16thC. Via French *tulipe* from Turkish *tülbend* (see TURBAN); from the shape of the expanded flower.]

tu·lip tree *n.* a tall deciduous North American tree of the magnolia family that has large tulip-shaped greenish-yellow flowers, and soft light wood. The tulip tree is the state tree of Indiana, Kentucky, and Tennessee. Latin name: *Liriodendron tulipifera.*

tu·lip·wood /to͞olip wo͝od/ *n.* the light soft wood of the tulip tree, or the striped wood of similar trees, used in making woodenware or in cabinetmaking

tulle /tool/ *n.* a thin netted, often stiffened, silk, nylon, or rayon fabric, used to trim hats and on ballet costumes and evening dresses and for veils [Early 19thC. Named for the French city *Tulle* where it was originally made.]

tul·li·bee /túllə bèe/ (*plural* **-bees** *or* **-bee**) *n.* ZOOL a cisco that lives in the Great Lakes in Canada [Late 18thC. Via Canadian French *toulibi* from Ojibwa *too-niebie*.]

Tul·sa /túlssə/ city in northeastern Oklahoma, on the Arkansas River, northeast of Oklahoma City. Population: 367,302 (1990).

tum·ble /túmb'l/ *v.* (**-bled, -bling, -bles**) **1.** *vti.* **FALL OR MAKE FALL OVER** to fall suddenly and awkwardly, especially rolling over and over, or cause something to fall in this way **2.** *vi.* **ROLL AROUND** to roll around, especially in play **3.** *vi.* **MOVE HASTILY** to move heedlessly or hastily ○ *The puppies tumbled from the room.* **4.** *vi.* GYMNASTICS **LEAP OR ROLL** to perform athletic or gymnastic leaps, rolls, or somersaults **5.** *vi.* **DROP STEEPLY** to fall quickly and by a significant amount ○ *Prices have tumbled on the stock market.* **6.** *vi.* **CASCADE OVER SOMETHING** to flow, fall, or spill out over something **7.** *vi.* **REALIZE SOMETHING** to realize the full significance of something, or see through a deceit (*informal*) ○ *She finally tumbled to it.* **8.** *vti.* **TOPPLE FROM POWER** to experience, or cause somebody to experience, a defeat or fall from power **9.** *vi.* **COME ACROSS BY CHANCE** to come across or stumble on something accidentally **10.** *vt.* **ROTATE IN TUMBLER** to roll or spin something in a drum or tumbler ■ *n.* **1.** **BAD FALL** an awkward or sudden fall ○ *He had a nasty tumble.* **2.** **DISORDERLY HEAP** a disorderly or disorganized heap or arrangement **3.** GYMNASTICS **ATHLETIC MOVEMENT** an athletic or gymnastic leap, roll, or somersault [13thC. From obsolete Low German *tummelen*.]

tum·ble·bug /túmb'l bùg/ *n.* a dung beetle of the scarab family that forms animal dung into balls, into which the female lays her eggs. The dung provides food for the larvae. Family: Scarabaeidae.

tum·ble·down /túmb'l dòwn/ *adj.* ruined or dilapidated and falling down

tum·ble-dry (**tum·ble-dried, tum·ble-dry·ing, tum·ble-dries**) *vt.* to dry wet laundry in the heated rotating drum of a clothes dryer —**tum·ble-dry·er** *n.*

tum·ble·home /túmb'l hòm/ *n.* the inward upward slope of a ship's topsides

tum·bler /túmblər/ *n.* **1.** HOUSEHOLD **DRINKING GLASS** a drinking glass with a thick flat bottom and no stem or handle **2.** HOUSEHOLD **ROUND-BOTTOMED GLASS** a drinking glass, used in the past, that had a rounded or pointed bottom and so could not be put down until it was empty **3.** **AMOUNT IN TUMBLER** the amount of liquid that a tumbler holds **4.** GYMNASTICS **ACROBAT** somebody who performs athletic or gymnastic leaps, rolls, and somersaults **5.** **PART OF LOCK** the part of a lock that must be engaged by a key in order to move the bolt **6.** = **tumbling barrel** **7.** MECH ENG **MACHINE PART** a part of a machine that moves or engages a gear **8.** ARMS **PART OF GUNLOCK** a lever in a gunlock that forces the hammer forward when a trigger is pressed **9.** **ROCKING TOY** a toy that is weighted so that it rocks when touched **10.** BIRDS **PIGEON THAT DOES SOMERSAULTS IN FLIGHT** a domestic pigeon that can perform backward somersaults in flight

tum·ble·weed /túmb'l wèed/ (*plural* **-weeds** *or* **-weed**) *n.* any densely branched plant such as the Russian thistle that grows in arid regions and in late summer withers and breaks from its roots to be blown about by the wind

tum·bling /túmbling/ *n.* the art, practice, or act of performing leaps, rolls, and somersaults

tum·bling bar·rel, tum·bling box *n.* a rotating drum for mixing, polishing, drying, or reducing something inside

tum·brel /túmbrəl/, **tum·bril** *n.* **1.** HIST **CART CARRYING PRISONERS TO BE GUILLOTINED** a cart used during the French Revolution to carry condemned prisoners to be executed by guillotine **2.** AGRIC **FARM CART** a tiltable farm cart used to carry manure **3.** ARMY **MILITARY CART** a covered cart formerly used to carry ammunition and equipment for the artillery [14thC. From Old French *tumberel*, from *tomber* "to fall."]

tu·me·fa·cient /to͞omə fáysh'nt/ *adj.* causing or tending to cause swelling [Late 19thC. From Latin, the present participle stem of *tumefacere* (see TUMEFY).]

tu·me·fac·tion /to͞omə fákshən/ *n.* **1.** **SWELLING OF TISSUE** the swelling of tissue as a result of a buildup of fluid within it **2.** **SWOLLEN PART** a swollen part or area [15thC. From French *tuméfaction*, from Latin *tumefacere* (see TUMEFY).]

tu·me·fy /to͞omə fì/ (**-fied, -fy·ing, -fies**) *vti.* to swell, or cause tissue to swell [Late 16thC. Via French *tuméfier* from Latin *tumefacere* "to make swollen," from *tumere* (see TUMOR) + *facere* "to make."]

tu·mes·cent /too méss'nt/ *adj.* swollen or showing signs of swelling, usually as a result of a buildup of blood or water within body tissues [Mid-19thC. From Latin, the present participle stem of *tumescere* "to become swollen," from *tumere* (see TUMOR).] —**tu·mes·cence** *n.*

tu·mid /to͞omid/ *adj.* **1.** MED **SWOLLEN** used to describe a body part or organ that is swollen **2.** **BULGING** bulging or sticking out **3.** **POMPOUS IN STYLE** having language or a style that is bombastic or inflated [Mid-16thC. From Latin *tumidus*, from *tumere* (see TUMOR).] —**tu·mid·i·ty** /too míddətee/ *n.* —**tu·mid·ness** *n.*

tumm·ler /túmmlər/ *n.* a man employed as a comedian and host to encourage audience participation, especially one hired to amuse guests at resorts in the Catskill Mountains, north of New York City [Mid-20thC. From American Yiddish, formed from Yiddish *tumlen* "to bustle."]

tum·my /túmmee/ (*plural* **-mies**) *n.* somebody's stomach (*informal*) [Mid-19thC. Babytalk alteration of STOMACH.]

tum·my but·ton *n.* *U.K.* the human navel (*informal*)

tum·my tuck *n.* a cosmetic surgical operation to

remove excess fat, skin, and tissue from the abdomen (*informal*)

tu·mor /to͞omər/ *n.* **1.** ABNORMAL MASS OF TISSUE an abnormal uncontrolled growth or mass of body cells, which may be malignant or benign and has no physiological function **2.** SWOLLEN PART any abnormal swelling in or on the body [15thC. From Latin, formed from *tumere* "to swell."] —**tu·mor·al** *adj.*

tu·mor·i·gen·ic /to͞omərə jénnik/ *adj.* used to describe a drug or other agent that may initiate or promote the growth of tumors —**tu·mor·i·gen·e·sis** *n.* —**tu·mor·i·ge·nic·i·ty** /to͞omərə jə níssətee/ *n.*

tu·mor ne·cro·sis fac·tor *n.* a protein that can cause the destruction of tumors. The gene encoding this factor has been used in gene therapy trials for cancer.

tump[1] /tump/ *n. U.K.* a small mound, hill, or clump, especially of vegetation (*regional*) [Late 16thC. Origin unknown.]

tump[2] /tump/ (**tumped, tump·ing, tumps**) *vti. Southern U.S.* to knock something over or tip over, especially accidentally [Late 19thC. Origin uncertain: perhaps an alteration of THUMP.]

tump·line /túmp lìn/ *n.* a band or strap strung across the forehead or chest to support a backpack [Late 18thC. *Tump* from Algonquian *mattump.*]

tu·mu·lar /to͞omyələr/ *adj.* resembling or in the form of a mound or tumulus

tu·mu·li plural of **tumulus**

tu·mu·lose /to͞omyə lōss/, **tu·mu·lous** /to͞omyələss/ *adj.* **1.** HAVING MOUNDS having many mounds or small hills **2.** LIKE A MOUND forming or resembling a mound —**tu·mu·los·i·ty** /to͞omyə lóssətee/ *n.*

tu·mult /to͞o mùlt/ *n.* **1.** NOISY COMMOTION a violent or noisy commotion **2.** EMOTIONAL UPHEAVAL a psychological or emotional upheaval or agitation [14thC. Directly or via French *tumulte* from Latin *tumultus* "commotion," from *tumere* (see TUMOR).]

tu·mul·tu·ar·y /too múlchoo èrree/ *adj.* marked by tumult or turbulence

tu·mul·tu·ous /too múlchoo əss, tə-/ *adj.* **1.** NOISY AND UNRESTRAINED noisy and unrestrained in a way that shows excitement or great happiness **2.** CONFUSED AND AGITATED involving great excitement, confusion, and emotional agitation —**tu·mul·tu·ous·ly** *adv.* —**tu·mul·tu·ous·ness** *n.*

tu·mu·lus /to͞omyələss/ (*plural* **-li** /-lī/) *n.* ARCHEOL = **barrow**[2] *n.* [15thC. From Latin, "mound," formed from *tumere* (see TUMOR).]

tun /tun/ *n.* **1.** CASK a large cask for beer or wine **2.** MEASURE OF VOLUME a measure of liquid volume, especially one for wine equal to 252 gallons/955 liters [Pre-12thC. From medieval Latin *tunna* (see TUNNEL).]

Tun. *abbr.* **1.** Tunisia **2.** Tunisian

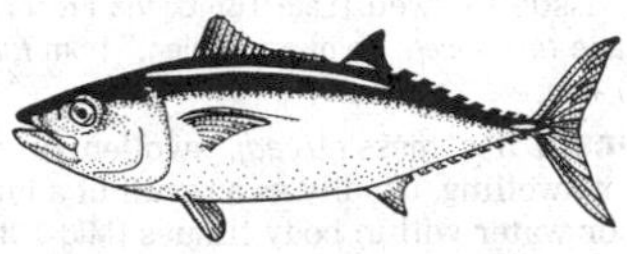

Tuna

tu·na[1] /to͞onə/ (*plural* **-na** *or* **-nas**) *n.* **1.** ZOOL LARGE EDIBLE FISH a large fast-swimming, widely distributed marine fish with a tapering body, large forked tail, and pointed head, found in warm and temperate waters. Genus: *Thunnus.* **2.** FOOD TUNA FLESH the firm meaty flesh of the tuna, used for food [Late 19thC. From American Spanish, of uncertain origin: probably via Spanish *atún* and Arabic *at-tún* from Latin *thunnus* (see TUNNY).]

tu·na[2] /to͞onə/ *n.* **1.** PLANTS PRICKLY PEAR CACTUS a tropical prickly pear cactus that has colored flowers and sweet edible fruit. Latin name: *Opuntia tuna.* **2.** FOOD TUNA CACTUS FRUIT the edible fruit of the tuna cactus [Mid-16thC. Via Spanish from Taino.]

tun·a·ble /to͞onəb'l/, **tune·a·ble** *adj.* capable of being tuned

tu·na fish *n.* = **tuna**[1] *n.* 2

tun·dra /túndrə/ *n.* the level or nearly level treeless plain between the ice cap and the timber line of North America and Eurasia that has permanently frozen subsoil [Late 16thC. Via Russian from Lappish *tundar.*]

tune /toon/ *n.* MUSIC **1.** SIMPLE MELODY a series of musical notes that make a simple melody **2.** SONG a melodious song or short piece of music ■ *vt.* (**tuned, tun·ing, tunes**) **1.** MUSIC ADJUST PITCH to adjust an instrument so that a note is at the required pitch **2.** ENG ADJUST ENGINE to adjust an engine or machine to make it run better **3.** BROADCAST ADJUST STATION OR CHANNEL to adjust a radio or television set to a particular station or channel (*usually passive*) **4.** ADAPT TO SOMETHING to bring yourself, somebody, or something into harmony or accord with something else **5.** ELECTRON ENG ADJUST ELECTRONIC INSTRUMENT to adjust an electronic device or instrument to the required frequency **6.** MUSIC SING to sing something (*archaic*) [14thC. Alteration of TONE.] ◇ **call the tune** to be in charge ◇ **change your tune** to change your attitude or opinion ◇ **in tune 1.** MUSIC played or sung at the appropriate pitch **2.** in accord or agreement with somebody or something **3.** ELECTRON ENG adjusted to the correct frequency ◇ **out of tune 1.** MUSIC played or sung at the wrong pitch **2.** out of harmony or in disagreement with somebody or something **3.** ELECTRON ENG not adjusted to the correct frequency ◇ **to the tune of something** to the stated exact or approximate amount

tune in *v.* **1.** *vti.* BROADCAST ADJUST RECEPTION OF BROADCAST to adjust a radio or television to receive a signal, program, or channel **2.** *vi.* PAY ATTENTION to be attentive or receptive to somebody or something

tune out *v.* **1.** *vt.* BROADCAST RID RECEPTION OF INTERFERENCE to adjust a radio or television set to eliminate the reception of something undesired such as interference **2.** *vi.* IGNORE SOMETHING to ignore or be unreceptive to somebody or something ○ *"The country was tuning out all things when suddenly there was focus on scandal."* (*U.S. News & World Report;* December 1998)

tune up *vti.* **1.** MUSIC ADJUST TO CORRECT PITCH to adjust one or more musical instruments to an accurate or common pitch **2.** PREPARE FOR SOMETHING to test and improve something as a preparation, e.g., for a competition or meeting

tune·a·ble *adj.* = **tunable**

tune·ful /to͞on fòol/ *adj.* having a pleasant melody —**tune·ful·ly** *adv.* —**tune·ful·ness** *n.*

tune·less /to͞onləss/ *adj.* unmusical, lacking a tune, or not producing a tune —**tune·less·ly** *adv.* —**tune·less·ness** *n.*

tun·er /to͞onər/ *n.* **1.** MUSIC SOMEBODY WHO TUNES INSTRUMENTS somebody who tunes musical instruments, especially pianos **2.** ELECTRON ENG DEVICE THAT RECEIVES SIGNALS a device, e.g., in a radio or television set containing one or more resonant circuits, used for selecting a desired signal from a mixture of signals

tune·smith /to͞on smìth/ *n.* a composer of popular songs or music (*informal*)

tune-up *n.* **1.** ENG ADJUSTMENTS TO ENGINE a set of adjustments to an engine to make it run better **2.** WARM-UP a preliminary trial or warm-up, e.g., a minor sporting event held before a major one

tung oil /túng-/ *n.* a quick-drying yellow oil extracted from the seeds of the tung tree, used in paints and varnishes to speed up drying, and also as a waterproofing agent [*Tung* from Chinese *tóng,* the name of the tree]

tung-oil tree *n.* = **tung tree**

tung·state /túng stàyt/ *n.* a salt or ester of tungstic acid. Many tungstates are found in the ores from which tungsten is extracted.

tung·sten /túngstən/ *n.* a hard lustrous gray metallic chemical element with a very high melting point that is used in various high-temperature alloys, lamp filaments, and high-speed cutting tools. Symbol **W** [Late 18thC. From Swedish, literally "heavy stone." Coined by its discoverer, the Swedish chemist Karl Wilhelm Scheele.]

tung·sten car·bide *n.* a fine, very hard, gray crystalline powder made by heating tungsten and carbon together, used in making dies, drill bits, cutting and abrasion tools, and wear-resistant machine parts

tung·sten lamp *n.* an incandescent electric lamp with a filament made of tungsten

tung·sten steel *n.* a hard heat-resistant steel containing between 1% and 20% tungsten, used in tools and high-temperature engineering equipment

tung·stic /túngstik/ *adj.* relating to or containing tungsten in its highest oxidation state. ◊ **tungstous**

tung·stic ac·id *n.* a yellow powder that is a weak acid, used in making textiles and plastics. Formula: H_2WO_4.

tung·stite /túng stìt/ *n.* a rare yellow-green oxide of tungsten that is found associated with ores of tungsten such as wolframite. Formula: WO_3.

tung·stous /túngstəss/ *adj.* relating to or containing tungsten in its low oxidation state. ◊ **tungstic**

tung tree *n.* a tree of eastern Asia whose large round fruit contain hard seeds that yield tung oil. Genus: *Aleurites.* [See TUNG OIL]

Tun·gus /to͝ong go͞oz, tùng go͞oz/ (*plural* **-gus** *or* **-gus·es**) *n.* PEOPLES = **Evenki** [Early 17thC. From Yakut.]

Tun·gus·ic /to͝ong go͞ozik/ *n.* LANG a group of languages spoken in northern parts of the People's Republic of China and eastern parts of Asiatic Russia. It forms a branch of the Altaic family of languages. Tungusic languages are spoken by about 50,000 people. —**Tun·gus·ic** *adj.*

tu·nic /to͞onik/ *n.* **1.** CLOTHES LOOSE GARMENT a loose wide-necked garment that extends to the hip or knee and is usually worn with a belt or gathered at the waist **2.** CLOTHES SHIRTLIKE GARMENT WORN IN PAST a shirtlike knee-length garment worn by men in ancient Rome, or a similar garment worn during the Middle Ages **3.** *U.K.* CLOTHES, MIL POLICE OR MILITARY JACKET a close-fitting high-collared jacket worn as part of a police or military uniform **4.** CLOTHES SPORTS DRESS a short belted dress worn when playing sports **5.** ANAT ENVELOPING MEMBRANE a covering or membrane that envelops an organ or part **6.** ZOOL FIBROUS MEMBRANE a layer of tissue that covers or lines a body part or organ, especially tubular parts such as the blood vessels **7.** BOT PAPERY COVERING ON BULB a dry, often brown and papery, covering around a bulb or corm such as of an onion **8.** RELIG = **tunicle** [Pre-12thC. Directly or via French *tunique* from Latin *tunica.*]

tu·ni·ca /to͞onikə/ (*plural* **-cae** /to͞oni kèe, -sèe/) *n.* = **tunic** *n.* 6 [Late 17thC. From Latin, "tunic."]

tu·ni·cate /to͞onikət, -kàyt/ *n.* MARINE BIOL MARINE ANIMAL a sac-shaped marine chordate animal such as a sea squirt or ascidian that has a tough leathery or rubbery outer coat. Subphylum: Urochordata. ■ *adj.* **1.** MARINE BIOL RELATING TO TUNICATES relating to or classified as a tunicate **2. tu·ni·cate, tu·ni·cat·ed** BOT WITH DRY PAPERY COVERING used to describe a bulb or corm that has a dry, often brown and papery, covering **3. tu·ni·cate, tu·ni·cat·ed** ANAT WITH COVERING OF TISSUE used to describe an organ or body part that is covered or lined with a layer of tissue [Mid-18thC. Via Latin *tunicatus* "covered with a tunic," from, ultimately, *tunica* (see TUNIC).]

tu·ni·cle /to͞onik'l/ *n.* in Christian worship, a short vestment worn over the alb by a subdeacon at a Mass, or under the dalmatic by a bishop or cardinal at other ceremonies [14thC. Directly or via Old French from Latin *tunicula,* literally "small tunic," from *tunica* (see TUNIC).]

tun·ing /to͞oning/ *n.* **1.** SET OF PITCHES the standard range of pitches to which a musical instrument is tuned **2.** MUSICAL INTONATION the degree to which musical instruments or the voices of a choir are adjusted to a standard norm

tun·ing fork *n.* an instrument consisting of a stem and two prongs that produces a constant pitch when struck, used to tune musical instruments and in acoustics

Tu·nis /tyo͞oniss/ capital city of Tunisia, situated on a shallow lake near the Gulf of Tunis. Population: 674,100 (1994).

Tu·nis, Gulf of arm of the Mediterranean Sea in northeastern Tunisia

Tu·ni·si·a /tyoo neezhə/ republic in North Africa, bordered by the Mediterranean Sea, Libya, and Algeria. Language: Arabic. Currency: Tunisian dinar. Capital: Tunis. Population: 9,245,284 (1997).

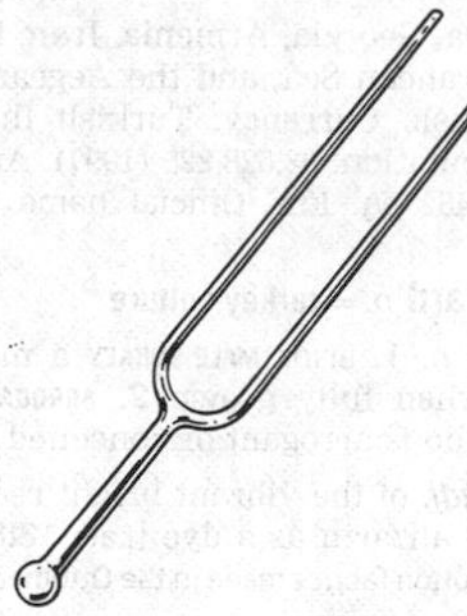

Tuning fork

Tunisia

Area: 63,482 sq. mi./164,418 sq. km. Official name **Republic of Tunisia** —**Tu·ni·si·an** *n., adj.*

tun·nel /túnn'l/ *n.* **1.** TRANSP **PASSAGEWAY UNDER OBSTRUCTION** a long passage that allows pedestrians or vehicles to proceed under or through an obstruction such as a river, mountain, or congested area **2.** ZOOL **ANIMAL'S UNDERGROUND PASSAGE** an underground passage or system of passages dug by a burrowing animal **3.** MINING **PART OF MINE** a corridor or working area in a mine **4. PASSAGE** any passage, channel, or route through or under something ■ *v.* **(-eled, -el·ing, -nels) 1.** *vti.* **MAKE TUNNEL** to make, burrow, or excavate a tunnel under or through something **2.** *vt.* **MAKE SOMETHING LIKE TUNNEL** to produce or dig something that resembles or is shaped like a tunnel [15thC. Via Old French *tonel*, literally "small barrel," from, ultimately, medieval Latin *tunna* "cask" (source of English *ton*), of uncertain origin: probably from Gaulish.] —**tun·nel·er** *n.*

tun·nel dis·ease *n.* = **ancylostomiasis** [*Tunnel* because it is caused by tunnel worms]

tun·nel ef·fect *n.* a quantum mechanical effect in which elementary particles can pass through an energy barrier such as a thin layer even if they do not have enough energy to do so

tun·nel·ing /túnn'ling/ *n.* = **tunnel effect**

tun·nel vault *n.* = **barrel vault**

tun·nel vi·sion *n.* **1.** OPHTHALMOL **RESTRICTED FIELD OF VISION** a condition in which peripheral vision is lost or severely limited, so that only objects directly in line with the eyes can be seen **2. CLOSE-MINDED THINKING** a very limited viewpoint or conception of things

Tun·ney /túnnee/, **Gene** (1898–1978) U.S. boxer. He was the world heavyweight boxing champion (1926–28). Real name **James Joseph Tunney**

tun·ny /túnnee/ (*plural* **-ny** *or* **-nies**) *n.* = **tuna**[1] *n.* **1** [Mid-16thC. Via French *thon* and Latin *thunnus* from Greek *thunnos*.]

tup /tup/ *vt.* **(tupped, tup·ping, tups)** *U.K.* AGRIC **MATE WITH A EWE** to copulate with a ewe ■ *n.* **1.** *Scotland, N England* AGRIC **RAM** a male sheep used for breeding **2.** MECH ENG **HEAD OF HAMMER** the head of a power hammer or a mechanism resembling a hammer [14thC. Origin unknown.]

tu·pek /tóopik/, **tu·pik** *n.* a tent made of animal skins, used in the summer by the Inuit in the Arctic [Mid-19thC. From Inuit *tupiq*.]

tu·pe·lo /tóopə lō/ (*plural* **-los**) *n.* **1. TREE WITH SOFT PALE WOOD** a North American or Asian deciduous tree that grows in swamps and on river banks and has soft pale wood. Genus: *Nyssa*. **2. TUPELO WOOD** the soft pale wood of the tupelo [Mid-18thC. From Creek *ito opilwa*, literally "swamp tree."]

Tu·pi /tóo peé/ (*plural* **-pi** *or* **-pis**) *n.* **1.** PEOPLES **MEMBER OF NATIVE S AMERICAN PEOPLE** a member of a group of Native South American peoples who live in the Amazon valley **2.** LANG **TUPI LANGUAGE** the language of the Tupi people. It belongs to the Tupi-Guarani language family. Tupi was once an important lingua franca in Brazil but is now only spoken by a few thousand people in the Amazon valley. [Mid-19thC. From Tupi, literally "comrade."] —**Tu·pi** *adj.*

tu·pik *n.* = **tupek**

tup·pence *n. U.K.* = **twopence**

tup·pen·ny *adj. U.K.* = **twopenny**

Tup·per /túppər/, **Sir Charles** (1821–1915) Canadian statesman. A longtime Conservative government official, he was one of the prime movers of Canadian federation, and negotiated Nova Scotia's entry into the Dominion of Canada (1867). He was prime minister of Canada for ten weeks in 1896.

tu·pu·na (*plural* **-na**), **ti·pu·na** (*plural* **-na**) *n. NZ* an ancestor or grandparent [From Maori]

tuque /took/, **toque** /tōk/ *n. Can* a cylindrical stocking cap of double-thickness wool or synthetic yarn, worn in winter [Late 19thC. Via Canadian French from French *toque* (see TOQUE).]

tu quo·que /too kwṓkwee, -kwō kwáy/ *interj.* used when accused of an offense to accuse the accuser of the same offense [Late 17thC. From Latin, literally "you too."]

Tur. *abbr.* **1.** Turkey **2.** Turkish

Tu·ra·ni·an /tōō ráynee ən, tə-/ *n.* **1.** PEOPLES **URAL-ALTAIC SPEAKER** a member of any of the peoples who speak a Ural-Altaic language **2.** LANG **OLD LANGUAGE GROUPING** a formerly accepted grouping of Asian languages roughly corresponding to the modern Altaic family with the addition of others (*dated*) ■ *adj.* PEOPLES **RELATING TO ANCIENT TURKISTAN** relating to ancient Turkistan, or its people or culture [Late 18thC. Formed from Persian *Tūrān* "Turkistan."]

tur·ban /túrbən/ *n.* **1. HEADDRESS** a man's headdress that consists of a long piece of fabric wrapped around the head or around a small cap, completely covering the hair, worn especially by Sikhs and Muslims **2. WOMAN'S HAT** a woman's hat that is similar in shape to a man's turban [Mid-16thC. Via obsolete French *turbant*, Italian *turbante*, and Turkish *tülbend* from Persian *dulband* (source also of English *tulip*).] —**tur·baned** *adj.*

tur·ba·ry /túrbəree/ *n.* an area of land where turf or peat may be cut or dug [14thC. Via Anglo-Norman *turberie* from, ultimately, French *tourbe* "turf," of Germanic origin.]

tur·bel·lar·i·an /tùrbə lérree ən/ *n.* a free-living flatworm such as a planarian that inhabits wet soil, freshwater, and marine environments. Turbellarians glide over stones and weeds by means of cilia on their undersurface and swim by undulating their bodies. Class: Turbellaria. [Late 19thC. From modern Latin *Turbellaria*, class name, from Latin *turbella*, literally "small commotion." From the little eddies created by its movement.] —**tur·bel·lar·i·an** *adj.*

tur·bid /túrbid/ *adj.* **1. MUDDY** opaque and muddy as when particles and sediment are stirred up **2. FOGGY** dense and cloudy or dark **3. CONFUSED** confused and muddled ○ *turbid thought processes* [Early 17thC. From Latin *turbidus* "troubled," from *turba* "disorder."] —**tur·bid·i·ty** /tur bíddətee/ *n.* —**tur·bid·ly** /túrbidlee/ *adv.* —**tur·bid·ness** /túrbidnəss/ *n.*

WORD KEY: USAGE

turbid or **turgid**? The two words are unrelated in form but curiously both describe water in their literal meanings (either "opaque and cloudy" in the case of ***turbid*** or "swollen and overflowing" in the case of ***turgid***), and both describe literary styles in their figurative meanings. ***Turgid*** is the more common and means "pompous, bombastic" (as in *turgid prose*), whereas ***turbid*** means "confused, muddled."

tur·bi·dim·e·ter /tùrbi dímmətər/ *n.* an instrument that determines the amount of material in suspension in a liquid or gas by measuring the decrease in light transmittance through the fluid —**tur·bi·di·met·ric** /tùrbidi méttrik/ *adj.* —**tur·bi·di·met·ri·cal·ly** /-méttrikəlee/ *adv.* —**tur·bi·dim·e·try** /tùrbi dímmətree/ *n.*

tur·bi·dite /túrbi dīt/ *n.* a sedimentary deposit laid down by a turbidity current, e.g., on the ocean floor at the bottom of the continental shelf

tur·bid·i·ty cur·rent *n.* a rapidly moving current containing dispersed sediments, sometimes started off by seismic shocks or slumping. The current arises from density differences created by the presence of the dispersed sediments.

tur·bi·nate /túrbinət, -nàyt/, **tur·bi·nal** /-n'l/ *adj.* **1.** ANAT **OF BONE IN NASAL PASSAGE** used to describe any of the three scroll-shaped bones found on the walls of the nasal passages of mammals **2. SPIRAL IN SHAPE** having a shape like a spiral or scroll **3.** ZOOL **SHAPED LIKE INVERTED CONE** used to describe a shell that spirals and is shaped like an inverted cone ■ *n.* **1.** ANAT **TURBINATE BONE** a turbinate bone in the nasal passage of mammals **2.** ZOOL **MOLLUSK SHELL** a turbinate mollusk shell [Mid-17thC. From Latin *turbinatus*, from the Latin stem *turbin-* (see TURBINE).] —**tur·bi·na·tion** /tùrbi náysh'n/ *n.*

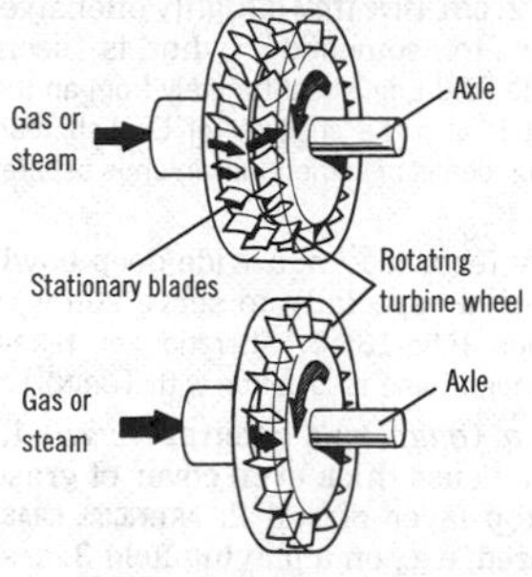

Turbine

tur·bine /túr bīn, -bin/ *n.* a machine in which a moving fluid such as steam acts upon the blades of a rotor to produce rotational motion that can be transformed to electrical or mechanical power. Electrical power is frequently produced from steam turbines. [Mid-19thC. From French, formed from the Latin stem *turbin-* "spiral, spinning-top."]

tur·bit /túrbit/ *n.* a domestic pigeon of a breed with a ruffed neck and breast [Late 17thC. Origin uncertain: perhaps formed from Latin *turbo* (see TURBO), from its shape.]

tur·bo /túr bō/ (*plural* **-bos**) *n.* a gastropod mollusk that has a whorled spiral shell. Genus: *Turbo*. [Mid-17thC. From Latin, "spiral, spinning-top."]

turbo- *prefix.* **1.** using the principle of a turbine, or driven by a turbine ○ *turbocharger* **2.** turbojet ○ *turboprop* [From TURBINE]

tur·bo·charg·er /túr bō chaarjər/ *n.* a specialized turbine driven by the exhaust gases of an engine that supplies air under pressure to the engine for combustion [Mid-20thC. Contraction of TURBO-SUPERCHARGER.] —**tur·bo·charged** *adj.*

tur·bo·fan /túr bō fàn/ *n.* **1. JET ENGINE AUGMENTED BY FANS** a jet engine in which fans driven by a turbine force air into the exhaust gases, thereby increasing the propelling thrust of the engine **2. AIRCRAFT WITH TURBOFAN ENGINES** a jet aircraft that has turbofan engines

tur·bo·jet /túr bō jèt/ *n.* **1. JET AIRCRAFT WITH ENGINES USING TURBINE** an aircraft powered by jet engine with a gas turbine that uses exhaust gases to provide the propulsive thrust **2. JET ENGINE USING TURBINE** a jet engine with a gas turbine that uses exhaust gases to provide the propulsive thrust for an aircraft

tur·bo·prop /túr bō pròp/ *n.* **1. AIRCRAFT USING TURBINE TO DRIVE PROPELLER** an aircraft whose propellers are driven by a gas turbine **2. TURBOJET ENGINE WITH PROPELLOR** a turbojet engine that powers a propellor

tur·bo·su·per·charg·er /tùr bō sóopər chaarjər/ *n.* = **turbocharger**

tur·bot /túrbət/ (*plural* **-bot** *or* **-bots**) *n.* **1. EUROPEAN FLATFISH** a European flatfish that is almost circular with bony tubercles on its body and both eyes on the left side. It is a prized food fish. Latin name: *Scophthalmus maximus*. **2. FLATFISH** a flatfish in the same family as the European turbot, e.g., the spotted turbot of the Pacific. Family: Pleuronectidae. [13thC. Via Old French from Old Swedish *törnbut*, literally "thorn-flatfish," from the spines on its back.]

tur·bu·lence /túrbyələns/, **tur·bu·len·cy** /túrbyələnsee/ *n.* **1. UNREST** a state of confusion characterized by unpredictability and uncontrolled change **2.** METEOROL **INSTABILITY IN ATMOSPHERE** an instability in the atmosphere that disrupts the flow of the wind, causing gusty, unpredictable air currents **3.** PHYS **EDDIES** eddies or secondary motion within a moving fluid

tur·bu·lent /túrbyələnt/ *adj.* **1. MOVING VIOLENTLY** full of violent motion and agitation ○ *turbulent rapids* **2. CHAOTIC AND RESTLESS** marked by disturbances, changes, and unrest ○ *a turbulent year in politics* **3.** METEOROL **ATMOSPHERICALLY UNSTABLE** atmospherically unstable, with variations in wind speed and direction [15thC. From Latin *turbulentus,* from *turba* "disorder."] —**tur·bu·lent·ly** *adv.*

tur·bu·lent flow *n.* a form of fluid flow in which particles of the fluid move with irregular local velocities and pressures

Tur·co·man *n., adj.* PEOPLES = **Turkmen**

turd /turd/ *n.* (*taboo offensive*) **1. OFFENSIVE TERM** an offensive term used to refer to a piece of excrement or dung **2. OFFENSIVE TERM** a highly offensive term used to refer to somebody who is seen as contemptible [Old English. Ultimately from an Indo-European word that is also the ancestor of English *tear* (verb). The underlying idea is of something which is separated from the body.]

tu·reen /tə reén, too͝-/ *n.* a wide deep bowl with a lid that is used especially to serve soups, stews, and casseroles [Mid-18thC. Alteration of TERRINE (perhaps partly through some association with TURIN).]

turf /turf/ *n.* (*plural* **turfs** *or* **turves** /turvz/) **1. DENSE LAYER OF GRASS** a dense thick even cover of grass and roots in the top layer of soil **2. ARTIFICIAL GRASS** artificial grass, used, e.g., on a playing field **3.** GARDENING **PIECE OF SOIL WITH GRASS** a piece of soil with grass growing in it **4. PEAT FOR FUEL** peat, especially when sold for fuel **5.** HORSERACING **HORSERACING** horseracing as a sport or industry **6.** HORSERACING **HORSERACING TRACK** a track where horses are raced **7. AREA OF EXPERTISE** an area in which somebody has authority or expertise (*informal*) **8. TERRITORY** a territory or geographical area (*informal*) **9. GANG TERRITORY** an area or territory that a gang claims as exclusively its own (*informal*) ■ *vt.* (**turfed, turf·ing, turfs**) **1. COVER WITH TURF** to cover an area with pieces of turf **2. FORCE SOMEBODY OUT** to force somebody or something to leave a position or location (*slang*) **3. TO KILL** to kill somebody (*slang*) [Old English. Ultimately from an Indo-European word that also produced German *Torf* "peat."] —**turf·y** *adj.*

Ivan Turgenev

Tur·ge·nev /toor gáynyəf/, **Ivan** (1818–83) Russian writer. His best known works include the novel *Fathers and Sons* (1862) and the play *A Month in the Country* (1855). Full name **Ivan Sergeyevich Turgenev**

tur·ges·cent /tur jéss'nt/ *adj.* **1.** MED **SWOLLEN** swollen or becoming swollen, usually as a result of an accumulation of blood or other fluids **2. POMPOUS** acting pompously, or feeling very self-important [Early 18thC. From Latin, the present participle stem of *turgescere* "to begin to swell," from *turgere* (see TURGID).] —**tur·ges·cence** *n.* —**tur·ges·cen·cy** *n.*

tur·gid /túrjid/ *adj.* **1. POMPOUS AND OVERCOMPLICATED** pompous, boring, and overcomplicated ○ *a turgid speech* **2.** MED **SWOLLEN** swollen or distended by a buildup of fluid [Early 17thC. From Latin *turgidus,* from *turgere* "to swell."] —**tur·gid·i·ty** /tur jíddətee/ *n.* —**tur·gid·ly** /túrjidlee/ *adv.* —**tur·gid·ness** /túrjidnəss/ *n.*

WORD KEY: USAGE

See Usage note at ***turbid.***

tur·gor /túrgər/ *n.* the normal rigid state of plant cells, caused by outward pressure of the water content of each cell on its membrane. The rigidity of plants relies on the turgor of the cells, a decrease in which leads to wilting. [Late 19thC. From late Latin, formed from *turgere* (see TURGID).]

Tu·rin /toor rín/ capital city of Turin Province, Piedmont Region, northwestern Italy. Population: 952,736 (1992).

Tur·ing /tyo͝oring/, **Alan** (1912–54) British mathematician. He was a major figure in the theoretical development of the computer. During World War II (1939–45) he worked as a British government cryptographer, and helped to break the German Enigma machine's code. Full name **Alan Mathison Turing**

Tur·ing ma·chine *n.* a mathematical model of a device that can modify its instructions and read from, write on, or erase a potentially infinite tape. It was instrumental in the evolution of computer theory. [Named for its inventor, Alan TURING]

Turk /turk/ *n.* **1.** PEOPLES **SOMEBODY FROM TURKEY** somebody who was born or raised in Turkey, or who has Turkish citizenship **2.** PEOPLES **MEMBER OF TURKISH ETHNIC GROUP** a member of the dominant, Turkish-speaking ethnic group in Turkey, or, in former times, in the Ottoman Empire **3.** LANG **TURKIC SPEAKER** a member of a people speaking a Turkic language **4.** RELIG **OFFENSIVE TERM** an offensive term used to refer to a Muslim (*archaic offensive*) **5. OFFENSIVE TERM** an offensive term used to refer to a cruel or tyrannical person (*archaic offensive*) [14thC. Via French *Turc* and medieval Latin *Turcus* from, ultimately, Turkish *Türk.*]

Turk. *abbr.* **1.** Turkey **2.** Turkish

Tur·ka·na, Lake /tur ka̋anə/ lake in northwestern Kenya, extending into Ethiopia at its northern end. Area: 2,700 sq. mi./7,100 sq. km. Former name **Rudolf, Lake**

Turkey

tur·key /túrkee/ (*plural* **-keys**) *n.* **1.** BIRDS **LARGE N AMERICAN BIRD** a large North American bird with a bare wattled head and neck and brownish feathers that is widely domesticated and raised as poultry. Latin name: *Meleagris gallopavo.* **2.** FOOD **TURKEY MEAT** the meat of the turkey used for food **3.** BIRDS **LARGE CENTRAL AMERICAN BIRD** a large bird of Central and northern South America, similar to the North American turkey. Latin name: *Agriocharis ocellata.* **4. FAILURE** something that fails or flops, especially a bad play or movie (*slang*) **5. OFFENSIVE TERM** an offensive term used to describe somebody regarded as unintelligent, incompetent, or socially inept (*slang insult*) **6.** SPORTS **THREE CONSECUTIVE BOWLING STRIKES** three strikes in a row in the sport of bowling (*informal*) [Mid-16thC. From its resemblance to the guinea fowl, which was named for TURKEY because it was imported through Turkish territory.]
◇ **talk turkey** to talk honestly and bluntly

Turkey

Tur·key /túrkee/ republic in southeastern Europe and southwestern Asia, bordered by Bulgaria, Greece, the Black Sea, Georgia, Armenia, Iran, Iraq, Syria, the Mediterranean Sea, and the Aegean Sea. Language: Turkish. Currency: Turkish lira. Capital: Ankara. Population: 63,528,225 (1997). Area: 300,948 sq. mi./779,452 sq. km. Official name **Republic of Turkey**

tur·key buz·zard *n.* = **turkey vulture**

tur·key cock *n.* **1.** BIRDS **MALE TURKEY** a male turkey, especially when fully grown **2. ARROGANT INDIVIDUAL** somebody who is arrogant or conceited (*insult*)

Tur·key red *adj.* of the vibrant bright red color produced using alizarin as a dye [Late 18thC. From the color used in cotton fabrics made in the Ottoman Empire.] —**Tur·key red** *n.*

tur·key shoot *n.* **1.** RIFLE SHOOTING **RIFLE FIRING CONTEST** a shooting contest in which rifles are fired at moving targets **2. SOMETHING VERY EASY** something easily accomplished (*slang*)

tur·key trot *n.* a round dance to ragtime music in which dancers walk springily and make birdlike movements with their shoulders and upper body

tur·key vul·ture *n.* a blackish-brown vulture of the Americas that has a bare wrinkled red head and neck and feeds on carrion. Latin name: *Cathartes aura.*

Turk·ic /túrkik/ *n.* LANG a group of languages spoken in western and central Asia, constituting a subfamily of the Altaic family of languages. As well as Turkish, it includes Azerbaijani, Kazakh, Kyrgyz, Tatar, Uighur, and Uzbek. —**Turk·ic** *adj.*

Turk·ish /túrkish/ *adj.* **1. OF TURKEY** relating to Turkey, or its people, or culture **2.** LANG **OF TURKISH** relating to the Turkish language ■ *n.* LANG **OFFICIAL LANGUAGE OF TURKEY** the official language of Turkey, also spoken in Cyprus and several European countries. It belongs to the Turkic branch of Altaic languages. Turkish is spoken by about 50 million people. Before 1928, when the Roman alphabet was adopted, it was written in Arabic script. —**Turk·ish·ness** *n.*

Turk·ish bath *n.* **1. STEAM BATH** a bath in which the bather sweats freely in hot air or steam, followed by a shower and often a massage **2. ESTABLISHMENT OFFERING TURKISH BATH** a commercial establishment where somebody can have a Turkish bath **3. HOT PLACE** a place that is very hot

Turk·ish cof·fee *n.* a strong coffee, usually sweetened, made by simmering finely ground coffee and serving the liquid with the grounds

Turk·ish de·light *n.* a candy made with flavored gelatin, cut in cubes and dusted with powdered sugar

Turk·ish to·bac·co *n.* an aromatic dark tobacco grown in southeastern Europe and Turkey

Turk·ish tow·el *n.* a large coarse-fibered cotton towel

Turk·ism /túr kìzzəm/ *n.* the culture and traditions of the Turks, or an example of these

Turk·i·stan /túrki stàn/, **Turk·e·stan** a mountainous region of central Asia that stretches from the Caspian Sea to the Gobi Desert. It is divided into three sections, Russian or Western Turkistan, which includes Kazakhstan, Kyrgyzstan, and Uzbekistan, Chinese or Eastern Turkistan, made up of the Xinjiang Uygor Autonomous Region of China, and Afghan Turkistan, consisting of the northeastern part of Afghanistan.

Turk·men /túrkmən/ (*plural* **-men** *or* **-mens**), **Tur·ko·man** /túrkəmən/ (*plural* **-mans**), **Tur·co·man** (*plural* **-mans**) *n.* **1.** PEOPLES **MEMBER OF CENTRAL ASIAN PEOPLE** a member of an originally nomadic Turkic-speaking people who now live mainly in Turkmenistan and Afghanistan **2.** LANG **TURKMEN LANGUAGE** the language spoken by the Turkmen people and the official language of Turkmenistan, belonging to the Turkic group of Altaic languages. Turkmen is spoken by about 4 million people. [Early 20thC. Via Persian *turkmān* from Turkish *türkmen.* The form *Turkoman* dates from the early 17thC, and a rare *Turkman* from the 15thC.] —**Turk·men** *adj.*

Turk·men·i·stan /tùrk menni stán, -sta̋an/ republic in the southwestern portion of Central Asia, bordered by Kazakhstan, Uzbekistan, Afghanistan, Iran, and the Caspian Sea. Language: Turkmen. Currency: manat. Capital: Ashgabat. Population: 4,229,249 (1997). Area: 188,500/488,100 sq. km. Official name **Republic of Turkmenistan**

Tur·ko·man *n., adj.* PEOPLES, LANG = **Turkmen**

Turkmenistan

Turks and Cai·cos Is·lands /tùrks ənd kàykoss-, -kīykōss-/ British dependency consisting of two island groups in the West Indies, southeast of the Bahamas. Capital: Cockburn Town. Population: 14,302 (1996). Area: 166 sq. mi./430 sq. km.

Turk's-cap lil·y /tùrks kàp-/ *n.* either of two lilies that have bright nodding flowers with petals that bend sharply backward. Latin name: *Lilium martagon* and *Lilium superbum.*

Turk's-head /túrks hèd/ *n.* a knot shaped like a turban, made by weaving a smaller rope around a larger rope or spar

tur·mer·ic /túrmərik/ *n.* **1.** BRIGHT YELLOW SPICE a yellow spice made from the dried rhizomes of an Asian plant and used as a condiment and as a yellow dye **2.** PLANT WITH YELLOW FLOWERS AND RHIZOMES a tropical Asian plant of the ginger family with yellow flowers and rhizomes that are dried to produce turmeric. Latin name: *Curcuma longa.* [Mid-16thC. From French *terre-mérite*, literally "worthy earth" (perhaps an alteration of Arabic *kurkum* "saffron").]

tur·mer·ic pa·per *n.* a paper impregnated with turmeric that turns brown in the presence of alkalis and red-brown in the presence of boric acid

tur·moil /túr mòyl/ *n.* **1.** CONFUSED DISTURBANCE a state of great confusion, commotion, or disturbance **2.** EVENT CAUSING CONFUSION a disruptive event that causes confusion, commotion, or disturbance ○ *a leader untroubled by the nation's turmoils* [Early 16thC. Origin unknown.]

turn /turn/ *v.* (**turned, turn·ing, turns**) **1.** *vti.* MOVE TO FACE DIFFERENT DIRECTION to move to face in a particular direction or toward a particular location, or move something so that it does this ○ *She turned to see what was happening.* ○ *turning his eyes skyward* **2.** *vti.* MOVE AROUND AN AXIS to move around an axis or point in a particular direction, or move something in this way ○ *Turn the handle to the left.* **3.** *vt.* USE CONTROL TO OPERATE SOMETHING to control something such as a machine or an appliance or some aspect of its performance by moving a knob, switch, or slider to a particular setting ○ *Turn the heat to high.* **4.** *vti.* TRAVEL IN NEW DIRECTION to go in a different direction when moving or traveling, or make a vehicle change direction ○ *Turn left at the crossroads.* **5.** *vt.* GO AROUND SOMETHING to change direction and go round something ○ *to turn a corner* **6.** *vi.* FOLLOW DIFFERENT COURSE to change direction and follow a different course ○ *The path turns uphill.* **7.** *vti.* MOVE PAGE OVER to move a page so that the other side, or another page, can be read or looked at ○ *He turned the pages slowly.* **8.** *vti.* CHANGE to change or be transformed, or change or transform somebody or something, into somebody or something different **9.** *vti.* CHANGE COLOR to change color, or cause something to change color **10.** *vti.* ALTER FOCUS OF SOMETHING to direct the focus of something toward something else, or be focused on something ○ *Her thoughts turned to the past.* **11.** *vi.* START DOING SOMETHING DIFFERENT to start doing something new or different, especially as a way of solving a problem or improving a situation **12.** *vi.* APPEAL to seek or appeal for help from somebody ○ *He turned to his mother for advice.* **13.** *vi.* CHANGE IN WEATHER to change to become a different temperature or type of weather ○ *It's turned cold again.* **14.** *vti.* MAKE SOMEBODY FEEL SLIGHTLY SICK to be sufficiently unpleasant or upsetting to make somebody feel nauseated, or respond with feelings of nausea ○ *The scenes of carnage turned his stomach.* **15.** *vt.* GYMNASTICS PERFORM CARTWHEEL to rotate the body to perform a physical action such as a cartwheel or somersault **16.** *vt.* MED TWIST ANKLE to injure the ankle or wrist by twisting or spraining it ○ *She turned her ankle getting off the bus.* **17.** *vt.* SEARCH EXTENSIVELY to search a place extremely thoroughly ○ *They turned the house upside down looking for the ticket.* **18.** *vt.* PASS TIME OR AGE to pass a particular age, time, or speed ○ *She's just turned sixty.* **19.** *vi.* BECOME SOUR to become sour (*refers to milk*) ○ *The milk has turned.* **20.** *vt.* PUT INTO CONDITION OR PLACE to cause or allow somebody or something to be in a particular condition or place ○ *The sight turned my blood cold.* ○ *He opened the gate and turned the horses loose.* **21.** *vi.* OCEANOG START TO EBB OR FLOW to reach high tide and ebb, or reach low tide and start to rise ○ *The tide has turned.* **22.** *vt.* WOODWORK, METALL SHAPE SOMETHING ON LATHE to shape or cut something on a lathe **23.** *vt.* FORM SOMETHING INTO ROUND SHAPE to shape clay or a pot into a rounded form with the hands or with tools **24.** *vt.* BUSINESS EARN MONEY to earn or achieve a monetary gain ○ *The business should turn a profit in this financial year.* **25.** *vti.* CHANGE SOMEBODY'S ALLEGIANCE to cause a change in somebody's allegiance, or undergo a change of allegiance ○ *a diplomat who turned spy* **26.** *vi.* CONVERT to convert to a religion **27.** *vt.* SAY OR WRITE SOMETHING WELL to give a distinctive or pleasing form to something said or written **28.** *vt.* GARDENING, AGRIC DIG UP LOWER LEVELS OF SOIL to dig soil so as to bring lower layers up to the surface **29.** *vt.* MIL PASS AROUND ENEMY to pass around an enemy in order to attack from the flank or rear **30.** *vt.* BLUNT A WEAPON to blunt the edge of a weapon (*archaic*) ■ *n.* **1.** CHANCE OR RIGHT TO DO SOMETHING a time when somebody gets an opportunity to do something or somebody is asked to do something, especially when this is rotated among other people ○ *It's your turn to clean up.* **2.** CHANGE OF DIRECTION a change of direction in something such as a road or the plot of a book ○ *Slow down for the turn in the road ahead.* **3.** JUNCTION a fork or corner at which a road or path divides **4.** MOVEMENT OF ROTATION a full or partial rotation ○ *Give the screw a few more turns.* **5.** WINDING a winding of something such as wire around something else **6.** PARTICULAR INCLINATION a particular inclination or tendency ○ *She has an academic turn of mind.* **7.** SUDDEN SCARE a sudden shock or scare ○ *It gave me quite a turn.* **8.** SPELL OF ILLNESS a short period of feeling unwell or faint ○ *She had a nasty turn but she's OK now.* **9.** SHORT OUTING a short walk, excursion, or dance (*dated*) ○ *They took a turn around the park.* **10.** END OF TIME PERIOD the point at which one period of time ends and another begins **11.** GOOD OR BAD DEED a deed that helps or harms another person ○ *a good turn* **12.** MUSIC MELODIC EMBELLISHMENT a melodic embellishment that is played around a given note, using one note above and one note below the principal note **13.** THEATER INDIVIDUAL THEATRICAL PERFORMANCE a short theatrical solo performance, e.g., in a cabaret **14.** STOCK EXCH STOCK MARKET TRANSACTION a stock market transaction that includes both a sale and a purchase **15.** MIL ADVANCE PASSING AROUND ENEMY a military advance that passes around an enemy in order to attack from the flank or rear **16.** *Southern U.S.* QUANTITY OF GRAIN the quantity of grain transported to a mill in one delivery **17.** *Southern U.S.* QUANTITY OF FIREWOOD the amount of firewood carried into a house at one time [Pre-12thC. Via Latin *tornare* "to turn on a lathe" from, ultimately, Greek *tornos* "lathe."] —**turn·able** *adj.* ◇ **at every turn** everywhere, or at every significant moment ◇ **be on the turn 1.** to be on the point of going sour **2.** to be on the point of changing **3.** to be at high or low tide and just about to ebb or return ◇ **by turns** one after the other, alternately ◇ **in turn** in a regular order, one after the other ◇ **to a turn** perfectly ○ *meat cooked to a turn*

WORD KEY: REGIONAL NOTE

Turn as in *turn of corn* (the amount of grain carried to the mill at one time) and *turn of wood* (the amount of firewood carried into the house) is a Southern term that once competed with *grist of corn* in the North and *jag of corn* in Pennsylvania and the North Midland region. In the Eastern States, Northern and Midland *armful of wood* contrasts with Southern *turn of wood.*

turn against *vti.* to stop approving of something or being friendly toward somebody and show definite disapproval or unfriendliness instead, or make somebody change attitude in this way

turn around *vt.* **1.** COMPLETE ALL NECESSARY PROCEDURES to carry out all the necessary procedures between receiving an order or task and shipping the order or completing the task ○ *How long will it take you to turn this work around?* **2.** PREPARE VEHICLE BETWEEN TRIPS to prepare an aircraft for its next flight or a ship for its next sailing **3.** IMPROVE SIGNIFICANTLY to cause a significant improvement in something, especially in the profits made by a company or organization ○ *moves to turn the debt around*

turn away *v.* **1.** *vti.* TURN TO FACE SOMEWHERE ELSE to change position so as to face away from somebody or something, or move somebody or something so as to face in another direction **2.** *vt.* REFUSE ADMISSION TO SOMEBODY to send somebody away, refusing to see, entertain, or accommodate him or her **3.** *vt.* REFUSE TO ACCEPT SOMETHING to refuse to listen to somebody or to what somebody wants to say or offer **4.** *vi.* REJECT to reject something as unworthy or undesirable ○ *to turn away from a life of sin*

turn back *v.* **1.** *vti.* REVERSE to reverse or cause something to reverse or go back **2.** *vti.* STOP GOING FORWARD AND RETURN to stop and return in the direction you have come from, or stop people or vehicles and make them return in the direction they have come from **3.** *vt.* FOLD BACK to fold something over and down ○ *turned back the top sheet on the bed*

turn down *vt.* **1.** REJECT to reject or refuse something such as an offer or application **2.** REDUCE VOLUME OR INTENSITY to make something less powerful, bright, loud, or hot, especially by moving a knob, switch, or slider **3.** FOLD SOMETHING DOWNWARD to fold something or the top part of something toward the bottom, so that a double layer is formed

turn in *v.* **1.** *vt.* RETURN SOMETHING AFTER USE to hand something over or give something back to its owner or to whoever is responsible for it ○ *turn in your key at the desk before leaving* **2.** *vt.* SUBMIT SOMETHING to hand in or send in something such as work assigned in school **3.** *vt.* TAKE SOMEBODY TO THE POLICE to hand over somebody or something to the police or other authorities **4.** *vi.* GO TO BED to go to bed at the end of the day (*informal*) **5.** *vt.* PRODUCE RESULT to achieve a particular outcome ○ *turned in a creditable performance* **6.** *vti.* FOLD INWARD to arrange something so that it bends or points inward, or be arranged in this way

turn off *v.* **1.** *vt.* OPERATE SWITCH TO STOP SOMETHING to make a machine or appliance stop working, or something stop flowing, by operating a control **2.** *vt.* SET TO OFF POSITION to move a device such as a button, knob, or lever so that a machine stops working or something stops flowing **3.** *vti.* DIMINISH ENTHUSIASM to diminish or destroy somebody's interest, enthusiasm, or sexual arousal, or lose interest or become unresponsive (*informal*) **4.** *vti.* GO IN A NEW DIRECTION to split off from a road or path and head a different way, or take a road or path that goes in a new direction

turn on *v.* **1.** *vt.* OPERATE SWITCH TO START SOMETHING to make a machine or appliance operate, or make something start flowing, by operating a control **2.** *vt.* SET TO ON POSITION to move a device such as a button, knob, or lever so that a machine starts working or something starts flowing **3.** *vt.* BEHAVE IN CALCULATED WAY to display a particular behavior or emotion in a way that people find calculated, irritating, or insincere ○ *He'll really turn on the charm if he thinks he's losing the sale.* **4.** *vt.* REACT AGGRESSIVELY OR VIOLENTLY to react aggressively or violently to somebody **5.** *vt.* MAKE SOMEBODY EXCITED to interest somebody greatly or fill somebody with pleasure, energy, or excitement (*informal*) **6.** *vt.* AROUSE to make somebody feel sexually excited (*informal*) **7.** *vti.* DRUGS TAKE ILLEGAL DRUGS to take drugs, especially a hallucinogenic drug, or cause somebody to take a hallucinogen or similar drug (*informal*)

turn out *v.* **1.** *vt.* SWITCH OFF to make an electric light go out by operating its power switch **2.** *vi.* COME TO EVENT to assemble in a particular place, especially for a special event or public occasion ○ *Hardly anybody turned out for the reunion.* **3.** *vt.* MAKE SOMEBODY LEAVE to force somebody to leave a room, building, or residence **4.** *vi.* HAPPEN IN PARTICULAR WAY to happen in a particular way, often in a way that was not expected **5.** *vi.* END UP to have a particular result ○ *The birthday party turned out OK, despite our fears.* **6.** *vt.* MAKE SOMETHING to create or produce something, especially in a consistent way or by mass production ○ *a factory that turns out tennis rackets* **7.** *vt.* DRESS SOMEBODY UP to clothe yourself or somebody else in a particular way **8.** *vti.* MIL SIGNAL GROUP TO ASSEMBLE to call an organized group of people, usually soldiers, to assemble for duty or for a military parade **9.** *vt.* EMPTY CONTENTS to take out the contents of a pocket or bag, usually to check or reorganize what is there **10.** *vti.* FOLD OUTWARD to be arranged so as to bend or point outward, or arrange something in this way **11.** *vi.* GET UP to get out of bed (*informal*)

turn over *v.* **1.** *vt.* TURN SOMETHING THE OTHER WAY UP to alter the position of the body or of an object, bringing the underside uppermost, or move so that the underside is uppermost **2.** *vt.* THINK ABOUT to give something slow and careful thought, considering different aspects or possibilities **3.** *vt.* GIVE TO SOMEBODY ELSE to hand something over to the police or other authorities, especially when required to do so **4.** *vt.* DELEGATE to give the responsibility for something to somebody else ○ *turned over some duties to her assistant* **5.** *vt.* PUT UNDER SOMEBODY'S RESPONSIBILITY to transfer the responsibility for somebody to another person or authority ○ *The principal turned him over to his parents.* **6.** *vti.* AUTOMOT START to start an engine or motor, or be started ○ *couldn't get it to turn over* **7.** *vt.* FIN HAVE SALES OF to have sales or other business transactions totaling a specified amount ○ *The firm turns over several million a month.* **8.** *vti.* COMM SELL AND RESTOCK GOODS to sell and restock all items for sale ○ *The produce usually turns over in 10 days time.*

turn to *vi.* to set to work, especially vigorously

turn up *v.* **1.** *vt.* INCREASE SOMETHING to make something louder, brighter, hotter, or more powerful, especially by operating its control **2.** *vti.* UNFOLD UPWARD to unfold something so that it stands up instead of lying in a flat double layer, or be capable of unfolding in this way **3.** *vt.* SEW SHORTEN GARMENT to fold and sew the bottom edge of a garment or piece of fabric, so as to shorten it **4.** *vi.* BE FOUND to reappear or be rediscovered after being lost or in an unknown place, often in a surprising or unexpected way ○ *It'll turn up sooner or later.* **5.** *vt.* FIND SOMETHING BY SEARCHING to uncover something that was hidden or previously unknown by investigating, hunting, or digging ○ *He didn't expect to turn up such an interesting story.* **6.** *vi.* ARRIVE to come or appear somewhere, especially in a casual or unplanned way ○ *She just turned up yesterday morning.* **7.** *vi.* HAPPEN to take place luckily or unexpectedly to settle matters or put things right ○ *They manage to get along somehow ... something always seems to turn up.*

turn·a·bout /túrnə bòwt/ *n.* **1.** ACT OF TURNING COMPLETELY AROUND the act of turning to face in the opposite direction **2.** TOTAL CHANGE IN OUTLOOK OR BEHAVIOR a shift from one situation, opinion, policy, or attitude to another that is the complete opposite

turn·a·round /túrnə ròwnd/ *n.* **1.** BUSINESS TIME TAKEN TO DO ENTIRE JOB the time it takes to carry out all the necessary procedures between receiving an order or task and the shipment of the order or completion of the task **2.** TRANSP PREPARATION OF VEHICLE BETWEEN TRIPS the process of unloading and reloading, refueling, and checking an aircraft, ship, or vehicle between journeys **3.** TRANSP TIME SPENT ON VEHICLE'S TURNAROUND the time taken on the process of unloading and reloading, refueling, and checking an aircraft, ship, or vehicle between journeys **4.** BIG IMPROVEMENT a dramatic improvement in a bad or unsatisfactory situation **5.** TRANSP PLACE FOR TURNING AUTOMOBILE AROUND a circular or curved driveway or section of road where vehicles can turn around **6.** = **turnabout** *n.* 1, **turnabout** *n.* 2

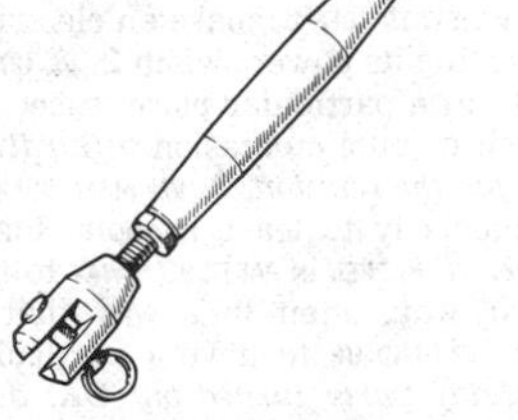

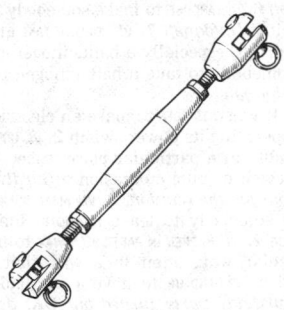

Turnbuckle

turn·buck·le /túrn bùk'l/ *n.* a device to tighten or loosen rope or wire, consisting of a sleeve through which the rope or wire is threaded and held so that the tension can be adjusted

turn·coat /túrn kōt/ *n.* somebody who abandons or betrays a group or cause and joins the opposing side

turn·down /túrn dòwn/ *n.* **1.** REJECTION a rejection of something such as an offer or application **2.** = **downturn** ■ *adj.* FOLDED DOWN folded down or over from the top

turned-on *adj.* (*slang*) **1.** SEXUALLY EXCITED sexually aroused or excited **2.** HIP aware of or involved in the most modern trends in culture and fashion **3.** HIGH ON DRUGS under the influence of a drug such as cannabis or LSD, or familiar with its effects as a result of having taken it

turn·er /túrnər/ *n.* **1.** SOMEBODY OR SOMETHING THAT TURNS somebody or something that turns or that is used for turning something else, e.g., a device for turning food while it is cooking ○ *a pancake turner* **2.** LATHE OPERATOR somebody whose job involves operating a lathe

Tur·ner /túrnər/, **J.M.W.** (1775–1851) English painter and watercolorist. His powerful landscape and seascape paintings used color to explore the effects of light, and influenced the French impressionists. His works include *Hannibal and his Army Crossing the Alps* (1812) and *Rain, Steam, and Speed* (1844). Full name **Joseph Mallord William Turner**

Tur·ner, John Napier (*b.* 1929) Canadian statesman. He was a Liberal member of the Canadian parliament (1962–75), and as leader of the Liberal Party (1984–90) was prime minister of Canada for 11 weeks in 1984.

Tur·ner, Lana (1920–95) U.S. actor. She is known for her roles in such Hollywood movies as *The Postman Always Rings Twice* (1946) and *The Bad and the Beautiful* (1952). Real name **Julia Jean Mildred Frances Turner**

Tur·ner, Nat (1800–31) U.S. leader of enslaved people. He led a brief rebellion (1831) of enslaved African Americans that ended in bloodshed. He fled, but after six weeks was captured and hanged.

Ted Turner

Tur·ner, Ted (*b.* 1938) U.S. business executive and philanthropist. He built Turner Broadcasting System into an international media empire. Full name **Robert Edward Turner III**

Tur·ner's syn·drome *n.* an inherited disorder affecting women, caused by an absence or abnormality of one of the two X chromosomes and resulting in an underdeveloped womb, vagina, and breasts, and infertility. It may also cause short stature, webbed neck skin, and irregularly shaped ears. [Mid-20thC. Named for Henry Hubert *Turner* (1892–1970), the U.S. physician who described the syndrome.]

turn·er·y /túrnəree/ (*plural* **-ies**) *n.* **1.** WORK ON LATHE the technique, art, or skill of forming and contouring using a lathe **2.** WORKSHOP a room or building where lathes are used

turn·ing /túrning/ *n.* **1.** *U.K.* = **turn** *n.* 3 **2.** DEVIATION a deviation from a straight or planned course **3.** = **turnery** *n.* 1 **4.** SEW FABRIC THAT FORMS HEM the amount of fabric that will be turned back to form a hem at the edge of a piece of sewing

turn·ing cir·cle *n. U.K.* = **turning radius**

turn·ing point *n.* **1.** IMPORTANT MOMENT OF CHANGE a particular time or incident that marks the beginning of a completely new, and usually better, stage in somebody's life or in the development of something **2.** MATH POINT ON CURVE a minimum or maximum point on a plane curve

turn·ing ra·di·us *n.* the smallest circle in which a vehicle can complete a 360-degree turn

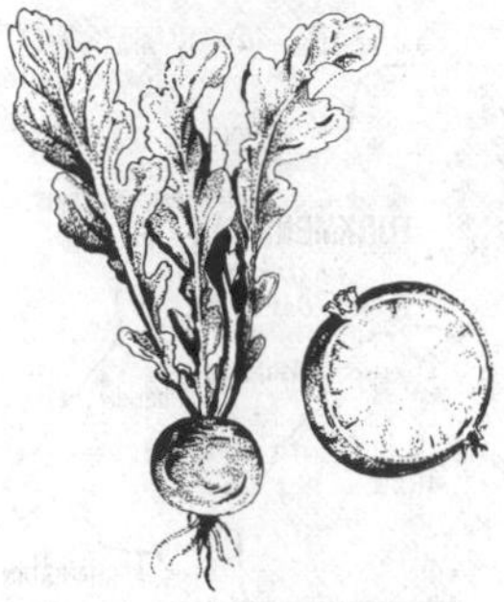

Turnip

tur·nip /túrnip/ *n.* **1.** PLANT WITH EDIBLE ROOT a plant belonging to the cabbage family, widely cultivated for its large white edible root. Latin name: *Brassica rapa.* **2.** ROOT VEGETABLE the white rounded fleshy root of the turnip that is eaten as a vegetable [Mid-16thC. Formed from *tur-* (of unknown origin) + Old English *nǣp* "turnip" (from Latin *napus*).]

tur·nip moth *n.* a brownish moth of Europe, Asia, and Africa whose caterpillar feeds on the stem base and roots of turnips, carrots, and similar plants. Latin name: *Agrotis segetum.*

turn·key /túrn kèe/ *adj.* READY TO USE complete and ready to use upon delivery or installation ○ *a turnkey operation* ■ *n.* (*plural* **-keys**) KEEPER OF KEYS a keeper of keys, especially in a jail (*archaic*)

turn·off *n.* **1.** SOMETHING DISGUSTING OR OFF-PUTTING somebody or something that causes a complete loss of interest, enthusiasm, or sexual arousal (*informal*) **2.** ROAD JUNCTION a junction formed by two roads, especially a larger and smaller one **3.** ROAD BRANCHING OFF MAIN ROAD a road that branches off a main road

turn-on *n.* somebody or something that causes sexual arousal (*informal*)

turn·out /túrn òwt/ *n.* **1.** ATTENDANCE the number of people who attend or take part in a particular event ○ *expecting a huge turnout for the homecoming game* **2.** POL NUMBER OF VOTERS the number or proportion of voters who register their vote in an election **3.** TRANSP WIDENED PART OF STREET a section where a narrow roadway is broader, allowing vehicles to pass each other, pull over, or park **4.** BUSINESS AMOUNT OF WORK PRODUCED the total quantity or amount produced, e.g., by a particular company or manufacturing process **5.** CLOTHES OUTFIT the clothes or equipment somebody is wearing ○ *a smart turnout* **6.** BALLET OUTWARD ROTATION OF DANCER'S LEGS the outward rotating movement from the hip sockets of a classical ballet dancer's legs

turn·o·ver /túrn ōvər/ *n.* **1.** COOK FILLED PASTRY a filled pastry, made by folding a square or circle of pastry in half over a filling to form a semicircle or triangle **2.** FIN AMOUNT OF BUSINESS the amount of business transacted over a given period of time, especially when expressed as gross revenue **3.** HR CHANGE IN EMPLOYEES the number of employees in an organization who leave and are replaced over a given period ○ *job dissatisfaction that results in high turnover* **4.** SPORTS LOSS OF POSSESSION in basketball and football, a loss of possession of the ball resulting from error or violation of rules ■ *adj.* ABLE TO BE FOLDED OVER designed to be turned or folded over

turn·pike /túrn pīk/ *n.* **1.** TRANSP TOLL ROAD a toll expressway or highway, usually a major long-distance one **2.** HIST ROAD BARRIER a gate formerly used to bar the way onto a section of road or a bridge until a toll had been paid **3.** HIST ROAD WITH TURNPIKE in former times, a road that travelers were only allowed to use after paying a toll at the turnpike [14thC. From TURN + PIKE[4].]

turn·sole /túrn sōl/ *n.* **1.** PLANTS MEDITERRANEAN PLANT YIELDING PURPLE DYE a Mediterranean annual plant that yields a purple dye. Latin name: *Chrozophora tinctoria.* **2.** INDUST PURPLE DYE the purple dye obtained from the turnsole plant [14thC. Via Old French *tournesole* from Old Italian *tornasole,* from *tornare* "to turn" + *sol* "sun."]

turn·stile /túrn stīl/ *n.* a mechanical barrier designed to let people pass through a narrow opening one at a time between bars that revolve around a central post

turn·stone /túrn stōn/ *n.* a wading bird with mottled black or tortoiseshell markings that breeds along Arctic coasts and migrates southward for the winter. Genus: *Arenaria.* [Late 17thC. From the way the bird turns over stones to expose the small creatures it feeds on.]

turn·ta·ble /túrn tàyb'l/ *n.* **1. REVOLVING PLATFORM ON PHONOGRAPH** the flat round revolving plate on which the record rests on a phonograph **2. PHONOGRAPH DECK** a phonograph deck, especially without the amplifier and speakers, and as distinct from a separate tape player, compact disk player, or tuner **3.** TRANSP **ROTATING PLATFORM** a rotating platform for turning around a vehicle such as a railroad locomotive, so that it is facing another direction

turn·up *n.* **1.** *U.K.* CLOTHES **FOLD AT BOTTOM OF TROUSER LEG** a fold of material that is turned up at the bottom of a trouser leg **2. SOMETHING TURNING UP** something that turns up or appears unexpectedly **3.** = **upturn** *n.* ■ *adj.* **FOR TURNING UP** designed to be folded or turned up

tur·pen·tine /túrpən tīn/ *n.* **1. SUBSTANCE FROM PINE TREES** a viscous substance obtained from coniferous trees and used to manufacture turpentine **2. STICKY SUBSTANCE FROM TEREBINTH TREE** a brownish-yellow sticky mixture of essential oil and resin that comes from the terebinth tree **3. OIL USED AS SOLVENT** a colorless, flammable, strong-smelling essential oil used as a paint solvent and in medicine ■ *vt.* (**-tined, -tin·ing, -tines**) **1. TREAT SOMETHING WITH TURPENTINE** to treat or thin something with turpentine **2. EXTRACT TURPENTINE FROM** to extract turpentine from trees [14thC. Via Old French *terbentine* "terebinth resin" from, ultimately, Greek *terebinthos* "terebinth tree."]

tur·pen·tine tree *n.* a tree such as the terebinth that yields turpentine

tur·pi·tude /túrpə tòod/ *n.* extreme immorality or wickedness (*formal or literary*) [15thC. Directly or via French from Latin *turpitudo,* from *turpis* "repulsive," of unknown origin.]

turps /turps/ *n.* (*informal*) **1. TURPENTINE** turpentine **2.** *Aus* BEVERAGES **ALCOHOL** beer or other alcoholic drink [Early 19thC. Shortening.]

tur·quoise /túr kwòyz, -kòyz/ *n.* **1. SEMIPRECIOUS STONE** a greenish-blue mineral form of aluminum and copper phosphate that occurs in igneous rocks and is used as a gemstone **2. GREENISH-BLUE COLOR** a bright greenish-blue color ■ *adj.* **GREENISH-BLUE** of a greenish-blue color [15thC. From Old French *(pierre) turqueise* "Turkish (stone)"; so called because the stone was first found in Turkestan.]

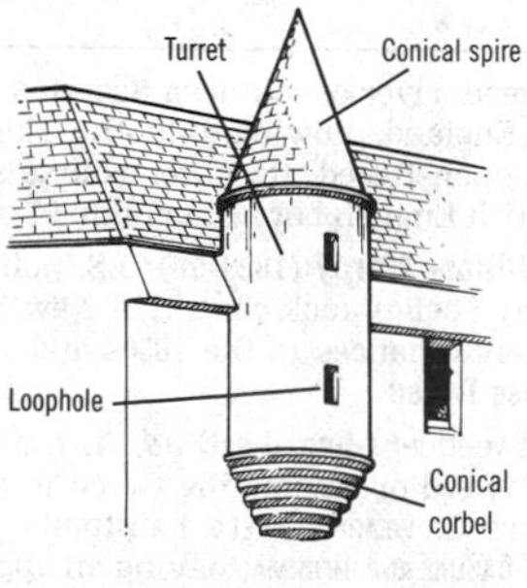

Turret

tur·ret /túrrət/ *n.* **1.** INDUST **DOME CONTAINING GUN** a rotating armored structure on a ship or tank, or a plexiglass dome projecting from the fuselage of an aircraft, containing one or more guns and a gun crew **2. SMALL TOWER** a small rounded tower that projects from a wall or corner of a large building such as a castle **3.** MECH ENG **PART OF LATHE** a device on a lathe, used for holding a range of tools [14thC. From Old French *tourete,* literally "small tower," from *tour* (see TOWER).]

tur·ret·ed /túrrətəd/ *adj.* **1. HAVING TURRETS** constructed or designed to include turrets **2.** ZOOL **WITH SPIRAL SHAPE** shaped like a long pointed spiral

tur·ret lathe *n.* a lathe for long work pieces, using a large number of tools carried on the revolving tool holder or turret

tur·tle[1] /túrt'l/ *n.* **1.** ZOOL **REPTILE WITH SHELL** a water- or land-dwelling reptile such as a tortoise or terrapin with a body protected by a bony shell **2.** *U.K.* ZOOL = **sea turtle 3.** FOOD **TURTLE MEAT** the flesh of any edible type of turtle [Mid-16thC. Origin uncertain: perhaps via

Turtle

French *tortue* "tortoise" from medieval Latin *tortuca,* of uncertain origin.] ◇ **turn turtle** to turn upside down

tur·tle[2] /túrt'l/ *n.* a turtledove (*archaic*) [Old English *turtla.* From Latin *turtur,* an imitation of the bird's voice.]

tur·tle·back /túrt'l bàk/ *n.* an arched cover for protecting the deck of a ship in heavy seas

tur·tle·dove /túrt'l dùv/ *n.* **1. DOVE WITH PURRING COO** a slender dove with black-and-chestnut upper parts, a pink breast, and a black-and-white neck, noted for its purring call. It breeds in northern Europe and winters in Africa. Latin name: *Streptopelia turtur.* **2. DEAR PERSON** a tender, faithful, and affectionate person or an affectionate address for somebody the speaker is very fond of (*archaic or literary*) **3.** = **mourning dove** [13thC. Formed from TURTLE[2].]

tur·tle·head /túrt'l hèd/ (*plural* **-heads** *or* **-head**) *n.* a perennial plant of eastern North America that bears clusters of white, purplish, greenish, or yellowish flowers and is found near running water. Genus: *Chelone.* [Mid-19thC. From the shape of the plant's flowers.]

tur·tle·neck /túrt'l nèk/ *n.* **1. HIGH TURNED-OVER COLLAR** a tight-fitting collar on a garment such as a sweater, reaching high up the neck and then folded down **2. SWEATER WITH TURTLENECK** a sweater or other garment that has a turtleneck

turves plural of **turf**

Tus·ca·loo·sa /tuskə lóossə/ city in western Alabama on the Black Warrior River, southwest of Birmingham. Population: 82,379 (1996).

Tus·can /túskən/ *adj.* **1. OF TUSCANY** relating to the Italian region of Tuscany, or its people or culture **2.** ARCHIT **OF STYLE OF ARCHITECTURE** relating to a classical order of architecture characterized by plain bases and capitals and unfluted columns ■ *n.* **1.** PEOPLES **SOMEBODY FROM TUSCANY** somebody who was born or lives in the Italian region of Tuscany **2.** LANG **STANDARD ITALIAN** the standard and literary form of Italian, principally based on the dialect of Florence [14thC. Via Old French from, ultimately, Latin *Tuscus* "Etruscan."]

Tus·ca·ny /túskənee/ region in northern Italy, a centre of culture during the Renaissance period. Capital: Florence. Population: 3,526,031 (1995). Area: 8,878 sq. mi./22,993 sq. km.

Tus·ca·ro·ra /tùskə ráwrə/ (*plural* **-ra** *or* **-ras**) *n.* PEOPLES a member of a Native North American people who originally occupied lands in North Carolina, and whose members now live mainly in New York State and Ontario. In 1722 the Tuscarora joined the Iroquois Confederacy, which then became known as the Six Nations. [Mid-17thC. From Iroquois, literally "hemp gatherer."]

tu·sche /tóoshə/ *n.* a thick black liquid that is used as a drawing medium in lithography and as a resist in silk-screen printing and etching [Late 19thC. From German, a back-formation from *tuschen* "to draw in ink," via French *toucher* from Old French *touchier* (see TOUCH).]

tush[1] /tòosh/ *n.* somebody's buttocks (*slang*) [Mid-20thC. Alteration of Yiddish *tokhes* (see TOKHES).]

tush[2] /tush/ *interj.* an expression of mild disapproval or disdain (*archaic*) [Mid-16thC. An imitation of a spontaneous exclamation.]

tush·er·y /túsharee/ *n.* an affected style of writing full of artificial and archaic-sounding expressions, such as "Tush!" (*literary*) [Late 19thC. Coined from TUSH[2] by Robert Louis STEVENSON.]

tush·y /túshee/ (*plural* **-ies**), **tush·ie** *n.* = **tush** (*slang*)

tusk /tusk/ *n.* **1.** ZOOL **ENLARGED TOOTH** an enlarged pointed front tooth that projects from the mouth in animals such as the elephant, walrus, and wild boar and is often used for fighting **2.** JOINERY **TENON JOINT** in joinery, a form of tenon that has a short projecting part to make it stronger ■ *vti.* (**tusked, tusk·ing, tusks**) **JAB TUSK INTO SOMEBODY OR SOMETHING** to use a tusk or tusks to attack, dig at, or stab somebody or something [Old English *tūsc, tux.* Ultimately from an Indo-European word meaning "tooth" that is also the ancestor of English *tooth* and *dental.*] —**tusked** *adj.*

Tus·ke·gee /tùskə jée/ city in eastern Alabama, east of Montgomery and west of Phenix City. Population: 11,504 (1996).

tusk·er /túskər/ *n.* a wild boar, elephant, or other animal with large tusks (*informal*)

tusk shell *n.* = **tooth shell**

tus·sah /tússə/ (*plural* **-sahs** *or* **-sah**) *n.* **1. SILKWORM** the silkworm of an Asian moth, from which a coarse silk is obtained. Latin name: *Antheraea paphia.* **2. SILK THREAD** the silk thread produced by the tussah silkworm **3. SILK FABRIC** the silk fabric woven from tussah. It is a coarse brownish or yellowish fabric with an attractive uneven surface. [Late 16thC. Via Hindi *tasar* from Sanskrit *tasaram* "shuttle," from the shape of the worm's cocoon.]

Tus·saud /tü sṓ, too-/, **Madame** (1760–1850) Swiss wax-modeler. She made death masks in Paris of victims of the French Revolution, which she exhibited in Great Britain, and founded Madame Tussaud's Exhibition in London (1835). Born **Marie Grosholtz**

tus·sis /tússiss/ *n.* a cough or coughing (*technical*) [From Latin] —**tus·sal** *adj.* —**tus·sive** *adj.*

tus·sle /túss'l/ *vi.* (**-sled, -sling, -sles**) **HAVE VIGOROUS FIGHT** to have a vigorous physical or verbal struggle with somebody ■ *n.* **VIGOROUS FIGHT** a vigorous physical or verbal struggle [15thC. Origin uncertain: probably formed from a northern English dialect word meaning "to pull about."]

tus·sock /tússək/ *n.* a small thick clump of growing vegetation, usually coarse grass or sedge [Mid-16thC. Origin uncertain.] —**tus·sock·y** *adj.*

tus·sock grass *n.* any of various grasses that grow in clumps

tus·sock moth *n.* a moth whose caterpillars are covered in tufts of brightly colored hairs. They often cause skin irritation if handled, and some are pests of crops and shade trees. Family: Lymantriidae.

tus·sore /tú sàwr/ (*plural* **-sores** *or* **-sore**) *n.* = **tussah** [Early 17thC. From Hindi *tasar* (see TUSSAH).]

tut /tut/, **tut-tut** *interj.* **EXPRESSION OF IRRITATION OR DISAPPROVAL** a clicking sound made with the tongue, or a spoken imitation of this sound, used as an expression of annoyance or disapproval, sometimes ironically ■ *vi.* (**tut·ted, tut·ting, tuts; tut-tut·ted, tut-tut·ting, tut-tuts**) **EXPRESS DISAPPROVAL** to make a clicking sound with the tongue to express annoyance or dissatisfaction, or to express these feelings in some other way [Early 16thC. An imitation of a spontaneous exclamation.]

Tutankhamen

Tu·tan·kha·men /tòot'n kaámən/, **Tu·tan·kha·mun** /tòot'n kaa móon/ (1343–1325 B.C.) Egyptian pharaoh. His sumptuously decorated tomb was discovered virtually intact in 1922.

tu·tee /too tée/ *n.* the student of a particular tutor, or somebody being tutored [Early 20thC. Formed from TUTOR + -EE.]

tu·te·lage /tóot'lij/ *n.* **1.** TEACHING instruction and guidance provided by somebody such as a tutor ○ *Under her tutelage, he became a first-rate marksman.*

2. SUPERVISION BY A TUTOR the condition of being supervised or protected by a tutor or guardian ○ *continued my studies under private tutelage* **3.** BEING A TUTOR the condition of being a tutor or guardian [Early 17thC. Formed from Latin *tutela* "guardianship," from *tut-*, the past participle stem of *tueri* "to watch over" (source of English *tutor*).]

tu·te·lar·y /tóot'l èrree/, **tu·te·lar** /tóot'lər/ *adj.* (*formal or literary*) **1.** ACTING AS PROTECTOR acting in the role of a protector or guardian ○ *tutelary saints* **2.** OF GUARDIAN relating to or belonging to a guardian ■ *n.* (*plural* **-ies**) GUARDING PRESENCE a tutelary being or person, especially a saint or deity (*literary*) [Early 17thC. From Latin *tutelarius*, from *tutela* (see TUTELAGE).]

tu·tor /tóotər/ *n.* **1.** TEACHER a teacher who instructs an individual student, or a small group of students, especially one teaching students in need of remedial work **2.** BRITISH UNIVERSITY TEACHER in British universities, an academic who is responsible for teaching and advising an allocated group of students **3.** LOW-RANKING U.S. UNIVERSITY TEACHER in some U.S. universities, a teacher ranking below an instructor ■ *v.* (**-tored, -tor·ing, -tors**) **1.** *vti.* ACT AS TUTOR to act as a tutor to somebody or in a particular discipline **2.** *vi.* RECEIVE PRIVATE LESSONS to study under a tutor [14thC. Via Anglo-Norman from Latin *tutor* "guardian," from *tut-*, the past participle stem of *tueri* "to watch over."] — **tu·tor·age** *n.* —**tu·tor·ship** *n.*

WORD KEY: SYNONYMS

See Synonyms at ***teach***.

tu·to·ri·al /too táwree əl/ *n.* **1.** LESSON FROM BOOK a chapter of a book or manual, or a section of a computer program, designed to provide instruction or training using exercises and assignments **2.** LESSON WITH TUTOR a teaching session spent individually or in a small group under the direction of a tutor ■ *adj.* RELATING TO TUTOR relating to or belonging to a tutor, or to the role and responsibilities of a tutor

Tut·si /tóotsee/ (*plural* **-si** *or* **-sis**) *n.* PEOPLES a member of a people living in Rwanda and Burundi, where they are one of the minority ethnic groups. ◊ **Hutu** [Mid-20thC. Of Bantu origin.]

tut·ti /tóotee/ *n.* the part of a concerto or other orchestral composition in which all the musicians play, as opposed to a solo section [Early 18thC. Via Italian from, ultimately, Latin *totus* (see TOTAL).]

tut·ti-frut·ti /tóotee fróotee/ (*plural* **tut·ti-frut·tis**) *n.* an ice cream, dessert, or type of candy containing a variety of chopped, usually dried or candied, fruit [Mid-19thC. From Italian, literally "all fruits."]

tut-tut *interj., vi.* = **tut**

tu·tu /tóo tòo/ *n.* a ballet dancer's skirt that is very short and made of layers of stiffened net so that it stands out from the body [Early 20thC. From French, a baby-talk alteration of *cucu*, from *cul* "buttocks," from Latin *culus* (source of English *culottes* and *recoil*).]

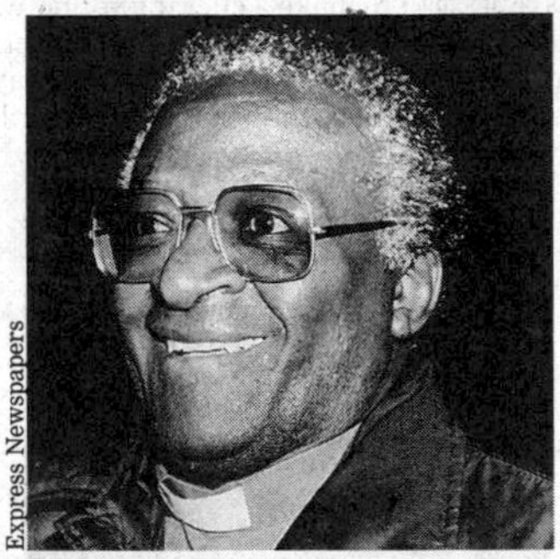

Express Newspapers

Desmond Tutu

Tu·tu /tóotoo/, **Desmond** (*b.* 1931) South African clergyman and political activist. A leader of the anti-apartheid movement, he became bishop of Johannesburg in 1984, and was archbishop of Cape Town (1986–96). In 1995 he was appointed chair of the Truth and Reconciliation Committee set up to investigate political and human rights crimes of the apartheid era. Full name **Desmond Mpilo Tutu**

Tu·va·lu /too vaáloo, tòova lóo/ small country consisting of coral islands in the western Pacific Ocean. Fiji and Samoa, each about 650 mi./1,050 km away, are the islands' nearest neighbors. Language: English, Tuvaluan. Currency: Australian dollar. Capital: Fongafale. Population: 10,297 (1997). Area:

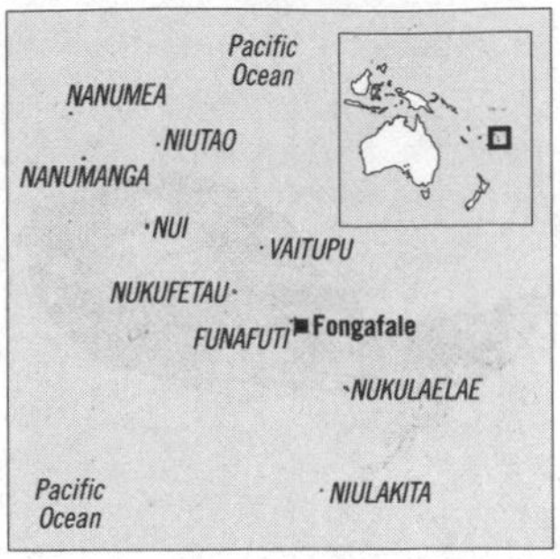

Tuvalu

10 sq. mi./26 sq. km. Former name **Ellice Islands** — **Tu·val·uan** /too vaáloo ən, tòova lóo ən/ *n., adj.*

tux /tuks/ *n.* a tuxedo (*informal*) [Early 20thC. Shortening.]

tux·e·do /tuk séedō/ (*plural* **-dos** *or* **-does**) *n.* **1.** MAN'S FORMAL JACKET an elegantly styled, usually black jacket worn by men to formal social occasions, especially as part of an outfit for evening wear **2.** MEN'S FORMAL CLOTHING a formal set of clothing for a man including a tuxedo jacket and matching trousers, usually with a band of silk down each leg, dress shirt, bow tie, and cummerbund [Late 19thC. Named for the town of *Tuxedo* Park, New York, where the garment was first worn at a country club.]

tu·yère /too yáir, twee yáir/, **twy·er** /twīr/ *n.* an opening in the refractory lining and shell of a furnace through which air is forced to promote combustion [Late 18thC. From French, formed from *tuyau* "pipe," of uncertain origin: probably from Germanic.]

TV[1] *n.* television or a television set (*informal*)

TV[2] *abbr.* transvestite (*informal*)

TVA *abbr.* Tennessee Valley Authority

TV din·ner *n.* a pre-cooked frozen or chilled meal that can be reheated in the oven or microwave and eaten straight from the tray or dish usually while watching TV

Tver /tvair/ city at the confluence of the Volga and Tvertsa rivers in western Russia. Population: 454,000 (1990). Former name **Kalinin** (1933–90)

TV mov·ie *n.* a movie that is made to be shown on television and is not usually released in theaters

TVP *n.* a high-protein product made from processed soya beans that are formed into chunks or ground and flavored to taste like meat. Full form **textured vegetable protein**

T-W *abbr.* three-wheeler (motorcycle)

twa /twaa/ *n. Scotland* two [Scots dialect variant of TWO]

twad·dle /twaád'l/ *n.* NONSENSE nonsensical or pretentious speech or writing (*informal*) ■ *vi.* (**-dled, -dling, -dles**) TALK TWADDLE to speak or write twaddle (*dated informal*) [Late 18thC. Origin uncertain.] — **twad·dler** /twaádlər/ *n.*

twain /twayn/ *npl.* two (*archaic or literary*) ○ *"Oh, East is East, and West is West, and never the twain shall meet."* (Rudyard Kipling, *The Ballad of East and West*) [Old English *twēgen*]

Library of Congress

Mark Twain

Twain /twayn/, **Mark** (1835–1910) U.S. writer. He wrote humorous travel books and the classic stories *The Adventures of Tom Sawyer* (1876) and *The Adventures of Huckleberry Finn* (1884). Pseudonym of **Samuel Langhorne Clemens**

twang /twang/ *n.* **1.** SOUND OF TIGHT STRING VIBRATING the sharp resonating noise made when something such as a tight string on an instrument is plucked or released **2.** LANG SOUND IN CERTAIN ACCENTS a nasal quality of voice associated with various accents ○ *a Texas twang* ■ *vti.* (**twanged, twang·ing, twangs**) **1.** VIBRATE WITH A TWANG to make a twang or cause something to make a twang **2.** MUSIC STRUM SOMETHING CARELESSLY to play a stringed instrument, or a tune on a stringed instrument, in a rough amateur style **3.** LANG SPEAK WITH A TWANG to speak or say something with a twang [Mid-16thC. An imitation of the sound.] —**twang·y** *adj.*

'twas /twuz, twəz/ *contr.* it was (*archaic or literary*)

twat /twot/ *n.* (*taboo offensive*) **1.** OFFENSIVE TERM a highly offensive term used to refer to a woman's vagina or genital area **2.** *U.K.* OFFENSIVE TERM a highly offensive term used to refer to somebody regarded as unintelligent, worthless, or detestable [Mid-17thC. Origin unknown.]

tway·blade /twáy blàyd/ *n.* an orchid that has only two leaves, arranged opposite each other, at the base. Genera: *Listera* and *Liparis* and *Ophrys.* [Late 16thC. Formed from an obsolete variant of TWAIN + BLADE.]

tweak /tweek/ *vt.* (**tweaked, tweak·ing, tweaks**) **1.** TWIST SOMETHING QUICKLY to take hold of something between the finger and thumb and twist it sharply **2.** ADJUST SOMETHING SLIGHTLY to make a slight adjustment or change in something, especially in order to improve it or fix it (*informal*) ○ *tweaked the engine to refine its performance* ■ *n.* **1.** SHARP PINCH a sharp pinch or twist **2.** SLIGHT ADJUSTMENT a slight adjustment or change in something, especially in order to improve it or fix it [Early 17thC. Origin uncertain: probably a variant of obsolete *twick*, from Old English *twiccian*.] —**tweak·y** *adj.*

twee /twee/ *adj. U.K.* dainty or pretty in an overdone and affected way [Early 20thC. Baby-talk alteration of SWEET.] —**twee·ly** *adv.* —**twee·ness** *n.*

tweed /tweed/ *n.* WOOLEN CLOTH a fairly rough, thick woolen fabric used for warm clothing and often made with several different shades of wool to give it a distinctive flecked appearance ■ **tweeds** *npl.* CLOTHES MADE OF TWEED a tweed suit, an outfit, or clothes made of tweed [Mid-19thC. Alteration of *tweel*, a Scottish variant of TWILL, under the influence of the name of the river *Tweed*.]

WORD KEY: ORIGIN

Early accounts date the coinage of ***tweed*** to 1831, and ascribe it to the London cloth merchant James Locke (although Locke himself in his book *Tweed and Don* (1860) does not make any such claim). The term was in general use by 1850, and it was registered as a trademark.

Tweed /tweed/ river of southern Scotland and northeastern England, flowing into the North Sea at Berwick-upon-Tweed. Its lower course runs along the Scottish-English border. Length: 97 mi./160 km.

Tweed, William Marcy (1823–78) U.S. politician. His Tammany Society took control of New York City's politics and finances in the 1850s and 1860s. Nickname **Boss Tweed**

tweed·y /tweédee/ (**-i·er, -i·est**) *adj.* **1.** TEXTILES OF TWEED made of tweed or resembling tweed in appearance or texture **2.** WEARING TWEED habitually dressed in tweed **3.** CASUAL AND INFORMAL having an appearance or manner that is casual and somewhat disordered, often associated with academics or people who are fond of the outdoors —**tweed·i·ness** *n.*

'tween /tween/ *contr.* between (*archaic or literary*) [13thC. Shortening.]

tweet /tweet/ *n.* SOUND MADE BY BIRD a light high-pitched note, especially one sung by a small bird ■ *vi.* (**tweet·ed, tweet·ing, tweets**) MAKE SOUND OF SMALL BIRD to make the light high-pitched sound of a small bird [Mid-19thC. An imitation of the sound.]

tweet·er /tweétər/ *n.* a loudspeaker used to reproduce high-frequency sounds, e.g., in a hi-fi system. ◊ **woofer**

tweeze /tweez/ (**tweezed, tweez·ing, tweez·es**) *vt.* to pull out or manipulate something using tweezers [Mid-20thC. Back-formation from TWEEZERS.]

tweez·ers /tweézərz/, **tweezer** /tweézər/ *npl.* a metal tool consisting of two narrow slightly curved arms joined at one end, typically used for extracting or holding small objects [Mid-17thC. Alteration of obsolete *tweeze* "tweezer case," from French *étuis*, plural of *étui* (see ÉTUI).]

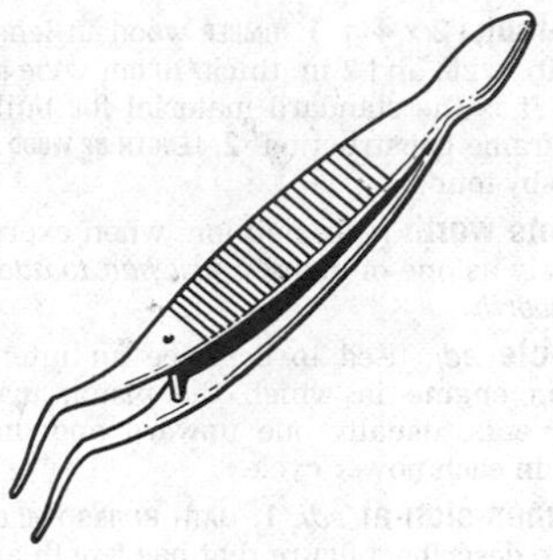

Tweezers

twelfth /twelfth/ *n.* one of twelve equal parts of something [Old English *twelfta.* Ultimately from the prehistoric Germanic base of English *twelve.*] —**twelfth** *adj., adv.*

Twelfth Day *n.* = **Epiphany**

Twelfth Night *n.* CALENDAR January 5, the day before Epiphany in the Christian calendar, or the evening of that day. It was formerly a time of special celebration at the end of the Christmas season.

twelve /twelv/ *n.* **1. NUMBER 12** the number 12 **2. SOMETHING WITH VALUE OF 12** something in a numbered series with a value of twelve **3. GROUP OF TWELVE** a group of twelve objects or people [Old English *twelf.* Ultimately from a prehistoric Germanic compound meaning literally "two left," that is "two left beyond ten."] —**twelve** *adj., pron.*

Twelve A·pos·tles, the Twelve *n.* eleven of the twelve followers originally chosen by Jesus Christ, according to the Bible, together with Matthias who was chosen to replace Judas

twelve-mile lim·it *n.* an offshore boundary 12 miles from a country's coast, claimed by some countries as marking the territorial limit of their jurisdiction in order to safeguard fishing rights and limit the approach of foreign vessels. ◊ **three-mile limit**

twelve·mo /twélv mō/ (*plural* **-mos**) *n.* = **duodecimo** [Early 18thC. Spelling of the abbreviation *12mo.*]

twelve·month /twélv mùnth/ *n.* a year (*archaic*) [Old English *twelf monaþ*]

twelve·pen·ny nail /twélv pènni-/ *n.* a nail that is $3\frac{1}{4}$ in./8.25 cm long [From the original cost of the nails per hundred]

twelve-step pro·gram *n.* a program for recovery from addiction, based on the methods of Alcoholics Anonymous and involving gradual self-improvement techniques

Twelve Ta·bles *n.* the earliest code of Roman law on civil, criminal, and religious matters, dating back to 451–450 B.C.

twelve-tone *adj.* MUSIC relating to or using compositional techniques based on strict sequences of notes selected from the 12 notes of the chromatic scale

twelve-tone row *n.* MUSIC = **tone row**

twen·ti·eth /twéntee əth/ *n.* one of twenty equal parts of something [Old English *twentigoþa*] —**twentieth** *adj., adv.*

twen·ty /twéntee/ *n.* (*plural* **-ties**) **1. NUMBER 20** the number 20 **2. GROUP OF 20** a group of twenty objects or people **3.** MONEY **$20 BILL** a bill worth twenty dollars ■ **twenties** *npl.* **1. NUMBERS 20 TO 29** the numbers 20 to 29, particularly as a range of temperature ○ *in the low twenties* **2. YEARS 1920 TO 1929** the years 1920 to 1929 ○ *in the late twenties* **3. PERIOD FROM AGE 20 TO 29** the period of somebody's life from the age of 20 to 29 ○ *when I was in my twenties* [Old English *twēntig,* ultimately from a prehistoric Germanic compound meaning literally "twice ten"] —**twen·ti·eth** *adj., pron.*

twen·ty-first *n.* somebody's 21st birthday

twen·ty-one *n.* = **blackjack**

twen·ty ques·tions *n.* a game in which one player imagines an object and others try to guess what it is by asking questions that can be answered only with "yes" or "no"

twen·ty-twen·ty, 20/20 *adj.* used to describe normal vision or eyesight [From the figures denoting normal eyesight at a distance of 20 feet]

.22 /twènti tóō/ *n.* a gun or rifle that uses a bullet with a diameter of .22 in., typically used for killing small game.

'twere /twur/ *contr.* it were (*archaic or literary*) [Early 17thC. Contraction.]

twerp /twurp/, **twirp** *n.* an offensive term used to refer to somebody who is seen as silly or insignificant (*slang insult*) [Late 19thC. Origin unknown.]

Twi /twee/ (*plural* **Twi** *or* **Twis**) *n.* **1.** PEOPLES **MEMBER OF GHANAIAN PEOPLE** a member of a people who live in southern Ghana **2.** LANG **TWI LANGUAGE** the language of the Twi people, belonging to the Kwa group of Niger-Congo languages, and now generally recognized as a dialect of Akan [Late 19thC. From Kwa.] —**Twi** *adj.*

twi·bill /twī bìl, twīb'l/ *n.* a double-edged battle-ax, formerly used as a weapon [Old English *twibil.* Formed from *twi-* "two" (ultimately) + *bill* "bladed weapon."]

twice /twīss/ *adv.* **1. TWO TIMES** on two occasions, or in two instances **2. DOUBLE** double in amount or degree [Old English *twige.* Ultimately from an Indo-European word that is also the ancestor of English *twilight, twine, bis,* and *di-.*]

twice-laid *adj.* used to describe ropes or cables that are made from previously used rope

twice-told *adj.* familiar or hackneyed through frequent repetition ○ *"Life is as tedious as a twice-told tale"* (William Shakespeare, *King John;* 1623)

twid·dle /twídd'l/ *vti.* (**-dled, -dling, -dles**) **1. TURN SOMETHING BACK AND FORTH** to turn something around or back and forth repeatedly ○ *twiddling the dial on the radio to get better reception* **2. TWIST OR TURN SOMETHING ABSENT-MINDEDLY** to keep twisting something or turning it around in a bored or absent-minded way ○ *sitting at a desk twiddling his pencil and staring out of the window* ■ *n.* **TWISTING ACTION** a to-and-fro turning or twisting action [Mid-16thC. Origin uncertain: perhaps a blend of TWIST and FIDDLE.] —**twid·dler** *n.* —**twid·dly** *adj.*

twig[1] /twig/ *n.* **1. SMALL BRANCH** a small branch or shoot, especially one from a tree or shrub **2. STRUCTURE RESEMBLING A BRANCH** a structure that resembles a branch, e.g., a minute offshoot of a nerve or blood vessel [Old English *twigge,* literally "forked branch." Ultimately from a prehistoric Germanic word.]

twig[2] /twig/ (**twigged, twigged, twig·ging, twigs**) *vti. U.K.* to understand or realize something (*informal*) ○ *finally twigged what was going on* [Mid-18thC. Origin uncertain: perhaps from Irish Gaelic *tuigim* "I understand."]

twig·gy /twíggee/ (**-gi·er, -gi·est**) *adj.* **1. THIN** very thin or fragile ○ *twiggy legs* **2. COVERED IN TWIGS** covered in twigs rather than branches or leaves ○ *a twiggy shrub*

twi·light /twī līt/ *n.* **1. TIME AFTER SUNSET** the time of day just after sunset or before dawn, when the Sun is below the horizon **2. HALF-LIGHT** the faint diffuse light that occurs at twilight. It is caused by the light from the Sun being refracted through the Earth's atmosphere. **3. FINAL PERIOD** the time when something is declining or approaching its end, especially in a gentle or peaceful way ○ *the twilight of the empire* [15thC. Formed from *twi-* "two, half" (from Old English; ultimately) + LIGHT.]

Twi·light of the Gods *n.* = **Götterdämmerung, Ragnarök** [Translation of German *Götterdämmerung*]

twi·light zone *n.* **1. UNCERTAIN STATE** an ambiguous or unsettled state or condition, especially between two opposing conditions **2.** OCEANOG **LOWEST PART OF THE SEA WITH LIGHT** the lowest layer of the sea that natural light can reach

WORD KEY: CULTURAL NOTE

The Twilight Zone, a television series (1959–65) created by U.S. writer Rod Serling. These dramatized fictional tales were the first adult television programs to present paranormal events in a serious and believable way. Staple topics included time travel, accidental journeys, premonitions, and encounters with the dead and with aliens. The series inspired a movie, *Twilight Zone – The Movie* (1983), and was revived sporadically from 1985–87, and run in syndication 1987–88. The expression *twilight zone* has long had the meaning "the lowest layer of the sea's photic zone." The show, however, popularized another preexisting meaning, "an ambiguous area, or gray area, between two opposing conditions, such as life and death, good and evil, or real and unreal."

twi·lit /twī lìt/ *adj.* lit by twilight or a similar kind of half-light, especially when this creates a feeling of mystery [Mid-19thC. Past participle of TWILIGHT, used as a verb.]

twill /twil/ *n.* **1. STRONG FABRIC** a strong woven material with diagonal ridges or ribs across its surface **2. TEXTILE WEAVE** the weave used to produce twill ■ *vt.* (**twilled, twill·ing, twills**) **WEAVE TWILL** to weave fabric with diagonal ridges or ribs across its surface [14thC. From a northern English dialect variant of Old English *twilic,* literally "having two threads." Ultimately from a prehistoric Germanic word.]

'twill /twil/ *contr.* it will (*archaic or literary*) [Mid-17thC. Contraction.]

twin /twin/ *n.* **1. EITHER OF TWO OFFSPRING BORN TOGETHER** either of two people or animals born to the same mother at the same time. Fraternal twins arise from different egg cells and are equivalent to ordinary siblings, while identical twins are derived from the same egg cell and are genetically identical. (*often used before a noun*) ○ *twin boys* **2. ONE OF TWO SIMILAR THINGS** somebody or something similar or identical to another, or unusually closely associated with another **3.** CHEM **COMPOUND CRYSTAL** a compound crystal consisting of two mirror-image crystals that share a common plane ■ *v.* (**twinned, twin·ning, twins**) **1.** *vti.* **PAIR PEOPLE OR THINGS** to group people or things in pairs, or to link them very closely **2.** *vi.* **HAVE TWINS** to give birth to twins [Old English *twinn.* Ultimately from an Indo-European word meaning "two by two" that is also the ancestor of English *binary.*]

twin bed *n.* either of a pair of matching single beds

twin·ber·ry /twín bèrree/ (*plural* **-ries**) *n.* **1.** = **partridgeberry 2. N AMERICAN SHRUB WITH PURPLE FLOWERS** a North American shrub of the honeysuckle family with purple flowers. Latin name: *Lonicera involucrata.*

twin bill *n.* **1.** SPORTS = **double-header 2.** CINEMA = **double feature**

Twin Cit·ies *npl.* the cities of Minneapolis and St. Paul, Minnesota.

twine /twīn/ *n.* **1. STRING** string or cord made from threads or strands that have been twisted together **2. SOMETHING MADE BY TWISTING** something that is formed by twisting or coiling separate strands together **3. TWISTING ACTION** a twisting or weaving action ■ *v.* (**twined, twin·ing, twines**) **1.** *vti.* **TWIST AROUND SOMETHING** to grow, wind, or twist around or together, or make something grow, wind, or twist around something else ○ *the ivy twining around the old oak tree* **2.** *vi.* **HAVE WINDING COURSE** to take or follow a winding route ○ *From the cabin door a path twines through the woods.* **3.** *vt.* **WEAVE SOMETHING** to make something by weaving or twisting separate strands together [Old English *twīn* "double thread." Ultimately from a prehistoric Germanic base that is also the ancestor of English *twice* and *twist.*] —**twin·er** *n.*

Twin Falls /twín fawlz/ city in southern Idaho, on the southern bank of the Snake River, northeast of Boise. Population: 31,989 (1996).

twin·flow·er /twín flòwr/ *n.* a creeping semi-woody North American plant of the honeysuckle family with opposite oval leaves and pairs of pinkish-white bell-shaped flowers. Latin name: *Linnaea borealis.*

twinge /twinj/ *n.* **1. BRIEF PAIN** a sudden brief stab of pain **2. BRIEF UNCOMFORTABLE EMOTION** a brief uncomfortable pang of an emotion such as guilt or fear ■ *vti.* (**twinged, twinge·ing** *or* **twing·ing, twing·es**) **FEEL A TWINGE** to feel a twinge, or make somebody feel a twinge, either physical or emotional [Old English *twengan* "to pinch." Ultimately from prehistoric Germanic.]

twi-night dou·ble-head·er /twī nīt dúbb'l hèddər/ *n.* two consecutive baseball games between the same teams, the first beginning in late afternoon and the last ending after dark [Blend of TWILIGHT and NIGHT]

twin·kle /twíngk'l/ *vi.* (**-kled, -kling, -kles**) **1. SHINE WITH FLICKER** to give out or reflect a bright but unsteady light, especially from a small or distant source **2. SHINE WITH AMUSEMENT** to be bright because of a feeling such as amusement, delight, or mischief (*refers to people's eyes*) ■ *n.* **1. FLICKERING SHINE** a bright unsteady light, especially one that is small or seen from a distance **2. BRIGHTNESS IN SOMEBODY'S EYES** a brightness in somebody's eyes, caused by a feeling such as amusement, delight, or mischief **3.** = **twinkling** [Old English *twinclian,* literally "to keep blinking," from *twincan* "to blink," ultimately from prehistoric Germanic] —**twin·kler** *n.* —**twink·ly** *adj.*

twin·kling /twíngkling/ *n.* **MOMENT** an instant of time ■ *adj.* **FLICKERING** giving out or reflecting light brightly but unsteadily, especially from a small or distant source ◇ **in the twinkling of an eye** very quickly or very soon

twin-lens re·flex *n.* a camera that has two forward-facing lenses, one for focusing through and one for taking pictures

twinned /twind/ *adj.* **1. EXISTING AS MATCHING PAIR** linked together as or like a couple **2.** CRYSTALS **SYMMETRICAL** used to describe a compound crystal consisting of two mirror-image crystals that share a common plane

Twins /twinz/ *n.* the constellation or zodiac sign Gemini

twin-screw *adj.* used to describe a ship that has two propellers

twin set *n.* a woman's matching short-sleeved pullover and cardigan designed to be worn together

twin-size, **twin-sized** *adj.* made to the size of a standard single bed, usually 39 x 75 in./99 x 190 cm

twirl /twurl/ *v.* (**twirled, twirl·ing, twirls**) **1.** *vti.* **SPIN AROUND QUICKLY** to turn lightly and rapidly around in a circle, or spin something so that it turns rapidly around and around ○ *twirled his partner around the dance floor* **2.** *vt.* **TURN SOMETHING AROUND** to fiddle with something by turning or spinning it between the fingers **3.** *vi.* **TURN AND FACE OTHER WAY** to turn around suddenly to face somebody or face the other way ○ *She twirled around, her eyes blazing.* **4.** *vti.* **PITCH A BASEBALL** in baseball, to pitch the ball ■ *n.* **1. QUICK SPINNING MOVEMENT** a quick turning or spinning movement, e.g., when somebody is dancing or modeling clothes **2. SPIRAL** a twisting or spiral shape, pattern, or line, especially something used for decoration [Late 16thC. Origin uncertain: probably influenced by *whirl*.] — **twir·ly** *adj.* —**twirl·er** *n.*

twirp *n.* = **twerp**

twist /twist/ *v.* (**twist·ed, twist·ing, twists**) **1.** *vti.* **MAKE ENDS TURN IN OPPOSITE DIRECTIONS** to make one part or end of something turn in the opposite direction from the other, or to turn in this way ○ *I twisted my handkerchief into a knot.* **2.** *vti.* **DISTORT SOMETHING** to distort the shape or position of something, or become distorted ○ *His face was twisted in a grimace of disgust.* **3.** *vti.* **WIND SOMETHING** to wind something, make something wind, or wind things together ○ *twisted the strands of fiber into a rope* **4.** *vt.* **INJURE PART OF BODY** to injure part of the body by turning or moving it out of position ○ *I've twisted my ankle.* **5.** *vti.* **ROTATE SOMETHING** to rotate, or turn something so that it rotates ○ *The lid just twists and comes off.* **6.** *vt.* **DISTORT MEANING** to distort the meaning of something ○ *keeps twisting what I'm saying to make it sound as if I agree* **7.** *vi.* **CONSTANTLY CHANGE DIRECTION** to change direction constantly instead of continuing in a direct or straight line **8.** *vi.* **SQUIRM** to squirm or wriggle ○ *a child twisting restlessly in her chair* **9.** *vi.* **DANCE** to dance the twist ■ *n.* **1. TWISTING MOVEMENT** the action or movement performed when somebody twists something ○ *a twist of the screw* **2. SOMETHING SHAPED BY BEING TWISTED** something that has been shaped, split, or gathered together by being twisted ○ *a twist of paper* **3. UNEXPECTED DEVELOPMENT** an unexpected development in a narrative or a sequence of events ○ *The story had a strange twist.* **4. BEND** a bend in something such as a road or river ○ *a road full of twists and turns* **5.** DANCE **1960S DANCE** a popular 1960s dance that involved twisting the hips **6.** BEVERAGES **SLICE OF LEMON** a thin slice of lemon, lime, or some other peel that is cut and twisted and added to a drink **7.** FOOD **BREAD OR ROLL** a roll or loaf of bread made by twisting pieces of dough **8. PAINFUL WRENCH** a painful wrench or pull in a wrist, ankle, or some other body part **9. LENGTH OF YARN OR THREAD** a length of yarn or thread whose strands have been twisted together **10.** PHYS **FORCE** a force that causes stress or strain by twisting **11.** SPORTS **SPIN GIVEN TO BALL** spin imparted to a hit, thrown, or pitched ball **12.** SPORTS **ROTATION OF THE BODY** a complete turn of the body around a vertical axis, e.g., in gymnastics or diving **13. DISTORTION** a contortion or distortion in the shape of something **14. QUIRK OF CHARACTER** an eccentricity or strange personal characteristic **15. CIGAR OR TOBACCO** a cigar made from three cigars twisted together, or chewing tobacco twisted into a roll [Mid-16thC. From Old English, "something split in two, twisted yarn." Ultimately from a prehistoric Germanic base that is also the ancestor of English *twine* and *twice*.] —**twist·a·bil·i·ty** /twìstə bíllətee/ *n.* —**twist·a·ble** /twístəb'l/ *adj.* — **twistingly** /twístinglee/ *adv.* —**twisty** /twístee/ *adj.*

WORD KEY: CULTURAL NOTE

Oliver Twist, a novel (1837–39) by the English writer Charles Dickens. It tells the tale of an abandoned child who runs away from his workhouse home to London, where he falls in with a band of criminals led by Fagin and his young assistant, a streetwise pickpocket called the Artful Dodger. The novel inspired a musical, *Oliver!* (1960) and several movies, most notably David Lean's 1948 adaptation.

twist drill *n.* a drill bit with one or more helical grooves along its axis to expel cuttings or swarf

twist·ed /twístəd/ *adj.* morally unacceptable ○ *What kind of twisted mind could think up a thing like that?*

twist·er /twístər/ *n.* **1. TORNADO** a tornado, cyclone, or whirlwind (*informal*) **2. SOMEBODY OR SOMETHING THAT TWISTS** a person or device that twists **3.** SPORTS **BALL WITH TWIST** a ball that has been thrown or hit with a twist

twist grip *n.* a control mounted in one of the handlebar grips of a motorcycle or bicycle, allowing the rider to change gear or accelerate by twisting the grip

twist-tie *n.* a piece of wire sealed in a paper or plastic strip, used as a fastener, especially for a plastic bag

twit /twit/ (**twit·ted, twit·ting, twits**) *n.* an offensive term used to refer to somebody who is seen as unthinking or silly (*slang insult*) [Mid-16thC. Shortening of Old English *ætwītan* "to find fault," from *æt-* AT + *wītan* "to reproach," ultimately from a prehistoric Germanic word.] — **twit·ter** *n.*

twitch /twich/ *v.* (**twitched, twitch·ing, twitch·es**) **1.** *vi.* **JERK SLIGHTLY** to move with a slight jerk, either once or repeatedly ○ *His eyebrow twitches when he's nervous.* **2.** *vt.* **PULL SOMETHING LIGHTLY AND QUICKLY** to give something a sudden light tug or jerk **3.** *vi.* **HURT SHARPLY** to hurt with a sharp or sudden pain ■ *n.* **1. JERKY MOVEMENT** a very quick jerky movement **2.** PHYSIOL **MUSCLE CONTRACTION** a brief, rapid contraction of a muscle. ◊ **tic 3.** VET **HORSE RESTRAINT** a restraint used on a horse during a veterinary procedure, consisting of a cord loop that can be pulled tight around the animal's upper lip [12thC. Origin uncertain: possibly from Low German.]

twitch grass *n.* = **couch grass** [Alteration of *quitch (grass)*]

twitch·y /twíchee/ (**-i·er, -i·est**) *adj.* **1. NERVOUS** nervous and jittery **2. TWITCHING** twitching frequently

twit·ter /twíttər/ *v.* (**-tered, -ter·ing, -ters**) **1.** *vi.* **CHIRP** to sing in a succession of light high-pitched chirping sounds (*refers to birds*) **2.** *vi.* **CHATTER** to chatter or giggle in an overexcited or nervous way **3.** *vti.* **USE SMALL HIGH VOICE** to sing or say something in a light shaky high-pitched voice **4.** *vi.* **TREMBLE** to quiver or move about nervously and quickly ■ *n.* **1. REPETITIVE HIGH-PITCHED SONG** a continuous light string of high sounds made by a small bird or other small animal **2. EXCITEMENT** a state of great agitation or excitement ○ *all of a twitter* [14thC. Originally an imitation of birds chirping.] —**twit·ter·er** *n.* —**twit·ter·y** *adj.*

'twixt /twikst/ *prep.* betwixt (*archaic*)

twiz·zle /twízz'l/ *vt.* (**-zled, -zling, -zles**) **TWIRL SOMETHING** to twirl or twist something vigorously ■ *n.* **TWIRLING MOVEMENT** a vigorous twirl or twist [Late 18thC. Origin uncertain: probably an alteration of TWIST or TWIRL.]

two /too/ (*plural* **twos**) *n.* **1. NUMBER 2** the number 2 **2. SOMETHING WITH VALUE OF 2** something in a numbered series, e.g., a playing card, with a value of 2 ○ *the two of clubs* **3. GROUP OF TWO** a group of two objects or people ○ *arrived in twos and threes* [Old English *twā*. Ultimately from the Indo-European word for "two"that is also the ancestor of English *dual*, *dyad*, and *binary*.] —**two** *adj.*, *pron.* ◇ **it takes two to tango** used to indicate that both of the people involved in an awkward or unpleasant situation, not just one, are responsible or to blame ◇ **put two and two together** to work something out from the available evidence ◇ **that makes two of us** used to indicate agreement with something expressed, or acknowledgment of something shared

two-bag·ger *n.* BASEBALL a two-base hit (*slang*)

two-base hit *n.* BASEBALL a hit that enables a batter to reach second base

two-bit *adj.* **1. CHEAP** of very low quality or importance (*informal*) **2. 25-CENT** costing or worth 25 cents (*archaic*)

two-by-four, **2 x 4** *n.* **1. TIMBER** wood in lengths that are 4 in. wide and 2 in. thick/10 cm wide and 5 cm thick. It is the standard material for buildings of wood-frame construction. **2. LENGTH OF WOOD** a length of two-by-four

two cents worth *n.* an opinion, when expressed assertively as one of many ○ *just had to add her two cents worth*

two-cy·cle *adj.* used to describe an internal-combustion engine in which the piston makes two movements, usually one upward and one downward, in each power cycle

two-di·men·sion·al *adj.* **1.** MATH **HAVING TWO DIMENSIONS** used to describe a figure that has length and width but no depth, e.g. a geometric figure on a single plane **2.** ARTS **DONE ON A FLAT SURFACE** used to describe works of art such as paintings and drawings that exist on a flat surface, as opposed to art forms such as sculpture that also have depth **3. HAVING NO DEPTH OF CHARACTER** lacking the emotional or psychological depth that creates the impression of realism ○ *a two-dimensional character* —**two-di·men·sion·al·i·ty** *n.* — **two-di·men·sion·al·ly** *adv.*

two-edged *adj.* **1. CUTTING TWO WAYS** having two sharp edges for cutting in opposite directions **2. WORKING TWO WAYS** having two effects, one positive and one negative, especially two possible and opposite interpretations or meanings

two-faced *adj.* **1. HYPOCRITICAL** insincere in dealings with people, especially by being outwardly friendly but secretly disloyal **2. HAVING TWO FACES** having two faces or surfaces —**two-fac·ed·ly** *adv.* —**two-fac·ed·ness** *n.*

two·fer /tóofər/ *n.* an offer of two items for the price of one, or a coupon giving entitlement to such a discount (*informal*) [Late 19thC. Alteration of *two for (one).*]

two-fist·ed *adj.* characterized by energy, enthusiasm, assertiveness, or aggression

two·fold /too fōld/ *adj.* **1. HAVING TWO ELEMENTS** consisting of two parts or elements **2. DOUBLE** twice as much or as many ■ *adv.* **DOUBLY** by the same amount over again

2,4-D *n.* a white crystalline compound used as a weedkiller. Formula: $C_8H_6Cl_2O_3$. [Mid-20thC. *D* from DI-.]

2,4,5-T /too fawr fīv tée/ *n.* a chemical weedkiller and plant hormone in a solid, crystalline, insoluble form. Formula: $C_8H_5Cl_3O_3$. [Mid-20thC. *T* from TRI-.]

two-four time *n.* a rhythm with two quarter-note beats to the measure

two-hand·ed *adj.* **1. USING TWO HANDS** using, or requiring the use of, two hands **2. DESIGNED FOR TWO** designed for two people, especially for two players or operators **3. AMBIDEXTROUS** able to use either the left or right hand with equal skill —**two-hand·ed·ly** *adv.* —**two-hand·ed·ness** *n.*

two-hand·er *n.* **1. TENNIS STROKE** a shot in tennis, usually a backhand, made with two hands gripping the handle of the racket **2. SOMEBODY WHO HITS TWO-HANDERS** somebody who uses a two-handed backhand in tennis

two-mast·er *n.* a sailing ship with two masts

two-name pa·per *n.* a commercial debt whose two signatories are jointly and individually responsible for it

two-pack *n.* a set of two identical products packaged together and sold as one

two·pence /túppəns/, **tup·pence** *n. U.K.* the value of two pence, especially two pennies in the pre-decimal British monetary system

two·pen·ny /túppənee, too pènnee/, **tup·pen·ny** /túp pənee/*adj.* **1. TWO-CENT** costing or worth two cents **2. CHEAP** cheap and of the poorest quality **3. BEING ONE INCH LONG** used to describe a nail that is one inch long

two-phase *adj.* used to describe an electrical system in which there are two alternating voltages of the same frequency, with a phase difference of 90° between them

two-piece *adj.* **BEING IN TWO PARTS** consisting of two parts or pieces, especially pieces of clothing ■ *n.* CLOTHES **SUIT IN TWO PARTS** a suit consisting of two garments such as a bikini

two-ply *adj.* consisting of two layers or strands

two-pot scream·er *n. Aus* somebody who becomes drunk very easily (*informal*) [Late 20thC. *Pot* in the Australian sense of "glass of beer," from the idea of having an extreme reaction to a small amount of alcohol.]

two-seat·er *n.* **1.** AUTOMOT **VEHICLE WITH TWO SEATS** a vehicle with seats for two people, especially a sports car **2.** FURNITURE **SEAT FOR TWO** a seat for two people, especially a couch

two-shot *n.* a movie or television shot in which two people more or less fill the screen

two-sid·ed *adj.* **1. HAVING TWO SURFACES** having two sides or surfaces **2. USING TWO SIDES** using both sides of a page **3. HAVING TWO CONTESTING SIDES** consisting of two contesting sides, e.g., two groups opposing each other, or two equally valid opinions

two·some /tóossəm/ *n.* **1. PAIR** a pair of people, especially two golfers paired to play together, a couple on a date together, or a team consisting of two players **2.** GOLF = **single** *n.* **5**

two-spot *n.* **1. GAME PIECE** a game piece such as a playing card or a domino with two marks on it **2.** MONEY **TWO-DOLLAR BILL** a two-dollar bill (*informal*)

two-step *n.* **1.** DANCE **BALLROOM DANCE** a ballroom dance in two-four time with sliding steps **2.** MUSIC **DANCE MUSIC** a piece of music written for the two-step ■ *vi.* (**two-stepped, two-step·ping, two-steps**) DANCE **DANCE TWO-STEP** to dance the two-step

two-stroke *adj. U.K.* = **two-cycle**

two-suit·er *n.* **1. SUITCASE** a suitcase designed to hold two suits and their accessories **2. BRIDGE HAND** a hand at bridge with two suits of five or more cards

two-tailed pa·sha *n.* a southern European butterfly that has brownish wings with an orange border. Latin name: *Charaxes jasius.*

two-tier *adj.* having two levels, especially two levels of administration or two standards of treatment or privilege

two-time (**two-timed, two-tim·ing, two-times**) *vt.* (*informal*) **1. BE UNFAITHFUL TO SOMEBODY** to be unfaithful to a romantic partner or sexual **2. DOUBLE-CROSS SOMEBODY** to deceive or betray a partner in an undertaking —**two-tim·er** *n.* —**two-tim·ing** *adj.*

two-toed sloth *n.* a mainly nocturnal Central and South American sloth with two digits on either forefoot. Latin name: *Choloepus didactylus.*

two-tone *adj.* consisting of two colors or two shades of the same color ○ *toe-tone shoes*

'twould /twŏŏd/ *contr.* it would (*archaic or literary*)

two-up *n. Aus* an Australian gambling game in which bets are placed on how two tossed coins will land

two-way *adj.* **1. MOVING IN BOTH DIRECTIONS** moving in opposite directions or allowing for movement in opposite directions **2.** SPORTS **INVOLVING TWO CONTESTANTS** involving two people or teams ○ *a two-way race* **3.** RADIO **ABLE TO TRANSMIT AND RECEIVE** able both to transmit and receive radio signals ○ *two-way radio* **4. RECIPROCAL** requiring cooperation between two people or groups **5.** BRIDGE **AMBIGUOUS AS BID** used to describe a bid at bridge that may have different meanings, to be clarified by later bids

two-way mir·ror *n. U.K.* = **one-way mirror**

two-wheel·er *n.* a vehicle with two wheels, especially a bicycle

twp. *abbr.* township

TWX *abbr.* teletypewriter exchange

TX *abbr.* Texas

Ty·cho /tī kō/ *n.* a crater on the south of the Moon that is the center of the Moon's most extensive ray system. It is 52 mi./84 km in diameter, 14,750 ft./4500 m high, and is surrounded by terraced walls.

ty·coon /tī kóon/ *n.* **1. SOMEBODY POWERFUL** somebody who has amassed great wealth and power, especially in business **2. SHOGUN** a shogun (*archaic*) [Mid-19thC. From Japanese *taikun* "great lord, shogun," from Chinese *dà* "great" + *jūn* "prince."]

ty·iyn /teè yeén/ (*plural* **-iyn** *or* **-iyns**) *n.* **1. SUBUNIT OF KYRGYZ CURRENCY** a subunit of currency in Kyrgyzstan, 100 of which are worth one som. See table at **currency** **2. COIN WORTH ONE TYIYN** a coin worth one tyiyn

tyke /tīk/, **tike** *n.* **1. NAUGHTY CHILD** a little child, especially one who is naughty or mischievous **2. MONGREL** a dog of mixed breed [14thC. From Old Norse *tík* "bitch."]

ty·lec·to·my /tī léktəmee/ (*plural* **-mies**) *n.* = **lumpectomy** [Late 20thC. Coined from Greek *tulos* "lump" + -ECTOMY.]

Ty·le·nol /tílə nàwl/ *tdmk.* a trademark for the painkiller acetaminophen

Ty·ler /tílər/, **Anne** (*b.* 1941) U.S. writer. Her novels include *Dinner at the Homesick Restaurant* (1982) and *The Accidental Tourist* (1985).

Library of Congress

John Tyler

Ty·ler, John (1790–1862) U.S. statesman and 10th president of the United States. He was William Henry Taft's vice president, and set a controversial historical precedent by assuming the presidency after Taft's death. As president (1841–45), his greatest achievement was the annexation of Texas (1844).

Ty·ler, Wat (*d.* 1381) English revolutionary leader. The leader of the Peasants' Revolt of 1381, he secured concessions from Richard II but was killed during negotiations.

tym·bal *n.* = **timbal**

tym·pan /tímpən/ *n.* **1.** PRINTING **PART OF PRINTING PRESS** a padding device that fits between the impression cylinder of a printing press and the paper to be printed so as to ensure a uniform image **2.** ARCHIT = **tympanum** *n.* **1** **3.** ACOUSTICS **VIBRATING MEMBRANE** a membrane or diaphragm that vibrates to produce or transmit sound, e.g., as the skin on a drum or the diaphragm in a telephone receiver [Pre-12thC. From Latin *tympanum* "drum" (see TYMPANUM).]

tym·pa·ni = **timpani**

tym·pan·ic /tim pánnik/ *adj.* relating to a tympanum

tym·pan·ic bone *n.* the part of the temporal bone that supports and partly surrounds the auditory canal

tym·pan·ic mem·brane *n.* the eardum (*technical*)

tym·pa·ni·tes /tìmpə níteez/ *n.* swelling of the abdominal wall caused by gas trapped in the intestines or peritoneal cavity [14thC. Via late Latin from Greek *tumpanitēs*, from *tumpanon* "drum" (see TYMPANUM).] —**tym·pa·nit·ic** /tìmpə níttik/ *adj.*

tym·pa·ni·tis /tìmpə nítiss/ *n.* inflammation of the eardrum [Mid-19thC. Formed from TYMPANUM.]

tym·pa·no·plas·ty /tímpənə plàstee/ (*plural* **-ties**) *n.* the surgical repair or reconstruction of the eardrum, usually in order to close a perforation [Mid-20thC. Formed from TYMPANUM.]

Tympanum

tym·pa·num /tímpənəm/ (*plural* **-nums** *or* **-na** /-nə/) *n.* **1.** ARCHIT **RECESSED SPACE** a recess, especially the recessed space between the top of a door or window and the arch above it, or between the cornices forming a classical triangular gable (**pediment**) **2.** ANAT **EAR PART** the eardum or the cavity of the middle ear (*technical*) **3.** INSECTS **INSECT ORGAN** a vibrating membrane in some insects that serves as a hearing organ **4.** = **tympan** *n.* **3** [Early 16thC. Via Latin from Greek *tumpanon* "drum." Ultimately from an Indo-European word denoting "something struck" that is also the ancestor of English *type*.]

tym·pa·ny /tímpənee/ *n.* = **tympanites** [Early 16thC. From Greek *tumpanias*, from *tumpanon* (see TYMPANUM).]

Tyn·dall ef·fect /tínd'l-/ *n.* the scattering of light by minute particles in its path, such as dust in the air [Early 20thC. Named for John *Tyndall* (1820–93), a British physicist who described the phenomenon.]

tyn·dal·lim·e·try /tìnd'l ímmətree/ *n.* the measurement of the concentration of particles suspended in a liquid by gauging the amount of light scattered by them [Formed from TYNDALL EFFECT]

typ. *abbr.* **1.** typographer **2.** typographic **3.** typographical **4.** typography

typ·al /típ'l/ *adj.* relating to a type or types

type /tīp/ *n.* **1. KIND OR SORT** a category of things or people whose members share some qualities **2. PERSON OR THING** somebody or something regarded as belonging to a group or category by virtue of having the main qualities associated with it ○ *the kerosene type of burner* **3. KIND OF PERSON** a person regarded as having the stated characteristics or temperament (*informal*) ○ *a gathering of bookish types* **4. SOMEBODY WHO APPEALS** somebody with the qualities that appeal to somebody else ○ *He's really not my type.* **5. TEMPLATE** something used as a pattern or template for making other things of the same kind **6.** PRINTING **PRINTING BLOCK** a small metal block with, on one of its sides, a raised figure that is the mirror image of a number or letter, used with others for printing **7.** PRINTING **SET OF PRINTING BLOCKS** printing blocks collectively **8.** PRINTING **PRINTED LETTERS** printed words, letters, or symbols on a page **9.** BIOL **REPRESENTATIVE GENUS OR SPECIES** a genus or species of plant or animal whose characteristics best represent the next higher category of taxonomic classification **10.** BIOL **REPRESENTATIVE ORGANISM** a plant or animal that represents its genus by having the main qualities that define it **11.** LING **LINGUISTIC UNIT** a letter, word, or other linguistic unit regarded as representing all units that are forms of it, as distinct from an individual form (**token**) **12.** PHILOS **GENERAL EXPRESSION** an expression regarded not as a physical object but as an abstract pattern that individual expressions can conform to **13.** CHR **SIGN OF SOMETHING TO COME** an event, figure, or sign taken as foreshadowing something in the future ■ *v.* (**typed, typ·ing, types**) **1.** *vti.* **KEY WORDS ON KEYBOARD** to key words using a computer keyboard, word processor, or typewriter **2.** *vt.* **CLASSIFY SOMETHING** to classify something, especially blood, according to its type **3.** *vt.* **TYPECAST SOMEBODY** to characterize somebody as being a person who plays a particular kind of role **4.** *vt.* CHR **FORESHADOW SOMETHING** to foreshadow a future event or fact [15thC. Via Latin from Greek *tupos* "blow, impression." Ultimately from an Indo-European base meaning "to strike." The sense "form, kind" evolved from "impression made by striking."]

WORD KEY: USAGE

See Usage note at *kind*.

WORD KEY: SYNONYMS

type, kind, sort, category, class, species, genre

CORE MEANING: a group having a common quality or qualities

type a group of people or things with strongly marked and readily defined similarities; **kind** a general word for a group of people or things that has been loosely defined according to their similarities; **sort** a general word used in the same way as "kind"; **category** a deliberately defined group, usually used to help sort or classify a larger group; **class** used in the same way as "category"; **species** used in the classification of living things to describe a specific group of animals, plants, insects, or other organisms; **genre** a formal word for a particular type of painting, writing, dance, or other art form.

type A *n.* a type of person who is anxious and hardworking, who has a strong drive to succeed, who overworks, and finds it hard to delegate or share tasks with colleagues

type B *n.* a personality type inclined toward patience and friendliness

type·bar /tīp baàr/ *n.* a lever operated by a typewriter key. Each lever has one or more printing blocks on the end that print characters on the paper.

type·case /tīp kàyss/ *n.* a tray or box for storing printer's type

type·cast /tīp kàst/ (**type·cast, type·cast·ing, type·casts**) *vt.* **1.** CAST SOMEBODY REPEATEDLY IN SIMILAR ROLES to give an actor a series of parts of the same type, to the extent that the performer becomes associated with that kind of role and is overlooked for others **2.** CAST ACTOR SUITABLY to give an actor a part that suits his or her physical or emotional type —**type·cast·er** *n.*

type·face /tīp fàyss/ *n.* **1.** STYLE OF PRINTED CHARACTERS a particular style of printed character such as Helvetica or bold **2.** PRINTING BLOCK SURFACE the side of a printing block that has the shape of the printed character on it

type foun·der *n.* a manufacturer of metal printing type —**type foun·dry** *n.*

type ge·nus *n.* the genus of a family or other higher taxonomic category that is most typical of it and usually bears the same name

type-high *adj.* as high as the standard height of a block of printer's type, 0.9186 in./23.3 mm

type I er·ror *n.* in statistics, the error of rejection of a null hypothesis when it is true

type II er·ror *n.* in statistics, the failure to reject a false null hypothesis

type lo·cal·i·ty *n.* a place where a rock formation or other geological feature was first found and described, and after which it is named

type met·al *n.* the alloy from which printing type is made, consisting mostly of lead, antimony, and tin

type·script /tīp skrìpt/ *n.* a typewritten document or other text [Late 19thC. Formed from TYPE + MANUSCRIPT.]

type·set /tīp sèt/ (**type·set, type·set·ting, type·sets**) *vt.* to prepare text for printing, either by the use of computers or by arranging blocks of type manually

type·set·ter /tīp sèttər/ *n.* **1.** PRINTER somebody who prepares text for printing **2.** TYPESETTING MACHINE a mechanical or electronic device that prepares text for printing

type·site *n.* an archeological site that is thought to typify a culture and that gives the culture its name

type spe·cies *n.* a species of plant or animal that is most typical of its genus and bears the same name or a related name

type spec·i·men *n.* an individual plant or animal that serves as the basis for the description of its species. Its name is usually taken as the name of the species.

type style *n.* = **typeface** *n.* 1

type·write /tīp rìt/ (**type·wrote** /-ròt/, **type·writ·ten** /-ritt'n/, **type·writ·ing, type·writes**) *vti.* to type (*dated*) [Late 19thC. Back-formation from TYPEWRITER.]

Typewriter

type·writ·er /tīp rìtər/ *n.* **1.** WRITING MACHINE an electrical or mechanical device for printing words on individual sheets of paper **2.** TYPEFACE a printing typeface that looks like characters produced by a typewriter

type·writ·ing /tīp rìting/ *n.* **1.** USE OF A TYPEWRITER the process or skill of writing on a typewriter **2.** OUTPUT OF TYPEWRITER the output of text produced on a typewriter

typh·li·tis /ti flītiss/ *n.* inflammation of the entrance to the large intestine (**cecum**) [Mid-19thC. Formed from Greek *tuphlon* "cecum," from *tuphlos* "sightless."] —**typh·lit·ic** /ti flíttik/ *adj.*

typh·lol·o·gy /ti flóllәjee/ *n.* the scientific study of sightlessness [Late 19thC. Formed from Greek *tuphlos* "blind."]

Ty·pho·eus /tī fée әss/ *n.* in Greek mythology, a monster with a hundred dragon heads who fought with Zeus and was thrown down into the ground under Mount Etna —**Ty·phoe·an** *adj.*

ty·phoid /tī fòyd/ *n.* INFECTIOUS DISEASE OF DIGESTIVE SYSTEM a serious and sometimes fatal bacterial infection of the digestive system, caused by ingesting food or water contaminated with the bacillus *Salmonella typhi.* It causes fever, severe abdominal pain, and sometimes intestinal bleeding. ■ *adj.* OF TYPHOID OR TYPHUS relating to typhoid or typhus —**ty·phoi·dal** /tī fóyd'l/ *adj.*

ty·phoid fe·ver *n.* = **typhoid**

Ty·phoid Mar·y /tī fòyd mèrree/ *n.* **1.** OFFENSIVE TERM an offensive term used to refer to somebody who spreads a disease or is held to be responsible for spreading it (*offensive*) **2.** OFFENSIVE TERM an offensive term used to refer to somebody who spreads something undesirable such as pessimism or bad news, and is generally avoided (*informal*) [Early 20thC. Nickname of *Mary* Mallon (died 1938), an Irish-born cook in the U.S. who was found to be a typhoid carrier.]

ty·phoon /tī fóon/ *n.* a violent tropical storm in the western Pacific and Indian oceans. ◊ **hurricane** [Late 16thC. Partly from Chinese (Cantonese) *toi fung,* literally "big wind," and partly via Portuguese *tufão,* Urdu *ṭūfān,* and Arabic from Greek *tuphōn.*] —**ty·phon·ic** /tī fónnik/ *adj.*

ty·phus /tīfәss/, **ty·phus fe·ver** *n.* an infectious disease that causes fever, severe headaches, a rash, and often delirium. It is spread by ticks and fleas carried by rodents. [Late 18thC. From Greek *tuphos* "smoke, stupor," from *tuphein* "to smoke." Ultimately from an Indo-European base that is also the ancestor of English *fume, dizzy,* and *deaf.*] —**ty·phous** *adj.*

typ·i·cal /típpik'l/ *adj.* **1.** REPRESENTATIVE having all or most of the characteristics shared by others of a type and therefore suitable as an example of the type **2.** CONFORMING TO EXPECTATION conforming to what is expected **3.** USUAL like what is usual **4.** BIOL RESEMBLING OTHERS IN TAXONOMIC GROUP used to describe an organism, species, or genus that has most of the characteristics that identify the larger taxonomic group to which it belongs [Early 17thC. Via French from, ultimately, Greek *tupikos,* from *tupos* (see TYPE).] —**typ·i·cal·i·ty** /tìppi kállәtee/ *n.* —**typ·i·cal·ness** *n.*

typ·i·cal·ly /típpikәlee/ *adv.* **1.** IN THE USUAL WAY with all or many of the usual or expected characteristics **2.** IN MOST CASES in most cases or on most occasions **3.** PREDICTABLY as is to be expected ○ *not her typically cheerful self today*

typ·i·fy /típpә fī/ (**typ·i·fied, typ·i·fy·ing, typ·i·fies**) *vt.* **1.** BE TYPICAL OF SOMETHING to have all or most of the characteristics of others of a type and therefore be a suitable example of the type **2.** EPITOMIZE SOMETHING to be a typical representation of something [Mid-17thC. Formed from Latin *typus* (see TYPE).] —**typ·i·fi·ca·tion** /tìppәfi káysh'n/ *n.* —**typ·i·fi·er** /típpә fīr/ *n.*

typ·ist /tīpist/ *n.* somebody who uses a typewriter, especially somebody whose job is producing documents using a typewriter or word processor

ty·po /tīpō/ (*plural* **-pos**) *n.* a typographical error (*informal*) [Early 19thC. Shortening.]

typo., **typog.** *abbr.* **1.** typographer **2.** typographic **3.** typographical **4.** typography

ty·pog·ra·pher /tī póggrәfәr/ *n.* a person or business engaged in preparing text for printing

ty·po·graph·i·cal /tìpә gráffik'l/, **ty·po·graph·ic** /-gráffik/ *adj.* **1.** OF TEXT PREPARATION relating to the activity of preparing texts for printing **2.** OF PRINTED CHARACTERS relating to the appearance of printed characters on the page

ty·po·graph·i·cal er·ror *n.* a printing error such as a misspelled word, that results from striking the wrong key or keys on a keyboard

ty·pog·ra·phy /tī póggrәfee/ *n.* **1.** PREPARATION OF TEXTS the activity or business of preparing texts for printing **2.** LOOK OF PRINTED MATTER the appearance of printed characters on the page [Early 17thC. Via French from modern Latin *typographia,* from Greek *tupos* (see TYPE) + *-graphia* (see -GRAPHY).]

ty·pol·o·gy /tī póllәjee/ *n.* **1.** CLASSIFICATION OF TYPES the study or systematic classification of types **2.** LING LANGUAGE STUDY the study of syntactic and morphological similarities in languages without regard to their history **3.** CHR STUDY OF RELIGIOUS TEXTS the study of religious texts for the purpose of identifying episodes in them that appear to prophesy later events [Mid-19thC. Coined from Greek *typos* (see TYPE) + -LOGY.] —**ty·po·log·ic** /tìpә lójjik/ *adj.* —**ty·po·log·i·cal** /-lójjik'l/ *adj.* —**ty·po·log·i·cal·ly** /-lójjikәlee/ *adv.* —**ty·pol·o·gist** /tī póllәjist/ *n.*

typw. *abbr.* **1.** typewriter **2.** typewritten

ty·ra·mine /tīrә meen/ *n.* an amine found in cheese, rotting meat, and mistletoe that results from the breakdown of the amino acid tyrosine, and has the effect of simulating sympathetic nervous system action. Formula: $C_8H_{11}NO$. [Early 20thC. Blend of TYROSINE and AMINE.]

ty·ran·ni·cal /ti ránnik'l/, **ty·ran·nic** /ti ránnik/ *adj.* **1.** POL RULING UNJUSTLY ruling with absolute power over a population cruelly kept submissive and fearful **2.** AUTHORITARIAN cruelly or irrationally insisting on complete obedience and giving harsh punishment to those who disobey [Mid-16thC. Via French *tyrannique* from, ultimately, Greek *turannikos,* from *turannos* (see TYRANT).] —**ty·ran·ni·cal·ly** *adv.* —**ty·ran·ni·cal·ness** *n.*

ty·ran·ni·cide /ti ránni sīd/ *n.* **1.** ASSASSINATION OF TYRANT the killing of a tyrant **2.** ASSASSIN OF TYRANT the killer of a tyrant [Mid-17thC. From Latin *tyrannicidium* "tyrant-killing" and Latin *tyrannicida* "tyrant-killer," both from *tyrannus* (see TYRANT) + *caedere* "to kill" (see -CIDE).] —**ty·ran·ni·cid·al** /ti rànni sīd'l/ *adj.*

tyr·an·nize /tírrә nīz/ (**-nized, -niz·ing, -niz·es**) *vti.* **1.** POL GOVERN CRUELLY to govern with extreme cruelty and harshness **2.** TREAT HARSHLY to treat somebody in a cruelly unfair way [15thC. Via French *tyranniser* from Old French *tyrant* (see TYRANT).] —**tyr·an·niz·er** *n.*

ty·ran·no·saur /ti ránnә sàwr/, **ty·ran·no·saur·us** /ti rànnә sáwrәss/, **ty·ran·no·saur·us rex** *n.* a large fierce flesh-eating dinosaur that walked on powerful hind legs and had small forelegs. It lived during the Jurassic and Cretaceous Periods and was the largest carnivore. [Early 20thC. From modern Latin *Tyrannosaurus,* genus name, from Greek *turannos* (see TYRANT) + *sauros* (see -SAUR).]

tyr·an·nous /tírrәnәss/ *adj.* **1.** POL RULING CRUELLY ruling cruelly and with absolute power **2.** TREATING OTHERS CRUELLY cruelly demanding complete obedience and punishing disobedience severely

tyr·an·ny /tírrәnee/ (*plural* **tyr·an·nies**) *n.* **1.** CRUEL USE OF POWER cruelty and injustice in the exercising of power or authority over others **2.** POL OPPRESSIVE GOVERNMENT oppressive government by one or more people who exercise absolute power cruelly and unjustly **3.** POL STATE RULED BY TYRANT a country or state under the power of an oppressive ruler **4.** CRUEL ACT an act of cruelty committed by somebody with great power [14thC. Via French from, ultimately, Greek *turannos* (see TYRANT).]

ty·rant /tīrәnt/ *n.* **1.** POL ABSOLUTE RULER an absolute ruler who exercises power cruelly and unjustly **2.** AUTHORITARIAN PERSON somebody who exercises authority unjustly and oppressively **3.** SOMETHING THAT OPPRESSES something that oppresses harshly or cruelly **4.** HIST ANCIENT GREEK RULER in ancient Greece, a ruler who took control of a state without legal sanction and governed with absolute power [13thC. Via Old French and Latin from Greek *turannos,* of uncertain origin; perhaps from Phrygian or Lydian.]

ty·rant fly·catch·er *n.* BIRDS = **flycatcher** *n.* 2 [Translation of modern Latin *Tyrannidae,* family name]

tyre /tīr/ *n.* U.K. = **tire**

Tyre /tīr/ town in southern Lebanon, on the Mediterranean Sea. It was the most important city of ancient Phoenicia. Population: 14,000 (1988).

Tyr·i·an /tírree әn/ *adj.* relating to the ancient Mediterranean port of Tyre, or its people or culture [Early 16thC. Coined from Latin *Tyrius,* from *Tyre,* an ancient Phoenician city, + -AN.]

Tyr·i·an pur·ple *n.* **1.** DEEP PURPLE DYE a deep purple dye extracted from mollusks **2.** COLORS RICH PURPLE COLOR a deep rich purple color tinged with crimson ■ *adj.* COLORS RICH PURPLE of a deep rich purple color tinged with crimson [Named for the city of TYRE, where the dye was made]

ty·ro /tīrō/ (*plural* **-ros**), **ti·ro** (*plural* **-ros**) *n.* somebody who is beginning to learn something [Early 17thC. Via medieval Latin, "squire," from Latin *tiro* "young soldier, recruit," of unknown origin.] —**ty·ron·ic** /tī rónnik/ *adj.*

WORD KEY: SYNONYMS

See Synonyms at ***beginner.***

ty·ro·ci·dine /tīrə sīd'n, -sī deen/, **ty·ro·ci·din** /tīrə sīd'n/ *n.* an antibiotic polypeptide extracted from a soil bacillus that is the main constituent of the antibiotic drug tyrothricin [Mid-20thC. Contraction of TYROTHRICIN + GRAMICIDIN + -INE.]

Ty·rol /tə rṓl, tī rṓl/ province in western Austria, lying within the Alps. Capital: Innsbruck. Population: 660,000 (1996). Area: 4,883 sq. mi./12,648 sq. km. —**Ty·ro·le·an** *n., adj.* —**Tyr·o·lese** *n., adj.*

Ty·ro·li·enne /ti rōlee én/ *n.* **1.** DANCE **FOLK DANCE** a lively folk dance that originated in the Tyrol **2.** MUSIC **DANCE MUSIC** a piece of music composed for a Tyrolienne, typically with yodeling [Late 19thC. From French *tyrolienne*, feminine of *tyrolien* "Tyrolean."]

ty·ros·i·nase /tī rósse nàyss, -nàyz/ *n.* a copper-containing enzyme that is important in the production of the skin pigment melanin. The absence of the enzyme results in albinism. [Late 19thC. Formed from TYROSINE.]

ty·ro·sine /tírə seen/ *n.* an amino acid that is the precursor of epinephrine, thyroxine, and other hormones and of melanin. Formula: $C_9H_{11}NO_3$. [Mid-19thC. Formed from Greek *turos* "cheese" (source of English *butter*). Ultimately from an Indo-European word meaning "to swell" that is also the ancestor of *tumor* and *tuber.*]

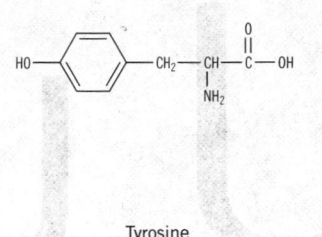

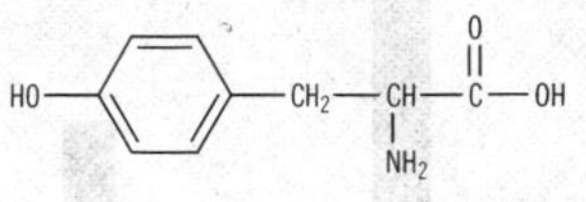

Tyrosine

ty·ro·thri·cin /tīrə thríss'n/ *n.* an antibiotic drug made from tyrocidine and gramicidin that is effective against gram-positive bacteria in local infections [Mid-20thC. Formed from modern Latin *Tyrothric-*, the stem of *Tyrothrix*, former genus name of a gram-positive bacterium, from Greek *turos* "cheese" + *thrix* "hair."]

Tyr·rhe·ni·an Sea /ti reenee ən-/ arm of the Mediterranean Sea, partially enclosed by the Italian Peninsula and the islands of Corsica, Sardinia, and Sicily. Area: 60,000 sq. mi./155,000 sq. km.

Ty·son /tíss'n/, **Mike** (*b.* 1966) U.S. boxer. He is the youngest heavyweight fighter to win a world title (1986). Real name **Michael Gerald Tyson**

tzad·dik /tsaádik/ (*plural* **-di·kim** /tsaádi kim/), **tsad·dik** (*plural* **-di·kim**), **zad·dik** (*plural* **-di·kim**) *n.* **1.** **RIGHTEOUS MAN** in Judaism, a righteous man **2.** = **rebbe** [Late 19thC. From Hebrew *ṣaddīq* "righteous."]

tzar /zaar, tsaar/ *n.* = **tsar**

tzet·ze fly *n.* = **tsetse fly**

tzi·gane /tsee gaán, see-/ *n.* PEOPLES a member of a Romany people, especially one from Hungary [Mid-18thC. Via French from Hungarian *czigany*.] —**tzi·gane** *adj.*

tzim·mes /tsímməss/ (*plural* **-mes**), **tsim·mes** (*plural* **-mes**) *n.* **1.** **CASSEROLE** a stew of meat, vegetables, and dried fruits, baked in a casserole **2.** **CONFUSION** a confused, muddled, or agitated state (*slang*) [Late 19thC. From Yiddish *tsimes*, of uncertain origin: perhaps from Middle High German *ze* "to, as" + *imbiz* "light meal".]

tzi·tzith /tsítsiss/, **tzi·tzit, tzi·tzes, tsi·tses** *n.* the fringes on the corners of a Jewish prayer shawl (**tallis**) to remind Jews of God's commandments (Num. 15:38). [Late 17thC. From Hebrew *ṣīṣṯ*.]

U u

u /yoo/ (*plural* **u's**), **U** (*plural* **U's** *or* **Us**) *n.* **1. 21ST LETTER OF ENGLISH ALPHABET** the 21st letter of the modern English alphabet **2.** PHON **SPEECH SOUND CORRESPONDING TO LETTER "U"** any of the speech sounds that correspond to the letter "U" **3. LETTER "U" WRITTEN** a written representation of the letter "U" **4. SHAPE LIKE "U"** the shape of the letter "U"

U[1] /yoo/ *pron.* a written form of "you" (*informal*) [Because the letter *U* and *you* are pronounced the same]

U[2] *symbol.* **1.** potential difference **2.** CHEM ELEM uranium **3.** Ⓤ kosher certification **4.** PHYS internal energy

U[3] *abbr.* **1. U, U.** university **2.** EDUC unsatisfactory **3. U, U.** united **4.** you (*informal*)

U[4] /yoo/ *n.* a title of respect for a man used in Myanmar (Burma), equivalent to "Mr" [Mid-20thC. From Burmese.]

u., U. *abbr.* **1.** upper **2.** unit **3.** uncle

U.A.E. *abbr.* United Arab Emirates

ua·ka·ri /waa kaaree/ (*plural* **-ri**) *n.* a South American short-tailed monkey that lives high in the forest canopy, seldom coming down onto the ground. Genus: *Cacajao.* [Mid-19thC. From Tupi.]

UAM *abbr.* underwater-to-air missile

UART *abbr.* COMPUT universal asynchronous receiver/transmitter

UAW, U.A.W. *abbr.* United Automobile Workers

U·ban·gi /yoo báng gee/ river in central Africa. The chief tributary of the Congo River, it is formed by the confluence of the Bomu and Uele rivers. Length: 660 mi./1,062 km.

U·ban·gi-Sha·ri /yoo bàng gi shaaree/ former name for **Central African Republic**

Ü·ber·mensch /óobər mènsh/ (*plural* **-mensch·en** /óobər mènshən/) *n.* a superior kind of human being, especially in Nietzschean philosophy or Nazi ideology (*literary*) [Late 19thC. From German, a back-formation from *übermenschlich* "superhuman."]

u·bi·e·ty /yoo bī ətee/ *n.* the condition of existing in a particular place (*literary*) [Late 17thC. From medieval Latin *ubietas*, from *ubi* "where" (source of English *ubiquitous.*)]

u·bi·qui·none /yoobi kwi nōn, -kí nōn/ *n.* a derivative of the compound quinone that acts as an electron carrier in reactions that occur in mitochondria during cellular respiration [Mid-20thC. Blend of UBIQUITOUS and QUINONE.]

u·biq·ui·tar·i·an·ism /yoo bìkwi táiree ə nìzzəm/ *n.* the Christian belief, held particularly by the Lutheran Church, that Jesus Christ is present in all places and at all times, not just in the Eucharist —**u·biq·ui·tar·i·an** *n., adj.*

u·biq·ui·tous /yoo bíkwitəss/ *adj.* present everywhere at once, or seeming to be [Mid-19thC. Formed from modern Latin *ubiquitas* "presence everywhere," from Latin *ubique* "everywhere," from *ubi* "where."] —**u·biq·ui·tous·ly** *adv.* —**u·biq·ui·tous·ness** *n.* —**u·biq·ui·ty** *n.*

U-boat *n.* a German submarine, especially one used during World Wars I and II [Early 20thC. Partial translation of German *U-Boot*, a shortening of *Unterseeboot*, literally "undersea boat."]

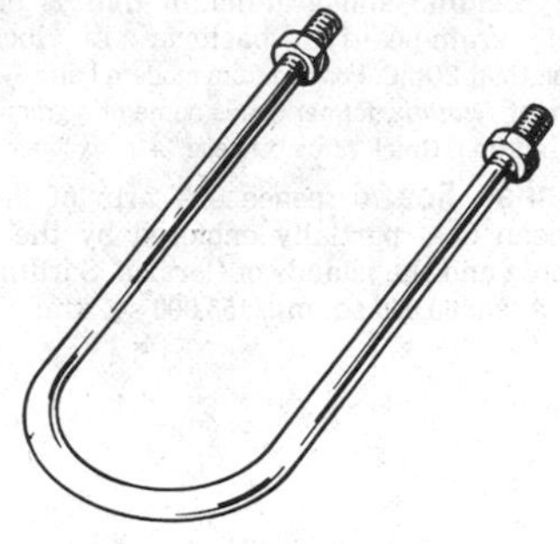

U-bolt

U-bolt *n.* a U-shaped bolt, threaded at the two ends

u·bun·tu /oo boon too/ *n.* *S Africa* humanity, compassion, and goodness, regarded as fundamental to the way Africans approach life [Late 20thC. From Xhosa.]

u.c. *abbr.* upper case

U·ca·ya·li /oo kaa yaalee/ river in eastern Peru, formed by the confluence of the Apurímac and Urubamba rivers. It is one of the headwaters of the Amazon River. Length: 1,200 mi./1,900 km.

UCC *abbr.* Uniform Commercial Code

UCLA *abbr.* University of California at Los Angeles

UCMJ *abbr.* Uniform Code of Military Justice

U·dai·pur /yoo dīpoor, yoo dīpoor/ city and administrative headquarters of Udaipur District, Rajasthan State, northwestern India. Population: 309,000 (1991).

ud·der /úddər/ *n.* a bag-shaped structure containing two or more milk-secreting glands, each with its own teat, found in mammals such as cows, sheep, and goats [Old English *ūder*. Ultimately from an Indo-European word meaning "udder," which is also the ancestor of English *exuberant.*]

Ud·murt /ood moort/ *n.* **1.** PEOPLES **MEMBER OF CENTRAL RUSSIAN PEOPLE** a member of a people who live mainly in Udmurtia in central Russia **2.** LANG **UDMURT LANGUAGE** the language spoken by the Udmurt people. It belongs to the Finno-Ugric family of languages and is spoken by about 500,000 people.

Ud·mur·ti·a /ood moortee ə/ republic in eastern European Russia between Tatarstan and Bashkortostan. Area: 16,300 sq. mi./42,100 sq. km.

u·do /oo dō/ (*plural* **u·dos**) *n.* a perennial Asian plant of the ginseng family whose tender shoots are cooked and eaten as a vegetable. Latin name: *Aralia cordata.* [Late 20thC. From Japanese.]

U·fa /oo faa/ industrial city in southeastern European Russia, situated at the confluence of the Ufa and Belaya rivers, on the western slopes of the Ural Mountains. Population: 1,097,200 (1992).

Uf·fi·zi /yoo fítsee/ *n.* a museum in Florence that contains one of the world's finest collections of Italian paintings. It is located in 16th-century buildings first used to house the Medici family's art collection, the nucleus of the museum's present holdings. [Mid-19thC. From Italian, literally "offices," because it was built to house the administrative center of the Florentine State, by order of Cosimo I MEDICI.]

UFO (*plural* **UFOs**) *n.* a flying object that cannot be identified and is thought by some to be an alien spacecraft [Mid-20thC. Acronym formed from *unidentified flying object.*]

u·fol·o·gy /yoo fólləjee/ *n.* the study of UFOs, especially the investigation of recorded sightings of them

Uganda

U·gan·da /yoo gándə/ republic in East Africa. It gained independence from Britain in 1962. Language: English. Currency: Uganda shilling. Capital: Kampala. Population: 19,136,000 (1996). Area: 91,134 sq. mi./236,036 sq. km. Official name **Republic of Uganda** —**U·gan·dan** *n., adj.*

U·ga·rit·ic /oogə ríttik/ *n.* LANG an ancient and extinct Semitic language once spoken in the region that is now northern Syria. It is closely related to Hebrew and Phoenician. [Mid-20thC. Formed from *Ugarit*, the name of an ancient city in northern Syria.] —**U·ga·rit·ic** *adj.*

ugh /ug, ookh, u/ *interj.* used as the written form of a grunting exclamation of disgust, strain, or horror [Mid-19thC. An imitation of an involuntary utterance.]

ugh boot *tdmk.* *Aus* a trademark for a sheepskin boot with a fleecy lining

Ug·li /ugglee/ *tdmk.* a trademark for a juicy West Indian citrus fruit that is a cross between a grapefruit and a tangerine

ug·li·fy /uggli fī/ (**ug·li·fied, ug·li·fy·ing, ug·li·fies**) *vt.* to make somebody or something physically unappealing —**ug·li·fi·ca·tion** /ugglifi káysh'n/ *n.* —**ug·li·fi·er** /uggli fīr/ *n.*

ug·li·ness /uggleenəss/ *n.* the quality of looking unattractive to look at

ug·ly /ugglee/ (**ug·li·er, ug·li·est**) *adj.* **1. UNATTRACTIVE** lacking appealing physical features, especially facial ones **2. ANGRY** characterized by anger or hostility ○ *an ugly mood* **3. POTENTIALLY VIOLENT** threatening or involving violence ○ *Things were turning ugly.* **4. UNPLEASANT** generally unpleasant ○ *a dull ugly afternoon* **5.** *Southern U.S.* **ILL-MANNERED** discourteous or rude [13thC. From Old Norse *uggligr* "frightful," from *uggr* "fear," of unknown origin.] —**ug·li·ly** *adv.* —**ug·li·ness** *n.*

ug·ly A·mer·i·can *n.* a loud, boorish, nationalistic American, especially one traveling abroad, who is regarded as conforming to a stereotype that gives Americans a bad reputation

ug·ly duck·ling *n.* **1. UNATTRACTIVE PERSON OR THING** somebody or something regarded as physically unappealing in comparison to others **2. UNDERVALUED PERSON OR THING** somebody or something whose true beauty or value is yet to be revealed or appreciated [From *The Ugly Duckling*, a children's story by Hans Christian Andersen in which a cygnet raised by a duck is considered ugly until it grows into a beautiful swan]

U·gri·an /o͞ogree ən, yo͞ogree ən/ *n.* PEOPLES a member of a group of peoples, including the Magyars and Voguls, who live in Hungary and parts of Siberia [Mid-19thC. Formed from Russian *Ugry* "Hungarians," of Turkic origin.] —**U·gri·an** *adj.*

U·gric /o͞ogrik, yo͞ogrik/ *n.* LANG one of the two branches of the Finno-Ugric family of languages. It includes the Hungarian language. [Mid-19thC. Formed from Russian *Ugry* "Hungarians" (see UGRIAN).] —**U·gric** *adj.*

uh /u/ *interj.* used as the written form of a grunting exclamation made to express surprise or request something to be said again [Early 17thC. An imitation of an inarticulate sound.]

UHF *n.* any or all radio frequencies between 300 and 3000 megahertz, typically used for television transmission. Full form **ultrahigh frequency**

uh-huh *interj.* used as the written form of a grunting exclamation made to express agreement or to answer affirmatively [An imitation of an inarticulate sound]

uh-oh *interj.* used as the written form of a grunting exclamation made to express apprehension [An imitation of an articulate sound]

UHT *adj.* sterilized and having a long shelf-life as a result of being heated to a very high temperature. Full form **ultra heat treated**

uh-uh *interj.* used as the written form of a grunting exclamation made to express disagreement or to answer in the negative [An imitation of an inarticulate sound]

u·hu·ru /oo ho͝o ro͞o/ *n.* freedom or national independence, especially for the people of East Africa [Mid-20thC. From Kiswahili.]

UI *abbr.* **1.** unemployment insurance **2.** COMPUT user interface

U-ie (*plural* **U-ies**) *n. Aus, U.K.* a U-turn (*informal*) [Late 20thC. Shortening and alteration of U-TURN.]

Ui·gur /wée go͝or/ (*plural* **Ui·gur** *or* **Ui·gurs**), **Ui·ghur** *n.* **1.** PEOPLES **MEMBER OF CHINESE PEOPLE** a member of a people who live in parts of western China, mainly in Xinjiang Uygur Autonomous Region in the far northwest, where they are the dominant ethnic group **2.** LANG **LANGUAGE OF UIGURS** the language spoken by the Uigurs people, belonging to the Turkic branch of the Altaic family of languages. Uigur is spoken by about 7 million people. [Mid-18thC. From Eastern Turkic.] —**Ui·gu·ri·an** /wee go͝oree ən/ *adj.* —**Ui·gu·ric** /wee go͝orik/ *adj.*

uil·leann pipes /íllən-/ *npl.* a type of Irish bagpipes played by squeezing the bellows under the arm [Early 20thC. From Irish *píob uilleann* "elbow pipe," from *uille* "elbow," from Old Irish *uilind*.]

u·in·ta·ite /yoo íntə ìt/ *n.* a bitumen mined in the Uinta mountains in Utah, used in manufacturing

U.K., **U.K.** *abbr.* United Kingdom

u·kase /yoo káyss, yo͞o kàyss/ *n.* **1. TSAR'S ORDER** in prerevolutionary Russia, an order from the tsar that had the force of law **2. RULING** any order or ruling, especially one handed down by a self-styled expert or guru [Early 18thC. From Russian *ukaz* "edict," from *ukazat'* "to show."]

uke /yook/ *n.* a ukulele (*informal*) [Early 20thC. Shortening.]

u·ke·le·le *n.* = **ukulele**

u·ki·yo-e /o͞okee ō áy/, **u·ki·yo-ye** /o͞okee ō yáy/ *n.* a movement in Japanese painting in which scenes and objects from ordinary life were depicted. It flourished from the 17th to 19th centuries. [Late 19thC. From Japanese, literally "transitory-world picture."]

U·kraine /yoo kráyn/ republic in eastern Europe, southwest of Russia, with a coastline on the Black Sea. Language: Ukrainian. Currency: hryvna. Capital: Kiev. Population: 51,639,000 (1995). Area: 233,090 sq. mi./603,700 sq. km.

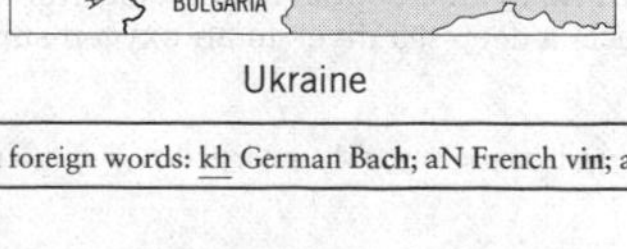

Ukraine

U·krain·i·an /yoo kráynee ən/ *n.* **1.** PEOPLES **SOMEBODY FROM UKRAINE** somebody who was born or raised in the Ukraine, or who has Ukrainian citizenship **2.** LANG **OFFICIAL LANGUAGE OF UKRAINE** the official language of the Ukraine, also spoken by some people in Poland and the Czech Republic. It belongs to the Balto-Slavic branch of the Indo-European family of languages. Ukrainian is spoken by aboout 45 million people. —**U·krain·i·an** *adj.*

u·ku·le·le /yo͞okə láylee/, **u·ke·le·le** *n.* an instrument like a small guitar with four strings, associated especially with Hawaiian music [Late 19thC. From Hawaiian *'ukulele*, literally "jumping flea," of uncertain origin: perhaps from the Hawaiian nickname of Edward Purvis, a British army officer who popularized the instrument.]

UL *abbr.* Underwriter's Laboratories (*on electrical appliances*)

U·laan·baa·tar = **Ulan Bator**

u·la·ma /o͞olə maá/, **u·le·ma** *npl.* a body of Islamic scholars who have jurisdiction over legal and social matters for the people of Islam [Late 17thC. Via Turkish *'ulemā* from Arabic *'ulamā'* "learned men."]

U·lan Ba·tor /o͞o laan baá tàwr/, **U·laan·baa·tar** capital city of the Republic of Mongolia, situated in the north central part of the country, on the Tuul River. Population: 600,900 (1992).

U·lan-U·de /o͞o laan oo dáy/ port city in southern Siberian Russia, located at the confluence of the Uda and Selenge rivers. Population: 366,000 (1992).

Ul·bricht /o͝ol brikht/, **Walter** (1893–1973) German statesman. He was the co-founder and secretary of the Socialist Unity Party (1950–71) and president of the German Democratic Republic (1960–73).

ul·cer /úlsər/ *n.* **1. INTERNAL SORE** a slow-healing sore on the surface of a mucous membrane, especially the membrane lining the stomach or other part of the digestive tract **2. EXTERNAL SORE** a suppurating sore on the skin that does not heal and results in the destruction of tissue **3. BAD INFLUENCE** a corrupting or debilitating influence [14thC. From Latin *ulcer-*, the stem of *ulcus* "a sore."]

ul·cer·ate /úlsə ràyt/ (**ul·cer·at·ed, ul·cer·at·ing, ul·cer·ates**) *vti.* to cause or undergo the formation of an ulcer or ulcers —**ul·cer·a·tive** *adj.*

ul·cer·a·tion /ùlsə ráysh'n/ *n.* **1. FORMING OF ULCER** the formation of an ulcer **2. ULCER** an ulcer or collection of ulcers

ul·cer·a·tive co·li·tis *n.* inflammation of the walls of the bowel accompanied by the formation of ulcers. The condition can result in permanent bowel damage.

ul·cer·a·tive gin·gi·vi·tis *n.* painful inflammation of the gums accompanied by the formation of ulcers. The condition is associated with bacterial infection and malnutrition.

ul·cer·ous /úlsərəss/ *adj.* affected with, causing, consisting of, or resembling ulcers

-ule *suffix.* small one, miniature ○ *lobule* [Via French from Latin *-ulus*]

u·le·ma *npl.* = **ulama**

-ulent *suffix.* having a great deal of something ○ *flocculent* [From Latin *-ulentus*]

ul·lage /úllij/ *n.* (*formal*) **1. VACANT CONTAINER SPACE** the amount or volume by which a container, especially one for liquids, is short of being full **2. LOST LIQUID** the amount of liquid lost from a container through evaporation or leakage [15thC. Via Anglo-Norman *ulliage* from Old French *ouillier* "to fill a barrel to the bunghole," from *oeil* "eye, bunghole," from Latin *oculus* "eye."]

Ulls·wa·ter /úlz wawtər/ the second largest lake in England, in the Lake District, northwestern England. Area: 3 sq. mi./8 sq. km.

ul·ma·ceous /ul máyshəss/ *adj.* belonging or relating to the family of temperate and tropical deciduous trees that includes the elms [Mid-19thC. Formed from modern Latin *Ulmaceae*, family name, from Latin *ulmus* "elm."]

ul·na /úlnə/ (*plural* **-nae** /úlnee/ *or* **-nas**) *n.* **1. BONE OF HUMAN FOREARM** the longer of the two bones in the human forearm, situated on the inner side **2. BONE OF LOWER FORELIMB OF ANIMAL** a bone in the lower forelimb of vertebrate animals, roughly corresponding to the human ulna [Mid-16thC. From Latin, "elbow, forearm." Ultimately from an Indo-European word that is also the ancestor of English *elbow*.] —**ul·nar** *adj.*

ul·nar nerve *n.* a major nerve of the arm that runs down the inner side of the upper arm and is situated just under the skin at the elbow

u·lot·ri·chous /yoo lóttrikəss/ *adj.* with hair that is naturally tightly curled, especially belonging to a group of people with this kind of hair [Mid-19thC. Coined from Greek *oulos* "crisp, curly" + *trikh-*, the stem of *thrix* "hair."]

ul·ster /úlstər/ *n.* a man's long heavy double-breasted overcoat [Mid-19thC. Named for ULSTER, where the original fabric (Irish frieze) for the coats was manufactured.]

Ul·ster /úlstər/ an informal name for Northern Ireland

ult. *abbr.* **1.** ultimate **2.** ultimo

ul·te·ri·or /ul téeree ər/ *adj.* **1. UNDERLYING** existing in addition to or being other than what is apparent or assumed **2. LYING OUTSIDE** lying beyond or outside a point or area **3. HAPPENING IN THE FUTURE** happening or expected in the future [Mid-17thC. From Latin, "further," formed from assumed *ulter* "beyond."] —**ul·te·ri·or·ly** *adv.*

ul·te·ri·or mo·tive *n.* a second and underlying motive, usually a selfish or dishonorable one

ul·ti·ma /últimə/ *n.* the final syllable of a word [Early 20thC. From Latin, a form of *ultimus* (see ULTIMATE).]

ul·ti·ma·ta plural of **ultimatum**

ul·ti·mate /últimət/ *adj.* **1. GREATEST** greatest, most nearly perfect, or highest in quality (*informal*) ○ *the ultimate home entertainment system* **2. FINAL** coming or expected as the very last ○ *our ultimate destination* **3. FUNDAMENTAL** existing as an underlying reality, when all other things are disregarded ○ *the ultimate truth* **4. FARTHEST AWAY** outermost or most remote ■ *n.* **GREATEST THING** the greatest or most nearly perfect thing (*informal*) ○ *seats that were the ultimate in passenger comfort* [Mid-17thC. Via late Latin *ultimatus*, past participle of *ultimare* "to be at an end," from Latin *ultimus* "last, final," from assumed *ulter* "beyond."] —**ul·ti·ma·cy** *n.* —**ul·ti·mate·ness** *n.*

ul·ti·mate·ly /últimətlee/ *adv.* **1. EVENTUALLY** in the end, as the culmination of a process or event **2. FUNDAMENTALLY** most importantly, when all things are considered

ul·ti·ma Thu·le /ùltimə tho͞olee/ *n.* (*literary*) **1. REMOTE PLACE** a distant or very remote place **2. FINAL GOAL** an ultimate or distant goal [Late 18thC. From Latin, "farthest Thule," the northernmost part of the inhabited world.]

ul·ti·ma·tum /ùlti máytəm/ (*plural* **ul·ti·ma·tums** *or* **ul·ti·ma·ta** /-tə/) *n.* a demand accompanied by a threat to inflict some penalty if the demand is not met [Mid-18thC. From modern Latin, formed from Latin *ultimatus* (see ULTIMATE).]

ul·ti·mo /últimō/ *adj.* used, especially in the past, in formal correspondence to refer to the previous month (*formal*) ○ *your letter of the 20th ultimo* [Late 16thC. From Latin *ultimo (mense)* "in the last (month)," from *ultimus* (see ULTIMATE).]

ul·ti·mo·gen·i·ture /ùltimō jéni cho͝or, -chər/ *n.* the principle of inheritance or succession by the youngest son [Late 19thC. Formed from Latin *ultimus* "last," on the model of *primogeniture*.]

ul·tra /últrə/ *adj.* **1. EXTREME** going beyond all else **2. HOLDING EXTREMIST VIEWS** holding extremist views, especially in religious or political matters **3. EXCELLENT** excellent or superior (*slang*) ■ *n.* **EXTREMIST** somebody with extremist views, especially in religious or political matters [Late 19thC. Via French from Latin, "beyond" (see ULTRA-).]

ultra- *prefix.* **1.** more than normal, excessively, completely ○ *ultrasophisticated* **2.** outside the range of ○ *ultrasound* [From Latin *ultra*, "beyond." Ultimately from an Indo-European base meaning "beyond," which is also the ancestor of English *alter, other, alias,* and *else*.]

ul·tra·ba·sic /ùltrə báyssik/ *adj.* **WITH HIGH IRON CONTENT** used to describe igneous rock that is high in iron and magnesium and contains no free quartz. ◊ **ultramafic** ■ *n.* **ULTRABASIC ROCK** a rock of ultrabasic composition. ◊ **ultramafic**

ul·tra·cen·tri·fuge /ùltrə séntri fyo͞oj/ *n.* **FAST CENTRIFUGE** a centrifuge for separating microscopic or submicroscopic particles by using a force many times greater than gravity ■ *vt.* (**ul·tra·cen·tri·fuged, ul·tra·cen·tri·fug·ing, ul·tra·cen·tri·fuges**) **SPIN FAST** to subject something to the action of an ultracentrifuge —**ul·tra·cen·trif·u·gal** /ùltrə sen trífyəgəl/ *adj.* —**ul·tra·cen·trif·u·gal·ly** /-trífyəgəlee/ *adv.* —**ul·tra·cen·trif·u·ga·tion** /ùltrə sentrifyə gaysh'n/ *n.*

ul·tra·con·ser·va·tive /ùltrəkən súrvətiv/ *adj.* **EXTREMELY CONSERVATIVE** extremely conservative in religious or political views ■ *n.* **SOMEBODY ULTRACONSERVATIVE** somebody who holds ultraconservative views

ul·tra·fiche /últrə feesh/ *n.* **1. SMALL MICROFICHE** a sheet of microfilm of similar size to a microfiche but with a much greater number of much smaller microcopied documents on it **2. VIEWING DEVICE** a device for viewing ultrafiches that has much greater magnification than a microfiche

ul·tra·fil·ter /últrə fíltər/ *n.* a filter for separating extremely small particles from a solution or colloid [Early 20thC. Back-formation from ULTRAFILTRATION.]

ul·tra·fil·trate /últrə fíl tràyt/ *n.* the material that is not filtered out and remains in the liquid phase after ultrafiltration

ul·tra·fil·tra·tion /ùltrəfil tráysh'n/ *n.* a filtration process that uses a porous membrane to isolate and remove particles such as bacteria and viruses. The process is used for water purification and in the pharmaceutical industry.

ul·tra heat treat·ed *adj.* full form of **UHT**

ul·tra·high fre·quen·cy *n.* full form of **UHF**

ul·tra·ism /últrə ìzzəm/ *n.* religious or political extremism —**ul·tra·ist** *n.* —**ul·tra·is·tic** /ùltrə ístik/ *adj.*

ul·tra·maf·ic /ùltrə máffik/ *adj.* **WITH HIGH FERROMAGNESIUM CONTENT** used to describe a dark igneous rock, over 90% of whose content consists of ferromagnesian minerals, including olivine and pyroxenes. ◊ **ultrabasic** ■ *n.* **ULTRAMAFIC ROCK** a rock of ultramafic composition. ◊ **ultrabasic**

ul·tra·ma·rine /ùltrəmə reen/ *n.* **1. BLUE PIGMENT** a deep blue pigment or dye, especially one made from the blue mineral lapis lazuli **2.** COLORS **DEEP BLUE COLOR** a brilliant deep blue color ■ *adj.* **1.** COLORS **OF A DEEP BLUE** of a brilliant deep blue color **2. BEYOND THE SEA** coming from or lying beyond the sea (*literary*) [Late 16thC. From medieval Latin *ultramarinus*, literally "beyond the sea."]

ul·tra·mi·crom·e·ter /ùltrə mī krómmətər/ *n.* a measuring device designed to measure spaces and thicknesses more minute than those measurable using a standard micrometer

ul·tra·mi·cro·scope /ùltrə mīkrə skòp/ *n.* a microscope that uses scattered light to make submicroscopic objects visible

ul·tra·mi·cro·scop·ic /ùltrə mīkrə skóppik/ *adj.* **1.** = **submicroscopic 2. USING AN ULTRAMICROSCOPE** involving the use of an ultramicroscope

ul·tra·mod·ern /ùltrə móddərn/ *adj.* more modern than anything comparable, especially in using the very latest designs or making use of the most advanced technology —**ul·tra·mod·ern·ism** *n.* —**ul·tra·mod·ern·ist** *n.*

ul·tra·mon·tane /ùltrə món tàyn, ùltrə mon táyn/ *adj.* **1. BEYOND MOUNTAINS** coming from or lying beyond mountains, especially beyond the Alps as viewed from ancient Rome **2.** CHR **SUPPORTING THE POPE** supporting the power and authority of the pope within the Roman Catholic Church ■ *n.* **1. DWELLER BEYOND MOUNTAINS** somebody who lives beyond mountains, especially beyond the Alps as viewed from ancient Rome **2.** CHR **PAPAL SUPPORTER** somebody who supports the power and authority of the pope in the Roman Catholic Church [Late 16thC. From medieval Latin *ultramontanus* "beyond the mountains."]

ul·tra·mon·ta·nism /ùltrə mónt'n ìzzəm/ *n.* in the Roman Catholic Church, the policy of investing all power and authority in the pope

ul·tra·mun·dane /ùltrə mun dáyn/ *adj.* (*literary*) **1. EXTRATERRESTRIAL** coming from or lying beyond the Earth or its solar system **2. SPIRITUAL** belonging or relating to heaven or to the realm of the spirit, and not to the physical world [Mid-16thC. From Latin *ultramundanus*, literally "beyond the world," from *ultra* "beyond" + *mundus* "world."]

ul·tra·na·tion·al·ism /ùltrə náshən'l ìzzəm, -náshnə lìzzəm/ *n.* nationalism that is so extreme as to be detrimental to international interests or cooperation —**ul·tra·na·tion·al·ist** *n.* —**ul·tra·na·tion·al·is·tic** /ùltrə nashən'l ístik, -nashnə lístik/ *adj.*

ul·tra-Or·tho·dox *adj.* supporting or practicing very strict observance of Orthodox Judaism —**ul·tra-Or·tho·dox·y** *n.*

ul·tra·red /ùltrə réd/ *n.*, *adj.* infrared (*dated*)

ul·tra·re·lig·ious /ùltrəri líjjəss/ *adj.* showing great devotion to religious rites and rituals

ul·tra·short /ùltrə shàwrt/ *adj.* **1.** RADIO **SHORTER THAN 10 M** used to describe wavelengths that are shorter than 10 m **2. EXTREMELY SHORT** extremely short in length or duration

ul·tra·son·ic /ùltrə sónnik/ *adj.* used to describe sound waves that have frequencies above the upper limit of the normal range of human hearing, which is about 20 kilohertz —**ul·tra·son·i·cal·ly** *adv.*

ul·tra·son·ics /ùltrə sónniks/ *n.* the study of sound waves that have frequencies above the upper limit of the normal range of human hearing, which is about 20 kilohertz (*takes a singular verb*)

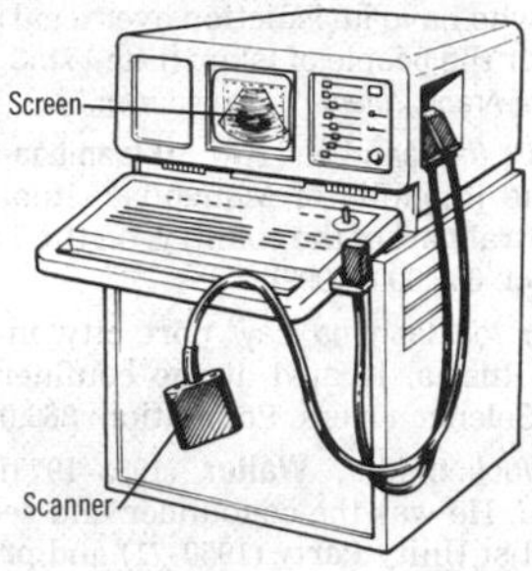

Ultrasonic testing

ul·tra·son·ic test·ing *n.* the scanning of surfaces with high-frequency sound waves in order to gauge their integrity and check for defects or to measure the thickness of materials

ul·tra·son·ic weld·ing *n.* the bonding of two components by bombarding them with ultrasonic waves to cause vibrations between them

ul·tra·son·o·gram /ùltrə sōnə gràm/ *n.* a picture made with ultrasound for the purpose of medical examination or diagnosis

ul·tra·sound /últrə sòwnd/ *n.* **1.** ACOUSTICS **HIGH-FREQUENCY SOUND** sound of a frequency above the upper limit of the normal range of human hearing, which is about 20 kilohertz **2.** MED **SOUND-WAVE TECHNOLOGY FOR MEDICAL EXAMINATIONS** an imaging technique that uses high-frequency sound waves reflecting off internal body parts to create images, especially of the fetus in the womb, for medical examination. Ultrasound vibrations can also be used to treat deep tissue disorders in physiotherapy, and can break up kidney stones.

ul·tra·struc·ture /últrə strùkchər/ *n.* the minute structure of an organic substance or object that becomes evident only under electron microscopy —**ul·tra·struc·tur·al** *adj.*

Ul·tra·suede /últrə swàyd/ *tdmk.* a trademark for a synthetic fabric that resembles suede

ul·tra·vi·o·let /ùltrə vī ələt/ *adj.* **RELATING TO INVISIBLE LIGHT** relating to or producing electromagnetic radiation of wavelengths from about 5 to about 400 nanometers, beyond the violet end of the visible light spectrum ■ *n.* **1. ULTRAVIOLET LAMP** a lamp or bulb that emits ultraviolet radiation **2. ULTRAVIOLET RADIATION** radiation with ultraviolet wavelengths. Radiation of this kind is a component of sunlight and is the light that makes exposed skin become darker.

ul·tra vi·res /ùltrə vīriz/ *adj.*, *adv.* beyond the legal capacity of a person, company, or other legal entity [From Latin, "beyond the powers"]

ul·tra·vi·rus /últrə vīrəss/ *n.* a virus small enough to pass through an ultrafilter —**ul·tra·vi·ral** /ùltrə vīrəl/ *adj.*

u·lu /oo loo/ *adj.* *Malaysia, Singapore* not economically or technologically advanced (*informal*)

ul·u·late /yoolyə làyt, úll-/ (**-lat·ed, -lat·ing, -lates**) *vi.* to howl or wail, in grief or in jubilation (*literary*) [Early 17thC. From Latin *ululare*, ultimately an imitation of the sound.] —**ul·u·la·tion** /yoolyə láysh'n, ùllyə-/ *n.*

Ul·u·ru /oolə roo/ the largest individual rock mass in the world, located in the south of the Northern Territory, Australia. Height: 1,100 ft./335 m. Former name **Ayers Rock**

U·lys·se·an /yoo líssee ən/ *adj.* **1. RELATING TO ULYSSES** relating to the mythological character Ulysses, called Odysseus by the Greeks **2. LIKE ULYSSES OR HIS STORY** like Ulysses, especially in being courageous or cunning, or like the life story of Ulysses, especially in involving a long journey full of adventure

U·lys·ses /yoo lísseez/ *n.* the name used by the Romans for the Greek hero Odysseus [Early 17thC. From Latin.]

um /um/ *interj.* a word used in writing to represent the kind of grunting sound that people make when they hesitate in speaking [Early 17thC. An imitation of an inarticulate sound.]

U·may·yad /oo mī àd/, **Om·mi·ad, O·may·yad** *n.* the family that dominated the politics and commercial economy of Mecca and later established a dynasty as rulers (**caliphs**) of Islam [Mid-18thC. From *Umayya*, the name of a cousin of Muhammad's grandfather.] —**U·may·yad** *adj.* —**Om·mi·ad** *adj.* —**O·ma·yad** *adj.*

um·bel /úmb'l/ *n.* an umbrella-shaped flower head in which the individual flowers are borne on short stems arising from the top of a main stem. It is typical of plants such as parsley, carrot, dill, and fennel. [Late 16thC. Directly or via Old French *umbelle*, from Latin *umbella* "parasol," from *umbra* "shade."] —**um·bel·lar** /um béllər/ *adj.* —**um·bel·late** /úmbə làyt, um béllət/ *adj.* —**um·bel·lat·ed** /úmbə làytəd/ *adj.*

um·bel·lif·er·ous /ùmbə líffərəss, -líffrəss/ *adj.* with flower heads shaped like an opened umbrella [Mid-17thC. Coined from Latin *umbella* "parasol" (see UMBEL) + -FEROUS.]

um·bel·lule /úmb'l yool, um bél-/ *n.* a small umbel that is part of, and has a similar arrangement to, a larger umbel [Late 18thC. From modern Latin *umbellula* "little umbel," from Latin *umbella* (see UMBEL).]

um·ber /úmbər/ *n.* **1. SOIL USED FOR PIGMENTS AND DYES** a kind of soil that contains oxides of iron and manganese and is used to make pigments and dyes. It is dark yellowish-brown in its natural state (**raw umber**), and dark reddish-brown when roasted, (**burnt umber**). **2. PIGMENT** pigment or dye made from umber **3.** ZOOL = **umber moth** ■ *adj.* COLORS **OF BROWN PRODUCED BY UMBER PIGMENT** of any of the shades of brown that are produced by umber pigment ■ *vt.* (**-bered, -ber·ing, -bers**) **PAINT SOMETHING WITH UMBER** to paint or dye something with umber, or generally to color something dark brown [Mid-16thC. Via French *terre d'ombre* or Italian *terra di ombre*, from Latin *umbra* "shadow."]

um·ber moth *n.* a dark brown moth whose markings make it difficult to pick out when it is resting on tree bark. Family: Geometridae.

Um·ber·to I /oom bértō/, **King of Italy** (1844–1900). Reigning from 1878, he sought to consolidate Italy as a unified country.

Um·ber·to II, King of Italy (1904–83). He abdicated in 1946, a month after becoming king, when Italy became a republic as a result of a referendum.

um·bil·i·cal /um bíllik'l/ *adj.* **1.** ANAT **OF THE UMBILICAL CORD** relating to or situated in the umbilical cord, the navel, or the area of the abdomen that surrounds the navel **2. RESEMBLING A NAVEL** resembling a navel (**umbilicus**) in appearance **3. PROVIDING A LIFELINE** providing a link to something essential, e.g., supplies or services in wartime, or connecting an astronaut to a spacecraft while outside of it ■ *n.* = **umbilical cord** [Mid-16thC. Via French from Latin *umbilicus* (see UMBILICUS).]

um·bil·i·cal cord *n.* **1. TUBE CONNECTING FETUS TO PLACENTA** the flexible, often spirally twisted tube that connects the abdomen of a fetus to the mother's placenta in the womb, and through which nutrients are delivered and waste expelled. It contains two arteries, which carry oxygen-depleted blood to the placenta, and one vein, which returns oxygen-rich blood to the fetus. **2. CABLE OR PIPE PROVIDING ESSENTIAL LINK** a cable, tube, or pipe attaching somebody or something to an essential supply, e.g., the tube that connects a deep-sea diver to an oxygen supply on a ship

um·bil·i·cate /um bíllikət, -kàyt/, **um·bil·i·cat·ed** /-kàytəd/ *adj.* **1.** ZOOL, BOT **WITH SOMETHING LIKE A NAVEL** with a mark, depression, or perforation that resembles a navel **2.** BIOL **NAVEL-SHAPED** shaped like a navel [Late 17thC. Formed from UMBILICUS.] —**um·bil·i·ca·tion** /um billi káysh'n/ *n.*

um·bil·i·cus /um bíllikəss/ (*plural* **-ci** /-sī/ *or* **-cus·es**) *n.* **1.** ANAT **NAVEL** a navel (*technical*) **2.** BIOL **HOLLOW RESEMBLING A NAVEL** a dip or hollow, e.g., the hollow at each end of the shaft of a feather, that resembles a navel [Late 17thC. From Latin. Ultimately from the Indo-European word for "navel," which is also the ancestor of English *navel* and *nave.*]

um·bo /úmbō/ (*plural* **-bo·nes** /-bṓneez/ *or* **-bos**) *n.* **1.** BIOL **BUMP ON PLANT OR ANIMAL PART** a small protuberance on a plant or animal part, e.g., the hump on the caps of some mushrooms, or the bump just above the hinge of a bivalve shell **2.** ANAT **SMALL HOLLOW IN THE EARDRUM** a small hollow in the center of the outer surface of the eardrum, at the point where the malleus joins it on the inside **3.** ARMS **KNOB ON SHIELD** a knob at the center of a round shield, especially a Saxon shield [Early 18thC. From Latin, "shield boss," related to *umbilicus* "navel" (see UMBILICUS.] —**um·bo·nal** *adj.* —**um·bo·nate** /-nàyt, -nət/ *adj.*

um·bra /úmbrə/ (*plural* **-bras** *or* **-brae** /úmbree/) *n.* **1.** PHYS **COMPLETE SHADOW** an area of complete shadow caused by light from all points of a source being prevented from reaching the area, usually by an opaque object **2.** ASTRON **DARKEST PART OF MOON'S SHADOW** the darkest portion of the shadow cast by a celestial body during an eclipse, especially that cast on the Earth during a solar eclipse **3.** ASTRON **DARK PART OF SUNSPOT** the inner, darker area of a sunspot [Late 16thC. From Latin, "shadow."] —**um·bral** *adj.*

um·brage /úmbrij/ *n.* **1.** OFFENSE resentment or annoyance arising from some offense ○ *took umbrage* **2.** **GIVER OF SHADE** something that gives shade, e.g., a tree (*literary*) **3.** **VAGUE SHAPE** a vague or shadowy shape, or simply an outline (*archaic*) [15thC. Via Old French, from, ultimately, Latin *umbra* "shadow."]

WORD KEY: ORIGIN

The Latin word *umbra*, from which ***umbrage*** is derived, is also the source of English *adumbrate*, *penumbra*, *somber*, *sombrero*, and *umbrella*.

um·bra·geous /um bráyjəss/ *adj.* **1.** **SHADY** providing shade and coolness (*literary*) **2.** **IRRITABLE** easily offended or likely to become irritated —**um·bra·geous·ly** *adv.* —**um·bra·geous·ness** *n.*

um·brel·la /um brélle/ *n.* **1.** **COLLAPSIBLE CANOPY THAT PROTECTS FROM RAIN** a round collapsible canopy of plastic or waterproof material on a frame at the top of a handle, held in the hand to protect somebody from rain or sun **2.** **OBJECT LIKE AN UMBRELLA** an object that looks like an open umbrella, or that collapses like an umbrella, e.g., the folding paper decoration sometimes served in cocktails **3.** ZOOL **JELLYFISH'S BODY** the rounded body of a jellyfish **4.** MIL **AIRCRAFT FLYING OVERHEAD FOR PROTECTION** a group of aircraft patrolling the sky above a place where troops are carrying out operations, to give them protection **5.** MIL **SHIELD OF GUNFIRE** gunfire used to suppress enemy fire and thus shield friendly forces making a movement or attack **6.** MIL **PARACHUTE** a parachute (*slang*) **7.** **SUPPORT OR AUTHORITY** something that gives support, protection, or authority ○ *under the umbrella of the United Nations* ■ *adj.* **1.** **UNIFYING MEMBER ORGANIZATIONS** acting to coordinate or protect a number of member organizations or bodies **2.** **INCLUDING SEVERAL THINGS** including or containing a number of things ○ *an umbrella term for a variety of plants* [Early 17thC. Via Italian *ombrella* from late Latin *umbrella*, an alteration of Latin *umbella* "parasol"(see UMBEL) under the influence of *umbra* "shadow."]

um·brel·la bird *n.* a bird of Central and South America with a large feathered crest that resembles an umbrella. Genus: *Cephalopterus.*

um·brel·la plant *n.* **1.** **PLANT WITH LEAVES LIKE UMBRELLA SPOKES** a plant of the sedge family, native to Africa, that has thin leaves radiating from the top of long stems. It is widely grown as a houseplant. Latin name: *Cyperus alternifolius.* **2.** *Midwest* **MAY APPLE** a May apple

um·brel·la stand *n.* an upright stand or rack for holding walking sticks and folded umbrellas

um·brel·la tree *n.* **1.** **MAGNOLIA TREE OF SE U.S.** a magnolia tree that grows in the southeastern United States

Umbrella bird

and has large leaves clustered around the ends of the branches. Latin name: *Magnolia fraseri* and *Magnolia tripetala.* **2.** **AUSTRALIAN TREE WITH UMBRELLA-SHAPED LEAVES** a small to medium-sized Australian tree with clusters of red flowers that grow on long spikes and long shiny leaves that grow in umbrella-shaped clusters around thick stalks. Latin name: *Schefflera actinophylla.*

Um·bri·a /úmbree ə/ agricultural region in central Italy, west of the Apennines. Population: 822,972 (1991). Area: 3,265 sq. mi./8,456 sq. km.

Um·bri·an /úmbree ən/ *n.* **1.** PEOPLES **SOMEBODY FROM UMBRIA** somebody who was born or raised in the Italian region of Umbria **2.** LANG **LANGUAGE OF ANCIENT UMBRIA** an extinct language spoken in ancient southern Italy. It belongs to the Italic branch of Indo-European languages. —**Um·bri·an** *adj.*

Um·bri·el /úmbree əl/ *n.* one of the five major moons circling the planet Uranus [Named for a sprite in the poem "The Rape of the Lock" by Alexander Pope]

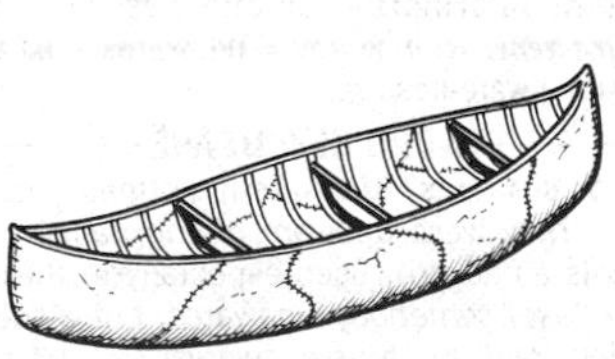

Umiak

u·mi·ak /óomee àk/ *n.* a large Inuit boat made of animal skins stretched across a wooden frame, larger and more open than a kayak and traditionally paddled by women [Mid-18thC. From Inuit (Eskimo) *umiaq.*]

um·laut /óom lòwt/ *n.* **1.** **CHANGE IN A VOWEL SOUND** in Germanic languages, a change in the way a vowel is pronounced, caused by the influence of another vowel in a syllable immediately after it **2.** **TWO DOTS ABOVE A VOWEL** the mark (¨) that is placed above a vowel in Germanic languages to show that it is pronounced differently from the way the vowel is usually pronounced ■ *v.* (**-laut·ed, -laut·ing, -lauts**) **1.** *vti.* **CHANGE A VOWEL SOUND** to change a sound, or make a vowel change its sound, because of other vowel sounds next to it **2.** *vt.* **MARK A VOWEL WITH TWO DOTS** to write or print a vowel with an umlaut above it [Mid-19thC. From German, from *um-* "around, change" + *Laut* "sound."]

um·ma /óomə/, **um·mah** *n.* within Islam, the community of the faithful that transcended long established tribal boundaries to create a degree of political unity [Late 19thC. From Arabic, "people, community."]

um·pire /úm pīr/ *n.* **1.** SPORTS **OFFICIAL ENFORCING A SPORT'S RULES** an official who supervises play and enforces the rules of the game in some sports such as baseball **2.** **SOMEBODY SETTLING A DISPUTE** somebody called in to settle a dispute ■ *vti.* (**-pired, -pir·ing, -pires**) **1.** SPORTS **ACT AS AN UMPIRE IN SPORT** to supervise play in a game or sport and enforce the rules **2.** **SETTLE A DISPUTE** to give a ruling on a dispute as an impartial arbitrator [Late 16thC. By false division from earlier *noumper*, from Old French *non per*, from *non* "not" + *per* "pair," literally "not one of a pair."]

ump·teen /úmp tèen, úm-/ *adj.* a large but unspecified number of (*informal*) [Early 20thC. Formed from *umpty*, a humorous formation after cardinal numbers; modeled on *thirteen*, *fourteen*, etc.] —**ump·teenth** *adj.*

Um·ta·ta /um taátə/ town in Eastern Cape Province, South Africa. Population: 67,000 (1995).

UMWA *abbr.* United Mine Workers of America

un /ən, 'n/, **'un** *pron.* a spelling of the pronoun "one" designed to reflect the way it is sometimes pronounced in informal speech (*informal*) [Early 19thC. Representing a pronunciation of ONE.]

UN, **U.N.** *abbr.* United Nations

un-[1] *prefix.* **1.** not ○ *unavoidable* **2.** opposite of, lack of ○ *unrest* [Old English]

WORD KEY: USAGE

un- or **non-** Many adjectives formed with *un-* have special (usually unfavorable) meanings, for example *unprofessional* and *unscientific*. In these cases neutral equivalents that mean simply "not . . ." are formed by means of ***non-***, for example *nonprofessional*, *nonscientific*.

un-[2] *prefix.* **1.** to do the opposite of, reverse ○ *unclose* **2.** to deprive of, remove something from ○ *unfrock* **3.** to release from ○ *unchain* **4.** completely ○ *unloose* [Old English *on-*, an alteration of *ond-* and- "against," under the influence of *un-*[1]"un-"]

un·a·bashed /ùnnə básht/ *adj.* not ashamed or embarrassed by something

un·a·bat·ed /ùnnə báytəd/ *adj.* still as forceful or intense as before —**un·a·bat·ed·ly** *adv.*

un·a·ble /un áyb'l/ *adj.* not able to do something

un·ac·com·mo·dat·ed /ùnnə kómmə dàytəd/ *adj.* (*formal*) **1.** **NOT ADAPTED** not adapted to or for something ○ *unaccommodated to the dryness of the desert* **2.** **WITHOUT ACCOMMODATIONS OR PROVISIONS** lacking accommodations, equipment, or supplies

un·ac·com·pa·nied /ùnnə kúmpəneed/ *adj.*, *adv.* **1.** **ALONE** alone, especially when a companion would be expected **2.** MUSIC **WITHOUT OTHER INSTRUMENTS OR VOICES** playing or singing alone, without any other instruments or voices

un·ac·com·plished /ùnnə kúmplisht/ *adj.* **1.** **NOT COMPLETED** not carried out or completed **2.** **LACKING SOCIAL OR INTELLECTUAL SKILLS** lacking talents or abilities, especially those abilities educated people may be expected to have

un·ac·count·a·ble /ùnnə kówntəb'l/ *adj.* **1.** **INEXPLICABLE** impossible to explain or give a reason for **2.** **NOT ANSWERABLE** not answerable or responsible to anyone —**un·ac·count·a·bil·i·ty** /ùnnə kòwntə bíllətee/ *n.*

un·ac·count·a·bly /ùnnə kówntəblee/ *adv.* for some unknown and usually puzzling reason

un·ac·count·ed-for *adj.* **1.** **MISSING** missing or absent, for unknown reasons **2.** **UNEXPLAINED** not explained or understood

un·ac·cred·it·ed /ùnnə krédditəd/ *adj.* **1.** **WITH NO SOURCE GIVEN** with the source or origin not given **2.** **NOT OFFICIALLY APPROVED** not officially declared to be of the required standard, or with no official status

un·ac·cus·tomed /ùnnə kústəmd/ *adj.* **1.** **NOT ACCUSTOMED** not used or accustomed to something **2.** **UNFAMILIAR** not usual or known before —**un·ac·cus·tomed·ness** *n.*

u·na cor·da /óonə káwrdə/ *adj.*, *adv.* in piano music, using only one string per pitch. This is achieved by depressing the soft pedal, causing the hammers to strike only one string and thus reducing the volume and changing the quality of the tone. [From Italian, literally "one string"]

un·a·dul·ter·at·ed /ùnnə dúltə ràytəd/ *adj.* **1.** **PURE** not mixed or diluted with something else **2.** **ABSOLUTE** free from any element that would spoil or detract from it —**un·a·dul·ter·at·ed·ly** *adv.*

un·ad·vised /ùnnəd vízd/ *adj.* **1.** **WITHOUT CAREFUL CONSIDERATION** done without being carefully considered **2.** **WITHOUT ASKING ADVICE** without asking the advice of others —**un·ad·vis·ed·ly** /-vízədlee/ *adv.* —**un·ad·vis·ed·ness** *n.*

un·af·fect·ed /ùnnə féktəd/ *adj.* **1.** **NOT AFFECTED BY SOMETHING** not influenced or affected by something **2.** **GENUINE** sincere and genuine, with no intention to mislead or deceive —**un·af·fect·ed·ly** *adv.* —**un·af·fect·ed·ness** *n.*

Un·a·las·ka /ùnnə láskə/ island in southwestern Alaska, between the Bering Sea and the Pacific Ocean. It is the most important and second largest of the Aleutian Islands. Area: 800 sq. mi./1,287 sq. km.

un·al·ien·a·ble /ùn áylee ənəb'l/ *adj.* not alienable

un·al·loyed /ùnnə lóyd/ *adj.* **1.** METALL **IN A PURE STATE** containing no impurities, and not mixed or alloyed with other metals **2. ABSOLUTE** not mixed with anything else, especially anything that would dilute it or any other feeling that would diminish it ○ *unalloyed pleasure*

un-A·mer·i·can *adj.* **1. NOT AMERICAN** at odds with the customs, traditions, or ways of the people of the United States ○ *It's practically un-American not to like apple pie.* **2. NOT LOYAL TO UNITED STATES** unpatriotic or disloyal to the United States

un·a·neled /ùnnə néeld/ *adj.* in the Roman Catholic Church, not having received the last rites given to people who are dying or very ill (*archaic*) [Early 17thC. Formed from UN- + *aneled*, past participle of obsolete *anele* "to anoint," literally "to put oil on," from Old English *ele* "oil," from Latin *oleum*.]

u·nan·i·mous /yoo nánnəməss/ *adj.* **1. AGREED ON BY EVERYONE** shared as a view by all of the people concerned, with nobody disagreeing **2. IN COMPLETE AGREEMENT** with all members in agreement with each other ○ *Board members were unanimous in their rejection of the proposed merger.* [Early 17thC. Formed from Latin *unanimus*, from *unus* "one" + *animus* "mind."] —**u·na·nim·i·ty** /yòonə nímmətee/ *n.* —**u·nan·i·mous·ly** /yoo nánnəməsslee/ *adv.*

un·an·swer·a·ble /un ánsərəb'l/ *adj.* **1. IMPOSSIBLE TO RESOLVE** impossible to answer or solve **2. IMPOSSIBLE TO CONTRADICT** so clearly true that nobody could contradict or deny it —**un·an·swer·a·ble·ness** *n.* —**un·an·swer·a·bly** *adv.*

un·an·tic·i·pat·ed /ùnnan tíssi pàytəd/ *adj.* **1. UNFORESEEN** not foreseen or prepared for in advance **2. UNEXPECTED** not expected or scheduled in advance

un·ap·peal·a·ble /ùnnə péeləb'l/ *adj.* used to describe a case or judgment that is not open to appeal —**un·ap·peal·a·bly** *adv.*

un·ap·peal·ing /ùnnə péeling/ *adj.* not attractive or likely to be enjoyable —**un·ap·peal·ing·ly** *adv.*

un·ap·proach·a·ble /ùnnə próchəb'l/ *adj.* **1. TOO UNFRIENDLY TO APPROACH OR CONTACT** characterized by a formal, unfriendly, or hostile manner that discourages communication **2. INACCESSIBLE** difficult to get to **3. UNRIVALED** so excellent that nothing or nobody else is nearly as good —**un·ap·proach·a·bil·i·ty** /ùnnə pròchəb'lnəss/ *n.* —**un·ap·proach·a·ble·ness** /ùnnə pròchə bíllətee/ *n.* —**un·ap·proach·a·bly** /-próchəblee/ *adv.*

un·ap·pro·pri·at·ed /ùnnə própree àytəd/ *adj.* **1. NOT YET MARKED FOR A PURPOSE** not yet set aside for a specific purpose and therefore still available or free **2. WITH OWNERSHIP OR CONTROL NOT DECIDED** not yet brought under the ownership or control of a particular person or organization

un·apt /un ápt/ *adj.* **1. NOT APPROPRIATE** lacking the qualities suitable or appropriate to a particular context **2. NOT LIKELY TO DO SOMETHING** not likely or liable to do something (*formal*) ○ *unapt to cause any problems* —**un·apt·ly** *adv.* —**un·apt·ness** *n.*

un·ar·gu·a·ble /un árgyoo əb'l/ *adj.* so clearly true or correct that nobody can argue with it or deny it

un·arm /un áarm/ (**-armed, -arm·ing, -arms**) *vt.* to take arms away from a country, armed force, or person

un·armed /un áarmd/ *adj.* **1.** ARMS **WITHOUT WEAPONS** not carrying or using weapons **2.** BIOL **WITH NO OBVIOUS MEANS OF SELF-DEFENSE** with no horns, claws, shells, thorns, prickles, or other means of self-protection **3.** MIL **UNABLE TO FIRE** used to describe a missile or projectile whose fuse or firing mechanism has been disabled

u·nar·y /yóonəree/ *adj.* used to describe a mathematical operation that is applied to only one member of a set at a time, e.g., squaring a number [Early 20thC. Formed from Latin *unus* "one."]

un·a·shamed /ùnnə sháymd/ *adj.* **1. NOT ASHAMED OR APOLOGETIC** not ashamed or embarrassed, and not feeling the need to apologize to others **2. UNRESTRAINED** not limited, restrained, or avoided out of a feeling of shame or embarrassment —**un·a·sham·ed·ly** /-sháymədlee/ *adv.* —**un·a·sham·ed·ness** *n.*

un·asked /un áskt/ *adj.* **1. NOT ASKED** not having been asked **2. NOT INVITED** coming to a gathering without an invitation **3. NOT ASKED FOR** providing something, e.g., assistance, that has not been asked for

un·as·sail·a·ble /ùnnə sáyləb'l/ *adj.* **1. IMPOSSIBLE TO CHALLENGE** so sound or well established that it cannot be challenged or overtaken ○ *an unassailable lead* **2. IMPOSSIBLE TO ATTACK** so strong or impregnable that it cannot be successfully attacked —**un·as·sail·a·bil·i·ty** /-saylə bíllətee/ *n.* —**un·as·sail·a·bly** /ùnnə sáyləblee/ *adv.*

un·as·sum·ing /ùnnə sóoming/ *adj.* acting in a way that does not assume superiority —**un·as·sum·ing·ly** *adv.* —**un·as·sum·ing·ness** *n.*

un·at·tached /ùnnə tácht/ *adj.* **1. WITHOUT A SPOUSE OR PARTNER** not married and not in a long-term romantic or sexual relationship **2. NOT JOINED** not joined or attached, especially to other or larger organizations or bodies **3.** LAW **NOT SEIZED FOR SECURITY** used to describe property that is not taken away from its owner for security under the orders of a court of law

un·at·tend·ed /ùnnə téndəd/ *adj.* **1. WITH NO ONE THERE** with no one present to listen, watch, or participate **2. NOT CARED FOR** not taken care of or seen to **3. NOT ESCORTED** not accompanied or escorted (*formal*) **4. NOT HEEDED** not listened to or heeded (*formal*) **5. NOT HAVING SOMETHING AS CONSEQUENCE** not accompanied by something, or not having something as a result or consequence (*formal*)

u·nau /yóo nòw, -nàw/ (*plural* **u·naus** *or* **u·nau**) *n.* = **two-toed sloth** [Late 18thC. Via French from Tupi *unáu*.]

un·a·vail·ing /ùnnə váyling/ *adj.* done but failing to achieve the desired result —**un·a·vail·ing·ly** *adv.*

un·a·void·a·ble /ùnnə vóydəb'l/ *adj.* that cannot be avoided —**un·a·void·a·bil·i·ty** /ùnnə vòydə bíllətee/ *n.* —**un·a·void·a·bly** /ùnnə vóydəblee/ *adv.*

un·a·ware /ùnnə wáir/ *adj.* **1. NOT AWARE** not conscious or aware of something **2. NOT KNOWLEDGEABLE** lacking important information or analysis ○ *a politically unaware generation* ■ *adv.* = **unawares** —**un·a·ware·ly** *adv.* —**un·a·ware·ness** *n.*

WORD KEY: USAGE

unaware or **unawares**? ***Unaware*** is normally used as an adjective, *They were unaware of the danger*, whereas ***unawares*** is an adverb, used especially in the idiom *to catch (or take) somebody unawares*, but also in other ways: *They crept up on us unawares.*

un·a·wares /ùnnə wáirz/ *adv.* **1. UNEXPECTEDLY** without any warning or anticipation ○ *His question caught me unawares.* **2. WITHOUT INTENDING TO** without planning or intending to do something ○ *He took the wrong coat, unawares.* [Mid-16thC. Coined from UNAWARE + -s, an adverbial ending originally meaning "of."]

WORD KEY: USAGE

See Usage note at ***unaware***.

unb. *abbr.* PUBL unbound

un·backed /un bákt/ *adj.* **1. NOT SUPPORTED OR BACKED** with no support or backing, especially financial backing **2.** FURNITURE **WITHOUT A BACK** used to describe a chair that has been made without a back **3.** RIDING **NEVER RIDDEN** used to describe a horse that has never been ridden ○ *an unbacked mare* **4.** GAMBLING **NOT BET ON** used to describe a horse that has had no bets placed on its performance

un·bal·ance /un bálləns/ *vt.* (**-anced, -anc·ing, -anc·es**) **1. KNOCK SOMETHING OFF BALANCE** to make something lose its balance or equilibrium **2. MAKE SOMEBODY PSYCHOLOGICALLY UNSTABLE** to make somebody psychologically or emotionally unstable ■ *n.* **STATE OF INSTABILITY** the state of being unstable and out of balance —**un·bal·ance·a·ble** *adj.*

un·bal·anced /un bállənst/ *adj.* **1. WITHOUT EQUILIBRIUM** lacking the proper distribution of weight or forces that would provide balance **2. PSYCHOLOGICALLY UNSTABLE** unable to make sound judgments **3. ONE-SIDED** done or provided from only one perspective ○ *unbalanced reporting* **4.** ACCT **WITH UNEQUAL DEBITS AND CREDITS** in which the totaled debits and credits are not equal

un·bar /un báar/ (**-barred, -bar·ring, -bars**) *vt.* **1. UNLOCK A DOOR** to unlock or open a door or gate **2. REMOVE BARS** to remove the bars or obstructions from something

un·bat·ed /un báytəd/ *adj.* lacking a protective button or guard on its point (*archaic*) ○ *an unbated sword* [Late 16thC. Formed from UN- + *bated*, the past participle of *bate* "to abate, blunt," a shortening of ABATE.]

unbd. *abbr.* PUBL unbound

un·bear·a·ble /un báirəb'l/ *adj.* difficult, unpleasant, or impossible to bear or tolerate —**un·bear·a·ble·ness** *n.* —**un·bear·a·bly** *adv.*

un·beat·a·ble /un béetəb'l/ *adj.* too good or favorable to be beaten or surpassed —**un·beat·a·bly** *adv.*

un·beat·en /un béet'n/ *adj.* **1. UNDEFEATED** never having been defeated or outdone **2.** COOK **NOT WHIPPED OR POUNDED** not subjected to pounding, whipping, or beating as part of the preparation for cooking or eating **3.** TRANSP **NOT TRAVELED** not made smooth from pedestrian or vehicular traffic

un·be·com·ing /un bi kúmming/ *adj.* **1.** CLOTHES **NOT FLATTERING** unsuitable or unattractive on the wearer **2. NOT RIGHT OR PROPER** not suitable, especially as not conforming with accepted attitudes or behavior —**un·be·com·ing·ly** *adv.* —**un·be·com·ing·ness** *n.*

un·be·known /ùnbi nón/, **un·be·knownst** /ùnbi nónst/ *adj.* **1. WITHOUT SOMEBODY KNOWING** happening without a particular person knowing about it **2. NOT KNOWN TO SOMEBODY** not known or familiar to somebody ■ *adv.* **un·be·knownst WITHOUT BEING SEEN** without being noticed or seen by anybody ○ *slipped away unbeknownst* [Mid-17thC. Formed from UN- + *beknown*, the past participle of obsolete *beknow*, literally "to know thoroughly," from KNOW.]

un·be·lief /ùnbi léef/ *n.* lack of religious or political belief

un·be·liev·a·ble /ùnbi léevəb'l/ *adj.* **1. IMPLAUSIBLE** too unrealistic or improbable to be believed **2. EXTRAORDINARY** used to emphasize that something is very great, or very good, bad, or impressive ○ *reacted with unbelievable agility* —**un·be·liev·a·bly** *adv.*

un·be·liev·er /ùnbi léevər/ *n.* somebody who does not believe in a particular religious faith or subscribe to conventional beliefs

un·be·liev·ing /ùnbi léeving/ *adj.* **1. SKEPTICAL** lacking belief or expressing disbelief about something **2. WITHOUT BELIEFS** with no religious faith or doctrinal beliefs —**un·be·liev·ing·ly** *adv.*

un·belt /un bélt/ (**-belt·ed, -belt·ing, -belts**) *vt.* **1. UNDO GARMENT'S BELT** to unfasten the belt on a garment **2. REMOVE SOMEBODY OR SOMETHING FROM BELT** to remove somebody or something from a supporting or restraining belt

un·bend /un bénd/ (**-bent** /-bént/, **-bent, -bend·ing, -bends**) *v.* **1.** *vti.* **MAKE OR BECOME RELAXED** to become, or make somebody become, more informal, relaxed, or friendly **2.** *vti.* **MAKE OR BECOME STRAIGHT** to become, or make something become, straight after being bent, twisted, or flexed **3.** *vt.* NAUT **UNFASTEN SAIL OR ROPE** to free a sail, rope, or mooring line that was fastened —**un·bend·a·ble** *adj.*

un·bend·ing /un bénding/ *adj.* **1. RESOLUTE** not willing to change opinions, beliefs, or attitudes **2. STRICTLY OBSERVED** strictly applied or observed **3. ALOOF** formal or unfriendly in manner or behavior —**un·bend·ing·ly** *adv.*

un·bent[1] /un bént/ *adj.* **1. NOT FORCED INTO SUBMISSION** not forced into submitting or giving in **2. STRAIGHT** not bent or twisted

un·bent[2] past tense, past participle of **unbend**

un·bi·ased /un bí əst/, **un·bi·assed** *adj.* **1. NOT BIASED** fair and impartial rather than biased or prejudiced **2.** STATS **WITH ZERO BIAS** with an expected value that is equal to the parameter being estimated —**un·bi·ased·ly** *adv.* —**un·bi·ased·ness** *n.*

un·bib·li·cal /un bíblik'l/ *adj.* opposed or in contrast to the teachings of the Bible, or not present or approved in biblical teaching

un·bid·den /un bídd'n/ *adj., adv.* (*literary*) **1. SPONTANEOUS** not wished for or willed **2. UNSOLICITED** not asked for or invited [Old English *unbeden*, formed from *beden*, the past participle of *biddan* "to ask for," an earlier form of BID]

un·bind /un bínd/ (**-bound** /-bównd/, **-bound, -bind·ing, -binds**) *vt.* (*literary*) **1. FREE SOMEBODY FROM RESTRICTIONS** to free somebody from something restraining or restricting, e.g., a duty or obligation **2. UNTIE** to untie a person or animal

un·bleached /un bléecht/ *adj.* not treated with a bleach or whitener

un·blessed /un blést/ *adj.* **1. WITHOUT A BLESSING** not given a blessing **2. UNFORTUNATE** unfortunate or wretched (*literary*) **3. REGARDED AS EVIL** in particular religions, regarded as behaving in unrighteous ways (*literary*) —**un·bless·ed·ness** /un bléssədnəss/ *n.*

un·blink·ing /un blíngking/ *adj.* 1. WITHOUT HESITATION showing no emotion, reluctance, or hesitation 2. WITHOUT BLINKING failing or unable to close and open the eyes in quick succession —**un·blink·ing·ly** *adv.*

un·blush·ing /un blúshing/ *adj.* feeling or showing no shame or embarrassment —**un·blush·ing·ly** *adv.* —**un·blush·ing·ness** *n.*

un·bolt /un bṓlt/ (**-bolt·ed, -bolt·ing, -bolts**) *vt.* to pull back the bolt or bolts on a door or gate, so that it can be opened

un·bolt·ed /un bṓltəd/ *adj.* 1. NOT FASTENED WITH BOLTS not fitted with bolts, or with bolts not fastened 2. UNSIFTED not having had the coarse particles sifted from the fine ones (*refers to flower or grain*)

un·born /un báwrn/ *adj.* 1. NOT BORN YET not yet born, but usually already conceived and gestating ○ *behavior that could benefit the unborn child* 2. NOT THOUGHT OF YET not thought of or begun yet (*literary*)

un·bos·om /un bŏŏzzəm/ (**-omed, -om·ing, -oms**) *v.* (*literary*) 1. *vti.* EXPRESS SOMETHING PREVIOUSLY HIDDEN to express something previously suppressed or hidden 2. *vr.* SAY WHAT IS ON YOUR MIND to reveal the thoughts, feelings, or secrets you have been keeping inside yourself

un·bound[1] *adj.* 1. WITHOUT A COVER not fastened inside a permanent cover 2. UNRESTRICTED having had restraints or fetters removed 3. SCI NOT IN CHEMICAL COMBINATION free from chemical or physical combination 4. LING CONSTITUTING A WORD used to describe a morpheme that can form a word on its own without any added elements

un·bound[2] past tense, past participle of **unbind**

un·bound·ed /un bówndəd/ *adj.* 1. NOT RESTRAINED not controlled or restrained in any way 2. WITHOUT RESTRICTIONS not subject to limits, boundaries, or restrictions —**un·bound·ed·ly** *adv.* —**un·bound·ed·ness** *n.*

un·bowed /un bówd/ *adj.* 1. UNDEFEATED having refused to submit or admit defeat 2. NOT BENT remaining in an erect position, not bent or bowed

un·brace /un bráyss/ (**-braced, -brac·ing, -brac·es**) *vt.* to make something less tense or strained (*literary*)

un·bred /un bréd/ *adj.* 1. NOT TRAINED not given training or instruction (*literary*) 2. NOT WELL BRED lacking refinement or breeding (*literary*) 3. AGRIC NOT YET MATED not yet mated with another animal

un·bri·dle /un brī́d'l/ (**-dled, -dling, -dles**) *vt.* 1. FREE SOMETHING FROM RESTRAINTS to take away the limits, controls, or restraints that apply to something 2. EQU REMOVE BRIDLE to take the bridle from a horse

un·bri·dled /un brī́d'ld/ *adj.* 1. OPENLY EXPRESSED freely and openly expressed 2. EQU WITHOUT BRIDLE not fitted with a bridle —**un·bri·dled·ly** *adv.* —**un·bri·dled·ness** *n.*

un·bro·ken /un brṓkən/ *adj.* 1. WITHOUT GAPS OR PAUSES with no gaps or pauses 2. NOT FRAGMENTED remaining intact or in one piece 3. ONGOING continued without interruption 4. UNDEFEATED not beaten or subdued 5. UNTAMED not yet having submitted to human control ○ *an unbroken horse* 6. NOT VIOLATED having remained viable or in force —**un·bro·ken·ly** *adv.* —**un·bro·ken·ness** *n.*

un·bun·dle /un búnd'l/ (**-dled, -dling, -dles**) *vt.* to sell or charge for related products and services separately, rather than as a unit

un·bur·den /un búrd'n/ (**-dened, -den·ing, -dens**) *v.* 1. *vr.* GET SOMETHING OFF YOUR MIND to relieve yourself of something that has been worrying you by telling somebody about it (*formal*) 2. *vt.* REMOVE PERSON'S OR ANIMAL'S LOAD to take off a load that a person or animal has been carrying (*literary*)

un·but·ton /un bútt'n/ (**-toned, -ton·ing, -tons**) *v.* 1. *vt.* UNDO CLOTHES WITH BUTTONS to undo a garment by unfastening the buttons 2. *vi.* RELAX to relax and become more talkative (*informal*)

un·caged /un káyjd/ *adj.* 1. RELEASED FROM A CAGE no longer restrained in a cage 2. NOT LIMITED TO A CAGE allowed to fly or roam freely

un·called-for /un káwld-/ *adj.* beyond what is necessary or expected, especially in being unjustifiably unkind or impolite

un·can·ny /un kánnee/ (**-ni·er, -ni·est**) *adj.* 1. EERIE too strange or unlikely to seem merely natural or human 2. KEEN unexpectedly accurate or precise ○ *an uncanny resemblance to the president* —**un·can·ni·ly** *adv.* —**un·can·ni·ness** *n.*

un·cap /un káp/ (**-capped, -cap·ping, -caps**) *vt.* to remove an upper limit or restriction from something

un·cared-for /ùn káird-/ *adj.* neglected and allowed to deteriorate

Un·cas /úngkəss/ (1588?–1683?) Native North American leader. He was a chief of the Mohegan (Mohican) people and sided with the British against other Native North American peoples.

un·ceas·ing /un seéssing/ *adj.* continuing without stopping, pausing, or diminishing —**un·ceas·ing·ly** *adv.* —**un·ceas·ing·ness** *n.*

un·cer·e·mo·ni·ous /un sèrrə mṓnee əss/ *adj.* 1. ABRUPT sudden and rude, with no concern for politeness or good manners 2. INFORMAL done without formality or ceremony —**un·cer·e·mo·ni·ous·ly** *adv.* —**un·cer·e·mo·ni·ous·ness** *n.*

un·cer·tain /un súrt'n/ *adj.* 1. WITHOUT KNOWLEDGE lacking clear knowledge or a definite opinion 2. NOT KNOWN OR SETTLED not yet known, or remaining undecided 3. CHANGEABLE likely to change, and therefore not reliable or stable 4. LACKING SELF-ASSURANCE lacking self-assurance or confidence —**un·cer·tain·ly** *adv.* —**un·cer·tain·ness** *n.*

WORD KEY: SYNONYMS

See Synonyms at ***doubtful***.

un·cer·tain·ty /un súrt'ntee/ (*plural* **-ties**) *n.* 1. FACT OF BEING UNCERTAIN the quality or state of being uncertain 2. UNPREDICTABLE THING something that nobody can predict or guarantee (*often plural*)

un·cer·tain·ty prin·ci·ple *n.* a principle in quantum mechanics holding that it is impossible to determine both the position and momentum of a particle at the same time

un·chain /un cháyn/ (**-chained, -chain·ing, -chains**) *vt.* 1. REMOVE CHAINS FROM SOMEBODY to take off the chain or chains holding a person or animal 2. FREE SOMETHING OR SOMEBODY FROM RESTRAINTS to take away the limits, controls, or restraints that apply to something or somebody

un·charged /un chaárjd/ *adj.* with no electric charge

un·char·i·ta·ble /un chérrətəb'l/ *adj.* lacking in kindness or mercy —**un·char·i·ta·bly** *adv.*

un·chart·ed /un chaártəd/ *adj.* 1. NOT MAPPED not surveyed or recorded on a map 2. UNKNOWN not previously encountered, experienced, or investigated

un·char·tered /un chaártərd/ *adj.* not officially authorized or permitted

un·checked /un chékt/ *adj.* 1. NOT CURBED not limited or controlled, especially when restraint or control is required 2. NOT TESTED remaining unverified or untested, especially for problems or imperfections

un·chris·tian /un krísch'n/ *adj.* 1. UNCHARITABLE unkind or selfish, and therefore against Christian principles and teachings 2. RELIG NON-CHRISTIAN not belonging to the Christian church

un·church /un chúrch/ (**-churched, -church·ing, -church·es**) *vt.* 1. EXCOMMUNICATE to expel somebody from a church 2. DECLARE TO BE NO LONGER A CHURCH to remove the status of being a church from a building

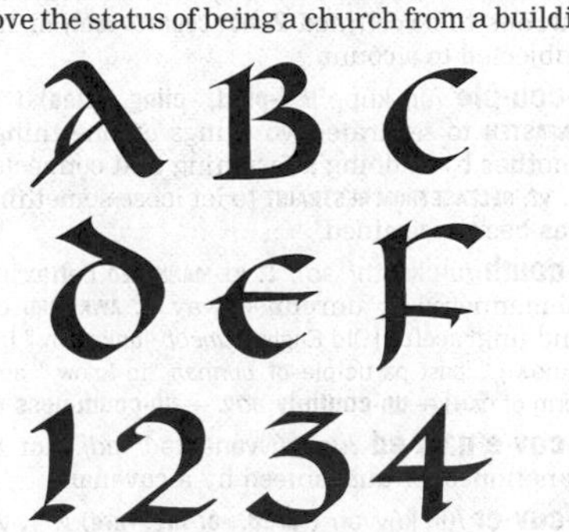

Uncial

un·cial /únshəl/ *n.* 1. STYLE OF LETTER USED IN MANUSCRIPTS a letter of the kind used in Greek and Latin manuscripts written between the third and ninth centuries that resembles a modern capital letter but is more rounded 2. MANUSCRIPT IN UNCIALS a manuscript written in uncials ■ *adj.* WRITTEN IN UNCIALS relating to or written in uncials [Mid-17thC. From late Latin *unciales (litterae)*, literally "inch-high (letters)," from *uncia* "twelfth part, inch."] —**un·cial·ly** *adv.*

un·ci·form /únsi fàwrm/ *adj.* BIOL HOOK-SHAPED shaped like a hook ■ *n.* ANAT BONE IN THE WRIST a small hook-shaped bone in the wrist, at the base of the third and little fingers [Mid-18thC. Formed from Latin *uncus* "hook."]

un·ci·nar·i·a·sis /ùnsinə rī́ əssiss/ *n.* infestation of the intestines with hookworms [Early 20thC. From modern Latin *Uncinaria*, name of a genus of hookworms, from Latin *uncus* "hook."]

un·ci·nate /únsinət, -nàyt/ *adj.* shaped like a hook at the end [Mid-18thC. From Latin *uncinatus*, from *uncus* "hook."]

un·ci·nus /un sī́nəss/ (*plural* **-ni** /-nī/) *n.* 1. ZOOL HOOKED PART OF AN ANIMAL'S BODY a small hooked body part, e.g., the hook-shaped tooth of a gastropod or a chitinous hook on the body of an annelid 2. METEOROL CIRRUS CLOUD a cirrus cloud that is curled in a hook shape at one of its elongated ends [Mid-19thC. From Latin, from *uncus* "hook."]

un·cir·cum·cised /un súrkəm sìzd/ *adj.* not having had the prepuce of the penis or clitoris removed —**un·cir·cum·ci·sion** /un sùrkəm sízh'n/ *n.*

un·civ·il /un sívv'l/ *adj.* 1. RUDE behaving in a way that is seen as hostile or indifferent 2. UNCIVILIZED lacking features thought to reflect a civilized society or individual (*archaic*) —**un·ci·vil·i·ty** /ùnsi víllətee/ *n.* —**un·civ·il·ly** /un sívv'l lee/ *adv.* —**un·civ·il·ness** /un sívv'lnəss/ *n.*

un·civ·i·lized /un sívv'l ìzd/ *adj.* 1. NOT CULTURALLY ADVANCED existing in a condition or behaving in ways that are thought to be socially or culturally primitive 2. REMOTE far from civilized or settled areas —**un·civ·i·lized·ly** *adv.* —**un·civ·i·liz·ed·ness** /-ìzəd nəss/ *n.*

un·clad /un klád/ *adj.* not wearing any clothes

un·clasp /un klásp/ (**-clasped, -clasp·ing, -clasps**) *vt.* 1. SEPARATE HANDS to separate hands previously held together 2. UNDO THE CLASP ON SOMETHING to unfasten the clasp holding something closed

un·clas·si·fied /un klássə fìd/ *adj.* 1. NOT ARRANGED SYSTEMATICALLY not arranged or grouped systematically 2. NOT SECRET remaining open for examination by anyone who wishes access

un·cle /úngk'l/ *n.* 1. PARENT'S BROTHER OR BROTHER-IN-LAW the brother of somebody's mother or father, or the husband of somebody's aunt (*capitalized before a name*) 2. KINDLY OLDER MAN an older male person who gives support, protection, and advice 3. PAWNBROKER a pawnbroker (*dated slang*) [13thC. Via Old French *oncle* from, ultimately, Latin *avunculus* "maternal uncle."] ◇ **cry uncle** surrender or admit defeat (*informal*)

Un·cle *n.* a name some children are encouraged to call a man friend of one or both of their parents

un·clean /un kleén/ *adj.* 1. DIRTY dirty or unsanitary 2. UNCHASTE sinful, especially involving or guilty of committing a sexual sin 3. RELIG RELIGIOUSLY OR RITUALLY IMPURE not pure according to religious rules or rituals [Old English *unclǣne*] —**un·clean·ness** *n.*

WORD KEY: SYNONYMS

See Synonyms at ***dirty***.

un·clean·ly *adj.* /un klénnlee/ = **unclean** (*formal or literary*) ■ *adv.* /un kleénlee/ IN UNCLEAN WAY in a way that is not clean [Old English *unclǣnic, unclǣnice*] —**un·clean·li·ness** /un klénleenəss/ *n.*

un·clear /un kleér/ *adj.* 1. NOT OBVIOUS not obvious or easy to understand 2. NOT SURE not sure or not free from doubt

Un·cle Sam *n.* 1. PERSONIFICATION OF THE UNITED STATES a personification of the government of the United States, shown in a tall thin man with a white beard, wearing red and white striped trousers, a blue tailcoat, and a stovepipe hat with a band of stars 2. UNITED STATES the United States or the American people [19thC. Invented from *U. S.*, abbreviation of *United States*.]

Un·cle Tom *n.* a highly offensive term used to describe a Black man who is thought to be too solicitous of or subservient to Caucasians (*insult*) [Mid-19thC. After a character in Harriet Beecher Stowe's novel *Uncle Tom's Cabin*.] —**Uncle Tom·ism** *n.*

un·clog /un klóg/ (**-clogged, -clog·ging, -clogs**) *vt.* to remove a blockage from something such as a pipe

un·close /un klṓz/ (**-closed, -clos·ing, -clos·es**) *vti.* **1.** MAKE OR BE OPEN to make or become open rather than closed **2.** DISCLOSE to reveal something, or to be revealed

un·closed /un klṓzd/ *adj.* not in a closed condition

un·clothe /un klṓth/ (**-clothed, -clothing, -clothes**) *vt.* to remove the clothes or covering from somebody or something —**un·clothed** *adj.*

un·co /úng kō/ *adv. Scotland* VERY very or extremely ■ *adj. Scotland* UNUSUAL unusual or unfamiliar [15thC. Variant of UNCOUTH.]

un·coil /un kóyl/ (**-coiled, -coil·ing, -coils**) *vti.* to release something, or be released, from a coiled or wound position

un·com·fort·a·ble /un kúmfərtəb'l, un kúmftərb'l/ *adj.* **1.** NOT PHYSICALLY COMFORTABLE feeling a lack of or not providing physical comfort **2.** AWKWARD OR UNEASY feeling or making others feel awkward and ill-at-ease —**un·com·fort·a·ble·ness** *n.* —**un·com·fort·a·bly** *adv.*

un·com·mer·cial /ùnkə múrsh'l/ *adj.* **1.** NOT CONCERNED WITH COMMERCE OR BUSINESS not involved in commerce, especially not operated or organized for profit **2.** AGAINST BUSINESS PRINCIPLES OR PRACTICES contrary to the way things are usually done in commerce or business **3.** UNPROFITABLE unappealing to consumers and so not likely to turn a profit

un·com·mit·ted /ùnkə míttəd/ *adj.* **1.** WITH NO SENSE OF COMMITMENT not dedicated to a particular principle, cause, or organization **2.** NOT PLEDGED not pledged to a particular cause, purpose, or course of action ○ *uncommitted funds*

un·com·mon /un kómmən/ *adj.* **1.** RARE appearing or happening infrequently **2.** VERY GREAT used to emphasize the great extent of something —**un·com·mon·ness** *n.*

un·com·mon·ly /un kómmənlee/ *adv.* **1.** SELDOM not frequently **2.** UNUSUALLY to a degree or extent that is unusual or rare

un·com·mu·ni·ca·tive /ùnkə myṓōnə kàytiv, ùnkə myṓōnəkətiv/ *adj.* not willing to say much or tending not to say much —**un·com·mu·ni·ca·tive·ly** *adv.* —**un·com·mu·ni·ca·tive·ness** *n.*

WORD KEY: SYNONYMS

See Synonyms at ***silent***.

un·com·pro·mis·ing /un kómprə mīzing/ *adj.* feeling or showing no willingness to compromise or back down —**un·com·pro·mis·ing·ly** *adv.* —**un·com·pro·mis·ing·ness** *n.*

un·con·cern /ùnkən súrn/ *n.* lack of concern or interest, especially where concern would be expected or thought appropriate

un·con·cerned /ùnkən súrnd/ *adj.* **1.** NOT ANXIOUS not worried or anxious, especially when this seems unexpected or unnatural **2.** INDIFFERENT lacking concern or interest or unwilling to become involved in something —**un·con·cern·ed·ly** /-súrnədlee/ *adv.* —**un·con·cern·ed·ness** /-súrnədnəss/ *n.*

un·con·di·tion·al /ùnkən dísh'n'l, -díshnəl/ *adj.* complete or guaranteed, with no conditions, limitations, or provisos attached ○ *unconditional love* —**un·con·di·tion·al·i·ty** /-dìshə nállətee/ *n.* —**un·con·di·tion·al·ly** /ùnkən dísh'n'lee, -díshnəlee/ *adv.*

un·con·di·tioned /ùnkən dísh'nd/ *adj.* **1.** WITHOUT CONDITIONS without any conditions or limits restricting or affecting it **2.** PSYCHOL NATURAL arising spontaneously and not as a result of learning or conditioning ○ *an unconditioned reflex* —**un·con·di·tioned·ness** *n.*

un·con·di·tioned stim·u·lus *n.* a stimulus that evokes a reflexive response without prior conditioning or learning

un·con·form·a·ble /ùnkən fáwrməb'l/ *adj.* **1.** UNWILLING TO CONFORM unwilling or unable to follow conventional social customs **2.** GEOL SHOWING GEOLOGIC UNCONFORMITY used to describe a layer of rock that lies directly on a much older stratum, indicating a period of erosion —**un·con·form·a·bil·i·ty** /-fàwrmə bíllətee/ *n.* —**un·con·form·a·bly** /ùnkən fáwrməblee/ *adv.*

un·con·for·mi·ty /ùnkən fáwrmətee/ (*plural* **-form·i·ties**) *n.* **1.** LACK OF CONFORMITY behavior or thinking that refuses to follow conventional social prescriptions **2.** GEOL BREAK IN CONTINUITY IN SEDIMENTARY ROCKS a break in the continuity of sedimentary rocks resulting from erosion or cessation of deposition **3.** GEOL SURFACE BETWEEN MISMATCHED STRATA the contact surface between two uncomformable strata, often marked by angular discordance

un·con·nect·ed /ùnkə néktəd/ *adj.* not related or connected to something else or each other ○ *The two incidents are entirely unconnected.* —**un·con·nect·ed·ly** *adv.* —**un·con·nect·ed·ness** *n.*

un·con·scion·a·ble /un kónshənəb'l/ *adj.* **1.** MORALLY UNACCEPTABLE shocking and morally unacceptable **2.** UNREASONABLE far beyond what is considered reasonable —**un·con·scion·a·ble·ness** *n.* —**un·con·scion·a·bly** *adv.*

un·con·scious /un kónshəss/ *adj.* **1.** MED EXPERIENCING LOSS OF SENSES unable to see, hear, or otherwise sense what is going on, usually temporarily and often as a result of an accident or injury **2.** UNAWARE not aware of something **3.** UNINTENTIONAL not intended, or not realized or recognized ○ *unconscious irony* ■ *n.* PSYCHOL MIND'S HIDDEN PART the part of the mind containing memories, thoughts, feelings, and ideas that the person is not generally aware of but that manifest themselves in dreams and dissociated acts —**un·con·scious·ly** *adv.* —**un·con·scious·ness** *n.*

un·con·sid·ered /ùnkən síddərd/ *adj.* done without being adequately thought about beforehand

un·con·sti·tu·tion·al /un kònstə tóōshən'l, -tóōshnəl/ *adj.* not allowed by or against the principles set down in a constitution, especially a nation's written constitution —**un·con·sti·tu·tion·al·i·ty** /un konstə tòōsh'n állətee/ *n.* —**un·con·sti·tu·tion·al·ly** /un konstə tóōshən'lee, -tóōshnəlee/ *adv.*

un·con·trol·la·ble /ùnkən trṓləb'l/ *adj.* **1.** TOO STRONG TO SUPPRESS too strongly felt to be suppressed **2.** TOO UNRULY TO CONTROL too unruly or wild to discipline or control —**un·con·trol·la·bil·i·ty** /-trōlə bíllətee/ *n.* —**un·con·trol·la·bly** /ùnkən trṓləblee/ *adv.*

un·con·ven·tion·al /ùnkən vénshən'l/ *adj.* different from what is regarded as normal or standard —**un·con·ven·tion·al·i·ty** /ùnkən vènshə nállətee/ *n.* —**un·con·ven·tion·al·ly** /ùnkən vénshən'lee/ *adv.*

un·cool /un kóōl/ *adj.* **1.** UNDESIRABLE unfashionable, undesirable, or unacceptable, especially in the opinion of young people (*slang*) **2.** UNRELAXED not suitably relaxed, casual, or self-assured, especially in the opinion of young people (*informal*)

un·co·or·di·nat·ed /un kō áwrd'n àytəd/ *adj.* **1.** CLUMSY IN MOVEMENT OR ACTION awkward when moving or doing something, as if different parts of the body were not acting in harmony **2.** NOT ORGANIZED with no organization or proper cooperation between individuals or groups

un·cork /un káwrk/ (**-corked, -cork·ing, -corks**) *vt.* **1.** REMOVE THE CORK FROM to open a bottle of something, especially wine, by taking out its cork **2.** UNLEASH to release something that has been restrained or repressed such as a strong emotion

un·count·a·ble /un kówntəb'l/ *adj.* **1.** NOT ABLE TO BE COUNTED too various or great in number to be counted **2.** GRAM NOT REFERRING TO AN INDIVIDUAL used to describe a noun that does not refer to a single object

un·count·ed /un kówntəd/ *adj.* **1.** INNUMERABLE too numerous to be counted **2.** NOT COUNTED not, or not yet, subjected to a count

un·cou·ple /un kúpp'l/ (**-pled, -pling, -ples**) *v.* **1.** *vti.* UNFASTEN to separate two things or one thing from another by undoing a fastening that connects them **2.** *vt.* RELEASE FROM RESTRAINT to let loose something that has been restrained

un·couth /un kóōth/ *adj.* **1.** ILL-MANNERED behaving in a ill-mannered or unrefined way **2.** AWKWARD clumsy and ungraceful [Old English *uncūþ* "unknown," from *cūþ* "known," past participle of *cunnan* "to know," an earlier form of CAN] —**un·couth·ly** *adv.* —**un·couth·ness** *n.*

un·cov·e·nant·ed /un kúvvənəntəd/ *adj.* not bound, sanctioned, or guaranteed by a covenant

un·cov·er /un kúvvər/ (**-ered, -er·ing, -ers**) *v.* **1.** *vti.* TAKE THE COVER OFF to remove a covering from something **2.** *vt.* EXPOSE to find, find out about, or reveal something secret or previously hidden ○ *uncover the truth about somebody* **3.** *vti.* TAKE OFF YOUR HAT to take off a hat or other head covering (*dated*)

un·cov·ered /un kúvvərd/ *adj.* **1.** WITH NO COVERING without any covering or protection **2.** INSUR NOT INSURED not protected by insurance or guaranteed by some security **3.** WITH THE HEAD BARE with a hat or other head covering removed, usually as a sign of respect (*dated*)

un·crit·i·cal /un kríttik'l/ *adj.* accepting or approving something without analyzing or questioning it or discriminating between good and bad —**un·crit·i·cal·ly** *adv.*

un·cross /un kráwss, un kross/ (**-crossed, -cross·ing, -cross·es**) *vt.* to straighten out from a crossed position ○ *She sat crossing and uncrossing her arms impatiently.*

un·crowned /un krównd/ *adj.* **1.** WITH POWER BUT NO TITLE possessing power, status, or wide respect but without an official title or recognition **2.** ROYAL BUT NOT YET CROWNED with royal rank but not yet crowned

unc·tion /úngkshən/ *n.* **1.** ANOINTING WITH OIL the rubbing or sprinkling of oil on somebody as part of a religious ceremony or medical treatment **2.** SUBSTANCE USED IN A RITE OR TREATMENT an oil, ointment, or salve used in religious rites or medical treatment **3.** REAL OR PRETENDED EARNESTNESS real or pretended earnestness or fervor, especially with regard to spiritual matters and especially when expressed in suitably solemn language **4.** FLATTERING EFFORTS TO CHARM excessively ingratiating efforts to charm or convince somebody **5.** SOMETHING SOOTHING something that soothes or comforts somebody [14thC. From Latin *unction-*, from *unguere* "to smear, anoint" (source of English *ointment* and *anoint*).]

unc·tu·ous /úngkchoo əss/ *adj.* **1.** EXCESSIVELY INGRATIATING attempting to charm or convince somebody in an unpleasantly suave, smug, or smooth way **2.** OILY, FATTY, OR GREASY resembling or containing oil, fat, or grease **3.** SOFT AND RICH soft and rich in texture and easily workable, especially through containing a high proportion of organic material [14thC. From medieval Latin *unctuosus*, from Latin *unctus* "anointing," from *unguere* (see UNCTION).] —**unc·tu·os·i·ty** /ùngkchoo óssətee/ *n.* —**unc·tu·ous·ly** /úngkchoo əsslee/ *adv.* —**unc·tu·ous·ness** /úngkchoo əssnəss/ *n.*

un·curl /un kúrl/ (**-curled, -curl·ing, -curls**) *vti.* to straighten something that was previously wound in a curl, coil, or spiral, or to become unwound or straight

un·cus /úngkəss/ (*plural* **-ci** /ún sī/) *n.* ANAT a body part shaped like a hook [Early 19thC. Via modern Latin from Latin, "hook."]

un·cut /un kút/ *adj.* **1.** NOT CUT with no part removed or divided by cutting **2.** COMPLETE not abridged, shortened, or censored **3.** NOT FACETED used to describe a gemstone in its original shape, before facets have been cut **4.** PUBL WITH UNSEPARATED PAGES with the edges of the pages not yet trimmed to separate them **5.** DRUGS NOT ADULTERATED in a pure and unadulterated form (*informal*)

un·damped /un dámpt/ *adj.* **1.** NOT DIMINISHED not subdued or discouraged **2.** PHYS ABLE TO OSCILLATE used to describe a scientific instrument or system that is allowed to oscillate unchecked

un·daunt·ed /un dáwntəd/ *adj.* not afraid or deterred by the prospect of defeat, loss, or failure —**un·daunt·ed·ly** *adv.* —**un·daunt·ed·ness** *n.*

un·dead /un déd/ *npl.* in fiction, especially vampire stories, people or other beings who are technically dead but still exist, move, and interact with the living in a physical form —**un·dead** *adj.*

un·de·bat·a·ble /ùndi báytəb'l/ *adj.* not open to debate or dispute —**un·de·bat·a·bly** *adv.*

un·dec·a·gon /un dékə gòn/ *n.* a plane figure with eleven sides and eleven angles [Early 18thC. Formed from Latin *undecim* "eleven" + -GON, on the model of DECAGON.]

un·de·ceive /ùndi sēev/ (**-ceived, -ceiv·ing, -ceives**) *vt.* to tell the truth to somebody who has been misled (*often passive*) —**un·de·ceiv·er** *n.*

un·de·cid·ed /ùndi sīdəd/ *adj.* **1.** NOT HAVING DECIDED not yet having made a choice or decision **2.** NOT FINALIZED not yet settled or resolved ■ *n.* SOMEBODY WITHOUT MIND MADE UP somebody who has not yet made a decision or choice about something ○ *She was counted among the undecideds.* —**un·de·cid·ed·ly** *adv.* —**un·de·cid·ed·ness** *n.*

un·de·fined /ùndi fīnd/ *adj.* **1.** WITHOUT FIXED LIMITS for which no definite limits have been decided **2.** NOT EXPLAINED not given a definition, meaning, or value

un·de·lete /ùndi léet/ (**-let·ed, -let·ing, -letes**) *vt.* COMPUT to reinstate text or a file that has been deleted on a computer

un·dem·o·crat·ic /un dèmmə kráttik/ *adj.* not in accordance with or not practicing democracy —**un·dem·o·crat·i·cal·ly** *adv.*

un·de·mon·stra·tive /ùndi mónstrətiv/ *adj.* tending not to show emotions openly —**un·de·mon·stra·tive·ly** *adv.* —**un·de·mon·stra·tive·ness** *n.*

un·de·ni·a·ble /ùndi nī́ əb'l/ *adj.* **1. BEYOND QUESTION** unquestionably true or real and beyond dispute **2. UNABLE TO BE REFUSED** not able to be refused because of its importance or impact **3. INDISPUTABLY WORTHY** with worth, merit, or quality that cannot be doubted ○ *a person of undeniable character* —**un·de·ni·a·ble·ness** *n.* —**un·de·ni·a·bly** *adv.*

un·der /úndər/ CORE MEANING: a grammatical word used to express the concept of being beneath or below something, e.g., in location, size, age, or price ○ (prep) *Johnny had the book hidden under his tunic.* ○ (prep) *The machine is under a foot high and will fit on to any work surface.* ○ (prep) *The toy should not be given to children under three years old.* ○ (prep) *It's the best meal you can get for under $5.* ○ (adv) *For one week only, kids five and under eat free.*
1. *prep.* **BELOW** directly below or underneath the base of something ○ *They were sheltering under a huge umbrella.* **2.** *prep.* **BENEATH** beneath a layer of something ○ *He had two sweaters on under his jacket.* **3.** *prep.* **LESS THAN** fewer in number than or less than something, e.g., in age, quantity, size, or price ○ *By the age of sixteen she was still under five feet tall.* **4.** *prep.* **SUBORDINATE TO** lower in rank or status than somebody ○ *I was under him in the company hierarchy.* **5.** *prep.* **SUBJECT TO** subject to the control or authority of somebody or something ○ *under existing legislation* ○ *working under a new boss* **6.** *prep.* **DURING THE RULE OF** during the rule of a person or government ○ *The crime rate had in fact gone down under the new mayor.* **7.** *prep.* **IN VIEW OF** in view of something or while something, especially conditions or circumstances, prevails ○ *Serious work is impossible under these conditions.* **8.** *prep.* **UNDERGOING A PROCESS** used to indicate that somebody or something is going through a particular process or experience ○ *The proposals have come under attack.* **9.** *prep.* **USING THE NAME OF** using a particular name, especially an assumed name ○ *traveling under a false name* **10.** *prep.* **CLASSIFIED WITHIN** classified as or in something ○ *You should find it in the filing cabinet under "Miscellaneous."* **11.** *prep.* **PLANTED WITH** planted with a particular crop ○ *That field will be under rye next year.* **12.** *prep.* **POWERED BY** powered or driven by something ○ *under sail* **13.** *prep.* **IN A SIGN OF THE ZODIAC** during a period in which the sun is in a particular position in the zodiac ○ *I was born under Saggitarius.* **14.** *adv.* **BELOW A SURFACE OR POINT** at or to a point or place at a lower level, especially one below a surface ○ *lifted the wire and crawled under* **15.** *adv.* **FEWER OR LESS** fewer or less than a previously given figure ○ *Employers with 50 employees or under are exempt.* **16.** *adv., adj.* **SUBSERVIENT** in or into a position of submissiveness or subservience (*informal*) ○ *policies designed to keep the masses under* **17.** *adv., adj.* **UNCONSCIOUS** in or into a state of unconsciousness or hypnosis (*informal*) ○ *could feel myself going under* [Old English *under.* Ultimately from an Indo-European word that is also the ancestor of English *inferior* and *inferno.*]

un·der·a·chieve /ùndərə chéev/ (**-chieved, -chiev·ing, -chieves**) *vi.* to fail to fulfill your potential or somebody's expectations —**un·der·a·chieve·ment** *n.*

un·der·a·chiev·er /ùndər ə chéevər/ *n.* **1. SOMEBODY WHO UNDERPERFORMS ACADEMICALLY** somebody who does less well in academic work than might have been expected, given the evidence of the person's intelligence and aptitude **2. UNDERPERFORMER** somebody or something that performs below expectations

un·der·act /ùndər ákt/ (**-act·ed, -act·ing, -acts**) *v.* **1.** *vti.* **ACT A ROLE POORLY** to fail to play a role with enough power or conviction **2.** *vt.* **PLAY DOWN EFFECTIVELY** to play a role in an understated way deliberately, for dramatic effect

un·der·age /ùndər áyj/ *adj.* **1. BELOW AGE** below the legal or required age for something **2. DONE BY PEOPLE UNDER THE LEGAL AGE** carried on by people who are below the age at which something is legally permitted

un·der·arm /úndər àarm/ *adj.* **1. BELOW THE ARM** below the arm or for use under the arm, especially the armpit **2. FROM WRIST TO ARMPIT** relating to the area along the underside of the arm from armpit to wrist **3.** *U.K.* SPORTS = **underhand** ■ *adv. U.K.* SPORTS = **underhand** ■ *n.* **AREA JUST BELOW THE ARM** the area below the arm on the body or on a garment, especially the armpit

un·der·bel·ly /úndər bèllee/ (*plural* **-lies**) *n.* **1.** ZOOL **LOWEST PART OF AN ANIMAL'S BELLY** the underside of an animal, normally the part of the belly that is closest to the ground **2. WEAK POINT** a weak or vulnerable part of something ○ *the soft underbelly of the regime* **3. SEAMY PART OF SOMETHING** a sordid area or aspect of something, especially one regarded as outside the experience of the average person **4. LOWER SURFACE** the underside of an object, especially an aircraft

un·der·bid /ùndər bíd/ *v.* (**-bid, -bid·ding, -bids**) **1.** *vti.* **OFFER LESS** to offer a lower price than somebody else in competitive bidding **2.** *vi.* **MAKE TOO LOW A BID** to make a very low bid or too low a bid to obtain something **3.** *vti.* CARDS **BID LESS THAN THE VALUE OF YOUR CARDS** to bid less than the full value of a hand in cards ■ *n.* **VERY LOW BID** a bid that is lower than somebody else's, or too low to obtain something —**un·der·bid·der** *n.*

un·der·bite /úndər bīt/ *n.* DENT a dental condition in which the lower incisor teeth overlap the upper. ◊ **overbite** [Late 20thC. Modeled on OVERBITE.]

un·der·bod·y /úndər bòddee/ (*plural* **-ies**) *n.* the underside of the body of a motor vehicle or of an animal

un·der·boss /úndər bòss/ *n.* a lesser or deputy boss in a criminal organization, especially the Mafia [Mid-20thC]

un·der·bred /ùndər bréd/ *adj.* **1. NOT PUREBRED** not bred from pure stock **2. NOT WELL-BRED** not raised well or well-mannered —**un·der·breed·ing** /úndər brèeding/ *n.*

un·der·brush /úndər brùsh/ *n.* = **undergrowth** *n.* 1

un·der·cap·i·tal·ize /ùndər káppit'l īz/ (**-ized, -iz·ing, -iz·es**) *vti.* to fail to supply an organization, especially a business, with enough capital to operate efficiently (*often passive*) —**un·der·cap·i·tal·i·za·tion** /ùndər kàppit'li záysh'n/ *n.*

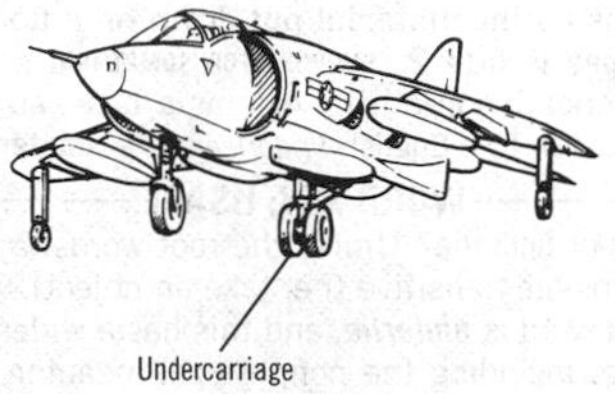

Undercarriage

un·der·car·riage /úndər kèrrij/ *n.* **1. WHEEL STRUCTURE FOR AN AIRCRAFT** the framework of struts and wheels on which an aircraft runs when it moves on the ground **2. SUPPORTING STRUCTURE UNDERNEATH A VEHICLE** the supporting framework underneath a vehicle, to which wheels, tracks, or other means of locomotion are attached

un·der·charge *v.* /ùndər chaárj/ (**-charged, -charg·ing, -charg·es**) **1.** *vti.* **NOT CHARGE SOMEBODY ENOUGH** to charge somebody too low a price for something **2.** *vt.* ARMS **INSERT TOO WEAK A CHARGE IN** to put an inadequate charge in a firearm ■ *n.* /úndər chaàrj/ **EXCESSIVELY LOW PRICE** a price charged that is too low

un·der·class /úndər klàss/ *n.* a social class consisting of people so underprivileged that they are seen as being excluded from mainstream society

un·der·class·man /úndər klássmən/ *n.* (*plural* **-men** /-mən/) somebody in either of the first two years of high school or college

un·der·clay /úndər klày/ *n.* a layer of fine-grained sedimentary clay found beneath a coal seam, containing the fossilized roots of the plants that became the coal

un·der·clothes /úndər klṑz, -klṑthz/ *npl.* = **underwear**

un·der·cloth·ing /úndər klṑthing/ *n.* = **underwear**

un·der·coat /úndər kṑt/ *n.* **1. COAT BENEATH THE FINAL PAINT COAT** a coat of paint or emulsion applied to a surface before a top coat is applied **2. PAINT TO BE COVERED** paint or emulsion designed to be used as an undercoat **3.** ZOOL **SHORT HAIRS UNDER AN ANIMAL'S COAT** a dense layer of short hairs, fur, or wool beneath the longer growth of an animal's outer coat **4.** CARS = **undercoating** ■ *vt.* (**-coat·ed, -coat·ing, -coats**) **1. PAINT WITH AN UNDERCOAT** to apply an undercoat to a surface **2.** CARS **APPLY A PROTECTIVE COATING TO A VEHICLE'S UNDERSIDE** to apply a waterproof coating on the underside of a motor vehicle in order to prevent rust and corrosion

un·der·coat·ing /úndər kṑting/ *n.* a coating of a waterproof material applied to the underside of a motor vehicle as protection against rust and corrosion

un·der·cool /ùndər kóol/ (**-cooled, -cool·ing, -cools**) *vt.* CHEM = **supercool**

un·der·cov·er /ùndər kúvvər/ *adj.* engaged in or involving the secret gathering of information, especially by somebody who disguises himself or herself as a member of the group whose activities are being investigated ○ *an undercover police officer* —**un·der·cov·er** *adv.*

un·der·croft /úndər kròft/ *n.* an underground room, especially the crypt of a church

un·der·cur·rent /úndər kùrrənt/ *n.* **1. UNDERLYING CURRENT** a current in a body of water or air that flows beneath another current or the surface **2. HIDDEN FEELING OR FORCE** a feeling, opinion, force, or tendency that is felt to be present in somebody, but that is not openly shown or expressed and often differs markedly from the person's outward reaction ○ *an undercurrent of resentment*

un·der·cut *v.* /ùndər kút/ (**-cut, -cut·ting, -cuts**) **1.** *vt.* BUSINESS **CHARGE A LOWER AMOUNT THAN** to charge less for something than somebody else **2.** *vt.* **REDUCE SOMETHING'S FORCE** to undermine something or detract from its force (*often passive*) **3.** *vt.* **CUT THE LOWER PART OF** to cut away or cut into the lower part of something, especially so as to leave a portion overhanging **4.** *vti.* SPORTS **HIT A BALL WITH BACKSPIN** to hit a ball with a downward oblique stroke, e.g., in golf or tennis, so that it has backspin ■ *n.* /úndər kùt/ **1. CUT MADE IN A LOWER PART** a cut made below another or into the lower part of something **2. SOMETHING CUT AWAY** a piece of material that has been cut away from the lower part of something **3.** FORESTRY **NOTCH IN A TREE TRUNK** a notch cut in a tree that is being felled that helps it make a clean break and directs its fall **4.** SPORTS **STROKE WITH BACKSPIN** a stroke that gives backspin to a ball

un·der·daks /úndər dàks/ *npl. Aus* underpants, especially men's underpants (*informal*) [Late 20thC. *Daks* from a proprietary name for a make of men's clothes, especially of pants.]

un·der·de·vel·oped /úndər di vélləpt/ *adj.* **1. NOT FULLY GROWN** not grown to a full or normal extent **2.** ECON **WITHOUT MEANS FOR ECONOMIC GROWTH** lacking the technology and capital to make efficient use of available resources **3.** PHOTOGRAPHY **NOT DEVELOPED ENOUGH** used to describe a photograph, negative, or film that was inadequately developed during processing, usually through being taken out of the developer too soon, and that lacks contrast as a result —**un·der·de·vel·op·ment** *n.*

un·der·dog /úndər dòg/ *n.* **1. EXPECTED LOSER** somebody who is expected to lose a fight or contest **2. SOMEBODY AT A DISADVANTAGE** somebody who tends to be unsuccessful in life

un·der·done /ùndər dún/ *adj.* **1. INADEQUATELY COOKED** not cooked as thoroughly as intended or required **2.** *U.K.* **RARE** cooked only lightly or partially to achieve a desired flavor or texture

un·der·dress *vi.* /ùndər dréss/ (**-dressed, -dress·ing, -dress·es**) **DRESS INADEQUATELY FOR AN OCCASION** to dress less fully or formally than an occasion or circumstance demands, e.g., in cold weather or for a social event (*often passive*) ◊ **dress down** ■ *n.* /úndər drèss/ **GARMENT WORN BENEATH OTHERS** a garment or set of garments worn beneath others, especially if designed to be seen when worn

un·der·em·pha·size /ùndər émfə sīz/ (**-sized, -siz·ing, -siz·es**) *vt.* to fail to give something the emphasis or importance it deserves —**un·der·em·pha·sis** /ùndər émfəssiss/ *n.*

un·der·em·ployed /ùndər im plóyd/ *adj.* **1. NOT USED FULLY** not being used to full capacity in a job **2. NOT WORKING FULL-TIME** working part-time but preferring full-time employment —**un·der·em·ploy·ment** *n.*

un·der·es·ti·mate /ùndər ésti màyt/ *v.* (**-mat·ed, -mat·ing, -mates**) 1. *vti.* **MAKE TOO LOW AN ESTIMATE** to make an estimate of something that is too low ○ *We underestimated the time it would take.* 2. *vt.* **MISJUDGE THE WORTH OF** to judge people or things as being inferior to their real value or ability ○ *Don't underestimate her – she's tougher than she looks.* ■ *n.* **TOO LOW AN ESTIMATE** an estimate that is too low, or a judgment that is too unfavorable to somebody or something —**un·der·es·ti·ma·tion** /ùndər esti máysh'n/ *n.*

un·der·ex·pose /ùndər ik spṓz/ (**-posed, -pos·ing, -pos·es**) *vt.* 1. PHOTOGRAPHY **EXPOSE FILM INADEQUATELY** to expose film to light for too short a time or to inadequate light 2. **PUBLICIZE INADEQUATELY** to fail to give somebody or something enough publicity —**un·der·ex·po·sure** /ùndər ik spṓzhər/ *n.*

un·der·feed /ùndər fééd/ (**-fed** /ùndər féd/, **-feed·ing, -feeds**) *vt.* 1. **FEED INADEQUATELY** to fail to give a person or animal enough to eat 2. **FUEL FROM UNDERNEATH** to fuel something, e.g., an engine or a furnace, from underneath

un·der·fi·nanced /ùndər fī́ nànst, -fi nánst/ *adj.* not provided with sufficient capital or funds to be able to run efficiently

un·der·floor /ùndər fláwr/ *adj.* locating beneath the flooring of a room or building ○ *underfloor heating*

un·der·flow /úndər flṑ/ *n.* the inability of a location in computer memory to handle data of an excessively small magnitude, or an instance of this. ◊ **overflow**

un·der·foot /ùndər fóot/ *adv.* 1. **BENEATH THE FEET** under the feet of a person or animal, on the ground, or between the feet and the ground ○ *It was muddy underfoot.* 2. **IN THE WAY** creating an obstacle or obstruction 3. **WITH ARROGANT DISREGARD OR DESTRUCTIVE INTENT** in a way that shows an arrogant or callous disregard or an intention to destroy ○ *trampled underfoot the feelings of everyone who worked for him*

un·der·fund /ùndər fúnd/ *vt.* to fail to provide adequate funding for something such as a project or program (*often passive*) ○ *It was an ambitious plan, hopelessly underfunded from the start.*

un·der·fund·ing /ùndər fúnding/ *n.* failure to make enough funds available for something ○ *The program eventually foundered after years of underfunding.*

un·der·fur /úndər fùr/ *n.* a soft layer of short fur beneath the outer, coarser fur of some animals such as the beaver

un·der·gar·ment /úndər gaàrmənt/ *n.* a piece of clothing worn beneath outer clothes, especially next to the skin, and not normally seen in public

un·der·gird /ùndər gúrd/ (**-gird·ed** *or* **-girt** /-gúrt/, **-gird·ed** *or* **-girt, -gird·ing, -girds**) *vt.* 1. **SUPPORT FROM BELOW** to support or secure something from below, e.g., with ropes passed underneath 2. **SUPPORT** to provide something with support or reinforcement of any kind

un·der·glaze /úndər glàyz/ *adj.* **APPLIED PRIOR TO GLAZING** used to describe decoration or pigment applied to a piece of pottery before the glaze is put on ○ *an underglaze pigment* ■ *n.* **SOMETHING APPLIED BEFORE GLAZING** something, especially a decoration or pigment, that is applied to a piece of pottery before the glaze is put on

un·der·go /ùndər gṓ/ (**-went** /-wént/, **-gone** /-gón/, **-go·ing, -goes**) *vt.* to experience or endure something, or have something happen to you ○ *You'll be obliged to undergo a thorough medical examination.* ○ *The city underwent a period of great change.*

un·der·grad /úndər gràd/ *n.* an undergraduate (*informal*) ○ *undergrad humor* [Early 19thC. Shortening.]

un·der·grad·u·ate /ùndər grájjoo ət/ *n.* a student at university or college who has not yet received a degree (*often used before a noun*) ○ *undergraduate courses*

un·der·ground *adj.* /úndər grównd/ 1. **BENEATH THE EARTH'S SURFACE** located, happening, or operating beneath the surface of the Earth 2. **COVERT** concealed and done in secret 3. **CONTRARY TO THE PREVAILING CULTURE** separate from a prevailing social or artistic environment, and often exercising a subversive influence ○ *The story had been circulating in the underground press for years.* ■ *n.* /úndər grównd/ 1. **RESISTANCE MOVEMENT** a secret movement that aims to overthrow a government or fight against an occupying enemy 2. **MOVEMENT CONTRARY TO THE PREVAILING CULTURE** a movement or group that is separate from the prevailing social or artistic environment and often exerts a subversive influence 3. *U.K.* = **subway** ■ *adv.* /ùndər grównd/ 1. **BELOW GROUND** below the surface of the ground 2. **SECRETLY** in secret or in hiding

un·der·ground rail·road *n.* a secret network or route by which a fugitive can be smuggled into or out of a country or moved around safely inside it

Un·der·ground Rail·road *n.* a secret organization that helped enslaved laborers flee from the southern United States to Canada or other places of safety prior to the abolition of slavery

un·der·grown /úndər grṑn/ *adj.* 1. **NOT FULLY GROWN** not grown to the expected size 2. **WITH UNDERGROWTH** having or covered with undergrowth

un·der·growth /úndər grṑth/ *n.* 1. **VEGETATION UNDER TREES** shrubs, small trees, or other vegetation growing beneath the trees in a forest 2. **STUNTED GROWTH** growth that is less than expected 3. ZOOL = **undercoat, underfur**

un·der·hand *adj.* /ùndər hánd/ 1. **SECRET AND DISHONEST** done secretively and dishonestly or with the intention to deceive or cheat somebody 2. SPORTS **WITH THE ARM BELOW THE SHOULDER** with the arm kept below shoulder height and usually close to the body when performing an action such as throwing, serving, or pitching a ball ■ *adv.* 1. **SECRETLY AND DISHONESTLY** in a secretive and dishonest way 2. **BELOW THE SHOULDER** with the arm kept below shoulder height [Late 16thC. Origin uncertain: possibly from a sleight of hand in gambling as in Old French *par sous main*, literally "by under hand."]

un·der·hand·ed /ùndər hándəd/ *adj., adv.* = **underhand** *adj.* 1, **underhand** *adv.* 1 —**un·der·hand·ed·ly** *adv.* —**un·der·hand·ed·ness** *n.*

un·der·hung /ùndər húng/ *adj.* 1. MED **JUTTING BEYOND THE UPPER JAW** used to describe a lower jaw that projects beyond the upper jaw 2. CONSTR **RUNNING ON A RAIL UNDERNEATH** running on a rail or track situated underneath ○ *underhung sliding doors*

un·der·in·sure /ùndərin shóor/ (**-sured, -sur·ing, -sures**) *vt.* to take out insufficient insurance to cover the value of the article that is being insured

un·der·lain past participle of **underlie**

un·der·lay[1] *vt.* /ùndər láy/ (**-laid** /-láyd/, **-lay·ing, -lays**) **PROVIDE WITH SOMETHING UNDERNEATH** to lay something underneath something else (*often passive*) ■ *n.* /úndər lày/ 1. **LAYER BENEATH CARPET** a layer of cushioning and insulating material put down on a floor before a carpet is laid 2. **SUPPORT FOR SOMETHING** something laid beneath something else as a base, support, or foundation [Old English *underleegan*] —**un·der·laid** *adj.*

WORD KEY: USAGE

underlay or **underlie**? Unlike the root words *lay* and *lie*, both verbs are transitive (i.e. take an object). The more common word is ***underlie***, and this has a wider range of meanings including the nonphysical meaning "to form the basis of": *This trend underlies all the social changes of recent times.* The primary meaning of ***underlay*** is "to cover the bottommost part of" (*We underlaid the carpet with felt*) and in this meaning it also acts as a noun (with the stress on the first syllable).

un·der·lay[2] past tense of **underlie**

un·der·let /ùndər lét/ (**-let, -let·ting, -lets**) *v.* 1. *vt.* **LET CHEAPLY** to let a property for less than its full value 2. *vti.* = **sublet**

un·der·lie /ùndər lī́/ (**-lay** /-láy/, **-lain** /-láyn/, **-ly·ing, -lies**) *vt.* 1. **LIE BENEATH** to lie or be put under something else 2. **BE THE FOUNDATION OF SOMETHING** to be the basis or cause of something ○ *the assumptions that underlie this argument* 3. FIN **HAVE FINANCIAL PRIORITY OVER** to take priority over other financial rights or securities ○ *This claim underlies yours.* [Old English *underliegan*]

WORD KEY: USAGE

See Usage note at ***underlay***[1].

un·der·line *vt.* /ùndər līn, úndər līn/ (**-lined, -lin·ing, -lines**) 1. **PUT LINE BELOW** to draw or type a line under something 2. **EMPHASIZE** to give emphasis or extra force to something ■ *n.* /úndər līn/ 1. **LINE BENEATH SOMETHING** a line drawn or typed under something 2. PRINTING **CAPTION UNDER AN ILLUSTRATION** a caption placed below an illustration

un·der·lin·en /úndər linnən/ *n.* underwear, especially when made of linen (*archaic*)

un·der·ling /úndərling/ *n.* a servant or subordinate of somebody else, especially one regarded as of little worth or importance

un·der·ly·ing /úndər lī ing/ *adj.* 1. **LYING UNDERNEATH** positioned beneath something else ○ *the underlying rock strata* 2. **HIDDEN AND SIGNIFICANT** present and important but not immediately obvious ○ *the underlying reasons for his odd behavior* 3. **ESSENTIAL** basic or fundamental to something ○ *at odds with the underlying ideology of the party* 4. FIN **FINANCIALLY MOST IMPORTANT** used to describe financial obligations or assets that take priority over others

un·der·mine /ùndər mī́n, úndər mīn/ (**-mined, -min·ing, -mines**) *vt.* 1. **ERODE** to weaken something by removing or wearing away material from its base or from beneath it ○ *The chalk cliffs are being gradually undermined by the waves.* 2. **WEAKEN GRADUALLY** to diminish or weaken something gradually ○ *Successive failures at job interviews began to undermine my confidence.* 3. **WEAKEN INSIDIOUSLY** to demoralize somebody or something by covert and malicious action

un·der·most /úndər mṑst/ *adj.* **LOWEST OF ALL** lowest or last in position, status, or level ■ *adv.* **IN THE LOWEST PLACE** in the lowest or last place

un·der·neath /ùndər néeth/ CORE MEANING: a grammatical word indicating that something is below or beneath another thing, and may be covered by it ○ (adv) *Underneath, on the floor, was what appeared to be a heap of black clothes.* ○ (prep) *I left the key underneath the doormat.*

1. *prep., adv.* **UNDERLYING SOMETHING** underlying something that is shown on the surface or openly expressed ○ (prep) *Underneath her confident exterior she was a very shy person.* ○ (adv) *There must be deeper problems underneath.* 2. *adv., adj.* **ON THE LOWER PART OF SOMETHING** on the bottom of something or the part that faces toward the ground ○ (adv) *brown with white feathers underneath* ○ (adj) *The underneath part is hard to reach.* 3. *n.* **THE LOWER PART OF SOMETHING** the bottom part of something or the part that faces toward the ground [Old English *underneoþan*, from UNDER + *neoþan* "beneath" (source of English *beneath*)]

un·der·nour·ish /ùndər núr ish/ (**-ished, -ish·ing, -ish·es**) *vt.* to fail to supply somebody with enough food or other resources to provide for proper development (*often passive*) —**un·der·nour·ish·ment** *n.*

un·der·pants /úndər pànts/ *npl.* briefs or shorts worn as underclothes (*takes a plural verb*)

un·der·pass /úndər pàss/ *n.* 1. **ROAD UNDER ANOTHER ROAD** a part of a road that crosses under another road or a railroad 2. **TUNNEL UNDER A ROAD** a tunnel for pedestrians beneath a road or railroad

un·der·pay /ùndər páy/ (**-paid** /-páyd/, **-paid, -pay·ing, -pays**) *vt.* to pay somebody less than he or she deserves or than is usual, or to fail to pay the full amount of something —**un·der·pay·ment** *n.*

un·der·per·form /ùndər pər fáwrm/ (**-formed, -form·ing, -forms**) *vi.* to do less well than expected or than something or somebody else ○ *underperforming investments* —**un·der·per·form·ance** *n.* —**un·der·per·form·er** *n.*

un·der·pin /ùndər pín/ (**-pinned, -pin·ning, -pins**) *vt.* 1. CONSTR **SUPPORT FROM BELOW** to support a weakened wall or structure by propping it up from below 2. **ACT AS SUPPORT FOR** to act as a support or foundation for something (*often passive*) ○ *the hard facts that underpin these assumptions*

un·der·pin·ning /úndər pínning/ *n.* 1. CONSTR **SUPPORTING STRUCTURE** a structure built to support a weakened wall or building 2. **FOUNDATION FOR SOMETHING** something that supports or acts as a foundation for something (*usually plural*)

un·der·play /ùndər pláy/ (**-played, -play·ing, -plays**) *v.* 1. *vti.* ARTS **ACT A ROLE SUBTLY** to act a role in a deliberately restrained or subtle way 2. *vt.* **DO SUBTLY** to present or deal with something in a deliberately restrained or subtle way 3. *vi.* CARDS **PLAY A LOWER CARD** to play a lower card while holding a higher one

un·der·plot /úndər plòt/ *n.* a secondary plot in a play, novel, or other work of fiction

un·der·price /ùndər prī́ss/ (**-priced, -pric·ing, -pric·es**) *vt.* 1. **SELL CHEAPLY** to put a price on something for sale that is less than its actual value 2. **SELL CHEAPER THAN A COMPETITOR** to sell something for a lower price than somebody else

un·der·priv·i·leged /ùndər prívvəlijd/ *adj.* **DENIED SOCIAL PRIVILEGES AND RIGHTS** deprived of many of the rights and privileges enjoyed by most people in society, usually as a result of poverty (*used euphemistically*)

■ *n.* UNDERPRIVILEGED PEOPLE underprivileged people considered as a social group (*used euphemistically*)

un·der·proof /ùndər pro͞of/ *adj.* used to describe an alcoholic drink that contains less alcohol than is standard or than is legally required

un·der·prop /ùndər próp/ (**-propped, -prop·ping, -props**) *vt.* to prop something up from underneath —**un·der·prop·per** *n.*

un·der·quote /ùndər kwṓt/ (**-quot·ed, -quot·ing, -quotes**) *v.* **1.** *vti.* SELL BELOW ITS ACTUAL VALUE to offer something for sale at a lower price than the market value **2.** *vt.* QUOTE A LOWER PRICE THAN to quote a price for something that is lower than that quoted by somebody else

un·der·rate /ùndər ráyt/ (**-rat·ed, -rat·ing, -rates**) *vt.* to judge the value, degree, or worth of somebody or something to be less than it really is ○ *a greatly underrated writer*

un·der·re·port /ùndər ri páwrt/ (**-port·ed, -port·ing, -ports**) *vt.* to declare or report a number or amount to be smaller than is actually the case

un·der·rep·re·sent /ùndər rèppri zént/ (**-sent·ed, -sent·ing, -sents**) *vt.* **1.** REPRESENT INADEQUATELY to contain a disproportionately small number of representatives of a particular population group or a particular type of thing (*often passive*) ○ *addressing the problem of women being underrepresented in government.* **2.** PRESENT SOMETHING AS LESS to present something as smaller, less widespread, or less important than it actually is —**un·der·rep·re·sen·ta·tion** /ùndər reppri zen táysh'n, -repprizən táysh'n/ *n.*

un·der·run /ùndər rún/ *v.* (**-ran** /ùndər rán/, **-run, -run·ning, -runs**) **1.** *vt.* MOVE UNDER to run, pass, or go under something **2.** *vti.* NAUT PASS SOMETHING OVER A BOAT FOR INSPECTION to pass something such as a net or cable over the deck of a boat, hauling it in on one side and putting it back into the water on the other, so that it can be inspected or repaired ■ *n.* **1.** FIN LOWER-THAN-ESTIMATED COST a cost or expense that is less than anticipated **2.** INDUST LOWER-THAN-REQUIRED PRODUCTION RUN a production run of a manufactured or printed item that is less than the quantity ordered

un·der·sat·u·rat·ed /ùndər sáchə ràytəd/ *adj.* **1.** GEOL LOW IN SILICA used to describe igneous rock that contains low levels of combined silica and no free silica **2.** CHEM = **unsaturated**

un·der·score *vt.* /ùndər skáwr/ (**-scored, -scor·ing, -scores**) **1.** DRAW A LINE UNDER to draw a line underneath something **2.** EMPHASIZE to give emphasis or extra force to something ■ *n.* /ùndər skàwr/ **1.** LINE UNDER SOMETHING a line drawn underneath something **2.** BACKGROUND MUSIC a piece of background music accompanying action or dialogue in a movie

un·der·sea /ùndər sée/ *adj.* RELATING TO THE AREA BELOW THE SEA existing, carried out, or designed for use below the surface of the sea ■ *adv.* **un·der·sea, un·der·seas** TO THE AREA BELOW THE SEA in or into the area below the surface of the sea

un·der·seal *n.* /ùndər sèel/ *U.K.* = **undercoating** ■ *vt.* /ùndər sèel/ (**-sealed, -seal·ing, -seals**) *U.K.* = **undercoat**

un·der·sec·re·tar·y /ùndər sékrə tèrree/ (*plural* **-ies**) *n.* **1.** ASSISTANT SECRETARY somebody who is immediately subordinate to a principal secretary in a government or bureaucratic organization **2.** *U.K.* SUBORDINATE OF A SECRETARY OF STATE a government minister who is subordinate to the secretary of state for a government department —**un·der·sec·re·tar·i·at** /ùndər sekrə térree ət/ *n.* —**un·der·sec·re·tar·y·ship** *n.*

un·der·sell /ùndər sél/ (**-sold** /-sṓld/, **-sold, -sell·ing, -sells**) *vt.* **1.** SELL BELOW ITS PROPER VALUE to sell something at a price below its full or usual value **2.** SELL MORE CHEAPLY THAN to sell something more cheaply than a competitor **3.** ADVERTISE WITH TOO LITTLE ENTHUSIASM to present the merits of something or somebody with too little enthusiasm or conviction or in too restrained or understated a way —**un·der·sell·er** *n.*

un·der·set *n.* /ùndər sèt/ OCEAN UNDERCURRENT an ocean undercurrent that runs in a direction contrary to the direction of the surface waves ■ *vt.* /ùndər sét/ (**-set, -set·ting, -sets**) PROVIDE A PROP FOR to support something from below

un·der·sexed /ùndər sékst/ *adj.* having less sex drive or less interest in sex than some other people

un·der·shirt /ùndər shùrt/ *n.* a collarless undergarment for the upper body, usually with short sleeves or no sleeves

un·der·shoot /ùndər sho͞ot/ (**-shot** /ùndər shót/, **-shot, -shoot·ing, -shoots**) *vti.* **1.** AIR LAND TOO SHORT to land an aircraft short of a landing area ○ *The pilot undershot the runway.* **2.** FIRE SHORT to shoot something, e.g., an arrow, so that it lands short of the target

un·der·shorts /ùndər shàwrts/ *npl.* shorts or briefs worn as underclothes by men and boys (*informal; takes a plural verb*)

un·der·shot /úndər shòt/ *adj.* **1.** = **underhung** *adj.* 1 **2.** DRIVEN BY WATER PASSING BENEATH used to describe a device, especially a waterwheel, that is driven by water flowing beneath it

un·der·shrub /ùndər shrùb/ *n.* = **subshrub**

un·der·side /ùndər sīd/ *n.* **1.** LOWER SIDE the lower side or bottom of something **2.** UNDESIRABLE SIDE an aspect of something that is undesirable or unpleasant and usually hidden

un·der·signed /ùndər sīnd/ *n.* (*plural* **-signed**) PERSON SIGNING BELOW the person who has signed a document below ■ *adj.* SUPPLYING SIGNATURES with their signatures appearing below

un·der·sized /ùndər sīzd/, **un·der·size** /-sīz/ *adj.* smaller than the prevailing or preferred size

un·der·skirt /úndər skùrt/ *n.* a skirt worn under another skirt

un·der·slung /ùndər slúng/ *adj.* suspended or supported from above, like a motor vehicle chassis that is suspended from the axles

un·der·soil /úndər sòyl/ *n.* = **subsoil**

undersold past tense, past participle of **undersell**

un·der·spend /ùndər spénd/ (**-spent** /-spént/, **-spend·ing, -spends**) *vi.* to spend less money than is required or expected —**un·der·spend** *n.*

un·der·staff /ùndər stáf/ (**-staffed, -staff·ing, -staffs**) *vt.* to provide a workplace or an organization with inadequate or insufficient staff

un·der·stand /ùndər stánd/ (**-stood** /-sto͝od/, **-stand·ing, -stands**) *v.* **1.** *vti.* GRASP THE MEANING OF SOMETHING to know or be able to explain to yourself the nature of somebody or something, or the meaning or cause of something ○ *I can't understand what all the fuss is about.* **2.** *vti.* COME TO KNOW SOMETHING to realize or become aware of something ○ *Only then did she understand the urgency of the situation.* **3.** *vt.* BE ABLE TO HANDLE to know and be able to use something such as a foreign language ○ *She thoroughly understood the workings of the system.* **4.** *vti.* KNOW AND SYMPATHIZE to recognize somebody's character or somebody's situation, especially in a sympathetic, tolerant, or empathetic way ○ *It's such a relief to find someone who understands.* **5.** *vt.* TAKE AS MEANT to interpret something in a particular way, or to infer or deduce a particular meaning from something ○ *I understood it as a peacemaking gesture.* ○ *Am I to understand from this that you are refusing our offer?* **6.** *vt.* TAKE AS SETTLED to believe something to be agreed, settled, or firmly communicated ○ *The bank was given to understand that you would repay the loan in six months.* **7.** *vt.* KNOW BY LEARNING OR HEARING to gather or assume something on the basis of having heard or been told it ○ *They're not due back, so I understand, until next Tuesday.* [Old English *understandan*, from UNDER + *standan*, an earlier form of STAND. The underlying idea is "to be close to."]

un·der·stand·a·ble /ùndər stándəb'l/ *adj.* **1.** ABLE TO BE UNDERSTOOD having a meaning or nature that can be understood ○ *Try to make it understandable to a nonspecialist.* **2.** REASONABLE able to be accepted as normal, reasonable, or forgivable ○ *Under the circumstances it was a perfectly understandable reaction.* —**un·der·stand·a·bil·i·ty** /ùndər stàndə bíllətee/ *n.* —**un·der·stand·a·bly** /-stándəblee/ *adv.*

un·der·stand·ing /ùndər stánding/ *n.* **1.** ABILITY TO GRASP A MEANING the ability to perceive and explain the meaning or the nature of somebody or something ○ *Surely even someone with a very limited understanding could see the logic in that.* **2.** INTERPRETATION OF SOMETHING somebody's interpretation of something, or a belief or opinion based on an interpretation of or inference from something ○ *It was my understanding that the costs would be shared equally.* **3.** MUTUAL COMPREHENSION an agreement, often an unofficial or unspoken one ○ *I'm sure we can come to an understanding about this.* **4.** KNOWLEDGE OF ANOTHER'S NATURE a sympathetic, empathetic, or tolerant recognition of somebody else's nature or situation ○ *I thought you of all people would show a little understanding.* ■ *adj.* **1.** SYMPATHETICALLY AWARE sympathetic, empathetic, or tolerant in recognizing somebody's or something's character and situation ○ *fortunate in having understanding parents* **2.** ABLE TO KNOW SOMETHING able to comprehend the sense or meaning of something (*archaic*) —**un·der·stand·ing·ly** *adv.*

un·der·state /ùndər stáyt/ (**-stat·ed, -stat·ing, -states**) *vt.* **1.** EXPRESS WITH RESTRAINT to express something in a deliberately less dramatic, emphatic, or emotional way than it seems to warrant, often in order to increase its actual effect or for the sake of irony **2.** STATE SOMETHING AS BELOW ITS TRUE AMOUNT to describe something as being smaller in quantity or number than it really is ○ *The official account understates the true costs of the delay.*

un·der·stat·ed /ùndər stáytəd/ *adj.* achieving its effect through restraint, subtlety, and good taste ○ *understated elegance* —**un·der·stat·ed·ness** *n.*

un·der·state·ment /ùndər stáytmənt, úndər stàytmənt/ *n.* **1.** RESTRAINED OR MUTED STATEMENT a statement, or a way of expressing yourself, that is deliberately less forceful or dramatic than the subject would seem to justify or require **2.** INCOMPLETE STATEMENT a statement that underrepresents or underreports something

un·der·steer *vi.* /ùndər stéer/ (**-steered, -steer·ing, -steers**) TURN TOO WIDE to turn less sharply than the turning of a steering wheel would lead the driver to expect ■ *n.* /úndər stèer/ TENDENCY TO TURN TOO WIDE a motor vehicle's tendency to turn less sharply than expected

un·der·stood[1] /ùndər sto͝od/ past tense, past participle of **understand**

understood[2] *adj.* agreed, assumed, or implied, especially without being openly or officially expressed

un·der·sto·ry /úndər stàwree/ (*plural* **-ries**) *n.* a layer of small trees and shrubs below the level of the taller trees in a forest

un·der·strap·per /úndər stràppər/ *n.* an underling or subordinate [Early 18thC. Formed from *strapper* in the sense of "person who straps or harnesses horses."]

un·der·strength /ùndər stréngth/ *adj.* having inadequate strength, especially less than usual or desirable number of personnel

un·der·stud·y /úndər stùddee/ *n.* (*plural* **-ies**) **1.** SUBSTITUTE ACTOR an actor who learns the role of another actor so as to be able to act as a replacement if necessary **2.** TRAINED SUBSTITUTE somebody who is trained to do the work of somebody else so as to be able to act as a replacement if necessary ■ *vti.* (**-ied, -y·ing, -ies**) BE A SUBSTITUTE ACTOR to learn the role of another actor so as to be able to replace him or her if necessary

un·der·sub·scribed /ùndər səb skrībd/ *adj.* with fewer than the expected number of people subscribing or showing an interest, often not enough people to make something viable ○ *We couldn't offer the course as it was undersubscribed.*

un·der·take /ùndər táyk/ (**-took** /-to͝ok/, **-tak·en** /-táykən/, **-tak·ing, -takes**) *v.* **1.** *vti.* MAKE A PLEDGE TO DO SOMETHING to make a commitment to do something ○ *Jo undertook to find out the cost of flights.* **2.** *vt.* SET ABOUT DOING to begin to do something or to set out on something ○ *They were prepared to undertake the work at the formerly agreed price.*

un·der·tak·er *n.* **1.** /úndər tàykər/ = **funeral director 2.** /ùndər táykər/ SOMEBODY WHO SETS ABOUT SOMETHING somebody who attempts or agrees to attempt a task

un·der·tak·ing /ùndər táyking/ *n.* **1.** TASK a task or project ○ *It was a colossal undertaking.* **2.** PLEDGE TO DO SOMETHING a promise or agreement to do something **3.** FUNERAL BUSINESS the business of preparing the dead for burial or cremation and arranging funerals

un·der-the-count·er *adj.* sold or obtained clandestinely or illegally (*not hyphenated after a verb*)

un·der-the-ta·ble *adj.* done or organized clandestinely and often illegally (*not hyphenated after a verb*)

un·der·things /úndər thingz/ *npl.* underwear, especially women's underwear

un·der·thrust /úndər thrùst/ *n.* GEOL a reverse fault in which a lower layer of rock is driven underneath a higher, relatively passive layer

UV

un·der·tint /úndər tìnt/ *n.* a slight or subtle tint

un·der·tone /úndər tòn/ *n.* **1. LOW TONE** a quiet, subdued, or background tone, especially of the voice ○ *He spoke in an undertone.* **2. UNDERLYING QUALITY OR ELEMENT** something that is suggested or implied rather than stated openly ○ *undertones of menace* **3.** COLORS **MUTED COLOR** a pale, subdued, or unobtrusive color

un·der·tow /úndər tò/ *n.* **1. SEAWARD PULL OF WATER** the seaward pull of water away from a shore after a wave has broken **2. OPPOSING UNDERCURRENT** an underlying tendency or force that runs in the opposite direction to the apparent one ○ *An undertow of dissatisfaction made it difficult to carry everyone with us.*

un·der·trick /úndər trìk/ *n.* CARDS in bridge, a trick short of the number declared by a player

un·der·trump /úndər trúmp, úndər trùmp/ (**-trumped, -trump·ing, -trumps**) *vi.* in cards, to play a trump that is lower than a trump that has already been played in a hand

un·der·val·ue /úndər vállyoo/ (**-ued, -u·ing, -ues**) *vt.* **1. APPLY TOO LOW A VALUE TO** to judge the value of something or somebody as being lower than it really is ○ *buy up stock that is undervalued* **2. HOLD IN LOW ESTEEM** to hold too low an opinion of something or somebody —**un·der·val·u·a·tion** /úndər vallyoo áysh'n/ *n.*

un·der·wa·ter *adj.* /úndər wáwtər, úndər wóttər/ **1. BELOW THE WATER SURFACE** existing, carried out, or designed for use below the surface of water **2. UNDER A SHIP'S WATERLINE** below the waterline in a ship ■ *adv.* **BELOW THE WATER SURFACE** in or to a place below the surface of a body of water ■ *n.* /úndər wàwtər, -wòttər/ **WATER UNDERNEATH THE SURFACE** the water beneath the surface of a river, lake, or sea

un·der way /úndər wáy/, **un·der·way** *adj.* **1. PROCEEDING** in motion or progress ○ *not long before the project was underway* **2. un·der·way, un·der weigh** NAUT **DONE WHILE MOVING** carried out while a ship is in motion, not in port or at anchor

WORD KEY: USAGE

under way or **underway**? Although the form ***underway*** is often seen, and has long been in use, ***under way*** is still widely preferred. The only exception to this is the rare adjectival use that precedes the noun: *The submarine received underway servicing.*

un·der·wear /úndər wàir/ *n.* clothes worn beneath outer clothes, usually next to the skin and not normally seen in public

un·der·weight /úndər wáyt, úndər wàyt/ *adj.* weighing less than is normal or required

un·der·went past tense of **undergo**

un·der·whelm /úndər wélm, -hwélm/ (**-whelmed, -whelm·ing, -whelms**) *vt.* to fail notably to impress or excite somebody (*humorous*) [Mid-20thC. Modeled on OVERWHELM.] —**un·der·whelm·ing** *adj.*

un·der·wing /úndər wìng/ *n.* **1.** INSECTS **HIND WING OF AN INSECT** a hind wing of an insect such as a beetle, especially when covered by a forewing while the insect is not in flight **2.** ZOOL **MOTH WITH BRIGHT WINGS** a moth that has brightly colored hind wings that become visible only in flight. Genus: *Catocala.* **3.** BIRDS **LOWER SIDE OF A BIRD'S WING** the underside of a bird's wing

un·der·wire /úndər wìr/ *n.* a wire sewn into the lining under each cup of a brassiere to provide support —**un·der·wired** *adj.*

un·der·wood /úndər wòòd/ *n.* = **undergrowth** *n.* 1

un·der·world /úndər wùrld/ *n.* **1. CRIMINAL SOCIETY** the part of society that lives by crime (*often used before a noun*) ○ *an underworld shooting* **2.** MYTHOL **ABODE OF THE DEAD** in classical mythology, the place beneath the earth where the souls of the dead go

un·der·write /úndər rìt, úndər rìt/ (**-wrote** /-ròt, -ròt/, **-writ·ten** /-rìtt'n, -rìtt'n/, **-writ·ing, -writes**) *v.* **1.** *vti.* INSUR **ISSUE INSURANCE** to insure somebody or something by accepting liability for specified losses, or to be in the business of doing this **2.** *vti.* STOCK EXCH **AGREE TO BUY UNSOLD SECURITIES** to guarantee the sale of an issue of securities at a fixed price **3.** *vti.* **SUBSIDIZE SOMETHING** to agree to provide funds for something and to cover any losses ○ *The tour was underwritten by an electronics company.* **4.** *vt.* **LEND SUPPORT TO** to give support to somebody or something, especially by signing a document **5.** *vt.* **WRITE BENEATH OTHER WRITING** to write something, or add a signature, underneath other written matter [15thC. Modeled on Latin *subscribere* "to write underneath, sign."]

un·der·writ·er /úndər rìtər/ *n.* **1.** INSUR **INSURER COVERING LIABILITIES** a person, firm, or organization that issues insurance and accepts liability for specified risks **2.** INSUR **SOMEBODY ASSESSING RISKS ON INSURANCE** somebody employed by an insurance company to assess risks and fix premiums **3.** STOCK EXCH **GUARANTOR OF A SECURITIES ISSUE** a person or organization that agrees to buy at a fixed price any unsold part of an issue of securities

un·de·scend·ed /úndi séndəd/ *adj.* used to describe a testicle that has remained in the inguinal canal and has not descended into the scrotum

un·de·served /úndi zúrvd/ *adj.* unfairly awarded or endured, or not merited on the basis of the facts —**un·de·serv·ed·ly** /úndi zúrvədlee/ *adv.*

un·de·sign·ing /úndi zìning/ *adj.* not trying to deceive or manipulate

un·de·sir·a·ble /úndi zìrəb'l/ *adj.* **NOT WANTED** not wanted, liked, or approved of ■ *n.* **SOMEBODY UNDESIRABLE** somebody or something regarded as undesirable —**un·de·sir·a·bil·i·ty** /-zìrə bíllətee/ *n.* —**un·de·sir·a·bly** /-zìrəblee/ *adv.*

un·de·ter·mined /úndi túrmind/ *adj.* **1. NOT SETTLED** not resolved, decided, or fixed **2. NOT KNOWN** unknown or undiscovered

un·de·vi·at·ing /un déevee àyting/ *adj.* remaining loyal or constant —**un·de·vi·at·ing·ly** *adv.*

un·did past tense of **undo**

un·dies /úndeez/ *npl.* underclothes, especially women's underclothes (*informal*) [Late 19thC. Formed from a shortening of UNDERCLOTHES, probably on the model of *frillies* "frilled underwear."]

un·dine /un déen, ún dèen/ *n.* a female spirit that lives in water, especially one that could become human by bearing the child of a human male [Early 19thC. From modern Latin *undina* (coined by Paracelsus), from Latin *unda* "wave" (see UNDULATE).]

un·dip·lo·mat·ic /un dìpplə máttik/ *adj.* lacking in tact and diplomacy —**un·dip·lo·mat·i·cal·ly** *adv.*

un·di·rect·ed /úndi réktəd/ *adj.* **1. PURPOSELESS** without a purpose or object **2. WITHOUT ADDRESS** not marked with an address in the proper way

un·dis·guised /úndiss gízd/ *adj.* expressed fully and openly —**un·dis·guis·ed·ly** /úndiss gízədlee/ *adv.*

un·dis·posed /úndiss pózd/ *adj.* **1. NOT DEALT WITH** not resolved or dealt with **2. NOT FAVORABLY INCLINED** not prepared or inclined to do something

un·dis·so·ci·at·ed /úndi sóshee àytəd/ *adj.* CHEM used to describe a molecule that has not been broken down into simpler molecules, atoms, or ions

un·dis·tin·guished /úndi stíngwisht/ *adj.* **1. MEDIOCRE** not very good or ever rising above the ordinary ○ *an undistinguished career* **2. COMMONPLACE** not at all striking or likely to stand out from others ○ *undistinguished appearance* **3. NOT MADE SEPARATE** not differentiated from others **4. NOT ATTRACTING NOTICE** not noticeable or noticed

un·dis·trib·ut·ed /úndi stríbbyətəd/ *adj.* **1.** BUSINESS **NOT PAID TO SHAREHOLDERS** not paid out as a dividend to stockholders, but invested back into the business ○ *undistributed profits* **2.** LOGIC **NOT REFERRING TO ENTIRE CLASS** used to describe a term that does not refer to all members of the class it designates. The term "dogs" is undistributed in the statement "Some dogs are unfriendly."

un·do /un dóò/ (**-did** /-díd/, **-done** /-dún/, **-do·ing, -does** /-dúz/) *v.* **1.** *vti.* **UNFASTEN** to open, unfasten, untie, or unwrap something ○ *I can't undo this button.* **2.** *vt.* **NULLIFY** to cancel or reverse the effect of an action ○ *What's done can't be undone.* **3.** *vt.* COMPUT **REVERSE AN ACTION** to cancel the effect of the last command or action done on a computer, restoring the material being worked on to its previous condition **4.** *vt.* **RUIN SOMEBODY** to bring somebody or something to ruin or disaster

un·dock /un dók/ (**-docked, -dock·ing, -docks**) *vi.* SPACE TECH to become detached from each other, a space station, or another spacecraft, in space

un·do·ing *n.* **1. ACT OF BRINGING TO RUIN** the ruin, downfall, or destruction of somebody or something, or something that causes this ○ *Pride was our undoing.* **2. ACT OF UNFASTENING** the opening, unfastening, untying, or unwrapping of something **3. ACT OF NULLIFYING SOMETHING'S EFFECT** the canceling or reversing of the effect of an action

un·done *adj.* **1. UNCOMPLETED** not yet done or completed **2. UNFASTENED** not tied or fastened **3. BROUGHT TO RUIN** ruined, destroyed, or brought to the brink of collapse

un·doubt·ed /un dówtəd/ *adj.* not subject to doubt or dispute

un·doubt·ed·ly /un dówtədlee/ *adv.* without any doubt or question

un·draw /un dráw/ (**-drew** /un dróò/, **-drawn** /un dráwn/, **-draw·ing, -draws**) *vt.* to draw back or open something such as a curtain

un·dreamed-of, **un·dreamt-of** *adj.* impossible to imagine in advance, usually through being so wonderful and so unlikely

un·dress /un dréss/ *v.* (**-dressed, -dress·ing, -dress·es**) **1.** *vti.* **TAKE CLOTHES OFF** to remove the clothes from somebody's body **2.** *vt.* **TAKE DRESSING OFF** to remove a dressing from a wound **3.** *vt.* **REMOVE ORNAMENTATION** to strip something of its decoration ■ *n.* **1. CONDITION OF HAVING NO CLOTHES ON** a condition of nakedness or of being scantily clothed **2. INFORMAL CLOTHING** informal attire or an everyday uniform. ◊ **dress** ■ *adj.* **INFORMAL** not full or formal in dress, or for which informal clothing can be worn ○ *an undress uniform*

un·dressed /un drést/ *adj.* **1. WITHOUT CLOTHES** naked or scantily clothed **2. UNTREATED** not processed or treated in some way ○ *undressed leather* **3. NOT READY FOR TABLE** not fully prepared for cooking or eating **4. WITHOUT DRESSING** not covered with a dressing or sauce **5. INFORMALLY DRESSED** appropriately but not formally dressed for an event or occasion **6. WITHOUT A BANDAGE** without a dressing or bandage ○ *an undressed wound*

WORD KEY: SYNONYMS

See Synonyms at ***naked***.

un·due /un dóò/ *adj.* **1. EXCESSIVE OR VERY INAPPROPRIATE** going beyond the limits of what is proper, normal, justified, or permitted ○ *using undue force to disperse the crowd* **2. NOT PAYABLE NOW** not owed or payable at present

un·du·lant /únjələnt/ *adj.* resembling waves in motion or form (*literary*) [Early 19thC. Formed from UNDULATE.]

un·du·lant fe·ver *n.* = **brucellosis**

un·du·late *v.* /únjə làyt, úndyə-/ (**-lat·ed, -lat·ing, -lates**) **1.** *vti.* **MOVE SINUOUSLY LIKE WAVES** to move, or cause something to move, in waves or in a movement resembling waves **2.** *vi.* **GO UP AND DOWN GRACEFULLY** to rise and fall gracefully in volume or pitch ■ *adj.* /-lət, -làyt/ **un·du·late, un·du·lat·ed** **WAVY IN APPEARANCE** with a wavy appearance, edge, or markings [Mid-17thC. From Latin *undulatus* "wavy," from *unda* "wave." Ultimately from an Indo-European word that is also the ancestor of English *water.*] —**un·du·la·to·ry** /únjələ tàwree, úndyələ-/ *adj.*

WORD KEY: ORIGIN

The Latin word *unda*, from which ***undulate*** is derived, is also the source of English *abound, inundate, redundant, sound,* and *surround.*

un·du·la·tion /únjə láysh'n, ùndyə-/ *n.* **1. WAVY MOVEMENT** a sinuous or wavy motion **2. CURVE** a curving form or outline, especially one in a series such as a wave

un·du·ly /un dóòlee/ *adv.* to a very great extent, or to an excessive, improper, or unjustifiable degree ○ *We were not unduly concerned.*

un·du·ti·ful /un dóòtif'l/ *adj.* **1. LACKING SENSE OF OBLIGATION** lacking a sense of moral or legal obligation **2. UNWILLING TO FULFILL OBLIGATIONS** unwilling to fulfill moral or legal obligations —**un·du·ti·ful·ly** *adv.* —**un·du·ti·ful·ness** *n.*

un·dy·ing /un dì ing/ *adj.* continuing forever

un·earned /un úrnd/ *adj.* **1. NOT GAINED BY WORK** not acquired by labor or service ○ *unearned income* **2. UNDESERVED** not deserved ○ *unearned criticism*

un·earned in·cre·ment *n.* an increase in property value resulting from factors other than labor or improvements made by the owner

un·earned run *n.* in baseball, a run that in the opinion of the official scorer would not have happened had it not been for errors or passed balls made by the defensive team

un·earth /un úrth/ (**-earthed, -earth·ing, -earths**) *vt.* **1. DIG SOMETHING UP** to bring something up out of the ground **2. DISCLOSE SOMETHING** to discover or disclose something, especially after an investigation **3. FIND**

SOMETHING LOST to find something that has been lost or hidden

un·earth·ly /un úrthlee/ *adj.* **1.** NOT FROM THIS WORLD not being or seeming to be from this world **2.** EERIE looking or sounding so strange as to be frightening **3.** COMPLETELY UNREASONABLE completely inappropriate or unreasonable ○ *She woke me up at some unearthly hour to tell me the news.* **4.** PERFECT embodying perfection —**un·earth·li·ness** *n.*

un·eas·y /un éezee/ (**-i·er, -i·est**) *adj.* **1.** ANXIOUS anxious or afraid **2.** UNCERTAIN not certain enough to let people relax completely ○ *an uneasy truce* **3.** ILL AT EASE awkward or lacking confidence **4.** RESTLESS not allowing somebody to rest properly ○ *Only towards dawn did he fall into an uneasy sleep.* —**un·ease** *n.* —**un·eas·i·ly** *adv.* —**un·eas·i·ness** *n.*

un·ec·o·nom·ic /un èkə nómmik, -èekə-/ *adj.* **1.** NOT MAKING PROFIT not making or not likely to make a profit **2.** **un·ec·o·nom·ic, un·ec·o·nom·i·cal** NOT EFFICIENT not efficient or worth the expense

un·ed·it·ed /un édditəd/ *adj.* **1.** NOT CORRECTED not corrected or revised **2.** NOT ADAPTED not adapted to a particular audience, purpose, or medium

un·ed·u·cat·ed /un éjjə kàytəd/ *adj.* lacking the learning that is usually acquired in schools

un·e·lect·a·ble /ùn i léktəb'l/ *adj.* certain to be defeated as a candidate for public office, e.g., because of extreme positions on controversial issues

un·e·mo·tion·al /ùnni mṓshən'l, -mṓshnəl/ *adj.* **1.** SHOWING NO FEELING showing little or no feeling **2.** REASONED AND OBJECTIVE involving reason or intellect rather than feelings —**un·e·mo·tion·al·ly** *adv.*

un·em·ploy·a·ble /ùnnim plóyəb'l/ *adj.* lacking the skills, education, or ability to get a job

un·em·ployed /ùnnim plóyd/ *adj.* **1.** JOBLESS not in paid employment **2.** NOT IN USE not being used ■ *npl.* JOBLESS PEOPLE people who are out of work

un·em·ploy·ment /ùnnim plóymənt/ *n.* **1.** JOBLESSNESS the condition of having no job **2.** NUMBER OF UNEMPLOYED the number of people who are unemployed in an area, often given as a percentage of the total labor force **3.** = **unemployment compensation**

un·em·ploy·ment com·pen·sa·tion, **un·em·ploy·ment** *n.* regular payments made to somebody who is out of work from a government insurance fund contributed to by employers

un·end·ing /un énding/ *adj.* continuing or seeming to continue forever

un·e·qual /un éekwəl/ *adj.* **1.** NOT MEASURABLY THE SAME not measurably the same, e.g., in size or number **2.** NOT OF SAME SOCIAL POSITION not of the same status, rank, or position in society **3.** NOT EVENLY MATCHED not evenly matched in competition **4.** VARIABLE uneven or variable in quality or character **5.** ASYMMETRICAL not evenly balanced **6.** UNABLE TO DO SOMETHING having less than the required ability to do something ○ *unequal to the task* **7.** UNFAIR not fair or just (*archaic*) ■ *n.* SOMEBODY NOT EQUAL TO ANOTHER somebody or something not equal to another —**un·e·qual·ly** *adv.*

un·e·qualed /un éekwəld/, **un·e·qualled** *adj.* without equal or parallel among things of its kind

un·e·quiv·o·cal /ùnni kwívvik'l/ *adj.* allowing for no doubt or misinterpretation —**un·e·quiv·o·cal·ly** *adv.*

un·err·ing /un érring/ *adj.* **1.** ACCURATE striking the mark or target without fail **2.** WITHOUT MISTAKES free of any mistakes —**un·err·ing·ly** *adv.*

UNESCO /yoo nés kṓ/, **Unesco** *abbr.* United Nations Educational, Scientific, and Cultural Organization

un·es·sen·tial /ùnni sénshəl/ *adj.* DISPENSABLE not absolutely needed ■ *n.* SOMETHING UNNECESSARY something that is not necessary or important

un·e·ven /un éevən/ *adj.* **1.** NOT LEVEL without a level or smooth surface **2.** VARYING varying and inconsistent, e.g., in quality, thoroughness, or duration **3.** NOT PARALLEL not straight or parallel **4.** NOT FAIRLY MATCHED not fairly matched in competition **5.** ODD not divisible by two **6.** NOT THE SAME SIZE unequal in number or measurement to another **7.** UNFAIR not just (*archaic*) [Old English *unefen*] —**un·e·ven·ly** *adv.* —**un·e·ven·ness** *n.*

un·e·vent·ful /ùnni véntfəl/ *adj.* not marked by any unusual or important occurrence —**un·e·vent·ful·ly** *adv.* —**un·e·vent·ful·ness** *n.*

un·ex·am·pled /ùnnig zámp'ld/ *adj.* without a similar case or occurrence

un·ex·cep·tion·a·ble /ùnnik sépshənəb'l/ *adj.* good enough to provide no reason for criticism or objection —**un·ex·cep·tion·a·bil·i·ty** /ùnnik sepshənə bíllətee/ *n.* —**un·ex·cep·tion·a·ble·ness** /ùnnik sépshənəb'lnəss/ *n.* —**un·ex·cep·tion·a·bly** /-sépshən əblee/ *adv.*

WORD KEY: USAGE

See Usage note at ***unexceptional***.

un·ex·cep·tion·al /ùnnik sépshən'l/ *adj.* **1.** NOT SPECIAL not special or unusual **2.** WITH NO EXCEPTIONS allowing no exception —**un·ex·cep·tion·al·ly** *adv.*

WORD KEY: USAGE

unexceptional or **unexceptionable**? The distinction in meaning corresponds to that between the positive forms *exceptional* and *exceptionable*. Something is described as ***unexceptional*** when it is ordinary or commonplace, and perhaps a little dull: *Her performance got a good review, but I thought it was unexceptional.* ***Unexceptionable*** comes close to this in meaning, but its strict meaning is "not open to criticism" and therefore "satisfactory, acceptable": *Their behavior has been unexceptionable so far.*

un·ex·cit·ed /ùnnik sítəd/ *adj.* **1.** NOT AROUSED not emotionally aroused **2.** PHYS AT LOWEST ENERGY LEVEL used to describe particles that remain at the lowest energy level

un·ex·pect·ed /ùnnik spéktəd/ *adj.* coming as a surprise —**un·ex·pect·ed·ly** *adv.* —**un·ex·pect·ed·ness** *n.*

un·ex·pe·ri·enced /ùnnik speéree ənst/ *adj.* **1.** NOT UNDERGONE BEFORE not having been known or undergone before **2.** INEXPERIENCED lacking experience

un·ex·pressed /ùnnik sprést/ *adj.* **1.** NOT MADE KNOWN not spoken or made known **2.** UNDERSTOOD WITHOUT SAYING ANYTHING understood without anything being said **3.** GENETICS WITH NO AFFECT ON ORGANISM used to describe a gene that does not have an observable effect on the organism that carries it

un·fail·ing /un fáyling/ *adj.* **1.** LIMITLESS never used up or exhausted **2.** ALWAYS RELIABLE able to be relied on at all times **3.** ALWAYS ACCURATE totally accurate and reliable —**un·fail·ing·ly** *adv.* —**un·fail·ing·ness** *n.*

un·fair /un fáir/ *adj.* **1.** NOT JUST not equal or just **2.** UNETHICAL IN BUSINESS not ethical in business dealings —**un·fair·ly** *adv.* —**un·fair·ness** *n.*

un·faith·ful /un fáythfəl/ *adj.* **1.** UNTRUE TO COMMITMENTS untrue to commitments, duties, beliefs, or ideals **2.** ADULTEROUS engaging in sexual relations with somebody other than one to whom monogamy has been pledged **3.** NOT LIKE ORIGINAL not true to the original **4.** WITH NO RELIGIOUS FAITH not having religious faith (*archaic*) —**un·faith·ful·ly** *adv.* —**un·faith·ful·ness** *n.*

un·fal·ter·ing /un fáwltəring/ *adj.* strong, steady, and not becoming weaker —**un·fal·ter·ing·ly** *adv.*

un·fa·mil·iar /ùn fə míllyər/ *adj.* **1.** NOT PREVIOUSLY KNOWN not previously known or recognized **2.** NOT ACQUAINTED with no previous knowledge or experience ○ *unfamiliar with the software.* —**un·fa·mil·iar·i·ty** /ùn fə mil yérrətee/ *n.* —**un·fa·mil·iar·ly** /ùn fə míllyərlee/ *adv.*

un·fash·ion·a·ble /un fásh'nəb'l/ *adj.* **1.** NOT POPULAR NOW not in the current style **2.** UNFAVORED SOCIALLY not socially approved of ○ *an unfashionable suburb* —**un·fash·ion·a·bly** *adv.*

un·fas·ten /un fáss'n/ (**-tened, -ten·ing, -tens**) *vt.* undo something that holds things together, e.g., the buttons of a garment

un·fath·om·a·ble /un fáthəməb'l/ *adj.* **1.** IMPOSSIBLE TO MEASURE too deep to be measured **2.** IMPOSSIBLE TO UNDERSTAND so mysterious or complicated that understanding is impossible —**un·fath·om·a·ble·ness** *n.* —**un·fath·om·a·bly** *adv.*

un·fa·vor·a·ble /un fáyvərəb'l/ *adj.* **1.** DISAPPROVING expressing disapproval or opposition **2.** NOT GOOD unlikely to be beneficial —**un·fa·vor·a·ble·ness** *n.* —**un·fa·vor·a·bly** *adv.*

un·feel·ing /un féeling/ *adj.* **1.** NOT SYMPATHETIC without caring or sympathy for somebody else's feelings **2.** NUMB unable to experience physical sensation [Old English *unfēlend*] —**un·feel·ing·ly** *adv.* —**un·feel·ing·ness** *n.*

un·fet·ter /un féttər/ (**-tered, -ter·ing, -ters**) *vt.* **1.** RELEASE SOMEBODY OR SOMETHING to release somebody or something from fetters **2.** FREE SOMEBODY FROM CONSTRAINTS to allow somebody to act without restraint

un·fet·tered /un féttərd/ *adj.* not subject to limits or restrictions

un·fin·ished /un fínnisht/ *adj.* **1.** NOT COMPLETED not completed satisfactorily **2.** NOT FINALLY TREATED not finally processed or treated with dye, varnish, paint, or bleach **3.** TEXTILES WITH SLIGHT NAP woven with a slight nap

un·fit /un fít/ (**un·fit·ted, un·fit·ting, -fits**) *adj.* **1.** UNSUITABLE unsuitable for a specific purpose **2.** UNQUALIFIED lacking the necessary skills or qualifications to perform a specific task adequately **3.** NOT HEALTHY not physically or mentally healthy —**un·fit·ly** *adv.* —**un·fit·ness** *n.* —**un·fit·ting·ly** *adv.*

un·fit·ted /un fíttəd/ *adj.* **1.** NOT SUITED not suited or adapted for a specific purpose **2.** NOT FITTED used to describe furniture that is not fitted

un·fit·ting /un fítting/ *adj.* not suitable or appropriate for somebody or something

un·fix /un fíks/ (**-fixed, -fix·ing, -fix·es**) *vt.* **1.** DETACH SOMETHING to loosen or detach something **2.** MAKE SOMETHING UNSTABLE to upset the certainty or stability of something

un·flag·ging /un flágging/ *adj.* remaining strong and unchanging —**un·flag·ging·ly** *adv.*

un·flap·pa·ble /un fláppəb'l/ *adj.* able to maintain composure under all circumstances —**un·flap·pa·bil·i·ty** /un flàppə bíllətee/ *n.* —**un·flap·pa·bly** /un fláppəblee/ *adv.*

un·fledged /un fléjd/ *adj.* **1.** BIRDS NOT HAVING FEATHERS FOR FLYING not having developed the feathers required for flight **2.** INEXPERIENCED young and inexperienced

un·flinch·ing /un flínching/ *adj.* strong and unhesitating —**un·flinch·ing·ly** *adv.*

un·fo·cused /un fṓkəst/, **un·fo·cussed** *adj.* **1.** NOT ADJUSTED not adjusted for a clear image **2.** WITH NO CLEAR PURPOSE lacking a clear purpose or objective

un·fold /un fṓld/ (**-fold·ed, -fold·ing, -folds**) *v.* **1.** *vti.* OPEN OUT to open something and spread it out, or to open and spread out **2.** *vti.* MAKE SOMETHING UNDERSTOOD to make something clear and understood by gradual exposure, or to become clear in this way **3.** *vi.* DEVELOP to develop or expand over time ○ *His talent unfolded as he grew older.* [Old English *unfealdan*]

un·fore·seen /ùnfər séen, ùn fawr séen/ *adj.* not expected beforehand

un·for·get·ta·ble /ùnfər géttəb'l/ *adj.* remarkable in a way that cannot be forgotten —**un·for·get·ta·bly** *adv.*

un·for·giv·a·ble /ùnfər gívvəb'l/ *adj.* so bad that it can never be forgiven —**un·for·giv·a·bly** *adv.*

un·for·giv·ing /ùnfər gívving/ *adj.* **1.** UNWILLING TO FORGIVE unwilling or unable to forgive **2.** PROVIDING NO MARGIN FOR MISTAKES providing little or no margin for mistakes or weakness —**un·for·giv·ing·ly** *adv.*

un·formed /un fáwrmd/ *adj.* **1.** WITH NO REAL SHAPE without coherent shape or structure ○ *the unformed restless desire in her mind* **2.** UNDEVELOPED not yet fully developed **3.** NOT CREATED not yet created

un·for·tu·nate /un fáwrchənət/ *adj.* **1.** UNLUCKY never experiencing good luck **2.** WITH BAD LUCK accompanied by or bringing bad luck **3.** INAPPROPRIATE not appropriate to a given situation ○ *The unfortunate comment was an example of his lack of social polish.* ■ *n.* POOR PERSON somebody who is pitied by others for having bad luck or inadequate resources —**un·for·tu·nate·ness** *n.*

un·for·tu·nate·ly /un fáwrchənətlee/ *adv.* **1.** USED TO EXPRESS REGRET used when somebody wishes something were not true ○ *I didn't get there before he left, unfortunately.* **2.** INAPPROPRIATELY in a way that is inappropriate to a given situation ○ *an unfortunately worded critique*

un·found·ed /un fówndəd/ *adj.* **1.** NOT SUPPORTED BY EVIDENCE not supported by evidence or facts **2.** NOT ESTABLISHED not yet established

un·freeze /un fréez/ (**un·froze** /-frṓz/, **un·froz·en** /-frṓz'n/, **-freez·ing, -freez·es**) *vt.* to remove controls or restrictions fixing wages, hiring, prices, or rents

un·fre·quent·ed /un fréekwəntəd, ùnfree kwéntəd/ *adj.* not often visited, especially by tourists or travelers

un·friend·ly /un fréndlee/ *adj.* **1.** HOSTILE behaving in an obviously cold or hostile way **2.** UNFAVORABLE not beneficial or advantageous —**un·friend·li·ness** *n.*

un·frock /un frók/ (**-frocked, -frock·ing, -frocks**) *vt.* **1.** RELIG REMOVE ORDAINED PERSON FROM OFFICE to remove an ordained person from office and duties as a punishment for doing something considered immoral or heretical **2.** TAKE AWAY SOMEBODY'S RIGHT to take away somebody's right to practice a profession **3.** REMOVE SOMEBODY FROM POSITION to remove somebody from an honorary or privileged position

un·fruit·ful /un fróotfəl/ *adj.* **1.** NOT FERTILE not bearing fruit or offspring (*literary*) **2.** UNSUCCESSFUL not having a successful outcome —**un·fruit·ful·ly** *adv.* —**un·fruit·ful·ness** *n.*

un·furl /un fúrl/ (**-furled, -furl·ing, -furls**) *vti.* to unroll or spread out something, or to become extended in this way

un·gain·ly /un gáynlee/ *adj.* **1.** LACKING GRACE lacking grace while moving **2.** AWKWARD awkward to handle **3.** GANGLY having an awkward long-limbed appearance ■ *adv.* CLUMSILY in a clumsy or graceless way (*archaic*) [Early 17thC. Formed from obsolete *gain* "straight, convenient," from Old Norse *gegn.* Ultimately from a prehistoric Germanic word meaning "against," which is also the ancestor of English *against* and *again.*]

Un·gava /óong gaávə/ region in northeastern Canada, situated east of Hudson Bay and north of the Eastmain River

Un·ga·va Bay /óong gàyvə-, -gaávə-/ bay in northeastern Quebec, Canada, opening into Hudson Strait

un·gen·er·ous /un jénnərəss/ *adj.* **1.** STINGY slow to give, forgive, or share things **2.** MEAN-SPIRITED mean-spirited and ignoble —**un·gen·er·ous·ly** *adv.*

un·glued /un glóod/ *adj.* **1.** SEPARATED having become separated or detached **2.** UPSET OR ANGRY emotionally upset and lacking composure (*informal*)

un·god·ly /un góddlee/ *adj.* **1.** RELIG NOT REVERING GOD not devoted to or obeying God **2.** WICKED behaving in a way thought to violate moral strictures **3.** UNREASONABLE not meeting standards for reasonableness (*informal*) ○ *woke me up at some ungodly hour* —**un·god·li·ness** *n.*

un·gov·ern·a·ble /un gúvvərnəb'l/ *adj.* incapable of being governed or restrained —**un·gov·ern·a·ble·ness** *n.* —**un·gov·ern·a·bly** *adv.*

un·gra·cious /un gráyshəss/ *adj.* **1.** ILL-MANNERED inconsistent with good manners **2.** NOT PLEASANT extremely unpleasant or difficult **3.** EVIL behaving in a way perceived as immoral or inappropriate (*archaic*) [13thC. The original underlying meaning was "lacking the grace of God."] —**un·gra·cious·ly** *adv.* —**un·gra·cious·ness** *n.*

un·grate·ful /un gráytfəl/ *adj.* **1.** NOT APPRECIATIVE not thankful or appreciative **2.** UNREWARDING unpleasant or unrewarding —**un·grate·ful·ly** *adv.* —**un·grate·ful·ness** *n.*

un·grudg·ing /un grújjing/ *adj.* without reluctance or reservation —**un·grudg·ing·ly** *adv.*

un·gual /úng gwəl/ *adj.* **1.** ANAT OF FINGERNAILS OR TOENAILS relating to or affecting the fingernails or toenails **2.** ZOOL OF NAIL, CLAW, OR HOOF relating to, occurring in, or supporting a nail, claw, or hoof [Mid-19thC. Formed from Latin *unguis* "nail, claw" (see UNGUIS).]

un·guard·ed /un gaárdəd/ *adj.* **1.** WITH NO PROTECTION lacking a guard or protection **2.** NATURAL free from pretense or guile **3.** NOT WARY showing a lack of thought or care —**un·guard·ed·ly** *adv.* —**un·guard·ed·ness** *n.*

un·guent /úng gwənt/ *n.* a healing or soothing ointment [15thC. From Latin *unguentum*, from *unguere* "to anoint" (source of English *ointment, anoint,* and *unctuous*).]

un·guis /úng gwiss/ (*plural* **un·gues** /úng gweez/) *n.* **1.** ZOOL NAIL, CLAW, OR HOOF a nail, claw, hook, or hoof on a digit or foot of an animal **2.** BOT CLAW-SHAPED BASE OF PETAL the claw-shaped base of some petals [Early 18thC. From Latin, "nail, claw" (source of English *ungulate*). Ultimately from an Indo-European word that is also the ancestor of English *nail* and *onyx.*]

un·gu·late /úng gyələt, úng gyə làyt/ *adj.* **1.** WITH HOOFS having hoofs **2.** SHAPED LIKE HOOF resembling a hoof in shape or function ■ *n.* HOOFED MAMMAL a mammal with hoofs, e.g., the horse, rhinoceros, hog, giraffe, deer, or camel [Early 19thC. From late Latin *ungulatus*, from Latin *ungula* "hoof, claw," literally "small claw," from *unguis* "nail" (see UNGUIS).]

un·gu·li·grade /úng gyəli gràyd/ *adj.* used to describe a mammal that walks on hoofs [Mid-19thC. Coined from Latin *ungula* "hoof" (see UNGULATE) + GRADE.]

un·hair /un háir/ (**-haired, -hair·ing, -hairs**) *vt.* to remove hair from something, especially a hide (*archaic*)

un·hal·lowed /un hállōd/ *adj.* **1.** NOT CONSECRATED not consecrated or blessed **2.** IRREVERENT lacking religious reverence **3.** IMMORAL not conforming to the standards of a religion [Old English *unhālgod*]

un·hand /un hánd/ (**-hand·ed, -hand·ing, -hands**) *vt.* to let somebody go by releasing a grasp

un·hand·y /un hándee/ (**-i·er, -i·est**) *adj.* **1.** NOT SKILLED WITH HANDS not skilled at working with the hands or with tools **2.** INCONVENIENTLY LOCATED in an inconvenient location **3.** DIFFICULT TO USE not easy to use or handle

un·hap·pi·ly /un háppilee/ *adv.* **1.** IN UNHAPPY WAY in an way that expresses or is characterized by unhappiness **2.** UNFORTUNATELY used to express a wish that something were not true (*dated*)

un·hap·py /un háppee/ (**-pi·er, -pi·est**) *adj.* **1.** SAD not cheerful or joyful **2.** UNFORTUNATE not bringing good luck **3.** INAPPROPRIATE done without proper thought or inappropriate in a specific context **4.** DISPLEASED not pleased or satisfied with somebody or something **5.** UNFAVORABLE not advantageous (*archaic*) —**un·hap·pi·ness** *n.*

un·har·ness /un haárnəss/ (**-nessed, -ness·ing, -ness·es**) *vt.* **1.** REMOVE HARNESS FROM HORSE to remove the harness from a horse **2.** RELEASE ENERGY OR PASSIONS to release energy or passions from restraints **3.** REMOVE ARMOR to remove the armor from somebody (*archaic*)

UNHCR *abbr.* United Nations High Commission for Refugees

un·health·y /un hélthee/ (**-i·er, -i·est**) *adj.* **1.** SICK affected by ill health **2.** BAD FOR HEALTH not good for the health **3.** SYMPTOMATIC OF ILL HEALTH showing the symptoms of or resulting from ill health **4.** HARMING CHARACTER harmful to the character **5.** CORRUPT morally corrupt or unwholesome ○ *an unhealthy interest in lurid crimes* **6.** RISKY taking unnecessary risks (*informal*) —**un·health·i·ly** *adv.* —**un·health·i·ness** *n.*

un·heard /un húrd/ *adj.* **1.** NOT HEARD not perceived by the ear **2.** NOT GIVEN A HEARING not listened to or given a hearing **3.** UNKNOWN unknown or obscure (*archaic*)

un·heard-of *adj.* **1.** UNKNOWN not previously known **2.** UNPRECEDENTED never having happened before **3.** OFFENSIVE extremely offensive or rude

un·hes·i·tat·ing /un hézzi tàyting/ *adj.* **1.** PROMPT without pause or indecision **2.** UNCHANGING without change or deviation —**un·hes·i·tat·ing·ly** *adv.*

un·hinge /un hínj/ (**-hinged, -hing·ing, -hing·es**) *vt.* **1.** REMOVE SOMETHING FROM HINGES to remove something from its hinges **2.** REMOVE HINGES to remove the hinges of something **3.** DISLOCATE SOMETHING to dislodge or detach something **4.** DISRUPT to throw something into confusion **5.** MAKE PSYCHOLOGICALLY UNSTABLE to cause somebody to become emotionally or mentally unstable

un·hip /un híp/ *adj.* not in keeping with popular fashions or ideas (*dated informal*)

un·hitch /un hích/ (**-hitched, -hitch·ing, -hitch·es**) *vt.* **1.** UNFASTEN SOMETHING to unfasten something that is tied up **2.** DIVORCE to divorce (*informal; usually passive*)

un·ho·ly /un hólee/ (**-li·er, -li·est**) *adj.* **1.** NOT BLESSED not blessed or consecrated by a church ritual **2.** DEFYING RELIGIOUS PRECEPTS deliberately defiant of specific religious precepts **3.** OUTRAGEOUS extremely annoying or disturbing ○ *This place is an unholy mess!* [Old English *unhālig*] —**un·ho·li·ness** *n.*

un·hook /un hóok/ (**-hooked, -hook·ing, -hooks**) *v.* **1.** *vt.* REMOVE SOMETHING FROM HOOK to remove something from a hook **2.** *vt.* UNDO HOOKS OF SOMETHING to unfasten the hooks of something **3.** *vti.* DETACH to separate somebody from a contract (*informal*)

un·hoped-for *adj.* not expected or anticipated ○ *an unhoped-for victory* [14thC. *Unhoped* formed from HOPED.]

un·horse /un háwrs/ (**-horsed, -hors·ing, -hors·es**) *vt.* **1.** KNOCK SOMEBODY FROM HORSE to knock or throw somebody from a horse **2.** BRING SOMEBODY DOWN FROM OFFICE to bring somebody down from a high office or position

un·hur·ried /un húrreed/ *adj.* done in a relaxed and deliberate way —**un·hur·ried·ly** *adv.*

uni- *prefix.* one, single ○ *unicellular* [From Latin, formed from *unus* "one." Ultimately from the Indo-European word for "one," which is also the ancestor of English *one, alone,* and *inch.*]

U·ni·at /yóonee àt, -ət/, **Uniate** *n.* MEMBER OF EASTERN CHRISTIAN CHURCH a member of any of the Eastern Christian Churches that recognize papal supremacy but keep their own liturgy, language, and canon law ■ *adj.* OF UNIAT CHURCHES relating to or typical of the Uniat Churches [Mid-19thC. From Russian *uniyat* and Polish *uniat*, from *unia* "union" (of the Roman Catholic and Greek Churches), ultimately from Latin *unio* (see UNION).]

u·ni·ax·i·al /yóonee áksee əl/ *adj.* **1.** CRYSTALS WITH SINGLE REFRACTION IN ONE DIRECTION used to describe a crystal or mineral that has one direction, parallel to the principal axis, along which single refraction occurs **2.** BOT WITH AN UNBRANCHED MAIN STEM used to describe a plant with an unbranched main stem —**u·ni·ax·i·al·ly** *adv.*

u·ni·cam·er·al /yóoni kámmərəl/ *adj.* having only one legislative chamber [Mid-19thC. Formed from Latin *camera* "chamber" (see CAMERA).] —**uni·cam·er·al·ism** *n.* —**uni·cam·er·al·ist** *n.* —**u·ni·cam·er·al·ly** *adv.*

UNICEF /yóoni sèf/, **Unicef** *n., abbr.* United Nations Children's Fund

u·ni·cel·lu·lar /yóoni séllyələr/ *adj.* consisting of a single cell —**uni·cel·lu·lar·i·ty** /-sellyə láiratee/ *n.*

u·ni·col·or /yóoni kúllər/ *adj.* composed of or containing only one color

Unicorn

u·ni·corn /yóoni kàwrn/ *n.* **1.** MYTHICAL ONE-HORNED HORSE a mythical animal usually depicted as a white horse with a single straight spiraled horn growing from its forehead **2.** BIBLE BIBLICAL HORNED ANIMAL a horned animal mentioned in the Bible, now believed to be a rhinoceros or aurochs [13thC. Via Old French from Latin *unicornis*, literally "one-horned," from *cornu* "horn" (see CORN). Translation of Greek *monokerōs.*]

u·ni·cos·tate /yóoni kó stàyt/ *adj.* BOT used to describe a leaf with one main rib

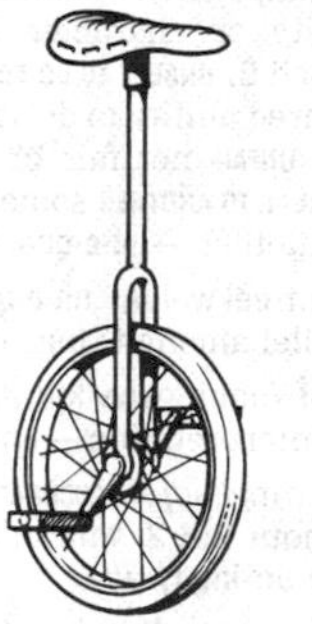

Unicycle

u·ni·cy·cle /yóoni sīk'l/ *n.* a vehicle having a single wheel with a seat mounted on a frame above it. It is steered and kept upright by balance and propelled by pedals. [Mid-19thC. Modeled on BICYCLE.] —**u·ni·cy·clist** *n.*

un·i·den·ti·fied /ùn ī dénti fīd/ *adj.* **1.** UNABLE TO BE NAMED unable to be recognized or given a name **2.** WANTING TO REMAIN ANONYMOUS wishing not to be associated with or held responsible for something

u·ni·di·rec·tion·al /yóoni di rékshən'l, -dī-/ *adj.* thinking, moving, or operating in only one direction

UNIDO /yóoni dō/, **Unido** *n., abbr.* United Nations Industrial Development Organization

u·ni·fac·to·ri·al /yóoni fak táwree əl/ *adj.* used to describe an inherited characteristic dependent on a single gene

u·ni·fi·ca·tion /yòonifi káysh'n/ *n.* **1.** ACT OF UNITING the act or process of uniting or joining together **2.** RESULT OF UNITING a result of uniting or joining

U·ni·fi·ca·tion Church *n.* a religious denomination founded in 1954 by the South Korean industrialist Sun Myung Moon

u·ni·fied field the·o·ry *n.* a single theory capable of defining the nature of the interrelationships among nuclear, electromagnetic, and gravitational forces

u·ni·fo·li·ate /yòoni fólee ət/ *adj.* with a single leaf or leaf-shaped part

u·ni·form /yóoni fàwrm/ *n.* **1.** DISTINCTIVE CLOTHES a distinctive set of clothes worn to identify somebody's occupation, affiliation, or status **2.** COMPLETE OUTFIT a single outfit of identifying clothes **3.** PARTICULAR IDENTIFYING LOOK a particular style or other feature that identifies somebody as a member of a certain group ■ *adj.* **1.** UNCHANGING always the same in quality, degree, character, or manner **2.** CONSISTENT conforming to one standard or rule **3.** LIKE ANOTHER being the same as another or others **4.** UNVARYING IN DESIGN unvarying in color, texture, or design ■ *vt.* **(-formed, -form·ing, -forms) 1.** PROVIDE PEOPLE WITH UNIFORMS to provide people or a group with uniforms **2.** MAKE SOMETHING THE SAME to make something homogeneous, unvarying, or consistent [Mid-16thC. Directly or via French from Latin *uniformis*, literally "having one form," from *forma* "shape" (source of English *form* and *formal*).] —**uniformed** /yóoni fáwrmətee/ *adj.* —**u·ni·for·mi·ty** /yòoni fàwrmlee/ *n.* —**u·ni·form·ly** *adv.*

U·ni·form *n.* COMMUNICATION a code word for the letter "U," used in international radio communications

u·ni·for·mi·tar·i·an·ism /yòoni fawrmi táiree ə nìzzəm/ *n.* the theory that the same geologic processes occurred in the past as occur today, and that geologic formations and structures can be interpreted by observing present-day actions —**u·ni·for·mi·tar·i·an** *adj., n.*

U·ni·form Re·source Lo·ca·tor *n.* full form of **URL**

u·ni·fy /yóoni fī/ **(-fied, -fy·ing, -fies)** *vt.* to bring people or things together to form a single unit or entity [Early 16thC. Via French *unifier* from Latin *unificare*, literally "to make one."] —**u·ni·fi·a·ble** *adj.* —**u·ni·fied** *adj.* —**u·ni·fi·er** *n.* —**u·ni·fy·ing** *adj.*

u·nij·u·gate /yoo níjjə gàyt, yòoni jóo-/ *adj.* used to describe a compound leaf with a single pair of leaflets [Mid-19thC. Formed from JUGUM.]

u·ni·lat·er·al /yòonə láttərəl/ *adj.* **1.** DECIDED BY ONE PARTY decided or acted on by only one involved party or nation irrespective of what the others do **2.** ACCOUNTING FOR ONE SIDE ONLY taking into account only one side of a subject **3.** BINDING ONLY ONE PARTY binding or at the insistence of only one party to a contract, obligation, or agreement **4.** MED AFFECTING ONLY ONE SIDE affecting or involving only one side of the body, only one of a pair of organs, or only one side of an organ **5.** BOT WITH PARTS ON ONLY ONE SIDE having parts that are arranged on only one side of a stem or other axis **6.** WITH ONE SIDE having only one side **7.** THROUGH ONE PARENT ONLY tracing lineage through one parent only —**u·ni·lat·er·al·ly** *adv.*

u·ni·lat·er·al·ism /yòonə láttərə lìzzəm/ *n.* the implementation of a foreign policy with little or no regard for the views of allies —**u·ni·lat·er·al·ist** *n.*

u·ni·lin·e·al /yòoni línnee əl/ *adj.* = **unilateral** *adj.* 7

u·ni·lin·e·ar /yòoni línnee ər/ *adj.* developing or evolving progressively through defined stages from primitive to advanced and excluding any variation on this course

u·ni·lin·gual /yòoni líng gwəl/ *adj.* using or knowing only one language

u·ni·lit·er·al /yòoni líttərəl/ *adj.* having only a single letter

u·ni·loc·u·lar /yòoni lókyələr/ *adj.* with a single loculus, cell, or cavity

un·i·mag·i·na·ble /ùnni májjənəb'l/ *adj.* beyond anything that could be imagined or described —**un·i·mag·i·na·bly** *adv.*

un·i·mag·i·na·tive /ùnni májjənətiv/ *adj.* **1.** UNABLE TO THINK OF NEW IDEAS unable to think of new or interesting ideas, plans, or situations **2.** BORING AND WITHOUT NEW IDEAS boring and ordinary, without any new ideas

U·ni·mak Is·land /yóonə mak-/ the largest of the Aleutian Islands, between the Bering Sea and the Pacific Ocean, southwestern Alaska

un·im·paired /ùnnim páird/ *adj.* not damaged by something unpleasant, dangerous, or different that happens

un·im·pas·sioned /ùnnim pásh'nd/ *adj.* unlikely to appeal to the emotions

un·im·peach·a·ble /ùnnim péechəb'l/ *adj.* **1.** IMPOSSIBLE TO DISCREDIT impossible to discredit or challenge **2.** FAULTLESS so good that it is beyond reproach —**un·im·peach·a·bly** *adv.*

un·im·por·tant /ùnnim páwrt'nt/ *adj.* of little or no significance —**un·im·por·tance** *n.*

un·im·proved /ùnnim próovd/ *adj.* **1.** NOT MADE BETTER not made better from an original condition **2.** WITHOUT IMPROVEMENTS not modified in a way that would increase value, e.g., by the addition of buildings, landscaping, or services ○ *an unimproved lot* **3.** NOT GETTING HEALTHIER not showing improvement in health **4.** NOT PUT TO GOOD USE not used to advantage

un·in·cor·po·rat·ed /ùnnin káwrpə ràytəd/ *adj.* **1.** NOT ORGANIZED AS ENTITY not organized into a corporation or municipality ○ *an unincorporated township* **2.** NOT INCLUDED not included or a part of something

un·in·form·a·tive /ùnnin fáwrmətiv/ *adj.* not providing adequate information —**un·in·form·a·tive·ly** *adv.*

un·in·formed /ùnnin fáwrmd/ *adj.* lacking facts or knowledge of a particular situation or subject

un·in·hab·it·a·ble /ùnnin hábbitəb'l/ *adj.* unfit as a habitation, especially for human beings —**un·in·hab·it·a·bil·i·ty** /-habbitə bílləteel *n.*

un·in·hab·it·ed /ùnnin hábbitəd/ *adj.* without human habitation

un·in·hib·it·ed /ùnnin híbbitəd/ *adj.* **1.** UNRESTRAINED expressing feelings or views without restraint **2.** UNCONSTRAINED not subject to social or other constraints —**un·in·hib·it·ed·ly** *adv.* —**un·in·hib·it·ed·ness** *n.*

un·in·i·ti·ate /ùnni níshee ət/ *adj.* without experience

un·in·i·ti·at·ed /ùnni níshee àytəd/ *adj.* WITHOUT KNOWLEDGE OF SUBJECT having no knowledge or experience of a particular subject ■ *npl.* PEOPLE UNKNOWLEDGEABLE IN SUBJECT people who have no knowledge or experience of a particular subject (*takes a plural verb*)

un·in·spired /ùnnin spírd/ *adj.* lacking originality or distinction

un·in·spir·ing *adj.* not arousing interest or excitement

un·in·stall /ùnnin stáwl/ **(-stalled, -stall·ing, -stalls)** *vt.* to remove software from a computer

un·in·struct·ed /ùnnin strúktəd/ *adj.* **1.** NOT EDUCATED not educated or informed **2.** NOT TOLD WHAT TO DO not informed how to proceed or vote

un·in·sur·a·ble /ùnnin shóorəb'l/ *adj.* considered too great a risk to cover by insurance —**un·in·sur·a·bil·i·ty** /-shoorə bíllətee/ *n.*

un·in·sured /ùnnin shóord/ *adj.* NOT COVERED BY INSURANCE not covered against some hazard by insurance ■ *npl.* SOMEBODY NOT INSURED a person or group not covered by insurance (*takes a plural verb*)

un·in·tel·li·gent /ùnnin téllijənt/ *adj.* **1.** LACKING INTELLIGENCE lacking or showing a lack of intelligence **2.** NOT HAVING ABILITY TO THINK not having a mind or the ability to think and reason —**un·in·tel·li·gent·ly** *adv.*

un·in·tel·li·gi·ble /ùnnin téllijəb'l/ *adj.* difficult or impossible to understand —**un·in·tel·li·gi·bil·i·ty** /-tellijə bíllətee/ *n.* —**un·in·tel·li·gi·bly** /-téllijəblee/ *adv.*

un·in·tend·ed /ùnnin téndəd/ *adj.* neither planned nor wanted

un·in·ten·tion·al /ùnnin ténshən'l/ *adj.* not on purpose or by plan —**un·in·ten·tion·al·ly** *adv.*

un·in·ter·est /un íntrəst, -íntərəst, -ín trèst/ *n.* a lack of interest or concern

un·in·ter·est·ed /un íntrəstəd, -íntərəstəd, -ín trèstəd/ *adj.* lacking interest or concern [Mid-17thC. The earliest meaning was "impartial, disinterested."] —**un·in·ter·est·ed·ly** *adv.* —**un·in·ter·est·ed·ness** *n.*

un·in·ter·est·ing /un íntrəsting, -íntərəsting, -ín trèsting/ *adj.* without interesting qualities —**un·in·ter·est·ing·ly** *adv.*

WORD KEY: SYNONYMS

See Synonyms at ***boring***.

un·in·ter·rupt·ed /ùnnintə rúptəd/ *adj.* **1.** WITH NO BREAK without interruption or break **2.** WITHOUT OBSTRUCTIONS free from obstructions ○ *an uninterrupted view* —**un·in·ter·rupt·ed·ly** *adv.*

u·ni·nu·cle·ate /yòoni nóoklee ət/ *adj.* having a single nucleus

un·in·vit·ed /ùnnin vítəd/ *adj.* not invited or welcome

un·in·vit·ing /ùnnin víting/ *adj.* not appealing or pleasant —**un·in·vit·ing·ly** *adv.*

un·in·volved /ùnnin vólvd/ *adj.* not participating in something

un·ion /yóonyən/ *n.* **1.** ACT OF JOINING TOGETHER the act of joining together people or things to form a whole **2.** RESULT OF BRINGING PEOPLE TOGETHER a result of bringing or joining together people or things **3.** = **labor union 4.** AGREEMENT agreement or unity of interests or opinions **5. un·ion, Un·ion** EDUC ORGANIZATION PROVIDING RECREATIONAL FACILITIES an organization that provides recreational facilities for students at a college or university **6. un·ion, Un·ion** EDUC BUILDING FOR RECREATION a building that houses recreational facilities for students at a college or university **7.** MARRIAGE the state of being married **8.** SEX sexual intercourse **9.** POLITICAL ALLIANCE an alliance formed by the joining of people or organizations for a common political purpose **10.** EMBLEM OF UNION an emblem of union used on a flag (*archaic*) **11.** CONSTR COUPLING a coupling for parts such as pipes and pipe fittings **12.** MATH SMALL SET OF ELEMENTS the smallest set that consists of all the elements of any or all of two or more given sets and no other elements. An element is counted only once even if it occurs in more than one of the given sets. **13.** TEXTILES FABRIC OF DIFFERENT YARNS a fabric made of two or more different yarns, e.g., cotton and linen [15thC. Directly or via French from the Latin stem *union-*, "oneness," from *unus* "one." Ultimately from an Indo-European word meaning "one," the ancestor of English *one, any, inch,* and *ounce*.]

Un·ion *n.* **1.** NORTHERN SIDE IN CIVIL WAR the side of the northern states in the Civil War, or its armed forces **2.** UNITED STATES OF AMERICA the United States of America **3.** UNION OF BRITAIN AND NORTHERN IRELAND the union of Great Britain and Northern Ireland since 1920

un·ion card *n.* a card signifying membership in a labor union

un·ion cat·a·log *n.* a library catalog combining the materials in more than one library or in branches of the same library

Un·ion Cit·y /yóonyən-/ **1.** residential and industrial city in western California, on Alameda Creek, near San Francisco Bay. Population: 53,762 (1990). **2.** city in northeastern New Jersey, on the Hudson River, adjoining Jersey City and opposite New York City. Population: 58,012 (1990).

Un·ion flag *n.* = **Union Jack**

un·ion·ism /yóonyə nìzzəm/ *n.* **1.** PRINCIPLES OF UNIONS the principles or policies of labor unions **2.** ADVOCACY OF UNIONS the advocacy of forming and joining labor unions —**un·ion·ist** *n.*

Un·ion·ism *n.* loyalty to the federal union during the Civil War —**Un·ion·ist** *n.*

un·ion·ize /yóonyə nīz/ **(-ized, -iz·ing, -iz·es)** *vti.* to organize workers into a labor union, or to join a labor union —**un·ion·i·za·tion** /yòonyəni záysh'n/ *n.* —**un·ion·iz·er** *n.*

Un·ion Jack, Union flag *n.* the flag of the United Kingdom, which united by superposition the flags of England, Scotland, and Ireland [*Union* because it represents the UNITED KINGDOM + *jack*[1] in the sense "ship's flag"]

un·ion la·bel *n.* a label identifying a product as having been made or produced by members of a labor union

union scale *n.* = **scale**[2]

un·ion shop *n.* a place of employment where a contract between the employer and a labor union requires employees to be or become members of the union within a specified time. ◊ **open shop**

un·ion suit *n.* a one-piece undergarment covering the entire body, arms, and legs, now considered old-fashioned

u·nip·a·rous /yoo níppərəss/ *adj.* **1.** HAVING ONE CHILD having given birth to only one child **2.** PRODUCING ONE OFFSPRING PER BIRTH producing a single offspring at each birth

u·ni·per·son·al /yòoni púrsən'l/ *adj.* **1.** EXISTING AS ONE PERSON existing or manifested in the form of only one person **2.** GRAM USED IN ONE PERSON existing as an inflected form in only one person, especially the third person singular

u·ni·pla·nar /yòoni pláynər/ *adj.* occurring or located in a single plane

u·ni·pod /yóoni pòd/ *n.* a one-legged stand, e.g., for a camera [Mid-20thC. Modeled on TRIPOD.]

u·ni·po·lar /yòoni pṓlər/ *adj.* **1.** PHYS **HAVING SINGLE POLE** operating by means of, having, or produced by a single electric or magnetic pole **2.** BIOL **BRANCHING OUT AT ONLY ONE END** used to describe a neuron that branches out at only one end **3.** PHYS **WITH ONE POLARITY** used to describe a transistor that has carriers with only one polarity —**u·ni·po·lar·i·ty** /yòoni pō lérrətee/ *n.*

u·ni·po·tent /yoo níppət'nt/ *adj.* capable of developing into only one type of cell or tissue

u·nique /yoo neék/ *adj.* **1. ONLY ONE** being the only one of its kind **2. BETTER THAN OTHERS** superior to all others **3. UNUSUAL** different from others in a way that makes something worthy of note ○ *a unique marketing opportunity* **4. LIMITED TO SOMEBODY OR SOMETHING** limited to a specific place, situation, group, person, or thing ○ *concerns that are unique to resettled refugees* [Early 17thC. Via French from Latin *unicus*, from *unus* "one" (see UNION).] —**u·nique·ly** *adv.* —**u·nique·ness** *n.*

WORD KEY: USAGE

Meaning trap: The use of ***unique*** in its weakened sense "remarkable, outstanding" is common in marketing and advertising (*Don't miss this unique offer*), and these uses have somewhat discredited what is arguably a routine development in meaning. Many dictionaries and usage guides argue that ***unique*** is an absolute concept, thereby rejecting the use of qualifying words such as *very* and *rather*, but in many cases this stricture seems a pedantic objection to what is a linguistic rather than a philosophical convention.

u·nique sell·ing prop·o·si·tion *n.* full form of **USP**

u·ni·ra·mous /yòoni ráyməss/ *adj.* used to describe an appendage without multiple branches [Late 19thC. Formed from Latin *ramus* "branch."]

u·ni·sep·tate /yòoni sép tàyt/ *adj.* with a single separating wall or membrane [Mid-19thC. Formed from SEPTUM.]

u·ni·ser·i·al /yòoni seéree əl/, **u·ni·se·ri·ate** /-àyt, -ət/ *adj.* arranged in or consisting of a single row or series

u·ni·sex /yóoni sèks/ *adj.* **1. SUITABLE FOR EITHER SEX** designed or suitable for people of either sex ○ *unisex fashions* **2.** BIOL **NOT DISTINCTLY MALE OR FEMALE** not distinctly of either the male or the female sex

u·ni·sex·u·al /yòoni sékshoo əl/ *adj.* **1. RELATED TO ONE SEX** related to or limited to one sex **2. WITH MALE OR FEMALE REPRODUCTIVE ORGANS** having either only male or only female reproductive organs —**u·ni·sex·u·al·i·ty** /-sèkshoo állətee/ *n.* —**u·ni·sex·u·al·ly** /-əlee/ *adv.*

u·ni·son /yóoniss'n, -z'n/ *n.* **1. NOTES AT SAME PITCH** two or more notes sharing the same pitch **2. PERFORMANCE OF PARTS** the performance of two or more parts at the same pitch or an octave apart [Late 16thC. Via Old French from, ultimately, late Latin *unisonus*, literally "having the same sound," from *sonus* "sound" (see SOUND).] ◇ **in unison 1.** in perfect agreement or harmony **2.** at the same time as somebody or something else

u·nit /yóonit/ *n.* **1. ONE PERSON, THING, OR GROUP** a single person, thing, or group, usually regarded as a whole part of something larger **2. DISCRETE PART** any of the individuals or discrete parts or elements into which something can be divided, especially for analysis **3. GROUP WITH SPECIFIC FUNCTION** a group of people with a specific function who are part of a larger organization ○ *the cancer research unit* **4. GROUP OF MILITARY PERSONNEL** a group of military personnel with a particular function organized as a subdivision of a larger body **5. COMPONENT OR ASSEMBLY OF COMPONENTS** a component or assembly of components that performs a specific function ○ *a kitchen unit* **6.** *U.S., Can, Aus, NZ* **RESIDENCE** one of a number of similar residences within a building or development **7.** EDUC **PART OF ACADEMIC COURSE** a part of an academic course that focuses on a particular theme **8.** EDUC **MEASURE OF ACADEMIC INSTRUCTION** a measure of academic instruction, usually based on the number of hours of classroom and laboratory work **9.** MEASURE **MEASUREMENT** a standard measurement, e.g., an inch, degree, calorie, volt, or hour, whose multiples are used in determining quantity **10.** MED **DRUG AMOUNT** an amount of an enzyme, hormone, drug, or other agent that produces a given effect, often as specified by an internationally agreed standard **11.** MATH **NATURAL NUMBER** the lowest positive natural number **12.** MATH **NUMBER LESS THAN TEN** the first digit to the left of the decimal point in decimal notation, representing a whole number less than ten. Broadly, the first place in a place-value number system, representing a whole number less than the base (**radix**) multiplied by the base raised to the zero power. **13.** LOGIC, MATH **SET WITH SINGLE NUMBER** a set having a single number [Late 16thC. Formed from Latin *unus* "one" (see UNION), on the model of *digit*.]

u·ni·tard /yóoni taàrd/ *n.* a one-piece stretchable garment with or without sleeves that covers the body from the neck to the feet [Mid-20thC. Coined from UNI- and LEOTARD.]

u·ni·tar·i·an /yòo ni táiree ən/ *n.* **1. SUPPORTER OF UNITY** a supporter of unity or a unitary system **2.** RELIG **SOMEBODY BELIEVING GOD IS ONE** somebody who believes that God is one being —**u·ni·tar·i·an·ism** *n.*

U·ni·tar·i·an *n.* **1.** RELIG **MEMBER OF UNITARIAN UNIVERSALIST CHURCH** somebody who believes in or practices the precepts of Unitarian Universalism **2.** RELIG **MONOTHEIST WHO IS NOT CHRISTIAN** somebody who believes in one god but who does not follow the precepts of a Christian church **3.** CHR **NONBELIEVER IN TRINITY** a Christian who does not believe in the Trinity —**Unitarian** *adj.*

Unitarian Universalism *n.* a religious doctrine that rejects the Christian doctrine of the Trinity, the divinity of Jesus Christ, and formal dogma but stresses reason and individual conscience in belief and practice —**Unitarian Universalist** *adj.*

u·ni·tar·y /yóoni tèrree/ *adj.* **1. RELATING TO UNIT** relating to or consisting of a unit **2. CHARACTERIZED BY UNITY** based on or characterized by unity **3. EXISTING AS UNIT** undivided and existing as a unit **4. OF CENTRALIZED GOVERNMENT** of or based on a system of government in which authority is centralized —**u·ni·tar·i·ly** *adv.*

u·nit cell *n.* the smallest structural unit of a crystal that has all its symmetry and by repetition in three dimensions makes up its full lattice

u·nit cost *n.* the cost of producing a single item

u·nite /yoo nít/ (**u·nit·ed, u·nit·ing, u·nites**) *v.* **1.** *vti.* **BRING THINGS TOGETHER** to bring things together or to come together to form or act as a unit **2.** *vti.* **UNIFY PEOPLE** to unify people or to become unified by a common interest or concern **3.** *vti.* **MARRY** to join a couple in marriage **4.** *vti.* **ADHERE** to adhere or cause things to adhere **5.** *vt.* **COMBINE QUALITIES** to combine qualities or traits [15thC. From Latin *unit-*, the past participle stem of *unire*, literally "to make one," from *unus* "one" (see UNION).] —**u·nit·er** *n.*

u·nit·ed /yoo nítəd/ *adj.* **1. COMBINED INTO ONE** combined into or made one **2. BY OR FROM UNION** formed by or resulting from the union of two or more persons or things **3. IN HARMONY** in agreement or harmony —**u·nit·ed·ness** *n.*

U·nit·ed *adj. Can* belonging to the United Church of Canada

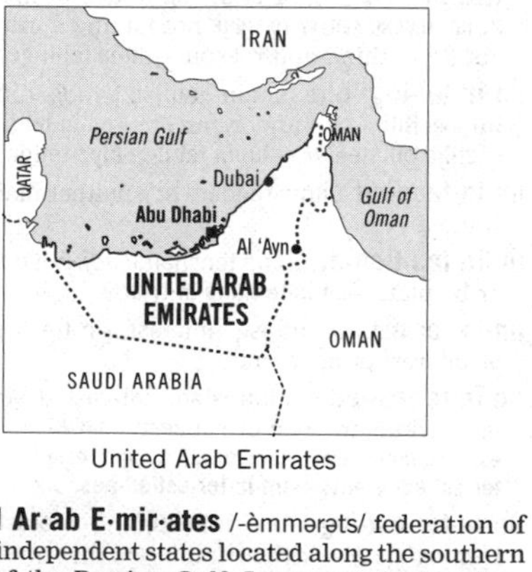

United Arab Emirates

U·nit·ed Ar·ab E·mir·ates /-èmmərəts/ federation of seven independent states located along the southern coast of the Persian Gulf. Language: Arabic. Currency: dirham. Capital: Abu Dhabi. Population: 2,500,000 (1996). Area: 30,000 sq. mi./77,700 sq. km. Former name **Trucial States**

U·ni·ted Ar·ab Re·pub·lic former independent union between Egypt and Syria, founded in 1958. It was disbanded when Syria left the union in 1961, although Egypt retained the name until 1971.

U·nit·ed Church of Can·a·da *n. Can* a large Protestant Christian church formed in 1926 by the amalgamation of most Presbyterian, Methodist, and Congregationalist congregations in Canada

U·nit·ed Church of Christ *n.* a Protestant denomination in the United States that was formed in 1957 by the merging of the Evangelical and Reformed Church and the Congregational Church

U·nit·ed King·dom constitutional monarchy in northwestern Europe, occupying the British Isles with the exception of most of the island of Ireland. It comprises the historic kingdoms of England and Scotland, the principality of Wales, and the province of Northern Ireland. Language: English. Currency: pound sterling. Capital: London. Population: 58,784,000 (1996). Area: 93,341 sq. mi./241,752 sq. km. Official name **United Kingdom of Great Britain and Northern Ireland**

U·nit·ed Na·tions *n.* **1. ORGANIZATION OF NATIONS** an organization of nations that was formed in 1945 to promote peace, security, and international cooperation **2.** HIST **ALLIANCE OF NATIONS** an alliance of nations that pledged in January 1942 to defeat the Axis powers in World War II

U·nit·ed States POL federal republic in the continent of North America, consisting of 50 states. Language: English. Currency: dollar. Capital: Washington, D.C. Population: 270,311,758 (1998). Area: 3,717,796 sq. mi./9,629,047 sq. km. Official name **United States of America**

u·ni·tive /yóonitiv/ *adj.* **1. ABLE TO UNITE** having the ability to unite or promoting unity **2. CHARACTERIZED BY UNION** characterized by union or unity [Early 16thC. From late Latin *unitivus*, from Latin *unit-* (see UNITE).]

u·nit of ac·count *n. U.K.* = **money of account**

u·nit op·er·a·tion *n.* an operation, e.g., mixing, filtration, chemical reaction, or distillation, that is common to the chemical process industries. The study of unit operations is the basis of chemical engineering.

u·nit price *n.* the price of goods per item or measure, e.g., per pound or dozen

u·nit rule *n.* the rule that a state's entire vote for nomination to office must go to the candidate preferred by the majority of its delegation to the political party's national convention

u·nit trust *n. U.K.* = **mutual fund**

u·ni·ty /yóonitee/ (*plural* **-ties**) *n.* **1. BEING ONE** the state of being one **2. COMBINING INTO ONE** the combining or joining of separate things or entities to form one **3. SOMETHING WHOLE** something whole or complete formed by combining or joining separate things or entities **4. HARMONY** harmony of opinion, interest, or feeling **5. SINGLENESS AMONG INDIVIDUALS** singleness or constancy among individuals or groups **6.** ARTS **ARRANGING OF ARTISTIC ELEMENTS AESTHETICALLY** the arranging of separate elements in a literary or artistic work to create an overall aesthetic impression **7.** ARTS **AESTHETIC IMPRESSION** the overall aesthetic impression produced by the arrangement of elements in an artistic or literary work **8.** THEATER **PRINCIPLE OF DRAMATIC STRUCTURE** any one of the three principles of dramatic structure derived from Aristotle's *Poetics*. These state that the action of a play should be limited to one plot (**unity of action**), one day (**unity of time**), and one location (**unity of place**). **9.** MATH **NUMBER ONE** a number by which a given element of a mathematical system can be multiplied with the result being equal to the value of the given element **10.** MATH = **identity element** [13thC. Via Old French *unite* from Latin *unitas*, literally "oneness," from *unus* "one" (see UNION).]

univ. *abbr.* university

u·ni·va·lent /yòoni váylənt/ *adj.* **1.** = **monovalent 2. REMAINING UNPAIRED DURING CELL DIVISION** used to describe a chromosome that remains unpaired during the cell division (**meiosis**) that precedes sex cell formation —**u·ni·va·len·cy** *n.*

u·ni·valve /yóoni vàlv/ *adj.* **1. WITH SINGLE-PIECE SHELL** having a shell that is a single piece or valve ○ *an univalve gastropod* **2. MADE OF SINGLE PIECE** used to describe a shell that is made of a single piece ■ *n.* **MOLLUSK** a mollusk or shell that is univalve

United Kingdom

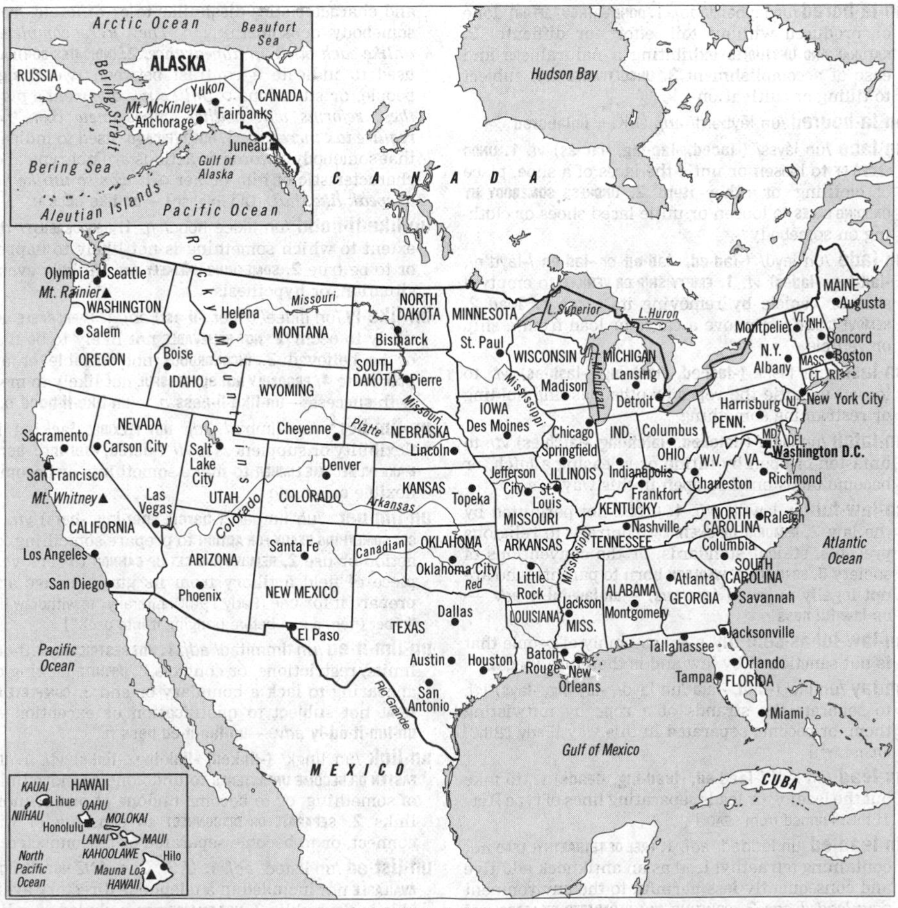

United States

u·ni·ver·sal /yòonə vúrs'l/ *adj.* **1.** AFFECTING THE WORLD affecting, relating to, or including the whole world or everyone in the world **2.** RELATING TO UNIVERSE relating to the universe or everything **3.** AFFECTING THOSE IN PARTICULAR GROUP affecting, relating to, or including everyone in a particular group or situation **4.** USED BY EVERYONE used or understood by everyone **5.** APPLICABLE TO ALL applicable to all situations or purposes ○ *a universal solution* **6.** PRESENT EVERYWHERE present or prevalent everywhere **7.** KNOWLEDGEABLE knowledgeable about or encompassing extensive skills, interests, activities, or subjects **8.** ADAPTABLE TO DIFFERENT SIZES adaptable to many uses or sizes **9.** LOGIC AFFIRMING OR DENYING EVERY MEMBER relating to a proposition that is true or false of every member of a class or group ■ *n.* **1.** COMMON CHARACTERISTIC a characteristic or behavior pattern common to everyone or all the people in a particular group or situation **2.** LOGIC TRUE OR FALSE PROPOSITION FOR ALL a proposition that is true or false for all members of a class or group **3.** PHILOSOPHY GENERAL TERM OR CONCEPT a general term or concept or that which it denotes **4.** PHILOSOPHY UNCHANGING METAPHYSICAL ENTITY a metaphysical entity that remains unchanged in character through a series of changing relations **5.** PHILOSOPHY PLATONIC IDEA OR ARISTOTELIAN FORM a Platonic idea or Aristotelian form **6.** LING GRAMMATICAL CHARACTERISTIC COMMON TO ALL LANGUAGES an actual or possible characteristic common to the grammatical description of all human languages —**u·ni·ver·sal·i·ty** /-vur sállətee/ *n.* —**u·ni·ver·sal·ly** /-vúrsəlee/ *adv.*

WORD KEY: SYNONYMS

See Synonyms at ***widespread***.

uni·ver·sal beam *n.* a strong steel beam suitable as a support, used either vertically or horizontally

uni·ver·sal class *n.* = **universal set**

uni·ver·sal cou·pling *n.* = **universal joint**

uni·ver·sal do·nor *n.* somebody with group O blood who can potentially donate blood to anyone, regardless of the recipient's blood group. ◊ **universal recipient**

uni·ver·sal gram·mar *n.* the set of actual or possible rules that form the grammatical description of all human languages

u·ni·ver·sal·ism /yòonə vúrs'l ìzzəm/ *n.* **1.** COMPREHENSIVE RANGE a comprehensive range of knowledge, interests, or activities **2.** UNIVERSAL FEATURE a universal characteristic or feature —**u·ni·ver·sal·ist** *n.* —**u·ni·ver·sal·is·tic** /-vursə lístik/ *adj.*

U·ni·ver·sal·ism *n.* the doctrine of salvation for all souls —**U·ni·ver·sal·ist** *n.*

u·ni·ver·sal·iz·a·bil·i·ty /yòonə vurs'l ìzə bíllətee/ *n.* **1.** UNIVERSAL APPLICATION OF MORAL JUDGMENT the thesis that any moral judgment must apply equally to all relevantly identical situations **2.** KANTIAN PRINCIPLE OF MORALITY the Kantian principle that any course of action that cannot be universally adopted must be morally impermissible

u·ni·ver·sal·ize /yòonə vúrs'l ìz/ (**-ized, -iz·ing, -iz·es**) *vt.* **1.** MAKE WIDESPREAD to make something universal in use or distribution, often within a certain field **2.** MAKE GENERAL to generalize a theory, proposition, or idea so that it applies to all people, instances, or situations —**u·ni·ver·sal·i·za·tion** /yòonə vursʼli záysh'n/ *n.*

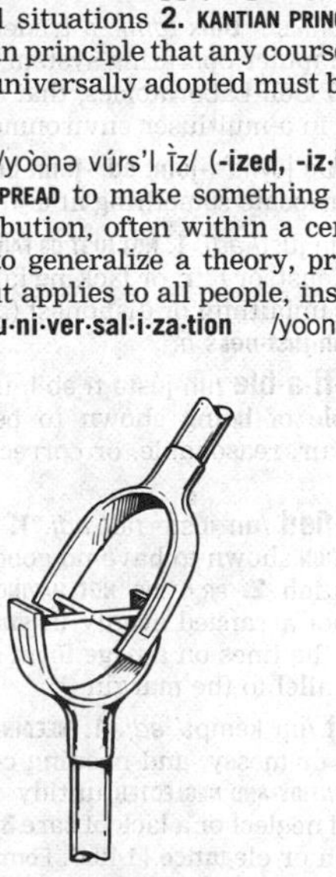

Universal joint

u·ni·ver·sal joint, u·ni·ver·sal coup·ling *n.* a coupling device between two rotating shafts in line with each other that permits rotation in three planes. It is commonly used in vehicle construction.

u·ni·ver·sal mo·tor *n.* an electric motor that runs with a relatively constant output speed on either alternating or direct current

U·ni·ver·sal Prod·uct Code *n.* a bar code containing a unique 12-digit number that identifies a commercial product

u·ni·ver·sal quan·ti·fi·er *n.* a word such as "all" and "every" in English and the logical operator or constant that performs the same function in symbolic, mathematical, or predicate logic

u·ni·ver·sal re·cip·i·ent *n.* somebody who belongs to the AB blood group and, as a result, can receive transfusions of blood of any ABO group. ◊ **universal donor**

u·ni·ver·sal set, **u·ni·ver·sal class** *n.* a mathematical set that contains all of the possible elements and all of the subsets relevant to the solution of a particular problem

u·ni·ver·sal time *n.* 1. = **Greenwich Mean Time** 2. **u·ni·ver·sal time, u·ni·ver·sal time co·ord·in·a·ted** INTERNATIONALLY ACCEPTED STANDARD FOR TIME an internationally accepted standard for calculating time based on International Atomic Time

u·ni·verse /yóonəvərs/ *n.* 1. ALL MATTER AND ENERGY IN SPACE the totality of all matter and energy that exists in the vastness of space, whether known to human beings or not 2. THE EARTH AND HUMANITY the earth along with the human race and the totality of human experience 3. SPHERE OF PERSON OR THING a sphere of activity or field that is centered on and includes everything associated with a person, place, or thing 4. = **universe of discourse** 5. = **population** *n.* 5 [14thC. Directly or via French from Latin *universum* "the whole world," from *universus* "whole," literally "turned into one," from *versus*, past participle of *vertere* "to turn" (source of English *versatile*).]

u·ni·verse of dis·course *n.* in logic, all of a set of objects implied by a specific discussion

u·ni·ver·si·ty /yoònə vúrsətee/ (*plural* **-ties**) *n.* 1. UNDERGRADUATE AND POSTGRADUATE EDUCATIONAL INSTITUTION an educational institution for higher learning that typically includes an undergraduate college and graduate schools in various disciplines, as well as medical and law schools and sometimes other professional schools 2. BUILDINGS HOUSING A UNIVERSITY the buildings, other facilities, and grounds of a university 3. STUDENTS AND FACULTY the students, teachers, and administrative and other staff of a university [14thC. Via French *université* from Latin *universitas* "the whole, society, guild," from *universus* (see UNIVERSE).]

u·niv·o·cal /yoo nívvək'l/ *adj.* UNAMBIGUOUS having only one meaning ■ *n.* UNIVOCAL WORD a word or term with only one meaning [Mid-16thC. Formed from Late Latin *univocus*, literally "having one voice," from *vox* "voice" (see VOICE).] —**u·niv·o·cal·ly** *adv.*

UNIX /yóoniks/, **Unix** *tdmk.* a trademark for a widely used computer operating system, developed in 1969 at AT&T Bell Laboratories, that can support multitasking in a multiuser environment

un·joint /un jóynt/ (**-joint·ed, -joint·ing, -joints**) *vt.* to cut off or dislocate something at a joint

un·just /un júst/ *adj.* 1. NOT JUST OR FAIR contrary to what is right, just, or fair, or lacking fairness or justice 2. FAITHLESS unfaithful or dishonest (*archaic*) —**un·just·ly** *adv.* —**un·just·ness** *n.*

un·jus·ti·fi·a·ble /un jústə fī əb'l, ùn justə fī əb'l/ *adj.* incapable of being shown to be, or defended as being, fair, reasonable, or correct —**un·jus·ti·fi·a·bly** *adv.*

un·jus·ti·fied /un jústə fīd/ *adj.* 1. HAVING NO ACCEPTABLE JUSTIFICATION shown to have no good or just reason or explanation 2. PRINTING NOT HAVING A STRAIGHT VERTICAL MARGIN not arranged evenly in such a way that the ends of the lines on a page form a straight vertical line parallel to the margin

un·kempt /un kémpt/ *adj.* 1. NEEDING GROOMING tangled, matted, or messy, and needing combing or grooming 2. UNTIDY AND NEGLECTED untidy or disorderly as a result of neglect or a lack of care 3. UNPOLISHED lacking in polish or elegance [14thC. Formed from *kempt*, past participle of *kemb* "to comb," from Old English *cemban*, from a prehistoric Germanic word that is also the ancestor of English *comb*.]

un·ken·nel /un kénn'l/ (**-neled, -nel·ing, -nels**) *vt.* 1. LET OUT OF KENNEL to let a dog out of a kennel 2. FORCE OUT OF LAIR to make an animal leave its den or lair 3. MAKE KNOWN to reveal or uncover something secret or hidden

un·kind /un kīnd/ *adj.* 1. LACKING KINDNESS lacking or resulting from a lack of kindness, sympathy, or consideration 2. HARSH severe, harsh, or inclement —**un·kind·ness** *n.* —**un·kind·ly** *adj.*

un·kind·ly /un kīndlee/ *adv.* CRUELLY in an unkind manner or without showing kindness ■ *adj.* NOT KINDLY lacking in kindliness

un·kink /un kíngk/ (**-kinked, -kink·ing, -kinks**) *v.* 1. *vti.* GET KINKS OUT OF to remove a kink or kinks from something, or to have a kink or kinks removed 2. *vi.* RELAX to become loose or relaxed

un·knit /un nít/ (**-knit** *or* **-knit·ted, -knit·ting, -knits**) *vti.* 1. UNDO OR BECOME UNDONE to unravel something or become unraveled 2. RELAX CONTRACTED EYEBROWS to allow the eyebrows to move back to a natural position after being drawn together, or to be moved apart in this way

un·know·a·ble /un nṓ əb'l/ *adj.* NOT KNOWABLE impossible to know, often because of lying outside human experience or being inaccessible to human understanding ■ *n.* SOMETHING NOT KNOWABLE something that cannot be known —**un·know·a·bil·i·ty** /un nṓ ə bíllətee/ *n.* —**un·know·a·ble·ness** /un nṓ əb'lnəss/ *n.* —**un·know·a·bly** /un nṓ əblee/ *adv.*

un·know·ing /un nṓ ing/ *adj.* 1. UNAWARE unwitting or lacking awareness 2. UNINTENTIONAL not intended —**un·know·ing·ly** *adv.*

un·known /un nṓn/ *adj.* 1. NOT KNOWN not forming part of somebody's knowledge or of knowledge in general 2. NOT IDENTIFIED undetermined or undiscovered 3. NOT WIDELY KNOWN not known to, or recognized by, many people ■ *n.* 1. SOMEBODY OR SOMETHING NOT KNOWN somebody or something that is not part of somebody's knowledge or of knowledge in general 2. SOMEBODY OR SOMETHING NOT WIDELY KNOWN somebody or something that is not known or recognized by many people 3. MATH VARIABLE TO BE DETERMINED a variable in an equation whose values are solutions of the equation

Un·known Sol·dier *n.* an unidentified soldier killed in battle and selected for burial with national honors to represent all those who died fighting for their country but could not be identified

un·la·bored /un láybərd/ *adj.* 1. DONE WITHOUT EFFORT done or produced without toil, effort, or difficulty 2. NATURAL AND UNSTUDIED exhibiting a naturalness and ease of accomplishment 3. UNCULTIVATED not subject to tilling or cultivation

un·la·boured /un láybərd/ *adj.* U.K. = **unlabored**

un·lace /un láyss/ (**-laced, -lac·ing, -lac·es**) *vt.* 1. UNDO LACES OF to loosen or untie the laces of a shoe, piece of clothing, or other item 2. UNDRESS SOMEBODY BY UNDOING LACES to loosen or untie laced shoes or clothing on somebody

un·lade /un láyd/ (**-lad·ed, -lad·ed** *or* **-lad·en** /-láyd'n/, **-lad·ing, -lades**) *vt.* 1. EMPTY SHIP OR VEHICLE to empty a ship or vehicle by removing its cargo or load 2. REMOVE CARGO to remove a cargo or load from a ship or vehicle

un·lash /un lásh/ (**-lashed, -lash·ing, -lash·es**) *vt.* to loosen or untie the ropes or other lashing holding or restraining something

un·latch /un lách/ (**-latched, -latch·ing, -latch·es**) *vti.* to unfasten or open by lifting or releasing a latch, or become unfastened or open in this way

un·law·ful /un láwf'l/ *adj.* 1. ILLEGAL not permitted by the law 2. IMMORAL OR UNETHICAL contrary to religious precepts, ethical standards, or the conventions of society 3. BORN OUT OF WEDLOCK born to parents who are not legally married (*archaic*) —**un·law·ful·ly** *adv.* —**un·law·ful·ness** *n.*

un·law·ful as·sem·bly *n.* an assembly of people that is not sanctioned by law and is therefore illegal

un·lay /un láy/ (**-laid, -laid** /un láyd/, **-lay·ing, -lays**) *vti.* to separate the strands of a rope by untwisting them, or become separated in this way [Early 18thC. From LAY[1].]

un·lead /un léd/ (**-lead·ed, -lead·ing, -leads**) *vt.* to take out the leading or leads separating lines of type [Late 16thC. Formed from LEAD.]

un·lead·ed /un léddəd/ *adj.* 1. FREE OF TETRAETHYL LEAD not containing tetraethyl lead as an antiknock additive and consequently less harmful to the environment ○ *unleaded gas* 2. PRINTING NOT SEPARATED BY LEADS not separated by spaces created by inserting leads between the lines of type ■ *n.* UNLEADED GASOLINE gasoline that does not contain tetraethyl lead as an antiknock additive

un·learn /un lúrn/ (**-learned** *or* **-learnt, -learn·ing, -learns**) *vt.* 1. RID MIND OF to rid the mind of the knowledge or memory of something 2. END PRACTICE OF to break the habit of something or end the practice of something

un·learn·ed /un lúrnəd/ *adj.* 1. LACKING EDUCATION not having received an education or schooling 2. DISPLAYING LACK OF EDUCATION showing or resulting from a lack of education 3. UNSKILLED OR UNFAMILIAR lacking a knowledge of, skills in, or familiarity with, a specified field 4. **un·learn·ed, un·learnt** NATURAL OR UNSTUDIED possessed or known without having been practiced, studied, or taught [15thC. Formed from LEARN.] —**un·learn·ed·ly** *adv.*

un·leash /un leésh/ (**-leashed, -leash·ing, -leash·es**) *vt.* 1. FREE FROM LEASH to set a person or animal free from a leash or other form of restraint or confinement 2. ALLOW SOMETHING TO HAVE FULL EFFECT to allow something, especially something previously held in check, to have its full effect

un·leav·ened /un lévvənd/ *adj.* not made with yeast or other raising agent

un·less /un léss/ *conj.* except under the circumstances that ○ *I won't go unless the weather improves.* [15thC. Formed from *on lesse than* "on a lower condition, except," of unknown origin.]

un·let·tered /un léttərd/ *adj.* 1. NOT WELL-EDUCATED lacking a good education or the knowledge and understanding that such an education can provide 2. ILLITERATE unable to read and write 3. NOT HAVING ANY LETTERING not containing or inscribed with any lettering [14thC]

un·li·censed /un líss'nst/ *adj.* 1. HAVING NO LICENSE lacking a required official license 2. UNSANCTIONED done without authorization or permission 3. WITHOUT ETHICAL INHIBITIONS lacking ethical or religious constraints

un·licked /un líkt/ *adj.* 1. NOT LICKED not licked, e.g., so as to moisten, clean, or dry 2. NOT FULLY FORMED not completely or properly formed or shaped (*archaic*) [Late 16thC. Formed from LICK.]

un·like /un lík/ *prep.* 1. DISSIMILAR having qualities and characteristics dissimilar to or different from somebody or something ○ *They were completely unlike each other in appearance.* 2. INDICATES CONTRAST used to indicate a contrast between two things, people, or situations ○ *Unlike my opponent's plan, these reforms will neither impose new costs nor require tax increases.* 3. NOT TYPICAL OF used to indicate that somebody's words or actions are not typical or characteristic of him or her ○ *It was so unlike her to speak like that.* [Old English] —**un·like·ness** *n.*

un·like·li·hood /un líklee hòod/ *n.* 1. IMPROBABILITY the extent to which something is not likely to happen or to be true 2. SOMETHING UNLIKELY an unlikely event, situation, or hypothesis

un·like·ly /un líklee/ (**-li·er, -li·est**) *adj.* 1. IMPROBABLE not likely to occur 2. NOT BELIEVABLE not likely to be true or be believed 3. INCONGRUOUS not suitable or appropriate 4. PROBABLY NOT SUCCESSFUL not likely to meet with success —**un·like·li·ness** *n.* —**un·like·li·hood** *n.*

un·lim·ber[1] /un límbər/ *adj.* NOT FLEXIBLE lacking in flexibility or suppleness ■ *vti.* (**-bered, -ber·ing, -bers**) MAKE OR BECOME LIMBER to make something, or become, flexible or supple

un·lim·ber[2] /un límbər/ (**-bered, -ber·ing, -bers**) *vti.* 1. GET SOMETHING READY FOR ACTION to prepare something for action or use 2. REMOVE AND SET UP CANNON to remove a piece of field artillery from its gun carriage and prepare it for use [Early 19thC. Literally "to withdraw the limber (from a gun before bringing it into use)."]

un·lim·it·ed /un límmitəd/ *adj.* 1. NOT RESTRICTED without limits, restrictions, or controls 2. INFINITE lacking or appearing to lack a boundary or end 3. COMPLETE OR TOTAL not subject to qualification or exception —**un·lim·it·ed·ly** *adv.* —**un·lim·it·ed·ness** *n.*

un·link /un língk/ (**-linked, -link·ing, -links**) *vti.* 1. UNFASTEN OR BECOME UNFASTENED to undo one or more links of something, or to become undone at one or more links 2. SEPARATE OR DISCONNECT to separate or disconnect, or to become separated or disconnected

un·list·ed /un lístəd/ *adj.* 1. *U.S., Can, ANZ* NOT PUBLICLY AVAILABLE not included in a telephone directory available to the public 2. NOT ON LIST not included on a list 3. NOT LISTED ON STOCK EXCHANGE not registered on a stock exchange and consequently not available for trading on that exchange

un·live /un lív/ (**-lived, -liv·ing, -lives**) *vt.* to reverse or undo the effects of an experience, action, or period of life

un·load /un lṓd/ (**-load·ed, -load·ing, -loads**) *vti.* **1. REMOVE CARGO OR LOAD FROM CARRIER** to take off or remove a cargo or load from a ship, truck, or pack animal **2. DISCHARGE** to discharge passengers or cargo **3. REMOVE CHARGE FROM GUN** to remove a charge or cartridge from a gun **4. SHARE TROUBLES** to find an outlet for worries or negative feelings by sharing them with somebody else **5. SELL SOMETHING UNWANTED** to get rid of something, especially by selling a large quantity of it **6. TRANSFER SOMETHING UNWANTED** to pass work, responsibility, or a problem on to somebody else **7. TAKE FILM OUT OF CAMERA** to remove a roll of film from a camera **8. HIT SOMETHING FORCEFULLY** to hit something with great force or power

un·lock /un lók/ (**-locked, -lock·ing, -locks**) *v.* **1.** *vti.* **OPEN OR BECOME OPEN AFTER LOCKING** to open a lock or something locked, or to become open after being locked **2.** *vt.* **GIVE ACCESS TO SOMETHING** to provide access to something previously unavailable **3.** *vti.* **RELEASE EMOTION** to release or unleash a pent-up feeling or emotion, or to be released or unleashed **4.** *vti.* **REVEAL OR BE REVEALED** to expose or explain something, or to be exposed or explained **5.** *vti.* **LOOSEN** to unclench something, or to be unclenched

un·looked-for /un lŏŏkt fàwr/ *adj.* not hoped for or expected

un·loose /un lŏŏss/ (**-loosed, -loos·ing, -loos·es**), **un·loos·en** /un lŏŏss'n/ (**-ened, -en·ing, -ens**) *vt.* **1. UNFASTEN** to untie or undo something, especially a knot **2. SET FREE BY UNTYING** to set a person or animal free by untying restraints **3. RELEASE FROM RESTRAINT OR CONFINEMENT** to restore freedom to somebody held under restraint or in confinement **4. MAKE LOOSER** to relax the tightness of something **5. MAKE SOMETHING LESS INTENSE** to reduce the intensity of something

un·love·ly /un lúvvlee/ (**-li·er, -li·est**) *adj.* **1. NOT BEAUTIFUL** not beautiful or pleasing to look at **2. NOT PLEASURABLE** not producing pleasure or delight —**un·love·li·ness** *n.*

un·luck·i·ly /un lúkilee/ *adv.* **1. UNFORTUNATELY** in an unfortunate manner **2. IN AN UNLUCKY WAY** in a way characterized by bad luck [Mid-16thC]

un·luck·y /un lúkee/ (**-i·er, -i·est**) *adj.* **1. HAVING BAD LUCK** not experiencing good luck or good fortune **2. FULL OF MISFORTUNE OR FAILURE** full of bad luck, misfortune, or failure **3. BRINGING MISFORTUNE** causing or heralding misfortune **4. DISAPPOINTING** producing disappointment or regret —**un·luck·i·ness** *n.*

un·made past tense, past participle of **unmake** ■ *adj.* **NOT MADE NEAT AND TIDY** not restored to a neat and tidy state after being slept in ○ *an unmade bed*

un·make /un máyk/ (**-made, -made** /un máyd/, **-mak·ing, -makes**) *vt.* **1. UNDO** to undo the effects of something **2. CHANGE COMPLETELY** to make a fundamental change or changes in something **3. REMOVE FROM POWER** to remove somebody from office or a position of authority

un·man /un mán/ (**-manned, -man·ning, -mans**) *vt.* **1. STRIP OF COURAGE** to cause somebody to lose a quality or qualities traditionally attributed to men, especially courage **2. EMASCULATE** to deprive a man or boy of the ability to have intercourse or father children

un·man·age·a·ble /un mánnəjəb'l/ *adj.* impossible or difficult to deal with —**un·man·age·a·bil·i·ty** /un mànnəjə bíllətee/ *n.* —**un·man·age·a·bly** *adv.*

un·man·ly /un mánlee/ (**-li·er, -li·est**) *adj.* **1. WEAK AND COWARDLY** not strong and brave in the way that a man is traditionally supposed to be **2. UNSUITABLE FOR A MAN** not appropriate for or typical of a man, according to traditional perceptions of masculinity —**un·man·li·ness** *n.*

un·manned /un mánd/ *adj.* not having any personnel, especially not having a pilot or crew [Mid-16thC. Formed from MAN.]

un·man·nered /un mánnərd/ *adj.* **1. NOT HAVING GOOD MANNERS** lacking or displaying a lack of good manners **2. WITHOUT AFFECTATION** having an easy, unaffected manner —**un·man·nered·ly** *adv.*

un·man·ner·ly /un mánnərlee/ *adj.* **LACKING GOOD MANNERS** lacking or displaying a lack of good manners ■ *adv.* **RUDELY** in a rude or discourteous manner —**un·man·ner·li·ness** *n.*

un·marked /un ma̋arkt/ *adj.* **1. WITHOUT MARK** not bearing any mark **2. LACKING IDENTIFYING MARKINGS** lacking identifying letters, numbers, or symbols ○ *an unmarked police car* **3. LACKING DISTINGUISHING QUALITY** having no particular distinguishing quality or character **4. UNSEEN** not seen or spotted

un·mar·ried /un mérreed/ *adj.* not joined to another person by marriage

un·mask /un másk/ (**-masked, -mask·ing, -masks**) *v.* **1.** *vti.* **TAKE MASK OFF** to remove a mask from somebody or somebody's face **2.** *vt.* **EXPOSE TRUE NATURE OF** to expose the true nature or identity of somebody or something **3.** *vi.* **LET TRUE NATURE BECOME KNOWN** to allow somebody's or something's true nature or identity to become known

un·matched /un mácht/ *adj.* **1. NOT MATCHING** not matching, especially not belonging to a matching pair **2. NOT EQUALED** having no equal or rival

un·mean·ing /un méening/ *adj.* **1. MEANINGLESS** lacking meaning or significance **2. UNINTENTIONAL** not intended or deliberate **3. UNINTELLIGENT** devoid of intelligence —**un·mean·ing·ly** *adv.*

un·meant *adj.* not intended

un·meas·ured /un mézhərd/ *adj.* **1. NOT DETERMINED BY MEASURING** not found out by measurement **2. NOT RESTRAINED** unrestrained, incautious, or ill-considered **3.** MUSIC **NOT DIVIDED INTO BARS** not marked with bar lines and therefore with no set rhythm

un·me·chan·i·cal /ùnmə kánnik'l/ *adj.* lacking the ability or skill to work with tools and machinery —**un·me·chan·i·cal·ly** *adv.*

un·meet /un méet/ *adj.* not proper, suitable, or becoming (*archaic or literary*) [Old English *unmǣte*, from MEET]

un·men·tion·a·ble /un ménshənəb'l/ *adj.* **NOT TO BE MENTIONED** not to be mentioned or discussed, especially in polite conversation ■ *n.* **THING NOT TO BE MENTIONED** something that should not be mentioned or discussed, especially in polite conversation ■ **un·men·tion·a·bles** *npl.* **UNDERWEAR** undergarments (*dated or humorous*) —**un·men·tion·a·ble·ness** *n.* —**un·men·tion·a·bly** *adv.*

un·mer·ci·ful /un múrsif'l/ *adj.* **1. NOT MERCIFUL** displaying no mercy or characterized by a lack of mercy **2. EXCESSIVE** going beyond what is reasonable —**un·mer·ci·ful·ly** *adv.* —**un·mer·ci·ful·ness** *n.*

un·met *adj.* not satisfactorily fulfilled

un·mind·ful /un mīndfəl/ *adj.* not aware, attentive, careful, or heedful of somebody or something —**un·mind·ful·ly** *adv.* —**un·mind·ful·ness** *n.*

un·mis·tak·a·ble /ùnmi stáykəb'l/ *adj.* easily recognized or understood —**un·mis·tak·a·bly** *adv.*

un·mit·i·gat·ed /un mítti gàytəd/ *adj.* **1. NOT LESSENED** not lessened or eased in any way **2. COMPLETE AND UTTER** absolute and unqualified —**un·mit·i·gat·ed·ly** *adv.* —**un·mit·i·gat·ed·ness** *n.*

un·mixed /un míkst/ *adj.* not mixed, especially not diminished by the presence or occurrence of something else

un·mold /un mṓld/ (**-mold·ed, -mold·ing, -molds**) *vt.* to remove something from a mold

un·mo·lest·ed /ùnmə léstəd/ *adj.* **NOT INTERFERED WITH** not bothered, interfered with, or stopped ■ *adv.* **WITHOUT INTERFERENCE** without being bothered, interfered with, or stopped

un·moor /un mŏŏr/ (**-moored, -moor·ing, -moors**) *v.* **1.** *vti.* **FREE OR BE FREED FROM MOORINGS** to free a ship or boat from its moorings, or to be freed from moorings **2.** *vt.* **LEAVE MOORED BY ONLY ONE ANCHOR** to leave a ship or boat moored by only one of its anchors

un·mor·al /un máwrəl/ *adj.* **1. AMORAL** lacking or displaying a lack of a moral sense **2. NONMORAL** not subject to morality or ethics —**un·mo·ral·i·ty** /ùnmə rállətee/ *n.* —**unmorally** /ùnmə rállee/ *adv.*

un·mo·ti·vat·ed /un mṓtə vàytəd/ *adj.* **1. LACKING MOTIVATION TO DO SOMETHING** not stimulated by interest or desire to do something **2. LACKING MOTIVE** not resulting from an understandable reason or motive

un·moved /un mŏŏvd/ *adj.* having or showing no emotional reaction to something

WORD KEY: SYNONYMS

See Synonyms at ***impassive***.

un·mov·ing /un mŏŏving/ *adj.* **1. STATIONARY** not in motion **2. EMOTIONALLY UNAFFECTING** not causing an emotional reaction

un·muf·fle /un múff'l/ (**-fled, -fling, -fles**) *vt.* to remove a muffle or something that muffles from something

un·mu·si·cal /un myŏŏzik'l/ *adj.* **1. UNMELODIC** lacking melodic qualities and consequently unpleasant to hear **2. HAVING NO EAR FOR MUSIC** having no ability for, or no interest in, music —**un·mu·si·cal·ly** *adv.* —**un·mu·si·cal·ness** *n.* —**un·mu·si·cal·i·ty** /un myŏŏzi kállətee/ *n.*

un·muz·zle /un múzz'l/ (**-zled, -zling, -zles**) *vt.* **1. FREE DOG FROM MUZZLE** to remove a muzzle from an animal, especially a dog **2. RESTORE FREEDOM OF SPEECH TO** to restore to a person or organization the right to say, publish, or broadcast something

un·my·e·lin·at·ed /un mī əli nàytəd/ *adj.* used to describe a nerve fiber that lacks a myelin sheath. Such fibers transmit nerve impulses more slowly than myelinated ones, and are found mainly in worms, insects, and other invertebrate animals. [Mid-20thC. Coined from MYELIN.]

un·name·a·ble /un náyməb'l/, **un·nam·a·ble** *adj.* incapable of being named, especially too terrible to name

un·named /un náymd/ *adj.* **1. NOT MENTIONED BY NAME** having a name but not specified by it **2. HAVING NO NAME** not yet assigned a name

un·nat·u·ral /un náchərəl/ *adj.* **1. CONTRARY TO LAWS OF NATURE** contrary to the physical laws of nature **2. NOT CONFORMING TO THE AVERAGE** behaving in ways that contradict conventional assumptions about what constitutes normal or acceptable human behavior **3. CONTRARY TO EXPECTED BEHAVIOR** contrary to a particular habit, custom, or practice **4. ARTIFICIAL** affected, artificial, contrived, or strained —**un·nat·u·ral·ly** *adv.* —**un·nat·u·ral·ness** *n.*

un·nec·es·sar·y /un néssə sèrree/ *adj.* **1. NOT NECESSARY** not essential, needed, or required **2. GRATUITOUS** gratuitous, unjustified, and hurtful —**un·nec·es·sar·i·ly** *adv.*

un·nerve /un núrv/ (**-nerved, -nerv·ing, -nerves**) *vt.* **1. CAUSE SOMEBODY TO LOSE NERVE** to deprive somebody of courage, resolve, or self-confidence **2. MAKE SOMEBODY NERVOUS** cause somebody to feel nervous —**un·nerv·ing** *adj.* —**un·nerv·ing·ly** *adv.*

un·no·tice·a·ble /un nṓtissəb'l/ *adj.* not easily noticed or observed —**un·no·tice·a·bly** *adv.*

un·no·ticed /un nṓtist/ *adv.* **WITHOUT BEING OBSERVED** without being seen or spotted by anybody ■ *adj.* **UNOBSERVED** not seen or spotted by anybody [Early 18thC]

un·num·bered /un númbərd/ *adj.* **1. NOT COUNTABLE** too many to be counted **2. LACKING IDENTIFYING NUMBER** not assigned or having an identifying number

UNO, U.N.O. *abbr.* United Nations Organization

un·ob·tru·sive /ùnnəb trŏŏssiv/ *adj.* not conspicuous, blatant, or assertive —**un·ob·tru·sive·ly** *adv.* —**un·ob·tru·sive·ness** *n.*

un·oc·cu·pied /un ókyə pīd/ *adj.* **1. NOT IN USE** not being used by anybody **2. NOT DOING ANYTHING** not doing anything or anything important **3. NOT INHABITED** not lived in by anybody **4. NOT UNDER FOREIGN MILITARY RULE** not under the control or military rule of a foreign country

WORD KEY: SYNONYMS

See Synonyms at ***vacant***.

un·of·fi·cial /ùnnə físh'l/ *adj.* **1. UNAUTHORIZED** not authorized or sanctioned by the proper official or other authority **2. NOT ACTING OFFICIALLY** not acting or employed in an official capacity or position **3. NOT DONE OR MADE OFFICIALLY** not done or made by somebody acting in an official capacity —**un·of·fi·cial·ly** *adv.*

un·op·posed /ùnnə pṓzd/ *adj., adv.* **1. MEETING WITH NO OPPOSITION** not fought, objected to, or resisted **2. HAVING NO OPPONENT** unchallenged by an official opponent in an election or competition

un·or·gan·ized /un áwrgə nīzd/ *adj.* **1. NOT DONE IN ORGANIZED WAY** not arranged or done in an orderly or systematic way **2. NOT ACTING IN ORGANIZED WAY** not acting, thinking, or working in an orderly or systematic manner **3. NOT UNIONIZED** not organized in a labor union or unions **4. NOT LIVING** lacking the characteristics of a living organism

un·o·rig·i·nal /ùnnə ríjjən'l/ *adj.* lacking in originality or creativity

un·or·tho·dox /un áwrthə dòks/ *adj.* **1.** UNCONVENTIONAL not following, or resulting from a failure to follow, conventional or traditional beliefs or practices **2.** NOT RELIGIOUSLY ORTHODOX not practicing or conforming to the accepted traditional form of a particular religion —**un·or·tho·dox·ly** *adv.* —**un·or·tho·dox·y** *n.*

unp. *abbr.* unpaged

un·pack /un pák/ (**-packed, -pack·ing, -packs**) *v.* **1.** *vt.* TAKE CONTENTS FROM SOMETHING to take the contents out of something **2.** *vti.* TAKE OUT PACKED THINGS to remove something that has been packed from its container or packaging **3.** *vt.* TAKE PACK OFF to take a pack or other burden from a person or animal that has been carrying it **4.** *vt.* REVEAL WHAT IS HIDDEN IN to reveal what is hidden, buried, or encoded within something

un·paged /un páyjd/, **un·pag·i·nat·ed** /un pájjə nàytəd/ *adj.* not marked with page numbers

un·paid /un páyd/ *adj.* **1.** NOT YET SETTLED awaiting payment or settlement **2.** NOT HAVING YET RECEIVED PAYMENT not yet in receipt of payment for work done **3.** WORKING FOR NO PAY working without wages or a salary **4.** NOT PAYING MONEY not paying wages or a salary

un·paired /un páird/ *adj.* **1.** NOT BELONGING TO PAIR not being one of a pair **2.** CHEM CONSISTING OF NO PAIRS characterized by a lack of pairs

un·pal·at·a·ble /un pállətəb'l/ *adj.* **1.** NOT TASTING GOOD having an unpleasant taste **2.** HARD TO ACCEPT not pleasant, agreeable, or acceptable —**un·pal·at·a·bil·i·ty** /un pàllətə bíllətee/ *n.* —**un·pal·at·a·bly** /un pállətəblee/ *adv.*

un·par·al·leled /un pérrə lèld/ *adj.* not equaled, matched, or paralleled in kind or quality

un·par·lia·men·ta·ry /ùn paarlə méntəree/ *adj.* not acceptable according to the practice of a parliament

un·peg /un pég/ (**-pegged, -peg·ging, -pegs**) *vt.* **1.** TAKE PEG FROM to take a peg or pegs from something **2.** RELEASE BY REMOVING PEG to release something by removing a peg or pegs **3.** STOP FIXING PRICES OR WAGES to allow something, especially prices or wages, to fluctuate freely by removing restrictions holding them at a fixed level

un·peo·ple /un peép'l/ (**-pled, -pling, -ples**) *vt.* = **depopulate**

un·peo·pled /un peép'ld/ *adj.* containing no people or inhabitants

un·per·son /ùn púrs'n/ *n.* somebody whose existence is not acknowledged officially, especially a public figure whose existence is, for political or ideological reasons, unrecognized by a totalitarian government and the news media it controls

un·per·turbed /ùnpər túrbd/ *adj.* not worried, concerned, or upset

un·pick /un pík/ (**-picked, -pick·ing, -picks**) *vt.* to undo something by pulling out a thread or threads

un·pile /un píl/ (**-piled, -pil·ing, -piles**) *vt.* to take or separate something from a pile

un·pin /un pín/ (**-pinned, -pin·ning, -pins**) *vt.* **1.** TAKE PIN FROM to take a pin or pins from something **2.** RELEASE BY REMOVING PIN to release or unfasten something by removing a pin or pins

un·placed /un pláyst/ *adj.* not assigned a particular place or position

un·planned /un plánd/ *adj.* **1.** NOT INTENDED not happening according to a plan **2.** LACKING AN OVERALL PLAN not following or structured according to an overall plan or program **3.** DONE SPONTANEOUSLY accomplished without advance planning

un·pleas·ant /un plézz'nt/ *adj.* **1.** NOT PLEASING not pleasing, enjoyable, or agreeable **2.** UNFRIENDLY unfriendly and nasty to somebody —**un·pleas·ant·ly** *adv.*

un·pleas·ant·ness /un plézz'ntnəss/ *n.* **1.** UNPLEASANT STATE OR QUALITY the state or quality of being unpleasant **2.** UNPLEASANT EXPERIENCES OR EVENTS experiences or events that are not pleasing or enjoyable **3.** UNFRIENDLINESS an unfriendly and nasty attitude or behavior **4.** UNPLEASANT SITUATION a situation that is not pleasing or enjoyable **5.** DISAGREEMENT an argument or disagreement

un·pleas·ant·ry /un plézz'ntree/ (*plural* **-ries**) *n.* an unfriendly and nasty remark or action (*often used in the plural*) [Mid-19thC]

un·plug /un plúg/ (**-plugged, -plug·ging, -plugs**) *vt.* **1.** TAKE STOPPER FROM to remove a stopper, cork, or other plug from something **2.** REMOVE BLOCKAGE FROM to remove a blockage, clog, or other obstruction from something **3.** PULL OUT OF ELECTRIC SOCKET to pull an electric plug out of a socket **4.** DISCONNECT ELECTRICAL APPLIANCE to disconnect an electrical appliance by pulling its plug out of a socket

un·plugged /un plúgd/ *adv.* WITHOUT AMPLIFIED INSTRUMENTS without the use of amplified musical instruments, especially guitars ■ *adj.* ACOUSTIC performed without the use of amplified musical instruments, especially guitars [Late 20thC]

un·plumbed /un plúmd/ *adj.* **1.** NOT CHECKED FOR VERTICALITY not checked for verticality with a plumb line **2.** NOT MEASURED FOR DEPTH not measured with a plumb line to determine depth **3.** NOT FULLY EXAMINED not thoroughly understood or investigated

un·pol·ished /un póllisht/ *adj.* **1.** NOT SHINY FROM POLISHING lacking a shiny surface produced by polishing **2.** LACKING IN REFINEMENT OR SOPHISTICATION not brought to a high level of refinement or sophistication

un·polled /un pṓld/ *adj.* **1.** NOT INVITED TO PARTICIPATE IN POLL not invited to participate in a survey of public opinion **2.** NOT VOTING not having cast a vote at an election **3.** NOT ON ELECTORAL ROLL not included in a list of electors

un·pop·u·lar /un póppyələr/ *adj.* not liked by, approved of, or acceptable to a person, a group of people, or the general public —**un·pop·u·lar·i·ty** /ùn poppyə lérrətee/ *n.* —**un·pop·u·lar·ly** /un póppyələrlee/ *adv.*

un·prac·ticed /un práktist/ *adj.* **1.** UNTRAINED OR INEXPERIENCED lacking in training or experience **2.** NOT DONE FREQUENTLY not done or not commonly done **3.** NOT REHEARSED not prepared and tried out beforehand

un·prec·e·dent·ed /un préssədəntəd/ *adj.* having no earlier parallel or equivalent

un·pre·dict·a·ble /ùnprə díktəb'l/ *adj.* not easily foreseen or predicted —**un·pre·dict·a·bil·i·ty** /ùnprə diktə bíllətee/ *n.* —**un·pre·dict·a·bly** /-díktəblee/ *adv.*

un·pre·med·i·tat·ed /ùnprə méddi tàytəd/ *adj.* done without advance planning or thought —**un·pre·med·i·tat·ed·ly** *adv.*

un·pre·pared /ùnprə páird/ *adj.* **1.** UNREADY not ready for something or not expecting something to happen **2.** NOT MADE READY not having been prepared as required or expected **3.** IMPROVISED done without any preparation —**un·pre·par·ed·ly** /-páirdlee, -páirədlee/ *adv.* —**un·pre·par·ed·ness** /-páirdnəss, -páirədnəss/ *n.*

un·pre·pos·sess·ing /ùnpripə zéssing/ *adj.* not producing a favorable impression —**un·pre·pos·sess·ing·ly** *adv.*

un·pre·tend·ing /ùnprə ténding/ *adj.* not pretentious or affected

un·pre·ten·tious /ùnprə ténshəss/ *adj.* not putting on a false or showy display of importance, wealth, or knowledge —**un·pre·ten·tious·ly** *adv.* —**un·pre·ten·tious·ness** *n.*

un·prin·ci·pled /un prínsəp'ld/ *adj.* lacking, or resulting from a lack of, moral or ethical principles —**un·prin·ci·pled·ness** *n.*

un·print·a·ble /un príntəb'l/ *adj.* not fit for publication, usually because obscene, libelous, or otherwise illegal or offensive

un·pro·duc·tive /ùnprə dúktiv/ *adj.* **1.** FRUITLESS not producing useful results, decisions, or achievements **2.** PRODUCING LITTLE not producing very much in terms of work or output —**un·pro·duc·tive·ly** *adv.* —**un·pro·duc·tive·ness** *n.*

un·pro·fessed /ùnprə fést/ *adj.* not freely or openly declared

un·pro·fes·sion·al /ùnprə féshən'l, -féshnəl/ *adj.* **1.** CONTRARY TO PROFESSIONAL STANDARDS being or behaving contrary to the expected standards of a profession **2.** AMATEURISH unworthy of a professional **3.** NOT BELONGING TO PROFESSION not having membership in a profession —**un·pro·fes·sion·al·ism** *n.* —**un·pro·fes·sion·al·ly** *adv.*

un·prof·it·a·ble /un próffitəb'l/ *adj.* **1.** MAKING NO PROFIT not producing a profit **2.** NOT HELPFUL OR USEFUL not producing a desirable result or having a useful purpose —**un·prof·it·a·bil·i·ty** /un pròffitə bíllətee/ *n.* —**un·prof·it·a·ble·ness** /un próffitəb'lnəss/ *n.* —**un·prof·it·a·bly** /un próffitəblee/ *adv.*

UN·PRO·FOR *abbr.* United Nations Protection Force

un·prom·is·ing /un prómmissing/ *adj.* **1.** UNLIKELY TO SUCCEED not likely to prove successful **2.** UNFAVORABLE not favorable —**un·prom·is·ing·ly** *adv.*

un·pro·nounce·a·ble /ùnprə nównsəb'l/ *adj.* very difficult or impossible to pronounce

un·pro·nounced /ùnprə nównst/ *adj.* **1.** NOT VERY NOTICEABLE not clear or easy to notice **2.** MUTE OR SILENT not sounded or pronounced

un·pro·pi·tious /ùnprə píshəss/ *adj.* not seeming to promise success —**un·pro·pi·tious·ly** *adv.*

un·pro·vid·ed /ùnprə vídəd/ *adj.* not supplied or furnished with something —**un·pro·vid·ed·ly** *adv.* ◇ **unprovided for** not provided with money or the means to live adequately

un·pub·lish·a·ble /un púbblishəb'l/ *adj.* not fit or feasible to publish, usually because of poor quality or expected poor sales

un·put·down·a·ble /un po͝ot dównəb'l/ *adj.* so interesting, entertaining, or exciting that the reader cannot stop reading (*informal*) [Mid-20thC. Coined by the U.S. writer Raymond Chandler.]

un·qual·i·fied /un kwóllə fìd/ *adj.* **1.** LACKING REQUIRED QUALIFICATIONS having no academic, professional, or vocational qualifications **2.** GIVEN WITHOUT RESERVATION not limited or modified by any condition or reservation **3.** TOTAL complete and absolute —**un·qual·i·fied·ly** *adv.* —**un·qual·i·fied·ness** *n.*

un·quench·a·ble /un kwénchəb'l/ *adj.* **1.** INSATIABLE impossible to satisfy **2.** INEXTINGUISHABLE impossible to extinguish **3.** UNDIMINISHING OR UNDYING impossible to suppress, stifle, or destroy —**un·quench·a·bly** *adv.*

un·ques·tion·a·ble /un kwéschənəb'l/ *adj.* **1.** IMPOSSIBLE TO DOUBT impossible to doubt, question, or dispute **2.** UNIVERSALLY RECOGNIZED AND ACKNOWLEDGED acknowledged as not subject to doubt or open to question —**un·ques·tion·a·bil·i·ty** /un kwèschənə bíllətee/ *n.* —**un·ques·tion·a·ble·ness** /un kwéschənəb'lnəss/ *n.* —**un·ques·tion·a·bly** /un kwéschənəblee/ *adv.*

un·ques·tioned /un kwéschənd/ *adj.* **1.** NOT ASKED QUESTIONS not asked a question or questions **2.** UNDISPUTED not open to questioning, doubt, or dispute

un·ques·tion·ing /un kwéschəning/ *adj.* not asking questions, expressing doubt, or hesitating because of questions or doubts —**un·ques·tion·ing·ly** *adv.*

un·qui·et /un kwí ət/ *adj.* **1.** NOISY OR TURBULENT full of noise or unrest **2.** ANXIOUS unsettled or restless, especially in thought or feeling ■ *n.* **1.** NOISE OR UNREST a state of noisiness or unrest **2.** ANXIETY restlessness or uneasiness —**un·qui·et·ly** *adv.* —**un·qui·et·ness** *n.*

un·quote /un kwṓt/ *adv.* used when speaking to indicate where the end of a quotation falls ○ *He said, quote, You're fired, unquote.* ◊ **quote**

un·quot·ed /un kwṓtəd/ *adj.* not listed or quoted on a stock exchange [Early 19thC]

un·raised /un ráyzd/ *adj.* **1.** UNLEAVENED made without yeast and therefore fairly flat and firm in consistency **2.** NOT LIFTED UP not moved, lifted, or increased to a raised position or level

un·rav·el /un rávv'l/ (**-eled, -el·ing, -els**) *v.* **1.** *vti.* UNDO STRANDS OF SOMETHING to undo the knitted or woven yarn, thread, or other strands of something, or to become undone by having the strands come apart **2.** *vti.* DISENTANGLE OR BECOME DISENTANGLED to separate something out from a tangle or other mass, or to become disentangled or separated out **3.** *vti.* MAKE OR BECOME UNDERSTANDABLE to make clear or understandable all the complex, baffling, or intricate elements or aspects of something, or to become clear or understandable **4.** *vi.* START TO FAIL to begin to fail or come to an end

un·reach·a·ble /un reéchəb'l/ *adj.* **1.** INACCESSIBLE impossible to travel to **2.** NOT CONTACTABLE impossible to contact, especially by telephone —**un·reach·a·bil·i·ty** /un reèchə bíllətee/ *n.* —**un·reach·a·bly** /un reéchəblee/ *adv.*

un·read /un réd/ *adj.* **1.** NOT READ not read, especially by a usual or intended reader **2.** NOT WELL READ having read very little and consequently lacking knowledge acquired from reading **3.** LACKING KNOWLEDGE OF SUBJECT not acquainted with a specific subject through reading

un·read·a·ble /un reédəb'l/ *adj.* **1.** ILLEGIBLE consisting of letters, words, or symbols that are difficult to identify **2.** NOT ENJOYABLE TO READ impossible to read because boring, badly written, or intellectually difficult 3. IMPOSSIBLE TO INTERPRET impossible to interpret or make sense of ○ *his unreadable face* —**un·read·a·bil·i·ty** /un rèedə bíllətee/ *n.* —**un·read·a·ble·ness** /un réedəb'lnəss/ *n.* —**un·read·a·bly** /un réedəblee/ *adv.*

un·read·y /un réddee/ *adj.* 1. UNAVAILABLE not available or prepared for use 2. NOT PREPARED TO DO SOMETHING not prepared or available to do something or to act 3. LACKING MENTAL ALERTNESS OR QUICKNESS lacking or displaying a lack of mental alertness or quickness —**un·read·i·ly** /un réddilee/ *adv.* —**un·read·i·ness** /un réddeenəss/ *n.*

un·re·al /un rée əl/ *adj.* 1. NOT EXISTING having no substance, reality, or existence 2. FALSE not true or genuine 3. IMAGINARY imaginary or dreamlike 4. EXCELLENT excellent or extremely good (*informal*) 5. INCREDIBLE difficult to believe (*informal*) —**un·re·al·ly** *adv.*

un·re·al·is·tic /un rèe ə lístik/ *adj.* not taking into account or based on the way the world actually is and how events are likely to happen —**un·re·al·is·ti·cal·ly** *adv.*

un·re·al·i·ty /ùnree állətee/ (*plural* **-ties**) *n.* 1. UNREAL QUALITY an unreal or seemingly unreal state or quality 2. UNREAL THING something that is not real, genuine, or true, or lacks substance 3. INABILITY TO FACE REALITY an inability to accept reality

un·re·al·ized /un rée ə līzd/ *adj.* not achieved, brought to fruition, or made real

un·rea·son /un réez'n/ *n.* lack of reason or rationality

un·rea·son·a·ble /un réezənəb'l/ *adj.* 1. NOT SUBJECT TO REASON not acting with or subject to reason 2. EXCESSIVE being or going beyond accepted or reasonable limits —**un·rea·son·a·ble·ness** *n.* —**un·rea·son·a·bly** *adv.*

un·rea·soned /un réez'nd/ *adj.* not resulting from sound reasoning

un·rea·son·ing /un réez'ning/ *adj.* lacking, or resulting from a lack of, sound judgment or reasoning —**un·rea·son·ing·ly** *adv.*

un·reck·on·a·ble /un rékənəb'l/ *adj.* impossible to calculate

un·re·con·struct·ed /un rèekən strúktəd/ *adj.* 1. CLINGING TO OUTDATED BELIEFS retaining beliefs, views, or practices that are outdated or associated with a particular place or group 2. NOT REBUILT not rebuilt, restored, or recreated [Mid-19thC. Originally in the meaning of "not willing to accept the Reconstruction after the Civil War."]

un·reel /un réel/ (**-reeled, -reel·ing, -reels**) *vti.* to unwind something from a reel, or to become unwound from it

un·reeve /un réev/ (**-reeved** *or* **-rove, -reeved** *or* **-rove** /un rṓv/, **-reev·ing, -reeves**) *vti.* to pull out a rope or cable from a block or thimble on a ship, or be pulled out from a block or thimble

un·re·fined /ùnri fínd/ *adj.* 1. NOT PROCESSED not processed to remove impurities 2. VULGAR not in accord with socially approved tastes

un·re·flect·ing /ùnri flékting/ *adj.* not engaging in or resulting from deep or serious thinking —**un·re·flect·ing·ly** *adv.*

un·re·flec·tive /ùnri fléktiv/ *adj.* not tending to think or reflect, or not resulting from thinking or reflection —**un·re·flec·tive·ly** *adv.*

un·re·gen·er·ate /ùnri jénnərət/ *adj.* 1. NOT REFORMED not reborn spiritually and not repentant 2. VIOLATING SOCIAL OR MORAL STRUCTURES behaving in a way regarded as violating particular social or moral structures 3. CLINGING TO OUTDATED BELIEFS retaining beliefs, views, or practices that are outdated or associated with a particular place or group 4. STUBBORN unyielding or stubborn —**un·re·gen·er·a·ble** *adj.* —**un·re·gen·er·a·cy** *n.* —**un·re·gen·er·ate·ly** *adv.*

un·re·lent·ing /ùnri lénting/ *adj.* 1. DETERMINED AND UNYIELDING unyielding or unswerving in determination or resolve 2. NOT WEAKENING OR EASING UP not weakening, easing up, or otherwise diminishing in strength, speed, or effort —**un·re·lent·ing·ly** *adv.*

un·re·li·a·ble /ùnri lí əb'l/ *adj.* not able to be relied on or trusted —**un·re·li·a·bil·i·ty** /ùnri lī ə bíllətee/ *n.* —**un·re·li·a·ble·ness** *n.* —**un·re·li·a·bly** *adv.*

un·re·marked /ùnri maárkt/ *adj.* not noticed or observed

un·re·mit·ting /ùnri mítting/ *adj.* continuing, persisting, or recurring without diminishing or ceasing —**un·re·mit·ting·ly** *adv.* —**un·re·mit·ting·ness** *n.*

un·re·quit·ed /ùnnri kwítəd/ *adj.* 1. NOT RECIPROCATED not felt in response, or not returned in the same way or to the same degree 2. UNAVENGED not avenged —**un·re·quit·ed·ly** *adv.*

un·re·serve /ùnnri zúrv/ *n.* a lack of reserve in showing and expressing feelings or opinions

un·re·served /ùnnri zúrvd/ *adj.* 1. NOT RESERVED FOR PARTICULAR USE not set aside or retained for a particular person or group of people to use 2. GIVEN WITHOUT QUALIFICATION not limited or modified by any condition or reservation 3. FRANK OR OPEN not cautious, restrained, or reticent —**un·re·serv·ed·ly** *adv.* —**un·re·serv·ed·ness** *n.*

un·rest /un rést/ *n.* 1. VIOLENT SOCIAL OR POLITICAL DISCONTENT strong social or political discontent or protest that disrupts the established order and is often violent but falls short of true rebellion 2. ANXIOUSNESS a disturbed, unsettled, or uneasy mental or emotional state

un·re·strained /ùnnri stráynd/ *adj.* 1. NOT CONTROLLED OR RESTRICTED not subject to control, restriction, or restraint 2. SPONTANEOUS natural and uninhibited —**un·re·strain·ed·ly** /ùnnri stráynədlee/ *adv.* —**un·re·strain·ed·ness** *n.*

un·re·straint /ùnnri stráynt/ *n.* lack of restraint in actions or behavior

un·rid·dle /un rídd'l/ (**-dled, -dling, -dles**) *vt.* to find a solution or explanation for something

un·ri·fled /un ríf'ld/ *adj.* having no spiral grooves (**rifling**) cut on the inside of the barrel

un·rig /un ríg/ (**-rigged, -rig·ging, -rigs**) *vt.* to remove the rigging from a ship

un·right·eous /un ríchəss/ *adj.* 1. SINFUL sinful, wicked, or evil 2. UNJUST not just, fair, or right —**un·right·eous·ly** *adv.* —**un·right·eous·ness** *n.*

un·rip /un ríp/ (**-ripped, -rip·ping, -rips**) *vt.* 1. RIP OPEN to open something by ripping 2. DISCLOSE to reveal or divulge something (*archaic*)

un·ripe /un rīp/ (**-rip·er, -rip·est**) *adj.* 1. NOT RIPE not yet ripe or mature 2. NOT FULLY READY not yet complete or fully developed 3. PREMATURE occurring too soon or too early (*archaic*) —**un·ripe·ness** *n.*

un·ri·valed /un rív'ld/, **un·ri·valled** *adj.* having no rival or equal

un·roll /un rṓl/ (**-rolled, -roll·ing, -rolls**) *vti.* 1. UNWIND OR BECOME UNWOUND to unwind, uncoil, or open up something that is rolled up, or become unwound, uncoiled, or opened up 2. DISCLOSE OR BECOME DISCLOSED to disclose something gradually and smoothly, or to become disclosed in this way

un·round /un równd/ (**-round·ed, -round·ing, -rounds**) *vt.* to pronounce a sound with the lips kept flat —**un·round** *adj.*

un·rove past tense, past participle of **unreeve**

UNRRA *abbr.* United Nations Relief and Rehabilitation Administration

un·ruf·fled /un rúff'ld/ *adj.* 1. CALM AND POISED calm and poised, especially in a crisis 2. SMOOTH having a smooth surface, especially one without ripples 3. HAVING NO RUFFLE lacking decorative ruffles or ruffling

WORD KEY: SYNONYMS

See Synonyms at ***calm***.

un·ru·ly /un róolee/ (**-li·er, -li·est**) *adj.* difficult to control, manage, discipline, or govern [15C. Formed from archaic *ruly* "disciplined, observing rules," from RULE.] —**un·ru·li·ness** *n.*

WORD KEY: SYNONYMS

unruly, intractable, recalcitrant, obstreperous, willful, wild, wayward

CORE MEANING: not submitting to control

unruly boisterous and disruptive and showing a mild resistance to discipline. Often used to describe children; **intractable** a formal word used for somebody who stubbornly refuses to be controlled or to submit to discipline; **recalcitrant** a formal word for somebody who is obstinate and defiant in refusing to submit to discipline or control; **obstreperous** noisy, difficult to control, and uncooperative; **willful** used for somebody who is stubbornly disobedient or who seems determined to do as he or she pleases; **wild** a fairly informal word used for somebody whose behavior shows a general lack of control or restraint. It can also be used to describe behavior or an event such as a party; **wayward** used for somebody who demonstrates an obstinate and unpredictable tendency to do what he or she wants or thinks is best, instead of following instructions or doing what everyone else is doing.

UNRWA *abbr.* United Nations Relief and Works Agency

uns. *abbr.* unsymmetrical

un·sad·dle /un sádd'l/ (**-dled, -dling, -dles**) *v.* 1. *vti.* TAKE SADDLE FROM HORSE to take a saddle from a horse 2. *vt.* UNHORSE SOMEBODY to throw a rider from a saddle (*refers to a horse*)

un·safe /un sáyf/ (**-saf·er, -saf·est**) *adj.* 1. DANGEROUS causing or exposing somebody to danger 2. BEING IN DANGER being in danger or at risk

un·said /un séd/ past tense, past participle of **unsay** ■ *adj.* NOT MENTIONED not spoken of or discussed, although thought about [Old English]

un·sat·is·fac·to·ry /un sàtiss fáktəree/ *adj.* not adequate, acceptable, or satisfying —**un·sat·is·fac·to·ri·ly** *adv.* —**un·sat·is·fac·to·ri·ness** *n.*

un·sat·u·rate /un sáchə ràyt/ *n.* an unsaturated chemical compound

un·sat·u·rat·ed /un sáchə ràytəd/ *adj.* 1. ABLE TO CONTINUE TO DISSOLVE able to dissolve more of a substance 2. ABLE TO FORM MORE CARBON BONDS having or able to form double and triple carbon bonds

un·sa·vor·y /un sáyvəree/ *adj.* 1. DISTASTEFUL not pleasant or agreeable 2. IMMORAL morally unacceptable 3. UNAPPETIZING tasting or smelling unappetizing —**un·sa·vor·i·ly** *adv.* —**un·sa·vor·i·ness** *n.*

un·say /un sáy/ (**-said** /-séd/, **-say·ing, -says**) *vt.* to take back something said as if it has never been said

un·say·a·ble /un sáy əb'l/ *adj.* difficult or impossible to say or speak about

un·scathed /un skáythd/ *adj.* not hurt, damaged, or harmed in any way

un·schooled /un skóold/ *adj.* 1. NOT EDUCATED not educated or trained 2. NOT ACQUIRED BY EDUCATION innate and not acquired by education or training

un·sci·en·tif·ic /ùn sī ən tíffik/ *adj.* 1. NOT SCIENTIFIC IN METHOD OR PRINCIPLE not following, or compatible with, the methods and principles of science 2. NOT INFORMED ABOUT SCIENCE not possessing knowledge about science and its methods and principles —**un·sci·en·tif·i·cal·ly** *adv.*

un·scram·ble /un skrámb'l/ (**-bled, -bling, -bles**) *vt.* 1. RESTORE ORDER TO to restore order to something jumbled or confused 2. MAKE UNDERSTANDABLE BY REVERSING SCRAMBLING to make a message understandable by undoing the effects of scrambling, especially electronic scrambling —**un·scram·bler** *n.*

un·screw /un skróo/ (**-screwed, -screw·ing, -screws**) *vti.* 1. REMOVE OR LOOSEN SCREWS OF to remove or loosen a screw or screws holding something in place, or to have a screw or screws removed or loosened 2. OPEN BY REMOVING THREADED LID to open something by turning and removing a threaded lid or cap, or to be opened in this way 3. TURN TO REMOVE OR ADJUST to remove or adjust something by rotating, or to be removed or adjusted by rotating

un·script·ed /un skríptəd/ *adj.* 1. WITHOUT A SCRIPT without a script that was written or agreed on in advance 2. UNPLANNED not planned or expected

un·scru·pu·lous /un skróopyələss/ *adj.* not restrained by moral or ethical principles —**un·scru·pu·lous·ly** *adv.* —**un·scru·pu·lous·ness** *n.*

un·seal /un séel/ (**-sealed, -seal·ing, -seals**) *vt.* 1. BREAK OR REMOVE SEAL OF to break or remove the seal of something, or to open something by breaking a seal or closure 2. FREE FROM RESTRICTION to free something from constraint or restriction [Old English] —**un·seal·a·ble** *adj.*

un·sealed road *n.* ANZ a dirt road that has no tar or bitumen surface

un·seam /un séem/ (**-seamed, -seam·ing, -seams**) *vt.* to unpick a seam or seams of something

un·search·a·ble /un súrchəb'l/ *adj.* not capable of being searched or investigated —**un·search·a·ble·ness** *n.* —**un·search·a·bly** *adv.*

un·sea·son·a·ble /un séez'nəb'l/ *adj.* 1. UNUSUAL FOR TIME OF YEAR not usual or appropriate for the time of year 2. NOT TIMELY not occurring at the right time or at a good time —**un·sea·son·a·ble·ness** *n.* —**un·sea·son·a·bly** *adv.*

un·sea·soned /un séez'nd/ *adj.* **1. NOT DRIED OUT** not dried, aged, or matured **2. NOT EXPERIENCED** lacking the skills or knowledge that experience provides **3. PREPARED WITHOUT SALT AND PEPPER** lacking salt and pepper, or other herbs or spices

un·seat /un séet/ (**-seat·ed, -seat·ing, -seats**) *vt.* **1. EJECT FROM SADDLE** to eject somebody from a seat, especially a saddle **2. REMOVE FROM OFFICE** to remove somebody from office or a position, especially by means of an election

un·se·cured /ùnsə kyŏŏrd/ *adj.* **1. NOT MADE SECURE** not fastened, held in place, or otherwise made secure **2. MADE WITHOUT SECURITY** not protected against financial loss **3. UNPROTECTED FROM BUGGING** not protected against electronic eavesdropping

un·seed·ed /un séedəd/ *adj.* SPORTS not assigned a position in a draw whereby the best players or teams can, in theory, avoid meeting until the later rounds

un·seem·ly /un séemlee/ *adj.* **1. NOT IN GOOD TASTE** contrary to accepted standards of good taste or appropriate behavior **2. INCONVENIENT** occurring at an inconvenient time or place ■ *adv.* **IN AN UNSEEMLY MANNER** in an improper or inappropriate manner —**un·seem·li·ness** *n.*

un·seen /un séen/ *adj.* **1. NOT SEEN** not observed, noticed, watched, or seen **2. DONE WITHOUT PRACTICE** done or comprehended without previous study or practice

un·se·lec·tive /ùnsə léktiv/ *adj.* choosing or chosen without regard for quality or value

un·self·con·scious /ùn self kónshəss/, **un·self-con·scious** *adj.* not affected, pretentious, or self-conscious —**un·self·con·scious·ly** *adv.* —**un·self·con·scious·ness** *n.*

un·sel·fish /un sélfish/ *adj.* putting the general good or the needs or interests of others first —**un·sel·fish·ly** *adv.* —**un·sel·fish·ness** *n.*

un·sell /un sél/ (**-sold, -sold** /un sṓld/, **-sell·ing, -sells**) *vt.* to convince somebody that something is false or worthless

un·set /un sét/ *adj.* **1. NOT HARDENED** not hardened or firm **2. NOT READY** not prepared or made ready **3. NOT MOUNTED** not mounted in a jewelry setting

un·set·tle /un sétt'l/ (**-tled, -tling, -tles**) *vt.* **1. DISRUPT** to disrupt the orderly, fixed, or established state of something **2. UPSET SOMEBODY** to make somebody ill at ease or insecure —**un·set·tle·ment** *n.*

un·set·tled /un sétt'ld/ *adj.* **1. LACKING ORDER OR STABILITY** characterized by a lack of order or stability ○ *an unsettled political climate* **2. CHANGEABLE** changing frequently within a given period of time ○ *unsettled weather* **3. BEING IN MOTION** not being in a state or position of rest ○ *unsettled sediment in the water* **4. NOT DECIDED** not resolved, determined, or decided ○ *an unsettled issue* **5. UNCERTAIN** not sure, or full of doubt ○ *He was unsettled about his future at the firm.* **6. UNINHABITED** not inhabited or colonized ○ *unsettled territory* **7. UNPAID** not paid or fulfilled ○ *an unsettled debt* **8. MOVING ABOUT** not regular or fixed ○ *an unsettled lifestyle* **9. NOT LEGALLY RESOLVED** not resolved as required by law ○ *an unsettled lawsuit*

un·set·tling /un séttling/ *adj.* producing a feeling of unease or insecurity

un·sex /un séks/ (**-sexed, -sex·ing, -sex·es**) *vt.* **1. MAKE LESS FEMININE OR MASCULINE** to strip away from somebody the qualities stereotypically associated with his or her sex ○ *"Come, you spirits /That tend on mortal thoughts, unsex me here"* (William Shakespeare, *Macbeth*; c. 1605) **2. CASTRATE** to deprive somebody of the ability to have sex [Early 17thC. Coined by William Shakespeare.]

UNSF *abbr.* United Nations Special Fund for Economic Development

un·shack·le /un shák'l/ (**-led, -ling, -les**) *vt.* **1. FREE FROM SHACKLES** to release somebody from shackles **2. FREE FROM RESTRICTIONS** to release somebody from restrictions or constraints

un·shak·a·ble /un sháykəb'l/, **un·shake·a·ble** *adj.* not subject to doubt or uncertainty —**un·shak·a·bly** *adv.*

un·shaped /un sháypt/, **un·shap·en** /un sháypən/ *adj.* **1. NOT YET GIVEN SHAPE** not yet shaped, formed, or finished **2. NOT PROPERLY FORMED** imperfect in its final or finished form or state

un·sheathe /un shéeth/ (**-sheathed, -sheath·ing, -sheathes**) *vt.* to remove a sword from a sheath

un·shell /un shél/ (**-shelled, -shell·ing, -shells**) *vt.* to remove something from a shell

un·shift /un shíft/ (**-shift·ed, -shift·ing, -shifts**) *vi.* to release the depressed shift key on the keyboard of a computer or typewriter

un·ship /un shíp/ (**-shipped, -ship·ping, -ships**) *vti.* **1.** SHIPPING **UNLOAD OR BE UNLOADED** to unload something from a ship, or to be unloaded **2.** NAUT **MOVE OR BE REMOVED FROM POSITION** to move something, or to be moved, out of its normal position on a ship

un·shod /un shód/ *adj.* not wearing shoes or horseshoes

un·shriv·en /un shrívv'n/ *adj.* not having confessed sins to a priest and been given absolution

un·sight·ed /un sítəd/ *adj.* not fitted with a sight or sights to help with aiming

un·sight·ly /un sítlee/ *adj.* not pleasant to look at —**un·sight·li·ness** *n.*

un·skilled /un skíld/ *adj.* **1. LACKING SKILL** lacking skill or the basic or proper skills **2. LACKING EDUCATION OR TECHNICAL TRAINING** lacking the skills acquired through technical training or higher education **3. NOT REQUIRING SPECIAL SKILLS** not requiring special training, education, or skill **4. DONE WITHOUT SKILL** done without skill, or displaying a lack of the basic or proper skills

un·skill·ful /un skílfəl/ *adj.* lacking or done without skill or expertise —**un·skill·ful·ly** *adv.* —**un·skill·ful·ness** *n.*

un·slak·a·ble /un sláykəb'l/, **un·slake·a·ble** *adj.* impossible to satisfy or quench [Early 19thC. Formed from SLAKE.]

un·slaked lime *n.* = **calcium hydroxide**

un·sling /un slíng/ (**-slung, -slung** /-slúng/, **-sling·ing, -slings**) *vt.* **1. REMOVE SOMETHING SLUNG** to remove something that has been slung, especially over the shoulder or shoulders **2. TAKE OUT OF SLING** to take something out of a sling **3.** NAUT **REMOVE SUPPORTING ROPES FROM** to remove the supporting ropes or chains (**slings**) from something

un·snag /un snág/ (**-snagged, -snag·ging, -snags**) *vt.* **1. FREE SOMETHING CAUGHT** to free something caught on an obstruction **2. MAKE SOMETHING PROGRESS OR DEVELOP FREELY** to remove a difficulty or difficulties impeding the progress or development of something

un·snap /un snáp/ (**-snapped, -snap·ping, -snaps**) *vt.* to release or open something by unfastening a snap or snaps

un·snarl /un snáarl/ (**-snarled, -snarl·ing, -snarls**) *vt.* to free something from a snarl or snarls

un·so·cia·ble /un sṓshəb'l/ *adj.* **1. PREFERRING OWN COMPANY** not liking or seeking the company of other people **2. NOT ENCOURAGING SOCIAL INTERACTION** not favoring or encouraging social interaction —**un·so·cia·bil·i·ty** /un sṓshə bíllətee/ *n.* —**un·so·cia·ble·ness** /un sṓshəb'lnəss/ *n.* —**un·so·cia·bly** /un sṓshəblee/ *adv.*

WORD KEY: USAGE

unsociable or **unsocial**? See Usage note at ***sociable***. Note that ***unsociable*** is less strong in force than *antisocial*, which denotes behavior or attitudes that are harmful to social order.

un·so·cial /un sṓsh'l/ *adj.* **1. PREFERRING OWN COMPANY** not liking or seeking the company of other people **2. OF UNSOCIAL PERSON** characterized or caused by a dislike of the company of other people **3. ANTISOCIAL** annoying, inconsiderate, or indifferent to the needs of others —**un·so·cial·ly** *adv.*

WORD KEY: USAGE

See Usage note at ***unsociable***.

un·sold *adj.* **NOT SOLD** not bought by anybody ■ past tense, past participle of **unsell**

un·so·lic·it·ed /ùnsə líssitəd/ *adj.* given, sent, or received without being requested

un·so·phis·ti·cat·ed /ùnsə fístə kàytəd/ *adj.* **1. NOT WORLDLY OR SOPHISTICATED** naive, inexperienced, and not wise in the ways of the world **2. CRUDE** simple and lacking in refinements, especially those required to solve a particular problem —**un·so·phis·ti·cat·ed·ly** *adv.* —**un·so·phis·ti·cat·ed·ness** *n.* —**un·so·phis·ti·ca·tion** /ùnsə fìstə káysh'n/ *n.*

WORD KEY: SYNONYMS

See Synonyms at ***naive***.

un·sought /un sáwt/ *adj.* not looked for or asked for

un·sound /un sównd/ *adj.* **1. UNHEALTHY** not in a healthy physical or psychological state **2. NOT SOLID OR FIRM** in a structurally poor or dangerous state ○ *unsound foundations* **3. NOT RELIABLE** not based on reliable facts, information, or reasoning ○ *an unsound conclusion* **4. FINANCIALLY INSECURE** not safe or secure financially ○ *an unsound investment* **5. DISTURBED AND NOT RESTFUL** characterized by periods of restlessness ○ *unsound sleep* —**un·sound·ly** *adv.* —**un·sound·ness** *n.*

un·spar·ing /un spáiring/ *adj.* **1. MERCILESS** harsh or without mercy **2. GENEROUS** not frugal or stingy with something —**un·spar·ing·ness** *n.* —**un·spar·ing·ly** *adv.*

un·speak /un spéek/ (**-spoke** /un spṓk/, **-spo·ken** /un spṓkən/, **-speak·ing, -speaks**) *vt.* = unsay (*archaic*)

un·speak·a·ble /un spéekəb'l/ *adj.* **1. NOT DESCRIBABLE IN WORDS** incapable of being described in words **2. EXTREMELY BAD OR AWFUL** so bad or awful as to be impossible to describe in words **3. NOT TO BE SPOKEN OF** not allowed to be spoken of, mentioned, or talked about —**un·speak·a·ble·ness** *n.* —**un·speak·a·bly** *adv.*

un·spe·cial·ized /un spésh'l ìzd/ *adj.* **1. WITHOUT SPECIAL PURPOSE** not having a special use or purpose **2. HAVING NO SPECIALIZATION** not concerned or involved with just one specialized area of knowledge or skill

un·sphere /un sféer/ (**-sphered, -spher·ing, -spheres**) *vt.* **1. REMOVE PLANET FROM SPHERE** to remove a planet or other celestial body from its sphere in the sky **2. REMOVE FROM SPHERE OF ACTIVITY** to remove somebody or something from a particular sphere of activity (*literary*)

un·spoiled /un spóyld/ *adj.* **1. UNCHANGED BY DEVELOPMENT** not changed for the worse by modern civilization, industry, or tourism **2. NOT DAMAGED** not damaged or physically harmed **3. UNFLAWED** not lessened or diminished by flaws or imperfections **4. NOT RUINED IN CHARACTER** not ruined in character as a result of success, wealth, or overindulgence

un·spoke past tense of **unspeak**

un·spo·ken /un spṓkən/ *adj.* **NOT MENTIONED** not uttered or talked about, although thought about ■ past participle of **unspeak**

un·sports·man·like /un spáwrtsmən lìk/ *adj.* being or acting contrary to fair play or the rules and spirit of a sport or of sport in general

un·spot·ted /un spóttəd/ *adj.* **1. NOT SPOTTED OR STAINED** not soiled with spots or stains **2. MORALLY UNBLEMISHED** not marred by moral or ethical lapses or failures **3. UNOBSERVED** not seen or observed —**un·spot·ted·ness** *n.*

un·sprung /un sprúng/ *adj.* having no springs or having the springs removed

un·sta·ble /un stáyb'l/ *adj.* **1. NOT FIXED** not firm, solid, or fixed ○ *unstable ground* **2. LIKELY TO FALL OR COLLAPSE** likely to fall, collapse, or sway ○ *unstable scaffolding* **3. LACKING EMOTIONAL OR PSYCHOLOGICAL STABILITY** lacking, or resulting from a lack of, emotional control or psychological stability ○ *unstable behavior* **4. CHANGEABLE** apt to change ○ *unstable weather* **5. UNSTEADY IN PURPOSE OR INTENT** unsteady or unsure in purpose or intent ○ *political support that is unstable* **6. IRREGULAR IN MOVEMENT OR RHYTHM** having a movement or rhythm that changes irregularly ○ *an unstable heartbeat* **7.** CHEM **APT TO DECOMPOSE** able or likely to change chemical or biological composition readily **8.** PHYS **HAVING SHORT HALF-LIFE** having a brief existence or half-life **9.** PHYS **SUBJECT TO SPONTANEOUS CHANGE** used to describe a particle that is subject to spontaneous change, such as radioactive decay —**un·sta·ble·ness** *n.* —**un·sta·bly** *adv.*

un·stead·y /un stéddee/ *adj.* **1. NOT FIXED** not firm, solid, or fixed **2. TOTTERING** staggering or tottering in walking **3. LIKELY TO MOVE** likely to move or shift position ○ *an unsteady ladder* **4. CHANGEABLE** subject to large and frequent changes ○ *unsteady financial markets* **5. IRREGULAR IN RHYTHM** irregular in movement, rhythm, or pitch ○ *a voice that is unsteady* **6. NOT CONSTANT OR RELIABLE** not constant in purpose or actions ■ *vt.* (**-ied, -y·ing, -ies**) **MAKE UNSTEADY** to cause something to become unsteady —**un·stead·i·ly** *adv.* —**un·stead·i·ness** *n.*

un·steel /un stéel/ (**-steeled, -steel·ing, -steels**) *vt.* to soften or weaken a firm or hard emotion or attitude

un·step /un stép/ (**-stepped, -step·ping, -steps**) *vt.* NAUT to take a mast out of its step or socket

un·stick /un stík/ (**-stuck, -stuck** /-stúk/, **-stick·ing, -sticks**) *vt.* to cause something to stop sticking

un·stint·ing /un stínting/ *adj.* given or giving generously [14thC. The word in its original sense of "unceasing" disappeared from the language; it was revived in its modern sense in the mid-19thC.] —**un·stint·ingly** *adv.*

un·stop /un stóp/ (**-stopped, -stop·ping, -stops**) *vt.* **1. REMOVE STOPPER FROM** to remove a stopper from something **2. UNBLOCK SOMETHING** to remove a blockage from something **3.** MUSIC **PULL OUT STOPS OF** to pull out the stops of an organ

un·stop·pa·ble /un stóppəb'l/ *adj.* not capable of being halted, or not easily halted —**un·stop·pa·bly** *adv.*

un·stopped /un stópt/ *adj.* **1. NOT BLOCKED OR STOPPERED** not blocked, closed, or stoppered **2. NOT HALTED** able to continue without being halted **3.** PHON **ARTICULATED WITH VOCAL ORGANS PARTLY OPEN** articulated without a complete closure of the vocal organs

un·strained /un stráynd/ *adj.* **1. NOT PUT THROUGH STRAINER** not put through a strainer to remove lumps **2. FREE FROM STRAIN** not subjected to strain

un·strap /un stráp/ (**-strapped, -strap·ping, -straps**) *vt.* to remove something by undoing a strap or straps

un·strat·i·fied /un stráttə fīd/ *adj.* **1. NOT FORMING LAYERS OR STRATA** not arranged in or forming layers or strata **2. NOT FORMING CLASSES OR RANKS** not arranged in or forming social classes, grades, or ranks

un·stressed /un strést/ *adj.* **1.** LING **NOT ACCENTED** not accented or emphasized in pronunciation **2. NOT UNDER PHYSICAL OR MENTAL PRESSURE** not subjected to physical, psychological, or emotional pressure

un·stri·at·ed /un strī àytəd/ *adj.* lacking transverse striations

un·string /un stríng/ (**-strung, -strung** /un strúng/, **-string·ing, -strings**) *vt.* **1. REMOVE OR LOOSEN STRINGS OF** to remove or loosen a string or strings of something **2. REMOVE FROM STRING** to remove something from a string or wire **3. UPSET SOMEBODY** to make somebody upset or nervous

un·struc·tured /un strúkchərd/ *adj.* **1. NOT ORGANIZED INTO HIERARCHY** not organized into a hierarchy or similar system **2. NOT ORDERED OR CONVENTIONALLY ARRANGED** not forced to conform to a particular order or arrangement, especially a conventional one **3.** CLOTHES **LOOSE AND FLOWING** not tailored to fit tightly, but flowing freely

un·strung past tense, past participle of **unstring** ■ *adj.* **1. UPSET** emotionally upset or nervous **2. LACKING STRINGS** with a string or strings missing, removed, or loosened **3. NOT ON STRING** not threaded on a string or wire

un·stuck past tense, past participle of **unstick** ■ *adj.* **FREED FROM BEING STUCK** freed from being stuck or adhering to something

un·stud·ied /un stúddəd/ *adj.* **1. NATURAL** natural or casual in manner **2. NOT LEARNED THROUGH STUDYING** not acquired through studying or training **3. NOT KNOWLEDGEABLE** lacking the knowledge and understanding of a particular field that is acquired through studying or training

un·sub·stan·tial /ùnsəb stánshəl/ *adj.* **1. IMMATERIAL** not having physical substance **2. FLIMSY** not strong or firm **3. NOT TRUE OR BASED ON FACT** having no basis in truth or fact —**un·sub·stan·ti·al·i·ty** /ùnsəb stanshee állətee/ *n.* —**un·sub·stan·tial·ly** /-stánshəlee/ *adv.*

un·sub·stan·ti·at·ed /ùnsəb stánshee àytəd/ *adj.* not proven factually [Late 18thC. Formed from *substantiated*, the past participle of SUBSTANTIATE.]

un·suc·cess /ùnsək séss/ *n.* a lack of success in achieving something

un·suc·cess·ful /ùnsək sésfəl/ *adj.* **1. NOT RESULTING IN SUCCESS** not resulting in success or turning out favorably **2. NOT ACHIEVING SUCCESS** not achieving an intended aim or goal —**un·suc·cess·ful·ly** *adv.* —**un·suc·cess·ful·ness** *n.*

un·suit·a·ble /un sóotəb'l/ *adj.* not appropriate or becoming —**un·suit·a·bil·i·ty** /un sòotə bíllətee/ *n.* —**un·suit·a·ble·ness** /un sóotəb'lnəss/ *n.* —**un·suit·a·bly** /un sóotəblee/ *adv.*

un·sung *adj.* **1. NOT PRAISED OR HONORED** not given the praise or honor that is due **2. NOT SUNG** not sung or to be sung

un·sup·port·a·ble /ùnsə páwrtəb'l/ *adj.* **1. INDEFENSIBLE** impossible to defend or excuse **2. INTOLERABLE** impossible to tolerate or endure **3. IMPOSSIBLE TO SUPPORT PHYSICALLY** impossible to support physically in order to prevent collapse

un·sure /un shóor/ *adj.* **1. UNCERTAIN** doubtful or uncertain about somebody or something **2. NOT CONFIDENT** lacking in confidence

WORD KEY: SYNONYMS

See Synonyms at ***doubtful***.

un·sur·pris·ing /ùnsər prízing/ *adj.* not causing surprise, usually because not unexpected —**un·sur·pris·ing·ly** *adv.*

un·sus·pect·ed /ùnsə spéktəd/ *adj.* **1. NOT SUSPECTED** not under suspicion of doing something **2. UNKNOWN** not known or believed to exist —**un·sus·pect·ed·ly** *adv.*

un·sus·pect·ing /ùnsə spékting/ *adj.* not suspicious of somebody or something —**un·sus·pect·ing·ly** *adv.*

un·swathe /un swáyth/ (**-swathed, -swath·ing, -swathes**) *vt.* to remove bindings or wrappings from somebody or something

un·swear /un swáir/ (**-swore** /-swáwr/, **-sworn** /-swáwrn/, **-swear·ing, -swears**) *vti.* to take back a sworn oath, especially by taking another oath (*archaic*)

un·swerv·ing /un swúrving/ *adj.* **1. STEADY AND UNCHANGING** firm and unchanging in intent or purpose **2. NOT TURNING TO THE SIDE** not turning to the side or otherwise altering the direction of movement —**un·swerv·ing·ly** *adv.*

un·swore past tense of **unswear**

un·sworn past participle of **unswear** ■ *adj.* **1. NOT STATED UNDER OATH** not stated under an oath to tell the truth **2. NOT HAVING TAKEN OATH** not having taken an oath to tell the truth [Early 16thC. Formed from *sworn*, the past participle of SWEAR.]

un·sym·met·ri·cal /ùnsi méttrik'l/ *adj.* lacking symmetry —**un·sym·met·ri·cal·ly** *adv.*

un·tan·gle /un táng g'l/ (**-gled, -gling, -gles**) *vt.* **1. FREE SOMETHING FROM TANGLES** to undo the tangles in something such as yarn or hair **2. STRAIGHTEN OUT SOMETHING COMPLEX** to clarify or resolve something that is intricate or puzzling **3. FREE SOMEBODY FROM BAD SITUATION** to remove somebody from a difficult or complicated situation

un·tapped /un tápt/ *adj.* **1. POTENTIALLY USABLE** not yet in use, but available ○ *untapped talents* **2. UNOPENED** not yet opened or tapped

un·taught *adj.* **1. UNEDUCATED** ignorant or not having had a formal education **2. NATURAL OR INNATE** arising from innate or natural talent or ability rather than from instruction [14thC]

un·teach /un teéch/ (**-taught, -taught** /un táwt/, **-teach·ing, -teach·es**) *vt.* **1. MAKE SOMEBODY FORGET SOMETHING** to cause somebody to forget something previously learned **2. TEACH THE OPPOSITE OF SOMETHING** to reverse somebody's opinion or belief about something previously learned

un·ten·a·ble /un ténnəb'l/ *adj.* **1. NOT DEFENDABLE** lacking the qualities, e.g., sound reasoning or high ground, that make defense possible ○ *an untenable position* **2. UNINHABITABLE** so shabby, filthy, or poorly built as to be unfit for human occupation (*archaic*) —**un·ten·a·bil·i·ty** /un tènnə bíllətee/ *n.* —**un·ten·a·ble·ness** *n.* —**un·ten·a·bly** *adv.*

un·teth·er /un té*th*ər/ (**-ered, -er·ing, -ers**) *vt.* **1. UNTIE SOMETHING** to free something from a restraining rope or other tie **2. EXPRESS EMOTION FULLY** to give vent to something such as an emotion after suppressing it

un·thank·ful /un thángkfəl/ *adj.* without feelings of gratitude —**un·thank·ful·ly** *adv.* —**un·thank·ful·ness** *n.*

un·think /un thíngk/ (**-thought** /un tháwt/, **-think·ing, -thinks**) *vt.* **1. STOP THINKING ABOUT SOMETHING** to stop thinking about something **2. REVERSE OPINION ABOUT** to change a view or opinion about something

un·think·a·ble /un thíngkəb'l/ *adj.* **1. OUT OF THE QUESTION** too strange or extreme even to be considered **2. INCONCEIVABLE** impossible even to conceive of **3. UNLIKELY TO HAPPEN** highly unlikely to happen or succeed [15thC] —**un·think·a·bil·ity** /un thìngkə bíllətee/ *n.* —**un·think·a·ble·ness** *n.* —**un·think·a·bly** /un thíngkəblee/ *adv.*

un·think·ing /un thíngking/ *adj.* **1. INCONSIDERATE** not thoughtful or considerate of other people **2. HEEDLESS** without proper attention to the effects of what is said or done **3. UNAWARE** unable or unwilling to think deeply about things —**un·think·ing·ly** *adv.* —**un·think·ing·ness** *n.*

un·thought past tense, past participle of **unthink**

un·thread /un thréd/ (**-thread·ed, -thread·ing, -threads**) *vt.* **1. REMOVE THREAD FROM** to remove the thread or threads from something **2. DISENGAGE FROM SITUATION** to remove somebody or something with difficulty from a demanding or complicated situation

un·throne /un thrṓn/ (**-throned, -thron·ing, -thrones**) *vt.* to dethrone somebody (*archaic*)

un·ti·dy /un tīdee/ *adj.* (**-di·er, -di·est**) **1. NOT NEAT** not neat or tidy **2. DISORDERED** not properly organized or ordered ■ *vt.* (**-died, -dy·ing, -dies**) **MESS SOMETHING UP** to mess up something that was tidy —**un·ti·di·ly** *adv.* —**un·ti·di·ness** *n.*

un·tie /un tī/ (**-tied, -ty·ing, -ties**) *v.* **1.** *vti.* **UNDO KNOT IN SOMETHING** to loosen or unfasten a knot or similar fastening in something such as a string, ribbon, or rope, or to be loosened or unfastened **2.** *vt.* **FREE SOMETHING FROM RESTRAINT** to release or free somebody or something that is tied up **3.** *vt.* **RESOLVE DIFFICULTY** to resolve a difficult or complicated situation [Old English *untīgan*]

un·til /un tíl/ *conj., prep.* **1. UP TO A TIME** up to a time or event but not afterward ○ (conj) *I lived with my grandparents until I was ten.* ○ (prep) *from the late 1980s until 1994* **2. BEFORE** before a time or event (*used with a negative*) ○ (conj) *She agreed not to write about the case until a verdict was reached.* ○ (prep) *He did not open his mail until Monday.* [12thC. From assumed Old Norse *und* "till" + TILL (the sense "till" thereby being duplicated).]

WORD KEY: USAGE

See Usage note at ***till***.

un·time·ly /un tīmlee/ *adj.* **1. OCCURRING AT A BAD TIME** happening or done at a bad or inconvenient time ○ *an untimely decision* **2. PREMATURE TIME** happening before the expected time ○ *his untimely death* ■ *adv.* (*old*) **1. AT AN INAPPROPRIATE TIME** at a bad or inappropriate time **2. PREMATURELY** earlier than wanted or expected —**un·time·li·ness** *n.*

un·tir·ing /un tīring/ *adj.* **1. NOT BECOMING TIRED** not growing weary or exhausted **2. GOING ON** continuing in spite of difficulty or frustration ○ *her untiring efforts* —**un·tir·ing·ly** *adv.*

un·ti·tled /un tīt'ld/ *adj.* **1. UNNAMED** not having a name or title **2. NOT BELONGING TO NOBILITY** possessing no aristocratic title **3. WITHOUT PROPER CLAIM** having no legitimate right or claim

un·to /úntoo/ *prep.* (*archaic*) **1. TO** used to indicate that something is said, given, or done to somebody ○ *the elders of Gilead said unto Jephthah* **2. UNTIL** used to indicate that something continues until a particular time ○ *faithful unto death* [13thC. Formed from UNTIL, with TO replacing TILL (the original, and still dialectal, sense of which was "to").]

un·told /un tṓld/ *adj.* **1. NOT REVEALED** not having been revealed or related **2. INDESCRIBABLE OR UNCOUNTABLE** too great or numerous to be properly described or counted [Old English *unteald*. Originally in the sense "uncounted, not enumerated."]

un·touch·a·ble /un túchəb'l/ *adj.* **1. NOT TO BE TOUCHED** not able or allowed to be touched **2. OUT OF REACH** completely out of reach **3. ABOVE CRITICISM** too well known or important to be investigated or criticized **4. DISAGREEABLE TO TOUCH** unpleasant or disagreeable to touch ■ *n.* **un·touch·a·ble, Un·touch·a·ble** INDIAN RELIG **OFFENSIVE TERM** an offensive term for a member of the hereditary Hindu class that was formerly segregated and regarded as ritually unclean by the four castes, and who performed tasks that were considered polluting (*offensive*) —**un·touch·a·bil·i·ty** /un tùchə bíllətee/ *n.* —**un·touch·a·bly** /un túchəblee/ *adv.*

un·touched /un túcht/ *adj.* **1. NOT TOUCHED** not touched or handled **2. UNEATEN** not eaten or consumed **3. UNINJURED** not injured, damaged, or harmed **4. UNALTERED** not changed or altered **5. EMOTIONALLY UNAFFECTED** emotionally unaffected by something **6. NOT MENTIONED** omitted from mention or discussion [14thC]

un·to·ward /un táwrd/ *adj.* **1. CAUSING MISFORTUNE** causing misfortune or disadvantage ○ *several untoward events* **2. INAPPROPRIATE** not appropriate or fitting ○ *untoward rudeness* **3. UNEXPECTED** beyond the ordinary or the expected ○ *an untoward piece of* *luck* [14thC. Originally in the sense "stubborn, disinclined."] —**un·to·ward·ly** *adv.* —**un·to·ward·ness** *n.*

un·tram·meled *adj.* not restricted or restrained

un·trav·eled /un trávv'ld/ *adj.* **1. INEXPERIENCED** not having wide knowledge or experience of the world **2. NOT OFTEN TRAVELED ON** never or rarely traveled along

un·tried /un trī́d/ *adj.* **1. NOT TESTED** not tried, tested, or proved **2.** LAW **NOT TRIED IN COURT** not tried in a court of law

un·trou·bled /un trúbb'ld/ *adj.* **1. NOT ANXIOUS OR DISTURBED** not bothered, uneasy, or distracted by something **2. CALM** tranquil and without disturbances ○ *untroubled sleep* —**un·trou·bled·ness** *n.*

un·true /un trōō/ *adj.* **1. WRONG OR FALSE** not in accordance with the facts or what is known **2. NOT PRECISE** not precise or accurate according to some standard or measure **3. UNFAITHFUL** not faithful or loyal to somebody [Old English *untrēowe* "unfaithful"] —**un·tru·ly** *adv.*

un·truth /un trōōth/ *n.* **1. LIE** something that is presented as being true but is actually false ○ *accused of telling untruths* **2. FALSENESS** a lack of truth, especially as a result of lying [Old English *untrēowþ* "disloyalty"]

WORD KEY: SYNONYMS

See Synonyms at *lie.*

un·truth·ful /un trōōthfəl/ *adj.* **1. UNTRUE** not in accordance with the facts or what is known **2. NOT TELLING THE TRUTH** lying or failing to tell the truth —**un·truth·ful·ly** *adv.* —**un·truth·ful·ness** *n.*

un·tu·tored /un tōōtərd/ *adj.* **1. UNTAUGHT** not formally educated or trained **2. UNSOPHISTICATED** without any awareness of or interest in what is socially acceptable behavior

un·un·qua·di·um /ùn un kwáydee əm/ *n.* **HEAVIEST CHEMICAL ELEMENT THOUGHT TO EXIST** the heaviest chemical element currently thought to exist. The first evidence for it was obtained in 1998 after bombarding plutonium atoms with calcium ions in a cyclotron. *Symbol* **Uuq**

un·used /un yōōzd, -yōōst/ *adj.* **1. NOT USED** never having been used ○ *unused matches* **2. NOT IN USE** not being put to use ○ *unused land* **3. UNFAMILIAR** not familiar with or accustomed to something ○ *Our dog is unused to city traffic.* [13thC]

un·u·su·al /un yōōzhoo əl/ *adj.* **1. RARE** not common or familiar **2. REMARKABLE** remarkable or out of the ordinary —**un·u·su·al·ly** *adv.* —**un·u·su·al·ness** *n.*

un·ut·ter·a·ble /un úttərəb'l/ *adj.* **1. UNABLE TO BE EXPRESSED** impossible to express or describe because of emotional intensity **2. UNPRONOUNCEABLE** impossible to pronounce or say —**un·ut·ter·a·ble·ness** *n.* —**un·ut·ter·a·bly** *adv.*

un·val·ued /un vállyood/ *adj.* **1. NOT VALUED** not regarded as valuable, especially when true value is being overlooked **2. NOT APPRAISED** not having had a value attached **3. PRICELESS** so valuable as to have no price in monetary terms (*archaic*)

un·var·nished /un vaárnisht/ *adj.* **1. NOT VARNISHED** having no protective or decorative coat of varnish **2. STRAIGHTFORWARD** said or presented without any attempt to disguise the truth ○ *the unvarnished facts*

un·veil /un váyl/ (**-veiled, -veil·ing, -veils**) *v.* **1.** *vti.* **REMOVE COVERING FROM** to take off a veil or other covering, especially from somebody's face or from a plaque, monument, or artwork during a formal ceremony **2.** *vt.* **EXPOSE SOMETHING SECRET** to reveal something that has been hidden or kept secret

un·veil·ing /un váyling/ *n.* **1. UNCOVERING CEREMONY** the formal removal of a covering that has hidden a plaque, monument, or artwork **2. REVELATION** the revelation of something for the first time, especially something kept secret

un·voice /un vóyss/ (**-voiced, -voic·ing, -voic·es**) *vt.* = **devoice**

un·voiced /un vóyst/ *adj.* **1. UNSPOKEN** not spoken or explicitly stated **2.** PHON **SPOKEN WITHOUT VOICING** pronounced without vibration of the vocal chords

un·war·rant·a·ble /un wáwrəntəb'l/ *adj.* unable to be justified or condoned —**un·war·rant·a·bly** *adv.*

un·war·rant·ed /un wáwrəntəd/ *adj.* not justified or deserved

un·war·y /un wáiree/ *adj.* failing to be alert and cautious —**un·war·i·ly** *adv.* —**un·war·i·ness** *n.*

un·washed /un wósht, -wáwsht/ *adj.* **1. NOT WASHED** not having been washed **2. OFFENSIVE TERM** offensive term meaning belonging to the lower social classes (*offensive*) [14thC] ◇ **the great unwashed** an offensive term used to refer to the mass of ordinary people (*offensive*)

un·watch·a·ble /un wóchəb'l/ *adj.* too bad to be worth watching, or too unpleasant and distressing to watch

un·wa·ver·ing /un wáyvəring/ *adj.* firm in your view or purpose and unable to be swayed or diverted from it —**un·wa·ver·ing·ly** *adv.*

un·wea·ried /un weéreed/ *adj.* **1. NEVER TIRING** performing a task or promoting a cause without ceasing **2. NOT TIRED** not tired, e.g., from working or playing —**un·wea·ried·ly** *adv.*

un·well /un wél/ *adj.* not in good health

un·wept *adj.* **1. NOT MOURNED** not cried for or mourned as a loss (*literary*) **2. SUPPRESSED** held back and not allowed to moisten the eyes ○ *unwept tears*

un·whole·some /un hṓlsəm/ *adj.* **1. UNHEALTHY** harmful to health ○ *unwholesome eating habits* **2. REGARDED AS HARMFUL TO MORALS** regarded as being harmful to character or morals **3. LOOKING UNHEALTHY** unhealthy in appearance ○ *an unwholesome pallor* —**un·whole·some·ly** *adv.* —**un·whole·some·ness** *n.*

un·wield·y /un weéldee/ *adj.* **1. NOT EASY TO HANDLE** hard to handle because of being large, heavy, or awkward **2. DIFFICULT TO MANAGE** too complex or extensive to be manageable [14thC. Originally in the sense "weak, lacking strength."] —**un·wield·i·ly** *adv.* —**un·wield·i·ness** *n.*

WORD KEY: USAGE

Spelling trap: This word is often incorrectly spelled and pronounced *unwieldly*, as if it were formed with the common adjective ending *-ly*.

un·willed /un wíld/ *adj.* involuntary rather than chosen or planned

un·will·ing /un wílling/ *adj.* **1. NOT WILLING** not willing to do something ○ *unwilling to participate* **2. RELUCTANT** given reluctantly or grudgingly ○ *unwilling assistance* [Old English *unwillende*] —**un·will·ing·ly** *adv.* —**un·will·ing·ness** *n.*

WORD KEY: SYNONYMS

unwilling, reluctant, disinclined, averse, hesitant, loath

CORE MEANING: lacking the desire to do something

unwilling used to describe somebody who states firmly that he or she is not prepared to do something; **reluctant** used to describe somebody who really does not want to do something, and will only do it if he or she has to; **disinclined** used to suggest that somebody has a lack of enthusiasm for something rather than a strong objection to it; **averse** a fairly formal word used to suggest that somebody has a mild dislike or distaste for something; **hesitant** used to describe somebody who is not keen to do something because he or she is uncertain about it; **loath** a fairly formal word used to suggest that somebody has strong objections to or reservations about doing something.

un·wind /un wī́nd/ (**-wound** /un wównd/, **-wound, -wind·ing, -winds**) *v.* **1.** *vti.* **UNCOIL** to undo something such as tape or cable by winding, or to come undone in this way **2.** *vt.* **UNTANGLE** to remove or undo the tangles in something **3.** *vti.* **RELAX** to relieve somebody of, or obtain relief from, tension or worry ○ *It's sometimes hard to unwind at the end of a busy day.*

un·wis·dom /un wízdəm/ *n.* lack of wisdom or thought [Old English *unwīsdōm*]

un·wise /un wī́z/ (**-wis·er, -wis·est**) *adj.* lacking wisdom, judgment, or good sense [Old English *unwīs*] —**un·wise·ly** *adv.*

un·wish /un wísh/ (**-wished, -wish·ing, -wish·es**) *vt.* **1. REVOKE A WISH** to undo or take back a wish **2. DESIRE SOMETHING NOT BE** to want something not to be or not to happen

un·wit·ting /un wítting/ *adj.* **1. UNKNOWING** unaware of what is happening in a particular situation **2. UNINTENTIONAL** said or done unintentionally [Old English *unwitende*, from the present participle of *witan* "to become aware of, learn," related to English *wit*] —**un·wit·ting·ly** *adv.*

un·wont·ed /un wáwntəd, -wṓnt-, -wúnt-/ *adj.* **1. UNUSUAL** not what is expected or usual (*literary*) **2. UNUSED TO** not used to or in the habit of doing something (*archaic*) —**un·wont·ed·ly** *adv.* —**un·wont·ed·ness** *n.*

un·work·a·ble /un wúrkəb'l/ *adj.* **1. NOT PRACTICAL** too complicated or ambitious to be accomplished or established **2.** INDUST **NOT ABLE TO BE WORKED** unable to be cut, shaped, or otherwise fashioned **3.** AGRIC **IMPOSSIBLE TO FARM** so hard or rocky that it is impossible to farm —**un·work·a·bil·i·ty** /un wùrkə bíllətee/ *n.* —**un·work·a·ble·ness** *n.* —**un·work·a·bly** *adv.*

un·world·ly /un wúrldlee/ *adj.* **1. NOT MATERIALISTIC** not interested in money or material goods **2. INEXPERIENCED** lacking experience of the world **3. NOT OF THIS WORLD** not concerned with or part of the material world —**un·world·li·ness** *n.*

un·worn *adj.* **1. NOT WORN** not previously or recently worn ○ *an unworn shirt* **2. LIKE NEW** in good condition, rather than worn out or ruined ○ *unworn tires* **3. FRESH** original rather than trite or stale

un·wor·thy /un wúrthee/ *adj.* **1. UNDESERVING** not deserving a particular benefit, privilege, or compliment ○ *They proved themselves unworthy of our trust.* **2. BENEATH SOMEBODY** not typical of somebody's usual standards of behavior ○ *Such conduct is unworthy of you.* **3. WITHOUT VALUE** lacking value or merit **4. VILE** bad or unpleasant and wholly undeserved [13thC] —**un·wor·thi·ly** *adv.* —**un·wor·thi·ness** *n.*

un·wound past tense, past participle of **unwind**

un·wrap /un ráp/ (**-wrapped, -wrap·ping, -wraps**) *vti.* to take off the wrapping from something, or to have the wrapping removed [14thC]

un·writ·ten /un rítt'n/ *adj.* **1. NOT WRITTEN DOWN** remaining unprinted or not written down **2. ACCEPTED THROUGH TRADITION** generally accepted and understood even though not formally recorded in writing ○ *unwritten laws* **3. BLANK** not marked or covered with writing

un·yield·ing /un yeélding/ *adj.* **1. STUBBORN** not giving in to persuasion, pressure, or force **2. INFLEXIBLE** hard or rigid rather than flexible —**un·yield·ing·ly** *adv.* —**un·yield·ing·ness** *n.*

un·yoke /un yṓk/ (**-yoked, -yok·ing, -yokes**) *vt.* **1. UNTIE SOMETHING** to release an animal such as a horse from a yoke **2. DISCONNECT SOMETHING** to separate two or more connected things **3. FREE** to set somebody free (*archaic or literary*) [Old English *ungeocian*]

un·zip /un zíp/ (**-zipped, -zip·ping, -zips**) *v.* **1.** *vti.* **UNDO ZIPPER OF** to open or unfasten something such as clothing or luggage by means of a zipper, or to become open or unfastened by this means **2.** *vt.* COMPUT **DECOMPRESS FILE** to decompress a computer file that has been compressed

up /up/ *adv., prep.* **AT A HIGHER LEVEL** in, at, or to a higher level or position ○ (adv) *Put your hand up if you know the answer.* ○ (prep) *We climbed up the hill.* ○ (adv) *Prices are going up all the time.* ○ (prep) *I went up the ladder as far as the second-floor window.* ■ *prep., adv.* **ALONG** along ○ (prep) *Go up the street until you come to a school.* ○ (adv) *You'll find her house up at the top of the street* ■ *adv.* **1. INDICATING COMPLETION** used to indicate thoroughness or the completion of an action ○ *I tore up all the photographs.* **2. UPRIGHT** in or to an upright position from a lower or prone position ○ *sitting up in bed* **3. COMING OUT** coming through or out of some medium ○ *The whales came up for air.* **4. OUT** in a way that detaches or removes ○ *Pulling up weeds isn't easy.* ○ *We drew up water from the well.* **5. RISING ABOVE** rising, or seeming to rise, above or over something ○ *When does the moon come up?* **6. INTO CONSIDERATION** so as to be discussed or mentioned ○ *The subject just didn't come up.* **7. IN NORTHERLY POSITION** toward or in a northerly position relative to the speaker ○ *Our cousins live up in Alaska.* **8. TO A HIGHER VALUE** to or at a higher amount or price ○ *The interest rate is going up again.* **9. TO A GREATER INTENSITY** with or to more intensity or higher pitch or volume ○ *His voice goes up when he's nervous.* ○ *Let's turn up the volume.* **10. NEAR** so as to move toward or closer to the speaker ○ *She ran up to me and gave me a big hug.* ○ *They came up to the door and knocked.* **11. EACH** with all participants equal ○ *The score is now 14 up.* ■ *adv., n.* **AHEAD** to the better or ahead ○ (adv) *Our team is up by two.* ○ (n) *Sales are on the up this month.* ■ *adj.* **1. INCREASED** more than before ○ *Your grades are up this semester.* **2. OUT OF BED** awake and out of bed ○ *She was already up when I called.* **3. FACING UPWARD** having the face or top side upward **4. RAISED UPWARD** in a raised or lifted position ○ *The switch is in the up position.* **5. GOING HIGHER OR NORTH** located in or moving toward a higher or northern direction ○ *The train is waiting at the* *up platform.* ○ *Take the up escalator.* **6. CHEERFUL** happy and feeling good ○ *We've been so up since hearing the news.* **7. HAPPENING** going on at a particular time (*informal*) ○ *What's up with you these days?* **8. BEING CONSIDERED** approaching a deadline for an action ○ *The contract is up for renewal.* **9. NOMINATED FOR SOMETHING** in the running for an office or professional achievement ○ *I hear she's up for a promotion.* **10. ON TRIAL** charged with an offense or called into a court of law ○ *The accused is up on murder charges.* **11. OVER** over or finished ○ *Your time is up.* **12. HAVING KNOWLEDGE** possessing up-to-date or accurate information ○ *I'm not up on the latest gossip.* **13. FUNCTIONING** able to operate or function ○ *Is the computer up?* **14.** BASEBALL **BATTING** taking a turn at bat in baseball ○ *Who's up first in this inning?* ■ *n.* **SOURCE OF GOOD FEELING** something that causes excitement or a feeling of euphoria (*informal*) ○ *The news was a real up for her.* ■ *v.* **(upped, up·ping, ups) 1.** *vt.* **RAISE** to raise or increase something ○ *The insurance company has upped our premiums again.* **2.** *vt.* **PROMOTE** to promote or raise somebody or something to a higher level or position (*usually passive*) ○ *He was upped to manager last week.* **3.** *vi.* **ACT SUDDENLY** to act suddenly or impulsively ○ *She just upped and left.* [Old English *up* "upward" and *uppe* "on high." Ultimately from an Indo-European word that is also the ancestor of English *above, eaves,* and *open.*] ◇ **up and around, up and about** active and on your feet again after an illness ◇ **be up to somebody** to be the duty, responsibility, or job of somebody ◇ **on the up and up** in an honest or legitimate way (*informal*) ◇ **up against it** facing difficulty or danger ◇ **ups and downs** changes of fortune or alternating spells of good and bad experiences ◇ **up to 1.** occupied with or involved in something, often in a way that arouses suspicion ○ *I knew what he was up to, but I couldn't do anything about it.* **2.** able to undertake or endure ○ *I don't think I'm up to the journey.* **3.** as many as, or as long as ◇ **up to your ears** *or* **elbows** *or* **eyes in something** deeply involved in or preoccupied with something ◇ **up yours** an offensive term used to show anger or resentment (*offensive*) ◇ **what's up** what's the matter?

WORD KEY: USAGE

See Usage note at ***back***.

UP *abbr.* underproof

up. *abbr.* upper

U.P. *abbr.* Upper Peninsula

up-and-com·ing *adj.* successful or improving, and showing signs of continuing to do so

up-and-down *adj.* (*not hyphenated when used after a verb*) **1. GOING UP AND DOWN** moving alternately upward and downward **2. VARIABLE** uneven or readily changing **3. VERTICAL** in a vertical position or direction ○ *up-and-down stripes*

U·pan·i·shad /oo pa̐ani shàad, -pánni shàd/ *n.* any of the sacred texts written in Sanskrit that form the basis for Hindu philosophy and doctrine. They date from 400 B.C. and represent the last stage in the tradition of the Vedas, the most ancient of Hindu scriptures. [Early 19thC. From Sanskrit *upaniṣad,* literally "a sitting down near (something)," from *upa* "near" + *ni-ṣad* "to sit down."] —**U·pan·i·shad·ic** /oo pa̐ani sha̐adik, -pànni sháddik/ *adj.*

u·pas /yóopəss/ (*plural* **u·pas·es** *or* **u·pas**) *n.* **1. TROPICAL TREE** a tropical and subtropical tree found in Southeast Asia with white bark and poisonous sap. Latin name: *Antiaria toxicaria.* **2. POISON FROM UPAS TREE** a poison made from the sap of the upas and used on arrows [Late 18thC. From Malay (*pohun*) *upas* "poison (tree)."]

up·beat /úp beet/ *n.* MUSIC **UNACCENTED BEAT** an unaccented beat in music, especially one that ends a bar ■ *adj.* **OPTIMISTIC** full of optimism or cheerfulness (*informal*) ■ *n.* **1.** MUSIC **GESTURE OF BATON** the upward movement of a conductor's baton that indicates an upbeat **2. IMPROVEMENT** an increase in happiness, prosperity, or favorable activity

up-bow *n.* the movement of the bow across the strings of an instrument in which the tip of the bow moves away from the instrument

up·braid /up bráyd/ (**-braid·ed, -braid·ing, -braids**) *vt.* to correct or criticize somebody in a harsh manner [Old English *upbrēdan,* of uncertain origin: probably literally "to throw something up (against someone as a fault)," formed from *bregdan* "to move quickly, throw"] —**up·braid·er** *n.* —**up·braid·ing·ly** *adv.*

up·bring·ing /úp bringing/ *n.* the way somebody has been brought up, or trained and educated early in life [15thC. Originally in the sense of "building."]

up·build /up bíld/ (**-built, -built** /up bílt/, **-build·ing, -builds**) *vt.* to build up, develop, or enlarge something —**up·build·er** *n.*

UPC *abbr.* Universal Product Code

up·cast *adj.* /úp kàst/ **CAST UPWARD** thrown, propelled, or looking upward ■ *n.* /úp kàst/ **1. SOMETHING THROWN UP** material that has been thrown up **2.** MINING **VENTILATION SHAFT** a ventilation shaft in a mine that brings air up

up·chuck /úp chùk/ (**-chucked, -chuck·ing, -chucks**) *vti.* to vomit (*slang*)

up·com·ing /úp kùmming/ *adj.* about to happen or coming soon

up·coun·try /úp kùntree/ *adj.* **COMING FROM THE INTERIOR** coming from, associated with, or located in an inland region of a country ■ *n.* **INLAND REGION** an inland area of a country ■ *adv.* **TOWARD THE INTERIOR** in, to, or toward the inland region of a country

up·date *vt.* /up dáyt/ (**-dat·ed, -dat·ing, -dates**) **PROVIDE NEW INFORMATION** to provide somebody or something with the most recent information, or with more recent information than was previously available ○ *The website is updated once a month.* ■ *n.* /úp dàyt/ **LATEST INFORMATION** the latest available information or more recent information [Mid-20thC]

Popperfoto

John Updike

Up·dike /úp dīk/, **John** (*b.* 1932) U.S. writer. He is best known for his novel *Rabbit, Run* (1960), and its sequels, two of which won Pulitzer Prizes. Full name **John Hoyer Updike**

up·draft /úp dràft/ *n.* a current of air that is moving upward

up·end /up énd/ (**-end·ed, -end·ing, -ends**) *v.* **1.** *vti.* **SET SOMETHING ON END** to place, stand, or turn something upward so that it is standing or resting on one end, or be turned over onto one end **2.** *vt.* **UPSET** to upset, disconcert, or disturb somebody or something to a serious degree

up-front *adj.* (*informal*) **1. STRAIGHTFORWARD** honest, frank, or straightforward **2. IN ADVANCE** paid in advance —**up front** *adv.* —**up-front·ness** *n.*

up·grade *v.* /up gràyd, up gráyd/ (**-grad·ed, -grad·ing, -grades**) **1.** *vt.* **PROMOTE** to promote somebody or increase the status of somebody's job or position **2.** *vti.* **IMPROVE QUALITY** to improve the quality, standard, or performance of something, especially by incorporating new advances ○ *upgrade a computer* **3.** *vti.* **TRADE UP** to exchange something for another of better quality ○ *upgrade a seat on a flight* **4.** *vt.* AGRIC **IMPROVE LIVESTOCK** to improve the quality of livestock by breeding with superior animals to introduce desirable traits into the offspring ■ *n.* /úp gràyd/ **1. IMPROVEMENT OF SOMETHING** an improvement in the quality or performance of something, e.g., computer hardware or software **2. SOMETHING THAT IMPROVES** something that improves the performance or quality of something else, or something that has better performance or qualities **3. UPWARD SLOPE** an upward slope or incline ■ *adj.* /úp gràyd/ **SLOPING UPWARD** going or sloping uphill ■ *adv.* /úp gràyd/ **UPHILL** up an incline, slope, or hill

up·growth /úp grōth/ *n.* the process of growing upward, or the result of such a process

up·heav·al /up heev'l/ *n.* **1. DISTURBANCE** a strong or sudden change in political, social, or living conditions **2.** GEOL **UPWARD MOVEMENT** a sudden raising of part of the earth's crust

up·heave /up heev/ (**-heaved** *or* **-hove** /up hṓv/, **-heaved, -heav·ing, -heaves**) *vti.* to lift something forcefully from underneath, or rise or be thrust upward

up·hill *adv.* /up híl/ **1. UP A SLOPE** up a slope or toward the top of a hill **2. WITH DIFFICULTY** against great resistance or in spite of difficulty ■ *adj.* /úp hìl/ **1. GOING HIGHER ON A SLOPE** going upward on a slope or to higher ground **2. ON HIGHER GROUND** located farther up on a slope or on higher ground **3. DIFFICULT** requiring a lot of effort ○ *an uphill struggle*

up·hold /up hṓld/ (**-held** /up héld/, **-held, -hold·ing, -holds**) *vt.* **1. MAINTAIN OR SUPPORT** to maintain or defend something, especially laws or principles, in the face of hostility **2. GIVE SOMEBODY SUPPORT** to provide somebody with moral support, or inspire somebody with confidence —**up·hold·er** *n.*

up·hol·ster /up hṓlstər, ə pṓl-/ (**-stered, -ster·ing, -sters**) *vt.* to fit chairs, couches, and similar items of furniture with stuffing, springs, and covering [Mid-19thC. Back-formation from UPHOLSTERY.] —**up·hol·ster·er** *n.*

up·hol·ster·y /up hṓlstəree, ə pṓl-/ *n.* **1. MATERIALS USED FOR UPHOLSTERING** the stuffing, cushions, fabric, and other materials used to upholster chairs and couches ○ *upholstery fabric* **2. WORK OF UPHOLSTERING** the craft, trade, or business of upholstering furniture [Mid-17thC. Formed from obsolete *upholster* "upholsterer."]

UPI *abbr.* United Press International

Up·john /úp jon/, **Richard** (1802–78) British-born U.S. architect. He was a leader of the gothic revival style in the United States. Full name **Richard Morris Upjohn**

up·keep /úp keep/ *n.* **1. MAINTENANCE** the maintenance of somebody or something in proper condition or operation **2. COST** the financial cost of providing maintenance for somebody or something

up·land /úplənd, úp lànd/ *n.* **1. HIGH LAND** land that has a high elevation, or a region of such land **2. INLAND REGION** a region that lies in the interior of a country ■ *adj.* **HIGH OR INLAND** relating to, located in, or native to a region that is at a high elevation or lies in the interior of a country

up·land cot·ton *n.* **1.** PLANTS **COTTON PLANT** a cotton plant that probably originated in Central America and is now grown widely for the wooly fiber that surrounds its seeds. Latin name: *Gossypium hirsutum.* **2.** TEXTILES **COTTON FIBER OR FABRIC** the wooly fiber of the upland cotton plant, or fabric made from it

up·land sand·pi·per, up·land plov·er *n.* a large sandpiper that lives in the fields and uplands of eastern North America and has brownish streaked plumage and a short bill. Latin name: *Bartramia longicauda.*

up·lift *vt.* /up líft/ (**-lift·ed, -lift·ing, -lifts**) **1. PHYSICALLY LIFT SOMETHING** to raise or lift somebody or something **2. SPIRITUALLY LIFT SOMEBODY** to help somebody attain a higher intellectual or spiritual level, or improve somebody's living conditions **3.** *NZ, S Africa, Scotland* **COLLECT** to pick up passengers or baggage ■ *n.* /úp lìft/ **1. SOMETHING IMPROVING** something that elevates somebody morally or spiritually, or improves somebody's living conditions **2. LIFTING UP** the lifting up of something, or the result of doing so **3.** GEOL **UPWARD MOVEMENT OF EARTH'S CRUST** the slow upward movement of large parts of stable areas of the earth's crust —**up·lift·er** /up líftər/ *n.*

WORD KEY: SYNONYMS

See Synonyms at ***raise.***

up·link /úp lingk/ *n.* a transmitter on the ground that sends radio or other signals to an aircraft or communications satellite

up·load /up lṓd/ (**-load·ed, -load·ing, -loads**) *vti.* to transfer data or programs, usually from a peripheral computer to a central, often remote computer

up·man·ship /úpmən shìp/ *n.* one-upmanship (*informal*) [Mid-20thC. Shortening.]

up·mar·ket *adj.* /úp maarkət/ **EXPENSIVE** intended or designed for wealthy consumers ■ *adv.* /úp maarkət, ùp maarkət/ **TOWARD MORE EXPENSIVE TASTES** toward a higher and more expensive standard that appeals to wealthy consumers ○ *The hotel seems to have gone upmarket.*

up·most /úp mōst/ *adj.* = **uppermost**

up·on /ə pón/ CORE MEANING: means the same as "on" but is more formal ○ *He stretched out his legs upon the sofa.* ○ *She climbed upon her father's knee.*
prep. **1. ON SURFACE** on or onto the surface of something (*formal*) ○ *The great beast bounced to a halt upon the parapet.* **2. ONE AFTER ANOTHER** used to indicate two occurrences of the same noun, referring to a large number ○ *They claimed that the report contained "innuendo upon innuendo."* **3. FOLLOWED BY** used to indicate that one event is followed immediately by another event ○ *Upon finding the relevant text, they stored it in their own electronic files.* **4. ABOUT TO HAPPEN** used to indicate that an event is imminent ○ *The holidays are upon us again.* [12thC. From UP + ON; modeled on Old Norse *upp á.*]

up·per /úppər/ *adj.* **1. HIGHER** located above another part of something ○ *the upper deck* ○ *a muscle in the upper arm* **2. MORE IMPORTANT** higher in social position or importance ○ *upper management* **3. MORE DISTANT** lying farther inland, upstream, or to the north ○ *the upper reaches of the river* **4.** GEOL **LATER** later in a named geologic formation, period, or system (*technical*) **5.** MATH **INDICATING A MATHEMATICAL LIMIT** indicating a limit or bound of a set of numbers equal to or greater than every member of the set ■ *n.* **1. THE ONE ABOVE** the higher of two people or objects **2.** CLOTHES **PART OF SHOE** the part of a boot or shoe that covers the upper surface of the foot **3.** DRUGS **STIMULANT** a drug such as an amphetamine that has a stimulating effect (*slang*) **4. GOOD EXPERIENCE** an experience that is exciting or produces euphoria (*slang*) ■ **up·pers** *npl.* **UPPER TEETH** the teeth of the upper jaw or of a top set of dentures (*informal*) [13thC. Formed from UP + -ER², being originally the comparative of UP.]

up·per at·mos·phere *n.* the part of the Earth's atmosphere above the troposphere, especially at heights unreachable by balloon

up·per bound *n.* a number that is greater than or equal to all the members of a set

Up·per Can·a·da former British province in Canada, corresponding to present-day southern Ontario

Up·per Car·bon·if·er·ous *n.* GEOL = **Pennsylvanian** *n.* 2

up·per·case /ùppər káyss/ *n.* **CAPITAL LETTERS** capital letters used in writing, typing, typesetting, or printing ○ *printed in uppercase* ■ *adj.* **IN CAPITAL LETTERS** belonging to, written, or printed in capital letters ■ *vt.* (**-cased, -cas·ing, -cas·es**) **CAPITALIZE SOMETHING** to write, type, typeset, or print something in capital letters [Mid-18thC. From typesetters having kept capital letters in the upper of a pair of type cases.]

up·per cham·ber *n.* = **upper house**

up·per cir·cle *n.* the gallery of seats at the top of a theater, above the dress circle

up·per class *n.* **1. HIGHEST SOCIAL CLASS** the highest social class, or the people in it **2.** EDUC **HIGH GRADE LEVEL** the group of students who belong to the junior or senior class of a high school, college, or university — **up·per-class** *adj.*

up·per·class·man /ùppər klássmən/ (*plural* **-men** /-mən/) *n.* a student who belongs to the junior or senior class of a high school, college, or university

up·per crust *n.* the upper class (*informal*)

up·per·cut /úppər kùt/ *n.* **BLOW** a swinging upward blow in which the fist is aimed at an opponent's chin ■ *vt.* (**-cut, -cut·ting, -cuts**) **STRIKE SOMEBODY** to hit or attempt to hit an opponent with an uppercut

up·per hand *n.* the controlling position in a situation

up·per house *n.* in a political system, the house in a two-house legislature that is smaller and less representative of the general population, e.g., the U.S. Senate

up·per·most /úppər mōst/ *adj.* **HIGHEST** highest in position, rank, or level ■ *adv.* **AT THE TOP** in, at, or toward the highest point, position, or rank

Up·per Pa·le·o·lith·ic *n.* the latest of the three periods of the Paleolithic era, about 40,000 to 14,000 years ago, when modern human beings first appeared —**Up·per Pa·le·o·lith·ic** *adj.*

Up·per Pen·in·su·la peninsula in northern Michigan between Lake Superior and Lake Michigan

up·per res·pi·ra·to·ry *adj.* relating to or affecting any of the air passages or associated structures that connect the lungs with the exterior, including the nasal passages, trachea, and bronchi

Up·per Vol·ta former name for **Burkina Faso**

up·per works *npl.* the parts of a boat or ship above the waterline when it is fully loaded

up·pi·ty /úppitee/ *adj.* behaving in a way that other people consider presumptuous and more suited to somebody belonging a higher social class or position (*informal*) [Late 19thC. Formed fancifully from UP.] —**up·pi·ty·ness** *n.*

Upp·sa·la /up sáalə/ city in eastern central Sweden, location of the country's oldest university. Population: 184,507 (1996).

up·raise /up ráyz/ (**-raised, -rais·ing, -rais·es**) *vt.* to raise something or cause something to rise, e.g., hands, prayers, or voices (*literary*)

up·rear /up reér/ (**-reared, -rear·ing, -rears**) *vti.* to rise, or to cause something to rise (*archaic or literary*) [13thC]

up·right /úp rìt/ *adj.* **1. ERECT** standing vertically or straight upward **2. RIGHTEOUS** behaving in a moral or honorable manner ■ *adv.* **VERTICALLY** straight upward rather than at an angle ■ *n.* **1. VERTICAL SUPPORT** something that stands upright, e.g., as a stake or post **2.** MUSIC = **upright piano** —**up·right·ly** *adv.* —**up·right·ness** *n.*

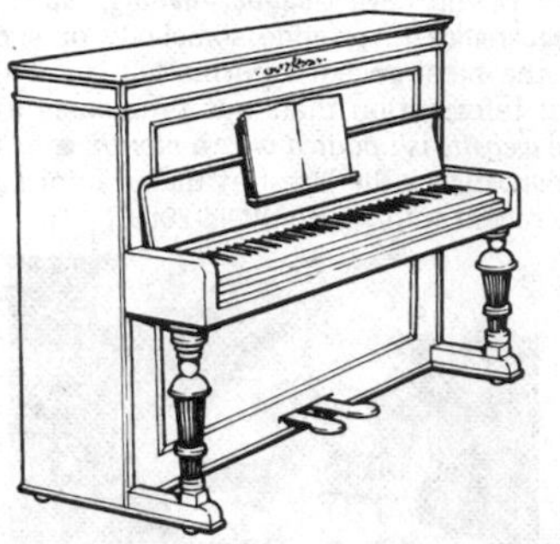

Upright piano

up·right pi·an·o, **up·right** *n.* a piano with a rectangular upright case in which the strings are mounted vertically, and a keyboard at right angles to the case

up·rise *vi.* /up ríz/ (**-rose** /-róz/, **-ris·en** /-rízz'n/, **-ris·ing, -ris·es**) **1. RISE UP** to stand or get up (*literary or archaic*) **2. MOVE UPWARD** to stand, go, or move in an upward direction (*literary or archaic*) **3. APPEAR** to rise up or come into view from below a horizon ■ *n.* /úp rìz/ **UPWARD SLOPE** an upward slope or incline

up·ris·ing /úp rìzing/ *n.* an act of rebellion or revolt against an authority

up·riv·er /úp rìvvər/ *adv., adj.* toward or closer to the source of a river

up·roar /úp ràwr/ *n.* **1. NOISY DISTURBANCE** a loud or noisy disturbance **2. ARGUMENT** a heated or intense controversy [Early 16thC. By folk etymology from Middle Low German *uprōr* or Dutch *oproer*, literally "stirring up," formed, respectively, from Middle Low German *rōr* "stirring, motion" and Dutch *roer*. Originally "insurrection."]

up·roar·i·ous /up ráwree əss/ *adj.* **1. TUMULTOUS** characterized by noisy confusion **2. HILARIOUS** extremely funny and causing people to laugh loudly **3. VERY LOUD** loud and boisterous —**up·roar·i·ous·ly** *adv.* —**up·roar·i·ous·ness** *n.*

up·root /up ro͞ot/ (**-root·ed, -root·ing, -roots**) *vt.* **1. PULL PLANT FROM SOIL** to pull a plant and its roots from the soil **2. REMOVE OR DESTROY** to remove or destroy something completely **3. DISPLACE** to displace somebody or something from a home or habitual environment ○ *I don't want to uproot the children and move to the other end of the country.* —**up·root·ed·ness** *n.* —**up·root·er** *n.*

up·rose past tense of **uprise**

up·rush /úp rùsh/ *n.* a sudden upward rush of something

up·sa·dai·sy *interj.* = **upsy-daisy**

up·scale /úp skàyl/ *adj., adv.* = **upmarket**

up·set *v.* /up sét/ (**-set, -set·ting, -sets**) **1.** *vti.* **TURN SOMETHING OVER** to turn or tip over, or knock or tip something over accidentally, usually scattering its contents **2.** *vt.* **DISTURB ORDER** to disrupt the usual order or course of something **3.** *vt.* **MAKE SOMEBODY UNHAPPY** to cause somebody emotional or mental distress **4.** *vt.* **NAUSEATE** to make somebody feel nauseous, or cause a disorder of the digestive system ○ *Spicy foods upset my stomach.* **5.** *vt.* SPORTS **DEFEAT UNEXPECTEDLY** to defeat a competitor or a team unexpectedly in a sports contest **6.** *vt.* METALL **THICKEN RIVET END** to make a heated bolt, rivet, or bar shorter and thicker by hammering one end ■ *n.* /úp sèt/ **1. DRAMATIC CHANGE** an unexpected problem that disturbs people or causes them to change their plans **2. UNEXPECTED RESULT** an unexpected result, e.g., in a sporting contest or an election **3. EMOTIONAL OR PHYSICAL DISTURBANCE** a mild illness of the stomach, or an unhappy experience **4.** METALL **TOOL** a tool used to make a rivet, bar, or other piece of heated metal shorter and thicker at one end **5.** METALL **RIVET** a rivet, bar, or other piece of metal that has been hammered and made shorter and thicker at one end ■ *adj.* /up sèt/ **1. OVERTURNED** overturned or spilled **2. DISTURBED OR SAD** unhappy, disappointed, or emotionally distressed because of something that has happened **3. DISORDERED** thrown into disorder or confusion — **up·set·ter** *n.*

up·set price *n. U.S., Can, Scotland* the lowest sale price at which something can be sold or auctioned. ◊ **reserve price**

up·set·ting /up sétting/ *adj.* emotionally distressing or disturbing —**up·set·ting·ly** *adv.*

up·shift /úp shìft/ (**-shift·ed, -shift·ing, -shifts**) *vi.* to shift a vehicle into a higher gear

up·shot *n.* the end result or outcome of something [Mid-16thC. Originally in the sense "final shot (in archery)."]

up·side /úp sìd/ *n.* **1. UPPER SIDE** the upper side or part of something **2. POSITIVE SIDE** the most favorable or positive aspect of a particular situation or event **3.** FIN **INCREASE IN VALUE** an increase in business profits or stock prices

up·side down *adv.* **1. IN AN INVERTED WAY** turned so that the part that should be higher is lower or the side that should be underneath is on top **2. IN DISORDER** in total confusion or great disorder ○ *We turned the house upside down looking for the keys.* —**up·side-down** *adj.*

up·side-down cake *n.* a sponge cake baked with a layer of fruit at the bottom, then inverted before it is served so that the caramelized fruit is on top

up·si·lon /úpsi lòn, yo͞opsi lòn/ *n.* the 20th letter of the Greek alphabet, represented in the English alphabet as "y" or "u" [Mid-17thC. From Greek *u psilon* "simple u" (named to distinguish it from the diphthong *oi*, which in late Greek had the same pronunciation), from *psilon*, a form of *psilos* "simple."]

up·spring /up spríng/ (**-sprang** /-spráng/, **-sprung** /-sprúng/, **-spring·ing, -springs**) *vi.* to come suddenly into existence or become visible (*archaic or literary*)

up·stage /up stáyj/ *vt.* (**-staged, -stag·ing, -stag·es**) **1. OUTDO SOMEBODY ELSE** to divert, or attempt to divert, attention away from somebody else **2.** THEATER **TURN ACTOR AWAY FROM AUDIENCE** to move toward the back of the stage in order to force another actor to turn his or her back to the audience **3. TREAT SOMEBODY DISDAINFULLY** to treat somebody in a haughty or disdainful manner (*informal*) ■ *adv.* THEATER **TOWARD REAR** in, at, or toward the rear part of a stage ■ *adj.* **1.** THEATER **LOCATED AT REAR** located in or relating to the rear part of a stage **2. ALOOF** distant from and disdainful of other people (*informal*) ■ *n.* THEATER **BACK OF STAGE** the rear part of the stage —**up·stag·er** *n.*

up·stairs *adv.* /up stáirz/ **1. UP THE STAIRS** to, toward, or on an upper level or floor **2. MENTALLY** in the mind or brain (*humorous*) ○ *not a lot happening upstairs* **3. TO A HIGHER JOB** to a higher level or job in an organization or hierarchy (*informal*) ■ *n.* /úp stàirz/ **UPPER FLOOR** an upper floor or the part of a building above the first floor (*often used before a noun*) ○ *an upstairs bathroom* ◇ **kick somebody upstairs** to promote somebody to a rank or position that is officially superior but in fact carries less power and opportunity for influence (*informal*)

up·stand·ing /up stánding, úp stànding/ *adj.* **1. VIRTUOUS** honest and socially responsible **2. VERTICAL** in an erect position (*archaic*) —**up·stand·ing·ness** *n.*

up·start /úp staart/ **SOMEBODY WITH NEWLY ACQUIRED STATUS** somebody who has suddenly acquired wealth, power, or status but is thought not to deserve it ■ *vi.* /up staárt/ (**-start·ed, -start·ing, -starts**) **RISE SUDDENLY** to rise or jump up suddenly or unexpectedly (*archaic*)

up·state /up stáyt, úp stàyt/ *adj.* **NORTHERN** relating to or living in the northern part of a state ■ *adv.* **NORTHWARD** in, to, or toward the northern part of a state ■ *n.* **NORTHERN PART** the northern area of a state —**up·stat·er** /up stáytər, úp stàytər/ *n.*

up·stream /up streém, úp streèm/ *adv.* **1. AGAINST THE CURRENT** in or toward the source of a river or stream **2. AGAINST TRADITION** contrary to popular opinion and customs (*informal*) **3.** BUSINESS **IN AN EARLY STAGE** of, for, or in an early stage of an industrial or commercial operation, e.g., during exploration in the oil industry **4.** GENETICS **IN OPPOSITE DIRECTION TO TRANSCRIPTION** in a direction along a strand of a DNA molecule counter to that in which transcription takes place. ◊ **downstream** ■ *adj.* **NEARER THE SOURCE** located farther toward the source of a stream or river

up·stroke /úp strōk/ *n.* **1. UPWARD STROKE** an upward or rising movement of a pen or brush, or the mark it makes **2.** MECH ENG **PISTON MOVEMENT** the upward movement of a piston in a reciprocating engine

up·surge *n.* /úp sùrj/ **INCREASE** a rapid increase in something ■ *vi.* /up súrj/ (**-surged, -surg·ing, -surg·es**) **SUDDENLY RISE** to rise or increase rapidly

up·sweep /úp sweèp/ *n.* **1. UPWARD SWEEP** an upward or curving line or motion **2.** HAIR **HAIRSTYLE** a hairstyle in which the hair is swept upward from the neck ■ *vti.* (**-swept** /-swèpt/, **-swept, -sweep·ing, -sweeps**) **MOVE UPWARD** to sweep, curve, or brush something upward

up·swing *n.* /úp swìng/ **1. INCREASE OR IMPROVEMENT** an increase or improvement, e.g., in business profits **2. UPWARD MOTION** a motion or swing upward ■ *vi.* /up swíng/ (**-swung** /-swùng, -swung/, **-swung, -swing·ing, -swings**) **SWING UPWARD** to swing or move upward (*archaic*)

up·sy-dai·sy /úpsee dàyzee/, **up·sa·dai·sy** /úpsə dàyzee/ *interj.* a reassuring expression usually addressed to a child being lifted or who has fallen or stumbled (*babytalk*) [Mid-19thC. Alteration of earlier *up-a-daisy*, from UP + *a-day*, expressing surprise, literally "(to) the day" (see LACKADAISICAL).]

up·take /úp tàyk/ *n.* **1. VENT** a passage such as a pipe or chimney, that draws up smoke or air **2.** BIOL **PHYSICAL ABSORPTION** the process of physically absorbing something into a living organism ◇ **be quick** *or* **slow on the uptake** to be quick or slow to understand things or realize what is happening (*informal*)

up·tem·po *n.* MUSIC **FAST TEMPO** a fast or lively musical tempo ■ *adj.* **EXCITING** fast-paced and exciting

up·throw /úp thrō/ *n.* the upward movement of one block of rock over another in a low-angle fault

up·thrust /úp thrùst/ *n.* **1. UPWARD PUSH** an upward push or thrust **2.** GEOL **FAULTED ROCK** a block of rock that has moved upward in a low-angle fault ■ *adj.* **RAISED UP** raised or lifted up

up·tick /úp tìk/ *n.* a small increase in something, especially in stock or bond prices

up·tight /up tīt/ *adj.* (*informal*) **1. TENSE** tense as a result of anger, fear, or annoyance in a way that is difficult to control **2. REPRESSED** unable or unwilling to show emotion —**up·tight·ness** *n.*

up·time /úp tīm/ *n.* the time during which a computer or other machine is operating or ready for use

up-to-date *adj.* (*not hyphenated when used after a verb*) **1. WITH LATEST KNOWLEDGE** including or possessing knowledge of the latest information **2. CURRENT** extending up to or reflecting the current time **3. FASHIONABLE** familiar with or knowledgeable about current fashions, styles, or ideas

up-to-the-min·ute *adj.* including or relating to the most recent events or things

up·town /úp tòwn/ *n.* **UPPER PART OF CITY** the upper or northern area of a city ■ *adv.* **TOWARDS UPPER PART OF CITY** to, toward, or in the upper part of a city ■ *adj.* (*informal*) **1. CONDESCENDING** pretentious or condescending in behavior or attitudes **2. FASHIONABLE** of the latest fashion or style —**up·town·er** /úp tòwnər, up tównər/ *n.*

up·trend /úp trènd/ *n.* an upward improving trend, especially in business or an economy

up·turn *v.* /úp tùrn, up túrn/ (**-turned, -turn·ing, -turns**) **1.** *vti.* **TURN OVER** to turn over or cause something to turn over, up, or upside down **2.** *vt.* **TURN UPWARD** to turn something upward, e.g., a face or gaze (*usually passive*) ■ *n.* /úp tùrn/ **IMPROVEMENT** an improvement in the economy or in business conditions [14thC. Originally in the sense "to overthrow."]

up·ward /úpwərd/ *adv.* **1. TOWARD A HIGHER LEVEL** in, to, or toward a higher place, level, or position ○ *She's working her way upward through the company hierarchy.* ○ *Keep going upward and you'll soon see the house.* **2. TOWARD INTERIOR OR SOURCE** toward the interior of a place, or toward an origin or source ○ *The hikers left the path and headed upward along the river.* **3. FROM SOME LESSER AMOUNT** toward a larger amount, degree, or position ○ *Sales have gone steadily upward during the last quarter.* ■ *adj.* **1. GOING TOWARD** going or directed toward a higher level or position ○ *a steep upward climb* **2. RISING** used to indicate that something is rising or becoming better ○ *an upward trend* —**up·ward·ly** *adv.* ◇ **upward of** more than

up·ward·ly mo·bile *adj.* **ASPIRING TO HIGHER CLASS** desiring and attempting to move to a higher social class or to obtain greater social or financial status ■ *npl.* **AMBITIOUS PEOPLE** those who are becoming richer or more powerful and moving up from a lower class

up·ward mo·bil·i·ty *n.* the ability or opportunity to move to a higher social class and acquire greater wealth, power, or status

up·wards /úpwərdz/ *adv.* U.K. = **upward** ◇ **upwards of, upward of** more than

up·well·ing /up wélling/ *n.* **1. EMERGENCE** a rising up from or as if from lower depths **2.** OCEANOG **RISING OF WATER TO SURFACE** a process in which cold nutrient-rich water rises to the surface from the ocean depths

up·wind *adv.* /up wínd/, *adj.* /úp wìnd/ **1. AGAINST WIND** against or into the wind **2. WINDWARD** on the side toward which the wind is blowing

Ur /ur/ ancient city of Mesopotamia, in the southeastern part of present-day Iraq. It was a major city-state of the Sumerian civilization by 2800 B.C.

ur-[1] *prefix.* = **uro-**[1] (*used before vowels*)

ur-[2] *prefix.* = **uro-**[2] (*used before vowels*)

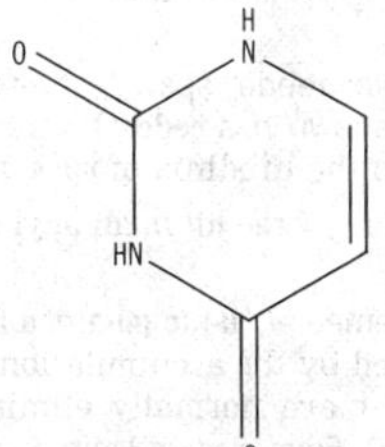

Uracil

u·ra·cil /yóorəssil/ *n.* a component of RNA that carries hereditary information in cells. Chemically, it is a pyrimidine derivative. Symbol **U** [Late 19thC. Origin uncertain: perhaps coined from UREA + ACETIC + *-il*, variant of -ILE.]

u·rae·mi·a *n.* = **uremia**

Barnaby's

Uraeus

u·rae·us /yoo reé əss/ *n.* the sacred serpent found on the headdresses of Egyptian rulers and divinities, representing sovereignty [Mid-19thC. Via modern Latin from Greek *ouraios* "cobra," of uncertain origin: perhaps an alteration (modeled on *ouraios* "of the tail") of an Egyptian word for "cobra."]

U·ral /yóorəl/ river of southern Russia and northwestern Kazakhstan, rising in the southern Ural Mountains, and flowing southward into the Caspian Sea. Length: 1,509 mi./2,428 km.

U·ral-Al·ta·ic *n.* LANG a hypothetical language group that was once proposed by scholars as containing the Uralic and Altaic language families —**U·ral-Al·ta·ic** *adj.*

U·ral·ic /yoo rállik/ *n.* LANG a family of languages spoken in northern and central Europe and western Siberia. There are two branches of the family, Finno-Ugric and Samoyed. —**U·ral·ic** *adj.*

u·ra·lite /yóorə līt/ *n.* a fibrous blue-green mixture of amphibole minerals, with no distinct composition. Uralite is produced by hydrothermal or low-grade metamorphic alteration of pyroxenes. [Mid-19thC. From German *Uralit*, from *Ural* "Ural Mountains" (where it was first found).]

U·ral Moun·tains /yóorəl-/ mountain system running from northern Russia southward to the Kirgiz Steppe in Kazakhstan. It is the traditional dividing line between Asia and Europe. Its highest point is Mount Narodnaya, 6,214 ft./1,894 m. Length: 1,500 mi./2,400 km.

uran- *prefix.* uranium ○ *uranous* [From URANIUM]

U·ra·ni·a /yoo ráynee ə/ *n.* in Greek mythology, the Muse of astronomy. ◊ **Muse**

u·ran·ic /yoo ránnik, -ráynik/ *adj.* derived from or containing uranium, especially in a higher valence state [Mid-19thC. Formed from Latin *uranus*, from Greek *ouranos* "the heavens."]

u·ra·ni·nite /yoo ráynə nīt/ *n.* a black mineral form of uranium oxide that contains thorium, radium, and lead and is a major ore of uranium [Late 19thC. Coined from German *Uranin* (from modern Latin *uranium* (see URANIUM) + -ITE.]

u·ra·nite /yóorə nīt/ *n.* any mineral that contains uranium [Late 19thC. Coined from URANIUM + -ITE[1].] —**u·ra·nit·ic** /yóorə níttik/ *adj.*

u·ra·ni·um /yoo ráynee əm/ *n.* a heavy silvery-white radioactive metallic chemical element that occurs in uraninite and pitchblende in three isotopes, one of which is used as a fuel in nuclear reactors and weapons. Symbol **U** [Late 18thC. From modern Latin, from *Uranus*, the name of the planet (discovered eight years before the element was identified).]

u·ra·ni·um 235 /-too thurtee fīv/ *n.* an isotope of uranium that has a mass number of 235 and is used as a source of nuclear energy because it readily undergoes fission when bombarded with neutrons

u·ra·ni·um 238 /-too thurtee áyt/ *n.* a stable isotope of uranium that has a mass number of 238 and is the most abundant isotope

u·ra·ni·um-lead dat·ing *n.* the determination of the age of a uranium-containing mineral by measuring the level of lead isotope produced by the radioactive decay of uranium, which occurs at a known rate

u·ra·nog·ra·phy /yóorə nóggrəfee/ *n.* the branch of astronomy that deals with making maps of the constellations [Mid-17thC. Formed from Greek *ouranographia*, literally "science of the skies."] —**u·ra·nog·ra·pher** *n.* —**u·ra·no·graph·ic** /yóorənə gráffik/ *adj.* —**u·ra·nog·ra·phist** /yóorə nóggrəfist/ *n.*

u·ra·nous /yóorənəss/ *adj.* derived from or containing uranium, especially in a lower valence state

U·ra·nus /yóorənəss, yoo ráynəss/ *n.* **1.** MYTHOL **GREEK GOD** in Greek mythology, the ruler of the heavens, husband of Gaia, and father of the Titans. He was dethroned by his son Cronus. **2.** ASTRON **7TH PLANET FROM SUN** the seventh smallest planet in the solar system and the seventh planet from the Sun. Uranus is blue-green in colour and has 17 satellites, all of which are named for characters in the plays of William Shakespeare. [Via Latin from Greek *Ouranos*, the name of the god]

u·ra·nyl /yóorə nil, yoo ráyn'l/ *n.* a compound containing the chemical group UO_2

u·rase *n.* = **urease**

u·rate /yóor àyt/ *n.* a salt of uric acid —**u·rat·ic** /yoo ráttik/ *adj.*

ur·ban /úrbən/ *adj.* relating or belonging to a city [Early 17thC. From Latin *urbanus*, from *urbs* "city" (source of English *suburb*).]

Ur·ban VIII /úrbən/, **Pope** (1568–1644). His reign (1623–44) was marked by diplomatic activity, reform of

Church affairs, and lavish artistic and architectural patronage. Real name **Maffeo Barberini**

Ur·ban·a /ur bánnə, ur baánə/ city in eastern Illinois, west of Danville and directly east of Champaign. The University of Illinois is located there. Population: 33,179 (1996).

ur·ban blues *n.* blues music that has a stronger beat than country blues, often played with electric instruments and featuring songs about life in the city (*takes a singular verb*)

Ur·ban·dale /úrbən dayl/ city in southern central Iowa, on Walnut Creek. It is a northwestern suburb of Des Moines. Population: 26,902 (1996).

ur·bane /ur báyn/ (**-ban·er, -ban·est**) *adj.* showing sophistication, refinement, or courtesy [Mid-16thC. Directly or via Old French *urbaine* "urban," from Latin *urbanus* (see URBAN). The modern meaning evolved from "urban" because city life was associated with sophistication.] —**ur·bane·ly** *adv.* —**ur·bane·ness** *n.*

ur·ban guer·ril·la *n.* somebody who lives in a city and carries out violent acts there to further a political cause

ur·ban·ism /úrbə nìzzəm/ *n.* **1.** CITY LIFE the typical way of life of people who live in a city or town **2.** STUDY OF CITIES the study of life in cities and towns

ur·ban·ist /úrbənist/ *n.* somebody who specializes in city planning and the study of cities —**ur·ban·is·tic** /ùrbə nístik/ *adj.* —**ur·ban·is·ti·cal·ly** *adv.*

ur·ban·ite /úrbə nìt/ *n.* somebody who lives in a city or town

ur·ban·i·ty /ur bánnətee/ *n.* (*plural* **-ties**) SOPHISTICATION the quality of being sophisticated, refined, or courteous ■ **ur·ban·i·ties** *npl.* COURTESY polite or courteous actions [Mid-16thC. Directly or via French *urbanité* from Latin *urbanitas*, from *urbanus* (see URBAN).]

ur·ban·ize /úrbə nìz/ (**-ized, -iz·ing, -iz·es**) *vt.* **1.** MAKE AREA INTO TOWN to make an area of countryside or villages into a town or part of one **2.** CAUSE COUNTRY PEOPLE TO BECOME URBAN to cause people who live in the countryside to migrate to a town or city **3.** MAKE SOMEBODY URBAN to accustom somebody to living in a town or city rather than in the country —**ur·ban·i·za·tion** /ùrbəni záysh'n/ *n.*

ur·ban myth *n.* a bizarre and untrue story that circulates in a society through being presented to people as something that actually happened, usually to a friend or relative of somebody the speaker knows

ur·ban plan·ning *n.* the planning of the physical and social development of a city through the design of its layout and the provision of services and facilities —**ur·ban plan·ner** *n.*

ur·ban re·new·al *n.* the redevelopment of urban areas that have become run down or impoverished, by demolishing or renovating old buildings or building new ones

ur·ban sprawl *n.* the expansion of an urban area into areas of countryside that surround it

ur·bi et or·bi /úrbee et áwrbee/ *adv.* a phrase used in a papal blessing, meaning "to the city of Rome and to the world" [From Latin]

ur·ce·o·late /úrssee ə làyt, ur seé ələt/ *adj.* shaped like an urn or pitcher, with a swollen middle and narrowing top [Mid-18thC. Formed from Latin *urceolus*, literally "little pitcher," from *urceus* "pitcher."]

ur·chin /úrchin/ *n.* **1.** MISCHIEVOUS CHILD a mischievous child, especially a young one who is unkempt in appearance **2.** SEA URCHIN a sea urchin **3.** ZOOL HEDGEHOG a hedgehog (*archaic*) [13thC. Via Old Northern French *herichon* from, ultimately, Latin *(h)ericius* "hedgehog," from *er*.]

Ur·du /óor doò, úr doò/ *n.* LANG the official language of Pakistan, spoken also in Bangladesh and in parts of India. It belongs to the Indic group of Indo-European languages and is closely related to Hindi. Urdu is spoken by about 40 million people. [Late 18thC. Via Persian and Urdu *(zabān i) urdū* "(language of the) camp," from, ultimately, Turkish *ordū* "camp" (source of English *horde*).] —**Ur·du** *adj.*

-ure *suffix.* **1.** process or condition, or something resulting from an action ○ *licensure* ○ *erasure* **2.** office or function, or a body performing a particular function ○ *prefecture* ○ *legislature* [Via Old French from Latin *-ura*]

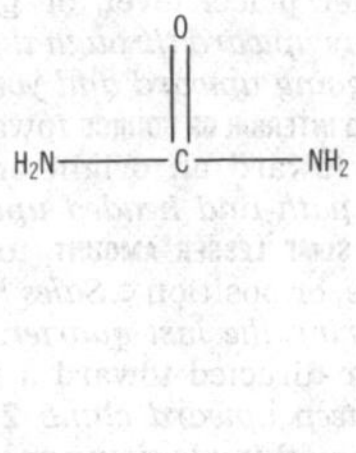

Urea

u·re·a /yoò reé ə/ *n.* a nitrogenous compound found in the urine of mammals and produced through protein decomposition. It is also produced synthetically and used in fertilizer, feeds, and in resin manufacturing. Formula: $CO(NH_2)_2$. [Early 19thC. From modern Latin, an alteration of French *urée*, from Old French *urine* (see URINE).] —**u·re·al** *adj.*

u·re·a-for·mal·de·hyde res·in *n.* a resin made from urea and formaldehyde, used in making electrical fittings and in cavity insulation

u·re·ase /yoóree àyss, -àyz/, **u·rase** /yoó ràyss/ *n.* an enzyme occuring in some bacteria and seeds, e.g., soybeans, that aids in the breakdown of urea to produce carbon dioxide and ammonia [Late 19thC. Coined from UREA + -ASE.]

u·re·din·i·o·spore *n.* = **uredospore** [Early 20thC. Coined from UREDINIUM + SPORE.]

u·re·din·i·um /yoòrə dínnee əm/ (*plural* **-a** /yoòrə dínnee ə/), **u·re·di·um** /yoò reédee əm/ (*plural* **-a** /yoò reédee ə/), **u·re·do·sor·us** /yə reédə sáwrəss/ (*plural* **-i** /yə reédə sáw rì/) *n.* a reddish or black mass of spores produced on a plant by a rust fungus [Early 20thC. Coined from Latin *uredin-* stem of *uredo* (see UREDO) + -IUM.]

u·re·do /yoò reé dō/ (*plural* **-di·nes** /-reédə neèz/) *n.* = **urticaria** [Early 18thC. From Latin, from *urere* "to burn."]

u·re·do·sor·us *n.* = **uredinium** [Early 20thC. Formed from UREDO.]

u·re·do·spore /yə reédə spàwr/, **u·re·din·i·o·spore** /yoòrə dínnee ə spàwr/ *n.* a reddish unicellular spore that develops in the uredinia of rust fungi

u·re·ide /yoóree ìd, yoóree id/ *n.* an acyl derivative of urea

u·re·mi·a /yoò reémee ə/, **u·rae·mi·a** *n.* a form of blood poisoning caused by the accumulation in the blood of products that are normally eliminated in the urine [Mid-19thC. From modern Latin, from Greek *ouron* "urine" (see URINE) + *aima* "blood."]

u·re·o·tel·ic /yoòree ə téllik/ *adj.* producing nitrogen-containing waste in the form of urea [Early 20thC. Coined from UREA + TELIC.] —**u·re·o·tel·ism** *n.*

u·re·ter /yoò reétər, yoórətər/ *n.* either of a pair of ducts that carry urine from the kidneys to the bladder in mammals or to the common cavity for wastes (**cloaca**) in lower vertebrate animals [Late 16thC. Via modern Latin from Greek *ourētēr*, from *ourein* "to urinate," from *ouron* "urine" (see URINE).] —**u·re·ter·al** /yoò reétərəl/ *adj.* —**u·re·ter·ic** /yoòrə térrik/ *adj.*

u·re·thane /yoórə thàyn/, **u·re·than** /yoórə thàn/ *n.* **1.** COLORLESS CRYSTALLINE COMPOUND a colorless odorless crystalline compound, the ethyl ester of carbamic ester, used in solvents, pesticides, and pharmaceuticals. Formula: $C_3H_7NO_2$. **2.** ESTER OF CARBAMIC ACID any ester of carbamic acid other than the ethyl ester **3.** = **polyurethane** [Mid-19thC. Coined from modern Latin *urea* + English ETHANE.]

u·re·thra /yoò reéthrə/ (*plural* **-thras** *or* **-thrae** /-ree/) *n.* the tube in mammals that carries urine from the bladder out of the body and in the male also carries semen during ejaculation [Mid-17thC. Via late Latin from Greek *ourēthra*, from Greek *ourein* "to urinate," from *ouron* "urine" (see URINE).] —**u·re·thral** *adj.*

u·re·thri·tis /yoòrə thrítiss/ *n.* inflammation of the urethra, usually caused by infection [Early 19thC. Coined from URETHRA + -ITIS.] —**u·re·thrit·ic** /yoòrə thríttik/ *adj.*

u·re·thro·scope /yoò reéthrə skòp/ *n.* a medical instrument for examining the inside of the urethra, consisting of a fine flexible tube fitted with lenses and a light [Mid-19thC. Coined from URETHRA+ -SCOPE.] —**u·re·thro·scop·ic** /yoò reèthrə skóppik/ *adj.* —**u·re·thros·co·py** /yoòri thróskəpee/ *n.*

u·ret·ic /yoò réttik/ *adj.* relating to, involving, or in urine [Mid-19thC. Via late Latin *ureticus* from Greek *ourētikos* from *ourein* "to urinate," from *ouron* "urine" (see URINE).]

U·rey /yoóree/, **Harold C.** (1893–1981) U.S. chemist. He won a Nobel Prize (1934) for his discovery of the isotope deuterium (**heavy hydrogen**). Full name **Harold Clayton Urey**

urge /urj/ *vt.* (**urged, urg·ing, urg·es**) **1.** ADVISE SOMEBODY STRONGLY to advise somebody strongly to do something ○ *urged his firm to reconsider* **2.** ADVOCATE SOMETHING EARNESTLY to recommend or advise something earnestly and with persistence ○ *urging restraint* **3.** ENCOURAGE SOMEBODY OR SOMETHING to encourage, drive, or force somebody or something to do something ○ *could hear the crowd urging her on* **4.** EXCITE SOMEBODY to excite or stimulate somebody (*archaic literary*) ■ *n.* STRONG NEED a strong need, wish, or impulse to do something ○ *the urge to travel* [Mid-16thC. From Latin *urgere* "to push, press, compel."] —**urg·er** *n.*

ur·gen·cy /úrjənssee/ (*plural* **-cies**) *n.* **1.** IMMEDIATE NEED FOR ACTION the fact or state of requiring immediate action ○ *a matter of urgency* **2.** IMMEDIATE ATTENTION immediate attention or speed **3.** EARNESTNESS a quality that conveys earnestness or the need for doing something quickly **4.** PRESSING NEED a pressing and immediate need [Mid-16thC. Formed from French *urgent* (see URGENT).]

ur·gent /úrjənt/ *adj.* **1.** REQUIRING IMMEDIATE ACTION calling for immediate action or attention **2.** SHOWING EARNESTNESS showing earnestness or the desire for something to be done quickly [15thC. Via French from the present participle stem of Latin *urgere* (see URGE).] —**ur·gent·ly** *adv.*

-urgy *suffix.* technique or art of working with something ○ *metallurgy* [Via modern Latin *-urgia* from, ultimately, Greek *-ourgos* "working," from *ergon* "work" (see ERG)]

-uria *suffix.* **1.** the condition of having a particular substance in the urine ○ *aciduria* **2.** the condition of having a particular kind of urine ○ *polyuria* [Via modern Latin from, ultimately, Greek *ouron* "urine"]

U·ri·ah /yoò rí ə/ *n.* in the Bible, a Hittite officer purposely killed in battle to allow King David to marry his wife, Bathsheba (2 Samuel 11:2–16)

u·ric /yoórik/ *adj.* relating to, involving, or found in urine [Late 18thC. Formed from Old French *urine* "urine" (see URINE).]

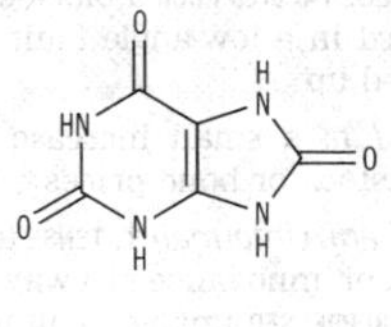

Uric acid

u·ric ac·id *n.* a slightly soluble acid present in urine and blood, produced by the body's breakdown of waste nitrogenous substances. Crystals of uric acid accumulate in the joints of people affected by gout. Formula: $C_5H_4N_4O_3$.

u·ri·dine /yoórə dìn/ *n.* a basic compound, pyrimidine nucleoside, that plays an important role in the metabolism of carbohydrates and consists of ribose and uracil. Formula: $C_9H_{12}N_2O_6$. [Early 20thC. Coined from URACIL + -IDINE.]

U·rim and Thum·mim /yoórim ənd thúmmim/ *npl.* oracles on the breastplate of the high priest of ancient Israel [*Urim* is an Anglicization of Hebrew *'ūrīm*; *Thummim* is an Anglicization of Hebrew *tummīm*]

urin- *prefix.* = **urino-** (*used before vowels*)

u·ri·nal /yoórən'l/ *n.* **1.** RECEPTACLE FOR MEN TO URINATE INTO a receptacle that is attached to a wall and plumbed in, used for men to urinate into **2.** PLACE WITH URINALS a room or building in which there are urinals **3.** PORTABLE CONTAINER FOR URINE a container used to transport urine [13thC. Via French from late Latin *urinalis* "urinary," from Latin *urina* (see URINE).]

u·ri·nal·y·sis /yŏŏrə nálləssiss/ (*plural* **-ses** /-seez/) *n.* analysis of the physical, chemical, and microbiological properties of urine, carried out to help diagnose disease, monitor treatment, or detect the presence of a specific substance [Late 19thC. Blend of URINE and ANALYSIS.]

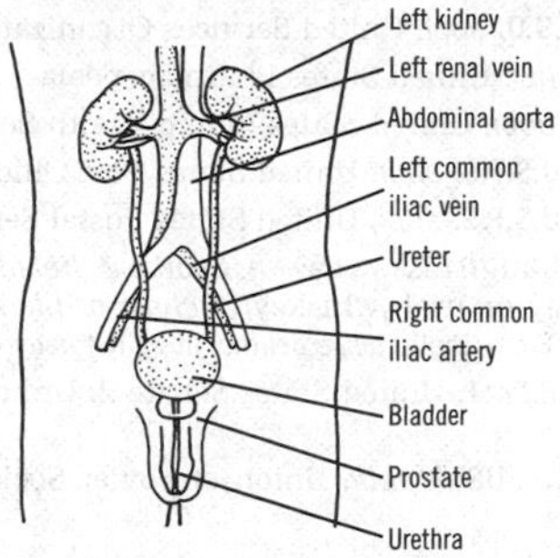

Urinary: Human male urinary system

u·ri·nar·y /yŏŏrə nèrree/ *adj.* relating to, involving, or affecting urine or the organs that form and discharge urine [Late 16thC. Formed from Latin *urina* (see URINE).]

u·ri·nar·y blad·der *n.* an expanding muscular sac in mammals and some other vertebrates in which urine collects before it is discharged from the body through the urethra

u·ri·nate /yŏŏrə nàyt/ (**-nat·ed, -nat·ing, -nates**) *vi.* to discharge urine from the body [Late 16thC. From the past participle stem of medieval Latin *urinare,* from Latin *urina* (see URINE).] —**u·ri·na·tion** /yŏŏrə náysh'n/ *n.* —**u·ri·na·tive** /yŏŏrə nàytiv/ *adj.* —**u·ri·na·tor** *n.*

u·rine /yŏŏrin/ *n.* the yellowish liquid containing waste products that is excreted by the kidneys and discharged through the urethra. In birds and reptiles it is semisolid. [14thC. Directly and via Old French from Latin *urina.*]

u·ri·nif·er·ous /yŏŏrə níffərəss/ *adj.* used to describe a tube that carries urine, especially the tubules of the kidneys [Mid-18thC. Coined from URINE + -FEROUS.]

urino- *prefix.* urine, urinary ○ *urinometer* [From Latin *urina* (see URINE)]

u·ri·no·gen·i·tal *adj.* = **urogenital**

u·ri·nom·e·ter /yŏŏrə nómmətər/ *n.* a hydrometer for measuring the specific gravity of urine [Mid-20thC. Coined from URINO- + -METER.]

u·ri·nous /yŏŏrənəss/, **u·ri·nose** /-nōss/ *adj.* relating to, resembling, or containing urine

URL *n.* an address identifying the location of a file on the Internet, consisting of the protocol, the computer on which the file is located, and the file's location on that computer. Full form **Uniform Resource Locator**

Ur·mi·a, Lake /úrmee ə/ large salt lake in northwestern Iran, west of Tabriz. Area: 1,815 sq. mi./4,700 sq. km.

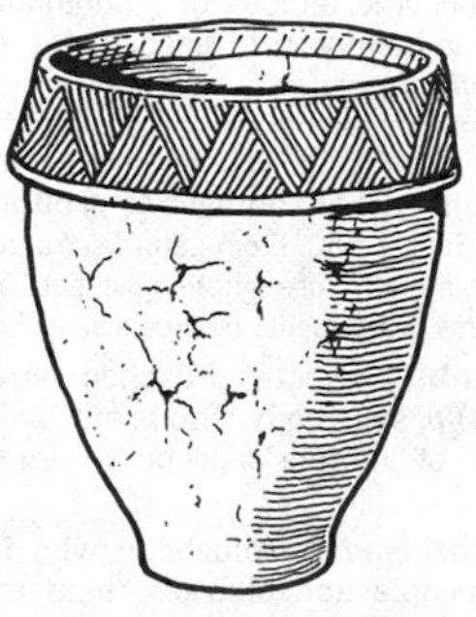

Urn

urn /urn/ *n.* **1. ORNAMENTAL VASE WITH PEDESTAL** an ornamental vase that usually has a foot or a pedestal **2. VASE FOR SOMEBODY'S ASHES** a sealed vase in which the ashes of somebody who has died and been cremated are kept **3. VESSEL FOR HOT DRINKS** a closed vessel in which a hot drink, especially tea or coffee, is made in a large quantity and poured out through a spigot **4. SPORE-PRODUCING PART OF MOSS CAPSULE** the part of a moss capsule where spores are produced [14thC. From Latin *urna.*]

WORD KEY: CULTURAL NOTE

Ode on a Grecian Urn, a poem by English writer John Keats (1819). It describes the poet's reaction to a Greek vase decorated with reliefs of joyful rural scenes. The urn becomes a symbol of the contrast between the permanence of art and the transience of human life, and inspires the poem's famous proclamation "Beauty is truth, truth beauty.".

uro-[1] *prefix.* **1.** urine, urinary tract ○ *uroscopy* ○ *urolithiasis* **2.** urea ○ *urease* [From Greek *ouron* "urine"]

uro-[2] *prefix.* tail ○ *uropod* [From Greek *oura*]

u·ro·chord /yŏŏrō kàwrd/ *n.* **1. SKELETAL ROD** a flexible skeletal rod (**notochord**) that supports the posterior part of the body in some marine animals, e.g., sea squirts **2. u·ro·chord, u·ro·chor·date** = **tunicate** [Late 19thC. Coined from Greek *oura* "tail" + CHORD.] —**u·ro·chor·dal** /yŏŏrə káwrd'l/ *adj.* —**u·ro·chor·date** *adj.*

u·ro·chrome /yŏŏrə krōm/ *n.* a yellow pigment that gives urine its normal color [Mid-19thC. Coined from URO- + CHROME.]

u·ro·dele /yŏŏrə deel/ *n.* an amphibian that has a tail throughout its adult life, a long body, and short limbs, e.g., the salamander or newt. Order: Caudata and Urodela. [Mid-19thC. Directly or formed via French *urodèle* from modern Latin *Urodela*, the order name, from Greek *oura* "tail" + *dēlos* "visible."] —**u·ro·dele** *adj.*

u·ro·gen·i·tal /yŏŏrō jénnit'l/, **u·ri·no·gen·i·tal** /yŏŏrə nō jénnit'l/ *adj.* relating to or involving the organs of the urinary tract and the reproductive organs when considered together [Mid-19thC. Coined from URO- + GENITAL.]

u·rog·e·nous /yŏŏ rójjənəss/ *adj.* producing, obtained from, or formed in urine

u·ro·gram /yŏŏrə gràm/ *n.* an X-ray picture of the urinary tract or some part of it

u·rog·ra·phy /yŏŏ róggrəfee/ *n.* X-ray photography of all or part of the urinary tract. It is performed after a patient has been given an opaque substance that highlights the various structures, in order to locate and diagnose urinary disorders. —**u·ro·graph·ic** /yŏŏrə gráffik/ *adj.*

u·ro·ki·nase /yŏŏrō kí nàyss, -rō kí-/ *n.* an enzyme in blood and urine, produced by the kidneys, that catalyzes the conversion of plasminogen to plasmin and is used medicinally to dissolve blood clots [Mid-20thC. Coined from URO- + KINASE.]

urol. *abbr.* **1.** urological **2.** urology

u·ro·lith /yŏŏrə lìth/ *n.* a stony mass (**calculus**) in the urinary tract —**u·ro·lith·ic** /yŏŏrə líthik/ *adj.*

u·ro·lith·i·a·sis /yŏŏrəli thí əssiss/ *n.* the formation or presence of stony masses in the urinary tract, or the medical condition resulting from this [Mid-19thC. Coined from URO- + LITHIASIS.]

u·rol·o·gy /yŏŏ róllәjee/ *n.* a branch of medicine that deals with the study and treatment of disorders of the urinary tract in women and the urogenital system in men —**ur·o·log·ic** /yŏŏrə lójjik/ *adj.* —**u·rol·o·gist** /yŏŏ róllәjist/ *n.*

u·ro·pod /yŏŏrə pòd/ *n.* either of a pair of flat appendages on the last abdominal segment of a crustacean, e.g., a lobster or shrimp [Late 19thC. Coined from Greek *oura* "tail" + -POD.] —**u·rop·o·dal** /yŏŏ róppəd'l/ *adj.*

u·ro·py·gi·al gland /yoorə pijjee əl-/ *n.* a gland in the skin at the base of the tail of most birds that secretes an oil used while preening to condition and waterproof their feathers [*Uropygial* formed from UROPYGIUM]

u·ro·py·gi·um /yŏŏrə píjjee əm/ *n.* the fleshy hindmost part of a bird's body from which the tail feathers grow [Late 18thC. Via medieval Latin from Greek *ouropugion.*] —**u·ro·py·gi·al** *adj.*

u·ros·co·py /yŏŏ róskəpee/ (*plural* **-pies**) *n.* the medical examination of urine in order to make a diagnosis —**u·ro·scop·ic** /yŏŏrə skóppik/ *adj.* —**u·ros·cop·ist** /yŏŏ róskəpist/ *n.*

u·ro·style /yŏŏrə stìl/ *n.* a fused flexible structure at the end of the spinal column of a toad, frog, or similar amphibian [Late 19thC. Coined from Greek *oura* "tail" + Greek *stylos* "pillar."]

-urous *suffix.* having a particular kind of tail ○ *anurous* [Formed from Greek *oura* "tail"]

Ur·quhart /ŏŏrkərt, -kaart/, **Sir Thomas** (1611?–60) Scottish author. A fighter for the royalist cause, he was a writer on a wide range of subjects and translator of Rabelais.

Ur·sa Ma·jor /úrssə-/ *n.* a conspicuous constellation in the sky of the northern hemisphere, near the North Pole, that contains the seven stars forming the Big Dipper

Ur·sa Mi·nor /úrssə-/ *n.* a small constellation in the sky of the northern hemisphere that contains the North Star

ur·sine /úr sìn, -seen/ *adj.* **1. TYPICAL OF BEARS** relating to or typical of bears, or belonging to the bear family **2. HAVING CHARACTERISTICS OF BEARS** having the characteristics usually associated with bears [Mid-16thC. From Latin *ursinus*, from *ursus* "a bear."]

Ur·su·line /úrssəlin, -lìn, -leen/ *n.* a member of a Roman Catholic order of nuns founded by St. Angela Merici in Brescia, Italy, in the 16th century and dedicated to teaching. [Late 17thC. Formed from *Ursula*, the name of the patron saint of the order's founder.] —**Ur·su·line** *adj.*

ur·ti·ca·ceous /ùrti káyshəss/ *adj.* used to describe a plant that belongs to the nettle family [Mid-19thC. Formed from Latin *urtica* "a nettle," from *urere* "to burn."]

ur·ti·cant /úrtikənt/ *adj.* **STINGING** stinging or causing itching ■ *n.* **AGENT CAUSING ITCHING** something that stings or causes itching [Late 19thC. From the present participle stem of medieval Latin *urticare* (see URTICATE).]

ur·ti·car·i·a /ùrti kérree ə/ *n.* a skin rash, usually occurring as an allergic reaction, that is marked by itching and small pale or red swellings and often lasts for a few days (*technical*) [Late 18thC. From modern Latin, from Latin *urtica* "a nettle."] —**ur·ti·car·i·al** *adj.* —**ur·ti·car·i·ous** *adj.*

ur·ti·cate /úrti kàyt/ *vi.* (**-cat·ed, -cat·ing, -cates**) **HAVE OR CAUSE URTICARIA** to be affected by or cause urticaria ■ *adj.* **CAUSING SMALL SWELLINGS AND ITCHING** producing wheals and itching [Mid-19thC. From the past participle stem of medieval Latin *urticare* "to sting," from Latin *urtica* "a nettle."]

ur·ti·ca·tion /ùrti káysh'n/ *n.* **1. DEVELOPMENT OF URTICARIA** the process by which somebody develops the condition urticaria **2. ITCHY SENSATION** an intensely itchy or burning sensation

Uru., Urug. *abbr.* Uruguay

Uruguay

U·ru·guay[1] /yŏŏrə gwì, -gwày/ republic in southeastern South America, south of Brazil, bordering the Atlantic Ocean. Language: Spanish. Currency: Uruguayan peso. Capital: Montevideo. Population: 3,238,952 (1996). Area: 68,037 sq. mi./176,215 sq. km. Official name **Oriental Republic of Uruguay** —**U·ru·guay·an** *n., adj.*

U·ru·guay[2] river in southeastern South America, rising in southern Brazil and entering the Atlantic Ocean through the Río de la Plata. Length: 990 mi./1,600 km.

U·rum·qi /ŏŏ rŏŏmchee/ capital city of Xinjiang Uygur Autonomous Region, northwestern China. Population: 1,046,898 (1991).

u·rus /yŏŏrəss/ *n.* = **aurochs** [Early 17thC. Via Latin from Greek *ouros.*]

u·ru·shi·ol /ŏŏ rŏŏshee àwl/ *n.* an oily poisonous irritant found in the resin and on the leaves and stems of poison ivy, the lacquer tree, and some related plants [Early 20thC. Coined from Japanese *urushi* "lacquer" + English -OL.]

us /uss/ *pron.* **1. SELF AND OTHER OR OTHERS** a pronoun used to refer to both yourself and another person or other people (*used after a verb or preposition*) ○ *He* *told us to go away.* ○ *This problem affects all of us.* **2.** ROYAL US used by a king or queen, or the editor of a newspaper, to mean "me" (*formal*) ○ *It gives us great pleasure to declare this building open.* **3.** OURSELVES ourselves (*regional informal*) (*used after a verb as the indirect object*) ○ *We'd better find us a place to sleep.* [Old English *ūs*, from, ultimately, prehistoric Germanic]

U.S., US *abbr.* **1.** Uncle Sam **2.** uniform system (*used of lens apertures*) **3.** United States **4.** United States highway

u.s. *abbr.* **1.** ubi supra **2.** ut supra

U/S *abbr.* unserviceable

USA, U.S.A. *abbr.* **1.** United States of America **2.** United States Army

us·a·ble /yóozəb'l/, **use·a·ble** *adj.* capable of being used —**us·a·bil·i·ty** /yòozə bíllətee/ *n.* —**us·a·ble·ness** /yóozəb'lnəss/ *n.* —**us·a·bly** /yóozəblee/ *adv.*

USAEUR *abbr.* United States Army, Europe

USAF, U.S.A.F. *abbr.* United States Air Force

us·age /yóossij, yóoz-/ *n.* **1.** ACT OR WAY OF USING SOMETHING the act of using something, the way something is used, or how much something is used **2.** ACCEPTED PRACTICE a customary and generally accepted practice or procedure **3.** WAY LANGUAGE IS ACTUALLY USED the way in which words and phrases are actually used in speech or writing **4.** EXAMPLE OF LANGUAGE USE an example of a particular use of language **5.** TREATMENT OF SOMETHING the handling or treatment of something [13thC. Via Old French from, ultimately, Latin *usus* (see USE).]

us·ance /yóoz'ns/ *n.* the customary length of time allowed for payment of a bill of exchange in foreign commerce [14thC. Via Old French from, ultimately, assumed Vulgar Latin *usare* "to keep on using," from Latin *uti* (see USE).]

USAR *abbr.* United States Army Reserve

U.S.C. *abbr.* LAW United States Code

U.S.C.A. *abbr.* LAW United States Code Annotated

USCG, U.S.C.G. *abbr.* United States Coast Guard

USDA *abbr.* United States Department of Agriculture

USDI *abbr.* United States Department of the Interior

use[1] *v.* /yooz/ (**used, us·ing, us·es**) **1.** *vt.* EMPLOY SOMETHING FOR SOME PURPOSE to employ something for some purpose or to put something into action or service ○ *use a hammer* **2.** *vt.* DO SOMETHING HABITUALLY to do something habitually ○ *use common sense* **3.** *vt.* CONSUME SOMETHING to expend or consume something, often until none is left ○ *All of the space on the disk has been used.* **4.** *vt.* MANIPULATE OR EXPLOIT SOMEBODY to exploit or manipulate somebody as a means to an end ○ *the type of person who uses others* **5.** *vti.* CONSUME DRUGS OR ALCOHOL REGULARLY to consume something regularly, especially drugs or alcohol **6.** *vt.* BEHAVE TOWARD SOMEBODY OR SOMETHING to behave toward somebody or something in a particular way ○ *used his employees poorly* **7.** *vt.* BENEFIT FROM SOMETHING to benefit or get satisfaction from something ○ *I could use a good night's sleep.* ■ *n.* /yooss/ **1.** ACT OF USING SOMETHING the act of using something for a particular purpose ○ *skilled in the use of computers* **2.** STATE OF BEING EMPLOYED FOR SOMETHING the state or fact of being employed for a particular purpose ○ *no longer in use* **3.** WAY OF EMPLOYING SOMETHING a way of employing something ○ *We admired the artist's use of color.* **4.** HABITUAL OR CUSTOMARY USAGE something done habitually or customarily (*literary or archaic*) **5.** RIGHT TO USE SOMETHING the right to use something or the benefit of using something **6.** ABILITY TO USE SOMETHING the power or ability to use something **7.** PURPOSE the purpose of something ○ *Put your education to good use.* **8.** USEFULNESS the quality of being useful **9.** THE NEED TO USE SOMETHING the occasion or need to use something **10.** LAW BENEFIT OF PROPERTY the benefit or profit of property held by one person for another **11.** LAW LEGAL ENJOYMENT OF PROPERTY the legal enjoyment of property in its employment, occupation, or practice **12.** RELIG MODIFIED LOCAL LITURGY a modified liturgical form or observance practiced in a particular church or religious order [13thC. Via Old French *user* "to use," from, ultimately, Latin *usus*, the past participle of *uti* (source of English *utensil*).] ◇ **have no use for somebody or something 1.** to have no need or purpose for somebody or something **2.** to have no liking or respect for somebody or something (*informal*) ◇ **make use of** to use something, often in a particular way ◇ **what's the use?** used to suggest that doing something is pointless (*informal*)

WORD KEY: USAGE

See Usage note at *utilize*.

WORD KEY: SYNONYMS

use, employ, make use of, utilize

CORE MEANING: to put something to use

use a general and widely used word, appropriate in most contexts to talk about the function or purpose something serves; **employ** a more formal word meaning to use something such as a tool or a resource in a particular way; **make use of** to use what is readily available, especially in a sensible or economical way; **utilize** a formal word meaning the same as *use*, often used to talk about using something particularly effectively and practically.

use up *vt.* to expend or consume something, often until none is left

use[2] /yooss/ *vi.* used to say that somebody or something habitually or usually did something ○ *We used to eat out more often.* ○ *He used not to be so grumpy.* ○ *Did you use to make your own bread?*

use·a·ble *adj.* = **usable**

used /yoozd/ *adj.* **1.** PREVIOUSLY OWNED having been owned by somebody else **2.** EXPENDED having been put to a purpose or expended

used to *adj.* accustomed to or familiar with something ○ *We're not used to this weather.*

use·ful /yóosfəl/ *adj.* **1.** SERVING A PURPOSE capable of being put to use or serving some purpose **2.** HAVING VALUE having value or benefit, or bringing some advantage —**use·ful·ly** *adv.* —**use·ful·ness** *n.*

use im·mu·ni·ty *n.* immunity from prosecution granted to a witness in return for testimony that cannot be used in any manner in any criminal prosecution against him or her

use·less /yóossləss/ *adj.* **1.** UNUSABLE not able to be used **2.** UNSUCCESSFUL unsuccessful, or unlikely to be worthwhile **3.** INEPT not able to do something properly (*informal*) —**use·less·ly** *adv.* —**use·less·ness** *n.*

Use·net /yóoz nèt/ *n.* a worldwide system that uses the Internet and other networks to distribute articles of news or information

us·er /yóozər/ *n.* **1.** PERSON OR THING THAT USES a person or thing that uses something ○ *computer users* **2.** DRUG TAKER somebody who takes illegal drugs (*informal*) **3.** LAW EXERCISE OF RIGHT the exercise of a right to do or use something

us·er-friend·ly (**us·er-friend·li·er, us·er-friend·li·est**) *adj.* easy to operate, understand, or deal with —**us·er-friend·li·ness** *n.*

us·er group *n.* a group of people with common interests in some aspect of computer hardware or software who share information among themselves and with the hardware manufacturer or software developer

us·er in·ter·face *n.* the part of the design of a computer or other device or program that accepts commands from and returns information to the user

USES *abbr.* United States Employment Service

USFS *abbr.* United States Forest Service

ush·er /úshər/ *n.* **1.** SOMEBODY WHO SEATS PEOPLE somebody who escorts people to their seats in a place such as a theater or church **2.** DOORKEEPER somebody who tends the door of a court, hall, or chamber **3.** OFFICER WALKING BEFORE SOMEBODY OF RANK an officer who walks in front of people of rank in a procession or who introduces strangers at formal events ■ *v.* (**-ered, -er·ing, -ers**) **1.** *vt.* ESCORT OR SEAT SOMEBODY to escort or conduct somebody to a place or from a place **2.** *vi.* ACT AS USHER to act as an usher [14thC. Via Anglo-Norman *usser* from, ultimately, Latin *ostarius* "door-keeper," from *ostium* "door."]

usher in *vt.* to introduce or lead up to something

ush·er·ette /ùshə rét/ *n.* a woman or girl who escorts people to their seats in a theater or church (*dated*) See usage note **-ette**

USIA *abbr.* United States Information Agency

Usk /usk/ river in southeastern Wales. It rises in Brecon Beacons National Park and flows to the Severn Estuary at Newport. Length: 60 mi./97 km.

USM *abbr.* underwater-to-surface missile

U.S.M. *abbr.* United States Mail

USMC, U.S.M.C. *abbr.* United States Marine Corps

USN, U.S.N. *abbr.* United States Navy

USNA, U.S.N.A. *abbr.* United States Naval Academy

us·ne·a /úsnee ə, úz-/ (*plural* **-ae** /úsnee èe, úznee èe/ *or* **-as**) *n.* a common lichen with a hanging body in which the root, stem, and leaf are not distinguished. Genus: *Usnea.* [Late 16thC. Via modern and medieval Latin from Arabic and Persian *ušna* "moss, lichen."]

USNR *abbr.* United States Naval Reserve

USO, U.S.O. *abbr.* United Services Organization

U.S.P. *abbr.* United States Pharmacopoeia

USPHS *abbr.* United States Public Health Service

USPO, U.S.P.O. *abbr.* United States Post Office

USPS, U.S.P.S. *abbr.* United States Postal Service

us·que·baugh /úskwə bàw/ *n. Scotland, Ireland* Scotch whiskey or Irish whiskey (*archaic or literary*) [Late 16thC. From Gaelic *uisge beatha*, literally "water of life."]

U.S.S. *abbr.* **1.** United States Senate **2.** United States Ship

U.S.S.R., USSR *abbr.* Union of Soviet Socialist Republics

Sir Peter Ustinov

U·sti·nov /yóosti nof/, **Sir Peter** (*b.* 1921) British writer, director and actor. A noted raconteur, he wrote or directed many plays and movies.

usu. *abbr.* usually

u·su·al /yóozhoo əl/ *adj.* NORMAL OR TYPICAL normal, customary, or typical of somebody or something ■ *n.* **1.** ORDINARY WAY the ordinary, normal, or customary way of things **2.** WHAT SOMEBODY CUSTOMARILY HAS what somebody customarily has, especially a drink in a bar (*informal*) [14thC. Directly or via Old French *usuel* from late Latin *usualis*, from Latin *usus* (see USE).] —**u·su·al·ly** *adv.* —**u·su·al·ness** *n.* ◇ **as usual** in a normal or customary way

WORD KEY: SYNONYMS

usual, customary, habitual, routine, wonted

CORE MEANING: often done, used, bought or consumed

usual a general word used to describe something that is very commonly done, used, bought, or consumed (and therefore predictable); **customary** a more formal word meaning the same as *usual*; **habitual** used to suggest that something has been done so often or repeatedly that the behavior or practice has become difficult to vary, change, or stop; **routine** used to describe something that is done commonly or often, especially to suggest that it has become tedious or monotonous; **wonted** a very formal or literary word used in the same way as *usual* or *habitual*.

u·su·fruct /yóozə frùkt, yóossə-/ *n.* the legal right to use and enjoy the advantages or profits of another's property [Early 17thC. From Latin *usufructus*, a variant of *ususfructus*, literally "use (and) enjoyment," from *usus* (see USE) + *fructus* "enjoyment" (source also of English *fruit*).]

u·su·fruc·tu·ar·y /yòozə frúkchoo èrree, yòossə-/ (*plural* **-ies**) *n.* somebody who is entitled by usufruct to the use of another's property —**u·su·fruc·tu·ar·y** *adj.*

u·su·rer /yóozhərər/ *n.* somebody who loans money to other people and charges them exorbitant or unlawful interest on it [13thC. Via Anglo-Norman from, ultimately, late Latin *usurarius*, from Latin "that pays interest," from *usura* (see USURY).]

u·surp /yoo súrp, -zúrp/ (**u·surped, u·surp·ing, u·surps**) *vti.* use something without the right to do so [14thC. Via Old French *usurper* from Latin *usurpare* "to seize for use," from, perhaps, *usus* "use" (see USE) + *rapere* "to seize" (source of English *rape*).] —**u·sur·pa·tion** /yòossər páysh'n, yòozər-/ *n.* —**u·sur·pa·tive** /yoo súrpətiv, -zúrpətiv/ *adj.* —**u·surp·er** *n.* —**u·surp·ing·ly** *adv.*

u·su·ry /yóozhəree/ (*plural* **-ries**) *n.* **1. LENDING AT EXORBITANT INTEREST** the lending of money at an exorbitant rate of interest **2. EXORBITANT INTEREST** an exorbitant rate of interest [14thC. Via assumed Anglo-Norman *usurie,* from, ultimately, Latin *usura* "use of money lent," hence "interest," from *usus* "use" (source also of English *use*).] —**u·su·ri·ous** /yoo zhóoree əss/ *adj.* —**u·su·ri·ous·ly** *adv.* —**u·su·ri·ous·ness** *n.*

USW *abbr.* RADIO ultrashort wave

ut /ut, oot/ *n.* MUSIC the note C, equivalent to "do" in the solmization system. It is the first note of the hexachord system devised by Guido d'Arezzo. [14thC. From Latin, the syllable sung to this note in a hymn to Saint John the Baptist.]

UT, Ut. *abbr.* **1.** universal time **2.** Utah

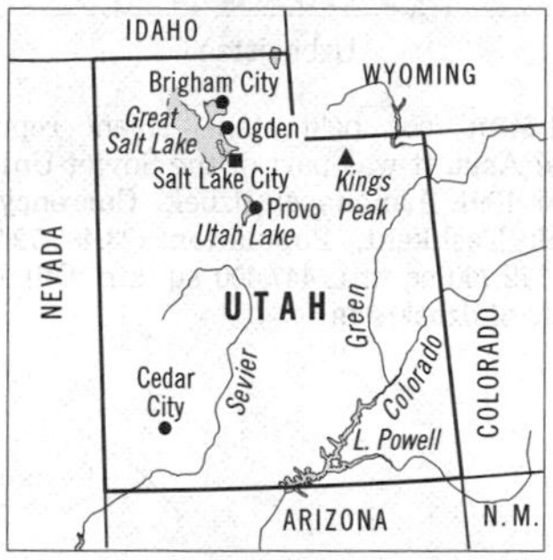

Utah

U·tah /yóot aa, -aw/ state in the western United States, bordered by Idaho, Wyoming, Colorado, Arizona, and Nevada. Capital: Salt Lake City. Population: 2,059,148 (1997). Area: 84,904 sq. mi./219,902 sq. km. —**U·ta·han** /yóot aan, -awn/ *n., adj.*

U·ta·ma·ro /ootaa maárō/ (1753–1806) Japanese artist. He was noted for his delicate portraits of women in teahouses, shops, and brothels. Full name **Kitagawa Utamaro**

UTC *abbr.* universal time coordinated

ut dict. /ùt díkt/ *abbr.* as directed (*used on prescriptions*) [Latin *ut dictum*]

ute /yoot/ *n. ANZ* a pickup truck (*informal*) [Mid-20thC. Shortening of *utility.*]

Ute /yóot/ (*plural* **Ute** *or* **Utes**) *n.* **1.** PEOPLES **MEMBER OF NATIVE N AMERICAN PEOPLE** a member of a Native North American people who originally lived in Colorado, Utah, and New Mexico. Most Ute continue to live in the same area. **2.** LANG **UTE LANGUAGE** the Uto-Aztecan language of the Ute people. About 2,500 people speak Ute. [Early 19thC. Shortening of Spanish *Yuta,* an Indian language.]

u·ten·sil /yoo ténss'l/ *n.* a tool or container, especially one used in a kitchen [14thC. Via Old French *utensile* from, ultimately, Latin *utensilis* "usable," from *uti* "to use" (source also of English *use*).]

u·ter·i plural of **uterus**

u·ter·ine /yóotərin, -rīn/ *adj.* **1. OF UTERUS** relating to, in, or affecting the womb **2. HAVING SAME MOTHER** related by having the same mother but a different father ○ *a uterine brother* [15thC. From late Latin *uterinus,* literally "from the same womb," from Latin *uterus* "womb" (see UTERUS).]

u·ter·us /yóotərəss/ (*plural* **-us·es** *or* **-i** /-rī/) *n.* **1. WOMB** a hollow muscular organ in the pelvic cavity of female mammals, in which the embryo is nourished and develops before birth (*technical*) **2. ORGAN SIMILAR TO MAMMALIAN WOMB** a structure in some animals that is similar to the mammalian womb, in which eggs or young develop [17thC. From Latin, "belly, womb." Ultimately from an Indo-European word that is possibly the ancestor of Greek *hustera* (source of English *hysteria*).]

U·ti·ca /yóotikə/ city in eastern New York, on the Mohawk River, east of Syracuse. Population: 61,368 (1996).

util. *abbr.* utility

u·til·i·tar·i·an /yoo tìllə térree ən/ *adj.* **1. BELIEVING VALUE LIES IN USEFULNESS** relating to, typical of, or advocating the doctrine that value is measured in terms of usefulness **2. PRACTICAL** designed primarily for practical use rather than beauty ■ *n.* **BELIEVER IN UTILITARIANISM** somebody who believes in the doctrine of utilitarianism

u·til·i·tar·i·an·ism /yoo tìllə térree ə nìzzəm/ *n.* **1. ETHICAL DOCTRINE** the ethical doctrine that the greatest happiness of the greatest number should be the criterion of the virtue of action **2. UTILITARIAN QUALITY** the quality of being designed primarily for practical use rather than beauty

u·til·i·ty /yoo tíllətee/ *n.* (*plural* **-ties**) **1. USEFULNESS** the quality or state of being useful for something **2. SOMETHING USEFUL** something that serves a useful purpose **3.** = **public utility 4. SERVICE PROVIDED BY PUBLIC UTILITY** a service such as electricity, gas, or water that is provided by a public utility **5. SATISFACTION DERIVED FROM CONSUMPTION** the amount of satisfaction or pleasure that somebody gains from consuming a commodity, product, or service. In classical economics this was considered to be an absolute measurement, but in modern economics it is considered to be merely a matter of relative preference. **6. u·til·i·ty, u·til·i·ty truck** *ANZ* **PICK-UP TRUCK** a pick-up truck ■ *adj.* **1. INTENDED FOR PRACTICAL USE** designed or intended for practical use rather than for show or appearance **2.** THEATER **ABLE TO PERFORM ANY SMALL ROLE** able to perform any small role in a theater production **3.** SPORTS **ABLE TO PLAY SEVERAL POSITIONS** able to substitute for other players in several different positions **4. DESIGNED FOR STRENGTH** built or designed for performing tasks that require strength and versatility ○ *a utility truck* **5.** AGRIC **RAISED FOR FARM USE** grown or raised to be used on a farm ○ *utility livestock* **6.** AGRIC **OF LOWEST GRADE** classified as the lowest grade of beef by the U.S. Government [14thC. Via French *utilité* from, ultimately, Latin *utilis* "usable," from *uti* "to use" (source also of English *use*).]

u·til·i·ty pro·gram *n.* a computer program that carries out routine tasks and supports the operation of the computer or another device, as compared to an application program

u·til·i·ty room *n.* a room in a house where there are large domestic appliances, e.g., a washing machine or furnace, and where many household tasks are done

u·til·i·ty truck *n. ANZ* = **utility** *n.* **6**

u·til·i·ty ve·hi·cle *n.* **1. SPORT-UTILITY VEHICLE** a sport-utility vehicle **2.** *NZ* **PICKUP TRUCK** a pickup truck

u·til·ize /yóot'l īz/ (**-ized, -iz·ing, -iz·es**) *vt.* to make use of or find a practical use for something [Early 19thC. Via French *utiliser* from, ultimately, Latin *utilis* (see UTILITY).] —**u·til·iz·a·ble** *adj.* —**u·til·i·za·tion** /yóot'li záysh'n/ *n.* —**u·til·iz·er** /-īzər/ *n.*

WORD KEY: USAGE

utilize or **use**? **Utilize** means "to use in a practical or effective way" and so it means something more than **use**, which is the general all-purpose word. **Utilize** is common in technical applications: *The device utilizes a special solderless plug-in connection.* It can also refer to using things in unusual or unintended ways, as a more formal equivalent of "make use of" : *When the fan belt broke we utilized an old pair of tights.* In business jargon and in other contexts **utilize** is often written when **use** is all that is intended, and this should be avoided: *Successful applicants will be able to utilize their skills and experience in this field.*

WORD KEY: SYNONYMS

See Synonyms at ***use***.

u·ti pos·si·de·tis /yoo tī possi deétiss/ *n.* INTERNAT LAW the principle in international law that land and property captured by belligerent parties in war remain their property unless a treaty rules otherwise (*formal*) [From late Latin, literally "as you possess"]

ut·most /út mōst/, **ut·ter·most** /úttər mōst/ *adj.* **1. AT THE EXTREMITY** at the most distant point or extremity **2. OF THE GREATEST DEGREE** of the greatest degree, number, or amount ■ *n.* **GREATEST DEGREE OR AMOUNT** the greatest degree, number, or amount of something, especially the greatest effort that somebody is capable of ○ *I did my utmost to persuade her.* [Old English *ūt(e)mest,* from an earlier form of English OUT + an earlier form of -MOST]

U·to-Az·tec·an /yóotō-/ *n.* **1.** LANG **N AND CENTRAL AMERICAN LANGUAGE FAMILY** a family of languages, including Ute and Nahuatl, spoken in the western United States and in Mexico **2.** PEOPLES **MEMBER OF UTO-AZTECAN PEOPLES** a member of one of the peoples who speak a language classified as Uto-Aztecan [*Uto* formed from UTE] — **U·to-Az·tec·an** *adj.*

u·to·pi·a /yoo tṓpee ə/, **U·to·pi·a** *n.* an ideal and perfect place or state, where everyone lives in harmony and everything is for the best [Mid-16thC. From modern Latin, imaginary island, described in Sir Thomas More's *Utopia* (1516), whose society is perfect in many respects. Literally, "noplace," formed from Greek *ou* "not" + *topos* "place."]

WORD KEY: CULTURAL NOTE

Utopia, a philosophical treatise by English writer and statesman Sir Thomas More (1516). It contrasts the moral decadence and disunity of contemporary Christian Europe with the tolerance and prosperity of More's imaginary ideal state of Utopia, which is run on secular, communist principles. More coined the state's name from the Greek words *ou* "not" and *topos* "place," literally meaning "the land of nowhere." The term itself has spawned a number of derivatives, such as *utopian, utopianism* and *utopianist.*

u·to·pi·an /yoo tṓpee ən/, **U·to·pi·an** *adj.* **1. IDEAL** belonging to or typical of an ideal perfect state or place **2. ADMIRABLE BUT IMPRACTICABLE** admirable but impracticable in real life **3. IMPRACTICALLY IDEALISTIC** tending to deal in admirable but impracticable ideas ■ *n.* **PROPOSER OF UTOPIAN REFORMS** somebody who proposes or advocates visionary but impractical social or political reforms

u·to·pi·an·ism /yoo tṓpee ə nìzzəm/, **U·to·pi·an·ism** *n.* **1. UTOPIAN IDEAS OR THEORIES** the principles, views, or aims of a utopian **2. BELIEF IN IDEAL SOCIETY** the belief that an ideal society can be achieved —**u·to·pi·an·ist** *n.*

u·to·pi·an so·cial·ism *n.* a form of socialism based on the belief that a socialist society can be brought about by peacefully persuading those in power to accept it

U·trecht /yóot rekt, -rekht, yoo trékt, -trékht/ historic university city in the central Netherlands. Population: 234,254 (1996).

u·tri·cle /yóotrik'l/, **u·tric·u·lus** /yoo tríkyələss/ (*plural* **-li** /yoo tríkyə lī/) *n.* **1. PART OF INNER EAR** the larger of two fluid-filled sacs in the labyrinth of the inner ear and into which the semicircular canals open **2. BLADDER-SHAPED FRUIT** the bladder-shaped fruit of some plants [Mid-18thC. Directly or via French *utricule* from Latin *utriculus,* literally "little leather bottle," from *uter* "leather bottle."] —**u·tric·u·lar** *adj.* —**u·tric·u·late** *adj.*

Ut·tar Pra·desh /óottər prə dáysh, -désh/ the most populous state in India, located in the northern part of the country, south of Nepal. Capital: Lucknow. Population: 139,112,287 (1991). Area: 113,673 sq. mi./294,413 sq. km.

ut·ter[1] /úttər/ (**-tered, -ter·ing, -ters**) *vt.* **1. SAY SOMETHING** to say or pronounce something **2. EMIT SOMETHING AS VOCAL SOUND** to emit something as a sound made by the voice **3. PUBLISH SOMETHING** to publish something, e.g., in a book or newspaper (*archaic*) ○ *You would not dare to utter this nonsense in print.* **4.** LAW **TO PUT SOMETHING INTO CIRCULATION** to put something into circulation, especially counterfeit money or a forgery, under the pretense that it is genuine (*formal*) [14thC. From Middle Dutch *ūteren* "to drive out, announce, speak," from Old Low German *ūt* "out."] — **ut·ter·a·ble** *adj.* —**ut·ter·er** *n.*

ut·ter[2] /úttər/ *adj.* at the most extreme point or of the highest degree [Old English *ūtera,* literally "further out," from *ūt,* an earlier form of OUT]

ut·ter·ance /úttərəns/ *n.* **1. SOMETHING SAID** something said or emitted as a vocal sound **2. EXPRESSION OF SOMETHING** the expression of something, especially in speech or vocal sound **3. WAY OF SPEAKING** a style, power, or way of speaking **4. ACT OF SAYING** the act of saying something ◇ **give utterance** to express something, especially in speech

ut·ter·ly /úttərlee/ *adv.* in an extreme or complete way

ut·ter·most *adj., n.* = **utmost**

U-turn *n.* **1. TURN MADE TO FACE OPPOSITE DIRECTION** a turn in the shape of a U made by a vehicle to reverse direction **2. REVERSAL OF ACTIONS OR POLICY** a complete reversal in opinion, actions, or policy

UV *abbr.* ultraviolet

u·va·rov·ite /oo vaárə vīt/ *n.* a bright emerald green mineral composed of calcium chromium silicate. It is a variety of garnet and is used as a gemstone. [Mid-19thC. Formed from the name of Count Sergei Semenovich *Uvarov* (1785–1855), a Russian statesman.]

u·ve·a /yŏovee ə/ *n.* the middle of the three layers of the eyeball, made up of the choroid, ciliary body, and iris surrounding the lens. It contains blood vessels and its pigmentation is responsible for eye color. [Early 16thC. Via medieval Latin from Latin *uva* (see UVULA).] —**u·ve·al** *adj.* —**u·ve·ous** *adj.*

u·ve·i·tis /yŏovee ítiss/ *n.* inflammation of the uvea of the eye

UV In·dex *n.* a scale used to indicate the intensity of the sun's ultraviolet rays

u·vu·la /yŏovyələ/ (*plural* **-las** *or* **-lae** /-lee/) *n.* a small fleshy V-shaped extension of the soft palate that hangs above the tongue at the entrance to the throat [14thC. From late Latin, literally "little grape," from Latin *uva* "grape," from its shape.]

u·vu·lar /yŏovyələr/ *adj.* **1. INVOLVING UVULA** relating to or involving the uvula **2. PRONOUNCED VIBRATING THE UVULA** pronounced with vibration of the uvula ■ *n.* **UVULAR SOUND** a uvular consonant —**u·vu·lar·ly** *adv.*

u·vu·li·tis /yŏovyə lítiss/ *n.* inflammation of the uvula

UW *abbr.* **1.** underwriter **2.** underwritten

ux. *abbr.* uxor [From Latin]

UXB *abbr.* unexploded bomb

ux·o·ri·al /uk sáwree əl/ *adj.* relating to, involving, or typical of a wife [Early 19thC. Formed from Latin *uxor* "wife."] —**ux·o·ri·al·ly** *adv.*

ux·o·ri·cide /uk sáwrə sīd/ *n.* **1. MURDER OF WIFE** murder of a wife by her husband **2. MAN WHO MURDERS WIFE** a man who murders his wife [Mid-19thC. Coined from Latin *uxor* "wife" + English -CIDE.] —**ux·o·ri·ci·dal** *adj.*

ux·o·ri·ous /uk sáwree əss/ *adj.* excessively devoted or submissive to your wife [Late 16thC. Formed from Latin *uxoriosus*, from *uxor* "wife."] —**ux·o·ri·ous·ly** *adv.* —**ux·o·ri·ous·ness** *n.*

Uz·bek /ŏoz bèk, úz bèk/ (*plural* **-bek** *or* **-beks**) *n.* **1.** PEOPLES **MEMBER OF PEOPLE LIVING IN UZBEKISTAN** a member of a people that live mainly in Uzbekistan, where they are the dominant ethnic group, and in parts of neighboring regions. The Uzbek people is made up mainly of descendents of Turkic-speaking nomads who settled in the region in the 15th century and Farsi-speaking inhabitants of the area. **2.** LANG **UZBEK LANGUAGE** a language spoken in Uzbekistan and central Asia, belonging to the Turkic branch of Altaic languages. About 16 million people speak Uzbek. [Early 17thC. Directly or via Persian or Russian *uzbek* from Turkish and Uzbek *özbek*.]

Uzbekistan

Uz·beki·stan /ŏoz béki stàn, -staàn/ republic in Central Asia. It was part of the Soviet Union from 1924 to 1991. Language: Uzbek. Currency: soum. Capital: Tashkent. Population: 23,467,724 (1997). Area: 172,700 sq. mi./447,400 sq. km. Official name **Republic of Uzbekistan**

V v

v[1] /vee/ (*plural* **v's**), **V** (*plural* **V's** *or* **Vs**) *n.* **1.** **22ND LETTER OF THE ENGLISH ALPHABET** the 22nd letter of the modern English alphabet **2.** **SPEECH SOUND CORRESPONDING TO THE LETTER "V"** the speech sound that corresponds to the letter "V" **3.** **LETTER "V" WRITTEN** a written representation of the letter "V"

v[2] (*plural* **v's**), **V** (*plural* **V's** *or* **Vs**) *symbol.* **1.** SCI image distance **2.** PHYS instantaneous potential difference **3.** PHYS instantaneous voltage **4.** PHYS specific volume

v[3] (*plural* **v's**), **V** (*plural* **V's** *or* **Vs**) *abbr.* **1.** PHYS vacuum **2.** vagrant **3.** vale **4.** MATH vector **5.** MED vein **6.** PHYS velocity component **7.** velocity speed **8.** MED ventilator **9.** ANAT, BOT ventral **10.** GRAM verb **11.** verbal **12.** verse **13.** versed **14.** verso **15.** versus **16.** vertical **17.** via **18.** CHEM vibrational quantum number **19.** CHR vicarage **20.** victory **21.** vide **22.** MUSIC violin **23.** MED virus **24.** METEOROL (abnormally good) visibility **25.** MED vision **26.** vocative **27.** voice **28.** GEOG volcano **29.** MEASURE voltage **30.** vowel

V[1], **v** *n.* the Roman numeral for five

V[2] *symbol.* **1.** PHYS electric potential **2.** PHYS electromotive force **3.** PHYS luminous efficiency **4.** PHYS potential **5.** PHYS potential efficiency **6.** PHYS potential energy **7.** vanadium

V[3] *abbr.* **1.** valine **2.** vanadium **3.** variable region **4.** MONEY vatu **5.** Venerable **6.** Very (*used in titles*) **7.** version **8.** vespers **9.** vicar **10.** vice **11.** victory **12.** village **13.** Viscount **14.** Viscountess **15.** volt **16.** voltmeter **17.** Volunteer **18.** Volunteers

V-1 (*plural* **V-1's**) *n.* a German robot bomb used in World War II, mainly against England [Abbreviation of German *Vergeltungswaffe eins*, literally "reprisal weapon one"]

V-2 (*plural* **V-2's**) *n.* a German liquid-fueled ballistic missile used in the latter part of World War II, chiefly against London [Abbreviation of German *Vergeltungswaffe zwei*, literally "reprisal weapon two"]

V6 (*plural* **V6's**) *n.* an internal-combustion engine with six cylinders arranged in a V shape

V8 (*plural* **V8's**) *n.* an internal-combustion engine with eight cylinders arranged in a V shape

va *abbr.* **1.** GRAM verbal adjective **2.** GRAM verb active **3.** MUSIC viola

VA *abbr.* **1.** ECON value-added **2.** value analysis **3.** MED ventricular arrhythmia **4.** Veterans' Administration **5.** CHR Vicar Apostolic **6.** NAVY Vice Admiral **7.** MAIL Virginia **8.** visual acuity **9.** visual aid **10.** Voice of America **11.** MEASURE volt-ampere **12.** MIL Volunteer Artillery **13.** Volunteers of America

Va. *abbr.* Virginia

V/A *abbr.* voucher attached

Vaal /vaal/ river in northeastern South Africa, a tributary of the Orange River. Length: 720 mi./1,160 km.

Vaa·sa /vaáss aa/ capital city and port of Vaasa Province, in western Finland. Population: 55,502 (1995).

vac *abbr.* **1.** vacancy **2.** vacant **3.** vacation **4.** vacuum **5.** vacuum cleaner

va·can·cy /váykənsee/ (*plural* **-cies**) *n.* **1.** **VACANT OFFICE OR POSITION** an office, position, or tenancy that is unfilled or unoccupied **2.** **MENTAL INACTIVITY** mental inactivity or lack of thought or intelligence **3.** the state of being vacant **4.** a period of leisure (*archaic*) **5.** PHYS **EMPTY SITE IN A CRYSTAL** an empty site, normally containing an atom or ion, in a crystal [Late 16thC. Formed from VACANT or from late Latin *vacantia*, from the present participle stem of Latin *vacare* (see VACATE).]

va·cant /váykənt/ *adj.* **1.** **WITHOUT AN OCCUPANT** having no occupant or contents ○ *There were several vacant seats on the bus.* ○ *a vacant lot* **2.** **UNOCCUPIED BY AN INCUMBENT OR OFFICIAL** not occupied by an incumbent, official, or possessor **3.** **LACKING EXPRESSION** showing no signs of thought, intelligence, or expression ○ *a vacant stare* **4.** **FREE FROM ACTIVITY** free from activity, business, or work ○ *a vacant afternoon* [13thC. Via Old French from the present participle stem of Latin *vacare* (see VACATE). It almost disappeared by 1400 but was reintroduced from Latin in the 16thC.] —**va·cant·ly** *adv.* —**va·cant·ness** *n.*

WORD KEY: SYNONYMS

vacant, unoccupied, empty, unfilled, void

CORE MEANING: lacking contents or occupants

vacant describes a house or room that has no occupants, often temporarily; **unoccupied** describes a building that has no one in it, especially when this has been the case for quite some time; **empty** describes something such as a container that has no contents or something such as a room that has no occupants; **unfilled** used to describe something such as a seat on an airplane or in a theater that has no one sitting in it because no one has bought a ticket for it; **void** a formal or literary word that emphasizes that something is completely empty.

va·cate /váy kàyt/ (**-cat·ed, -cat·ing, -cates**) *vt.* **1.** **EMPTY OF OCCUPANTS** to empty something of incumbents or occupants **2.** **GIVE UP OCCUPANCY OF** to relinquish the possession, or occupancy of something ○ *vacate the premises* **3.** **RESIGN FROM** to withdraw from or surrender possession of an office or post ○ *vacate a legislative seat* **4.** LAW **MAKE INVALID** to make something legally void [Mid-17thC. From the past participle stem of Latin *vacare* "to be empty" (source also of English *void*).] —**va·cat·a·ble** *adj.*

va·ca·tion /vay káysh'n, və-/ *n.* **1.** **FIXED HOLIDAY PERIOD** a scheduled period during which the activities of courts, schools, or other regular businesses are suspended **2.** **BREAK FROM WORK** a period of time devoted to rest, travel, or recreation **3.** **ACT OR INSTANCE OF VACATING** an act or an instance or vacating something ■ *vi.* (**-tioned, -tion·ing, -tions**) **TAKE A VACATION** to take or spend a vacation [14thC. Via Old French from, ultimately, the past participle of Latin *vacare* (see VACATE).]

va·ca·tion·er /vay káysh'nər, və-/, **va·ca·tion·ist** /vay káysh'nist, və-/ *n.* a person who takes or is on a vacation

va·ca·tion·land /vay káysh'n lànd, və-/ *n.* an area with many attractions and facilities for vacationers [Early 20thC]

vac·ci·nal /váksən'l, vak seén'l/ *adj.* relating to a vaccine or vaccination

vac·ci·nate /váksə nàyt/ (**-nat·ed, -nat·ing, -nates**) *vt.* to inoculate a person or animal with a vaccine to produce immunity —**vac·ci·na·tor** *n.* —**vac·ci·na·to·ry** /váksənə tàwree/ *adj.*

vac·ci·na·tion /váksə náysh'n/ *n.* inoculation with a vaccine to produce immunity [Early 19thC. Formed from VACCINE or from VACCINATE.]

vac·cine /vak seén, vák seèn/ *n.* **1.** MED **INOCULATION** a preparation containing weakened or dead microbes of the kind that cause a particular disease, administered to stimulate the immune system to produce antibodies against that disease **2.** COMPUT **PROTECTIVE SOFTWARE** a program that protects a system against a computer virus [Late 18thC. From Latin *vaccinus* "of a cow," from *vacca* "cow," because it was originally applied to the cowpox virus and its use to prevent smallpox.]

WORD KEY: ORIGIN

Vaccine was used by the British physician Edward Jenner at the end of the 18th century in the terms *vaccine disease*, meaning "cowpox," and hence *vaccine inoculation*, meaning the technique he developed of preventing smallpox by injecting people with cowpox virus. There is no evidence of the use of ***vaccine*** as a noun to denote the inoculated material until the 1840s.

vac·ci·nee /vàksə neé/ *n.* somebody who receives or has received a vaccination [Late 19thC. Formed from VACCINATE.]

vac·cin·i·a /vak sínnee ə/ *n.* a skin eruption in reaction to inoculation with the weakened cowpox virus that was once used to vaccinate people against smallpox [Early 19thC. Via modern Latin from Latin *vaccinus* (see VACCINE).] —**vac·cin·i·al** *adj.*

va·cher·in /vásh ràN, vash ráN/ *n.* a soft cow's-milk cheese from France or Switzerland [Mid-20thC. From French.]

vac·il·lant /vássələnt/ *adj.* wavering indecisively [Early 16thC. From the present participle stem of Latin *vaccillare* (see VACILLATE).]

vac·il·late /vássə làyt/ (**-lat·ed, -lat·ing, -lates**) *vi.* **1.** to be indecisive or irresolute **2.** to sway from side to side [Late 16thC. From the past participle stem of Latin *vaccillare* "to sway, totter."] —**vac·il·la·tion** /vàssə láysh'n/ *n.* —**vac·il·la·tor** /vássə làytər/ *n.*

WORD KEY: SYNONYMS

See Synonyms at ***hesitate***.

vacua plural of **vacuum**

va·cu·i·ty /va kyoo itee/ (*plural* **-ties**) *n.* (*formal*) **1.** **EMPTINESS** the condition, state, or quality of being empty of all contents **2.** **EMPTY SPACE** an empty area or space **3.** **MEANINGLESS STATE OR THING** a thing or condition that is inane or devoid of any meaningful content ○ *legislative vacuity* [Mid-16thC. Directly or via French *vacuité* from, ultimately, Latin *vacuus* "empty" (source of English *vacuum*).]

vac·u·o·lar mem·brane /vakyoo ōlər-, vàkyoo ələr-/ *n.* a membrane containing fluid in the cytoplasm of a cell

vac·u·o·late /vákyoo ō làyt, vákyoo ōlət/, **vac·u·o·lat·ed** /vákyoo ō làytəd/ *adj.* having small holes —**vac·u·o·la·tion** /vàkyoo ō láysh'n/ *n.* —**vac·u·o·li·za·tion** /vàkyoo ōli záysh'n/ *n.*

vac·u·ole /vákyoo ōl/ *n.* **1.** **CAVITY IN TISSUE** a small cavity in tissue **2.** **COMPARTMENT IN THE CYTOPLASM OF CELL** a membrane-bound compartment containing fluid that is found in the cytoplasm of a cell [Mid-19thC. From French, literally "little empty (space)," from Latin *vacuus* "empty" (source of English *vacuum*) + French *-ole* "little."] —**vac·u·o·lar** /vakyoo ōlər, vàkyoo ələr/ *adj.*

vac·u·ous /vákyoo əss/ *adj.* **1.** **LACKING CONTENT** having no content **2.** **EMPTY OF MEANING** lacking ideas or intelligence **3.** **IDLE** lacking serious occupation **4.** MATH, LOGIC **NULL** null [Mid-17thC. Formed from Latin *vacuus* "empty" (see VACUUM).] —**vac·u·ous·ly** *adv.* —**vac·u·ous·ness** *n.*

vac·u·um /vákyoo əm, vákyəm/ *n.* (*plural* **-ums** *or* **-a** /vákyoo ə/) **1.** PHYS **SPACE EMPTY OF MATTER** a space completely empty of matter but not achievable in practice on Earth **2.** PHYS **SPACE WITH ALL THE GAS REMOVED** a space from which all air or gas has been extracted **3.** **EMPTINESS CAUSED BY ABSENCE** an emptiness caused by somebody or something's absence or removal ○ *Her death left a vacuum in his life.* **4.** **ISOLATION FROM THE OUTSIDE WORLD** isolation from external influences ○ *You can't live in a vacuum.* **5.** = **vacuum cleaner** ■ *vti.* (**-umed, -um·ing, -ums**) **CLEAN SOMETHING USING A VACUUM CLEANER** to clean an area or object using a vacuum cleaner [Mid-16thC. From the neuter of Latin *vacuus* "empty."]

vac·u·um ac·tiv·i·ty *n.* innate behavior manifested in the absence of the usual stimulus

vac·u·um bot·tle *n.* a bottle with two walls enclosing a vacuum, used for keeping the contents at a constant temperature

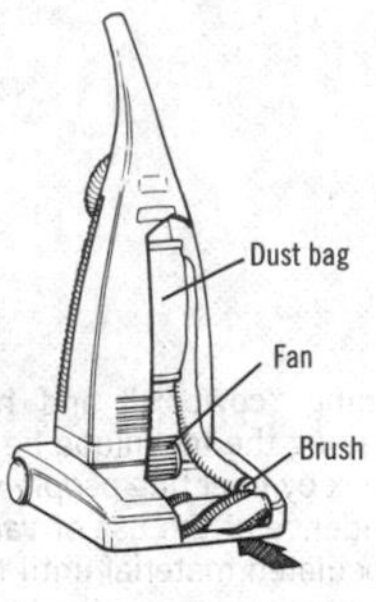

Vacuum cleaner

vac·u·um clean·er *n.* an electrical appliance that cleans surfaces such as floors, upholstery, and window coverings by sucking dirt and other material into a bag

vac·u·um dis·til·la·tion *n.* a process of distilling liquid at low pressure so that it boils at a lower boiling point

vac·u·um dry·ing *n.* the removal of liquid from a solution or mixture at reduced air pressure so that it dries at a lower temperature than it would at full pressure

vac·u·um flask *n.* = **vacuum bottle**

vac·u·um form·ing *n.* the process of shaping sheets of heated thermoplastic by placing them in a mold and removing air by suction

vac·u·um gauge *n.* an instrument that measures pressures below atmospheric pressure

vac·u·um-packed *adj.* packed in an airtight container or package under low pressure in order to prevent the contents from spoiling or corroding

vac·u·um pan *n.* a device with a vacuum pump that removes moisture quickly by boiling a substance at a low temperature under reduced pressure

vac·u·um pump *n.* **1.** DEVICE FOR REMOVING AIR a device that creates a partial vacuum **2.** = **pulsometer**

vac·u·um tube *n.* an electron tube that is either evacuated or filled with low-pressure gas and in which electrons are pulled from the cathode by an applied anode voltage. It is used to produce effects such as amplification and oscillation.

va·da *n. S Asia* = **wada**

va·de me·cum /vàydee méekəm, vaàdee-/ *n.* **1.** USEFUL BOOK a guidebook, handbook, or manual, especially one carried around or designed to be carried around constantly and referred to often **2.** USEFUL OBJECT an object that a person carries constantly because it is useful [Early 17thC. From Latin, literally "go with me."]

V.Adm., **VADM** *abbr.* Vice Admiral

Va·do·da·ra /vaa dṓdaaraa/ industrial city in Gujarat State, western India. Population: 1,115,265 (1991).

va·dose /váy dṑss/ *adj.* used to describe or relating to water in the unsaturated zone of the Earth's crust that is above the level of ground water [Late 19thC. From Latin *vadosus*, from *vadum* "shallow piece of water."]

va·dose zone *n.* the unsaturated zone between the ground surface and the water table through which ground water can percolate

Va·duz /fa dŏŏts/ town and capital of the principality of Liechtenstein, central Europe. Population: 5,085 (1995).

vag- *prefix.* = **vago-** (*used before vowels*)

vag·a·bond /vággə bònd/ *n.* **1.** HOMELESS WANDERER somebody who has no permanent place to live and wanders from place to place **2.** BEGGAR somebody who survives by asking for food or money ■ *adj.* OF VAGABONDS relating to or characteristic of a vagabond ■ *vi.* (**-bond·ed, -bond·ing, -bonds**) BE A VAGABOND to wander from place to place [15thC. Via French from Latin *vagabundus*, from *vagari* "to wander" (source of English *vagrant*).] —**vag·a·bond·age** *n.* —**vag·a·bond·ism** *n.*

va·gal /váyg'l/ *adj.* relating to the tenth pair of cranial nerves (**vagus nerves**) —**va·gal·ly** *adv.*

va·ga·ry /váygəree/ (*plural* **-ries**) *n.* an unpredictable or eccentric change, action, or idea ○ *the vagaries of the weather* [Late 16thC. From Latin *vagari* (see VAGABOND).] —**va·gar·i·ous** /vay gérree əss, və gérree əss/ *adj.* —**va·gar·i·ous·ly** *adv.*

va·gi plural of **vagus**

vag·ile /vájjəl/ *adj.* able to move around within a specific environment [Early 20thC. Formed from VAGUS.] —**va·gil·i·ty** /və jíllətee/ *n.*

va·gi·na /və jī́nə/ (*plural* **-nas** *or* **-nae** /-nee/) *n.* **1.** PART OF THE FEMALE REPRODUCTIVE TRACT in female mammals, a lubricated muscular tube connecting the cervix of the womb to the vulva. It receives the penis during copulation and expands to expel the fetus during birth. **2.** PLANT OR ANIMAL SHEATH a plant or animal part that forms a sheath, e.g., that formed by a leaf around a stem [Late 17thC. From Latin, "sheath, scabbard" (source of English *vanilla*).] —**vag·i·nal** /vájjən'l/ *adj.* —**vag·i·nal·ly** /vájjənəlee/ *adv.*

vag·i·nate /vájjənət, vájjə nàyt/, **vag·i·nat·ed** /vájjə nàytəd/ *adj.* having, forming, or resembling a sheath

vag·i·nec·to·my /vàjjə néktəmee/ (*plural* **-mies**) *n.* **1.** REMOVAL OF THE VAGINA the removal of all or part of the vagina by surgery **2.** REMOVAL OF THE TESTIS MEMBRANE the removal by surgery of all or part of the smooth moist membrane that encloses the testis and epididymis

vag·i·nis·mus /vàjjə nízməss/ *n.* a painful and often prolonged contraction of the vagina in response to the vulva or vagina being touched. It may have a psychological cause, or be due to physical factors such as injury, ulceration, or inflammation.

vag·i·ni·tis /vàjjə nī́tiss/ *n.* inflammation of the vagina. caused by infection, an ill-fitting contraceptive device, or hormonal deficiency. Its typical symptoms include irritation, vaginal discharge, and painful urination.

vago- *prefix.* vagus ○ *vagotomy* [From VAGUS]

va·got·o·my /və góttəmee/ (*plural* **-mies**) *n.* the surgical cutting of the tenth pair of cranial nerves (**vagus nerves**) or any of their branches, performed to control duodenal ulcers by decreasing acid secretion of the stomach

va·go·to·ni·a /vàygə tṓnee ə/ *n.* a pathological condition in which overactivity of the tenth pair of cranial nerves (**vagus nerves**) affects bodily functions controlled by these nerves, such as those in blood vessels and the gut. Symptoms may include sweating, constipation, and slowed heartbeat. [Early 20thC. Coined from VAGO- + Greek *tonos* "stretching, tension" (source of English *tone*).] —**va·go·ton·ic** /vàygə tónnik/ *adj.*

va·go·tro·pic /vàygə tróppik/ *adj.* used to describe a drug that has an effect on the tenth pair of cranial nerves (**vagus nerves**)

va·gran·cy /váygrənsee/ (*plural* **-cies**) *n.* **1.** HOMELESSNESS the state of wandering and having no permanent place to live **2.** LAW VAGRANCY AS A LEGAL OFFENSE the legal offense of living on the street without money or a place to live and, in some jurisdictions, begging **3.** LAPSE IN THINKING a lapse in thinking

va·grant /váygrənt/ *n.* **1.** HOMELESS WANDERER somebody who wanders from one place to another and has no permanent place to live **2.** WANDERER somebody who never stays in one place for long **3.** LAW SOMEBODY GUILTY OF THE OFFENSE OF VAGRANCY somebody guilty of the legal offense of vagrancy **4.** BIRDS BIRD OFF THE NORMAL MIGRATION ROUTE a migratory bird or insect that deviates from its normal migration route ■ *adj.* **1.** HOMELESS wandering from one place to another and having no permanent place to live **2.** WANDERING never staying in one place for long **3.** WAYWARD wayward or capricious in nature **4.** RANDOM acting or done in a random way **5.** BOT GROWING IN AN UNCONTROLLED WAY used to describe plants that grow in a lush uncontrolled way [15thC. From Anglo-Norman *varagarant*, of uncertain origin: ultimately, perhaps from (influenced by French *vaguer* "to wander"), Old French *walcrer* "to walk," from Germanic.] —**va·grant·ly** *adv.* —**va·grant·ness** *n.*

va·grom /váygrəm/ *adj.* vagrant (*archaic*) [Late 16thC. Alteration of VAGRANT. Coined by William Shakespeare.]

vague /vayg/ (**vagu·er, vagu·est**) *adj.* **1.** NOT EXPLICIT not clear in meaning or intention ○ *a vague proposal* **2.** NOT DISTINCTLY SEEN not having a clear or perceptible form ○ *a vague form in the shadows* **3.** UNVERIFIED not properly validated or having no clear or identifiable source **4.** UNCLEAR IN THINKING unclear or incoherent in thinking or expression **5.** NOT CLEARLY PERCEIVED IN THE MIND not clearly felt, understood, or recalled ○ *I have a vague recollection of it.* [Mid-16thC. Directly or via French from Latin *vagus* "wandering, inconstant" (source of English *vagus*).] —**vague·ly** *adv.* —**vague·ness** *n.*

va·gus /váygəss/ (*plural* **-gi** /váy gī, -jī/), **va·gus nerve** *n.* either of the tenth pair of cranial nerves that carry sensory and motor neurons serving the heart, lungs, stomach, intestines, and various other organs [Mid-19thC. From Latin *vagus* (see VAGUE).]

VAH *abbr.* Veterans' Administration Hospital

vai·dya /vī́dee ə/ *n. S Asia* an Ayurvedic Hindu physician [Mid-20thC. From Hindi, from *vaidy* "export of Ayurvedic medicine."]

vain /vayn/ *adj.* **1.** EXCESSIVELY PROUD excessively proud, especially of your appearance **2.** UNSUCCESSFUL failing to have or unlikely to have the intended or desired result ○ *a vain attempt at persuading them* **3.** EMPTY OF SUBSTANCE devoid of substance or meaning [14thC. Via Old French from Latin *vanus* "empty, without substance" (source of English *evanescent* and *vanish*).] —**vain·ly** *adv.* —**vain·ness** *n.* ◇ **in vain** fruitlessly, pointlessly, or unsuccessfully ○ *We searched in vain for a solution.*

WORD KEY: SYNONYMS

vain, empty, hollow, idle

CORE MEANING: without value or worth

vain emphasizes that something such as a hope or ambition is unlikely to be fulfilled; **empty** describes something such as a threat or a promise that seems to lack substance and is therefore unlikely to be carried through; **hollow** a more literary word meaning "empty"; **idle** emphasizes that something such as a threat lacks purpose or seems unlikely to be effective.

vain·glo·ri·ous /vàyn gláwree əss/ *adj.* excessively proud or boastful (*literary*) —**vain·glo·ri·ous·ly** *adv.* —**vain·glo·ri·ous·ness** *n.*

vain·glo·ry /váyn glàwree/ (*plural* **-ries**) *n.* (*literary*) **1.** EXCESSIVE PRIDE excessive pride in or boastfulness about yourself, your achievements, or your abilities **2.** VAIN DISPLAY an excessive display of something in order to draw attention to it [12thC. Via Old French from Latin *vana gloria*, literally "empty glory."]

vair /vair/ *n.* **1.** FUR TRIMMING FOR ROBES fur used as a trimming on medieval robes **2.** HERALDRY FUR USED ON HERALDIC SHIELDS a blue-and-white fur used on heraldic shields. ◊ **ermine** [14thC. Via Old French from Latin *varius* "speckled, changeable" (source of English *various*).]

Vais·a·kha /vīss aàkə/ *n.* in the Hindu calendar, the second month of the year, made up of 29 or 30 days and falling in approximately April to May

Vaish·na·va /vī́shnəvə/ *n.* a member of a group devoted to the worship of the Hindu god Vishnu or one of his incarnations [Late 18thC. From Sanskrit *vaiṣṇava*, literally "relating to Vishnu."] —**Vaish·na·vism** *n.*

Vais·ya /vī́ssyə, vī́sh-/ *n.* **1.** HINDU MERCHANT CASTE the third of the four Hindu castes, the members of which were merchants and farmers **2.** MEMBER OF THE HINDU MERCHANT CASTE a member of the Vaisya caste [Mid-17thC. From Sanskrit *vaiśya* "farm laborer, tradesman."]

va·kil /və kéel/, **va·keel, wa·kil** *n. S Asia* a lawyer or legal representative in a court of law in the Indian subcontinent [Early 17thC. Via Persian and Urdu *wakīl* and Turkish *vakīl* from Arabic *wakīl*.]

val. *abbr.* **1.** GEOL valley **2.** FIN valuation **3.** COMM value

val·ance /vállǝns, váylǝns/ *n.* **1.** COVER FOR A CURTAIN ROD a

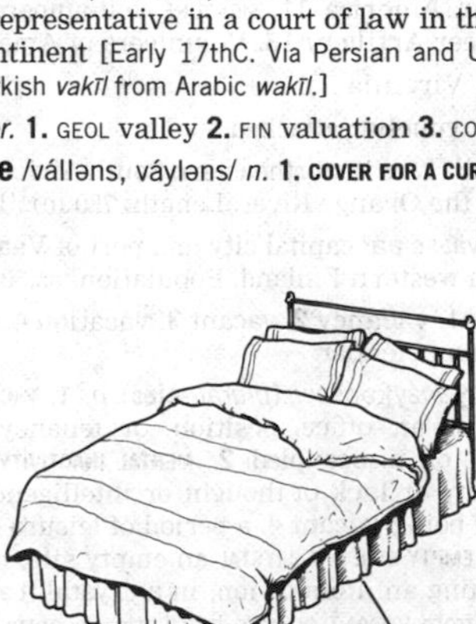

Valance

short decorative piece of drapery or wood hung across a window to cover the rod from which curtains hang **2.** FABRIC COVER FOR A BED BASE a plain, pleated, or gathered fabric cover that hangs from a shelf or is used to cover up the base of a bed from mattress to floor [15thC. Origin uncertain: perhaps ultimately from Old French *(a)valer* "go down."] —**val·anced** *adj.*

Val·dez /val deéz/ city in southeastern Alaska, on the shore of an inlet of Prince William Sound. Population: 4,309 (1996).

Val-d'Or /val dáwr/ city in southwestern Quebec, Canada. It was a gold-rush town in the 1930s. Population: 32,648 (1996).

vale[1] /vayl/ *n.* a valley or dale, often one that has a stream running through it (*literary*) (*often used in place names*) [14thC. Via French from Latin *valles* (see VALLEY).] ◇ **vale of tears** the world considered as a place full of sadness or unhappiness (*literary*)

vale[2] /vaá lày, váylee/ *interj.* FAREWELL a Latin expression of farewell ■ *n.* SAYING FAREWELL an act of saying farewell or adieu [Mid-16thC. From Latin, literally "be well," a form of *valere* "to be strong or well."]

val·e·dic·tion /vàllə díkshən/ *n.* (*formal*) **1.** SAYING GOODBYE the act of saying goodbye or an instance of leave-taking **2.** FAREWELL SPEECH a statement, speech, or letter of farewell [Mid-17thC. Formed from Latin *valedicere* "to say goodbye," on the model of BENEDICTION.]

val·e·dic·to·ri·an /vàllə dik táwree ən/ *n.* the student who delivers the valedictory address at graduation

val·e·dic·to·ry /vàllə díktəree/ *n.* (*plural* **-ries**) **1.** FAREWELL SPEECH a statement or speech of farewell (*formal*) **2.** = **valedictory address** ■ *adj.* SAYING GOODBYE performing the function of saying farewell (*formal*)

val·e·dic·to·ry ad·dress *n.* a speech delivered at graduation by the student with the best academic record

va·lence /váyləns/ *n.* **1. va·lence, va·len·cy** CHEM COMBINING POWER OF ATOMS the chemical combining power of atoms or groups measured by the number of electrons the atom or group will receive, give up, or share in forming a compound **2. va·lence, va·len·cy** IMMUNOL COMBINING ANTIGENIC DETERMINANTS the number of different antigenic determinants with which a single antibody molecule can combine **3.** GRAM COMBINING POWER OF A VERB the ability of a verb to combine grammatically with noun phrases in a given clause [Late 19thC. Variant of VALENCY.]

va·lence e·lec·tron *n.* an electron in an outer shell of an atom that can be lost to or shared with another atom to form a molecule

va·lence shell *n.* the outer electron shell of an atom consisting of one or more electrons (**valence electrons**) that are available to form bonds with other atoms to form molecules

Va·len·ci·a /və lénshee ə, və lénssee ə/ **1.** capital city of Valencia Province and the autonomous region of Valencia, in eastern Spain. The city was founded in Roman times. Population: 763,308 (1995). **2.** city in northern Venezuela, on the Cabriales River. Population: 1,034,033 (1992).

Va·len·ci·ennes[1] /və lènsee én, và laaN syén/ *n.* a fine lace made with bobbins that is usually floral in design and is now made of cotton instead of the original linen [Early 18thC. Named for VALENCIENNES, where the lace was originally produced.]

Va·len·ci·ennes[2] /vallènssee én, va laaNss yen/ city in the Nord-Pas-de-Calais Region, northern France, and administrative center of the Nord Department. Population: 39,276 (1990).

va·len·cy *n.* = **valence** [Mid-19thC. From Latin *valentia* "power, competence," from *valere* "to be powerful."]

va·len·cy gram·mar *n.* a type of grammar where verbs are considered in terms of their ability to combine with noun phrases

-valent *suffix.* having a particular valence or valences ○ *divalent* [Formed from VALENCE]

val·en·tine /vállən tīn/ *n.* **1.** VALENTINE'S DAY CARD a greeting card or gift sent, traditionally anonymously, to somebody on Valentine's Day as a token of love **2.** RECIPIENT OF A VALENTINE the person to whom somebody sends a card or gift on Valentine's Day as a token of love [15thC. Named for St. VALENTINE.]

Val·en·tine's Day *n.* February 14, the Christian feast day of St. Valentine and the traditional day for sending a romantic card or gift, especially anonymously, to somebody you love.

Rudolph Valentino

Val·en·ti·no /vàllən teénō/, **Rudolph** (1895–1926) Italian-born U.S. actor. His passionate roles in silent movies made him a romantic screen idol. Real name **Rodolpho Guglielmi di Valentina d'Antonguolla**

va·le·ri·an /və léeree ən/ (*plural* **-ans** *or* **-an**) *n.* **1.** PLANTS EURASIAN PLANT WITH MEDICINAL ROOT a plant of Europe and Asia with small sweet-smelling white or pinkish flowers and a root that is used medicinally. Genus: *Valeriana.* **2.** MED SEDATIVE MADE FROM VALERIAN a sedative made from the dried roots of valerian plants [15thC. Via Old French from medieval Latin *valeriana,* named for *Valeria,* a Roman province.]

va·ler·ic ac·id /və leérik-, və lèrrik-/ *n.* a pungent colorless liquid used in flavorings and manufacturing. Formula: $C_5H_{10}O_2$. [*Valeric* formed from VALERIAN]

Va·lé·ry /vàlle reé, vaa lay reé/, **Paul** (1871–1945) French poet and critic. He was considered to be one of France's greatest 20th-century poets, and his prolific early output was followed by a 20-year silence, during which he worked mainly on mathematics and philosophical meditations. His later work was heavily influenced by the symbolists. Full name **Paul Ambroise Valéry**

val·et *n.* /vállət, vá lày, va láy/ **1.** MAN SERVANT a male personal servant of a man, whose duties include looking after his employer's clothes and providing his meals **2.** SOMEBODY PERFORMING CAR PARKING SERVICE somebody employed to park the cars of people arriving at a hotel, restaurant, or airport and bring the cars back for them on departure **3.** MALE HOTEL OR PASSENGER SHIP EMPLOYEE a man employee whose duties include cleaning the clothes of hotel guests or passengers on ships ■ *v.* /vállət/ (**-et·ed, -et·ing, -ets**) **1.** *vti.* WORK AS A VALET to work as a valet or provide valet services to somebody **2.** *vt.* CLEAN A CAR to clean somebody's car in return for payment [15thC. Via French from, ultimately, assumed medieval Latin *vassus* "servant to a knight" (source of English *vassal*).]

va·le·ta *n.* DANCE = **veleta**

val·et de cham·bre /vàllay də shaáNbrə/ (*plural* **val·ets de cham·bre**) *n.* = **valet** *n.* 1 [French, literally "valet of the room"]

val·et park·ing *n.* a service provided by some hotels, restaurants, and airports whereby an employee parks people's cars for them on arrival and brings the cars back for them on departure

val·e·tu·di·nar·i·an /vàllə tood'n érree ən/, **val·e·tu·di·nar·y** /vàllə tood'n èrree/ *n.* (*plural* **-ies**) **1.** SOMEBODY WITH POOR HEALTH somebody who has persistent ill health **2.** SOMEBODY OBSESSED WITH HEALTH somebody who is excessively concerned with his or her own health ■ *adj.* **1.** OF A VALETUDINARIAN relating to or being a valetudinarian **2.** OF POOR HEALTH relating to, characterized by, or arising from poor health —**val·e·tu·di·nar·i·an·ism** /vàllə tood'n érree ə nìzzəm/ *n.*

val·e·tu·di·nar·y *n., adj.* = **valetudinarian** [Late 16thC. From Latin *valetudinarius* "in ill health," from *valetudo* "state of health," from *valere* "to be well."]

val·gus /válgəss/ *adj.* MED TWISTED OUTWARD used to describe a deformity in which a body part such as the knee or foot is bent or twisted outward away from the midline of the body. ◊ **varus** ■ *n.* MED STATE OF BEING TWISTED OUTWARD the position or state in which a bone or body part is bent or twisted outward away from the midline of the body. ◊ **varus** [Early 19thC. From Latin, "knock-kneed."] —**val·goid** /vál gòyd/ *adj.*

Val·hal·la /val hállə, vaal haálə/, **Wal·hal·la, Wal·hall** *n.* in Norse mythology, the great hall where the souls of heroes killed in battle spend eternity [Late 17thC. Via modern Latin from Old Norse *valhall,* literally "hall of the slain," from *valr* "those slain in battle" (source of English *Valkyrie*).]

val·iant /vállyənt/ *adj.* **1.** COURAGEOUS brave and steadfast **2.** DONE COURAGEOUSLY characterized by or performed with bravery but often ending in failure ○ *despite a valiant attempt at rescue* ■ *n.* SOMEBODY COURAGEOUS a brave and steadfast person [14thC. Via Old French from Latin *valent-,* the present participle stem of *valere* "to be strong."] —**val·iance** *n.* —**val·ian·cy** *n.* —**val·iant·ly** *adv.* —**val·iant·ness** *n.*

val·id /vállid/ *adj.* **1.** JUSTIFIABLE having a solid foundation or justification ○ *It's a perfectly valid argument.* **2.** EFFECTIVE bringing about the results or ends intended **3.** LAW LEGALLY BINDING having binding force in law **4.** LAW LEGALLY ACCEPTABLE acceptable under law **5.** UNEXPIRED usable or acceptable until a specified expiration date or under specified conditions of use ○ *a valid passport* **6.** LOGICAL having premises from which the conclusion follows logically **7.** HEALTHY having good health (*archaic*) [Late 16thC. Directly or via French from Latin *validus* "strong," from *valere* "to be strong."] —**va·lid·i·ty** /və líddətee/ *n.* —**va·lid·ly** /vállidlee/ *adv.* —**va·lid·ness** /vállidnəss/ *n.*

WORD KEY: SYNONYMS

valid, cogent, convincing, reasonable, sound

CORE MEANING: being worthy of acceptance or credence

valid describes something such as an argument or an excuse that is acceptable on the strength of the evidence it supplies; **cogent** a fairly formal word describing an argument that is forceful and weighty; **convincing** describes something such as an argument or an excuse that seems likely to overcome the doubts and win the support of those who hear it; **reasonable** describes an argument or excuse that seems worthy of consideration but not necessarily ultimately convincing; **sound** emphasizes that something such as an argument is based on truth and contains no errors or falsehoods.

val·i·date /válli dàyt/ (**-dat·ed, -dat·ing, -dates**) *vt.* **1.** CONFIRM THE TRUTHFULNESS OF to confirm or establish the truthfulness or soundness of something **2.** LAW MAKE LEGAL to declare or render something legal or binding ○ *validate a passport* **3.** REGISTER SOMETHING FORMALLY to register something formally and have its use officially sanctioned [Mid-17thC. From Latin *validare* "render legally valid," from *validus* (see VALID).] —**val·i·da·tion** /vàlli dáysh'n/ *n.* —**val·i·da·to·ry** /vállidə tàwree/ *adj.*

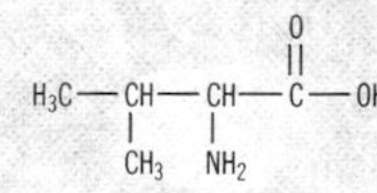

Valine

val·ine /vá leèn, váy-/ *n.* an amino acid essential to normal animal growth, produced from pyruvic acid or during the hydrolysis of some proteins. Formula: $C_5H_{11}NO_2$. [Early 20thC. Coined from VALERIC ACID + -INE.]

va·lise /və leéss/ *n.* a small piece of luggage [Early 20thC. Via French from Italian *valigia,* of unknown origin.]

Val·i·um /vállee əm/ *tdmk.* a trademark for diazepam, a tranquilizer

Val·kyr·ie /val keéree, válkəree/, **Wal·kyr·ie, Val·kyr** /válkər/ *n.* in Norse mythology, one of the 12 handmaids of Odin who ride their horses over the field of battle and escort the souls of slain heroes to Valhalla [Mid-18thC. From Old Norse *Valkyrja,* literally "chooser of the slain," from *valr* "those slain in battle."] —**Val·kyr·i·an** /val keéree ən/ *adj.*

val·la plural of **vallum**

Val·la·do·lid /vàallə do líd/ capital city of Valladolid Province, northern Spain. It was the capital of Spain before Madrid. Population: 334,820 (1995).

val·late /vá làyt/ (**-lat·ed, -lat·ing, -lates**) *vt.* to plan or build earthworks for defense [Late 19thC. Back-formation from VALLATION.]

val·la·tion /va láysh'n/ *n.* **1.** DEFENSIVE EARTHWORK a defensive fortification or embankment made of earth **2.** CONSTRUCTION OF DEFENSIVE EARTHWORKS the planning or building of defensive fortifications or embankments made of earth [Mid-17thC. Via Latin *vallatio* from, ultimately, *vallare* "to protect," from *vallum* "rampart" (source of English *wall* and *circumvallate*).]

val·lec·u·la /va lékyələ/ (*plural* **-lae** /-lee/) *n.* a shallow groove, depression, or furrow in an animal or plant body such as that between the hemispheres of the cerebellum in the brain [Mid-19thC. From Latin *vallicula*, from *valles* (see VALLEY).] —**val·lec·u·lar** *adj.* —**val·lec·u·late** /və lékyələt, və lékyə làyt/ *adj.*

Val·le d'A·os·ta /vaallay daa óstə/ region in northern Italy on the border with France and Switzerland. It contains the Alpine peaks of the Matterhorn and Mont Blanc. Population: 117,208 (1991). Area: 1,260 sq. mi./3,262 sq. km.

Val·les Ma·ri·ner·is /và less merri náiriss/ *n.* a system of valleys and canyons in the equatorial region of Mars 2,500 mi./4,000 km long, up to 150 mi./240 wide, and 4 mi./6.5 km deep

val·ley /vállee/ (*plural* **-leys**) *n.* **1.** GEOG LOW-LYING AREA a long low area of land, often with a river or stream running through it, that is surrounded by higher ground **2.** GEOG LOW-LYING LAND AROUND A RIVER a large area of low-lying land around a river and its tributaries **3.** GEOG VALLEY-SHAPED HOLLOW a long sunken area or groove shaped like a valley **4.** BUILDING ANGLE BETWEEN ROOF SLOPES the angle formed where two slopes of a roof intersect [13thC. Via Old French *valee* from, ultimately, Latin *valles* "valley" (source of English *vale*).] —**val·leyed** *adj.*

val·ley fe·ver *n.* = **coccidioidomycosis** [Named for the San Joaquin Valley in California]

Val·ley Forge /vállee fàwrj/ historic site in Pennsylvania, northwest of Philadelphia on the Schuylkill River, where George Washington kept his winter quarters during the Revolution

Val·ley of the Kings gorge on the western bank of the Nile River, southern Egypt. It was the burial site of pharaohs of the New Kingdom (1570–1070 B.C.).

Val·lis Al·pes /vàlliss ál pèz/ *n.* a valley on the Moon northeast of Mare Imbrium, running approximately from west to east and cutting across Montes Alpes

val·lum /válləm/ (*plural* **-lums** *or* **-la** /-ə/) *n.* an ancient Roman fortification or embankment, built for military defense [Early 17thC. From Latin, from *vallus* "palisade, stake."]

Hulton-Deutsch Collection/Corbis

Dame Ninette de Valois

Val·ois /válwaa/, **Dame Ninette de** (*b.* 1898) Irish-born British dancer and choreographer. She was a cofounder in 1931 of the Royal Ballet and Royal Ballet School in London. Real name **Edris Stannus**

va·lo·ni·a /və lṓnee ə/ *n.* the dried acorn cups and unripe acorns of a Eurasian oak, used in the tanning industry and in the manufacture of inks and dyes [Early 18thC. Via Italian from, ultimately, Greek *balanos* "acorn."]

val·or /vállər/ *n.* courage, especially that shown in war or battle [Late 16thC. Via Italian *valore* from Latin *valor*, from *valere* "to be strong."]

val·or·ize /vállə rīz/ (**-ized, -iz·ing, -iz·es**) *vt.* to set and maintain the price of a commodity at an artificially high level through government action [Early 20thC. Via Portuguese *valorizar*, from *valor* "value," from late Latin (see VALOR).] —**val·or·i·za·tion** /vàllərі záysh'n/ *n.*

val·or·ous /vállərəss/ *adj.* having or showing courage, especially in war or battle —**val·or·ous·ly** *adv.* —**val·or·ous·ness** *n.*

val·our /vállər/ *n.* U.K. = valor

Val·pa·rai·so /vàlpə rāyzō, -rī́zō/ **1.** city and port in central Chile. It is the capital city of Valparaiso Region. Population: 274,228 (1992). **2.** city in northwestern Indiana, south of Lake Michigan and southwest of Michigan City. Population: 25,804 (1996).

Val·po·li·cel·la /vaal pōlə chéllə/ *n.* a light red Italian wine from the northern province of Verona [Early 20thC. Named for the district of *Valpolicella* in northwestern Italy, where it is made.]

val·pro·ate /val prṓ àyt/, **val·pro·ic ac·id** /val prṓ ik-/ *n.* a drug used to help control epileptic convulsions [Late 20thC. Coined from *valproic acid* (from VALERIC ACID + PROPYL) + -ATE.]

Val·sal·va ma·neu·ver /val sálvə-/ *n.* MED **1.** FORCING OF AIR INTO THE MIDDLE EAR the action of attempting to breathe out when the mouth is closed and the nostrils are held shut, thereby forcing air into the middle ear via the eustachian tubes. It can be used to test if the eustachian tubes are blocked and to counteract increased external pressure on the eardrum. **2.** INCREASING OF PRESSURE IN THE THORACIC CAVITY the action of attempting to breathe out against a closed glottis, which increases pressure in the thoracic cavity and hinders the return of venous blood to the heart. When the breath is released the trapped blood flows rapidly through the heart, causing a brief increase followed by a brief decrease in heart rate. [Named for Antonio Maria *Valsalva* (1666–1723), an Italian anatomist]

valse /vaals/ *n.* a waltz, especially one written by a French composer or given a French title [Late 18thC. Via French from German *Walzer* (see WALTZ).]

val·u·a·ble /vállyoo əb'l/ *adj.* **1.** WORTH A GREAT DEAL OF MONEY having significant monetary value **2.** USEFUL having great importance or usefulness ○ *a valuable insight* **3.** HELD DEAR cherished or esteemed because of personal qualities **4.** RARE highly prized because of being in short or limited supply **5.** ABLE TO BE VALUED capable of being assigned a value ■ *n.* VALUABLE ITEM a possession, especially a piece of jewelry, that has significant monetary value —**val·u·a·ble·ness** *n.* —**val·u·a·bly** *adv.*

val·u·a·ble con·sid·er·a·tion *n.* in English contract law, something given or undertaken as part of an agreement between two parties that has some objective value and so makes the agreement a valid contract. For example, to form a valid contract for the sale of a car, valuable consideration is the money paid to the person selling the car.

val·u·ate /vállyoo àyt/ (**-at·ed, -at·ing, -ates**) *vt.* to value something

val·u·a·tion /vàllyoo áysh'n/ *n.* **1.** APPRAISAL OF COST the act of determining the value or price of something, especially property **2.** PRICE the price of something established by appraisal of its quality, condition, and desirability, or of the cost of replacement **3.** ESTIMATE OF IMPORTANCE an estimate of the importance or usefulness of something —**val·u·a·tion·al** *adj.* —**val·u·a·tion·al·ly** *adv.*

val·u·a·tor /vállyoo àytər/ *n.* somebody who assesses the value of objects such as jewelry or works of art

val·ue /vállyoo/ *n.* **1.** MONETARY WORTH an amount expressed in money or another medium of exchange that is thought to be a fair exchange for something ○ *goods to the value of $500* **2.** FULL RECOVERED WORTH the adequate or satisfactory return on or recompense for something ○ *it's value for money* **3.** WORTH OR IMPORTANCE the worth, importance, or usefulness of something to somebody ○ *a ring with great sentimental value* **4.** LING MEANING the exact meaning or significance of a word **5.** MATH NUMERICAL QUANTITY a numerical quantity assigned to a mathematical symbol **6.** MUSIC LENGTH OF A NOTE the length of time that a note or pause is held **7.** ARTS SHADE OF A COLOR in painting and drawing, the lightness or darkness of a color **8.** PHON SOUND REPRESENTED the quality or tone of a speech sound that a letter or written character represents, especially in a particular context when in isolation it can represent more than one sound ■ **val·ues** *npl.* PRINCIPLES OR STANDARDS the accepted principles or standards of an individual or a group ■ *vt.* (**-ued, -u·ing, -ues**) **1.** ESTIMATE THE VALUE OF SOMETHING to estimate or determine the value of something ○ *the painting was valued at $5,000* **2.** RATE SOMETHING to rate something according to its perceived worth, importance, or usefulness **3.** REGARD HIGHLY to regard somebody or something as important or useful ○ *I value her as a friend.* [14thC. From Old French, from *valoir* "to be worth," from Latin *valere* "to be powerful."]

val·ue add·ed *n.* the amount by which the value of a product increases as it proceeds through the various stages of its manufacture and distribution

val·ue-add·ed *adj.* relating to the increasing value of a product as it proceeds through the various stages of its manufacture and distribution

val·ue-add·ed tax *n.* full form of **VAT**

val·ue date *n.* in the calculation of exchange rates, the date on which a transaction is judged to have occurred

val·ued pol·i·cy *n.* an insurance policy in which the amount payable for a valid claim is established when the policy is issued and is independent of the value of a loss subsequently incurred

val·ue-free *adj.* not affected by or based on value judgments

val·ue judg·ment *n.* a judgment of the worth, appropriateness, or importance of somebody or something made on the basis of personal beliefs, opinions, or prejudices rather than facts

val·ue·less /vállyooləss/ *adj.* having no value —**val·ue·less·ness** *n.*

val·ue sys·tem *n.* a set of personal principles and standards

val·u·ta /və lóotə/ *n.* the value of one nation's currency in terms of its exchange rate with another currency [Late 19thC. From Italian, "value."]

val·val /válvəl/, **val·var** /válvər/ *adj.* = **valvular**

val·vate /vál vàyt/ *adj.* **1.** WITH VALVES having valves or parts similar to valves **2.** BOT NOT OVERLAPPING IN BUD used to describe sepals or petals that touch but do not overlap in the bud. ◊ **imbricate 3.** BOT TAKING PLACE BY MEANS OF VALVES used to describe the splitting open of the seed capsules of the iris or lily that takes place by means of valves [Early 19thC. From Latin *valvatus* "having folding doors," from *valva* (see VALVE).]

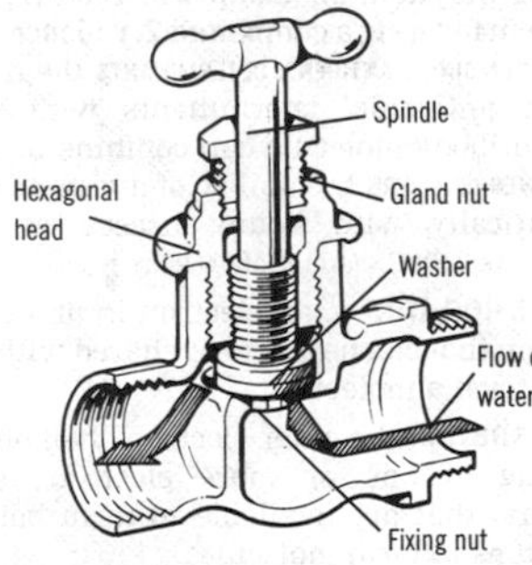

Valve

valve /valv/ *n.* **1.** ENG DEVICE THAT CONTROLS LIQUID FLOW a device that controls the movement of liquids or gases through piping or other passages by opening or closing ports and channels **2.** MUSIC PART ON A BRASS INSTRUMENT a device in some brass instruments that diverts air down tubes of varying length, thereby altering the pitch **3.** *U.K.* ELECTRON ENG = **vacuum tube 4.** ANAT CLOSABLE FLAP IN AN ORGAN a membranous structure in a hollow organ or vessel such as the heart or a vein that prevents the return flow of fluid passing through it by folding or closing **5.** BOT PART OF A SEED POD any of the segments of the wall of a seed pod or other fruit that splits apart to reveal the contents **6.** BOT ANTHER FLAP a flap that acts like a lid in some types of anthers **7.** BOT PART OF THE CELL WALL either of the two parts of the silica-impregnated cell wall of a type of alga (**diatom**) that fit together like the lid and base of a box **8.** ZOOL SEPARABLE PART OF A SHELL a hinged part of the shell of a brachiopod or some mollusks **9.** ZOOL SINGLE-UNIT SHELL the single-unit shell of a snail and some other mollusks **10.** DOOR LEAF a leaf of a double or folding door (*archaic*) [15thC. From Latin *valva* "leaf of a folding door," of uncertain origin.] —**valve·less** *adj.*

valve gear *n.* a mechanical device that controls the valves of a reciprocating engine

valve-in-head en·gine *n.* an internal-combustion engine with its inlet and exhaust valves in the cylinder head, not in the engine block

valve spring *n.* **1.** SPRING HOLDING A VALVE CLOSED a spiral spring that holds a valve closed in the cylinder head of an internal-combustion engine **2.** SPRING THAT CLOSES A VALVE a spring that closes an opened valve

val·vu·la /válvyələ/ (*plural* **-lae** /-lèe/) *n.* ANAT = **valvule** *n.* 1 [Early 17thC. From modern Latin, from Latin *valva* (see VALVE).]

val·vu·lar /válvyələr/ *adj.* **1.** RELATING TO VALVES relating to, having, or acting like a valve or set of valves **2.** AFFECTING VALVES involving or affecting a valve or set of valves

val·vule /vál vyoo͞l/ *n.* **1.** ANAT SMALL VALVE a small valve or a part that functions or looks like one **2.** BOT = **palea** [Mid-18thC. Variant of VALVULA.]

val·vu·li·tis /vàlvyə lítiss/ *n.* inflammation of a valve in the body, especially one in the heart, often caused by rheumatic fever

val·vu·lo·plast·y /válvyələ plàstee/ (*plural* **-plas·ties**) *n.* plastic surgery performed to repair a valve in the body, especially one in the heart [Mid-20thC. Coined from VALVULE + -PLASTY.]

vam·brace /vám bràyss/ *n.* a piece of armor worn over the forearm as protection [14thC. Via Anglo-Norman *vauntbras* from Old French *avantbras*, from *avant* "before" + *bras* "arm" (source of English *brace*).]

va·moose /va mo͞oss, və mo͞oss/ (**-moosed, -moos·ing, -moos·es**) *vi.* to leave in a hurried way (*slang*) [Mid-19thC. From Spanish *vamos* "let us go."]

WORD KEY: REGIONAL NOTE

The term ***vamoose*** is now widespread through the United States, spreading into general currency from Texas to California and further strengthened with the recent accelerated influx of Mexican-Americans across the country.

vamp[1] /vamp/ *n.* SEDUCTIVE WOMAN a woman who is believed to use her sexual attractiveness for the seduction and manipulation of others ■ *v.* (**vamped, vamp·ing, vamps**) **1.** *vti.* SEDUCE SOMEBODY to seduce and manipulate somebody by appearing to offer sexual intercourse **2.** *vi.* ACT LIKE VAMP to act like or play the role of a vamp [Early 20thC. Shortening of VAMPIRE.] —**vamp·er** *n.* —**vamp·ish** *adj.* —**vamp·ish·ly** *adv.* —**vamp·y** *adj.*

vamp[2] /vamp/ *n.* **1.** CLOTHES UPPER PART OF A SHOE the upper part of a shoe that covers the front part of the foot **2.** SOMETHING PATCHED UP something repaired so as to appear new **3.** REHASHING OF SOMETHING a reworking of something already used or available, especially a book or article **4.** MUSIC IMPROVISED MUSICAL INTRODUCTION an improvised musical introduction or accompaniment that is repeated as necessary until the entry of the solo line ■ *v.* (**vamped, vamp·ing, vamps**) **1.** *vt.* CLOTHES PUT A VAMP ON A SHOE to put a vamp on a shoe **2.** *vti.* MUSIC IMPROVISE A MUSICAL INTRODUCTION OR ACCOMPANIMENT to improvise a musical introduction or accompaniment for a solo line [14thC. Shortening of Old French *avantpié*, from *avant* "before" + *pié* "foot."] —**vamp·er** *n.*

vamp up *vt.* **1.** REPAIR to rework or renovate something **2.** FABRICATE to make something up or improvise something

vam·pire /vám pīr/ *n.* **1.** MYTHOL BLOODSUCKING EVIL SPIRIT in European folklore, a dead person believed to rise each night from the grave and suck blood from the living for sustenance **2.** SOMEBODY PREDATORY somebody who preys on other people for financial or emotional gain **3.** ZOOL = **vampire bat 4.** THEATER TRAPDOOR a trapdoor on the floor of a stage (*technical*) [Mid-18thC. Via French or German from Serbo-Croat *vampir*, of uncertain origin: perhaps via Russian from Kazan Tatar *ubyr* "witch."] —**vam·pir·ic** /vam peérik/ *adj.* —**vam·pir·i·cal** /-peérik'l/ *adj.* —**vam·pir·ish** /vám pīrish/ *adj.*

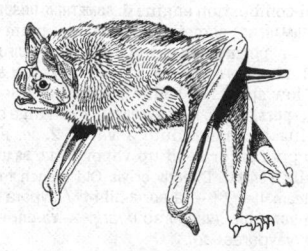

vam·pire bat *n.* a bat found in tropical and subtropical Central and South America that bites the skin of birds or other mammals and laps the blood. It takes relatively little blood from its victims but can transmit serious diseases such as rabies. Family: Desmodontidae.

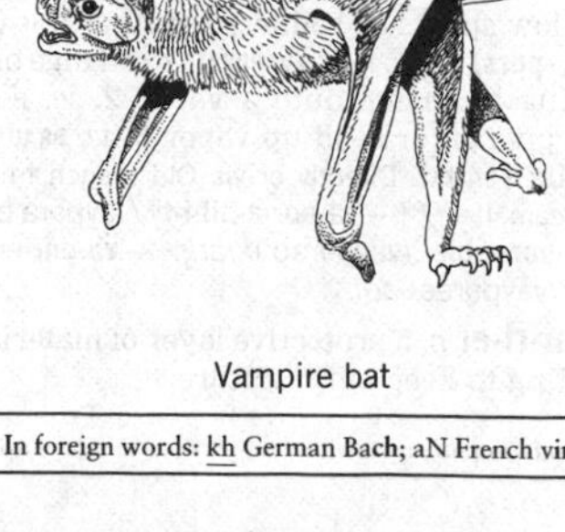

Vampire bat

vam·pir·ism /vám pī rìzzəm/ *n.* **1.** BELIEF IN VAMPIRES the belief that corpses can leave their graves at night and suck the blood of living people **2.** STATE OF BEING A VAMPIRE the supposed state or practices of a vampire **3.** FINANCIAL OR EMOTIONAL EXPLOITATION the act of preying on other people for financial or emotional gain

van[1] /van/ *n.* **1.** AUTOMOT ENCLOSED MOTOR VEHICLE a motor vehicle that has rear or side doors or sliding side panels and is used for transporting goods or people **2.** *U.K.* RAIL RAILROAD CAR a closed railroad car for goods, or the section of the car for the conductor, luggage, packages, or mail ■ *v.* (**vanned, van·ning, vans**) TRANSP **1.** *vt.* TRANSPORT BY VAN to move something from one place to another by van **2.** *vi.* TRAVEL IN A VAN to drive or travel in a van [Early 19thC. Shortening of CARAVAN.]

van[2] /van/ *n.* **1.** AGRIC WINNOWING DEVICE a device used for winnowing grain (*archaic*) **2.** BIRDS WING a bird's wing (*archaic or literary*) [15thC. Originally a dialect form of FAN.]

van[3] /van/ *n.* the leading position [Early 17thC. Shortening of VANGUARD.]

Van /van, vaan/ city in eastern Turkey, the capital of Van Province. It lies on the eastern shore of Lake Van, about 50 mi./80 km west of the Turkish-Iranian border. Population: 153,111 (1990).

Van, Lake saltwater lake in eastern Turkey, between the sources of the Euphrates and Tigris rivers, at an altitude of 5,643 ft./1,720 m. Area: 1,453 sq. mi./3,763 sq. km.

van. *abbr.* vanilla

van·a·date /vánnə dàyt/ *n.* a salt or ester of vanadium [Mid-19thC. Formed from VANADIUM.]

va·na·dic /və náydik, -náddik/ *adj.* consisting of or containing high-valence vanadium. ◊ **vanadous** [Mid-19thC. Formed from VANADIUM.]

va·na·di·nite /və náyd'n īt, və nádd'n-/ *n.* a rare lead and vanadium mineral, brown, red, or yellow in color, that is found with other lead minerals and is a source of vanadium. Formula: $Pb_5(VO_4)_3Cl$. [Mid-19thC. Formed from VANADIUM.]

va·na·di·um /və náydee əm/ *n.* a poisonous silvery-white metallic chemical element used in making tough steel alloys and as a catalyst. Symbol **V** [Mid-19thC. Via modern Latin from Old Norse *Vanadis*, a Scandinavian goddess.]

va·na·di·um pent·ox·ide *n.* a yellow or red crystalline compound used in glass-making and as a catalyst. Formula: V_2O_5.

va·na·di·um steel *n.* a low-alloy steel containing the element vanadium for added strength

va·na·dous /və náydəss, vánnədəss/ *adj.* consisting of or containing low-valence vanadium. ◊ **vanadic** [Mid-19thC. Formed from VANADIUM.]

Van Al·len /van állən/, **James** (*b.* 1914) U.S. physicist. A pioneer in high altitude and space research, he discovered (1958) two radiation belts that encircle the Earth. Full name **James Alfred Van Allen**

Van Al·len belt, **Van Al·len ra·di·a·tion belt** *n.* either of two belts surrounding the Earth and containing charged particles held there by the Earth's magnetic field [Mid-20thC. Named for James VAN ALLEN.]

van·as·pa·ti /və náspətee/ *n.* a hydrogenated vegetable oil commonly used in Indian cooking instead of butter [Mid-20thC. From Sanskrit *vanas-pati*, literally "lord of the plants."]

Van Bu·ren /-byo͞orən/, **Martin** (1782–1862) U.S. statesman and 8th president of the United States. As president (1837–41) he supported the war against the Seminoles in Florida but opposed the annexation of Texas. Known as **Little Magician, Red Fox of Kinderhook**

Vance /vanss/, **Cyrus** (*b.* 1917) U.S. statesman. He resigned as Jimmy Carter's secretary of state (1977–80) after a failed attempt to rescue U.S. hostages in Iran. He subsequently worked as an international peace negotiator, notably in Bosnia (1992–93). Full name **Cyrus Roberts Vance**

Van·cou·ver /van ko͞ovər/ city and port in southwestern British Columbia, Canada, opposite Vancouver Island. Population: 514,008 (1996).

Van·cou·ver, Mount peak of St. Elias Range in southwestern Yukon Territory, Canada. Height: 15,840 ft./4,828 m.

Van·cou·ver, George (1757–98) British naval officer and explorer. He sailed with Captain James Cook and later was the first European to circumnavigate Vancouver Island, during a surveying expedition.

Van·cou·ver Is·land island off the southwestern coast of British Columbia, Canada. It is the largest island off western North America. Area: 12,079 sq. mi./31,284 sq. km.

van·da /vándə/ (*plural* **-das** *or* **-da**) *n.* an orchid native to East Asia and Australia with strap-shaped leaves and flowers that are typically flattened with a spur on the lip. There are many cultivated varieties and hybrids. Genus: *Vanda*. [Early 19thC. Via modern Latin from Sanskrit *vandā*.]

van·dal /vánd'l/ *n.* somebody who maliciously and deliberately defaces or destroys somebody else's property [Mid-16thC. From Latin *Vandalus*, of Germanic origin (see VANDAL).] —**van·dal·ish** *adj.*

Van·dal *n.* a member of an ancient Germanic people who originated in Jutland, now in Denmark. They swept through Roman Europe during the 3rd and 4th centuries A.D., conquering Gaul, Spain, Rome, and parts of North Africa, before being defeated at Carthage in 533. [Old English *Wendlas* (plural) "Vandals," from prehistoric Germanic] —**Van·dal·ic** /van dállik/ *adj.* —**Van·dal·ism** /vánd'l ìzzəm/ *n.*

van·dal·ism /vánd'l ìzzəm/ *n.* the malicious and deliberate defacement or destruction of somebody else's property —**van·dal·is·tic** /vànd'l ístik/ *adj.*

van·dal·ize /vánd'l īz/ (**-ized, -iz·ing, -iz·es**) *vt.* to deface, destroy, or otherwise damage private or public property maliciously and deliberately —**van·dal·i·za·tion** /vànd'li záysh'n/ *n.*

van·da or·chid *n.* = **vanda**

van de Graaff gen·er·a·tor /ván də graf-/ *n.* an electrostatic machine that produces electrical discharges at extremely high voltages, used in particle accelerators and for testing electrical insulators. The electric charge from a source of direct current accumulates on a high-speed belt inside an insulated metal sphere filled with Freon™ or nitrogen gas under high pressure. [Named for R. J. *van de Graaff* (1901–67), U.S. physicist.]

Van·den·berg /vándən bùrg/, **Arthur H.** (1884–1951) U.S. statesman. A senator from 1928, he was influential in setting up the United Nations (1945). Full name **Arthur Hendrick Vandenberg**

Van·der·bilt /vándər bilt/, **Cornelius** (1794–1877) U.S. industrialist. He made a fortune from his steamship company. In 1862 he began investing in the railroads that he consolidated in 1872 as the New York Central. He was reputed to be the richest man in the United States when he died. Known as **Commodore Vanderbilt**

van der Waals' e·qua·tion /vàn dər wáalz-, vàn dər wáwlz-/ *n.* a modified equation of state describing the physical behavior of gases that takes into account the volumes of molecules and the interactions between them. It explains the difference in behavior between a real gas and an ideal gas that obeys the gas laws. [Named for Johannes *van der Waals* (1837–1923), Dutch physicist]

van der Waals' force *n.* a weak attractive force between atoms or molecules resulting from the positioning of the electrons within the interacting particles [See VAN DER WAALS' EQUATION]

Van Die·men's Land /van deémənz-, vaan-/ former name for **Tasmania**

Van Dor·en /-dáwrən/, **Mark** (1894–1972) U.S. poet and critic. His *Collected Poems 1928–38* (1939) won a Pulitzer Prize. Full name **Mark Albert Van Doren**

Van·dyke /van dīk/ *n.* **1.** = **Vandyke beard 2.** CLOTHES = **Vandyke collar 3.** V-SHAPE a V-shape forming part of a decorative border on material or clothing **4.** DECORATIVE BORDER a decorative border on material or clothing made up of V-shaped points [Mid-18thC. Named for Sir Anthony *Van Dyck* (1599–1641), Flemish painter, in reference to various characteristic features of his paintings.] —**van·dyked** *adj.*

Van·dyke beard *n.* a short, neatly trimmed, pointed beard

Van·dyke brown *adj.* DARK BROWN of a deep rich brown

color (*hyphenated before a noun*) ■ *n.* **BROWN COLOR OR PIGMENT** a deep rich brown color or pigment

Van·dyke col·lar *n.* a large white collar of linen or lace that has a deeply indented edge

Van·dyke stitch *n.* a V-shaped variation of cross stitch, used as a filling stitch to form a solid decoration

vane /vayn/ *n.* **1. ROTATING BLADE** a flat blade mounted as part of a set in a circle so as to rotate under the action of wind or liquid. Windmill sails and turbine blades are examples. **2.** METEOROL **WEATHERVANE** a weathervane **3.** ARMS **STABILIZER ON A MISSILE** a stabilizing or guiding blade on a missile **4.** BIRDS **BLADE OF A FEATHER** the flat part of a feather, consisting of interlocking rows of barbs. Each feather has two vanes, one on each side. **5. PART OF A LEVELING ROD** the moving part on a leveling rod **6.** COMPASS **COMPASS OR QUADRANT SIGHT** a sight on a compass or quadrant [15thC. Originally a dialect form of FANE.] —**vaned** *adj.*

Vä·nern, Lake /vénnərn, váynərn/ the largest lake in Sweden, situated in the southwest of the country. Area: 2,156 sq. mi./5,584 sq. km.

Van Fleet /-fleet/, **James A.** (1892–1992) U.S. soldier. A veteran of both World Wars, he was field commander (1951–53) of United Nations forces during the Korean War. Full name **James Alward Van Fleet**

vang /vang/ *n.* a guy rope forming part of a pair that extend from a gaff to the deck [Mid-18thC. Variant of FANG.]

van Gogh /vaan kháwkh, van gṓ, -gáwkh/, **Vincent** (1853–90) Dutch painter. His highly expressive canvases are characterized by their bright colors and vigorous brushstrokes. Full name **Vincent Willem van Gogh**

van·guard /ván gaard/ *n.* **1. LEADING POSITION OR PEOPLE** the leading position of a movement, field, or cultural trend, or the people who are foremost in a movement, field, or cultural trend **2.** MIL **ADVANCE TROOPS** the military divisions of an army or navy that lead the advance into battle [15thC. Shortening of French *avant-garde*, from *avant* "before" + *garde* "guard."] —**van·guard·ism** *n.* —**van·guard·ist** *n.*

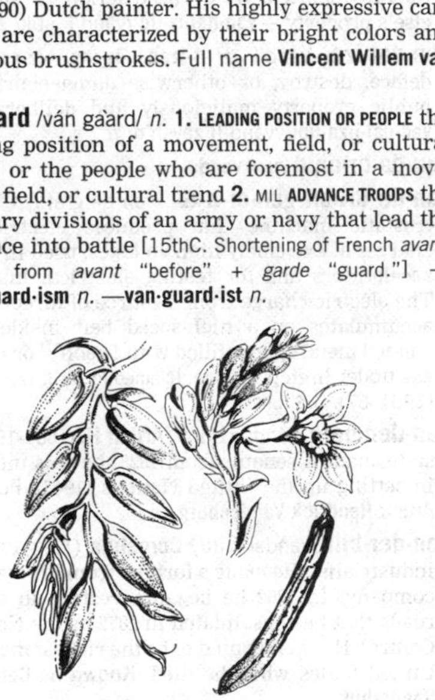

Vanilla

va·nil·la /və níllə/ *n.* **1.** PLANTS **VINE WITH SEED PODS USED AS FLAVORING** a tropical American vine of the orchid family cultivated for its seed pods, from which a popular flavoring is produced. Genus: *Vanilla.* **2.** PLANTS **VANILLA POD** the long, narrow, fleshy seedpod of the vanilla vine **3.** COOK **VANILLA FLAVORING** a flavoring extracted from the seed pods of the vanilla vine and used in cooking ■ *adj.* **1.** COOK **FLAVORED WITH VANILLA** flavored with vanilla, or having a flavor of vanilla **2. PLAIN OR DULL** lacking outstanding or interesting characteristics ○ *vanilla software* [Mid-17thC. From Spanish *vainilla*, literally "small sheath," from *vaina* "sheath," from Latin *vagina*. From the shape of the vanilla seed pod.]

va·nil·la bean *n.* = **vanilla** *n.* 2

va·nil·la plant *n.* a plant used commercially as a source of vanilla pods. Latin name: *Vanilla planifolia.*

va·nil·lic /və níllik/ *adj.* resembling, containing, or derived from vanilla or vanillin

va·nil·lin /və níllin, vánnəlin/ *n.* a white aldehyde obtained from vanilla or prepared synthetically and used as a flavoring and in perfumes. Formula: $C_8H_8O_3$.

Va·nir /vaa neer/ *npl.* in Norse mythology, a race of peace-loving gods [From Old Norse, of uncertain origin: probably ultimately from an Indo-European word meaning "to desire," which is also the ancestor of English *win* and *venerate*]

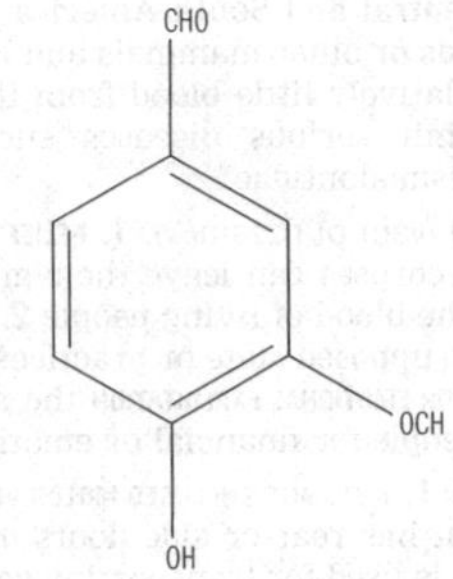

Vanillin

van·ish /vánnish/ (**-ished, -ish·ing, -ish·es**) *vi.* **1. DISAPPEAR SUDDENLY** to disappear suddenly or inexplicably ○ *It can't just have vanished!* **2. STOP EXISTING** to cease to exist **3.** MATH **BECOME ZERO** to assume or be given the value of zero (*refers to a function or variable*) [14thC. From the Old French stem *esvaniss-*, from *esvanir*, from Latin *evanescere* "to die out, pass away," from, ultimately, *vanus* "empty" (see VAIN).] —**van·ish·er** *n.* —**van·ish·ing·ly** *adv.* —**van·ish·ment** *n.*

van·ish·ing point /vánnishing-/ *n.* **1. APPARENT MEETING POINT OF PARALLEL LINES** a point in a drawing or painting at which parallel lines seem to meet as represented in perspective **2. POINT WHERE SOMETHING DISAPPEARS** a point at which something disappears or ceases being

van·i·ty /vánnətee/ (*plural* **-ties**) *n.* **1. EXCESSIVE PRIDE** excessive pride, especially in your appearance ○ *She is entirely free of personal vanity.* **2. SOMETHING SOMEBODY IS VAIN ABOUT** an instance or source of excessive pride **3. FUTILITY** the state or fact of being futile, worthless, or empty of significance **4. SOMETHING FUTILE** something that is considered futile, worthless, or empty of significance **5.** = **vanity case 6.** = **dressing table 7.** *U.S., NZ* **CABINET HOLDING A SINK** a cabinet that holds a sink and its plumbing, usually with drawers or shelves under the sink for storage [13thC. Via Old French from Latin *vanitas*, from *vanus* "empty" (see VAIN).]

van·i·ty case, van·i·ty *n.* **1. SMALL COSMETICS CASE** a small case or bag in which somebody carries cosmetics **2.** ACCESSORIES **COMPACT** a compact (*dated*)

Van·i·ty Fair, van·i·ty fair *n.* a place, especially a very large city or the world in general, considered to be frivolous and full of idle worthless amusements (*literary*) [Coined by John BUNYAN in his *Pilgrim's Progress* (1678)]

van·i·ty plate *n.* a license plate for a motor vehicle for which the owner has paid extra to be able to choose its numbers and letters

van·i·ty pub·lish·er, van·i·ty press *n.* a publishing house that publishes an author's work in return for payment from the author. Vanity publishers do not typically market or distribute their publications.

van·i·ty pub·lish·ing *n.* the business of publishing books at the author's expense

van·i·ty ta·ble *n.* = **dressing table**

van·i·ty tel·e·phone num·ber *n.* a telephone number consisting of numbers chosen by the customer, usually so as to spell some mnemonic on the standard telephone dial

van·i·ty u·nit *n. U.K.* = **dressing table**

van·load /ván lṑd/ *n.* the amount of goods or passengers that a van can transport at one time

Van Loon /-lo͝on, -lṓn/, **Hendrick Willem** (1882–1944) Dutch-born U.S. historian. He is known for his bestselling *The Story of Mankind* (1921) and other works of popular history.

van·pool /ván po͞ol/ *n.* **VAN-SHARING ARRANGEMENT FOR COMMUTERS** an arrangement by which a number of people travel together to and from work in a shared van ■ *vi.* (**-pooled, -pool·ing, -pools**) **COMMUTE IN A SHARED VAN** to convey somebody to and from work in a shared van, or to be conveyed in this way [Late 20thC. *Van* from VAN[1].]

van·quish /vángkwish/ (**-quished, -quish·ing, -quish·es**) *vt.* **1. DEFEAT IN BATTLE** to defeat an opponent or opposing army in a battle or fight **2. DEFEAT IN COMPETITION** to prove convincingly superior to somebody in a contest, competition, or argument **3. OVERCOME EMOTION** to overcome, suppress, or subdue an emotion, feeling, or idea [14thC. Formed from Old French *venquis*, from *veintre*, from Latin *vincere* "conquer" (source of English *convince, victory,* and *evict*).] —**van·quish·a·ble** *adj.* —**van·quish·er** *n.* —**van·quish·ment** *n.*

WORD KEY: SYNONYMS

See Synonyms at ***defeat***.

Van Rens·se·laer /-rènssə leer, -rénssələr/, **Stephen** (1764–1839) U.S. soldier and politician. A major landowner in New York State, he commanded the New York militia during the War of 1812 and also promoted educational and development projects.

van·tage /vántij/ *n.* **1. ADVANTAGEOUS POSITION** a position that provides an advantage **2. SUPERIORITY IN A CONTEST** superiority in a contest or competition **3.** = **vantage point** [14thC. From Old French *avantage* (see ADVANTAGE).] —**van·tage·less** *adj.*

van·tage point *n.* **1. van·tage point, van·tage POSITION GIVING A GOOD VIEW** a position or location that provides a broad view or perspective of something **2. PERSONAL STANDPOINT** a personal point of view

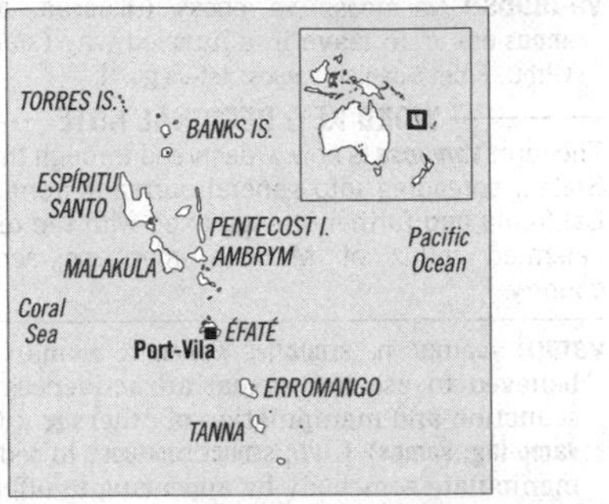

Vanuatu

Van·u·a·tu /vaannoo aa too/ republic in the southwestern Pacific Ocean, comprising approximately 80 islands. Language: English, French. Currency: vatu. Capital: Port-Vila. Population: 172,000. Area: 4,707 sq. mi./12,190 sq. km. Official name **Republic of Vanuatu**. Former name **New Hebrides**

van·ward /vánwərd/ *adj.* **AT THE FRONT** in or at the front or edge of something ■ *adv.* **MOVING TOWARD THE FRONT** moving toward the front or edge of something

Van·zet·ti /van zéttee/, **Bartolomeo** (1888–1927) Italian-born U.S. anarchist. With Nicola Sacco, he was convicted of murder in 1921 and executed in 1927 despite a lengthy appeal and worldwide protests that the verdict was politically motivated. The case continued to generate controversy, and modern scholars believe that Vanzetti was probably innocent.

vap·id /váppid/ *adj.* **1. DULL** lacking interest or liveliness **2. INSIPID** lacking strength, taste, or flavor [Mid-17thC. From Latin *vapidus* "insipid."] —**va·pid·i·ty** /və píddətee/ *n.* —**vap·id·ly** /váppidlee/ *adv.* —**vap·id·ness** /váppidnəss/ *n.*

va·por /váypər/ *n.* **1.** PHYS **GASEOUS SUBSTANCE** a gaseous substance at a temperature lower than that at which it can be liquefied or solidified by an appropriate increase in pressure alone **2.** PHYS **MOISTURE PARTICLES** moisture or some other matter visible in the air as mist, clouds, fumes, or smoke **3.** PHYS **GASEOUS STATE OF A SUBSTANCE** the gaseous state of a liquid or solid at a temperature below its boiling point **4.** CHEM **VAPORIZED SUBSTANCE** a substance prepared for military, industrial, or medical use in vaporized form **5.** ENG **GAS AND AIR MIXTURE** a combination of air with a gaseous substance such as that of air and gasoline in an internal-combustion engine **6. SOMETHING UNSUBSTANTIAL AND IMPERMANENT** something without material existence or permanence (*archaic*) **7. FANCIFUL IDEA** a fanciful idea (*archaic*) ■ **va·pors** *npl.* **LOW SPIRITS** a bout of low spirits or sadness (*archaic*) ■ *v.* (**-pored, -por·ing, -pors**) **1.** *vti.* PHYS **EVAPORATE** to change or cause something to change into a vapor **2.** *vi.* PHYS **EMIT VAPOR** to give off or send up vapor **3.** *vi.* **BRAG** to talk boastfully [14thC. Directly or via Old French from Latin *vapor* "steam, heat."] —**va·por·a·bil·i·ty** /vàypərə bíllətee/ *n.* —**va·por·a·ble** /váypərəb'l/ *adj.* —**va·por·er** *n.* —**va·por·y** /váypəree/ *adj.*

va·por bar·ri·er *n.* a protective layer of material used in building to keep out moisture

va·por den·si·ty *n.* the density of a gas or vapor in relation to that of hydrogen

va·por·es·cence /vàypə réssəns/ *n.* the formation or creation of vapor —**va·por·es·cent** *adj.*

va·por·et·to /vàypəréttō/ (*plural* **-ti** /-réttee/ *or* **-tos**) *n.* a motorboat for transporting passengers along the canals in Venice, Italy [Early 20thC. From Italian, literally "small steamboat," from *vapore*, from Latin *vapor* (see VAPOR).]

va·por·if·ic /vàypə ríffik/ *adj.* **1. PRODUCING VAPOR** producing, causing, or becoming vapor **2. BEING VAPOR** being, containing, or resembling vapor **3. VOLATILE** capable of changing easily from a liquid or solid state into vapor

va·por·ize /váypə rīz/ (**-ized, -iz·ing, -iz·es**) *vti.* **1. CHANGE INTO VAPOR** to change into or cause something to change into vapor **2. VANISH OR MAKE VANISH** to vanish or cause somebody or something to vanish **3. ANNIHILATE OR BE ANNIHILATED** to destroy somebody or something so completely that the person or object is turned into a gas or vapor, or to be destroyed in this way —**va·por·iz·a·ble** *adj.* —**va·por·i·za·tion** /vàypəri záysh'n/ *n.*

va·por·iz·er /váypə rīzər/ *n.* something used to produce a vapor, especially a device used to vaporize a medication so that it can be inhaled

va·por lock *n.* a bubble of vaporized gasoline that blocks the normal flow of fuel in the line that supplies the carburetor of an internal-combustion engine

va·por·ous /váypərəss/ *adj.* **1. BEING VAPOR** being, containing, or resembling vapor **2. PRODUCING VAPOR** producing, causing, or becoming vapor **3. VOLATILE** capable of changing easily from a liquid or solid state into vapor **4. UNSUBSTANTIAL** lacking material existence or permanence **5. FANCIFUL** of a fanciful, ridiculous, or implausible nature **6. OBSCURED BY VAPOR** made hard to see because of being obscured by mist or vapor —**va·por·os·i·ty** /vàypə róssətee/ *n.* —**va·por·ous·ly** /váypərəsslee/ *adv.* —**va·por·ous·ness** /-rəssnəss/ *n.*

va·por pres·sure, va·por ten·sion *n.* the pressure exerted by a vapor, particularly a vapor in contact with its liquid form

va·por trail *n.* a visible trail of condensed vapor left by an aircraft flying at high altitude

va·por·ware /váypər wàir/ *n.* new software that has been announced or advertised but has not yet been, and may never be, produced [Late 20thC. Formed from VAPOR, on the model of SOFTWARE.]

va·pour /váypər/ *n., vti.* U.K. = **vapor**

va·que·ro /vaa kérrō/ (*plural* **-ros**) *n. Southwest U.S.* a cowboy [Early 19thC. From Spanish, from *vaca* "cow."]

WORD KEY: REGIONAL NOTE

Vaquero is primarily a Texas word, where it contrasts in social usage with two other terms, the Anglicized *buckaroo* and the Mexican-Spanish loan *charro* ("rude, tasteless farm laborer"). In Texas, ***vaquero*** applies mainly to a working cowboy, especially a bachelor, *buckaroo* to a married working cowboy, and *charro* to an ostentatiously dressed pretender, a dude.

var *abbr.* volt-ampere reactive

VAR[1] /vaar/ *n.* a retail seller of computers who adds products to computers produced by manufacturers or performs services such as product integration or customization before selling the computers to customers. Abbr of **value-added reseller**

VAR[2] *abbr.* **1.** visual aural range **2.** volt-ampere reactive

var. *abbr.* **1.** variable **2.** variant **3.** variation

va·ra /vaárə/ *n.* a unit of length used in Spain, Portugal, and Latin America that can be from 32 in./80cm to 43 in./108 cm in length [Late 17thC. Via Spanish, "rod, yardstick," from Latin, "forked pole, trestle," from *varus* "bent."]

va·rac·tor /və ráktər/ *n.* a semiconductor diode with a capacitance that varies according to the voltage applied to it, used to regulate the frequency of electronic circuits in amplifiers [Mid-20thC. Contraction of VARIABLE + REACTOR.]

Va·ra·na·si /və raánəssee/, **Vā·rā·na·si** city in Uttar Pradesh State, northern India, on the Ganges River. It is an important place of pilgrimage for Hindus. Population: 925,962 (1991). Former name **Benares**

Va·ran·gi·an /və ránjee ən/ *n.* a member of any of the Scandinavian peoples who invaded and settled in Russia between the 8th and the 11th centuries [Late 18thC. Via medieval Latin *Varangus* and medieval Greek *baraggos* from, ultimately, Old Norse *Væringi*, from *vár* "pledge."] —**Va·ran·gi·an** *adj.*

Va·ran·gi·an Guard *n.* **1. SCANDINAVIAN FORCE GUARDING A BYZANTINE EMPEROR** the body of Scandinavian soldiers who were the Byzantine emperor's bodyguard in the 10th and 11th centuries **2. MEMBER OF THE VARANGIAN GUARD** a Scandinavian soldier in the Varangian Guard

var·ec /vérrək/ *n.* kelp [Late 17thC. From French.]

Mario Vargas Llosa

Var·gas Llo·sa /vaárgəss yṓssə/, **Mario** (*b.* 1936) Peruvian writer and critic. Many of his works deal with issues of social change and political corruption. Full name **Jorge Mario Pedro Varga Llosa**

vari- *prefix.* = **vario-** (*used before vowels*)

var·i·a /vérree ə/ *npl.* a collection, especially one of diverse literary works [Mid-20thC. From Latin, literally "various things."]

var·i·a·ble /vérree əb'l/ *adj.* **1. ABLE TO CHANGE** able or liable to change, especially suddenly and unpredictably **2.** METEOROL **LIKELY TO BLOW DIFFERENTLY** used to describe a wind that is likely to change direction or intensity **3. INCONSISTENT** inconsistent or uneven in quality or performance ○ *a variable performance* **4. FICKLE** inconstant and capricious in nature or character **5.** ELECTRON ENG **WITH RESISTANCE THAT VARIES** used to describe an electrical device that has a resistance that varies **6.** BIOL **DIFFERING FROM THE SPECIES NORM** used to describe a species that tends to differ in some characteristic from a recognized or known type **7.** MATH **WITH NO FIXED NUMERICAL VALUE** not having a fixed numerical value ■ *n.* **1. SOMETHING THAT CAN VARY** something capable of changing or varying **2.** ENG **FLUCTUATING DESIGN CRITERION** a parameter of an engineering design criterion whose value may fluctuate over a wide range, e.g., the dynamic load on a bridge caused by traffic **3.** MATH **SYMBOL FOR AN UNSPECIFIED QUANTITY** a symbol that represents an unspecified or unknown quantity, such as "x, y, z" or "a, b, c" **4.** MATH **RANGE OF VALUES** a range of values, any one of which is a solution to an algebraic expression **5.** LOGIC **LOGIC SYMBOL** a symbol, especially "x," "y," or "z," that is used usually in connection with quantifiers to represent individuals in a universe of discourse **6.** ASTRON = **variable star 7.** METEOROL **VARIABLE WIND** a wind that is likely to change in direction or intensity ■ **var·i·a·bles** *npl.* METEOROL **REGION OF VARIABLE WINDS** a region where variable winds are likely to be encountered [14thC. Via Old French from Latin *variabilis*, from *variare* (see VARY).] —**var·i·a·bil·i·ty** /vèrree ə bíllətee/ *n.* —**var·i·a·ble·ness** /vérree əb'lnəss/ *n.* —**var·i·a·bly** /vérree əblee/ *adv.*

var·i·a·ble cost *n.* a cost that varies directly in relation to output

var·i·a·ble-ge·om·e·try *adj.* used to describe an aircraft with wings that are hinged so that in flight they can move backward or forward. The wings are swept back to give low drag in supersonic flight and are moved forward for takeoff and landing.

var·i·a·ble-in·ter·val sched·ule *n.* PSYCHOL in operant conditioning, a rule for delivering reinforcements after varying amounts of time, e.g., at intervals averaging one minute. ◊ **variable-ratio schedule**

var·i·a·ble-rate mort·gage *n.* = **adjustable-rate mortgage**

var·i·a·ble-ra·tio sched·ule *n.* PSYCHOL in operant conditioning, a rule for delivering reinforcement after a varying number of responses, e.g., after every 10 responses on average. ◊ **variable-interval schedule**

var·i·a·ble star *n.* a star whose brightness changes at regular or irregular intervals

var·i·a·ble-sweep *adj.* AEROSP = **variable-geometry**

var·i·ance /vérree əns/ *n.* **1. CHANGE IN SOMETHING** a change that occurs in something **2. DIFFERENCE BETWEEN THINGS** a difference between two or more things **3. DISAGREEMENT** a difference of opinion or attitude ○ *The project failed because of variances of opinion about the next step.* **4.** LAW **DISCREPANCY IN SOMETHING** a discrepancy between two statements, documents, or steps in a legal proceeding **5.** LAW **LEGAL DISPENSATION** a dispensation to ignore a rule or law **6.** ACCT **DIFFERENCE IN COST** a difference between actual costs and the usual costs of production **7.** STATS **SQUARE OF STANDARD DEVIATION** a statistical measure of the spread or variation of a group of numbers in a sample, equal to the square of the standard deviation. Other measures of the spread are the ratio of the squared standard deviation to the sample size (**population variance**), and the ratio of the squared standard deviation to the sample size minus one (**sample variance**). [14thC. Via Old French from Latin *variantia*, from *variare* (see VARY).]

var·i·ant /vérree ənt/ *adj.* **1. DIFFERING SLIGHTLY** having or showing a difference from the norm ○ *variant pronunciations of common words* **2. CHANGEABLE** tending or likely to change ■ *n.* **1. SLIGHTLY DIFFERENT FORM** something that differs slightly from the norm **2.** LING **DIFFERENT FORM OR SPELLING OF WORD** a different form or spelling of a word or phrase from the standard one **3.** STATS = **random variable** [14thC. Via French, from *varier* "to vary," from Latin *variare* (see VARY).]

var·i·ate /vérree it, -àyt/ *n.* = **random variable** [Late 19thC. From Latin *variatus*, the past participle stem of *variare* (see VARY).]

var·i·a·tion /vèrree áysh'n/ *n.* **1. ACT OF VARYING** the act or a result of varying **2. STATE OF DIFFERING** the state or fact of differing, e.g., from a former state or value, from others of the same type, or from a standard **3. DEGREE OF DIFFERENCE** the degree to which something differs, e.g., from a former state or value, from others of the same type, or from a standard ○ *There is a variation of several points in the test scores.* **4. SOMETHING DIFFERING SLIGHTLY** something that differs slightly from the norm **5.** MUSIC **ALTERED VERSION OF A MUSICAL THEME** an altered version of an original musical theme or melody, such that the rhythm or harmony is varied or melodic embellishment is added. Variations are often found in sets, where a theme is followed by several variations. **6.** MUSIC **REPETITION OF A MUSICAL THEME** the repetition of a musical theme with modifications of melody, rhythm, or harmony **7.** MATH **MATHEMATICAL FUNCTION** a mathematical function that relates the values of one variable to those of other variables **8.** BIOL **BIOLOGICAL DEVIATION** a significant deviation from the normal biological form, function, or structure **9.** BIOL **LIVING ORGANISM THAT DIFFERS** a living organism that differs from the normal form for its kind **10.** BALLET **SOLO DANCE** a dance performed by a single dancer **11.** ASTRON **CHANGE IN ORBIT** a change in or deviation from the average motion or orbit of a celestial body **12.** ASTRON **TERM IN EQUATION DESCRIBING THE MOON'S MOTION** a term representing the gravitational attraction of the Sun on the Earth-Moon system in the mathematical equation for the Moon's motion **13.** PHYS = **magnetic declination 14.** LING **LINGUISTIC CHANGE** a change in conjugation, declension, inflection, or vowel form [14thC. Via French or directly from the Latin stem *variation-*, ultimately from *variare* (see VARY).] —**var·i·a·tion·al** *adj.* —**var·i·a·tion·al·ly** *adv.*

varic- *prefix.* = **varico-** (*used before vowels*)

var·i·ce·al /vérri seél/ *adj.* relating to or caused by a dilated blood vessel (**varix**) or blood vessels [Mid-20thC. Coined from VARICO- on the model of such words as CORNEAL and LARYNGEAL.]

var·i·cel·la /vèrri séllə/ *n.* chickenpox (*technical*) [Late 18thC. From modern Latin, literally "lesser smallpox," from *variola* (see VARIOLA).] —**va·ri·cel·lar** *adj.* —**var·i·cel·lous** *adj.*

var·i·cel·late /vèrri séllət, -sé làyt/ *adj.* used to describe a gastropod's shell that has small longitudinal ridges on its surface [Mid-20thC. Formed from modern Latin *varicella*, literally "little pustule," from medieval Latin *variola* (see VARIOLA), from the ridged surface.]

var·i·cel·la-zos·ter vi·rus /verri sèllə zóstər-/ *n.* a herpes virus that is responsible for chickenpox and shingles

var·i·ces plural of **varix**

varico- *prefix.* varix, varicose vein ○ *varicotomy* [From Latin *varic-*, the stem of *varix*]

var·i·co·cele /vérri kō seel/ *n.* a swelling of the veins in the spermatic cord of the scrotum. It may cause only slight discomfort but can affect fertility, so that surgical correction is required.

var·i·col·ored /vérri kùllərd/ *adj.* consisting of or having many colors

var·i·col·oured *adj.* U.K. = **varicolored**

var·i·cose /vérri kōss/, **var·i·cosed** *adj.* **1.** SWOLLEN swollen, knotted, or distended to a greater extent than normal **2.** MED WITH VARICOSE VEINS affected with or having varicose veins **3.** PRODUCING SWELLING relating to or producing swelling **4.** ZOOL RIDGED LIKE A GASTROPOD SHELL resembling a small longitudinal ridge on the shell of some gastropods [15thC. From Latin *varicosus*, from *varix* "varix."]

var·i·cos·es plural of **varicosis**

var·i·cose vein *n.* SWOLLEN VEIN a vein that has become abnormally swollen and knotted as a result of defective valves ■ **var·i·cose veins** *npl.* CONDITION WITH SWOLLEN VEINS a condition in which the surface veins, especially of the legs, become knotted and swollen, as a result of defects in the valves of the affected veins. The tendency to develop the condition may be inherited, while other causes include injury, inflammation, or thrombosis.

var·i·co·sis /vèrri kōssiss/ (*plural* **-ses** /-seez/) *n.* **1.** MED CONDITION WITH SWOLLEN VEINS a condition in which a vein or veins become swollen or knotted **2.** ZOOL FORMATION OF RIDGES ON A GASTROPOD SHELL the formation of small longitudinal ridges on the surface of a gastropod shell

var·i·cos·i·ty /vèrri kóssətee/ (*plural* **-ties**) *n.* **1.** SWOLLEN STATE the state of being abnormally swollen or knotted (**varicose**) **2.** VARICOSE VEIN a varicose vein (*technical*) **3.** HAVING SWOLLEN VEINS the condition of suffering from or having abnormally swollen or enlarged veins

var·i·cot·o·my /vèrri kóttəmee/ (*plural* **-mies**) *n.* a surgical incision into a swollen vein, usually performed to treat varicose veins

var·ied /vérreed/ *adj.* **1.** DIVERSE showing or characterized by many different forms or kinds **2.** CHANGED having undergone change or alteration **3.** WITH MANY COLORS consisting of or having many colors —**var·ied·ly** *adv.* —**var·ied·ness** *n.*

var·ied thrush *n.* a North American thrush that looks like the robin but has a black band on its breast. Latin name: *Ixoreus naevius.*

var·i·e·gate /vérree ə gàyt, vérri-/ (**-gat·ed, -gat·ing, -gates**) *vt.* **1.** CHANGE LOOK OF SOMETHING to change the way something looks, especially by adding different colors **2.** ADD VARIETY to add variety to something [Mid-17thC. From Latin *variegare* "to make varied," from *varius* "diverse" (source of English *various*).] —**var·i·e·ga·tion** /vèrree ə gáysh'n, vérri-/ *n.* —**var·i·e·ga·tor** /vérree ə gàytər, vérri-/ *n.*

var·i·e·gat·ed /vérree ə gàytəd, vérri-/ *adj.* **1.** WITH PATCHES OF DIFFERENT COLORS marked with or containing patches of different colors **2.** BOT WITH PATCHES OF LIGHTER COLOR marked with or containing patches of lighter color **3.** DIVERSE showing or characterized by many different forms or kinds

va·ri·e·tal /və rī́ ət'l/ *adj.* **1.** BIOL TYPICAL OF BIOLOGICAL VARIETY relating to, typical of, or being a variety of something, especially a biological variety **2.** WINE MADE FROM SINGLE GRAPE VARIETY made entirely or principally from a single variety of grape ■ *n.* WINE WINE MADE FROM SINGLE GRAPE VARIETY a wine that is made entirely or principally from a single variety of grape, and is usually known by the name of the grape variety —**va·ri·e·tal·ly** *adv.*

va·ri·e·ty /və rī́ ətee/ (*plural* **-ties**) *n.* **1.** QUALITY OF BEING VARIED the quality of being varied or diversified ○ *It's easy to get bored if there's no variety in your work.* **2.** PARTICULAR TYPE a particular type or kind within a general group ○ *a new variety* **3.** COLLECTION OF VARIED THINGS a collection of varied things, often belonging to the same general group **4.** THEATER ENTERTAINMENT MADE UP OF DIFFERENT ACTS entertainment made up of a number of different kinds of acts **5.** BOT SUBDIVISION OF SPECIES a rank used in classifying living things, especially plants, that is subordinate to species but superior to form. Varieties of a species generally have certain distinguishing characteristics, such as a particular flower color, and may arise naturally or through deliberate plant breeding. [Mid-16thC. Via Old French from the Latin stem *varietat-*, from *varius.* See VARIOUS.]

va·ri·e·ty meat *n.* **1.** ORGAN MEAT any meat taken from a slaughtered animal other than flesh removed from the skeleton, especially organ meat **2.** PROCESSED MEAT any meat that is processed, e.g., sausage

va·ri·e·ty show *n.* a theatrical show made up of a number of short performances of different kinds, such as singing, comic sketches, dancing, and magic acts

va·ri·e·ty store *n.* a retail store that sells a wide range of inexpensive items

var·i·fo·cal /vèrri fṓk'l/ *adj.* WITH MANY FOCUSING DISTANCES used to describe composite eyeglass lenses with varying focal length that allow different focusing distances for near, far, and intermediate vision ■ **var·i·fo·cals** *npl.* VARIFOCAL EYEGLASSES eyeglasses with composite lenses for distant, intermediate, and near vision

var·i·form /vérri fàwrm/ *adj.* existing in different shapes or forms [Mid-17thC. Coined from VARIOUS + -FORM.] —**var·i·form·ly** *adv.*

vario- *prefix.* variation, variance, difference ○ *variolite* [From Latin *varius* "speckled, variegated"]

va·ri·o·la /vèrree ṓlə/ *n.* smallpox (*technical*) [Early 19thC. From late Latin, literally "pustule," from Latin *varius* (see VARIOUS).]

var·i·o·late /vérree ə làyt/ *vt.* (**-lat·ed, -lat·ing, -lates**) INOCULATE WITH SMALLPOX VIRUS to inoculate somebody with the smallpox virus (*dated*) ■ *adj.* PITTED OR SCARRED with a pitted or scarred appearance, like the skin of somebody who has had smallpox —**var·i·o·la·tion** /vèrree ə láysh'n/ *n.*

var·i·ole /vérree ōl/ *n.* any of the small rounded masses that cause the pockmarked surface in the rock variolite [Early 19thC. From late Latin *variola* (see VARIOLA).]

var·i·o·lite /vérree ə līt/ *n.* a rock that has a pockmarked surface caused by rounded fibrous crystalline masses that are embedded in it [Late 18thC. Coined from VARIOLA + -ITE.] —**var·i·o·lit·ic** /-líttək/ *adj.*

var·i·o·loid /vérree ə lòyd/ *adj.* LIKE SMALLPOX having the characteristics of smallpox ■ *n.* MILD FORM OF SMALLPOX a mild form of smallpox that affects people who are partially immune because of having been inoculated or having had smallpox already

va·ri·o·lous /və rī́ ələss/ *adj.* relating to, like, or affected by smallpox

var·i·om·e·ter /vèrree ómmətər/ *n.* **1.** PHYS MAGNETIC FIELD INSTRUMENT an instrument used to measure magnetic fields, especially variations in Earth's magnetic field **2.** AIR RATE-OF-CLIMB INDICATOR an instrument used to measure the rate of climb of an aircraft such as a glider

var·i·o·rum /vèrree áwrəm/ *adj.* **1.** WITH VARIOUS ANNOTATIONS with commentary or notes written by various editors or scholars **2.** WITH DIFFERENT VERSIONS OF TEXT containing different versions or readings of a text ■ *n.* VARIORUM EDITION an edition of a text with commentary or notes written by various editors or scholars, or with various different versions or readings [Early 18thC. From Latin *editio cum notis variorum*, "edition with notes of various (commentators)"; *variorum*, genitive plural of *varius* (see VARIOUS).]

var·i·ous /vérree əss/ *det.* ASSORTED many different ■ *adj.* **1.** OF DIFFERENT KINDS of different kinds or categories **2.** INDIVIDUAL individual or separate **3.** BEING AN ASSORTMENT being an assortment or variety **4.** CHANGING changing rather than constant (*archaic*) [Mid-16thC. Formed from Latin *varius*, "variegated, diverse."] —**var·i·ous·ly** *adv.* —**var·i·ous·ness** *n.*

var·i·sized /vérri sīzd/ *adj.* being or consisting of different sizes

var·is·tor /və rístər/ *n.* a two-element semiconductor with nonlinear resistance in which the resistance drops as the applied voltage increases. Varistors are often used as a safety device to short circuit transient high voltages in electronic circuits. [Mid-20thC. From VARIABLE + RESISTOR.]

var·ix /vérriks/ (*plural* **-i·ces** /-seez/) *n.* **1.** MED SWOLLEN OR KNOTTED VEIN an abnormally swollen or knotted vessel, especially a vein **2.** ZOOL RIDGE ON GASTROPOD SHELL a ridge along the length of the shell of a gastropod mollusk [14thC. From Latin, literally "dilated vein, varicose vein."]

var·let /vaárlət/ *n.* (*archaic*) **1.** RASCAL a rogue or rascal **2.** SERVANT a servant or attendant **3.** KNIGHT'S PAGE a knight's page [15thC. From Old French *vaslet* (see VALET).]

var·mint /vaármint/ *n.* a troublesome, unpleasant, or despicable person or animal (*regional*) [Mid-16thC. Dialectal variant of VERMIN.]

WORD KEY: REGIONAL NOTE

Used of animals, the term recurs across the rural South, the Lower Southwest, and even into the Middle Rocky Mountain states.

Var·na /vaárnə/ city, port, and tourist center in eastern Bulgaria, on the Black Sea. Population: 301,421 (1996).

var·nish /vaárnish/ *n.* **1.** INDUST TRANSPARENT RESIN SOLUTION a solution of a resin in oil or spirits, applied to a surface to give it a protective gloss **2.** INDUST SMOOTH COATING OF VARNISH a coating of varnish, applied to something to give it a protective gloss **3.** SUPERFICIALLY ATTRACTIVE MANNER OR APPEARANCE a superficially or deceptively attractive manner or appearance ■ *vt.* (**-nished, -nish·ing, -nish·es**) **1.** INDUST APPLY VARNISH to coat something with varnish **2.** GIVE SOMETHING A SMOOTH SURFACE to give something a smooth and usually glossy surface **3.** MAKE SOMETHING SUPERFICIALLY ATTRACTIVE to make something superficially or deceptively attractive [14thC. Via Old French *vernis* from medieval Latin *vernicium*, "sandarac," from Greek *Berenikē*, "Berenice," a city in Cyrenaica, where varnish was first used.] —**var·nish·er** *n.*

var·nish tree *n.* a tree such as the lacquer tree that when tapped yields a juice that may be used as a varnish or lacquer

Var·ro /várrō/, **Marcus Terentius** (116–27 B.C.) Roman scholar. He was one of the most learned Romans of his day, and the author of more than 70 known works on a variety of subjects from farming to the Latin language. Little of his work survives.

var·si·ty /vaársətee/ *n.* (*plural* **-ties**) **1.** SPORTS TEAM the principal team representing a university, college, or high school, especially in sports competitions **2.** *U.K.* UNIVERSITY a university (*dated*) ■ *adj.* INVOLVING A UNIVERSITY belonging to or involving a university, e.g., a sports competition or team [Mid-19thC. Dialectal variant of "versity," shortening of UNIVERSITY.]

var·us /vérrəss/ *adj.* used to describe an abnormality in which a body part such as the foot is turned or displaced inward toward the midline of the body or limb [Late 18thC. From Latin, literally "bent, crooked."]

varve /vaárv/ *n.* a layer or series of layers of sediment deposited annually in a still body of water, e.g., by a glacier. Varves can be counted back to date a particular layer. [Early 20thC. From Swedish *varv*, "layer, turn."]

var·y /vérree/ (**-ied, -y·ing, -ies**) *v.* **1.** *vti.* UNDERGO OR MAKE SOMETHING UNDERGO CHANGE to undergo or make something undergo a change in appearance or characteristics **2.** *vi.* BE DIFFERENT to be different **3.** *vt.* GIVE VARIETY TO SOMETHING to give variety or diversity to something [14thC. Via Old French *varier* from Latin *variare*, derived from *varius* (see VARIOUS).] —**var·y·ing** *adj.* —**var·y·ing·ly** *adv.*

WORD KEY: SYNONYMS

See Synonyms at ***change***.

var·y·ing hare *n.* = **snowshoe hare**

vas /vass/ (*plural* **va·sa** /vássə, váyssə, váyzə/) *n.* a vessel or duct in the body of a human or animal [Mid-17thC. From Latin, literally "vessel."] —**va·sal** /váyss'l, váyz'l/ *adj.*

vas- *prefix.* = **vaso-** (*used before vowels*)

va·sa plural of **vas**

vas·cu·lar /váskyələr/ *adj.* relating to, involving, typical of, or having fluid-carrying vessels, e.g., blood vessels in animals or the sap-carrying vessels in plants [Mid-17thC. From modern Latin *vascularis*, formed from VASCULUM.] —**vas·cu·lar·i·ty** /vàskyə lérrətee/ *n.* —**vas·cu·lar·ly** /váskyələrlee/ *adv.*

vas·cu·lar bun·dle *n.* any of the many strands of tissue that contain the xylem and phloem vessels, responsible for conducting sap through the stems and branches of a plant. They are most prominent in annual and young plants, and in perennial and woody plants they become part of an inner cylinder of vascular tissue.

vas·cu·lar cyl·in·der *n.* = **stele**

vas·cu·lar·i·za·tion /vàskyələri záysh'n/ *n.* the development of vessels, especially blood vessels, in an organism or tissue

vas·cu·lar tis·sue *n.* plant tissue that is specialized for conducting sap. It comprises phloem, which conveys chiefly dissolved sugars, and xylem, which conveys water and dissolved minerals.

vas·cu·la·ture /váskyələ choo̅r, váskyələchər/ *n.* the arrangement of blood vessels in the body or in a particular organ or tissue

vas·cu·li·tis /vàskyə lítiss/ *n.* inflammation of a blood vessel or lymph vessel

vas·cu·lum /váskyələm/ (*plural* **-la** /-lə/) *n.* a small box or case used by botanists in the field for storing collected plants or other specimens [Mid-19thC. From Latin, literally "little vessel," from VAS.]

vas def·er·ens /vàss déffərənz, -rènz/ (*plural* **va·sa def·er·en·ti·a** /vàssə deffə rénshə, -deffə rénshee ə/) *n.* either of a pair of ducts that carry sperm from the testes to the urethra during ejaculation. Contraction of its thick muscular wall propels sperm rapidly through the duct, which forms part of the spermatic cord. [Late 19thC. From Latin, literally "carrying-away vessel."]

vase /vayss, vayz, vaaz/ *n.* an open container, usually tall and rounded, used for displaying cut flowers or as an ornament [Mid-16thC. Via French from Latin *vas*, "vessel."]

va·sec·to·mize /və séktə mīz/ (**-mized, -miz·ing, -miz·es**) *vt.* to perform a vasectomy on somebody

va·sec·to·my /və séktəmee/ (*plural* **-mies**) *n.* a surgical operation in which the vas deferens from each testis is cut and tied to prevent transfer of sperm during ejaculation [Late 19thC. Coined from VAS DEFERENS + -ECTOMY.]

Vas·e·line /vássə leen/ *tdmk.* a trademark for medical petroleum jelly and other products such as lip balm and hand lotion

vaso- *prefix.* **1.** blood vessels, vascular ○ *vasodilation* **2.** vas deferens ○ *vasectomy* [From Latin *vas* "vessel"]

va·so·ac·tive /vàyzō áktiv/ *adj.* making blood vessels contract or dilate —**va·so·ac·tiv·i·ty** /vàyzō ak tívvə tee/ *n.*

va·so·con·stric·tion /vàyzō kən stríkshən/ *n.* narrowing of the blood vessels with consequent reduction in blood flow or increased blood pressure

va·so·con·stric·tor /vàyzō kən stríktər/ *n.* AGENT THAT NARROWS BLOOD VESSELS any agent such as a nerve or hormone that narrows the blood vessels, which in turn increases resistance to blood flow and raises blood pressure. Vasoconstrictors such as the hormone epinephrine and various drugs are used medically to maintain or raise blood pressure in circulatory disorders or during surgery, or to counteract shock. ■ *adj.* NARROWING BLOOD VESSELS causing narrowing of the blood vessels —**vas·o·con·stric·tive** *adj.*

va·so·dil·a·tion /vàyzō dī láysh'n, -di láysh'n/, **va·so·dil·a·ta·tion** /vàyzō dìllə táysh'n, -dìllə táysh'n/ *n.* widening of the blood vessels, especially the arteries, leading to increased blood flow or reduced blood pressure

va·so·di·la·tor /vàyzō dī láytər, -di láytər/ *n.* AGENT THAT WIDENS BLOOD VESSELS an agent, such as a nerve or hormone that widens the blood vessels, which in turn decreases resistance to blood flow and lowers blood pressure. Drugs that act as vasodilators are used medically to treat high blood pressure and various other circulatory disorders. ■ *adj.* WIDENING BLOOD VESSELS causing widening of the blood vessels —**va·so·di·la·to·ry** /vàyzō díllə tàwree/ *adj.*

va·so·in·hib·i·tor /vàyzō in híbbitər/ *n.* something that depresses or stops the activity of the nerves that control widening or narrowing of the blood vessels —**va·so·in·hib·i·to·ry** *adj.*

va·so·mo·tor /vàyzə mōtər/ *adj.* causing or influencing changes in the diameter of blood vessels

va·so·pres·sin /vàyzō préssin/ *n.* a hormone produced by the pituitary gland that causes narrowing of the arteries and raises blood pressure. It also reduces the volume of urine excreted by the kidneys. [Early 20thC. Originally a trademark.]

va·so·pres·sor /vàyzō préssər/ *adj.* RAISING BLOOD PRESSURE causing or promoting the narrowing of blood vessels, which in turn raises blood pressure ■ *n.* SOMETHING THAT RAISES BLOOD PRESSURE something that has the effect of raising blood pressure

va·so·spasm /váyzō spàzzəm/ *n.* sustained contraction of the muscular walls of the blood vessels with a resultant reduction in blood flow. In Raynaud's disease there is vasospasm of the arteries of the fingers, which causes cold or numb fingers. —**va·so·spas·tic** /vàyzō spástik/ *adj.*

va·so·va·gal /vàyzō váyg'l/ *adj.* relating to, or involving the influence of the vagus nerve on circulation. Stimulation of the vagus reduces heart rate and, consequently, the amount of blood being pumped by the heart. [Early 20thC. Coined from VASO- + VAGAL.]

vas·sal /váss'l/ *n.* **1.** DEPENDENT LANDHOLDER IN FEUDAL SOCIETY somebody who was obliged to show loyalty and homage to a feudal lord in return for being allowed to occupy land belonging to the lord and receiving his protection **2.** SLAVE a bondsman or slave **3.** PERSON OR NATION DEPENDENT ON ANOTHER a person, nation, or group that is dependent on or subordinate to another [14thC. Via Old French from medieval Latin *vassallus*, from *vassus*, "servant," from the assumed Celtic stem *wass-*, "young man, squire."] —**vas·sal** *adj.*

vas·sal·age /váss'lij/ *n.* **1.** CONDITION OF BEING VASSAL the dependent condition of being somebody's vassal **2.** DEPENDENT CONDITION any condition of being dependent on or subordinate to somebody or something else (*literary*)

vast /vast/ *adj.* VERY GREAT IN SIZE OR AMOUNT very great in number, size, amount, extent, or degree ■ *n.* IMMENSE SPACE the immense expanse of space (*literary*) [Late 16thC. From Latin *vastus*, "immense, empty."] —**vast·ly** *adj.* —**vast·ness** *n.* —**vas·ti·tude** *n.* —**vas·ti·ty** /vástətee/ *n.*

vast·y /vástee/ (**-i·er, -i·est**) *adj.* vast (*archaic or literary*)

vat /vat/ *n.* **1.** LARGE CONTAINER FOR LIQUID a large container used to hold or store liquid **2.** PREPARATION OF DYE a preparation of weakly colored soluble dye (**vat dye**) ■ *vt.* (**vat·ted, vat·ting, vats**) TREAT OR PUT SOMETHING IN VAT to treat, store, or put something in a vat [12thC. Alteration of *fat*, from Old English *fæt* "vessel."]

VAT, V.A.T *n.* a tax added to the estimated value of a product or material at each stage of its manufacture or distribution, in the end paid by the consumer. Full form **value-added tax**

Vat. *abbr.* Vatican

vat dye *n.* any of a class of dyes that are made insoluble and fixed by oxidation after being taken up by fibers —**vat-dyed** *adj.*

vat·ic /váttik/ *adj.* relating to, involving, or typical of a prophet [Early 17thC. Formed from Latin *vates*, "prophet, seer."]

Vat·i·can /váttikən/ *n.* **1.** POPE'S RESIDENCE the palace in the Vatican City that is used as the official residence of the Pope and the administrative center of the papacy **2.** POPE'S AUTHORITY the authority and jurisdiction of the Pope [Mid-16thC. From Latin (*mons*) *Vaticanus*, "Vatican (hill)."]

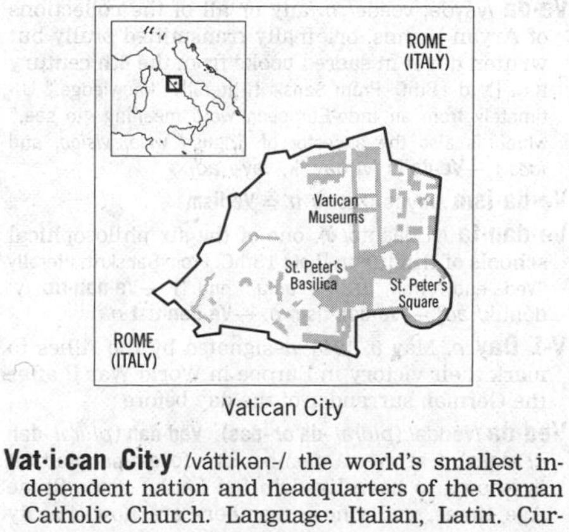

Vatican City

Vat·i·can Cit·y /váttikən-/ the world's smallest independent nation and headquarters of the Roman Catholic Church. Language: Italian, Latin. Currency: lira. Population: 850 (1996). Area: 110 acres/44 hectares. Official name **State of Vatican City**

Vat·i·can·ism /váttikə nìzzəm/ *n.* the policies and authority of the Pope, especially the idea of absolute papal authority

va·tic·i·nate /və tíss'n àyt/ (**-nat·ed, -nat·ing, -nates**) *vti.* to prophesy something [Early 17thC. From Latin *vaticinari*, derived from *vates*, "prophet, seer", + *canere*, "to sing."] —**va·tic·i·nal** /və tíssin'l/ *adj.* —**va·tic·i·na·tion** /və tìss'n áysh'n/ *n.* —**va·tic·i·na·tor** /-àytər/ *n.*

va·tu /vaá too/ (*plural* **-tu**) *n.* a unit of currency in Vanuatu. See table at **currency**

Vau·ban /vō baáN/, **Sebastien le Prestre de** (1633–1707) Marshal of France. He was a specialist in siegecraft and fortifications during the reign of Louis XIV. He directed the sieges of Mons (1691) and Namur (1692).

vaude·ville /váwd vìl, váwdə-/ *n.* **1.** THEATER POPULAR ENTERTAINMENT a type of entertainment popular in the late 19th and early 20th centuries consisting of a variety of singing, dancing, and comic acts **2.** VAUDEVILLE SHOW a vaudeville show **3.** COMIC PLAY WITH SONGS a comic play with songs and dances **4.** MUSIC SATIRICAL POPULAR SONG a satirical popular song of the type performed in cabarets in the 19th and 20th centuries [Mid-18thC. From Old French *vaudevire*, a shortening of *chanson du Vau de Vire*, "song of the Valley of Vire," a region of Calvados, Normandy, noted for satirical folksongs.]

WORD KEY: ORIGIN

In 15th-century France there was a fashion for songs from the valley of the Vire, in the Calvados region of Normandy (particularly popular, apparently, were the satirical songs composed by a local fuller, Olivier Basselin). The geographic connection had been lost by the time English acquired the word, and the element *-vire* had been replaced with *-ville* "town." The semantic transition from "popular song" to "light theatrical entertainment" is not recorded until the early 19th century.

vaude·vil·lian /vàwd víllee ən, vàwdə-/ *n.* VAUDEVILLE COMPOSER OR PERFORMER somebody who performs in or composes for vaudeville shows ■ *adj.* TYPICAL OF VAUDEVILLE typical of, suitable for, or used in vaudeville

Vau·dreuil /vō drő ee/, **Philippe de Rigaud de Vaudreuil de Cavagnal, Marquis de** (1698–1778) French soldier and colonial administrator. He was governor of New France (now Canada) from 1755 to 1760, when he was forced to surrender to British forces during the French and Indian War.

Sarah Vaughan

Vaughan /vawn/, **Sarah** (1924–90) U.S. jazz singer. Performing with Earl Hines, Billy Eckstine, Count Basie, and other leading jazz musicians, she was a major international star known for her complex harmonization and vocal improvisation. Full name **Sarah Lois Vaughan**

Vaughan Wil·liams /vawn wíllyəmz/, **Ralph** (1872–1958) British composer. He developed a British national style of music from choral tradition and folksong. His works include nine symphonies and many choral works.

vault[1] /vawlt/ *n.* **1.** ARCHIT ARCHED CEILING an arched structure of stone, brick, wood, or plaster that forms a ceiling or roof **2.** ARCHIT ROOM WITH ARCHED CEILING a room, especially an underground room, with an arched ceiling **3.** BUILDING STRENGTHENED ROOM FOR VALUABLES a strengthened room or compartment used for the safe storage of valuables, especially one in a bank **4.** BURIAL CHAMBER a burial chamber, usually underground **5.** SOMETHING ARCHING OVERHEAD something that arches overhead, especially the sky (*literary*) **6.** ANAT ARCHED PART OF BODY a part of the body with an arched

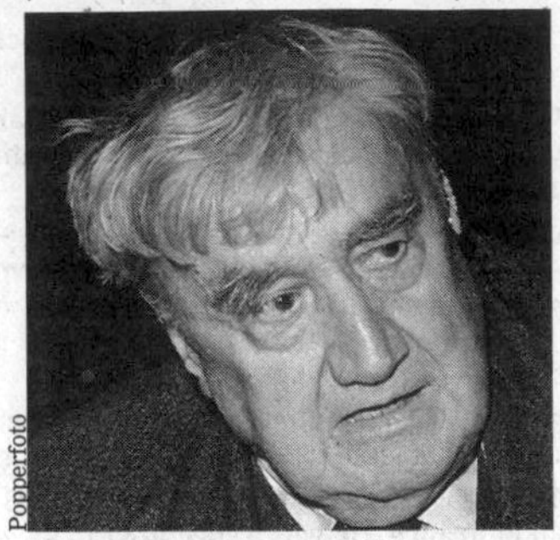

Ralph Vaughan Williams

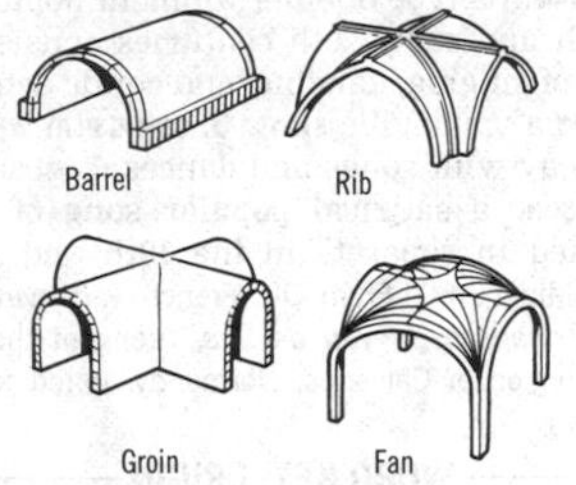

Vault

shape ■ *v.* (**vault·ed, vault·ing, vaults**) **1.** *vt.* ARCHIT **PUT ARCHED STRUCTURE OVER SOMETHING** to cover a building with an arched ceiling or roof **2.** *vt.* ARCHIT **BUILD SOMETHING AS VAULT** to build something in the shape of a vault **3.** *vi.* **FORM VAULT** to arch or curve like a vault [14thC. From Old French *vaute*, from assumed Vulgar Latin *volvita*, "turn, vault," from Latin *voluta*, feminine past participle of *volvere*, "to turn."]

vault[2] /vawlt/ *v.* (**vault·ed, vault·ing, vaults**) **1.** *vti.* **SPRING OVER OBJECT** to leap or spring over something, especially by pushing on it with the hands or using a pole **2.** *vi.* **MOVE WITH A BOUND** to move with a leap or bound **3.** *vi.* **RISE SUDDENLY TO PROMINENCE** to arrive somewhere or achieve something suddenly ○ *She vaulted to fame with the publication of her first novel.* **4.** *vti.* DRESSAGE **PERFORM CURVET** to perform a curvet in dressage or to make a horse perform a curvet ■ *n.* **1. ACT OF VAULTING** an act of vaulting **2.** DRESSAGE = **curvet** [Mid-16thC. Via Old French *volter*, ultimately from assumed Vulgar Latin *volvitare*, literally "to roll repeatedly," from Latin *volvere*, "to roll."] —**vault·er** *n.*

vault·ed /váwltəd/ *adj.* built with one or more vaults

vault·ing[1] /váwlting/ *n.* ARCHIT the structural use of brick, stone, or reinforced concrete to form a ceiling or roof over a space

vault·ing[2] /váwlting/ *adj.* aspiring or confident, especially in an excessive way (*literary*) ○ *vaulting ambition*

vault·ing horse *n.* a piece of gymnastic equipment with four legs and a solid leather-covered oblong body, used for exercises and especially for vaulting over

vaunt /vawnt/ *v.* (**vaunt·ed, vaunt·ing, vaunts**) **1.** *vt.* **BE BOASTFUL ABOUT SOMETHING** to boast or act boastfully about something such as achievements or possessions **2.** *vi.* **BOAST** to boast or brag (*literary*) ■ *n.* **A BOAST** a boast, or display of boasting [14thC. Via Old French *vanter* from late Latin *vanitare*, "to be vain," from *vanus*, "empty," (see VAIN).] —**vaunt·er** *n.* —**vaunt·ing·ly** *adv.*

vaunt-cour·i·er *n.* a person or thing sent in advance of another (*archaic or literary*) [Mid-16thC. From French *avant* "before" + COURIER, modeled on French *avant-coureur.*]

vaunt·ed /váwntəd/ *adj.* boasted about or praised in an ostentatious way

vav /vaav/, **waw** /waw/ *n.* the sixth letter in the Hebrew alphabet, usually transliterated as "v" or "w" [Early 19thC. From Hebrew *wāw*, "hook."]

vav·a·sor /vávvə sàwr, vávvə sòor/, **vav·a·sour** *n.* a feudal lord or knight who has power over vassals but is himself a vassal of a more powerful lord [14thC. Via Old French from medieval Latin *vavassor*, of uncertain origin: perhaps a contraction of *vassus vassorum*, "vassal of vassals." See VASSAL.]

vb. *abbr.* **1.** verb **2.** verbal

V.C. *abbr.* **1.** vice-chairman **2.** vice chancellor **3.** vice consul **4.** Victoria Cross **5. V.C., VC** Vietcong

VCR *n.* a tape recorder that can record and play videocassettes through a standard television receiver. It can capture live television programs for later replay and also play back prerecorded cassettes. Full form **videocassette recorder**

VD, **V.D.** *abbr.* venereal disease

v.d. *abbr.* **1.** vapor density **2.** various dates

V-Day *n.* Victory Day

VDR *abbr.* **1.** videodisk recorder **2.** videodisk recording

VDT *abbr.* video display terminal

've /v, əv/ *contr.* a contracted form of "have"

veal /veel/ *n.* meat from a young calf, light in color and texture with a delicate flavor [14thC. Via Old French from Latin *vitellus*, a diminutive of *vitulus*, "calf."]

veal calf *n.* a calf reared for veal

veal·er /véelər/ *n. ANZ, Can, U.S.* a veal calf

Veb·len /vébblən/, **Thorstein** (1857–1929) U.S. economist. An unorthodox thinker, he criticized modern industrial society in works such as *The Theory of the Leisure Class* (1899). He coined the phrase "conspicuous consumption." Full name **Thorstein Bunde Veblen**

vec·tor /véktər/ *n.* **1.** MATH **QUANTITY WITH DIRECTION AND MAGNITUDE** a quantity, e.g., force or velocity, made up of components of both direction and magnitude **2.** MATH **ELEMENT OF VECTOR SPACE** an element of a vector space **3.** AIR **COURSE OF AIRCRAFT** the course taken by an aircraft or a missile **4.** MED, VET **DISEASE-TRANSMITTING ORGANISM** an organism such as a mosquito or tick that transmits disease-causing microorganisms from infected individuals to other persons, or from infected animals to human beings **5.** GENETICS **GENE TRANSFER AGENT** an agent such as a plasmid or bacteriophage that is used in genetic engineering to transfer a segment of foreign DNA into a bacterium or other cell. The foreign DNA is spliced into the vector's DNA, which contains the genes necessary for switching on replication and transcription of the foreign DNA in its new setting. **6.** COMPUT **COMPUTER ARRAY** in computing, an array of any length but only one dimension ■ *vt.* (**-tored, -tor·ing, -tors**) AIR **1. DIRECT AIRCRAFT BY RADIO** to direct an aircraft in flight, or its pilot, by radio, often from the ground **2. CHANGE THRUST DIRECTION OF AIRCRAFT ENGINE** to change the direction of the thrust of an aircraft engine as a means of steering the aircraft [Early 18thC. From Latin, literally "carrier," from *vectus*, past participle of *vehere*, "to carry."] —**vec·to·ri·al** /vek táwree əl/ *adj.* —**vec·to·ri·al·ly** /-táwree əlee/ *adv.*

vec·tor prod·uct *n.* the result of multiplying two vectors. It is perpendicular to the vectors and its magnitude equals the product of their magnitudes multiplied by the sine of the included angle.

vec·tor space *n.* a mathematical set of vectors associated with a field of scalars comprising a commutative group under addition and in which multiplication of a vector and a scalar is a vector

vec·tor sum *n.* the result of adding two vectors, obtained graphically as the directed diagonal of the parallelogram whose sides are the given vectors

Ve·da /váydə, véedə/ *n.* any or all of the collections of Aryan hymns, originally transmitted orally but written down in sacred books from the 6th century B.C. [Mid-18thC. From Sanskrit, literally "knowledge." Ultimately from an Indo-European word meaning "to see," which is also the ancestor of English *wise, vision*, and *idea.*] —**Ve·da·ic** /vi dáy ik, vay-/ *adj.*

Ve·da·ism /váydə ìzzəm/ *n.* = **Vedism**

Ve·dan·ta /vi daántə/ *n.* one of the six philosophical schools of Hinduism [Late 18thC. From Sanskrit, literally "Veda-end," from VEDA + *anta*, "end."] —**Ve·dan·tic** /vi dántik/ *adj.* —**Ve·dan·tism** *n.* —**Ve·dan·tist** *n.*

V-E Day *n.* May 8, 1945, designated by the Allies to mark their victory in Europe in World War II after the German surrender of the day before

Ved·da /véddə/ (*plural* **-da** *or* **-das**), **Ved·dah** (*plural* **-dah** *or* **-dahs**) *n.* PEOPLES a member of a forest-people that is known to have lived in Sri Lanka since Stone Age times, and whose members are now mainly integrated with the Sinhalese [Late 17thC. From Sinhalese *vaddā* "hunter."] —**Ved·doid** *adj.*

ve·dette /və dét/ *n.* **1. ve·dette, vi·dette FORWARD SCOUT** a mounted soldier posted forward of a larger force to serve as a scout **2. ve·dette, ve·dette boat SMALL FAST SCOUTING VESSEL** a small fast boat posted forward of a larger seaborne force to serve as a scout [Late 17thC. Via French from Italian *vedetta*, alteration (influenced by *vedere*, "to see") of *veletta*, from Spanish *vela*, "watch," from Latin *vigilare*, "to watch," from *vigil*, "awake." See VIGIL.]

Ve·dic /váydik, véedik/ *adj.* **1.** INDIAN RELIG **IN THE VEDAS** contained in or referring to the Vedas **2.** INDIAN RELIG **BELONGING TO CULTURE THAT PRODUCED VEDAS** belonging to or typical of the Hindu culture that produced the Vedas **3.** LANG **IN ANCIENT SANSKRIT** relating to, in, or typical of the ancient form of Sanskrit in which the Vedas are written ■ *n.* LANG **ANCIENT SANSKRIT** the ancient form of Sanskrit in which the Vedas are written

Ve·dism /váy dìzzəm/ *n.* the Hindu religious theory and practice contained in, or based on, the Vedas

vee /vee/ *n.* the letter "V," or something with a similar shape [Late 19thC. From the pronunciation of the letter's name.]

vee-jay *n.* a video jockey (*informal*)

veep /veep/ *n.* a vice president (*slang*) [Mid-20thC. Formed from VP.]

veer[1] /veer/ *v.* (**veered, veer·ing, veers**) **1.** *vti.* **CHANGE DIRECTION SUDDENLY** to change direction, especially suddenly, or to make something do this **2.** *vi.* **CHANGE FROM ONE OPINION TO ANOTHER** to change from one opinion or state of mind to another, especially when this is sudden or extreme **3.** *vi.* METEOROL **SHIFT IN CLOCKWISE DIRECTION** to shift in a clockwise direction (*refers to a wind*) **4.** *vti.* NAUT **SAIL AWAY FROM WIND** to change course in a sailing vessel away from the wind, or to make a vessel do this ■ *n.* **CHANGE IN DIRECTION** a change in direction or course [Late 16thC. From French *virer*, "to turn," of uncertain origin: perhaps ultimately from Latin *gyrare* "to turn around," influenced by Latin *viriae* (plural) "bracelets."]

veer[2] /veer/ (**veered, veer·ing, veers**) *vt.* to let out a cable or chain or to make it go slack [15thC. From Middle Dutch *vieren*, "to let out."]

vee·ry /véeree/ (*plural* **-ries**) *n.* a thrush that lives in the woodland and dense brush of the eastern United States, with tawny upper parts and a spotted breast. Latin name: *Catharus fuscescens.* [Mid-19thC. Origin uncertain: perhaps an imitation of its call.]

veg /vej/ *vi.* = **veg out**

Ve·ga /véegə, váygə/ *n.* the brightest star in the constellation Lyra, and one of the brightest in the northern hemisphere

Ve·ga /lṓpay də váygə/, **Lope de** (1562–1635) Spanish playwright and poet. He is considered the founder of Spanish national drama. More than 400 of his 2,000 plays survive. Full name **Lope Félix de Vega Carpio**

veg·an /véegən, véjjən/ *n.* somebody who does not eat meat, dairy products, or eggs [Mid-20thC. Contraction of VEGETARIAN.] —**veg·an** *adj.* —**veg·an·ism** *n.*

Veg·e·mite /véjjə mīt/ *tdmk. ANZ* a trademark for a savory yeast extract that is eaten as a spread

veg·e·ta·ble /véjjətəb'l/ *n.* **1.** FOOD **EDIBLE PLANT** any plant with edible parts, especially leafy or fleshy parts that are used mainly for soups and salads and to accompany main courses **2.** PLANTS **ANY PLANT** any member of the plant kingdom, as opposed to the animal or mineral kingdoms **3. OFFENSIVE TERM** a highly offensive term referring to somebody in whom normal functions are severely reduced or absent, often due to injury to the brain (*slang offensive*) **4. INACTIVE PERSON** a term that deliberately insults somebody's personality or level of activity (*slang insult*) ■ *adj.* **CONSISTING OF VEGETABLES** consisting of, made from, using, or like vegetables [14thC. Via Old French from medieval Latin *vegetabilis*, "animating, able to grow," from Latin *vegetare* (see VEGETATE).]

veg·e·ta·ble i·vor·y (*plural* **veg·e·ta·ble i·vor·ies**) *n.* **1. HARD SUBSTANCE SIMILAR TO IVORY** a hard pale material like ivory, used to make decorative items and accessories. It comes from the endosperm of a South American palm nut (**ivory nut**). **2.** = **ivory nut**

veg·e·ta·ble mar·row *n. U.K.* PLANTS = **marrow** *n.* 5

veg·e·ta·ble oil *n.* oil that has been extracted from a plant or the seeds of a plant, e.g., olive oil, sunflower oil, sesame oil, and canola oil

veg·e·ta·ble oy·ster *n.* = **salsify**

veg·e·ta·ble wax *n.* a waxy material that forms part of the thin film covering the surfaces of most plants and helps reduce their loss of water through evaporation. It is obtained commercially from certain palms, such as the carnauba.

veg·e·tal /véjjət'l/ *adj.* **1.** TYPICAL OF VEGETABLES relating to, involving, or typical of vegetables or other plants **2.** INVOLVING GROWTH, NOT SEXUAL REPRODUCTION used to describe processes concerned with the maintenance or growth and development of an organism, rather than sexual reproduction [14thC. Via Old French *vegeter*, "to grow," from Latin *vegetare* (see VEGETATE).]

veg·e·tal pole *n.* the end of an animal egg that contains the greatest concentration of yolk, lying opposite to the animal pole

veg·e·tar·i·an /vèjjə térree ən/ *n.* SOMEBODY NOT EATING MEAT OR FISH somebody who does not eat meat or fish but eats vegetables, fruits, grains, seeds, and sometimes eggs and dairy products ■ *adj.* EXCLUDING MEAT AND FISH not eating or including meat and fish, but sometimes eating or including dairy products and eggs [Mid-19thC. Formed from VEGETABLE + *-arian*.] —**veg·e·tar·i·an·ism** *n.*

veg·e·tate /véjjə tàyt/ (**-tat·ed, -tat·ing, -tates**) *vi.* **1.** BOT GROW OR SPROUT LIKE PLANT to grow or sprout like a plant **2.** BEHAVE IN DULL OR INACTIVE WAY to live or behave in a dull, inactive, or undemanding way **3.** MED PRODUCE FLESHY OUTGROWTHS to grow or spread, especially by producing fleshy outgrowths [Early 17thC. From late Latin *vegetare* "to grow," from Latin *vegere*, "to quicken."]

veg·e·ta·tion /vèjjə táysh'n/ *n.* **1.** PLANTS IN GENERAL plants in general or the mass of plants growing in a particular place **2.** PROCESS OF VEGETATING the process of vegetating **3.** MED ABNORMAL OUTGROWTH an abnormal outgrowth from a body part such as on the membranes surrounding the heart —**veg·e·ta·tion·al** *adj.*

veg·e·ta·tive /véjjə tàytiv/ *adj.* **1.** CONCERNED WITH PLANTS relating to, involving, typical of, or like vegetation, plants, or plant growth **2.** INVOLVING GROWTH, NOT SEXUAL REPRODUCTION relating to, involving, or typical of processes in the maintenance or growth and development of an organism, rather than sexual reproduction **3.** REPRODUCING FROM BODY CELLS OF PARENT used to describe a method of reproduction, especially in plants, in which new individuals originate from the body cells of the parent rather than from specialized sex cells. Organs of vegetative reproduction in plants include bulbs, corms, tubers, and rhizomes. **4.** DULL OR INACTIVE dull, inactive, and undemanding in lifestyle **5.** OFFENSIVE TERM an offensive term referring to somebody in whom normal functions are reduced or absent due to injury to the brain —**veg·e·ta·tive·ly** *adv.* —**veg·e·ta·tive·ness** *n.*

veg·gie /véjjee/, **veg·ie** *n.* (*informal*) **1.** VEGETABLE a vegetable **2.** VEGETARIAN somebody who is a vegetarian [Mid-20thC. Shortening.] —**veg·gie** *adj.*

veg·gie·bur·ger /véjjee bùrgər/ *n.* a flat cake made from vegetables and legumes, fried or grilled, and often served in the same way as a hamburger

veg out, veg *vi.* to relax, be idle, or loaf, e.g., while watching television (*informal*) [Late 20thC. "Veg" from VEGETATE.]

ve·he·ment /vée əmənt/ *adj.* **1.** WITH CONVICTION expressed with, or showing conviction or intense feeling **2.** DONE FORCEFULLY done with vigor or force [15thC. Via Old French from the Latin stem *vehement-*, "forceful, violent," of unknown origin.] —**ve·he·mence** *n.* —**ve·he·ment·ly** *adv.*

ve·hi·cle /vée ìk'l, vée hìk'l/ *n.* **1.** TRANSP MEANS OF LAND TRANSPORT a usually wheeled conveyance used on land for carrying people or goods, most often by road or rail **2.** SPACE TECH STRUCTURE FOR TRANSPORT IN SPACE a powered structure, device, or rocket used to transport a payload or another craft through space **3.** COMMUNICATION MEDIUM a medium for communicating, expressing, or accomplishing something **4.** ARTS PERFORMANCE FOR PARTICULAR PERFORMER a film, play, show, or other performance designed or used to show off the talents of a particular performer **5.** PAINTING MIXTURE FOR PAINT PIGMENT a substance or mixture such as linseed oil or an acrylic vinyl polymer in which a pigment is mixed for painting **6.** PHARM SUBSTANCE BLENDED WITH DRUG an inactive substance with which a drug is blended to make it easier to apply, administer, or take [Early 17thC. Via French *véhicule* from Latin *vehiculum*, from *vehere* "to carry."]

ve·hic·u·lar /vi híkyələr/ *adj.* relating to, involving, or for use by vehicles, especially motor vehicles [Early 17thC. From late Latin *vehicularis*, from Latin *vehiculum* (see VEHICLE).]

veil /vayl/ *n.* **1.** CLOTHES FACE COVERING WORN BY WOMEN a length of fabric, usually sheer, worn by women over the head and face as a concealment or for protection **2.** CLOTHES NETTING ATTACHED TO WOMAN'S HAT a piece of netting or other sheer fabric attached to a woman's hat and covering the eyes. This was especially popular as a millinery style in the 1950s. **3.** CHR NUN'S HEADDRESS a part of a nun's headdress covering the sides and back of the head **4.** CHR NUN'S VOWS OR LIFE the vows that a nun takes or the life that she leads **5.** SOMETHING LIKE CURTAIN something that acts like a curtain in hiding, disguising, or obscuring something else, or separating one thing from another **6.** BOT COVERING MEMBRANE OF YOUNG MUSHROOM a thin membrane that covers the stalk and cap of an immature mushroom. It ruptures as the mushroom matures, leaving remnants at the base of the stalk, and some tissue flecks at the crown of the cap. **7.** ANAT = **caul** **8.** CHR = **humeral veil** ■ *v.* (**veiled, veil·ing, veils**) **1.** *vt.* COVER SOMETHING WITH A VEIL to cover something such as a person's face with a veil **2.** *vt.* HIDE OR DISGUISE to hide or disguise something, or separate something from something else **3.** *vi.* WEAR A VEIL to put on or wear a veil [12thC. Via Old French *veile* from Latin *vela*, "covering," the plural of *velum*, "sail."] ◇ **draw a veil over something** to ignore something deliberately or refrain from mentioning it, in order to be discreet

veiled /vày'ld/ *adj.* **1.** WEARING A VEIL covered with or wearing a veil **2.** DISGUISED not open or direct but disguised or suggested —**veiled·ly** /váylədlee/ *adv.*

veil·ing /váyling/ *n.* **1.** FABRIC FOR VEILS fabric used for veils **2.** VEIL a veil

vein /vayn/ *n.* **1.** ANAT VESSEL CARRYING BLOOD TO HEART any of the blood vessels that carry blood to the heart. All carry oxygen-depleted blood, except the pulmonary vein, which carries oxygenated blood from the lungs. **2.** ANY BLOOD VESSEL any of the vessels that carry blood around the body (*not used technically*) **3.** BOT SAP-CONDUCTING LEAF STRAND a distinct strand in a leaf that contains the sap-conducting vessels. It comprises one of several bundles of vessels and associated tissues (**vascular bundles**), and forms part of a network, arranged in a characteristic pattern. **4.** GEOL LAYER OF MINERAL a layer of a mineral in rock, especially an ore or a metal **5.** PARTICULAR QUALITY a particular recurrent quality or characteristic **6.** STREAK OF DIFFERENT COLOR a streak of different color or material within a substance such as marble, wood, or cheese **7.** INSECTS SUPPORTING STRUCTURE IN INSECT WING any of a network of hollow supporting structures in the wing of an insect that carry inside them blood vessels, nerves, and air tubes supplying the wing. The pattern of veins is characteristic for particular types of insect, and is useful in identifying and classifying new species. **8.** GEOL FISSURE FILLED WITH MATERIAL a fissure, crack, or channel in rock or ice that has been filled with a crystallized mixture of minerals **9.** DISPOSITION a disposition, tone, or mood ■ *vt.* (**veined, vein·ing, veins**) **1.** FORM VEINS IN SOMETHING to form veins or things like veins in something **2.** STREAK SOMETHING to streak or suffuse something of one color or material with another [13thC. Via Old French *veine* from Latin *vena*, "blood vessel, vein of metal, mine."] —**vein·al** *adj.*

veined /vaynd/ *adj.* **1.** HAVING VEINS with veins **2.** HAVING STREAKS with streaks that resemble veins in it

vein·ing /váyning/ *n.* a distribution or pattern of veins or streaks

vein·let /váynlət/ *n.* a small vein

vein·stone /váyn stōn/ *n.* = **gangue**

vel. *abbr.* **1.** vellum **2.** velocity

ve·la plural of **velum**

Ve·la /véelə/ *n.* a constellation in the sky of the southern hemisphere lying across the Milky Way, located between Centaurus and Puppis [Mid-19thC. Latin, literally "sails," from the shape of the constellation (see VEIL).]

ve·la·men /və láymən/ (*plural* **-mi·na** /-lámmənə/) *n.* PLANTS the spongy layer that covers the aerial roots of some plants such as tree-dwelling orchids. It helps to protect the plant and assists in absorbing moisture from the air. [Late 19thC. From Latin, literally "covering," from *velare*, "to cover," from *velum*, "sail."]

ve·lar /véelər/ *adj.* **1.** PHON WITH TONGUE NEAR SOFT PALATE spoken with the back of the tongue close to, or in contact with, the soft palate (**velum**) **2.** OF A VELUM relating to, involving, or typical of a velum ■ *n.* PHON VELAR CONSONANT a velar consonant [Early 18thC. From modern Latin *velaris*, from Latin *velum* "sail."]

ve·lar·i·um /və láiree əm/ (*plural* **-a** /-ə/) *n.* a large awning used in an amphitheater, e.g., the one used at the Coliseum in Rome, to shade an audience [Mid-19thC. From Latin, "awning" or "curtain," from *velum* "sail."]

ve·lar·ize /véelə rìz/ (**-ized, -iz·ing, -iz·es**) *vt.* to pronounce a speech sound by bringing the back of the tongue close to or against the soft palate (**velum**) —**ve·lar·i·za·tion** /vèeləri záysh'n/ *n.*

ve·late /véelət, -làyt/ *adj.* with or covered by a velum [Mid-19thC. Coined from VELUM + -ATE.]

Ve·láz·quez /be láath keth, ve láass kayss, və láaskez/, **Diego** (1599–1660) Spanish painter. Court painter to Philip IV, he is noted for his portraits, kitchen scenes, and interior schemes. *Las Meniñas* (1656) is considered to be his masterpiece. Full name **Diego Rodríguez de Silva y Velázquez**

Vel·cro /vél krō/ *tdmk.* a trademark for a fastener consisting of two strips, one with a dense layer of hooks and the other of loops, used especially on outerwear, athletic shoes, and luggage

veld /velt/, **veldt** *n.* a broad high grassland, especially in southern Africa [Early 19thC. Via Afrikaans from Dutch *veld* "field."]

veldskoen /vélt skoon/ *n. S Africa* a shoe or boot made of rough hide [Early 19thC. From Afrikaans, by folk etymology (from *veld* "veld") from earlier *velskoen*, "skin shoe," from *vel* "skin."]

ve·le·ta /və léetə/, **va·le·ta** *n.* a ballroom dance in triple time in which partners sometimes dance side by side and sometimes do a quick waltz

ve·li·ger /véelәjər, vélləjər/ *n.* a larva of some mollusks, e.g., limpets and mussels, that has a protective shell and a ciliated flap-shaped foot used for swimming and feeding [Late 19thC. Formed from VELUM + Latin *gerere*, "to carry, bear."]

vel·le·i·ty /və lée atee, ve-/ (*plural* **-ties**) *n.* **1.** THE WEAKEST LEVEL OF WILL volition or desire at its weakest level (*literary*) **2.** SLIGHT WISH a vague wish or desire [Early 17thC. Via the medieval Latin stem *velleitat-* from Latin *velle*, "to wish."]

vel·lum /véllәm/ *n.* **1.** HIGH QUALITY PARCHMENT OF ANIMAL SKIN high quality parchment made from calfskin, kidskin, or lambskin **2.** MANUSCRIPT ON VELLUM a manuscript written or printed on vellum **3.** PAPER RESEMBLING VELLUM an off-white heavy paper resembling vellum [15thC. From French *vélin*, literally "of a calf," from *veel* "calf" (see VEAL).] —**vel·lum** *adj.*

ve·lo·ce /və lóchee/ *adv.* to be played or performed rapidly (*used as a musical direction*) [Early 19thC. Via Italian from the Latin stem *veloc-* (see VELOCITY).]

ve·lo·cim·e·ter /vèllə símmətər, véelō-/ *n.* an instrument used to measure the speed of a fluid or sound

ve·loc·i·pede /və lóssə peed/ *n.* any of various early forms of bicycle or tricycle, including some that had pedals attached to the front wheel or were propelled by pushing the feet along the ground [Early 19thC. From French *vélocipède*, "bicycle," from the Latin stem *veloc-*, "swift," + the stem *ped-*, "foot."] —**ve·loc·i·pe·dist** *n.*

ve·loc·i·ty /və lóssətee/ (*plural* **-ties**) *n.* **1.** SPEED the speed at which something moves, happens, or is done **2.** RATE OF CHANGE IN POSITION a measure of the rate of change in position of something with respect to time, involving speed and direction **3.** = **speed** *n.* 2 (*not used technically*) [Mid-16thC. From Latin *velocitat-*, from the stem *veloc-*, "quick, swift."]

ve·loc·i·ty of cir·cu·la·tion *n.* the rate at which money circulates throughout an economy during a particular period, usually a year

ve·lo·drome /véllə drōm/ *n.* a stadium that has a banked track for bicycle races [Late 19thC. From French, formed from VELOCIPEDE + -DROME.]

ve·lour /və lŏor/, **ve·lours** (*plural* **-lours**) *n.* a fabric with a thick pile, similar to velvet, often used in upholstery and clothing [Early 18thC. Via Old French *velous*, from Latin *villosus*, "shaggy," from *villus*, "shaggy hair, wool."]

ve·lou·té /və lŏo táy/ *n.* a white sauce made from chicken, veal, or fish stock that has been thickened with a butter and flour roux and cream. Velouté sauce is often used on poultry or vegetables. [Mid-19thC. From French, literally "velvety," from Old French *vellute*, from *velous* (see VELVET).]

ve·lum /veéləm/ (*plural* **-la** /-lə/) *n.* ANAT a layer of tissue or other part that covers something like a veil, such as the muscular soft palate in the roof of the mouth [Late 18thC. From Latin, literally "sail, covering" (source of English *veil*).]

ve·lure /və lŏor/ *n.* velvet, or a fabric with a similar thick soft pile (*archaic*) [Late 16thC. From Old French *velour*, variant of *velous* (see VELOUR).]

ve·lu·ti·nous /və lŏot'nəss/ *adj.* densely covered with short soft hairs [Early 19thC. From modern Latin *velutinus*, "velvety," from medieval Latin *velutum* "velvet," from assumed Vulgar Latin *villutus*. See VELVET.]

vel·vet /vélvət/ *n.* **1.** TEXTILES **FABRIC WITH SOFT LUSTROUS PILE** a cotton, silk, or nylon fabric with a dense soft usually lustrous pile and a plain underside **2. SOMETHING LIKE VELVET** something that is smooth and soft like velvet **3.** ZOOL **FURRY COVERING ON DEER ANTLERS** the furry layer that covers the growing antlers of deer and is sloughed off when the antlers stop growing and harden **4.** GAMBLING **GAMBLING WINNINGS** winnings from gambling (*slang*) **5.** FIN **UNEXPECTEDLY LARGE GAIN OR PROFIT** a gain or profit that is unexpectedly large (*slang*) ■ *adj.* **1.** TEXTILES **MADE OF VELVET** made of or covered with velvet **2. LIKE VELVET** like velvet, especially in being or looking soft, smooth, or lustrous [14thC. From Old French *veluotte*, from *velu*, literally "shaggy (cloth)," from medieval Latin *villutus*, from Latin *villus*, "shaggy hair, wool."]

vel·vet ant *n.* any one of various wasps with bodies covered in soft hair. The females are generally wingless and have a potent sting. Family: Mutillidae.

vel·vet·een /vèlvə teén/ *n.* a brushed fabric with a soft pile like velvet [Late 18thC. Formed from VELVET + "-een," a variant of -INE.]

vel·vet glove *n.* kind, careful, or gentle treatment, especially when this disguises strength or determination

vel·vet shank *n.* an edible mushroom that grows in Europe and North Africa in clusters on hardwood trees, has a yellow cap, and a velvety dark brown stalk. It has a mild flavor and is sometimes cultivated. Latin name: *Flammulina velutipes*.

vel·vet·y /vélvətee/ *adj.* **1. FEELING LIKE VELVET** soft and smooth in a way that suggests the feel of velvet **2. SMOOTH** smooth and mellow —**vel·vet·i·ness** *n.*

Ven. *abbr.* **1.** CHR Venerable **2.** Venezuela

ven- *prefix.* = **veno-** (*used before vowels*)

ve·na /veénə/ (*plural* **-nae** /-nee/) *n.* a vein (*technical*) [14thC. From Latin.]

ve·na ca·va /-káyvə, -kaávə/ (*plural* **ve·nae ca·vae** /-káyvee, -kaávee/) *n.* one of two major veins that carry circulating blood into the right atrium of the heart. One carries blood returning from the upper body and head (**superior vena cava**) and the other brings that from below the chest (**inferior vena cava**). [Late 16thC. From Latin, literally "hollow vein."] —**ve·na·ca·val** *adj.*

ve·nal /veén'l/ *adj.* **1. OPEN TO BRIBERY** open to persuasion by corrupt means, especially bribery **2. CORRUPT** characterized by corruption **3. ABLE TO BE BOUGHT** able to be bought, especially in an illegal or unfair way [Mid-17thC. From Latin *venalis*, from *venum* "something for sale."] —**ve·nal·i·ty** /vee nállətee/ *n.* —**ve·nal·ly** /veén'lee/ *adv.*

WORD KEY: USAGE

venal or **venial**? The two words are derived from entirely different Latin roots: ***venal*** comes from *venum* meaning "thing for sale" and ***venial*** from *vena* meaning "forgiveness." ***Venial***, meaning "forgivable," is used in connection with minor faults or transgressions: *He was inclined to be thoughtless but that was a venial fault in one so young.* In Roman Catholic theology, a *venial sin* is one that does not deprive the soul of divine grace, as opposed to a *mortal sin*, which does. ***Venal***, meaning "liable to corruption," describes people as well as processes and organizations: *The political system is so venal that bribery is commonplace.*

ve·nat·ic /və náttik/, **ve·nat·i·cal** /və náttik'l/ *adj.* involving, connected with, or taking part in hunting (*formal*) [Mid-17thC. From Latin *venaticus*, from *venari*, "to hunt."] —**ve·nat·i·cal·ly** *adv.*

ve·na·tion /vee náysh'n/ *n.* **1. PATTERN OF VEINS** the pattern formed by the network of veins in an insect's wing or in a leaf. It is often useful in identifying or classifying specimens. **2. NETWORK OF VEINS** all the veins making up a network —**ve·na·tion·al** *adj.*

vend /vend/ (**vend·ed, vend·ing, vends**) *v.* **1.** *vt.* **SELL SOMETHING FROM VENDING MACHINE** to sell something from a vending machine **2.** *vti.* **SELL IN STREET** to sell something, especially in the street, or make a living doing this [Early 17thC. From Latin *vendere*, "to sell."]

Ven·da[1] /véndə/ (*plural* **-da** *or* **-das**) *n.* **1.** PEOPLES **MEMBER OF SOUTHERN AFRICAN PEOPLE** a member of a people who live in southern Africa, mainly in northern parts of Transvaal in South Africa **2.** LANG **VENDA LANGUAGE** a language spoken mainly in Transvaal in South Africa. It belongs to the Bantu group of Benue-Congo languages. About 750,000 people speak Venda. [Early 20thC. From Bantu.] —**Ven·da** *adj.*

Ven·da[2] /véndə/ former homeland in South Africa. Abolished in 1994, it is now part of Northern Province.

vend·a·ble *adj.* = **vendible**

ven·dace /véndəss/ (*plural* **-dac·es** *or* **-dace**) *n.* a whitefish of northwest Europe and Russia, found mainly in freshwater lakes, with a streamlined body and leading lower jaw. It is dark greenish blue above and silvery below. Genus: *Coregonus*. [Late 17thC. Origin uncertain: probably from Old French *vendoise*, of Celtic origin.]

vend·ee /ven deé/ *n.* somebody who buys something

Ven·dé·mi·aire /vàN dem yáir/ *n.* the first month of the year in the French Revolutionary calendar, corresponding to September 23 to October 22 in the Gregorian calendar [Late 18thC. From French, from *vendémi*, from Latin *vindemia*, "vintage" (see VINTAGE).]

vend·er *n.* = **vendor**

ven·det·ta /ven déttə/ *n.* **1. BLOOD FEUD BETWEEN FAMILIES** a feud between families started by the killing of a member of one family that is then avenged by a killing of a member of the other family **2. PROLONGED FEUD** a prolonged bitter feud or quarrel [Mid-19thC. From Italian, from Latin *vindicta*, "vengeance." See VINDICTIVE.]

vend·i·ble /véndəb'l/, **vend·a·ble** *adj.* **FIT TO BE SOLD** suitable or fit to be sold ■ *n.* **SOMETHING THAT CAN BE SOLD** something that can be sold or is available for sale —**vend·i·bil·i·ty** /vèndə bíllətee/ *n.* —**vend·i·ble·ness** /véndəb'lnəss/ *n.*

vend·ing ma·chine *n.* a machine from which people can buy such items as packaged food or drinks by inserting money

Ven·dôme /vaaN dṓm/, **Louis Joseph, duc de** (1654–1712) French soldier. He commanded forces in a number of battles during the War of the Spanish Succession (1701–14).

ven·dor /véndər/, **vend·er** *n.* **1. SELLER** somebody who sells something **2. VENDING MACHINE** a vending machine

ven·due /ven dŏo, vén dŏo/ *n.* a public sale or auction [Late 17thC. Via Dutch *vendu* from French *vendue*, perfect participle of *vendre*, "to sell, vend" (see VEND).]

ve·neer /və neér/ *n.* **1.** INDUST **THIN LAYER AS SURFACE** a thin layer of a material fixed to the surface of another material that is of inferior quality or less attractive **2.** INDUST **LAYER OF PLYWOOD** any of the layers of wood that are glued together to make plywood **3.** INDUST, BUILDING **OUTER LAYER** an outer layer fixed to something for decoration or protection, e.g., a facing of stone on a brick building **4. DECEPTIVE APPEARANCE** an outward appearance that is meant to please or impress others but that is false or only superficial ■ *vt.* (**-neered, -neer·ing, -neers**) **1.** INDUST **FIX VENEER TO SOMETHING** to fix a veneer to a surface **2.** INDUST, WOODWORK **GLUE LAYERS TO MAKE PLYWOOD** to glue layers of wood together to make plywood **3. HIDE SOMETHING BEHIND DECEPTIVELY PLEASANT APPEARANCE** to hide or disguise something behind a deceptively pleasant or impressive appearance [Early 18thC. Earlier "fineering, faneering," from German *Fournierung*, "inlay, veneer," from French *fournir* (see FURNISH).] —**ve·neer·er** *n.*

ve·ne·punc·ture *n.* MED = **venipuncture**

ven·er·a·ble /vénnərəb'l/ *adj.* **1. WORTHY OF RESPECT** worthy of respect as a result of great age, wisdom, remarkable achievements, or similar qualities **2.** RELIG **REVERED** revered for qualities such as great age or holiness **3. ANCIENT** extremely old **4.** CHR **USED AS TITLE BEFORE CANONIZATION** used by the Roman Catholic Church to describe somebody who has died and attained the first of the three degrees of canonization **5.** CHR **USED AS ARCHDEACON'S TITLE** used as a title to describe an archdeacon in the Church of England [15thC. Directly or via French from Latin *venerabilis*, from *venerari* (see VENERATE).] —**ven·er·a·bil·i·ty** /vènnərə bíllətee/ *n.* —**ven·er·a·bly** /vénnərəblee/ *adv.*

ven·er·ate /vénnə ràyt/ (**-at·ed, -at·ing, -ates**) *vt.* **1. RESPECT SOMEBODY** to regard somebody with profound respect **2. HONOR SOMETHING OR SOMEBODY** to honor something or somebody as sacred or special [Early 17thC. From Latin *venerat-*, past participle stem of *venerari*, from *vener-*, stem of *venus* "love, desire" (source of English *venereal*).] —**ven·er·a·tor** *n.*

ven·er·a·tion /vènnə ráysh'n/ *n.* **1. FEELING OF RESPECT** a feeling of great respect or reverence for somebody or something **2. EXPRESSING OF RESPECT** the expression of respect or reverence for somebody or something in words or actions **3. BEING RESPECTED** the condition of being respected or revered —**ven·er·a·tion·al** *adj.*

WORD KEY: SYNONYMS

See Synonyms at ***regard***.

ve·ne·re·al /və neéree əl/ *adj.* **1. PASSED ON THROUGH SEX** used to describe an infection or disease that is caught or transmitted through sexual intercourse **2. ASSOCIATED WITH SEXUALLY TRANSMITTED DISEASE** associated with, symptomatic of, or infected with a sexually transmitted disease **3. GENITAL** affecting or originating in the genitals **4. ABOUT SEX** relating to sex acts or sexual desire (*archaic or literary*) [15thC. Formed from Latin *venereus*, from *vener-*, the stem of *venus* "love" (see VENERATE).]

ve·ne·re·al dis·ease *n.* a disease that is caught or transmitted through sex acts, e.g., syphilis or gonorrhea (*dated*)

ve·ne·re·ol·o·gy /və neéree óllәjee/ *n.* the branch of medicine involving the study and treatment of sexually transmitted diseases [Late 19thC. Coined from VENEREAL + -LOGY.] —**ve·ne·re·o·log·i·cal** /və neéree ə lójjik'l/ *adj.* —**ve·ne·re·ol·o·gist** /və neéree óllәjist/ *n.*

ven·er·y[1] /vénnəree/ *n.* the pursuit of or indulgence in sexual pleasure (*archaic*) [15thC. From medieval Latin *veneria*, from Latin *vener-*, the stem of *venus* "love, desire" (see VENERATE).]

ven·er·y[2] /vénnəree/ *n.* GAME the sport or practice of hunting, or the animals hunted (*archaic*) [14thC. Via French from, ultimately, Latin *venari* "to hunt" (source of English *venison*).]

ven·e·sec·tion /vènnə sékshən, vénnə sèk-/ *n.* = **phlebotomy** [Mid-17thC. From medieval Latin *venae sectio*, literally "cutting of a vein."]

Ven·e·ti /vénnə tī/ *npl.* an ancient people that inhabited northeastern Italy and neighboring areas from around the 10th century B.C. [Early 17thC. From Latin.]

Ve·ne·tian /və neésh'n/ *adj.* PEOPLES **OF VENICE** relating to the Italian city of Venice, or its people or culture ■ *n.* PEOPLES **SOMEBODY FROM VENICE** somebody who lives in or was born or raised in the city of Venice, Italy [15thC. From Old French, from Latin *Venetia* "Venice."]

Ve·ne·tian blind, **ve·ne·tian blind** *n.* a window blind

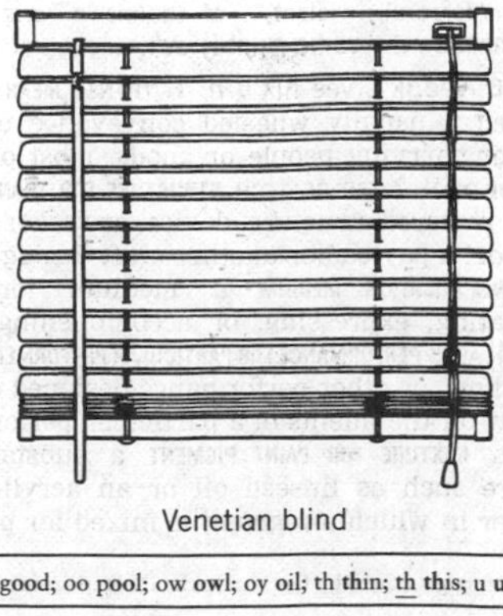

Venetian blind

consisting of narrow horizontal slats whose angle can be adjusted to let in more or less light

Ve·ne·tian glass *n.* delicate glassware, often with colorful ornamentation, made in or around Venice, especially at Murano

venetian red *n.* **1.** RED PIGMENT a dark red pigment made from a natural or synthetic iron oxide **2.** REDDISH-BROWN COLOR a strong reddish-brown color ■ *adj.* REDDISH-BROWN of a strong reddish-brown color

Ve·net·ic /və néttik/ *n.* a language once spoken in northwestern Italy by the Veneti people

Venez. *abbr.* Venezuela

Venezuela

Ve·nez·ue·la /vènnə zwáylə/ republic in northeastern South America, north of Brazil, on the Caribbean Sea and the Atlantic Ocean. Language: Spanish. Currency: bolívar. Capital: Caracas. Population: 22,311,000 (1996). Area: 352,144 sq. mi./912,050 sq. km. Official name **Republic of Venezuela** —**Ven·e·zue·lan** *n., adj.*

Ven·e·zue·la, Gulf of inlet of the Caribbean Sea, northwestern Venezuela. It is connected to Lake Maracaibo to the south by a narrow strait.

venge /venj/ (**venged, veng·ing, veng·es**) *vt.* to avenge somebody or something (*archaic*) [13thC. Via Old French *vengier* from Latin *vendicare* (see VINDICATE).]

ven·geance /vénjəns/ *n.* punishment that is inflicted in return for a wrong [13thC. Via Old French from, ultimately, Latin *vendicare* "to avenge" (see VINDICATE).] ◇ **with a vengeance** in an extreme or intense manner

venge·ful /vénjfəl/ *adj.* **1.** WANTING REVENGE having or showing a strong desire for revenge **2.** AVENGING serving the purpose of revenge or resulting from somebody's desire for revenge —**venge·ful·ly** *adv.* —**venge·ful·ness** *n.*

V-en·gine *n.* an internal-combustion engine with cylinders arranged in two rows to form a V-shaped angle

veni- *prefix.* = **veno-**

ve·ni·al /veénee əl, veényəl/ *adj.* easily forgiven or excused [13thC. Via Old French from, ultimately, Latin *venia* "forgiveness."] —**ve·ni·al·i·ty** /veénee állətee/ *n.* —**ve·ni·al·ly** /veénee əlee, veényəlee/ *adv.*

WORD KEY: USAGE

See Usage note at ***venal.***

ve·ni·al sin *n.* in the Roman Catholic Church, a sin that does not deprive the soul of divine grace, either because it was not serious or because it was committed without intent or without understanding its seriousness. ◊ **mortal sin**

Ven·ice /vénniss/ historic city and seaport in northeastern Italy, built on islands in a lagoon on the coast of the Adriatic Sea. Population: 298,915 (1995).

ven·i·punc·ture /vénni pùngkchər, veéni-/, **ve·ne·punc·ture** *n.* the puncturing of a vein for any medical purpose, e.g., to take blood, to feed somebody intravenously, or to administer a drug

ve·ni·re /və nīree, və neéree/, **ve·ni·re fa·ci·as** /və nīree fáyshəss, -neéree-/ *n.* a judicial writ ordering the summoning of jurors [Mid-17thC. From medieval Latin *venire facias* "you should cause to come."]

ve·ni·re·man /və nīreemən, -neéreemən/ (*plural* **-men**) *n.* a citizen summoned for jury duty under a venire

ven·i·son /vénniss'n, -z'n/ *n.* **1.** DEER MEAT the meat of a deer used as food, especially for stewing or roasting. Venison is dark in color and rich in flavor. **2.** GAME MEAT the meat of any animal hunted as game (*archaic*) [13thC. Via Old French from the Latin stem *venation-* "hunting," from *venari* "to hunt" (source of English *venery*²).]

Ve·ni·te /və nītee, -neétee/ *n.* **1.** CHR 95TH PSALM AS INVITATION TO PRAYER the 95th Psalm from the Bible sung as an invitation to morning prayer **2.** MUSIC MUSICAL SETTING OF 95TH PSALM a musical setting of the 95th Psalm [13thC. From Latin, "come ye," the first word of the psalm.]

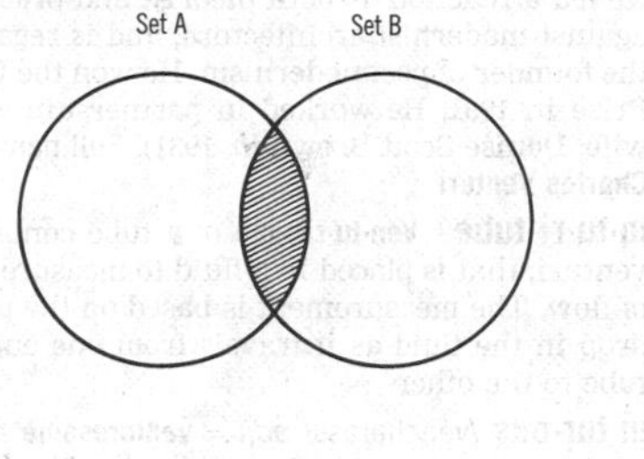

Venn diagram

Venn di·a·gram /vén-/ *n.* a mathematical diagram representing sets as circles, with their relationships to each other expressed through their overlapping positions, so that all possible relationships between the sets are shown [Early 20thC. Named for the English logician John *Venn* (1834–1923).]

veno- *prefix.* vein, venous ○ *venogram* [From Latin *vena* "vein" (source of English *vein*)]

ve·no·gram /veénə gràm/ *n.* an X-ray photograph of a vein or network of veins, taken after injecting a substance that absorbs X-rays and so makes the veins visible

ve·nog·ra·phy /vi nóggrəfee/ *n.* the examination of somebody's veins by taking an X-ray photograph (**venogram**) after injecting a substance that absorbs X-rays

ven·om /vénnəm/ *n.* **1.** BIOL POISONOUS FLUID INJECTED BY ANIMAL a poisonous fluid produced by an animal and injected by a bite or sting in order to immobilize prey or defend itself. Venoms are produced by a wide range of animals, including snakes, scorpions, spiders, and fish. **2.** MALICE something that is full of malice, spite, or vicious hostility **3.** POISON any kind of poison (*archaic*) [13thC. Via Old French *venim* from, ultimately, Latin *venenum* "poison."]

ven·om·ous /vénnəməss/ *adj.* **1.** BIOL PRODUCING VENOM producing venom and capable of inflicting a poisonous bite or sting **2.** MALICIOUS full of malice, spite, or extreme hostility **3.** POISONOUS full of or containing poison —**ven·om·ous·ly** *adv.* —**ven·om·ous·ness** *n.*

ve·nose /veé nōss/ *adj.* with veins, especially many branched veins e.g., an insect's wing or the leaf of a plant [Mid-17thC. From Latin *venosus*, from *vena* "vein."]

ve·nos·i·ty /vi nóssətee/ *n.* **1.** EXCESSIVE AMOUNT OF BLOOD an excessive amount of blood in the veins, or in an organ or other body part **2.** HIGH NUMBER OF VEINS an unusually large number of veins in an organ or other body part **3.** QUALITY OF VENOUS BLOOD the deoxygenated state of venous blood **4.** VEINED CONDITION the presence or possession of veins, especially many branched veins

ve·nous /veénəss/ *adj.* **1.** OF VEINS relating to or involving the veins **2.** RELATING TO BLOOD IN VEINS used to describe blood in the veins, which is returning to the heart, as opposed to blood in the arteries, which is leaving the heart **3.** WITH VEINS containing or full of veins [Early 17thC. Formed from Latin *vena* "vein" (source of English *vein*).] —**ve·nous·ly** *adv.* —**ve·nous·ness** *n.*

vent¹ /vent/ *n.* **1.** OPENING FOR AIR a small opening that allows fresh air to enter or stale air, gas, smoke, or steam to escape **2.** ZOOL OPENING IN ANIMAL'S BODY the external opening through which all waste material and eggs pass in fish, amphibians, reptiles, birds, and primitive mammals **3.** WAY OF RELEASING STRONG FEELINGS a way of releasing or expressing strong feelings, or a chance to do so ○ *a vent for his anger* **4.** GEOL OPENING IN EARTH'S CRUST an opening in the Earth's crust from which gases or volcanic material escape **5.** ARMS OPENING IN GUN BREECH a small opening in the breech of an old muzzle-loading gun through which the charge is ignited ■ *vt.* (**vent·ed, vent·ing, vents**) **1.** RELEASE EMOTIONS to release or forcefully express strong feelings or emotions **2.** LET OUT AIR to let out smoke, gases, steam, or stale air through a vent **3.** MAKE VENT to provide a vent for something [14thC. Via Old French *esventer* "to let out air" from assumed Vulgar Latin *exventare*, from Latin *ventus* "wind" (source of English *ventilate*).] —**vent·less** *adj.* ◇ **give vent to something** to express a strong feeling or emotion freely

vent² /vent/ *n.* SEW VERTICAL SLIT IN SEAM OF JACKET a vertical slit at the bottom of a seam in a jacket or other garment, that provides room for movement ■ *vt.* (**vent·ed, vent·ing, vents**) SEW ADD VENT TO JACKET to put a vent in a jacket or other garment [15thC. Alteration of earlier *fent*, via Old French *fente* "slit" from, ultimately, Latin *findere* "to split" (source of English *fission*).] —**vent·ed** *adj.* —**vent·less** *adj.*

vent·age /véntij/ *n.* **1.** MUSIC FINGER HOLE IN WIND INSTRUMENT a finger hole in a recorder or other wind instrument **2.** SMALL VENT a small opening or vent [Early 17thC. Formed from VENT¹.]

ven·tail /vén tàyl/ *n.* a movable covering for the neck or lower face on a medieval helmet [14thC. Via Old French from, ultimately, Latin *ventus* "wind" (source of English *vent*¹).]

ven·ter /véntər/ *n.* **1.** ANAT, ZOOL BELLY OF ANIMAL WITH BACKBONE the abdomen of a vertebrate **2.** ZOOL BODY PART RESEMBLING ABDOMEN the part of the body in lower animals that corresponds to the abdomen in mammals **3.** ANAT SOFT PART OF MUSCLE the soft fleshy area that forms the main part of a muscle **4.** ANAT HOLLOW OR CAVITY a hollow or cavity, e.g., on a bone **5.** BOT FEMALE PLANT PART in plants such as mosses and ferns, the swollen lower part of the female sex organ (**archegonium**) where the ovum develops **6.** LAW WOMB in law, a woman's womb. The term is used, e.g., with reference to an unborn child. (*technical*) [Mid-16thC. Directly or via law French and French *ventre* from Latin *venter* "belly."]

ven·ti·fact /véntə fàkt/ *n.* a rock, stone, or pebble that has been shaped, cut, or polished by wind-blown sand [Early 20thC. Formed from Latin *ventus* "wind," on the model of "artifact."]

ven·ti·late /vént'l àyt/ (**-lat·ed, -lat·ing, -lates**) *vt.* **1.** PROVIDE FRESH AIR to provide a room or other enclosed space with fresh air or a current of air **2.** PROVIDE VENT to provide an enclosed space with a vent or other means of letting fresh air in and stale air out **3.** EXPOSE SOMETHING TO MOVING AIR to expose something to moving fresh air, e.g., in order to dry, cool, or preserve it **4.** PUBLICLY EXAMINE QUESTIONS to examine freely and publicly or discuss grievances, opinions, or questions **5.** PHYSIOL SUPPLY OXYGEN TO BLOOD to oxygenate or aerate the blood through the blood vessels of the lungs [15thC. From Latin *ventilat-*, the past participle stem of *ventilare* "to fan," from *ventilus* "fan," from *ventus* "wind."]

ven·ti·la·tion /vènt'l áysh'n/ *n.* **1.** CIRCULATION OF AIR the movement or circulation of fresh air **2.** MEANS OF SUPPLYING FRESH AIR the means of supplying fresh air to an enclosed space, e.g., an opening or equipment installed in a building **3.** PUBLIC DISCUSSION the public discussion or examination of a particular issue

ven·ti·la·tor /vént'l àytər/ *n.* **1.** DEVICE FOR CIRCULATING FRESH AIR a device that circulates fresh air in an enclosed space **2.** MED MACHINE THAT HELPS SOMEBODY BREATHE a machine that keeps air moving in and out of the lungs of a patient who cannot breathe normally

ven·ti·la·to·ry /vént'lə tàwree/ *adj.* relating to or used for breathing or for oxygenating the blood

Ven·tôse /vaN tớwz/ *n.* the sixth month of the year in the French Revolutionary calendar, corresponding to February 20 to March 21 in the Gregorian calendar [Early 19thC. From French, literally "windy."]

ventr- *prefix.* = **ventro-** (*used before vowels*)

ven·trad /vén tràd/ *adv.* toward the ventral surface or side

ven·tral /véntrəl/ *adj.* **1.** ZOOL OF LOWER BODY AT FRONT located on or affecting the lower surface of an animal's body, or the front of the human body **2.** ANAT OF OR CLOSE TO ABDOMEN relating to or situated in, on, or near the abdomen **3.** BOT FACING AXIS used to describe the upper side of a leaf or other surface that faces toward the stem ■ *n.* ZOOL = **ventral fin** [Mid-18thC. Formed from the Latin stem *ventr-* "belly, abdomen" (source of English *ventriloquism*).] —**ven·tral·ly** *adv.*

ven·tral fin, **ven·tral** *n.* a fin on the underside of a fish, especially a pelvic fin or anal fin. ◊ **dorsal fin**

ven·tral root *n.* the spinal nerve root emerging from the lower surface of the spinal cord in animals and the front surface in humans, and that in mammals consists of motor nerve fibers

ven·tri·cle /véntrik'l/ *n.* **1.** PHYSIOL **HEART CHAMBER** either of the two lower chambers of the heart that receives blood from the upper chambers **(atria)** and pumps it into the arteries by contraction of its thick muscular walls **2.** PHYSIOL **BRAIN CAVITY** any of the four interconnected cavities in the brain that are enlargements of the central canal of the spinal cord and contain cerebrospinal fluid **3. HOLLOW IN BODY PART** a small cavity or chamber in the body or in an organ [14thC. From Latin *ventriculus*, literally "little belly" (see VENTRICULUS).]

ven·tri·cose /véntri kòss/ *adj.* **1.** MED **SWOLLEN ON ONE SIDE** used to describe a body part or plant part that is swollen, distended, or protruding on one side **2. CORPULENT** carrying a lot of weight, especially around the midsection (*formal*) [Mid-18thC. From modern Latin *ventricosus*, from Latin *venter* "belly" (source of English *ventriloquism*).] —**ven·tri·cos·i·ty** /vèntri kóssətee/ *n.*

ven·tric·u·lar /ven tríkyələr/ *adj.* involving, affecting, or relating to a ventricle or a ventriculus

ven·tric·u·lar fib·ril·la·tion *n.* an often fatal heartbeat irregularity in which the muscle fibers of the ventricles work without coordination, resulting in loss of effective pumping action of the heart

ven·tric·u·lus /ven tríkyələss/ (*plural* **-li** /-lī/) *n.* **1.** INSECTS **INSECT GUT** the part of an insect's gut where digestion takes place **2.** BIRDS **GIZZARD OF BIRD** the part of a bird's stomach where digestion takes place **3.** MARINE BIOL **SPONGE DIGESTIVE SYSTEM** the digestive cavity of a sponge [Early 18thC. From Latin, literally "little belly," from *venter* "belly" (source of English *ventriloquism*).]

ven·tril·o·quism /ven tríllə kwìzzəm/, **ven·tril·o·quy** /-tríllәkwee/ *n.* the art or skill of producing vocal sounds that seem to come from something other than the speaker [Late 18thC. Formed from *ventriloquy*, from modern Latin *ventriloquium*, literally "speaking from the stomach," from Latin *venter* "stomach" + *loqui* "to speak" (source of English *locution*).] —**ven·tri·lo·qui·al** /vèntri lőkwee əl/ *adj.* —**ven·tri·lo·qui·al·ly** /-lőkwee əlee/ *adv.* —**ven·tril·o·quist** /ven trílləkwist/ *n.* —**ven·tril·o·quis·tic** /-kwístik/ *adj.* —**ven·tril·o·quis·ti·cal·ly** /-kwístikəlee/ *adv.*

ven·tril·o·quize /ven tríllə kwīz/ (**-quized, -quiz·ing, -quiz·es**) *vi.* to produce vocal sounds that seem to come from something other than the speaker

ven·tril·o·quy *n.* = **ventriloquism** [Late 16thC. See VENTRILOQUISM.]

ventro- *prefix.* ventral, having to do with the belly ○ *ventromedial* [From Latin *venter* "belly" (source of English *ventral, ventricle*, and *ventriloquism*)]

ven·tro·dor·sal /vèn trō dáwrs'l/ *adj.* = **dorsoventral** *adj.* 2 —**ven·tro·dor·sal·ly** *adv.*

ven·tro·lat·er·al /vèn trō láttərəl/ *adj.* relating to or extending between the ventral and lateral surfaces of something such as an animal or organ —**ven·tro·lat·er·al·ly** *adv.*

ven·tro·me·di·al /vèn trō méedee əl/ *adj.* located near or facing the middle of a ventral surface on something such as an animal or organ —**ven·tro·me·di·al·ly** *adv.*

ven·ture /vénchər/ *n.* **1. RISKY PROJECT** a risky or daring undertaking that has no guarantee of success **2. NEW BUSINESS ENTERPRISE** a business enterprise that involves risk but could lead to profit **3. MONEY RISKED** the money or property risked in a business venture ■ *v.* (**-tured, -tur·ing, -tures**) **1.** *vi.* **MAKE DANGEROUS TRIP** to make a trip that is unpleasant or dangerous ○ *I ventured out into the storm to close the barn doors.* **2.** *vt.* **RISK DANGERS** to undertake the risks or dangers of a particular task or project **3.** *vt.* **MAKE SUGGESTION** to offer or express something tentatively at the risk of being contradicted, embarrassed, or ignored **4.** *vi.* **DARE TO DO SOMETHING** to presume or dare to do something **5.** *vt.* FIN **PUT MONEY AT RISK** to expose money or property to risk by committing it to a particular project [15thC. Shortening of ADVENTURE.] —**ven·tur·er** *n.*

ven·ture cap·i·tal *n.* money used for investment in projects that involve a high risk but offer the possibility of large profits —**ven·ture cap·i·tal·ist** *n.*

ven·ture·some /vénchərsəm/ *adj.* (*formal*) **1. ADVENTUROUS** willing to take risks or have new experiences **2. RISKY** involving risk or danger —**ven·ture·some·ly** *adv.* —**ven·ture·some·ness** *n.*

ven·tu·ri /ven tóoree/ *n.* **1. CONSTRICTION IN TUBE** a constriction in a tube designed to cause a pressure drop when a liquid or gas flows through it **2. CARBURETOR AIR INLET** a restricted air inlet in a carburetor that produces a drop in pressure, causing fuel vapor to be drawn out of the carburetor bowl [Late 19thC. Named for the Italian physicist Giovanni Battista *Venturi* (1746–1822), who described the relationship between velocity and pressure in moving fluids.]

Ven·tu·ri /ven tóoree/, **Robert** (*b.* 1925) U.S. architect. He led a reaction as both theorist and practitioner against modernist architecture, and is regarded as the founder of postmodernism. He won the Pritzker Prize in 1991. He worked in partnership with his wife, Denise Scott Brown (*b.* 1931). Full name **Robert Charles Venturi**

ven·tu·ri tube, **Ven·tu·ri tube** *n.* a tube containing a venturi, that is placed in a fluid to measure its rate of flow. The measurement is based on the pressure drop in the fluid as it travels from one end of the tube to the other.

ven·tur·ous /vénchərəss/ *adj.* = **venturesome** *adj.* 1 —**ven·tur·ous·ly** *adv.* —**ven·tur·ous·ness** *n.*

ven·ue /vén yoo/ *n.* **1. SCENE** a scene or setting in which something takes place **2. PLACE WHERE EVENT IS HELD** a place where an event such as a sports competition or a concert is held, especially one where events are often held **3.** LAW **SCENE OF CRIME** the place in which a crime takes place or a cause of action arises **4.** LAW **PLACE OF TRIAL** a county or other area from which a jury is selected and in which a trial is held **5.** LAW **STATEMENT** a statement that a case is being brought to the proper court or authority [Mid-16thC. From Old French, past participle of *venir* "to come," from Latin *venire*. Ultimately from an Indo-European word that is also the ancestor of English *come, basis*, and *juggernaut*.]

ven·ule /vén yool/ *n.* **1. SMALL BLOOD VESSEL** a small blood vessel, especially one that transfers blood from the capillaries to the veins **2. BRANCHING VEIN** a small branching vein in a leaf or an insect's wing [Mid-19thC. From Latin *venula*, literally "small vein," from *vena* "vein" (source of English *vein*).] —**ven·u·lar** *adj.*

Ve·nus /véenəss/ *n.* **1.** MYTHOL **ROMAN GODDESS OF LOVE** in Roman mythology, the goddess of love and beauty. She was the mother of Aeneas and Cupid. Greek equivalent **Aphrodite 2.** ASTRON **PLANET 2ND FROM THE SUN** the fourth smallest planet in the solar system and the second planet from the Sun. Seen from the Earth as a bright morning or evening star, Venus has a high surface temperature and is covered by clouds of carbon dioxide gas. See table at **planet** [Pre-12thC. From Latin, from *venus* "love, desire."]

Ve·nus fly·trap *n.* = **Venus's flytrap**

Ve·nus·hair *n.* = **Venus's-hair**

Ve·nu·sian /və nóosh'n, vi nóoshee ən/ *adj.* **OF PLANET VENUS** relating or belonging to the planet Venus ■ *n.* **INHABITANT OF VENUS** an inhabitant of the planet Venus, as portrayed in science fiction

Ve·nus's flow·er bas·ket *n.* a deep-sea sponge of the western Pacific and Indian oceans with a skeleton of glassy slender pointed structures **(spicules)** that intersect to form a geometrically patterned surface. Genus: *Euplectella*.

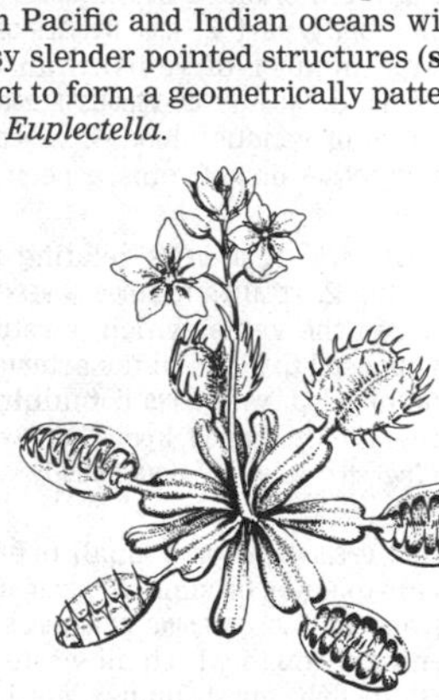

Venus's flytrap

Ve·nus's fly·trap, **Venus flytrap** *n.* an insect-eating plant native to North and South Carolina that has leaves ending in hinged lobes that spring shut, entrapping the insect. Latin name: *Dionaea muscipula*.

Ve·nus's gir·dle *n.* a marine animal **(ctenophore)** that lives in warm seas and has a long virtually transparent belt-shaped body with rows of cilia along the top and bottom edges. Latin name: *Cestum veneris*.

Ve·nus's-hair /véenəss háir/, **Ve·nus·hair** *n.* a delicate fan-shaped fern that is native to wet limestone areas of the southern United States and tropical America and is widely grown as an ornamental plant. Latin name: *Adiantum capillus-veneris*.

Ve·nus shell *n.* a common marine mollusk that has a hinged shell with rounded ribbed valves. Family: Veneridae.

Ve·nus's-look·ing-glass *n.* an annual plant that has hairy oval leaves and purple flowers. It grows on cultivated and bare land in parts of Eurasia and North Africa. Latin name: *Legousia hybrida*.

ver. *abbr.* **1.** verse **2.** version

ve·ra·cious /və ráyshəss/ *adj.* **1. HONEST** honest or truthful **2. TRUE** true or accurate (*formal or literary*) [Late 17thC. Formed from Latin *verac-*, the stem of *verax*, from *verus* "true" (source of English *verify, verdict*, and *aver*.] —**ve·ra·cious·ly** *adv.* —**ve·ra·cious·ness** *n.*

ve·rac·i·ty /və rássətee/ (*plural* **-ties**) *n.* **1. TRUTH** the truth, accuracy, or precision of something ○ *They questioned the veracity of our claims.* **2. TRUTHFULNESS** the truthfulness or honesty of a person **3. TRUE STATEMENT** a truth or true statement [Early 17thC. Directly or via French from medieval Latin *veracitas*, from *verax* "truthful" (see VERACIOUS).]

Ve·ra·cruz /vèrrə króoz/ city and port in eastern Mexico, located on the Gulf of Mexico. Population: 328,607 (1990).

ve·ran·da /və rándə/, **ve·ran·dah** *n.* a porch, usually roofed and sometimes partly enclosed, that extends along an outside wall of a building [Early 18thC. Via Hindi *varaṇḍā* from Portuguese *varanda* "railing, balcony," of unknown origin.] —**ve·ran·daed** *adj.*

WORD KEY: REGIONAL NOTE

To refer to a large porch, especially with a suggestion of luxury, ***veranda*** is most common in the Middle and South Atlantic States. In the Gulf states, *piazza*, especially in Lower Alabama, and *gallery*, which dominates the Lower Mississippi Valley out of New Orleans, recur much more frequently than does ***veranda***.

ve·ra·pa·mil /və ráppəmil/ *n.* a drug used to treat heart and circulatory disorders, including angina pectoris, hypertension, and irregular heartbeat. It works by inhibiting the movement of calcium ions across membranes, especially in muscle cells. [Mid-20thC. From *v(al)er(ic)* + *am(ino-)* + *(nitr)il(e)* (with inserted "p"), its chemical name.]

ve·rat·ri·dine /və ráttrə deen, -din/ *n.* a poisonous yellowish-white substance obtained from sabadilla seeds and used in insecticides and formerly in medicine. Formula: $C_{36}H_{51}NO_{11}$. [Early 20thC. Formed from VERATRUM.]

ver·a·trine /vérrə treen, -trin/, **ver·a·trin** /-trin/ *n.* a poisonous mixture of alkaloids including veratridine, formerly used in medicine to relieve inflammation [Early 19thC. Formed from VERATRUM.]

verb /vurb/ *n.* **1. WORD INDICATING ACTION OR STATE** a word used to show that an action is taking place, or to indicate the existence of a state or condition, or the part of speech to which such a word belongs **2. PREDICATE OF SENTENCE** the part of a clause or sentence that includes the verb but excludes the subject of the verb [14thC. Via Old French from Latin *verbum* "word." Ultimately from an Indo-European base meaning "to speak," which is also the ancestor of English *word* and *irony*.]

ver·bal /vúrb'l/ *adj.* **1. USING WORDS RATHER THAN PICTURES** expressed in or using words or language, especially as opposed to pictorial representation ○ *a verbal picture of the scene outside* **2. USING WORDS RATHER THAN ACTION** relating to or consisting of words rather than physical action or confrontation ○ *verbal protest* **3. ORAL RATHER THAN WRITTEN** relating to or consisting of spoken rather than written words ○ *They made a verbal agreement.* **4. USING WORDS WITHOUT MEANING** using words without conveying meaning or making any meaningful distinctions ○ *a purely verbal distinction rather than anything more fundamental* **5. INVOLVING SKILL WITH WORDS** involving skill in the use and understanding of words and language ○ *verbal dexterity* **6.** GRAM **RELATING TO VERBS** derived from or relating to a verb, or to verbs in general **7.** GRAM **FORMING VERBS** used to form verbs **8. VERBATIM** corresponding word for word (*archaic*) ■ *n.* GRAM **WORD FORMED FROM VERB** a word formed from a verb, especially one used as a noun or an adjective, such as a gerund or participle [15thC. Via Old French from, ultimately, Latin *verbum* (see VERB).]

WORD KEY: SYNONYMS

verbal, spoken, oral

CORE MEANING: expressed in words

verbal indicates that something such as an apology or request is expressed in words, usually spoken words, but sometimes in writing; **spoken** indicates that communication is expressed by means of speech rather than writing; **oral** a more formal word meaning the same as *spoken.*

ver·bal ad·jec·tive *n.* a verb participle ending in -ing or -ed that is used as an adjective

ver·bal·ism /vúrb'l ìzzəm/ *n.* **1. VERBAL EXPRESSION** something expressed in words **2. LONG-WINDED EXPRESSION** a wordy expression that has little meaning or relevance **3. USE OF TOO MANY WORDS** the uncritical or undisciplined use of words, especially without any attempt to analyze their meaning or value **4. WAY SOMETHING IS EXPRESSED** the manner in which something is expressed or communicated

ver·bal·ist /vúrb'list/ *n.* **1. SOMEBODY SKILLED WITH WORDS** somebody who is skilled in the use of words and language **2. SOMEBODY WHO CONCENTRATES ON WORDS** somebody who tends to concentrate on words or language rather than on things such as facts, feelings, or ideas —**ver·bal·is·tic** /vùrb'l ístik/ *adj.*

ver·bal·ize /vúrb'l ìz/ (**-ized, -iz·ing, -iz·es**) *v.* **1.** *vt.* **EXPRESS SOMETHING IN WORDS** to express feelings, thoughts, or ideas in words **2.** *vt.* GRAM **MAKE WORD INTO VERB** to make a word that is another part of speech, e.g., a noun or adjective, into a verb **3.** *vi.* **BE VERBOSE** to speak or write in a way that uses too many words —**ver·bal·i·za·tion** /vùrb'li záysh'n/ *n.* —**ver·bal·iz·er** /vúrb'l ìzər/ *n.*

ver·bal noun *n.* a form of a verb ending in "-ing" used as a noun, e.g., "dancing" in "he teaches dancing"

ver·ba·tim /vər báytim/ *adj.* **USING IDENTICAL WORDS** corresponding word for word with something else ■ *adv.* **IN IDENTICAL WORDS** repeated, written down, or copied word for word [15thC. From medieval Latin, from Latin *verbum* "word."]

ver·be·na /vər béenə/ *n.* a common plant or shrub, native mainly to North and South America, that bears clusters of small tubular five-lobed flowers and is widely grown for ornament. Genus: *Verbena.* [Mid-16thC. From Latin. Ultimately from an Indo-European base meaning "to bend," which is also the ancestor of English *warp, reverberate,* and *rhombus.*]

ver·bi·age /vúrbee ij/ *n.* **1. EXCESS OF WORDS** an excess of words, especially in writing or speech with little or no meaning **2. WORDING** the style of language in which something is expressed ○ *bureaucratic verbiage explaining the regulations* [Early 18thC. Via French from, ultimately, Latin *verbum* "word."]

ver·bid /vúrbid/ *n.* LING = **verbal** *n.*

verb·i·fy /vúrbi fì/ (**-fied, -fy·ing, -fies**) *vt.* = **verbalize** *v.* 2 (*archaic or formal*) —**verb·i·fi·ca·tion** /vùrbifi káysh'n/ *n.*

ver·big·er·ate /vər bíjjə ràyt/ (**-at·ed, -at·ing, -ates**) *vi.* to repeat the same words or phrases obsessively as a symptom of a psychiatric disorder [Late 19thC. From Latin *verbigerat-*, the past participle stem of *verbigerare* "to chat," from *verbum* "word" + *gerare* "to keep carrying on."] —**ver·big·er·a·tion** /vər bìjjə ráysh'n/ *n.*

ver·bose /vər bṓss/ *adj.* expressed in or using language that is too long-winded or complicated [Late 17thC. From Latin *verbosus*, from *verbum* "word."] —**ver·bose·ly** *adv.* —**ver·bose·ness** *n.*

WORD KEY: SYNONYMS

See Synonyms at *wordy.*

ver·bo·ten /vər bṓt'n, fər-/ *adj.* forbidden or prohibited [Early 20thC. From German.]

verb phrase *n.* a grammatical construction consisting of a verb and any direct and indirect objects and modifiers linked to it, but not including the subject of the verb

Ver·cheres /vúrchərəss/, **Marie-Madeleine Jarret de** (1678–1747) French-Canadian colonist. She is known for defending her family's fort against an attack by the Iroquois in 1692.

ver·dant /vúrd'nt/ *adj.* **1. WITH LUSH GREEN GROWTH** green with vegetation or foliage **2.** COLORS **GREEN** green in color **3. NAIVE** lacking experience or sophistication (*literary*) [Late 16thC. Via Old French *verdeant*, literally "becoming green," from, ultimately, Latin *viridis* "green" (source of English *vireo*).] —**ver·dan·cy** *n.* —**ver·dant·ly** *adv.*

verd an·tique /vùrd an téek/, **verde an·tique** *n.* **1. GREEN VEINED MARBLE** a dark-green mottled or veined variety of serpentine marble that is used in decoration **2. GREEN STONE** a green marble or stone that resembles verd antique **3.** = **verdigris** *n.* 1 [From obsolete French, literally "antique green"]

Verde, Cape /vurd/ **1.** peninsula in western central Senegal. Its tip is the westernmost point of the African mainland. **2.** ◆ **Cape Verde**

Ver·di /váirdee/, **Giuseppe** (1813–1901) Italian composer. He was one of the greatest operatic composers of all time. His works include *Rigoletto* (1851), *La Traviata* (1853), *Aida* (1871), *Otello* (1887), and *Falstaff* (1893). Full name **Guiseppe Fortunino Francesco Verdi**

ver·dict /vúrdikt/ *n.* **1.** LAW **JURY DECISION** the finding of a jury on the matter that has been submitted to it in a trial **2. DECISION OR OPINION ABOUT SOMETHING** a judgment, opinion, or conclusion that is expressed about something [13thC. From Anglo-Norman *verdit*, literally "true speech," from *ver* "true" + *dit* "speech, saying."]

ver·di·gris /vúrdi grèess, vúrdi grìss, -grèe/ *n.* **1. GREEN DEPOSIT ON COPPER** a green or greenish-blue deposit (**patina**) that forms on copper, brass, and bronze through the atmospheric corrosion of copper carbonates **2. GREENISH COPPER POWDER** a green or greenish-blue poisonous powder that is used as a paint pigment and fungicide. It is formed by the action of acetic acid on copper and consists of one or more basic copper acetates. [14thC. From Old French *vert de Grece*, literally "green of Greece."]

ver·din /vúrd'n/ *n.* a small bird of the southwestern United States and Mexico, with gray plumage, a white breast, and a yellow head and throat. Latin name: *Auriparus flaviceps.* [Late 19thC. Via French from, ultimately, Latin *viridis* "green."]

ver·di·ter /vúrditər/ *n.* a basic copper carbonate that is used as a blue or green pigment. The blue variety contains azurite, the green variety contains malachite. [Early 16thC. From Old French *verd de terre*, literally "green of the earth."]

Ver·dun /vur dún/ town in northeastern France. One of the longest and bloodiest battles of World War I was fought around the town during 1916. Population: 23,427 (1990).

ver·dure /vúrjər/ *n.* **1. VIVID GREEN OF PLANTS** the green color associated with lush vegetation **2. VEGETATION** extremely lush vegetation **3. FRESHNESS** a fresh, healthy, or flourishing condition [14thC. Via French from, ultimately, Latin *viridis* "green."] —**ver·dured** *adj.* —**ver·dure·less** *adj.* —**ver·dur·ous** *adj.* —**ver·dur·ous·ness** *n.*

ve·re·cund /vérrə kùnd/ *adj.* shy or modest (*archaic*) [Mid-16thC. From Latin *verecundus*, from *vereri* "to respect" (source of English *revere*).]

Vereenig·ing /və réeniking/ industrial city in Gauteng Province, South Africa. Population: 71,255 (1991).

verge[1] /vurj/ *n.* **1. POINT BEYOND WHICH SOMETHING HAPPENS** the point beyond which something happens or begins ○ *He was on the verge of tears.* **2. BOUNDARY** a line, belt, or strip that acts as a boundary or edge **3. EDGE** the edge, rim, or margin of something **4.** *U.K.* TRANSP **ROADSIDE BORDER** a narrow border that runs alongside a road **5.** ARCHIT **ROOF EDGE** the edge of a sloping roof where it extends beyond the gable **6. CLOCK SPINDLE** the spindle of a balance wheel in early clock and watch mechanisms **7.** HIST **ROD HELD BY TENANT** a rod held by a feudal tenant when swearing an oath of loyalty to his lord **8. ROD AS SYMBOL OF OFFICE** a rod or staff carried as a symbol of authority or an emblem of office ■ *vi.* (**verged, verg·ing, verg·es**) **1. APPROACH A STATE OR QUALITY** to approach or come close to a particular quality, state, or condition ○ *verging on brilliance* **2. BORDER ON AN AREA** to border on or be on the edge of a particular place or area [14thC. Via French, "rod" (symbolizing the office of Lord High Steward and the limits of his jurisdiction), from Latin *virga* (source of English *virgule*).]

verge[2] /vurj/ (**verged, verg·ing, verg·es**) *vi.* **1. MOVE IN PARTICULAR DIRECTION** to move or lean in a particular direction or toward a certain condition **2. CHANGE GRADUALLY** to change gradually from one thing to another (*literary*) **3. SINK FROM VIEW** to descend toward the horizon (*literary*) [Early 17thC. From Latin *vergere* "to bend, incline" (source of English *converge* and *diverge*). Ultimately from an Indo-European word meaning "to turn," which is also the ancestor of English *wrench* and *wrinkle.*]

ver·gence /vúrjənss/ *n.* the inward or outward turning of both eyes when focusing on a near or distant object [Early 20thC. Back-formation from CONVERGENCE and DIVERGENCE.]

verg·er /vúrjər/ *n. U.K.* **1. CHURCH OFFICIAL** a church official who acts as a caretaker and attendant and looks after the inside of a church, usually including the furnishings and the vestments **2. OFFICIAL WHO CARRIES STAFF** a church official who carries the staff of office (**verge**) in front of somebody such as a bishop or dean during ceremonies and processions [15thC. Via Anglo-Norman from Old French *verge* "rod of office" (see VERGE[1]).]

Ver·gil = **Virgil**

ver·glas /vair glaá/ *n.* a thin coating of ice found on rock or exposed ground [Early 19thC. From French, from *verre* "glass" + *glas* "ice."]

ve·rid·i·cal /və ríddik'l/ *adj.* (*formal*) **1. TRUTHFUL** telling the truth **2. REAL** corresponding to facts or to reality, and therefore genuine or real [Mid-17thC. Formed from Latin *veridicus*, literally "truth-speaking," from *verus* "true" + *dicere* "to say."] —**ve·rid·i·cal·i·ty** /və rìddi kállətee/ *n.* —**ve·rid·i·cal·ly** /və ríddiklee/ *adv.*

ver·i·fi·ca·tion /vèrrəfi káysh'n/ *n.* **1. ESTABLISHMENT OF TRUTH** the establishment of the truth or correctness of something by investigation or evidence **2. EVIDENCE** the evidence that proves something true or correct **3.** INTERNAT LAW **CONFIRMATION OF PROCEDURES** in international law, the process of confirming that procedures laid down in an agreement such as a weapons limitation treaty are being followed **4.** LAW **AFFIDAVIT** in law, an affidavit swearing to the accuracy of a pleading **5.** LAW **CONFIRMATORY EVIDENCE** evidence or testimony that confirms something —**ver·i·fi·ca·tive** /vérrəfi kàytiv/ *adj.*

ver·i·fi·ca·tion·ism /vèrrəfi káysh'n ìzzəm/ *n.* the view that every meaningful proposition is capable of being shown to be true or false

ver·i·fi·ca·tion prin·ci·ple *n.* the principle that a proposition or sentence is meaningful only if it is possible to establish whether it is true or false by experience or observation

ver·i·fy /vérrə fì/ (**-fied, -fy·ing, -fies**) *vt.* **1. PROVE SOMETHING** to prove that something is true **2. CHECK WHETHER SOMETHING IS TRUE** to check whether or not something is true by examination, investigation, or comparison **3.** LAW **SWEAR SOMETHING UNDER OATH** in law, to swear or affirm under oath that something is true **4.** LAW **ATTEST TO TRUTH BY AFFIDAVIT** in law, to support the truth of a pleading by affidavit [14thC. Via French *verifier* from medieval Latin *verificare*, literally "to make true," from *verus* "true" (source of English *very*) + *facere* "to make."] —**ver·i·fi·a·bil·i·ty** /vèrrə fì ə bíllətee/ *n.* —**ver·i·fi·a·ble** /vérrə fì əb'l, vèrrə fí əb'l/ *adj.* —**ver·i·fi·a·bly** /vérrə fì əblee, vèrrə fí əblee/ *adv.* —**ver·i·fi·er** /vérrə fìr/ *n.*

ver·i·ly /vérrəlee/ *adv.* in truth (*archaic*) ○ *Verily, he has admitted it.* [13thC. Formed from VERY, in the sense "true."]

ver·i·sim·i·lar /vèrrə símmilər/ *adj.* appearing to be true or real (*literary*) [Late 17thC. Formed from Latin *verisimilis*, literally "like the truth," from *verus* "true" and *similis* "like."] —**ver·i·sim·i·lar·ly** *adv.*

ver·i·si·mil·i·tude /vèrrə si míllə tòod/ *n.* (*formal*) **1. APPEARANCE OF BEING TRUE** the appearance of being true or real **2. SOMETHING THAT ONLY SEEMS TRUE** something that only appears to be true or real, e.g., a statement that is not supported by evidence [Early 17thC. From Latin *verisimilitudo*, from *verisimilis* (see VERISIMILAR).] —**ver·i·si·mil·i·tu·di·nous** /vèrrə simmilə tóod'nəss/ *adj.*

ver·ism /vé rìzzəm/ *n.* strict realism or naturalism in art and literature [Late 19thC. Formed from Latin *verus* or Italian *vero* "true."] —**ver·ist** *n.* —**ve·ris·tic** /və rístik/ *adj.*

ve·ris·mo /və ríz mō/ *n.* a late 19th-century movement in Italian opera that advocated the use of themes drawn from real life and naturalistic portrayal of characters and events. Puccini was one of the principal members of this movement. [Early 20thC. From Italian, "verism."]

ver·i·ta·ble /vérrətəb'l/ *adj.* **1.** ABSOLUTE indicating that something being referred to figuratively is as good as true **2.** TRUE true as a declaration or statement (*archaic*) [15thC. Via French from, ultimately, Latin *veritas* "truth" (see VERITY).] —**ver·i·ta·ble·ness** *n.* —**ver·i·ta·bly** *adv.*

ver·i·ty /vérrətee/ (*plural* **-ties**) *n.* (*formal*) **1.** TRUTH OR REALITY the quality of being true or real **2.** SOMETHING TRUE something that is true, especially a statement or principle that is accepted as a fact [14thC. Via French from Latin *veritas*, from *verus* "true" (source of English *very, verify*, and *verdict*).]

ver·juice /vúr jòoss/ *n.* **1.** LIQUID FROM SOUR FRUIT an acid liquid made from crab apples or other sour or unripe fruit, formerly used in cooking instead of vinegar **2.** UNPLEASANTNESS sourness of temper, attitude, or expression [14thC. From Old French *vertjus*, from *verd* "green" + *jus* "juice."]

Ver·laine /ver láyn, ver lén/, **Paul** (1844–96) French poet. He wrote *Songs Without Words* (1874) while in prison for shooting his friend Arthur Rimbaud. His later symbolist verse influenced the development of French poetry. Full name **Paul Marie Verlaine**

Ver·meer /vər meér, -máir/, **Jan** (1632–75) Dutch artist. A major painter of the Dutch Golden Age, he painted domestic interiors of great serenity. Only 35 of his paintings survive.

ver·meil /vúrm'l, vúr màyl/ *n.* **1.** GILDED METAL gilded silver, bronze, or copper **2.** VERMILION the color vermilion (*literary*) [14thC. Via Old French from late Latin *vermiculus*, kermes insect from which red dye was made, literally "little worm," from Latin *vermis* "worm" (see VERMI-).]

vermi- *prefix.* worm ○ *vermivorous* [From Latin *vermis* "worm" (source of English *vermicelli* and *vermin*). Ultimately from an Indo-European word that is also the ancestor of English *worm*.]

ver·mi·cel·li /vùrmə séllee, -chéllee/ *n.* a kind of pasta in long fine threads, often used in soups [Mid-17thC. From Italian, literally "little worms," from, ultimately, Latin *vermis* "worm."]

ver·mi·cide /vúrmi sìd/ *n.* **1.** CHEM CHEMICAL WORM KILLER a substance used to kill worms **2.** MED REMEDY FOR PARASITIC WORMS a chemical substance that expels parasitic worms from the small intestines —**ver·mi·cid·al** /vùrmi síd'l/ *adj.*

vermicomposting *n.* = **vermiculture**

ver·mic·u·lar /vər míkyələr/ *adj.* **1.** WAVY in wavy lines like the movements, shape, or tracks of worms **2.** OF WORMS relating to worms [Late 17thC. From medieval Latin *vermicularis*, from Latin *vermiculis*, literally "little worm," from *vermis* "worm."] —**ver·mic·u·lar·ly** *adv.*

ver·mic·u·late *vt.* /vər míkyə làyt/ (**-lat·ed, -lat·ing, -lates**) DECORATE SOMETHING WITH WAVY LINES to decorate something with wavy lines or patterns (*formal*) ■ *adj.* /vər míkyələt, -làyt/ **1.** WITH WAVY LINES with wavy lines like the movements, shape, or tracks of a worm **2.** SINUOUS with many twists and turns (*formal*) **3.** LOOKING WORM-EATEN with a worm-eaten appearance (*literary*) [Early 17thC. From Latin *vermiculat-*, the past participle stem of *vermiculari* "to be full of worms," from *vermiculus* (see VERMICULAR).]

ver·mic·u·la·tion /vər mìkyə láysh'n/ *n.* **1.** MOVEMENT IN WAVES movement in waves, e.g., the muscular contractions of the intestines (**peristalsis**) **2.** WAVY DECORATION decorative wavy lines, patterns, or carvings **3.** WORM INFESTATION infestation by worms, or the resulting worm-eaten condition

ver·mic·u·lite /vər míkyə lìt/ *n.* a hydrous silicate of aluminum, magnesium, or iron, resulting from the alteration of the mineral constituents of basic rocks. It is used for insulation, as a lubricant, and as a medium for starting or growing plants. [Early 19thC. Formed from Latin *vermiculus* "little worm" (see VERMICULAR), because of the way flakes of it expand and writhe in long shapes when heated.]

ver·mi·cul·ture /vúrmi kùlchər/, **ver·mi·com·post·ing** /vúrmi kòmpōsting/ *n.* the use of specially bred worms to convert organic matter into compost

ver·mi·form /vúrmi fàwrm/ *adj.* resembling a worm in shape

ver·mi·form ap·pen·dix, ver·mi·form proc·ess *n.* ANAT = **appendix** *n.* 1

ver·mi·fuge /vúrmi fyòoj/ *n.* a drug or other substance that causes worms or other parasites to be expelled from the intestines —**ver·mif·u·gal** /vər míffyəg'l, vùrmi fyòog'l/ *adj.*

ver·mil·ion /vər míllyən/, **ver·mil·lion** *n.* **1.** RED PIGMENT a bright red pigment made from mercuric sulfide or created artificially **2.** COLORS BRIGHT RED COLOR a bright red color, sometimes tinged with orange ■ *adj.* OF A BRILLIANT RED of a bright red color [13thC. From Old French *vermeillon*, from *vermeil* (see VERMEIL).]

ver·min /vúrmin/ (*plural* **-min**) *n.* **1.** DESTRUCTIVE ANIMALS OR INSECTS small animals or insects that harm people, livestock, property, or crops and are difficult to control, e.g., rats, weasels, fleas, or cockroaches **2.** OFFENSIVE TERM an offensive term for a person or group considered to be extremely unpleasant or undesirable (*slang insult*) [13thC. Via Old French from assumed Vulgar Latin *verminum* "noxious life forms," from Latin *vermis* "worm."]

ver·mi·na·tion /vùrmi náysh'n/ *n.* the spreading of or infestation with vermin, especially parasites

ver·min·ous /vúrminəss/ *adj.* **1.** OF OR WITH VERMIN relating to or infested with vermin **2.** CAUSED BY VERMIN OR WORMS caused by vermin or parasitic worms **3.** DISGUSTING extremely unpleasant or offensive —**ver·min·ous·ly** *adv.* —**ver·min·ous·ness** *n.*

ver·mis /vúrmiss/ *n.* the middle lobe of the brain that connects the two hemispheres of the cerebellum [Late 19thC. From Latin, "worm."]

ver·miv·o·rous /vər mívvərəss/ *adj.* used to describe birds or other animals that feed on worms

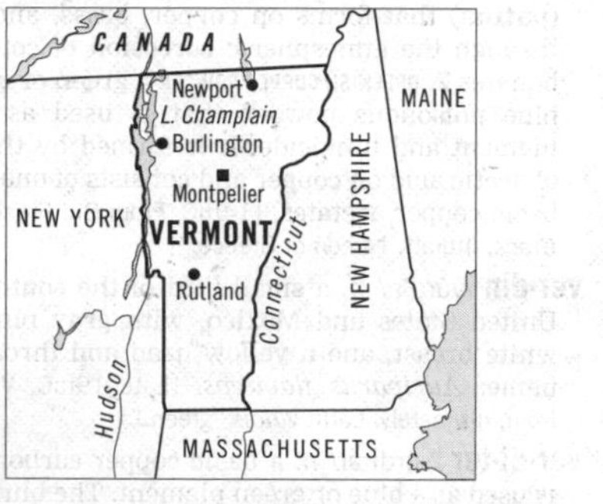

Vermont

Ver·mont /vur mónt/ state in the northeastern United States, bordered by Canada, New Hampshire, Massachusetts, and New York State. Capital: Montpelier. Population: 588,978 (1997). Area: 9,615 sq. mi./24,903 sq. km. —**Ver·mon·ter** *n.*

ver·mouth /vər mòoth/ *n.* a wine flavored with aromatic herbs [Early 19thC. Via French from German *Wermut* "wormwood," with which it was originally flavored.]

ver·nac·u·lar /vər nákyələr/ *n.* **1.** LANG ORDINARY LANGUAGE the everyday language of the people in a particular country or region, as opposed to official or formal language **2.** LANG SPOKEN LANGUAGE the common spoken language of a people as opposed to formal written or literary language **3.** LANG LANGUAGE OF PARTICULAR GROUP the distinctive vocabulary or language of a particular profession, group, or class **4.** BIOL COMMON NAME a common name of a plant, animal, or other organism as opposed to its scientific name **5.** ARCHIT ORDINARY BUILDING STYLE the architecture of a particular place or people, especially the architectural style that is used for ordinary houses as opposed to large official or commercial buildings ■ *adj.* **1.** LANG USING ORDINARY LANGUAGE belonging to, relating to, or using the everyday language of the people in a particular country or region, as opposed to official or formal language **2.** LANG IN ORDINARY SPOKEN LANGUAGE belonging to, relating to, or using the common spoken language of a people as opposed to formal written or literary language **3.** BIOL RELATING TO COMMON NAME used to describe the common name of a plant, animal, or other organism as opposed to its scientific name **4.** ARCHIT BUILT IN COMMON STYLE built in the style of architecture used for the ordinary houses of a particular place or people, as opposed to the style used for large official or commercial buildings [Early 17thC. Formed from Latin *vernaculus* "native," from *verna* "native-born slave," of uncertain origin: possibly from Etruscan.] —**ver·nac·u·lar·ly** *adv.*

ver·nac·u·lar·ism /vər nákyələ rìzzəm/ *n.* **1.** ORDINARY WORD OR PHRASE a word or phrase from the everyday language of the people in a particular country or region, as opposed to official or formal language **2.** USE OF ORDINARY LANGUAGE the use of everyday language, as opposed to official or formal language

ver·nac·u·lar·ize /vər nákyələ rìz/ (**-ized, -iz·ing, -iz·es**) *vt.* to make a word or phrase a part of ordinary everyday language

ver·nal /vúrn'l/ *adj.* **1.** IN THE SPRING appearing or happening in the season of spring **2.** YOUTHFUL having the freshness or energy associated with being young (*literary*) [Mid-16thC. From Latin *vernalis*, from *vernus* "of the spring," from *ver* "spring."]

ver·nal e·qui·nox *n.* **1.** TIME BEGINNING OF SPRING the time when the sun crosses the celestial equator and day and night are of equal length, marking the beginning of spring. In the northern hemisphere this is around March 21, in the southern hemisphere around September 23. **2.** ASTRON INTERSECTION OF CELESTIAL EQUATOR AND ECLIPTIC the point on the celestial sphere where the path of the sun (**ecliptic**) crosses the celestial equator, in the constellation of Pisces

ver·nal·ize /vúrn'l ìz/ (**-ized, -iz·ing, -iz·es**) *vt.* to expose plant seeds or seedlings to artificially cold temperatures in order to promote development and flowering. For example, seeds of winter cereals can be vernalized to mimic the passing of winter and allow them to germinate and grow successfully when sown in the spring. —**ver·nal·i·za·tion** /vùrn'li záysh'n/ *n.*

ver·na·tion /vər náysh'n/ *n.* the way that young leaves are arranged in a bud [Late 18thC. From the modern Latin stem *vernation-*, from Latin *vernare* "to grow in the spring," from *vernus* "of the spring" (see VERNAL).]

Verne /vurn/, **Jules** (1828–1905) French writer. His novels, which included *20,000 Leagues Under the Sea* (1870) and *Around the World in 80 Days* (1873), were pioneering works of science fiction.

ver·ni·cle /vúrnək'l/ *n.* CHR = **veronica**^{2} *n.* 1 [14thC. From Old French *veronicle*, variant of *veronique* (see VERONICA).]

ver·ni·er /vúrnee ər/ *n.* **1.** SMALL SCALE FOR PRECISE READINGS a small movable graduated scale parallel to a larger graduated scale, used to obtain smaller or more precise readings from the main scale **2.** DEVICE FOR MAKING FINE ADJUSTMENTS an auxiliary device used to make fine adjustments to a precision instrument ■ *adj.* WITH A VERNIER relating to or fitted with a vernier [Mid-18thC. Named for the French mathematician Pierre *Vernier* (1580–1637).]

ver·ni·er rock·et *n.* = **thruster** *n.* 1 [Mid-20thC. See VERNIER.]

ver·nis·sage /vùrni saázh/ *n.* a private showing or preview before the public opening of an art exhibition [Early 20thC. From French, literally "varnishing," because it was originally the day before a public exhibition, when exhibitors varnished paintings after they were in place.]

Ver·non /vúrnin/ city in southern British Columbia, Canada. Population: 55,359 (1996).

Ve·ro·na /və rṓnə/ capital city of Verona Province, Veneto Region, northern Italy. Population: 254,145 (1995). —**Ver·o·nese** /vèrrə neéz, -neéss/ *n.*, *adj.*

ve·ron·i·ca^1 /və rónnikə/ *n.* a perennial or annual plant or shrub of the figwort family, e.g., the speedwell, that bears clusters of small, typically blue flowers. Genus: *Veronica.* [Early 16thC. From modern Latin, genus name, of uncertain origin: possibly an alteration of Greek *berenikion*.]

ve·ron·i·ca^2 /və rónnikə/ *n.* **1.** IMPRESSION OF JESUS CHRIST'S FACE the impression of Jesus Christ's face believed by some to have been miraculously left on the cloth with which Saint Veronica wiped it on his way to his crucifixion **2.** CLOTH THAT WIPED JESUS CHRIST'S FACE the cloth with which Saint Veronica is said to have wiped Jesus Christ's face on his way to his crucifixion **3.** CLOTH WITH JESUS CHRIST'S FACE a cloth bearing a representation of Jesus Christ's face, sometimes worn by pilgrims [Late 17thC. Origin uncertain: possibly an alteration (influenced by the name of Saint Veronica) of medieval Latin *vera iconica*, literally "true image."]

ve·ron·i·ca^3 /və rónnikə/ *n.* a move in bullfighting in which the bullfighter stands in place and slowly swings the cape away from the bull as it charges [Mid-19thC. From Spanish *verónica*, named for Saint *Veronica*, from the gesture involved in wiping Jesus Christ's face.]

Ver·raz·za·no /vèrrə zaánō, -raa tsaá-/, **Ver·ra·za·no, Giovanni da** (1480?–1527?) Italian explorer. He explored the eastern coast of North America and was the first European to sail into New York Bay.

ver·ru·ca /və ro͝okə/ (*plural* **-cae** /və ro͝okee/) *n.* **1. WART ON FOOT** a wart that grows on the foot, usually on the sole **2. GROWTH RESEMBLING A WART** a wart-shaped growth or projection on a plant or the skin of an animal [Mid-16thC. From Latin, "wart." Ultimately from an Indo-European word meaning "bump," which is also the ancestor of English *wart* and *varicose*.]

ver·ru·cose /vérrə kòss/, **ver·ru·cous** /-kəss/ *adj.* covered with warts or similar growths or projections [Late 17thC. From Latin *verrucosus*, from *verruca* "wart" (see VERRUCA).] —**ver·ru·cos·i·ty** /vèrrə kóssətee/ *n.*

vers *abbr.* versed sine

Ver·sailles /vər sí/ *n.* a large and elaborately decorated palace near Paris, France, built for Louis XIV in the mid-17th century. It is now a museum. The Treaty of Versailles was signed there in 1919, ending World War I.

ver·sant /vúrs'nt/ *n.* **1. MOUNTAIN SLOPE** the slope of a mountain or mountain range **2. AREA SLOPE** the slope of a particular region [Mid-19thC. From French, the present participle of *verser* "to turn over," from Latin *versare* (see VERSATILE).]

ver·sa·tile /vúrsət'l/ *adj.* **1. WITH MANY USES** able or meant to be used in many different ways **2. MOVING EASILY BETWEEN TASKS** able to move easily from one subject, task, or skill to another **3. CHANGEABLE** subject to rapid or unpredictable change **4.** ZOOL **FREE-MOVING** used to describe a body part or joint that can turn or move freely in more than one direction, e.g., an insect's antenna **5.** BOT **ATTACHED LOOSELY** used to describe an anther that is attached to the filament by a small area, allowing it to move more freely [Early 17thC. From Latin *versatilis*, from *versat-*, the past participle stem of *versare*, literally "to keep turning or changing," from *vertere* (see VERSE[1]).] —**ver·sa·tile·ly** *adv.* —**ver·sa·til·i·ty** /vùrsə tíllətee/ *n.*

vers de so·cié·té /vùr də sōssyə táy/ *n.* verse or poetry written in a light witty sophisticated style [From French, literally "society verse"]

verse[1] /vurs/ *n.* **1.** MUSIC, POETRY **GROUP OF SONG OR POEM LINES** a section of a poem or song consisting of a number of lines arranged together to form a single unit **2.** JUD-CHR **NUMBERED DIVISION OF BIBLE CHAPTER** any of the numbered subdivisions into which the chapters of the Bible are divided **3.** POETRY **POETRY** poetry as opposed to prose **4.** POETRY **BODY OF POETRY** a body of poetry, e.g., by a single author or from a particular country or period ○ *an anthology of 19th-century verse* **5.** POETRY **KIND OF POETRY** a particular form of poetry **6.** POETRY **BAD POETRY** poetry that is trivial in content or inferior in quality ○ *It's not poetry at all, it's just verse.* **7.** POETRY **SHORT POEM** a poem, especially a short one **8.** POETRY **LINE OF A POEM** a single line of a poem, arranged rhythmically in metrical feet ■ *vt.* **(versed, vers·ing, vers·es) VERSIFY PROSE CONTENT** to turn something from prose into poetry (*archaic*) [Pre-12thC. Directly and via Old French *vers* from Latin *versus* "turning (of a plow), furrow, line," from *vertere* "to turn").]

WORD KEY: ORIGIN

The Latin word *vertere*, from which **verse** is derived, is also the source of English *adverse, advertise, controversy, conversation, convert, diverse, invert, obverse, pervert, prose, reverse, subvert, universe, versatile, version, versus, vertebra, vertical,* and *vertigo.*

verse[2] /vurs/ **(versed, vers·ing, vers·es)** *vt.* to instruct somebody in something (*archaic or literary*) [Back-formation from VERSED]

versed /vurst/ *adj.* very knowledgeable about or skilled in something [Early 17thC. Directly or via French *versé* from Latin *versatus*, the past participle of *versari* "to occupy oneself with," from *versare* "to keep turning" (see VERSATILE).]

versed co·sine *n.* a trigonometric function equal to one minus the sine of the specified angle [Modeled on VERSED SINE]

versed sine *n.* a trigonometric function equal to one minus the cosine of the specified angle [Translation of modern Latin *sinus versus*, literally "turned sine"]

ver·set /vúrsət/ *n.* a short verse, especially one from a sacred book [Early 17thC. From French, literally "short verse," from *vers* "line" (see VERSE[1]).]

ver·si·cle /vúrsik'l/ *n.* **1.** CHR **SHORT SENTENCE IN LITURGY** a short sentence spoken or chanted by the minister during a liturgical service and responded to by the congregation or choir **2.** POETRY **VERSE** a short verse (*literary or archaic*) [14thC. From Latin *versiculus*, literally "short verse," from *versus* "line" (see VERSE[1]).] —**ver·sic·u·lar** /vər síkyələr/ *adj.*

ver·si·col·or /vúrsi kùllər/, **ver·si·col·ored** /-kùllərd/ *adj.* **1. MULTICOLORED** having various colors **2. OF CHANGEABLE COLOR** varying or changing in color [Early 17thC. From Latin *versicolor*, from *versus*, the past participle of *vertere* "to turn, change" (see VERSE[1]), + *color* "color."]

ver·si·fi·ca·tion /vùrsifi káysh'n/ *n.* **1. ART OF VERSE-WRITING** the art or practice of writing verse **2. METRICAL FORM** the metrical form or structure of a poem **3. TURNING PROSE INTO VERSE** the conversion of prose into verse, or the recounting of something in verse **4. VERSION IN POETRY** a poetic or metrical version of a prose work

ver·si·fy /vúrsi fì/ **(-fied, -fy·ing, -fies)** *v.* **1.** *vt.* **CHANGE PROSE INTO POETRY** to turn prose into verse **2.** *vt.* **TELL STORY IN POETRY** to recount something in verse **3.** *vi.* **WRITE POETRY** to compose verse [14thC. Via French from Latin *versificare*, literally "to make verses," from *versus* "line" (see VERSE[1]).] —**ver·si·fi·er** *n.*

ver·sine /vúr sìn/ *n.* MATH = **versed sine**

ver·sion /vúrzh'n/ *n.* **1. ACCOUNT OF SOMETHING** an account of something, given from a particular point of view **2. PARTICULAR FORM OF SOMETHING** a particular form or variety of something that is different from others or from the original **3. ADAPTATION OF SOMETHING** an adaptation of something for another medium, e.g., a book made into a play or film **4. TRANSLATION OF SOMETHING** a translation of something into another language **5. ver·sion, Ver·sion BIBLE TRANSLATION** a particular translation of the Bible **6.** MED **MANIPULATION OF FETUS** the manipulation of a fetus to change its position in the womb, e.g., so it can be delivered safely **7.** MED **TILTED CONDITION OF ORGAN** a condition in which an internal organ, especially the womb, is abnormally tilted or turned [Late 16thC. Via French from the Latin stem *version-*, from *vers-*, the past participle stem of *vertere* "to turn" (see VERSE[1]).] —**ver·sion·al** *adj.*

vers li·bre /vùr leébrə/ *n.* = **free verse** [From French]

ver·so /vúr sō/ (*plural* **-sos**) *n.* **1.** PUBL **BACK OF PRINTED PAGE** the back of a page or other printed sheet. ◊ **recto 2.** PUBL **LEFT-HAND PAGE** any of the left-hand pages of a book, usually printed with an even page number. ◊ **recto 3.** COINS = **reverse** *n.* 3 [Mid-19thC. From Latin *verso (folio)* "(with the page) turned," from *versus*, the past participle of *vertere* "to turn" (see VERSE[1]).]

verst /vurst/ *n.* a Russian measure of length equal to 0.66 mi./1.07 km [Mid-16thC. Via French *verste* or German *Werst* from Russian *versta* "line."]

ver·sus /vúrsəss/ *prep.* **1. AGAINST** against, especially in a competition or court case ○ *The United States versus Canada* **2. ALTERNATIVE TO** as opposed to or contrasted with ○ *such considerations as money versus job satisfaction* [15thC. From medieval Latin, "against," from the past participle of Latin *vertere* "to turn" (see VERSE[1]).]

vert /vurt/ *n.* **1.** HERALDRY **GREEN COLOR** in heraldry, the color green **2.** LAW **RIGHT TO CUT WOOD OR VEGETATION** in former times, the right to cut living wood or green vegetation in a forest **3.** HIST **WOOD OR VEGETATION** in former times, living wood or green vegetation in a forest ■ *adj.* HERALDRY **GREEN** in heraldry, green in color [15thC. Via Old French, literally "green," from Latin *viridis* (source of English *verdant* and *vireo*).]

vert. *abbr.* vertical

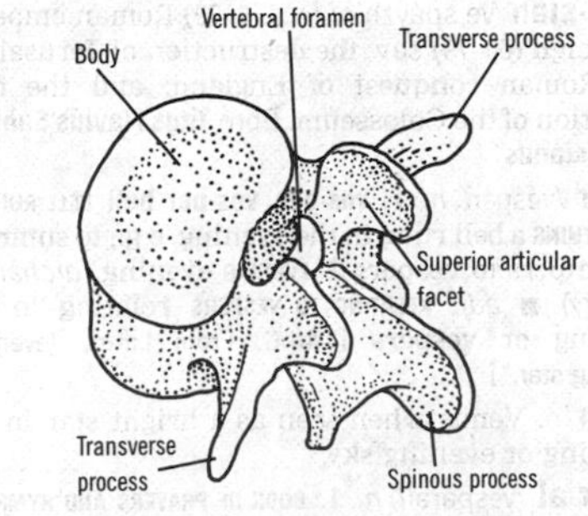

Vertebra

ver·te·bra /vúrtəbrə/ (*plural* **-brae** /-brày, -bree/ *or* **-bras**) *n.* a bone of the spinal column, typically consisting of a stout body, a bony arch enclosing a hole for the spinal cord, and stubby projections that connect with adjacent bones. In humans the spinal column contains 33 vertebrae, including the fused lower vertebrae that form the sacrum and coccyx. [Early 17thC. From Latin, formed from *vertere* "to turn" (see VERSE[1]).] —**ver·te·bral** *adj.* —**ver·te·bral·ly** *adv.*

ver·te·bral ca·nal *n.* = **spinal canal**

ver·te·bral col·umn *n.* = **spinal column**

ver·te·brate /vúrtəbrət, -bràyt/ *n.* an animal with a segmented spinal column and a well-developed brain, e.g., a mammal, bird, reptile, amphibian, or fish [Early 19thC. From Latin *vertebratus* "having joints," from *vertebra* (see VERTEBRA).] —**ver·te·brate** *adj.*

ver·te·bra·tion /vùrtə bráysh'n/ *n.* the formation of or division into vertebral segments, or segments resembling vertebrae, during the development of an embryo

ver·tex /vúr tèks/ (*plural* **-ti·ces** /-ti seèz/ *or* **-tex·es**) *n.* **1. APEX** the highest point of something **2.** ANAT **TOP OF THE HEAD** the highest point of a body part, especially the top or crown of the head **3.** GEOM **POINT OPPOSITE THE BASE** the point opposite the base of a figure **4.** GEOM **POINT WHERE SIDES OF ANGLE MEET** the point where two sides of a plane figure or an angle intersect **5.** GEOM **POINT WHERE PLANES OF SOLID MEET** the point where three or more planes of a solid figure intersect **6.** ASTRON **POINT TOWARD WHICH STARS MOVE** a point on the celestial sphere toward which or from which a group of stars appears to move [Late 16thC. From Latin, "whirl, spiral of hair at the top of the head," from *vertere* "to turn" (see VERSE[1]).]

ver·ti·cal /vúrtik'l/ *adj.* **1. AT RIGHT ANGLE TO HORIZON** at a right angle to the horizon **2. UPRIGHT** extending or standing in an upright position, or running straight up or down something such as a piece of paper **3. OVERHEAD** at the vertex or directly overhead **4.** ECON **INVOLVING ALL STAGES OF PRODUCTION** relating to or involving all the consecutive stages in the production of goods, from design to sale **5.** ANAT **AT THE TOP OF THE HEAD** at or relating to the highest point of a body part, especially the top or crown of the head **6. MADE UP OF MANY LEVELS** involving or made up of successive or many levels ○ *a vertical management structure* ■ *n.* **1. SOMETHING VERTICAL** a vertical structure, line, surface, or part **2. VERTICAL POSITION** a position that is upright or at a right angle to the horizon [Mid-16thC. Directly or via French from late Latin *verticalis* "overhead," from Latin *vertex* (see VERTEX).] —**ver·ti·cal·i·ty** /vùrti kállətee/ *n.* —**ver·ti·cal·ly** /vúrtikəlee/ *adv.*

ver·ti·cal an·gle *n.* either of the pair of equal angles formed on opposite sides of the point at which two lines intersect. The sides of either of the pair of vertical angles are the extensions of those of the other angle.

ver·ti·cal cir·cle *n.* a great circle on the celestial sphere whose plane is perpendicular to the horizon and passes through the zenith and the nadir

ver·ti·cal file *n.* a collection of miscellaneous resource materials e.g., in a library, stored separately from the main collection [Because stored vertically, in suspension files]

ver·ti·cal mo·bil·i·ty *n.* the movement of people or groups in society either upward or downward in terms of class or status

ver·ti·cal sta·bi·liz·er *n.* = **fin**[1] *n.* 4

ver·ti·cal un·ion *n.* = **industrial union**

ver·ti·ces plural of **vertex**

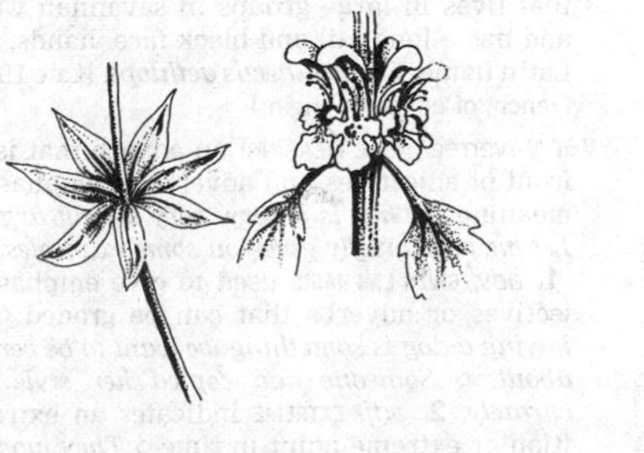

Verticil: Two verticil plants

ver·ti·cil /vúrtəssìl/ *n.* a circular arrangement of similar parts around a central point [Early 18thC. From Latin *verticillus* "whorl of a spindle."]

ver·ti·cil·las·ter /vùrtəssi lástər/ *n.* a flower cluster that looks like a whorl of flowers but actually consists of two crowded clusters (**cymes**) arising opposite each other, as in many mints [Mid-19thC. Formed from Latin *verticullus* "whorl of a spindle" + -ASTER.] —**ver·ti·cil·las·trate** /vùrtəssi lá strāyt, -lástrət/ *adj.*

ver·ti·cil·late /vùrtə síllət, -làyt/ *adj.* arranged in whorls, or forming a whorl —**ver·ti·cil·late·ly** *adv.* —**ver·ti·cil·la·tion** /vùrtəssi láysh'n/ *n.*

ver·tig·i·nous /vur tíjjənəss/ *adj.* **1.** DIZZYING causing dizziness, especially because of being very high or exposed ○ *the mountain's vertiginous summit* **2.** SUFFERING FROM VERTIGO relating to or suffering from the whirling or tilting sensation of vertigo **3.** ROTARY whirling or spinning on an axis **4.** FICKLE tending to change frequently or suddenly —**ver·tig·i·nous·ly** *adv.* —**ver·tig·i·nous·ness** *n.*

ver·ti·go /vúrti gō/ (*plural* **-ti·goes** *or* **-ti·gos** *or* **-tig·i·nes** /vər tíjjə neez/) *n.* **1.** CONDITION MARKED BY WHIRLING SENSATIONS a condition in which somebody feels a sensation of whirling or tilting that causes a loss of balance. It is most often caused by disease of the inner ear or of the parts of the brain concerned with balance, or it may precede an epileptic episode. **2.** INSTANCE OF VERTIGO an instance or episode of vertigo [15thC. From Latin (stem *vertigin-*), "whirling about, giddiness," from *vertere* "turn."]

WORD KEY: CULTURAL NOTE

Vertigo, a movie by English director Alfred Hitchcock (1958). One of Hitchcock's most highly regarded films, it is both a typically suspenseful thriller and a powerful study of obsession. When former policeman Scottie Fergusson is asked to shadow a friend's wife, he first falls in love with her and then, after her suicide, becomes infatuated with a woman who appears to be her double.

ver·tu *n.* = **virtu**

Ver·tum·nus /vur túmnəss/ *n.* the Roman god of gardens

ver·vain /vúr vàyn/ *n.* a herbaceous plant with small blue, white, or purple flowers and square stems, especially one with lilac flowers that grows wild in temperate regions. Genus: *Verbena.* [14thC. Via French *verveine* from Latin *verbena* (see VERBENA).]

verve /vurv/ *n.* **1.** CREATIVE ENTHUSIASM enthusiasm, energy, or spirit, especially in the expression of artistic ideas **2.** VITALITY lively vigorous spirit [Late 17thC. Via French, "vigor, fanciful expression," from Latin *verba* "whimsical words," literally "words," plural of *verbum* "word" (source of English *verb* and *verbal*).]

Vervet

ver·vet /vúrvət/, **ver·vet mon·key** *n.* an African monkey that lives in large groups in savannah woodlands and has a long tail and black face, hands, and feet. Latin name: *Cercopithecus aethiops.* [Late 19thC. From French, of unknown origin.]

ver·y /vérree/ CORE MEANING: an adverb that is used in front of adjectives and adverbs to emphasize their meaning ○ *That is a very, very strong argument.* ○ *Let me very briefly give you some examples.*

1. *adv.* GIVES EMPHASIS used to give emphasis to adjectives or adverbs that can be graded ○ *I think buying a dog is something we want to be very careful about.* ○ *Someone had copied her style very accurately.* **2.** *adj.* EXTREME indicates an extreme position or extreme point in time ○ *They moved to the very back of the set, smiling at the technicians.* **3.** *adj.* RIGHT exactly the right or appropriate person or thing, or exactly the same person or thing ○ *Hello! The very person I wanted to see!* ○ *He died this very day in 1986.* **4.** *adj.* EMPHASIZES IMPORTANCE used before nouns to emphasize seriousness or importance ○ *An event like this can't help but shake the boxing world to its very foundation.* [13thC. Via Old French *verrai* from, ultimately, Latin *verax* "truthful," from *verus* "true" (source of English *verdict, verisimilitude,* and *verify*).] ◇ **very much so** an emphatic way of saying yes to something or indicating that it is true or correct ○ *"He was a good man, brave and honest." "Yes, very much so."* ◇ **very well** indicates that somebody agrees to do something or accepts what somebody has said

ver·y high fre·quen·cy *n.* the radio frequency band between 30 and 300 megahertz, reserved for the transmission of television and FM radio signals

Ver·y light /vérree-/ *n.* a colored flare fired from a pistol, used as a signal [Early 20thC. Named for the U.S. naval officer Edward W. *Very* (1847–1910).]

very low fre·quen·cy *n.* the radio frequency band between 3 and 30 kilohertz

Ver·y pis·tol /vérree-, véeree-/ *n.* a pistol used for firing colored flares [Early 20thC. See VERY LIGHT.]

Ver·y Rev·er·end *n.* the title of religious officials below the rank of bishop or abbot

Ve·sey /véezee/, **Denmark** (1767?–1822) U.S. freedman. Having purchased his own freedom he planned an uprising to free all the enslaved laborers in South Carolina (1822), but the plot was discovered and he was hanged.

ve·si·ca /və síkə, və séekə, véssikə/ (*plural* **-cae** /və síkee, və síssee, və séekee, və séessee/) *n.* **1.** ANAT BLADDER a bladder, especially the urinary bladder (*technical*) **2.** ARTS OVAL a pointed oval shape used in medieval art and sculpture, especially to enclose a figure of Jesus Christ or the Virgin Mary [Mid-17thC. From Latin, "bladder, blister."]

ves·i·cal /véssik'l/ *adj.* occurring in or relating to a bladder, especially the urinary bladder ○ *vesical veins* [Late 18thC]

ves·i·cant /véssikənt/, **ves·i·ca·to·ry** /véssikə tàwree/ *n.* (*plural* **-ries**) BLISTERING SUBSTANCE a substance that causes blisters, especially a substance such as mustard gas used in chemical warfare ■ *adj.* CAUSING BLISTERING causing blisters to form [Mid-17thC]

ves·i·cate /véssi kàyt/ (**-cat·ed, -cat·ing, -cates**) *vti.* to cause or be affected by blisters [Mid-17thC. Formed from VESICA.] —**ves·i·ca·tion** /vèssi káysh'n/ *n.*

ves·i·cle /véssik'l/ *n.* **1.** MED FLUID-FILLED CYST a small sac or hollow organ in the body, especially one containing fluid **2.** MED FLUID-FILLED BLISTER a very small blister filled with clear fluid (**serum**) **3.** GEOL SPHERICAL CAVITY WITHIN A ROCK a bubble-shaped cavity in an igneous rock, formed by the expansion of gases trapped in lava and often later filled with minerals deposited from percolating solutions **4.** BOT CAVITY IN AN AQUATIC PLANT a cavity filled with air in a seaweed or aquatic plant [Late 16thC. Directly or via French *vésicule* from Latin *vesicula* "small vesica," from *vesica* "bladder, blister."]

ve·sic·u·lar /və síkyələr/ *adj.* resembling, having, or made up of vesicles —**ve·sic·u·lar·ly** *adv.*

ve·sic·u·late *vti.* /və síkyə làyt/ (**-lat·ed, -lat·ing, -lates**) FORM OR BECOME A VESICLE to form blisters or vesicles in something, or to become like a vesicle ■ *adj.* /və síkyələt, və síkyə làyt/ HAVING VESICLES having or resembling blisters or vesicles —**ve·sic·u·la·tion** /və sìkyə láysh'n/ *n.*

Ves·pa·sian /ve spáyzh'n/ (A.D. 9–79) Roman emperor His reign (69–79) saw the destruction of Jerusalem, the Roman conquest of England, and the construction of the Colosseum. Born **Titus Flavius Sabinus Vespasianus**

ves·per /véspər/ *n.* **1.** **ves·per, ves·per bell** BELL RUNG IN THE EVENING a bell rung in the evening, e.g., to summon worshipers to vespers **2.** EVENING evening (*archaic or literary*) ■ *adj.* RELATING TO VESPERS relating to the evening or vespers [14thC. From Latin, "evening, evening star."]

Ves·per *n.* Venus when seen as a bright star in the morning or evening sky

ves·per·al /véspərəl/ *n.* **1.** BOOK OF PRAYERS AND HYMNS a book that contains the prayers and hymns used at vespers **2.** ALTAR CLOTH COVERING a covering for an altar cloth

ves·pers /véspərz/, **Ves·pers** *n.* EVENING WORSHIP an evening church service, particularly evensong (*takes a singular or plural verb*) ■ *npl.* SIXTH CANONICAL HOUR the sixth of the seven canonical hours or a service held on Sundays and holy days at this time, especially in the Roman Catholic Church (*takes a singular or plural verb*) [14thC. Via Old French *vespres* (plural) from, ultimately, Latin *vespera* (singular) "evening," from *vesper* "evening star."]

ves·per spar·row *n.* a North American sparrow that is found in grasslands and pastures, has white outer feathers on a notched tail, and is known for its evening song. Latin name: *Pooecetes gramineus.*

ves·per·til·i·o·nid /vèspər tíllee ənid/ *n.* a common, insect-eating, long-tailed bat. Family: Vespertilionidae. [Late 19thC. From modern Latin *Vespertilionidae*, family name, ultimately from Latin *vespertilio* "bat," from *vesper* "evening."]

ves·per·tine /véspər tīn/ *adj.* **1.** BOT OPENING IN THE EVENING used to describe a flower that opens in the evening **2.** ZOOL ACTIVE IN THE EVENING tending to be most active in the evening **3.** ASTRON APPEARING IN THE EVENING appearing or setting in the evening [Early 16thC]

ves·pi·ar·y /véspee èrree/ (*plural* **-ies**) *n.* a nest or colony of social wasps or hornets [Early 19thC. Formed from Latin *vespa* "wasp" on the model of APIARY.]

ves·pid /véspid/ *n.* INSECT OF THE WASP AND HORNET FAMILY an insect of the family that includes wasps and hornets. Family: Vespidae. ■ *adj.* BELONGING TO THE WASP AND HORNET FAMILY belonging or related to the family of insects that includes wasps and hornets [Early 20thC. Formed from Latin *vespa* "wasp."]

ves·pine /vé spīn/ *adj.* relating to or resembling wasps [Mid-19thC. Formed from Latin *vespa* "wasp."]

Ves·puc·ci /ves pōochee/, **Amerigo** (1454–1512) Italian explorer. He claimed to be the first European to reach the mainland of the Americas (1497–98). "America" is named for him.

ves·sel /véss'l/ *n.* **1.** RECEPTACLE a hollow receptacle, especially one that is used as a container for liquids **2.** NAUT LARGE WATERCRAFT a ship or large boat **3.** AIR AIRSHIP a flying craft, especially an airship **4.** ANAT TUBULAR STRUCTURE CONDUCTING BODY FLUID a duct that carries fluid, especially blood or lymph, around the body **5.** BOT TUBE CONDUCTING WATER IN A PLANT a tube that carries water and dissolved minerals through a plant, forming part of the sap-conducting tissue (**xylem**). Vessels consist of a longitudinal series of fused cylindrical cells whose end walls have broken down, and are found in most flowering plants and some ferns. **6.** SOMEBODY WHO EMBODIES A QUALITY somebody seen as the recipient or embodiment of a quality [14thC. Via Anglo-Norman from Latin *vascellum* "small dish or vase, ship," from *vas* "dish, vase" (source of English *vase*).]

vest /vest/ *n.* CLOTHES **1.** *U.S., Can, Aus* SLEEVELESS GARMENT a man's or woman's sleeveless and collarless waist-length garment, usually with buttons down the front, worn over a shirt and traditionally worn by men under a suit jacket **2.** *U.K., NZ* = **undershirt** ■ *v.* (**vest·ed, vest·ing, vests**) **1.** *vt.* CONFER POWER ON to bestow a power on somebody or something (*usually passive*) ○ *The governor was vested with certain powers.* **2.** *vti.* CONFER RIGHTS ON to settle or confer property, power, or rights on somebody, or to be a part of somebody's property, power, or rights ○ *by the authority vested in me* **3.** *vti.* CLOTHE OR PUT ON CLOTHES to clothe somebody or to put on clothes, especially vestments [15thC. From Old French *vestu*, past participle of *vestir* "to clothe," from Latin *vestire*, from *vestis* "clothing, garment" (source of English *invest, travesty,* and *vestry*).]

Ves·ta /véstə/ *n.* **1.** MYTHOL ROMAN GODDESS the Roman goddess of the hearth. Greek equivalent **Hestia** **2.** ASTRON LARGE BRIGHT ASTEROID the brightest and third largest of the asteroids that orbit the sun [From Latin]

ves·tal /vést'l/ *adj.* **1.** CHASTE chaste, or not having experienced sexual intercourse **2.** MYTHOL OF VESTA relating to the Roman goddess Vesta ■ *n.* **1.** VIRGIN a woman who is a virgin (*literary*) **2.** NUN a nun (*literary*) **3.** = **vestal virgin** [15thC]

ves·tal vir·gin *n.* a celibate woman who tended the sacred fire in the temple of Vesta in ancient Rome. There were originally four, and later six vestal virgins, who were vowed to 30 years of service.

vest·ed /véstəd/ *adj.* **1.** HAVING RIGHTS TO SOMETHING having an unquestionable right to the possession of property or a privilege **2.** CLOTHED wearing clothes, especially religious vestments **3.** CLOTHES INCLUDING A VEST coming with a vest as part of the whole ○ *a vested suit*

vest·ed in·ter·est *n.* **1.** RIGHT TO POSSESS SOMETHING a right to the present or future possession of property **2.** SPECIAL INTEREST a person's particular concern in maintaining or promoting an issue or situation for reasons of private gain **3.** INDIVIDUAL OR GROUP HAVING A VESTED INTEREST an individual or group with a vested interest in maintaining or promoting something (*often plural*)

ves·ti·ar·y /véstee èrree/ *n.* (*plural* **-ies**) DRESSING ROOM a dressing room or storeroom for clothes ■ *adj.* OF CLOTHES relating to clothes (*formal*) [13thC. Via Old French *vestiarie* from Latin *vestiarium* "clothes chest, wardrobe," later "vestry," from, ultimately, *vestis* (see VEST).]

ves·tib·u·lar /ve stíbbyələr/ *adj.* relating to a vestibule

ves·tib·u·lar nerve *n.* a branch of the acoustic nerve that carries nerve impulses from the semicircular canals and other organs in the inner ear, conveying information about posture and balance

ves·ti·bule /vésti byo͞ol/ *n.* **1.** ARCHIT ENTRANCE HALL a small room or hall between an outer door and the main part of a building **2.** ANAT BODY CAVITY a cavity or space in the body that serves as the entrance to another cavity or canal, e.g., the part of the mouth between the teeth and lips **3.** ANAT MIDDLE CAVITY OF THE INNER EAR the middle cavity of the inner ear between the cochlea and the semicircular canals **4.** TRANSP ENCLOSED AREA AT A RAIL CAR ENTRANCE an enclosed area at the entrance to a railroad car [Early 17thC. Directly or via French from Latin *vestibulum*.]

ves·ti·bule school *n.* a school organized in a factory where workers can go to learn specific skills

ves·ti·bu·lo·coch·le·ar nerve /ve stìbbyəlō kòklee ər-/ *n.* either of the eighth pair of cranial nerves, critical to the sense of hearing [*Vestibulocochlear* formed from Latin *vestibulum* "entrance" + *cochlear* (see COCHLEA)]

ves·tige /véstij/ *n.* **1.** TRACE OF SOMETHING GONE a trace or sign of something that is no longer present **2.** SLIGHTEST AMOUNT the slightest amount ○ *There wasn't a vestige of truth in what she wrote.* **3.** BIOL RUDIMENTARY BODY PART an organ or part of the body that is now rudimentary and no longer functions, but that was fully developed and useful in the past [Early 17thC. Via French from Latin *vestigium* "sole of the foot, footprint, trace."]

ves·tig·i·al /ve stíjjee əl/ *adj.* **1.** BEING A TRACE remaining after nearly all the rest has disappeared or dwindled ○ *a vestigial stirring of passion* **2.** BIOL NO LONGER FUNCTIONAL having become degenerate or functionless in the course of time ○ *the vestigial muscles of the ear* —**ves·tig·i·al·ly** *adv.*

vest·ing /vésting/ *n.* the granting of certain pension rights to an employee, usually after a specified period of employment, with the pension given either when the job is terminated or at retirement

vest·ment /véstmənt/ *n.* **1.** ROBE a garment, especially a robe worn to show rank or office **2.** RELIGIOUS ROBE a ceremonial robe worn by members of the clergy during a religious ceremony [13thC. Via Old French *vestiment* from Latin *vestimentum*, from *vestire* (see VEST).] —**vest·men·tal** /vest mént'l/ *adj.* —**vest·ment·ed** /véstməntəd/ *adj.*

vest-pock·et *adj.* small enough to fit into the pocket of a vest ○ *a vest-pocket edition*

vest-pock·et park *n.* a small park in an urban area

ves·try /véstree/ (*plural* **-tries**) *n.* **1.** ROOM FOR VESTMENTS a room attached to a church, where vestments or sacred objects are kept **2.** MEETING ROOM a room in a church where meetings or classes are held **3.** MEETING OF CHURCH MEMBERS in the Anglican church, a meeting of church members or their representatives [14thC. From an Anglo-Norman form of Old French *vestiarie* (see VESTIARY).] —**ves·tral** *adj.*

ves·try·man /véstreemən/ (*plural* **-men** /-mən/) *n.* a member of a church vestry [Early 17thC]

ves·ture /véschər/ *n.* CLOTHING clothing, or something that covers like clothing (*archaic*) ■ *vt.* (**-tured, -tur·ing, -tures**) CLOTHE SOMEBODY OR SOMETHING to clothe or cover somebody or something (*archaic*) [14thC. From Old French, from, ultimately, Latin *vestire* (see VEST).] —**ves·tur·al** *adj.*

ve·su·vi·an /və so͞ovee ən/ *n.* a slow-burning match used especially for lighting cigars (*archaic*) [Late 17thC. Named for Mount VESUVIUS in Sicily.]

Ve·su·vi·an *adj.* **1.** RELATING TO VESUVIUS relating to or like the volcano Vesuvius **2. Ve·su·vi·an, ve·su·vi·an** VOLATILE marked by volatile sudden outbursts

ve·su·vi·an·ite /və so͞ovee ə nìt/ *n.* a green, brown, or yellow crystalline mineral that is a complex silicate of calcium and aluminum with magnesium and iron. It occurs in some marbles and is used as a gemstone. [Late 19thC. Named for Mount VESUVIUS in Sicily.]

Ve·su·vi·us, Mount /və so͞ovee əss/ active volcano overlooking the Bay of Naples, southern Italy. An eruption in A.D. 79 destroyed the Roman cities of Pompeii and Herculaneum. Height: 4,190 ft./1,277 m.

vet[1] /vet/ *n.* VETERINARIAN a veterinarian ■ *v.* (**vet·ted, vet·ting, vets**) **1.** *vt.* CHECK UP ON SOMEBODY OR SOMETHING to subject somebody or something to a careful examination or scrutiny, especially when this involves determining suitability for something **2.** *vt.* VET EXAMINE AN ANIMAL to examine or treat an animal **3.** *vi.* VET PRACTICE VETERINARY MEDICINE to practice as a veterinarian [Mid-19thC. Shortening of VETERINARY or VETERINARIAN.]

vet[2] /vet/ *n.* somebody who has served in the armed forces, especially in a particular conflict (*informal*) ○ *Vietnam vets* [Mid-19thC]

vet. *abbr.* **1.** veteran **2.** veterinarian **3.** veterinary

vetch /vech/ *n.* **1.** PLANT WITH SMALL FLOWERS a leguminous plant with small flowers that is often used for silage or fodder. Genus: *Vicia.* **2.** PLANT LIKE VETCH a plant related to or similar to vetch, e.g., the kidney vetch [14thC. Via Old Northern French *veche* from Latin *vicia*.]

vetch·ling /véchling/ *n.* a plant with yellow flowers that is related to vetch. Latin name: *Lathyrus pratensis.* [Late 16thC. Formed from VETCH.]

vet·er·an /véttərən/ *n.* **1.** SOMEBODY WITH EXPERIENCE somebody who has had considerable experience of a particular activity **2.** MIL SOMEBODY WHO HAS SERVED IN THE ARMED FORCES somebody who has served in the armed forces **3.** MIL EXPERIENCED SOLDIER somebody who has been a member of one of the armed forces for many years and has seen a great deal of active service ○ *a veteran of three foreign wars* ■ *adj.* MIL **1.** EXPERIENCED having a great deal of experience in a particular endeavor or skill, often built up over the whole of the working life **2.** OF VETERANS relating to a veteran or veterans [Early 16thC. Directly or via French *vétéran* from Latin *veteranus*, from *vetus* "old" (source of English *inveterate*).]

Vet·er·ans Day *n.* a legal holiday celebrated on November 11 to honor former members of the armed forces. It began as a commemoration of the end of World War I and was originally called Armistice Day.

vet·er·i·nar·i·an /vèttərə náiree ən, vèttrə-/ *n.* somebody trained and qualified in the medical treatment of animals [Mid-17thC. From Latin *veterinarius* (see VETERINARY).]

vet·er·i·nar·y /véttərə nèrree, véttrə-/ *adj.* relating to diseases of animals and their treatment [Late 18thC. From Latin *veterinarius*, from *veterinus*, "concerning cattle (literally at least one year old)," from *veter-*, stem of *vetus* "old."]

vet·er·i·nar·y med·i·cine *n.* the branch of medicine dealing with the health of animals and the diagnosis and treatment of their diseases and injuries

vet·i·ver /véttəvər/ *n.* **1.** TALL INDIAN GRASS a tall grass that grows in India, the leaves of which are used to make screens and fans. Latin name: *Vetiveria zizanioides.* **2.** ROOTS OF VETIVER the roots of the vetiver, which produce an oil that is used to make perfume [Mid-19thC. Via French *vétiver* from Tamil *veṭṭivēr*, from *vēr* "root."]

ve·to /veétō/ *n.* (*plural* **-toes**) **1.** RIGHT TO REJECT LEGISLATION the power of one branch of government to reject the legislation of another **2.** EXERCISE OF THE RIGHT TO REJECT MEASURES the exercise of the power or right to reject something, especially a political measure **3.** PROHIBITION an order prohibiting something ■ *vt.* (**-toed, -to·ing, -toes**) **1.** REJECT A MEASURE to reject something such as a measure or government bill by veto **2.** PROHIBIT SOMETHING to refuse to consent to or approve something ○ *My teacher vetoed the idea.* [Early 17thC. From Latin, "I forbid," a formula used in ancient Rome by the Tribunes of the People when they opposed measures taken by either the Senate or the magistrates.] —**ve·to·er** *n.*

vex /veks/ (**vexed, vex·ing, vex·es**) *vt.* **1.** ANNOY SOMEBODY to make somebody annoyed or upset **2.** AGITATE to cause somebody anxiety or distress **3.** CONFOUND to confuse or puzzle somebody [15thC. Via French *vexer* from Latin *vexare* "to shake, disturb."] —**vex·ing·ly** *adv.*

WORD KEY: SYNONYMS

See Synonyms at ***annoy.***

vex·a·tion /vek sáysh'n/ *n.* **1.** STATE OF BEING VEXED the state of being provoked to irritability or anxiety **2.** ACT OF VEXING the act of provoking somebody to irritability or anxiety **3.** SOMETHING THAT VEXES something that provokes irritability or anxiety

vex·a·tious /vek sáyshəss/ *adj.* **1.** CAUSING TROUBLE provoking irritation or anxiety by causing trouble **2.** LAW BROUGHT WITH THE INTENTION OF ANNOYING put forward on insufficient grounds and with the intention of causing annoyance to the defendant —**vex·a·tious·ly** *adv.* —**vex·a·tious·ness** *n.*

vexed /vekst/ *adj.* **1.** IRRITATED provoked to irritability or anxiety **2.** DEBATED being the subject of much debate —**vex·ed·ly** /véksədlee/ *adv.* —**vex·ed·ness** /véksədnəss/ *n.*

vex·il·lol·o·gy /vèksə lóllәjee/ *n.* the study of flags —**vex·il·lo·log·ic** /vèksələ lójjik/ *adj.* —**vex·il·lo·log·i·cal** /-lójjik'l/ *adj.* —**vex·il·lol·o·gist** /vèksə lólləjist/ *n.*

vex·il·lum /vek sílləm/ (*plural* **-la** /vek síllə/) *n.* in ancient Rome, a military standard or the troops serving under a separate standard [Early 18thC. From Latin, "flag, banner," from *vex-*, a stem of *vehere* "to carry."]

VF, V.F. *abbr.* **1.** visual field **2.** TV video frequency

VFD *abbr.* volunteer fire department

VFR *abbr.* AEROSPACE visual flight rules

VFW, V.F.W. *abbr.* Veterans of Foreign Wars

vg *abbr.* very good

V.G. *abbr.* Vicar General

VGA *n.* a widely used specification for video display controllers used in personal computers. Abbr of **video graphics array**

VHF, vhf *abbr.* TV very high frequency

VHS *tdmk.* a trademark for a system for recording television programs in the home

VI, V.I. *abbr.* **1.** Vancouver Island **2.** Virgin Islands

v.i., vi *abbr.* **1.** GRAM verb intransitive **2.** vide infra

vi·a /vî ə, veé ə/ *prep.* **1.** THROUGH by way of or through ○ *Can you come home via the post office?* **2.** BY MEANS OF using the means or agency of ○ *removed the obstruction via surgery* [Early 17thC. From Latin, literally "by way of," a form of *via* "way, road."]

vi·a·ble /vî əb'l/ *adj.* **1.** PRACTICABLE OR WORTHWHILE able to be done or worth doing ○ *a viable proposition* **2.** BIOL ABLE TO GROW able to germinate or develop normally **3.** MED ABLE TO SURVIVE OUTSIDE THE WOMB used to describe a fetus that can survive outside the womb. This now generally applies to a fetus after about 24 weeks of gestation. [Early 19thC. Via French *vie* from Latin *vita* "life" (source of English *vitamin, vivid,* and *vital*).] —**vi·a·bil·i·ty** /vî ə bíllətee/ *n.* —**vi·a·bly** /vî əblee/ *adv.*

Vi·a Do·lo·ro·sa /veè ə dollə rṓssə, -dōlə-/ *n.* **1.** JESUS CHRIST'S ROUTE TO CALVARY the route taken by Jesus Christ to Calvary to be crucified **2. Vi·a Do·lo·ro·sa, vi·a do·lo·ro·sa** DIFFICULT EXPERIENCE a difficult or distressing course or experience [From Latin, literally "sorrowful way"]

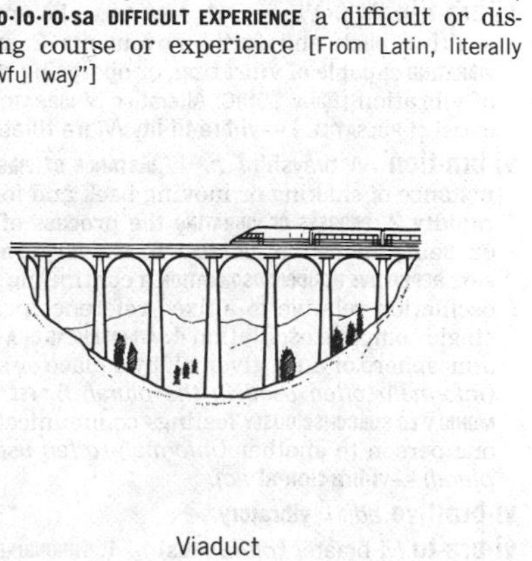

Viaduct

vi·a·duct /vî ə dùkt/ *n.* a bridge that consists of a series of short masonry or concrete arched spans supported on towers. Viaducts usually take a road or railroad over a wide valley. [Early 19thC. Formed from Latin *via* "way, road" on the model of AQUEDUCT.]

Vi·ag·ra /vī ággrə/ *tdmk.* a trademark for an enzyme-inhibiting drug, sildenafil citrate, that is used to treat impotence in men

vi·al /vī əl/ *n.* a small glass bottle, especially one for medicines [14thC. Alteration of PHIAL.]

vi·a me·di·a /vī ə meédee ə, -méddee ə/ *n.* a middle course or choice between extreme possibilities (*literary*) [From Latin]

vi·and /vī ənd/ *n.* (*formal*) **1. ARTICLE OF FOOD** an article of food **2. PROVISIONS** a store or collection of food, especially the food that makes up a meal or a feast (*often used in the plural*) [14thC. Via French *viande* "food" (now "meat") from, ultimately, Latin *vivenda* "things for living," from *vivere* "to live."]

vi·at·i·cum /vī áttikəm, vee-/ (*plural* **-ca** /-áttikə/ *or* **-cums**) *n.* **1.** CHR **HOLY COMMUNION GIVEN TO SOMEBODY DYING** Holy Communion given to somebody who is dying or in danger of dying **2. PROVISIONS FOR A JOURNEY** provisions or money for a journey (*literary*) [Mid-16thC. From Latin "provision for a journey," from *via* "way, road."]

vibe /vīb/ *n.* a particular kind of atmosphere, feeling, or ambience (*slang*) ○ *The new decor has a kind of 50s vibe to it.* [Mid-20thC. Shortening.]

vibes /vībz/ *npl.* (*slang*) **1. SOMETHING SENSED** the atmosphere, feeling, or ambience that somebody senses from a person or thing ○ *I'm picking up really negative vibes from this group.* **2.** MUSIC **VIBRAPHONE** a vibraphone [Mid-20thC. Shortening.]

vib·ist /vībist/ *n.* somebody who plays the vibraphone (*slang*)

Vi·borg /veé bawrg/ capital city of Viborg County, north central Jutland, Denmark. Population: 39,395 (1990).

vi·bra·harp /víbrə haàrp/ *n.* = **vibraphone** [Mid-20thC. On the model of VIBRAPONE.]

vi·brant /víbrənt/ *adj.* **1. PULSATING WITH ENERGY** seeming to quiver or pulsate with energy or activity **2. RESONANT** having a full rich sound that tends to continue for some time **3. BRIGHT** dazzling or radiantly bright ○ *awash in vibrant reds and oranges* **4. VIBRATING** vibrating very rapidly [Mid-16thC. From Latin *vibrant-*, past participle stem of *vibrare* (see VIBRATE).] — **vi·bran·cy** /víbrənssee/ *n.* —**vi·brant·ly** *adv.*

vi·bra·phone /víbrə fōn/ *n.* a percussion instrument with electrically driven resonators beneath a set of metal bars that are struck with small mallets or sometimes played with a bow, causing vibration [Early 20thC. Formed from the stem of VIBRATE + PHONE.] — **vi·bra·phon·ist** *n.*

vi·brate /vī bràyt/ (**-brat·ed, -brat·ing, -brates**) *v.* **1.** *vti.* **MAKE SMALL MOVEMENTS RAPIDLY** to shake or move back and forth rapidly, or make something move in this way ○ *The traffic made the whole room vibrate.* **2.** *vti.* PHYS **OSCILLATE** to oscillate or to make something oscillate with a continuing periodic change relative to a fixed reference point **3.** *vi.* **RESONATE** to make a full rich tone that tends to continue for some time **4.** *vi.* **THRILL** to experience a rush of emotion in response to something [Early 17thC. From Latin *vibrat-*, past participle stem of *vibrare* "to shake." Ultimately from an Indo-European word that is also the ancestor of English *whip* and *weave*.]

vi·bra·tile /víbrət'l/ *adj.* **1. VIBRATING** showing rapid shaking back and forth movements **2. CAPABLE OF VIBRATING** capable of vibrating, or operating by means of vibration [Early 19thC. Alteration of VIBRATORY on the model of PULSATILE.] —**vi·bra·til·i·ty** /vìbrə tíllətee/ *n.*

vi·bra·tion /vī bráysh'n/ *n.* **1. INSTANCE OF VIBRATING** an instance of shaking or moving back and forth very rapidly **2. PROCESS OF VIBRATING** the process of moving or being moved back and forth very rapidly **3.** PHYS **REPETITIVE PERIODIC OSCILLATION** a continuing periodic oscillation relative to a fixed reference point, or a single complete oscillation **4. ATMOSPHERE OF A PLACE** the atmosphere or aura given off by a place or situation (*informal*) (*often used in the plural*) **5. FEELINGS COMMUNICATED SUBCONSCIOUSLY** feelings communicated from one person to another (*informal*) (*often used in the plural*) —**vi·bra·tion·al** *adj.*

vi·bra·tive *adj.* = **vibratory**

vi·bra·to /vi braàtō/ (*plural* **-tos**) *n.* **1. THROBBING EFFECT IN A MUSICAL INSTRUMENT** a throbbing effect in the playing of a stringed or wind instrument made by rapidly varying the pitch **2. THROBBING EFFECT IN SINGING** a throbbing effect in singing produced by rapidly varying the breath pressure or the pitch [Mid-19thC. From Italian, literally "vibrated."]

vi·bra·tor /vī bràytər/ *n.* **1. VIBRATING DEVICE** an electric device that vibrates, e.g., one used to give a massage or as a sexual aid **2. SOMETHING THAT VIBRATES** something that vibrates or makes something vibrate **3.** ELEC ENG **DEVICE CONVERTING DIRECT TO ALTERNATING CURRENT** an electromechanical device, often used in bells and buzzers, that interrupts a direct current to convert it into an alternating current

vi·bra·to·ry /víbrə tàwree/, **vi·bra·tive** /víbrətiv/ *adj.* **1. VIBRATING** shaking or moving back and forth very rapidly **2. CAUSING VIBRATION** making something shake or move back and forth rapidly

vib·ri·o /víbbree ō/ (*plural* **-os** *or* **-on·es** /víbbree ōneez/) *n.* a bacterium shaped like a comma or like the letter S. Genus: *Vibrio.* [Mid-19thC. Via modern Latin from Latin *vibrare* (see VIBRATE).] —**vib·ri·oid** /víbbree òyd/ *adj.*

vib·ri·o·sis /vìbbree ṓssiss/ *n.* an infectious disease, especially of sheep, cattle, and goats, characterized by the death of a developing fetus and caused by a vibrioid bacterium. Latin name: *Vibrio fetus.* [Mid-20thC. Formed from VIBRIO.]

vi·bris·sa /vī bríssə/ (*plural* **-sae** /-see/) *n.* **1. SENSITIVE HAIR ON A MAMMAL** a mammal's hair or whisker, usually on the face or limbs, that vibrates when touched, stimulating nervous tissue in the animal's skin **2.** BIRDS **FEATHER NEAR THE BEAK** a feather that is like a bristle, near the beak of an insect-eating bird [Late 17thC. From Latin, formed from *vibrare* (see VIBRATE).] — **vib·ris·sal** *adj.*

vi·bron·ic /vī brónnik/ *adj.* relating to the electronic and vibrational energy states of elementary particles and atoms [Mid-20thC. Coined from VIBRATIONAL + ELECTRONIC.]

vi·bro·tron /víbrə tròn/ *n.* a triode electron tube in which the anode can be vibrated by an external force

vi·bur·num /vī búrnəm/ *n.* a shrub or small tree with flat or rounded clusters of white flowers sometimes tinged with pink. The guelder rose, blackhaw, and nannyberry are all types of viburnum. Genus: *Viburnum.* [Mid-18thC. From modern Latin, from Latin, "wayfaring tree."]

vic. *abbr.* **1.** RELIG vicar **2.** vicinity

Vic. *abbr.* Victoria

vic·ar /víkər/ *n.* **1. ANGLICAN PRIEST** a priest in the Anglican Church who is in charge of a parish and receives a salary but not the tithes **2. MEMBER OF THE ANGLICAN CLERGY** a member of the Anglican clergy who acts in place of a rector or bishop at Communion **3. ROMAN CATHOLIC PRIEST** a Roman Catholic priest who represents or deputizes for a bishop **4. EPISCOPAL CHURCH CLERIC** a cleric in the Episcopal Church who is in charge of a chapel **5. SUBSTITUTE** somebody who acts as a substitute for somebody else (*archaic*) [14thC. Via Anglo-Norman *vicare* from, ultimately, Latin *vicarius* "substitute," from the stem *vic-* "change, place" (source of English *vicissitude*); because the vicar acted as a substitute for the rector.] —**vic·ar·ly** *adj.* —**vic·ar·ship** *n.*

vic·ar·age /víkərij/ *n.* **1. VICAR'S RESIDENCE** the residence of a vicar **2. VICAR'S POSITION** the office or duties of a vicar

vic·ar ap·os·tol·ic (*plural* **vic·ars ap·os·tol·ic**) *n.* a titular bishop or missionary in the Roman Catholic Church

vic·ar·ate *n.* = **vicariate**

vic·ar gen·er·al (*plural* **vic·ars gen·er·al**) *n.* **1. ROMAN CATHOLIC BISHOP'S ASSISTANT** a priest acting as an assistant to a Roman Catholic bishop **2. ANGLICAN CHURCH BISHOP'S ASSISTANT** a lay official assisting an Anglican bishop with administrative or judicial duties

vi·car·i·al /vī káiree əl, vi káiree əl/ *adj.* **1. BEING VICAR** being or acting as a vicar **2. OF VICAR** relating to a vicar **3.** = **vicarious** *adj.* 3

vi·car·i·ate /vī káiree ət, -àyt, vi-/, **vic·ar·ate** /víkərət, víkə ràyt/ *n.* **1. OFFICE OF VICAR** the office or authority of a vicar **2. DISTRICT OF A VICAR** the district that falls under the care of a vicar

vi·car·i·ous /vī káiree əss, vi-/ *adj.* **1. EXPERIENCED THROUGH ANOTHER BY IMAGINING** experienced through another person rather than at first hand, by using sympathy or the power of the imagination **2. ENDURED FOR SOMEBODY ELSE** done or endured by somebody as a substitute for somebody else **3. DELEGATED** delegated to somebody else or performing a function that has been delegated **4.** MED **OCCURRING IN AN UNEXPECTED PART OF BODY** occurring in or performed by an unexpected part of the body, e.g., menstrual bleeding in the breasts, nose, or sweat glands [Mid-17thC. Formed from Latin *vicarius* (see VICAR).] —**vi·car·i·ous·ly** *adv.* — **vi·car·i·ous·ness** *n.*

Vic·ar of Christ *n.* the Roman Catholic pope

vice[1] /vīss/ *n.* **1. IMMORAL HABIT** an immoral or wicked habit or characteristic **2. DEPRAVITY** immoral conduct **3. PROSTITUTION** a form of immoral conduct, especially prostitution **4. MILD DEFECT IN CHARACTER** a mild failing or defect in somebody's behavior or character **5. FAULT IN AN ANIMAL** a fault or undesirable habit in a horse or other domestic animal [13thC. Via French from Latin *vitium* (source of English *vitiate* and *vituperate*).]

vi·ce[2] /vísee, víssə/ *prep.* in place of or instead of somebody or something [Late 18thC. From Latin *vice* "in place of," from the stem *vic-* (see VICAR).]

vice[3] *n.*, *vt.* U.K. = **vise**

vice ad·mi·ral *n.* an officer in the navy ranking below admiral and above rear admiral —**vice-ad·mi·ral·ty** *n.*

vice chair·per·son *n.* somebody who takes the place of a chairperson in his or her absence —**vice-chair·man·ship** *n.*

vi·ce chan·cel·lor *n.* **1.** UNIV **ASSISTANT CHANCELLOR OF A UNIVERSITY** a deputy or assistant chancellor in a university **2.** POL **DEPUTY CHANCELLOR** a deputy for the chancellor of a country **3.** LAW **JUDGE** a U.S. judge ranking below a chancellor, or an English judge who runs the Chancery Division of the High Court —**vice-chan·cel·lor·ship** *n.*

vice con·sul *n.* an officer who acts as the deputy for the official representing a country's commercial interest in an overseas country —**vice-con·su·lar** *adj.*

vice·ge·rent /vīss jeérənt/ *n.* a deputy appointed to act on the authority of a ruler or magistrate, especially in administrative duties [Mid-16thC. From medieval Latin, "deputy," literally "one carrying on in place of," from Latin *gerent-*, present participle stem of *gerere* "to carry on."] —**vice·ge·ral** *adj.* —**vice·ge·ren·cy** *n.*

vic·e·nar·y /víss'n èrree/ *adj.* **1. RELATING TO 20** being, based on, or relating to the number 20 **2. NUMBER SYSTEM BASED ON 20** relating or belonging to a number system that has 20 as its base [Early 17thC. From Latin *vicenarius*, from, ultimately, *viginti* "twenty."]

vi·cen·ni·al /vī sénnee əl/ *adj.* lasting for or occurring every 20 years [Mid-18thC. From Latin *vicennium* "period of twenty years," from *vic-*, stem of *vicies* "twenty times."]

Vi·cen·za /vi chénzə/ capital of Vicenza Province, Veneto Region, northern Italy. Population: 107,786 (1995).

vice pres·i·dent *n.* an official who ranks immediately below a president and who can take the president's place if necessary —**vice-pres·i·den·cy** *n.* —**vice-pres·i·den·tial** *adj.*

vice·re·gal /vīss reég'l/ *adj.* relating to a viceroy — **vice·re·gal·ly** *adv.*

vice·re·gent /vīss reéjənt/ *n.* a deputy for the regent of a country —**vice·re·gen·cy** *n.*

vice·reine /vīss ràyn/ *n.* a viceroy who is a woman, or the wife of a viceroy [Early 19thC. From French, literally "vice-queen."]

vice·roy /vīss ròy/ *n.* **1.** POL **GOVERNOR REPRESENTING A SOVEREIGN IN A COLONY** a governor who represents a sovereign in a province, colony, or country **2.** ZOOL **ORANGE-AND-BLACK BUTTERFLY** a brightly colored orange-and-black butterfly of North America that resembles the monarch butterfly. Latin name: *Limenitis archippus.* [Early 16thC. From French, literally "vice-king."] —**vice·roy·ship** *n.*

vice·roy·al·ty /vīss róy əltee, vīss ròy əltee/ (*plural* **-ties**) *n.* **1. OFFICE OF VICEROY** the office, term of office, or authority of a viceroy **2. DISTRICT GOVERNED BY A VICEROY** a district that is governed by a viceroy

vi·ce squad *n.* a police division in charge of enforcing laws relating to prostitution, gambling, and drugs

vi·ce ver·sa /vīss vúrssə, vīssə-/ *adv.* the other way around [From Latin, literally "the position being reversed"]

Vi·chy /veéshee/ city in central France, the site of important mineral springs. It was the seat of a French government that collaborated with the Germans during World War II. Population: 28,048 (1990).

vi·chys·soise /víshee swaáz, veéshee-/ *n.* a creamy soup made from leeks, potatoes, and onions, often served chilled [Mid-20thC. Shortening of French *crème vichyssoise glacée,* literally "iced cream soup from Vichy."]

Vi·chy wa·ter /víshee-, víshee-/, **Vi·chy** *n.* a natural sparkling mineral water from Vichy, France, or a similar sparkling water

vic·i·nage /víss'nij/ *n.* **1. NEIGHBORHOOD** a neighborhood, or the people living in it (*archaic*) **2. VICINITY** the area immediately surrounding a place [14thC. Via Old French *vis(e)nage* from, ultimately, Latin *vicinus* (see VICINITY).]

vic·i·nal /víssən'l/ *adj.* **1. NEIGHBORING** adjacent or neighboring **2. LOCAL** relating to or restricted to a local area **3.** CHEM **OF CONSECUTIVE POSITIONS ON A CARBON CHAIN** relating to two or more adjacent positions on a carbon ring or chain [Early 17thC. Directly or via French from Latin *vicinalis,* from *vicinus* (see VICINITY).]

vi·cin·i·ty /və sínnətee/ (*plural* **-ties**) *n.* **1. SURROUNDING REGION** a neighborhood, or the surrounding region of a place ○ *Homes in the vicinity of the fire were evacuated.* **2. PROXIMITY** an area near something else **3. APPROXIMATION** an approximate amount ○ *something in the vicinity of 1,000 miles* [Mid-16thC. From Latin *vicinitas,* from *vicinus* "neighbor," from *vicus* "village, homestead."]

vi·cious /víshəss/ *adj.* **1. FEROCIOUS** showing fierce violence **2. DANGEROUS AND AGGRESSIVE** dangerous because of being aggressive ○ *a vicious dog* **3. MALICIOUS** intended to do harm **4. WICKED AND IMMORAL** displaying or tending to immoral behavior **5. UNSOUND** incorrect or showing faulty logic [14thC. Formed from VICE¹.] —**vi·cious·ly** *adv.* —**vi·cious·ness** *n.*

vi·cious cir·cle *n.* **1. SITUATION WORSENED BY ATTEMPTS TO SOLVE IT** a situation in which attempts to solve one problem lead to further problems that only make the original position worse **2.** LOGIC **REASONING BASED ON AN UNPROVEN ASSUMPTION** a form of reasoning that bases a conclusion on a statement assumed to be true but not proven independently **3.** MED **LINKING OF TWO DISEASES** a situation in which two diseases or conditions are linked so that each leads to or aggravates the other

WORD KEY: USAGE

vicious circle or **vicious cycle**? Until quite recently the invariable choice was ***vicious circle.*** Perhaps influenced by such phrases as *the cycle of welfare dependency,* however, the variant ***vicious cycle*** has been gaining ground, to the point that it is now seen almost as frequently as ***vicious circle,*** in virtually indistinguishable contexts.

vi·cis·si·tude /vi síssi tood/ *n.* **VARIABILITY** the fact of being variable (*literary*) ■ **vi·cis·si·tudes** *npl.* **UNEXPECTED CHANGES** unexpected changes, especially in a person's fortunes [Mid-16thC. Directly or via French from Latin *vicissitudo,* from *vicissim* "by turns," from the stem *vic-* (see VICAR).] —**vi·cis·si·tu·di·nar·y** /vi sìssi tood'n èrree/ *adj.* —**vi·cis·si·tu·di·nous** /və sìssi tood'nəss/ *adj.*

Vicks·burg /víks bùrg/ city in western Mississippi. In 1863 during the Civil War the city was besieged for 47 days before falling to Union forces led by General Ulysses S. Grant. Population: 20,908 (1990).

vi·comte /vee kóNt/ *n.* a French nobleman who is equal in rank to a British viscount [Mid-19thC. From French, from Old French *vi(s)conte* (see VISCOUNT).]

vi·com·tesse /vee koN téss/ *n.* a French noblewoman who is equal in rank to a British viscountess [Late 18thC. From French, from *vicomte.*]

vic·tim /víktim/ *n.* **1. SOMEBODY HURT OR KILLED** somebody who is hurt or killed by somebody or something **2. SOMEBODY OR SOMETHING HARMED** somebody or something harmed by an act or circumstance ○ *a victim of her own success* **3. SOMEBODY DUPED** somebody who is tricked or taken advantage of **4. CREATURE USED FOR SACRIFICE** a living creature used as a sacrifice or in a religious rite **5. HELPLESS PERSON** somebody who experiences misfortune and feels helpless to do anything about it [15thC. From Latin *victima* "animal offered as a sacrifice." Later meanings did not develop until the 17thC and 18thC.] —**vic·tim·hood** *n.* ◇ **fall victim to** to be affected, harmed, or deceived by somebody or something

vic·tim·ize /víktə mìz/ (**-ized, -iz·ing, -iz·es**) *vt.* **1. TREAT UNFAIRLY** to single somebody out unfairly for punishment or ill treatment **2. MAKE INTO A VICTIM** to cause somebody to become a victim —**vic·tim·i·za·tion** /vìktəmi záysh'n/ *n.* —**vic·tim·iz·er** /víktə mìzər/ *n.*

vic·tim·less crime /víktəmləss/ *n.* an illegal act such as prostitution or drug use in which there is no obvious injured party

vic·tor /víktər/ *n.* **1. WINNER** a winner in a contest or battle **2.** COMMUNICATION **CODE WORD FOR V** a code word for the letter "V," used in international radio communications [14thC. Directly, or via Anglo-Norman, from Latin, from *vic-,* past participle stem of *vincere* "to conquer."]

Vic·tor Em·man·u·el III /víktər i mánnyoo əl/, **King of Italy** (1869–1947). Reigning from 1900, he accepted fascist rule in Italy from 1922. After defeat in World War II he abdicated (1946).

vic·to·ri·a /vik táwree ə/ *n.* a horse-drawn carriage with four wheels and a folding hood, accommodating two passengers [Mid-19thC. Named for Queen VICTORIA.]

Vic·to·ri·a /vik táwree ə/ **1.** state in southeastern Australia. Capital: Melbourne. Population: 4,561,000 (1996). Area: 87,884 sq. mi./227,620 sq. km. **2.** capital city of British Columbia, Canada, on the southern tip of Vancouver Island. Population: 71,228 (1991). **3.** capital city of the Republic of Seychelles, situated on the northeastern coast of Mahé island. Population: 25,000 (1993).

Vic·to·ri·a, Queen of the United Kingdom (1819–1901). She reigned longer than any other British monarch (1837–1901), and was empress of India (1876–1901). As queen she exhibited an alert and informed understanding of government affairs, and set a national example of domestic harmony and morality in her marriage to Prince Albert (1840–61).

Vic·to·ri·a, Lake the largest lake in Africa, shared between Tanzania, Uganda, and Kenya. Area: 26,828 sq. mi./69,482 sq. km.

Vic·to·ri·a Cross *n.* a decoration in the form of a bronze cross, given to members of British and Commonwealth armed forces for conspicuous bravery. It was instituted by Queen Victoria in 1856.

Vic·to·ri·a Day *n.* a Canadian statutory holiday held on the Monday of or preceding May 24 to commemorate the birthday of Queen Victoria

Victoria Falls

Vic·to·ri·a Falls falls on the Zambezi River in south central Africa, on the border between Zambia and Zimbabwe. Height: 355 ft./108 m.

Vic·to·ri·a Is·land the second largest island in Canada, divided between Nunavut and the Northwest Territories, located in the Arctic Archipelago. Area: 83,896 sq. mi./217,290 sq. km.

Vic·to·ri·a Land region of Antarctica, west of Ross Sea and east of Wilkes Land

Vic·to·ri·an /vik táwree ən/ *adj.* **1. CHARACTERISTIC OF THE TIME OF QUEEN VICTORIA** relating to, belonging to, or typical of the reign of the British Queen Victoria **2. CONVENTIONAL, HYPOCRITICAL, OR PRUDISH** showing or typical of attitudes commonly associated with the Victorian era, especially prudery or conventionalism **3.** ARCHIT **ARCHITECTURALLY ELABORATE** in or typical of the elaborate style of architecture popular in Victorian Britain **4. FROM VICTORIA** relating to or from the state of Victoria in Australia, or the cities of Victoria in Canada or the Seychelles ■ *n.* **1.** HIST **SOMEBODY LIVING IN VICTORIA'S REIGN** somebody who lived in the reign of Queen Victoria **2. SOMEBODY FROM VICTORIA** somebody who lives in or comes from the state of Victoria in Australia, or the cities of Victoria in Canada or the Seychelles **3.** ARCHIT **VICTORIAN HOUSE** a house in Victorian architectural style —**Vic·to·ri·an·ism** *n.*

Vic·to·ri·a·na /vik tàwree ánnə, -aánə/ *npl.* collectible objects dating from the time of Queen Victoria

Vic·to·ri·a Nile section of the upper Nile River in Uganda, between lakes Victoria and Albert

Vic·to·ri·a Peak mountain on Hong Kong Island, overlooking Hong Kong Harbor. Height: 1,818 ft./554 m.

vic·to·ri·ous /vik táwree əss/ *adj.* **1. HAVING WON** having won something such as a contest or a battle **2. CHARACTERIZED BY VICTORY** typical of or showing a sense of victory —**vic·to·ri·ous·ly** *adv.* —**vic·to·ri·ous·ness** *n.*

vic·to·ry /víktəree/ (*plural* **-ries**) *n.* **1. DEFEAT OF OPPONENT** defeat of an enemy or opponent **2. SUCCESS** success attained over a difficult situation or opponent [14thC. Via Anglo-Norman *victorie* from Latin *victoria,* from *victor* (see VICTOR).]

vict·ual /vítt'l/ *n.* **PROVISIONS** provisions of food (*archaic or formal*) ■ **vict·uals** *npl.* **FOOD** food or other provisions (*often used humorously*) ■ *v.* (**-ualed** *or* **-ualled, -ual·ing, -uals**) (*archaic or formal*) **1.** *vt.* **FEED SOMEBODY OR SOMETHING** to give food to people or animals **2.** *vi.* **ASSEMBLE PROVISIONS** to collect a store of food [14thC. Via Old French *vitaille* from Latin *victualia* (which later influenced the spelling of the English word), from *victus* "livelihood, food" from *vivere* "to live."]

vict·ual·er, vict·ual·ler (*plural* **-ers** *or* **-lers**) *n.* **1. SUPPLIER OF PROVISIONS** somebody who supplies food or other provisions (*archaic or formal*) **2. INNKEEPER** an innkeeper, especially one licensed to sell spirits (*archaic or formal*) **3. SHIP CARRYING STORES** a ship carrying food or other provisions

Vicuña

vi·cu·ña /vī koónyə, vī koónə, vi-/, **vi·cu·na** *n.* **1.** ZOOL **S AMERICAN MAMMAL** a tawny-colored South American mammal with a silky fleece. It is related to the llama and lives high in the Andes mountains. Latin name: *Vicugna vicugna.* **2.** CLOTHES **CLOTH MADE FROM VICUÑA WOOL** cloth made from the wool of the vicuña, or an imitation of it [Early 17thC. Via Spanish from Quechua *wikúña.*]

vid /vid/ *n.* a video cassette (*informal*)

Vi·dal /vi daál/, **Gore** (*b.* 1925) U.S. writer. His novels, critical works, and essays are often sharply critical of U.S. politics and culture. They include *The City and the Pillar* (1948) and the semifictional study *Lincoln* (1984). Full name **Eugene Luther Gore Vidal**

Vi·dal·ia on·ion /vi dáylyə-/ *n.* a large sweet onion that has a delicate flavor and is grown in Georgia [Named for the city of Vidalia in Georgia, USA]

vi·de /vídee, veé dày/ *vt.* a word used to refer a reader to another place in a text, or tell a musician to skip to a place further ahead in the score (*formal*) [Mid-16thC. From Latin, literally "see!", a form of *videre* "to see."]

vi·de in·fra *vt.* a term used to refer a reader to a place further on in a text [From Latin, "see below"]

vi·del·i·cet /və déllə sèt/ *adv.* full form of **viz.** (*formal*) [15thC. From Latin, from *vide,* stem of *videre* "to see" + *licet* "it is permissible."]

vid·e·o /víddee ō/ *n.* (*plural* **-os**) **1. VISUAL PART OF TELEVISION** the visual part of a television broadcast **2. VIDEOCASSETTE** videotape, or a videocassette (*informal*) ○ *now available to rent or buy on video* **3. SOMETHING RECORDED ONTO VIDEOTAPE** something, especially a movie that has been recorded onto video tape **4. TELEVISION** television when considered as a broadcasting medium ■ *adj.* **1. RELATING TO TELEVISION** relating to television, especially the reproduction or broadcasting of televised images **2. RELATING TO VIDEO FREQUENCIES** relating to or using video frequencies [Mid-

20thC. Formed from Latin *videre* "to see" on the model of AUDIO.]

vid·e·o ar·cade *n.* a place where people pay to play video games

vid·e·o cam·er·a *n.* a camera that records onto videotape

vid·e·o·cas·sette /víddee ō kə sèt/ *n.* a flat rectangular plastic cassette containing two tape reels and a magnetic videotape

vid·e·o·cas·sette re·cord·er *n.* full form of **VCR**

video·con·fer·enc·ing /víddee ō kònfərənsing/ *n.* the holding of a meeting in which participants are in different places, connected by audio and video links [Late 20thC] —**video·con·fer·ence** *n.*

vid·e·o·disk /víddee ō dìsk/, **vid·e·o·disc** *n.* = **optical disk**

vid·e·o dis·play ter·mi·nal *n. U.S., ANZ* a device used to display data from and enter data into a computer, consisting of a visual display such as a cathode-ray tube and a keyboard, mouse, or touchscreen

vid·e·o fre·quen·cy *n.* a frequency in the range of signals used to carry the image and synchronizing pulses in a television broadcasting system. Frequencies range from the very high to the ultra high in the United States and are found in two ultra high bands in Europe.

vid·e·o game *n.* an electronic or computerized game, usually controlled by a microprocessor, played by making images move on a computer or television screen or, for hand-held games, on a liquid-crystal display

vid·e·og·ra·phy /vìddee óggrəfee/ *n.* the art or practice of using a video camera to make films or programs [Late 20thC. Formed from VIDEO + -GRAPHY.] —**vid·e·og·ra·pher** *n.*

vid·e·o jock·ey *n.* somebody who plays videos, especially music videos, especially on television

vid·e·o·phile /víddee ō fìl/ *n.* somebody who has an enthusiastic interest in watching or making video recordings

vid·e·o·phone /víddee ō fòn/ *n.* a communications device that can transmit and receive both video and audio signals, allowing people having a telephone conversation to see as well as hear each other [Mid-20thC]

vid·e·o re·cord·er *n.* = **VCR**

vid·e·o·tape /víddee ō tàyp/ *n.* = **video cassette** ■ *vt.* **(-taped, -tap·ing, -tapes)** RECORD SOMETHING ON VIDEOTAPE to make a recording of something on videotape

vid·e·o·tape re·cord·er *n.* a tape recorder that can record and play back visual images and sound using magnetic tape

vid·e·o ter·mi·nal *n.* = **video display terminal**

vid·e·o·text /víddee ō tèkst/ *n.* a communications service linked to an adapted television receiver or video display terminal by telephone or cable television lines to allow access to pages of information. Sytems can be one-way, allowing only for the display of selected information, or on-line or interactive, allowing for two-way communication. [Late 20thC]

vid·e·o vér·i·té *n.* the use in video documentaries of the realistic, unrehearsed portrayal of people and situations [*Vérité* from French, "truth," on the model of CINÉMA VÉRITÉ]

vi·de su·pra *vt.* a term used to refer a reader to an earlier place in a text [From Latin, "see above"]

vi·dette *n.* = **vedette** *n.* 1

vid·i·con /víddi kòn/ *n.* a light-sensitive television camera tube in which an image is stored on a photoconductive plate as an electric charge pattern that is scanned by an electron beam and transmitted. These tubes have been replaced by more reliable solid-state television cameras using semiconductor charge-coupled devices. [Mid-20thC. Coined from VIDEO + ICONOSCOPE.]

Vi·dor /vée dàwr/, **King** (1894–1982) U.S. movie director. His movies spanned the period from the silent era to the television age. Full name **King Wallis Vidor**

vie /vī/ **(vied, vy·ing, vies)** *vi.* to strive for superiority or compete with somebody or something for something [Mid-16thC. Shortening of Middle English *envien*, from Old French *envier* "to raise the bid (at cards), challenge," from Latin *invitare* "to entertain, feast" (source of English *invite*).] —**vier** *n.*

Vi·en·na /vee énnə/ capital city of Austria, located in the east of the country, on the Danube River. Population: 1,539,848 (1991). —**Vi·en·nese** /vèe ə néez, -néess/ *n., adj.*

Vi·en·na cir·cle /vee ènnə-/ *n.* the leading school of logical positivists of the 1920s and 1930s [Because the group was based at Vienna University]

Vi·en·na sau·sage *n.* a small, spicy sausage like a frankfurter, often served as a snack or hors d'oeuvre

Vien·tiane /vyen tyáan/ capital city of Laos, in the central part of the country, on the Mekong River. Population: 178,203 (1985).

Viet. *abbr.* **1.** Vietnam **2.** Vietnamese

Viet·cong /vee èt káwng, vyèt-/ (*plural* **-cong**), **Viet Cong** (*plural* **Viet Cong**) *n.* **1.** COMMUNIST GUERRILLA IN VIETNAM a member or supporter of the Communist-led armed forces of the National Liberation Front of South Vietnam that fought to unite the country with North Vietnam between 1954 and 1976 **2.** VIETNAMESE GUERRILLA somebody, especially a guerrilla soldier, who belonged to or supported the Vietcong during the Vietnam War [Mid-20thC. From Vietnamese *Việt-cộng*, a shortening of *Việt-Nam Cộng Sam* "Vietnamese Communist."]

Viet·minh /vee èt mín, vyèt-/ (*plural* **-minh**), **Viet Minh** (*plural* **Viet Minh**) *n.* **1.** COMMUNIST-DOMINATED VIETNAMESE NATIONALIST MOVEMENT the Vietnamese armed forces led by Ho Chi Minh that resisted and defeated first the Japanese and then the French between 1941 and 1954. The Vietminh operated from a base in southern China during World War II and employed guerrilla tactics similar to the Maoists in China. **2.** VIETNAMESE SOLDIER FIGHTING FOR INDEPENDENCE a member or supporter of the Vietnamese armed forces led by Ho Chi Minh that resisted and defeated first the Japanese and then the French between 1941 and 1954 [Mid-20thC. From Vietnamese *Việt Minh*, a shortening of *Việt-Nam Dôc-Lâp Dông-Minh* "Vietnam Independence Federation."]

Vietnam

Viet·nam /vee èt náam/ country in Southeast Asia, on the South China Sea, south of China and east of Cambodia and Laos. Language: Vietnamese. Currency: new dông. Capital: Hanoi. Population: 75,123,880 (1997). Area: 128,066 sq. mi./331,690 sq. km. Official name **Socialist Republic of Vietnam**

Viet·nam·ese /vee ètnə méez, vyètnə-, -méess/ *adj.* PEOPLES OF VIETNAM relating to or typical of Vietnam, or its people or culture ■ *n.* (*plural* **-ese**) **1.** PEOPLES SOMEBODY FROM VIETNAM somebody who was born or raised in Vietnam, or who has Vietnamese citizenship **2.** LANG OFFICIAL LANGUAGE OF VIETNAM the official language of Vietnam, belonging to the Austro-Asiatic language family. Vietnamese is spoken by the majority of people living in Vietnam.

Vi·et·nam·ese pot·bel·lied pig *n.* a small domesticated pig with a rounded shape and a dark skin with a lighter band running around its middle. It is sometimes kept as a pet.

Viet·nam War *n.* a conflict in which the Communist forces of North Vietnam and guerrillas in South Vietnam fought against the non-Communist forces of South Vietnam and the United States. It began in 1954 and ended in 1975 in a Communist victory.

view /vyoo/ *n.* **1.** ACT OF LOOKING AT SOMETHING an act of looking at or inspecting something **2.** RANGE OF VISION the range or extent of somebody's ability to see something **3.** SCENE a scene or an area that can be seen from a particular place, especially one that is pleasing or impressive **4.** PICTORIAL REPRESENTATION a painting, drawing, or photograph of a particular scene or building **5.** PERSPECTIVE a particular position or angle from which somebody can look at something **6.** OPINION somebody's opinion on or interpretation of something such as politics or religion **7.** SURVEY a general survey of a particular subject ■ *v.* **(viewed, view·ing, views) 1.** *vt.* OBSERVE SOMETHING to see or look at something, especially with interest **2.** *vt.* INSPECT SOMETHING to make an inspection or examination of something **3.** *vt.* CONSIDER SOMETHING to think over or consider something, especially a range of things **4.** *vt.* THINK OF SOMEBODY OR SOMETHING to regard or assess somebody or something, especially in a particular way **5.** *vti.* WATCH TELEVISION to watch television, or watch something on television [15thC. From Old French *vëue*, past participle of *vëoir* "to see," from Latin *videre* "to see" (source of English *vision* and *voyeur*).] —**view·less** *adj.* ◇ **in view of something** because of something, or bearing something in mind ◇ **on view** put somewhere so as to be seen ◇ **take a dim view of somebody** *or* **something** to disapprove of somebody or something ◇ **with a view to something** with the aim, intention, or hope of doing or achieving something

WORD KEY: CULTURAL NOTE

A Room with a View, a novel by English writer E.M. Forster (1908). It describes how a young Englishwoman's visit to Italy and her encounter there with a young, unconventional expatriate encourages her to rebel against the emotionally stifling conventions of her upper-class background. It was made into a movie by Ismail Merchant and James Ivory in 1985.

view·a·ble /vyoó əb'l/ *adj.* **1.** ABLE TO BE SEEN able to be seen or inspected **2.** FIT TO BE WATCHED of a good enough standard, or in a good enough condition, to be watched

view·er /vyoó ər/ *n.* **1.** SOMEBODY WHO WATCHES somebody who watches something such as television, a movie, or an event **2.** OPTICAL DEVICE any optical device for illuminating and magnifying a photographic transparency, videotape, or motion picture film **3.** SOMEBODY WHO MAKES A FORMAL INSPECTION somebody appointed, especially by a court, to inspect something such as property —**view·er·ship** *n.*

view·find·er /vyoó fìndər/ *n.* a device on a camera that lets the user see what is being photographed

view hal·loo /vyoó hə lóo/ *interj.* USED TO SHOW FOX IS SIGHTED used during a fox hunt as a shout to signal that the fox has been seen breaking cover ■ *n.* HUNTER'S CRY a shout of "view halloo!"

view·ing /vyoó ing/ *n.* **1.** ACT OF WATCHING an act or the practice of watching, seeing, or inspecting something **2.** TV SHOWS COLLECTIVELY television programs as a body or type

view·point /vyoó pòynt/ *n.* **1.** POINT OF VIEW a personal perspective from which somebody considers something **2.** VIEWING LOCATION a place or position from which people can look at something

vig /vig/ *n.* = **vigorish** *n.* 1 (*slang*)

vi·ges·i·mal /vī jéssəm'l, vi-/ *adj.* based on or reckoned in units of the number twenty [Mid-17thC. Formed from Latin *vigesimus*, variant of *vicesimus* "twentieth," from *viginti* "twenty."]

vi·gi·a /vi jée ə, vee hée ə/ *n.* NAUT something marked on a chart as a hazard to navigation, although its existence, position, and nature are unconfirmed [Mid-19thC. From Portuguese, "lookout," ultimately from Latin *vigilia* (see VIGIL).]

vig·il /víjjəl/ *n.* **1.** NIGHT WATCH a period spent in doing something through the night, e.g., watching, guarding, or praying **2.** FESTIVAL EVE the eve of some festivals and holy days, spent in prayer ■ **vig·ils** *npl.* RELIGIOUS SERVICES AT NIGHT religious services or prayers at night, especially on the eve of a festival or holy day [13thC. Via Old French *vigile* from medieval Latin *vigilia*, "eve of a holy day," from Latin, "watchfulness," from *vigil* "awake, alert."]

vig·i·lance /víjjələns/ *n.* the condition of being watchful and alert, especially to danger

vig·i·lance com·mit·tee *n.* a group of people who pursue and punish suspected or alleged criminals without having the legal authority to do so

vig·i·lant /víjjələnt/ *adj.* watchful and alert, especially to danger or to something that is wrong —**vig·i·lant·ly** *adv.*

WORD KEY: SYNONYMS

See Synonyms at ***cautious***.

vig·i·lan·te /vìjji lántee/ *n.* **1. LAW-ENFORCING CITIZEN** somebody who punishes lawbreakers personally and illegally rather than relying on the legal authorities **2. VIGILANCE COMMITTEE MEMBER** a member of a vigilance committee [Mid-19thC. From Spanish, "watchman," ultimately from Latin *vigilant-*, the present participle of *vigilare* "to watch," from *vigil* (see VIGIL).]

vign *abbr.* vignette

vig·ne·ron /véenyə ráwn, -ráwN/ *n.* somebody who grows grapes for use in making wine [15thC. From French, from *vigne* (see VINE).]

vi·gnette /vin yét/ *n.* **1. BRIEF SCENE** a brief scene from a movie or play **2.** LITERAT **SHORT ESSAY** a short descriptive piece of literary writing **3.** ARTS **UNBORDERED PICTURE** a painting, drawing, or photograph that has no border but is gradually faded into its background at the edges **4.** PRINTING **DESIGN ON A BOOK PAGE** a small decorative design printed at the beginning or end of a book or chapter of a book, or in the margin of a page **5.** ARCHIT **ARCHITECTURAL ORNAMENTATION** a carved architectural decoration in the form of tendrils and leaves ■ *vt.* **(-gnet·ted, -gnet·ting, -gnettes) 1.** ARTS **FINISH PICTURE OFF BY SOFTENING EDGES** to finish a painting, drawing, or photograph by gradually fading it into its background at the edges rather than giving it a border **2.** LITERAT **DESCRIBE SOMETHING BRIEFLY** to describe something in a brief but elegant way [Mid-18thC. From French, literally "small vine" (from such decorations on the margins of pages in early books), from *vigne* (see VINE).] —**vi·gnet·ter** *n.* —**vi·gnet·tist** *n.*

Vi·go /véegō/ city and port in the autonomous region of Galicia, northwestern Spain, on the Atlantic Ocean. Population: 290,582 (1995).

vig·or /víggər/ *n.* **1. VITALITY** great physical or mental strength and energy **2. INTENSITY** intensity or forcefulness in the way something is done **3. ABILITY TO GROW** the ability of plants or animals to survive, grow, and thrive **4. LEGAL VALIDITY** legal validity or force [14thC. Via Old French *vigour* from Latin *vigor* "liveliness, energy," from *vigere* "to be lively."]

vig·o·rish /víggərish/ *n.* (*slang*) **1. ADDITIONAL PAYMENT** any additional payment that somebody is forced to make, e.g., a bribe or interest paid to a usurer **2. BETTING CHARGE** a sum of money that a bookmaker or gambling establishment charges a customer for accepting a bet [Early 20thC. Earlier "viggresh," of uncertain origin: perhaps via Yiddish from Russian *vyigrysh* or Ukrainian *vygrash* "winnings, profit."]

vig·o·ro·so /vìggə róssō/ *adv.* to be played with intensity and liveliness (*used as a musical direction*) [Early 18thC. From Italian, literally "vigorous," from medieval Latin *vigorosus*, from Latin *vigor* (see VIGOR).] —**vi·go·ro·so** *adj.*

vig·or·ous /víggərəss/ *adj.* **1. VERY HEALTHY** extremely strong and active, physically and mentally **2. ENERGETIC** displaying or using great energy —**vig·or·ous·ly** *adv.* —**vig·or·ous·ness** *n.*

vig·our *n.* U.K. = **vigor**

Vi·ja·ya·wa·da /vèej ī yə waádə/ town in Krishna District, Andhra Pradesh State, southern India. Population: 701,351 (1991).

Vi·king /víking/ *n.* **1.** PEOPLES **MEMBER OF ANCIENT SCANDINAVIAN PEOPLE** a member of any of the Scandinavian peoples who carried out seaborne raids and invasions of various parts of northwestern Europe from the 8th to 11th centuries A.D. They usually came by sea in longships, raiding mainly coastal regions, and often settled in the areas they invaded, as in Britain. **2. Vi·king, vi·king SEAFARER** any plundering seafarer or pirate **3. SPACE PROBE TO MARS** either of two identical, highly instrumented, uncrewed U.S. space probes to Mars, launched in 1975. The probes' orbiters photographed the surface of Mars and its satellites and mapped water vapor and surface temperature variations while the landers transmitted color pictures and meteorological and soil data. [Early 19thC. From Old Norse *víkingr*, either from *vík* "creek, inlet" (literally "person coming from inlets of the sea") or Old English *wīc* "camp" (from their temporary encampments on raids).]

vil. *abbr.* village

vile /vīl/ **(vil·er, vil·est)** *adj.* **1. DISGUSTING** causing disgust or abhorrence **2. WICKED** very evil or shameful **3. VERY UNPLEASANT** extremely unpleasant to experience **4. WORTHLESS** of little or no worth (*archaic*) **5. DEGRADING** so despicable or undesirable as to be degrading [13thC. Via Old French from Latin *vilis* "of little value, cheap, base."] —**vile·ly** *adv.* —**vile·ness** *n.*

WORD KEY: SYNONYMS

See Synonyms at ***mean***.

vil·i·fy /víllə fī/ **(-fied, -fy·ing, -fies)** *vt.* to make malicious and abusive statements about somebody [15thC. From late Latin *vilificare* "to hold cheap," from Latin *vilis* "worthless."] —**vil·i·fi·ca·tion** /vìlləfi káysh'n/ *n.* —**vil·i·fi·er** /víllə fīr/ *n.*

WORD KEY: SYNONYMS

See Synonyms at ***malign***.

vil·i·pend /víllə pènd/ **(-pend·ed, -pend·ing, -pends)** *vt.* (*literary*) **1. TREAT SOMEBODY WITH CONTEMPT** to treat or view somebody with contempt **2. MALIGN SOMEBODY** to make malicious or contemptuous statements about somebody [15thC. Via Old French *vilipender* from Latin *vilipendere*, literally "to consider base," from *vilis* "base, cheap."]

vill *abbr.* **vill.** village

vil·la /víllə/ *n.* **1. EXPENSIVE HOUSE** a large, luxurious house in the country **2. VACATION HOME** a house rented for a vacation **3. ROMAN HOUSE** a country house in ancient Rome or one of its colonies, with living quarters, farm buildings, and a courtyard [Early 17thC. Via Italian from Latin, "country home, farm."]

Vil·la /vée yə/, **Pancho** (1878–1923) Mexican revolutionary leader. He helped overthrow two Mexican dictators in 1911 and 1914. He was later assassinated. Real name **Francisco Villa**. Born **Doroteo Arango**

vil·lage /víllij/ *n.* **1. RURAL COMMUNITY** a group of houses and other buildings in a rural area, smaller than a town but larger than a hamlet **2. INHABITANTS OF VILLAGE** all of the people who live in a village **3. SMALL INCORPORATED COMMUNITY** in some U.S. states, a community that is smaller than a town but that is similarly incorporated **4. TEMPORARY COMMUNITY** a place where people live temporarily as a community, e.g., an apartment complex for the use of athletes taking part in Olympic games **5. ANIMAL DWELLINGS** a group of bird or animal dwellings [14thC. Via Old French from Latin *villaticum* "farmstead," from *villa* (see VILLA).]

vil·lag·er /víllijər/ *n.* somebody who lives in a village

Vi·lla·her·mo·sa /vèe ə hair mósə/ city and capital of Tabasco State, northeastern Mexico. Population: 261,231 (1990).

vil·lain /víllən/ *n.* **1. EVIL CHARACTER** an evil character in a novel, movie, play, or other story, especially one who is the main enemy of the hero **2. CONTEMPTIBLE PERSON** any person regarded as evil or otherwise contemptible (*old or humorous*) **3.** = **villein** [14thC. Via Old French *vilein* "feudal serf," from late Latin *villanus* "farmhand," from Latin *villa* (see VILLA).]

vil·lain·age *n.* = **villeinage**

vil·lain·ess /víllənəss/ *n.* **1. EVIL WOMAN CHARACTER** an evil woman character in a novel, movie, play, or other story, especially one who is the main enemy of the hero **2. CONTEMPTIBLE WOMAN** any woman regarded as evil or otherwise contemptible (*old or humorous*)

vil·lain·ous /víllənəss/ *adj.* **1. WICKED** typical of an evil or contemptible person **2. UNDESIRABLE** obnoxious or unpleasant —**vil·lain·ous·ly** *adv.* —**vil·lain·ous·ness** *n.*

vil·lain·y /víllənee/ *n.* **1. EVIL CONDUCT** behavior typical of an evil or contemptible person **2. STATE OF BEING EVIL** the state of being evil or contemptible **3.** (*plural* **-ies**) **EVIL ACT** an evil or immoral act

Vil·la-Lo·bos /vèelyaa lṓbōosh, vèelaa lṓbōs/, **Heitor** (1897–1959) Brazilian composer. His prolific output was much influenced by the popular music of Brazil and by Native South American Music.

vil·la·nelle /villə nél/ *n.* a 19-line poem, originally French, that uses only two rhymes and consists of five three-line stanzas and a final quatrain. The first and third lines of the first stanza are alternately repeated as a refrain that closes the following stanzas, and joined as a final couplet of the quatrain. [Late 16thC. Via French from Italian *villanella* "old rustic (Italian) song," ultimately from *villano* "peasant," from medieval Latin *villanus* (see VILLAIN).]

Vil·la·no·van /villə nṓv'n/ *adj.* **BELONGING TO IRON AGE CULTURE** belonging to or typical of an early Iron Age culture that existed near Bologna, Italy, in which bronze was used and also, in a primitive way, iron ■ *n.* **MEMBER OF VILLANOVAN CULTURE** a member of the Villanovan culture [Early 20thC. Named after *Villanova*, a town in northeastern Italy near Bologna, where archeological finds were made.]

Vil·la Park /villə paárk/ village in northeastern Illinois, west of Elmhurst. It is a western suburb of Chicago. Population: 22,563 (1996).

vil·lein /víllən/, **vil·lain** *n.* a feudal serf who had the status of a freeman except in relation to his lord, to whom he owed dues and services in exchange for land [14thC. Variant of VILLAIN.]

vil·lein·age /víllənij/, **vil·lain·age** *n.* **1. STATUS OF VILLEIN** the status of being a villein in feudal society **2. LAND TENURE OF VILLEIN** the form of feudal tenure by which a villein held land

vil·li plural of **villus**

vil·li·form /víllə fàwrm/ *adj.* in the form of or resembling a minute projection (**villus**) [Mid-19thC. Formed from VILLUS.]

Vil·lon /vee yóN/, **François** (1431?–63?) French poet. He wrote lyric poetry notable for its fresh interpretation of medieval verse forms and its frank expression of feeling. He was repeatedly arrested for criminal acts, and nothing is known of him after he was banished from Paris in 1463. Real name **François de Montcorbier, François des Loges**

vil·lose *adj.* = **villous** [Early 18thC. From Latin *villosus* (see VILLOUS).]

vil·los·i·ty /vi lóssətee/ (*plural* **-ties**) *n.* **1. HAIRINESS** the condition of being covered in long shaggy hairs **2. BEING COVERED WITH MINUTE PROJECTIONS** the condition of being covered with minute projections **3. COATING OF FINE PROJECTIONS** a surface or coating of very fine projections resembling hairs **4. PART RESEMBLING HAIR** a fine projection that resembles a hair

vil·lous /vílləss/, **vil·lose** /ví lòss/ *adj.* **1. HAIRY** covered with long shaggy hairs **2. WITH MINUTE PROTUBERANCES** relating to, resembling, or covered with minute protuberances [14thC. From Latin *villosus* "shaggy," from *villus* "shaggy hair."] —**vil·lous·ly** *adv.*

vil·lus /vílləss/ (*plural* **-li** /ví lī/) *n.* **1. MINUTE PROTUBERANCE** any of many vascular protuberances growing out from some mucous membranes, e.g., from that of the small intestine of some vertebrates or from the chorion that surrounds an embryo **2. PLACENTAL GROWTH** a finger-shaped protuberance that contributes to the formation of the placenta in mammals **3. OUTGROWTH ON PLANT** a fine part resembling a hair, growing from the surface of a plant [Early 18thC. From Latin, literally "shaggy hair."]

Vil·ni·us /vílnee əss/ capital city of Lithuania, situated in the southeast of the country, near the border with Belarus. Population: 580,100 (1997).

vim /vim/ *n.* exuberant vitality and energy (*informal*) [Mid-19thC. Origin uncertain: probably from Latin, a form of *vis* "power, strength" (source of English *violent*).]

vin *abbr.* vinegar

VIN /vin/ *abbr.* vehicle identification number

vin- *prefix.* = **vini-**

vi·na /vée naà/ *n.* a stringed instrument used in the Indian subcontinent, similar to the sitar. It has a long fretted fingerboard with resonating gourds at both ends and is played by plucking. [Late 18thC. From Sanskrit *vīṇā*.]

vi·na·ceous /vī náyshəss, vi-/ *adj.* **1. LIKE WINE** of the nature of or containing wine **2. REDDISH** of the color of red wine [Late 17thC. Formed from Latin *vinaceus*, from *vinum* "wine."]

vin·ai·grette /vìnnə grét/ *n.* **1. SALAD DRESSING** a salad dressing made with vinegar, oil, salt, pepper, and sometimes other seasonings **2. SMALL CONTAINER** a small bottle or box with a perforated cap, used to hold aromatic substances such as smelling salts or vinegar [Late 17thC. From French, literally "little vinegar," from *vinaigre* (see VINEGAR).]

vi·nasse /vi náss, vī-/ *n.* the residue left in a still after the distillation of an alcoholic beverage, especially brandy. It is used as a fertilizer and is a source of potassium salts. [Via French from Provençal *vinassa*, ultimately from Latin *vinaceus* (see VINACEOUS)]

vin·blas·tine /vin blás teen/ *n.* an alkaloid drug extracted from the Madagascar periwinkle, used in the treatment of some cancers. It works by blocking cell division (**mitosis**) and is highly toxic. Formula:

$C_{46}H_{58}N_4O_9$. [Mid-20thC. Formed from modern Latin *Vinca*, genus name (see VINCA), + LEUKOBLAST + -INE.]

vin·ca /víngkə/ *n.* = **periwinkle**[2] *n.* [Mid-19thC. From modern Latin, genus name, from late Latin *pervinca* (see PERIWINKLE).]

Vin·cennes /vin sénz/ city in southwestern Indiana, on the Wabash River. Population: 19,312 (1996).

Vin·cent de Paul /vaN sàN də páwl, vínsənt-/, **St.** (1581–1660) French priest. He was the founder of the Congregation of the Mission (1625), also called the Vincentians.

Vin·cent's an·gi·na /vínsənts-/, **Vin·cent's in·fec·tion** *n.* a painful mouth inflammation with ulcers and gum damage. Two organisms that are normally present cause the condition only when somebody has a vitamin B deficiency or an immune deficiency. [Early 20thC. Named for Jean Hyacinthe *Vincent* (1862–1950), French physician who discovered the disease.]

vin·ci·ble /vínsəb'l/ *adj.* able to be defeated or conquered (*archaic*) [Mid-16thC. From Latin *vincibilis*, from *vincere* "to conquer."] —**vin·ci·bil·i·ty** /vìnsə bíllətee/ *n.* —**vin·ci·ble·ness** /vínsəb'lnəss/ *n.*

vin·cris·tine /vin krís teen/ *n.* an alkaloid drug produced from the Madagascar periwinkle, used to treat acute leukemia and lymphomas. It works by blocking cell division (**mitosis**) and is highly toxic. Formula: $C_{46}H_{56}N_4O_{10}$. [Mid-20thC. Formed from modern Latin *Vinca*, genus name (see VINCA), + Latin *crista* "crest" + -INE.]

vin·cu·lum /víngkyələm/ (*plural* **-lums** *or* **-la** /-lə/) *n.* **1.** MATH **RAISED LINE CONNECTING MATHEMATICAL TERMS** a horizontal line above two or more members of a compound mathematical expression, used like parentheses to show that the expression is to be treated as a single term. Parentheses, brackets, and braces are used more frequently for this purpose than is the vinculum. **2.** ANAT **BAND OF TISSUE** a band of tissue, especially a ligament [Mid-17thC. From Latin, literally "fetter, bond," from *vincire* "to tie, fasten."]

vin·da·loo /víndə lōō/ (*plural* **-loos**) *n.* a very hot curry sauce made with coriander, red chili, ginger, and other spices, or a dish cooked in this [Late 19thC. From Konkani *vindalu*, ultimately from Portuguese *vinho de alho*, a wine and garlic sauce, literally "wine of garlic."]

vin·di·ca·ble /víndikəb'l/ *adj.* able to be vindicated or justified [Mid-17thC. From medieval Latin *vindicabilis*, from Latin *vindicare* (see VINDICATE).] —**vin·di·ca·bil·i·ty** /vìndikə bíllətee/ *n.*

vin·di·cate /víndi kàyt/ (**-cat·ed, -cat·ing, -cates**) *vt.* **1. SHOW SOMEBODY OR SOMETHING IS BLAMELESS** to clear somebody or something of blame, guilt, suspicion, or doubt **2. JUSTIFY SOMEBODY OR SOMETHING** to show that somebody or something is justified or correct **3. UPHOLD SOMETHING** to defend or maintain something such as a cause or rights [Mid-16thC. From Latin *vindicatus*, perfect participle of *vindicare* "to claim, set free, avenge," from the stem *vindic-* "avenger."] —**vin·di·ca·tor** *n.*

vin·di·ca·tion /vìndi káysh'n/ *n.* **1. BEING VINDICATED** the act of vindicating somebody or something, or the condition of being vindicated **2. REASON FOR VINDICATING SOMEBODY OR SOMETHING** evidence or an argument used to vindicate somebody or something

vin·di·ca·to·ry /víndikə tàwree/ *adj.* providing something such as facts or an argument that justifies a belief, conclusion, or action

vin·dic·tive /vin díktiv/ *adj.* **1. VENGEFUL** looking for revenge or done through a desire for revenge **2. SPITEFUL** feeling, showing, or done through a desire to hurt somebody **3.** LAW **MEANT TO PUNISH** used to describe damages awarded by a court that are set higher than the amount necessary to compensate the victim, in order to punish the defendant [Early 17thC. Formed from Latin *vindicta* "revenge."]

vine /vīn/ *n.* **1. CLIMBING PLANT** a plant that supports itself by climbing, twining, or creeping along a surface **2. STEM** the weak flexible stem of a vine **3.** = **grapevine** *n.* 1 **4. GRAPEVINES COLLECTIVELY** grapevines considered collectively ■ *vi.* (**vined, vin·ing, vines**) **GROW LIKE VINE** to form or grow like a vine [13thC. Via Old French *vigne* from Latin *vinea* "vine, vineyard," from *vinum* "wine" (source of English *wine* and *vinegar*).] —**vin·y** *adj.*

vine·dress·er /vīn drèssər/ *n.* somebody who tends and prunes grapevines

vin·e·gar /vínnəgər/ *n.* **1. SOUR-TASTING LIQUID** a sour-tasting liquid used to flavor and preserve foods. It is a dilute acetic acid made by fermenting beer, wine, or cider. **2. ILL TEMPER** sourness or ill-tempered behavior or speech **3. VITALITY** exuberant energy and enthusiasm [13thC. From Old French *vyn egre* "sour wine," from Latin *vinum acre*.] —**vin·e·gar·ish** *adj.*

vin·e·gar eel, **vin·e·gar worm** *n.* a very small nematode worm that feeds on bacteria that cause fermentation, especially in vinegar. Latin name: *Anguillula aceti*.

vin·e·gar·y /vínnəgəree/ *adj.* **1. SOUR-TASTING** with a sour taste or smell like vinegar **2. IRRITABLE** showing an unpleasant, irritable disposition —**vin·e·gar·i·ness** *n.*

vin·er·y /vínəree/ (*plural* **-ies**) *n.* an area or building, especially a greenhouse, in which grapevines are grown

vine·yard /vínnyərd/ *n.* **1. PLACE WHERE GRAPES ARE GROWN** a piece of land where grapevines are grown **2. SPHERE OF ENDEAVOR** any sphere of mental, physical, or spiritual endeavor

vingt-et-un /vàN tay úN/ *n.* CARDS the game of blackjack [Late 18thC. From French, literally "twenty-one."]

vini- *prefix.* wine, grapes ○ *viniculture* [From Latin *vinum*]

vin·i·cul·ture *n.* = **viticulture** —**vin·i·cul·tur·al** /vìnni kúlchərəl/ *adj.* —**vin·i·cul·tur·ist** /vìnni kúlchərist/ *n.*

vin·i·fi·ca·tion /vìnnəfi káysh'n/ *n.* the process by which a liquid is fermented into wine (*technical*)

vin·i·fy /vínnə fī/ (**-fied, -fy·ing, -fies**) *vt.* to ferment grape juice, or another liquid, into wine

Vin·land /vínlənd/ part of North America, now northern Newfoundland, first seen by the Norse voyager Bjarni Herjólfsson during a voyage from Iceland to Greenland in about A.D. 986. The Icelandic explorer Leif Ericson explored the Newfoundland and Labrador coasts several years later.

vi·no /veenō/ *n.* wine, especially cheap wine (*informal*) [Late 19thC. From Italian, "wine."]

vin or·di·naire /vàN áwrdee náir/ (*plural* **vins or·di·naires** /vàNz áwrdee náir/) *n.* cheap table wine, especially from France [Early 19thC. From French, literally "ordinary wine."]

vi·nos·i·ty /vī nóssətee/ *n.* the distinctive and essential character of wine, including qualities such as body, color, and taste

vi·nous /vínəss/ *adj.* **1. OF WINE** relating to, typical of, or containing wine **2. WINE-DRINKING** tending to drink a lot of wine, or caused by wine-drinking **3. WINE-COLORED** of the color of red wine [Mid-17thC. Formed from Latin *vinum* "wine."] —**vi·nous·ly** *adv.* —**vi·nous·ness** *n.*

Vin·son /vínssən/, **Frederick M.** (1890–1953) U.S. jurist. He served as chief justice of the U.S. supreme court (1946–53). Full name **Frederick Moore Vinson**

Vin·son Mas·sif /vìnssən máss eef/ the highest mountain in Antarctica, in the central Ellsworth Mountains. Height: 16,864 ft./5,140 m.

vin·tage /víntij/ *n.* **1. WINE PRODUCTION YEAR** the year in which the grapes used in making a particular wine were harvested **2. WINE FROM A PARTICULAR YEAR** wine made from a particular harvest of grapes **3. GRAPE HARVESTING** the harvesting of grapes for wine **4. WINE** a wine, especially an excellent one **5. PERIOD** the period of time when something appeared or began, or when somebody was born or flourished ○ *Depression-vintage furniture* **6. GROUP SHARING CHARACTERISTICS** a group of people or things that are similar or belong to the same period of time (*informal*) ■ *adj.* **1. GOOD FOR WINE** produced from or characterized by a good harvest of grapes for wine-making, so that the wine does not have to be improved by blending with wine from another harvest **2. OF THE BEST** representing what is best or most typical of somebody or something **3. CLASSIC** recognized as being of high quality and lasting appeal **4. OUT OF DATE** no longer fashionable or modern [14thC. Alteration (influenced by *viniter* "vintner") of *vendage*, from Old French *vendange*, from Latin *vindemia* "grape-gathering," from *vinum* "wine" + *demere* "to take away."]

vin·tage car *n.* an old car, especially one built between 1919 and 1930

vin·tag·er /víntijər/ *n.* somebody who takes part in harvesting grapes and making wine

vin·tage year *n.* **1. YEAR OF GOOD WINE** a year in which the wine that is made is of excellent quality **2. OUTSTANDING YEAR** a year of extraordinary accomplishment or success

vint·ner /víntnər/ *n.* **1. WINE MERCHANT** somebody who sells wine **2. WINEMAKER** somebody who makes wine [15thC. Via Old French *vinetier* from medieval Latin *vinetarius*, from Latin *vinetum* "vineyard," from *vinum* "wine."]

vi·nyl /vín'l/ *n.* **1. CHEMICAL GROUP** a univalent unsaturated chemical group or radical that is formed when one hydrogen atom is removed from ethylene. Formula: CH_2CH. (*often used before a noun*) **2. COMPOUND USED IN PLASTICS** a reactive compound that contains the vinyl radical, usually in polymerized form, used in making plastics (*often used before a noun*) **3. PLASTIC MATERIAL** a plastic material, made from a vinyl polymer **4. PLASTIC RECORDS** phonograph records made of a vinyl polymer, as opposed to compact disks ■ *adj.* **MADE OF VINYL** made of or containing a vinyl polymer [Mid-19thC. Formed from VIN- + -YL.] —**vi·nyl·ic** /vī níllik/ *adj.*

vi·nyl chlo·ride *n.* a colorless, carcinogenic, explosive, flammable gas used in organic synthesis, particularly in making polyvinyl chloride, and in adhesives. Formula: CH_2:CHCl.

vi·nyl·i·dene /vī níllee deen/ *n.* a bivalent chemical group or radical, made when two hydrogen atoms are removed from one carbon atom of ethylene. Formula: CH_2:C.

vi·nyl pol·y·mer, **vi·nyl res·in** *n.* any odorless and tasteless thermoplastic material made by polymerizing compounds containing vinyl groups. PVC is a typical example.

vi·ol /ví əl/ *n.* **1. STRINGED INSTRUMENT** a stringed instrument popular during the 16th and 17th centuries with a fretted fingerboard, a flat-backed body, and six strings, played with a curved bow. It is a member of a family of stringed instruments that preceded the violin family. **2.** = **viola da gamba** [15thC. Via Old French *viole* from Old Provençal *viola*, of uncertain origin: perhaps from medieval Latin *vitula* (see VIOLA[1]).]

vi·o·la[1] /vee ṓlə/ *n.* **1. STRINGED INSTRUMENT** a stringed instrument slightly larger than a violin held under the chin and played with a long slender bow. It is tuned an octave above the cello and is the alto of the violin family. **2.** = **viola da gamba** [Late 18thC. Via Italian from Old Provençal *viola*, from medieval Latin *vitula* "stringed instrument" (source of English *fiddle*).]

vi·o·la[2] /vī ṓlə, vee-, ví ələ/ *n.* a plant related to the violets and pansies, especially one with small white, yellow, or purple flowers. Genus: *Viola*. [15thC. From Latin, "violet" (source of English *violet*).]

vi·o·la·ble /ví ələb'l/ *adj.* capable of being disregarded or treated with disrespect —**vi·o·la·bil·i·ty** /vī ələ bíllətee/ *n.* —**vi·o·la·ble·ness** *n.* —**vi·o·la·bly** /ví ələblee/ *adv.*

vi·o·la·ceous /vī ə láyshəss/ *adj.* relating to, belonging to, or typical of the family of plants that includes violets and pansies [Mid-17thC. Formed from Latin *violaceus* "violet-colored," from *viola* "violet."]

vi·o·la da brac·cio /vee ṑlə də bráachō/ (*plural* **vi·o·las da brac·cio**) *n.* an old stringed instrument of the viol family, held against the shoulder when played [Mid-19thC. From Italian, literally "viol for (the) arm."]

vi·o·la da gam·ba /vee ṑlə də gáambə, -gámbə/ (*plural* **vi·o·las da gam·ba**) *n.* an old stringed bass instrument of the viol family, with a range similar to a cello [Late 16thC. From Italian, literally "viol for (the) leg."]

vi·o·la d'a·mo·re /vee ṑlə daa máw rày/ (*plural* **vi·o·las d'a·mo·re**) *n.* a fretless stringed instrument of the viol family with six or seven strings and a second set of strings that are not played but are made to vibrate by the first set (**sympathetic strings**) [Late 17thC. From Italian, literally "viol of love."]

vi·o·late /ví ə làyt/ (**-lat·ed, -lat·ing, -lates**) *vt.* **1. DISREGARD SOMETHING** to act contrary to something such as a law, contract, or agreement, especially in a way that produces significant effects **2. RAPE SOMEBODY** to rape or sexually assault somebody **3. DISTURB SOMETHING** to disturb or interrupt something in a rude or violent way **4. DEFILE SOMETHING** to treat something sacred with a lack of respect [15thC. From Latin *violatus*, perfect participle of *violare* "to treat with violence, injure," of uncertain origin.] —**vi·o·la·tive** *adj.* —**vi·o·la·tor** *n.*

vi·o·la·tion /vī ə láysh'n/ *n.* **1.** ACT OF VIOLATING the act or an example of violating somebody or something **2.** CRIME OR INFRINGEMENT OF RULE a crime or infringement of a law or rules, especially one less serious than a misdemeanor or a foul in sports

vi·o·lence /vī ələns/ *n.* **1.** PHYSICAL FORCE the use of physical force to injure somebody or damage something ○ *threats of violence* **2.** ILLEGAL FORCE the illegal use of unjustified force, or the effect created by the threat of this ○ *robbery with violence* **3.** DESTRUCTIVE FORCE extreme, destructive, or uncontrollable force, especially of natural events ○ *the violence of the storm* **4.** FERVOR intensity of feeling or expression ○ *the violence of her response to our suggestion* ◇ **do violence to something** to violate, harm, or damage something

vi·o·lent /vī ələnt/ *adj.* **1.** USING PHYSICAL FORCE using physical force to hurt somebody or damage something ○ *violent crime* **2.** EMOTIONALLY INTENSE showing emotional intensity or strong feeling ○ *his violent objections to the plan* **3.** SHOWING DESTRUCTIVE FORCE showing extreme, destructive, or uncontrollable force ○ *a violent thunderstorm* **4.** INTENSE very intense or strong ○ *a violent headache* **5.** CAUSED BY FORCE caused by force rather than natural causes ○ *met a violent death* **6.** DISTORTING distorting or misinterpreting the meaning of something ○ *a violent interpretation of the poem* [14thC. From Latin *violentus* "forcible, vehement," of uncertain origin.] —**vi·o·lent·ly** *adv.*

vi·o·lent storm *n.* a storm that causes widespread damage with winds of force 11 on the Beaufort scale, reaching speeds of 64–72 mph/103–117 kph

Violet

vi·o·let /vī ələt/ *n.* **1.** FLOWERING PLANT a low-growing, perennial plant with irregular flowers that are usually but not always a purplish blue. Genus: *Viola.* **2.** PLANT RESEMBLING A VIOLET any of several plants such as the African violet that are like the violet but are not necessarily related to it **3.** PURPLISH-BLUE COLOR a deep purplish-blue color like that of a violet flower ■ *adj.* PURPLISH-BLUE of a deep purplish-blue color like a violet flower [14thC. From Old French *violete*, a diminutive of *viole*, from Latin *viola* "violet."]

vi·o·lin /vī ə lín/ *n.* **1.** STRINGED INSTRUMENT PLAYED WITH BOW a wooden musical instrument with four strings and an unfretted fingerboard, held under the player's chin and played with a bow. The violin has the highest range in the family of stringed instruments to which it gives its name. **2.** VIOLINIST a musician who plays a violin, especially in an orchestra [Late 16thC. From Italian *violino*, a diminutive of *viola* (see VIOLA[1]).]

vi·o·lin·ist /vī ə línnist/ *n.* somebody who plays the violin

vi·o·lin so·na·ta *n.* a sonata for solo violin, usually with piano accompaniment

vi·o·list[1] /vī əlist, vee ṓlist/ *n.* somebody who plays the viola

vi·o·list[2] /vī əlist/ *n.* somebody who plays the viol

vi·o·lon·cel·lo /vèe ələn chéllō, vī-/ (*plural* **-los**) *n.* a cello (*formal*) [Early 18thC. From Italian, a diminutive of *violone* (see VIOLONE).]

vi·o·lo·ne /vèe ə lṓ nàỳ/ *n.* the double-bass viol, larger and with a deeper range than the viola da gamba [Early 18thC. From Italian, literally "large viola," from *viola* (see VIOLA[1]).]

VIP *abbr.* very important person

vi·pas·sa·na, Vi·pas·sa·na *n.* Theravada Buddhist meditation that aims at concentrating the mind on the body

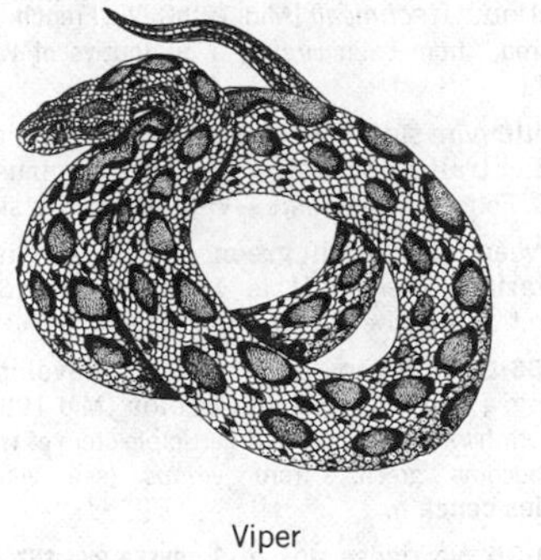

Viper

vi·per /vípər/ *n.* **1.** POISONOUS SNAKE a snake with hollow fangs that it uses to inject venom into its victim when it bites. Vipers are found in Europe, Asia, and Africa. Family: Viperidae. **2.** = **adder**[2] *n.* **3.** POISONOUS SNAKE NOT OF VIPER FAMILY a poisonous snake such as the horned viper belonging to a family other than the vipers proper **4.** PIT VIPER a pit viper **5.** OFFENSIVE TERM an offensive term used to refer to somebody who is considered to be malicious, treacherous, or ungrateful (*offensive*) **6.** = **adder** [Early 16thC. Via Old French *vipere* from Latin *vipera* "snake," a contraction of assumed *vivipera* "live-bearing" (from the ancient belief that snakes bore live young), from *vivus* "alive."]

vi·per·ine *adj.* = **viperous**

vi·per·ish /vípərish/ *adj.* **1.** MALICIOUS malicious or spiteful **2.** = **viperous** —**vi·per·ish·ly** *adv.*

vi·per·ous /vípərəss/, **vi·per·ine** /vípə rìn, vípərin/ *adj.* typical of or like a viper —**vi·per·ous·ly** *adv.*

vi·per's bu·gloss *n.* a weed that is native to Europe and Asia and is naturalized in other areas. It has spikes of blue tubular flowers and rough foliage. Latin name: *Echium vulgare.*

Vir *abbr.* **1.** Virgil **2.** Virgo

vir- *prefix.* = **viro-** (*used before vowels*)

vi·ra·go /vi ráagō/ (*plural* **-goes** *or* **-gos**) *n.* **1.** OFFENSIVE TERM an offensive term that deliberately insults a woman's temperament or behavior (*insult offensive*) **2.** COURAGEOUS WOMAN a woman who is strong and brave (*archaic*) [Pre-12thC. From Latin, from *vir* "man, husband" (source of English *virile*).] —**vi·rag·i·nous** /vi rájjənəss/ *adj.*

vi·ral /vírəl/ *adj.* relating to, typical of, or caused by a virus —**vi·ral·ly** *adv.*

vi·ral pneu·mo·nia *n.* an infection of the lungs caused by a virus

Vir·chow /féerkō/, **Rudolf** (1821–1902) German pathologist and anthropologist. His textbook on cellular pathology (1850) was the foundation text of the field. He also published significant works in anthropology and archaeology. Full name **Rudolf Carl Virchow**

vir·e·lay /véerə lày/ *n.* an old French verse form consisting of short lines arranged in stanzas with two rhymes. The end rhyme is repeated as the first line of the next stanza. [14thC. From French *virelai*, an alteration (influenced by *lai* "lay, song") of obsolete *vireli*, of uncertain origin: perhaps a nonsense word used in the refrain of a song.]

vi·re·mi·a /vī réemee ə/ *n.* the presence of viruses in the bloodstream [Mid-20thC. From modern Latin, from VIRUS + -EMIA.] —**vi·re·mic** *adj.*

vir·e·o /véeree ō/ (*plural* **-os**) *n.* a small insect-eating songbird that lives in the Americas and has grayish or greenish plumage. Genus: *Vireo.* [Mid-19thC. From modern Latin, genus name, from Latin, a bird (probably the greenfinch), from *virere* "to be green."]

vi·res plural of **vis**

vi·res·cence /vi réss'ns, vī-/ *n.* the state of being green or the process of becoming green, especially the abnormal development of green coloration in plant parts that are not normally green, as a result of disease

vi·res·cent /vi réss'nt, vī-/ *adj.* **1.** GREENISH having or developing a green or greenish color **2.** ABNORMALLY GREEN used to describe plant parts that are not normally green but are turned green by disease [Early 19thC. From Latin *virescent-*, present participle stem of *virescere* "to become green."]

vir·ga /vúrgə/ (*plural* **-ga**) *n.* vertical trails of rain, snow, or ice from the underside of a cloud that evaporate before reaching the ground [Mid-20thC. From Latin, literally "rod, staff, twig."]

vir·gate /vúrgət, vúr gàyt/ *adj.* long and thin like a rod [Early 19thC. From Latin *virgatus*, from *virga* "rod, staff."]

Vir·gil /vúrjəl/, **Ver·gil** (70–19 B.C.) Roman poet. Regarded as the finest Latin poet of his age, he wrote pastoral verse before composing his great mythological epic *Aeneid*, which tells the story of the seven-year wanderings of Aeneas after the fall of Troy. Full name **Publius Vergilius Maro** —**Vir·gil·i·an** /vur jíllee ən/ *adj.*

vir·gin /vúrjin/ *n.* **1.** SOMEBODY WHO HAS NOT HAD SEX somebody, especially a woman, who has never had sexual intercourse **2.** RELIG RELIGIOUS WOMAN COMMITTED TO CHASTITY a woman who has taken a vow of chastity for religious reasons **3.** ZOOL FEMALE ANIMAL a female animal that has never copulated **4.** INSECTS FEMALE INSECT a female insect that produces fertile eggs without the help of a male ■ *adj.* **1.** OF A VIRGIN relating to, typical of, or being a virgin **2.** PURE in a pure, natural, or clean state **3.** ENVIRON NOT TOUCHED BY HUMANS never having been explored or exploited by humans **4.** FIRST first or happening for the first time **5.** FOOD FROM FIRST PRESSING used to describe vegetable oils that come from the first pressing of fruit, leaves, or seeds without the use of heat **6.** METALL PRODUCED DIRECTLY FROM ORE used to describe metals produced directly from an ore, not from scrap metal **7.** MINERALS UNALLOYED found in a pure, unmixed state **8.** PHYS NEVER HAVING COLLIDED used to describe a neutron that has never been in a collision and therefore retains the energy with which it started [12thC. Via Old French *virgine* from Latin *virgin-*, the stem of *virgo* "maiden."]

Vir·gin /vúrjən/ *n.* **1.** CHR = **Virgin Mary 2.** ZODIAC = **Virgo**

vir·gin·al[1] /vúrjin'l/ *adj.* **1.** CHASTE relating to, typical of, or appropriate for somebody, especially a woman, who has never had sexual intercourse **2.** LIVING CHASTELY living in a state of virginity **3.** PURE not corrupted or spoiled in any way

vir·gin·al[2] /vúrjin'l/ *n.* a smaller, often legless, oblong version of the harpsichord, popular in the 16th and 17th centuries [Early 16thC. Directly or via French from Latin *virginalis* (see VIRGIN), perhaps because the instrument was played by young girls.] —**vir·gin·al·ist** *n.*

Vir·gin Birth *n.* the Christian doctrine that Jesus Christ was born as the son of God rather than of a human father and that his mother was a virgin

Vir·gin·ia[1] /vər jínnyə/, **vir·gin·ia** *n.* a type of tobacco originally grown in the state of Virginia

Virginia

Vir·gin·ia[2] /vər jínnyə/ state of the eastern United States, bordered by Maryland, the Atlantic Ocean, North Carolina, Tennessee, Kentucky, and West Virginia. Capital: Richmond. Population: 6,733,996 (1997). Area: 42,326 sq. mi./109,624 sq. km. Official name **Commonwealth of Virginia** —**Vir·gin·ian** /vər jínnyən/ *n., adj.*

Vir·gin·ia Beach the largest city in Virginia, situated in the southeastern part of the state, on the Atlantic Ocean and Chesapeake Bay, near the border with North Carolina. Population: 430,295 (1994).

Vir·gin·ia cow·slip, Vir·gin·ia blue·bell *n.* a plant that grows in eastern North America and has clusters of blue flowers. Latin name: *Mertensia virginica.*

Vir·gin·ia creep·er *n.* a climbing plant with leaves made up of five leaflets and bluish-black berries. Latin name: *Parthenocissus quinquefolia.*

Vir·gin·ia deer *n.* = **white-tailed deer**

Vir·gin·ia fence *n.* = **worm fence**

Vir·gin·ia ham *n.* a kind of lean, hickory-smoked ham with dark reddish meat

Vir·gin·ia rail *n.* a small North American bird of the rail family with a long, slender bill. Latin name: *Rallus limicola.*

Vir·gin·ia reel *n.* an American country dance in which a caller instructs couples facing each other in long lines to perform various steps

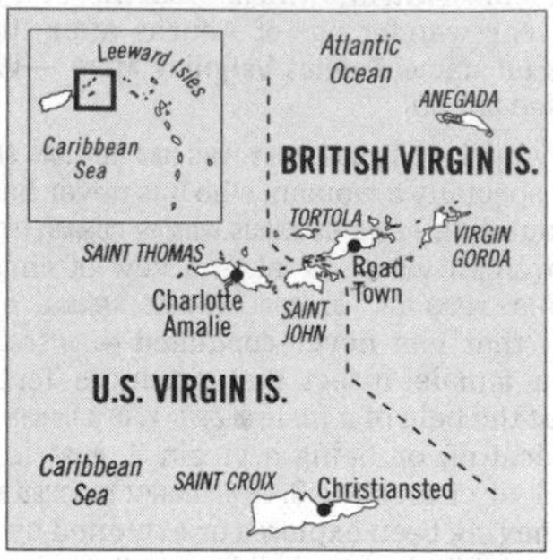

British Virgin Islands and U.S. Virgin Islands

Vir·gin Is·lands, British /vùrjin-/ dependent territory of the United Kingdom consisting of 36 islands in the West Indies, east of Puerto Rico. Capital: Road Town. Population: 13,195 (1996). Area: 59 sq. mi./153 sq. km.

Vir·gin Is·lands Na·tion·al Park national park on the islands of St. John and Hassel, in the U.S. Virgin Islands. It was established in 1956. Area: 23 sq. mi./59.5 sq. km.

Vir·gin Is·lands of the U·ni·ted States unincorporated external territory of the United States in the eastern Caribbean Sea, consisting of three main islands and over 60 smaller islands and islets. Capital: Charlotte Amalie. Population: 97,120 (1996). Area: 135 sq. mi./349 sq. km.

vir·gin·i·ty /vər jínnətee/ *n.* **1. VIRGIN STATE** the state of being a virgin **2. UNSPOILED STATE** the state of being untouched, unexplored, or unspoiled

vir·gin·i·um /vər jínnee əm/ *n.* an old name for the element francium (*archaic*) [Early 20thC. Formed from VIRGINIA[2] + -IUM.]

Vir·gin Mar·y *n.* in Christian tradition, the mother of Jesus Christ

Vir·gin Queen *n.* a name used for Elizabeth I, Queen of England

vir·gin's bow·er *n.* a clematis of eastern North America that has clusters of small white flowers. Latin name: *Clematis virginiana.*

vir·gin soil *n.* soil that has not yet been used for cultivation

vir·gin wool *n.* wool that has not already been used to make something

Vir·go /vúrgō/ (*plural* **-gos**) *n.* **1.** ASTRON **LARGE CONSTELLATION** a constellation located on the celestial equator between Leo and Libra that contains the binary star Spica. The Virgo cluster, which lies near the North Galactic Pole about 16 billion light-years from the Earth, contains about 3,000 galaxies. **2.** ZODIAC **ASTROLOGICAL SIGN** the sixth sign of the zodiac, represented by a virgin and lasting from approximately August 23 to September 22. Virgo is classified as an earth sign and its ruling planet is Mercury. **3. Vir·go, Vir·go·an SOMEBODY BORN UNDER VIRGO** somebody whose birthday falls between August 23 and September 22 **4. PERSON BORN UNDER VIRGO** a person born under the sign of Virgo [Pre-12thC. From Latin (see VIRGIN).] —**Vir·go** *adj.*

vir·go in·tac·ta /vùrgō in táktə/ *n.* a girl or woman whose hymen remains unbroken [From Latin, literally "intact virgin"]

vir·gu·late /vúrgyələt, -làyt/ *adj.* shaped like a rod [Mid-19thC. From Latin *virgula*, a diminutive of *virga* "rod, staff, twig."]

vir·gule /vúr gyo͞ol/ *n.* a diagonal mark used to separate alternatives, as in "and/or," to stand for the word per, as in "miles/hours," and to show the line breaks in verse printed continuously. For example, "The expense of spirit in a waste of shame/Is lust in action." (*technical*) [Mid-19thC. Via French, "comma, little rod," from Latin *virgula*, a diminutive of *virga* "rod, staff."]

vi·ri·cide /vírə sìd/, **vi·ru·cide** *n.* a drug or other agent that neutralizes or destroys a virus or viruses [Mid-20thC. Formed from VIRUS.] —**vi·ri·cid·al** /vìrə síd'l/ *adj.*

vir·id /vèerid/ *adj.* bright green, or covered with green vegetation (*literary*) [Late 16thC. From Latin *viridis* "green," a derivative of *virere* "to be green."]

vir·i·des·cent /vèeri déss'nt/ *adj.* developing or having a green or greenish color [Mid-19thC. From late Latin *viridescent-*, present participle stem of *viridescere* "to become green," from *viridus* (see VIRID).] — **vir·i·des·cence** *n.*

vi·rid·i·an /və ríddee ən/ *n.* **1. GREEN PIGMENT** a green pigment made of a form of chromic oxide **2. BLUISH-GREEN COLOR** a bluish-green color —**vi·rid·i·an** *adj.*

vi·rid·i·ty /və ríddətee/ *n.* (*literary*) **1. GREENNESS** the state of being green **2. INNOCENCE** the state of being inexperienced

vir·ile /vèerəl, ví rìl/ *adj.* **1. MASCULINE** relating to or having the characteristics of an adult male **2. POTENT** able to carry out the male sexual function **3. STRONG** showing strength and forcefulness [15thC. From Latin *virilis*, from *vir* "man, husband" (source of English *virtue*).]

vir·il·ism /vèerə lìzzəm/ *n.* the development of male secondary sex characteristics culturally considered to be unusual in a woman, e.g., body hair or a deep voice

vi·ril·i·ty /vi ríllətee/ *n.* the state of being male, having male characteristics, or male sexual potency

vir·i·lo·cal /vèeri lṓk'l/ *adj.* used to describe a form of marriage or the custom where, after the wedding, the bride moves to her new husband's family home [Mid-20thC. Formed from Latin *virilis* "of a man" (see VIRILE) + LOCAL.]

vi·ri·on /vìree òn, vèe-/ *n.* the form taken by a virus when it is outside living cells and capable of causing infection. It consists of a core of DNA or RNA surrounded by a protein coat, sometimes covered by an outer envelope. [Mid-20thC. From French, formed from *virien* "viral" + -ON.]

viro- *prefix.* virus, viral ○ *virology* [From VIRUS]

vi·roid /ví ròyd/ *n.* an infectious RNA particle that is like a virus but smaller. It causes diseases in plants. [Mid-20thC. Coined from VIRUS + -OID.]

vi·rol·o·gy /vī róllәjee/ *n.* the scientific study of viruses and the diseases caused by them [Mid-20thC. Formed from VIRUS.] —**vi·ro·log·ic** /vìrə lójjik/ *adj.* — **vi·ro·log·i·cal** /-lójjik'l/ *adj.* —**vi·ro·log·i·cal·ly** /-lójjikəlee/ *adv.* —**vi·rol·o·gist** /vī róllәjist/ *n.*

vir·tu /vər to͞o/, **ver·tu** *n.* a love of or taste for fine art objects or curios [Early 18thC. From Italian, literally "virtue."]

vir·tu·al /vúrchoo əl/ *adj.* **1. BEING SOMETHING IN PRACTICE** being something in effect even if not in reality or not conforming to the generally accepted definition of the term **2.** PHYS **HYPOTHETICAL** used to describe a particle whose existence is suggested to explain observed phenomena but is not proven or directly observable **3.** COMPUT **GENERATED BY COMPUTER** simulated by a computer for reasons of economics, convenience, or performance **4.** COMPUT **RELATING TO DATA STORAGE MANAGEMENT TECHNIQUE** used to describe a technique of moving data between storage areas or media to create the impression that a computer has a storage capacity greater than it actually has [14thC. From medieval Latin *virtualis*, from Latin *virtus* (see VIRTUE). The meaning of "so in effect" developed from "having power."]

vir·tu·al as·sis·tant *n.* somebody who uses computer and phone connections to work from a distance as a personal assistant to somebody else, instead of working in the same office or building ○ *"There are many reasons why home-based business owners are hiring virtual assistants."* (*Washington Post*; December 1998)

vir·tu·al com·mu·ni·ty *n.* a group of people communicating with each other via the Internet

vir·tu·al fo·cus *n.* the point from which divergent reflected or refracted light rays seem to originate

vir·tu·al im·age *n.* an image from which reflected or refracted light rays appear to diverge. It cannot be projected onto a screen or a photographic emulsion.

vir·tu·al·i·ty /vùrchoo állətee/ *n.* the inherent ability or potential to come into existence

vir·tu·al·ly /vúrchoo əlee/ *adv.* **1. PRACTICALLY** in effect even if not in fact **2. NEARLY** almost but not quite

vir·tu·al ma·chine *n.* a program running on a computer that creates a self-contained operating environment and presents the appearance to the user of a different computer. A virtual machine simulates at a minimum the instruction set of the computer it emulates.

vir·tu·al mem·o·ry, **vir·tu·al stor·age** *n.* a technique for creating the illusion that a computer has more memory than it really has by swapping blocks or pages of data between memory and external storage

vir·tu·al re·al·i·ty *n.* **1. COMPUTER SIMULATION** a technique by which a computer simulates a three-dimensional physical environment using visual and auditory stimuli with and within which people can interact to affect what happens in the simulation **2. SIMULATED REALITY** a computer-generated environment that simulates three-dimensional reality

Vir·tual Re·al·i·ty Mod·el·ing Lan·guage *n.* full form of **VRML**

vir·tue /vúrchoo/ *n.* **1. GOODNESS** the quality of being morally good or righteous ○ *a paragon of virtue* **2. GOOD QUALITY** a particular quality that is morally good ○ *Patience is a virtue.* **3. ADMIRABLE QUALITY** a particular quality that is good or admirable, but not necessarily in terms of morality **4. CARDINAL OR THEOLOGICAL MORALITY** any of the cardinal virtues, such as justice or moderation, or of the theological virtues, such as hope or charity **5. CHASTITY** the moral quality of being chaste, especially in a woman **6. WORTH** the worth, advantage, or beneficial quality of something ○ *knew the virtue of thrift* **7. EFFECTIVE FORCE** the power or efficacy that something contains to do something (*archaic*) ■ **vir·tues** *npl.* CHR **ORDER OF ANGELS** the fifth of the nine traditional orders in the hierarchy of angels [12thC. Via Old French *vertu* from the Latin stem *virtut-* "manliness, excellence, worth," from *vir* "man, husband."] —**vir·tue·less** *adj.* ◇ **by virtue of** because of, through the power of, or by the authority of something ◇ **make a virtue of necessity** to do something with good grace, when you are obligated to do it anyway

vir·tu·o·sa /vùrchoo ṓssə, vùrchoo ṓzə/ *n.* a woman musician who shows exceptional ability, technique, or artistry [Mid-17thC. From Italian, feminine of *virtuoso* (see VIRTUOSO).]

vir·tu·o·si plural of **virtuoso**

vir·tu·os·i·ty /vùrchoo óssətee/ *n.* **1. OUTSTANDING SKILL** great skill or technique shown by somebody who excels at doing something, especially performing music **2. ENJOYMENT OF ART OBJECTS** interest in, or knowledge and appreciation of, fine art objects

vir·tu·o·so /vùrchoo ṓssō/ (*plural* **-sos** /-ṓssee/ *or* **-si**) *n.* **1. EXCEPTIONAL PERFORMER** a musician who shows exceptional ability, technique, or artistry **2. TALENTED PERSON** somebody who shows exceptional technique or ability in something **3. CONNOISSEUR** somebody who cultivates an interest in, or knowledge and appreciation of, fine art objects [Early 17thC. From Italian, literally "skillful, versed," from late Latin *virtuosus* "good," from Latin *virtus* (see VIRTUE).] —**vir·tu·o·sic** /-óssik/ *adj.* —**vir·tu·o·si·cal·ly** /-óssikəlee/ *adv.*

vir·tu·ous /vúrchoo əss/ *adj.* **1. WITH MORAL INTEGRITY** having or showing moral goodness or righteousness **2. CHASTE** not having sexual intercourse with anyone except a partner in marriage, especially a husband —**vir·tu·ous·ly** *adv.* —**vir·tu·ous·ness** *n.*

vi·ru·cide *n.* = **viricide**

vir·u·lence /vèeryələnss, vèerə-/, **vir·u·len·cy** /vèeryələnsee, vèerə-/ *n.* **1. POISONOUSNESS** the quality of being extremely poisonous, infectious, or damaging, or the extent to which a disease or toxin possesses this quality **2. BITTERNESS** the quality of being bitter, malicious, or hostile [Early 17thC]

vir·u·lent /vèeryələnt, vèerə-/ *adj.* **1. VERY POISONOUS** extremely poisonous, infectious, or damaging to organisms **2. MALICIOUS** showing great bitterness, malice, or hostility ○ *virulent criticism* **3. IRRITATING** extremely obnoxious or harsh [14thC. From Latin *virulentus* "poisonous," from *virus* "poison, venom" (source of English *virus*).] —**vir·u·lent·ly** *adv.*

vir·u·lif·er·ous /vèeryə líffərəss, vèerə-/ *adj.* used to describe an organism that contains or carries a virus [Mid-20thC. Formed from VIRULENT + -IFEROUS.]

vi·rus /vírəss/ *n.* **1.** BIOCHEM **SUBMICROSCOPIC ENTITY** a minute particle that lives as a parasite in plants, animals, and bacteria and consists of a nucleic acid core within a protein sheath. Viruses can only replicate within living cells and are not considered to be independent living organisms. **2.** MED **VIRAL DISEASE** a disease caused by a virus **3.** COMPUT **CONTAGIOUS COMPUTER PROGRAM** a computer program that is part of another and inserts copies of itself. A virus travels with the program that contains it and may damage the integrity of stored data. ◊ **Trojan horse, worm 4. SOMETHING THAT CORRUPTS** anything that has a corrupting or poisonous effect, especially on people's minds [Late 16thC. From Latin, literally "poison, venom, medicinal liquid."]

vis[1] /viss/ (*plural* **vi·res** /ví reez/) *n.* force or power (*literary*) [Early 17thC. From Latin.]

vis[2] *abbr.* **1.** viscosity **2. vis, VIS** visibility **3.** visible **4.** visual

Vis. *abbr.* **1.** Viscount **2.** Viscountess

vi·sa /veezə/ *n.* **1. PASSPORT INSERTION** an official endorsement in a passport authorizing the bearer to enter or leave, and travel in or through, a particular country or region **2. AUTHORIZATION** any mark of official authorization ■ *vt.* **(-saed, -sa·ing, -sas) 1. SUPPLY DOCUMENT WITH VISA** to insert a visa in a passport or other document **2. GIVE SOMEBODY A VISA** to provide somebody with a visa [Mid-19thC. Via French from Latin *visa*, "things seen," the perfect participle of *videre* "to see."]

vis·age /vízzij/ *n.* **1. FACE** somebody's face or facial expression (*literary*) **2. APPEARANCE** the appearance or look of something [13thC. From Old French, from *vis* "face, appearance," from Latin *visus*, perfect participle of *videre* "to see."]

vis-à-vis /veezə veé/ *prep.* **1. REGARDING** in relation to **2. OPPOSITE** opposite to or face to face with ■ *adv.* **FACE TO FACE** face to face, or opposite each other ■ *n.* (*plural* **vis-à-vis**) **1. SOMEBODY OR SOMETHING FACING** somebody or something that is face to face with another **2. COUNTERPART** somebody who is the counterpart of somebody else **3. HORSE-DRAWN CARRIAGE** a horse-drawn carriage in which people sit facing each other [Mid-18thC. From French, literally "face to face," from Old French *vis* (see VISAGE).]

Vis·by /vízbee/ port on the western coast of the island of Gotland, Sweden. It was an important member of the Hanseatic League in the Middle Ages. Population: 57,110 (1990).

visc *abbr.* viscosity

Visc. *abbr.* **1.** Viscount **2.** Viscountess

visc- *prefix.* = **visco-** (*used before vowels*)

vis·ca·cha /vi skaáchə/, **viz·ca·cha** *n.* a burrowing, gregarious South American rodent with black and white markings on its face, related to and resembling the chinchilla. Latin name: *Lagostomus maximus.* [Early 17thC. Via Spanish from Quechua *(h)uiscacha*.]

vis·cer·a /víssərə/ *npl.* the internal organs of the body, especially those of the abdomen such as the intestines [Early 18thC. From Latin, "internal organs, entrails," of uncertain origin: perhaps originally "coil."]

vis·cer·al /víssərəl/ *adj.* **1. INSTINCTUAL** proceeding from instinct rather than from reasoned thinking **2. EMOTIONAL** characterized by or showing basic emotions **3.** ANAT **OF INTERNAL ORGANS** relating to or affecting one or more internal organs of the body [Late 18thC] — **vis·cer·al·ly** *adv.*

vis·cer·o·mo·tor /vìssərō mṓtər/ *adj.* relating to the nervous control of gut movements, especially to disorders of bowel movement

vis·cid /víssid/ *adj.* **1. THICK AND STICKY** thick and sticky in consistency **2.** BOT **COVERED WITH STICKY SUBSTANCE** used to describe a leaf or other plant part that is covered with a sticky substance [Mid-17thC. From late Latin *viscidus*, from Latin *viscum* (see VISCOUS).] —**vis·cid·i·ty** /vi síddətee/ *n.* —**vis·cid·ness** /víssidnəss/ *n.* —**vis·cid·ly** /víssidlee/ *adv.*

visco- *prefix.* viscosity ○ *viscoelastic* [From VISCOUS]

vis·co·e·las·tic /vìskō i lástik/ *adj.* used to describe asphalt and many polymers that exhibit both viscous and elastic properties when deformed —**vis·co·e·las·tic·i·ty** /-ee las tíssətee/ *n.*

vis·com·e·ter /vi skómmətər/, **vis·co·sim·e·ter** /viskō símmətər/ *n.* an instrument used to measure the viscosity of a substance [Late 19thC. Coined from late Latin *viscosus* (see VISCOUS) + -METER.] —**vis·co·met·ric** /vìskə méttrik/ *adj.* —**vis·co·met·ri·cal** /-méttrik'l/ *adj.* —**vis·com·e·try** /vi skómmətree/ *n.*

vis·cose /vís kòss/ *n.* **1. CELLULOSE USED IN MAKING RAYON** a cellulose solution of thick consistency used in making rayon **2. RAYON MADE FROM VISCOSE** a type of rayon with a soft silky feel made from a viscose solution [Late 19thC. Coined from late Latin *viscosus* (see VISCOUS) + -OSE.]

vis·co·sim·e·ter /vìskə símmətər/ *n.* = **viscometer**

vis·cos·i·ty /vis kóssətee/ (*plural* **-ties**) *n.* **1. THICKNESS AND STICKINESS** a thick and sticky consistency or quality **2.** PHYS **PROPERTY OF FLUID THAT RESISTS FLOWING** the property of a fluid or semifluid that causes it to resist flowing **3.** PHYS **MEASURE OF SUBSTANCE'S RESISTANCE TO MOTION** a measure of the resistance of a substance to motion under an applied force

vis·cos·i·ty in·dex *n.* an arbitrary scale for lubricating oils that is used to indicate how much the viscosity of the oil varies according to its temperature

vis·count /ví kòwnt/ *n.* **1. BRITISH NOBLEMAN** a British nobleman below an earl and above a baron in rank **2. COUNT'S SON OR YOUNGER BROTHER** in European countries other than the United Kingdom, especially France, somebody whose father or elder brother is a count **3. COUNT'S REPRESENTATIVE** in medieval Europe, somebody acting for or representing a count [14thC. From Anglo-Norman *viscounte*, ultimately from the medieval Latin *vicecomes*, from late Latin *vice-* (see VICE-) + *comes* "count" (see COUNT.] —**vis·count·cy** *n.* —**vis·count·y** *n.*

vis·count·ess /ví kòwntəss/ *n.* **1. WOMAN WITH RANK OF VISCOUNT** a woman who holds a rank equivalent to viscount **2. VISCOUNT'S WIFE OR WIDOW** a woman who is or was married to a viscount

vis·cous /vískəss/ *adj.* **1. THICK AND STICKY** thick and sticky, reluctant to flow, and difficult to stir **2.** PHYS **HAVING RELATIVELY HIGH VISCOSITY** used to describe a fluid that has a relatively high resistance to flow [14thC. From late Latin *viscosus* "sticky," from Latin *viscum* "mistletoe, birdlime made from mistletoe berries," of uncertain origin.] —**vis·cous·ly** *adv.* —**vis·cous·ness** *n.*

Visct. *abbr.* **1.** Viscount **2.** Viscountess

vis·cus /vískəss/ *n.* singular of **viscera**

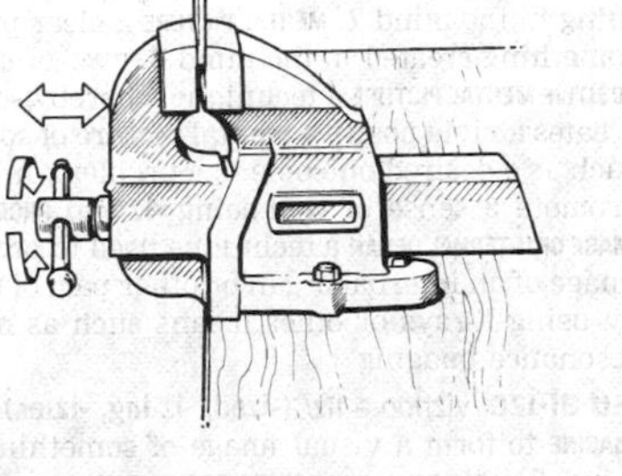

Vise

vi·se /vīss/ *n.* **TOOL FOR KEEPING THINGS IMMOBILE** a tool with two jaws that close by a lever or screw that is used to hold an object immobile so that it can be worked on ■ *vt.* **(vi·sed, vised, vis·ing, vi·ses) HOLD IN VISE** to hold something tightly in a vise [13thC. Via Old French *vis* "screw" from Latin *vitis* "vine." Ultimately from an Indo-European word meaning "wind" that is also the ancestor of English *wire*.] —**vise·like** *adj.*

Vi·sha·kha·pat·nam /vi shaákə pútnəm/ city and port on the Bay of Bengal, in Andhra Pradesh State, southeastern India. Population: 750,024 (1991).

Vish·nu /vísh noō/ *n.* a Hindu god called the Preserver, the second member of the triad that includes Brahma the Creator and Shiva the Destroyer [Mid-17thC. From Sanskrit *Viṣṇu*.]

vis·i·bil·i·ty /vìzzə bíllətee/ *n.* **1. ABILITY TO BE SEEN** the fact of being able to be seen **2. DISTANCE IT IS POSSIBLE TO SEE** the distance it is possible to see under the prevailing atmospheric or weather conditions **3. CLEAR VIEW** the ability to provide somebody, especially the driver of a vehicle, with a good view of what is around him or her, or the view obtained from a particular position **4. PUBLIC PROMINENCE** the degree to which somebody or something is easily noticed by and catches the attention of the public or a particular group of people ○ *the comparatively low visibility of the board of directors*

vis·i·ble /vízzəb'l/ *adj.* **1. ABLE TO BE SEEN** capable of being seen by, or perceptible to, the human eye ○ *the visible spectrum* **2. IN SIGHT** in somebody's sight at a particular time ○ *The building became visible again as soon as she turned the corner.* **3. OBVIOUS** easily noticeable ○ *the very visible results of the recent floods* **4. DETECTABLE** capable of being discovered by means of the mental faculties ○ *no visible prospect of a solution to the problem* **5. OFTEN SEEN PUBLICLY** frequently in the public eye ○ *the company's very visible head of public relations* **6. DESIGNED TO KEEP SOMETHING IN VIEW** designed to keep information or an item in view or able to be readily brought to view ○ *a visible index* [14thC. From, ultimately, Latin *visibilis*, from *vis-*, past participle stem of *videre* "to see" (source of *evident* and *survey*).] —**vis·i·ble·ness** *n.* —**vis·i·bly** *adv.*

vis·i·ble ra·di·a·tion *n.* radiation such as sunlight that falls within the range of wavelengths that can be detected by the human eye

vis·i·ble speech *n.* **1. SYMBOLS REPRESENTING MOUTH POSITION IN SPEECH** a set of phonetic symbols intended to represent the position of the lips, tongue, and other speech organs in creating sounds **2. VISUAL RECORD OF SPEECH** a visual representation of speech using a spectrograph that disperses radiation into a spectrum and photographs it

Vis·i·goth /vízzi gòth/ *n.* PEOPLES a member of an ancient Germanic people who invaded and conquered parts of the Roman Empire during the 5th century A.D. They destroyed Rome in 410 and took over parts of Spain and southern France, where they established a powerful kingdom that lasted until the beginning of the 8th century. ◊ **Ostrogoth** [Mid-16thC. From late Latin *Visigothi* "Visigoths," of uncertain origin: perhaps literally "West Goths").] —**Vis·i·goth·ic** *adj.*

vi·sion /vízh'n/ *n.* **1. EYESIGHT** the ability to see **2. MENTAL PICTURE** an image or concept in the imagination ○ *visions of power and wealth* **3. SOMETHING SEEN IN DREAM OR TRANCE** an image or series of images seen in a dream or trance, often interpreted as having religious, revelatory, or prophetic significance **4. FAR-SIGHTEDNESS** the ability to anticipate possible future events and developments **5. TELEVISION PICTURE** the picture on a television screen **6. SOMEBODY OR SOMETHING BEAUTIFUL** a beautiful or pleasing sight [13thC. From, ultimately, the Latin stem *vision-*, from *vis-* (see VISIBLE).] —**vi·sion·al** *adj.* —**vi·sion·al·ly** *adv.*

vi·sion·ar·y /vízh'n èrree/ *adj.* **1. FULL OF FORESIGHT** characterized by unusually acute foresight and imagination **2. IMAGINARY** produced by, resulting from, or originating in the imagination **3. INCAPABLE OF BEING REALIZED** so idealistic or unrealistic as to be unrealizable in practice **4. GIVEN TO DREAMINESS** tending by nature to be dreamy or to have impractical schemes and ideas **5. RELATING TO MYSTICAL VISIONS** relating to or seen in a mystical vision **6. HAVING VISIONS** given to seeing mystical visions ■ *n.* (*plural* **-ies**) **1. SOMEBODY WITH MUCH FORESIGHT** somebody of unusually acute foresight and imagination **2. SOMEBODY WHO HAS VISIONS** somebody who has mystical visions **3. DREAMER** somebody who tends by nature to be dreamy or who is given to impractical schemes and ideas —**vi·sion·ar·i·ness** *n.*

vi·sion quest *n.* a personal spiritual search undertaken by an adolescent Native North American boy in order to learn by means of a trance or vision the identity of his guardian spirit

vis·it /vízzit/ *v.* **(-it·ed, -it·ing, -its) 1.** *vti.* **GO TO SEE SOMEBODY** to go to see and spend time with somebody, especially as an act of affection or friendship ○ *Nobody visited him in hospital.* **2.** *vt.* **STAY WITH SOMEBODY** to go to stay with somebody for a time as a guest in his or her home ○ *I'm going to visit my family over the vacation.* **3.** *vti.* **GO TO SEE PLACE** to go to see or stay at a place for a time, e.g., as a tourist **4.** *vt.* **GO TO INSPECT PLACE** to go to a place as an official inspector **5.** *vi.* **CHAT WITH SOMEBODY** to engage in amiable or casual conversation with somebody **6.** *vt.* **INFLICT SOMETHING ON SOMEBODY** to inflict something unpleasant such as punishment or vengeance on somebody (*archaic*) ○ *visited them with plagues* ■ *n.* **1. SOCIAL CALL** a trip to see somebody and a period of time spent in his or her company **2. STAY IN A PLACE** an extended temporary stay in a place, e.g., as somebody's guest or as a tourist **3. CHAT** an amiable or casual conversation **4. OFFICIAL INSPECTION** an official call paid for the purpose of inspection **5.** LAW **BOARDING OF SHIP** the boarding of a ship on the high seas to carry out a search for contraband [12thC. Directly or via French from Latin *visitare* "to go to see," literally "to view repeatedly," from *visare* "to view," from *vis-* (see VISIBLE).] —**vis·it·a·ble** *adj.*

vis·i·tant /vízzit'nt/ *n.* **1.** BIRDS = **visitor** *n.* 2 **2. VISITOR** a visitor (*archaic*) **3.** PARANORMAL **VISITING SPIRIT** a being thought to visit from the spirit world ■ *adj.* **MAKING VISIT** paying a visit to somebody or something

vis·i·ta·tion /vìzzi táysh'n/ *n.* **1. OFFICIAL VISIT** an official visit for inspection or examination **2.** LAW **VISIT WITH CHILD GRANTED TO PARENT** the right of a divorced parent to have access to a child for a specified period of time, or a period of time with the child granted by this right **3. SOCIAL VISIT** a social visit to somebody's home, especially if it is unwelcome or lasts too long (*humorous*) **4.** RELIG **PUNISHMENT FROM GOD** a punishment or, sometimes, a benefit received, especially one believed to be sent by God **5.** PARANORMAL **APPEARANCE FROM SPIRIT WORLD** a supposed appearance made by a supernatural being —**vis·i·ta·tion·al** *adj.*

Vis·i·ta·tion *n.* **1. VIRGIN MARY'S VISIT TO ELIZABETH** the visit made by the Virgin Mary after the Annunciation to her cousin Elizabeth **2. CHRISTIAN FESTIVAL** a Christian festival held on July 2 to celebrate the Visitation of the Virgin Mary to Elizabeth [15thC. Shortening of *the Visitation of our Lady.*]

vis·it·ing card *n. U.K.* = **calling card**

vis·it·ing fire·man *n.* an important visitor who is entertained lavishly and impressively

vis·it·ing hours *npl.* the period of time during which patients in a hospital may have visitors

vis·it·ing nurse *n.* a nurse employed to provide medical care to the sick in their homes

vis·it·ing pro·fes·sor *n.* a professor from one college or university who teaches at another for a semester or academic year

vis·it·ing teach·er *n.* a teacher employed by a public school system to teach children in their homes if they have medical conditions that prevent them from attending school

vis·i·tor /vízzitər/ *n.* **1. SOMEBODY VISITING** somebody who visits a person or place **2.** BIRDS **MIGRATORY BIRD APPEARING TEMPORARILY** a migratory bird that regularly spends a short time in a place

vis·i·tor cen·ter *n.* a building offering information and services to visitors in a city or at a historical or archeological site, a park, or a nature reserve

vis·i·tors' book *n.* a book in which visitors, e.g., to a house, guesthouse, hotel, or art gallery, write their names, their home addresses, and often their comments on the visit

vi·sive /vívssiv/ *adj.* relating to vision (*archaic*)

vis·na /víssnə/ *n.* a chronic progressive pneumonia of sheep and goats [Mid-20thC. From Old Norse "to wither."]

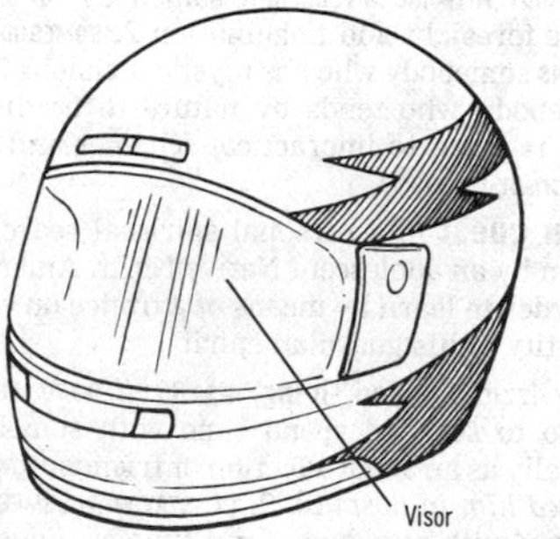

Visor

vi·sor /vízər/, **vi·zor** *n.* **1. TRANSPARENT FRONT OF HELMET** a hinged front part of a helmet, made of transparent or tinted plastic and designed to protect the face or eyes, especially on helmets worn by motorcyclists or welders **2.** HIST **FRONT OF MEDIEVAL HELMET** a hinged metal front part of a medieval helmet in a suit of armor designed to protect the face and having slits for the eyes to see through **3. EYESHADE** a shade for the eyes attached to a band worn around the head **4.** CARS **FLAP OVER A WINDSHIELD FOR GLARE** a flap mounted above the windshield inside an automobile used to shield the eyes from glare **5.** CLOTHES **CAP BRIM** the front brim of a cap [13thC. From Anglo-Norman *viser,* from French *vis* (see VISAGE).] —**vi·sored** *adj.*

vis·ta /vístə/ *n.* **1. SCENIC VIEW** a scenic or panoramic view **2. VIEW THROUGH NARROW OPENING** a view seen through a long narrow opening, e.g., between rows of trees or buildings **3. MENTAL PICTURE** a mental picture covering a wide range of objects or a long succession of events in the past or future ○ *open up vistas of expansion into hitherto untapped markets* [Mid-17thC. From Italian, "view," from the past participle of *vedere* "to see," from Latin *videre* (see VISIBLE).]

VISTA /vístə/ *abbr.* Volunteers in Service to America

Vis·tu·la /víschələ, víschōōlə/ the longest river of Poland, flowing northward from the Carpathian Mountains in the southwest of the country, through Cracow, Warsaw, and Torun, before emptying into the Baltic Sea at the Gulf of Gdansk. Length: 675 mi./1,090 km.

vi·su·al /vízhoo əl/ *adj.* **1. OF VISION** relating to vision or sight **2. VISIBLE** able or intended to be seen by the eyes, especially as opposed to being registered by one of the other senses or by a machine ○ *visual humor* **3. OPTICAL** of or relating to sight **4. PERCEPTIBLE BY THE MIND'S EYE** able to be perceived as a picture in the mind rather than as an abstract idea ○ *a visual memory* **5. DONE BY SIGHT ONLY** done by sight only and without the use of scientific instruments or equipment ○ *visual navigation* ■ *n.* **1.** = **visual aid 2. PIECE OF ILLUSTRATIVE MATERIAL** a photograph, picture, chart, or graph that displays information or promotional material in a way that appeals to the eye [15thC. From late Latin *visualis,* from Latin *visus* "sight," from the past participle of *videre* (see VISIBLE).] —**vi·su·al·ly** *adv.* —**vi·su·al·ness** *n.*

vi·su·al a·cu·i·ty *n.* acuteness of vision as determined by a comparison with the normal ability to identify letters at a distance of 20 ft./6 m

vi·su·al aid *n.* something such as a model, chart, or movie that is looked at as a complement to a lesson or presentation

vi·su·al arts *npl.* arts such as painting or sculpture that are perceived by sight

vi·su·al bi·na·ry *n.* a star that can be seen to be a double star either with the naked eye or when viewed through a telescope

vi·su·al field *n.* = **field of vision**

vi·su·al·i·za·tion /vìzhoo əli záysh'n/ *n.* **1. CREATION OF MENTAL PICTURE** the creation of a clear picture of something in the mind **2. MENTAL PICTURE** a clear picture of something created in the mind **3.** PSYCHOL **CREATION OF POSITIVE MENTAL PICTURE** a technique whereby somebody creates a vivid positive mental picture of something such as a desired outcome to a problem, in order to promote a sense of well-being **4.** MED **PRODUCTION OF IMAGE OF INTERNAL ORGAN** a technique used to produce an image of an internal organ or other part of the body by using X-rays or other means such as magnetic resonance imaging

vi·su·al·ize /vízhoo ə lìz/ (**-ized, -iz·ing, -iz·es**) *v.* **1.** *vti.* **IMAGINE** to form a visual image of something in the mind **2.** *vti.* PSYCHOL **CREATE POSITIVE MENTAL PICTURE** to create a vivid positive mental picture of something such as a desired outcome to a problem, in order to promote a sense of well-being **3.** *vt.* MED **MAKE IMAGE OF INTERNAL ORGANS** to produce an image of an internal organ or other part of the body by using X-rays or other means such as magnetic resonance imaging —**vi·su·al·iz·er** *n.*

vi·su·al·ly im·paired *adj.* having reduced vision, especially having eyesight so poor that it interferes with the ability to perform day-to-day activities effectively

vi·su·al-mo·tor co·or·di·na·tion *n.* the coordination of the body's visual and motor systems, as shown, e.g., in reaching for something being looked at

vi·su·al pur·ple *n.* = **rhodopsin**

vi·su·o·mo·tor /vìzhoo ō mṓtər/ *adj.* relating to or involving motor processes that are linked to vision, e.g., the coordination of movements

vi·ta /veétə/ (*plural* **-tae** /-tee/) *n.* **1.** = **curriculum vitae 2. SHORT BIOGRAPHY OR AUTOBIOGRAPHY** a brief account of somebody's life [Mid-20thC. From Latin, "life."]

vi·tal /vít'l/ *adj.* **1. CRUCIAL** extremely important and necessary, or indispensable to the survival or continuing effectiveness of something **2. LIVELY** full of animation or vigor **3. OF LIFE** relating to life **4. NEEDED FOR LIFE** required for the continuation of life [14thC. From, ultimately, Latin *vitalis,* from *vita* "life."] —**vi·tal·ness** *n.*

WORD KEY: SYNONYMS

See Synonyms at ***necessary.***

vi·tal ca·pac·i·ty *n.* a measure of the air that can be exhaled from the lungs after maximum inhalation

vi·tal·ism /vít'l ìzzəm/ *n.* a doctrine that maintains that life and the functions of a living organism depend on a nonmaterial force or principle separate from physical and chemical processes. ◊ **dynamism, mechanism** —**vi·tal·is·tic** /vìt'l ístik/ *adj.* —**vi·tal·is·ti·cal·ly** /-ístəkəlee/ *adv.*

vi·tal·i·ty /vī tállətee/ *n.* **1. LIVELINESS** abundant physical and mental energy usually combined with a wholehearted and joyous approach to situations and activities **2. DURABILITY** the ability of something to live and grow or to continue in existence **3. VITAL PRINCIPLE** the nonmaterial force that, according to vitalism, distinguishes the living from the nonliving

vi·tal·ize /vít'l ìz/ (**-ized, -iz·ing, -iz·es**) *vt.* **1. GIVE SOMEBODY OR SOMETHING LIFE** to cause somebody or something to live **2. ENERGIZE SOMEBODY OR SOMETHING** to make somebody or something lively —**vi·tal·i·za·tion** /vìt'li záysh'n/ *n.* —**vi·tal·iz·er** /vít'l ìzər/ *n.*

vi·tal·ly /vít'lee/ *adv.* extremely or indispensably [Late 17thC]

vi·tals /vít'lz/ *npl.* **1. ORGANS ESSENTIAL TO LIFE** the internal organs of the body that are essential to life, especially the stomach and intestines **2. GENITALS** the genitals, especially those of a man (*humorous*) **3. ESSENTIALS** the essential parts of something [Early 17thC. From Latin *vitalia,* literally "vital things," from a form of *vitalis* (see VITAL).]

vi·tal signs *npl.* the signs that indicate life, namely pulse, body temperature, breathing, and blood pressure

vi·tal stain·ing *n.* the process of using a substance that colors only live cells in order to study the fate of certain cells in embryonic development

vi·tal sta·tis·tics *npl.* **1. STATISTICS ABOUT HUMAN LIFE** statistics of human births, deaths, marriages, and health **2. BODY MEASUREMENTS** the measurements of a woman's bust, waist, and hips (*dated informal*) (*considered offensive by many people*)

vi·ta·min /vítəmin/ *n.* **1. ORGANIC SUBSTANCE ESSENTIAL TO NUTRITION** any of various organic substances essential in small quantities to the nutrition and normal metabolism of most animals. Vitamins are found in minute quantities in food, in some cases are produced by the body, and are also produced synthetically. **2. VITAMIN PILL** a vitamin in a pill or capsule form [Early 20thC. From German *Vitamine,* from Latin *vita* "life" + AMINE. From the former belief that vitamins contained amino acids.] —**vi·ta·min·ic** /vìtə mínnik/ *adj.*

vi·ta·min A *n.* a fat-soluble vitamin found in green and yellow vegetables and animal products such as egg yolk and milk. Vitamin A is important to the health of the outer layer of cells in the skin and organs. A deficiency leads to roughening of the skin and night blindness.

vi·ta·min A_2 *n.* a type of vitamin A obtained from fish liver

vi·ta·min B *n.* **1.** = **vitamin B complex 2.** = **thiamine**

vi·ta·min B_1 *n.* = **thiamine**

vi·ta·min B_2 *n.* = **riboflavin**

vi·ta·min B_6 *n.* = **pyridoxine**

vi·ta·min B_{12} *n.* a complex water-soluble vitamin obtained from liver, milk, eggs, fish, oysters, and clams that is important to growth, normal blood formation, and neural function. A deficiency of it causes pernicious anemia.

vi·ta·min B com·plex *n.* a group of water-soluble vitamins found in yeast, seed germs, eggs, liver, and vegetables

vi·ta·min C *n.* a water-soluble vitamin found in fruits and leafy vegetables or made synthetically and used as an antioxidant. Lack of this vitamin causes scurvy.

vi·ta·min D *n.* any of several fat-soluble vitamins that occur in fish-liver oils and are often added to milk. They are essential for the formation of bones and teeth. Lack of vitamin D causes rickets.

vi·ta·min D_2 *n.* a dietary supplement used in the treatment of rickets, prepared by the ultraviolet irradiation of ergosterol. Formula: $C_{28}H_{43}OH$.

vi·ta·min D_3 *n.* a form of vitamin D that occurs in fish-liver oils and has a slightly different molecular structure from vitamin D_2

vi·ta·min E *n.* a pale yellow viscous fluid occurring in vegetable oils, butter, eggs, and cereal grains that is important for fertility in humans and as an antioxidant

vi·ta·min G *n.* = **riboflavin**

vi·ta·min H *n.* = **biotin**

vi·ta·min K *n.* any of three fat-soluble vitamins essential for the clotting of blood

vi·ta·min K_1 *n.* a yellowish oily liquid that is found in leafy vegetables, rice, bran, and pork liver and is essential for the clotting of blood

vi·ta·min K_2 *n.* a form of vitamin K that is found in fish meal

vi·ta·min P *n.* = **bioflavonoid**

vi·tel·lar·i·um /vìt'l áiree əm, vitt'l-/ (*plural* **-a** /-áiree ə/ *or* **-ums**) *n.* the part of the ovary in some invertebrates that produces yolk-filled cells providing nourishment to the developing eggs

vi·tel·lin /vi téllin, vī-/ *n.* a protein found in the yolk of eggs

vi·tel·line /vi téllin, vī-, -té leen/ *adj.* **1. OF EGG YOLK** relating to egg yolk **2. YELLOW** of a yellow color, like an egg yolk [From medieval Latin *vitellinus*, from Latin *vitellus* (see VITELLUS)]

vi·tel·line mem·brane *n.* the membrane that encloses a fertilized egg

vi·tel·lus /vi télləss, vī télləss/ (*plural* **-lus·es** *or* **-li** /-té lī/) *n.* the yolk of an egg [Early 18thC. From Latin, "yolk of an egg," of uncertain origin: probably literally "small calf," from *vitulus* "calf" (source of English *veal*).]

vi·ti·ate /víshee àyt/ (**-at·ed, -at·ing, -ates**) *vt.* **1. MAKE SOMETHING INEFFECTIVE** to destroy or drastically reduce the effectiveness of something, or make it invalid **2. MAKE SOMETHING DEFECTIVE** to cause something to become defective **3. DEBASE SOMETHING** to degrade something morally [Mid-16thC. From, ultimately, Latin *vitiare*, from *vitium* "fault" (see VICE[3]).] —**vi·ti·a·ble** *adj.* —**vi·ti·a·tion** /vìshee áysh'n/ *n.* —**vi·ti·a·tor** /víshee àytər/ *n.*

vit·i·cul·ture /vítti kùlchər, víti-/, **vin·i·cul·ture** /vínni-/ *n.* the science or practice of growing grapevines, especially for wine making [Late 19thC. Coined from Latin *vitis* (see VISE) + CULTURE.] —**vit·i·cul·tur·al** /vìtti kúlchərəl/ *adj.* —**vit·i·cul·tur·al·ly** /-kúlchərəlee/ *adv.* —**vit·i·cul·tur·ist** /-kúlchərist/ *n.*

vit·i·li·go /vìtt'l í gō/ *n.* a skin disorder in which smooth whitish patches appear on the skin [Late 16thC. From Latin, "skin eruption."]

Vi·to·ri·a /vi táwree ə/ capital city of the Basque Country in northern Spain. Population: 204,961 (1991).

Vi·tó·ri·a /vi táwree ə/ city and port on an island in Espírito Santo Bay, eastern Brazil. Population: 258,245 (1991).

vitr- *prefix.* = **vitri-**

vit·rain /ví tràyn/ *n.* a narrow glassy band found in bituminous coal [Early 20thC. Coined from VITREOUS + *-ain* on the model of *fusain* "charcoal crayon."]

vit·rec·to·my /vi tréktəmee/ (*plural* **-mies**) *n.* a surgical operation to remove some or all of the vitreous humor of the eye

vit·re·ous /víttree əss/ *adj.* **1. SIMILAR TO GLASS** having the characteristics or appearance of glass **2. OF GLASS** relating to, consisting of, or derived from glass **3. OF VITREOUS HUMOR** relating to the vitreous humor of the eye [Mid-17thC. From Latin *vitreus*, from *vitrum* "glass," of uncertain origin: perhaps related to *vitrum* "woad," from the bluish-green color of glass.] —**vit·re·os·i·ty** /vìttree óssətee/ *n.* —**vit·re·ous·ness** /víttree əssnəss/ *n.*

vit·re·ous bod·y *n.* the transparent gel that fills the main cavity of the eyeball, between the lens and the retina

vit·re·ous e·nam·el *n.* an opaque glassy coating applied to steel or other metals through firing

vit·re·ous hu·mor *n.* the fluid component of the gel (**vitreous body**) that fills the main cavity of the eye between the lens and retina

vit·re·ous sil·i·ca *n.* a type of glass made solely from silica

vi·tres·cent /vi tréss'nt/ *adj.* capable of being made into glass [Mid-18thC. Coined from Latin *vitrum* (see VITREOUS) + -ESCENT.]

vitri- *prefix.* glass ○ *vitrify* [From Latin *vitrum*]

vit·ric /víttrik/ *adj.* having the characteristics or appearance of glass [Early 20thC. Coined from Latin *vitrum* (see VITREOUS) + -IC.]

vit·ri·fi·ca·tion /vìttrəfi káysh'n/ *n.* **1. CONVERSION INTO GLASS** the process of converting materials to glass **2.** CERAMICS **POINT WHERE FIRED POT LOSES POROSITY** the point at which a pot loses its porosity during a firing

vit·ri·form /víttrə fàwrm/ *adj.* having the form or appearance of glass [Late 18thC. Coined from Latin *vitrum* (see VITREOUS) + -FORM.]

vit·ri·fy /víttrə fī/ (**-fied, -fy·ing, -fies**) *vti.* to become changed into glass, or to change materials into glass [Late 16thC. From French *vitrifier* or directly from Latin *vitrum* (see VITREOUS).] —**vit·ri·fi·a·bil·i·ty** /vìttrə fī ə bíllətee/ *n.* —**vit·ri·fi·a·ble** /víttrə fī əb'l/ *adj.*

vi·trine /vi tréen/ *n.* a cabinet or case with glass walls for displaying specimens or art objects [Late 19thC. From French, from *vitre* "glass," from Latin *vitrum* (see VITREOUS).]

vit·ri·ol /víttree àwl/ *n.* **1. BITTER HATRED** extreme bitterness and hatred toward somebody or something, or an expression of this feeling in speech or writing **2.** CHEM **GLASSY METALLIC SULFATE** a glassy metallic sulfate such as copper sulfate or iron sulfate **3.** CHEM **SULFURIC ACID** sulfuric acid (*archaic*) [14thC. From, ultimately, medieval Latin *vitriolum*, from Latin *vitrum* "glass" (see VITREOUS). From its glassy appearance.]

vit·ri·ol·ic /vìttree óllik/ *adj.* **1. EXPRESSING BITTER HATRED** filled with or expressing violent and bitter hatred toward somebody or something **2. LIKE METALLIC SULFATE** resembling a glassy metallic sulfate —**vit·ri·ol·i·cal·ly** *adv.*

vit·ta /vítta/ (*plural* **-tae** /-tee/) *n.* **1.** BOT **OIL-CONTAINING TUBE IN PLANT** a tube or cavity containing oil in the carpels of the family of plants that includes carrot, parsley, and celery **2.** ZOOL **COLORED STRIPE ON ANIMAL'S BODY** a stripe or band of color on the body of an animal [Late 17thC. From Latin, "headband," originally "something that twists."] —**vit·tate** *adj.*

vit·tles /vítt'lz/ *npl.* food or other provisions (*archaic or humorous*) [Variant of VICTUAL]

vi·tu·line /víchə lìn, víchəlin/ *adj.* relating to or resembling a calf or veal [Mid-17thC. From Latin *vitulinus*, from *vitulus* "calf" (source of English *veal*).]

vi·tu·per·ate /vī tóopə ràyt, vi-/ (**-at·ed, -at·ing, -ates**) *vti.* to attack somebody in harshly abusive or critical language [Mid-16thC. From, ultimately, Latin *vituperare*, from *vitium* (see VICE[3]) + *parare* (see PREPARE).] —**vi·tu·per·a·tor** *n.* —**vi·tu·per·a·to·ry** *adj.*

vi·tu·per·a·tion /vī tòopə ráysh'n, vi-/ *n.* **1. OUTBURST OF ABUSE** an outburst of violently abusive or harshly critical language **2. ACT OF VITUPERATING** the use of violent abuse or extremely harsh criticism —**vi·tu·per·a·tive** /vī tóopərətiv, -ràytiv, vi-/ *adj.*

vi·va[1] /véevə, vée vaa/ *interj.* used to express support for somebody whose success or life is hoped will continue ○ *Viva the president!* [Mid-17thC. From Italian, "may he, she, or it live," a present subjunctive form of *vivere* "to live," from Latin (see VIVID).]

vi·va[2] /vívə, véevə/ *n. U.K.* an examination, especially one taken as part of a university or college degree, in which a student is asked and answers questions in a spoken interview rather than on paper [Late 19thC. Shortening of VIVA VOCE]

vi·va·ce /vi vaá chày, -vaáchee/ *adv.* **IN A LIVELY WAY** in a lively and spirited manner (*used as a musical direction*) ■ *n.* **VIVACE PIECE OF MUSIC** a piece of music, or a section of a piece, played vivace [Late 17thC. From Italian, "lively," from the Latin stem *vivac-* (see VIVACIOUS).] —**vi·va·ce** *adj.*

vi·va·cious /vi váyshəss/ *adj.* exhibiting or characterized by liveliness and high-spiritedness [Mid-17thC. From the Latin stem *vivac-* "lively, long-lived," from *vivus* (see VIVID).] —**vi·va·cious·ly** *adv.* —**vi·va·cious·ness** *n.*

vi·vac·i·ty /vi vássətee/ *n.* liveliness and high-spiritedness

Vi·val·di /vi vaáldee, -váwl-/, **Antonio** (1678–1741) Italian composer. His music epitomizes the Italian baroque style, his concertos being particularly influential on later composers. Full name **Antonio Lucio Vivaldi**

vi·van·dière /vée vaaN dyáir/ *n.* in former times, a woman who followed an army and sold food and drink to the soldiers [Late 16thC. From French, feminine of *vivandier*, from, ultimately, late Latin *vivenda* (see VIAND).]

vi·var·i·um /vī vérree əm/ (*plural* **-a** /-ə/ *or* **-ums**) *n.* a transparent enclosure in which small animals are kept so that their behavior can be studied [Early 17thC. From Latin, "game preserve, fish pond," from a form of *vivarius* "of living things," from *vivus* (see VIVID).]

vi·va vo·ce /vìvə vṓssee, véevə-/ *adv.* by word of mouth [Mid-16thC. From medieval Latin, literally "with the living voice."]

vi·vax ma·lar·i·a /vī vaks-/, **vi·vax** *n.* a form of malaria marked by convulsions that occur every 48 hours and that is caused by the parasite *Plasmodium vivax*

vi·ver·rid /vī vérrid, vi-/ *n.* a civet, mongoose, or other similar small carnivorous mammal with a long slender body. Family: Viverridae. [Early 20thC. From modern Latin *Viverridae* (plural), from the genus name *Viverra* (singular), from Latin, "ferret."] —**viverrid** *adj.*

viv·id /vívvid/ *adj.* **1. VERY BRIGHT** strikingly bright or intense in color **2. EXTREMELY CLEAR AND FRESH** characterized by striking clarity, distinctness, or truth to life when perceived either by the eye or the mind ○ *a vivid image* **3. GRAPHIC** producing strong and distinct mental images **4. INVENTIVE** active and inventive ○ *a vivid imagination* **5. LIVELY** characterized by spirit and animation [Mid-17thC. From Latin *vividus*, from *vivere* "to live."] —**viv·id·ly** *adv.* —**viv·id·ness** *n.*

viv·i·fy /vívvə fī/ (**-fied, -fy·ing, -fies**) *vt.* **1. GIVE LIFE TO SOMEBODY OR SOMETHING** to cause somebody or something to come to life **2. GIVE LIVELINESS TO** to give liveliness or vividness to something [14thC. Via French *vivifier* from late Latin *vivificare*, literally "to make alive," from Latin *vivus* (see VIVID).] —**viv·i·fi·ca·tion** /vìvvəfi káysh'n/ *n.* —**viv·i·fi·er** /vívvə fīr/ *n.*

vi·vip·a·rous /vi vípparəss/ *adj.* **1.** ZOOL **BEARING LIVE YOUNG** bearing live young rather than eggs **2.** BOT **PRODUCING PLANTLETS** used to describe a plant, e.g., the spider plant, that produces plantlets or bulbils from the flower stem **3.** BOT **PRODUCING SEEDLINGS ON PLANT** used to describe a plant, e.g., a mangrove, with seeds that germinate and develop into seedlings before being shed from the parent plant [Mid-17thC. Formed from Latin *viviparus*, literally "bringing forth alive," from *vivus* (see VIVID).] —**vi·vip·a·rous·ly** *adv.* —**vi·vip·a·rous·ness** *n.*

viv·i·sect /vívvi sèkt/ (**-sect·ed, -sect·ing, -sects**) *vti.* to perform operations on living animals that involve cutting into their bodies in order to gain knowledge of pathological or physiological processes [Mid-19thC. Back-formation from VIVISECTION.] —**viv·e·sec·tive** *adj.* —**viv·i·sec·tor** *n.*

viv·i·sec·tion /vìvvi sékshən/ *n.* the practice of operating on living animals in order to gain knowledge of pathological or physiological processes [Early 18thC. From Latin *vivus* (see VIVID) + SECTION on the model of DISSECTION.] —**viv·i·sec·tion·al** *adj.* —**viv·i·sec·tion·al·ly** *adv.* —**viv·i·sec·tion·ist** *n.*

viv·i·sec·to·ri·um /vìvvi sek táwree əm/ (*plural* **-ums** *or* **-a** /-ə/) *n.* an establishment where vivisection is practiced [Late 20thC. Coined from VIVISECTION + Latin *-orium*, neuter of *-orius* "-ory," on the model of EMPORIUM.]

vi·vo /vée vō/ *adv.* in a lively and energetic manner (*used as a musical direction*) [Mid-18thC. Via Italian from Latin *vivus* "alive."]

vix·en /víksən/ *n.* **1.** ZOOL **FEMALE FOX** a female fox **2. OFFENSIVE TERM** an offensive term that deliberately insults a woman regarded as vindictive and bad-tempered (*insult*) [15thC. Dialect variant of earlier *fixen*, from Old English *fyxe*, feminine of *fox* (see FOX).] —**vix·en·ish** *adj.* —**vix·en·ish·ly** *adv.* —**vix·en·ish·ness** *n.* —**vix·en·ly** *adj., adv.*

viz. /viz/ namely. Abbr of **vide licet** [From Latin *videlicet*, literally "it is permitted to see" (because it is used to introduce lists), from *vide-*, the stem of *videre* "to see" + *licet* "it is permitted"]

viz·ard /vízzərd/ *n.* a mask or or other form of disguise for the face (*archaic*) [Mid-16thC. Variant of VISOR by folk etymology from words ending in -ARD.] —**viz·ard·ed** *adj.*

viz·ca·cha *n.* = **viscacha**

Víz·cai·no /bith kīnō, biss-/, **Sebastían** (1550?–1615) Spanish explorer. He was the first European to systematically explore the Pacific coast of the United States.

vi·zier /vi zéer/ *n.* a high-ranking government officer in various Islamic countries and especially in the former Ottoman empire [Mid-16thC. Via French or

Spanish *visir* from Turkish *vezir*, from Arabic *wazīr* "vizier," earlier "helper, assistant."] **—vi·zier·ate** /vi zéerət, vi zí ràyt/ *n.* **—vi·zier·i·al** /vi zéeree əl/ *adj.* **—vi·zier·ship** /-zeer shìp/ *n.*

vi·zor *n.* = visor

Vizsla

vizs·la /vízhlə, vízh làa/ *n.* a medium-sized hunting dog of a Hungarian breed with a short, smooth, reddish coat [Mid-20thC. Origin uncertain: perhaps named for *Vizsla*, town in Hungary, from the breed's Hungarian origin.]

VJ *abbr.* video jockey

V-J day *n.* August 15, 1945, the day of the Japanese surrender in World War II

vl *abbr.* a variant reading [From Latin *varia lectio*]

VL *abbr.* Vulgar Latin

VLA *n.* a system of radio telescopes at the National Radio Astronomy Observatory, New Mexico. Abbr of **Very Large Array**

Vlach /vlaak, vlak/ *n.* **1.** PEOPLES **MEMBER OF BALKAN PEOPLE** a member of a people of southeastern Europe who in the 13th century established the principalities of Wallachia and later Moldavia. These later merged to become Romania. Vlachs now live mainly in the mountainous regions of the Balkans, e.g. in northern Greece, Macedonia, or Albania. **2.** LANG **ROMANCE DIALECT** any of the languages of the Romance family that are spoken in southeastern Europe, particularly those of the traditionally nomadic Vlachs of northern Greece and Albania [Mid-19thC. From Bulgarian and Serbo-Croat, from, ultimately, a prehistoric Germanic word meaning "foreign."] **—Vlach** *adj.*

Vla·di·mir /vláddə meer, vlə dyée meer/ city and capital of Vladimir Oblast in western Russia. Population: 353,000 (1990).

Vla·di·vos·tok /vlàddəvə stók/ city and major port in southeastern Russia, on Golden Horn Bay, an inlet of the Sea of Japan. It is the eastern terminus of the Trans-Siberian Railway. Population: 648,000 (1991).

VLCC *abbr.* INDUST very large crude carrier

vlei /flay, vlay/ (*plural* **vleis**) *n. S Africa* a stretch of low-lying ground that is either permanently marshy or is flooded in the rainy season to form a shallow lake [Late 18thC. Via Afrikaans from Dutch *wallei* "valley."]

VLF, vlf *abbr.* RADIO very low frequency

V-neck *n.* **1. V-SHAPED NECKLINE** a neckline shaped like a letter "V" **2. GARMENT WITH V-SHAPED NECKLINE** a garment, especially a sweater or T-shirt, with a v-shaped neckline **—V-necked** *adj.*

VO *abbr.* **1.** verbal order **2.** very old (*used on labels for bottles of brandy, whiskey, or port*) **3.** voice-over

vo. *abbr.* verso

VOA *abbr.* Voice of America

VOC *abbr.* volatile organic compound

voc. *abbr.* **1.** vocational **2.** vocative

vo·cab /vṓ kàb/ *n.* vocabulary (*informal*) [Early 20thC. Shortening.]

vo·ca·ble /vṓkəb'l/ *n.* **WORD AS MERELY SOUNDS OR LETTERS** a single word considered only as a grouping of sounds or letters, not in terms of its meaning (*dated formal*) ■ *adj.* **CAPABLE OF BEING SPOKEN** capable of being pronounced or spoken (*formal*) [Mid-16thC. Directly or via French from Latin *vocabulum* "name," from *vocare* "to call, name" (source of English *vouch, advocate,* and *provoke*).] **—vo·ca·bly** *adv.*

vo·cab·u·lar /vō kábbyələr, və-/ *adj.* relating to words [Early 17thC. Formed from Latin *vocabulum* (see VOCABLE).]

vo·cab·u·lar·y /vō kábbyə lèrree, və-/ (*plural* **-ies**) *n.* **1.** LANG **WORDS KNOWN** all the words used by or known to a particular person or group, or contained in a language as a whole **2.** LANG **LIST OF WORDS** an alphabetical list of words and phrases supplied with definitions or translations **3.** ARTS **RANGE OF EXPRESSIVE TECHNIQUES** a repertoire of expressive forms or techniques used by an artist or in a particular art form [Mid-16thC. From medieval Latin *vocabularium*, literally "of words," from Latin *vocabulum* (see VOCABLE).]

WORD KEY: SYNONYMS

See Synonyms at ***language***.

vo·cal /vṓk'l/ *adj.* **1. SPOKEN** uttered with the voice **2. OF THE VOICE** relating to the voice **3. HAVING VOICE** having a voice or using a voice to produce speech or sound **4. OUTSPOKEN** using frank, forthright, or insistent speech **5.** MUSIC **OF OR FOR SINGING** composed or arranged for singing, or relating to the art or techniques of singing **6. NOISY WITH VOICES** full of the sound of voices **7.** PHON = **vocalic** ■ *n.* MUSIC **1. SUNG PART** the sung part of a piece of pop music or jazz **2. POP OR JAZZ SONG** a song in the pop or jazz style [14thC. From Latin *vocalis*, from the stem of *vox* "voice" (source of English *voice, vowel,* and *equivocal*).] **—vo·cal·i·ty** /vō kállətee/ *n.* **—vo·cal·ly** /vṓk'lee/ *adv.* **—vo·cal·ness** /vṓk'lnəss/ *n.*

vo·cal cords *npl.* a pair of fibrous sheets of tissue that span the cavity of the voice box (**larynx**) and produce sounds by vibrating. Muscles tighten the cords, narrowing the gap between them, and as air is expelled from the lungs they vibrate.

vo·cal folds *npl.* a pair of folds in the wall of the voice box (**larynx**) situated just above the vocal cords. They are not involved in producing sound.

vo·cal·ic /vō kállik/, **vo·cal** *adj.* PHON **1. RELATING TO VOWELS** relating to or containing vowels **2. ACTING AS VOWEL** used or acting as a vowel **—vo·cal·i·cal·ly** *adv.*

vo·cal·ise /vṓk'l ees/ *n.* **1. SINGING EXERCISE** a voice training exercise in which a singer sings using only vowel sounds, especially one single vowel sound **2. VOCAL COMPOSITION USING ONLY VOWEL SOUNDS** a passage or composition for performance in which a singer sings only vowel sounds, especially one single vowel sound [Late 19thC. From French, from *vocaliser* "to vocalize."]

vo·cal·ism /vṓk'l ìzzəm/ *n.* **1. USE OF VOICE** the use of the voice in producing speech, singing, or other sounds **2.** MUSIC **ART OF SINGING** the art or technique of singing **3.** PHON **VOWELS OF A LANGUAGE** the range of vowels used in a specific language **4.** PHON **VOWEL** a vowel sound

vo·cal·ist /vṓk'list/ *n.* a singer, especially of pop music or jazz **—vo·cal·is·tic** *adj.*

vo·cal·ize /vṓk'l ìz/ (**-ized, -iz·ing, -iz·es**) *v.* **1.** *vti.* **EXPRESS** to use the voice to express something **2.** *vti.* PHON **TRANSFORM INTO A VOWEL** to transform a consonant into a vowel sound in speaking, or to be transformed into a vowel **3.** *vt.* PHON = **voice** *v.* 3 **4.** *vt.* = **vowelize** **5.** *vi.* MUSIC **SING WITHOUT WORDS** to sing without words, using only one or more vowel sounds, especially as a vocal exercise to warm up the voice **—vo·cal·i·za·tion** /vṑk'li záysh'n/ *n.* **—vo·cal·iz·er** /vṓk'l ìzər/ *n.*

vo·cal score *n.* the score of a vocal work, especially an opera, that gives the vocal parts in full with the orchestral parts transcribed for piano

vo·cal tic *n.* a sudden noise or shout produced involuntarily, especially as a symptom of Tourette's syndrome or a similar neurological condition

vocat. *abbr.* vocative

vo·ca·tion /vō káysh'n/ *n.* **1. SOMEBODY'S JOB** somebody's work, job, or profession, especially a type of work demanding special commitment **2. URGE TO FOLLOW A PARTICULAR CAREER** a strong feeling of being destined or called to undertake a particular type of work, especially a sense of being chosen by God for religious work or a religious life [15thC. From, ultimately, the Latin stem *vocation-*, from vocat-, the past participle stem of *vocare* (see VOCABLE).]

WORD KEY: ORIGIN

The Latin word *vocare*, from which ***vocation*** is derived, is also the source of English *advocate, convoke, evoke, invoke, provoke, revoke, vocabulary, vocative,* and *vouch.*

vo·ca·tion·al /vō káyshən'l, -káyshnəl/ *adj.* **1. RELATING TO JOB OR CAREER SKILLS** relating to education designed to provide the necessary skills for a particular job or career **2. OF SOMEBODY'S VOCATION** relating to somebody's vocation **—vo·ca·tion·al·ly** *adv.*

vo·ca·tion·al guid·ance *n.* guidance in the form of interviews and tests to see which job or career would best suit somebody's individual abilities and personality

vo·ca·tion·al school *n.* a secondary school at which students are trained in a trade or skill to be pursued as a career

voc·a·tive /vókətiv/ *adj.* **INDICATING SOMEBODY OR SOMETHING ADDRESSED** used to describe a grammatical case or a form of a word that indicates that somebody or something is being directly addressed by the speaker. In Julius Caesar's dying words "et tu, Brute," "Brute" is the vocative form of the name "Brutus." ■ *n.* **1. VOCATIVE CASE** the vocative case (*informal*) **2. WORD IN THE VOCATIVE** a word or form in the vocative case [15thC. From, ultimately, Latin *vocativus*, from the stem *vocat-* (see VOCATION).] **—voc·a·tive·ly** *adv.*

voc-ed *abbr.* vocational education

vo·cif·er·ate /vō síffə ràyt/ (**-at·ed, -at·ing, -ates**) *vti.* to shout something out loudly [Late 16thC. From, ultimately, Latin *vociferari*, literally "to carry voice," from the stem *voc-* (see VOCAL) + *ferre* (see -FER).] **—vo·cif·er·a·tion** /vō sìffə ráysh'n/ *n.* **—vo·cif·er·a·tor** /-síffə ràytər/ *n.* **—vo·cif·er·ant** /vō síffərənt/ *adj.*

vo·cif·er·ous /vō síffərəss/ *adj.* **1. SHOUTING NOISILY** shouting in a noisy and determined way **2. FULL OF NOISY SHOUTING** characterized by noisy and determined shouting [Early 17thC. Coined from Latin *vociferari* (see VOCIFERATE) + -OUS.] **—vo·cif·er·ous·ly** *adv.* **—vo·cif·er·ous·ness** *n.*

vo·cod·er /vṓ kòdər/ *n.* an electronic device or computer program that converts speech into digital form and resynthesizes it at a later time or after transmission as artificial speech. Originally developed to encode speech signals for more efficient electronic transmission, vocoders are now used in audio response units and voice recognition systems. [Mid-20thC. Coined from VOICE + CODE + -ER.]

vod·ka /vódkə/ *n.* a colorless distilled liquor originally from Russia that is made from a grain such as rye or wheat or from potatoes [Early 19thC. From Russian, literally "small water," from *voda* "water." From the belief that vodka is as essential to life as water.]

vo·doun /vō dóon/, **vo·dun** *n.* = **voodoo** [Late 19thC. From Fon *vodū* (see VOODOO).]

voet·sak /fóot sàk/ *interj. S Africa* used to tell somebody to go away or to express disbelief (*slang*) [Mid-19thC. From Afrikaans *voertsek*, from Dutch *voort zeg ik* "be off, I say."]

voet·stoots /fóot stòots/ *adv. S Africa* with the seller having no responsibility for any defects in the item sold or for any other problems arising from the sale [Late 20thC. From Afrikaans.] **—voet·stoots** *adj.*

vogue[1] /vōg/ *n.* **1. PREVAILING FASHION** the prevailing fashion at a particular time **2. POPULARITY** the state of being widely popular and fashionable at a particular time ○ *in vogue* ■ *adj.* **FASHIONABLE** currently popular or fashionable [Late 16thC. From French, literally "rowing," hence "smooth, fashionable course," from *voguer* "to row," of uncertain origin: probably from assumed Old Low German *wogon* "to float."]

vogue[2] /vōg/ (**vogued, vogu·ing** *or* **vogue·ing, vogues**) *vi.* DANCE to dance to music imitating the poses struck by fashion models [Late 20thC. Named for *Vogue*, a fashion magazine.] **—vogu·ing** *n.*

vogu·ish /vṓgish/ *adj.* **1. STYLISH** elegantly fashionable and stylish in appearance **2. BRIEFLY POPULAR** enjoying brief or sudden popularity **—vogu·ish·ly** *adv.* **—vogu·ish·ness** *n.*

Vo·gul /vṓ gòol/ (*plural* **-gul** *or* **-guls**) *n.* PEOPLES a member of a people from the regions around the western tributaries of the Ob River and the central and northern Ural mountains in Russia [Late 18thC. From Russian *vogul*.]

voice /voyss/ *n.* **1. SOUND MADE USING VOCAL ORGANS** the sound produced by using the vocal organs, especially the sound used in speech **2.** MUSIC **SOUND OF SINGING** the musical sound produced in singing **3. ABILITY TO USE VOICE** the ability to produce vocal sounds for speaking or singing ○ *have a good voice* **4. SOUND LIKE HUMAN VOICE** a sound similar to a human voice ○ *listen to the voice of the wind* **5. RIGHT TO STATE OPINION**

a right to express an opinion ○ *sections of society that feel they have no voice* **6.** **EXPRESSED OPINION** an expressed opinion or desire ○ *hear the voice of the people* **7.** **REPRESENTATIVE EXPRESSION** a medium of communication or expression for somebody or something ○ *the voice of reason* **8.** MUSIC **SINGER** a singer taking a part in a musical composition **9.** MUSIC **SINGING PART** a sung part in a musical composition **10.** PHON **VIBRATION OF VOCAL CORDS IN SPEAKING** the passing of air across the vocal cords so as to create audible vibrations **11.** GRAM **FORM OF VERBS** the form of a verb that indicates the relation of the subject to the verb. In the active voice, the subject performs the action, as in "I hit him," while in the passive voice the subject suffers the effect of the action, as in "he was hit." ■ *vt.* (**voiced, voic·ing, voic·es**) **1.** **SPEAK SOMETHING** to express a sentiment or opinion verbally ○ *voice an opinion* **2.** MUSIC **REGULATE THE TONE OF AN ORGAN** to regulate the tone of an organ pipe in order to produce the desired sound **3.** PHON **PRONOUNCE SOMETHING USING THE VOCAL CORDS** to pronounce a consonant or vowel by passing air across the vocal cords so as to create audible vibrations [13thC. Via Old French *vois* from Latin *vox* (see VOCAL).] ◇ **be in (good) voice** to be singing well or speaking well ◇ **with one voice** simultaneously or unanimously

voice box *n.* = **larynx**

voiced /voyst/ *adj.* PHON used to describe a consonant or vowel pronounced by passing air across the vocal cords to create audible vibrations, as for the "s" sound in the word "his" —**voic·ed·ness** /vóyssədnəss/ *n.*

voice·ful /vóysfəl/ *adj.* having a loud or ringing voice (*literary*) —**voice·ful·ness** *n.*

voice·less /vóyssləss/ *adj.* **1.** **SAYING NOTHING** maintaining a silence **2.** **HAVING NO SAY** having no vote or influence **3.** **HAVING NO VOICE** not endowed with a voice **4.** PHON **PRONOUNCED WITHOUT VIBRATION OF VOCAL CORDS** used to describe a consonant or vowel pronounced without passing air across the vocal cords and creating audible vibrations, as in the "s" sound in the word "hiss" —**voice·less·ly** *adv.* —**voice·less·ness** *n.*

voice mail *n.* an electronic communications system that stores digitized recordings of telephone messages for later playback (*hyphenated when used before a noun*)

voiceo·ver *n.* the voice of, or the words spoken by, an unseen narrator, commentator, or character in a motion picture or television program

voiceprint /voyss print/ *n.* a representation in graph form of the frequencies that make up somebody's voice. Each person's voiceprint is unique, and can be used to identify an individual. [Mid-20thC. From VOICE + FINGERPRINT.]

voic·er /vóyssər/ *n.* **1.** **SOMEBODY WHO VOICES** somebody who voices something such as an opinion or objection **2.** **SOMEBODY WHO REGULATES TONE OF ORGAN** somebody whose job is to regulate the tone of an organ pipe in order to produce the desired sound

voice rec·og·ni·tion *n.* **1.** = **speech recognition** **2.** **DETERMINING SPEAKER BY COMPUTER** a computer function that enables the machine to recognize a particular voice or voices speaking into a microphone attached to it. Like password verification, it is a means for determining the identity of somebody trying to use a computer and controlling access to it.

voice vote *n.* a vote taken in a parliament or other legislative body in which voters cry out "aye" or "no," or "yea" and "nay," with the louder cry winning the vote

void /voyd/ *adj.* **1.** LAW **NOT LEGALLY VALID** having no legal force ○ *declared the will null and void* **2.** **POINTLESS** ineffective or useless **3.** **DEVOID** totally lacking in something (*formal*) ○ *a personality void of all compassion* **4.** **NOT CONTAINING ANYTHING** having no contents **5.** **VACANT** having no incumbent, occupant, or holder **6.** CARDS **HAVING NO CARDS IN A SUIT** lacking any cards in a particular suit ■ *n.* **1.** **VACUUM** an empty space, especially a large empty space **2.** **PRIVATION** a state of loss or privation, or a feeling of loneliness and emptiness **3.** **GAP** a gap or opening **4.** CARDS **LACK OF CARDS IN A SUIT** a complete lack of cards in a particular suit ○ *a void in spades* ■ *v.* (**void·ed, void·ing, voids**) **1.** *vt.* LAW **MAKE SOMETHING LEGALLY INVALID** to deprive something of legal force **2.** *vt.* **EMPTY CONTENTS OF SOMETHING** to empty out the contents of something or empty something of its contents **3.** *vti.* **EMPTY BOWELS OR BLADDER** to empty the bowels or bladder [13thC. From Old French *voide* "empty," ultimately from assumed Vulgar Latin *vocitus*, alteration of Latin *vocivus*.] —**void·er** *n.* —**void·ness** *n.*

WORD KEY: SYNONYMS

See Synonyms at ***vacant***.

void·a·ble /vóydəb'l/ *adj.* capable of being deprived of legal force —**void·a·ble·ness** *n.*

void·ance /vóyd'ns/ *n.* **1.** LAW **INVALIDATION OF CONTRACT** the act of depriving a contract of legal force **2.** **ACT OF EMPTYING** the act of voiding or emptying something **3.** **VACANCY** the situation of having no incumbent or occupant, e.g., no bishop in a diocese

void deck *n.* in Malaysia and Singapore, the empty ground floor of an apartment block, used for social events by people living in the block

void·ed /vóydəd/ *adj.* in heraldry, having the center and a narrow surrounding area removed or left empty

Voight /voyt/, **Jon** (*b.* 1938) U.S. movie actor. He won an Academy Award for best actor for *Coming Home* (1977).

voi·là /vwaa laá/ *interj.* used to bring somebody's attention to something, especially in order to elicit appreciation or approval [Mid-18thC. From French, from *voi*, imperative of *voir* "to see" + *là* "there."]

voile /voyl/ *n.* a crisp lightweight translucent fabric made from cotton, synthetic fibers, or wool [Late 19thC. From French, "veil," from Latin *vela*, plural of *velum* (see VEIL).]

voir dire /vwaar deér/ *n.* the preliminary examination of a witness or juror to determine his or her competency to give or hear evidence [Late 17thC. From Law French, from Old French *voir* "truth" + *dire* "to speak."]

voix cé·leste /vwaà say lést/ *n.* an organ stop that gives a light wavering otherworldly quality to the notes played [Late 19thC. From French, from *voix* "voice" + *céleste* "heavenly." From the belief that the tone produced resembled heavenly voices.]

vol. *abbr.* **1.** volcano **2.** volume **3.** volunteer

Vo·lans /vṓ lànz/ *n.* a small constellation in the sky of the southern hemisphere between Carina and Hydrus, east of the Large Magellanic Cloud

vo·lant /vṓlənt/ *adj.* **1.** HERALDRY **HAVING WINGS SPREAD** in heraldry, having the wings outspread as in flight **2.** **ABLE TO FLY** flying or having the power of flight **3.** **NIMBLE** moving quickly, lightly, and easily (*literary*) [Early 16thC. From French, present participle of *voler* "to fly," from Latin *volare* (see VOLATILE).]

Vo·la·pük /vṓlə pòok, vóllə-/ *n.* LANG a language based on English and German, invented by Johann Martin Schleyer in 1880 [Late 19thC. From *vol*, alteration of WORLD, + *pük* "speech," alteration of SPEAK.]

vo·lar /vṓlər/ *adj.* relating to the palm of the hand or the sole of the foot [Early 19thC. Formed from *vola* "hollow of the hand or foot," from Latin, "sole, palm."]

vol·a·tile /vóllət'l/ *adj.* **1.** **CHANGING SUDDENLY** characterized by or prone to sudden change **2.** **UNSTABLE AND POTENTIALLY DANGEROUS** apt to become suddenly violent or dangerous **3.** **UNPREDICTABLE OR FICKLE** changeable in mood, temper, or desire **4.** CHEM **PRONE TO EVAPORATION** changing into a vapor at a relatively low temperature **5.** **SHORT-LIVED** continuing for only a short time **6.** COMPUT **LOSING DATA WHEN POWER IS OFF** used to describe a computer memory that does not store data when the power is turned off. Random access memory (**RAM**) is volatile, while read-only memory (**ROM**) is not. ■ *n.* CHEM **VOLATILE SUBSTANCE** a substance that changes into a vapor at a relatively low temperature [Late 16thC. From, ultimately, Latin *volatilis*, from *volat-*, past participle stem of *volare* "to fly."] —**vol·a·tile·ness** *n.* —**vol·a·til·i·ty** /vòllə tíllətee/ *n.*

vol·a·tile or·gan·ic com·pound *n.* an organic compound, e.g., ethylene, propylene, benzene, or styrene, that changes into a vapor at a relatively low temperature and contributes to air pollution and ozone formation

vol·a·til·ize /vóllət'l ìz/ (**-ized, -iz·ing, -iz·es**) *vti.* to change into a vapor or to cause a solid or liquid to be changed into a vapor —**vol·a·til·iz·a·ble** *adj.* —**vol·a·til·i·za·tion** /vòllət'li záysh'n/ *n.* —**vol·a·til·iz·er** /vóllət'l ìzər/ *n.*

vol-au-vent /vàwlə vaáN/ *n.* a small light pastry shell filled with meat, fish, game, or fowl in a sauce and baked [From French, literally "flight in the wind," probably from the lightness of the pastry]

vol·can·ic /vol kánnik/ *adj.* **1.** **OF VOLCANOES** relating to or originating from a volcano **2.** GEOL **CONSISTING OF VOLCANOES** made up of or coming from volcanoes **3.** **SUDDEN AND VIOLENT** characterized by sudden violent outbursts —**vol·can·i·cal·ly** *adv.*

vol·can·ic arc *n.* = **island arc**

vol·can·ic bomb *n.* a lump of lava ejected from a volcano that has acquired a characteristic form as a result of its solidification while traveling through the air

vol·can·ic cone *n.* a cone-shaped mass of material that has built up around the crater of a volcano

vol·can·ic dust *n.* fine particles of ash that are suspended in the atmosphere after a volcanic eruption

vol·can·ic glass *n.* natural glass formed when molten lava from a volcano cools too quickly to crystallize

vol·can·ic·i·ty /vòlkə níssətee/, **vul·can·ic·i·ty** /vùlkə-/ *n.* the tendency or likelihood of a volcano or group of volcanoes to erupt [Mid-19thC. From French *volcanicité*, from *volcan* (see VOLCANO).]

vol·can·ic plug, **vol·can·ic neck** *n.* a massive cylindrical formation of solidified lava that once blocked the vent of a volcano, now exposed after erosion of softer surrounding material

vol·ca·nism /vólkə nìzzəm/, **vul·ca·nism** /vúlkə-/ *n.* the processes involved in the formation of volcanoes, and in the transfer of magma and volatile material from the interior of the earth to its surface

vol·ca·nize /vólkə nìz/ (**-nized, -niz·ing, -niz·es**) *vt.* to cause something to change as a result of volcanic activity —**vol·ca·ni·za·tion** /vòlkəni záysh'n/ *n.*

MAJOR VOLCANOES OF THE WORLD

Cotopaxi *Ecuador*
Elevation [**19,347 ft / 5,897 m**]
World's highest active volcano

Mauna Loa *Hawaii*
Elevation [**13,680 ft / 4,170 m**]
Major eruption 1984

Erebus *Antarctica*
Elevation [**12,448 ft / 3,794 m**]
Major eruptions 1970s

Cameroon *Cameroon*
Elevation [**13,435 ft / 4,095 m**]
Major eruption 1982

Etna *Italy*
Elevation [**10,902 ft / 3,323 m**]
Over 90 recorded eruptions

Ruapehu *New Zealand*
Elevation [**9,177 ft / 2,797 m**]
Major eruptions 1995, 1996

Saint Helens *United States*
Elevation [**8,365 ft / 2,550 m**]
Major eruption 1980

Vesuvius *Italy*
Elevation [**4,190 ft /1,277 m**]
Major eruption 79 AD — destroying Roman Pompeii

Soufriere Hills *Montserrat*
Elevation [**3,002 ft / 915 m**]
Major eruption 1997 — much of island left uninhabitable

Krakatau *Indonesia*
Elevation [**2,667 ft / 813 m**]
Major eruption 1883 — tidal waves from eruption estimated to have caused over 30,000 deaths

vol·ca·no /vol káy nō/ (*plural* **-noes** *or* **-nos**) *n.* **1.** **OPENING IN EARTH'S CRUST** a naturally occurring opening in the surface of the Earth through which molten, gaseous, and solid material is ejected **2.** **MOUNTAIN** a mountain created by the deposition and accumulation of materials ejected from a vent in a central crater [Early 17thC. Via Italian from Latin *Volcanus, Vulcanus* VULCAN, the Roman god of fire.] —**vol·ca·ni·an** *adj.*

WORD KEY: CULTURAL NOTE

Under the Volcano, a novel by English writer Malcolm Lowry (1947). Set in Mexico on the annual Day of the Dead, it describes the last hours of British consul Geoffrey Firman, who, depressed by the failure of his marriage and the onset of war, slowly drinks himself to death. A harrowing psychological study, it can also be read as an allegory of the disintegration of Western values.

vol·ca·nol·o·gy /vòlkə nóllәjee/, **vul·ca·nol·o·gy** /vùlkә-/ *n.* the scientific study of volcanoes, including their formation, signs of an eruption, and other aspects of volcanic activity —**vol·ca·no·log·ic** /vòlkәnә lójjik/ *adj.* —**vol·ca·no·log·i·cal** /-lójjik'l/ *adj.* —**vol·ca·nol·o·gist** /-nóllәjist/ *n.*

Vole

vole[1] /vōl/ (*plural* **voles** *or* **vole**) *n.* a small rodent found mostly in North America and Eurasia, similar to mice and rats but with a shorter tail and legs and a stocky body. Genus: *Microtus.* [Early 19thC. Originally "vole mouse," from Norwegian *voll mus* "field mouse."]

vole[2] /vōl/ *n.* a taking of all the tricks in a single hand in a card game such as bridge. Extra points are scored for this. [Late 17thC. From French, probably from *voler* "to fly," from Latin *volare* (source of English *volatile* and *volley*).]

Vol·ga /vólgә, váwlgә/ the longest river in Europe, in western Russia. It rises northwest of Moscow and flows southeast and south to empty into the Caspian Sea. Length: 2,194 mi./3,531 km.

Vol·go·grad /vólgә gràd, vṓlgә-/ industrial and port city in southwestern Russia, on the Volga River. It is an important rail junction and inland port. In World War II the city was subjected to a long seige by German forces that proved to be one of the turning points of the war. Population: 1,006,100 (1992). Former name **Stalingrad** ((1925–61))

vol·i·tant /vóllәt'nt/ *adj.* **1.** ZOOL **ABLE TO FLY** flying or capable of flight **2. MOVING QUICKLY** moving about rapidly or constantly [Early 17thC. From Latin *volitare* "to keep on flying," from *volare* "to fly."]

volitation /vòllә táysh'n/ *n.* the act of flying or the ability to fly (*formal*) [Mid-17thC. From medieval Latin *volitation-*, the stem of *volitatio*, from *volitare*, literally "to keep on flying," from *volare* "to fly."] —**vol·i·ta·tion·al** *adj.*

vo·li·tion /vә lísh'n/ *n.* **1. CHOOSING** the act of exercising the will **2. ABILITY TO CHOOSE** the ability to make conscious choices or decisions **3. CHOICE MADE** the result of exercising the will **4.** PHILOS **ACT OF WILL** an act of will distinguished from the intended physical movement it causes [Early 17thC. Directly or via French from Latin *volitio*, from *vol-* (see VOLUNTARY).] —**vo·li·tion·al** *adj.* —**vo·li·tion·al·ly** *adv.* —**vo·li·tion·ar·y** *adj.*

vol·i·tive /vóllәtiv/ *adj.* **1. OF THE WILL** relating to or beginning in the will **2.** GRAM = **desiderative** [15thC. From medieval Latin *volitivus*, from the Latin stem *volition-* (see VOLITION).]

volk /fawlk, fōk/ *n. S Africa* a people or nation, especially the nation of Afrikaners [Late 19thC. Via Afrikaans from Dutch, "nation, people."]

Volks·lied /fáwlks leèd, fṓks-/ (*plural* **-lie·der** /-leèdәr/) *n.* a traditional German folk song [Mid-19thC. From German, literally "people's song."]

vol·ley /vóllee/ *n.* **1.** SPORTS **SWING AT A BALL** a swing, kick, or hit at a ball, e.g., in tennis or soccer, before it touches the ground or court **2.** ARMS **FIRING OF WEAPONS** a simultaneous discharge of several weapons, especially firearms **3.** ARMS **MISSILES FIRED** a discharge of missiles or other projectiles fired simultaneously **4. SIMULTANEOUS EXPRESSION OF SOMETHING** a simultaneous rapid expression of something, e.g., curses or protests **5.** MINING **ROCK BLASTING** a simultaneous explosion of several blastings of rock ■ *v.* (**-leyed, -ley·ing, -leys**) **1.** *vti.* SPORTS **STRIKE A BALL BEFORE IT LANDS** to hit or kick a ball before it reaches the ground, e.g., in tennis or soccer **2.** *vti.* ARMS **FIRE SIMULTANEOUSLY** to fire weapons simultaneously **3.** *vti.* **SAY RAPIDLY** to say something forcefully or loudly and rapidly, or to be spoken forcefully and rapidly **4.** *vi.* **MOVE RAPIDLY** to move or rush rapidly or loudly [Late 16thC. Via French *volée* from, ultimately, Latin *volare* "to fly."] —**vol·ley·er** *n.*

Popperfoto

Volleyball: Players jump to block a smash

vol·ley·ball /vóllee bàwl/ *n.* **1. TEAM SPORT** a sport played on a rectangular court, in which two teams can each use up to three hits to pass a large ball over a high net **2. LARGE INFLATED BALL** a large, usually white inflated ball used to play volleyball —**vol·ley·ball·er** *n.*

vo·lost /vṓ lòst/ *n.* **1. RURAL SOVIET** a rural elected council in the former Soviet Union **2. FORMER PEASANT COMMUNITY IN RUSSIA** in tsarist Russia, a peasant community made up of several villages [Late 19thC. From Russian.]

vol·plane /vól plàyn/ *vi.* (**vol·planed, vol·plan·ing, vol·planes**) **1. GLIDE TO THE GROUND** to glide toward the ground in an airplane with the engine turned off **2. MOVE BY GLIDING** to travel or move by gliding ■ *n.* **ACT OF GLIDING** a glide toward the ground in an aircraft with the engine turned off [Early 20thC. From French *vol plané*, literally "planed flight."]

vols. *abbr.* volumes

Vol·sci /váwlskee, vól sī, vólshee/ *npl.* PEOPLES an ancient people who occupied lands in Latium, a region of central Italy. Their territory was progressively taken over by the Romans during the 5th and 4th centuries B.C.

volt[1] /vōlt/ *n.* the unit of electromotive force and electric potential difference equal to the difference between two points in a circuit carrying one ampere of current and dissipating one watt of power. Symbol **V** [Late 19thC. Named for Alessandro VOLTA , the inventor of the electric battery.]

volt[2] /vōlt/, **volte** *n.* **1.** DRESSAGE **CIRCULAR MOTION BY HORSE** a circular movement executed by a horse in dressage **2.** FENCING **SUDDEN MOVE** a sudden leap made in fencing to elude an opponent's thrust [Late 16thC. Via French *volte* from Italian *volta* (see VOLTA).]

vol·ta /vṓltә, vóltә/ (*plural* **-te** /-tày/) *n.* **1.** DANCE **ITALIAN DANCE** a very fast dance popular in Italy during the 16th and 17th centuries **2.** MUSIC **VOLTA MUSIC** a piece of music written for the volta or in the triple-time rhythm of the dance **3.** MUSIC **ONE PLAYING OF A MUSICAL PASSAGE** a single playing of a passage of music that may then be repeated [Late 16thC. From Italian, "a turn," from *volgere* "to turn," from Latin *volvere* "to roll" (source of English *volume*).]

Vol·ta /vóltә, vṓltә/ river in Ghana, formed by the confluence of the Black Volta and White Volta rivers in the central part of the country. Length: 930 mi./1,500 km.

Vol·ta /vṓltә/, **Alessandro, Count** (1745–1827) Italian physicist. He developed the first electric battery (1800).

volt·age /vṓltij/ *n.* electric potential expressed in volts

volt·age di·vid·er *n.* a series of resistors or a single resistor used to provide various voltages that are fractions of the source voltage

vol·ta·ic /vol táy ik, vōl-/ *adj.* relating to or denoting direct electric current produced by chemical action [Early19thC. Formed from the name of Alessandro *Volta* (see VOLT[1]).]

Vol·ta·ic /vol táy ik/ *adj.* **1.** PEOPLES **OF BURKINA-FASO** relating to or typical of Burkina-Faso, formerly called Upper Volta, or its people or culture **2.** LANG **OF GUR LANGUAGES** relating to the Gur group of languages, spoken chiefly in Burkina-Faso and Ghana [Mid-20thC. From the name of the River *Volta* in West Africa.]

vol·ta·ic bat·ter·y *n.* an electric battery made up of one or more primary cells

vol·ta·ic cell *n.* = **primary cell**

vol·ta·ic cou·ple *n.* two different metals immersed in an electrolyte that produce a potential difference due to chemical action

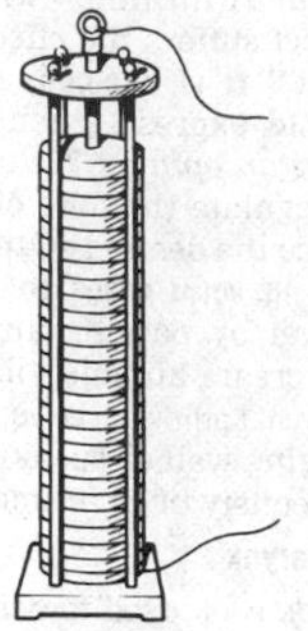

Voltaic pile

vol·ta·ic pile *n.* a stack of dissimilar metal disks separated by a porous material soaked in electrolyte that acts as a battery

Vol·taire /vōl táir/ (1694–1778) French writer and philosopher. A leading figure in the Enlightenment, he produced a range of literary works embodying his radical spirit and religious ideas. They include *Philosophical Letters* (1734), *Candide* (1759), and the *Dictionnaire Philosophique* (1764). Real name **François Marie Arouet**

vol·ta·ism /vóltә ìzzәm, vṓltә-/ *n.* = **galvanism**

volte *n.* = **volt**[2]

volte-face /vawlt fáass, vàwltә-/ *n.* **1. ABOUT-FACE** a sudden reversal in opinion or policy **2. POSITION CHANGE** a change in position so as to be facing the opposite direction [Early 19thC. Via French from Italian *voltafaccia*, literally "a turn of the face."]

volt·me·ter /vṓlt meètәr/ *n.* an instrument calibrated in volts that measures the electromotive force or potential difference between two points in a circuit

vol·u·ble /vóllyәb'l/ *adj.* **1. TALKING A GREAT DEAL** talking or spoken easily and at length **2.** BOT **TWINING** twining or twisting [14thC. Directly or via French from Latin *volubilis*, from, ultimately, *volvere* "to roll."] —**vol·u·bil·i·ty** /vòllyә bíllәtee/ *n.* —**vol·u·ble·ness** /vóllyәb'lnәss/ *n.* —**vol·u·bly** /vóllyәblee/ *adv.*

vol·ume /vóllyәm, -yoòm/ *n.* **1. LOUDNESS** the loudness of a sound **2. SPACE INSIDE AN OBJECT** the size of a three-dimensional space enclosed within or occupied by an object. Volume is measured in cubic units. Symbol **V** **3. SOUND CONTROL** the knob or button on a radio, television, or audio player that controls loudness **4. AMOUNT** the total amount of something **5.** PUBL **BOOK** a bound collection of printed or written pages **6.** PUBL **BOOK OF A SET** a single book that belongs to a set of books **7.** PUBL **CONSECUTIVE MAGAZINE ISSUES** a set of issues of a periodical spanning one calendar year **8.** HIST **SCROLL** a roll of parchment or papyrus ■ *adj.* **INVOLVING LARGE QUANTITIES** using or involving large amounts or quantities ○ *The factory is offering volume discounts on carpet sales.* [14thC. Via Old French *volum* from Latin *volumen* "roll, scroll, book," from *volvere* "to roll." The sense "loudness" evolved from "certain size of book" via "size," hence "size of sound."] ◇ **speak volumes** to be highly expressive or significant

vol·umed /vóllyәmd, -yoòmd/ *adj.* **1.** PUBL **IN A SET OF BOOKS** published in a series or set of a specified number of books (*usually used in combination*) ○ *three-volumed set* **2. IN A ROUND MASS** forming or rolling in a rounded mass (*literary*)

vol·u·me·ter /vә loòmәtәr, vollyә meètәr/ *n.* an instrument used to measure the volume of a solid, liquid, or gas

vol·u·met·ric /vòllyә méttrik/ *adj.* of, relating to, or using measurement by volume —**vol·u·met·ri·cal·ly** *adv.*

vol·u·met·ric a·nal·y·sis *n.* **1. CHEMICAL ANALYSIS OF LIQUIDS** an analysis of liquids using measured volumes of standard chemical reagents **2. ANALYSIS OF GAS** an analysis of gas by volume

vo·lu·mi·nous /və lóomənəss/ *adj.* **1. LARGE** having great size, capacity, or fullness **2. EXTREMELY LONG** very lengthy and taking up many pages or books ○ *a voluminous report* **3. PROLIFIC** producing a large amount of creative work ○ *a voluminous novelist* **4. WINDING** winding or coiling (*archaic*) [Early 17thC. Directly or via late Latin *voluminosus* "with many coils," from Latin *volumen* (see VOLUME).] —**vo·lu·mi·nos·i·ty** /və lòomə nóssətee/ *n.* —**vo·lu·mi·nous·ly** /və lóomənəslee/ *adv.* —**vo·lu·mi·nous·ness** /-lóomənəssnəss/ *n.*

vol·un·ta·rism *n.* **1.** PUBLIC ADMIN **RELIANCE ON VOLUNTARY CONTRIBUTIONS** the use of or dependence on voluntary contributions rather than government funds to keep an institution such as a school or church in existence **2.** PHILOS **PHILOSOPHICAL THEORY** the theory that regards the will, rather than the intellect, as the essential principle of the individual or cosmos —**vol·un·ta·rist** *n.* —**vol·un·ta·ris·tic** /vòlləntə rístik/ *adj.*

vol·un·tar·y /vóllən tèrree/ *adj.* **1. OF FREE WILL** arising, acting, or resulting from somebody's own choice or decision rather than because of external pressure or force **2. WITHOUT PAY** performing, working, or done without financial reward **3. USING VOLUNTEERS** composed of, functioning, or requiring volunteers **4. HAVING WILL** having the capacity required to make conscious choices or decisions **5.** LAW **WITHOUT LEGAL OBLIGATION** not involving legal obligation, coercion, or persuasion **6.** LAW **DONE ON PURPOSE** performed or carried out with intention rather than accidentally **7.** LAW **GIVEN WITHOUT PAYMENT IN RETURN** done or given freely with no promise of money or other recompense in return ■ *n.* (*plural* **-ies**) **1.** MUSIC **SHORT COMPOSITION** a short musical composition, often played on a solo instrument, that introduces a longer work **2.** MUSIC **CHURCH MUSIC** a piece of music or improvisation for the organ, played before, during, or at the end of a church service **3. VOLUNTEER** a volunteer for something, particularly to join the army (*archaic*) [14thC. From Latin *voluntarius*, from *voluntas* "will, choice," from *vol-*, stem of *velle* "to wish."] —**vol·un·tar·i·ly** /vóllən tèrəlee/ *adv.* —**vol·un·tar·i·ness** *n.*

vol·un·tar·y·ism /vóllən terree ìzzəm/ *n.* = **vol·un·ta·rism** —**vol·un·tar·y·ist** *n.*

vol·un·tar·y mus·cle *n.* a muscle, usually made up of striated fibers, that is consciously controlled by the individual

vol·un·teer /vòllən téer/ *n.* **1. SOMEBODY WHO WORKS FOR FREE** somebody who works without being paid **2. SOMEBODY WHO DOES SOMETHING VOLUNTARILY** somebody who does something, especially something undesirable, without being forced to do it **3.** MIL **VOLUNTARY RECRUIT TO ARMED FORCES** somebody who has offered to serve in one of the armed services rather than being required to join by law **4.** BOT **CULTIVATED PLANT GROWING NATURALLY** a cultivated plant, especially a crop plant, that grows without having been intentionally sown or planted **5.** LAW **SOMEBODY ACTING WITHOUT LEGAL OBLIGATION** somebody who performs an act or participates in a transaction without being legally bound to do so and without expecting to be paid **6.** LAW **SOMEBODY GIVEN PROPERTY** somebody who receives property without having to pay for it or give anything in return ■ *v.* (**-teered, -teer·ing, -teers**) **1.** *vti.* **OFFER FREE HELP** to do charitable or helpful work without receiving pay for it ○ *volunteers his time* **2.** *vti.* **DO SOMETHING BY CHOICE** to perform or offer to perform work of your own free will ○ *volunteered to work the night shift* **3.** *vt.* **TELL SOMETHING WITHOUT BEING ASKED** to tell somebody something or give information without being asked ○ *to volunteer information* **4.** *vt.* **OFFER SOMEBODY ELSE'S HELP** to suggest somebody else as a helper ○ *volunteered her secretary for a few days* **5.** *vi.* MIL **OFFER TO DO MILITARY SERVICE** to offer to serve in one of the armed services without being required to join by law [Late 16thC. Via French *volontaire* from Latin *voluntarius* (see VOLUNTARY).]

WORD KEY: REGIONAL NOTE

Volunteer is used of a second or unplanted crop, often one that develops from seed left the year before, throughout the Mid-Atlantic rural South. It can be a noun (*harvest the volunteers*), adjective (*volunteer tomatoes*), or adverb (*came up volunteer*).

vol·un·teer ar·my *n.* an army that relies on recruiting people who enlist voluntarily rather than conscripting recruits by law

vol·un·teer·ism /vòllən téer ìzzəm/ *n.* the practice of using volunteer workers in community service organizations and programs

Vol·un·teers of A·mer·i·ca *n.* a religious organization founded in 1896 by Ballington Booth that is committed to social reform and relieving need

vol·un·teer va·ca·tion *n.* a vacation in which somebody does volunteer work such as environmental clean-up or housing construction and repair

vo·lup·tu·ar·y /və lúpchoo èrree/ (*plural* **-ies**) *n.* somebody whose life is devoted to enjoying luxury and the pleasures of the senses [Early 17thC. From Latin *voluptuarius*, from *voluptas* "pleasure."]

vo·lup·tu·ous /və lúpchoo əss/ *adj.* **1. SENSUAL** sensual in appearance **2. SENSUAL** providing sensual pleasure **3. INDULGENT** inclined or devoted to a luxurious sensual life [14thC. Directly or via French *voluptueux* from Latin *voluptuosus*, from *voluptas* "pleasure."] —**vo·lup·tu·ous·ly** *adv.* —**vo·lup·tu·ous·ness** *n.*

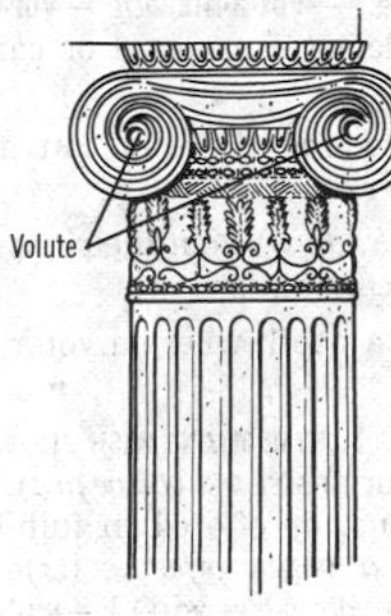

Volute

vo·lute /və lóot/ *n.* **1. SPIRAL SHAPE** a spiral form or structure, e.g., the whorl in the shell of a snail **2.** ARCHIT **DECORATIVE SCROLL** a carved spiral decoration, usually on an Ionic capital **3.** MARINE BIOL **TROPICAL MOLLUSK** a gastropod mollusk that lives in tropical waters and has a spiral shell with colorful markings. Family: Volutidae. ■ *adj.* **SPIRALING** moving in or following a spiral path [Mid-16thC. Directly or via French from Latin *voluta*, feminine past participle of *volvere* "to roll."]

WORD KEY: ORIGIN

The Latin word *volvere*, from which ***volute*** is derived, is also the source of English *convolution, convolvulus, devolution, evolution, involve, revolt, revolution, revolve, vault, voluble*, and *volume*.

vol·u·tin /vóllyətin, və lóot'n/ *n.* an easily stained substance found in the cytoplasm of some bacterial and fungal cells that serves to store phosphates for the energy needs of the cell [Early 20thC. From modern Latin *Spirillum volutans*, "rolling spirillum," the species of bacterium in which it was first found, from Latin *volutare* "to keep rolling around," from *volvere* (see VOLUTE).]

vo·lu·tion /və lóosh'n/ *n.* **1. SPIRAL** a shape that coils, twists, or turns around a center **2.** ZOOL **WHORL** any of the spiral segments of a gastropod's shell [15thC. From late Latin *volutio*, from Latin *volvere* "to roll."]

vol·va /vólvə/ *n.* a cup-shaped structure that encircles the base of the stalk of some mushrooms [Mid-18thC. From modern Latin, from Latin *volvere* "to roll."] —**vol·vate** /vólvət, -vàyt/ *adj.*

vol·vox /vól vòks/ *n.* freshwater green algae that form communities made up of hollow multicellular spheres. Genus: *Volvox*. [Late 18thC. From modern Latin, from Latin *volvere* "to roll."]

vol·vu·lus /vólvyələss/ (*plural* **vol·vu·li** /vólvyə lī/) *n.* an abnormal twisting of the digestive tract that leads to partial or complete obstruction and a reduction in blood supply. Gangrene is a possible consequence. [Late 17thC. From medieval Latin, from Latin *volvere* "to roll."]

vo·mer /vṓmər/ *n.* a thin plate of bone that forms part of the septum dividing the nasal passages inside the nose [Early 18thC. From Latin, literally "ploughshare"; so called because of its shape.] —**vo·mer·ine** /vṓmə rīn/ *adj.*

vom·it /vómmit/ *vti.* (**-it·ed, -it·ing, -its**) **1. THROW UP STOMACH CONTENTS** to expel the contents of the stomach through the mouth as a result of a series of involuntary spasms of the stomach muscles **2. GUSH FORTH** to send something out in a forceful stream, or to be ejected forcefully ○ *to vomit curses* ■ *n.* **1. EXPELLED STOMACH CONTENTS** the stomach contents expelled through the mouth. Technical name **vomitus** **2. ACT OF VOMITING** the act of expelling the stomach contents through the mouth [15thC. Directly or via Anglo-French from Latin *vomitus*, past participle of *vomere* "to eject or vomit."] —**vom·it·er** *n.*

vom·i·to·ry /vómmi tàwree/ *adj.* **vomitory, vomitive** MED **CAUSING VOMITING** causing the vomiting of stomach contents (*dated*) ■ *n.* (*plural* **-ries**) **1. OPENING** an opening through which matter is ejected **2.** ARCHIT, HIST **ANCIENT ROMAN PASSAGEWAY** a passageway, usually in an amphitheater or stadium, connecting a tier of seats with an outside entrance [Early 17thC. From Latin *vomitorius*, from *vomitus* (see VOMIT).]

vom·i·tu·ri·tion /vòmmichə rísh'n/ *n.* failure to bring up the contents of the stomach in spite of forceful attempts to do so (*dated*) [Mid-19thC. Coined from VOMIT and *micturition* "urination," from MICTURATE.]

vom·i·tus /vómmitəss/ *n.* vomited contents of the stomach (*technical*) [Early 20thC. From Latin (see VOMIT).]

Von Braun /fən brówn, von-/, **Wernher** (1912–77) German engineer. He developed the V2 rocket for Germany during World War II. He later worked in the United States on developing the launch vehicle used in the Moon landing program.

Vo Ngu·yen Giap /vṑ nóoyen yáp, -záp, -ngóoyen-/ (*b.* 1912) Vietnamese military leader. In Vietnam, he led communist fighters against the Japanese (1945), the French (1954), and the United States (1964–73).

Von·ne·gut /vónni gət/, **Kurt** (*b.* 1922) U.S. writer. He is known for his satirical novels, including *Slaughterhouse Five* (1969). Full name **Kurt Vonnegut, Jr.**

von Neu·mann /von nóy maan/, **John** (1903–57) Hungarian-born U.S. mathematician. Working in both pure and applied mathematics, he invented game theory and contributed to the development of the nuclear bomb and early computers. Born **Johann von Neu·mann**

Von Stern·berg /von stúrnburg/, **Josef** (1894–1969) Austrian-born U.S. movie director. His interest in visual style is a notable element in his films. Born **Jonas Sternberg**

Von Stro·heim /von strṓ hīm/, **Erich** (1885–1957) Austrian-born U.S. actor and movie director. In Hollywood after 1914, he directed films of unparalleled realism and psychological intensity, including his masterpiece, *Greed* (1925). His budget overruns ended his directing career after only eight movies, and his later years were devoted to acting. Full name **Erich Oswald Stroheim**

voo·doo /vóo doo/ *n.* (*plural* **voo·doos**) **1. CARIBBEAN RELIGION** a religion practiced throughout Caribbean countries, especially Haiti, that is a combination of Roman Catholic rituals and the animistic beliefs of Dahomean enslaved laborers, involving magic and communication with ancestors **2. PRACTITIONER OF VOODOO** somebody who practices voodoo **3. SOMETHING MAGIC** a charm, spell, or fetish regarded by those who practice voodoo as having magical powers **4. SOMETHING WITHOUT BASIS** a belief, theory, or method that lacks sufficient evidence or proof ■ *vt.* (**voo·dooed, voo·doo·ing, voo·doos**) **CAST A SPELL ON SOMEBODY** to cast a voodoo spell on somebody [Early 19thC. Via Louisiana French *voudou* from Fon *vodū* "fetish."]

voo·doo·ism /vóo doo ìzzəm/ *n.* **1. VOODOO AS RELIGION** the practices and beliefs of voodoo **2. MAGIC** an attempt to control or affect the world by using magic or sorcery —**voo·doo·ist** *n.* —**voo·doo·is·tic** /vòo doo ístik/ *adj.*

voop /voop/ *n.* *Carib* **WILD SWING AT CRICKET BALL** in cricket, a wild uncontrolled swing at the ball by a batsman ■ *vi.* (**vooped, voop·ing, voops**) *Carib* **MAKE WILD SWING AT BALL** in cricket, to make a wild uncontrolled swing at the ball when batting

voorkamer /fáwr kaamər/ *n.* *S Africa* the front room of a house, especially of a Cape Dutch house or farmhouse [Late 18thC. Via Afrikaans from Dutch, literally "front room."]

Voortrekker /fáwr trèkər/ *n.* *S Africa* a member of a band of Afrikaner pioneers who, in the early 19th century, left the British-ruled Cape for the eastern

Cape and the interior of South Africa [Late 19thC. Via Afrikaans from Dutch, literally "before-trekker."]

VOR *abbr.* very-high-frequency omnidirectional radio range

vo·ra·cious /vaw ráyshəss, və-/ *adj.* 1. VERY HUNGRY desiring or consuming food in great quantities ○ *a voracious appetite* 2. ESPECIALLY EAGER unusually eager or enthusiastic about an activity ○ *a voracious reader* [Mid-17thC. From the Latin stem *vorac-*, from *vorare* "to devour."] —**vo·ra·cious·ly** *adv.* —**vo·ra·cious·ness** *n.* —**vo·rac·i·ty** /vaw rássətee, və-/ *n.*

Vor·la·ge /fáwr laàgə/, **vor·la·ge** *n.* a skiing position in which a skier leans forward from the ankle but keeps his or her heels on the skis [Mid-20thC. From German, literally "forward position."]

Vo·ro·nezh /və ráwnish/ city and capital of Voronezh Oblast in western Russia. Population: 895,000 (1990).

-vorous *suffix.* eating, having a particular kind of food ○ *herbivorous* [Formed from Latin *-vorus*, from *vorare* "to swallow" (source of English *devour*)]

Vor·ster /fáwrstər/, **John** (1915–83) South African statesman. He was prime minister (1966–78) and president (1978–79) of South Africa. His career ended after he was implicated in a financial scandal. Real name **Balthazar Johannes Vorster**

vor·tex /váwr tèks/ (*plural* **vor·tex·es** *or* **vor·ti·ces** /-tə seèz/) *n.* 1. WHIRLING MASS a whirling mass of something, especially water or air, that draws everything near it toward its center 2. SOMETHING OVERWHELMING a situation or feeling that seems to swamp or engulf everything else [Mid-17thC. From Latin, a variant of *vertex* (see VERTEX).]

vor·ti·cal /váwrtik'l/ *adj.* relating to or moving in a vortex [Mid-17thC. From Latin *vortic-*, stem of *vortex* (see VORTEX).] —**vor·ti·cal·ly** *adv.*

vor·ti·cel·la /vàwrti séllə/ (*plural* **-lae** /-séllee/ *or* **-las**) *n.* an underwater protozoan with a bell-shaped body. It is usually attached to something such as a plant by a slender stalk. Genus: *Vorticella.* [Late 18thC. From modern Latin, literally "little vortex," from Latin *vortic-* (see VORTICAL).]

vor·ti·cism /váwrti sìzzəm/ *n.* a short-lived early 20th-century British movement in art and literature that was both abstract and concerned about the future and the machine age [Early 20thC. Formed from Latin *vortic-* (see VORTICAL). So called from Ezra Pound's idea of an image as a whirling center "from which ideas are constantly rushing."] —**vor·ti·cist** *n.*

vor·tic·i·ty /vawr tíssətee/ *n.* the state of a fluid moving in a vortex [Late 19thC. From Latin *vortic-* (see VORTICAL).]

vor·ti·cose /váwrti kòss/ *adj.* = **vortical** *adj.*

vor·tig·i·nous /vawr tíjjənəss/ *adj.* vortical (*formal*) [Late 17thC. From Latin *vortigin-*, stem of *vortigo*, variant of *vertigo* (see VERTIGO).]

Vosges /vōzh/ mountain range in northeastern France that extends 120 mi./190 km from south to north, parallel to the Rhine River. The highest summits in the southern portion rise to about 4,672 ft./1,424 m above sea level, and the northern peaks average about 3,000 ft./910 m.

Vos·tok /vó stòk/ *n.* any of seven numbered spacecraft launched by the former Soviet Union, beginning in April 1961 [Mid-20thC. From Russian.]

vo·ta·ry /vṓtəree/ (*plural* **-ries**), **vo·ta·rist** /vṓtərist/ *n.* 1. NUN OR MONK somebody who has taken a vow to dedicate his or her life to religious worship or service 2. DEVOTEE somebody who has devoted himself or herself to something such as a religion or cause [Mid-16thC. From Latin *vot-*, past participle stem of *vovere* "to vow."]

vote /vōt/ *n.* 1. FORMAL CHOICE FOR OR AGAINST SOMETHING a formal indication of somebody's choice or opinion, especially in an election or referendum 2. ACT OF CHOOSING the act of making a choice or stating a preference to determine the outcome of something 3. BALLOTS CAST the total number of ballots cast by eligible voters ○ *They got 83 percent of the vote.* 4. SUFFRAGE the right to express opinions and preferences by casting a ballot ○ *Women struggled for many years to get the vote.* 5. MEANS OF EXPRESSING A VOTE the ticket, ballot, or other method by which somebody expresses a vote 6. RESULT OF BALLOTING the outcome of an election or referendum ○ *Yesterday's vote indicates that people are tired of being lied to.* 7. OPINION EXPRESSED the preference of a group of people as indicated by a ballot ○ *Politicians can no longer ignore the youth vote.* 8. POTENTIAL VOTERS all the people eligible to cast their ballots in an election or for a referendum ○ *Volunteers worked day and night to get out the vote.* ■ *v.* (**vot·ed, vot·ing, votes**) 1. *vti.* INDICATE FORMAL PREFERENCE to express an opinion or preference in an election or for a referendum ○ *How did you vote in the last election?* 2. *vt.* VOTE FOR OR AGAINST SOMEBODY to decide the outcome of an election by voting for or against somebody ○ *It's difficult to vote an incumbent out of office.* 3. *vt.* VOTE TO MAKE SOMETHING AVAILABLE to create something or make something available by casting a vote ○ *The city council refused to vote additional funds for the new building.* 4. *vt.* VOTE FOR SOMEBODY TO WIN to vote for a candidate to win a competition or title ○ *He was voted "Waiter of the Year."* 5. *vt.* SHOW OPINION ON SOMETHING to agree on how successful or enjoyable something is (*informal*) ○ *The meal was voted a great success.* 6. *vt.* SUGGEST SOMETHING to make a suggestion ○ *I vote that we eat out.* 7. *vt.* USE AS A GUIDE to use something such as the conscience to determine how to vote ○ *Citizens often vote their pocketbooks, not their conscience.* [13thC. From Latin *votum* "a vow," from *vovere* "to vow," later "to desire" (source of English *vow*). The underlying sense is of expressing a desire.] —**vot·a·ble** *adj.* —**vot·er** *n.*

vote down *vt.* to defeat a proposal or candidate in a vote

vote get·ter *n.* somebody who can attract large numbers of voters

vote·less /vṓtləss/ *adj.* without the right to choose or express a political opinion

vot·ing booth *n.* a booth where a voter casts a vote in an election

vo·tive /vṓtiv/ *adj.* 1. SYMBOLIZING WISH showing or symbolizing a wish or desire ○ *a votive prayer* 2. FULFILLING A VOW given, done, or offered in fulfillment of an oath or vow ○ *a votive offering* [Late 16thC. From Latin *votivus*, from *votum* (see VOTE).] —**vo·tive·ly** *adv.* —**vo·tive·ness** *n.*

Vot·yak /vṓtee àk/ (*plural* **-yak** *or* **-yaks**) *n.* 1. PEOPLES MEMBER OF FINNISH PEOPLE IN RUSSIA a member of a Finnish people living in eastern central European Russia, especially in the Udmurt Autonomous Region 2. LANG = **Udmurt** [Mid-19thC. From Russian.] —**Vot·yak** *adj.*

vou. *abbr.* voucher

vouch /vowch/ (**vouched, vouch·ing, vouch·es**) *v.* 1. *vi.* PROVIDE SUPPORTING EVIDENCE to provide supporting evidence for the quality of somebody or something 2. *vt.* CITE AUTHORITY to cite somebody such as an authority in support of something (*archaic*) 3. *vt.* DECLARE SOMETHING to assert or declare something (*archaic*) [14thC. Via French *voucher* "to summon" from, ultimately, Latin *vocare* "to call." The meaning developed from "to summon someone as a witness or an authority."]

vouch·ee /vow cheé/ *n.* somebody for whom another person vouches

vouch·er /vówchər/ *n.* 1. SUBSTITUTE FOR MONEY WHEN BUYING SOMETHING a card, token, or other document that can be exchanged for goods and services in place of money 2. DOCUMENTARY EVIDENCE a document that provides supporting evidence for a claim, e.g., a receipt proving that a purchase was made 3. GUARANTOR somebody or something that guarantees or provides proof of something

vouch·safe /vòwch sáyf, vówch sàyf/ (**-safed, -saf·ing, -safes**) *vt.* 1. CONDESCEND TO GIVE SOMETHING to undertake or deign to grant or give something, especially a reply 2. PROMISE SOMETHING to promise, agree, or allow something (*formal*) [14thC (originally as two words)]

vous·soir /voo swaár/ *n.* a wedge-shaped brick or stone used to form the curved parts of an arch or vault [14thC. Via French from, ultimately, Latin *volvere* "to roll."]

Vou·vray /voo vráy/ *n.* a dry white wine produced in the Loire Valley of France [Late 19thC. Named for the village of *Vouvray* in Inde-de-Loire, France.]

vow /vow/ *n.* SOLEMN PLEDGE a solemn promise to perform a certain act, carry out an activity, or behave in a given way ■ **vows** *npl.* RELIGIOUS PROMISE a solemn promise to join a religious order and live in accordance with its rules ■ *v.* (**vowed, vow·ing, vows**) 1. *vt.* PLEDGE SOMETHING to promise something solemnly and seriously 2. *vti.* DEDICATE SOMEBODY to promise somebody to a pledge, task, or to somebody such as a deity 3. *vt.* ASSERT SOMETHING to assert or declare something [13thC. Via Old French *vou* from Latin *votum* (see VOTE).] —**vow·er** *n.*

vow·el /vów əl/ *n.* a speech sound produced by the passage of air through the vocal tract, with relatively little obstruction, or the corresponding letter of the alphabet [14thC. Via Old French *vouel* from, ultimately, Latin *vocalis* (see VOCAL).]

vow·el gra·da·tion *n.* = **ablaut**

vow·el·ize /vów ə līz/ (**-ized, -iz·ing, -iz·es**) *vt.* to mark the vowel points in a Hebrew or Arabic text — **vow·el·i·za·tion** /vòw əli záysh'n/ *n.*

vow·el mu·ta·tion *n.* = **umlaut**

vow·el point *n.* a diacritical mark placed above or below a consonant to show a preceding or following vowel, used especially in languages such as Arabic and Hebrew that lack symbols for vowel sounds

vox an·gel·i·ca /vòks an jéllikə/ *n.* a quiet organ stop, usually with vibrato, that enriches the tone of other quiet stops [From Latin, literally "angelic voice"]

vox hu·ma·na /-hyoo maánə, -hyoo máynə/ *n.* an organ reed stop that produces a tone resembling the human voice [From Latin, literally "human voice"]

vox pop·u·li /-póppyə lī/ *n.* popular public opinion ○ *Let's see if we can detect the vox populi.* [From Latin, literally "voice of the people"]

voy·age /vóy ij/ *n.* 1. LONG TRIP a journey by sea or air, especially one to a distant place 2. AEROSP SPACE JOURNEY a journey into space 3. JOURNEY EVENTS the events of an exploratory trip regarded as a story (*literary*) 4. NARRATIVE a story of an exploratory trip ■ *vti.* (**-aged, -ag·ing, -ag·es**) TRAVEL to make a long journey to, through, or over a place [13thC. Via Old French *voiage* from, ultimately, Latin *viaticus* "of a road or journey," from *via* "road."] —**voy·ag·er** *n.*

Voy·ag·er /vóy ijər/ *n.* the name of two U.S. spacecraft, Voyager 1 and Voyager 2, designed for exploring the outer planets of the solar system without a crew and launched in 1977

voy·a·geur /vòyə júr, vwaàyə zhúr/ *n.* *Can* a boatman, woodsman, trapper, or explorer hired by fur companies to carry furs and supplies from one remote station to another, especially in Canada and the northwestern United States [Late 18thC. From French, literally "voyager."]

Voy·a·geurs Na·tion·al Park /vòy ə júrz-/ national park in northern Minnesota, established in 1975. Area: 218,035 acres/88,236 hectares.

voy·eur /voy yúr, vwaà yúr/ *n.* 1. SOMEBODY WHO WATCHES FOR SEXUAL PLEASURE somebody who is sexually excited by looking, especially secretly, at other people's naked bodies or the sexual acts in which they participate 2. PERSISTENT OBSERVER OF MISERY OR SCANDAL somebody who is fascinated with, or persistently observes, distressing, sordid, or scandalous topics or events [Early 20thC. From French, literally "one who sees," from *voir* "to see," from Latin *videre.*] —**voy·eur·ism** *n.* —**voy·eur·is·tic** /vòy yə rístik/ *adj.* —**voy·eur·is·ti·cal·ly** /-rístikəlee/ *adv.*

Voy·sey /vóyzee/, **Charles** (1857–1941) British architect and designer. A member of the Arts and Crafts movement, he designed furniture, wallpapers, textiles, tiles, and country houses. Full name **Charles Francis Annesley Voysey**

VP, **V.P.** *abbr.* 1. verb phrase 2. Vice President

vr *abbr.* verb reflexive

VR *abbr.* 1. variant reading 2. virtual reality 3. Volunteer Reserve

vrai·sem·blance /vràv saaN blaáNs/ *n.* the quality of seeming to be true or likely [Early 19thC. From French, literally "true appearance."]

VRM *abbr.* variable-rate mortgage

VRML *n.* a computer-graphics programming language used to create images of three-dimensional scenes. Abbr of **Virtual Reality Modeling Language**

vroom /vroom/ *n.* LOUD ENGINE NOISE the loud noise of an engine when it is being revved up or is running at high speed (*informal*) ■ *vi.* (**vroomed, vroom·ing, vrooms**) MOVE NOISILY to move noisily at high speed ■ *interj.* USED TO IMITATE NOISY ENGINE used to imitate an engine running at high speed [Mid-20thC. An imitation of the sound.]

vs., **v.** *abbr.* versus

v.s. *abbr.* vide supra

V-shaped *adj.* having the shape of a "V"

V sign *n.* **V-sign** a hand sign that indicates victory, approval, or solidarity, made by holding up the index and middle fingers so that they form a "V," palm outward

VSO *adj.* used to indicate that brandy or port is between 12 and 17 years old. Abbr of **very superior old**

VSOP /veé sòp/ *adj.* used to indicate that brandy or port is between 20 and 25 years old. Abbr of **very special old pale, very superior old pale**

vss. *abbr.* **1.** verses **2.** versions

V/STOL /veé stawl/ *abbr.* vertical and short takeoff and landing

vt *abbr.* verb transitive

VT *abbr.* **1.** vacuum tube **2.** variable time **3.** Vermont

Vt. *abbr.* Vermont

VTOL /veé tàwl/ (*plural* **VTOLs**) *n.* **1. AIRCRAFT VERTICAL TAKEOFF SYSTEM** a system used by some aircraft that enables them to take off and land vertically. Abbr of **vertical takeoff and landing 2. AIRCRAFT CAPABLE OF VERTICAL TAKEOFF** an aircraft capable of vertical takeoff and landing

VTR *n.* (*plural* **VTRs**), *abbr.* video-tape recorder

vug /vug, vŏŏg/ *n.* a small hole in a rock or vein that often contains a mineral lining that differs from that of the surrounding matrix [Early 19thC. From Cornish *vooga*.] —**vug·gy** *adj.*

Vuil·lard /vwee yaár/, **Édouard** (1868–1940) French painter. He designed theater sets and textiles in addition to the intricately patterned paintings of domestic interiors for which he is best known. Full name **Jean Édouard Vuillard**

Vul. *abbr.* Vulgate

Vul·can /vúlkən/ *n.* in Roman mythology, the god of fire. Greek equivalent **Hephaestus** —**Vul·ca·ni·an** /vul káynee ən/ *adj.*

vul·ca·ni·an /vul káynee ən/ *adj.* **1.** GEOL **RELATING TO VOLCANIC ERUPTION** relating to or caused by a type of explosive volcanic eruption resulting when the pressure of gases trapped in viscous magma is sufficient to blow off overlying solidified material **2. OF METALWORKING** relating to or consisting of metalworking or metal craft

vul·can·ic·i·ty *n.* = **volcanicity** [Late 18thC. From French *vulcanicité*, variant of *volcanicité* (see VOLCANICITY).]

vul·ca·nism *n.* = **volcanism**

vul·ca·nite /vúlkə nīt/ *n.* a hard rubber produced by vulcanizing natural rubber with large amounts of sulfur [Mid-19thC. Named for VULCAN.]

vul·ca·nize /vúlkə nīz/ (**-nized, -niz·ing, -niz·es**) *vt.* to strengthen a material such as rubber by combining it with sulfur and other additives and then applying heat and pressure —**vul·ca·niz·a·ble** *adj.* —**vul·ca·niz·er** *n.*

vul·ca·nol·o·gy *n.* = **volcanology**

vulg. *abbr.* **1.** vulgar **2.** vulgarly

Vulg. *abbr.* vulgate

vul·gar /vúlgər/ *adj.* **1. CRUDE AND INDECENT** crude or obscene, particularly about sex or bodily functions **2. TASTELESSLY OSTENTATIOUS** showing a lack of taste or reasonable moderation **3. LACKING REFINEMENT** lacking in courtesy and manners **4.** LANG **OF ORDINARY PEOPLE'S LANGUAGE** relating to a form of a language spoken by ordinary people **5. OF ORDINARY PEOPLE** characteristic of or associated with the majority of ordinary people (*archaic*) ■ *npl.* **ORDINARY PEOPLE** ordinary people regarded or spoken of as a group ○ *She believes that fine food and wine are beyond the taste of the vulgar.* [14thC. From Latin *vulgaris*, from *vulgus* "the common people."] —**vul·gar·ly** *adv.*

vul·gar frac·tion *n.* = **simple fraction**

vul·gar·i·an /vul gérree ən/ *n.* somebody who is wealthy but tasteless or overly ostentatious

vul·gar·ism /vúlgə rìzzəm/ *n.* **1. CRUDE TERM** a crude or indecent word or phrase **2. TERM IN ORDINARY PEOPLE'S LANGUAGE** a word or phrase from the language spoken by ordinary people, as contrasted with a more formal or refined usage **3.** = **vulgarity**

vul·gar·i·ty /vul gérrətee/ (*plural* **-ties**) *n.* **1. BEING VULGAR** a vulgar state or way of behaving **2. SOMETHING CRUDE OR INDECENT** a crude or tasteless joke, remark, or act

vul·gar·ize /vúlgə rīz/ (**-ized, -iz·ing, -iz·es**) *vt.* **1. DEBASE SOMETHING** to make something less refined or reduce the quality of something **2. MAKE SOMETHING ACCESSIBLE** to present or treat something in a way that makes it accessible to ordinary people —**vul·gar·i·za·tion** /vùlgəri zάysh'n/ *n.* —**vul·gar·iz·er** /vúlgə rīzər/ *n.*

Vul·gar Lat·in *n.* LANG the form of Latin that was the common spoken language of the western Roman Empire

vul·gate /vúl gàyt, -gət/ *n.* **1.** LING **ORDINARY SPEECH** the everyday informal use of a language **2.** LITERAT **ACCEPTED VERSION** a text generally accepted among experts as being the best or most accurate version [Early 16thC. From Latin *vulgatus*, past participle of *vulgare* "to make public or common," from *vulgus* (see VULGAR).]

Vul·gate *n.* a Latin version of the Bible produced by Saint Jerome in the 4th century [Early 17thC. From Latin *vulgata editio* "edition made public, edition for ordinary people," from *vulgatus* (see VULGATE).]

vul·ner·a·ble /vúlnərəb'l/ *adj.* **1. WITHOUT ADEQUATE PROTECTION** open to emotional or physical danger or harm **2.** MIL **OPEN TO ATTACK** exposed to an attack or possible damage **3. EXTREMELY SUSCEPTIBLE** easily persuadable or liable to give in to temptation **4. PHYSICALLY OR PSYCHOLOGICALLY WEAK** unable to resist illness, debility, or failure **5.** BRIDGE **LIABLE TO INCREASED STAKES** liable to higher penalties as well as bonuses, having won one game of a rubber [Early 17thC. From late Latin *vulnerabilis*, from *vulnerare* "to wound," from *vulnus* "wound, injury."] —**vul·ner·a·bil·i·ty** /vùlnərə bíllətee/ *n.* —**vul·ner·a·ble·ness** /vúlnərəb'lnəss/ *n.* —**vul·ner·a·bly** /vúlnərəblee/ *adv.*

vul·ner·ar·y /vúlnə rèrree/ *adj.* MED **HEALING** capable of or used for healing wounds (*archaic*) ■ *n.* (*plural* **-ies**) PHARM **HEALING AGENT** a drug or other agent used in treating and healing wounds (*archaic*) [Late 16thC. From Latin *vulnerarius*, from *vulnus* "wound, injury."]

Vul·pec·u·la /vul pékyələ/ *n.* a constellation in the sky of the northern hemisphere between Cygnus and Sagitta [From Latin, diminutive of *vulpes* "fox"]

vul·pine /vúl pīn/ *adj.* **1. TYPICAL OF A FOX** typical of or resembling a fox **2. HAVING A TRAIT ATTRIBUTED TO FOXES** having or displaying a trait that is commonly associated with foxes such as cunning [Early 17thC. From Latin *vulpes* "fox."]

Vulture

vul·ture /vúlchər/ *n.* **1. BIRD OF PREY** a large bird of prey found in Africa, Eurasia, and the Americas. It has dark plumage and broad wings and feeds on carrion. Family: Accipitridae and Cathartidae. **2. PREDATOR** somebody who waits or looks eagerly for opportunities to take advantage of somebody else, especially somebody weak or helpless [14thC. Via Anglo-Norman *vultur* or Old French *voltour* from, ultimately, Latin *vultur*.]

vul·tur·ine /vúlchə rīn/ *adj.* **1. TYPICAL OF VULTURE** typical of or resembling a vulture **2. vul·tur·ine, vul·tur·ous GREEDY** having a trait commonly associated with vultures, e.g., opportunism or greed

vul·va /vúlvə/ (*plural* **-vae** /-vee/ *or* **-vas**) *n.* the external female genitals. These include two pairs of fleshy folds, the labia majora and labia minora, that surround the opening of the vagina and the clitoris. [14thC. From Latin, variant of *volva* "womb," from *volvere* "to roll."] —**vul·val** *adj.* —**vul·var** *adj.* —**vul·vi·form** /vúlvə fàwrm/ *adj.*

vul·vec·to·my /vul véktəmee/ (*plural* **-mies**) *n.* the surgical removal of all or part of a woman's external genitals

vul·vi·tis /vul vítiss/ *n.* painful swelling and redness of the vulva

vul·vo·vag·i·ni·tis /vùl vō vajjə nítiss/ *n.* painful swelling and redness of the vulva and vagina

vum /vum/ *interj.* *New England* used to express surprise or puzzlement (*dated*) [Late 18thC. Alteration of VOW.]

vv. *abbr.* **1.** verses **2.** MUSIC (first and second) violins **3.** volumes

v.v. *abbr.* vice versa

VW *abbr.* very worshipful

VX *n.* an oily, liquid, highly lethal, nerve gas

vy. *abbr.* very

vy·ing present participle of **vie**

Ww

W /dúbb'l yŏŏ/ (*plural* **w's**), **W** (*plural* **W's** *or* **Ws**) *n.* **1.** **23RD LETTER OF ENGLISH ALPHABET** the 23rd letter of the modern English alphabet **2.** **SPEECH SOUND CORRESPONDING TO LETTER "W"** the speech sound that corresponds to the letter "W" **3.** **LETTER "W" WRITTEN** a written representation of the letter "W" **4.** **SOMETHING SHAPED LIKE "W"** something that has the shape of the letter "W"

W[1] *symbol.* **1.** tungsten **2.** ELEC watt **3.** PHYS weight **4.** PHYS work

W[2] *abbr.* **1.** West **2.** women's (*used of clothing sizes*)

W. *abbr.* **1.** MEASURE width **2.** TIME week **3.** wife **4.** with

W. *abbr.* **1.** West **2.** Western **3.** CALENDAR Wednesday **4.** Warden **5.** Wales **6.** Welsh

w/ *abbr.* with

W3 *abbr.* World Wide Web

WA *abbr.* **1.** Washington (State) **2.** Western Australia **3.** INSUR with average

WAAC /wak/ *abbr.* Women's Army Auxiliary Corps

Waal /vaal/ the largest and southernmost of the three branches of the Rhine River in the Netherlands. Length: 52 mi./84 km.

Wa·bash /wáw bash, wáa-/ river in northern central United States. It rises in Ohio, and forms the Indiana-Illinois border, before flowing into the Ohio River. Length: 512 mi./815 km.

wab·bit /wábbit/ *adj.* *Scotland* weary or exhausted [Late 19thC. Origin unknown.]

wab·ble *n.*, *vti.* = **wobble** *n.*, **wobble** *v.* 1

WAC /wak/ *abbr.* Women's Army Corps ■ *n.* (*plural* **WACs**) **WAC MEMBER** a member of the Women's Army Corps

wack /wak/ *n.* an offensive term used to refer to somebody who is regarded as unconventional or unpredictable (*slang insult*) [Mid-20thC. Back-formation from WACKY.]

wack·o /wákō/ (*plural* **wack·os** *or* **wack·oes**), **whack·o** /hwákō/ (*plural* **-os** *or* **-oes**) *n.* an offensive term for somebody or something regarded as unconventional, unpredictable, or unusual (*slang insult*) [Late 20thC. From WACKY.]

wack·y /wákee/ (**-i·er, -i·est**), **whack·y** /wákee, hwákee/ (**-i·er, -i·est**) *adj.* **1.** **OFFENSIVE TERM** an offensive term used to describe somebody regarded as unconventional or unpredictable (*slang insult*) **2.** **SILLY** entertainingly silly (*informal*) [Mid-19thC. Origin uncertain: probably from the phrase *out of whack* "out of order" (see WHACK).] —**wack·i·ly** *adv.* —**wack·i·ness** *n.*

Wa·co /wáykō/ city on the Brazos River in central Texas. In 1993, 84 people were killed when federal agents stormed the compound of a religious group just outside the city. Population: 105,892 (1994).

wad /wod/ *n.* **1.** **SOFT MATERIAL** a small rounded mass of soft material, usually used to pack or stuff something ○ *The vase was carefully packed in wads of cotton.* **2.** **BUNDLE** a roll or small bundle of paper money ○ *a wad of notes* **3.** **COMPRESSED MATERIAL** a rounded compressed lump of something soft, especially tobacco or gum for chewing **4.** **MANY** a large quantity of something (*informal*) ○ *She has a wad of friends.* **5.** FIN **A LOT OF MONEY** a large amount of money (*informal*) **6.** ARMS **POWDER PLUG** a plug of material such as paper or cloth used to hold the powder charge in a muzzle-loading gun or cannon **7.** ARMS **DISK IN SHOTGUN CARTRIDGE** a disk made of felt or paper, used to hold the powder or shot in a shotgun cartridge **8.** MINERALS **MINERAL MIXTURE IN BOGGY GROUND** a fine-grained mixture of hydrated barium manganese oxide and other hydrated oxide minerals precipitated from water and poorly drained boggy ground ■ *v.* (**wad·ded, wad·ding, wads**) **1.** *vti.* **COMPRESS** to form or compress something into a small mass ○ *He wadded up the speeding ticket and threw it away.* **2.** *vt.* **PUT WADDING INTO SOMETHING** to stuff or plug something with wadding ○ *She wadded her ears so she wouldn't hear the noise.* **3.** *vt.* ARMS **KEEP CHARGE IN PLACE** to hold a charge of powder or shot in place **4.** *vt.* ARMS **INSERT WADDING INTO GUN** to insert a piece of wadding into a gun [Mid-16thC. Origin unknown.] —**wad·der** *n.* ◇ **shoot your wad** to use all your resources in achieving something and be unable to achieve anything more

wa·da /vaádə/, **va·da** *n.* *S Asia* a fried lentil ball eaten as a popular snack, particularly in South India [From Hindi *vaḍā*]

wad·die *n.* = **waddy**

wad·ding /wódding/ *n.* **1.** **SOFT PROTECTIVE MATERIAL** soft material used to protect something, especially in packaging **2.** ARMS **GUN WADS** material used to hold powder or shot in a gun or cartridge **3.** *U.K.* TEXTILES = **batting**[2] *n.*

wad·dle /wódd'l/ *vi.* (**-dled, -dling, -dles**) **WALK WITH SIDE-TO-SIDE GAIT** to walk with short steps, causing the body to tilt slightly from one side to the other ■ *n.* **DUCKLIKE GAIT** a way of walking, taking short steps with the body tilting slightly from one side to the other with each step [Late 16thC. From WADE.] —**wad·dler** *n.* —**wad·dly** *adj.*

wad·dy /wóddee/ (*plural* **-dies**), **wad·die** *n.* (*regional*) **1.** **COWBOY** a cowboy **2.** **RUSTLER** a cattle thief [Late 19thC. Origin unknown.]

wade /wayd/ *v.* (**wad·ed, wad·ing, wades**) **1.** *vti.* **WALK IN WATER** to walk against the pressure of water or mud **2.** *vi.* **GO THROUGH SOMETHING WITH DIFFICULTY** to read through something with difficulty, especially because it is very long or boring ■ *n.* **WALK TAKEN IN SHALLOW WATER** an act or instance of walking in shallow water [Old English *wadan*. Ultimately from an Indo-European word meaning "to go" that is also the ancestor of English *invade* and *vamoose*.] —**wad·a·ble** *adj.*

wade in *vti.* **1.** **INTERRUPT** to interrupt somebody forcefully or with determination **2.** **INTERVENE** to intervene in a situation in an attempt to help or restore order

Wade /wayd/, **Virginia** (*b.* 1945) British tennis player. She won the U.S. Open (1968), Italian Open (1971), French Open (1972), Australian Open (1972), and Wimbledon (1977). Full name **Sarah Virginia Wade**

wad·er /wáydər/ *n.* **1.** **SOMEBODY WHO WADES** somebody who or something that wades through water **2.** = **wading bird** ■ **wad·ers** *npl.* **WATERPROOF BOOTS OR PANTS** waterproof boots or combined boots and pants that reach to the hips or chest, worn as protection while fishing

wa·di /waádee/ (*plural* **wa·dis** *or* **wa·dies**), **wa·dy** (*plural* **wa·dies**) *n.* **1.** **MAINLY DRY WATER COURSE** a steep-sided water course in arid regions of North Africa and southern Asia through which water flows only after heavy rainfalls **2.** **OASIS** an oasis, especially in North Africa [Early 17thC. From Arabic *wādī* "valley, river bed."]

wad·ing bird *n.* a long-legged bird such as a crane, heron, or stork that stands in water and hunts for its food that includes fish, frogs, invertebrates, certain, and algae

wad·ing pool *n.* a shallow pool, sometimes near a larger pool, provided for small children's water play

wad·mal /wódməl/ *n.* a dense coarse woolen fabric once made in Orkney and Shetland and used for outer garments [14thC. From Old Norse *vaðmál* "cloth measure."]

Wad Me·da·ni /waad mi daánee/ capital city of El Gezira Province, central Sudan. Population: 218,714 (1993).

WAF /waf/ (*plural* **WAFs**), **Waf** (*plural* **Wafs**) *n.* formerly, a member of the women's section of the Air Force [Acronym, formed from *Women in the Air Force*]

Wafd /waaft/ *n.* an Egyptian nationalist party that emerged after an Egyptian delegation was refused a hearing at the Versailles Treaty negotiations following World War I. Negotiations eventually led to limited Egyptian independence beginning in 1922.

wa·fer /wáyfər/ *n.* **1.** **THIN CRISP COOKIE** a thin, crisp, and sometimes sweetened cookie, usually in a rectangular, fan, or cone shape, often eaten with ice cream **2.** CHR **BREAD IN CHRISTIAN COMMUNION SERVICE** a very thin disk of unleavened bread used to represent the body of Jesus Christ in the Christian Eucharist **3.** ELECTRON ENG = **chip** *n.* 4 **4.** **ADHESIVE MATERIAL** a small thin disk of adhesive material, used to seal letters and formal documents **5.** PHARM **MEDICINE CASING** a piece of rice paper or dried flour paste formerly used to encase a powdered medicine (*archaic*) ■ *vt.* (**-fered, -fer·ing, -fers**) **1.** **FASTEN WITH WAFER** to fasten something such as a letter or formal document with a wafer **2.** PHARM **ENCASE MEDICINE** to encase a powdered medicine in rice paper or dried flour paste (*archaic*) [14thC. Via Anglo-Norman *wafre*, variant of French *gaufre*, from Middle Low German *wāfel*, from a prehistoric Germanic word that is also the ancestor of English *waffle*[1].]

wa·fer-thin *adj.* extremely thin or narrow

waf·fle[1] /wóff'l/ *n.* a thick light pancake, crisp on the outside, that is baked in a waffle iron to give a pattern of indentations on both sides [Mid-18thC. From Dutch *wafel* (see WAFER).]

waf·fle[2] /wóff'l/ *vi.* (**-fled, -fling, -fles**) **BE INDECISIVE** to be unable to make a decision (*informal*) ■ *n.* **VERBIAGE THAT WAFFLES** speech or writing that is indecisive and vague (*informal*) [Late 17thC. From *waff* "to yelp or bark," an imitation of the sound; literally "to keep on waffing."] —**waf·fly** *adj.*

waf·fle iron *n.* an appliance used to bake waffles that has hinged indented plates that press a grid design into both sides of the waffle as it cooks

waft /woft/ *vti.* (**waft·ed, waft·ing, wafts**) **FLOAT GENTLY** to float gently through the air, or move something gently through the air ■ *n.* **1.** **SOMETHING CARRIED THROUGH AIR** something such as a scent carried on the air or by a breeze **2.** **WAVING MOTION** a gentle waving or fluttering motion **3.** **LIGHT BREEZE** a brief gentle gust of air **4.** NAUT **SIGNALING FLAG** a hoisted flag formerly used for signaling at sea (*archaic*) **5.** NAUT **SIGNAL USING FLAGS** a signal formerly sent at sea using flags (*archaic*) [Early 16thC. Back-formation from *wafter* "an armed ship used to guard a convoy," from Dutch *wachter*, from *wachten* "to guard." The meaning developed via "to sail."]

wag[1] /wag/ *v.* (**wagged, wag·ging, wags**) **1.** *vti.* **MOVE SOMETHING RAPIDLY TO AND FRO** to move part of the body to and fro, or move to and fro ○ *The dog wagged its tail.* **2.** *vi.* **GOSSIP** to gossip about somebody or other people, especially disapprovingly ○ *tongues are wagging* ■ *n.* **MOTION GOING TO AND FRO** a motion that goes to and fro [Old English. From or related to *wagian* "to move backward and forward." Ultimately from a prehistoric Germanic word.]

wag[2] /wag/ (**wagged, wag·ging, wags**) *n.* a humorous or witty individual (*informal*) [Mid-16thC. Originally used as an affectionate term for a mischievous boy. Origin uncertain: probably a shortening of *waghalter* "somebody who swings in a noose," that is, somebody likely to be hanged.] —

wag·ger·y *n.* —**wag·gish** *adj.* —**wag·gish·ly** *adv.* —**wag·gish·ness** *n.*

wage /wayj/ *n.* **PAYMENT FOR WORK** a sum of money paid to a worker in exchange for services, especially for work performed on an hourly, daily, or weekly basis, or by the piece (*often used in the plural*) ■ *vt.* (**waged, wag·ing, wag·es**) **ENGAGE IN FIGHT** to engage in war or in a serious fight to achieve an end ○ *wage war* [14thC. From Anglo-Norman or Old Norman French. Ultimately from a prehistoric Germanic word meaning "pledge" (the original sense in English), which is also the ancestor of English *gage* and *wed*.] —**wage·less** *adj.* —**wage·less·ness** *n.*

WORD KEY: SYNONYMS

wage, salary, pay, fee, remuneration, emolument, honorarium, stipend

CORE MEANING: money given for work done

wage a fixed regular payment made on a weekly or daily basis, especially to manual workers; **salary** a fixed regular payment, often made on a monthly or biweekly basis, especially when made to white-collar or professional workers. It is usually expressed in terms of the amount earned per year; **pay** an informal general word for "wage" or "salary"; **fee** the payment made to a professional person by a client; **remuneration** a more formal word for "pay," that may also include fringe benefits; **emolument** a formal word for any profit made from a job or office; **honorarium** a formal word for money given in exchange for services for which there is normally no charge; **stipend** a regular payment or allowance.

wage dif·fer·en·tial *n.* any difference in wages between workers with different skills working in the same industry or workers with similar skills working in different industries or regions

wage earn·er *n.* **1. HOUSEHOLD SUPPORTER** somebody in a family or household who is earning a wage or salary **2. PERSON PAID WAGES** somebody who works by the hour, day, or week for wages contrasted with somebody who is paid a fixed salary regardless of the hours worked

wage in·cen·tive *n.* additional money paid to a worker in order to improve that person's productivity

wa·ger /wáyjər/ *n.* **1.** GAMBLING **BET ON OUTCOME** an agreement between two people that whoever loses a bet on an uncertain outcome will pay the other a specified amount or some other form of compensation **2.** GAMBLING **AMOUNT BET** a sum of money, property, or other compensation to be paid to the person who wins a bet **3.** HIST **PLEDGE** a pledge to engage in combat, especially in order to establish guilt or innocence by single combat ■ *vt.* (**-gered, -ger·ing, -gers**) GAMBLING **BET MONEY** to risk or bet money or property on the outcome of a game, event, or uncertain situation [14thC. From Anglo-Norman *wageure*, from *wagier* "to pledge," from *wage* (see WAGE).] —**wa·ger·er** *n.*

wag·es /wáyjəz/ *n.* a just reward or recompense for something (*literary; takes a singular verb*) ○ *the wages of sin*

wage scale *n.* a scale of the different wages paid to employees who are performing different jobs within a single company or industry

wage slave *n.* somebody who relies on earning money in order to live (*informal*)

wag·gle /wágg'l/ *vti.* (**-gled, -gling, -gles**) **MOVE BACK AND FORTH** to move rapidly back and forth, or make something move rapidly back and forth ■ *n.* **WOBBLING MOTION** a quick shaking or wobbling motion [Late 16thC. From WAG[1], literally "to keep on wagging."] —**wag·gly** *adj.*

Wag·ner /vaágnər/, **Richard** (1813–83) German composer. He developed both the form and content of opera, notably in his opera cycle *The Ring of the Nibelungs* (1852–74), and was a major influence on orchestral composers of the late romantic period.

AKG London

Richard Wagner

Wag·ner /wágnər/, **Robert F.** (1877–1953) German-born U.S. politician. He took the lead in passing progressive legislation while representing New York in the U.S. Senate (1927–49). Full name **Robert Ferdinand Wagner**

Wag·ner·i·an /vaag neéree ən/ *adj.* **1.** MUSIC **RELATING TO RICHARD WAGNER** resembling or relating to the dramatic musical compositions of Richard Wagner **2.** MUSIC **POWERFUL** having a voice powerful enough to perform in one of Wagner's musical compositions, with their heavy orchestration **3. JUNOESQUE** used to describe a woman with an imposing statuesque figure or a domineering manner ■ *n.* **Wagnerian, Wagnerite** MUSIC **RICHARD WAGNER FOLLOWER** somebody who believes in and follows the musical theories of Richard Wagner, or who loves his music

wag·on /wággən/ *n.* **1. WHEELED VEHICLE** a rectangular vehicle that is used to carry heavy loads and is pulled by an animal or tractor or is motor-powered **2. DELIVERY VEHICLE** a light automotive vehicle used to sell or deliver something **3. POLICE PATROL WAGON** a van or truck used by the police to transport suspects or criminals **4. CHILD'S FOUR-WHEELED CART** a low four-wheeled cart with a long handle a child can use to pull the cart or to control the direction of the front wheels **5. SERVING CART** a four-wheeled rectangular cart used to display or serve food or drink **6.** *U.K.* **FREIGHT CAR** a railroad car for goods, particularly an open one [15thC. From Dutch *wagen*. Ultimately from a prehistoric Germanic word that is also the ancestor of English *wain*.] —**wag·on·er** *n.* ◇ **be off the wagon** to resume drinking alcoholic beverages after a period of abstinence ◇ **be on the wagon** to abstain from drinking any alcoholic beverage

wag·on·ette /wàggə nét/ *n.* a light four-wheeled horse-drawn vehicle with two lengthwise seats facing each other behind a crosswise driver's seat

wa·gon-lit /vaà goN leé/ (*plural* **wag·on-lits** *or* **wag·ons-lits** /vaà goN leé/) *n.* **1. SLEEPING CAR** a sleeping car on a European railroad **2. COMPARTMENT** an individual compartment in a railroad sleeping car [From French, formed from *wagon* "railroad coach" + *lit* "bed"]

wag·on·load /wággən lòd/ *n.* the amount that a wagon does or can hold

wag·on train *n.* a line of two or more animal-drawn wagons traveling cross-country and carrying people, food supplies, or goods

wag·on vault *n.* ARCHIT = **barrel vault**

Wa·gram /vaág raam/ village in northeastern Austria. It was the site of the Battle of Wagram in which Napoleon defeated the Austrians in July 1809.

wag·tail /wág tàyl/ *n.* a songbird, found in Europe, Asia, and Africa, with a long tail that bobs up and down when it walks and especially when it lands. Family: Motacillidae.

Wag the Dog syn·drome *n.* a situation in which a U.S. President uses military attacks on other nations as a diversionary tactic to deflect intense public and media scrutiny from a personal scandal (*slang*) ○ *"Was the bombing of Iraq really a result of Wag the Dog syndrome?"* (*Vanity Fair*; March 1999) [Late 20thC. *Wag the Dog* from a movie.]

WORD KEY: CULTURAL NOTE

Wag the Dog, a movie by Tribeca Productions and screenplay by Hilary Henkin and David Mamet (1997). Based on a novel by Larry Beinhart titled *American Hero*, the movie depicts a fictional U.S. President's advisors starting a phony war in order to deflect media attention from a scandal. The movie's premiere in early 1998 coincided with a grand jury investigation of U.S. President Bill Clinton, a sex scandal involving him and a former White House intern, and an impeachment trial (which later ended in acquittal). During this period the President responded to military aggression and terrorist acts affecting the United States by launching cruise missiles against Iraq, Sudan, and Afghanistan. The U.S. media and the pop culture soon drew a figurative connection between the movie and the Presidential scandal, leading to such expressions as "Is it Wag the Dog?", "Was it a Wag the Dog scenario?", and the phrase *Wag the Dog syndrome*.

Wah·ha·bi /wə haábee, waa-/ (*plural* **-bis**), **Wa·ha·bi** (*plural* **Wahabis**) *n.* a member of a very conservative Islamic group that rejects any innovation that occurred after the 3rd century of Islam. It flourishes primarily in Arabia. [Early 19thC. From Arabic *wahhābī*, named for Muhammad ibn bd-al- *Wahhāb* (1703–92), who founded the sect.] —**Wah·ha·bism** *n.*

wa·hi·ne /waa heénee, -này/ *n.* **1.** *Hawaii, NZ* **HAWAIIAN OR MAORI WOMAN** a Hawaiian or Maori woman or wife **2.** *Hawaii* **WOMAN SURFER** a young woman surfer (*informal*) [Late 18thC. From Hawaiian or Maori.]

wa·hoo[1] /waa hoó, waá hoó/ (*plural* **-hoos**) *n.* a deciduous shrub or small tree of eastern North America, with dark purple flowers that open to expose the seed's scarlet arils. Latin name: *Euonymus atropurpureus*. [Mid-19thC. From Dakota *wa hu*, literally "arrow-wood."]

wa·hoo[2] /waa hoó, waá hoó/ (*plural* **-hoos**) *n.* a small elm tree of the southeastern United States, with hairy reddish fruits and twigs with corky projections resembling wings. Latin name: *Ulmus alata*. [Late 18thC. Origin unknown.]

wa·hoo[3] /waa hoó, waá hoó/ (*plural* **-hoos**) *n.* a large fast-swimming fish of the mackerel family that lives in tropical seas worldwide and weighs up to 120 pounds. Latin name: *Acanthocybium solanderi*. [Early 20thC. Origin unknown.]

wa·hoo[4] /waa hoó/ *interj.* **YIPPEE** used to express happy excitement ■ *n.* (*plural* **-hoos**) **SHOUT OF HAPPINESS** a rowdy cry of excitement (*regional*)

wah-wah /waá waá/, **wa-wa** *n.* **1. WAVERING SOUND OF WIND INSTRUMENT** the wavering sound made by alternately covering and uncovering the bell of a trumpet or trombone **2. ELECTRONIC SOUND** a sound similar to the wah-wah of a trumpet or trombone created electronically for guitars, keyboards, and other electronic instruments **3. ELECTRONIC DEVICE** an electronic device attached to a musical instrument for producing a wavering wah-wah sound [Early 20thC. An imitation of the sound.]

wah-wah ped·al *n.* a foot pedal attached to an electronic musical instrument such as an electric guitar, used to create a wavering sound

waif /wayf/ *n.* **1. ABANDONED CHILD** a homeless or friendless person, especially an abandoned child **2. STRAY ANIMAL** a stray animal whose owner is unknown **3. THIN YOUNG PERSON** somebody, usually a young person, with a thin fragile appearance who looks needy **4. UNCLAIMED ITEM** any item found whose owner is unknown (*literary*) **5.** NAUT = **waft** *n.* **5** [14thC. From Anglo-Norman *weyf*, earlier *gwayf*, "lost property," from Scandinavian. The sense of "abandoned child" evolved from "unclaimed property" through "lost thing" and "lost child."]

Wai·ka·to /wīkaátō/ the longest river in New Zealand. It rises in Lake Taupo in the center of the North Island and empties into the Tasman Sea south of Waiuku. Length: 270 mi./434 km.

Wai·ki·ki /wī kee keè, wī kee keé/ beach resort northeast of Honolulu, Oahu Island, Hawaii

wail /wayl/ *v.* (**wailed, wail·ing, wails**) **1.** *vti.* **MAKE MOURNFUL CRY** to express pain, grief, or misery in a long mournful high-pitched cry or in words uttered in a mournful way ○ *He could only wail when he heard the news.* **2.** *vi.* **MAKE LONG HIGH-PITCHED NOISE** to make a long loud high-pitched sound ○ *The sirens wailed.* **3.** *vt.* **LAMENT** to express grief over somebody or something (*archaic*) ■ *n.* **1. LONG HIGH-PITCHED SOUND** a long loud high-pitched sound or cry **2. PROTEST** a loud plaintive expression of protest, resentment, or disappointment [13thC. From an Old Norse word that was formed from *vei*, "woe."] —**wail·ful** *adj.* —**wail·ful·ly** *adv.*

Wail·ing Wall *n.* = **Western Wall**

wain /wayn/ *n.* a farm wagon or cart (*archaic or literary*) [Old English *wæ(g)n*, of prehistoric Germanic origin]

wain·scot /wáynskət, -skòt/ *n.* **1. WOODEN PANELS LINING ROOM** a lining for the walls of a room, especially one made of wood paneling **2. LOWER PART OF WALL OF ROOM** the lower part of the wall of a room, especially when it is paneled in wood or finished differently from the upper part **3. OAK PANELING** a fine grade of oak used as wall paneling ■ *vt.* (**-scot·ed, -scot·ing, -scots**) **COVER WALL WITH PANELING** to cover a wall, especially with wood paneling [14thC. From Middle Dutch *waghenscote* or Middle Low German *wagenschot*, literally "wagon-boarding."]

wain·scot·ing /wáynskəting, -skòtting/, **wain·scot·ting** *n.* **1.** = **wainscot** *n.* 1 **2. WOOD FOR COVERING WALL** the material, especially wood, used to cover a wall

wain·wright /wáyn rīt/ *n.* somebody who makes and repairs wagons

Wai·ra·ra·pa, Lake /wī raa ráapə/ lake in the southern part of the North Island, New Zealand. Area: 50 sq. mi./80 sq. km.

Wai·rau /wír ow/ river in the northern part of the South Island, New Zealand. It rises in the Southern Alps and empties into the Cook Strait near Blenheim. Length: 105 mi./169 km.

waist /wayst/ *n.* **1.** ANAT **BODY AREA BETWEEN RIBS AND HIPS** the part of the human trunk between the ribcage and the hips, usually narrower than the rest of the trunk **2.** CLOTHES **PART OF CLOTHING** the part of a garment that fits around the waist of the body **3. NARROW PART** the narrow middle part of something, e.g., the middle of a violin **4.** SHIPPING **MIDDLE OF DECK** the middle part of a ship or a ship's deck between the raised sections at the bow and stern **5.** AIR **MIDDLE OF AIRPLANE** the middle section of an aircraft's fuselage **6.** INSECTS **MIDDLE OF INSECT** the narrow part of an insect's body between the thorax and the abdomen [14thC. Origin uncertain: perhaps from an Old English word meaning "girth to which somebody has grown," from a prehistoric Germanic word meaning "to grow" (ancestor of English *wax*).] —**waist·less** *adj.*

waist·band /wáyst bànd/ *n.* a band of fabric in a piece of clothing, e.g., at the top of a skirt or pair of pants, that circles the waist

waist·cloth /wáyst klòth, -klàwth/ *n.* a loincloth (*archaic*)

waist·coat /wáyst kōt/ *n.* **1.** *U.K., ANZ* **SLEEVELESS UPPER GARMENT WORN OVER SHIRT** a man's or woman's sleeveless and collarless waist-length garment, usually with buttons down the front, worn over a shirt and traditionally worn by men under a suit jacket **2.** HIST **GARMENT WORN UNDER DOUBLET** a man's sleeveless garment reaching to the hips or knees, worn under a doublet in the 16th century —**waist·coat·ed** *adj.*

waist·ed /wáystəd/ *adj.* made with a waist or a part that resembles a waist

waist·line /wáyst līn/ *n.* **1. MEASUREMENT OF WAIST** the measurement around the narrowest part of the waist **2.** CLOTHES **MEETING OF BODICE AND WAIST** the level, usually near the waist, where the bodice and skirt of a dress meet ○ *a low waistline*

wait /wayt/ *v.* (**wait·ed, wait·ing, waits**) **1.** *vi.* **DO NOTHING EXPECTING SOMETHING TO HAPPEN** to stay in one place or do nothing for a period of time until something happens or in the expectation or hope that something will happen ○ *I'll wait for you here until noon.* **2.** *vi.* **STOP SO SOMEBODY CAN CATCH UP** to stop or slow down in order to allow somebody else to catch up ○ *Wait for me!* **3.** *vi.* **BE HOPING FOR SOMETHING** to be hoping for something or on the lookout for something ○ *He is waiting for a job opportunity.* **4.** *vi.* **BE DELAYED OR IGNORED FOR NOW** to be postponed or put off until later ○ *Fame would just have to wait.* **5.** *vi.* **BE READY OR AVAILABLE** to be ready or available for somebody to take or use ○ *Your mail is waiting for you.* **6.** *vt.* **DELAY SOMETHING** to delay something, especially a meal, because somebody is expected to arrive soon ○ *We waited dinner for you.* **7.** *vti.* **BE A WAITER** to work as a waiter ○ *She waits tables at the hotel.* ■ *n.* **TIME SPENT WAITING** a period of time spent while expecting something to happen ○ *The wait seemed to go on forever.* ■ **waits** *npl.* MUSIC **BAND OF MUSICIANS** a band of musicians who play and sing Christmas carols in the streets (*archaic*) [12thC. Via Old Northern French *waitier*, "to spy, prepare to ambush," from Frankish.] ◇ **lie in wait for somebody** *or* **something** be waiting to catch or attack somebody

wait on *vt.* **1. SERVE SOMEBODY BY BRINGING REQUESTED ITEMS** to go and get the things that somebody asks for, usually continuously for a period of time ○ *It's nice to be waited on for a change.* **2. SERVE SOMEBODY AT TABLE** to bring food and drink to people sitting at a table, usually in a restaurant **3. SERVE RETAIL CUSTOMER** to attend to a customer's purchasing needs **4. WAIT FOR SOMEBODY** to wait for somebody or something (*informal*) **5. VISIT SOMEBODY** to pay a formal visit to somebody (*archaic*)

wait out *vt.* to stay in one place or do nothing until something ends ○ *We decided to wait out the storm.*

wait up *vi.* **DELAY BEDTIME** to delay going to bed to await an event or somebody's arrival ○ *I'll be home late; don't wait up.* ■ *interj.* **WAIT** used to tell somebody to stop while somebody else catches up (*informal*)

wait upon *vt.* = **wait on** *v.* 1, **wait on** *v.* 2, **wait on** *v.* 3, **wait on** *v.* 5

Wai·ta·ki /wī tákee/ river in the southeastern part of the South Island, New Zealand. It rises in Lake Benmore and empties into the Pacific Ocean near the town of Waitaki. Length: 130 mi./209 km.

Wai·tang·i /wī táangee/ historic site in the northern part of the North Island, New Zealand. A treaty between the Maori people and the British government was signed there in February 1840.

Waite /wayt/, **Morrison Remick** (1816–88) U.S. jurist. He served as chief justice of the United States (1874–88).

Wai·te·ma·ta Har·bour /wìtə màtə-/ arm of the Pacific Ocean on the northeastern coast of the North Island, New Zealand. Auckland is situated on part of it.

wait·er /wáytər/ *n.* **1. SOMEBODY WHO SERVES AT TABLES** somebody employed to bring food and drink to people, usually in a restaurant **2. TRAY** a tray for carrying dishes or serving food [14thC. Via Anglo-Norman, "attendant, watchman," from Old Northern French, or directly formed from WAIT.]

wait·ing game *n.* a tactic whereby somebody delays taking any action or making a move in a contest or negotiation, hoping that his or her position will improve with the passage of time

wait·ing list *n.* a list of people waiting for something that is not immediately available, e.g. a table in a restaurant, a place in a school, or an out-of-stock product

wait·ing room *n.* a room in which people may wait, e.g., for a doctor's appointment

Wai·to·mo Caves /wī tōmō-/ limestone cave system in the western part of the North Island, New Zealand, noted for its large colonies of glowworms

wait·per·son /wáyt pùrss'n/ (*plural* **waitpeople** /-peep'l/ *or* **wait·per·sons**) *n.* a man or woman employed to serve at tables, usually in a restaurant

wait·ress /wáytrəss/ *n.* a woman who serves food or drink at tables, usually in a restaurant

wait·ron /wáytrən/ *n.* somebody who serves at tables (*slang*) [Late 20thC. Blend of WAITER or WAITRESS and AUTOMATON, suggesting mechanical, repetitive work.]

wait·staff /wáyt stàf/ *n.* the group of waitpersons in a café or restaurant

wait state *n.* a period of time during which a central processing unit in a computer sits idle while a slower computer component such as a memory or a bus performs its function

waive /wayv/ (**waived, waiv·ing, waives**) *vt.* **1. SURRENDER CLAIM** to give something up voluntarily, especially a right or claim ○ *She waived her right to remain silent.* **2. NOT ENFORCE SOMETHING** to refrain from enforcing or applying something in a particular instance ○ *They decided to waive the restrictions.* **3. TEMPORARILY DELAY SOMETHING** to put off something for a time **4.** SPORTS **MAKE PLAYER AVAILABLE TO OTHER TEAM** to remove a professional ball player from a team's roster, thereby making the player available to other teams [13thC. From Anglo-Norman *weyver*, "to make a waif of, abandon," from *weyf*. See WAIF.]

waiv·er *n.* **1. RELINQUISHMENT OF RIGHT** a voluntary giving up of a right or claim **2. DOCUMENT CONTAINING WAIVER** a document or formal statement relinquishing a right or claim, or an action indicating an intention to waive something **3.** SPORTS **ACT OF GIVING UP CLAIM ON PLAYER** the act of a sports team in giving up the right to claim a professional ball player who has been removed from another team's roster

wa·ka·me /waa káamee/ (*plural* **-mes** *or* **-me**) *n.* a brown seaweed native to the coasts of Japan, China, and Korea, often dried and used in Japanese and Chinese cooking. Latin name: *Undaria pinnatifida.* [Mid-20thC. From Japanese.]

wa·kan·da /waa káandə/ *n.* in the religion of the Sioux, the great supernatural power that lies behind the whole of the natural world

Wa·kash·an /waa kásh'n, wàakə shàn/ *n.* a family of languages spoken by Native North American peoples in British Columbia and Washington State. About 3,000 people speak one of the Wakashan languages. [Late 19thC. From Nootka *waukash*, "good." Said to have been applied to these peoples by CAPTAIN COOK.] —**Wa·kash·an** *adj.*

Wa·ka·ti·pu /wàakə típpoo/ lake in the southwestern part of the South Island, New Zealand. The town of Queenstown is located on its northern shore. Area: 113 sq. mi./293 sq. km.

Wa·ka·ya·ma /wàakə yàamə/ seaport and capital city of Wakayama Prefecture, southwest of Osaka, Japan. Population: 396,553 (1990).

wake[1] /wayk/ *v.* (**woke** /wōk/ *or* **waked, wok·en** /wṓkən/ *or* **waked, wak·ing, wakes**) **1.** *vti.* **END SOMEBODY'S OR YOUR OWN SLEEP** to come back, or bring somebody back, to a conscious state after sleeping ○ *I woke suddenly at dawn.* **2.** *vti.* **END INACTIVITY** to become alert and active, or make somebody alert and active, after being inactive, in a daydream, or preoccupied **3.** *vti.* **MAKE SOMEBODY REALIZE SOMETHING** to make somebody aware of something ○ *Their pleas woke us to the situation.* **4.** *vi.* **WATCH OVER CORPSE** to hold a vigil over the body of somebody who has died **5.** *vi.* **STAY AWAKE** to be or to remain awake ○ *"Fled is that music – Do I wake or sleep?"* (John Keats, *Ode to a Nightingale*; 1819) **6.** *vti.* **KEEP WATCH** to keep watch over somebody or something (*archaic*) ■ *n.* **1. WATCH KEPT OVER CORPSE** a watch or vigil held over a corpse before burial or cremation **2. FESTIVE GATHERING AROUND FUNERAL** a social gathering held after a funeral or, in Ireland, often after the death but before the funeral. Traditionally people drink and talk about the dead person, and there is a happy jovial atmosphere. **3.** *U.K.* CHR **BRITISH CHURCH FESTIVAL** in Great Britain, the festival for the patron saint of a parish church or one held to commemorate its dedication (*regional*) [Old English *wacan*, "to become awake." Ultimately from the same Indo-European word meaning "be active or lively" as English *vigilance, wait, vigor*, and *watch*.] —**wak·er** *n.*

WORD KEY: USAGE

See Usage note at ***awake.***

WORD KEY: CULTURAL NOTE

Finnegan's Wake, a novel by Irish author James Joyce (1939). Joyce's last novel recounts a single night in the life of a Dublin barkeeper, Humphrey Chimpden Earwicker, and his family. An extraordinary multilayered work consisting chiefly of extended interior monologues, it is crammed with multilingual puns, poetry, and literary and historical allusions that emphasize the universal and cyclical nature of human experience.

wake up *vti.* = **wake**[1] *v.* 1, **wake**[1] *v.* 2, **wake**[1] *v.* 3 ◇ **wake up and smell the coffee** used to tell somebody that he or she is wrong about a particular situation and that it is time to acknowledge the reality (*informal*)

wake[2] /wayk/ *n.* **1.** NAUT **TRACK IN WATER** the track left in water by a vessel or any other body moving through it **2. DISTURBED AIR BEHIND VEHICLE** the stream of turbulence in the air left by an aircraft or land vehicle passing through it **3. POSITION BEHIND SOMEBODY** a position or the area behind somebody or something that is moving ahead fast ○ *left the rest of the field trailing in her wake* **4. AFTEREFFECTS** the aftermath or aftereffects of a dramatic event or powerful thing ○ *The bomb left destruction in its wake.* [15thC. Via Middle Low German from Old Norse *vok* "hole in ice (made by a boat)."]

wake·board·ing *n.* a water sport in which somebody riding a single board is pulled behind a motor boat and performs jumps while crisscrossing the wake of the boat [Late 20thC. Modeled on SKATEBOARDING.]

Wake·field /wáyk fèeld/ town in northeastern Massachusetts, southeast of Lake Quannapowitt, east of Woburn, and north of Boston. Population: 24,756 (1996).

wake·ful /wáykfəl/ *adj.* **1. NOT SLEEPING** unable to sleep **2. SLEEPLESS** passed without sleep ○ *a wakeful night* **3. ALERT** awake, especially while watching or guarding something ○ *promised to remain wakeful* —**wake·ful·ly** *adv.* —**wake·ful·ness** *n.*

Wake Is·land /wáyk-/ group of three islets comprising a coral atoll in the central Pacific Ocean. It was occupied by the U.S. in 1898 and held by the Japanese in World War II between 1941 and 1945. Population: 126 (1997). Area: 3 sq. mi./8 sq. km.

wake·less /wáykləss/ *adj.* uninterrupted by waking, or spent in uninterrupted sleep

wak·en /wáykən/ (**-ened, -en·ing, -ens**) *vti.* to become, or make somebody, conscious after sleeping, active after being inactive, or aware after being unaware (*formal*) —**wak·en·er** *n.*

WORD KEY: USAGE

See Usage note at ***awake***.

wake-rob·in /-ròbbin/ (*plural* **wake-rob·ins** *or* **wake-rob·in**) *n.* **1.** = **trillium 2.** = **cuckoopint 3. ARUM PLANT** a member of a group of early-blooming North American arums, e.g., the arrow arum

wake-up call *n.* **1. CALL TO AWAKEN GUEST** a telephone call or a personal visit made to awaken somebody, especially a telephone call from or arranged by hotel staff made at an agreed-upon time to awaken a guest **2. FRIGHTENING EXPERIENCE** a frightening experience that is interpreted as a sign that a major change is needed in the way somebody lives or conducts business

wa·kil = **vakil**

Waks·man /wáksmən/, **Selman A.** (1888–1973) Russian-born U.S. microbiologist. He was the pioneer researcher of streptomycin, and was the first person to use the term "antibiotics." He was awarded a Nobel Prize in physiology and medicine (1952). Full name **Selman Abraham Waksman**

Wa·la·chi·a /wə láykee ə/ fomer region in southeastern Europe, in present-day southern Romania. Founded as a principality toward the end of the 13th century, it was ruled by Turkey from 1387 until it joined Moldavia to form Romania in 1861. —**Wa·la·chi·an** *n., adj.*

Wal·cott /wáwlkət/, **Derek** (*b.* 1930) St. Lucian writer. His Caribbean-based novels and plays are characterized by a vivid use of language. He won a Nobel Prize in literature (1992).

Wald /wawld/, **George** (1906–97) U.S. biologist. He shared a Nobel Prize in physiology or medicine (1967) for his work on vision. He was an outspoken opponent of the arms race and the Vietnam War.

Wald, Lillian D. (1867–1940) U.S. nurse and social worker. She founded the Henry Street Settlement for social work (1893) in New York City and promoted the need for public health services.

Wal·de·mar I /vaáldə maar/, **King of Denmark** (1131–82). Having gained sole control of the Danish throne (1157–82), he established a dynastic rule in Denmark. Known as **Waldemar the Great**

Wal·de·mar II, King of Denmark (1170–1241). He was the son of Waldemar I. As king (1202–41), he extended Danish territory and instituted legal and administrative reforms. Known as **Waldemar the Conqueror**

Wal·den·ses /wol dén seez/ *npl.* the members of a small Christian denomination, originating in southern France, that broke with the Roman Catholic Church in the 12th century and experienced much persecution. In the 16th century the Waldenses joined the Reformation and adopted Calvinist doctrines. [Mid-16thC. From medieval Latin, from *Waldensis*, a variant of Peter *Valdes* (d. 1205), who founded the movement.] —**Wal·den·sian** /wol dénssee ən/ *adj.*

Wald·heim /wáwld hīm, vaált-/, **Kurt** (*b.* 1918) Austrian statesman. He was secretary general of the United Nations (1972–81) and president of Austria (1986–91). During his presidency it was alleged he had been complicit in Nazi war crimes.

Wal·dorf sal·ad /wáwl dawrf-/ *n.* a salad made of diced raw apples, celery, and walnuts with a mayonnaise dressing [Early 20thC. Named for the *Waldorf*-Astoria Hotel in New York, where this salad was first served.]

wale /wayl/ *n.* **1. SKIN WELT** a raised mark on the skin made by a blow, particularly with a whip **2.** TEXTILES **RIDGE ON FABRIC** a ridge on the surface of a woven fabric such as corduroy **3.** TEXTILES **WEAVE OF FABRIC** the weave or texture of a fabric with ribs **4.** KNITTING **VERTICAL ROW OF KNITTING** a vertical row of stitches in knitting **5.** NAUT **WOOD FORMING SIDES OF SHIP** any of the strong horizontal planks forming the sides of a wooden ship ■ *vt.* (**waled, wal·ing, wales**) **1. RAISE WELT ON SKIN** to raise a red swollen mark on the skin by striking a blow, particularly with a whip **2.** TEXTILES **WEAVE RIDGED FABRIC** to weave fabric with ridges [Old English *walu*, "ridge," from prehistoric Germanic]

Wales /waylz/ principality in Great Britain, part of the United Kingdom of Great Britain and Northern Ireland. Once a separate kingdom, it was united with England in 1536. It voted in 1997 to have its own assembly, giving it a degree of self-government. Capital: Cardiff. Population: 2,921,000 (1996). Area: 8,018 sq. mi./20,766 sq. km.

Wal·hal·la *n.* = **Valhalla**

walk /wawk/ *v.* (**walked, walk·ing, walks**) **1.** *vi.* **MOVE ON FOOT** to move or travel on legs and feet, alternately putting one foot a comfortable distance in front of, or sometimes behind, the other and usually proceeding at a moderate pace. When walking, as opposed to running, one of the feet is always in contact with the ground, the one being put down as or before the other is lifted. ○ *a toddler just learning to walk* **2.** *vt.* **TRAVEL THROUGH PLACE ON FOOT** to travel along or through something on foot ○ *walking the coastal path* **3.** *vt.* **TAKE ANIMAL FOR EXERCISE BY WALKING** to lead or exercise an animal, usually a dog on a leash ○ *walked the dog* **4.** *vt.* **WALK WITH SOMEBODY TO SOMETHING** to accompany somebody on foot as far as a particular place such as a home or car ○ *walking a friend home* **5.** *vt.* **CAUSE SOMEBODY TO WALK** to help or force somebody to walk by holding and pushing from behind ○ *We kept walking him till he was able to stand on his own.* **6.** *vti.* **MOVE LARGE OBJECT BY ROCKING** to move, or move something, in a way that suggests walking, e.g., by pivoting a large heavy object alternately on its corners and swinging the other side forward ○ *The bureau's too heavy to lift; we'll have to walk it into the bedroom.* **7.** *vt.* **MEASURE SOMETHING BY WALKING** to measure or inspect something by walking over or along it, especially the boundaries of an area or piece of property ○ *walk the west property line* **8.** *vi.* **BE STOLEN** to disappear or be stolen (*informal*) ○ *The petty cash seems to have walked.* **9.** *vi.* **GO ON STRIKE** to go out on strike (*slang*) ○ *threatened to walk* **10.** *vi.* **LEAVE IN PROTEST** to quit a job, event, or meeting to express disagreement (*slang*) ○ *You better apologize, or I'm walking!* **11.** *vi.* **BE FREED FROM JAIL OR ACQUITTED** to be released from prison or found innocent of a crime (*slang*) ○ *I couldn't believe they walked after what they did!* **12.** *vi.* BASEBALL **GO TO FIRST BASE** to proceed to first base on four balls **13.** *vt.* BASEBALL **ALLOW BATTER ON FIRST** to allow a batter to go to first base on four balls **14.** *vi.* BASKETBALL **TAKE STEPS ILLEGALLY** to take more than two steps in basketball without dribbling while holding the ball ■ *n.* **1. JOURNEY ON FOOT** a journey made on foot, especially for pleasure or exercise ○ *a walk in the woods.* **2. DISTANCE OR TIME OF FOOT JOURNEY** the distance traveled or the time it takes to go somewhere on foot ○ *a four-mile walk* ○ *a ten-minute walk from home* **3.** EQU **HORSE'S SLOWER GAIT** a relatively slow-paced way of moving for a horse or other four-legged animal, in which two feet are always on the ground ○ *The mare started at a walk, then broke into a trot.* **4. WAY OF WALKING** somebody's characteristic way of walking ○ *She's got a graceful walk.* **5. PLACE FOR PEDESTRIANS** a place designed or set aside for the use of people on foot **6. ROUTE FOR PEOPLE WALKING** a route or path for travelers on foot ○ *The miner's trail is an easy scenic walk.* **7.** SPORT **TRACK RACE** a track race in which the competitors walk a specified distance **8. AREA FOR ANIMALS** an enclosed area for exercising or pasturing domestic animals such as horses **9. ROWS OF TREES** a plantation of widely spaced trees or shrubs **10. SPACE BETWEEN ROWS** the space between rows of widely spaced trees or shrubs **11.** BASEBALL **ACT OF REACHING FIRST BASE** in baseball, the act of reaching first base on four balls **12.** BASKETBALL **ILLEGAL HOLDING INSTEAD OF DRIBBLING** in basketball, an illegal taking of steps while holding the ball **13. SOMETHING VERY EASY** something that is very easy to do (*informal*) [Old English *wealcan* "to roll, toss" and *wealcian* "to roll up," from a prehistoric Germanic word (ancestor of English *gauche*). The meaning developed via "move about," "go on a journey."] —**walk·a·ble** *adj.* ◇ **walk all over somebody** to ignore somebody's rights or feelings ◇ **walk tall** to feel and display self-confidence and pride in your achievements

walk away *vi.* **1. ABANDON PROBLEM** to refrain from becoming, or refuse to become, involved in a situation or problem **2. HAVE MINOR INJURIES** to survive an accident uninjured or with few and minor injuries and be able to walk from the scene **3. DEFEAT SOMEBODY** to defeat or outdo another person or team easily **4. WIN SOMETHING** to win or achieve something ○ *She walked away with the first prize.*

walk off *v.* **1.** *vi.* **LEAVE ABRUPTLY** to leave a place abruptly ○ *She walked off without a word.* **2.** *vt.* **CURE SOMETHING BY WALKING** to get rid of something such as an injury or feeling of sickness by walking

walk off with *vt.* **1. STEAL SOMETHING** to steal something ○ *walked off with all the jewels* **2. WIN EASILY** to win something effortlessly

walk out *vi.* **1. LEAVE WITHOUT EXPLANATION** to leave, especially in anger or protest, without explanation **2. GO ON STRIKE** to go out on strike **3. LEAVE SOMEBODY PERMANENTLY** to leave a spouse, partner, or family permanently

walk out on *vt.* to leave or abandon somebody (*informal*) ○ *My wife walked out on me last summer.*

walk over *vt.* to win or defeat an opponent easily (*informal*) ○ *That horse will walk over the rest.*

walk through *vt.* **1.** ARTS **REHEARSE OR PERFORM A PLAY SKETCHILY** to rehearse something in a simple, unelaborate way, mainly practicing basic moves and positions, or perform something in a perfunctory, uncommitted way, as if still in rehearsal **2.** TV **REHEARSE WITHOUT CAMERAS** to rehearse a television program without cameras

walk·a·bout /wáwkə bòwt/ *n.* **1.** *Aus* **JOURNEY THROUGH BUSH** an extended journey through a remote area made by an Australian Aboriginal wishing to experience or return to a traditional way of life and to traditional beliefs **2. WALK** a walking trip (*informal*) ◇ **go walkabout 1.** *Aus* go for an extended journey on foot in remote country, traditionally alone and living off the land (*informal*) **2.** *Aus* leave your normal surroundings (*informal*)

walk·a·way /wáwkə wày/ *n.* **1. SOMETHING EASILY WON** an easily won contest or victory (*slang*) ○ *The election was a walkaway.* **2. SOMETHING EASILY DONE** something that can be easily done or accomplished (*informal*)

walk·er /wáwkər/ *n.* **1. SOMEBODY WHO WALKS** somebody who walks, especially regularly for exercise or in competition **2. SUPPORT FOR BABY** a lightweight framework on wheels that surrounds a baby, used to help a baby learn to walk **3. WALKING SUPPORT** a lightweight waist-high framework, usually with four legs and rubber feet, used to help somebody who cannot walk without support **4.** CLOTHES **WALKING SHOE** a shoe designed for walking

Alice Walker

Wal·ker /wáwkər/, **Alice** (*b.* 1944) U.S. writer. Her novels, including the Pulitzer Prize-winning *The Color Purple* (1982), are concerned largely with the experience of African American women. Full name **Alice Malsenior Walker**

Wal·ker, John George (*b.* 1952) New Zealand athlete. He won the 1,500 meters at the 1976 Olympic Games and was the first person to run a mile in less than 3 minutes 50 seconds (1975).

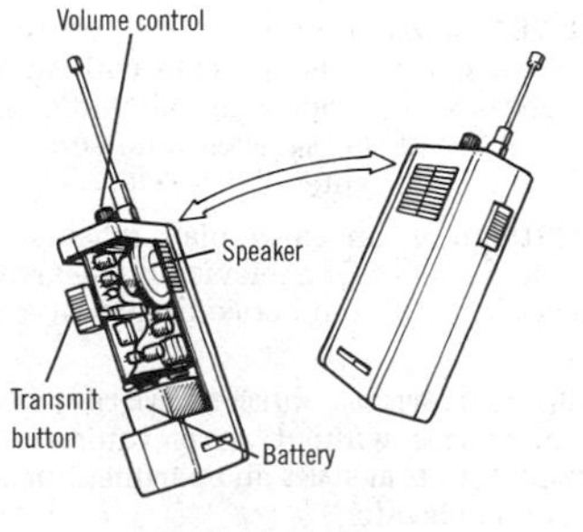

Walkie-talkie

walk·ie-talk·ie /wàwki táwkee/, **walk·y-talk·y** (*plural* **walk·y-talk·ies**) *n.* a hand-held battery-operated radio transmitter and receiver often used by emergency personnel to communicate with one another [Mid-20thC. A playful variant of WALK and TALK.]

walk-in /wáwk ìn/ *adj.* **1. LARGE ENOUGH TO ENTER** large and spacious enough to enter **2. LOCATED ON STREET** having direct access from the street ○ *a walk-in apartment* ■ *n.* **1. COLD STORAGE ROOM** a cold storage room or a refrigerator or freezer large enough to enter **2.** EASY VICTORY an easily won victory **3.** CUSTOMER WITHOUT APPOINTMENT somebody who requires a service and enters a place of business, e.g., a barber shop or doctor's office, without an appointment (*informal*) **4.** INTERNAT REL DEFECTOR somebody who walks into a foreign embassy or consulate wanting to leave his or her country

walk·ing /wáwking/ *adj.* **1.** ABLE TO WALK capable of walking **2.** FOR WALKING used or designed for the purpose of walking ○ *walking shoes* **3.** OF WALKING that involves traveling on foot ○ *a walking tour* ◇ **a walking dictionary** *or* **encyclopedia** somebody who is very knowledgeable

walk·ing bass /-bàyss/ *n.* a bass accompaniment, usually consisting of small steps or intervals up and down the scale in 4/4 time

walk·ing cat·fish *n.* a freshwater catfish native to tropical Asia with special organs that enable it to breathe on land for short periods while it moves to another body of water. Latin name: *Clarius batrachus.*

walk·ing del·e·gate *n.* a labor-union representative appointed to visit local unions and their employers to insure compliance with contracts and sometimes to represent the local union in negotiations

walk·ing fern *n.* a fern of eastern North America whose long arching fronds take root at the tip, sprouting new plants. Latin name: *Camptosorus rhizophyllus.*

walk·ing horse *n.* = **Tennessee walking horse**

walk·ing leaf *n.* **1.** = **walking fern 2.** = **leaf insect**

walk·ing pa·pers *npl.* official notification that somebody has been fired from a job or dismissed from military service (*informal*)

walk·ing stick *n.* **1.** STICK THAT HELPS WALKING a cane or stick used to assist in walking **2.** INSECTS INSECT RESEMBLING TWIG any of various long brown or green phasmid insects that resemble twigs, especially a North American species that feeds on leaves. Latin name: *Diapheromera femorata.*

walk·ing wound·ed *npl.* CASUALTIES WHO CAN WALK casualties of war, terrorism, or disaster who are able to walk despite their injuries ■ *n.* PEOPLE WHO HAVE BEEN HURT people who continue to be affected by great emotional pain experienced during their lives

Walk·man /wáwkmən/ *tdmk.* a trademark for a small portable cassette player with earphones

walk of life *n.* somebody's occupation or social or economic class ○ *people from all walks of life*

walk-on *n.* **1.** SMALL PART IN PLAY OR MOVIE a small part, usually a nonspeaking one, in a stage or movie production **2.** SOMEBODY WITH BRIEF PART somebody who has a small part, usually a nonspeaking one, in a stage or movie production

walk·out /wáwk òwt/ *n.* **1.** EMPLOYEE STRIKE an organized strike by employees in which workers walk out of the building or off the premises **2.** ACT OF LEAVING AS PROTEST a departure in protest or anger about something

walk·o·ver /wáwk òvər/ *n.* **1.** EASY VICTORY an easy victory or one that is obtained without a contest, e.g., because the opposing side did not show (*informal*) **2.** RACE WITH ONE HORSE a horserace in which only one horse is entered

walk-through *n.* an early play rehearsal without props or costumes, or a television rehearsal without cameras, usually to practice basic moves and positions

walk-up *n.* **1.** BUILDING WITHOUT ELEVATOR a building of several stories without an elevator (*informal*) **2.** APARTMENT REACHED BY STAIRS an apartment in a building without an elevator

walk·way /wáwk wày/ *n.* a specially constructed path for pedestrians

Wal·kyr·ie *n.* = **Valkyrie**

walk·y-talk·y *n.* = **walkie-talkie**

wall /wawl/ *n.* **1.** FLAT SIDE OF BUILDING OR ROOM a vertical structure forming an inside partition or an outside surface of a building **2.** STANDING STRUCTURE THAT SURROUNDS OR BLOCKS a narrow upright structure, usually built of stone, wood, plaster, or brick, that acts as a boundary or keeps something in or out **3.** SOMETHING IMPENETRABLE something similar to a wall in appearance or impenetrability ○ *met with a wall of reporters* **4.** SOMETHING THAT PREVENTS COMMUNICATION an obstacle to understanding or communication between people **5.** ANAT BODY MEMBRANE OR LINING a membrane or lining enclosing or bounding an organ, blood vessel, or cavity of the body ○ *the uterine wall* **6.** MOUNTAINEERING ROCK FACE a vertical or nearly vertical rock face ○ *a sheer wall of granite* **7.** BUILDING DEFENSIVE STRUCTURE a structure of earth or stone built for defensive purposes **8.** CIV ENG BARRIER TO FLOODING a structure built as a barrier to flooding **9.** SOCCER LINE OF DEFENSIVE PLAYERS in soccer, a line of defensive players who must stand at least ten yards from a free kick and who try to block a shot on goal **10.** BIOL RIGID COVERING FOR CELLS a rigid covering over the outer membranes of plant cells and of some prokaryotic animal cells ■ **walls** *npl.* BARRIERS TO INTIMACY protective behavior used by somebody to keep others from getting too close ■ *vt.* (**walled, wall·ing, walls**) **1.** SURROUND SOMETHING WITH WALLS to fortify or surround something or somebody with a wall ○ *They walled in the back yard.* **2.** SEPARATE SOMETHING WITH WALLS to put up a wall to separate one area from another **3.** CLOSE SOMETHING WITH WALL to close an opening with a wall ○ *wall up the passage* **4.** TRAP OR BURY BEHIND WALLS to seal somebody or something in a space with a wall [Pre-12thC. From Latin *vallum*, "rampart," from *vallus*, "stake" (source also of English *interval*).] —**walled** *adj.* ◇ **be climbing the wall** *or* **walls** to be extremely bored or frustrated (*informal*) ◇ **drive somebody up the wall** to annoy or irritate somebody extremely (*informal*) ◇ **go to the wall** to be destroyed or ruined, especially financially

wal·la *n.* = **wallah**

Wallaby

wal·la·by /wáaləbee/ (*plural* **-bies**) *n.* any of various marsupials of Australia and New Guinea that resemble small kangaroos. Family: Macropodidae. [Early 19thC. From Dharuk *walabi* and *waliba*.]

Barnaby's

Edgar Wallace

Wal·lace /wólləss/, **Edgar** (1875–1932) British writer. He wrote more than 170 popular crime novels and thrillers, beginning with *The Four Just Men* (1905). Full name **Richard Horatio Edgar Wallace**

Wal·lace /wólliss/, **Henry A.** (1888–1965) U.S. agriculturalist and statesman. With his father, Henry Cantwell Wallace, he developed the first successful hybrid seed maize. He became vice president during Franklin D. Roosevelt's third term (1941–45), and ran for president as a progressive in 1948. Full name **Henry Agard Wallace**

Wal·lace, Lew (1827–1905) U.S. writer and statesman. A veteran of the Mexican War and the Civil War, he was governor of New Mexico (1878–81) and minister to Turkey (1881–85). He wrote *Ben Hur* (1880). Full name **Lewis Wallace**

Barnaby's

Sir William Wallace: Commemorative statue near Melrose, Scotland

Wal·lace, Sir William (1272?–1305) Scottish patriot. He led a rebellion against the English (1297), but was defeated by Edward I (1298). He was later captured and executed.

Wal·lace's line /wólləssəz-/ *n.* a hypothetical boundary in the southwestern Pacific separating the Oriental and Australian biogeographic regions and their distinctive types of wildlife. The line runs between Bali and Lombok in the Indonesian island chain and north through the Makassar Strait, passing south of the Philippines. [Mid-19thC. Named for Alfred Russel *Wallace* (1823–1913), the English naturalist who defined this boundary.]

wal·lah /wóllə/, **wal·la** *n.* somebody in charge of a specified thing or associated with a particular service or occupation (*dated informal*) ○ *a legal wallah* [Late 18thC. Via Hindi *-vālā*, "(somebody) responsible for something or some duty," from Sanskrit *pālaka*, "keeper."]

wal·la·roo /wòllə ro͞o/ (*plural* **-roos** *or* **-roo**) *n.* either of two species of large and sturdy kangaroo found throughout rocky upland areas of mainland Australia. Latin name: *Macropus robustus* and *Macropus bernardus.* [Early 19thC. From Dharuk *walaru*.]

wall bars *npl.* a series of horizontal bars attached to a wall and used for exercises

wall·board /wáwl bàwrd/ *n.* = **plasterboard**

wall creep·er *n.* a songbird of rocky mountainous regions of Europe and Asia that has a long slender beak and black wings with scarlet markings. It is related to the nuthatch. Latin name: *Tichodroma muraria.*

Wal·ler /wóllər/, **Fats** (1904–43) U.S. singer, pianist, and composer. He wrote and performed many jazz classics such as "Ain't Misbehavin" (1929). Real name **Thomas Wright Waller**

wal·let /wóllət/ *n.* **1.** POCKET-SIZED FOLDED CASE FOR MONEY a small flat folding case usually made of leather or plastic that holds paper money and credit cards and is usually carried in a pocket or purse **2.** COMPUT SOFTWARE FOR ON-LINE PURCHASES a software program that is used to carry out transactions for on-line purchases made on the Internet **3.** FOLDER a folder for holding items such as papers, photographs, or maps [14thC. Origin uncertain: probably via an Anglo-Norman word for "traveling pack," from a Germanic word for "roll."]

wall·eye /wáwl ī/ (*plural* **walleye** *or* **wall·eyes**) *n.* **1.** ZOOL FRESHWATER FISH OF N AMERICA a large predatory freshwater fish of northeastern North America that has large eyes and is related to the perch. Latin name: *Stizostedion vitreum.* **2.** OPHTHALMOL EYE THAT APPEARS WHITE an eye with a white or streaked iris, giving the appearance of a pale ring around the pupil **3.** OPHTHALMOL WHITE IN CORNEA an eye with an opaque white cornea, or the condition that causes this opacity **4.** OPHTHALMOL OUTWARD TURNING EYES a form of squint (**strabismus**) in which one or both eyes turn outward [Early 16thC. Back-formation from WALLEYED.]

wall·eyed /wáwl īd/ *adj.* **1.** OPHTHALMOL HAVING WALLEYE having any of the medical conditions known as walleye **2.** WITH BULGING EYES having bulging or staring eyes [14thC. From a Scandinavian word meaning "speckle-eyed."]

wall·eyed pike *n.* ZOOL = **walleye** *n.* **2**

wall·eyed pol·lack *n.* an important northern Pacific food fish of the cod family that resembles the pollack. Latin name: *Theragra chalcogramma.*

wall·flow·er /wáwl flòwr/ *n.* **1.** PLANTS **SPRING-FLOWERING GARDEN PLANT** a common garden plant with rather woody erect stems and fragrant yellow, orange, or brownish flowers clustered at the top of the stem, that blooms in early spring. Genera: *Cheirantus* and *Erysimum*. **2.** PLANTS **PLANT WITH FRAGRANT COLORFUL FLOWERS** a plant originally from southern Europe with fragrant colorful flowers, often found growing on walls, rocks, and cliffs. Latin name: *Cheiranthus cheiri*. **3. SOMEBODY UNNOTICED AT SOCIAL EVENT** a shy or retiring person who remains unnoticed at social events, especially a woman without a dance partner (*informal*)

wall hang·ing *n.* a tapestry or other large flat object hung on a wall as a decoration

Wal·lis and Fu·tuna Is·lands /wòlliss ənd foo tóonə-/ island group situated in the southwestern Pacific Ocean, northeast of Fiji. It is an overseas territory of France. Capital: Mata Utu. Population: 13,705 (1988). Area: 77 sq. mi./200 sq. km.

wall liz·ard *n.* a lizard that can be found on walls and rocks. Family: Lacertidae.

wall mus·tard *n.* = **wall rocket**

wall of sound *n.* a type of recorded sound on pop records achieved by overdubbing or layering many different instruments around a pop tune

Wal·loon /wo lóon, wə-/ *n.* **1.** PEOPLES **FRENCH-SPEAKING BELGIAN** a member of a French-speaking people living in southern Belgium, mainly in the autonomous region of Wallonia, and in neighboring parts of France. ◊ **Fleming 2.** LANG **BELGIAN DIALECT OF FRENCH** the dialect of French spoken in southern Belgium and nearby areas of France [Mid-16thC. Via French *Wallon* from the medieval Latin stem *wallo(n)-*, "foreigner," ultimately from the same prehistoric Germanic word as English *Welsh*.] —**Wal·loon** *adj.*

wal·lop /wólləp/ *vt.* (**-loped, -lop·ing, -lops**) (*informal*) **1. HIT SOMEBODY VERY HARD** to strike something or somebody with great force ○ *She can really wallop the ball.* **2. BEAT SOMEBODY** to give somebody a sound physical beating **3. DEFEAT SOMEBODY DECISIVELY** to defeat a person or team decisively ■ *n.* (*informal*) **1. HARD HIT** a powerful blow **2. ABILITY TO HIT HARD** the ability to strike a powerful blow ○ *He's got a wallop that could make him heavyweight champion.* **3. ABILITY TO IMPRESS** the ability to create a powerful impression on others [14thC. From Old French *waloper*, variant of *galoper*, "to gallop" (source of English *gallop*), literally "to run well," from the prehistoric Germanic ancestors of English *well* and *leap*.]

wal·lop·ing /wólləping/ *n.* (*informal*) **1. BEATING** a sound physical beating **2. DECISIVE DEFEAT** a decisive defeat or victory ■ *adj.* **BIG** very large or impressive (*informal*) ○ *The angler came back with a walloping catch.* ■ *adv.* **VERY** to an extreme degree (*informal*) ○ *a walloping big lie*

wal·low /wóllō/ *vi.* (**-lowed, -low·ing, -lows**) **1. ROLL IN SOMETHING** to lie down and roll around in something ○ *hogs wallowing in mud* **2. HEAVILY INDULGE IN SOMETHING** to immerse yourself in something, e.g., an emotion or material wealth, in a self-indulgent way **3. HAVE HUGE AMOUNT OF SOMETHING** to be amply or overly supplied with something ○ *We suddenly found ourselves wallowing in kittens.* **4. WALK WITH DIFFICULTY** to move clumsily, as if in mud ■ *n.* **1. ACT OF WALLOWING** an instance of wallowing in something such as mud, emotion, or material luxury **2.** ZOOL **PLACE WHERE ANIMALS ROLL** a muddy, wet, or dusty place which animals use to roll around in **3.** ZOOL **DEPRESSION FORMED BY ANIMAL** a sunken area in the ground made by a rolling animal **4. CONDITION OF DEPRAVITY** a state of degradation or low behavior [Old English *wealwian*, "to roll." Ultimately from the same Indo-European ancestor as English *revolve, waltz, helix*, and *wallet*.] —**wal·low·er** *n.*

wall·pa·per /wáwl pàypər/ *n.* **1. PAPER TO DECORATE WALLS** paper, usually printed with a pattern, that is pasted on walls and sometimes ceilings **2.** COMPUT **BACKGROUND PATTERN FOR COMPUTER** the graphic background pattern for a computer screen ■ *vti.* (**-pered, -per·ing, -pers**) **PUT UP WALLPAPER** to cover a surface with wallpaper

wall plug *n.* a receptacle in the wall connected to an electric circuit, into which appliances can be plugged

wall rock *n.* the rock that surrounds a vein, mineral deposit, or fault

wall rock·et *n.* either of two cruciferous plants bearing yellow flowers that are native to Europe and grow on walls and waste ground. Latin name: *Diplotaxis muralis* and *Diplotaxis tenuifolia.*

wall rue *n.* a small delicate fern that grows in fan-shaped clusters on walls or in rocky crevices. Latin name: *Asplenium ruta-muraria.*

Wall Street *n.* **1. NEW YORK STREET OF STOCK EXCHANGE** the street in Manhattan, New York City, where the New York Stock Exchange and many major financial institutions of the United States are located **2. U.S. FINANCIAL MARKET** the U.S. financial market, especially as represented by the publicly traded companies comprising the stock markets

wall-to-wall *adj.* **1. FROM ONE WALL TO ANOTHER** completely covering a floor or floors ○ *wall-to-wall carpeting* **2. CROWDED WITH SOMETHING** completely filling, covering, or pervading something, or occurring nonstop (*informal*) ○ *fed up with wall-to-wall pop music* ■ *n.* **FITTED CARPET** a carpet that completely covers a floor

wal·ly /wóllee/ (*plural* **-lies**) *n. U.K.* an offensive term that deliberately insults somebody's intelligence or common sense (*slang*) [Mid-20thC. Origin uncertain: perhaps from the name *Wally*, from *Walter*.]

wal·nut /wáwl nùt, -nət/ *n.* **1.** TREES **TREE VALUED FOR NUTS AND WOOD** a large deciduous tree with fragrant compound leaves and drooping catkins, grown worldwide for its shade, wood, and nuts. Genus: *Juglans.* **2.** FOOD **NUT OF WALNUT TREE** the edible nut of a walnut tree, which has a deeply wrinkled surface and is enclosed in a hard shell and a thick leathery husk **3.** INDUST **WALNUT WOOD** the wood of a walnut tree used in cabinetry, for paneling, and veneer (*often used before a noun*) **4.** COLORS **LIGHT-BROWN COLOR** a light yellowish-brown color like that of the wood of the walnut tree ■ *adj.* COLORS **OF LIGHT-BROWN COLOR** of a light yellowish-brown color [14thC. From Old English *wealhnutu*, literally "foreign nut," from *wealh*, "foreign, Welsh, Celtic."]

WORD KEY: ORIGIN

The prehistoric Germanic peoples regarded the ***walnut*** as the "foreign nut" because it did not originally grow in northern Europe but was introduced from Gaul and Italy, the lands of the Celts and the Romans (the Germans' own native nut was the hazel).

Wal·pole /wáwlpōl, wól-/ town in eastern Massachusetts, west of Stoughton and southwest of Boston. Population: 22,251 (1996).

Wal·pole /wáwl pōl/, **Sir Robert, 1st Earl of Orford** (1676–1745) British statesman. He became a Whig member of Parliament in 1701. From 1721 to 1742 he wielded considerable political power as chief minister to George I and George II. Although he himself repudiated the title, which did not become official until much later, he is regarded as Britain's first prime minister.

Wal·pur·gis night /vaal póorgiss nīt/, **Wal·pur·gis Night** *n.* **1. WITCH'S FESTIVAL** the eve of May Day, believed in German folklore to be the witch's feast night on the Brocken in the Harz mountains **2. WILD OR SCARY EVENT** a wild celebration or a nightmarish situation [Early 19thC. Translation of German *Walpurgisnacht*, named for *Walpurga*, an 8thC Anglo-Saxon saint, venerated by Christians on this date (the night before her remains were buried at Eichstätt in Germany).]

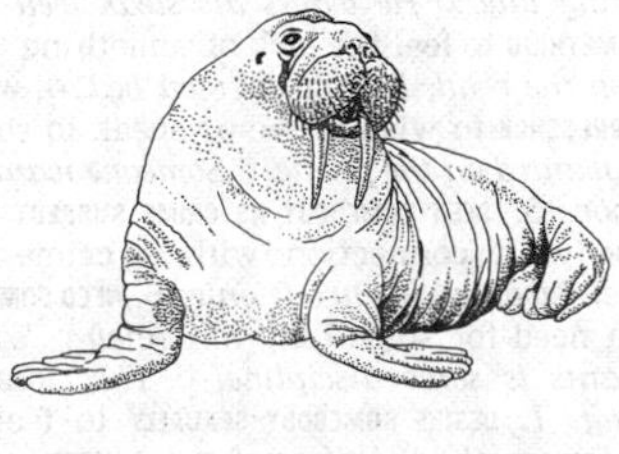

Walrus

wal·rus /wáwlrəss/ (*plural* **-rus** *or* **-rus·es**) *n.* a large Arctic sea mammal related to seals and sea lions, with tough wrinkled skin, large tusks, and bristly whiskers. Latin name: *Odobenus rosmarus.* [Early 18thC. From Dutch *walrus, walros*, literally "whale-horse," from *walvis(ch)*, "whale."]

wal·rus mus·tache *n.* a thick drooping mustache resembling a walrus's whiskers

Wa·łę·sa /waa lénssə, vaa wénssə/, **Lech** (*b.* 1943) Polish trade unionist and statesman. At the head of Solidarity after 1980, he led Poland's independent labor movement and was instrumental in ending Communist rule there. He won the Nobel Peace Prize in 1983. He was the president of Poland from 1990 to 1995.

Wal·ter /vaáltər, wáwl-/, **Bruno** (1876–1972) German-born U.S. conductor. As chief conductor of several orchestras of international renown, he was best known for his interpretations of the music of Mozart, Bruckner, and Mahler. Real name **Bruno Walter Schlesinger**

Wal·ter Mit·ty /wàwltər míttee/ (*plural* **Wal·ter Mit·ties**) *n.* an ordinary person who daydreams about great personal adventure and success [Mid-20thC. Named for the hero of "The Secret Life of Walter Mitty," a 1939 short story by James Thurber, about such a daydreamer.] —**Wal·ter Mit·ty·ish** *adj.*

Popperfoto

Barbara Walters

Wal·ters /wáwltərz/, **Barbara** (*b.* 1931) U.S. television journalist. As a reporter and host of television news magazines and celebrity interview shows, she established a reputation for eliciting candid answers to difficult questions from public figures.

Wal·tham /wáwlthəm, wólthəm/ city in eastern Massachusetts, southwest of Arlington. Founded in 1636, it is a western suburb of Boston. Population: 57,214 (1996).

Wal·ton /wáwltən/, **Ernest T. S.** (1903–95) Irish physicist. He helped develop a particle accelerator, which led to the first artificial nuclear reaction. He shared a Nobel Prize in physics (1951). Full name **Ernest Thomas Sinton Walton**

Wal·ton /wáwlt'n/, **Izaak** (1593–1683) English writer. He is remembered for his contemplation on fishing and the charms of pastoral life, *The Compleat Angler* (1653).

Wal·ton, Sir William (1902–83) British composer. He wrote orchestral works, an opera, and movie scores including the music for Laurence Olivier's adaptations of Shakespeare's plays. Full name **Sir William Turner Walton**

waltz /wawlts/ *n.* (*plural* **waltz·es**) **1.** DANCE **DANCE FOR COUPLES IN TRIPLE TIME** a ballroom dance in triple time in which the couple turns continuously while moving around the dance floor **2.** MUSIC **MUSIC FOR WALTZ** a piece of music for a waltz, in triple time **3. SOMETHING EASY** something that can be accomplished effortlessly (*informal*) ■ *v.* (**waltzed, waltz·ing, waltz·es**) **1.** *vti.* DANCE **DANCE WALTZ** to dance or lead somebody in a waltz **2.** *vi.* **MOVE IN RELAXED MANNER** to move in a relaxed and confident manner (*informal*) ○ *She just waltzed right in and demanded more money.* **3.** *vi.* **GO THROUGH SOMETHING EASILY** to accomplish something effortlessly [Late 18thC. From German *Walzer*, from *walzen*, "to waltz, roll, revolve." Ultimately from the same Indo-European ancestor as English *wallow* and *revolve*.]

waltz Matilda *v. Aus* to wander around looking for work carrying one's belongings in a pack (*dated slang*)

Waltz·ing Ma·til·da /wàwltsing mə tíldə/ *n.* a traditional Australian song that tells the story of a vagrant worker (**swagman**) who commits suicide at a waterhole to avoid being arrested for sheep-stealing (*informal*) [Because of the dancing motion of a pack carried on somebody's shoulder; Matilda "personal pack, bundle," from the name]

Wal·vis Bay /wàwlviss-/ town and port in western Namibia, on the Atlantic coast. It was a former enclave of South Africa until 1994. Population: 16,652 (1985).

Wam·pa·no·ag /wòmpə nṓ àg/ (*plural* **-ag** *or* **-ags**) *n.* a member of a Native North American people who once occupied lands in Rhode Island and Massachusetts [Late 17thC. From Narragansett, literally "easterners."] —**Wam·pa·no·ag** *adj.*

wam·pum /wómpəm/, **wam·pum·peag** /wómpəm peeg/ *n.* **1. DECORATIVE BEADS USED AS MONEY** small polished beads made from shells, threaded on string, used by some Native North Americans as decoration, for ceremonial purposes, or formerly for money **2. MONEY** money (*dated slang*) [Mid-17thC. Shortening of *wampumpeag*, from Algonquian, literally "white strings," from *wap*, "white" + *umpe*, "string."]

wan /won/ *adj.* (**wan·ner, wan·nest**) **1. PALE** unhealthily pale, especially from illness or grief **2. INDICATIVE OF LOW SPIRITS** suggesting ill health or unhappiness ○ *He gave me a wan look.* **3. FAINT** lacking brightness ○ *a wan star* ■ *vti.* (**wanned, wan·ning, wans**) **MAKE OR BECOME PALE OR ILL** to make something pale, or become pale or unhealthy (*literary*) [Old English *wann*, "dark, dusky, gray," of unknown origin] —**wan·ly** *adv.* —**wan·ness** *n.*

WAN /wan/ *abbr.* wide area network

Wan·a·ma·ker /wónnə màykər/, **John** (1838–1922) U.S. merchant. He began a clothing business in Philadelphia (1861), which expanded to become one of the leading department store chains in the United States.

wand /wond/ *n.* **1. ROD WITH MAGICAL POWERS** a thin rod believed to possess magical powers, used by supposed magicians, wizards, and supernatural beings **2. STAFF SHOWING AUTHORITY** a thin staff carried as a symbol of office **3.** HOUSEHOLD **VACUUM CLEANER PART** an attachment between the hose and cleaning tool of a vacuum cleaner that resembles a pipe **4.** COMPUT **BAR-CODE SCANNER** a hand-held optical scanning device used to read and enter bar-code information into a computer **5.** MUSIC **BATON** a conductor's baton **6.** BOT **SLENDER PLANT SHOOT** a slender bendable shoot of a shrub or tree (*archaic*) [12thC. Via Old Norse *vondr*, "straight flexible stick" from a prehistoric Germanic word meaning "turn" (ancestor of English *wander* and *went*).]

wan·der /wóndər/ *v.* (**-dered, -der·ing, -ders**) **1.** *vti.* **TRAVEL WITHOUT A DESTINATION** to move from place to place, either without a purpose or without a known destination ○ *They wander the countryside looking for work.* **2.** *vi.* **LEAVE A FIXED PATH** to stray from a particular course ○ *Don't wander far from the path.* **3.** *vi.* **DAYDREAM** to lose the ability to concentrate on or listen to a particular thing ○ *My mind was wandering.* **4.** *vi.* **TAKE A CURVING PATH** to follow a winding course ○ *The river wandered through the meadows.* **5.** *vi.* **STROLL SOMEWHERE** to go somewhere at a leisurely pace **6.** *vi.* **FAIL TO THINK OR SPEAK CLEARLY** to lose the ability to think, speak, or write in an organized and coherent way ■ *n.* **AIMLESS STROLL** an aimless or leisurely moving from place to place [Old English *wandrian*, from a prehistoric Germanic word meaning "turn," which also produced English *wand*] —**wan·der·er** *n.* —**wan·der·ing** *adj.* —**wan·der·ing·ly** *adv.*

wan·der·ing al·ba·tross *n.* a large albatross of southern seas with a white body and black wings and tail that spends most of its life in flight at sea. Latin name: *Diomedea exulans.*

wan·der·ing Jew *n.* any of three tropical American trailing plants widely grown as houseplants for their variegated foliage and white or rose-red flowers. Latin name: *Tradescantia fluminensis* and *Tradescantia albiflora* and *Zebrina pendula.*

Wan·der·ing Jew *n.* in medieval legend, a Jewish man, sometimes named as Ahasuerus, condemned to remain alive wandering the earth until Judgment Day for having mocked Jesus Christ on the day of the Crucifixion

wan·der·lust /wóndər lùst/ *n.* a strong desire to travel [Early 20thC. From German, literally "desire to travel."]

wane /wayn/ *vi.* (**waned, wan·ing, wanes**) **1. SHOW LESS LIGHTED AREA** to show a decreasing illuminated surface between a full moon and new moon (*refers to the moon or a planet*) **2. GET SMALLER OR LESS** to decrease gradually in intensity or power ○ *His interest was waning.* **3. FINISH** to draw to a close ○ *Winter is waning at last.* ■ *n.* **1. DECREASE IN INTENSITY** a gradual lessening of power or intensity **2. TIME DURING MOON'S WANE** the period during which the moon's visible illuminated surface is decreasing in size **3. PERIOD OF LESSENING** a period of gradual decrease **4. END OF PERIOD** the conclusion of a time or season ○ *the wane of summer* **5.** WOODWORK **IRREGULARITY ON PLANK'S EDGE** a defective edge left on a rough-sawn plank [Old English *wanian*, "to lessen," from a prehistoric Germanic word meaning "lacking"] ◇ **be on the wane** decrease or pass out of fashion

Wang·a·nu·i /wòngə nōō ee/ river in the southwestern part of the North Island, New Zealand. It rises on Mount Tongariro and flows southward through the city of Wanganui to the Cook Strait. Length: 180 mi./290 km.

wan·gle /wáng g'l/ *vt.* (**-gled, -gling, -gles**) **1. GET SOMETHING DEVIOUSLY** to get something using indirect and sometimes deceitful methods (*informal*) ○ *I'm trying to wangle some time off work.* **2. FALSIFY ACCOUNTS** to manipulate accounts or records, usually deceitfully ■ *n.* **DISHONEST METHOD** a devious means of accomplishing something [Late 19thC. Origin uncertain: perhaps a variant of WAGGLE. The meaning "to get something deviously" evolved from printer's slang, "to manipulate type to achieve a desired appearance."] —**wang·ler** *n.*

wan·i·gan /wónnigən/ *n.* **1.** *Northeast U.S., Northwest U.S.* **BOAT OR CHEST OF LUMBER SUPPLIES** a boat or chest equipped with supplies for a lumber camp **2.** *Northeast U.S., Northwest U.S.* **CAMP SUPPLIES** supplies for a camp or cabin **3. LIVING QUARTERS ON RUNNERS** a cabin on runners towed behind a trailer used as living quarters in Alaska for a work crew (*regional*) **4. TRAILER HOUSE ADDITION** an addition built on a trailer house in Alaska for extra space (*regional*) [Mid-19thC. From Montagnais *atawangan*, from *atawan*, "to buy or sell."]

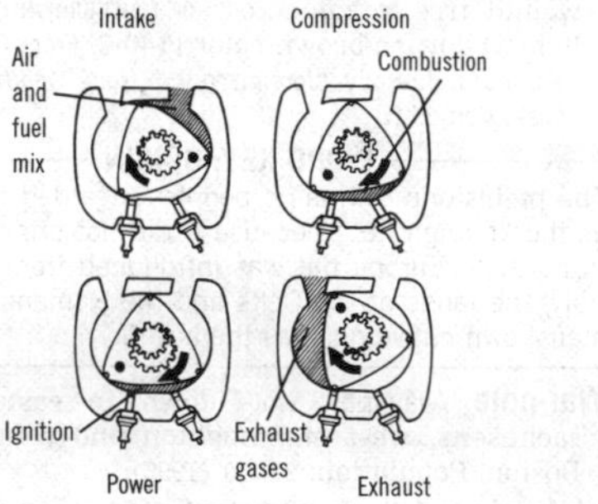

Wankel engine

Wan·kel en·gine /wángk'l-/ *n.* an internal-combustion engine in which an approximately triangular rotor inside an elliptical combustion chamber replaces the pistons of a conventional engine, thus reducing the number of moving parts [Mid-20thC. Named for Felix *Wankel* (1902–88), the German engineer who invented it.]

wan·na /wónnə/ *vt.* want to (*nonstandard*) ○ *I wanna go!* [Late 19thC. Alteration of *want to.*]

wan·na·be /wónnəbee/ *n.* somebody who is trying to be like another person or to belong to a particular group (*informal disapproving*) [Late 20thC. Alteration of *want to be.*]

want /wont/ *vt.* (**want·ed, want·ing, wants**) **1. DESIRE SOMETHING** to feel a need or desire for something ○ *We want a new car.* **2. WISH SOMETHING DONE** to desire to do something or that something be done ○ *I don't want you being late.* ○ *He wants his steak well done.* **3. MISS SOMETHING** to feel the lack of something ○ *After a week on the road, I want my own bed.* **4. WISH SOMEBODY'S PRESENCE** to wish to see or speak to somebody ○ *He's wanted on the phone.* ○ *Someone wants you at the door.* **5. SEEK SOMEBODY AS CRIME SUSPECT** to seek somebody in connection with a crime (*usually passive*) ○ *wanted for two felonies* **6. NEED SOMETHING** to have a need for something (*informal*) ○ *What that kid wants is some discipline!* ○ *The closets want cleaning.* **7. DESIRE SOMEBODY SEXUALLY** to feel sexual desire for somebody (*informal*) ■ *n.* **1. NEED** something that somebody desires or needs (*usually used in the plural*) ○ *All your wants can be easily supplied.* **2. LACK OF SOMETHING** an absence or shortage of something ○ *There's been no want of snow for the skiers this winter.* **3. POVERTY** the state of being poor ○ *Freedom from want is a fundamental human right.* [12thC. Via Old Norse *vanta*, "to be lacking," from a prehistoric Germanic word meaning "lacking" (ancestor of English *wane* and *wanton*).] —**want·er** *n.* ◇ **for want of** through the lack of something ○ *No one should be left behind for want of opportunity.*

WORD KEY: SYNONYMS

want, desire, wish, long, yearn, covet, crave

CORE MEANING: to seek to have, do, or achieve something

want a fairly informal and general word meaning to seek to have, do, or achieve something; **desire** a more formal and often stronger alternative to "want." It can be used specifically to talk about sexual attraction; **wish** a more formal alternative to "want," often suggesting that the thing wanted will be very difficult or impossible to attain; **long** emphasizes that somebody wants something very much; **yearn** to want something very much, especially when it seems unlikely that it can ever be obtained; **covet** often used for wanting something that belongs to another person. It can also be used to indicate that somebody wants something very much; **crave** to desire something very much, especially when this desire is physical.

want for *vt.* to experience the lack of something ○ *The family wants for nothing.*

want in *vi.* (*informal*) **1. WANT TO BE INCLUDED** to wish to be included in something, especially to want to invest in a business deal ○ *Do you want in?* **2. WANT TO ENTER** to wish to go inside a place ○ *See if the cat wants in.*

want out *vi.* (*informal*) **1. WISH NOT TO TAKE PART** to wish to be excluded from or to leave something, especially a business deal ○ *We want out before we get into trouble.* **2. DESIRE TO GET OUTSIDE** to wish to go outside a building ○ *The dog wants out.*

want ad *n.* a classified advertisement in a newspaper or magazine (*informal*)

want·ing /wónting/ *adj.* not meeting expectations or requirements ○ *found wanting in the area of security*

wan·ton /wóntən/ *adj.* **1. SEXUALLY INDISCRIMINATE** without restraint, or inhibition especially in sexual behavior **2. RANDOM** without reason or provocation ○ *wanton violence and destruction* **3. DESIRING TO DO HARM** done out of a desire to cause harm **4. EXCESSIVE** unrestrained, heedless of reasonable limits, or characterized by greed and extravagance ○ *wanton indulgence* **5. UNRULY** lacking discipline **6. LUSH** growing luxuriantly (*archaic*) **7. PLAYFUL** engaged in play that is carefree (*archaic*) ■ *n.* **1. SOMEBODY WITHOUT SEXUAL RESTRAINT** somebody who is lascivious or sexually uninhibited **2. SOMEBODY PLAYFUL** a playful person (*archaic*) **3. SOMEBODY GROWING UNRULY** an undisciplined person (*archaic*) ■ *vi.* (**-toned, -ton·ing, -tons**) **BE WANTON** to behave in a wanton manner (*archaic*) [14thC. From Old English *wan-*, "un+" + *togen*, "disciplined," from *tēon*, "to train, discipline, pull."] —**wan·ton·ly** *adv.* —**wan·ton·ness** *n.*

wap·i·ti /wóppitee/ (*plural* **-tis** *or* **-ti**) *n.* a large North American deer, found especially in the mountainous west, that has tall branched antlers and lives in herds. Latin name: *Cervus elaphus.* [Early 19thC. From Shawnee *wapiti*, literally "white rump."]

Wap·pin·ger /wóppinjər/ (*plural* **-ger** *or* **-gers**) *n.* a member of a Native North American people who formerly occupied lands along the Hudson River in New York State, and whose members dispersed following wars with Dutch settlers in the 17th century

war /wawr/ *n.* **1. ARMED FIGHTING BETWEEN GROUPS** an armed conflict between countries or groups that involves killing and destruction ○ *The two countries are at war.* **2. PERIOD DURING WAR** a period of armed conflict ○ *during the Vietnam War* **3. METHODS OF WARFARE** the techniques or the study of the techniques of armed conflict **4. CONFLICT** any serious struggle, argument, or conflict between people ○ *The candidates are at war.* **5. SERIOUS EFFORT TO END SOMETHING** an effort to eradicate something harmful ○ *a war against drugs* ■ *vi.* (**warred, war·ring, wars**) **1. MAKE WAR** to engage in an armed conflict with somebody **2. BE IN A STRUGGLE** to be involved in a serious disagreement with somebody or a struggle to combat or eradicate something [12thC. Via Old Northern French *werre* from Old French *guerre*, ultimately from a prehistoric Germanic word meaning "strife, confusion."]

WORD KEY: SYNONYMS

See Synonyms at ***fight.***

WORD KEY: CULTURAL NOTE

War and Peace, a novel by Russian writer Leo Tolstoy (1865–69). This monumental work is set in Russia during and after the Napoleonic Wars (1805–14). Though it focuses on five fictional families, the story incorporates historical accounts and philosophical essays to create an extraordinarily comprehensive portrait of Russian society that touches on almost every aspect of human experience from love and happiness to grief and war.

---

war. *abbr.* warrant

war ba·by *n.* a baby born or conceived during a war

War Be·tween the States *n.* = **Civil War** *n.* 1

war·ble[1] /wáwrb'l/ *vti.* (**-bled, -bling, -bles**) **1. SING NOTES WITH TRILLS** to sing a song or note with trills or other vocal modulations ○ *a songbird warbling outside my window* **2. SING SOMETHING** to sing, or express something in song ○ *warble a tune* ■ *n.* **1. MODULATED SINGING** singing with trills or other vocal modulations **2. MODULATED SOUND** a sound with trills or quavers [14thC. Via Old Northern French *werbler,* "to sing with trills," from a Frankish word for "whirl, trill."]

war·ble[2] /wáwrb'l/ *n.* **1.** VET **SWELLING IN HORSES AND CATTLE** a swelling under the skin that forms usually on the back in horses and cattle, caused by the warble fly maggot **2.** INSECTS **WARBLE FLY OR ITS LARVAE** the warble fly, or the maggot of the warble fly **3.** VET **LUMP ON HORSE'S BACK FROM SADDLE** a hard tumorous lump of tissue on the back of a riding horse caused by the rubbing of the saddle [Late 16thC. Origin uncertain: perhaps from Scandinavian.]

war·ble fly *n.* a large hairy fly, the larvae of which form painful swellings under the skin of cattle and horses. Family: Oestridae.

war·bler /wáwrblər/ *n.* **1.** BIRDS **SMALL SINGING BIRD** a small American songbird that eats insects and is often brightly colored. Family: Parulidae. **2.** BIRDS **THRUSH RELATIVE** a songbird of Europe and Asia that is related to the thrush. Family: Sylviidae. **3. SOMEBODY WHO WARBLES** somebody who warbles or sings

war·bling vir·e·o *n.* a small gray North American bird with a distinctive warbling song. Latin name: *Virio gilvus.*

war bon·net *n.* a ceremonial headdress decorated with feathers, worn by some Native North American warriors

war bride *n.* a woman who meets and marries a serviceman during wartime, especially one from another country

war chest *n.* funds collected to pay for a war or a campaign of any sort

war clouds *npl.* signs of impending war

war cor·re·spon·dent *n.* a journalist reporting from a war

war crime *n.* a crime committed during wartime that is in violation of international agreements concerning the conventions of war, e.g., the mistreatment of prisoners or genocide (*often used in the plural*) —**war crim·i·nal** *n.*

war cry *n.* = **battle cry** *n.* 1

ward /wawrd/ *n.* **1.** POL **CITY DIVISION** an administrative or electoral division of an area such as a city, town, or county **2.** MED **ROOM IN HOSPITAL** a room in a hospital, especially one for several patients being given similar treatment **3. PRISON DIVISION** a division in a prison **4.** LAW **SOMEBODY UNDER OFFICIAL CARE** somebody, especially a child or young person, who is under the care of a guardian or a court **5.** BUILDING **AREA IN CASTLE** an open area within the walls of a castle **6.** LAW **CUSTODY** a state of official custody or protection **7. DEFENSE MOVEMENT** a movement or stance used as a means of protection, e.g., in fencing **8.** RELIG **LATTER-DAY SAINTS' ADMINISTRATIVE DIVISION** in the Church of Jesus Christ of Latter-day Saints, an administrative division presided over by a bishop and two counselors **9. LOCK OR KEY FEATURE** a ridge or groove in a key or a lock that makes one fit the other ■ *vt.* (**ward·ed, ward·ing, wards**) **GUARD** to guard or protect somebody or something (*archaic*) [Old English *weard,* from a prehistoric Germanic word meaning "to be on guard," which is also the ancestor of English *guard, aware,* and *wary*]

ward off *vt.* **1. REPEL** to parry or repel a blow or attack **2. AVERT SOMETHING BAD** to keep away or avert something bad

Ward /wawrd/, **Aaron Montgomery** (1843–1913) U.S. merchant. He pioneered mail-order merchandising (1872) with a catalog offering low-cost goods to people in rural areas.

Ward, Artemus (1834–67) U.S. humorist. In the persona of an uneducated traveling showman, he wrote newspaper pieces and lectures combining humor, satire, and basic common sense. Pseudonym of **Charles Farrar Browne**

-ward *suffix.* **1.** in a particular direction, or toward a particular place ○ *earthward* **2.** lying or occurring in a particular direction ○ *rightward* ○ *windward* [Old English *-weard.* Ultimately from an Indo-European base meaning "to turn," which is also the ancestor of English *avert.*]

war dance *n.* a dance performed as a ceremony before a battle or to celebrate victory, e.g., by Native North Americans

ward·ed /wáwrdəd/ *adj.* used to describe locks or keys that have grooves or ridges

war·den /wáwrd'n/ *n.* **1. PRINCIPAL PRISON OFFICER** the principal officer in charge of a prison **2. OFFICIAL CONCERNED WITH REGULATIONS** an official, e.g., an air-raid warden, who makes sure that regulations are enforced **3.** *U.K.* **SOMEBODY IN CHARGE OF INSTITUTION** somebody who is in charge of an institution such as a college or school **4.** CHR = **churchwarden** *n.* 1 **5.** FORESTRY = **ranger** *n.* 1 [12thC. From Anglo-Norman *wardein,* from a prehistoric Germanic word meaning "to be on guard" (see WARD).] —**war·den·ship** *n.*

ward·er /wáwrdər/ *n.* *U.K.* a prison officer [14thC. From Anglo-Norman *wardere,* from Old Northern French *warder* "to guard," variant of French *garder* (see GUARD).]

ward heel·er *n.* somebody who carries out minor tasks for a powerful local or city politician (*informal*)

ward·robe /wáwrd ròb/ *n.* **1.** CLOTHES **PLACE FOR CLOTHES** a large closet or freestanding cupboard with a rail or shelves for clothes and shoes **2.** CLOTHES **CLOTHES COLLECTION** all the clothes that belong to a particular person **3.** CLOTHES **CLOTHES FOR A PURPOSE** a collection of clothes for a particular season or purpose **4.** THEATER **THEATER COSTUMES** the costumes used by a theatrical company **5.** THEATER **PLACE FOR COSTUMES** a place in a theater where costumes are kept **6. ROYAL DEPARTMENT** the department in a royal or noble household in charge of robes and jewels [14thC. From Old Northern French *warderobe,* variant of French *garderobe,* from French *garder* "to guard" + *robe* "robe."]

ward·robe mis·tress *n.* a woman in charge of the costumes in a theater or on a movie set

ward·robe trunk *n.* a large upright trunk with a rail for on which clothes can be hung

ward·room /wáwrd ròom, -ròom/ *n.* **1. SHIP'S OFFICERS' ROOM** a room on a warship used by all the officers except the captain **2. WARSHIP'S OFFICERS** the officers on a ship who can use the wardroom

-wards *suffix.* = **-ward**

ward·ship /wáwrd shìp/ *n.* **1. GUARDIANSHIP** the state of being in the care of a guardian appointed by parents or a court **2. BEING A WARD** the state of being a ward

ware[1] /wair/ *n.* **1. SIMILAR THINGS** similar things, or things that are made of the same material (*usually used in combination*) **2. CERAMICS** ceramic articles of a particular kind or made by a particular manufacturer ○ *delftware* ■ **wares** *npl.* **1. THINGS FOR SALE** articles offered for sale **2. MARKETABLE SKILLS** skills or talents offered as a service or a commodity [Old English *waru,* of uncertain origin: probably from the same word as WARD, with the underlying idea "something taken care of"]

ware[2] /wair/ *vti.* (**wared, waring, wares**) **BEWARE** to beware (*archaic*) ■ *adj.* **WARY** wary or prudent (*archaic*) [Old English *warian,* from a prehistoric Germanic word meaning "to be on guard" (see WARD)]

Ware·ham /wáirəm/ town in southeastern Massachusetts, on an inlet of Buzzards Bay, south of Plymouth and northeast of New Bedford. Population: 19,545 (1996).

ware·house /wáir hòwss/ *n.* (*plural* **-hous·es** /wàir hówsez/) **1. STORAGE BUILDING** a large building in which goods, raw materials, or commodities are stored **2. BIG STORE** a large store, especially one where goods are sold wholesale ■ *vt.* (**-housed, -hous·ing, -hous·es** /wáir hòwzəz/) **1. STORE IN A WAREHOUSE** to store materials, goods, or commodities in a warehouse **2. ABANDON IN AN INSTITUTION** to leave somebody in an institution that does not provide adequate care or treatment (*informal*) —**ware·hous·er** /wáir hòwzər/ *n.*

ware·house·man /wáir hòwssmən/ (*plural* **-men** /-mən/) *n.* somebody who works in or owns a warehouse

ware·hous·ing /wáir hòwzing/ *n.* the accumulation of a particular security in the hope that demand will push the price up as the result of the reduced supply on the open market

ware·room /wáir ròom, -ròom/ *n.* a room where goods are kept or displayed for sale

war·fare /wáwr fàir/ *n.* **1. WAGING OF WAR** the act or fact of engaging in a war **2. CONFLICT** conflict or struggle ○ *economic warfare*

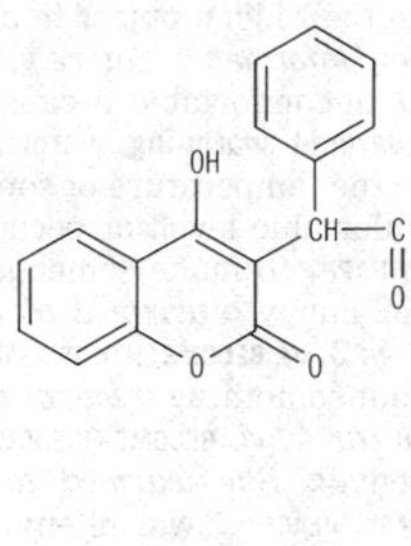

Warfarin

war·fa·rin /wáwrfərin/ *n.* a colorless crystalline compound that is used as a rat poison and, usually in the form of its sodium salt, medicinally as an anticoagulant. Formula: $C_{19}H_{16}O_4$. [Mid-20thC. Formed from the initial letters of *Wisconsin Alumni Research Foundation* and the ending of COUMARIN.]

war game *n.* **1.** MIL **MILITARY EXERCISE** a military exercise that simulates battle conditions **2. PLAYING AT WAR** a game in which models of soldiers, battlefields, and equipment are used to refight historical battles

war-game (**war-gamed, war-gam·ing, war-games**) *v.* **1.** *vi.* **BE IN WAR GAME** to take part in a war game **2.** *vt.* **TEST MILITARY STRATEGY** to try out a military operation or strategy using simulation —**war-gam·er** *n.*

war·head /wáwr hèd/ *n.* the part of a bomb, ballistic or guided missile, rocket, or torpedo that contains the biological, chemical, explosive, incendiary, or nuclear material intended to damage the enemy

AKG London

Andy Warhol

War·hol /wáwr hawl, -hōl/, **Andy** (1928–87) U.S. artist. His stylized multiple depictions of mass-produced objects and celebrities made him a leader of the pop art movement. He also produced a series of movies that reproduced the banalities of life. Born **Andrew Wahola**

war·horse /wáwr hàwrs/ *n.* **1.** MIL **HORSE IN BATTLE** a horse ridden in battle **2. SURVIVOR OF A CONFLICT** somebody who has taken part in and survived many conflicts (*informal*) **3.** ARTS **STANDARD WORK** a play or a piece of music that is familiar and hackneyed because of too frequent performance (*informal*)

war·i·son /wáirəss'n/ *n.* a note played on a bugle as a sign for soldiers to attack [13thC. From Old French, variant of *garison* "provision" (see GARRISON).]

war·like /wáwr lìk/ *adj.* **1. HOSTILE** hostile and inclined to fight **2. RELATING TO WAR** relating to war or warfare **3. MARTIAL** martial or military

war·lock /wáwr lòk/ *n.* a male sorcerer or wizard [Old English *wærloga* "oath-breaker," from *wær* "oath, pledge" + *-loga* "liar"]

war·lord /wáwr làwrd/ *n.* a military leader, especially a powerful one operating outside the control of government —**war·lord·ism** *n.*

warm /wawrm/ *adj.* **1. QUITE HOT** moderately or comfortably hot **2. PROVIDING WARMTH** providing warmth or protection against cold **3. WITH TOO MUCH HEAT** having or feeling an undesirable amount of heat, from exertion or ambient temperature **4. FRIENDLY** showing or feeling kindness and friendliness ○ *a warm person.* **5. PASSIONATE** showing passion or liveliness **6. ENTHUSIASTIC OR ARDENT** showing or feeling great enthusiasm **7. QUICK TO ANGER** excitable or easily angered **8.** COLORS **SUGGESTING WARMTH** with a color that suggests warmth, especially yellow or red **9.** PHYSIOL **HEATED BY METABOLISM** giving off the heat that arises normally in warm-blooded creatures **10.** HUNT **FRESH** used to describe a scent in hunting that is fresh and strong **11. CLOSE** close to the hidden object in a game or to guessing a secret (*informal*) ○ *You're getting warm.* **12. UNCOMFORTABLE** uncomfortable because of danger (*informal*) ■ *v.* (**warmed, warm·ing, warms**) **1.** *vti.* **MAKE WARM** to increase the temperature of something to a desirable or comfortable level, or become warm **2.** *vt.* **MAKE SOMEBODY HAPPY** to make somebody or something cheerful or happy ○ *warmed by the presence of all their children* **3.** *vi.* **BECOME ENTHUSIASTIC** to become enthusiastic about something ○ *warmed to the idea of buying a new car* **4.** *vi.* **BECOME FRIENDLY** to become fond of somebody ○ *She warmed to him.* ■ *n.* (*informal*) **1. WARM PLACE** a warm environment **2. GETTING WARM** an act of making something warm or becoming warm [Old English *wearm.* Ultimately from an Indo-European word that is also the ancestor of English *furnace, fornication,* and *thermometer.*] —**warm·ness** *n.*

warm down *vi.* to get back to a normal level of activity after strenuous physical exertion in a way that avoids cramping, usually by gentle exercising (*informal*)

warm over *vt.* **1. REHEAT** to reheat food **2. SUGGEST SOMETHING NOT NEW** to suggest something again, without having greatly altered it

warm up /wáwrm ùp/ *v.* **1.** *vi.* **PREPARE FOR EXERCISE** to prepare for physical exercise by stretching or practicing **2.** *vi.* **PREPARE FOR SOMETHING** to prepare for something that is going to happen **3.** *vti.* **GET WARM** to become, or make something become, warm or warmer **4.** *vti.* **GET TO OPERATING TEMPERATURE** to run something such as an engine to bring it to a temperature at which it works efficiently, or reach this condition **5.** *vti.* **GET ANIMATED** to become, or make somebody, enthusiastic, animated, or eager

war ma·chine *n.* the combined military resources with which a country can fight a war

warm-blood·ed *adj.* **1.** ZOOL **WITH CONSTANT BODY TEMPERATURE** maintaining a nearly constant body temperature, usually higher than, and independent of, the environment **2. PASSIONATE** passionate, impetuous, and enthusiastic —**warm-blood·ed·ness** *n.*

warm·boot /wáwrm bo͝ot/ (**-boot·ed, -boot·ing, -boots**) *vt.* to restart a computer without switching it off, e.g., by pressing the control, alt, and delete keys together. ◊ **coldboot**

warmed-o·ver *adj.* **1. REHEATED** reheated, having been cooked before ○ *warmed-over rice and beans* **2. UNORIGINAL** not fresh or original ○ *a warmed-over version of their original proposal*

warm·er /wáwrmər/ *n.* something that makes or keeps something warm

warm front *n.* the gently sloping advancing edge of a warm air mass that displaces colder air, bringing a temperature increase and heavy rain where the front contacts the ground

warm-heart·ed *adj.* having or showing a kind and sympathetic nature —**warm-heart·ed·ly** *adv.* —**warm-heart·ed·ness** *n.*

warm·ing pan *n.* a long-handled metal pan that in the past was filled with hot coals and placed in a bed to warm it

warm·ly /wáwrmlee/ *adv.* **1. ENTHUSIASTICALLY** with enthusiasm, fondness, or passion **2. WITH WARM CLOTHES** in a way that will keep somebody warm ○ *dressed warmly*

war·mon·ger /wáwr mùng gər, -mòng-/ *n.* somebody who is eager for war or tries to start a war —**war·mon·ger·ing** *n.*

war·mouth /wáwr mòwth/ (*plural* **-mouths** /-mòwthz, -mòwths/), **war·mouth bass** (*plural* **war·mouth bass**) *n.* an olive-colored freshwater sunfish with a large mouth, found in the eastern and midwestern United States. Latin name: *Lepomis gulosus.* [Late 19thC. Origin unknown.]

warm sec·tor *n.* a wedge of warm air within the low-pressure region between the cold front and warm front of a storm

warmth /wawrmth/ *n.* **1. WARM STATE** the feeling, quality, or state of being warm **2. AFFECTION** affection and kindness **3. AMOUNT OF HEAT** a moderate amount of heat present in something **4. EXCITEMENT** strong emotion, especially anger or zeal **5. EFFECT OF COLOR** the effect gained from using colors such as red and yellow

warm-up /wáwrm ùp/, **warm·up** *n.* **1. EXERCISE BEFORE EVENT** an exercise, or period spent exercising, before a contest or event **2.** CLOTHES **CLOTHES FOR WARMING UP** an outfit, e.g., a tracksuit, worn while warming up (*often used in the plural*)

warn /wawrn/ (**warned, warn·ing, warns**) *v.* **1.** *vti.* **TELL OF RISK** to tell somebody about something that might cause injury or harm **2.** *vt.* **TELL SOMEBODY IN ADVANCE** to tell somebody about something in advance **3.** *vt.* **SCOLD SOMEBODY** to admonish somebody **4.** *vt.* **KEEP SOMEBODY FROM DOING SOMETHING** to tell somebody to desist from doing something or going somewhere ○ *warned us off driving over the pass in the storm* [Old English *war(e)nian,* from a prehistoric Germanic word meaning "to be cautious"] —**warn·er** *n.*

warn·ing /wáwrning/ *n.* **1. SIGN OF SOMETHING BAD COMING** a threat or a sign that something bad is going to happen **2. ADVICE TO BE CAREFUL** advice to be careful or to stop doing something ○ *If you're late again, you'll get a written warning.* **3. NOTICE** a notice (*archaic*) ■ *adj.* **MEANT TO WARN** intended to warn somebody —**warn·ing·ly** *adv.*

warn·ing col·or·a·tion *n.* markings on an animal warning predators that it is poisonous or dangerous. Many insects and amphibians have warning coloration.

warn·ing shot *n.* a shot fired deliberately off target as a threat to somebody to stop doing something,

war of nerves *n.* a conflict in which psychological tactics are used against an opponent

warp /wawrp/ *v.* (**warped, warp·ing, warps**) **1.** *vti.* **GET TWISTED** to become or make something twisted out of shape **2.** *vti.* **CHANGE FOR WORSE** to change something so that it no longer follows its usual course, or become distorted or strange **3.** *vti.* SHIPPING **MOVE SHIP BY PULLING ON ROPES** to move a ship by pulling on ropes fastened to a dock or fixed buoy, or move in this way **4.** *vt.* TEXTILES **ARRANGE THREADS** to arrange threads to form the warp in a loom ■ *n.* **1. DISTORTION** a twist or distortion in something, e.g., in wood that curls when dried **2. PERVERSION** a deviation or perversion of mind or character **3.** TEXTILES **THREADS RUNNING LENGTHWISE** the threads that run lengthwise on a loom or in a piece of fabric. ◊ **weft** *n.* 1 **4.** NAUT **ROPE FOR TOWING** a rope used to warp a vessel [Old English *weorpan,* from a prehistoric Germanic word meaning "to throw," of uncertain origin: probably ultimately from an Indo-European word meaning "to turn"] —**warp·age** *n.* —**warp·er** *n.*

war paint *n.* **1. PAINT FOR DECORATING WARRIORS** paint used to decorate the body before a battle, e.g., that formerly used by some Native North American peoples **2. MAKEUP** face makeup (*informal*)

warp and woof *n.* the foundation or base of something

war par·ty *n.* **1. GROUP OF FIGHTERS** a group of people, especially Native North Americans in the past, engaged in fighting or attacking an enemy **2. PARTY FAVORING WAR** a political party that supports or wants war

war·path /wáwr pàth/ *n.* in the past, a route taken by Native North Americans on the way to war ◇ **on the warpath** angry and in the mood for a confrontation (*informal*)

war·plane /wáwr plàyn/ *n.* an aircraft used in war

war·rant /wáwrənt/ *n.* **1. AUTHORIZATION** something that authorizes somebody to do something **2. WRITTEN AUTHORIZATION** a written authorization or certifying document **3.** LAW **DOCUMENT AUTHORIZING POLICE TO DO SOMETHING** a document that gives police particular rights or powers, e.g., the right to search or arrest somebody **4.** FIN **OPTION TO BUY STOCK** a document authorizing a stockholder to buy shares from a company at a later date and at a given price **5.** MIL **WARRANT OFFICER'S CERTIFICATE** a warrant officer's certificate of appointment ■ *vt.* (**-rant·ed, -rant·ing, -rants**) **1. SERVE AS A REASON** to serve as a justifiable reason to do, believe, or think something **2. GUARANTEE** to guarantee something such as the truth or dependability of something or somebody **3. AUTHORIZE** to give authority to somebody **4.** LAW **GUARANTEE TITLE** to guarantee the title to property **5. STATE CONFIDENTLY** to state something with the confidence that it is true or will happen (*archaic*) [12thC. From Old Northern French *warant,* variant of Old French *guarant* (source of English *guarantee*), from, ultimately, a prehistoric Germanic word meaning "to be on guard" (see WARD).] —**war·rant·er** *n.*

war·rant·a·ble /wáwrəntəb'l/ *adj.* able to be justified or permitted —**war·rant·a·bil·i·ty** /wàwrəntəbíllətee/ *n.* —**war·rant·a·bly** /wáwrəntəblee/ *adv.*

war·ran·tee /wàwrən tée/ *n.* somebody to whom a warrant is given or a warranty is made

war·rant of·fi·cer *n.* an officer in the armed services ranking between a commissioned and a noncommissioned officer

war·ran·tor /wáwrəntər, -tàwr/ *n.* somebody who gives a warranty to somebody

war·ran·ty /wáwrəntee/ (*plural* **-ties**) *n.* **1.** COMM **GUARANTEE** a guarantee on purchased goods that they are of the quality represented and will be replaced or repaired if found defective **2.** LAW **INSURED PERSON'S UNDERTAKING** a condition in an insurance contract in which the insured person guarantees that something is the case **3.** LAW **GUARANTEE OF TITLE** a covenant guaranteeing the security of the title to property being sold **4. JUSTIFICATION** a justification or authorization for an action

war·ran·ty deed *n.* a deed that binds a seller of property to defend the security of the title against any claims that may arise against the buyer

war·ren /wáwrən/ *n.* **1. RABBIT HABITAT** a group of connected burrows where rabbits live and breed **2. RABBIT COLONY** a colony of rabbits **3. CROWDED BUILDING OR AREA** an area or building that is crowded or has a complicated layout **4. AREA FOR GAME ANIMALS** a piece of ground where game animals are kept and bred [14thC. From Anglo-Norman *warenne* "enclosed area for breeding game," of uncertain origin: perhaps ultimately from assumed Gaulish *warenna* "fenced-off area," from assumed *warros* "post."]

War·ren /wáwrən/, **Earl** (1891–1974) U.S. Supreme Court judge. He was governor of California (1943–53). As Supreme Court chief justice (1953–69) he presided over a liberal court that desegregated public schools and articulated the rights of criminal suspects.

War·ren, Joseph (1741–75) U.S. patriot. A noted leader among the anti-British protesters in pre-Revolutionary Boston, he died in the Battle of Bunker Hill.

War·ren, Robert Penn (1905–89) U.S. author and poet. He is best known for the Pulitzer Prize-winning political novel *All the King's Men* (1946).

war·ren·er /wáwrənər/ *n.* a gamekeeper or keeper of a rabbit warren

War·ren Re·port *n.* the 1964 report of the Commission, headed by Chief Justice Earl Warren, that officially investigated the assassination of President John F. Kennedy.

war·ri·or /wáwree ər/ *n.* somebody who fights or is experienced in warfare [13thC. From Old Northern French *werreior,* ultimately from *werre* "war" (see WAR).]

Warr·nam·bool /wáwrnəm bo͝ol/ city in southwestern Victoria, Australia. It is a commercial and industrial center. Population: 26,052 (1996).

War·rum·bun·gle Range /wòrrəm bung g'l-/ range of volcanic peaks in northern New South Wales, Australia. Highest peak: 4,028 ft./1,228 m.

war·saw /wáwr sàw/ *n.* a large sea bass found off the southeastern coast of the United States. Latin name: *Epinephelus nigritus.* [Mid-20thC. From American Spanish *guasa.*]

War·saw /wáwr sàw/ capital city of Poland, located in the center of the country, on the Vistula River. Population: 1,638,300 (1995).

war·ship /wáwr shìp/ *n.* an armored ship that is equipped with weapons and is used in war

war sto·ry *n.* a narrative of personal experience involving conflict or hardship ○ *frightening the interns with emergency-room war stories*

wart /wawrt/ *n.* **1.** MED **SMALL LUMP ON SKIN** a small benign rough lump that grows usually on the hands, feet, or genitals, caused by a virus. ◊ **verruca 2.** BOT **GROWTH ON PLANT** any abnormal growth that looks like a wart and is found on a plant [Old English *wearte.* Ultimately from an Indo-European word meaning "raised spot."] — **wart·ed** *adj.* —**wart·y** *adj.* ◇ **warts and all** including any flaws, faults, or disadvantages (*hyphenated when used before a noun*)

Wart hog

wart hog *n.* a wild hog that lives in Africa south of the Sahara. It has tusks, a coarse mane, and wartlike growths on its face. Latin name: *Phacochoerus aethiopicus.*

war·time /wáwr tìm/ *n.* a period during which a war is being fought

war-torn *adj.* disrupted by war, especially war between different groups from one country

war whoop *n.* a yell made when attacking, used in the past by Native North American warriors

War·wick /wáwr wik/ town in eastern Rhode Island on Narragansett Bay, at the mouth of the Providence River. Population: 84,514 (1996).

war·y /wáiree/ (**-i·er, -i·est**) *adj.* **1. CAUTIOUS** cautious and watchful ○ *wary of hidden rocks in the water* **2. SHOWING CAUTION** showing caution or watchfulness ○ *a wary approach* [15thC. Formed from WARE[2].]

WORD KEY: SYNONYMS

See Synonyms at ***cautious.***

was /(stressed) woz, wuz, (unstressed) wəz/ past tense of **be** (*used with I, he, she, it, and singular nouns*) [Old English *wæs*, a form of *wesan* "to be." Ultimately from an Indo-European word meaning "to stay, dwell," which is also the ancestor of English *wassail.*]

wa·sa·bi /waássəbee/ *n.* **1. JAPANESE CONDIMENT** a green powder or paste from the root of an herb, used as a condiment in Japanese cooking. It has a strong sharp taste similar to horseradish or mustard. **2.** (*plural* **wasabis** *or* **wasabi**) **HERB CULTIVATED FOR ITS ROOT** an Asian herb whose root is ground to make wasabi powder or paste. Latin name: *Eutrema wasabi.* [Early 20thC. From Japanese.]

wash /wosh/ *v.* (**washed, wash·ing, wash·es**) **1.** *vt.* **CLEAN SOMETHING** to clean something with water, usually with added soap or detergent **2.** *vti.* **REMOVE SOMETHING BY WASHING** to remove something with water and usually with soap, or be removed in this way ○ *couldn't get the stain to wash out* **3.** *vr.* **CLEAN YOURSELF** to clean yourself, especially your hands or face, with soap and water **4.** *vi.* **BE WASHABLE** to be capable of being washed without fading or being damaged (*refers to garments or fabrics*) ○ *curtains that wash well* **5.** *vti.* **LICK TO CLEAN** to clean something by licking ○ *The cat washed her kittens.* **6.** *vi.* **WASH CLOTHES** to clean clothes in soap and water or in a washing machine ○ *spent the morning washing* **7.** *vt.* **MOISTEN** to wet or moisten something (*literary*) ○ *lashes washed with tears* **8.** *vt.* **FLOW OVER SOMETHING** to flow over the surface of something ○ *washed by the tides* **9.** *vt.* **ERODE SOMETHING WITH WATER** to erode something by the action of water **10.** *vt.* **MOVE SOMETHING ON WATER** to carry something along or away on water, or as if on water **11.** *vt.* **PURIFY** to remove something corrupting ○ *the power to wash away sins* **12.** *vt.* MINING **SEPARATE SOMETHING BY WASHING** to separate something such as precious stones or valuable minerals by sifting ore or gravel through water **13.** *vt.* **APPLY THIN COATING TO SOMETHING** to brush a thin coating or layer over something **14.** *vi.* **BE CONVINCING** to be convincing or believable (*informal*) ○ *That story won't wash.* **15.** *vt.* CHEM **PUT GAS THROUGH LIQUID** to pass a gas or vapor through a liquid to remove contaminants ■ *n.* **1. ACT OF WASHING** the act or process of washing something or somebody **2. QUANTITY OF CLOTHES** a quantity of clothes that have been or are to be washed **3.** INDUST **THIN LIQUID COATING** a thin or weak liquid, especially one used to rinse or coat something **4. SKIN TREATMENT** a lotion, antiseptic, or cosmetic that is applied to the skin **5. FLOW OF WATER** the flow of water against a surface, or the sound made by this **6.** *Southwest U.S.* **DRY STREAM BED** the dry bed of a stream that flows only after heavy rains, often found at the bottom of a canyon **7.** PAINTING **LAYER OF COLOR** a thin layer of color applied with a brush **8.** PAINTING **PAINTING TECHNIQUE** the technique of using washes in painting **9.** PAINTING = **wash drawing 10. SURGE OF DISTURBED WATER OR AIR** the surge of disturbed water, air, or other fluid caused by something such as an oar, propeller, or jet engine moving through the fluid **11.** AGRIC **REMOVAL OF SOIL** removal of soil by the action of flowing water **12.** GEOL **SEDIMENT** alluvial material carried and left by the movement of water. When washed down the side of a mountain, the sediment forms fans and cone-shaped deposits. **13.** GEOG **LAND PERIODICALLY COVERED BY WATER** land that is periodically covered by a sea or river, e.g., by a tide **14.** MINING **ORE** material such as gravel from which precious stones and valuable minerals can be extracted by washing **15.** *U.K.* = **swill** *n.* 1 **16.** BEVERAGES **FERMENTED MALT** the liquor from fermented malt before it is distilled **17. EVEN OUTCOME** a situation in which the losses and gains are balanced (*informal*) ○ *We sold a lot at the crafts fair, but our expenses were so high that in the end it was a wash.* [Old English *wæscan*, from a prehistoric Germanic word that is also the ancestor of English *water*]

wash down *vt.* **1. WASH SOMETHING COMPLETELY** to wash something thoroughly and completely ○ *had to wash down the kitchen walls afterward* **2. DRINK AFTER DRINKING OR EATING SOMETHING** to follow something drunk or eaten with another drink ○ *washed down the cake with a glass of milk*

wash out *v.* **1.** *vt.* **CLEAN INSIDE OF SOMETHING** to clean something by washing the inside **2.** *vti.* **REMOVE BY WASHING** to come out or get something out by washing **3.** *vt.* **CANCEL** to cancel something because of rain **4.** *vti.* **MOVE AWAY ON WATER** to carry away something, or be carried away, on water ○ *washed out to sea* **5.** *vti.* **WEAR AWAY** to wear something away, or be worn away, by water **6.** *vt.* **EXHAUST SOMEBODY** to make somebody exhausted (*informal*) **7.** *vt.* **END SOMETHING** to bring something to an end (*informal*) ○ *"Baltimore washed out the Indians' six-game win streak with an 8–3 win."* (*Major League Baseball News, ESPN Sports Zone*; 1997)

wash over *v.* **1.** *vt.* **FLOW OVER** to cover something in a flowing or overflowing manner, as a liquid does **2.** *vi.* **FILL SOMEBODY WITH EMOTION** to well up in somebody (*refers to feelings*) ○ *A wave of homesickness washed over him.*

wash up *v.* **1.** *vi.* **WASH FACE AND HANDS** to wash your face and hands **2.** *vti.* **ARRIVE BY WATER** to deposit something on the shore, or land on the shore from tidal or wave action ○ *Look what the tide washed up!* **3.** *vt.* **ELIMINATE BY WASHING** to get rid of something by washing ○ *wash up that spilled coffee* **4.** *vti. U.K.* **WASH DISHES** to wash the dishes after a meal

Wash. *abbr.* Washington

wash·a·ble /wóshəb'l/ *adj.* capable of being washed without being damaged —**wash·a·bil·i·ty** /wòshə bíllətee/ *n.*

wash-and-wear *adj.* easily washed and dried and needing little or no ironing

wash·ba·sin /wósh bàyss'n/ *n.* a bowl or basin for washing the face and hands or small articles

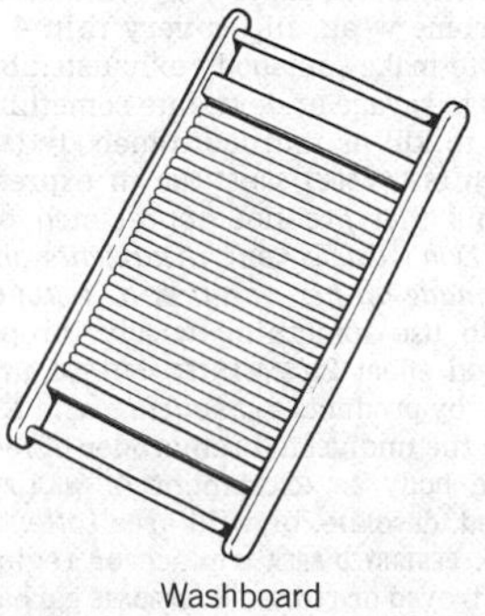

Washboard

wash·board /wósh bàwrd/ *n.* **1. RIDGED BOARD** a board with a corrugated surface on which clothes being washed can be rubbed to help get them clean **2.** MUSIC **MUSICAL INSTRUMENT** a board similar to a washboard used as a musical instrument to produce a scratching sound **3.** TRANSP **ROUGH ROAD** a road or section of road with bumpy ridges **4.** BUILDING = **baseboard** *n.* 2 **5.** NAUT **PROTECTIVE FEATURE ON A BOAT** a thin plank on the gunwale of a boat to stop water from splashing over the side ■ *adj.* **MUSCULAR** used to describe a man's stomach that has well-defined muscles

wash·bowl /wósh bōl/ *n.* = **washbasin**

wash·cloth /wósh klàwth/ *n.* a small piece of absorbent fabric, usually terry cloth, for washing the face or body

wash·day /wósh dày/ *n.* a day when clothes are washed, usually the same day each week

wash draw·ing *n.* a drawing made in ink to which a wash of color is applied, or a painting made using washes

washed-out, **washed out** *adj.* **1. FADED** faded or without color **2. EXHAUSTED** exhausted or lacking vitality and strength

washed-up, **washed up** *adj.* no longer likely to continue or succeed (*informal*)

wash·er /wóshər/ *n.* **1. SMALL RING** a small disk or ring used to keep a screw or bolt secure or prevent leakage at a joint **2.** HOUSEHOLD **WASHING APPLIANCE** an appliance used for washing, especially a washing machine **3. SOMEBODY WHO WASHES** somebody who washes something **4.** *Aus* **WASHCLOTH** a washcloth (*informal*)

wash·er-up (*plural* **wash·ers-up**) *n. U.K.* somebody who is employed to wash dishes (*informal*)

wash·er·wom·an /wóshər wŏŏmmən/ (*plural* **-en** /-wìmmin/), **wash·wom·an** /wósh wŏŏmmən/ (*plural* **-en** /-wimmən/) *n.* a woman who is employed to wash clothes (*dated*)

wash house *n.* a building where laundry or other washing is done

wash·ing /wóshing/ *n.* **1. CLOTHES FOR WASHING** clothes to be washed, being washed, or washed just before **2. DOING LAUNDRY** the act or process of washing clothes **3.** INDUST **THIN COAT** a thin coat of something ○ *a washing of silver* **4. LIQUID USED FOR WASHING** the liquid that has been used to wash something (*often used in the plural*)

wash·ing ma·chine *n.* a machine for washing clothes, usually an electric one

wash·ing so·da *n.* a crystalline form of sodium carbonate used for washing and cleaning

Washington

Wash·ing·ton /wóshingtən/ state of the northwestern United States, bordered by British Columbia, Idaho, Oregon, and the Pacific Ocean. Capital: Olympia. Population: 5,610,362 (1997). Area: 70,637 sq. mi./182,949 sq. km. —**Wash·ing·to·ni·an** /wòshing tṓnee ən/ *n., adj.*

Washington, D.C. capital city of the United States. The city of Washington has the same boundaries as the District of Columbia, a federal territory established in 1790 as the site of the new nation's permanent capital. Located at the confluence of the Potomac and Anacostia rivers, it is bordered by Maryland and Virginia. Population: 543,000 (1996).

Wash·ing·ton /wóshingtən/, **Booker T.** (1856–1915) U.S. educator. As the first president of Alabama's Tuskegee Institute (1881–1915), he urged African Americans to attempt to uplift themselves through educational attainments. Real name **Booker Taliaferro**

George Washington

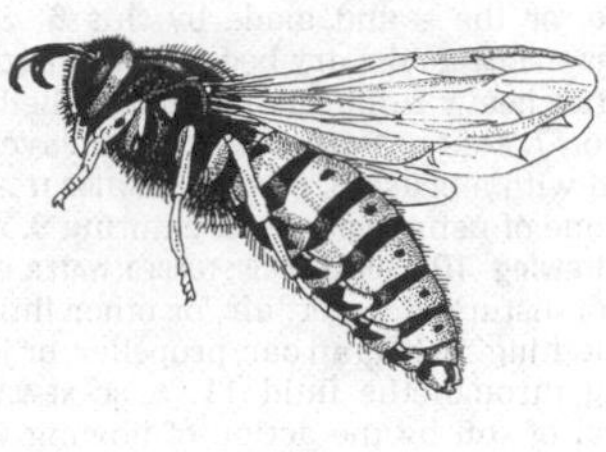

Wasp

Wash·ing·ton, George (1732–99) U.S. statesman and 1st president of the United States. Commander in chief of the American forces during the Revolution (1775–83), and president of the second Constitutional Convention, he was the first president of the newly independent United States (1789–97).

Wash·ing·ton's birth·day *n.* February 22, the birthday of George Washington. It is observed as an official holiday in the United States on Presidents' Day, the third Monday in February.

wash·ing-up liq·uid *n. U.K.* = **dishwashing liquid**

wash·out /wósh òwt/ *n.* **1. FAILURE** a complete failure or fiasco (*informal*) **2. OFFENSIVE TERM** an offensive term that deliberately insults somebody's competence or achievements (*informal insult*) **3.** GEOL **EROSION CAUSED BY RUNNING WATER** erosion caused by running water, e.g., during a flash flood **4.** GEOL **CHANNEL WASHED OUT** a hole or channel made by floodwater

wash·room /wósh ròom, -ròom/ *n.* **1. PUBLIC WASHING FACILITY** a room, especially in a public place, with toilet and washing facilities **2. PUBLIC TOILET** a euphemism for a public toilet

wash sale *n.* **1. ILLEGAL STOCK TRADING** near-simultaneous buying and selling of a particular stock to give the impression that the stock is being actively traded. The practice is illegal. **2. RAPID SALE OF STOCK** the repurchase of stock sold within 30 days of the time it was sold. Capital losses on such a sale are not tax deductible.

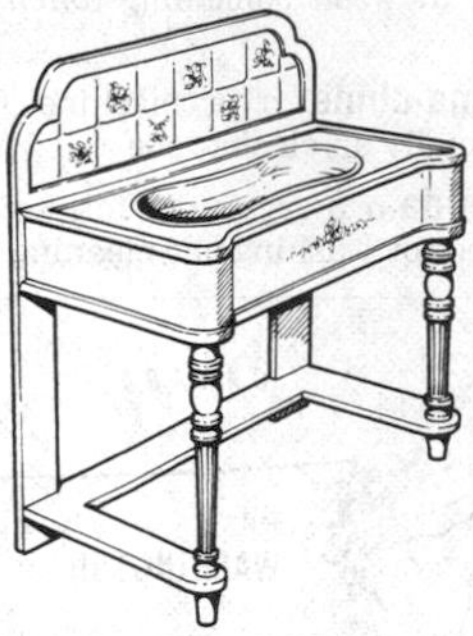

Washstand

wash·stand /wósh stànd/ *n.* a stand on which a basin and jug can be placed for washing the face and hands

wash·tub /wósh tùb/ *n.* a large container in which clothes can be washed

wash-up *n. Aus* the outcome of a process or series of events

wash·wom·an /wósh wòomən/ (*plural* **-en** /wósh wìmmən/) *n.* = **washerwoman**

wash·y /wóshee/ (**-i·er, -i·est**) *adj.* **1. WEAK** watery or weak **2. PALE** faint or faded **3. NOT FORCEFUL** without intensity or vitality —**wash·i·ly** *adv.* —**wash·i·ness** *n.*

was·n't /wúzz'nt, wózz'nt/ *contr.* was not

wasp /wosp/ *n.* INSECTS a slender black-and-yellow striped social stinging insect that typically has well-developed wings, biting mouthparts, and a narrow stalk connecting the abdomen and thorax. Family: Vespidae and Sphecidae. [Old English *wæsp*. Ultimately from an Indo-European word meaning "to weave," which is also the ancestor of English *web* and *weave*. The name probably refers to the fact that wasps' build nests.]

Wasp /wosp/, **WASP** *n.* an offensive term used to refer to a Caucasian, who has a Protestant Anglo-Saxon background, and is viewed as belonging to the dominant and most powerful level of society (*informal insult*) [Mid-20thC. Acronym formed from *White Anglo-Saxon Protestant*.] —**Wasp·ish** *adj.* —**Wasp·ish·ness** *n.* —**Wasp·y** *adj.*

wasp·ish /wóspish/, **wasp·y** /wóspee/ (**-i·er** /wóspee/, **-i·est**) *adj.* **1. OF WASPS** like a wasp, or relating to wasps **2. EASILY IRRITATED** easily irritated or annoyed **3. SPITEFUL** showing spite —**wasp·ish·ly** *adv.* —**wasp·ish·ness** *n.*

wasp moth *n.* = **clearwing**

wasp waist *n.* a very slender waist, or one that is corseted to make it appear slender —**wasp waist·ed** *adj.*

wasp·y /wóspee/ (**-i·er, -i·est**) *adj.* = **waspish**

was·sail /wóss'l, wó sàyl/ *n.* (*archaic*) **1. FESTIVE SALUTATION** a salutation or drinking toast made during festivities **2. FESTIVE OCCASION** a festive occasion at which people drink a great deal **3.** BEVERAGES **ALCOHOLIC DRINK** an alcoholic drink, usually mulled wine or ale, drunk on a festive occasion **4.** MUSIC **DRINKING OR CHRISTMAS SONG** a drinking song or a song sung at Christmas ■ *v.* (**-sailed, -sail·ing, -sails**) **1.** *vi.* **DRINK IN CELEBRATION** to celebrate by drinking (*archaic*) **2.** *vi. U.K.* **SING CHRISTMAS SONGS** to go from house to house at Christmas, singing carols and greeting people (*regional archaic*) **3.** *vt.* **TOAST SOMEBODY** to drink to somebody's health (*archaic*) [12thC. From Old Norse *ves heill*, literally "be healthy," *heill* from a prehistoric Germanic word that is also the ancestor of English *hale* and *health*.] —**was·sail·er** *n.*

Was·ser·mann test /wáassərmən-/, **Was·ser·man re·ac·tion** *n.* a test for syphilis infection, based on determining the presence in a blood sample of antibodies to the syphilis bacterium [Named for the German bacteriologist August Paul *Wassermann* (1866–1925)]

wast (*stressed*) /wost/; (*unstressed*) /wəst/ 2nd person past singular of **be** (*archaic*)

wast·age /wáystij/ *n.* **1. AMOUNT WASTED** an amount that is lost or wasted **2. LOSS** loss caused when something is used, is worn, decays, or leaks **3.** *U.K.* **REDUCTION IN NUMBERS** the reduction in numbers of people working in a place because of deaths and resignations, rather than from layoffs

waste /wayst/ *v.* (**wast·ed, wast·ing, wastes**) **1.** *vt.* **USE SOMETHING CARELESSLY** to use something or use something up carelessly, extravagantly, or without effect **2.** *vt.* **FAIL TO USE SOMETHING** to fail to make use of something such as an opportunity **3.** *vti.* **GET WEAK OR ILL** to become weak, ill, or very thin, or make somebody become weak, ill, or very thin **4.** *vt.* **EXHAUST SOMEBODY** to make somebody exhausted **5.** *vt.* **DESTROY SOMETHING** to ravage or devastate something **6.** *vt.* **KILL SOMEBODY** to kill or murder somebody (*slang*) **7.** *vt.* **SPEAK POINTLESSLY ABOUT SOMETHING** to express ideas or arguments that are not appreciated or have no effect ○ *Don't waste your arguments on her; she's already made up her mind!* ■ *n.* **1. ACT OF WASTING** a failure to use something wisely, properly, fully, or to good effect **2. UNWANTED MATERIAL** unwanted or unusable by-products ○ *chemical waste* **3.** PHYSIOL **FOOD REMAINDER** the undigested remainder of food expelled from the body as excrement **4. WILD AREA** an uncultivated, desolate, or wild area (*often used in the plural*) **5. DESTROYED AREA** a place or region that has been destroyed or ruined **6. GARBAGE** garbage or trash ○ *household waste* **7.** ENG **USED OR CONTAMINATED WATER** used or contaminated water from domestic, industrial, or mining applications **8.** MINING **ROCK ASSOCIATED WITH A MINERAL** enclosing rock mined with a mineral, or ore with insufficient mineral content to justify further processing ■ **wastes** *npl.* **WILD AREA** an uncultivated, desolate, or wild area or region ○ *the frozen wastes of the tundra* ■ *adj.* **1. NOT NEEDED** superfluous, useless, or not needed **2. UNPRODUCTIVE** unproductive, uninhabited, or uncultivated ○ *waste ground* **3.** PHYSIOL **REJECTED FROM BODY** expelled from the body as unwanted and indigestible ○ *waste matter* **4. FOR WASTE** used to carry off or store waste [12thC. Via Old Northern French from, ultimately, Latin *vastus* "empty" (source of English *devastate* and *vast*).] —**wast·a·ble** *adj.* ◇ **lay something (to) waste** to destroy or devastate something

waste·bas·ket /wáyst bàskət/ *n.* a small container into which people can throw trash, especially paper

wast·ed /wáystəd/ *adj.* **1. NOT USED** not used or exploited **2. USELESS** useless because it achieves nothing **3. WITHERED** shrunken or ravaged **4. EXHAUSTED** exhausted from exertion (*slang*) **5. INTOXICATED** under the influence of drink or drugs (*slang*)

waste dis·pos·al, **waste dis·pos·al u·nit** *n. U.K.* = **garbage disposal**

waste·ful /wáystf'l/ *adj.* **1. EXTRAVAGANT** using resources unwisely **2. CAUSING WASTE** causing waste or devastation —**waste·ful·ly** *adv.* —**waste·ful·ness** *n.*

waste heat re·cov·er·y *n.* the reclaiming of heat that would otherwise be unused, from such sources as furnaces, kilns, or engines, for use in another process, e.g., preheating air or water

waste·land /wáyst lànd/ *n.* **1. DESOLATE LAND** an area of land that is desolate or barren and not used **2. BARREN PLACE OR TIME** an environment that is thought to be spiritually or intellectually barren ○ *the wasteland of daytime TV*

WORD KEY: CULTURAL NOTE

The Waste Land, a poem by U.S.-born British poet T.S. Eliot (1922). One of the 20th century's major poetic works, it portrays the disintegration of western values, the soullessness of modern society, and humankind's desperate search for salvation. It consists of five seemingly disconnected sections made up of fragmented verses written in a variety of styles but linked by imagery, symbols, and diverse literary and historical references.

waste·lot /wáyst lòt/ *n. Can* an area of wasteland in a city

waste man·age·ment *n.* activities that deal with waste before and after it is produced, including its minimization, transfer, storing, separating, recovering, recycling, and final disposal

waste·pa·per /wáyst pàypər/ *n.* paper that is not needed and has been thrown away

waste·pa·per bas·ket *n.* = **wastebasket**

waste pipe *n.* a pipe that carries excess or used fluids from a container such as a sink or bathtub

waste prod·uct *n.* a useless or unwanted by-product of a process

wast·er /wáystər/ *n.* **1. ONE WHO WASTES** somebody who wastes something **2. SOMETHING THAT WASTES** something that destroys or wastes something **3. RUINED ARTICLE** an article that has been spoiled during manufacture, especially a ceramic piece

waste·wa·ter /wáyst wòwtər/ *n.* water that has been used

wast·ing /wáysting/ *adj.* taking away strength and energy —**wast·ing·ly** *adv.*

wast·ing as·set *n.* an asset, especially a natural resource such as a mine, that cannot be renewed and that loses its value over time

wast·rel /wáystrəl/ *n.* **1. OFFENSIVE TERM** an offensive term that deliberately insults somebody for being wasteful or spendthrift **2. OFFENSIVE TERM** an offensive term that deliberately insults somebody for being lazy [Late 16thC. Formed from WASTE + *-rel* an ending indicating "little" or derogatory sense.]

wat /wot/ *n.* a Buddhist monastery or temple in Thailand, Cambodia, or Laos [Mid-19thC. Via Thai from Sanskrit *vāṭa* "enclosure."]

wa·tap /wa taap/ *n.* a stringy thread formerly made by some Native North Americans from conifers. It was used for sewing and weaving. [Mid-18thC. Via North American French from Ojibwa.]

watch /woch/ *n.* **1. PERSONAL CLOCK** a small clock worn on the wrist or carried in a pocket **2. TIME SPENT OBSERVING** a period of time spent observing something closely **3.** NAUT **DUTY ON SHIP** a fixed period of a day spent on duty on board a ship **4.** NAUT **CREW ON DUTY**

the members of a ship's crew who are on duty at a particular time **5.** TIME **DIVISION OF NIGHT** one of the periods of time into which the night was divided in the past **6. GUARD'S DUTY** the period during which a guard is on duty **7. PERSON'S DUTY** a period when a particular person is in charge of something **8.** METEOROL **WEATHER ALERT** an official notice from meteorological authorities that weather of a particular kind is likely to develop in an area ○ *a tornado watch* **9. PEOPLE WATCHING** a person or group that guards or observes something, especially at night ○ *posted a watch around the house, day and night* ■ *v.* (**watched, watch·ing, watch·es**) **1.** *vti.* **LOOK CAREFULLY** to look at something carefully or closely **2.** *vi.* **BE ALERT** to be vigilant or alert **3.** *vi.* **KEEP LOOKOUT** to keep a lookout for something that might appear or happen **4.** *vti.* **GUARD SOMETHING** to guard or keep something or somebody under observation **5.** *vi.* **KEEP VIGIL** to stay awake and keep a vigil [Assumed Old English *wæccan* "to keep watch, be awake," from a prehistoric Germanic word that is also the ancestor of English *wake*] ◇ **be on the watch for somebody** *or* **something** to look out for somebody or something ◇ **watch it** to be careful

watch out *vi.* **1. BE CAREFUL** to be careful, alert, or wary **2. LOOK** to look and wait for something or somebody

watch over *vt.* to look after, supervise, or guard somebody or something

watch·a·ble /wóchəb'l/ *adj.* **1. OBSERVABLE** apparent or capable of being observed **2. ENJOYABLE** interesting and enjoyable to watch ○ *a very watchable detective series* —**watch·a·bil·i·ty** /wòchə bíllətee/ *n.*

watch·band /wóch bànd/ *n. U.S., Can, Aus* a strap for a wristwatch

watch cap *n.* a dark-blue close-fitting knitted woolen cap worn in cold weather, especially by sailors in the Navy

watch·case /wóch kàyss/ *n.* the protective casing for a watch mechanism

watch·dog /wóch dōwg/ *n.* **1.** DOMESTIC **DOG FOR GUARDING** a dog used for guarding property or people **2.** PUBLIC ADMIN **GUARD AGAINST UNDESIRABLE PRACTICES** a person or organization guarding against illegal practices, unacceptable standards, or inefficiency ○ *a government watchdog* ■ *vti.* (**-dogged, -dog·ging, -dogs**) **BE A WATCHDOG** to act as a watchdog on something

watch·er /wóchər/ *n.* **1. SOMEBODY WHO WATCHES OR LOOKS** a person who watches or observes somebody or something or who looks for somebody or something's appearance or occurrence **2. SOMEBODY WHO GUARDS** somebody who acts as a guard or guardian **3. SOMEBODY KEEPING VIGIL** somebody who keeps a vigil, especially at the bed of an ill person

watch·eye /wóch ī/ *n.* = **walleye** *n.* 2, **walleye** *n.* 3, **walleye** *n.* 4

watch fire *n.* a fire kept burning at night either as a signal or for the comfort of somebody keeping watch

watch·ful /wóchfəl/ *adj.* **1. OBSERVING CLOSELY** carefully observant or alert ○ *watchful for signs of recovery* **2. AWAKE** not asleep (*archaic*) —**watch·ful·ly** *adv.* —**watch·ful·ness** *n.*

watch glass *n.* **1.** = **crystal** *n.* 8 **2.** SCI **SHALLOW DISH** a shallow round glass dish used to evaporate liquids or to cover something

watch·mak·er /wóch màykər/ *n.* somebody who makes or repairs watches

watch·man /wóchmən/ (*plural* **-men** /-mən/) *n.* somebody employed to patrol or guard buildings or an area

watch night *n.* **1. DECEMBER 31** the night of December 31, celebrated in some Protestant churches with a special nighttime service that takes in the midnight transition from the old year to the new **2. DECEMBER 24** the night of December 24, celebrated in some Protestant churches with a special nighttime service to welcome Jesus Christ to the world, and the arrival of Christmas, at midnight

watch pock·et *n.* a small pocket for a watch in a vest or pants

watch·strap /wóch stràp/ *n. U.K., NZ* a strap for a wristwatch. ◊ **watchband**

watch·tow·er /wóch tòwər/ *n.* a high tower in which sentries keep watch for the approach of an enemy

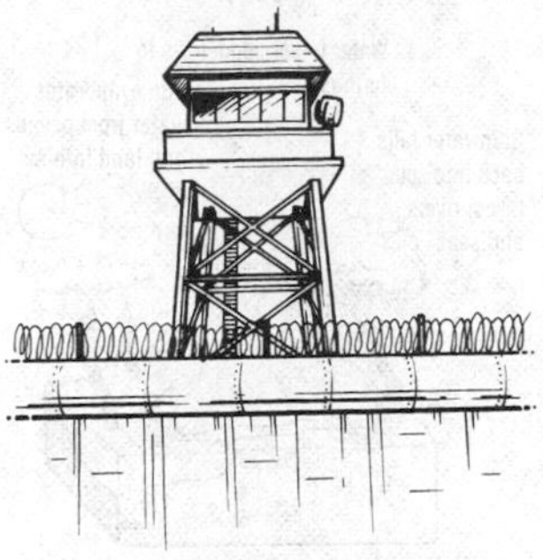

Watchtower

watch·word /wóch wùrd/ *n.* **1. SLOGAN** a word or slogan that encapsulates a mode of action, a set of beliefs, or membership of a group **2. PASSWORD** a word or phrase that somebody has to say to prove a right to be in a particular place

wa·ter /wáwtər/ *n.* **1. LIQUID OF RAIN AND RIVERS** the clear liquid, essential for all plant and animal life, that occurs as rain, snow, and ice, and forms rivers, lakes, and seas. Pure water is odorless, colorless, and tasteless. Naturally occurring water picks up color and taste from substances in its environment. Formula: H_2O. **2.** GEOG **AREA OF WATER** an area or body of water, e.g., a river, stream, lake, or sea **3. SURFACE OF WATER** the surface of a body of water ○ *swim under water* **4.** PHILOS **ELEMENT** in ancient and medieval philosophy, one of the four elements **5.** TRANSP **TRANSPORT OVER WATER** a means of transport over or through water, especially a boat ○ *can only get there by water* **6.** UTIL **WATER SUPPLY** a supply of water to a house, town, or region **7. SOLUTION OF SUBSTANCE IN WATER** a solution of a specified chemical or substance in water ○ *lavender water* **8.** PHYSIOL **BODY FLUID** any watery fluid present in or secreted by the body, e.g., urine, sweat, saliva, or tears **9.** PHYSIOL **FLUID SURROUNDING FETUS** the amniotic fluid that surrounds the fetus in the womb (*often used in the plural*) **10.** TEXTILES **WAVY PATTERN** a lustrous wavy pattern on the surface of some fabrics, e.g., silk **11. BRIGHTNESS** the quality of brightness of a gem. ◊ **first water** ■ **wa·ters** *npl.* **1. PARTICULAR AREA OF SEA** a particular region of sea, e.g., that belonging to a specific nation ○ *territorial waters* **2. WATER CONTAINING MINERALS** naturally occurring water containing minerals, e.g., that found at a spa and used for health reasons ■ *v.* (**-tered, -ter·ing, -ters**) **1.** *vt.* **SPRINKLE OR SOAK SOMETHING WITH WATER** to sprinkle, wet, or soak something with water **2.** *vt.* AGRIC **IRRIGATE LAND** to take water to crops or fields **3.** *vti.* **GIVE OR GET WATER** to give drinking water to an animal, or get or take water as an animal does **4.** *vi.* **FILL WITH TEARS WHEN IRRITATED** to fill with tears, especially because of irritation (*refers to eyes*) **5.** *vi.* **PRODUCE SALIVA** to produce saliva, particularly in pleasant anticipation of food (*refers to the mouth*) **6.** *vi.* NAUT **TAKE ON WATER SUPPLY** to take on a supply of water **7.** *vt.* TEXTILES **GIVE WAVY SHEEN** to give a lustrous wavy pattern to material, especially silk [Old English *wæter*. Ultimately from the Indo-European word meaning "water" that is also the ancestor of English *hydro-*, *whiskey*, and *vodka*.] —**wa·ter·er** *n.* ◇ **be dead in the water** to have no chance of success or survival ◇ **be water under the bridge** to be something that is in the past and that cannot be altered ◇ **hold water** to be well-founded, or stand up under scrutiny ◇ **in deep water** in severe difficulties ◇ **in hot water** in trouble or in a difficult or embarrassing situation ◇ **pour** *or* **throw cold water on** *or* **onto** *or* **over something** to discourage a plan or idea by showing a lack of interest in it or rejecting it as impractical ◇ **tread water 1.** to keep afloat without moving forward, by moving the legs and arms **2.** to make no progress but manage to keep a situation the same for a period of time ◇ **water off a duck's back** something said that has absolutely no effect on the attitude or behavior of the person to whom it is said

WORD KEY: CULTURAL NOTE

Water Music, an orchestral suite by German-born British composer George Frederic Handel (1717). It consists of three separate suites for strings and wind instruments. The exact circumstances of its composition are not known, but it was first performed to accompany a royal barge trip along the Thames River from Whitehall to Chelsea on July 17, 1717.

water down *vt.* **1. DILUTE** to weaken or dilute something by adding water to it **2. REDUCE DIFFICULTY OR OFFENSIVENESS OF SOMETHING** to moderate or attenuate something in order to make it less difficult, offensive, or controversial ○ *The producers want to water down her original script.* —**wa·tered-down** *adj.*

wa·ter ar·um *n.* an aquatic plant native to cool northern temperate regions and cultivated for its glossy heart-shaped leaves and large white funnel-shaped cone surrounding the flower spike. Latin name: *Calla palustris.*

wa·ter ash *n.* TREES = **stinking ash**

wa·ter bag *n.* **1. BAG FOR CARRYING WATER** a bag made of leather, canvas, or similar material used for carrying water **2.** ANAT **FLUID-FILLED SAC SURROUNDING FETUS** the thin protective sac (**amnion**) around the growing fetus, and the watery fluid (**amniotic fluid**) it contains that is expelled just before or during childbirth

wa·ter bal·let *n.* the performance of dance movements in water

wa·ter bear *n.* = **tardigrade**

Wa·ter Bear·er *n.* ASTRON = **Aquarius**

wa·ter bed *n.* a bed with a special mattress filled with water

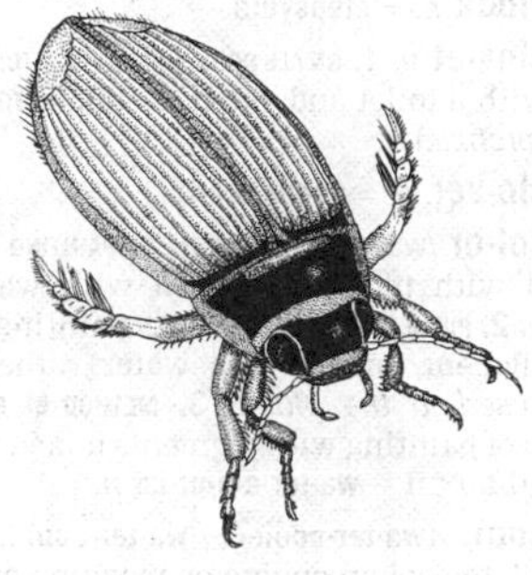

Water beetle

wa·ter bee·tle *n.* a member of a group of beetles that live mainly in water. Some have broad hind legs for swimming; others crawl over aquatic vegetation. Family: Hydrophilidae.

wa·ter bird *n.* a bird that lives mainly near, and wades in or swims on, water, especially fresh water

wa·ter bis·cuit *n.* a thin plain cracker made from flour and water, often served with cheese

wa·ter blis·ter *n.* a blister that contains clear watery fluid without blood or pus

wa·ter bloom *n.* a growth of algae on a body of water such as a lake

wa·ter boat·man (*plural* **wa·ter boat·men**) *n.* **1. POND BUG** any of various bugs that live mainly at the bottom of ponds and have oarlike flattened hind legs that they use for swimming. Most water boatmen are good fliers. Family: Corixidae. **2.** = **backswimmer**

wa·ter·borne /wáwtər bàwrn/ *adj.* **1.** TRANSP **CARRIED BY WATER** traveling on or transported by water ○ *a waterborne vessel* **2.** MED **TRANSMITTED BY WATER** transmitted or transported by water, as certain infectious agents are

wa·ter boy *n.* somebody who keeps a group of people, e.g., athletes, supplied with drinking water

wa·ter brash *n.* the sudden filling of the mouth with acidic juices from the stomach, usually accompanied by heartburn and often resulting from indigestion. It is common in pregnancy but may also be an indication of a disorder of the digestive tract.

wa·ter·buck /wáwtər bùk/ (*plural* **-bucks** *or* **-buck**) *n.* a large antelope of southern Africa with a shaggy dark-gray or reddish coat, found in grassland and woodland near open water. Latin name: *Kobus ellipsiprymnus.*

wa·ter buf·fa·lo *n.* a large buffalo native to swamplands of Southeast Asia but widely domesticated, with a gray-black coat and long backward-curving horns. Domestic breeds are more docile, have shorter horns, and are used as draft animals and for milk. Latin name: *Bubalus bubalis.*

wa·ter bug *n.* an aquatic insect, e.g., the water boatman or water strider

wa·ter·bus /wáwtər bùss/ *n.* a boat carrying passengers in a regular service across a river or lake

wa·ter butt *n. U.K.* = **rain barrel**

wa·ter cal·trop *n.* = **water chestnut**

wa·ter can·non *n.* an apparatus usually mounted on a truck that produces a jet of high-pressure water and is used to disperse crowds

Wa·ter Car·ri·er *n.* ASTRON = **Aquarius**

wa·ter chest·nut *n.* **1.** PLANTS **AQUATIC PLANT** an annual aquatic plant that forms rosettes of diamond-shaped floating leaves, has feathery submerged leaves, and bears hard spiny dark-gray fruit containing edible seeds. It is native to Europe and Asia. Latin name: *Trapa natans.* **2.** PLANTS **CHINESE PLANT WITH AN EDIBLE STEM** a Chinese sedge that produces edible stems (**corms**). Latin name: *Eleocharis tuberosa.* **3.** FOOD **CRUNCHY NUTLIKE CORM IN ASIAN COOKING** the round white crunchy stem (**corm**) of the Chinese water-chestnut plant. Water chestnuts are common in Asian cooking, and are used in food manufacture to add crunchiness to processed foods.

water chin·qua·pin *n.* an American aquatic plant that resembles a water lily and has fragrant cup-shaped pale-yellow flowers. Latin name: *Nelumbo lutea.*

wa·ter clock *n.* = **clepsydra**

wa·ter clos·et *n.* **1. SMALL ROOM CONTAINING TOILET** a small room with a toilet and, often, a sink **2. TOILET** a flush toilet (*archaic*)

wa·ter clo·ver *n.* = **pepperwort**

wa·ter·col·or /wáwtər kùllər/ *n.* **1. PAINTING** a painting created with pigments mixed with water rather than oil **2. PIGMENT MIXED WITH WATER** painting pigments, or a pigment, mixed with water rather than oil (*often used in the plural*) **3. METHOD OF PAINTING** the method of painting with pigments mixed with water rather than oil —**wa·ter·col·or·ist** *n.*

wa·ter-cool (**wa·ter-cooled, wa·ter-cool·ing, wa·ter-cools**) *vt.* to cool an engine or machine by means of water, typically by circulating water in a water jacket or by pipes

wa·ter cool·er *n.* a device that dispenses cooled drinking water

wa·ter·course /wáwtər kàwrss/ *n.* **1. CHANNEL FOR FLOWING WATER** a river or stream channel, or an artificial channel, through which water flows **2. STREAM** the water of a river or stream that flows along a water-course

wa·ter·craft /wáwtər kràft/ *n.* **1. BOAT OR SHIP** a vessel used for traveling on water (*formal*) **2. SKILL IN WATER-RELATED ACTIVITIES** skill in swimming, handling boats, or other water-related activities

Watercress

wa·ter·cress /wáwtər krèss/ *n.* a perennial aquatic plant of Europe and Asia that is widely cultivated for its peppery-flavored leaves and stems, used in salads. Latin name: *Nasturtium officinale.*

wa·ter cure *n.* a session of treatment by hydrotherapy or hydropathy (*dated*)

wa·ter cy·cle *n.* the constant circulation of water between atmosphere, land, and sea by evaporation, precipitation, and percolation through soils and rocks

wa·ter dog *n.* **1.** ZOOL **DOG AT HOME IN WATER** a dog that likes water, especially one trained to hunt or retrieve game in water **2. SOMEBODY WHO LIKES THE WATER** somebody who likes being in, on, or near water, e.g., a sailor or swimmer (*informal*)

wa·ter·fall /wáwtər fàwl/ *n.* a vertical stream of water that occurs where a river or stream falls over the edge of a steep place

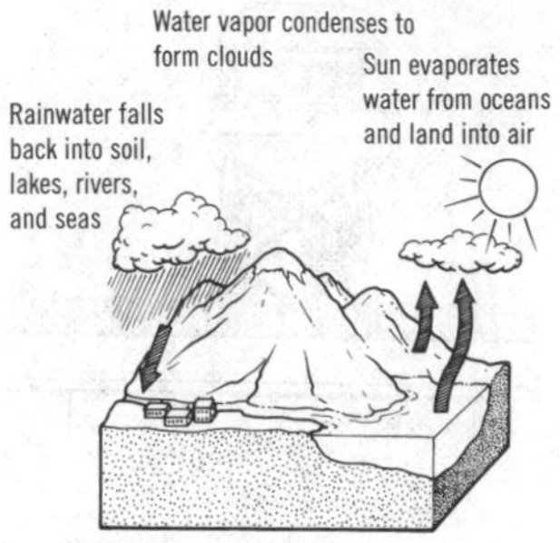
Water vapor condenses to form clouds
Sun evaporates water from oceans and land into air
Rainwater falls back into soil, lakes, rivers, and seas

Water cycle

WORLD'S HIGHEST WATERFALLS

1	Angel Falls	Height [3,212 ft / 979 m*] (also single largest leap, [2,647 ft / 807 m*])	Location Venezuela
2	Tugela Waterfall	Height [3,110 ft / 948 m*]	Location South Africa
3	Mtarazi Waterfall	Height [2,500 ft / 762 m*]	Location Zimbabwe
4	Yosemite Falls	Height [2,425 ft / 739 m*]	Location United States
5	Cuquenán Waterfall	Height [2,000 ft / 610 m*]	Location Venezuela
6	Sutherland Falls	Height [1,904 ft / 580 m*]	Location New Zealand
7	Kile Waterfall	Height [1,840 ft / 561 m*]	Location Norway
8	Kahiwa Waterfall	Height [1,748 ft / 533 m*]	Location United States
9	Mardal Waterfall	Height [1,696 ft / 517 m*]	Location Norway
10	Takakkaw Falls	Height [1,650 ft / 503 m*]	Location Canada

* Total height may include more than one leap

wa·ter fern *n.* = **mosquito fern**

wa·ter fil·ter *n.* an appliance or fitting for removing unwanted matter from water, especially bacteria or harmful chemicals from drinking water

wa·ter·find·er /wáwtər fìndər/ *n.* = **dowser**

wa·ter flea *n.* a tiny crustacean that swims with rapid jerky movements, using its large forked antennae. Suborder: Cladocera.

wa·ter·fowl /wáwtər fòwl/ *n.* (*plural* **-fowl** *or* **-fowls**) **AQUATIC BIRD** any of various birds that swim on water ■ *npl.* **SWIMMING GAME BIRDS** swimming game birds such as ducks, considered collectively

wa·ter·front /wáwtər frùnt/ *n.* **1. PART OF TOWN ALONGSIDE WATER** the part of a town that lies alongside a body of water **2. SHORE** land beside an area of water

wa·ter gap *n.* a deep valley through a mountain ridge, in which water flows

wa·ter gas *n.* a toxic mixture of carbon monoxide and methane generated by the passage of steam through an incandescent bed of coal. It is used for industrial heating, as an illuminant, and as a gas-engine fuel.

wa·ter gate *n.* **1.** = **floodgate 2. GATE INTO AREA OF WATER** a gate that gives access to an area of water

Wa·ter·gate /wáwtər gàyt/ *n.* **1.** HIST **1972 U.S. POLITICAL SCANDAL** a political scandal stemming from a break-in by Republican operatives at the 1972 U.S. Democratic National Committee headquarters, which were in the Watergate complex in Washington, D.C. The scandal led to the resignation of President Nixon and the conviction and imprisonment of a number of his closest aides. **2. PUBLIC SCANDAL** a public scandal involving politicians or officials abusing power, especially if a cover-up is also attempted

wa·ter gauge *n.* a device that indicates the quantity or level of water in a tank, boiler feed, reservoir, or stream

wa·ter glass *n.* **1.** HOUSEHOLD **DRINKING GLASS** a drinking glass, especially for water **2.** CHEM **THICK CHEMICAL SOLUTION** an extremely viscous solution of sodium silicate used as a waterproof coating, a cement, a fireproofing agent, and for preserving eggs **3. GLASS GAUGE** a water gauge consisting of a glass tube **4. DEVICE FOR EXAMINING UNDERWATER OBJECTS** an instrument such as an open box or tube with a glass bottom, used for looking at objects under the water's surface

wa·ter gun *n.* a toy gun that squirts water

wa·ter ham·mer *n.* a hammering or stuttering sound in a pipeline that sometimes accompanies a sudden and significant change in the flow rate of the fluid through the pipeline

wa·ter hem·lock *n.* any of various poisonous, highly scented plants found in marshy areas of the northern hemisphere that have compound leaves and dense flat-topped clusters of small white flowers. All parts of the plants, especially the tuberous roots, contain a toxic chemical. Genus: *Cicuta.*

wa·ter hen *n.* a bird that lives near water, e.g., a rail or a coot. Family: Rallidae.

wa·ter hole *n.* a natural hollow in the ground containing water, especially one where animals drink

wa·ter hy·a·cinth *n.* a perennial aquatic plant, native to the subtropical Americas but also found elsewhere, that has glossy rounded leaves with bulbous stalks, and lilac-blue flowers. Widely cultivated as an ornamental, it has become a troublesome weed of waterways in many subtropical regions, including Australia, Africa, and Southeast Asia. Latin name: *Eichhornia crassipes.*

wa·ter ice *n.* a frozen dessert of sweet-flavored ice

wa·ter·ing can *n.* a container with a handle and a spout, often with a perforated nozzle, used to water plants

wa·ter·ing hole *n.* **1. BAR SERVING DRINKS** a place such as a bar where people meet socially to drink (*informal*) **2.** = **water hole**

wa·ter·ing place *n.* **1.** = **water hole 2.** = **watering hole** *n.* 1 **3. HEALTH RESORT** a place where people go to drink or bathe in the local water for health reasons

wa·ter·ing pot *n.* = **watering can**

wa·ter·ish /wáwtərish/ *adj.* somewhat watery

wa·ter jump *n.* a place in a race where the runners or horses have to jump over an obstacle that includes a stream, ditch, or pool

wa·ter·leaf /wáwtər lèef/ *n.* any of various woodland plants of western North America with deeply toothed leaves and bell-shaped flowers. Genus: *Hydrophyllum.*

wa·ter·less /wáwtərləss/ *adj.* **1. WITHOUT WATER** lacking water **2. NOT NEEDING WATER** not needing water in the making or use of something

wa·ter lev·el *n.* **1.** GEOG **HEIGHT OF WATER SURFACE** the level of the surface of a body of water **2.** SHIPPING = **water line** *n.* 1 **3.** GEOL = **water table** *n.* 1

Water lily

wa·ter lil·y *n.* a perennial aquatic plant with roundish leaves that float on the water and showy cup-shaped often fragrant flowers. Family: Nymphaeaceae.

WORD KEY: CULTURAL NOTE

Water Lilies, the title of a number of paintings by French artist Claude Monet (1899–1925). In his later years, Monet retired to his house at Giverny near Paris, where he painted numerous studies of the water lilies in his garden pond. While tending toward abstraction, many of these works, for example, the enormous panels now in the Orangerie in Paris, succeed brilliantly in capturing the evanescent quality of natural phenomena.

wa·ter line *n.* **1.** SHIPPING **LINE ON HULL** a line on a ship's hull indicating the level to which the ship can sink into the water under various conditions **2. LINE OF EDGE OF WATER** the line to which a body of water rises or reaches

wa·ter·logged /wáwtər làwgd/ *adj.* **1. SOAKED WITH WATER** saturated with water ○ *a waterlogged field* **2.** NAUT **HARD TO STEER BECAUSE OF WATER** filled with water and therefore hard to steer —**wa·ter·log** *vt.*

Wa·ter·loo[1] /wátər lo͞o, wàtər lo͞o/ **1.** town in central Belgium, about 10 mi./16 km south of Brussels. It was the site of the Battle of Waterloo on June 18, 1815, where Napoleon was decisively defeated by British and Prussian forces. Population: 27,860 (1991). **2.** city in northeastern Iowa, northwest of Cedar Rapids and southeast of Cedar Falls. Population: 65,022 (1996).

Wa·ter·loo[2] /wáwtər lo͞o, wáwtər lo͞o/ (*plural* **-loos**), **wa·ter·loo** (*plural* **-loos**) *n.* a crushing or decisive defeat ◇ **meet your Waterloo** to be decisively defeated or overcome

wa·ter main *n.* a large underground pipe supplying water

wa·ter·man /wáwtərmən/ (*plural* **-men** /-mən/) *n.* somebody who works on or rents out boats

wa·ter·mark /wáwtər maàrk/ *n.* **1.** PAPER **HIDDEN MARK IN PAPER** a design or mark in paper that can be seen when the paper is held up to the light, or the metal tool used to make such a design **2.** SHIPPING = **water line** *n.* 2 **3. LINE LEFT BY WATER** a line showing where the edge or surface of water has been ■ *vt.* (**-marked, -mark·ing, -marks**) PAPER **PUT WATERMARK OR PATTERN IN PAPER** to put a watermark into paper while it is being made, or impress a particular pattern as a watermark

wa·ter meas·ur·er *n.* INSECTS = **marsh treader**

wa·ter·mel·on /wáwtər mèllən/ *n.* **1.** FOOD **LARGE FRUIT WITH SWEET JUICY FLESH** a large oval or round fruit with a hard green skin and sweet and very juicy pink, red, or yellow flesh usually with many black seeds **2.** PLANTS **AFRICAN PLANT PRODUCING WATERMELON FRUIT** an annual climbing plant native to Africa but widely cultivated that has deeply lobed hairy leaves, yellow flowers, and bears the watermelon fruit. Latin name: *Citrullus lanatus.*

wa·ter me·ter *n.* a device that records the amount of water that passes through a pipe, usually for billing purposes

wa·ter mil·foil *n.* any of various perennial aquatic plants that have submerged leaves made up of many feathery segments and bear slender spikes of tiny flowers above the water surface. Genus: *Myriophyllum.*

wa·ter mill *n.* a mill that has machinery powered by moving water

wa·ter mint *n.* a perennial plant of swampy areas with toothed hairy leaves, a hairy stem, and whorls of lilac-pink flowers. It emits a strong scent when crushed. Latin name: *Mentha aquatica.*

wa·ter moc·ca·sin *n.* **1. POISONOUS N AMERICAN SNAKE** a venomous semiaquatic snake belonging to the pit viper family and inhabiting wetlands of the southern United States that has an olive to brownish back and indistinct black bars. It feeds on water birds, fish, and other reptiles, and shows the white insides of its mouth when threatened. Latin name: *Agkistrodon piscivorus.* **2. HARMLESS WATER SNAKE** a snake that resembles a venomous water moccasin but is harmless. Genus: *Nerodia.*

wa·ter mold *n.* any of various fungi that inhabit fresh or brackish water and feed mainly on dead organic material but are sometimes parasitic on fish, plants, and other living organisms. Order: Saprolegniales.

wa·ter nymph *n.* in folklore and classical mythology, a nymph that lives in water

wa·ter oak *n.* an oak of the southern United States that favors wet locations. Latin name: *Quercus nigra.*

wa·ter of crys·tal·li·za·tion *n.* molecules of water incorporated in a crystalline substance and responsible for its properties and structure

wa·ter of hy·dra·tion *n.* molecules of water chemically incorporated in a substance but removable without affecting the essential composition of the substance

wa·ter on the brain *n.* MED = **hydrocephalus**

wa·ter on the knee *n.* the accumulation of watery fluid in or around the knee indicating disease or injury of the knee joint

wa·ter o·pos·sum *n.* = **yapok**

wa·ter ou·zel *n.* BIRDS = **dipper** *n.* 2

wa·ter part·ing *n.* GEOG = **divide** *n.* 2

wa·ter pen·ny *n.* any of various circular beetle larvae that cling like tiny suction cups to rocks in swift streams. Family: Psephenidae.

wa·ter pen·ny·wort *n.* a creeping plant thats grows in water or moist places. Genus: *Hydrocotyle.*

wa·ter pep·per *n.* an annual plant widely distributed in damp places that has lance-shaped leaves, a hot peppery taste, and slender spikes of inconspicuous pink or greenish flowers. Latin name: *Polygonum hydropiper.*

wa·ter pipe *n.* **1.** CONSTR **PIPE FOR CONVEYING WATER** a pipe for transporting water from one place to another **2.** DRUGS **WATER-FILLED SMOKING PIPE** a pipe for smoking something, especially marijuana, that is filled with water in order to cool the smoke by drawing it through the water

wa·ter pis·tol *n.* a toy gun that squirts water

wa·ter plan·tain *n.* a perennial plant found in water or wet places, with a rosette of pointed oval leaves and branching heads of pinkish or white flowers. Genus: *Alisma.*

wa·ter po·lo *n.* a game played in a swimming pool by two teams of seven players whose object is to score by sending a large ball into the opposing team's goal

wa·ter pow·er *n.* **1. POWER GENERATED BY FORCE OF WATER** power, usually generated from an elevated water supply, that is converted to electricity through the use of hydraulic turbines **2. FALL OF WATER THAT GENERATES POWER** the descent of a watercourse capable of or providing water power

wa·ter·proof /wáwtər pro͞of/ *adj.* **IMPERVIOUS TO WATER** treated or constructed so as to be impenetrable or unaffected by water ■ *n.* **1.** *U.K.* **ITEM OF WATERPROOF CLOTHING** an item of waterproof clothing, e.g., a plastic cape **2.** TEXTILES **TEXTILE IMPERVIOUS TO WATER** a textile that has been made or treated so as to be impenetrable or unaffected by water ■ *vt.* (**-proofed, -proof·ing, -proofs**) **MAKE SOMETHING WATERPROOF** to make something such as a house or an item of clothing impenetrable by water

wa·ter purs·lane *n.* a creeping annual plant growing in moist places with fleshy rounded leaves and small purplish flowers at the leaf base. Latin name: *Lythrum portula.*

wa·ter rail *n.* a Eurasian bird of marshes and other wet places with a long red bill, gray underparts with black-striped flanks, and mottled brown back and wings. Latin name: *Rallus aquaticus.*

wa·ter rat *n.* **1.** = **muskrat 2. RAT WITH FEET ADAPTED FOR SWIMMING** any of various large amphibious rats, native to Australia, New Guinea, and the Philippines, that have broad paddle-shaped hind feet for swimming. Subfamily: Hydromyinae. **3. WATERFRONT THUG** a criminal, loafer, or hooligan who often frequents waterfront areas (*slang*)

wa·ter-re·pel·lent, **wa·ter-re·sis·tant** *adj.* treated or constructed so as to prevent water being absorbed into it or passing through it

wa·ter right *n.* **1.** AGRIC **RIGHT TO USE A WATER SOURCE** the right to use a water source, especially for irrigation (*often plural*) **2.** NAUT **RIGHT TO SAIL SOMEWHERE** the right to sail on particular rivers, lakes, or seas

Wa·ters /wáwtərz/, **Ethel** (1900–77) U.S. singer and actor. A noted blues singer, she was one of the most prominent African American performers of stage and screen in the 1930s and 1940s.

Wa·ters, Muddy (1915–83) U.S. musician. He was a country blues singer who originated the Chicago blues style in the 1950s, and was a leading figure in the revival of folk-blues music in the 1960s. Real name **McKinley Morganfield**

wa·ter sap·phire *n.* a blue form of the mineral cordierite, found in river gravel and used as a gemstone

wa·ter·scape /wáwtər skàyp/ *n.* a view or picture of an expanse of water

wa·ter scav·en·ger bee·tle *n.* any of various smooth dark aquatic beetles that are found worldwide in marshes and ponds and eat algae and decaying organic matter. Family: Hydrophilidae.

wa·ter scor·pi·on *n.* an aquatic insect that lies submerged in water breathing through a long tubular siphon, and that catches prey by using the front pair of legs. Family: Nepidae.

wa·ter seal *n.* water that lies in a waste pipe and forms a seal that prevents the escape of unpleasant smells

wa·ter·shed /wáwtər shèd/ *n.* **1.** GEOG = **divide** *n.* 2 **2.** GEOG **REGION DRAINING INTO RIVER OR OCEAN** the land area that drains into a particular lake, river, or ocean **3. TURNING POINT** an important period, time, event, or factor that marks a change or division [Early 19thC. Anglicization of German *Wasserscheide*, literally "water divide."]

wa·ter shield *n.* **1. AQUATIC PLANT WITH PURPLE FLOWERS** a widely distributed perennial aquatic plant with purple flowers and floating leaves that are purple underneath and covered in a layer of clear jelly. Latin name: *Brasenia schreberi.* **2. AQUATIC PLANT WITH DISTINCTIVE LEAVES** any of various aquatic plants with roundish floating leaves or finely divided needle-shaped submerged leaves. Genus: *Cabomba.* [Because the leaves are shaped like shields]

wa·ter-sick *adj.* used to describe land that has been made unproductive by excessive irrigation

wa·ter·side /wáwtər sīd/ *n.* **LAND BY WATER** land alongside an area of water ■ *adj.* **LIVING OR WORKING BESIDE WATER** living or working beside an area of water

wa·ter sign *n.* any one of the three signs of the zodiac, Pisces, Cancer, or Scorpio, that are associated with emotional sensitivity

wa·ter ski *n.* a type of ski designed for skiing over water

Barnaby's

Water-ski

wa·ter-ski (**wa·ter-skied, wa·ter-ski·ing, wa·ter-skis**) *vi.* to ski over water while being towed by a boat —**wa·ter-ski·er** *n.* —**wa·ter-ski·ing** *n.*

wa·ter snake *n.* **1. SNAKE LIVING IN WATER** a snake that lives in or near water **2. NONPOISONOUS MARSH SNAKE** a nonvenomous snake found in North America, Europe, and Asia especially Southeast Asia, that lives in marshes and other wet places. Genus: *Natrix.*

wa·ter soft·en·er *n.* **1. APPARATUS FOR REMOVING HARDNESS FROM WATER** a device that removes or reduces hardness in water, usually by means of ion-exchange resins **2. CHEMICAL FOR REDUCING HARDNESS OF WATER** a substance used to reduce hardness of water, e.g., by precipitating out the minerals causing the hardness

wa·ter-sol·u·ble *adj.* capable of being dissolved completely by water

wa·ter span·iel *n.* any of several breeds of dog that have thick curly water-resistant coats and that were developed for retrieving from water

wa·ter sports *npl.* SPORTS ASSOCIATED WITH WATER sports carried out on or in water ■ *n. U.K.* TABOO OFFENSIVE TERM a euphemism used to describe sexual activity in which urine or the act of urination provides gratification (*taboo offensive*)

wa·ter·spout /wáwtər spòwt/ *n.* **1.** METEOROL **TORNADO OVER WATER** a funnel-shaped tornado, sometimes hundreds of feet wide, extending from the surface of the sea or a lake to the cloud base and caused by violent circulation of air **2.** BUILDING **SPOUT FROM ROOF GUTTER** a hole or spout through which water flows, e.g., from the gutter of a building

wa·ter sprite *n.* in folklore and classical mythology, a sprite that lives in water

wa·ter star·wort *n.* an aquatic plant that can form rosettes of rounded floating leaves at the base of which develop tiny male or female flowers. The underwater leaves are less rounded, and the form of the plant can vary markedly, depending on its location. Genus: *Callitriche.*

wa·ter stick in·sect *n.* an aquatic bug with a long slender body and a long siphon used for breathing underwater that catches prey by using its front legs. Although winged, it has poorly developed flight muscles and cannot fly. Latin name: *Ranatra linearis.*

wa·ter strid·er *n.* an aquatic insect that walks on water with long legs and feeds on dead insects. Family: Gerridae.

wa·ter sup·ply *n.* **1.** **WATER DISTRIBUTED TO PLACE** the water distributed to a town, community, or region **2.** **WATER SOURCE OR DELIVERY SYSTEM** the source or delivery system supplying water to an area, e.g., reservoirs, pipes, or purification plants

wa·ter sys·tem *n.* **1.** GEOG **RIVER AND TRIBUTARIES** a river with all its tributaries **2.** UTIL **SYSTEM FOR DELIVERING WATER** a system for delivering water to a group of users or a town or region

wa·ter ta·ble *n.* **1.** GEOL **GROUNDWATER LEVEL** the upper surface of groundwater, below which pores in the rocks are filled with water **2.** ARCHIT **BAND DIVERTING RAINWATER** a molding or band that projects from a wall and is intended to divert rainwater

wa·ter tax·i *n.* a motorboat used to ferry passengers between destinations separated by water for a fare

wa·ter thrush *n.* either of two small North American songbirds of the wood warbler family that have markings similar to the thrush and live near streams, ponds, and swampy ground. Genus: *Seiurus.*

wa·ter·tight /wáwtər tìt/ *adj.* **1.** **KEEPING WATER IN OR OUT** not allowing water to pass in, out, or through **2.** **STANDING UP TO SCRUTINY** without loopholes or flaws ○ *a watertight argument* —**wa·ter·tight·ness** *n.*

Wa·ter·ton-Gla·cier In·ter·na·tion·al Peace Park /wàwtərtən glàysər-/ national park established in 1932 by linking the U.S. Glacier National Park with the Canadian Waterton Lakes National Park. Area: 203 sq. mi./526 sq. km.

wa·ter tor·ture *n.* a form of torture in which water is used, especially one in which water is dripped steadily onto somebody's forehead

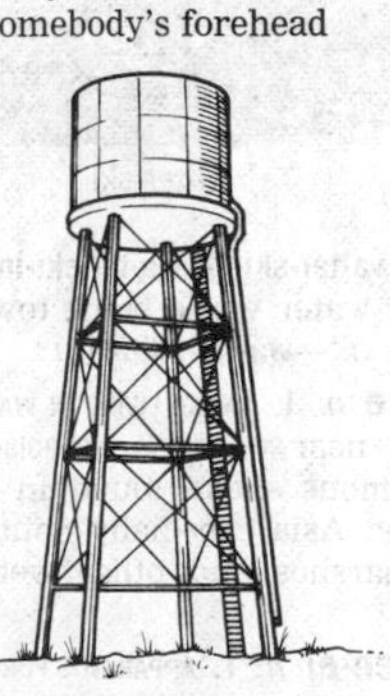

Water tower

wa·ter tow·er *n.* **1.** **WATER STORAGE TOWER** a tower for water storage where the prevailing water pressure is not sufficient for either firefighting or general distribution **2.** **FIREFIGHTING APPARATUS FOR RAISING WATER** a firefighting apparatus for lifting hoses to high levels

Wa·ter·town /wáwtər town/ **1.** city in eastern Massachusetts, on the Charles River. Founded in 1630, it is a western suburb of Boston. Population: 32,490 (1996). **2.** city in northern New York, on the Black River, northeast of Syracuse. Population: 28,700 (1996). **3.** city in eastern South Dakota, on the Big Sioux River, north of Sioux Falls. Population: 19,619 (1996).

wa·ter turk·ey *n.* = **anhinga**

wa·ter va·por *n.* water in the form of a vapor but usually below boiling point

wa·ter-vas·cu·lar sys·tem *n.* a system of water-filled vessels connecting the tube feet of echinoderms such as starfish

Wa·ter·ville /wáwtər vìl/ city in southwestern Maine, on the western bank of the Kennebec River, southwest of Bangor and northeast of Augusta. It is home to Colby College. Population: 17,173 (1990).

wa·ter·way /wáwtər wày/ *n.* **1.** GEOG **RIVER OR CANAL** a navigable channel such as a river or canal used by boats or ships **2.** SHIPPING **DRAIN ON DECK** a drain for water at the edge of the deck of a boat

wa·ter·weed /wáwtər wèed/ *n.* any of various plants such as pondweed that grow profusely in ponds, rivers, and other areas of fresh water

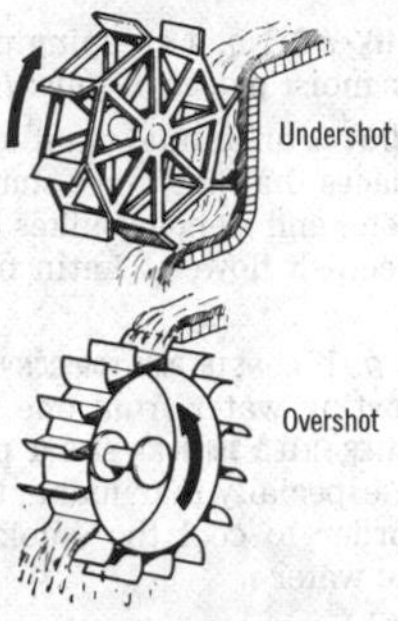

Water wheel

wa·ter wheel *n.* **1.** **WATER-DRIVEN WHEEL POWERING MACHINERY** a simple wheel driven by water flowing or falling onto vanes or into buckets on the edges of the wheel, used to power machinery **2.** **WHEEL FOR LIFTING WATER** a wheel with buckets fixed to its rim, used for lifting water

wa·ter wings *npl.* a pair of air-filled supports that fit closely around the upper arms of a swimmer, especially a child learning to swim

wa·ter witch *n.* = **dowser**

wa·ter·works /wáwtər wùrks/ *n.* (*plural* **-works**) **1.** **SYSTEM FOR SUPPLYING WATER** the entire system of treating, storing, supplying, and managing the distribution networks of pumps and pipes that provide water to a community or region (*takes a singular or plural verb*) **2.** **COMPONENT OF WATER SYSTEM** a single component of a waterworks system such as a pumping station **3.** **DISPLAY OF MOVING WATER** a display of water that has been made to move artificially, e.g., a fountain ■ *npl.* **TEARS** a display of crying (*informal*) (*takes a plural verb*)

wa·ter·worn /wáwtər wàwrn/ *adj.* smoothed or eroded by the action of water

wa·ter·y /wáwtəree/ *adj.* **1.** **RELATING TO OR CONTAINING WATER** relating to, containing, soaked with, or like water **2.** **HAVING EXCESSIVE WATER** containing too much water ○ *watery coffee* **3.** **FILLED WITH TEARS** filled with tears, from either emotion or physical irritation ○ *watery eyes* **4.** **LACKING FORCE** lacking the usual full force and appearing thin or weak ○ *A watery sun hung in the autumn sky.* **5.** **WEAK** lacking strength or sincerity ○ *a watery smile* **6.** **FULL OF FLUID** discharging, secreting, or filled with a watery fluid ○ *watery blister* —**wa·ter·i·ness** *n.*

WATS /wawts/ *abbr.* Wide-Area Telecommunications Service

Wat·son /wóts'ən/, **Chris** (1867–1941) Chilean-born Australian statesman. The leader of the Labor Party, he was prime minister of Australia in 1904. Full name **John Christian Watson**

Wat·son, James D. (*b.* 1928) U.S. biochemist. His work with Francis Crick and Maurice Wilkins in exploring the structure of the DNA molecule won them a shared Nobel Prize in physiology or medicine (1962). Full name **James Dewey Watson**

Wat·son-Crick mod·el /-krík-/ *n.* the three-dimensional double-helix model of the DNA molecule proposed by James Watson and Francis Crick in 1953 [Mid-20thC. Named for J. D. WATSON and F. H. C. *Crick,* a British biochemist (born 1916).]

watt /wot/ *n.* the international (**SI**) unit of power equal to the power produced by a current of one ampere acting across a potential difference of one volt. Symbol **W** [Late 19thC. Named for James WATT.]

Watt /wot/, **James** (1736–1819) British inventor. He improved the steam engine and, in partnership with Matthew Boulton, developed a pumping engine and rotative engine. The metric unit of power is named for him.

watt·age /wóttij/ *n.* electrical power measured in watts

watt-hour *n.* a unit of electrical energy equal to that of one watt operating for one hour

wat·tle /wótt'l/ *n.* **1.** BUILDING **STAKES INTERWOVEN WITH BRANCHES** stakes or poles interwoven with branches and twigs, used for walls, fences, and roofs **2.** INDUST **MATERIAL FOR WATTLE** material such as branches or stakes used to make wattle **3.** ZOOL **SKIN HANGING FROM ANIMAL'S THROAT** a loose, often highly colored fold of bare skin hanging from the throat or cheek of birds and lizards. It is used in courtship and other displays. **4.** TREES **AUSTRALIAN ACACIA TREE** any of various Australian trees and shrubs that put out leaves with many leaflets, bear heads of tiny flowers, and produce useful timber. Now used mainly as shade and ornamental trees, wattles were originally used to make fences, while the bark was used for tanning. Genus: *Acacia.* ■ *vt.* (**-tled, -tling, -tles**) BUILDING **1.** **MAKE FROM WATTLE** to construct something from wattle **2.** **WEAVE BRANCHES INTO WATTLE** to weave branches or twigs into wattle [Old English *watul,* of uncertain origin] —**wat·tled** *adj.*

wat·tle and daub *n.* building material consisting of wattle covered with mud or clay, often containing lime, dung, or straw

wat·tle·bird /wótt'l bùrd/ *n.* a slender-bodied gray-brown or olive-brown Australian bird with a long bill, a brush-tipped tongue for lapping nectar, and wattles on the cheeks. Genus: *Anthochaera.*

watt·me·ter /wótt meetər/ *n.* an instrument designed to measure the magnitude of the power in an electric circuit. It may be scaled in watts, kilowatts, or megawatts.

Evelyn Waugh

Waugh /waw/, **Evelyn** (1903–66) British novelist. His early novels satirizing high society gave way to the more serious later work such as *Brideshead Revisited* (1945) that reflected his preoccupation with Roman Catholicism. Full name **Evelyn Arthur St. John Waugh**

Wau·ke·gan /waw kéegən, wáwkəgən/ city in northeastern Illinois, on the shore of Lake Michigan, north of Chicago. Population: 74,166 (1996).

wave[1] /wayv/ (**waved, wav·ing, waves**) *v.* **1.** *vti.* **MOVE HAND REPEATEDLY AS SIGNAL** to move the hand or arm from side to side or up and down as a greeting, farewell, or signal **2.** *vti.* **MOVE SOMETHING REPEATEDLY IN AIR** to move or to cause something such as a flag to move from side to side or up and down ○ *The flag waved in the wind.* **3.** *vt.* **DIRECT SOMEBODY OR SOMETHING BY WAVING** to direct somebody or something by waving a hand, arm, or object ○ *The police waved the traffic around the procession.* **4.** *vti.* **MAKE INTO OR BE IN UNDULATIONS** to make something into or be in the form of swells, ridges, or swirls ○ *a field of grain waving in the wind* **5.** *vi.* **MOVE IN WAVES** to move in a series of swells (*refers to water*) **6.** *vti.* HAIR **BE OR MAKE SLIGHTLY CURLED** to be slightly or gently curled, or make hair slightly curled **7.** *vt.* TEXTILES **GIVE MATERIAL A RIPPLED PATTERN** to create a rippled pattern in a fabric such as silk [Old English *wafian*. From a prehistoric Germanic base meaning "to move back and forth," which is also the ancestor of English *waver* and *wobble*.]

wave aside *vt.* to dismiss something or somebody as trivial or inconsequential

wave down *vt.* to stop a vehicle by waving to the driver to halt

wave[2] /wayv/ *n.* **1. MOVING RIPPLE ON LIQUID OR OCEAN** any of a series of ripples moving across the surface of a liquid, especially a large raised ridge of water moving across the surface of the sea **2. ACT OF WAVING THE HAND** an instance of moving the hand or arm as a signal or greeting **3. LINE CURVING IN ALTERNATING DIRECTIONS** a line, shape, surface, or pattern that curves in one direction and then another, especially one with repeated curves **4. UNDULATING MOTION** a movement on a surface or edge that is similar to a wave ○ *The wind made waves across the field of grain.* **5. SUDDEN REPETITION OF EVENTS** a sudden occurrence of repeated activity ○ *a crime wave* **6. OVERWHELMING FEELING** a sudden overwhelming feeling ○ *a wave of sorrow* **7. INCOMING GROUP** an advancing or incoming group of people ○ *a wave of immigrants* **8.** HAIR **LOOSE CURVE IN HAIR** a soft, usually large, curve or ripple in the hair where the lie of the hair changes direction, either naturally or after setting **9.** PHYS **OSCILLATION OF ENERGY** an oscillation that travels through a medium by transferring energy from one particle or point to another without causing any permanent displacement of the medium ○ *sound waves* **10.** TEXTILES **RIPPLED PATTERN** a rippled pattern in material such as silk **11.** SPORTS **CONTINUOUS RIPPLING MOVEMENT BY SPORTS CROWD** the rippling effect produced by rows of spectators at a sporting event standing up, raising their arms, and then sitting down again ■ **waves** *npl.* **SEA** the waves of the ocean, or the ocean itself [15thC. Alteration of obsolete *waw* under the influence of the verb WAVE[1].] ◇ **make waves** to cause a disturbance or trouble, e.g., by suggesting or introducing changes or making criticisms

Wave /wayv/ *n.* a member of the WAVES

wave·band /wáyv bànd/ *n.* a range of radio frequencies within which transmissions occur

wave e·qua·tion *n.* an equation, usually a partial differential equation, that defines the propagation of a wave through a medium. The form of the equation is determined by the medium, the method by which the wave is transmitted, and the circumstance of its propagation.

wave·form /wáyv fàwrm/ *n.* the profile or shape of a wave, especially the graphic representation of one of its characteristics, e.g., frequency or amplitude, relative to time

wave·front /wáyv frùnt/ *n.* a line or surface that joins points of the same phase in a wave traveling through a medium

wave func·tion *n.* an equation that shows how a wave's amplitude varies in space and time

wave·guide /wáyv gīd/ *n.* a transmission line consisting of a hollow metal conductor used as a path to convey microwave energy along its length. It is used in radar systems to convey transmitted microwave energy from the transmitter to the antenna and received energy from the antenna back to the receiver.

wave·length /wáyv lèngth/ *n.* **1.** PHYS **LENGTH OF WAVE CYCLE** the distance between two points on adjacent waves that have the same phase, e.g., the distance between two consecutive peaks or troughs. Symbol λ **2.** BROADCAST **BROADCASTING WAVELENGTH** the wavelength of the fundamental radio wave used by a broadcasting station ◇ **be on the same wavelength** to have the same opinions, attitudes, or tastes

wave·let /wáyvlit/ *n.* a small wave, e.g., a ripple

wa·vel·lite /wáyvə līt/ *n.* a soft light gray, yellow, or brown mineral form of hydrated aluminum phosphate, usually in the form of clusters of radiating crystals in slates and shales [Early 19thC. Named for William *Wavell* (d. 1829), the English physician who discovered the substance.]

wave me·chan·ics *n.* a form of quantum theory in which happenings on the atomic scale are explained in terms of interactions between systems of waves, represented by wave functions (*takes a singular verb*)

wave·me·ter /wáyv meetər/ *n.* an instrument for measuring wavelengths

wave num·ber *n.* the number of waves in a given unit distance. Wave number is the reciprocal of wavelength. Symbol σ

wave-par·ti·cle du·al·i·ty *n.* a fundamental concept of quantum theory holding that energy sometimes behaves like particles and sometimes behaves like waves, so that descriptions of energy as one or the other are inadequate

wave pool *n.* a public swimming pool equipped with a device to produce waves

wa·ver /wáyvər/ *vi.* (**-vered, -ver·ing, -vers**) **1. FLUCTUATE BETWEEN POSSIBILITIES** to go back and forth between possibilities, or be indecisive in making a choice **2. BEGIN TO CHANGE OPINION** to become unsure or begin to change from a previous opinion **3. MOVE IN DIFFERENT DIRECTIONS** to move one way and then another in an irregular pattern **4. FLUCTUATE, ESPECIALLY IN TONE** to vary or fluctuate, as, e.g., the voice does from emotion **5. FLICKER** to go on and off, especially due to burning unsteadily (*refers to a light or a flame*) ■ *n.* **ACT OF WAVERING** an instance or act of wavering [14thC. From Old Norse *vafra*.] —**wa·ver·er** *n.* —**wa·ver·ing·ly** *adv.*

WORD KEY: SYNONYMS

See Synonyms at ***hesitate***.

WAVES /wayvz/ *n.* NAVY the women's branch of the U.S. Naval Reserve that was organized in World War II. It no longer exists as a separate entity. Full form **Women Accepted for Volunteer Emergency Service**

wave the·o·ry *n.* the theory that the behavior of light or any other electromagnetic radiation can be explained by assuming that it travels in waves. ◊ **corpuscular theory**

wave train *n.* a series of similar waves produced at equal intervals and traveling in the same direction

wav·ey /wáyvee/ (*plural* **-eys**) *n. Can* a snow goose or other wild goose

wav·y /wáyvee/ (**-i·er, -i·est**) *adj.* **1. REPEATEDLY CURVING** forming a series of smooth curves that go in one direction and then another **2.** HAIR **HAVING SOFT CURVES** having loose open waves ○ *wavy hair* **3. CONTAINING WAVES** full of waves or having a surface covered by waves **4. MOVING LIKE A WAVE** moving with an up-and-down or side-to-side motion **5. WAVERING** wavering or changeable —**wav·i·ly** *adv.* —**wav·i·ness** *n.*

waw *n.* = **vav** [Mid-19thC. Variant of VAV.]

wa·wa /waá waa/ *n. Can* = **wavey** [Mid-19thC. Variant of WAVEY.]

wa-wa *n.* = **wah-wah**

wa-wa ped·al *n.* = **wah-wah pedal**

wax[1] /waks/ *n.* **1.** INDUST **NATURALLY-OCCURRING GREASY SUBSTANCE** any of various hard or soft and moldable substances of animal, plant, or mineral origin that feel slightly greasy or oily to the touch **2.** DOMESTIC **PREPARATION FOR POLISHING** a preparation containing wax used to polish floors, cars, and other surfaces **3.** INDUST = **beeswax 4.** PHYSIOL = **earwax 5.** MED = **bone wax 6.** INDUST **RESINOUS MIXTURE USED IN SHOEMAKING** a resinous mixture rubbed onto thread used in shoemaking **7. SOMETHING EASILY MOLDED** somebody who or something that is readily molded, shaped, or manipulated **8.** RECORDING **RECORD** a phonograph record (*dated informal*) ■ *vt.* (**waxed, waxed** *or* **wax·en** *archaic* /wáksən/, **wax·ing, wax·es**) **1. POLISH SOMETHING WITH WAX** to coat or polish something such as a floor or car with wax **2.** COSMETICS **REMOVE HAIR WITH WAX** to remove unwanted hair from the skin using heated wax that is left to dry and then removed [Old English *wæx* from prehistoric Germanic] —**wax·er** *n.*

wax[2] /waks/ (**waxed, wax·ing, wax·es**) *vi.* **1.** ASTRON **APPEAR LARGER EACH NIGHT** to show a gradually increasing illuminated surface, as does the Moon between its new and full phases (*refers to the Moon or a planet*) **2. INCREASE** to increase in size, power, or intensity (*literary*) **3. BECOME SOMETHING STATED** to get into a particular emotional or behavioral state (*literary*) ○ *waxed philosophical* [Old English *weaxan*. Ultimately from an Indo-European base meaning "to increase," which is also the ancestor of English *augment* and *eke*.]

wax bean *n.* a variety of string bean that is yellow

wax·bill /wáks bìl/ *n.* small brightly colored African finch with a red conical bill. Waxbills feed on seeds and insects and build roofed nests of grass. Family: Estrildidae.

wax cap *n.* a mushroom with a cap that has waxy gills. Family: Hygrophoraceae.

waxed pa·per *n.* = **wax paper**

wax·en[1] /wáks'n/ *adj.* **1. LIKE WAX** resembling wax in texture and color **2. MADE OF WAX** covered with, permeated with, or made of wax **3. PALE AND UNHEALTHY-LOOKING** lacking the rosy glow of life or health ○ *a waxen face* **4. EASY TO SHAPE** easily shaped, changed, or manipulated

wax·en[2] past participle of **wax** (*archaic*)

wax in·sect *n.* any of various scale insects that secrete a wax. Superfamily: Coccoidea.

wax light *n.* a candle or taper made of wax

wax moth *n.* a small brownish moth whose larvae develop inside beehives, feeding on the honeycombs and covering them with silken tunnels. Latin name: *Galleria mellonella*.

wax mu·se·um *n.* a museum containing wax models of famous people

wax myr·tle *n.* = **bayberry** *n.* **1**

wax palm *n.* = **carnauba** *n.* **1**

wax pa·per *n.* paper that does not allow oil or grease to soak into it or pass through it and is used especially in cooking, preparing, or wrapping food.

wax plant *n.* an Asian and Australian evergreen climbing plant or shrub that is related to milkweed and bears waxy white flowers. Genus: *Hoya*.

wax tree *n.* a Southeast Asian tree that was formerly cultivated especially in Japan for its fruits, used as a source of candle wax, and for its resin, used for lacquer. Latin name: *Rhus succedanea*.

wax vine *n.* = **wax plant**

wax·wing /wáks wìng/ *n.* a bird of northern regions that is marked by a crest, buff-brown plumage, and waxy-looking red tips on the upper flight feathers. Genus: *Bombycilla*.

wax·work /wáks wùrk/ *n.* **1. WAX MODEL** a realistic model, usually of a famous person, made from wax **2. WAX OBJECT** an object made of wax, especially an ornament **3. ART OF USING WAX FOR MODELING** the art of using wax as a modeling or expressive medium

wax·y /wáksee/ (**-i·er, -i·est**) *adj.* **1. LIKE WAX** resembling wax in appearance, color, texture, or pliability **2. COVERED WITH WAX** covered with, having a lot of, or made of wax **3.** MED **HAVING HARD DEPOSITS LIKE WAX** containing deposits of a hard waxlike substance resembling wax (**amyloid**) resulting from tissue degeneration —**wax·i·ness** *n.*

way /way/ *n.* **1. MANNER OR METHOD** a means, manner, or method of doing or achieving something ○ *You do it your way, I'll do it mine.* **2. EXAMPLE** a feature, aspect, or example of something ○ *In some ways, my sisters are very similar.* **3. CONDITION** the state or condition of somebody or something, especially with regard to health or finances ○ *He was in a bad way after the accident.* **4. PREFERENCE** something somebody wants to happen or to do ○ *You can't always get your own way.* **5. CHARACTERISTIC ASPECT OF BEHAVIOR** a usual, characteristic, or distinctive activity or style of behavior ○ *How do you put up with those irritating ways of theirs?* **6. TRADITION OR CUSTOM** the customary style or practices of somebody's life ○ *the way of the Sufi* **7. TYPICAL HAPPENING** the usual occurrence or pattern of events ○ *Isn't it usually the way that all the cabs are taken when you're late?* **8. PATH** a path or physical means of getting from one place to another ○ *The way out is through here.* **9. DOOR OR OPENING** a door or opening leading or providing access to or from somewhere ○ *Come in the front way.* **10. JOURNEY OR ROUTE** a particular journey or the route followed or to be followed ○ *on my way to the office* **11. PROGRESS THROUGH LIFE** progress or a path through life and its experiences or difficulties **12. DIRECTION** a direction such as left, right, up, or down **13. MANNER OF PLACING** the manner in which something is placed, packed, or arranged, or the direction it faces **14. SPACE FOR ACTION** path, room, territory, or space allowing movement, progress, or action ○ *Excuse me, you're in my way.* **15. AREA** an area or district, e.g., around somebody's home (*informal*) ○ *out our way* **16. DISTANCE** a distance away in space or time ○ *Graduation is still a long way off.* **17. AMOUNT** the extent or amount to which somebody does something ○ *He's fallen for her in a big way.* **18. way, Way STREET** a street (*often used in place names*) **19. SUBPART** each of a particular number of parts into which something divides or is split ○ *They're going to split the prize four ways.* **20.** MECH ENG **GUIDE OR SUPPORT** a surface used to guide or provide support to moving parts of a machine tool such as a lathe (*often used in the plural*) **21.** SHIPPING **MOVEMENT THROUGH WATER** movement or speed of a ship through water ○ *have some way on* ■ *adv.* **1. VERY MUCH** to a considerable extent or at a considerable distance (*informal*) ○ *That's way out of our price range.* **2. VERY** to a great extent (*slang*) [Old English *weg.* Ultimately from an Indo-European base meaning "to go," which is also the ancestor of English *wagon* and *vehicle.*] ◇ **be under way** to be in progress ◇ **by the way** used to introduce something that is not strictly part of the subject at hand ◇ **by way of something** as a means of or for the purpose of something ◇ **every which way 1.** in all directions **2.** in every way possible (*informal*) ◇ **give way** to collapse or break under pressure ◇ **go out of your way to do something** to do more than is usual or necessary ◇ **have a way with somebody** *or* **something** to be good at dealing with somebody or something ◇ **have it both ways** to have the benefits of opposing situations or actions ◇ **in a way** from a certain point of view ◇ **make way (for somebody** *or* **something)** to move aside to make room for somebody or something ◇ **make your way 1.** to go somewhere, especially when getting there requires overcoming some obstacle, e.g., finding the route or some transport **2.** to become successful ◇ **no way** used as an emphatic negative ◇ **way to go** used to congratulate somebody on something that he or she has done (*informal*)

way·bill /wáy bìl/ *n.* a document that gives information about goods being shipped or carried

way·far·er /wáy fàirər/ *n.* a traveler, especially somebody who makes a journey on foot (*literary*) —**way·far·ing** *n., adj.*

way·far·ing tree *n.* a shrub that is found in Europe and western Asia and has white flowers and red berries that turn black. Latin name: *Viburnum lantana.* [Probably because it can provide the traveler with shade]

Way·land /wáylənd/, **Way·land Smith, Way·land the Smith** *n.* in northern European folklore, a magical smith who was the king of the elves [From Old Norse *Völundr.* First mentioned in the 13thC *Poetic Edda.*]

way·lay /wáy lày/ (**-laid** /-làyd/, **-laid, -lay·ing, -lays**) *vt.* **1. LIE IN WAIT FOR SOMEBODY** to lie in wait for somebody, especially as part of an attack or ambush **2. STOP SOMEBODY** to stop or accost somebody, e.g., in order to talk —**way·lay·er** *n.*

way·leave /wáy lèev/ *n.* the right of way over somebody else's property, for which payment is usually made

Wayne /wayn/, **Anthony** (1745–96) American soldier. As a general in the Revolution (1775–83), he led a brilliant victory at Stony Point (1779) and contributed to the British defeat at Yorktown (1781). Known as **Mad Anthony**

John Wayne

Wayne, John (1907–79) U.S. actor. He starred as the rugged hero in numerous westerns, including the Academy Award-winning *True Grit* (1969). Real name **Marion Michael Morrison.** Known as **the Duke**

Way of the Cross *n.* a series of pictures representing Jesus Christ's progress on the road to Calvary

way-out *adj.* **1. UNUSUAL OR PECULIAR** unusual, peculiar, or unconventional (*informal*) **2. WONDERFUL** excellent or exciting (*dated informal*)

way·point /wáy pòynt/ *n.* a point on a journey or route where a traveler can stop or change course

ways /wayz/ *n.* **1. DISTANCE** a distance traveled or to be traveled (*informal*) (*takes a singular verb*) ○ *The next gas station is quite a ways from here.* **2.** SHIPPING **LAUNCH TRACKS FOR SHIP** the tracks a ship slides down to be launched (*takes a singular or plural verb*)

-ways *suffix.* in a particular direction or position ○ *edgeways* [Old English *weges,* a form of *weg* "way," literally "of (such a) way"]

ways and means *npl.* **1. METHODS OF GETTING OR ACCOMPLISHING SOMETHING** methods of accomplishing or achieving something, especially finding a way of paying for something **2. METHODS OF RAISING MONEY FOR GOVERNMENT** methods, e.g., legislation, used by a government to raise money

Ways and Means *npl.* a legislative committee in charge of methods of raising money for government

way·side /wáy sìd/ *n.* **SIDE OF ROAD** the side of a road or path ■ *adj.* **SITUATED AT SIDE OF ROAD** situated at the side of a road or path ◇ **fall by the wayside** to fail to continue or complete something ○ *Several students fell by the wayside after the first few weeks.* ◇ **go by the wayside** to be abandoned because of other commitments or interests

way sta·tion *n.* **1. SMALL RAILROAD STATION** a station between the major stations on a railroad **2. STOPPING PLACE ON ROUTE** a point or stopping place on a route

way·ward /wáywərd/ *adj.* **1. WILLFUL** characterized by willfulness or disobedience **2. ERRATIC OR UNPREDICTABLE** behaving in an erratic, apparently perverse, or unpredictable manner [14thC. Alteration of earlier *awayward.*] —**way·ward·ly** *adv.* —**way·ward·ness** *n.*

WORD KEY: SYNONYMS

See Synonyms at **unruly**.

way·worn /wáy wàwrn/ *adj.* worn out or weary from traveling

wayz·goose /wáyz gòoss/ *n. U.K.* formerly, an annual outing for people working at a printing house (*archaic*) [Mid-18thC. Alteration of earlier *waygoose,* of unknown origin.]

wa·zoo /wə zóo/ (*plural* **-zoos**) *n.* an offensive term used to refer to the anus or buttocks (*slang offensive*) [Origin uncertain; perhaps an alteration of KAZOO] ◇ **up the wazoo** used to indicate an abundance of something (*sometimes considered offensive*)

Wb *symbol.* weber

w.b. *abbr.* **1.** water ballast **2. w.b., W.B.** waybill **3.** westbound

WBA *abbr.* World Boxing Association

WBC *abbr.* **1.** BIOL white blood cell **2.** BOXING World Boxing Council

WbN *abbr.* west by north

W bo·son *n.* PHYS = **W particle**

WbS *abbr.* west by south

w.c. *abbr.* without charge

W.C. *abbr.* water closet

WCC, W.C.C. *abbr.* World Council of Churches

WCTU, W.C.T.U. *abbr.* Women's Christian Temperance Union

WD, W.D. *abbr.* War Department

wd. *abbr.* **1.** word **2.** HEALTH ward **3.** wood

WDM, wdm *abbr.* wavelength division multiplex

wdth. *abbr.* width

we /wee/ *pron.* **1. REFERS TO SPEAKER AND OTHERS** refers to the speaker or writer and at least one other person (*first person plural personal pronoun, used as the subject of a verb*) ○ *We are going on vacation.* ○ *We grown-ups should protect our children's rights.* ○ *We all want our children to have a better future.* **2. REFERS TO PEOPLE IN GENERAL** refers to all people or to people in general ○ *We are getting closer to the election.* **3. USED INSTEAD OF "I"** used by a writer or speaker to include the listener or speaker in what is being said, used especially to talk about how a book or talk is organized ○ *We will now consider the causes of World War I.* **4. USED INSTEAD OF "YOU"** used sarcastically or condescendingly by a speaker ○ *How are we today? Are we getting better?* [Old English *wē.* Ultimately from an Indo-European word of the same meaning that is also the ancestor of German *wir* and, in a variant form, English *us.*]

weak /week/ *adj.* **1. NOT STRONG OR FIT** not physically or mentally strong **2. EASILY DEFEATED** easily overcome or defeated **3. LACKING STRENGTH OF CHARACTER** not having strength of character **4. NOT INTENSE** not powerful or intense ○ *weak winter sunshine* **5. LACKING SKILLS OR ABILITIES** not having particular skills or abilities **6. WATERY OR TASTELESS** watery or lacking flavor ○ *weak tea* **7. NOT WORKING TO FULL CAPACITY** not working as well as normal **8. UNCONVINCING** not persuasive or convincing ○ *a weak argument* **9. NOT STRONG POLITICALLY** not politically strong or powerful **10.** POETRY **UNSTRESSED** used to describe a syllable or word that is not stressed or accented **11.** POETRY **HAVING ACCENT ON NORMALLY UNSTRESSED SYLLABLE** used to describe verse that has the accent on a syllable that is normally unstressed **12.** GRAM **CHARACTERIZED BY REGULAR INFLECTIONAL ENDINGS** used to describe a verb whose forms are characterized by regular inflectional endings, not by vowel changes **13.** FIN **CHARACTERIZED BY FALLING PRICES** falling in price, or characterized by falling prices ○ *a weak market* **14.** PHOTOGRAPHY **LACKING IN CONTRAST** not having much contrast between tones [13thC. From Old Norse *veikr* "pliant." Ultimately from a prehistoric Germanic word that is also the ancestor of German *weich* and Dutch *week* "soft."]

WORD KEY: SYNONYMS

weak, feeble, frail, infirm, debilitated, enervated, decrepit

CORE MEANING: lacking physical strength or energy

weak lacking strength or energy, either temporarily, or as part of the person's constitution; **feeble** describes somebody who is very weak, either temporarily or as part of his or her constitution; **frail** used to suggest physical delicacy or weakness, either as part of somebody's physical constitution or as a result of illness or advancing years; **infirm** lacking strength as a result of advanced years or illness, especially when it seems unlikely that this condition will improve; **debilitated** made weak by something such as illness or physical exertion, especially when this condition is likely to be temporary; **enervated** made weak and tired by something such as extreme heat or physical exertion; **decrepit** a formal or literary word used to describe somebody who has been made very weak by advancing years. It is sometimes used humorously.

weak·en /wéekən/ (**-ened, -en·ing, -ens**) *vti.* to make somebody or something weak or weaker, or become weak or weaker —**weak·en·er** *n.*

weak·er sex *n.* an highly offensive term used by men to refer to women as a group (*dated offensive*)

weak·fish /wéek fish/ (*plural* **-fish** *or* **-fish·es**) *n.* = **sea trout** *n.* 1 [Late 18thC. From obsolete Dutch *weekvisch,* literally "soft fish," from *week* "soft" + *visch* "fish."]

weak force /wéek fáwrs/ *n.* = **weak interaction**

weak in·ter·ac·tion *n.* the fundamental interaction between elementary particles that is mediated by the W and Z particles. It is involved in radioactive decay which occurs by electron production, and particle decay. One of the four fundamental interactions, it is only effective at distances of less than 10^{-15} meters and is a trillion times weaker than the strong interaction.

weak-kneed *adj.* easily persuaded or intimidated —**weak-kneed·ly** *adv.* —**weak-kneed·ness** *n.*

weak·ling /wéekling/ *n.* somebody who lacks physical strength or strength of character

weak·ly /wéeklee/ *adj.* (**-li·er, -li·est**) **SICKLY** sickly or delicate ■ *adv.* **WITHOUT STRENGTH OR FORCE** with little strength or force ○ *She nodded weakly.* —**weak·li·ness** *n.*

weak-mind·ed *adj.* **1. OFFENSIVE TERM** an offensive term used to refer to somebody considered to be of low intelligence (*offensive*) **2. EASILY PERSUADED** easily persuaded or convinced (*disapproving*) —**weak-mind·ed·ly** *adv.* —**weak-mind·ed·ness** *n.*

weak·ness /wéekniss/ *n.* **1. LACK OF STRENGTH OR DETERMINATION** lack of strength, power, or determination **2. WEAK POINT** a weak point or flaw in something ○ *Unfortunately, the escape plan had a serious weakness.* **3. CHARACTER FLAW** a failing or defect in somebody's character **4. FONDNESS** a strong liking for something ○ *a weakness for chocolate* **5. OBJECT OF DESIRE** an irresistible object of desire ○ *My weakness is action movies.*

weak sis·ter /wéek sístər/ *n.* (*informal insult*) **1. OFFENSIVE TERM** an offensive term for a weak or unreliable member or component of a group **2. OFFENSIVE TERM** an offensive term for somebody timid or cowardly

weak-willed *adj.* not having a strong will

weal[1] /weel/ *n.* = **wheal**

weal[2] /weel/ *n.* **1. STATE OF WELL-BEING** a general state of well-being, prosperity, and happiness (*literary*) **2. PROSPERITY** fortune or prosperity (*archaic*) **3. BODY**

POLITIC the state or the body politic (*archaic*) [Old English *wela*. Ultimately from an Indo-European base meaning "to wish," which is also the ancestor of English *will* and *well*.]

weald /weeld/ *n. U.K.* open or wooded country (*archaic*) [Old English. Variant of *wald* (see WOLD).]

wealth /welth/ *n.* **1.** LARGE AMOUNT OF MONEY a large amount of money or possessions **2.** STATE OF HAVING MUCH MONEY the state of having plenty of money or possessions ○ *came from a background of great wealth* **3.** ABUNDANCE OF SOMETHING an abundance or great quantity of something ○ *quoted a wealth of statistics to prove the point* **4.** ECON VALUE OF ASSETS the value of assets owned by an individual or a community ○ *need to determine the family's wealth* **5.** WELL-BEING well-being or prosperity (*archaic*) [13thC. Formed from WEAL[2].]

WORD KEY: CULTURAL NOTE

The Wealth of Nations, a philosophical treatise by Scottish economist and philosopher Adam Smith (1776). One of the earliest and most comprehensive analyses of economic systems, it began as a study of the relationship between human nature and social evolution. Smith's assertion that the natural outcome of this evolution is an economy based on open markets and driven by competition inspired many modern-day laissez-faire capitalist philosophies.

wealth·y /wélthee/ (**-i·er, -i·est**) *adj.* **1.** RICH having a large amount of money or possessions **2.** CHARACTERIZED BY ABUNDANCE enjoying an abundance or great quantity of something —**wealth·i·ly** *adv.* —**wealth·i·ness** *n.*

wean /ween/ (**weaned, wean·ing, weans**) *v.* **1.** *vti.* GIVE FOOD OTHER THAN MOTHER'S MILK to start feeding a baby or young animal food other than its mother's milk **2.** *vt.* STOP SOMEBODY FROM HAVING SOMETHING to cause somebody to go without something that has become a habit or that is much liked **3.** *vt.* ACCUSTOM SOMEBODY TO SOMETHING FROM CHILDHOOD to accustom somebody to something from an early age ○ *children weaned on computer games and videos* [Old English *wenian* "to accustom." Ultimately from a prehistoric Germanic base that is also the ancestor of German *gewöhnen* "to accustom" and English *wont* "accustomed."] —**wean·ed·ness** /weénidniss, weéndniss/ *n.*

wean·er /weénər/ *n.* **1.** WEANED ANIMAL a young animal that has recently been weaned, especially a hog **2.** MEANS OF WEANING AN ANIMAL somebody who weans animals, or something used in weaning animals

wean·ling /weénling/ *n.* RECENTLY WEANED CHILD OR ANIMAL a child or young animal that has just been weaned ■ *adj.* JUST WEANED newly weaned ○ *a weanling lamb*

weap·on /wéppən/ *n.* **1.** DEVICE DESIGNED TO INJURE OR KILL a device designed to inflict injury or death on an opponent **2.** SOMETHING USED TO GAIN ADVANTAGE something used as a way of getting an advantage in a situation ○ *A teacher's best weapon can be humor.* **3.** ZOOL ANIMAL'S PROTECTIVE PART an animal part, e.g., claws, used for defense or attack ■ *vt.* (**-oned, -on·ing, -ons**) ARM SOMEBODY to provide somebody with weapons [Old English *wæpen*. Ultimately from prehistoric Germanic.] —**weap·oned** *adj.* —**weap·on·less** *adj.*

weap·on·eer /wèppə neér/ *n.* **1.** SOMEBODY WHO HELPS DETONATE NUCLEAR WEAPON somebody who prepares a nuclear weapon for detonation **2.** DESIGNER OF NUCLEAR WEAPONS somebody who designs nuclear weapons

weap·on·ry /wéppənree/ *n.* **1.** WEAPONS all the weapons possessed by an individual, group, or nation **2.** PRODUCTION OF WEAPONS techniques for producing weapons

weap·ons sys·tem (*plural* **weap·ons sys·tems** *or* **weap·on sys·tems**) *n.* a weapon consisting of two or more major components, e.g., a missile and its ground-based radar guidance

wear[1] /wair/ *v.* (**wore** /wawr/, **worn** /wawrn/, **wear·ing, wears**) **1.** *vt.* USE TO COVER OR ADORN BODY to have something on all or part of the body as clothing, jewelry, protection, or for another purpose, e.g., to aid sight or hearing, either temporarily or habitually **2.** *vt. Malaysia, Singapore* PUT ON to put on a piece of clothing **3.** *vt.* DISPLAY ON FACE to display, show, or present an expression or physical manifestation of an emotion on the face ○ *wear a smile* **4.** *vti.* DAMAGE BY USING OR RUBBING to damage or alter something by using or rubbing it, or be damaged or altered in this way **5.** *vti.* PRODUCE BY USING OR RUBBING to produce something, especially a hole, through continued use, pressure, or friction, or be produced in this way ○ *had worn a hole in his sweater* **6.** *vti.* RUB OFF to rub something off or away, or be rubbed off or away **7.** *vt.* TIRE OUT to tire somebody out, or become exhausted **8.** *vi.* LAST IN SAME CONDITION to last in the same, especially good, condition with much use ○ *That fabric doesn't look as if it would wear well.* **9.** *vti.* PASS SLOWLY to pass time slowly, or be passed slowly ○ *We wore the evening away worrying about him.* **10.** *vt.* SHIPPING FLY FLAG to fly a particular flag or colors as a ship's identification ■ *n.* **1.** ACT OF WEARING the act of wearing something, or the condition of being worn **2.** DAMAGE FROM BEING USED damage or deterioration from something being used **3.** ABILITY TO LAST the ability to last without deteriorating **4.** CLOTHES CLOTHING OF PARTICULAR KIND clothing, especially clothing of a particular kind (*often used in combination*) ○ *beachwear* [Old English *werian*. Ultimately from a prehistoric Germanic word that is also the ancestor of Icelandic *varinn* "clad."] —**wear·er** *n.* ◇ **the worse for wear 1.** in a poor condition because of much use **2.** looking unwell, especially because of being tired ◇ **wear thin 1.** to weaken or fail ○ *My patience is wearing thin.* **2.** to become unacceptable or implausible because of excessive use ○ *That excuse is beginning to wear a little thin.*

wear down *vti.* to overcome or weaken somebody or something by a gradual process, or be overcome or weakened in this way

wear off *vi.* to lose effectiveness or strength gradually ○ *Let me know when the anesthetic wears off.*

wear out *v.* **1.** *vti.* USE SOMETHING HEAVILY to use something heavily or for a long time until it is no longer useful, or to become useless through long use **2.** *vt.* EXHAUST to tire somebody out

wear[2] /wair/ (**wore** /wawr/, **worn** /wawrn/, **wear·ing, wears**) *vti.* to bring a ship about by turning the stern to windward, or come about in this way [Early 17thC. Origin unknown.]

wear·a·ble /wáirəb'l/ *adj.* SUITABLE FOR WEAR suitable and in a condition to be worn ■ *n.* WEARABLE ITEM OF CLOTHING an item of clothing that can be worn —**wear·a·bil·i·ty** /wàirə bíllətee/ *n.*

wear and tear /-táir/ *n.* damage caused by using something over a period of time

wea·ri·ful /weérif'l/ *adj.* **1.** TEDIOUS AND ANNOYING tedious and causing annoyance or fatigue **2.** TIRED tired and weary —**wea·ri·ful·ly** *adv.* —**wea·ri·ful·ness** *n.*

wea·ri·less /weériliss/ *adj.* not feeling or showing tiredness —**wea·ri·less·ly** *adv.*

wear·ing /wáiring/ *adj.* **1.** TIRING tiring or tedious ○ *found the long journey very wearing* **2.** MADE TO BE WORN made or designed to be worn ○ *wearing apparel* —**wear·ing·ly** *adv.*

wea·ri·some /weérisəm/ *adj.* physically or mentally tiring and tedious ○ *a wearisome task* —**wea·ri·some·ly** *adv.* —**wea·ri·some·ness** *n.*

wear·proof /wáir proof/ *adj.* able to withstand normal wear or use

wea·ry /weéree/ *adj.* (**wea·ri·er, wea·ri·est**) **1.** TIRED tired, especially in having run out of strength, patience, or endurance **2.** TIRING tiring or exhausting **3.** SHOWING TIREDNESS showing or characterized by tiredness ■ *vti.* (**wea·ried, wea·ry·ing, wea·ries**) BECOME OR MAKE TIRED OR IMPATIENT to become or cause somebody to become tired or impatient [Old English *wērig*. Ultimately from a prehistoric Germanic base that also produced Old English *wōrian* "to wander."] —**wea·ri·ly** *adv.* —**wea·ri·ness** *n.* —**wea·ry·ing** *adj.* —**wea·ry·ing·ly** *adv.*

wea·sand /weézənd/ *n.* the throat, especially the windpipe or the gullet (*archaic*) [Old English *wāsend*. Ultimately from prehistoric West Germanic.]

wea·sel /weéz'l/ *n.* (*plural* **-sels** *or* **-sel**) **1.** ZOOL SMALL MAMMAL WITH LONG BODY a small carnivorous mammal with a long body and tail, short legs, and brown fur that in northern species may turn white in winter. Genus: *Mustela*. **2.** SOMEBODY SLY somebody who is regarded as sly or underhanded (*insult*) **3.** TRANSP VEHICLE USED ON SAND OR SNOW a vehicle designed for use on sand, snow, or ice ■ *vi.* (**-seled** *or* **-selled, -sel·ing** *or* **-sel·ling, -sels**) BE EVASIVE to be evasive or try to mislead others [Old English *wesule*. Ultimately from prehistoric Germanic.] —**wea·sel·ly** *adj.*

Weasel

weasel out *vi.* to try to get out of an obligation or commitment, especially in a cowardly way (*informal*)

wea·sel words *npl.* deliberately misleading or ambiguous language (*informal*) —**wea·sel-word·ed** *adj.*

weath·er /wéthər/ *n.* METEOROL **1.** STATE OF THE ATMOSPHERE the state of the atmosphere with regard to temperature, cloudiness, rainfall, wind, and other meteorological conditions **2.** BAD WEATHER adverse weather such as a storm, or the effects of this ○ *protection from the weather* ■ *adj.* **1.** METEOROL USED IN WEATHER FORECASTING used in or relating to weather forecasting **2.** NAUT WINDWARD toward the wind ■ *v.* (**-ered, -er·ing, -ers**) **1.** *vt.* COME SAFELY THROUGH A CRISIS to come safely through a crisis or difficult time **2.** *vi.* ENDURE THE EFFECTS OF THE WEATHER to endure the damaging effects of the weather **3.** *vti.* EXPOSE SOMETHING TO THE WEATHER to expose something to the weather, or to be exposed to it **4.** *vti.* CHANGE BECAUSE OF EXPOSURE TO WEATHER to change color or become worn because of prolonged exposure to the weather, or to cause such a change **5.** *vt.* NAUT SAIL WINDWARD OF SOMETHING to sail on the windward side of something **6.** *vt.* CONSTR SLANT SOMETHING TO KEEP OFF RAIN to give a slope to something such as a roof to keep off rain [Old English *weder*. Ultimately from an Indo-European base meaning "to blow," which is also the ancestor of English *wind* and *vent*.] —**weath·er·a·bil·i·ty** /wèthərə bíllətee/ *n.* —**weath·er·er** /wéthərər/ *n.* ◇ **be** *or* **feel under the weather** to be *or* feel slightly unwell ◇ **make heavy weather of something** to make a task that is quite easy to do seem more difficult than it is

weath·er bal·loon *n.* a balloon used to carry meteorological instruments

weath·er-beat·en *adj.* damaged, worn, or marked by exposure to the weather ○ *a weather-beaten face*

weath·er·board /wéthər bàwrd/ *n.* **1.** CONSTR = **clapboard 2.** NAUT WINDWARD SIDE the windward side of a ship **3.** *ANZ* ARCHIT = **weatherboard house**

weath·er·board house *n. ANZ* a house clad with clapboards

weath·er·board·ing /wéthər bàwrding/ *n.* clapboards collectively

weath·er-bound /wéthər bòwnd/ *adj.* delayed or kept from functioning by bad weather ○ *a weather-bound plane*

weath·er·cast /wéthər kàst/ *n.* = **weather forecast** [Mid-19thC. Contraction of WEATHER FORECAST.] —**weath·er·cast·er** *n.*

weath·er·cock /wéthər kàwk/ *n.* **1.** WEATHER VANE a weather vane shaped like a rooster **2.** SOMEBODY FICKLE somebody who changes opinion or allegiance frequently ■ *vi.* (**-cocked, -cock·ing, -cocks**) AIR TURN IN THE DIRECTION OF THE WIND to tend to turn in the direction of the wind (*refers to aircraft*)

weath·er deck *n.* an open deck on a ship

weath·ered /wéthərd/ *adj.* **1.** WORN BY EXPOSURE TO WEATHER worn, damaged, or seasoned by exposure to the weather **2.** GIVEN A WEATHERED APPEARANCE given an artificial appearance of having been exposed to weather **3.** GEOL ERODED BY WEATHER used to describe rocks that have been eroded or changed by the action of the weather **4.** CONSTR WITH A SLOPING SURFACE having a sloping surface so that rain can run off ○ *a weathered roof*

weath·er eye *n.* **1.** ALERTNESS TO CHANGE alertness or watchfulness, especially an alertness to change (*informal*) **2.** EYE TRAINED TO WATCH THE WEATHER the eye of somebody trained to watch for changes in the weather ◇ **keep a weather eye open, keep a weather eye on, keep a weather eye out** to be alert and watchful for any change or development in something

weath·er fore·cast *n.* a radio or television broadcast announcing weather conditions —**weath·er fore·cast·er** *n.*

weath·er·glass /wéthər glàss/ *n.* an instrument such as a barometer used to indicate changes in atmospheric conditions

weath·er·ing /wéthəring/ *n.* GEOL **1.** EFFECT OF THE WEATHER the effect of prolonged exposure to the weather on, e.g., a building **2.** EFFECT OF WEATHER ON ROCKS the disintegration and decomposition of rocks and minerals by natural processes such as the action of frost or percolating groundwater. Weathering makes rock susceptible to erosion.

weath·er·ize /wéthə rìz/ (**-ized, -iz·ing, -iz·es**) *vt.* to take action to protect something such as a building against cold weather

weath·er·ly /wéthərlee/ *adj.* capable of sailing close to the wind

weath·er·man /wéthər màn/ (*plural* **-men** /-mèn/) *n.* a man who works as a weather forecaster (*dated*)

weath·er map *n.* a map or chart showing the meteorological conditions over a large area

weath·er·per·son /wèthər púrss'n/ *n.* somebody who works as a weather forecaster

weath·er·proof /wéthər pro͞of/ *adj.* ABLE TO WITHSTAND BAD WEATHER able to withstand exposure to rain or bad weather ■ *vt.* (**-proofed, -proof·ing, -proofs**) MAKE WEATHERPROOF to make something able to withstand exposure to rain or bad weather —**weath·er·proof·ness** *n.*

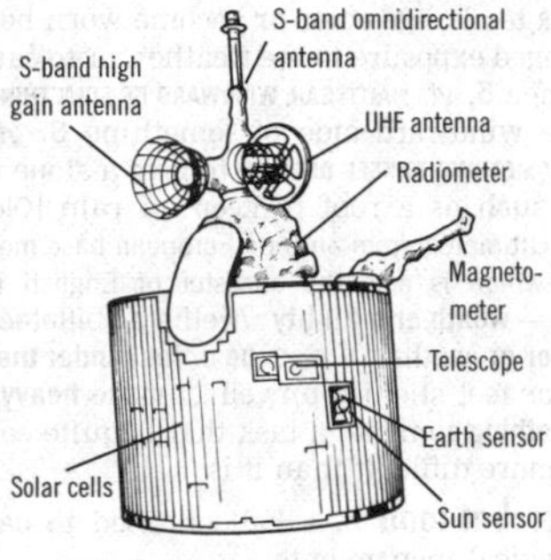

Weather satellite

weath·er sat·el·lite *n.* a satellite that records cloud distribution and temperature to help in predicting weather patterns

weath·er ship *n.* a ship that collects meteorological information

weath·er sta·tion *n.* an observation post where meteorological conditions are observed and recorded

weath·er strip *n. U.K.* = **weather stripping**

weath·er·strip /wéthər strìp/ (**weath·er·stripped, weath·er·strip·ping, weath·er·strips**) *vt.* to put weather stripping around a door or window

weath·er strip·ping *n.* a thin piece of material fitted around a door or window to stop wind, rain, and cold from coming through

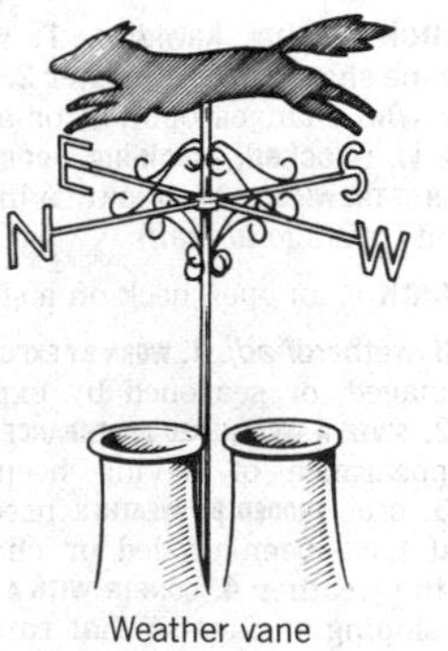

Weather vane

weath·er vane *n.* a device, usually mounted on a roof, that turns to point in the direction the wind is blowing

weath·er win·dow *n.* a period of time in which weather conditions are suitable for a particular activity

weath·er-wise *adj.* **1.** METEOROL GOOD AT PREDICTING THE WEATHER good at predicting what the weather will be **2.** GOOD AT PREDICTING PUBLIC OPINION good at predicting what public opinion will be

weath·er·worn /wéthər wàwrn/ *adj.* worn or damaged by exposure to the weather

weave[1] /weev/ *v.* (**wove** /wōv/ *or* **weaved, wo·ven** /wṓvən/ *or* **weaved, weav·ing, weaves**) **1.** *vti.* MAKE CLOTH to make cloth by interlacing threads vertically and horizontally, especially on a loom **2.** *vt.* MAKE SOMETHING BY INTERLACING STRANDS to make something by interlacing strands or strips of any material **3.** *vti.* SPIN A WEB to spin something such as a spider's web **4.** *vt.* CONSTRUCT A STORY to construct something such as a story by combining separate elements **5.** *vt.* INTRODUCE ELEMENTS INTO SOMETHING LARGER to introduce separate elements into something larger ○ *weaving new elements into the plot* ■ *n.* WAY IN WHICH SOMETHING IS WOVEN the way in which something is woven and the pattern formed by it ○ *a fabric with an open weave* [Old English *wefan.* Ultimately from a prehistoric Germanic word that is also the ancestor of German *weven.*]

weave[2] /weev/ (**weaved, weav·ing, weaves**) *vi.* to move forward on a zigzag course [Late 16thC. Origin uncertain: perhaps from Old Norse *veifa.* Ultimately from an Indo-European base meaning "to move quickly" that is also the ancestor of English *whip* and *vibrate.*]

weav·er /wéevər/ *n.* somebody who weaves, especially as a livelihood

weav·er·bird /wéevər bùrd/, **weaver** /wéevər/, **weaver finch** *n.* a gregarious finch of Africa and Asia, known for its communal woven nest. Family: Ploceidae.

web /web/ *n.* **1.** ZOOL SPIDER'S CONSTRUCTION a delicate structure of threads woven by a spider or other arachnid to catch prey **2.** COMPLEX NETWORK a complex structure, network, or design ○ *a web of interconnecting wires* ○ *a web of deceit* **3.** ZOOL MEMBRANE BETWEEN ANIMAL TOES a membrane of skin joining the digits of an animal's foot, especially the foot of a bird or amphibian **4.** CRAFT WOVEN FABRIC a piece of fabric created by weaving **5.** TECH THIN METAL PLATE a thin plate or strip of metal such as the blade of a saw **6.** BIRDS BARBS ON THE SHAFT OF A FEATHER the barbs on either side of the shaft of a feather **7.** ARCHIT RIBBED SURFACE IN A VAULT a ribbed surface within a vaulted structure **8.** PRINTING PRINTING PAPER a roll of paper that is used on a rotary printing press ■ *vi.* (**webbed, web·bing, webs**) FORM A WEB to form or produce a web [Old English. Ultimately from an Indo-European base meaning "to weave" that is also the ancestor of English *weave* and *weft.*]

Web /web/ *n.* the World Wide Web (*informal*)

webbed /webd/ *adj.* joined by a membrane or membranes of skin ○ *webbed feet* [Mid-17thC]

web·bing /wébbing/ *n.* **1.** TEXTILES STRONG COARSE FABRIC strong coarse fabric used in belts and harnesses and for supporting upholstery **2.** ZOOL SKIN OF THE FOOT the membrane of skin joining the digits of an animal's foot, especially the foot of a bird or amphibian **3.** SOMETHING FORMING A WEB something that forms a web

Web brows·er, web brows·er *n.* a program used for displaying and viewing pages on the World Wide Web

Web·cam /wéb kàm/, **web·cam** *n.* a video camera recording pictures that are broadcast live on the Internet [Late 20thC. Blend of WORLD WIDE WEB + CAMERA.]

Web·cast /wéb kàst/, **web·cast** *n.* a broadcast made on the World Wide Web ○ *"... they spent $5 million promoting the live Webcast of their Spring Fashion Show ..."* (*The New York Times*; April 1999) [Late 20thC. Blend of WORLD WIDE WEB + BROADCAST.]

Web·cast·ing /wéb kàsting/, **web·cast·ing** *n.* the use of the World Wide Web for broadcasting information [Late 20thC. Blend of WORLD WIDE WEB + BROADCASTING.]

Web crawl·er, web crawl·er *n.* a program used to search through pages on the World Wide Web in order to locate documents containing a particular set of words, a phrase, or a topic

Web·er /wébbər, váybər/ *n.* the SI unit of magnetic flux, equal to 1 joule per ampere or 1 volt-second. Symbol **Wb** [Late 19thC. Named for Wilhelm Eduard *Weber* (1804–91), a German physicist known for his work on magnetism.]

We·ber /váybər/, **Carl Maria von** (1786–1826) German composer. His orchestral works and operas are important in the growth of early romanticism.

Web·er /wébbər/, **Max** (1881–1961) Russian-born U.S. artist. His vivid pictures combine cubist, expressionist, and fauvist styles.

web·foot /wéb fo͝ot/ (*plural* **web·feet** /-fèet/) *n.* ZOOL **1.** FOOT WITH TOES JOINED BY WEBBING a foot that has the toes joined by a membrane of skin **2.** ANIMAL WITH WEBBED FEET an animal with webbed feet —**web·foot·ed** *adj.*

Web·head /wéb hèd/, **web·head** *n.* a frequent user of the World Wide Web (*slang*) [Late 20thC. Blend of WORLD WIDE WEB + HEAD.]

Web·i·sode /wébbi s-d/, **web·i·sode** *n.* an episode, preview, or promotion of a movie, television program, or music video on a World Wide Web site (*slang*) [Late 20thC. Blend of WORLD WIDE WEB + EPISODE.]

Web·li·og·ra·phy /wèbblee óggrəfee/ (*plural* **-phy**), **web·li·og·ra·phy** (*plural* **-phy**) *n.* a list of particular documents available on the Web [Late 20thC. Blend of WORLD WIDE WEB + BIBLIOGRAPHY.]

Web·mas·ter /wéb mastər/, **web·mas·ter** *n.* somebody who creates, organizes, or updates the information content of a World Wide Web site

web mem·ber *n.* a brace that links the top and bottom flanges of a lattice girder or truss

web off·set *n.* offset printing carried out on a web press

Web page, web page *n.* a computer file, encoded in HyperText Markup Language (**HTML**) and containing text, graphics files, and sound files, that is accessible through the World Wide Web. Every Web page has a unique Uniform Resource Locator (**URL**), or address.

web press *n.* a printing press that is fed paper from a large roll [Late 19C. See WEB.]

Web ring, web ring *n.* a series of interlinked World Wide Web sites that are visited in sequential order, eventually returning to the original site

Web serv·er, web serv·er *n.* a program such as a Web browser that serves up Web pages when requested by a client

Web site /wéb sìt/, **web·site** *n.* a group of related Web pages. Approximately 85 percent of all Web pages are in English.

web spin·ner *n.* an insect that spins a web, especially one with glands that produce a kind of silk used to construct a web. Order: Embioptera.

web·ster /wébstər/ *n.* a weaver (*archaic*) [Old English *webbestre*]

Web·ster /wébstər/ town in southern Massachusetts, north of the Connecticut border and south of Worcester. Population: 16,089 (1996).

Web·ster, John (1580?–1623?) English playwright. His plays *The White Devil* (1612) and *The Duchess of Malfi* (1614?) are outstanding examples of the revenge tragedies of their time.

Web·ster, Noah (1758–1843) U.S. lexicographer. He is known for institutionalizing the differences between American and English grammar, pronunciation, and spelling in his *American Dictionary of the English Language* (1828).

web-toed *adj.* having a membrane of skin tissue between the toes

web·worm /wéb wùrm/ (*plural* **-worms** *or* **-worm**) *n.* a caterpillar, especially a tiger moth caterpillar, that spins a web in which it feeds or rests

Wechs·ler A·dult In·tel·li·gence Scale-Re·vised /wèkslər-/ *n.* an individually administered IQ test for adults developed by the psychologist David Wechsler. It incorporates subtests of both verbal and performance abilities. [Late 20thC]

Wech·sler In·tel·li·gence Scale for Chil·dren *n.* an individually administered IQ test for children, developed by the psychologist David Wechsler and measuring a wide variety of abilities [Mid-20thC]

wed /wed/ (**wed·ded** *or* **wed, wed·ding, weds**) *v.* **1.** *vt.* MARRY to marry somebody (*formal or literary*) **2.** *vi.* GET MARRIED to become married to somebody **3.** *vt.* JOIN A COUPLE IN MARRIAGE to join two people in marriage **4.** *vt.* UNITE THINGS to bring two things together or regard them as linked ○ *The two concepts had become wedded in his mind.* [Old English *weddian.* Ultimately from an Indo-European base meaning "pledge" that is also the ancestor of English *engage* and *wager.*]

we'd /weed/ *contr.* **1.** we had **2.** we would

Wed. *abbr.* Wednesday

wed·ded /wéddəd/ *adj.* **1. MARRIED** united in marriage **2. OF MARRIAGE** relating to marriage ○ *wedded bliss* **3. COMMITTED TO SOMETHING** strongly attached or committed to something ○ *wedded to the idea of reform* [Old English]

Wed·dell Sea /wédd'l-, wə dél-/ arm of the South Atlantic Ocean, south of Cape Horn and the Falkland Islands

wed·der /wéddər/ *n.* = **wether**

wed·ding /wédding/ *n.* **1. MARRIAGE CEREMONY** a marriage ceremony, or the act of marrying (*often used before a noun*) ○ *a wedding veil* **2. WEDDING ANNIVERSARY** the anniversary of a marriage (*used in combination*) ○ *a silver wedding* **3. UNITING OF TWO THINGS** the bringing together of two things ○ *the wedding of form and function* [Old English *weddung*]

wed·ding band *n.* = **wedding ring**

wed·ding cake *n.* a cake decorated with icing, usually white, and arranged in tiers, served at a wedding reception

wed·ding-cake *adj.* characterized by an extremely ornate style of architecture

wed·ding dress *n.* a dress worn by a bride at her wedding

wed·ding march *n.* a piece of music in march time played during a marriage ceremony, usually when the bride enters

wed·ding ring *n.* a ring, usually a gold band, worn on the third finger of the left hand by somebody who is married

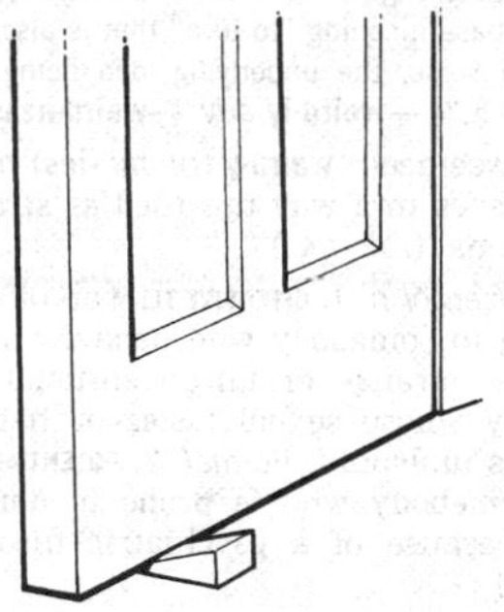

Wedge

wedge /wej/ *n.* **1. TAPERING BLOCK** a solid block that is thick at one end and thin at the other, used to secure or separate two objects **2. WEDGE-SHAPED OBJECT** an object that has a wedge shape ○ *a wedge of cake* **3. SOMETHING THAT ACTS AS A WEDGE** something that acts as a wedge, e.g., by causing division ○ *drove a wedge between the two families* **4.** CLOTHES = **wedge heel 5.** GOLF **GOLF CLUB** a golf club with a markedly slanted head, used to hit the ball along a high arcing trajectory **6. STROKE IN CUNEIFORM WRITING** a wedge-shaped stroke used in cuneiform writing ■ *v.* (**wedged, wedg·ing, wedg·es**) **1.** *vt.* **FORCE APART WITH A WEDGE** to force something apart or open with a wedge **2.** *vt.* **SECURE WITH A WEDGE** to secure or tighten something with a wedge **3.** *vti.* **SQUEEZE** to squeeze or pack something into a small space, or to be squeezed or packed in this way ○ *Hundreds of people were wedged into the room.* [Old English *wecg.* Ultimately from a prehistoric Germanic base, which probably came from an Indo-European word meaning "plowshare, wedge" that is also the probable ancestor of English *vomer.*] —**wedg·y** *adj.*

wedge heel *n.* **1. SHOE HEEL** a shoe heel shaped like a wedge, forming a solid extension of the sole so that there is no gap under the instep **2. SHOE** a shoe with a wedge heel

wedg·ie /wéjjee/ *n.* = **wedge heel**

Wedg·wood /wéj wŏŏd/, **Josiah** (1730–95) British potter. He developed a distinctive pottery inspired by ancient Greek ware, and established a highly successful pottery business.

Wedg·wood blue *adj.* pale gray blue in color [Early 20thC. Named for Josiah WEDGWOOD.] —**Wedg·wood blue** *n.*

wedg·y /wéjjee/ (*plural* **-ies**) *n.* an uncomfortable intrusion of clothing, usually briefs, up into the crack between the buttocks (*informal*) ○ *his new underpants gave him a wedgy*

wed·lock /wéd lòk/ *n.* the state of being married [12thC. By folk etymology from earlier *wedlac*, literally "action of pledging," from *wed* "pledge," by association with LOCK.] ◇ **born out of wedlock, conceived out of wedlock** born to *or* or conceived by parents who are not married (*dated*)

Wednes·day /wénz dày, -dee/ *n.* the third day of the week, coming after Tuesday and before Thursday [Old English *wōdnesdæg*, literally "Odin's day," from *Woden* "Odin" (chief deity of the Germanic peoples) + *dæg* "day," a translation of Latin *Mercurii dies* "Mercury's day"]

Wednes·days /wénz dàyz, -deez/ *adv.* every Wednesday ○ *Wednesdays I leave a little early.*

wee /wee/ *adj.* **TINY** very small ■ *n. Scotland* **SHORT TIME** a brief period of time ○ *bide a wee* [Old English *wēg* "weight." The modern meaning evolved via its use in phrases such as *little wee* "small weight."]

weed[1] /weed/ *n.* **1. UNWANTED PLANT** a plant, especially a wild plant, growing where it is not wanted **2. UNWANTED PLANTS** weeds in general (*often used before a noun*) ○ *weed control* **3. PLANT GROWING IN WATER** a plant that grows in water, especially seaweed **4. MARIJUANA** marijuana for smoking as a drug (*slang*) **5. TOBACCO** tobacco or cigarettes (*slang*) **6. INFERIOR ANIMAL** an inferior animal, especially a horse that cannot be bred ■ *v.* (**weed·ed, weed·ing, weeds**) **1.** *vt.* **REMOVE WEEDS FROM THE GROUND** to clear an area of weeds ○ *to weed the garden* **2.** *vi.* **PULL UP WEEDS** to pull up and remove weeds ○ *spent several hours weeding* [Old English *wēod.* Ultimately from a prehistoric Germanic plant name.] —**weed·er** *n.*

weed out *vt.* to separate out or remove somebody or something undesirable or unwanted ○ *a test to weed out unsuitable candidates*

weed[2] /weed/ *n.* **SOMETHING WORN AS A SIGN OF MOURNING** something worn as a sign of mourning, especially a black band around a sleeve or hat ■ **weeds** *npl.* **1. WIDOW'S CLOTHES** the black clothes once traditionally worn by widows (*archaic or literary*) **2. CLOTHES** clothes in general (*archaic*) [Old English *wǣd.* Ultimately from a prehistoric Germanic base meaning "garment."]

weed·kill·er /wéed kìllər/ *n.* a chemical that kills plants by attacking the root, leaf, or vascular system

weed·y /wéedee/ (**-i·er, -i·est**) *adj.* **1. FULL OF WEEDS** filled with or containing many weeds ○ *a weedy patch of ground* **2.** BOT **LIKE A WEED** resembling or having the characteristics of a weed ○ *weedy plants* **3. THIN** strikingly thin and weak-looking (*insult*) —**weed·i·ly** *adv.* —**weed·i·ness** *n.*

wee hours *npl.* = **wee small hours**

week /week/ *n.* **1. 7-DAY PERIOD** a period of seven consecutive days **2. CALENDAR WEEK** a period of seven days beginning from a particular day, usually Sunday ○ *the middle of the week* **3. WORKING WEEK** the days of the week on which somebody works, or the time that is spent working ○ *goes to bed early during the week* **4. SPECIAL WEEK** a week containing a particular holiday, or dedicated to a particular cause ○ *Easter week* ■ *adv. U.K.* **ONE WEEK AFTER A PARTICULAR DAY** one week after or before a particular day ○ *arranged to meet on Thursday week* [Old English *wice.* Ultimately from a prehistoric Germanic word meaning "series, succession," which is also the ancestor of German *Woche.*]

week·day /wéek dày/ *n.* a day of the week other than Saturday or Sunday ○ *only open on weekdays* [Old English *wicdæg*]

week·end /wéek ènd/ *n.* **FROM FRIDAY EVENING TO SUNDAY EVENING** the end of the week, from Friday evening, or sometimes Saturday morning, until Sunday evening ■ *vi.* (**-end·ed, -end·ing, -ends**) **SPEND THE WEEKEND SOMEWHERE** to spend a weekend or weekends in a particular place

week·end bag *n.* a bag or small suitcase used to carry clothes and other items needed for a short trip or vacation

week·end·er /wéek èndər/ *n.* **1. SOMEBODY SPENDING A WEEKEND SOMEWHERE** somebody spending a weekend somewhere, especially on a regular basis **2.** = **weekend bag 3.** *Aus* **VACATION HOME** a vacation house (*informal*)

week·ends /wéek èndz/ *adv.* on or during the weekend (*informal*)

week·long /wéek làwng/ *adj.* lasting for a whole week

week·ly /wéeklee/ *adj.* **1. HAPPENING ONCE A WEEK** happening, produced, or done once a week or every week **2. CALCULATED BY THE WEEK** worked out by the week ○ *weekly pay* ■ *adv.* **1. ONCE A WEEK** once each week ○ *does the shopping weekly* **2. EVERY WEEK** every single week **3. BY THE WEEK** by the week ○ *gets paid weekly* ■ *n.* (*plural* **-lies**) **SOMETHING PUBLISHED ONCE A WEEK** a newspaper or magazine published once a week

week·night /wéek nìt/ *n.* the evening or night of a weekday ○ *I'm not letting you go out on a weeknight.*

Weems /weemz/, **Parsons** (1759–1825) U.S. clergyman and writer. His fictionalized biography of George Washington (1800) was a bestseller for decades. Full name **Mason Locke Weems**

ween /ween/ (**weened, ween·ing, weens**) *vt.* to think, believe, or suppose something (*archaic*) [Old English *wēnan.* Ultimately from an Indo-European base meaning "to desire" that is also the ancestor of English *wish* and *venereal.*]

ween·ie /wéenee/ *n.* **1.** = **wiener** (*informal*) **2. OFFENSIVE TERM** an offensive term referring to somebody regarded as weak or insignificant (*slang insult*) **3. OFFENSIVE TERM** an offensive term for a penis (*slang offensive*)

ween·sy *adj.* = **weeny** (*informal*)

wee·ny /wéenee/ (**-ni·er, -ni·est**), **ween·sy** /wéenzee/ (**-si·er, -si·est**) *adj.* very small (*informal*) [Late 18thC. Formed from WEE on the model of *tiny.*]

wee·ny-bop·per /wéenee bòpər/ *n.* a child, especially a young girl, who is fond of pop music and the latest fashions (*informal*) ◊ **teenybopper**

weep /weep/ *v.* (**wept, wept** /wept/, **weep·ing, weeps**) **1.** *vi.* **CRY** to shed tears ○ *They walked behind the coffin, weeping silently.* **2.** *vt.* **EXPRESS SOMETHING WHILE CRYING TEARS** to express something while crying or by crying tears **3.** *vti.* **MOURN SOMEBODY** to lament or cry tears for somebody or something (*literary*) **4.** *vti.* **LEAK FLUID** to leak, drip, or ooze drops of liquid ○ *The eye was inflamed and weeping* ■ *n.* **SPELL OF CRYING** a period of time spent crying [Old English *wēpan.* Ultimately from a prehistoric Germanic word of uncertain origin: perhaps an imitation of the sound of weeping.]

weep·er /wéepər/ *n.* **1. SOMEBODY WHO WEEPS** somebody who weeps, especially somebody hired to weep at a funeral **2. SOMETHING WORN AS A SIGN OF MOURNING** something that is worn as a sign of mourning such as a black armband or a veil **3.** BUILDING **HOLE FOR WATER TO ESCAPE** a hole in a wall or foundation that allows accumulated water to escape **4.** CINEMA, LITERAT = **weepie** (*informal*) ■ **weep·ers** *npl.* **SIDEBURNS** long sideburns (*informal*)

weep·ie /wéepee/, **weep·er** /wéepər/ *n.* a movie, play, or book that tends to move people to tears, especially one that is blatantly sentimental in tone (*informal*)

weep·ing /wéeping/ *adj.* **1.** BOT **WITH DROOPING BRANCHES** having slender drooping branches ○ *a weeping birch* **2. CRYING** shedding tears **3. LEAKING FLUID** leaking, dripping, or oozing drops of liquid [Old English *wepende*] —**weep·ing·ly** *adv.*

weep·ing fig *n.* a small tree of the mulberry family that has glossy leaves and is often grown as a houseplant. Latin name: *Ficus benjamina.*

Weeping willow

weep·ing wil·low *n.* an ornamental willow tree, originally from China with long drooping branches and narrow leaves. Latin name: *Salix babylonica.*

weep·y /wéepee/ (**weep·i·er, weep·i·est**) *adj.* **1. TEARFUL** inclined to weep (*informal*) **2. MOVING PEOPLE TO TEARS** tending to make people cry —**weep·i·ly** *adv.* —**weep·i·ness** *n.*

wee small hours *npl.* the early hours of the morning, especially those just after midnight

wee·ver /wéevər/, **wee·ver·fish** /wéevər fish/ (*plural* **-fish·es** *or* **-fish**) *n.* a small marine fish with a single long spine on each gill cover and several on its back. Family: Trachinidae. [Early 17thC. Origin uncertain: probably from Old North French *wivre* (see WYVERN).]

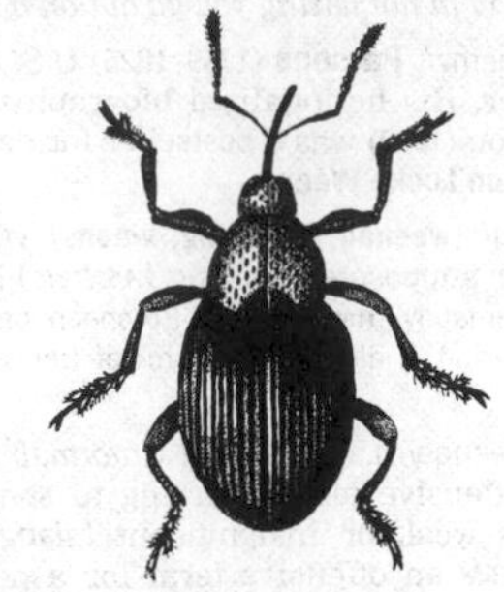

Weevil

wee·vil /wéev'l/ *n.* **1. DESTRUCTIVE BEETLE WITH A SNOUT** a beetle with a long head that forms a snout or rostrum. Many are pests, destroying plants and grain. Family: Curculionidae. **2. PEA OR BEAN PEST** a beetle whose larvae live in the seeds of peas and beans. Family: Bruchidae and Lariidae. **3. BEETLE LIKE A WEEVIL** any beetle similar to a weevil including many that are pests. Family: Rhynchophora. [Old English *wifel* "beetle." Ultimately from an Indo-European base meaning "to move quickly" that is also the ancestor of English *weave*[2] and *whip*.] —**wee·vi·ly** *adj.*

wee-wee *n.* (*informal babytalk*) **1. ACT OF URINATING** an act or instance of urinating **2. URINE** urine (*offensive in some contexts*) ■ *vi.* (**wee-weed, wee-wee·ing, wee-wees**) **URINATE** to urinate (*babytalk*) (*offensive in some contexts*) [Repetition of WEE]

weft /weft/ *n.* **1. HORIZONTAL THREADS** the horizontal threads of a woven fabric or a tapestry. ◊ **warp** *n.* 3 **2. YARN FOR THE WEFT** yarn used for the weft **3. SOMETHING WOVEN** an article or piece of woven fabric [Old English. Ultimately from an Indo-European base meaning "to weave" that is also the ancestor of English *weave* and *web*.]

Wehr·macht /váir maàkt, váir maàkht/ *n.* the German armed forces, especially the army between 1935 and 1945 [Mid-20thC. From German, literally "defense force."]

wei·ge·la /wī jéelə, wī géelə, wíjələ, wígələ/ *n.* a shrub native to Asia with bell-shaped pink, white, or red flowers. Genus: *Weigela*. [Mid-19thC. From modern Latin *Weigela*, the name of the genus, named for Christian E. *Weigel* (1748–1831), German physician.]

weigh[1] /way/ (**weighed, weigh·ing, weighs**) *v.* **1.** *vt.* **FIND THE WEIGHT OF SOMETHING** to find out the weight of somebody or something ○ *he weighed himself regularly* **2.** *vi.* **BE A PARTICULAR WEIGHT** to be of a particular weight **3.** *vt.* **MEASURE BY WEIGHT** to measure or distribute something by weight ○ *weighed out two pounds of onions* **4.** *vt.* **EVALUATE** to consider or evaluate something, especially so as to be able to come to a decision or choice ○ *had to weigh all possible options* **5.** *vi.* **HAVE IMPORTANCE** to have importance or be influential **6.** *vt.* **GUESS THE WEIGHT OF** to hold something in the hand in order to assess its weight **7.** *vi.* **BE BURDENSOME** to be burdensome, oppressive, or worrying to somebody ○ *The problem weighed heavily on my mind.* **8.** *vti.* SHIPPING **RAISE ANCHOR** to raise the anchor of a vessel [Old English *wegan* "to weigh, carry." Ultimately from an Indo-European base meaning "to carry" that is also the ancestor of English *wagon*.] —**weigh·a·ble** *adj.* —**weigh·er** *n.*

weigh down *vt.* **1. OPPRESS SOMEBODY** to be oppressive or burdensome to somebody ○ *weighed down by grief* ○ *weighed down with extra paperwork* **2. PRESS SOMETHING DOWN** to press somebody or something down by exerting weight ○ *trees weighed down with fruit*

weigh in *vi.* **1.** SPORTS **BE WEIGHED FOR A RACE OR CONTEST** to be weighed before or after a race or contest such as a boxing match or horserace **2. HAVE BAGGAGE WEIGHED** to have baggage weighed before a flight **3. CONTRIBUTE A COMMENT** to contribute or produce something such as an argument or comment, especially in an assertive way (*informal*)

weigh[2] /way/ *n.* = **way** *n.* 21 [Late 18thC. By folk etymology from WAY by association with WEIGH[1] in *weigh anchor*.] ◇ **under weigh** SHIPPING = **under way**

weigh-in *n.* the weighing of a competitor before or after a race or contest

weight /wayt/ *n.* **1. HEAVINESS** the heaviness of somebody or something ○ *Just feel the weight of it!* **2. MEASURE OF SOMEBODY'S HEAVINESS** the specific amount that a person or animal weighs ○ *I had lost 10 pounds in weight.* **3. SYSTEM FOR MEASURING HEAVINESS** a system of standard measures of weight **4.** PHYS **FORCE CAUSED BY GRAVITY** the vertical force experienced by a mass because of gravity. Symbol *W* **5.** MEASURE **UNIT OF WEIGHT** a unit used as a measure of weight **6. HEAVY OBJECT** a heavy object used to hold something down **7. MENTAL BURDEN** a mental or moral burden or load **8. HEAVY LOAD** a heavy load to carry ○ *had to put him down since he was a heavy weight* **9. IMPORTANCE** importance or significance ○ *a motion that did not carry much weight with the judge* **10. GREATER PART** the preponderance or greater part of something **11.** PRINTING **HEAVINESS OF TYPEFACE** the heaviness or thickness of a typeface **12.** GYM **OBJECT USED IN WEIGHTLIFTING** a heavy object used in weightlifting or for exercise (*often used in the plural*) **13.** TEXTILES **THICKNESS OF CLOTH** the heaviness or thickness of cloth (*often used in combination*) ■ *vt.* (**weight·ed, weight·ing, weights**) **1. ADD WEIGHT TO** to add weight or weights to something **2. OPPRESS OR BURDEN** to oppress or burden somebody, e.g., with problems or cares ○ *The responsibility weighed on him.* **3. BIAS** to slant something in somebody's favor or assign additional importance to something such as a test or part of one ○ *The choice of candidate was heavily weighted in her favor.* **4.** TEXTILES **INCREASE DENSITY OF FABRIC** to treat fabric so as to increase its density **5.** SPORTS **ASSIGN A HORSE A HANDICAP WEIGHT** to assign a handicap weight to a horse [Old English *wiht*. Ultimately from an Indo-European base that is also the ancestor of English *weigh*.] —**weight·er** *n.* ◇ **be worth its** *or* **your weight in gold** to be extremely valuable ◇ **to gain** *or* **lose weight** become heavier or lighter in body weight ◇ **pull your weight** to do your fair share of work or take your fair share of responsibility ◇ **throw your weight around** to be domineering

weight·ed /wáytəd/ *adj.* adjusted by the addition of a statistical value

weight·less /wáytləss/ *adj.* having no weight, especially by virtue of being in an atmosphere in which there is no gravitational pull —**weight·less·ly** *adv.* —**weight·less·ness** *n.*

weight·lift·er /wáyt liftər/ *n.* somebody who lifts heavy weights as a sport

weight·lift·ing /-/ *n.* the sport of lifting heavy weights, either for exercise or in competition

weight train·ing *n.* physical training using weights to strengthen the muscles

Weight·watch·ers /wáyt wòchərz/ *tdmk.* a trademark for an organization that helps people who want to lose weight (*takes a singular verb*)

weight·y /wáytee/ (**-i·er, -i·est**) *adj.* **1. HEAVY** weighing a great deal **2. IMPORTANT** of an important or serious nature ○ *discussing weighty matters* **3. INFLUENTIAL** able to exert influence **4. OPPRESSIVE** oppressive or burdensome ○ *a weighty responsibility* —**weight·i·ly** *adv.* —**weight·i·ness** *n.*

Weil /vayl/, **Simone** (1909–43) French philosopher and mystic. Her major writings, reflecting her Christian mysticism, were published posthumously and include *Waiting for God* (1950).

Weill /vīl, wīl/, **Kurt** (1900–50) German-born U.S. composer. His work, including *The Threepenny Opera* (1928) which he wrote with Bertold Brecht, was banned by the Nazis. After settling in the United States (1935) he wrote successful Broadway musicals. Full name **Kurt Julian Weill**

Weil's dis·ease /vílz-, wílz-/ *n.* a severe form of leptospirosis, usually resulting from contact with the urine of infected animals such as rats. Symptoms include jaundice, anemia, hemorrhaging, fever, and meningitis. [Late 19thC. Named for H. Adolf *Weil* (1848–1916), the German physician who described the disease.]

Wei·mar /wí maar/ city in Thuringia State, east central Germany, southwest of Leipzig. It was a major cultural center in the 18th and 19th centuries. Population: 61,583 (1990).

Wei·mar·an·er /wímə raanər/ *n.* a large hunting dog of a breed with a short-haired silver-gray coat, originally bred in Germany [Mid-20thC. Named for WEIMAR, where the dog was first bred.]

Wei·mar Re·pub·lic /w-maar/ *n.* the government of Germany between 1919 and 1933, so named because

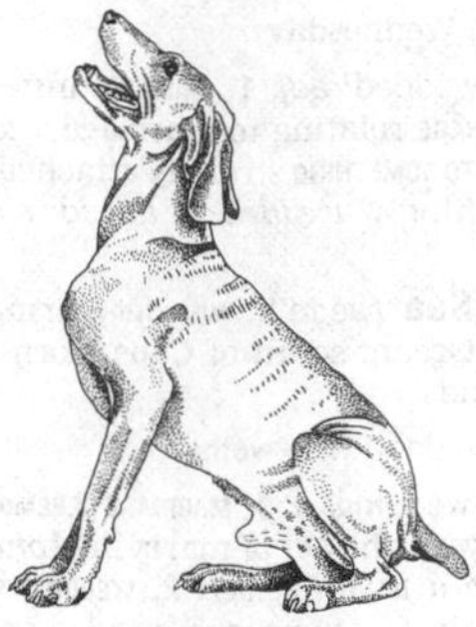

Weimaraner

the National Assembly met in Weimar in 1919 to establish a new republic and draw up a constitution

weir /weer/ *n.* **1. DAM** a dam built across a river to regulate the flow of water, divert it, or change its level **2.** ANGLING **BARRICADE FOR FISH** a fence placed in a stream to catch fish [Old English *wer*. Ultimately from an Indo-European base meaning "to cover" that is also the ancestor of English *garage* and *warn*.]

Weir /weer/, **Peter** (*b.* 1944) Australian movie director. After achieving international success with the Australian-made *Picnic at Hanging Rock* (1975), he established himself as a leading Hollywood director. Full name **Peter Lindsay Weir**

weird /weerd/ *adj.* **1. ODD** strange or unusual **2. SUPERNATURAL** belonging to or suggesting the supernatural **3. OF FATE** relating to or influenced by fate (*archaic*) [Old English *wyrd* "fate." Ultimately from an Indo-European base meaning "to turn" that is also the ancestor of English *verse*, the underlying idea being "that which comes about."] —**weird·ly** *adv.* —**weird·ness** *n.*

weird·ie /wéerdee/, **weird·y** (*plural* **-ies**) *n.* somebody who behaves in a way regarded as strange or unconventional (*informal*)

weird·o /wéerdō/ *n.* **1. OFFENSIVE TERM** an offensive term referring to somebody who behaves in a way regarded as strange or unconventional, especially somebody whose sexual tastes or habits are regarded as unusual (*informal*) **2. POTENTIALLY DANGEROUS PERSON** somebody who is prone to dangerous behavior because of a psychiatric disorder (*slang offensive*)

weird sis·ters, Weird Sisters *npl.* **1.** MYTHOL **FATES** the Fates **2.** MYTHOL = **the Norns** **3.** THEATER **WITCHES IN *MACBETH*** the three witches in Shakespeare's play *Macbeth* [*Weird* from WEIRD in the meaning of "having the power to control fates"]

Weir·ton /wéertən/ city in the northern panhandle of northern West Virginia, on the Ohio River, north of Wheeling. Population: 21,813 (1996).

weis·en·hei·mer *n.* = **wisenheimer** (*informal*)

Weis·mann·ism /wísmə nìzzəm/ *n.* the principle that the inherited characteristics of any organism are determined solely by material (**germ plasm**) contained in the male and female sex cells from which the organism develops. This theory excludes any role for the body cells in inheritance and rules out the inheritance of characters acquired during an organism's lifetime. It remains a fundamental tenet of modern genetics. [Late 19thC. Named for August F. L. *Weismann* (1834–1914), the German biologist who propounded this principle.]

Weiz·mann /vīts maan, wítsmən/, **Chaim** (1874–1952) Russian-born Israeli chemist and statesman. He helped to secure the Balfour Declaration (1917), which committed Britain to Zionism, and served as the first president of modern Israel (1948–52). Full name **Chaim Azriel Weizmann**

we·ka /wéekə, wáykə/ *n.* a flightless fast-running bird with mainly brown and black plumage, found in the scrubland and forest margins of New Zealand. Latin name: *Gallirallus australis*. [Mid-19thC. From Maori, an imitation of the sound of the bird's call.]

welch *vi.* = **welsh**

wel·come /wélkəm/ *adj.* **1. RECEIVED GLADLY** received or entertained glady and generously ○ *a welcome gift* **2. EAGERLY AND DELIGHTEDLY ACCEPTED** accepted or anticipated with delight and eagerness, often because it answers a need ○ *It was a welcome break after two solid weeks of writing.* **3. FREELY INVITED OR PERMITTED** freely and willingly invited or permitted ○ *You're* *welcome to stay for dinner.* **4.** WITH NOTHING EXPECTED IN RETURN with no obligation incurred by a courtesy, favor, gift, or something else given ○ *You're very welcome, it was no trouble.* ■ *n.* **1.** ACKNOWLEDGMENT OF SOMEBODY'S ARRIVAL a greeting or reception given to somebody upon arrival or being met ○ *a warm welcome to their guests* **2.** REACTION TO SOMETHING a particular response or reaction to something ○ *Local authorities have extended a cautious welcome to the new proposals* ■ *vt.* (**-comed, -com·ing, -comes**) **1.** RECEIVE IN A PARTICULAR WAY to greet, receive, or entertain somebody in a particular way **2.** ACCEPT IN A PARTICULAR WAY to accept or receive something in a particular way ○ *We welcome any feedback from our customers.* ■ *interj.* USED TO GREET SOMEBODY used to express a friendly or courteous greeting to somebody who has just arrived or is a stranger [Old English *wilcuma*, originally a noun meaning "welcome guest" (influenced by WELL[2] and either Old Norse *velkominn* or Old French *bien venu*), from *willa* (see WILL[2]) + *cuma* "comer"] — **wel·come·ly** *adv.* —**wel·come·ness** *n.* —**wel·com·er** *n.* ◇ **be welcome to something** used to indicate that the speaker is happy for somebody to have something (*often used ironically*) ◇ **wear out** *or* **outstay** *or* **overstay your welcome** to stay longer than is polite or accept somebody's hospitality for too long

wel·come mat *n.* a doormat, especially one with the word "welcome" on it ◇ **put out** *or* **roll out the welcome mat for somebody** to make somebody feel very welcome (*informal*)

wel·come page *n.* ONLINE = **home page**

Wel·come Wag·on *tdmk.* a trademark for an organization whose members welcome newcomers to a neighborhood, distribute small gifts, give information about the community, and offer samples of locally available merchandise

weld[1] /weld/ *v.* (**weld·ed, weld·ing, welds**) **1.** *vti.* FUSE MATERIAL BY HEATING to join together pieces or parts of some material by heating, hammering, or using other pressure, or to be joined in this way ○ *to weld two pieces of iron together* **2.** *vt.* REPAIR OR CONSTRUCT SOMETHING BY FUSING to repair or construct something by heating its pieces or parts so that they fuse together ○ *to weld a metal sculpture* **3.** *vti.* ASSOCIATE OR BECOME ASSOCIATED to join or become joined in a union or a close association ■ *n.* **1.** FUSION OF PARTS the union or fusion of parts or pieces **2.** JOINT FORMED BY FUSION a joint where pieces or parts have been fused together [Late 16thC. Alteration of WELL[1] (verb) in the obsolete meaning of "to liquefy by heating"; influenced by its past participle *welled*.] —**weld·a·bil·i·ty** /wèldə bíllətee/ *n.* —**weld·a·ble** /wéldəb'l/ *adj.*

weld[2] /weld/ *n.* **1.** BOT = **dyer's rocket** **2.** YELLOW DYE a yellow dye extracted from the dyer's rocket plant, widely used from ancient times until the modern era to color wool and other fabrics [Origin uncertain: perhaps from obsolete Low German *walde, wolde*; or perhaps from assumed Old English *w(e)ald*]

weld·er /wéldər/ *n.* **1.** SOMEBODY WHO WELDS SOMETHING somebody who welds, especially somebody who earns a living by welding metal **2.** SOMETHING THAT WELDS a device, machine, or other apparatus that is used to make metal welds

weld·ment /wéldmənt/ *n.* something that has been assembled by welding its parts or pieces together

wel·fare /wél fàir/ *n.* **1.** PHYSICAL, SOCIAL, AND FINANCIAL WELL-BEING the physical, social, and financial conditions under which somebody may live satisfactorily **2.** AID TO PEOPLE IN NEED financial aid and other benefits for people who are unemployed, below a specified income level, or otherwise requiring assistance, especially when provided by a government agency or program **3.** = **welfare work** ■ *adj.* **1.** AIDING PEOPLE IN NEED concerning or designed to aid people who are poor, unemployed, or in need of assistance in some other way ○ *a welfare agency* **2.** RECEIVING GOVERNMENT AID OWING TO NEED receiving government financial aid or benefits because of income level, unemployment, or other conditions that create a need for assistance ○ *welfare clients* [14thC. Contraction of *well fare* "fare well."]

wel·fare state *n.* **1.** GOVERNMENT RESPONSIBILITY FOR SOCIAL WELFARE a political system in which a government assumes the primary responsibility for assuring the basic health and financial wellbeing of all its citizens through programs and direct assistance **2.** NATION FULLY ASSUMING CITIZENS' WELFARE a nation whose government assumes primary responsibility for the social welfare of its citizens

wel·fare work, **wel·fare** *n.* the organized efforts of an organization, community, or agency to improve the living conditions and economic status of its socially disadvantaged members, residents, or citizens — **wel·fare work·er** *n.*

wel·far·ism /wél fài rìzzəm/ *n.* the policies, practices, and beliefs that characterize the welfare state (*disapproving*) [Mid-20thC] —**wel·far·ist** *n.*

wel·kin /wélkin/ *n.* the sky, heaven, or the upper air (*archaic or literary*) [Old English *weolcen, wolc(e)n* "cloud, firmament." From a prehistoric Germanic word that is also the ancestor of Dutch *wolk* and German *Wolke* "cloud."]

Wel·kom /wélkəm, vélk-/ town in Free State, central South Africa. It is the center of a gold-mining region. Population: 185,500 (1985).

Well

well[1] /wel/ *n.* **1.** HOLE MADE TO DRAW UP FLUIDS a hole or shaft that is dug or drilled into the ground in order to obtain water, brine, petroleum, or natural gas ○ *an oil well* **2.** SPRING OF WATER a place where water comes out of the ground as a natural source ○ *get their water from a well* **3.** SOURCE OF SOMETHING a source of a freely and abundantly available supply of something ○ *a well of information* **4.** CONTAINER FOR LIQUID a container or sunken area for holding ink or another liquid ○ *a well on a cutting board* **5.** VERTICAL PASSAGE IN A BUILDING a vertical space within or enclosed by a building, often used as a passageway for stairs or elevators or for air and light **6.** ENCLOSURE FOR A SHIP'S PUMPS an enclosed area in the hold of a ship in which the pumps are located **7.** SHIPBOARD CONTAINER FOR FISH a compartment in a fishing boat in which freshly caught fish are held **8.** ENCLOSING COMPARTMENT a compartment that encloses or is used to store something temporarily such as the retracted wheels of an aircraft in flight ■ *v.* (**welled, well·ing, wells**) **1.** *vti.* RISE OR BRING TO THE SURFACE to rise or flow to the surface from inside the earth or the body, or to cause something to do this ○ *Tears welled up in his eyes.* ○ *The fountain welled a stream of clear water into the basin below.* **2.** *vi.* GROW STRONGER to surge from within or grow stronger so as to threaten to burst forth ○ *Fear welled up inside me.* **3.** *vi.* BECOME FILLED WITH LIQUID to become filled with a pool of water, tears, or another liquid ○ *My eyes welled with tears.* [Old English *wella* "spring of water" and *wellan* "to boil." Ultimately from an Indo-European word meaning "to turn," which also produced English *walk, wallet, waltz*, and *welter*.]

well[2] /wel/ (**bet·ter** /béttər/, **best** /best/) CORE MEANING: a grammatical word indicating that something is satisfactory or is performed in a satisfactory way ○ *She did very well on her test.*

1. *adv.* PLEASINGLY OR DESIRABLY in an efficient, satisfying, or otherwise desirable way (*often used in combination*) ○ *I thought the party went very well.* **2.** *adv.* ETHICALLY OR PROPERLY in an ethical, proper, or courteous way ○ *He always treated the children very well.* **3.** *adv.* SKILLFULLY OR EXPERTLY with proficiency, skill, or expertise (*often used in combination*) ○ *She plays tennis really well.* **4.** *adv.* JUSTLY AND APPROPRIATELY with justice and good reason ○ *I could not very well refuse her request.* **5.** *adv.* COMFORTABLY in ease and comfort (*often used in combination*) ○ *I just want to be rich enough to live well.* **6.** *adv.* ADVANTAGEOUSLY in a way that promotes somebody's advantage and well-being (*often used in combination*) ○ *She married well – her husband is a wealthy pig-farmer.* **7.** *adv.* CONDUCIVE TO GOOD HEALTH in a way that promotes health and physical well-being (*often used in combination*) ○ *Both mother and baby are doing well.* **8.** *adv.* CONSIDERABLY to a considerable extent, distance, or degree (*often used in combination*) ○ *I was well prepared for the exams.* **9.** *adv.* FULLY AND THOROUGHLY in a complete and thorough way (*often used in combination*) ○ *Stir the mixture well, then turn it out onto a baking sheet.* **10.** *adv.* WITH CERTAINTY with no doubt whatever about something ○ *As you well know, I will not tolerate any laziness* **11.** *adv.* FAMILIARLY AND INTIMATELY in a familiar and intimate way ○ *I knew them well when they were students.* **12.** *adv.* GOOD-NATUREDLY taking something in a tolerant or good-humored way ○ *I teased him but he took it well.* **13.** *adj.* IN GOOD HEALTH mentally and physically healthy ○ *I'm feeling much better.* **14.** *adj.* PROPER OR APPROPRIATE suitable, proper, or appropriate in the circumstances ○ *It is as well that you apologized to her.* **15.** *adj.* HIGHLY SATISFACTORY in a good, pleasing, or satisfying condition ○ *Is everything well with you?* **16.** *interj.* USED TO EXPRESS EMOTION used to express surprise, agreement, indignition, disapproval, or some other emotion ○ *Well! You've finally come back!* **17.** *interj.* USED TO INTRODUCE OR RESUME SOMETHING used to introduce a comment or statement, or to resume a conversation ○ *Well, it looks as if we'll be waiting a while.* [Old English *wel(l)*. Ultimately from an Indo-European base meaning "to wish," which is also the ancestor of Latin *velle* (source of English *benevolent* and *voluntary*) and English *wealth*.] ◇ **as well** in addition to something ○ *The members were mostly young couples, but there were several grandparents as well.* ◇ **as well as** to an equal degree or extent ○ *Banking, as well as other businesses, will take the demographics into consideration.* ◇ **be as well to do something** to be advisable or sensible to do something ○ *It would be as well to look at a variety of mutual funds before investing your savings.* ◇ **be well out of something** to be fortunate in having escaped from a difficult or unhappy situation ○ *You're well out of it – they weren't treating you very well in that job* ◇ **that's** *or* **it's just as well** used to indicate that something is fortunate ○ *It's just as well that she's going to be a little late, because we're not quite ready.* ◇ **well and good** indicating qualified approval ○ *If he wants to come with us, well and good, but he'll have to pay his share.*

we'll /weel, wil/ *contr.* **1.** we will **2.** we shall

well-ad·just·ed *adj.* (*not hyphenated after a verb*) **1.** ALTERED ACCORDINGLY successfully adapted to prevailing conditions **2.** EMOTIONALLY STABLE content with your own self and life and therefore emotionally and psychologically stable

well-ad·vised *adj.* acting with good sense (*not hyphenated after a verb*) ○ *You would be well-advised to leave before the storm hits.*

Wel·land Ca·nal /wèllənd-/, **Wel·land Ship Ca·nal** canal system in Ontario, Canada, linking Lake Ontario and Lake Erie. It is part of the St. Lawrence Seaway, and bypasses the Niagara Falls. Length: 28 mi./44 km.

well-ap·point·ed *adj.* equipped, furnished, or arranged with whatever is necessary or desired (*not hyphenated after a verb*)

well·a·way /wéllə wày/ *interj.* used as a cry of sorrow, distress, or regret (*archaic*) [Old English *wei lā wei*, an alteration (influenced by WELL[2] and Old Norse *vei* "woe") of *wā lā wā*, literally "woe lo woe"]

well-bal·anced *adj.* (*not hyphenated after a verb*) **1.** ORGANIZED WITH THE PARTS IN PROPORTION organized, conducted, or constructed so that all the parts are appropriately and sensibly proportioned or coordinated **2.** SENSIBLE AND RATIONAL psychologically or emotionally stable

well-be·haved *adj.* behaving, operating, or occurring properly and as expected (*not hyphenated after a verb*)

well-be·ing *n.* a good, healthy, or comfortable state

well-be·lov·ed *adj.* (*not hyphenated after a verb*) **1.** DEARLY LOVED truly and dearly loved **2.** RESPECTED highly respected or honored ■ *n.* (*plural* **well-be·lov·ed**) DEARLY LOVED PERSON somebody who is truly and dearly loved

well·born /wèl báwrn, wél bàwrn/ *adj.* BELONGING TO A RESPECTED FAMILY born into an aristocratic, highly respected, or wealthy family ■ *n.* PEOPLE FROM ESTEEMED FAMILIES people who were born in aristocratic, highly respected, or wealthy families (*takes a plural verb*) [Old English *welboren*]

well-bred *adj.* (*not hyphenated after a verb*) **1. WITH GOOD MANNERS** possessing or displaying good manners or other marks of a good upbringing **2.** ZOOL **WITH A DESIRABLE PEDIGREE** born as an animal from a good breed or of good stock

well-built *adj.* (*not hyphenated after a verb*) **1. PHYSICALLY BIG AND STRONG** having a sturdy and strong physique **2. PROPERLY CONSTRUCTED** of strong or sound construction

well-cho·sen *adj.* selected carefully so as to be suitable or appropriate (*not hyphenated after a verb*)

well-con·nect·ed *adj.* having relatives, friends, or acquaintances in important or influential positions who can provide help when necessary (*not hyphenated after a verb*)

well-de·fined *adj.* **1. STATED PRECISELY AND CLEARLY** stated or described with clarity and without ambiguity (*not hyphenated after a verb*) **2. WITH A DISTINCT OUTLINE OR FORM** having a clearly observable outline or form (*not hyphenated when used after a verb*)

well-dis·posed *adj.* feeling or inclined to be approving, friendly, kindly, or sympathetic and potentially helpful (*not hyphenated after a verb*) ○ *She seemed well disposed toward us.*

well-done *adj.* (*not hyphenated after a verb*) **1. PERFORMED CORRECTLY AND WELL** carried out or performed correctly, properly, or skillfully **2. COOKED THROUGH** cooked right through to the center

well-earned *adj.* fully deserved, especially as a result of hard work or effort (*not hyphenated after a verb*) ○ *sat down for a well-earned rest*

well-en·dowed *adj.* (*not hyphenated after a verb*) **1. OFFENSIVE TERM** an offensive term meaning having a large penis or large breasts (*informal*) **2. AFFLUENT** provided with substantial property, a sizable income, or a good source of income **3. NATURALLY EXCELLENT** talented or capable as a result of a natural gift

Orson Welles

Welles /welz/, **Orson** (1915–85) U.S. actor and director. Although *Citizen Kane* (1941) garnered enormous critical respect, Hollywood's mistrust of his maverick talents prevented him from producing more than a handful of movies. Full name **George Orson Welles**

Welles·ley /wélzlee/ town in eastern Massachusetts, southwest of Boston. It is home to Wellesley College. Population: 26,809 (1996).

Welles·ley, Arthur, 1st Duke of Wellington (1769–1852) British general and statesman. He led the British forces that helped defeat Napoleon at the Battle of Waterloo (1815) and was prime minister (1828–30).

well-fa·vored *adj.* good-looking (*dated or formal*) (*not hyphenated after a verb*)

well-fed *adj.* (*not hyphenated after a verb*) **1. WITH A GOOD DIET** having a diet that provides proper nourishment **2. OVERWEIGHT** overweight, especially as a result of having eaten a great deal of good or rich food

well-fixed *adj.* provided with a sizable income or substantial property (*informal*) (*not hyphenated after a verb*)

well-formed *adj.* fully conforming to the rules of grammar and syntax in a language (*not hyphenated after a verb*) —**well-formed·ness** *n.*

well-found *adj.* properly and fully fitted out or equipped (*not hyphenated after a verb*)

well-found·ed *adj.* based on sound reasons, information, or evidence or on indisputable facts (*not hyphenated after a verb*)

well-groomed *adj.* (*not hyphenated after a verb*) **1. TAKING CARE WITH YOUR APPEARANCE** clean, neat, and well-dressed **2. CAREFULLY TENDED** carefully cleaned, brushed, or tended

well-ground·ed *adj.* (*not hyphenated after a verb*) **1. FAMILIAR WITH ESSENTIAL KNOWLEDGE** encompassing or thoroughly familiar with the essential details or knowledge of a subject **2.** = **well-founded**

well·head /wél hèd/ *n.* **1. SOURCE OF A SPRING OR STREAM** the place where a spring emerges from the earth or a stream begins **2. SOURCE OF SOMETHING** a principal or primary source of something **3. STRUCTURE ON TOP OF A WELL** a structure or enclosure at the upper end of a water, oil, or natural-gas well, e.g., one containing pipes and pumping equipment [14thC]

well-heeled *adj.* having a large income or substantial property (*informal*) (*not hyphenated after a verb*)

well-hung *adj.* (*not hyphenated after a verb*) **1. OFFENSIVE TERM** an offensive term meaning having a large penis or a large penis and testicles (*slang offensive*) **2. HANGING AS DESIRED OR REQUIRED** suspended or attached so as to hang in a way that is desired or required **3. HUNG FOR THE PROPER TIME** hung up long enough to mature and be good to eat ○ *he liked his venison well hung*

well-in·formed *adj.* having a broad and detailed knowledge of something, especially of the world and current events or of a particular subject (*not hyphenated after a verb*)

Wel·ling·ton /wéllingtən/ capital city of New Zealand, built around a deep harbor at the southern end of the North Island. Population: 335,051 (1996).

Wel·ling·ton, Mount mountain near Hobart in southern Tasmania, Australia. Height: 4,167 ft./1,270 m.

wel·ling·ton boot, wel·ling·ton *n. U.K.* **1. LOOSE RUBBER BOOT FOR WET CONDITIONS** a loose waterproof rubber boot extending to the knee or just below it and worn in wet weather or muddy conditions **2. BOOT CUT LOWER AT THE BACK** a leather boot that reaches to the top of or above the knee in the front but is cut lower in the back [Early 19thC. Named for Arthur WELLESLEY, the first Duke of Wellington.]

well-in·ten·tioned *adj.* intended to be helpful or useful in some way but producing a negative effect or result (*not hyphenated after a verb*)

well-kept *adj.* (*not hyphenated after a verb*) **1. CAREFULLY LOOKED AFTER** carefully maintained or looked after **2. CAREFULLY PRESERVED AND CONFIDENTIAL** not revealed to anyone or to only a few people

well-knit *adj.* (*not hyphenated after a verb*) **1. BOUND BY CLOSE TIES** bound or joined together by close relationships or ties **2. FIRMLY CONSTRUCTED** constructed or produced in such a way that the parts are firmly joined together or are integrated well **3. COMPACT IN PHYSIQUE** with a compact and strong physique

well-known *adj.* (*not hyphenated after a verb*) **1. WIDELY KNOWN** known to many people **2. FULLY UNDERSTOOD** fully known or understood

well-man·nered *adj.* behaving with politeness and courtesy (*not hyphenated after a verb*)

well-mean·ing *adj.* trying to be helpful or useful in some way, but often producing a negative effect or result (*not hyphenated after a verb*)

well-meant *adj.* arising from a desire to be helpful or useful, but often producing a negative effect (*not hyphenated after a verb*)

well·ness /wélnəss/ *n.* physical well-being, especially when maintained or achieved through good diet and regular exercise

well-nigh *adv.* nearly or almost ○ *well-nigh impossible*

well-off *adj.* **1. FAIRLY WEALTHY** having a good income or enough money to live comfortably (*not hyphenated after a verb*) **2. FAVORABLY PLACED** in a good or favorable situation or circumstances ○ *It's not a good idea to change jobs, you're better off where you are.* **3. WITH PLENTY** having a good supply of something ○ *well off for fuel right now*

well-oiled *adj.* (*not hyphenated after a verb*) **1. FUNCTIONING SMOOTHLY** functioning, operating, or carried out efficiently **2. DRUNK** having drunk too much alcohol (*informal*)

well-or·dered *adj.* (*not hyphenated after a verb*) **1. PROPERLY ORGANIZED** arranged or organized so that things are in the proper place or run smoothly **2.** MATH **WITH FIRST NUMERICAL ELEMENT** having the property that every subset with members has an element that precedes all other elements in that subset

well-pad·ded *adj.* (*not hyphenated after a verb*) **1. OVERWEIGHT** having a greater bodyweight than is desirable or advisable (*informal*) **2. HAVING MONEY** having money or access to a ready source of it

well-pre·served *adj.* in good condition or maintaining a good appearance or good health in spite of advanced age (*not hyphenated after a verb*)

well-read *adj.* knowing much about many things or a particular field from having read widely and thoroughly (*not hyphenated after a verb*)

well-round·ed *adj.* (*not hyphenated after a verb*) **1. WITH EXPERIENCE IN MANY AREAS** having abilities, experience, or achievements in a wide and balanced variety of fields **2. COMPREHENSIVE AND VARIED** encompassing or including a wide, desirable, and balanced variety of subjects or activities **3. SHAPELY** having a rounded or otherwise pleasingly shaped body

Wells /welz/ city in Somerset, southwestern England. It is known for its medieval cathedral. Population: 10,000 (1993).

Wells, H. G. (1866–1946) British writer. A prolific writer of history and science books, he is remembered for his science fiction novels, including *The Time Machine* (1895) and *The Shape of Things to Come* (1933). Full name **Herbert George Wells**

well-set *adj.* (*not hyphenated after a verb*) **1. WITH A POWERFUL PHYSIQUE** strong and solid in physique **2. FIRMLY SET** solidly established or fixed

well-spo·ken *adj.* (*not hyphenated after a verb*) **1. REFINED** speaking clearly, articulately, and in a refined accent **2. EXPRESSED APPROPRIATELY** selected or expressed appropriately

well·spring /wél sprìng/ *n.* **1. SPRING OR STREAM SOURCE** a source of a spring or stream **2. PLENTIFUL SOURCE OF SOMETHING** a plentiful source or supply of something ○ *a wellspring of artistic talent* [Old English *welspryng, wylspring*]

well-stacked *adj.* an offensive term meaning having large breasts (*slang offensive*)

well-tak·en *adj.* based on sound reasons, information, or evidence or on indisputable facts (*not hyphenated after a verb*)

well-tem·pered *adj.* tuned so as to permit playing in any key (*not hyphenated after a verb*)

well-thought-of *adj.* regarded with respect or esteem or enjoying a good reputation (*not hyphenated after a verb*)

well-thought-out *adj.* carefully and skillfully planned (*not hyphenated after a verb*)

well-timed *adj.* done or occurring at an appropriate or opportune moment (*not hyphenated after a verb*)

well-to-do *adj.* having a good income or enough money to live comfortably

well-turned *adj.* (*not hyphenated after a verb*) **1. GRACEFULLY OR ATTRACTIVELY SHAPED** having a graceful or attractive shape ○ *a well-turned ankle* **2. SKILLFULLY STATED** skillfully expressed or worded ○ *a well-turned phrase* **3. MANUFACTURED WITH A GRACEFUL SHAPE** turned on a lathe or formed so as to have a pleasing, graceful shape

well-wish·er *n.* somebody who expresses good wishes for another's success or who shows good will toward somebody or something —**well-wish·ing** *adj., n.*

well-worn *adj.* (*not hyphenated after a verb*) **1. SHOWING WEAR** showing signs of wear as a result of much use **2. OVERUSED** trite or hackneyed as result of being used too often in speech or writing **3. CARRIED BECOMINGLY** becomingly worn or borne, especially with grace, style, or dignity ○ *well-worn celebrity*

wels /velss/ (*plural* **wels**) *n.* a large Central and Eastern European freshwater catfish. Latin name: *Silurus glanis.* [Late 19thC. From German.]

Wels·bach burn·er /wélz bàk-, -baak-/ *tdmk.* a trademark for a gas burner consisting of a Bunsen burner equipped with a gauze mantle impregnated with cerium oxide and thorium oxide that emits a greenish light when ignited

welsh /welsh/ (**welshed, welsh·ing, welsh·es** /welsh/), **welch** (**welched, welch·ing, welch·es**) *vi.* **1. FAIL TO REPAY A DEBT** to fail to pay money owed as a debt or lost in a wager (*informal*) **2. OFFENSIVE TERM** an offensive term meaning to fail to fulfill or honor an obligation entered into or incurred (*informal offensive*) [Mid-19thC. Origin uncertain: probably from WELSH.] —**welsh·er** *n.*

Welsh /welsh/ *npl.* PEOPLES **PEOPLE OF WALES** the people of Wales ■ *n.* LANG **CELTIC LANGUAGE** a language spoken in Wales belonging to the Celtic group of Indo-European languages. About 500,000 people speak Welsh. ■ *adj.* **1.** PEOPLES **OF WALES** relating to Wales or its people or culture **2.** LANG **OF WELSH** relating to the Welsh language [Old English *Wēlisc, Wǣlisc,* from *W(e)alh* "Briton, Celt, Welshman" (literally "foreigner"), via a prehistoric Germanic word meaning "foreign" (ancestor of English *walnut*) from Latin *Volcae* "Celtic people of southern Gaul"]

Welsh cob *n.* a horse with a strong neck, powerful shoulders, and compact body, used as a saddle and harness horse. It is descended from the Welsh mountain pony.

Welsh cor·gi *n.* = **corgi** [*Welsh* from the fact that it originated in Wales]

Welsh Eng·lish *n.* the variety of English spoken in Wales

WORD KEY: WORLD ENGLISH

Welsh English is the English language as used in Wales where it is the majority language, coexisting with Welsh, the surviving Celtic language with the largest number of speakers but a minority language in its homeland. It can be categorized in three overlapping ways. The first is influenced by Welsh, mainly in the northern counties (often referred to as "Welsh Wales"). The second is related to dialects in neighboring counties of England. The third is influenced by school and the media. The Welsh are often said to have a "singsong" accent, perhaps because of their use of a rising-and-falling tone at the end of sentences (rather than a simple fall), and because of their full vowels and stress on usually weak syllables such as the "den" in *garden*. ***Welsh English*** is generally non-rhotic (i.e., "r" is not pronounced in words such as *art, door,* and *worker*). Two sounds from Welsh are common, especially in names: the "ll" of *Llangollen*, pronounced as /hl/, and the "ch" in *bach* (dear), pronounced as /kh/. Native speakers of English in South Wales, like some dialect speakers in England, generally do not pronounce an initial "h" (as in *hat* and *home*), whereas residents of North Wales do because it occurs in Welsh. A general influence from Welsh is notable in such usages as "Comin back soon she is" for "She's coming back soon" and *there* in exclamations such as "There's kind he is!" for "How kind he is!" The catchall question tag *isn't it?* has long been common, as in "They'll be here soon, isn't it?" (as opposed to standard *won't they?*). Some words of Welsh origin are *bugaboo, corgi, crag, flannel,* and *flummery,*.

Welsh harp *n.* a harp with three rows of strings that allow the production of a chromatic scale

Welsh·man /wélshmən/ (*plural* **-men** /-mən/) *n.* PEOPLES a man who was born or raised in Wales, or who has Welsh ancestry [Old English]

Welsh moun·tain po·ny *n.* a pony of a breed native to the Welsh hills that has tiny pointed ears and a compact body. It is popular for harness work and as a child's pony.

Welsh po·ny *n.* a pony descended from crosses between Welsh cobs and Welsh mountain ponies, slightly larger than the latter. It is used for jumping and riding.

Welsh pop·py *n.* a poppy of western Europe that forms branching tufts of deeply divided compound leaves and has yellow flowers borne singly on long slender stems. Latin name: *Meconopsis cambrica.*

Welsh rare·bit /-ráirbit/, **Welsh rab·bit** /-rábbit/ *n.* a dish made of hard cheese melted with seasoning, mustard, and a little beer or milk, then spread on toast and grilled until bubbling and golden [Late 18thC. Alteration of WELSH RABBIT, perhaps from a popular association of Wales with cheese, or in the former meaning "inferior"; *rabbit* perhaps because cheese was commonly substituted for meat.]

Welsh spring·er span·iel *n.* a spaniel of a breed with a thick silky coat that is chiefly white with large reddish patches. It is very similar to but smaller than the English springer spaniel. [*Welsh* from the fact that it originated in Wales]

Welsh ter·ri·er *n.* a wire-haired terrier of a breed originally developed for hunting. It resembles an Airedale and has a long, thick, typically black-and-tan coat. [*Welsh* from the fact that it originated in Wales]

Welsh·wom·an /wélsh wòomən/ (*plural* **-en** /-wìmmin/) *n.* a woman who was born or raised in Wales, or who has Welsh ancestry [15thC]

welt /welt/ *n.* **1. RIDGE ON THE SKIN** a raised ridge or bump on the skin caused by a lash from a whip, a scratch, or a similar blow **2. LASH FROM A WHIP CAUSING A RIDGE** a lash from a whip or a similar blow that causes a raised ridge or bump on the skin **3.** CLOTHES **STRIP SEWN INTO A SHOE** a strip of leather or other material that is sewn into a shoe or boot between the upper and the sole in order to strengthen the seam **4.** SEW **REINFORCEMENT FOR A SEAM** a folded strip of cloth, sometimes wrapped around a cord, that is sewn into a seam in a garment or pillow as a reinforcement or decoration ■ *vt.* (**welt·ed, welt·ing, welts**) **1. BEAT SOMEBODY SEVERELY** to beat or hit somebody severely, especially with a whip or switch **2. RAISE SMALL RIDGES ON THE SKIN** to cause raised ridges or bumps on the skin as a result of a lash from a whip or switch **3. STITCH SOMETHING REINFORCING OR DECORATIVE** to stitch or supply something with a strip of material as a reinforcement or decoration [15thC. Origin uncertain: perhaps from assumed Old English *wealt, wælt,* of unknown origin.]

Welt·an·schau·ung /vélt aan shòw òong/ (*plural* **-ung·en** /-òongən/) *n.* a comprehensive and usually personal conception or view of humanity, the world, or life [Mid-19thC. From German, literally "world view," from *Welt* "world" + *Anschauung* "view."]

wel·ter /wéltər/ *n.* **1. CONFUSED MASS** a confused or jumbled mass of something **2. CONFUSED CONDITION** a state of confusion or chaos or a disorderly or chaotic situation **3. SURGING MOTION OF WATER** a surging, rolling, or heaving motion made by the sea or waves **4.** SPORTS **WELTERWEIGHT** a welterweight (*informal*) ■ *vi.* (**-tered, -ter·ing, -ters**) **1. WALLOW IN SOMETHING** to wallow or roll around in something **2. LIE DRENCHED WITH LIQUID** to lie soaked or bathed in water, blood, or some other liquid **3. BE COMPLETELY IMMERSED IN SOMETHING** to be completely or deeply involved, absorbed, or entangled in something **4. SURGE OR ROLL IN WATER** to surge, roll, or heave in the sea or waves [14thC. From Middle Dutch or Middle Low German *welteren* "to roll."]

wel·ter·weight /wéltər wàyt/ *n.* a sports contestant ranked by body weight between a lightweight and a middleweight, especially a professional boxer weighing between 135 lb./61 kg and 147 lb./66.5 kg [Early 19thC. "Welter-" came from *welter* "heavyweight rider or boxer," of uncertain origin: perhaps formed from the verb WELT.]

Welt·schmerz /vélt shmùrts/, **welt·schmerz** *n.* sadness felt at the imperfect state of the world, especially at the behavior of human beings [Late 19thC. From German, from *Welt* "world" + *Schmerz* "pain."]

CORBIS/Philip Gould

Eudora Welty

Wel·ty /wéltee/, **Eudora** (*b.* 1909) U.S. writer. Her novels, set in her native Mississippi, include the Pulitzer Prize-winning *The Optimist's Daughter* (1969).

wen[1] /wen/ *n.* a cyst containing material secreted by a sebaceous gland of the skin, usually on the scalp or genitals. It may grow to an appreciable size and become infected. [Old English *wen(n).* Origin uncertain.]

wen[2] /wen/ *n.* = **wynn**

Wen·ces·las IV /wénsəss làwss, -làass/, **King of Bohemia and Holy Roman Emperor** (1361–1419). Anarchy and unrest marked his reign as Holy Roman Emperor (1378–1400) and he was deposed in 1400, though he remained King of Bohemia until his death.

Wen·ces·laus /wénsəss làwss/, **St., Duke of Bohemia** (907?–929). The patron saint of Czechoslovakia, he encouraged Bohemia's conversion to Christianity. He was murdered by his pagan brother. Known as **Good King Wenceslaus**

wench /wench/ *n.* **1. SERVANT GIRL** a girl or young woman who works at a paid job, usually as a servant or on a farm (*archaic*) **2. COUNTRY GIRL** a girl or young woman who lives in a rural area (*archaic*) **3. OFFENSIVE TERM** an offensive term for a prostitute or a woman who is regarded as sexually promiscuous (*offensive*) **4. OFFENSIVE TERM** an offensive term referring to a young woman (*offensive*) ■ *vi.* (**wenched, wench·ing, wench·es**) **HAVE SEX WITH PROSTITUTES** to engage in sex with prostitutes or with women considered to be promiscuous (*archaic offensive*) [13thC. Shortening of obsolete *wenchel* "child, enslaved laborer, prostitute," from Old English *wencel* "child," of uncertain origin: perhaps ultimately from a prehistoric Germanic base meaning "to falter."] —**wench·er** *n.*

wend /wend/ (**wend·ed, wend·ing, wends**) *vti.* to proceed along a course or route ○ *The boat wended its way through the reefs.* [Old English *wendan* "to turn, proceed," from a prehistoric Germanic base meaning "to turn," which is also the ancestor of English *wand* and *wander*]

Wend /wend/ *n.* a member of a Slavic people that occupied large parts of northeastern Germany in medieval times. A group descended from the Wends survive today and are known as Sorbs. [Late 18thC. From German *Wende.* The related Old English word was *Winedas* "Wends." Both of unknown origin.]

wen·di·go /wéndi gō/ (*plural* **-gos** *or* **-goes**), **win·di·go** /wíndi gō/ (*plural* **-gos** *or* **-goes**) *n. Can* a demonic creature who according to Cree and Algonquian folklore eats people or possesses them and turns them into cannibals [Early 18thC. From Ojibwa *wintiko.*]

Wend·ish /wéndish/ *n.* LANG a language spoken in some districts of eastern Germany belonging to the Slavic group of Indo-European languages. About 100,000 people speak Wendish. —**Wend·ish** *adj.*

Wen·dy house /wéndee-/ *n. U.K.* = **playhouse** [Mid-20thC. Named for the house built around the character *Wendy* in the play *Peter Pan* (1904) by J. M. Barrie.]

wen·ge /wéng gày/ *n.* the dark brown wood of an African tree, often used as a veneer for furniture. Latin name: *Millettia laurentii.* [Mid-20thC]

Wens·ley·dale /wénzlee dàyl/ *n.* **1. ENGLISH HARD CHEESE** a white crumbly English hard cheese with a slightly tangy flavor **2. SHEEP WITH MOTTLED LEGS** one of a breed of sheep, native to northern England, that has a blue-gray head and ears and dark mottled legs and is raised for its long fleece [Late 19thC. Named for *Wensleydale*, a valley in North Yorkshire, England, where the sheep originated and where the cheese is chiefly made.]

went past tense of **go**

wen·tle·trap /wént'l tràp/ *n.* a marine gastropod mollusk with a spiral prominently ribbed shell that is typically white but is sometimes tinged with brown. Family: Epitoniidae. [Mid-18thC. From Dutch *wenteltrap*, literally "winding stair," from the appearance of the shells.]

wept past tense, past participle of **weep**

were (*stressed*) /wur/; (*unstressed*) /wər/ past tense of **be** [Old English *wǣron* (plural past indicative), *wǣren* (plural past subjunctive), and *wǣre* (2nd person singular past indicative and singular past subjunctive), forms of *wesan* "to be" (see WAS)]

we're /weer/ *contr.* we are

were·gild *n.* = **wergild**

were·n't /wurnt/ *contr.* were not

were·wolf /wáir wòolf, wúr-/ (*plural* **-wolves** /-wòolvz/), **wer·wolf** (*plural* **-wolves**) *n.* somebody who is believed to have been transformed into a wolf, or who is believed to be able to change into a wolf and then back into a human being [Old English *werewulf*, from *were-* "man" + *wulf* "wolf." Ultimately from an Indo-European word meaning "man," which is also the ancestor of English *virile* and *world*.]

wer·gild /wúr gìld/, **were·gild, wer·geld** /wúr gèld/ *n.* in Anglo-Saxon and Germanic law, the amount of compensation paid to the relatives of somebody slain, calculated on the basis of the person's rank in society [Old English *wergeld*, from *wer* "man" (see WEREWOLF) + *gield* "payment," an earlier form of YIELD (noun)]

wer·ner·ite /wúrnə rìt/ *n.* MINERALS = **scapolite** [Early 19thC. Named in honor of Abraham Gottlob *Werner* (1750–1817), a German mineralogist.]

Wer·nick·e-Kor·sa·koff syn·drome /vàirnikee káwrssəkòf-, váirnikə-/ *n.* a form of brain damage occurring in long-term alcoholics that results from severe nutritional deficiencies [Mid-20thC. Named for Karl *Wernicke* (1848–1905), German neurologist, and Sergei Sergeevich *Korsakov* (1854–1900), Russian psychiatrist, who independently described it.]

wert past tense of **be** (*archaic*)

Wert·heim·er /váirt hìmər/, **Max** (1880–1943) Czech-born U.S. psychologist. He taught at the New School for Social Research (1933–43) and was one of the founders of Gestalt theory.

wer·wolf *n.* = **werewolf**

We·ser /váyzər/ river in northwestern Germany. Formed by the confluence of the Werr and Fulda rivers, it flows northwestward through Lower Saxony and empties into the North Sea near Bremerhaven. Length: 300 mi./400 km.

wes·kit /wéskit/ *n.* a waistcoat (*regional*) [Mid-19thC. Alteration of WAISTCOAT.]

Wes·ley /wésslee, wéz-/, **John** (1703–91) British religious leader. He founded Methodism in 1739, and thereafter preached tirelessly to huge crowds and published hymns and other religious works for mass distribution.

Wes·ley·an /wésslee ən, wéz-/ *adj.* BASED ON WESLEY'S TEACHING based on, consisting of, or resembling the teachings, practices, and beliefs of the Christian preacher John Wesley and his brother Charles, or of Methodism. ◊ **Methodist** ■ *n.* FOLLOWER OF WESLEY a follower of the Christian preacher John Wesley and his brother Charles, or a believer in their teachings or those of Methodism —**Wes·ley·an·ism** *n.*

west /west/ *n.* **1.** DIRECTION IN WHICH THE SUN SETS the direction that lies directly ahead of somebody facing the setting sun or that is located toward the left-hand side of a conventional map of the world **2.** COMPASS POINT OPPOSITE EAST the compass point that lies directly opposite east **3. west, West** AREA IN THE WEST the part of an area, region, or country that is situated in or toward the west **4. west, West** POSITION EQUIVALENT TO WEST the position equivalent to west in any diagram consisting of four points at 90-degree intervals ■ *adj.* **1.** IN THE WEST situated in, facing, or coming from the west of a place, region, or country **2.** BLOWING FROM WEST blowing from the west ○ *a west wind* ■ *adv.* TOWARD THE WEST in or toward the west [Old English. Ultimately from an Indo-European word meaning "evening, night," which also produced Greek *hesperos* "evening" (source of English *Hesperian*) and Latin *vesper* (source of English *vespers*).] ◇ **go west** to die, disappear, or be destroyed (*informal*)

West /west/, **west** *n.* **1.** EUROPE AND THE AMERICAS the countries of Europe and North and South America. ◊ **western hemisphere 2.** COUNTRIES WITH GRECO-ROMAN AND CHRISTIAN TRADITIONS those countries of the world, especially in Europe and North and South America, whose culture and society are most influenced by traditions rooted in Greek and Roman culture and in Christianity **3.** NON-COMMUNIST COUNTRIES IN THE COLD WAR the non-Communist countries of Europe and North and South America during the Cold War **4.** WESTERN UNITED STATES the part of the United States west of the Mississippi River or west of the Allegheny Mountains during early phases of the country's history

West /west/, **Benjamin** (1738–1820) U.S. artist. His historical and portrait paintings include *The Death of General Wolfe* (1770).

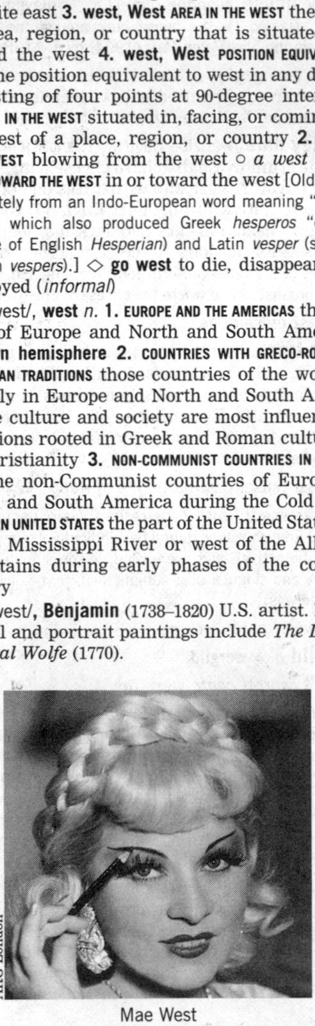

Mae West

West, Mae (1892–1980) U.S. actor and comedian. She was known for her irreverent wit and disdain for conventional morals. Her movies include *She Done Him Wrong* (1933), *I'm No Angel* (1933), and *Klondike Annie* (1936).

West, Nathanael (1903–40) U.S. writer. The four novels he wrote before his early death, which include *The Day of the Locust* (1939), satirize contemporary society. Real name **Nathan Wallenstein Weinstein**

West, Dame Rebecca (1892–1983) British writer. She wrote noted studies of the Nuremberg war crimes trials and novels including *The Thinking Reed* (1936). Pseudonym of **Cicily Isabel Andrews**. Born **Cicily Isabel Fairfield**

West, Thomas, 3rd Baron De La Warr ➧ **De La Warr**

West Bank

West Bank territory in the Middle East on the western bank of the Jordan River, bordered by Israel and Jordan. Once part of Palestine, it was annexed by Jordan in 1950 and occupied by Israel in 1967. As a result of peace agreements between 1993 and 1997 much of it was transferred to Palestinian administration. Population: 1,600,000 (1996). Area: 2,263 sq.mi./5,860 sq. km.

West Ben·gal state in northeastern India. Capital: Calcutta. Population: 73,600,000 (1994). Area: 33,920 sq. mi./87,853 sq. km.

West Ber·lin western part of the city of Berlin. It was officially part of West Germany between 1945 and 1990, when the rest of the city was designated East German territory. —**West Ber·lin·er** *n.*

west·bound /wést bòwnd/ *adj.* leading, going, or traveling toward the west

west by north *n.* the direction or compass point midway between west and west-northwest —**west by north** *adj., adv.*

west by south *n.* the direction or compass point midway between west and west-southwest —**west by south** *adj., adv.*

West Coast 1. region comprising the coastal areas of California, Oregon, and Washington on the Pacific coast of the United States **2.** region comprising the western area of British Columbia between the mountains and the sea, including coastal areas, Vancouver Island, the Gulf Islands, and the Queen Charlotte Islands

West Des Moines /-də móyn, -móynz/ city in south central Iowa. It is a western suburb of Des Moines. Population: 40,380 (1996).

west·er /wéstər/ *n.* WEST WIND a wind blowing from the west, especially one blowing ahead of or with a storm ■ *vi.* (**-ered, -er·ing, -ers**) MOVE WEST to move or appear to move across the sky to the west (*refers to the sun, moon, or other celestial bodies*) [Late 16thC]

west·er·ly /wéstərlee/ *adj.* **1.** IN THE WEST situated in or toward the west **2.** METEOROL COMING FROM THE WEST blowing from the west ■ *n.* (*plural* **-lies**) WIND FROM THE WEST a wind blowing from the west ■ *adv.* **1.** FROM THE WEST from the west **2.** TOWARD THE WEST toward the west [15thC] —**west·er·li·ness** *n.*

Wes·ter·ly /wéstərlee/ town in southwestern Rhode Island, on the Connecticut border, southwest of South Kingstown. Population: 22,773 (1996).

west·ern /wéstərn/ *adj.* **1.** IN THE WEST situated in the west of a region or country **2.** FACING WEST situated in or facing the west ○ *The house has a western aspect.* **3. west·ern, West·ern** OF THE WEST typical of or native to the west of a region or country **4.** COMING FROM THE WEST blowing from the west ○ *a western wind* **5.** WEST OF THE PRIME MERIDIAN lying west of the prime meridian [Old English *westerne*, from WEST + a suffix denoting direction] —**west·ern·ness** *n.*

West·ern, west·ern *adj.* **1.** INFLUENCED BY GRECO-ROMAN AND CHRISTIAN TRADITIONS found in or typical of countries, especially in Europe and North and South America, whose culture and society are greatly influenced by traditions rooted in Greek and Roman culture and in Christianity **2.** OF NON-COMMUNIST COUNTRIES IN THE COLD WAR found in or belonging to the non-Communist countries of Europe and North and South America during the Cold War **3.** TYPICAL OF THE AMERICAN WEST found in or relating to the part of the United States west of the Mississippi River or west of the Allegheny Mountains during early phases of the country's history **4.** FOUND IN EUROPE AND AMERICAS located in or relating to Europe and North and South America **5.** CATHOLIC AND PROTESTANT based on, consisting of, or resembling the practices, and beliefs of Roman Catholicism and Protestantism, as opposed to those of the Eastern churches ■ *n.* MOVIE OR BOOK ON THE AMERICAN WEST a movie, radio or television program, novel, or story set in the western part of the United States, usually during the second half of the 19th century —**West·ern·ness** *n.*

West·ern Aus·tra·lia state occupying the western part of Australia. Founded as a British colony in 1829, it is the largest state in Australia. Capital: Perth. Population: 1,766,000 (1996). Area: 975,100 sq. mi./2,525,500 sq. km.

West·ern blot, West·ern blot·ting *n.* a technique in which a mixture of proteins is separated in a gel by electrophoresis, then absorbed by a nylon membrane blotted onto its surface to identify its constituents [Modeled on *Southern blot*]

West·ern Can·a·da region comprising the Canadian provinces of Manitoba, Saskatchewan, Alberta, and British Columbia

West·ern Cape province in southwestern South Africa, formerly part of Cape Province. Capital: Cape Town. Population: 4,055,000 (1996). Area: 49,943 sq. mi./129,386 sq. km.

West·ern Church *n.* the Christian Church as found in or influenced by that of Europe, especially the Roman Catholic Church

west·ern·er /wéstərnər/, **West·ern·er** *n.* **1.** SOMEBODY FROM THE WEST somebody who lives in or comes from the western part of a country or region **2.** SOMEBODY FROM WESTERN CANADA somebody who lives in or comes from Western Canada

West·ern Eu·ro·pe·an Time *n.* the standard time in the time zone centered on 0° longitude (**the prime meridian**), which includes the United Kingdom. It is the same time as Universal Coordinated Time.

West·ern Eur·o·pe·an Un·ion *n.* an association of European countries, inaugurated in 1955, whose main function is to coordinate defense, economic, and social policy

West·ern Front *n.* the battle line between the French and British armies and the German armies in western Europe during World War I. It extended from Belgium to the Swiss border.

West·ern Ghats mountain range in southern India, forming the western edge of the Deccan plateau. The highest peak is Doda Betta, 8,652 ft./2,637 m.

west·ern hem·i·sphere *n.* the half of the earth that is to the west of the prime meridian, including North and South America and portions of western Europe and Africa

west·ern hem·lock *n.* a coniferous tree that is native to western North America but widely grown as an ornamental for its attractive drooping foliage, and for lumber. Latin name: *Tsuga heterophylla.*

west·ern hon·ey mes·quite *n.* a mesquite that grows in the southwestern United States and Mexico and has pods with a high sugar content. Latin name: *Prosopis glandulosa.*

west·ern·ism /wéstər nìzzəm/, **West·ern·ism** *n.* **1.** AMERICAN OR EUROPEAN CUSTOM a custom or practice typical of the countries of Europe and North and South America **2.** TERM USED IN THE WEST a word or idiom chiefly used in the western part of a country or region, especially the western United States

west·ern·ize /wéstər nìz/ (**-ized, -iz·ing, -iz·es**) *v.* **1.** *vti.* ADOPT WESTERN CUSTOMS to adopt or cause a person, country, or culture to adopt the customs, practices, or beliefs of the people of Europe or North and South America **2.** *vt.* **CHANGE SOMETHING TO RESEMBLE WESTERN PRACTICE** to change a law, custom, practice, or belief so that it resembles or is replaced by its European or North American counterpart —**west·ern·i·za·tion** /wèstərnə záysh'n/ *n.*

west·ern larch *n.* a tall coniferous tree, native to western North America, that has purplish-gray, deeply fissured bark. Latin name: *Larix occidentalis.*

west·ern·most /wéstərn mōst/ *adj.* situated farthest west

west·ern om·e·let *n.* an omelet made with diced ham, green pepper, and onion

west·ern red ce·dar *n.* **1. CONIFER OF WESTERN NORTH AMERICA** a coniferous tree native to the Pacific coast of North America but widely grown for lumber. It has a narrow conical crown with an erect tip. Latin name: *Thuja plicata.* = **red cedar 2. WESTERN RED CEDAR WOOD** the wood of the western red cedar tree

west·ern roll *n.* a high jump in which the body is half-turned over the bar

west·ern sad·dle, **West·ern sad·dle** *n.* = **stock saddle**

West·ern Sa·ha·ra region in northwestern Africa formerly ruled by Spain. It was partitioned between Morocco and Mauritania in 1976 and fully occupied by Morocco in 1979. Area: 103,000 sq. mi./267,000 sq. km. Former name **Spanish Sahara**

West·ern Sa·mo·a former name for **Samoa** (until 1997)

west·ern sand·wich *n.* a sandwich whose filling is an omelet made with diced ham, green pepper, and onion

West·ern Stan·dard Time *n.* a time zone lying west of the 120th meridian and including the whole of Western Australia. It is seven to nine hours ahead of GMT.

west·ern swing *n.* a type of country and western music played on guitars, steel guitars, fiddles, and other instruments that incorporates elements of swing music

west·ern tan·a·ger *n.* a medium-sized forest songbird similar to an oriole of western North America, Mexico, and Central America. Males are yellow with black wings and a red head. Latin name: *Piranga ludoviciana.*

West·ern Wall *n.* a wall in Jerusalem believed to be part of the Second Temple, destroyed in A.D. 70 by the Romans. It is used by some Jewish people as a place for prayer and lamentation.

West·ford /wéstfərd/ town in northeastern Massachusetts, southwest of Chelmsford and northwest of Bedford. Population: 18,642 (1996).

West Ger·man·ic *n.* a subgroup within the Germanic languages that consists of English, German, Yiddish, Dutch, Flemish, Afrikaans, and Frisian

West Ger·ma·ny republic of western Europe from 1945 to 1990, formed from the territories of Germany occupied by the U.S., British, and French forces at the end of World War II. In 1990 it was reunited with East Germany. Area: 95,976 sq. mi./248,577 sq. km. Official name **Federal Republic of Germany** —**West Ger·man** *n., adj.*

West Goth *n.* PEOPLES = **Visigoth**

West High·land ter·ri·er, **West High·land white ter·ri·er** *n.* a small terrier of a hardy long-haired breed with a pure white coat, originally bred for hunting small mammals but now kept as a pet [From its having originated in the West Highlands of Scotland]

West In·di·an *n.* somebody who was born or raised in the West Indies, who has citizenship of one of the islands of the West Indies, or whose ancestors lived in or came from the West Indies —**West In·di·an** *adj.*

West In·di·an ce·dar *n.* = **cigar box cedar**

West In·di·an eb·on·y *n.* = **cocuswood**

West In·dies /wèst ín dèez/ chain of islands that separate the Caribbean Sea from the Atlantic Ocean. They consist of three main island groups, the Greater Antilles, the Lesser Antilles, and the Bahamas, that extend from the southeastern tip of Florida to the coast of Venezuela.

west·ing /wésting/ *n.* **1. DISTANCE WEST** the distance due west between two points on a course heading in a westward direction **2. TRAVEL WESTWARD** travel or progress in a westward direction

West·ing·house /wésting hòwss/, **George** (1846–1914) U.S. engineer and industrialist. He invented the air brake (1869), which revolutionized the railroad industry, and founded the Westinghouse Electric Company (1886).

Westm. *abbr.* Westminster

West Mem·phis city in eastern Arkansas near the Mississippi River, a western suburb of Memphis, Tennessee. Population: 26,894 (1996).

West·min·ster /wést mĭnstər/ city in north central Maryland on the northern branch of the Monocacy River, northwest of Baltimore. Population: 15,073 (1996).

West·min·ster Ab·bey *n.* a large Gothic church in London, England, originally a Benedictine abbey, in which British monarchs are traditionally crowned

West·mont /wést mònt/ town in northeastern Illinois, southwest of La Grange. It is a western suburb of Chicago. Population: 22,366 (1996).

west-north·west *n.* **COMPASS POINT BETWEEN W AND NW** the direction or compass point midway between west and northwest ■ *adj., adv.* **IN THE WEST-NORTHWEST** in, from, facing, or toward the west-northwest —**west-north·west·er·ly** *adv.*

Edward Weston: Photographed in 1923 by Tina Modotti

Wes·ton /wést'n/, **Edward** (1886–1958) U.S. photographer. His sharp, semiabstract photographs often magnify details of natural objects.

Wes·ton stan·dard cell *n.* a portable, highly accurate, voltage source used as a standard for calibration purposes [Early 20thC. Named for Edward *Weston* (1850–1936), English-born electrical engineer.]

West Pak·i·stan western area of Pakistan from 1947 to 1971, when the nation was geographically divided. West Pakistan comprised the provinces of Baluchistan, North-West Frontier Province, Punjab, and Sind, and it became the state of Pakistan in 1971 after East Pakistan seceded to become independent Bangladesh.

West·pha·lia /west fáylyə, -fáylee ə/ former province in northeastern Germany, in the present-day state of North-Rhine Westphalia. The Peace of Westphalia, marked the end of the Thirty Years' War. signed at Münster and Osnabrück in 1648, marked the end of the Thirty Years' War.

West·pha·lian /west fáylyən, -fáylee ən/ *n.* somebody who lives in or was born or raised in Westphalia [Early 17thC] —**West·pha·lian** *adj.*

West·pha·lian ham *n.* German ham that is cured and eaten raw, very thinly sliced

West Point *n.* the site of the United States Military Academy, on the Hudson River in New York State, or the Academy itself

West·port /wést pàwrt/ town on the northwestern coast of the South Island, New Zealand. It is the commercial center of a coal-mining region. Population: 4,236 (1996).

West Sax·on *n.* **1.** LANG **WESSEX DIALECT OF OLD ENGLISH** the dialect of Old English in use in Wessex during Anglo-Saxon times and the main literary dialect of the language. ◊ **Anglian, Kentish 2.** PEOPLES **SOMEBODY FROM ANGLO-SAXON WESSEX** somebody who was born in or lived in Wessex during Anglo-Saxon times —**West Sax·on** *adj.*

west-south·west *n.* **COMPASS POINT BETWEEN W AND SW** the direction or compass point midway between west and southwest ■ *adj., adv.* **IN THE WEST-SOUTHWEST** in, from, facing, or toward the west-south-west —**west-south·west·er·ly** *adv.*

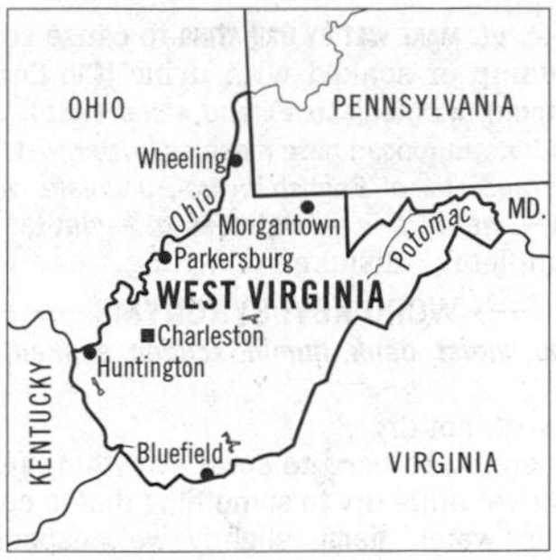

West Virginia

West Vir·gin·ia state of the eastern United States bordered by Ohio, Pennsylvania, Maryland, Virginia, and Kentucky. Capital: Charleston. Population: 1,815,787 (1997). Area: 24,232 sq. mi./62,761 sq. km. —**West Vir·gin·ian** *n., adj.*

west·ward /wéstwərd/ *adj.* **IN THE WEST** toward or in the west ■ *adv.* **TOWARD THE WEST** in a westerly direction ■ *n.* **POINT IN THE WEST** a direction toward or a point in the west [Old English *westweard*] —**west·ward·ly** *adv., adj.* —**west·wards** *adv.*

WORD KEY: USAGE

westward or **westwards**? ***Westward*** is the only form available for the adjective: *in a westward direction.* In American English it is also more common than ***westwards*** for the adverb: *The ship was moving slowly westward.*

West War·wick town in Rhode Island, southwest of Providence and west of Warwick. Population: 29,120 (1996).

Vivienne Westwood

West·wood /wést wŏŏd/, **Vivienne** (*b.* 1941) British fashion designer. She was a pioneer of punk fashion in the late 1970s and is known for her unconventional costumes.

wet /wet/ *adj.* **1. SOAKED WITH WATER** covered, soaked, or dampened with water or some other liquid **2. NOT YET DRY** not completely dry **3. NOT YET SET** not yet firm or solidified ○ *wet cement* **4. RAINY, SHOWERY, MISTY, OR FOGGY** characterized by rain, showers, mist, or fog ○ *Come in out of the wet.* **5. WITH RAINY WEATHER** subject to frequent heavy rain, showers, mist, or fog ○ *a wet climate* **6. USING OR DONE WITH LIQUID** using or done in water or another liquid **7. ALLOWING LIQUOR SALES** allowing the legal manufacture, storage, transportation, and sale of alcoholic beverages (*informal*) ○ *a wet town* **8. FAVORING LIQUOR SALES** favoring the legal manufacture, storage, transportation, and sale of alcoholic beverages (*informal*) ○ *a wet representative* **9.** *U.K.* **UNASSERTIVE** regarded as weak and lacking resolution or decisiveness (*insult*) ■ *n.* **1. LIQUID OR MOISTURE** water or another liquid, or moisture from it **2. RAINY OR DAMP WEATHER** rainy, showery, misty, or foggy weather ○ *Come in out of the wet.* **3.** *Aus* **NORTHERN AUSTRALIAN WET SEASON** the wet season in northern Australia that lasts from December to March **4. SUPPORTER OF LEGAL LIQUOR SALES** somebody who supports the legal manufacture, storage, transportation, and sale of alcoholic beverages (*informal*) **5.** *U.K.* **UNASSERTIVE PERSON** somebody who is regarded as weak and lacking in resolution or decisiveness (*insult*) **6.** *U.K.* **LIBERAL CONSERVATIVE** a Conservative politician whose policies some other Conservatives consider not to be sufficiently pure or doctrinaire (*informal*) ■ *v.* (**wet** *or* **wet·ted, wet·ting, wets**) **1.** *vti.* **MAKE OR BECOME WET** to become or cause something to become damp or soaked with water or some other liquid 2. *vt.* MAKE WET BY URINATING to cause something to be damp or soaked with urine [Old English *wǣt*, *wǣta* (noun), *wǣt* (adjective), and *wǣtan* (verb). Ultimately from an Indo-European base meaning "water, wet," which is also the ancestor of English *hydro-*, *undulate*, *vodka*, and *winter*.] —**wet·ly** *adv.* —**wet·ness** *n.* —**wet·ter** *n.* ◇ **all wet** completely mistaken or wrong

WORD KEY: SYNONYMS

wet, damp, moist, dank, humid, sodden, soaked, soaking, sopping

CORE MEANING: not dry

wet a general word used to cover everything from paint that is not yet quite dry to something that is completely covered in water; **damp** slightly wet, especially undesirably so; **moist** slightly wet, especially desirably so; **dank** describes a place that is unpleasantly damp and cold and that usually also has a bad smell; **humid** describes something such as air that is damp, often also suggesting accompanying heat; **sodden** extremely wet; **soaked** an informal word meaning extremely wet; **soaking** an informal word meaning extremely and undesirably wet; **sopping** an informal word emphasizing that something is extremely and undesirably wet.

wet·back /wét bàk/ *n.* a highly offensive term referring to a Mexican person recently arrived in the United States, especially somebody who has entered the country illegally to work as a laborer (*taboo insult*) [Early 20thC. From Mexican immigrants having waded or swum across the Rio Grande river to enter the United States.]

wet bar *n.* a small bar equipped with a sink in a house or hotel room, used for mixing alcoholic drinks

wet blan·ket *n.* somebody who spoils or reduces other people's enthusiasm or enjoyment (*informal*) [From the use of wet blankets to smother small fires]

wet-bulb ther·mom·e·ter *n.* a thermometer that records the temperature at which pure water must be evaporated to saturate a given volume of air

wet cell *n.* a primary cell that contains a free-flowing electrolyte. ◊ **dry cell**

wet dream *n.* (*offensive in some contexts*) 1. EROTIC DREAM RESULTING IN EJACULATION a dream that has sexual content and leads to the ejaculation of semen 2. PLEASANT FANTASY an overly optimistic and highly unrealistic idea or image

wet fish *n. U.K.* fresh fish for sale, as distinguished from frozen or cooked fish

wet fly *n.* a fishing lure resembling a fly that slips beneath the surface of the water after it is cast. ◊ **dry fly**

weth·er /wéth̲ər/ *n.* a male sheep or goat that has been castrated before becoming sexually mature [Old English *weþer*, from prehistoric Germanic]

wet·land /wét lànd/ *n.* a marsh, swamp, or other area of land where the soil near the surface is saturated or covered with water, especially one that forms a habitat for wildlife (*often used in the plural*)

wet look *n.* 1. GLOSSY FINISH ON MATERIAL a glossy finish on a material that gives an appearance of wetness 2. GLOSSY SHEEN ON THE HAIR a glossy sheen given to the hair by the use of a special hair gel that gives an appearance of wetness —**wet-look** *adj.*

wet nurse *n.* a woman who breast-feeds and takes care of another woman's baby

wet-nurse (**wet-nursed, wet-nurs·ing, wet-nurs·es**) *vt.* 1. BREAST-FEED ANOTHER'S BABY to breast-feed and take care of another woman's baby 2. GIVE SOMEBODY EXCESSIVE CARE to bestow excessive care or attention on somebody (*informal disapproving*)

wet pack *n.* a piece or pieces of material dampened with hot or cold water and wrapped around a patient's body for therapeutic purposes

wet suit *n.* a tight-fitting garment worn by a diver, made of foam neoprene rubber or a similar material. It traps a thin insulating layer of water near the skin.

wet·ta·ble /wéttəb'l/ *adj.* 1. ABLE TO BE MADE WET capable of being made wet 2. ALLOWING LIQUID TO SPREAD ACROSS SURFACE able to make a liquid spread easily across the surface of a solid by reducing surface tension —**wet·ta·bil·i·ty** /wèttə bíllətee/ *n.*

wet·ting a·gent *n.* a chemical agent that makes the surface of a substance less repellent to a liquid and allows the liquid to spread across it more easily

Wey·mouth /wáyməth/ town in eastern Massachusetts, south of Boston. Population: 54,013 (1990).

wf, **w.f.** *abbr.* PRINTING wrong font

wff *abbr.* LOGIC well-formed formula

WFTU *abbr.* World Federation of Trade Unions

w.g. *abbr.* 1. water gauge 2. wire gauge

WH *abbr.* watt-hour

wh. *abbr.* white

whack /wak, hwak/ *vti.* (**whacked, whack·ing, whacks**) 1. HIT WITH A LOUD SHARP BLOW to hit somebody or something with a swift sharp blow that produces a loud noise 2. CUT OR CHOP SOMETHING to cut or chop something with a swift sharp blow ■ *n.* 1. SHARP BLOW a swift sharp blow 2. SOUND OF A SHARP BLOW the sound made by a swift sharp blow 3. ATTEMPT AT SOMETHING an attempt at doing something (*informal*) ○ *That looks like fun – can I take a whack at it?* 4. SHARE OF SOMETHING a share or portion of something, especially one deserved or due (*informal*) [Early 18thC. Origin uncertain: probably an imitation of the sound, but perhaps an alteration of THWACK.] —**whack·er** *n.* ◇ **at one** *or* **a (single) whack** quickly and on a single occasion (*informal*) ◇ **out of whack** not working properly, especially because of being out of order or alignment (*informal*)

whack off *vti.* 1. OFFENSIVE TERM an offensive term meaning to masturbate (*taboo offensive; refers to men*) 2. FORCIBLY SEVER SOMETHING to remove or separate something suddenly and forcefully

whacked /wakt, hwakt/ *adj.* 1. *U.K., Can* EXTREMELY TIRED very tired or exhausted (*informal*) 2. UNDER THE INFLUENCE OF DRUGS relaxed, excited, or euphoric as a result of taking drugs, especially marijuana (*slang*)

whacked-out *adj.* 1. = **whacked** (*informal*) 2. = **stoned** (*slang*)

whack·ing /wáking, hwáking/ *adj. U.K.* HUGE very large or impressive (*informal*) ■ *adv. U.K., Can* EXTREMELY to an extreme degree (*informal*)

whack·o *n., adj.* = **wacko**

whack·y *adj.* = **wacky**

whak·a·pa·pa /fáakə pùppə/ (*plural* **-pa**) *n. NZ* a Maori term for the genealogy of an individual or family

Wha·ka·ta·ne /fáakə táa này/ coastal town in the northeastern part of the North Island, New Zealand. It is a commercial center for an agricultural and timber region. Population: 17,493 (1996).

whale[1] /wayl, hwayl/ *n.* 1. BIG MARINE MAMMAL a large marine mammal that breathes through a blowhole on the top of its head and has front flippers, no hind limbs, and a flat horizontal tail. Its body is insulated by a thick layer of fatty blubber beneath the skin, and many species live in social groups, communicating by sound. Order: Cetacea. 2. IMPRESSIVE EXAMPLE OF SOMETHING an impressive, very large, or very enjoyable example of something (*informal*) ■ *vi.* (**whaled, whal·ing, whales**) HUNT WHALES to hunt for and kill whales [Old English *hwæl*. Related to German *Wal*.]

whale[2] /wayl, hwayl/ (**whaled, whal·ing, whales**) *v.* 1. *vt.* THRASH SOMEBODY to beat somebody severely as a punishment 2. *vt.* HIT SOMETHING FORCEFULLY to hit or strike somebody or something with great force 3. *vi.* BE HIGHLY CRITICAL to be critical of somebody or something in a severe way ○ *whaling away at her detractors* 4. *vt.* DEFEAT SOMEBODY CONVINCINGLY to defeat somebody soundly or completely [Late 18thC. Origin uncertain: perhaps a variant of WALE.]

whale·back /wáyl bàk, hwáyl-/ *n.* 1. LARGE AND ROUNDED OBJECT something large and rounded like the back of a whale, e.g., an ocean wave or a small hill 2. NAUT SHIP WITH A ROUNDED DECK a cargo vessel with a rounded bow and arched upper deck designed to allow the water from waves breaking on it to run off more easily

whale·boat /wáyl bōt, hwáyl-/ *n.* a long, narrow, easily maneuvered boat with a pointed bow and stern, originally rowed in pursuit of whales but now often powered and used as a lifeboat

whale·bone /wáyl bōn, hwáyl-/ *n.* 1. = **baleen** 2. PIECE OF MATERIAL FROM WHALES a piece or strip of a hard elastic material found in some whales, formerly used in making corset stays and whips [13thC. Originally in the sense "ivory from an animal confused with a whale such as a walrus."]

whale·bone whale *n.* = **baleen whale**

whale catch·er *n.* a boat with a harpoon launcher mounted in its bow, used for pursuing and catching whales

whale·fish /wáyl fish, hwáyl-/ (*plural* **whale·fish** *or* **whale·fish·es**) *n.* a small and rare deep-sea fish that has orange or red markings on a black body, a large mouth, and extremely weak eyes. Family: Cetomimidae.

whale·head /wáyl hèd, hwáyl-/ *n.* = **shoebill**

Whale Is·land uninhabited volcanic island in the Bay of Plenty off the northeastern coast of the North Island, New Zealand. Area: 2 sq. mi./4 sq. km.

whale oil *n.* a yellowish oil manufactured by rendering the blubber of whales, formerly used as a lamp fuel and in making soap and candles

whal·er /wáylər, hwáylər/ *n.* 1. SOMEBODY ENGAGED IN WHALING INDUSTRY somebody who hunts or harpoons whales or who processes killed whales 2. SHIP FOR HUNTING OR PROCESSING WHALES a ship used for hunting whales or processing killed whales 3. = **whaleboat**

whale shark *n.* the largest of all sharks, found in warm oceanic waters worldwide, with a white-spotted dark body up to 50 ft./15 m in length. It feeds near the surface on small fish and invertebrates and is not aggressive. Latin name: *Rhincodon typus.*

whal·ing /wáyling, hwáyling/ *n.* the activity or industry of hunting and processing whales

wham /wam, hwam/ *n.* (*informal*) 1. FORCEFUL BLOW a solid forceful blow or impact 2. SOUND OF FORCEFUL BLOW the loud noise produced by a solid forceful blow ■ *vti.* (**whammed, wham·ming, whams**) HIT SOMETHING WITH LOUD NOISE to hit or crash into somebody or something with a loud noise (*informal*) ○ *The car whammed into the brick wall.* ■ *interj.* USED TO INDICATE THE SOUND OF BLOW used to imitate the sound of a forceful blow or impact (*informal*) ■ *adv.* SUDDENLY AND FORCEFULLY with a startling or jarring suddenness (*informal*) ○ *I ran wham right into my ex-husband.* [Early 20thC. An imitation of the sound.]

wham·mo /wámmō, hwámmō/ *adv.* = **wham** (*informal*)

wham·my /wámmee, hwámmee/ (*plural* **-mies**) *n.* (*informal*) 1. JINX a jinx or hex 2. SEVERE SETBACK something with unpleasant or damaging consquences [Mid-20thC. Origin uncertain.]

whang[1] /wang, hwang/ *n.* 1. OFFENSIVE TERM an offensive term for a penis (*slang offensive*) 2. THONG a thong, especially a thong made from leather 3. UNTANNED ANIMAL HIDE untanned hide from cattle or other animals ■ *vt.* (**whanged, whang·ing, whangs**) 1. HIT SOMEBODY SEVERELY to beat, whip, or thrash somebody 2. HIT SOMETHING WITH FORCE to hit or kick something with enough force to dislodge it (*informal*) [Early 16thC. Alteration of *thwang*, a variant of THONG.]

whang[2] /wang, hwang/ *n.* 1. RESOUNDING BLOW a blow that resounds when it hits something 2. SOUND OF RESOUNDING BLOW the sound produced by a heavy blow when it hits something ■ *vti.* (**whanged, whang·ing, whangs**) HIT WITH RESOUNDING SOUND to hit something and produce a loud resounding sound [Early 19thC. An imitation of the sound.]

Whang·a·rei /fáangə ráy/ coastal town in the northern part of the North Island, New Zealand. It is a commercial and tourist center. Population: 45,892 (1996).

whang·ee /wang gée, hwang-/ *n.* 1. PLANTS CHINESE BAMBOO PLANT a bamboo plant, native to China, whose stems are used to make canes and walking sticks. Genus: *Phyllostachys.* 2. BAMBOO WALKING STICK a walking stick or cane made from a piece of whangee bamboo [Late 18thC. From Chinese (Beijing) *huang* "bamboo sprouts too old for eating, bamboo."]

whap *n., vt.* = **whop**

wharf /wawrf, hwawrf/ *n.* (*plural* **wharves** /wawrvz, hwawrvz/ *or* **wharfs**) 1. LANDING PLACE FOR SHIPS a structure built alongside or out into the water as a landing place for boats and ships, sometimes with a protective covering or enclosure 2. SHORE a riverbank or seashore (*archaic*) ■ *v.* (**wharfed, wharf·ing, wharfs**) 1. *vti.* MOOR A BOAT AT A WHARF to moor a vessel at a wharf, or to be moored there 2. *vt.* UNLOAD OR STORE CARGO ON A WHARF to unload cargo onto or store it on a wharf 3. *vt.* EQUIP A PLACE WITH A WHARF to provide a place with a wharf or wharves [Old English *hwearf* "embankment, wharf," via a prehistoric Germanic word (source also of German *Werft* "shipyard") from a base meaning "to turn," which also produced English *warp*]

wharf·age /wáwrfij, hwáwrfij/ *n.* **1.** USE OF A WHARF the use of a wharf or wharves **2.** FEE TO USE A WHARF a fee that is paid for the use of a wharf or wharves **3.** WHARVES wharves collectively, especially the wharves in a particular location [15thC]

wharf·ie /wáwrfee, hwáwrfee/ *n. Aus* a worker at a dock or wharf (*informal*)

wharf·in·ger /wárfinjər, hwárfinjər/ *n.* somebody who owns or supervises the running of a wharf or group of wharves [Mid-16thC. Alteration of obsolete *wharfager* (perhaps on the model of *harbinger, messenger,* or *passenger*), from WHARFAGE.]

AKG London

Edith Wharton

Whar·ton /wáwrt'n, hwáwrt'n/**, Edith** (1862–1937) U.S. writer. She wrote on everything from interior decorating to the art of writing but is best known for her novels, particularly the Pulitzer Prize-winning *The Age of Innocence* (1920). Born **Edith Newbold Jones**

wharve /wawrv, hwawrv/ *n.* a wheel or similar part on a spindle, used as a pulley on a spinning machine or as a flywheel on a spinning wheel [Old English *hweorfa*, from *hweorfan* "to turn." Ultimately from a prehistoric Germanic base that is also the ancestor of English *whirl*.]

wharves plural of **wharf**

what /wot, hwot/ CORE MEANING: a grammatical word used in direct and indirect questions to request further information, e.g., about the identity or nature of somebody, or about the purpose of something ○ (adj) *What time do you make it?* ○ (adj) *I'm not sure what kind of sauce goes best with this dish.* ○ (pron) *What are they doing?* ○ (pron) *Do you know what she does for a living?*

1. *adj., pron.* THAT WHICH the person or persons that, or the thing or things that ○ (adj) *we spent what money we did have* ○ (pron) *picking their way through what remained of the house* **2.** *adj.* EMPHASIZING A REACTION used in exclamations to emphasize a reaction or opinion ○ *What fantastic news!* ○ *What a miserable day it's been.* **3.** *adv.* HOW in what respect or to what degree ○ *What does it matter now that they've gone?* **4.** *adv.* AT A GUESS used to indicate a guess or approximation of an amount or value ○ *It must be, what, ten years since we first met.* **5.** *interj.* EXCLAMATION used as an exclamation when expressing an emotion such as suprise, anger, or disappointment ○ *The plane will be delayed by two hours. – What?* [Old English *hwæt.* Ultimately from an Indo-European word that also produced Latin *quot* "how many" (source of English *quote*) and English *how*.] ◇ **give somebody what for** to scold or punish somebody severely (*informal*) ◇ **what about . . . 1.** used to suggest that somebody or something be taken into consideration ○ *What about all the money we've already paid then?* **2.** used to suggest that somebody might like to do something ○ *What about going on a fishing trip?* ◇ **what for** asking the reason for or the purpose of something ◇ **what have you** other things similar to those just mentioned ◇ **what if 1.** used to make a suggestion about a possible course of action **2.** used to ask what might or would happen in a given situation ◇ **what of it?** used to suggest that something is not important ◇ **what's what** the true facts or actual situation (*informal*) ◇ **what with** used to introduce the reason or reasons for something ○ *I didn't get there until ten, what with all the traffic and setting out late.*

what all *pron.* = **whatnot** (*informal*)

what·cha·ma·call·it /wòchəmə káwlit, hwòchəmə-/ (*plural* **-its** *or* **-um** /-káwləm/) *n.* something whose name is forgotten or is not known [Early 20thC. From a pronunciation of *what you may call it*.]

what·ev·er /wot évvər, hwot-/ CORE MEANING: a grammatical word used to refer to everything of a particular type, without limitation ○ (pron) *Feel free to say whatever you like.* ○ (adj) *He lost whatever interest he may have had in it.*

1. *pron., adj.* NO MATTER WHAT being the case in all circumstances ○ (pron) *She always seems to succeed, whatever she does.* ○ (adj) *Whatever problem you come up with they'll deal with.* **2.** *pron.* EMPHATIC "WHAT" an emphatic form of "what" used to express an emotion such as suprise or perplexity ○ *Whatever is the matter now?* **3.** *adv.* OF ANY KIND used for emphasis ○ *I can see no reason whatever why you shouldn't go.* **4.** *adv.* EXPRESSING MILD DISAGREEMENT used to indicate that the speaker disagrees with what has just been said but is not prepared to argue (*informal*) ○ *OK, if that's what you think, whatever.* [14thC] ◇ **or whatever** used to refer generally to something else of the same kind ○ *any tool such as a hoe, fork, or spade, or whatever*

what-if *n.* a problem, difficulty, or obstacle that could arise in the future and needs to be considered or anticipated now (*informal*)

what·ness /wótnəss, hwótnəss/ *n.* PHILOS = **quiddity** [Early 17thC. Translation of medieval Latin *quidditas* (source of English *quiddity*), from Latin *quid* "what."]

what·not /wót nòt, hwót-/ *n.* **1.** SOMEBODY THE SAME OR SIMILAR something of the same or a similar kind **2.** FURNITURE SET OF SHELVES a set of light shelves for displaying small ornamental items **3.** SOMETHING UNIMPORTANT something nondescript, trivial, or unimportant [Late 16thC. From *what not?* Originally in the sense "everything."]

what's /wots, hwots/ *contr.* **1.** what is **2.** what has **3.** what does

whats·her·name /wótsər nàym, hwótsər-/ *pron.* a woman or girl whose name you have forgotten or do not know (*informal*)

whats·his·name /wótsiz nàym, hwótsiz-/ *pron.* a man or boy whose name has been forgotten or is not known (*informal*)

what·sis *n.* = **whatsit** (*informal*) [Contraction and alteration of *what-is-it*]

whats·it /wótsit, hwótsit/, **whats·is** /wótsiss, hwótsiss/ *n.* something whose name you have forgotten or do not know (*informal*) [Contraction of *what-is-it*]

whats·its·name /wótsits nàym, hwótsits-/ *pron.* something whose name you have forgotten or do not know (*informal*)

what·so·ev·er /wòtsō évvər, hwòtsō-/ *adv.* AT ALL used to emphasize a negative statement, after words such as "none," "no one," and "anyone" ○ *Did you have any doubts? – None whatsoever.* ■ *pron., adj.* WHATEVER whatever (*archaic*) [13thC]

wheal /weel, hweel/ *n.* **1.** RED MARK a raised reddened area on the skin caused by a blow, scratch, or pressure **2.** MED ITCHY SWELLING ON SKIN a temporary raised area on the skin, often red and itchy, caused, e.g., by a nettle or insect sting or by exposure to an allergen [Early 19thC. Origin uncertain: probably an alteration of WALE by association with obsolete *wheal* "pustule, pimple" (from assumed Old English *hwele*).]

wheat /weet, hweet/ *n.* **1.** GRASS WITH EDIBLE GRAIN an annual grass, native to southwestern Asia and the Mediterranean, some types of which are widely cultivated in temperate regions for their edible grains. The numerous varieties of cultivated wheat are based on three main species: bread wheat, durum or hard wheat, and emmer. Genus: *Triticum.* **2.** GRAIN HARVESTED FROM THE WHEAT PLANT the grain harvested from the wheat plant, which is ground into flour and used to make bread, pasta, and other foods **3.** PALE YELLOW COLOR a pale yellow or light yellow color ■ *adj.* PALE YELLOW pale or light yellow in color [Old English *hwǣte*, literally "that which is white." Ultimately from an Indo-European word meaning "white," which also produced English *white*; from the "white" flour produced from the grain.]

wheat bread *n.* a bread that is made from a blend of white flour and whole-wheat flour

wheat·ear /weet èer, hweet-/ *n.* a small thrush found in North America, Europe, Asia and Africa, typically having a white rump and black face. Genus: *Oenanthe.* [Late 16thC. Back-formation from *wheatears*, probably (by folk etymology from WHEAT + EAR) from assumed *whiteeres*, literally "(bird with a) white ass" (with white feathers on its rump).]

wheat·en /weet'n, hweet'n/ *adj.* **1.** FOOD MADE FROM WHEAT made from or with wheat or milled wheat flour **2.** COLORS PALE YELLOW pale or light yellow in color ■ *n.* COLORS PALE YELLOW COLOR a pale yellow or light yellow color [Old English *hwǣten*]

wheat·en ter·ri·er *n.* a terrier of a medium-sized breed that has a soft, wavy, wheat-colored coat and a docked tail

wheat germ *n.* the embryonic center of the wheat grain, rich in B vitamins, that is sold milled finely and sometimes toasted for sprinkling over cereals or use in cooking

wheat·grass /hweet fràss/ *n.* wheat grains sprouted to a height of around 7 in./17 cm, cut and pulped to produce a highly nutritious juice that is drunk in very small quantities

Wheat·ley /weetlee, hweetlee/**, Phillis** (1753?–84) African-born U.S. poet. Sold into slavery to the Wheatley family as a child, she started writing poetry at an early age and gained recognition in the United States and Britain for her neoclassical verse. She is regarded as the first important African American poet.

Whea·ton /weetən, hweetən/ city in northeastern Illinois, southwest of Addison. It is a western suburb of Chicago and home to Wheaton College. Population: 54,173 (1996).

wheat rust *n.* **1.** FUNGAL DISEASE OF WHEAT a disease of wheat caused by various fungi and marked by blackish, brownish, or yellowish streaks on the leaves and stems **2.** FUNGUS CAUSING WHEAT DISEASE a fungus that causes rust in wheat

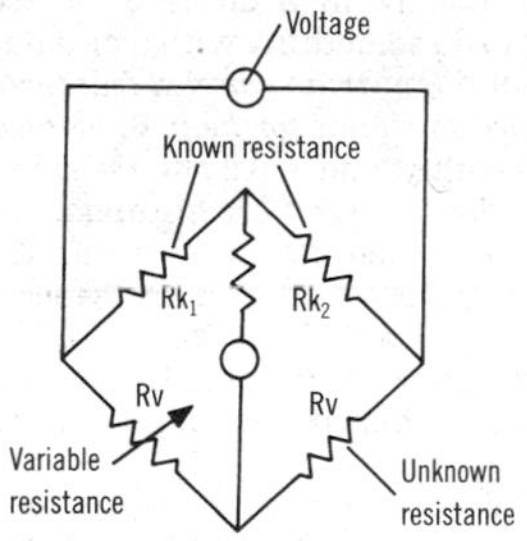

Wheatstone bridge

Wheat·stone bridge /weet stōn-, hweet-/ *n.* a device consisting of an electrical circuit, three known resistances, and a galvanometer that is used for measuring an unknown resistance [Late 19thC. Named for its inventor, Sir Charles *Wheatstone* (1802–75), an English physicist.]

wheat·worm /weet wùrm, hweet-/ (*plural* **-worms** *or* **-worm**) *n.* a small nematode worm that lives as a parasite on and is destructive to wheat. Latin name: *Anguina tritici.*

whee /wee, hwee/ *interj.* used to express exhilarating or unrestrained joy, pleasure, or excitement [Early 20thC. Natural exclamation.]

whee·dle /weed'l, hweed'l/ (**-dled, -dling, -dles**) *v.* **1.** *vti.* COAX SOMEBODY to coax or try to persuade somebody to do something using flattery, guile, or other indirect means **2.** *vt.* OBTAIN SOMETHING BY WHEEDLING to obtain something from somebody by coaxing, flattery, guile, or other indirect means of persuasion [Mid-17thC. Origin uncertain: perhaps from German *wedeln* "to fawn, cringe, wag the tail," from *Wedel* "tail, fan," or from Old English *wædlian* "to beg."] —**whee·dler** *n.* —**whee·dling·ly** *adv.*

wheel /weel, hweel/ *n.* **1.** ROTATING ROUND PART a ring or disk that revolves or is turned by a central shaft or pin, sometimes having a central hub with radiating spokes attached to a circular rim (*often used in combination*) ○ *a wagon wheel* **2.** MECH ENG ROUND MACHINE PART THAT TURNS ANOTHER a rotating circular part of a mechanism, often with projections on the outer edge, used to turn another part **3.** STEERING WHEEL a steering wheel (*informal*) **4.** SPINNING WHEEL a spinning wheel (*informal*) **5.** CASTER a small rotating or swiveling circular part fitted to the base of something such as a piece of furniture or luggage to make it easier to move **6.** POTTER'S WHEEL a potter's wheel (*informal*) **7.** MEDIEVAL TORTURE DEVICE a medieval instrument of torture in the form of a large wheel to which the victim was tied. The outstretched arms and legs of the victim were usually broken with a metal bar. **8.** ROTATING FIREWORK a flat round or coiled firework that spins as it burns (*often used in combination*) **9.** WHEEL OF FORTUNE an imaginary wheel said to be spun by fate **10.** GAMBLING ROUND FRAME SPUN IN GAMBLING a circular device that is spun in games of chance such as roulette in order to determine who wins in a random way **11.** SOMETHING RESEMBLING A WHEEL something that resembles a wheel in shape, form, or function **12.** TURN a turn or revolution **13.** MOVEMENT IN A CIRCLE a turning, spinning, pivoting, or circular movement **14.** MIL MILITARY FORMATION a military formation in which the inner unit remains in one place, as a pivot, while the outer units change direction and make an arc around it. It is used in marching performances by a troop of soldiers and displays by a fleet of ships. **15.** MIL ROUND MILITARY CAP a round cap with a visor, worn by members of the armed forces (*slang*) **16.** POETRY SET OF RHYMING LINES a group of rhyming lines that end a stanza of verse. They are usually shorter than the other lines and often occur in a group of four. **17.** BICYCLE a bicycle (*informal*) ■ **wheels** *npl.* **1.** CAR a car, especially for personal use (*slang*) **2.** DRIVING FORCE OR WORKINGS the system or influences controlling the way something functions or operates ○ *the wheels of government* ■ *v.* (**wheeled, wheel·ing, wheels**) **1.** *vti.* MOVE ON WHEELS to push something that has wheels or to roll along ○ *wheeled her bicycle up the steep hill* **2.** *vt.* TRANSPORT SOMEBODY IN A WHEELED OBJECT to move or carry somebody or something in a conveyance with wheels such as a cart or wheelchair ○ *wheeled the patient out of the room* **3.** *vt.* PROVIDE SOMETHING WITH WHEELS to fit something with a wheel or wheels **4.** *vi.* TURN QUICKLY to move quickly in a circle **5.** *vi.* MAKE A CIRCULAR MOVEMENT to do something with a circular or curving movement ○ *Her arms wheeled frantically in the air as she tried to signal for help.* **6.** *vi.* MOVE SMOOTHLY to move smoothly and easily ○ *He wheeled through the gathering, making all his appointed stops.* [Old English *hwēol*. Ultimately from an Indo-European word meaning "to go around," which is also the ancestor of English *cycle* and *encyclopedia*.] —**wheel·less** *adj.* ◇ **wheel and deal** to use complex and skillful, sometimes slightly dishonest, negotiating techniques in order to secure something

wheel around *vi.* **1.** TURN AROUND QUICKLY to turn around quickly or suddenly **2.** CHANGE A FORMERLY FIRM OPINION to reverse or radically change an opinion, position, or belief

wheel in *vi.* to approach or enter a place quickly and confidently (*informal*)

wheel out *v.* **1.** *vt.* BRING SOMEBODY OR SOMETHING FORWARD to present somebody or use something readily or repeatedly **2.** *vi.* LEAVE QUICKLY to leave a place quickly (*informal*)

wheel and ax·le *n.* a simple machine, often used to raise or lower loads, typically consisting of a cylindrical drum and wheel mounted on the same axle with ropes wound around each. Depending on the relative diameters of the drum and wheel, various levels of mechanical advantage are achieved.

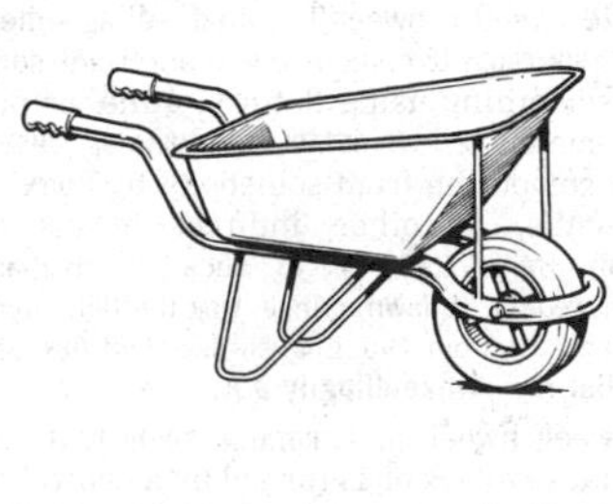

Wheelbarrow

wheel·bar·row /wéel bèrrō, hwéel-/ *n.* CONTAINER WITH A WHEEL AND HANDLES a small cart used to transport things, usually in the form of an open container with a single wheel at the front and two handles at the back ■ *vt.* (**-rowed, -row·ing, -rows**) MOVE SOMETHING IN A WHEELBARROW to move or transport something in a wheelbarrow

wheel·base /wéel bàyss, hwéel-/ *n.* the distance between the front axle and the rear axle of a motor vehicle, usually measured in inches. It determines how sharply the vehicle can turn in a given direction.

wheel bug *n.* a large and powerful insect belonging to the assassin bug family that preys on other insects and has an outgrowth on its back resembling a gear. Latin name: *Arilus cristatus*.

wheel·chair /wéel chàir, hwéel-/ *n.* a chair with two small wheels at the front and two large wheels at the sides, used as a way of moving around by somebody who cannot walk. Wheelchairs may be propelled by turning the large wheels, by somebody pushing from behind, or by a small motor.

wheel·chair hous·ing *n.* houses and apartments designed or adapted for people who use wheelchairs to enable them to move around easily

wheel clamp *n. U.K.* = **Denver boot**

wheeled *adj.* equipped with wheels or a particular number of wheels (*often used in combination*) ○ *a three-wheeled vehicle*

wheel·er /wéelər, hwéelər/ *n.* **1.** AUTOMOT WHEELED VEHICLE a vehicle that has a particular number of wheels (*used in combination*) ○ *an eighteen-wheeler* **2.** SOMEBODY WHO WHEELS somebody or something that wheels or pushes something with wheels **3.** WHEELMAKER OR REPAIRER somebody who makes or repairs wheels, especially the wheels of carriages or wagons used in former times

wheel·er-deal·er *n.* somebody who uses complex and skillful and perhaps slightly dishonest negotiating techniques to obtain what he or she wants, especially in business or politics (*informal*)

wheel horse *n.* a steady, diligent, and reliable worker, especially in a political organization

wheel·house /wéel hòwss, hwéel-/ (*plural* **-houses** /-hòwzəz, -hòwzəz/) *n.* NAUT = **pilothouse**

wheel·ie /wéelee, hwéelee/ *n.* a maneuver performed on a moving or stationary bicycle or motorcycle in which the rider raises the front wheel off the ground and balances on the back wheel

Wheel·ing /wéeling, hwéeling/ city in northern West Virginia, on the Ohio border, south of Weirton. Population: 33,311 (1996).

wheel lock *n.* in some old firearms, a firing mechanism in which a steel spring-wound wheel strikes sparks from a piece of iron pyrites

wheel·man /wéelmən, hwéel-/ (*plural* **-men** /-mən/), **wheels·man** /hwéelzmən/ (*plural* **-men**) *n.* **1.** DRIVER OF VEHICLE somebody who drives a car or other motor vehicle, especially for a criminal activity **2.** BICYCLE OR MOTORCYCLE RIDER somebody who rides a motorcycle or bicycle **3.** NAUT = **helmsman** [Mid-19thC]

wheel of for·tune, **Wheel of For·tune** *n.* a revolving wheel said to determine random changes in the course of somebody's life, used as a symbol of the inconstancy of fortune

wheels·man *n.* NAUT = **helmsman**

wheel-thrown *adj.* made by being turned on a potter's wheel

wheel·work /wéel wùrk, hwéel-/ *n.* an arrangement of interlocking wheels or gears within a machine or other device, e.g., the geartrain in a mechanical timepiece

wheel·wright /wéel rìt, hwéel-/ *n.* somebody who makes or repairs wheels, especially the wheels of carriages and wagons

wheesh /weesh, hweesh/, **wheesht** /weesht, hweesht/ *interj. Scotland* CALL FOR SILENCE used to command a person or a group to be silent (*informal*) ■ *vti.* (**wheeshed, wheesh·ing, wheeshes; wheeshted, wheesht·ing, wheeshts**) *Scotland* BE SILENT to silence somebody or something, or become or remain silent ■ *n. Scotland* SILENCE the state or condition of making no noise (*informal*) [Imitative of the sound of hushing somebody]

wheeze /weez, hweez/ *v.* (**wheezed, wheez·ing, wheez·es**) **1.** *vi.* BREATHE WITH A HOARSE WHISTLING SOUND to breathe with an audible whistling sound and with difficulty, usually because of a respiratory disorder such as asthma **2.** *vt.* SAY SOMETHING WITH A NOISY WHISTLING SOUND to say or express something while breathing noisily and with difficulty **3.** *vi.* MAKE A WHISTLING OR PUFFING SOUND to make a noisy whistling or puffing sound that resembles wheezing ○ *The old locomotive wheezed and puffed up the steep slope.* ■ *n.* **1.** NOISY BREATHING SOUND noisy and difficult breathing, or the hoarse whistling sound of this **2.** OFTEN REPEATED JOKE a hackneyed story, joke, or saying (*informal*) [15thC. Origin uncertain: perhaps from Old Norse *hvæsa* "to hiss." Ultimately an imitation of the sound.] —**wheez·er** *n.* —**wheez·i·ly** *adv.* —**wheez·i·ness** *n.* —**wheez·y** *adj.*

whelk[1] /welk, hwelk/ (*plural* **whelk** *or* **whelks**) *n.* a predatory marine gastropod mollusk with a conical spiraling shell. Some kinds of whelk are edible. Family: Buccinidae. [Old English *weoloc*, altered perhaps by association with WHELK[2]]

whelk[2] /welk, hwelk/ *n.* a raised spot or mark on the skin such as a pimple, boil, or wheal [Old English *hwylca* "pustule, tumor"] —**whelk·y** *adj.*

whelm /welm, hwelm/ (**whelmed, whelm·ing, whelms**) *vt.* (*literary*) **1.** COVER WITH WATER to engulf or submerge something in water **2.** OVERWHELM to overpower or overburden somebody or something [14thC. Origin uncertain: probably an alteration of Old English *āhwylfan* "to cover over, submerge," influenced by *helmian* "to cover."]

whelp /welp, hwelp/ *n.* **1.** YOUNG ANIMAL a young animal, especially the young of carnivorous mammals such as wolves, lions, bears, and dogs **2.** RUDE YOUNG MAN a boy or young man regarded as showing inappropriate boldness or lack of deference (*insult*) **3.** CHILD a child or young person **4.** NAUT RIDGE ON CAPSTAN OR WINDLASS a projection on the barrel of a capstan or windlass **5.** MECH ENG TOOTH ON A WHEEL a tooth on a sprocket wheel ■ *vti.* (**whelped, whelp·ing, whelps**) BEAR YOUNG to give birth to young (*refers to animals, especially carnivores*) [Old English *hwelp*, of prehistoric Germanic origin]

when /wen, hwen/ CORE MEANING: an adverb used to ask at what time or at what point things happen ○ *When can we expect you?* ○ *When should you use your rearview mirror?*

1. *conj.* WHILE at or during the time that ○ *When I was a child, I lived in the country.* **2.** *conj.* AS SOON AS as soon as somebody does something or something happens ○ *Call me when you get home.* **3.** *conj.* AT SOME POINT at some point during an activity, event, or circumstance ○ *We got him when he was still a pup.* **4.** *conj.* EACH TIME each time something happens ○ *When it thunders the whole house shakes.* **5.** *conj.* IF considering the fact that ○ *Why walk when you can ride?* **6.** *conj.* ALTHOUGH in spite of the fact that ○ *They think I'm really easygoing, when in fact I'm not.* **7.** *adv.* AT OR DURING WHICH TIME used to indicate a time at or during which something happens ○ *He remembered a time when he could run a mile without any difficulty.* **8.** *n.* UNSPECIFIED TIME PERIOD used to refer to the time that something happened or will happen (*often used in the plural*) ○ *We're having trouble determining the whens and hows of the thing.* [Old English *hwonne, hwænne*. Ultimately from an Indo-European base that is also the ancestor of Latin *quando* (source of English *quandary*).]

WORD KEY: USAGE

See Usage note at ***if***.

when·as /wen áz, hwen-/ *conj.* (*archaic*) **1.** WHENEVER at such time as **2.** WHILE at or during the time that **3.** ALTHOUGH in spite of the fact that

whence /wenss, hwenss/ *adv.* FROM WHERE from what place or source (*formal*) ○ *Can we know whence comes this good luck?* ■ *pron.* WHICH PLACE the place or thing previously referred to (*formal*) ○ *that envy whence comes hate* ■ *conj.* AS A RESULT from which cause or origin (*formal*) ○ *You have treated her badly, whence her anger.* [13thC. From earlier *whennes*, literally "of or from when."]

WORD KEY: USAGE

whence or **from whence**? Both uses now sound old-fashioned or literary in tone, but ***from whence***, as an attempt to bring it up to date, fits rather better in the structures of modern English. In everyday English, however, the word can normally be avoided altogether: *They did not know from whence they came* can easily be recast as *They did not know where they came from.*

whence·so·ev·er /hwènssō évvər, wènsō évvər/ *adv., conj.* from whatever cause, origin, or source (*archaic*) ○ *accept the gifts whencesoever they come*

when·e'er /wen áir, hwen-/ *adv., conj.* whenever (*literary*)

when·ev·er /wen évvər, hwen-/ *conj.* **1.** AT ANY TIME at whatever time ○ *Whenever you need me I'll be there.* **2.** EACH AND EVERY TIME at every time or occurrence ○ *Whenever you're around, the dog growls.* ■ *adv.*

when·ev·er, when ev·er WHEN used as an intensive form of "when" (*informal*) ○ *Whenever will you learn?*

when·so·ev·er /w-nssō évvər, hwènssō-/ *adv., conj.* used as an intensive form of "whenever"

whe·nu·a /fénnoo ə/ *n. NZ* land [From Maori]

where /wair, hwair/ CORE MEANING: an adverb used to ask a question about the place somebody or something is in, at, coming from, or going to ○ *Where are my keys?* ○ *Where are you going?* ○ *Guess where I've been. – Where?*

1. *adv.* **IN OR TO A PLACE** used to indicate the place in which something is located or happens ○ *I want to live where it's warm.* ○ *Nobody really knew where she had gone.* ○ *They went to the beach, where they spent the afternoon* 2. *adv.* **WHAT PURPOSE** used to ask questions about the purpose or goal of something ○ *Where will all your hard work get you?* 3. *adv.* **IN ANY SITUATION** in any situation in which ○ *Where there's life, there's hope.* ○ *They're at a stage where they can now talk about their problems.* 4. *n.* **UNKNOWN PLACE** used to refer to an unspecified place or event (*usually used in the plural*) ○ *Let us know the wheres and whens of your itinerary.* [Old English *hwær, hwar.* Ultimately from an Indo-European base that is also the ancestor of English *who, when,* and *why.*]

where·a·bouts /wáir ə bòwts, hwáir-/ *adv.* **IN WHAT PLACE** in, at, or near what location ○ *Do you know whereabouts the hotel is?* ○ *I've forgotten whereabouts I parked the car.* ■ *n.* **LOCATION OF SOMEBODY OR SOMETHING** the approximate place where somebody or something is ○ *Could you give us any information regarding the whereabouts of your brother?*

where·af·ter /wair áftər, hwair-/ *adv.* after which time or event (*formal*) ○ *She left, whereafter he also departed.*

where·as /wair áz, hwair-/ *conj.* 1. **WHILE IN CONTRAST** while on the other hand ○ *She was saving money, whereas you were living in the fast lane.* 2. **BECAUSE** for the reason that (*formal*) ○ *Whereas you've proven your worth, you're welcome to join the team.* 3. **CONNECTING SERIES** used to introduce each clause in a series (*formal*)

where·at /wair át, hwair-/ *adv.* **TO OR AT WHICH PLACE** toward or at which place (*archaic*) ■ *conj.* **BECAUSE OF WHICH** because or as a consequence of which (*archaic*)

where·by /wair bī́, hwair-/ *adv.* by means of or through which ○ *the invention whereby he made his millions*

where'er /wair áir, hwair-/ *adv.* wherever (*literary*)

where·fore /wáir fàwr, hwáir-/ *n.* **REASON** a reason or purpose for something ○ *I don't want to know the whys or the wherefores of your decision.* ■ *adv.* (*archaic*) 1. **THEREFORE** for the foregoing reason 2. **FOR WHAT REASON** for what reason or purpose

where·from /wair fróm, hwair-/ *adv.* from what place or origin (*archaic*) ○ *Do we know wherefrom this stranger comes?*

where·in /wair ín, hwair-/ *adv.* (*archaic*) 1. **HOW** in what particular way or respect ○ *Wherein did I misspeak myself?* 2. **WHERE** in which particular place ○ *the country wherein they dwelled* 3. **DURING WHICH** during the time which ○ *the years wherein we were ignorant and happy*

where·in·to /wair íntoo, hwair-/ *adv.* into which place or thing (*archaic*)

where·of /wair óv, hwair-/ *adv.* of or about what thing or person (*formal or archaic*) ○ *Do you know whereof you speak?*

where·on /wair ón, hwair-/ *adv.* on which thing or place (*archaic or formal*) ○ *the couch whereon she lay*

where·so·ev·er /wàirssō évvər, hwàirssō-/ *adv., conj.* used as an emphatic form of "wherever" (*archaic*)

where·to /wair tóo, hwair-/, **where·un·to** /wair úntoo, hwair-/ *adv.* where or to which (*archaic formal*) ○ *the place whereto you've brought me*

where·up·on /wáirə pòn, hwàirə-/ *conj.* **AT WHICH POINT** at which time or as a result of (*formal*) ○ *The rain began to come down hard, whereupon we ran for the house.* ■ *adv.* **ON WHICH** on or upon which (*archaic or formal*) ○ *the pillow whereupon she laid her head*

wher·ev·er /wair évvər, hwair-/ *adv.* 1. **TO ANY PLACE** in, at, or to any place ○ *I'll go wherever you go.* 2. **NO MATTER WHERE** at or in an indefinite place ○ *I'll sleep on the couch, the floor, wherever.* 3. **AT AN UNKNOWN PLACE** to, in, or at an unknown or unidentified place or position 4. **wher·ev·er, where ev·er WHERE INDEED** used as an emphatic form of *where* ○ *Wherever have my glasses gone?* ■ *conj.* **EVERY TIME OR PLACE THAT** on every occasion or in every place that ○ *Take exercise wherever possible.* ○ *I crossed the fields wherever there was a gate.*

where·with /wair wíth, hwair-/ *adv.* with or by means of which (*archaic*) ○ *the tool wherewith the deed was done*

where·with·al /wáirwi thòl, hwáirwi-, -thòl/ *n.* the money or resources required for a purpose

wher·ry /wérree, hwérree/ (*plural* **-ries**) *n.* 1. **LIGHT ROWBOAT** a small light rowboat used in inland waters 2. **ENGLISH COMMERCIAL BARGE** a small barge, once used for commercial purposes in parts of England, now used largely for pleasure cruises [15thC. Origin unknown.] —**wher·ry·man** *n.*

whet /wet, hwet/ *vt.* (**whet·ted, whet·ting, whets**) 1. **STIMULATE SOMETHING** to make a feeling, sense, or desire more keen or intense ○ *The thought of easy money whetted my enthusiasm for the undertaking.* 2. **SHARPEN A TOOL OR WEAPON** to sharpen the cutting edge or blade of a tool or weapon, usually by rubbing it on a stone ■ *n.* 1. **SHARPENING OR INTENSIFYING** an act of sharpening, intensifying, or stimulating something 2. **SHARPENING BLOCK** something that sharpens a cutting edge 3. **SOMETHING THAT WHETS THE SENSES** something that stimulates a feeling, sense, or desire, especially a small amount that makes somebody want more (*informal*) [Old English *hwettan* "to sharpen." Ultimately from a prehistoric Germanic word meaning "sharp."] —**whet·ter** *n.*

wheth·er /wéthər, hwéthər/ *conj.* 1. **INTRODUCES ALTERNATIVES** used to indicate alternatives in an indirect question or a clause following a verb that expresses or implies doubt or the possibility of choice ○ *We should try to meet them whether it's raining or not.* 2. **INTRODUCES AN INDIRECT QUESTION** used to introduce an indirect question ○ *I wonder whether it's worth the effort.* 3. **EITHER** used to introduce doubt regarding two equal possibilities ○ *She said she'd get here whether by car or by train.* [Old English *hwæþer, hweþer.* Ultimately from an Indo-European word that is also the ancestor of English *where* and *other.*] ◇ **whether or no** whatever the circumstances might be

whet·stone /wét stòn, hwét-/ *n.* a stone used to sharpen the cutting edge or blade of a tool or weapon by rubbing [Old English *hwetstān*]

whew /fyoo, hyoo/ *interj.* used to express great relief, surprise, or discomfort [15thC. An imitation of the sound.]

whey /way, hway/ *n.* the watery liquid that separates from the solid part of milk when it turns sour or when enzymes are added in cheesemaking [Old English *hwæg, hweg,* of prehistoric Germanic origin] —**whey·ey** *adj.*

whey·face /wáy fàyss, hwáy-/ *n.* 1. **PALE FACE** a very pale face (*informal*) 2. **SOMEBODY WITH VERY PALE FACE** somebody whose face is regarded as too pale (*insult*) —**whey·faced** *adj.*

whf. *abbr.* wharf

which /wich, hwich/ CORE MEANING: used to ask for something to be identified from a known larger group or range of possibilities ○ (adj) *Which part of it don't you understand?* ○ (pron) *Which would you like?* ○ (pron) *Which of the colors do you prefer?* ○ (pron) *At which stage do we start to cut our losses?*

1. *pron.* **INTRODUCES A RELATIVE CLAUSE** used to introduce a clause that provides additional information about something previously mentioned ○ *The cabin, which we bought last spring, sits high on the dunes.* ○ *A success for which she is to be congratulated.* 2. *pron.* **THAT** used to introduce a relative clause that provides necessary information about its antecedent ○ *Please return the money which I loaned to you.* 3. *pron.* **REFERS BACK TO A PHRASE OR SENTENCE** used to refer back to an entire verb phrase or sentence ○ *Swimming after eating, which I've told you not to do, can be very dangerous.* 4. *adj., pron.* **ONE FROM KNOWN SET** one of a range of things or possibilities specified or implied by the immediate context ○ (adj) *I can't decide which activity would be the most fun.* ○ (pron) *He decided which to buy and paid the money.* 5. *adj., pron.* **INDICATES CHOICE** used to indicate one or any number of things ○ (adj) *Use which method best suits you.* ○ (pron) *Take which you prefer.* [Old English *hwilc,* literally "of what form, like what." Ultimately from a prehistoric Germanic word that is also the ancestor of English *like* and *such.*]

WORD KEY: USAGE

See Usage note at ***that.***

which·ev·er /wich évvər, hwich-/ *adj., pron.* used to refer to any one or any number of items in a class ○ (adj) *Whichever job you take, starting out will be hard.* ○ (pron) *I'll buy whichever you think best.*

which·so·ev·er /wìchsō évvər, hwìchsō-/ *pron., adj.* whichever (*archaic*)

whick·er /wíkər, hwíkər/ (**-ered, -er·ing, -ers**) *vi.* to neigh softly [Mid-17thC. An imitation of the sound.] —**whick·er** *n.*

whid·ah *n.* BIRDS = **whydah**

whiff /wif, hwif/ *n.* 1. **SLIGHT OR BRIEF ODOR** a faint smell of something, pleasant or unpleasant, often perceived briefly ○ *a whiff of disinfectant* 2. **TRACE OF SOMETHING** a slight sign or trace of something ○ *a whiff of corruption* 3. **GENTLE GUST OR PUFF** a short light gust, puff, or breath of wind 4. **SNIFF OF SOMETHING** a sniff, smell, or brief inhalation of something ○ *took one whiff of the concoction and started coughing* 5. *U.K.* NAUT **SMALL SKIFF** a narrow skiff for one rower 6. BASEBALL **STRIKEOUT** an instance of swinging at and missing the third strike in a turn at bat 7. GOLF **COMPLETE MISS** a swing that completely misses the golfball ■ *v.* (**whiffed, whiff·ing, whiffs**) 1. *vti.* **WAFT OR PUFF** to come or send something in short light gusts or puffs ○ *The smoke whiffed and curled around the room.* 2. *vt.* **SNIFF SOMETHING** to sniff, smell, or inhale something ○ *The hyena whiffed the night air for predators.* 3. *vti.* BASEBALL **STRIKE OUT** to strike out a batter or to strike out ○ *That pitcher whiffed all the batters this inning.* 4. *vi.* GOLF **FAIL TO HIT A BALL** to swing at and miss a ball completely [Late 16thC. Thought to suggest a light puff of wind that carries a smell.] —**whiff·er** *n.*

whif·fle /wíff'l, hwíff'l/ (**-fled, -fling, -fles**) *v.* 1. *vi.* **BEHAVE ERRATICALLY** to be indecisive or unpredictable in thought or action 2. *vti.* **BLOW GENTLY** to blow or move in short light variable gusts or puffs, or to blow or move something in this way 3. *vi.* **WHISTLE** to whistle softly [Late 17thC. Formed from WHIFF.]

whif·fler /wíflər, hwíflər/ *n.* somebody who vacillates or is evasive

whif·fle·tree /wíff'l trèe, hwíff'l-/ *n. Northeast U.S.* a horizontal crossbar used to attach the harness traces of a draft animal that is then attached to a vehicle or device [Mid-19thC. Variant of WHIPPLETREE.]

Whig /wig, hwig/ *n.* 1. **MEMBER OF 19C U.S. POLITICAL PARTY** a member of a 19th-century U.S. political party that favored loose interpretation of the Constitution and opposed the Democratic Party 2. **SUPPORTER OF THE REVOLUTION AGAINST BRITISH CONTROL** somebody who supported the American side against the British in the American Revolution 3. *U.K.* **MEMBER OF A FORMER BRITISH POLITICAL PARTY** a member of a reforming English political party that supported the aristocracy and later the business community, finally becoming the core of the Liberal Party 4. *U.K.* **CONSERVATIVE IN THE BRITISH LIBERAL PARTY** a conservative member of the Liberal Party in the United Kingdom 5. *U.K.* **SUPPORTER OF FREE ENTERPRISE** somebody who opposes government regulation of commerce and the economy 6. *Scotland* **SCOTTISH PRESBYTERIAN** a 17th-century Presbyterian in Scotland [Mid-17thC. Shortening of obsolete Scots dialect *whiggamaire,* literally "horse driver."] —**Whig·ger·y** *n.* —**Whig·gism** *n.* —**Whig·gish** *adj.* —**Whig·gish·ly** *adv.* —**Whig·gish·ness** *n.*

WORD KEY: ORIGIN

The Scots word ***Whig*** seems originally to have been used as a contemptuous term for a country dweller, but by the middle of the 17th century it was being applied to Presbyterian supporters in Scotland. It was later adopted as a name for those who opposed the succession of the Catholic King James II of England, and by 1689 it had established itself as the title of one of the two main British political parties, opposed to the Tories.

while /wīl, hwīl/ *conj.* 1. **AT OR DURING SAME TIME** at or during the same time that ○ *We can talk while I fix supper.* 2. **EVEN THOUGH** in spite of the fact that ○ *While I admire your tenacity, I cannot support your aims.* 3. **BUT IN CONTRAST** and on the contrary ○ *An older car would be cheaper to buy while a newer one might be more reliable.* ■ *n.* **PERIOD OF TIME** a period of time or some interval ○ *It's been a while since I saw her.* [Old English *hwīl* "period of time." Ultimately from an Indo-European word meaning "rest, period of rest," which is also the ancestor of English *tranquil* and *quiet.*] ◇ **once in a**

while very occasionally ◇ **worth (somebody's) while** **1.** deserving somebody's time, money, or support **2.** rewarding in terms of money or advantage

while away *vt.* to pass time in an idle, leisurely, and usually pleasant way

whiles /wīlz, hwīlz/ *conj.* while (*archaic*)

whi·lom /hwíləm/ *adv.* **FORMERLY** at or during some past time (*archaic*) ■ *adj.* **FORMER** having been at an earlier time (*archaic*) [Old English *hwīlom*, a form of *whīl* (see WHILE)]

whim /wim, hwim/ *n.* **1. PASSING IMPULSE** a sudden thought, idea, or desire, especially one based on impulse rather than reason or necessity **2.** MINING **HORSE-DRAWN WINCH** a winch used to lift ore or water from a mine, drawn by a horse [Mid-17thC. Origin uncertain: perhaps a shortening of WHIMSY or WHIM-WHAM. The main modern meaning evolved from "pun" via "quaint idea."]

whim·brel /wímbrəl, hwímbrəl/ (*plural* **-brel** *or* **-brels**) *n.* a large shorebird that has a long downward curving bill and breeds in the Arctic. It is related to but smaller than the curlew. Latin name: *Numenius phaeopus.* [Mid-16thC. Origin uncertain: formed from obsolete dialect *whimp* "to whimper" (with reference to the bird's cry), or from WHIMPER.]

whim·per /wímpər, hwímpər/ *v.* (**-pered, -per·ing, -pers**) **1.** *vi.* **SOB SOFTLY** to make repeated weak plaintive crying or whining sounds of pain, distress, or fear **2.** *vi.* **COMPLAIN PEEVISHLY** to complain in a weak, whining, or irritated manner **3.** *vt.* **SAY SOMETHING PLAINTIVELY** to say something in a plaintive or whining voice ■ *n.* **1. WHINE** a weak plaintive cry or whine **2. COMPLAINT** a feeble or peevish complaint [Early 16thC. Formed from earlier *whimp* "to whimper," of imitative origin.] —**whim·per·ing·ly** *adv.*

whim·si·cal /wímzik'l, hwímzik'l/ *adj.* **1. FANCIFUL** imaginative and impulsive **2. AMUSING** slightly odd, old-fashioned, or playful, especially in an endearing way ○ *He gave me that whimsical smile of his.* **3. ERRATIC OR UNPREDICTABLE** behaving in such a way as to be impossible to predict ○ *She distrusted his whimsical nature.* [Mid-17thC. Formed from WHIMSY.] —**whim·si·cal·i·ty** /wìmzi kálləteе, hwìmzi-/ *n.* —**whim·si·cal·ly** *adv.* —**whim·si·cal·ness** *n.*

whim·sy /wímzee, hwímzee/ (*plural* **-sies**), **whim·sey** (*plural* **-seys,** *comparative* **-si·er,** *superlative* **-si·est**) *n.* **1. ENDEARING QUAINTNESS OR ODDITY** the quality of being quaint, odd, or playfully humorous, especially in an endearing way ○ *There's a touch of whimsy about the old cottage.* **2. IMPULSIVE NOTION** an idea that has no immediately obvious reason to exist ○ *We can't always be catering to their whimsies.* [Early 17thC. Origin uncertain: probably based on WHIM-WHAM, perhaps modeled on words like *dropsy.*]

whim-wham *n.* a quaint, odd, or fanciful object such as an ornament, toy, or device (*archaic*) ○ *some whim-wham he bought somewhere* [Origin uncertain: perhaps thought to suggest something frivolous]

whin[1] /win, hwin/ (*plural* **whin** *or* **whins**) *n.* = **gorse** [15thC. Origin uncertain: probably from a Scandinavian word related to Old Danish *hvinegræs*, literally "rough grass."]

whin[2] /win, hwin/ *n.* = **whinstone**

whin·chat /wín chàt, hwín-/ (*plural* **-chat** *or* **-chats**) *n.* a small songbird of the thrush family, native to Asia and Europe, that has mottled brown and white plumage and a streaky reddish brown breast. It is found in meadows. Latin name: *Saxicola rubetra.* [Late 17thC. From WHIN[2] + CHAT "warbler."]

whine /wīn, hwīn/ *v.* (**whined, whin·ing, whines**) **1.** *vi.* **MAKE A HIGH SORROWFUL SOUND** to cry, moan, or plead with a long, plaintive, high-pitched sound **2.** *vi.* **GRUMBLE PEEVISHLY** to complain or protest about something, often in an annoyingly plaintive voice **3.** *vt.* **UTTER SOMETHING IN A WHINING VOICE** to say something in a plaintive high-pitched voice **4.** *vi.* **MAKE A HIGH-PITCHED SOUND** to make a continuous high-pitched sound ○ *The wind whined and moaned through the trees.* ■ *n.* **1. HIGH-PITCHED CRY** a long, plaintive, high-pitched cry **2. PEEVISH COMPLAINT** a complaint or protest, especially one made repeatedly in a whining voice **3. CONTINUOUS HIGH-PITCHED SOUND** a long or continuous high-pitched sound ○ *The whine of the jet engines woke me up.* [Old English *hwīnan* "(of an arrow) to whistle through the air." Ultimately of imitative origin.] —**whin·er** *n.* —**whin·ing·ly** *adv.* —**whin·y** *adj.*

WORD KEY: SYNONYMS

See Synonyms at ***complain.***

whinge /winj, hwinj/ (**whinged, whinge·ing, whing·es**) *vi. U.K., Aus* to complain annoyingly or continuously about something perceived as relatively unimportant (*informal*) [Old English *hwinsian* "to whine." Ultimately an imitation of the sound of a whining dog.] —**whing·er** *n.*

whinge·ing Pom /wìnjing póm, hwìnjing-/ *n. Aus* an English person, especially one perceived as constantly complaining, particularly about life in Australia (*insult*)

whin·ny /wínnee, hwínnee/ *v.* (**-nied, -ny·ing, -nies**) **1.** *vi.* **NEIGH** to neigh softly **2.** *vi.* **MAKE A NEIGHING SOUND** to make a neighing sound, especially when laughing **3.** *vt.* **UTTER WITH A NEIGHING SOUND** to say or express something with a neighing sound ■ *n.* (*plural* **-nies**) **NEIGHING SOUND** a soft neigh or neighing sound [Mid-16thC. An imitation of the sound.]

whin·stone /wín stòn, hwín-/ *n.* a hard, dark, fine-grained rock such as basalt or chert [Early 16thC. From WHIN[2] + STONE.]

whip /wip, hwip/ *v.* (**whipped, whip·ping, whips**) **1.** *vt.* **LASH SOMEBODY OR SOMETHING** to strike a person or animal repeatedly with a flexible rod, length of rope, thin strip of leather attached to a handle, or something similar, especially as a punishment **2.** *vti.* **STRIKE AGAINST SOMETHING SHARPLY** to strike something or somebody very hard, sharply, or repeatedly ○ *The icy rain whipped our faces.* **3.** *vt.* **CRITICIZE SOMEBODY SEVERELY** to criticize or reproach somebody very strongly or severely **4.** *vti.* **MOVE RAPIDLY** to move very quickly, forcefully, or suddenly, or to make something move in this way ○ *She whipped around guiltily as I came in.* **5.** *vt.* **MOVE SOMETHING WITH RAPID ACTION** to move, remove, or produce something very quickly, suddenly, or forcefully **6.** *vt.* **DEFEAT SOMEBODY** to defeat, overcome, or outdo somebody (*informal*) **7.** *vt.* COOK **BEAT LIQUID UNTIL STIFF** to make a food substance such as batter or whipping cream stiff and creamy by adding air to it with short quick movements using a fork, whisk, or electric beater **8.** *vt.* **BIND THE END OF A ROPE** to wind thread, cord, or twine around the end of a rope or cable to keep it from fraying or raveling **9.** *vt.* NAUT **LIFT SOMETHING BY A ROPE AND PULLEY** to lift something by means of a device consisting of a rope passed through a single pulley **10.** *vt.* SEW **SEW SOMETHING IN WHIPSTITCH** to sew the edge of a piece of fabric using whipstitch ■ *n.* **1. INSTRUMENT FOR INFLICTING PAIN** a flexible rod, a length of rope, or a thin strip of leather attached to a handle, used to strike people or animals **2. LASHING STROKE OR BLOW** a stroke or blow with a whip or something similar ○ *a whip across the face* **3. SOMETHING RESEMBLING A WHIP** something that resembles a whip in form, motion, or flexibility **4. SOMEBODY WHO USES A WHIP** somebody who is experienced or skilled in the use of a whip, e.g., the driver of a horse-drawn carriage **5.** POL **SOMEBODY IN CHARGE OF PARTY DISCIPLINE** an elected representative in a legislative body such as Congress or the U.K. Parliament who has special responsibility for ensuring discipline and attendance among his or her party's representatives **6.** POL **CALL FOR PARTY SOLIDARITY** a call issued to a party's elected legislators to ensure they attend for an important vote and vote the party line **7.** FOOD **SWEET DISH** a light creamy dessert made from whipped cream with added sweetening and flavoring **8.** NAUT **HOISTING APPARATUS** a device that consists of a rope, a pulley, and a snatch block, used to raise heavy cargo **9.** MUSIC **FLEXIBLE PERCUSSION INSTRUMENT** a percussion instrument with two flexible strips of wood attached in the shape of a V that make a loud clapping sound when they are waved in the air **10.** HUNT = **whipper-in** **11. WINDMILL VANE** a sail or arm of a windmill **12. FAIRGROUND AMUSEMENT** a ride at an amusement park with small cars that travel with sudden rapid jerking movements around a track **13.** WRESTLING **WRESTLING THROW** in wrestling, a throw in which an opponent is seized by an outstretched arm and thrown to the floor **14. LONG FLEXIBLE BRANCH** a long, slender, flexible branch of some trees such as some willows ○ *furniture made of willow whips* [13thC. Origin uncertain: probably from Middle Low German or Middle Dutch *wippen* "to swing," from, ultimately, a prehistoric Germanic base meaning "to move quickly" (ancestor also of English *wipe*).] ◇ **crack the whip** a children's game in which they join hands in a line and pull each other around sharply

whip in *vt.* POL to keep the members of a political party in line with the party's aims

whip through *vt.* to do something very quickly (*informal*)

whip up *vt.* **1. EXCITE SOMETHING OR SOMEBODY** to arouse or provoke a strong feeling or reaction in a group of people **2. MAKE SOMETHING RISE UP** to stir or disturb something with force so that it rises or flies up **3. PREPARE SOMETHING RAPIDLY** to make something quickly, especially an impromptu meal (*informal*)

whip·cord /wíp kàwrd, hwíp-/ *n.* **1. STRONG FABRIC** a strong cotton or woolen fabric woven with diagonal ribs **2. CORD USED TO MAKE A WHIP** a tough twisted cord used for the flexible part of a whip

whip graft *n.* a way of grafting two plants by inserting the cut end of a scion into a similar cut in a rootstock and tying them securely together until they join

whip hand *n.* **1. MOST POWERFUL POSITION** the most powerful or advantageous position in a particular situation ○ *She has the whip hand.* **2. HAND HOLDING A WHIP** a hand that holds a whip, especially one used to drive horses

whip·lash /wíp làsh, hwíp-/ *n.* **1. FLEXIBLE PART OF A WHIP** the flexible part of a whip **2.** MED **INJURY TO THE NECK** an injury to the muscles, ligaments, vertebrae, or nerves of the neck caused when the head is suddenly thrown forward and then sharply back **3. LASHING STROKE OR BLOW** a stroke or blow from a whip, or something that resembles this in motion, speed, or force

whip·per-in /wìppər-, hwìppər-/ (*plural* **whip·pers-in**) *n.* POL = **whip** *n.* **5**

whip·per·snap·per /wíppər snàppər, hwíppər-/ *n.* somebody who is impudent and unimportant, especially a young person (*dated*) [Late 17thC. Origin uncertain: perhaps from WHIP + SNAPPER, modeled on earlier *snipper-snapper* "somebody who cracks whips."]

whip·per snip·per /wíppər snìppər, hwippər-/ *n. Aus* a machine for trimming the edges of lawns

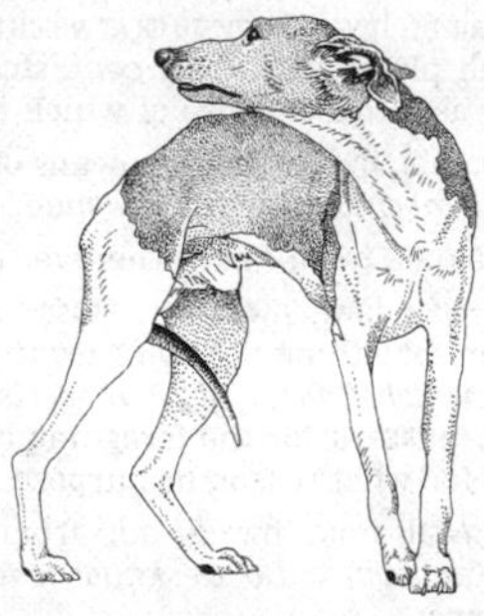

Whippet

whip·pet /wíppət, hwíppət/ *n.* a fast slender short-haired dog of a breed that resembles but is smaller than a greyhound. They are bred in the British Isles for racing. [Mid-16thC. Formed from WHIP in the sense "to move quickly."]

whip·ping /wípping, hwípping/ *n.* **1. PUNISHMENT** a beating, spanking, or flogging with a whip or something similar **2. CORD BINDING** thread, cord, or twine wound around the end of a rope or cable to keep it from fraying or raveling **3.** SPORTS **DEFEAT** a convincing defeat (*informal*) ○ *They really gave us a whipping in that last game.*

whip·ping boy *n.* somebody who takes the blame or punishment for the mistakes or wrongdoings of more important people [Originally, this referred to a boy raised and educated with a prince. If the prince misbehaved, the whipping boy would be punished in his place (typically by whipping).]

whip·ping cream *n.* a heavy cream containing a high proportion of butterfat, which causes it to stiffen when whipped

Whip·ple /wípp'l, hwípp'l/, **William** (1730–85) American patriot. Representing New Hampshire, he signed the Declaration of Independence (1776) and fought in the Revolution (1775–83).

whip·ple·tree /wípp'l tree, hwípp'l-/ *n.* = **whiffletree** [Mid-18thC. *[Whipple]* formed from WHIP. The underlying idea is of a springy, flexible wooden pole.]

whip·poor·will /wíppər wìl, hwíppər-/ *n.* a common North American nocturnal bird of the nightjar family, with spotted dark plumage and a distinctive song from which its name is derived. Latin name: *Caprimulgus vociferus.*

whip·ray /wíp rày, hwíp-/ *n.* a marine fish of the ray family that has a flat body, long whip-shaped tail, and venomous spines

whip·saw /wíp sàw, hwíp-/ *n.* NARROW CROSSCUT SAW a narrow crosscut saw for use by two people ■ *vt.* (**-sawed, -sawed** *or* **-sawn** /-sàwn/, **-saw·ing, -saws**) **1.** CUT WITH WHIPSAW to saw something with a whipsaw **2.** GAMBLING WIN TWO BETS AT ONCE to win two bets simultaneously from one person **3.** DEFEAT IN TWO WAYS SIMULTANEOUSLY to defeat somebody or win in two ways at the same time

whip scor·pi·on *n.* a terrestrial invertebrate related to the scorpion but having a whip-shaped appendage at the end of its abdomen. Order: Uropygi.

whip snake *n.* a fast-moving nonpoisonous snake that pursues its prey, found in North America, Asia, Europe, and Africa. Genus: *Coluber.*

whip·stall /wíp stàwl, hwíp-/ *n.* a maneuver in a small aircraft in which it goes into a vertical climb, pauses briefly, then drops toward the earth nose first

whip·stitch /wíp stich, hwíp-/ *n.* OVERSEWING STITCH a small stitch that passes over the edge of a piece of fabric, used to finish the edge or baste two pieces of fabric together ■ *vt.* (**-stitched, -stitch·ing, -stitch·es**) SEW IN WHIPSTITCH to sew the edge of a piece of fabric using a whipstitch

whip·stock /wíp stòk, hwíp-/ *n.* the handle of a whip

whip·tail /wíp tàyl, hwíp-/ *n.* a lizard with a long thin tail found in South America and Mexico. Genus: *Cnemidophorus.*

whip·worm /wíp wùrm, hwíp-/ *n.* a nematode worm found in human intestines. Its presence usually produces no symptoms but a severe infection with this parasite can cause diarrhea. Latin name: *Trichuris trichiura.*

whir /wur, hwur/, **whirr** *vti.* (**whirred, whir·ring, whirs; whirred, whir·ring, whirrs**) MAKE A WHIRLING OR VIBRATING SOUND to make a continuous soft buzzing or humming sound, usually by vibrating or turning very quickly, or to cause something to make such a sound ■ *n.* WHIRLING OR VIBRATING SOUND a continuous soft buzzing or humming sound like that of something vibrating or turning very quickly [14thC. Origin uncertain: probably from a Scandinavian source.]

whirl /wurl, hwurl/ *v.* (**whirled, whirling, whirls**) **1.** *vti.* TURN OR SPIN RAPIDLY to turn or spin very quickly, or to make something revolve in this way **2.** *vti.* MOVE WHILE TURNING QUICKLY to move along while turning or spinning very quickly, or to make something move along in this way ○ *The dancers whirled around the floor.* **3.** *vi.* FEEL DIZZY OR CONFUSED to seem to spin with dizziness, confusion, or excitement ○ *So much information at one time made my head whirl.* **4.** *vti.* MOVE VERY FAST to move very quickly or make something move very quickly on a straight or curved course ○ *Cars whirled past on the highway.* ■ *n.* **1.** SPINNING MOTION a rapid turning or spinning movement ○ *gave the prayer wheel a whirl* **2.** SOMETHING THAT WHIRLS something that moves or is moved with a rapid circular or spiral motion ○ *Whirls of dust filled the air.* **3.** SENSATION OF SPINNING a spinning sensation caused, e.g., by confusion, excitement, or dizziness ○ *So much good luck had my head in a whirl.* **4.** THINGS HAPPENING IN QUICK SUCCESSION the bustling activity of an endless series of events or engagements ○ *the whirl and bustle of a large city* **5.** BRIEF TRIP OR RIDE a short trip, ride, or dance (*informal*) ○ *Let's go for a whirl in my new car.* [13thC. Origin uncertain: probably from Old Norse *hvirfla.* Ultimately from an Indo-European base meaning "to turn around."] —**whirl·er** *n.* —**whirl·y** *adj.* ◇ **give it** *or* **something a whirl** to have a try at something (*informal*)

whirl·a·bout /wúrl ə bòwt, hwúrl-/ *n.* a turn, spin, or revolution

whirl·i·gig /wúrli gìg, hwúrli-/ *n.* **1.** SPINNING TOY any toy that spins or turns very quickly **2.** MERRY-GO-ROUND a merry-go-round or carousel **3.** SOMETHING THAT WHIRLS something that revolves rapidly or changes continuously ○ *Her life's a whirligig since she took over the business.* **4.** INSECTS = **whirligig beetle** [15thC. From *whirling* or *whirly* (see WHIRL) + GIG "spinning top."]

whirl·i·gig bee·tle *n.* an aquatic insect with a smooth, oval, flattened body, usually seen spinning around on the surface of calm freshwater in groups. Family: Gyrinidae.

whirl·ing der·vish /wùrling-, hwùrling-/ *n.* somebody who busily does many things in quick succession ○ *Once we sent out the invitations, he became a whirling dervish, cleaning, shopping, and cooking.* ◊ **dervish**

whirl·pool /wúrl pòol, hwúrl-/ *n.* **1.** SPIRALING CURRENT OF WATER a spiraling current of water in a stream or river **2.** SOMETHING RESEMBLING A WHIRLPOOL something that has or seems to have the action, motion, or power of a whirlpool ○ *a whirlpool of despair* **3.** POOL OR TUB WITH WATER JETS a bathtub or pool with underwater jets that keep the water constantly moving or swirling

whirl·wind /wúrl wìnd, hwúrl-/ *n.* **1.** METEOROL SPINNING COLUMN OF AIR a column of air rotating rapidly around a core of low pressure **2.** SOMETHING HAPPENING OR CHANGING SWIFTLY something that happens very quickly, or a rapid succession of events (*often used before a noun*) ○ *a whirlwind romance* ○ *a whirlwind visit* **3.** SOMETHING VERY DESTRUCTIVE something having a terrible destructive force ○ *swept up in the whirlwind of war* [14thC. From Old Norse *hvirfilwindr.*]

whirl·y·bird /wúrlee bùrd, hwúrlee-/ *n.* a helicopter (*informal*)

whirr *vti., n.* = **whir**

whish /wish, hwish/ *v.* (**whished, whish·ing, whish·es**) **1.** *vi.* MAKE OR MOVE WITH A RUSHING SOUND to make the soft smooth rushing sound of something moving quickly through the air, or to move with such a sound ○ *Water whished along the boat as we rowed upstream.* **2.** *vt.* MOVE SOMETHING QUICKLY WITH RUSHING SOUND to cause something to make or move with a whishing sound ○ *the dog whished its tail* ■ *n.* WHISHING SOUND OR MOVEMENT a soft whistling or rushing sound, or a movement that makes such a sound ○ *the whish of the windshield wipers* ■ *adv.* WITH A WHISHING SOUND moving or falling with a whishing sound ○ *Whish, the branch came down.* [Early 16thC. An imitation of the sound.]

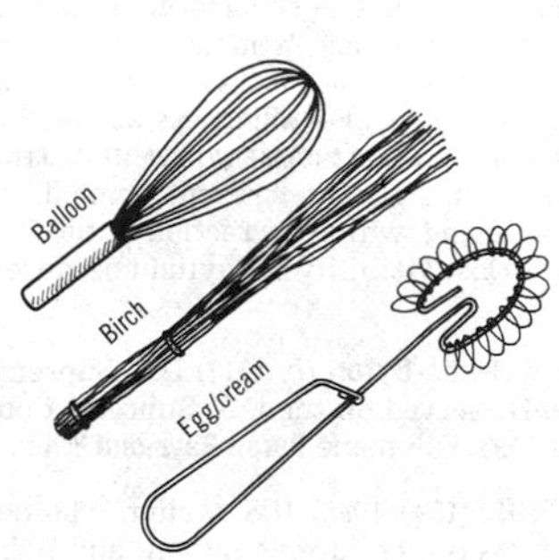

Whisk

whisk /wisk, hwisk/ *n.* **1.** COOK UTENSIL FOR WHIPPING SOMETHING a kitchen tool, usually with curved or coiled wires attached to a handle, used with short quick movements to aerate a soft or liquid substance and make it thick and frothy **2.** BRUSHING MOVEMENT a quick light brushing or sweeping movement ○ *He wiped the table with a whisk of his hand.* **3.** SOMETHING USED TO SWEEP THINGS AWAY a small brush or similar implement made of a bundle of twigs, straw, or grass, used to sweep or stir things ■ *v.* (**whisked, whisk·ing, whisks**) **1.** *vt.* MAKE THICK AND SMOOTH to make a soft or liquid substance thick and smooth by beating it with a fork, whisk, or other device to create air bubbles in the mixture **2.** *vt.* BRUSH AWAY LIGHTLY to remove something with a quick light sweeping movement ○ *He whisked the crumbs from the table.* **3.** *vt.* PLACE WITH A SWEEPING MOTION to move or place something somewhere with a quick light sweeping motion **4.** *vti.* MOVE QUICKLY to move or take somebody or something somewhere very quickly or suddenly ○ *They whisked her off to the hospital.* [14thC. Of Scandinavian origin.]

whisk·broom /wísk bròom, hwísk-/ *n.* a small short-handled broom with stiff bristles, used to clean small areas

whisk·er /wískər, hwískər/ *n.* **1.** HAIR NEAR ANIMAL'S MOUTH a long stiff hair growing near the mouth of some mammals, e.g., cats, mice, and rabbits **2.** HAIR ON SOMEBODY'S FACE a short stiff hair growing on somebody's face, especially on the cheeks, chin, or upper lip **3.** SMALL MARGIN a very small amount or margin ○ *We came within a whisker of losing everything.* **4.** **whisk·er, whisk·er boom** NAUT LIGHT POLE a light pole used for extending the corners of a sail **5.** CHEM THIN CRYSTAL a strong thin hair-shaped crystal of a metal or mineral, used to strengthen composite material ■ **whisk·ers** *npl.* SOMEBODY'S FACIAL HAIR a short growth of hair growing on somebody's cheeks, chin, or upper lip [15thC. Formed from WHISK. Originally used for "something that whisks or sweeps," the main modern meaning evolved because of the supposed resemblance to a small brush.] —**whisk·ered** *adj.* —**whisk·er·y** *adj.*

whis·key /wískee, hwískee/ (*plural* **-keys**), **whis·ky** (*plural* **-kies**) *n.* **1.** ALCOHOLIC SPIRIT an alcoholic beverage made from a fermented grain, such as corn, rye, or barley, that is sometimes aged or blended **2.** DRINK OF WHISKEY a drink or measure of whiskey [Early 18thC. From Scottish Gaelic *usquebea, usque beatha,* literally "water of life," from *usque* "water" and *bethu* "life."]

WORD KEY: USAGE

whiskey or **whisky**? ***Whisky*** is the spelling used for the Scottish drink and in British English generally; ***whiskey*** is used for the drink produced in Ireland and in American English generally.

Whis·key *n.* a code word for the letter "W," used in international radio communications

whis·key jack *n.* = **gray jay** [From earlier *whiskey john,* by folk etymology from Cree *wiskatjan*]

whis·key sour *n.* a mixed drink containing whiskey, lemon juice, and sugar

whis·ky *n.* = **whiskey**

whis·per /wíspər, hwíspər/ *v.* (**-pered, -per·ing, -pers**) **1.** *vti.* BREATHE WORDS VOICELESSLY to speak or say something very softly, without using the vocal cords **2.** *vti.* SPEAK OR SUGGEST SOMETHING SECRETLY to speak or say something in a confidential or furtive manner, often to spread gossip, reveal a secret, or conspire with somebody ○ *Whisper so that no one else hears.* **3.** *vi.* RUSTLE SOFTLY to make a soft rustling sound ■ *n.* **1.** VERY LOW VOICE a soft speaking sound that uses the breath but not the vocal cords ○ *She spoke in a whisper.* **2.** SOMETHING SAID IN SOFT VOICE something said in a whisper **3.** RUSTLING SOUND a soft rustling sound **4.** FAINT HINT a hint or trace of something ○ *a whisper of perfume* **5.** RUMOR a rumor expressed confidentially or furtively ○ *Ignore the whispers of the crowd.* [Old English *hwisprian.* Ultimately from a prehistoric Germanic base, imitative of a hissing sound, which is also the ancestor of English *whistle.*] —**whis·per·er** *n.*

whis·per·ing cam·paign /wíspəring-, hwíspəring-/ *n.* the spreading of scandalous rumors in order to damage or destroy the reputation of a person or group

whis·per·ing gal·ler·y *n.* a space or gallery beneath a dome or vault in which whispers can be heard clearly in other parts of the building

whist /wist, hwist/ *n.* a card game in which two pairs of people try to take a majority of the tricks and the trump suit is determined by the last card dealt. Whist is a forerunner of bridge. [Mid-17thC. Origin uncertain: perhaps a variant of WHISK (because your cards are "whisked" away after your turn), or perhaps from *whist* in the sense "be quiet!" (because silence was expected during play).]

whis·tle /wíss'l, hwíss'l/ *v.* (**-tled, -tling, -tles**) **1.** *vi.* MAKE A SHRILL SOUND THROUGH PURSED LIPS to make a shrill or musical sound by forcing the breath through a small gap between the lips or the teeth **2.** *vi.* PRODUCE A SHRILL SOUND to produce a shrill sound or signal by forcing steam or air through a narrow opening (*refers to trains, kettles, etc.*) ○ *heard the train whistle as it came around the bend* **3.** *vi.* MOVE WITH A SHRILL SOUND to move at great speed through the air, making a shrill sound ○ *bullets whistling by overhead* **4.** *vi.* PRODUCE SOUND WHEN WIND RUSHES BY to make a sound, especially a high-pitched one, when moving through a narrow opening ○ *wind whistling through the rafters* **5.** *vt.* MAKE A MUSICAL SOUND BY WHISTLING to produce music or give a signal by whistling ○ *whistling a tune* **6.** *vti.* ISSUE A CALL OR ORDER BY WHISTLING to express a summons or order to a person or animal by whistling **7.** *vi.* EMIT A SHRILL CHARACTERISTIC CALL to make a characteristically shrill sound, using the mouth or throat or by other means (*refers to birds or animals*) ■ *n.* **1.** DEVICE PRODUCING A SHRILL SOUND a device or instrument that produces a shrill or musical sound when air or breath is forced through it **2.** WHISTLING SOUND a sound or signal made by a person, animal, or object whistling ○ *He let out a low whistle.* **3.** ACT OF WHISTLING an act of whistling [Old English *hwistlian*, from a prehistoric Germanic word meaning "to whistle, hiss" that is also the ancestor of English *whisper* and *whine*] —**whis·tling** *adj.* ◇ **blow the whistle (on somebody** *or* **something)** to report somebody for doing something wrong or illegal, especially within an organization ◇ **wet your whistle** to have a drink, especially of alcohol (*dated informal*) ◇ **whistle in the dark** to attempt to or pretend to keep up your courage when afraid

whistle for *vt.* to expect something that is not going to happen or be given (*dated informal*)

whis·tle-blow·er *n.* somebody who exposes wrongdoing, especially within an organization [From the idea of a police officer sounding the alarm when witnessing a crime] —**whis·tle-blow·ing** *n.*

whis·tle pig *n.* a woodchuck (*regional*) [From the chirping sound it makes when threatened]

whis·tler /wísslər, hwísslər/ *n.* **1.** WHISTLING PERSON OR OBJECT somebody or something that whistles **2.** RADIO RADIO DISTURBANCE an interference signal in a radio receiver, resembling a whistling sound of decreasing pitch and caused by lightning or other electromagnetic disturbance **3.** BIRDS WHISTLING AUSTRALIAN FLYCATCHER an often brightly colored Australian flycatcher with a particularly melodious whistling call. Genus: *Pachycephala.* **4.** ZOOL = **hoary marmot** **5.** VET HORSE WITH A RESPIRATORY PROBLEM a horse with a breathing defect that causes it to make a whistling noise when it breathes in [Old English *hwistlere*]

AKG London

James Abbott McNeill Whistler

Whist·ler /wísslər, hwísslər/, **James Abbott McNeill** (1834–1903) U.S. artist. Influenced by both European and Japanese art, he was renowned for his etchings, subtle landscapes, and portraits such as the one popularly known as *Whistler's Mother* (1871).

whis·tle stop *n.* **1.** SMALL RAILROAD STATION a town or railroad station where trains stop only when signaled to do so **2.** SMALL TOWN a small town or community (*slang*) **3.** SHORT STOP a short stop to make a brief public appearance, especially one made by a political candidate during an election campaign, traditionally from a train's observation car

whis·tle-stop *adj.* HAVING FREQUENT STOPS conducted very rapidly with frequent brief stops or visits, especially in order to make public appearances or deliver election speeches ○ *a whistle-stop tour of the state* ■ *vi.* (**whis·tle-stopped, whis·tle-stop·ping, whis·tle-stops**) **1.** TOUR SMALL TOWNS to make a rapid tour that features many stops in small towns **2.** MAKE A BRIEF STOP to make a short stop in a place as part of a rapid tour, especially as a political candidate

whis·tling duck *n.* a long-legged upright duck found in tropical waters. Genus: *Dendrocygna.* [From the whistling calls made by most of the ducks]

whit /wit, hwit/ *n.* used with verbs in the negative to refer to the smallest imaginable degree or amount (*dated informal*) ○ *I don't care a whit whether they succeed or fail.* [15thC. Alteration of WIGHT[1].]

white /wīt, hwīt/ *adj.* (**whit·er, whit·est**) **1.** SNOW-COLORED having the color of fresh snow or milk, which results from the reflection of nearly all light from all visible wavelengths **2.** LACKING COLOR lacking any color or hue **3. white, White** CAUCASIAN belonging to a people with naturally pale skin **4. white, White** OF CAUCASIAN PEOPLE of, for, or relating to a pale-skinned people ○ *a white problem* **5.** COMPARATIVELY LIGHT light in color in comparison with others of the same kind ○ *white cabbage* **6.** WINE MADE FROM WHITE GRAPES made from pale-skinned grapes **7.** LACKING PIGMENT used to describe hair that has lost most or all of its pigment, usually as a result of aging **8.** HAVING A VERY PALE COMPLEXION unusually pale in the face, e.g., from fright or shock **9.** ZOOL HAVING WHITE PARTS OR COLORINGS used with the names of plants or animals to indicate the presence of light or white parts or colorings ○ *white bass* **10.** FOOD, TECH WITHOUT BRAN OR GERM used to describe wheat flour that has had the bran and germ removed **11.** COOK MADE FROM WHITE FLOUR made using white flour **12.** BEVERAGES SERVED WITH MILK served with milk added **13.** UNMARKED BY WRITING not written on or printed on **14.** PURE unblemished, especially in character **15.** WEARING WHITE dressed in white or characterized by the wearing of white ○ *a white wedding* **16. white, White** HIST, POL POLITICALLY CONSERVATIVE conservative in political outlook. ◊ **red** **17.** INCANDESCENT heated to such a high degree that the substance turns white in color **18.** HAVING SNOW accompanied or characterized by the presence of snow ○ *a white Christmas* **19.** MUSIC LACKING TONAL WARMTH relating to a pure musical tone that lacks warmth, color, and resonance ■ *n.* **1.** COLORS COLOR OF SNOW the color of fresh snow or milk **2.** PAINTING WHITE PAINT a paint or dye that is or is near to the color of fresh snow **3.** WHITE OBJECT a white object, substance, or fabric, or the part of something that is white, e.g., an unprinted area on a page **4.** WHITE CLOTHING clothing that is white (*usually used in the plural*) **5. white, White** CAUCASIAN PERSON a member of a people with pale skin **6.** FOOD PART OF EGG the transparent liquid that surrounds the yolk of an egg and turns white when the egg is cooked **7.** ANAT PART OF EYE the part of the eyeball surrounding the iris **8.** ARCHERY PART OF TARGET the white outermost ring of an archery target or a shot that lands in it **9.** BOARD GAMES GAME PIECE OR PLAYER a white or light-colored piece or set of pieces in a game such as in chess or checkers, or the player using them **10.** INSECTS BUTTERFLY a butterfly that is predominantly white in color. Family: Pieridae. ■ *v.* (**whit·ed, whit·ing, whites**) **1.** *vt.* LEAVE BLANK SPACES IN to make or leave blank spaces in something, especially something printed **2.** *vti.* WHITEN to become or cause something to become white (*archaic*) [Old English *hwīt*. Ultimately from an Indo-European base meaning "to shine," which is also the ancestor of English *wheat* and *Whitsunday*.] —**white·ness** *n.* —**whit·ish** *adj.*

white out *v.* **1.** *vt.* COVER MISTAKE WITH WHITE CORRECTION FLUID to cover a mistake in written, printed, or typed material using white correction fluid **2.** *vi.* LOSE VISIBILITY to lose visibility in daylight because of snow or fog

White /wīt, hwīt/, **Byron** (*b.* 1917) U.S. Supreme Court justice. He served on the U.S. Supreme Court from 1962 to 1993. Full name **Byron Raymond White**

White, E. B. (1899–1985) U.S. writer. The author of popular essays, children's fiction, and light verse, he is best known for the children's classic *Charlotte's Web* (1952). Full name **Elwyn Brooks White**

White, Edward Douglass (1845–1921) U.S. Supreme Court justice. He was an associate justice (1894–1910) and chief justice (1910–21) of the U.S. Supreme Court.

Popperfoto

Patrick White

White, Patrick (1912–90) British-born Australian writer. His works, mainly set in Australia, include plays, poems, short stories, and novels. He won a Nobel Prize in literature in 1973. Full name **Patrick Victor Martindale White**

White, Stanford (1853–1906) U.S. architect. A specialist in adapting older styles, especially Italian Renaissance, he designed Madison Square Garden (1889) and the Washington Arch in Washington Square Park (1895), both in New York. His murder by millionaire Harry Kendall Thaw, with whose wife he was having an affair, was a social cause célèbre.

White, William Allen (1868–1944) U.S. writer and newspaper editor. The small-town paper he owned and edited, the *Emporia Gazette*, became known across the United States and enjoyed great political influence. Known as **the Sage of Emporia**

white ad·mi·ral *n.* **1.** BROWN BUTTERFLY WITH WHITE MARKS a butterfly of Europe and Asia that has brown wings with white marks. Latin name: *Limenitis camilla.* **2.** BLUISH BUTTERFLY WITH WHITE BAND a North American butterfly that has bluish-black wings with a large white band on them. Latin name: *Limenitis arthemis.*

white al·ka·li *n.* a whitish deposit of mineral salts that is sometimes seen on the surface of very alkaline soils

white ant *n.* = **termite**

white ash *n.* **1.** N AMERICAN ASH TREE a North American ash tree that has leaves with a paler silvery underside. Latin name: *Fraxinus americana.* **2.** WOOD OF THE WHITE ASH TREE the wood of the white ash tree, used especially for making oars [From the pale color of the undersides of its leaves]

white·bait /wīt bàyt, hwīt-/ (*plural* **-bait**) *n.* any small young fish fried and eaten whole, especially a young herring [Mid-18thC. *White* from the silvery color of most of the fish.]

white·bark pine /wīt baàrk-, hwīt-/ *n.* a pine tree with small purplish cones that is native to the Pacific Northwest. Latin name: *Pinus albicaulis.* [*Whitebark* from its whitish-gray bark]

white bass *n.* an edible silvery freshwater fish of the bass family, native to the Great Lakes and the Mississippi valley. Latin name: *Morone chrysops.*

white·beam /wīt bèem, hwīt-/ *n.* a deciduous tree native to Europe and Asia related to the rowan and the service trees that has leaves with pale and hairy undersides. Latin name: *Sorbus aria.* [Early 18thC. From the white undersides of its leaves.]

white bear *n.* = **polar bear**

white belt *n.* MARTIAL ARTS **1.** BEGINNER'S BELT the belt worn by a beginner in a martial art such as karate or judo **2.** BEGINNER AT MARTIAL ART a martial arts novice

white birch *n.* a birch tree with whitish or grayish bark such as the European silver birch or the North American paper birch. Genus: *Betula.*

white blood cell *n.* a common large blood cell that has no pigmentation. It helps protect the body against infection in the immune response, and also plays a role in inflammation and allergic reactions.

white·board /wīt bàwrd, hwīt-/ *n.* a board for writing on, similar to a chalkboard or blackboard but with a white plastic surface that is written on with erasable marker pens, used in teaching and in giving presentations [Mid-20thC. Formed from WHITE, on the model of *blackboard*.]

white book *n.* in some countries, an official government report published in a white binding

white bread *n.* bread made from flour that has had the bran and wheat germ removed

white-bread *adj.* (*informal*) **1.** CAUCASIAN AND MIDDLE-CLASS relating to, belonging to, or considered typical of middle-class North American Caucasians **2.** BLAND bland, conventional, and unimaginative [From the idea that white bread symbolizes something overrefined, soulless, and unexciting]

white bry·o·ny *n.* a climbing plant with lobed leaves and reddish-black berries, belonging to the gourd family and native to Europe, Asia, and North Africa. Genus: *Bryonia.* [From its greenish-white flowers]

white·cap /wīt kàp, hwīt-/ *n.* the white crest of a breaking wave

white ce·dar *n.* **1.** N AMERICAN CONIFER either of two coniferous trees of eastern North America with leaves resembling scales and light-colored durable wood. Latin name: *Chamaecyparis thyoides* and *Thuja occidentalis.* **2.** WOOD OF WHITE CEDAR TREES the wood from either white cedar, the one used in boatbuilding and the other for telephone poles [From the light color of their wood]

white cell *n.* = **white blood cell**

white chip *n.* **1.** GAMBLING **BETTING TOKEN** a betting chip with the lowest possible value **2. SOMETHING WORTHLESS** a thing of little value

white choc·o·late *n.* a cream-colored confection containing the same ingredients as chocolate but lacking cocoa powder

white Christ·mas *n.* a Christmas when there is snow, especially a Christmas day

white cloud, white cloud moun·tain fish *n.* a small brightly colored Asian freshwater fish that belongs to the minnow family and is a popular aquarium fish. Latin name: *Tanichthys albonubes.* [Mid-20thC. Named for *White Cloud*, the English name of a mountain northeast of Guangzhou (Canton), China, where the fish was discovered.]

white clo·ver *n.* a perennial Eurasian plant naturalized in North America, grown with grass as pasture for livestock. It has small white flowers that attract honey bees. Latin name: *Trifolium repens.*

white coal *n.* flowing water considered as a source of hydroelectric power

white·coat /wīt kōt, hwīt-/ *n. Can* a young harp seal, before its fine white coat has turned brown. Latin name: *Phoca groenlandica.*

white-col·lar *adj.* relating to jobs that are usually salaried and do not involve manual labor. ◊ **blue-collar, pink-collar** [From the white shirts traditionally worn by people in such jobs]

white-col·lar crime *n.* crime committed in the workplace by white-collar workers, e.g., embezzlement and fraudulent accounting practices

white cor·pus·cle *n.* = **white blood cell**

white crab *n.* = **ghost crab**

white crap·pie *n.* an edible silvery North American fish of the sunfish family that is found in muddy waters. Latin name: *Pomoxis annularis.*

white-crowned spar·row *n.* a sparrow with black-and-white bands on its head, found in western and northern North America. Latin name: *Zonotrichia leucophrys.*

white cur·rant *n.* **1. SHRUB PRODUCING EDIBLE WHITE BERRIES** a shrub of the same family as black and red currants that produces small edible white berries. Latin name: *Ribes sativum.* **2. BERRY OF WHITE CURRANT SHRUB** the edible white fruit of the white currant shrub, usually eaten raw instead of being used for jellies

whit·ed sep·ul·cher /wītəd-, hwītəd-/ *n.* a hypocrite, especially somebody who is falsely righteous or pious [From the Bible (Matthew 23:27), which compares such people to whitewashed tombs, appearing "... beautiful outward, but ... within full of dead men's bones ..."]

white dwarf *n.* a small, dim, extremely dense star that has collapsed on itself and is in the final stages of its evolution [From its color]

white el·e·phant *n.* **1. SOMETHING COSTLY TO MAINTAIN** an expensive and often rare or valuable possession whose upkeep is a considerable financial burden **2. POSSESSION OF QUESTIONABLE VALUE** something with a questionable or at least very limited value **3. CONSPICUOUS FAILED VENTURE** a much publicized or keenly anticipated venture that proves to be a spectacular flop **4. DISCARDED OBJECT** an unwanted object of possible use to somebody else (*dated*) (*hyphenated before a noun*) **5. ALBINO ELEPHANT** a rare albino Indian elephant regarded as sacred in India and in neighboring parts of Southeast Asia [Said to derive from the practice of the King of Siam of giving a white elephant to troublesome courtiers, who would be ruined by the cost of keeping the animal]

white-eye *n.* a small green or greenish-brown songbird with a ring of white feathers around the eye that is found in tropical and subtropical regions. Family: Zosteropidae.

white·face /wīt fāyss, hwīt-/ *n.* white makeup for the face, used, e.g., by clowns

white-faced *adj.* **1. HAVING AN UNUSUALLY PALE FACE** having a face that has turned pale through fear, anger, or some other strong emotion **2.** ZOOL **HAVING WHITE MARKINGS** having white markings on the face, especially when this distinguishes one species from other similar species

White·field /wīt fēeld, wīt-, hwīt-, hwīt-/, **George** (1714–70) British-born U.S. evangelist. As leader of the Calvinist Methodists, he ignited the Great Awakening religious revival of the late 1730s.

white fish *n. U.K.* any or all edible marine fish with whitish flesh, including cod, hake, and whiting, as distinct from flat fish such as plaice and oily fish such as mackerel

white·fish /wīt fish, hwīt-/ (*plural* **-fish·es** *or* **-fish**) *n.* any edible North American freshwater fish with large scales, a small mouth, and pale flesh, or its flesh used as food. Family: Coregonidae.

white flag *n.* a white cloth or improvised flag waved as an international sign of truce or surrender

white flight *n.* the exodus of white people from neighborhoods where nonwhites are settling

white·fly /wīt flī, hwīt-/ (*plural* **-flies** *or* **-fly**) *n.* a minute insect with a white waxy coating on the body. Many species suck the sap from garden and house plants. Family: Aleyrodidae.

white-foot·ed mouse *n.* a mouse with small white feet and undersides, native to North and Central America. Latin name: *Peromyscus leucopus.* ◊ **deer mouse**

white fox *n.* the Arctic fox in its white winter coat. Its coat is dark gray in summer.

white fri·ar, White Fri·ar *n.* a member of the Carmelite order of monks [From the white habits of the monks]

white gas·o·line *n.* gasoline that contains no tetraethyl lead, used especially as a fuel in stoves in the early 20th century [From the fact that it lacks the yellow color of regular gasoline]

white gold *n.* a silvery-looking gold alloy that contains gold mixed with palladium, nickel, or sometimes zinc and is typically used in jewelry

white goods *npl.* **1. HOUSEHOLD APPLIANCES** large household appliances such as refrigerators, stoves, and dishwashers, typically finished with white enamel **2. HOUSEHOLD LINEN** household goods made of fabric, e.g., bedlinens, towels, and tablecloths

white-haired *adj.* having hair that has become white with advanced age

White·hall /wīt hàwl, hwīt-/ *n.* **1. CENTRAL LONDON STREET** a street in central London, England, between Trafalgar Square and the Houses of Parliament, containing the main offices of the British civil service **2. BRITISH GOVERNMENT** a collective term for the administration and civil service departments of the British government, many of which are located in Whitehall **3. TRINIDADIAN PRIME MINISTER'S RESIDENCE** the official residence of the prime minister of Trinidad

white·head /wīt hèd, hwīt-/ *n.* a small pimple with a whitish top formed when a sebaceous gland becomes blocked. Technical name **milium** [Mid-20thC. Modeled on *blackhead*.]

White·head /wīt hed/, **Alfred North** (1861–1947) British mathematician and philosopher. He wrote *Principia Mathematica* (1910 13) with Bertrand Russell.

white-head·ed *adj.* **1. WITH WHITE MARKINGS** having white markings on the feathers, hair, or fur of the head, especially when this distinguishes one species from other similar species **2. FAVORED AND LUCKIER** favored over others and considered blessed by luck

white heat *n.* **1. VERY HIGH TEMPERATURE** an extremely high degree of heat characterized by the emission of white light **2. INTENSE EXCITEMENT** a state of intense excitement or activity

white hole *n.* a hypothetical region in space from which stars, light, and other forms of energy explosively emerge [Modeled on *black hole*]

White·horse /wīt hōwrss, hwīt-/ capital city of the Yukon Territory, Canada, located on the Yukon River, just off the Alaska Highway. Population: 21,808 (1996).

white-hot *adj.* **1. EXTREMELY HOT** so hot that white light is emitted **2. EXTREMELY EXCITED** characterized by intense excitement or activity

White House *n.* **1. OFFICIAL RESIDENCE OF U.S. PRESIDENT** the large white mansion in Washington, D.C. that is the official residence of the president of the United States. It was built between 1792 and 1800 in the classical Palladian style. **2. EXECUTIVE BRANCH OF THE U.S. GOVERNMENT** the executive branch of the U.S. government **3. RUSSIAN PARLIAMENT BUILDING** the Russian parliament building in central Moscow

Barnaby's

White House, Washington, D.C.

white hunt·er *n.* a Caucasian man hunting big game professionally or working as a safari guide, especially in Africa in former times

white knight *n.* **1. RESCUING HERO** somebody who rescues a person or situation from disaster **2.** FIN **FINANCIAL SAVIOR** a person or organization that rescues a business company, especially from an undesirable takeover

white-knuck·le, white-knuck·led *adj.* causing or characterized by fear, apprehension, nervousness, or uncertainty [From the appearance of nervously clenched fists]

white-knuck·le ride *n.* **1. TERRIFYING TIME OR EXPERIENCE** a situation, experience, or encounter that causes fear, anxiety, or uncertainty **2. FAST FAIRGOUND RIDE** a frightening or exhilarating fairground ride, especially a rollercoaster

white la·dy *n.* a cocktail made with gin, Cointreau™, and lemon juice

white lead *n.* **1. POISONOUS LEAD COMPOUND** lead carbonate in the form of a poisonous heavy white powder, used as a pigment in paints and in putty. Formula: $2PbCO_3.Pb(OH)_2$. **2. PUTTY** putty made from white lead suspended in boiled linseed oil

white leath·er *n.* soft leather treated with salt and alum for a white finish

white lie *n.* a lie perceived or intended not to harm, but told in order to avoid distress or embarrassment [From WHITE in the sense "benign"]

WORD KEY: SYNONYMS

See Synonyms at ***lie***.

white light *n.* light such as sunlight that contains all the wavelengths from red to violet at approximately equal intensity

white light·ning *n.* strong, illegally distilled alcohol, usually whiskey (*regional*) [*White* because it is usually colorless]

white line *n.* a white line along the middle or edge of a road, used to mark the edge of a road or to separate lanes of traffic, especially ones moving in opposite directions

white list *n.* a list of people, organizations, or items deemed acceptable. ◊ **blacklist** [Modeled on *blacklist*] —**white-list·ed** *adj.*

white-liv·ered *adj.* = **lily-livered** (*literary*)

white·ly /wītlee, hwītlee/ *adv.* showing a face pale with anger, fear, or shock

white mag·ic *n.* supposed magic practiced for good purposes or as an antidote to evil [Modeled on *black magic*]

White·man /hwītmən/, **Paul** (1890–1967) U.S. bandleader. He was an exponent of "sweet jazz," and became celebrated for commissioning *Rhapsody in Blue* (1924) from George Gershwin.

white man's bur·den *n.* the supposed responsibility of Europeans and their descendants to impose their allegedly advanced civilization on the non-Caucasian original inhabitants of the territories they colonized

white mar·lin *n.* a large marine fish with a light-colored belly, found in the western Atlantic. It is one of the smaller species of marlin. Latin name: *Tetrapturus albidus.*

white mat·ter *n.* the whitish nerve tissue of the brain and spinal cord, consisting mostly of myelinated nerve fibers. ◊ **gray matter**

white meat *n.* a light-colored meat, especially chicken, turkey, or pork, that is usually lower in fat than red meat, more tender, more delicate in flavor, and requires a shorter cooking time

white met·al *n.* a light-colored alloy, especially one with a high tin or lead content such as pewter or babbitt

white mi·ca *n.* = **muscovite**

White Moun·tain peak in the Sierra Nevada, east central California. Height: 14,246 ft./4,345 m.

White Moun·tains mountain range in northern New Hampshire and southwestern Maine, part of the Appalachian Mountains. The highest peak is Mount Washington, 6,288 ft./1,917 m.

white mul·ber·ry *n.* **1. CHINESE TREE** a mulberry tree of Chinese origin with edible whitish berries. Its leaves are used as food for silkworms. Latin name: *Morus alba.* **2. FRUIT OF WHITE MULBERRY TREE** the edible berry of the white mulberry tree

white mus·tard *n.* a Eurasian mustard plant with yellow flowers. Its seeds are used to make mustard and mustard oil. Latin name: *Brassica hirta.*

whit·en /wít'n, hwít'n/ (**-ened, -en·ing, -ens**) *vti.* to become or cause something to become white or lighter in color

whit·en·er /wít'nər, hwít'nər/ *n.* **1. WHITE COLORING SUBSTANCE** any substance used to color something white or enhance its whiteness, e.g., a dye for sports shoes or bleach **2. MILK SUBSTITUTE** a substance added to tea or coffee as a substitute for milk, usually in powder form and lower in calories or with a longer shelf life than milk

White Nile the section of the Nile river from near the Sudan-Uganda border to its junction with the Blue Nile at Khartoum. Length: 500 mi./805 km.

white noise *n.* low-volume electrical or radio noise of equal intensity over a wide range of frequencies [By analogy with white light, which contains light from the whole range of visible frequencies]

white oak *n.* **1. OAK WITH PALE WOOD** a variety of oak tree with evenly lobed, hairless leaves and pale-colored wood. It is native to eastern North America. Latin name: *Quercus alba.* **2.** = **roble** *n.* 1 **3. WOOD OF WHITE OAK TREE** the wood of the white oak tree (*hyphenated when used before a noun*)

white·out /wít òwt, hwít-/ *n.* **1. LOSS OF VISIBILITY** an atmospheric condition in which low clouds merge with a snow-covered landscape, greatly restricting visibility, and only darker objects are discernible **2. BLIZZARD** a blizzard that is so severe it reduces visibility to virtually zero [Mid-20thC. Modeled on BLACKOUT.]

white pag·es *npl.* the part of a telephone book that alphabetically lists names of individuals and businesses, gives their street addresses and telephone numbers, is printed on white paper, and has little or no advertising

white pa·per *n.* **1. OFFICIAL GOVERNMENT REPORT** in many countries, an official report setting out government policy on a particular issue to be voted on by the country's legislature. ◊ **green paper 2. AUTHORITATIVE REPORT** an official, authoritative, or heavily researched report on a topic, e.g., a report produced by a group of journalists [From the fact that such reports are customarily printed as white pamphlets]

white pep·per *n.* light-colored pepper made from peppercorns that have had their dark husk removed

white perch *n.* a silver-colored edible fish that is a variety of sea bass. It is found in the western Atlantic and in freshwater streams of eastern North America. Latin name: *Morone americana.*

white pine *n.* **1. N AMERICAN PINE** a fast-growing pine tree native to eastern North America that is grown for its soft durable wood. Latin name: *Pinus strobus.* **2. WOOD OF WHITE PINE TREE** the wood of the white pine tree (*hyphenated when used before a noun*) **3. SIMILAR PINE TREE** any of a number of other pines resembling the white pine, particularly in having five-needle clusters [*White* from its light-colored wood]

White Plains /wìt pláynz, hwìt-/ city in southeastern New York, northeast of Yonkers. It is a northern suburb of New York City. Population: 48,653 (1996).

white pop·lar *n.* **1. POPLAR WITH WHITE WOOLY LEAVES** a Eurasian poplar tree with white wooly leaves. Latin name: *Populus alba.* **2. WOOD OF WHITE POPLAR TREE** the straight-grained wood of the white poplar tree (*hyphenated when used before a noun*)

white po·ta·to *n.* the edible tuber of a potato with whitish flesh, or the plant that it grows on

white rat *n.* an albino variety of the brown rat, used widely in scientific research. Latin name: *Rattus norvegicus.*

white rice *n.* rice that has had both the outer husk and the bran layer removed. ◊ **brown rice**

white room *n.* = **clean room**

White Rus·sian *n.* **1. VODKA COCKTAIL** a cocktail made from vodka, coffee liqueur, and cream **2.** = **Belarusian**

whites /wits, hwits/ *npl.* **1. WHITE LAUNDRY** white or light-colored laundry, usually washed separately from colored laundry items **2. SPORTS CLOTHES** white or off-white clothing of a particular kind, especially as worn by sportspeople such as tennis players **3. WHITE DRESS MILITARY UNIFORM** the white dress uniform of a military service such as that of the U.S. Navy or Coast Guard **4.** MED **LEUKORRHEA** leukorrhea (*informal*) **5. WHITE-COLORED PRODUCTS** products such as flour, sugar, or salt that are white in color

white sale *n.* a sale of household linen

white sap·phire *n.* a colorless variety of the mineral corundum, used as a gemstone

white sauce *n.* a pale milk sauce, thickened with butter and flour or cornstarch and variously seasoned or flavored

White Sea arm of the Barents Sea, forming an indentation in the coast of northwestern Russia and partly enclosed on the north by the Kola Peninsula. Area: 36,700 sq. mi./794,500 sq. km.

white shark *n.* = **great white shark**

white slave *n.* a Caucasian girl or woman sold into prostitution against her will —**white slav·er** *n.* —**white slav·er·y** *n.*

white·smith /wít smìth, hwít-/ *n.* **1. WORKER WITH METAL** somebody who makes or repairs objects made of metal, especially tin and other white metals **2. METAL POLISHER** somebody whose job is smoothing and polishing metal articles that have been forged [14thC. Modeled on BLACKSMITH.]

white snake·root *n.* a poisonous plant native to eastern North America with heart-shaped leaves and clusters of small white flowers. Latin name: *Eupatorium rugosum.*

white space *n.* an area of a page or other printed surface where no text or pictures appear

white spruce *n.* **1. N AMERICAN SPRUCE** a North American spruce tree with short blue-green needles and non-drooping branches. Latin name: *Picea glauca.* **2. WOOD OF WHITE SPRUCE TREE** the soft wood of the white spruce tree [*White* from its silvery-brown bark]

white squall *n.* a violent tropical or subtropical storm that stirs up the surface of the sea into whitecaps, but is limited to a very localized area, often with no storm clouds present

white stork *n.* a Eurasian stork with black-and-white plumage, reddish feet, and a reddish bill. Latin name: *Ciconia ciconia.*

white stur·geon *n.* a sturgeon of the North American Pacific coast that is fished commercially and for sport. It is the largest freshwater fish in the United States. Latin name: *Acipenser transmontanus.* [*White* from its grayish-white color]

white su·prem·a·cy *n.* the view that Caucasian people are supposedly genetically and culturally superior to all other people or races and should therefore rule over them —**white su·prem·a·cist** *n.*

white-tailed deer /wít tòyl, hwít-/, **white·tail** *n.* a North American deer with a grayish or reddish-brown coat and a tail that is white on the underside. Latin name: *Odocoileus virginianus.*

white·throat /wít thròt, hwít-/ *n.* **1.** = **white-throated sparrow 2. SMALL SONGBIRD WITH WHITE THROAT** a small songbird with a white throat, native to Europe, Asia, and North Africa. Genus: *Sylvia.*

white-throat·ed spar·row *n.* a North American sparrow with a prominent white throat and black-and-white bands on its head. Latin name: *Zonotrichia albicollis.*

white tie *n.* **1. WHITE BOW TIE** a white bow tie worn as part of a man's formal evening dress. ◊ **black tie 2. MAN'S EVENING CLOTHES** a man's full formal evening clothes, consisting of a black suit with a tailcoat and a white bow tie

white-tie *adj.* requiring evening dress for women and full formal evening clothes for men, with tailcoats and white bow ties. ◊ **black-tie**

white trash *n.* an offensive term used to refer to a Caucasian person or group of Caucasian people considered as possessing the stereotypical characteristics of a member or members of a lower-income group in society (*slang offensive*)

white vit·ri·ol *n.* = **zinc sulfate**

white·wall /wít wòwl, hwít-/, **white·wall tire** *n.* a vehicle tire with a band of white on the outside sidewall

white wal·nut *n.* = **butternut** [*White* from the fact that its wood is lighter in color than that of the black walnut]

white·wash /wít wòsh, hwít-/ *n.* **1. WHITE PAINTING SOLUTION** lime suspended in water, often with glue or sizing, and used like paint for whitening walls **2. COVERUP** a coordinated attempt to hide unpleasant facts, especially in a political context (*informal*) **3. THOROUGH DEFEAT** a resounding defeat, especially one in which the losing player or team does not score at all (*informal*) ■ *v.* (**-washed, -wash·ing, -wash·es**) **1.** *vt.* **PAINT SOMETHING WITH WHITEWASH** to paint something, usually a wall, with whitewash **2.** *vti.* **HIDE TRUTH ABOUT** to conceal the unpleasant facts about something **3.** *vt.* **DEFEAT SOMEBODY DECISIVELY** to defeat an opposing player or team resoundingly, especially by preventing the player or team from scoring at all —**white·wash·er** *n.* —**white·wash·ing** *n.*

white wa·ter *n.* **1. FAST-FLOWING WATER** fast-flowing water with a foamy, choppy surface (*hyphenated when used before a noun*) **2. SHALLOW WATER** lighter-colored sea water visible in shallow areas

white wed·ding *n.* a wedding that takes place in a Christian church, with the bride wearing a traditional white dress

white whale *n.* a small white fish-eating whale with a bulbous head that lives mainly in Arctic waters. Latin name: *Delphinapterus leucas.*

white-winged dove *n.* a dove with white patches on its wings, native to the southern United States and Mexico. Latin name: *Zenaida asiatica.*

white-winged sco·ter *n.* a North American sea duck that is mostly black with a white patch on each wing. Latin name: *Melanitta fusca.*

white witch *n.* a witch whose supposed magic is designed to do good or to counter evil magic [*White* because such a witch practices white magic]

white·wood /wít wòod, hwít-/ *n.* **1. TREE WITH LIGHT WOOD** a deciduous tree such as the tulip tree, the cottonwood, or the basswood, with pale-colored wood **2. WOOD OF WHITEWOOD TREE** the wood of a whitewood tree

whit·ey /wítee, hwítee/ (*plural* **-eys**), **whit·y** (*plural* **-ies**) *n.* an offensive term used to refer contemptuously to a white person (*slang offensive*)

whith·er /wíthər, hwíthər/ *adv.* **1. TO WHAT PLACE** to what place (*archaic or literary*) **2. INTO WHAT STATE** to what state, condition, outcome, or degree (*literary or humorous*) [Old English *hwider*, from a prehistoric Germanic base that is also the ancestor of English *who*, *when*, and *where* (see WHO)]

whith·er·so·ev·er /wìthər sō évvər, hwìthər-/ *adv.* to whatever place, or to any place whatever (*archaic*)

whith·er·ward /wíthərwərd, hwíthər-/, **whith·er·wards** /wíthərwərdz, hwíthər-/ *adv.* to what place or in what direction (*archaic*)

whit·ing[1] /wíting, hwíting/ (*plural* **-ing**) *n.* **1. EUROPEAN**

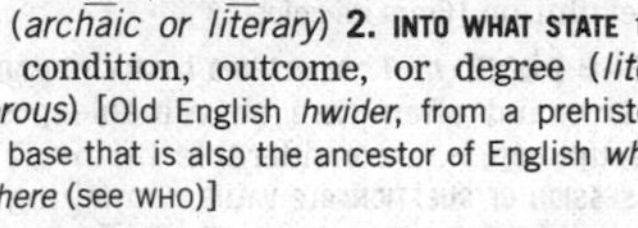

Whiting

FISH a small edible European sea fish related to the cod, with a silvery underside and white flesh. It is an important commercial food fish throughout Europe. Latin name: *Merlangus merlangus.* **2. PACIFIC AND ATLANTIC FISH** a commercially important Pacific and Atlantic fish such as the American silver hake or corbina similar to the European whiting. Genera: *Merluccius* and *Menticirrhus.* [15thC. From Dutch *wijting,* from *wijt* "white."]

whit·ing[2] /wíting, hwíting/ *n.* pure powdered chalk used as an ingredient in various commercial preparations such as putty and whitewash [15thC. Formed from WHITE.]

whit·low /wítlō, hwítlō/ *n.* a pus-filled infection on the skin at the side of a fingernail or toenail [14thC. Alteration of earlier *whitflawe,* from WHITE (of uncertain origin: possibly from Middle Dutch *vijt* "abscess") + FLAW.]

Library of Congress

Walt Whitman

Whit·man /wít mən, hwítmən/, **Walt** (1819–92) U.S. poet and essayist. He is known for his free verse, best exemplified in the stylistically revolutionary collection *Leaves of Grass* (1855–89). Real name **Walter Whitman**

Whit·mon·day *n.* the Monday after Whitsunday, an official holiday in England, Ireland and Wales [Modeled on WHITSUNDAY]

Whit·ney, Mount /wítnee, hwít-/ mountain in eastern California, a peak of the Sierra Nevada. Height: 14,494 ft./4,418 m.

Whit·ney /wítnee, hwítnee/, **Eli** (1765–1825) U.S. inventor. His cotton gin, a machine for separating the seeds from the fiber of the cotton plant, revolutionized the cotton industry.

Whit·sun /wíts'n, hwíts'n/ *adj.* relating to or happening on Whitsuntide or Whitsunday [13thC. Back-formation from WHITSUNDAY, understood as "Whitsun day."]

Whit·sun·day /wít sùndee, -day, hwít-/ *n.* = **Pentecost** [Old English *hwīta sunnandæg* "white Sunday," because of the white robes the priests wear on this day]

Whit·sun·tide /wíts'n tīd, hwíts'n-/ *n.* the days around and including Whitsunday [13thC. From WHITSUN + TIDE in the obsolete sense of "period of time."]

Whit·ta·ker /wíttəkər, hwít-/, **Charles Evans** (1901–73) U.S. Supreme Court justice. He served as an associate justice on the U.S. Supreme Court (1957–62).

Whit·tier /wíttee ər, hwíttee-/, **John Greenleaf** (1807–92) U.S. poet and abolitionist. His strong Quaker beliefs, which underlie his poetry, prompted him to oppose slavery.

whit·tle /wítt'l, hwítt'l/ (**-tled, -tling, -tles**) *vti.* to carve something out of wood, usually something small enough to hold in the hand, by cutting away small pieces of wood [Mid-16thC. From *whyttel* "knife," a variant of *thwitel,* literally "tool for paring," ultimately from Old English *þwītan* "to pare, cut."] —**whit·tler** *n.* —**whit·tling** *n.*

whittle away *vt.* to deplete something by using or spending a little of it at a time

whittle down *vt.* to reduce or diminish something gradually by taking away a little of it at a time

whit·tlings /wíttlingz, hwíttlingz/ *npl.* pieces of wood that have been whittled off a larger piece and discarded

whit·y (*plural* **-ies**) *n.* = **whitey**

whiz /wiz, hwiz/, **whizz** *v.* (**whizzed, whiz·zing, whiz·zes**) **1.** *vi.* **HUM** to make a humming, hissing, or buzzing noise **2.** *vti.* **MOVE WITH A HUMMING NOISE** to move swiftly with a humming, hissing, or buzzing noise, or to cause something to move in this way ○ *bullets whizzing past* **3.** *vi.* **MOVE QUICKLY** to move or travel somewhere rapidly ○ *whizz down to the store* **4.** *vt.* **THROW SOMETHING** to throw something, especially with a spin, or cause something to move and rotate (*informal*) ○ *He whizzed the ball right past the catcher.* **5.** *vi.* **OFFENSIVE TERM** an offensive term meaning to urinate (*slang*) ■ *n.* (*plural* **whiz·zes**) **1. HUMMING SOUND** a humming, hissing, or buzzing sound **2. whiz, whizz, wiz** (*plural* **wiz·zes**) **EXPERT** somebody who is very skilled in a particular field (*informal*) ○ *a computer whiz* **3. FAST MOVEMENT** a fast movement, often accompanied by a humming, hissing, or buzzing sound **4. OFFENSIVE TERM** an offensive term used to refer to an act of urinating (*slang*) [Mid-16thC. An imitation of the sound.]

whiz-bang, whizz-bang *n.* (*informal*) **1. SOMEBODY OR SOMETHING EXCELLENT** somebody or something that is outstandingly successful or effective, loud, or fast **2. ARMS ARTILLERY SHELL** a lightweight artillery shell used in World War I ■ *adj.* **EXCELLENT, FAST, OR LOUD** outstandingly successful or effective, loud, or fast (*informal*) ○ *a whiz-bang presentation*

whiz kid, whizz kid, wiz kid *n.* a young and exceptionally talented and successful person in a given field (*informal*) [Possibly an alteration of Quiz Kid, a contestant on an early radio quiz program]

who /hoo/ *pron.* **1. INTRODUCES A QUESTION** used to introduce a question asking about the name or identity of a person or people ○ *Who's that at the door?* ○ *Who did you see there?* **2. INTRODUCES A RELATIVE CLAUSE** used to introduce a relative clause giving information about a person or people ○ *meals for people who are too busy to cook* [Old English *hwā.* Ultimately from an Indo-European base meaning "who, what" that is also the ancestor of English *what, how, quote,* and *quantity.*]

WORD KEY: USAGE

See Usage note at ***whom.***

WHO *abbr.* World Health Organization

whoa /wō, hwō/ *interj.* used to order an animal, or humorously, a person, to stop [Mid-19thC. Variant of HO.]

who'd /hood/ *contr.* **1.** who had **2.** who would [Mid-17thC]

who·dun·it /hoo dúnnit/, **who·dun·nit** *n.* a novel, movie, or play centering on the solving of a crime, usually a murder [Mid-20thC. Alteration of "who done it?".]

who·ev·er /hoo évvər/ *pron.* **1. INTRODUCES AN EMPHATIC QUESTION** used to introduce an emphatic question indicating surprise or disbelief ○ *Whoever would do such a thing?* **2. ANY PERSON WHO** used to indicate a person or people whose identity is not known ○ *Whoever takes over from her will have difficult decisions to make.* ■ *conj.* **NO MATTER WHO** used to indicate a person or people whose identity is not important ○ *You can bring whoever you like to the party.*

WORD KEY: USAGE

whoever or **whomever**? ***Whoever*** is a relative pronoun used in statements or commands: *Whoever made this has done a good job. Ask whoever you like.* The objective case ***whomever,*** though strictly correct in the last example, is falling out of use just as ***whom*** is and ***whoever*** is generally considered acceptable.

whole /hōl/ *adj.* **1. ENTIRE** complete, including all parts or aspects, with nothing left out **2. UNDIVIDED** not divided into parts or not regarded as consisting of separate elements **3. RELATING TO DURATION OR EXTENT** relating to or representing the full duration or extent of something ○ *stayed up the whole night* **4. UNBROKEN** not damaged or broken ○ *not a single item of furniture left whole* **5. UNIMPAIRED** not wounded, impaired, or incapacitated ○ *no longer a whole man* **6. HEALED OR HEALTHY** healed or restored to health physically or psychologically ○ *made him whole again* **7. HAVING COMMON PARENTS** having both parents in common with your siblings ○ *a whole sister* **8. NOT FRACTIONAL** containing no fractions or decimals ■ *adv.* **1. AS A SINGLE PIECE** in a single piece rather than in several pieces ○ *Many snakes swallow their food whole.* **2. COMPLETELY** completely and in every way (*informal*) ○ *a whole different approach* ■ *n.* **1. SOMETHING COMPLETE** something that is complete and has no parts missing **2. SINGLE ENTITY OR UNIT** something regarded as a single and complete unit or entity, as opposed to a set of components [Old English *hāl* (source of English *hale*). Ultimately from an Indo-European word meaning "sound, propitious."] ◇ **as a whole** as a single and complete entity ◇ **a whole lot** very much or a great deal (*informal*) ◇ **on the whole 1.** as a rule or in general **2.** taking all relevant factors into account

WORD KEY: ORIGIN

The prehistoric Germanic precursor of ***whole*** is also the source of English *hail, hallow, heal, health,* and *holy.*

whole cloth *n.* complete fiction or fabrication ○ *an explanation made out of whole cloth* [From the sense "untrimmed cloth as it comes directly from the manufacturer." The underlying meaning is "cut from new material, in any shape you please."]

whole·food /hṓl fòod/ *n. U.K.* food that has undergone very little processing and has been grown or produced without the use of synthetic pesticides or fertilizers

whole gale *n.* a wind of force 10 on the Beaufort scale, travelling at 55 to 63 mi./87 to 102 km per hour and capable of causing considerable structural damage

whole·heart·ed /hòl haártəd/ *adj.* characterized by enthusiasm, passion, or commitment —**whole·heart·ed·ly** *adv.* —**whole·heart·ed·ness** *n.*

whole hog *adv.* in every way or to the fullest extent (*informal*) [Origin uncertain: perhaps from HOG in the archaic sense "shilling," thus "to spend the whole shilling all at once"]

whole·meal /hṓl meel/ *adj. U.K.* = **whole-wheat** [Early 17thC]

whole milk *n.* cow's milk from which no fat has been removed

whole note *n.* the longest musical note in common use, equal in length to four quarter notes or two half notes. It is written as an open note-head with no stem or tail. [*Whole* from the fact that it lasts for one full measure]

whole num·ber *n.* a positive or negative number, including zero, that does not contain a fraction or decimal

whole·sale /hṓl sàyl/ *n.* **TRADE IN QUANTITY** the business of buying and selling goods in quantity at discounted prices, usually direct from manufacturers or distributors, in order to sell them on to the consumer ■ *adj.* **1. OF TRADE IN QUANTITY** relating to the buying and selling of goods in quantity at discounted prices **2. DONE ON LARGE SCALE** done on a large scale and indiscriminately ■ *adv.* **1. IN BULK** on a large scale and at a discounted price **2. INDISCRIMINATELY** as a whole, without exercising any judgment or taking individual cases into account ■ *v.* (**-saled, -sal·ing, -sales**) **1.** *vti.* **BUY OR SELL GOODS WHOLESALE** to buy or sell goods in large quantities at a discounted price, especially selling to retailers, instead of direct to the consumer, or to be bought or sold in this way **2.** *vi.* **TO BE SOLD WHOLESALE** to participate in selling things wholesale, or to be sold in such a way [15thC. From the phrase "by whole sale," that is, sold in a single lot for redistribution at retail.] —**whole·sal·er** *n.*

whole·some /hṓlsəm/ *adj.* **1. HEALTH-GIVING** beneficial to physical health, usually by virtue of being fresh and naturally produced **2. MORALLY BENEFICIAL** leading to or promoting improved moral well-being **3. SENSIBLE** based on openness, honesty, and common sense **4. HEALTHY AND FIT** having a fit, healthy appearance that suggests clean living [Assumed Old English *hālsum*] —**whole·some·ly** *adv.* —**whole·some·ness** *n.*

whole step *n.* a musical interval consisting of two half steps, such as exists between the notes D and E or A and B

whole-wheat *adj.* **1. NOT HAVING HAD BRAN REMOVED** not having had the bran and wheatgerm taken out **2. MADE WITH WHOLE-WHEAT FLOUR** made using whole-wheat flour

who'll /hool/ *contr.* **1.** who shall **2.** who will

whol·ly /hṓlee, hṓl lee/ *adv.* **1. COMPLETELY AND ENTIRELY** totally and in every way or to the fullest extent **2. SOLELY AND EXCLUSIVELY** solely and to the exclusion of all other things

whom /hoom/ *pron.* (*formal*) **1. INTRODUCES A QUESTION** used to introduce a question asking about the name or identity of a person or people ○ *Whom did you expect to see?* **2. INTRODUCES A RELATIVE CLAUSE** used to introduce a relative clause giving information about a person or people ○ *Birch and her colleagues studied 162 infants, none of whom were born prematurely.* [Old

English *hwæm*, from a prehistoric Germanic word that is also the ancestor of English *who*]

WORD KEY: USAGE

who or **whom**? Although ***whom*** is the correct form when it is the object of a verb or preposition, it has fallen into disuse in many contexts, and constructions with ***who*** are taking its place. A sentence of the type *Do you remember whom you saw?* would be expressed as *Do you remember who you saw?*, and *The man to whom I was talking* as *The man I was talking to* (often with ellipsis of the relative pronoun, as in the last example). Note that ***whom*** is incorrectly used in sentences of the type *The woman whom we thought was dead is still alive*, since the relative pronoun is the subject of *was* (not *is*) and not the object of *thought*.

whom·ev·er /hoom év̇vər/ *pron.* a formal word for "whoever" when used as the object of a verb or preposition (*formal*)

WORD KEY: USAGE

See Usage note at ***whoever***.

whomp /womp, hwomp/ *v.* (**whomped, whomp·ing, whomps**) **1.** *vti.* **STRIKE** to hit somebody or something with great force, especially noisily **2.** *vt.* **DEFEAT SOMEBODY** to subject somebody to a crushing defeat (*informal*) ■ *n.* **BLOW OR NOISE OF BLOW** a heavy blow or the loud deep sound it makes [Early 20thC. An imitation of the sound.]

whomp up *vt.* to arouse, incite, or stir up interest or enthusiasm (*archaic*)

whom·so·ev·er /hoom sō évvər/ *pron.* an emphatic form of "whomever" (*formal*)

whoop /hoop, whoop/ *v.* (**whooped, whoop·ing, whoops**) **1.** *vi.* **CRY OUT** to make a loud howling cry of excitement or joy **2.** *vt.* **EXCLAIM SOMETHING** to exclaim something loudly and with great excitement **3.** *vt.* **URGE OR DRIVE SOMEBODY FORWARD** to urge somebody on, chase after somebody, or drive a person or animal forward with a whooping call **4.** *vi.* MED **WHEEZE** to breathe in with the sharp wheezing sound associated with whooping cough ■ *n.* **1. LOUD CRY** a loud howling cry of excitement or joy **2. BATTLE CRY** a cry uttered before a battle or hunt, by a warrior, soldier, or hunter **3. CALL MADE BY BIRD OR ANIMAL** a loud call or hoot, e.g., from a bird or animal **4.** MED **WHEEZING SOUND** a sharply wheezing inhalation associated with whooping cough [14thC. Ultimately an imitation of the sound.] ◇ **whoop it up 1.** to have fun or celebrate in an extravagant or noisy way (*informal*) **2.** to express and try to arouse enthusiasm for somebody or something (*informal*)

whoop-de-do /ho͝op di do͞o, hwo͝op-/, **whoop-de-doo** *n.* (*informal*) **1. PARTY** a large-scale party or celebration that is lively or noisy **2. PUBLICITY** noisy activity meant to attract attention ○ *the whoop-de-do surrounding the movie's release* **3. FUSS** a noisy public commotion or outcry ■ *interj.* **EXPRESSING EXCITEMENT** used to express excitement (*informal*) (*often used ironically*) [Mid-20thC. Expressive alteration of WHOOP, perhaps under the influence of TO-DO.]

whoop·ee /wo͝oppee, wo͝oppee, hwo͝oppee, hwo͝opee/ *interj.* used to express great and sudden excitement (*informal*) (*often used ironically*) [Mid-19thC. Alteration of WHOOP.] ◇ **make whoopee 1.** to celebrate noisily and exuberantly (*dated informal*) **2.** to engage in sexual activity (*dated informal*)

whoop·ee cush·ion *n.* a practical joker's toy in the form of an inflatable cushion with a small opening, designed to make a noise resembling flatulence when somebody sits on it

whoop·er /hoopər, hwo͝opər/ *n.* **1.** = **whooping crane 2.** = **whooper swan**

whoop·er swan *n.* a large white Eurasian swan with a yellow and black bill, straight neck, and loud whooping cry in flight. Latin name: *Cygnus cygnus.*

whoop·ing cough /hooping-, hwo͝oping-/ *n.* an infectious bacterial disease that causes violent coughing spasms followed by sharp, shrill inhalation. It affects children particularly. Latin name: *Bordetella pertussis.* Technical name **pertussis**

whoop·ing crane *n.* a large white North American crane with black wingtips that makes a loud whooping cry in flight and is now an endangered species. Latin name: *Grus americana.*

whoops /hoops, hwoops/, **woops** *interj.* used to express surprise, concern, or embarrassment at making a mistake or having a slight accident [Mid-20thC. Origin uncertain: possibly a variant of OOPS.]

whoosh /woosh, hwoosh/ *n.* **1. NOISE OF RUSHING AIR OR WATER** the sound made by rushing air or rushing water **2. SWIFT MOTION OR RUSH** a swift motion, spurt, or rush ■ *vi.* (**whooshed, whoosh·ing, whoosh·es**) **1. MAKE RUSHING SOUND** to make the sound of rushing air or rushing water **2. MOVE FAST** to move rapidly, with a whooshing sound ○ *whooshed into the room* [Mid-19thC. An imitation of the sound.]

whop /wop, hwop/, **whap** *vt.* (**whopped, whop·ping, whops; whapped, whap·ping, whaps**) (*informal*) **1. HIT SOMEBODY OR SOMETHING** to strike somebody or something forcefully **2. DEFEAT SOMEBODY DECISIVELY** to subject an opponent to a crushing defeat ■ *n.* **BLOW OR NOISE OF BLOW** a heavy blow or the loud dull sound it makes [14thC. Variant of *wap* "to strike, slap," also "a blow," of unknown origin.]

whop·per /wóppər, hwóppər/ *n.* (*informal*) **1. SOMETHING BIG** something that is much bigger than others of its kind **2. BIG LIE** a blatant and outrageous lie [Late 18thC. Formed from WHOPPING.]

whop·ping /wópping, hwópping/ *adj.* **BIG** very big or great (*informal*) ■ *adv.* **VERY** extremely (*informal*) [Early 18thC. Formed from WHOP.]

whore /hawr/ *n.* **1. OFFENSIVE TERM** an offensive term used to refer to a prostitute (*offensive*) **2. OFFENSIVE TERM** an offensive term used to refer to somebody regarded as being sexually indiscriminate (*taboo insult offensive*) **3. OFFENSIVE TERM** an offensive term used to refer to somebody who is regarded as willingly setting aside principles or personal integrity in order to obtain something, usually for selfish motives (*insult offensive*) ■ *vi.* (**whored, whor·ing, whores**) (*offensive*) **1. OFFENSIVE TERM** an offensive term meaning to work as a prostitute **2. OFFENSIVE TERM** an offensive term meaning to be a regular customer of prostitutes [Old English *hōre*. Ultimately from an Indo-European base meaning "to desire" that is also the ancestor of English *cherish, caress,* and *Kama Sutra.*]

whore after *vt.* an offensive term meaning to pursue something desperately, making whatever sacrifices of principles or personal integrity are necessary (*offensive*)

whore·dom /háwrdəm/ *n.* **1. OFFENSIVE TERM** an offensive term used to refer to the state, status, or job of a prostitute (*literary offensive*) **2.** BIBLE **IDOLATRY** the worship of idols (*literary*) [12thC. Origin uncertain: either formed from WHORE, or from Old Norse *hórdómr.*]

whore·house /háwr hòwss/ (*plural* **-hous·es** /-hòwzəz/) *n.* an offensive term used to refer to a brothel or other place of prostitution (*informal offensive*)

whore·mon·ger /háwr mùnggər, -mònggər/ *n.* an offensive term used to refer to a sexually indiscriminate man, especially one who frequents prostitutes (*archaic insult offensive*) —**whore·mon·ger·y** *n.*

whore·son /háwrss'n/ *n.* (*archaic insult offensive*) **1. OFFENSIVE TERM** an offensive term used to refer to a boy or man whose paternity is unknown or has not been established **2. OFFENSIVE TERM** an offensive term used to refer to a man regarded as dishonest, treacherous, or otherwise disreputable ■ *adj.* **OFFENSIVE TERM** an offensive term meaning contemptible or loathsome (*archaic offensive*) [14thC. Translation of Anglo-Norman *fiz a putain.*]

Whorf hy·poth·e·sis *n.* = **Sapir-Whorf hypothesis**

whor·ish /háwrish/ *adj.* (*offensive*) **1. OFFENSIVE TERM** an offensive term used to refer to traits of character or behavior stereotypically ascribed to prostitutes **2. OFFENSIVE TERM** an offensive term meaning relating to prostitutes or prostitution —**whor·ish·ly** *adv.* —**whor·ish·ness** *n.*

whorl /wawrl, wurl, hwawrl, hwurl/ *n.* **1. SOMETHING SPIRAL-SHAPED** something in the shape of a spiral, coil, or curl **2.** ANAT, CRIMINOL **PATTERN ON FINGER OR IN FINGERPRINT** a series of concentric circular or elliptical ridges in the pattern of lines on the gripping surface of a finger or thumb, or this shape seen in a fingerprint **3.** BOT **CIRCLE OF PLANT PARTS** a circular arrangement of three or more leaves, petals, or other plant parts arising at the same level on a stem or other axis, like spokes on a wheel **4.** ZOOL **SPIRAL IN SHELL** any of the turns or coils of a mollusk's shell [15thC. Alteration of WHIRL under the influence of *wharve* "spindle-whorl" (from the same prehistoric Germanic base as *whirl*).]

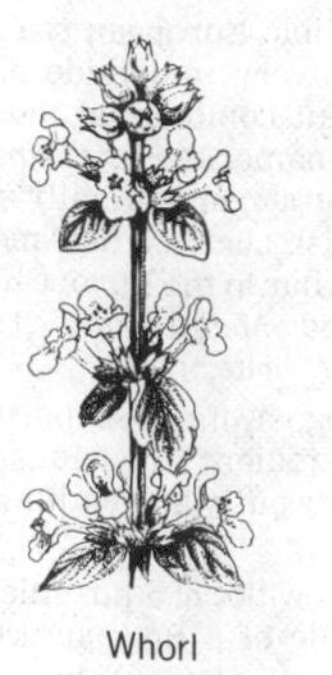

Whorl

whorled /wawrld, wurld, hwawrld, hwurld/ *adj.* in the shape of a whorl or having a pattern of whorls

whor·tle·ber·ry /wúrt'l bèrree, hwúrt'l bèrree/ (*plural* **-ries**) *n.* **1. PLANT WITH EDIBLE BERRIES** a low-growing European plant of the heather family, found in heathland and mountainous areas. It has greenish-pink flowers and tiny sweet blue-black edible fruit. Latin name: *Vaccinium myrtillus.* **2. PLANT RELATED TO THE WHORTLEBERRY** any of several plants related to the whortleberry that have edible berries, e.g., the blueberry **3.** FOOD **BERRY OF WHORTLEBERRY PLANT** the edible blue-black fruit of any whortleberry plant [Late 16thC. Dialect variant of *hurtleberry.*]

who's /hooz/ *contr.* **1.** who is **2.** who has

WORD KEY: USAGE

See Usage note at ***whose***.

whose /hooz/ *pron., adj.* a grammatical word used to talk or ask about the person or thing something belongs to ○ *Whose are these boots?* ○ *"It wasn't my idea." – "Well, whose was it then?"* ○ *a theatre whose doors will always be open to such a talented performer* ○ *Whose car shall we use?* ○ *He wanted to know whose the scarf was.* [Old English *hwæs*, the genitive of the pronouns *hwa* (masculine) "who" (see WHO) and *hwæt* (neuter) "what" (see WHAT). Influenced in Middle English by *who* and *whom.*]

WORD KEY: USAGE

whose or **who's**? ***Whose*** means "of whom" or "of which" and denotes possession or association: *These are the children whose father we saw yesterday. There was a church whose steeple had been struck by lightning.* (Some people dislike the use of ***whose*** to mean "of which," but it is a well established use and the alternatives are usually awkward.) ***Who's*** is a contraction of *who is* or *who has*: *She's the one who's coming to dinner next week. Who's got my pen?*

who·so·ev·er /hoosso év̇vər/ *pron., adj.* whoever (*literary or archaic*) [12thC]

who's who *n.* a list of or guide to the most important people in a place or field of activity ○ *The guest list to her party reads like a who's who in the publishing world.*

Who's Who *tdmk.* a trademark for a reference work giving brief biographical sketches for notable people

WH-ques·tion *n.* a question that starts with *who, what, where, when, why,* or *how.* It cannot be answered by "yes" or "no."

whs. *abbr.* warehouse

whsle. *abbr.* wholesale

whump /wump, hwump/ *n.* **MUFFLED SOUND** the sound of a dull thump or muffled explosion ■ *vti.* (**whumped, whump·ing, whumps**) **THUMP** to make the sound of a dull thump or muffled explosion, or to hit somebody or something with such a sound [Late 19thC. An imitation of the sound.]

whup /wup, wo͝op, hwup, hwo͝op/ (**whupped, whup·ping, whups**) *vt.* **1. DEFEAT SOMEBODY** to subject an opponent to a crushing defeat (*informal*) **2.** *Southern U.S.* **WHIP SOMEBODY** to beat somebody with a whip [Late 19thC. Dialect variant of WHIP; from Scots dialect.]

why /wī, hwī/ CORE MEANING: an adverb used to ask or talk about the reason, purpose, or cause of something ○ *Why didn't you call?* ○ *I wish you'd tell me why you're so unhappy.* ○ *He could not say why he'd done it.* ○ *It seems clear to me why.*

1. *adv.* **BECAUSE OF** for or on account of which ○ *There's* *no reason why you shouldn't go.* **2.** *interj.* EXCLAMATION an exclamation used to express surprise, shock, or indignation ○ *Why, John, how could you!* [Old English *hwȳ,* the instrumental case form of *hwæt* "what" (see WHAT)] ◇ **why not** used to express agreement with a suggestion or proposed course of action ○ *"Would you like another coffee?" – "Why not?"*

Why·al·la /wī állə/ city and port on the Spencer Gulf in South Australia. It is a center of iron and steel production. Population: 23,382 (1996).

whyd·ah /wíddə, hwíddə/ (*plural* **-ah** *or* **-ahs**), **whid·ah** (*plural* **-ahs** *or* **-ah**) *n.* an African weaverbird the male of which has long black tail feathers during the breeding season. Genus: *Vidua.* [Late 18thC. Named for *Ouidah,* a West African town where the bird is found. Perhaps influenced by WIDOW, because of the black coloration of the males.]

whys and where·fores *n.* all the reasons and explanations for something ○ *Without going into all the whys and wherefores, let's just say the wedding's off.*

WI *abbr.* Wisconsin

W.I. *abbr.* **1.** West Indian **2.** West Indies

WIA *n., abbr.* wounded in action

Wic·ca /wíkə/ *n.* religious practice involving nature-worship and witchcraft [Mid-20thC. A deliberate revival of Old English *wicca* (see WITCH).]

Wic·can /wíkən/ *n.* somebody who practices Wicca —**Wic·can** *adj.*

Wich·i·ta[1] /wíchi tàw/ (*plural* **-ta** *or* **-tas**) *n.* PEOPLES a member of a Native North American people that originally lived in lands that are now in Kansas, Oklahoma, and Texas. Its members now live mainly in Oklahoma. [Mid-19thC. From Caddo.]

Wich·i·ta[2] /wíchi tàw/ city in south central Kansas, on the Arkansas River, southwest of Emporia. Population: 320,395 (1996).

wick /wik/ *n.* **1.** MATERIAL HOLDING FUEL THAT BURNS a string or piece of fabric that uses capillary action to draw the fuel to the flame in a candle, oil lamp, or cigarette lighter **2.** MED MATERIAL THAT DRAWS UP LIQUID any piece of material that draws liquid up by capillary action, e.g., a strip of gauze put into a wound to drain it ■ *vti.* (**wicked, wick·ing, wicks**) MOVE LIQUID BY CAPILLARY ACTION to take in or transfer liquid by capillary action, or to be taken in or transferred in this way ○ *synthetic materials that wick moisture away from the skin* [Old English *wēoc.* The word has relatives in Dutch and German, but is of unknown origin.]

wick·ed /wíkid/ *adj.* **1.** VERY BAD very wrong or very bad **2.** MISCHIEVOUS liking to tease people playfully or cause them slight trouble, but without upsetting them seriously ○ *a wicked sense of humor* **3.** MEAN liking to say very unpleasant things to people ○ *She has a really wicked tongue sometimes!* **4.** VERY GOOD very impressive or very skillful (*slang*) ○ *He plays a wicked game of tennis.* **5.** DANGEROUS capable of causing harm to somebody ○ *a knife with a wicked blade* **6.** DISTRESSING causing discomfort, distress, or disappointment (*informal*) ○ *I've got a wicked headache.* **7.** DISGUSTING tasting or smelling disgusting and repulsive ■ *npl.* BAD PEOPLE people who do very bad things [13thC] —**wick·ed·ly** *adv.* —**wick·ed·ness** *n.*

wick·er /wíkər/ *n.* **1.** = **wickerwork** *n.* 1 **2.** TWIG, CANE, OR REED any one of the twigs, canes, or reeds woven together to make such things as baskets or chairs **3.** SOMETHING MADE OF WICKER something such as a basket made of twigs, canes, or reeds [14thC. From Scandinavian. Ultimately from an Indo-European base meaning "to bend" that is also the ancestor of English *weak* and *vicar.*]

wick·er·work /wíkər wùrk/ *n.* **1.** WOVEN TWIGS, CANES, OR REEDS thin twigs, canes, or reeds woven together to make objects such as baskets and chairs **2.** THINGS MADE OF WICKER objects such as baskets and chairs made by weaving together thin twigs, canes, or reeds

wick·et /wíkit/ *n.* **1.** SMALL DOOR OR GATE a small door or gate, especially one close to or forming part of a larger one **2.** SMALL OPENING FOR COMMUNICATION a small opening or window in a wall or door through which people can communicate. Wickets are often fitted with glass, a grating, or a sliding panel. **3.** ENG GATE CONTROLLING WATER FLOW a gate used to control the flow of water at a lock or water wheel **4.** SPORTS CROQUET HOOP any of the hoops through which the ball is hit in croquet **5.** CRICKET UPRIGHT STICKS DEFENDED BY CRICKET BATSMAN in cricket, either of two sets of three upright sticks (**stumps**) on which are balanced two shorter sticks (**bails**) and in front of which the batsman or batswoman stands **6.** CRICKET PART OF CRICKET PITCH the part of a cricket pitch between the two sets of stumps, which are placed 22 yd./20 m apart **7.** CRICKET TURN OF BATTING in cricket, a batsman's or batswoman's turn of batting, or that of a pair of batsmen or batswomen **8.** CRICKET ENDING OF TURN OF BATTING in cricket, the ending of somebody's turn of batting, e.g., by knocking down the stumps or catching the ball [13thC. Via Old Northern French *wiket,* from prehistoric Germanic. Ultimately from an Indo-European word meaning "to bend" (see WICKER).]

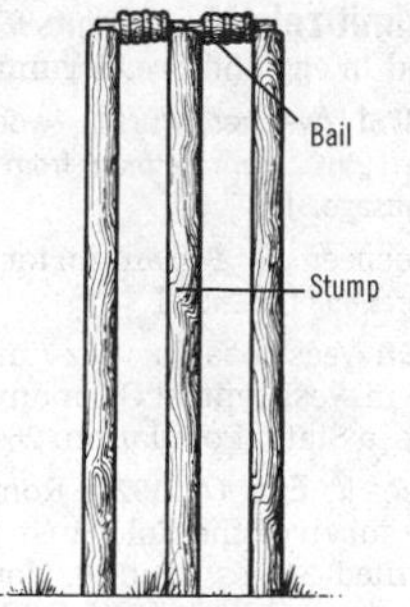

Wicket

wick·et·keep·er /wíkit keèpər/ *n.* in cricket, the player positioned behind the wicket to catch the ball or knock the bails off the stumps

wick·ing /wíking/ *n.* INDUST material used to make wicks

wick·i·up /wíkee ùp/, **wik·i·up** *n.* a hut made by Native North Americans of the southwestern United States by covering a framework of arched poles with mats of bark, grass, or branches [Mid-19thC. From Fox *wikiapi.* Ultimately from the same prehistoric Algonquian base as WIGWAM.]

Wick·low Moun·tains /wíklō-/ mountain range in Wicklow County, on the eastern coast of the Republic of Ireland. The highest point is Lugnaquill, 3,039 ft./926 m.

wick·y /wíkee/ (*plural* **-ies**) *n.* = **sheep laurel**

wic·o·py /wíkəpee/ (*plural* **-pies**) *n.* = **leatherwood** [Late 18thC. From Algonquian.]

wid·der·shins /wíddər shìnz/ *adv. Scotland* = **withershins** (*literary*) [Early 16thC. Via Middle Low German *weddersin(ne)s* from Middle High German *widersinnes,* literally "against the direction," from *sinnes,* a form of *sin* "direction, way."]

wide /wīd/ *adj.* (**wid·er, wid·est**) **1.** WITH SIDES OR EDGES FAR APART having a relatively large distance or space between one side or edge and the other **2.** BEING A SPECIFIED DISTANCE APART having a specified distance between one side or edge and the other ○ *three inches wide* **3.** OPENED TO GREAT EXTENT opened to a great extent or as far as possible ○ *staring at him with wide eyes* **4.** WITH MANY TYPES OR CHOICES including many varieties, offering many choices, or having a large range ○ *a wide selection of cheeses* **5.** INVOLVING MANY PEOPLE from, involving, or given to many people ○ *wide support for the plan* **6.** LARGE IN SCOPE with a large scope ○ *a very wide gap between living standards here and in developing countries* **7.** NOT HITTING TARGET going some distance away from the intended, expected, or correct place **8.** GOING BEYOND SPECIFIC DETAILS looking beyond the particular issue involved toward the more general aspects of something rather than the details ○ *We need to look at the wider implications of these proposals.* **9.** FITTING LOOSELY not fitting tightly round the body **10.** BASEBALL = **outside** 5 **11.** PHON = **lax** *adj.* 4 ■ *adv.* (**wid·er, wid·est**) **1.** TO GREAT EXTENT to a great extent or as much as possible ○ *Stand with your legs wide apart.* **2.** OVER LARGE AREA over an extensive area ○ *scattered far and wide* **3.** TO SIDE OF TARGET to one side of the intended target ○ *A few shots were fired but they all went wide.* [Old English *wīd.* Ultimately from an Indo-European base meaning "apart" that is also the ancestor of English *with.*] —**wide·ness** *n.* —**wid·ish** *adj.*

-wide *suffix.* effective throughout a particular place ○ *statewide* ○ *storewide* [From WIDE]

wide-an·gle *adj.* PHOTOGRAPHY **1.** GIVING WIDE ANGLE OF VIEW used to describe a camera lens that gives an unusually wide field of view by making things appear smaller or further away than they really are **2.** USING WIDE-ANGLE LENS relating to or using a camera lens with an unusually wide field of view ○ *a wide-angle shot*

wide-ar·e·a net·work *n.* a network of computers and peripheral devices linked by cable over a broad geographic area

wide-a·wake *adj.* **1.** FULLY AWAKE completely awake and alert (*not hyphenated when used after a verb*) **2.** ALERT very aware of surroundings and watching for advantageous possibilities (*informal*) ○ *a wide-awake young go-getter* ■ *n.* **wide-a·wake, wide-a·wake hat** CLOTHES FELT HAT a soft felt hat with a wide brim and a low crown —**wide-a·wake·ness** *n.*

wide-bod·ied, wide-bod·y *adj.* AIR with a fuselage wide enough to have three sets of passenger seats in a row, separated by two aisles running the length of the airplane

wide-eyed *adj.* **1.** WITH EYES WIDE OPEN with eyes that are wide open, e.g., in amazement or fear **2.** EASILY FOOLED lacking experience, wisdom, or common sense and therefore easily fooled by other people

wide·ly /wídlee/ *adv.* **1.** WITH SPACE BETWEEN with a relatively large distance between ○ *Plant them fairly widely apart.* **2.** MAKING SOMETHING SPREAD OR OPEN WIDE in such a way as to make something open or spread as much as possible or to a great extent ○ *smiling a little too widely* **3.** OVER LARGE AREA over an extensive area ○ *She is very widely travelled.* **4.** OVER LARGE RANGE so as to cover an extensive range ○ *The conversation ranged widely, from politics to bee-keeping.* **5.** BY MANY PEOPLE by a large number of people ○ *It is not widely known that he was once an acrobat.* **6.** GREATLY to a great degree ○ *widely different examples of this phenomenon*

wide-mouthed /wīd mówthd, -mówtht/ *adj.* **1.** WITH WIDE MOUTH with a mouth that is notably wider than average **2.** WITH MOUTH OPEN WIDE with the mouth open wide, e.g., in surprise

wid·en /wíd'n/ (**-ened, -en·ing, -ens**) *vti.* to become wider or to make something wider —**wid·en·er** *n.*

wide-o·pen *adj.* (*not hyphenated when used after a verb*) **1.** OPEN TO GREAT EXTENT open to a great extent, or as much as possible ○ *The door was wide open.* **2.** UNPREDICTABLE not as yet decided or even predictable in outcome ○ *The match is still wide open.* **3.** VULNERABLE TO ATTACK unprotected and therefore able to be attacked easily **4.** WITHOUT LAWS OR LAW ENFORCEMENT with few laws regulating such things as prostitution, gambling, or the sale of alcohol, or not stringently enforcing the laws that do exist (*informal*)

wide-rang·ing *adj.***1.** DEALING WITH DIFFERENT THINGS dealing with a great variety of matters **2.** AFFECTING MANY PEOPLE OR THINGS affecting a large number of people or things ○ *a decision that has wide-ranging implications*

wide re·ceiv·er *n.* in football, a player who positions himself to the side of the offensive formation, and whose role is to catch long passes from the quarterback

wide-screen *adj.* **1.** CINEMA VERY WIDE used to describe a type of film projection in which the image is substantially wider than it is tall **2.** VERY LARGE used to describe a television whose screen is notably larger than average

wide·spread /wīd sprèd/ *adj.* **1.** COMMON existing or happening in many places, or affecting many people **2.** SPREAD FAR APART spread or extending far apart ○ *with arms widespread*

WORD KEY: SYNONYMS

widespread, prevalent, rife, epidemic, universal

CORE MEANING: occurring over a wide area

widespread a general word that describes both concrete and abstract things that occur over a wide area; **prevalent** a more formal word than *widespread,* often used to suggest that something occurring over a wide area is also dominant in that area. It can be used to describe both concrete and abstract things; **rife** describes something undesirable that occurs frequently or in great numbers over a wide area, especially when it appears to be uncontrollable; **epidemic** indicates the widespread occurrence of something, especially disease, in an area at a particular time; **universal** describes something that occurs worldwide. It is also used to mean extremely widespread.

---

wid·geon /wíjjən/ (*plural* **-geons** *or* **-geon**), **wi·geon** (*plural* **-geons** *or* **-geon**) *n.* **1.** DUCK OF EUROPE AND ASIA a freshwater duck of Europe and Asia that has a white patch on each wing. Latin name: *Anas penelope.* **2.** N AMERICAN DUCK a North American duck the male of which has a white crown. Latin name: *Anas americana.* [Early 16thC. Origin uncertain: perhaps ultimately an imitation of the bird's call.]

wid·get /wíjjit/ *n.* **1.** UNNAMED DEVICE any little device or mechanism, especially one whose name is unknown or forgotten (*humorous*) **2.** OBJECT a hypothetical manufactured object, considered to represent the typical product of a manufacturer [Early 20thC. Origin uncertain: perhaps an alteration of GADGET.]

wid·ow /wíddō/ *n.* **1.** WOMAN WHOSE HUSBAND HAS DIED a woman whose husband has died, especially when she has not remarried **2.** WOMAN LEFT BEHIND a woman whose partner regularly goes away from her to take part in a particular activity (*only used in combination*) ○ *a golf widow.* ◊ **grass widow 3.** PRINTING SHORT FINAL LINE OF PARAGRAPH a short line at the end of a paragraph, especially when occurring as the top line of a page or column of text. The text is usually altered so that this is removed. ◊ **orphan 4.** CARDS EXTRA HAND OF CARDS an extra hand of cards dealt out in some card games ■ *vt.* (**-owed, -ow·ing, -ows**) MAKE SOMEBODY WIDOW OR WIDOWER to cause somebody to become a widow or widower (*usually passive*) ○ *She was widowed a year ago.* [Old English *widuwe.* Ultimately from an Indo-European base meaning "to separate" that is also the ancestor of English *divide.*] —**wid·ow·hood** *n.*

wid·ow·bird /wíddō bùrd/ (*plural* **-birds** *or* **-bird**) *n.* = **whydah** [Late 18thC]

wid·ow·er /wíddō ər/ *n.* a man whose wife has died, especially when he has not remarried —**wid·ow·er·hood** *n.*

wid·ow·mak·er /wíddō màykər/ *n.* something that is so dangerous that it might kill anyone who uses it or tries it

wid·ow's cruse *n.* a source that provides an unending supply of something [From the miracle of the widow's cruse of oil that supplies Elijah during a famine in the *Bible* ((I Kings 17:8–16))]

wid·ow's mite *n.* a contribution that, although small, is generous because it comes from somebody who has very little to give [From the poor widow's contribution of two copper coins to the treasury in the *Bible* (Mark 12:42)]

wid·ow's peak *n.* a V-shaped line across the top of a person's forehead behind which the hair grows [From the superstition that this feature portends early widowhood]

wid·ow's walk *n.* a walkway with a rail around it on the rooftop of a house, especially one that was used in the past to keep watch for incoming ships [Said to be so named because, while pacing along it, anxious wives commonly looked in vain for signs of their husbands returning from sea]

wid·ow's weeds *npl.* the black clothes once traditionally worn by widows (*archaic or literary*)

wid·ow wom·an *n.* a widow (*archaic*)

width /width, witth/ *n.* **1.** DISTANCE ACROSS the distance from one side or edge of something to the other **2.** STATE OF BEING WIDE the fact of being wide or how wide something is **3.** SEW MATERIAL OF FULL WIDTH a piece of material of its full width

width·wise /width wìz, witth-/, **width·ways** /-wàyz/ *adv.* from one side or edge to the other [Late 19thC (WIDTHWAYS: late 18thC)]

wield /weeld/ (**wield·ed, wield·ing, wields**) *vt.* **1.** HAVE AND EXERCISE SOMETHING to have and be able to use something, especially power or authority ○ *the immense economic power wielded by large companies* **2.** USE WEAPON OR TOOL to hold and use a weapon or tool [Old English *wieldan* "to rule," a variant of *wealden.* Ultimately from an Indo-European base meaning "to be strong" that is also the ancestor of English *valiant* and *valid.*] —**wield·a·ble** *adj.* —**wield·er** *n.*

wie·ner /wéenər/ *n.* = **frankfurter** [Late 19thC. Shortening of WIENERWURST.]

Wie·ner /wéenər/, **Norbert** (1894–1964) U.S. mathematician. His work on the mathematics and theories underlying communication and electronic machines founded the science of cybernetics.

Wie·ner schnit·zel /véenər shnìts'l/ *n.* a thin slice of veal coated in egg and breadcrumbs and fried

wie·ner·wurst /wéenər wùrst, -wo͝orst/ *n.* = **frankfurter** [Late 19thC. From German, from *Wiener* "of Vienna" + *Wurst* "sausage."]

wie·nie /wéenee/ *n.* a frankfurter (*informal*) [Mid-19thC. Alteration of WIENER.]

Wies·ba·den /véess bàad'n, véez-/ industrial city and spa resort in west central Germany. It is the capital city of Hesse State. Population: 266,400 (1995).

Wie·sel /vées'l/, **Elie** (*b.* 1928) Romanian-born U.S. writer. He survived the Holocaust, and after settling in the United States in 1956, devoted himself to writing and speaking about it. He won a Nobel Peace Prize in 1986. Full name **Eliezer Wiesel**

wife /wīf/ (*plural* **wives** /wīvz/) *n.* **1.** WOMAN MARRIED TO A PARTICULAR MAN the woman to whom a particular man is married **2.** *U.K.* MARRIED WOMAN a woman, especially a married one (*archaic*) **3.** *U.K.* MATURE WOMAN a woman, especially a mature woman (*regional*) [Old English *wīf* "woman, wife," of unknown origin, but with related forms in other Germanic languages] —**wife·hood** *n.*

wife·ly /wíflee/ (**-li·er, -li·est**) *adj.* showing the attitudes or behavior stereotypically expected of a wife [Old English *wīflic*] —**wife·li·ness** *n.*

wig[1] /wig/ (**wigged, wig·ging, wigs**) *n.* **1.** FALSE HAIR a covering of hair or something resembling hair worn on the head for adornment, ceremony, or to cover baldness **2.** TOUPEE a toupee (*informal*) [Late 17thC. Shortening of PERIWIG.] —**wigged** *adj.*

wig[2] /wig/ (**wigged, wig·ging, wigs**) *vt. U.K.* to speak sternly to somebody who has done something wrong (*dated informal*) [Early 19thC. From WIG[1].]

wig out *vti.* to become enthusiastic or anxious about something, or to make somebody enthusiastic or anxious (*slang*) ○ *He wigged out from the stress of his new job.*

wig·an /wíggən/ *n.* a tough fabric used for stiffening clothes [Mid-19thC. Named for the town in Lancashire, England, where the material was first made.]

wi·geon *n.* = **widgeon**

wigged-out *adj.* experiencing an extreme emotional or psychological state such as nervousness or anxiety (*slang*) ○ *wigged-out from staying up all night*

wig·gle /wígg'l/ *vti.* (**-gled, -gling, -gles**) MAKE SMALL BACK AND FORTH MOVEMENTS to move side to side in small quick movements, or to make something move in this way ■ *n.* **1.** INSTANCE OF WIGGLING a small quick side to side movement **2.** WAVY LINE a line with irregular curves in it [13thC. From Low German or Dutch *wiggelen,* from a prehistoric Germanic base.]

wig·gler /wígglər/ *n.* **1.** SOMEBODY OR SOMETHING THAT WIGGLES somebody or something that moves side to side in small quick movements **2.** INSECTS MOSQUITO LARVA the larva or pupa of a mosquito [Mid-19thC]

wig·gly /wígglee/ (**-gli·er, -gli·est**) *adj.* **1.** MAKING WIGGLING MOVEMENTS moving side to side with small quick movements, or able to be moved in this way (*informal*) **2.** WAVY with many irregular curves ○ *a wiggly line*

wig·gy /wíggee/ (**-gi·er, -gi·est**) *adj.* (*slang*) **1.** UNCONVENTIONAL tending to behave in an unconventional or unpredictable way **2.** UNINHIBITED behaving in an extremely excited and uninhibited way [Mid-20thC. Formed from WIG[2] in the sense "to lose control of your emotions."]

wight[1] /wīt/ *n.* a living being, especially a human being (*archaic*) [Old English *wiht* (source of English *nought* and *whit*), from a prehistoric Germanic word of unknown origin]

wight[2] /wīt/ *adj.* brave and strong (*archaic*) [13thC. From Old Norse *vígt,* a form of *vígr* "skilled in arms."]

wig·let /wígglət/ *n.* a small hairpiece for a woman, worn as an addition to a hairstyle rather than covering the head

wig·mak·er /wíg màykər/ *n.* somebody who makes wigs for a living

Wig·ner /wígnər/, **Eugene Paul** (1902–95) Hungarian-born U.S. physicist. He shared a Nobel Prize (1963) for his research in nuclear physics.

wig·wag /wíg wàg/ *vti.* (**-wagged, -wag·ging, -wags**) **1.** MOVE FROM SIDE TO SIDE to wave or swing from side to side in an arc around a fixed point, or to make something such as a flag move in this way **2.** NAUT SIGNAL BY WAVING SOMETHING to send a message by waving something such as an arm or a flag ■ *n.* NAUT **1.** PROCESS OF WIGWAGGING the method of communicating by waving an arm or a flag **2.** MESSAGE SENT BY WIGWAGGING a message communicated by the moving of arms or flags [Late 16thC. Reduplication of WAG.] —**wig·wag·ger** *n.*

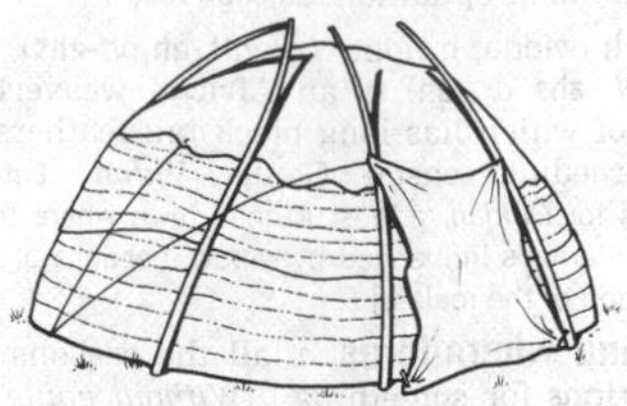

Wigwam

wig·wam /wíg wòm/ *n.* **1.** NATIVE N AMERICAN HUT a Native North American hut made by covering a conical or dome-shaped framework of poles with woven rush mats or sheets of bark. Wigwams were used by the Algonquian-speaking Native North Americans of the northeastern United States. **2.** CHILD'S TOY a light tent in the shape of a wigwam for a child to play in [Early 17thC. From Abenaki *wikewam.* Ultimately from the same prehistoric Algonquian base as WICKIUP.]

wik·i·up *n.* = **wickiup**

wik·i·wik·i /wíkee wìkee/ *adv. Hawaii* quickly

Wil·ber·force /wílbər fawrss/, **William** (1759–1833) British politician and political reformer. His campaign to end the slave trade resulted in its abolition in the West Indies in 1807, and in the Slave Abolition Act of 1833.

wil·co /wíl kō/ *interj.* used to indicate that you understand what has just been said in a radio message and will do what is necessary [Mid-20thC. Blend and shortening of *will comply.*]

Wil·cox·on test /wíl kòks'n-/ *n.* a statistical test of the equality of similar or matched groups of data, without any assumptions about the underlying distribution patterns, to determine whether they differ significantly from one another [Mid-20thC. Named for Frank *Wilcoxon* (1892–1965), the Irish statistician who developed the test.]

wild /wīld/ *adj.* **1.** NOT TAME OR DOMESTICATED not kept as a pet or used for display, work, or experimentation, but living freely in a natural habitat **2.** NOT CULTIVATED growing in a natural state rather than being cultivated in fields, parks, or gardens ○ *picking wild strawberries* **3.** PRODUCED BY WILD ANIMALS produced by animals living freely rather than by domesticated animals ○ *wild honey* **4.** ROUGH, DESOLATE, AND BARREN not inhabited or able to be inhabited by humans because of being barren, remote, or rugged **5.** ENTHUSIASTIC OR EAGER feeling enthusiastic or eager or showing enthusiasm or eagerness ○ *I'm not wild about the idea.* **6.** OFFENSIVE TERM an offensive term used to describe a people or its culture or customs as being supposedly culturally inferior (*offensive*) **7.** OVERWHELMED BY EMOTION overwhelmed by or showing a strong emotion such as anger, grief, or desire ○ *wild with grief.* **8.** STORMY rough and stormy, with a strong wind **9.** UNRULY lively and showing a disregard for rules ○ *The kids next door are really wild.* **10.** UNRESTRAINED marked by a lack of restraint or prudence, especially in things considered to be vices ○ *a really wild party* **11.** MESSY not neat or well-groomed ○ *His hair was wild.* **12.** NOT CAREFULLY THOUGHT OUT not based on rational thought, evidence, or probability ○ *I just made a wild guess.* **13.** SPORTS POORLY AIMED not carefully aimed ○ *throwing wild punches* **14.** UNCONVENTIONAL unconventional, exciting, and slightly irrational (*informal*) ○ *a wild idea* **15.** EXCELLENT excellent (*dated slang*) ○ *Hey, man, that's really wild!* **16.** CARDS WITH VALUE ASSIGNED BY PLAYER used to describe a playing card that has any value that the player using it wishes to give it ○ *Jokers are wild.* ■ *adv.* **1.** IN UNCULTIVATED WAY in a natural state rather than being cultivated in fields, parks, or gardens ○ *flowers that grow wild in the fields* **2.** IN UNCONTROLLED WAY in an uncontrolled, unpredictable, or unplanned way ○ *She just lets her kids run wild.*

3. *Ireland* **EXTREMELY** to an extreme degree (*informal*) ○ *That was wild stupid.* ■ *n.* **UNDOMESTICATED STATE** the natural, free state of an undomesticated animal ○ *Most people have never actually seen a panda in the wild.* ■ *n.* **wild, wilds** *npl.* **UNINHABITED AREA** an area that is completely uninhabited or only very sparsely populated because it is remote or rugged ○ *They live somewhere out in the wilds.* [Old English *wilde.* Ultimately from an Indo-European word meaning "wild, woods" that is also the ancestor of English *wold* and *vole.*] —**wild·ish** *adj.* —**wild·ness** *n.*

WORD KEY: SYNONYMS

See Synonyms at ***unruly.***

wild ber·ga·mot *n.* a North American mint that has fragrant leaves and a round cluster of purple flowers. Latin name: *Monarda fistulosa.*

wild boar *n.* a wild pig of Europe and Asia that has a coat ranging from pale gray to black, dense bristles, a thin body, and small tusks. Domestic swine were developed from it. Latin name: *Sus scrofa.*

wild bri·er *n.* = **wild rose**

wild card *n.* **1. SOMEBODY OR SOMETHING UNPREDICTABLE** somebody or something that is important to a plan or course of action, but whose behavior cannot be predicted (*informal*) **2.** SPORTS **EXTRA PLAYER OR TEAM IN COMPETITION** an extra player or team selected to take part in a competition although not technically qualified to do so **3.** CARDS **CARD OF NO FIXED VALUE** in card games, a card that can have whatever value its player assigns it **4.** COMPUT **COMPUTER SYMBOL REPRESENTING ANY CHARACTER** a symbol, usually *, that can be used to represent any character that may appear in the same position in a computer search argument

wild car·rot *n.* = **Queen Anne's lace**

Wildcat

wild·cat /wīld kàt/ *n.* (*plural* **-cats** *or* **-cat**) **1. WILD EUROPEAN OR ASIAN CAT** a cat of Europe, Asia, and Africa that resembles the domestic tabby but is heavier and has a bushy tail. It is regarded as the ancestor of the domestic cat. Latin name: *Felis sylvestris.* **2. MEDIUM-SIZED WILD FELINE** any of several medium-sized wild felines such as the bobcat, caracal, lynx, and ocelot **3. QUICK-TEMPERED PERSON** somebody who tends to get angry quickly **4.** INDUST, UTIL **SPECULATIVE OIL OR GAS WELL** an exploratory or speculative well drilled in an area not yet known to be productive of oil or gas **5.** COMM **FINANCIALLY UNSOUND BUSINESS** a financially unsound business ■ *adj.* **NOT FINANCIALLY SAFE** practicing unethical or financially risky business methods, or characteristic of such methods ○ *wildcat stocks* ■ *vti.* (**-cat·ted, -cat·ting, -cats**) INDUST, UTIL **DRILL EXPLORATORY WELL** to drill an exploratory well or take samples in an area not yet known to have any reserves of what is being sought, especially oil or gas —**wild·cat·ting** *n., adj.*

wild·cat strike *n.* a sudden strike not authorized by the labor union that the strikers belong to

wild·cat·ter /wīld kàttər/ *n.* **1.** INDUST, UTIL **PROSPECTOR** somebody who prospects for oil in areas not yet known to be productive (*informal*) **2.** COMM **UNETHICAL BUSINESSPERSON** somebody who develops or promotes risky or fraudulent business ventures **3. WILDCAT STRIKE PARTICIPANT** somebody who participates in a sudden strike not authorized by the labor union he or she belongs to

wild cel·er·y *n.* = **tape grass**

wild cher·ry *n.* = **gean**

wild dog *n.* any wild member of the dog family, especially the dingo, the African hunting dog, or the dhole

AKG London

Oscar Wilde

Wilde /wīld/, **Oscar** (1854–1900) Irish writer and wit. His works include the plays *Lady Windermere's Fan* (1892) and *The Importance of Being Earnest* (1895) and the novel *The Picture of Dorian Gray* (1891). His flamboyance and legendary wit made him a leading figure in society, but he was convicted of sodomy and sentenced to two years' hard labor in 1895. Full name **Oscar Fingal O'Flahertie Wills Wilde**

wil·de·beest /wíldə bèest/ (*plural* **-beests** *or* **-beest**) *n.* = **gnu** [Early 19thC. From Afrikaans, literally "wild beast."]

wil·der /wíldər/ (**-dered, -der·ing, -ders**) *vti.* (*archaic*) **1. GO OR LEAD ASTRAY** to go astray or lead somebody or something astray **2. BEWILDER** to become confused by a number of complex options, or to confuse somebody in this way [Early 17thC. Origin uncertain: perhaps a back-formation from WILDERNESS.] —**wil·der·ment** *n.*

Wil·der /wíldər/, **Billy** (*b.* 1906) Austrian-born U.S. movie director. At home in a wide variety of movie genres, he made several Hollywood classics, including *Sunset Boulevard* (1950) and *Some Like It Hot* (1959). Real name **Samuel Wilder**

Wil·der, Thornton (1897–1975) U.S. writer. His Pulitzer Prize-winning works include the novel *The Bridge of San Luis Rey* (1927) and the play *Our Town* (1938). Full name **Thornton Niven Wilder**

wil·der·ness /wíldərnəss/ *n.* **1. NATURAL UNCULTIVATED LAND** a mostly uninhabited area of land such as a forest or mountainous region in its natural uncultivated state, sometimes deliberately preserved like this **2. BARREN AREA** an area that is empty or barren ○ *in the vast wilderness of outer space* **3. DELIBERATELY UNCULTIVATED LAND IN GARDEN** a piece of land, e.g., in a garden, that is deliberately not cultivated but is left to grow wild **4. UNCOMFORTABLE SITUATION** a place, situation, or multitude of people or things that makes somebody feel confused, overwhelmed, or desolate ○ *the wilderness of the big city* [Old English *wilddēornes,* formed from *wilddēor* "wild beast," from *wilde* "wild" + *dēor* "animal" (see DEER)] ◇ **be (a voice) crying in the wilderness** to be giving advice or suggestions that are very unlikely to be followed

wil·der·ness ar·e·a *n.* a protected area set aside for preservation in as natural a state as possible, with restrictions on most human activity, except for nonmotorized forms of outdoor recreation ○ *backpacking in the wilderness areas*

wild-eyed *adj.* **1. WITH EYES WIDE WITH EMOTION** with eyes that are wide and glaring because of fear, anger, or psychological disorder **2. EXTREME** marked by or advocating ideas that are so extreme and far-fetched as to be completely impracticable

wild·fire /wīld fīr/ *n.* **1. RAPIDLY SPREADING FIRE** a fierce fire that spreads rapidly, especially in an area of wilderness **2.** = **will-o'-the-wisp** **3. LIGHTNING WITHOUT THUNDER** lightning that occurs without audible thunder **4.** HIST, MIL **INFLAMMABLE MATERIAL AS WEAPON** any of various inflammable materials used in warfare in the past, e.g., against enemy ships [Old English] ◇ **like wildfire** very rapidly

wild·flow·er /wīld flòwr/ *n.* a flowering plant growing in a natural, uncultivated state, or the flower of such a plant

wild·fowl /wīld fòwl/ (*plural* **-fowl**) *n.* a bird that is hunted for food or sport, e.g., a duck, goose, pheasant, or quail [Old English] —**wild·fowl·er** *n.* —**wild·fowl·ing** *n.*

wild ge·ra·ni·um *n.* a North American geranium with deeply divided leaves and rosy purple flowers. Latin name: *Geranium maculatum.*

wild gin·ger *n.* a North American herb that has two heart-shaped leaves, a single reddish-brown flower, and an aromatic root. Latin name: *Asarum canadense.*

wild-goose chase *n.* a futile search for something that there is no chance of finding, especially because it does not exist [Originally the expression referred to following someone or something along an irregular course, as wild geese follow one another in their patterned flight]

wild hy·a·cinth *n.* = **bluebell** *n.* **1**

wild in·di·go *n.* a North American plant of the legume family that has three-lobed leaves and bright yellow flowers. Genus: *Baptisia.*

wild·ing /wīlding/ *n.* **1. WILD PLANT OR TREE** a plant that grows wild or one that has escaped from cultivation, especially a wild crab-apple tree **2. FRUIT** the fruit of a plant that grows wild or that has escaped from cultivation, especially a wild crab apple **3. WILD ANIMAL** a wild animal ■ *adj.* **UNCULTIVATED** uncultivated or undomesticated

wild·life /wīld līf/ *n.* wild animals, birds, and other living things, sometimes including vegetation, living in a natural undomesticated state

wildlife park *n.* = **safari park**

wild·life ref·uge *n.* a protected area set aside to preserve habitats for particular types of wild animals, especially migratory waterfowl, and in which people are allowed to view wildlife in a natural setting

wild·ling /wīldling/ *n.* = **wilding**

wild·ly /wīldlee/ *adv.* **1. WITH ENTHUSIASM** in a very enthusiastic way ○ *cheering wildly* **2. WITHOUT CAREFUL THOUGHT** not considering something carefully **3. VERY** to a great extent (*informal*) ○ *not wildly enthusiastic about the idea* **4. IN WAY THAT SHOWS FEAR** in an uncontrolled way that betrays fear or anxiety, and often with eyes that are wide and staring ○ *looking wildly in all directions* **5. STRONGLY** in a fierce and rough way ○ *The wind blew wildly through the trees.*

wild man *n.* an offensive term used to refer to a man regarded as supposedly being culturally inferior (*archaic offensive*)

wild mus·tard *n.* = **charlock**

wild oat *n.* a weedy annual grass of temperate regions that resembles cultivated oats. Latin name: *Avena fatua.* ◇ **sow your wild oats** to behave in an uncontrolled way, especially sexually, while young

wild ol·ive *n.* a tree that resembles the olive tree and bears fruit that resemble olives

wild pink *n.* a perennial plant of the eastern United States that has pink or whitish flowers. Latin name: *Silene caroliniana.*

wild pitch *n.* a baseball pitch that a catcher could not have caught and that results in a runner advancing to the next base. ◊ **passed ball**

wild rice *n.* **1. TALL N AMERICAN GRASS** a tall perennial aquatic grass of North America that yields an edible grain. Latin name: *Zizania aquatica.* **2.** FOOD **GRAIN OF WILD RICE** the dark grain of the wild rice plant, used as food

wild rose *n.* any wild-growing rose such as the dog rose and sweetbrier

wild rub·ber *n.* rubber obtained from uncultivated rubber trees

wild rye *n.* a perennial grass of temperate regions that has flat leaves, paired ears, and somewhat resembles cultivated rye. Genus: *Elymus.*

wild silk *n.* **1. SILK FROM WILD SILKWORMS** silk fiber obtained from wild silkworms **2.** TEXTILES **FABRIC MADE OF WILD SILK** fabric woven from the silk of wild silkworms, or an imitation of this made with short silk fibers

wild type *n.* the form of an organism, strain, or gene that results from natural breeding, as opposed to mutant forms or those resulting from selective breeding

Wild West show *n.* a form of entertainment involving the demonstration of skills associated with the Wild West, e.g., shooting, riding, and roping cattle, especially performed by people dressed as cowboys

wild·wood /wīld wòod/ *n.* natural uncultivated woodland [Old English]

wile /wīl/ *n.* **TRICK** a trick or cunning ruse ■ **wiles** *npl.* **TRICKERY MEANT TO PERSUADE** trickery intended to persuade somebody to do something, especially in

W-Z

the form of insincere charm or flattery ■ *vt.* (**wiled, wil·ing, wiles**) PERSUADE SOMEBODY BY WILES to trick or entice somebody into doing or not doing something [12thC. Origin uncertain: perhaps from or related to Old Norse *vél* "artifice."]

wile away *vi.* = **while away**

wil·ful *adj.* = **willful**

WORD KEY: SYNONYMS

See Synonyms at ***unruly.***

Wil·helms·ha·ven /vìl helmz haávən, vìl helms haáfən/ city and port in northwestern Germany. It was formerly an important naval base. Population: 89,900 (1989).

Wilkes /wilks/, **Charles** (1798–1877) U.S. naval officer and explorer. He charted the coastlines of northwestern North America, the Antarctic, and numerous South Pacific islands (1838–42). In the Civil War, he was court-martialed for violating neutral ships in pursuit of Confederate ships.

Wil·kins /wílkinz/, **Roy** (1901–81) U.S. civil rights leader. He headed the National Association for the Advancement of Colored People (NAACP) (1955–77).

will[1] /wil/ CORE MEANING: a modal verb used to indicate future time ○ *Delegates from all over Europe will attend the forum.* ○ *Will you ever be able to forgive him?* ○ *Your suit will be ready for collection tomorrow.*

vi. **1.** POLITE QUESTIONS used in questions to make polite invitations or offers ○ *Will you sit down please?* ○ *Will you have more coffee?* **2.** REQUESTS used in questions to make requests ○ *Will you take the washing out for me please?* ○ *Phone the garage, will you?* **3.** COMMANDS used when ordering somebody to do something ○ *You will do exactly as I say.* ○ *Students will not start writing until told to do so.* **4.** CUSTOMARY BEHAVIOR used to indicate the way that something usually happens or the way that somebody usually does something ○ *The wetter the road conditions, the harder it will be for a vehicle to stop.* ○ *When they're out together they will shop till they drop!* **5.** WILLINGNESS used to indicate that somebody is willing to do something ○ *I will mail your letters for you.* ○ *I will not tolerate this kind of behavior.* **6.** ABILITY used to indicate the ability or capacity of something ○ *That wardrobe will not fit in your bedroom.* ○ *The truck will carry loads of up to 10 tons.* **7.** EXPECTATION used to express surmise or likelihood ○ *That will be them at the door now.* ○ *He will have left the country by now.* **8.** INCLINATION used to indicate the inevitability of something happening or being true ○ *She will stay up till all hours in front of the TV.* [Old English *wyllan.* Ultimately from an Indo-European base that is also the ancestor of German *wollen* and Latin *velle.*]

WORD KEY: USAGE

See Usage note at ***shall.***

will[2] /wil/ *n.* **1.** PART OF MIND THAT MAKES DECISIONS the part of the mind with which somebody consciously decides things **2.** POWER TO DECIDE the power to make decisions ○ *This lawnmower seems to have a will of its own!* **3.** PROCESS OF MAKING DECISIONS the use of the mind to make decisions about things **4.** DETERMINATION the determination to do something ○ *She has lots of ability but she lacks the will to succeed.* **5.** DESIRE OR INCLINATION a desire or inclination to do something **6.** ATTITUDE TOWARD SOMEBODY ELSE the attitude or feelings somebody has toward somebody or something **7.** SOMETHING DESIRED BY SOMEBODY TO HAPPEN what a person or group, especially one in authority, wants to happen (*formal*) ○ *It was her will that he should never be told the truth.* **8.** LAW STATEMENT DETERMINING DISTRIBUTION OF DECEASED'S PROPERTY a statement of what somebody wants to happen to his or her property after he or she dies, or a legal document containing this statement. ◊ **living will** ■ *vt.* (**willed, will·ing, wills**) **1.** TRY TO CAUSE SOMETHING BY THOUGHTS to make or try to make something happen or somebody do something by the power of the mind ○ *He willed himself to stay awake.* ○ *Her parents were watching her run, willing her on.* **2.** LAW LEAVE SOMEBODY SOMETHING IN WILL to give something officially to somebody by declaring it in a will **3.** WANT OR DECIDE SOMETHING to want something to happen or to decide that something will happen (*archaic or formal*) ○ *It shall be as God wills.* [Old English *willa* (noun), *wyllan* (verb), and *willian* (verb from the base of the noun). Ultimately from an Indo-European base meaning "to will, wish."] —**will·er** *n.* ◇ **at will** when somebody wishes (*formal*) ○ *They are free to come and go at will.* ◇ **with the best will in the world** used to indicate that somebody cannot do something however much he or she wishes or tries to do it ○ *With the best will in the world we won't be able to supervise her all the time.*

will·able /wílləb'l/ *adj.* able to be done or decided by the force of willpower [15thC. Formed from WILL².]

Wil·lam·ette /wə lámmit/ river in western Oregon that flows north into the Columbia River near Portland. Length: 309 mi./497 km.

Wil·lard /wíllərd/, **Frances** (1839–98) U.S. reformer and educator. She headed the Women's Christian Temperance Union (1879–98) and the National Council of Women (1890–98). Full name **Frances Elizabeth Caroline Willard**

Wil·lard, Jess (1881–1968) U.S. boxer. He beat Jack Johnson for the heavyweight world title (1915), which he held until he was defeated by Jack Dempsey (1919).

wil·lem·ite /wíllə mìt/ *n.* a colorless brown, green, or red mineral form of zinc sulfate that occurs with some zinc ores and fluoresces in ultraviolet light [Mid-19thC. Named for the king of the Netherlands, *Willem* I (1772–1843).]

wil·let /wíllit/ *n.* a large gray North American shore bird that has a long straight moderately stout bill, long legs, and a distinctive black-and-white wing pattern. Latin name: *Catoptrophorus semipalmatus.* [Mid-19thC. An imitation of the sound made by the bird.]

will·ful /wílfəl/, **wil·ful** *adj.* **1.** DELIBERATE done deliberately, especially with the intention of harming somebody or in spite of knowing that it will harm somebody **2.** STUBBORN always determined to act on a desire, regardless of the opinions or advice of others (*disapproving*) —**will·ful·ly** *adv.* —**will·ful·ness** *n.*

WORD KEY: SYNONYMS

See Synonyms at ***unruly***

Wil·liam /wíllyəm/, **Prince of the United Kingdom** (*b.* 1982). The first child of Prince Charles and Diana, Princess of Wales, he is second in line to the British throne.

Wil·liam I, King of England (1028?–87). A Norman, he invaded England and defeated Harold II at the Battle of Hastings (1066), subsequently imposing a new ruling aristocracy on England. The *Domesday Book* was compiled during his reign. Known as **William the Conqueror**

Wil·liam II, King of England (1056?–1100). The son and successor of William I, he seized territory in Normandy and Scotland. He was killed, probably accidentally, while hunting in the New Forest. Known as **William Rufus**

Wil·liam III, King of England, Scotland, and Ireland (1650–1702) Dutch-born English monarch. He was the grandson of Charles I and the husband of James II's daughter Mary. He and Mary replaced James II on the English throne after the Revolution of 1689. Known as **William of Orange**

Wil·liam IV, King of the United Kingdom (1765–1837). He succeeded his brother George IV on the throne after a 50-year naval career, and during his reign (1830–37) was the last monarch to exercise the royal prerogative. Known as **the Sailor King**

Wil·liams /wíllyəmz/, **Hank** (1923–53) U.S. musician. He developed a wide audience for country music through his recordings and performances on radio and at the Grand Ole Opry. His songs include "Your Cheatin' Heart." Real name **Hiram Williams**

Wil·liams, Robin (*b.* 1952) U.S. comedian and actor. Originally known for his standup comedy, he went on to perform both comic and serious roles in many Hollywood movies.

Wil·liams, Roger (1603–83) American colonial clergyman. A Puritan who held unorthodox views on the toleration of other faiths, he left Massachusetts to establish a colony (1636) in what would become Rhode Island.

Wil·liams, Ted (*b.* 1918) U.S. baseball player. A Boston Red Sox outfielder (1939–60), he was one of the game's greatest hitters, batting .406 in 1941 and compiling a lifetime average of .344. Full name **Theodore Samuel Williams**

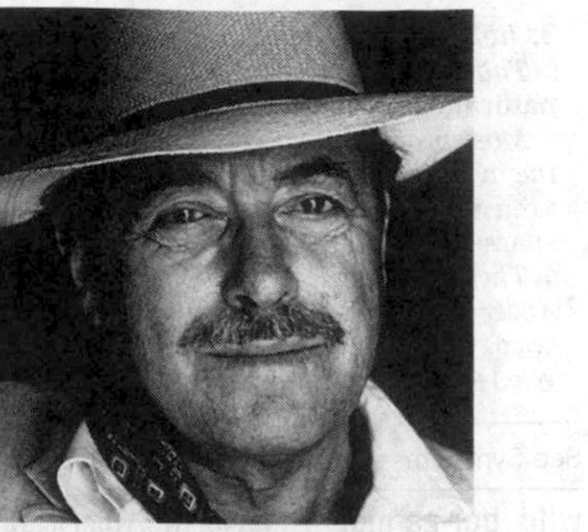

New Directions Publishing Corp.

Tennessee Williams

Wil·liams, Tennessee (1911–83) U.S. playwright. His plays are largely set in the American South, and he won Pulitzer Prizes for *A Streetcar Named Desire* (1947) and *Cat on a Hot Tin Roof* (1955). Real name **Thomas Lanier Williams**

Wil·liams, William (1731–1811) American patriot. Representing Connecticut, he signed the Declaration of Independence (1776), and raised funds and equipment for the Continental Army.

Wil·liams, William Carlos (1883–1963) U.S. writer. While practicing as a doctor (1910–51) he produced poetry and novels concerned with everyday American life, including the epic poem *Paterson* (1946–58).

Wil·liams·burg /wíllyəmz bùrg/ city in southeastern Virginia. The central part of the city has been restored along colonial lines and is an important tourist center. Population: 11,530 (1990).

wil·lie *n.* = **willy**

wil·lies /wílliz/ *npl.* an uncomfortable, anxious, or fearful feeling (*informal*) [Late 19thC. Origin unknown.]

will·ing /wílling/ *adj.* **1.** READY TO DO SOMETHING VOLUNTARILY ready to do something without being forced **2.** HELPFUL cooperative and enthusiastic **3.** OFFERED VOLUNTARILY offered or given by somebody readily and enthusiastically [Old English] —**will·ing·ly** *adv.* —**will·ing·ness** *n.*

Wil·lis /wílləss/, **Bruce** (*b.* 1955) U.S. actor. Specializing in tough-guy roles, he made his name in Hollywood movies such as the *Die Hard* trilogy (1988–95). Real name **Walter Willison**

wil·li·waw /wílli wàw/ *n.* **1.** GUST OF WIND a sudden gust of wind **2.** COLD WIND BLOWING SEAWARD a violent gust of cold wind blowing down from a mountainous region to the coast and out to sea, especially in the Straits of Magellan and in Alaska **3.** TURMOIL a state of confusion or turmoil [Mid-19thC. Origin unknown.]

will-o'-the-wisp /willə thə wísp/ *n.* **1.** LIGHT FROM BURNING MARSH GAS a phosphorescent light sometimes seen at night over marshy ground, caused by the spontaneous combustion of gases given off by rotting organic matter **2.** SOMEBODY OR SOMETHING ELUSIVE somebody or something that is misleading or elusive, e.g., a false hope [From *Will,* a shortening of the forename *William,* + OF + THE + WISP] —**will-o'-the-wisp·ish** *adj.*

wil·low /wíllō/ *n.* **1.** TREES TREE WITH LONG FLEXIBLE BRANCHES a tree or shrub with long flexible branches, narrow leaves, and catkins containing small flowers without petals. Some species are valued for their wood, twigs, and tanbark. Genus: *Salix.* **2.** INDUST WILLOW WOOD the wood of the willow tree **3.** INDUST MACHINE FOR CLEANING FIBROUS MATERIALS a machine with a revolving spiked cylinder inside a box that is also fitted with spikes, used to clean or loosen fibrous materials such as cotton, wool, or rags [Old English *welig.* Perhaps ultimately from an Indo-European base meaning "to turn" that is the ancestor of English *well* and *helix.*] —**wil·low·ish** *adj.*

WORD KEY: CULTURAL NOTE

The Wind in the Willows, a children's story by the British writer Kenneth Grahame (1908). Originally written as a bedtime story for Grahame's son, it recounts the mishaps that befall four animals – Mole, Water Rat, Toad, and Badger – when they venture outside their natural habitats. Much loved by children, the tales are also enjoyed by adults as entertaining allegories of human behavior.

wil·low grouse *n. U.K.* = **willow ptarmigan**

wil·low herb *n.* = **fireweed**

wil·low oak *n.* an oak of North America that has narrow leaves and hard wood. Latin name: *Quercus phellos.*

wil·low pat·tern *n.* a pattern used to decorate china, usually blue on a white background, featuring a Chinese landscape with a willow tree, pagoda-style buildings, a bridge, and two swallows

wil·low ptar·mi·gan *n.* a plump ground bird of the grouse family found in northern North America, Europe, and Asia that turns from mottled brown to white in the winter. Latin name: *Lagopus lagopus.*

wil·low tit *n.* a black-capped member of the tit family found in forest and scrub in northern Europe and Asia. Latin name: *Parus montanus.*

Barnaby's

Willowware

wil·low·ware /wíllō wàir/ *n.* china decorated with the willow pattern

wil·low·y /wíllō ee/ (**-i·er, -i·est**) *adj.* **1.** GRACEFUL used to describe somebody who is slim, graceful, and elegant, partly because of being tall **2.** FLEXIBLE able to be bent easily, and springing back into place **3.** COVERED BY WILLOWS covered or shaded by willow trees

will·pow·er /wíl pòwr/ *n.* a combination of determination and self-discipline that enables somebody to do something despite the difficulties involved

Wills /wilz/, **Helen** (1906–98) U.S. tennis player. She won the U.S. women's singles title seven times between 1923 and 1931, and was eight times Wimbledon singles champion. Known as **Helen Wills Moody**. Born **Helen Newington Wills**

wil·ly /wíllee/ (*plural* **-lies**), **wil·lie** *n. U.K.* an offensive term for a penis (*informal offensive*) [Early 20thC. Formed from a shortening of the proper name *William.*]

wil·ly-nil·ly /wílli níllee/ *adv.* **1.** NOT CONTROLLABLY whether or not somebody wants it to happen ○ *He won't be rushed willy-nilly into a quick decision.* **2.** HAPHAZARDLY in a disorganized or unplanned way ○ *Totally confused by now, I handed out the invitations willy-nilly.* ■ *adj.* **1.** HAPPENING WITHOUT CHOICE happening or existing without plan or choice **2.** HAPHAZARD lacking direction or organization [Early 17thC. From the phrase "will I, nill I" "whether I wish it or do not wish it."]

willy-willy *n. Aus* a dust storm or whirlwind [Late 19thC. From Aboriginal Australian.]

Wil·mette /wil mét/ village in northeastern Illinois on the shore of Lake Michigan, north of Evanston. It is a northern suburb of Chicago. Population: 26,036 (1996).

Wil·ming·ton /wílmingtən/ city in northern Delaware. Situated on the Delaware River, it is the largest city in the state. Population: 71,529 (1990).

Wil·son, Mount /wílss'n/ mountain in southern California, home to Mount Wilson Observatory, an astronomical observatory. Height: 5,710 ft./1,740 m.

Wil·son, Alexander (1766–1813) British-born U.S. ornithologist. He conducted the first major studies of North American birds, and wrote and illustrated *American Ornithology* (1808–13).

Wil·son, Edmund (1895–1972) U.S. literary critic. One of the leading essayists of his generation, he wrote critical studies across a broad spectrum of literature and social thought, including a volume on the Civil War, *Patriotic Gore* (1962).

AKG London

Harold Wilson

Wil·son, Harold, Baron Wilson of Rievaulx (1916–95) British statesman. He served two terms as Labour prime minister (1964–70, 1974–76). He sought to bolster Britain's economy and introduced the first antiracist legislation.

Wil·son, James (1742–98) British-born U.S. jurist. He signed the Declaration of Independence (1776), and served on the U.S. Supreme Court (1789–98).

Library of Congress

Woodrow Wilson

Wil·son, Woodrow (1856–1924) U.S. statesman and 28th president of the United States. A Democratic president (1913–21), he brought the United States into World War I in 1917 and negotiated the peace treaty in 1918, making the League of Nations a part of the treaty. He was awarded the Nobel Peace Prize in 1919. Full name **Thomas Woodrow Wilson** —**Wil·so·ni·an** *adj.*

Wil·son's dis·ease /wílss'nz-/ *n.* a rare hereditary disease resulting from an inability to metabolize copper and marked by cirrhosis of the liver, damage to other organs, and psychiatric disorder [Early 20thC. Named for S. A. Kinnier *Wilson* (1878–1937), English neurologist.]

Wil·son's pet·rel (*plural* **Wil·son's pet·rels** *or* **Wil·son's pet·rel**) *n.* = **Wilson's storm petrel**

Wil·son's phal·a·rope *n.* a small swimming shorebird with a long thin bill, similar to the sandpiper, found in western North American wetlands. Latin name: *Phalaropus tricolor.* [Early 19thC. Named for Alexander *Wilson.*]

Wil·son's Prom·on·to·ry peninsula in southeastern Victoria, Australia. It is the most southerly point on the Australian mainland.

Wil·son's storm pet·rel, **Wil·son's pet·rel** *n.* a small dark seabird of southern oceans that breeds in Antarctica but sometimes wanders to the northern Atlantic. Latin name: *Oceanites oceanicus.*

wilt[1] /wilt/ *v.* (**wilt·ed, wilt·ing, wilts**) **1.** *vti.* BOT DROOP OR SHRIVEL to droop or shrivel, or make a plant droop or shrivel through lack of water, too much heat, or disease **2.** *vi.* BECOME WEAK to become weak and tired, e.g., because of heat **3.** *vti.* LOSE CONFIDENCE to lose confidence, composure, or enthusiasm, or to make somebody do this ■ *n.* **1.** BOT DROOPING OR SHRIVELING the drooping of plants or shriveling of leaves because of a lack of water, too much heat, or disease **2.** BOT PLANT DISEASE a plant disease caused by fungi, bacteria, or viruses that make plants droop and leaves shrivel **3.** ACT OF WILTING an instance of wilting or the condition of having wilted [Late 17thC. Origin uncertain: perhaps a dialect variant of obsolete *welk*, probably of Low Dutch origin.]

wilt[2] /wilt/ *vti.* 2nd person present singular of **will** (*archaic*)

Wil·ton /wílt'n/ *n.* carpet with a thick velvety pile [Late 18thC. Named for a town in the British county of Wiltshire, known for its carpet industry.]

wi·ly /wílee/ (**-li·er, -li·est**) *adj.* skilled at using clever tricks to deceive people —**wil·i·ly** *adv.* —**wil·i·ness** *n.*

wim·ble /wímb'l/ *n.* BORING TOOL a hand-held tool used for boring holes ■ *vt.* (**-bled, -bling, -bles**) MAKE HOLE WITH WIMBLE to bore a hole with a wimble [13thC. From Anglo-Norman, probably from Middle Dutch *wimmel* "augur."]

wimp /wimp/ *n.* an offensive term used to refer to somebody who is regarded as weak, timid, unassertive, or ineffectual (*insult offensive*) [Early 20thC. Origin uncertain: perhaps a shortening of WHIMPER.] —**wimp·ish** *adj.* —**wimp·y** *adj.*

wimp out *vi.* to fail to do or finish doing something because of fear or a weakness of character (*slang*)

WIMP[1] /wimp/ *n.* a graphical user interface for computers designed to make them more user-friendly that includes windows, icons, mice, and pull-down menus. Full form **windows, icons, mice, and pull-down menus**

WIMP[2] /wimp/ *n.* a hypothetical nonbaryonic subatomic particle that has been proposed as a possible form of dark matter. Full form **weakly interacting massive particle**

wim·ple /wímp'l/ *n.* **1.** WOMAN'S HEAD COVERING a cloth covering for a woman's head and neck. The wimple was common in medieval Europe and it is still worn by some orders of nuns. **2.** FOLD IN CLOTH a fold or pleat in a piece of cloth ■ *v.* (**-pled, -pling, -ples**) **1.** *vi.* RIPPLE to form small undulating waves **2.** *vt.* DRESS SOMEBODY IN WIMPLE to put a wimple on somebody (*archaic*) [Old English *wimpel.* Perhaps from the Indo-European base meaning "to turn" that is the ancestor of English *wipe* and *vibrate.*]

win /win/ *v.* (**won** /wun/, **won, win·ning, wins**) **1.** *vti.* ACHIEVE VICTORY to beat any or every opponent or enemy in a competition or fight **2.** *vt.* GET SOMETHING FOR DEFEATING OTHERS to get something as a prize by beating other competitors using skill, effort, or luck ○ *proud of the cups he had won for shooting* **3.** *vt.* MAKE SOMEBODY SUCCEED IN GETTING SOMETHING to be the reason why somebody is first in something or receives something as a prize ○ *That photo is sure to win you a prize.* **4.** *vt.* GAIN SOMETHING to gain something such as respect or friendship, e.g., because of something done or said or an ability shown, or to make somebody do this ○ *His attitude won him few friends in the company.* **5.** *vt.* GET SOMETHING to obtain something by hard work (*literary*) ○ *winning his livelihood by the sweat of his brow* **6.** *vt.* REACH PLACE WITH EFFORT to arrive somewhere by great effort or with difficulty (*literary*) **7.** *vt.* CAPTURE SOMETHING USING FORCE to capture something such as a city using force (*formal*) **8.** *vt.* GAIN SUPPORT to persuade somebody to do something or agree to something, or to gain somebody's sympathy or support **9.** *vt.* EARN THE LOVE OF SOMEBODY to persuade somebody to love or marry you **10.** *vt.* MINING GET SOMETHING BY MINING to mine coal, oil, or ore from a source **11.** *vt.* MINING PREPARE LODE FOR MINING to discover a source of coal, oil, or ore and prepare it for mining **12.** *vt.* MINING EXTRACT SOMETHING FROM ORE to extract a metal or mineral from its ore ■ *n.* **1.** VICTORY success in a competition, game or bet ○ *The team has had six wins in a row.* **2.** AMOUNT OF MONEY WON the amount of money won, e.g., in a bet **3.** SPORTS FIRST PLACE the position of first place in a race. ◊ **place, show** [Old English *winnan.* Ultimately from an Indo-European base meaning "to desire" that is also the ancestor of English *wish* and *Venus.*] —**win·less** *adj.* —**win·na·ble** *adj.* ◇ **(you) win some, (you) lose some** used to indicate philosophically or humorously that in life everyone has some successes and some failures

win out *vi.* to be successful or dominant after a struggle

win over *vt.* to persuade somebody to agree with you, support you, or give you permission

wince /winss/ *vi.* (**winced, winc·ing, winc·es**) **1.** MOVE BODY BACK SLIGHTLY to make an involuntary movement away from something because of pain or fear **2.** MAKE PAINED EXPRESSION to make an expression of pain with the face because of seeing or thinking of something unpleasant or embarrassing ■ *n.* **1.** EXPRESSION OF PAIN a facial expression to pain **2.** SLIGHT MOVEMENT AWAY a slight movement away from something because of pain or fear **3.** EXPRESSION OF DISPLEASURE OR EMBARRASSMENT a facial reaction to seeing or thinking of something unpleasant or embarrassing [13thC. From Anglo-

Norman, a variant of Old French *guencir* "to turn aside," from Germanic.] —**winc·er** *n.*

WORD KEY: SYNONYMS

See Synonyms at ***recoil***.

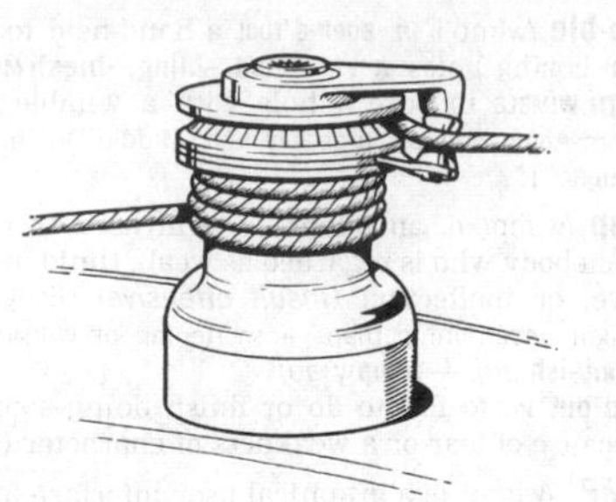

Winch

winch /winch/ *n.* **1.** LIFTING MACHINE a machine for lifting loads by means of a rope or chain that is wound around a cylinder turned by an engine or by hand **2.** CRANK OR HANDLE the handle used to turn a machine ■ *vt.* (**winched, winch·ing, winch·es**) MOVE SOMETHING WITH WINCH to lift or pull something by means of a winch [Old English *wince.* Ultimately from the prehistoric Germanic base that is the ancestor of English *wink.*] —**winch·er** *n.*

Win·ches·ter /winchestər/ city in Hampshire, southern England. It was the capital of the Anglo-Saxon kingdom of Wessex. Population: 34,700 (1994).

Win·ches·ter ri·fle *tdmk.* a trademark for a rifle first produced in the late 19th century that can fire several shots before it has to be reloaded [Late 19thC. Named for Oliver *Winchester* (1810–80), the U.S. manufacturer of the rifle.]

winch·man /winchmən/ (*plural* **-men** /-mən/) *n.* somebody who operates a winch

wind[1] /wind/ *n.* **1.** MOVING AIR air moving across the surface of the planet or through the atmosphere at a speed fast enough to be noticed **2.** AIR MOVED ARTIFICIALLY air that is being made to move by a device such as a fan **3.** POWER TO BREATHE the power to breathe, especially when making an effort such as running **4.** BREATH the breath of normal breathing and talking **5.** INFORMATION HINTING AT SOMETHING news that brings information of something intended to be secret ○ *If wind of this gets out, we've had it.* **6.** MUSIC MUSICAL INSTRUMENTS the group of musical instruments that require a flow of air to produce a sound. These include both woodwind and brass instruments. ○ *the wind section of the orchestra* **7.** SOCIAL OR ECONOMIC FORCE a force or movement bringing something such as change or destruction (*formal*) ○ *"The wind of change is blowing through the continent."* (Harold Macmillan, *speech to South African parliament*; Feb 3, 1960) **8.** HUNT AIR CARRYING A SCENT the air on which a scent, e.g., that of a hunter, is carried **9.** PHYSIOL STOMACH GAS gas that builds up in the stomach and intestines while food is being digested **10.** ASTRON FLOW OF PARTICLES INTO SPACE a flow of particles ejected into space from the surface of the Sun or a star **11.** IDLE TALK talk that is empty and meaningless **12.** VANITY boastful vanity **13.** DIRECTION OF WIND the direction from which the wind blows (*literary*) ■ **winds** *npl.* MUSIC PLAYERS OF WIND INSTRUMENTS the musicians in an ensemble, especially an orchestra, who play wind instruments ■ *v.* (**wind·ed, wind·ing, winds**) **1.** *vt.* MAKE SOMEBODY SHORT OF BREATH to make somebody unable to breathe in enough air, e.g., because of too much exertion or by a blow to the abdomen **2.** *vt.* LET HORSE REST to allow a horse to rest after exertion **3.** *vti.* HUNT SMELL SOMEBODY OR SOMETHING to get a scent of somebody or something in the air **4.** *vt.* HUNT PURSUE ANIMAL BY SCENT to pursue an animal in a hunt by following its scent **5.** *vt.* EXPOSE SOMETHING TO WIND to expose something to the wind, e.g., in order to dry it [Old English. Ultimately from an Indo-European base meaning "to blow" that is also the ancestor of English *weather* and *vent.*] ◇ **be in the wind** to be about to happen or be likely to happen ◇ **get wind of something** to hear indirectly about something ◇ **get your second wind** to recover your natural breathing pattern, and your usual energy levels, after a period of breathlessness and great effort ◇ **sail close to the wind** to come very close to breaking the law or a rule ◇ **see which way** *or* **how the wind blows** to wait and find out the nature of a situation before making a decision ◇ **swing** *or* **twist in the wind** to be left in a difficult or unpleasant situation without any help or support from other people (*informal*) ◇ **take the wind out of somebody's sails** to make somebody feel deflated, silly, or embarrassed, or put somebody at a disadvantage

WORD KEY: CULTURAL NOTE

Gone With the Wind, a movie (1939) by U.S. director Victor Fleming and producer David O. Selznick. Based on Margaret Mitchell's extremely popular novel (1936), this idealized portrait of the antebellum American South focuses on the relationship between dashing rake Rhett Butler (Clark Gable) and resourceful, prewar plantation belle and postwar "Iron Magnolia" Scarlett O'Hara (Vivien Leigh).

wind[2] /wīnd/ *v.* (**wound** /wownd/, **wound, wind·ing, winds**) **1.** *vti.* GO ALONG PATH WITH BENDS to move along a course with many bends and twists in it, or to make a route with many bends and twists in it ○ *The river winds lazily through the valley.* ○ *The procession wound its way slowly up the hill.* **2.** *vi.* FOLLOW SPIRAL PATH to go in a spiral path ○ *smoke winding slowly up into the air* **3.** *vti.* GO OR PUT AROUND to go around something in a coil or coils, or to wrap something around something else in a coil or coils ○ *winding the thread onto the bobbin* **4.** *vt.* WRAP SOMETHING WITH COILS to cover or decorate something by wrapping something else around it in coils ○ *She wound the injured arm with a scarf.* **5.** *vt.* MOVE SOMETHING UP OR DOWN to move or lift something by turning a handle or pressing a button ○ *I wound the car window down.* **6.** *vti.* MOVE SOMETHING BACKWARD OR FORWARD to move something such as film forward or backward by turning a handle or pressing a button, or to be moved in this way ○ *Let's wind the tape back and see that part again.* **7.** *vt.* MAKE SOMETHING REVOLVE to turn something such as a crank with a circular motion **8.** *vt.* MAKE A CLOCKWORK MECHANISM WORK to turn a key or handle in a clock or clockwork device in order to make the mechanism operate, usually by means of a spring that tightens on being wound **9.** *vt.* INTRODUCE SOMETHING SLYLY to introduce something into something else in a sly way ■ *n.* **1.** CURVE OR BEND a bend or twist in something such as a river or a path **2.** ACT OF WINDING SOMETHING the act of winding something such as a clock or motor, or a single turn in this process [Old English *windan.* Ultimately from a prehistoric Germanic base that is also the ancestor of English *wander* and *wend.*]

wind down *v.* **1.** *vi.* GO MORE SLOWLY to operate more and more slowly and then stop because the spring by which a mechanism works is losing or has lost its tension **2.** *vi.* RELAX to relax after a period of feeling stressed or tense **3.** *vti.* STEADILY REDUCE WORK to gradually reduce the amount of work done before stopping completely

wind up *v.* **1.** *vt.* FINISH ACTIVITY to conclude something or to bring an activity to an end **2.** *vi.* END UP to come to be in a particular place or situation as a result of, or at the end of, a series of earlier events (*informal*) **3.** *vt.* MAKE SOMEBODY TENSE to make somebody nervous or irritated, usually deliberately (*informal*) (*often passive*) **4.** *vi.* BASEBALL PREPARE TO PITCH to make a windup in preparation for pitching the ball in baseball

wind[3] /wīnd, wind/ (**wind·ed** *or* **wound, wind·ed** *or* **wound** /wownd/, **wind·ing, winds**) *v.* **1.** *vti.* BLOW SOMETHING to blow a horn or bugle to create a sound **2.** *vt.* MAKE SIGNAL BY BLOWING to make a signal by blowing a horn [14thC. From WIND[1]. Originally in the meaning of "to follow by scent."]

wind·age /windij/ *n.* **1.** DEFLECTION CAUSED BY WIND the amount of deflection the wind will produce in a projectile **2.** ALLOWANCE MADE FOR WIND DEFLECTION the amount needed to adjust the aim of a projectile to counter wind deflection **3.** DIFFERENCE BETWEEN BORE AND PROJECTILE the amount by which the bore of a gun is larger than the bullet or shell it fires, so that gases can escape **4.** SAILING PART OF SHIP ABOVE WATER the part of a ship's body that is above the water and consequently causes wind resistance **5.** MECH ENG FRICTION BETWEEN AIR AND MOVING PARTS the friction between air and the moving parts of a machine, which tends to slow the machine. For example, in an electric generator, the windage is the friction between the rotating element, the rotor, and the surrounding air.

wind·bag /wind bàg/ *n.* **1.** BORING TALKER somebody who talks a great deal but has very little of interest or value to say (*informal*) **2.** MUSIC BAG IN MUSICAL INSTRUMENT the bag in a set of bagpipes into which air is forced by the player's lungs or a set of bellows and from which it flows to produce sound

wind·bell *n.* BELL RUNG BY WIND a light bell that rings when the wind moves it ■ **wind·bells** *npl.* WIND CHIMES a set of wind chimes

wind·blast /wínd blàst/ *n.* the harmful effect of air friction on a pilot who has ejected from an aircraft traveling at high speed

wind·blown /wínd blōn/ *adj.* **1.** BLOWN BY THE WIND blown about by the wind ○ *They came back from their walk looking a bit windblown.* **2.** GROWING IN SHAPE CAUSED BY WIND growing in a shape caused by the action of the prevailing winds **3.** *NZ* BLOWN DOWN blown down by the wind

wind·borne *adj.* carried or dispersed by the wind

wind·bound /wínd bòwnd/ *adj.* unable to sail because the wind is blowing in the wrong direction

wind·break /wínd bràyk/ *n.* something such as a wall or hedge that breaks the force of the prevailing wind

Wind·break·er /wínd bràykər/ *tdmk.* a trademark for a jacket of nylon or other wind-resistant fabric, usually gathered at the waist and wrist, and sometimes with a hood

wind·bro·ken *adj.* used to describe a horse that has impaired breathing, e.g., because of heaves

wind·burn /wínd bùrn/ *n.* redness and inflammation of the skin caused by exposure to harsh wind —**wind·burned** *adj.*

Wind Cave Na·tion·al Park national park in the Black Hills of southwestern South Dakota, established in 1903. It is noted for its limestone caverns. Area: 44 sq. mi./114 sq. km.

wind·cheat·er /wínd chèetər/ *n. U.K.* a warm windproof outer jacket with tight-fitting neck, cuffs, and waistband, and sometimes with a hood

wind chest *n.* a compartment in an organ that stores wind from the bellows under pressure before it goes to the pipes

wind·chill fac·tor /wìnd chill-/, **windchill** *n.* a temperature in calm conditions that has the equivalent effect on exposed skin as the combination of a given temperature and wind speed

wind chime *n.* a musical decoration consisting of objects such as beads or metal tubes suspended on strings so that they will make a pleasant noise when moved by the wind

wind cone *n.* = **windsock**

wind·ed /wíndəd/ *adj.* unable to breathe easily because of exertion or a blow to the abdomen

win·der /wíndər/ *n.* **1.** MECH ENG SOMETHING THAT WINDS UP a key, knob, or other device that is used to wind up a spring-powered mechanism such as a clock **2.** SOMEBODY OR SOMETHING THAT WINDS SOMETHING a person or device that winds thread or textiles around a spool, cone, or tube **3.** OBJECT FOR WINDING SOMETHING AROUND a spool or bobbin around which something such as thread is wound **4.** BUILDING STEP IN SPIRAL STAIRCASE a step in a spiral staircase or at the turn of a staircase that is narrower at the inside of the curve

wind·fall /wínd fàwl/ *n.* **1.** MONEY OBTAINED UNEXPECTEDLY something good that is received unexpectedly, especially a sum of money **2.** SOMETHING BLOWN DOWN BY WIND something that the wind has blown down, especially a piece of ripe fruit blown off a tree

wind farm *n.* an area of land with a large number of electricity-generating windmills or wind turbines

wind·flaw /wínd flàw/ *n.* = **flaw**[1] *n.* 1 [Early 20thC. Formed from WIND + FLAW.]

wind·flow·er /wínd flòwr/ *n.* an anemone plant such as the wood anemone

wind·gall /wínd gàwl/ *n.* a fluid-filled swelling around the fetlock joint of a horse, usually not associated with loss of function or lameness

wind gap *n.* a shallow pass or gap in a mountain ridge, often originally a water gap

wind gauge *n.* **1.** METEOROL = **anemometer** **2.** ARMS GUNSIGHT ATTACHMENT SHOWING ALLOWANCE FOR WIND an attachment to the sight on a musket or rifle showing how much the aim should be adjusted to allow for the effect of the wind on the bullet

wind harp *n.* = **aeolian harp**

Wind·hoek /wínd ho͝ok, wínt-, vínt-/ capital city of Namibia, located in the center of the country. Population: 125,000 (1990).

win·di·go *n.* = **wendigo** [Early 18thC. From Ojibwa *wintiko.*]

wind·ing /wínding/ *adj.* **1. TWISTING AND CURVING** made up of many consecutive curves or twists **2. SPIRALING** arranged or moving in a spiral ■ *n.* **1. SOMETHING WOUND** something wound or coiled around an object, or a single turn of it **2. ACT OF COILING** the act or process of coiling something **3. CURVING COURSE** the bending or curving course that something follows **4.** ELEC ENG **WIRE COIL CARRYING ELECTRICITY** a wire coil designed to have an electric current passing through it, forming part of numerous electrical devices such as electric motors and transformers [Old English *windung*] — **wind·ing·ly** *adv.*

wind·ing drum *n.* a revolving drum with a wire rope coiled around it that acts as the lifting mechanism of a hoist or winch

winding sheet, **winding-sheet** *n.* a sheet that a corpse is wrapped in before it is buried

wind in·stru·ment *n.* a musical instrument such as a trumpet or flute played by causing the air in the instrument to vibrate by blowing into or across the air tube

wind·jam·mer /wínd jàmmər/ *n.* a large sailing ship, especially a large and fast merchant ship [Late 19thC. So called because of its huge sail area.]

wind·lass /wíndləss/ *n.* **REVOLVING LIFTING DEVICE** a device that uses a rope or cable wound around a revolving drum to pull and lift things, especially the mechanism on a ship to raise and lower the anchor ■ *vt.* **(-lassed, -lass·ing, -lass·es) LIFT SOMETHING WITH WINDLASS** to raise or pull something using a windlass [14thC. Alteration of Old Norse *vindáss*, from *vinda* "to wind" + *áss* "pole."]

win·dle·straw /wínd'l strāw/ *n. U.K.* **1. DRY GRASS STALK** a thin dry stalk of grass (*regional*) **2. WEAK-WILLED PERSON** somebody who is regarded as lacking in strength of character (*regional archaic or literary*) [Old English *windelstrēaw*, from *windan* "to wind" + *strēaw* "straw"]

wind ma·chine *n.* **1.** THEATER **THEATRICAL DEVICE SIMULATING WIND** a device used backstage in a theater to simulate the sound of wind blowing, or a large fan that simulates windy weather on a movie set **2.** AGRIC **MACHINE PRODUCING STRONG CURRENT OF AIR** a machine that creates a strong current of air, e.g., a device that produces warm air to protect crops from frost

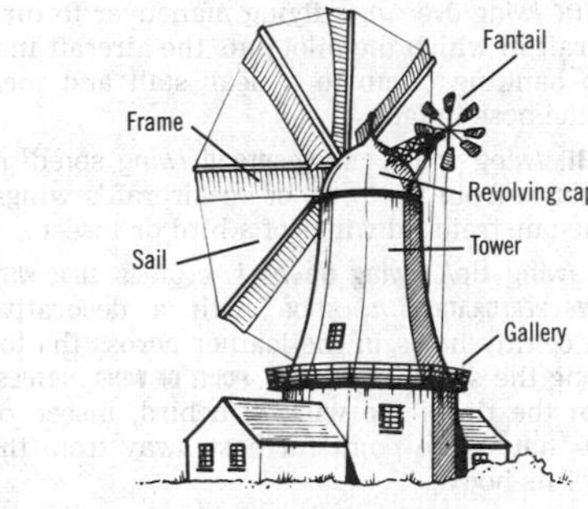

Windmill

wind·mill /wínd mìl/ *n.* **1. BUILDING WITH REVOLVING BLADES** a building with a set of wind-driven revolving sails or blades attached to the site of its roof that drive a grinding machine inside **2. REVOLVING BLADES OR GRINDING MECHANISM** the set of revolving sails or blades on a windmill, or the grinding mechanism inside the building **3. DEVICE HARNESSING WIND POWER** a building or device fitted with a set of revolving blades designed to harness the power of the wind, e.g., to pump water or generate electricity ■ *v.* **(-milled, -mil·ling, -mills) 1.** *vti.* **SPIN LIKE WINDMILL** to spin or turn like the sails of a windmill, or to be spun or turned in this way **2.** *vi.* **ROTATE UNPOWERED** to rotate solely by wind force and with no engine power ◇ **tilt at windmills** to struggle against imagined enemies or opponents

win·dow /wíndō/ *n.* **1. GLASS-COVERED OPENING IN BUILDING** an opening in a wall of a building, usually with an inner frame of wood or metal with glass fitted in it, to let in light or, when opened, air **2. GLASS-COVERED OPENING LETTING LIGHT IN** any glass-covered opening designed to let in light or, when opened, air, e.g., in a vehicle **3.** = **windowpane 4. DISPLAY IN STORE WINDOW** the area immediately behind a large window in the wall of a store, where merchandise is put on display **5. OPENING WHERE SOMETHING IS DISPENSED** an opening above a counter where somebody provides information or goods or services to customers **6. OPENING SIMILAR TO WINDOW** an opening that makes it possible to see something behind or underneath, e.g., the opening on some envelopes **7. PERIOD OF AVAILABLE TIME** a period of free time in a schedule available for use, or a limited time during which conditions are right for something to take place **8. OPPORTUNITY TO EXPERIENCE SOMETHING** an opportunity to see or experience something **9.** COMPUT **SECTION ON COMPUTER SCREEN** any of the rectangular frames into which a computer display can be divided and in which images output by application programs can be displayed, moved around the screen, or resized **10.** PHYS **PART OF ELECTROMAGNETIC SPECTRUM** the range of the electromagnetic spectrum that a given medium will allow to pass through it **11.** AIR FORCE = **chaff**[1] [Pre-12thC. From Old Norse *vindauga*, from *vindr* "wind" + *auga* "eye."] ◇ **be** *or* **go out the window** to be lost for good (*informal*)

win·dow box *n.* **1.** GARDENING **PLANTER ON WINDOW LEDGE** a soil-filled box on a window ledge with plants growing in it, or a box made to be used in this way **2. SPACE IN SASH WINDOW'S FRAME** either of the spaces in the sides of the frame of a sash window that conceal the weights, ropes, and pulleys that raise and lower the window's separate sections

win·dow dress·ing *n.* **1. DISPLAY IN STORE WINDOWS** a display of merchandise for sale in a store window **2. DECEPTIVELY APPEALING PRESENTATION** deceptively appealing presentation of something, intended to conceal flaws

win·dow en·ve·lope *n.* an envelope with a transparent panel at the front, making it possible to see the address to which the letter is being sent on the letter inside

win·dow·pane /wíndō pàyn/ *n.* a sheet of glass that forms part of a window

win·dow seat *n.* **1.** ARCHIT **INDOOR SEAT UNDER WINDOW** an indoor seat attached to a wall under a window, especially a window that is set into a recess **2.** TRANSP **SEAT BY WINDOW** a seat by a window in a plane, train, or bus

win·dow shade *n.* a shade for a window, e.g., a flexible fabric shade on a roller

win·dow-shop **(win·dow-shopped, win·dow-shop·ping, win·dow-shops)** *vi.* to look at goods displayed in store windows without a serious intention of buying anything —**win·dow-shop·per** *n.*

win·dow·sill /wíndō sìl/ *n.* the shelf on the bottom edge of a window, either a projecting part of the window frame or the bottom of the wall recess that the window fits into

wind·pipe /wínd pìp/ *n.* = **trachea**

wind-pol·li·nat·ed *adj.* pollinated by pollen that is carried to the plant by the wind

wind pow·er *n.* the force of the wind harnessed by windmills and wind turbines that convert it into electricity, or the electricity produced in this way

wind·proof /wínd pro͞of/ *adj.* resisting the force of the wind

wind·puff /wínd pùff/ *n.* = **windgall**

wind rose *n.* a circular diagram indicating the range of wind speeds and directions for a particular place over a given time period

wind·row /wínd rō/ *n.* **1. ROW OF DRYING HAY** a long thin pile of cut hay or grain designed to catch the wind and dry quickly **2. PILE BLOWN TOGETHER BY WIND** a long thin pile of things, especially leaves or snow, heaped up by the wind ■ *vt.* **(-rowed, -row·ing, -rows) GATHER HAY INTO WINDROWS** to gather cut grass, hay, or other crop material into windrows for a drying — **wind·row·er** *n.*

wind·sail /wínd sàyl/; *nautical* /wíndss'l, wínss'l/ *n.* **1.** SAILING **VENTILATION TUBE** a tube or funnel of sailcloth rigged over a companionway or hatch to catch breezes and provide ventilation for a ship **2. WINDMILL SAIL** a sail on a windmill

wind scale /wínd-/ *n.* a scale for measuring the strength of a wind, e.g., the Beaufort Scale

wind·screen /wínd skrēen/ *n.* **1. SCREEN PROTECTING SOMETHING FROM WIND** a screen used to protect somebody or something from the wind, e.g., by sunbathers on a beach or gardeners protecting plants **2.** *U.K.* = **windshield**

wind shake *n.* a crack between the growth rings of a tree, thought to be caused when the tree bends violently in the wind

wind shear *n.* the amount by which the speed of the wind varies at different altitudes, often causing difficulties for aircraft

wind·shield /wínd shēeld/ *n.* **1.** the pane of glass or plastic that forms the front window of a motor vehicle **2.** *U.K.* = **windscreen**

wind·shield wip·er *n.* a motorized device consisting of a rubber blade on a metal arm that is attached just below a vehicle's windshield, used for wiping rain and snow off the windshield

wind·sock /wínd sòk/ *n.* a fabric tube or cone attached at one end to the top of a pole, so that it blows like a flag to show which way the wind is blowing

Wind·sor /wínzər/ **1.** the southernmost city in Canada, situated directly southeast of Detroit, Michigan, in the province of Ontario. Population: 278,685 (1996). **2.** town in southern England, on the Thames River. Windsor Castle, located in the town, has been a royal residence for over 900 years. Population: 27,400 (1995). **3.** town in southeastern New South Wales, Australia. Founded in 1810, it is one of Australia's oldest settlements. Population: 21,317 (1996).

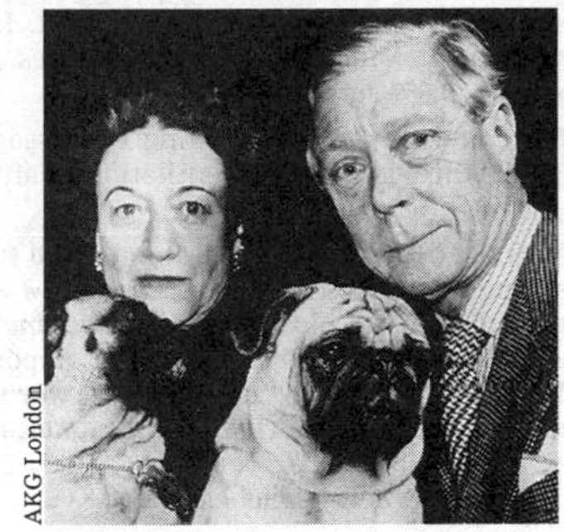

Duke and Duchess of Windsor

Wind·sor, Duke of the title granted to Edward VIII after his abdication from the British throne in 1936 and subsequent marriage to Wallis Simpson in June 1937. ➧ **Edward VIII**

Wind·sor chair *n.* a wooden chair that traditionally has a back formed of spindles, a saddle-shaped seat, and splayed legs [Mid-18thC. Named for the town of WINDSOR in southern England, where it originated.]

Wind·sor knot *n.* a large triangular knot in a man's necktie, made by putting an extra turn on each side of the loop that lies beneath the knot [Mid-20thC. Origin uncertain: probably named for the Duke of *Windsor*.]

Wind·sor tie *n.* a broad necktie loosely knotted with a double bow

wind·storm /wínd stàwrm/ *n.* a storm consisting of very strong winds and little or no rain or other precipitation

wind·suck·ing /wínd-/ *n.* the habit some horses have of biting the edge of a stall or fence while gulping air or sucking in air by making certain head and neck movements —**wind·suck·er** *n.*

wind·surf /wínd sùrf/ **(-surfed, -surf·ing, -surfs)** *vi.* to ride and steer a sailboard fitted with a movable sail —**wind·surf·er** *n.*

wind·surf·ing /wínd sùrfing/ *n.* the sport of riding and steering a sailboard

wind·swept /wínd swèpt/ *adj.* **1. EXPOSED TO WIND** exposed to the wind and usually very windy **2. DISHEVELED** disheveled in appearance as a result of exposure to the wind

wind tee *n.* a T-shaped weather vane at an airfield that shows which way the wind is blowing

wind tun·nel *n.* a tunnel-shaped chamber through which air can be passed at a known speed in order to test the aerodynamic properties of an object such as an aircraft or automobile placed inside it

wind·up /wínd ùp/ *adj.* **OPERATED BY TURNING HANDLE** made to work by turning a handle or key that winds an internal spring ■ *n.* **1. ENDING OF SOMETHING** the bringing to a close of something such as a meeting, dis-

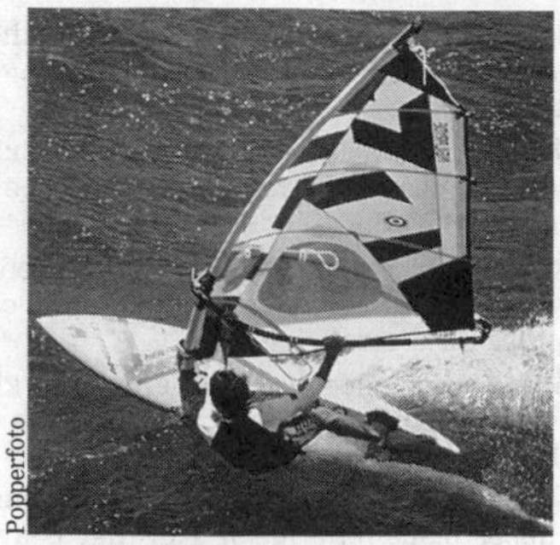
Popperfoto

Windsurfing

cussion, or electoral campaign **2.** BASEBALL **PITCHER'S PREPARATION TO THROW** a pitcher's preparation to pitch in baseball including pulling the arm back just before releasing the ball

wind·ward /wíndwərd/ *adj.* **FACING THE WIND** facing the wind, or on the side of something, especially a boat, that is facing the wind ■ *adv.* **INTO THE WIND** toward where the wind is coming from ■ *n.* **SIDE FACING WIND** the side facing the wind, or the direction that the wind is blowing from

Wind·ward Is·lands /wíndwərd-/ group of islands in the eastern Caribbean Sea, at the southern end of the Lesser Antilles. It includes Martinique and the independent island states of Dominica, St. Lucia, Grenada, and St. Vincent and the Grenadines. Area: 1,412 sq. mi./3,657 sq. km.

wind·way /wínd wày/ *n.* an opening or passage allowing air through, e.g., a ventilation shaft in a mine

wind·y /wíndee/ (**-i·er, -i·est**) *adj.* **1. WITH WIND BLOWING** with strong winds blowing **2. WHERE WINDS BLOW** where strong winds tend to blow ○ *a high and windy hill* **3. FULL OF EMPTY WORDS** full of long and important-sounding though largely meaningless words designed to impress people (*informal*) **4. FLATULENT** suffering from flatulence (*informal*) [Old English *windig*] —**wind·i·ly** *adv.* —**wind·i·ness** *n.*

wine /wīn/ *n.* **1. ALCOHOL FERMENTED FROM GRAPES** an alcoholic drink made by fermenting the juice of grapes **2. ALCOHOL FERMENTED FROM OTHER FRUIT** an alcoholic drink made by fermenting the juice of fruit other than grapes, or the juice of other plants **3. SOMETHING STIMULATING OR INTOXICATING** something that has a stimulating or intoxicating effect resembling that of wine (*literary*) **4.** COLORS **DARK PURPLISH-RED COLOR** a dark purplish-red color, like that of red wine ■ *adj.* COLORS **DARK PURPLISH-RED** of a dark purplish-red color, like that of red wine [Old English *wīn*, from Latin *vinum* (source of English *vine* and *vinegar*). Ultimately from a pre-Indo-European word that is also the ancestor of Greek *oinos* (source of *oenophile*).] ◇ **wine and dine** to enjoy, be treated, or treat somebody to an expensive meal out

wine bar *n. U.K.* a bar that specializes in serving wine, although beer and liquor may also be served

wine cel·lar *n.* **1. CELLAR FOR STORING WINE** a cellar where wine is stored, or any dark cool room used for storing wine **2. WINE SUPPLY** a stock of wine

wine cool·er *n.* **1.** HOUSEHOLD **CONTAINER FOR KEEPING WINE COOL** a container filled with ice or a refrigerant and used to keep one or more bottles of wine cool **2.** BEVERAGES **BOTTLED WINE COCKTAIL** a mixture of wine and fruit juice, sometimes with carbonated water, sold in bottles

wine·glass /wīn glàss/ *n.* a glass suitable for drinking wine, with a bowl mounted on a stem and usually a rounded base

wine grow·er *n.* somebody who grows grapes for making wine, especially the owner or manager of a vineyard who also oversees the winemaking

wine palm *n.* a palm tree whose fermented sap is used to make palm wine

wine·press /wīn prèss/ *n.* a piece of winemaking equipment that squeezes the juice from grapes

win·er·y /wīnəree/ (*plural* **-ies**) *n.* a place where wine is made

wine·skin /wīn skìn/ *n.* a container for wine made from the skin of a sheep or goat sewn into a bag

wine·tast·ing /wīn tàysting/ *n.* **1. SAMPLING OF WINE** the sampling of a variety of wines, either as a preliminary to buying wine or as instruction in the appreciation of wine **2. GATHERING TO SAMPLE WINES** a gathering to sample, learn about, and enjoy drinking a variety of wines

Win·frey /wínfree/, **Oprah** (*b.* 1954) U.S. talk show host and actor. Hosting *The Oprah Winfrey Show* from 1986, she pioneered television programs in which people publicly discuss their intimate problems. Full name **Oprah Gail Winfrey**

wing /wing/ *n.* **1.** BIRDS **BIRD'S LIMB FOR FLYING** either of a bird's feather-covered limbs that are typically used for flying **2.** ZOOL **INSECT'S OR BAT'S LIMB FOR FLYING** any of the large membrane-covered limbs on an insect or a bat that it uses for flying. Many insects have two pairs of wings. **3.** AIR **FLAT SURFACE PROJECTING FROM AIRCRAFT'S SIDE** either of the large flat surfaces sticking out from the sides of an aircraft's body that provide the aircraft's main source of lift. Although most modern aircraft have only one pair of wings, it was not unusual for earlier aircraft to have two pairs set one above the other. **4. FLAT PROJECTING PART** either of a pair of flat parts that stick out from the main body of something, e.g., the outgrowths of a wind-dispersed seedcase or the ends of an old-fashioned collar **5. FLIGHT** a means or manner of flying **6.** ARCHIT **PART OF BUILDING PROJECTING FROM MIDDLE** one of the parts of a building that project from the main part **7.** SPORTS **LONGER SIDE OF SPORTS FIELD** either of the longer sides of the field of play in some sports, at right angles to the sides where the goals are **8.** SPORTS **OFFENSIVE PLAYER ON SIDE OF FIELD** an offensive player who plays down one side of the field in some team sports such as soccer and field hockey, or the position the person plays **9.** POL **SUBDIVISION OF POLITICAL GROUP** a faction within a political party or movement, especially either of two broad factions, one more conservative, the other more liberal **10. SUBSIDIARY GROUP** a group attached and subordinate to a parent organization **11.** AIR FORCE **AIR FORCE UNIT** an air force unit that is larger than a group but smaller than a division **12.** MIL **PART OF MILITARY FORMATION** the left or right part of a large military formation such as a field army or a fleet **13.** THEATER **SCENERY PIECE AT SIDE OF STAGE** a piece of scenery at the side of the stage **14.** *U.K.* AUTOMOT = **fender** ■ **wings** *npl.* **1.** THEATER **SIDE OF THEATER STAGE** the areas of a theater to the sides of the stage, unseen by the audience **2.** AIR **QUALIFIED PILOT'S BADGE** a badge with a design in the shape of wings, worn by a trained and qualified pilot ■ *v.* (**winged, wing·ing, wings**) **1.** *vti.* **MOVE SWIFTLY** to move or travel somewhere swiftly, or send something with great speed **2.** *vt.* **WOUND BIRD BY HITTING WING** to wound a bird superficially by hitting it on its wing **3.** *vt.* **WOUND SOMEBODY, OR DAMAGE SOMETHING, SUPERFICIALLY** to wound somebody superficially, especially in the arm or leg, or cause only superficial damage to something [12thC. Of Scandinavian origin. Ultimately from an Indo-European base meaning "to blow" that is also the ancestor of English *wind, weather, ventilate,* and *nirvana.*] ◇ **be (waiting) in the wings** to be ready and prepared to do something, or available for use when needed ◇ **take somebody under your wing** to look after or protect somebody ◇ **with wings** to be taken away rather than consumed on the premises (*informal*) ○ *one cappuccino with wings* ◇ **wing it** to improvise (*informal*)

wing and wing *adv.* NAUT with sails extended on each side

wing·back /wíng bàk/ *n.* an offensive back in football who lines up outside an end, or the position taken by this player

wing bar *n.* a short white band on the wing of a bird, visible when the wing is folded

wing case *n.* INSECTS = **elytron**

wing chair *n.* an armchair with a high back and large side panels

wing col·lar *n.* a high stiff collar on a man's shirt, worn with the points at the upper corner turned down over the tie as part of formal dress

wing com·mand·er *n.* an officer of middle rank in some air forces, or the rank itself

wing cov·ert *n.* a small feather on a bird's wing, covering the base of the wing quills

wing·ding /wíng dìng/ *n.* **1. NOISY PARTY** a party or celebration, especially a noisy and boisterous one (*dated*) **2. VIOLENT OUTBURST** a wild or violent outburst such as a fit of anger (*slang*) [Early 20thC. Origin unknown.]

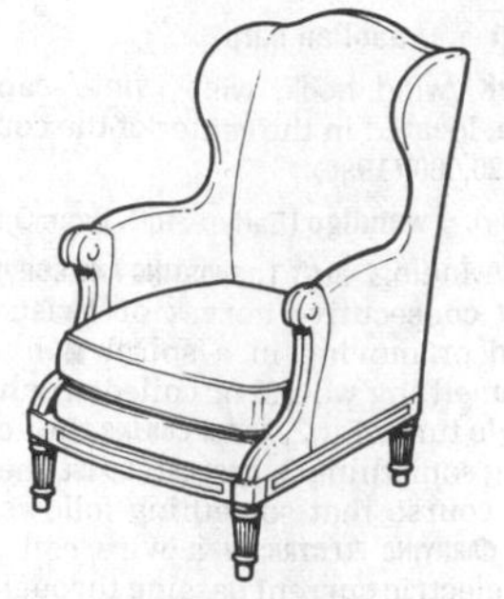

Wing chair

winged /wingd/ *adj.* **1. CAPABLE OF FLIGHT** able to fly because having wings **2. MOVING SWIFTLY** moving swiftly in a manner resembling flying (*literary*)

winged bean *n.* = **asparagus pea**

wing·er /wíngər/ *n.* SPORTS = **wing** *n.* 8

wing-foot·ed *adj.* moving swiftly in a manner resembling flying (*archaic or literary*)

wing·less /wíngləss/ *adj.* without wings or having only very small wings that are not used for flying. Certain parasitic flies and other primitive insects such as springtails and bristletails are described as wingless. —**wing·less·ness** *n.*

wing·man /wíng màn/ (*plural* **-men** /-mèn/) *n.* AIR a pilot who flies in a position behind, and to the side of, the leader of a flying formation

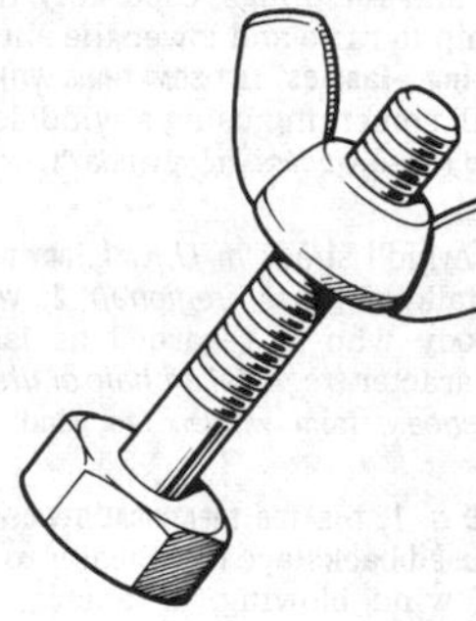

Wing nut

wing nut *n.* a nut that has flat projections on its sides for the fingers to grip

wing·o·ver /wíng ōvər/ *n.* a flying maneuver to turn an aircraft in which the pilot puts the aircraft into a steep banking climb to a near stall and then allows the nose to fall

wing·span /wíng spàn/, **wing·spread** /wíng sprèd/ *n.* the distance from tip to tip of an aircraft's wings, or of the outstretched wings of a bird or insect

wing·tip /wíng tìp/, **wing tip** *n.* **1.** CLOTHES **SHOE WITH DECORATIVE PERFORATIONS** a shoe with a decorative pattern of tiny holes in the leather across the toe and along the sides **2.** AIR, ZOOL **POINT OF WING FURTHEST FROM BODY** the tip of the wing of a bird, insect, or aircraft that is the point furthest away from the center of its body

wink /wingk/ *v.* (**winked, wink·ing, winks**) **1.** *vti.* **GESTURE BY CLOSING ONE EYE BRIEFLY** to close one eye briefly, usually either as a friendly greeting or to show that something just done or said is a joke or a secret **2.** *vi.* **SHINE INTERMITTENTLY** to shine intermittently or faintly ■ *n.* **1. BRIEF CLOSING OF ONE EYE** a brief closing of one eye as a greeting or signal **2. TWINKLING LIGHT** a twinkling or faintly flashing light **3. SHORT TIME** the briefest period of time **4. SHORT NAP** a brief nap or very short period of being asleep (*informal*) [Old English *wincian* "to close one's eyes"]

wink at *vt.* to pretend not to notice an offense or wrongdoing (*informal*)

wink·er /wíngkər/ *n.* **1. SOMEBODY WHO WINKS** somebody or something that winks **2. EYE OR PART OF EYE** an eye, or a part of the eye such as an eyelid or eyelash (*informal*) ■ **winkers** *npl.* **BLINKERS** a racehorse's blinkers

win·kle /wíngk'l/ (**-kled, -kling, -kles**) *n.* a small edible mollusk with a spirally coiled shell that lives in coastal waters. Genus: *Littorina.* [Late 16thC. Shortening of PERIWINKLE[1].]

Win·ne·ba·go[1] /wìnnə báygō/ (*plural* **-go** *or* **-gos** *or* **-goes**) *n.* **1.** PEOPLES **NATIVE N AMERICAN** a member of a Native North American people who formerly inhabited areas around Wisconsin and Illinois, and whose members now live principally in Wisconsin and Nebraska **2.** LANG **WINNEBAGO LANGUAGE** the Siouan language spoken by the Winnebago people [Mid-18thC. From Algonquian *winepyekoha*, literally "person of the dirty water."]

Win·ne·ba·go[2] (*plural* **-gos** *or* **-goes**) *tdmk.* a trademark for a large motor vehicle with cooking and sleeping facilities

Win·ne·ba·go, Lake /wìnnə báy gō/ the largest lake in Wisconsin, in the eastern part of the state. It forms part of the course of the Fox River. Area: 215 sq. mi./557 sq. km.

win·ner /wínnər/ *n.* **1. SOMEBODY OR SOMETHING WINNING COMPETITION** somebody or something that wins a competition or contest **2. SOMEBODY OR SOMETHING SUCCESSFUL** a very successful or popular person or thing, or one that seems likely to become successful or popular

win·ner's cir·cle *n.* an enclosure at a racetrack where the winning horses are unsaddled and prizes awarded to owners, trainers, and jockeys

Win·net·ka /wi nétkə/ village in northeastern Illinois, on the shore of Lake Michigan, north of Wilmette. It is a northern suburb of Chicago. Population: 11,940 (1996).

win·ning /wínning/ *adj.* **1. VICTORIOUS** victorious or bringing victory **2. CHARMING** very charming, to the extent that people are won over ■ **win·nings** *npl.* **MONEY WON** money or other valuables that are won, especially from gambling —**win·ning·ly** *adv.* —**win·ning·ness** *n.*

win·ning·est /wínningəst/ *adj.* winning the highest number of victories or prizes, or the most prize money (*informal*)

win·ning gal·ler·y *n.* an opening in a side wall of a court tennis court into which the ball is hit from the other side of the net in order to win a point

Win·ni·peg /wínni pèg/ capital city of Manitoba, Canada, located in the southern part of the province. Population: 666,700 (1996).

Win·ni·peg, Lake freshwater lake in central Manitoba, Canada. Its greatest depth is 60 ft./18m. Area: 9,417 sq. mi./24,390 sq. km.

Win·ni·peg couch *n. Can* a couch with no back or arms that opens out to form a double bed [Mid-20thC. Named for WINNIPEG.]

Win·ni·pe·go·sis, Lake /wìnnipi gṓssiss/ lake in western Manitoba, southern Canada, that drains into Lake Manitoba. Area: 2,103 sq. mi./5,447 sq. km.

Win·ni·pe·sau·kee, Lake /wìnnəpi sáwkee/ lake in central New Hampshire, near the southern extremity of the White Mountains. It contains more than 300 islands and is surrounded by wooded hills. Area: 72 sq. mi./186 sq. km.

win·now /wínnō/ *v.* (**-nowed, -now·ing, -nows**) **1.** *vti.* AGRIC **USE AIR TO REMOVE CHAFF** to separate grain from its husks (**chaff**) by tossing it in the air or blowing air through it **2.** *vt.* **EXAMINE SOMETHING TO REMOVE BAD PARTS** to examine something in order to remove the bad, unusable, or undesirable parts ■ *n.* **PROCESS OF WINNOWING** the process of separating grain from chaff, or a device used to do this [Old English *windwian*, from *wind* "wind"] —**win·now·er** *n.*

win·o /wí nō/ (*plural* **-os**) *n.* an offensive term used to refer to somebody who is addicted to alcohol, especially wine, and is usually homeless (*informal insult offensive*)

win·some /wínssəm/ *adj.* charming, especially because of a naive, innocent quality [Old English *wynsum* "pleasant," formed from *wynn* "joy." Ultimately from an Indo-European base meaning "to desire" that is also the ancestor of English *win, wish,* and *venerate.*] —**win·some·ly** *adv.* —**win·some·ness** *n.*

win·ter /wíntər/ *n.* **1. YEAR'S COLDEST SEASON** the coldest season of the year, which comes between autumn and spring and runs in the northern hemisphere from around November or December to February or March and in the southern hemisphere from June to August **2. CLOSING PERIOD OR PERIOD OF INACTIVITY** the closing part or period of something, or a period of decline or inactivity **3. A YEAR** one of a number of years, especially a great number (*literary*) ■ *v.* (**-tered, -ter·ing, -ters**) **1.** *vi.* **SPEND WINTER SOMEWHERE** to spend the winter in a particular place, especially away from home **2.** *vt.* **KEEP SOMETHING SOMEWHERE IN WINTER** to keep something, especially farm animals, in a particular place during the winter [Old English. Ultimately from an Indo-European base meaning "wet" that is also the ancestor of English *water, hydro-, inundate,* and *vodka.*]

win·ter ac·o·nite *n.* a low-growing plant of the buttercup family that is native to Europe and Asia and has a single yellow flower that blooms in winter or early spring. Latin name: *Eranthis hyemalis.*

win·ter·ber·ry /wíntər bèrree/ (*plural* **-ries** *or* **-ry**) *n.* a North American shrub of the holly family that has bright red berries and deciduous leaves that turn black in autumn. Latin name: *Ilex verticillata.*

win·ter·bourne /wíntər bàwrn/ *n.* a stream that flows only or mostly in winter, after heavy rains [Old English *winterburna*]

win·ter cher·ry *n.* **1. PLANT WITH BERRIES IN PAPERY CASES** a Eurasian plant of the nightshade family that has red berries enclosed in papery orange cases resembling Chinese lanterns. Latin name: *Physalis alkekengi.* **2. BERRY OF WINTER CHERRY PLANT** the fruit of the winter cherry

win·ter·cress /wíntər krèss/ *n.* a yellow-flowered plant of the mustard family, formerly used as a winter salad. Genus: *Barbarea.*

win·ter·feed /wíntər fēed/ (**-fed, -fed** /-fèd/, **-feed·ing, -feeds**) *vt.* to feed livestock in winter, e.g., on hay or silage, when there is little or no grazing

win·ter floun·der *n.* a reddish-brown flounder that lives in the northwestern Atlantic and is a popular food fish in winter. Latin name: *Pseudopleuronectes americanus.*

win·ter gar·den *n.* **1. GARDEN CONTAINING EVERGREEN PLANTS** a garden planted with evergreen plants, to give growth even in winter **2. GREENHOUSE CONTAINING WINTER PLANTS** a greenhouse or conservatory that contains winter plants

win·ter·green /wíntər grēen/ (*plural* **-greens** *or* **-green**) *n.* **1. LOW-GROWING EVERGREEN FLOWERING PLANT** a low-growing evergreen flowering plant with small leaves. Latin name: *Gaultheria procumbens.* **2.** = **oil of wintergreen** [Mid-16thC. Translation of Dutch *wintergroen.*]

win·ter·ize /wíntə rīz/ (**-ized, -iz·ing, -iz·es**), **winter·ise** *vt.* to prepare something, especially a house or an automobile, to withstand cold winter conditions —**win·ter·i·za·tion** /wìntərə záysh'n/ *n.*

win·ter·kill /wíntər kìl/ *vti.* (**-killed, -kill·ing, -kills**) **KILL PLANT BY EXPOSURE TO WINTER** to die, or cause a plant to die, from lack of adequate protection from winter weather conditions ■ *n.* **EXPOSURE TO LETHAL WINTER WEATHER** exposure to harsh winter weather that kills unprotected plants

win·ter mel·on *n.* a variety of fragrant melon similar to the honeydew and cantaloupe that keeps well when stored and has unusually smooth skin. Latin name: *Cucumis melo inodorus.*

Win·ter O·lym·pics, Win·ter O·lym·pic Games *npl.* an international gathering of athletes competing in a variety of winter sports, held every four years

win·ter purs·lane *n.* a North American annual flowering plant whose fleshy leaves are sometimes used in salad. Latin name: *Montia perfoliata.*

win·ter sports *npl.* sports such as skiing and ice skating performed on snow and ice

win·ter squash *n.* a slow-maturing squash that grows on long trailing vines, has a tough skin, and stores well. ◊ **summer squash**

win·ter·tide /wíntər tīd/ *n.* wintertime (*archaic or literary*)

win·ter·time /wíntər tīm/ *n.* the season of winter

win·ter·weight /wíntər wàyt/ *adj.* made of thick heavy fabric and designed to protect somebody or something from cold weather

win·ter wheat *n.* a variety of wheat planted in autumn, left in the ground over winter, and harvested the following spring or early summer

win·ter wren *n.* the common wren, a very small brownish bird with a short tail and a powerful warbling call. Latin name: *Troglodytes troglodytes.*

Win·throp /wínthrəp/, **John** (1588–1649) English-born American colonial governor. For most of the years between 1629 and 1649, he presided over the Massachusetts Bay Colony, exerting a decisive influence in shaping it as a Puritan commonwealth.

Win·throp, John (1606–76) English-born American colonial governor. The son of John Winthrop, he followed his father to Massachusetts and was commissioned to settle Saybrook Colony, Connecticut. He was governor of Connecticut (1657–76).

win·try /wíntree/ (**-tri·er, -tri·est**), **win·ter·y** /wíntəree/ (**-teri·er, -teri·est**) *adj.* **1. RELATING TO WINTER** relating to or typical of winter, especially in being cold **2. BLEAK** cheerless or unfriendly ○ *She gave him a wintry smile.* —**win·tri·ly** *adv.* —**win·tri·ness** *n.*

win-win *adj.* used to describe a situation in which all parties benefit in some way ○ *a win-win scenario*

win·y /wínee/ (**-i·er, -i·est**) *adj.* like wine in taste or appearance

winze /winz/ *n.* a steeply inclined or vertical shaft between levels in a mine [Mid-18thC. Alteration of obsolete *winds*, of uncertain origin: probably formed from WIND[2].]

wipe /wīp/ *v.* (**wiped, wip·ing, wipes**) **1.** *vt.* **RUB SOMETHING WITH LIGHT STROKES** to rub something with long light strokes with a soft material, or rub something lightly on a soft material ○ *wiped their hands on the towel* **2.** *vti.* **REMOVE OR BE REMOVED BY RUBBING** to remove something such as dirt with long light rubbing strokes, usually with a soft material, or be removed in this way ○ *The mark wiped off easily.* **3.** *vt.* **REMOVE RECORDING FROM TAPE** to remove recorded material from an audio- or videotape **4.** *vt.* **REMOVE SOMETHING** to remove something or get rid of it as if by wiping ○ *wiped from my memory* **5.** *vt.* **APPLY SOMETHING WITH LIGHT RUBBING** to apply something, especially a liquid or cream, by rubbing it on lightly, e.g., with a cloth or the hand ■ *n.* **1. LIGHT RUBBING STROKE** one or more long light rubbing strokes **2. DISPOSABLE CLEANING CLOTH** a soft disposable cloth or tissue soaked with a cleansing liquid, used for cleaning something such as the skin ○ *"Remember trash bags, wipes, and napkins. It's no fun sitting next to banana peel for five hours."* (*Washington Post*; July 1998) **3.** CINEMA, TV **ONE PICTURE PUSHING OTHER OFF SCREEN** an effect in which one picture on the screen appears to be pushed off the side of the screen by another, often used to move from scene to scene [Old English *wīpian*. Ultimately from an Indo-European base meaning "to move back and forth," which is also the ancestor of English *whip* and *vibrate.*]

wipe out *v.* **1.** *vt.* **DESTROY SOMETHING IN LARGE NUMBERS** to destroy large numbers of things or kill large numbers of people, especially suddenly and violently (*informal*) **2.** *vt.* **MURDER SOMEBODY** to murder or assassinate somebody (*slang*) **3.** *vi.* SPORTS **FALL FROM SURFBOARD** to fall from a surfboard, either because of losing control or because of being knocked off by a wave, or fall or crash in some other sport (*informal*)

wiped out *adj.* (*slang*) **1. VERY TIRED** thoroughly exhausted **2. INTOXICATED** intoxicated by drugs or alcohol

wipe·out /wíp owt/ *n.* (*informal*) **1.** SPORTS **FALL IN SURFING** a fall from a surfboard, or a fall or crash in other sports, e.g., skiing and cycling **2. FAILURE OR DEFEAT** a total failure or a crushing defeat **3.** RADIO **RECEIVING OF RADIO SIGNAL MASKING OTHERS** the receiving of a radio signal that is so strong it makes receiving other signals impossible

wip·er /wípər/ *n.* **1.** AUTOMOT = **windshield wiper** **2.** MECH ENG **CAM PROJECTING FROM SHAFT** a cam that projects from a rotating shaft and is designed to move, dislodge, or lift another component **3.** ELEC ENG **ELECTRICAL DEVICE MOVING CONDUCTING ARM** an electrical device in which a conducting arm may be rotated or moved over a row of contacts, e.g., a rheostat

WIPO /wípō/, **Wipo** *abbr.* World Intellectual Property Organization

wire /wīr/ *n.* **1. STRAND OF METAL** metal in the form of thin flexible strands, or a single strand of it **2.** ELEC **METAL STRAND CARRYING ELECTRIC CURRENT** a strand of metal, usually copper, that is encased in plastic or another insulating material and is used to carry an electric current **3.** TELECOM **CABLE PROVIDING TELECOMMUNICATIONS LINK** a cable that provides a telecommunications link **4. MESH STRUCTURE** a mesh made of strands of metal, or a structure such as a fence made of the mesh **5.** HORSERACING **RACETRACK FINISH LINE** the finish line on a racetrack **6. ANY END OR FINISH** the end of anything, or the time when something ends (*informal*) ○ *writing in their blue books right down to the wire* **7. ELECTRONIC LISTENING DEVICE** a small electronic listening device concealed in somebody's clothes (*slang*) **8.** TELECOM **TELEGRAM OR TELEGRAPH** a telegram or the telegraph system ■ *vt.* (**wired, wir·ing, wires**) **1. FASTEN SOMETHING WITH WIRE** to use wire to fasten or secure something **2. CONNECT ELECTRICAL EQUIPMENT** to connect a piece of electrical equipment to a power source or to another piece of equipment **3. PROVIDE A PLACE WITH NECESSARY EQUIPMENT** to provide a place with the equipment, especially electrical or electronic equipment, needed to give it a particular facility or capability **4. FIT SOMEBODY WITH A LISTENING DEVICE** to fit somebody or a place with a concealed electronic listening device (*slang*) **5. SEND A TELEGRAM** to send a telegram to somebody, or send something to somebody by means of a telegram [Old English *wīr* "metal thread." Ultimately from an Indo-European base meaning "to twist," which is also the ancestor of English *withy* and *garland*.] ◇ **go to the wire** to risk your reputation, job, or life in order to help somebody (*informal*) ◇ **have** *or* **get your wires crossed** have a misunderstanding

wire brush *n.* a brush with short stiff wires instead of bristles

wire cloth *n.* a flexible mesh of soft fine wires woven closely together, used to make strainers and some types of screening

wired /wīrd/ *adj.* **1. SUPPORTED BY WIRE** supported or strengthened by wire **2.** COMPUT **EQUIPPED FOR INTERNET** having computer equipment that allows use of the Internet (*informal*) ○ *"Ireland has seen Dublin go wired."* (*Newsweek*; November 1998) **3. FITTED WITH LISTENING DEVICES** fitted with one or more concealed electronic listening devices (*slang*) **4. NERVOUS** full of nervous energy, especially because under the influence of drugs (*slang*)

wire·draw /wīr dràw/ (**-drew** /-dròo/, **-drawn** /-dràwn/, **-draw·ing, -draws**) *vt.* **1.** METALL **MAKE WIRE FINER** to reduce the diameter of a wire by pulling it through successively smaller dies **2. SPIN SOMETHING OUT** to spin something out to great lengths, overrefining it and treating it with excessive subtlety [Late 16thC. Back-formation from earlier *wiredrawer* "somebody skilled in drawing metal into threads."]

wire en·tan·gle·ment *n.* a barrier of barbed wire used to keep enemy troops back

wire fox ter·ri·er *n.* a fox terrier with a wirehaired coat

wire·free /w-r frèe/ *adj.* used especially to describe telephones that do not use electrical wires in order to operate ○ *"Today, more than 1.7 million people subscribe to our wirefree services."* (*Marketing Week*; December 1998)

wire gauge *n.* **1. GAUGE MEASURING WIRE THICKNESS** a gauge used to measure the thickness of wire or sheet metal **2. SYSTEM OF MEASURING WIRE** a standard system of sizes for measuring wire

wire gauze *n.* a fine mesh of thin wires woven closely together

wire glass *n.* glass reinforced with a sheet of wire mesh embedded in it

wire grass *n.* a coarse grass with tough wiry roots

wire·hair /wīr hàir/ *n.* = **wire fox terrier**

wire·haired /wīr hàird/ *adj.* having a coat of coarse stiff hair

wire·less /wīrləss/ *n.* **RADIO** a radio or a radio set (*dated*) ■ *adj.* **WITHOUT WIRES** lacking wires

wire·less te·leg·ra·phy *n.* a system that sends telegrams using radio signals, as opposed to a system connected by wires

wire·man /wīr man/ (*plural* **-men** /-men/) *n.* **1. INSTALLER OF CABLES** somebody who installs or repairs electrical or telecommunications cables **2. ELECTRONIC LISTENING DEVICES EXPERT** an expert at installing and operating electronic listening devices (*slang*)

wire net·ting *n.* mesh made of medium to thick wire that is stronger, less flexible, and has larger spaces than wire gauze

wir·er /wīrər/ *n.* somebody who uses snares to catch animals (*informal*)

wire re·cord·er *n.* an early type of magnetic recorder that used stainless steel wire instead of magnetic tape to record sound

wire rope *n.* strong thick rope made of twisted strands of wire

wire ser·vice *n.* a news agency that sends out syndicated news items to various media by means of wire or satellite

wire·tap /wīr tàp/ *vti.* (**-tapped, -tap·ping, -taps**) **TAP A TELEPHONE LINE** to make a wire connection to a telephone line in order to listen in secret to somebody's conversations ■ *n.* **SECRET CONNECTION TO A TELEPHONE LINE** a connection made to a telephone line in order to listen secretly to somebody's conversations —**wire·tap·per** *n.*

wire wheel *n.* **1.** AUTOMOT **VEHICLE WHEEL WITH WIRE SPOKES** a motor vehicle wheel that has wire spokes connecting the hub to the rim **2.** INDUST **WIRE POLISHING DISK ON POWER TOOL** a disk of coarse wires designed to be attached to a power tool and used for rubbing down metal

wire·work /wīr wùrk/ *n.* **1. LAYOUT OF WIRES** an arrangement or system of wires **2. SOMETHING MADE OF WIRE** something made by shaping or weaving wire **3.** ARTS **TIGHTROPE ACROBATICS** acrobatics performed on a tightrope

wire·works /wīr wùrks/ (*plural* **-works**) *n.* a factory where wire is made, or where wire articles are made

wire·worm /wīr wùrm/ *n.* the long thin hard-bodied larva of various kinds of beetle that feeds on plant roots and is a serious agricultural pest

wir·ing /wīring/ *n.* a network of electrical wires

wir·y /wīree/ (**-i·er, -i·est**) *adj.* **1. SLIM BUT STRONG** slim but muscular and strong **2. COARSE** stiff and coarse like wire **3. PRODUCED BY VIBRATING WIRES** produced by or sounding as though produced by vibrating wires —**wir·i·ly** *adv.* —**wir·i·ness** *n.*

wis /wiss/ (**wissed** *or* **wist** /wist/, **wiss·ing, wiss·es**) *vti.* to know, think, or suppose something (*archaic*) [Old English *wissian*]

Wis. *abbr.* Wisconsin

Wisconsin

Wis·con·sin /wi zkónssin/ state of the northern central United States, bordered by Lake Superior, Michigan, Lake Michigan, Illinois, Iowa, and Minnesota. Capital: Madison. Population: 4,891,769 (1990). Area: 65,500 sq. mi./169,644 sq. km. —**Wis·con·sin·ite** *n.*

Wisd. *abbr.* Wisdom of Solomon

wis·dom /wízdəm/ *n.* **1. GOOD SENSE** the knowledge and experience needed to make sensible decisions and judgments, or the good sense shown by the decisions and judgments made **2. ACCUMULATED LEARNING** accumulated knowledge of life or in a particular sphere of activity that has been gained through experience **3. OPINION WIDELY HELD** an opinion that almost everyone seems to share or express **4. SAYINGS** ancient teachings or sayings [Old English *wīsdōm*, formed from *wīs* (see WISE)]

Wis·dom lit·er·a·ture *n.* a speculative or didactic form of religious writing, exemplified in the Bible by the books of Job, Proverbs, and Ecclesiastes, and the Apocryphal books the Wisdom of Solomon and Ecclesiasticus

Wis·dom of Je·sus, the Son of Sir·ach /-sí ràak/ *n.* BIBLE = **Ecclesiasticus**

Wis·dom of Sol·o·mon *n.* an Apochryphal book of the Bible expounding Jewish doctrines in the terminology of Greek philosophy. It was probably written in the 1st century B.C.

wis·dom tooth *n.* one of the four teeth at the back of each side of the upper and lower jaw of human beings. They are the last teeth to come in. [Translation of Latin *dens sapientiae*; so called because the wisdom teeth usually appear in young adulthood]

Wis·dom writ·ings *n.* = **Wisdom literature**

wise[1] /wīz/ (**wis·er, wis·est**) *adj.* **1. KNOWING MUCH FROM EXPERIENCE** able to make sensible decisions and judgments on the basis of knowledge and experience **2. SENSIBLE** showing good sense or good judgment **3. LEARNED** knowledgeable about many subjects **4. SHREWD** capable of achieving some purpose or goal by cunning **5. DISRESPECTFUL** behaving in a way that is perceived as disrespectful or impudent (*informal*) ○ *Don't get wise with me!* **6. SKILLED IN OCCULT PRACTICES** skilled in magic or fortunetelling (*archaic*) [Old English *wīs*. Ultimately from an Indo-European base meaning "to see, know," which is also the ancestor of English *wit, vision,* and *idea*.] ◇ **be** *or* **get wise (to something)** to be or become aware of something, usually something dishonest or secret (*informal*) ◇ **put somebody wise (to something)** to let somebody know about something, or give somebody information about something (*informal*)

wise up *vti.* to become, or make somebody, aware or informed (*informal*)

wise[2] /wīz/ *n.* a way or manner (*archaic*) [Old English *wīse*. From a prehistoric Germanic word meaning "shape, form," literally "something seen."]

Wise /wīz/, **Isaac Mayer** (1819–1900) Bohemian-born U.S. rabbi. A leader in establishing Reform Judaism in the United States, he formed the Central Conference of American Rabbis (1889).

Wise, Stephen Samuel (1874–1949) Hungarian-born U.S. Zionist. Outspoken on behalf of labor and other liberal causes, he was one of the founders of the Federation of American Zionists (1893).

-wise *suffix.* in a particular manner or direction ○ *crabwise* ○ *coastwise* [Old English *-wīsan*, formed from *wīse* "manner" (see WISE[2])]

wise·a·cre /wīz àykər/ *n.* **1. ANNOYINGLY AUTHORITATIVE OR SELF-ASSURED PERSON** somebody who speaks with an authority or self-assurance that people find irritating, especially somebody who is not genuinely knowledgeable (*dated informal*) **2. INSOLENT SARCASTIC PERSON** somebody who is insolent and given to making wisecracks (*informal*) [Late 16thC. Alteration of Middle Dutch *wijsseggher* "soothsayer."]

wise·crack /wīz kràk/ *n.* **FLIPPANT REMARK** a flippant or sarcastic remark (*informal*) ■ *vi.* (**-cracked, -crack·ing, -cracks**) **MAKE WISECRACKS** to make flippant or sarcastic remarks (*informal*) —**wise·crack·er** *n.*

wise guy *n.* somebody inclined to make impudent or sarcastic remarks (*informal*)

wise man *n.* **1. LEARNED MAN** a scholar or a very learned man **2. ANCIENT PRACTITIONER OF OCCULT ARTS** a man who, in ancient times, practiced any of the occult arts such as magic or astrology (*archaic*) **3. SPECIAL ADVISER** a man chosen as a special senior adviser to a government or other authority (*informal*) **4.** BIBLE **ONE OF MAGI** one of the three Magi who came to pay homage to the infant Jesus Christ

wis·en·heim·er /wīz'n hīmər/, **weis·en·heim·er** *n.* somebody inclined to make impudent or sarcastic remarks (*informal*) [Early 20thC. Formed from WISE[1], on the model of surnames such as *Oppenheimer* and *Guggenheimer*.]

wi·sent /vée zènt, véez'nt/ *n.* the bison that is native to Europe. Its head is smaller and higher than that of the North American bison. Latin name: *Bison bonasus*. [Mid-19thC. Via German from, ultimately, Old High German *wisunt*. Ultimately from an Indo-European word that is also the ancestor of English *bison*.]

wise·wom·an /wīz wòomən/ (*plural* **-en** /-wimmin/) *n.* a woman who is skilled in the art of using herbs to heal people and ease the pains of childbirth

wish /wish/ *v.* (**wished, wish·ing, wish·es**) **1.** *vt.* **DESIRE SOMETHING** to have a strong desire for something **2.** *vt.* **DEMAND SOMETHING** to want or demand something ○ *I wish you to leave him alone.* **3.** *vti.* **EXPRESS DESIRE** to express or feel a desire that something is true or will come to pass ○ *They wished me a safe journey.* ○ *We only wish for peace* **4.** *vt.* **WANT SOMETHING TO BE OTHERWISE** to desire somebody or something to be in a particular state ○ *We all wish it were different.* **5.** *vt.* **GREET SOMEBODY** to greet somebody in a particular way ○ *She wished me good afternoon as I left.* ■ *n.* **1. YEARNING** a desire or strong yearning for something ○ *I certainly had no wish to speak to him.* **2. EXPRESSION OF DESIRE** an expression of a desire or longing for something **3. SOMETHING WISHED** something that is desired **4. HOPE** a hope for somebody's welfare or health (*usually plural*) ○ *Give him our best wishes.* **5. POLITE REQUEST** a polite request (*formal*) (*often plural*) [Old English *wȳscan*. Ultimately from an Indo-European base meaning "to desire," which is also the ancestor of English *win* and *venerate*.] —**wish·er** *n.*

WORD KEY: SYNONYMS

See Synonyms at ***want***.

wish on *vt.* to wish that something, usually something unpleasant, would happen to somebody ○ *I wouldn't wish that on my worst enemy.*

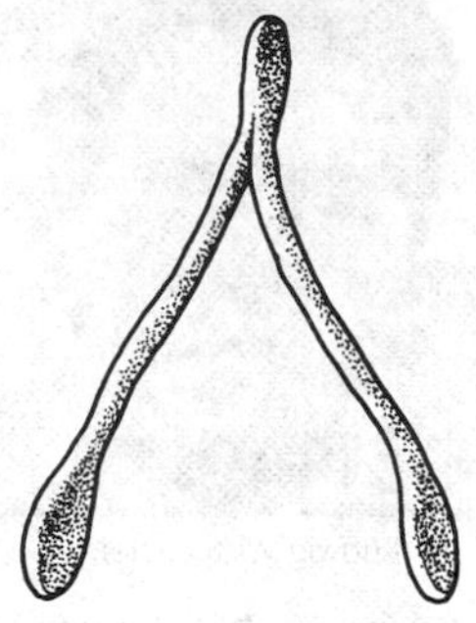

Wishbone

wish·bone /wísh bōn/ *n.* the V-shaped bone, actually two fused collarbones, found between the breasts of a chicken or other bird. Traditionally two people pull the bones apart and the person left holding the larger piece has a wish granted. Technical name **furcula**

wish·bone boom *n.* the boom on a sailboard that a windsurfer holds on to. It has two curving arms, one on either side of the sail, joined at the ends.

wishbone-T *n.* in football, a variant of the T-formation in which the halfbacks line up further from the line of scrimmage than the fullback

wish·ful /wíshfəl/ *adj.* wishing for something, or expressing a wish or longing —**wish·ful·ly** *adv.* —**wish·ful·ness** *n.*

wish ful·fill·ment *n.* in psychoanalytic theory, the process by which unconscious desires are realized in the imagination, mainly through dreams and fantasies

wish·ful think·ing *n.* the unrealistic belief that something that is wished for is actually true or will be realized

wish list *n.* an often informal list of things somebody would like to have or would like to happen

wish-wash *n.* (*archaic*) **1. WEAK DRINK** an unpleasantly weak or tasteless drink **2. DULL TALK OR WRITING** uninteresting and uninspiring talk or writing [Late 18thC. Doubling of WASH, in the sense "thin, weak."]

wish·y-wash·y /wìshee wáwshee/ *adj.* (*informal*) **1. INCAPABLE OF MAKING FIRM DECISIONS** changeable or fluctuating in character, especially unable to make firm decisions or develop clear opinions **2. LACKING STRENGTH OR COLOR** weak, lacking taste, or unattractively pale [Late 17thC. Doubling of *washy* "thin, watery," from WASH.] —**wish·y-wash·i·ly** *adv.* —**wish·y-wash·i·ness** *n.*

wisp /wisp/ *n.* **1. SOMETHING RESEMBLING THREAD** something that is thin and delicate like thread, especially a lock of hair, a piece of straw, or a streak of smoke **2. SOMEBODY SLENDER AND DELICATE** somebody or something that is slender and delicate ○ *a wisp of a child* **3. SOMETHING INSUBSTANTIAL** something that is vague and fleeting ○ *a wisp of a memory* **4. BUNDLE** a bundle of something, especially a bundle of hay or straw ■ *v.* (**wisped, wisp·ing, wisps**) **1.** *vt.* **BUNDLE STRAW OR HAY** to make a handful of straw or hay into a bundle **2.** *vi.* **MOVE LIKE WISP** to float like something delicate or faint [14thC. Origin unknown.] —**wisp·i·ly** *adv.* —**wisp·i·ness** *n.* —**wisp·y** *adj.*

wist (*archaic*) **1.** past participle, past tense of **wis 2.** past participle, past tense of **wit**

Wis·ter /wístər/, **Owen** (1860–1938) U.S. writer. His novel about cowboy life, *The Virginian* (1902), became the archetype for the Western.

wis·ter·i·a /wi stéeree ə/ (*plural* **-as** *or* **-a**) *n.* a deciduous climbing shrub native to North America and Asia, with blue, pink, or white flowers that hang down in clusters. Genus: *Wisteria*. [Early 19thC.

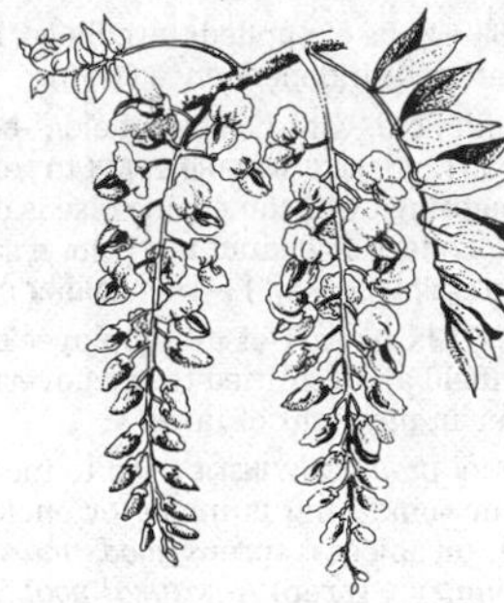

Wisteria

From modern Latin, genus name, from the name of the U.S. anatomist Caspar *Wistar* (1761–1818).]

wist·ful /wístfəl/ *adj.* deep in sad thoughts, especially thoughts of something yearned for or lost, or expressing this sad yearning [Early 17thC. Formed from obsolete *wistly* "intently," of uncertain origin.] —**wist·ful·ly** *adv.* —**wist·ful·ness** *n.*

wit[1] /wit/ *n.* **1. INGENIOUS HUMOR** apt, clever, and often humorous association of words or ideas, or a capacity for this **2. SPEECH OR WRITING SHOWING WIT** speech or writing that shows an apt, clever, and often humorous association of words **3. WITTY PERSON** somebody known for using wit **4. INTELLIGENCE** mental acumen, intelligence, or reasoning power ■ **wits** *npl.* **SHREWDNESS** mental acumen, shrewdness, or reasoning power [Old English *wit* "mind, understanding." Ultimately from an Indo-European base meaning "to see, know," which is also the ancestor of English *wisdom, vision,* and *idea*.] ◇ **be at your wits' end** to be in despair as to how to cope with something ◇ **live by your wits** to use cunning and ingenuity in order to survive

wit[2] /wit/ (**wist** /wist/, **wist, wit·ting,** *1st person present singular* **wot** /wot/, *3rd person present singular* **wits** *or* **wot**) *vti.* to know or become aware of something (*archaic*) [Old English *witan*; ultimately related to WIT[1]] ◇ **to wit** that is to say

wit·an /wí taàn/ *n.* an assembly of the king's counselors in Anglo-Saxon England [Early 19thC. Revival of Old English, "counselors," from *wita* "counselor," literally "one who knows"; ultimately related to WIT[1].]

Wit·bank /wít bàngk/ town in Mpumalanga Province, northeastern South Africa. Population: 83,400 (1998).

wit·blits /vít blits/ *n.* *S Africa* illegally distilled alcoholic liquor, usually made from grapes [Mid-20thC. From Afrikaans, literally "white lightning."]

witch /wich/ *n.* **1. SOMEBODY WITH MAGIC POWERS** somebody, especially a woman, who is supposed to have magical or wonder-working powers that are most often used malevolently **2. FOLLOWER OF NATURE RELIGION** a follower of Wicca, a pre-Christian natural religion **3. OFFENSIVE TERM** an offensive term that deliberately insults a woman regarded as ugly, vicious, or malicious (*insult*) **4. SEDUCTIVE WOMAN** an alluring or seductive woman (*offensive in some contexts*) ■ *vt.* (**witched, witch·ing, witch·es**) **EXERCISE WITCHCRAFT** to cause or change something by witchcraft [Old English *wicce* "witch" and *wicca* "wizard," both ultimately related to WAKE[1] and WATCH]

witch·craft /wích kràft/ *n.* **1. EXERCISE OF MAGICAL POWERS** the art or exercise of magical powers **2. EFFECT OF MAGICAL POWERS** the effect or influence of magical powers **3. SEDUCTIVE CHARM** alluring or seductive charm or influence (*informal*)

witch doc·tor *n.* **1. TRIBAL HEALER OR MAGICIAN** in tribal societies, somebody who practices healing, divining, or other magical powers **2. HUNTER OF WITCHES** in some African cultures, somebody who detects or identifies supposed witches

witch elm *n.* = **wych elm**

witch·er·y /wíchəree/ *n.* **1. PRACTICE OF MAGIC** the practice of witchcraft or magic (*dated or literary*) **2. BEWITCHING CHARM** charm or influence that has a bewitching quality or effect

witch·es' brew *n.* **1. DIABOLICAL MIXTURE** a malevolent or diabolical mixture of different things ○ *an article that was a witches' brew of spite and innuendo* **2. POTION** a potion concocted by a witch or witches

witch·es' broom *n.* an abnormal tufted growth of shoots on a tree or woody plant, usually caused by parasitic fungi. The fungi usually responsible are of the genus *Taphrina*.

witch·es' but·ter *n.* = **jelly fungus**

witch·es' Sab·bath *n.* a midnight assembly for devil-worship or other rites

witch grass *n.* **1. GRASS WITH CREEPING ROOTS** a North American grass with creeping roots. Latin name: *Panicum capillare*. **2.** = **couch grass** [Origin uncertain: probably an alteration of QUITCH GRASS]

witch ha·zel *n.* **1. TREES SHRUB WITH YELLOW FLOWERS** a tree or shrub with toothed, egg-shaped leaves and small yellow flowers. There are several species, the best-known being *Hamamelis virginiana* of eastern North America, which is related to the sweet gum and witch alder and blooms in late autumn. **2. PHARM SOOTHING LOTION** a mixture of alcohol, water, and extract from the bark and dried leaves of the witch hazel tree, used as an astringent and in the treatment of sprains and bruises [Alteration of earlier *wych*]

witch-hunt, witch hunt *n.* **1. CAMPAIGN AGAINST DISSENTERS** an intensive systematic campaign directed against those who have done something wrong or who hold different views **2. HIST PERSECUTION OF WITCHES** a persecution of people believed to be witches —**witch-hunt·er** *n.*

witch·ing /wíching/ *adj.* **1. SUITABLE FOR WITCHCRAFT** suitable for or resembling witchcraft (*archaic*) **2. BEWITCHING** bewitching (*literary*) ■ *n.* **WITCHCRAFT** witchcraft or sorcery (*archaic*)

witch·ing hour *n.* midnight, said to be the time when witches appear

witch·weed /wích wèed/ *n.* a parasitic plant with small red flowers, native to South Africa and introduced into the southern United States. Genus: *Striga*.

wit·e·na·ge·mot /wítt'nəgə mōt/ *n.* = **witan** [Old English *witena gemōt* "assembly of wise men," from *wita* (see WITAN) + *gemōt* "assembly" (source of English *moot*)]

Wite-Out /wít òwt/ *tdmk.* a trademark for a white fluid used to cover up mistakes in writing, typing, or printing

with /with, with/ *prep.* **1. IN THE COMPANY OF** used to indicate that somebody is accompanying or is in the company of another person or people, or that something is accompanying something else ○ *at the amusement park with their children* ○ *Do you still want me to go with you?* **2. USED TOGETHER** used together or at the same time ○ *She brought ice cream to go with dessert.* **3. INVOLVING** involving that person or people ○ *He organized the meeting together with a professor from the university.* **4. AGAINST** in opposition to ○ *students competing with each other for a limited number of spaces* **5. BY MEANS OF** by the means of or using a particular object, substance, or system ○ *After 18 months, all the rats treated with the altered virus were healthy.* **6. CARRYING** carrying or having in one's possession ○ *He came into the office with a box full of files.* **7. HAVING** having as a possession, attribute, or feature ○ *The movie is in French with English subtitles.* **8. BECAUSE OF** in a particular condition as a result of something ○ *I felt heartsick and faint with anxiety.* **9. ON OR IN** used to indicate that something has a substance or things on or in it ○ *brightly painted walls covered with photographs of Italy* **10. CONCERNING** used to indicate the person or thing that a state, quality, or action relates to or affects ○ *not happy with the service provided* **11. IN THIS WAY** used to indicate the way something is done, or the degree to which it is done ○ *sitting with her head on his shoulder* **12. ACCOMPANIED BY** used to indicate the feeling, gesture, sound, or facial expression that accompanies or causes an action ○ *walks with a limp* **13. IN THE LIGHT OF** in the light of or given the situation mentioned ○ *With all the problems you have, the last thing you need is a lawsuit.* **14. IN SPITE OF** in spite of the situation mentioned ○ *With all his charm and good breeding, he's a man not to be trusted.* **15. AT TIME OF** at the same time as ○ *He woke with the alarm and hurriedly dressed.* **16. FOLLOWING THE DIRECTION OF** in the same direction as ○ *They were to sail with the tide the next day.* **17. ACCORDING TO** used to indicate that something happens or is true according to something else ○ *how much the risk of death increases with age* **18. AFTER** following on from ○ *With a final wave goodbye she turned the corner.* [Old English *wiþ* "with, against." Ultimately from an Indo-European word meaning "apart," which is also the ancestor of English *wide*.] ◇ **be with it 1.**

to be fashionable or up to date with fashion (*informal*) **2.** to be able to understand what is going on in a situation (*informal*) ◇ **be with somebody 1.** to understand somebody **2.** to approve of or support somebody ○ *Are you with us or not?*

with·al /wi*th* áwl/ *adv.* (*archaic*) **1.** MOREOVER along with the rest or in addition **2.** NEVERTHELESS in spite of that ■ *prep.* WITH with (*archaic*) [12thC. Formed from WITH + ALL.]

with·draw /wi*th* dráw, with-/ (**-drew** /-dróo/, **-drawn** /-dráwn/, **-draw·ing, -draws**) *v.* **1.** *vt.* REMOVE SOMETHING to remove or take back something that was previously provided or in place **2.** *vt.* RETRACT STATEMENT to deny the truth or validity of something that was previously stated **3.** *vi.* RETREAT FROM POSITION to retreat or retire from a position **4.** *vt.* TAKE MONEY FROM ACCOUNT to take money out of an account [Literally "to pull away from"] —**with·draw·able** *adj.* —**with·drawer** *n.*

with·draw·al /wi*th* dráw əl, with-/ *n.* **1.** TAKING MONEY FROM BANK the act of taking money from a bank account, or the amount of money taken out **2.** PERIOD OF FIGHTING ADDICTION a period during which somebody addicted to a drug or other addictive substance stops taking it, causing the person to experience painful or uncomfortable symptoms **3.** TAKING SOMETHING AWAY the act or condition of taking something away or no longer taking part in something **4.** RETREAT OF ARMY retreat or retirement of an army or other military force from an area in which it was fighting

with·drawn /wi*th* dráwn/ *adj.* **1.** INTROVERTED not friendly or sociable but quiet and thoughtful, especially to an unusual or abnormal degree **2.** REMOVED FROM MARKET removed from circulation, competition, or activity ■ past participle of **withdraw** —**with·drawn·ness** *n.*

with·drew past tense of **withdraw**

withe /with, wi*th*, wī*th*/ *n.* **1.** FLEXIBLE STEM a strong flexible twig or stem used to bind something **2.** FLEXIBLE TOOL HANDLE a shock-absorbing flexible handle for a tool ■ *vt.* (**withed, with·ing, withes**) BIND SOMETHING WITH WITHES to bind something with withes [Old English *wiþþe*. Ultimately from an Indo-European base meaning "to twist, bend," which is also the ancestor of English *withy* and *wire*.]

with·er /wí*th*ər/ (**-ered, -er·ing, -ers**) *v.* **1.** *vti.* SHRIVEL to shrivel or dry up as part of the process of dying, or make something, especially a plant or part of a plant, shrivel in this way **2.** *vi.* FADE AWAY to fade or lose freshness or vitality **3.** *vti.* MAKE SOMEBODY LOSE CONFIDENCE to make somebody feel embarrassed, foolish, or incapable of activity as the object of scorn or contempt, or lose confidence in the face of somebody's scorn [14thC. Origin uncertain: probably a variant of WEATHER in the sense "to expose to the elements."] —**with·ered** *adj.* —**with·er·er** *n.*

with·er·ing /wí*th*əring/ *adj.* expressing scorn or contempt with the intention of causing somebody to feel embarrassed or foolish ○ *"When he assumed this attitude in the courtroom, ears were always pricked up, as it usually foretold a flood of withering sarcasm."* (Willa Cather, *The Troll Garden*; 1905) —**with·er·ing·ly** *adv.*

with·er·ite /wí*th*ə rìt/ *n.* a rare grayish-white barium carbonate mineral found in veins associated with lead ore, used as a barium ore [Late 18thC. Named for the English scientist William *Withering* (1741–99), who first described the mineral.]

withe rod *n.* a viburnum that has tough flexible shoots. Latin name: *Viburnum cassinoides* and *Viburnum nudum*.

with·ers /wí*th*ərz/ *npl.* the ridge between the shoulder bones of a horse, sheep, ox, or similar four-legged animal, forming the highest part of its back [Early 16thC. Origin uncertain: probably ultimately from Old English *wiþer* "against."]

with·er·shins /wí*th*ər shìnz/, **wid·der·shins** /wíddər-/ *adv.* (*literary*) **1.** *Scotland* IN THE WRONG DIRECTION in the direction that is contrary to the natural course **2.** *U.K.* COUNTERCLOCKWISE counterclockwise or in the direction that is contrary to the course of the sun [Early 16thC. Alteration of Middle Low German *weddersinnes*, from Middle High German *widersinnes*, from *wider* "against, opposite" + *sin* "sense, direction."]

With·er·spoon /wí*th*ər spòon/, **John** (1723–94) British-born U.S. clergyman and educator. As president of the College of New Jersey, now Princeton University (1768–94), he expanded the college. He signed the Declaration of Independence (1776).

with·hold /with hṓld, wi*th*-/ (**-held** /-héld/, **-held, -hold·ing, -holds**) *v.* **1.** *vti.* HOLD SOMETHING BACK to refuse to do or give something until something else is done **2.** *vt.* DEDUCT TAX to collect or deduct tax from a salary [Literally "to hold against or away"] —**with·hold·er** *n.*

with·hold·ing tax *n.* part of an employee's wage or salary withheld and remitted to the government by an employer in payment of taxes

with·in /wi*th* ín/ *prep., adv.* INSIDE used to indicate that somebody or something is inside or enclosed by a place, area, or object ○ (prep) *goods manufactured within a country* ○ (prep) *A natural pool lay within a grove of young trees.* ○ (adv) *The door was locked from within.* ■ *prep.* NOT BEYOND not beyond the scope, experience, range, time, or distance of ○ *regulations requiring that all accidents be reported within 48 hours* ■ *prep., adv.* HAPPENING INSIDE happening inside an organization, system, or society ○ (prep) *keeping companies within a given industry technologically competitive* ○ (adv) *A lot of our Internet development activity is coming from within.* ■ *prep.* INSIDE LIMITS OF inside the limits or rules of ○ *Try to keep within your budget and avoid overspending.* ■ *prep., adv.* INSIDE YOURSELF inside the body or mind ○ (adv) *Her new-found happiness was from within.* ○ (prep) *He needed to find the strength within him to carry on.* ■ *adv.* INDOORS indoors (*literary*) [Old English *wiþinnan* "on the inside," from WITH + *innan* "from within"]

with·in·doors /wi*th* ìn dáwrz/ *adv.* indoors (*archaic*)

with-it *adj.* fashionable and modern in dress and behavior (*dated informal*)

with·out /wi*th* ówt/ *prep.* **1.** NOT HAVING used to indicate that somebody or something does not have the thing mentioned ○ *left without proper tools to finish the job* **2.** NOT ACCOMPANIED BY not with somebody, or not having the involvement of somebody ○ *We can't really make any decisions without him.* **3.** NOT HAPPENING used to indicate that something does not happen or occur ○ *The bill was passed without a dissenting voice.* **4.** LACKING lacking a feeling of ○ *The accused engaged in physical abuse without remorse or intent to change.* ■ *prep., adv.* OUTSIDE on, at, or to the outside of somewhere (*regional or archaic*) ○ (prep) *Without the town the air was fresher.* ○ (adv) *She knocked and waited without.* ■ *prep.* BEYOND beyond (*archaic*) ■ *conj.* UNLESS unless (*nonstandard*) [Old English *wiþūtan* "on the outside of," from WITH + *ūtan* "from the outside"] ◇ **be** *or* **do without** to manage in spite of not having something considered necessary or desirable ○ *a form of power he could not buy or do without*

with·out·doors /wi*th* òwt dáwrz/ *adv.* outdoors (*archaic*)

with·stand /with stánd, wi*th*-/ (**-stood** /-stóod/, **-stood, -stand·ing, -stands**) *vti.* to be strong enough to stand up to somebody or remain unchanged by something such as extremes of heat or pressure [Literally "to stand against"] —**with·stand·er** *n.*

with·y /wí*th*ee/ *n.* (*plural* **-ies**) **1.** = **withe 2.** WILLOW TREE a willow tree, especially an osier ■ *adj.* TOUGH AND PLIABLE tough and pliable, like withes (*dated*) [Old English *wīþig* "willow." Ultimately from an Indo-European base meaning "to twist, bend," which is also the ancestor of English *withe* and *wire*.]

wit·less /wítləss/ *adj.* lacking intelligence or common sense —**wit·less·ly** *adv.* —**wit·less·ness** *n.*

wit·ling /wíttling/ *n.* somebody who aspires to be witty (*literary insult*)

wit·ness /wítnəss/ *n.* **1.** SOMEBODY WHO SEES SOMETHING somebody who saw or heard something that happened and gives evidence about it **2.** LAW SIGNATORY OF A DOCUMENT somebody who signs a document to show that it, or a signature on it, is genuine **3.** CHR SOMEBODY WHO TESTIFIES TO CHRISTIAN BELIEFS somebody who publicly testifies to strong personal Christian beliefs **4.** CHR PUBLIC STATEMENT OF CHRISTIAN BELIEFS a public statement of strong personal Christian beliefs ■ *v.* (**-nessed, -ness·ing, -ness·es**) **1.** *vt.* LAW SEE SOMETHING HAPPEN to see something happen, especially a crime or an accident **2.** *vt.* LAW COUNTERSIGN A DOCUMENT to affirm the authenticity of a document or a signature on a document by signing it **3.** *vt.* EXPERIENCE IMPORTANT EVENTS to experience important events or changes, or be the time in which they occur **4.** *vt.* BE SIGN OF SOMETHING to be a sign or proof of something that is happening **5.** *vi.* CHR SPEAK PUBLICLY ABOUT RELIGIOUS BELIEFS to talk in public about strong personal Christian beliefs [Old English *witnes*, formed from *wit* (see WIT[1])] —**wit·ness·a·ble** *adj.* —**wit·ness·er** *n.* ◇ **bear witness, bear witness to something** to be evidence or prove that something is true or that something happened

wit·ness box *n. U.K.* = **witness stand**

wit·ness stand *n.* the enclosed place in a courtroom where witnesses give evidence

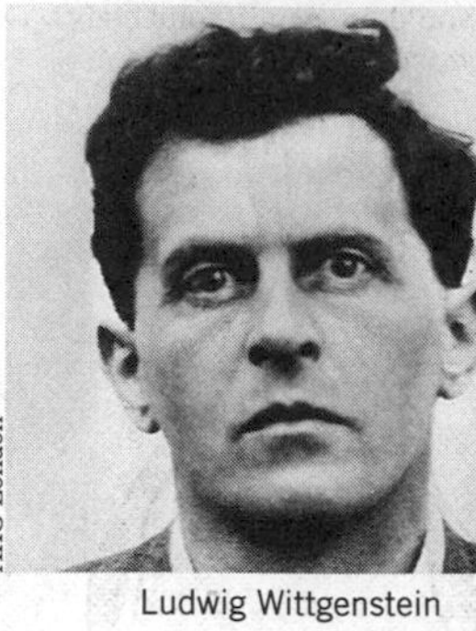

AKG London

Ludwig Wittgenstein

Witt·gen·stein /vítgən shtìn, -stìn/, **Ludwig** (1889–1951) Austrian-born British philosopher. He is considered one of the most important thinkers of the 20th century. His *Tractatus Logico-philosophicus* (1921) and *Philosophical Investigations* (1953) represent distinct phases in his work in analytic and linguistic philosophy. Full name **Ludwig Josef Johann Wittgenstein**

wit·ti·cism /wítti sìzzəm/ *n.* a witty or clever remark [Late 17thC. Coined by the poet John Dryden; a blend of WITTY and CRITICISM.]

wit·ting /wítting/ *adj.* **1.** DELIBERATE done deliberately or intentionally **2.** RESPONSIBLE responsible and fully aware —**wit·ting·ly** *adv.*

wit·ty /wíttee/ (**-ti·er, -ti·est**) *adj.* **1.** USING WORDS CLEVERLY using words in an apt, clever, and amusing way **2.** CLEVERLY DONE strikingly clever, stylish, or original in design or execution —**wit·ti·ly** *adv.* —**wit·ti·ness** *n.*

WORD KEY: SYNONYMS

See Synonyms at ***funny***.

Wit·wa·ters·rand /wit wáwtərz rànd/ rocky ridge in northeastern South Africa. Commonly known as the Rand, it is the most productive gold-mining area in the world. Johannesburg is located near its center. Length: 60 mi./100 km.

wive /wīv/ (**wived, wiv·ing, wives**) *v.* (*archaic*) **1.** *vti.* MARRY WOMAN to marry a woman **2.** *vt.* GIVE SOMEBODY WIFE to supply somebody with a wife [Old English *wīfian*, formed from *wīf* (see WIFE)]

wi·vern *n.* = **wyvern**

wives plural of **wife**

wiz[1] /wiz/ (*plural* **wiz·zes**) *n.* a wizard (*informal*) [Shortening]

wiz[2] *n.* = **whiz** *v.* 3 (*informal*)

wiz·ard /wízzərd/ *n.* **1.** MALE WITCH a man who is supposed to have magical or wonder-working powers **2.** SOMEBODY WHO IS EXCELLENT AT SOMETHING somebody who is extremely clever at or knowledgeable about something (*informal*) [15thC. Variant of earlier *wisard*, from WISE.] —**wiz·ard·ly** *adj.*

WORD KEY: CULTURAL NOTE

The Wizard of Oz, a movie by U.S. producer David O. Selznick and director Victor Fleming (1939). This enchanting musical, based on a novel by L. Frank Baum (1900), tells the story of Dorothy, a young Kansas girl who dreams she is transported to the magical world of Oz, a utopian place without disease, poverty, or political discussion "except in the outlying districts." Evading the Wicked Witch of the West, she sets off along the yellow brick road in search of the mysterious Wizard. The words *Oz* (a magical, unreal, even bizarre place or situation), *Wicked Witch of the West* (evil person) and *munchkin* (from the elflike Munchkins in the movie, now meaning also an elflike person, a young child, or a minor goverment official) have established a place in the English language.

wiz·ard·ry /wízzərdree/ *n.* **1.** ART OF WIZARDS the art, activities, or accomplishments of a wizard **2.** SKILL extreme skill or accomplishment

wiz·en[1] /wízz'n/ (**-ened, -en·ing, -ens**) *vti.* to wither or dry up, or make something wither or dry up [Old English *wisnian*]

wiz·en[2] /wízz'n/ *adj.* withered or dried up [Late 18thC. Alteration of WIZENED.]

wiz·ened /wízz'nd/ *adj.* looking wrinkled, shriveled, or dried up

wk *abbr.* **1.** week **2.** work **3.** weak

wkly *abbr.* weekly

WL *abbr.* **1. WL, w.l.** INSUR water line **2.** ELEC wavelength

Wm. *abbr.* William

wmk. *abbr.* watermark

WMO *abbr.* World Meteorological Organization

WNW *abbr.* west-northwest

WO, W.O. *abbr.* MIL warrant officer

w/o *abbr.* without

woad /wōd/ *n.* **1. PLANT THAT YIELDS BLUE DYE** a European plant that was formerly cultivated for the blue dye extracted from its leaves. Latin name: *Isatis tinctoria.* **2. BLUE DYE** the blue dye obtained from the woad plant and used in ancient times as a body paint [Old English *wād.* From a prehistoric Germanic word of unknown origin.]

woad·wax·en /wṓd wàks'n/ (*plural* **-ens** *or* **-en**) *n.* = **dyer's greenweed** [14thC. Alteration (influenced by *woad*) of *woodwaxen*, from Old English *wuduweaxe*, from *wudu* "wood" + *weaxan* "to grow."]

w.o.b. *abbr.* INSUR washed overboard

wob·ble /wóbb'l/, **wab·ble** *v.* (**-bled, -bling, -bles**) **1.** *vti.* **MOVE FROM SIDE TO SIDE** to move or cause something to move in a swaying, shaking, or trembling way **2.** *vi.* **QUAVER** to vary uncertainly in pitch or volume **3.** *vi.* **BE UNABLE TO DECIDE** to be unable or unwilling to reach a decision ■ *n.* **WOBBLING EFFECT** a wobbling movement or sound [Mid-17thC. Origin uncertain: probably from Low German *wabbeln*; ultimately from a prehistoric Germanic word that is also the ancestor of English *wave* and *waver.*] —**wob·bler** *n.* —**wob·bling·ly** *adv.*

wob·bler syn·drome *n.* a condition in horses and dogs characterized by an unsteady gait and sometimes falling, due to a misalignment of vertebrae in the neck, which impinges on the spinal cord

wob·bly /wóbblee/ (**-bli·er, -bli·est**), **wab·bly** /wábblee/ *adj.* **1. UNSTEADY** moving unsteadily from side to side **2. FEELING WEAK** feeling weak and unable to keep balanced (*informal*) —**wob·bli·ness** *n.*

Wob·bly /wóbblee/ (*plural* **-blies**) *n.* a member of the Industrial Workers of the World (*informal*) [Early 20thC. Origin unknown.]

P. G. Wodehouse

Wode·house /wŏŏd hòwss/, **P. G.** (1881–1975) British writer. He wrote over 100 novels, many of which feature the fictional characters Bertie Wooster and his "gentleman's gentleman," Jeeves. He became a U.S. citizen in 1955. Full name **Sir Pelham Grenville Wodehouse**

Wo·den /wṓd'n/ *n.* an Anglo-Saxon god, the equivalent of the Norse Odin

wodge /woj/ *n. U.K.* a large lump or chunk of something (*informal*) ○ *They caught him stuffing wodges of banknotes into his pockets.* [Mid-19thC. Blend of WAD and WEDGE.]

woe /wō/ *n.* **1. UNFORTUNATE HAPPENING** a serious affliction or misfortune **2. GRIEF** grief or distress resulting from a serious affliction or misfortune ■ *interj.* **EXPRESSING GRIEF** used to express grief or distress (*archaic or literary*) [Old English *wā*, from a prehistoric Germanic base that is also the ancestor of English *wail*; ultimately from an Indo-European exclamation] ◇ **woe betide somebody** used as a threat to indicate that somebody is going to regret something or be punished in some way ○ *Woe betide him if he turns up late for work again.* ◇ **woe is me** used to indicate that the speaker is in distress or feels unhappy or unfortunate (*literary or humorous*)

woe·be·gone /wṓ bi gàwn/ *adj.* feeling or looking distressed or sorrowful [13thC. Formed from WOE + *begon* "beset" (ultimately from Old English *gān*; see GO).]

woe·ful /wṓf'l/ *adj.* **1. UNHAPPY** feeling or expressing great distress or sorrow **2. CAUSING GRIEF** bringing or causing great distress or sorrow **3. PATHETICALLY BAD** pitifully or regrettably bad —**woe·ful·ly** *adv.* —**woe·ful·ness** *n.*

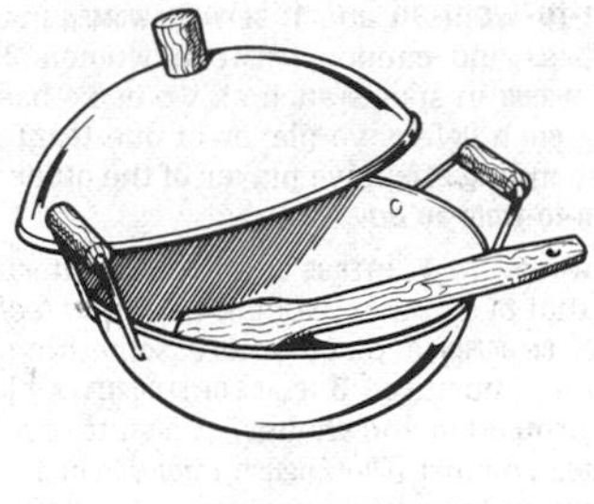
Wok

wok /wok/ *n.* a large thin metal pan with a curved base, used for stir-frying, steaming, and braising food, especially in Chinese and other Far Eastern cookery [Mid-20thC. From Chinese (Cantonese).]

woke past tense of **wake**

wok·en past participle of **wake**

wold /wōld/ *n.* upland or rolling country, especially when treeless (*literary*) [Old English *wald, weald* "forest." Ultimately from an Indo-European word meaning "wild," which is also the ancestor of English *wild* and *wilderness.*]

Wolf

wolf /wŏŏlf/ *n.* (*plural* **wolves** /wŏŏlvz/) **1. CARNIVORE THAT HUNTS IN PACKS** any one of several predatory animals of North America and Eurasia that are related to the dog and hunt in packs, especially the gray wolf. Genus: *Canis.* **2. ANIMAL RESEMBLING WOLF** an animal that resembles a wolf but is not of the dog family, e.g., the Tasmanian wolf **3. FUR OF WOLF** the fur of the wolf **4. GREEDY AND CRUEL PERSON** somebody who is greedy and cruel **5. MAN WHO PURSUES WOMEN** a sexually aggressive or predatory man (*informal*) **6.** INSECTS **DESTRUCTIVE LARVA** the destructive larva of several moths and beetles that sometimes infests granaries **7.** MUSIC **DISCORD** an unpleasant discord produced on a string or keyboard instrument (*often used before a noun*) ■ *vt.* (**wolfed, wolf·ing, wolfs**) **EAT SOMETHING QUICKLY AND GREEDILY** to eat food quickly and greedily or in gulps [Old English *wulf.* Ultimately from an Indo-European word that is also the ancestor of English *lupus, lycanthropy,* and *alyssum.*] ◇ **a wolf in sheep's clothing** somebody who looks harmless or pleasant but is in fact dangerous or unpleasant ◇ **cry wolf** to give a false alarm or cry for help too many times, so that when help is really needed, no one will give it ◇ **keep the wolf from the door** to be enough to prevent hunger or starvation ◇ **throw somebody to the wolves** to abandon somebody to be destroyed by enemies in order to save yourself

Wolf /wŏŏlf/ *n.* ASTRON = **Lupus**

Wolf /vawlf/, **Hugo** (1860–1903) Austrian composer. He is noted especially for several hundred songs exploring a wide range of themes and moods. Full name **Hugo Philipp Jakob Wolf**

wolf·ber·ry /wŏŏlf bèrree/ (*plural* **-ries**) *n.* a North American shrub that has gray leaves, pinkish flowers, and white berries. Latin name: *Symphoricarpos occidentalis.*

wolf dog *n.* **1. DOG USED TO HUNT WOLVES** a dog used to hunt wolves **2. OFFSPRING OF WOLF AND DOG** an offspring of a wolf and a dog

James Wolfe

Wolfe /wŏŏlf/, **James** (1727–59) British general. The second in command of British troops in North America, he is most famous for his capture of Quebec (1759) from the French in the French and Indian War (1756–63). He was fatally wounded in the attack.

Wolfe, Thomas (1900–38) U.S. writer. His novels, including *Look Homeward, Angel* (1929) and *You Can't Go Home Again* (1940), are heavily autobiographical. Full name **Thomas Clayton Wolfe**

wolf eel *n.* a large long fish with a pointed tail found in Pacific coastal waters of North America. Latin name: *Anarrhicthys ocellatus.* [So called because it is a species of wolffish]

wolf·er *n.* = **wolver**

Wolff·i·an bod·y /wŏŏlfee ən-/ *n.* ANAT, ZOOL = **mesonephros** [Mid-19thC. Named for the German embryologist K. F. *Wolff* (1733–94), who first described the structure.]

wolf·fish /wŏŏlf fish/ (*plural* **-fish** *or* **-fish·es**) *n.* a large northern Atlantic fish that has large sharp teeth and no pelvic fins. Genus: *Anarhichas.* [*Wolf* from the fish's voracious appetite]

wolf·hound /wŏŏlf hòwnd/ *n.* a large dog of a breed that was originally bred to hunt wolves

wolf·ish /wŏŏlfish/ *adj.* resembling or characteristic of a wolf —**wolf·ish·ly** *adv.*

wolf pack *n.* **1. GROUP OF WOLVES** a group of wolves that hunt together **2.** MIL **GROUP OF SUBMARINES** a group of submarines engaged in hunting and attacking enemy convoys during World War II

wolf·ram /wŏŏlfrəm/ *n.* tungsten (*archaic*) [Mid-18thC. From German, "wolframite," from *Wolf* "wolf" + German dialect *Rahm* "soot, dirt."]

wolf·ram·ite /wŏŏlfrə mìt/ *n.* a brownish-black crystalline mineral consisting of a tungstate of iron and manganese. It is the chief ore of tungsten. [Mid-19thC. From German (see WOLFRAM).]

wolfs·bane /wŏŏlfs bàyn/ (*plural* **-banes** *or* **-bane**) *n.* any of several wild or cultivated poisonous plants with yellow or purplish-blue flowers, sometimes used for medicinal purposes. Genus: *Aconitum.* [Mid-16thC. Translation of Greek *lukoktonon*, literally "wolf-killer," from the poison found in the plants]

Wolfs·burg /wŏŏlfs bùrg, váwlfs bŏŏrk/ industrial city in Lower Saxony State, north central Germany. Population: 126,800 (1995).

wolf spi·der *n.* a ground spider that hunts its prey instead of using a web. Family: Lycosidae.

wolf whis·tle *n.* a whistle given to signal sexual interest or admiration in somebody (*considered offensive by some people*)

wolf-whis·tle *vti.* to make a wolf whistle at somebody, especially a woman passer-by

wol·las·ton·ite /wŏŏllәstə nìt/ *n.* a gray-white calcium silicate mineral that occurs as fibrous masses in metamorphosed limestones [Early 19thC. Named for the English physicist William Hyde *Wollaston* (1766–1828).]

Wol·lon·gong /wŏŏlləng gòng/ coastal city in eastern New South Wales, Australia. It is an industrial center and the site of a university. Population: 219,761 (1996).

Mary Wollstonecraft: Portrait (1790) by John Opie

Woll·stone·craft /wŏŏstən kràft/, **Mary** (1759–97) British feminist. Her *Vindication of the Rights of Woman* (1792), advocating the equality of the sexes, is an important early document of modern feminism.

Wo·lof /wō̆ lòf/ (*plural* **-lof** *or* **-lofs**) *n.* **1.** PEOPLES **MEMBER OF W AFRICAN PEOPLE** a member of a people who live in West Africa, mainly in Senegal, but also with sizable communities in the Gambia and Mauritania **2.** LANG **NIGER-CONGO LANGUAGE** a language spoken in Senegal and the Gambia, belonging to the Niger-Congo language family. About two million people speak Wolof. [Early 19thC. From Wolof.] —**Wo·lof** *adj.*

Wol·sey /wŏŏlzee/, **Thomas** (1475–1530) English clergyman and statesman. As Henry VIII's Lord Chancellor (1515–29), he exercised great power both in England and abroad. He was impeached for failing to secure Henry's divorce from Catherine of Aragon. Known as **Cardinal Wolsey**

wol·ver /wŏŏlvər/, **wol·fer** /wŏŏlfər/ *n.* somebody who hunts wolves

wol·ver·ine /wŏŏlvə reen/ (*plural* **-ines** *or* **-ine**) *n.* a strong dark-furred usually solitary carnivore of the weasel family, chiefly found in northern Eurasian and North American forests. Latin name: *Gulo gulo.* [Late 16thC. Origin uncertain: probably from WOLF.]

wolves plural of **wolf**

wom·an /wŏŏmmən/ (*plural* **-en** /wímmin/) *n.* **1. FEMALE ADULT** an adult female human being **2. WOMEN AS GROUP** women collectively or in general **3. FEMININITY** feminine qualities or feelings **4. DOMESTIC EMPLOYEE** a woman who is a domestic employee **5. WIFE OR GIRLFRIEND** a wife, female lover, or girlfriend (*informal*) (*offensive to some people*) [Old English *wimman*, a variant of *wīfman*, from *wīf* "woman, wife" + *man* "person"] ◇ **to a woman** used to indicate that every one of a group of women does or thinks something, without any exceptions

WORD KEY: USAGE

See Usage note at ***girl***. See Usage note at ***person***.

WORD KEY: CULTURAL NOTE

Little Women, a novel by Louisa May Alcott (1868–69). An abidingly popular family saga set in 1860s New England, it recounts the emotional and intellectual development of four sisters – Meg, Jo, Beth, and Amy – as they progress through adolescence to adulthood. It was followed by two sequels, *Little Men* (1871) and *Jo's Boys* (1886).

wom·an·ful·ly /wŏŏmmənfəlee/ *adv.* in a way that shows or is characteristic of womanly spirit or energy [Early 19thC. Modeled on MANFULLY.]

wom·an·hood /wŏŏmmən hŏŏd/ *n.* **1. CONDITION OF BEING WOMAN** the state or condition of being a woman **2. WOMEN** women in general, or as a group

wom·an·ish /wŏŏmmənish/ *adj.* an offensive term for a man perceived to have qualities stereotypically attributed to women, e.g., weakness or fussiness (*insult*) —**wom·an·ish·ly** *adv.* —**wom·an·ish·ness** *n.*

wom·an·ist /wŏŏmmənist/ *adj.* having a respect for and a belief in the abilities and talents of women [Late 20thC. Modeled on *humanist*.]

wom·an·ize /wŏŏmmə nīz/ (**-ized, -iz·ing, -iz·es**) *vi.* to be constantly in search of casual sex with women (*disapproving; refers to men*) —**wom·an·iz·er** *n.*

wom·an·kind /wŏŏmmən kīnd/, **wom·en·kind** /wímmin-/ *n.* women collectively or in general

wom·an·ly /wŏŏmmənlee/ *adj.* having positive characteristics or qualities, especially warmth, calmness, and competence, attributed to mature women — **wom·an·li·ness** *n.*

wom·an of the house *n.* a woman who is in charge of or who is the primary woman of a household

wom·an of the world (*plural* **wom·en of the world**) *n.* a socially experienced and sophisticated woman

wom·an·pow·er /wŏŏmmən pòwr/ *n.* **1. WOMEN IN WORKFORCE** women as part of the workforce in society **2. INFLUENCE OF WOMEN** the influence and impact of women in society [Early 20thC. Modeled on MANPOWER.]

wom·an suf·frage *n.* = **women's suffrage**

wom·an-to-wom·an *adj.* **1. BETWEEN WOMEN** marked by directness and candor between women **2.** SPORTS **PLAYER PAIRING** in sports such as women's basketball, having each defensive player of one team guard a corresponding offensive player of the other team — **wom·an-to-wom·an** *adv.*

womb /woom/ *n.* **1. UTERUS OF WOMAN** the uterus, especially that of a human woman (*not used technically*) **2. PLACE OF ORIGIN** a place where something is conceived and nurtured **3. PLACE OF SECURITY** a place that offers protection and shelter, or a state of mind that provides comfort [Old English *wamb*, from a prehistoric Germanic word of unknown origin]

Wombat

wom·bat /wóm bàt/ *n.* any of several Australian burrowing marsupials that are short, robust, covered in dense wiry hair, and have a stumpy tail and wide blunt snout. Latin name: *Vombatus ursinus* and *Lasiorhinus latifrons.* [Late 18thC. From Dharuk (an Australian Aboriginal language) *wambaty*.]

womb·like /woom līk/ *adj.* resembling a womb, especially in being reassuring, all-enclosing, and giving a feeling of security

wom·en plural of **woman**

wom·en·folk /wímmin fōk/, **wom·en·folks** /wímmin fōks/ *n.* women collectively, or a particular group of women, especially those belonging to the same family or society (*dated*)

wom·en·kind *n.* = **womankind**

wom·en's lib *n.* women's liberation (*informal disapproving*) —**wom·en's lib·ber** *n.*

wom·en's lib·er·a·tion *n.* a political movement intended to free women from oppression, or the act of a woman's freeing herself

wom·en's move·ment *n.* a movement seeking to promote and improve the position of women in society

wom·en's ref·uge *n. U.K.* = **women's shelter**

wom·en's room *n.* a public toilet for women and girls to use

wom·en's shel·ter *n.* a place where women and children can stay after leaving home to escape domestic violence

wom·en's stud·ies *npl.* a course of study examining the historical, economic, and cultural roles and achievements of women (*takes a singular or plural verb*)

wom·en's suf·frage *n.* the right of women to vote in elections

wom·ens·wear /wímminz wàir/ *n.* clothing and accessories for women

wom·er·a *n.* = **woomera**

won[1] /won/ (*plural* **won**) *n.* **1. UNIT OF KOREAN CURRENCY** the main unit of currency in North and South Korea, worth 100 chon. See table at **currency 2. BILL WORTH ONE WON** a bill worth one won [Mid-20thC. From Korean *wǎn*.]

won[2] past participle, past tense of **win**

won·der /wúndər/ *n.* **1. AMAZED ADMIRATION** amazed admiration or awe, especially at something very beautiful or new **2. SOMETHING MARVELOUS** a miracle or other cause of intense admiration or awe ■ *adj.* **EXTRAORDINARILY GOOD** exciting admiration or amazement by virtue of being outstandingly good, effective, or unusual ■ *v.* (**-dered, -der·ing, -ders**) **1.** *vti.* **SPECULATE ABOUT SOMETHING** to speculate or be curious to know about something **2.** *vi.* **BE AMAZED** to be in a state of amazed admiration or awe [Old English *wundor*, from a prehistoric Germanic word of unknown origin] —**won·der·er** *n.* ◇ **no wonder, small wonder, little wonder** used to indicate that something is not surprising ◇ **work wonders, perform wonders, do wonders** to achieve remarkable results or be very effective in solving a problem

Won·der /wúndər/, **Stevie** (*b.* 1950) U.S. singer and songwriter. He released his first album at age 13, began an international career, and won numerous Grammy awards for a succession of recordings of Motown rhythm and blues. He often used synthesizers and advanced technology, performing all the instrumental and vocal parts himself. Real name **Steveland Judkins**

won·der·ful /wúndərfəl/ *adj.* **1. OUTSTANDING** of a quality that excites admiration or amazement **2. EXCEEDINGLY PLEASING** suiting somebody perfectly —**won·der·ful·ly** *adv.* —**won·der·ful·ness** *n.*

won·der·land /wúndər lànd/ *n.* a land where wonderful things happen or exist

WORD KEY: CULTURAL NOTE

Alice's Adventures in Wonderland, a children's story by English writer Lewis Carroll (1865). This extraordinarily inventive and immensely popular tale was based on stories that the author made up to entertain his friends' children. A girl called Alice dreams that she falls down a rabbit hole into a surreal world inhabited by eccentric characters including the Mad Hatter, the March Hare, and the King and Queen of Hearts. The expressions "Curiouser and curiouser!" and "Oh my fur and whiskers!" are direct quotations from this book. The oft-used expressions "grin like a Cheshire cat," "wild as a March hare," and "mad as a hatter" have associations with characters in the book.

won·der·ment /wúndərmənt/ *n.* **1. AMAZED ADMIRATION** amazed admiration or awe **2. PUZZLEMENT** puzzled surprise

won·der·work /wúndər wùrk/ *n.* something made or done that arouses amazed admiration or awe — **won·der·work·er** *n.*

won·drous /wúndrəss/ *adj.* **EXCITING WONDER** so good or admirable as to inspire wonder or awe (*literary*) ■ *adv.* **AMAZINGLY** wondrously or extraordinarily (*literary*) [15thC. Alteration (influenced by MARVELOUS) of obsolete *wonders*, from WONDER.] —**won·drous·ly** *adv.* — **won·drous·ness** *n.*

wonk /wongk/ *n.* somebody who is regarded as boringly, narrowly, or obliviously preoccupied with something, especially work (*informal*) [Early 20thC. Origin unknown.]

won·ky /wóngkee/ *adj.* (**-ki·er, -ki·est**), *adv. U.K.* not to be relied on to be steady or secure or to function correctly (*informal*) [Early 20thC. Origin uncertain: perhaps ultimately from Old English *wancol* "unsteady."]

wont /wawnt, wōnt/ *adj.* **ACCUSTOMED TO SOMETHING** accustomed or likely to do something (*formal*) ○ *He is wont to be rather quick of temper when tired.* ■ *n.* **SOMEBODY'S CUSTOM** a habit or custom followed by a particular person or group of people (*formal*) ■ *vti.* (**wont** *or* **wont·ed, wont·ing, wonts**) **BE ACCUSTOMED** to have or give somebody the habit of doing something (*archaic*) [12thC. From the past participle of Old English *wunian* "to be accustomed." Ultimately from an Indo-European base meaning "to desire," which is also the ancestor of English *win* and *wean*.]

WORD KEY: SYNONYMS

See Synonyms at ***habit***.

won't /wōnt/ *contr.* will not

wont·ed /wáwntəd, wóntəd/ *adj.* usual or typical (*formal*) —**wont·ed·ly** *adv.* —**wont·ed·ness** *n.*

WORD KEY: SYNONYMS

See Synonyms at ***usual***.

won ton /wòn tón/ *n.* **1.** CHINESE DUMPLING in Chinese cooking, a small dumpling made from a square of noodle dough with a little filling in the middle, boiled in soup or deep-fried **2. won ton, won ton soup** SOUP WITH DUMPLINGS Chinese soup with boiled small dumplings in it [Mid-20thC. From Chinese (Cantonese) *wān t'ān*.]

woo /woo/ (**wooed, woo·ing, woos**) *v.* **1.** *vti.* SEEK WOMAN'S LOVE to seek the affection or love of a woman in order to marry her (*dated or literary*) **2.** *vti.* SEEK SOMETHING to try to please in order to gain something, especially acceptance, fame, or approval **3.** *vt.* CAUSE SOMETHING UNPLEASANT to bring about something unpleasant as a result of action taken (*formal*) ○ *wooing their own destruction* [Old English *wōgian*, of unknown origin] —**woo·ing·ly** *adv.*

wood /wŏŏd/ *n.* **1.** SUBSTANCE OF TREES a hard fibrous substance that chiefly composes shrubs and trees and is found beneath their bark **2.** FUEL OR BUILDING MATERIAL wood from trees, cut and dried then used as a fuel or a building material or in other areas of craft and manufacture **3.** = **woods** *npl.* 1 **4.** GOLF GOLF CLUB a golf club with a head formerly made of wood, but now usually made of stainless steel or titanium ■ *adj.* **1.** OF WOOD made of or used for wood **2.** AMONG TREES located or living in a forested area ■ *v.* (**wooded, wood·ing, woods**) **1.** *vt.* COVER AREA WITH TREES to cover an area of land with trees **2.** *vti.* FUEL SOMETHING WITH WOOD to supply somebody or something or be supplied with wood as fuel [Old English *wudu*] ◇ **be out of the woods** to be out of danger or difficulty (*informal*) ◇ **knock on wood** used to express a wish for good fortune in some particular respect to continue ○ *It never snows in May, but knock on wood.*

WORD KEY: ORIGIN

The ancestral meaning of ***wood*** is probably "collection of trees, forest." The meanings "tree" (now obsolete) and "substance from which trees are made" are secondary developments. It has been suggested that the word ***wood*** may go back to an Indo-European source meaning "separate," in which case it would originally have denoted a "separated" or "remote" piece of territory, near the outer edge or borders of known land. Since such remote, uninhabited areas were usually wooded, the word came to denote "forest."

Wood /wŏŏd/, **Grant** (1892–1942) U.S. artist. His paintings of his native Iowa are influenced by the formal early Dutch and Flemish style. His best known work is *American Gothic* (1930).

Wood, Leonard (1860–1927) U.S. soldier. After achieving fame as a commander in the Cuban campaign in the Spanish-American War (1898), he became a strong advocate of "military preparedness" on the eve of World War I.

wood al·co·hol *n.* = **methanol**

wood a·nem·o·ne *n.* any of several anemones in North America and Europe with divided leaves and a single showy flower that can be white to crimson. Latin name: *Anemone quinquefolia*. Latin name: *Anemone nemorosa*.

wood ant *n.* a large reddish European ant that builds huge domed colonies of wood chips. Latin name: *Formica rufa*.

wood bet·o·ny *n.* an eastern North American lousewort that has yellow or reddish flowers. Latin name: *Pedicularis canadensis*.

wood·bine /wŏŏd bīn/ (*plural* **-bines** *or* **-bine**) *n.* **1.** CLIMBING PLANT WITH FRAGRANT FLOWERS a honeysuckle of Eurasia and North Africa that has fragrant yellow flowers. Latin name: *Lonicera periclymenum*. **2.** = **Virginia creeper** [Old English *wudubinde*, from *wudu* "wood" + *bindan* "to bind"; so called because the plant grows around trees]

wood·block /wŏŏd blòk/ *n.* **1.** = **woodcut** *n.* 1 **2.** MUSIC PERCUSSION INSTRUMENT a hollow block of wood used as a percussion instrument in an orchestra or band **3.** BUILDING FLOOR TILE a small flat piece of wood laid in a pattern with others to make a floor surface

wood·bor·er /wŏŏd bàwrər/ *n.* a medium sized moth with a stocky body that, as a large fleshy larva, bores into wood, causing considerable damage. Family: Cossidae.

Wood Buf·fa·lo Na·tion·al Park /wŏŏd bùffəlō-/ national park and preserve in central Canada, on the Alberta-Northwest Territories border, established in 1922. Area: 17,298 sq. mi./44,802 sq. km.

wood·carv·ing /wŏŏd kaarving/ *n.* **1.** CARVING WOOD the art of carving wood **2.** SOMETHING CARVED FROM WOOD a decorative article carved from wood

wood·chat /wŏŏd chàt/ (*plural* **-chats** *or* **-chat**), **wood·chat shrike** *n.* a European and North African songbird of the shrike family that has black-and-white plumage and a reddish-brown crown. Latin name: *Lanius senator*.

wood·chop /wŏŏd chòp/ *n.* a wood-chopping competition held at country fairs in Australia

wood·chop·per /wŏŏd chòppər/ *n.* somebody who chops wood, especially somebody who chops down trees

wood·chuck /wŏŏd chùk/ (*plural* **-chucks** *or* **-chuck**) *n.* a heavy-set short-legged marmot common to northern North America, with brownish fur streaked with gray. Latin name: *Marmota monax*. [Late 17thC. By folk etymology from an Algonquian word.]

wood coal *n.* **1.** = **lignite 2.** = **charcoal**

wood·cock /wŏŏd kòk/ (*plural* **-cocks** *or* **-cock**) *n.* either of two small ground-dwelling birds related to the snipe, with short legs and rounded wings, a stocky body, and a disproportionately long bill. Genus: *Scolopax*.

wood·craft /wŏŏd kràft/ *n.* **1.** SKILL IN MAKING THINGS FROM WOOD skill in carving or making objects from wood **2.** SKILL IN THINGS CONCERNING WOODS skill in traveling, living, or working in the woods or forests —**wood·craft·er** *n.* —**wood·crafts·man** *n.*

wood·creep·er /wŏŏd kreepər/ (*plural* **-ers** *or* **-er**) *n.* a Central or South American forest bird that clings to tree trunks with its short strong legs and probes for insects with its bill. Family: Dendrocolaptidae.

wood·cut /wŏŏd kùt/ *n.* **1.** BLOCK OF WOOD FOR MAKING PRINTS a block of wood carved with a picture or design and from which prints are made **2.** PRINT MADE WITH WOODCUT a print made by pressing a woodcut into a coloring substance and then onto paper

wood·cut·ter /wŏŏd kùttər/ *n.* **1.** OCCUPATIONS LUMBERJACK somebody who chops down trees **2.** CRAFT SOMEBODY WHO MAKES PRINTS somebody who makes woodcuts, and prints from woodcuts

wood duck *n.* a crested North American duck that nests in tree cavities near water. The male has black, chestnut, green, purple, and white plumage. Latin name: *Aix sponsa*.

wood·ed /wŏŏddəd/ *adj.* covered with or consisting of woodland or trees

wood·en /wŏŏdd'n/ *adj.* **1.** MADE OF WOOD made or consisting of wood **2.** UNGAINLY lacking flexibility, relaxation, and grace **3.** INEXPRESSIVE lacking animation, emotion, or responsiveness ○ *a wooden prose style* **4.** DULL IN SOUND making a dull unresonant sound ○ *spoke in a toneless, wooden voice* —**wood·en·ly** *adv.* —**wood·en·ness** *n.*

wood en·grav·ing *n.* **1.** ART OF ENGRAVING ON WOOD the art or process of engraving a picture or design with a burin on a block of wood **2.** PRINT FROM ENGRAVING ON WOOD an engraving made with a burin on a block of wood, or a print from one —**wood en·grav·er** *n.*

wood·en·head /wŏŏdd'n hèd/ *n.* somebody who is considered very unintelligent (*informal insult*) —**wood·en·head·ed** *adj.* —**wood·en·head·ed·ly** *adv.* —**wood·en·head·ed·ness** *n.*

Wood·en Horse *n.* = **Trojan horse** *n.* 1

wood·en In·di·an *n.* a carved wooden figure of a Native American, formerly used as an advertisement outside tobacco shops

wood·en·ware /wŏŏdd'n wàir/ *n.* dishes or utensils made from wood

wood frog *n.* an eastern North American frog that lives in woodlands and is light brown with darker markings on the head. Latin name: *Rana sylvatica*.

wood·grain /wŏŏd gràyn/ *n.* a material or finish that imitates the natural grain of wood

wood grouse *n.* = **capercaillie**

wood hoo·poe *n.* a tropical African bird that has dark glossy plumage, a long tail, and a slender curved bill. Genus: *Phoeniculus*.

Wood·hull /wŏŏd hùl/, **Victoria** (1838–1927) U.S. feminist. She was the first woman to run for the U.S. presidency (1872). Born **Victoria Claflin**

wood hy·a·cinth *n.* = **bluebell**

wood i·bis *n.* **1.** AFRICAN STORK WITH YELLOW BILL an African stork with white plumage, a bare red face, and a yellow bill. Latin name: *Mycteria ibis*. **2.** = **wood stork**

wood·ie *n.* CARS = **woody** *n.*

wood·land /wŏŏdlənd/ *n.* land that is covered with trees, shrubs, or bushes —**wood·land·er** *n.*

wood·lark /wŏŏd laark/ (*plural* **-larks** *or* **-lark**) *n.* a small Eurasian lark noted for its song in flight. Latin name: *Lullula arborea*.

wood·lot /wŏŏd lòt/ *n.* a privately owned tract of woodland where trees are grown for fuel, posts, timber, or pulpwood

wood louse /wŏŏd lòwss/ *n.* any of several small land-dwelling crustaceans that live in damp woody places and are capable of rolling into a ball. Genera: *Oniscus* and *Porcellio*.

wood·man *n.* = **woodsman**

wood mouse *n.* a small mouse that lives in woodlands in western and central Europe and North Africa. Latin name: *Adopdemus sylvaticus*.

wood·note /wŏŏd nōt/ *n.* a natural musical note, call, or song, e.g., that made by a wild bird (*literary*)

wood nymph *n.* **1.** MYTHOL WOODLAND NYMPH a nymph that lives in woodlands, e.g., a dryad **2.** INSECTS BUTTERFLY any one of several brown butterflies, especially one with a broad yellow band and black-and-white eyespots on each front wing. Family: Satyridae. **3.** HUMMINGBIRD a Central or South American hummingbird. Genus: *Thalurania*.

wood o·pal *n.* wood impregnated and fossilized by silica and displaying the preserved wood grain

wood owl *n.* = **tawny owl**

Woodpecker

wood·peck·er /wŏŏd pèkər/ *n.* a tree-climbing bird that has boldly patterned plumage, a stiff tail, and a hard bill for hammering against wood and extracting insects. Family: Picidae.

wood pi·geon *n.* a pigeon that has a white patch on each side of the neck and lives in woodlands. Latin name: *Columba palumbus*.

wood·pile /wŏŏd pīl/ *n.* a heap or stack of firewood

wood pitch *n.* the sticky residue left after wood tar has been distilled

wood·print /wŏŏd prìnt/ *n.* = **woodcut** *n.* 1

wood pulp *n.* wood that has been mechanically and chemically broken down for use in making paper and paper products

wood puss·y *n.* a skunk (*humorous informal*) [Pussy "cat," for POLECAT]

wood rab·bit *n.* = **cottontail**

wood rat *n.* = **pack rat**

Wood·roffe, Mount /wŏŏdrəf/ mountain in South Australia, the highest peak in the state. Height: 4,721 ft./1,439 m.

wood·ruff /wŏŏd rùf/ (*plural* **-ruffs** *or* **-ruff**) *n.* any of several plants with sweet-scented flowers used in perfumery and for flavoring wines and liqueurs. Genera: *Asperula* and *Galium*. [Old English *wudurofe*, from *wudu* "wood" + *rofe*, of unknown meaning and origin]

Wood·ruff key /wŏŏd ruff-/ *n.* a self-aligning key that is semicircular in cross-section, designed to fit into the recess of a shaft [Late 19thC. Named for the *Woodruff*

Manufacturing Co. in Hartford, Connecticut, which developed the key.]

wood·rush /wŏŏd rŭsh/ *n.* a plant that grows in cold and temperate areas of the northern hemisphere and has flat leaves fringed with hairs. Genus: *Luzula.*

woods /wŏŏdz/ *npl.* **1. FORESTED AREA** a forested or wooded area or region **2.** MUSIC **WOODWIND** the woodwind instruments of an orchestra

Express Newspapers

Tiger Woods

Woods /wŏŏdz/, **Tiger** (*b.* 1975) U.S. golfer. At 21, he became the youngest player ever to win the U.S. Masters championship (1997). Real name **Eldrick Woods**

wood sage *n.* a downy aromatic European plant found in woods and heaths. Latin name: *Teucrium scordonia.*

wood·screw /wŏŏd skrōō/ *n.* a tapered metal screw that can be driven into wood by a screwdriver

wood·shed /wŏŏd shĕd/ *n.* an outbuilding or connected room in which firewood and tools are stored

wood·si·a /wŏŏdzee ə/ (*plural* **-as** *or* **-a**) *n.* a small fern that has wiry fronds and is found in northern often mountainous regions. Genus: *Woodsia.* [Mid-19thC. From modern Latin, genus name, in honor of the English botanist Joseph *Woods* (1776–1864).]

woods·man /wŏŏdzmən/ (*plural* **-men** /-mən/), **wood·man** /wŏŏdmən/ (*plural* **-men** /-mən/) *n.* somebody who is skilled at living, working, or traveling in the woods

wood sor·rel *n.* an herb that has a creeping stem, heart-shaped leaves, and white flowers with colored veins. Genus: *Oxalis.* [Translation of obsolete French *sorrel de boys*, from the plant's sour taste, resembling sorrel, and the fact that it grows in woodland]

wood spir·it *n.* = **methanol**

Wood·stock /wŏŏd stŏk/ **1.** town in New York State. It is best known for a rock music festival in 1969, although the site of the festival was moved beforehand to nearby Bethel. Population: 6,290 (1990). **2.** city in southern Ontario, Canada, on the Thames River. Population: 30,075 (1991). **3.** town in Oxfordshire, England. Blenheim Palace, home of the Dukes of Malborough, is located there. Population: 2,898 (1991).

wood stork *n.* a large stork with a long heavy bill, bare head, white plumage, and black wingtips found in wooded marshes in North, Central, and South America. Genus: *Mycteria americana.*

wood sug·ar *n.* = **xylose**

wood·swal·low /wŏŏd swŏllō/ *n.* a medium-sized, long-winged Australian bird that has a black-tipped bill and feeds on insects while on the wing. Genus: *Artamus.* [Mid-19thC]

Woods·worth /wŏŏdz wùrth/, **James Shaver** (1874–1942) Canadian clergyman. He led the Cooperative Commonwealth Federation and, as a gospel minister, advocated democratic socialism.

woods·y /wŏŏdzee/ (**-i·er, -i·est**) *adj.* relating to or reminiscent of the woods, especially in scent (*informal*)

wood tar *n.* a black viscous tar produced as a by-product in the destructive distillation of wood, used as a protective coating for rope and timber

wood thrush *n.* a large thrush that lives in wooded areas of eastern North America and has a reddish-brown head, a pale spotted breast, and a melodious call. Latin name: *Hylocichla mustelina.*

wood tick *n.* a tick of western North America that transmits the pathogenic microorganism that causes Rocky Mountain spotted fever. Genus: *Dermacentor.*

wood vin·e·gar *n.* = **pyroligneous acid**

wood war·bler *n.* **1. BRIGHTLY COLORED AMERICAN SONGBIRD** a small, insect-eating, often brightly colored bird found throughout North and South America that has a distinctive song. Family: Parulidae. **2. SMALL EUROPEAN WOODLAND WARBLER** a small yellowish-green European songbird that lives in woods. Latin name: *Phylloscopus sibilatrix.*

Wood·ward /wŏŏdwərd/, **Robert B.** (1917–79) U.S. chemist. He won a Nobel Prize (1965) for his work in chemical synthesis, notably of quinine (1944), cholesterol (1951), and cortisone (1951). Full name **Robert Burns Woodward**

wood·wax·en /wŏŏd wăks'n/ *n.* = **dyer's greenweed**

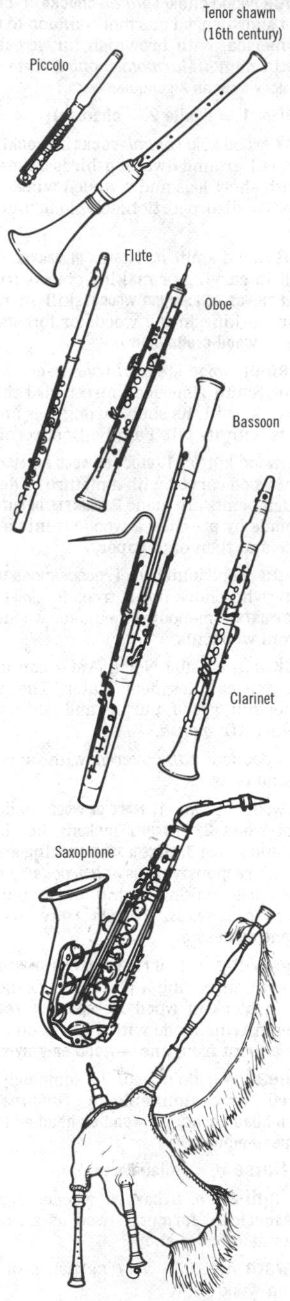

Woodwind instruments

wood·wind /wŏŏd wìnd/ *n.* **1. MUSICAL INSTRUMENT** a wind instrument, originally made of wood, belonging to the family of instruments that includes the flute, clarinet, oboe, and bassoon **2. WOODWINDS OF ORCHESTRA** the woodwinds of an orchestra, considered collectively (*takes a singular verb*) ■ *adj.* **RELATING TO WOODWIND** relating to or consisting of a woodwind [Late 19thC]

wood·work /wŏŏd wùrk/ *n.* **1.** *U.K.* = **woodworking** *n.* **2. ITEMS MADE FROM WOOD** items or components made from wood, especially the interior parts of a building, e.g., the frames of windows, staircases, and doors ◇ **crawl** *or* **come out of the woodwork** to appear suddenly and unexpectedly in large numbers (*slang*) ○ *It's amazing how many relatives crawl out of the woodwork when a rich man dies.*

wood·work·ing /wŏŏd wùrking/ *n.* **MANUFACTURE OF WOODEN ITEMS** the skill or craft of making items or parts out of wood ■ *adj.* **RELATING TO WOODWORKING** relating to woodworking or used in making things from wood

wood·worm /wŏŏd wùrm/ *n.* **1.** INSECTS **WOOD-BORING LARVA** a worm or insect larva that bores into and weakens wood, e.g., in joists or stairs inside a building **2. DAMAGE TO WOOD BY WOOD-BORING INSECTS** the damaged condition of wood from its infestation by wood-boring insects, especially larvae

wood·y /wŏŏdee/ *adj.* (**-i·er, -i·est**) **1. HAVING MANY TREES** containing or covered with many trees **2. RELATING TO WOODS** relating to, typical of, or situated in the woods **3. MADE OF WOOD** made of or containing wood or a material resembling wood **4. RESEMBLING WOOD** resembling wood in some way, e.g., in appearance, texture, or smell ■ *n.* (*plural* **-ies**) **wood·y** (*plural* **-ies**), **wood·ie** CARS **WOOD-PANELED CAR** a wood-paneled station wagon (*dated*)

wood·y night·shade *n. U.K.* = **bittersweet**

woof[1] /wŏŏf, woof/ *n.* **SOUND OF BARKING DOG** the sound made by a dog when it barks ■ *interj.* **REPRESENTATION OR IMITATION OF BARKING** a representation or imitation of the sound made by a barking dog ■ *vi.* (**woofed, woof·ing, woofs**) **MAKE BARKING SOUND** to produce a woof [Early 19thC. An imitation of the sound.]

woof[2] /wŏŏf/ *n.* TEXTILES a woven fabric or its texture [Old English *owef*, literally "to weave on," from *wefan* "to weave." Ultimately from an Indo-European word that is also the ancestor of English *web* and *wave*.]

woof·er /wŏŏffər/ *n.* a loudspeaker used to reproduce low-frequency sounds. ◊ **tweeter** [Mid-20thC. As a metaphor from WOOF[1].]

wool /wŏŏl/ *n.* **1.** TEXTILES **YARN USED TO MAKE CLOTHES** yarn spun from the short curly hair of sheep or other mammals, used in knitting or weaving **2.** ZOOL **SHEEP'S HAIR** the short curly overlapping hair of sheep and some other mammals, e.g., the llama and the alpaca, used to make wool **3.** TEXTILES **WOOLLEN MATERIAL** material knitted or woven using wool **4.** INSECTS **HAIR OF INSECT LARVA** the furry hair of some insect larvae, e.g., caterpillars (*informal*) **5.** BOT **HAIRS GROWING ON PLANT** a mass of soft hairs that grows on some plants ■ *adj.* TEXTILES **MADE FROM WOOL** knitted or woven using wool [Old English *wull*. Ultimately from an Indo-European word that is also the ancestor of Latin *lana* (source of English *lanolin*).] ◇ **pull the wool over somebody's eyes** to deceive or trick somebody

wool class·er *n. ANZ* somebody who grades sheep fleeces —**wool class·ing** *n.*

wool·ed /wŏŏld/, **wool·led** *adj.* having wool, especially of a particular kind ○ *a fine-wooled breed of sheep*

wool·en /wŏŏllən/, **wool·len** *adj.* **1. MADE FROM WOOL** knitted or woven using wool **2. PRODUCING WOOL OR WOOLEN ITEMS** relating to the production of wool or items made from wool ■ *n.* **WOOLEN GARMENT** a garment made from wool, especially one with a fleecy surface

Corbis/Bettmann

Virginia Woolf

Woolf /wŏŏlf/, **Virginia** (1882–1941) British novelist and critic. The psychological depth of her stream-of-consciousness technique and the poetic language of novels such as *To the Lighthouse* (1927) profoundly influenced the 20th-century English novel. Born **Virginia Adeline Stephen**

wool fat *n.* = **lanolin**

wool·gath·er·ing /wŏŏl gàthəring/ *n.* daydreaming or absent-mindedness [Mid-16thC. Originally used to mean "gathering the bits of wool torn from sheep by bushes," the underlying idea being "wasting time."] —**wool·gath·er** *vi.* —**wool·gath·er·er** *n.*

wool grease *n.* a fatty wax that coats the fibers of sheep's wool and yields lanolin

wool·grow·er /wŏŏl grō ər/ *n.* somebody who keeps sheep in order to sell their wool —**wool·grow·ing** *n.*

woolled /wŏŏld/ *adj.* = **wooled**

wool·len /wŏŏllən/ *adj., n.* = **woolen**

Wool·ley /wŏŏllee/, **Mary Emma** (1863–1947) U.S. educator. A leading educator of women, she was president of Mount Holyoke College (1900–37), and was a leading advocate for women's rights and world peace.

wool·ly /wŏŏllee/, **wool·y** *adj.* (**-li·er, -li·est; -i·er, -i·est**) **1.** TEXTILES **MADE OF WOOL** knitted or woven using wool. ◊ **woolen 2.** INSECTS **COVERED WITH INSECT HAIR** used to describe an insect larva, e.g., a caterpillar, that is covered with furry hair resembling wool **3. CONFUSED** confused, vague, and lacking focus ○ *woolly thinking* **4.** BOT **COVERED WITH PLANT HAIRS** used to describe a stem, leaf, or other plant part that is covered with long, soft white hairs **5. UNCIVILIZED AND UNRULY** rough and boisterous in a way that is reminiscent of the frontier days of the American West (*informal*) ○ *wild and woolly* ■ *n.* (*plural* **-lies;** *plural* **-ies**) **WOOLEN GARMENT** a garment made from wool (*informal*) —**wool·li·ly** *adv.* —**wool·li·ness** *n.*

wool·ly a·phid *n.* a tiny insect that secretes a waxy substance in long filaments that gives it a woolly appearance. Family: Aphididae.

wool·ly bear *n.* the caterpillar of various moths, especially the tiger moth, that has a coat of dense woolly hairs

wool·ly-head·ed *adj.* **1. HAVING THICK CURLY HAIR** having thick curly hair that looks or feels like wool **2. CONFUSED** confused, vague, and lacking focus

wool·ly mam·moth *n.* an extinct mammoth with a shaggy coat that lived in cold regions across North America and Eurasia during the Ice Age. Genus: *Mammuthus primigenius.*

wool·pack /wŏŏl pàk/ *n.* **1. MATERIAL FOR WRAPPING BALE OF WOOL** the coarse material, usually jute or canvas, used to wrap a bale of wool **2. CONTAINER FOR BALE OF WOOL** a package in which a bale of raw wool is transported

wool·sack /wŏŏl sàk/ *n.* a sack for holding wool

wool·shed /wŏŏl shèd/ *n.* ANZ a building or group of buildings in which sheep are sheared and their wool is prepared and packed for market

wool·skin /wŏŏl skìn/ *n.* the skin of a sheep with the wool still on it

wool-sort·er *n.* somebody who sorts wool into different grades

wool-sort·er's dis·ease *n.* pulmonary anthrax resulting from the inhalation of spores of an anthrax bacterium that contaminates wool

wool sta·pler *n.* **1.** = **wool-sorter 2. WOOL DEALER** somebody who deals in wool

Wool·worth /wŏŏl wùrth/, **Frank W.** (1852–1919) U.S. retailer. In 1879 he opened what was to prove the first of a chain of more than 1,000 five-and-ten-cent stores across the United States and Great Britain. Full name **Frank Winfield Woolworth**

wool·y *adj., n.* = **woolly**

woom·er·a /wŏŏmmərə, wŏŏm-/ (*plural* **-as**), **woom·er·ah** (*plural* **-ahs**), **wom·er·a** *n.* a wooden stick with a notch at one end, used by Australian Aboriginals to launch a spear. The stick provides extra leverage and force. [Early 19thC. From Dharvk, the Aboriginal language of the Port Jackson area in Australia.]

Woon·sock·et /woon sókit/ city in northeastern Rhode Island, on the Massachusetts border, northwest of Providence. Population: 41,817 (1996).

woops *interj.* = **whoops** (*informal*)

Woop Woop /wŏŏp wŏŏp/ *n.* Aus a remote town or area that is regarded as lacking the facilities and sophistication of the city (*informal humorous*) [Early 20thC. Mock Australian Aboriginal.]

wooz·y /wŏŏzee/ (**-i·er, -i·est**) *adj.* **1. WEAK AND DIZZY** weak and unsteady or dizzy **2. CONFUSED** confused or unable to think clearly [Late 19thC. Origin uncertain: perhaps coined from OOZY or BOOZY.] —**wooz·i·ly** *adv.* —**wooz·i·ness** *n.*

wop /wop/ *n.* a highly offensive term referring to an Italian person (*slang offensive*) [Early 20thC. Via Italian dialect *guappo* "tough, bold" from Spanish *guapo* "dandy," of uncertain origin: perhaps from Middle French *vape* "insipid," from Latin *vappa* "wine gone flat."]

wop-wops /wóp wòps/ *n.* NZ an offensive term referring to a rural or isolated region (*insult*)

Worces·ter /wŏŏstər/ **1.** city and administrative center of Worcestershire, west central England. Population: 91,100 (1995). **2.** city in central Massachusetts, west of Boston. Population: 169,759 (1990).

Worces·ter chi·na, **Worces·ter por·ce·lain, Worces·ter** *n.* fine china made in Worcester, England, since 1751, or the articles made from this china

Worces·ter·shire sauce /wŏŏstər sheer-/ *n.* a thin pungent table sauce flavored with soy, tamarind, and spices, originally made in Worcestershire, England

word /wurd/ *n.* **1. MEANINGFUL UNIT OF LANGUAGE SOUNDS** a meaningful sound or combination of sounds that is a unit of language or its representation in a text **2. BRIEF UTTERANCE** a brief comment, announcement, discussion, or conversation ○ *Could I have a word with you in my office, please?* **3. INFORMATION** information or news about somebody or something ○ *Is there any word on your daughter?* **4. RUMOR** rumor or gossip ○ *The word is that she's leaving the company.* **5. PROMISE** a promise, assurance, or guarantee ○ *I give you my word.* **6. COMMAND** a command, order, or authorization ○ *He gave the word to attack.* **7. PASSWORD** a password or verbal signal ○ *Don't let anyone in unless they give the word.* **8.** COMPUT **FIXED NUMBER OF PROCESSED BITS** a number of bits, e.g., 32, 48, or 64, processed as a single unit by a computer ■ **words** *npl.* **1. ANGRY TALK** angry or quarrelsome speech ○ *had words with him over the shoddy merchandise he sold us* **2.** MUSIC **TEXT OF SONG** the text or lyrics of a song, musical, or opera ■ *vt.* (**word·ed, word·ing, words**) **PHRASE SOMETHING** to express something in words [Old English. Ultimately from an Indo-European word that is also the ancestor of Latin *verbum* (source of English *verb*) and Greek *rhētôr* "public speaker" (source of English *rhetoric*.] ◇ **a man of his word, a woman of her word** somebody who keeps his or her promise ◇ **be as good as your word** to do as promised ◇ **be the last word in something** to be the best, greatest, most fashionable, or most up-to-date instance of something ◇ **eat your words** to admit humbly that you were wrong or mistaken (*informal*) ◇ **in a word** briefly or very concisely expressed ◇ **my word** used to express surprise or astonishment (*dated*) ◇ **put in** *or* **say a good word for somebody** to speak well of or recommend somebody ◇ **put words in somebody's mouth** to say that somebody has said something when in fact he or she did not say it

Word *n.* CHR **1. DIVINE REASON** in Christian theology, the divine rational principle as epitomized by Jesus Christ **2. Word, Word of God CHRISTIAN HOLY SCRIPTURES** in Christianity, the Bible or Scriptures, considered as revealing divine truth

word·age /wúrdij/ *n.* **1. NUMBER OF WORDS** the number of words in a text **2. WORDS COLLECTIVELY** words considered as a group **3. WORDINESS** the use of too many words to express something **4. WORDING OF SOMETHING** the choice of words made by a writer or speaker

word as·so·ci·a·tion *n.* a method of assessing somebody's mental state or personality by asking the person to respond with the first word that comes to mind when a given word is heard

word blind·ness *n.* = **alexia** —**word-blind** *adj.*

word·book /wúrd bŏŏk/ *n.* a dictionary, vocabulary, or lexicon

word·break /wúrd bràyk/ *n.* the point in a word where it can be divided if there is insufficient room at the end of a line for the entire word

word class *n.* a category of words that have the same form or function, e.g., parts of speech

word count *n.* the calculation of the number of words in a piece of text, or the result of such a calculation

word deaf·ness *n.* the loss of the capacity to understand spoken words, especially when caused by a cerebral lesion —**word-deaf** *adj.*

word·ed /wúrdəd/ *adj.* expressed in words, especially in a particular way ○ *a carefully worded reply*

word find·er *n.* a book that lists words according to meaning or subject, designed to help users find the word that best expresses the meaning they want to convey

word for word *adv.* **1. IN SAME WORDS** in exactly the same words as originally used **2. LITERALLY** by translating each word used in a spoken or written piece of foreign language individually ■ *adj.* **word-for-word 1. USING SAME WORDS** using exactly the same words as the original spoken or written text **2. LITERAL** translating each word used in a spoken or written piece of foreign language individually

word game *n.* **1. GAME TO CONSTRUCT OR FIND WORDS** a game in which players have to construct, find, or change the form of words **2. CRAFTY LANGUAGE** disingenuous language intended to mislead, misrepresent, conceal, or put a spin onto a usually awkward situation or issue (*slang*) (*often plural*) ○ *Please stop the word games and give me a truthful answer*

word-hoard *n.* the total number of words that somebody is able to use or understand

word·ing /wúrding/ *n.* the choice of words made by a writer or speaker

word·less /wúrdləss/ *adj.* **1. NOT USING WORDS** communicating without the use of speech **2. UNABLE TO SPEAK** incapable of speech, especially temporarily —**word·less·ly** *adv.* —**word·less·ness** *n.*

word·mon·ger /wúrd mùng gər, -mòng-/ *n.* somebody who uses words pretentiously or merely for effect (*dated*)

Word of God *n.* = **Word** *n.* 2

word of hon·or *n.* a solemn promise or undertaking to do something

word of mouth *n.* communication using the spoken word, as distinct from written communication

word-of-mouth *adj.* made by using oral communication, not written ○ *A small business thrives on word-of-mouth recommendation.*

word-per·fect *adj.* **1.** *U.K.* = **letter-perfect 2. ABSOLUTELY CORRECT** accurate in every detail

word pic·ture *n.* a vivid description of something in words

word·play /wúrd plày/ *n.* the witty, subtle, or ingenious use of words, e.g., in taking advantage of their multiple meanings

word proc·ess·ing *n.* the creation, retrieval, storage, and printing of text using a computer or other electronic equipment (*hyphenated when used before a noun*)

word proc·es·sor *n.* **1. MACHINE FOR MANIPULATING TEXT** a piece of electronic equipment that has a keyboard and video display unit and is used to create, retrieve, store, and print text. It is usually not as advanced as a personal computer. **2. COMPUTER PROGRAM FOR MANIPULATING TEXT** a computer program that is used to create, retrieve, store, and print text **3. SOMEBODY PROCESSING WORDS** somebody who does word processing

word·smith /wúrd smìth/ *n.* somebody such as a professional writer or journalist who uses words skillfully —**word·smith** *vti.*

word square *n.* a puzzle consisting of a square grid to be constructed of words that read the same vertically and horizontally

word stress *n.* the placing of stress on the syllables of a word, or an instance of this

Words·worth /wúrdz wùrth/, **William** (1770–1850) British poet. *Lyrical Ballads* (1798), written with Samuel Taylor Coleridge, was the seminal work of English romantic poetry. His greatest work is the autobiographical epic *The Prelude* (1850). —**Words·worth·i·an** *adj.*

word wrap, **word wrap·ping** *n.* COMPUT a feature of word-processing programs in which a word that causes a preset line length to be exceeded is moved automatically to the beginning of the next line

word·y /wúrdee/ (**-i·er, -i·est**) *adj.* **1.** USING TOO MANY WORDS using an excessive number of words in writing or speech **2.** RELATING TO WORDS relating to or consisting of words [Old English *wordig*] —**word·i·ly** *adv.* —**word·i·ness** *n.*

WORD KEY: SYNONYMS

wordy, verbose, long-winded, rambling, prolix, diffuse

CORE MEANING: too long or not concisely expressed

wordy an informal word used to describe speech or writing that is too long, especially when it contains ideas or concepts that are not concisely expressed; **verbose** a more formal word meaning the same as *wordy*; **long-winded** used to describe speech or writing that is excessively long to the point of tedium; **rambling** used to describe speech or writing that is excessively long and badly ordered, making it difficult to follow; **prolix** a formal word meaning the same as *long-winded*; **diffuse** a formal word meaning the same as *rambling*.

wore past tense of **wear**

work /wurk/ *n.* **1.** PAID JOB paid employment at a job **2.** DUTIES OF JOB the duties or activities that are part of a job or occupation ○ *Much of my work involves talking on the phone.* **3.** SOMEBODY'S PLACE OF EMPLOYMENT the place where somebody is employed ○ *spends all her time at work* **4.** TIME SPENT AT PLACE OF EMPLOYMENT the time that a person spends carrying out his or her job ○ *meet you after work* **5.** PURPOSEFUL EFFORT the physical or mental effort directed at doing or making something ○ *It was a lot of work, but it was worth it.* **6.** SOMETHING MADE OR DONE that which has been made or done as part of a job or as a result of effort or activity requiring skill (*often used in combination*) ○ *Your work is satisfactory.* **7.** ARTS ARTISTIC OR INTELLECTUAL CREATION an artistic or intellectual composition, e.g., a book, treatise, painting, sculpture, film, or piece of music (*often used in the plural*) **8.** PHYS MEANS FOR ENERGY TRANSFER the transfer of energy, measured as the product of the force applied to a body and the distance moved by that body in the direction of the force. Symbol *W* **9.** SOMETHING MANUFACTURED that which has been or is in the process of being worked on or manufactured ■ *v.* (**worked** *or* **wrought** *archaic* /rawt/, **worked** *or* **wrought** *archaic*, **work·ing, works**) **1.** *vi.* HAVE JOB to have a paid job **2.** *vti.* EXERT OR CAUSE EFFORT to exert or make somebody exert physical or mental effort in order to do, make, or accomplish something **3.** *vti.* FUNCTION to function or operate or cause something to function or operate ○ *The television doesn't work.* **4.** *vi.* BE SUCCESSFUL to be effective or achieve a desired result ○ *Our relationship just isn't working.* **5.** *vti.* WORK IN SPECIFIC PLACE to carry on an operation or activity in a particular place or area ○ *You'll be working the southern region.* **6.** *vi.* EXERT INFLUENCE to produce results or exert an influence **7.** *vti.* SHAPE SOMETHING to shape, bend, form, or forge a material, or to be shaped, bent, formed, or forged in a specified way **8.** *vt.* CULTIVATE LAND to cultivate land in order to grow crops on it **9.** *vt.* ACHIEVE SOMETHING to effect something or bring something about ○ *Attention to detail can work wonders.* **10.** *vti.* ATTAIN SPECIFIED CONDITION to attain or cause something to attain a specified condition slowly or gradually ○ *Sometimes the screw just seems to work itself loose.* **11.** *vti.* MOVE SLOWLY AND WITH EFFORT to move or progress slowly and with effort, or to cause something to move or progress in this way ○ *He worked his way through the crowd.* **12.** *vt.* SOLVE MATHEMATICAL PROBLEM to solve a mathematical problem or puzzle **13.** *vti.* EXERCISE to move or exercise a muscle or part of the body **14.** *vt.* PROVOKE EMOTIONAL RESPONSE IN SOMEBODY to arouse or stir up emotions in somebody ○ *The crowd seemed to work itself into a frenzy.* **15.** *vt.* SEW MAKE SOMETHING IN NEEDLEWORK to make or decorate something by hand in needlework or embroidery **16.** *vi.* MECH ENG MOVE LOOSELY to move in a loose way that results in friction and wear (*refers to machinery*) **17.** *vt.* ARRANGE SOMETHING to arrange or exploit something in order to gain an advantage (*informal*) ○ *He managed to work it so that he got every other Friday off.* **18.** *vt.* CHARM SOMEBODY to use charm and personal influence on somebody in order to attain popularity or acclaim ○ *The politician really knew how to work a crowd.* **19.** *vti.* FERMENT to ferment or cause something to ferment **20.** *vi.* NAUT STRAIN SLIGHTLY IN ROUGH WATER to give slightly in rough water so that the joints move slightly and the fastenings become looser (*refers to ships*) **21.** *vi.* SAILING SAIL INTO WIND to sail against the wind [Old English *weorc*. Ultimately from an Indo-European word that is also the ancestor of English *energy, organ*, and *orgy*.] ◇ **at work 1.** engaged in employment **2.** in operation ◇ **do somebody's dirty work** to do something unpleasant, dishonest, or immoral on behalf of somebody else ◇ **have your work cut out (for you)** to be faced with a difficult task ◇ **make short work of somebody** *or* **something** to dispose of or deal with somebody or something very quickly

WORD KEY: USAGE

See Usage note at ***wrought***.

WORD KEY: SYNONYMS

work, labor, toil, drudgery

CORE MEANING: sustained effort required to do or produce something

work the physical and mental effort employed to do or achieve something. It can be used to talk about animals and machines as well as people; **labor** strenuous work, usually physical; **toil** tiring, often tedious, physical work; **drudgery** work that is strenuous and not at all rewarding. Used especially of work that is sustained over a long period.

work back *vi. Aus* to stay on late at work, with or without payment

work in *vt.* **1.** ADD SOMETHING GRADUALLY to add something gradually while blending it with another substance **2.** ARRANGE TO INCLUDE SOMETHING to arrange a time or place for something in a given situation ○ *I'll see if I can work you in on Friday.*

work off *vt.* **1. work off, work at** PAY DEBT BY WORKING to pay back a debt by doing work rather than by paying the money owed **2.** USE SOMETHING UP BY WORKING to use up or get rid of something by the effort of working

work on *vt.* **1.** AFFECT SOMEBODY OR SOMETHING to influence or attempt to influence somebody or something **2.** MAKE OR FIX SOMETHING to spend time making, improving, or fixing something **3.** USE SOMETHING AS BASIS to use something as a starting point for further investigation or inquiry

work out *v.* **1.** *vi.* EXERCISE to train or take part in strenuous physical exercise as a way of keeping in shape **2.** *vi.* END SATISFACTORILY to have a satisfactory or successful result **3.** *vi.* END IN PARTICULAR WAY to have a particular result **4.** *vt.* RESOLVE DIFFICULTY to resolve differences or find a way of dealing with a difficulty **5.** *vt.* THINK SOMETHING UP to devise something, especially a course of action **6.** *vt.* SOLVE OR CALCULATE SOMETHING to solve a problem or find an answer to a question by reasoning or calculation **7.** *vi.* MAKE TOTAL to come to a particular amount ○ *That works out to $100.* **8.** *vt.* COMPREHEND SOMEBODY OR SOMETHING to understand somebody or something fully **9.** *vt.* ACHIEVE SOMETHING BY EFFORT to succeed in doing something after working long and hard at it **10.** *vt.* = **work off** *v.* 1 **11.** *vt.* EXHAUST MINE BY EXTRACTION to extract all the valuable material from a mine or deposit

WORD KEY: SYNONYMS

See Synonyms at ***deduce***.

work over *vt.* **1.** GIVE SOMEBODY A BEATING to give somebody a severe beating or subject somebody to severe physical punishment (*informal*) **2.** REDO SOMETHING to do something again **3.** EXAMINE SOMETHING THOROUGHLY to work at or examine something thoroughly and in detail

work through *vt.* to deal with an emotional problem by thinking about it often until it is understood or its impact is lessened

work up *v.* **1.** *vt.* EXCITE EMOTIONS IN SOMEBODY to arouse or stir up emotions in somebody **2.** *vt.* CREATE SOMETHING to create something or cause it to grow ○ *working up a sweat* **3.** *vt.* IMPROVE SOMETHING to develop, refine, or improve something **4.** *vi.* BECOME MORE INTENSE to grow or develop in intensity **5.** *vt.* MED EXAMINE A PATIENT THOROUGHLY to subject a patient to a thorough diagnostic examination

work up to *vt.* to gradually reach a particular level by effort

work·a·ble /wúrkəb'l/ *adj.* **1.** ABLE TO BE DONE able to be accomplished or carried out ○ *The plan is not workable.* **2.** ABLE TO BE WORKED ON capable of being operated or handled ○ *workable steel* —**work·a·bil·i·ty** /wùrkə bíllətee/ *n.* —**work·a·ble·ness** /wúrkəb'lnəss/ *n.* —**work·a·bly** /w/ *adv.*

work·a·day /wúrkə dày/, **work·day** /wúrk dày/ *adj.* **1.** ROUTINE AND COMMONPLACE ordinary or part of the experience of most people **2.** APPROPRIATE FOR WORK suitable for work or for a working day [Mid-16thC. Origin uncertain: perhaps from WORK + DAY.]

work·a·hol·ic /wùrkə hóllik/ *n.* somebody who displays a compulsive need to work hard and for very long hours [Mid-20thC. Coined from WORK + -AHOLIC.]

work·bag /wúrk bàg/, **work·bas·ket** /wúrk bàskit/ *n.* a bag for holding materials and tools for work, especially sewing or knitting

work·bench /wúrk bènch/ *n.* a table or surface on which work is done, e.g., by a carpenter or mechanic

work·boat /wúrk bōt/ *n.* a boat that is used solely for work, e.g., for fishing or transporting cargo

work·book /wúrk bòòk/ *n.* **1.** STUDENT'S EXERCISE BOOK a book of exercises and questions for students, usually with spaces for answers to be written in **2.** INSTRUCTION BOOK a book of instructions on how to do or operate something **3.** RECORD OF WORK a book in which a record is kept of work done or to be done

work camp *n.* **1.** CAMP FOR VOLUNTEER WORKERS a camp where volunteers, especially young people or members of a religious organization, work on a project of benefit to the community **2.** PRISON CAMP a camp in which prisoners are forced to work

work·day /wúrk dày/ *n.* **1.** DAY FOR WORKING a day on which people work, usually but not always a weekday **2.** HOURS SPENT WORKING the part of a day during which somebody works ■ *adj.* = **workaday**

worked /wurkt/ *adj.* produced, decorated, or treated with craft and skill [Late 16thC. Originally "that has been worked on."]

worked up *adj.* full of anger or other strong emotion (*informal*)

work·er /wúrkər/ *n.* **1.** PERSON OR THING THAT WORKS a person, animal, or device that is engaged in or used for a task of some kind **2.** EMPLOYEE somebody who is an employee, not an employer or manager **3.** INDUST MEMBER OF WORKING CLASS somebody who belongs to the working class, especially a factory employee or manual laborer **4.** INSECTS INSECT THAT WORKS a member of a colony of social insects, especially sterile females, that carry out all the work, e.g., gathering food or feeding larvae

work·er par·tic·i·pa·tion *n.* the involvement of ordinary employees in making decisions at all levels in a business

work·er-priest *n.* a Roman Catholic priest who also has a secular job

work·ers' com·pen·sa·tion *n.* **1.** PROGRAM COMPENSATING INJURED WORKERS a form of insurance required from employers that provides money as compensation for workers who are injured at work or who contract an occupational disease **2.** PAYMENT FOR INJURY AT WORK money paid as compensation to a worker who is injured at work or contracts an occupational disease

work eth·ic *n.* a dedication to work, or belief in the moral value of hard work ○ *hasn't got much of a work ethic*

work·fare /wúrk fàir/ *n.* a government program that obliges unemployed people to do community work or attend training courses in return for welfare payments [Mid-20thC. Blend of WORK and WELFARE.]

work farm *n.* a farm on which short-term prisoners are confined and forced to work

work·flow /wúrk flō/ *n.* the progress or rate of progress of work done by a business, department, or individual

work force /wúrk fàwrs/, **work·force** *n.* **1.** ALL WORKERS IN COMPANY all of the workers employed in a company or industry **2.** ALL PEOPLE EMPLOYED OR EMPLOYABLE all of the people who are employed or able to work, e.g., in a country

work func·tion *n.* the minimum energy needed to remove an electron from within a solid to a point outside its surface in a vacuum. Symbol Φ

work-hard·en *vt.* to increase the hardness or strength of a metal by subjecting it to compression, tension, or another mechanical process

work·horse /wúrk hàwrss/ *n.* **1.** HARD-WORKING PERSON somebody who works hard and diligently, often assuming extra duties (*informal*) **2.** RELIABLE TOOL OR MACHINE something such as a machine that performs well over long periods **3.** AGRIC HORSE USED FOR HEAVY WORK a horse used for heavy work such as hauling, rather than for riding

work·house /wúrk hòwss/ (*plural* **-hous·es** /-hòwzəz/) *n.* **1. FORMER INSTITUTION FOR THE POOR** formerly, a publicly run institution in Britain in which people living in poverty were given food and accommodations in return for unpaid work **2. PRISON FOR MINOR OFFENDERS** a type of prison in which prisoners guilty of minor violations work at manual labor

work·ing /wúrking/ *adj.* **1. FUNCTIONING** capable of being used or operated **2. WORN AT WORK** suitable for use while at work **3. HAVING PAID JOB** engaged in doing paid work **4. SPENT AT WORK** taken up with work ○ *all his working life* **5. GIVEN OVER TO WORK** spent doing work at a time when work is not normally done ○ *a working lunch* **6. ADEQUATE** good enough for a purpose, though not perfect or complete ○ *a working knowledge of Italian* **7. PROVIDING BASIS** usable as a basis for further work ○ *a working theory* ■ *n.* **1. PROCESS OF SHAPING SOMETHING** the shaping, bending, forming, or forging of a material **2. JERKING MOTION** the convulsive, involuntary motion of a part of the body, caused by excitement or tension (*formal*) ■ *npl.* **1. work·ings FUNCTIONING OF SOMETHING** the operation of something or the way in which it operates **2. workings USED PARTS OF MINE** the parts of a mine or quarry in which work is carried on

work·ing cap·i·tal *n.* **1. MONEY AVAILABLE TO COMPANY** the money that a business has available for use **2. CURRENT ASSETS MINUS LIABILITIES** the amount of current assets that remains after current liabilities are deducted

work·ing class *n.* **1. HOURLY WORKERS** the part of society made up of people who work for hourly wages, not salaries, especially manual or industrial laborers **2. MARXIST PROLETARIAT** in Marxist theory, the proletariat or revolutionary class

work·ing-class *adj.* relating to or belonging to the part of society made up of people who work for hourly wages, not salaries, especially manual or industrial laborers ○ *a working-class neighborhood*

work·ing day *n. U.K.* = **workday**

work·ing dog *n.* a dog that is kept in order to do work, e.g., herding, guarding, or guiding. Among breeds of working dogs are the collie, Doberman pinscher, German shepherd, and husky.

work·ing draw·ing *n.* a detailed scale drawing of something, for use as a guide in building or manufacturing

work·ing girl *n.* **1. YOUNG WOMAN WITH A PAID JOB** a young woman who works for a living (*informal*) **2. WOMAN PROSTITUTE** a woman who is a prostitute (*slang*)

work·ing hours *npl.* the part of the day during which most people normally work and shops and offices are open

work·ing·man /w/ *n.* a man who works for wages, especially at manual labor

work·ing mem·o·ry *n.* the contents of a person's consciousness at the present moment

work·ing pa·per *n.* a document created as a basis for discussion rather than as an authoritative text

work·ing pa·pers *npl.* official documents showing that somebody, e.g., an alien or a minor, is legally permitted to work

work·ing stor·age *n.* the amount of storage in a computer's memory that is assigned for data stored only while a program is running

work·ing sub·stance *n.* a substance, especially a fluid, that undergoes changes in form or degree that are used to operate something such as an engine

work·ing ti·tle *n.* the provisional title by which a project, especially a movie or novel, is known while it is still being worked on

work·ing week *n. U.K.* = **workweek**

work·ing·wom·an /wúrking wŏŏmmən/ (*plural* **-en** /-wìmmin/) *n.* a woman who works for wages, especially in a manual job

work-in-pro·gress (*plural* **works-in-pro·gress**) *n.* a piece of artistic work, e.g., a novel or musical composition, that has not yet been finished but may be printed, exhibited, or performed

work·less /wúrkləss/ *adj.* having no job (*dated*) — **work·less·ness** *n.*

work·load /wúrk lōd/ *n.* **1. AMOUNT OF WORK MACHINE DOES** the amount of work that a machine does or can do in a particular period **2. AMOUNT OF WORK FOR SOMEBODY** the amount of work assigned to a person or a group, and that is to be done in a particular period

work·man /wúrkmən/ (*plural* **-men** /-mən/) *n.* **1. MAN JUDGED ON WORKING ABILITY** a man described or judged according to his skill or diligence as a worker ○ *a tidy workman* **2. CRAFTSMAN** somebody who works as a craftsman or artisan [Old English]

work·man·like /wúrkmən lìk/, **work·man·ly** /wúrkmən lee/*adj.* done in a way that is thorough and satisfactory, without being imaginative or exciting

work·man·ship /wúrkmən shìp/ *n.* **1. ART OR SKILL OF WORKER** the skill or craft of a worker or artisan **2. QUALITY OF SKILL** the level of skill used in making or doing something **3. PRODUCT OR RESULT OF WORKER'S SKILL** the product or result of the skill of a worker or artisan

work·mate /wúrk màyt/ *n.* somebody who works with or in the same place as another

work of art *n.* **1. PAINTING OR SCULPTURE** a piece of fine art, e.g., a painting or sculpture **2. SOMETHING MADE OR DONE WELL** something made or done exceptionally well ○ *The second touchdown was an absolute work of art.*

work·out /wúrk òwt/ *n.* **1. STRENUOUS EXERCISE SESSION** a session of strenuous physical exercise or the practicing of physical skills intended as a way of keeping in shape or as practice for a game or athletic competition **2. RIGOROUS TEST** a tough practical test of the capability or performance of a person, animal, or device [Early 20thC]

work·peo·ple /wúrk peèp'l/ *npl. U.K.* hourly workers, especially those with manual jobs

work·piece /wúrk peèss/ *n.* something that has been, or is in the process of being, worked on or manufactured

work·place /wúrk plàyss/ *n.* the place where somebody works, e.g., a factory or office

work plane *n.* a simple, wheeled desk that can be used in various work sites by several employees using the same desk at different times in a flexible workplace [Late 20thC]

work print *n.* a print of a movie used in various stages of editing and as a guide in cutting the original negative from which the final commercial prints are made

work-re·lease *n.* a system of allowing prisoners to perform paid work outside prison while serving their sentences

work·room /wúrk ròom, -ròom/ *n.* a room in which work is done, especially one equipped for manual work

works /wurks/ *n.* (*plural* **works**) **1. PLACE FOR INDUSTRIAL PRODUCTION** a place where industrial work, especially manufacturing, is done ○ *an engineering works* **2. EVERYTHING** all things that are available (*informal*) ○ *A hot dog with the works, please.* **3. SYRINGE FOR INJECTING NARCOTICS** a syringe used to inject narcotics (*slang*) **4. BAD BEATING** a severe beating or punishment (*slang*) ■ *npl.* **1. COLLECTED COMPOSITIONS** all of the compositions created by an artist, writer, or musician ○ *the complete works of Shakespeare* **2. INNER MECHANISMS** the interior moving parts of a mechanism ○ *the works of the clock are rusty* **3. ACTS** deeds or actions ◇ **in the works** being prepared or worked on

work·sheet /wúrk sheèt/ *n.* **1. SHEET OF QUESTIONS FOR STUDENTS** a sheet of questions or tasks for students on a recent lesson **2. SHEET RECORDING WORK** a sheet of paper used for keeping a record of work done or scheduled **3. SHEET FOR DRAFT** a sheet of paper used for making a rough draft or preliminary notes

work·shop /wúrk shòp/ *n.* **1. PLACE WHERE MANUAL WORK IS DONE** a place where manual work is done, especially manufacturing or repairing **2. GROUP WORKING TOGETHER** a group of people working on a creative project, discussing a topic, or studying a subject ○ *a songwriting workshop*

work song *n.* a song sung by people working, usually with a repetitive rhythm that guides the rhythm of the work being done

work·space /wúrk spàyss/ *n.* an area set aside for an individual worker or a business

work·sta·tion /wúrk stàysh'n/ *n.* **1. WORKING AREA** a small area in a workplace assigned to one worker, especially a desk with a computer **2. COMPUT TERMINAL OF NETWORK OR MAINFRAME** a computer terminal, usually connected to a network in a business environment, that runs application programs and serves as an access point to the network **3. COMPUT POWERFUL SPECIALIZED COMPUTER** a powerful stand-alone computer, often with a high-resolution display, used for computer-aided design and other complex and specialized applications

work stop·page *n.* an occasion when a group of employees stop work, often as a protest or as a bargaining tool

work-stud·y *adj.* combining an academic program with paid employment in which students gain practical experience in the workplace

work sur·face *n.* a rigid flat area on which work is done, e.g., a tabletop or kitchen counter

work·ta·ble /wúrk tàyb'l/ *n.* a table at which work is done, e.g., writing or drawing

work·top /wúrk tòp/ *n.* a rigid flat surface on which work is done, especially the top of a kitchen counter, used when preparing food

work to rule (**worked to rule, work·ing to rule, works to rule**) *vi. U.K., Can* to take part in a labor protest in which workers make a point of adhering strictly to the rules of the workplace so that work will slow down

work-to-rule *n. U.K., Can* a type of labor protest in which workers make a point of adhering strictly to the rules of the workplace so that work will slow down

work·up /wúrk ùp/ *n.* a complete diagnostic medical examination

work·wear /wúrk wàir/ *n.* clothes worn at work, especially at manual work

work·week /wúrk weèk/, **work week** *n.* the amount of hours or days worked in a week

world /wurld/ *n.* **1. PLANET EARTH** the planet Earth **2. EARTH AND EVERYTHING ON IT** the Earth, including all of its inhabitants and the things upon it **3. HUMAN RACE** all of the human inhabitants of the Earth ○ *Soon, the world would know the truth.* **4. SOCIETY** human society ○ *in the eyes of the world* **5. PART OF EARTH** a particular part of the Earth, considered in terms of time or space ○ *the western world* **6. AREA OF ACTIVITY** a specified area of human activity and the people involved in it ○ *the world of fashion* **7. UNIVERSE** all the galaxies that are known or thought to exist in space **8. DOMAIN** a sphere, realm, or domain ○ *the world of reptiles* **9. INHABITED BODY** an astronomical body considered to be inhabited, e.g., a planet **10. EVERYTHING IN SOMEBODY'S LIFE** all that relates to or makes up the life of an individual ○ *Her entire world collapsed.* **11. CONDITION OF EXISTENCE** a condition or state of existence ○ *the world of tomorrow* **12. GREAT DEAL OR AMOUNT** a very large amount, degree, or distance ○ *They're still worlds apart.* ○ *in a world of hurt* **13. SECULAR EXISTENCE** secular life and its ways ○ *a man of the world* ■ *adj.* **1. OF THE ENTIRE WORLD** relating to the entire world ○ *the world champions* **2. EXERTING INFLUENCE GLOBALLY** exerting influence over the whole of the world ○ *a world figure* **3. AFFECTING WHOLE WORLD** involving or affecting the whole of the Earth ○ *a world crisis* [Old English *woruld* "human existence, age, Earth." Ultimately from a prehistoric Germanic compound meaning "age of man" that is also the ancestor of English *old* and *werewolf*.] ◇ **be out of this world** to be extraordinarily good in some way (*informal*) ◇ **for all the world** exactly and in every detail ◇ **have the best of both worlds** to have the advantage of the best features of two different situations ◇ **in the world** used to express puzzlement, surprise, or dismay, or to give emphasis to a statement ○ *What in the world have you done?* ◇ **not for the world** no matter what happens ○ *Not for the world would I think of doing such a thing* ◇ **think the world of somebody** to be extremely fond of somebody

World Bank *n.* a specialized agency of the United Nations established in 1944 that guarantees loans to member nations for the purpose of reconstruction and development. Full form **International Bank for Reconstruction and Development**

world-beat·er *n.* one that is the best in a particular field

world-beat·ing *adj.* surpassing all others in a particular field

world-class *adj.* ranked among the best or most prominent in the world ○ *a world-class downhill racer* ○ *a world-class liar*

World Coun·cil of Church·es *n.* an international ecumenical organization founded in 1948 that links Protestant and Eastern churches from around the world for the purpose of coordinated and cooperative action in religious and secular areas

World Court *n.* = **International Court of Justice**

World Cup *n.* a sports tournament, especially in soccer, contested by the national teams of qualifying countries, that has been held every four years on a different continent and in a different country

world e·con·o·my *n.* the economy of the world, considered as an international exchange of goods and services

World Eng·lish *n.* the English language in all its varieties as it is spoken and written over the world

World Health Or·gan·i·za·tion *n.* a specialized agency of the United Nations that helps countries to improve their health services and coordinates international action against diseases

World Her·i·tage Site *n.* an area or structure designated by UNESCO as being of global significance and conserved by a country that has signed a United Nations convention pledging its protection

world lan·guage *n.* **1. LANGUAGE USED IN MANY COUNTRIES** a language that is used in many countries, e.g., English, Spanish, or Arabic **2. INTERNATIONAL ARTIFICIAL LANGUAGE** a language created for international use, e.g., Esperanto or Interlingua

world lead·er *n.* **1. LEADER OF POWERFUL COUNTRY** a leader of a politically and economically powerful country **2. SOMETHING BIGGEST OR BEST IN WORLD** a company, organization, or country that is the biggest or best in a particular field

world line *n.* the path of a particle in time and space, which is straight if the particle moves in a uniform way

world·ling /w/ *n.* somebody more interested in everyday material things than in spiritual matters

world·ly /wúrldlee/ *adj.* **1. EXPERIENCED IN LIFE** experienced in and knowledgeable about human society and its ways **2. BELONGING TO PHYSICAL WORLD** relating to everyday material existence **3. MATERIALISTIC** much more interested in everyday materialistic concerns than in the spiritual side of life

world·ly-mind·ed *adj.* = **worldly** *adj.* 1, **worldly** *adj.* 3

world·ly-wise *adj.* = **worldly** *adj.* 1

world mu·sic *n.* popular music from or influenced by countries outside the western world and its traditions

world pow·er *n.* a country or alliance of countries powerful enough to influence events on a global scale

World Se·ries *tdmk.* a trademark for a series of baseball games played between the winners of the American League and the National League to decide the major league championship

world's fair *n.* an exhibition of commercial and cultural products from many different countries

world-shak·ing *adj.* = **earthshaking**

world soul *n.* a spirit believed to animate the world in the same way that the human soul animates the body

world-view, world·view *n.* a comprehensive interpretation or image of the universe and humanity

world war *n.* a war involving a number of countries on each side, with fighting spread over much of the world

World War I *n.* a war fought mainly in Europe from 1914 to 1918, in which an alliance including Great Britain, France, Russia, Italy, and the United States defeated the alliance of Germany, Austria-Hungary, Turkey, and Bulgaria

World War II *n.* a war fought in Europe, Africa and Asia from 1939 to 1945, in which an alliance including Great Britain, France, the Soviet Union, and the United States defeated the alliance of Germany, Italy, and Japan

world-wea·ry *adj.* tired of or bored with life —**world-wear·i·ness** *n.*

world·wide /wúrld wīd/ *adj.* **RELATING TO WHOLE WORLD** affecting or found throughout the entire world ■ *adv.* **OVER WHOLE EARTH** all over the world

World Wide Web *n.* the very large set of linked documents and other files located on computers connected through the Internet and used to access, manipulate, and download data and programs

UNESCO WORLD HERITAGE SITES: AUSTRALIA, CANADA, NEW ZEALAND, THE UNITED KINGDOM, AND THE UNITED STATES

Australia

1981 Great Barrier Reef
1981 Kakadu National Park
1981 Willandra Lakes Region
1982 Tasmanian Wilderness
1982 Lord Howe Island Group
1987 Uluru National Park
1987 Central Eastern Australian Rainforest Reserves
1988 Wet Tropics of Queensland
1991 Shark Bay
1992 Fraser Island
1994 Australian Fossil Mammal Sites (Riversleigh/Naracoorte)
1997 Heard and McDonald Islands
1997 Macquarie Island

Canada

1978 L'Anse aux Meadows National Historic Park
1978 Nahanni National Park Reserve
1979 Dinosaur Provincial Park
1981 Anthony Island
1981 Head-Smashed-In Buffalo Jump Complex
1983 Wood Buffalo National Park
1984 Rocky Mountain Park
1985 Québec (Historic Area)
1987 Gros Morne National Park
1995 Lunenburg Old Town

New Zealand

1990 Tongariro National Park
1990 Te Wahipounamu — South West New Zealand
1998 New Zealand Sub-Antarctic Islands

United Kingdom

1986 Giant's Causeway and Causeway Coast
1986 Durham Castle and Cathedral
1986 Ironbridge Gorge
1986 Studley Royal Park, including the Ruins of Fountains Abbey
1986 Stonehenge, Avebury, and Associated Sites
1986 Castles and Town Walls of King Edward in Gwynedd
1986 Saint Kilda
1987 Blenheim Palace
1987 City of Bath
1987 Hadrian's Wall
1987 Westminster Palace, Westminster Abbey, and Saint Margaret's Church
1988 Henderson Island
1988 Canterbury Cathedral, Saint Augustine's Abbey, and Saint Martin's Church
1988 Tower of London
1995 Old and New Towns of Edinburgh
1995 Gough Island Wildlife Reserve
1997 Maritime Greenwich

United States

1978 Mesa Verde National Park
1978 Yellowstone National Park
1979 Grand Canyon National Park
1979 Everglades National Park
1979 Independence National Historic Park
1980 Redwood National Park
1981 Mammoth Cave National Park
1981 Olympic National Park
1982 Cahokia Mounds State Historic Park
1983 Great Smoky Mountains National Park
1983 La Fortaleza and San Juan Historic Site in Puerto Rico
1984 Statue of Liberty
1984 Yosemite National Park
1987 Monticello and University of Virginia in Charlottesville
1987 Chaco Culture National Historical Park
1987 Hawaii Volcanoes National Park
1992 Taos Pueblo
1995 Carlsbad Caverns National Park

worm /wurm/ *n.* **1.** ZOOL **LONG CYLINDRICAL INVERTEBRATE** an invertebrate that has a slender, soft, cylindrical or flat body and no apparent appendages, especially an annelid, nematode, or flatworm (*often used in combination*) **2.** INSECTS **INSECT LARVA** the larva of an insect, e.g., a caterpillar, grub, or maggot **3. ANIMAL LOOKING OR MOVING LIKE WORM** an animal that looks or moves like a worm, e.g., the shipworm or the slowworm **4. OFFENSIVE TERM** a term that deliberately insults somebody regarded as contemptible, especially somebody who behaves in a groveling way (*insult*) **5. SOMETHING THAT TORMENTS** something that torments, undermines, or corrupts a person from within ○ *a worm of discontent* **6.** MECH ENG **THREADED SHAFT** a shaft with a helical thread that is the part of a gear that meshes with a toothed wheel **7. SPIRAL CONDENSER IN STILL** a spiral pipe in a still in which alcohol condenses **8.** COMPUT **INVASIVE COMPUTER PROGRAM** a computer program that invades computers on a network, replicates itself to prevent deletion, and interferes with the host computer's operation ■ *v.* (**wormed, worm·ing, worms**) **1.** *vt.* **PROCEED DEVIOUSLY** to make progress deviously or obsequiously ○ *How is he going to worm his way out of trouble this time?* **2.** *vt.* **OBTAIN SOMETHING DEVIOUSLY** to obtain something from somebody by devious or underhand means ○ *They wormed his secret formula out of him.* **3.** *vt.* VET, MED **TREAT SOMEBODY FOR PARASITIC WORMS** to treat a person or animal in order to remove an infestation of parasitic worms **4.** *vt.* **WIND YARN AROUND ROPE** to wind yarn around a rope so as to give it a smooth surface **5.** *vi.* **MOVE LIKE WORM** to move in a slow, slithering way **6.** *vi.* **SEARCH FOR EARTHWORMS** to search for earthworms, especially for use as fishing bait [Old English *wurm*. Ultimately from an Indo-European word that is also the ancestor of Latin *vermis* (source of English *vermin*), and English *wrap*, the underlying idea being "twisting."] —**worm·er** *n.* —**worm·ish** *adj.*

WORM /wurm/ *n.* a computer storage medium, usually optical, in which data cannot be changed after it is stored but can be read. Full form **write once read many (times)**

worm·cast /wúrm kàst/ *n.* a small spiral mound of earth or sand that has been excreted by a burrowing earthworm or lugworm

worm-eat·en *adj.* **1. EATEN INTO BY WORMS** weakened by worms burrowing into it **2. DECAYED** affected by decay or rot **3. DILAPIDATED** old or worn-out

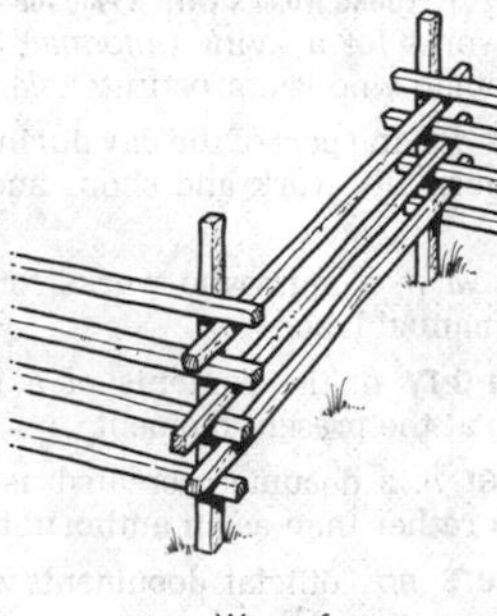

Worm fence

worm fence *n.* a fence consisting of crossed poles that support interlocking rails in a zigzag pattern

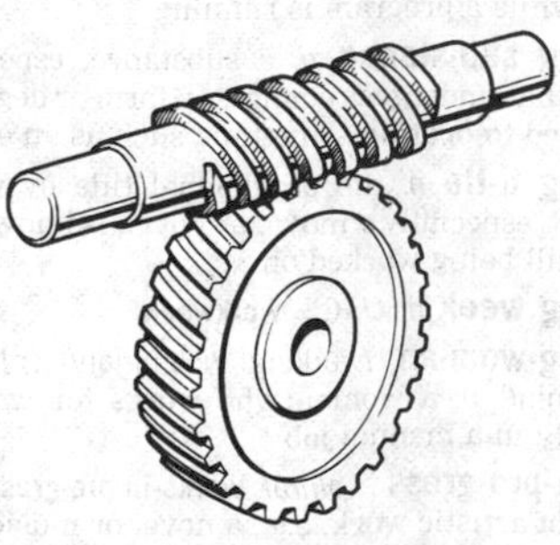

Worm gear

worm gear *n.* **1. GEAR WITH THREADED SHAFT** a gear consisting of a shaft with a helical thread that meshes a toothed wheel to transfer rotary motion between two shafts at right angles to one another **2.** = **worm wheel**

worm grass *n.* = **pinkroot**

worm·hole /wúrm hōl/ *n.* **1. HYPOTHETICAL PASSAGE BETWEEN PARTS OF UNIVERSE** a hypothetical passage in space-time connecting widely separated parts of the universe **2. HOLE MADE BY WORM** a hole made by a burrowing worm, e.g., in wood —**worm·holed** *adj.*

worm liz·ard *n.* = **amphisbaena**

worms /wurmz/ *n.* an infestation of parasites, especially pinworms or tapeworms, affecting the intestines or other parts of a person's or animal's body (*takes a singular verb*) [Old English (see WORM)]

Worms /wurmz, vawrmz/ historic city in Rhineland-Palatinate State, southwestern Germany. Population: 78,415 (1993).

worm·seed /wúrm seed/ *n.* a plant whose seeds or other parts are used as a treatment for infestation by parasitic worms

worm's-eye view *n.* a view of somebody or something from a lower or inferior position

worm snake *n.* a small nonvenomous snake with vestigial eyes, found in the central and eastern United States. Genus: *Carphophis.*

worm wheel *n.* the toothed wheel that meshes with the threaded shaft in a worm gear

worm·wood /wúrm wŏŏd/ *n.* **1. BITTER-TASTING PLANT** a plant that yields a bitter extract used to flavor absinthe and formerly as a medicine for intestinal worms. Genus: *Artemisia.* **2. CAUSE OF BITTERNESS** something that causes somebody to feel bitter (*literary*) ○ *Her ingratitude was wormwood to him.* [14thC. By folk etymology from Old English *wermod*, by association with WORM, because the plant was used as medicine for intestinal worms.]

worm·y /wúrmee/ *adj.* **1. INFESTED BY WORMS** full of or eaten into by worms **2. RESEMBLING WORM** resembling or characteristic of a worm —**worm·i·ness** *n.*

worn /wawrn/ past participle of **wear** ■ *adj.* **1. SHOWING EFFECTS OF WEAR** weakened or frayed by use **2. SHOWING EFFECTS OF FATIGUE** showing the effects of fatigue, worry, illness, or age **3. HACKNEYED** used so much as to have lost meaning [15thC (see WEAR)] —**worn·ness** *n.*

worn-out *adj.* (*not hyphenated when used after a verb*) **1. DAMAGED OR WEAKENED BY LONG USE** so damaged or affected by prolonged use as to be no longer usable **2. EXHAUSTED** very tired **3. OUTDATED** no longer relevant, useful, or fashionable

wor·ri·ment /wúrimənt/ *n.* anxiety or something that causes anxiety (*dated*)

wor·ri·some /wúrissəm/ *adj.* **1. CAUSING WORRY** causing anxiety or distress **2. TENDING TO WORRY** having a tendency to worry —**wor·ri·some·ly** *adv.*

wor·ry /wúree/ *v.* (**-ried, -ry·ing, -ries**) **1.** *vti.* **BE OR MAKE ANXIOUS** to feel anxious or to cause another person to feel anxious about something unpleasant that may have happened or may happen **2.** *vt.* **ANNOY ANOTHER** to annoy another person by making insistent demands or complaints **3.** *vt.* **TRY TO BITE ANIMAL** to try to wound or kill an animal by biting it ○ *a dog suspected of worrying sheep* **4.** *vt.* = **worry at 5.** *vi.* **PROCEED DESPITE PROBLEMS** to proceed persistently despite problems or obstacles ○ *worried the project along despite continued delays* **6.** *vt.* **TOUCH SOMETHING REPEATEDLY** to touch, move, or interfere with something repeatedly ○ *Stop worrying that button or it'll come off.* ■ *n.* (*plural* **-ries**) **1.** (*plural* **worries**) **ANXIOUSNESS** a feeling of anxiety or concern **2. CAUSE OF ANXIETY** something that causes anxiety or concern **3. PERIOD OF ANXIETY** a period spent feeling anxious or concerned [Old English *wyrgan.* Originally in the sense "to strangle." Its modern meaning developed perhaps via the idea of dogs or wolves harrassing their prey by seizing it by the throat.] —**wor·ried** *adj.* —**wor·ried·ly** *adv.* —**wor·ried·ness** *n.* —**wor·ri·er** *n.* —**wor·ry·ing** *adj.* —**wor·ry·ing·ly** *adv.* ◇ **not to worry** used to tell somebody that something is not important and need not be a cause of concern ○ *Not to worry. We'll do better next time.* ◇ **no worries** *ANZ* used to say that something is no trouble or is not worth mentioning (*informal*)

WORD KEY: SYNONYMS

worry, unease, care, anxiety, angst, stress

CORE MEANING: lack of peace of mind

worry describes a troubled state of mind resulting from concern about current or potential difficulties; **unease** is a more formal word meaning the same as *worry,* often also suggesting discontent or dissatisfaction; **care** is a more formal word meaning the same as *worry;* **anxiety** describes nervous apprehension about a future event or a general fear of possible misfortune; **angst** describes nonspecific chronic anxiety about the human condition or the state of the world; **stress** describes the worry and nervous apprehension related to a particular situation or event, for example, a job or the process of relocation.

worry at, wor·ry *vt.* to shake or tear at something with the teeth

wor·ry beads *npl.* a string of beads for fingering or playing with when feeling tense

wor·ry·guts /wúri gùts/ (*plural* **-guts**) *n. U.K.* = **worrywart** (*informal*)

wor·ry·wart /wúri wàwrt/ *n.* somebody who tends to worry needlessly (*informal*)

worse comparative of **bad, badly, ill** ■ *adj.* **1. LESS GOOD THAN SOMETHING ELSE** less good in quality or effect than before or than somebody or something else ○ *did a worse job on the painting than the previous workers* **2. MORE SEVERE** more severe than before or than something else of the same kind ○ *The patient's fever is worse this morning.* **3. SICKER** more ill than before ○ *The patient is worse today.* ■ *adv.* **TO A WORSE DEGREE** to a degree worse than before ■ *n.* **SOMETHING WORSE** somebody or something that is worse than another ○ *Of the two of them, this one's the worse.* [Old English *wyrsa.* From a prehistoric Germanic word that is also the ancestor of English *war,* the underlying idea being of things thrown into confusion or deteriorating.] ◇ **be none the worse for something** to experience no harm or ill effects from something

wors·en /wúrss'n/ (**-ened, -en·ing, -ens**) *vti.* to become or cause something to become worse

wors·er /wúrssər/ comparative of **bad** (*nonstandard*) [15thC]

wor·ship /wúrship/ *v.* (**-shiped** *or* **-shipped, -ship·ing** *or* **-ship·ping, -ships**) **1.** *vti.* RELIG **TREAT SOMEBODY OR SOMETHING AS DEITY** to treat somebody or something as divine and show respect by engaging in acts of prayer and devotion **2.** *vt.* **LOVE SOMEBODY DEEPLY** to love, admire, or respect somebody or something greatly and perhaps excessively or unquestioningly **3.** *vi.* RELIG **TAKE PART IN RELIGIOUS SERVICE** to take part in a religious service ■ *n.* **1.** RELIG **RELIGIOUS ADORATION** the adoration, devotion, and respect given to a deity **2.** RELIG **RELIGIOUS RITES** the rites or services through which people show their adoration, devotion, and respect for a deity **3. GREAT DEVOTION** great or excessive love, admiration, and respect felt for somebody or something [Old English *weortscipe,* literally "condition of worth," from *weorth* "worth" (source of English *worth*)] —**wor·ship·er** *n.*

Wor·ship *n. U.K., Can* a title of respect for a mayor, magistrate, or other similar dignitary ○ *His Worship, the Mayor*

wor·ship·ful /wúrshipfəl/ *adj.* **1. SHOWING WORSHIP** showing or expressing deep reverence and devotion **2.** **wor·ship·ful, Wor·ship·ful** *U.K.* **DISTINGUISHED** used as the honoring adjective in the titles of some dignitaries, e.g., mayors, and of the ancient guild companies of the City of London —**wor·ship·ful·ly** *adv.* —**wor·ship·ful·ness** *n.*

worst /wurst/ superlative of **bad, badly, ill** ■ *adj.* **LEAST GOOD** least good, most unpleasant, or most unfavorable ○ *your worst enemy* ■ *adv.* **LEAST WELL** in the least good, most unpleasant, or most unfavorable way ■ *n.* **LEAST GOOD THING** the least good, least pleasant, or least favorable aspect or part of something, or the worst thing that could happen or be done ○ *fear the worst* ○ *The worst was over.* ■ *vt.* (**wor·sted, worst·ing, worsts**) **DEFEAT SOMEBODY** to get the better of or defeat an opponent [Old English *wyrsta.* Ultimately from an Indo-European base meaning "to confuse," which is also the ancestor of English *wurst.*] ◇ **get the worst of it** to be defeated, or to get the least benefit from something ◇ **(in) the worst way** very much, very badly, or very intensely

worst case *n.* the least desirable, most disastrous situation or result that can be envisioned (*hyphenated when used before a noun*) ○ *the worst-case scenario*

wor·sted /wúrstəd/ *n.* **1. SMOOTH WOOLEN CLOTH** smooth closely-woven woolen cloth without a nap, made from tightly twisted yarn **2. YARN FOR WORSTED** the tightly twisted yarn, made from long-fibered wool, from which worsted cloth is made [13thC. Named for the village of *Worstead* in Norfolk, England, where it was originally made.]

wort[1] /wurt, wawrt/ *n.* BOT a medicinal plant. This word survives mainly in plant names, e.g., "liverwort" and "woundwort." (*usually used in combination*) [Old English *wyrt.* Ultimately from an Indo-European base meaning "branch, root," which is also the ancestor of English *root.*]

wort[2] /wurt, wawrt/ *n.* BEVERAGES a sugary liquid produced from crushed malted grain and water, to which yeast and hops are added in the brewing of beer [Old English *wyrt* (see WORT[1])]

worth /wurth/ *n.* **1. VALUE IN MONEY** the value of something, especially in terms of money **2. AMOUNT EQUALING GIVEN VALUE** the amount of something that can be bought for a particular sum of money or that will last for a particular length of time ○ *get your money's worth* **3. MORAL OR SOCIAL VALUE** the goodness, usefulness, or importance of something or somebody, irrespective of financial value or wealth ○ *A diploma from that place has little worth.* **4. WEALTH** the wealth of a person, group, organization, or other entity ○ *your aunt's net worth* ■ *adj.* **1. EQUAL IN VALUE TO STATED AMOUNT** equivalent in value to the amount stated ○ *How much is it worth?* ○ *a painting worth thousands* **2. IMPORTANT ENOUGH TO JUSTIFY SOMETHING** important, large, or good enough to justify something ○ *His friendship is not worth having.* [Old English *weorþ.* Ultimately from an Indo-European base meaning "to turn," which is also the ancestor of English *verse*[1].] ◇ **for all you are worth** as fast, energetically, or enthusiastically as possible ◇ **for what it's worth** used to suggest that what you say may not be true or of much value ○ *Here's my opinion on the issue, for what it's worth.*

worth·less /wúrthləss/ *adj.* **1. HAVING NO VALUE** having no financial or other value or usefulness **2. LACKING GOOD, ATTRACTIVE, OR ADMIRABLE QUALITIES** bad, incompetent, or totally lacking good, attractive, or admirable qualities —**worth·less·ly** *adv.* —**worth·less·ness** *n.*

worth·while /wùrth wīl, wúrth wīl, -hwīl/ *adj.* rewarding or beneficial enough to justify the time taken or the effort made [Mid-17thC. Shortening of "worth the while."]

wor·thy /wúrthee/ *adj.* (**-thi·er, -thi·est**) **1. DESERVING** fully deserving something, usually as a suitable reward for merit or importance ○ *That remark is not worthy of a reply.* **2. RESPECTABLE** morally upright, good, and deserving respect **3. GOOD BUT DULL** having good qualities, good intentions, or the best of motives, but boring and pedestrian ■ *n.* (*plural* **-thies**) **SOMEBODY GOOD OR MORAL** somebody who is good or morally upright and therefore deserves respect (*often used ironically*) ○ *studied the lives of the colonial governors and other 18th-century worthies* —**wor·thi·ly** *adv.* —**wor·thi·ness** *n.*

wot 1st person present singular, 3rd person present singular of **wit** (*archaic*)

Wo·tan /vṓ taan/ *n.* in Germanic mythology, the supreme god and the god of war. He corresponds to Odin in Norse mythology.

would /wŏŏd/ CORE MEANING: used to express the sense of "will" in reported speech or when referring to an event that has not happened yet ○ *Susan didn't think she would pass.* ○ *It would be wrong to suggest otherwise.*

vi. **1. USED WITH "IF" CLAUSES** used in stating what will, or suggesting what might, happen under the circumstances described in the conditional clause ○ *You would know him if you saw him.* ○ *My mother would be annoyed if I were to come home late.* **2. POLITE REQUEST** used in making polite requests or offers ○ *Would you mind closing the window?* ○ *Would you like more coffee?* **3. HABITUAL ACTION** used to indicate that a past action was habitual ○ *Every Sunday we would drive out to Coney Island.* ◇ **would that** used to introduce a strong desire or wish, usually one that is not expected to be fulfilled (*formal*) ○ *Would that we had never met.*

WORD KEY: USAGE

See Usage note at ***should.***

would-be *adj.* **HOPING TO DO OR BE SOMETHING** who hopes, or is trying, to do or be something ○ *a would-be poet* ■ *n.* **PERSON ASPIRING TO SOMETHING** a person who is hoping or trying to become something or achieve the status of something (*informal*) ○ *The reception was attended by all the major candidates for office and other would-bes.*

would·n't /wo͝od'nt/ *contr.* would not

would·'ve /wo͝odəv/ *contr.* would have

Woulfe bot·tle /wo͝olf-/ *n.* a vessel with more than one neck, in which gases can be bubbled through liquids [Named for the English chemist Peter *Woulfe* (1727?–1803)]

wound[1] /woond/ *n.* **1. INJURY TO BODY** an injury in which the skin, tissue, or an organ is broken by some external force, e.g., a blow or surgical incision, with damage to the underlying tissue **2. EMOTIONAL INJURY** a lasting emotional or psychological injury ○ *still recovering from the wounds of a bitter divorce* **3. INJURY TO PLANT** damage to plant tissue caused by an external agent such as wind or frost ■ *vti.* (**wound·ed, wounded, wound·ing, wounds**) **1. INJURE** to cause a wound in the body of somebody or something, especially using a knife, gun, or other weapon ○ *He was wounded in the leg.* **2. CAUSE EMOTIONAL WOUND** to cause somebody emotional or psychological distress by saying or doing something ○ *cutting remarks intended to wound* [Old English *wund*. Ultimately from an Indo-European base meaning "to beat," which is also the ancestor of English *wen*[1].] —**wound·a·ble** *adj.* —**wound·ed** *adj.* —**wound·er** *n.* —**wound·ing** *adj.* —**wound·ing·ly** *adv.* —**wound·less** *adj.*

WORD KEY: SYNONYMS

See Synonyms at ***harm***.

wound[2] /wownd/ past participle, past tense of **wind**[2]

Wound·ed Knee /wo͞ondəd nee/ village in South Dakota. In 1890 it was the site of a massacre of Native North Americans in which between 150 and 370 Sioux people were killed, most of them unarmed.

wound·wort /wo͞ond wùrt, -wàwrt/ (*plural* **-worts** *or* **-wort**) *n.* **1. HEALING PLANT OF MINT FAMILY** betony or a related plant of the mint family, formerly used to treat wounds. Genus: *Stachys*. **2. PLANT FOR TREATING WOUNDS** any plant formerly used to treat wounds

wove past tense of **weave**

wo·ven past participle of **weave** ■ *adj.* **CREATED BY WEAVING** made or manufactured by the process of weaving ○ *woven synthetic textiles* ■ *n.* **SOMETHING MADE BY WEAVING** a textile or other material that is created by weaving ○ *a factory making cotton and other wovens*

wove pa·per *n.* paper made using a roller with a fine mesh that leaves a faint mesh imprint

Wo·vo·ka /wə vṓkə/ (1856?–1932) U.S. prophet. A member of the Paiute people, he developed the ritual of the Ghost Dance. Many of his followers were killed by federal troops at Wounded Knee (1890). Known as **Jack Wilson**

wow[1] /wow/ *interj.* **EXPRESSING SURPRISE** used to express surprise, admiration, wonder, or pleasure (*informal*) ■ *vt.* (**wowed, wow·ing, wows**) **IMPRESS SOMEBODY GREATLY** to impress or delight somebody greatly (*informal*) ○ *The acrobats wowed the audience with their daring moves.* ■ *n.* **GREAT SUCCESS** a great success or an object of great admiration (*informal*) [Early 16thC. A natural interjection.]

wow[2] /wow/ *n.* RECORDING a distortion in recorded sound in the form of slow fluctuations in the pitch of long notes, caused by variations in the speed of the reproducing or recording equipment [Mid-20thC. An imitation of the acoustic effect.]

wow·ser /wówzər/ *n.* *ANZ* (*informal*) **1. PURITANICAL PERSON** somebody with a puritanical disposition who disapproves of activities such as drinking and dancing **2. KILLJOY** somebody who disrupts or ruins the fun of others [Late 19thC. Origin uncertain: perhaps from English dialect *wow* "to waul."]

WP *abbr.* **1.** weather permitting **2.** word processing **3.** word processor **4.** LAW without prejudice

WPA *abbr.* HIST Work Projects Administration

W par·ti·cle *n.* an elementary particle with a relatively large mass and either positively or negatively charged, believed to mediate weak interactions between other particles in which the charges on the particles change

WPGA *abbr.* Women's Professional Golfers' Association

WPI *abbr.* wholesale price index

wpm, w.p.m. *abbr.* words per minute

wpn. *abbr.* weapon

wrack[1] /rak/, **rack** *n.* **1. DESTRUCTION** the complete destruction of something ○ *wrack and ruin* **2. REMNANT OF SOMETHING DESTROYED** a fragment or remnant of something that has been destroyed (*literary*) [Old English *wræc* "misery"]

wrack[2] /rak/ *n.* **1.** MARINE BIOL **MARINE VEGETATION** seaweed floating in the sea or growing on the shoreline **2.** MARINE BIOL **BROWN SEAWEED** any brown seaweed, e.g., bladderwrack. Family: Fucaceae. **3.** NAUT **WRECKED SHIP** a wrecked ship, especially one driven onto the shore (*archaic*) **4. WRECKAGE** wreckage or a piece of wreckage (*archaic*) ■ *vti.* (**wracked, wrack·ing, wracks**) **WRECK OR BE WRECKED** to wreck something or be wrecked [14thC. From Dutch *wrak* "wreck."]

wraith /rayth/ (*plural* **wraiths**) *n.* PARANORMAL **1. GHOST** the ghost of a dead person, or any ghostly and insubstantial apparition **2. APPARITION OF SOMEBODY SOON TO DIE** a vision of a person still alive, said to appear as a premonition of that person's death [Early 16thC. Origin unknown.]

Wran·gel Is·land /ráng g'l-/ island in the Arctic Ocean, northeastern Russia, between the East Siberian Sea and the Chukchi Sea. Area: 1,800 sq. mi./4,660 sq. km.

Wran·gell Moun·tains /ráng g'l-/ mountain range in southeastern Alaska, near the border with the Yukon Territory, Canada. The highest peak is Mount Blackburn, 16,390 ft./4,996 m.

Wran·gell-St. E·li·as Na·tion·al Park and Pre·serve /ràng g'l saynt i lī əss-/ the largest national park in the United States, in southeastern Alaska, established in 1980. It is noted for its high peaks, glaciers, and wildlife. Area: 13,017 sq. mi./33,716 sq. km.

wran·gle /ráng g'l/ *v.* (**-gled, -gling, -gles**) **1.** *vi.* **ARGUE NOISILY** to argue noisily and persistently ○ *wrangled for hours over the wording of the agreement* **2.** *vt.* **GET SOMETHING BY PERSISTENT ARGUMENT** to obtain something or persuade somebody by arguing persistently (*informal*) ○ *managed to wrangle a commitment to peace out of the opposing side* **3.** *vt.* AGRIC **HERD ANIMALS** to herd horses or cattle ■ *n.* **LONG ARGUMENT** a lengthy or noisy and bad-tempered argument or dispute [14thC. From a prehistoric Germanic word which is related to the ancestor of English *wring*.]

wran·gler /ráng glər/ *n.* **1.** AGRIC **SOMEBODY WHO LOOKS AFTER HORSES** somebody who takes care of saddle horses on a ranch **2. SOMEBODY INVOLVED IN LENGTHY ARGUMENT** somebody who argues noisily and persistently or is involved in a lengthy argument [Early 16thC]

wrap /rap/ *v.* (**wraps, wrapped, wrap·ping, wraps**) **1.** *vt.* **COVER SOMETHING UP** to cover something up by winding or folding a pliable material such as cloth or paper around it ○ *The package was wrapped in plain brown paper.* **2.** *vti.* **COIL AROUND SOMETHING** to wind, fold, or clasp something, oneself, or itself around somebody or something else ○ *He wrapped his arms around the pole and wouldn't let go.* **3.** *vt.* **GIVE SOMETHING AURA** to surround something with a particular type of atmosphere or quality such as secrecy or scandal ○ *The whole affair was wrapped in secrecy.* **4.** *vt.* **ENGROSS SOMEBODY** to occupy the mind and attention of somebody fully ○ *wrapped in thought* **5.** *vi.* CINEMA **FINISH FILMING** to finish filming or videotaping something ○ *We're scheduled to wrap at the end of the month.* **6.** *vt.* **ENVELOP SOMETHING** to envelop and obscure or conceal something ○ *Fog wrapped the harbor.* **7.** *vt.* **FOLD SOMETHING UP** to fold or roll something up into a compact bundle ○ *linen napkins neatly wrapped* **8.** *vi.* **FINISH** to come to an end ○ *"The government's antitrust case ... was supposed to wrap by the end of the year."* (*Newsweek*; November 1998) **9.** *vti.* COMPUT **TAKE SOMETHING OVER TO NEXT LINE** to take a word or piece of text over to the next line automatically on reaching the margin, or to be taken over in this way ■ *n.* **1.** CLOTHES **OUTER GARMENT** an outer garment such as a shawl, cloak, or coat to be wrapped or folded around the wearer **2.** INDUST **MATERIAL USED TO WRAP SOMETHING** material, or a piece of material, used to wrap something **3.** CINEMA **COMPLETION OF FILMING** the completion of filming or videotaping something ○ *All right, everybody, that's a wrap!* **4.** FOOD **FILLED TORTILLA SANDWICH** a sandwich consisting of fillings enclosed in a tortilla **5.** *Aus* **PIECE OF PRAISE** a praising comment or assessment of something (*informal*) [14thC. Origin unknown.] ◇ **keep something under wraps** to keep something secret ○ *Our new product is being kept under wraps for the moment.*

wrap up *vt.* **1. COMPLETE SOMETHING** to complete something or bring it to an end (*informal*) ○ *We'll wrap up the editing phase of the project next week.* **2. SUMMARIZE SOMETHING** to give a short final summary of something such as the news **3. COVER SOMETHING WITH MATERIAL** to cover something completely with material such as paper, plastic, or foil **4.** *Aus* **PRAISE SOMEBODY** to sing somebody's praises (*informal*) ◇ **be wrapped up in somebody** *or* **something** to be completely absorbed by or preoccupied with somebody or something ○ *She is completely wrapped up in her career.*

wrap·a·round /ráppə równd/ *adj.* **1.** CLOTHES **DESIGNED FOR WRAPPING AROUND BODY** designed to be worn wrapped around the body and tied in position with one edge overlapping the other rather than fastened with buttons or a zipper **2. CURVING AROUND SIDES** curving around the sides of whatever it is attached to ■ *n.* **1.** CLOTHES **WRAPAROUND GARMENT** a wraparound skirt or other piece of clothing **2. WRAPAROUND CABINET** a cabinet that is shaped to curve around the sides of something **3.** COMPUT **COMPUTER FUNCTION AUTOMATICALLY STARTING NEW LINE** a function of a computer program or visual display unit that makes text automatically begin a new line as soon the last character space in the previous line is filled **4.** PUBL **PAPER STRIP AROUND BOOK'S DUST JACKET** a strip of paper fastened around the dust jacket of a book, e.g., to announce a price reduction **5.** PRINTING **PLATE FOR ATTACHING TO PRESS CYLINDER** a plate of flexible material that can be attached to the cylinder of a rotary press

wrap·o·ver /rápp ṑvər/ *n. U.K.* = **wraparound** *adj.* 1

wrapped /rapt/ *adj. Aus* extremely pleased (*informal*) [Mid-20thC. A blend of *wrapped (up in)* "deeply interested in" and RAPT "enraptured."]

wrap·per /ráppər/ *n.* **1. MATERIAL WRAPPED AROUND SOMETHING** the paper, plastic, or other material wrapped around something that is sold **2. PAPER AROUND MAGAZINE OR NEWSPAPER** a piece of paper wrapped around a magazine or newspaper sent through the mail **3. TOBACCO LEAF FORMING OUTSIDE OF CIGAR** a tobacco leaf wrapped around a cigar to form its outer skin **4.** PUBL = **dust jacket** **5.** CLOTHES **LOOSE LOUNGING GARMENT** a garment such as a dressing gown that wraps loosely around the body **6. SOMEBODY WHO WRAPS PACKAGES IN STORE** an employee whose job is to wrap up packages in a store or to wrap manufactured products in a factory

wrap·ping /rápping/ *n.* the paper, plastic, or other material used to wrap something

wrap-up *n.* **1. SHORT FINAL SUMMARY** a short summary at the end of something such as a news bulletin **2.** *Aus* **PIECE OF PRAISE** a praising comment or assessment of something (*informal*)

wrasse /rass/ (*plural* **wrass·es** *or* **wrasse**) *n.* a fish with protruding lips and well developed canine teeth that lives in temperate and tropical seas worldwide. Wrasses are found in various sizes and are often brightly colored. Family: Labridae. [Late 17thC. From Cornish *wrah* "old woman."]

wrath /rath/ *n.* **1. GREAT ANGER** fury often marked by a desire for vengeance **2.** RELIG **DIVINE RETRIBUTION** God's punishment for sin **3. VENGEANCE** the vengeance, punishment, or destruction wreaked by somebody in anger (*literary*) ■ *adj.* **FURIOUS** full of anger (*archaic or literary*) [Old English *wrǣþþu*. From *wrāþ* "angry" (see WROTH).] —**wrath·less** *adj.*

WORD KEY: SYNONYMS

See Synonyms at ***anger***.

wrath·ful /ráthfəl/ *adj.* extremely or violently angry, or expressing one's anger —**wrath·ful·ly** *adv.* —**wrath·ful·ness** *n.*

Wray /ray/, **Fay** (*b.* 1907) Canadian-born U.S. actor. She starred in several movies of the early sound era, most notably *King Kong* (1933). Full name **Vina F. Wray**

wreak /reek/ (**wreaked, wreak·ing, wreaks**) *vt.* **1. CAUSE HAVOC OR DESTRUCTION** to cause something violent and destructive ○ *a storm that wreaked vast destruction* **2. INFLICT REVENGE** to inflict something violent, especially revenge or punishment, on somebody **3. EXPRESS ANGER OR HATRED** to express anger, hatred, or another violent emotion in action against somebody (*literary*) [Old English *wrecan* "to drive out"] —**wreak·er** *n.*

WORD KEY: USAGE

See Usage note at ***wrought***.

wreath /reeth/ (*plural* **wreaths** /reeths, reethz/) *n.* **1. CIRCULAR ARRANGEMENT OF FLOWERS** a circular arrangement of flowers and greenery placed as a memorial on a grave, hung up as a decoration, or put on somebody's head as a sign of honor **2.** **REPRESENTATION OF WREATH** a representation of a circular arrangement of flowers, vines, or other things, e.g., in a carving or on a coat of arms **3.** **CIRCULAR SHAPE** a hollow circular shape formed by something such as smoke [Old English *wriþa*. From *wrīþan* (see WRITHE).] —**wreath·less** *adj.*

wreathe /reeth/ (**wreathed, wreath·ing, wreathes**) *v.* **1.** *vt.* **PUT WREATH ON OR AROUND SOMETHING** to encircle, surround, or cover something with a wreath or wreaths or a similar type of decoration **2.** *vt.* **MAKE SOMETHING INTO WREATH BY INTERTWINING** to make things into a wreath by twisting and intertwining them **3.** *vti.* **WRITHE OR COIL** to move, or to cause something to move, in coils, curves, or spirals [Mid-16thC. Partly formed from WREATH and partly a back-formation from *wrethen* "twisted."]

wreck /rek/ *vt.* (**wrecked, wreck·ing, wrecks**) **1.** **DESTROY OR DAMAGE SOMETHING** to destroy something completely or damage it beyond repair **2.** **DESTROY SHIP** to cause a ship to sink or run aground and be destroyed ■ *n.* **1.** = **crash**[1] *n.* 1 **2.** **SOMETHING BADLY DAMAGED** something that is in very poor condition, damaged, or dilapidated **3.** **REMAINS OF SOMETHING DESTROYED** something that has been totally destroyed, or its shattered remains **4.** NAUT **BADLY DAMAGED SHIP** a very badly damaged or sunken ship **5.** NAUT **DESTRUCTION OF SHIP** the sinking or destruction at sea of a ship from accidental causes **6.** **CARGO FROM WRECKED SHIP** cargo or other goods that are washed ashore after a shipwreck **7.** **DESTRUCTION** the ruin or destruction of something **8.** **SOMEBODY LOOKING OR FEELING TERRIBLE** somebody who is physically or emotionally exhausted or broken down [13thC. From Anglo-Norman *wrec*, of Scandinavian origin.]

wreck·age /rékij/ *n.* **1.** **REMAINS AFTER DESTRUCTION** the broken pieces left after something has been extremely badly damaged or destroyed **2.** **PROCESS OF WRECKING** the wrecking, ruining, or destruction of something (*formal*)

wrecked /rekt/ *adj.* **1.** **EXHAUSTED** very tired or exhausted (*informal*) **2.** **INTOXICATED** in an intoxicated or drugged state (*slang*) [Early 18thC]

wreck·er /rékər/ *n.* **1.** AUTOMOT **TRUCK FOR TOWING** a truck with a hoisting mechanism used to tow away damaged cars or other vehicles **2.** **SOMEBODY DEMOLISHING BUILDINGS OR DISMANTLING CARS** somebody whose job is to demolish buildings or dismantle old cars for salvage **3.** **SOMEBODY WHO WRECKS** somebody who destroys or spoils something, especially deliberately, maliciously, or with pleasure ○ *He's a wrecker of others' dreams.* **4.** **SOMEBODY LURING SHIPS TO DESTRUCTION** somebody who, in the past, lured ships onto rocks in order to steal the cargo or other goods on board

wreck·er's ball *n.* = **wrecking ball**

wreck·fish /rék fìsh/ (*plural* **-fish** *or* **-fish·es**) *n.* = **stone bass** [Late 19thC. So called from its habit of following wreckage.]

wreck·ing ball *n.* a heavy ball attached by a cable to a crane and swung to knock down parts of buildings that are being demolished

wreck·ing bar *n.* a short crowbar forked at one end and bent at the other to provide leverage

Wren

wren /ren/ *n.* a small songbird found in North and South America and Eurasia with a long slender downturned bill, usually brown feathers, and a short upright tail. Family: Troglodytidae. [Old English *wrenna*]

Wren /ren/ *n.* a member of the British Women's Royal Naval Service [Early 20thC. Back-formation from the acronym formed from WRNS.]

AKG London

Sir Christopher Wren: Portrait medal by G. D. Gaab

Wren /ren/, **Sir Christopher** (1632–1723) English architect, scentist, and mathematician. The founder of the English baroque style, he designed St. Paul's Cathedral, London (1675–1710) and 50 other English churches. He was also a noted mathematician and inventor, and a founding member of the Royal Society.

wrench /rench/ *v.* (**wrenched, wrench·ing, wrench·es**) **1.** *vti.* **PULL AND TWIST SOMETHING AWAY** to pull something away forcefully, often using a twisting movement ○ *He angrily wrenched the bag away from the cashier and left the store.* **2.** *vt.* **INJURE SOMETHING BY TWISTING** to injure part of the body by twisting it suddenly and forcibly **3.** *vi.* **MOVE WITH TWISTING MOVEMENT** to move with a forceful twisting movement **4.** *vt.* **DISTRESS SOMEBODY** to make somebody feel very sad or distressed **5.** *vt.* **SKEW MEANING OR FUNCTION** to distort something in order to make it mean or appear to be something different ■ *n.* **1.** **TOOL USED TO GRASP AND TURN** a hand or power tool with fixed or movable jaws, used to seize, turn, or twist objects such as nuts and bolts **2.** **SPRAIN CAUSED BY TWISTING** a sprain caused by a sudden forceful twisting movement of a part of the body **3.** **FORCEFUL TWISTING PULL** a forceful twisting pull at something, especially to free it **4.** **SURGE OF EMOTION** a sudden surge of emotion, e.g., pity or empathy ○ *the wrench we felt when viewing film footage of the flood's devastation* **5.** **SADNESS AND LOSS ON PARTING** a difficult parting from a person or place, or the feelings of sadness and loss that accompany such a parting ○ *Leaving New York was a terrible wrench after having lived there for 30 years.* [Old English *wrencan*. Ultimately from an Indo-European base meaning "to turn" that is also the ancestor of English *converge*.]

wrest /rest/ *vt.* (**wrest·ed, wrest·ing, wrests**) **1.** **GAIN CONTROL OR POWER** to take something such as control or power from somebody in the face of opposition or resistance **2.** **PULL SOMETHING AWAY FORCIBLY** to seize something with the hands and take it away from somebody by using physical force **3.** **GET SOMETHING WITH EFFORT** to get or extract something with an effort or struggle **4.** **ALTER SOMETHING'S MEANING** to change or twist the meaning of something ■ *n.* **FORCEFUL PULL** a sharp wrench or pull at something [Old English *wrǣstan*. From a prehistoric Germanic base that is also the ancestor of English *wrist*.] —**wrest·er** *n.*

wres·tle /réss'l/ *v.* (**-tled, -tling, -tles**) **1.** *vti.* **FIGHT BY GRIPPING AND PUSHING** to fight somebody using special holds and moves in an attempt to force his or her shoulders onto a mat **2.** *vti.* **HAVE A STRUGGLING FIGHT** to fight with somebody by gripping and pushing rather than hitting him or her **3.** *vi.* **HAVE DIFFICULTY** to struggle to deal with something difficult or intractable ○ *I spent the evening wrestling with my accounts.* **4.** *vti.* **MANEUVER SOMETHING AWKWARD** to struggle to lift or move something ○ *We wrestled the trunk down the hall.* ■ *n.* **1.** **FIGHT BETWEEN WRESTLERS** a wrestling match or a fight in which people wrestle rather than hit each other **2.** **A STRUGGLE WITH SOMETHING DIFFICULT** a struggle to deal with something difficult or intractable [Old English. From *wrǣstan* (see WREST).] —**wres·tler** *n.*

wres·tling /réssling/ *n.* **1.** **SPORT WITH TWO CONTESTANTS FIGHTING** a sport in which two contestants fight by gripping each other using special holds, each trying to force the other's shoulders onto a mat **2.** **ACTION OF STRUGGLING WITH SOMEBODY** the action of having a struggling fight with somebody [Old English *wrǣstlunge*]

wretch /rech/ *n.* **1.** **SOMEBODY MISERABLE** somebody who is in trouble or distress and evokes pity in others **2.** **ANNOYING PERSON** somebody who provokes mild irritation or annoyance (*humorous*) **3.** **DESPICABLE PERSON** somebody who provokes contempt or disapproval (*formal*) [Old English *wrecca*. Related to the source of English *wreak*.]

wretch·ed /réchəd/ *adj.* **1.** **UNHAPPY OR ILL** feeling very unhappy or ill **2.** **APPEARING MISERABLE OR DEPRIVED** in a state of great hardship, deprivation, and hopelessness and arousing sympathy in others ○ *living in wretched conditions* **3.** **INADEQUATE OR OF LOW QUALITY** seriously inadequate or of very low quality **4.** **IRRITATING** provoking irritation or anger ○ *The wretched car won't start!* —**wretch·ed·ly** *adv.* —**wretch·ed·ness** *n.*

wri·er comparative of **wry**

wri·est superlative of **wry**

wrig·gle /rígg'l/ *v.* (**-gled, -gling, -gles**) **1.** *vti.* **TWIST AND TURN** to make quick small twisting and turning movements with the body, or to cause the body to make these movements **2.** *vi.* **MOVE WHILE TWISTING AND TURNING** to move by making quick twisting and turning movements ○ *managed to wriggle out of the sleeping bag* ■ *n.* **1.** **TWISTING OR TURNING MOVEMENT** a short twisting or turning movement **2.** **TWISTING PASSAGE OR COURSE** a twisting passage or line [14thC. Origin uncertain: probably from Middle Low German *wriggelen*, from *wriggen* "to turn."] —**wrig·gly** *adj.*

wriggle out of *vt.* to avoid doing something or suffering the consequences of something by making excuses or using deception

wrig·gler /rígglər/ *n.* = **wiggler**

Wright /rīt/, **Fanny** (1795–1852) British-born U.S. social reformer. Her interest in the abolition of slavery included the founding of a controversial and short-lived settlement in Tennessee in the 1820s intended to demonstrate the practicability of emancipation. Full name **Frances Wright**

Library of Congress

Frank Lloyd Wright

Wright, Frank Lloyd (1869–1959) U.S. architect. The clean lines of his designs, his use of new materials, and his consideration of the environment around his buildings made him one of the most influential modern architects.

Wright, Richard (1908–60) U.S. writer. A campaigner against racism, he achieved considerable success with his autobiographical novel, *Black Boy* (1945). Full name **Richard Nathaniel Wright**

Library of Congress

Wilbur (right) and Orville Wright

Wright, Wilbur (1867–1912) U.S. inventor. With his brother **Orville Wright** (1871–1958), he made the first successful flight of a powered aircraft at Kitty Hawk, North Carolina (1903).

wring /ring/ *vt.* (**wrung, wrung** /rung/, **wring·ing, wrings**) **1. TWIST AND COMPRESS SOMETHING** to twist and compress something in order to force liquid out of it ○ *wring the towel out and hang it up to dry* **2. FORCE OUT LIQUID BY TWISTING** to force liquid out of something by twisting and compressing it **3. EXTRACT SOMETHING WITH DIFFICULTY** to extract something from somebody with great difficulty ○ *finally managed to wring an answer out of him* **4. TWIST SOMETHING FORCIBLY AND PAINFULLY** to twist something forcefully, e.g., an animal's neck, usually causing pain or death **5. CAUSE DISTRESS** to cause somebody emotional pain and distress ■ *n.* **TWIST GIVEN TO WET MATERIAL** a twist or squeeze given to wet material in order to force out water or other liquid [Old English *wringen.* Ultimately from a prehistoric Germanic base that is also the ancestor of English *wrong.*]

wring·er /ríngər/ *n.* a machine with two rollers set close together that can be turned by a handle so that wet clothes fed between them have the water forced out of them (*dated*) ◇ **put somebody through the wringer** to subject somebody to a very difficult or stressful experience (*informal*)

wring·ing wet *adj.* extremely wet

wrin·kle /ríngk'l/ *n.* **1. FACIAL LINE FROM AGING** a line or crease between small folds of skin that forms on the face as a result of aging or exposure to the sun **2. SMALL FOLD IN MATERIAL** a small messy or unintentional fold in cloth or paper **3. PROBLEM** something that causes trouble or inconvenience ○ *We need to iron out the wrinkles in the plan before implementing it.* **4. NEW FEATURE** an ingenious trick, method of doing something, or feature of something (*informal*) ○ *We've added a couple of new wrinkles to the policy.* ■ *vti.* (**-kled, -kling, -kles**) **1. MAKE OR GET SMALL MESSY FOLDS** to make small messy or unintentional folds in something, or to come to have messy folds ○ *This fabric wrinkles easily.* **2. MAKE OR GET LINES ON SKIN** to develop lines or to cause lines to develop in the skin as a result of aging or exposure to the sun **3. CONTRACT PART OF FACE** to tighten the muscles in part of the face so that it contracts or creases [14thC. Origin uncertain: possible from, ultimately, Old English *gewrinclian* "to wind."] —**wrin·kled** *adj.* —**wrin·kle·less** *adj.*

wrin·kly /ríngklee/ (**-kli·er, -kli·est**) *adj.* covered with wrinkles

wrist /rist/ *n.* **1.** ANAT **JOINT AT BASE OF HAND** the lower end of the forearm or the joint between the forearm and the hand together with the tissue surrounding it **2.** CLOTHES **PART OF GARMENT OVER WRIST** the part of a sleeve or glove that covers the wrist ■ *vt.* SPORTS **HIT WITH TWISTING STROKE** to hit a ball with a lot of wrist movement to make the ball spin [Old English. Ultimately from a prehistoric Germanic base that is also the ancestor of English *wrest.*]

wrist·band /ríst bànd/ *n.* **1. ABSORBENT BAND WORN AROUND WRIST** an absorbent band of material worn around the wrist to keep sweat from running onto the hand **2. WATCH STRAP** the strap of a wristwatch **3. IDENTIFICATION BAND WORN AROUND WRIST** an identification band worn around the wrist, e.g., when in the hospital **4.** CLOTHES **PART OF SOMETHING COVERING WRIST** a band of material that fits over the wrist, e.g., at the end of a long sleeve or on a glove

wrist-drop *n.* inability to move the muscles that raise the wrist and move the fingers, caused by damage to or compression of the radial nerve

wrist·let /rístlət/ *n.* a close-fitting band of material worn around the wrist, especially a decorative one that is attached to the top of a glove or the end of a sleeve

wrist·lock /ríst lòk/ *n.* a hold in wrestling in which the wrist is held and twisted, rendering an opponent helpless

wrist pin *n.* a pin in a piston of an internal-combustion engine attaching to the little end of a connecting rod

wrist·watch /ríst wòch/ *n.* a watch on a band that is worn around the wrist

wrist·y /rístee/ (**-i·er, -i·est**) *adj.* using a lot of wrist movement when hitting a ball

writ[1] /rit/ *n.* **1.** LAW **WRITTEN COURT ORDER** a written court order demanding that the addressee do or stop doing whatever is specified in the order **2. WRITTEN TEXT** a piece of written text (*archaic*) [Old English "something written." Formed from *wrītan* "to write."]

writ[2] past tense, past participle of **write** (*archaic*)

write /rīt/ (**wrote** /rōt/ *or* **writ** *archaic*, **writ·ten** /rítt'n/ *or* **writ** *archaic*, **writ·ing, writes**) *v.* **1.** *vti.* **PUT WORDS ON PAPER** to put words, letters, numbers, or musical notation on a surface using a pen, pencil, or similar instrument **2.** *vti.* **CREATE BOOK, POEM, OR MUSIC** to create or compose something for others to read or listen to, e.g., a letter or note, an article, a poem, or a piece of music **3.** *vt.* **SPELL SOMETHING** to spell a word or words ○ *two words that are written the same but mean different things* **4.** *vti.* **COMPOSE AND SEND LETTER** to compose and send a letter to somebody ○ *I wrote her a long letter.* **5.** *vi.* **COMPOSE MATERIAL FOR PUBLICATION** to create books, poems, or newspaper articles for publication, often as part of a job **6.** *vt.* **FILL IN FORM** to fill in the details on a form such as a check, prescription, or other document and, usually, sign it ○ *I had to write 20 checks this morning.* **7.** *vt.* **TELL SOMETHING IN WORDS** to say something in a letter, book, or article ○ *He wrote that he would be home on Tuesday.* **8.** *vi.* **WORK AS WRITING TOOL** to function as a writing instrument ○ *There's something wrong with this pen: it won't write.* **9.** *vti.* **USE CURSIVE SCRIPT** to employ a cursive script when setting down words **10.** *vt.* **DISPLAY SOMETHING** to reveal or exhibit something clearly ○ *She had glee written all over her face.* **11.** *vt.* INSUR = **underwrite** *v.* 1 **12.** *vt.* **PREDETERMINE SOMETHING** to ordain or prophesy what will happen in the future (*usually passive*) ○ *It is written: your future is preordained* **13.** *vt.* COMPUT **STORE COMPUTER DATA** to transfer data to a storage medium such as a magnetic or optical disk or tape **14.** *vt.* COMPUT **DISPLAY SOMETHING ON SCREEN** to display text or images on a computer monitor [Old English *wrītan* "to score, draw, write." Ultimately from a prehistoric Germanic base meaning "to tear," of unknown origin.]

WORD KEY: ORIGIN

The notion underlying ***write*** is of "cutting" or "scratching" (it is related to German *reissen* "to tear"). The earliest form of writing involved cutting marks on hard materials such as stone and wood and the same word was carried over when the technique of writing moved on to pen and ink.

write away *vt.* to send off an order for goods of some kind to a distant supplier ○ *wrote away for new upholstery materials*

write down *vt.* **1. RECORD SOMETHING IN WORDS** to record something in writing, usually so that the information is not lost or forgotten ○ *I wrote down her address.* **2. OVERSIMPLIFY SOMETHING FOR UNSOPHISTICATED AUDIENCE** to write in simplified language for the benefit of an audience considered to be unsophisticated, inexperienced, or unintelligent **3. WRITE DISPARAGINGLY ABOUT SOMEBODY** to write slightingly or disparagingly about somebody **4. REDUCE THE ENTERED VALUE OF SOMETHING** to reduce the price or value of something, especially the value of an asset as entered in the accounts of a business

write in *v.* **1.** *vi.* **WRITE TO AN ORGANIZATION** to send a letter to an organization **2.** *vt.* POL **ADD NAME TO BALLOT** to add somebody's name to a ballot in an election in order to vote for that person **3.** *vt.* **WRITE DETAILS IN FORM** to write additional words into a text or document ○ *wrote in all the personal health data required*

write off *vt.* **1. DECIDE SOMEBODY OR SOMETHING IS WORTHLESS** to dismiss somebody or something as worthless or unsuccessful and not worth continued attention or performance (*informal*) **2.** *U.K.* **DAMAGE VEHICLE TOO BADLY TO REPAIR** to damage a vehicle so badly that it is not economical to repair it **3.** ACCT **REDUCE VALUE OF SOMETHING** to reduce the estimated value of an asset for accounting purposes **4.** ACCT **REMOVE BAD DEBT OR VALUELESS ASSET** to remove a debt considered irrecoverable or an asset with no value from the accounts of a business

write out *vt.* **1. WRITE SOMETHING IN COMPLETE FORM** to write something in its complete form ○ *write out your name* **2. SAY SOMETHING IN WRITING** to express something in written form **3.** BROADCAST **REMOVE A CHARACTER FROM A SERIES** to remove a regular character from a radio or television series ○ *He's been written out of the show.*

write up *vt.* **1. WRITE SOMETHING FROM EARLIER NOTES** to write a report or account of something from notes made earlier **2. WRITE REVIEW OF SOMETHING** to write a review of something such as a new play or book **3. UPDATE JOURNAL OR DIARY** to bring something such as a journal or log up to date by writing additional entries **4. REPORT SOMEBODY FOR UNLAWFUL ACT** to report somebody in writing for violating a law or rule ○ *wrote the motorist up for illegal parking* **5.** ACCT **OVERVALUE ASSETS** to overvalue corporate assets

write-down *n.* a reduction in the value of an asset as entered in the books of a business

write-in *n.* POL **1. VOTE ADDING CANDIDATE TO BALLOT** a vote cast in an election by adding somebody's name to the ballot **2. CANDIDATE ADDED TO BALLOT** a candidate added to a ballot by a voter

write-off *n.* **1.** ACCT **REDUCTION IN VALUE** a reduction in the estimated value of an asset **2.** ACCT **SOMETHING REDUCED IN VALUE** an asset that has had its estimated value reduced **3.** ACCT **AMOUNT OF REDUCTION IN VALUE** the monetary amount by which something such as a corporate asset has been reduced in value ○ *The corporation took a $5 million write-off in the second quarter.* **4.** *U.K.* AUTOMOT **VEHICLE DAMAGED BEYOND REPAIR** something, especially a vehicle, that is so badly damaged that it is not economical to repair it

write-pro·tect·ed *adj.* used to describe computer storage space that cannot be altered or erased

writ·er /rītər/ *n.* **1. SOMEBODY WHO WRITES AS PROFESSION** somebody who writes books or articles as a profession **2. PERSON WHO WROTE DOCUMENT** the person who wrote a particular text or document **3. SOMEBODY WHO CAN WRITE** somebody who is able to write, who writes well, or who enjoys writing **4. SCRIBE** a scribe (*archaic*) [Old English *wrītere*]

writ·er's block *n.* an inability on the part of a writer to start a new piece of writing or continue an existing one

writ·er's cramp *n.* a muscular spasm that results from a prolonged period of writing and affects the muscles of the forearm, hand, and fingers, causing temporary cramping and pain

write-up *n.* **1.** PUBL **REVIEW OF MATERIAL** a written account of material, especially a published review of a new play, book, or movie **2.** ACCT **OVERVALUATION OF ASSETS** a deliberate overvaluation of company assets

writhe /rīth/ *v.* (**writhed, writh·ing, writhes**) **1.** *vi.* **TWIST OR SQUIRM** to make violent twisting and rolling movements with the body, especially as a result of severe pain ○ *writhing in agony* **2.** *vti.* **MOVE IN TWISTING WAY** to move in a twisting, squirming way, or to cause the body to move in this way **3.** *vi.* **EXPERIENCE STRONG EMOTION** to feel a particular emotion, especially embarrassment or shame, very strongly, and experience internal stress as a result of it ■ *n.* **WRITHING MOVEMENT** a twisting or squirming movement [Old English *wrīþan.* Ultimately from a prehistoric Germanic base that is also the ancestor of English *wrest* and *wreath.*] —**writh·er** *n.*

writ·ing /rīting/ *n.* **1. WORDS WRITTEN DOWN** words or other symbols, e.g., hieroglyphics, written down as a means of communication **2. WRITTEN MATERIAL** written material, especially considered as the product of a writer's skill **3. ACTIVITY OF CREATING BOOKS** the activity of creating written works, especially as a job **4. STYLE OF LETTERS IN WRITING** the letters and words formed on a page by somebody using a pen or pencil, or the style in which somebody writes ○ *I can't read your writing.* ■ **writ·ings** *npl.* **ALL AUTHOR'S WRITTEN OUTPUT** all the publications and written work of a writer ○ *Churchill's writings on the war*

writ·ing desk *n.* **1. DESK FOR WRITING** a desk with a surface for writing on and compartments for holding paper, envelopes, and other writing materials **2. PORTABLE CASE WITH WRITING SURFACE** a portable case used for carrying writing materials that often has a hard surface for writing

writ·ing pa·per *n.* paper of a quality good enough to write on with ink

Writ·ings /rítingz/ *npl.* = **Hagiographa** (the)

writ of e·lec·tion *n.* an order to hold an election, particularly a special election to fill a vacancy, issued by a governor or other controlling authority

writ of er·ror *n.* a writ that directs and empowers an appellate court to review, and if necessary correct, a prior proceeding or ruling of a lower court

writ of pro·hi·bi·tion *n.* a writ made by a higher court to a lower court ordering the lower court to stop proceeding in a matter outside its jurisdiction

writ·ten past participle of **write**

Writ·ten Law *n.* JUDAISM = **Torah** *n.* 2

WRNS, W.R.N.S. *abbr.* Women's Royal Naval Service

wrnt. *abbr.* warrant

Wroc·law /vráwt slaaf/ city and port in southwestern Poland, on the Oder River. Population: 644,000 (1992).

wrong /rawng/ *adj.* **1.** INCORRECT not correct or accurate ○ *That's the wrong answer.* **2.** MISTAKEN holding an incorrect opinion about a person, thing, or matter ○ *I thought it would be fun, but I was wrong.* **3.** NOT MEANT not the intended or desired one ○ *It was sent to the wrong address.* **4.** NOT IN NORMAL STATE not in the normal satisfactory state ○ *What's wrong with you today?* **5.** NOT CONFORMING TO ACCEPTED STANDARDS not in accordance with law, morality, or with people's sense of fairness, justice, and what is acceptable behavior ○ *It's wrong to steal.* **6.** UNSUITABLE unsuitable, or showing poor judgment on the part of the person who chooses, does, or says it ○ *It's the wrong time of year to be planting seeds.* **7.** NOT WORKING not functioning correctly ○ *There's something wrong with the washing machine.* **8.** REVERSED OR INVERTED opposite to the normal, proper, or intended side, way or direction ○ *This picture is the wrong way up.* ■ *adv.* **1.** INCORRECTLY incorrectly or in a way that leads to failure or a different result from the one intended ○ *You've spelled that wrong.* **2.** IN WRONG DIRECTION in a direction that is different from or opposite to the right or intended direction ■ *n.* **1.** ACTION NOT CONSIDERED MORAL an action or situation that does not conform to ideas of morality or justice **2.** UNACCEPTABLE BEHAVIOR behavior that is morally or socially unacceptable ○ *Children have to be taught the difference between right and wrong.* **3.** LAW = **tort 4.** LAW INFRINGEMENT OF SOMEBODY'S LEGAL RIGHTS an infringement, abridgment, or violation of another party's rights under the law ■ *vt.* (**wronged, wrong·ing, wrongs**) **1.** TREAT SOMEBODY UNJUSTLY to judge or treat somebody unjustly ○ *He felt he had been wronged.* **2.** DISCREDIT SOMEBODY to discredit somebody by saying malicious but untrue things about him or her **3.** BRING DISHONOR ON A WOMAN to seduce a woman and thereby bring about her dishonor (*archaic*) [Old English *wrange* "wrongful act." The adjective *wrang* probably existed in Old English, but is not found before the 12thC. The adjective and probably the noun are of Scandinavian origin.] —**wrong·er** *n.* —**wrong·ly** *adv.* —**wrong·ness** *n.* ◇ **be in the wrong 1.** to be to blame for something **2.** to be mistaken ◇ **get something wrong** to make a mistake in an answer or calculation ◇ **get something wrong, get somebody wrong** to misunderstand something or somebody ◇ **go wrong 1.** to go badly or not according to plan **2.** to make a mistake **3.** to fail to conform to ideas of morality or justice ◇ **go wrong with** to develop a malfunction or error ○ *something's gone wrong with the television*

wrong·do·ing /ráwng do͞o ing/ *n.* behavior or an action that fails to conform to standards of law or morality —**wrong·do·er** *n.*

wrong-foot (**wrong-foot·ed**) *vt.* to cause an opponent to anticipate wrongly the direction in which a move is going to be made or a ball hit or kicked

wrong·ful /ráwngfəl/ *adj.* **1.** UNLAWFUL not done according to the law ○ *brought a suit alleging wrongful arrest* **2.** UNJUST not just or fair —**wrong·ful·ly** *adv.* —**wrong·ful·ness** *n.*

wrong·ful death ac·tion *n.* LAW an action provided by statute or constitution to recover or obtain remedy from a party that is judged to have contributed to or caused the death of another person

wrong-head·ed *adj.* **1.** IRRATIONAL completely contrary to reason or good sense **2.** OBSTINATELY UNREASONABLE obstinately sticking to a false belief, opinion, or course of action —**wrong-head·ed·ly** *adv.* —**wrong-head·ed·ness** *n.*

wrong num·ber *n.* an incorrectly dialed telephone number that connects the caller with the wrong person

wrote past tense of **write**

wroth /roth/ *adj.* extremely angry (*archaic or literary*) [Old English *wrāþ*. Ultimately from a prehistoric Germanic base that is also the ancestor of English *wreath* and *wrath*.]

wrought past tense, past participle of **work** (*archaic*) ■ *adj.* **1.** MADE CAREFULLY OR DECORATIVELY made in a skillful or decorative way (*often used in combination*) ○ *a delicately wrought ebony screen* **2.** RELATING TO DECORATIVE METALWORK used to describe decorative metalwork shaped by hammering and welding

WORD KEY: USAGE

Correct and incorrect contexts: As the term *wrought iron* suggests, ***wrought*** is a past tense not of *wreak* but of *work*. Confusion is perhaps inevitable, because *wreak* means "inflict, vent, cause," and *work*, too, can mean "cause," among many other things. Furthermore, *work* has the additional, and far more common, past tense *worked*. ***Wrought*** is seen in only a few, rather specialized situations such as ones relating to metalwork, and the set phrase *What hath God wrought* (used by Samuel Morse in the first successful test of the telegraph). *Wrought havoc*, however, is not correct; it should be *wreaked havoc*.

Barnaby's

Wrought iron

wrought i·ron *n.* a highly refined form of iron that is easy to shape but is strong and fairly resistant to rust, widely used for decorative metalwork. Wrought iron contains only 1 to 3 % of silicate slag distributed in fibers within the iron, thus making it very malleable. —**wrought-i·ron** *adj.*

wrought-up, wrought up *adj.* tensely nervous, agitated, or excited

wrung past tense, past participle of **wring**

wry /rī/ (**wri·er** *or* **wry·er, wri·est** *or* **wry·est**) *adj.* **1.** AMUSING AND IRONIC combining, or expressing a mixture of, mild amusement and irony ○ *a wry remark* **2.** CHARACTERIZED BY IRONIC ACCEPTANCE characterized by or showing a slightly ironic acceptance of something not particularly pleasant or desirable ○ *a wry grin* **3.** TWISTED out of shape or twisted to one side [Old English *wrīgian* "to turn." Ultimately from an Indo-European base meaning "to turn" that is also the ancestor of English *invert*.] —**wry·ly** *adv.* —**wry·ness** *n.*

wry·bill /rī bil/ *n.* a New Zealand shorebird of the plover family whose bill is bent to one side so that it can search for food beneath pebbles. Latin name: *Anarhyncus fontalis.*

wry·neck /rī nèk/ *n.* **1.** BIRD OF WOODPECKER FAMILY a European and Asian bird of the woodpecker family with mottled brown plumage and a short sharp bill. The wryneck eats insects and lives in holes but does not drill into trees. Latin name: *Jynx torquilla* and *Jynx ruficollis.* **2.** MED = **torticollis**

WS *abbr.* Western Samoa

WSW *abbr.* west-southwest

wt. *abbr.* weight

WTA *n., abbr.* Women's Tennis Association

WTO *abbr.* World Trade Organization

Wu /woo/ *n.* LANG a group of Chinese dialects belonging to the Sino-Tibetan language family of the Chinese group. It is spoken mainly in the Jiangsu and Zhejiang provinces of China and is the colloquial language of Shanghai. About 90 million people speak Wu. [Early 20thC. From Chinese *wú*.]

Wu·han /wo͞o h-n/ capital city of Hubei Province, central China. Population: 3,860,000 (1993).

wul·fen·ite /wo͞olfə nīt/ *n.* an orange, yellow, or brown mineral consisting of lead molybdate, used as a source of molybdenum [Mid-19thC. Named for the Austrian scientist F. X. von *Wulfen* (1728–1805).]

wun·der·kind /vo͞ondər kìnd, wúnd-/ (*plural* **-kind·er** /-kìndər, wúndər kìndər/ *or* **-kinds**) *n.* **1.** YOUNG SUCCESSFUL PERSON somebody who is extremely successful at a young age **2.** CHILD PRODIGY a child who is unusually talented at something [Late 19thC. From German, literally "wonder child."]

Wup·per·tal /vo͝oppər taal/ city in North Rhine-Westphalia State, northwestern Germany. It is situated about 20 mi./32 km east of Düsseldorf. Population: 382,400 (1995).

wurst /wurst, woorst/ *n.* **1.** SAUSAGE sausage of any kind **2.** *U.K.* GERMAN SAUSAGE a type of sausage made in Germany and Austria, especially a large sausage intended to be sliced and eaten cold [Mid-19thC. From German *Wurst* "sausage." Ultimately from an Indo-European base meaning "to confuse" that is also the ancestor of English *worst*.]

Würz·burg /vúrts burg, vürts berk/ city in northeastern Bavaria State, southern Germany. Population: 127,700 (1995).

wu·shu /wo͞o sho͞o/, **wu shu** *n.* Chinese martial arts considered collectively [Late 20thC. From Chinese *wǔ shù*, literally "military technique."]

wuss /wuss/ *n.* a term that deliberately insults somebody regarded as weak or ineffectual (*slang insult*) [Late 20th C. Origin unknown.] —**wuss·y** *adj.*

WV *abbr.* **1.** West Virginia **2.** (Windward Islands) St. Vincent.

WWF *abbr.* **1.** World Wide Fund for Nature **2.** World Wrestling Federation

WWI *abbr.* World War One

WWII *abbr.* World War Two

WWW *abbr.* World Wide Web

WY, Wy *abbr.* Wyoming

Wy·an·dot /wī ən dòt/ (*plural* **-dot** *or* **-dots**), **Wy·an·dotte** (*plural* **-dotte** *or* **-dottes**) *n.* PEOPLES a member of a Native North American people that originally occupied lands in Ohio and parts of neighboring states, and whose members now live mainly in Oklahoma [Mid-18thC. Via French *Ouendat* from Huron *Wendat*.]

Wy·an·dotte /wī ən dòt/ *n.* a medium-sized North American domestic chicken [Late 19thC. Variant of WYANDOT.]

Wy·att /wī ət/, **Sir Thomas** (1503–42) English courtier and poet. His service at Henry VIII's court included diplomatic missions. His poems, published in 1557, introduced Italian verse forms into England.

wych elm /wích èlm/, **witch elm** *n.* an elm with a rounded crown, long pointed leaves, and clusters of winged green fruit. Latin name: *Ulmus glabra.* [Old English *wice*. Ultimately from an Indo-European base meaning "to bend, be pliant," which is also the ancestor of English *wicker, vetch, weak,* and *vicar*.]

Wych·er·ley /wíchər lee/, **William** (1640?–1716) English playwright. His comedies include *The Country Wife* (1675) and *The Plain Dealer* (1677).

Wy·cliffe /wíklif/, **Wy·clif, Wi·cliff, John** (1330?–84) English philosopher and religious reformer. He supervised the first English translation of the Bible, published posthumously in 1388. He rejected the doctrine of transubstantiation and denounced abuses in the Roman Catholic Church, anticipating the Protestant Reformation. —**Wyc·liff·ite** *n., adj.*

wye /wī/ *n.* **1.** LETTER "Y" the letter "y" **2.** SOMETHING WITH SHAPE OF LETTER "Y" something that has a shape resembling the letter "Y" [Mid-19thC. Origin uncertain: perhaps a variant pronunciation of *ui*, from the letters "V" plus "I," analyzed as components of the letter "Y."]

Popperfoto

Andrew Wyeth (right)

Wy·eth /wī əth/, **Andrew** (*b.* 1917) U.S. artist. The son of N. C. Wyeth, he typically depicted rural scenes with a strong emotional charge in paintings such as *Christina's World* (1948). Full name **Andrew Newell Wyeth**

Wy·eth, N. C. (1882–1945) U.S. artist. A leading illustrator and muralist, he produced illustrations for many children's classics, notably *Treasure Island* (1924). Full name **Newell Convers Wyeth**

Wy·ler /wílər/, **William** (1902–81) German-born U.S. movie director. His Academy Award-winning movies include *Mrs. Miniver* (1942) and *Ben-Hur* (1959).

Wy·lie /wílee/, **Elinor** (1885–1928) U.S. writer. She achieved success with both poetry and fiction, especially *The Orphan Angel* (1926), a fantasy on the life of the poet Shelley. Full name **Elinor Morton Wylie**

wynd /wīnd/ *n. Scotland* a narrow lane in a town [15thC. Origin uncertain: Probably formed from WIND[2].]

wynn /win/, **wyn** *n.* a runic letter used in Old English [Old English *wyn*, literally "joy." Runes were named using words beginning with their sound.]

Wyo. *abbr.* Wyoming

Wy·o·ming /wī ōming/ state of the northwestern United States, bordered by Montana, South Dakota, Nebraska, Colorado, Utah, and Idaho. Capital: Cheyenne. Population: 528,964 (1997). Area: 97,819 sq. mi./253,350 sq. km. —**Wy·o·min·gite** *n.*

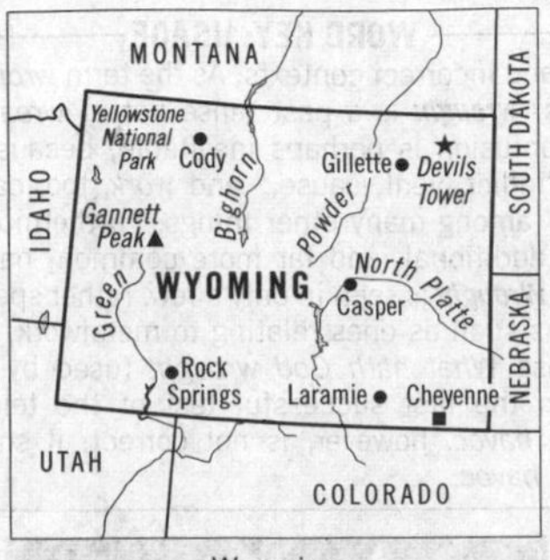

Wyoming

WYSIWYG /wízzi wig/ *adj.* used to describe any technology that enables the user to see an image of text and graphics on a computer display exactly as it will appear when printed. Full form **what you see is what you get** [Late 20thC. Acronym.]

Wythe /with/, **George** (1726–1806) American patriot and jurist. Representing Virginia, he signed the Declaration of Independence (1776). His greatest influence came through his work training lawyers at the College of William and Mary (1779–90).

Wyvern

wy·vern /wívərn/, **wivern** *n.* in heraldry, a mythical creature depicted as having two legs, a dragon's head, wings, and a long tail [Late 16th C. Via Old French *wivre* from Latin *vipera* (see VIPER).]

X x

x[1] /eks/, **X** *n.* (*plural* **x's**; *plural* **X's** *or* **Xs**) **1.** **24TH LETTER OF ENGLISH ALPHABET** the twenty-fourth letter of the modern English alphabet **2.** **SPEECH SOUND CORRESPONDING TO LETTER "X"** the speech sound that corresponds to the letter "X" **3.** **LETTER "X" WRITTEN** a written representation of the letter "X" **4.** **"X"-SHAPED SYMBOLIC MARK** an "X"-shaped mark used in place of a signature by somebody who cannot write, to indicate a vote, to show that something is incorrect, or to represent a kiss **5.** **SYMBOL USED TO REPRESENT AN UNKNOWN** a letter "X" or an "X"-shaped mark used to represent an unknown quantity, an unnamed person, or any unknown or unspecified factor or thing ■ *vt.* (**x-ed** *or* **x'ed**, **x-ing** *or* **x'ing**, **x-es** *or* **x'es**; **X-ed** *or* **X'ed**, **X-ing** *or* **X'ing**, **X-es** *or* **X's**) **MARK OR SIGN WITH "X"** to mark or sign something with an "X"

X out *vt.* to cross something out

x[2] *symbol.* **1.** by (*used when giving the dimensions of something*) **2.** MATH multiplied by **3.** MATH an algebraic variable **4.** MATH a Cartesian coordinate along the x-axis **5.** BRIDGE any card that is not an honor **6.** COMM, FIN ex

x[3] *abbr.* TELECOM, BUSINESS extension

X[1] /eks/, **x** *n.* the Roman numeral for ten

X[2] *symbol.* PHYS, ELECTRON ENG reactance

Xan·a·du /zánnə dòo/ (*plural* **-dus**) *n.* an idyllically beautiful place [Mid-20thC. From Samuel Taylor Coleridge's poem *Kubla Khan* (1816), in which it is the name of a residence of Kubla Khan (1216–94). An alteration of *Shang-tu.*]

xanth- *prefix.* = **xantho-**

xan·than gum /zánthən-/ *n.* a natural gum with a high molecular weight that is produced by the fermentation of glucose and is used in the food industry as a stabilizer [Mid-20thC. "Xanthan" formed from modern Latin *Xanthomonas*, a bacterium, coined from XANTHO- + MONAD.]

xan·thate /zán thàyt/ *n.* a chemical compound that is a salt or ester of xanthic acid. Xanthates are used in the chemical extraction of metals such as copper and gold and in the manufacture of rayon. [Mid-19thC. Formed from XANTHIC ACID.]

xan·thene /zán thèen/ *n.* a yellow crystalline compound used as a fungicide. Its structure forms the basis of a range of organic dyes such as fluoroscein. Formula: $CH_2(C_6H_4)_2O$. [Late 19thC]

xan·thic ac·id /zànthik-/ *n.* an unstable organic sulfur-containing acid. Formula: ROC(S)SH where R is an organic group.

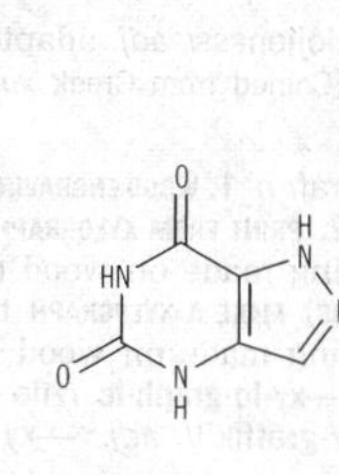

Xanthine

xan·thine /zán thèen, -thin/ *n.* **1.** **CRYSTALLINE COMPOUND** a yellow-white crystalline compound found in blood and urine and in some plants. It is the precursor of uric acid. Formula: $C_5H_4N_4O_2$. **2.** **XANTHINE DERIVATIVE** a derivative of xanthine such as caffeine, theophylline, or theobromine [Mid-19thC]

xantho- *prefix.* **1.** yellow ○ *xanthopterin* **2.** xanthic acid ○ *xanthate* [From Greek *xanthos* "yellow"]

xan·tho·ma /zan thṓmə/ (*plural* **-mas** *or* **-ma·ta** /-mətə/) *n.* a yellow lipid-filled lesion on the skin, especially on the eyelids, that indicates a disorder of fat metabolism —**xan·thom·a·tous** /zan thómmətəss/ *adj.*

xan·tho·ma·to·sis /zànthəmə tṓssiss/ *n.* the presence of multiple xanthomas on the skin

xan·thone /zán thōn/ *n.* a colorless crystalline compound that is the basis of certain dyes. Formula: $C_{13}H_8O_2$.

xan·tho·phyll /zànthə fìl/ *n.* a yellow oxygen-containing pigment found with chlorophyll in the tissue of plants. Some xanthophylls are responsible for the colors of autumn leaves. —**xan·tho·phyl·lic** /zànthə fíllik/ *adj.*

Xan·thus /zánthəss/ ancient capital city of Lycia in southern Asia Minor, in present-day southwestern Turkey. Destroyed by the Persians in 546 B.C. and the Romans in 42 B.C., the remains of the city and numerous artworks were discovered by Sir Charles Fellows in 1838. —**Xan·th·i·an** *n., adj.*

Xa·vi·er /záyvee ər, ig záy-/, **St. Francis** (1506–52) Spanish missionary. He helped St. Ignatius of Loyola to found the Jesuits, and established missions in India, Japan, and parts of Southeast Asia. Known as **the Apostle of the Indies**

x-ax·is *n.* **1.** **AXIS IN THREE-DIMENSIONAL COORDINATE SYSTEM** an axis in the three-dimensional Cartesian coordinate system, conventionally the horizontal one **2.** **AXIS IN TWO-DIMENSIONAL COORDINATE SYSTEM** the horizontal axis in a two-dimensional coordinate system

XC, **X-C** *abbr.* SPORTS cross-country

X-cer·tif·i·cate *adj. U.K.* = **X-rated**

X-chro·mo·some, **X chromosome** *n.* a chromosome present in both sexes that plays a role in determining the sex of an individual. Female mammals carry two X chromosomes and males carry one. ◊ **Y chromosome**

x-co·or·di·nate *n.* the position of a point in space with reference to the x-axis in the Cartesian coordinate system, defined in conjunction with the y- and z-coordinates

XD, **x-div.** *abbr.* STOCK EXCH ex dividend

Xe *symbol.* xenon

xe·bec /zée bèk/, **ze·bec** *n.* a small Mediterranean ship with three masts rigged with both square and triangular sails [Mid-18thC. Via French *chebec* from, ultimately, Arabic *šabbāk*.]

xen- *prefix.* = **xeno-** (*used before vowels*)

xe·ni·a /zéenee ə, zéenyə/ *n.* the effect of genes carried by pollen on the food storage tissue (**endosperm**) of the pollinated seed [Late 19thC. Via modern Latin from Greek, formed from *xenos* (see XENO-).]

xeno- *prefix.* foreign, strange, different ○ *xenophile* ○ *xenolith* [Via modern Latin from Greek *xenos* "stranger, foreigner"]

xen·o·bi·ot·ic /zènnə bī óttik, zèenə-/ *adj.* **FOREIGN TO BODY** used to describe a chemical compound, e.g., a drug or pesticide, that is foreign to the body of a living organism ■ *n.* **FOREIGN COMPOUND** a xenobiotic chemical compound

xen·o·cryst /zénnə krìst, zéenə kríst/ *n.* a crystal in an igneous rock introduced from an external source and not crystallized from the magma [Late 19thC. Formed from an abbreviation of XENO- + CRYSTAL.]

xen·o·di·ag·no·sis /zènnō dī əg nṓssiss, zèenō-/ (*plural* **-nos·es** /-nṓ seez/) *n.* the diagnosis of a parasitic infection by allowing a noninfected disease-carrying organism, e.g., a mosquito, to feed on an infected person's blood and then examining the organism for infection —**xen·o·di·ag·nos·tic** /zènnō dī əg nóstik, zèenō-/ *adj.*

xen·o·ge·ne·ic /zènnəjə née ik, -náy ik, zèenə-/ *adj.* coming from or derived from a different species [Mid-20thC. Modeled on SYNGENEIC.]

xen·o·gen·e·sis /zènnə jénnəsiss, zèenə-/ *n.* BIOL **1.** **PRODUCTION OF OFFSPRING DIFFERENT FROM PARENTS** the supposed production of offspring completely different from either parent **2.** **ALTERNATION OF GENERATIONS** the existence in the life cycle of an organism of two or more alternating forms or reproductive modes, e.g., sexual and asexual cycles —**xen·o·ge·net·ic** /zènnə jə néttik, zèenə-/ *adj.*

xen·o·graft /zénnə gràft, zèenə-/ *n.* = **heterograft**

xen·o·lith /zénnə lìth, zèenə-/ *n.* a fragment of rock that is different in origin from the igneous rock in which it occurs —**xen·o·lith·ic** /zènnə líthik, zèenə-/ *adj.*

xe·non /zée nòn/ *n.* a heavy colorless odorless gaseous chemical element that is relatively inert, found in minute quantities in air, and used in electronic tubes and specialized lamps. Symbol **Xe** [Late 19thC. From Greek *xenon*, the neuter of *xenos* (see XENO-).]

Xe·noph·a·nes /zə nóffə neez/ (*fl.* late 6th-early 5th centuries B.C.) Greek philosopher and poet. He ridiculed the polytheistic beliefs of earlier Greek poets and is thought to have founded the Eleatic school of philosophy.

xen·o·phile /zénnə fìl, zèenə-/ *n.* somebody who likes foreign people, their customs and culture, or foreign things —**xen·o·phil·i·a** /zènnə fíllee ə, zèenə-/ *n.* —**xe·noph·i·lous** /ze nóffələss, zə-/ *adj.*

xen·o·phobe /zénnə fōb, zèenə-/ *n.* somebody who fears or dislikes foreign people, their customs and culture, or foreign things

xen·o·pho·bi·a /zènnə fṓbee ə, zèenə-/ *n.* an intense fear or dislike of foreign people, their customs and culture, or foreign things —**xen·o·pho·bic** /zènnə fṓbik, zèenə-/ *adj.*

Xen·o·phon /zénnəf'n, -fon/ (430?–355? B.C.) Greek historian and soldier. A disciple of Socrates, he participated in the attack on Persia by Cyrus the Younger (401 B.C.) and led the 10,000-strong Greek force to safety on the Black Sea, an episode he described in his *Anabasis.*

xe·no·pus /zénnəpəss/ *n.* an aquatic frog found in pools and streams in southern Africa. Genus: *Xenopus.* [Late 19thC. Via modern Latin, name of the genus, from Greek *xeno-* (see XENO-) + *pous* "foot."]

xen·o·trans·plan·ta·tion /zènnō trans plan táysh'n, zèenō-/ *n.* the process of transplanting organs from one species to another, especially from animals to humans [Late 20thC. Coined from XENO- + *transplantation.*]

xer- *prefix.* = **xero-** (*used before vowels*)

xer·ic /zérrik, zír-/ *adj.* relating to or living in a dry habitat —**xer·i·cal·ly** *adv.*

Xe·ri·scape /zérri skàyp/ *tdmk.* a trademark for a method of water conservation by landscaping, used in areas with an arid climate

xero- *prefix.* dry, dryness ○ *xerothermic* [From Greek *xēros*]

xer·o·der·ma /zèerō dúrmə/, **xe·ro·der·mi·a** /-dúrmee ə/ *n.* a mild form of the hereditary disorder ichthyosis, marked by discolored dry hard scaly skin —**xe·ro·der·mat·ic** /zèerō dur máttik/ *adj.* —**xe·ro·der·ma·tous** /-dúrmətəss/ *adj.*

xer·o·der·ma pig·men·to·sum /zèerō dúrmə pìgmən tṓssəm/ *n.* a rare and often fatal hereditary condition beginning in infancy in which the skin and eyes are damaged by sunlight. It results in freckles, discolored patches, and skin cancers.

xe·rog·ra·phy /zi róggrəfee/ *n.* a method of photocopying in which the image is formed by attracting a resinous powder to an electrostatically charged plate, then transferred to paper and fixed by heating —**xe·rog·ra·pher** *n.* —**xer·o·graph·ic** /zèerə gráffik/ *adj.* —**xer·o·graph·i·cal·ly** /-gráffikəlee/ *adv.*

xe·ro·mor·phic /zèerə máwrfik/ *adj.* used to describe plants or plant parts that are adapted for survival in dry conditions, e.g., spiny leaves that reduce surface area and therefore water loss [Early 20thC. Ultimately from Greek *xēros* "dry."]

xe·roph·i·lous /zi róffələss/ *adj.* thriving in or adapted for a hot dry habitat —**xe·ro·phile** /zèerə fìl/ *n.* —**xe·roph·i·ly** /zi róffəlee/ *n.*

xer·oph·thal·mi·a /zèeròf thálmee ə/ *n.* an eye disease caused by vitamin A deficiency, marked by dryness and ulceration of the conjunctiva and cornea. If untreated, it may cause blindness. —**xer·oph·thal·mic** *adj.*

xer·o·phyte /zèerə fìt/ *n.* a plant that is adapted for a dry habitat, e.g., a cactus —**xer·o·phyt·ic** /zèerə fíttik/ *adj.* —**xer·o·phyt·i·cal·ly** /-fíttikəlee/ *adv.* —**xe·ro·phyt·ism** /zèerə fì tìzzəm/ *n.*

xe·ro·ra·di·og·ra·phy /zèerə ràydee óggrəfee/ *n.* a type of high-definition X-ray photography in which the image is first made on a specially coated metal plate then transferred to paper. It is often used in screening for breast cancer. [Mid-20thC. Coined from Greek *xēro-* "dry," from *xēros* + RADIOGRAPHY.]

xe·ro·sis /zi rṓssiss/ *n.* abnormal dryness of the skin and mucous membranes of the eye, caused by thickening of the membranes —**xe·rot·ic** /zi róttik/ *adj.*

xe·ros·to·mi·a /zèerə stṓmee ə/ *n.* an abnormal lack of saliva in the mouth, caused by disease, poisoning, or some drugs

xe·ro·ther·mic /zèerə thúrmik/ *adj.* very hot and having little rainfall ○ *a xerothermic climate*

Xer·ox /zèe ròks/ *tdmk.* a trademark for a photocopying process

Xer·xes I /zúrk sèez/, **King of Persia** (519?–465 B.C.). As king (486–465 B.C.), he led a huge army into Greece (480 B.C.), defeating the Greeks at Thermopylae and burning Athens, but his fleet was defeated at Salamis. He was assassinated by his palace guard. Known as **Xerxes the Great**

x-height *n.* the height of the lowercase letter x in a particular typeface, used as a measure of the height of the main body of all lowercase letters in that typeface

Xho·sa /kṓssə, kṓzə/ (*plural* **-sa** *or* **-sas**), **Xo·sa** *n.* **1.** PEOPLES **MEMBER OF A S AFRICAN PEOPLE** a member of a Bantu people of South Africa **2.** LANG **XHOSA LANGUAGE** the language of the Xhosa people, belonging to the Bantu group of the Bene-Congo family of languages. Xhosa is spoken by about 7 million people and is closely related to Zulu. [Early 19thC. From Nguni.]

xi /zī, ksī/ (*plural* **xis**) *n.* the 14th letter of the Greek alphabet, represented in the English alphabet as "x." See table at **alphabet**

Xia·men /shyaà mén/ city and seaport on Xiamen Island in Fujian Province, southeastern China. It lies in the Taiwan Strait, west of Taiwan. Population: 470,000 (1993).

Xi'an /shyaan/ capital city of Shaanxi Province in eastern China. One of China's oldest cities, it is home to some major archeological sites, including one found to contain a vast army of life-sized soldiers made of terrcotta. Population: 2,790,000 (1992).

Xiang·tan /shyàang taàn/ city in southern China, in Hunan Province. It is an inland port and industrial center on the Xiang River. Population: 411,000 (1988).

xi hy·per·on, **xi particle** *n.* a neutral or negatively charged elementary particle present in cosmic rays and in high-energy collisions in particle accelerators [Mid-20thC. *Xi* is the name of the Greek letter used to represent such a particle.]

Xi Jiang /shèe jyaàng/ river in southern China that rises in Yunnan Province and flows east to the South China Sea. Length: 1,300 mi./2,100 km.

Xi·ning /shèe níng/ capital city of Qinghai Province, in central China, northeast of Lanzhou. Population: 551,776 (1990).

Xin·jiang Uy·gur /shìn jyaàng wèegər/ autonomous region in northwestern China. With one sixth of China's land, it is the country's largest region. Capital: Urumqi. Population: 15,550,000 (1991). Area: 618,000 sq. mi./1,600,000 sq. km.

xiph·i·ster·num /zìffi stúrnəm/ (*plural* **-na** /-nə/) *n.* the third and lowest segment of the breastbone (**sternum**) in humans. It consists of a flat plate of cartilage that gradually changes into bone during life.

xiph·oid /zí fòyd/ *adj.* **1.** **SWORD-SHAPED** shaped like a sword **2.** **OF THE XIPHISTERNUM** relating to the xiphisternum ■ *n.* **xiph·oid, xiph·oid proc·ess** = **xiphisternum**

XL *abbr.* extra large (*used of clothing sizes*)

X·mas /krísməss, éksməss/ *n.* Christmas (*informal*) [Mid-16thC. *X* represents the Greek letter *chi*, an abbreviation of Greek *Khristos* "Christ."]

Xn. *abbr.* Christian

Xnty. *abbr.* Christianity

xo·a·non /zṓ ə nòn/ (*plural* **-na** /-nə/) *n.* an image of a god that has been carved out of wood [Early 18thC. From Greek *xoanon* "carved statue."]

Xo·chi·mil·co /kòchi mílkō/ city in south central Mexico. It is a suburb of Mexico City, and is famous for its precolonial canals and floating gardens. Population: 271,020 (1990).

X-ra·di·a·tion *n.* **1.** **EXPOSURE TO X-RAYS** exposure to X-rays or medical treatment by means of X-rays **2.** **X-RAY RADIATION** radiation in the form of X-rays

X-rat·ed *adj.* **1.** **SEXUALLY EXPLICIT** containing explicit sex scenes or descriptions of sex (*informal*) **2.** **NOT VIEWABLE BY YOUNG PEOPLE** used in the past to describe a movie not allowed to be viewed by people under the age of 17, usually because of its sexual or violent content [Late 20thC. From "X" rating given to such material.]

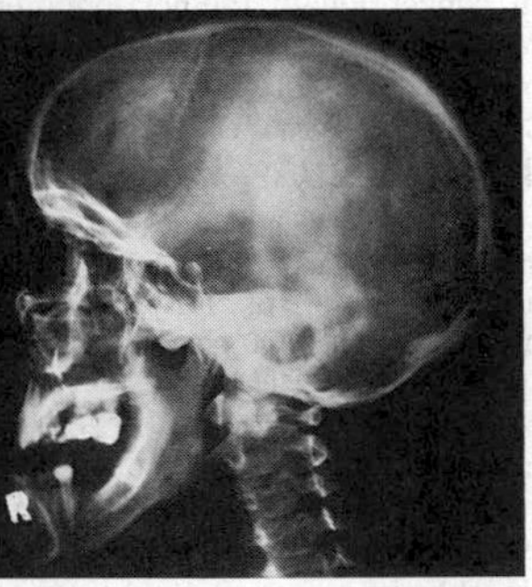

X-ray: Image of a human skull

X-ray, **X ray, x-ray, x ray** *n.* **1.** **ELECTROMAGNETIC RADIATION** a high-energy electromagnetic radiation. It has a wavelength between 0.01 and 10 nanometers, which is between gamma rays and ultraviolet light, and can penetrate solids and ionize gas. **2.** **PHOTOGRAPHIC IMAGE USING X-RAYS** an image produced on photographic film by X-rays passing through objects or parts of the body, often used in medicine and science as a diagnostic tool. Dense parts such as bones absorb the X-rays and so appear as lighter regions on the developed film. **3.** COMMUNICATION **CODE WORD FOR THE LETTER "X"** a code word for the letter "X," used in international radio communications ■ *vt.* (**X-rayed, X-ray·ing, X-rays**) **1.** **PHOTOGRAPH SOMETHING USING X-RAYS** to expose something, e.g., a part of the body, to X-rays in order to obtain a photographic image of it **2.** **EXAMINE PATIENT USING X-RAYS** to examine or treat somebody using X-rays [Late 19thC. Translation of German *X-Strahl*, the name given by Röntgen, who discovered the rays, *x* signifying "unknown."]

X-ray as·tron·o·my *n.* the branch of astronomy in which the properties of celestial bodies are determined using the X-rays they emit. Because the Earth's atmosphere is opaque to X-rays, observations are made using rockets or satellites.

X-ray crys·tal·log·ra·phy *n.* the study of crystal structures using the diffraction patterns produced by scattered X-rays

X-ray dif·frac·tion *n.* the diffraction of X-rays produced by the atoms within a crystal, used to determine information about the crystal's structure

X-ray star, **X-ray source** *n.* a celestial object that emits X-rays in addition to other types of radiation

X-ray ther·a·py *n.* the medical application of X-rays in treating illnesses such as cancer

X-ray tube *n.* a vacuum tube in which a stream of high-energy electrons is made to strike a metal target to produce X-rays

XS *abbr.* extra small (*used of clothing sizes*)

Xt. *abbr.* Christ

Xtian. *abbr.* Christian

Xty. *abbr.* Christianity

xu /soo/ (*plural* **xu**) *n.* **1.** **SUB-UNIT OF VIETNAMESE CURRENCY** a sub-unit of currency in Vietnam, 100 of which are worth a dong. See table at **currency** **2.** **COIN WORTH XU** coin worth one xu [Mid-20thC. Via Vietnamese from French *sou* (see SOU).]

xyl- *prefix.* = **xylo-** (*used before vowels*)

xy·lan /zí làn, zílən/ *n.* a yellow gummy polysaccharide (**pentosan**) found in plant cell walls and woody tissue such as straw husks that yields xylose when subjected to hydrolysis

xy·lem /zíləm/ *n.* plant tissue that carries water and dissolved minerals from the roots through the stem and leaves. It also helps to support the plant and is the main constituent of wood. [Late 19thC. From German, formed from Greek *xulon* "wood."]

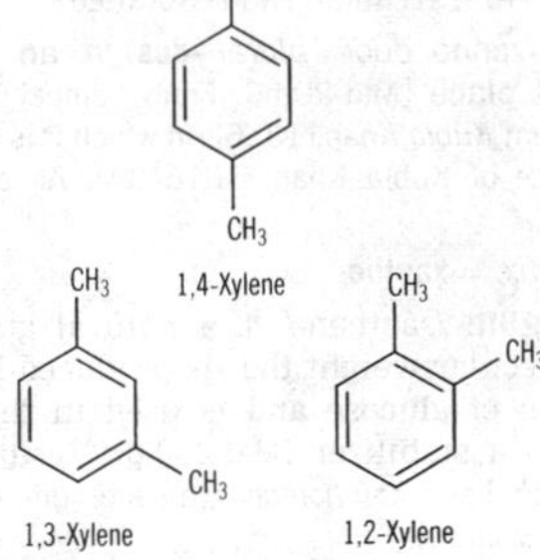

Xylene

xy·lene /zí lèen/ *n.* any of three isomeric hydrocarbons that are flammable volatile colorless liquids obtained from petroleum or natural gas and are used as solvents and in making aviation fuel, resins, and dyes. Formula: C_8H_{10}.

xy·li·dine /zílə dèen, zíllə-, zíləd'n, zílləd'n/ *n.* any of six toxic amines derived from xylene and used in dyes and in organic synthesis. Formula: $C_8H_{11}N$.

xylo- *prefix.* **1.** wood ○ *xylograph* **2.** xylene ○ *xylidine* [From Greek *xulon* "wood"]

xy·log·e·nous /zī lójjənəss/ *adj.* adapted to or living in or on wood [Coined from Greek *xulo-* "wood," from *xulon* + -GENOUS]

xy·lo·graph /zílə gràf/ *n.* **1.** **WOOD ENGRAVING** an engraving made on wood **2.** **PRINT FROM XYLOGRAPH** a print made from an engraving made on wood ■ *vt.* (**-graphed, -graph·ing, -graphs**) **MAKE A XYLOGRAPH** to take a print from an engraving made on wood —**xy·log·ra·pher** /zī lóggrəfər/ *n.* —**xy·lo·graph·ic** /zìlə gráffik/ *adj.* —**xy·lo·graph·i·cal** /-gráffik'l/ *adj.* —**xy·lo·graph·i·cal·ly** /-gráffikəlee/ *adv.*

xy·log·ra·phy /zī lóggrəfee/ *n.* the art of engraving on and printing from wooden blocks

xy·loid /zí lòyd/ *adj.* relating to or resembling wood

xy·lol /zí lòl, -lōl/ *n.* = **xylene** [Mid-19thC. Coined from XYLO- + -OL.]

xy·loph·a·gous /zī lóffəgəss/ *adj.* feeding on or living in wood —**xy·lo·phage** /zílə fàyj/ *n.*

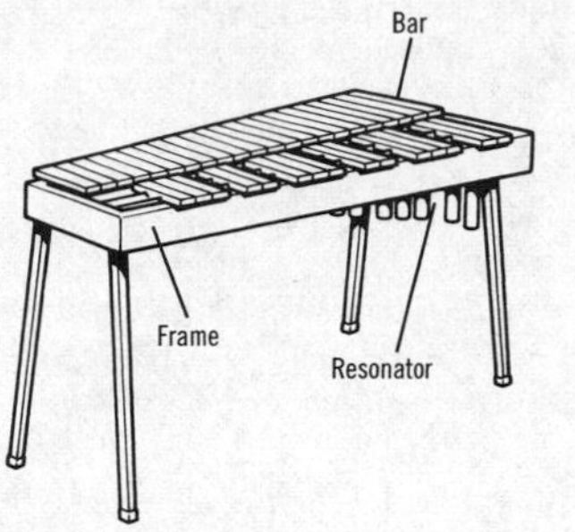

Xylophone

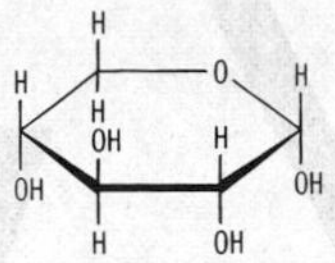

Xylose

xy·lo·phone /zílə fōn/ *n.* a musical instrument consisting of a row of wooden bars of different lengths that are laid out like a keyboard and produce a tone when struck with a mallet —**xy·lo·phon·ist** /zílə fōnist/ *n.*

xy·lose /zí lōss/ *n.* a white crystalline combustible sugar obtained from xylan and used in diabetic foods and in dyeing and tanning. Formula: $C_5H_{10}O_5$.

xys·tus /zístəss/ (*plural* **-tus·es**), **xyst** /zist/ *n.* **1.** ANCIENT GREEK COVERED EXERCISE AREA in ancient Greece, a long walkway with a roof supported by pillars, used for athletics **2.** ANCIENT ROMAN PATH in ancient Rome, a covered or open path in a garden, lined with trees or pillars [Mid-17thC. Via Latin from Greek *xustos* "covered colonnade," literally "smooth" (from its polished floor), from *xuein* "to scrape."]

Y y

y[1] /wī/ (*plural* **y's**), **Y** (*plural* **Y's** *or* **Ys**) *n.* **1.** **25TH LETTER OF ENGLISH ALPHABET** the 25th letter of the modern English alphabet **2.** **SPEECH SOUND CORRESPONDING TO LETTER "Y"** the speech sound that corresponds to the letter "Y" **3.** **LETTER "Y" WRITTEN** a written representation of the letter "Y" **4.** **SOMETHING SHAPED LIKE Y** a Y-shaped object or group of objects

y[2] *abbr.* NAVY yeoman

y[3] (*plural* **y's**) *symbol.* **1.** y-axis **2.** a coordinate along the y-axis **3.** an algebraic variable **4.** yocto-

Y[1] *symbol.* **1.** ELEC admittance **2.** an unknown factor **3.** yotta- **4.** yttrium

Y[2] *abbr.* **1.** yen **2.** yuan **3.** YMCA (*informal*) **4.** YWCA (*informal*) **5.** YMHA (*informal*) **6.** YWHA (*informal*)

y. *abbr.* year

-y[1], **-ey** *suffix.* **1.** consisting of or characterized by ○ *muddy* **2.** somewhat, like ○ *chilly* ○ *wintry* **3.** tending toward ○ *sleepy* [Old English *-ig*]

-y[2] *suffix.* **1.** condition, state, or quality ○ *infamy* **2.** an activity ○ *chandlery* **3.** the place where an activity is carried on, or the result or product of an activity ○ *colliery* ○ *laundry* **4.** body or group ○ *soldiery* [Via Old French *-ie* from Latin *-ia*]

-y[3] *suffix.* = **-ie**

Y2K *abbr.* **1.** year 2000 ○ *Y2K-compliant software* **2.** millennium bug

YA *abbr.* young adult

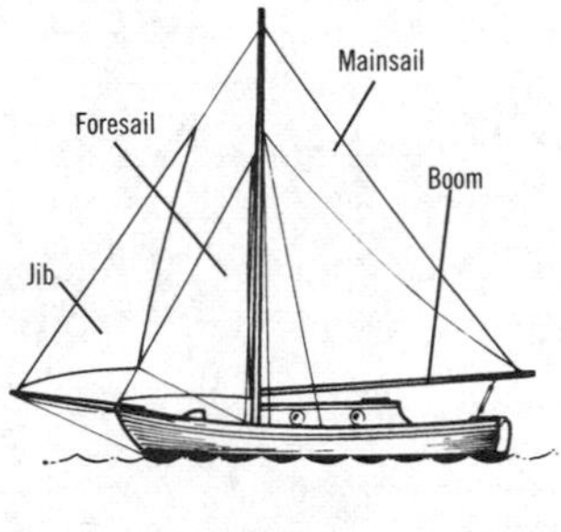

Yacht

yacht /yot/ *n.* **1.** **SAILBOAT** a sailboat, often one that has living quarters and is used for cruising or racing. Most sailing yachts have a motor as an alternative or extra means of power. **2.** **MOTORBOAT FOR CRUISING** a large motorboat used for cruising ■ *vi.* (**yacht·ed, yacht·ing, yachts**) **SAIL IN YACHT** to sail in a yacht for leisure or sport [Mid-16thC. From obsolete Dutch *jaghte*, a shortening of *jaghtschip* "chasing ship."]

WORD KEY: SYNONYMS

See Synonyms at ***boat***.

yacht·ie /yóttee/ *n.* somebody who owns a yacht or enjoys sailing, cruising, or racing in yachts (*informal*)

yacht·ing /yótting/ *n.* the sport or pastime of sailing a yacht

yachts·man /yótsmən/ (*plural* **-men** /-mən/) *n.* somebody who owns or sails a yacht —**yachts·man·ship** /yótsmən shìp/ *n.*

yachts·wom·an /yóts wŏŏmmən/ (*plural* **-en** /-wìmmin/) *n.* a woman who owns or sails a yacht

yack *vi., n.* = **yak**[2] (*informal*)

yack·e·ty-yak /yàkkətee yák/ *vi.* (**yack·e·ty-yakked, yack·e·ty-yak·king, yack·e·ty-yaks**), *n.* = **yak**[2] (*informal*) [Mid-20thC. An imitation of the sound.]

yad·da yad·da yad·da /yàddhə yàddhə yáddhə/ *n.* **VACUOUS CHATTER** boring, trite, superficial, unending talk (*slang*) ○ *just a lot of yadda yadda yadda on the talk shows tonight* ■ *interj.* **USED AS FILLER OR INDICATOR** used in speaking as a filler for unstated material or to indicate boredom or distaste for things others are saying or have just said (*slang*) ○ *We chewed it over forever ... yadda yadda yadda, you know, nothing important* [Late 20thC. Origin uncertain.]

Yad·kin /yád kin/ river in central North Carolina. It joins the Uharie River to form the Pee Dee River, flows through South Carolina, and empties into the Atlantic Ocean. Length: 202 mi./325 km.

YAG /yag/ *n.* a mineral made synthetically from yttrium, aluminum, and garnet. It is used in infrared lasers and as a gemstone. [Mid-20thC. Acronym formed from *yttrium, aluminum* and *garnet.*]

ya·gi /yaágee, yággee/ (*plural* **-gis**) *n.* a directional radio or television antenna consisting of several elements arranged in line [Mid-20thC. Named for Hidetsugu *Yagi* (1886–1976), Japanese electrical engineer.]

ya·hoo[1] /yaá hŏŏ, yaa hŏŏ/ (*plural* **-hoos**) *n.* an offensively crude or brutish person (*insult*) [Early 18thC. Named for the *Yahoos* in Jonathan Swift's *Gulliver's Travels* (1726).] —**ya·hoo·ism** *n.*

ya·hoo[2] /yaá hŏŏ, yaa hŏŏ/ *interj.* **EXPRESSING ENTHUSIASM** used to express enthusiasm, approval, or celebration (*informal*) ○ *Yahoo! Let's go!* ■ *n.* (*plural* **-hoos**) **ENTHUSIASTIC CRY** a cry of yahoo (*informal*)

Yahr·zeit /yaár tsīt/ *n.* in Judaism, the anniversary of somebody's death, celebrated by near relatives with the lighting of a memorial candle and the saying of the kaddish [Mid-19thC. From Yiddish *yortsayt*, literally "year's time."]

Yah·weh /yaá wày/, **Yah·veh** /yaá vày/, **Jah·veh, Jah·weh** *n.* a name of God, expanded from the four letters, YHWH (**Tetragrammaton**), that form the proper name of God in Hebrew [Late 19thC. From Hebrew.]

Yah·wism /yaá wìzzəm/, **Yah·vism** /yaá vìzzəm/ *n.* the use of "Yahweh" to represent the name of God or to worship God

Yah·wist /yaáwist/, **Yah·vist** /yaáv-/ *n.* the unknown writer of the parts of the Old Testament of the Bible in which a set of four letters (**Tetragrammaton**) is used to refer to God

Yah·wis·tic /yaa wístik/, **Yah·vis·tic** /-víst-/ *adj.* relating to Yahweh, Yahwism, or the Yahwist

yak[1] /yak/ (*plural* **yaks** *or* **yak**) *n.* a large long-haired ox of the Tibetan highlands that has long curved horns and is found both wild and domesticated. Latin name: *Bos grunniens.* [Late 18thC. From Tibetan *gyag.*]

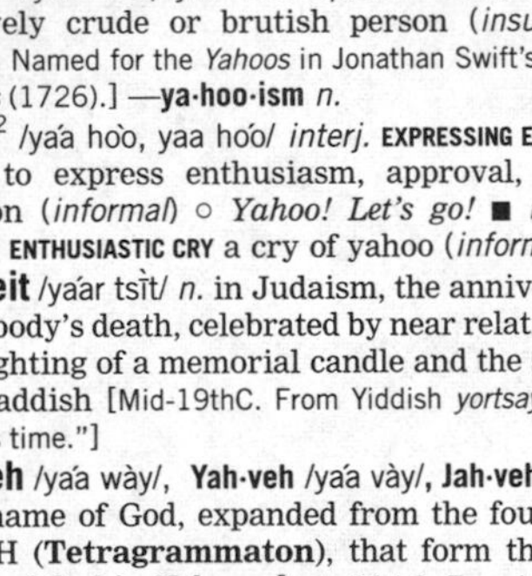

Yak

yak[2] /yak/, **yack** *vi.* (**yakked, yak·king, yaks; yacked, yack·ing, yacks**) **CHATTER CONTINOUSLY** to talk continuously, usually about unimportant matters (*informal*) ■ *n.* **CONTINUOUS CHATTER** continuous talking, usually about unimportant matters, or an instance of this (*informal*) [Mid-20thC. An imitation of the sound.]

Ya·ka·ma /yákəmə/ (*plural* **-ma** *or* **-mas**) *n.* **1.** PEOPLES **MEMBER OF NATIVE N AMERICAN PEOPLE** a member of a Native North American people of south-central Washington **2.** LANG **YAKAMA LANGUAGE** the Penutian language spoken by the Yakama. It is spoken by about 3,000 people. [Mid-19thC. From Sahaptin.]

ya·ki·to·ri /yaák táwree/ *n.* a dish of Japanese origin consisting of small pieces of grilled chicken that are basted on skewers with a sauce of soy, stock, sugar, and mirin [Mid-20thC. From Japanese, literally "grilling fowl."]

yak·ka /yákə/, **yak·ker** /yákər/, **yack·er** *n.* *ANZ* work (*informal*) [Late 19thC. Origin unknown.]

Ya·kut /yaa kŏŏt, yə-/ (*plural* **-kut** *or* **-kuts**) *n.* **1.** PEOPLES **MEMBER OF SIBERIAN ETHNIC GROUP** a member of an ethnic group that lives in northeastern Siberia, mainly in the Russian republic of Sakha **2.** LANG **YAKUT LANGUAGE** the language of the Yakut people, belonging to the Turkic branch of the Altaic family of languages. Yakut is spoken by about 300,000 people. [Mid-18thC. Via Russian from Yakut.] —**Ya·kut** *adj.*

Ya·kutsk /yə kŏŏtsk/ capital city of the autonomous region of Sakha, northeastern Russia. Population: 197,600 (1992).

ya·ku·za /yaá koo zaá, yaa kŏŏzə/ (*plural* **-za**) *n.* **1.** **JAPANESE CRIME SYNDICATE** a Japanese criminal organization involved in illegal activities such as drug-dealing, extortion, and prostitution **2.** **YAKUZA MEMBER** a member the yakuza [Mid-20thC. From Japanese "gambler," formed from *ya* "eight" + *ku* "nine" + *-za* "three," the worst hand in a card game.]

Yale /yayl/, **Elihu** (1649–1721) U.S. merchant and philanthropist. He grew wealthy as an East India Company agent in India (1670–99), and made large gifts to the Collegiate School in Connecticut, which was named Yale College in his honor (1718).

Yale lock *tdmk.* a trademark for a type of padlock operated with a key

y'all *contr.* *Southern U.S.* = **you all** (*informal*)

Yal·lourn /yál awrn/ town in southern Victoria, Australia. It is a major coal-mining center. Population: 15,512 (1996).

Yal·ta /yáltə, yóltə/ town and resort in Crimea Region, southern Ukraine. Situated on the Black Sea, it was the site of a conference in 1945 between Joseph Stalin, Franklin Roosevelt, and Winston Churchill that determined the areas of Germany that each of the great powers would administer after World War II. Population: 89,000 (1991).

Ya·lu /yaá lŏŏ/ river in East Asia, forming most of the boundary between North Korea and China. Length: 490 mi./790 km.

yam /yam/ *n.* **1.** = **sweet potato, sweet potato** *n.* 2 **2.** **ROOT VEGETABLE** a vegetable that resembles a large white floury potato and is the root of a tropical vine **3.** **TROPICAL VINE** a tropical vine that produces yams. Genus: *Dioscorea.* [Late 16thC. Via Portuguese *inhame*

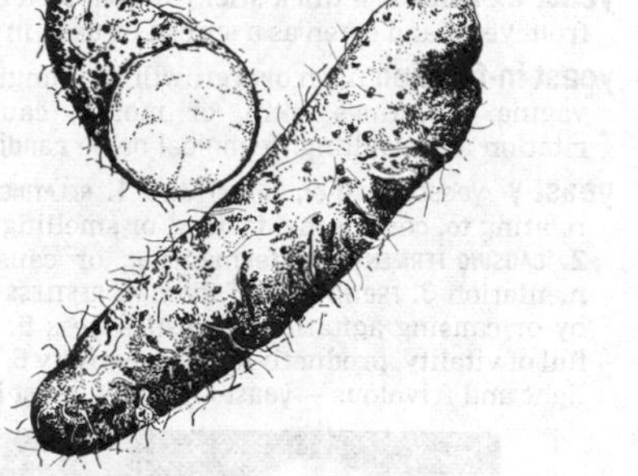

Yam

or Spanish *iñame*, of West African origin (related to Fulani *nyami* "to eat").]

WORD KEY: REGIONAL NOTE

In the sense "sweet potato," **yam** was formerly largely restricted to the South, where its use was universal. Now, through commercial usage, the term recurs virtually everywhere in the United States.

ya·men /yaámən/ *n.* in the Chinese Empire, the home or office of a mandarin or other public official [Early 19thC. From Chinese *yámen*, from *yá* "office" + *mén* "gate."]

yam·mer /yámmər/ *vi.* **(-mered, -mer·ing, -mers)** (*informal*) **1.** TALK LOUDLY AND AT LENGTH to talk, chat, or chatter noisily and continuously **2.** WHINE to whine or complain persistently about something **3.** HOWL OR WAIL to make repeated howling sounds of pain or distress ■ *n.* (*informal*) **1.** NOISY CHATTERING noisy continuous talk, chat, or chattering **2.** COMPLAINT a whining sound or persistent complaint [15thC. Origin uncertain: probably from Middle Dutch *jammeren* "to mourn."] —**yam·mer·er** *n.*

Ya·mous·sou·kro /yàmmoō sóokrō/ capital city of Côte d'Ivoire, in the central part of the country. Population: 100,000 (1988).

Yan'an /yàn án/ town in northern Shaanxi Province, northeastern China. The terminus of the Long March, Yan'an was used by communist forces as a base between 1936 and 1949. Population: 113,277 (1990).

yan·cha /yánchə/ *n. Hong Kong* the social practice of going to a teahouse (*dated*)

yang /yang/, **Yang** *n.* the principle of light, heat, motivation and masculinity in Chinese philosophy that is the counterpart of yin. The dual, opposite, and complementary principles of yin and yang are thought to exist in varying proportions in all things. ◊ **yin** [Late 17thC. From Chinese *yáng* "sun, positive."]

Yan·gon /yang gón/ capital city of Myanmar, in the south of the country. Population: 2,513,023 (1983). Former name **Rangoon** (until 1989)

Yang·tze /yáng see, yáng ts-/, **Yang·zi** the longest river in China. It rises in the Kunlun Mountains, and flows southward and then eastward to enter the East China Sea directly north of Shanghai. Length: 3,400 mi./5,470 km.

yank /yangk/ *v.* **(yanked, yank·ing, yanks) 1.** *vti.* PULL SHARPLY to pull or jerk somebody or something suddenly and sharply **2.** *vt.* REMOVE SOMEBODY OR SOMETHING SWIFTLY to remove somebody or something suddenly and quickly ■ *n.* SHARP PULL a sudden sharp pull or jerk [Early 19thC. Origin unknown.]

WORD KEY: SYNONYMS

See Synonyms at ***pull***.

Yank /yangk/ *n.* PEOPLES a Yankee (*informal; offensive in some contexts*) [Late18thC. Shortening of YANKEE.]

Yan·kee /yángkee/ *n.* **1.** PEOPLES SOMEBODY FROM UNITED STATES somebody who is from the United States (*offensive in some contexts*) **2.** PEOPLES SOMEBODY FROM A NORTHERN STATE somebody born or living in a northern state of the United States, especially a soldier fighting on the side of the Union during the Civil War (*offensive in some contexts*) **3.** PEOPLES SOMEBODY FROM NEW ENGLAND somebody who was born or raised in one of the states of New England (*offensive in some contexts*) **4.** COMMUNICATION CODE WORD FOR LETTER "Y" a code word for the letter "Y," used in international radio communications [Mid-18thC. Origin uncertain: perhaps from Dutch *Janke* "Johnny."] —**Yan·kee·dom** *n.*

Yan·kee Doo·dle *n.* **1.** POPULAR AMERICAN SONG a song first popular during the American Revolutionary War **2.** PEOPLES YANKEE a Yankee (*informal; offensive in some contexts*) [In the meaning of "Yankee," from the idea that the song is typically national]

Yan·kee·ism /yángkee ìzzəm/ *n.* an expression or other characteristic considered typical of Yankees

Yank·ton /yángktən/ city in southeastern South Dakota, southwest of Sioux Falls and northwest of Sioux City, Iowa. Population: 13,884 (1996).

yan·qui /yaángkee/ (*plural* **-quis**) *n.* an offensive term used by some members of Spanish-speaking American communities to refer disparagingly to an English-speaking U.S. citizen [Early 20thC. Spanish phonetic spelling of YANKEE.]

Ya·oun·dé /yaa oōnd ay/ capital city of Cameroon, in the southwestern part of the country. Population: 800,000 (1992).

yap /yap/ *vi.* **(yapped, yap·ping, yaps) 1.** CHATTER ANNOYINGLY to talk continuously about trivial things, often in a loud or high-pitched voice (*informal*) **2.** MAKE HIGH BARKING SOUND to make a short loud high-pitched barking noise ■ *n.* **1.** MOUTH somebody's mouth (*slang*) **2.** SHORT HIGH-PITCHED BARK a short, loud, high-pitched bark **3.** TRIVIAL CONVERSATION a trivial or meaningless conversation (*informal*) **4.** OFFENSIVE TERM an offensive term that deliberately insults somebody regarded as vulgar and unintelligent (*slang insult*) [Early 19thC. An imitation of a dog's bark.] —**yap·per** *n.* —**yap·py** *adj.*

Yap /yap/ group of islands, islets, and atolls in the western Pacific Ocean. Part of the Caroline Islands, the group comprises one of the states of Micronesia. Population: 10,886 (1991). Area: 46 sq. mi./119 sq. km.

ya·pok /yə pók/ (*plural* **-poks** *or* **-pok**) *n.* an amphibious nocturnal opossum of tropical Central and South America that has dense fur, webbed hind feet, a long tail, and feeds on aquatic organisms such as shrimp. Latin name: ***Chironectes minimus.*** [Early 19thC. Named for the river *Oyapok*, which forms the border between northern Brazil and French Guiana.]

ya·pon *n.* = **yaupon**

Ya·qui /yaákee/ (*plural* **-qui** *or* **-quis**) *n.* **1.** PEOPLES MEMBER OF NATIVE N AMERICAN PEOPLE a member of a Native North American people of Arizona and Sonora, Mexico **2.** LANG YAQUI LANGUAGE the Uto-Aztecan language of the Yaqui people. Yaqui is spoken by about 20,000 people. [Early 19thC. Via Spanish from Yaqui *Hiaki*.] —**Ya·qui** *adj.*

yar·bor·ough /yaárbərō, -bərə/, **Yar·bor·ough** *n.* a hand in bridge or whist consisting of 13 cards each of which has a value lower than ten [Late 19thC. Named for Charles Anderson Worsley (1809–97), Second Earl of *Yarborough*, who allegedly bet 1000 to 1 against the occurrence of such a hand.]

yard[1] /yaard/ *n.* **1.** IMPERIAL UNIT OF LENGTH a unit of length equal to 3 ft./0.9144 m **2.** = **yardstick** *n.* 2 **3.** SPAR SUPPORTING SAIL a long spar that supports the head of a square sail, lugsail, or lateen **4.** ONE HUNDRED DOLLARS one hundred dollars (*slang*) [Old English *gerd* "rod"] ◇ **the whole nine yards** the totality or full extent of something (*informal*)

yard[2] /yaard/ *n.* **1.** LAND AROUND A HOUSE the area of land immediately surrounding a house, often covered with grass or landscaping **2.** ENCLOSED PAVED PIECE OF LAND an area of ground that is usually paved and enclosed, and is next to or surrounded by a building or buildings **3.** AREA USED FOR BUSINESS OR ACTIVITY an area of ground, sometimes with associated buildings, used for a particular purpose (*often used in combination*) ○ *a lumber yard* **4.** RAILROAD STORAGE AREA an area of railroad tracks used for storing cars or locomotives and for making up trains **5.** LIVESTOCK ENCLOSURE an enclosed area of land for livestock **6.** WINTER GRAZING AREA an area of land where deer, moose, or other animals graze in winter ■ *vt.* **(yard·ed, yard·ing, yards)** KEEP LIVESTOCK IN A YARD to put or keep livestock in a yard [Old English *geard* "enclosure, garden"]

yard·age[1] /yaárdij/ *n.* measurement in yards, or an amount measured in yards

yard·age[2] /yaárdij/ *n.* **1.** USE OF A LIVESTOCK YARD use of a livestock yard for storing animals before transporting them **2.** FEE CHARGED FOR USING A YARD a fee charged for storing livestock in a yard

yard·arm /yaárd aàrm/ *n.* an end of the yard used to support a sail

yard·bird /yaárd bùrd/ *n.* **1.** SOLDIER ASSIGNED MENIAL DUTIES a soldier who is assigned menial tasks or is confined to a limited area, usually as a punishment (*informal*) **2.** CONVICT a convict or prisoner (*dated informal*) **3.** INEPT RECRUIT an untrained and inept military recruit (*dated informal*) [Mid-19thC. Modeled on JAILBIRD.]

yard broom *n. Southern U.S.* a push broom that will stand up to outdoor use

WORD KEY: REGIONAL NOTE

The term ***yard broom*** is mainly Southern. The Coastal Southern term is *stick broom*; the Northern and Western term is *corn broom*.

yard goods *npl.* = **piece goods**

yard grass *n.* a coarse annual grass with ground-hugging leaves and grouped spikes that grows widely as a weed. Latin name: ***Eleusine indica.***

Yard·ie /yaárdee/ *n.* a member of a criminal syndicate that originated in Jamaica

yard-long bean *n.* the long thin edible pod of the cowpea of southern Asia, which reaches up to a yard in length. Latin name: ***Vigna unguiculata sesquipedalis.***

yard·man /yaárdmən/ (*plural* **-men** /-mən/) *n.* **1.** SOMEBODY EMPLOYED IN A YARD somebody who works in a yard, especially a railroad yard or a lumberyard **2.** GARDENER somebody hired to care for a lawn or yard

yard·mas·ter /yaárd màstər/ *n.* somebody in charge of a railroad yard

yard of ale *n.* **1.** YARD-LONG GLASS a long narrow drinking glass, sometimes shaped like a horn, approximately one yard long and holding two to three pints of beer **2.** CONTENTS OF A YARD OF ALE the contents of a yard of ale

yard sale *n.* a sale at which personal possessions and household items are sold, usually held in the yard of somebody's house

yard·stick /yaárd stìk/ *n.* **1.** YARD-LONG MEASURING STICK a measuring stick one yard long, usually marked in feet and inches **2.** STANDARD OF COMPARISON a standard used to judge the quality, value, or success of something

yard work *n.* tending a yard as a profession, chore, or hobby

yare /yair/ *adj.* **1.** EASY TO HANDLE used to describe a ship that is easy to handle and responsive **2.** READY ready or prepared (*archaic*) **3.** QUICK quick or lively (*archaic*) ■ *adv.* QUICKLY quickly or nimbly (*archaic*) [Old English *gearo* "ready"] —**yare·ly** *adv.*

yar·mul·ke /yaármәlkə, yaáməlkə/, **yar·mel·ke, yar·mul·ka, yar·mul·kah** *n.* a small round cap worn by Jewish men and boys. Orthodox Jews wear the yarmulke at all times, while Conservative Jews wear it for prayer or on ceremonial occasions only. [Mid-20thC. Via Yiddish from Polish *jarmułka*, of uncertain origin: probably from, ultimately, Turkish *yağmur* "rain."]

yarn /yaarn/ *n.* **1.** THREAD a continuous twisted strand of wool, cotton, or synthetic fibers, usually used for knitting or weaving **2.** STRAND OF GLASS OR METAL a continuous strand of a material such as glass or metal **3.** LONG STORY a long or involved tale, especially one that relates exciting or incredible events (*informal*) ■ *vi.* **(yarned, yarn·ing, yarns)** TELL A YARN to relate a long tale full of incredible events (*informal*) [Old English *gearn*. Ultimately from an Indo-European base meaning "entrail" that is also the ancestor of English *hernia* and *cord*.]

yarn-dyed *adj.* dyed in the form of yarn before being woven or knitted

Ya·ro·slavl /yaáro slaávəl/ city and capital of Yaroslavl Oblast, central European Russia. It is situated on the Volga River. Population: 636,000 (1990).

Yar·ra /yárrə/ river in southern Victoria, Australia. Length: 155 mi./250 km.

yar·row /yá rō/ (*plural* **-rows** *or* **-row**) *n.* a European and Asian composite plant with leaves resembling ferns and broad flat clusters of flower heads. Latin name: ***Achillea millefolium.*** [Old English *gearwe*]

yash·mak /yaash maák, yásh màk/, **yash·mac** *n.* a veil worn by some Muslim women in public [Mid-19thC. From Turkish *yaşmak*.]

yat·a·ghan /yáttə gàn, -gən/, **yat·a·gan, at·a·ghan** /áttə gàn, -gən/ *n.* a Turkish sword with no handle guard and a single-edged blade that curves inward then outward [Early 19thC. From Turkish *yatağan*.]

ya·tra /yáttrə/ *n.* a holy pilgrimage for Hindus [Early 19thC. From Sanskrit *yātrā*, which was formed from *yā* "to undertake a trip."]

yaup *vi., n.* = yawp

yau·pon /yáw pòn/ (*plural* **-pons** *or* **-pon**), **ya·pon** (*plural* **-pons** *or* **-pon**) *n.* an evergreen holly of the southeastern United States that has red fruit and smooth bitter leaves that are made into a tea for their emetic and purgative properties. Latin name: *Ilex vomitoria*. [Early 18thC. From Catawba *yápa*, literally "tree leaf."]

yau·ti·a /yow tée ə/ (*plural* **-as** *or* **-a**) *n.* **1.** PLANT YIELDING EDIBLE TUBERS a West Indian plant of the arum family cultivated for its edible tuber. Genus: *Xanthosoma*. **2.** EDIBLE TUBER the brown starchy tuber of the yautia plant, cooked and eaten as a vegetable [Early 20thC. Via Spanish from Taino.]

yaw /yaw/ *vti.* (**yawed, yaw·ing, yaws**) **1.** TURN AROUND A VERTICAL AXIS to turn around the vertical axis, or to make an aircraft turn in this way. ◊ **pitch, roll 2.** GO OR PUT OFF COURSE to deviate from a straight course, or to make a boat or ship do this **3.** ZIGZAG to move unsteadily on a zigzag course, or to make somebody or something advance in this way ■ *n.* DEVIATION FROM COURSE the deviation of a ship from a straight course [Mid-16thC. Origin unknown.]

yawl /yawl/ *n.* **1.** SAILING VESSEL a sailing vessel rigged fore-and-aft with a large mainmast and a smaller mizzenmast toward the stern **2.** SHIP'S ROWING BOAT a small boat kept on a ship, rowed by four or six people [Mid-17thC. From Dutch *jol*, of unknown origin.]

yawn /yawn/ *v.* (**yawned, yawn·ing, yawns**) **1.** *vi.* OPEN MOUTH WIDE to open the mouth wide and take a long deep breath, usually involuntarily, because of tiredness or boredom **2.** *vt.* SAY SOMETHING WHILE YAWNING to say something while yawning, or in a tired or bored voice **3.** *vi.* BE WIDE OPEN to open wide or be wide open, especially in a threatening or alarming manner ■ *n.* **1.** ACT OF YAWNING an involuntary response to tiredness or boredom in which the mouth is opened wide and a long deep breath is taken **2.** SOMEBODY OR SOMETHING BORING a boring person, thing, or event (*informal*) [Old English *ginian*] —**yawn·ing** *adj.* —**yawn·ing·ly** *adv.*

yawn·er /yáwnər/ *n.* **1.** = yawn *n.* 2 (*informal*) **2.** SOMEBODY YAWNING somebody who yawns

yawp /yawp/, **yaup** *vi.* (**yawped, yawp·ing, yawps; yauped, yaup·ing, yaups**) (*informal*) **1.** TALK COARSELY to talk or complain loudly, coarsely, and sometimes meaningless **2.** UTTER A YELP to utter a sharp loud yelp ■ *n.* (*informal*) **1.** YELP a sharp, loud yelp **2.** COARSE TALK loud, coarse, and sometimes meaningless talk [14thC. Origin uncertain: perhaps related to YELP.] —**yawp·er** *n.*

yaws /yawz/ *n.* an infectious tropical disease marked initially by red skin eruptions and later by joint pains. It mainly affects children and is caused by the bacterium *Treponema pertenue*. (*takes a singular or plural verb*) [Late 17thC. From Carib *yaya*.]

y-ax·is *n.* **1.** VERTICAL AXIS the vertical axis in a two-dimensional coordinate system such as a graph **2.** AXIS IN THREE-DIMENSIONAL COORDINATE SYSTEM one of the axes in the three-dimensional Cartesian coordinate system, conventionally the vertical one

Yb *symbol.* ytterbium

YB *abbr.* yearbook

Y chro·mo·some, Y-chro·mo·some *n.* the sex chromosome that determines the male sex in humans and other mammals. The body cells of males each possess one Y chromosome paired with one X chromosome. ◊ **X chromosome**

y·clept /i klépt/ *adj.* called by the name of (*archaic or humorous*) [Old English *geclipod*, past participle of *geclipian* "to call"]

yd. *abbr.* MEASURE yard

yea /yay/ *adv., n.* YES yes (*archaic*) ■ *adv.* INDEED indeed (*archaic*) ○ *"Yea, though I walk through the valley of the shadow of death, I will fear no evil" (Psalm 23, King James Bible)* [Old English *gēa* "yes"]

yeah /ye ə, yaa/ *interj.* yes (*informal*) [Early 20thC. Variant of YEA.]

yean /yeen/ (**yeaned, yean·ing, yeans**) *vti.* to give birth to a young sheep or goat (*archaic*) [14thC. From an assumed Old English *geēanian* "to give birth to young."]

yean·ling /yéenling/ *n.* a young sheep or goat (*archaic*)

year /yeer/ *n.* **1.** TWELVE-MONTH PERIOD FROM JANUARY 1 a period of 365 days (or 366 in a leap year), measured from January 1 to December 31 **2.** TWELVE-MONTH PERIOD FROM ANY DATE a period of 365 or 366 days, measured exactly or approximately from any date ○ *The company's financial year ends on July 31.* **3.** SOLAR YEAR the time it takes the Earth to orbit the Sun, approximately 365.25 days **4.** TIME OF PLANET'S ORBIT AROUND SUN the time taken for a planet to orbit once around the Sun **5.** PERIOD OF PARTICULAR ACTIVITY the time occupied by a particular activity within a twelve-month period ○ *academic year* **6.** AGE BAND IN SCHOOL OR COLLEGE a group of students, usually of approximately the same age, who start school or college at the same time and study together in one or more classes ■ **years** *npl.* **1.** LONG TIME a very long time (*informal*) ○ *It's years since I last saw him.* ○ *We haven't been back for years.* **2.** AGE age, especially advanced age ○ *a man of his years* **3.** TIME IN GENERAL time in the past, present, or future ○ *in years to come* **4.** PARTICULAR PERIOD OF TIME a particular period of time, usually in the past ○ *her early years* [Old English *gēar*]

year·book /yéer bòok/ *n.* **1.** BOOK COMMEMORATING A SCHOOL YEAR a book compiled by members of a graduating class of a high school or college, commemorating their school year and usually including photographs of the students **2.** ANNUAL RECORD OF EVENTS a book published annually containing details of events in the previous year, usually within a particular organization or field of interest

year-end *n.* END OF A YEAR the end of a financial year or calendar year ■ *adj.* DONE AT THE YEAR-END occurring or done at the end of a financial year or calendar year

year·ling /yéerling/ *n.* **1.** YOUNG ANIMAL an animal, e.g., a calf or deer, between one and two years of age **2.** YEAR-OLD RACEHORSE a racehorse that is one year old, as reckoned from January 1 in the year after it was born

year·long /yéer láwng, yéer làwng/ *adj.* lasting for a year or continuing throughout a year

yearly /yéerlee/ *adj.* **1.** ANNUAL happening, done, appearing, or published once a year or every year **2.** RELATING TO ONE YEAR relating to or lasting for a period of twelve months ■ *adv.* **1.** ONCE A YEAR once every year **2.** PER YEAR during each year ■ *n.* (*plural* **year·lies**) ANNUAL EVENT OR ISSUE something that happens or appears once a year, especially an annual publication [Old English *gēarlīc*]

yearn /yurn/ (**yearned, yearn·ing, yearns**) *vi.* **1.** LONG FOR to want somebody or something very much, often with a feeling of sadness because of the difficulty or impossibility of fulfilling the desire **2.** FEEL AFFECTION to feel affection, tenderness, or compassion [Old English *giernan*. Ultimately from an Indo-European base meaning "to want" which is also the ancestor of English *greedy* and *charisma*.] —**yearn·er** *n.*

WORD KEY: SYNONYMS

See Synonyms at ***want***.

yearn·ing /yúrning/ *n.* a very strong desire, often tinged with sadness [Old English *gierninge*] —**yearn·ing·ly** *adv.*

year of grace, year of our Lord *n.* a particular year of the Christian era

year-round *adj.* LASTING THROUGHOUT THE YEAR existing, continuing, or operating throughout the year ■ *adv.* THROUGHOUT THE YEAR throughout the year —**year-round·er** *n.*

yea-say·er *n.* **1.** SOMEBODY OPTIMISTIC somebody who is always confident and optimistic **2.** SOMEBODY AGREEING SUBMISSIVELY somebody who always agrees submissively with a superior

yeast /yeest/ *n.* **1.** PREPARATION FOR BAKING a commercial preparation used in brewing, baking, and as a source of vitamins and protein **2.** SMALL SINGLE-CELLED FUNGUS a small single-celled fungus that ferments sugars and other carbohydrates, and reproduces by budding. It is the source of yeast. Genus: *Saccharomyces*. **3.** FROTH the yellowish froth that forms on the surface of a fermenting liquid such as beer, contains yeast cells and carbon dioxide, and promotes fermentation **4.** FOAM any foam or froth, e.g., on sea waves **5.** CAUSE OF FERMENT OR ACTIVITY somebody or something that causes ferment, activity, or unrest ■ *vi.* (**yeast·ed, yeast·ing, yeasts**) FERMENT to ferment, froth, or foam [Old English *gist*]

yeast ex·tract *n.* a thick sticky brown food obtained from yeast and eaten as a spread or used in cooking

yeast in·fec·tion *n.* an overgrowth of a fungus in the vagina, intestines, skin, or mouth, causing irritation and swelling. Technical name **candidiasis**

yeast·y /yéestee/ (**-i·er, -i·est**) *adj.* **1.** RELATING TO YEAST relating to, containing, tasting, or smelling of yeast **2.** CAUSING FERMENTATION fermenting, or causing fermentation **3.** FROTHY full of foam **4.** RESTLESS marked by or causing agitation or restlessness **5.** ENERGETIC full of vitality, productivity, or creativity **6.** FRIVOLOUS light and frivolous —**yeast·i·ly** *adv.* —**yeast·i·ness** *n.*

William Butler Yeats

Yeats /yayts/, **William Butler** (1865–1939) Irish poet and dramatist. A leader of the Irish Renaissance, he is considered to be one of the greatest poets of the 20th century. His poetry incorporates a complex personal mythology. He wrote plays for Dublin's Abbey Theatre, which he cofounded. He won the Nobel Prize in literature (1923).

yech /yek, yekh/, **yecch** *interj.* used to express disgust (*informal*) [Mid-20thC. A natural exclamation.]

yegg /yeg/ *n.* a burglar, especially a safecracker (*slang*) [Early 20thC. Origin unknown.]

Ye·ka·ter·in·burg /yə kàttərin bùrg/ industrial city in central Russia, on the Iset River, on the eastern slopes of the Ural Mountains. Population: 1,280,000 (1995).

yell /yel/ *vti.* (**yelled, yell·ing, yells**) SHOUT LOUDLY to shout or scream something, or to speak in a very loud voice ■ *n.* **1.** LOUD CRY a loud shout, scream, or cry **2.** CHEER OF SUPPORT a rhythmic word or phrase chanted together by people to give support or encouragement [Old English *giellan*. Ultimately from an Indo-European base meaning "to call" which is also the ancestor of English *nightingale*.] —**yell·er** *n.*

Yell /yel/ the second largest of the Shetland Islands of Scotland. Population: 1,075 (1991). Area: 81 sq. mi./210 sq. km.

yel·low /yéllō/ *adj.* **1.** OF THE COLOR OF BUTTER having or being near the color of butter or ripe lemons **2.** OFFENSIVE TERM an offensive term referring to people from or born in Asia (*offensive*) **3.** COWARDLY cowardly or afraid (*informal insult*) **4.** SENSATIONALIST using scandalous or sensational material, often greatly exaggerating or distorting the truth. ◆ **yellow journalism** ■ *n.* **1.** YELLOW COLOR a color such as that of butter or ripe lemons that lies between orange and green on the visible spectrum and is one of the three primary colors of pigment. Yellow is also one of the three primary colors used in printing and photographic processing. **2.** YELLOW PIGMENT a yellow pigment or dye **3.** YELLOW FABRIC yellow clothing or fabric ○ *dressed in yellow* **4.** YELLOW OBJECT a yellow object or substance **5.** EGG YOLK the yolk of an egg ■ **yel·lows** *npl.* PLANT DISEASE a plant disease marked by a yellowing of foliage that may be caused by a mineral deficiency, virus, or some other infectious agent ■ *vti.* (**-lowed, -low·ing, -lows**) BECOME YELLOW to become or make something yellow or yellowish, especially as a result of age [Old English *geolu*. Ultimately from an Indo-European base meaning "to shine" which is also the ancestor of English *gleam* and *gold*.] —**yel·low·ish** *adj.* —**yel·low·ish·ness** *n.* —**yel·low·ly** *adv.* —**yel·low·ness** *n.* —**yel·low·y** *adj.*

WORD KEY: SYNONYMS

See Synonyms at ***cowardly***.

yel·low-bel·lied *adj.* **1.** COWARDLY cowardly or afraid (*informal insult*) **2.** YELLOW UNDERNEATH with a yellow underside

yel·low-bel·lied sap·suck·er *n.* a small North American woodpecker that feeds on sap and insects. The male has a yellowish belly and bright red crown and throat. Latin name: *Sphyrapicus varius.*

yel·low·bel·ly /yéllō bèllee/ *n.* a cowardly person (*informal insult*)

yel·low bile *n.* = **choler** (*archaic*)

yel·low birch *n.* **1. TREE WITH YELLOWISH BARK** a North American birch with yellowish peeling bark. Latin name: *Betula alleghaniensis.* **2. YELLOW BIRCH WOOD** the hard, light-reddish-colored wood of the yellow birch, used in building and furniture making

yel·low·bird /yéllō bùrd/ *n.* a bird with yellow plumage, e.g., the goldfinch or yellow warbler

yel·low brain fun·gus *n.* a type of jelly fungus

yel·low-breast·ed chat *n.* a common North American songbird with a bright yellow breast and white marks over the eyes. Latin name: *Icteria virens.*

yel·low·cake /yéllō kàyk/ *n.* the concentrated semi-refined oxide of uranium ore

yel·low card *n.* in soccer, a card shown by the referee to a player guilty of serious or persistent foul play as an indication that the player has been cautioned. ◊ **red card**

yel·low cress *n.* a cress with yellow flowers that is related to watercress, but is not limited to growing at water margins

yel·low-dog *adj.* so cowardly and mean as to be beneath contempt (*insult*)

yel·low-dog con·tract *n.* an employment contract in which the employee agrees not to join a labor union. Such contracts are no longer legal.

yel·low fe·ver *n.* an infectious, often fatal viral disease of warm climates, transmitted by mosquitoes and marked by high fever, hemorrhaging, vomiting of blood, liver damage, and jaundice

yel·low·fin tu·na /yéllō fin-/, **yel·low·fin** (*plural* **-fins** *or* **-fin**) *n.* a small, widely distributed tuna inhabiting warm seas. It has yellowish fins and is an important food fish. Latin name: *Thunnus albacares.*

yel·low-green al·ga *n.* an alga that lives in soil and other moist environments and contains brown and bright yellow pigments that mask the chlorophyll. Division: *Chrysophyta.*

yel·low·ham·mer /yéllō hàmmər/ *n.* **1. EUROPEAN SONGBIRD** a stout-billed European songbird of the bunting family. The male has a bright yellow head, neck, and breast. Latin name: *Emberiza citrinella.* **2.** = **yellow-shafted flicker** [Mid-16thC. By folk etymology from earlier *yelambre*, from *yelwe* "yellow" + *-amber*, of uncertain origin: perhaps from Old English *amore*, a type of bird.]

yel·low jack *n.* **1. YELLOW FEVER** yellow fever (*archaic*) **2. YELLOWISH ATLANTIC FOOD FISH** a large yellowish food fish that lives off the Atlantic coast of North, South, and Central America. Latin name: *Caranx bartholomaei.*

yel·low jack·et *n.* a social wasp with black-and-yellow bands on its body. It nests in the ground or in the hollows of trees, and can sting repeatedly. Family: Vespidae.

yel·low jer·sey *n.* in the Tour de France, the jersey awarded to the cyclist with the fastest elapsed time at a completed stage of the race

yel·low jes·sa·mine /yèllō jéssəmin/, **yel·low jas·mine** *n.* = **Carolina jasmine**

yel·low jour·nal·ism *n.* a style of journalism that makes unscrupulous use of scandalous, lurid, or sensationalized stories to attract readers [Late 19thC. A reference to the yellow ink of the *Yellow Kid* cartoons appearing in the sensationalistic *New York World*.]

Yel·low·knife /yéllō nīf/ capital city of the Northwest Territories, Canada. It is situated on the northern shore of the Great Slave Lake. Population: 15,179 (1991).

yel·low·legs /yéllō lègz/ (*plural* **-legs**) *n.* either of two large American shorebirds, the greater yellowlegs or the lesser yellowlegs, of the sandpiper family that have bright yellow legs, mottled brown plumage, and white underparts. Genus: *Tringa.*

yel·low o·cher *n.* a yellow-brown inorganic pigment that contains iron and is used in artist's colors

Yel·low Pag·es *tdmk.* a trademark for a telephone directory printed on yellow paper and containing names, addresses, and telephone numbers of businesses and other organizations listed according to the products or services offered

yel·low perch *n.* a bony North American freshwater fish that has a yellow body with greenish brown vertical bars and orange fins, and is valued as a food and sport fish. Latin name: *Perca flavescens.*

yel·low per·il, **Yel·low Per·il** *n.* a highly offensive term reffering to the perceived threat to Western nations posed by the nations of eastern Asia, especially China (*dated offensive*)

yel·low pine *n.* **1. N AMERICAN PINE** a North American pine tree, e.g., the longleaf pine, shortleaf pine, or the Ponderosa pine **2. YELLOW PINE WOOD** the strong yellowish wood of various kinds of pine tree, especially the North American shortleaf and longleaf pines

yel·low pop·lar *n.* **1.** = **tulip tree 2.** = **tulipwood**

yel·low press *n.* collectively, the newspapers that make unscrupulous use of scandalous, lurid, or sensationalized stories to attract readers. ◆ **yellow journalism**

yel·low rain *n.* a fungal toxin that occurs as a form of precipitation in Southeast Asia. It has been attributed by different sections of the scientific community to residue from chemical warfare or to the excrement of wild honeybees.

yel·low rat·tle *n.* a plant found in both Europe and North America that has yellow flowers whose seeds rattle in their pouches when they are shaken. Latin name: *Rhinanthus minor.*

Yel·low Ri·ver /yèllō-/ = **Huang He**

Yel·low Sea arm of the Pacific Ocean bordered on the west and north by China and on the east by the Korean Peninsula. It merges with the East China Sea to the south.

yel·low-shaft·ed flick·er *n.* a large woodpecker of eastern North America that has shafts of yellow on the underside of its wings and tail and a red spot on its nape. Latin name: *Colaptes auratus.*

yel·low spot *n.* OPHTHALMOL = **macula**

Yel·low·stone /yéllō stōn/ river in the western United States, rising in northwestern Wyoming, and flowing into the Missouri River in North Dakota. Length: 692 mi./1,110 km.

Yel·low·stone Na·tion·al Park /yèllōstōn–/ the world's first national park, established in 1872 in parts of Wyoming, Montana, and Idaho. It is noted for its geysers, hot springs, and the Yellowstone Falls. Area: 3,468 sq. mi./8,983 sq. km.

yel·low streak *n.* a tendency to be cowardly (*insult*)

yel·low·tail /yéllō tàyl/ (*plural* **-tail** *or* **-tails**) *n.* **1. MARINE FISH WITH YELLOWISH TAIL** a marine game fish with a yellowish tail, found in the coastal waters of California and Mexico. Latin name: *Seriola lalandei.* **2. AUSTRALIAN BAIT FISH** a small greenish fish with silver underparts and a yellow tail and fins found in southern Australian and New Zealand waters and commonly used as bait. Latin name: *Trachurus novaezelandiae.*

yel·low·throat /yéllō thrōt/ *n.* a small American warbler that nests in dense undergrowth and has a yellow breast and throat, a black mask, and a brownish back. Latin name: *Geothylpis trichas.*

yel·low-throat·ed war·bler *n.* a small songbird of the warbler family that has a bright yellow throat and inhabits the eastern United States. Latin name: *Dendroica dominica.*

yel·low war·bler *n.* a common North American warbler that has bright yellow plumage with brown streaks along its sides. Latin name: *Dendroica petechia.*

yel·low·wood /yéllō wòŏd/ (*plural* **-woods** *or* **-wood**) *n.* **1. U.S. TREE WITH YELLOW WOOD** a tree of the southern United States that has yellow wood, yields a yellow dye, and bears drooping clusters of showy white flowers. Latin name: *Cladastris lutea.* **2. WOOD OF YELLOWWOOD TREE** the yellow-colored wood of the yellowwood tree

yelp /yelp/ *v.* (**yelped, yelp·ing, yelps**) **1.** *vi.* **BARK OR CRY SHARPLY** to utter a short sharp high-pitched bark or cry, usually of pain **2.** *vt.* **UTTER SOMETHING WITH YELPING SOUND** to say something in a sharp high-pitched voice ■ *n.* **SHORT BARK OR CRY** a short high-pitched bark or cry [Old English *gelpan* "to boast." Ultimately from an Indo-European base meaning "to call" which is also the ancestor of English *yell*.] —**yelp·er** *n.*

Yel·tsin /yéltsin/, **Boris** (*b.* 1931) Russian statesman. He was the first democratically elected Russian president (1991), and was instrumental in planning the country's transition from communism to a market economy. Full name **Boris Nikolayevich Yeltsin**

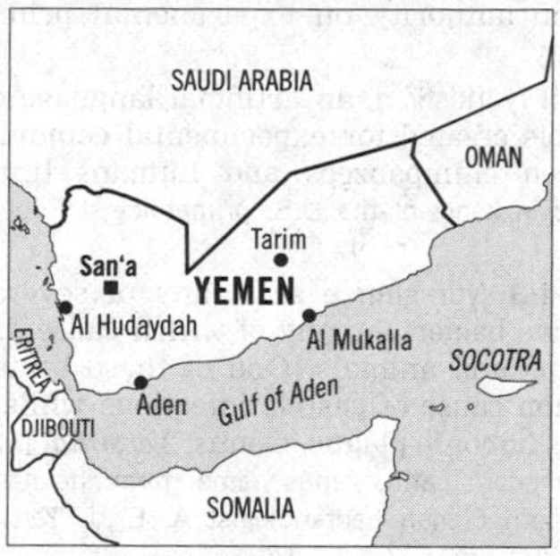

Yemen

Ye·men /yémmən, yáy-/ country on the Arabian peninsula, in southwestern Asia, on the Red Sea. The country was created in 1990 by the unification of the Yemen Arab Republic, or North Yemen, and the People's Democratic Republic of Yemen, or South Yemen. Language: Arabic. Currency: Yemeni riyal. Capital: San'a. Population: 16,600,000 (1996). Area: 207,285 sq. mi./536,869 sq. km. Official name **Republic of Yemen** —**Yem·e·ni** *n., adj.*

yen[1] /yen/ (*plural* **yen**) *n.* **1. UNIT OF JAPANESE CURRENCY** a unit of currency in Japan, worth 100 sen. See table at **currency 2. BILL WORTH A YEN** a bill worth a yen [Late 19thC. Via Japanese *en* from Chinese *yuán*, literally "round."]

yen[2] /yen/ *n.* **YEARNING** a strong yearning for something ■ *vi.* (**yenned, yen·ning, yens**) **HAVE YEARNING** to have a strong yearning for something [Early 20thC. Origin uncertain: probably from Chinese (Cantonese) *yăn*.]

Ye·ni·sey /yénnə sày/ river in central Siberian Russia. It is formed in the Sayan Mountains in southern Siberia by the union of the Greater Yenisey and the Little Yenisey, and flows northward into the Kara Sea. Length: 2,540 mi./4.090 km.

yen·ta /yéntə/, **yen·te** *n.* an offensive term that deliberately insults a woman's temperament or behavior (*slang insult*) [Mid-20thC. Formed from Yiddish *yente*, from the feminine name *Yente*, from, ultimately, Latin *gentilis* "of the same family."]

yeo. *abbr.* NAVY yeoman

yeo·man /yṓmən/ *n.* (*plural* **-men** /-mən/) **1. NAVY MEMBER WITH CLERICAL DUTIES** an enlisted member of the U.S. Navy whose duties are mostly clerical **2. LOYAL WORKER** a loyal, reliable, or diligent worker **3. FARMER WITH SMALL FREEHOLDING** a member of a former class of English commoners who owned and cultivated their own land **4. SHERIFF'S ASSISTANT** an assistant to a sheriff or other official in the past **5. ATTENDANT TO NOBILITY OR ROYALTY** a servant or minor official employed in the past in a royal or noble household **6. YEOMAN OF THE GUARD** a yeoman of the guard ■ *adj.* **PERFORMED DILIGENTLY** characterized by loyalty, diligence, and reliablility ○ *performed yeoman service in completing the task on time* [13thC. Origin uncertain: perhaps a contraction of earlier *yongman* "young man."]

yeo·man·ly /yṓmənlee/ *adj.* **1. RELATING TO YEOMAN** relating to or characteristic of a yeoman or yeomen **2. STAUNCH AND DEPENDABLE** dependable, loyal, and brave (*archaic or literary*) ■ *adv.* **BRAVELY** in a brave and loyal way

yeo·man of the guard (*plural* **yeo·men of the guard**) *n.* a member of a British royal guard who perform ceremonial duties, especially as guards of the Tower of London

yeo·man·ry /yṓmənree/ *n.* **1. FARMERS WITH SMALL FREEHOLDINGS** a former class of English commoners who owned and cultivated their own land **2. FORMER BRITISH CAVALRY FORCE** a British cavalry force organized as a home guard in 1761 that became part of the Territorial Army in 1907

yep /yep/ *adv.* yes (*informal*) [Late19thC. Alteration of YES, possibly on the model of nope.]

YER *abbr.* BANKING yearly effective rate

yer·ba /yáirbə, yúrbə/, **yer·ba ma·té** *n.* = **maté** [Early 19thC. From Spanish "herb."]

Ye·re·van /yèrrə vaán/ capital and largest city of Armenia, on the Hrazdan River, in the west of the country. Population: 1,202,000 (1990).

Yer·kes /yúrkiz/, **Robert Mearns** (1876–1956) U.S. psychobiologist. He developed intelligence tests and was an authority on experimental primate psychology.

Yerk·ish /yúrkish/ *n.* an artificial language of visual symbols created for experimental communication between chimpanzees and humans [Late 20thC. Named in honor of the U.S. primatologist Robert Mearns YERKES.]

yer·sin·i·a /yur sínnee ə/ *n.* any of several gram-negative bacteria, many of which cause disease in humans and animals. One of these bacteria is a common cause of gastric infections while another causes bubonic plague. Genus: *Yersinia.* [Mid-20thC. From modern Latin, genus name, from the name of the Swiss-born French bacteriologist A. E. J. *Yersin* (1863–1943).]

yer·sin·i·o·sis /yur sìnni óssəss/ *n.* a condition, mainly found in children and young adults, caused by a bacterium and characterized by intestinal pain and symptoms that resemble appendicitis [Late 20thC. Formed from YERSINIA, the bacterium that causes the disease.]

yes /yess/ *adv.* **1.** ASSENT INDICATOR used especially in speech to indicate assent, agreement, or affirmation ○ *"Do you mean it's all over?" "Yes, I suppose I do."* ○ *97 percent of respondents answered yes, a ringing endorsement of one of his central beliefs.* **2.** INDICATES CONTRADICTION used to indicate contradiction in response to a negative proposition ○ *"He won't believe you." "Oh yes he will."* **3.** MARK OF ATTENTION used to indicate that somebody is ready to give his or her attention to somebody who has asked for it ○ *"Doctor?" "Yes?"* **4.** ACCEPTANCE used to accept an offer or a request ○ *"Would you like some tea?" "Yes, please."* ■ *n.* **1. yes** (*plural* **yes·es** *or* **yes·ses**) AFFIRMATIVE RESPONSE an affirmative response to a question ○ *Was that a yes or a no?* **2.** AFFIRMATIVE VOTER somebody who votes in the affirmative ○ *The yeses have 65 percent and the noes 35 percent, so the motion is carried.* [Old English *gēse*, from *gēa* (see YEA) + *sīe* "may it be (so)," a form of the verb *to be*]

ye·shi·va /yə sheévə/ (*plural* **-vas** *or* **-vot** /yə sheé vot, -vōt/ *or* **-voth**), **ye·shi·vah** (*plural* **-vahs** *or* **-vot** *or* **-voth**) *n.* a seminary for orthodox Jewish, usually unmarried, men where they study the primary source of Jewish law, the Talmud [Mid-19thC. From Hebrew *yəšīḇāh*, from *yāšaḇ* "to sit."]

yes man, yes-man *n.* somebody who agrees enthusiastically with the ideas and views of a superior without offering any criticism

yes/no ques·tion *n.* a question that can be answered with "yes" or "no" and that in English begins with an actual or implied verb

yes·sir /yéssər/, **yess·ir·ee** /yéssəreé/ *interj.* used, often ironically or humorously, to express submissive assent or obedience (*informal*) [Early 20thC. Representing a casual pronunciation of *yes, sir.*]

yes·ter /yéstər/ *adj.* happening or belonging to yesterday (*archaic; usually used in combination*) ○ *yesteryear* [Late 16thC. Backformation for *yesterday.*]

yester- *prefix.* used to refer to a time in the past denoted by the suffix ○ *yestermorning* [Old English *geostran*]

yes·ter·day /yéstər day, -dee/ *n.* **1.** DAY BEFORE TODAY the day before this one **2.** PAST a time in the past ■ *adv.* **1.** ON THE PREVIOUS DAY on the day before today **2.** IN THE PAST at a time in the past [Old English *geostran dæg*]

yes·ter·eve·ning /yéstər eévning/ *adv.* DURING YESTERDAY EVENING yesterday in the evening (*archaic or literary*) ■ *n.* YESTERDAY'S EVENING the evening of yesterday (*archaic or literary*)

yes·ter·morn·ing /yéstər màwrning/ *adv.* DURING YESTERDAY MORNING yesterday in the morning (*archaic or literary*) ■ *n.* YESTERDAY'S MORNING the morning of yesterday (*archaic or literary*)

yes·ter·night /yéstər nìt/ *adv.* DURING LAST NIGHT yesterday at night (*archaic or literary*) ■ *n.* LAST NIGHT the night of yesterday (*archaic or literary*) [Old English *gystran niht*]

yes·ter·year /yéstər yeér/ *n.* **1.** THE PAST the not very recent past **2.** LAST YEAR the year before this one [Late 19thC. Coined by the poet Dante Gabriel ROSSETTI to translate French *antan.*]

yet /yet/ *adv.* **1.** SO FAR so far, or up to now (*often used with a negative or interrogative*) ○ *The information has not yet been analyzed.* **2.** NOW now, as opposed to later (*often used with a negative*) ○ *I can't come over just yet.* **3.** EVEN even or still (*often used with a comparative*) ○ *He spurred her on to yet greater efforts.* **4.** IN SPITE OF EVERYTHING used to indicate that it is still possible that something will happen despite everything ○ *We'll solve this problem yet.* **5.** UP TO NOW used with superlatives to indicate that something is, e.g., the best, worst, or most impressive up to now (*often used after a superlative*) ○ *This study is the largest yet – a 14-year study of 87,000 nurses.* **6.** FOR LONGER used to indicate that something will go on happening for a specified time ○ *It would take hours yet for the space telescope photos to arrive on Earth and be processed.* **7.** NEVER UP TO NOW used to indicate that somebody has not done something up to now ○ *She's been there several weeks and we have yet to hear from her.* ■ *conj.* NEVERTHELESS however or nevertheless ○ *They can't find the cause, yet the researchers agree that one must be found.* [Old English *gīet*, of uncertain origin] ◇ **as yet** up to now or up to the time being spoken about (*often used with a negative*)

WORD KEY: USAGE

Did she go yet? In the simple past tense ***yet*** is used in this way in informal English rather than the perfect tense: *Has she gone yet?* In some meanings, ***yet*** and *still* are largely interchangeable: *This has still to be decided* or *This has yet to be decided.*

ye·ti /yéttee/ (*plural* **-tis**) *n.* a mysterious hairy humanoid animal said to live in the Himalayas [Mid-20thC. Origin uncertain: perhaps from Tibetan *yeh-teh* "small manlike animal," or an alteration of Tibetan *miti*, from *mi* "person" + *ti* "kind of animal."]

Yev·tu·shen·ko /yèvtə shéngkō/, **Yevgeny Aleksandrovich** (*b.* 1933) Russian poet. His works such as *Zima Junction* (1956) and *Babi Yar* (1961) were critical of the post-Stalinist U.S.S.R., and were widely read in the Soviet Union and the West, although officially condemned by Soviet authorities.

Yew

yew /yoo/ *n.* **1.** EVERGREEN TREE an evergreen tree or shrub that has flat dark green needles and red cones that resemble berries. Most parts of the tree are considered poisonous. Genus: *Taxus.* **2.** YEW WOOD the fine-grained wood of the yew **3.** YEW BOW an archer's bow made from yew [Old English *īw*]

Yez·i·di /yézzədee/ *n.* a member of a Kurdish religious group, founded by an Islamic mystic in the 12th century but incorporating many elements of Iranian myth and tradition. The group has been branded as heretical by orthodox Muslims and has been the object of intense persecution. [Early 19thC. Origin unknown.] —**Yez·i·dism** *n.*

Ygg·dra·sil /ígdrəss'l/, **Yg·dra·sil** *n.* in Norse mythology, the great ash tree that overshadows the world, binding together earth, heaven, and hell [From Old Norse]

YHWH, YHVH, JHVH, JHWH *n.* the transliteration of the four letters (**tetragrammaton**) representing the name of God in the Bible. This transliteration was only ever pronounced by the high priest in the Temple. ◊ **Adonai, Yahweh**

Yi /yee/ *n.* a Korean dynasty that ruled Korea from 1392, following a period of Mongol invasions, until 1910, and that restored aristocratic dominance and Chinese influence

yid /yid/ *n.* a highly offensive term referring to a Jewish person (*taboo offensive*) [Late 19thC. Via Yiddish from Middle High German *jüde* "Jew," ultimately from Latin *Judaeus* (see JEW).]

Yid·dish /yíddish/ *n.* LANG a language written in Hebrew script and spoken by Jewish people in many European countries, in Israel, and in some parts of North and South America. Mainly derived from medieval German dialect, it includes many elements from Hebrew, Aramaic, and other languages, especially Slavonic languages. [Late 19thC. From Yiddish *yidish (daytsh)*, literally "Jewish (German)," from Middle High German *jüdisch diutsch*, from *jüde* "Jewish person," ultimately from Latin *Judaeus.*] —**Yid·dish** *adj.*

yield /yeeld/ *v.* (**yield·ed, yield·ing, yields**) **1.** *vt.* AGRIC PRODUCE SOMETHING to produce something naturally or as a result of cultivation ○ *The field yields a good crop.* **2.** *vt.* GIVE SOMETHING AS RESULT to produce something as the result of work, activity, or calculation ○ *The research has yielded some interesting results.* **3.** *vt.* FIN GIVE PROFIT to gain an amount as a return on an investment ○ *bonds that yield 9 percent* **4.** *vi.* GIVE WAY to give way or give up further resistance ○ *She refused to yield despite our pleas.* **5.** *vt.* GIVE SOMETHING UP TO SOMEBODY to give something up to somebody else or concede it ○ *He eventually yielded control of the company to his daughter.* **6.** *vi.* GIVE WAY TO PRESSURE to move or bend under pressure or with the application of force ○ *The window was painted shut and wouldn't yield.* **7.** *vi.* SURRENDER to admit defeat and surrender **8.** *vi.* BE REPLACED BY SOMETHING to be replaced by something else ○ *Older houses and gardens were gradually yielding to modern apartments.* **9.** *vi.* TRANSP LET ANOTHER PASS to slow down or stop in order to let another vehicle pass ○ *yield to traffic on the right* ■ *n.* **1.** AGRIC AMOUNT PRODUCED the amount of something, especially a crop, produced by cultivation or labor ○ *Yields per acre were slightly lower than last year.* **2.** FIN RETURN ON INVESTMENT a part of a return on investment coming from the receipt of interest or dividends ○ *The yield on the account was disappointing.* **3.** CHEM PRODUCT FROM A CHEMICAL REACTION the quantity of product resulting from a chemical reaction or process, often expressed as a percentage of the amount that is theoretically obtainable **4.** PHYS EXPLOSIVE FORCE the amount of energy released in a nuclear explosion expressed as the amount of TNT that would have the same explosive force [Old English *geldan* "to pay." Ultimately from a prehistoric Germanic base meaning "to pay," which is also the ancestor of English *guild.*] —**yield·a·bil·i·ty** /yeèldə bílləte/ *n.* —**yield·a·ble** /yeéldəb'l/ *adj.* —**yield·er** *n.*

WORD KEY: SYNONYMS

yield, capitulate, submit, succumb, surrender

CORE MEANING: to give way

yield to give way to something such as force, pressure, entreaty, or persuasion; **capitulate** to cease to resist a superior force, especially one that seems invincible, sometimes without having offered much active opposition; **submit** to accept somebody else's authority or will, especially reluctantly or under pressure; **succumb** to give in to something due to weakness or a failure to offer much active opposition; **surrender** to give way to the power of another and stop offering resistance, usually after active opposition.

yield up *vt.* to reveal something formerly hidden or secret

yield·ing /yeélding/ *adj.* **1.** SOFT AND BENDING inclined to give or bend under pressure **2.** COMPLIANT tending to obey others **3.** PRODUCING productive of a good or bad yield or crop —**yield·ing·ly** *adv.* —**yield·ing·ness** *n.*

yikes /yīks/ *interj.* used when suddenly startled (*informal*) [Late 20thC. Origin uncertain: perhaps an alteration of YOICKS.]

yin /yin/ *n.* the principle of darkness, negativity, and femininity in Chinese philosophy that is the counterpart of yang. The dual, opposite, and complementary principles of yin and yang are thought to exist in varying proportions in all things. ◊ **yang** [Late 17thC. From Chinese *yīn* "shade, feminine, moon."]

Ying·lish /yínglish/ *n.* LANG a type of English with a heavy overlay of Yiddish words and syntax, as spoken by early Jewish immigrants to the United States [Mid-20thC. Blend of YIDDISH and ENGLISH.] —**Ying·lish** *adj.*

yip /yip/ *vi.* (**yipped, yip·ping, yips**) **BARK** to give a high-pitched bark ■ *n.* **SHRILL BARK** a high-pitched bark [15thC. Originally "to cheep," used of birds; ultimately an imitation of the sound.]

yipe /yīp/ *interj.* used to express fear or alarm (*informal*) [Mid-20thC. Origin uncertain.]

yip·ee /yi pée/, **yip·pee** *interj.* used to express joy and excitement (*usually used by or to children*) [Early 20thC. A natural exclamation.]

yip·pie /yíppee/ *n.* a politically radical hippie during the late 1960s and early 1970s in the United States [Mid-20thC. Coined from *Y(outh) I(nternational) P(arty)*, on the model of HIPPIE.]

yips /yips/ *npl.* nervousness that impairs the performance of a sportsman or sportswoman, especially a golfer [Mid-20thC. Origin unknown.]

Yiz·kor /yíz kawr/ *n.* a memorial prayer for deceased relatives recited in synagogue on Festivals and Yom Kippur [Mid-20thC. From Hebrew *yizkōr*, literally "may He remember."]

-yl *suffix.* a group of atoms forming a radical ○ *carbonyl* [Via French *-yle* from Greek *hulē* "wood, organic matter"]

y·lang-y·lang /ée laáng ée laáng/, **i·lang-i·lang** *n.* a tropical tree native to Asia and North Australia with flowers that yield a fragrant oil used in perfumery. Latin name: *Cananga odorata*. [Late 19thC. From Tagalog *ilang-ilang*.]

y·lem /ílәm/ *n.* hypothetical matter that, according to the big bang theory of the origin of the universe, was the substance from which the chemical elements were formed. ◊ **big bang theory** [Mid-20thC. Via medieval Latin *hylem* "universal matter" from, ultimately Greek *hulē* "wood, matter."]

Y-lev·el *n.* a rotatable level mounted on a Y-shaped frame, used in surveying

YMCA, **Y.M.C.A.** *abbr.* Young Men's Christian Association ■ *n.* (*plural* **YMCAs;** *plural* **Y.M.C.A.s**) **YMCA CENTER** a building or other center where social, sports, or educational facilities are provided by the YMCA for its members

YMHA (*plural* **YMHAs**), **Y.M.H.A.** (*plural* **Y.M.H.A.s**) *abbr.* Young Men's Hebrew Association

Y·mir /ée meér/ *n.* the forefather of all the giants of Norse mythology. Ymir was killed by Odin and his brothers, and the world was formed from his body, the heavens from his skull, and the water from his blood.

yo /yō/ *interj.* used as a greeting or to get somebody's attention [15thC. Natural exclamation.]

yob /yob/ *n. U.K.* a young hooligan (*informal*) [Mid-19thC. Backward spelling of BOY.] —**yob·ber·y** *n.* —**yob·bish** *adj.*

YOB *abbr.* year of birth

yob·bo /yóbbō/ (*plural* **-bos**) *n.* = **yob** (*informal*) [Early 20thC. Formed from YOB.]

yod /yod/, **yodh** *n.* the tenth letter of the Hebrew alphabet, represented in the English alphabet as "y" or "j." See table at **alphabet**

yo·del /yṓd'l/, **yo·dle** *vi.* (**-deled, -del·ing, -dels; -dled, -dling, -dles**) **SING HIGH** to sing, changing rapidly between a normal and falsetto voice. It is a feature of Alpine folk music and of some U.S. country and western music. ■ *n.* **YODELING SONG** a song or passage that features yodeling [Early 19thC. From German *jodeln*, literally "to utter JO"; ultimately an imitation of the sound.] —**yo·del·er** *n.*

yodh *n.* = **yod**

yo·dle *vi., n.* = **yodel**

yo·ga /yṓgә/ *n.* **1. HINDU DISCIPLINE** any of a group of related Hindu disciplines that promote the unity of the individual with a supreme being through a system of postures and rituals **2. SYSTEM OF EXERCISE** a system or set of breathing exercises and postures derived from or based on Hindu yoga [Late 18thC. From Sanskrit *yogaḥ*, literally "union." Ultimately from an Indo-European word meaning "to join," which is also the ancestor of English *yoke*, *join*, and *zygo-*.]

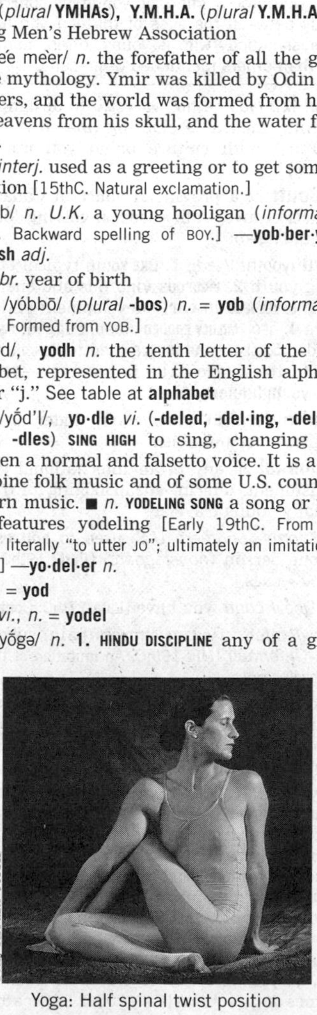

Yoga: Half spinal twist position

yogh /yōg/ *n.* a letter ʒ used in Middle English, usually represented in modern English as "gh" or "y" [13thC. Origin uncertain.]

yo·ghurt *n.* = **yogurt**

yo·gi /yṓgee/ (*plural* **-gis**), **yo·gin** /yṓgәn/ *n.* **1. YOGA PRACTITIONER** somebody who practices yoga **2. STUDENT OF GURU** somebody who studies under a guru or other spiritual teacher of Indian religion [Early 17thC. From Sanskrit *yogī*, from *yogaḥ* "yoga."]

yo·gurt /yṓgәrt/, **yo·ghurt, yo·ghourt** *n.* milk fermented by bacteria to give a tangy or slightly sour flavor and a lightly set or thick and creamy consistency. It is sometimes sweetened and flavored, usually with fruit. [Early 17thC. From Turkish *yoğurt*.]

Yog·ya·kar·ta /yòggyә kaártә, jàwk yaa-/ city in southwestern Indonesia, on the island of Java. Population: 412,059 (1990).

yo-heave-ho *interj.* used formerly by sailors as a rhythmic accompaniment to hauling work

Yo·ho Na·tion·al Park /yṓhō-/ national park in the Rocky Mountains of southeastern British Columbia, Canada. Area: 507 sq. mi./1,313 sq. km.

yoicks /yoyks/ *interj.* used to encourage hounds in a foxhunt [Mid-18thC. Origin uncertain.]

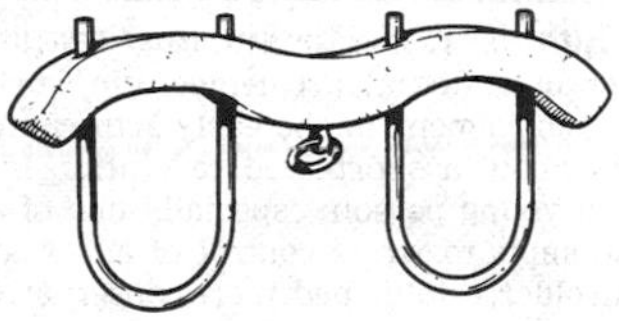

Yoke

yoke /yōk/ *n.* **1. ANIMAL HARNESS** a wooden frame for harnessing two draft animals **2. FRAME FOR CARRYING LOADS** a frame designed to fit across somebody's shoulders with balanced loads suspended at either end **3. RESTRICTIVE BURDEN** something that is oppressive and restrictive **4.** CLOTHES **FITTED PART OF A GARMENT** the fitted part of a garment, usually around the shoulders or waist, from which an unfitted part is suspended **5. BOND** a bond or tie that keeps people together ○ *the yoke of marriage* **6.** HIST **CROSSED SPEARS** an archway made of crossed spears under which defeated enemies of the ancient Romans were forced to march **7. JOINED ANIMALS** two animals joined by a yoke **8.** NAUT **RUDDER CROSSBAR** a crossbar fitted to the top of a rudder and connected to the front of a boat by ropes or cables for steering **9.** ELECTRON ENG **CATHODE RAY DEVICE** a device fitted to the neck of a cathode ray tube to control the scanning motion of the electron beam **10.** RECORDING **EQUIPMENT FOR MULTI-TRACK RECORDING** equipment for recording or reproducing sounds or music on more than one track simultaneously, by joining together two or more magnetic recording heads **11.** AIR **AIRCRAFT PART** the handle of the steering mechanism for an airplane's ailerons ■ *vt.* (**yoked, yok·ing, yokes**) **1. FIT ANIMALS WITH A YOKE** to put a yoke on two draft animals **2. CONNECT AN ANIMAL TO A VEHICLE** to connect a draft animal to a plow or vehicle **3. LINK THINGS TOGETHER** to join or link two things forcibly or surprisingly ○ *Ranchers were yoked together with farmers on the issue.* [Old English *geoc*. Ultimately from an Indo-European word meaning "to join," which is also the ancestor of English *join*, *zygo-*, and *yoga*.]

yoke·fel·low /yṓk fèllō/ *n.* a mate, associate, or companion (*archaic*)

yo·kel /yṓk'l/ *n.* an offensive term regarding to somebody regarded as lacking intelligence or other qualities perceived as urbane or superior (*insult offensive*) [Early 19thC. Origin uncertain: perhaps from a dialect word meaning "green woodpecker, yellowhammer."] —**yo·kel·ish** *adj.*

yolk /yōk/ *n.* **1. YELLOW OF EGG** the round yellow portion of a bird's or reptile's egg, containing protein and fats that provide nourishment for the developing young. Yolks are virtually absent from the eggs of mammals, whose embryos absorb nutrients from the mother. **2. OILY SUBSTANCE IN WOOL** a greasy substance from the skin of sheep that collects in wool [Old English *geol(o)ca*, from *geolu* (see YELLOW)] —**yolk·y** *adj.*

yolk sac *n.* a thin yolk-containing membrane that is attached to the embryos of birds, fish, and reptiles, or a membrane containing no yolk in marsupials and mammals and functioning primarily in placental formation

yolk stalk *n.* a narrow tube or duct attaching the yolk sac to an embryo and allowing the passage of yolk to the embryo's elementary digestive tract

Yom Kip·pur /yawm kíppәr/ *n.* the holiest day of the Jewish year, falling on the tenth day of Tshiri, in September or October, on which Jewish people fast and say prayers of penitence [From Hebrew *Yōm Kippūr* "day of atonement"]

yom tov /yáwm tàwv/ (*plural* **ya·mim to·vim** /yaa meém taw veém/) *n.* a Jewish term for a religious festival [Directly and via Yiddish *yontef* from Hebrew *yōm ṭōb*, literally "good day"]

yon /yon/ *adv.* **YONDER** yonder, over there (*regional*) ■ *adj.* **THAT OR THOSE** that or those over there (*regional*) [Partly a shortening of YONDER, and partly from Old English *geon* "that one"]

yond /yond/ *adv.* yonder, over there (*archaic or literary*) [Old English *geond*, *geondan* (source of English *beyond*). Ultimately from an Indo-European base meaning "that one," which is also the ancestor of *yon*.]

yon·der /yóndәr/ *adv.* **OVER THERE** over there (*regional*) ■ *adj.* **THAT** that over there (*regional*) [14thC. Formed from YOND.]

yo·ni /yṓnee/ (*plural* **-nis**) *n.* in Hinduism, a representation of the female genitals regarded as a manifestation of the feminine principle [Late 18thC. From Sanskrit *yoniḥ* "womb," of unknown origin.]

Yon·kers /yóngkәrz/ city in southeastern New York, on the Hudson River. It is a northern suburb of New York City. Population: 190,316 (1996).

yoo-hoo /yoó hoó/ *interj.* **HELLO** used to get somebody's attention, especially when the speaker is at a distance ■ *vti.* (**yoo-hooed, yoo-hoo·ing, yoo-hoos**) **SAY YOO-HOO** to say or shout "yoo-hoo" to attract somebody's attention [Early 20thC. Natural exclamation.]

yore /yawr/ *n.* time long past (*literary*) [Old English *geāra*, of uncertain origin: perhaps a variant of *gēara*, literally "of years," from *gēar* (see YEAR)]

York /yawrk/ city in Yorkshire, northern England. Originally a Celtic settlement, under the Romans it became an important regional center. Population: 105,500 (1991).

Yorke Pen·in·su·la /yàwrk-/ peninsula in South Australia, situated between the Gulf of St. Vincent and the Spencer Gulf. Length: 160 mi./160 km.

york·ie /yáwrkee/, **York·ie** *n.* a Yorkshire Terrier (*informal*) [Early 19thC. Shortening.]

York·ist /yáwrkәst/ *n.* **YORK SUPPORTER** somebody who was loyal to or connected with the House of York that ruled England from 1461 to 1485 ■ *adj.* **OF YORK** supporting or connected with the House of York

York rite *n.* a masonic ceremony that confers different degrees at different levels of the membership [Late 19thC. Named for the city of YORK in England.]

York·shire /yàwrkshәr/ former county in northern England, at one time the largest in the country. Traditionally divided into the East, West, and North Ridings, it has been an important region since Roman times.

York·shire Dales area of wild moorlands divided by fertile valleys in the mid-Pennines, northern England

York·shire pud·ding *n.* a flour-based batter that is traditionally cooked in the drippings of roast meat. It was originally served with gravy before roast meat with the intention of satisfying appetites so that a small amount of meat would go a long way. [Mid-18thC. Named for YORKSHIRE.]

Yorkshire terrier

York·shire ter·ri·er *n.* a very small long-haired terrier with a long silky brown and gray coat [Late 19thC. Named for YORKSHIRE, where the breed was developed.]

York·ton /yáwrktən/ town in Saskatchewan, Canada, northeast of Regina. Population: 17,713 (1996).

Yo·ru·ba /yáwrəbə/ (*plural* **-ba** *or* **-bas**) *n.* **1.** PEOPLES **MEMBER OF WEST AFRICAN PEOPLE** a member of a West African people living mostly in Nigeria **2.** LANG **YORUBA LANGUAGE** a language spoken in southwestern Nigeria, Benin and Togo. It belongs to the Niger-Congo language family and is spoken by about 20 million people. **3. REGION OF CITY-STATES IN NIGERIA** a region of city-states that developed in northern Nigeria around A.D. 1200, notable for the population's animistic religion and their artistic work, in particular wood and bronze pieces [Mid-19thC. From Yoruba.] —**Yoruba** *adj.* —**Yo·ru·ban** *adj.*

Yo·se·mi·te Falls /yō sèmmətee-/ falls in the Yosemite National Park, California. Consisting of the Upper Yosemite Falls and the Lower Yosemite Falls, it is one of the highest falls in the world, with a total drop of 2,245 ft./739 m.

Yo·sem·i·te Na·tion·al Park national park in central California in the Sierra Nevada, established in 1890. It is noted for its giant sequoia trees and falls. Area: 1,189 sq. mi./3,079 sq. km.

you *(stressed)* /yoo/; *(unstressed)* /yə/ *pron.* **1. PERSON BEING ADDRESSED** refers to the person or people being addressed or written to ○ *I'm fine – how about you?* **2. PERSON OR PEOPLE UNSPECIFIED** refers to an unspecified person or people in general ○ *You have to see it to believe it.* ○ *You mix all the dry ingredients together in a bowl.* **3. THOSE BEING REFERRED TO** used to refer to the person you are talking to, as well as other people of the same type or class (*used before a plural*) ○ *Isn't it time you kids were in bed?* **4. PERSONALITY OF PERSON ADDRESSED** refers to the personality of the person addressed or something's suitability to express it (*informal*) ○ *Don't buy that suit, it's not really you!* **5. YOURSELF** yourself (*informal*) ○ *You'll have to get you a job.* [Old English *ēow*, from *gē* (see YE)]

WORD KEY: USAGE

See Usage note at ***yourself.***

you-all /yawl/, **y'all** *pron. Southern U.S.* used to address more than one person (*informal*)

WORD KEY: REGIONAL NOTE

This is Southern usage. Unlike Northern *youse*, which is limited to nonstandard usage, the Southern form recurs among all social groups, virtually never used in the singular except in bad imitations by people of other regions.

you'd /yood/ *contr.* you had or you would [Early 17thC. Contraction.]

you'll /yool/ *contr.* you will or you shall [Late 16thC. Contraction.]

young /yung/ *adj.* **1. NOT VERY OLD** having lived or been in existence a relatively short time **2. OF YOUTH** relating to somebody's youth **3. YOUTHFUL** looking or behaving like a young or younger person **4. FOR YOUNG PEOPLE** designed for or appropriate to young people **5. RECENTLY BEGUN** recently begun or in an early stage **6.** GEOL **NOT SIGNIFICANTLY ERODED** in a relatively early stage of landscape formation and therefore steep and largely uneroded ■ *npl.* **1. OFFSPRING** offspring, especially when still completely dependent on parents **2. YOUNG PEOPLE** young people in general [Old English *geong*. Ultimately from an Indo-European word meaning "youth, vigor," which is also the ancestor of English *youth* and *juvenile*.] —**young·ish** *adj.* —**young·ness** *n.*

Young /yung/, **Brigham** (1801–77) U.S. religious leader. He succeeded Joseph Smith as the leader of the Church of Jesus Christ of Latter-Day Saints (1844–77). He organized the church members' migration from Illinois to Utah (1845–46), where he founded Salt Lake City.

Young, Cy (1867–1955) U.S. baseball player. He was the first player in major league history to pitch a perfect game (1904), and an annual award for the best major league pitcher was established in his honor. Real name **Denton True Young**

Young, Whitney M., Jr. (1921–71) U.S. civil rights leader and social worker. He directed the National Urban League (1961–71) and advised President Lyndon B. Johnson on antipoverty programs. Full name **Whitney Moore Young, Jr.**

young·ber·ry /yúng bèrree/ (*plural* **-ries**) *n.* **1. HYBRID BRAMBLE** a trailing bramble, native to the southwestern United States, that is a hybrid of the blackberry and dewberry, with large, sweet, dark purple fruit **2. FRUIT OF YOUNGBERRY** the edible berry of the youngberry [Early 20thC. Named for the U.S. horticulturist B. M. *Young*, who developed the shrub.]

young blood *n.* fresh, new, and vigorous ideas or people

young·ling /yúngling/ *n.* a young person or a young animal [Old English *geongling*]

young of·fend·er *n. U.K.* = **youthful offender**

young·ster /yúngstər/ *n.* **1. CHILD** a child or young person **2. YOUNG HORSE** a young horse **3. SECOND-YEAR NAVAL CADET** a second-year student in the U.S. Naval Academy

WORD KEY: SYNONYMS

See Synonyms at ***youth.***

Young Turk *n.* **1. TURKISH NATIONALIST REVOLUTIONARY** a member of a liberal pro-democratic Turkish nationalist movement in the early 20th century that brought about a short-lived revolution in 1908 **2. UPSTART** a young person, especially one of a group, who attempts to wrest control of an organization from an older, established, more conservative group

young'un /yúngən/ *n.* an infant or child (*informal*) [Early 20thC. Contraction of *young one.*]

youn·ker /yúngkər/ *n.* (*archaic*) **1. YOUNG MALE** a young man **2. CHILD** a child [Early 16thC. From Middle Dutch *jonckher*, from *jonc* "young" + *hēre* "lord."]

your *(stressed)* /yawr, yoor/; *(unstressed)* /yər/ *adj.* **1. BELONGING TO PERSON SPOKEN TO** refers to something that belongs to or relates to an addressee ○ *What's your phone number?* **2. BELONGING OR RELATING TO SOMEBODY** refers to something that belongs or relates to an unspecified person or people in general ○ *The house is on your left as you come down the street.* ○ *not just your average dancer* **3. INDICATES TOPIC** refers to somebody or something as an example or topic (*informal*) [Old English *ēower*, from *gē* (see YE)]

Marguerite Yourcenar

Your·ce·nar /yoórsə naar/, **Marguerite** (1903–87) Belgian-born French and U.S. writer. Many of her works, including *Memoirs of Hadrian* (1951), follow historical themes. Pseudonym of **Marguerite de Crayencour**

you're *(stressed)* /yoor, yawr/; *(unstressed)* /yər/ *contr.* you are [Late 16thC. Contraction.]

yours /yawrz, yoorz/ *pron.* **1. INDICATES BELONGING** refers to something that belongs or relates to the person or people being addressed ○ *This idea of yours is very interesting.* **2. yours, Yours LETTER ENDING** used at the end of letters before somebody signs his or her name ○ *Sincerely yours, Marcia Klein* [14thC. Formed from YOUR.] ◇ **Yours sincerely, Yours faithfully, Yours truly** used at the end of a letter before somebody signs his or her name ○ *Yours sincerely, John Smith*

your·self /yawr sélf, yoor-, yər-/ (*plural* **-selves** /-sélvz/) *pron.* **1. SOMEBODY BEING ADDRESSED** refers to the person or people being addressed or written to ○ *Be careful not to hurt yourself.* **2. MAKING REFERENCE TO SOMEBODY SPOKEN TO** refers emphatically or politely to the person or people being addressed or written to ○ *"Consider," he replied, "how you yourself really feel about such things."* **3. YOUR NORMAL SELF** your normal or usual self ○ *You are not yourself tonight.*

WORD KEY: USAGE

Grammar: The primary uses of ***yourself*** are as a reflexive pronoun (*Don't hurt yourself*) and as a reinforcing pronoun (*Can you do it yourself?*). It should not be used as an alternative for *you* in sentences of the type *That's up to you* (not: *That's up to yourself*).

yours tru·ly *pron.* me, myself, or I ○ *Of course, everyone's going to be there except yours truly.*

youse /yooz/, **yous** *pron.* used to address more than one person (*regional nonstandard*) [Late 19thC. Formed from YOU.]

youth /yooth/ *n.* **1. TIME WHEN SOMEBODY IS YOUNG** the period of human life between childhood and maturity **2. BEING YOUNG** the state of being young **3. YOUNG PERSON** a young person, especially a boy or young man **4. EARLY STAGE** an early stage of something **5.** GEOL **EROSION STAGE** the first stage in landscape formation in which fast-flowing streams travel down steep mountain valleys ■ *npl.* **YOUNG PEOPLE** young people in general [Old English *geoguþ*, from a prehistoric Germanic word]

WORD KEY: SYNONYMS

youth, child, kid, teenager, youngster

CORE MEANING: somebody who is young

youth a man or boy who is in his teens or early twenties; **child** between birth and the onset of puberty; **kid** an informal word for a child or young person; **teenager** somebody between the ages of thirteen and nineteen; **youngster** somebody who is young, often, humorously, younger than others mentioned or present.

youth·an·ize /yoóthə nīz/ *vt.* COMM to design or alter something such as a clothing line so that it will appeal to youth culture or to youthful buyers (*informal*)

Youth Court *n.* a provincial court in Canada with jurisdiction over all cases involving offenders under the age of 18

youth·ful /yoóthf'l/ *adj.* **1. LIKE YOUTH** typical of or possessing youth **2. VIGOROUS** vigorous and energetic **3. NOT FULLY DEVELOPED** in early development and not yet mature **4.** GEOL **MILDLY ERODED** steep, rugged, relatively uneroded **5.** GEOG **NEAR SOURCE** used to describe a fast-flowing stream close to its source —**youth·ful·ly** *adv.* —**youth·ful·ness** *n.*

youth·ful of·fend·er *n.* somebody under 18 who has committed a criminal act

youth hos·tel *n.* any of an international group of establishments offering cheap lodging for travelers, especially young travelers

you-uns *pron. Southern U.S.* used to address more than one person (*nonstandard*) [Early 19thC. Formed from YOU + ONES.]

you've /yoov/ *contr.* you have [Late 17thC. Contraction.]

yow /yow/ *interj.* used to express pain, surprise, or alarm (*informal*) [Mid-19thC. An imitation of the sound of an involuntary cry.]

yowl /yowl/ *vi.* (**yowled, yowl·ing, yowls**) **UTTER A HOWL** to cry out mournfully or as an expression of pain ■ *n.* **SAD CRY** a long mournful wail [12thC. Origin uncertain: probably an imitation of the sound.] —**yowl·er** *n.*

yo-yo /yṓ yō/ *n.* (*plural* **yo-yos**) **1. TOY WITH STRING WOUND ON SPOOL** a toy consisting of a long string wound onto a spool that is dropped and raised repeatedly using the force of gravity and momentum to unwind and rewind the string **2. FLUCTUATING THING** something that repeatedly goes up and down or fluctuates between one extreme and another **3. OFFENSIVE TERM** an offensive term used to refer to somebody regarded as silly or unintelligent (*slang insult*) ■ *vi.* (**yo-yoed, yo-yo·ing, yo-yos**) **FLUCTUATE** to fluctuate between two extremes or directions [Early 20thC. Earlier a trademark,

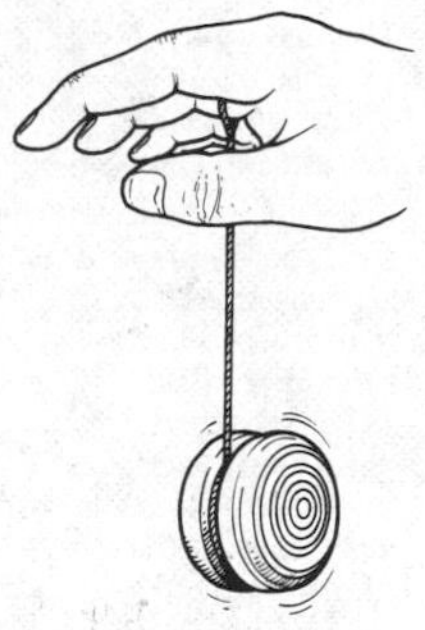

Yo-yo

of uncertain origin: probably the name of a Philippine toy, from a language of the Philippines.]

yo-yo diet·ing *n.* a situation in which somebody repeatedly loses weight and then regains the weight that he or she has lost

yr. *abbr.* **1.** year **2.** younger **3.** your

Yrs. *abbr.* Yours (*used at end of letter*)

Y.T. *abbr.* Yukon Territory

YTD *abbr.* year to date

yt·ter·bi·a /i túrbee ə/ *n.* = **ytterbium oxide** [Late 19thC. Named after *Ytterby* (see YTTERBIUM).]

yt·ter·bi·um /i túrbee əm/ *n.* a soft silvery metal belonging to the lanthanide group of rare earth elements, used to strengthen steel, in laser devices, and in portable X-ray units. Symbol **Yb** [Late 19thC. Formed from earlier *ytterbite*, a mineral containing the element, which was named for *Ytterby*, a Swedish quarry where it was found.] —**yt·ter·bic** *adj.*

yt·ter·bi·um ox·ide *n.* a colorless oxide of ytterbium used in certain alloys and ceramics. Formula: Yb_2O_3.

yt·tri·a /íttree ə/ *n.* = **yttrium oxide** [Early 19thC. Named for *Ytterby*, a Swedish quarry, because a mineral (gadolinite) was found there from which the compound was obtained.]

yt·trif·er·ous /i tríffərəss/ *adj.* yielding or containing yttrium

yt·tri·um /íttree əm/ *n.* a silvery gray metallic element occurring in many uranium and rare-earth ores, used in superconducting alloys and in permanent magnets. Symbol **Y** [Early 19thC. Formed from YTTRIA.] —**yt·tric** *adj.*

yt·tri·um met·al *n.* a metal in the group that includes yttrium and related rare earth elements such as holmium, erbium, thulium, ytterbium, and lutetium

yt·tri·um ox·ide *n.* a yellowish powder with several industrial applications, notably in glass, ceramics, lasers, and microwave components. Formula: Y_2O_3.

yu·an /yoo aán/ (*plural* **-an**) *n.* **1. UNIT OF CHINESE CURRENCY** the main unit of currency in China, worth 10 jiao. See table at **currency 2. BILL WORTH ONE YUAN** a bill worth one yuan [Early 20thC. From Chinese *yuán*, literally "round" (source of English *yen*[1]).]

Yu·ca·tán /yòokə tán, -taán/ peninsula in Central America consisting of three Mexican states, Belize, and part of northern Guatemala. Area: 70,000 sq. mi./181,300 sq. km.

Yuc·a·tec /yóokə tèk/ (*plural* **-tec** *or* **-tecs**) *n.* **1.** PEOPLES **MEMBER OF MAYAN PEOPLE IN YUCATAN** a member of a Mayan people of the Yucatan Peninsula **2.** LANG **YUCATEC LANGUAGE** a Mayan language of southern Mexico, spoken by about half a million people [Mid-19thC. From Spanish *yucateco*, from *Yucatán* "Yucatan."] —**Yu·ca·tec** *adj.*

yuc·ca /yúkə/ *n.* an evergreen plant native to the southwestern United States and Mexico but widely grown for its sharp lance-shaped leaves and clusters of white flowers that grow in vertical spikes. Genus: *Yucca*. [Mid-16thC. Via Spanish *yuca* from Taino. One of the first Native American words ever recorded (by Amerigo Vespucci).]

yuc·ca moth *n.* a small white North American moth that pollinates the yucca plant and lays its eggs in the ovaries of the yucca's flowers. Latin name: *Tegeticula alba*.

yuck /yuk/, **yuk** *interj.* used to express disgust or revulsion (*informal*) [Mid-20thC. An imitation of the sound of vomiting.]

yuck·y /yúkee/ (**-i·er, -i·est**), **yuk·ky** (**-ki·er, -ki·est**) *adj.* disgusting or unpleasant (*informal*) —**yuck·i·ness** *n.*

Yug. *abbr.* Yugoslavia

yu·ga /yóogə/ *n.* in Hinduism, any one of the four stages in each cycle of history, each worse than the one before [Late 18thC. From Sanskrit *yugam* "yoke, era."]

Yugo. *abbr.* Yugoslavia

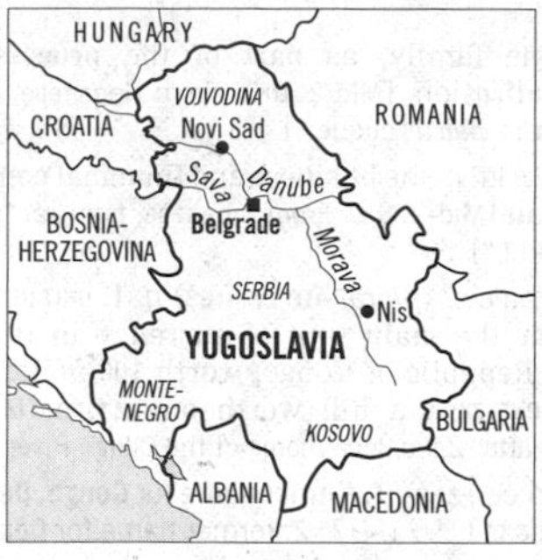

Yugoslavia

Yu·go·sla·via /yòogō slaávee ə/ republic in the Balkans, southeastern Europe, consisting of Serbia and Montenegro, two of the six republics that made up the former Federal People's Republic of Yugoslavia. Language: Serbo-Croatian. Currency: Yugoslav new dinar. Capital: Belgrade. Population: 10,574,000 (1996). Area: 39,449 sq. mi./102,173 sq. km. Official name **Federal Republic of Yugoslavia** — **Yu·go·slav** /yóogō slaav/ *n., adj.*

yuk[1] *interj.* = **yuck**

yuk[2] /yuk/ *n.* **LAUGH** a laugh or chortle (*slang*) ■ *vi.* (**yukked, yuk·king, yuks**) **LAUGH** to produce a laugh (*slang*) [Mid-20thC. Origin uncertain: perhaps an imitation of the sound of laughing.]

yuk·ky *adj.* = **yucky**

Yu·kon /yóok on/ river in North America, flowing through Canada and Alaska and into the Bering Sea. Length: 1,979 mi./3,185 km.

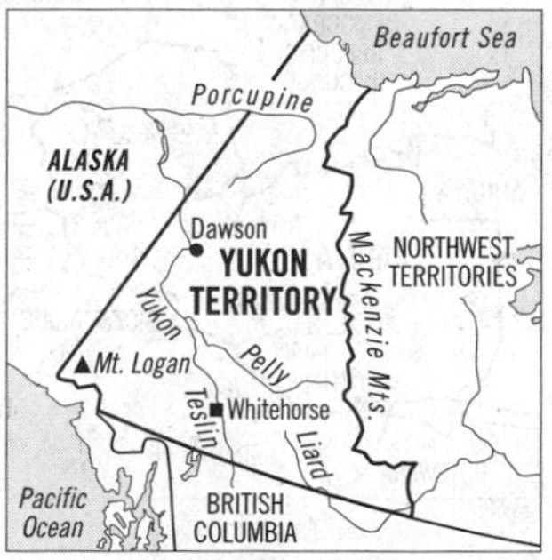

Yukon Territory

Yu·kon Ter·ri·to·ry territory in northwestern Canada. It was the site of the Klondike gold rush between 1896 and 1899. Capital: Whitehorse. Population: 30,766 (1996). Area: 186,660 sq. mi./483,450 sq. km.

Yu·kon Time *n.* the time observed in the Yukon Territory and in a section of more or less equivalent longitude extending southward from there, being nine hours earlier than Greenwich Mean Time

yu·lan /yóo laan, -lan/ *n.* a deciduous spreading tree or shrub of the magnolia family, native to China, that has masses of fragrant white cup-shaped flowers that appear in spring before the leaves. Latin name: *Magnolia denudata*. [Early 19thC. From Chinese *yùlán*, literally "jade orchid."]

Yule /yool/, **yule** *n.* Christmas day or the Christmas season (*archaic literary*) [Old English *gēol* "mid-winter festival, Christmas," of prehistoric Germanic origin]

yule log *n.* a large log traditionally placed on the hearth fire on Christmas eve

Yule·tide /yóol tīd/ *n.* the Christmas season

Yu·ma[1] /yóomə/ *n.* PEOPLES a member of a Native North American people of southwestern Arizona and neighboring areas [Early 19thC. From Pima *yumĭ*.] — **Yu·ma** *adj.*

Yu·ma[2] /yóomə/ city in the southwestern corner of Arizona, on the Arizona-California border, southwest of Phoenix. Population: 60,519 (1996).

Yu·man /yóomən/ *n.* LANG a family of languages spoken in the southwestern U.S. and in northern Mexico. Yuman languages are spoken by about 4,000 people. [Late 19thC. Formed from YUMA.] —**Yu·man** *adj.*

yum·my /yúmmee/ (**-mi·er, -mi·est**) *adj.* very appealing to taste or smell [Late 19thC. Formed from *yum*, an imitation of the sound of smacking the lips.] —**yum·mi·ness** *n.*

Yun·nan /yoo nán/ province in southern China, on the southwestern border of the country. Capital: Kunming. Population: 39,390,000 (1994). Area: 150,600 sq. mi./390,000 sq. km.

Yün Shou·p'ing /yǜn shō píng/ (1633–90) Chinese artist. He is known for his landscapes and flower paintings.

yup /yup/ *adv.* yes (*informal*) [Early 20thC. Representing a casual pronunciation of YES.]

Yu·pik /yóo pik/ (*plural* **-pik** *or* **-piks**) *n.* **1.** PEOPLES **INUIT PEOPLE** an Inuit people of Western Alaska and parts of coastal Siberia **2.** LANG **YUPIK LANGUAGE GROUP** the group of languages spoken by the Yupik people [Mid-20thC. From Alaskan Yupik *Yup'ik*, literally "real person."] —**Yu·pik** *adj.*

yup·pie /yúppee/ *n.* a young educated city-dwelling professional, especially when regarded as materialistic [Late 20thC. Coined from *y(oung) u(rban) p(rofessional)*, on the model of HIPPIE and YIPPIE.]

yup·pie flu, **yup·pie disease** *n.* chronic fatigue syndrome (*informal*)

yup·pi·fy /yúppə fī/ (**-fied, -fy·ing, -fies**) *vt.* to cause an area to be increasingly populated by young educated city-dwelling professionals or to modify something with the values ascribed to yuppies — **yup·pi·fi·ca·tion** /yùppəfə káysh'n/ *n.*

Yu·rok /yóor ok/ (*plural* **-rok** *or* **-roks**) *n.* PEOPLES a member of a Native North American people that live in California, mainly along the northwestern coast and in the lower Klamath River valley [Mid-19thC. From Karok *yúruk* "downstream."] —**Yu·rok** *adj.*

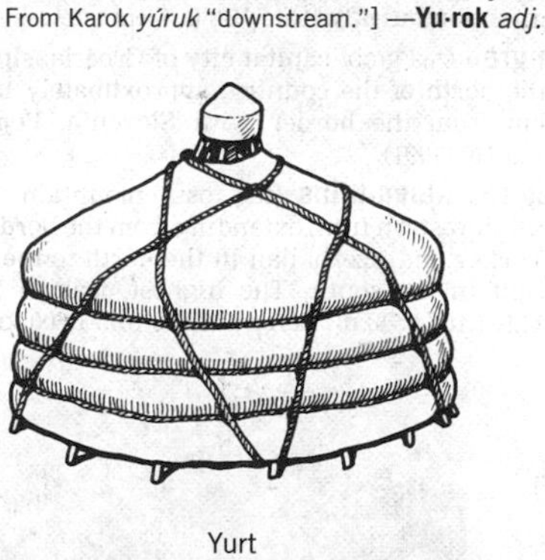

Yurt

yurt /yurt/ *n.* a collapsible circular tent of skins stretched over a pole frame, used by central Asian nomadic peoples [Late 18thC. Via Russian *yurta* from, ultimately, Turkic *jurt*.]

YWCA, **Y.W.C.A.** *abbr.* Young Women's Christian Association ■ *n.* **YWCA CENTER** a building or other center where social, sports, or educational facilities are provided by the YWCA for its members

YWHA, **Y.W.H.A.** *abbr.* Young Women's Hebrew Association

Z z

z[1] /zee/, **Z** *n.* (*plural* **z's**; *plural* **Z's** *or* **Zs**) **1. 26TH LETTER OF ENGLISH ALPHABET** the 26th and final letter of the modern English alphabet **2. SOUND CORRESPONDING TO LETTER "Z"** the speech sound that corresponds to the letter "Z" **3. LETTER "Z" WRITTEN** a written representation of the letter "Z" **4. SOMETHING Z-SHAPED** something shaped like a "Z" ■ **z's** *npl.* **SLEEP** sleep, from the traditional transcription of the sound of snoring (*informal*)

z[2] *symbol.* **1.** MONEY zaire **2.** MATH a Cartesian coordinate along the z-axis **3.** MATH an algebraic variable **4.** zepto-

Z[1], **z.** *abbr.* GEOG zone

Z[2], **z.** *symbol.* **1.** PHYS impedance **2.** CHEM atomic number **3.** zetta-

Zaan·stad /zaan shtát/ city in North Holland Province, western Netherlands. Population: 133,817 (1996).

za·ba·gli·o·ne /zaàb'l yṓnee/ *n.* a dessert made of egg yolks, sugar, and Marsala wine beaten over hot water until pale and foamy. It is served hot with sponge finger biscuits. [Late 19thC. From Italian, variant of *zabaione*, of uncertain origin.]

Za·cyn·thus /zə sínthəss, -kínth-/ the most southerly of the Ionian Islands, in southwestern Greece. Population: 30,014. Area: 155 sq. mi./401 sq. km.

zad·dik *n.* = **tzaddik**

zaf·fer /záffər/, **zaf·fre** *n.* an impure form of cobalt oxide that is added to glass and ceramics to make them blue [Mid-17thC. Directly or via Italian *zaffera* from French *safre*, of uncertain origin.]

zaf·tig /zaáf tig/, **zof·tig** *adj.* with a full-figured body [Mid-20thC. Via Yiddish from Middle High German *saftec* "juicy," from *saft* "juice."]

zag /zag/ *n.* **OPPOSITE DIRECTION TO ZIG** a direction or segment of a course running opposite to a zig ■ *vi.* (**zagged, zag·ging, zags**) **TURN ABRUPTLY** to change direction quickly [Late 18thC. From ZIGZAG.]

Za·greb /zaá greb/ capital city of Croatia, situated in the north of the country, approximately 15 mi./25 km from the border with Slovenia. Population: 726,770 (1991).

Zag·ros Moun·tains /zàg ross-/ mountain range in southwestern Iran, extending from the borders with Turkey and Azerbaijan in the north to the Persian Gulf in the south. The highest peak is Sabalan, 14,921 ft./4,548 m. Length: 1,000 mi./1,600 km.

Babe Didrikson Zaharias

Za·har·i·as /zə háiriee əss, -hárriee-/, **Babe Didrikson** (1913–56) U.S. athlete. She excelled in basketball, swimming, track and field, and golf. Born **Mildred Didrikson**

zai·bat·su /zī bat sóō/ (*plural* **-su**) *n.* a large industrial combine created in Japan in the 1890s, usually by a single family, as part of the process of industrialization [Mid-20thC. From Japanese, from *zai* "wealth" + *batsu* "clique."]

zai·kai /zī kī/ *n.* the business and financial community of Japan [Mid-20thC. From Japanese, from *zai* "wealth" + *kai* "world."]

za·ïre /zaa éer/ (*plural* **-ïre** *or* **-ïres**) *n.* **1. UNIT OF CONGOLESE CURRENCY** the main unit of currency in the Democratic Republic of Congo, worth 100 makuta **2. BILL WORTH ONE ZAÏRE** a bill worth one zaïre [Mid-20thC. Named after *Zaire*, local name of the Congo River.]

Za·ire /zí éer, zaa-/ **1.** former name for **Congo, Democratic Republic of** (1971–97) **2.** former name for **Congo, River**

Za·ir·e·an /zaa éerree ən/ *adj.* PEOPLES relating to Zaire, now the Democratic Republic of Congo, or its people or culture

za·kat /zə kaát/ *n.* a tax that goes to charity, obligatory for all Muslims, set traditionally at 2.5 per cent of somebody's annual income and capital [Early 19thC. Via Persian and Urdu *zakā(t)* or Turkish *zekât* from Arabic *zakā(t)* "almsgiving."]

za·kus·ki /zə kóōskə/, **za·kus·ka** /-kaa/ *npl.* a variety of blinis and breads with savory toppings, especially caviar and other accompanying tidbits, served in Russia with vodka. Traditionally, it is an alternative to the first course of a meal but sometimes it provides a pre-theater supper, followed by the main meal after the show. [Late 19thC. From Russian, plural of *zakuska* "hors d'oeuvre."]

Zam·be·zi /zam beézee/ river in southern Africa, flowing through Zambia, Angola, Botswana, Zimbabwe, and Mozambique, and into the Indian Ocean. Length: 2,200 mi./3,540 km.

Zambia

Zam·bi·a /zámbee ə/ republic in south central Africa. It became independent from the United Kingdom in 1964. Language: English. Currency: kwacha. Capital: Lusaka. Population: 9,715,000 (1996). Area: 290,586 sq. mi./752,614 sq. km. Official name **Republic of Zambia** —**Zam·bi·an** *n., adj.*

Zam·bo·ni /zam bṓnee/ *tdmk.* a trademark for a machine that resurfaces the ice on hockey and skating rinks

za·mi·a /záymee ə/ *n.* a small tropical tree (**cycad**) that looks like a palm tree, with a short thick trunk, spiky leaves, and upright woody cones that contain seeds. It is a modern representative of a group of trees that is largely extinct. Genus: *Zamia.* [Early 19thC. Via modern Latin, genus name, ultimately from a misreading of Latin *azaniae* "pine cones."]

zam·in·dar /zámmən daàr, zə meén-/, **zem·in·dar, ja·min·dar** *n.* **1. TAX COLLECTOR IN MOGUL INDIA** a collector of property taxes in Mogul India **2. TAXPAYER IN BRITISH COLONIAL INDIA** a landlord in British colonial India liable for tax on his holdings **3. LANDOWNER IN INDIA OR PAKISTAN** somebody who has traditionally owned land in India or Pakistan [Late 17thC. Via Urdu from Persian *zamīndār*, from *zamīn* "land" + *dār* "holder."]

zam·in·dar·i /zàmmən daáree, zə meén-/ (*plural* **-is**), **zem·in·dar·y** (*plural* **-ies**), **jam·in·dar·i** (*plural* **-is**) *n.* the system of traditional land ownership in India or Pakistan, or the area of land owned [Mid-18thC. Via Urdu from Persian *zamīndārī*, from *zamīndār* (see ZAMINDAR).]

za·na·na /zə naánə/ *n.* **1. WOMEN'S QUARTERS IN TRAINS** in southern Asia, an area reserved for women in some trains and waiting rooms in railroad stations **2.** = **zenana** [Mid-18thC. From Persian and Urdu *zanānah*, from *zan* "woman." Ultimately from the Indo-European word for "woman" that is also the ancestor of English *queen*, *gyno-*, and *banshee*.]

zan·der /zándər/ (*plural* **-der** *or* **-ders**) *n.* a central European freshwater fish in the perch family, harvested for food. Latin name: *Stizostedion lucioperca*. [Mid-19thC. Via German from Low German *sandāt*, of unknown origin.]

zan·do·li /zán dṓlee/ *n.* *Carib* a largish brown and green lizard that lives in holes

za·ny /záynee/ *adj.* (**-ni·er, -ni·est**) **AMUSINGLY UNCONVENTIONAL** entertainingly strange or amusingly unusual ■ *n.* (*plural* **-nies**) **1. CLOWN** a fool, buffoon, or clown **2.** THEATER **STOCK CHARACTER** a stock character in Renaissance comedies who mimicked other characters [Late 16thC. Via French *zani* from, ultimately, Italian dialect *Zanni*, a variant of *Gianni*, pet form of *Giovanni*, the character in the commedia dell'arte who tried to mimic the clown.] —**za·ni·ly** *adv.* —**za·ni·ness** *n.* —**za·nism** *n.*

Zan·zi·bar /zánzi baar/ island of Tanzania, in the Indian Ocean, approximately 22 mi./35 km off the eastern coast of Africa. Population: 375,539 (1988). Area: 637 sq. mi./1,650 sq. km.

zap /zap/ *v.* (**zapped, zap·ping, zaps**) (*informal*) **1.** *vt.* **DESTROY SOMEBODY OR SOMETHING** to kill or finish somebody or something off with sudden force **2.** *vti.* **CHANGE TV CHANNELS USING REMOTE CONTROL** to change channels on a television set using a remote control device, especially to change channels rapidly **3.** *vi.* **MOVE QUICKLY** to move about or accomplish something very rapidly **4.** *vt.* **COOK SOMETHING IN MICROWAVE** to cook something in a microwave oven ○ *I'll just zap this for a minute and then we can eat.* **5.** *vt. Malaysia, Singapore* **PHOTOCOPY** to photocopy something ■ *n.* (*informal*) **1. ENERGY** energy and excitement **2. TIME IN MICROWAVE** a short period of time in a microwave oven ■ *interj.* **EXPRESSION OF FORCEFUL ACTION** used especially in comic books to indicate sudden and violent force (*informal*) [Early 20thC. An imitation of the sound of a lightning strike or electric sparks.]

Za·pa·ta /saa paátaa, zə-tə/, **Emiliano** (1879–1919) Mexican revolutionary. He took part in a number of uprisings, and redistributed land among the Native Central Americans in southern Mexico.

Za·pa·ta mus·tache *n.* a thick mustache that curves down around the edges of the mouth [Mid-20thC. Named for Emiliano ZAPATA, who wore such a mustache.]

za·pa·te·a·do /zàppətee aádō/ (*plural* **-dos**), **za·pa·te·o** /zàppə táy ō/ (*plural* **-os**) *n.* a Spanish or Latin American dance involving rhythmic tapping of the feet [Mid-19thC. From Spanish, from *zapatear* "to tap with the shoe," from *zapato* "shoe."]

Za·po·pan /zaápō pan/ city in southwestern Mexico near Guadalajara. Population: 668,323 (1990).

Za·po·rizhzh·ya /zə pa rózhyə/ city in southeastern Ukraine. It is situated about 135 mi./217 km west of Donetsk. Population: 897,000 (1993).

Za·po·tec /zàpə ték/ (*plural* **-tec** *or* **-tecs**) *n.* **1.** PEOPLES **NATIVE CENTRAL AMERICAN PEOPLE** a Native Central American people who before the arrival of the Spanish in the 16th century had developed one of the most advanced civilizations in Mesoamerica. Today, most Zapotec live in the highlands of Oaxaca, Mexico. **2.** LANG **OTO-MANGUEAN LANGUAGE** a language belonging to the Oto-Manguean family that is spoken in Oaxaca, Mexico. About 500,000 people speak Zapotec and it is one of the most widely-spoken Native American languages. [Late 18thC. Via Spanish *zapoteco* from, ultimately, Nahuatl *tzapotecatl*, literally "person from the place of the sapotilla."] —**Za·po·tec·an** *adj.*

zap·per /záppər/ *n.* (*informal*) **1. REMOTE CONTROL** a remote control for a television or other home entertainment device **2. INSECT-KILLING DEVICE** a device that attracts and electrocutes insects

zap·py /záppee/ (**-pi·er, -pi·est**) *adj.* lively and forcefully impressive (*informal*)

Za·ra·go·za /zàrrə gṓzə, tha ra gṓth a/ capital of Zaragoza Province in the autonomous region of Aragon, northeastern Spain. Population: 607,900 (1995).

Zar·a·thu·stra /zèrrə thóostrə/ = **Zoroaster**

za·ra·tite /zérrə tīt/ *n.* an amorphous green mineral consisting of hydrated nickel carbonate [Mid-19thC. From Spanish *zaratita*, from the surname *Zarate*.]

za·re·ba /zə réebə/ *n.* an outdoor enclosure, especially one made of thorn bushes and used as protection around a campsite or village in various parts of North Africa [Mid-19thC. From Arabic *zarība* "cattle pen."]

zarf /zaarf/ *n.* a metal frame for holding a cup, used in the Middle East [Mid-19thC. From Arabic *ẓarf* "vessel."]

za·ri /záa ree/, **ja·ri** *n.* *S Asia* gold brocade used to decorate clothes [Mid-20thC. Via Urdu from Persian *zarī*, from *zar* "gold."]

Za·ri·a /záaree ə/ city in Kaduna State, north central Nigeria. Population: 345,200 (1992).

zar·zue·la /zaar zwáylə/ *n.* a type of Spanish musical theater, usually comic, combining dialogue, music, and dance [Late 19thC. From Spanish, of uncertain origin.]

zax /zaks/ *n.* a tool similar to a hatchet used for cutting and shaping slate [Mid-17thC. Variant of *sax*, from Old English *seax* "knife." Ultimately from an Indo-European base meaning "to cut," that is also the ancestor of English *saw*, *sickle*, and *section*.]

z-ax·is *n.* one of the axes of the Cartesian coordinate system that provides a reference in three-dimensional space

za·yin /záa yin/ *n.* the seventh letter of the Hebrew alphabet, represented in the English alphabet as "Z" [Early 19thC. From Hebrew, literally "weapon."]

za·zen /záa zen/ *n.* a form of meditation in Zen, practiced sitting in a prescribed position [Early 18thC. From Japanese, "sitting zen."]

ZBB *abbr.* zero-based budgeting

Z bo·son *n.* = **Z particle**

Z chart *n.* a chart used in business and industry to illustrate production data

z-co·or·di·nate *n.* one of three numbers that provide a reference to a position in three-dimensional space, conventionally the vertical one

zeal /zeel/ *n.* energetic and unflagging enthusiasm, especially for a cause or idea [14thC. Via late Latin *zelus* from Greek *zēlos* "eager rivalry" (source also of English *jealous*).]

Zea·land /zéelənd/ = **Sjaelland**

zeal·ot /zéllət/ *n.* somebody who shows excessive enthusiasm for a cause, particularly a religious cause [Mid-16thC. Via late Latinfrom Greek *zēlōtēs*, from *zēloun* "to be jealous,"from *zēlos* (see ZEAL).] —**zeal·ot·ry** *n.*

Zeal·ot /zéllət/ *n.* a member of a group of Jewish rebels who attempted the military overthrow of Roman rule in Palestine in the 1st and 2nd centuries A.D.

zeal·ous /zélləss/ *adj.* actively and unreservedly enthusiastic [Early 16thC. From medieval Latin *zelosus*, from *zelus* (see ZEAL).] —**zeal·ous·ly** *adv.* —**zeal·ous·ness** *n.*

ze·a·tin /zée ətin/ *n.* a naturally occurring growth promoter found in many plants, first isolated from kernels of the maize plant [Mid-20thC. Coined from modern Latin *Zea*, genus name of the corn plant (see ZEIN) + -IN.]

ze·bec *n.* = **xebec**

Ze·be·dee /zébbə dee/ *n.* in the Bible, a fisherman, and the father of the apostles, James and John (Matthew 4:21)

Zebra

ze·bra /zéebrə/ *n.* **1. STRIPED ANIMAL RESEMBLING HORSE** an animal resembling a horse that is native to Africa, has a black and white or brown and white striped hide, and is found in small family groups that sometimes make up larger herds. Genus: *Equus.* **2.** = **zebra butterfly** [Early 17thC. From Italian, Spanish, or Portuguese, originally "wild ass," of uncertain origin.] —**ze·bra·ic** /zə bráy ik/ *adj.* —**ze·brine** /zée brīn, -brən/ *adj.* —**ze·broid** *adj.*

ze·bra but·ter·fly *n.* a butterfly of the southern United States with a black body marked with distinctive yellow stripes. Latin name: *Heliconius chairtonius.*

ze·bra da·ni·o *n.* = **zebra fish**

ze·bra finch *n.* an Australian finch found throughout inland areas that has a reddish-orange bill, gray head and back, and a black-and-white striped tail. Zebra finches are popular cage birds and now exist in a variety of colors not found in the wild. Latin name: *Poephila guttata.*

ze·bra fish *n.* a small freshwater fish native to India and popular in aquariums, with a blue body and longitudinal silvery or gold stripes. Latin name: *Brachydanio rerio.*

ze·bra mus·sel *n.* a European and Asian freshwater mussel regarded as a nuisance in the Great Lakes and surrounding waterways where it was accidentally introduced. Latin name: *Dreissena polymorpha.*

ze·bra plant *n.* a tropical South American evergreen plant with green and purple striped leaves. Latin name: *Calathea zebrina.*

ze·bra·wood /zéebrə wòod/ *n.* **1. HARDWOOD TREE WITH STRIPED WOOD** a tropical hardwood tree producing wood in distinct dark and light colored bands, used to make decorative furniture. Latin name: *Connarus guianensis.* **2. TREE WITH STRIPED WOOD** any tropical tree producing wood in two distinct color bands **3. STRIPED WOOD** wood from a zebrawood tree

ze·bu /zée boo/ (*plural* **-bu** *or* **-bus**) *n.* a domesticated ox of Asia and India with a humped back, curving horns, floppy ears, and a large dewlap. Latin name: *Bos indicus.* [Late 18thC. From French *zébu*, of unknown origin.]

zec·chi·no /ze kéenō/ (*plural* **-ni** /ze kéenee/ *or* **-nos**) *n.* = **sequin** [Early 17thC. From Italian (see SEQUIN).]

Zech·a·ri·ah /zèkə rī́ ə/ *n.* **1. HEBREW PROPHET** in the Bible, a Hebrew priest and prophet of the 6th century B.C. He was the husband of Elisabeth, and father of John the Baptist. **2. BOOK IN BIBLE** a book in the Bible containing the prophecies of Zechariah, including his visions of the rebuilding of the Temple in a restored Jerusalem. See table at **Bible**

zed /zed/ *n.* = **zee** [15thC. Via French *zède* and Latin *zeta* from Greek *zēta*.]

Zed·e·ki·ah /zèddə kī́ ə/ *n.* in the Bible, the last king of Judah (597 B.C.–586 B.C.). After rebelling against Nebuchadnezzar, he was imprisoned in Babylon, where he died in captivity (2 Kings 24–25) (2 Chronicles 36).

zed·o·ar·y /zéddō èree/ (*plural* **-ies**) *n.* **1. AROMATIC PLANT** an Indian plant with yellow flowers and starchy aromatic rhizomes that when dried are used as a condiment, in cosmetics, in perfume, and medicinally as a stimulant. Latin name: *Curcuma zedoaria.* **2. ZEDOARY POWDER** an aromatic powder obtained from crushing dried zedoary roots [15thC. Via medieval Latin *zedoarium* from Persian *zadwār*.]

ze·donk /zə dóngk/ *n.* the offspring of a male zebra and a female donkey [Late 20thC. Coined from ZEBRA + DONKEY.]

zee /zee/ *n.* a written representation of the sound of the letter "Z" [Late 17thC. Alteration of Latin *zeta*, under the influence of *b*, *p*, etc.]

Zee·brug·ge /zée bròogə/ port in northwestern Belgium, in northwestern Flanders Province

Zee·land /zéelənd/ province in the southwestern Netherlands. Population: 367,400 (1996). Area: 695 sq. mi./1,800 sq. km.

Zee·man ef·fect /záy maan-/ *n.* the splitting of single lines in a spectrum into two, three, or more polarized lines when the source of the spectrum is placed in a magnetic field [Late 19thC. Named for the Dutch physicist Pieter *Zeeman* (1865–1943), who described the phenomenon.]

Express Newspapers

Franco Zeffirelli

Zef·fi·rel·li /zèffəréllee/, **Franco** (*b.* 1923) Italian movie, stage, and opera director. His movies include versions of Shakespeare and adaptations of operas.

ze·in /zée in/ *n.* a powder of proteins obtained from corn, with various applications in industry and manufacturing [Early 19thC. Coined from modern Latin *Zea*, genus name of the corn plant, via Latin *zea* "emmer" from Greek *zeia*, a kind of wheat.]

Zeit·geist /zī́t gīst, tsī́t-/, **zeit·geist** *n.* the ideas prevalent in a period and place, particularly as expressed in literature, philosophy, and religion [Mid-19thC. From German, literally "spirit of the time."]

zel·ko·va /zélkəvə/ *n.* an Asian tree especially cultivated for its resistance to Dutch elm disease. Genus: *Zelkova.* [Late 19thC. Via modern Latin, genus name, from, ultimately, a Caucasian source.]

zem·in·dar *n.* = **zamindar**

zem·in·dar·y *n.* = **zamindari**

zem·stvo /zém stvō/ (*plural* **-stvos**) *n.* an elected provincial legislature that existed in Russia between 1864 and 1917 [Mid-19thC. From Russian, from obsolete *zem* "land." Ultimately from an Indo-European base meaning "earth," which is also the ancestor of English *chthonic*, *humble*, and *bridegroom*.]

Zen /zen/, **Zen Bud·dhism** *n.* a major school of Buddhism originating in 12th century China that emphasizes enlightenment through meditation and insight [Early 18thC. Via Japanese *zen* and Chinese *chán* from, ultimately, Sanskrit *dhyānam* "meditation," literally "watching."]

ze·na·na, **za·na·na** *n.* in southern Asia, the part of the house reserved for women and girls in a Muslim household [Mid-18thC. From Persian and Urdu *zanānah*, from *zan* "woman." Ultimately from an Indo-European word that is also the ancestor of English *queen*, *gyno-*, and *banshee*.]

Zen Bud·dhism *n.* = **Zen**

Zend /zend/ *n.* **1.** = **Zend-Avesta** **2.** LANG = **Avesta**

Zend-A·ves·ta /-ə véstə/ *n.* the canonical writings of Zoroastrianism, preserved in the Pahlavi language [Mid-17thC. Via French from Persian *zand-awastā*, literally "Avesta with interpretation," from Middle Persian *zend* "interpretation" + *Awastā* (see AVESTA).]

ze·ner di·ode /zeénər-/ *n.* a type of semiconductor used as a voltage regulator because of its ability to maintain a constant voltage during fluctuating current conditions [Mid-20thC. Named for the U.S. physicist Clarence M. *Zener* (1905–93), whose research led to the device.]

Zeng·er /zéng ər, -gər/, **John Peter** (1697–1746) German-born U.S. newspaper publisher. His acquittal on a charge of sedition libel was a milestone in press freedom.

ze·nith /zeénith/ *n.* **1.** ASTRON **POINT STRAIGHT UP** the point of the celestial sphere that is directly over the observer and 90 degrees from all points on that person's horizon **2. HIGHEST POINT** the high point or climax of something [14thC. Via Old French and medieval Latin from, ultimately, Arabic *samt (ar-ra's)* "path (over the head)" (source also of English *azimuth*).] —**ze·nith·al** *adj.*

ze·nith·al pro·jec·tion *n.* a type of map projection of the Earth onto a plane tangential to a point on the surface of the Earth such as the North Pole or the Equator

Ze·no of E·le·a /zeénō əv eélee ə/ (*fl.* 5th century B.C.) Greek mathematician and philosopher. The paradoxes for which his philosophy is known were designed to discredit the information conveyed by the senses. Aristotle regarded him as the inventor of dialectical reasoning.

ze·o·lite /zeé əlīt/ *n.* one of a large group of amorphous hydrated aluminum silicate minerals that may also contain sodium, calcium, barium, and potassium, occurring in cavities in weathered igneous rocks and hydrothermal veins. The ion exchange properties of zeolites have application in water purification. [Late 18thC. Coined from Greek *zein* "to boil" (source of English *eczema*).] —**ze·o·lit·ic** /zeé ə líttik/ *adj.*

Ze·pha·ni·ah /zèffə nī ə/ *n.* **1. HEBREW PROPHET** in the Bible, a minor Hebrew prophet of the 7th century B.C. **2. BOOK IN THE BIBLE** a book in the Bible, traditionally attributed to Zephaniah. It urges repentance by the people of Judah, and predicts a day of judgment.

zeph·yr /zéffər/ *n.* **1. MILD WIND** a light warming breeze **2.** TEXTILES **DELICATE FABRIC** a delicate usually woolen fabric or garment [Pre-12thC. Via Latin from Greek *zephuros* "west wind."]

zeph·yr lil·y *n.* a tropical American plant with clump-forming bulbs, narrow leaves, and single funnel-shaped colorful flowers. Genus: *Zephyranthes.* [From the fact that the plant is native to warm regions]

Zeph·y·rus /zéffərəss/ *n.* in Greek mythology, the god who personified the west wind and was always mild and gentle in character. ◊ **Boreas**

zep·pe·lin /zéppələn/ *n.* a rigid cylindrical airship consisting of a covered frame and a suspended compartment for engines and passengers [Early 20thC. Named for Count Ferdinand von *Zeppelin* (1838–1917), who constructed the first such airship.]

Zer·matt /zúr màt, tsur mát/ town and ski resort in Valais Canton, southwestern Switzerland. Population: 4,200 (1989).

ze·ro /zeérō/ *n.* (*plural* **-ros** *or* **-roes**) **1. SYMBOL 0** the numerical symbol 0, representing the absence of any quantity or magnitude **2. NUMBER WITH THE VALUE OF 0** the number that, when added to another number, results in that number, e.g., 0 + 4 = 4 **3. STARTING POINT FOR VALUES ON GAUGE** the starting or center point for values on a counter, scale, or gauge ○ *Set the counter to zero.* **4. LOW TEMPERATURE** the temperature indicated by 0 on a thermometer scale, especially that corresponding to the freezing point of water on the Celsius scale ○ *It got down to zero last night.* **5. LOW POINT** the lowest possible point or degree ○ *Her spirits are at zero.* **6. NOTHING** nothing or nil ○ *They beat us five to zero.* **7. FAILURE** somebody who is regarded as a complete failure (*insult*) **8.** LING **ABSTRACT REALIZATION OF A MORPHEME** a variant form of a morpheme (**allomorph**) that is purely abstract and does not exist in any physical phonetic form. An example of a zero allomorph in English is the plural marker of "sheep." Compare "two cats," "two dogs," and "two sheep." **9.** ARMS **SETTING ON A GUN SIGHT** a setting on a gun sight indicating the center of a target ■ *vt.* (**-roed, -ro·ing, -roes**) **SET TO ZERO** to set an instrument, gauge, counter, or similar measuring device to zero ■ *adj.* **1. COMPLETELY WITHOUT SOMETHING** utterly lacking a particular thing (*informal*) **2.** METEOROL **WITH LIMITED VISIBILITY** used to describe a level of visibility limited to 50 ft./15 m vertically or 165 ft./50 m horizontally [Early 17thC. Via French and Italian from, ultimately, Arabic *ṣifr* "emptiness" (source of English *cipher*).]

zero in *vi.* **1.** MIL **LOCATE A TARGET AND AIM AT IT** to find the precise position of a target and move toward it or aim a weapon at it, threateningly or inexorably **2. IDENTIFY SOMETHING AND CONCENTRATE ON IT** to identify something precisely and concentrate all efforts on dealing with it ○ *The report zeroed in on the weaknesses inherent in the management structure.* [From the technique of setting a gun sight exactly on a target by canceling out the effects of elevation and wind deflection]

ze·ro-base, ze·ro-based *adj.* relating to a budget or budgeting that considers each item on its merits without reference to previous practice or expenditure

ze·ro-cou·pon *adj.* FIN not paying interest but sold at a discount and redeemable at maturity ○ *a zero-coupon bond*

ze·ro-de·fect *adj.* with no defects or flaws

ze·ro grav·i·ty *n.* PHYS a condition of apparent weightlessness resulting from the centrifugal force on an object counterbalancing the gravitational force attracting it

ze·ro growth *n.* no increase in the growth or development of something, especially when an increase might have been expected and where any increase is measured as a percentage ○ *predictions of zero growth in the economy*

ze·ro hour *n.* **1.** MIL **SCHEDULED START OF A MILITARY OPERATION** the time set for the start of a military operation **2. TIME WHEN SOMETHING IMPORTANT WILL OCCUR** the time or date when something important is due to happen

ze·ro op·tion *n.* an offer to limit the number of short-range nuclear missiles or remove them altogether if an opposing side agrees to do the same

ze·ro pop·u·la·tion growth *n.* a situation in which the number of new births is no greater than the number of people dying, so that the overall population size remains the same

ze·ro-sum *adj.* relating to a situation in which a gain by one side or person requires any other side or person involved in it to sustain a corresponding loss

ze·roth /zí rōth/ *adj.* preceding number one in a series [Late 19thC. Coined from ZERO + -TH.]

ze·ro tol·er·ance *n.* the absence of any leniency or exception in the enforcement of a law, rule, or regulation, especially a law against antisocial behavior

ze·ro-ze·ro *adj.* AIR used to describe flying conditions in which cloud is so thick and low that the pilot can see nothing ahead and nothing above or below the aircraft [Shortening of *zero ceiling, zero visibility*]

ze·ro-ze·ro op·tion *n.* = **double-zero option**

zest /zest/ *n.* **1. HEARTY ENJOYMENT** lively enjoyment and enthusiasm ○ *zest for life* **2. EXCITING ELEMENT ADDING TO ENJOYMENT** an exciting or interesting quality that makes something particularly enjoyable **3.** COOK **CITRUS PEEL USED AS FLAVORING** the thin outer rind of the peel of a citrus fruit that is cut, scraped, or grated to yield a sharp fruity flavoring for foods and drinks **4. PIQUANT FLAVOR** a pleasantly sharp flavor ■ *vt.* (**zest·ed, zest·ing, zests**) **1.** COOK **GRATE THE SKIN OF CITRUS FRUIT** to cut, grate, or scrape the rind of a citrus fruit in order to flavor foods and drinks **2. MAKE SOMETHING MORE STIMULATING AND ENJOYABLE** to make an experience more enjoyable by adding excitement or interest to it [15thC. Originally in the meaning of "orange or lemon peel," from French, of unknown origin.] —**zest·y** *adj.*

zest·er /zéstər/ *n.* a small utensil with a row of tiny sharpened holes or edges at its tip for cutting strips of zest from oranges, lemons, or other citrus fruits

zest·ful /zéstfəl/ *adj.* full of or showing lively enjoyment and enthusiasm —**zest·ful·ly** *adv.* —**zest·ful·ness** *n.*

ze·ta /záytə, zeétə/ *n.* the sixth letter of the Greek alphabet, written in the English alphabet as Z [Early 18thC. From Greek *zēta*, of Phoenician origin.]

Ze·thus /zeéthəss/ *n.* in Greek mythology, a son of Zeus and Antiope and the twin of Amphion. The brothers became joint kings of Thebes.

zeug·ma /zóogmə/ *n.* a figure of speech in which an adjective or verb is used with two nouns but is appropriate to only one of them or has a different sense with each. The sentence "During the race he broke the record and a leg" is a zeugma. [Late 16thC. Via Latin from Greek, literally "joining."] —**zeug·mat·ic** /zoog máttik/ *adj.* —**zeug·mat·i·cal·ly** /-máttiklee/ *adv.*

Zeus /zooss/ *n.* in Greek mythology, the god of the sky, ruler of the Olympian gods, and spiritual father of gods and mortals. Roman equivalent **Jupiter**

Zhang·jia·kou /jaáng jyaá kṓ/ city in northeastern China in Hebei Province, situated at one of the gates of the Great Wall of China. Population: 529,136 (1990).

Zhang Zhi·dong /jaáng jeédáwng/ (1837–1909) Chinese reformer and statesman. A modernizer in the Qing administration, he reformed the Chinese educational system.

Zhao Meng·fu /jòw məng fóo/ (1254–1322) Chinese artist. He is known for his realistic animal pictures and for his expressive landscapes and studies of bamboo.

Zhe·jiang /jè jáng/ province in China on the East China Sea. Capital: Hangzhou. Population: 42,940,000 (1994). Area: 38,600 sq. mi./100,000 sq. km.

Zhen·ghe ex·pe·di·tions /júng hə-/ *npl.* a series of seven overseas trade expeditions under the Ming emperor Yunglo between 1405 and 1423 that were the last Chinese attempt to create a worldwide trading empire [Named for *Zhenghe*, the court eunuch who led the expeditions]

Zheng·zhou /jùng jṓ/ capital city of Henan Province, located on the Yellow River between Taiyuan and Wuhan, in eastern China. Population: 1,710,000 (1991).

zho *n.* ZOOL = **dzo**

Zhou /jō/ *n.* a Chinese dynasty that ruled from the 12th to the 3rd centuries B.C., during which China was divided into feudal states and the religions of Confucianism and Taoism arose [Late 18thC. From Chinese *zhòu*.]

zib·e·line /zíbbə leén, -līn/, **zib·el·line** *n.* a thick soft fabric with a long nap, made of wool, especially mohair or alpaca, or of the hair of another animal such as a camel [Late 16thC. Via French from Italian *zibellino* "sable," of Slavic origin.]

zib·et /zíbbit/ *n.* a civet native to Southeast Asia. Latin name: *Viverra zibetha.* [Late 16thC. Via medieval Latin *zibethum* or Italian *zibetto* from Arabic *zabād* "musky perfume obtained from civets" (source of English *civet*).]

zi·do·vu·dine /zi dṓvyoo deén/ *n.* = **AZT** [Late 20thC. Origin uncertain: probably an alteration of AZIDOTHYMIDINE.]

CORBIS/Bettmann

Florenz Ziegfeld

Zieg·feld /zíg fèld/, **Florenz** (1869–1932) U.S. theater producer. He launched the Ziegfeld Follies, an annual musical revue (1907), and produced extravagant musicals in New York.

zig /zig/ *n.* **ONE DIRECTION OF A ZIGZAG** a sharp line, direction, movement, or course that forms part of a zigzag ■ *vi.* (**zigged, zig·ging, zigs**) **FORM PART OF A ZIGZAG** to move in a sharp line, direction, movement, or course that forms part of a zigzag [Mid-20thC. Back-formation from ZIGZAG.]

zig·gu·rat /zíggə ràt/ *n.* an ancient Mesopotamian pyramid-shaped tower with a square base, rising in stories of ever-decreasing size, with a terrace at each story and a temple at the very top. It is thought that the Tower of Babel referred to in the Bible was a tower of this kind. [Late 19thC. From Assyrian *ziqqurratu* "pinnacle."]

zig·zag /zíg zàg/ *n.* **1. LINE TAKING ALTERNATING TURNS** a line going at an angle first one way, then sharply the opposite way, then back the first way, and so on,

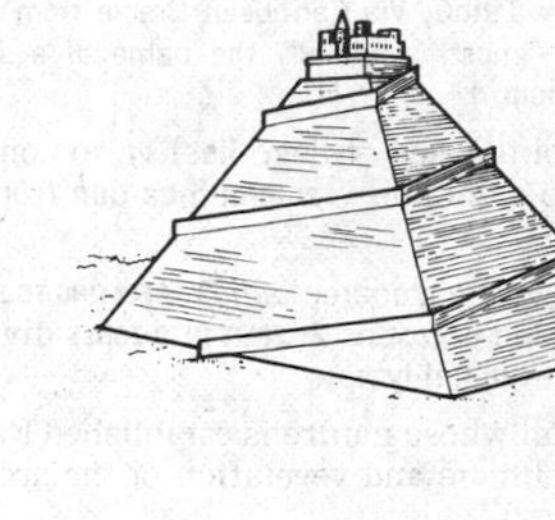

Ziggurat

like the outline of a saw's teeth **2.** SOMETHING REPEATEDLY SWITCHING DIRECTIONS SHARPLY something that follows a sharply alternating line or course, e.g., a road with sharp bends alternating right and left ■ *adv.* IN SHARPLY ALTERNATING DIRECTIONS along a sharply alternating line or course ■ *v.* **(-zagged, -zag·ging, -zags) 1.** *vti.* PROCEED IN A SHARPLY ALTERNATING PATH to follow a sharply alternating line or course, moving rapidly ○ *They zigzagged across the field, dodging enemy bullets.* **2.** *vt.* SEW MAKE A SHARPLY ALTERNATING PATTERN to make a pattern of sharply alternating lines or directions, e.g., by sewing something with herringbone stitches [Early 18thC. Via French from German *Zickzack*, of uncertain origin: perhaps formed from *Zacke* "tooth."] —**zig·zag·ged·ness** /zíg zàggədnəss/ *n.*

zig·zag fence *n. Northeast U.S.* a fence made of split rails each resting on and set at angles to the next, forming a zigzag

WORD KEY: USAGE

This term belongs to Upper New England. It occupies much the same territory as *snake fence*; together, they contrast with the Pennsylvania and North Midland *worm fence*. In the South and the West, *rail fence* prevails, with scattered instances of the Eastern forms, as well as *log fence*, *split-rail fence*, and *stake-and-rider fence*.

zi·la *n.* = **zillah**

zilch /zilch/ *pron.* zero or nothing at all (*informal*) ○ *They take all the profits and we're left with zilch.* [Mid-20thC. Origin unknown.]

zill /zil/ *n.* either one of a pair of tiny cymbals that belly dancers hold in their fingers and play in time to their dancing [From Turkish *zil* "cymbals"]

zil·lah /zíllə/, **zil·la, zi·la** /zeélə/ *n.* an administrative district in India when the country was under British rule [Early 19thC. Via Persian and Urdu from Arabic *ḍila'* "division."]

zil·lion /zíllyən/ *adj.* HUGE NUMBER OR QUANTITY a number or quantity so huge it cannot be counted or determined (*informal*) ○ *I had a zillion things to do.* ■ *pron.* HUGE NUMBER OF PEOPLE OR THINGS a number of people or quantity of things so huge it cannot be counted or determined (*informal*) ○ *Zillions preferred the new model to the old one.* [Mid-20thC. Modeled on *million* and *billion*, with *z* representing the last in a series.]

zil·lion·aire /zìllyə náir, zíllyə nàir/ *n.* somebody who is extremely wealthy (*informal*) [Mid-20thC. Modeled on *millionaire*.]

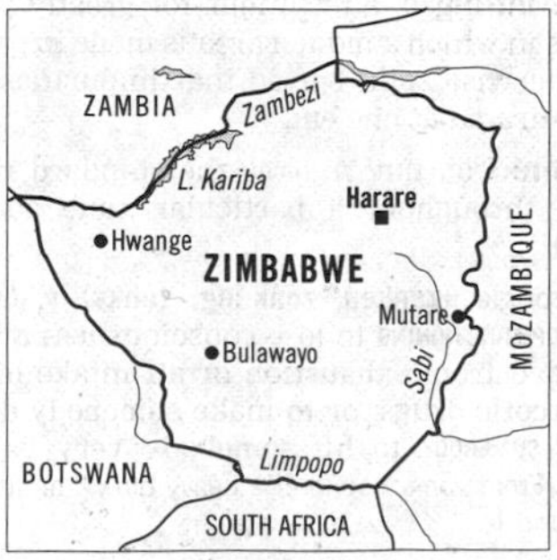

Zimbabwe

Zim·bab·we /zim baábwee, -baáb way/ republic in southern Africa. Language: English. Currency: Zimbabwe dollar. Capital: Harare. Population: 11,515,000 (1996). Area: 150,873 sq. mi./390,759 sq. km. Official name **Republic of Zimbabwe**. Former name **Rhodesia** —**Zim·bab·we·an** *n., adj.*

zinc /zingk/ *n.* BLUISH METALLIC ELEMENT USED AS ANTI-CORROSIVE a bluish-white metallic chemical element that is used in alloys such as brass and German silver and as a protective corrosion-resistant coating for other metals, especially steel and iron. Symbol **Zn** ■ *vt.* **(zinced** *or* **zincked, zinc·ing** *or* **zinck·ing, zincs)** INDUST COAT WITH ZINC to cover a metal, especially iron or steel, with a protective corrosion-resistant coating of zinc [Mid-17thC. From German *Zink*, of unknown origin.] —**zin·cic** *adj.* —**zinck·y** *adj.* —**zin·coid** *adj.*

zinc·ate /zíng kàyt/ *n.* a salt derived from zinc hydroxide

zinc blende *n.* MINERALS = **sphalerite**

zinc chlo·ride *n.* a poisonous soluble salt used as a wood preservative, an antiseptic, and a catalyst in chemical reactions. Formula: $ZnCl_2$.

zin·cif·er·ous /zing kíffərəss/ *adj.* containing or yielding zinc, especially as an ore

zinc·ite /zíng kìt/ *n.* a reddish-orange mineral form of zinc oxide

zinck·en·ite *n.* MINERALS = **zinkenite**

zinc·o·graph /zíngkə gràf/ *n.* **1.** ZINC PRINTING PLATE WITH AN ETCHED SURFACE a printing plate made of zinc that has the design to be printed etched into its surface **2.** PRINT TAKEN FROM A ZINC PLATE a print taken from a printing plate made of zinc that has the design to be printed etched into its surface [Late 19thC. Back-formation from ZINCOGRAPHY.]

zinc·og·ra·phy /zing kóggrəfee/ *n.* the art or business of making zinc printing plates with the designs to be printed etched into their surfaces [Mid-19thC. Coined from modern Latin *zincum* "zinc" + -GRAPHY.] —**zinc·og·ra·pher** *n.* —**zinc·o·graph·ic** /zìngkə gráffik/ *adj.*

zinc oint·ment *n.* a soothing antiseptic ointment containing zinc oxide in a base of petroleum jelly or lanolin, used to treat skin conditions

zinc ox·ide *n.* an odorless water-insoluble white powder that is used as an astringent in cosmetics, an antiseptic in ointments, and a pigment in paints and inks. Formula: ZnO.

zinc sul·fate *n.* a colorless crystalline powder that is used as a pigment in paints and inks, as an emetic in pharmaceuticals, and in wood preservatives and crop sprays. Formula: $ZnSO_4$.

zinc sul·fide *n.* a crystalline white or yellowish powder used as a pigment and as a phosphor on X-ray and television screens. Formula: ZnS.

zinc white *n.* zinc oxide used as a white pigment in paint

Zin·der /zíndər/ city in south central Niger. Situated about 70 mi./113 km north of the border with Nigeria, it was Niger's capital until 1926. Population: 119,838 (1988).

zine /zeen/ *n.* a self-published paper, Internet magazine, or other periodical, issued at irregular intervals with limited means and usually appealing to a specialist readership (*informal*) [Mid-20thC. Shortening of MAGAZINE.]

zin·fan·del /zínfən dèl/, **Zinfandel** *n.* **1.** PLANTS VARIETY OF GRAPE a variety of black grape used, especially in California, to make a light fruity red or rosé wine **2.** WINE WINE MADE FROM ZINFANDEL GRAPE a light-bodied fruity red or rosé wine, or less commonly a hearty red wine, made from the zinfandel grape, especially in California [Mid-19thC. Origin unknown.]

zing /zing/ *n.* **1.** SHARP SINGING SOUND a short high-pitched humming or buzzing sound, e.g., the sound of a bullet whizzing through the air **2.** LIVELY AND EXCITING QUALITY a lively exciting aspect of something that makes it particularly enjoyable (*informal*) ○ *The rhythm guitar gives the tune extra zing.* ■ *v.* **(zinged, zing·ing, zings)** (*informal*) **1.** *vi.* MAKE A HUMMING NOISE to make or move with a short high-pitched humming or buzzing noise **2.** *vt.* ATTACK WITH WORDS to criticize somebody sharply, especially in a swift and clever way [Early 20thC. An imitation of the sound.] —**zing·y** *adj.*

zing·er /zíngər/ *n.* (*informal*) **1.** CLEVER REMARK SKILLFULLY DELIVERED a remark delivered with great skill and speed, especially a sharp and perfectly timed witticism or criticism **2.** SHOCKING AND UNEXPECTED HAPPENING a shocking and unexpected turn of events such as an abrupt shift in the plot of a movie, play, or book **3.** SOMEBODY OR SOMETHING ENERGETIC AND SURPRISING somebody who or something that is energetic and produces startling results [Early 20thC. Formed from ZING.]

zin·jan·thro·pus /zin jánthrəpəss/ (*plural* **-pi** /-pì/ *or* **-pus·es**) *n.* a hominid fossil found in 1959 at Olduvai Gorge in East Africa. Originally classified as a distinct genus and species, it is now recognized as an australopithecine. [Mid-20thC. From modern Latin, former genus name, from medieval Arabic *Zinj* "East Africa" + Greek *anthrōpos* "person."] —**zin·jan·thro·pine** *adj., n.*

zink·en·ite /zíngkə nìt/, **zinck·en·ite** *n.* a dark gray mineral consisting of antimony and a sulfide of lead [Mid-19thC. Named for the German mineralogist J. K. L. *Zincken* (1790–1862).]

Zinnia

zin·ni·a /zínnee ə/ (*plural* **-as** *or* **-a**) *n.* a plant of the daisy family native to Mexico and adjacent areas that is widely grown as a garden plant for its large colorful flower heads. It is the state flower of Indiana. Genus: *Zinnia.* [Mid-18thC. From modern Latin, genus name, named for the German physician and botanist Johann Gottfried *Zinn* (1727–59).]

Zins·ser /zínsər/, **Hans** (1878–1940) U.S. bacteriologist. A pioneer of immunology, he worked on typhus, cholera, and other bacterial diseases.

Zi·on /zí ən/ *n.* **1.** JUDAISM MOUNTAIN NEAR JERUSALEM one of the hills of Jerusalem, in Biblical times emblematic of the house or household of God and later by extension the Jewish people and their religion **2.** CHR PLACE OF CHRISTIAN LIFE AND WORSHIP in Christian belief, the place where God lives and is worshiped on earth or in the kingdom of heaven [Pre-12thC. Via late Latin and Greek from Hebrew *ṣīyôn*.]

Zi·on·ism /zí ə nìzzəm/ *n.* a worldwide movement, originating in the 19th century, that sought to establish and develop a Jewish nation in Palestine. Since 1948 its function has been to support the state of Israel.

Zi·on·ist /zí ənist/ *n.* **1.** JUDAISM SUPPORTER OF A JEWISH STATE a supporter of 19th-century Zionism, or a modern supporter of the state of Israel **2.** *S Africa* CHR CHRISTIAN WITH TRADITIONAL AFRICAN BELIEFS a member of an independent Christian church in South Africa that incorporates traditional African beliefs and forms of worship —**Zi·on·ist** *adj.* —**Zi·on·is·tic** /zì ə nístik/ *adj.*

Zi·on Na·tion·al Park park in southwestern Utah, characterized by canyons, mesas, and cliffs. Its main feature is Zion Canyon. Area: 229 sq. mi./593 sq. km.

zip /zip/ *n.* **1.** LIVELY AND EXCITING QUALITY a lively exciting aspect of something that makes it particularly enjoyable (*informal*) **2.** BRIEF HISSING SOUND a brief sibilant sound such as the sound of a bullet whizzing through the air **3.** *U.K., Can* = **zipper 4.** ZERO nothing at all (*informal*) **5.** = **zip code** ■ *v.* **(zipped, zip·ping, zips) 1.** *vti.* FASTEN WITH ZIPPER to fasten something, or to be fastened, with a zipper **2.** *vi.* MAKE OR MOVE WITH HISSING SOUND to make or move with a rapid sibilant sound (*informal*) **3.** *vti.* GO OR MOVE VERY FAST to go somewhere or move something somewhere very fast (*informal*) **4.** *vt.* COMPUT COMPRESS A FILE to compress a computer file for storage or transmission [Late 19thC. An imitation of the sound.]

ZIP code, zip code *n.* a sequence of five or nine digits forming part of all postal addresses that is used to identify each postal district in the United States [An acronym formed from *Zone Improvement Program*]

zip file *n.* a computer file with the extension .ZIP containing data that has been compressed for storage or transmission.

zip gun *n.* a homemade pistol, especially one that uses a spring or a rubber band as the firing mechanism (*slang*)

zip·less /zípplәss/ *adj.* **1. WITH NO ZIPPER** not fitted with, or fastened using, a zipper **2. PASSIONATE** passionate and lasting only a short time [Late 20thC. In the sense of "passionate," from the idea of clothes coming off suddenly, without the awkward undoing of zippers.]

Zip·loc /zíp lòk/ *tdmk.* a trademark for a small transparent plastic storage bag that is sealed by pressing together the specially prepared edges of the opening

zip·per /zíppәr/ *n.* a fastener for clothes, bags, or garments consisting of two rows of interlocking metal or plastic teeth with an attached sliding tab pulled to open or close the fastener [Early 20thC. Originally a trademark.]

zip·pered /zíppәrd/ *adj.* fitted with or fastened using a zipper

zip·po /zíppō/ *n.* = **zip** *n.* 4 (*informal*)

Zip·po *tdmk.* a trademark for a sturdy metal cigarette lighter [Mid-20thC]

zip·py /zíppee/ (**-pi·er, -pi·est**) *adj.* showing or having spirit or energy (*informal*)

Zir·ca·loy /zúrkә lòy/ *tdmk.* a trademark for an alloy of zirconium with tin, chromium, and nickel that is resistant to heat and corrosion, making it a useful material in the nuclear power industry

zir·con /zúr kòn/ *n.* zirconium silicate, a very hard crystalline mineral that is the main source of zirconium. In its colorless varieties it is used as a substitute for diamonds in jewelry. [Late 18thC. From German *Zirkon*, via Arabic from, ultimately, Persian *āzargūn* "fire color."]

zir·co·ni·a /zur kṓnee ә/ *n.* = **zirconium oxide** [Late 18thC. Formed from ZIRCON.]

zir·co·ni·um /zur kṓnee әm/ *n.* a grayish-white metallic chemical element used as a coating for the fuel rods in nuclear reactors because of its very high resistance to corrosion and its low absorption of neutrons. Symbol **Zr** —**zir·con·ic** /zur kónnik/ *adj.*

zir·co·ni·um ox·ide *n.* a heavy water-insoluble white powder used as a pigment for paints, as an abrasive, and in making heat-resistant materials and ceramics. Formula: ZrO_2.

zit /zit/ *n.* a pimple on the skin (*slang*) [Mid-20thC. Origin unknown.] —**zit·ty** *adj.*

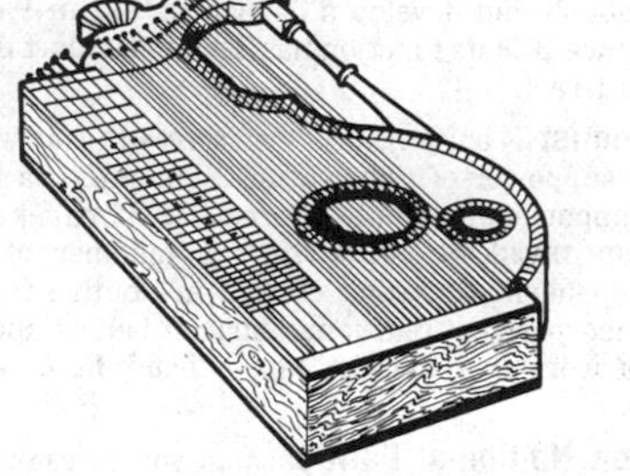

Zither

zith·er /zíthәr, zíthәr/ *n.* a musical instrument consisting of a flat shallow sound box with up to forty-five metal strings stretched across it that are plucked with the fingers or a plectrum [Mid-19thC. Via German from Latin *cithara* (see CITHARA).] —**zith·er·ist** *n.*

zi·ti /zée tée/ *n.* pasta in the form of medium-sized tubes, longer and thicker than macaroni [Mid-19thC. From Italian, plural of *zito*, literally "boy."]

Zl *abbr.* zloty

Z line *n.* a narrow dark line across striated muscle fibers that marks the boundaries between adjacent segments [*Z* from the initial letter of German *Zwischenscheibe* "intervening disk"]

zlo·ty /zlóttee/ (*plural* **-ties** *or* **-ty**) *n.* **1. UNIT OF POLISH CURRENCY** the main unit of currency in Poland, worth 100 groszy. See table at **currency 2. COIN WORTH A ZLOTY** a coin worth one zloty [Early 20thC. From Polish *złoty*, literally "golden," from *złoto* "gold." Ultimately from an Indo-European word that is also the ancestor of English *gold* and *guilder*.]

Zn *symbol.* zinc

zo *n.* = **dzo**

zo- *prefix.* = **zoo-** (*used before vowels*)

zo·ar·i·um /zō áiree әm/ (*plural* **-ums** *or* **-a** /-ә/) *n.* a collection of distinct organisms that together form a compound organism [Late 19thC. Formed from Greek *zōion* "animal" (see -ZOON).]

zod. *abbr.* zodiac

zo·di·ac /zṓdee àk/ *n.* **1.** ASTRON **PART OF THE SKY CONTAINING THE MAJOR CONSTELLATIONS** a narrow band in the sky in which the movements of the major planets, Sun, and Moon take place, astrologically divided into twelve sections named for the major constellations **2.** ZODIAC **ASTROLOGER'S CHART** a chart linking twelve constellations to twelve divisions of the year, used as the astrologer's main tool for analyzing character and predicting the future **3. RECURRING SET** a set of things or sequence of events that repeats itself cyclically (*literary*) [14thC. Via French and Latin from Greek *zōidiakos kuklos*, literally "circle of animal figures," from *zōidion* "small animal," from *zōion* "living being" (see -ZOON).] —**zo·di·a·cal** /zō dī́ әk'l/ *adj.*

zo·di·a·cal con·stel·la·tion *n.* any of the twelve constellations that a sign of the zodiac is named for. The constellations are Aries, Taurus, Gemini, Cancer, Leo, Virgo, Libra, Scorpio, Sagittarius, Capricorn, Aquarius, and Pisces.

zo·di·a·cal light *n.* a faint glow in the sky, seen before sunrise to the east and after sunset to the west and caused by small particles reflected in sunlight

zof·tig *adj.* = **zaftig** (*slang*)

Zo·har /zṓ haar/ *n.* a 13th-century Jewish mystical text that is the primary text of cabalistic writings [Late 17thC. From Hebrew *zōhar*, literally "light, splendor."]

-zoic *suffix.* **1.** relating to a particular geologic era ○ *Mesozoic* **2.** having a particular kind of animal existence [Formed from Greek *zōē* "life." Ultimately from an Indo-European base meaning "to live," which is also the ancestor of English *quick, vital*, and *biology*.]

zoi·site /zóy sīt/ *n.* a gray or green hydrated calcium aluminosilicate mineral found in metamorphic rocks [Early 19thC. Named for the Slovenian scholar Baron Sigismund *Zois* von Edelstein (1747–1819), who discovered it.]

AKG London

Émile Zola

Zo·la /zṓlә, zṓ laa/, **Émile** (1840–1902) French novelist. The leading French novelist of the 19th century, he employed a scientifically based technique of naturalism in his epic 20-novel cycle *Les Rougon-Macquart* (1871–93). He is also known for "J'Accuse" (1898), a defense of Alfred Dreyfus. Full name **Émile Édouard Charles Antoine Zola**

Zoll·ver·ein /tsáwlfә rīn, záwl-/ *n.* **1.** HISTORY **19C GERMAN CUSTOMS UNION** a customs union formed in the 19th century by a number of German states to establish uniform import tariffs from other countries and free trade among themselves **2. CUSTOMS UNION** any customs union formed to establish uniform import tariffs [Mid-19thC. From German, literally "tariff union."]

zom·bie /zómbee/, **zom·bi** *n.* **1. SOMEBODY UNRESPONSIVE OR UNTHINKING** somebody who lacks energy, enthusiasm, or the ability to think independently (*informal*) **2. DEAD BODY GIVEN LIFE BY VOODOO** in voodoo, a soulless dead body brought back to life again **3. VOODOO SPIRIT REVIVING A DEAD BODY** in voodoo, a spirit that brings a soulless dead body back to life again **4.** RELIG **SNAKE GOD OF VOODOO** a snake god of West Indian, Brazilian, and West African voodoo religions **5.** BEVERAGES **VERY STRONG RUM COCKTAIL** a very strong alcoholic cocktail made with various kinds of rum **6.** HIST **ARMY CONSCRIPT ASSIGNED FOR HOME DEFENSE** in Canada, a conscripted soldier assigned to home defense during World War II (*slang*) [Early 19thC. Via Caribbean Creole from Kimbundu *n-zumbi* "ghost," originally the name of a snake god.] —**zom·bi·ism** *n.*

zom·bi·fy /zómbi fī/ (**-fied, -fy·ing, -fies**) *vt.* to convert somebody into a zombie —**zom·bi·fi·ca·tion** /zòmbifi káysh'n/ *n.*

zo·nal /zṓn'l/, **zo·na·ry** /zṓnәree/ *adj.* **1. RELATING TO ZONES** relating to a zone or zones **2. SPLIT INTO ZONES** divided up into zones —**zo·nal·ly** *adv.*

zo·nal soil *n.* soil whose nature is established by the action of the climate and vegetation of the area in which it is found

zo·na pel·lu·di·ca /zṓnә pә lóossidә/ *n.* a thick transparent envelope that surrounds a developing ovum, allowing only one sperm cell through to fertilize the ovum [From modern Latin, literally "transparent band"]

zo·na·ry *adj.* = **zonal**

zo·nate /zṓ nàyt/, **zo·nat·ed** /zṓ nàytәd/ *adj.* **1. ARRANGED IN ZONES** divided up into zones **2. MARKED BY ZONES** distinguished by zones, e.g., of color or texture

zo·na·tion /zō náysh'n/ *n.* the division of something into separate zones

zone /zōn/ *n.* **1. SEPARATE AREA WITH A PARTICULAR FUNCTION** an area regarded as separate or kept separate, especially one with a particular use or function ○ *a loading zone* **2. SUBSECTION OF A PARTICULAR AREA** one of the smaller, usually named or numbered sections that a particular area is divided into, e.g., those of a transportation network or an athletic field **3.** METEOROL **HORIZONTAL CLIMATIC BAND AROUND THE EARTH** one of five horizontal bands across the Earth's surface, separated by the Arctic Circle, the Tropic of Cancer, the Tropic of Capricorn, and the Antarctic Circle, that marks climates. The zones are called the North Frigid Zone, the North Temperate Zone, the South Frigid Zone, the South Temperate Zone, and the Torrid Zone. **4.** TIME **TIME ZONE** a time zone **5.** ECOL **AREA WITH DISTINCT PLANTS AND ANIMALS** an area with characteristic types of organisms determined largely by its environment, e.g., any of the belts of vegetation on a mountain **6.** GEOL **UNIT OF ROCK FORMATION WITH FOSSILS** a unit of a rock formation characterized by its fossil content **7.** MATH **PART OF A SPHERE** the portion of a sphere included between two parallel planes meeting the sphere, one of which may be tangent to the sphere or both of which may intersect it ■ *vti.* (**zoned, zon·ing, zones**) **1. SPLIT INTO ZONES** to divide up an area into zones **2. DESIGNATE AREA FOR SOMETHING** to declare officially that an area is to be used for a particular purpose or to be developed in a particular way (*often passive*) ○ *The canal areas have been zoned for leisure and recreation.* [15thC. Via French and Latin from Greek *zōnē* "belt, girdle."] —**zon·ing** *n.*

zone de·fense *n.* a system of defense in sports, especially in basketball and football, in which each defender is responsible for guarding a portion of the playing area

zone melt·ing *n.* = **zone refining**

zone of sat·u·ra·tion *n.* an area of soil or rock below the level of the water table where all the voids are filled with water

zone re·fin·ing *n.* a technique for greatly purifying metals in which a molten area is made to pass along an otherwise solid bar so that impurities become concentrated at one end

zone·time /zṓn tīm/ *n.* NAVIG the standard time that exists throughout a particular time zone [Early 20thC]

zonk /zongk/ (**zonked, zonk·ing, zonks**) *v.* (*slang*) **1.** *vti.* **STOP FUNCTIONING** to lose consciousness or become stupefied from exhaustion or an intake of alcohol or narcotic drugs, or to make somebody do this **2.** *vt.* **HIT SOMEBODY** to hit somebody very hard [Early 20thC. From *zonk* "sound of a heavy blow," an imitation of the sound.]

zonked /zonkt/, **zonked out** *adj.* unconscious, stupefied, or sleeping, especially as a result of the effects of alcohol or a drug (*slang*) [Mid-20thC]

Zon·ti·an /zóntee әn/ *n.* a member of Zonta International, founded in 1919 as a worldwide society for business and professional women. Each chapter organizes or takes part in community events. [Early 20thC. Formed from Lakota *zœta* "trustworthy."]

zon·ule /zṓn yŏŏl/ *n.* a small zone, band, or belt —**zon·u·lar** /zṓnyələr/ *adj.*

zoo /zoo/ (*plural* **zoos**) *n.* **1.** PARK DISPLAYING LIVE ANIMALS IN ENCLOSURES a park where live wild animals from different parts of the world are kept in cages or enclosures for people to come and see, and where they are bred and studied by scientists **2.** CHAOTIC PLACE a place characterized as being full of noisy obstreperous people creating confusion and disorder (*informal*) [Mid-19thC. Shortening of ZOOLOGICAL GARDEN.]

zoo- *prefix.* **1.** animal, animal kingdom ○ *zootoxin* **2.** motile organism ○ *zoospore* [From Greek *zōion* (see -ZOON)]

zo·o·flag·el·late /zṑ ə flájjələt, -làyt/ *n.* a colorless protozoan that ingests organic matter, is often parasitic, and has one or more flagella

zo·o·ge·og·ra·phy /zṑ ə jee óggrəfee/ *n.* the scientific study of the areas where different animals live and the causes and effects of such distribution, especially distributions on a large or global scale —**zo·o·ge·og·ra·pher** *n.* —**zo·o·ge·o·graph·ic** /zṑ ə jee ə gráffik/ *adj.*

zo·o·gle·a /zṑ ə glée ə/ (*plural* **-as** *or* **-ae** /-ée/), **zo·o·gloe·a** (*plural* **-as** *or* **-ae**) *n.* a colony of microbes embedded in a gelatinous matrix [Late 19thC. From modern Latin *zoogloea*, from Greek *zōion* "animal" + *gloios* "glutinous substance."] —**zo·o·gle·al** *adj.*

zo·og·ra·phy /zō óggrəfee/ *n.* a branch of zoology that deals with describing animals and their habitats —**zo·og·ra·pher** *n.* —**zo·o·graph·ic** /zṑ ə gráffik/ *adj.*

zo·oid /zṓ òyd/ *n.* an individual invertebrate animal that reproduces nonsexually by budding or splitting, especially one that lives in a colony in which each member is joined to others by living material, e.g., a coral [Mid-19thC. Coined from ZOO- + -OID.] —**zo·oid·al** *adj.*

zoo·keep·er /zóo keèpər/ *n.* somebody whose job is taking care of the animals in a zoo

zool. *abbr.* **1.** zoological **2.** zoology

zo·ol·a·try /zō óllətree, zə wól-/ *n.* **1.** ANIMAL WORSHIP in some ancient cultures, the worshiping of animals **2.** EXTREME DEVOTION TO ANIMALS excessive devotion to animals, especially domestic pets (*humorous*) —**zo·ol·a·ter** *n.* —**zo·ol·a·trous** *adj.*

zo·o·log·i·cal /zṑ ə lójjik'l/ *adj.* **1.** OF SCIENTIFIC STUDY OF ANIMALS relating to the scientific study of animals **2.** ABOUT ANIMALS relating to or about animals

zo·o·log·i·cal gar·den *n.* a zoo (*formal*)

zo·ol·o·gist /zō óllәjist, zə wól-/ *n.* somebody who studies animals and animal behavior scientifically

zo·ol·o·gy /zō óllәjee, zə wól-/ (*plural* **-gies**) *n.* **1.** SCIENTIFIC STUDY OF ANIMALS the branch of biology that involves the scientific study of animals and all aspects of animal life **2.** ANIMALS LIVING IN REGION the animal life of a particular region **3.** ANIMAL'S OR ANIMAL GROUP'S CHARACTERISTICS the physical and biological characteristics of a particular animal or group of animals [Mid-17thC. Via modern Latin from Greek *zoologia*, literally "the study of life," from *zōion* "life form" (see -ZOON).]

zoom /zoom/ *v.* (**zoomed, zoom·ing, zooms**) **1.** *vi.* MOVE SPEEDILY to move very fast, especially while emitting a loud low-pitched buzzing noise **2.** *vi.* INCREASE SUDDENLY to rise or increase suddenly and significantly **3.** *vi.* MAKE LOUD BUZZING NOISE to emit a loud low-pitched buzzing or humming noise **4.** *vti.* AIR CARRY OUT STEEP CLIMB IN AIRCRAFT to make an aircraft climb rapidly at a very steep angle, or to be piloted in this way ■ *n.* **1.** ACT OF VERY RAPID MOVEMENT an act of moving or performing an activity at great speed **2.** PHOTOGRAPHY = **zoom lens 3.** LOUD BUZZING NOISE a loud low-pitched buzzing noise, especially one caused by rapid movement **4.** CINEMA SHOT WITH ZOOM LENS a shot in which a zoom lens is used to make the object in focus appear to move closer or farther away while the camera itself stays still [Late 19thC. An imitation of the sound.]

zoom in *vi.* to make an object appear bigger or closer, or to decrease the area in view, by use of a zoom lens or a graphic imaging device

zoom out *vi.* to make an object appear smaller or further away, or to increase the area in view, by use of a zoom lens or a graphic imaging device

zo·om·e·try /zō ómmətree/ *n.* the branch of zoology that deals with the sizes and proportions of animals —**zo·o·met·ric** /zṑ ə méttrik/ *adj.* —**zo·o·met·rist** *n.*

zoom lens, **zoom** *n.* a camera lens assembly with adjustable focal lengths that make an object being photographed or filmed appear closer or farther away than it really is

zo·o·mor·phism /zṑ ə máwr fìzzəm/ *n.* **1.** ATTRIBUTION OF ANIMAL FORMS TO GODS the representation of gods as animals, or the attributing of animal characteristics to gods **2.** ARTS USE OF ANIMALS IN ART the use of animal figures in art and design, or of animal symbols in literature —**zo·o·mor·phic** *adj.*

-zoon *suffix.* animal, zooid ○ *epizoon* [Via modern Latin from Greek *zōion* "living being, animal." Ultimately from an Indo-European base meaning "to live," which is also the ancestor of English *quick, vital, biology*, and *whiskey*.]

zo·on·o·sis /zō ónnəssiss/ (*plural* **-ses** /-seèz/) *n.* a disease, e.g., rabies, anthrax, or ringworm that can be transmitted from vertebrate animals to humans [Late 19thC. Coined from ZOO- + Greek *nosos* "disease."] —**zo·on·o·tic** /zṑ ə nóttik/ *adj.*

zo·oph·a·gous /zō óffəgəss/ *adj.* feeding on animals

zo·o·phil·ia /zṑ ə fíllee ə/ *n.* a sexual attraction to animals

zo·o·phil·ic *adj.* = **zoophilous**

zo·oph·i·lism /zō óffə lìzzəm/ *n.* a strong affinity for animals and a devotion to protecting or rescuing them from human activities, e.g., vivisection, that exploit or endanger them

zo·oph·i·lous /zō óffələss/, **zo·o·phil·ic** /zṑ ə fíllik/ *adj.* **1.** DEVOTED TO ANIMALS very fond of animals **2.** BOT POLLINATED BY ANIMALS using the actions of animals other than insects in pollinating a plant

zo·o·pho·bi·a /zṑ ə fṓbee ə/ *n.* an unusually intense fear of animals —**zo·o·phobe** /zṓ ə fōb/ *n.* —**zo·o·pho·bous** /zō óffəbəss/ *adj.*

zo·o·phyte /zṓ ə fìt/ *n.* an invertebrate animal that looks like a plant, e.g., the sea anemone, coral, or sponge [Early 17thC. Via modern Latin from Greek *zōiophuton*, literally "animal-plant," from *zōion* "animal" + *phuton* "plant."] —**zo·o·phyt·ic** /zṑ ə fíttik/ *adj.*

zo·o·plank·ton /zṑ ə plángktən/ *n.* plankton that is made up of microscopic animals, e.g., protozoans. ◊ **phytoplankton**

zo·o·plas·ty /zṓ ə plàstee/ *n.* the surgical transplantation of an animal organ, e.g., a pig's heart, into a human body —**zo·o·plas·tic** /zṑ ə plástik/ *adj.*

zo·o·sperm /zṓ ə spùrm/ *n.* = **spermatozoon** —**zo·o·sper·mat·ic** /zṑ ə spur máttik/ *adj.*

zo·o·spo·ran·gi·um /zṑ əspə ránjee əm/ (*plural* **-a** /-ə/) *n.* an organ of a fungus or plant that produces spores that can swim —**zo·o·spo·ran·gi·al** *adj.*

zo·o·spore /zṓ ə spàwr/ *n.* a spore of some algae and fungi that is capable of independent movement —**zo·o·spo·ral** /zṑ ə spáwrəl/ *adj.* —**zo·o·spor·ic** /-spáwrik/ *adj.*

zo·os·ter·ol /zō óstə ròl/ *n.* a sterol that is produced by an animal, e.g., cholesterol

zo·ot·o·my /zō óttəmee/ *n.* **1.** STUDY OF ANIMAL ANATOMY the study of the anatomy of animals, especially comparative anatomy **2.** ANIMAL DISSECTION the dissection of animals [Mid-17thC. Formed from ZOO-, on the model of "anatomy."] —**zo·o·tom·ic** /zṑ ə tómmik/ *adj.* —**zo·o·tom·i·cal·ly** /-tómmikəlee/ *adv.* —**zo·ot·o·mist** *n.*

zo·o·tox·in /zṑ ə tóksin/ *n.* a poisonous substance produced by an animal, e.g., snake venom —**zo·o·tox·ic** *adj.*

zoot suit /zóot-/ *n.* a man's suit, popular in the 1940s, that had a long jacket heavily padded at the shoulders and baggy high-waisted trousers tapering to narrow bottoms. A long watch chain was also sometimes worn looping across the trousers. [*Zoot* of uncertain origin: probably a rhyming formation from SUIT] —**zoot suit·er** *n.*

zoo TV *n.* a type of television program that encourages emotional and often uncontrolled reactions from the participants such as those featuring debates or personal disclosures in front of live audiences (*slang*)

zoot·y /zóotee/ *adj.* ostentatious in a showy or gaudy way (*dated slang*)

zo·o·xan·thel·la /zṑəzən théllə/ (*plural* **-lae** /-lee/) *n.* a microscopic yellow-green alga that lives symbiotically within the cells of some marine invertebrates, especially corals [Late 19thC. From modern Latin, literally "small yellow animal," from Greek *zōion* "animal" + *xanthos* "yellow."]

zo·ri /záwree/ (*plural* **-ri** *or* **-ris**) *n.* a simple Japanese sandal with a flat sole and a single thong, originally made of straw but now also made of rubber or felt [Early 19thC. From Japanese, literally "straw sole."]

zo·ril·la /zə ríllə/, **zor·ille** /záwrril/, **zor·il** *n.* a carnivorous African mammal of the weasel family that looks like a skunk and has long black-and-white fur. Latin name: *Ictonyx striatus.* [Late 18thC. Via French and modern Latin from Spanish *zorilla*, literally "little fox," from *zorro* "fox."]

Zo·ro·as·ter /záwrō àstər/ (630?–550? B.C.) Persian prophet. He founded Zoroastrianism, a religion based on revelations he received from Ahura Mazda, the "Lord Wisdom."

Zo·ro·as·tri·an·ism /zàwrō ástree ə nìzzəm/ *n.* an ancient religion founded by the Persian prophet Zoroaster the principal belief of which is in a supreme deity and in a cosmic contest between two spirits, one good and one evil. The sacred writings of Zoroastrianism are collected in the Zend-Avesta. —**Zo·ro·as·tri·an** *n., adj.*

zos·ter /zóstər/ *n.* **1.** MED SHINGLES shingles (*technical*) **2.** ARCHEOL ANCIENT GREEK BELT a belt worn by men, especially soldiers, in ancient Greece [Early 18thC. Via Latin from Greek *zōstēr* "girdle"; from the fact that the blisters often appear in a band across the body.]

Zou·ave /zoo áav, zwaav/ *n.* **1.** ALGERIAN INFANTRYMAN IN FRENCH ARMY UNIT a member of a former French infantry unit composed of Algerian soldiers, noted for their colorful uniforms and precision drill **2.** MEMBER OF UNIT IMITATING FRENCH ZOUAVES a member of an army unit imitating the uniform of the French Zouaves, especially those on the Union side during the U.S. Civil War [Mid-19thC. Via French from Kabyle *Zouaoua*, the name of a tribe in Algeria.]

zouk /zook/ *n.* a style of dance music originating in Guadeloupe and Martinique played with guitars and synthesizers that combines a strong fast disco beat and Caribbean rhythms [Late 20thC. Via French from Antillean Creole.]

zounds /zowndz/ *interj.* a mild expression of surprise or annoyance (*archaic*) [Late 16thC. Shortening of *by God's wounds!*]

zow·ie /zów ee/ *interj.* used to express surprise, admiration, or pleasure (*dated informal*) [Early 20thC. Natural exclamation.]

zoy·sia /zóyssee ə/ *n.* a low-growing grass plant often used for lawns in its native Asia and other regions. Genus: *Zoysia.* [Mid-20thC. From modern Latin, genus name, named for the Austrian botanist Carl von *Zoys* zu Laubach (1756–1800?).]

Z par·ti·cle *n.* a short-lived electrically neutral elementary particle considered to mediate the weak interaction between other elementary particles

ZPG *abbr.* zero population growth

Zr *symbol.* zirconium

zuc·chet·to /zoo kéttō/ (*plural* **-tos**) *n.* a small round skullcap worn by members of the Roman Catholic clergy that varies in color depending on the rank of the person wearing it. The pope wears a white one, cardinals red, bishops purple, and priests black. [Mid-19thC. Alteration of Italian *zucchetta*, literally "headlet," from *zucca* "gourd, head" (see ZUCCHINI).]

zuc·chi·ni /zoo keènee/ (*plural* **-ni** *or* **-nis**) *n. Aus, Can, U.S.* **1.** PLANTS SMALL SUMMER SQUASH a small variety of summer squash that is shaped like a cucumber and has a smooth thin dark-green or yellow skin. It is eaten as a vegetable. U.K. = **courgette 2.** ZUCCHINI PLANT the plant on which zucchini grow [Early 20thC. From Italian, plural of *zucchino* "zucchini," literally "small gourd," from *zucca* "gourd," from late Latin *cucutia*, a variant of Latin *cucurbita* (source of English *gourd*).]

zug·zwang /tsóok tsvaàng/ *n.* DISADVANTAGEOUS CHESS SITUATION a chess situation in which a player is forced into making a disadvantageous move, especially one that involves the loss of a piece ■ *vt.* (**-zwanged, -zwang·ing, -zwangs**) FORCE INTO BAD CHESS POSITION to force a chess opponent into a disadvantageous situation, especially one that involves the loss of one of the opponent's pieces [Early 20thC. From German, literally "being forced to move."]

Zui·der Zee /zídər zeé, zàydər-/ former inlet of the North Sea, south of the West Friesian Islands and occupying a deep indentation in the coast of the Netherlands. After completion of the IJsselmeer Dam in 1932, parts of it were drained, and the remainder now forms the IJsselmeer.

Zuk·er·man /zóokər mən, zóokər-/, **Pinchas** (*b.* 1948) Israeli-born U.S. violinist. His performance of both the classical repertoire and 20th-century works established his reputation as the outstanding violinist of his generation.

Zu·lu /zóo loo/ (*plural* **-lu** *or* **-lus**) *n.* **1.** PEOPLES **MEMBER OF SOUTH AFRICAN PEOPLE** a member of a people of South Africa who live mainly in the northern part of the province of Natal, where they were the dominant people during the 19th century. They fiercely resisted Boer incursions into their lands and, under their chief, Cetewayo, fought and won several battles against British forces before being comprehensively defeated in 1879. **2.** LANG **BENUE-CONGO LANGUAGE** a language spoken in eastern South Africa that belongs to the Bantu group of Benue-Congo languages, closely related to Xhosa. Zulu is spoken by about 8 million people. **3.** COMMUNICATION **CODE WORD FOR LETTER "Z"** a code word for the letter "Z," used in international radio communications [Early 19thC. From Zulu *umzulu*.] —**Zulu** *adj.*

Zu·lu·land /zóoloo land/ historic region in South Africa. Now incorporated into KwaZula-Natal Province, it is the homeland of the Zulu people.

Zu·ni /zóonee/ (*plural* **-ni** *or* **-nis**), **Zu·ñi** /zóonyee, zóonee/ (*plural* **-ñi** *or* **-ñis**) *n.* **1.** PEOPLES **MEMBER OF A NATIVE N AMERICAN PEOPLE** a member of a Native North American Pueblo people of western New Mexico **2.** LANG **ZUNI LANGUAGE** the language spoken by the Zuni people of New Mexico. It is a linguistically isolated language with no identified relatives. Zuni is spoken by about 5,000 people. [Mid-19thC. From American Spanish, of Keresan origin.] —**Zu·ni** *adj.*

Zu·rich /zóorik/, **Zü·rich** the largest city in Switzerland and capital of Zurich Canton. Population: 353,361 (1994).

Zu·rich, Lake of lake in northern Switzerland, predominantly in Zurich Canton. Area: 34 sq. mi./88 sq. km.

Zwick·au /zwík ow, tsvík ow/ city in Saxony, eastern Germany. Population: 103,900 (1995).

zwie·back /swée bàk/ *n.* a piece of bread, sliced and baked again until crisp and dry [Late 19thC. From German, literally "twice-bake."]

Zwing·li·an /zwínglee ən, swínglee ən/ *adj.* **RELATING TO ZWINGLI OR HIS DOCTRINE** relating to the life, works, or beliefs of the Swiss Protestant theologian Ulrich Zwingli, who believed that the Communion wafer and wine were only symbolic of Christ's body and blood ■ *n.* **FOLLOWER OF ZWINGLI** a follower of the Swiss Protestant theologian Ulrich Zwingli or a believer in his doctrines —**Zwing·li·an·ism** *n.*

zwit·ter·i·on /zwíttə rī ən, swíttə-/ *n.* an ion that has both a negative and a positive pole [Early 20thC. From German, literally "hybrid ion."]

Zwol·le /zwóllə/ capital city of Overijssel Province, in the north central Netherlands. Population: 100,835 (1996).

Zwor·y·kin /zwáwr i kin/, **Vladimir** (1889–1982) Russian-born U.S. inventor. He was largely responsible for the development, during the 1920s and 1930s, of the television camera and television tube. Full name **Vladimir Kosma Zworykin**

zy·de·co /zídə kō/ *n.* a style of dance music originating in Louisiana that is usually played on accordion, guitar, and violin and combines traditional French melodies with Caribbean and blues influences [Mid-20thC. Origin uncertain: probably from Louisiana creole *Les haricots (sont pas salé)*, literally "the beans (are not salted)," the name of a well-known dance tune.]

zyg- *prefix.* = **zygo-** (*used before vowels*)

zygo- *prefix.* **1.** yoke, pair ○ *zygomorphic* **2.** union, reproduction ○ *zygogenesis* [From Greek *zugon* "yoke, pair." Ultimately from an Indo-European word meaning "to join," which is also the ancestor of English *yoke, join, adjust,* and *yoga.*]

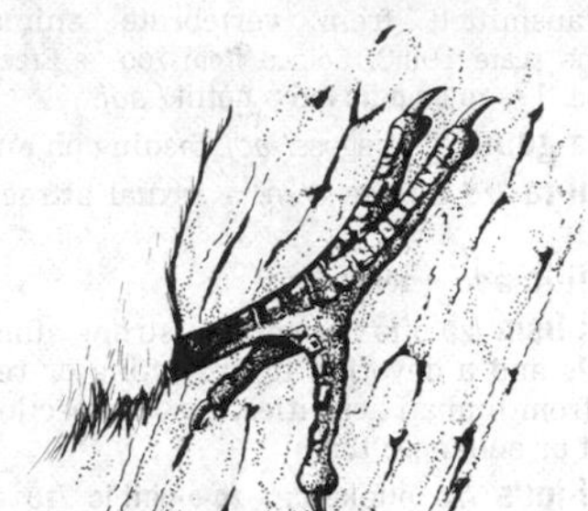

Zygodactyl

zy·go·dac·tyl /zīgə dákt'l/ *adj.* **zy·go·dac·tyl, zy·go·dac·ty·lous** **WITH TWO PAIRS OF TOES** with toes arranged in pairs, two facing forward and two backward, like those found on woodpeckers ■ *n.* **BIRD WITH TWO PAIRS OF TOES** a bird that has two pairs of toes, e.g., the woodpecker —**zy·go·dac·tyl·ism** *n.*

zy·go·gen·e·sis /zīgō jénnəssiss/ *n.* reproduction involving the fusion of male and female nuclei —**zy·go·ge·net·ic** /zīgōjə néttik/ *adj.*

zy·go·ma /zī gṓmə/ (*plural* **-ma·ta** /-mətə/ *or* **-mas**) *n.* **1.** **CHEEKBONE** a cheekbone (*technical*) **2.** = **zygomatic arch 3.** = **zygomatic process** [Late 17thC. From Greek *zugōma*, literally "joining," from *zugoun* "to join."] —**zy·go·mat·ic** /zīgə máttik/ *adj.*

zy·go·mat·ic arch *n.* a slender bar of bone connecting the cheekbone with the temporal bone on the side of the skull

zy·go·mat·ic bone *n.* a cheekbone (*technical*)

zy·go·mat·ic proc·ess *n.* a bony projection that forms part of the zygomatic arch and is joined to the cheekbone

zy·go·mor·phic /zīgə máwrfik/ *adj.* producing identical halves only when divided along a vertical axis —**zy·go·mor·phism** *n.* —**zy·go·mor·phy** /zígə màwrfee/ *n.*

zy·go·sis /zī gṓssiss/ *n.* BIOL = **conjugation** *n.* **6** [Late 19thC. From Greek *zugōsis*, from *zugoun* "to join."] —**zy·gose** /zī gṑss/ *adj.*

zy·gos·i·ty /zī góssətee/ *n.* a particular characterization of a genetic trait, zygote, or embryo, e.g., whether twins have resulted from the division of one zygote or from two different zygotes (*often used in combination*) [Mid-20thC. Formed from ZYGOSIS.]

zy·go·spore /zígə spàwr/ *n.* a thick-walled sexual spore formed from the union of two gametes in some fungi and green algae —**zy·go·spor·ic** /zígə spáwrik/ *adj.*

zy·gote /zí gòt/ *n.* an ovum that has been fertilized by a spermatozoon [Late 19thC. From Greek *zugōtos* "joined," from *zugoun* "to join."] —**zy·got·ic** /zī góttik/ *adj.* —**zy·got·i·cal·ly** /-góttikəlee/ *adv.*

zy·go·tene /zígə tèen/ *n.* a stage of the first meiotic cell division in which homologous chromosomes are paired [Early 20thC. From French *zygotène*, from *zygo-* "zygo-" and *-tène* "ribbon" (from Latin *taenia*).]

-zygous *suffix.* having a particular kind of zygotic constitution ○ *hemizygous* [Formed from Greek *zugos* "yoked, paired," which in turn was formed from *zugon* "yoke" (see ZYGO-)]

zym- *prefix.* = **zymo-** (*used before vowels*)

zy·mase /zí màyss, -màyz/ *n.* an enzyme or complex of enzymes obtained from yeast that makes sugars ferment [Late 19thC. Coined from Greek *zumē* "leaven" (see ZYMO-) + -ASE.]

zymo- *prefix.* **1.** fermentation ○ *zymology* **2.** enzyme ○ *zymogen* [Via modern Latin from Greek *zumē* "leaven" (source also of English *enzyme*). Ultimately from an Indo-European word meaning "to mix," which is also the ancestor of English *juice.*]

zy·mo·gen /zímәjən/ *n.* = **proenzyme**

zy·mo·gen·e·sis /zìmə jénnəssiss/ *n.* the transformation of a zymogen into an enzyme

zy·mo·gen·ic /zìmə jénnik/, **zy·mo·ge·net·ic** /zìməjə néttik/, **zy·mog·e·nous** /zī mójjənəss/ *adj.* **1.** **RELATING TO ZYMOGENS** relating to a zymogen **2.** **CAUSING FERMENTATION** causing or producing fermentation [Late 19thC]

zy·mol·o·gy /zī móllәjee/ *n.* a branch of biochemistry that studies fermentation, in particular the behavior of enzymes during it —**zy·mo·log·ic** /zìmə lójjik/ *adj.* —**zy·mol·o·gist** *n.*

zy·mol·y·sis /zī mólləssiss/ *n.* the action of enzymes in the process of fermentation (*technical*) —**zy·mo·lyt·ic** /zìmə líttik/ *adj.*

zy·mom·e·ter /zī mómmətər/ *n.* an instrument that measures how much or how efficiently fermentation has taken place, by measuring the level of carbon dioxide produced

zy·mo·sis /zī mṓssiss/ *n.* = **zymolysis** [Early 18thC. From Greek *zumōsis* "fermentation," from *zumoun* "to leaven," from *zumē* (see ZYMO-).]

zy·mot·ic /zī móttik/ *adj.* relating to, producing, or produced by fermentation [Mid-19thC. From Greek *zumōtikos* "causing fermentation," from *zumōsis* (see ZYMOSIS).] —**zy·mot·i·cal·ly** *adv.*

zy·mur·gy /zí mùrjee/ *n.* the scientific study of the process of fermentation in brewing and distilling [Mid-19thC. Formed from ZYMO-, on the model of "metallurgy."] —**zy·mur·gic** /zī múrjik/ *adj.*

zzz /zz/ (*plural* **zzz's**) *n.* a representation of the sound made by somebody sleeping or snoring, often used in cartoons (*humorous*)

TABLES, CHARTS, AND COMPOSITE PICTURES

The following tables, charts, and composite pictures can be found at their alphabetical entry:

Airport codes
Aircraft
Alphabets
Angles
Astrological signs
Automobiles
Bible, Books of the
Boats
Braille
Brass instruments
Bridges
Calendars
Cards
Cloud formations
Crosses
Currencies
Deserts
Diacritical marks
Domains (used in e-mail)
Emoticons
European Union
Fungi
El Niño
Geometry
Gulf Stream
Gymnasium equipment
Herbs
Hats
Keyboard instruments
Knots
Lakes
Leaf shapes
Map projections
Measurements
Military ranks
Mountains
Musical notation
National Parks
Oceans and seas
Percussion instruments
Periodic table
Phases of the Moon
Presidents of the United States
Prime ministers of Canada, Britain, Australia, and New Zealand
Proofreaders' marks
Registration of automobiles
Rivers
Roofs
Runes
San Andreas Fault
Semaphore
Shoes
Stars
Stringed instruments
Time zones
Triangles
Trigrams
Volcanoes
Waterfalls
Weather symbols
Woodwind instruments
World Heritage Sites

Subject Labels for Specialist Areas

ACCESSORIES	Accessories (clothing)
ACCT	Accounting
ACOUSTICS	Acoustics
AERON	Aeronautics
AEROSP	Aerospace
AGRIC	Agriculture
AIR	Aircraft
AIR FORCE	Air Force
ALGEBRA	Algebra
ALTERN MED	Alternative Medicine
AMPHIB	Amphibians
ANAT	Anatomy
ANGLING	Angling
ANTHROP	Anthropology
ANTIQUES	Antiques
ARCHEOL	Archeology
ARCHERY	Archery
ARCHIT	Architecture
ARITH	Arithmetic
ARMS	Arms
ARMY	Armed Forces
ART	Art
ARTS	Arts
ASTROL	Astrology
ASTRON	Astronomy
ASTROPHYS	Astrophysics
AUTOMOT	Automotive
BACKGAMMON	Backgammon
BALLET	Ballet
BALLROOM	Ballroom Dancing
BANKING	Banking
BASEBALL	Baseball
BASKETBALL	Basketball
BETTING	Betting
BEVERAGES	Beverages
BIBLE	Biblical terms
BIOCHEM	Biochemistry
BIOL	Biology
BIRDS	Birds and ornithology
BOARD GAMES	Board Games
BOBSLED	Bobsledding
BOT	Botany
BOWLING	Bowling
BOXING	Boxing
BRIDGE	Bridge (card game)
BROADCAST	Broadcasting and Media
BUDDHISM	Buddhism
BUILDING	Building
BUSINESS	Business
CALENDAR	Calendar Terms
CARDS	Card Games
CARS	Cars
CELL BIOL	Cell Biology
CERAMICS	Ceramics and Pottery
CHEM	Chemistry
CHEM ELEM	Chemical Elements
CHEM ENG	Chemical Engineering
CHESS	Chess
CHR	Christianity
CINEMA	Cinema
CIV ENG	Civil Engineering
CLIMBING	Climbing
CLOTHES	Clothing and Costume
COINS	Coins and Coin collecting
COLLECTING	Collecting
COLORS	Colors
COMM	Commerce
COMM LAW	Commercial Law
COMMUNICATIONS	Communications
COMPASS	Compass points
COMP SCI	Computer science
COMPUT	Computers
CONSTR	Construction
COOK	Cooking
COSMETICS	Cosmetics
COSMOL	Cosmology
COUNSELING	Counseling
CRAFT	Crafts
CRICKET	Cricket
CRIMINAL LAW	Criminal Law
CRIMINOL	Criminology
CRYSTALS	Crystals and Crystallography
CUE GAMES	Cue Games
CYCLING	Cycling
DANCE	Dance
DARTS	Darts
DENT	Dentistry
DERMAT	Dermatology
DESIGN	Design
DRAWING	Drawing
DRESSAGE	Dressage
DRUGS	Drugs
EASTERN RELIG	Eastern Religions
ECOL	Ecology
ECON	Economics
EDUC	Education
ELEC	Electricity
ELEC ENG	Electrical Engineering
ELECTRON ENG	Electronic Engineering
EMBRYOL	Embryology
EMERGENCIES	Emergency Services
ENERGY	Energy
ENG	Engineering
ENVIRON	Environment
EQU	Equestrianism
ETHICS	Ethics
ETHNOL	Ethnology
FASHION	Fashion
FENCING	Fencing
FIN	Finance
FISHING	Fishing
FITNESS	Fitness
FOOD	Food
FOOD TECH	Food Technology
FOOTBALL	Football
FORESTRY	Forestry
FREEMASONRY	Freemasonry
FREIGHT	Freight
FUNGI	Fungi
FURNITURE	Furniture
GAMBLING	Gambling
GAMES	Games
GARDENING	Gardening
GENETICS	Genetics
GEOG	Geography
GEOL	Geology
GEOM	Geometry
GOLF	Golf
GRAM	Grammar
GYM	Gymnastics
GYN	Gynecology
HAIR	Hairdressing
HEALTH	Health
HERALDRY	Heraldry
HIKING	Hiking
HIST	History
HOCKEY	Hockey
HOME MAINTENANCE	Home maintenance
HORSERACING	Horseracing
HOUSEHOLD	Household
HR	Human Resources
HUNT	Hunting
ICE SKATING	Ice Skating
ILLNESS	Illness
INDIAN RELIG	Indian Religions
INDUST	Industry
INSECTS	Insects
INSUR	Insurance
INTERNAT LAW	International Law
ISLAM	Islam
JOINERY	Joinery
JUDAISM	Judaism
JUD-CHR	Judeo-Christian
KNITTING	Knitting
LACROSSE	Lacrosse
LANG	Languages
LAW	Law
LEGEND	Legend
LEISURE	Leisure
LIBRARIES	Libraries
LING	Linguistics
LITERAT	Literature
LOGIC	Logic
MAIL	Mail and Postal services
MANAGEMT	Management
MANUF	Manufacturing
MAPS	Maps and Cartography
MARINE BIOL	Marine Biology
MARKETING	Marketing
MARTIAL ARTS	Martial Arts
MATH	Mathematics
MEASURE	Measurement
MECH ENG	Mechanical Engineering
MED	Medicine
METALL	Metallurgy
METEOROL	Meteorology
MICROBIOL	Microbiology
MIL	Military
MINERALS	Minerals and Mineralogy
MONEY	Currencies
MOTOR SPORTS	Motor Sports
MOTORCYCLES	Motorcycles
MOUNTAINEERING	Mountaineering
MUSIC	Music
MYTHOL	Mythology
NAUT	Nautical
NAVIG	Navigation
NAVY	Navy
NUCLEAR PHYS	Nuclear Physics
OBSTET	Obstetrics
OCEANOG	Oceanography
ONLINE	Online
OPHTHALMOL	Ophthalmology
OPTICS	Optics
PAINTING	Painting
PALEONT	Paleontology
PAPER	Paper manufacturing
PATHOL	Pathology
PENSIONS	Pensions
PEOPLES	Peoples
PHARM	Pharmacology
PHILOS	Philosophy
PHON	Phonetics
PHOTOGRAPHY	Photography
PHYS	Physics
PHYSIOL	Physiology
PLANTS	Plants
POETRY	Poetry
POL	Politics
PREHIST	Prehistory
PRESS	Press and Journalism
PRINTING	Printing
PROPERTY LAW	Property Law
PSYCHIAT	Psychiatry
PSYCHOANAL	Psychoanalysis
PSYCHOL	Psychology
PUBL	Publishing
PUBLIC ADMIN	Public Administration
QUANTUM PHYS	Quantum Physics
RACKET GAMES	Racket Games
RADIO	Radio
RAIL	Railroads
RECORDING	Recording
RELIG	Religion
RIDING	Riding
RIFLE SHOOTING	Rifle Shooting
ROLLER SKATING	Roller Skating
ROWING	Rowing
RUGBY	Rugby
SAILING	Sailing
SCI	Science
SCOUTING	Scouting
SCULPTURE	Sculpture
SEISMOL	Seismology
SEW	Sewing
SHIPPING	Shipping
SHOWJUMPING	Showjumping
SKIING	Skiing
SOC SCI	Social Science
SOC WELFARE	Social Welfare
SOCCER	Soccer
SOCIOL	Sociology
SOFTBALL	Softball
SPACE TECH	Space Technology
SPORTS	Sports
STAMPS	Stamps
STATS	Statistics
STOCK EXCH	Stock Exchange
SURG	Surgery
SWIMMING	Swimming
TECH	Technology
TELECOM	Telecommunications
TENNIS	Tennis
TEXTILES	Textiles
THEATER	Theater
TIME	Time
TRANSP	Transport
TREES	Trees
TV	Television
UNIV	University
UTIL	Public Utilities
VET	Veterinary Medicine
VIDEO	Video
WINE	Wine and Winemaking
WOODWORK	Woodworking
WRESTLING	Wrestling
ZODIAC	Zodiac
ZOOL	Zoology

Illustration Credits

Wyf of Bath © Popperfoto
First Folio of Shakespeare © Corbis
Samuel Johnson © Popperfoto
Noah Webster © Corbis
Samuel Beckett © John Haynes